# IF ELECTED...

IDAHO
FOR PRESIDENT NIXON
UTAH

# IF ELECTED...

## Presidential Campaigns From Lincoln to Ford

As Reported By

The New York Times

Edited By
Arleen Keylin
and
Eve Nelson

ARNO PRESS
RANDOM HOUSE
NEW YORK • 1976

**A Note to the Reader**
Original copies of *The New York Times* were not available to the publisher. This volume, therefore, was created from 35mm microfilm.



Frontispiece photograph courtesy of United Press International.

**Library of Congress Cataloging in Publication Data**
Main entry under title:
if elected.
1. United States—Politics and government—1865-1900—Sources. 2. United States—Politics and government— 20th century—Sources. 3. Presidents—United States—Election—History—Sources. I. Keylin, Arleen. II. Nelson, Eve, 1952- III. New York times.
E661.E43 329'023'73 76-12599
ISBN 0-405-09188-5

Assistant to the Editors: Arlene Fleischer

Manufactured in the United States of America

2 3 4 5 6 7 8 9 10

# Contents


**ELECTION OF 1860** 1

Republicans At Cooper Institute; Address By Hon. Abraham Lincoln Of Illinois
Charleston Convention: Triumph Of The Douglas Party
Abraham Lincoln Of Illinois, Nominated For President
Nomination Of Douglas And Fitzpatrick
Mass Meeting In Union Square
The Election: How The Result Is Received
The Republican Success
The New Federal Administration

**ELECTION OF 1864** 9

Unanimous Renomination Of President Lincoln
Chicago Convention: McClellan Nominated For President
Victory: Election Of Lincoln And Johnson
The Inauguration
President Lincoln Shot By An Assassin
The Succession: Mr. Johnson Inaugurated As President

**ELECTION OF 1868** 16

Gen. Grant For President And Gov. Fenton For Vice-President
Impeachment: The President Acquitted Of The Offences Charged
Grant And Colfax; The Republican Candidates For President And Vice-President
Ex-Gov. Horatio Seymour Nominated For President
Victory: Gen. Grant Elected President Of The United States
Washington: A Day Of General Excitement At The Capital

**ELECTION OF 1872** 23

Greeley Nominated!
The Republican Candidates: Gen. Grant Officially Notified Of His Renomination
Gen. Wilson's Letter Accepting The Philadelphia Nomination

**ELECTION OF 1872** (Cont.)

Last Act Of The Democratic Bedlamites; They Gulph Down Greeley And Brown
The Infamous Alliance: Tammany Responds To Greeley
Victory! A Sweeping Republican Triumph
The Inauguration

**ELECTION OF 1876** 30

The Political Campaign
Hayes And Wheeler: An Invincible Combination
Tilden Nominated
The Republican Campaign
The Victory In The Nation
The Organization Of The Electoral Tribunal
The Counting Of The Vote
The Counting Of The Vote
Succession To The Presidency
The Presidential Count
Hayes President: The Great Contest In Congress Ended
The New Administration

**ELECTION OF 1880** 43

The Political Campaign
Voice Of Massachusetts: Blaine And Sherman Thrown Completely Aside
The Presidential Race
Gen. Grant For President
Garfield And Arthur
The Republican Ticket
Mr. Tilden Withdraws
The Bourbons Stampeded
Garfield And Arthur The Choice Of The Nation
A New Chief Magistrate: Garfield And Arthur Reap The Fruits Of Victory
President Garfield Shot By An Assassin
The President Dead: The Oath Administered; Gen. Arthur Made President

**ELECTION OF 1884** 57

Arthur's Home Hostile
H. B. Payne For President

**ELECTION OF 1884 (Cont.)**

Is This The Dark Horse
The Convention's Choice: Blaine And Logan To Bear The Republican Standard
Mr. Tilden Will Not Run
Cleveland The Favorite
Balloting At Midnight
Cleveland And Hendricks The Democratic Nominees
Gov. Cleveland Elected
The Reform President

**ELECTION OF 1888** 68

A Persistent Candidate: John Sherman's Work To Gain The Presidency
Cleveland And Thurman
Cleveland Renominated
Harrison Has The Lead
The Blaine Men's Scheme
Harrison And Morton
The Republican National Ticket Victorious
Under A New President: Harrison Assumes The Reins Of Office

**ELECTION OF 1892** 77

Voters Favor Cleveland
Where Cleveland Leads
Harrison Fears Sherman
Harrison's Great Day
Harrison Wins The Prize
Cleveland And Stevenson: Two Strong Leaders For All Democrats To Follow
The Republican Issues
Mr. Cleveland's Victory
President Once Again

**ELECTION OF 1896** 86

Democrats Think Money Is The Great Issue
McKinley And Hobart Of New-Jersey
New Yorkers Are Firm
Bryan, Free Silver, And Repudiation
Palmer And Buckner: Probably Nominees Of The True Democrats
Palmer And Buckner Nominated At Indianapolis
McKinley Elected
The Inaugural Address

**ELECTION OF 1900** 95

Populists' Plans At Kansas City: Expect To Dominate The Democratic Convention
Bryan And Towne Populists' Choice
McKinley And Roosevelt: Ticket Nominated By The Republican Convention
Bryan Nominated; 16 To 1 Platform
Adlai E. Stevenson For Vice President
Gov. Roosevelt Formally Accepts
McKinley Re-Elected
Mr. McKinley Begins His Second Term
President Shot At Buffalo Fair
Mr. McKinley Dies After A Brave Fight
Mr. Roosevelt Is Now the President

**ELECTION OF 1904** 107

Roosevelt And Fairbanks Named
Bryan Crushed In Test Of Strength
Parker Nominated In First Ballot
Parker Accepts For Single Term
Democrats Arriving At Saratoga Springs
Parker Barred the Trusts From Democratic Fund
Roosevelt: Sweeps North And West And Is Elected President
Roosevelt Hero of Brilliant Day

**ELECTION OF 1908** 115

Bryan Plans To Be Roosevelt's Heir
Taft Named: First Ballot
Sherman Goes On Taft Ticket
Bryan Named: First Ballot
Bryan And Kern Put On Ticket
Taft Wins
Taft Is Sworn In Senate Hall

**ELECTION OF 1912** 123

Roosevelt Triumphant In Ohio
Taft Men Confident of Victory; Sherman Not To Be On Ticket
Roosevelt, Beaten, Taft's Nomination Seems Assured
Taft Renominated By The Republican Convention
Bryan, Repulsed, To Open Bitter Fight
Woodrow Wilson Is Nominated For President
Thousands Hear Wilson Accept
Maniac In Milwaukee Shoots Col. Roosevelt
Wilson Wins
Wilson Sworn In As President

**ELECTION OF 1916** 134

America Ready To Join A Peace League, Says Wilson
Hughes Accepts Republican Nomination For President
Democrats At Midnight Renominate Wilson and Marshall
Roosevelt Will Indorse Hughes
Great Throng In Garden Hears Wilson Appeal For Justice To All Mankind
Election Close. Wilson 264, Hughes 251
With 272 Electoral Votes, Wilson Wins
President Inaugurated, Calls For A United Nation

**ELECTION OF 1920** 142

Debs In Prison Garb Takes Nomination For President
Harding Nominated For President On The Tenth Ballot
M'Adoo Leads And Bryan Defeated
Democratic Ticket Is Cox And Roosevelt
Cox Stirs High Enthusiasm As He Speaks Twice
Harding Wins; Million Lead Here
Harding Inaugurated
President Harding Dies Suddenly; Calvin Coolidge Is President

**ELECTION OF 1924** 153

State Democrats Put Smith In The Race
Borah Agreed Upon As Vice Presidential Nominee
Coolidge And Dawes Nominated
Convention, By One Vote, Defeats Plank Naming Klan
M'Adoo Frees Delegates For Meredith
Democrats Nominate Davis And C. W. Bryan
Coolidge Wins, 357 To Davis's 136
Coolidge Is Inaugurated With Simple Ceremonies

**ELECTION OF 1928** 161

Hoover Comes Out For The Presidency
Hoover Named On First Ballot By 837
Senator Curtis Named For Vice President
Hoover Formally Notified
Smith For State Control Of Liquor Traffic, Changes In 18th Amendment And Volstead Law
Throng Of 22,000 In The Garden Hears Hoover Assail Smith's Policies
Hoover Wins 407 To 69
Hoover Inaugurated Before Throng Of 50,000

**ELECTION OF 1932** 170

Convention Adopts Hoover Dry-Wet Plank
Hoover, Curtis Renamed On First Ballots
Roosevelt Decides On Fight To Finish
Democrats Pledge Party To Repeal Of The Dry Law
Roosevelt Nominated On Fourth Ballot
Roosevelt Puts Economic Recovery First, Garner For Vice President By Acclamation
Roosevelt Winner In Landslide!
Assassin Fires Into Roosevelt Party At Miami; President-Elect Uninjured
Roosevelt Inaugurated

**ELECTION OF 1936** 180

Smith Expected To Lead Open Fight On Roosevelt
Republicans Name Landon Unanimously
Knox Nominated For Vice President
Democrats Adopt Platform Continuing New Deal
Roosevelt Nominated By Acclamation
Roosevelt Hailed By Throngs In Acceptance Ceremony; Garner Named
Great Crowds Acclaim Roosevelt
City Throngs Cheer Roosevelt And Landon
Roosevelt Sweeps The Nation
Roosevelt Pledges Warfare Against Poverty

**ELECTION OF 1940** 190

Republicans Nominate Wendell Willkie For The Presidency
Republicans Name M'Nary For Vice President
Roosevelt Leaves Third Term To Party
Roosevelt Renominated On First Ballot
Roosevelt, Accepting, Feels He Must Serve With Others In Crisis
Lewis Declares For Willkie
Roosevelt Elected President
Roosevelt Inaugurated For The Third Time

**ELECTION OF 1944** 198

Dewey And Bricker Named On 1st Ballot
Roosevelt Agrees To Run For A Fourth Term
Wallace Left To Delegates By Roosevelt
Roosevelt Nominated For Fourth Term
Truman Nominated For Vice Presidency
Roosevelt Wins Fourth Term
Roosevelt Sworn In For Fourth Term
President Roosevelt Is Dead
Truman Is Sworn In The White House

**ELECTION OF 1948** 207

Truman And M'Arthur Will Accept Nomination For The Presidency
Socialists Name Norman Thomas A Sixth Time For The Presidency
Dewey Unanimous Republican Choice
Warren Wins Second Place On Ticket
Truman, Barkley Named By Democrats
Truman Wins With 304 Electoral Votes
Truman, 32nd President, Is Inaugurated

**ELECTION OF 1952** 214

Truman Announces He Will Not Run Again
Eisenhower Nominated On The First Ballot; Nixon Chosen As His Running Mate
Stevenson Is Nominated On The Third Ballot
Sparkman Chosen By Democrats As Running Mate For Stevenson
Nixon Leaves Fate To G.O.P. Chiefs
Eisenhower Calls Nixon Vindicated
Eisenhower Would 'Go To Korea'
Eisenhower Wins In A Landslide
Eisenhower Sworn

**ELECTION OF 1956** 224

Eisenhower Says He Will Seek A 2nd Term
Nixon Decides He Will Run; Eisenhower Is 'Delighted'
Kefauver Withdraws From Race, Throwing Support To Stevenson
Democratic Keynote Talk Assails Nixon As 'Hatchet Man' Of G.O.P.
Stevenson Nominated On The First Ballot
Kefauver Nominated For Vice President; Beats Kennedy
Eisenhower And Nixon Are Renominated
Eisenhower By A Landslide
Eisenhower, In Second Inaugural

**ELECTION OF 1960** 233

Kennedy In Race
Kennedy Beats Humphrey
Rockefeller Available For Presidential Draft
Johnson Enters Race Officially
Kennedy Nominated On The First Ballot
Johnson Is Nominated For Vice President
Nixon Is Given Nomination By Acclamation
Lodge Is Nominated For Vice-Presidency
Nixon And Kennedy Clash On TV
Kennedy's Victory Won By Close Margin
Kennedy Sworn In
Kennedy Is Killed By Sniper
Johnson Sworn In On Plane

**ELECTION OF 1964** 247

Lodge Victor In New Hampshire
Goldwater Clings To Thin Lead
Scranton Enters G.O.P. Contest
Rockefeller Gives Up Race; Aids Scranton
Goldwater Is Nominated On First Ballot
Goldwater Promises Program To Make Communism 'Give Way'
Democratic Ticket: Johnson And Humphrey
Goldwater Exhorts 18,000 In Garden 'Victory' Rally
Johnson Swamps Goldwater
Johnson, Taking Oath

**ELECTION OF 1968** 257

Johnson Says He Won't Run
Humphrey Joins Presidency Race
McCarthy Beats Kennedy In Oregon Primary Upset; Nixon Is A Strong Winner
Kennedy Shot And Gravely Wounded
Kennedy Is Dead
Rockefeller And Reagan Struggle To Deny Nixon Victory On First Ballot
Nixon Is Nominated On The First Ballot
Nixon Selects Agnew As His Running Mate
Senator McGovern Ready To Run Against Humphrey
Humphrey Nominated On The First Ballot
Humphrey: Muskie On His Ticket
Gen. Lemay Joins Wallace's Ticket As Running Mate
Nixon Wins By A Thin Margin
Nixon, Sworn, Dedicates Office To Peace

**ELECTION OF 1972** 272

Democratic Race Widens
M'Govern Winner In Wisconsin, Wallace, Humphrey Vie For 2nd

**ELECTION OF 1972** (Cont.)

Wallace Is Shot; Condition Serious
Humphrey And Muskie Yield To M'Govern
M'Govern Nominated On The First Ballot
M'Govern Names Eagleton Running Mate
Eagleton Tells Of Shock Therapy On Two Occasions
Eagleton Quits At Request Of M'Govern
Shriver Is Chosen By M'Govern
Nixon Is Renominated
Nixon: Agnew Is Renamed As Running Mate
Nixon Elected In Landslide
Nixon Inaugurated For His Second Term
Agnew Quits Vice Presidency
Gerald Ford Named By Nixon As The Successor To Agnew
Ford Sworn As Vice President
Nixon Resigns
Ford Sworn In As President
Ford Gives Pardon To Nixon
Rockefeller Sworn In As Vice President

**ELECTION OF 1976** 293

Rockefeller Bars Race On Ford Ticket
Ford Edges Past Reagan By 1,300 In New Hampshire
Jackson Beats Wallace And Udall, Carter Is 4th In Massachusetts Vote
Ford Defeats Reagan In Florida; Carter Is Winner Over Wallace
Ford Decisively Defeats Reagan In Illinois Voting; Carter Is A Solid Winner
Reagan Tops Ford In N. Carolina; Carter Easily Defeats Wallace
Jackson First In New York; Carter Tops Udall In Wisconsin
Carter Is Victor In Pennsylvania; Udall Is Next

# Introduction

Our national leaders affect each of us each day. Their decisions — whether to act or not and when, what to say if anything, where to lead and when to follow events — do much to determine the national agenda and the climate of public reaction to specific problems and policies. It is impossible to avoid this impact.

Today, twenty-five percent of the Gross National Product is spent directly by the federal government (a $400 billion budget in a $1600 billion economy). About 4.8 million people are directly employed by the federal government — over 2 million in the Armed Services alone. The direction, the tone and the responsiveness of this immense mechanism are entrusted to 537 elected men and women; of these 535 comprise the Legislative Branch and two — the President together with his Vice President — are associated with the Executive Branch. All others are appointed. The leaders of the Executive Branch are elected directly by the people every four years. The leaders of the Legislative Branch are elected by the 535 Members of Congress. The leaders of each branch are our national leaders.

It is in this perspective that we must judge the role and the effectiveness of each branch in formulating national policy. Our judgment of their performance must take account of the fact that Congress during this past decade has abandoned its passive role in exercising its constitutional responsibilities; it has insisted upon sharing the responsibility for significant national directions. This resurgence has been specifically translated into the structural changes embodied in the new Congressional Budget and Impoundment Act — establishing in the Congress for the first time a mechanism to gain a perspective on and control of its $400 billion annual responsibility — and the War Powers Act — assuring Congress of a role in war making, now that declarations of war have become outmoded in practice.

These and other actions evidence an attitude of healthy Congressional assertiveness over the spectrum of federal responsibility. With their newly assertive role, the Members of Congress might in the future establish new criteria in electing their leaders — criteria designed to fulfill a specific role in national leadership. The criteria for national leadership, whether Executive or Legislative, will determine the qualities of those selected.

This volume contains a fascinating record of the events that effected the selection of the President and Vice President over the past century as observed by **The New York Times.** The lessons from this history might prove useful in the selection of the Presidential candidates and, perhaps, of the leaders of the Legislative Branch as well.

The Presidential nominating process has been remarkably static over the past 100 years. There have, however, been significant modifications. The Republicans expanded the electoral vote basis for the selection of delegates to provide bonus delegates for states with stronger party performance in 1916 [the Democrats did the same in 1944]. The Democrats reduced from two-thirds to a majority the number of votes required for nomination (1936). The majority rule facilitated more direct popular appeal for the nomination by a candidate, minimizing the need for a harmonious choice among a wider spectrum of the party.

Presidential primaries are a highlight of this volume. This 20th century phenomenon was born of the frustration of the Progressives of the Republican Party at the turn of the century. The primaries have always appeared to be the best route for outsiders to gain a foothold in the party from outside the establishment. The primaries have enjoyed their greatest popularity during the "reform" periods. But before World War II, the Presidential primary usually served only to eliminate rather than elect nominees. Teddy Roosvelt won nine out of 10 Presidential primaries against President Taft in 1912 including Taft's home state of Ohio, but he did not get the nomination. It was that setback which prompted a movement for a nationwide Presidential primary. Interest in Presidential primaries faltered in 1916 and they remained largely dormant until after World War II when Harold Stassen revived the process to challenge the Old Guard in 1948. The advent of television and the need for "media events" will probably prevent future retrenchment of the use of Presidential primaries.

Most fascinating is the comparison this volume provides between the popular perception of Presidents as candidates and their subsequent performance in office. Woodrow Wilson, the scholar who would bring reason to public policy, was unable to understand the process of compromise; Franklin Roosevelt, the champion of the balanced budget, saved the economy and probably the Republic by the wise use of deficit spending; Harry Truman, perceived as unable to cope with the complications of national, let alone international, crises, brought to the office a capacity for judgment and a capacity to act comparable with any President, at least during this century; Dwight D. Eisenhower, a military leader, demonstrated the greatest control over the military budget of any modern President and the confidence of judgment to forestall military options in emergent international crises; Lyndon B. Johnson, a Southern conservative, fulfilled the promise of the Emancipation Proclamation and of the New Deal by identifying residual national problems for which the federal government should assume active responsibility; Richard Nixon, the Cold War warrior and legal pragmatist, abandoned ideology in accepting the realities of the new China, only to be consumed by an arrogant disregard of the law. If anything stands out in this period, it is the notion that what you see is not always what you get.

More productive might be a search for the basic premises of our candidates, what their real interests are now and have been through life — their assumptions about people and their relationship to each other and to property; the issues that have generated their emotional involvement, not just how they have voted on issues in the past, if such a public record is available, but issues on which they have chosen to give their personal attention and expended their personal reputation. Different leaders react differently and for different reasons. Often, the "right" decision is arrived at for the "wrong" reasons.

When we select national leaders we hope that in their use of the immense power of these offices, they will set a decent tone and create a good climate for public policy decisions. To do so, they must retain a healthy perspective of where we have been and what role each part our system of checks and balances needs to play in the formulation of national policy.

**Charles D. Ferris**
General Counsel
United States Senate
Democratic Policy

# IF ELECTED...

ABRAHAM LINCOLN

# The New-York Times.

VOL. IX—NO. 2633. NEW-YORK, TUESDAY, FEBRUARY 28, 1860. PRICE TWO CENTS.


## REPUBLICANS AT COOPER INSTITUTE.

## Address by Hon. Abraham Lincoln, of Illinois.

### Remarks of Messrs. Wm. Cullen Bryant, Horace Greeley, Gen. Nye and J. A. Briggs.

The announcement that Hon. ABRAHAM LINCOLN, of Illinois, would deliver an address in Cooper Institute, last evening, drew thither a large and enthusiastic assemblage. Soon after the appointed hour for commencing the proceedings, DAVID DUDLEY FIELD, Esq., arose and nominated as Chairman of the meeting Mr. WILLIAM CULLEN BRYANT. The nomination was received with prolonged applause, and was unanimously approved.

SPEECH OF WM. CULLEN BRYANT.

Mr. BRYANT, after the applause had subsided, said: It is a grateful office that I perform in introducing to you at this time an eminent citizen of the West, whom you know—whom you have known hitherto—only by fame, and who has consented to address a New-York assemblage this evening. The great West, my friends, is a potent auxiliary in the battle we are fighting, for Freedom against Slavery; in behalf of civilization against barbarism; for the occupation of some of the fairest region of our Continent on which the settlers are now building their cabins. I see a higher and wiser agency than that of man in the causes that have filled with hardy people the vast and fertile regions which form the northern part of the valley of the Mississippi—a race of men who are not ashamed to till their acres with their own hands, and who would be ashamed to subsist on the labor of the slave. [Applause.] These children of the West, my friends, form a living bulwark against the advance of Slavery, and from them is recruited the vanguard of the armies of liberty. [Applause.] One of them will appear before you this evening in person—a gallant soldier of the political campaign of 1856—[applause]—who then rendered good service to the Republican cause, and who has been since the great champion of that cause in the struggle which took place two years later for the supremacy of the Republicans in the Legislature of Illinois; who took the field against Senator DOUGLAS, and would have won in the conflict but for the unjust provisions of the law of the State, which allowed a minority of the people to elect a majority of the Legislature [Applause.] I have only, my friends, to pronounce the name of ABRAHAM LINCOLN of Illinois—[cheers]—I have only to pronounce his name to secure your profoundest attention. [Prolonged applause, and cheers for LINCOLN.]

Mr. LINCOLN advanced to the desk, and smiling graciously upon his audience, complacently awaited the termination of the cheering and then proceeded with his address as follows:

SPEECH OF MR. LINCOLN.

MR. PRESIDENT AND FELLOW-CITIZENS OF NEW-YORK: The facts with which I shall deal this evening are mainly old and familiar; nor is there anything new in the general use I shall make of them. If there shall be any novelty, it will be in the mode of presenting the facts, and the inferences and observations following that presentation.

In his speech last Autumn, at Columbus, Ohio, as reported in the NEW-YORK TIMES, Senator DOUGLAS said:

"Our fathers, when they framed the Government under which we live, understood this question just as well, and even better, than we do now."

I fully indorse this, and I adopt it as a text for this discourse. I so adopt it because it furnishes a precise and an agreed starting point for a discussion between Republicans and that wing of the Democracy headed by Senator DOUGLAS. It simply leaves the inquiry: "What was the understanding those fathers had of the question mentioned?"

What is the frame of Government under which we live?

The answer must be: "The Constitution of the United States." That Constitution consists of the original, framed in 1787 (and under which the present Government first went into operation,) and twelve subsequently framed amendments, the first ten of which were framed in 1789.

Who were our fathers that framed the Constitution? I suppose the "thirty-nine" who signed the original instrument may be fairly called our fathers who framed that part of the present Government. It is almost exactly true to say they framed it, and it is altogether true to say they fairly represented the opinion and sentiment of the whole nation at that time. Their names, being familiar to nearly all, and accessible to quite all, need not now be repeated.

I take these "thirty-nine," for the present, as being "our fathers who framed the Government under which we live."

What is the question which, according to the text, those fathers understood just as well, and even better than we do now?

It is this: Does the proper division of local from Federal authority, or anything in the Constitution, forbid our Federal Government to control as to Slavery in our Federal Territories?

Upon this, DOUGLAS holds the affirmative, and Republicans the negative. This affirmative and denial form an issue; and this issue—this question—is precisely what the text declares our fathers understood better than we.

Let us now inquire whether the "thirty-nine" or any of them, ever acted upon this question; and if they did, how they acted upon it—how they expressed that better understanding.

In 1784—three years before the Constitution—the United States then owning the Northwestern Territory, and no other—the Congress of the Confederation had before them the question of prohibiting Slavery in that Territory; and four of the "thirty-nine" who afterward framed the Constitution were in that Congress, and voted on that question. Of these, ROGER SHERMAN, THOMAS MIFFLIN and HUGH WILLIAMSON voted for the prohibition—thus showing that, in their understanding, no line dividing local from Federal authority, nor anything else, properly forbade the Federal Government to control as to Slavery in Federal territory. The other of the four—JAMES MCHENRY—voted against the prohibition, showing that, for some cause, he thought it improper to vote for it.

In 1787, still before the Constitution, but while the Convention was in session framing it, and while the Northwestern Territory still was the only Territory owned by the United States—the same question of prohibiting Slavery in the Territory again came before the Congress of the Confederation; and three more of the "thirty-nine" who afterward signed the Constitution were in that Congress, and voted on the question. They were WILLIAM BLOUNT, WILLIAM FEW and ABRAHAM BALDWIN; and they all voted for the prohibition—thus showing that, in their understanding, no line dividing local from Federal authority, nor anything else, properly forbade the Federal Government to control as to Slavery in Federal territory. This time the prohibition became a law, being a part of what is now well known as the Ordinance of '87.

The question of Federal control of Slavery in the Territories seems not to have been directly before the Convention which framed the original Constitution; and hence it is not recorded that the "thirty-nine," or any of them, while engaged on that instrument, expressed any opinion on that precise question.

In 1789, by the first Congress which sat under the Constitution, an act was passed to enforce the Ordinance of '87, including the prohibition of Slavery in the Northwestern Territory. The bill for this act was reported by one of the "thirty-nine," THOMAS FITZSIMMONS, then a member of the House of Representatives from Pennsylvania. It went through all its stages without a word of opposition, and finally passed both branches without Yeas and Nays, which is equivalent to a unanimous passage. In this Congress there were sixteen of the "thirty-nine" fathers who framed the original Constitution. They were:

| | | |
|---|---|---|
| John Langdon, | Thos. Fitzsimmons, | Richard Bassett, |
| Nicholas Gilman, | William Few, | George Read, |
| Wm. S. Johnson, | Abraham Baldwin, | Pierce Butler, |
| Roger Sherman, | Rufus King, | Daniel Carroll, |
| Robert Morris, | William Patterson, | James Madison, |
| | George Clymer. | |

This shows that, in their understanding, no line dividing local from Federal authority, nor anything in the Constitution, properly forbade Congress to prohibit Slavery in the Federal territory; else both their fidelity to correct principle, and their oath to support the Constitution, would have constrained them to oppose the prohibition.

Again, GEORGE WASHINGTON, another of the "thirty-nine," was then President of the United States, and as such approved and signed the bill, thus completing its validity as a law, and thus showing that, in his understanding, no line dividing local from Federal authority, nor anything in the Constitution, forbade the Federal Government to control as to Slavery in Federal territory.

No great while after the adoption of the original Constitution, North Carolina ceded to the Federal Government the country now constituting the State of Tennessee; and a few years later Georgia ceded that which now constitutes the States of Mississippi and Alabama. In both deeds of cession it was made a condition by the ceding States that the Federal Government should not prohibit Slavery in the ceded country. Beside this, Slavery was then actually in the ceded country. Under these circumstances, Congress, on taking charge of these countries, did not absolutely prohibit Slavery within them. But they did interfere with it—take control of it—even there, to a certain extent. In 1798, Congress organized the Territory of Mississippi. In the act of organization they prohibited the bringing of slaves into the Territory, from any place without the United States, by fine, and giving freedom to slaves so brought. This act passed both branches of Congress without Yeas and Nays. In that Congress were three of the "thirty-nine" who framed the original Constitution. They were, JOHN LANGDON, GEORGE READ and ABRAHAM BALDWIN. They all, probably, voted for it. Certainly they would have placed their opposition to it upon record, if, in their understanding, any line dividing local from Federal authority, or anything in the Constitution, properly forbade the Federal Government to control as to Slavery in Federal authority.

In 1803, the Federal Government purchased the Louisiana country. Our former territorial acquisitions came from certain of our own States; but this Louisiana country was acquired from a foreign nation. In 1804, Congress gave a Territorial organization to that part of it which now constitutes the State of Louisiana. New-Orleans, lying within that part, was an old and comparatively large city. There were other considerable towns and settlements, and Slavery was extensively and thoroughly intermingled with the people. Congress did not, in the Territorial act, prohibit Slavery; but they did interfere with it—in a more marked and extensive way than they did in the case of Mississippi. The substance of the provision therein made, in relation to slaves, was:

*First*—That no slave should be imported into the Territory from foreign parts.

*Second*—That no slave should be carried into it who had been imported into the United States since the first day of May, 1798.

*Third*: That no slave should be carried into it, except by the owner, and for his own use as a settler; the penalty in all the cases being a fine upon the violator of the law, and freedom to the slave.

This act also was passed without yeas and nays. In the Congress which passed it, there were two of the "thirty-nine." They were ABRAHAM BALDWIN and JONATHAN DAYTON. As stated in the case of Mississippi, it is probable they both voted for it. They would not have allowed it to pass without recording their opposition to it, if, in their understanding, it violated either the line properly dividing local from Federal authority, or any provision of the Constitution.

In 1819-20, came, and passed, the Missouri question. Many votes were taken, by Yeas and Nays, in both branches of Congress, upon the various phases of the general question. Two of the "thirty-nine"—RUFUS KING and CHARLES PINCKNEY—were members of that Congress. Mr. KING steadily voted for Slavery prohibition and against all compromises, while Mr. PINCKNEY as steadily voted against Slavery prohibition, and against all compromises. By this Mr. KING showed that, in his understanding, no line dividing local from Federal authority, nor anything in the Constitution, was violated by Congress prohibiting Slavery in Federal territory; while Mr. PINCKNEY, by his votes, showed that in his understanding there was some sufficient reason for opposing such prohibition in that case.

The cases I have mentioned are the only acts of the "thirty-nine," or of any of them, upon the direct issue, which I have been able to discover.

To enumerate the persons who thus acted, as being four in 1784, three in 1787, seventeen in 1789, three in 1798, two in 1804, and two in 1819-20; there would be thirty-one of them. But this would be counting JOHN LANGDON, ROGER SHERMAN, WM. FEW, RUFUS KING, and GEORGE READ, each twice, and ABRAHAM BALDWIN four times. The true number of those of the "thirty-nine" whom I have shown to have acted upon the question, which, by the text, they understood better than we, is twenty-three, leaving sixteen not shown to have acted upon it in any way.

Here, then, we have twenty-three of our "thirty-nine" fathers who framed the Government under which we live, who have, upon their official responsibility and their corporal oaths, acted upon the very question which the text affirms they "understood just as well and even better than we do now;" and twenty-one of them—a clear majority of the whole "thirty-nine"—so acting upon it as to make them guilty of gross political impropriety, and wilful perjury, if, in their understanding, any proper division between local and Federal authority, or anything in the Constitution they had made themselves, and sworn to support, forbade the Federal Government to control as to Slavery in the Federal Territories. Thus the twenty-one acted; and, as actions speak louder than words, so actions under such responsibility speak still louder.

Two of the twenty-three voted against Congressional prohibition of Slavery in the Federal Territories, in the instances in which they acted upon the question. But for what reasons they so voted is not known. They may have done so because they thought a proper division of local from Federal authority, or some provision or principle of the Constitution, stood in the way; or they may, without any such question, have voted against the prohibition on what appeared to them to be sufficient grounds of expediency. No one who has sworn to support the Constitution, can conscientiously vote for what he understands to be an unconstitutional measure, however expedient he may think it; but one may and ought to vote against a measure which he deems constitutional, if, at the same time, he deems it inexpedient. It, therefore, would be unsafe to set down even the two who voted against the prohibition, as having done so because, in their understanding, any proper division of local from Federal authority, or anything in the Constitution, forbade the Federal Government to control as to Slavery in Federal Territory.

The remaining sixteen of the "thirty-nine," so far as I have discovered, have left no record of their understanding upon the direct question of Federal control of Slavery in the Federal Territories. But there is much reason to believe that their understanding upon that question would not have appeared different from that of their twenty-three compeers, had it been manifested at all.

For the purpose of adhering rigidly to the text, I have purposely omitted whatever understanding may have been manifested by any person, however distinguished, other than the thirty-nine fathers who framed the original Constitution; and, for the same reason, I have also omitted whatever understanding may have been manifested by any of the "thirty-nine" even, on any other phase of the general question of Slavery. If we should look into their acts and declarations on those other phases, as the foreign slave trade, and the morality and policy of Slavery generally, it would appear to us that on the direct question of Federal control of Slavery in Federal Territories, the sixteen, if they had acted at all, would probably have acted just as the twenty-three did. Among that sixteen were several of the most noted anti-Slavery men of those times—as DR. FRANKLIN, ALEXANDER HAMILTON and GOUVERNEUR MORRIS—while there was not one now known to have been otherwise, unless it may be JOHN RUTLEDGE, of South Carolina.

The sum of the whole is, that of our "thirty-nine" fathers who framed the original Constitution, twenty-one—a clear majority of the whole—certainly understood that no proper division of local from Federal authority, nor any part of the Constitution, forbade the Federal Government to control Slavery in the Federal Territories; while all the rest probably had the same understanding. Such, unquestionably, was the understanding of our fathers who framed the original Constitution; and the text affirms that they understood the question better than we.

But, so far, I have been considering the understanding of the question manifested by the framers of the original Constitution. In, and by, the original instrument, a mode was provided for amending it; and, as I have already stated, the present frame of Government under which we live consists of that original, and twelve amendatory articles framed and adopted since. Those who now insist that Federal control of Slavery in Federal Territories violates the Constitution, point us to the provisions which they suppose it thus violates; and, as I understand, they all fix upon provisions in these amendatory articles, and not in the original instrument. The Supreme Court, in the Dred Scott case, plant themselves upon the fifth amendment, which provides that "no person shall be deprived of property without due process of law;" while Senator DOUGLAS and his peculiar adherents plant themselves upon the tenth amendment, providing that "the powers not granted by the Constitution, are reserved to the States respectively, and to the people."

Now, it so happens that these amendments were framed by the first Congress which sat under the Constitution—the identical Congress which passed the act already mentioned, enforcing the prohibition of Slavery in the Northwestern Territory. Not only was it the same Congress, but they were the identical, same individual men who, at the same session, and at the same time within the session, had under consideration, and in progress toward maturity, these Constitutional amendments and this act prohibiting Slavery in all the territory the nation then owned. The Constitutional amendments were introduced before and passed after the act enforcing the Ordinance of '87; so that during the whole pendency of the act to enforce the Ordinance, the Constitutional amendments were also pending.

That Congress, consisting in all of seventy-six members, including sixteen of the framers of the original Constitution, as before stated, were preeminently our fathers who framed that part of the Government under which we live which is now claimed as forbidding the Federal Government to control Slavery in the Federal Territories.

Is it not a little presumptuous in any one at this day to affirm that the two things which that Congress deliberately framed, and carried to maturity at the same time, are absolutely inconsistent with each other? And does not such affirmation become impudently absurd when coupled with the other affirmation, from the same mouth, that those who did the two things alleged to be inconsistent, understood whether they really were inconsistent better than we—better than he who affirms that they are inconsistent?

It is surely safe to assume that the "thirty-nine" framers of the original Constitution, and the seventy-six members of the Congress which framed the amendments thereto, taken together, do certainly include those who may be fairly called "our fathers who framed the Government under which we live." And so assuming, I defy any man to show that any one of them ever in his whole life declared that, in his understanding, any proper division of local from Federal authority, or any part of the Constitution, forbade the Federal Government to control as to Slavery in the Federal Territories. I go a step further. I defy any one to show that any living man in the whole world ever did, prior to the beginning of the present century, (and I might almost say, prior to the beginning of the last half of the present century,) declare that, in his understanding any proper division of local from Federal authority, or any part of the Constitution, forbade the Federal Government to control as to Slavery in the Federal Territories. To those who now so declare, I give, not only "our fathers who framed the Government under which we live," but with them all other living men within the century in which it was framed, among whom to search, and they shall not be able to find the evidence of a single man agreeing with them.

Now, and here, let me guard a little against being misunderstood. I do not mean to say we are bound to follow implicitly in whatever our fathers did. To do so would be to discard all the lights of current experience—to reject all progress—all improvement. What I do say is, that if we would supplant the opinions and policy of our fathers in any case, we should do so upon evidence so conclusive, and argument so clear, that even their great authority, fairly considered and weighed, cannot stand; and most surely not in a case whereof we ourselves declare they understood the question better than we.

If any man, at this day, sincerely believes that a proper division of local from Federal authority, or any part of the Constitution, forbids the Federal Government to control as to Slavery in the Federal Territories, he is right to say so, but to enforce his position by all truthful evidence and fair argument which he can. But he has no right to mislead others, who have less access to history and less leisure to study it, into the false belief that "our fathers, who framed the Government under which we live," were of the same opinion—thus substituting falsehood and deception for truthful evidence and fair argument. If any man at this day sincerely believes "our fathers, who framed the Government under which we live," used and applied principles, in other cases, which ought to have led them to understand that a proper division of local from Federal authority, or some part of the Constitution, forbids the Federal Government to control as to Slavery in the Federal Territories, he is right to say so. But he should, at the same time, brave the responsibility of declaring that, in his opinion, he understands their principles better than they did themselves, and especially should he not shirk that responsibility by asserting that they "understood the question just as well, and even better, than we do now."

But enough. Let all who believe that "our fathers, who framed the Government under which we live, understood this question just as well, and even better than we do now," speak as they spoke, and act as they acted upon it. This is all Republicans ask—all Republicans desire—in relation to Slavery. As those fathers marked it, so let it be again marked, as an evil not to be extended, but to be tolerated and protected only because of and so far as its actual presence among us makes that toleration and protection a necessity. Let all the guarantees those fathers gave it be, not grudgingly, but fully and fairly, maintained. For this Republicans contend, and with this, so far as I know or believe, they will be content.

And now, if they would listen—as I suppose they will not—I would address a few words to the Southern people.

I would say to them: You consider yourselves a reasonable and a just people; and I consider that in the general qualities of reason and justice you are not inferior to any other people. Still, when you speak of us Republicans, you do so only to denounce us as reptiles, or, at the best, as no better than outlaws. You will grant a hearing to pirates or murderers, but nothing like it to "Black Republicans." In all your contentions with one another, each of you deems an unconditional condemnation of "Black Republicanism" as the first thing to be attended to. Indeed, such condemnation of us seems to be an indispensable prerequisite—license, so to speak—among you to be admitted or permitted to speak at all.

Now, can you, or not, be prevailed upon to pause, and to consider whether this is quite just to us, or even to yourselves?

Bring forward your charges and specifications, and then be patient long enough to hear us deny or justify.

You say we are sectional. We deny it. That makes an issue, and the burden of proof is upon you. You produce your proof, and what is it? Why, that our party has no existence in your section—gets no votes in your section. The fact is substantially true; but does it prove the issue? If it does, then, in case we should, without change of principle, begin to get votes in your section, we should thereby cease to be sectional. You cannot escape this conclusion; and yet, are you willing to abide by it? If you are, you will probably soon find that we have ceased to be sectional, for we shall get votes in your section this very year. You will then begin to discover, as the truth plainly is, that your proof does not touch the issue. The fact that we get no votes in your section is a fact of your making, and not of ours. And if there be fault in that fact, that fault is primarily yours, and remains so until you show that we repel you by some wrong principle or practice. If we do repel you by any wrong principle or practice, the fault is ours; but this brings you to where you ought to have started—to a discussion of the right or wrong of our principle. If our principle, put in practice, would wrong your section for the benefit of ours, or for any other object, then our principle, and we with it, are sectional, and are justly opposed and denounced as such. Meet us, then, on the question of whether our principle, put in practice, would wrong your section; and so meet it as if it were possible that something may be said on our side. Do you accept the challenge? No? Then you really believe that the principles which our fathers who framed the Government under which we live, thought so clearly right as to adopt it, and indorse it again and again, upon their official oaths, is, in fact, so clearly wrong as to demand your condemnation without a moment's consideration.

Some of you delight to flaunt in our faces the warning against sectional parties given by WASHINGTON in his Farewell Address. Less than eight years before WASHINGTON gave that warning, he had, as President of the United States, approved and signed an act of Congress, inforcing the prohibition of Slavery in the Northwestern Territory, which act embodied the policy of the Government upon that subject, up to and at the very moment he penned that warning; and about one year after he penned it he wrote LA FAYETTE that he considered that prohibition a wise measure, expressing in the same connection his hope that we should some time have a confederacy of Free States.

Bearing this in mind, and seeing that sectionalism has since arisen from this same subject, is that warning a weapon in your hands against us, or in our hands against you? Could WASHINGTON himself speak, would he cast the blame of that sectionalism upon us, who sustain his policy, or upon you who repudiate it? We respect that warning of WASHINGTON, and we commend it to you, together with his example pointing to the right application of it.

But you say you are conservative—eminently conservative—while we are revolutionary, destructive, or something of the sort. What is conservatism? Is it not adherence to the old and tried, against the new and untried? We stick to, contend for the identical old policy on the point in controversy which was adopted by our fathers who framed the Government under which we live; while you with one accord reject, and scout, and spit upon that old policy, and insist upon substituting something new. True, you disagree among yourselves as to what that substitute shall be. You have considerable variety of new propositions and plans, but you are unanimous in rejecting and denouncing the old policy of the fathers. Some of you are for reviving the foreign Slave-trade; some for a Congressional Slave Code for the Territories; some for Congress forbidding the Territories to prohibit Slavery within their limits; some for maintaining Slavery in the Territories through the Judiciary; some for the "gur-reat pur-rinciple" that "if one man would enslave another, no third man should object," fantastically called "Popular Sovereignty;" but never a man among you in favor of Federal prohibition of Slavery in Federal Territories, according to the practice of our fathers who framed the Government under which we live. Not one of all your various plans can show a precedent or an advocate in the century within which our Government originated. Consider, then, whether your claim of conservatism for yourselves, and your charge of destructiveness against us, are based on the most clear and stable foundations.

Again, you say we have made the Slavery question more prominent than it formerly was. We deny it. We admit that it is more prominent, but we deny that we made it so. It was not we, but you, who discarded the old policy of the fathers. We resisted, and still resist, your innovation; and thence comes the greater prominence of the question. Would you have that question reduced to its former proportions? Go back to that old policy. What has been will be again, under the same conditions. If you would have the peace of the old times, readopt the precepts and policy of the old times.

You charge that we stir up insurrections among your slaves. We deny it; and what is your proof? Harper's Ferry! JOHN BROWN! JOHN BROWN was no Republican; and you have failed to implicate a single Republican in the Harper's Ferry enterprise. If any member of our party is guilty in that matter, you know it or you do not know it. If you do know it, you are inexcusable to not designate the man and prove the fact. If you do not know it, you are inexcusable to assert it, and especially to persist in the assertion after you have tried and failed to make the proof. You need not be told that persisting in a charge which one does not know to be true, is simply malicious slander.

Some of you admit that no Republican designedly aided or encouraged the Harper's Ferry affair; but still insist that our doctrines and deliberations necessarily lead to such results. We do not believe it. We know we hold to no doctrines, and make no declarations, which were not held to and made by our fathers who framed the Government under which we live. You never dealt fairly by us in relation to this affair. When it occurred, some important State elections were near at hand, and you were in evident glee with the belief that, by charging the blame upon us, you could get an advantage of us in those elections. The elections came, and your expectations were not quite fulfilled. Every Republican man knew that, as to himself at least, your charge was a slander, and he was not much inclined by it to cast his vote in your favor. Republican doctrines and declarations are accompanied with a continual protest against any interference whatever with your slaves, or with you about your slaves. Surely, this does not encourage them to revolt. True, we do, in common with our fathers, who framed the Government under which we live, declare our belief that Slavery is wrong; but the slaves do not hear us declare even this. For anything we say or do, the slaves would scarcely know there is a Republican Party. I believe they would not, in fact, generally know it but for your misrepresentations of us in their hearing. In your political contests among yourselves, each faction charges the other with sympathy with Black Republicanism; and then, to give point to the charge, defines Black Republicanism to simply be insurrection, blood and thunder among the slaves.

Slave insurrections are no more common now than they were before the Republican Party was organized. What induced the Southampton insurrection, twenty-eight years ago, in which at least three times as many lives were lost as at Harper's Ferry. You can scarcely stretch your very elastic fancy to the conclusion that Southampton was got up by Black Republicanism. In the present state of things in the United States, I do not think a general, or even a very extensive slave insurrection, is possible. The indispensable concert of action cannot be attained. The slaves have no means of rapid communication; nor can incendiary free men, black or white, supply it. The explosive materials are everywhere in parcels; but there neither are, nor can be supplied, the indispensable connecting trains.

Much is said by Southern people about the affection of slaves for their masters and mistresses; and a part of it, at least, is true. A plot for an uprising could scarcely be devised and communicated to twenty individuals before some one of them, to save the life of a favorite master or mistress, would divulge it. This is the rule; and the slave-revolution in Hayti was not an exception to it, but a case occurring under peculiar circumstances. The gunpowder plot of British history, though not connected with slaves, was more in point. In that case, only about twenty were admitted to the secret; and yet one of them, in his anxiety to save a friend, betrayed the plot to that friend, and, by consequence, averted the calamity. Occasional poisonings from the kitchen, and open or stealthy assassinations in the field, and local revolts extending to a score or so, will continue to occur as the natural results of Slavery; but no general insurrection of slaves, as I think, can happen in this country for a long time. Whoever much fears, or much hopes, for such an event, will be alike disappointed.

In the language of Mr. JEFFERSON, uttered many years ago, "It is still in our power to direct the process of emancipation, and deportation, peaceably, and in such slow degrees, as that the evil will wear off insensibly; and their places be, *pari passu*, filled up by free white laborers. If, on the contrary, it is left to force itself on, human nature must shudder at the prospect held up."

Mr. JEFFERSON did not mean to say, nor do I, that the power of emancipation is in the Federal Government. He spoke of Virginia; and, as to the power of emancipation, I speak of the Slaveholding States only.

The Federal Government, however, as we insist, has the power of restraining the extension of the institution—the power to insure that a slave insurrection shall never occur on any American soil which is now free from Slavery.

JOHN BROWN's effort was peculiar. It was not a slave insurrection. It was an attempt by white men to get up a revolt among slaves, in which the slaves refused to participate. In fact, it was so absurd that the slaves, with all their ignorance, saw plainly enough it could succeed. That affair, in its philosophy, corresponds with the many attempts, related in history, at the assassination of kings and emperors. An enthusiast broods over the oppression of a people, till he fancies himself commissioned by Heaven to liberate them. He ventures the attempt, which ends in little else than his own execution. ORSINI's attempt on LOUIS NAPOLEON, and JOHN BROWN's attempt at Harper's Ferry were, in their philosophy, precisely the same. The eagerness to cast blame on old England in the one case, and on New-England in the other, does not disprove the sameness of the two things.

And how much would it avail you, if you could, by the use of JOHN BROWN, HELPER's book, and the like, break up the Republican organization? Human action can be modified to some extent, but human nature cannot be changed. There is a judgment and a feeling against Slavery in this nation, which cast at least a million and a half of votes. You cannot destroy that judgment and feeling—that sentiment—by breaking up the political organization which rallies around it. You can scarcely scatter and disperse an army which has been formed into order in the face of your heaviest fire, but if you could, how much would you gain by forcing the sentiment which created it out of the peaceful channel of the ballot-box into some other channel? What would that other channel probably be? Would the number of John Browns be lessened or enlarged by the operation?

But you will break up the Union, rather than submit to a denial of your Constitutional rights.

That has a somewhat reckless sound; but it would be palliated, if not fully justified, were we proposing, by the mere force of numbers, to deprive you of some right, plainly written down in the Constitution. But we are proposing no such thing.

When you make these declarations, you have a specific and well-understood allusion to an assumed Constitutional right of yours, to take slaves into the Federal Territories, and to hold them there as property. But no such right is specifically written in the Constitution. That instrument is literally silent about any such right. We, on the contrary, deny that such a right has any existence in the Constitution, even by implication.

Your purpose, then, plainly stated, is, that you will destroy the Government, unless you be allowed to construe the Constitution as you please, on all points in dispute between you and us. You will rule or ruin in all events.

This, plainly stated, is your language to us. Perhaps you will say the Supreme Court has decided the disputed Constitutional question in your favor. Not quite so. But, waiving the lawyer's distinction between dictum and decision, the Court have decided the question for you in a sort of way. The Court have substantially said, it is your Constitutional right to take Slaves into the Federal Territories, and to hold them there as property.

When I say the decision was made in a sort of way, I mean it was made in a divided Court by a bare majority of the Judges, and they not quite agreeing with one another in the reasons for making it; that it is so made as that its avowed supporters disagree with one another about its meaning; and that it was mainly based upon a mistaken statement of fact—the statement in the opinion that "the right of property in a slave is distinctly and expressly affirmed in the Constitution."

An inspection of the Constitution will show that the right of property in a slave is not distinctly and expressly affirmed in it. Bear in mind the Judges do not pledge their judicial opinion that such right is impliedly affirmed in the Constitution; but they pledge their veracity that it is distinctly and expressly affirmed there—"distinctly"—that is, not mingled with anything else—"expressly"—that is, in words meaning just that, without the aid of any inference, and susceptible of no other meaning.

If they had only pledged their judicial opinion that such right is affirmed in the instrument by implication, it would be open to others to show that neither the word "slave" nor "slavery" is to be found in the Constitution, nor the word "property," even, in any connection with language alluding to the things slave, or slavery, and that wherever in that instrument the slave is alluded to, he is called a "person;" and wherever his master's legal right in relation to him is alluded to, it is spoken of as "service or labor due," as a "debt" payable in service or labor. Also, it would be open to show, by cotemporaneous history, that this mode of alluding to slaves and Slavery, instead of speaking of them, was employed on purpose to exclude from the Constitution the idea that there could be property in man.

To show all this is easy and certain.

When this obvious mistake of the Judges shall be brought to their notice, is it not reasonable to expect that they will withdraw the mistaken statement, and reconsider the conclusion based upon it?

And then it is to be remembered that "our fathers, who framed the Government under which we live"—the men who made the Constitution—decided this same constitutional question in our favor, long ago—decided it without a division among themselves, when making the decision; without division among themselves about the meaning of it after it was made, and so far as any evidence is left without basing it upon any mistaken statement of facts.

Under all these circumstances, do you really feel yourselves justified to break up this Government, unless such a Court decision as yours is shall be at once submitted to as a conclusive and final rule of political action?

But you will not abide the election of a Republican President. In that supposed event, you say, you will destroy the Union; and then, you say, the great crime of having destroyed it will be upon us!

That is cool. A highwayman holds a pistol to my ear, and mutters through his teeth, "Stand and deliver, or I shall kill you, and then you will be a murderer!"

To be sure, what the robber demanded of me—my money—was my own; and I had a clear right to keep it; but it was no more my own than my vote is my own; and the threat of death to me, to extort my money, and the threat of destruction to the Union, to extort my vote, can scarcely be distinguished in principle.

A few words now to Republicans. It is exceedingly desirable that all parts of this great Confederacy shall be at peace, and in harmony, one with another. Let us Republicans do our part to have it so. Even though much provoked, let us do nothing through passion and ill temper. Even though the Southern people will not so much as listen to us, let us calmly consider their demands, and yield to them if, in our deliberate view of our duty, we possibly can. Judging by all they say and do, and by the subject and nature of their controversy with us, let us determine, if we can, what will satisfy them.

Will they be satisfied if the Territories be unconditionally surrendered to them? We know they will not. In all their present complaints against us, the Territories are scarcely mentioned. Invasions and insurrections are the rage now. Will it satisfy them if, in the future, we have nothing to do with invasions and insurrections? We know it will not. We so know because we know we never had anything to do with invasions and insurrections; and yet this total abstaining does not exempt us from the charge and the denunciation.

The question recurs, what will satisfy them? Simply this: We must not only let them alone, but we must, somehow, convince them that we do let them alone. This, we know by experience, is no easy task. We have been so trying to convince them from the very beginning of our organization, but with no success. In all our platforms and speeches, we have constantly protested our purpose to let them alone; but this has had no tendency to convince them. Alike unavailing to convince them is the fact that they have never detected a man of us in any attempt to disturb them.

These natural and apparently adequate means all failing, what will convince them? This, and this only: cease to call Slavery *wrong*, and join them in calling it *right*. All this must be done thoroughly—done in *acts* as well as in *words*. Silence will not be tolerated—we must place ourselves avowedly with them. DOUGLAS' new sedition law must be enacted and enforced, suppressing all declarations that Slavery is wrong, whether made in politics, in presses, in pulpits, or in private. We must arrest and return their fugitive slaves with greedy pleasure. We must pull down our Free-State Constitutions. The whole atmosphere must be disinfected from the taint of opposition to Slavery, before they will cease to believe that all their troubles proceed from us.

I am quite aware they do not state their case precisely in this way. Most of them would probably say to us, "Let us alone, do nothing with us, and say what you please about Slavery." But we do let them alone—have never disturbed them—so that, after all, it is what we say which dissatisfies them. They will continue to accuse us of doing until we cease saying.

I am also aware they have not, as yet, in terms, demanded the overthrow of our Free-State Constitutions. Yet those Constitutions declare the wrong of Slavery, with more solemn emphasis than do all other sayings against it: and when all these other sayings shall have been silenced, the overthrow of these Constitutions will be demanded, and nothing be left to resist the demand. It is nothing to the contrary that they do not demand the whole of this just now. Demanding what they do, and for the reason they do, they can voluntarily stop nowhere short of this consummation. Holding, as they do, that Slavery is morally right, and socially elevating, they cannot cease to demand a full national recognition of it, as a legal right, and a social blessing.

Nor can we justifiably withold this on any ground save our conviction that Slavery is wrong. If Slavery is right, all words, acts, laws, and Constitutions against it, are themselves wrong, and should be silenced, and swept away. If it is right, we cannot justly object to its nationality—its universality; if it is wrong, they cannot justly insist upon its extension—its enlargement. All they ask, we could readily grant, if we thought Slavery right; all we ask, they could as readily grant, if they thought it wrong. Their thinking it right, and our thinking it wrong, is the precise fact upon which depends the whole controversy. Thinking it right, as they do, they are not to blame for desiring its full recognition, as being right; but thinking it wrong, as we do, can we yield to them? Can we cast our votes with their view, and against our own? In view of our moral, social, and political responsibilities, can we do this?

Wrong as we think Slavery is, we can yet afford to let it alone where it is, because that much is due to the necessity arising from its actual presence in the nation; but can we, while our votes will prevent it, allow it to spread in the National Territories, and to overrun us here in these Free States?

If our sense of duty forbids this, then let us stand by our duty, fearlessly and effectively. Let us be diverted by none of those sophistical contrivances wherewith we are so industriously plied and belabored—contrivances such as groping for some middle ground between the right and the wrong, vain as the search for a man who should be neither a living man nor a dead man—such as a policy of "don't care" on a question about which all true men do care—such as Union appeals beseeching true Union men to yield to Disunionists, reversing the Divine rule, and calling, not the sinners, but the righteous to repentance—such as invocations of WASHINGTON, imploring men to unsay what WASHINGTON said, and undo what WASHINGTON did.

Neither let us be slandered from our duty by false accusations against us, nor frightened from it by menaces of destruction to the Government, nor of dungeons to ourselves. Let us have faith that right makes might; and in that faith, let us, to the end, dare to do our duty, as we understand it.

When Mr. LINCOLN had concluded his address, during the delivery of which he was frequently applauded, three rousing cheers were given for the orator and the sentiments to which he had given utterance. There were then loud calls for Mr. GREELEY, who came forward and assured the audience that the orator of the occasion was a specimen of what free labor and free expression of ideas could produce He was followed by Gen. NYE, who was called for a long time before he appeared; and when he did appear it was only to say that he could not allow himself to disturb the effect of the address to which they had listened, by any remarks of his. By and by there would be a more appropriate occasion, and when it came he promised to express his sentiment freely.

After a few words from Hon. JAS. A. BRIGGS and Judge CULVER, the audience separated.

## NEWS BY TELEGRAPH.

### THE LOSS OF THE HUNGARIAN.

#### Tardy Preparations for Visiting the Wreck.

FACTS ABOUT SUPPOSED PASSENGERS.

HALIFAX, Monday, Feb. 27—8 P. M.

Not another word, as yet, has been heard from the steamship *Hungarian*.

The revenue cutter *Daring* has not yet arrived at the scene of the wreck.

A party of divers has left here in the schooner *Ospray* to render assistance.

A hat-box marked "WM. BOULLENHOUSE, Sackville," has been washed ashore.

TORONTO, C. W., Monday, Feb. 27.

Letters received by the *Europa* by the friends of Mr. MCKELLAR, M. P. P., state that he did not sail by the *Hungarian*, as was supposed.

ST. CATHERINES, C. W., Monday, Feb. 27.

Letters per the steamship *Europa* state that Hon. Mr. MERRITT, M. P. P., was not a passenger by the *Hungarian*, he being prevented by business from coming in her.

THE CATASTROPHE AT PORTLAND.

*From the Portland Advertiser, Feb. 27.*

We have no recollection of any catastrophe that has thrown such a gloom over our city as this. Many of those on board had connections or intimate frends here, and the anxiety of these connections and friends, and those who sympathize with them, has been heightened by the delay in the reception of news, and the mystery in which everything in regard to the disaster seems enveloped. Rev. Mr. GOSNER, of Montreal, who occupied the pulpit of the Park-street Church, and Rev. Dr. SHAILER, of the Federal-street Baptist Church, preached sermons yesterday specially upon the subject; and it was alluded to with much feeling in the sermons or devotional exercises in most of the other pulpits in the city.

The steamer *Bohemian*, which sailed from this port on Saturday for Liverpool, took in tow a large schooner, the *Sarah*, Capt. UPTON, and with a strong crew on board, accompanied by Capt. CRAWFORD, the efficient agent of the steamship line at this port; and from this source, if from no other, we hope eventually to get all the particulars that can be gleaned of the shocking catastrophe.

#### South Carolina Items.

MOVEMENTS OF ARCHBISHOP HUGHES—OBITUARY—BURNING OF A RICE MILL.

CHARLESTON, Monday, Feb. 27.

Archbishop HUGHES and Rev. Father MATHEWS have arrived here from New-York.

Capt. DESPERJOLS, of the French bark *Palmier*, just arrived from Pointpetre, Guadaloupe, died suddenly in a fit yesterday. He was a native of Bordeaux.

The *South Carolinian*, of yesterday, announces the death, by apoplexy, of Col. J. H. IRBY, formerly a Congressman.

The Canonsboro' Rice Mill, with 5,000 bushels of rice, was destroyed by fire yesterday. The mill was the oldest in the city. The residence of EDWARD LUCAS was also much damaged. The property was generally insured.

#### Excitement at Louisville, Ky.

ATTEMPT TO LYNCH A PRISONER.

LOUISVILLE, Ky., Monday, Feb. 27.

A man calling himself JOHN HASKELL, hailing from Massachusetts, (but others say an Englishman, a sailor recently from New-Orleans,) 42 years old, was arrested on Saturday last for an unnatural crime. His examination, to-day, was postponed on account of the illness of one of the witnesses. This forenoon a crowd gathered about the Court-house, increasing till 2 o'clock, when the Mayor ordered the steam fire-engine to the spot, to drive away the crowd. This was temporarily successful, but towards dark the crowd swelled to several thousands, and an attack on the jail and the hanging of the prisoner were apprehended. The military were ordered to hold themselves in readiness. Two cannons were placed inside the jail, and the police marshaled, keeping the square in front of it clear, and arresting several intoxicated and turbulent persons. At 5 o'clock this afternoon Judge BULLOCK addressed the crowd, urging moderation, and saying that the persons interested in the prosecution desired no riotous conduct, but were willing that the prisoner should be dealt with by the law.

The crowd is now (9:30 P. M.) gradually dispersing, and although great indignation exists against the prisoner, the fears of an attack upon the jail to-night are subsiding.

#### Stand of Colors for the Seventh Regiment.

WASHINGTON, Monday, Feb. 27.

Both branches of the Common Council to-nigh passed, unanimously, resolutions of thanks to the military who visited the City on the occasion of the recent inauguration of the statue of WASHINGTON, and specially to the Seventh Regiment, National Guard, of New-York. They also voted to present to the latter in the name of the city a handsome stand of colors. Mr. WARD introduced the resolution.

#### From Texas.

REPORT OF THE RIO GRANDE COMMISSIONERS—ADJOURNMENT OF THE TEXAS LEGISLATURE.

WASHINGTON, Monday, Feb. 27.

The New-Orleans *Picayune*, of Wednesday, is received by Adams' Express.

The Galveston *Civilian*, of the 17th, says that Gov. HOUSTON has transmitted to the President the result of the labors of the Texas Commissioners on the Rio Grande. He says that unless immediate steps are taken for the efficient protection of the frontier of Texas, he will himself move to repel the present invasion and prevent a recurrence of the measures progressing in and out of Texas, looking to a protectorate in Northern Mexico. The Commissioners report that there is no certainty of quiet without a partial occupation of Mexico.

The Texas Legislature adjourned on the 13th inst., without action on the South Carolina resolutions.

#### The Marietta and Cincinnati Railroad.

SALE OF THE ROAD AND RECONSTRUCTION OF THE COMPANY.

BUFFALO, Monday, Feb. 27.

The Marietta and Cincinnati Railroad, with the property and effects belonging to it, was sold at Chillicothe yesterday by ORLANDO SMITH, in accordance with a decree of the Court. The property was purchased in the name of NOAH L. WILSON, DAVID GIBSON and others, Trustees under a compromise-agreement for capitalization. The effect of the sale will be the reorganization of the Company free of debt, as the value of the property is to be represented entirely by the capital stock, all the mortgages being wiped out. The property was sold for the minimum fixed by the Court, two hundred thousand dollars.

#### Important Patent Decision.

PATERSON, N. J., Monday, Feb. 27.

Judge DICKERSON, of the United States Circuit Court, New-Jersey, this day granted an injunction at the suit of CHARLES GOODYEAR and the New-York Belting and Packing Company, restraining DUNBAR & JOSLIN, of Trenton, from making billiard strips, car springs, and other articles of India-rubber, in violation of the patent of CHARLES GOODYEAR. The defence was, that the defendants had patents for using sulphurates and shale; but it was proved, and not denied, that rubber cannot be vulcanized without the use of free sulphur.

#### Accident to the Steamer Jura.

BOSTON, Monday, Feb. 27.

The Cunard steamer *Jura*, from Liverpool on the 11th inst., put into New-Bedford this afternoon, having on Thursday, the 23d, broke her engine off Georges' Shoal. She will await the arrival of a steam-tug to tow her to New-York.

[It is needless to say that the dispatch in the morning papers of yesterday announcing the arrival of the *Jura* at this port was incorrect.—ED. TIMES.]

#### Fire in Philadelphia.

PHILADELPHIA, Monday, Feb. 27.

A fire broke out this evening in the drug warehouse of CHARLES ELLIS & Co., originating in the explosion of a can of ether in the packing-room, and seriously burning a female employe. The fire was extinguished with little damage to the building, but the extensive stock received much injury from the water.

#### Loss of the Steamboat Portsmouth.

ST. JOSEPH, Monday, Feb. 27.

The steamboat *Portsmouth*, of the Hannibal and St. Joseph Railroad Line, which left here on Saturday, bound for Kansas City, with a cargo of lumber and other stuff, struck a snag and sunk near Leavenworth on Sunday. She went down in twelve feet of water, and is a total loss. She is insured. Most of the cargo will be recovered.

#### Later from Minatitlan.

NEW-ORLEANS, Monday, Feb. 27.

Minatitlan dates of the 12th inst. are received. They state that the Mexican war-steamer *Fire* arrived there on the 7th, dismantled the fort and took the guns to Vera Cruz, by order of JUAREZ.

The United States Marines at Tehuantepec had interfered to prevent Americans from being driven out.

#### Adjournment of the Alabama Legislature.

MONTGOMERY, Ala., Monday, Feb. 27.

The State Legislature adjourned this morning. The Governor failed to approve the Convention bill.

Mr. JACKSON, ex-Speaker of the House of Representatives, died at Autauga on Sunday.

#### Arrest of an Alleged Counterfeit Money Dealer.

BOSTON, Monday, Feb. 27.

ALONZO P. BURRILL, a broker at No. 16 State-street, was arrested to-day upon the charge of dealing in counterfeit and broken bank-bills. Several hundred dollars of the stuff were found in his possession.

#### Murder in Georgia.

AUGUSTA, Ga., Monday, Feb. 27.

The Rome (Ga.) *Courier* of Saturday reports the brutal murder of ROBERT THOMPSON and his wife on the previous Tuesday. Mr. THOMPSON was a merchant and Postmaster of Sugar Valley, Ga.

#### Death of Dr. John Barker.

MEADVILLE, Pa., Monday, Feb. 27.

Dr. JOHN BARKER, President of the Alleghany College in this place, died suddenly at 2 o'clock on Sunday afternoon.

#### North River Opening.

RONDOUT, N. Y., Monday, Feb. 27.

The ferry between this place and Rhinebeck station is now running regularly, connecting with all trains on the Hudson River Railroad.

#### Markets by Telegraph.

PHILADELPHIA, Monday, Feb. 27.

FLOUR firm, at \$5 75@\$6 25 for superfine. WHEAT 2c.@3c. higher; sales of 4,500 bushels, at \$1 55@\$1 57 for white and \$1 40 for red. CORN dull; sales of 3,000 bushels yellow at 75c.@76c. OATS 43c.@44½c. PORK—Mess, \$18 75; Prime, \$13@\$15. WHISKY dull, at 23½c.@25c.

BALTIMORE, Monday, Feb. 27.

FLOUR quiet and firm; Howard-street, \$5 50; Ohio City Mills held at \$5 37½. WHEAT active; Red, \$1 30@\$1 33; White, \$1 40@\$1 50. CORN active and firmer, at 69c.@71c. by measure, and 73c.@74c. for White and Yellow, by weight. PORK steady; Mess at \$18@\$18 25; Prime advanced 50c., sales at \$14@\$14 50. WHISKY dull, at 24½c.

CHARLESTON, Monday, Feb. 27.

COTTON unchanged; sales to-day 1,700 bales.

SAVANNAH, Monday, Feb. 27.

COTTON—Sales to-day 650 bales, with more sellers than buyers, and holders pressing on the market.

AUGUSTA, Monday, Feb. 27.

COTTON—Sales unimportant, with little inquiry, and prices weak.

CINCINNATI, Monday, Feb. 27.

FLOUR dull and unchanged. WHISKY steady at \$6 37½. PROVISIONS generally unchanged. LARD a shade easier. BACON and bulk meats—a small business doing, but held firmly. MESS PORK—no sales; offered at \$17@\$17 50.

NEW-ORLEANS, Monday, Feb. 27.

COTTON firm; sales to-day 10,500 bales. SUGAR steady, at 7⅛c.@7½c. MOLASSES, 38c.@39c. CORN firm; yellow, 75c.@78c.; white, 80c.@85½c. PROVISIONS firm; Mess Pork, \$13 30@\$16 75. Freights and Exchange unchanged.

#### Exchanges.

CINCINNATI, Monday, Feb. 27.

Money market firm, and the demand fully up to the supply. Sight Exchange on New-York unchanged.

#### Outrages on the Indians on the Mendocino Reservation.

If accounts that reach us from the Mendocino Reservation, says the Petaluma *Argus* of Feb. 4, are reliable, the villanies that are there perpetrated are exceeded only by the exploits of the valorous heroes of the North, and the whole affair is an outrage upon the Indians, and a swindle against the Government. Our information is direct, and comes to us under such circumstances as compel us to believe that it is reliable. Parties who have contracts for furnishing the Indians with beef and blankets are continually receiving money from the Government for articles the Indians never obtain. While the Indians are dispersed over the country, earning their own living and getting nothing from these contractors, the Government is daily charged for supplies that would be adequate to support every Indian on the Reservation. The blankets furnished the Indians, and for which the Government is charged at a high rate, are absolutely worthless—so rotten and damaged that they are of no value whatever. Nor is this all. The women are not protected against the abuses of unprincipled white men, but are subjected to indignities too revolting to describe, while the children are often sold to those who think they can make them serviceable. If these things are true, it is time this infamous system was abolished, and something else instituted in its place. For the sake of humanity we hope these things are not true; yet, in the face of so many acts of perfidy and cruelty on the part of those who are attempting to make money out of the Indians, nothing need surprise us.

# The New-York Times.

VOL. IX—NO. 2683. NEW-YORK, THURSDAY, APRIL 26, 1860. PRICE TWO CENTS.


## CHARLESTON CONVENTION.

### PROCEEDINGS OF THE THIRD DAY.

### THE WOOD DELEGATION EXCLUDED.

### TRIUMPH OF THE DOUGLAS PARTY.

### Douglas and Orr to be the Candidates.

### THE CINCINNATI PLATFORM REPUDIATED.

Special Dispatch to the New-York Times.

CHARLESTON, Wednesday, April 25.

Ex-Gov. ROBINSON, of Vermont, died of apoplexy at the Mills House last night.

The vote on the New-York case is as follows: Twenty-three against WOOD, and seven for him, three not voting. North Carolina, Georgia, Alabama, Mississippi, Texas, Arkansas and California voted for him. Oregon and Louisiana dodged. New-York, of course, did not vote.

During the afternoon session, Mr. BURNETT, of Alabama, made a speech, reflecting bitterly on the fact that the New-York and Illinois delegations had been allowed to vote on the proceedings of the Convention before the difficulties in their midst had been settled.

Judge CRUMP, of Missouri, as the Chairman of the Committee on Credentials, reported upon the contested seats, in favor of the sitting members. Messrs. DOHERTY and CHAPIN, of Massachusetts; LANAHAN and BRANDT, of Maryland; the Richardson delegation from Illinois, and the Richmond delegation from New-York, are entitled to vote in the Convention. This announcement was received with applause. Mr. BROOKS, of Alabama, presented a minority report signed by Messrs. Brooks, Dudley, Manning, Green, Partridge and Barry, from Alabama, California, Arkansas, Texas, Georgia, and Mississippi.

After dragooning the vote of Louisiana this morning it was cast in favor of the Majority Report. BROOKS, of Alabama, raised a tremendous hubhub by claiming the floor for the purpose of arguing the case. He was instantly interrupted by Mr. WHITLEY, of Delaware, who insisted on the right of the majority to be heard. The previous question was called. Mr. WHITLEY pledged himself to demand it when he closed, and thus obtained the floor when Mr. BROOKS closed. When Mr. WHITLEY's time was up the hammer fell, and he had forgot to call the previous question. He felt badly about it, and appealed to the clemency of the Chair. Mr. CUSHING said that he could not supply memory to the delegates.

The Minority Report suggested that both delegations be allowed seats upon the floor; though entitled to but thirty-five votes, each to cast seventeen votes, and the odd one to be thrown in alternation.

Mr. WHITLEY took the floor to reply. He spoke fifteen minutes. He urged the members by their sense of honor and their love of justice to cast WOOD from them, and to embrace the other wing. He was frequently interrupted, but in spite of the storm maintained his position, and made a strong, effective argument. The debate became conversational and personal. The excitement was intense. Mr. BARRY, from Mississippi, was particularly vehement in his denunciation of the majority, and was very violent in his manner. He asked members to correct him if he made misstatements, and taking him at his word, they crowded around him, and all order was lost sight of.

At the end of his fifteen minutes, it required all the skill and authority of the Chair to recall the House to a sense of its propriety. The question was then taken on the minority report, which was rejected by 55 yeas to 210½ nays. The result was received with prolonged applause.

Mr. NORTH, of Pennsylvania, offered a resolution tendering honorary seats to WOOD and his delegation upon the floor of the House. This suited neither party. The minority would accept no courtesy; the majority would yield none.

Mr. LAWRENCE, of Louisiana, jumped upon the chair, and began a stump-speech against the resolution. Fifty cries of order roused his ire. Mr. NORTH appealed to him to yield the floor, that he might withdraw the resolution. He declined. Mr. BARRY, of Mississippi, and other Southern members continually posted him as to points. Frequent points of order were taken, but invariably ruled out. Twilight came on. Everybody crowded around the speaker. Anger, contempt, mirth and exultation were alternately visible in the faces around, and at one time the prospects for a row cheered us considerably.

District-Attorney WATERBURY, of New-York, finally choked him off by a Parliamentary dodge, which put off the further consideration of the subject till to-morrow. The Hall has been crowded to suffocation all day.

Mr. COCHRANE made allusions as usual to his bachelorhood, and the joyous welcome which he would extend to the ladies if they could favor his side of the Hall with their presence. A long and somewhat tedious running fire was kept up by him and a Missouri member on the same subject, till by a vote of the House they were laid on the table together.

The Wood Delegation had the New-York steamer detained until 7 o'clock this evening, that they might avail themselves thereof.

Mr. WATERBURY telegraphed to New-York to have a hundred guns fired on account of WOOD's defeat.

Much amusement was created on the arrival of the New-York papers, at the two columns of telegraph matter from Charleston, when it was patent that not half of it passed the wires.

Douglas stock is on the rise. He has thirty votes now in the New-York Delegation. They probably will not be able to vote solid on the first ballot; but bets are high—in some cases three to one—in favor of a unit for DOUGLAS on the second ballot. Even bets are offered for the first ballots.

Judge SMALLEY's arrangements produce great dissatisfaction. No one is suited; everybody is inconvenienced.

The weather, to-day, has been delightfully cool, and the rush for the Hall by the people who desire to see the magnates in council was fairly terrific.

The Platform Committee are in trouble. They want to please all sides, but they cannot do it. Trouble in the camp is certain, unless they embody the Slave code, and defeat is certain in November, if they do.

Private hospitalities are constant. The citizens of Charleston vie with each other in endeavoring to disabuse the mind of the public of the impression made thereon by the reports of the extra charges and closed doors.

The Convention adjourned at 6 o'clock, to follow the body of Gov. ROBINSON, of Vermont, to the boat.

HOWARD.

From the Associated Press.

CHARLESTON, Wednesday, April 25.

The Convention met at 10 o'clock.

The gallery was crowded with ladies, and on motion several hundred who were crowding outside, were admitted to the floor of the Convention, occasioning much good feeling.

The resolution restricting speakers to fifteen minutes, and but once on the same subject, was taken up, debated and rejected, ayes 120, nays 121.

Mr. ROBINSON, Chairman of the Vermont delegation, died of apoplexy this morning.

A resolution relative to debate, restricting speakers to fifteen minutes on all subjects except the Platform was then introduced.

A Southern delegate demanded that there should be no gag-law on any subject.

At 11 o'clock the resolution was adopted limiting speaking to fifteen minutes on all subjects except the platform, and on that the rule of the House of Representatives will apply, limiting each speaker to one hour.

The Committee on Credentials announced that they would be ready to make their report this afternoon.

The Convention then, on motion, adjourned at noon until 4 o'clock.

The Committee on Credentials will report in favor of the Dean Richmond Delegation. The Wood Delegation received but six votes, being those of Mississippi, Texas, Alabama, North Carolina, Georgia and California.

The Committee on Platform have just repudiated the Cincinnati Platform, by a vote of 17 to 15, the Southern delegates demanding a platform that will not be liable to two constructions.

The nomination of Mr. DOUGLAS is considered certain. The entire New-York, and a part of the South Carolina delegation, will vote for him.

The Convention met at 4 o'clock.

A resolution to appoint a National Committee to act for the next four years was discussed and finally referred to a Select Committee, to inquire into the propriety of giving the National Committee power to name both the time and place of holding the Convention.

The Committee on Credentials reported that the sitting delegates from New-York, Illinois, Massachusetts and Maryland, (the latter T. M. LANNAHEN and ROBERT J. BRENT,) are entitled to their seats.

The report of the minority of the Committee was presented. It is signed by the members of the Committee from Alabama, California, Arkansas, Texas, Georgia and Mississippi, and recommends that one half of each of the New-York contestants be admitted to the Convention, each to cast 17 votes.

The debate on the report of the Committee on Credentials was continued until 6 o'clock, when it was closed by the previous question being called.

A vote was first taken on the Illinois question, and the Douglas delegates were admitted.

The vote was next taken on the Maryland question, and Messrs. BRANDT and LANAHAN were awarded seats.

A vote was then taken by States on the minority report of the Committee to divide the votes between the two New-York delegations.

The States that voted aye were: North Carolina, 5; Georgia, 10; Virginia, 3½; Missouri, 1; Alabama, 9; Mississippi, 7; Texas, 4; Tennessee, 9; California, 3½; Arkansas, 3. Ayes 55; nays 210—so the Dean Richmond delegates were admitted and the Wood delegates excluded.

The announcement of the result was received with cheers and great excitement.

A resolution to admit the Wood delegates to honorable seats on the floor added to the excitement, but the resolution was finally laid over, under the rule, until to-morrow.

Mr. MONTGOMERY moved that the resolution for appointing a National Committee be laid over until after the nomination of candidates for the Presidency.

The death of Gov. ROBINSON, of Vermont, was announced to the Convention, and a resolution of condolence with his family was adopted. It was also resolved to accompany the remains from the Mills House to the boat, immediately after the adjournment.

The Convention then, at 7 o'clock, adjourned.

There appears to be a better feeling between the North and South, and the Committee on Platforms are laboring for harmony. The large vote on excluding the Wood Delegation is regarded as favorable to DOUGLAS. No one but the extreme Southerners now dispute his nomination.

## FROM MISSOURI.

### Missouri Democratic Convention—Buchanan Platform—Douglas Delegates—The State Ticket—Claib. Jackson Candidate for Governor—Thomas C. Reynolds Candidate for Lieutenant-Governor—Prospects of the Opposition Party.

*Correspondence of the New-York Times.*

ST. LOUIS, Tuesday, April 24, 1860.

The last National Democratic Convention of this State afforded a most charming illustration of the difference between principle and practice. The platform, which they adopted with a reasonable degree of harmony for so heterogeneous an assembly, most decidedly condemned the heresy of squatter sovereignty, and cordially indorsed the administration of JAMES BUCHANAN as wise, efficient, and truly Democratic. The State nominations were made in the same spirit, all Douglas men were most carefully eschewed, and the friends of GREEN and BUCHANAN were elevated to the chief places in the true church. So unsatisfactory, indeed, were the proceedings the first two or three days of the Convention, to the ardent admirers of "the Little Giant," that the editorial correspondent of the *Republican* telegraphed home that the Convention was packed, and that all hopes were lost.

But a change came over the assembled wisdom of the party when the nomination for delegates to Charleston became the order of the day. Then more than half the delegation was composed of Douglas men, who had all, however, voted for a declaration of political faith, in which every line condemns the abominable heresies of their chosen chief.

The Democratic State ticket is not a strong ticket, although with their overwhelming vote in the rural districts they could afford to put a comparatively weak force in the field. CLAIBORNE F. JACKSON, the nominee for the Gubernatorial chair, now so worthily filled by his erratic Excellency BOB STEWART, first rendered himself conspicuous in Missouri by his opposition to BENTON. He introduced the so-called Calhoun resolution into the Legislature, and thereby incurred the bitter enmity of one of the best haters of his day and generation. BENTON made the hills and valleys of Missouri ring with his denunciation of a foe whom this notice alone prevented from being contemptible. Thanks to the imprudence of the great man, and the indefatigable industry of the little man, the defection from BENTON grew from a cloud smaller than a man's hand to the storm which hurled the veteran statesman from "his ancient, solitary reign."

Apart from his successful contest with BENTON, CLAIB JACKSON, as he is familiarly called, has occupied no very prominent place in the public eye. He has been Bank Commissioner of the State, and his policy in that office will be one of the issues of the canvass. He stands in a somewhat equivocal position upon the great question of Missouri—the railroad system of the State—having been opposed previous to his nomination to any further grant of State aid to the roads, but having also pledged himself to the St. Louis delegation to the Democratic Convention to advocate a railroad bill if he were nominated. JACKSON is a good stump speaker, which is a prime requisite in the candidate for Governor in a State where the aspirant for executive honors is expected personally to address from the hustings his fellow citizens in every portion of the State. In this department of his canvass, JACKSON will be very efficiently assisted by the gentleman who fills the candidacy for ornamental position of Lieutenant-Governor on the ticket, THOMAS C. REYNOLDS, Esq., of St. Louis. Mr. REYNOLDS, although not possessed of any very great intellectual vigor, has a mind of considerable activity and sprightliness. He has had the advantage of a thorough culture by books, travel and society, and he alone can give to the Democratic ticket whatever of scholarly flavor it may possess. Mr. REYNOLDS was entitled to this honorary distinction, since he is one of the few martyrs to Democratic principles in Missouri. He was the unsuccessful opponent of FRANK BLAIR for Congress from this District four years ago, and not only suffered a defeat at the ballot-box, but in one of the little incidents of the canvass, was compelled to stand in imminent peril of life and limb from the pistol of Mr. B. GRATZ BROWN, the then editor of the *Democrat*. REYNOLDS escaped unscathed, while BROWN with a bullet in his leg, was borne limping from the field of honor.

If the Opposition in Missouri are aided by the Republicans nominating any conservative man at Chicago, and more particularly if EDWARD BATES be the nominee, and if they should make a judicious selection of a standard-bearer, say ROLLINS, for the State canvass, Missouri, despite Senators GREEN and POLK, and an entire National Democratic delegation in the lower House, may be considered next August and November as among the very doubtful States on the Democratic slate. Should, however, SEWARD be nominated, or any other Republican leader who stands upon an "irrepressible conflict" platform, the result would not only be an overwhelming Democratic victory, but the Emancipation or Free Democratic Party of St. Louis would be fearfully crippled, and the Americans and Conservatives would add to the Democratic strength by casting their votes for some harmless and impossible candidate.

While I am indulging in these surmises and speculations the Charleston Convention is about organizing, and upon its action will depend, in good part, not only the probable course of the Chicago Convention, but the conduct of the canvass in Missouri, and every other State in the Union.

Q.

## FROM WASHINGTON.

### THE FUGITIVE SLAVE-LAW DISCUSSED.

### Entertaining Speech of Mr. Corwin of Ohio.

WASHINGTON, Wednesday, April 25.

As the first legislative step on the subject which has been privately discussed during the past six months, Mr. MORRIS, of Illinois, will urge the passage of a joint resolution appointing Mr. ORR, of South Carolina; Gen. DONIPHAN, of Missouri; and Gov. WOOD, of Illinois, Commissioners, to negotiate with the Mormons for the sale of their possessions, on the express condition that they remove within a reasonable time from the limits and jurisdiction of the United States. The Commissioners are to make their report to the President by the next session of Congress. The ground for this movement is to prevent a recurrence of war and bloodshed, as the history of the Mormons in Missouri and Illinois shows that they cannot, owing to their peculiarities, live on terms of peace and good neighborhood with contiguous settlements. It is also treated as a question of economy to the Treasury.

Mr. BURLINGAME, from the Committee on Foreign Affairs, will report a bill in accordance with his resolution providing for a first-class mission to Sardinia, the Envoy to receive $12,000, and the Secretary of Legation $1,800 per annum. The Sardinian *Chargé d'Affaires* is delighted with the movement.

Railroad officials state that a large amount of bills on the Clinton Bank of Westernport, Md., a broken concern, are being forced upon the unwary, and it is believed that a still larger amount has been sent into the West.

### HOUSE OF REPRESENTATIVES.

WASHINGTON, Wednesday, April 25.

Mr. COLFAX, of Indiana, (Rep.,) introduced, by mutual consent, a bill providing that the regular dealers in newspapers and periodicals may receive packages by mail at *pro rata* rates. Maps, engravings, phonographic paper and envelopes, books, bound and unbound; blank or printed cards to go through the mails at one cent per ounce under 1,500 miles, now charged letter postage, by a recent decision of the Department; and the present California postage to apply on letters carried by the overland mail from the Atlantic States to the Pacific coast, even if under 3,000 miles.

Mr. COLFAX, of Indiana, (Rep.,) stated that he would call up the bill when the House was full.

The House went into Committee of the Whole on the State of the Union.

Mr. FLORENCE, of Pennsylvania, (Dem.,) briefly explained his tariff substitute. Simple in the details, it avoids the perplexities and complications of the main bill; it is free from compound duties; has no minimums; gives specific duties for our country's staples; leaving for further legislation any extension of the system. He appealed to all true friends of the measure to discard party and vote for the bill, which, in his judgment, can succeed, and not join in the vain search for what cannot reasonably be expected by its most sanguine advocates.

Mr. CURTIS, of Iowa, (Rep.,) gave notice that, at an early day, he intended to bring the Pacific Railroad bill before the House for discussion and passage.

Mr. ELIOT, of Massachusetts, (Rep.,) in the course of his remarks, said that it would be the happiest day of his life when, at the proper time and under proper surroundings, and at a proper request of the citizens of the District of Columbia, he could aid them to strike off the shackles of the slaves here. If he were to say outside what he was now saying in this hall, what security would he have that he would not be put under bonds to keep the peace? The doctrines of the Republican platform were recognized by the fathers of the Republic. There is not one doctrine of his party which does not find its root and beginning from them. On the contrary, the doctrine of the Democratic Party was subject to Slavery, which has arrayed itself against the theory and practice of the leading statesmen, North and South, from the beginning of the Government down to the time of CALHOUN.

Mr. CORWIN, of Ohio, (Rep.,) at the conclusion of Mr. ELIOT's speech, rose to an explanation. He understood the gentlemen from Massachusetts to say that he (Mr. CORWIN) was in favor of all the provisions of the law of 1858 for the capture and rendition of fugitive slaves.

Mr. ELIOT—Yes, Sir.

Mr. CORWIN—The gentleman, then, misunderstood his opinions upon that point, notwithstanding he had endeavored to be very clear and explicit upon it; and lest others might also have misunderstood him, he would reply to the remarks of the gentleman. He had unmistakably stated, upon a thousand occasions, in public assemblies, in that hall, and various other places, that he did not agree with all the provisions of that act. That was the extent to which he had gone. He had stated that he had some doubts as to the constitutionality of that law, although better lawyers than he was, had expressed their opinion on its constitutionality.

Mr. ELIOT was glad to find the gentleman went farther than he had known him to do before on this point. A few steps further, and he thought he would be able to shake hands with the gentleman from Ohio, for that, then, they should occupy the same platform.

Mr. CORWIN—It had become fashionable for gentlemen in this as well as in the other hall of the Legislature, to set themselves right, and to pay great regard for what was called the "record." Now, he thought that it would be well for some among them if there was no record of their acts. [Laughter.] And, if he was to be interpreter, and his acts recorded according to these interpretations, it would be well for him, humble as his acts were, if his were never to be recorded. [Continued laughter.] In order, therefore, once for all, to make himself perfectly understood upon this point, he wished to say—first, as to what he had often asserted, that he was opposed to the power being placed in the hands of the President of putting his construction upon the laws, from the fact that there was the danger of that power falling into the hands of a President unfriendly to the institutions of the country. In 1848, when Gen. TAYLOR was elected to the Presidency, this opinion of his became to be an opinion very popularly entertained, especially with the old Whig Party of that day. In consequence of this, during the canvass of 1848 this opinion was very universally inculcated by himself and his friends in the Northwestern States, who advocated the election of General TAYLOR, which opinion was that the President of the United States should not exercise the veto power except in cases where the act presented for his approval was clearly unconstitutional—that the power of construing the law rested with the people and their representatives in either branch of the Legislature—that it was the right of Congress alone, elected by the people of all the States, to determine the policy and propriety of the laws—and that the President was not bound to affix his signature to any law which he believed was unconstitutional. Very likely that principle was carried to an extreme; but it was upon that hypothesis that very generally the voice of the Whig Party were cast for Gen. TAYLOR as President and for Mr. FILLMORE as Vice-President. It so happened that he was a member of that Administration, and the principle was well understood, and acted upon, during the whole of that Administration, that neither the President nor his Cabinet were the proper persons to put a construction upon the laws, but that the whole people, here assembled, were to determine this question, and not the President or his Cabinet. He was a member of the Senate when the law of 1850 for the recapture and rendition of fugitive slaves, which was a compromise of the law of 1793, was introduced, and he at that time more than once mentioned to the gentleman who had introduced the Fugitive Slave law, that he was greatly mistaken if he thought by that means of securing to the people of the South greater facilities for recapturing their runaway slaves than was afforded by the law of 1793. Events since then had proved that he was right in his judgment, for there had been more runaway slaves recaptured by the act of 1793 than had been recaptured by the amended act of the law of 1850. He believed still, as he believed then, that it was a great mistake to replace the law of 1793 by that of 1850. He did at the present time, and always had entertained doubts as to the constitutionality of that part of the law relating to the appointment of Court Commissioners under the Fugitive Slave law. He was, indeed, very much disappointed that the law did not provide that the Commissioners should be appointed by the President, with the consent of the Senate, for he thought then, as he did now, that the Commissioners acted, not in a ministerial character altogether, but in some sort in a judicial capacity, and therefore the necessity that those parties should have been selected by the President, with the consent of the Senate. That was the doubt he had as to the constitutionality of the law, which he yielded to the opinions of his colleagues in the Cabinet. Under these circumstances, he was willing, though as he had often declared that he did not see the necessity or expediency of it, seeing that the Constitution itself provided in some shape or other for the recapture of runaway negroes owing labor and service to a master, that the President should give his sanction to the bill. That the Constitution did in some way provide for the recapture of runaway slaves he thought none would deny. Now, what would they gain by having a written Constitution if they did not abide by the fundamental principles of that Constitution? The Fathers of the Republic, as they called the old men who bequeathed to them the Constitution, knowing how uncertain a thing would be a traditionary constitution, determined that the instrument which secured to the people the rights of free men should be written down, and printed, and transmitted to them as the embodiment of the principles of their organic law. That was the great idea. They secured it against the changes which the great charter of the English Constitution suffered during the reigns of the Henrys and Edwards, the Plantagenets, the Tudors and the Stuarts. They knew that the traditionary Constitution of England changed with every fresh reign, just as the will of the monarch desired; therefore it was that they determined that the Constitution they had formed, and which they bequeathed to us, should be fixed and stable, and remain so forever. When a change becomes necessary, the Constitution itself provides how that change should be effected. The men who framed the Constitution enacted the law known as the act of 1793, and under that law, and under that Constitution, they had lived and prospered for fifty or sixty years. For his own part, he humbled himself before these old men, the fathers of the Republic, and acknowledged that they knew better than he did what was necessary for the future government of a great country. And what did they say? They said that if a man owing labor and service to another, should escape from the State where such labor or service was due, he should be returned to his master, according to the law of the State from whence he fled. The words are: "That he shall be returned and delivered up." Now, he thought that the provisions of the Constitution were all-sufficient to meet the wants and demands of Southern gentlemen, without any amendment of the act of 1793, by the enactment of the Fugitive Slave law of 1850. For his own part, if he owned slaves, and they escaped from him into another State, he would ask no other law than that of 1793 in his hands to follow his slaves into any other State of the Union and demand their rendition. Everybody knew that by a "man owing labor and service to another," he meant in fact a slave. If that slave fled from Virginia into Ohio, his master could follow him, lay hold of him, and, under the Constitution, demand that he be delivered up to him, and none would be found to dispute his right. The Constitution, to this extent, recognizes the man owning service and labor as property—qualified property. But if a man claiming property in a slave follows him into Ohio, whither he may have fled, and attempts to carry him off with violence, then he subjects himself to the operation of the common law. But, under the Constitution, a runaway slave must be delivered up by the person to whom he owes labor and service proving his claim to him, and this without any specific law such as that of 1850. The Judge before whom the case would be brought would hardly pronounce the Constitution unconstitutional and refuse to deliver the runaway up. The Constitution does not say that such a man shall be discharged; no, but that he shall be delivered up; and, therefore, he asserted that it was a great mistake in Southern men to suppose that the Fugitive Slave law was necessary to the security of their rights in this respect. If a man owed service and labor, and he escaped from the master to whom such labor and service were due, then I say the Constitution provided for his recovery, and when captured he must be delivered up to his master. That was his opinion. He might be wrong, but all he had to say was that the Constitution so provided, and so had the law decided; and in that respect he did not think the Constitution was unconstitutional. [Laughter.] Now, surely, in the year 1860, they were not going back, and to say that the several States should legislate for or against that law. He thought it hardly necessary that he should remind his friends of the propriety of being consistent; not that it was necessary that men should be consistent, but it looked better. [Laughter.] But when men come to speak of Slavery as a thing that Congress can interfere with, they go right back from the traditions and principles of the fathers of the Republic. If the fathers were right fifty years ago, seeing the Constitution appears to prohibit the extension of Slavery, was it not as likely that they were right in enacting the law of 1793 for the rendition of runaway negroes who owed labor and service to their masters? If the arguments in favor of one view of the case were worth anything, they must be of equal force in support of the other view. Now, the argument of the Republican Party which it was most difficult for the gentlemen from the South to get over was, that the men who framed the Constitution construed it in that way. It was not, therefore, consistent to say that any of the fathers of the Republic, the framers of the Constitution, did anything favoring Slavery. Now the first construction put upon the Constitution by the very men who framed it he thought was the best and most reliable, and they held that it was the right of Congress to make laws for the recapture of runaway slaves.

Mr. CARTER, of New-York, (Rep.)—Do I understand the gentleman to say that a master can lay hold of a black man whom he calls his slave? Can he lay hold of him in Ohio and take him solely on the ground that the slave was his property?

Mr. CORWIN—If he had time to write in his own office an answer to the question, he would answer him at once in the affirmative; but he answered now with this qualification—That the master could do so, and was entitled to retake his slave, because the Constitution says that the man who escapes, owing labor and service to another, shall, on being recaptured, be delivered up, and the master shall take him back to the place from whence he fled.

Mr. CARTER asked, if a slave was brought into a Free State by his master, and that he there made his escape, would he be subject to the same law, and liable to be recaptured and delivered up to his master?

Mr. CORWIN—No, Sir. He understood the gentleman to ask him whether, if a master took his slave voluntarily from Kentucky to Ohio, that then he would be as much a slave as before, and subject to the same law of rendition. In that case, he answered, no. When he spoke of the slave as property, he meant qualified property, as described in the Constitution—a man who owed service and labor to another. He held that Slavery was the creature of local law. He knew that the right of a white man to work a black man, and hold the descendants of that man as slaves, was the creature of local law, or laws of local usage. The framers of the Constitution knew very well that these black fellows would run away whenever they got the chance, and they provided a means whereby he could be recovered. The Constitution does not provide for the recovery of runaway horses in Ohio, because the law which regulated this description of property was well understood everywhere, and was decided by the common law everywhere. If it could be supposed that the negro was property everywhere, and that he could be seized everywhere, it would be perfect nonsense to provide a law for his recovery, providing that the master can follow him and take him back.

Mr. CARTER asked whether it was in consequence of the negro being property that the master could take him back, or whether it was merely in consequence of his violating the sovereign law of the State from which he had fled?

Mr. CORWIN thought that on this point none could misunderstand him. If a negro is property in Virginia, and he runs away from labor and service he owes his master, the constitution says the master can follow him into Ohio, whither he has fled, and take him back; but if the master brings him voluntarily into Ohio, as he explained before, then the man had not escaped, had not violated any law in that way, and he was free. That was the law of Ohio.

Mr. ELIOT reported that the Constitution confers no power on Congress to legislate thereon, and in support of his position quoted the remark of Mr. WEBSTER in 1850, who said he always thought that part of the Constitution addressed itself to the Legislature of each State.

Mr. CORWIN replied that as all departments of the Government have recognized the power of Congress to pass a law for the recapture of fugitive slaves they must regard that as the true reading, otherwise we may lose the benefits of a written constitution. The law of 1793 was just as effectual as that of 1850, without the constitutional objections.

Messrs. CARTER, of New-York, (Rep.,) ELIOT and DAWES, of Massachusetts, (Rep.,) controverted the positions of Mr. CORWIN, who, in his further remarks, kept the audience in remarkably good humor. When his hour expired there was a general acquiescence that he should continue his speech.

Mr. CURTIS wished to know how much time he wanted.

Mr. CORWIN thought he would get through before the Chicago Convention. [Laughter.]

He made some good-natured hits at the South, which were all received in a similar spirit.

He said, among other things, that some would dissolve the Union to-morrow because their negroes run so fast they cannot catch them; but they ought to recollect that these negroes have to run through Slave States before they get to the Free. Why not kill the negroes South because they don't catch the fugitive? [Laughter.] JOHN BROWN got up a scheme in Chatham to operate in Virginia, contrary to our laws. Why not call on the British Government to deliver up those engaged in the transaction? If there was no other reason why this was not done it was because Great Britain wants our Cotton, and we don't desire to go to war with her. [Laughter.] It would not be long before Massachusetts, following the example of Indiana, would pass a law preventing free negroes coming thither, and so it would be with other Free States, when they found that they were going to have a negro pauper population. The Republican Party are not opposed to the recovery of fugitive negroes. There was not one in a hundred thousand who would undertake to repeal the present law, and substitute State legislation. Every body knows that we would not be in our present position if it had not been for the repeal of the Missouri Compromise.

His speech was generally moderate and conciliatory.

The Committee rose, and the House adjourned.

### WASHINGTON MATTERS.

#### FRANKING DOCUMENTS—THE TARIFF BILL—THE ART COMMISSION—HOW DO THE SECRET PROCEEDINGS OF THE COVODE COMMITTEE GET PUBLIC?—THE TOWN—LITERARY.

*Correspondence of the New-York Times.*

WASHINGTON, D. C., Monday, April 23, 1860.

A brief visit to the Executive Committee Rooms of the Democrats and Republicans, this evening well repaid the time and trouble of the excursion. Besides portraying the extreme interest felt in the proceedings at Charleston, we had an opportunity to view the "mill" which grinds out opinions for men all over the country. Several thousand speeches, of different stamps, from that of LOVEJOY and VAN WYCK, down the Republican scale, to that of HICKMAN and Senator PUGH, were piled on a long table in the Republican rooms. Around these tables were seated four or five Senators, and at least a dozen members of the House, working like beavers, franking documents. There must be several millions go through the Post-office from these two speech-dépôts. Of course, this is done to "disseminate knowledge among the poor people in the country." The Democrats are even worse than the Republicans in this respect. The Department has recently notified Members of Congress that documents cannot pass unless the frank upon them is genuine, and the practice which has heretofore prevailed of deputizing that business is therefore broken up. The Democrats to-night look exceedingly anxious, especially the friends of Mr. DOUGLAS. With them it is life and death. There were several bets of large amounts offered to-night by Anti-Douglas men on the nomination, but no takers were found. Up to the closing of the mail, not a word has been heard from there. Rumors of a row between the New-York delegations are afloat, and have created some sensation.

As the Pacific Railroad bill will be up soon in the House for consideration, financial and business men will be likely to pay considerable attention to it. When it comes up, Col. LANDER's bill proposing to build four hundred miles of the Eastern part of the road for $6,000 per mile from the Government, will be put in either as an amendment to Col. CURTIS' bill or as an original proposition. This may succeed if properly amended, as it is a practicable method of commencing this great enterprise.

Mr. SHERMAN gave notice in the House to-day of his intention to press a vote upon the Tariff bill at the earliest practicable moment. You will recollect that it comes up in the shape of a Treasury Note Loan, and upon that necessity the friends of the measure intend to press it through the Senate. It is a question of great importance, and the debate upon it will be protracted. The peculiarities of the measure have already been pointed out in this correspondence.

Mr. BROWN, Chairman of the National Art Commission, left this City to-night for Columbia, S. C., whither he goes to execute a large marble statue, for which he received the order and worked the model some time since. The report of the Commissioners upon the decoration of the public buildings and grounds in this city has been before Congress some time, but no action has been taken upon it. Mr. LAMBDEN, the second on the Commission, is also absent, and Mr. KENSETT is the only one who remains.

There was an attempt this morning, in the House, to discover the means by which the evidence respecting the letter of BUCHANAN to WALKER, and the testimony of the latter and SCHNABLE, in regard to affairs in Kansas, before the Covode Investigating Committee, were made public. Mr. COVODE did not seem to fancy the idea that the action of his Committee cannot be kept secret. It is certain that the Committee did not make public the details, so that it must have been done by the witnesses themselves or some outside party who was previously cognizant of the facts, and had them all in possession. But Mr. COVODE was not permitted to explain, on the ground that newspapers were not legitimate subjects for discussion in the House. We hope, therefore, that they will now be allowed, in future, to go on making public whatever is proper for the people to know without interference or molestation. With regard to this matter, it is probably the best thing the Democrats could do to hush it up.

The town is nearly deserted—nearly all the members have sent home their families, and more than half are absent themselves. Many of the Democrats are at Charleston. Some of them and very many Republicans are paired off and gone home. When they return from Charleston the Opposition men must go to Baltimore, and the next week nearly all the Republicans will spend in Chicago. When they return it will be oppressively hot here, so that about all the business, except the general and necessary appropriation bills, has been done that will be this session. This fact has taken off many outsiders, lobbyists, claimants and fashionable people.

Senator BAYARD received a dispatch from Charleston, and very soon after left for that place. It is thought that he has gone there to throw his weight into the balance in favor of the nomination of a Southern man. Of course, his presence there will be interpreted as having given up all hopes, himself, that he will be taken up.

Mr. DOUGLAS' house is crowded with visitors, day and evening, seeking news from the seat of war.

Half-a-million copies of Mr. SEWARD's late speech have recently been ordered for circulation in Pennsylvania and New-Jersey. One million of that and his Rochester speech have already been distributed in the former State alone.

Occasionally we have here a literary emanation although this is no latitude for them. We have just received one. Miss HARRIET FANNY REED has issued a novel, based upon historical facts, and a romance entitled the *Haunted Student*. It is an eccentric title and a still more eccentric work. I understand that it succeeds much better than was anticipated. Its emanation is at least a slight respite from the continual din of politics which reigns here.

H.

## LATE FROM ARIZONA.

### A Provisional Government Convention in Session—Constitution Adopted—Election of a Governor—Two Days' Proceedings Entire.

*Correspondence of the New-York Times.*

TUCSON, Tuesday, April 3, 1860.

A Convention of delegates from all parts of Arizona, called for the purpose of forming a Provisional Government, assembled in this place yesterday morning. The move originated with citizens of Eastern Arizona, who *modestly* apportioned the delegates in a manner that would insure them a controlling vote on any question that might come up. The citizens of Western Arizona were almost unanimously opposed to the measure, but sent delegates to represent their interests, with instructions to protest against any action inconsistent with the Constitution of the United States.

The Convention, which consisted of thirty-two delegates, thirteen from Western Arizona and nineteen from Eastern Arizona, was organized by the election of JAS. A. LUCAS, of Mesilla, as President, and GRANVILLE OURY as Secretary. It having been asserted that the design of the Convention was contrary to the spirit of the Constitution, a resolution was proposed to the effect that the members of the body be required to take the usual oath to support the Constitution. This was finally carried, after meeting with some opposition from those who looked upon the movement as not only unconstitutional but treasonable, while, singular to say, it was advocated by those who most strongly urged the Provisional Government. A Committee of seven was appointed to present a Constitution for the consideration of the body, which contained but one member of the minority. The Chairman, who evidently is a novice in parliamentary practice, pursued the same plan throughout, and gave the minority no opportunity to claim a fair hearing. This was not done from design, it is generally believed, but through inexperience.

The Committee reported a preamble and constitution at the afternoon session of the first day, and in order to afford every facility for inspection it was decided to lay the consideration of it over till Tuesday. Meanwhile the objections of the delegates from Western Arizona were stated, and a long discussion took place, involving the question of constitutionality. It was urged by the friends of the measure that Congress, having failed to legislate in our behalf, we had no other course left; that it was a step designed only for temporary use, to cease the moment we were provided with a government by Congress; that it was not designed to wrest the country from the American eagle, but only to meet our wants in a manner that would secure law and order. By its adoption we were securing for ourselves a protection essential to every well-constituted society, which we had always been without, and that we were merely making a temporary provision for supplying the neglect of Congress till such time as that body may see proper to listen to our petitions, when the Provisional Government will cease.

These arguments, backed as they are by the great necessity existing for the establishment of law and order, had great weight with the Opposition, and it was evident on the morning of the second day that the measure would be adopted with little if any opposition. The day was mostly spent in debating the Constitution proposed before the Convention, but it finally received sundry amendments, and was at length adopted with but one dissenting voice. A brief abstract of this document will be interesting to your readers. The preamble reads as follows:

"We, the people of Arizona, in order to form a Government, establish justice, insure domestic tranquility, and provide for the common defence, do ordain and establish this Constitution; Provided, that this Constitution shall remain in force till Congress shall organize a Territorial Government, *and no longer*."

Sec. 1 of Art. 1, That there shall be and hereby is created for Arizona a Provisional Government, which said Government shall be divided into three separate and distinct departments, viz.: Legislative, Executive, and Judicial."

The boundaries of the Territory are the same proposed for Arizona in the bill before Congress, comprising an area of 90,000 miles, which are divided into four counties, for local purposes.

The Senate is to consist of nine members, the House of eighteen—the whole of whom are elected for one year, and an additional clause provides "that no session shall continue longer than thirty days."

American citizens acquire eligibility to any office in the gift of the people by a residence of six months.

The legislative power extends only to "all rightful subjects of legislation consistent with the provisions of the Constitution of the United States, and not inconsistent with this Constitution."

The present existing laws of New Mexico, as far as consistent with the provisions of this Constitution, are declared in full force and effect, until such time as the Provisional Legislature of the Territory shall alter, amend or repeal them.

The Executive authority is vested in a Governor the first of whom is made elective by the Convention. He holds his seat for one year, and all subsequent elections are to be made by the people.

The Governor is invested with extraordinary powers. He has an absolute veto power over all and every act of the Territorial Legislature, from which there is no appeal; is made Commander-in-Chief of the military of the Territory; may grant pardons for offences against the laws of the Territory, and is otherwise invested with the usual authority of executive officers. He is also empowered to appoint, by advice and consent of the Senate, a Lieutenant-Governor, Secretary of State, a Comptroller, a Treasurer, Marshal, three District Judges, and an Attorney-General.

It is provided that the Legislature shall have no power to levy any direct tax upon the people of the Territory.

The election for county officers, members of the Legislature, etc., will take place on the first Monday in May next.

Such is a brief synopsis of the Constitution for the Provisional Government of Arizona, as adopted by the Convention this day, with but one dissenting voice. A schedule to accompany it will be reported to-morrow. An effort will also be made to submit it to a vote of the people for ratification. The Government, without unanimity, is worthless. No Provisional Government can enforce laws unless supported heartily by the grand majority. There can be no doubt, however, from the great harmony prevailing in the Convention, that it will be cordially received by the mass, if submitted to a popular vote. The only objection that can be urged against it is that it would cause a delay in the organization, and our present necessities admit of no procrastination. The Constitution is defective—it bears the impress of our hasty legislation in almost every clause; but with well-digested amendments by the Legislature, it will meet our present necessities.

A ballot was entered into for the office of Governor of Arizona, under the Constitution. Dr. L. S. OWINGS, of Mesilla, was nominated, and elected by a unanimous vote. The Governor elect, who is an affable gentleman, of ability and moderation, was selected without reference to any political proclivities, and the other officers provided for by the Constitution will be filled in the same manner. As all will have the pleasure of working without salaries, I presume we shall secure the services of the most efficient men, and those long tried for ability, integrity and honor. We have taken a decisive step—I hope for the better—and will labor sedulously to open a brighter future for Arizona.

This evening the Hall in which the sessions of the Constitutional Convention are held, is the scene of a grand Gubernatorial Ball, given in honor of his Excellency Gov. OWINGS. "Gay women and brave men are gathered there," and "joy reigns supreme."

To-morrow's session will be important. The schedule will be reported, the seat of Government decided upon, county lines adopted, and, perhaps, an "inaugural address" from the Governor.

TUCSON, Arizona, Friday, April 6, 1860.

The Constitutional Convention for the formation of a Provisional Government, concluded its labors yesterday. The third day was occupied almost entirely in considering the schedule to accompany the Constitution. After sundry amendments it was finally adopted. Its great length forbids the attempt at copying, and time will scarcely admit of even a brief abstract of its leading provisions.

The first session of the Legislature will be held in Tucson on the first Monday in March, 1861. The Schedule fixes compensation of members and mileage.

The duties and privileges of the judiciary, the judicial districts, and regulations pertaining to the courts are next defined. The officers under the Constitution—their duties, salaries, &c. A provision is made for taking a census of the people prior to the session of the Legislature.

The names and boundaries of the counties as described in the schedule, for the convenience of map publishers, I will quote entire:

SECTION 1. The County of Doña Ana shall comprise all that portion of territory lying east of the Rio Grande.

SEC. 2. The County of Mesilla is hereby established, with the following boundaries—viz.: the Rio Grande on the east, the Chiricuhui Mountains on the west.

SEC. 3. The County of Ewell comprises all that portion of territory lying between the Chiricunui Mountains, on the east, and the longitudinal line which crosses what is known as the "Little Desert," near the centre thereof, on the west.

SEC. 4. The County of Castle Dome comprises all that portion of the Territory lying west of the western boundary of Ewell County.

SEC. 5. It is understood that the above specified boundary lines of counties above defined, traverse the entire Territory from north to south, crossing the St. Louis and San Francisco Overland Mail Route at the points above specified; *provided*, that the Rio Grande shall be the permanent boundary between Dona Ana and Mesilla Counties.

SEC. 6. The people of the different counties shall, at the first Territorial election, to be held on the first Monday in May next, fix the place for holding the different Courts in their respective counties.

The mode of amending the Constitution is definite, and provision is made for the punishment of offences against the Provisional Government.

The Schedule concludes with an exposition of the militia system, which creates nearly two hundred officers and four regiments of troops.

The proceedings yesterday were unimportant. The Governor-elect was duly inaugurated, and the following appointments were announced by his Excellency:

*Lieutenant-Governor*—Ygnatio Orrantia, of Mesilla.
*Secretary of State*—Jas. A. Lucas, of Mesilla.
*Territorial Treasurer*—M. Aldrich, of Tucson.
*Marshal*—Samuel G. Bean, of Mesilla.
*Comptroller*—J. Howard Wells, Tucson.
*Attorney-General*—Benjamin F. Neal, of Gila City.
*Chief Justice*—Granville H. Oury, of Tucson.
*District Judges*—Samuel W. Cozzins and Edward McGowan.

These gentlemen, together with other officers of minor rank, upon being commissioned, took the following oath, as prescribed by the Schedule:

"I, ———, do solemnly swear (or affirm) that I will faithfully discharge and perform all the duties incumbent upon me as ——— of the Provisional Government of the Territory of Arizona, according to the best of my skill and ability, agreeably to the Constitution and laws of the United States and of this Territory."

The enrolled Constitution and schedule was signed by the members of the Convention, and the following resolution was presented for adoption. As it explains itself, I will merely remark that it passed by acclamation:

"Be it resolved by the Delegates of the people of Arizona, in Convention assembled, that we earnestly and particularly protest against the removal of any United States troops now stationed in Arizona or the breaking up of any United States military post now established in said Territory, and particularly do we protest against the removal of Fort Fillmore, upon the Rio Grande, and Fort Buchanan at the head of the Sonoita, as the citizens of those portions of the Territory are left entirely without protection, and exposed to the depredations of hostile Indians who infest that region of country."

Several other resolutions were passed, one of which was highly complimentary to Hon. SYLVESTER MOWRY, our delegate, to whom a vote of thanks was tendered by the Convention.

The delegates mostly left to-day, and the capital has resumed its usual state. The Convention concluded its labors in the most harmonious manner, and nothing occurred during the session to mar the good feeling which prevailed. I have no time to indulge in reflections, as the stage is expected every moment.

HESPERIAN.

### From Hayti.

#### AN EARTHQUAKE AT ST. MARKS.

The schooner *Sarah Burton*, at Boston, and the brig *Baltimore*, at this port, bring advices from St. Marks, Hayti, to the 16th. They report that on the 8th inst., a very heavy shock of an earthquake was felt at that place. Several buildings were thrown down and much damage done in different parts of the town. Up to the 12th inst. several slight shocks had occurred, which so alarmed the inhabitants that they abandoned the houses and slept in the street. It was supposed that a large amount of damage was sustained in other parts of the Island. The shocks were felt on board the vessels lying in the harbor, causing their masts to shake violently.

The body of a child about a year old has been exhumed at Port Republic, N. J., by orders of the Coroner, and an examination has revealed the presence of a large quantity of pounded window glass in the intestines. The jury returned a verdict of "death from the administration of pounded glass, by the hands of the girl's step-father." He was duly committed to jail, at May's Landing, to await his trial in September.

# The New-York Times.

VOL. IX---NO. 2703. NEW-YORK, SATURDAY, MAY 19, 1860. PRICE TWO CENTS—WITH A SUPPLEMENT.


## FROM CHICAGO.

### THE REPUBLICAN TICKET FOR 1860.

### Abram Lincoln, of Illinois, Nominated for President.

The Late Senatorial Contest in Illinois to be Re-Fought on a Wider Field.

### Hannibal Hamlin, of Maine, the Candidate for Vice-President.

### Disappointment of the Friends of Mr. Seward.

### INTENSE EXCITEMENT AND ENTHUSIASM

### Reception of the Nominations in this City.

### How They are Hailed Throughout the North.

Special Dispatch to the New-York Times.

CHICAGO, Friday, May 18.

The work of the Convention is ended. The youngster who, with ragged trousers, used barefoot to drive his father's oxen and spend his days in splitting rails, has risen to high eminence, and ABRAM LINCOLN, of Illinois, is declared its candidate for President by the National Republican Party.

This result was effected by the change of votes in the Pennsylvania, New-Jersey, Vermont, and Massachusetts Delegations.

Mr. SEWARD's friends assert indignantly, and with a great deal of feeling, that they were grossly deceived and betrayed. The recusants endeavored to mollify New-York by offering her the Vice-Presidency, and agreeing to support any man she might name, but they declined the position, though they remain firm in the ranks, having moved to make LINCOLN's nomination unanimous. Mr. SEWARD's friends feel greatly chagrined and disappointed.

Western pride is gratified by this nomination, which plainly indicates the departure of political supremacy from the Atlantic States.

The prominent candidates for Vice-Presidency were Messrs. HICKMAN, BANKS, CLAY and REEDER. Pennsylvania desired HICKMAN. New-York, in order to resent the conduct of Pennsylvania, Massachusetts and Kentucky, favored Mr. HAMLIN, of Maine; and on the second ballot cast her whole strength for him, and it was owing to this, and the desire to conciliate New-York, that his nomination was so promptly secured.

Immense enthusiasm exists, and everything here would seem to indicate a spirited and successful canvass. The city is alive with processions, meetings, music and noisy demonstrations. One hundred guns were fired this evening.

The Convention was the most enthusiastic ever known in the country, and if one were to judge from appearances here, the ticket will sweep the country.

Great inquiry has been made this afternoon into the history of Mr. LINCOLN. The only evidence that he has a history as yet discovered, is that he had a stump canvass with Mr. DOUGLAS, in which he was beaten. He is not very strong at the West, but is unassailable in his private character.

Many of the delegates went home this evening by the 9 o'clock train. Others leave in the morning.

A grand excursion is planned to Rock Island and Davenport, and another to Milwaukee and Madison, and still another over the Illinois Central, over the prairies. These will detain a great many of the delegates and the editorial fraternity.

The Wigwam is as full as ever—filled now by thousands of original LINCOLN men, who they "always knew" would be nominated, and who first suggested his name, who are shouting themselves hoarse over the nomination. "What was it WEBSTER said when TAYLOR was nominated?" ask the opponents of LINCOLN. "What was the result of the election?" retort LINCOLN's friends.

Thirty-three guns were fired from the top of the Tremont House.

The dinner referred to in Tuesday evening's dispatch was a private one, and I regret that inaccurate reading of it should have misrepresented the position of the delegation as regards Mr. GREELEY. His right to act as he deemed best politically, was not denied, and consequently there was no defence of his career needed.

Massachusetts delegates, with their brass band, are parading the streets, calling at the various headquarters of the other delegations, serenading and bidding them farewell. "Hurrah for LINCOLN and HAMLIN—Illinois and Maine!" is the universal shout, and sympathy for the bottom dog is the all-pervading sentiment.

The "Wide-Awakes," numbering about two thousand men, accompanied by thousands of citizens, have a grand torch-light procession. The German Republican Club has another. The office of the *Press and Tribune* is brilliantly illuminated, and has a large transparency over the door, saying, "For President, Honest Old ABE." A bonfire thirty feet in circumference burns in front of the Tremont House, and illumines the city for miles around. The city is one blaze of illumination. Hotels, stores and private residences, shining with hundreds of patriotic dips. ENOUGH. HOWARD.

### PROCEEDINGS OF THE CONVENTION.

From the Associated Press.

CHICAGO, Friday, May 18.

The Wigwam was closely packed for a full hour before the Convention assembled this morning. The interest in the proceedings appears on the increase as the time for balloting approaches. A crowd, numbered by thousands, has been outside the building since 9 o'clock, anxiously awaiting intelligence from the inside. Arrangements have been made for passing the result of the ballots up from the platform to the roof of the building and through the sky-light—men being stationed above to convey speedily the intelligence to the multitude in the streets.

A large procession was formed by the various delegations to march to the Hall, preceded by bands of music. New-York being by far the most numerous. As ... entered the platform, several distinguished men were greeted with rounds of applause by the audience.

The opening prayer was delivered by Rev. Mr. GREEN, of the Tabernacle Baptist Church.

Three or four meetings were held at a distance outside, and during the silence of the prayer in the Convention the roars and shouts of these meetings could be distinctly heard in the Wigwam.

The President, on opening the proceedings, begged the audience to refrain as much as possible from applause, and to preserve as far as consistent the decorum and dignity of the meeting.

The President announced an invitation for an excursion over the Chicago and Galena Railroad; also, a communication from the workingmen of Brooklyn, Williamsburgh and Greenpoint, New-York, in favor of bestowing the Government lands on actual settlers, and for arresting the further sale of the public lands.

Both communications were ordered to be entered on the record.

The President announced the motion pending to be, to take a ballot for a candidate for President of the United States.

Mr. BLAIR, of Maryland, announced that in consequence of the adoption by the Convention of the rule restricting the vote of Maryland to the number of Delegates present, the delegation had last evening filled up its number, and asked leave to present the credentials of five new Delegates to fill the number from that State.

Mr. SARGEANT, of California, inquired whether the five additional votes now added would increase the vote to sixteen or leave it at eleven, which was the number of votes assigned to that State by the report of the Committee on Credentials. If it designed to increase the vote above eleven, he was opposed to it.

W. T. COLE, of Maryland, said that Maryland had been entitled to eleven votes only because the necessary number of delegates for the sixteen votes were not present. The delegation had power, by the action of the State Convention, to fill vacancies. They had now done so, under that authority, and claimed right to cast a full vote.

The President said he understood the rule adopted in the report of the Committee on Credentials to have restricted Maryland to eleven votes. The additional delegates would not entitle them to a greater vote.

Mr. BLAIR, of Maryland, desired to correct the error of the Chair. As he understood, the number was only limited because the delegates were not present. The delegation had a right to fill vacancies, and had done so in consequence of the rule adopted yesterday by the Convention.

Mr. ARMOUR, of Maryland, protested against the reception of the credentials of new delegates. Eleven representatives only were present from his State. The delegation had met without his knowledge, and without the knowledge of at least more than one delegate, and filled up their numbers with men who lived, God only knows where. A resident of the State had been refused admission to the delegation, and what object his colleagues had in filling the delegation with non-residents he did not know. He hoped the motion to admit these delegates would be voted down.

The motion to admit the extra delegates was lost amidst applause.

The Convention then voted to proceed to ballot for a candidate for President of the United State.

WM. M. EVARTS, of New-York, did not rise for the purpose of making a speech, but only to ask if at this time it is in order to put candidates in nomination.

THE PRESIDENT—The Chair considers it in order to name candidates without debate.

A delegate from Pennsylvania drew attention to the fact that delegates' seats were occupied by outsiders.

A VOICE—The same here in Ohio.

THE PRESIDENT—This affords an opportunity to the Chair to read a communication just received from the doorkeepers. The communication stated that Delegates as soon as they got into the hall passed their tickets out to friends. The officers, therefore, found it impossible to prevent the admission of outsiders, but the fault rested with the Delegates.

The President suggested that the only method to pursue would be for each delegate to claim his own seat with vigor.

After some delay, occasioned by the clearing of the platform and distributing ballots, the Convention proceeded to ballot.

WM. M. EVARTS rose and said: I beg leave to offer the name of WM. H. SEWARD as a candidate before this Convention for the nomination of President of the United States.

This nomination was received with loud and long continued applause.

Mr. JUDD, of Illinois, rose and said: Mr. President, I beg leave to offer as a candidate before this Convention for President of the United States the name of ABRAM LINCOLN, of Illinois.

The crowded audience greeted this nomination with perfectly deafening applause, the shouts swelling into a perfect roar, and being continued for several minutes, the wildest excitement and enthusiasm prevailing. At the close of the applause some hisses were heard, but the pressure for LINCOLN was tremendous.

Mr. DUDLEY, of New-Jersey, presented the name of WM. E. DAYTON. [Light applause.]

Gov. REEDER, of Pennsylvania—The State of Pennsylvania desires to present as her candidate the name of SIMON CAMERON. [Applause.]

Mr. CARTER, of Ohio, put forward the name of SALMON P. CHASE, of Ohio. [Loud applause.]

Mr. SMITH, of Maryland—I am instructed by the State of Indiana to second the motion of ABRAM LINCOLN. [Another outburst of enthusiastic applause from the body of the hall, mingled with some hisses.]

FRANCIS P. BLAIR, of Missouri, nominated EDWARD BATES, of Missouri. [Applause.]

Mr. BLAIR, of Michigan, said on the part of Michigan—I desire to say that the Republicans of that State second the nomination of WM. H. SEWARD for the Presidency.

Tremendous applause followed this speech, thousands of those present rising and waving their hats and handkerchiefs, and swelling the applause to a thundering roar through several minutes. This was followed by some hisses and loud applause for LINCOLN, when the friends of SEWARD again rallied, determined not to be put down in applause by the friends of LINCOLN. At this second trial of the lungs, however, it was evident that the crowd was more divided than at first appeared, and the Lincoln men apparently had the majority.

TOM CORWIN, of Ohio, nominated JOHN MCLEAN, of Ohio, for the Presidency. [Loud applause.]

CARL SCHURZ, of Wisconsin, on the part of his State, here rose and seconded the nomination of WM. H. SEWARD.

Upon this another scene of the greatest enthusiasm and tumultuous excitement ensued.

Mr. NORTH, of Minnesota, also seconded, on the part of Minnesota, the nomination of Mr. SEWARD. [Tremendous applause.]

Mr. WILSON, of Kansas—The delegates and people of Kansas second the nomination. [Renewed cheers.]

Mr. DELANO, of Ohio—On the part of a large number of people of Ohio, I desire to second the nomination of the man who can split rails and maul Democrats, ABRAM LINCOLN. [Rounds of applause by Lincoln men.]

A Delegate from Iowa also seconded the nomination of Mr. LINCOLN, on the part of that State, amid renewed excitement and applause.

A VOICE—ABE LINCOLN has it by the sound now. Let us ballot.

Cheers and hisses.

Judge LOGAN, of Illinois—Mr. President, in order or out of order, I propose this Convention and audience give three cheers for the man who is evidently their nominee.

Hisses and cries of "No," "No;" "Call the roll."

THE PRESIDENT—If the Convention will get over this irrepressible excitement, the roll will be called.

After some further excitement, the calling of the roll commenced, the applause at the different announcements being with difficulty checked.

When Maryland was called, the Chairman of the delegation cast the vote of the State for BATES, two Delegates claiming their right to individual votes.

After some discussion, the Convention rejected the votes as cast by the Chairman, and received the votes of the Delegates separately.

FIRST BALLOT.

The first ballot resulted as follows:

FOR MR. SEWARD.

| State | Votes | State | Votes | State | Votes |
|---|---|---|---|---|---|
| Maine | 10 | N. Hampshire | 1 | Massachusetts | 21 |
| New-York | 70 | Pennsylvania | 1½ | Maryland | 3 |
| Virginia | 8 | Kentucky | 5 | Michigan | 12 |
| Texas | 4 | Wisconsin | 10 | Iowa | 2 |
| California | 8 | Minnesota | 8 | Kansas | 6 |
| Nebraska | 2 | Dis. of Col. | 2 | | |
| Total | | | | | 173½ |

FOR MR. LINCOLN.

| State | Votes | State | Votes | State | Votes |
|---|---|---|---|---|---|
| Maine | 6 | N. Hampshire | 7 | Massachusetts | 4 |
| Connecticut | 2 | Pennsylvania | 4 | Virginia | 14 |
| Kentucky | 6 | Ohio | 8 | Indiana | 26 |
| Illinois | 22 | Iowa | 2 | Nebraska | 1 |
| Total | | | | | 102 |

FOR MR. BATES.

| State | Votes | State | Votes | State | Votes |
|---|---|---|---|---|---|
| Rhode Island | 1 | Connecticut | 7 | Maryland | 8 |
| Delaware | 6 | Missouri | 18 | Texas | 2 |
| Iowa | 1 | Oregon | 5 | | |
| Total | | | | | 48 |

FOR MR. CAMERON.

| State | Votes | State | Votes | State | Votes |
|---|---|---|---|---|---|
| Pennsylvania | 47½ | Virginia | 1 | Iowa | 1 |
| Nebraska | 1 | | | | |
| Total | | | | | 50½ |

FOR MR. M'LEAN.

| State | Votes | State | Votes | State | Votes |
|---|---|---|---|---|---|
| Rhode Island | 5 | Pennsylvania | 1 | Kentucky | 1 |
| Ohio | 4 | Iowa | 1 | | |
| Total | | | | | 12 |

FOR MR. CHASE.

| State | Votes | State | Votes | State | Votes |
|---|---|---|---|---|---|
| N. Hampshire | 1 | Rhode Island | 1 | Connecticut | 2 |
| Kentucky | 8 | Iowa | 1 | Ohio | 34 |
| Nebraska | 2 | | | | |
| Total | | | | | 49 |

FOR MR. WADE.

| State | Votes | State | Votes |
|---|---|---|---|
| Connecticut | 1 | Kentucky | 2 |
| Total | | | 3 |

FOR MR. DAYTON.

New-Jersey ... 14

FOR MR. READ.

Rhode Island ... 1

FOR MR. FREMONT.

New-Hampshire ... 1

FOR MR. COLLAMER.

Vermont ... 10

FOR MR. SUMNER.

Kentucky ... 1

Whole number of votes ... 465

Necessary to a choice ... 233

SECOND BALLOT.

The second ballot was then taken.

Mr. CAMERON's name was withdrawn.

FOR MR. LINCOLN.

| State | Votes | State | Votes | State | Votes |
|---|---|---|---|---|---|
| N. Hampshire | 9 | Vermont | 10 | R. Island | 3 |
| Pennsylvania | 48 | Delaware | 6 | Kentucky | 9 |
| Ohio | 14 | Iowa | 5 | | |
| Total | | | | | 181 |

FOR MR. SEWARD.

| State | Votes | State | Votes | State | Votes |
|---|---|---|---|---|---|
| Massachusetts | 22 | New-Jersey | 4 | Pennsyl'va. | 2½ |
| Kentucky | 7 | Texas | 6 | Nebraska | 3 |
| Total | | | | | 184½ |

SCATTERING.

Bates, 35; McLean, 8; Chase, 42½; Cameron, 2; Dayton, 10; C. M. Clay, 2.

THIRD BALLOT.

The third ballot was taken amidst excitement, and cries of "the ballot." Intense feeling existed during the ballot, each vote being awaited in breathless silence and expectancy.

FOR MR. LINCOLN.

| State | Votes | State | Votes | State | Votes |
|---|---|---|---|---|---|
| Massachusetts | 8 | Rhode-Island | 5 | New-Jersey | 8 |
| Penn. (appl.) | 52 | Maryland | 9 | Kentucky | 13 |
| Ohio, (appl.) | 29 | Oregon | 4 | | |

This gave LINCOLN 230½ votes, or within 1½ of a nomination.

Mr. ANDREWS, of Massachusetts, then rose and corrected the vote of Massachusetts, by changing four votes and giving them to LINCOLN, thus nominating him by 2½ majority.

The Convention immediately became wildly excited.

A large portion of the delegates who had kept tally, at once said the struggle was decided, and half the Convention rose cheering, shouting, and waving hats.

The audience took up the cheers, and the confusion became deafening.

State after State rose, striving to change their votes to the winning candidate, but the noise and enthusiasm rendered it impossible for the delegates to make themselves heard.

Mr. MCCRILLIS, of Maine, making himself heard, said that the young giant of the West is now of age. Maine now casts for him her 16 votes.

Mr. ANDREWS, of Massachusetts, changed the vote of that State, giving 18 to Mr. LINCOLN and 8 to Mr. SEWARD.

Intelligence of the nomination was now conveyed to the men on the roof of the building, who immediately made the outside multitude aware of the result. The first roar of the cannon soon mingled itself with the cheers of the people, and at the same moment a man appeared in the hall bringing a large painting of Mr. LINCOLN. The scene at this time beggars description—11,000 inside and 20,000 or 30,000 outside were yelling and shouting at once. Two cannon sent forth roar after roar in quick succession. Delegates tore up the sticks and boards bearing the names of the several States and waved them aloft over their heads, and the vast multitude before the platform were waving their hats and handkerchiefs. The whole scene was one of the wildest enthusiasm.

WM. M. EVARTS, of New-York, having obtained a hearing, said: Mr. Chairman, can New-York have the silence of the Convention? [Cries, "Yes! yes!"] I ask if the vote has yet been announced. [Cries, "Not yet."] Then, Sir, I wait to be in order.

Mr. BROWN, of Missouri, desired to change 18 votes of Missouri for the gallant son of the West, ABRAM LINCOLN. Iowa, Connecticut, Kentucky and Minnesota also changed their votes. The result of the third ballot was then announced:

Whole number of votes cast ... 466

Necessary to a choice ... 234

Mr. Abram Lincoln received ... 354

And was declared duly nominated.

The States still voting for SEWARD were Massachusetts, 8; New-York, 70; New-Jersey, 5; Pennsylvania, ½; Maryland, 2; Michigan, 12; Wisconsin, 10; California, 3. Total, 110½.

Mr. DAYTON received one vote from New-Jersey, and MCLEAN half a vote from Pennsylvania.

The result was received with renewed applause.

When silence was restored WM. M. EVARTS came forward on the Secretary's table and spoke as follows:

MR. CHAIRMAN, GENTLEMEN OF THE NATIONAL CONVENTION: The State of New York, by a full delegation, wishing complete unanimity in purpose at home, came to this Convention and presented its choice—one of its citizens who had served the State from boyhood up, and labored for it and loved it. We came here a great State, with, as we thought, a great statesman, [applause,] and our love of the great Republic from which we are all delegates. The great Republic of the American Union, and our love for the great Republican Party of the Union, and our love of our Statesman and candidate, made us think we did our duty to the country, and the whole country, in expressing our preference and love for him. [Applause.] But, gentlemen, it was from Gov. SEWARD that most of us learned to love Republican principles and the Republican Party. [Cheers.] His fidelity to the country, the Constitution and the laws—his fidelity to the party and the principle that majorities govern—his interest in the advancement of our party to its victory, that our country may rise to its true glory, induce me to declare that I speak his sentiments, as I do the united opinion of our delegation, when I move, Sir, as I do now, that the nomination of ABRAM LINCOLN, of Illinois, as the Republican candidate for the suffrages of the whole country, for the office of Chief Magistrate of the American Union, be made unanimous. [Applause, and three cheers for New-York.]

A life-size portrait of ABRAM LINCOLN was here exhibited from the platform amidst renewed cheers.

Mr. ANDREWS, of Massachusetts, on the part of the united delegation of that State, seconded the motion of the gentleman of New-York, that the nomination be made unanimous. After declaring the devotion of Massachusetts to the principles of freedom and equality, he extolled Gov. SEWARD as a statesman and patriot, and pledged the State to roll up over 100,000 majority, and give the 18 (13?) electoral votes to the candidates.

Eloquent speeches, indorsing the nominee, were also made by CARL SCHURZ, F. P. BLAIR, of Missouri, and Mr. BROWNING, of Illinois—all of which breathed a spirit of confidence and enthusiasm.

At the close, three hearty cheers were given for New-York, and the nomination of Mr. LINCOLN was made unanimous.

With loud cheers for LINCOLN, the Convention adjourned till 5 o'clock.

### AFTERNOON SESSION.

The Convention reassembled at 5 o'clock.

A large banner was brought on the platform by Pennsylvania, bearing the inscription—"Pennsylvania good for 20,000 majority for the People's Candidate, ABE LINCOLN." It was received with loud applause.

At 5½ o'clock order was obtained, and the President announced the business before the Convention to be a ballot for Vice President.

Mr. WILDER, of Kansas, named JOHN HICKMAN, of Pennsylvania.

Mr. SAUPE, of Pennsylvania, seconded the nomination. [Applause.]

Mr. CARTER, of Ohio, named HANNIBAL HAMLIN, of Maine.

Mr. BOUTWELL, of Massachusetts, named N. P. BANKS, of Massachusetts. [Loud applause.]

Mr. SMITH, of Indiana, named CASSIUS M. CLAY. [Loud applause.]

Mr. LOWREY, of Pennsylvania, named Gov. REEDER, of Pennsylvania.

A ballot was then taken with the following result:

FOR HANNIBAL HAMLIN.

| State | Votes | State | Votes | State | Votes |
|---|---|---|---|---|---|
| Maine | 16 | New-Jersey | 6 | Illinois | 2 |
| New-Hamp're | 10 | Pennsylvania | 11 | Wisconsin | 5 |
| Vermont | 10 | Maryland | 8 | Iowa | 6 |
| Massachusetts | 3 | Delaware | 2 | Minnesota | 6 |
| Rhode Island | 8 | Ohio | 46 | Oregon | 1 |
| Connecticut | 8 | Indiana | 8 | | |
| New-York | 35 | Michigan | 8 | Total | 191 |

FOR CASSIUS M. CLAY.

| State | Votes | State | Votes | State | Votes |
|---|---|---|---|---|---|
| Connecticut | 3 | New-York | 9 | New-Jersey | 1 |
| Penn. | 4½ | Maryland | 2 | Delaware | 3 |
| Virginia | 23 | Kentucky | 23 | Indiana | 18 |
| Michigan | 4 | Illinois | 1 | Wisconsin | 5 |
| Minnesota | 1 | Nebraska | 1 | Dist. of Col. | 2 |
| Total | | | | | 101½ |

FOR JOHN HICKMAN.

| State | Votes | State | Votes | State | Votes |
|---|---|---|---|---|---|
| Massachusetts | 1 | Delaware | 1 | Minnesota | 1 |
| Connecticut | 3 | Missouri | 9 | Oregon | 3 |
| New-York | 1 | Illinois | 8 | Kansas | 6 |
| Pennsylvania | 7 | California | 8 | Nebraska | 5 |
| Maryland | 1 | | | | |
| Total | | | | | 58 |

FOR GOV. REEDER.

| State | Votes | State | Votes | State | Votes |
|---|---|---|---|---|---|
| Massachusetts | 1 | New-Jersey | 7 | Illinois | 16 |
| New-York | 2 | Pennsylvania | 24 | Iowa | 1 |
| Total | | | | | 51 |

FOR N. P. BANKS.

| State | Votes | State | Votes | State | Votes |
|---|---|---|---|---|---|
| Massachusetts | 20 | Pennsylvania | 2½ | Oregon | 1 |
| Connecticut | 1 | Missouri | 9 | | |
| New York | 4 | Iowa | 1 | Total | 38½ |

FOR HENRY WINTER DAVIS.

New York ... 8

FOR SAM. HOUSTON.

Texas ... 6

FOR WM. L. DAYTON.

——— ... 3

FOR MR. READ, OF PENNSYLVANIA.

——— ... 1

Total ... 461

Necessary to a choice ... 232

SECOND BALLOT.

The second ballot was then taken. Massachusetts withdrew the name of Mr. BANKS and cast 26 votes for Mr. HAMLIN.

Pennsylvania withdrew the name of Gov. REEDER and cast 54 votes for Mr. HAMLIN.

New-York cast 70 votes for Mr. HAMLIN.

The result of the vote was announced as follows:

Hamlin ... 367

Clay ... 86

Hickman ... 13

The result was received with tumultuous applause.

When order was restored, Mr. BLAKELY, of Kentucky, said, "Mr. Chairman, on behalf of that gallant son of Freedom, CASSIUS M. CLAY and friends, I move that the nomination be made unanimous; and in retiring from the Convention, at the close of the proceedings, allow me to tender to you on the part of the friends of Mr. CLAY our thanks for your liberal support. In presenting his name to you we presented the name of one who rolls the end of freedom under his tongue, while on his lips sweet liberty loves to linger. [Laughter and applause.]

Mr. BRUSH, of Indiana, seconded the motion, and made an eloquent speech in support of the nomination, and in eulogy of WM. H. SEWARD.

Mr. MCCRILLIS, of Maine, on the part of the people of Maine, expressed thanks for the honor done the State by the nomination, and declared that Maine would cast her vote for LINCOLN, HAMLIN, Union and Victory. [Loud cries for CORWIN.]

Mr. CARTER explained that Mr. CORWIN was confined to his house by sickness, but he had sent his hearty indorsement of the proceedings of the Convention.

AMOS TUCK, of New-Hampshire, moved that the President of the Convention and Chairmen of the several Delegations be a Committee to inform Messrs. LINCOLN and HAMLIN of their nomination. Adopted.

Mr. GIDDINGS moved the following:

*Resolved*, That we deeply sympathize with those men who have been driven, some from their native States, and others from the States of their adoption, and are now exiled from their homes on account of their opinions, and we hold the Democratic Party responsible for the gross violation of that clause of the Constitution which declares that citizens of each State shall be entitled to all the privileges and immunities of citizens of the several States.

Adopted.

Mr. LANE, of Indiana, took the floor, and made an eloquent speech in favor of the whole ticket, and pledged Indiana for 10,000 majority, and his honor for the redemption of the pledge.

Loud cries were here made for GREELEY, which were met by applause and hisses.

Mr. GOODRICH, of Minnesota, announced that a triumphal procession would parade the streets to-night and march to the Wigwam, where a grand ratification meeting would be held. [Loud cheers.] Mr. GOODRICH moved a vote of thanks to the ladies and gentlemen of Chicago for the liberality displayed in building and decorating the Wigwam. Carried unanimously.

The Convention accepted the invitation of the Rock Island and Chicago and Galena railroads, to excursion rides on their roads.

Mr. ASHLEY, of Ohio, moved the following:

*Resolved*, That the Republican National Committee appointed by the Convention, be and they are hereby instructed to prescribe uniform rules that shall operate equally in all the States and Territories, whereby in the future the wishes and preferences of the electors in the Republican organization in the choice of candidates for President and Vice-President may be fully and fairly ascertained, and that the basis of the nominating vote be fixed as near as may be in proportion to the number of Republican electors found to reside at the last general State election preceding said nomination in each Congressional District throughout the Union. After some skirmishing, laid on the table.

Mr. WASHBURN, of Vermont, moved a vote of thanks of the Convention to the President for the ability and courtesy with which he discharged the duties of the office. Carried unanimously. A vote of thanks was also passed to the other officers of the Convention, especially Recording Secretary PRATT, of Indiana.

The following was announced as the National Committee for the ensuing four years—Pennsylvania alone unfilled:

Maine—C. J. Gillman. Indiana—S. Meredith.
N. Hampshire—G. G. Fogg. Missouri—Asa S. Jones.
Vermont—L. Brainard. Michigan—Austin Blair.
Mass.—J. Z. Goodrich. Illinois—N. B. Judd.
R. Island—Thos. G. Turner. Texas—D. Henderson.
Conn.—Gideon Wells. Wisconsin—Carl Schurz.
N. Y.—Edwin D. Morgan. Iowa—A. J. Stevens.
N. Jersey—Denning Duer. Califor.—D. W. Cheeseman.
Md.—James T. Wagner. Minnesota—J. McCusick.
Delaware—N. B. Smithers. Oregon—W. C. Johnson.
Virginia—Alfred Caldwell. Kansas—Wm. A. Phillips.
Kentucky—C. M. Clay. Nebraska—O. H. Irish.
Ohio—Thomas Spooner. Dist. Colum.—J. Gerhardt.

Mr. ASHMUN then, in short remarks, returned thanks to the Convention for the kind assistance extended him in the discharge of the duties of the Chair. He congratulated them on the gratifying auspices of the result of their labors. He indorsed the character and ability of both the nominees, with whom he had enjoyed a long association in public life, and expressed the conviction that victory must crown the efforts of the party in November.

The Convention then adjourned *sine die*, with nine cheers for the ticket.

Immediately on the adjournment 100 guns were fired from the roof of the Tremont House.

The entire Press are under great obligations to the Western Union Telegraph Line, and connecting lines, for the promptness and accuracy with which the long reports have been forwarded, and especially to the Chicago office, for facilities and accommodations afforded the reporters.

### HOW THE NOMINATIONS WERE RECEIVED IN THE CITY.

OPENING OF THE PRESIDENTIAL CAMPAIGN—MEETINGS AT THE REPUBLICAN HEAD-QUARTERS AND IN SEVERAL WARDS—SPEECHES, RESOLUTIONS AND MUSIC—MR. SEWARD'S FRIENDS, THOUGH SORROWING, DO NOT DESPAIR OF THE UNION.

The announcement that the National Republican Convention at Chicago had nominated ABRAM LINCOLN for President, on the third ballot, was published in the City at 1 o'clock, and, as it spread, was received by the friends of Senator SEWARD with some show of disappointment. They had been informed by the Republican organ, in the morning, that the opposition to Mr. SEWARD could not be united, and that therefore his prospect of receiving the nomination was very good. Therefore, many of them were unprepared to hear of his defeat soon, if at all, they had not anticipated such a result until after a protracted struggle. The result was that the nomination was not received with enthusiasm. During the morning, the only Republicans who seemed pleased with the result, who were inclined to talk, were those of the old friends of HENRY CLAY, who had joined the Republican Party. Some of them showed great delight, not so much because Mr. LINCOLN had received the nomination, as that Mr. SEWARD had been defeated. They claimed that in his defeat he had received full pay for having defeated HENRY CLAY in the very same manner and under similar circumstances. The Democracy appeared jubilant. They said they saw in the action of the Republican Convention the same unfortunate element that destroyed the old Whig Party. The old doctrine of availability had ruled, they said, and it would ruin, as it had done before. They pretended great indignation that the Republicans should have sacrificed their representative man in the present campaign, as the Whigs did in the case of HENRY CLAY and of DANIEL WEBSTER, and resolved to punish them by electing a Democratic President in November next. Later in the day many of the Republicans came to speak of the nomination as a very good one, although they coupled with the remark an expression of regret that Mr. SEWARD had not been made their candidate. At about 4 o'clock one hundred guns were fired in the City Hall Park, and some of the several hundred present spoke cheeringly of the nomination of Mr. LINCOLN. In the evening several meetings were held, which are reported below.

#### YOUNG MEN'S REPUBLICAN UNION.

A special meeting of this Association was called to assemble at their head-quarters, the Stuyvesant Institute, where at 8 o'clock our reporter found a band of music discoursing favorite national airs to an audience which about half filled the hall. The President and Vice-President of the Association being both absent, Mr. CEPHAS BRAINARD assumed the Chair, and called the meeting to order. He said they had assembled to respond to the nomination which had just been made by the Chicago Convention, and, as he was not much of a speaker himself, he would introduce to the audience Mr. ELLIOT F. SHEPARD, who would favor them with a speech.

Mr. SHEPARD said he could not but be struck with the loyalty of the New-York Republican Union in thus promptly responding to the nomination of their party. The principles of the organization descended from the founders of the Republic, and the character of the members of the Republican Party would compare favorably with that of any other party. It was not strange that such a party, composed of honest men, should have selected a man for their candidate whose Christian name signified "honest." They knew their candidate and were proud of him. They remembered when he confronted the "Little Giant" of the Democratic Party eighteen months ago, and defeated him in his own State on the popular vote. It was only owing to the false apportionment of Representatives that DOUGLAS was elected over him to the Senate of the United States. Mr. LINCOLN had been trying ever since to get an appeal to the Courts from the fraud that cheated him out of the Senatorship without success. But now the people of the United States summon DOUGLAS, or whoever may be the nominee of the opposition, to the supreme tribunal, the people of the country. The speaker continued at considerable length to speak of liberty and the rights of free labor, &c., alluding to the noble platform of the party, and closing by a reference to the enthusiasm that attended the proceedings of the Chicago Convention, and which he hoped would be imitated by the party in this City.

At the close of his speech, the Chairman proposed three cheers for LINCOLN, which were faintly responded to, and the band struck up the "Star-spangled Banner." Mr. CENTAR was next introduced, and spoke of spoke of the good old campaign of 1856, and the part which he took in the same. The party was then new, and composed of different elements, while they had a foe to contend with well organized and united. Now, however, the case was different; their foe was divided and broken up—his party was gone, and all the Republicans had to do, was to march on to victory. After referring to the deception practiced by the Democrats in the last Presidential campaign, the final showing of the cloven-foot, and the present demoralized and disunited condition of the party, he asked "how a party thus divided and disgraced could withstand the onset of us honest Republicans?" They cannot," said he; "they must be swept down; the country demands it, and you and I will help do it. [Applause.] When I heard that LINCOLN had been nominated by our Representatives in Convention, I felt ready to bow to the decision, take my coat off and go to work. [Loud applause.] He had yet to hear of a Republican who would refuse to support the nomination. To be sure, Mr. SEWARD—[three cheers were proposed for WM. H. SEWARD, which were given with tremendous force,]—had great merits, and he had not been rewarded as he deserved; but, thank God, said he, there is a future, and Mr. SEWARD will remain embalmed in our memory. But, however that may be,—[three more cheers were here proposed for Mr. SEWARD, and responded to with great enthusiasm]—Republicans are not going to back down because they have not got the man of their choice, Mr. LINCOLN, was among the foremost men of talent and ability in the country. His public life had been honorable, although he had not held so many and different public offices as many other men. It was well, perhaps, that he had not, for if he had he might have become contaminated by long associations with politicians and office-seekers. He was a fresh man, and just such a man as would sweep that young country like a whirlwind. After dwelling at some length upon the points of difference in the principles of the Republican Party, and then of their opponents, he concluded by saying that although he was not a prophet, nor the son of a prophet, yet he ventured to predict that the Democratic Party would get its marching orders in November next, and would never be heard of more. [Applause.] The band then played "Hail Columbia," after which Mr. MCCORMICK offered for adoption a series of resolutions indorsing the nomination of LINCOLN for President and HAMLIN for Vice-President, enlarging their eminent qualification and fitness for the offices for which they were nominated, and pledging the Young Men's Republican Union to their support. The resolutions, as they were read, received the indorsement of faint cheers. Mr. WHEELER then offered a resolution, thanking the New-York Delegation in the Convention for the faithful manner in which they stood by the New-York candidate, the greatest statesman of the present age—WM. H. SEWARD. The resolution was received with cheers, and immediately adopted. DEXTER A. HAWKINS, Esq., then took the stand, and spoke at considerable length in praise of the nominees, particularly of Mr. HAMLIN, whom he said he knew well, having spent a portion of his life under the same roof with him. During his speech, a delegation of fifteen representatives from the Twenty first Ward Campaign Club entered the room, which by this time had become nearly two-thirds full.

At the conclusion of Mr. HASKIN's remarks, Mr. MCDERMOTT took the floor, and announced himself from Greenpoint, where, he said, Mr. LINCOLN was nominated a long time since, and he was glad to find that he had now been indorsed by the Chicago Convention. After saying a few words in his praise, and claiming the credit of the nomination for Greenpoint, he commenced reading a sketch of his life from the *New-York Tribune*. This seemed rather too slow business for the audience, which manifested great impatience, and finally choked him off. He then resumed his remarks, and said that he had only one favor to ask of Mr. LINCOLN, when he became President, and that was that he would appoint W. H. SEWARD Secretary of State.

A VOICE—Is that a Greenpoint nomination too?

Yes, that is a Greenpoint nomination, and if he will only do that, we will leave the rest to his discretion. [Laughter and Applause.]

Mr. D. T. T. MARSHALL, one of the delegation from the Twenty-first Ward Campaign Club, was then called upon, and briefly responded, saying that the Club from which he was a delegate had met that evening, and changed its name to the Lincoln and Hamlin Campaign Club, indorsed the nominations with great enthusiasm, and appointed himself and his associates to come down and congratulate the Republican Young Mens' Union upon the bright prospects before them. They had reason to feel proud of their candidate—he was a man of the people. Born in a Slave State, God Almighty had given him a long pair of legs, with which he made tracks for that young Territory of Illinois, which the immortal JEFFERSON had rescued from the curse of Slavery. [Prolonged applause.]

The Chairman then called upon LUTHER R. MARSH, Esq., another of the Twenty-first Ward delegates, who excused himself from making a speech by saying he had not yet got warmed up to a speaking condition. He felt, however, that the nominations were eminently worthy, and although they might not perhaps meet the expectations of the Republicans of this City and State, yet they should yield their individual preferences to the choice of the majority, and go in heartily for the support of the candidates.

Mr. J. B. DUTCHER then addressed the assembly, eulogizing WM. H. SEWARD, and recommending the Republicans to support the nomination of the Convention for the sake of their principles.

Several other speakers followed, and the meeting broke up at a late hour. The only enthusiasm displayed throughout the meeting, was when the name of WM. H. SEWARD was mentioned. The house was not more than two-thirds full at any time, and a great portion of those present appeared to have dropped in mainly for curiosity—and to have remained mainly to hear the music of the band which filled up the interval between the speeches, and performed its part well.

#### THE REPUBLICAN CENTRAL CAMPAIGN CLUB.

Soon after 8 o'clock about one hundred persons met at the rooms of the Republican Campaign Club, and after some conversation, in which regret that WM. H. SEWARD had not received the nomination, was most prominent, a meeting was organized—DANIEL ULLMAN, Esq., President of the Club, in the Chair. Mr. ULLMAN, on taking the Chair, advised all to be of good cheer, and go into the canvass with a determination to be victorious. For himself, he considered the nomination of ABRAM LINCOLN a sure guarantee of the success of the Republican Party in the coming contest. He believed that the Republicans, would put aside their preferences for the good of the cause, and rally at the polls in November next.

When Mr. ULLMAN had concluded, Mr. DALTON offered a resolution to the effect that the nomination of ABRAM LINCOLN for President, and HANNIBAL HAMLIN for Vice-President, is worthy the hearty support of every Republican, and that the Central Campaign do promise it a hearty support. The resolution was adopted unanimously.

J. W. WHARTON was the first speaker. He approved of the nomination of ABRAM LINCOLN; he was the man of his choice. He admired him both for his republicanism and for his boldness. He (LINCOLN) had met DOUGLAS face to face in Illinois, and he would meet him again and conquer. He referred to Mr. LINCOLN as a self-made man, a perfectly honest and honorable man, a profound lawyer, and as a statesman, incorruptible—in fact, just the man to honor the Presidential Chair. In conclusion, he expressed his entire confidence in the success of the Presidential ticket.

Mr. F. C. HILLS, of the *Evening Post*, was the next speaker. He said it was enough for him to know that ABRAM LINCOLN had been nominated to make him sure of a great Republican victory. The Convention by which he was nominated was a Convention of the wisdom of the country, and the decision of that Convention was, as he believed, final and binding upon all good Republicans. For himself, he had no grievances to complain of; in fact he rejoiced in the nomination. He believed it was the wisest nomination that could have been made. He ratified it with his whole soul, and would support it with all his might. [Applause.] What a contrast there was between the Convention at Chicago and the late Convention at Charleston. In the Republican Convention all was harmony and good feeling, while in the Democratic Convention the worst passions prevailed. All was discordant, and the result was secession and utter failure. So it would be on the day of the election. The Republicans would march up to the polls in one solid and harmonious phalanx, while the Democracy would be distracted, broken, and utterly routed. [Applause.]

Mr. RUFUS SANDERS, who spoke next, said he had the same hearty approval of the nomination of Mr. LINCOLN as had been expressed by the previous speaker. Mr. LINCOLN was the man of his choice. He was the strongest man that could have been presented for the suffrages of the Republican Party. He was sure, in his own mind, that at the next election the Republicans would poll vastly more votes than would be necessary to elect LINCOLN. [Applause.]

Mr. A. F. DOW was the next speaker. He was not disappointed as were some of the previous speakers, at the nomination of Mr. LINCOLN. He was gratified. The Chicago Convention had, in his opinion, made the wisest nomination that could have been made under the circumstances. The Republicans of every State that had sent its delegates to that Convention would come out on the next election day in their full strength to ratify such nominations. He was proud to say that WM. H. SEWARD was the man of his choice, as he was of hosts of other Republicans; but, with equal proudness, he believed that he did not believe that it was his duty to say that WM. H. SEWARD had at the present time sufficient strength to carry the Republican Party to victory. It was an old proverb that one man shook the bush and another gathered the birds. It was true that WILLIAM H. SEWARD had shaken the bush. He had shaken it well; he had shaken it satisfactorily, but ABRAM LINCOLN had got the bird. Whatever their feelings as to a particular candidate might be—whatever their prejudices—he deemed it the duty of every true Republican to drown those feelings and wage those prejudices in harmonious action for the success of the candidate of the party. A better day was coming. The march of freedom was onward. Right principles were now getting the upper hold—principles of freedom and humanity against oppression and Slavery.

Following the conclusion of Mr. DAVIS' speech, the President asked if any brother present had a heart overflowing and desired to speak. Any such one he asked to rise in his place and let himself be heard.

Mr. A. N. COFFIN said he was not overflowing with anxiety to speak, but he had a bit of news to tell them as to how the nominations at Chicago were received in the upper part of the City. He was a member of the Twenty-first Ward Republican Association, and he had just come from a meeting of the Association. The meeting was one of intense enthusiasm for Mr. LINCOLN. Their preference had been for Mr. SEWARD; but as Mr. LINCOLN had been nominated, they had accepted him as their man, and they should fight for him to the best of their united ability. [Applause.]

Mr. A. F. DOW stated that the Republican Association of the Ninth Ward was in favor of the nomination of Mr. SEWARD or any other candidate, but they should drop Mr. SEWARD for the present and come up to the battle for Mr. LINCOLN. They might depend upon it that at the next election the Ninth Ward would come up right side up with care—their care being to do their best toward the election of the Chicago nominee.

Mr. DITTENHOFF, in an animated speech, gave the views of the German Republicans of the City touching the nomination of Mr. LINCOLN. He knew the Republicans among the Germans would accept the nomination and give it their full support, and he prophesied their entire vote for Mr. Lincoln.

Mr. E. WEBSTER stated that Gov. BANKS was his first choice for the Presidency, Mr. WADE his next choice, Mr. SEWARD his next, and Mr. LINCOLN the last on the list. Notwithstanding the name of Mr. LINCOLN was the last man on his slate, he should now be the first in receiving his support. [Applause.]

Mr. ULLMANN said a great battle had got to be fought and he hoped they would all be fully armed to meet the enemy.

With three times three cheers for ABRAM LINCOLN and HANNIBAL HAMBLIN, the meeting adjourned till Monday evening.

#### THE FEELING IN THE SEVERAL WARDS.

Late in the evening there were gatherings at the Republican Head Quarters, in several Wards, for the purpose of talking over the Chicago nominations. Excepting where the gatherings were regularly organized, the conversation was carried on in a very moderate tone of voice. All expressed their astonishment and sore disappointment because of the failure of WILLIAM H. SEWARD to receive the nomination. With him they were confident they could have carried the State of New York, and, with that, the Union. However, ABRAM LINCOLN was a good Republican, and a strong man. So was HANNIBAL HAMLIN, and with them they would go into the fight, and win if they could. The largest Ward meeting was held in the Ninth Ward, where speeches were made by Mr. DOW and others, all expressing disappointment because Mr. SEWARD had not been nominated; but concluding, after, as Mr. DOW expressed it looking all through the matter and all around the matter, that the nomination of Mr. LINCOLN was a good one, and that if the people would enter warmly into the contest, in his fancy he would certainly be elected. A resolution, ratifying the nomination of Mr. LINCOLN, was passed, and the meeting adjourned. Soon after the adjournment the news of the nomination of HANNIBAL HAMLIN, for the Vice Presidency, was received, and those who remained, said they would have ratified that too, if they had known it in time.

There was a regularly organized meeting in the Twenty-first Ward, at which Mr. A. N. COFFIN, and others made speeches. They were the same in substance as those delivered elsewhere in the City. They all expressed disappointment and regret because of the failure of Mr. SEWARD to receive the nomination, but considered the nomination of Mr. LINCOLN a good one, and determined to support it. A resolution ratifying the nomination was passed unanimously, and the meeting adjourned. There, as in the Ninth Ward, the nomination of HANNIBAL HAMLIN was not known until after the adjournment, but they all promised it a hearty support.

In the other upper Wards there were no demonstrations of joy. Nearly all the Republicans expressed disappointment and regret freely, though but few of them expressed a determination not to support the ticket. In the lower Wards there was nothing done by way of joyous demonstration except in the City Hall Park, during the afternoon, where one hundred guns were fired, in the presence of several hundred persons.

In Wall-street, when the news of the nomination of Mr. LINCOLN was made known, the Republicans there either declined to talk at all on the subject, or expressed dissatisfaction with the result, nor did they, when the time came for leaving the street, appear to have changed their minds, or to have improved in spirits.

### THE NOMINATIONS ELSEWHERE.

NEW-YORK.

ALBANY, Friday, May 18.

One hundred guns are now being fired by some of the enthusiastic Republicans of this city, in honor of the nomination of LINCOLN for President. The greatest excitement prevails in the city. The streets are alive with politicians, and groups are gathered on State-street and Broadway discussing the subject of the nomination. The announcement of the nomination was entirely unexpected by the Republicans of this city. They were confident that WM. H. SEWARD was to be the man, and when it was announced that LINCOLN was the nominee a feeling of disappointment was manifest. At first the intelligence was not credited, but these doubts were of short duration. This feeling still exists, but they say that they will abide by the decision of the Convention, and give LINCOLN a hearty and cordial support.

ALBANY, Friday, May 18—9 P. M.

The Republicans of this city are now fairly waked up, and the wildest excitement prevails in regard to the nomination of LINCOLN. State-street is a perfect sea of fire from burning tar-barrels. The whole heavens are illuminated with a red glare, while cannon is firing, music is playing, and the people shouting on State-street and Broadway. Both streets are literally jammed with men of all parties, who are earnestly discussing the action of the Convention.

The Republicans of the City are now more reconciled to the nomination, and unite in hearty approval of it. They consider that while LINCOLN may not be as strong in the State as SEWARD, he will be less objectionable throughout the Union.

Since the reception of the news of the successful laying of the Atlantic cable, no more animated scene has ever been witnessed in this city than has been seen this evening. The firing of guns and the illumination of the principal thoroughfares have called out thousands of people, and the excitement is at the highest pitch.

ALBANY, Friday, May 18—11 P. M.

The Republicans here seem determined to keep up the excitement. They have just had a great pyrotecnic display on State-street. It is the intention of the Republicans here to extend a formal reception to the New-York delegation on their return from the Convention. A dispatch has been forwarded to them to this effect.

BUFFALO, Friday, May 18.

A salute was fired here, this afternoon, upon the receipt of the news of the nomination of LINCOLN and HAMLIN. No other evidences of mad enthusiasm, however, were manifested.

ROCHESTER, Friday, May 18.

A salute of 100 guns was fired this afternoon by the Republicans, in honor of the nomination of ABRAM LINCOLN.

ILLINOIS.

CHICAGO, Friday, May 18.

The nomination of Mr. LINCOLN for President by the Republican National Convention has been received by Illinois and the Northwest with an enthusiasm unparalleled since the days of 1840. The excitement which was centered in the Wigwam in the last three days was scattered throughout the city this evening. The "Wide Awakes" are marching in a procession numbering over 2,000 torch-lights, with banners, transparencies, &c.

The German Republicans formed also a large procession. The city is wild with excitement. All appear to have laid aside their gravity, and become boys again. Bonfires blaze at the corners of the streets. Meetings are being held in front of the Tremont and Metropolitan Hotels. A large and enthusiastic meeting is also being held in the Wigwam. Speeches were made by Mr. J. R. GIDDINGS and other prominent men, delegates of the Convention.

The *Press and Tribune* establishment, whose publication of the debates of the DOUGLAS and LINCOLN Senatorial Campaign of 1858 gave the latter much of his national reputation, is splendidly illuminated in honor of the success of their favorite candidate, with a large transparency at their front

"*For President*—Honest Old Abe."

"*For Vice-President*—Hannibal Hamlin."

A large number of other buildings in the City were also brilliantly illuminated.

SPRINGFIELD, Ill., Friday, May 18.

At noon to-day Mr. LINCOLN received the an-

[*Concluded on Eighth Page.*]

# The New-York Times.

VOL. IX—NO. 2731. | NEW-YORK, MONDAY, JUNE 25, 1860. | PRICE TWO CENTS.


## PRESIDENTIAL.

### The Proceedings of the Disunited Democracy.

### TWO TICKETS NOMINATED.

### Nomination of Douglas and Fitzpatrick by the Regulars.

### Breckinridge and Lane the Candidates of the Seceders.

### What is Thought of the Nominations.

Special Dispatch to the New-York Times.

BALTIMORE, Sunday, June, 24.

We have assurances from persons who ought to know that both BRECKINRIDGE and LANE will accept their nominations by the Convention of seceders.

It is the game of the Southern wing to defeat an election by the people and carry it into Congress, where they think they are reasonably certain of electing BRECKINRIDGE. The Douglas men here speak openly of preferring LINCOLN's election to such a result.

YANCEY and other extremists are delighted at the prospect. They say that they can either elect BRECKINRIDGE in the House and thus perpetuate their control over the Government, or else elect LINCOLN, which will give them an opportunity to rally the South in favor of dissolution.

The city is entirely deserted. H.

Dispatch to the Associated Press.

BALTIMORE, Sunday, June 24.

The nominations of both the Democratic and the Seceders Conventions, were received well here by their respective friends, but all the outside enthusiasm is for DOUGLAS. There was much excitement last night about the ballots. The nomination of the Seceding Convention was tendered to Mr. GUTHRIE's friends, as well as to Mr. HUNTER's, but both candidates declined. It is understood that Mr. BRECKINRIDGE will accept.

A challenge has been sent by A. SMITH, of California, to Mr. NESBITT, of Illinois, who was the Delegate who declared in the Convention, during Mr. SMITH's offensive remarks, that if Mr. CUSHING, the President, would not protect the members, they would protect themselves.

A large number of persons went to Washington to-day, both the friends of BRECKINRIDGE and DOUGLAS. Most of the New-York delegation return to-night.

### PROCEEDINGS OF THE CONVENTION.

FIFTH DAY.

BALTIMORE, Saturday, June 23.

The theatre is again crowded to-day.

The Douglas delegates from Louisiana and Alabama have taken seats.

Prayer was delivered by Rev. Mr. CUMMINGS.

Mr. DODGE, of Iowa, moved to dispense with the reading of the journal. Agreed to.

Mr. GARRETT, of Alabama, moved to have the names of the delegates from Alabama corrected according to the list sent up.

Mr. CALDWELL, of Kentucky, stated that after the withdrawal of the delegation last evening they held a meeting and reassembled again this morning. The circumstances in which they were placed were exceedingly embarrassing, and they were unable to come to a harmonious conclusion. The result is that ten delegates will withdraw from the Convention and nine remain. Those that withdraw beg leave to submit a paper stating their reasons for withdrawal. Five others desire for the present to suspend action with the Convention without taking part in any other body. In suspending their action with the Convention they hope there may yet arise an opportunity to act harmoniously with the Convention, and therefore retain their seats and the right to act with the Convention should such an opportunity arise. It is the wish of the ten that withdraw, and they request that their votes may not be cast by any other party. The action on their part has been taken without anger or bitterness, and in the deepest sorrow. They do not cast censure anywhere; it was not for them to question the action of any independent sovereignty. But it was felt to be their duty and policy to return to their constituents, and leave them free to act should there be two candidates in the field. He now withdrew the name of that disinterested patriot, Mr. GUTHRIE, from before this Convention as a candidate for the Presidency. He then presented papers from those who withdrew and those who suspend action, and also a communication from Hon. JAMES G. LEACH, one of the retiring delegates, stigmatizing the action of the Convention in harsh terms as unfair, undemocratic, irregular and attacking the majority in violent language.

The latter paper was read first, and after it had been read, Mr. PAINE, of Ohio, moved to return the paper immediately to the gentleman who presented it, with the intimation that the Convention declined to receive it.

Cries of "Yes!" "Yes!" "That's right!"

Mr. PAINE did not recognize the right of delegates seceding from the Convention to insult the majority, or to impugn the action of the Convention because a majority pass on the credentials of those claiming seats in the Convention.

Mr. CALDWELL assured the Convention that he had no knowledge of the contents of the paper just read. It had been handed to him while on the floor. The other papers would be found perfectly respectful in language and temper.

Mr. PAINE moved that the paper be handed back to its author.

Mr. SAYLES, of Rhode Island, hoped the motion would prevail. The paper was a direct insult to the Convention, as impugning the Convention, and a direct insult also to the Douglas delegates who had taken seats in the Convention. He trusted that the paper would be instantly separated from the others, and returned to the writer. He acquitted Mr. CALDWELL of all knowledge of the contents of the paper, and he felt certain that he would not have presented it if he had known its true character.

Mr. KAYE, of Missouri, hoped that the paper would be received. He desired to defend and justify the action of this Convention on the stump, and this paper was the best argument against the seceders.

Mr. RICHARDSON, of Illinois, suggested that the reading of the other papers be completed first.

Mr. LEACH, of Kentucky, disclaimed any intention to offer an insult to the Convention, or any of its members. He believed that the facts stated in his paper were incontrovertible, and believing them true, he had stated them plainly, but without any intent to insult the Convention.

The reception of the paper was unanimously declined, and it was returned to the writer.

Mr. WEST, of Connecticut, called for the question on proceeding to ballot for candidates. This is the sixth day of the proceedings of this Convention, and the country is weary of them.

Mr. REID, of Kentucky, on the part of a portion of the Kentucky delegation, declared that they had seen no cause why Kentucky should desert a Democratic Convention and the Democratic Party. The doomed city was to be saved if five true men could be found therein. Here were five delegates from Kentucky who intended to redeem and save that State. They recognize the Convention as the only Convention of the National Democratic Party. They will have no sectionalism of the North or the South, but will stand here as a pillar of fire between the men of both extremes. They were not going to abandon the Convention because one great leader whose pathway from Washington to the Great West had been lighted by gallant deeds was to be nominated. [Loud applause.] The people of the country would not leave the party, but would step forth in might and rescue it from the hands of politicians and out of the hands of the present Administration. [Immense applause, continued for several minutes.] The State of Kentucky would come up to the support of the nominee of the Convention, whoever he may be, and the five delegates present would stand by the action of the Convention, though the heavens fall. His colleague had withdrawn the name of Mr. GUTHRIE from before the Convention, but he, (REID,) on his part, begged to present that name again.

Mr. CLARK, of Missouri, desired to say that he would announce the action of the Missouri delegation after consultation.

Mr. KING, of Missouri, hoped that his colleague would say a part of the Missouri delegation, because some here do not wish the idea to go forth that consultation is necessary.

Mr. CLARK, of Missouri, said that such was the fact. A portion of the delegation desire to retire for consultation. Two had agreed to withdraw out of eighteen. The remainder will stay here where their constituents sent them, with the National Democratic Party of the Union.

Mr. HILL, of North Carolina, announced that while he found nothing in the action of the Convention to cause any man to withdraw, he yet felt that he should probably be doing injustice to his constituents if he remained to act any longer with the Convention when a majority of the delegates from his State had withdrawn.

Mr. MOORE, of Delaware, attempted to take the floor, but objections were made with loud calls for the question.

Mr. JONES, of Tennessee, said only thirteen delegates from Tennessee had withdrawn. It was represented that nineteen delegates had withdrawn, but six were simply appointed by the others, and had no delegated authority.

Cries of "Question, question."

Mr. COOPER, of Tennessee, rose to a question of privilege, and a scene of excitement ensued. He desired to reply to Mr. JONES, but the latter disclaimed any allusion to Mr. COOPER, and the Convention drowned their voices by cries of "Question," "Question."

Mr. JONES, of Pennsylvania, raised a point of order. This was no place to settle private quarrels.

The President decided that all remarks are out of order. He desired to present to the Convention two papers, one from Mr. STRAUMAN, of Arkansas, the other from the delegates from the State of Georgia.

Mr. PAINE, of Ohio, moved to suspend the reading and lay it on the table.

After some skirmishing this course was agreed to.

RESIGNATION OF THE PRESIDENT.

Loud calls for the "question" were then made, when the President then rose and said:

I beg the indulgence of the Convention to say, that whilst deeply sensible of the honor done me by the Convention in placing me in this chair, I was not less deeply sensible of the difficulties, general and personal, looming up in the future to environ my path. Nevertheless, in the solicitude to maintain the harmony and the union of the Democratic Party, and in the face of the retirement of the delegations of several of the States, I continued at my post laboring to that end, and in that sense had the honor to meet you, gentlemen, here at Baltimore. But circumstances have since transpired which compel me to pause. The delegations of a majority of the States have, either in whole or in part, in one form or another, ceased to participate in the deliberations of this Convention. At no time would any consideration of candidates have affected me, gentlemen, as to my duty, and I came here prepared, regardless of all personal preferences, cordially to support the nominee of this Convention, whomsoever they might be. But in the present circumstances I deem it a duty to self-respect, and I deem it still more a duty to this Convention as at present organized—I say I deem it my duty in both relations, whilst tendering my most grateful acknowledgments to all sides, and especially to those gentlemen who may have differed with me in opinion in any respect, whilst tendering my acknowledgments to all gentlemen for the cordial and honest support they have given the Chair when differing with him in his ruling; whilst tendering my respects to all, I deem it my duty to resign my seat as presiding officer of the Convention. [Tremendous applause.] I deem it my duty to resign my place as presiding officer of the Convention in order to take my place on the floor as a member of the delegation from Massachusetts, and to abide whatever may be the result of its future deliberations. [Loud applause.] I deem this a duty to the members of the Convention, in view of the circumstances in which it is placed. [Loud applause.]

The applause continued several moments, and as Mr. CUSHING left the chair the whole Convention rose, waving their hats and handkerchiefs and clapping their hands, mingled with cries of "Good," "Good," "Now we shall have a fair man in the chair."

Mr. TODD, of Ohio, Vice-President of the Convention, then took the chair, amidst loud applause. He briefly addressed the Convention, declaring that for over thirty years he had fought under the Democratic banner in the Giddings district, and he should not flinch from duty now. He asked the indulgence of the Convention while endeavoring to discharge the duties which had devolved upon him.

Mr. BUTLER, of Massachusetts, rose to speak, but the Convention refused to listen to him, when a scene of the utmost confusion and excitement ensued.

The Chair appealed to the honor of the Convention to keep quiet, when order once more became restored.

Several attempts subsequently were made to interrupt the proceedings, but the Chair quietly and steadily insisted on the preservation of order, and an immediate vote on the motion on which the previous question had been ordered since last evening.

THE BALLOTING FOR A CANDIDATE FOR PRESIDENT.

The resolution to proceed at once to ballot for a candidate for President was then adopted.

The roll was called, and when Massachusetts was reached,

Mr. BUTLER again claimed the floor to explain the position of the delegation from Massachusetts.

Objections were made; but the Chair decided that when a State was called the Chairman of the delegation had a right to explain the vote or position of the delegation.

Mr. BUTLER then, on the part of a portion of the delegation, presented a protest against the unjust exclusion of one of their number from the Convention, and withdrew from further action with the Convention.

Loud applause followed this, with cries of "Good," "Good," "Go along," "Go along."

Mr. BUTLER resumed, saying that he desired to place the withdrawal on the ground that a majority of the States had seceded, and he desired to say that he could not act with a Convention in which a gentleman had advocated the reopening of the African Slave-trade. [Loud laughter, yells and hisses.]

Mr. BUTLER then retired, with others from the Massachusetts delegation, amidst derisive applause from the Convention and galleries.

The call of the roll proceeded.

Mr. DAWSON, of Pennsylvania, asked leave for that delegation to retire for consultation. (Cries of "No," "no.") He desired to say they only wished to consult as to the candidate.

When Massachusetts was called, Mr. STEVENS, of that State, said, although he was not yet ready to cast the vote of the State, he would not let his name be called twice without a response. The action of those who rejected their duties and the party would be indignantly repudiated and reprobated by the democracy of the whole State. (Cheers.) The people are pledged over and over again for the principles of non-intervention, and there were those who have retired from this hall who were elected as delegates only because they pledged themselves to vote for Judge Douglas.

Messrs. BRENT, of Maryland, HOGE, of Virginia, and GAULDEN, of Georgia, in turn denounced the secessionists from their States, and signified their intention to act with the National Democratic Convention.

Mr. PARSONS, of Alabama, denounced the secession movement as one of disunion, and when they declared opposition to disunion, they only spoke the sentiments of a large majority of the people of Alabama. This fight had been anticipated. They were prepared for it—prepared to see a violent effort made to break up the Democratic Party, so that the bonds of this Union may be severed. Shall this effort succeed? [Cries of "No," "no."] Shall it be said that 1860 shall see the grave of the Union opened? No. They would find that one voice would come up from the Gulf States—from the cotton States of the South. The heart of the whole South will throb with enthusiasm when called on to rally to the support of the Union. The Convention had been told that the delegates now present from Alabama did not represent the people of Alabama. He appealed to the ballot-box for a refutation of this statement. They were prepared to meet the seceders now on the issue of disunion they now make, as they met them on the same issue in 1851. He cast the vote of Alabama as a unit for STEPHEN A. DOUGLAS. [Tremendous applause.]

Mr. SOULE, of Louisiana, next addressed the Convention when that State was called. He was hailed with round after round of applause.

When the State of Louisiana was called Hon. PIERRE SOULE rose and was received with enthusiastic cheers and applause. After silence had been restored the gentleman proceeded as follows:

Mr. PRESIDENT: I am appalled, truly appalled, by the ejaculations which the welcome which has just been extended to me seems to signify. I am the last man in this Convention from whom anything deserving these manifestations could be expected; and it is at once with a deep feeling of gratitude for what kindness there was in them, and of great diffidence, that I attempt to address you on this most solemn and momentous occasion. Be not afraid, however, that I shall trespass long upon your kindness and your attention. But a few remarks from me will lay the foundation for the vote which I shall cast for the noble State which I have the honor in part to represent in this body. I have not been at all discouraged by the emotion which has been attempted to be created in this body by those who have seceded from it. We from the farthest South were prepared. We had heard around us the rumors which were to be mitiatory of the acts which you have witnessed this day, and we knew that the conspiracy which had been brooding for months past would break out on this occasion and for the purposes which are obvious to every member. Sirs, there are in political life men who were once possessed of popular favor and consider that the favor has become to them an inalienable property, and who clung to it as something that can no longer be wrested from their hands; political fossils, so much enervated in office that there is hardly any power that can extract them. [Applause.] They saw that the popular voice was clearly manifesting to this glorious nation who was to be the next ruler. More than eight or ten months before the Convention assembled the name of that future ruler of these States has been thrown into the canvass and was before the people. Instead of bringing a candidate to oppose him, instead of creating before the people issues upon which the choice of the nation could be enlightened, instead of principles discussed, what have we seen? An unrelenting war against the individual presumed to be the favorite of the nation. (Applause.) A war waged by an army of unprincipled and unscrupulous politicians leagued with a power which could not be exerted on their side without disgracing itself and disgracing the nation. [Renewed applause.] When this Convention assembled at Charleston, the idea had not yet struck their minds that a movement of the nature of the one which has been effected could be based upon the doctrines of the distinguished gentleman from Alabama, Mr. YANCEY, who has fathered this secession. It was presumed by these political intriguers outside of the Convention who were manœuvering the measures through by which the destruction of the Democratic Party was to be effected—it was presumed by them that it would be in their power, after raising the storm, to master and guide it, but it will be found before forty-eight hours have elapsed that in that storm they are bound eventually to sink and disappear. [Loud applause.] For it is idle for Southern men to disguise the true object of that movement. Secession from the Democratic Party can be nothing else than a disruption of that party at the very moment when the hopes of the whole nation are hanging upon its continuing in power. [Applause.] Secession is a word intended to conceal another word of more significancy. If secession was to find an echo among the people of this great confederacy, then no longer could this Republic boast that the structure which our fathers erected with so much sacrifice and so much toil was a noble experiment. Secession must beget disunion. Upon what pretence must secession have been predicted? I will not do those distinguished gentlemen who stepped out of this room this morning the injustice to suppose that they truly parted from you because of your having decided the question of internal organization in a manner that did not agree with their views. They may give this, give this as a pretence; they may use it as a cloak to cover their desertion from the party, but the truth cannot be disguised. Whether deluded or not, they are tools in the hands of intriguers, and their course must necessarily tend to disunion [Applause.]

Sirs, it is said that they carry with them out of this Convention, the sympathies of the South, believe it not. [Renewed applause.] Believe it not; and I have in my own experience of the past, certain stray reasons why I cannot bring my mind to the supposition that the South, under present circumstances, can respond to that movement, and I will briefly lay them before you. In 1849 and 50, when California was about being admitted into this Union, the South rose against her admission, passed resolutions and impressed upon the minds of the North, that if the outrage was perpetrated she would secede from the Union. Many of us, who were then the representatives of the South in the National Councils, believing that the South was in earnest, and considering ourselves bound to follow in her footsteps, bought the battle not with the view of creating the contingency contemplated, but to defend the rights of the South and oppose the introduction of California into the councils of the nation. That at that time was to the South the great wrong and the creating of a great danger, because not only was California coming into the Union with a Constitution obliterating the Missouri Compromise not only was she coming into the Union without passing through the ordeal in Territorial existence;—not only was she coming into the Union organized by the military forces of the Federal Government;—but her entrance into the Union was going to destroy that power of numbers which was the last bulwarks of our protection in the Senate. In the higher House of Congress we fought against that wrong—we engaged in the battle to maintain our rights to the last, but when the question came to the last, one after the other, we saw the States of the South receding from their position—disowning every effort we had made to maintain our rights, and, let me say it with sorrow, dragging us into the very gutter for the very devotion we had shown them. And why did the South do this? There is no ungrateful breast at the South. It could not be that she was inclined to disown the services of those who had stood by her to the last; but it was because she considered, and truly considered, that even an impending wrong was not to be put in the scale with the preservation of this glorious Confederacy—[great applause]—and we, in obedience to their wishes, out of deference to their convictions, surrendered. We considered that we were in duty bound to abide by your own decisions; and perhaps it may not be improper for me here to refer to the considerations upon which those decisions were predicted. The only compensation which the South could find in the measures generally known as the Compromise measures, was the doctrine of non-intervention then claimed. [Applause.] That was the only boon offered to us in those days as a compensation for the great sacrifice which was asked at our hands, and the South accepted the compromise, and the compromise became the law of the nation, certainly of the party as far as the question of Slavery was concerned. I am surprised at the extreme sensitiveness exhibited by men of the South at this day upon that question of non-intervention. JOHN C. CALHOUN, when the famous compromise tendered by Mr. CLAYTON of Delaware was being discussed in the United States Senate, considered that the proffer to place in the hands of one federal tribunal the question of the extent of power in the Territories, was to the South a sufficient guaranty to make acceptable the compromise tendered, and where Mr. CALHOUN could stand a Southern man need not fear to stand. [Applause.] I have said, in the very unconnected remarks that I have had the honor to submit to you, that secession meant disunion, and I will go on now to show you you what considerations that opinion of mine is predicated. That is the question at issue. On the one hand, Northern Abolitionists claim intervention for the purpose of excluding Slavery from the Territories; on the other hand Southern men claim intervention on the part of Congress for purpose of protecting Slavery in the Territories. Now I ask Southern gentlemen, here and elsewhere, are you serious, when the battle is thus drawn—when the lines are thus drawn out—when the whole strength of the North is combined with the great strength on the part of the West, to exclude Slavery from the Territories? Are you, my friends of the South, in earnest when you ask to submit the protection of your property to the keeping of such men as may be sent from the North and West to constitute the majority in your Congress? There is not a paper in the South which is not teeming with denunciations that Congress has became a rotten body, that the majority in both Houses is in heart, to all intents and purposes opposed to Slavery, and yet these men who set up the pretension of being the exclusive friends of Slavery at the South, ask that the protection of Slavery shall be put in the keeping of that very power which is represented as being bent upon its destruction. [Applause.] I say whatever be the views that they take of the manner in which that power might eventually be exerted; from the moment that the power is recognized as existing in Congress, from that moment there is not a Southern heart, which does not beat to the conviction that Slavery is gone. And if that should be the ultimatum of the issue, is the South ready now for it? Have they prepared their armor? Are they ready for the battle? Sirs, they are not, and the reasons are very obvious. The gentlemen who have seceded from the Convention know that the masses of the people at home will not respond to the call which they have made upon them; and the best proof of it is that in no State whose delegations have seceded did the seceders call a fair Convention of the people, to put to the test the innovation which they have attempted. [Applause.] I perceive that I have detained the Convention longer than I have intended—[cries of "go on," "go on,"]—and my own strength is nearly exhausted Mr. President, though Louisiana is mindful of what she owes to her sisters of the South, and is even ready to act in concert with them when actual oppression shall call for actual resistance, still Louisiana is unwilling to risk her future and the future of this Union upon impracticable issues, and purely theoretical abstractions. (Applause.) She cannot be so far oblivious of the past and recent services to disown that fearless and indomitable champion of popular rights, and of State equality; him who, in that great and memorable struggle which, in his own State, initiated that war which has been waged against him so unrelentingly; him who has vindicated the rights of the South so victoriously against his infuriated opponents; him who will yet enable us to triumph over the enemies of the South, the Black Republicans, who are arrayed against us—Louisiana casts her entire vote for STEPHEN A. DOUGLAS, of Illinois. [Vociferous cheers and applause.]

Mr. STRAUMAN, of Arkansas, here signified his intention as an individual member of a delegation representing half a vote, to withdraw.

Several delegates rose as different States were called, and gave in their allegiance to Judge Douglas.

In announcing the vote of Pennsylvania, Mr. DAWSON stated that nine delegates refused to vote.

One delegate cast a vote for HORATIO SEYMOUR, of New-York.

Dr. BISSELL, of New-York immediately arose and read a letter from Mr. SEYMOUR, peremptorily withdrawing his name, and refusing to be a candidate for any office on the ticket. He stated he had this letter in his possession at Charleston, and it had been the intention of Governor SEYMOUR to withdraw whenever his name was mentioned. He should not have stated this had not a paper, with whose name he blushed to pollute his lips, the New-York Herald, persisted in the silly falsehood that Mr. SEYMOUR was a candidate.

FIRST BALLOT.

The first ballot was then announced, as follows:

| | | | |
|---|---|---|---|
| Douglas | 173½ | Bocock | 1 |
| Guthrie | 9 | Wise | 1 |
| Breckinridge | 5 | Dickinson | 1 |
| Horatio Seymour | 1 | Blank | 21 |

Whole number of votes ........ 212½

Every State was represented in the vote except Delaware, South Carolina, Florida, Mississippi, Texas, California and Oregon. Georgia was represented in part, but did not vote.

Mr. CHURCH, of New-York, offered the following:

*Resolved*, That STEPHEN A. DOUGLAS, having received two-thirds of all the votes cast in this National Democratic Convention, is, according to the rules of this Convention and the usages of the Democratic Party, declared nominated for the office of President of the United States.

Mr. FLOURNOY, of Arkansas, wished another ballot might be taken. They would make the vote stronger next time.

Mr. CHURCH—You can make it as strong as you please after the adoption of the resolution.

Several delegates rose to speak, but after considerable excitement and confusion the point of order was raised that the resolution was not in order, as it changed the rule of the Convention.

Mr. CHURCH agreed that, according to the decision of the former chairman at Charleston the resolution only interpreted the rule, and did not change it.

The President ruled the resolution in order.

Mr. CHURCH explained the position of New-York in this contest. She had been willing to yield all except personal honor, and the honor of her constituents, to conciliate and harmonize the Democratic party. But when approached and told they must yield the candidate who was chosen, and who was the choice of the democracy of the State, and in addition admit unconditionally to the Convention men who had seceded without any just cause, they had spurned the overtures. They would now go home and sweep the State of New-York as a whirlwind. [Loud applause.] They had at Charleston voted to construe the two-thirds rule to mean two-thirds of the vote of the Electoral College, at the request of the South, who remained with them on the pledge that if they so voted the South would remain with the Convention. A portion of the South had broken the pledge, and now this wrong construction of the rule was no longer a peace offering. New-York was prepared to take all responsibility for the resolution he now offered. A portion of the South had seceded only for the avowed reason that a majority of the Convention chose to decide on the contested seat questions against the wishes of the minority, and if such action was indorsed by the party there would be an end of all conventions.

Mr. DUNNING, of Indiana, made a stirring speech in favor of DOUGLAS as the choice of nineteen twentieths of the Democrats throughout the Union. He should be the unanimous nominee of the Democratic Convention, as he is of the Democracy of the Union.

Mr. GITTINGS, of Maryland, spoke against the resolution. He desired to ballot.

Mr. CHURCH then withdrew the resolution for another ballot, Mr. HOGE, of Virginia, declaring he would move the nomination be unanimous as soon as the next vote was declared.

Mr. SAYLES, of Rhode Island, made an eloquent address, declaring that firm adherence to Judge DOUGLAS and his principles had alone enabled Rhode Island to wipe out five thousand majority on the Black Republican side and carry the State by two thousand majority.

DAVID L. SEYMOUR, on the part of the Dickinson men of the New-York delegation, said they stood in a peculiar position. They had used all honorable means to secure the nomination of the great son of New-York, DANIEL S. DICKINSON. [Applause.] But he was now ready on their behalf to acknowledge that a great majority of the people of the State were in favor of the nomination of DOUGLAS, and with one voice the friends of DANIEL S. DICKINSON would rally to the support of the nominee.

Mr. MASON, of Kentucky, gave in his allegiance to DOUGLAS, while expressing his preference for Mr. GUTHRIE.

THE SECOND BALLOT.

The second ballot was then announced, DOUGLAS getting 181½ votes—the balance scattering.

Subjoined is the vote on the second ballot in detail:

| | Breckinridge. | Guthrie. | Douglas. |
|---|---|---|---|
| Maine | — | — | 7 |
| New-Hampshire | — | — | 5 |
| Vermont | — | — | 5 |
| Massachusetts | — | — | 10 |
| Rhode Island | — | — | 4 |
| Connecticut | ½ | — | 3½ |
| New-York | — | — | 31 |
| New Jersey | — | — | 2½ |
| Pennsylvania | 10 | 2½ | 10 |
| Maryland | — | — | 2½ |
| Virginia | — | — | 3 |
| North Carolina | — | — | 1 |
| Alabama | — | — | 9 |
| Arkansas | — | — | 1½ |
| Missouri | — | — | 4½ |
| Tennessee | — | — | 3 |
| Kentucky | — | 1½ | 3 |
| Ohio | — | — | 23 |
| Indiana | U | — | 12 |
| Illinois | — | — | 11 |
| Michigan | — | — | 6 |
| Wisconsin | — | — | 6 |
| Iowa | — | — | 4 |
| Minnesota | — | — | 4 |

Whole number of votes ........ 194½.

Seven of the Pennsylvania delegates declined voting.

NOMINATION OF STEPHEN A. DOUGLAS FOR PRESIDENT.

Messrs. HOGE, of Virginia, and CLARK, of Missouri, then simultaneously seconded the resolution of Mr. CHURCH, declaring Judge DOUGLAS nominated, according to the usages of the Democratic Party and the rules of the Convention, by a two-thirds vote.

The resolution was adopted unanimously.

A scene of excitement then ensued that evinced the violence of the feelings so long pent up. The cheers were deafening, every person in the theatre rising, waving hats, handkerchiefs, and evincing the utmost enthusiasm. The scene could not be exceeded in excitement. From the upper tier banners long kept in reserve were unfurled and waved before the audience. On the stage appeared banners, one of which was borne by the delegation from Pennsylvania, bearing the motto, "Pennsylvania good for 40,000 majority for the Douglas." Cheers for the "Little Giant," and responded to until all was in a perfect roar inside the building and outside.

After considerable time, something like order being restored, the President said: With heartfelt satisfaction, as presiding officer of this Convention, I declare STEPHEN A. DOUGLAS, by unanimous vote, the candidate of the Democratic Party of the Union for President of these United States, and may God, in his infinite mercy, protect him and the Union he represents.

The Convention again rose *en masse*, and the scene of excitement was renewed, cheer after cheer being sent forth for the nominee.

Mr. DAWSON, of Pennsylvania, being called, took the floor, and in an eloquent speech gave the indorsement of Pennsylvania to the nominee, declaring admiration for his ability, gallantry and devotion to the Democracy and the Union.

Mr. SIBLY, of Maine, followed in an able speech.

JOHN COCHRANE, of New-York, on behalf of the Guthrie men of that State, warmly indorsed Judge DOUGLAS, admitting he was, above all others, the choice of the Democracy of New-York, and declaring their intentions to support him with the utmost enthusiasm.

Loud applause followed each address, and at the close the Convention took a recess till 7 P. M.

### EVENING SESSION.

NOMINATION OF BENJAMIN FITZPATRICK, OF ALABAMA, FOR VICE-PRESIDENT.

On the reassembling of the Convention, BENJAMIN FITZPATRICK, of Alabama, was unanimously nominated for Vice-President on the first ballot.

On motion, the Democratic National Committee for four years was appointed, the member from New-York being Mr. AUGUST BELMONT.

Mr. RICHARDSON, of Illinois, then made a speech, thanking the Convention for the high honor conferred on his State in selecting for the candidate for the Presidency her favorite son. Alluding to the seceders, he said that if the Democratic Party should be defeated and perpetually ruined, they, the seceders, must bear the responsibility, not DOUGLAS or his friends. In this connection he produced a letter from Mr. DOUGLAS, dated Washington, the 20th inst., authorizing and requesting his friends to withdraw his name if in their judgment harmony could be restored to the Democratic ranks. Mr. RICHARDSON then said that the course of the seceders had placed it out of the power of the friends of Mr. DOUGLAS to make any use of the letter. He concluded by saying that when the Government fails to accomplish the object for which it was formed let it go down.

LETTER FROM MR. DOUGLAS.

The following is the letter of Mr. DOUGLAS:

WASHINGTON, June 20—1 P. M.

MY DEAR SIR: I learn there is imminent danger that the Democratic Party will be demoralized, if not destroyed, by the breaking up of the Convention. Such a result would inevitably expose the country to the perils of sectional strife between the Northern and Southern partisans of Congressional intervention upon the subject of Slavery in the Territories. I firmly and conscientiously believe that there is no safety for the country, no hope for the preservation of the Union except by a faithful and rigid adherence to the doctrine of non-intervention by Congress with Slavery in the Territories. Intervention means disunion. There is no difference in principle between Northern and Southern intervention. The one intervenes for Slavery, and the other against Slavery; but each appeals to the passions and prejudices of his own section against the peace of the whole country and the right of self-government by the people of the Territories. Hence the doctrine of non-intervention must be maintained at all hazards. But while I can never sacrifice the principle even to obtain the Presidency, I will cheerfully and joyfully sacrifice myself to maintain the principle. If, therefore, you and my other friends who have stood by me with such heroic firmness at Charleston and Baltimore, shall be of the opinion that the principle can be preserved, and the unity and ascendancy of the Democratic Party maintained, and the country saved from the perils of Northern Abolitionism and Southern disunion by withdrawing my name and uniting with some other non-intervention Union-loving Democrat, I beseech you to pursue that course. Do not understand me as wishing to dictate to my friends; I have implicit confidence in yours and their patriotism, judgment and discretion. Whatever you may do in the premises will meet my hearty approval. But I conjure you to act with a single eye to the safety and welfare of the country, and without the slightest regard to my individual interest or aggrandizement. My interest will be best promoted, and my ambition gratified, and motives vindicated, by that course on the part of my friends which will be most effectual in saving the country from being ruled or ruined by a sectional party. The action of the Charleston Convention, by sustaining me by so large a majority on the platform, and designating me as the first choice of the party for the Presidency, is all the personal triumph I desire. This letter is prompted by the same motives which induced my dispatch four years ago, withdrawing my name from the Cincinnati Convention. With this knowledge of my opinions and wishes you and your other friends must act upon your own convictions of duty.

Very truly, your friend,

S. A. DOUGLAS.

To Hon. WM. A. RICHARDSON, Baltimore, Md.

Mr. WICKLIFFE, of Louisiana offered the following, which he said would give DOUGLAS 40,000 in his State:

*Resolved*, That it is in accordance with the Cincinnati Platform, that during the existence of Territorial Governments the measure of restriction, whatever it may be, imposed by the Federal constitution on the power of the Territorial legislature over the subject of the domestic relations, as the same has been or shall hereafter be finally determined by the Supreme Court of the United States should be respected by all good citizens, and enforced with promptness and fidelity by every branch of the General Government.

Mr. PAINE, of Ohio, called for the previous question, when the resolution was adopted.

The Convention, then, after the passage of several unimportant resolutions, adjourned *sine die*.

### THE SECEDERS' CONVENTION.

BALTIMORE, Saturday, June 23.

The Seceders' Convention met at noon to-day, in the Maryland Institute, which was crowded to its utmost capacity.

The Convention was called to order by Mr. EWING, of Tennessee.

Mr. RUSSELL, of Virginia, was chosen temporary Chairman, and addressed the Convention as follows:

GENTLEMEN OF THE NATIONAL DEMOCRATIC CONVENTION: I do not know of anything on which the honor in selecting me Chairman of this Democratic Convention is based, except it is the honor to the ancient and loyal Commonwealth of Virginia, whose interest I here represent. The first official act of this Convention since it assembled at this place has been to signify that it will be governed by the usages, principles and spirit which have governed the National State Rights Democracy of Virginia. The Convention which has assembled elsewhere, and from which you have withdrawn, has lost all title to the designation of national. It cannot perform the functions of a National Democratic Convention, and every one believes that all true Democrats will unite to declare it unsound in national relations. You and those you represent are a majority of the people, of the Democracy and of Democratic States. They will look to you to perform the functions of a National Democratic Convention; and you will be so recognized alike by the North and South, the East and the West. [Loud and enthusiastic cheers.] I have every confidence that you will stand upon the principles and will be able to defend the Democratic Party, protect the rights of all the States, and maintain the Constitution against all enemies, open or insidious. With this brief reliance upon you and confidence in the justice of our course, I am prepared to perform, in a humble and imperfect way, the duties you have confided to me.

Mr. JOHNSON, of Maryland, and Mr. CRAWSBY, of Oregon, were elected Secretaries.

A Committee on Permanent Organization was then appointed, when the Convention adjourned until 5 o'clock this evening.

The following States are represented in the Convention, wholly or in part:

| | |
|---|---|
| Virginia, | Louisiana, |
| North Carolina, | Mississippi, |
| South Carolina, | Texas, |
| Missouri, | Tennessee, |
| California, | Kentucky, |
| Oregon, | Arkansas. |
| Florida, | |

The Wood delegation to the Charleston Convention will claim admission here.

The South Carolina delegates did not feel authorized to come to Baltimore; but they are with the seceders.

AFTERNOON SESSION.

The Seceders' Convention reassembled at 5 P. M.

The hall was densely crowded in every part. There were fully three thousand persons present, and the greatest enthusiasm was manifested.

On motion of Mr. DAVIS, of Mississippi, the ladies were invited to occupy the vacant seats on the floor.

The CHAIR then requested the several delegations to hand up the list of members.

The roll was called and the following States responded.

Vermont, one delegate.
Massachusetts, sixteen delegates.
New York responded.
Pennsylvania responded.
Delaware responded.
Maryland responded.
Virginia, twenty-four.
North Carolina, nineteen and a half delegates.
Georgia, twenty-eight delegates.
Florida responded that all the delegates from that State were not here, but all will be soon.
Alabama, twenty-nine.
Louisiana, all the delegates.
Texas, all the delegates.
Mississippi, fourteen delegates.
Arkansas responded.
Missouri, two delegates.
Tennessee, nineteen delegates.
Kentucky, ten delegates.
Iowa was responded to by Mr. HEATH, of that State.
Minnesota responded.
California responded, her whole electoral vote.
Oregon, all her delegates.

Mr. WALKER, from the Committee on Permanent Organization, reported Hon. CALEB CUSHING for permanent President of the Convention.

This announcement was received with tremendous cheering.

The Committee also reported Vice-Presidents from each State represented.

The Committee also recommended that the rules and regulations of the Democratic Conventions of 1852 and 1856 be adopted, with the qualification that in making the nominations for President and Vice-President, two-thirds of the votes of all the States represented be necessary; that each delegate in the Convention shall cast the vote to which he is entitled, and that each State shall only cast the number of votes to which it may be entitled by actual representation in the Convention. This was adopted unanimously.

Mr. LEVERING moved the appointment of a Committee on Credentials to whom the credentials of Delegates should be submitted, but he accepted the amendment of Mr. JOHNSON, of Maryland, that the credentials be referred to the Committee on Credentials already appointed, (referring to those members of the said Committee who seceded from the regular Convention.)

Mr. HENRY, of Pennsylvania, moved that a Committee be appointed to inform Mr. CUSHING of his election as President, and request him to resume his seat.

The motion was greeted with loud applause.

Presently the Committee appeared, conducting Mr. CUSHING through the densely-packed hall. His appearance was greeted with immense cheering, the whole body rising in a mass to their feet and giving cheer after cheer.

When quietness had become somewhat restored, Mr. RUSSELL kindly greeted Mr. CUSHING and handed him to the platform, when the cheering was again renewed.

As soon as silence was restored Mr. RUSSELL said, turning to Mr. CUSHING:

GENTLEMEN OF THE CONVENTION—Your chosen President needs no introduction from me, for you have already acknowledged him as one who is now, as he has been before, the President of the National Democratic Convention. (Tremendous cheering.)

Mr. CUSHING, on taking the Chair, said:

GENTLEMEN—We are reassembled here as delegates to the National Democratic Convention, duly accredited from more than twenty States, for the purpose of annunciating the principles of the party, and for the purpose of continuing and reestablishing the principles of the party, of upholding the Constitution and the Union, and the coequal rights of the several States. [Loud cheering.]

The Chair then announced that the Convention will now proceed to business.

The Committee on Credentials reported that no person from North Carolina was present or authorized to say whether they were prepared to act with the Convention or not. They reported that 110 delegates were present, including two from New-York, (Messrs. BARTLETT and SCHELL,) one from Vermont, and two from Missouri.

The report of the Committee on Credentials was then adopted.

Mr. HUNTER, of Louisiana, offered a resolution, which was adopted, inviting the delegates from North Carolina and Florida, accredited to Richmond, to unite with their brethren of the National Democratic Convention, assembled at the Maryland Institute Hall, upon the same platform and principles with themselves, provided they feel authorized to do so.

Mr. H. H. HEATH, of Iowa, presented a paper signed by himself and another, stating that no election of delegates had been made by the National State Rights Democrats of Iowa, but knowing the sentiments and wishes of the democracy of that State, they came here to consult in the deliberations of this Convention.

Objection was made to the reception of the paper, and it was subsequently referred to the Committee on Credentials.

Mr. SEWALL moved that the Iowa delegates be invited to retain their seats until the Committee on Credentials reported whether they were entitled to them. Adopted.

Mr. J. D. C. ATKINSON, of Tennessee, moved that the Chairman of each delegation on the floor at once report to the Chairman of the Committee on Credentials the names of the delegates entitled to vote, so that the Convention can at once proceed to make nominations. He thanked God that he was at length on a floor where he could speak without being hissed at.

Mr. RUSSELL proposed the appointment of a committee to report the names of candidates for President and Vice-President to the Convention, but subsequently withdrew it.

Mr. BUTLER, of Massachusetts, as a member of the Committee on Resolutions in the Charleston Convention, now on this floor resigned his place in the Committee, and nominated Hon. BENJAMIN F. HALLETT, of Massachusetts, to fill the vacancy. Agreed to.

On motion of Mr. FISHER, of Virginia the Chair was directed to appoint a committee of five to prepare an address to the Democracy of the Union upon the principles which have governed this body in making nominations for the Presidency and Vice-Presidency, and in vindication of the principles of the party.

Mr. HOWARD, of Tennessee, moved that Hon. CALEB CUSHING, President of the Convention, be Chairman of said Committee.

The motion was unanimously adopted with great applause.

Mr. AVERY, of North Carolina, reported from the Committee on Resolutions the platform of the Seceders at Charleston without crossing a t or dotting an i. He then moved the previous question, which was ordered, and the platform adopted.

Mr. CHAPMAN, of Alabama, moved to reconsider the vote and to lay that motion on the table. Carried.

Mr. MATHEWS, of Mississippi, moved that the National Democratic Committee be instructed not to issue tickets to any delegates whose seats are contested to a National Convention. Adopted.

Mr. GREEN, of North Carolina, moved that all the States in the Union be invited to run an electoral ticket for the candidates of this Convention. Carried.

Mr. WALKER moved an informal recess of fifteen minutes.

Cries of "No," "No," when the motion was withdrawn.

A resolution was adopted that the National Committee be appointed by the delegations naming a member for each State.

A resolution was also adopted that the next Convention be held at Philadelphia.

Mr. BARKSDALE, of Mississippi, moved that the Convention now proceed to nominate candidates for President and Vice-President of the United States.

Motion carried.

Mr. FISHER, of Virginia, moved that the chairman of each delegation be requested to collect a sum of money from each delegate and hand it to the Maryland delegation.

A VOICE—How much.

Mr. JOHNSON, of Maryland, here rose and begged leave to state that the Maryland delegation claimed the privilege of paying for the use of the hall.

Mr. BRADFORD said in Pennsylvania there were several districts only represented by one delegate. He wished to know if they were to cast one vote or half a vote?

Mr. BUTLER, of Massachusetts, said that only half a vote should be cast, that being all each delegate was entitled to at Charleston.

The President said that if the balloting was to be the same as in the Democratic Convention, each must vote half a vote.

Mr. YANCEY thought each Congressional district entitled to one vote. If two were here they might cast but one vote, but when one only was here he should cast the whole vote of the district.

After debate it was decided that a whole vote should be cast by each single representative.

Mr. HUNTER of Louisiana, said that his delegation was entitled to the whole vote of the State as the majority directs. The whole delegation was not here, but he should claim the right to cast the whole vote of the State.

Mr. LORING, of Massachusetts, made several attempts to obtain the floor, but was eventually cut off by a motion for the previous question.

The President announced that he had received a dispatch from two delegates from Minnesota not here, asking that Mr. JOHNSON, of Maryland, might cast their votes.

Mr. AVERY rose to a point of order. He thought it a dangerous precedent to allow these votes to be cast by proxy by a delegate from another State.

Mr. STEVENS, of Oregon, moved that Mr. JOHNSON, of Maryland, be entitled to cast the vote of the delegates from Minnesota.

This was agreed to.

NOMINATION OF JOHN C. BRECKINRIDGE FOR PRESIDENT.

Mr. LORING, of Massachusetts, addressed the Convention, pledging Massachusetts to stand by the South in her struggle for constitutional right. The delegates from Massachusetts had no personal prejudices. They desired only to present the name of a man who had "no friends to reward or enemies to punish." They claimed the right, on behalf of the Democracy of Massachusetts, to present the name of the gallant son of Kentucky, JOHN C. BRECKINRIDGE.

Loud and enthusiastic cheering greeted this nomination.

Mr. DENNY, of Pennsylvania, on behalf of those present, seconded the nomination.

Mr. WARD, of Alabama, nominated R. M. T. HUNTER, of Virginia. (Applause.)

Mr. EWING, of Tennessee, with appropriate remarks, nominated DANIEL S. DICKINSON, of New-York lauding him as an able statesman, who had ever stood by the Constitution and true Democratic principles. (Applause.)

Mr. STEVENS, of Oregon, desired to nominate a man who had for the last half-century had practical experience in the active life of our growing country. He alluded to his achievements in Mexico to his worth as a statesman, as a man of unblemished honor, and presented the name of Gen. JOSEPH LANE, of Oregon. (Applause.)

Mr. MATHEWS, of Mississippi, desired to say his delegation was instructed to present the name of one of her distinguished sons as a candidate—the distinguished lawyer, statesman and orator, JEFFERSON DAVIS. But the Mississippi delegation, for the sake of harmony and peace, withdrew his name. They had won a glorious victory on the platform, and that was enough. They would now join in support of the man indicated as the choice of the Convention, and go home satisfied that though they had yielded their candidate, they had secured his principles.

Mr. RUSSELL, of Virginia, desired to express the thanks of his State to Alabama for nominating her favorite son for a high office. They might take the assurance of the delegation that he was heart and hand with them. He could see nothing so well calculated to secure the success of their principles as this organization, but he desired to say that the difficult circumstances surrounding the Democratic Party are such that Mr. HUNTER cannot now accept any nomination at the hands of either Convention. He therefore requested Alabama to withdraw his name.

Mr. WARD, of Alabama, withdrew the name, as requested, expressing profound admiration for Virginia.

Mr. STEVENS, of Oregon, in order to secure harmony of action, begged to withdraw the name of Gen. LANE, of Oregon.

Mr. BARTLETT of New-York, when the name of New-York was called, said he was not at Charleston, but came here as a substitute, and entered the delegation under the unit rule. After one day's session he became satisfied the State had been filled, and he was placed, with others, in the minority. He enlarged upon what he considered the injustice of this rule, and stated that, though some who sympathized with them were not here, yet a few were here to express devotion to the principles of the platform adopted here to-day, and sympathy with the South, pledging themselves to stand by that Platform.

An attempt was made to nominate without a ballot by acclamation, but failed.

When the roll was called the whole number of votes cast were 105, of which Mr. BRECKINRIDGE received 81, and DICKINSON 24.

The States which had cast their votes for DICKINSON then withdrew, giving the full vote of the Convention, 105, for BRECKINRIDGE.

The President announced the result, when the Convention rose and applauded enthusiastically, giving several rounds of applause.

NOMINATION OF JOSEPH LANE FOR VICE-PRESIDENT.

Loud calls were made for YANCEY, but Mr. GREEN, of North Carolina, nominated JOSEPH LANE for Vice-President.

Loud cries of "Vote," "Vote."

Mr. SCOTT, of California, seconded the nomination, with appropriate remarks.

Mr. ADKINS, of Tennessee, moved to make the nomination by acclamation.

Cries of "No," "No," "Call the roll."

On the first ballot, the whole 105 votes were for JOSEPH LANE, and he was declared nominated amidst loud applause.

Deafening calls were then made for YANCEY, who took the platform amidst cheers. He addressed the Convention in an eloquent and brilliant speech, congratulating the Convention on the nomination of a representative of the State Rights Democracy, who was prepared to maintain their rights and the Constitution. He begged them to accept these congratulations at the hands of a man who had some reputation as a factionist and a disunionist—of a man who was, right or wrong, ten years ago an advocate of disunion, because he saw the constitutional rights of the South invaded by the admission of California, by "Squatter sovereignty," and by the interference with the Slave-trade in the District of Columbia. He had gone before the State of Alabama and asked them to secede—to secede. He had been then voted down by States, and had not since advocated disunion. Those men then, who said he had, uttered a falsehood; but he was prepared to advocate secession from the Union whenever he saw the constitutional rights of the South invaded. He was neither for the Union nor against it. He should watch for aggression on the sovereign rights of the States. He should be prepared to throw away the shell that was no longer valuable. The Union would then be a failure. When Government fails to accomplish the end for which it was formed let it go down. There was hope for the country yet: but he was sorry to say it depended only on the power of this organization here to-day to carry its principles aloft to triumph. He should not have made these remarks had he not been attacked in the Senate of the United States by the candidate who had been to-day nominated by the Squatter Sovereignty faction. He would have liked to have met the man who thus attacked him in his own arena. But this was not allowed him, and so he deemed it just to those associated with him in this movement to set his position right before the world. He preferred his position should be defined by himself, rather than by the great enemy of the Democracy. He reviewed the action of the Democratic Convention, and declared that, after what it had done, it must be damned to immortality as a political faction. He recounted the history of the secession at Charleston, holding that the constituents of the several delegations had indorsed the action of their representatives, and designating the action of the Convention as an outrage. Who, he said, was the leader of the bogus delegation in the Convention? He said it in

[Concluded on Eighth Page.]

# The New-York Times.

VOL. IX—NO. 2752. NEW-YORK, TUESDAY, JULY 17, 1860. PRICE TWO CENTS.


## PRESIDENTIAL.

### Mass Meeting in Union-Square.

### Americans and Old-Line Whigs for Lincoln and Hamlin.

### Speeches by Hons. Horace Greeley, Daniel Ullman, and R. F. Andrews.

### Letters from Hon. R. S. Baldwin, Hon. James O. Putnam, Willis Hall, and Truman Smith.

Something more than two thousand persons gathered in Union Square, near Washington Statue, last evening, in response to a call upon "citizens, irrespective of party, who believe that the best interests of our country, the stability of the Union, the success of our free institutions, will be best served and promoted by the election of ABRAHAM LINCOLN to the Presidency," to meet in Union Square. Added to the call was the statement that Horace Greeley, Thomas Corwin, James O. Putnam, Roger S. Baldwin, Truman Smith, Geo. R. Babcock, Daniel Ullmann, R. F. Andrews, E. L. Snow, Geo. G. Bellows, and Ex-Mayor Hall, had been invited and were expected to address the meeting. At 8 o'clock, Mr. MERWIN R. BREWER called the meeting to order, and the organization was completed by the election of the following officers:

President—Judge WILLIAM MITCHELL.

VICE-PRESIDENTS.

| | | |
|---|---|---|
| Willis Hall, | Benj. F. Camp, | Am. C. Kingsland, |
| Dr. J. W. French, | A. B. Brinckerhoff, | Shepherd Knapp, |
| A. J. Williamson, | John Newhouse, | Geo. E. Deane, |
| Wm. Stokley, | John Paine, | Thos. McCormick, |
| M. R. Brewer, | Dr. S. R. Kirby, | Samuel Strong, |
| S. B. Wycoff, | An. Lambrecht, | Horatio Reed, |
| Hiram Corwin, | Noah Worrall, | Harvey Hart, |
| Graham Roberts, | James McDonald, | Abraham Lent, |
| Wm. Welsh, | Alex. Spaulding, | Wm. Tucker, |
| Wm. H. Riblet, | Jas. G. Elliott, | C. S. Hoffman, |
| J. Berrian, | Dr. F. S. Harris, | Peter V. Husted, |
| Geo. W. Perkins, | J. M. Andrews, | B. F. Weymouth, |
| T. W. Gladding, | B. R. Sutcliffe, | Jos. Southworth, |
| A. W. Griswold, | N. S. Husted, | Peter Coutant, |
| J. O. Marshall, | E. Warner, | A. S. Hope, |
| J. S. Jones, | A. J. Steward, | John Welsh, |
| G. M. Simpson, | Wm. V. Brady, | R. M. Minturn, |
| Zenas Wheeler, | J. M. Patterson, | Edwin V. Price, |
| Nathan C. Ely, | W. H. Albertson, | L. L. Johnson, |
| Sam'l Sotaling, | Chas. Boome, | Floyd Smith, Jr., |
| J. H. Pinckney, | G. M. Bucklin, | C. E. Gildersleeve, |
| J. Comerford, | David S. Jarvis, | Joel W. Mason, |
| Gil't C. Deane, | Peter Palm, | Sewel Dodge, |
| Francis Godine, | A. L. Wood, | J. B. Dunham, |
| J. Quackenbush, | D. F. Bacon, | C. N. Decker, |
| Henry A. Burr, | John H. Brady, | John Ridley, |
| Henry B. Cook, | Dr. J. W. Ranney, | Allan Hay, |
| Henry Smith, | Chas. McNeil, | Edwin Ferguson, |
| John M. Read, | J. W. Currier, | Thomas E. Smith, |
| John B. Fry, | John B. Webb, | A. D. Fry, |
| A. H. Gale, | W. R. Havens, | John Sheridan, |
| Dr. Clarke Wright, | W. Boardman, Jr., | Wm. S. Wood, |
| John E. Briggs, | John Delemater, | Daniel Herrick, |
| Andrew Oats, | H. S. Smith, | Henry Skinner, |
| Chas. B. Tappen, | James Owens, | E. C. Johnson, |
| John Fershay, | Dennis McCabe, | James M. Murray, |
| Geo W Quintard, | Wm. G. Michel, | Wm. S. Davison, |
| Chas. L. Frost, | Isaac J. Oliver, | John P. Hone. |

SECRETARIES.

| | | |
|---|---|---|
| J. W. Winegar, | Robt. F. Mather, | J. B. Pollock, |
| Chas. E. Swords, | Jas. A. Rodney, | C. S. Van Orden, |
| A. E. Hemphill, | J. L. Tonelly, | L. Harney, |
| John Cooper, | Joseph Flock, | E. King, |
| W. Ryan, | C. H. Whitaker, | F. J. Tucker, |
| J. W. Denman, | Aug. P. Greene, | S. J. Pollock, |
| E. Ainslee, | J. W. Thompson, | S. Johnson, |
| John Shea, | John E. Burns, | James Connor, |
| W. Lyons, | E. Finsh, | W. M. Gillespie, |
| S. Koppman. | | |

RESOLUTIONS.

The following resolutions were then read by Mr. ALEXANDER SPAULDING:

*Whereas*, a Presidential election once more approaches, whereof the issue is already manifest; therefore,

*Resolved*, That the election of ABRAHAM LINCOLN to the Presidency, now morally certain, will fitly close an era of prodigality, imbecility and sectional discord, and usher in the rule of integrity, economy and nationality, restoring the golden age of the Republic.

*Resolved*, That we call upon our citizens without distinction of party to rally around the standard of LINCOLN and HAMLIN in the full assurance that their election will insure renewed and most needed attention to the great industrial and commercial interests of the country, too long made the sport of faction and the plaything of reckless ambition.

*Resolved*, That we call upon the electors of our City and State to surround and sustain the Administration of ABRAHAM LINCOLN with a Congress of able, experienced, discreet and incorruptible men, who will cordially and earnestly labor to restore the Era of Liberty, Honesty and National Prosperity.

When the resolutions had been read, the following letters were announced and read by the same gentleman:

POLICY AND DUTY OF THE FILLMORE MEN OF 1856 —LETTER FROM HON. JAMES O. PUTNAM.

FREDONIA, July 13, 1860.

GENTLEMEN: Engagements already made for the ensuing week prevent my acceptance of your invitation to attend and address a mass meeting at Union Park on the 16th inst., of citizens, irrespective of party, who believe that the prosperity of our Union will be advanced by the election of Mr. LINCOLN to the Presidency.

You say it is to be more particularly under the auspices of gentlemen, "many of whom have heretofore supported HENRY CLAY and MILLARD FILLMORE, and are not now connected with any political organization."

To meet with and confer with those who have always acted as I have, with the conservative school, prepared to follow where duty and patriotism lead, whether under a CLAY, a FILLMORE, or a LINCOLN, or whomsoever the time shall designate, would afford me great pleasure.

You will allow me to refer briefly to our past political history.

The friends of Mr. CLAY who sustained the Compromise measures of 1850, naturally yielded their support to Mr. FILLMORE in 1856, whose Administration was distinguished for its fidelity to those measures. Not that they necessarily preferred the disposition made of that series of questions to some other, had such other been possible; but they accepted them as, under the circumstances, best calculated to give repose to a distracted country. They believed it was best to give and take—to win peace among brethren by concession, rather than to force it by conquest.

We saw the storm of opposition to that settlement fast yielding to the general conviction that, on the whole, it was wisest and best, and the country congratulated itself on a "final settlement" of the Slavery question.

In an evil hour, STEPHEN A. DOUGLAS opened the question afresh, and plunged us into that sea of troubles in which we have been wandering, rayless and pathless, and at times hopeless, for the past six years. The Missouri Compromise, the great achievement of Mr. CLAY's life—a compact which had all the sacredness of a constitutional obligation—a compact cherished in the hearts of twenty millions of American citizens as a new charter of humanity—was trodden under foot as a worthless thing, and civil war invoked to settle anew the question of free or servile labor in the Territories.

And now the author of all this harvest of mischief asks a grateful country to reward him with the highest trust in its gift!

"Conservative" men must find relations in some of the organizations which now ask their alliance, and there is a wide latitude for choice. I know nothing in the Republican Party which turns a "Conservative," whether he be such from temperament or education, into an Abolitionist, a Disunionist, or a hater of his brethren. "Friends of Mr. CLAY and Mr. FILLMORE," to use the language of your letter, have never had much sympathy with any branch of the Democratic Party. They saw it calumniate Mr. CLAY down to the grave from the time of the election in 1824. He was ever the target for all their hunters, and he went into his grave covered with their poisoned arrows. He was hardly at rest in his tomb before it undid the most glorious act of his life.

From my stand-point, I cannot see how any friend of Mr. CLAY can vote for either of the Democratic candidates.

Where then shall we go? Two paths are open before us. We can support Mr. LINCOLN, and seek to inaugurate a Republican policy in the Government, under his auspices, or we can support Mr. BELL. Now, gentlemen, I yield my unqualified assent to every eulogium that has been pronounced on Mr. BELL and Mr. EVERETT. Their names are synonyms of every public and private virtue. The Republic has no worthier men. But this fact stares us in the face. In them, able and worthy as they are, the hour and the men for success do not meet. Nobody believes, no sane or insane man pretends, that in the State of New-York they can command a tenth of the popular vote. A vote for them in any Northern State is a vote thrown away. If I lived in a Southern State, where a Lincoln ticket is not in the field, I would give my best energies to the Baltimore Union ticket. And if a Lincoln ticket were in the field, but only nominally so, where to support it would be practical neutrality in the contest, then I would vote for BELL and EVERETT, as the best thing I could do to defeat the Democracy, and as eminently fitting and proper in itself.

But here we can do an efficient, and a fitting and proper service, only by a support of LINCOLN. And yet, strange to say, there are men, once "friends of CLAY and FILLMORE," who advise a support of DOUGLAS, if necessary to defeat LINCOLN in New-York—not to do DOUGLAS any service, but to defeat an election by the College, and throw it into Congress.

The friends of BRECKINRIDGE are looking to the same result to take the election over the House to the [illegible] Senate, [illegible] may make a Presi[dent] [illegible] [illegible] a [illegible] for [illegible] [illegible], and the Presidency may be [illegible] for in the Congressional ring.

[If] our "Union" friends shall succeed, and make a President in LANE by their pains, they will learn by experience a lesson I will learn at a cheaper rate.

Now, let me ask, why should we not vote for LINCOLN [illegible]

[illegible] To preserve it [illegible] [illegible] [illegible]. In other words, to adhere to the principles of Mr. CLAY, as declared by him in his memorable speech in 1850. It makes no retrograde movement in all that pertains to human progress. It does not propose to interfere with Slavery in the States, but the contrary. It has some Abolitionists in its body,—so had the old Whig Party. But it is no more an Abolition Party, and from the strong conservative element in it, can no more become so than can the Baltimore Union Party. Every liberal-minded man knows this. If it is sectional, because its ticket is made from the North, and its main support is in the North, the responsibility of this lies at the door of the Democratic Party, for it has established a reign of terror all over the South which renders it unsafe for men to coöperate with the organization.

Now who, and what, is Mr. LINCOLN, that Conservative men should shrink from him as from contagion? I have read him carefully, and have not been able to find a sentiment in all his frank, unreserved discussions, which does not accord with what Mr. CLAY has uttered over and over again. He is opposed to making Free Territory Slave. So was Mr. CLAY. He looks hopefully to the extinction of the institution, and the substitution of a more humane and just relation of labor to capital, and that by the parties interested, and in lawful and proper ways. So did Mr. CLAY. He is no fanatic, bawling after equal social and political right for the negro with the white race. Read his debate with Senator DOUGLAS for the most sound and common-sense views on all this class of questions. He does believe the negro to be a man, and not a thing, and that the broad humanity of our Declaration of Independence, which declares that all men are entitled to life, liberty, and the pursuit of happiness, as the free gift of God, is a universal principle, as good at the tropics as in the temperate latitudes. Did Mr. CLAY think otherwise? I see nothing in Mr. LINCOLN's political character which repels me from his support.

In his personal character I find much that is attractive. It is the universal testimony, it comes from political foe and friend alike, who know him, that he has kept his heart sound in all his life battle. So preëminent is his integrity, so deep-rooted is his justice in public confidence, that his familiar appellation is a *sobriquet* indicative of that confidence.

Few men win this in any country. ARISTIDES did, and he was banished from Athens because he was "honest."

We are not immaculate, but I do not believe we are yet prepared to banish our Aristides because he is called "the Just." Very respectfully,

JAMES O. PUTNAM.

THE TAYLOR MEN OF 1848.—LETTER FROM TRUMAN SMITH.

NEW-YORK CITY, No. 49 Wall street, June 10, 1860.

GENTLEMEN: I have this moment received your note of yesterday's date, in which, acting as a Committee in behalf of citizens of New-York, you invite me to address a public meeting to be held at the Union-square, in this City, on Monday evening, July 16th inst., to be composed in a large degree of the friends of HENRY CLAY and MILLARD FILLMORE, not at present particularly connected with any political organization, but who are convinced that the best interests of our country, the stability of the Union, and the success of our free institutions, will be best subserved and promoted by the elevation of ABRAHAM LINCOLN to the Presidency. Fully sympathizing with you and those you represent in the object indicated, nothing would afford me more satisfaction than to take some part, however humble it might be, on such an occasion; but I regret to be obliged to say that, having within the last three or four weeks experienced serious indisposition, from which I am not as yet fully restored, I cannot undertake to address a public assembly, in the open air, at so early a date as the 16th instant, and will only add that I fully believe that were HENRY CLAY now living he would in some marked form assert the principles and maintain the cause which you yourselves propose to assert and maintain by sustaining Mr. LINCOLN for the Presidency; and therefore possibly (such as is now contemplated) at a more advanced stage of the canvass, (particularly if assembled indoors,) should you and other friends desire it. With sentiments of high respect, I am faithfully and truly yours,

TRUMAN SMITH.

M. R. BREWER and R. F. ANDREWS, Esqs., Committee.

LETTER FROM ROGER S. BALDWIN, OF CONNECTICUT.

NEW-HAVEN, July 14, 1860.

GENTLEMEN: Your favor of the 9th, inviting me to attend and address the Mass Meeting of citizens, irrespective of party, who believe that the prosperity of our Union will be advanced by the election of ABRAHAM LINCOLN to the Presidency, to be held at Union-square, in the City of New-York, on Monday evening, arrived during my absence from the State. Regretting that it will not be in my power to be present on that occasion, I avail myself of the earliest leisure moment since my return to-day, to express to you my cordial sympathy and concurrence in the patriotic purposes of the meeting, and to tender to you my congratulations on the auspicious indications from every part of the country, that the sectional oligarchy, which, under the specious name of Democracy, has so long and so grievously misgoverned the nation, is destined to a sure and speedy overthrow, to be succeeded, I confidently trust, by an Administration imbued with the spirit and conducted on the principles upon which our Government was founded and administered, and our glorious Union cemented, by the Fathers of the Republic.

Thanking you for the honor of your invitation, I am, with great respect, your obedient servant,

ROGER S. BALDWIN.

To M. R. BREWER and R. F. ANDREWS, Esqs., Committee, No. 40 Park-row.

THE OLD CLAY GUARD—LETTER FROM WILLIS HALL.

NEW-YORK, July 12, 1860.

GENTLEMEN: I have just received your note of yesterday, requesting me to preside at a mass meeting to be held at Union-square on Monday evening next, of citizens, irrespective of party, who believe that the prosperity of our Union will be advanced by the election of ABRAHAM LINCOLN to the Presidency.

I could conscientiously join in such a meeting as you propose, owing to events which have occurred within the last three months, and should feel myself very highly honored to preside over its deliberations; but I am reluctantly compelled to decline. The state of my health renders it quite impossible.

Accept, gentlemen, for yourselves and for those whom you represent, my very cordial thanks for the honor you have intended me.

With high regard, I am your friend and servant,

WILLIS HALL.

When all the letters had been read, the President announced Mr. GREELEY as the first speaker.

REMARKS OF HON. HORACE GREELEY.

Mr. GREELEY said he believed he was addressing an audience composed largely of old Whigs, and believing so, he proposed to speak to them in favor of that old Whig, ABRAHAM LINCOLN, as against STEPHEN A. DOUGLAS. He was not surprised that at the last Presidential election many old Whigs preferred to vote for Mr. FILLMORE, who had always been a Whig, rather than to vote for Col. FREMONT, who had always been a Democrat; but he could not see any reason why old Whigs should favor the election of Mr. DOUGLAS, who had never been a Whig, and oppose Mr. LINCOLN, who was a Whig, while the Whig Party had a recognized existence. In this State there were some men, claiming to be Whigs, who were working against Mr. LINCOLN, on the alleged ground that he was a sectional man, holding sectional principles. Now he proposed to test the principles of Mr. LINCOLN, by the standard of acknowledged Whig doctrine; and in doing so he should, for that occasion, consider Mr. BROOKS, who was the most ardent opponent of Mr. LINCOLN in the City, an authority as to what Whig doctrine was. In 1847, Mr. JAMES BROOKS was a member of a Convention, and was appointed a member of the Committee on Resolutions. On that occasion Mr. Brooks drew the resolutions which were presented to the Convention, and among them was one strongly opposed to the conversion of Free territory into Slave territory. That was Whig doctrine, acknowledged as such, and as such was written by Mr. BROOKS. Now, he would ask whether Mr. LINCOLN or the Republican Party had ever gone further than that? He was positive they never had. That was good Republican doctrine; it was good Whig doctrine, and it was written by Mr. BROOKS. Then there was another man who was working actively against Mr. LINCOLN, and that man was WASHINGTON HUNT. He (Mr. GREELEY) proposed to try Mr. LINCOLN by Mr. HUNT's standard of Whig doctrine. In 1848, he (Mr. G.) went to Congress, and there found Mr. HUNT and Mr. LINCOLN; and, lately, he had been comparing their records, on all points of Whig doctrine that were voted on during that session. He had found them precisely the same—always voting together, except in one case, and that case was a resolution prohibiting the Slave-trade in the District of Columbia. When the resolution came up, a motion was made to lay it on the table. Mr. LINCOLN voted in favor of laying it on the table, while Mr. HUNT, with Mr. GREELEY voted against—so that the only difference in their records showed Mr. LINCOLN to be the most conservative man. Mr. LINCOLN did not favor laying the resolution on the table because he was in favor of the Slave-trade, by any means, but because he deemed it inexpedient to raise the question at that time. How was it, then, that WASHINGTON HUNT was talking against Mr. LINCOLN on the ground of sectionalism? Mr. HUNT, during the time referred to, voted in every instance with the Northern Whigs. On every question touching that of Slavery in the Territories Mr. HUNT voted with Mr. GREELEY and the other Northern Whigs; and they all acted in accordance with the Whig doctrine laid down by Mr. BROOKS. How was it, then, that Mr. BROOKS and Mr. HUNT were now found helping Mr. DOUGLAS, the breaker down of the Missouri Compromise? Why was it they had turned against their old Whig friend, Mr. LINCOLN, and were found aiding Mr. DOUGLAS? On all questions of Slavery, Mr. HUNT voted with Mr. LINCOLN to let Slavery alone in the States where it existed, and to keep it out of the Territories. But they said Mr. LINCOLN was sectional, because in one of his speeches he had said he did not believe the United States would always be divided on the Slavery question; that he believed they would at some time be either all Slave or all Free States. If that doctrine was sectional, it was the doctrine held and declared by HENRY CLAY, and he believed Mr. CLAY was indorsed by Mr. BROOKS and Mr. HUNT. In conclusion, Mr. GREELEY referred to the time when the Chamber of Commerce of this City sent a protest to Congress against a proposition to let every State make its own improvements in its rivers and harbors, and tax the vessels of other States using those waters for commerce for the outlay. That bill, he claimed, would, if it had passed, have crippled the commerce of the States with each other, and proved greatly injurious to the country; and that was the policy proposed and advocated by Mr. DOUGLAS—it was Mr. DOUGLAS, who proposed to erect State toll-gates across the highways of commerce, and Messrs. BROOKS and HUNT were helping Mr. DOUGLAS. Now, if the people wanted a government favorable to, and which would encourage commerce, they must elect Mr. LINCOLN on his old Whig doctrine. [Applause.] They must not help Mr. DOUGLAS as a means of electing Mr. BELL, for even if they could elect him (and he did not think it possible) he would have a Democratic Congress against him, and be voted down on every question. In short, if the people wanted a good Government they must elect Mr. LINCOLN, and have honest men to support him—such men as could be found in the State of New-York.

RUFUS S. ANDREWS, the former candidate of the American Party for Corporation Counsel, was the next speaker. He said he wished to call upon the friends of HENRY CLAY, DANIEL WEBSTER and MILLARD FILLMORE to vote for ABRAHAM LINCOLN for President. Under some circumstances it would have given him pleasure to vote for JOHN BELL and EDWARD EVERETT for President and Vice-President of the United States. But as things stood now he considered that a vote for them was a vote thrown away. The platform of that party, as drawn by Mr. ERASTUS BROOKS, was "the Union, the Constitution and the Laws." Now, was there anybody or any party in the country that was not in favor of the Union, the Constitution and the laws? Is there anybody here who is in favor of Disunion? [A Voice—"Yes."] The people would not be satisfied with this brief and general platform. It would not do for Mr. BELL and Mr. EVERETT to say that they were in favor of the Union and the Constitution without also telling the people whether they believed the Constitution gave Congress the control over the territories of the United States. JAMES BROOKS and WASHINGTON HUNT intend to sell the people. Now, what about STEPHEN A. DOUGLAS? [Three cheers were here given for Mr. DOUGLAS.] Your cheers will be groans in November. Now, if you will keep still a moment, I will tell you what a miserable devil you are supporting. The speaker then referred to the course of Mr. DOUGLAS in the repeal of the Missouri Compromise, and denounced him as a miserable traitor to his country. He then referred to that branch of the Democratic Party represented by BRECKINRIDGE and LANE, whom he took it for granted the people of the City could not support. In conclusion, he dwelt upon the eminent fitness of Mr. LINCOLN as the candidate of the old friends of CLAY, WEBSTER, and FILLMORE, and exhorted his audience to come up heartily to his support.

Loud calls were here made for "CORWIN," when the President announced that Mr. CORWIN was not and would not be present, and in his stead he would introduce to the audience a man well known to all of them—Hon. DANIEL ULLMANN.

Mr. ULLMANN said he proposed to speak of some things that were of interest to his old friends, with whom he had acted in times gone by. He should speak in all kindness, but at the same time distinctly and fearlessly. He had been severely criticised by many old friends for whom he entertained great respect, and he hoped they were there to-night to hear what he had to say. If the 400,000 voters of the North who, in 1856, cast their votes against the Democratic Party, had united with the 2,200,000 voters who so nearly coincided with them upon the great principles at issue, the country would have been spared the deep mortification, humiliation, and disgrace of the administration of JAMES BUCHANAN. The audience well knew that he had heretofore acted with the American Party. They also knew that for the last two years he had tried his best to bring about an honorable union between the American and Republican Parties. He had long felt that these two parties agreed so nearly in sentiment upon the great principles at issue before the country, that it was a shame that they could not unite and relieve the country from the blighting effects of Democracy. But his efforts had been unavailing until now, when the American Party had not, as he believed, an organization in any State in the Union. The cause of this breaking up of the American Party was to be found in the vital principle that lay at the foundation of our Government. It was the same cause that had rent asunder the old Democratic Party. In June, 1855, the American Party of the United States held a great National Council in the city of Philadelphia, and then for two weeks this great vital principle raged as furiously as it did at Baltimore in June last. This principle was the Slavery question and the power of Congress over Slavery in the Territories. He proposed to read the famous Twelfth Section of the platform of the American Party which caused the controversy in the National Council at Philadelphia. [Some one in the audience here shouted, "Don't expose them, Mr. ULLMANN," which so disconcerted the speaker that he lost his temper, and threatened to call an officer if the man who made the remark dared to open his head again.]

He then proceeded to read the twelfth section, wherein, among other things, it was declared by the Council to be expedient to "pretermit" any expression of opinion with regard to the power of Congress on the subject of Slavery in the Territories. After ridiculing the far-fetched word "pretermit," which, he said, meant to "evade" and "dodge," he said that the Council, for the sake of harmony, and in order to conciliate the South, consented to pass over the question. This action of the National Council lost the party nearly the whole of New-England and the greater part of New-York. "If," said he, "the American Party in June, 1855, instead of evading this question, had taken high and honorable and constitutional ground, they would this day have been able to control the Government." Now Mr. LINCOLN occupied to-day, upon this ground, precisely the same position that HENRY CLAY occupied all his life time.

The speaker here read long extracts from a speech made by Senator BENJAMIN, of Louisiana, in May last, wherein, in comparing the discussion between LINCOLN and DOUGLAS in the campaign for the United States Senatorship in Illinois, he gives as his opinion that Mr. LINCOLN is a far more conservative man than Mr. DOUGLAS.

During the reading of these extracts a large portion of the audience left the ground.

Having finished Mr. BENJAMIN's speech, he next replied to the old Clay Whigs who now criticized his position as a Republican, and declared that in voting for LINCOLN he was supporting an Abolitionist. He read the oft-quoted declaration of HENRY CLAY, that no earthly power would ever compel him to vote for the extension of Slavery over one foot of territory now free, and drew the conclusion that Mr. CLAY was as much of an Abolitionist as ever LINCOLN was, and that those who criticized him for his support of LINCOLN, had themselves deserted the principles of their great leader, HENRY CLAY.

He next proceeded to read from a letter of Hon. EDWARD BATES, of Missouri, but had hardly commenced before it began to sprinkle, and the audience, which was already small, hastily dispersed, and left the stand almost deserted. Mr. ULLMAN drew his remarks abruptly to a close, intimating that he had much more to say, and would take some other opportunity to give the people of New-York his views at length.

## POLITICAL MOVEMENTS.

### Decapitation in the New-York Custom-House for Opinion's Sake.

*To the Editor of the New-York Times:*

On Monday last the following note was sent to me by the Collector of this port.

CUSTOM HOUSE, NEW-YORK, July 7, 1860.

SIR: You are hereby informed that your services as a Weigher of the Customs are no longer required. Respectfully, AUGUSTUS SCHELL, Collector.

To JAMES P. DUNN.

Being aware that no charges had been, or could be, made against me for neglect of duty or incompetency, immediately upon the receipt of the above, I called at the Collector's Office for the purpose of ascertaining the cause of my summary dismissal, and, although the Collector was disengaged, he refused to grant me an interview. The only alternative left me was to make the inquiry of the Surveyor, which I accordingly did, by addressing him the following letter:

*Hon. E. B. Hart, Surveyor of the Port of New-York*

DEAR SIR: On Monday last I received a note from the Collector of this Port, informing me that my services as a Weigher of the Customs were no longer required.

That I may know upon what grounds my removal, by an Administration I have so faithfully supported, is predicated, permit me to ask you, as the head of the Department of which I was a subaltern, if you ever had cause to believe me derelict in the discharge of my duties, or guilty of any act unbecoming the character of an officer.

My object in addressing you is to ask you, as the Surveyor of the Port of New-York, whether any complaints have been made to you against me, relative to the discharge of my duties as a Weigher of the Customs, or whether you had preferred any charges against me to the Collector which would warrant my removal on account of neglect or incompetency to discharge my official duties? Having been refused an audience by the Collector, for an explanation of the cause of my removal, in justice to myself I respectfully request from you a reply to this note.

Very respectfully, your ob't serv't,

NEW-YORK, July 11, 1860. JAS. P. DUNN.

To which I received the following reply:

CUSTOM HOUSE, NEW-YORK SURVEYOR'S OFFICE, Nos. 27 and 29 Pine-street, July 12, 1860.

DEAR SIR: In reply to yours of yesterday, I have to say that no complaints for dereliction of duty or conduct unbecoming an officer, have been made to me, nor have I preferred any charges against you to the Collector; had I done so, you would have had, as is always the custom of this office, an official notice of the same. Very truly, &c.,

To JAMES P. DUNN. E. B. HART.

From the correspondence and particularly from the curt and peremptory note of the Collector, I leave it to an unbiased public, to decide whether my removal, so evidently without cause given by me, is not a direct proscription for opinion's sake. If those who have been the warm supporters of the present Administration are thus to be ostracised because they dare manfully and openly to proclaim their choice for the succession, it is high time that the Democratic Party were made aware of it. My choice was and is Judge DOUGLAS for the Presidency, and while exposing the proscriptive policy of the present dynasty, I glory in the cause for the support of which I have thus called vindictive punishment upon my head.

Very respectfully, JAMES P. DUNN.

NEW-YORK, July 16, 1860.

### Mr. Douglas at Hartford.

HIS RECEPTION BY THE DEMOCRACY—DIFFERENT METHODS OF REPORTING THE SAME MATTER.

COURANT OFFICE, HARTFORD, Conn., Monday, July 16.

Mr. DOUGLAS arrived in this city at 7½ o'clock this evening. The Douglas wing of the Democratic party had arranged to receive and escort him to his quarters at the United States Hotel, where he was to have received his friends. The Breckinridge wing of the party have quietly been at work for a couple of days, headed by A. E. BURR, publisher of the Hartford *Times*, to take the reception in their own hands. The result was that they met Mr. D. at the dépôt, with Colt's Armory Band and Guards, and a carriage drawn by four horses, to escort him to the State-house, where he was welcomed. 100 guns were fired, church bells rung, and a large crowd turned out.

Mr. DOUGLAS expressed himself grateful for the reception given him. He denounced the Republican and Breckinridge Parties, calling them sectional, and claimed that he and his party occupied the middle and true ground, and were the regular Democratic Party, and the only party which could save the country. Mr. DOUGLAS is the guest of Mayor DEMING. A. E. BURR, who has refused to support DOUGLAS, rode in the carriage with him, while those who have worked faithfully, early and late, and claimed to be leaders of the Douglas wing, were allowed the privilege of staying out in the cold. It was the coolest operation ever witnessed in this city, and has occasioned much comment and merriment.

OFFICE OF THE HARTFORD POST, HARTFORD, Monday, July 16, 1860.

Senator DOUGLAS had a most glorious reception in this city this evening. There was a liberal outpouring of the masses. He was escorted from the dépôt by a company of military, headed by a band of music. A salute of 100 guns was fired in honor of his visit, and bells were rung, and the wildest demonstrations of enthusiasm made.

Mr. DOUGLAS was introduced to the vast multitude by Hon. R. D. HUBBARD, and made a short speech from the steps of the Phenix Bank, which was received with vociferous applause.

A noticeable feature of the reception was that it was shared in by the leading Democratic politicians who have not hitherto been favorable to Mr. DOUGLAS, and prominent amongst them was A. E. BURR, Esq., of the Hartford *Times*.

Mr. DOUGLAS leaves to-morrow for Boston. During his stay here he will be the guest of the Mayor of the City.

OFFICE OF THE HARTFORD TIMES, Monday, July 16, 1860.

Senator DOUGLAS arrived here this evening, on his way to Boston. He was received at the cars by two military companies, and guns were fired in the Park in his honor. He was also handsomely met by a large concourse of people without regard to party. He was escorted to State-House-square, where he was welcomed to the city by Hon. R. D. HUBBARD, who introduced him as standing on middle ground, politically,—between the Arctic and the Antarctic extremes, where the olive and the vine grow spontaneously.

Mr. DOUGLAS replied that he did occupy that ground, and claimed that non-intervention was the true policy of the country, to prevent angry disputes and unhappy results. The large crowd of five or six thousand were orderly and quiet. Mr. DOUGLAS is the guest of his Honor Mayor DEMING.

Mr. DOUGLAS leaves for Boston to-morrow noon.

### Politics in Missouri.

ST. LOUIS, Sunday, July 15.

A large gathering was held last night to ratify the nomination of FRANCIS P. BLAIR, Jr., for Congress. Mr. BLAIR made an eloquent address, after which a variety of brilliant fireworks, including one piece in which was shown the name of "FRANK BLAIR," were exhibited.

ST. LOUIS, Monday, July 16.

The Democratic County Convention to-day nominated a full ticket, including J. R. BARRETT for Congress, by acclamation; Gen. FROST for State Senator. Col. BOOE, the principal competitor of Gen. FROST, withdrew, and made a Breckinridge speech to the outside crowd, and announced himself an independent candidate. The Convention was not harmonious.

### Politics in Arkansas.

FAYETTEVILLE, Ark., Saturday, July 14.

An enthusiastic ratification meeting was held here to-day, to indorse the nomination of BRECKINRIDGE and LANE. Hon. G. W. TAYLOR, elector, addressed the meeting, advocating the claims of the South with great zeal. Senator LATHAM arrived at 4 o'clock, and was introduced to the meeting, and delivered a very effective speech in favor of BRECKINRIDGE and LANE.

### Politics in Pennsylvania.

HARRISBURGH, Pa., Monday, July 16.

A call has been issued by Mr. HALDEMAN, of the National Democratic Committee, protesting against the action of the Democratic State Committee, calling a mass and delegate Convention, to meet at Harrisburgh, July 26, to form a straight Douglas Electoral ticket.

### Politics in Iowa.

DAVENPORT, Iowa, Monday, July 16.

A call appears this morning for a BRECKINRIDGE and LANE mass meeting, to be held here on the 15th of August. It is signed by Messrs. AUSTIN CORBIN, JOHN JONES, GEORGE H. PARKER and many other prominent Democrats of the State.

### Politics in Illinois.

BELLVILLE, Ill., Sunday, July 15.

Judge TRUMBULL was welcomed home by the Bellville Republicans last evening in an enthusiastic manner.

### A Vice-President on his Travels.

SPEECH OF THE HON. J. C. BRECKINRIDGE, IN BALTIMORE.

The Baltimore *American*, of the 14th, gives the following report of the speech delivered by Mr. BRECKINRIDGE in that city:

FELLOW-CITIZENS: I beg leave to render you my grateful acknowledgments for the cordial reception which I have met with in your beautiful city. This, however, is not the first time that I have visited it, for I have wandered over its suburbs many years ago. Twenty years since I visited it, and I only hope that it may continue to increase in prosperity—[applause]—and meet your largest expectations. Without entering into our political history, it becomes us to consider how our institutions can be best preserved. The State of Maryland is a border State, and to your citizens it is a matter of moment as to the welfare and prosperity of our common country. [Applause.] I know full well that you are always anxious to support the Union, and will do so at all hazards. [Applause.] It becomes us, my fellow citizens, to pay strict fidelity to the Constitution and the Union; it is the only guarantee that we have for a perpetuation of the unity of these States, and it is the surest guarantee of peace and happiness for our entire land. [Loud applause.] If at any time we throw away the principles of the Constitution, the only safeguard of our liberties, the only source of national happiness, we merely drift away from the very foundation of our Government, and effect a radical change in the very Constitution itself. This is not to be desired, and should be averted by every true patriot of our land. This, I am sure, will be done by the lovers of the Constitution and the Union. [Loud applause.] The Constitution, as formed by our fathers, we have all lived happily under, and may we not say the form of Government suited to the fathers is certainly suited to the children? Let us keep the form of our fathers. If it was good enough for them, it is certainly good enough for us. The Constitution is good enough for us. The rights there laid down meet our approval. Among the few things that are not assailed stand the rights of conscience, and if they were, I know that such rights would need no defenders on the soil of Maryland, a State which has been distinguished for its Union and patriotic sentiments. [Loud applause.] But, my friends, the Constitution has been assailed, and it becomes us to defend it. [Applause.] There is a point which, if not as clearly defined as it might be, is still paramount. It is the equality of the States. [Applause.] They were equal before they formed the solemn compact of Union. That is inviolable, and the Constitution points out clearly the protection of persons and property. And I tell you now, that if the principles of the Constitution are violated, it can only result in a change of this Government—a change much to be deplored, and the end of which can only result in inevitable ruin. But, fellow-citizens, the equality of the States is the leading principle to be established, and we must maintain it; and if we adhere to this principle, there can only be a happy and peaceful termination to the present sectional differences. [Applause.] My friends, allow me to wish that your great and prosperous city may continue in its present course of prosperity; that the Union of the States may be preserved; and let me hope that the principles cherished by the Fathers of the Republic may long continue to prosper in our land. [Applause.] In conclusion, permit me to again tender you my grateful acknowledgments for the kind reception with which I have been greeted, and although my remarks may have been somewhat inappropriate, I could not refrain from expressing my views thus briefly to my fellow-citizens of this great and prosperous city. [Applause.] At the conclusion of the remarks of Mr. BRECKINRIDGE, he was greeted with loud applause, and was repeatedly called on to again address the crowd, who remained about the hotel until a late hour.

### Letter from Hon. Silas Seymour in favor of Douglas.

PIERMONT, N. Y., Monday, July 9, 1860.

*Col. John W. Forney, Philadelphia:*

MY DEAR SIR: I embrace the first leisure moment, since the adjournment of the Baltimore Convention, to congratulate you upon the nomination of Hon. STEPHEN A. DOUGLAS as the candidate of the Democratic Party for the office of President of the United States.

Perhaps no one knows better than myself the disinterestedness of your motives and efforts in bringing about this important result; and also the personal sacrifices and indignities to which you have submitted while defending the great principle of *Popular Sovereignty*, from its first inception to its triumphant indorsement by the regular Democratic Convention at Baltimore.

I may also say, without wishing to flatter you, that to no one more than yourself do I feel indebted for the confirmation of my present views and convictions upon the great questions now at issue between the North and South in relation to the subject of Slavery, and the intervention of Congress for its protection or prohibition in the Territories of the United States.

Since the exciting Presidential contest of 1856, I have become satisfied that unless before another Presidential campaign some solid middle ground could be discovered by our political navigators, upon which the conservative people of the North and South could rally and meet as friends, our glorious Union must either be dissolved or rendered practically useless for all the great political and commercial purposes for which it was originally established.

Ever since my first political recollections there has been a constant warfare waged between the North and South upon the subject of slavery. And it seems to me that at least three-fourths of every session of Congress, and nine-tenths of every political speech that has been made either in or out of Congress, has been devoted to this prolific scheme. The only result that I can discover is the formation of two great sectional parties, one for the North, and one for the South, whose antagonisms are so bitter that each would prefer the dissolution of the Union to the success of the other.

The effect of all this has been to retard the prosperity and development of our country and its resources to such an extent, that I sometimes think that, unless this *eternal* Slavery question can be forever put at rest, it would be better for us all if a dividing line could be peacefully drawn between the Free and Slave States, and a separate Government and laws established for each. The Government of the Northern, or Free States, could then improve her harbors for the protection of her commerce, and establish a tariff that would protect her labor and develop her resources, without being subject to the constant and united opposition of the Southern States. And we could then have a Pacific Railroad immediately commenced and constructed, as it should be, by the General Government, upon the *best natural route*, and without reference to the supposed sectional benefits that its construction upon any particular route would confer, either upon the North or South—whereas all these, and many other great measures, are now prevented by bitter sectional jealousies.

But how much better will it be if the people of all the States will consent that this vexed and most profitless question be driven out and kept out of Congress, and out of our general politics; and the people of each State and Territory not only allowed, but *compelled*, to settle it in their own way among themselves, without the interference of Congress or the Executive? This I understand to be *Popular Sovereignty*, as expounded by Judge DOUGLAS.

The more I reflect upon this great principle, and follow it out to its legitimate results as affecting the internal peace and prosperity of our country, the more fully am I impressed with the profound sagacity and statesmanship of its author and expounder. I can see no other way, in the present crisis, to save the Union intact, and, at the same time, restore its members to that feeling of concord and fraternity which is so necessary to our growth and prosperity.

I am, and always have been, opposed to the extension of Slavery, and in favor of Freedom, in its largest and most comprehensive sense. I do not consider it material, so far as the true policy involved in this question is concerned, whether Congress has or has not the power, under the Constitution, to prohibit or protect Slavery in the Territories. Neither am I particularly impressed with the solemnity or importance of Supreme Court decisions upon this grave question, because I believe that its final solution should, and is to be, one of *expediency* rather than of law; and that it is far above and beyond the reach of all these powers combined. And here allow me to quote, as expressive of my own views, the eloquent language of Mr. WEBSTER, in his great speech "for the Constitution and the Union," delivered in the United States Senate in 1850:

"And I now say, Sir, as the proposition upon which I stand this day, and upon the truth and firmness of which I intend to act until it is overthrown, that there is not at this moment within the United States, or any Territory of the United States, a single foot of land the character of which, in regard to its being free territory or slave territory, is not fixed by some law, and some irrepealable law beyond the power of the action of the Government. I mean the law of Nature, of physical geography—the law of the formation of the earth; and I would not take pains uselessly to reaffirm an ordinance of Nature, nor to reënact the will of God."

The Conservative men of the Republican Party say "we claim the right to legislate against the extension of Slavery; but we never intend to do so; the South need not be alarmed; *we are only fighting for a principle*." And the Southern men tell us of the North that "you must not feel alarmed, for although we claim and mean to maintain our right to establish and protect Slavery in the Territories, yet we never intend to exercise it, *we are only fighting for a principle*." And thus, while these rival factions are fighting for an abstract principle which, in my opinion, neither of them, if they had the power, would dare carry into effect, the material interests of the country are suffering from the want of proper and efficient legislation, and the Union itself is threatened with dissolution.

The beautiful consistency of such a suicidal course was exemplified by an engineer who undertook to build a bridge of one span, upon a new *principle* which he had invented, across the Delaware river, at a point where at least two spans were required. The bridge stood very well until it was completed, and the false or temporary work, upon which it had rested, taken from under it, when, as almost every one had predicted, it fell into the river. The engineer, upon being asked what he now thought of the bridge, replied that "he did not care a d—n about the bridge, *but the principle was there*." Would it not be well for some of our leading politicians to apply the moral, and abandon a useless and dangerous principle before it is too late?

But I have already written much more than I intended, or than was necessary, in order to assure you that I am with you heart and soul in this contest; and that there are thousands of others in this State who, like myself, have not heretofore acted or voted with the Democratic Party; but who, now that it has cut loose from the dictation and control of a corrupt Administration, and the disunion faction of the South, will have their hearty and efficient support to the regular candidates of the Baltimore Convention.

I have known Judge DOUGLAS long and well, and believe him to be a statesman of great integrity and ability. If elected by the American people, as I trust he will be, to the highest office in their gift, I have no doubt that his Administration will reflect the highest honor both upon himself and the country.

Yours, sincerely, SILAS SEYMOUR.

### Political Miscellany.

Hon. T. G. DAVIDSON, Representative from the Third Congressional District of Louisiana, has taken the stump for BRECKINRIDGE and LANE.

Senator LATHAM left St. Louis for California on the 12th, *via* the Southern Overland Mail route. He was serenaded by his friends on the evening before his departure.

Hon. JOHN W. NOELL, of Missouri, having declared for Mr. DOUGLAS, CHARLES JONES, Esq., of Franklin County, has come out as a Breckinridge candidate for Congress in opposition to him.

The Republicans in Illinois have difficulty in finding a candidate for Lieutenant-Governor. Mr. HOFFMAN, of Chicago, was first nominated, but he declined the honor, and now Mr. VITAL JARROT, of St. Clair County, has done likewise.

Hon. W. E. BOULIGNY, of Louisiana, who, last Winter, announced his intention of supporting Mr. DOUGLAS, has declared for BELL and EVERETT. This divides the Louisiana delegation to Congress, as Mr. BOULIGNY's colleague is a supporter of Mr. DOUGLAS.

The campaign in Georgia is sufficiently spirited. The Augusta *Chronicle and Sentinel* reports the proceedings of meetings to ratify the nomination of Messrs. BELL and EVERETT, and DOUGLAS and JOHNSON, and gives notice of a third meeting at which the claims of BRECKINRIDGE and LANE would be presented.

The Nashville *Banner* announces that Hon. M. P. GENTRY, Hon. CHARLES READY, Hon. BARCLAY MARTIN and STERLING R. COCKRILL, Esq., of Tennessee, have left the Bell and Everett ranks, and declared for BRECKINRIDGE and LANE.

The "Wide Awakes" of Newark are to make an excursion to Hartford and New-Haven, Conn., on the 16th, by steamboat. They will first go to Hartford, where they will spend Thursday night. On Friday they will be at New-Haven, returning home on Saturday.

The Washington *States and Union* contradicts the statement which has been in circulation, that with the retirement of Maj. HEISS the paper passed under the control of the Douglas National Democratic Committee. The proprietorship of the *States* is the same as when it was founded.

Mr. O. JENNINGS WISE has telegraphed the editor of the Montgomery (Ala.) *Daily Advertiser* that there is no truth in the rumor that Mr. BRECKINRIDGE signed a petition to Gov. WISE for the pardon of "Old JOHN BROWN." His telegram is based on information from the office of the Secretary of the Commonwealth of Virginia.

The Philadelphia *Argus* learns from "a reliable source that JOHN G. BRENNER, Esq., Col. WM. C. PATTERSON, F. A. SERVER, Esq., and several other gentlemen on the Democratic Electoral ticket, have already forwarded to Mr. WELSH, Chairman of the Democratic State Committee, a pledge in accordance with the resolution adopted by the Committee on the 2d inst.

The Alton (Ill.) *Courier* sets at rest the story that Rev. PETER CARTWRIGHT, the noted Methodist preacher, had beaten Mr. LINCOLN twice in contests for a seat in the State Legislature. According to Mr. CARTWRIGHT's autobiography, he was a candidate for the Legislature in 1826 and 1827, when Mr. LINCOLN was only 17 or 18 years of age.

Mr. DOUGLAS passed through New-Haven on Saturday. A large crowd assembled at the dépôt to greet him, but all he had time to do was to mount a chair, in obedience to the calls of his friends, to tell them that the cars were going, and that he was going with them; and that he would be back on Monday, when he hoped to have more time at his disposal.

The Charleston *Mercury* is inclined to repudiate the proposed coalition. All propositions of this sort, it says, are based on the supposition that there is no principle worth regarding in the schism between the Northern and Southern Democrats. The people of the Southern States are gradually forced to the conviction that they must rely upon themselves, and themselves only, to maintain their right. It was an egregious folly, the *Mercury* thinks, even to have supposed otherwise.

Hon. HORACE MAYNARD, of Tennessee, spoke at Knoxville on the 7th. No candid man, he said, believed that there was a remote chance of electing either BRECKINRIDGE or DOUGLAS. While he regarded the chances of LINCOLN as decidedly good for an election, and would deplore such an event, he maintained that if the Democrats and Conservative men, North and South, would rally to the support of the BELL and EVERETT ticket, as they ought to do, the Constitutional Union ticket would be successful.

The following is an extract from a letter written by Hon. HIRAM WARNER, of Georgia, to the editor of the *Southern Confederacy*: "I shall vote for the nominees of the regular National Democratic Convention, DOUGLAS and JOHNSON; am opposed to Congressional intervention with the question of Slavery in the Territories. Shall stand firmly by that great fundamental Democratic principle of *non-intervention* by Congress with the question of Slavery; stand by my friends in this State who maintain that great fundamental principle, whether they be in the minority or majority, because it is *right*, and in my judgment the *only* safe policy for the South."

The Chicago *Press and Tribune*, of the 13th, says that so far the campaign has been carried on in that State guerilla fashion. On the 10th, however, it states: "The State Central Committee met at Springfield on Tuesday last, and in conjunction with the Presidential electors and the Republican nominees for State officers, arranged a plan for a systematic and vigorous campaign, so far as it could be done at the present time. In accordance with this programme appointments were made for Judge TRUMBULL, Mr. YATES, Mr. SWETT, CARL SCHURZ, Judge HASSAUREK and others, extending to the middle or last of August. It was justly deemed advisable by the Committee to expend their force first in those Democratic localities in the centre and South, where, according to all accounts, the people are beginning to think that Republicans are not all insurrectionists and cut-throats, and are anxious to hear something in behalf of freedom."

Regarding the position of Senator BROWN, of Mississippi, the *Constitution* of Saturday morning says: "Upon the authority of an intimate personal and political friend of Hon. A. G. BROWN, whose peculiar relations with him justify the utmost confidence in what he asserts, we deny the report that that distinguished Senator intends opposing the election of BRECKINRIDGE and LANE. The last conversation had by Gov. BROWN previous to his departure from this city, on Thursday morning, was with the gentleman alluded to. *He clearly avowed his determination to support our ticket*, though it is true he could not agree with the letter of acceptance of Mr. BRECKINRIDGE, in so far as it embraces him in the general expression that "the friends of constitutional equality do not and never did, demand a slave code." In view of the fact that Gov. BROWN spoke at the Breckinridge and Lane ratification meeting in this city on Monday night last the statement is scarcely necessary, except that the letter of acceptance alluded to has appeared since.

Col. M. C. GALLAWAY, Editor of the Memphis (Tenn.) *Avalanche*, recently published the following paragraph in regard to Mr. YERGER, a political opponent and prominent lawyer of Memphis: "YERGER is a lawyer and nothing else. He has no experience in statesmanship, and is by nature and habit a very poor politician. As a lawyer he is learned, profound, and without a peer. As a politician he makes small speeches and puts stings in their tails. He has a nervous organization and is good at saucy repartee. He is audacious in appearance and in fact, and in speaking he throws his head back, so that a scorpion from the ceiling could light on his chin, and feel as much at home as on the knot of a sturdy hickory." When this paragraph appeared, Mr. YERGER was absent from the city. He returned, however, on the 11th, and met Col. GALLAWAY in the parlor of the Guyoso House on the evening of the same day. Some words passed between them, when Col. GALLAWAY withdrew and went down stairs. Intercepting Mr. YERGER, who soon followed, he told him that he had insulted him. Another altercation ensued, which terminated in Mr. YERGER's being stabbed twice. The parties were then separated, and Mr. YERGER's wounds, which were not considered dangerous, were attended to.

Col. CAREW, Capt. B. H. RUTLEDGE, Hon. WM. PORCHER MILES, and Hon. R. B. RHETT spoke at a Breckinridge ratification meeting held in Charleston, S. C., on the 9th inst. The following passage occurs in Mr. RHETT's speech: "If the Black Republicans succeed in electing LINCOLN and HAMLIN, who openly advocate that Slavery be abolished throughout the whole world, then we have to look to ourselves. HAMLIN is what we call a mulatto. He has black blood in him, and let me tell you that it is his nomination that has a remarkable peculiarity. The Northern people take that man in consequence of that peculiarity. I see it stated in the papers that he is a mulatto. I can only say that some state it as a reason why that man is taken up, is in consequence of the spite and malignity manifested towards him. But they design to place over the South a man who has negro blood in his veins. They put a renegade Southerner on one side for President, for LINCOLN is a native Kentuckian, and they put a man of colored blood on the other side of the ticket for Vice-President of the United States. This was a sectional Convention. It nominated men upon a sectional principle, with not a single Southern State represented among them. They proposed a platform of principles utterly inconsistent with the Constitution of the United States, by which their rulers should be governed. The question is, will you submit to such a nomination, if effectual? Mr. RHETT urged his hearers to act, and to stop passing resolutions and talking. They should unite under a banner inscribed with the motto, "Equality of the South in the Union, or Independence out of it."

Messrs. TIMOTHY RUSS and JOHN A. HARMAN have issued an address to the Democracy of Virginia, reviewing the transactions of the State Central Committee, which was in session at Richmond on the 10th. They claim that they went as far as honor would permit in endeavoring to reconcile the two factions of the party, and conclude their address as follows: "No friend of BRECKINRIDGE and LANE has yet been so bold as to aver that their election can be made by the people. Their entire effort is to carry him before the House of Representatives. Is that Democratic usage? Has the contest between JEFFERSON and BURR been forgotten? Has the struggle between CRAWFORD, ADAMS and JACKSON been forgotten? Surely these warnings should teach Democrats a sad lesson. If not, what elements in the present House of Representatives are so enticing as to induce a Democrat to subject the claims of a favorite of his party to that body? Have they forgotten the election of the Speaker? Don't they know that the Black Republicans can carry or defeat any measure? We cannot believe that the people desire that such a House shall select a President for them. Then what shall be done? The undersigned, after much reflection and consultation with Democrats of distinction for their talents and service in the cause of Democracy, concur in the plan suggested for a mass Convention of National Democrats, who adhere to the usages and nominees of the regular organization, to be held at Staunton on the 16th of next August. In our opinion, this is the only way which will secure the election of the nominees of the National Democracy, and defeat the election of LINCOLN by the people.

The New-York Times.

VOL. X.—NO. 2851. NEW-YORK, FRIDAY, NOVEMBER 9, 1860. PRICE TWO CENTS.

# THE ELECTION.

## HOW THE RESULT IS RECEIVED.

### Demonstrations and Speculations at Lincoln's Home.

### CONJECTURES ABOUT THE CABINET.

### The President's Policy to be Conservative—Disunion Scouted.

### Sentiment of the South for and against Disunion.

### State of Feeling at the National Capital.

### Probable Course of Southern Federal Office-Holders.

### Comments of the Press North and South.

### ADDITIONAL ELECTION RETURNS.

Special Dispatch to the New-York Times.

SPRINGFIELD, Ill., Thursday, Nov. 8.

Speculation is rife among prominent politicians most intimate with the President elect and supposed therefore to be well-informed as to his probable course. The composition of his Cabinet is freely canvassed, and the following are the names most prominently mentioned:

FOR SECRETARY OF STATE.

WILLIAM H. SEWARD.................New-York.
SIMON CAMERON.....................Pennsylvania.
WILLIAM C. RIVES..................Virginia.

FOR SECRETARY OF THE INTERIOR.

JOHN BELL..........................Tennessee.

FOR SECRETARY OF WAR.

CASSIUS M. CLAY....................Kentucky.

FOR POSTMASTER-GENERAL.

SCHUYLER COLFAX....................Indiana.
——— CHANDLER.......................Michigan.

FOR SECRETARY OF THE NAVY.

JOHN MINOR BOTTS...................Virginia.

FOR ATTORNEY-GENERAL.

HENRY WINTER DAVIS.................Maryland.

It is hoped that the Union Congressmen will work with the Republicans, thus securing a Republican majority in the House of Representatives.

Mr. LINCOLN is continually receiving applications from Southerners for office, and every train brings politicians. Mr. LINCOLN receives his friends freely at the Executive rooms, but visitors must tell short stories.

Preparations are in progress for a grand demonstration in Springfield, with illuminations, a parade, a mass meeting and speeches.

The idea of secession is scouted here by all parties. It is believed that Mr. LINCOLN will be conservative, even at the risk of offending his own party, and that he will administer the Government without regard to his election by our section.

The State returns indicate that the lower House is sure for the Republicans, and the Senate probably, which inspires confidence in the reelection of Senator TRUMBULL. The State election is highly important also, in view of the efforts of the Republicans to secure a fair apportionment, so that a majority of the popular vote will give a majority of the Legislature. The present apportionment is unfavorable to the Republicans; as instanced in 1858, when Mr. LINCOLN received a majority over Mr. DOUGLAS, but failed to secure the Legislature. Mr. LINCOLN appears to take more interest in the State returns than in his own success.

O., JR.

### Alarm at Washington—Silence of President Buchanan—Gen. Lane Ridicules the Idea of Secession—No Resignations.

Special Dispatch to the New York Times.

WASHINGTON, Thursday, Nov. 8.

There is evidently great alarm here at the position of affairs in the South, the most serious difficulty being apprehended from the resignation of Federal officers, particularly those connected with the collection of the revenue. The Collector of the port of Charleston has already tendered his resignation, and the Department apprehends that his subordinates will do likewise. "What's to be done?" seems to be a puzzling question with the Administration—and, strange to say, Mr. BUCHANAN still maintains an unbroken silence on the subject—not even expressing an opinion to any member of his Cabinet. In Cabinet meeting to-morrow it is anticipated that he will indicate his views. A rumor current on the street this morning, that the President had already determined to issue a proclamation, has no foundation in truth, as I learn from reliable authority.

Gen. LANE, who ridicules the idea of secession or disunion, had a long interview this morning with the Secretary of War, in company with Gov. STEVENS. The General claims that a suspicion of secession is an imputation upon the intelligence of the Southern States. He looks as calm and good-humored as if defeat had not overtaken the Democratic Party.

I am happy to announce that there is no probability of the wheels of the Federal Government stopping at this point in consequence of resignations. Many promised to resign, but none have done so—not even Secretary COBB.

Our whole population condemn the outrage perpetrated on the *Era* office by a few outlaws. Several have been arrested and severe punishment awaits them.

Q.

Dispatch to the Associated Press.

WASHINGTON, Thursday, Nov. 8.

Numerous letters, from respectable sources, continue to be received by the Administration, communicating statements respecting the condition of affairs in the South, and asserting that, according to present indications, South Carolina will certainly secede from the Union. As yet, there has been no formal consideration of the subject in the Cabinet, and therefore no course of action, in view of such a contingency, has been adopted. Notwithstanding the reserve of Cabinet officers, it is known that, on the distinctive legal question of secession, they do not all agree. This difference among them has revived the rumor that Secretaries COBB and THOMPSON are on the eve of resigning their positions, but there is authority for saying that it is without foundation.

No troops have recently been sent to Southern posts, nor is any movement of this character contemplated.

### The Feeling in the South—The Secession Sentiment not generally Popular—Message from the Governor of Georgia—No Movement in South Carolina.

Special Dispatch to the New-York Times.

BALTIMORE, Thursday, Nov. 8.

Members of the Brokers' Board here had dispatches to-day from prominent parties in South Carolina and other Southern States, which give assurances that there will be no secession or disunion at present, or under BUCHANAN'S Administration, nor at any other time, unless overt acts are committed by Mr. LINCOLN.

The excitement is cooling down in Virginia. The general sentiment is in favor of awaiting the issue, and testing the Republican Administration. The same feeling gains strength everywhere in Maryland with all parties.

I have indirect information from Charleston, to the effect that the steamer *Keystone*, running between Philadelphia and Charleston, on arriving in the latter city to-day, was met at the wharf by an excited crowd, and the captain was requested to lower his colors, which he did. This seems doubtful. No prominent citizens participated.

The South Carolina Legislature has done nothing definite yet regarding secession. The rumored resignation of the Federal officers in Charleston, is not credited.

The Governor of Georgia has issued a message making numerous suggestions for Southern protection, the protection of slaves and the enforcement of the Fugitive Slave law, but he does not advocate secession or disunion. He thinks a very critical moment is at hand, requiring great wisdom, forbearance, &c., to prevent the disruption of the Confederacy, and the insufferable encroachments on sacred Southern rights.

So far as Southern feeling can be ascertained, there is a positive division of opinion amongst the people of the Cotton States on the absorbing question of disunion and secession. A Charleston merchant told me to-day that his interests compelled him to support the Union, and that a large conservative body in the State agreed with him.

There was some excitement in Charleston, to-day, about a Boston ship arriving in the harbor with the Palmetto flag flying. The people supposed it was done to conciliate good will.

W.

### The Sentiment in Virginia—Comments of the Press—No Probability of Any Movement towards Secession.

Special Dispatch to the New-York Times.

RICHMOND, Va., Thursday, Nov. 8.

Large majorities are coming in for BRECKINRIDGE, and two to one is bet on the State going for him.

In regard to secession, the Richmond *Examiner*, of this morning, has the following:

"The denial of the right of any State to leave the Union will at once prevent any reunion of the States. The attempt to coerce one will lead to a general civil war, and that once commenced, no man can pretend to guess at its direction or its results. Let no man think that he or his State can lie idle and avoid this approaching conflict. Firm, wise, resolute and prompt action can alone avert the disastrous catastrophe of war. We entreat all Virginians to put an end to these angry partisan conflicts, and to take counsel as to the action they must pursue."

Neutral in politics, the Petersburgh *Express*, of this date, has the most sensible article of any, which says:

"To drop metaphor, the people must now consider what their interests and welfare require them to do in a crisis big with the fate of the Republic. Statesmen and patriots must now come forward and take cousel together upon public affairs. This is no time for heartless politicians and crazy fanatics and infuriated declaimers to be permitted to have their way."

The Petersburgh *Bulletin* dissolved the Union this morning, but in doing so dissolved itself. *Vide* the two paragraphs below:

"With this number of the paper the publication of the *Bulletin* will be discontinued for the present. The Federal Union in effect no longer exists. It was virtually dissolved last Tuesday, by the election of a Black Republican to the Presidency. We are on the brink of a revolution, of which none can say what the issue may be. Let us hope for the best."

The following I take from the Richmond *Enquirer* of this date:

"It will be seen that the South Carolina Legislature is now engaged in considering the question of calling a State Convention with the view of adopting measures for seceding from the Union and arming the State. Other States will doubtless pursue a similar course. What will be the final result none but He who watches over the destinies of the world, and thus far has vouchsafed to us peace, prosperity and happiness, can foretell. Let us hope for the best;—sufficient for the day is the evil thereof."

The Richmond *Whig*, speaking of the result, says:

"It now seems to us clear, too, that if the Democratic Convention at Charleston had dealt justly and fairly with Judge DOUGLAS, had given him the nomination to which he was entitled, and had yielded him the hearty and zealous support they have been accustomed to give their candidates—he would have rallied to his standard a host that would have borne him triumphantly into the Presidency. To the Breckinridgeites, led on by YANCEY, and to the corruption of the Buchanan Administration, we attribute the election of LINCOLN, more than to the influence of the Slavery question. YANCEY and BUCHANAN have done the deed. Would that they only had to meet its consequences; but these will fall upon the country and upon each individual citizen. We pray heaven that the country and they may pass them unscathed!"

Mr. GLASS, Post-master of Lynchburgh, and Editor of the *Republican*, in a card in his paper, says "he will not hold office any longer than BUCHANAN'S term, and if any Lincolnite wants it now, he can have it by saying so." There are plenty of others who would take it.

The much talked of Cavalry encampment commenced yesterday. There are fifteen companies in the encampment.

LINCOLN'S election has been confirmed, and from what I can gather about secession from the sovereign people, opinions are about divided. If, in case LINCOLN does not commit an overt act, it is put to the people, the Union men will be largely in the majority.

News from South Carolina is anxiously looked for.

RICHMOND, Thursday, Nov. 8—P. M.

The vote of the State, as far as heard from, gives BRECKINRIDGE a majority of 2,065. There are 70 counties yet to hear from, which gave LETCHER a majority of 325.

There is very little excitement now about the election of LINCOLN. We are all waiting to hear from South Carolina.

S.

### Prospect of the Secession of South Carolina—Action of the Legislature—The Resigned Federal Officeholders, &c.

COLUMBIA, S. C., Thursday, Nov. 8.

The Speaker of the House last night received a dispatch from Virginia, tendering the services of a volunteer corps in the event of South Carolina's secession.

EDMUND RUFFIN spoke last night. He said Southern independence had been his life-long study, and he thought it could only be secured by the secession of South Carolina. His speech was rapturously applauded. Other stirring addresses were made.

Efforts were made yesterday in the Legislature to wait for Southern coöperation, but failed. *A State Convention is to be called.* The election of delegates will probably be ordered on the 4th of December, and the Convention meet on the 17th.

Messrs. BOYCE, BONHAM and KEITT urge the call for a Convention and immediate action.

CHARLESTON, Thursday, Nov. 8.

A large body of citizens called on the resigned Federal officers last night. They were greeted with enthusiasm. The officials returned thanks in spirited addresses.

A dispatch in the *Courier*, from Washington, says BUCHANAN will resist nullification, but not secession.

The bark *James Gray*, owned by CUSHING'S Boston Line, lying at our wharves, under instructions from her owners, has hoisted the Palmetto flag, and fired a salute of fifteen guns.

JAMES CONNER, District-Attorney, has resigned. Messrs. COLCOCK, Collector, and JACOBS, Deputy-Collector, have notified the President of their resignations.

### Message of the Governor of Georgia—He Does Not Approve of Calling a Southern Convention—Important Recommendations.

MILLEDGEVILLE, Ga., Thursday, Nov. 8.

Gov. BROWN, in a special message to the Legislature, thinks but few States will meet the Southern Convention, and does not recommend the appointment of delegates from Georgia. He thinks the constitutional rights of the people of Georgia have been violated by several non-slaveholding States to the extent of justifying, in the judgment of civilized nations, the adoption of any measures necessary for the restoration or the future protection of their rights. He refers to the patriotic spirit in the origin of our Government, and portrays the series of unconstitutional and unfriendly acts. Subsequently he is pointedly severe on Massachusetts laws, and says if the laws of Massachusetts cause plunder from Georgia citizens, that State must be compelled to compensate them. He advises reprisals, and says, let us meet unjust aggression and unconstitutional State legislation with just retaliation. He recommends the enactment of laws authorizing the seizing of such amount of money or property of any citizen of such offending and faithless State for indemnifying the losses of the citizens of Georgia. He recommends legislation to drive the manufactured articles of such offending States from Georgia. He says Georgia has the right, as soon as Northern goods are brought into Georgia, to tax them as she deems proper. He advises the passage of a law taxing goods and merchandise twenty-five *per centum* introduced after the 1st of January, if manufactured in, or brought from Massachusetts, Vermont, Michigan, Maine, Rhode Island, New-York, Wisconsin or other unfriendly States, and the tax to be remitted when the unfriendly legislation is repealed. Should such legislation prove ineffectual, he recommends the repeal of all parts of the penal and civil code, protecting the lives, liberties and properties of the citizens of the States where such unfriendly laws exist. He says, in my opinion the time for bold and decided action has arrived, and he is unworthy the confidence of the people of Georgia, who refuses to vindicate her power at any cost, and maintain her Constitutional rights at every hazard. He believes the legislation recommended will tend to strengthen rather than weaken the ties of the Union of the States. It will destroy sectional controversy, and narrow down the issue to a contest between individual States. He says if the Legislature fails to enact laws, he recommends that the people should rise in their might, and at the ballot-box demand their enactment.

The Governor entertains no doubt of the right of each State to decide to act for herself. So long as al the States abide in good faith by the Constitutional obligations, no State can withdraw from the Union without being guilty of bad faith to the other. Any violation of the compact relieves all parties. The right of secession for cause was only denied by those who deny the sovereignty of the States.

The message fills twenty-two closely printed octavo pages. A full review of offensive Northern legislation concludes thus: For the purpose of putting the State in a defensive condition as fast as possible, and preparing for the emergency which must be met sooner or later, he recommends that the sum of a million of dollars be immediately appropriated as a military fund for the ensuing year, and prompt provision made for raising such portion of the money as may not be in the Treasury, as fast as the public expenditure require. Millions for defence, not one cent for tribute, should be the future motto of the Southern States. To every demand for further concession or compromise of our rights, we should reply: "The argument is exhausted, and we now stand on our arms."

MASS MEETINGS IN SAVANNAH AND AUGUSTA—DISUNION RESOLUTIONS ADOPTED.

SAVANNAH, Thursday, Nov. 8.

The mass meeting of the citizens to-night was the largest ever held here. Capt. JOHN W. ANDERSON was chosen President, and CHARLON H. WAY, Secretary. The following resolutions were moved by Capt. T. S. BARTON, seconded by Col. HENRY R. JACKSON, and supported in an eloquent and patriotic speech by Hon. W. LAW BELL, Elector of the State at Large, and were adopted unanimously with great enthusiasm.

We, the citizens of the County of Chatham, ignoring all party names and issues, cordially unite in the following resolutions:

1. *Resolved*, That the election of LINCOLN and HAMLIN to the Presidency and Vice-Presidency of the United States ought not and will not be submitted to.

2. *Resolved*, That we request the Legislature to announce this opinion by resolution, at the earliest practicable moment, to communicate to our Senators and Representatives in Congress, and to coöperate with the Governor in calling a Convention of the people, to determine on the mode and measure of redress.

3. *Resolved*, That we respectfully recommend the Legislature to take into immediate consideration the passage of such laws as will be likely to alleviate any unusual embarrassment of commercial interests of the State consequent upon the present political emergency.

4. *Resolved*, That we respectfully suggest to the Legislature to take immediate steps to organise and arm the forces of the State.

*Resolved*, That copies of the foregoing resolution be sent without delay to our Senators and Representatives in the General Assembly of the State, who are hereby requested to lay them before the Houses of which they are respectively members.

The colonial flag of Georgia was raised this afternoon on Green's Monument, Johnson's-square, in the presence of an immense multitude. Addresses were made, and great excitement prevailed. Capt. BARLOW, Col. JACKSON, Mayor JONES, and others, are now addressing an immense crowd of citizens in Johnson's-square.

AUGUSTA, Ga., Thursday, Nov. 8.

A large and enthusiastic meeting was held to-night for the formation of a club of minute men. Spirited addresses were made, and a large number enrolled.

### Great Wide-Awake Demonstration to be Made in Hartford.

Special Dispatch to the New-York Times.

HARTFORD, Thursday, Nov. 8.

At a large and enthusiastic meeting of the original Wide-Awakes, held this evening, it was decided to make the State demonstration on Wednesday evening, Nov. 14, to which every Wide-Awake Republican Club of the State is invited. Several companies from other States will also be present.

H.

### Formation of Minute Men in New-Orleans.

NEW-ORLEANS, Thursday, Nov. 8.

Placards are posted about the city calling a Convention of those favorable to the organization of a corps of "Minute Men."

## SOUTHERN SENTIMENT.

### Comments of the Executive Organ on the Election of Lincoln.

*From the Constitution, Nov. 7.*

From the returns which have reached us we are forced to the lamentable conclusion that ABRAHAM LINCOLN has been elected President of the United States from the 4th of next March.

We declare this opinion as to the eventful result of yesterday with sorrow which has no source in party defeat. The people of the Northern States, by an apparently overwhelming majority, have rendered their verdict on an issue fully made up, and after full deliberation, and that verdict says that *they deny that fifteen States of the Union are entitled to equality in the Union; and that the future policy of the Federal Government shall be based on active deadly hostility to the South and her institutions.* What the effect of that verdict, immediate or ultimate, will be, we do not intend to prophesy. We see in the immediate future gloom and storm, and much to chill the heart of every patriot in the land. We can understand the effect that will be produced in every Southern mind when he reads the news this morning—that he is now called on to decide for himself, his children, and his children's children, *whether he will submit tamely to the rule of one elected on account of his hostility to him and his, or whether he will make a struggle to defend his rights, his inheritance, and his honor.*

A SECOND ARTICLE ON THE SAME SUBJECT.

*From the Constitution, Nov. 8.*

THE DEMANDS OF THE CRISIS.—When we received the indisputable evidence early yesterday morning that ABRAHAM LINCOLN had been elected President of the United States from the 4th of next March, we stated briefly the issue that had been decided by that action of a majority of the people of the Northern States, and the manner in which that action was likely to be viewed by the people of the South.

We have watched the progress of the contest with anxious care and deep solicitude. We were enabled to judge, separated as we have been from the excited contestants of both sections, with calmness and unbiased observation. We have endeavored earnestly and faithfully to counsel that action on the part of the whole people which we felt would allay the strife and give continued peace and happiness to the country, and we deplore with bitter sorrow that our advice has been rejected, and that the present crisis has been permitted to occur. We knew what vast interests were involved in the struggle. We regarded it not as one between political parties, but as one on the issue of which depended considerations, which, in the estimation of every sincere patriot, transcended immeasurably partisan success or personal interests.

The crisis has come. A sectional majority of the North have pronounced judgment, and we have already stated how the men of the South will be likely to regard that decision. To ignore the danger is to resist the evidence of our senses. To mis-state, or rather to understate, the issue, is to criminally mislead public opinion. It is best that the men of the North and of the South should look the facts, startling as they may be, squarely in the face, and guide their future conduct with a perfect knowledge of the case they have to meet. We have not attempted to suggest what that conduct ought to be, nor have we indicated what course or policy the South ought to pursue with a view to redressing her wrongs or insuring her safety. *We can only hope that that course and policy will be well considered, cool and wise; that the men who will have to act will discard passion, anger and excitement, and take counsel only from their sense of justice, their honor, and that patriotism which every true-hearted American must feel.*

We are not without hope that, although the political horizon is now apparently bounded on all sides by dark and lowering clouds, portentous of coming tempest, a bright spot will yet appear and the danger be averted. But if that hope, so dear, so precious to every friend of this country and its institutions, is to be realized, it is not by the continuance of the taunts, threats, and boasted possession of superior numerical strength on the one side, nor by hasty, passionate and inconsiderate action on the other. It is not in the hour of heated exultation at a victory won, or of anger at defeat sustained, that we can look for that wisdom and coolness which alone can devise a successful adjustment of the present momentous difficulty. If adjustment be possible, it will not be found in force, nor in precipitate acts of hostility. It will be found in the patriotism, statesmanship, and sagacity of the American people, who, if honor and safety will permit, will use every exertion and consent to any sacrifice rather than destroy a Union and institutions which have been the source of so much happiness, so much prosperity, and which, if preserved, promise to our country a career of power and wealth beyond the power of human imagination to conceive.

*The attempt to distort our remarks into a recommendation of disunion is as unjust as the effort to hold others responsible for our language is disreputable.* In the silent hour of the night we gave expression to the honest impulses of a heart full of sympathy with a section of our country threatened with wrong and danger.

### Treason in South Carolina—Message of Gov. Gist.

EXECUTIVE DEPARTMENT,
COLUMBIA, S. C., Nov. 5, 1860.

*Gentlemen of the Senate and House of Representatives:*

The Act of Congress, passed in the year 1846, enacts that the Electors of President and Vice President shall be appointed on the Tuesday next after the first Monday of the month of November, of the year in which they are to be appointed. The annual meeting of the Legislature of South Carolina, by a constitutional provision, will not take place until the fourth Monday in November inst. I have considered it my duty, under the authority conferred upon me, to convene the Legislature on extraordinary occasions, to convene you that you may, on to-morrow, appoint the number of Electors of President and Vice President to which this State is entitled.

Under ordinary circumstances your duty could be soon discharged by the election of Electors representing the choice of the people of the State, but in view of the threatening aspect of affairs, and the strong probability of the election to the Presidency of a sectional candidate, by a party committed to the support of measures which, if carried out, will inevitably destroy our equality in the Union, and ultimately reduce the Southern States to mere provinces of a consolidated despotism, to be governed by a fixed majority in Congress hostile to our institutions, and fatally bent upon our ruin, I would respectfully suggest that the Legislature remain in session, and take such action as will prepare the State for any emergency that may arise.

That an exposition of the will of the people may be obtained on a question involving such momentous consequences, I would earnestly recommend that, in the event of ABRAHAM LINCOLN'S election to the Presidency, *a Convention of the people of this State be immediately called, to consider and determine for themselves the mode and measure of redress.* My own opinions of what the Convention should do are of little moment; but, believing that the time has arrived when every one, however humble he may be, should express his opinions in unmistakable language, I am constrained to say *that the only alternative left, in my judgment, is the secession of South Carolina from the Federal Union.* The State has, with great unanimity, declared that she has the right, peaceably, to secede, and no power on earth can rightfully prevent it.

If, in the exercise of arbitrary power and forgetful of the lessons of history, the Government of the United States should attempt coercion, *it will become our solemn duty to meet force by force*; and whatever may be the decision of the Convention, representing the sovereignty of the State, and amenable to no earthly tribunal, it shall, during the remainder of my administration, be carried out to the letter, regardless of any hazards that may surround its execution. I would also respectfully recommend a thorough reorganization of the militia, so as to place the whole military force of the State in a position to be used at the shortest notice and with the greatest efficiency. Every man in the State, between the ages of eighteen and forty-five, should be well armed with the most efficient weapons of modern warfare, and all the available means of the State used for that purpose.

In addition to this general preparation, I would also recommend that the services of ten thousand volunteers be immediately accepted; that they be organized and drilled by officers chosen by themselves, and hold themselves in readiness to be called on upon the shortest notice. With this preparation for defence, and with all the hallowed memories of past achievements, with our love of liberty and hatred of tyranny, and with the knowledge that we are contending for the safety of our homes and firesides, we can confidently appeal to the Disposer of all human events, and safely trust our cause in His keeping.

WM. H. GIST.

### Demonstration at the Capital of South Carolina.

PUBLIC MEETING AT COLUMBIA—SPEECHES BY SENATOR CHESNUT, R. BARNWELL RHETT, GOV. ADAMS AND OTHERS.

COLUMBIA, (S. C.,) Monday, Nov. 5, 1860.

A serenade was given to Senator CHESNUT, Representative BONHAM, and some members of the General Assembly, this evening, by over one thousand citizens. Eloquent replies were made by Messrs. CHESNUT and BONHAM. Mr. CHESNUT spoke in substance as follows:

He thanked them for the cordiality with which they had received him. Often he had spoken as a representative of the people in the halls of the Legislature, and sometimes in primary assemblies, but always with the earnestness and conviction which became an honest man and a patriot, but never had he spoken to the ear of his countrymen with that deep sense of the obligations which now pressed upon him. If he did not speak to them with that exaltation of feeling, which unclouded hope and an undoubted prosperity alone can inspire, he trusted that he would be far, very far, from addressing them under the influence of an unmanly despair. *Before the setting of to-morrow's sun, in all human probability, the destiny of this Confederated Republic would be decided.* He solemnly thought, in all human probability, that the Republican Party of this country would triumph in the election of LINCOLN as President. In that event, the lines of our enemies seem to be closing around us, but they must be broken. They might see in the hurried paths of these starched men of livery the funeral cortege of the Constitution of the country. Peace, hope, independence, liberty, power, and the prosperity of sovereign States may be draped as chief mourners, still in the rear of this procession there is the light of the glorious past, from which they might rekindle the dying blaze of their own altars. We see it all—know it all—feel it all. It was evident we had arrived at the initial point of a new departure. We have two ways before us, in one of which, whether we will or not, we must tread; for, in the event of this issue, there would be no repose. In both lie dangers, difficulties and troubles, which no human foresight can foreshadow or perceive, but they are not equal in magnitude. One is beset with humiliation, dishonor, emeutes, rebellions, with submission, in the beginning, to all, and at all times, and confiscation and slavery in the end. The other, it is true, has its difficulties and trials, but no disgrace. Hope, duty and honor shine along the path. Hope beckons you at the end. Before deciding, consider well the ancient and sacred maxim, "Stand upon the ancient way—see which is the right, good way, and walk in it." He then referred to the fearless conduct of the American Colonies eighty-five years ago, when the British undertook to bind them down without their consent or the authority of the British Constitution. All knew the result. Thirteen free and independent States were ushered into the family of nations. He alluded to the insignificant causes of that Revolution, as compared with the issue now before the country. That issue now was: *shall New-Englanders—avowed enemies, without the Constitution, without their consent—bind Carolina and determine for the people in all cases, whatsoever?* [Cries of "Never," "Never."] Or shall Carolina be governed by Carolinians? [Cries, "Yes! yes!"] This covered all questions which now press for immediate solution. That it is the settled purpose of the Northern States and will of Congress under rule of the Black Republican Party to govern them in all cases whatsoever, in violation of the Constitution and without their consent, was apparent from the past conduct in their multiform claims, arrogant pretensions and avowed intention. For forty years, under the formation of Societies they have continued to agitate, to disturb the peace and endanger the lives of Southern people. They had broken their oaths, under the Constitution, and the plighted faith made therein, by seducing and keeping Southern property; had passed laws making it criminal in their own citizens to do that which the Constitution enjoins as a duty. Deep solicitude was felt here and throughout South Carolina as to the great and important events now transpiring, and he came among them to meet their agents and contribute his humble mite in the way of counsel, and to take his share of the responsibility which every public man in South Carolina should be prepared to do. He spoke of the election of a Black Republican Speaker, of the Democratic Party, to rend asunder which, the true men had been separated from the untrue. South Carolina supported BRECKINRIDGE and LANE with a few true men of the North who stand by her side. But the question now was would the South submit to a Black Republican President and a Black Republican Congress, which will claim the right to construe the Constitution of the country and administer the Government in their own hands, not by the law of the instrument itself, nor by those fathers of the country, or by the practices of those administered seventy years ago, but by rules drawn from their own blind consciences and crazy brain? They call us inferiors, semi-civilized barbarians, and claim the right to possess our lands and to give them to the destitute of the Old World and the profligates of this. They claim the dogmas of the Delaration of Independence, as part of the Constitution, and that it is their right and duty so to administer the Government as to give full effect to them. The people now must choose whether they would be governed by enemies or govern themselves. For himself he would unfurl the Palmetto flag, fling it to the breeze, and with the spirit of a brave man determine to live and die as became our glorious ancestors, and ring the clarion notes of defiance in the ears of an insolent foe. He then spoke of the undoubted right to withdraw their delegated powers, and it was their duty, in the event contemplated, to withdraw them. It was their only safety.

Mr. C. *favored separate State action*, saying the rest would flock to our standard. They should be just to themselves, just to the great cause in hand, just to posterity, and the God of Justice would stand by their side—peril all, and trust in God. In past times, their altars had been altars to a well-ordered and enlightened liberty; it behoved them to rescue their land from the relentless foe, put aside all minor consequences, and resolve upon the great event, and if true, strike for their altars and their firesides, "Strike for the green graves of your sires, God and your native land."

Gen. BONHAM followed in a spirited address, in which *he deprecated delay in the assertion of the separate secession of the State of South Carolina from the Federal Union in the contingency of Lincoln's election.* Her action would, in his judgment, be the signal of a combined Southern movement, that would inevitably be crowned with brilliant success.

Hon. R. BARNWELL RHETT referred, in thrilling tones, to the illustrious deceased, with whom he had acted in the incipiency of the measures which were now so rapidly ripening. They were not dead; their spirits, their example, called us to rise to the level of the great duty before us. That duty he had long counseled; it was to escape the fanaticism, the injustice, the greed, and the shameless effrontery of our foes, by taking our destiny into our hands. The question to be decided was, whether we would submit to be ruled by the North, or whether we would, like men and freemen, resolve to govern ourselves. Mr. RHETT very happily *ridiculed the idea of any invasion of our soil*, and in any event called upon the country to stand fast by right and duty. South Carolina had a history—had bred a noble race of statesmen and patriots—had nurtured a people brave, intelligent, of immaculate honor, of unsullied integrity. She was to this country what Athens had been to Greece, and she owed it to herself to interpose her sovereignty in this great crisis in behalf of regulated liberty.

EX-GOV. ADAMS showed that every class of our people were equally and vitally interested in the decision of this matter. His advice was, to *try the virtue of the great principle of State Rights, and the remedy of separate State action.* His faith in the doctrine had increased with the necessity for its exercise. The contest was upon us, and nothing but the most active measures could take us safely through it. *Gov. Adams scouted the idea of coercion.* The accession of States to the present Government was not the result, in any degree, of force; their withdrawal, in spite of the empty threats of DOUGLAS at Norfolk, where he pandered to the Black Republicans, could not be prevented by force.

Mr. WARREN, of Camdem, and J. D. TRADEWELL, of this city, followed in effective efforts.

### Speech from a Judge of the Supreme Court.

At a railroad celebration in Savannah, Ga., on the 2d, in response to a toast complimentary to the Supreme Court of the United States and to Chief-Justice TANEY, Judge WAYNE, one of the Judges, made the following remarks:

MR. MAYOR: As one of your constituents, I thank you for having brought together so many of the citizens of South Carolina upon the present occasion. No man can feel more pleasure in their society than I do, and none can congratulate the communities of Charleston and Savannah upon the completion of this enterprise more than I do. The forbearance which a judicial officer must observe will restrain me from saying much that I would otherwise say, and that will be said—and upon a proper occasion. [Great applause.] I am to thank you, Mr. Mayor and Aldermen of the City of Savannah, for thinking of the Supreme Court of the United States. This day week I left in Washington our venerable leader, in the enjoyment of better health than he has had for many years, and in the unclouded possession of his great faculties. But I will say to yourselves, and to the respected Mayor and Aldermen of the City of Charleston present, that *what that Court has determined she means to enforce.* [Thunders of applause.] And, moreover, that *we look with calm indifference upon all threats made to reorganise that Court.* What it has said it will adhere to; and if it is not enforced, it will not be because they have not called upon the proper authorities. [Renewed applause.] I beg to be excused from saying more. I feel, however, the compliment paid to the Court, and to our venerable senior it will, I know, be peculiarly gratifying. [Applause.]

### Speech by one of Mr. Buchanan's Office-holders.

At the same railroad celebration referred to above, W. F. COLCOCK, Esq., United States Collector for the port of Charleston, responded to a toast complimentary to South Carolina. After returning his thanks, and speaking of the coming triumph of the Republican Party, he went on to say that if they asked him what South Carolina intended to do, he believed, taking the present state of feeling in South Carolina, that she *does intend to secede from the Union.* [Great applause and cheering.] I am no prophet, said he, nor the son of a prophet; but I know this; and I beg you to remember that it is only my own individual opinion. Our Legislature meets on the 5th of November next. On the 6th they will vote for Electors. It is the purpose of our Legislature not to adjourn until the close of the annual session. As soon as it is known that LINCOLN is elected, they will call a Convention of the people of South Carolina, to meet together before he goes into office, *for the purpose of putting the State out of the Union.* [Applause.] When you ask me, "Do you believe your people are in favor of separate State action?" I tell you that I believe that when the State of South Carolina decides to go out of the Union, she will do so *in the confident hope and expectation that she will have the assistance of Georgia, Alabama, Mississippi and Florida.* [A Voice—"They will," and applause.] We have been in correspondence, in South Carolina, with the leading men in these States; at *first we found considerable divisions of sentiment; but now I believe we have good ground to hope that these States will follow and sustain South Carolina. One thing Georgia can do. Her Legislature meets on* the 7th inst. Allow me to say, as a citizen of South Carolina, that you could impart confidence to my State by passing a joint resolution declaring that the Representatives of Georgia assure the people of South Carolina, knowing the sentiments of her people that if she goes out of the Union her people will follow. [Applause.] We met on Monday, you met on Wednesday. On Wednesday send a messenger over (we will receive the message on Saturday), assuring South Carolina that if she goes out of the Union, Georgia will stand beside her. *We do not want to take the first step.* We have waited ten, twenty years, and have not yet obtained what we want. If you go out first, it is certain that we will join you. If we go out first, there is some doubt whether you will send the message to us. It is no easy matter to pull down one Government and build up another. I tell you that it is a work that requires the courage and wisdom of the bravest and most intelligent people. When you dissolve this Union, you will undertake a work that is worthy of you. If you undertake it, prepare for danger. If you advance you will meet danger; if you stand still you are certain to meet death. I tell you the best plan is for Georgia to take the lead, and for South Carolina to follow.

### The Plots on Foot in Washington.

*From the Pennsylvanian.*

WASHINGTON, Wednesday, Nov. 7.

I could startle you with information that I possess in regard to the men who are pledged never to submit to the inauguration of LINCOLN. Consideration for Mr. BUCHANAN may prevent any decided overt act until LINCOLN'S inauguration; but the latter is destined to meet the issue on the very threshold of his Administration. As there are no more elections to affect, people may begin to believe, presently. I assure you of my belief, founded on good reasons, that the Union of these States will not exist on the 4th of March next.

The effect of the election on the people of this city is very strong. The anticipations of the slave population are not less noticeable, they believing yesterday that they were to be freed to-day. I learn that the same impression prevailed among the negroes of Georgetown and Alexandria. The slaves in *the towns* are believed to be pretty generally corrupted by intercourse with free negroes and disguised Abolitionists.

A distinguished military man now in this city has authorized a telegram to Gov. GIST, of South Carolina, tendering his sword in aid of a secession movement in that State.

All business in the Departments, save the preparation of the annual reports for Congress, is about suspended.

### Taxation for Disunion Resisted in Alabama.

Last Winter the Alabama Legislature passed a bill authorizing a tax of $200,000 to be raised to defray the expense of arming the State, and giving the Governor power to appoint two Commissioners from each county, with power to determine the course which the State should take in the event of the Lincoln election. The tax-gatherers of Alabama are now collecting this tax from the poor and rich alike in that State; and a portion of the citizens of Madison County, Ala., have assembled together, and solemnly resolved to resist its collection. Here are their resolutions:

*Resolved*, That we, as freemen, abhor the Military Law passed by our Legislature, and now, in this public manner, *denounce the law as unconstitutional, and subversive of our liberties as freemen.*

*Resolved*, That *we will resist this military tax by all lawful means*, let it be attempted to be enforced in any manner or shape.

*Resolved*, That we recommend to all citizens and freemen of the State of Alabama to do as we have done—take a bold and legal stand against the enforcement of this Military law.

*Resolved*, That when our State requires our property and lives in defence of what we may consider her honor and the safety of her citizens and their property, we will freely give both; but we are not willing to surrender up our property, liberty and lives to an unconstitutional and intolerant act of our Legislature.

### The Financial Stringency.

The Charleston *Courier* attributes the present scarcity of money in the South to the fact that the cotton crop is not yet paid for, and to the alarm of large numbers of citizens of Southern States in Europe and in the Northern States. These travelers it estimates spend annually $300,000. The *Courier* remarks in conclusion:

"The election of LINCOLN will, in all probability, destroy the present Confederation. If it does not, it will certainly shake it to its centre. It becomes prudent men, therefore, so to shape their course as to meet the shock with as much preparation and as little at stake as possible. This has led to the shortening of the time on which drafts would be taken on Northern acceptors. In case of difficulty, it would be better that they should not have the cotton and the money too. It is the period when we will be out of debt to them, and it would be best that we should not have an account more than square. Our crops are coming rapidly forward, and are bringing good prices. Both the North and Europe must have our cotton, and if we will not take their paper they will bring us their money; and the Banks will soon be in a condition to extend all the necessary facilities for the legitimate purposes of trade

The commercial community of this city, although sorely pressed by the curtailment to a somewhat greater extent than usual of those facilities to which they have been accustomed to look, are, nevertheless, as sound and reliable, at this time, as at any other period. But we would make one suggestion, which seems to us apparent, and that is, that our business men have been accustomed to rely too entirely on Bank facilities for their permanent capital, and employ too little of their own means in their business."

### The Union Sentiment in Virginia.

At a recent meeting of the citizens of Virginia, in Rockbridge County, the following resolutions, among others, were adopted:

*Resolved*, That the allegation that Virginia "is so hitched to the Southern States that they can drag her into a common destiny with them, no matter what may be the desire of her people," is a foul calumny and aspersion on this noble old Commonwealth, and a gross insult to her people.

*Resolved*, That we verily believe that *nine-tenths of the people of this State will be opposed to resisting the General Government, so long as it may be administered in conformity to the Constitution, and the common benefit of all the States.*

*Resolved*, That Virginia owes no "duty to the South," or any other quarter of the world, except to discharge those Constitutional obligations resting on her as a member of the Union, and such as every civilized community owes to every other; and that she has the ability and resolution to maintain her rights, from whatever quarter they may be assailed.

### Gov. Houston on the Troubles in Texas and Disunion.

A correspondent of the Galveston *News*, writing from Independence, Texas, on the 21st, gives the following sketch of a speech delivered there by Gov. HOUSTON:

"In regard to the recent raid and incendiarism in Texas, he said it had been exaggerated and misrepresented by the letters of 'that man PRYOR, of Dallas,' the brother, he said, of ROGER A. PRYOR, of Virginia, who had some time since sent a certain challenge. *The fact was, there had been but one white man hung in Texas for incendiarism*—HEARDON, of Henderson—and two negroes; and there never had been a vial or bottle of poison found in the possession of any other negroes in this State—thus intimating very clearly that the others, that were punished, were unjustly punished.

As to the house-burnings, it had been reported at one time that there were fourteen houses burned in the City of Austin, when in fact, there was only a shanty or shed in the outskirts of the city burned; and he accounted for the burning of that by the carelessness of the Dutch, who were lounging and smoking there at the time.

He said that this Pryor letter had injured and was greatly injuring our country; its effects were being felt everywhere; our lands depreciating in value; persons from other States were afraid to immigrate

[Concluded on Eighth Page.]

# The New-York Times.

VOL. X.—NO. 2852. NEW-YORK, SATURDAY, NOVEMBER 10, 1860. PRICE TWO CENTS.


## THE REPUBLICAN SUCCESS.

### Interesting from Mr. Lincoln's Home—The Latest Cabinet.

### THE QUESTION OF DISUNION.

### A More Healthy Tone of Feeling in the South.

### Doubts About the Secession of South Carolina.

### DISCUSSION OF THE MATTER IN THE CABINET.

### President Buchanan Thinks there will be No Secession During his Term.

### TONE OF THE SOUTHERN PRESS.

### Stampede of Southern Students in New-York.

Special Dispatch to the New-York Times.

SPRINGFIELD, Ill., Friday, Nov. 9.

I find that Mr. LINCOLN is not insensible to any uneasiness in the minds of candid men, nor to any commercial or financial expression of disturbance in the country. If there be such still, he does, so far as at present advised, deem it unnecessary for him to make or authorize any public declaration. He thinks candid men need only examine his views already before the public.

Leading Republicans here are opposed to giving the secessionists any satisfaction as to what will be LINCOLN's course. They say: "What is the use of letting your enemy know what you will do when he attacks you? Why tell him, if he strikes you, where you are going to hit him? Why should LINCOLN put his enemies on their guard? Is it not better that the Secessionists should be in the dark as to how they will be treated?"

Mr. LINCOLN is still receiving all who choose to call at the Executive Room. The Sucker State is well represented. Honest farmers, sturdy ploughboys, eminent lawyers, judges, drovers—all are received cordially, and authorized to keep calling him Uncle ABE.

Mr. LINCOLN laughs good-naturedly at the various Cabinets made up for him by the newspapers. His attention was directed to-day to Mr. CURTIS NOYES' Wall-street speech, suggesting RIVES, BOTTS, BELL and WINTER DAVIS for Cabinet positions. He laughed, and said he thought that was enough for the South. He said that some were not content with giving him one name, but mentioned two or three for each office. He continues to receive applications for office from Southern men.

The following Cabinet was made up for him to-day by the Democracy of this place:

*Secretary of State*..........WM. H. SEWARD.
*Secretary of War*..........F. P. BLAIR, JR.
*Secretary of the Navy*..........H. W. DAVIS.
*Secretary of the Treasury*..........JOHN SHERMAN.
*Postmaster-General*..........H. ETHERIDGE.
*Attorney-General*..........S. T. LOGAN.
*Secretary of the Interior*..........JOHN HICKMAN.

O. J.

### Feeling at Washington—Meeting of the Cabinet—The Question of Secession Discussed—The President thinks there will be nothing done before the 4th of March.

Special Dispatch to the New-York Times.

WASHINGTON, Friday, Nov. 9.

The Cabinet had a protracted session to-day, during which the present unfortunate State of affairs in the South was freely discussed. President BUCHANAN expressed himself as confident that South Carolina would leave the Confederacy, whether it be called nullification, secession or revolution. On this point all agreed, but the President did not believe that secession would actually occur during his term. He anticipated that things will go on as they are until the fourth of March; but should the issue be precipitated before that time, he thinks it would be madness to attempt coercion, as the slightest collision would disrupt the whole country, and involve us in irretrievable ruin.

The hope was generally entertained by the Cabinet that the cool judgment of the best men of the South would prevent secession on the part of other States, unless some conflict should occur—Secretary COBB alone excusing the extreme position of South Carolina.

The message of Gov. BROWN, of Georgia, was severely criticised, that portion suggesting a repeal of the penal laws being pronounced the ravings of a lunatic. The commercial policy recommended by him was approved, and pronounced by several members of the Cabinet to be the proper remedy for the evils complained of; but should South Carolina hasten matters and annul the resolutions adopting the Federal Constitution, she will be let alone by the present Administration.

No effort will be made at present to fill the vacancy occasioned by the resignation of the Federal Judges. If South Carolina does not desire the Federal Courts, the President thinks no one should complain; and as the Collector at Charleston has *not* resigned, as rumored, there is no embarrassment felt here.

The whole number of Federal troops, from Maryland to Florida, is less than 1,000, 500 of whom are in the Artillery School of Fort Monroe—the rest being a few scattered Companies, three of them at Fort Moultrie, in Charleston harbor. Nearly the entire military force is employed at present West of the Mississippi River.

President BUCHANAN will act on the idea of the constitutional right of a State to secede, but at the same time will offer in his Annual Message an argument disapproving of it. On this point the Cabinet are divided.

Should peaceable secession not take place prior to the 4th of March, the opinion was expressed in the Cabinet to-day that a conflict would be certain, and a dissolution of the Union inevitable.

It is much regretted by all influential men here that Mr. LINCOLN did not come out with a conservative *pronunciamiento* when called on for a speech. His reference to previous speeches is regarded as unfavorable.

Gen. JOHNSON, having selected the Department of California in preference to that of Texas, has been assigned to that command, and Maj-Gen. TWIGGS to Texas. Q.

Dispatch to the Associated Press.

WASHINGTON, Friday, Nov. 9.

No apprehension exists in official quarters that any efforts will be made to seize the forts or other public property in the South, as no such movement would be tolerated by the authorities of the States in which they are located. The questions which now distract the people of that section being of great delicacy, nothing will be done by executive authority which would tend to exasperate the public mind against the General Government at this juncture, while, however, the President will perform his duty of duly enforcing the laws.

The resignation of the Federal officers at Charleston being contingent on the acceptance by the President, time will be allowed them to reconsider their action.

An erroneous report has prevailed that the President intends issuing a proclamation, but it will be remembered that Gen. JACKSON did not pursue such a course until South Carolina had passed the nullifying ordinance.

The Cabinet to-day held their first meeting since the Presidential election, but no question in connection with Southern events required formal action.

### The Feeling in Virginia—Disunion Discountenanced—One County in the Old Dominion for Lincoln.

Special Dispatch to the New-York Times.

RICHMOND, Friday, Nov. 9.

The Southern Press continues to discuss the question of secession, *pro* and *con*. It will in the end amount to nothing but talk, if no aggressions are made on the rights of the South.

The news from South Carolina is viewed with indifference. If she wants to go out of the Union she can go peaceably. Virginia will not go with her, that is certain. Before she is out one year she will find what a great mistake she has made, and undoubtedly will fall into the traces again.

The Goldsboro, (N. C.,) *Tribune* proves itself to be a false prophet when it says: "We do not believe that this Union will endure three months. The announcement of the Republican victory of the North sounded to our ears like a death-knell of this United Confederacy."

The Raleigh, (N. C.,) *Press* is also an evil conjecturer. Hear what it says: "We repeat what we said a short time ago—there is no more hope for the Union as it has existed than there is for the dead and the lost." Its neighbor, the *Register*, is of a different opinion altogether, and vehemently opposes disunion under any circumstances.

The Richmond *Examiner* still continues to agitate for disunion. Does the *Examiner* wish to precipitate the South into scenes of bloodshed, carnage and revolution?

The Richmond *Whig* opposes secession and disunion; and agrees with the New-Orleans *Picayune*, which ventures to affirm that Louisiana will neither lead nor follow in any secession movement. She acknowledges a fealty to the Constitution, and regards her own honor too highly to favor extreme measures before they become the last alternative. In the words of the illustrious JACKSON, whose memory she reveres, "compared to disunion, all other evils yet experienced are light; because that brings with it an accumulation of all."

The Petersburg *Express* opposes disunion in the following strong language. I indorse every word of it, as every good citizen will:

"As long as this Union can be preserved with honor—as long as there is the faintest hope or chance or prospect of the present unhappy and fearful dissensions being appeased or moderated—it is the sacred duty of every citizen to do all in his power to effect that end. We are for the South. Part and parcel of her, our interests are identified with her interests, and her fortunes are our fortunes. There breathes not within her beautiful sunny borders a soul more devoted to her rights and welfare than ours. Yet at the same time we have such a veneration for the Union which our fathers handed down to us,—such a deep solicitude for the cause of free institutions, which must perish if the fabric in which they are enshrined in our land is broken up—that we cannot contemplate without emotions of horror the approach or imminence of a calamity so appalling."

Returns from little Tennessee give BRECKINRIDGE a gain of 2,500.

A letter to the *Whig*, to-day, states that the scattering returns from Hancock County (Va.) show that the county has gone for LINCOLN.

DOUGLAS' vote in Virginia will not exceed 12,000.

It is rumored that JOHN BELL will have a Cabinet office, and that Mr. BOTTS will be Secretary of State. Should Mr. LINCOLN make these appointments, he will do a great deal to harmonize the Southern antipathy to his rule, and at the same time allay sectional feelings. S.

### The Feeling in Maryland and Elsewhere in the South—No Probability of Disunion—Calmness Returning.

Special Dispatch to the New-York Times.

BALTIMORE, Friday, Nov. 9.

The feeling here to-day is feverish under the exciting advices from South Carolina, Georgia and other Southern States, but confidence in the ultimate result continues strengthening. Stocks of all kinds declined, but mainly owing to moneyed operators taking advantage of the crisis to demand call loans. The money market is feverish, banks acting cautiously, and refusing large offerings from merchants and others. There is no real scarcity of capital, but capitalists are indisposed to let it out until public sentiment assumes a more settled basis, which is confidently anticipated when the first flush of disappointment subsides.

You can safely say that Maryland is uncompromisingly opposed to disunion. The Union feeling strengthens hourly in all parts of the State.

A dispatch from Columbia this afternoon informs me that the Senate has just passed a bill, with only one dissenting vote, providing for the calling of a State Convention to consider the subject of secession, and fixing the 8th of January as the day of electing members thereto, and the 16th of January for the Convention to assemble. It is generally believed that the House will demand an election, and the meeting of the Convention at an earlier day.

Extreme politicians continue much excited, and disposed towards absolute secession, but others counsel moderation and cautious action. The feeling in Charleston and other Southern cities is less violent—the people finding two sides to the question with influential parties.

The sentiment in New-Orleans is decidedly adverse to secession or a disturbance of the Federal compact, without a better pretext than the constitutional election of a President. The *Picayune* has a decided conservative article; also the *Bulletin* and other papers.

Prominent journals South generally advise patience, calmness and reasonable submission, rather than dangerous, inconsiderate haste. This is especially so throughout Virginia and most of North Carolina.

It is believed that South Carolina's disposition to postpone the question until January, indicates a conviction against precipitate action. Gentlemen from Washington, to-night, say that matters there are less excited. W.

### The Feeling in Georgia—Formation of Companies of Minute Men—A Highly-Colored and Somewhat Amusing Dispatch.

AUGUSTA, Ga., Thursday, Nov. 8.

The telegraph lines are down south of Augusta, and we have nothing, in consequence, from Milledgville.

Meetings are being held all over Georgia for forming Minute Men corps. A meeting has been called for Augusta to-morrow night. It will be managed by the most talented and conservative citizens, and decided measures, loooking to the secession of Georgia, will be adopted.

A highly exciting scene occurred in this city this afternoon. A Northern man, named THAYER, a homœopathic doctor and former resident, recently returned, was charged with uttering Abolition sentiments. Thursday night he was ordered to leave the city. Refusing, he was waited on by a crowd this afternoon. The crowd, which increased to several hundred, was addressed by several citizens, some urging summary treatment, and others a milder course. While the crowd was engaged listening, THAYER was conveyed off to the rear of the hotel and escaped. The citizens aided his safety in consequence of the entreaties of THAYER's wife and children. It is presumed he is off safe.

The feeling is gradually widening and deepening into hostility to the Yankees among all parties.

A Military Convention of the State will be held next Tuesday at Milledgeville.

Gov. BROWN's special message has been approved. During its reading in the Legislature there was warm applause.

Delegations of South Carolinians are visiting Georgia. Sedate and conservative Georgians have mounted cockades. The South is in earnest, depend on it.

We have not a line from Charleston.

N. H. T. WALKER, Brevet-Lieutenant in the Army, who is reported to have resigned his commission, will be a candidate for Colonel of the Augusta Volunteer Battalion. The election will be held on Saturday night.

It is reliably reported that several hundred thousand Minute men are already enrolled South, and the enrollment continues.

There is much excitement in Charleston consequent upon orders to remove the arms deposited in the Citadel to Fort Moultrie—said removal being unauthorized by the Secretary of War. The arms will probably remain at the Citadel.

Reports are circulating in the South about the burning of the Astor House, *Tribune* office, and battles in New-York with the Republicans and Democrats.

LINCOLN was burnt in effigy in Florida near the Navy-yard, yesterday. The wildest extravagances are reported and measurably accredited.

Palmetto flags are floating from many streets in Charleston.

The *Key Stone State* steamer had to haul down the United States flag and put up the Palmetto flag before arrival at the port of Charleston. It is so reported here by the passengers.

It is reported here that cotton in a Boston steamer was unloaded in consequence of a determination of the people of Charleston not to allow cotton to go to Boston. Other kinds of extravagances and reports are afloat.

### NEWSPAPER INDICATIONS.

### How the Election of Mr. Lincoln is Received at the South.

#### IN VIRGINIA.

The Petersburgh (Va.) *Express* says:

"The great national or *sectional*, battle has been fought, and although the official report of it has not been completed, there can be no manner of doubt that victory has perched upon the Black Republican banner. The issue has been disastrous to the Union cause; for the triumph of sectionalism has laid the foundation for all the mischiefs and ills to the country which were predicted and deprecated by WASHINGTON in his Farewell Address. It is a gloomy exercise of the mind to contemplate the new aspect of things, but the people must look at it and ponder it. It is time now for the wisest heads and most patriotic hearts in the land to enlist in the great work of adjusting matters in such a way as to save the Republic, if possible, from the almost certain perdition which stares it in the face. * * *

To drop metaphor—the people must now consider what their interest and welfare require them to do in a crisis big with the fate of the Republic. Statesmen and patriots must now come forward and take counsel together upon public affairs. This is no time for heartless politicians, and crazy fanatics, and infuriated declaimers to be permitted to have their way. *They* have been the men to precipitate the country into the sectional strife which has just culminated in the issue of life or death to our institutions, which now stares us in the face. To their inflammatory and detestable appeals to the popular passions is alone attributable the calamitous condition of the country.

Let the people then summon up their energies and grapple at once with the danger that is upon them. Let them with composure, firmness and dignity meet the trial which has befallen them. In moments of imminent peril, *coolness* and *self-possession* are the greatest of reliances. On the other hand, wild excitement and despair are sure leaders to destruction. At all events, they certainly make matters worse. Let these considerations be laid to heart, and let them be the guides of action.

The *Express* has the following paragraph elsewhere: "EDMUND RUFFIN, Esq., of Hanover, the distinguished agriculturist and champion for Southern rights, passed through the city on Tuesday evening, *en route* for South Carolina. Mr. RUFFIN, it will be remembered, purchased a number of old JOHN BROWN's pikes, last December, and presented one to each Governor of the Southern States. He is an ardent defender of the rights of the South, and his visit to South Carolina is looked upon as indicative of something connected with the present political furore."

The Alexandria *Gazette* of Thursday says: "The election of LINCOLN, as next President, has, at least, not taken the country by surprise. The result was expected as well as dreaded. It has long been seen that the organization of his friends in all the Northern and Northwestern States was so thorough as to give him the majority not only over any other party, but over all other parties combined. * * * The crisis is upon us, and we must *continue* to do our duty to our country! Rashness, recklessness and wildness are not now to be thought of, or countenanced. Wisdom, moderation and patriotism must now prevail, or the direst consequences may follow. Brawling demagogues must not be suffered to pervert the public judgment, or lead the people to their own destruction."

The old Norfolk (Va.) *Herald* is actively contending against the ultraists and their extreme measures, proposed in that section of the State. It meets them at every turn, and denounces their efforts to overturn the Government, or resort, at this time, to revolutionary proceedings.

Gov. LETCHER having refused to arm the Light Dragoons of Petersburgh, Va., with Colt's revolvers, as was anticipated, they have determined to arm themselves with carbines. On yesterday, four of the officers of the company waited upon the citizens to aid them in the purchase, and in less than two hours secured the sum of $1,450. The purchase will require some $1,600.

The Richmond correspondent of the Petersburgh *Express* writes on the 7th:

"I understand that a dispatch was received at the Executive Department of this State, to-day, from South Carolina, announcing that the Palmetto State is no longer considered by her citizens a member of the Confederate Government. All the United States officers have resigned. This intelligence is said to have created considerable excitement here, and particularly among those who deem the election of LINCOLN just cause for a dissolution of the Union.

Great crowds have assembled around the bulletin boards of the various newspaper offices, to-day, and the intelligence has proved anything but welcome to the great body of our citizens. The election of LINCOLN is truly a national calamity. May God avert the storm which seems to be now impending."

*Correspondence of the Baltimore American.*

RICHMOND, Wednesday, Oct. 31, 1860.

The sensation stories which the New-York *Herald* is publishing from Virginia and Washington, under flaming captions, such as "Virginia is Arming Herself," "Immense Excitement in Richmond," "Preparations for Secession and for Civil War," "Organization of Committees of Safety and Minute Men in Virginia and the South," may possibly astonish those Northern readers, if there are any such, who do not understand the "*Herald's* style," but they can astonish nobody as much as they do the people of Virginia. There is not the slightest foundation for a single one of these statements, except that a small county meeting on the seaboard adopted Ex-Gov. WISE's resolutions in favor of the organization of Committees of Safety and of Minute Men. Saturday last, which one of the *Herald's* correspondents alleges was a day of terrific military and sectional excitement in this city, was the dullest and flattest day I have seen this year.

It was the last day of the annual Virginia Agricultural Fair, which had begun on the Monday previous, and which had drawn together by far the greatest crowd ever seen in Richmond upon that or any similar occasion. This vast assemblage, composed of the flower of our Virginia population—of our fair women and brave men—poured out day after day to the Fair grounds, excited by the bright skies and the beautiful and peaceful spectacle, and the interchanges of social courtesies and kindnesses, which none appreciate more highly than our Virginians, but *not* excited about political subjects, nor permitting even an apprehension of disunion to cloud the mirror of the universal gayety and happiness. Saturday was the breaking-up day, the city was deserted by the strangers, and instead of "immense excitement," there was that apathy and lassitude which always follows a period of extraordinary exhilaration and enjoyment.

As to the stories of "Virginia Arming Herself," "Batteries of Rifled Cannon about to arrive in Richmond," they has no other foundation than the steps which have been taken by the State authorities, in obedience to an act of the Legislature, passed last Winter, appropriating half a million for changes in the State armory, and providing for the better arming and defence of the State. This act was the product of the JOHN BROWN raid, and was adopted with the view of defending the State from such incursions in future. It had no connection whatever with the plans of disunion, in any shape or form. The act was passed long before the meeting of any of the Presidential Nominating Conventions, and the arms have been obtained from time to time, in pursuance of that act. If any rifled cannon are on their way to Richmond, of which I have no other knowledge than the *Herald's* statement, and if other arms have been contracted for, the explanation is that which I have given.

It is pretended by some of these sensation letter-writers that Gov. LETCHER, of this State, is preparing to put Virginia in a fighting position, in the event of LINCOLN's election to the Presidency. There is not a word of truth in the assertion. The writer of this has known Gov. LETCHER well for the last twenty years, and has conversed with him lately on the absorbing topic of public interest. *He has no affiliation whatever with the Secessionists.* A good thing was said lately in a conversation of Gov. LETCHER with a Southern Governor, who was overflowing with fire and combativeness, on the subject of fugitive slaves. The Virginia Governor asked the Southern fire-eater if *his* State had suffered much from the running off of slaves to the North? "No," was the answer, "but we sympathize with *you*." "*I wish you would show your sympathy in some other manner,*" Gov. LETCHER replied. How absurd to impute to such a man disunionism, or any policy looking towards it. He is one of the calmest and soundest minds in the State, belongs to a District where in none of the three parties can there be found a disunion man, and is himself a firm supporter of DOUGLAS.

*The largest slaveholders in this State are at this moment the most conservative and Union men in it.* That is a fact to which I challenge contradiction from any quarter. Nay more, *it is true of South Carolina.* I heard only a few days ago, from one of our most estimable and reliable Democratic citizens, that one of the wealthiest, probably *the* wealthiest and largest slaveholder in South Carolina, who is able to equip and arm at his own expense several regiments of soldiers, was solicited by Mr. RHETT to give his support to the secession cause. His reply was this: "Mr. RHETT, every one knows that I began life here a poor man. I made all my money in the Union, bought all my negroes in the Union, raised all my cotton in the Union, sold it and got the proceeds of it in the Union, and I think the Union is good enough for me. *I desire to live and die in the Union, and I shall exhort my children to do the same.*" Mr. RHETT told this story himself to my informant. *And such is the general sentiment of the largest slaveholders in the South.* It is the sentiment of men who know their rights, and who consider it no more necessary to proclaim eternally their intention to defend their property than their intention to protect their lives, their wives, or children, if attacked by robbers and ruffians. When that attack comes, depend upon it, they will be heard from, but their "tongue" will be in "their swords."

I beg to mention a significant circumstance in connection with the wonderful stories of the *Herald's* correspondents about Minute-Men and organized rebellion in Virginia. A gentleman of this city, of the Yancey school, has caused a badge to be made like the cockade now worn in South Carolina, and this emblem of secession has been exposed for sale in one of our most conspicuous shop windows for a week past. During that week, in addition to the large population of our city, there has been an immense accession of strangers from all parts of Virginia, and in all that time, and with all that crowd, *only one of these secession cockades has been sold.* From these facts, your readers may judge what amount of reliance is to be placed in the flaming stories which the New-York *Herald* is daily publishing about vast excitement and preparations for military resistance in Virginia. The whole State is as calm as a Summer's morning, calm in its conscious strength and courage, and impregnable in its devotion to the Union.

#### IN SOUTH CAROLINA.

PROCEEDINGS OF THE LEGISLATURE—THE QUESTION OF CALLING A CONVENTION.

*From the Charleston Courier.*

COLUMBIA, Tuesday, Nov. 6, 1860.

Mr. BUIST, of Charleston, called for the special order which had been made for 1 o'clock, viz.: So much of the Governor's message as relates to the call for a Convention, the reorganization of the Militia and defence of the State; also the resolutions in relation to the appropriation, made at the last session, of $100,000 for militia contingencies.

Mr. BUIST addressed the House, and spoke in substance as follows:

He said that the subjects embraced in the Message of his Excellency the Governor, and made the special order for this hour, as perhaps is well known to the members of the House who have examined the journal of proceedings, are the recommendations as to the call of a Convention of the people of the State, and the practical measures to be taken with regard to the defence of the State, and also the resolution of his friend and colleague from Charleston, (Mr. CUNNINGHAM.) He proposed to direct his attention alone to the subject of the Governor's Message. The matters therein referred to, he could well say, were such as required grave consideration. By directing attention, however, to that document, it would be seen that the recommendations of his Excellency were predicated upon a contingency, namely, the result of the election for President and Vice-President of the United States, and the untoward consummation of that great national contest, which is upon this day agitating our great country throughout its length and breadth. Inasmuch as such was the case, his own opinion was that it would be impolitic for the House to take any action upon the subject of the recommendations until the result became known; but if it be so, as we have every reason to expect and anticipate, that the consummation will be untoward, and that Mr. LINCOLN will receive a majority of the votes of the Electoral College, then he might be permitted to remark that it was his individual opinion that the time for action had come—and that action should be immediate, unqualified, effective and decisive. The reasons which influenced him in pronouncing this judgment it would be inappropriate at that time to set forth. He might, however, claim the attention of the House on some future occasion. The views which he had indicated were the result of a calm deliberation upon this question, and with a view of directing the attention of the House to it, and of affording an opportunity of disposing of the recommendations, he would propose the following order:

*Ordered*, That so much of the special order as relates to the call of a Convention of the people of the State, the reorganization of the Militia, and the defence of the State, as referred to in message number one, of his Excellency the Governor, be discharged, and that the said matters be made the special order for Thursday, the 8th inst., at 1 o'clock.

Mr. CUNNINGHAM's resolution, authorizing the Governor to use the $100,000 appropriated at the last session for purposes of common defence, was passed and sent to the Senate for concurrence.

DEMONSTRATION AT COLUMBIA—SPEECH OF MR. BOYCE.

COLUMBIA, Tuesday, Nov. 6—P. M.

Hon. W. W. BOYCE was serenaded, this evening, by a large concourse of citizens, and replied in substance as follows:

I thank you for this manifestation of kindness, and attribute it to the deep interest which you take in the present condition of affairs; and, indeed, the condition of our country is such as to demand the earnest consideration of every lover of his country. In all human probability the nominee of the Black Republican Party is at this moment elected President of the United States.

From this fact arises the greatest question which we, the people of South Carolina, can possibly be called upon to decide—one which I hope we will consider and determine among ourselves in a spirit of fraternal kindness, with all due allowances for the opinions of all classes of our people, whatever their opinions may be. In my opinion *the South cannot submit to the election of Lincoln*, because he is the nominee of a sectional party—a party confined altogether to the Northern section of this Confederacy.

It was not into such a Union that our ancestors entered—it was not a Union of one section dominant over another, that WASHINGTON, MADISON, RUTLEDGE, and other great men entered, and if there is no other objection, this alone would be sufficient. Why stay in a Union where we are to be subjected to another section? This is not the only objection to this party. Besides being sectional, it is a party filled with animosity to the South and her institutions—it is a party which hates us and would delight in our ruin—a party which would rejoice to see the torch applied to our dwellings.

To such a party why should we submit? If we submit to this, we will submit to even greater evils. It is a party founded upon a system destructive to our whole social fabric, and which would reduce the beautiful South to a howling wilderness. Can we submit to such a party? In my opinion, we should not ask if that party hates us. I tell you, in proof of what I say, you can refer to their societies. Look to their Press, their public speakers, look to their sympathy expressed, not only by mobs and violence, but by Representative bodies, in their Courts of Justice, as evidence of this. There you find the John Brown feeling. The bells toll with all the pomp and circumstances of pageantry, as if a great martyr had suffered.

When we remember what BROWN intended, we understand their sympathy towards us. The question then is, what are we to do? In my opinion, the South ought not to submit. If you intend to resist, the way to resist in earnest is to act; the way to enact revolution is to stare it in the face. I think the only policy for us is to arm as soon as we receive authentic intelligence of the election of LINCOLN. It is for South Carolina, in the quickest manner and by the most direct means, to withdraw from this Union. Then we will not submit, whether the other Southern States will act with us or our enemies.

They cannot take sides with our enemies: they must take sides with us. When an ancient philosopher wished to inaugurate a great revolution, his motto was to dare! to dare!! My motto, then, is that our policy is to dare, to dare!

Mr. BOYCE was followed by Gen. WM. E. MARTIN, Col. CUNINGHAM, SIMPSON, RICHARDSON, and others, who contended that to submit to the election of LINCOLN is to consent to a lingering death.

#### IN MARYLAND.

THE SOUTH MUST REMAIN IN THE UNION.

*From the Baltimore Sun, Nov. 9.*

The fact is now beyond peradventure. And an exclusively sectional candidate has been elected to the chief magistracy of the country. He is expected to take the reins of government, and rule with authority over the people of sovereign States who reject his principles and avowed policy as in direct conflict with their constitutional rights, their institutions, their interests, their equality in the general confederacy, their honor, dignity and self-respect.

In the very flush of such an offensive triumph as this, when in her perplexity the South is at a loss what to do for her own safety, she is taunted with the purpose of treason, and her citizens who talk of escaping from consequences which they believe threaten her integrity, are already branded as traitors by the minions of this newly fledged and unhallowed power. The treason is not with the South. In her Federal compact she was supposed to be secure in constitutional rights and the perfect equality of the States. But she is taught by bitter experience, under the exercise of a mere popular majority in one section of the Union, that she may be reduced and subjugated at will.

It is, in this extremity, her obvious duty to consider wisely, temperately and fearlessly, the crisis of the hour, and to act decidedly and harmoniously. The treachery which assails her is not of her provoking. She has meditated no wrong against the North; has devised no aggression and sanctified no crusade against her fellow-citizens. The North has originated, nursed, cherished, and finally invested with the power of Government, the hostile spirit of disloyalty to the Constitution. And the issue thus presented to the acceptance of the South, while it denies the right to escape from her avowed adversary, and stigmatizes such a purpose as treason, leaves her no alternative but submission.

Under all these circumstances, and which we are by no means disposed to consider in all their odiousness of character, the South needs the utmost measure of forbearance, and of such devotion to the Union as she has never in all her trials been required to exercise before, to govern and guide her in this emergency. The act of deliberate secession, and which has been ascribed to her as a thing of choice, will be, should the necessity ever occur, most repugnant to her. And it was to avert an apparent necessity which threatened her that the man, who, of all others, has been stigmatized as the embodiment of secession, has within the past month or two traversed the North, and made appeal after appeal to the reason, intelligence and patriotism of his fellow-citizens there; but, unfortunately, so far as the result is indicative, without avail.

We can but insist, therefore, at such a crisis as this, upon common decency in the treatment of States and people occupying so anomalous a position as the South must do, in the Union or out of it. In the Union she must remain for a time, at least, subject to a power she can neither recognize civilly, socially, nor politically. And in all that time, with an uncertain future before her, must live on the hope of her emancipation from the most odious thraldom that could be inflicted upon her. Out of the Union she could only exist burdened with regrets as an unwilling separatist, having chosen an undesirable political independence because her first choice has been rudely and offensively denied to her, with an equality of the rights and honors of Confederation.

#### IN THE NATIONAL CAPITAL.

THE ADMINISTRATION ORGAN LETTING ITSELF DOWN GRADUALLY.

*From the Constitution, Nov. 9.*

We would suggest, in perfect good humor, to those of our city cotemporaries who are so troubled about our course, who lament with such touching sincerity our want of common sense, and fervently desire that we shall "cool off," that it is "love's labor lost."

We may be very treasonable, or very foolish, because we cannot entertain the opinion that Southern men are likely to accept Mr. LINCOLN's election without murmur, complaint or remonstrance, yet we confess that we cannot do so, and we believe, further, that we are not singular in our opinion. It will be terrible to receive the ignominious punishment of traitors with which one of our neighbors threatens us, and it is lamentable to feel that another pities our folly and want of common sense. But we must bear both the future and present calamities, if there is no other escape than by abandoning the belief that Mr. LINCOLN's election is fraught with extreme danger to the Republic.

We have no ambition to find favor in the sight of Mr. LINCOLN. We announce now our determination to earn his disfavor, and thus leave the field open to others who are less foolish and are endowed with more common sense than ourselves. If others have discovered the transcendent merits of Mr. LINCOLN within the last two days, and are convinced that his rule will be beneficent, just, and acceptable to the South, they have the perfect right to sing his praises and declare their convictions from every housetop. But let them not express their gratitude that they are so much better and wiser than their neighbors. We shall never dispute their title to the high places in the Lincoln synagogue, nor feel the least envy if they receive the highest rewards he can bestow.

Whoever charges us with recommending disunion states what he knows to be an infamous slander; and as we now solemnly assert that we shall never bid for Mr. LINCOLN's patronage, there is no need for its repetition by those who seek to conciliate the President elect.

WHAT A SOUTHERN CONVENTION SHOULD DO.

*From the States and Union, Nov. 9.*

The Message of Gov. GIST to the Legislature of South Carolina, which we print elsewhere, is calculated to excite not only the people of the Palmetto State, but those of other States, North as well as South, from different causes. When the Executive of a sovereign State feels it his duty to write such a message, it must command attention. It is true that the continuously protesting position occupied by the State, the feelings of which it would appear Gov. GIST expresses, will detract somewhat in the minds of many from the importance of the document, and the position of South Carolina. Still we cannot overcome evils by underrating them.

It is needless for us to say that in our opinion, Gov. GIST takes an unconstitutional view of the issue—hence his necessity for means outside of the Constitution to meet it. While insinuating an idea that his action is guided by the State-rights doctrine, he virtually does not recognize it; for, if he did, he would not fear the incoming of ABRAHAM LINCOLN, or any other worse individual to the Presidential chair. To the firm State-rights believer and practical advocate, the Federal power has no danger and conveys no fear. It is the error of the Secessionists that they argue like inhabitants of provinces desirous to rebel against a recognized despotism, instead of citizens of free sovereign States, having and sharing equal rights in a Confederacy of equal States. The mode of protestations in which their leaders indulge does not partake of that temper which is the accompaniment of conscious equality. It is pitched in a key of rebuke or remonstrance, which, to one not used to the ebbs and flows of political resources, would indicate that the States represented by them were either above or beneath the others in the Confederacy—one of which is quite as absurd as the other.

The State-rights doctrine gives to every State its own destiny. Under such a faith, and in the practice of it, the State is as independent of Federal intrusion as a private family.

The Convention suggested by Gov. GIST ought not to be confined to the State of South Carolina. For the facilitation of peace and an expression of the whole opinion of the Southern States, we would like to see them meet together—as some such movement appears to be necessary. Let them come calmly together—let good, sound, mature men, representing their best interests and their dearest rights meet in council—as their fathers did when founding the Independence now so recklessly trifled with, and when almost all of the old thirteen were Slave States. Let them be actuated by a desire for the public welfare, and the same abnegation of self-interest—let them meet as the representatives of living, breathing, and patriotic people; not as the mere representatives of themselves and their own views and own ends; and let them determine, like the noble men who entered the old State House of Philadelphia, on the night of the 3d of July, 1776—to come to an understanding, to yield their personal frenzies to the popular voice, as indicated by the will of the majority; and though they go into council with differing views and policies, to come out with a united faith, and an identity of purpose suitable for the defence and preservation of the identity of interests they represent.

Such a convention—if held in a spirit of wisdom—if convened not for the purpose of issuing inflammatory manifestoes and the display of pyrotechnic speeches, but to ponder on the best means of self-preservation instead of suicide—would, we firmly believe, result in a healthy consolidation of conservative opinion, such as would be a standing barrier in the way of all wild and treasonable projects in future.

## SECESSION IN NEW-YORK.

### Meeting of Southern Medical Students—Resolutions to Return Home Adopted.

### Speeches by Mr. Clinton, of Mississippi, Dr. Marion Sims, Col. Dick, of Maryland, Gen. Bynum, of Tennessee, and Others.

In the papers of Friday morning, Nov. 9, a call appeared for the Southern Medical Students attending lectures in this City, to meet at the hall of the Medical College on Fourteenth-street, to take action as to their course in remaining here or going home, since the result of the election of Tuesday. The Faculty, however, being unwilling that the hall should be used for political purposes, refused to open it for the meeting, and consequently the place of meeting was changed to the Democratic Head-quarters on Broadway, opposite Astor-Place.

The room was nearly filled with Southerners from nearly every State south of Mason & Dixon's line.

The hour of meeting was 8 o'clock, but it was half-past 8 before the house was called to order. The meeting was organized by appointing a Chairman; also four Secretaries, and a committee of three from among the students, on resolutions.

At this juncture it was announced that the Reporters of the *Herald* and *Express* would be allowed to remain, but that those of the other City papers were requested to withdraw.

Hon. Mr. CLINTON, of Mississippi, was then introduced to the meeting, who prefaced his remarks by saying that he would say nothing to them that he would not say to his brother or his only son. He stated that before last Tuesday he was a firm Union man, and that for three months he had been traveling through the North, at his own expense, striving to open the eyes of the people of the North, and to lead them to a right decision, but that since the election of ABRAHAM LINCOLN to the highest office in the gift of the people he was for disunion, and the sooner the better. The Union at first contained but one free State, and twelve slave States, and the slave States had been yielding to the demands of the free States till they exposed themselves to ridicule by further concessions. He was ready to make sacrifice of his property, prospects, and even his wife and children for the sake of Southern honor. He closed by advising the young gentlemen immediately to return to their Southern homes, and withdraw their patronage from Northern institutions.

Previous to Mr. CLINTON's speech, Mr. CHARLES W. ASHBY, of Culpepper Court-house, attempted to make a few remarks in favor of moderation and calmness, but was hissed, and finally only allowed to proceed upon his avowing himself a friend to the South and Southern institutions.

Dr. MARION SIMS, of this City, next was called for. He assured the gentlemen that he had a right to speak to them, as he was bound by the tenderest ties to nearly every Southern State. He did not wish to talk politics, but to address them a few words of tenderness. He counseled the students to remain here, as the opportunities for learning from actual observation were much greater than in any Southern city. They were surrounded by friends, not enemies. Most of the Medical Faculty were Southern men, or men with Southern preferences. He advised the young men to wait till their respective States seceded, and then be ready to go to their assistance.

Dr. SIMS was followed by Capt. ST. CLAIR MORGAN of Nashville, Tenn. He said that till last Tuesday he was a Union man, and had organized, trained and commanded the body-guard of the Union candidate—JOHN BELL—but now he was for immediate disunion. Dr. SIMS had said that when any State *had* seceded, then it would be time for Southern students to leave. He held in his hand a telegraphic dispatch which he read:

*Richmond, Friday, Nov. 9.*

*Southern students, welcome to Richmond. South Carolina has seceded.*

He advised every Southern medical student to leave immediately for his home.

Col. DICK, of Maryland, was next introduced as "the man who gave BROOKS the cane to whip SUMNER with." He said the young men should not wait for their States to secede, but should go home and urge them to secede.

The Committee on Resolutions then presented the following report:

*Whereas*, The people of the North, by the election of ABRAHAM LINCOLN as President and HANNIBAL HAMLIN as Vice-President of these United States, have signified their hostility to the South in thus elevating to office sectional candidates—

*Resolved*, 1. That we withdraw our patronage from Northern institutions.

2. That we leave immediately for our Southern homes.

3. That we thank the people of this City for the stand they have taken for the Union and the Constitution, and shall always remember them with gratitude.

These resolutions called forth remarks from various persons, after which Gen. BYNUM, of Chattanooga, Tenn., took the stand. He agreed with the gentlemen who had spoken, advising the students to go home, for since the Black Republicans, under the lead of SEWARD, GREELEY, CHASE and GIDDINGS, had made the decision they had at the late election, Southerners would expose themselves to ridicule were they to remain here.

Mr. CLINTON came forward to state that he was not a New-York Southerner, but a Mississippi Southerner, and as such he had given his advice to the young men.

One of the students attempted to indorse Dr. SIMS' views, but was hissed down by the rest.

Dr. SIMS offered as an amendment to the first and second resolutions:

"*Resolved*, That we leave this City for our homes as soon as any State secedes."

A VOICE—"South Carolina, the little palmetto, has already seceded."

Mr. ASHBY called the attention of the audience to the fact that the dispatch was not dated in South Carolina, but in Richmond, Va., and that if South Carolina *had* seceded, it would be known in New-York as soon as in Richmond.

The question of the amendment being called for, the amendment was adopted by a large majority. The impression, however, prevailing that many had voted in the affirmative, supposing they were voting for the first resolution, a division of the house was called for, which was made.

Throughout the meeting, the speakers who advocated disunion and secession, were loudly applauded, while those advocating moderation and deliberate action, were hissed, and in every manner embarrassed in their speaking.

### ADDITIONAL ELECTION RETURNS.

#### NEW-HAMPSHIRE.

CONCORD, Friday, Nov. 9.

The State, except thirteen small towns, gives Lincoln 37,052; Douglas, 23,257; Breckinridge, 2,072 Bell, 398. Lincoln over all, 9,295.

#### PENNSYLVANIA.

WAYNE COUNTY.—[Official.]—Republican, 2,857; Democrat, 2,318; Bell vote, 2.

#### VIRGINIA.

BALTIMORE, Friday, Nov. 9.

The *American* has the following special: "One hundred and ten Counties in Virginia give Breckinridge's majority 600. The Counties not heard from gave Letcher a majority of 300."

ALEXANDRIA, Friday, Nov. 9.

The *Gazette* in summing up the returns from 106 Counties, claims that Breckinridge gains over Letcher's vote 8,310, and Bell over Goggin's 12,532.

RICHMOND, Friday, Nov. 9.

Returns from 13 Counties in the Southwest give Breckinridge 2,700 majority. Democratic gain, 3,300. The State is now considered certain for Breckinridge.

#### GEORGIA.

AUGUSTA, Friday, Nov. 9.

Thirty counties in this State give Bell 19,000, Breckinridge 17,000, and Douglas 6,000.

The indications are in favor of a considerable plurality for BRECKINRIDGE, and perhaps a majority over all.

WASHINGTON, Friday, Nov. 9.

The official majorities of sixty-seven counties in Georgia give Breckinridge 30,000; Bell, 29,500; Douglas, 9,000.

MILLEDGEVILLE, Friday, Nov. 9.

Seventy-nine counties (official) give Breckinridge 35,130; Bell, 34,180; Douglas, 10,104.

The State Senate has refused to bring on the election of a U. S. Senator, by a large majority.

#### FLORIDA.

MONTGOMERY, Ala., Friday, Nov. 9.

The *Mail* publishes a dispatch from Apalachicola stating that McQueen McIntosh, Federal Judge for Florida, will not hold office under LINCOLN.

#### LOUISIANA.

Breckinridge's plurality will be about 3,000.

#### MISSISSIPPI.

Returns from Mississippi show Breckinridge gains.

### Rejoicings of the Republicans.

ALBANY, Friday, Nov. 9.

The Republicans held a grand jubilee to-night in honor of the election of ABRAHAM LINCOLN. It is a perfect gala night. The Wide-Awakes are out in full force, bearing handsome banners and transparencies. Cannon firing, music playing, letting off of fireworks and bonfires is the order of the evening. The Capitol, Congress Hall, the *Evening Journal* office, the Delavan House and a large number of private dwellings are brilliantly illuminated and present a handsome appearance. All is excitement and rejoicing in the streets.

BOSTON, Friday, Nov. 9.

There was an immense meeting of Republicans in Music Hall to-night, congratulatory of the election of LINCOLN and HAMLIN. CHAS. W. SLACK presided. Among the speakers were HENRY WILSON, ANSON P. BURLINGAME, RICHARD WARREN, of New-York, and CHARLES A. PHELPS.

# The New-York Times.

VOL. X....NO. 2950 | NEW-YORK, WEDNESDAY, MARCH 6, 1861. | PRICE TWO CENTS.


## HIGHLY IMPORTANT NEWS.

### THE NEW FEDERAL ADMINISTRATION.

### The Cabinet and its Confirmation by the Senate.

### What is Thought of the Inaugural Address

### Visits of the State Delegations to the President, Secretary of State, and Others.

### Speeches of Mr. Lincoln and Mr. Seward.

### IMPORTANT DISPATCHES FROM THE SOUTH

### Capt. Hill Prepared to Defend Fort Brown.

### THE TEXANS CONCENTRATING TROOPS.

### General Twiggs' Treason Indorsed in New-Orleans.

### SEIZURE OF ANOTHER REVENUE CUTTER.

### Exciting Session of the Virginia Convention.

#### OUR WASHINGTON DISPATCHES.

WASHINGTON, Tuesday, March 5.

THE CABINET NOMINATIONS CONFIRMED.

The Cabinet appointments, as sent to the Senate, and immediately confirmed to-day, are as follows:

*Secretary of State*—WM. H. SEWARD.
*Secretary of the Treasury*—S. P. CHASE.
*Secretary of the Interior*—CALEB B. SMITH.
*Postmaster-General*—MONTGOMERY BLAIR.
*Secretary of War*—SIMON CAMERON.
*Secretary of the Navy*—GIDEON WELLES.
*Attorney-General*—EDWARD BATES.

The Cabinet nominations were all confirmed without objection except in the case of Messrs. BATES and BLAIR, against whom some Southern Senators voted. No other nominations came in, nor have any others been decided upon. The new Cabinet meets to-morrow.

As soon as the confirmation of the members of the Cabinet was made public, the office-seekers began a raid upon them, of course with no view but to pay their respects.

I hear again to-night, under circumstances which lead me to put some faith in it, that Mr. CHASE may resign the Treasury after all. The question is expected to be decided early to-morrow forenoon.

THE LOCAL APPOINTMENTS.

Some of the Congressional delegations met to-day to discuss and argue, as far as possible, upon the men for the important offices in their respective States. It is understood that Hon. J. Z. GOODRICH, the present Lieutenant-Governor of Massachusetts, will be recommended for Collector of Boston. Mr. HUMPHRIES, ex-member of Congress from New-York, is strongly urged by his friends to apply for and accept the Surveyorship of New-York. He would prefer to go abroad.

In his reply to the Massachusetts Delegation, Mr. SEWARD said he could not speak for the Administration, but hoped and believed that before the close of the present Administration, Massachusetts and South Carolina would again grasp the right hand of fellowship.

The Treasury will not pay anything until Mr CHASE assumes his position. A large amount of claims have passed since Friday last, when Mr. DIX declined to pay anything more, and they have been accumulating. The claimants are exceedingly anxious to get their dues and leave the place.

It is probable that Mr. TUCK, of New-Hampshire, will be tendered the Chief Clerkship in the Treasury Department, by Mr. CHASE, if he will accept it. He would prefer a Foreign appointment. This is one of the first places that must be filled.

From remarks made by the President to-day, it is evident that he regards the departments as having become so corrupt that an entire change of officials, from first to last, is necessary.

Mr. LINCOLN wrote to Mr. CAMERON requesting him to appoint Col ELLSWORTH chief clerk of the War Department, if there was no reason why the present incumbent should not be changed. And it is apparently settled that Col. ELLSWORTH will be installed as such as soon as it can with propriety be done.

There was quite an animated discussion this morning at the White House as to the propriety of placing Mr. BATES on the Supreme Court Bench and Mr. GILMER in the Cabinet.

Mr. GREELEY and Mr. GRIMES, of Iowa, had a protracted interview with Mr. LINCOLN, to night, on the questions of internal policy. Mr. GREELEY availed himself of the occasion to press Col. FREMONT for the French mission, and received assurances that there would be no trouble on that point.

MR. SEWARD AND THE ILLINOIS DELEGATION.

I happened in at Mr. SEWARD's to-night, just as he was replying to the address from the Illinois citizens who are in town, who called to pay their respects. I could not get near enough to hear distinctly, but caught the following significant sentiment:

"Gentlemen: If you want to save this Administration, and have it successful and profitable to the country, I implore you to remember that the battle for Freedom has been fought and won. Henceforth forget that Freedom ever was in danger, and exert your best influence now to save the Union. Let it not be said that the Republican Party of the United States won its first, last and only victory over the dissolution of the Union."

The scene which followed when the delegation took its leave, was a touching demonstration of respect and affection entertained for Mr. SEWARD. Great, stalwart, grey-haired men, whose faces seemed of iron mould, gave way to tears as they shook him by the hand, and said "Farewell,"—each adding some peculiar expression of his hopes and wishes for the Administration.

One man, as he came up, said:

"Governor, I want the integrity of the Republican Party maintained."

Mr. SEWARD instantly responded: "Remember, that the way to maintain the integrity of the Republican Party is by maintaining the Union. Remember, the point at which the enemy strikes is always the point where you should defend."

Mr. LOVEJOY, of Illinois, standing near, interposed—"And remember that the Union is worth nothing except so long as there is freedom in it."

Mr. SEWARD responded: "Freedom is always in the Union."

During the day Mr. SEWARD was also visited by delegations from Pennsylvania, Massachusetts, New-Jersey and Iowa. He is quite hoarse from such constant speaking. The last few days have greatly increased the number of his warm friends, by means of his intercourse with so many strangers, for all who come within his influence, for ever so brief a period, go away captivated.

SOUTHERN POLITICIANS AND THE INAUGURAL.

The Inaugural Address is the subject of much excited comment among Southern politicians here. Hon JOHN BELL is said to pronounce it a declaration of war, and to declare that he shall urge Tennessee to prepare for conflict. This is very doubtful. Some Southern men consider it a hostile paper clothed in the most pacific and conciliatory language, or, in other words, that it presents a basis for either war or peace. Some contend that the declaration concerning the collection of the revenue and the defence of the forts was made to satisfy the ultra Republicans, while the pacific tone of the Inaugural would afford a basis on which Senator SEWARD could diplomatize through our national difficulties and finally restore harmony.

While the objectionable portion of the Inaugural was being delivered yesterday, several Southern gentlemen telegraphed to Gov. PICKENS advising against any attack on Fort Sumter until action could be had by the Confederated States.

ARRIVAL OF A SOUTHERN COMMISSIONER.

Hon. MARTIN J. CRAWFORD has arrived here and taken private lodgings. He is one of the Commissioners from the Southern Confederacy, who are to demand its recognition as announced in Monday's TIMES.

RUMORS.

Mr. SEWARD was summoned to the White House at a late hour to-night, and the impression outside is that the call relates to news from Fort Sumter; but nothing has yet transpired on the subject. Another surmise is that Commissioner CRAWFORD has indicated his demand. The hour is too late to verify the reports.

THE PRESIDENT AND HIS FAMILY.

Mr. LINCOLN is very well to-day. Mrs. LINCOLN has a severe cold. ROBERT returned to College this afternoon.

Col. and Mrs. BAKER, Miss EDWARDS, and others of the President's household, attended the promenade concert to-night, where the ladies were the recipients of marked attention.

Mr. LINCOLN's first public reception will be given on Friday night.

THE DEPARTURE OF THE EX-PRESIDENT.

Except for the quickstep music of the military band, one might have mistaken the procession escorting Mr. BUCHANAN to the cars to-day for a funeral. First came a corps of cavalry and sappers and miners; then several carriages, containing the Ex-President and suite, followed by the District Union Regiment Militia. No citizens joined the *cortege*.

CAPT. POPE'S COURT-MARTIAL DISCONTINUED BY MR. BUCHANAN.

Mr. BUCHANAN, yesterday, ordered the proceedings for the Court-martial of Capt. POPE to be discontinued. The reason he assigns for so doing is that he don't think the Captain's reflections upon him in the Cincinnati lecture did him any harm. That is pretty good.

THE COMMISSION OF CAPT. SCHAEFFER STILL WITHHELD.

The report that Capt. SCHAEFFER, of the District Militia, had received his commission, turns out to be untrue. Mr. BUCHANAN, on an appeal being made to him, ordered it to be delivered, but the Secretary still refused on account of Capt. SCHAEFFER's refusal to say he would maintain his oath to support the Constitution under all circumstances. The President, not desiring to make an issue with a member of his Cabinet, allowed the commission to remain suspended. This resulted in the resignation of Hon. ROBERT OULD, who had just been appointed Brigadier General of the Militia, and the appointment of Mr. BOTELER, of this city, as his successor, has created such general dissatisfaction among the volunteer companies that serious difficulties are anticipated.

STRANGERS LEAVING.

It is estimated that four thousand persons left town by the cars to-day. Four heavy trains left this afternoon loaded to their utmost capacity, yet the hotel lobbies are so full that it is difficult to pass. The horde of office-seekers is remarkable for number and pertinacity.

OFFICIAL DISPATCHES FROM MEXICO.

Official dispatches from the City of Mexico, dated Feb. 16, say that Gen. URAGA has been appointed Envoy Extraordinary and Minister Plenipotentiary to Washington. Gen. URAGA was formerly the Mexican Minister to Prussia, and subsequently lost his leg at the battle of Guadalajara. Gens. ZUOLAGA and VICARIO, commanding remnants of the Church-party Army, were defeated at Cuautla. The difficulties with the English Minister had been settled. The *conducta* taken by Gen. DEGOLLADO, at Lagos, is to be paid back in four months, and the British bondholders' money, which was taken in the City of Mexico, is to be paid out of the property of the persons who authorized the seizure of these funds, the property being already attached for that purpose.

The difficulties with France have been satisfactorily arranged, and the best feeling exists between the French Minister and the Government. The affair with Spain for the expulsion of Señor PACHECO remains in an unsettled condition. The Presidential election will probably be determined by Congress, no one of the candidates having received a majority of the whole vote cast.

There came near being a serious difficulty in Mexico growing out of the convent question. The Government having determined to require the nuns to occupy only as many Convents in the city as might be necessary for their comfortable accommodation and retire from the others, some twenty in number, with a view to their sale on public account, the priests attempted to get up a revolt, but failed. Several of these Convents cover a square of ground each, and are occupied by less than a dozen nuns. The Government is taking active steps to encourage immigration, and the several departments are earnestly striving to restore prosperity to the country. Gen. URAGA may arrive in the *Tennessee* on her next trip from Vera Cruz.

DISPATCH TO THE ASSOCIATED PRESS.

WASHINGTON, Monday, March 4.

Several State delegations this morning, at different times, paid their respects to President LINCOLN. Prominent among them were those from Pennsylvania and Massachusetts. The latter, as did the former, assembled in the East room, when Mr. LINCOLN making his appearance, Mr. HANSCOMB, introduced Hon. CHARLES R. TRAIN, who, in briefly addressing Mr. LINCOLN, said Massachusetts had read his Inaugural, and would stand by it, and that from none would it meet with a more cordial support than from the old Bay State.

Mr. LINCOLN replying, said substantially:

"I am thankful for this renewed assurance of kind feeling and confidence and support of the old Bay State, in so far as you, Mr. Chairman, have expressed, in behalf of those whom you represent, your sanction of what I have enunciated in my inaugural address. This is very grateful to my feelings. The subject was one of great delicacy. In presenting my views at the opening of an Administration, under the peculiar circumstances attending my entrance upon the official duties connected with the Government, I studied all the points with great anxiety, and presented them with whatever of ability and sense of justice I could bring to bear. If it meet the approbation of our good friends in Massachusetts I shall be exceedingly gratified while I hope it will meet the approbation of friends everywhere. I am thankful for the expressions of those who have voted with us, and like every other man of you, I like them, certainly, as I do others [Laughter.] As President, in the administration of the Government, I hope to be man enough not to know one citizen of the United States from another, [cries of "Good,"] nor one section from another. I shall be gratified to have the good friends of Massachusetts, and others who have thus far supported me in these national views, still to support me in carrying them out."

Mr. LINCOLN excused himself from further remarks on account of pressing business, and, therefore, retired without further ceremony than a farewell bow.

Gen. SCOTT and Secretary HOLT were also visited. To the greetings of the Pennsylvania Delegation, Gen. SCOTT made a brief, patriotic and friendly speech. Mr. HOLT expressed himself honored by the visit, and his regret that the brief time he had occupied in the War Department had not enabled him to do more for the country in this time of troubles.

Major ANDERSON, up to the 4th of March, has continued to speak of his condition as safe, and to express the opinion that reinforcements had better not be sent to him.

The point of difference between the two Houses on the bill reorganizing the Patent Office, was with reference to the extension of patents. The House had amended it, providing that no patent should be reissued when the Commissioner was satisfied that both the inventor and assignee had netted one hundred thousand dollars. The Senate amended this by confining that amount of profit to the inventor alone. The Committee of Conference consisted of Messrs. Douglas, Cameron and Fitch, of the Senate, and Cox, Frank and Barr, of the House, who adopted, in place of what is above stated, the following: "All patents hereafter granted shall remain in force for seventeen years from the date of issue, and all extensions of such patents is hereby prohibited."

The bill was thus passed. It stops all the corruption and intrigue as to present patents in Congress, and all patents granted after its passage cannot be renewed at the patent office.

The drafts drawn by Ex Secretary DIX on the Assistant Treasurer at New-Orleans, to pay for work done on the Custom house, and also the drafts by Ex-Postmaster General KING, on the same officer, in connection with the postal service, amounting to between two and three hundred thousand dollars, have been returned unpaid.

The resignations to Mr. BUCHANAN of his Cabinet officers were to take effect on the 4th of March, or not until their successors were appointed, consequently they have been attending to the business, until closing hours, of their respective departments, to-day.

Gen. DIX will return to New-York on Thursday.

Judge BLACK will not leave Washington for the present. He remains on private and professional business, and will probably continue to practice the law here.

Ex-President BUCHANAN departed on his journey to Wheatland this afternoon. He was escorted to the railroad station by two mounted and two infantry companies, together with the Committee from that locality and prominent citizens of Washington. He exchanged many farewell hand-shakings, appearing to be deeply affected by the manifestations of friendship; and when he bowed adieu to the large crowds, as the train was about to start, they further testified their respect by vigorous cheers.

The resignation of Mr. PRESTON, Minister to Spain, was this morning filed in the State Department.

Capt LAY, of Virginia, by local rank a Brevet Lieutenant Colonel, as an aid to Lieut.-Gen. SCOTT, has resigned.

The Republican Senators held a caucus this morning to arrange the Standing Committees.

A large number of citizens of Kentucky and Indiana are here urging the promotion of Major ROBERT ANDERSON, as Brigadier General, *vice* Gen. TWIGGS, stricken from the roll as recently officially published, for treachery.

State delegations have all day been calling on the President and Gen. SCOTT, and other distinguished gentlemen. Gen. SCOTT, in addressing the Illinoisans this afternoon, exhorted them to stand by the Union, and to cherish feelings of fraternity towards all citizens.

Representative LOVEJOY, who occupies apartments in the same house with Gen. SCOTT, was called out, and said, among other things, that SCOTT saved the Union in 1832 and 1860, paying an eloquent tribute to his bravery and patriotism.

The newly confirmed Cabinet are overcrowded to-night with visitors.

MARTIN J. CRAWFORD, one of the Commissioners from the Southern Confederacy, accredited to negotiate with the Administration, has arrived here.

The Border Slave States men almost generally condemn the Inaugural There is, however, a difference of opinion among them, some saying it is capable of two constructions, war or peace, and that it remains to be seen what policy Mr. LINCOLN will pursue. The Republicans indorse the Inaugural nearly all enthusiastically. Other classes regard the Inaugural favorably.

#### THIRTY-SEVENTH CONGRESS.

UNITED STATES SENATE—EXTRA SESSION.

WASHINGTON, Tuesday, March 5.

The floor of the Senate chamber was densely crowded to-day before the members were called to order.

The utmost anxiety was everywhere expressed to learn the formation of the Cabinet.

The galleries were about two-thirds filled.

The Senate met at 1 P. M.

A prayer was offered up by the Chaplain especially in behalf of the President of the United States.

On motion of Mr. HALE, of New-Hampshire, (Rep.) a Committee of Two was appointed to wait on the President and inform him that the Senate was ready to receive any communication he might be pleased to make.

Messrs. HALE and DOUGLAS were appointed such Committee, and immediately proceeded to perform their duty.

The Senate here took a recess till 4½ P. M.

On the Senate again coming to order, Mr. HALE reported that the Committee had performed their duty, and that the President had informed them that he would forthwith communicate a Message in writing.

After a short interview, Mr. NICOLAY, the Private Secretary of the President, appeared with the message, when, on motion of Mr. HALE, the Senate went into Executive session at 4½ o'clock.

The following gentlemen were confirmed as members of Mr LINCOLN's Cabinet:

Hon. WM. H. SEWARD, Secretary of State.
Hon. SALMON P. CHASE, Secretary of the Treasury.
Hon. SIMON CAMERON, Secretary of War.
Hon. GIDEON WELLES, Secretary of the Navy.
Hon. MONTGOMERY BLAIR, Postmaster General.
Hon. CALEB B. SMITH, Secretary of the Interior.
Hon EDWARD BATES, Attorney General.

The votes were unanimous for all except Messrs. BATES and BLAIR, four or five votes being cast against each of these gentlemen, that many objecting to them because they were unwilling that any one from the Slave States should go into the Cabinet.

A large crowd assembled around the doors, anxious to hear the result of the session.

MR. CRITTENDEN'S FAREWELL SPEECH.

The following is the latter portion of Mr. CRITTENDEN's farewell speech, delivered on Sunday night, March 3:

Now, in regard to the South and the Border States, I would have them trust to the Union and to the people. The North has given assurances of their sympathy for them, and justice will be done. I believe it. There are assurances given of kindness and patriotism that will be redeemed; that sympathy and that kindness which exists in the North will attract others to it its standard of Liberty and Justice will be raised from one end of the country to the other, and the people will crowd around it until States shall come and make peace offerings to their brethren. That day will come, and it will be a happy day. I believe this, and I would have the South and the Border States believe it. Our Northern fellow-citizens have entitled themselves to confidence by their action upon these very resolutions; thousands and tens of thousands have come here with petitions in their favor; States have petitioned for them; and in all this I recognize a spirit of kindness which should bind the hearts of Southern men. I will say, I am for the Union; I am not for secession. No, Sir. And as to my native State, I will say to her, more than to others, I desire to see you stand by the Union of the country. Do not go off unless an imperious necessity forces you. You have given to the world long-continued evidences of your consistency, your patriotism, and your fidelity to the Union. Stand by it. You have stood there heretofore; why not now? You have literally founded your State upon a rock. Yes, Sir, upon a rock that State is founded, and you have engraven on a rock your testimony to the Union. The stone you sent to be a portion of the monument to WASHINGTON bore upon its Kentucky marble front these words: "Kentucky was the first to enter the Union after the adoption of the Constitution; she will be the last to leave it." That sentiment she has engraved upon marble, and it now stands sanctified still more by forming a portion of the monument to GEORGE WASHINGTON. I want to see her true to that great and noble sentiment. It swells the heart within me. There is nothing, it seems to me in all the hope of triumph—nothing of the manly and heart-swelling character of the feelings which this noble and patriotic sentiment has called forth! Let her stand there with us; and stand by those sentiments. Let her be the last to leave the Union which is covered with so much glory, so much of triumph, and so much of blessing. This is the only Government on earth under which man can control his action, can speak his own thoughts, and where no man is imprisoned unlawfully from one end to the other—from San Francisco to Portland. What if our Treasury is empty and our money spent, and our Government badly administered? Still, with all these faults, it is the best Government in the world. It is here only, in the arms of this great and mighty Empire, that Liberty was presented to the world, in all her might and all her glory, and all her usefulness. In the little Republics in the Alpine hills of Europe, whose little territories are too small to attract the ambition or cupidity of imperial power, there Liberty is kept as a thing to be looked at and petted; but here she stands in all her majesty and might, with her arms stretching across a continent. Who does not love this great country, with its mighty benefits to every citizen? The name of his country goes before him like a host, and is a shield over him. The very name contains a charm and a spell which attaches to him in every region of the world; and its greatness and blessing is magnified still more every day. I say I hope Kentucky will stand for the Union. Try it, and try it again! If one Congress does not judge rightly and does not act rightly, another will; it is a principle of our Government that these frequent changes will give us justice, and every State in the Union should exercise patience and forbearance. Let us wait; and when, if it be our sad fate, rebellion and revolution shall have passed over the whole land, I want to see old Kentucky standing up, even in that day of dissolution—standing up with unabated strength and with the Flag of our Union in her hand—standing upon her conquered fields like the last soldier of a brave and gallant band; and then, when the Union is no more, and she stands the image of patriotism, honor, heroism and fidelity to the Union to the last; then, and not till then, I would have her consider what next is to be done for herself My principle is, take care of the Union; compromise—do anything for it It is the Palladium of Government. Take care of it, and it will take care of you.

Mr. President, I have occupied more of your time than I intended. I am about to part from all my friends here, whom I shall be sorry to leave. If I have offended or grieved the heart of any man, I never so intended. I have spoken what in soberness and truth I believe, and what to some extent, coming from the region which I do, I may say I know as a fact. I have endeavored to give you warning, but not to threaten. I have long ago learned not to threaten. I may warn; it is one of the duties of brotherhood; it is one of the duties of my place in the Senate to warn you of any danger I see approaching our common country. I have endeavored to do so. To-morrow, after to-morrow, and each succeeding to-morrow, brings with it new fears and new apprehensions. To my mind, rebellion and revolution seem to be epidemic in the land, and some remedy must be devised.

Mr. CRITTENDEN closed with an appeal to the Senate to pass some measure, "not of compromise, but of policy," which should bring peace to the country and allow the sunshine once more to break through the clouds and make us once again the brethren of one common family.

#### THE VIRGINIA STATE CONVENTION.

RICHMOND, Tuesday, March 5.

Mr. COX, of Chesterfield, introduced a resolution, instructing the Committee on Federal Relations to report without delay, a plan for a Convention of the Border Slave States at the earliest practicable day; also to report on the subject of the coercion of the seceded States by the Government.

Mr. LEAK, of Goochland, offered a substitute, instructing the Committee, in view of the coercive policy indicated by the President, and a long list of aggressions, to report an ordinance for Virginia to reassume all the powers she delegated to the Government, and declare herself independent, and then call a Convention of the Slaveholding States to determine what new Constitution would be necessary for the protection of their rights in a Confederacy of Slave States, and such Free States as were willing to come in.

Mr. HARVIE, of Amelia, introduced an amendment instructing the Committee to report in effect, that,

*Whereas*, It is plain that it is Mr. LINCOLN's purpose to plunge the country into civil war by his coercive policy, which Virginia will resist,

*Resolved*, That the Legislature be requested to make the needful appropriations of means, and provide the necessary forces to resist and repel every attempt of the Federal authorities to hold, occupy and possess the property and places of the United States in any of the seceded States or those that may withdraw, or collect duties on imports in the same.

Mr. GOODE read a series of resolutions against coercive measures for the collection of the Revenue, etc; that Virginia would repel such attempts; requesting the coöperation of the Border Slave States in effecting a plan for uniting with the South, with the hope of restoring harmony to the Union, and of reforming the United States upon the basis of the Constitution modified to protect the rights of person and property in the Territories for all time; that in the event of a separation of Virginia from the Union, the Government property in Virginia ought to be resumed by her, as well for the defence of her citizens and property in particular locations, as for purposes of general defence; that while Virginia remains a member of the Union she will assume no hostile attitude towards the Government, but be prepared to repel any assaults made upon her.

The debate exhibited the effect of the inaugural to some extent. The Union men, including Messrs Cox and GOODE, urged that some action was necessary, as all Virginia's previous efforts had failed. They want the opinion of the Border Slave States before determining, but contemplate no Union with the North on unequal terms.

Mr. DORMAN, of Rockbridge, though regretting Mr. LINCOLN's position thinks the Union men should work all the harder to oppose coercion.

The Secessionists are "death" on the Inaugural, and are for hard blows, and this feeling is apparent among the people; but the Union men will prevent hasty action in the Convention, and perhaps prevent the passage of the Ordinance of Secession.

There was great excitement in the Convention all day, but an adjournment was had without taking action. The Secessionists are in better spirits.

#### INAUGURATION DAY.

A Brief Resume of its Happenings and a Briefer Account of the Highly Successful Inauguration Ball.

From Our Special Correspondent.

NATIONAL HOTEL, WASHINGTON,
Tuesday, March 5, 1861—3 o'clock A. M.

Though the streets of the city are deserted, and no noise, save that of the occasional rapping of the watchman's club, is heard, the busy feet of the merry dancers still trip gaily on the floor of the Inauguration ball-room. Monday was, as you may imagine, an exciting day, and as well an interesting one, particularly to those who have sympathized with Republican movements, and who, being National men, were anxious that everything should pass off pleasantly and peaceably.

A brief resume of what has fallen under the eye of your correspondent may be of interest to the readers of the TIMES, who have not found all that they require under the telegraphic announcement of this evening.

For several days past the heat has been most extraordinary, the dust has been intolerably thick, and the wind remarkable for its stirring up proclivities and relentless persecution of the dust aforesaid. Old ladies versed in signs have prognosticated that on Monday the windows of heaven would be opened, and that the rain which for so long a time has been but a memory in the minds of the Washingtonians, would descend upon the head of ABRAHAM and scatter incontinently the hosts who would assemble at the Capitol to do him honor. This prophecy bid fair to eventuate in entire fulfillment, for on Monday morning clouds filled the air, dense masses of watery vapor sailed slowly across the sky, and it was very evident that a wet time might be expected. Umbrellas and overshoes were in great demand, and surtouts, which for weeks had been laid off as cumbersome articles of clothing, were hunted up, brushed up, and gotten ready for use and service Thank Heaven the rain was withheld, the clouds are dispersed, and by nine o'clock the sun had so gained the bright ascendency as to render it certain that the day on which ABRAHAM LINCOLN was to be inaugurated President of the United States was to be bright, cheerful, sunny, and peaceful.

The two events of the day were, of course, the inauguration ceremonies and the ball in honor of the President, in the evening. Rumors of war, of insurrection, of conspiracy, of treason, of murder and assassination, had been rife for weeks. It was certain to the eyes of many a good old man and woman that he would certainly be shot or stabbed as he rode to the Senate Chamber, and it was equally certain to the eyes of the military chieftains here in charge, that trouble might be apprehended, so much so that soldiers clad in all the panoply of war, surrounded the city, promenaded the avenues, and aided greatly in keeping up the feelings of insecurity and danger that were so prevalent among the white residents of the city. It was certain also to the minds of others that of all times in the world, this was to be the jolliest kind of a time for a row of the first water. These three classes,—the timid, the warriors and the roughs had created a public sentiment here which was prepared for anything and everything disagreeable. Still, in spite of all this preparatory state, the storm of passion was blown over, even as was the storm of rain which early in the morning had brooded over the city.

After breakfast I sauntered up towards Willard's. On the road I met hundreds of people who were hastening toward the Capitol, anxious to get seats or standing places at the Capitol steps, where the inauguration was to take place some five hours after. All sorts of men—all kinds of people—all races, all colors, all tongues, were represented in the throngs of human beings who rushed frantically up the avenue. At Willard's there was a vast collection of individuals—specimens of all sorts and conditions of men—most of whom wanted office, and if they did not their friends did for them, which is just as bad and harder to manage. The ladies were there dressed in their prettiest, arrayed most gorgeously, and all on tip-toe for what was yet to happen.

Mr. LINCOLN, the object of all solicitude and the object of all curiosity, was in his room To it no one was admitted save his immediate family, his particular friends, and Gov. SEWARD. The Senate had held over from Sunday night until Monday at noon. It was important that he should know what they had done concerning the matter at issue before the people ere he completed his Inaugural or appointed his Cabinet. At last word had been brought to him, that beyond the passing of a certain compromising measure, nothing would be done, and he at once proceeded to put the finishing touches to the Inaugural, which was looked for with much interest by thousands of people on both sides of the broad Atlantic, and which ere now has been flashed along the telegraphic wire to every hamlet in the Union, and has been read by every man, woman and child who is old enough to know the difference between Major ANDERSON and Gen TWIGGS.

Soon the sound of brass and leather announced that President BUCHANAN was approaching, and sure enough, looking from the window, we saw the old man in his barouche, surrounded by soldiers of a sanguinary appearance. In a few moments Mr. LINCOLN was with him, promptness and exact obedience to engagement being with him imperative rules of life. As he took his seat in the barouche, Mr. BUCHANAN occupying the seat of honor, Mr. LINCOLN was saluted with cheers of the most enthusiastic nature, which were continued the whole ride from the hotel to the Capitol.

The procession was like all other similar performances, gotten up for the delectation of some grand or chief marshal, and the prospective tickling of an indefinite number of assistant marshals and aids, and so on. There was a good band, a car-load of pretty girls, thirty-four in all, each one of whom personated a State; militia-men, who walked like country paupers on a semi-diluted spree, and that climax of absurdities, "citizens in carriages." However, the road was lined with people, was crowded with people, and every place was occupied by some man more or less distinguished in the world of science, politics, learning, or nothing. The brass band exhausted its capabilities and the endurance of the throats of the musicians. Patriotic airs were generally played, though I noticed that "Way down South in Dixie" was a great favorite with anybody who knew what a good tune was, and, as slowly the procession moved on, the President elect was obliged, in response to repeated calls, to rise and bow with hat in hand.

In the meantime I cut across lots, so to speak, and encountered a stern old codger at the doorway of an immense temporary corridor, built expressly for the admission of the biggest kind of bugs. I knew that I was not clearly entitled to a classification of that stamp, but I also knew that the readers of the TIMES would look to me for an account of the affair, so I "pitched in." I attempted to bribe the door-keeper, but he was utterly incorruptible; and at last, as a forlorn hope, I went to the house of Senator FOOTE, the Chairman of the Committee, whose bell I had rung for the past hour. After a little coaxing, Mr FOOTE gave me a pass to no place, or any place, as I might prefer, and at once I dashed on, to the astonishment of sundry keepers, who are not accustomed to frolicsome oysters, or habits of individuals who are determined to get all that is properly within their reach. The result was, that in about five minutes I found myself on the floor of the Senate of the United States.

The Senate was in session for the last time. Many of the members were to leave their seats forever—others were ready to take them, and the Vice-President was ready to take his farewell, to resign the insignia of his office, and to reassume his position as Senator—a position to which Kentucky has just reëlected him for the term of six years. There were but few people there, few speeches, and dry ones at that, were made, until BRIGHT, of Indiana, commenced a long rigmarole about some gas company, located in some untraveled region, whose merits he argued at length, and until the striking of the noon-day hour announced that the moment of adjournment had arrived.

I will pass over the affecting scene that followed, when Mr. BRECKINRIDGE made his farewell speech, and swore in his successor, HAMLIN; an account of the jolly old coves, the animated mummies who compose the Supreme Tribunal of our land; the inauguration, so grand, so simple, so effective and so eminently gratifying, and the many pleasing and singular incidents of the day—that I may indulge for a few moments in a description of the Inauguration Ball.

The Inauguration Ball was a success, and not only a success, but a complete success. It was a victory achieved by a few hard-working and reliable Republicans over caste, prejudice and scoffings on one side, and fear, forebodings and disinclination on the other. A large hall, capable of accommodating say three thousand people, was erected especially for the purpose, connecting conveniently with the City Hall, whose Committee-rooms and Council-chambers were of great service for dressing-apartments and sundry other domestic purposes. The hall, which was shaped like a parallelogram, was beautifully decorated with red and white muslin, while around the walls were a number of shields, bearing the arms of the United States. A ball is a ball, and but little can be said of one that is not equally true of another, save the mentioning of the *personnel* thereof, and a description of toilettes, elegant and rare, for the delight of the ladies.

At 5 o'clock in the morning, after a hard day's work and an evening of telegraphing, I do not propose at any extended length to enter upon the details of the affair; but as the chief interest of the occasion centered upon Mr. and Mrs LINCOLN, and a few of their friends, I will give a short account of them and their appearance.

The hall was well filled by 11 o'clock with dancers impatient for the signal to commence "the mazy," but as Mr. LINCOLN had not yet arrived, it was not considered etiquette to begin A little while longer and the youngsters impatient for the pastime, started the band and at it they went. Soon, however, it was noised about that the party had arrived Dancing was for a moment suspended, and all eyes turned in the direction of the door. Presently the President appeared, leaning on the arms of Vice-President HAMLIN and Senator ANTHONY, of Rhode Island. His entrance was, of course, the signal for applause, and the band struck up "Hail Columbia." Behind the President came a couple, the sight of whom was singular and yet eminently gratifying; singular, because so wholly unexpected, and gratifying, because it was an indication of the beginning of an era of good feeling

The parties were Mrs LINCOLN and Senator DOUGLAS. Mrs. LINCOLN appeared remarkably well; she wore a very tasteful and becoming head-dress, and a low-necked lavender silk, (I think,) of exquisite shade, perfect fit, and evident richness. Her lace was point, her jewelry was the simple diamond, and her attire such as commended itself to the good taste, the sense of propriety and the love of the beautiful of every person in the room. It was a general remark that LINCOLN was an infinitely better-looking man than he was represented, and that Mrs. LINCOLN was evidently a lady of refinement, of tact and of taste.

Of the ladies who were with her, Miss EDWARDS, of Springfield, was the most noticeable. She dressed with great elegance and equal simplicity. —what the name of the material is, I do not pretend to say or know. It was very thin, gauzy and white, looked as if it would burn very easily, and had a long row of beautiful bouquets down the front of it. That's not a very technical description of a lady's ball-dress, but it may answer every purpose just as well.

Mrs. BAKER was also dressed very elegantly. She wore a white silk, in which were embroidered flowers of exquisite color. She wore a head-dress to match, and looked well

Mrs. SEDGWICK and Miss BEAN, of New-York; Miss WILLIAMS and Miss CAMERON, of Pennsylvania; Miss CHASE, of Ohio; Miss DIXON, of Connecticut, and Miss BLAIR, of Maryland, were also "bright, particular stars" There were many others there deserving of notice, but time forbids.

They danced, talked, flirted, chatted, supped most bounteously, had a splendid time, and all that sort of thing, affording a series of items unrivaled for sketches, but as the cars are soon to go, I must close by stating that this Inauguration Ball is considered to have been one of the pleasantest and most enjoyable of any ever given in this good City of Washington HOWARD.

#### RECEPTION OF THE INAUGURAL ADDRESS.

IN RICHMOND.

RICHMOND, Va., Tuesday, March 5.

The *Whig* (conservative) says: The policy indicated towards the seceding States will meet the stern and unyielding resistance of the united South.

The *Enquirer* (secessionist) says: No action of our Convention can now maintain peace. Virginia must fight.

The *Dispatch* remarks: "Every Border State ought to go out of the Union in 24 hours."

Dispatches from Staunton state that the Inaugural was received with universal dissatisfaction Resistance to coercion is the feeling of all parties.

The Inaugural creates intense excitement. The Secessionists regard it as equivalent to a declaration of war. The Union men say but little, but evidently are disappointed.

IN PETERSBURGH, VA.

PETERSBURGH, Tuesday, March 5.

There was intense excitement on the reception of the Inaugural Hundreds, hitherto for the Union, avowed boldly for revolution, if the Convention does not immediately pass the secession ordinance.

IN ALEXANDRIA.

ALEXANDRIA, Va., Tuesday, March 5.

The *Gazette* (Union) says the Inaugural is not such a one as it wished; nor such as will probably conciliate or satisfy those whom Mr. LINCOLN speaks of as dissatisfied in the South

The *Sentinel* (secession) says the positions taken are a declaration of war, laying down doctrines which would reduce the Southern section to the unquestioned dominion of the North as a section.

IN LOUISVILLE AND ELSEWHERE.

LOUISVILLE, Ky., Tuesday, March 5.

The opinions on the Inaugural at Nashville are unfavorable. It is believed that Mr. LINCOLN is determined to retake the forts and forcibly collect the revenue. Opinions are unsettled by its reception at Washington. The people are awaiting the document in full.

At Jackson and Columbus, Miss., and Tuscumbia, Ala., it is considered a declaration of war.

At Vicksburgh, it is regarded unfavorably, and generally considered a silly production.

At New-Orleans, it is most generally condemned.

In this city, the Union men are rather favorably im-

[Continued on Eighth Page.]

# The New-York Times.

VOL. XIII—NO. 3966. NEW-YORK, THURSDAY, JUNE 9, 1864. PRICE THREE CENTS.


# PRESIDENTIAL.

## Lincoln & Johnson.

### Proceedings of the National Union Convention Yesterday.

### Unanimous Renomination of President Lincoln.

### Gov. Andy Johnson, of Tennessee, for Vice-President.

### THE LOYAL PLATFORM.

### Slavery Must Perish by the Constitution.

### Emancipation, the Monroe Doctrine, Economy and the Pacific Railroad.

### Enthusiastic Scenes at the Nomination.

### THE FINAL ADJOURNMENT

BALTIMORE, Wednesday, June 8.

The Convention reassembled at 10 o'clock this morning, President DENISON in the Chair.

A prayer was offered up by Rev. Mr. GADDIS, a delegate from Hamilton County, Ohio.

The hall was, if possible, more crowded than on yesterday, every nook and corner being occupied.

REPORTS OF COMMITTEES.

The President called for reports from the Committees.

The Committee on the Order of Business by its Chairman, Mr. DAY, of Connecticut, reported a set of rules to control the convention in the transaction of its business, which were read, amended and adopted.

THE COMMITTEE ON CREDENTIALS.

PRESTON KING, of New-York, said: The Committee on Credentials, after a patient hearing of the representations made by gentlemen who have appeared as delegates to this convention, wherever there has been a question of their right to a seat here, from whatever cause that question may have arisen, have come to conclusions, which they report as the report of the committee, upon the main questions of which there has been entire unanimity. But upon some points there will be a minority report. There will also be two or three points upon which I differ from the report, but desiring that it should be regarded as the report of the committee, I concluded to agree to it as such, but to move to amend the report on my individual responsibility as a member of the convention. The report of the majority of the committee was in substance, as follows:

*First*—That the delegations from the States of Maine, New-Hampshire, Massachusetts, Connecticut, Vermont, Rhode Island, New-York, New-Jersey, Pennsylvania, Delaware, Maryland, Ohio, Kentucky, Indiana, Illinois, Iowa, Minnesota, Oregon, California, Kansas and West Virginia are all regular, and are admitted to seats, with the rights and privileges of members, except one district of Pennsylvania, which had elected four instead of two members. The committee admit the two who received the largest number of votes as delegates, and the other two as alternates.

*Second*—That there being two delegations from the State of Missouri claiming seats, the committee recommend that those styling themselves the Union Radical delegation be awarded the seats. [Applause and cheering.]

*Third*—That the delegates from Virginia, Tennessee, Louisiana and Arkansas be admitted to all the privileges of the floor, except that of voting.

*Fourth*—That the persons presenting themselves as delegates from the State of South Carolina are not entitled to the rights of delegates on the floor.

Mr. KING then asked that the convention receive the report of the minority of the committee, after which he would make his motion to amend the report.

Mr. E. STEVENSON, of West Virginia—I desire to state that this minority report was prepared very hurriedly this morning. The committee deliberated until long after midnight, and I have not been able to obtain the signatures to report that I expected to obtain.

The minority report was then read as follows:

The undersigned concur in the report of the majority of the Committee on Credentials, except that portion which proposes to exclude from the privilege of voting in the convention the delegates from the States of Virginia, Louisiana, Arkansas, Tennessee and Florida, and from the Territories of Colorado, Nevada, New-Mexico, Dakotah and Montana; therefore, the undersigned recommend that the delegates from the said States and Territories be entitled to vote on all questions brought before the convention.

Which is respectfully submitted,

W. E. STEVENSON, West Virginia.
HIRAM SMITH, Oregon.

PRESTON KING—I am informed that the minority were not entirely agreed, but that the member from Kansas desires also to submit a minority report. I ask that he be allowed to submit that report.

A. H. INSLEY, of Kansas, presented the following minority report:

The undersigned respectfully desires to present a minority report from the Committee on Credentials, of which he is a member, in relation to the admission of the delegates from the Territories of Nebraska, Colorado, and Nevada, to seats and votes in this convention. Differing with the majority of the committee only on this point, it is fitting that I present my reasons for the course herein urged. The first and foremost is the fact that the three Territories named are about to pass from the territorial condition of dependence on the General Government, to that of State Sovereignties, subordinate only to the supreme law and necessities of the nation. The present Congress having passed enabling acts whereby these Territories receive a pledge of admission into the Federal Union, provided only they come clothed in the robes of freedom, and the people of those Territories having gladly accepted the supreme condition, are even now engaged in the work of State organization, with a fair prospect of completing the same in time to wheel into line with the other loyal States, and by voting for the nominees of the Union party, and politically as they have already done materially and by arms in the establishment of the national authority and securing the perpetuity of the Union.

*Secondly*—The recognition of the delegates from these Territories by the Convention will very materially aid the party of nationality and freedom in these communities. Our interests lie with the movements now being made under the authority of Congress for their organization and admission. It is our duty, both as loyal men seeking the supreme good of the nation, and as members of a great party, having that end for its primary purpose, to give all the aid and strength we legitimately may for the furtherance of that object. It is believed that the recognition of these delegates will materially benefit our cause as well as the State movements now pending. The loyalty of these Territories none can question. Nebraska has sent her citizens to the field, and from Donelson to Chattanooga their courage and sacrifices have been freely offered. Colorado makes the proud boast of never having had a Copperhead in her Territorial Legislature. She has a prouder boast than this in that New-Mexican campaign, where her volunteers won such imperishable honors, saving thereby the immensely important mountain Territories of the far West from being overrun by the Texan rebels, and securing uninterrupted our communication with the Pacific. For Nevada, let the Treasury of the Sanitary Commission speak in praise. Under the wise rule of Gov. NYE that distant Territory is emerging as not only one of the richest, but one of the most loyal of States. For this reason I urge the admission of these gentlemen with all the rights of delegates into this convention. Let me refer you as a precedent for such action to the course taken in relation to that State (Kansas) which I have the honor in part to represent here. The Republican Convention of 1856 admitted its delegates to seats and votes. It was then seeking admission into the Union under what was known as the Topeka Constitution. Again at Chicago, in 1860, was the same course adopted. Its admission was pending before Congress, nor was it recognized as a State until the party of freedom, under the lead of ABRAHAM LINCOLN, obtained power. It will not do in this hour, with this precedent, with the facts before us, and strong probability presented by these Commissioners of being enabled to swell the vote of the next President of the United States, ABRAHAM LINCOLN, by the welcome addition of three members to the Electoral College, to ignore the claims of Nebraska, Colorado and Nevada.

Mr. PRESTON KING—There was scarcely a proposition in the report of the majority of the committee from which some member did not dissent. There were three propositions on which I dissented, and I move to amend the report, to substitute for the proposition of the majority report, that the delegation known as the Unconditional Union Delegation from Missouri, be admitted as delegates with the Radical Union Delegation from that State; that when the delegates agree they cast the vote to which the State is entitled, and when they do not agree the vote of the State shall not be cast. The majority report proposes to admit the delegates without voting, and in my amendment I propose also to give to all the delegates admitted the rights and privileges of delegates without any exception, but that the District of Columbia and the territories shall be entitled to two votes only, and that no State, or District, or Territory, be allowed to cast more votes than they have delegates present in the Convention, or in any case more than they are entitled to under the rules of the Convention. I move this proposition as a substitute for the report of the Committee on these subjects.

A member requested that the amendment should be divided so as to take a motion upon the different propositions separately.

Mr. KING—I prefer that they should be taken together. But any member of the Convention has a right to call for a division.

Mr. SCHOLES, of Wisconsin—In order that we may have a properly constituted convention, I would suggest that, before we proceed to vote upon these disputed questions, that portion of the report of the committee which is unanimously presented, be adopted by this convention. That will admit as delegates all who come here without question, and will give us the power to vote upon any questions that may arise.

The President stated that there was a pending question, which he ruled to be susceptible of division.

Mr. REEDER, of Pennsylvania—I suggest to the Chairman of the committee to withdraw his motion to allow the report of the majority, as far as it is unanimous, to be adopted, so that we delegates from uncontested States may be admitted, that we may know who shall be entitled to vote should there be a call of the States making. I prefer not to withdraw this motion, but I will modify my own motion so as to make that the first clause of my amendment.

The majority report, so far as it related to uncontested States, was adopted by the convention.

Mr. KING—The second portion of my amendment is to that portion of the report relating to the State of Missouri, which determines that the Radical Union delegation from that State shall be admitted, and they only, as the delegates to be from that State. The original clause is this: That the delegation known as the Radical Union delegation from Missouri be admitted as the delegates to represent that State. My motion is to amend by substituting that the delegation from Missouri be admitted with the delegates of the Radical Union delegation, and that where the delegations agree, they shall cast the vote of the State, and where they do not agree, the vote of the State shall not be cast. I think that the suggestion of this proposition is all that is required by this convention. Unless this suggestion is such as meets their approbation, no argument could carry it through. I make the motion in the spirit of brotherhood, and union and harmony, and in the determination to strike down every common enemy, and to strike down nobody else. I suppose it was wisest and best to admit these delegates as brethren. I would not have offered this proposition that I have made in ordinary times. I do not propose that it shall be a precedent. I hope we shall never again be in a condition of affairs in this country, and I do not believe we ever shall be, when an action now may be quoted as a precedent. This is my proposition. I will not debate it. There is a right and a wrong in that case. There is a delegation here duly accredited, and there is but one, and it is the duty of the convention to ascertain which of these contesting delegations is that duly credited delegation holding credentials from an organized party association in that State. I aver from facts which none will dispute, that the radical delegation is the only true delegation here, and that the Unconditional Union delegation has no constituency in that State embracing any considerable element in the natural history of that State. The Radical delegation represent the only Republican organization which existed at the time the Convention was called to send delegates to this National Convention. There was no other organization except a rebel organization existing in the State of Missouri.

Mr. BRECKINRIDGE—I wish to move an amendment to the amendment to suit both parties, that the rule be that they shall divide. I move to amend the amendment offered by the gentleman from New-York, to the effect that, instead of silencing both parties from Missouri, when they cannot agree, that they may then divide the vote.

VOICES—"Question," "question."

Dr. BRECKINRIDGE—The gentleman from Connecticut has made a statement of facts at second-hand, and he has no personal knowledge of them except as they were told to the committee, of which he was a member. I also live remotely from Missouri. But Kentucky is a great deal nigher Missouri than Connecticut, and I suppose he will admit that Kentucky and Missouri thought not exactly alike, are more alike than Missouri and Connecticut. I therefore suppose that my knowledge is as good as his. With the greatest possible respect, both for his statements of facts and his statements of inference, I have not a particle of doubt, but say to you to-day, if I were in the profession of the law, I would risk my head upon making twelve of you find everything he has stated is either unfounded or wrongly considered. If you pursue the course undertaken to be recommended by that gentleman, you will get Missouri into a condition, if possible, worse than it has already been in. But for compromise sake, if you choose to admit both delegations without asking whether this or that is radical, then it appears to me that as it is perfectly certain that one or the other is entitled to vote, it is absurd in us to undertake to silence a State that is truly represented here by somebody, and that the proper course will be for them, if they will, to agree to take half of the vote of the State from each delegation. I think this is the only way to do under the circumstances. My object is, if you let both in, not to silence both, but to let them divide this vote so that we can get the votes of the State; for undoubtedly the State is entitled to representation by somebody.

Mr. DORSEY, of Ohio, said—I want simply to call attention to the fact that this convention for the purpose of deciding questions which could not be decided in mass convention, appointed a Committee on Credentials, because they knew they could better judge of facts which would be presented by a small number of men to such committee than a mass convention could judge of the same facts. Under the lead of its excellent chairman, the gentleman from New-York, that committee had a prolonged session of many hours, and had brought before it gentlemen representing both sides of the contest in the State of Missouri, and with great deliberation they weighed the arguments of both contesting parties. The result from the deliberations of that committee, based upon the statements of the contesting parties, the convention has, in the report of the majority, and I beg leave to say to this convention, with all respect for the honorable chairman, and without violation of any of the proprieties of that committee rule, that the very same proposition presented here before the convention this morning, was presented before that committee and voted down. Why so? Is it proper then to present the same question to this convention? The question having been decided in the committee ought not to be brought up here.

The Committee voted down the very proposition which the honorable Chairman now proposes to the Convention.

Mr. BRECKINRIDGE, of Missouri, was announced as having the floor.

Mr. LANE, of Kansas—Who is Mr. BRECKINRIDGE, of Missouri?

VOICES—He is not a delegate.

[Mr. BRECKINRIDGE was one of the excluded delegates.]

Mr. CURTIS, of New-York—I submit that this convention is at present composed only of those delegates who are here without any contest.

The Chair said that the gentleman from New-York was correct.

Mr. CURTIS said the Missouri question was no new question either to this convention or to the country. It is a question which is almost coeval with that of the most profound reverence for our eminent friend from Kentucky (BRECKINRIDGE,) which is well known and understood all over the country. The Missouri question is one which must be met and settled, and nowhere can it be so well met and conclusively settled as in this National Convention of Union men. [Applause.] We yesterday appointed a committee, as the gentleman from Ohio has so well stated, for the purpose of making these inquiries of details which it was impossible for this convention to make. We have the report of that committee, which is unanimous, with the exception of my honored friend from New-York, that the Radical delegation from Missouri shall be admitted, with the privilege of voting and with every other privilege. The question has been settled and reported on by that committee, why should we admit the Radical delegation? I take my words from the mouth of my most honored friend from New-York, who here introduced this question. It is because we wish to strengthen the Union sentiment of the country. [Applause.] It is because we wish to strengthen the brave men who have bared their breasts in battle and who have stood firm since the outbreak of this war. It is for that reason that I implore you to give no uncertain sound. My most eminent friend says we have also been true. I freely confess we have not had the bitter sufferings they have had in the Border States, but that we may be strengthened at home and that the army all along the line with SHERMAN and GRANT may hear of no uncertain sound from us at the rear. As a practical contest there is no man in this convention who does not know that the admission of the Radical delegates from Missouri is the practical settlement of this question, and the practical adhesion of the great national party of this country to the policy and measures which will save the country.

Mr. MACE, of Indiana, moved that the proposed amendment be laid upon the table.

Mr. SMITHERS, of Delaware—I call for the previous question.

Mr. STEVENS, of Pennsylvania—Do I understand the previous question to be called upon the whole proposition, or only upon this amendment.

VOICES—Only on the amendment.

Mr. STEVENS—Then Pennsylvania seconds the amendment.

VOICES—Read the amendment.

CHAIRMAN—The amendment is that where two sets of delegates from Missouri cannot agree, that instead of not voting at all they shall divide the vote.

The question on the amendment to the report was lost.

CHAIRMAN—The question now is on adopting the report of the majority on the Missouri question.

After further debate Mr. BRANSAGE moved the previous question on the Missouri case.

YEAS—Maine, 14; New-Hampshire, 10; Vermont, 10; Massachusetts, 24; Rhode Island, 8; Connecticut, 12; New-York, 88; New-Jersey, 14; Pennsylvania, 49; Delaware, 6; Maryland, 14; Kentucky, 21; Ohio, 42; Indiana, 26; Illinois, 32; Michigan, 16; Wisconsin, 16; Minnesota, 8; California, 10; Oregon, 6; Western Virginia, 10; Kansas, 6.

NAYS—Pennsylvania, 3; Kentucky, 1.

Total—Yeas, 440; Nays, 4.

Then said the President, the Radical delegation of Missouri are admitted as full delegates to the Convention. The question is now upon the second clause of the amendment.

Mr. KING—The second clause is that the delegates from Virginia, Tennessee, Louisiana, Florida, Arkansas, and from all the Territories and the District of Columbia, who shall be admitted to this Convention shall be allowed all the privileges of delegates, including that of voting. But that the Territories and the District of Columbia shall be allowed two votes, and no State, or Territory, shall be allowed to cast more votes than it has delegates here, or more than it is entitled to under the rules of the Convention.

Mr. STEVENS, of Pennsylvania, moved the previous question, and the main question was ordered to be taken.

Mr. KING—The remainder of the report, which has not been adopted, is as follows: That the delegations from Virginia, Tennessee, Louisiana, Florida and Arkansas be admitted with all the rights and privileges of delegates to this committee, except that of voting; that the delegation asking admission from South Carolina be not admitted to the convention; that the delegations from the organized Territories and the District of Columbia be admitted to the convention, with all the rights and privileges of delegates, except that of voting.

Mr. LANE, of Kansas, asked for a division of the question, so as to take the vote separately upon Tennessee, Arkansas, Louisiana, Nebraska, Colorado and Nevada.

Subsequently he modified his demand for a division, so that the question should first be taken on the three States—Tennessee, Louisiana and Arkansas.

Mr. ELDEN, of Indiana, demanded a further division, so as to take the vote on Tennessee separately.

The question was stated to be upon admitting the delegation from Tennessee.

A call for a vote by States was made and the House voted, Yeas 310, Nays 153, as follows:

YEAS—Maine 3, Vermont 2, Rhode Island 2, Connecticut 10, New-York 66, New-Jersey 14, Pennsylvania 31, Delaware 1, Maryland 1, Missouri 19, Kentucky 4, Ohio 42, Indiana 24, Illinois 32, Michigan 2, Wisconsin 15, Iowa 9, Minnesota 1, California 10, Oregon 6, West Virginia 10, Kansas 6.

NAYS—Maine 11, New-Hampshire 10, Vermont 8, Massachusetts 24, Rhode Island 6, Connecticut 2, Pennsylvania 21, Delaware 4, Maryland 13, Missouri 3, Indiana 2, Michigan 14, Wisconsin 1, Iowa 7, Minnesota 7.

Mr. LANE, of Kansas, now moved that Kansas and Louisiana be admitted by acclamation.

Mr. STEVENS, of Pennsylvania, objected.

The question was stated to be upon admitting the delegation from Arkansas and Louisiana, with the right of voting.

Mr. STEVENS demanded that the vote be taken by States, and the demand was seconded. The vote resulted—ayes, 307; nays, 167.

The question was then taken upon that portion of the report as amended, and it was agreed to.

The question was stated upon admitting the delegations of the Territories of Colorado, Nebraska and Nevada, with the right of voting.

That portion of the report was then agreed to as amended.

Mr. SCAMMON, of Illinois—What is to be done with Virginia, South Carolina and Florida?

PRESTON KING—The only portion of the report which remains is that which relates to admitting the delegates from Virginia and Florida, without the right of voting; the rejection of the delegation from South Carolina, and admitting the delegates of the territories other than those already passed upon, and of the District of Columbia without the right to vote.

The remaining portion of the report was agreed to, amid great applause.

THE PLATFORM.

Mr. RAYMOND, of New-York, from the Committee on Resolutions, reported the following resolutions:

*Resolved*, That it is the highest duty of every American citizen to maintain against all their enemies the integrity of the Union, and the paramount authority of the Constitution and laws of the United States, and that laying aside all differences and political opinions, we pledge ourselves as Union men, animated by a common sentiment and aiming at a common object, to do everything in our power to aid the Government in quelling by force of arms the rebellion now raging against its authority, and in bringing to the punishment due to their crimes the rebels and traitors arrayed against it. [Prolonged applause.]

*Resolved*, That we approve the determination of the Government of the United States not to compromise with rebels or to offer any terms of peace except such as may be based upon an "unconditional surrender" of their hostility and a return to their just allegiance to the Constitution and laws of the United States: and that we call upon the Government to maintain this position and to prosecute the war with the utmost possible vigor to the complete suppression of the rebellion, in full reliance upon the self-sacrifices, the patriotism, the heroic valor and the undying devotion of the American people to their country and its free institutions. [Applause.]

*Resolved*, That as Slavery was the cause, and now constitutes the strength of this rebellion, and as it must be always and everywhere hostile to the principles of Republican Government, justice and the national safety demand its utter and complete extirpation from the soil of the Republic; [applause,] and that we uphold and maintain the acts and proclamations by which the Government, in its own defence, has aimed a death-blow at this gigantic evil. We are in favor, furthermore, of such an amendment to the Constitution, to be made by the people in conformity with its provisions, as shall terminate and forever prohibit the existence of Slavery within the limits or the jurisdiction of the United States. [Applause.]

*Resolved*, That the thanks of the American people are due to the soldiers and sailors of the army and the navy, [applause,] who have periled their lives in defence of their country and in vindication of the honor of the flag; that the nation owes to them some permanent recognition of their patriotism and their valor, and ample and permanent provision for those of their survivors who have received disabling and honorable wounds in the service of the country; and that the memories of those who have fallen in its defence shall be held in grateful and everlasting remembrance. [Loud applause.]

*Resolved*, That we approve and applaud the practical wisdom, the unselfish patriotism and unswerving fidelity to the Constitution and the principles of American liberty with which ABRAHAM LINCOLN has discharged, under circumstances of unparalleled difficulty, the great duties and responsibilities of the Presidential office; that we approve and indorse, as demanded by the emergency and essential to the preservation of the nation, and as within the Constitution, the measures and acts which he has adopted to defend the nation against its open and secret foes; that we approve especially the proclamation of emancipation and the employment as Union soldiers of men heretofore held in slavery [applause]; and that we have full confidence in his determination to carry these and all other constitutional measures essential to the salvation of the country into full and complete effect.

*Resolved*, That we deem it essential to the general welfare that harmony should prevail in the national councils, and we regard as worthy of public confidence and official trust those only who cordially indorse the principles proclaimed in these resolutions, and which should characterize the administration of the Government. [Applause.]

*Resolved*, That the Government owes to all men employed in its armies, without regard to distinction of color, the full protection of the laws of war, [applause] and that any violations of these laws, or of the usages of civilized nations in the time of war, by the rebels now in arms, should be made the subject of full and prompt redress. [Prolonged applause.]

*Resolved*, That the foreign immigration which in the past has added so much to the wealth and development of resources and increase of power to this nation—the asylum of the oppressed of all nations—should be fostered and encouraged by a liberal and just policy.

*Resolved*, That we are in favor of the speedy construction of the railroad to the Pacific.

*Resolved*, That the national faith pledged for the redemption of the public debt must be kept inviolate, and that for this purpose we recommend economy and rigid responsibility in the public expenditures, and a vigorous and just system of taxation; that it is the duty of every loyal State to sustain the credit and promote the use of the national currency. [Applause.]

*Resolved*, That we approve the position taken by the Government that the people of the United States can never regard with indifference the attempt of any European Power to overthrow by force or to supplant by fraud, the institutions of any Republican Government on the Western Continent; [prolonged applause;] and that they will view with extreme jealousy, as menacing to the peace and independence of this our country, the efforts of any such Power to obtain new footholds for Monarchical Governments, sustained by a foreign military force in near proximity to the United States. [Long-continued applause.]

The reading of the resolution elicited the wildest outbursts of enthusiasm, especially the emancipation and Anti-Slavery sentiments enunciated.

The mention of the name of ABRAHAM LINCOLN was received with tremendous cheering, the whole house rising and waving hats and handkerchiefs.

The resolution indorsing the Monroe doctrine was also received with great applause.

On motion of Mr. BUSHNELL, of Connecticut, the resolutions were adopted by acclamation.

THE NOMINATIONS.

Mr. DELANO, of Ohio—I move that this convention now proceed to the nomination of candidates for President and Vice President of the United States.

The Chairman stated the motion.

Mr. CAMERON—I move the following as a substitute for the motion of the gentleman from Ohio.

The Chairman directed the Secretary to read the resolution.

*Resolved*, That ABRAHAM LINCOLN, of Illinois, be declared the choice of the Union party for President, [applause,] and HANNIBAL HAMLIN, of Maine, be the candidate for Vice President of the same party.

Cries of "No, no."

A VOICE—Divide the resolution.

Mr. CRESWELL, of Maryland—I call for a division.

Mr. STONE, of Iowa—I ask if I can make an amendment to that resolution.

The Chairman said the resolution of Mr. CAMERON was now the question before the convention.

Mr. STONE—I move to lay it on the table. Carried.

Mr STONE—I now move that ABRAHAM LINCOLN, of Illinois, be the unanimous nominee of the convention.

Cries of "Question" and great confusion.

THE CHAIRMAN—Will the gentleman listen for one moment. The gentleman from Iowa moved that a resolution offered by the gentleman from Pennsylvania (CAMERON) be laid on the table. That has been carried. The Chair then recognized Mr. COOK, of Illinois, as having the floor.

Mr. STEVENS, of Pennsylvania—I called for the vote by States before the vote was declared to the House.

Mr. STONE, of Iowa, claimed the floor.

Mr. STEVENS—I have not yielded the floor.

THE CHAIRMAN—Does the gentleman from Pennsylvania insist upon a call of the States, upon the motion to lay on the table the resolution of Mr. CAMERON?

MANY VOICES—State the question.

THE CHAIR—The gentleman from Iowa moved to lay upon the table the substitute offered by Gen. CAMERON, of Pennsylvania, and Mr. STEVENS informs the Chair that before that motion was put to the convention he moved a call of the States under the rules. Before the announcement of a vote, a delegate has a right to move a call by States, that being so the convention will now come to the question of laying on the table the substitute offered by Mr. CAMERON. Upon that the States were ordered to be called.

Mr. CRESSWELL, of Maryland—I call for a division of the question.

Mr. GOLDSBOROUGH, of Maryland, also called for a division.

THE CHAIRMAN—The question is shall the resolution offered by Gen. CAMERON as a substitute be laid upon the table. The Secretary will proceed with the call.

Mr. BRECKINRIDGE—I wish to make a motion concerning the whole of this subject, and I hope the house will hear me for one moment. I want to modify it so as to lay the resolution on the table for the purpose of declaring ABRAHAM LINCOLN the nominee by acclamation.

Mr. STEVENSON, of Indiana—I desire to know what has become of the vote to lay the substitute of Mr. CAMERON on the table.

THE CHAIRMAN—That is now before the convention. The Secretary will call the roll of the States for the purpose of knowing whether it will be laid upon the table.

Mr. LANE, of Kansas—I appeal to the gentleman from Pennsylvania, with the consent of the convention, to withdraw his resolution. It places us in a very awkward predicament. I hope Gen. CAMERON, consulting the best wishes of the country, will withdraw his resolution. Let us vote upon the motion put by the gentleman from Iowa.

Mr. STONE, of Iowa—Hurrah for LINCOLN.

Mr. CAMERON—To save all this trouble to gentlemen who seem to wish to show their hands here I will withdraw it. [Applause.]

THE CHAIRMAN—Mr. COOK, of Illinois, has the floor.

Mr. CAMERON, of Pennsylvania—I will withdraw it, or amend by moving that this convention nominate by acclamation ABRAHAM LINCOLN for a second term.

Mr. STONE, of Iowa—The gentleman is cheating me out of my motion; I object.

Laughter—Cries of "order," "order," "question," "question."

Mr. LANE, of Kansas—Hurrah for STONE.

THE CHAIRMAN—Mr. CAMERON's motion to amend is not in order. It must be an absolute withdrawal, or none at all. Does he withdraw his resolution.

Mr. CAMERON—I will modify my resolution to make it "nominate ABRAHAM LINCOLN by acclamation."

Mr. STONE, of Iowa—That won't do. You must withdraw.

THE CHAIRMAN—The gentleman from Pennsylvania has not answered the question of the Chair. Has the resolution been withdrawn or not?

Mr. CAMERON—I want to modify.

THE CHAIRMAN—That is not a definite answer, and cannot be recognized as such by the Chair. The question before the convention is upon the resolution offered by Mr. CAMERON. A call of the States is demanded.

Mr. RAYMOND, of New-York—I understand that the question before the convention is the substitute offered by Gen. CAMERON for one which he offered and afterward withdrew, and that the motion now is that ABRAHAM LINCOLN be nominated for the Presidency. I desire to say one word upon the manner in which it is proposed to be done. I believe that there is no man in this convention who will not, however the vote may be taken, give his vote in just one way. It can therefore, be from no apprehension of the result of the vote that this particular way of taking it should be proposed, therefore, we may as well look to other considerations in deciding how we will take it. It is very well known that attempts have been made, though with no very great success, to create the impression that the nomination of ABRAHAM LINCOLN has to be pushed through this convention by some demonstration that will not look to the exercise of individual influence. Is it wise under these circumstances to take a vote by acclamation? It cannot possibly change the result. It can add no weight whatever to its earnestness, and it may give rise to false impressions. I suggest, and will move as a substitute a resolution embodying my view. I suggest that the wisest course would be to allow the roll of the States represented in this convention to be called, and let every delegation declare its vote. I believe there will be a unanimous vote from every delegation precisely to the same effect. I think the effect of that vote will be greater than one taken by acclamation. It can be reinforced, as it will be reinforced, by this convention, and throughout the country by the loud acclamations of the American people; and now I move, as a substitute for the motion of the gentleman from Pennsylvania, that the roll of the States be called, and that each delegation be called upon to record its vote. [Applause.]

Mr. CAMERON—I accept the modification.

Mr. COOK, of Illinois—Mr. President, the State of Illinois again presents to the loyal people of this nation, for President of the United States, ABRAHAM LINCOLN—God bless him!

Mr. CAMERON—I desire to accept the modification of the gentleman of New-York.

Cries of "Roll, roll." "Question," &c.

THE CHAIR—The gentleman from Ohio moved that this convention proceed to the nomination of candidates for President and Vice-President. Upon that a resolution was offered by Gen. CAMERON that has been discussed. Upon that the gentleman from New-York (RAYMOND) moves we proceed to the nomination of a candidate for President alone. I ask the gentleman from Ohio whether he accepts that as a substitute for his motion.

Mr. DELANO—It was in full comprehension of the necessity of having an individual expression of opinion in favor of ABRAHAM LINCOLN that I made my motion, and that there should be no misapprehension, and no claim that he had been nominated by clamor, that public sentiment had been suppressed, that I desired the nomination as indicated by my resolution. For no man desires his nomination more than I. I accept the resolution offered by the gentleman from New-York as a substitute for my own.

The Chair stated that the question was to proceed to a nomination for President by a call of the States.

After further debate, and great confusion, the question was put on Mr. RAYMOND's substitute, which was adopted.

The convention then proceeded to ballot for President, which resulted as follows:

*For Mr. Lincoln*—Maine, 14; New-Hampshire, 10; Vermont, 10; Massachusetts, 24; Rhode Island, 8; Connecticut, 12; New-York, 66; New-Jersey, 14; Pennsylvania, 52; Delaware, 6; Maryland, 14; Louisiana, 14; Arkansas, 10; Tennessee, 15; Kentucky, 22; Ohio, 42; Indiana 26; Illinois, 32; Michigan, 16; Wisconsin, 16; Iowa, 16; Minnesota, 8; California, 10; Oregon, 6; West Virginia, 10; Kansas, 6; Nebraska, 6; Colorado, 6; Nevada, 6. Total, 497.

*For Gen. Grant*—Missouri, 22.

On motion of Mr. HUME, of Missouri, the vote was declared unanimous.

The enthusiasm was perfectly indescribable, the whole convention being on their feet, shouting, and the band playing "Hail Columbia."

After the nomination the Chairman read a dispatch from the Secretary of War, giving the good news from Gen. HUNTER, which was received with great cheering.

The convention resolved to proceed to vote for a candidate for Vice-President.

The following names were presented:

DANIEL MACE, of Indiana, presented the name of ANDREW JOHNSON, of Tennessee.

Mr. STONE, of Iowa, seconded the motion.

Mr. CAMERON, of Pennsylvania, offered the name of HANNIBAL HAMLIN.

Mr. TREMAINE, of New-York, in behalf of a portion of the delegation, presented DANIEL S. DICKINSON.

Mr. MAYNARD, of Tennessee, advocated the claims of ANDREW JOHNSON.

Mr. TREMAINE, of New-York, made an eloquent appeal in favor of the nomination of DANIEL S. DICKINSON. His remarks were received with great enthusiasm.

Great impatience was manifested to vote.

The President announced the following names as being before the convention:

ANDREW JOHNSON, of Tennessee.
HANNIBAL HAMLIN, of Maine.
L. H. ROUSSEAU, of Kentucky.
DANIEL S. DICKINSON, of New-York.

The House then proceeded to ballot.

Maine, New-Hampshire, Vermont, Connecticut, New-York, New-Hampshire, New-Jersey, Pennsylvania, Delaware, Maryland, Louisiana, Arkansas, Missouri, Kentucky, Ohio, Indiana, Illinois, Michigan, Iowa, California, Oregon, West Virginia, Kansas, Nebraska, Colorado and Nevada voted entire for Johnson. Massachusetts voted Johnson 21; Dickinson 3. Rhode Island, Johnson, 7; Dickinson, 1. Wisconsin, Johnson, 2; Dickinson, 10; Hamlin, 4. Minnesota, Dickinson, 3; Hamlin, 5. The total vote was Johnson, 492; Dickinson, 17; Hamlin, 9. Previous to the vote being announced, Johnson had 200; Dickinson, 113; Hamlin, 145; Butler, 28; Rosseau, 21; Burnside, 2; Colfax, 6; Col. Colt, 2; Tod, 2, and King, 1; but the States changed their votes before the announcement was made.

The Chair announced the next business in order was the election of a National Committee, and the States were called to name the same, as follows:

NATIONAL COMMITTEE.

Maine, Samuel F. Hersey; New-Hampshire, John B. Clark; Vermont, Abraham B. Gardner; Massachusetts, William Claflin; Rhode Island, Thomas G. Turner; Connecticut, N. J. Sperry, New-York, H. J. Raymond; New-Jersey, Marcus L. Ward; Pennsylvania, not appointed yet; Delaware, N. B. Smithers; Maryland, H. W. Huffman; Virginia, W. H. Wallace; Florida, Calvin S. Robinson; Louisiana, Cuthbert Bullit; Arkansas, Jas. S. Johnston; Missouri, S. H. Boyd; Tennessee, Jos. S. Fowler; Kentucky, R. K. Williams; Ohio, G. V. Senter; Indiana, J. D. Defrees; Illinois, Burt C. Cook; Michigan, R. Giddings; Wisconsin, S. Judd; Iowa, D. B. Stubbs; Minnesota, Thomas Simpson; California, not named yet; Oregon, Erasmus D. Shattuck; West Virginia, A. W. Campbell; Kansas, James H. Lane; Colorado, James P. Taylor; Nebraska, W. H. H. Waters; Nevada, H. D. Morgan; Dacotah, S. M. Binney; New-Mexico, John W. Kerr; Montana, N. P. Lankford; Washington, Arthur A. Denin; Idaho, W. H. Wallace; Arizona, James S. Turner; District of Columbia, James T. Combs.

Mr. KING, of New-York, offered a resolution returning thanks to the President and officers of the convention for the able and satisfactory manner in which they had performed the duties assigned them.

The resolution was adopted.

A resolution was also adopted returning thanks to the Mayor and City Council of Baltimore for the excellent arrangements they had made for the accommodation of the convention.

On a motion for a final adjournment being made, the President in a few eloquent remarks congratulated the convention on the happy conclusion of their labors, and returned his thanks for the complimentary resolution that had been passed.

The convention then adjourned *sine die*.

### The Union National Committee.

BALTIMORE, Wednesday, June 8.

The Union National Committee appointed by the convention met at BARNUM's hotel, this evening.

On motion of Gen. LANE, of Kansas, Henry J. RAYMOND, of New-York, was elected Chairman, and E. MCPHERSON, of Pennsylvania, Secretary.

The committee adjourned to meet in Washington on Friday.

### Mass Meeting in Baltimore.

BALTIMORE, Wednesday, June 8—Evening.

A great mass meeting to ratify the nominations is now being held in Monument-square. The Mayor of the city is presiding, and Messrs. MAYNARD and BROWNLOW, of Tennessee; GADDIS, of Ohio; Ex-Mayor SWAN, and others, are the speakers. Resolutions were adopted cordially indorsing and ratifying the nomination of President, and commencing the same to the loyal voters throughout the country.

## THE DRAFT.

### Report of Provost-Marshal-General Fry—Recommendation that the $300 Clause be Repealed.

WASHINGTON, Wednesday, June 8.

The following was laid by the Speaker before the House to-day, and was referred to the Committee on Military Affairs:

*To the Senate and House of Representatives:*

I have the honor to submit, for the consideration of Congress, a letter and inclosure from the Secretary of War, with my concurrence in the recommendation therein made.

(Signed) ABRAHAM LINCOLN.

WASHINGTON, D. C., June 8, 1864.

WAR DEPARTMENT, WASHINGTON CITY, June 7, 1864.

*To the President:*

SIR: I beg leave to submit to you a report made to me by the Provost-Marshal-General, showing the result of the draft now going on to fill the deficiency in the quotas of certain States, and recommending a repeal of the clause in the Enrollment Act, commonly known as "the three hundred dollar clause." The recommendation of the Provost-Marshal-General is approved by this Department; and I trust that it will be recommended by you to Congress.

The recent successes that have attended our arms leads to the hope that by maintaining our military strength and giving it such increase as the extended field of operations may require, an early termination of the war may be attained. But to accomplish this it is absolutely necessary that efficient means be taken with vigor and promptness to keep the army up to its strength and supply deficiencies occasioned by the losses in the field.

To that end resort must be had to a draft. But ample experience has now shown that the pecuniary exemption from service frustrates the object of the Enrollment Law by furnishing money instead of men.

An additional reason for repealing the exemption clause is, that it is contemplated to make the draft for comparatively a short term. The burden of military service will therefore be lightened. But its certainty of furnishing troops is an absolute essential to success.

I have the honor to be your obedient servant,

(Signed) EDWIN M. STANTON, Secretary of War.

WAR DEPARTMENT, PROVOST-MARSHAL-GENERAL'S OFFICE, WASHINGTON, D. C., June 6, 1864.

*To Hon. Edwin M. Stanton, Secretary of War:*

SIR: In accordance with the amended Enrollment Act, approved Feb. 24, 1864, and your orders on the subject, I am now conducting a draft in various subdistricts for their respective deficiencies on quotas of troops heretofore assigned. The results of this draft, so far as showing the reports to this date, are worthy of attention. They are briefly as follows:

| | |
|---|---|
| Number of drafted men examined | 14,741 |
| Number exempted for physical disability | 4,374 |
| Number exempted for other causes | 2,632 |
| Total number exempted | 7,016 |
| Number paid commutation money | 5,050 |
| Number who have furnished substitutes | 1,416 |
| Number held for personal service | 1,259 |

The last includes some who may yet pay commutation money.

| | |
|---|---|
| Total not exempted | 7,725 |

These reports come from sub-districts in eight different States.

I invite your attention to the small proportion of soldiers being obtained under the existing law. I see no reason to believe that the army can be materially strengthened by draft so long as the $300 clause is in force; nor do I think it safe to assume that the commutation paid by a drafted man will enable the Government to procure a volunteer or substitute in his place.

I do not think that large bounties, by the United States, should be again resorted to for raising troops. I recommend that the $300 clause, as it is known, be repealed.

I am, Sir, very respectfully your obedient servant,

(Signed) JAMES B. FRY, Provost-Marshal-General.

### Turf Record.

THE PATERSON, N. J. RACING MEETING—SECOND DAY—WEDNESDAY.

The brilliant success which attended the opening of the Spring meeting of the Passaic County Agricultural Society on Tuesday found no abatement yesterday. All the leading patrons, both of the running and trotting turf, were again present in full force, whilst those who have no direct interest in racing, but love it simply for the gratification that the keen contests of that noblest of animals—the horse—affords them, were nearly as largely represented as on the previous, the Derby Day. The 8 and 10 o'clock A. M. trains brought down ample living freights of sporting humanity, and the 11:45 special was literally jammed throughout its lengthy proportions; whilst the delightful ride over the fine turnpike road from Hoboken tempted numbers to adopt that method of reaching the course, and there was a splendid display of fast teams, buggies, barouches, tandems, four in hands, &c., mixed up with the humbler vehicles ordinarily met with on the Jersey roads.

The ladies, who in other lands are enthusiastic patrons of the sports of the turf, were, as on the previous day, present in large numbers.

Too much praise cannot be awarded to the Executive Committee of the Passaic Club—its energetic Chairman, Mr. COLT, and indefatigable Secretary, Mr. CHRISWELL—for the truly admirable manner in which all the arrangements of the meeting have thus far been carried out; the strictest punctuality in the time of starting has been observed—the strictest decorum preserved, and absolute exclusion of all improper or obnoxious characters stringently adhered to—detectives traveling with each train, and immediately sending back to New-York any persons whose presence would not be desirable or agreeable to the respectable classes of society. The course is kept absolutely free from intrusion during the running of the different races—no gambling has been permitted either on the track or its vicinity.

COPY.

PASSAIC COUNTY AGRICULTURAL SOCIETY, Wednesday, June 8, 1864.

MEETING OF EXECUTIVE COMMITTEE.

It appearing there has been collusion and fraud in relation to the running of the colt *Norfolk*, in the Jersey Derby, perpetrated by JAMES L. EOFF, with the knowledge, or by the collusion of CHARLES MARSH. It is unanimously resolved that the said JAMES L. EOFF, *be ruled off this track forever*; that CHARLES MARSH be censured for his complicity in the affair, and that the colt *Norfolk* be not allowed to start again on this track until the further order of this committee.

E. BOUDINOT COLT, Chairman Executive Committee.

R. B. CHISWELL, Secretary.

WEDNESDAY'S RACING.

The sports of the turf commenced to-day with the *Underwood*, a one-mile dash, for all ages, named in honor of Dr. UNDERWOOD, a gentleman whose name and fame are patent on every race course, North and South.

SUMMARY.

WEDNESDAY, June 8.

PREMIUM—The Underwood gift of $200, for all ages, one mile dash.

Mr. W. H. RENFRO, enters b f sister to *Tipperary*, 4 years old ... 1

Mr. JOHN HUNTER, enters b c *Copeck* by *Lexington*, dam *Rosette* by imp. *Yorkshire*, 4 years old ... 2

The betting was all in favor of the filly, viz.: 100 to 80 on her. She had the inside place and was admirably ridden by "Honest old Abe," GILPATRICK tooling *Copeck*. In a good start the filly had a slight advantage, and took a decided lead as she rounded the turn, increasing it past the quarter to the half-mile, where *Copeck* vainly struggled to get up to her. The filly continued her lead round the turn, and up the home stretch was never approached in the run in, and won as she pleased, by two or three lengths.

Time—Quarter, 0:26½; half-mile, 0:51½; mile, 1:47¼.

SECOND RACE—SUMMARY.

SAME DAY.—The Nursery Stakes, a sweepstake premium of $200, for two-year olds; $100 entrance, $50 forfeit; three-quarter mile dash; to carry 90 pounds; four or more nominations to fill. Entries to be made on or before January 1, 1864. Free to all colts or fillies foaled in 1862. Closed with the following entries:

1. Mr. John Hunter enters ch. c. Waxlight by Colossus dam Waxwing by Wagner ... dr.
2. Mr. John Hunter enters b. f. Alexandria by imp. Sovereign, dam Miss Duke by imp. Glencoe dr.
3. Mr. John Hunter enters blk. f. La Noir by imp. Knight of St. George, dam Blonde by imp. Glencoe ... 1
4. Mr. John Hunter enters ch. c. by imp. Knight of St. George, dam sister to Tangent by Wagner dr.
5. Mr. James S. Watson enters b. c. by Lexington, dam Miss Julia by imp. Glencoe ... dr.
6. Mr. James S. Watson enters br. f. by Slasher, dam Pasta, by Revenue ... 2

This race was reduced to a match between the pick of the two stables, Mr. HUNTER selecting his black filly, *La Noir*, and Mr. WATSON his *Revenue* filly—that excellent colored rider, ABE, having justly the mount on the black; and, as will be seen, again defeating his white rival, Jockey GILPATRICK, on Mr. WATSON's nomination, which was thought to be so good a thing that in the betting, $100 to $50, and ultimately 100 to 40 was freely laid on her. The story of the race is soon told. In a good start *La Noir* was first on her legs, and soon took a lead of a length, which she increased to two on reaching the quarter; from this point she opened the gap wider and wider to the turn into the home stretch, which she came up pulling hard, and passing the score the easiest of winners by four lengths. Time, 1.23. The first quarter was ran in 0.52½, which is the fastest quarter ever done on this track.

THIRD RACE.

SAME DAY.—Premium of $400 for all ages; three-mile dash.

Mr. James S. Watson enters b. c. Capt. Moore, by imp. Bairownie, dam Jenny Rose, by imp. Glencoe ... Walked over.

FOURTH RACE.

SAME DAY.—Selling race of $300, for all ages, one and a quarter mile dash. Horses entered to be sold for $1,500, (no entries for a higher price,) to carry their proper weights; those entered to be sold for $1,000, allowed 7 pounds; if for $600, 14 pounds; if for $300, 21 pounds. The winner to be sold at auction immediately after the race. All over the price named in the entry to go to the society. The owner to retain his horse if he should not bring the price named in the entry. No penalties for other races won.

1. Mr. T. O. Smith enters b. h. Bill Davis, dam Rally, by Trustee, 5 years old. Price $600 ... 0
2. Messrs. Bowie & Hall enter ch. h. by Red Eye, dam Scione, 5 years old. Price $1,000 ... 0
3. Mr. W. H. Strong enters ch. h. Punch, by Mahomet, dam by Yorkshire, 5 years old. Price $600 ... 3
4. Mr. James S. Watson enters br. f. Miss Hays, by Lexington, dam Kate Hays, by imp. Albion, 4 years old. Price $600 ... 2
5. Mr. H. Hogans enters Zig-Zag, by Rurie, dam by Zenith, 4 years old. Price $1,300 ... 0
6. Mr. John Hunters b. c. Copeck, by Lexington, dam Rosette, by imp. Yorkshire, 4 years old. Price $1,000 ... 1

Time—2:18¾. The first quarter was done in 00:27¼, and the last mile in 1:51¼.

To-day, the last of the meeting, three races are on the cards, which are likely to be prolific of first-class running. In the post stake the renowned *Thunder* meets *Captain Moore* and *Fleetwing*.

### From Fortress Monroe.

FORTRESS MONROE, Tuesday, May 7.

Lieut. PAYSON, Aid-de-Camp to Gen. DEVENS, arrived at Chesapeake Hospital last evening, wounded.

The steamer *Metamora* arrived at 1 P. M. from the White House with a few "sick" officers. They had not been in the front for several days, and brought no news whatever.

4 P. M.—The steamer *John A. Warner* Capt. CONE has arrived from Bermuda Hundreds. She reports no fighting was reported there.

No news had been received from Gen. GRANT. No cannonading had been heard.

DEATHS IN THE CHESAPEAKE HOSPITAL JUNE 5, 1864.

| | |
|---|---|
| David Noakes, 13th Ind. | Wm A Goddard, 9th Maine. |
| James Goodrich, 14th N Y. | Henry M Park, 40th Mass. |

DEATHS IN THE HAMPTON HOSPITAL, JUNE 5.

| | |
|---|---|
| Corp Dan C Storrs, 11th Ct. | John Sellers, 96th Penn. |
| Thos D Cook, 11th Me. | Martin Russell, 115th N Y |
| John Smith, 97th Penn. | Wm H Jones, 7th South Carolina—rebel. |
| Chas H Smith, 4th N H. | Albert Rozier, 11th South Carolina—rebel. |
| Clark Eastman, 3d N H. | |
| Wm Hull, 67th Ohio. | |

JUNE 6.

| | |
|---|---|
| Albert E Littlefield, 24th Massachusetts | James A Mager, 115th N Y. |
| Sergt James H Harman, 9th Maine. | Chas McNab, 117th N Y. |
| Daniel Beaman, 11th Me. | Isaac McHarner, 55th, Pa. |
| | Corp Lewis Hengle, 18th Pennsylvania. |

### Shot by a Soldier.

ALBANY, Wednesday, June 8.

A young man named JAMES MURRAY, of Brooklyn, was shot by a soldier at the depot in East Albany this evening, while getting off the cars.

# The New-York Times.

VOL. XIII.---NO. 4037. NEW-YORK, THURSDAY, SEPTEMBER 1, 1864. PRICE FOUR CENTS.


## THE SITUATION.

### The Surrender of Fort Morgan.

### DETAILS OF THE CAPITULATION

### Five Hundred and Eighty-one Prisoners Captured.

### THE GUNS SPIKED BY THE REBELS.

### WAR THUNDER FOR COPPERHEADS

[OFFICIAL.]

WASHINGTON, Wednesday, Aug. 31.

*To Maj.-Gen. Dix, New-York:*

This Department has received from Gen. GRANT a rebel account of the surrender of Fort Morgan, taken from the Richmond papers:

CITY POINT, Aug. 30.

The following is from the Richmond *Inquirer* of this morning:

MOBILE, Aug. 26, 1864.

The flag of truce boat returned last evening. The Yankees say Fort Morgan capitulated at 2 o'clock last Tuesday. On Monday afternoon they concentrated their fire on the fort, when the bombardment was renewed spiritedly.

In the meanwhile the enemy succeeded in getting their howitzers into position and the line of skirmishers along the glacis of the fort, and opened a heavy fire on our guns and gunners, and with the assistance of the mortar fleet succeeded in damaging several gun carriages. The fort did not fire Tuesday. Gen. PAIGE destroyed everything in the fort, and spiked his guns. He and the garrison, numbering 581 men, were sent to New-Orleans. Seventeen were killed; the number of wounded is unknown. None of the non-combatants were allowed to visit the city. The enemy have a strong force of 4,000 on the mainland at Grant's Pass.

SECOND DISPATCH.

MOBILE, Sunday, Aug. 28.

There is no change of affairs at this point. All is quiet.

U. S. GRANT, Lieutenant-General.

Unofficial reports represent FORREST, WHEELER and MORGAN as having joined their forces and operating against Gen. SHERMAN's communications between Chattanooga and Nashville, but no report has been received from Gen. SHERMAN.

Gen. SHERIDAN is still, with his force, at Charlestown.

No operations have taken place, since my last telegram, in front of Petersburgh.

EDWIN M. STANTON, Secretary of War.

### Our Losses in the Recent Battles—How the Rebels are Said to be Getting Around the Break in the Weldon Road.

HEADQUARTERS ARMY OF THE POTOMAC, Monday, Aug. 29—Evening.

The reports in some of the newspapers that the losses in the Fifth Corps, in the battles of the 18th, 19th and 21st inst. reach 5,000, greatly exaggerate the facts. It is now definitely known that they do not exceed 3,500; and as stragglers and others continue to come in, and the sick are all accounted for, it is believed that the aggregate loss will not exceed 3,500.

The loss of the Second Corps in Thursday's fight will not exceed 1,500, according to the official statement, and it is hoped and believed that when all within our lines report, the entire loss will fail to 1,200.

The rebels are said to be using the Weldon Railroad below Ream's Station, and running their supplies thence to Petersburgh around our left by wagon. As this requires a large force to guard the trains and defend the road against our cavalry, it cannot be either a very profitable or pleasant means of communication, without taking into consideration the loss of time involved.

Arrangements have been made for burying the rebel dead left on the field of last Thursday's battle. The fact that the enemy did not do this, and also that they did not carry off their wounded, is palpable evidence that, although they drove back our Second Corps, they did not achieve a complete or creditable victory.

To-day nothing of interest has occurred. Cannonading and picket-firing is rather more brisk and continuous this evening, but without result.

### The Fight at Ream's Station—Lee's Official Dispatch.

HEADQUARTERS ARMY OF NORTHERN VIRGINIA, Aug. 26, 1864.

*Hon. J. A. Seddon, Secretary of War:*

Gen. A. P. HILL attacked the enemy in his intrenchments at Ream's Station, yesterday evening, and at the second assault carried his entire line.

COOKE's and MCCRAE's North Carolina brigades, under Gen. HETH, and LANE's North Carolina brigade of WILCOX's division, under Gen. CONNOR, with PEGRAM's artillery, composed the assaulting column.

One line of breastworks was carried by the cavalry under Gen. HAMPTON with great gallantry, who contributed largely to the success of the day.

Seven stands of colors, two thousand prisoners and nine pieces of artillery are in our possession.

The loss of the enemy in killed and wounded is reported to be heavy—ours relatively small.

Our profound gratitude is due to the Giver of all victory, and our thanks to the brave men and officers engaged.

R. E. LEE.

### The Quota of Pennsylvania.

PHILADELPHIA, Wednesday, Aug. 31.

A special to the *Bulletin* says:

WASHINGTON, Wednesday, Aug. 31.

Reports here place Pennsylvania in the lead as to the number of recruits raised under the last call. Reinforcements have been going forward to the Army of the Potomac at the rate of about 4,000 per week, and this amount, it is expected, will be largely increased before the 5th inst.

### Legality of the Soldiers' Voting Bill Established.

CONCORD, N. H., Wednesday, Aug. 31.

The Judges of the Supreme Court of New-Hampshire, to whom the question was referred, have affirmed the constitutionality of the bill allowing soldiers to vote.

### The Congressional Committee on Defences.

PORTLAND, Me., Wednesday, Aug. 31.

The Congressional Committee on the Defences have concluded their excursion and dispersed.

### The Europa Outward Bound.

HALIFAX, N. S., Wednesday, Aug. 31.

The Royal mail steamship *Europa* sailed at 12 o'clock at noon for Liverpool.

## KENTUCKY AND TENNESSEE.

### Wheeler's Forces Threatening Gallatin.

### MOVEMENTS OF GUERRILLAS

LOUISVILLE, Ky., Tuesday, Aug. 30.

Passengers by the Nashville train say that the rebel Gen. WHEELER with his entire force, appeared at the head of the Cumberland River, three miles below Gallatin, captured a company of Federal troops and was attempting to cross the river this morning for an advance upon Gallatin.

WHEELER's force is variously estimated at from 5,000 to 12,000. The former number is probably nea correct.

A report has reached Cave City, Ky., that the Colonel commanding the Federal forces at Gallatin ordered the depot to be burned, as it was without the range of his guns.

JESSEY's gang of guerrillas went into Ghent, Ky., last night, after having shot thirteen negroes in the suburbs. The Vevay Indiana Home Guards shelled the rebels out of Ghent from the opposite side of the river.

JAKE BENNETT's squad of seventeen guerrillas went into Owensboro, Ky., on Saturday afternoon, and captured and shot Capt. WATERS, of the Third Kentucky Cavalry. They also captured ten negro soldiers, seven of whom they shot. The three others escaped, and concealed themselves on the wharf boat. The rebels set the boat on fire and then left. The citizens afterward extinguished the flames.

Twenty guerrillas, under Capt. PRATT, attacked Taylorsville, Ky., on Sunday night, and were repulsed by ANDERSON with twenty Home Guards.

Last Tuesday the guerrillas, under DAPASTER, robbed DAVID HENRY's house, neary Bradbury. They shot Mr. HENRY, and afterward demolished his furniture.

## NEWS FROM WASHINGTON.

Special Dispatches to the New-York Times.

WASHINGTON, Wednesday, Aug. 31.

POLITICAL DOCUMENTS.

The Union Congressional Committee will immediately issue the following documents for distribution: First, "McClellan's Military Career Reviewed and Exposed;" second, "Geo. H. Pendleton, His Disloyal Record and Antecedents;" third, "The Chicago Copperhead Convention; the Men who Composed It;" fourth, "Base Surrender of the Copperheads to the Rebels in Arms;" fifth, "The Military Situation and the Glorious Achievements of our Soldiers and Sailors;" sixth, "A Few Plain Words with the Heroic Private Soldier;" seventh, "The History of MCCLELLAN's Arbitrary Arrest of the Maryland Legislature;" eighth, "What LINCOLN's Administration has Done." These documents will be printed in English and German, and sent for $2 per one hundred copies. Let loyal men everywhere send orders to Hon. JAMES HARLAN, Washington, D. C.

DEATHS OF NEW-YORK SOLDIERS.

The following deaths of New-York soldiers were reported to-day: John Pfeaster, Company C, 7th Infantry; Harry Staeter, Company F, 151st Infantry; Daniel Rodgers, Company B, First Artillery; W. H. Morse, Company H, 147th Infantry; Reuben Taylor, Company G, 9th Artillery; Henry J. Dunham, Company B, 10th Cavalry.

HOW THE CHICAGO NOMINATION IS RECEIVED.

The nomination of MCCLELLAN and PENDLETON created no enthusiasm or excitement whatever in this city, even among the representatives of ardent and active Democracy. The selection of these gentlemen, and the adoption of such a platform, at a time when the rebellion is upon its last legs, and the rebel leaders are robbing both the cradle and the grave for soldiers for post and garrison duty, to enable them to send the last able-bodied man to the front, is regarded as nothing more nor less than an offer to subject our army, navy and Government to the dictation of JEFF. DAVIS.

THE RUMORED FOREIGN LOAN.

The statements so persistently made by certain sensation journals in New-York and Philadelphia, respecting a foreign loan of one thousand millions, or any other loan, are manufactured entirely out of whole cloth. The Treasury Department was first advised that German bankers were proposing to take charge of our finances, when its attention was called to those dispatches. The simple fact that such a loan is unauthorized by law, is of itself a sufficient reason why the "shent per shent" gentry will not make such a proposition, or the Secretary of the Treasury entertain it. The programme, with all its elaborate details, is heartily ridiculed, and regarded as gotten up solely to operate upon the stock market.

A SPEECH BY THE PRESIDENT.

The President this afternoon addressed the One Hundred and Forty-eighth Ohio, who called on him on their way home to be mustered out of service. After thanking them on behalf of the country, he went on to say that they were embarked in the cause of equal rights, not only for themselves, but to be transmitted to their children; rights which the enemies of the Government are trying to destroy; that they should not allow themselves to be led astray from their allegiance to the Union, and from the question of its restoration and permanency by any of the arguments of those who continually assault the Government, and who seemed more willing to destroy than to uphold it. His remarks were received with much enthusiasm by the troops and were loudly cheered at the close.

PUNISHED FOR USING BORROWED PASSES.

Two citizens of Maine, who have been found guilty by a Military Commission of going to the front upon passes belonging to other persons, have been fined two hundred dollars and five hundred dollars respectively; and to be imprisoned until the fines is paid. It is the intention of the military authorities to deal promptly and severely with all detected in the commission of this crime.

Dispatches to the Associated Press.

WASHINGTON, Wednesday, Aug. 31.

SPANISH NAVAL REGULATION.

The State Department is in receipt of an official circular from the Spanish Government introducing some favorable modifications of the rules observed at Tarifa and Isla Verde, to oblige vessels navigating the jurisdictional waters of those fortresses to hoist the flag of their nation, which practice they often neglect, alleging a very improbable ignorance in vessels so repeatedly passing through the Straits.

Every vessel which, on crossing the line of the the fortresses within the range of either does not show the flag of her nation, is to be reminded of her neglect by the discharge of a cannon loaded with powder only. If after the lapse of ten minutes she does not hoist her flag, a shot will be fired across her bow. After a further delay of ten minutes, if she still omits to hoist a flag, a shot will be fired at her masts. Her Catholic Majesty's Minister of Foreign Affairs says the Queen, in bringing the preceding dispositions to the knowledge of our Government, flatters herself that the Cabinet of Washington will find in the measures adopted a fresh proof of the sentiments of deference which her Government entertains for the American nation.

## CHICAGO CONVENTION.

### McClellan Nominated for President.

### Pendleton, of Ohio, for Vice-President.

### Vallandigham Moves to Make the Nomination Unanimous.

### A PEACE HORSE AND A WAR HORSE.

### ADJOURNMENT OF THE CONVENTION.

### It is Resolved Into a Permanent Body.

CHICAGO, Wednesday, Aug. 31.

The National Democratic Convention reassembled at 10 o'clock this morning.

The Wigwam is again densely packed, and the crowd outside is greater than ever.

Immediately after the convention had been called to order, a prayer was offered up by Rev. Dr. HALSEY, of Chicago.

Mr. WICKLIFFE then rose and said that the delegates from the West were of the opinion that circumstances may occur between now and the 4th of March next for the Democracy of the country to meet in convention again. He therefore moved the following resolution which was unanimously adopted:

*Resolved*, That this convention shall not be dissolved by adjournment at the close of its business, but shall remain organized, subject to the call at any time and place that the Executive National Committee shall designate.

The following communication was then received from the National Democratic Committee, and was presented by Mr. LAWRENCE, of Rhode Island:

At a meeting of the National Democratic Committee, held at the Sherman House, at the City of Chicago, on the 31st day of August, 1864, the following resolution was adopted:

*Whereas*, A respectful devotion to the memory of STEPHEN A. DOUGLAS, the great statesman of the West, was the crowning motive which induced the committee to concur in calling the convention in the City of Chicago; now, therefore, it is the deliberate conviction of this committee, that had his life been spared his gigantic grasp of mind, taken in connection with his declaration that "War is Disunion," a declaration which time has proved the wisdom of, would long since have restored the power of the Federal compact, and avoided that terrible loss of life for which nothing can compensate, and that bitterness of feeling so much to be deplored, which is the great barrier to the restoration of peace and union.

THOMAS B. FLORENCE, Chairman.

WM. FLINN,
F. A. AIKEN, } Secretaries.

The President then stated the question before the convention to be on ordering the previous question, (nominating a candidate for the Presidency,) and it was ordered without dissent.

The vote was then taken by States, the Chairman of each delegation announcing the vote when the States were called.

Connecticut and Ohio having been passed for the moment, the vote stood as follows:

For McClellan ........ 162
Scattering ........ 64

The different delegations now began to change their votes, and the final result was announced as follows:

*Maine*—Seven for McClellan.
*New-Hampshire*—Five for McClellan.
*Vermont*—Five for McClellan.
*Massachusetts*—Twelve for McClellan.
*Rhode Island*—Four for McClellan.
*Connecticut*—Six for McClellan.
*New-York*—Thirty-three for McClellan.
*New-Jersey*—Seven for McClellan.
*Pennsylvania*—Twenty-six for McClellan.
*Delaware*—Three for Thomas H. Seymour.
*Maryland*—Seven for Thomas H. Seymour.
*Kentucky*—Eleven for McClellan.
*Ohio*—Fifteen for McClellan, six for Thomas H. Seymour.
*Indiana*—Nine and a half for McClellan; three and a half for Thomas H. Seymour.
*Illinois*—Sixteen for McClellan.
*Michigan*—Eight for McClellan.
*Missouri*—Seven for McClellan; four for Thomas H. Seymour.
*Minnesota*—Four for McClellan.
*Wisconsin*—Eight for McClellan.
*Iowa*—Eight for McClellan.
*Kansas*—Three for McClellan.
*California*—Five for McClellan.
*Oregon*—Three for McClellan.

TOTAL.

McClellan ........ 202½ | Thos. H. Seymour .... 23½

In announcing the vote of New-York Mr. SANFORD E. CHURCH said, that New-York regretted to pass by her favorite son, but she stands now as she has ever stood, ready to sacrifice her dearest personal preferences for the public good, holding it her duty above all others to do all in her power to rescue the country from the tyranny that oppresses it. Having full confidence in the Democracy, ability and patriotism of Gen. GEORGE B. MCCLELLAN, New-York gives him her entire electoral vote.

Several delegations having cast their votes for HORATIO SEYMOUR when the call of the States had been gone through with, Gov. SEYMOUR remarked that some gentlemen had done him the honor to name him for the nomination. It would be affectation to say that their expressions of preference did not give him pleasure, but he owed it to himself to say that many months ago he advised his friends in New-York that, for various reasons, private and public, he could not be a candidate for the Chicago nomination. Having made that announcement, he would lack the honor of a man, he would do great injustice to those friends to permit his name to be used now. As a member of the New-York delegation, he personally thought it advisable to support an eminent jurist of that State for the nomination, but he was not actuated in this by any doubt of the ability or patriotism of the distinguished gentleman who has been placed in nomination. He knew that Gen. MCCLELLAN did not seek the nomination. He knew that that able officer had declared that it would be more agreeable to him to resume his position in the army, but he will not honor any the less the high position assigned him by the great majority of the country, because he has not sought it. He desired to add a few words in reference to Maryland and her honored delegates here. Yesterday he did an act of injustice to a distinguished member of that delegation, (Mr. HARRIS,) because he (SEYMOUR) did not understand the purport of his remarks, and he now desired to say that he was fully satisfied that that high-toned gentleman was incapable of taking a position in this convention, participating in its deliberations and refusing to abide by its decisions. We are now appealing to the American people to unite and save our country. Let us not look back. It is with the present that we have to deal. Let by-gones be by-gones. He could say for our gallant nominee that the man's heart will grieve more than his will for any wrong done Maryland. As one who did not support him in my delegation, and as one who knows the man well, he felt bound to do him this justice. He (Gov. SEYMOUR) would pledge his life that when Gen. MCCLELLAN is placed in the Presidential Chair, he will devote all his energies to the best interests of his country, and to securing, never again to be invaded, all the rights and privileges of the people under the laws and the Constitution.

The President then announced the vote, which was received with deafening cheers, the delegates and the vast audience rising, the band playing, and the cheering lasting for several minutes.

Immediately after the nomination a banner on which is painted a portrait of MCCLELLAN, and bearing as a motto, "If I cannot have command of my own men let me share their fate in the field of battle," was run up behind the President's platform, and was welcomed by the wild enthusiastic cheers of the multitude.

A communication was received from the Chairman of the German People's Association of New-York, claiming to represent 200,000 citizens, and accompanied by resolutions pledging the members of the association to the support of the Chicago nominees. The communication was filed.

Mr. VALLANDIGHAM said that from the first moment he had been animated by but one sentiment in this convention—peace, to the end that there might be peace in the land. He then moved that the nomination of Gen. GEORGE B. MCCLELLAN be the unanimous sense of the convention.

Mr. MCKEON, of New-York, seconded the motion, and remarked that we were in the midst of a bloody revolution; that if the present Administration should be continued no man of note here would be safe in his liberty or life. He expected all to join with one heart and as one man in the effort to overthrow it.

Gov. POWELL also briefly addressed the convention, pledging his most earnest efforts for the success of the ticket, and expressing the firm conviction that the ticket would come out of the contest triumphant, with the liberties of the people restored, and the prosperity and happiness of the country secured.

Judge ALLEN, of Ohio, Mr. BOGG, of Missouri, JAS. S. THAYER, of New-York, followed in brief speeches, reviewing the history of the country under Democratic rule, in comparison with the acts of the present Administration; promising the return of lasting peace and national happiness with the success of MCCLELLAN.

The question was then taken on making the nomination unanimous, and it was declared carried. The shout that responded was deafening.

Mr. WICKLIFFE offered a resolution to the effect that Kentucky expects the first act of MCCLELLAN, when elected, in March next, to be open Lincoln's prison doors, and set the captives free. Carried unanimously.

Mr. WICKLIFFE said that many of the best and most loyal citizens of Kentucky, among them twenty or thirty ladies, were now imprisoned in Louisville, in damp and dirty cells, with only straw to lay upon and the coarsest prison fare to eat; and the newspapers of Louisville were forbidden to make the slightest allusion to this terrible state of affairs. He now proclaimed it at the risk of his liberty—perhaps of his life.

Mr. S. S. COX moved that the convention proceed to the nomination of a candidate for Vice-President, without debate or other business. Carried.

Judge Allen nominated George H. Pendleton, of Ohio.

Mr. McDowell nominated D. W. Voorhees, of Indiana.

Mr. Hughes nominated Geo. W. Cass, of Pennsylvania.

Mr. Dickey, of Vermont, nominated James Guthrie, of Kentucky.

Mr. Henry nominated Augustus Dodge, of Iowa.

Mr. Hickox nominated James D. Caton, of Illinois.

Gov. Hunt, of New-York, seconded the nomination of James Guthrie.

Mr. Saulsbury nominated Gov. Powell, of Kentucky.

The Missouri delegation nominated John S. Phelps, of Missouri.

The New-Jersey delegation seconded the nomination of Mr. Pendleton.

The first vote for Vice-President resulted, as follows:

| | | | |
|---|---|---|---|
| James Guthrie | 65½ | J. D. Caton | 16 |
| Geo. H. Pendleton | 54½ | Governor Powell | 32½ |
| Daniel W. Voorhees | 13 | John S. Phelps | 8 |
| George W. Cass | 26 | Blank | 1½ |
| Augustus Dodge | 9 | | |

On the second ballot, when New-York was called, Judge PARKER said that having cast her thirty-three votes for JAMES GUTHRIE against his wishes, she now gave them cheerfully to GEORGE H. PENDLETON, of Ohio.

The other candidates were then withdrawn, and GEORGE H. PENDLETON, of Ohio, received the unanimous vote of the convention as their candidate for Vice-President.

Mr. PENDLETON being loudly called for, he said that he had no language in which to express his thanks for this evidence of kindness and confidence. He could only promise to devote himself in the future, as in the past, with entire devotion to the great principles which lie at the foundation of our Government—the rights of the States and the liberties of the people. In the future, as in the past, he would be faithful to the great principles of Democracy, and strong in their cause, with the hearts of millions of freemen with them, they would again build up the shattered fragments of the Union, and hand it down to the next generation as it was received from the last.

On motion, a committee of one from each State was appointed to inform the candidates of their nomination, and request their acceptance thereof.

On motion, it was resolved that one person from each State, selected by the delegates thereof, be appointed to form the National Executive Committee.

On motion, it was resolved that 100,000 copies of the proceedings of the convention be printed.

Mr. TILDEN moved that the same ratio of representation which prevailed in this convention be the ratio of the next convention. Adopted.

On motion, it was resolved that the Democracy of the country be requested to meet in the different cities, and hold mass ratification meetings on the 17th of September, the anniversary of the adoption of the Federal Constitution.

A vote of thanks to the officers of the convention, was adopted.

With nine cheers for the ticket, the convention adjourned, subject to the call of the National Committee.

### THE CONVENTION.

#### Affairs on Monday—A Great Crowd—Vallandigham Worship.

*Correspondence of the New-York Times.*

CHICAGO, Monday, Aug. 29, 1864—A. M.

The cry is still they come. Last night and this morning, every train that has arrived has been filled with the sovereigns coming up to this great Babel.

The excitement continued all day yesterday. Toward evening a large crowd gathered in the Court-house-square, and were addressed most energetically by a gentleman whose name I did not learn, but he was evidently one of those who did not believe in Sabbaths in revolutionary times.

Many attended church. But the great majority remained in the streets and hotels. Thousands visited DOUGLAS' grave, and perhaps took a look at the objects of their sympathy, who are confined in Camp Douglas by "LINCOLN's minions." The day passed off good naturedly, and everybody appeared to be in the best of spirits. BURLEIGH, of the Boston *Journal*, "improved" the occasion by preaching in the First Baptist Church in the morning, and the Wabash-avenue Methodist Episcopal Church in the evening.

The Sherman House is the Headquarters. Passing among the delegates there last evening, it was evident that the out-and-out peace, anti-MCCLELLAN men, had taken courage from some quarter, and were confident that they should be able to defeat the nomination of the second NAPOLEON. His friends, too, appeared less confident; but I think still there is no doubt as to the result.

THE CONVENTION.

The convention is held in a large amphitheatre, located on the lake shore, about a mile south of the hotels. It has been erected by the Democrats of Chicago, at a cost of some $7,000, and is well adapted for the purpose, and capable of accommodating 15,000 people. A portion has been reserved for the delegates, and another section for their friends, for which tickets are necessary, in order to secure an admission. There is a ladies' gallery. These sections are seated. But the great presence chamber of the sovereigns is unseated, so that the people will have to stand "packed in a jam," while the leaders are hatching out a candidate and a set of principles for them to swear by.

Arrangements have been made on an extensive scale by the "Invincible Club," of this city, for a grand ratification demonstration on the evening of the day upon which the nomination is made. There is to be a torchlight procession, and every other kind of proceeding which will serve to make night hideous.

At 10 o'clock an immense crowd gathered in front of the Sherman House, which is the headquarters of the ultra peace men, and commenced calling for VALLANDIGHAM. The whole matter was doubtless prearranged, as there was a fugleman upon the balcony, acting as master of ceremonies, telling the unterrified when to cheer and when to call.

After the usual delirium, VALLANDIGHAM made his appearance, and hats swung in the air, and lungs gave out their loudest notes. When this part of the programme had been gone through with, VALLANDIGHAM bowed and put himself on his blandest, and expressed his grateful emotions at this compliment from the people. He then exhorted to peace, harmony and union, everything for the cause, and told them that when the work of the convention was over, when a Democratic candidate, who was to rescue the Constitution and restore the liberties of the nation, was in the field, he should make it his business, in season and out of season, to address assemblages of his Democratic fellow-citizens in all parts of the country, until a glorious victory crowned their efforts.

Having thus delivered himself, he bowed himself back into the hotel. The crowd called for several other "distinguished" gentlemen, but they were not forthcoming.

I forgot to mention, in connection with the "Conservative Democratic National Convention," that that eminent man of peace, ISAIAH RYNDERS, formerly leader of the Empire Club of your City, was present as a delegate, and his name is printed in the list. I could not help but think how those eminent Conservatives *per se* of your State—Granger, Duer, Kidd, Burrows, Noxon, Fillmore, &c.—would turn up their Conservative noses at even the political proximity of this redoubtable shoulder-hitter.

### Nomination of McClellan.

OGDENSBURGH, Wednesday, Aug. 31.

The nomination of MCCLELLAN was received here with great rejoicing. Thirty-four guns were fired on the receipt of the news. This evening guns are firing, bands playing, bonfires blazing, rockets ascending, processions moving and people rejoicing. The *Democrat* office and many private residences are brilliantly illuminated. Prominent citizens are addressing the crowds.

POUGHKEEPSIE, Wednesday, Aug. 31.

A salute of one hundred guns was fired here this afternoon in honor of the nomination of MCCLELLAN and PENDLETON.

ALBANY, Wednesday, Aug. 31.

The nomination of MCCLELLAN caused great enthusiasm in this city. A hundred guns were fired at noon, and a hundred more at sunset. This evening a procession preceded by a band of music, and bearing torches and transparencies, is parading the streets. Banners bearing the name of MCCLELLAN, are displayed at different points. Speeches were made from the Capitol steps by Hon. J. V. L. PRUYN and Gen. VANDERPOOL.

PORTLAND, Wednesday, Aug. 31.

The Democrats of Portland fired 150, and those of Westbrook 100, guns in honor of the nomination of MCCLELLAN.

SPRINGFIELD, Mass., Wednesday, Aug. 31.

One hundred guns were fired in this city this evening, in honor of the Chicago nominations. There was also a grand display of fireworks.

BOSTON, Wednesday, Aug. 31.

A salute of one hundred guns was fired by the Constitutional Club in honor of MCCLELLAN's nomination. The Boston *Post* office was brilliantly illuminated in the evening.

TROY, Wednesday, Aug. 31.

The Democracy of this city fired 100 guns this evening, in honor of MCCLELLAN's nomination. An impromptu procession paraded the streets, with two bands of music. Many private dwellings were illuminated. Subsequently a large public meeting was organized, and addresses were made in front of the Court-house steps.

BUFFALO, Wednesday, Aug. 31.

The news of MCCLELLAN's nomination was received with great enthusiasm by the Democrats here. One hundred guns were fired this afternoon; a band of music played at the *Courier* office and elsewhere, and in the evening fireworks were displayed, and speeches made. A great crowd assembled around the Democratic Association Rooms to hear and see the celebration.

NEWARK, N. J., Wednesday, Aug. 31.

A large and enthusiastic meeting was held this evening at the Democratic Headquarters, Hon. MOSES BIGELOW presiding, to ratify the nomination of Gen. MCCLELLAN for President. The hall was filled, and outside stands surrounded, forming one of the largest meetings held here. A grand procession marched through the streets after the meeting adjourned. A salute of thirteen guns was fired.

BORDENTOWN, Wednesday, Aug. 31.

Bordentown is alive to-night. About three thousand people are assembled together in front of the Railroad House, cheering for MCCLELLAN, and have been addressed by Col. G. S. CANNON and Col. WM. R. MURPHY.

BURLINGTON, N. J., Wednesday, Aug. 31.

The Democrats of this place responded to the nomination of Gen. MCCLELLAN by a salute and torchlight procession. Ex-Senator WALL delivered an address.

### From the Pacific Coast.

SAN FRANCISCO, Monday, Aug. 22.

Heavy earthquake shocks have been experienced in the mountains during the week.

Money is quiet at 1½ per cent.

The receipts of bullion for the last ten days amount to $1,500,000.

Currency bills on New-York are at 143 per cent. premium.

Coin bills are at 3½@4 per cent. premium.

Legal tender notes are weak at 39½c. on the dollar.

Public opinion seems to be changing in Nevada as to the propriety of adopting a State constitution. It may now be adopted in order to get rid of the obnoxious territorial officers.

Sandwich Island dates to July 25 report slow progress of the Constitutional Convention. Much time has been consumed in discussing the powers of the convention. The Government is accused of revolutionary designs.

Sailed, bark *Chalgrove*, for Hong Kong, with quicksilver to the value of $32,000 and nearly $506,000 in bullion.

SAN FRANCISCO, Saturday, Aug. 27.

The last steamer from Oregon and British Columbia brought over $700,000 in bullion. The Northern mines are increasing in productiveness. Great trade is springing up with this city.

The Indian war on the northern coast of California is at an end.

In the fair of the Christian Commission about $12,000 in gold are received daily.

Business is improving. Mining stock market dull. Wheat and Barley $1½@$1⅝.

SAN FRANCISCO, Monday, Aug. 29.

Arrived steamer *Constitution*, from Panama.

SAN FRANCISCO, Tuesday, Aug. 30.

Arrived ship *Intrepid*, from New-York; steamer *Sierra Nevada*, with about $150,000 in treasure from the Northern mines.

The Union State Convention organized at Sacramento this afternoon. After nominating the Presidential electors, the convention will divide into three district conventions, and nominate their congressional candidates. What is called the Anti-Conness wing of the party seems to be in the majority.

### Chased by a Supposed Pirate.

BALTIMORE, Wednesday, Aug. 31.

The bark *Adelaide*, Capt. WILLIAMS, arrived here from Rio Janeiro, reports Aug. 8, lat. 7° 40', lon. 45° 50', was chased by a schooner resembling a pilot-boat, supposed to be a pirate.

### Canal Break.

ALBANY, Wednesday, Aug. 31.

The bottom of one of the locks this side of Schoharie Creek Aqueduct gave out on Sunday night. It will require four days to repair the damage. No boats have come in from the canal this morning.

## GEN. SHERMAN'S DIVISION.

### The Raid Upon the Communications.

### The Raids Under Stoneman and McCook.

### Jeff. Davis Reported to be at Macon.

### SPECULATIONS UPON THE CAMPAIGN.

OUR SPECIAL ARMY CORRESPONDENCE.

#### The Recent Raids—Kilpatrick's Demonstration—The Rebel Editors' Utterances Miscellaneous.

NEAR ATLANTA, Thursday, Aug. 18, 1864.

THE RAID ON OUR REAR.

If you have received my letter, dated the 15th inst., you will have perceived that my anticipations of disturbances in our rear have unhappily been realized.

You will recollect that I learned from a deserter that a squad of picked men from different rebel regiments had been detailed to cut our rear in obscure places, in the vicinity of Calhoun. The road was cut on Monday afternoon in that vicinity, in three places, about a dozen rails being removed in each place.

While this work of destruction was going on, WHEELER, with between four and five thousand men, and ten pieces of cannon, appeared in front of Dalton, one of the most important points upon the road, and commenced a "siege." Upon each side of the eastern pike he planted his pieces, and gave the national officer in command notice that at an appointed time he should assault the town. The national officer responded by saying that it was a rebel town, and that if he wanted to shell it, he could shell and be —. But WHEELER didn't shell Dalton. Neither did he frighten out our officer in command, who had three infantry regiments well located, and a battery of artillery in position. All the trains were in the meantime ordered back to Chattanooga north and Resaca south, and up to the present time no cars, supplies or mails have been destroyed. WHEELER's forces were composed of cavalry and mounted infantry, a portion of whom he sent a short distance north of Dalton, with orders to destroy a bridge and as much of the road as possible. This cut off all communication by rail and by telegraph between Chattanooga and Dalton, but Gen. STEEDMAN, commanding at the former city, had been informed of the affair previously, and was already upon the march with two white regiments and six full companies of negroes.

Gen. STEEDMAN's forces arrived at an early hour Tuesday morning, and before daylight he drove off the road the force employed in its destruction, and immediately after attacked WHEELER, near Dalton. From the Adjutant-General of Gen. SCHOFIELD I learn that STEEDMAN had quite a fight, and that he drove the enemy nearly two miles. Before he arrived, the force dispatched to destroy the road had succeeded in tearing up over five miles of rails, which they heated and bent. They also burned a small bridge a few miles from Dalton, but which can be replaced in a very short time. We have received no mail in three days, but it is reported that the road will be in running order before Saturday. At the time of the raid, nearly all our construction trains were south of Resaca or at Nashville. At last accounts here, there were no rebels within several miles of the road.

We have been expecting a rebel demonstration of this nature for a long time, and have strong bodies of men at all the important points upon the road. The using up of STONEMAN and the partial destruction of MCCOOK's command by the enemy's cavalry has given it a chance to annoy us, and a speedy advantage was taken of our situation. But unless the rebels have been strongly reinforced in the cavalry arm, WHEELER will no doubt be recalled, for, as I write, we have sent out a tremendous raiding party under KILPATRICK, who has orders to attack the enemy's rear in its most vital parts. He is expected to return in a few days, and there are no apprehensions as regards his safety felt at headquarters. The enemy has a large body of cavalry, but it is divided up pretty well, and located at great distances from Atlanta, in many cases.

When HOOD took command he not only promised to hold Atlanta, whip the Federal army and drive it in disorder across the Chattahoochee, but he expressed his determination to cut our rear, and, if possible, to wholly destroy our lines of communication.

There are three very large bridges upon the road between Chattanooga and Atlanta, respectively spanning the Oostenaula, Etowa and Chattahoochee rivers. The most important structure upon the road is the tunnel, ten miles north of Dalton. At all these places we have very large forces and formidable works, with a sufficiency of artillery for all ordinary purposes.

But, of course, there are hundreds of important places upon the road, any of which, probably, might be successfully attacked by a large rebel force. On the whole, however, the entire road is well guarded, and an attack anywhere where much harm could be done, would be attended by great risks.

M'COOK'S FIGHT.

Large and small bodies of Gen. MCCOOK's unsuccessful raiding party return daily, his losses already having been reduced to less than a thousand men. I saw a rebel paper on Tuesday, in which a correspondent gives a full report of MCCOOK's fight, and, according to his account, the rebel forces far outnumbered our own. MCCOOK had but one small division, numbering less than three thousand men, while he was attacked, at different times, by six divisions. At one time he fought ARMSTRONG's and ROSS' divisions; and the rebel correspondent says he (MCCOOK) stood his ground and fought bravely against great odds for a long time. Instead of surrendering, our forces broke and ran, and in a short time encountered HUME's division, near a place called Newman's Station. At one time MCCOOK was completely surrounded, but he managed to cut his way out.

The report in the rebel newspaper made two

# The New-York Times.

VOL. XIV.—NO. 4096. NEW-YORK, WEDNESDAY, NOVEMBER 9, 1864. PRICE FOUR CENTS


# VICTORY!

## GLORIOUS RESULT YESTERDAY.

### Election of Lincoln and Johnson.

### Terrible Defeat of McClellan.

### THE UNION TRIUMPHANT.

### New-England a Solid Phalanx.

### New-York for Lincoln and Fenton

### Defeat of Governor Seymour and His Friends.

### Gain of Five Union Congressmen in the State.

### Election of Raymond, Dodge, Darling, Conklin and Humphrey.

### Pennsylvania Union on the Home Vote.

### HEAVY UNION GAINS.

### MARYLAND AND DELAWARE ALL RIGHT.

### Heavy Union Gains in New-Jersey.

### The Great Northwest Solid for Lincoln.

DETAILS OF THE RETURNS.

## THE VOTE OF THE CITY.

PRESIDENT AND GOVERNOR.

| Ward | District | PRESIDENT. Lincoln | McClellan | GOVERNOR. Fenton | Seymour |
|---|---|---|---|---|---|
| 1st Ward | 1 | [illegible] | [illegible] | [illegible] | 602 |
| | 2 | [illegible] | [illegible] | [illegible] | 493 |
| | 3 | [illegible] | [illegible] | [illegible] | 634 |
| | 4 | [illegible] | [illegible] | [illegible] | 97 |
| | 5 | [illegible] | [illegible] | [illegible] | 307 |
| Total | | [illegible] | [illegible] | [illegible] | 2138 |
| 2d Ward | 1 | [illegible] | [illegible] | [illegible] | 140 |
| | 2 | [illegible] | [illegible] | [illegible] | 195 |
| Total | | [illegible] | [illegible] | [illegible] | 335 |
| 3d Ward | 1 | [illegible] | [illegible] | [illegible] | 224 |
| | 2 | [illegible] | [illegible] | [illegible] | 120 |
| | 3 | [illegible] | [illegible] | [illegible] | 112 |
| | 4 | [illegible] | [illegible] | [illegible] | 44 |
| Total | | [illegible] | [illegible] | [illegible] | 500 |
| 4th Ward | 1 | [illegible] | [illegible] | [illegible] | 296 |
| | 2 | [illegible] | [illegible] | [illegible] | 502 |
| | 3 | [illegible] | [illegible] | [illegible] | 281 |
| | 4 | [illegible] | [illegible] | [illegible] | 336 |
| | 5 | [illegible] | [illegible] | [illegible] | 256 |
| | 6 | [illegible] | [illegible] | [illegible] | 319 |
| | 7 | [illegible] | [illegible] | [illegible] | 352 |
| Total | | [illegible] | [illegible] | [illegible] | 2422 |
| 5th Ward | 1 | [illegible] | [illegible] | [illegible] | 398 |
| | 2 | [illegible] | [illegible] | [illegible] | 363 |
| | 3 | [illegible] | [illegible] | [illegible] | 282 |
| | 4 | [illegible] | [illegible] | [illegible] | 238 |
| | 5 | [illegible] | [illegible] | [illegible] | 364 |
| | 6 | [illegible] | [illegible] | [illegible] | 286 |
| | 7 | [illegible] | [illegible] | [illegible] | 263 |
| | 8 | [illegible] | [illegible] | [illegible] | 374 |
| Total | | [illegible] | [illegible] | [illegible] | 2680 |
| 6th Ward | | [illegible] | [illegible] | [illegible] | [illegible] |
| 7th Ward | | [illegible] | [illegible] | [illegible] | [illegible] |
| 8th Ward | | [illegible] | [illegible] | [illegible] | [illegible] |
| 9th Ward | | [illegible] | [illegible] | [illegible] | [illegible] |
| 10th Ward | | [illegible] | [illegible] | [illegible] | [illegible] |
| 11th Ward | | [illegible] | [illegible] | [illegible] | [illegible] |
| 12th Ward | | [illegible] | [illegible] | [illegible] | [illegible] |

| Ward | District | Lincoln | McClellan | Fenton | Seymour |
|---|---|---|---|---|---|
| 13th Ward | 1 | 109 | 368 | 106 | 369 |
| | 2 | 173 | 414 | 172 | 419 |
| | 3 | 123 | 525 | 123 | 519 |
| | 4 | 117 | 409 | 117 | 411 |
| | 5 | 153 | 306 | 147 | 304 |
| | 6 | 139 | 267 | 133 | 265 |
| | 7 | 58 | 183 | 63 | 181 |
| | 8 | 142 | 297 | 137 | 301 |
| Total | | 1,106 | 2,767 | 1,077 | 2,769 |
| 14th Ward | 1 | 59 | 187 | .... | .... |
| | 2 | 29 | 670 | 20 | 678 |
| | 3 | 102 | 620 | 76 | 634 |
| | 4 | 41 | 609 | 37 | 38 |
| | 5 | 130 | 363 | 129 | 30 |
| | 6 | 139 | 366 | 136 | 366 |
| | 7 | 115 | 259 | 114 | 252 |
| | 8 | 80 | 319 | 80 | 382 |
| | 9 | 82 | 561 | 80 | 511 |
| | 10 | 82 | 285 | 78 | 267 |
| Total | | 859 | 4229 | .... | .... |
| 15 Ward | 1 | 289 | 260 | 275 | 262 |
| | 2 | 271 | 275 | 263 | 276 |
| | 3 | 137 | 294 | 131 | 290 |
| | 4 | 341 | 225 | 343 | 219 |
| | 5 | 161 | 88 | 162 | 85 |
| | 6 | 273 | 127 | 268 | 130 |
| | 7 | 150 | 85 | 162 | 82 |
| | 8 | 251 | 285 | — | — |
| | 9 | 209 | 160 | — | — |
| | 10 | 153 | 171 | — | — |
| Total | | 2244 | 1970 | — | — |
| 16th Ward | 1 | 307 | 278 | 302 | 280 |
| | 2 | 302 | 464 | 305 | 451 |
| | 3 | 303 | 351 | 360 | 470 |
| | 4 | 303 | 351 | — | — |
| | 4 | 183 | 393 | 294 | 378 |
| | 6 | 434 | 382 | — | — |
| | 7 | 211 | 463 | 211 | 456 |
| | 8 | 29 | 125 | — | — |
| | 9 | 387 | 275 | 390 | 276 |
| | 10 | 235 | 287 | 237 | 285 |
| Total | | 2,665 | 3,869 | — | — |
| 17th Ward | 1 | 251 | 248 | 238 | 256 |
| | 2 | 264 | 377 | 250 | 374 |
| | 3 | 252 | 352 | 243 | 354 |
| | 4 | 257 | 358 | 253 | 361 |
| | 5 | 319 | 409 | 319 | 408 |
| | 6 | 287 | 228 | 293 | 223 |
| | 7 | 403 | 327 | 400 | 324 |
| | 8 | 104 | 364 | 103 | 365 |
| | 9 | 61 | 489 | 47 | 502 |
| | 10 | 66 | 210 | 67 | 209 |
| | 11 | 108 | 412 | 108 | 411 |
| | 12 | 141 | 426 | 133 | 430 |
| | 13 | 165 | 290 | 161 | 283 |
| | 14 | 43 | 451 | 44 | 450 |
| | 15 | 96 | 404 | 89 | 402 |
| | 16 | 213 | 361 | 208 | 362 |
| | 17 | 99 | 435 | 99 | 433 |
| | 18 | 106 | 449 | 360 | 444 |
| | 19 | 211 | 441 | 208 | 448 |
| Total | | 3425 | 7031 | 3613 | 7647 |
| 18th Ward | 1 | 356 | 214 | 370 | 210 |
| | 2 | 452 | 371 | — | — |
| | 3 | 488 | 287 | 479 | 286 |
| | 4 | 178 | 124 | 177 | 122 |
| | 5 | 176 | 154 | 184 | 152 |
| | 6 | 216 | 365 | 215 | 353 |
| | 7 | 181 | 290 | 181 | 284 |
| | 8 | 87 | 200 | 90 | 197 |
| | 9 | 158 | 243 | 157 | 214 |
| | 10 | 68 | 306 | 67 | 308 |
| | 11 | 154 | 317 | 143 | 321 |
| | 12 | 46 | 346 | 46 | 312 |
| | 13 | 31 | 428 | 31 | 475 |
| | 14 | 36 | 318 | 34 | 390 |
| | 15 | 58 | 411 | 54 | 467 |
| Total | | 2673 | 4424 | — | — |
| 19th Ward | 1 | 203 | 507 | 208 | 502 |
| | 2 | 157 | 434 | 153 | 425 |
| | 3 | 247 | 392 | 251 | 383 |
| | 4 | 240 | 467 | 239 | 472 |
| | 5 | 163 | 298 | 163 | 295 |
| | 6 | 302 | 348 | 266 | 382 |
| | 7 | 191 | 467 | 188 | 412 |
| | 8 | 191 | 281 | 198 | 276 |
| | 9 | 247 | 369 | 252 | 362 |
| Total | | 1941 | 3674 | 1918 | 3675 |
| 20th Ward | 1 | 92 | 440 | 276 | 848 |
| | 2 | 189 | 303 | 122 | 303 |
| | 3 | 273 | 848 | — | — |
| | 4 | 173 | 360 | — | — |
| | 5 | 101 | 566 | 102 | 566 |
| | 6 | 328 | 216 | 326 | 216 |
| | 7 | 321 | 224 | 311 | 220 |
| | 8 | 161 | 419 | 162 | 416 |
| | 9 | 170 | 474 | 168 | 474 |
| | 10 | 169 | 347 | 169 | 346 |
| | 11 | 224 | 507 | 228 | 573 |
| | 12 | 186 | 336 | 184 | 337 |
| | 13 | 182 | 357 | 189 | 362 |
| | 14 | 311 | 437 | 318 | 431 |
| Total | | 2874 | 5553 | — | — |
| 21st Ward | 1 | 160 | 310 | 156 | 303 |
| | 2 | 127 | 428 | 132 | 419 |
| | 3 | 184 | 414 | 152 | 418 |
| | 4 | 141 | 446 | 140 | 441 |
| | 5 | 125 | 437 | 127 | 431 |
| | 6 | 84 | 278 | 82 | 277 |
| | 7 | 66 | 334 | 61 | 333 |
| | 8 | 188 | 146 | 190 | 145 |
| | 9 | 205 | 256 | 208 | 250 |
| | 10 | 238 | 309 | 241 | 323 |
| | 11 | 247 | 258 | 297 | 250 |
| | 12 | 290 | 264 | 298 | 201 |
| | 13 | 376 | 185 | 393 | 181 |
| | 14 | 340 | 176 | 321 | 275 |
| Total | | 2,767 | 4,177 | 2,788 | 42,29 |
| 22d Ward | 1 | 136 | 396 | 139 | 389 |
| | 2 | 248 | 420 | 247 | 419 |
| | 3 | 248 | 394 | 263 | 389 |
| | 4 | 281 | 290 | 275 | 284 |
| | 5 | 169 | 227 | 166 | 232 |
| | 6 | 137 | 165 | 131 | 161 |
| | 7 | 144 | 278 | 141 | 262 |
| | 8 | 200 | 218 | 198 | 229 |
| | 9 | 232 | 366 | 228 | 360 |
| | 10 | 163 | 314 | 153 | 310 |
| | 11 | 187 | 434 | 200 | 433 |
| | 12 | 60 | 300 | 86 | 307 |
| | 13 | 78 | 216 | 78 | 215 |
| | 14 | 70 | 138 | 74 | 128 |
| Total | | 2360 | 4136 | 2340 | 4130 |

### New-York City Recapitulated.

| Ward. | Lincoln. | McClellan |
|---|---|---|
| First | 213 | 2,162 |
| Second | 186 | 838 |
| Third | 207 | 500 |
| Fourth | 435 | 2,379 |
| Fifth | 1,022 | 2,038 |
| Sixth | 326 | 3,457 |
| Seventh | 1,230 | 4,090 |
| Eighth | 1,619 | 3,202 |
| Ninth | 3,468 | 3,745 |
| Tenth | 1,690 | 2,347 |
| Eleventh | 1,928 | 5,482 |
| Twelfth | 1,365 | 2,490 |
| Thirteenth | 1,106 | 2,767 |
| Fourteenth | 859 | 4,229 |
| Fifteenth | 2,244 | 1,970 |
| Sixteenth | 2,746 | 3,478 |
| Seventeenth | 3,425 | 7,031 |
| Eighteenth | 2,678 | 4,424 |
| Nineteenth | 1,941 | 3,574 |
| Twentieth | 2,874 | 5,553 |
| Twenty-first | 2,767 | 4,177 |
| Twenty-second | 2,366 | 4,127 |
| Total | 36,912 | 73,769 |

### The Vote for Governor.

The vote for Governor by Ward Districts is incomplete. The following is the total in the several wards:

| Ward. | Fenton. | Seymour. | Ward. | Fenton. | Seymour. |
|---|---|---|---|---|---|
| 1 | 207 | 2,133 | 12 | 1,273 | 2,486 |
| 2 | 188 | 336 | 13 | 1,077 | 2,769 |
| 3 | 221 | 800 | 14 | 800 | 4-247 |
| 4 | 397 | 2,422 | 15 | 2,247 | 1,980 |
| 5 | 1,012 | 2,680 | 16 | 2,804 | 3,428 |
| 6 | 349 | 3,429 | 17 | 3,613 | 7,047 |
| 7 | 1,199 | 4,061 | 18 | 2,261 | 4,370 |
| 8 | 1,620 | 3,274 | 19 | 1,918 | 3.676 |
| 9 | 3,685 | 2,714 | 20 | 3,071 | 5,689 |
| 10 | 1,619 | 2,361 | 21 | 2,788 | 4,228 |
| 11 | 1,948 | 5,533 | 22 | 2,340 | 4,130 |
| Totals | | | | 36,555 | 73,717 |
| Seymour's majority | | | | | 37,162 |

### Lieutenant-Governor.

| Ward. | Alvord. | Jones. | Wards. | Alvord. | Jones. |
|---|---|---|---|---|---|
| 1 | 207 | 2133 | 12 | 1268 | 2483 |
| 2 | 188 | 334 | 13 | 1078 | 2770 |
| 3 | 221 | 498 | 14 | 810 | 4246 |
| 4 | 396 | 2422 | 15 | 2228 | 1968 |
| 5 | 1010 | 2030 | 16 | 2852 | 3421 |
| 6 | 346 | 3435 | 17 | 3355 | 7043 |
| 7 | 1196 | 4060 | 18 | 2247 | 4348 |
| 8 | 1518 | 3276 | 19 | 1913 | 3592 |
| 9 | 3496 | 3820 | 20 | 3055 | 5694 |
| 10 | 1621 | 2268 | 21 | 2767 | 4148 |
| 11 | 1950 | 5538 | 22 | 2342 | 4133 |
| Total | | | | 36069 | 72790 |

### Canal Commissioner.

The vote for Canal Commissioner in this city stands Alberger, Union, 36,081; Lord, Democrat, 73,757.

### State Prison Inspector.

The vote for State Prison differs but little from that of Canal Commissioner—*Forrest*, Union, receiving 36,092, and McNeil, Democrat, 73,722.

### Fourth Congressional District.

William Walsh, 5,099; Carolin O'Brien Bryant, 1,628; Morgan Jones, 8,445.

The First District of the First Ward, First, Second and Fourth District of the Sixth Ward are missing.

Jones is elected.

### Fifth Congressional District.

Nelson Taylor.......... 9,144
Wm. B. McCay.......... 4,174
E. E. Ellery.......... 3,948

### Sixth Congressional District.

Ninth and Fifteenth Wards complete, with Sixteenth Ward, except Third District:
Henry J. Raymond, 7,156.
Elijah Ward, 6,640.
E. P. Morton, 438.
R. C. Hawkins, 129.

### Seventh Congressional District.

Chandler, 9,461.
Boardman, 4,711.
The First, Second, Third, Ninth, Eleventh and Eighteenth Districts of the Seventeenth Ward are Missing.
Chandler is elected.

### Eighth Congressional District.

W. B. Dodge.......... 6,573
James Brooks.......... 6,329
T. J. Barr.......... 3,302

1st and 2d District, 18th Ward; 1st, 9th, 11th and 14th, of the 20th Ward, and 1st, 5th, 11th and 14th, of the 21st Ward, are missing.

### Ninth Congressional District.

Darling..........5,201 Henrick..........3,667
Wood..........4,408 Smith.......... 240

The Third District of the Twelfth Ward is missing. Darling is elected.

### New-York Congressmen Elected.

| Dis. | | Dis. | |
|---|---|---|---|
| 1 | S. Tabor, Dem. | 17 | C. T. Hulburd, Union. |
| 2 | T. G. Bergen, Dem. | 18 | |
| 3 | J. Humphrey, Union. | 19 | D. Hubbard, jr., Un. |
| 4 | M. Jones, Dem. | 20 | A. H. Laflin, Union. |
| 5 | N. Taylor, Dem. | 21 | R. Concklin, Union. |
| 6 | H. J. Raymond, Un. | 22 | S. T. Holmes, Union. |
| 7 | J. W. Chanler, Dem. | 23 | T. T. Davis, Union. |
| 8 | Wm. E. Dodge, U. | 24 | T. M. Pomeroy, Union. |
| 9 | Wm. A. Darling, U. | 25 | D. Morris, Union. |
| 10 | W. Radford, Dem. | 26 | G. W. Hotchkiss, Union |
| 11 | J. A. Ketcham Un. | 27 | H. Ward, Union. |
| 12 | | 28 | R. Hart, Union. |
| 13 | E. N. Hubbell, Dem. | 29 | B. Van Horn, Union. |
| 14 | C. Goodyear, Dem. | 30 | |
| 15 | J. C. Griswold, Union. | 31 | H. Van Aernam, Union |
| 16 | O. Kellogg, Union. | | |

### Assemblymen Probably Elected.

First District—Jacob L. Smith, Dem.
Second District—Bryan Gaughan, Dem.
Third District—Geo. Leutrell, Dem.
Fourth District—Joel Sammis, Union.
Fifth District—Chas. T. Polhemus, Union.
Sixth District—Wm. Higgins, Union.
Seventh District—Thomas E. Stewart, Union.
Eighth District—Jacob Geebacher, Dem.
Ninth District—Samuel C. Reed, Union.
Tenth District—Patrick McGrave, Dem.
Eleventh District—Robert Usher, Union.
Twelfth District—Joseph A. Lyons, Dem.
Thirteenth District—Joel W. Mason, Union.
Fourteenth District—Michael N. Salmon, Dem.
Fifteenth District—Col. J. B. Van Buren, Union.
Sixteenth District—Henry Arcularius, Dem.
Seventeenth District—S. P. Ingraham, Jr. Union.
Union, 8; Dem. 9. Union gain of 6 over last year.

### County Ticket Election.

SHERIFF—John Kelly.
COUNTY CLERK—Wm. C. Conner, (probable.)
DISTRICT ATTORNEY—A. Oakey Hall.
CITY JUDGE—Abm. D. Russell.
SUPERVISOR—John Fox.
CORONERS—Cr. Schimer, Robert Gamble, John Wildey, Wm. C. Gover.

### THE TOTAL VOTE AND THE REGISTRY.

The following table shows the total vote in each of the wards of the city on President and its total registration. It will be readily seen that the wards, which polled such a heavy increase of the Democratic vote, are those in which the vote exceeds the registration—undoubtedly the work of fraud.

| Wards. | Total vote. | No. registered. |
|---|---|---|
| 1 | 2380 | 2122 |
| 2 | 524 | 603 |
| 3 | 727 | 993 |
| 4 | 2813 | 3162 |
| 5 | 3060 | 3457 |
| 6 | 3788 | 4142 |
| 7 | 5320 | 6138 |
| 8 | 4821 | 4992 |
| 9 | 7263 | 8057 |
| 10 | 4067 | 5010 |
| 11 | 7822 | 8731 |
| 12 | 3868 | 4228 |
| 13 | 3873 | 4629 |
| 14 | 5088 | 3829 |
| 15 | 4214 | 4670 |
| 16 | 6224 | 7099 |
| 17 | 10456 | 12756 |
| 18 | 7102 | 8283 |
| 19 | 5615 | 6779 |
| 20 | 7622 | 9409 |
| 21 | 6944 | 8306 |
| 22 | 6492 | 6877 |
| Total | 109,663 | 124,591 |

No returns have been received from two districts. The registration in six districts was not reported.

## NEW-YORK STATE.

### Kings County Election Returns.

| Wards. | Dis. | M'Clellan. | Lincoln. | Wards. | Dis. | M'Clellan. | Lincoln. |
|---|---|---|---|---|---|---|---|
| I. | 1 | 252 | 239 | | 5 | 173 | 336 |
| | 2 | 335 | 140 | XII. | 1 | 687 | 52 |
| II. | 1 | 400 | 96 | | 2 | 736 | 126 |
| | 2 | 653 | 257 | XIII. | 1 | 278 | 385 |
| III. | 1 | 208 | 311 | | 2 | 276 | 465 |
| | 2 | 290 | 398 | | 3 | 307 | 460 |
| | 3 | 207 | 478 | | 4 | 278 | 490 |
| IV. | 1 | 287 | 375 | XIV. | 1 | 575 | 90 |
| | 2 | 419 | 424 | | 2 | 532 | 280 |
| | 3 | 244 | 343 | | 3 | 376 | 176 |
| V. | 1 | 545 | 84 | | 4 | 247 | 218 |
| | 2 | 487 | 227 | XV. | 1 | — | — |
| V. | 3 | 402 | 242 | | 2 | 409 | 542 |
| | 4 | 469 | 203 | XVI. | 1 | — | — |
| VI. | 1 | 774 | 304 | | 2 | 368 | 415 |
| | 2 | 354 | 295 | | 3 | — | — |
| | 3 | 573 | 369 | | 4 | 548 | 241 |
| VII. | 1 | 317 | 232 | XVII. | 1 | 472 | 464 |
| | 2 | — | — | | 2 | 311 | 465 |
| | 3 | 240 | 238 | XVIII. | 1 | 261 | 163 |
| | 4 | 177 | 276 | | 2 | 209 | 260 |
| VIII. | 1 | 367 | 255 | XIX. | 1 | 120 | 152 |
| | 2 | 511 | 263 | | 2 | 183 | 333 |
| IX. | 1 | 741 | 260 | | 3 | 283 | 290 |
| | 2 | 240 | 215 | XX. | 1 | 150 | 235 |
| | 3 | 488 | 419 | | 2 | 242 | 532 |
| | 4 | 205 | 200 | | 3 | 332 | 451 |
| X. | 1 | 238 | 343 | | 4 | 167 | 240 |
| | 2 | 568 | 270 | New Lotts | | — | — |
| | 3 | 302 | 343 | Flatbush | | — | — |
| XI. | 1 | 351 | 351 | Flatlands | | — | — |
| | 2 | 538 | 213 | New Utrecht | | 299 | 126 |
| | 3 | 181 | 289 | Gravesend | | 136 | 98 |
| | 4 | 656 | 316 | | | — | — |
| Total | | | | | | 23,515 | 18,191 |

Flatbush, Lincoln 191; McClellan, 214.
Flatlands, Lincoln 164; McClellan 119.

The election in Brooklyn passed off quietly. Nothing whatever occurred to warrant the interference of the police authorities. A large vote was polled resulting in the election of the following officers:

Congress—2d District—Tunis G. Bergen, Dem.
Congress—3d District—James Humphrey, Rep., by about 300 majority.
Register—Hugh McLaughlin, Dem.
County Clerk—John J. White, Dem.
Coroner—James Devaucene, Dem.
Superintendent of Poor—Joseph Attebram, Dem.
Justice of Sessions—Stephen I. Voorhis, Dem.
Police Justice—James H. Cornwell, Dem., prob'ly.
Justice of Peace, First District—Michael Walsh, Dem.
Justice of Peace, Second District—James Buckley, Dem.
Assembly, First District—Jarvis Whitman, Dem.
Assembly, Second District—William D. Veeder, Dem.
Assembly, Third District—Stephen Haynes, Dem., probably.
Assembly, Fourth District—Patrick Burns, Dem.
Assembly, Fifth District—John Perry, Rep.
Assembly, Sixth District—Henry C. Boswell, Dem.
Assembly, Seventh District—Jacob Worth, Rep., probably.

ALDERMEN.

Second Ward—Daniel McLaughlin, Dem.
Fourth Ward—Lewis F. Newman, Dem.
Sixth Ward—George P. Willey, Rep., probably.
Eighth Ward—Joseph Wilson, Democrat.
Tenth Ward—Francis Kelly, Democrat.
Twelfth Ward—Dennis O'Keefe, Democrat.
Fourteenth Ward—Edward Murphy, Democrat, probably.
Sixteenth Ward—John A. Saal, Democrat.
Eighteenth Ward—Fred. W. Kalbfleisch, Democrat.
Twentieth Ward—John K. Bulmer, Republican.

SUPERVISORS.

First Ward—Alex. Maggrothy, Rep., probably.
Third Ward—John J. Studwell, Republican.
Fifth Ward—William H. Furey.
Seventh Ward—E. W. Bloom, Dem., probably.
Ninth Ward—George G. Herman, Democrat.
Eleventh Ward—John Lawrence, Dem., probably.
Thirteenth Ward—Charles W. Cheshire, probably.
Fifteenth Ward—Charles C. Talbott, Republican.
Seventeenth Ward—Stephen Clark, Republican.
Nineteenth Ward—Fred. W. Sholes, Republican.

RICHMOND COUNTY.

Middletown, Second District, 473 majority for McClellan, and 487 for Seymour.

Sixth Districts gave McClellan 1,058 majority.

The returns from Richmond County indicate that the Democrats have carried it by from 1,500 to 1,600 Democratic majority.

WESTCHESTER COUNTY.

West Farms—McClellan, 58 majority; Seymour 36; Radford, Dem., for Congress, 53 majority. Strong, Union, for Assembly, has 12 majority.

Yonkers gives McClellan, 233 majority; Seymour, 214 majority; Radford, Dem., for Congress, 194 majority.

Vote of New Rochelle complete. McClellan, 381; Lincoln, 239.

East Chester, First District, Lincoln, 269; McClellan 318. Fenton, 269; Seymour, 367. Radford, Democrat, for Congress has 97 majority. Second District, McClellan 92 majority.

Pelham 78 Union majority.
Tarrytown, 4 for Lincoln.
Beckmantown, McClellan 71 majority.
Machattan, 314 Democratic majority.
Peekskill, 22 Democratic majority.
Mamaroneck, McClellan's majority, 25; Seymour's 24.
Portchester—Dem. majority, 111; Seymour's, 108; Radford for Congress, 114.
Sing Sing gives McClellan 134 majority.
Brandreth, (Union,) is probably elected to the Assembly.

CHAUTAUQUA COUNTY.

Sheridan, 79 Union majority; Fenton, 92 majority.
Fredonia, 173 Lincoln majority; Fenton, 168 majority.
Randolph, Lincoln, 116 majority.
Jamestown, Lincoln, 649 majority.
Westfield, Lincoln, 231 majority.
Chautauqua, Lincoln, 172 majority.
Ripley, Lincoln, 92 majority.
Portland, Lincoln, 87 majority.
Forrestville, 47 Union majority.
Perrysburgh, 130 Union majority.

DUTCHESS COUNTY.

Pawlings, Lincoln 278; McClellan, 154; Fenton, for Governor, 281; Seymour, 150; Ketcham, (Rep.,) for Congress, 283; Nelson, (Dem.,) 145; Howard, (Rep.,) for Assembly, 284; Hopkins, (Dem.,) 144.

Rhinebeck, 86 Union majority; Fenton, 96 majority; Ketcham, Union, for Congress, 67 majority.

Poughkeepsie City—Lincoln's majority, 249; Fenton's majority, 247; Ketchum, (Union,) for Congress, 305 majority.

Armenia—Lincoln, 311; McClellan, 221; Fenton, 312; Seymour, 211; Ketcham, for Congress, Republican, 333; Nelson, for Congress, Democrat, 195.

North Salem—Lincoln, 236; McClellan, 110; Fenton, 236; Seymour, 110; Brandeth, Republican, 129 majority.

Northeast—McClellan, 188; Lincoln, 136; Seymour, 187; Fenton, 136; Nelson, Democrat, for Congress, 183; Ketchan, Republican, 236.

ALLEGANY COUNTY.

Cuba, Lincoln, 116 majority.
Belvidere, Lincoln, 14 majority.
Harsdale, Lincoln, 33 majority.
Angelica, Lincoln, 180 majority.
Phillipsville, 154 Union majority.
Frenchville, 122 Union majority.
Scio, 26 Union majority.
Alfred, 24 Union majority.
Andover, 210 Union majority.
Alleghany, 78 Democratic majority.

CATTARAUGUS COUNTY.

Little Valley, Lincoln 74 majority.

STEUBEN COUNTY.

Cameron, Lincoln, 127 majority.
Addison, Lincoln, 10 majority.
Canisheo, Lincoln, 174 majority.
Adrian, 76 Union majority.
Hornellsville, 65 Democratic majority.
Rathboneville, 76 Union majority.
Bath, 278 Republican majority. Fenton, 286.
Campbell, Rep., majority 176.
Condorton, Rep., majority 71.
Wayland, Dem., majority 79; Seymour 81.

ORANGE COUNTY.

Newburgh, 150 Union majority.
Goshen, 196 Dem. majority.
Blooming Grove, 123 Union majority.
Southfield, 55 Union majority.
Mount Hope, 40 Union majority.
Deerpark, 102 Dem. majority: Seymour, 112 majority; Winfield, Dem., for Congress, 76 majority.

TOMPKINS COUNTY.

Trumansburgh, 54 Union majority.
Ithaca, 43 Union majority.
Danbury, 150 Union majority.

CORTLAND COUNTY.

Homer, 480 Union majority.
Homer, 460 Union majority.
Cortland, 485 Union majority.
Scott, 172 Union majority.
Marsipoa, 125 Union majority.

ONONDAGA COUNTY.

Syracuse, 72 Union majority.

All three of the Union members of the Assembly are elected. Hon. I. T. Davis is reelected to Congress. Returns from towns give Union majorities as follows: Dewitt, 79; Fabius, 283; Gedder, 34; Lafayette, 55; two districts of Manlius, 224; Lysander 236; one district of Clay, 146; Camelius, 10; Union gain, 16. First district of Onondaga, 127; first district of Pompey, 64; Van Buren, 71; Spofford, first district, Lincoln's majority, 70; Fenton, 74. The county has given over 2,700 Union majority.

CHEMUNG COUNTY.

ELMIRA, Tuesday, Nov. 8.

This city goes Lincoln—162 majority.
Afton Union majority 80.
Bainbridge Union majority 150.
Sixteen towns give a Union majority of 1,190. The remaining towns will make it 1,350.

WYOMING COUNTY.

Athica, 14 Union majority.
Warsaw, Democratic majority, 170.
Wyoming County gives Lincoln 1,579 majority.

MONROE COUNTY.

Rochester City, complete, 62 Democratic majority. Union gain over last year 137 and 290 over 1862. Hart, Union, is elected to Congress.

LIVINGSTON COUNTY.

Lima, 59 Union majority.
Springwater, 270 Union majority.
Livonia, 219 Republican majority.
Leroy, Republican majority, 71.
Alexander, Union majority, 164.

ORLEANS COUNTY.

Two-thirds of the county give a gain for the Union ticket thus far over last year, when the majority in the county was 1,164. This indicates a majority in the county of 1,300.

SULLIVAN COUNTY.

Mount Hope 4 Democrat majority. The following is the vote for Gov.—Seymour 193; Fenton, 193—a tie. Morvin for assembly has one majority.

Cochecton, Democratic majority 293.

QUEENS COUNTY.

Newtown, Second District, Lincoln 218; McClellan, 353.

Flushing, McClellan, 365 majority; Seymour, 374 majority; Turner, (Democrat,) for Assembly, 331 majority; Faber, (Democrat,) for Congress, 300 majority; Hunter's Point, McClellan, 231 majority Seymour, 231 majority.

Jamaica—McClellan's majority 234; Seymour's, 237. Hempstead—Lincoln's majority 338.

Newtown, Dem. majority, 576.

North Hempstead, Union majority, Fenton, 109. Queens County complete will probably give 1,000 Dem. majority.

WAYNE COUNTY.

Palmyra, Union majority 40.
Arcadia, Second District, Union majority 78, Fenton 79.
Walworth, Union majority 179.
Marion, Union majority 326.
Savannah, Union majority, 122.
Fenton's majority, 119.
Rutler, Union majority, 104.
Lyons, Democratic majority, 94.
Arcadia, third district, McClellan majority, 15.
Williamson, Union majority, 195.
Macedon, Union majority, 108.

GENESEE COUNTY.

Batavia, Union majority 117, Fenton 121 majority.

MADISON COUNTY.

Lennox, Union majority 209.
Hamilton, Lincoln 291; McClellan 135. Fenton 293; Seymour 136.
Eaton, Union majority 138; Union gain 23.
Brookfield, Lincoln, 577; McClellan, 348. Fenton, 578; Seymour, 350.

ST. LAWRENCE COUNTY.

Potsdam, 786 Union majority.
Lawrence, 364 Union majority.
Oswegatchie, 275 Union majority.
Madrid, 267 Union majority.
These towns show a Union gain of 75 over last year.
Chateauquay, 20 Dem., majority; Union gain, 64.
Constable, 62 Lincoln majority; Union gain 63.

ERIE COUNTY.

Official returns from 16 out of 25 towns in this county give 1,098 Democratic majority against 685 Republican majority; nine towns yet to hear from. Democratic majority in the county will be from 500 to 600.

Tonawanda, McClellan, 353; Lincoln, 171.

The Democratic majority in Erie County will be about 400 or a trifle less. The towns of Clarence and Newstead give about 250 Republican gain, which uses up the Democratic gains in the strong towns.

Alden, Democratic majority, 114; Seymour, 109.
Perry, Union majority, 330.

COLOMBIA COUNTY.

Hudson City—210 Democratic majority.
The Town of Claversack—4 Democratic majority, a Union gain of 57.
Greenport—39 Democratic, a Union gain of 35.
Stockport—69 Union majority, a Union gain of 26.
Gallatin—51 Union majority.
Ghent—69 Union majority, a Union gain of 65.
Germantown—47 Union majority, a Union gain of 51.
Livingston—3 Union majority.
Laghkanic—148 Democratic majority.
Hillsdale—26 Democratic majority.
Copake—14 Democratic majority.
Ancram—53 Democratic majority.
New-Lebanon—Democratic majority, 31.
Town of Ghent—McClellan, 246; Lincoln, 333; Seymour, 267; Fenton, 331.
Town of Austerlitz—Lincoln, 214; McClellan, 140. Fenton, 212; Seymour, 143.

RENSSELAER COUNTY.

City of Troy—Democratic majority, 758.
Berlin—Union majority, 2.
Schaghticoke—Union majority, 13.
Poistenkill—Democratic majority, 55.
Brunswick—Union majority, 3.
Lansingburg—Union majority, 277.
Greenbush—Democratic majority, 261.
Schodack—Democratic majority, 116.
Sandlake, First District, Union majority, 69.
North Greenbush, Dem. majority, 59.
Grafton, Union majority, 73.
Troy city complete. McClellan over Lincoln, 788. Seymour over Fenton, 802. Van Alstyne, (Dem.,) for Congress, over Griswold, 713. Democratic Assembly, Bartlett by 650 majority.

McClellan's majority in this county is probably 300. A portion of the Republican county ticket is probably elected. Griswold is elected to Congress in the district of Rensselaer over Van Alstyne.

ONEIDA COUNTY.

Rome, 471 majority for McClellan, Seymour's 475, Kernan for Congress 469.

Utica City—Democratic majority, 259; Union gain over last year, 21.

Oneida County will give Lincoln from 1,300 to 1,500 majority, and Fenton 100 better. Roscoe Conkling (Union) has probably 800 majority for Congress, defeating Francis Kernan, the present member. For Assembly, A. B. Weaver and T. D. Penfield, Democratic, and Lorenzo Rowe and G. W. Cole, Union, are elected.

HERKIMER COUNTY.

German Flats, Union majority 6, Fenton 10.
Herkimer, Democratic majority 164.
Richfield, Union majority 126.
Warren, Democratic majority 40.
Columbia, Union majority 94.
Stark, Union majority 49.
Little Falls, Democratic majority 228.
Manheim, Democratic majority 60.

MONTGOMERY COUNTY.

St. Johnsville, Democratic majority 95.
Winden, Union majority 81.
Canajoharie, Democratic majority 11.
Root, Democratic majority 172.
Palestine, Democratic majority 156.
Mohawk, Democratic majority 53.
Amsterdam, Union majority 125.

OSWEGO COUNTY.

Oswego City and ten towns in the county, give a Union majority of 1,702. The remainder will probably increase this to 2,500. Three Union members of Assembly are elected.

FRANKLIN COUNTY.

Malone, 523 Union majority; gain over 1860 of 260.

OSWEGO COUNTY.

Volney, Union majority, 109.
Granby, Union majority, 102.
Palermo, Union majority, 264.
Schroppel, Union majority, 73

BROOME COUNTY.

Lisle, 270 Union majority.
Triangle, 160 Union majority.

SCHENECTADY COUNTY.

City of Schenectady, Democratic majority 229.

CHENANGO COUNTY.

Greene, Democratic majority 23.
Oxford, Union majority 34; Fenton's majority 37.
Norwich, Union majority 3; Fenton's majority 10.
Sherburne, Lincoln 457; McClellan 312.
Smyrna, Lincoln 318; McClellan 82.
Columbus, Lincoln 266; McClellan 60. Fenton 265; Seymour 62.

ALBANY COUNTY.

Albany City—The vote in this city is as follows: McClellan, 7,540; Lincoln, 5,066. Majority for McClellan, 2,476. Seymour, 7,541; Fenton, 5,078. Seymour's majority 2,463. The Democrats elect three of the four members of Assembly. Goodyear, (Dem.,) for Congress, has about the same majority as Seymour.

SCHOHARIE.

Wright, Democratic majority, 73; Seymour, 78.
Fulton, Democratic majority, 256.
Middleburgh, Democratic majority, 241.
Broome, Democratic majority, 18.

ULSTER COUNTY.

Kingston—Democratic majority, 526; majority Seymour, 511.

PUTNAM COUNTY.

Four towns give Lincoln 78 majority and Seymour 79. The Dem. majority in the county will be about 250.

Town of Patterson, Lincoln, 90 majority; Fenton, 100 majority; Larkin, for Congress, 80 majority; Penny, (Rep.,) for Assembly, 131 majority.

Town of Southeast: McClellan, 26 majority; Radford, 28 majority.

DELAWARE COUNTY.

Tomphins—Union majority, 115; Fenton's, 114. Gain of 46.
Sanford—Dem. majority, 3.

SUFFOLK COUNTY.

River Head, Union majority, 79.
Southold, Union majority, 164.
Southampton, Union majority, 283.
Easthampton, Union majority, 9.
Shelter Island, Union majority, 26.

SENECA COUNTY.

Seneca Falls, Democratic majority, 200.
Waterloo, Democratic majority, 171.

CAYUGA COUNTY.

Auburn City, Union majority, 281.

ULSTER COUNTY.

Saugerties, McClellan, 123 majority; Democratic gain, 89. Seymour, 60 majority. Bubbell, Democrat, for Congress, is elected. Booksleaver, Democrat, for Assembly, is elected.

SCHOHARIE COUNTY.

Experience gives 63 Republican majority.

SCHENECTADY COUNTY

Complete, gives McClellan 62 majority. The Republican county ticket is elected. Page, Democrat, for Congress, has 50 majority. Stanfield, Union, for Assembly, is probably elected.

DUTCHESS COUNTY.

Complete gives Lincoln 559 majority. Fenton, 725 majority. Ketchum, Union, for Congress 860 majority, electing him by over 1,000 in the district over Nelson, the present incumbent. Howard and Nilbur, both Union, all elected to the Legislature.

### The State—Reported and Estimated.

| | Lincoln. | | McClellan. |
|---|---|---|---|
| Chatauqua | 5,000 | New-York | 36,857 |
| Allegany | 3,500 | Kings | 4,300 |
| Orleans | 1,400 | Albany | 2,500 |
| Monroe | 1,050 | Richmond | 1,500 |
| Columbia | 200 | Schoharie | 1,500 |
| Delaware | 1,000 | Ulster | 800 |
| Suffolk | 300 | Herkimer | 1,200 |
| Livingston | 2,000 | Rensselear | 500 |
| Cortland | 2,200 | Erie | 550 |
| Onondaga | 2,800 | Queens | 1,500 |
| Broome | 2,100 | Seneca | 500 |
| Wayne | 2,000 | Schenedtady | 62 |
| Madison | 2,800 | Sullivan | 500 |
| Montgomery | 200 | Westchester | 2,100 |
| Genesee | 1,500 | Rockland | 1,000 |
| Oswego | 2,500 | Putnam | 400 |
| Franklin | 1,000 | Green | 800 |
| St. Lawrence | 7,000 | Orange | 200 |
| Chenango | 1,350 | | 55,369 |
| Oneida | 1,400 | | |
| Wyoming | 1,579 | | |
| Cayuga | 3,200 | | |
| Steuben | 2,000 | | |
| Washington | 2,200 | | |
| Jefferson | 2,500 | | |
| Cattaraugus | 2,000 | | |
| Essex | 1,000 | | |
| Lewis | 500 | | |
| Ontario | 1,300 | | |
| Saratoga | 1,000 | | |
| Schuyler | 500 | | |
| Tioga | 800 | | |
| Tompkins | 1,300 | | |
| Yates | 1,000 | | |
| Otsego | 600 | | |
| Warren | 500 | | |
| Dutchess | 550 | | |
| Niagara | 500 | | |
| Clinton | 200 | | |
| Chemung | 200 | | |
| Fulton and H | 200 | | |
| Total | 66,129 | | |

## NEW-JERSEY.

MILBURN, N. J., Tuesday, Nov. 8.

Lincoln, 141; McClellan, 88.

Theodore Little, (Union,) for Congress, 141; Andrew J. Rogers, (Dem.,) 89.

Legislature—Rufus F. W. Harrison, (Union,) 142; Joel D. Mead, (Dem.,) 88.

SUMMIT, N. J., Tuesday, Nov. 8.

New-Providence township gives Lincoln 98; McClellan, 136.

For Congress—Charles Scranton, Union, 97; Charles Sitgreaves, Dem., 137.

For Assembly—Joseph T. Crowell, Union, 96; Scudder, Dem., 138.

Delaware Township, in Camden County, Union majority, 97; gain, 52.

Morris Township, McClellan 80 majority. Rogers, Dem., for Congress, 53 majority. Treadwell, Dem., for Assembly, 48 majority.

Mercer County, West Windsor Township, Dem. 166; Rep. 150.

Elizabeth City—Democratic majority, 265. Rahway City gives 113 majority to the Union ticket. Plainfield—Union majority, 162. Cape Island—One township gives 88 Union majority.

Chatham Township, McClellan 9 majority. Little, Union, for Congress, 2 majority. For Assembly, Democratic 19.

Mendham Township, in Morris County, Lincoln 10 majority; Little, 18 majority; Gage, Union, for Assembly, 36 majority.

Newark—Full returns from four wards give a Union majority of 108.

Newark—Later—Nine out of fourteen wards show a Republican gain of 358. The Democrats carry the city by reduced majorities.

Morris, Union and Essex Counties—The returns show indecisive Republican gains.

Springfield—McClellan, 25 majority; Sitgreaves, Democrat, for Congress, 25 majority; Scudder, Democrat, for Assembly, 7 majority.

Returns from Pequannock, Morris County, are as follows:

Lincoln 259 majority.
Little, (Republican,) for Congress, 362 majority.

GLOUCESTER COUNTY.

Two townships give 156 Union majority.

CUMBERLAND COUNTY.

Melville, Union majority, 115. Stave, for Congress, 111.

NEWARK, Tuesday, Nov. 8.

Essex County has gone Union by over 150, making a Union gain of over 1,000 over last year. The Legislative delegation is six Union to three Democrats.

Camden County, 500 Union majority.
Trenton, 255 Democratic majority.
Bordentown, 146 Democratic majority.
Middlesex gives a Democratic majority of 775.
New-Brunswick gives McClellan 146 majority.

MERCER COUNTY.

McClellan's majority, 110; Middleton for Congress 91 majority.

Trenton—McClellan's majority, 255; Democratic Assemblyman, 117 majority. The whole Democratic County ticket is elected.

CAMDEN COUNTY.

Union majority, 360.

CUMBERLAND COUNTY.

Union majority, 400.

BURLINGTON, Wednesday, Nov. 9—A. M.

BURLINGTON COUNTY.—Wright, Union, is elected Senator. Stockton, Healings, Quick and Lathrop, all Union, are elected to the Assembly. Union gain in the Senate, 1; in the Assembly, 3. The county gives 1,800 Union majority.

## PENNSYLVANIA.

### GLORIOUS PHILADELPHIA.

*Special Dispatch to the National Union Committee.*

PHILADELPHIA, Tuesday, Nov. 8.

Philadelphia gives LINCOLN 11,000 majority—4,000 gain on October. Lancaster 5,400 majority—1,400 gain on October. Pittsburgh large gains.

### FROM HARRISBURGH.

Dispatch from Gen. Cameron.

HARRISBURGH, Tuesday, Nov. 8.

*Hon. H. J. Raymond:*

Returns indicate large Union gains in the State. S. CAMERON.

CHESTER COUNTY.

Nine districts shows Union gain of 120.


*(Continued on the Eighth Page.)*

# The New-York Times.

VOL. XIV......NO. 4194. NEW-YORK, SUNDAY, MARCH 5, 1865. PRICE FOUR CENTS.


## THE INAUGURATION.

### A Stormy Morning but a Clear Afternoon.

### THE PROCESSION TO THE CAPITOL.

### Imposing Display---Enthusiasm Among the People.

### THE INAUGURATION CEREMONIES.

### Vice-President Johnson Sworn in by Mr. Hamlin.

### President Lincoln takes the Oath for the Second Term.

### HIS INAUGURAL ADDRESS.

### The Changes of Four Years---Both Sides Disappointed at the Length of the War.

### THE SITUATION VERY HOPEFUL.

### Our Object a Just and Lasting Peace Among Ourselves and with Others.

**The Inauguration of President Lincoln.**
Dispatches to the Associated Press.
WASHINGTON, Saturday, March 4.

The procession is now forming, though a heavy rain is falling, and the streets are almost impassable with mud.

The avenue is filled with a dense mass of people.

The ceremonies will take place in the Senate Chamber.

SECOND DISPATCH.

The procession reached the Capitol at about quarter to twelve o'clock, escorting the President elect.

At a subsequent period, the President and Vice-President, together with the Justices of the Supreme Court, Members and Ex-Members of Congress, Foreign Ministers, and other persons of distinction, assembled in the Senate Chamber.

There the Vice-President elect took the oath of office, preceding it by an address.

Chief Justice CHASE administered the oath of office on the eastern portico, when the President delivered his Inaugural Address.

There was a very large attendance, and the scene was one of marked interest.

THIRD DISPATCH.

The rain has ceased, and the procession is now passing down the avenue. This display is exceedingly grand. The sidewalks are jammed with people, and every window and house-top was filled with ladies and gentlemen, who are waving handkerchiefs and hats with great enthusiasm.

The visiting Philadelphia Fire Department and ours, attract great attention by their beautifully adorned apparatus.

Many bands of music are interspersed throughout the whole procession, and the line is one continual ring of music.

The *Chronicle* is represented in the procession by a large truck with a press upon it printing a *Chronicle Junior*, and scattering them to the dense mass of humanity.

The procession was one hour passing a given point, and the length of it is probably over a mile.

The Navy-yard delegation has a monitor in line, with the turret turning.

The streets are almost in an impassable condition, which makes the display not as magnificent as it would have been, though it is exceedingly beautiful.

One feature in the procession is the colored troops and the Odd-Fellows, with their band of music.

FOURTH DISPATCH.

The weather has cleared off bright and beautiful.

The President and others reached the platform. The band played "Hail to the Chief." Salutes were fired, and the President was cheered by an immense throng, composed of civilians and the military.

After delivering the Inaugural Address he was again cheered, salutes were fired, and the band played.

#### THE INAUGURAL ADDRESS.

*Fellow-Countrymen:*

At this second appearing to take the oath of the Presidential office, there is less occasion for an extended address than there was at the first. Then a statement somewhat in detail of a course to be pursued seemed very fitting and proper. Now, at the expiration of four years, during which public declarations have been constantly called forth on every point and phase of the great contest which still absorbs the attention and engrosses the energies of the nation, little that is new could be presented.

The progress of our arms, upon which all else chiefly depends, is as well known to the public as to myself, and it is, I trust, reasonably satisfactory and encouraging to all. With high hope for the future, no prediction in regard to it is ventured.

On the occasion corresponding to this four years ago, all thoughts were anxiously directed to an impending civil war. All dreaded it; all sought to avoid it. While the inaugural address was being delivered from this place, devoted altogether to saving the Union without war, insurgent agents were in the city seeking to destroy it without war—seeking to dissolve the Union and divide the effects by negotiation. Both parties deprecated war, but one of them would make war rather than let the nation survive, and the other would accept war rather than let it perish, and the war came.

One-eighth of the whole population were colored slaves, not distributed generally over the Union, but localized in the Southern part of it. These slaves constituted a peculiar and powerful interest. All knew that this interest was somehow the cause of the war. To strengthen, perpetuate and extend this interest, was the object for which the insurgents would rend the Union by war, while the Government claimed no right to do more than to restrict the territorial enlargement of it.

Neither party expected for the war the magnitude or the duration which it has already attained. Neither anticipated that the cause of the conflict might cease, or even before the conflict itself should cease. Each looked for an easier triumph, and a result less fundamental and astounding.

Both read the same Bible and pray to the same God, and each invokes His aid against the other. It may seem strange that any men should dare to ask a just God's assistance in wringing their bread from the sweat of other men's faces, but let us judge not, that we be not judged. The prayers of both should not be answered. That of neither has been answered fully. The Almighty has his own purposes. Woe unto the world because of offences, for it must needs be that offences come, but woe to that man by whom the offence cometh. If we shall suppose that American slavery is one of these offences, which in the Providence of God must needs come, but which having continued through His appointed time, He now wills to remove, and that He gives to both North and South this terrible war as the woe due to those by whom the offence came. Shall we discern there is any departure from those Divine attributes which the believers in a living God always ascribe to him? Fondly do we hope, fervently do we pray, that this mighty scourge of war may speedily pass away. Yet, if God wills that it continue until all the wealth piled by the bondman's two hundred and fifty years of unrequited toil shall be sunk, and until every drop of blood drawn with the lash shall be paid by another drawn with the sword, as was said three thousand years ago; so, still it must be said, that the judgments of the Lord are true and righteous altogether.

With malice toward none, with charity for all, with firmness in the right, as God gives us to see right, let us finish the work we are in, to bind up the nation's wounds, to care for him who shall have borne the battle and for his widow and his orphans, to do all which may achieve and cherish a just and a lasting peace among ourselves and with all nations.

#### ANOTHER ACCOUNT.

WASHINGTON, Saturday, March 4.

President LINCOLN was inaugurated for another term of four years at twelve o'clock, noon, to-day.

Overhead the weather was clear and beautiful, and on account of the recent rains the streets were filled with mud. Despite this fact the crowd that assembled was exceedingly large, and thousands proceeded to the capital to witness the inauguration ceremonies.

The procession moved from Sixteenth-street and Pennsylvania-avenue at about 11 o'clock.

President LINCOLN had been at the capital all day, and consequently did not accompany the procession to the scene of the interesting ceremonies.

Several bands of music, two regiments of the Invalid Corps, a squadron of cavalry, a battery of artillery, and four companies of colored troops, formed the military escort.

The Mayor and Councilmen of Washington, visiting Councilmen from Baltimore, the firemen of this city and the visiting firemen from Philadelphia, the Good Will, Franklin and Perseverance companies, each company drawing its engine along, were also in the procession.

Among the benevolent societies present were Lodges of Odd Fellows and Masons, including a colored Lodge of the latter fraternity.

The public and principal private buildings along Pennsylvania-avenue were gaily decorated with flags, and every window was thronged with faces to catch a glimpse of the President elect.

The oath to protect and maintain the Constitution of the United States, was administered to Mr. LINCOLN by Chief-Justice CHASE, in the presence of thousands, who witnessed the interesting ceremony while standing in mud almost knee-deep.

The Inaugural was then read, after which a national salute was fired by a battery stationed east of the Capitol.

The procession then again moved up Pennsylvania-avenue, the President being conveyed in an open barouche. Seated with him was his son and Senator FOSTER, of the Committee of Arrangements.

The President was escorted to the White House; after which, the procession separated.

Everything passed off in a most quiet and orderly manner, and although thousands participated in the ceremonies, not an accident occurred to mar the pleasures of the day.

#### FROM MISSISSIPPI.

**Gen. Forrest Recounts his Exploits—He Warns his Soldiers to Prepare for Renewed Action.**

CAIRO, Friday, March 3.

The Jackson, Miss., papers of the 18th ult. contain an address of the rebel Gen. FORREST to his troops, recounting the result of his operations during the past year. He says they have fought fifty battles, killed and captured sixteen thousand of the enemy, captured two thousand horses and mules, sixty-seven pieces of artillery, fourteen transports, twenty barges, three hundred wagons, fifty ambulances, one hundred and five stands of arms, forty blockhouses, destroyed thirty-six railroad bridges, two thousand miles of railroad, six locomotives, and one hundred cars, amounting to fifteen millions of property.

In accomplishing this he admits they were occasionally sustained by other troops, but says their regular number never exceeded five thousand. Two thousand had been killed or wounded and two thousand taken prisoners.

He tells them to prepare for renewed actions and warns them against being allured by syren songs of peace, for there can be no peace save upon their seperate independent nationality.

The river is still rapidly rising here. Much of the low land between Cairo, Mound City, and portions of the latter place are submerged, interfering with operations on ships and Navy-yard.

Hon. F. C. COLLIETT, Assistant Special Agent of the Transportation Department at Memphis, has been appointed Supervisor and Special Agent for the first special agency, comprising that part of the Mississippi Valley lying west of the Allegheny Mountains, east of the mouth of the Tennessee, and extending south to such parts of Alabama, Georgia, North Carolina and Virginia as is, or shall be occupied by the national forces operating from the North.

Gen. GHOLSON is in command of all the rebel military prisoners in Georgia, Alabama and Mississippi.

Great scarcity of breadstuffs is said to exist. RODDY's division has been breaking up distilleries so that grain may be procured by suffering families and soldiers. Whisky is regarded as a worse enemy than the Yankees.

Gen. WIRT ADAMS has ordered all gins and cotton on the Big Black River to be removed.

#### Contemplated Rebel Raid on Oswego and Rochester.

OSWEGO, Saturday, March 4.

Maj. GRANT has received a dispatch from Gov. FENTON stating that the War Department at Washington had received information from Halifax that the rebels in the provinces are contemplating a raid on Oswego and Rochester. A public meeting is to be held in this city this afternoon to take such action in the matter as may be necessary.

#### Dry Goods Sale.

PHILADELPHIA, Saturday, March 4.

An immense sale of dry goods will take place here on March 9, when MYERS & Co. will dispose of 2,000 entire cases of domestic and foreign dry goods for cash.

#### Salute Fired in Boston.

BOSTON, Saturday, March 4.

A salute was fired at noon to-day and bells rung in honor of the late victories, and the inauguration of President LINCOLN. A heavy rain-storm prevails.

## ADJOURNMENT OF CONGRESS.

### Both Houses in Session All Night.

### The Army Appropriation Bill Finally Passed.

### Pay to the Illinois Central Railroad Refused.

### The Bankrupt Bill Passed Over Without Notice.

### Disagreement on the Civil Appropriation Bill.

### THE BILL DEFEATED FOR WANT OF TIME.

### CLOSING SCENES IN BOTH HOUSES.

### Reorganization and Extra Session of the Senate.

Special Dispatches to the New-York Times.
WASHINGTON, Saturday, March 4.

CLOSING SCENES IN CONGRESS.

[The following is the continuation of the dispatch published in Saturday morning's TIMES.—ED.]

At 6 o'clock and five minutes A. M., another motion for a recess is made, but the House still refuse and grumble audibly at the Senate for its delay.

Gen. SCHENCK, from the Military Committee, then made a report upon the subject of the order which requires colored men to have passes before they can leave the District of Columbia. It was accompanied by a joint resolution declaring the order an improper practice, and requesting its abrogation. Discussion followed, but the Democrats are mostly asleep, and he resolution is adopted.

At 6:35 A. M., it is announced that the Senate has finished the "omnibus," having loaded it down with new amendments, rendering the labors of the Conference Committee herculean. Three of the most energetic members of the House are appointed to meet the elephant. HENRY WINTER DAVIS, D. C., LITTLEJOHN, and JAMES S. ROLLINS; and they go at it.

A few more unimportant matters come up; are speedily disposed of, and at 7:15 A. M., the House takes a recess until 9 A. M.

The scene in the Senate during the small hours of the night was interesting, and many times amusing. Eight patriotic ladies in the gallery bravely kept their bright eyes beaming upon the Senators until day-dawn, while fifty or sixty male spectators listened, slept and yawned in the gentlemens' gallery.

SECOND DISPATCH.

9 A. M.—My dispatch for this morning's edition of the TIMES left off as the clock, which is my *vis-a vis*, pointed the hour of 4 A. M. But the proceedings of the two Houses did not leave off there, by any means. The House had cleared the Speaker's desk of all important bills and amused itself by acting on unfinished business going over to the next session, while the members impatiently awaited the issue between the Senate and the House on the Miscellaneous Appropriation Bill.

At 5:35 A. M., the Committee of Conference reported another disagreement on the clause of the Army Appropriation Bill relating to the Illinois Central Rail road. The Senate would hear to nothing but striking out the clause which singles out this road as an exception to the general rule of payment. Mr. MORRILL moved that the House recede, as a last resort, pending which, several fiery speeches were made, but the motion prevailed, 62 to 47.

The time, thence to 3:45 A. M., was spent on various small bills coming up from the Speaker's tables, or reports of Conference Committee coming in.

Mr. STEVENS then moved a recess until 9 A. M., but it was voted down, because it gave no time for the appointment and meeting of the committee, which was the only hope of saving the important bill which the Senate had been laboring on all night.

The business on the Speaker's desk was proceeded with. Mr. SUMNER's bill, providing that color shall not be a disqualification for carrying the mails, when last before the House, was dropped from want of a quorum vote with the previous question pending. It came up now under the operation of the previous question, and was finally passed with few or no dissenting votes.

8 A. M.—The Appropriation Bill was most severely handled in the Senate, much to the disgust of the most earnest member there. Mr. SHERMAN, who finally gave up all hope of saving anything of the bill, save the light-house appropriations, and a few other commercial matters. Millions of dollars were added in various appropriations, but the great sticking point was the Winter Davis military arrest amendment. The Senate, after rejecting a substitute, rather milder in its form, offered by Mr. TRUMBULL, finally resolved to strike it it out entirely. Among other things adopted in Committee of the Whole was a proposition which was soon recognized as an old customer, to wit: To purchase for each member of Congress one set of certain volumes of Congressional debates of sessions twenty or thirty years ago. This is known as the "Seaton Job," and would involve an expense of many thousands of dollars, and was rejected last Winter. It went through the Committee of the Whole, but when amendments came up for final adoption, Mr. CLARK demanded a separate vote on this, and it was rejected. The proposition to pay $1,000,000 to Missouri for expenses incurred in arming her militia, and $700,000 to Pennsylvania to reimburse her for moneys expended in repelling EARLY's last invasion, were also tacked on. Indeed, the majority of the Senate seemed to think no demand too enormous, and at least $7,000,000 or $8,000,000 were thus arranged for when it was positively certain that there was not a moment's time for a proper scrutiny of these items. To the credit of Senator SHERMAN be it said, that he protested earnestly against this style of legislation, but it was of no avail. At length the Senate consented to forego any further patchwork, and the Committee of Conference was soon at work on it. The Senate, at 7:15, then took a recess until 10 o'clock.

10 A. M.—The House did not meet very promptly, an hour and a half being too little time for members to get breakfast, and to refresh themselves for the duties of the day. It must be said that they bore the trying ordeal of the night with a far greater degree of equanimity, good feeling, and dignity than is usual on such occasions. It was reserved for the closing hour of the session to give birth to a series of disgraceful proceedings, and to perpetrate, at the very last moment of the constitutionally limited term, a scene of partisan filibustering that should cause shame and humiliation in the hearts of every one who promoted it.

At 10:20 A. M., Mr. HENRY WINTER DAVIS made a report from the Committee on Conference on the Miscellaneous Appropriation Bill, and reported that the committee had compromised everything but the section known as the Winter Davis Amendment; that could not be surmounted. The Senate insisted that it should not pass as a part of that bill, as that was no place for it; that body would be willing to receive it as a separate proposition, though the committee doubted if, in the present temper of the Senate on the subject, it could pass.

The House Committee are willing to make it a separate matter, but as they have no hope of effecting its passage in that way, Mr. DAVIS moves that the House insist, and on that motion makes a speech, which brings applause from the Democratic side. Mr. LITTLEJOHN, also a member of the Committee of Conference, speaks to the same effect, and the ball opens.

It is twenty minutes to eleven. The Democrats, headed mainly by Mr. ELDRIDGE, of Wisconsin, distinguished for nothing except the guerrilla warfare he has carried on against all Government measures, show signs of mischief.

Mr. ELDRIDGE rises in his seat and moves to adjourn.

The motion is declared out of order by Mr. GARFIELD, who is in the chair.

A motion is made to recede from the amendment, and the previous question demanded, and seconded, so the Chair states, when a message from the President (who is in his room in the Capitol, and where he seldom comes except on such an occasion as this,) is announced, and he communicates the fact that he has signed certain important bills.

Now comes confusion. Mr. ELDRIDGE says the previous question, which was pending, was not seconded.

Mr. COLFAX, (resuming the chair,) settles the matter, when Mr. PENDLETON moves to adjourn, on which Mr. ELDRIDGE demands the ayes and noes, and the demand being sustained, the clerk calls the roll.

It is eleven o'clock; the clerk proceeds rapidly, and at twenty minutes past eleven it is announced that the House will not adjourn.

Mr. ELDRIDGE moves to reconsider the vote by which the House refused to adjourn, and on that motion demands the ayes and noes; the demand is again sustained, and the clerk again calls the roll.

At eleven forty it is announced that the House refuses to reconsider.

Mr. KASSON, of Iowa, with characteristic good sense and a sincere desire to bring this matter to a conclusion, begs that unanimous consent may be given to strike out everything in the bill but the appropriations for the deaf and dumb and for the light-houses, for if these fail there will be suffering, shipwreck and loss of life.

This meets with a sentiment of apparent favor; but Mr. WINTER DAVIS rises in his seat, and says: "Mr. Speaker, I am in earnest, and not a single item of this bill shall pass if this amendment does not."

Mr. LITTLEJOHN says: "I agree with my colleague; the whole of the bill shall pass, or none."

It is now 11:45. The Conference Committee on the paper duty question make a report, fixing the duty at ten cents; and on a motion to recede from the House proposition to fix it at three cents, the yeas and nays are demanded, and the clerk once more calls the roll.

It is ten minutes of twelve. The call proceeds the clear sharp voice of the clerk ringing out above the confusion in the hall. And as the dial indicates the hour of twelve, the speaker orders the call suspended, and the term of the Thirty-eighth Congress expires, by constitutional limitation, in the midst of a call of the ayes and noes.

The Appropriation Bill is thus lost. Missouri and Pennsylvania get no reimbursements for militia expenses; the deaf and dumb starve; the light-houses are no beacon to the mariner; a hundred useful and necessary, and a few very suspicious and unworthy objects, are thus thrown overboard.

But perhaps it is best this Congress neglected its duty early in the session, or else this bill would have had ample consideration.

Speaker COLFAX rises from his chair, and the hall and galleries are breathless. In a brief but most felicitous speech, he returns thanks for the compliment paid him in the resolution of last evening, to the members for their courtesy, and with an eloquent allusion to the ceremony of the inauguration, which they are about to witness, he declares the House of Representatives of the Thirty-eighth Congress adjourned *sine die*.

## THIRTY-EIGHTH CONGRESS.

### SECOND SESSION.

### SENATE.

WASHINGTON, Saturday, March 4.

The following is a continuation of the Senate proceedings from the point where they broke off at an early hour this morning:

CIVIL APPROPRIATION BILL.

The debate being long-continued on the Civil Appropriation Bill,

Mr. GRIMES, of Iowa, (Union,) interrupted Mr. COWAN, who was speaking, and intimated that Mr. COWAN, as a member of the Committee on Finance, charged with the management of this bill, was endangering its passage.

Mr. CLARK, of New-Hampshire, (Union) warned the Senate that lengthened discussion would soon prove fatal to the bill, and begged that the question might be taken on its passage. It was now nearly three o'clock, and the bill was to be engrossed, and much business had yet to be concluded. He hoped the Senate would come to a vote at once.

The Civil Appropriation Bill was then informally laid aside.

ENROLLMENT BILL PASSED.

Mr. WILSON, of Massachusetts, (Union,) made a report from the Committee of Conference on the Amendatory Enrollment Bill, which was concurred in.

TRIALS BY COURT-MARTIAL.

Mr. TRUMBULL, of Illinois, (Union,) then took the floor upon the amendment of Mr. LANE, of Indiana, to the Civil Appropriation bill, and offered a further amendment to include persons "employed" as well as "drafted or enlisted" who should be subject to trial by court-martial.

This was adopted.

The amendment as thus amended was then agreed to by yeas 22, nays 13, as follows:

YEAS—Messrs. Anthony, Brown, Chandler, Clark, Conness, Doolittle, Farwell, Foster, Grimes, Harlan, Harris, Howard, Lane of Indiana, Morgan, Morrill, Nye, Ramsey, Sherman, Stewart, Sumner, Wilkinson and Wilson—22.

NAYS—Messrs. Buckalew, Cowan, Hale, Hendricks, Johnson, McDougal, Nesmith, Powell, Riddle, Sprague, Trumbull, Van Winkle and Wade—13.

So the section was stricken out.

ARMY APPROPRIATION BILL.

Mr. HARRIS, of New-York, (Union,) here obtained leave to make a report of the Committee of Conference on the Army Appropriation Bill, saying the Senate Committee could not agree with the House Committee.

The Senate insisted on its action.

PENNSYLVANIA CLAIMS.

Mr. COWAN offered an amendment to the pending bill, the Civil or "Omnibus" Appropriation Bill, providing for the claim of Pennsylvania for money paid to the troops of that State, called out in 1863 to oppose the advance of Gen. LEE.

The amendment was adopted, by yeas 18, nays 16.

REPAIRS TO THE NAVAL ACADEMY.

An amendment was offered by Mr. GRIMES, providing for repairs at the Naval Academy at Annapolis, which was adopted.

NAVIGATION OF LAKE MICHIGAN.

Mr. CHANDLER, of Michigan, (Union,) offered an amendment appropriating $84,000 for improving the navigation of Lake Michigan, which was lost.

CIVIL APPROPRIATION BILL PASSED.

After acting upon several minor amendments, the bill was passed at 6 o'clock A. M.

EXECUTIVE SESSION.

After the passage of several private bills, at 6:45 A. M. the Senate went into Executive Session.

WASHINGTON, Saturday, March 4.

The Senate reassembled at 10 o'clock.

THREE-CENT PIECES.

Mr. CLARK called up a bill to authorize the coinage of three-cent pieces and for other purposes, which was passed.

THE ARKANSAS SENATORS.

Mr. LANE, of Kansas, at 11 o'clock moved to take up a resolution for the admission of Senators from Arkansas.

Mr. SUMNER objected, and the resolution was not taken up.

EXTENDING COMMITTEES.

Mr. SPRAGUE, called up the joint resolution from the House authorizing the Committee on Commerce of both Houses, to sit after the 4th of March to investigate the subject of trade with the rebel States.

Mr. POWELL said the present Congress had no right to provide for the sitting of a committee after 12 o'clock to-day, and moved that the resolution be laid upon the table, which motion prevailed.

COLORED PEOPLE AS TRAVELERS.

Mr. CONNESS called up the bill to regulate commerce between the several States.

The pending question was on Mr. WILSON's amendment forbidding the exclusion of any citizen of the United States from any railroad-car, steamboat, or other conveyance, on account of any State law.

Mr. HALE moved, as an amendment to the amendment, to add that no citizen of the United States shall be excluded from any meeting-house, church or hotel, on account of any State law, or any regulation of any corporation. [Laughter.]

Mr. HALE's amendment was adopted.

The vote was then taken on Mr. WILSON's amendment as amended, and was decided in the affirmative, as follows:

YEAS—Messrs Brown, Clark, Collamer, Cowan, Dixon, Doolittle, Farwell, Foster, Grimes, Henderson, Lane of Kansas, Morrill, Nesmith, Pomeroy, Sumner, Ten Eyck, Wade, Willey, Wilson, and Wright—21.

NAYS—Messrs Chandler, Davis, Howard, Howe, Lane, of Indiana, McDougall, Morgan, Nye, Powell, Ramsey, Sherman, Sprague, Stewart, and Trumbull—14.

Mr. NESMITH moved to refer the bill to the Committee on the Conduct of the War, which was decided in the negative.

YEAS—Messrs Clark, Collamer, Cowan, Davis, Dixon, Hale, Lane, of Indiana, McDougall, Morrill, Nesmith, Powell, Ten Eyck, Trumbull, and Wright—14.

NAYS—Messrs Brown, Chandler, Howard, Lane of Kansas, Morgan, Nye, Pomeroy, Ramsey, Sherman, Sprague, Stewart, Sumner, Wade, Wilkinson, and Wilson—15.

Mr. MORRILL moved the indefinite postponement of the bill, which was disagreed to—YEAS 14, NAYS 21.

WAITING UPON THE PRESIDENT.

Mr. SHERMAN moved that a committee of three be appointed to wait upon the President and inquire if he had any further communication to make to the Senate. Carried.

Messrs. SHERMAN, COLLAMER and POWELL were appointed said committee.

INSTALLING THE NEW VICE-PRESIDENT.

At 11:45 Vice-President HAMLIN escorted the Vice-President elect into the Senate Chamber, and a few moments afterward Messrs. SEWARD, STANTON and SPEED entered, and seated themselves to the left of the chair. The judges of the Supreme Court entered immediately afterward, and seated themselves to the right of the chair.

At 12 o'clock Mr. HAMLIN briefly addressed the Senate, thanking the members for the kindness and consideration that had been shown to him on all occasions.

It was impossible to hear the speech of Mr. HAMLIN distinctly, owing to the confusion and conversation continually kept up between the women in the galleries.

Mr. JOHNSON, before taking the oath of office, made a short speech, which, as in the case of Mr. HAMLIN, was nearly inaudible, owing to the want of order which prevailed among the women in the galleries. By the choice of the people, he said, he had been made presiding officer of this body, and, in presenting himself here in obedience to the behests of the Constitution of the United States, it would, perhaps, not be out of place to remark just here what a striking thing the Constitution was. It was the Constitution of the people of the country, and under it, here to-day, before the American Senate, he felt that he was a man and an American citizen. He had a proud illustration of the fact that, under the Constitution, a man could rise from the ranks to occupy the second place in the gift of the American people and of the American Government. Those of us who have labored our whole lives for the establishment of a free Government knew how to cherish its great blessings. He would say to Senators and others before him—to the Supreme Court which sat before him, that they all got their power from the people of this country. Turning toward Mr. CHASE, Mr. JOHNSON said, And your exaltation and position depend upon the people. Then turning toward the Cabinet, he said, And I I will say to you, Mr. Secretary SEWARD, and to you, Mr. Secretary STANTON, and to you, Mr. Secretary—(to a gentleman near by, sotto voice, Who is Secretary of the Navy? the person addressed replied in a whisper, Mr. WELLS)—and to you, Mr. Secretary WELLS, I would say, you all derive your power from the people. Mr. JOHNSON then remarked that the great element of vitality in this Government was its nearness and proximity to the people. He wanted to say to all who heard him, in the face of the American people, that all power was derived from the people. He would say, in the hearing of the Foreign Ministers, for he was going to tell the truth here to-day, that he was a plebeian—he thanked God for it. It was the popular heart of this nation that was beating to sustain Cabinet officials and the President of the United States. It was a strange occasion that called forth a plebeian like him to tell such things as these. Mr. JOHNSON next adverted to affairs in Tennessee, and the abolition of slavery there. He thanked God Tennessee was a State in the Union, and had never been out. The State Government had been discontinued for a time—there had been an interregnum, a hiatus—but she had never been out of the Union. He stood here to-day as her representative. On this day she would elect a Governor and a Legislature, and she would very soon send Senators and members to Congress.

Mr. JOHNSON then took the oath of office, and Mr. HAMLIN declared the Senate adjourned *sine die*.

### U. S. SENATE—EXTRA SESSION.

WASHINGTON, Saturday, March 4.

After the above proceedings, the proclamation convening the Senate in extra session was read by the Secretary, Mr. FORNEY.

The President's inaugural address was then read.

The Senators elect were next sworn in, after which the procession was formed, and proceeded to the east front of the Capitol building.

### HOUSE OF REPRESENTATIVES.

WASHINGTON, Saturday, March 4.

CONCLUSION.

The following is the conclusion of the House proceedings from where our report broke off this morning:

MILITARY BUSINESS.

The report of Mr. GARFIELD on the disagreeing votes to the bill relating to various military subjects, was adopted by a vote of 71 to 57.

Much miscellaneous business was transacted.

STRUGGLE FOR PRECEDENCE.

[It is now 3 o'clock A. M. Almost every member has some little bill to be passed, and there were continuous struggles for the floor to offer their several measures. The galleries were nearly deserted. The ladies admitted to the floor had retired.]

COAL LOTS ON THE PUBLIC LANDS.

The House passed a bill to dispose of the coal lots on the public domain.

Some of the members exhausted by the long session had retired to sleep on the sofas.

DEPRIVING DESERTERS OF HOMESTEAD PRIVILEGES.

Mr. ALLISON, from the Committee on Public Lands, asked, but was refused permission, to report a bill to prevent deserters and others who may shirk military service from acquiring public lands under the Homestead law.

SUBSISTENCE DEPARTMENT.

Mr. SCHENCK, of Ohio, (Union,) made a report from the Committee of Conference, on the bill reorganizing the Subsistence Department, and it was adopted.

THANKS TO GEN. THOMAS.

Mr. SCHENCK reported back the joint resolution of thanks to Major-Gen. THOMAS, with the Senate's amendment thereto, which was disagreed to.

PRINTING CERTAIN REPORTS.

Mr. AMBROSE W. CLARK, from the Committee on Printing, reported in favor of printing 35,000 copies of the report of the commission on flax and hemp, 20,000 copies of the amended Internal Revenue Act, and 35,000 copies of the Agricultural Report for 1864, and it was agreed to.

EXTENSION OF TIME.

The House passed a bill extending the time for locating the Virginia military land warrants.

A RECESS REFUSED.

Mr. DAVIS, of Maryland, at 4 o'clock, moved to take a recess until 4 o'clock.

The Speaker deemed it his duty to say that if the House did so, two of the general Appropriation Bills would probably be lost.

The House refused to take a recess.

The business on the Speaker's table was taken up.

THE REBEL DEBT.

The House concurred in the Senate's joint resolution that this Government will never recognize the rebel debt on any conditions.

DUTY ON PRINTING PAPER.

The House then, by a vote of 53 against 67, non-concurred in the Senate's amendment to the joint resolution changing from three to fifteen per centum ad valorem the duty on printing paper used for books and newspapers exclusively. The House then, by a vote of 47 against 62, refused to lay the resolution on the table, and asked a committee of conference of the Senate.

THE ILLINOIS RAILROAD CLAIM.

Mr. THAYER, of Massachusetts, (Union,) made a report from the Conference Committee on the Army Appropriation Bill. He said the Senate struck out the proviso inserted by the House prohibiting any part of the money being paid to the Illinois Central Railroad Company. The difficulty seemed to rise on a point of law. Hence, he proposed an amendment in order that the question may be settled by the Supreme Court of the United States as to whether that company is, by the Land Grant Law of 1850, bound to transport, free of charge, the troops, munitions, and other property of the United States.

Mr. KERNAN, of New-York, (Dem.,) did not think a further conference would adjust the difficulty between the two Houses.

Mr. MORRILL, of Vermont, (Union,) said it was now 5 o'clock in the morning. He thought the contest had continued as long as it was proper. When the land was granted, no one thought that such an extensive use would be made of the road. No man would inforce such a contract against his neighbor. It is the letter that killeth, but the spirit which maketh alive.

Mr. WASHBURNE, of Illinois, (Union,) thought that the amendment of Mr. THAYER would be received in a spirit of compromise. He was surprised that his friend from Vermont should make such arguments in favor of the company. That company had made twenty-five per cent. more by the war than if the war had not gone on. The war had been a blessing to the road. The company was interested in this bill to the extent of a million and a half of dollars.

Mr. WOODBRIDGE, of Vermont, (Union,) opposed Mr. THAYER's amendment, and in reply to Mr. WASHBURNE, said if it had not been for foreign capital, the Western railroads never would have been built. He maintained that in equity the company should be paid.

Mr. THAYER expressed his surprise that Mr. WOODBRIDGE should characterize his proposition as absurd, and that the gentleman, so swift to make the assertion, should sustain it by so weak an argument.

Mr. MORRILL moved that the House recede from its amendment concerning the Illinois Central Railroad, and this was agreed to by a vote of 62 against 47.

ARMY APPROPRIATION BILL PASSED.

The difficulty between the two Houses was thus removed, and the bill was passed.

RECESS AGAIN DENIED.

Mr. STEVENS, of Pennsylvania, (Union,) moved, at half-past five, that the House take a recess till nine o'clock.

This was disagreed to.

COLOR QUALIFICATION REPEALED.

The House took up the Senate bill removing all disqualification of color in carrying the mails.

Mr. ELDRIDGE moved that the bill be laid on the table, which was disagreed to by a vote of 30 against 65.

The bill was then passed.

NO PASSPORTS FOR COLORED PERSONS.

Mr. SCHENCK, from the Committee on Military Affairs, to whom was referred the letter of the Secretary of War on the subject, reported a resolution that in the judgment of the House, the order of Maj.-Gen. AUGUR, issued on 12th Jan., 1864, directing that no colored man be allowed to leave Washington, going north, without a pass, is a regulation which makes an odious discrimination, for a law of the United States has declared free alike all citizens and residents of the District of Columbia, and the President be requested to direct that the order be at once abrogated.

The resolution was agreed to by Ayes, 75; Nays, 24.

A STORM EXCITEMENT.

About 6:30 o'clock a heavy rain and wind storm broke over the Capitol, rattling on the glass and ceiling and causing a fierce whistling noise throughout the building.

This storm came up so suddenly and created so much noise that it alarmed many of the members of the House, who, affrighted, fled toward the doors.

The excitement and confusion, however, was soon quieted by the calm announcement of the Speaker that it was merely "a storm."

PENSION FOR A WIDOW.

A bill giving a pension to a widow being under consideration,

Mr. INGERSOLL earnestly spoke of the military services of the deceased husband, and sent up to be read some patriotic verses as illustrative of his argument.

At the conclusion of the reading members loudly and laughingly applauded them.

A RECESS AT LAST.

The House then, at 7:15 A. M., took a recess until 9 o'clock.

SATURDAY MORNING 9 o'clock.

GOVERNMENT FOR THE INDIAN TERRITORY.

The House, on re-assembling, took up the Senate bill to establish a Civil Government for the Indian Territory.

It provides for the appointment of a Governor, Secretary of State, Judges, and all the other necessary machinery. Indians are to be elected to the Legislative Council. Involuntary servitude is forever prohibited, except as a punishment for crime. It also provides for the election of an Indian Delegate to Congress.

Mr. HOLMAN, of Indiana, (Dem.,) objected to the consideration of the bill.

MISCELLANEOUS WORK.

Much routine and miscellaneous business was then transacted, and questions were taken by yeas and nays on a number of private bills.

It was now 10 o'clock.

LANDS IN UTAH.

Mr. KINNEY, of Utah, unsuccessfully moved to suspend the rules in order to consider a bill confirming the citizens of Great Salt Lake in the possession of their lands.

CIVIL APPROPRIATION BILL DEFEATED.

The Committee of Conference on the Miscellaneous or Civil Appropriation Bill made a report.

Mr. DAVIS, of Maryland, (Union,) explained what had been done by the committee. They had struck out some of the provisions of the bill, including that to pay the Pennsylvania Volunteers, but retaining the section to pay the Missouri Volunteers.

The question left unsettled was that heretofore introduced by Mr. DAVIS, of Maryland, exempting civilians from trial by court-martial and military commissions.

Mr. LITTLEJOHN, of New-York, (Union,) owing to the few remaining minutes left to the House, moved that the report of the committee be concurred in, with the above exception.

Mr. ELDRIDGE moved to reconsider the vote by which the previous question was ordered.

Mr. PENDLETON, of Ohio, (Dem.,) moved that the House adjourn.

Thereupon Mr. HARDING called for the yeas and nays, which were ordered, and, being taken, the question was determined in the negative.

It was now 11 o'clock.

Mr. MALLORY, of Kentucky, (Dem.,) moved to lay the whole subject upon the table.

Mr. ELDRIDGE demanded the yeas and nays upon the motion, which were ordered.

It was now ten minutes to twelve o'clock.

The Clerk here commenced calling the roll, and when he had reached that of Mr. KNAPP, the hour of twelve had arrived.

THE PRESIDENT HAS NO MORE TO SAY.

The committee appointed to wait on President LINCOLN reported that they had performed that duty, and he had informed them that he had no further communication to make.

THE SPEAKER'S FAREWELL—CLOSE OF THE THIRTY-EIGHTH CONGRESS.

Mr. COLFAX, in taking leave of the members of the House, said:

GENTLEMEN OF THE HOUSE OF REPRESENTATIVES: The parting hour has come, and yonder clock, which takes note of time, will soon announce that the Congress of which we are members has passed into history. Honored by your votes with this responsible position, I have faithfully strive to perform its always complex and often perplexing duties without partizan bias, and with the sincerest impartiality. Whether I have realized the true ideal of a just presiding officer, aiding on the one hand the advance of the public business, with the responsibility of which the majority is charged, and on the other hand allowing no trespass on the parliamentary rights of the minority, must be left for others to decide. But looking back now over the entire Congress, I cannot remember a single word addressed to you which, "dying, I would wish to blot." On this day, which, by spontaneous consent, is being observed wherever our flag floats, as a day of national rejoicing, with a roar of cannons greeting the rising sun on the rock-bound coast of Maine, rechoed and rechoed by answering volleys from city to city, and from mountain peak to mountain peak, till from the golden gate they die away

*Continued on Eighth Page.*

# The New-York Times.

VOL. XIV......NO. 4230. NEW-YORK, SATURDAY, APRIL 15, 1865. PRICE FOUR CENTS

## AWFUL EVENT.

## President Lincoln Shot by an Assassin.

### The Deed Done at Ford's Theatre Last Night.

### THE ACT OF A DESPERATE REBEL

### The President Still Alive at Last Accounts.

### No Hopes Entertained of His Recovery.

### Attempted Assassination of Secretary Seward.

### DETAILS OF THE DREADFUL TRAGEDY.

[OFFICIAL.]

WAR DEPARTMENT, WASHINGTON, April 15—1:30 A. M.

*Maj.-Gen. Dix:*

This evening at about 9:30 P. M., at Ford's Theatre, the President, while sitting in his private box with Mrs. LINCOLN, Mrs. HARRIS, and Major RATHBURN, was shot by an assassin, who suddenly entered the box and approached behind the President.

The assassin then leaped upon the stage, brandishing a large dagger or knife, and made his escape in the rear of the theatre.

The pistol ball entered the back of the President's head and penetrated nearly through the head. The wound is mortal. The President has been insensible ever since it was inflicted, and is now dying.

About the same hour an assassin, whether the same or not, entered Mr. SEWARD's apartments, and under the pretence of having a prescription, was shown to the Secretary's sick chamber. The assassin immediately rushed to the bed, and inflicted two or three stabs on the throat and two on the face. It is hoped the wounds may not be mortal. My apprehension is that they will prove fatal.

The nurse alarmed Mr. FREDERICK SEWARD, who was in an adjoining room, and hastened to the door of his father's room, when he met the assassin, who inflicted upon him one or more dangerous wounds. The recovery of FREDERICK SEWARD is doubtful.

It is not probable that the President will live throughout the night.

Gen. GRANT and wife were advertised to be at the theatre this evening, but he started to Burlington at 6 o'clock this evening.

At a Cabinet meeting at which Gen. GRANT was present, the subject of the state of the country and the prospect of a speedy peace was discussed. The President was very cheerful and hopeful, and spoke very kindly of Gen. LEE and others of the Confederacy, and of the establishment of government in Virginia.

All the members of the Cabinet except Mr. SEWARD, are now in attendance upon the President.

I have seen Mr. SEWARD, but he and FREDERICK were both unconscious.

EDWIN M. STANTON,
Secretary of War.

### DETAIL OF THE OCCURRENCE.

WASHINGTON, Friday, April 14—12:30 A. M.

The President was shot in a theatre to-night, and is, perhaps, mortally wounded.

Secretary SEWARD was also assassinated.

SECOND DISPATCH.

WASHINGTON, Friday, April 14.

President LINCOLN and wife, with other friends, this evening visited Ford's Theatre for the purpose of witnessing the performance of the "American Cousin."

It was announced in the papers that Gen. GRANT would also be present, but he took the late train of cars for New-Jersey.

The theatre was densely crowded, and everybody seemed delighted with the scene before them. During the third act, and while there was a temporary pause for one of the actors to enter, a sharp report of a pistol was heard, which merely attracted attention, but suggesting nothing serious, until a man rushed to the front of the President's box, waving a long dagger in his right hand, and exclaiming "*Sic semper tyrannis*," and immediately leaped from the box, which was in the second tier, to the stage beneath, and ran across to the opposite side, making his escape amid the bewilderment of the audience from the rear of the theatre, and, mounting a horse, fled.

The screams of Mrs. LINCOLN first disclosed the fact to the audience that the President had been shot, when all present rose to their feet, rushing toward the stage, many exclaiming "Hang him! hang him!"

The excitement was of the wildest possible description, and of course there was an abrupt termination of the theatrical performance.

There was a rush toward the President's box, when cries were heard: "Stand back and give him air." "Has any one stimulants." On a hasty examination, it was found that the President had been shot through the head, above and back of the temporal bone, and that some of the brain was oozing out. He was removed to a private house opposite to the theatre, and the Surgeon-General of the army, and other surgeons sent for to attend to his condition.

On an examination of the private box blood was discovered on the back of the cushioned rocking chair on which the President had been sitting, also on the partition and on the floor. A common single-barreled pocket pistol was found on the carpet.

A military guard was placed in front of the private residence to which the President had been conveyed. An immense crowd was in front of it, all deeply anxious to learn the condition of the President. It had been previously announced that the wound was mortal; but all hoped otherwise. The shock to the community was terrible.

The President was in a state of syncope, totally insensible, and breathing slowly. The blood oozed from the wound at the back of his head. The surgeons exhausted every effort of medical skill, but all hope was gone. The parting of his family with the dying President is too sad for description.

At midnight, the Cabinet, with Messrs. SUMNER, COLFAX and FARNSWORTH, Judge CURTIS, Gov. OGLESBY, Gen. MEIGS, Col. HAY, and a few personal friends, with Surgeon-General BARNES and his immediate assistants, were around his bedside.

The President and Mrs. LINCOLN did not start for the theatre until fifteen minutes after eight o'clock. Speaker COLFAX was at the White House at the time, and the President stated to him that he was going, although Mrs. LINCOLN had not been well, because the papers had announced that Gen. GRANT and they were to be present, and, as Gen. GRANT had gone North, he did not wish the audience to be disappointed.

He went with apparent reluctance and urged Mr. COLFAX to go with him; but that gentleman had made other engagements, and with Mr. ASHMAN, of Massachusetts, bid him good bye.

When the excitement at the theatre was at its wildest height, reports were circulated that Secretary SEWARD had also been assassinated.

On reaching this gentleman's residence a crowd and a military guard were found at the door, and on entering it was ascertained that the reports were based on truth.

Everybody there was so excited that scarcely an intelligible word could be gathered, but the facts are substantially as follows.

About 10 o'clock a man rang the bell, and the call having been answered by a colored servant, he said he had come from Dr. VERDI, Secretary SEWARD's family physician, with a prescription, at the same time holding in his hand a small piece of folded paper, and saying in answer to a refusal that he must see the Secretary, as he was entrusted with particular directions concerning the medicine.

He still insisted on going up, although repeatedly informed that no one could enter the chamber. The man pushed the servant aside, and walked heavily toward the Secretary's room, and was then met by Mr. FREDERICK SEWARD, of whom he demanded to see the Secretary, making the same representation which he did to the servant. What further passed in the way of colloquy is not known, but the man struck him on the head with a "billy," severely injuring the skull and felling him almost senseless. The assassin then rushed into the chamber and attacked Major SEWARD, Paymaster of the United States army and Mr. HANSELL, a messenger of the State Department and two male nurses, disabling them all, he then rushed upon the Secretary, who was lying in bed in the same room, and inflicted three stabs in the neck, but severing, it is thought and hoped, no arteries, though he bled profusely.

The assassin then rushed down stairs, mounted his horse at the door, and rode off before an alarm could be sounded, and in the same manner as the assassin of the President.

It is believed that the injuries of the Secretary are not fatal, nor those of either of the others, although both the Secretary and the Assistant Secretary are very seriously injured.

Secretaries STANTON and WELLES, and other prominent officers of the government, called at Secretary SEWARD's house to inquire into his condition, and there heard of the assassination of the President.

They then proceeded to the house where he was lying, exhibiting of course intense anxiety and solicitude. An immense crowd was gathered in front of the President's house, and a strong guard was also stationed there, many persons evidently supposing he would be brought to his home.

The entire city to-night presents a scene of wild excitement, accompanied by violent expressions of indignation, and the profoundest sorrow—many shed tears. The military authorities have dispatched mounted patrols in every direction, in order, if possible, to arrest the assassins. The whole metropolitan police are likewise vigilant for the same purpose.

The attacks, both at the theatre and at Secretary SEWARD's house, took place at about the same hour—10 o'clock—thus showing a preconcerted plan to assassinate those gentlemen. Some evidence of the guilt of the party who attacked the President are in the possession of the police.

Vice-President JOHNSON is in the city, and his headquarters are guarded by troops.

### ANOTHER ACCOUNT.

Special Dispatch to the New-York Times.

WASHINGTON, Friday, April 14, 11:15 P. M.

A stroke from Heaven laying the whole of the city in instant ruins could not have startled us as did the word that broke from Ford's Theatre a half hour ago that the President had been shot. It flew everywhere in five minutes, and set five thousand people in swift and excited motion on the instant.

It is impossible to get at the full facts of the case, but it appears that a young man entered the President's box from the theatre, during the last act of the play of "Our American Cousin," with pistol in hand. He shot the President in the head and instantly jumped from the box upon the stage, and immediately disappeared through the side scenes and rear of the theatre, brandishing a dirk knife and dropping a kid glove on the stage.

The audience heard the shot, but supposing it fired in the regular course of the play, did not heed it till Mrs. LINCOLN's screams drew their attention. The whole affair occupied scarcely half a minute, and then the assassin was gone. As yet he has not been found.

The President's wound is reported mortal. He was at once taken into the house opposite the theatre.

As if this horror was not enough, almost the same moment the story ran through the city that Mr. SEWARD had been murdered in his bed.

Inquiry showed this to be so far true also. It appears a man wearing a light coat, dark pants, slouch hat, called and asked to see Mr. SEWARD, and was shown to his room. He delivered to Major SEWARD, who sat near his father, what purported to be a physician's prescription, turned, and with one stroke cut Mr. SEWARD's throat as he lay on his bed, inflicting a horrible wound, but not severing the jugular vein, and not producing a mortal wound.

In the struggle that followed, Major SEWARD was also badly, but not seriously, wounded in several places. The assassin rushed down stairs, mounted the fleet horse on which he came, drove his spurs into him, and dashed away before any one could stop him.

Reports have prevailed that an attempt was also made on the life of Mr. STANTON.

MIDNIGHT.

The President is reported dead. Cavalry and infantry are scouring the city in every direction for the murderous assassins, and the city is overwhelmed with excitement. Who the assassins were no one knows, though every body supposes them to have been rebels.

SATURDAY MORNING—1 O'CLOCK.

The person who shot the President is represented as about 30 years of age, five feet nine inches in height, sparely built, of light complexion, dressed in dark clothing, and having a genteel appearance. He entered the box, which is known as the State box, being the upper box on the right hand side from the dress-circle in the regular manner, and shot the President from behind, the ball entering the skull about in the middle, behind, and going in the direction of the left eye; it did not pass through, but apparently broke the frontal bone and forced out the brain to some extent. The President is not yet dead, but is wholly insensible, and the Surgeon-General says he cannot live till day-break. The assassin was followed across the stage by a gentleman, who sprang out from an orchestra chair. He rushed through the side door into an alley, thence to the avenue and mounted a dark bay horse, which he apparently received from the hand of an accomplice, dashed up F, toward the back part of the city. The escape was so sudden that he effectually eluded pursuit. The assassin cried "*sic sempre*" in a sharp, clear voice, as he jumped to the stage, and dropped his hat and a glove.

Two or three officers were in the box with the President and Mrs. LINCOLN, who made efforts to stop the assassin, but were unsuccessful, and received some bruises. The whole affair, from his entrance into the box to his escape from the theatre, occupied scarcely a minute, and the strongest of the action found everybody wholy unprepared. The assault upon Mr. SEWARD appeares to have been made almost at the same moment as that upon the President. Mr. SEWARDS wound is not dangerous in itself, but may prove so in connection with his recent injuries. The two assassins have both endeavored to leave the city to the northwest, apparently not expecting to strike the river. Even so low down as Chain Bridge, cavalry have been sent in every direction to intercept them.

SATURDAY, 1:30 o'clock A. M.

The President still lies insensible. Messrs. STANTON, WELLS, MCCULLOCH, SPEED and USHER are with him, as also the Vice-President, the Surgeon-General, and other Surgeons.

There is a great throng about the house, even at this hour.

2 o'clock A. M.

The President still lives, but lies insensible, as he has since the first moment, and no hopes are entertained that he can survive.

The most extravagant stories prevail, among which one is to effect, that Gen. GRANT was shot while on his was to Philaphia, of course this is not true.

Another is, that every member of Mr. SEWARD's family was wounded in the struggle with the assassin there. This also is untrue. Mr. FRED. SEWARD, the Assistant Secretary, and Major CLARENCE SEWARD, of the army, were wounded, neither of them dangerously.

### THE CONDITION OF THE PRESIDENT.

WASHINGTON, April 15—2:12 A. M.

The President is still alive; but he is growing weaker. The ball is lodged in his brain, three inches from where it entered the skull. He remains insensible, and his condition is utterly hopeless.

The Vice-President has been to see him; but all company, except the members of the Cabinet and of the family, is rigidly excluded.

Large crowds still continue in the street, as near to the house as the line of guards allows.

### THE SIEGE OF MOBILE.

**Fierce Bombardment of the Spanish Fort—Mobile Papers Announce the Capture of Selma.**

NEW-ORLEANS, Saturday, April 8, via CAIRO, Friday, April 14.

A special dispatch to the New-Orleans *Times*, from the Spanish Fort, dated April 5, says:

"A furious fire was opened on the rebel forts last night from our entire line. During the bombardment a small magazine in the Spanish Fort exploded. The damage is unknown. Quiet prevailed on the 5th. Deserters report from 16,000 to 20,000 troops in and about Mobile, including all the State Reserves, and about 2,000 in the Spanish Fort. The loss outside the Spanish Fort up to the 4th instant amounted to about 500 killed and wounded. The rebel loss exceeds ours."

Adjt.-Gen. THOMAS arrived at New-Orleans on the morning of the 7th.

Mobile papers of the 4th inst. announce the capture of Selma, Alabama, with 23 pieces of artillery, and a large amount of Government property.

**Fort Sumter Celebration in Bangor.**

BANGOR, Me., Friday, April 14.

The restoration of the Old Flag to Fort Sumter was celebrated here to-day by a national salute at noon, by a display of all the flags on public and private buildings, and by the raising of the Stars and Stripes one thousand feet above the city by means of a monster kite bearing the name of U. S. GRANT.

The Madrid *Bulea* says if the Pope should leave Rome, Spain would confer upon him the Balearic Isles.

The *Politica* says the Pope would rather inhabit the Montpensier Palace at Seville.

## EUROPEAN NEWS.

### TWO DAYS LATER BY THE EUROPA.

### The Insult to Our Cruisers by Portugal.

### The American Minister at Lisbon Demands Satisfaction.

### Dismissal of the Commander of Fort Belan Requested.

### Further Advance in Five-Twenties.

### FINANCIAL AND COMMERCIAL.

HALIFAX, Friday, April 14.

The steamship *Europa*, from Liverpool on the 1st, via Queenstown on the 2d inst., arrived here at 2 o'clock this morning. She has 43 passengers for this port, and 30 for Boston. Her dates are two days later than those already received.

The steamship *Cuba*, from New-York, arrived at Liverpool at noon on the 1st inst.

THE STONEWALL AFFAIR.

A Lisbon dispatch, of the 31st of March, says that the American Minister at Lisbon has demanded satisfaction of the Portuguese Government for the firing upon the *Niagara* and *Sacramento* by the Portuguese forts. He also requests the dismissal of the Commander of Fort Belan, and a salute of twenty-one guns to the American flag.

Nothing as yet has been decided in regard to the matter.

A PROPHECY FROM RICHMOND.

The correspondent of the London *Times*, writing from Richmond on the 4th of March, says:

"I am daily more convinced that if Richmond falls and LEE and JOHNSTON are driven from the field, it is but the first stage of this colossal revolution which will then be completed. There will ensue a time when every important town of the South will require to be held by a Yankee garrison, when exultation in New-York will be exchanged for soberness and right reason, and when it will be realised that the closing scenes of this mightiest revolutionary drama will not be played out, save in the times of our children's children."

#### GREAT BRITAIN.

Parliamentary proceedings on the 30th ult. were unimportant.

In the House of Commons, on the 31st, Lord C. PAGET said that the Admiralty had received no proposal for sanctioning or supporting any fresh attempt to reach the North Pole. He was, therefore, unable to say what course the government would take if such a proposal were made.

Mr. NEWDEGATE put some questions as to the idea of the Pope taking up his residence in England, as indicated in some foreign journals.

Lord PALMERSTON replied that the government respected the Pope personally very much, but for him to come to England would be both an anachronism and a solecism.

The revenue returns for the financial year, ending March 31, show a net increase of over £104,000 on the year. Notwithstanding the great reductions in taxation, the revenue exceeds by nearly half a million sterling the estimates of Mr. GLADSTONE.

Messrs. BARING's circular says that large business has been done in 5-20 bonds, and that prices advanced early in the week to 57½@58, but have since relapsed to 56¾@57—the demand being chiefly from the continent.

On *Friday*, the telegrams per the steamship *Cuba* were received, and 5 20s again advanced to 57¾@58¼. Erie and Illinois Central Shares have also attracted attention, and have again advanced.

The Bank of England on the 30th ult. reduced its rate of discount to 4 per cent., at which there is a fair demand for money. This movement strengthened the English funds, and Consols are buoyant and advancing.

KELSON, TRITTON & Co., East India and general merchants, have suspended payment. Their liabilities are estimated at £900,000 sterling.

Another provincial bank has suspended, the Portsmouth and South Hants Banking Company. Their liabilities are about £170,000 sterling.

The Birmingham and Joint Stock Banking Company had agreed to take up the business of Atwood & Spooner's Bank, which lately suspended at Birmingham, and to pay the creditors 11s. 3d. on the pound.

The West India Mail steamer had arrived, with over two and a quarter millions of dollars in specie. She also brought several Captains of blockade-runners, whose occupations were gone.

THE ATLANTIC TELEGRAPH.

The French Government will probably send one or two steamers to accompany the two that are sent by the English Government with the *Great Eastern* across the Atlantic, at the time of laying the Atlantic cable, and it is hoped that the United States Government will do the same.

#### FRANCE.

Weekly returns from the Bank of France show an increase of cash on hand of over ten and a half millions francs.

In the French Chambers of the 30th, M. JULES FAVRE spoke upon the necessity for political liberty, but was interrupted by the President and declined to finish his speech. The amendment was rejected.

The amendment in favor of the liberty of the press was debated, but rejected by a large majority.

It is stated that NAPOLEON will leave Paris early in May, not returning until November. His physicians have recommended seven months' absence in the country air.

The Bourse is firm, 67.45.

#### SPAIN.

The *Epoca* states that the Minister of War tendered his resignation, and that Gen. LERSUNDI refused to place him.

A later dispatch says the Minister of War resigned from ill health.

Gen. RIVERA succeeded to the office.

#### DENMARK.

The King relieved M. HELLSEN, Minister of Justice, of his functions. HELLSEN represented the alliance between the Reactionary and extreme Democratic parties. It is supposed that all members of the late Cabinet will return to their posts.

#### ITALY.

In the allocutions delivered at the last consistory the Pope expressed surprise and sorrow at the sad events which have recently taken place in Mexico. His Holiness hoped MAXIMILIAN would abandon the course upon which he had entered, and satisfy the just desires of the Holy See. The Pope further thanked the Bishops of the Catholic world, especially those of Italy, for defending the religion and liberties of the Church, despite the decrees of the secular authorities.

#### PRUSSIA.

In the Military Committee of Chambers, the Deputies amendment was introduced with the object of effecting a reconciliation between the government and chamber, and proposing a maximum strength of the army at 180,000 men, which was rejected by 11 to 8. The committee also rejected the general military estimates and navy estimates and amendments, thus refusing the whole military and naval proposals of the government.

#### AUSTRIA.

Count MENSDORFF had made some ministerial explanation in the Lower House Reichsrath. He said the views of the government on the question of the Duchies would be communicated to the Federal Diet on the 6th of April.

As regards relations with Italy, he said the government desired to promote the material interests of the two countries, but that Italy maintained a hostile attitude to the government. He desired to economize, but must maintain the position of Austria as a great Power.

#### INDIA.

A private Calcutta telegram of March 27 reports commercial affairs in much the same state as on the 25th, when slight improvement had taken place.

#### BRAZIL.

LONDON, Sunday, April 2.

The Brazilian mail has reached Lisbon, bringing the following dates:

RIO DE JANEIRO, Saturday, March 11.

Exchange 25¾@26¼.

COFFEE.—Sales of good firsts at 6s10s. Shipments 100,000 bags. Stock, 100,000 bags. Freights [illegible].

BAHIA, Saturday, March 11.

Exchange 26¼.

Cotton nominal.

PERNAMBUCO, Saturday, March 11.

Exchange 26¾@27.

Montivedeo has surrendered to Gen. FLORES. The Brazilians now occupy the city.

#### LATEST VIA LIVERPOOL.

LIVERPOOL, Saturday Evening, April 1, 1865.

The *Times* to-day has an editorial on the amended tariff law of the United States. It says: "It is impossible to find an excuse for it. Tried by the light of reason or by the results of experience it is alike condemned."

It ironically credits the framers of the scheme with peculiar wisdom in selecting the 1st of April for its inauguration.

The *Army & Navy Gazette* says: "The work of the United States Navy has now been accomplished, and it must be confessed that in the hands of FARRAGUT and PORTER, the high reputation which the officers and seamen of that Power established soon after the national existence of itself, has been greatly enhanced."

#### LATEST VIA QUEENSTOWN.

LONDON, Saturday, April 1.

There is no news of importance this morning.

PARIS, Friday, March 31—P. M.

The Bourse is steady. The Rentes closed at 67f. 30c.

#### COMMERCIAL.

LIVERPOOL MARKET.

LIVERPOOL, April 31.—Evening.

The Market report was received per *Moravian*.

COTTON—The stock of Cotton in port is 560,000 bales by actual count, being 13,000 bales below the estimates, of which amount 42,000 bales are American.

TRADE REPORT.

The Manchester market was firmer with an upward tendency.

BREADSTUFFS—The market is easier. Messrs. RICHARDSON, SPENCE & Co., and others, report: Flour dull and easier. Wheat quiet and quotations are barely maintained; red Western 8s.@8s. 9d. Corn inactive, mixed 27s. 6d.

PROVISIONS—The market is downward. WAKEFIELD, NASH & Co., and others, report: Beef has a downward tendency. Pork heavy and declined 2s. 6d. Bacon firmer and holders demand an advance. Lard dull and easier at 58s.@61s. Butter flat and declining. Tallow downward.

PRODUCE.—Ashes easier at 29s. 6d. for Pots, and 30s. for Pearls. Sugar, flat. Coffee, quiet and steady. Rice, quiet and steady. Clover Seed, firmer. Jute, 10s.@30s. lower. Cod Oil, quiet at 57s. Sperm Oil, no sales. Linseed Oil, steady. Resin, very dull. Spirits Turpentine, quiet at 65s.@66s.

PETROLEUM—SOCIY. ENGLISH & BRANDON report: Petroleum firm, at 1s. 11d.@2s. for refined; no crude in market.

LONDON MARKETS.

FLOUR firm; WHEAT steady. IRON advancing; bars and rails, £6 10s.@£6 15s; Scotch pig, 55s. 3d. SUGAR inactive. COFFEE active at a decline of 1s.@2s. TEA steady at 10¾d. for common Congou. RICE steady. SPIRITS TURPENTINE firm at 47s. PETROLEUM steady at £18 for crude, 2s. for refined. SPERM OIL nominal at £92. TALLOW downward, at 40s.@43s. LINSEED OIL flat.

#### LATEST COMMERCIAL.

LIVERPOOL, Saturday, April 1—Evening.

COTTON—Sales to-day 6,000 bales, including 2,000 bales to speculators and exporters. The market is less firm but quiet and unchanged.

BREADSTUFFS—The market is quiet and steady.

PROVISIONS—The market is dull.

PRODUCE—The market is quiet and steady. Petroleum firm at 2s. @2s. 0½d. for refined.

LONDON, Saturday, April 1—Evening.

CONSOLS closed at 89⅞@90, for money.

AMERICAN STOCKS—Illinois Central Railroad 61¾@62¼; Erie Railroad 34¾@35¼; United States Five-twenties 57⅞@58¼.

**Gen. Lee in Richmond—The Oath of Allegiance.**

BALTIMORE, Friday, April 14.

The Richmond *Whig* of yesterday contains little of importance. It announces the arrival of Gen. LEE on the night previous.

The *Whig* publishes the oath of allegiance, which it says citizens will be required to swear and subscribe to. The Provost-Marshal's office is crowded with people anxious to take it, and the only question among citizens seems to be who shall be first to renew their citizenship.

**Rejoicings at Cincinnati.**

CINCINNATI, Friday, April 14.

Business was entirely suspended to-day. The city was universally decorated with flags, and great enthusiasm prevailed. The procession was an immense affair, comprising the entire police force, Gens. HOOKER and WALLICH, with their staffs, four regiments of National Guards, discharged veterans, ward organizations, the Fenian Brotherhood, the Fire Department, and a large number of colored citizens. All the bells in the city were rung, and salutes were fired at 6 o'clock this evening. To-night the city is brilliantly illuminated, and there is generally a display of fireworks.

**Fire.**

ROCHESTER, N. Y., Friday, April 14.

The cabinet warehouse of JAMES E. HAYDON, of this city, was partially destroyed by fire this morning. The stocks of HUMPHREY REEDY & Co., stove dealers, HASTINGS & MCVEAN, paper dealers, S. B. ROBY, saddlery and hardware dealers, and the agency of the American Tract Society, were damaged. Total loss, [illegible]; insurance, [illegible]. The origin of the fire is unknown.

**The Funeral of Gen. T. A. Smyth.**

WILMINGTON, Del., Friday, April 14.

The remains of Brig.-Gen. T. A. SMYTH arrived here to-day at 1 o'clock, and will be interred on Monday afternoon with appropriate ceremonies.

**An Unseaworthy War Steamer.**

*To the Editor of the New-York Times:*

UNITED STATES STEAMER MUSCOOTA,
HAMPTON ROADS, Va., Wednesday, April 12, 1865.

This vessel has returned to this port, having made her fourth attempt to make a cruise to the Pacific. On each occasion she has proved herself to be an unsafe sea boat. On her last trial she narrowly escaped being lost in the Gulf Stream. Inclosed you will find a list of her officers; please publish.

Respectfully, &c.,

ARTHUR BURTIS, Jr., Paymaster.

List of officers attached to the U. S. steamer Muscoota, one thousand tons, 10 guns:

Commander GEO. H. RANSOM, Lieut. Thos. S. Spencer, Ass't Paymaster Arthur Burtis, Jr., Ass't Surgeon Dan'l. McMurtrie, Act'g Master Geo. E. Durand, Act'g Ensigns Robt. H. Clark, Jno. Courtney, John D. Thomas, Chas. A. Stewart, Second Ass't Engineers Robert H. Gunnell, Jos. H. Greener, Henry Snyder, Act'g Third Ass't Engineers Robt. L. Cass, Geo. Taylor, Geo. Westinghouse, Jr., Masters Fred'k. A. Beatie, A. L. Spinney, Wm. Merrill, Captain's Clerk Geo. S. Dane, Paymasters Clerk P. B. Hathaway.

**Arrivals in the City.**

Gov. Jos. A. Gilmore, Concord, N. H., is stopping at the Fifth-avenue Hotel.

Hon. O. N. Shannon, Cincinnati; Gen. B. F. Stringfellow, Atchison; Dr. N. Greene, Louisville, and Wm. D. Griswold, Terre Haute, are stopping at the Metropolitan Hotel.

COLLISION.—The steamship *La Favorite*, while returning from a trial trip and passing up the East River, collided with the Catharine Ferry-boat *Monhassett*, as she was entering her slip on the Brooklyn side, doing considerable damage to the *Monhassett*, by tearing away a portion of the gentlemen's cabin, and somewhat injuring the hull. Fortunately nobody was hurt.

ANDREW JOHNSON

# The New-York Times.

VOL. XIV......NO. 4230. NEW-YORK, SUNDAY, APRIL 16, 1865. PRICE FOUR CENTS


# OUR GREAT LOSS.

## Death of President Lincoln.

### The Songs of Victory Drowned in Sorrow.

### CLOSING SCENES OF A NOBLE LIFE.

### The Great Sorrow of an Afflicted Nation.

### Party Differences Forgotten in Public Grief.

### Vice-President Johnson Inaugurated as Chief Executive.

### MR. SEWARD WILL RECOVER.

### John Wilkes Booth Believed to be the Assassin.

### Manifestations of the People Throughout the Country.

## OFFICIAL DISPATCHES.

WAR DEPARTMENT, WASHINGTON, April 15—4:10 A. M.

*To Major-Gen. Dix:*

The President continues insensible and is sinking.

Secretary SEWARD remains without change.

FREDERICK SEWARD's skull is fractured in two places, besides a severe cut upon the head.

The attendant is still alive, but hopeless. Maj. SEWARD's wound is not dangerous.

It is now ascertained with reasonable certainty that two assassins were engaged in the horrible crime, WILKES BOOTH being the one that shot the President, and the other companion of his whose name is not known, but whose description is so clear that he can hardly escape. It appears from a letter found in BOOTH's trunk that the murder was planned before the 4th of March, but fell through then because the accomplice backed out until "Richmond could be heard from." BOOTH and his accomplice were at the livery stable at six o'clock last evening, and left there with their horses about ten o'clock, or shortly before that hour.

It would seem that they had for several days been seeking their chance, but for some unknown reason it was not carried into effect until last night.

One of them has evidently made his way to Baltimore—the other has not yet been traced.

EDWIN M. STANTON,
Secretary of War.

WAR DEPARTMENT, WASHINGTON, April 15.

*Major-Gen. Dix:*

ABRAHAM LINCOLN died this morning at twenty-two minutes after seven o'clock.

EDWIN M. STANTON,
Secretary of War.

WAR DEPARTMENT, WASHINGTON, April 15—3 P. M.

*Maj.-Gen. Dix, New-York:*

Official notice of the death of the late President, ABRAHAM LINCOLN, was given by the heads of departments this morning to ANDREW JOHNSON, Vice-President, upon whom the constitution devolved the office of President. Mr. JOHNSON, upon receiving this notice, appeared before the Hon. SALMON P. CHASE, Chief Justice of the United States, and took the oath of office, as President of the United States, assumed its duties and functions. At 12 o'clock the President met the heads of departments in cabinet meeting, at the Treasury Building, and among other business the following was transacted:

*First*—The arrangements for the funeral of the late President were referred to the several Secretaries, as far as relates to their respective departments.

*Second*—WILLIAM HUNTER, Esq., was appointed Acting Secretary of State during the disability of Mr. SEWARD, and his son, FREDERICK SEWARD, the Assistant Secretary.

*Third*—The President formally announced that he desired to retain the present Secretaries of departments of his Cabinet, and they would go on and discharge their respective duties in the same manner as before the deplorable event that had changed the head of the government.

All business in the departments was suspended during the day.

The surgeons report that the condition of Mr. SEWARD remains unchanged. He is doing well.

No improvement in Mr. FREDERICK SEWARD.

The murderers have not yet been apprehended.

EDWIN M. STANTON,
Secretary of War.

## THE ASSASSINATION.

### Additional Details of the Lamentable Event.

WASHINGTON, Saturday, April 15.

The assassin of President LINCOLN left behind him his hat and a spur.

The hat was picked up in the President's box and has been identified by parties to whom it has been shown as the one belonging to the suspected man, and accurately described as the one belonging to the suspected man by other parties, not allowed to see it before describing it.

The spur was dropped upon the stage, and that also has been identified as the one procured at a stable where the same man hired a horse in the evening.

Two gentlemen who went to the Secretary of War to apprise him of the attack on Mr. LINCOLN, met at the residence of the former a man muffled in a cloak, who, when accosted by them, hastened away.

It had been Mr. STANTON's intention to accompany Mr. LINCOLN to the theatre, and occupy the same box, but the press of business prevented.

It therefore seems evident that the aim of the plotters was to paralyze the country by at once striking down the head, the heart and the arm of the country.

As soon as the dreadful events were announced in the streets, Superintendent RICHARDS, and his assistants, were at work to discover the assassin. In a few moments the telegraph had aroused the whole police force of the city.

Maj WALLACH and several members of the City Government were soon on the spot and every precaution was taken to preserve order and quiet in the city.

Every street in Washington was patrolled at the request of Mr. RICHARDS.

Gen. AUGUR sent horses to mount the police.

Every road leading out of Washington was strongly picketed, and every possible avenue of escape was thoroughly guarded.

Steamboats about to depart down the Potomac were stopped.

The Daily *Chronicle* says:

"As it is suspected that this conspiracy originated in Maryland, the telegraph flashed the mournful news to Baltimore and all the cavalry was immediately put upon active duty. Every road was picketed and every precaution taken to prevent the escape of the assassin. A preliminary examination was made by Messrs. RICHARDS and his assistants. Several persons were called to testify and the evidence as elicited before an informal tribunal, and not under oath, was conclusive to this point. The murderer of President LINCOLN was JOHN WILKES BOOTH. His hat was found in the private box, and identified by several persons who had seen him within the last two days, and the spur which he dropped by accident, after he jumped to the stage, was identified as one of those which he had obtained from the stable where he hired his horse.

This man BOOTH has played more than once at Ford's Theatre, and is, of course, acquainted with its exits and entrances, and the facility with which he escaped behind the scenes is well understood.

The person who assassinated Secretary SEWARD left behind him a slouched hat and an old rusty navy revolver. The chambers were broken loose from the barrel, as if done by striking. The loads were drawn from the chambers, one being but a rough piece of lead, and the other balls smaller than the chambers, wrapped in paper, as if to keep them from falling out.

## CLOSING SCENES.

### Particulars of His Last Moments—Record of His Condition Before Death—His Death.

WASHINGTON, Saturday, April 15—11 o'clock A. M.

The *Star* extra says:

"At 7:20 o'clock the President breathed his last, closing his eyes as if falling to sleep, and his countenance assuming an expression of perfect serenity. There were no indications of pain, and it was not known that he was dead until the gradually decreasing respiration ceased altogether.

Rev. Dr. GURLEY, of the New-York-avenue Presbyterian Church, immediately on its being ascertained that life was extinct, knelt at the bedside and offered an impressive prayer, which was responded to by all present.

Dr. GURLEY then proceeded to the front parlor, where Mrs. LINCOLN, Capt. ROBERT LINCOLN, Mrs. JOHN HAY, the Private Secretary, and others, were waiting, where he again offered a prayer for the consolation of the family.

The following minutes, taken by Dr. ABBOTT, show the condition of the late President throughout the night:

11 o'clock—Pulse 44.
11:05 o'clock—Pulse 45, and growing weaker.
11:10 o'clock—Pulse 45.
11:15 o'clock—Pulse 42.
11:20 o'clock—Pulse 45; respiration 27 to 29.
11:25 o'clock—Pulse 42.
11:32 o'clock—Pulse 48, and full.
11:40 o'clock—Pulse 45.
11:45 o'clock—Pulse 45; respiration 22.
12 o'clock—Pulse 48; respiration 22.
12:15 o'clock—Pulse 48; respiration 21—echmos both eyes.
12:30 o'clock—Pulse 45.
12:32 o'clock—Pulse 60.
12:35 o'clock—Pulse 66.
12:40 o'clock—Pulse 69; right eye much swollen, and echmoses.
12:45 o'clock—Pulse 70.
12:55 o'clock—Pulse 80; struggling motion of arms.
1 o'clock—Pulse 86; respiration 30.
1:30 o'clock—Pulse 95; appearing easier.
1:45 o'clock—Pulse 86—very quiet, respiration irregular.
Mrs. LINCOLN present.
2:10 o'clock—Mrs. LINCOLN retired with ROBERT LINCOLN to an adjoining room.
2:30 o'clock—President very quiet—pulse 54—respiration 28.
2:52 o'clock—Pulse 48—respiration 30.
3 o'clock—Visited again by Mrs. LINCOLN.
3:25 o'clock—Respiration 24 and regular.
3:35 o'clock—Prayer by Rev. Dr. GURLEY.
4 o'clock—Respiration 26 and regular.
4:15 o'clock—Pulse 60—respiration 25.
5:50 o'clock—Respiration 28—regular—sleeping
6 o'clock—Pulse failing—respiration 28.
6 30 o'clock—Still failing and labored breathing.
7 o'clock—Symptoms of immediate dissolution.
7:22 o'clock—Death.

Surrounding the death-bed of the President were Secretaries Stanton, Welles, Usher, Attorney-General Speed, Postmaster-General Dennison, M. B Field, Assistant Secretary of the Treasury; Judge Otto, Assistant Secretary of the Interior; Gen. Halleck, Gen. Meigs, Senator Sumner, R. F Andrews, of New-York; Gen. Todd, of Dacotah; John Hay, Private Secretary; Gov. Oglesby, of Illinois; Gen. Farnsworth, Mrs. and Miss Kenney, Miss Harris, Capt. Robert Lincoln, son of the President, and Doctors E. W. Abbott, R. K. Stone, C. D. Gatch, Neal Hall, and Mr. Lieberman. Secretary McCulloch remained with the President until about 5 o'clock, and Chief-Justice Chase, after several hours' attendance during the night, returned early this morning.

Immediately after the President's death a Cabinet meeting was called by Secretary STANTON, and held in the room in which the corpse lay. Secretaries STANTON, WELLES and USHER, Postmaster-General DENNISON, and Attorney-General SPEED, were present. The results of the conference are as yet unknown.

### Removal of the Remains to the Executive Mansion—Feeling in the City.

WASHINGTON, Saturday, April 15.

The President's body was removed from the private residence opposite Ford's Theatre to the executive mansion this morning at 9:30 o'clock, in a hearse, and wrapped in the American flag. It was escorted by a small guard of cavalry, Gen. AUGUR and other military officers following on foot.

A dense crowd accompanied the remains to the White House, where a military guard excluded the crowd, allowing none but persons of the household and personal friends of the deceased to enter the premises, Senator YATES and Representative FARNSWORTH being among the number admitted.

The body is being enbalmed, with a view to its removal to Illinois.

Flags over the department and throughout the city are at half-mast. Scarcely any business is being transacted anywhere either on private or public account.

Our citizens, without any preconcert whatever, are draping their premises with festoons of mourning.

The bells are tolling mournfully. All is the deepest gloom and sadness. Strong men weep in the streets. The grief is wide-spread and deep and in strange contrast to the joy so lately manifested over our recent military victories.

This is indeed a day of gloom.

Reports prevail that Mr. FREDERICK W. SEWARD, who was kindly assisting the nursing of Secretary SEWARD, received a stab in the back. His shoulder blade prevented the knife or dagger from penetrating into his body. The prospects are that he will recover.

A report is circulated, repeated by almost everybody, that BOOTH was captured fifteen miles this side of Baltimore. If it be true, as asserted, that the War Department has received such information, it will doubtless be officially promulgated.

The government departments are closed by order, and will be draped with the usual emblems of mourning.

The roads leading to and from the city are guarded by the military, and the utmost circumspection is observed as to all attempting to enter or leave the city.

AUTOPSY UPON THE BODY OF ABRAHAM LINCOLN.

WASHINGTON, Saturday, April 15.

An autopsy was held this afternoon over the body of President LINCOLN by Surgeon-General BARNES and Dr. STONE, assisted by other eminent medical men.

The coffin is of mahogany, is covered with black cloth, and lined with lead, the latter also being covered white satin.

A silver plate upon the coffin over the breast bears the following inscription:

ABRAHAM LINCOLN.
SIXTEENTH PRESIDENT OF THE UNITED STATES.
Born July 12, 1809.
Died April 15, 1865.

The remains have been embalmed.

A few locks of hair were removed from the President's head for the family previous to the remains being placed in the coffin.

## THE ASSASSINS.

### Circumstances Tending to Inculpate G. H. Booth—Description of his Confederate in the Crime.

WASHINGTON, Saturday, April 15.

There is no confirmation of the report that the murderer of the President has been arrested.

Among the circumstances tending to fix a participation in the crime on BOOTH, were letters found in his trunk, one of which, apparently from a lady, supplicated him to desist from the perilous undertaking in which he was about to embark, as the time was inauspicious, the mine not yet being ready to be sprung.

The *Extra Intelligencer* says: "From the evidence obtained it is rendered highly probable that the man who stabbed Mr. SEWARD and his sons, is JOHN SURRATT, of Prince George County, Maryland. The horse he rode was hired at NAYLOR's stable, on Fourteenth-street. SURRATT is a young man, with light hair and goatee. His father is said to have been postmaster of Prince George County."

About 11 o'clock last night two men crossed the Anacostia Bridge, one of whom gave his name as BOOTH, and the other as SMITH. The latter is believed to be JOHN SURRATT.

Last night a riderless horse was found, which has been identified by the proprietor of one of the stables previously mentioned as having been hired from his establishment.

Accounts are conflicting as to whether BOOTH crossed the bridge on horseback or on foot; but as it is believed that he rode across it, it is presumed that he had exchanged his horse.

From information in the possession of the authorities it is evident that the scope of the plot was intended to be much more comprehensive.

The Vice-President and other prominent members of the Administration were particularly inquired for by suspected parties, and their precise localities accurately obtained; but providentially, in their cases, the scheme miscarried.

A boat was at once sent down the Potomac to notify the gunboats on the river of the awful crime, in order that all possible means should be taken for the arrest of the perpetrators.

The most ample precautions have been taken, and it is not believed the culprits will long succeed in evading the overtaking arm of justice.

The second extra of the *Evening Star* says:

"Col. INGRAHAM, Provost-Marshal of the defences north of the Potomac, is engaged in taking testimony to-day, all of which fixes the assassination upon J. WILKES BOOTH.

Judge OLIN, of the Supreme Court of the District of Columbia, and Justice MILLER, are also engaged to-day, at the Police Headquarters, on Tenth-street, in taking the testimony of a large number of witnesses.

Lieut. TYRELL, of Col. INGRAHAM's staff, last night proceeded to the National Hotel, where BOOTH had been stopping, and took possession of his trunk, in which was found a Colonel's military dress-coat, two pairs of handcuffs, two boxes of cartridges and a package of letters, all of which are now in the possession of the military authorities.

One of these letters, bearing the date of Hookstown, Md., seems to implicate BOOTH. The writer speaks of "the mysterious affair in which you are engaged," and urges BOOTH to proceed to Richmond, and ascertain the views of the authorities there upon the subject. The writer of the letter endeavors to persuade BOOTH from carrying his designs into execution at that time, for the reason, as the writer alleges, that the government had its suspicions aroused. The writer of the letter seems to have been implicated with BOOTH in "the mysterious affair" referred to, as he informs BOOTH in the letter that he would prefer to express his views verbally; and then goes on to say that he was out of money, had no clothes, and would be compelled to leave home, as his family were desirous that he should dissolve his connection with BOOTH. This letter is written on note paper, in a small, neat hand, and simply bears the signature of "Sam."

At the Cabinet meeting yesterday, which lasted over two hours, the future policy of the government toward Virginia was discussed, the best feeling prevailed. It is stated that it was determined to adopt a very liberal policy, as was recommended by the President. It is said that this meeting was the most harmonious held for over two years, the President exhibiting throughout that magnanimity and kindness of heart which has ever characterized his treatment of the rebellious States, and which has been so illy requited on their part.

One of the members of the Cabinet remarked to a friend he met at the door, that "The government was to-day stronger than it had been for three years past."

WASHINGTON, Saturday, April 15—2:30 P. M.

To-day no one is allowed to leave the city by rail conveyance, or on foot, and the issuing of passes from the Headquarters of the Department of Washington has been suspended by Gen. AUGUR.

### Probable Attempt of the Assassins to Escape into Canada—Order from the War Department.

[CIRCULAR.]

WAR DEPARTMENT,
PROVOST MARSHAL GENERAL'S BUREAU,
WASHINGTON, D. C.—9.40 A. M., April 15.

It is believed that the assassins of the President and Secretary SEWARD are attempting to escape to Canada. You will make a careful and thorough examination of all persons attempting to cross from the United States into Canada, and will arrest all suspicious persons. The most vigilant scrutiny on your part, and the force at your disposal, is demanded. A description of the parties supposed to be implicated in the murder will be telegraphed you to-day. But in the meantime be active in preventing the crossing of any suspicious persons.

By order of the Secretary of War.

N. L. JEFFERS, Brevet Brig. Gen.,
Acting Provost-Marshal General.

## MR. SEWARD AND SON.

### Secretary Seward will Recover—Frederick Seward Still Very Low.

Special Dispatch to the New-York Times.

WASHINGTON, Saturday, April 15.

Mr. SEWARD will recover.

FREDERICK SEWARD is still unconscious. He breathes calmly and has an easy pulse. His head is dreadfully contused and lacerated.

An invalid soldier nurse saved Mr. SEWARD's life.

## GEN. GRANT'S MOVEMENTS.

PHILADELPHIA, Saturday, April 15.

Gen. GRANT arrived in this city late last night on his way to Jersey, but was intercepted on his way to Walnut-street wharf, by a dispatch from the office of the Associated Press, and it is supposed he returned to Washington immediately.

### His Return to Washington—Dispatch from Mrs. Grant.

BURLINGTON, N. J., Saturday, April 15.

Lieut.-Gen. GRANT left Burlington for Washington, at 6 o'clock this morning.

MRS. U. S. GRANT.

WASHINGTON, Saturday, April 15.

Gen. GRANT, who left yesterday for New-Jersey, and who was informed of the assassination as he was leaving Philadelphia this morning, arrived here in a special train about noon, and immediately proceeded to the President's house.

### The Theatres.

Dispatches from Boston announce that all the theatres in that city will be closed until further notice.

In this city a movement of the same kind has been inaugurated. Fox's Old Bowery Theatre will be closed this evening.

## THE SUCCESSION.

### Mr. Johnson Inaugurated as President.

### The Oath Administered by Secretary Chase.

### He Will Perform His Duties Trusting in God.

WASHINGTON, Saturday, April 15—12 A. M.

ANDREW JOHNSON was sworn into office as President of the United States by Chief-Justice CHASE, to-day, at eleven o'clock.

Secretary MCCULLOUGH and Attorney-General SPEED, and others were present.

He remarked:

"The duties are mine. I will perform them, trusting in God.

SECOND DISPATCH.

WASHINGTON, Saturday, April 15.

At an early hour this morning, Hon. EDWIN M. STANTON, Secretary of War, sent an official communication to Hon. ANDREW JOHNSON, Vice-President of the United States, that in consequence of the sudden and unexpected death of the Chief Magistrate, his inauguration should take place as soon as possible, and requesting him to state the place and hour at which the ceremony should be performed.

Mr. JOHNSON immediately replied that it would be agreeable to him to have the proceedings take place at his rooms in the Kirkwood House as soon as the arrangements could be perfected.

Chief Justice CHASE was informed of the fact and repaired to the appointed place in company with Secretary MCCULLOUGH, of the Treasury Department, Attorney-General SPEED, J. P. BLAIR, Sr., Hon. MONTGOMERY BLAIR, Senators FOOT, of Vermont, RAMSAY, of Minnesota, YATES, of Illinois, STEWART, of Nevada, HALE, of New Hampshire, and Gen. FARNSWORTH, of Illinois.

At eleven o'clock the oath of office was administered by the Chief Justice of the United States, in his usual solemn and impressive manner.

Mr. JOHNSON received the kind expressions of the gentlemen by whom he was surrounded in a manner which showed his earnest sense of the great responsibilities so suddenly devolved upon him, and made a brief speech, in which he said:

"The duties of the office are mine. I will perform them. The consequences are with God. Gentlemen, I shall lean upon you. I feel that I shall need your support. I am deeply impressed with the solemnity of the occasion and the responsibility of the duties of the office I am assuming.

Mr. JOHNSON appeared to be in remarkably good health, and has a high and realizing sense of the hopes that are centred upon him. His manner was solemn and dignified, and his whole bearing produced a most gratifying impression upon those who participated in the ceremonies.

It is probable that during the day President JOHNSON will issue his first proclamation to the American People.

It is expected, though nothing has been definitely determined upon, that the funeral of the late President LINCOLN will take place on or about Thursday next. It is supposed that his remains will be temporarily deposited in the Congressional Cemetery.

## FROM RICHMOND.

WASHINGTON, Saturday, April 15.

The Richmond *Whig* of yesterday, contains the following:

HEADQUARTERS DEPARTMENT OF VIRGINIA,
RICHMOND, Va., April 13, 1865.

Owing to recent events, the permission for the reassembling of the gentlemen recently acting as the Legislature of Virginia, is rescinded. Should any of the gentlemen come to the city under the notice of reassembling already published, they will be furnished passports to return to their homes. Any of the persons named in the call signed by J. A. CAMPBELL and others, who are found in the city, twelve hours after the publication of this notice, will be subject to arrest, unless they are residents of this city.

E. O. C. ORD, Maj.-Gen.,
Commanding the Department.

HEADQUARTERS DEPARTMENT OF VIRGINIA,
ARMY OF THE JAMES, RICHMOND, Va., April 13, 1865.

GENERAL ORDERS No. 37.—Provost-Marshals will grant no passes to citizens from the North or to officers to come to this city, except on orders from the President, the Secretary of War, Lieut.-Gen. GRANT or the Department Commander.

Officers and soldiers now in the city will return to their respective commands at once, or be subject to arrest and confinement.

The Provost-Marshal-General is charged with the execution of this order.

By command of Maj.-Gen. ORD.

E. W. SMITH, Assistant Adjutant-General.

The *Whig* says: Maj.-Gen. GODFREY WEITZEL, commanding the Twenty-fourth Army Corps and Commander of the forces occupying Richmond, has been relieved from his command, and assigned to Petersburgh and vicinity. Maj.-Gen. E. O. C. ORD, commanding the Army of the James, assumes command of this department.

The report that Gen. R. E. LEE arrived in this city on Wednesday evening, was incorrect. The statement originated in the fact that Gen. CURTIS LEE had reached the city on a visit to his mother, Mrs. R. E. LEE. CURTIS LEE is a prisoner in the hands of the Union army, and, being at City Point, was kindly permitted to come to this city to see his mother, who was reported to be in ill-health.

The whereabouts of Gen. ROBERT E. LEE is not known here—at least, not outside of official circles. He is daily expected at Richmond.

### Personal.

ST. LOUIS, Friday, April 14.

Maj.-Gen. BANKS and family left this morning for New-Orleans.

## THE NATIONAL CALAMITY.

### Popular Feeling in New-York and the Country.

### REMARKABLE MEETING IN WALL-STREET

### Speeches of Representative Men.

### Doings of the City Council and Other Public Bodies

### Public Expression Throughout the Country.

### Sympathy of the Nova Scotia Parliament.

### A Rebel Flag Ordered to be Hauled Down.

### PROCLAMATION BY GOV. FENTON.

EXECUTIVE CHAMBER, ALBANY, April 15.

The fearful tragedy at Washington has converted an occasion of rejoicing over national victory into one of national mourning. It is fitting, therefore, that the 20th of April, heretofore set apart as a day of thanksgiving, should now be dedicated to services appropriate to a season of national bereavement. Bowing reverently to the Providence of God, let us assemble in our places of worship on that day to acknowledge our dependence on Him who has brought sudden darkness on the land in the very hour of its restoration to Union, Peace and Liberty.

In witness whereof, I have hereunto set my hand and affixed the privy seal of the State, at the City of Albany, this 15th day of April, in the year of our Lord one thousand eight hundred and sixty-five.

(Signed,) R. E. FENTON.

By the Governor,
GEORGE S. HASTINGS, Private Secretary.

### The State Legislature.

SENATE.

ALBANY, Saturday, April 15.

After an impressive prayer by Rev. Mr. SELKIRK, Mr. HUMPHREY said:

Mr. President—I understand that His Excellency the Governor is about to send a communication to this body, announcing the terrible calamity that has befallen our country. I move, therefore that no business be transacted until the reception of the communication from the Governor.

Subsequently Col. HASTINGS, the Governor's Private Secretary, appeared within the bar of the Senate and delivered the following message:

STATE OF NEW-YORK, EXECUTIVE CHAMBER,
ALBANY, April 15, 1865.

*To the Legislature:*

It becomes my painful duty to announce to the Legislature the death of ABRAHAM LINCOLN, President of the United States. It is with emotions of profoundest sorrow that I make this announcement to your honorable body. Such an event is a national calamity, and under the circumstances now attending the bereavement, the nation weeps with heightened anguish. To be deprived of his wisdom, experience and counsel at a time when most important to return to the United States peace, fraternity and prosperity—at a time when the gigantic war which confronted him at the threshold of his Administration is about drawing to a close, and a final deliverance obtained from our civil disturbances for which we have sacrificed so much, is a calamity that will cause the deepest sorrow and gloom to the millions of our land, and to the friends of freedom throughout the world.

This is the third time in our history that the Republic has been subjected to this trial, but it is hoped that our good cause and country, watered by a nation's tears and sanctified by its prayers, will pass in safety through the ordeal to a higher life and destiny. I have also to communicate to you the sad intelligence that our noble Secretary of State, and honored, favored son of New-York, WILLIAM H. SEWARD, was likewise a victim of the tragic plot of the assassins, and now lies in an unconscious condition. May God spare his life to this nation.

R. E. FENTON, Governor.

Mr. FOLGER moved the following resolution, which was adopted by consent, in silence:

*Resolved*, If the Assembly concur, that the message of his Excellency, the Governor, be referred to a joint committee of five from the Senate and seven from the Assembly, which was adopted and transmitted to the Assembly, when a recess was taken until 11:30 o'clock.

The President announced the committee on the part of the Senate: Messrs. Folger, Murphy, Andrews, Cook and Shafer.

Subsequently the committee reported the following through Mr. FOLGER:

The Joint Committee of the two Houses on the message of His Excellency the Governor, this day transmitted to the Legislature, makes the following report:

The Committee having in mind that the funeral ceremonies of the late President of the United States will probably take place on some early day in the next week, and that such day will be observed throughout the whole country as a day of solemn recognition of the tragic and awful event which now fills all thoughts, and that the Legislature will join in that observance, do unanimously recommend that on the day which shall be appointed for such obsequies, the two Houses of the Legislature do meet in their respective chambers, at the hour appointed for such funeral ceremonies, and that then, the two Houses being opened with prayer by clergymen especially selected for that service, resolutions appropriate to the occasion be offered. That the Joint Committee of the two Houses be now empowered to sit again to draft such resolutions, and report them on that day to the respective Houses, and do report the following resolution:

*Resolved by the Senate, if the Assembly concur*, That viewing this unexampled and solemn event as demanding a cessation of legislative business, do now adjourn until Tuesday of next week, at 11 o'clock A. M.

CHARLES J. FOLGER,
Chairman of the Senate Committee.
THOMAS B. VAN BUREN,
Chairman of the Assembly Committee.

The report of the Committee was adopted, and the Senate adjourned until Tuesday morning, at 11 o'clock.

## NEW YORK CITY.

### Proclamation by the Mayor.

MAYOR'S OFFICE, NEW-YORK, April 15, 1865.

*Citizens of New York:*

The death of the President of the United States may well excite your profound grief and amazement. I respectfully recommend that business be suspended, and that a public mourning for the departed Chief Magistrate be observed throughout the city.

C. GODFREY GUNTHER, Mayor.

### Expressions of Sorrow.

But few words are needed to express the condition of our city since the reception of the news of President LINCOLN's assassination. All men sorrow, all hearts are grieved and sickened at the great calamity which oppresses the nation, and universal gloom attests the sincerity of those

[Continued on Eighth Page.]

The New-York Times.

VOL. XVII......NO. 5107. NEW-YORK, THURSDAY, FEBRUARY 6, 1868. PRICE FOUR CENTS.

# TELEGRAMS.

## John Bright Demands Church Legislative Reform for Ireland.

## The Singing of a Papal Te Deum Prohibited in Italy.

## Entente Cordiale Between Italy and Prussia.

### THE IRISH QUESTION.

**John Bright's Views of Reform in Ireland and Opinion of its Probable Effects.**

LONDON, Wednesday, Feb. 5.

At a great meeting at Birmingham yesterday JOHN BRIGHT made a speech. He pleaded the wrongs of Ireland in part extenuation of the late Fenian outrages, and begged for Church legislative reform. Mr. BRIGHT said that there was nothing that the United States Government could do if Ireland were part and parcel of the United States, that England might not do also if she would.

### GREAT BRITAIN.

**Comments of the British Press upon the arrest of Mr. Train—His Imprisonment "a Mistake."**

LONDON, Wednesday, Feb. 5.

The London *Times* has an editorial to-day on the arrest of Irish-Americans. It admits that the imprisonment of Mr. TRAIN at Cork was a mistake; but says it should be distinguished from the arrest of Irishmen who come over here from the United States with the secret intention of creating a revolt against the Government.

**An Intended Fenian Attack Upon Macroom Castle Frustrated—Attempted Murder.**

CORK, Wednesday, Feb. 5.

Early this morning a considerable body of men, supposed to be Fenians, were discovered in the vicinity of Macroom Castle, about twenty miles west of this city. They appeared to be preparing to make an attack upon the Castle, and the authorities of the town of Macroom were notified of the danger. A strong force of police were forthwith ordered to the ground, and as soon as they appeared the Fenians dispersed in all directions.

LONDON, Wednesday, Feb. 5—Evening.

A man named CHATTERTON was shot in the street to-day and badly, if not fatally, wounded. The assassin was instantly arrested, and gave his name as JEM. MEDDLES. From his declarations it seems that he mistook CHATTERTON for JAMES BIRD, the milkman, who is an important witness for the Government in the affair of the Clerkenwell explosion, and who at the examination of the prisoners before the Police Court identified one of them as the man that fired the powder.

It is said that MEDDLES is a half-witted fellow, and the belief is general that he is the tool of other parties, who prompted him to commit the deed.

The pistol shot took effect in the throat of Mr. CHATTERTON, where it made a very ugly wound. He still lives, but his recovery is doubtful.

**Continuance of the Strike of Liverpool Cabmen.**

LIVERPOOL, Wednesday, Feb. 5.

The strike of the cabmen in this city still continues to the great inconvenience of all classes. At present there is no prospect of a compromise.

### ITALY AND ROME.

**Royal Prohibition of Religious Ceremonies in Celebration of the Papal Victory—Riots in Padua.**

FLORENCE, Wednesday, Feb. 5.

The Pope recently ordered the Catholic clergy to have a *Te Deum* sung in all the churches of Italy for the victory of the Papal arms at Mentana. King VICTOR EMMANUEL has issued a proclamation prohibiting the holding of religious ceremonies for such a purpose within the Kingdom.

Popular tumults are reported to have broken out in Padua yesterday. The Government is using every means to restore order.

### PRUSSIA AND ITALY.

**Reception of the Italian Ambassador—Evidence of an Entente-Cordiale.**

PARIS, Wednesday, Feb. 5.

The *Moniteur* gives an account of the reception of Signor BEREDUTTI, the new Italian Minister to Berlin, by the King of Prussia. The King warmly welcomed him as the first Ambassador from Italy accredited to the North German Confederation, and congratulated him upon his appointment, declaring that it was a new pledge of peace.

**Destructive Fire at Scranton, Penn.**

SCRANTON, Penn., Wednesday, Feb. 5.

The buildings Nos. 322, 324, 326, 328 and 330 Lackawanna-avenue, were burned to-night. Loss over $100,000; insurance about $65,000. Geo. H. Wilson, hatter; Darby Melvin, liquor-dealer; Dale & Keene, produce commission merchants; D. Morris, merchant tailor; Geo. Blake & Co., books and fancy goods; Crandall & Co., of the *Daily Republican;* Miss Jane Coolbough and H. M. Klein, are the principal losers. The *Republican* saved its engine and two cylinder presses; everything else is as good as a total loss. Blake & Co.'s stock on the first floor of No. 322 was not burned, but very badly injured by water and plundering. In all the other buildings the loss was total. Eight or ten families in the upper parts of the buildings lost everything.

**Great Storm and Loss of Life.**

HARBOR GRACE, N. F., Wednesday, Feb. 5.

One of the most severe and terrific storms ever known in Newfoundland has been experienced within the last two or three days. On the 3d inst. a most fearful gale prevailed, driving the falling snow furiously before it. It is reported that thirty people have perished from the cold and in the snow. Mr. MACKAY, the Superintendent of the Newfoundland Telegraph Line, nearly perished between Heart's Content and this place.

**Arrest of a United States Teller.**

LOUISVILLE, Ky., Wednesday, Feb. 5.

Joseph BLOOMGART, Assistant Teller United States Depository, in this city, was arrested yesterday for embezzling Government money to the amount of over $12,000. BLOOMGART made a written statement, acknowledging his guilt, and says the money has been spent.

**The Army of the Cumberland.**

CINCINNATI, Wednesday, Feb. 5.

A meeting of the officers of the Army of the Cumberland will be held here to-morrow, for the purpose of organizing a Society of the Army of the Cumberland. Lieut.-Gen. SHERMAN, Major-Gen. THOMAS and staff, and a large number of other distinguished officers will be present. The proceedings will close on Saturday with a grand banquet.

**The National Commercial Convention.**

BOSTON, Wednesday, Feb. 5.

The National Commercial Convention assembled at Mechanics' Hall, at 11 o'clock this morning.

CHARLES C. NAZRO, President of the Boston Board of Trade, called the delegates to order and delivered the opening address.

FREDERICK FRALEY, of Philadelphia, was then chosen temporary President, and a committee from each Board of Trade represented was appointed on permanent organization and rules.

A recess was then taken.

A permanent organization of the Commercial Convention was made as follows:

*President*—E. W. Fox, of St. Louis.

*Vice-Presidents at Large*—W. Merrill and George F. Daggett; by States—F. S. Sage, of New-York; G. H. Thurston, of Pennsylvania; J. Y. Munn, of Illinois; J. V. Lee, of Virginia; C. A. King, of Ohio; A. W. Fagin, of Missouri; W. D. Medberry, of Wisconsin; D. C. Hersey, of Maine; A. Dewitt, of California; S. S. Lobdell, of Delaware; C. G. Nazro, of Massachusetts; R. Blakely, of Minnesota; T. W. Barleywaite, of Iowa; Julius Dow, of Kentucky.

*Secretaries*—H. A. Hill, of Boston; J. F. Beatty, of Illinois; Jason Parker, of Buffalo; Thomas A. Winan, of Cincinnati; J. C. Sage, of Ohio; Edward Butts, of Delaware.

President FOX was conducted to the chair by Gen. HIRAM WALBRIDGE, of New-York, and made a short address stating that the duty of the Convention was to do what it could to invite the commercial and industrial interests of the country in bonds of alliance for public good.

The rules governing the United States House of Representatives were adopted, with the exception that speeches should be limited to ten minutes, and no member should speak but once on any subject.

After completing other preliminary business the Convention adjourned to 10 o'clock to-morrow morning.

After the adjournment the delegates accepted an invitation to a sleigh-ride, about the city and suburbs, followed by a concert in Music Hall. To-morrow afternoon the ladies of the delegates will have a sleigh ride, and in the evening a banquet will take place in the Music Hall by invitation of the city authorities.

**Special Order by Gen. Hancock—Removal from Office of Street Commissioner Baker, of New-Orleans.**

NEW-ORLEANS, Wednesday, Feb. 5.

Gen. HANCOCK, in Special Order No. 26, issued to-day, directs the investigation of the charges of malfeasance in office against Street Commissioner BAKER to be stopped; directs the District-Attorney to take charge of the matter, and take such action as may be proper and necessary, proceeding by due course of law.

BAKER was removed from office and GEO. D. FIELD appointed in his place.

The same order appoints ARTHUR GASTINEL as Recorder of the Second District, he having been declared by the Supreme Court ineligible when elected, but now eligible.

**North Carolina Conservative Convention.**

RALEIGH, N. C., Wednesday, Feb. 5.

The Conservative Convention met at Tucker's Hall to-day. About fifty counties were represented by about three hundred delegates.

R. H. SMITH, Esq., of Halifax, was chosen temporary chairman. Hon. W. A. GRAHAM, of Orange, was elected permanent President of the Convention with thirteen Vice-Presidents. The several editors in attendance were chosen Secretaries.

The best of spirit prevails, and many of the ablest men in the State are present.

**Democratic Caucus at Trenton, N. J.**

TRENTON, N. J., Wednesday, Feb. 5.

The joint Democratic caucus was held to-night to nominate State and County officers. None have yet been made. They passed the following resolutions, unanimously, recommending the nomination of Gov. PARKER for the Presidency:

*Resolved*, That the maintenance of the rights of the States, the protection of the liberties of the citizens the financial management, executive ability and enlarged patriotism that distinguished the administration of Hon. JOEL PARKER, late Governor of this State, in the most trying period of her history, will ever be gratefully remembered by the Democracy of New-Jersey.

*Resolved*, That, in view of the high personal character and unsullied political record of Ex-Gov. PARKER, we believe that his nomination for the office of President of the United States by the National Democratic Convention would unite the conservative elements of the country and secure the success of the Democracy in the approaching Presidential election.

**The Western Massachusetts Mechanics' Fair.**

SPRINGFIELD, Mass., Wednesday, Feb. 5.

The Western Massachusetts Mechanics' Fair opened at the City Hall in this city this evening, with very flattering indications, the number of machines and inventions exhibited being very large. The fair will continue four days, and many mechanics and inventors are arriving in the city.

HOLMES, the insurance agent, was tried at New-Haven this morning for abduction and acquitted.

**Suspension of Payment of the Gayoso Savings Institution of Memphis—Outrage.**

MEMPHIS, Wednesday, Feb. 5.

The Gayoso Savings Institution, the oldest bank in the city, suspended to-day. It is understood its liabilities will exceed $500,000.

WILLIS HALL, a fireman, was arrested yesterday at the instance of his wife, for raping his step-daughters, aged 11 and 12 years. He was committed to-day in default of $200 bail.

**Explosion at Pittsburg—One Man Killed.**

PITTSBURG, Penn., Wednesday, Feb. 5.

An explosion occurred at 5 o'clock this morning in the tin works of JOHN D. GRAY, at Frankstown Station, near Pittsburg, by which JOHN HARRIS, the engineer, was instantly killed, and his son, the fireman, seriously injured. The works were partially destroyed. The cause of the explosion is unknown.

**Accident on the New-Haven Railroad.**

PORTCHESTER, Wednesday, Feb. 5.

This afternoon about 4 o'clock THOMAS ARMSTRONG, a painter, formerly of Carmansville, N. Y., was found on the track of the New-Haven Railroad, near this station. It is supposed he had been struck and instantly killed by the Boston express train. The body was brought to this station and the Coroner notified.

**Appointment of Canal Engineers.**

ALBANY, Wednesday, Feb. 5.

At a meeting of the Canal Board to-day the following Division Engineers were appointed on the State canals: Eastern Division, E. H. CROOKER, in place of O. L. WETMORE; Middle Division, M. S. KIMBALL, in place of W. H. H. GERE; Western Division, DAN'L RICHMOND, to fill vacancy.

**Formation of a Grant Club at Wilmington, Del.**

WILMINGTON, Del., Wednesday, Feb. 5.

A large meeting was held this evening to organize a Republican GRANT Club. A large club was organized, and H. M. JENKINS, of the *Daily Commercial*, elected President. A mass meeting is to be held hereafter.

FIRE IN THIRD-AVENUE.—At 1:15 o'clock yesterday morning a fire occurred in the confectionary store of Mrs. FRANCIS KALF, at No. 960 Third-avenue, resulting in a damage of $1,000, covered by an insurance of $2,500 in the Brooklyn and Lafayette Companies. The plumber's shop of GILLROY & REYNOLDS, adjoining, was damaged to the extent of $200; covered by insurance. T. HOGANS, tinsmith, sustained a loss of $100. The building is damaged to the extent of about $600; insured.

# NEW-YORK.

## Proceedings of the Republican State Convention.

## Gen. Grant for President and Gov. Fenton for Vice-President.

**Speeches by C. H. Van Wyck, Lieut.-Gov. Woodford, Horace Greeley, Lyman Tremaine, and Others.**

SYRACUSE, Wednesday, Feb. 5.

The Republican State Convention, to nominate delegates to the Chicago National Republican Convention, met to-day at Shakespearean Hall, and was called to order soon after noon by HAMILTON HARRIS, Chairman of the State Central Committee. Mr. E. M. MADDEN nominated for temporary Chairman Mr. JOSHUA M. VAN COTT, of Kings County. Carried. Messrs. MADDEN and BARKER, of Schuyler, were appointed to conduct him to the chair. Mr. VAN COTT addressed the Convention.

Mr. VAN WYCK nominated Gen. JAMES S. HALL for Secretary. Carried.

Messrs. CALDWELL, JACOB C. CUTLER and H. C. WATKINS were appointed additional Secretaries.

HAMILTON HARRIS moved that the rules of the Assembly be adopted as the rules of this body.

The motion to adopt the rules of the Senate was then put and lost, and the rules of the Assembly adopted.

The list of delegates was then called, and it was found that each county was fully represented.

On the call of the New-York delegates, Mr. R. W. ANDREWS handed up a list of contestants, approved by the signatures of E. DELAFIELD SMITH, THOMAS MURPHY and A. G. PLUMB.

Mr. WM. G. WEED moved the appointment of two from each judicial district on contested seats. Carried.

Mr. E. DELAFIELD SMITH said that when it is seen that the contesting delegations do not come here to to make dissensions, nor even to insist upon seats in this body, he thought it would be admitted by all that it is not asking too much to ask this Convention to direct a reorganization of our party in the City. It cannot be denied that the party in New-York City is in a state of disorganization. Neither organization there has the confidence of our party there, or in the State. Then let this Committee just ordered report a resolution ordering a reorganization, and thus secure harmony of action there, and confidence in us throughout the State. [Applause.]

Mr. SMITH—I don't want to be applauded, but to be heard.

Mr. CHARLES S. SPENCER—You had better first get applauded by somebody besides your own delegation.

M. SMITH—There was a time when my friend would have applauded me instead of throwing stones, but I ask for the adoption of a resolution such as I have indicated. Let us go into this campaign not only united in purpose, but thoroughly satisfied on all hands. It should be remembered that our organization is the old original ground of the Republican Party in the city, and if some of us have strayed, it was due only to fidelity to one who, for many years, was the chosen leader of our party, and such fidelity ought to commend itself to this body, for such fidelity will always find admiration in the hearts of frank, fair-dealing minds. We are united against JOHNSON. We are united for GRANT. Let us then be united in our labors to punish the one and honor and exalt the other.

In concluding Mr. SMITH offered the following:

*Resolved*, That the Committee on Credentials be instructed to report a resolution providing for a reorganization of the Republican Party in the City and County of New-York, under the joint supervision and direction of Hon. FREEMAN J. FITHIAN and Hon. THOMAS MURPHY.

Mr. CHAS. S. SPENCER read from the NEW-YORK TIMES the resolution adopted by the Murphy organization, and published previously to the last gubernatorial election approving of the reconstruction policy of President JOHNSON, and pledging their hearty support to the election of JOHN T. HOFFMAN and ROBERT H. PRUYN. [Laughter.] He also quoted from the NEW-YORK TIMES the remarks of RUFUS H. ANDREWS, published two weeks ago, against holding this Convention thus early, charging it upon Gov. FENTON as being at the bottom of the election of State Committees, and threatening another convention in April to choose contesting delegates for Chicago. His friend said his delegation represented the old Republican Guards, but he forgot to liken that guard to the Old Guard of NAPOLEON, which died, but never surrendered. His old guard, though dead, will not surrender. [Laughter.] Why, it is only a few days ago that one of the most distinguished members of that organization told ANDREW JOHNSON that he was the only man who stood faithfully to the Constitution, [laughter,] and yet these are the men who are asking us to reorganize in New-York for their benefit. Sir, they cannot add anything to our vote. It will be large and triumphant without them—larger if we keep our skirts clear than if we listen to this seductive invitation to be shorn of our strength. We may be sick, but if we are we will take Plantation Bitters for our medicine, and the ten doses that we will take will be sure to carry us safely through.

Mr. THOMAS B. VAN BUREN was not at all surprised at the tone adopted by the gentleman last up. It was characteristic, and was calculated to cover reason and sense with sound. A member of the contesting organization, it would not have been strange if the gentleman, with his audacity of speech, had arraigned him too for some shortcoming; but it was out of his power to do so. He Mr. (VAN BUREN) claimed to be pretty radical, and he came here not as a dissatisfied member of either organization, but in the hope of being able in some way to help in bringing about a thorough reorganization of the party in the City of New-York. That there is dissatisfaction there, and consequently weakness, cannot be denied, and now, of all other times, is the opportunity to remedy the evil. It has been charged that some of those acting with our delegation once supported certain Democratic nominees. Well, their offence in that respect is not so fresh as is the offence of certain leading gentlemen on the other side, who, to his positive knowledge, supported at the last Mayoralty election FERNANDO WOOD instead of Mr. DARLING—the result being that Mr. DARLING received but 18,000 votes, while years before, when he (VAN BUREN) ran for Recorder, he received nearly 40,000 votes. These are facts that cannot be ignored. But he (VAN BUREN) firmly believed that it was in the hands of this Convention to bring about perfect unity where discord and dissension now reign, and that unity once secured and confidence restored in the City and State, New-York will be sure for at least 50,000 Republican majority in the contest next Fall.

Mr. F. G. FITHIAN opposed the resolution, believing it inexpedient. It was his firm conviction that instead of adding to our strength it would weaken us, for it would be sure to make sore the hearts of 25,000 Republicans in the City of New-York, who have always stood firmly and fearlessly by all our principles and against all our enemies. If these gentlemen mean what they say, let them join our party. There is but one true Republican organization in New-York, and every honest Republican can join it cheerfully, and will be gladly received. But there are gentlemen belonging to the contestants who are not honest in their professions, and such will not join us in any way save to cheat and injure. It is of these that we must beware, and they are the men who are most urgent for a reënrollment.

Mr. RUFUS W. ANDREWS said that if these gentlemen are competent to run the Republican Party, why is it that our vote in the City of New York has dwindled under their management from 40,000 down to 18,000? If we are to indulge in recriminations, why has it been forgotten that HORACE GREELEY, with his *Tribune*, opposed our nominee, Mr. MARSHALL O. ROBERTS, for Mayor, and supported a thorough Copperhead? That cannot be denied. It has been charged that I recently had a conversation with President JOHNSON, in which I said that he was the only man who had stood up for the Constitution. He (ANDREWS) never had such a conversation with President JOHNSON, and it was simply the villification of a reporter. His pleasant interview with Gen. GRANT has been almost as grossly misrepresented—but he (ANDREWS) did not like those personalities. If we have strength, and it is admitted by all who are seeking to repulse us, why not say to us unite, and let us work together. We are anxious for unity—anxious to work hard and harmoniously. You have need for money. We have time and time again contributed more than all the rest of you put together. Can you afford, then, to reject our work and our means.

Mr. A. N. COLE moved the following substitute, moving, at the same time, the "previous question" upon it:

*Whereas*, The last Republican State Convention fully and freely heard and determined the contest between the Radical and Conservative Republican organizations of the City of New-York, and unanimously declared in favor of the Radical organization: and

*Whereas*, The same contest is again presented here, unchanged: therefore,

*Resolved*, That the delegates to this Convention credentialed by the Radical Republican organization of the City of New-York, and headed by NATHAN KINGSLEY, be and are hereby admitted to seats in this Convention.

*Resolved*, That the Conservative Delegation from New-York be, and they are hereby invited to occupy seats upon the floor of this Convention.

Amid cries of question and decisions on points of order, the previous question was ordered.

Mr. E. MADDEN asked to be excused, for the reason that when dissension was going on, he attempted to speak, but was choked off, and the talking was all done by the members of the worrying city factions. He was in favor of giving the contesting delegation a chance to make good their boast that if an opportunity is offered them to secure harmonious action in the City, they will see to it that our vote there is increased ten to fifteen thousand.

A Delegate—I call the gentleman to order.

The Chair—The gentleman, under cover of being excused from voting, is giving his reasons why he should vote on one side and against the other. He is, therefore, out of order. He will proceed in order.

Mr. MADDEN would only repeat that he was in favor of the Convention so acting as to harmonize and unite its true organization, and then work in the great campaign before us.

The Convention refused the excuse, and he voted no.

The vote on the substitute stood 295 yeas to 86 nays.

Mr. CHARLES S. SPENCER moved that a committee of two from each Judicial District be appointed to report permanent officers.

Mr. C. M. SCHOFIELD moved to amend that the temporary officers be the permanent officers.

Mr. E. MADDEN opposed the motion to amend. It was lost, and SPENCER's motion carried.

Mr. LYMAN TREMAINE moved a committee of two from each Judicial District to report resolutions, the said resolutions to lay on the table until after the permanent organization. Carried.

The Chair announced the following Committee on Permanent Organization: Charles S. Spencer, J. V. Gridley, Hamilton Harris, S. L. Penfield, A. C. Churchill, S. P. Remington, Bemen Brockway, Wm. H. Lamport, A. M. Grier, Charles S. Morton, Isaac Holloway, John J. Woocott, B. F. Hoppin, T. J. Chatfield.

Recess for one hour.

The Convention reconvened at 4:30 o'clock P. M.

Mr. CHAS. SPENCER, from the Committee on Permanent Organization, reported the following, which was adopted unanimously:

*President*—Mr. CHARLES H. VAN WYCK.

*Vice-Presidents*—Messrs. Horace Greeley, Waldo Hutchins, Wm. H. Gleason, Volney Green, Lorenzo D. Collins, F. S. Thayer, B. W. Judson, George P. Batchelder, Joseph A. Sherman, A. P. Hart, W. W. Campbell, Giles W. Hotchkiss, Hiram Schutt, Geo. Arnold, Seth Clark and H. C. Fiske.

*Secretaries*—Messrs. Joseph F. Ellory, Isaac J. Oliver, Alfred Wagstaff, Stephen C. Hutchins, Robt. Horder, Chas. G. Ellis, J. W. Kimball, W. Strong, J. R. Stebbins, Luther Caldwell, Wm. L. Bostwick, Robt. H. Wiley, Joseph A. Stull, Wm. B. Sirritt and T. E. Ellsworth.

Messrs. WALDO HUTCHINS and CHAS. S. SPENCER were appointed to conduct Mr. VAN WYCK to the chair, on taking which he said:

MR. VAN WYCK'S SPEECH.

Although the battle has been fought and victory won, yet the victors and vanquished are engaged in another struggle—one to preserve, the other to destroy the fruits of that victory. We are called upon once again to marshal the grand army of the Union. The same Providence has decreed the length and fierceness of the conflict at the ballot-box, as he did with the bayonet, and for the same glorious result—equal and exact justice to all men. The nation required four years of war to be taught in what direction lay the path of justice and duty. They may need four years of struggle to teach them boldly to walk in it. We have passed our Red Sea in triumph. The horse and rider have been thrown in the sea. We have rejoiced upon our timbrel and harp, and are now passing through the wilderness. Yet, the bow of promise still shines in the heavens above us. How true it is, that "the price of liberty is eternal vigilance!" that the sentinel does not slumber at the outpost, nor the watchman lie at ease in his tower! After the war was ended we could look back and discover the great errors committed, and as Time is bearing us away from one and another of the civil contests, we find that serious mistakes in war and in peace have been the same—too much forgiveness and too great leniency to rebel criminals. The war was waged for years with the determination not to disturb the institutions which produced the rebellion, and not to harm those who were striving to overthrow the pillars of the Republic. We are yet told we must conciliate; otherwise the men who sought to destroy and failed, will come not back again. That *rôle* has been played. Their crime deserved confiscation of property and death. They were only asked to accept citizenship on a higher plane of civilization to which their treason had forced the nation; to recognize those principles which have given courage to our heroes and inspiration to our poets; to resume forfeited rights on condition of equal rights, which a broader Christian civilization has granted the oppressed; to aid in administering State Governments which they overthrew, only securing the same privileges to those who fought to sustain them. All such propositions they have spurned. JOHNSON has taught them that they were masters of the situation—had power indefinitely to delay the work of reconstruction. Congress was told to vote $1,000,000 to feed the suffering poor. It would be the "open sesame" to rebel hearts and renew their devotion to the old flag. From that day they have manifested more determination in their opposition to the demands of the nation. The patriots of the Revolution did not attempt to subdue by love those who had been Tories. They proclaimed no general amnesty. Every State save one disfranchised them. Many were driven to Canada and England. The Legislature of New-York, as late as November, 1781, prohibited all Tory lawyers from practicing in the courts of this State. Who has delayed so long the work of reconstruction? The rebels say there shall be none unless upon the terms which they approve. JOHNSON says there shall be none except as dictated by his policy. But the loyal men, the great mass of the population, insist that reconstruction shall be based upon the issues settled by the war; upon the principles illustrated by the death of 300,000 patriots, and the martyrdom of the great LINCOLN; upon such a basis as will not reproach the living soldier, nor blast the memory of the dead; on such a foundation that the future of this Republic may never be cursed again with treason's bloody hand. As this nation has spoken, so shall it be done; as they trampled on the rebellion and its cause, so will they on all who oppose them now. Through this delay, the nation has been growing to full manhood of the crisis. We were told let the Government be magnanimous and release the head of the rebellion. Let prominent men of the North sign the bail bond and have a love-feast with the rebel chief, and the heart of treason will soften and, forsooth, forgive us the humiliation of their defeat. Yet the very act seems only to have intensified the bitterness of their feelings, and DAVIS, released from the pretended torture of his prison, left proudly defiant, went to Canada, publicly thanked that people that they had furnished an asylum for his gangs of desperadoes, who during the war had met within their border to organize arson, rapine, murder and the scattering seed of pestilence. So that other rebel chief, who indulged the hope that he would call the roll of his slaves at the foot of Bunker Hill Monument, and who by reason of his infamous treason had earned the title to be a fugitive all the days of his life. But through this mistaken leniency, which is to change the tiger heart, he was allowed to return. The allies of JOHNSON's rebellion are the same as of DAVIS'. The Copperheads are still advising their friends in the South to their hurt. They counseled them early to resistance, promised them aid and a division among the men of the North, and so did those of Connecticut, that no regiments should cross the State to invade the South; that the grass should grow in the streets of our cities; that our currency would become worthless, and the national bonds not worth the paper they were printed on; that individual property would be swept away for taxes, and the nation made bankrupt. Yet the country has been obstinately prosperous, and they had not decent respect for their own prophecies to grow for themselves. In their judgement laws to raise revenue and conscripts were unconstitutional, and they organized mobs to resist, burn and murder, and who, when LINCOLN, stood as did Moses—his face shining as though his heart had been with God on the mount, amid the thunders of battle—wrote on the tables of the nation's remembrance the great law which the Almighty was giving, and issued the Proclamation of Emancipation, striking the chains from four millions of slaves. How bitter the denunciation—how malignant the slanders. Not only was it unconstitutional, but these prophets of Baal aspired to contemplate the piety of the act, pronounced it unchristian, worse than unloosing savages, in warfare on defenceless women and children, and actually implored the interposition of foreign nations, when on the 4th day of July the then Democratic Governor of the State, in a speech in New-York City, insulted the nation by prophesying our defeat; mocking and taunting, by exclaiming, where are the victories you promised—even that very day his treasonable shrieks were answered by the roar of cannon as the rebel works were crumbling at Vicksburg, and his unholy utterances were drowned in the proud hurrah of our army as they pulled LEE from his defences and broke the rebellion at Gettysburg. Blind to their own destruction, despised for their treasonable prophesies, and signal failure in 1864, they declared in National Convention, the war a failure, demanding a cessation of hostilities and withdrawal of our troops, while SHERMAN was marching through Georgia from Atlanta to the sea, FARRAGUT fighting from the shrouds of his ship at Mobile, GRANT drawing the anaconda folds around Richmond, SHERIDAN throwing himself against the tide of defeat and rolling back waves of victory. Every act of Congress during the war and since they have denounced—during all that time no Democratic Convention spoke harshly of the rebellion or its leaders, and failed to malign the action of their own Government. To-day they are living in the hope that JOHNSON may accomplish what DAVIS failed, and show the world that the war has been a failure; and the Democratic Party, which would fain, on now bended knees, by any device pretend a regard for the soldier it once despised, and always during the war, where it had the power, denied to him in the field the privilege of the elective franchise. It said of the soldier then, as it says of the negro to-day, that it was not safe to trust the ballot in his hands; and when it had no power, true to its affinities, from every bush and brake, where it wound its slimy length, its poisoned fangs would hiss out bitter denunciations by calling them "LINCOLN's minions, hirelings and dogs." Well might he exclaim, "Is my servant a dog that he should do this thing?" The continued resistance of the rebels has satisfied the nation of their unfitness to exercise the rights they forfeited. They refused the amendments to the Constitution, and it became evident that freedom would not be safe in their hands, and as a guarantee negro suffrage was demanded. "How true it is," as the faithful SHERIDAN has said, "the contest is not yet over." The result cannot be doubted. Storms may gather around us as they did during the war. We know that beyond the clouds the sun is shining brightly; we know that the blood of three hundred thousand patriots has not been shed in vain; that they never fail who die in a great cause. Rest assured that JOHNSON has met an Antietam and Gettysburgh, and is now only struggling in the defences around Richmond. Time is pointing clearly to the object of JOHNSON's rebellion. While Congress has been triumphantly sustained the object, and purpose of his life has been to thwart the legislation of the country. See his position to-day. Against the people, against Congress, against the prominent Generals of the nation and the military commanders of his own appointment. In his way stood one of the purest of American patriots as well as one of the ablest of American statesmen, to whom the nation is largely indebted for the great victory of the war and the preservation of the fruits of the conflict. History will yield the meed of praise while coming generations will revere the name of STANTON, yet the purity, ability, long and valuable services of his War Minister were obnoxious to JOHNSON, and in defiance of the law and wishes of the nation, he usurped the power and removed him. The victory over the people was short, thanks to the patriotism of the great Captain of the age, whose loyalty to the nation taught him obedience to the law. GRANT, SHERIDAN and SICKLES, who were between him and the restoration of rebels to power, he reprimands and attempts to disgrace. These military Commanders whom the people delight to honor, he brands as monarchs, satraps, and tyrants; his own organ at Washington saying that SHERIDAN exercised a despotism which far exceeded in atrocity any tyranny in the old world. SHERIDAN, SICKLES, THOMAS and POPE were all Democrats, but they loved their country better than party; they could not reproach the memory of their buried comrades by restoring to power those who would dance with fiendish hate upon their graves. What better commentary and what severer condemnation of JOHNSON's policy than the necessity to relieve his best officers to appease rebel wrath. The issue will not admit of compromise or conservatism; we want no leaders or standard-bearers who cannot defend our principles and carry our banner and wear our uniform. JOHNSON has been playing the part he contemplated a year ago, when he said he might make himself dictator; he has been significantly emphasizing the question of SEWARD, "Will you have this man President or King?" The mission of the Republican Party is not yet completed. With Radical Republicans overthrown and Democratic conservatism in power, where is the prospect of further deliverance to English subjects? How can the German hope that the liberty he here enjoys may one day bless his fatherland? And how would fade away every generous Irishman's prospects that EMMET's epitaph could be written, for he enjoined his countrymen, with the grave opening before him, "When my country shall take her stand among the nations of the earth, then and not till then, let my epitaph be written." Banish Radicalism from the continent and the history of the last Republic in Europe has been written. Why should any boast themselves of conservatism? Has it not always stood in the way of the world's progress? No reformer or discoverer but has found it soiled in his path. To-day, Conservatives in England and America are using the same argument—distrust of the masses; and to-day in both countries Radicalism is rejoicing in the same victory. It boldly asserts that six thousand years of the world's education has not fitted all men and all nations for freedom; that its simplest rights can not be enjoyed, nor its highest duties exercised except as the result of great mental culture and the highest type of intellect. Well may we despair if in this age of the world the humblest of men are not fitted to enjoy the sweets of human liberty. For humanity to-day, white conservatism is distrustful, scowling and shaking its head, we rejoice that under the leadership of that grand old statesman, JOHN BRIGHT, eight hundred thousand white men on English soil have been elevated from hewers of wood and drawers of water to the full rights of English citizenship even in this Republic. Years ago the Democratic Party in this State put the black man where Conservatism wanted to keep the white man, and they themselves settled for all time the right of the black man to vote by securing it in the Constitution of only annexing the property qualifications. To that organization which ground the rebellion to powder will the people look to remove all the evils JOHNSON has inflicted, when by their votes the incubus is removed. May we expect quiet and confidence to be restored, laws to be enforced in their spirit, economy and reform everywhere inaugurated, corrupt officials removed, faith in the currency and bonds of the nation, return labor encouraged, industry protected, equal distribution of burthens and equal taxation of all property, expenses of the Government removed, taxes taken from the necessities and retained only on the luxuries of life, where it shall wake to profitable activity again the grant of the spindle and loom, which is sleeping to-day. JOHNSON may hinder, but not stop, the work of reconstruction. When peace came he did not then recognize the then existing governments in the rebel States. To the United States belonged the duty, as by the Constitution they were enjoined, to guarantee republican governments. But JOHNSON felt as did LOUIS XIV., "I am the State," and without consulting the people or their representatives; by the breath of his power declaring committees without governments, ordering conventions, decreeing wherein constitutions shall be amended, confiscating property, disfranchising large classes, prescribing the qualifications and who shall be voters. When another branch of the Government exercise its legitimate prerogatives in the same direction, he interposes obstacles. He has a right to interpose his veto, for that was a part of the United States, but when two-thirds of Congress overrule his veto, that was a greater part of the United States to which obedience was exacted in the oath that he should take care that the laws be faithfully executed. The work of reconstruction will go on as Congress has ordered. Any impediment JOHNSON throws in the way will be removed from time to time by a supplemental bill, and Congress propose to continue the supplemental work until the end is consumated. State after State will follow the example of Tennessee and wheel into line with shouts of praise that the loyal men of the nation, when storms and clouds gathered, held on an even course, and exacted a restoration to power by engraving on the foundation-stones of each, "All men are created equal," and the topmost arch in radiant light, that patriots oppressed by other countries may take courage, proclaim liberty through all the land and to all the inhabitants thereof. Are we to be censured because JOHNSON has endeavored to mar the beauty and symmetry of the work, as well as upbraid the sculptor? If some vandal should attempt to deface the marble with the face half formed, or the architect; if some evil spirit should seek to undermine the foundations; force upon him untempered mortar instead of imperishable granite; for pillars porous sandstone, which shifting winds and storms and sun would crumble. Hostility to reconstruction was invited by the address of the weeping Convention of Philadelphia in 1867. Within a few days JOHNSON, by his prophet Senator, (DOOLITTLE,) in the Senate Chamber again encouraged the exercised spirit of rebellion by declaring that those of the South will gather on their knees around the family altar to curse this Government, and in the name of prayer to call on God to curse it. In seeking a prophet to pronounce the curse they would probably find another Balaam. Let them be admonished by the story of sacred history, when Balaak wanted to "Curse me this people for they are too mighty for me," and thrice from the mountain-top, and once with face toward the wilderness, Balaam said: "Here shall I curse whom God has not not cursed, and here shall I defy whom the Lord has not defied." Then will JOHNSON, DOOLITTLE & Co. say as did Balaak, trembling: "I took thee to curse my enemies, and behold thou hast blest them altogether." Beseechingly, neither curse them at all, nor bless them at all. Defiant and threatening when his anger was kindled after a third failure: "I thought to promote thee to honor, but this Lord hath kept thee back from great honor." How many times has JOHNSON, when his anger was kindled, reviled the truth, the faithful, the honest. And in the same spirit as Balaak, "I thought to promote thee to great honor," while indulging the vagaries of the circle, SEWARD claimed that JOHNSON was following the policy of LINCOLN. So says DOOLITTLE in his recent speech a few months ago. JOHNSON was present at the dedication of the cemetery at Antietam and there made a speech. Although standing on one of the great battle-fields of the rebellion, a stranger could not have told whether he came to dedicate to rebel or Union aded. Save the last sentence containing a general allusion to the flag, the speech could as well have been spoken by DAVIS. The clustering memories and thrilling associations of the thousand graves around him did not awaken a sentiment or kindle an inspiration to embalm the memory of the dead; no thanks to the living soldiers, no expression of gratitude to the nation for its sacrifice of millions of treasure and thousands of lives, no reference to the dead, except to malign their memory and to burn still deeper into the hearts of the survivors the recollection of their griefs. The world will little note or long remember what we say here, but it can never be forgot what they did here. It is for us, the living, rather to be dedicated here to the unfinished work that they have thus far so nobly carried on; it is rather for us to be here dedicated to the great task remainining before us, that from these honored dead we take increased devotion to the cause for which they here gave up the last full measure of devotion; that we here highly resolve that the dead shall not have died in vain; that the nation shall, under God, have a new birth of freedom, and that the Government of the people, by the people and for the people, shall not perish from the earth." To-day we stand by the utterances of the departed statesmen, rather than the cold sympathy toward rebels of the deceiver, JOHNSON. LINCOLN dedicated himself; he dedicated us of this generation to their unfinished work, so that the dead shall not have died in vain, while by the eye of inspiration he caught glimpses of the coming glory, while be could only indulge the hope and breathe the prayer, "We, if faithfully and fearlessly discharging our duty, may, in our time, rejoice in the fruition and the complete realization that government of the people, by the people, shall not perish from the earth."

Before concluding, Mr. VAN WYCK's voice gave out, and on motion of Gen. COCHRANE it was resolved that he be requested to furnish the concluding part for publication.

Mr. COCHRANE moved the following:

*Resolved*, That a committee be appointed of one from each Congressional District, by the delegates from each Congressional District to report the names of four delegates and four alternates from the State at large, and two delegates and two alternates from each Congressional District, to represent the State in the National Republican Union Convention at Chicago, and that said Committee be directed to report to this Convention for such delegates and alternates from the Congressional Districts, such names as shall be nominated to them by the delegates to this Convention from such Congressional Districts, or a majority of said Congressional Districts, the said Committee shall present to this Convention such names for delegates and alternates.

Mr. CHARLES S. SPENCER moved the following as a substitute, but it was voted down, and Mr. COCHRANE's resolution was adopted:

*Resolved*, That four delegates at large be chosen by a *vive voce* vote, and that the respective delegations from the Congressional districts choose and report to the Convention two delegates and two alternates to Chicago.

Mr. LYMAN TREMAINE called up the resolution for the appointment of a Committee on Resolutions, which was adopted, and the President announced the Committee as follows: *First District*—Horace Greeley, John Cochrane; *Second District*—A. W. Palmer, G. Hilton Scribner; *Third District*—Lyman Tremaine, Robert Kram; *Fourth District*—Charles Hughes, George Yost; *Fifth District*—J. R. Stebbins, Joseph Avery; *Sixth District*—W. W. Campbell, S. M. Barker; *Seventh District*—Thomas Underdonk, J. H. Butler; *Eighth District*—Joseph E. Ewell, M. A. Hall.

The following committee to select delegates to the National Convention was announced by the respective delegations:

Henry W. Eastman, Jonathan Moore, F. T. Parsons, F. Polhemus, Wm. H. McKinney, James W. Howe, John Cochrane, Cummings H. Tucker, Cooper C. Van Vorst, Jas. W. Husted, Edward M. Madden, H. T. Eastman, Geo. A. Sharpe, Hamilton Harris, Jas. C. Clark, Bloomfield Usher, Jas. W. Horton, Sheffield Harrington, Bemin Brockway, Albert Bickford, T. Kingsford, Daniel P. Wood, T. G. Yeoman, W. H. Simpson, Chas. H. Thompson, Ben. Field, D. D. Wait, Alvias Snyder, Seth Clark, Chas. L. Morton.

Mr. A. C. PULLMAN, of New-York, said that the question of representation in Republican Conventions had long been a mooted question, and on that question he moved the following resolution:

*Resolved*, That the Convention of the Republican Union Party of this State shall hereafter consist of delegates apportioned as follows: First—One delegate from each Assembly District; Second—One additional delegate for every one thousand Republican votes, and fractional part of one thousand, which shall be five hundred or over, from each district casting such vote—the basis for such representation to be the vote cast for Governor at the election preceding such Convention, all the delegates to be elected in the same manner as at present.

Referred to the State Committee, with power to report to the State Convention in the Fall.

While waiting for the Committees to report Lieut.-Gov. WOODFORD accepted an invitation and addressed the Convention briefly. He warmly eulogized the Congressional plan of reconstruction and urged the Republican Party not to look back, but to press forward and onward to the certain victory that awaits it in the great campaign of 1868.

LYMAN TREMAIN was next invited to the platform, and addressed the Convention at considerable length on political topics of the day.

Mr. HORACE GREELEY next responded to loud and repeated calls, and said he understood that the two Committees were now ready to report; let us hear from them and then he would say a few words.

Mr. LYMAN TREMAIN, of the Committee on Resolutions, reported the following:

*Resolved*, That the Union Republican Party of New-York hereby reaffirms its devotion to the principles of justice, equality, and nationality, which were triumphantly vindicated in the late war; that it declares its approval of the reconstruction measures adopted by Congress, and its unalterable purpose to maintain untarnished and inviolate the public faith and national credit, to lessen the burden of taxation by cutting off all useless expenditures and insisting upon the most thorough economy in the administration of the Government, and confidently anticipate that at an early day the Union will be completely restored on the solid basis of liberty, loyalty and genuine republicanism.

*Resolved*, That feeling assured that ULYSSES S. GRANT is in full accord with the loyal people of the country upon all the political issues that have sprung up between a hostile Executive and a patriotic Congress; regarding his splendid military record with unfeigned admiration; having full faith in his wisdom, integrity, prudence and firmness, and believing him to be emphatically the man for the times, this Convention declares its preference in favor of his nomination for the office of President of the United States.

*Resolved*, That REUBEN E. FENTON is the first choice of the Union Republican party in this State for the office of Vice-President. His early and consistent identification with the cause of human freedom, his patriotic services in Congress, the fidelity and sagacity he has displayed in the office of chief magistrate of the State, his earnest and uniform devotion to the wants and interests of the soldiers, his popularity, as attested by being twice elected Governor over strong antagonists, as well as his great prudence and firmness, give assurance that his nomination would inspire universal confidence and enthusiasm, and be followed by the triumphant success of the whole ticket.

*Resolved*, That the delegates elected by this Convention are authorized to fill all vacancies that may occur in their number, and they are hereby instructed to vote as a unit in the Chicago Convention, and are requested to employ all honorable and proper means to secure the nomination of Gen. GRANT and Gov. FENTON for the offices of President and Vice-President.

*Resolved*, That the reverses of 1867, with the formidable attempt now everywhere making to disseminate and commend the principles of rebellion and repudiation, admonish us that our adversaries are preparing for the most vehement and desperate efforts to regain the control of the Government and virtually reverse the triumph consummated at the Appomattox Court-house, and we exhort our fellow Republicans throughout the State to organize for the systematic diffusion of intelligence by journals and otherwise, and for a vigorous, persistent and efficient canvass henceforth to the close of the polls in November next.

*Resolved*, That this Convention expresses thanks to the soldiers and sailors of the Republic, to whom, under Providence, the nation is so much indebted for the preservation of its liberties and the perpetuation of its power, and that their heroic sacrifices and services in the suppression of the rebellion will forever be remembered with gratitude by the people of the country which has been saved through their valor and patriotism.

Adopted by acclamation.

The report of the Committee to nominate delegates to the National Union Republican Convention, was then made, as follows:

DELEGATES AT LARGE.

Maj.-Gen. Daniel E. Sickles, of New-York; Lyman Tremaine, of Albany; Charles Andrews, of Onondaga; D. D. S. Brown of Monroe. *Alternates*—John E. Williams, of New-York; Gilbert Robinson, Jr., of Rensselaer; Wm. W. Campbell, of Otsego; John Allen, Jr., of Erie.

CONGRESSIONAL DISTRICT DELEGATES.

*First District*—Alfred Wagstaff, Suffolk; L. Bradford Prince, Queens. Alternates—Albert R. Wilcox, Richmond; Samuel Smith, Queens.

*Second District*—Charles W. Godard, Kings; Archibald M. Bliss, Kings. Alternates—James A. Van Brunt, Kings; Wm. H. Burleigh, Kings.

*Third District*—Joshua M. Van Cott, Kings; Joseph Reeve, Kings. Alternate—Andrew R. Hodges, Kings.

*Fourth District*—Charles J. Lowrie, Kings; F. J. Fithian, New-York.

*Fourth District*—Joshua G. Abbey, New-York. Alternates—James Winterbottom, New-York; Nathan Kingsley, Sr., New-York.

*Fifth District*—Moses H. Grinnell, New-York; E. D. Culver, New-York. Alternates—Joseph F. Ellery, New-York; Thomas Mulligan.

*Sixth District*—Charles S. Spencer, New-York; John D. Lawson, New-York. Alternates—Jacob L. Dodge, New-York; George F. Merkies, New-York.

*Seventh District*—John Cochrane, New-York; W. F. Ashman, New-York. Alternates—Stephen H. Knapp, New-York; Simon Haselton, New-York.

*Eighth District*—W. R. Stewart, New-York; John D. Ottowell, New-York. Alternates—E. Harrison Hood, New-York; John Webber, New-York.

*Ninth District*—James W. Culver, New-York; Charles H. Cooper, New-York. Alternates, Jonathan Wilson, New-York; Nelson Berriman, New-York.

*Tenth District*—H. D. Robertson, Westchester; C. M. Depew, Westchester. Alternates, James F. Hall, Putnam; Charles H. Gillis, Westchester.

*Eleventh District*—George Clark, Orange; R. Low, Sullivan. Alternates, Halstead Sweet, Orange; John Waller, Sullivan.

*Twelfth District*—B. Platt Carpenter, Dutchess; Jacob W. Hogadrate, Columbia. Alternates—H. P. Eastman, Dutchess; Ezra Waterbury, Columbia.

*Thirteenth District*—George H. Sharp, Ulster; Rufus H. King, Greene. Alternates—Jacob Lefever, Ulster; Jno. B. Bronk, Greene.

*Fourteenth District*—Hamilton Harris, Albany; Berden H. Mills, Albany. Alternates—Wm. G. Weed, Albany; Weedman Demmick, Schoharie.

*Fifteenth District*—Robert M. Hasbrouck, Rensselaer; Alexander Barclay, Washington. Alternates—Joseph H. Satterhall, Rensselaer; Joseph Patten, Washington.

*Sixteenth District*—William Rockwell, Warren; Eli W. Rogers, Essex. Alternates—Robert Widdell, Warren; William E. Caulkins, Essex.

*Seventeenth District*—Calvin Hubbard, Sr., Lawrence; William Gillis, Franklin.

*Eighteenth District*—Truman G. Younglove, Saratoga; Seymour Sexton, Fulton. Alternates—Charles Stanford, Schenectady; Abram Hoffman, Montgomery.

*Nineteenth District*—Ebenezer Blakely, Oswego; Lewis Kingsley, Chenango. Alternates—Matthew Griffin, Delaware; Fred. Julian, Chenango.

*Twentieth District*—Wm. Dewey, Jefferson; E. B. Livingstone, Lewis. Alternates—James F. Foster, Herkimer; Allen Campbell, Jefferson.

*Twenty-first District*—Ellis H. Roberts, Oneida; George B. Anderson, Oneida. Alternates—Chas. M. Schofield, Oneida; Pat. C. Costello, Oneida.

*Twenty-second District*—Benjamin B. Bowen, Oswego; Delos W. Cameron, Madison. Alternates—J. W. Merchant, Madison; John H. Swann, Oswego.

*Twenty-third District*—Frank Hiscock, Onondaga; R. Holland Duell, Cortland. Alternates—C. R. Harmon, Onondaga; David Hibbard, Onondaga.

*Twenty-fourth District*—John S. Fowler, Cayuga; A. D. Baker, Seneca. Alternates—L. G. Yeomans, Wayne; Simeon Holton, Seneca.

*Twenty-fifth District*—Peter S. Bonesdale, Ontario; Isaac L. Endress, Livingston. Alternates—Geo. B. Dusenbury, Onondaga; W. H. Kelsey, Livingston.

*Twenty-sixth District*—Jeremiah W. Dwight, Tompkins; Thomas J. Chatfield, Tioga. Alternates—Alonzo H. B. Cornell, Tompkins; Wm. Smith, Tioga.

*Twenty-seventh District*—Stephen T. Hoyt, Steuben; Luther Caldwell, Chemung. Alternates—Chas. D. Robinson, Steuben; John H. Butler, Steuben.

*Twenty-eighth District*—E. L. Pitts, Orleans; O. O. Wildes, Monroe. Alternates—Joshua Benjamin, Orleans; Daniel Kingsley, Monroe.

*Twenty-ninth District*—John Fisler, Genesee; Andrew W. Branan, New-York.

*Thirtieth District*—T. K. Bass, Erie; Fred. H. Jones, Erie. Alternates—Isaac Holloway, Erie; Seth Yanner, Erie.

*Thirty-first District*—Geo. S. Barker, Chautauqua; Patrick H. Jones, Cattaraugus. Alternates—C. L. Horton, Chautauqua; H. Van Armen, Cattaraugus.

Mr. GREELEY being called for, said he wanted to warn the Convention against the danger of over confidence. Strong candidates had been nominated, but they could not win without strong supporters. The struggle is not yet terminated. If we consider that by spouting and hurrahing we shall be victorious we will find ourselves mistaken. We must make a canvass reaching every school district. We have formidable obstacles to overcome. The strongest vote ever polled in the State was polled against us last Fall. We need not have been beaten last Fall; we must not be beaten this Fall. We must circulate light and truth everywhere. I mean to do my part in this canvass. I hope you will incite your friends and neighbors to vigorous effort. We must work with a will and then we will win.

Adjourned *sine die*.

**Rights of American Citizens.**

ALBANY, Wednesday, Feb. 5.

Tweddle Hall was packed to-night in response to a call for the maintenance of the rights of naturalized citizens. Mayor THATCHER presided, speeches were made by Senator Henry C. Murphy of Brooklyn, Attorney-General Champlain, Hon. Patrick Corbett of Syracuse, Hon. S. D. Kiernan of New-York, Hon. John W. Murphy of Buffalo, and Hon. Francis H. Woods of Albany. Letters were read from Mayor Hoffman, Amasa J. Parker and Senator Folger. The resolutions were reported by William Cassidy.

**Proceedings of the State Legislature—The Election of Police Commissioner—New Measures Proposed.**

From Our Own Correspondent.

ALBANY, Wednesday, Feb. 5.

There was a slim attendance in either House this morning. A large proportion of the leading Republicans are absent at Syracuse, attending the State Convention.

Only one committee made a report in the Senate, and that was the bill which passed the House, giving an extension of three months on licenses now about to expire in the Metropolitan District. The Senate amends it by directing and obliging the Commissioners to give a license for three months to those who shall pay one-quarter of the regular yearly fee. Applications must be made previous to May 1, 1868. As amended, the bill was considered in Committee of the Whole, read a third time and passed. It is understood that the House will concur and the Governor sign—the temperance men of the two branches having acquiesced in the bill as it passes the Senate.

THE ELECTION OF POLICE COMMISSIONER

will probably be fixed for the 12th inst.—one week from to-day—Senator TWEED offering a resolution to that effect this morning, which went over under the rule.

The New-York delegation have canvassed the matter, and by a unanimous vote decided to go for Ex-Comptroller BRENNAN, and that I suspect fixes the thing. Brooklyn is "nowhar," as I suspected would be the end. BRENNAN was here in person to look after his interests; so also was Congressman MORRISSEY; but the laboring oar was taken by Senator TWEED, under whose practical hand the thing went along smooth enough. Grant is Tammany, and TWEED is the prophet.

IN THE ASSEMBLY,

this morning the third reading of bills was the regular order, under the ninth joint rule. That and the reading of the journal occupied about forty minutes.

Then the boys went in with a few whereases and therefores and those kind of things.

The Attorney of the Excise Commissioners was directed to report under oath, on or before the 15th of February, how many suits he has brought, how much money he has received, (they shrewdly omit to ask him what he has done with it, and what he proposes to do with it,) which will doubtless involve Mr. BLISS in a small expenditure for clerical labor, as it is understood that he has commenced what will prove to be no end of litigation They are evidently after the attorney, but I suspect he will prove equal to this, as he has to two or three other emergencies whereof I have had experience.

The Assembly also want the Commissioners for the opening of Worth-street to tell why they don't close up that little job. It is intimated that the Commissioners were seen, and not the opening of the street. It is a terrible wicked portion of the world, that City of New-York, if any reliance is to be placed upon the assertions, insinuations and conclusions of these inquiring individuals.

The Superintendent of Public Instruction was also required to report how much money had been received and expended in the payment of school officers. The odds are in favor of a bet that at least two centuries and a half must elapse before any embryo Superintendent will answer that question. The present occupant of that chair (and I believe I can truthfully say he occupies the entire superficial dimensions thereof,) is also a leading officer in a prominent life insurance company—but I don't believe the company would agree to underwrite his corporal existence until he has answered the Assembly. The mortality tables don't furnish any data for such a risk.

And at 12 o'clock precisely both Houses had adjourned. The several and sundry members thereof had gone up and down the hill, and by 12:15 a large proportion of the power of the upper and lower branches had resolved itself down to hunting ye tiger—an animal that prevails muchly in this locality, about now. LEO.

### STATE LEGISLATURE.

SENATE....ALBANY, Wednesday, Feb. 5.

BILLS INTRODUCED.

By Mr. GENET—To fix the compensation of Registers and Poll Clerks in New-York and Kings Counties; also, in relation to obstructions on railroads.

By Mr. PIERCE—To amend the charter of the Brooklyn Trust Company.

By Mr. NICHOLS—To amend the charter of the Niagara Suspension Bridge Company.

By Mr. CREAMER—To suppress the sale of adulterated and explosive oils in New-York and Brooklyn.

BILLS PASSED.

To amend the charter of the Mechanics' Savings Bank of Rochester.

For an additional Justice of the Peace in Syracuse.

An act supplementary of chapter 578, Laws of 1866, to regulate the sale of intoxicating liquors within the Metropolitan Police District.

ASSEMBLY.

MOTIONS AND RESOLUTIONS.

By Mr. KIERNAN—Calling upon the Superintendent of Public Instruction to furnish the House with the amount of money appropriated from the Common School Fund for the payment of school officers throughout the different counties of the State. Adopted.

By Mr. D. BURNS—Requesting the Clerk of the Assembly to demand an answer from the Metropolitan Board of Excise to a resolution passed Jan. 21, calling for a statement of the amount of fees received by the Attorney of said Board. Tabled.

By Mr. P. BURNS—That the Commissioners for the extension of Worth-street, New-York, be requested to report the cause of the unusual delay in completing said extension; also, the cost other than that to be paid for property taken. Adopted.

By Mr. DAYTON—Calling upon the Canal Commissioner of the Western Division to report what improvements are necessary to secure an adequate supply of water during the season of navigation. Adopted.

By Mr. WILEY—That the Treasurer of the Metropolitan Board of Health report in detail the sums collected or received by said Board or said Treasurer, for penalties, and all sums received or collected by suit, and the uses and purposes, specifically and in detail, to which said sums have been applied. Adopted.

By Mr. MCKIEVER—For a similar statement from the Attorney of the Metropolitan Board of Excise. Adopted.

THE CANAL FRAUDS.

Mr. JACOBS offered the following:

*Resolved*, That the honorable the Senate be respectfully requested to transmit to this House the testimony, or a copy thereof, taken by the Joint Committee of the Senate and Assembly, appointed to inquire into the management of the canals of the State, the departments thereof, and the conduct of any person now or hereafter connected with said canals; also to inquire into the acts of the Canal Contracting Board, and into the awards made for canal damages, and in reference to canal breaks, and the non-performance of contracts; and also the testimony, or a copy thereof, taken by the Senate Committee charged with the duty of inquiring into the management of the canals, and that the same be referred to a select committee of five, with instructions to inquire and report whether sufficient cause is shown for the impeachment of any canal officer or officers under the Constitution of this State, and if such cause, in the opinion of said Committee, is shown, that the said Committee present such officer or officers for impeachment, and that the said Committee, in prosecution of said inquiry, have leave to take such further evidence as they may deem expedient; and that they have power to send for persons and papers.

Adopted. Adjourned.

### THE STATE CONSTITUTIONAL CONVENTION.

ALBANY, Wednesday, Feb. 5.

Mr. ALVORD offered the following resolutions, which went over under the rule:

*Resolved*, That the Committee on Revision and Arrangement be instructed to make their final report on Wednesday, the 12th inst., immediately after the reading of the journal, and that the same be immediately considered in the Convention.

*Resolved*, That the Constitution passed by the Convention be signed by the members thereof, on Friday, the 14th inst., at 11 o'clock A. M.

*Resolved*, That the Convention do adjourn without day on Friday, the 14th inst.

Mr. SMITH introduced a resolution providing for the appointment of a committee to prepare the amended Constitution, and have the same printed and distributed throughout the State. Laid over under the rule.

The article on adulterated and intoxicating liquors was rejected.

The report on official corruption was then taken up.

Recess.

EVENING SESSION.

The Convention, in the evening session resumed the consideration of the report on official corruption.

# The New-York Times.

VOL. XVII......NO. 5193. NEW-YORK, SUNDAY, MAY 17, 1868. PRICE FIVE CENTS.


# IMPEACHMENT.

## Final Vote in the Senate on the Eleventh Article.

## The President Acquitted of the Offences Charged.

## Adjournment of the Court Without a Further Vote.

## An Investigation to be Made of the Bribery and Corruption Charges.

Special Dispatch to the New-York Times.

WASHINGTON, Saturday, May 16.

The great impeachment drama is practically at an end, and the President stands acquitted of the principal charge. Nineteen votes against thirty-five—just enough, and no more, to turn the scale of verdict. Twelve Democrats and seven Republicans—that magical number of seven—against thirty-five Republicans! My calculations since Tuesday are fully verified. Thirty-six was the best vote the friends of conviction could possibly count upon after Tuesday, and ever since then the fight has been to get the one necessary vote for acquittal on the one side and to keep the one necessary vote for conviction on the other. The debate of Monday developed the fact that the President had five Republican votes sure. Senator FOWLER's course developed the fact on Tuesday that he had six. It has been the work of the week to get the seventh man, and EDMUND G. ROSS, of Kansas, was secured. When Gen. THOS. EWING, Jr., said yesterday that Ross would vote for acquittal *if* necessary to secure it, he knew whereof he spoke.

The excitement last night on the revival of the prospect of conviction was so great that it survived the night, and this morning pervaded the minds of such people as went to bed early to hear of it. While the confidence of both sides were thus great, however, a few busy working spirits were still contesting the great question of the only still wanting vote. The man who bore the brunt of the contest was Mr. ROSS. Conviction had him to dinner last night, and pledged him sure; but Acquittal slept with him over night, and this morning he was weak and vacillating, and the few who talked with him gave him up. Two hours before the vote was taken it was known precisely how it would stand.

The morning opened with the most agreeable atmosphere we have yet had in this cold, chilly month of May. Possessors of tickets started early for the Capitol, and before 11 o'clock the best seats were all taken. Senators made their appearance very slowly. At 11:30 o'clock, when the Senate was called to order scarce a quorum was present. They dropped in one by one, seeming loth to step up to the task. The friends of conviction were heavy-hearted, for they knew the last condition of Ross. The friends of acquittal were light hearted for they also knew his last condition.

At 12 o'clock the galleries were crowded. Every ticket was in use. The diplomatic box overflowed as it rarely does. The reporters gallery was as usual, inundated by the friends of easy natured Mr. WADE, representing unheardof advocates of his aspirations. The day was propitious for fine toilettes, and the dramatic effect was brilliant. outside. Thousands lingered in the corridors or strolled in the beautiful grounds, inhaling the fresh odor of new-mown hay, waiting to catch the first vibration of the result. Down on the streets many more thousands waited in groups and in crowds, to hear the first note from the Capitol. The printing presses stood still, with a hand to the lever that should start the cylinder on the first exciting extra; the lightning quivered under the key of the telegraph, ready to put the news round the earth like a girdle in a minute. Everywhere and everything, and everybody but time, waited on impeachment.

Twelve o'clock rang out from the city bells, and the black-robed Chief Justice assumed the chair, while BEN. WADE assumed his Senatorial seat with a determination fully aroused to vote or die. The sick Senators had begun to arrive. CONKLING, pale, but straight and firm and dignified, as he always is, sat erect in his chair. MORTON was also there, determined and sincere, promising to be the statesman of the Senate. HOWARD was brought in leaning on the arms of friends, walking very feebly, and tottering into his chair with a heavy shawl thrown around him. Mr. GRIMES was brought in by four men in an invalid's chair, and allowed to recline on his side without taking his seat. Mr. FESSENDEN had just begun to be nervous about him, and had moved a half-hour postponement, when he came in. On the floor were SICKLES, Gen. HOLT, ANTHONY TROLLOPE, and a score more of notables.

At 12:15 o'clock the House of Representatives were announced, every man of them who is in the city being present. The galleries, the chamber, the Senate, and the court were now all full. The Managers sat at their table and Mr. EVARTS, Mr. GROESBECK and Mr. NELSON at theirs. All eagerly and anxiously awaited the calling of the roll. It had been resolved in consultation last night, however, that the eleventh article, being the strongest, should be voted on first, and this necessitated a little preliminary business, for it was necessary to take it up, and then necessary to agree to it, which necessitated two roll-calls. The result on these motions was thirty-four to nineteen, Mr. GRIMES not voting, which was immediately conceded to be a test vote, and to indicate acquittal, Messrs. ROSS and WILLEY voting against the change. But now comes the vote. The Chief Justice rises in his seat, and in grave tones enjoined the galleries to the strictest observance of order. The galleries bow in silent assent, and are reminded that the injunction is unnecessary, for in each aisle stands three muscular policemen with drawn batons ready to cleave the skull of the first person who shall demonstrate unseemly. Even the reporters' gallery is not exempt. As if to be sure that none escape the insult, a policeman, with club in hand and revolver in belt, stands at each end of the rows of desks. The Sergeant-at-Arms disclaims the responsibility for this exhibition, and says Senators demand it. Let Senators employ some of this brute force occasionally in carrying debauchees from its floor, and the reporters will not complain.

The eleventh article is now read. The Clerk calls "Mr. ANTHONY." Mr. ANTHONY rises in his seat, and the Chief Justice says, "Mr. Senator ANTHONY—How say you, is ANDREW JOHNSON' President of the United States, guilty or not guilty of a high misdemeanor, as charged in this article?" Mr. ANTHONY, with the poise of self-possession and the demeanor of an elegant gentleman, answers in clear, decided tones, "Guilty." A suppressed murmur of approbation runs through the galleries, and doubts about Mr. ANTHONY are scattered to the wind. BAYARD and BUCKALEW were called in quick succession, and responded in indistinct undertones "not guilty." Then came the long list of "C's." First the shrewd CAMERON, who pronounced his judgment of guilty almost before the question was asked. Then by the merchants CHANDLER and CATTELL, past COLE, to the able lawyer and graceful man CONKLING, past CONNESS and CORBETT to the matter-of-fact Mr. CRAGIN, all answering with gravity, deliberation and decision, "guilty." Then came the garrulous Mr. DAVIS, and sarcastic smiles when the conscientious Mr. DOOLITTLE and the precise Mr. DIXON announced their votes of "not guilty." Next the fiery Mr. DRAKE, "guilty," clear and strong. Then EDMUNDS and FERRY, calm and dignified with their verdict of "guilty." Then all eyes turned to the centre of the Chamber, as the tall form of the frail and fracile FESSENDEN arose at the call of his name and with graceful demeanor, but visible agitation, responded very decidedly, "not guilty." Then came FOWLER, who, with agitation staggered from his seat, stumbled on his chair, and was lost quite a minute before he recorded his vote, "not guilty," amid suppressed execrations. Next the classic FRELINGHUYSEN, grave but calm, silenced all doubts by his vote of "guilty." The next name was Mr. GRIMES, who, from his reclining position, reinforced his argument against conviction with his vote. After him the phlegmatic Mr. HARLAN put his convictions into affirmative shape. Next Mr. HENDERSON shot from his seat trembling with agitation, but sending his "not guilty" to the corners of the Chamber by his clear prompt tones. Next feeble Mr. HOWARD, rising in his seat with visible fatigue, replied in an emphatic "guilty." After him, Mr. HOWE, pale but unconcerned, on the side of "guilty." Next Mr. JOHNSON gruffly, and Mr. MCCREERY sharply, "not guilty." All eyes next turned on the merchant prince and Senator from New-York, Mr. MORGAN, who pronounced his verdict of "guilty," in behalf of the business of the country as well as his own convictions. Then the two MORRILLS of Maine and Vermont, and MORTON, bold and defiant, followed on the same side. After them the quiet Mr. NORTON, scarcely heard, so faint was his vote of "not guilty." Next, Mr. NYE, full and strong, and after him the cultivated Mr. PATTERSON, of New-Hampshire, both "guilty." Then, came the President's son-in-law, Mr. PATTERSON, of Tennessee, quickly and with evident pleasure responded "not guilty." After him, POMEROY and RAMSEY, prompt and positive "guilty." Then a thousand pair of eyes shot into the very heart of the modest, quiet little man who rises, at the call of the name of Ross. Nervously and quickly he responds, "not guilty." A suppressed condemnation is heard on all hands, and the fate of impeachment is sealed. The remaining votes cannot save it. The call goes quickly on down by SHERMAN, SPRAGUE, SUMNER to TRUMBULL, who winces under the flashing of indignant eyes, past him to old BEN WADE, who redeems his promise to vote without squirming, then to WILLEY, who was doubtful, but who sits grey-bearded in his chair, like an ironbound Puritan and responds, "Guilty." Then to the foot of the list and the result is flashed to the ends of the earth, the President is acquitted, thirty-five to nineteen, not two-thirds, by just exactly one vote too much and no more.

In an instant a motion is made to adjourn, as agreed upon in caucus before the Senate met, to Tuesday, the 26th inst. Cool-headed men feel that this is foolish and absurd. Let us finish this work at once, they say. But the rash men are the strongest. The rest of the articles are postponed, and the President, though practically acquitted, is left hanging by the eyelids, to the disgust of the entire country.

The indignation centres terribly and almost wholly upon poor Ross, and he has a hard position to occupy. Five times, once in writing, as his colleague POMEROY says, he can swear he has promised to vote for conviction. So late as last night at dinner at the latters house he promised. Until within two or three days he has never been doubted. He was not outspoken except to his friends, to whom he frankly stated ten days ago that his opinion was that the President was guilty. So much evidence of this kind is in existence that his friends are overwhelmed with shame and grief at his alleged duplicity.

Dispatches to the Associated Press.

SENATOR ROSS.

The following has been received here directed to Senators POMEROY and ROSS, of Kansas:

LEAVENWORTH, Kansas, May 14.

Kansas has heard the evidence and demands the conviction of the President. Signed by

D. R. ANTHONY,
and 1,000 others.

To the above Senator Ross has sent the following reply:

WASHINGTON, D. C., May 15.

GENTLEMEN: I do not recognize your right to demand that I shall vote either for or against conviction. I have taken an oath to do impartial justice according to the Constitution and laws, and trust that I shall have the courage and honesty to vote according to the dictates of my judgment, and for the highest good of my country.

Signed: E. G. ROSS.

To D. R. ANTHONY, and others.

SENATOR HENDERSON.

The Missouri Congressional delegation have replied to Senator HENDERSON's recent letter to them. In their letter they say they are placed in a false position. But the misstatement of facts and inferences they are confident was entirely unintentional on his part.

Senator HENDERSON has replied to them. In narrating what took place at the interview, he says:

"It was at this point that I promised to ascertain whether I must resign or not. I did not want time ty consider whether I could change my vote or sit silent, or commit perjury; but simply whether there would be a conviction regardless of my vote. These things were done on the spur of the moment, and almost without counsel on my part, and to me, under a sense of humiliation which I cannot describe. So soon as I had time to reflect on the subject I determined to remain in my seat and do my duty. If my constituents, honest, intelligent, brave and reliable, shall in a body condemn me, I will give up my seat, when it can be done with self-respect."

## THE IMPEACHMENT TRIAL.

The Senate met at 11:30 o'clock. The galleries were full, and policemen standing in the aisles.

WASHINGTON, Saturday, May 16.

At 12 o'clock precisely the Chief Justice, wearing the silk robe of office, entered and took his seat as presiding officer of the Court of Impeachment, and directed the Sergeant-at-Arms to make proclamation.

The proclamation was made in the usual form.

The Secretary then proceeded to read the journal of the last day's proceedings in the case of the United States against ANDREW JOHNSON, President.

When the reading was concluded Mr. EDMUNDS called up the order heretofore submitted in the following words:

*Ordered*, That the Chief Justice, in directing the Secretary to read the several articles of impeachment, shall direct him to read the eleventh article first, and the question shall be taken on that article, and thereafter on the other ten successively as they stand.

Before taking it up, Mr. EDMUNDS offered the following order:

*Ordered*, That the Secretary be directed to inform the House of Representatives that the Senate, sitting for the trial of the President on the articles of impeachment, are now ready to receive them in the Senate Chamber.

Which was adopted.

Senator JOHNSON inquired whether the order of Senator WILLIAMS was debatable?

The Chief Justice replied that it was not.

Senator JOHNSON said that he would like to make a motion on it.

Senator CONNESS objected.

The question was then put on taking up Senator WILLIAMS' order for action, and it was decided yeas 34, nays 19:

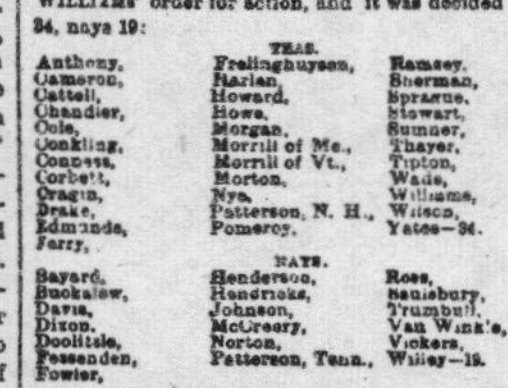

YEAS.

| | | |
|---|---|---|
| Anthony, | Frelinghuysen, | Ramsey, |
| Cameron, | Harlan, | Sherman, |
| Cattell, | Howard, | Sprague, |
| Chandler, | Howe, | Stewart, |
| Cole, | Morgan, | Sumner, |
| Conkling, | Morrill of Me., | Thayer, |
| Conness, | Morrill of Vt., | Tipton, |
| Corbett, | Morton, | Wade, |
| Cragin, | Nye, | Williams, |
| Drake, | Patterson, N. H., | Wilson, |
| Edmunds, | Pomeroy, | Yates—34. |
| Ferry, | | |

NAYS.

| | | |
|---|---|---|
| Bayard, | Henderson, | Ross, |
| Buckalew, | Hendricks, | Saulsbury, |
| Davis, | Johnson, | Trumbull, |
| Dixon, | McCreery, | Van Winkle, |
| Doolittle, | Norton, | Vickers, |
| Fessenden, | Patterson, Tenn., | Willey—19. |
| Fowler, | | |

Senator WADE voted for the first time, and voted in the affirmative.

Senator GRIMES was not present.

The question was then taken on the adoption of the order, and it was carried by the same—yeas 34, nays 19.

While the votes were being taken the members of the House of Representatives were announced as at the bar of the Senate. They entered, headed by Mr. WASHBURNE, of Illinois, and attended by their Clerk and Doorkeeper. Most of the members had preceded them, and had taken seats on the floor of the Senate Chamber and in the galleries.

Mr. FESSENDEN rose to make a motion to postpone the vote for an hour, on account of the absence of Mr. GRIMES, but on being informed that that Senator was in the Capitol he did not make the motion.

Mr. GRIMES immediately afterward entered the Chamber and took his seat in one of the side aisles.

Mr. EDMUNDS then submitted an order that the Senate do now proceed to vote on the articles according to the rules of the Senate, which was agreed to.

The Chief Justice, rising, said by direction of the Senate: The Chief Justice desires to admonish the citizens and strangers in the galleries that absolute silence and perfect order is required. It will be a subject of infinite regret if any violation of the order of the Senate will necessitate the execution of the further order, that the persons guilty of disturbance be immediately removed. Then addressing the Senators, the Chief Justice said: Senators, in conformity to the order of the Senate, the Chief Justice will now proceed to take the vote on the eleventh article as directed by the rule.

The eleventh article was read by the Clerk as follows:

ARTICLE ELEVEN.

That said ANDREW JOHNSON, President of the United States, unmindful of the high duties of his office and of his oath of office, and in disregard of the Constitution and laws of the United States, did heretofore, to wit: on the 18th day of August, 1866, at the City of Washington, and the District of Columbia, by public speech, declare and affirm in substance, that the Thirty-ninth Congress of the United States was not a Congress of the United States authorized by the Constitution to exercise legislative power under the same; but, on the contrary, was a Congress of only part of the States, thereby denying and intending to deny that the legislation of said Congress was valid or obligatory upon him, the said ANDREW JOHNSON, except in so far as he saw fit to approve the same, and also thereby denying and intending to deny the power of the said Thirty-ninth Congress to propose amendments to the Constitution of the United States; and, in pursuance of said declaration, the said ANDREW JOHNSON, President of the United States, afterward, to wit: on the 21st day of February, 1868, at the City of Washington, in the District of Columbia, did unlawfully and in disregard of the requirements of the Constitution, that he should take care that the laws be faithfully executed, attempt to prevent the execution of an act entitled "An act regulating the tenure of certain civil offices," passed March 2, 1867, by unlawfully devising and contriving, and attempting to devise and contrive means by which he should prevent EDWIN M. STANTON from forthwith resuming the functions of the office of Secretary of the Department of War, notwithstanding the refusal of the Senate to concur in the suspension therefore made by said ANDREW JOHNSON, of said EDWIN M. STANTON from said office of Secretary of the Department of War, and also by further unlawfully devising and contriving, and attempting to devise and contrive means then and there to prevent the execution of an act entitled "An act making appropriations for the support of the army for the fiscal year ending June 30, 1868, and for other purposes," approved March 2, 1867, and also to prevent the execution of an act entitled "An act to provide for the more efficient government of the rebel States," passed March 2, 1867; whereby the said ANDREW JOHNSON, President of the United States, did then, to wit: on the 21st day of February, 1868, at the City of Washington, commit and was guilty of a high misdemeanor in office.

The first name on the rollcall of Senator ANTHONY, being called, that Senator rose in his place, and the Chief Justice, also standing, addressed to him this formula:

Mr. Senator ANTHONY: How say you; is the respondent, ANDREW JOHNSON, President of the United States, guilty or not guilty of a high misdemeanor, as charged in this article?

Senator ANTHONY responded "guilty," and so the vote went on till the Senators had responded—the vote summing up, yeas 35, nays 19, as follows:

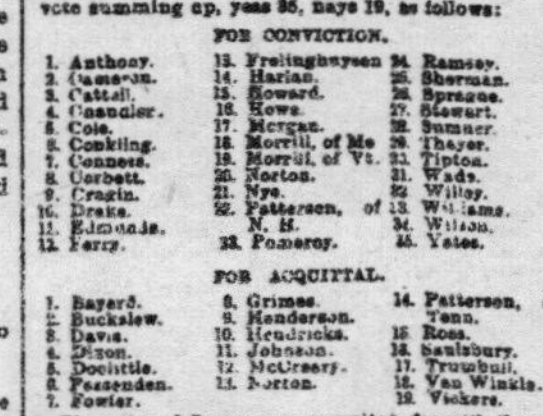

FOR CONVICTION.

| | | |
|---|---|---|
| 1. Anthony. | 13. Frelinghuysen | 24. Ramsey. |
| 2. Cameron. | 14. Harlan. | 25. Sherman. |
| 3. Cattell. | 15. Howard. | 26. Sprague. |
| 4. Chandler. | 16. Howe. | 27. Stewart. |
| 5. Cole. | 17. Morgan. | 28. Sumner. |
| 6. Conkling. | 18. Morrill, of Me | 29. Thayer. |
| 7. Conness. | 19. Morrill, of Vt. | 30. Tipton. |
| 8. Corbett. | 20. Norton. | 31. Wade. |
| 9. Cragin. | 21. Nye. | 32. Willey. |
| 10. Drake. | 22. Patterson, of N. H. | 33. Williams. |
| 11. Edmunds. | | 34. Wilson. |
| 12. Ferry. | 23. Pomeroy. | 35. Yates. |

FOR ACQUITTAL.

| | | |
|---|---|---|
| 1. Bayard. | 8. Grimes. | 14. Patterson, of Tenn. |
| 2. Buckalew. | 9. Henderson. | 15. Ross. |
| 3. Davis. | 10. Hendricks. | 16. Saulsbury. |
| 4. Dixon. | 11. Johnson. | 17. Trumbull. |
| 5. Doolittle. | 12. McCreery. | 18. Van Winkle. |
| 6. Fessenden. | 13. Norton. | 19. Vickers. |
| 7. Fowler. | | |

The votes of Senators were waited for with the utmost anxiety, though nothing more than a general motion, as of suspense relieved, was made manifest when the vote of a doubtful Senator was given. It was noticed that Senator CAMERON voted ahead of time. The Chief Justice had not concluded the formal question before the Senator's vote of guilty was pronounced.

Senators FESSENDEN, FOWLER, GRIMES, ROSS, TRUMBULL and VAN WINKLE, among the Republican Senators, voted "not guilty." Senator WADE, when his name was called, stood up unhesitatingly and voted "guilty."

Before the result of the vote was announced, but when it was known, Senator WILLIAMS rose and moved that the Senate, sitting as a Court of Impeachment, adjourn until Tuesday, the 26th of May, at 12 o'clock.

Senator JOHNSON addressed the Chief Justice.

The Chief Justice said that debate was not in order.

Senator JOHNSON—Is it in order to adjourn the Senate when it has already decided on one of the articles?

The CHIEF JUSTICE—The precedents are, except in one case—the case of HUMPHREY—that the announcement was not made until the end of the cause. The Chair will, however, take the direction of the Senate. If the Senate desire the announcement to be made now, it will be made.

Senator SHERMAN—The announcement of the vote had better be made.

Senator DRAKE—I submit as a question of order, that a motion to adjourn is pending, and that that motion takes precedence of all other things.

The CHIEF JUSTICE—The Senator from Missouri is perfectly right. A motion to adjourn has been made and that motion takes precedence.

Mr. HENDRICKS—The motion to adjourn cannot be made pending a vote, and the vote is not complete until it is announced.

Mr. CONKLING—A motion cannot be made pending the roll call.

Several Senators—Certainly not; let the vote be announced.

Senator JOHNSON—I ask that the vote be announced.

The CHIEF JUSTICE—The vote will be announced. The Clerk will read the roll.

The roll having been read by the Clerk, the Chief Justice rose and announced the result in the following words:

"On this article there are 35 Senators who have voted 'Guilty,' and 19 Senators who have voted 'Not guilty.' The President is, therefore, acquitted on this article."

No manifestation of sentiment was made on either side of the question. Whatever were the feelings of the Senators, members and spectators, they were thoroughly suppressed.

Mr. WILLIAMS' motion to adjourn until Tuesday, the 26th inst., was then taken up.

Mr. HENDRICKS submitted as a question of order, that the Senate was now executing an order already made which was in the nature and had the effect of the previous question. Therefore the motion to adjourn otherwise than simply to adjourn was not in order.

Calls of "Question," "Question."

The CHIEF JUSTICE—The motion that when the Senate adjourn, it adjourn to meet at a certain date, cannot now be entertained, because the Senate is in process of executing an order. A motion to adjourn to a certain day seems to the Chair to come under the same rule. The Chair will, therefore, decide the motion not in order.

Senator CONNESS—From that decision of the Chair I appeal.

The Chief Justice put the question, and directed the Clerk to read the order adopted to-day on motion of Senator EDMUNDS, as follows:

*Ordered*, That the Senate do now proceed to vote on the articles according to the rules of the Senate.

Senator HOWARD called for the yeas and nays on the question, whether the decision of the Chair should be sustained.

The vote was taken, and resulted, yeas 24, nays 30, as follows:

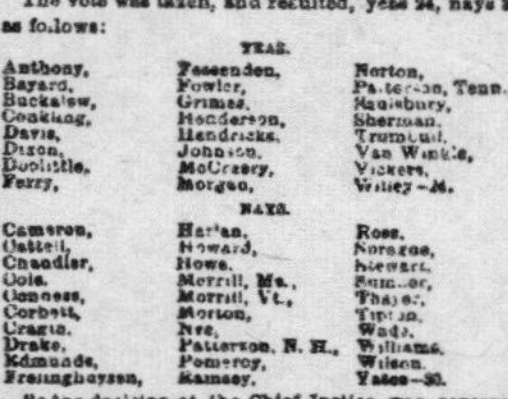

YEAS.

| | | |
|---|---|---|
| Anthony, | Fessenden, | Norton, |
| Bayard, | Fowler, | Patterson, Tenn., |
| Buckalew, | Grimes, | Saulsbury, |
| Conkling, | Henderson, | Sherman, |
| Davis, | Hendricks, | Trumbull, |
| Dixon, | Johnson, | Van Winkle, |
| Doolittle, | McCreery, | Vickers, |
| Ferry, | Morgan, | Willey—24. |

NAYS.

| | | |
|---|---|---|
| Cameron, | Harlan, | Ross, |
| Cattell, | Howard, | Sprague, |
| Chandler, | Howe, | Stewart, |
| Cole, | Morrill, Me., | Sumner, |
| Conness, | Morrill, Vt., | Thayer, |
| Corbett, | Morton, | Tipton, |
| Cragin, | Nye, | Wade, |
| Drake, | Patterson, N. H., | Williams, |
| Edmunds, | Pomeroy, | Wilson, |
| Frelinghuysen, | Ramsey, | Yates—30. |

So the decision of the Chief Justice was reversed, and the order to adjourn over was ruled to be in order.

Mr. HENDERSON moved to amend the order by striking out the words 26th inst., and inserting in lieu thereof the words "Wednesday the 1st day of July next."

The amendment was rejected, yeas 20, nays 34, as follows:

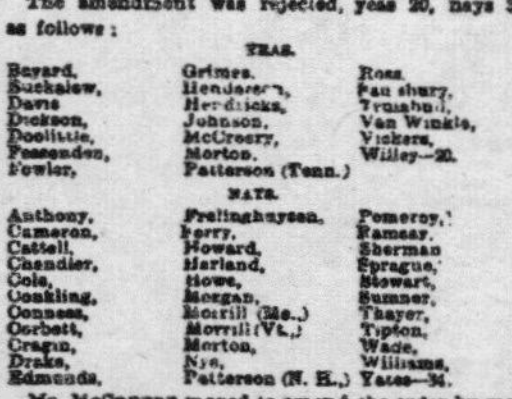

YEAS.

| | | |
|---|---|---|
| Bayard, | Grimes, | Ross, |
| Buckalew, | Henderson, | Saulsbury, |
| Davis, | Hendricks, | Trumbull, |
| Dickson, | Johnson, | Van Winkle, |
| Doolittle, | McCreery, | Vickers, |
| Fessenden, | Norton, | Willey—20. |
| Fowler, | Patterson (Tenn.) | |

NAYS.

| | | |
|---|---|---|
| Anthony, | Frelinghuysen, | Pomeroy, |
| Cameron, | Ferry, | Ramsey, |
| Cattell, | Howard, | Sherman, |
| Chandler, | Harland, | Sprague, |
| Cole, | Howe, | Stewart, |
| Conkling, | Morgan, | Sumner, |
| Conness, | Morrill (Me.) | Thayer, |
| Corbett, | Morrill (Vt.) | Tipton, |
| Cragin, | Morton, | Wade, |
| Drake, | Nye, | Williams, |
| Edmunds, | Patterson (N. H.) | Yates—34. |

Mr. MCCREERY moved to amend the order by making it read to adjourn without day.

The question was taken, and the amendment was rejected—yeas 6, nays 47—as follows:

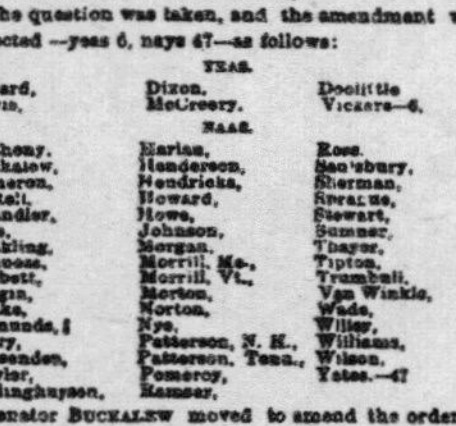

YEAS.

| | | |
|---|---|---|
| Bayard, | Dixon, | Doolittle |
| Davis, | McCreery, | Vickers—6. |

NAYS.

| | | |
|---|---|---|
| Anthony, | Harlan, | Ross, |
| Buckalew, | Henderson, | Saulsbury, |
| Cameron, | Hendricks, | Sherman, |
| Cattell, | Howard, | Sprague, |
| Chandler, | Howe, | Stewart, |
| Cole, | Johnson, | Sumner, |
| Conkling, | Morgan, | Thayer, |
| Conness, | Morrill, Me., | Tipton, |
| Corbett, | Morrill, Vt., | Trumbull, |
| Cragin, | Morton, | Van Winkle, |
| Drake, | Norton, | Wade, |
| Edmunds, | Nye, | Willey, |
| Ferry, | Patterson, N. H., | Williams, |
| Fessenden, | Patterson, Tenn., | Wilson, |
| Fowler, | Pomeroy, | Yates.—47 |
| Frelinghuysen, | Ramsey, | |

Senator BUCKALEW moved to amend the order by providing for an adjournment till Monday, the 25th inst.

Rejected without division.

The question recurred on the order as originally offered by Senator WILLIAMS, to adjourn the Court till Tuesday, 26th inst. The vote was taken, and resulted—yeas 32, nays 21—as follows:

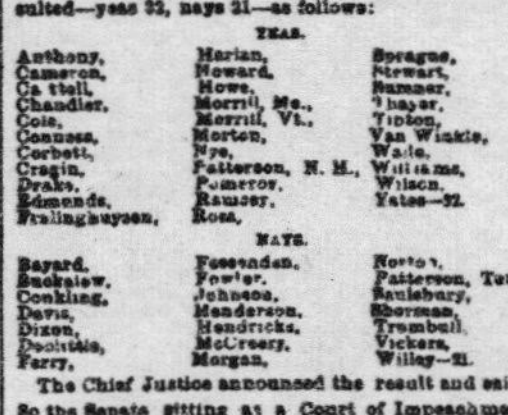

YEAS.

| | | |
|---|---|---|
| Anthony, | Harlan, | Sprague, |
| Cameron, | Howard, | Stewart, |
| Cattell, | Howe, | Sumner, |
| Chandler, | Morrill, Me., | Thayer, |
| Cole, | Morrill, Vt., | Tipton, |
| Conness, | Morton, | Van Winkle, |
| Corbett, | Nye, | Wade, |
| Cragin, | Patterson, N. H., | Williams, |
| Drake, | Pomeroy, | Wilson, |
| Edmunds, | Ramsey, | Yates—32. |
| Frelinghuysen, | Ross, | |

NAYS.

| | | |
|---|---|---|
| Bayard, | Fessenden, | Norton, |
| Buckalew, | Fowler, | Patterson, Tenn., |
| Conkling, | Johnson, | Saulsbury, |
| Davis, | Henderson, | Sherman, |
| Dixon, | Hendricks, | Trumbull, |
| Doolittle, | McCreery, | Vickers, |
| Ferry, | Morgan, | Willey—21. |

The Chief Justice announced the result and said: So the Senate sitting as a Court of Impeachment, stands adjourned till Tuesday, the 26th inst., at 12 o'clock.

The Chief Justice then left the chair, and the members of the House retired to their own chamber. The spectators who had filled every seat and standing place in the galleries, immediately began to pour out into the halls and corridors, and the curtain fell for ten days on the national drama of impeachment. The closing scene was not marked by the slightest breach of decorum or good order.

### The Reception of the News in the City—Telegraphic Reports from other Places.

The result of the vote on the impeachment articles was awaited with the liveliest interest by all classes in this City and vicinity yesterday. The matter had been figured down so closely by the Washington correspondents, and shown to depend upon a single doubtful vote, that the not-headed of the two political parties felt little disposed to count their chickens prematurely, and did not venture their opinions so freely even as the comparatively small body of disinterested, thinking men who, while nominally adherents of either party, are essentially non-partisan and conscientious, express themselves according to their honest convictions, and constitute the balance of power whose weight, thrown in either scale, determines the final judgment of the people on election day. These had not been so doubtful during the past few days of the final result.

The principal scenes of excitement were around the bulletin boards of the TIMES and other newspaper offices. Here, for several hours before it was possible for any news to be received from Washington, crowds congregated, talking over the probabilities of conviction and acquittal, making bets of more or less magnitude, and watching with eager eyes for the first intelligence to be made public. When it was known that the acquittal extended only to the eleventh article, and as very few of those who read the news remembered what the eleventh article was, the Johnsonites became exultant, and the Radicals correspondingly depressed. Soon, however, further news came, showing that the eleventh article carried the whole, and that the President was virtually acquitted. As a general thing the news appeared to give satisfaction, which, however, was expressed in a very undemonstrative manner. There was no shouting, no waving of hats. The Democrats grasped hands, and congratulated each other that WADE was not yet in the White House, while the Radicals turned away with glum faces but silent lips. In Broad and Wall streets the news was received with equal quietness, and after satisfying themselves that impeachment had virtually failed, brokers and merchants returned to their avocations. Never, perhaps, was the announcement of the decision of any great question affecting the interests of the country the cause of so little excitement as that of impeachment.

BOSTON, Saturday, May 16.

The friends of President JOHNSON expressed their satisfaction with the verdict to-night by a salute of one hundred guns on the Common.

Considerable excitement was manifested to-day preceding the result of the impeachment question being known, but immediately after the news was bulletined, and the vote printed in the papers, it quietly subsided. The people seem generally to have anticipated the verdict, and appear glad that the long-pending and exciting question has been so far decided.

BALTIMORE, Saturday, May 16.

Large crowds assembled about the bulletin boards of all news offices, while the result of the proceedings in the Senate was being announced by telegraph. The result of the vote on the eleventh article was received in the most quiet manner. There was no enthusiastic demonstration of any kind.

MEMPHIS, Saturday, May 16.

The news of the President's acquittal on the eleventh article created great excitement here, and universal enthusiasm prevailed throughout the afternoon.

## FORTIETH CONGRESS.

### SECOND SESSION.

SENATE....WASHINGTON, Saturday, May 16.

The Senate met at 11.30 o'clock A. M.

ARKANSAS AS A STATE.

Mr. TRUMBULL, from the Committee on the Judiciary, reported favorably the bill to admit Arkansas as a State.

Mr. HENDRICKS announced his intention of making a minority report.

Mr. TRUMBULL thought it would hardly be proper, since the majority of the Committee had made no written report.

The Senator expressed his views.

Mr. DRAKE submitted an amendment, which was ordered to be printed.

Some further trifling legislative business was done before 12 o'clock, at which hour the Chief Justice assumed the chair and called the Senate to order.

The Senate having adjourned as a Court, and the President *pro tempore* having resumed the chair, the concurrent resolution of the House for a recess until Monday, the 25th instant, was taken up. This gave rise to a discussion.

The concurrent resolution was supported by Messrs. MORRILL, of Vermont, HENDRICKS and SUMNER, and opposed by Messrs. CONKLING, MORRILL, of Maine, and NYE.

Mr. NYE said he had enough experience in this body to know that it was useless to oppose an adjournment for a week, a day, or an hour. He thought the President would be able to take care of himself, with his new recruits. He thought a little embarrassment to the President would not be unprofitable. Let Arkansas come in to-day; let us have a birth with a death; let us pass a concurrent resolution admitting the State of Arkansas, and relieve him of his embarrassment by not sending it to him at all, to have it sent back here at the end of ten days with another defiant veto. We have had enough of them. Let us admit Arkansas before the man is down; let the President have another sweet morsel to roll under his tongue.

Mr. SUMNER favored a recess on the ground that it would be beneath the dignity of the Senate to continue to transact business with the President of the United States. He had always felt it to be unbecoming in the Senate to transact business with him while he was on trial for high crimes and misdemeanors. The President might go forth nominally acquitted, but he would go forth, nevertheless, a blasted public functionary. That was his inevitable destiny, but until acquittal was entered on the record, the Senate would consult its own character by abstaining from any further interchange of messages between Congress and the President. For this reason he favored a recess.

Mr. MORTON thought it rather late in the day to act on that idea, having gone on up to this time transacting business with the President.

Mr. YATES was opposed to a recess, because he wanted more bills for the protection of human liberty to be presented to the President for his action between now and the final articles of impeachment.

Senator WILSON opposed a recess on the same general grounds as Senator NYE did.

Mr. DOOLITTLE favored the recess.

Mr. HENDERSON took Mr. SUMNER to account for reflection on the President. If nothing else should cause Senators to abstain from such remarks, a decent sense of self-respect should restrain them. No associate had a right, either in Senate or in the Court, to reflect on the conduct of any other Senator. No man had a higher respect for his constituents than himself, but his constituents could not enlighten him on the question of impeachment. It was a matter for his own conscience, and nothing could ever drive him from the performance of his duty. If his constituents disapproved of his course, he was in their hands, and they might do with him as they wished; but he was not to be told by his party to turn his back on law and justice. It was no use in trying to make impeachment a party question. It was no party question, and the moment a party should put itself in the position that its members must perjure themselves, that party ought to, and would, crumble into dust. For his own part he regretted that the subject of impeachment had ever been brought into the Senate, and he believed it never ought to have been. He thought as long as the President was not convicted it would not injure them to send a bill to him.

Mr. DRAKE asked if any Senator had assailed his colleague for his course in the Court of Impeachment.

Several Senators—No one.

Mr. HENDERSON inquired when his colleague had become the guardian of his character.

Mr. DRAKE replied that here and elsewhere he considered himself in duty bound to defend it when assailed.

Mr. MORTON raised the question of order that it was improper to assail Senators for voting one way or the other.

Mr. DRAKE suggested that when that Senator called another to order, he should do it at the time that disorderly words are spoken, and not take the floor from a Senator speaking in order. He confessed his surprise that his colleague, (Mr HENDERSON,) under the supposition that some general aspersions had been made upon the seven Senators who had voted for acquittal, had been called upon individually to defend himself from that general aspersion.

Mr. HENDERSON pointed out that a remark had been made deprecating intercourse with "this great criminal" whom the Senate had voted to acquit.

Mr. SUMNER disclaimed any allusion to the Senator in that remark, but, said he, listening to Senator, he will pardon me if I say that I was reminded of a proverb, which seemed to me to be very applicable to his case, as he presented it—it is this: "Who so excuses himself, accuses himself." The swiftness with which he rushed to self-defence, brought to my mind this ancient maxim. Mr. SUMNER went on to repeat his argument that it would be unbecoming in the Senate to interchange messages, &c., with the President while the impeachment is pending. A vote, he continued, has been taken on one article, but there are ten to be acted upon, and on the article acted upon we all know that the acquittal was only by one vote. He was saved, as the saying is, "by the skin of his teeth." I call it a nominal acquittal on that one article. I allude to that now, because it has been acted upon. There is a judgment against him; a judgment.——

Mr. HENDRICKS—I wish to inquire what decision the Chair made on the point of order made by my colleague.

The PRESIDENT *pro tem.*—The Chair did not make any.

Mr. HENDRICKS—Then I ask a decision on that point of order, as applicable to the remarks of the Senator from Massachusetts.

Mr. SUMNER—I ask the Senator to put it in writing.

The PRESIDENT *pro tem.*—The Senator must put it in writing.

Mr. HENDRICKS—I make the point of order that the line of argument made by the Senator is not in order.

Mr. SUMNER said he knew of no rule that dictates to a Senator what course of argument he can pursue, and he proceeded with his remarks, in the course of which he said he knew there were Senators who, since the impeachment question has been agitated, have continued in personal relations with the President, and others who have sought official appointments at his hands, and who have frequented his house. He had no criticism to make, but he could not have done so himself.

Mr. STEWART favored an adjournment on the ground that subjects must otherwise come up connected with the admission of the lately rebellious States, upon which opinions would be expressed that should be reserved until the question of impeachment is decided. He reminded the Senate that it was not a judicial trial only, as had been claimed, involving judicial issues and consequences, when

Mr. WILLEY raised the point of order, that it was improper to raise the question of impeachment in debate while it is pending.

The Chair ruled that no course of debate can be dictated by any question of order.

Mr. JOHNSON appealed from the decision of the Chair.

After some talk on the point of order, Mr. MORROW moved to adjourn, which was not agreed to.

The Chair stated the question to be on sustaining the decision of the Chair, whereupon Mr. JOHNSON withdrew the appeal, saying it had been made under a misapprehension of the point made.

Mr. STEWART concluded his remarks, holding that during the pending of this trial, questions involving the admission and reconstruction of States and the condition of the South and its people could not be freely discussed, and that, therefore, the best course was to adjourn.

Another motion to adjourn, made by Mr. CAMERON, was voted down.

The question was then stated to be on the motion to include the Senate in the resolution of the House.

It was agreed to by a vote of 26 to 20; and the question recurring on the resolution, as amended, it was rejected by the following vote:

YEAS—Messrs. Anthony, Bayard, Buckalew, Cole, Conness, Corbett, Davis, Dixon, Doolittle, Fowler, Hendricks, Johnson, McCreery, Morrill of Vermont, Norton, Patterson of New Hampshire, Patterson of Tennessee, Saulsbury, Sprague, Stewart, Sumner, Van Winkle, Vickers, Williams—24.

NAYS—Messrs. Cameron, Chandler, Conkling, Cragin, Drake, Edmunds, Ferry, Fessenden, Harlan, Howe, Morgan, Morrill of Maine, Morton, Nye, Pomeroy, Ramsey, Ross, Sherman, Thayer, Tipton, Trumbull, Wade, Willey, Wilson and Yates—25.

After an unavailing attempt by Mr. MORRILL, of Maine, to call up the Deficiency bill, at 3:45 the Senate adjourned.

HOUSE OF REPRESENTATIVES.

CHAPLAIN BOYNTON PRAYS.

The Chaplain, Rev. Dr. BOYNTON on the opening of the House, made the following prayer:

Almighty God, Thou art alone the righteous Judge. Thou art alone the hearer and answerer of prayer, and we come to Thee anew through our High Priest and Mediator, with worship, thanksgiving and prayer. We beseech Thee, O God, to prepare us and this whole country to meet with a firm and steadfast spirit whatever this day may bring forth. We pray Thee, O Lord, that Thou wilt Thyself preside in the most solemn assembly to-day and give direction to the thoughts, feelings and decisions of men. May they have a clear consciousness of what great responsibilities rest on each to-day. We pray Thee, Almighty God, that Thou wilt have mercy on this whole country to-day, and that Thou wilt cause every man in whose hands, especially, the destiny of the land is for the hour, to remember that a time is coming when all human praise will have faded away, when all human censure will be as nothing; when all present advantage will be as dust and ashes, and each one must meet the result of this day's doings at the solemn bar, where the award will bring unto every one eternal consequences. We pray Thee to enlighten each conscience; guide each mind, and O God of all grace and mercy, vindicate the right to-day, not according to our shortsightedness, but according to Thine own infinite wisdom; and we will give Thee all the praise forever. Amen.

A MESSAGE

having been received from the Senate that that body was now prepared to receive the members of the House at its bar, the House proceeded thither as a Committee of the Whole, headed by Mr. WASHBURNE, of Illinois, as Chairman, and the Clerk and Doorkeeper of the House.

MR. WASHBURNE'S REPORT.

When the members returned from the impeachment to their hall, Mr. WASHBURNE, of Illinois, as Chairman of the Committee of the Whole, responded that the House, according to order, have attended the trial by the Senate of the impeachment of ANDREW JOHNSON, President of the United States, that the respondent has been declared not guilty of the 11th article by a vote of 35 in the affirmative and 19 in the negative, and that the Senate, sitting for the said trial, had adjourned until Tuesday, the 26th instant, at noon.

SENATOR HENDERSON AND THE HOUSE.

Mr. ELDRIDGE offered as a question of privilege the following:

*Whereas*, It appears by the following letter, purporting to have been written and addressed by seven members of this House to one of the Senators of the United States, and which he published in the daily *National Intelligencer* of this city, to wit:

WASHINGTON, May 13, 1868.

*Hon. J. B. Henderson, U. S. Senate:*

SIR: On a consultation of the Republican members of the House of Representatives from Missouri, in view of your position on the impeachment articles, we ask you to withhold your vote on any article upon which you cannot vote affirmatively. This request is made because we believe the safety of the loyal people of the United States demands the immediate removal of ANDREW JOHNSON from the office of President of the United States.

Respectfully, George W. Anderson, William A. Pile, C. A. Newcomb, Joseph W. McClurg, Benjamin F. Loan, John F. Bingham, Joseph L. Grenety.

That an indecent and corrupt combination of the Representatives aforesaid has been entered into, to influence the Senator aforesaid in his judgment and decision in the impeachment now pending, and undetermined in the Senate; therefore, be it

*Resolved*, That a select committee of seven be appointed to investigate the matter of the writing of the said letter; the motive and purpose of said members in writing said letter; whether the same was written to corrupt or improperly influence the judgment and decisions of said Senator and what action the House ought to take with reference thereto, and that said committee be authorized to send for persons and papers.

Mr. MAYNARD inquired whether that was a question of privilege.

The Speaker replied that the gentleman from Wisconsin had so presented it.

After examining the paper, the Chair said the gentleman did not directly charge corrupt purposes, but made use of the words. Therefore, in the opinion of the Chair, as the letter did not embody any corrupt offer, it was not a question of privilege; but he would submit the question to the determination of the House itself.

Mr. ELDRIDGE said that he was desirous that the Missouri members should be either exculpated or convicted, as the facts might warrant.

Mr. BLAINE inquired whether it was in order to move that the paper be not received.

The Speaker replied that it was not yet before the House.

After further proceedings, the House by a party vote—yeas, 28; nays, 82—decided that the paper did not present a question of privilege.

Mr. BENJAMIN, of Missouri, asked leave to make a personal explanation not exceeding five minutes.

Mr. ELDRIDGE objected.

THE IMPEACHMENT ARTICLES.

Mr. ROBINSON gave notice that at the next assembling after recess he would renew his resolution heretofore offered directing the managers to withdraw their articles of impeachment.

The Speaker said that he would rule when that question shall be brought before the House.

LEAVE OF ABSENCE.

Mr. ROSS, of Illinois, in behalf of his colleague from the Galena District, moved that his colleague have leave of absence to travel in Europe, and have his expenses paid, as during last Summer.

The Speaker said that leave of absence could be granted on the request only of the gentleman desiring it.

Mr. WASHBURNE, of Illinois, reminded his colleague (Mr. ROSS) that he would attend to his own personal matters. He would not call on any Knight of the Golden Circle to serve him.

Mr. ROSS hoped that his colleague would take no offence. He had made the request in consideration of the onerous duties which devolved on his colleague.

ACCUSATION OF BRIBERY.

Mr. BINGHAM, from the Impeachment Managers, reported a preamble stating that information has come to them which seems to furnish them probable cause to believe that improper or corrupt means have been used to influence the determination of the Senate upon the articles of impeachment; therefore be it resolved that the Managers be directed and instructed to summon and examine witnesses, and send for persons and papers, and take testimony on the subject.

The House, by a vote of 73 to 24, agreed to receive the resolution reported by the Managers, and Mr. BINGHAM proceeded to state the reasons for it.

Various private bills were adopted and acted upon.

Mr. BENJAMIN said that the resolution of Mr. ELDRIDGE not having been received as a question of privilege, an impression might go abroad that this disposition of the resolution was at the instance of the Missouri delegation who signed the letter which had been read at the Clerk's desk. He was not satisfied that such an impression should be made for himself, and he believed he also spoke for his colleagues. They desired the fullest investigation into all the facts in relation to the matter mentioned, and they asked that a special committee of the House be appointed for the purpose. There were other facts within his knowledge and others, which would enter largely into the privileges of one of the Senators. They would not interpose any obstacles, but render every aid in their power which the House or the Committee might require. They desired that there should be a full investigation, and that all the facts should go to the country. They knew they had nothing to fear; they had neither done or said anything dishonorable or which would not bear the light of day before the country at large.

Mr. ELDRIDGE desired to know whether the gentleman thought it was right for the whole Missouri delegation to call on one of the Senators from that State, who was then considering a case judicially, and ask him to withhold his vote on one of the articles of impeachment.

Mr. BENJAMIN said that in view of the circumstances preceding the writing of the letter, he would reply "yes," emphatically.

Mr. ELDRIDGE further asked, whether on the principles of justice and right, it was proper to interfere with the deliberation of the Court when the question was pending.

Mr. BENJAMIN left that for the Committee to judge, and the House can then assent or dissent to what they may report.

Mr. BIGBY asked the gentleman the question whether they did not think they were right if they supposed there was to be a corrupt proceeding.

Mr. CHANLER demanded that the words of the gentleman from California be taken down by the Clerk.

THE SPEAKER—With reference to the objection thus made, these words did not come within the parliamentary law, for the reason that the Senate forms a part of Congress. It was the Senate, although presided over by the Chief Justice. The rules prohibited offensive remarks toward the proceedings of either branch, although the question of the gentleman from California was hypothetic. The Chair thought it did not come within the parliamentary law. The presumption of the gentleman was that the Senate could make a corrupt decision.

Mr. BIGBY said he did not charge anything of that kind.

Mr. ELDRIDGE observed the gentleman from Missouri (Mr. BENJAMIN) had made no such charge himself.

Mr. CHANLER demanded that the rules of the House be fully carried out.

Mr. BENJAMIN, resuming, said that the Missouri delegation had no idea in the world, nor did they throw out any suspicion whatever that the Senator (HENDERSON) would act corruptly, or that any influence beyond what was evidence disclosed, would be brought to bear upon him. They explicitly negatived such an inference. They charged nothing corrupt. It was stated on the floor that the Senator requested the presentation of such a letter to him.

CORRUPT INFLUENCES.

Mr. BINGHAM said he was instructed by the Impeachment Managers to report the following resolution, and ask that it be put on its passage:

*Whereas*, Information has come to the Managers which seems to them to furnish probable cause to believe that improper or corrupt influences have been used to influence the determination of the Senate upon the articles of impeachment exhibited to the Senate by the House of Representatives against the President of the United States, therefore,

*Resolved*, That for the further and more efficient prosecution of the impeachment of the President, the Managers be directed and instructed to summon and examine witnesses under oath; to send for persons and papers; to employ a stenographer and to appoint sub-committees to take testimony, the expenses thereof to be paid from the contingent fund of the House.

Mr. ROSS rose to a question of order and stated it to be that the House had no power to try Senators.

The Speaker replied that the resolution did not propose to try Senators.

Mr. BINGHAM said the resolution proposed no such thing.

Mr. ROBINSON made a point that the Managers appointed by the House to conduct the prosecution had discharged their duty; and, therefore, had nothing further to do; judgment in part having been rendered, they could not be further heard any more than counsel could after a case had been submitted to the Court.

The Speaker overruled the point of order on the ground that the duty of the Managers have not been fully discharged, and as the House reserved to itself the right to present any further articles of impeachment.

Mr. CHANLER raised the question that the proposition of the gentleman from Ohio charged corrupt motives, and could not, therefore, be entertained.

Mr. ROBINSON took an appeal.

The Speaker said the appeal was too late, after another point had been made.

Mr. ELDRIDGE said the point was, the resolution was a reflection upon the Senate, and it was not, therefore, proper to be entertained by the House.

The Speaker said the resolution was open to the same objection as that of the gentleman from Wisconsin, (Mr. ELDRIDGE.) There was no direct charge of corruption. The language was that the information which had come to the Managers seemed to furnish probable cause. The uniform ruling had been that vague charges could not be construed as questions of privilege, but specific charges could be. The Managers, apart from this, had a right to report at any time, not as a question of privilege, but as a matter of right under the order of the House. The proposition, however, was open to the same objection, and the question could be asked whether the House would consider it.

Mr. PHELPS understood that the resolution charged, at least, that unworthy and corrupt considerations had entered into the verdict of the Senate.

Mr. KELSEY objected to the gentleman proceeding with his remarks.

Mr. PHELPS said he considered such insinuations out of order.

Mr. BINGHAM replied that the resolution did not insinuate.

The Speaker remarked that the remedy of the gentleman from Maryland (Mr. PHELPS) would be by his vote on the question pending.

The House then agreed to consider the resolution; yeas 78, nays 26—a strict party vote.

Mr. BINGHAM said it was not his purpose to delay the House except for a moment or two, inasmuch as a question of order had been raised, and it had been intimated that this was an attempt on the part of the House to exercise a power not warranted by the Constitution. He desired to say for himself, and he believed he could speak in behalf of all the Managers, that the resolution expressly declared that its purpose was the further and more efficient prosecution of the impeachment of the President, predicated on information communicated to the Managers that corrupt influences had been employed to prevent a successful prosecution by the House.

Mr. MUNGEN rose to a point of order, namely, that after the Managers appointed to conduct the prosecution against the President had discharged their duty, it was improper for them to look to articles of impeachment against Senators, that being for the Senate itself to undertake.

The Speaker overruled the point, because the House had resolved to consider the resolution.

Mr. JOHNSON would ask the honorable Managers whether they had the consent of the High Court of Impeachment to reopen the case, and present new evidence.

Mr. BINGHAM replied that the gentleman ought to have understood it, if he attended to the case in the Senate, that when the counsel of the President asked the question after the argument was formally closed, he, (Mr. BINGHAM,) in behalf of the Managers, notified the Senate that the House of Representatives did not surrender its right at any time before judgment to present additional testimony, and, as it would be seen by the record, to present additional articles. He desired to state the other matter, that the Constitution having vested in this House the sole power of impeachment, (that was the language,) it clothed this House with the power until the day of judgment to investigate all appliances of corruption to prevent a decision of this question according to the law and the evidence. They were acting within the scope of the authority devolving upon them. They had no doubt that when the House undertook impeachment all the power with which the Constitution invested them for a just, proper and legal impeachment should be employed from time to time. This was all that the resolution contemplated—to see whether justice could be obstructed by the President, or any of his hired agents. It was a power which no man could successfully challenge. The *habeas corpus* could not control it. He did not say the truth of the information brought to the Managers would be sustained by proof, but it would be the duty of the Managers to investigate it.

Mr. BROOKS—I ask the gentleman from Ohio to state what course the Managers mean to pursue in this investigation.

Mr. BINGHAM—We intend simply to pursue the line of investigation that [illegible] in the [illegible].

Mr. BROOKS—With open doors or with shut doors?

Mr. BINGHAM—(repeating the words)—With open doors or with shut doors. [Laughter.] We intend to obey the order of the House, Sir.

Mr. BROOKS—But is it to be *ex parte*—what people generally call an inquisition—or is it to be a public examination?

Mr. BINGHAM—The gentleman need not inquire of me any further; he seems to be in pursuit of knowledge under difficulties.

Mr. BROOKS—Very great difficulties.

Mr. BINGHAM—Very great difficulties. Nearly ever since he was born, this thing, which he calls inquisition, was practised by that party of which he professes to-day to be the chief leader without challenge. "Out of his own mouth I condemn him." [Laughter.] Never, Sir, did your Democratic organization, when it controlled this House, proceed with an investigation touching the privileges of the House, or the rights of the people, in any other mode than we proceed with it to-day.

Mr. ELDRIDGE—I rise to a question of order. I insist that the gentleman from Ohio shall not address this side of the House, but shall address the Chair. He is looking round here so savagely that he has nearly driven us all out of our seats. [Laughter.]

The SPEAKER—By the rules the gentleman must address the Chair.

Mr. BINGHAM—I shall be glad, within the rules, to have the privilege of looking at the gentleman smilingly.

Mr. ELDRIDGE—I should like to see the gentleman smile once, for I have not seen him smile since the commencement of the impeachment matter. [Laughter.]

Mr. BINGHAM—The point of order is so stout on the gentleman's case; that is what we call "point-no-point." [Laughter.]

The Speaker—The gentleman from Ohio will proceed with his remarks.

Mr. CHANLER addressed the Speaker.

The Speaker asked Mr. BINGHAM whether he yielded to the gentleman from New-York.

Mr. BINGHAM—No, Sir. I believe I have said all that was needful for me to say. I merely state that the Managers, on the part of the House, propose, by leave of the House, to prosecute this impeachment in good faith, in accordance with the powers given under the Constitution, until the day of judgment. [Laughter on the Democratic side of the House.]

Mr. JOHNSON—On all the articles?

Mr. BINGHAM—I do not answer any further questions. I move the previous question.

Mr. ROBINSON moved that the resolution be laid on the table.

Mr. ROSS moved that the House adjourn.

The House refused to adjourn—yeas 22, nays 70.

The House refused to lay the resolution on the table—yeas 11, nays 87.

Mr. BARNUM—I ask to make a suggestion, in one word, to the gentleman from Ohio. Would he not let this subject go to a select committee, or, at all events, to some committee that has on it a representative of the Democratic Party, which we claim to be the majority of the people of the North? Is it not a mockery to send it to a committee on which there is no representative of that party?

Mr. BINGHAM—I insist on the previous question.

Mr. PRUYN—With the consent of the gentleman from Ohio, I should like to ask a question and to make a suggestion.

Mr. BINGHAM declined to yield.

Mr. PRUYN—I was not here when the discussion took place.

Mr. BINGHAM insisted on the previous question; it was seconded, and the resolution was adopted; yeas, 88; nays, 19.

The House, then, at 4:15 o'clock, adjourned till Monday next, the Senate having disagreed to the concurrent resolution for a week's recess.

# The New-York Times.

VOL. XVII......NO. 5198. NEW-YORK, FRIDAY, MAY 22, 1868. PRICE FOUR CENTS.

## GRANT AND COLFAX.

### The Republican Candidates for President and Vice-President.

### Gen. Grant Nominated on the First Ballot.

### An Exciting Contest for the Vice-Presidency.

### Schuyler Colfax Nominated on the Fourth Ballot.

### The Platform Received and Indorsed Amid Much Enthusiasm.

Special Dispatch to the New-York Times.

CHICAGO, Thursday, May 21.

Every one was astir betimes this morning. The bright, clear May atmosphere invigorated the body, and sharp, vigorous discussion cleared the intellect. There was more excitement and a deeper interest than has yet been seen. The Committee on Platform had been quietly at work all night, and reported progress. At 8 o'clock the Sub-Committee had reported to the full Committee, and the prospect was that they would be able to report to the Convention by 11 o'clock.

The canvass for Vice-President was more active than ever, and WADE and FENTON were said to be neck and neck. New-Yorkers were jubilant, for they had labored long and well with the Southern delegations, and had been rewarded with bright promise of success. WILSON, who has had most of the Southern delegations, had fallen behind, because of the inroads made by FENTON's active workers. COLFAX maintained a positive though fluctuating strength from the sheer magnetism of his name. HAMLIN and CURTIN were only incidentally mentioned, and when the ballot comes the candidates will stand about as above indicated.

PROCEEDINGS IN THE CONVENTION.

At 10 A. M. the Convention was opened with prayer. The Opera House was crowded to its utmost capacity, from pit to dome. There being no business in order but the report of the Committee on Resolutions, there was an hour for evil or for good. True to the firebrand spirit, Mr. CHAS. S. SPENCER, of New-York, proposed that the resolutions of the Union League of America, adopted at the council held on Tuesday, be recalled from the Committee on Resolutions, to which they had been referred, and read and spread upon the records of the Convention. This was acceded to as an act of courtesy, and the reading of the resolutions was proceeded with. The point proved, as might have been expected, that the denunciation of the seven Senators was what was aimed at. When these allusions were read, a wild frantic burst of applause followed, breaking out not generally, but in spots here and there, according to the feeling. When read Mr. JONES, of Ohio, boldly moved that the recall being a matter of discourtesy to the Committee, the whole subject be laid on the table. This was greeted with emphatic shouts of "Good," "That's right," "Question," &c. SPENCER frantically protested, but he was overborne by an overwhelming vote, and the matter went to the table. He gave notice that he would call the subject up again at another time, but that will require two-thirds under the rules adopted.

Pending the report of the Committee speeches were made by FRED. HASSAUREK, Esq., of Cincinnati, and Gen. JOHN M. PALMER, of Illinois. The latter, in alluding to impeachment, said that though impeachment had failed, the people believed the President guilty, and that he should have been removed, because he was an obstruction to the peace and dangerous to the safety of the country. This was applauded to the very echo. He then said that they did not propose to indict the President here, but to again arraign him before the tribunal of the people for a violation of duty, principle and law. This sentiment was also received with tremendous enthusiasm, and indicated that the spirit of the Convention was taking the right direction.

Music followed, and at 11:40 the Committee on Platform appeared and made their report through Hon. R. W. THOMPSON, of Indiana, the Chairman. He appeared on the platform gray haired and venerable, and proceeded to read in fine voice. As one point after another was revealed and the expectations of the Convention were gratified, applause followed, rising sometimes to a terrific storm and then falling to a tremulous approval as some new feature revealed itself. The resolutions on reconstruction and the national credit were received with the greatest enthusiasm, and when the arraignment of ANDREW JOHNSON came, people held their breath to see how the warm struggle in the Committee had resulted. When it was seen that the resolutions arraigned JOHNSON and indorsed the House of Representatives by declaring him justly impeached, and that he was properly found guilty by the votes of thirty-five Senators, without expressing any opinion or impugning the motives and conduct of those who voted for acquittal, every one accepted it as a gratifying compromise, and the friends of conscience and the right of private judgment thanked God it was no worse.

At the conclusion of the reading, Gen. COCHRANE moved to insert after the words "properly found guilty by the votes of thirty-five Senators," the words "improperly acquitted by the votes of nineteen Senators." This was received with such a storm of opposition that he speedily withdrew it, and the previous question being ordered the resolutions were adopted without debate, by the Convention rising to its feet, and with a terrific shout of "aye!" and amid the waving of hats and handkerchiefs the platform was adopted by acclamation.

A resolution by Gen. SCHURZ in favor of removing the disabilities of such Southern men as rendered loyal aid in reconstruction, was received with so much favor that it was unanimously made a part of the platform. A resolution making the Convention a permanent body, subject to the call of the Chairman, was then adopted, and the quidnuncs immediately had it.

GEN. GRANT NOMINATED.

Mr. FRENCH, of North Carolina, then moved that the Convention proceed to nominate a candidate for President. Gen. LOGAN took the floor, and in a brief and eloquent speech placed in nomination Gen. ULYSSES S. GRANT. To describe the scenes which followed for the next hour is simply impossible. The roll-call began, and as the Chairman of each delegation responded with its unanimous vote, the enthusiasm was tremendous. Spirits rose higher and higher. Various witty, eloquent and spirited sentiments accompanied the delivery of each vote. Each Chairman formed a fine oratorical period amid merriment and cheers, and the vote went rapidly on until the column footed up 650 votes for ULYSSES S. GRANT. Then the Opera House rang from floor to ceiling, from balcony to curtain, and from stage to gallery, with the wildest cheers ever heard in response to any nomination since 1860, when the wigwam resounded with the tumultuous applause which followed the nomination of ABRAHAM LINCOLN. The entire audience of three thousand people rose to their feet and gave three times three, and repeated it until it seemed as though the roof itself must give way under the volume and sound which surged upward to the ceiling.

A dramatic surprise, little expected by the large majority present, followed, and added to the delight of the spectators. A dove, representing the national colors, and the harbinger of peace, flew from one of the proscenium boxes, and made the passage of the vast audience room several times, until it landed at the rear of the stage. The band struck up "Hail to the Chief," and at a given moment the bunting which covered the rear of the stage was pulled aside, and NAST's splendid new picture, illustrative of GRANT's candidacy, appeared in view and received the unbounded applause of people already wild with delight. The scene covered the entire rear of the stage and represents the portico on the White House, with a large pedestal on the right, with GRANT seated thereon in uniform, and the base of it indorsed "Chicago nominee, 1868;" and on the left of the portico is another pedestal, but vacant, on which is painted "Democratic nominee, New-York, 1868." By the side of GRANT, with one hand pointing to him and the other to the vacant platform, stands the figure of Columbia, and over all the significant words "Match him

The enthusiasm now reached its highest point, and it was many minutes before the Convention could proceed with its work. This was the first real burst of genuine feeling which had yet been felt in the Convention. The soldiers present struck up, "Rally round the flag," the audience joined in the chorus, and then a glee club sang a new campaign song, entitled "Hurrah for Grant," with fine effect.

THE VICE-PRESIDENCY.

After order was restored, Mr. SCOFIELD, of New-York, moved that the Convention proceed to the nomination of a candidate for Vice-President, which being carried, the candidates were at once put in nomination. Virginia opened with the nomination of Gen. WILSON, in a speech from Mr. PIERCE; Lieut.-Gov. CLAFLIN, of Massachusetts, seconded it amid loud cheers. Then Ex-Senator LANE arose and put in nomination Hon. SCHUYLER COLFAX, and the moment the name was mentioned, it was easy to see where the popular heart lay. A perfect storm of applause greeted the nomination, continued for some minutes, and the result was that he became the strongest man from that very moment, no matter what his vote might be on the first ballot. CORTLAND PARKER, Esq., of New-Jersey, seconded the nomination followed by MICHIGAN, and then by BROWN, of Pittsburg, who said without regard to his delegation, but representing ten thousand majority in Alleghany County he should cast his one vote for SCHUYLER COLFAX.

WADE came next, and his friends gave him an enthusiastic reception, ranking him next to COLFAX in popular support. Ohio proposed him and North Carolina seconded the nomination.

Then Hon. LYMAN TREMAIN, in a spirited speech, brought forward the name of Gov. FENTON, and the New-Yorkers made good their claim to the third position in popular favor, and developed a feeling for FENTON which surprised those who did not know the industry of his friends. Louisiana and part of Illinois promptly seconded the nomination with much enthusiasm.

Then followed Pennsylvania for CURTIN, through FORNEY and MCCLURE; Maine and part of Wisconsin, for HAMLIN, while South Carolina closed the lists for WILSON.

Then came the first ballot. Alabama divided between WADE, WILSON, FENTON and KELLY, with one for COLFAX. Arkansas threw nine for WILSON, and most of the Southern States followed suit, except Louisiana, which went solid for FENTON, and North Carolina, which was solid for WADE. FENTON scattered through California, Connecticut, Florida, Mississippi and Nevada, and got his first solid vote, after Louisiana, from New-York, and then eleven from Tennessee and six from Wisconsin. WADE showed strongest on the first ballot, getting North Carolina, Minnesota and Ohio solid, and a heavy vote in Missouri and Illinois. COLFAX scattered down the list lightly until he touched his own solid Indiana, which renewed the *furore* now increasing every moment. Michigan added to it, New-Jersey added nine, Oregon came in with her quota from the Pacific coast, while Tennessee, Vermont and Wisconsin aided to swell up the total beyond the expectations of his warmest friends.

The result stood: WILSON, 119; WADE, 149; COLFAX, 118; FENTON, 132; CURTIN, 53; HAMLIN, 30.

On the second ballot COLFAX took Delaware from WILSON, divided Kentucky with WADE, broke into Ohio's solid front, increased his hold on Pennsylvania, and made a lodgment in the two Virginias. His net gain was 31. WILSON held his own very well, losing but six votes. On the ballot WADE gained in Georgia, took three-fifths of Kentucky, the most of Maryland, part of Texas, but lost in Ohio and North Carolina.

His net gain on the ballot was 21. FENTON gained in Iowa, and took a fraction of Texas from WILSON. His net gain was eight. The ballot closed; WILSON, 113; WADE, 170; FENTON, 140; COLFAX, 149; CURTIN, 45; HAMLIN, 30. This decided gain for COLFAX was received with cheers, while the friends of WADE also felt elated at his progress. Loud demands for another vote followed, and the third ballot went on. WILSON's net loss on this was twelve votes in Connecticut and Rhode Island; Massachusetts and the South still stood by him. WADE gained eight votes net in California, Illinois, Louisiana and Pennsylvania, losing a few scattering in other States. FENTON lost but one. COLFAX gained in Iowa, Ohio, Kentucky, Virginia, and Rhode Island went back to him; net gain fifteen votes. Result—Wilson, 101; Wade, 178; Fenton, 139; Colfax, 164; Hamlin, 25, and Curtin, 40.

The name of Mr. CURTIN was now withdrawn, and great interest was manifested on the fourth ballot to see where Pennsylvania would go to. Wilson brought up with a nett loss of 12. Votes mostly in Southern States. WADE remained steady until Pennsylvania was called, when she threw 35 for WADE, and 14 for COLFAX, being a nett gain of 26 for the former, and 9 for the latter. This caused a shout for WADE, but COLFAX followed him close, and showed a nett gain of 24. FENTON stood steady, gaining 4; the result was WILSON, 89; WADE, 24; FENTON, 144; COLFAX, 186; HAMLIN, 24.

On the 5th ballot there was no important change until Pennsylvania was called, when she took thirteen from WADE and three from FENTON, and gave thirty to COLFAX, all told, amid applause which made the building shake. Tennessee followed by repudiating her first love, and give COLFAX fourteen and WADE three. Wisconsin increased her vote by four, and the *furore* increased.

Then came the grand rush to be first in piling honors upon the successful candidate. Gen. DODGE who had been with difficulty holding Iowa back even between FENTON and COLFAX for two ballots now set the ball in motion and threw sixteen votes solid for the favorite candidate. Pennsylvania then jumped to her feet and changed her vote in a like manner, which was greeted with such storms of applause that business was interrupted for several minutes. Louisiana and Connecticut next went over bodily and Massachusetts followed with cheers. Then Tennessee, Kentucky and South Carolina in the order named, then Maine and Minnesota and Wisconsin with shout after shout. There were now so many chairmen of delegations on the floor demanding that their votes be changed to COLFAX, that it was impossible to recognize any one in the confusion. Finally Mississippi, Virginia, Nevada, Kansas, California and Nebraska, in one grand rush, and lastly Illinois, were put down solid for COLFAX, and when the terrific applause had somewhat subsided the vote was announced—COLFAX, 522; FENTON, 75; WADE, 42, and WILSON, 11.

Gen. SICKLES now moved to make it unanimous, and Ohio seconded the motion, which was carried with three times three for the whole ticket. The National Committee for the next four years was elected. Thanks were returned to the officers, the Committee of Arrangements, and the people of Chicago, and the Convention adjourned.

The nomination of COLFAX gives the greatest satisfaction on all hands, and is conceded to be the strongest that could be made. The manner in which the strength of the Convention combined upon him was a splendid tribute to his worth as a man and his standing as a Republican.

The hotels are crowded to-night with enthusiastic crowds, and two ratification meetings are in progress. The *Tribune* office is brilliantly illuminated, and the best of feeling prevails. The platform is generally accepted as satisfactory in all respects. The financial and suffrage features are especially comly commended as prudent, sagacious and sound. The impeachment feature is not quite so mild as the Conservative men hoped for; but it is much better than was feared. There was a very warm fight in the committee on this, and it had to be accepted as a compromise to save a worse resolution from being sprung upon the Convention in case the platform did not allude to it. It was only adopted in committee by a vote of 19 to 18, and was carried by the votes of Southern States and Territories, the Territory of Colorado overruling the voice of the great State of New-York on this important question. The following are all the States that voted against it but four: Maine, Vermont, Rhode Island Connecticut, New-Jersey, New-York, Pennsylvania, Ohio, Indiana, Michigan, Wisconsin, Iowa, Tennessee and North Carolina. Massachusetts, Illinois, Missouri, California, Nevada and Nebraska, with thirteen Southern States and Territories, voted for it.

The business of the Convention has been done with great expedition. It was exceedingly harmonious and enthusiastic beyond precedent. Thousands of delegates and visitors have already left for their homes.

### THE ASSOCIATED PRESS REPORT.

The Convention was called to order at 10:15 o'clock.

Prayer was offered by Rev. Dr. GULLIVER, of Chicago.

The President announced that the Committee on Resolutions had just sent word that they would not be ready to report before 11 o'clock.

THE UNION LEAGUE RESOLUTIONS.

Mr. CHARLES S. SPENCER, of New-York—I move, Sir, that the resolutions of the National Council of the Union League of America, which were yesterday presented to this Convention, and by the temporary Chairman referred to the Committee on Resolutions, take the same direction as the resolutions and proceedings of the Soldiers' and Sailors' Convention, and be spread on the record as part of our proceedings. I think that this courtesy is due the National Council of the Union League of America, which to-day is insuring Republican ascendancy in the South, and upon whose efficiency we depend for the Southern Republican preservation in the coming election, and which, if any Northern State shall falter, will supply its place by Radical South Carolina.

Mr. THOMAS W. CONWAY, of Louisiana, moved that the resolutions be read.

DELEGATE FROM MICHIGAN—How can these resolutions be acted upon by this Convention until reported back by the Committee, when the rules require their reference without debate?

Mr. SPENCER—There may be misapprehension. In entering these resolutions upon our record we shall by no means adopt them, but will only perform an act of courtesy by reciting in our proceedings the fact that they sent us such resolutions. That is a matter of fact which has transpired which should not be ignored.

Mr. CONWAY—I call for the reading of the resolutions.

The PRESIDENT—The Secretary will read the resolutions.

The Secretary proceeded to read the resolutions adopted by the National Council of America, in session at Chicago, May 19, 1868, as follows:

*Resolved*—*First*, That we deem the Union League of America of vital importance to the success of the Republican Party, and the maintenance of loyalty, liberty and equal rights in the Union, and urge its being vigorously sustained and reorganized in all the States as the right arm of the Union Party.

*Second*, That we pledge the loyal people of the North to uphold, protect and defend the loyal people of the South from injurious oppression and assassination, and to this end will use all the means in our power, even the resort to arms, if requisite, in defence of their right to life, liberty and the pursuit of happiness.

*Third*, That we would express our high appreciation of the sublime patience, forbearance and magnanimity of the negroes of the South, and their devotion as soldiers throughout the Union during the war of the rebellion, and of their hearty loyalty, zeal and becoming deportment since, showing that under all circumstances they have justified the reposing in their hands the highest boon of an American citizen, the ballot, and illustrated the truth that it is eminently wise and always safe to act with equity and justice to all men, without regard to race or color.

*Fourth*, That impartial suffrage is a cardinal principle of the Republican Party, and should not be abandoned: and that we urge upon the several States, and upon Congress, the adoption of such measures as will secure the right of suffrage to every American citizen impartially.

*Fifth*, That we fully indorse the action of Congress, and consider that the hour is past for hesitation, compromise and leniency toward those who support and defend traitors, and endeavor to restore them to power; and that the loyal people of the country are unanimous in the sentiment that all who defy and trample under foot the acts of Congress for the maintenance of the principles our gallant soldiers and sailors fought and died to secure, ought to be hurled from power by the use of every loyal and constitutional means that can be devised, and that any man, whoever he may be, who has been recreant to his duty in securing this, failed to meet the expectations of the loyal people of the country, and will be marked by men, and will deserve the indignation and censure he so richly merits, and will be denounced in thunder tones as an unworthy servant, whose place should be filled by a true patriot; and we especially feel called upon to condemn the traitorous conduct of the Senators who disappointed the hopes of every loyal heart in the land in voting for the acquittal of ANDREW JOHNSON, whom they knew to be guilty of the crime charged, and who deserted their country in the hour of its peril; and we class them with those traitors to their party and country—COWAN, DIXON, DOOLITTLE and ANDREW JOHNSON—with the assurance that a traitor's doom awaits them.

*Sixth*—That we respectfully recommend to the Union National Convention the nomination of that tried soldier, judicious man and reliable loyalist, ULYSSES S. GRANT, for President, and of an undoubted Republican and a proved, experienced statesman for Vice-President. With such men we feel confident of victory, as our cause is eminently that of Truth, Justice and Equal Rights, and must be approved.

Mr. JONES, of Ohio, urged that the rules of the Convention required the reference of all resolutions without debate, and opposed bringing these resolutions back to the Committee for discussion before the judgment of the Convention in regard to them had been heard. If that practice should be sanctioned, it would obstruct the business of the Convention. He hoped the rules would be observed. Perhaps the Committee would report the very thing proposed. He moved to lay the whole matter on the table.

Gen. COCHRANE, of New-York, called for a division of the original motion, asking the vote first on recalling the resolutions and then entering them in the proceedings. But the question was taken on the motion to lay on the table, which prevailed.

Mr. SPENCER, of New-York, moved that the resolutions just laid on the table be now taken from the table. ["No, no."] I propose to give some reasons why they should be taken from the table.

A DELEGATE—The motion is to table the motion to send for resolutions.

Mr. SPENCER—I move the whole subject be taken from the table. [Cheers.]

The PRESIDENT—Does the gentleman move to reconsider the vote just taken?

Mr. SPENCER—I cannot, because I voted in the negative; [laughter;] but when a subject is on the table I suppose it is within the power of the Convention to take it therefrom.

A DELEGATE—It is not in order now.

The PRESIDENT—I suppose not, for this reason: that no business has been intervened.

Mr. SPENCER—I will wait then until some does. [Applause.]

A DELEGATE—I move we hear from Mr. HASSAUREK, of Ohio.

The PRESIDENT—Will the Convention hear Mr. HASSAUREK, of Ohio? ["Yes, yes," cheers.]

REMARKS OF MR. HASSAUREK.

Mr. HASSAUREK then proceeded to address the Convention in an eloquent manner. He pictured the demoralized condition of the South, socially, politically and morally, and said that it was one of the chief duties of the Republican Party to see that the reconstruction of the late rebellious States was conducted in such manner as to secure to one and all—Northern men, Southern men and freedmen—protection to life, liberty and property. He continued: We protect our citizens in foreign lands—why not also protect them at home? If we do that, there must be peace, and security must be established, demanded, and maintained, only by keeping a party in power which will do it. The power of the Federal Government must not be intrusted to the hands of those who brought all these troubles on the country. Those who would unbend anarchy and remove all checks and restraints from the Southern men of our country, at a time when they most need the protecting care of the Federal Government. The power of the nation must not be intrusted to the Democratic Party, which is, and always has been, the party of lawlessness turbulance and violence. It must not be entrusted to the party which, having been an advocate and defender of slavery, is identified with all its excesses, and by keeping alive the spirit of rebellion and insurrection shares with ANDREW JOHNSON the blame and responsibility for the present affairs in the South. The sacred duty of protecting helpless and defenceless freedmen must not be intrusted to the hands of those who are daily preaching hatred of the race, and arousing the mob by appeals to its lowest prejudices and fiercest passions. The wolf must not be made custodian of the lamb, nor must the fox be appointed the protector of the hen-roost.

The speaker continued to discuss at great length the policy of the Republican Party past, present and to come. His remarks were received with much applause.

The speaker concluded as follows:

The peace and tranquility, business and common interests of the country, its future greatness and prosperity, its obligations of honor, justice and good faith, its position in the eyes of the civilized world, demand that the organization which alone can defeat the Democratic Party be put in possession of the Executive branch of the Government for the next four years. The policy of the Republican Party has not had a fair trial since the death of ABRAHAM LINCOLN. In possession of legislative power it could enact laws, but a hostile Executive defeated their purposes, or barely complied with the letter of Congressional enactments, while he endeavored to defeat the spirit of it. Had it not been for the determined opposition of ANDREW JOHNSON the time of Congress might have been more profitably occupied, and its work of reconstruction would now be complete; but, as it is, the great task still remains to be accomplished, and it ought to be left in the hands of those who begun it, and with whom alone it will be safe. Do not forget that a change of administration would not be a change of individuals, but a change of principles. Do not, therefore, call upon those to complete the restoration of the Union, who have done their utmost to destroy it. Let not the history of the last seven years be written in vain. Let not the memory of our dead be forgotten. Let us not desert the cause for which they have suffered and died. Let us not abandon our friends or carelessly, impiously sacrifice the fruits of such a costly war. Let us not give up the building to destruction on the verge of its successful completion. Let us place the ship of State under the guidance of him who has led the hosts of the Union to victory and glory, and he will safely pilot her into the harbor of peace, good will and justice to all men. [Cheers.]

Mr. SPALDING, of Ohio, as the Committee on Resolutions was not yet ready, moved to suspend the rules and proceed to nominate Gen. GRANT for the Presidency. [Loud cries of "No! no!"]

The Chairman of the delegation from Kentucky moved to lay the motion on the table.

Mr. SPALDING withdrew his motion.

On motion of the delegate from Kentucky, the soldier, statesman and patriot, Gen. JOHN M. PALMER, was called out and received with much enthusiasm.

GEN. PALMER'S SPEECH.

He spoke as follows:

MR. PRESIDENT AND GENTLEMEN OF THE REPUBLICAN CONVENTION: I attended this Convention to witness and observe its earnest action without any disposition on my part to contribute to the volume of words that usually attend assemblages like this, as you will see I have outlived in a great measure the estimate that young men place upon a mere speech. [Applause and cries of "Good!"] Years ago, when the great questions before the country were matters of argument and deliberation, I endeavored as best I could to contribute my share to their peaceful solution. In 1861 it was resolved by a portion of the people of this country that the problems of the hour were to be settled in a more stern and decisive manner. In my way—to the extent of the power I possessed—I contributed to the settlement of those problems. [Applause.] It seemed to me at the close of the war, and it seems to me now, that the matters of dispute between the different sections of the country were settled upon the battle-field; and that all I have desired since that time is that the logic of the battle-field should be recognized, and the decisions there made should be carried into effect. [Applause.] Years ago, in the beginning of the country, the question was whether men in all parts of the Republic should be allowed to speak. I valued freedom of speech—not much speech, but free speech. [Laughter and applause.] While I commanded no large share of the popular gift, I did insist that those who loved speaking should be allowed to do it. It was denied, not only in the South, but in many districts in the North. At that time it was insisted, not only that men should speak as they please, and for themselves and ourselves. [Applause.] I believe that while every man should be allowed to speak freely, and speak for himself; that all men should be allowed to act freely, and act for themselves; that while every man should be allowed to own himself, he should be allowed to own not only himself, but to own his own wife and his own children. This question has been decided by the arbitrament of the sword, and not only was that great fundamental essential doctrine established, but it was also settled as conclusively as any question could be settled, that hereafter men should not only be free in their own persons, but they should be a little free and equal before the law, everywhere in this great Republic; [applause;] and the issue of the Republican Party today is not to discuss theories, but to give practical effect to the great doctrines established upon the battle-field. [Applause.] Not for the loyal men alone. Not for North. Not for the South. But for men everywhere within the limits of the Republic. Not for white men. Not for red men. Not for black men. But for all men. ["That's so!" and applause.] And we supposed that the voice of the American people during the progress of the war, and at the close of the war, seemed to indicate that hereafter there would be no difficulty that these doctrines would be accepted—at least by the Republican Party—everywhere. Six months ago, what man supposed that there remained any further obstructions to the execution of the popular will, and that we were still to struggle on in vindication of these great principles? We have triumphed during the war, at the Presidential election of 1864, at the close of the war, in the greater conflict of 1866. When JOHNSON appealed from Congress to the people, and the people reiterated their determination that these great doctrines should be hereafter American doctrines everywhere, [cheers,] the public voice was spoken in language not to be misunderstood. It was supposed then that every man who accepted the name of Republican, recognized those great essential doctrines, and that they were hereafter not to be resisted, at least by the members of the Republican Party. There was but one thing then in the pathway of the people. In 1864, by one of those signal blunders which seemed like the dispensations of the Almighty in his wrath, we elected ANDREW JOHNSON Vice-President. Thoughtless men may characterize it as a blunder, but thoughtful men may well wonder whether what we deemed a mistake was not the judgment of the Almighty inflicted on the country for some sin; and certainly, except the war itself, no curse could be heavier than the election of ANDREW JOHNSON. [Cheers.] In 1866 the distinct issue was presented to the American people, whether that curse should be removed. The people of Illinois, by a majority unheard of in history, instructed its representatives upon that question. Iowa spoke out, Kansas spoke out, other States spoke out upon this question. There was no positive room for mistaking the will of the people of the country; there was but one way by which all the departments of the Government could be brought in harmony. A demand was made to impeach the President, but it has failed. It is not for me to speak of the reasons of that failure! it is enough for me to deplore that result. The removal of ANDREW JOHNSON was demanded by the national safety. We may talk about it, we may discuss it as a judicial or political question, but, as a question of common sense, it is that ANDREW JOHNSON stood in the way of the peace of the country, and ought to have been removed. [Prolonged cheers.] Impeachment is the substitute of modern civilization for old-fashioned resistance and decapitation; that is all there is of it. [Cheers, and cries of "Good, good."] Sir, in old times, among barbarous people, when the ruler stood in the way of the people, they took off his head. In America, under the influence of civilization and Christianity, when the ruler stands in the pathway of principles and the prosperity of the country, it is by impeachment that we take off his political head. [Cheers and applause.] Nice captious questions borrowed from a Police Court have no application here. It is enough that the interests of the millions of American people demanded that this obstruction should be taken out of the way, and it ought to have been done, [cheers,] or, to use a lawyer's phrase, JOHNSON ought to have been indicted. He should have been tried before the common courts, convicted and removed. Mr. President and gentlemen of the Convention, there remains for us but this remedy. Impeachment is a failure. There is a tribunal that cannot be corrupted. [A voice, "What of TRUMBULL?"—cries of "Go on! Go on!"—a hiss.] I leave the man to that tribunal of which I am about to speak. [Cries of "Good! Good!"] There is a tribunal that cannot be corrupted. [Cheers.] We propose at this Convention not to indict men but to again submit these great questions to the American people for their decision. [Cheers and cries of "Right! Right!"] We expect to summon the old anti-Slavery man who has struggled on amid the storm and the sunshine, amid persecution and success, the man who stood by the flag of freedom when many of us were still halting by the way. We expect to ask him to go to the ballot-box and deposit his vote for the right. [Cheers.] We expect to place the great Captain who led the armies of the Republic through the war. [Cheers.] And we expect to summon those gallant soldiers who followed him down the Mississippi, who were present at Vicksburg; we expect to summon those gallant men who saw the flag as it ascended Missionary Ridge and witnessed the flight of BRAGG and his host; we expect to summon those who marched from Atlanta to the sea, and those who so many years struggled between Washington and Richmond, and at last saw the rebel flag go down upon the Appomattox. We may expect to summon all these to rally under the flag of the great Captain, and we expect then a vote which shall place these questions where they will be disturbed no more in our history and age. [Cheers.] Gentlemen, I have said to you that I have no fondness for words; I trust your committee are prepared to report resolutions for your consideration, which shall have no uncertain sound. [Prolonged cheers.] Let us make an issue just as clear and distinct as the stars upon the flag; so distinct that upon this political fight we can do as we did upon the battle-field, when we saw the stars and stripes; we knew there were friends there. Let us have a distinct, clear, well defined platform. I do not want any mistake as to the issues to be decided in this contest. We mean to make ULYSSES S. GRANT President of the United States, [applause,] as you did ABRAHAM LINCOLN in 1860; and let me beg of you not to offer a continued, perpetual temptation and reward to the hands of the assassin that his life may be taken. Let me beg that you do not make a Vice-President whose character will offer a temptation for the assassination of GRANT. [Applause and cheers.] We want him to live out four years, and if the country demands his services, we desire his reëlection. If the country shall then prefer some other public man, we wish that he may retire and live to a good old

(Continued on Eighth Page.)

The New-York Times.

VOL. XVII......NO. 5240. NEW-YORK, FRIDAY, JULY 10, 1868. PRICE FOUR CENTS.

# THE DEMOCRATIC CONVENTION

## Unanticipated Result of the Five Days' Struggle.

## Ex-Gov. Horatio Seymour Nominated for President.

## Gen. Francis P. Blair Proposed for Vice-President.

## How the People of the Country Receive the Nominations.

## The Republicans Pleased and the Democrats Astonished.

## The Candidates to be Notified at Tammany Hall To-night.

The management of the great show at Tammany Hall had very elastic ideas as to the capacity of any given space, and hence persisted in issuing about 2,000 more tickets for admission to the Convention than the hall will comfortably hold. Yesterday the jam was terrible—no milder word will properly describe it. The general belief that a decision of the great conflict would be reached, had a powerful attractive force, and everybody who could manage to secure a ticket or a badge hurried at an early hour to the new shrine of the new dispensation. Thanks to the arrangements for ingress and egress so admirably enforced by Capt. CAMERON, of the Eighteenth Precinct, there was no detention or discomfort outside, but the vast crowd speedily and decently effected an entrance to the hall. Once there, however, and they experienced a martyrdom, resulting only from that sanguine hope that two persons could be put into the space required for one, and not from any want of skill and activity upon the part of Sergeant-at-Arms MOORE and his assistants. These latter officials had anything but an easy task. Hundreds were constantly demanding impossibilities in the way of accommodation, and being refused, vented their rage upon the poor ushers. These latter could do nothing more than protest, struggle, perspire in vain endeavors to satisfactorily discharge their duties. It was evident that the session was to be protracted suffering upon the part of those compelled by duty to remain within the hall. The ladies were out again in full force, and nearly the same persons as on the previous day occupied the wing seats, where there was a comparatively fresh atmosphere, and so managed to look upon the backs of the gentlemen standing in the aisles—which was all the view they had—with some degree of comfort. Why they should continue to crush their way into the hall remained a marvel. They could see nothing of the Convention, save a stray glimpse occasionally as the crowd of standers parted for a moment, and they would have heard nothing whatever had it not been for that wonderful voice of Secretary PERRIN.

Among the delegates, the hour before the session opened passed without incident. The members gathered as on previous occasions in knots among the benches, discussing the situation and anxiously inquiring as to the future. There had been something done during the previous evening, but exactly what, had not transpired. The Chase men had talked buoyantly, and shaken their heads knowingly into the late watches of the night. There had been a meeting of prominent gentlemen at the Manhattan Club, which was generally supposed to have arranged matters; but how, nobody knew. Hence, there was an eager expectancy everywhere throughout the hall. Men knew they stood upon a prepared mine that could be exploded at any moment, but who was to fire the train, and what would be the consequences of the explosion, were points only the event itself could determine. The bitter antagonism between the East and West was still apparent, and while everybody knew that some one must be found upon whom the warring factions could unite, none could imagine how the feat was to be accomplished. The conviction had grown stronger since the previous night that the prospects of the party were being frittered away in the fruitless balloting, and that some determination must be reached at once if any hope of success in November was to remain. Hence the Convention was in a condition that a bold, adroit move in any direction was almost certain of success, provided it would lead to decisive results.

Thus the vast throng waited the arrival of the appointed hour for the session to begin, all hoping that the rap of the President's gavel then to be sounded would be the last; some, perhaps, knowing of a prepared programme, but very few indeed believing the event the morning was to produce to be within the range of the possible.

### Fifth Day's Proceedings.

The Convention was called to order at 10:30 o'clock, Hon. THOMAS L. PRICE in the chair.

The following prayer was then offered by Rev. Dr. PLUMMER, of South Carolina:

THE PRAYER.

Holy, Holy, Holy, Lord God of Hosts! Creation abounds in the monuments and memorials of Thy being, wisdom, power, glory, justice, goodness and truth. Thy nature is infinite, eternal and unchangeable. Thou hast supreme claims to our love and homage—our submission and thanksgiving. Thou hast done great things for us, whereof we would make adoring mention. Thou madest man a little lower than the angels; and when he had sinned Thou didst provide a Redeemer. Thou hast also greatly favored our country. In days gone by thou didst bring a vine out of distant land. Thou didst cast out the heathen. Thou preparedst room before it and did cause it take deep root, and it filled the land. The hills were covered with the shadow of it, and the boughs thereof were like the goodly cedars. She sent out her boughs unto the sea and other branches unto the river. Why, then, hast Thou broken down her hedges, so that all they who pass by the way do pluck her? The boar out of the wood doth waste it, and the wild beast of the field doth devour it. Return, we beseech Thee, O God of Hosts; look down from Heaven and visit this vine. Thou hast for some time sorely afflicted us. The grievousness of war was long upon us; countless myriads of our people, as loving and magnanimous as those who survive them, prematurely sleep the long sleep of death. If we went into the field, behold the slain! If we went into the city, behold Rachael weeping for her children, and refusing to be comforted because they were not. Our great men have conceived chaff and brought forth stubble. Our land is full of widows and orphans. Even stout hearts among us have often been ready to fail for looking after those things, which were thought to be coming upon us. We have hoped for succor, and behold sadness for salvation, and behold perplexity. Thou that dwellest between the cherubim shine forth before all our tribes, stir up Thy strength and come and save us. Feed us no longer with the bread of tears. Let the love and fear of God rule all hearts. Let us cease from man, whose breath is in his nostrils. Let us no more pervert our blessings to the nourishing of our personal or national vanity, nor to malevolence, worldliness or ungodliness. Compass our land with Thy power, as with a shield. Let not our bruise be incurable nor our wound immedicable. Let our children be as aforetime and our people be established before Thee. Be not Thou as a man as to need, as a mighty man that cannot save. Implant and nourish in all our people a genuine love of country. Purely purge away our dross and take away our sin. Thou only canst heal our breaches, or make us dwell in safety. Let not lots again be cast for our honorable men, nor our great men be bound with chains. Feed our hungry, clothe our naked; make the widow's heart to sing for joy; in Thee let the fatherless find mercy; pity all who are tossed with tempest and not comforted; let not the rod of the wicked rest upon the lot of the righteous. Thou, blessed and only Potentate, canst make men to be of one mind and of the same judgment. O Thou, which hast showed us great and sore troubles, wilt Thou not quicken us again, and bring us up again from these low depths? Do Thou, the glorious Lord, be unto us a place of broad rivers and streams, wherein shall go no galley with oars, neither shall gallant ship pass thereby. Let the future history of our Government be as a morning without clouds. Let our sun no more go down, nor our moon refuse to give her light. Let North and South, East and West, henceforth see eye to eye, feel heart to heart, and join inseparable bonds in love and peace, with joy and singing.

And to the King eternal, immortal, invisible, the only wise God, our Saviour, be honor and glory, dominion and power, salvation and blessing, through Jesus Christ, forever and ever. Amen and Amen.

OPENING PROCEEDINGS.

Mr. SLADE, of Missouri—Mr. President

The CHAIRMAN—The first business in order is the reading of the proceedings of yesterday.

Mr. BLACK, of Indiana—I move that the reading of the journal be dispensed with.

The CHAIRMAN—It will be so ordered unless objection is made. It is so ordered.

Mr. SLADE, of Missouri—I rise to a privileged question. This Convention has adopted a resolution inviting the delegates to the Soldiers' and Sailors' Convention to seats upon this floor. Numerous complaints, however, have been made in my hearing, and some of them personally to myself, that that rule is disregarded, and some of the delegates are refused admission.

The PRESIDENT—The Secretary will state the proceedings with regard to the delegates to the Soldiers' and Sailors' Convention.

The SECRETARY—In conformity with the resolution of the Convention inviting the delegates to the Soldiers' and Sailors' Convention to seats upon this floor tickets have been issued by the National Executive Committee through their officers and sent to their hall for distribution. This hall is limited in capacity, and the Committee have endeavored to extend the courtesy just as far as the seats will permit.

Mr. SLADE—I learn that delegates have presented their tickets and have been refused admission.

The CHAIRMAN—Those were the tickets that were issued for a previous day. The tickets were changed yesterday, and new tickets were sent to the officers of that Convention.

Mr. SLADE—I move that the explanation be entered upon the record.

The CHAIRMAN—It will be so ordered unless there is objection. It was so ordered.

MISSOURI NOMINATES F. P. BLAIR.

Mr. BRODHEAD, of Missouri—We have now reached the fifth day of our session without any successful result. I now ask leave to present to the Convention another name for their consideration. I will nominate Gen. FRANCIS P. BLAIR, of Missouri. It is not necessary, in this Convention, that I should attempt to repeat his honorable services as a soldier or a statesman, for they are known to the whole country, without desiring to disparage the qualifications of any other of the distinguished gentlemen whose names are presented for the consideration of this Convention. I will only say that Gen. BLAIR is eminently possessed of those qualities most needed at this time—firmness of purpose, moral courage and indomitable will. He will not be readily turned from a purpose once deliberately formed, although another coördinate department of the Government may place itself in the way of its performance; and, as President of the United States, he would preserve, protect and defend the Constitution; and he would give to it a living meaning which, in the absence of any judicial interpretation to the contrary, gives to the President the right and imposes upon him the duty of refusing to execute unconstitutional laws. [Applause.] If we would meet the demands of this crisis, if we would not shirk from the issues of this hour, we must by some tangible form of action maintain the independence of the Executive. Congressional despotism is the great evil against which we have to contend. It is the fruitful source of all our troubles. It is that which is riving asunder the framework of our Government and substituting the views of faction for the requirements of the Constitution. We want a man at the head of the Government who knows the duties of the Executive station, and knowing dare maintain them. Such a man is the gentleman whose name I now present to the consideration of this Convention.

The CHAIRMAN—Mr. BRODHEAD, of the Missouri delegation, in behalf of that delegation, puts in nomination for President FRANCIS P. BLAIR, Sr., of Missouri.

PENNSYLVANIA HITS NEW-YORK.

Mr. MILLER, of Pennsylvania—I rise, Sir, to a privileged question. I notice, Sir, by the report of the proceedings of this Convention yesterday, that it is rather made a matter of congratulation by a portion of the Press that the superior shrewdness, or "sharpness," (for I believe that is the word used,) of certain politicians, the rules of this Convention can be utterly ignored. Now, Sir, I allude to the announcement of the change in the vote of the delegation from New-York, and I insist upon it, Sir, that upon a delegation voting for its candidate, or in changing its vote, even if its vote is changed from ANDREW JOHNSON or SALMON P. CHASE, [thunders of applause, long continued,] it shall content itself with simply voting. [Renewed cheers for CHASE, and confusion.] In order that the Chairman give the lie to the intimations that shrewdness and sharpness, emanating from where it may, can override the prevailing order of this Convention—[Great confusion.]——

The CHAIRMAN—Will the gentleman submit his motion?

Mr. MILLER—I make no motion; I simply rise to a privileged question to call attention to the fact that it is alleged that the orders of this Convention cannot be enforced because some people are smart enough to avoid them. [Great confusion, and cries of order.]

The CHAIRMAN—The first business in order will be the calling of the roll for the nineteenth ballot.

CALIFORNIA NOMINATES JUDGE FIELD.

Mr. ROSE, of California—Mr. President, I rise for the purpose of placing before the Convention the name of an eminent gentleman and statesman—a gentleman of accomplished education; of brilliant talents; one who has distinguished himself in the service of his State and the nation; a gentleman who has occupied the highest position of the judiciary of California; who from that position was transferred to the Supreme Court of the United States; occupying that position, it was his province to stand up like a wall of fire against the encroachment of Radical domination, and stand as the guardian of the Constitution of his country against all the power of the Radical Party at Washington; to vindicate the charter of our liberties at a time when it required some one of ability to raise his voice and his pen against Radical misrule, I allude, Sir, to STEPHEN J. FIELD, of the Supreme Court. [Great Applause.]

A DELEGATE—Mr. Chairman——

The CHAIRMAN—The Clerk will announce the nomination—wait until the nomination of the candidate is regularly announced and recorded.

Mr. PERRIN—Mr. ROSE, of California, places in nomination for President, STEPHEN J. FIELD, of California. [Cheers.]

Mr. VALLANDIGHAM, of Ohio—I have a communication in writing to make to this Convention. By permission of the Chair, I will read it from the stand. [Applause, during which Mr. VALLANDIGHAM made his way to the rostrum.]

The CHAIR—Mr. VALLANDIGHAM, of Ohio, will make a communication to the Convention.

Mr. VALLANDIGHAM—The following is the communication to which I refer:

PENDLETON'S LETTER.

CINCINNATI, July 2, 1868.

*Washington McLean, Fifth Avenue Hotel, New York:*

MY DEAR SIR: You know better than anyone the feelings and principles which have guided my conduct since the suggestion of my name for the Presidential nomination.

You know that while I covet the good opinion of my countrymen, and would feel an honest pride in so distinguished a mark of their confidence, I do not desire it at the expense of one single electoral vote, [great applause,] or of the least disturbance of the harmony of our party. I consider the success of the Democratic Party in the next election of far greater importance than the gratification of any personal ambition, however pure and lofty it might be. [Loud cheers.]

If, therefore, at any time a name shall be suggested, which, in the opinion of yourself and those friends who have shared our confidences, shall be stronger before the country, or which can more thoroughly unite our own party, I beg that you will instantly withdraw my name, and pledge to the Convention my hearty and zealous and active support for its nominee. Very truly yours,

GEO. H. PENDLETON.

[Great Cheering.]

Mr. VALLANDIGHAM—At the request of the gentleman to whom this letter is addressed I submit it to this Convention. It was his desire that it should have been done very early in the afternoon of yesterday, but the earnest zeal and fidelity of the Ohio delegation, and the distinguished son of Ohio whom they had presented to the Convention for the office of President, precluded their consent to any such proposition. This morning his request has been renewed, and in conformity with it I have produced and read the letter, and submit that the spirit of magnanimity, unselfishness and patriotic devotion to the interests of the country speak in terms of far higher eulogy in behalf of this distinguished gentleman than any words I could utter. [Great applause.] Pursuant, therefore, to the authority of Mr. McLEAN, and acting under the advice of Mr. PENDLETON, I withdraw his name, with hearty thanks to the multitude of earnest, zealous and devoted friends who have adhered to him with so great fidelity. [Applause long continued and cheers for PENDLETON.]

The CHAIRMAN.—Mr. VALLANDIGHAM, by the instructions of the Ohio delegation, withdraws the name of GEO. H. PENDLETON as a candidate for the Presidency before this Convention, and he does so by the direction of Mr. PENDLETON himself.

We will now proceed with the nineteenth ballot.

NINETEENTH BALLOT.

The Secretary called the roll with the following result:

Alabama—Eight for Gen. Hancock. [Applause.]

Arkansas—Five for Gen. Hancock.

California—Three for Judge Field, one and one-half for Hendricks, and one-half for Salmon P. Chase.

Connecticut—Six for Mr. English.

Delaware—The Chairman of the Delegation—As the favorite candidate of the State of Delaware has been withdrawn, Delaware casts her votes for Gen. Hancock. [Great applause.]

Florida—Three for Hendricks.

Georgia—Nine for Hancock.

Illinois—Sixteen for Hendricks.

Mr. MULLANY, of Illinois—Mr. Chairman ——.

Cries of "Order!" "Out of order!" "Put him out!"

The CHAIRMAN—The gentleman must come to order.

Mr. MULLANY—Mr. Chairman, I rise to a privileged question.

Mr. DAWSON, of Pennsylvania—Mr. Chairman, there can be no privileged question while the roll is being called. I insist, therefore, upon the enforcement of the rule. This is no place for mere exhibition.

Mr. CHAIRMAN—The opinion of the gentleman from Pennsylvania coincides with the opinion of the Chair; and the Chair must consider the gentleman from Illinois, (Mr. MULLANY,) out of order.

A delegate moved that Mr. MULLANY have permission to make an explanation.

Cries of "No," "No," "Out of order."

The CHAIRMAN—The gentleman from Illinois cannot proceed without suspending the rule of this Convention. I therefore hope he will take his seat and let us proceed with the balloting.

The Clerk will proceed.

Indiana—Thirteen for Hendricks.

Iowa requests to be passed by for the present.

Kansas—Two for Hendricks and one for Hancock.

Kentucky takes time.

Louisiana—Seven for Hancock.

Maine—Four and a half for Hancock, two and a half for Hendricks. [Applause.]

Maryland—Three for Blair, three for Hancock, one for Hendricks.

Massachusetts—Twelve for Gen. Winfield Scott Hancock. [Applause.]

Michigan—Eight for Thomas A. Hendricks.

Minnesota—Two and a half for Hendricks, one for Hancock and one-half for Thomas H. Seymour of Connecticut. [Applause; three cheers proposed for Thomas H. Seymour, but were not given.]

Mississippi—Seven for Hancock.

Missouri—Ten and a half for Blair, one-half for Hancock.

Nebraska—Three for Hendricks.

Nevada—Three for Judge Field.

New-Hampshire—Half for Thomas A. Hendricks, and four and a half for Gen. Hancock. [Applause.]

New-Jersey—Seven for Judge Field, of California.

New-York—Thirty-three for Thomas A. Hendricks. [Great applause.]

North Carolina—Nine for Gen. Hancock. [Applause.]

Ohio—Twenty-one for Judge Packer, of Pennsylvania. [Laughter, followed by applause.]

Oregon—Two for Field, and one for Packer.

Pennsylvania—Mr. WOODWARD—Mr. President, I beg that the vote of Pennsylvania may be passed for the present, and that her delegation have leave to retire. [Voices, "No," "No."]

Mr. PRICE in the Chair—The proposition of the gentleman from Pennsylvania to retire for consultation will be agreed upon without objection. It is so agreed.

The delegation from Pennsylvania thereupon withdrew.

Rhode Island—Four for Jas. R. Doolittle.

South Carolina—Six for Gen. Hancock. [Applause.]

Tennessee—Ten for Hancock. [Applause.]

Texas—Six for Hancock.

Vermont—Five for Thomas A. Hendricks.

Virginia—Ten for Hancock. [Applause.]

West Virginia—Five for Hendricks.

Wisconsin—Eight for Doolittle.

Iowa—Eight for Thomas A. Hendricks, of Indiana. [Applause.]

Kentucky—Three and a half votes for Hendricks; three votes for Gen. Hancock; three and a half votes for Charles A. Seymour, of Connecticut, one vote not voting.

Pennsylvania—Mr. WOODWARD—Pennsylvania casts twenty-six votes for Gen. Hancock. [Loud applause.]

The Secretary announced the result of the nineteenth ballot as follows: Whole number of votes cast, 316.

| | | | |
|---|---|---|---|
| J. E. English | 6 | F. P. Blair | 13½ |
| Gen. Hancock | 135½ | Field | 15 |
| Packer | 22 | Chase | ½ |
| J. R. Doolittle | 12 | Thos. H. Seymour | 4 |
| Thos. A. Hendricks | 107½ | | |

Before the announcement of the result, Mr. MULLANY, of Illinois, rose and said he had a resolution he desired to offer.

The CHAIRMAN—The Chair would state to the gentleman from Illinois that the order of the Convention is that when proceeding to a ballot no resolution is in order.

TWENTIETH BALLOT.

The Secretary then proceeded with the call of the States for the twentieth ballot, as follows:

Alabama—Eight for Hancock.

Arkansas—One for Hancock; four for Hendricks.

California—Three for Field; one and a half for Hendricks; one-half for Hancock.

Connecticut—Six for English.

Delaware—Three for Hancock.

Florida—Three for Hendricks.

Georgia—Nine for Hancock.

Illinois—Sixteen for Hendricks.

Indiana—Thirteen for Hendricks.

Iowa—Eight for Hendricks.

Kansas—Two for Hancock, one for Hendricks.

Louisiana—Seven for Hancock.

Maine—Four and a half for Hancock and two and a half for Hendricks.

Maryland—Three for Blair; three for Hancock; one for Hendricks.

Michigan—Eight for Hendricks.

Minnesota—Three and a half for Hendricks; one-half for Hancock.

Mississippi—Seven for Hancock.

Missouri—Three for Hendricks.

Nevada—Three for Field.

New-Hampshire—One half for Hendricks, four and a half for Hancock.

New-Jersey—Seven for Hendricks.

New-York—Thirty-three for Hendricks. [Cheers.]

North Carolina—Nine votes for Hancock.

Ohio—Passed at the request of the Chair.

Oregon—Three for Field.

Pennsylvania—Twenty-six for Hancock. [Cheers.]

Rhode Island—Four for Doolittle.

South Carolina—Six for Gen. Hancock.

Tennessee—Ten for Hancock.

Texas—Six for Hancock.

Vermont—Five for Hendricks.

Virginia—Ten for Hancock.

West Virginia—Five for Hendricks.

Missouri—Eight for Doolittle.

Kentucky—Three and a half for Thomas H. Seymour; one-half not voting.

Massachusetts—The Chairman of the Delegation—The State of Massachusetts asks leave to retire for fifteen minutes for consultation. It is the first time we have made the request. I believe we have always been ready to vote when called upon.

The CHAIRMAN—There being no objection, the request is granted.

Ohio—Ten for James E. English, eleven for Gen. Hancock. [Applause.]

The SECRETARY—The call will be suspended fifteen minutes, waiting for the Massachusetts delegation.

Gen. MCCOOK—I ask the same leave for Ohio.

The CHAIRMAN—Leave is granted. I would suggest that, inasmuch as two large delegations have retired for fifteen minutes, we take a recess for fifteen minutes.

A recess for fifteen minutes was accordingly taken by the Convention.

On the return from recess, and when order was restored, the Secretary proceeded with the call.

Massachusetts—Eleven votes for Gen. Hancock, one voter declining to vote. [Applause.]

The Secretary announced the result of the twentieth ballot as follows:

Whole number of votes cast, 318½.

| | | | |
|---|---|---|---|
| English | 16 | Blair | 13 |
| Hancock | 142½ | Field | [illegible] |
| Doolittle | 12 | Thomas H. Seymour, | 2 |
| Hendricks | 121 | | |

TWENTY-FIRST BALLOT.

The SECRETARY—The Convention will now proceed to take the twenty-first ballot.

Alabama—Eight for Gen. Hancock. [Applause.]

Arkansas—Five for Thomas A. Hendricks. [Applause.]

California—Three for Field, one for Hendricks and one for English.

Connecticut—Six for English.

Delaware—Three for Gen. Hancock. [Applause.]

Florida—Three for Thomas A. Hendricks. [Applause.]

Georgia—Nine for Hancock. [Applause.]

Illinois—Sixteen for Hendricks. [Applause.]

Indiana—Thirteen for Hendricks. [Applause.]

Iowa—Eight for Hendricks. [Applause.]

Kansas—Two for Hendricks, and one for Gen. Hancock.

Kentucky—The Chairman of the Delegation—Pass Kentucky; we are not ready.

The SECRETARY—We will pass Kentucky.

Louisiana—Seven for Hancock. [Applause.]

Maine—Four and a half for Hancock, and two and a half for Hendricks.

Maryland—Six for Hancock and one for Hendricks. [Applause.]

Massachusetts—The Chairman of the Delegation—Massachusetts is not ready.

The SECRETARY—We will pass Massachusetts.

Michigan—Eight for Thomas A. Hendricks.

Minnesota—Three and a half votes for Hendricks, one-half for Hancock.

Mississippi—Seven for Hancock. [Applause.]

Missouri—Four for Hendricks, six for Hancock and one for English. [Applause.]

Nebraska—Three for Hendricks.

Nevada—The Chairman of the Delegation—Pass Nevada.

New-Hampshire—One-half for Hendricks, four and a half for Hancock.

New-Jersey—Seven for Hendricks.

New-York—Thirty-three for Hendricks.

North Carolina—Eight for Hancock, one for Hendricks.

Ohio—Eleven for Hancock, ten for James E. English.

Oregon—Two for Field, one for English.

Pennsylvania—Twenty-six for Hancock.

Rhode Island—Four for James R. Doolittle.

South Carolina—Six for Hancock.

Tennessee—Five for Johnson, two and a half for Hancock, one-half for Hendricks, one-half for McClellan, two and a half not voting.

Texas—Six for Hancock.

Vermont—Five for Hendricks.

Virginia—Ten for Hancock.

West Virginia—Five for Hendricks.

Wisconsin—Eight for Doolittle.

Kentucky—Three and a half for Hancock, seven for Hendricks, and one-half for Seymour, of New-York.

Massachusetts—Five for Hendricks, of Indiana; four for Salmon P. Chase, of Ohio [illegible] and long-continued applause, followed by a few hisses,] and six votes for Hancock.

Nevada—Three for Field.

The Clerk announced the vote as follows:

Whole number of votes cast, 316½.

| | | | |
|---|---|---|---|
| English | 19 | Field | 8 |
| Hancock | 135½ | Chase | 4 |
| Doolittle | 12 | McClellan | ½ |
| Johnson | 5 | Hoffman | ½ |
| Hendricks | 132 | | |

PROPOSITION TO ADJOURN TO ST. LOUIS.

Mr. HUNTER, of Missouri—I desire to offer a resolution in reference to an adjournment to St. Louis, in September next. [Great confusion.] I will send it to the desk to be read. I rather think sometimes that I have not got into a Democratic Convention. I therefore present the resolution, in order that it may be read.

The CHAIRMAN—The resolution is not now in order. The Clerk will proceed to call the roll.

TWENTY-SECOND BALLOT.

Alabama—Eight for Hancock.

Arkansas—Five for Hendricks.

California—Five for Hendricks. [Applause.]

Connecticut—Six for English.

Delaware—Three for Hancock.

Florida—Three for Hendricks.

Georgia—Nine for Hancock. [Applause.]

Illinois—Sixteen for Hendricks. [Applause.]

Nevada—Thirteen for Hendricks.

Iowa—Eight for Hendricks.

Kansas—Two for Hendricks, one for Hancock.

Kentucky—The Chairman of the Delegation—Pass Kentucky.

Louisiana—Seven for Hancock.

Maine—Four and a half for Hancock, two and a half for Hendricks.

Maryland—Six for Hancock, one for Hendricks.

Massachusetts—The Chairman of the Delegation—Pass Massachusetts.

Michigan—Eight for Hendricks.

Minnesota—Four for Hendricks.

Mississippi—Seven for Hancock.

Missouri—Two and a half for Hancock, eight for Hendricks, one for English.

Nebraska—Three for Hendricks.

Nevada—Three for Hendricks.

New-Hampshire—One-half for Hendricks, four and a half for Hancock.

New-Jersey—Seven for Hendricks.

New-York—Thirty-three for Hendricks. [Cheers.]

South Carolina—Nine for Hendricks. [Applause.]

THE BEGINNING OF THE END.

Ohio was called, and Gen. McCOOK rose to his feet. There was a hush of expectancy throughout the hall. The State was known to have been merely waiting for time on the previous vote, and some movement of importance was expected. With a loud, clear voice, heard everywhere in the vast assemblage, the Ohioan spoke:

Mr. CHAIRMAN—I arise at the unanimous request and the demand of the delegation from Ohio, and with the consent and approval of every public man in the State, including Hon. GEORGE H. PENDLETON, to again place in nomination against his inclination, but no longer against his honor, the name of HORATIO SEYMOUR, of New-York. [Loud cheers and long-continued applause.] Let us vote, Mr. Chairman and gentlemen of the Convention, for a man whom the Presidency has sought, but who has not sought the Presidency. [Applause.] I believe in my heart that it is the solution of the problem which has been engaging the minds of the Democratic and conservative men of this nation for the last six months. ["Good, good."] I believe it will have a solution which will drive from power the vandals who now possess the Capitol of the nation. [Applause.] I believe it will receive the unanimous assent and approval of the great belt of States, from the Atlantic—New-York, New-Jersey, Pennsylvania, Ohio, Indiana, Michigan, Illinois and Missouri, and away West, for quantity, to the Pacific Ocean. [Applause.] I say that he has not sought the Presidency; and I ask—not demand—I ask that this Convention shall demand of him that, sinking his own inclination and the well-known desires of his heart, he shall yield to what we believe to be the almost unanimous wish and desire of the delegates to this Convention. [Great applause and loud cheers.] In my earnestness and enthusiasm I had almost forgotten to cast the twenty-one votes of Ohio for HORATIO SEYMOUR.

As McCOOK sat down audience and Convention rose up, and tremendous cheers leaped from almost every throat. The gallery, as it had done throughout, permeated its whole duty, and the air was freighted with this sudden manifestation of SEYMOUR's popularity. In the midst of it HORATIO SEYMOUR stepped forward to the President's place, which had been occupied by Gen. PRICE, of Missouri. Mr. SEYMOUR was evidently deeply agitated; his lip quivered, his face in every line betrayed his deep emotion, and for a moment his voice was tremulous and husky. When the thunders that his appearance evoked had subsided he addressed the Convention.

SPEECH OF MR. SEYMOUR.

GENTLEMEN OF THE CONVENTION: [Cheers.] The motion just made by the gentleman from Ohio excites in my mind the most mingled emotions. [Applause.] I have no terms in which to express my gratitude [cheers] for the magnanimity of his State, and for the generosity of this Convention. [Cheers.] I have no terms in which to tell of my regret that my name has been brought before this Convention. God knows that my life and all that I value most in life I would give for the good of my country, which I believe to be identified with the interests of the Democratic Party. [Applause and cries of "Take the nomination then."] I do not stand here as a man, proud of his opinions, or obstinate in his purposes, but upon a question of honor I must stand upon my own convictions against the world. [Applause, and a voice "God bless you, HORATIO SEYMOUR."]

Gentlemen: When I said here at an early day, that honor forbade my accepting a nomination by this Convention, I meant it. When, in the course of my intercourse with those of my own delegation, and my friends, I said to them that I could not be a candidate, I meant it. And now permit me here to say, that I know, after all that has taken place, I could not receive the nomination without placing not only myself, but the great Democratic Party in a false position. [Great applause.] But gentlemen of the Convention, more than that, we have had to-day an exhibition, from the distinguished citizen of Ohio, that has touched my heart, as it has touched yours. [Cheers.] I thank God, and I congratulate this country, that there is in the great State of Ohio, whose magnificent position gives it so great a control over the action of our country, a young man, rising fast in the estimation of his countrymen, and whose future is all glorious; who has told the world that he could tread beneath his feet every other consideration than that of duty, and when he expressed to his delegation and expressed in more direct terms, that he was willing that I should be nominated, who stood in such a position of his own nomination. I should feel a dishonored man if I could not tread the same honorable path which he has marked out. [Great applause.] Gentlemen, I thank you, and may God bless you for your kindness to me; but your candidate I cannot be. [Three cheers for HORATIO SEYMOUR.]

SPEECH OF MR. VALLANDIGHAM.

Mr. VALLANDIGHAM, of Ohio—Mr. President: In times of great public exigency, and especially in times of great public calamity, every personal consideration must be yielded to the public good. [Applause.] The safety of the people is the supreme law, and the safety of the American Republic demands the nomination of HORATIO SEYMOUR, of New-York. [Cheers.] Ohio cannot, Ohio will not, accept his declination, and her twenty-one votes shall stand recorded on his name, [cries of "good, good" and cheers,] and now I call upon the delegations from all the States represented on this floor; upon the delegations from all the States of this Union, from the Atlantic to the Pacific, from the Great Lakes to the Gulf, disregarding those minor considerations which, justly it may be, properly I know, tend to sway them in casting their ballots to make this nomination unanimous; and, before God, I believe that in November the judgment of this Convention will be confirmed and ratified by the people of all the United States. [Applause.] Let the vote of Ohio stand recorded then—twenty-one votes for HORATIO SEYMOUR. [Applause.]

SPEECH OF MR. KIERNAN.

Mr. KIERNAN, of New-York—Mr. President: Belonging to the delegation from the State of New-York, and coming from the district where the President of this Convention lives, I cannot, as an individual delegate, refrain from asking the indulgence of this Convention in making one or two observations; and in order that we may relieve everybody, in order that we may relieve our Chairman from every bit of sensitiveness on the question of honor, I desire to say on behalf of the delegation from the State of New-York, that they have had neither lot nor part in the motion, which in our hearts we yet rejoice to hear, from the State of Ohio. [Applause.] We heard but recently that some such movement was thought, by wise and good men, necessary for the safety of our country. But our hearts were coerced out of deference to the sensitiveness of the gentleman who presides over this Convention, and we told them we could have neither lot nor part in it, unless others would overcome that which we had never been able to do. Now, Sir, let me say another word. We have balloted two or three days; we have balloted, thank God, in the best of temper, and of spirits; we have resolved, and we required the judgment of two-thirds of the delegates of this Convention for our nominee, to the end that we might be sure, for the sake of our country, that we would have a majority of the electors next November. And after striving hard, after striving long, and after consulting as well as we could in reference to the various names brought before us, we have not been able yet to convince the judgment of two-thirds of the Convention for the candidates we have supported. New-York has steadily voted her judgment, with kind feelings to other candidates. We have pronounced as our second choice for a distinguished citizen of Indiana. But it seems to me that after this long struggle, and in this crisis of our affairs, and in view of what is so important to every man, woman and child in this Union, that we should succeed in November; it seems to me now, in reference to our distinguished Chairman, that his honor is entirely safe. No one can doubt that he has steadily and in good faith declined; but now his honor is safe, and his duty is to his country; his duty to his fellow-citizens, to all that shall come after us, requires that he shall let the judgment of the delegates of this Convention prevail; and if it should select him as the standard-bearer we are most certain in their

The New-York Times.

VOL. XVIII .....NO. 5340. NEW-YORK, WEDNESDAY, NOVEMBER 4, 1868. PRICE FOUR CENTS.

# VICTORY!

## Magnificent and Overwhelming Republican Triumph.

## Gen. Grant Elected President of the United States.

### He Will Have More Than a Two-Thirds Majority in the Electoral College.

### Massachusetts Gives Him 75,000; Maine, 40,000; Illinois, 60,000; Ohio, 45,000; Vermont, 30,000; Indiana, 15,000 Majority.

### California and Nevada Probably Republican.

### New-York State Elects Hoffman by About 12,000 Majority.

### The Democratic Electoral Ticket Probably Successful.

## NEW-YORK STATE.

REPORTED AND ESTIMATED MAJORITIES.

| Counties. | Grant. | Counties. | Seymour. |
|---|---|---|---|
| Alleghany | 3,800 | New-York | 60,000 |
| Broome | 2,000 | Kings | 12,500 |
| Cattaraugus | 2,500 | Albany | 1,900 |
| Cayuga | 3,500 | Columbia | 300 |
| Chautauque | 5,000 | Greene | 700 |
| Chemung | 300 | Putnam | 200 |
| Chenango | 1,800 | Queens | 1,400 |
| Clinton | 500 | Richmond | 800 |
| Cortland | 2,000 | Rockland | 800 |
| Delaware | 2,000 | Schoharie | 1,200 |
| Dutchess | 1,500 | Seneca | 500 |
| Erie | 500 | Sullivan | 600 |
| Essex | 1,400 | Ulster | 400 |
| Franklin | 1,200 | Westchester | 1,800 |
| Fulton and Ham. | 500 | | |
| Genesee | 1,600 | Total | 88,300 |
| Herkimer | 1,600 | | |
| Jefferson | 3,600 | | |
| Lewis | 800 | | |
| Livingston | 1,500 | | |
| Madison | 2,500 | | |
| Monroe | 1,600 | | |
| Montgomery | 300 | | |
| Niagara | 800 | | |
| Oneida | 1,500 | | |
| Onondaga | 4,000 | | |
| Ontario | 1,800 | | |
| Orange | 300 | | |
| Orleans | 1,600 | | |
| Oswego | 3,200 | | |
| Otsego | 500 | | |
| Rensselaer | 1,200 | | |
| St. Lawrence | 9,000 | | |
| Saratoga | 1,600 | | |
| Schenectady | 200 | | |
| Schuyler | 800 | | |
| Steuben | 2,500 | | |
| Suffolk | 300 | | |
| Tioga | 1,400 | | |
| Tompkins | 1,600 | | |
| Warren | 700 | | |
| Washington | 3,000 | | |
| Wayne | 2,000 | | |
| Wyoming | 1,600 | | |
| Yates | 1,600 | | |
| Total | 81,300 | | |

### The Vote by Towns.

The following table shows the vote by towns so far as heard from. The gains and losses are computed on the Gubernatorial vote of 1866, when the Republican majority in the State was about 13,800:

[illegible]

Ketcham, Republican, is elected to Congress, and Hegeman, Republican, to the Assembly.

Stuyvesant, Columbia Co.—Second District gives Seymour 53 majority; Democratic gain 51. Hoffman, for Governor, has 94 majority. Wheaton, for Congress, has 103 majority, and Tilden, for Assembly, has 100 majority.

Eastchester, Westchester Co.—Potter, Democrat, for Congress, has 290 majority. Lawrence, Democrat, for Assembly, has 300 majority.

The City of Lockport gives Hoffman 1,287. Griswold, 1,186.

Nineteen towns in Chautauque County give Grant 4,097 majority.

Gifford, Oneida County, gives Grant 152 majority, and Preston gives Seymour two majority.

Oneida County—Norwich, Second District, Griswold, 374; Hoffman. 275. North Norwich, Second District, Grant, 47; Seymour, 26. Plymouth, Grant's majority, 86.

Rockland County gives Seymour 900 majority.

Chemung County gives 25 majority for Grant.

Eleven townships in Cattaraugus County gives Grant 425 majority; Griswold 412 majority. The county is claimed for the Republicans by 2,200 to 2,500 majority.

Orange County—Newburgh City, Grant 192 majority; Republican gain, 191.

Washington County—Greenwich, First and Third Districts, Grant, 478; Seymour, 228.

Town of Richmond, Schoharie County, Seymour, 9 majority. Worcester—First District—Grant, 218; Seymour, 198. Second District—Grant, 171; Seymour, 90.

Wyoming County, complete, gives Grant 1,640 majority; Griswold, 1,600 majority.

Chesterfield—Grant, 60 majority.

Moriat—Grant, 508; Seymour, 427.

City of Syracuse—Grant, 618 majority; Griswold, 514 majority; McCarthy, for Congress, 417. Grant's majority over Fenton's in 1866 is 515.

The Republicans claim Erie County by a small majority. The electoral and State ticket is very close in this city. D. L. Bennett is undoubtedly elected to Congress. The Republicans elect 9 out of 13 Aldermen.

Griswold's majority in Rensselaer County is 500. Grant's majority, 200.

Southfield—First District—Grant, 78; Seymour, 103; Griswold, 74; Hoffman, 108; Wood, 72; Reeves, 108; Hawkins, 70; Declair, 78; Marsh, 29. Second District—Grant, 164; Seymour, 393; Griswold, 150; Hoffman, 407; Wood, 230; Reeves, 282; Hawkins, 183; Declair, 180; Marsh, 296.

Westfield—First District—Grant, 204; Seymour, 161; Griswold, 205; Hoffman, 163.

Columbia County, complete, gives Seymour 250 majority; Hoffman, 300. Elects two Democratic members of the Assembly, the First District by 550 majority and the Second District by 150. Wheaton, Dem., for Congress, is elected by 200 majority. The entire Democratic county ticket is elected.

Austerlitz gives 75 Republican majority.

Ghent gives 61 Republican majority.

Chatham—First District gives 74 Republican majority.

New-Lebanon gives Seymour 229, Grant 194, Hoffman 235, Griswold 191.

Putnam County—Horton (Democrat) is elected to the Assembly.

Franklin County—Thirteen towns give Grant, 1,141 majority, a gain of 445 over last year's vote. Four small towns to hear from.

Ontario County—Seneca complete gives Grant 120 majority.

Twelve towns in Oneida County give Grant 772 majority—a net Republican gain of 128 as compared with 1866. Bailey is elected to Congress.

Cayuga County, complete, all but four towns, gives 2,986 majority for Grant; the remaining four towns will increase this to about 3,450 majority.

Newburgh City—Orange County, Griswold, 1,269; Hoffman, 1,155; Van Wyck, for Congress, 1,266; Greene, 1,150; Davis, for Assembly, Republican, 1,207; Corwin, Democratic, 1,168.

Chemung County gives Grant about 25 majority; Patrick, Democrat, probably elected Member of Assembly.

Troy City complete gives a majority for Seymour of 685; Hoffman, 577; Bascom over Barclay, 801; O'Neil, 783; Osgood, Dem., for Congress, 914. Two Democratic Assemblymen are elected—Flagg from the First and Howard from the Third District. Flagg's majority is 820; Howard's, 100. Aiken, Rep., is elected in the Second District.

The following is the total vote of Monroe County: Grant, 11,677; Seymour, 10,089; Grant's majority, 1,588. Griswold, 11,550; Hoffman, 10,318; Griswold's majority, 1,232.

The total vote of the City of Rochester is as follows: Grant, 5,406; Seymour, 5,147; Griswold, 5,314; Hoffman, 5,240.

Eleven towns in Monroe County give Grant 3,680; Seymour, 2,782; Griswold, 3,546; Hoffman, 2,777. Grant's majority in this county will be fully 1,600; Griswold's about 1,300. Bradstreet, Dem., was elected by 417 majority. Wright, Rep., is elected to the Assembly in the First District, and Barnard, Rep., in the Third. Davis, Rep., is elected to Congress by over 2,500 majority in the district.

Westchester County—Gibbons, Assemblyman, is elected by a small majority.

Five districts in Flushing, complete, (one estimated,) Democratic majority for President, 360; for Governor, 440; Assembly, 230. Democratic majority last year, 564.

### Republican Triumph in the Twenty-Third District.

Special Dispatch to the New-York Times.

SYRACUSE, N. Y., Tuesday, Nov. 3.

This city gives 631 Republican majority. The county, as far as heard from, shows a probable Republican majority of 4,000. The news from the adjoining counties is gratifying, showing large Republican gains in nearly every city. Oswego gives 450 majority for GRANT. We elect in this District a Republican Representative in Congress—DENNIS MCCARTHY, and three Republican members of Assembly. GRISWOLD runs a little behind his ticket.

### New-York—The New Assembly.

| Probable Republican. | | Probable Democratic. | |
|---|---|---|---|
| Allegany | 1 | New-York | 21 |
| Broome | 1 | Kings | 8 |
| Cataragus | 2 | Albany | 4 |
| Cayuga | 2 | Chemung | 1 |
| Chatauque | 2 | Columbia | 2 |
| Chenango | 1 | Erie | 2 |
| Clinton | 1 | Greene | 1 |
| Courtland | 1 | Monroe | 1 |
| Delaware | 2 | Oneida | 1 |
| Dutchess | 2 | Orange | 1 |

[illegible]

### The Vote of New-York City.

[illegible]

| | | | | | | | |
|---|---|---|---|---|---|---|---|
| XXI | 8499 | 8369 | 11166 | 1870 | .... | 2580 | 4068 |
| XXII | 3436 | 8451 | 10849 | 3068 | .... | 3415 | 4962 |
| Total | 47960 | 107860 | 108948 | 59807 | 107 | 83492 | 80677 |

Seymour over Grant........59,400
Total vote of the City........155,860
Total vote of the City, November, 1866........114,255
Total vote of the City, November, 1867........112,007
Hoffman over Fenton, November, 1866........47,185

### The Vote for Governor in the City.

The returns of the vote for Governor from the following wards only reach us before going to press:

GOVERNOR.

| | Griswold. | Hoffman | | Griswold. | Hoffman |
|---|---|---|---|---|---|
| 1 | 281 | 2649 | 12 | 2201 | 4230 |
| 2 | 187 | 812 | 13 | 1384 | 4419 |
| 3 | 252 | 791 | 14 | 726 | 4626 |
| 4 | 460 | 3830 | 15 | 3276 | 3541 |
| 5 | 874 | 2709 | 16 | .... | .... |
| 6 | 359 | 5006 | 17 | 3813 | 11026 |
| 7 | 1275 | 6884 | 18 | 3261 | 6944 |
| 8 | 1720 | 5087 | 19 | 3245 | 6409 |
| 9 | 4058 | 5290 | 20 | .... | .... |
| 10 | 1571 | 4411 | 21 | 2992 | 6168 |
| 11 | 1981 | 8840 | 22 | 3209 | 6824 |

The estimate of the vote for Governor in this City, based on the incomplete returns received, gives HOFFMAN 69,000 majority.

### Assemblymen Elected.

| Dists. | Dists. |
|---|---|
| 1st—Murphy, Dem. | 12th—Woltman, Dem. |
| 2d—Burns, Dem. | 13th—Halpin, Dem. |
| 3d—Cavenagh, Dem. | 14th—Whalen, Dem. |
| 4th—Galvin, Dem. | 15th—Frear, Dem. |
| 5th—Mitchell, Dem. | 16th—Irving, Dem. |
| 6th—Campbell, Dem. | 17th—Plunkett, Dem. |
| 7th—Richmond, Rep. | 18th—Kiernan, Dem. |
| 8th—Witt, Dem. | 19th—Porter, Dem. |
| 9th—Bergen, Dem. | 20th—Keegan, Dem. |
| 10th—Hartman, Dem. | 21st—Hitchman, Dem. |
| 11th—Tainor, Dem. | |

### New-York—Congress.

The Republicans have probably carried nineteen Congressmen and the Democrats twelve Congressmen, of the New-York delegation of thirty-one members, as follows:

| Dis. Rep. | Dis. Dem. |
|---|---|
| 11. Van Wyck. | 1. Reeves. |
| 12. Ketcham. | 2. Slocum. |
| 15. Tanner. | 3. Shumaker. |
| 16. Ferris. | 4. Fox. |
| 17. Wheeler. | 5. Morrissey. |
| 18. Sandford. | 6. Cox. |
| 19. Knapp. | 7. Calkins. |
| 20. Laflin. | 8. Brooks. |
| 21. Bailey. | 9. Wood. |
| 22. Churchill. | 10. Potter. |
| 23. McCarthy. | 13. Griswold. |
| 24. Cowles. | 14. Mayhew. |
| 25. Kelsey. | |
| 26. Hotchkiss. | |
| 27. Ward. | |
| 28. Davis. | |
| 29. Fisher. | |
| 30. Bennett. | |
| 31. Sheldon. | |

## IN BROOKLYN.

With the exception of a quarrel or two of trifling importance the election in Brooklyn passed off as quietly as it did in New-York. The following are the returns:

### City of Brooklyn—For President.

| Wards and Towns. | Rep. Grant. | Dem. Seymour. | Registry. Seymour. |
|---|---|---|---|
| I | 826 | 724 | 1809 |
| II | 375 | 1536 | 2108 |
| III | 1295 | 726 | 2130 |
| IV | 1214 | 1263 | 2808 |
| V | 746 | 2600 | 3361 |
| VI | 1527 | 3292 | 6190 |
| VII* | 1173 | 1163 | 3761 |
| VIII | 509 | 960 | 1878 |
| IX | 624 | 1580 | 2340 |
| X* | 1842 | 3284 | 6036 |
| XI | 1629 | 2979 | 4092 |
| XII | 365 | 2619 | 3820 |
| XIII* | 1585 | 1188 | 3751 |
| XIV | 868 | 3670 | 3813 |
| XV | 1402 | 1340 | 3925 |
| XVI | 1830 | 2329 | 4208 |
| XVII* | 1178 | 1266 | 3067 |
| XVIII | 619 | 813 | 1483 |
| XIX | 1126 | 860 | 2270 |
| XX | 2114 | 1866 | 3844 |
| XX | 16.8 | 1968 | 3883 |
| XXII | 822 | 1054 | 1930 |
| Total | 26,589 | 36,865 | 68,307 |

Seymour's majority, 10,076.

* In the foregoing table there are five districts not heard from in the Seventh, Tenth, Thirteenth and Seventeenth Wards.

The total vote thus far is 62,854.

From the returns already received, the indications are that the following candidates for city and county offices are elected:

County Treasurer—Thomas A. Gardner.
District Attorney—Samuel D. Morris.
Comptroller—Evan M. Johnson.
Auditor—James O'Brien.
City Treasurer—Cortland A. Sprague.
Collector of Taxes—Isaac Badeau.
Justices of Sessions—Stephen J. Voorhis, William H. Hoyt.
Coroner, First District—Dr. Joseph B. Jones.
Coroner, Second District—Lawrence A. Whiteall.
Superintendent Poor, Third District—Henry Seiler.
Superintendent Poor, Fifth District—Cornelius Ferguson.
Police Justice—Andrew Walsh.
Justice, First District—John Delmar.
Justice, Third District—James Buckley.
Justice Peace, Sixth District—John Lynch.
The following Assemblymen are elected:

[illegible]

James B. Allaben is the only Republican Assemblyman known to be surely elected. The entire Brooklyn City Democratic ticket is elected.

### Kings County.

| | Grant. | Seymour. |
|---|---|---|
| New-Lots | 416 | 804 |
| Flatbush | 283 | 337 |
| Flatlands | 170 | 170 |
| Gravesend | 100 | 185 |
| New-Utrecht | 178 | 321 |

The Governor's ticket is just the same.

## NEW-JERSEY.

### The Returns Incomplete—The State Probably Republican by a Small Majority.

A dispatch to the Western Union Telegraph Company says: Returns from New-Jersey come in very slowly, but it is believed that the State has gone for Grant and Colfax by a small majority, while Randolph, Democrat, is elected Governor.

The following returns have been received:

Paterson City gives 324 Republican majority. Plainfield gives Grant 182 majority; Blair, for Governor, 175, and Clark, for Congress, 178. The following are the majorities in Orange:

First Ward—Grant, 107; Blair, 103; Hill, 108; Leed, 107; Peck, 115—a Republican gain of 27.

Second Ward—Seymour, 63; Randolph, 69; Rafferty, 61; Booth, 63; Rush, 73.

Third Ward—SEYMOUR, 209; BLAIR, 218; RAFFERTY, 223; Rush, 294; Booth, 219.

In West Orange Township Seymour received 79 majority; Randolph, 80; Rafferty, 77; Rush, 86; Booth, 76.

East Orange Township gives Grant 333 majority; Blair, 328; Hill, 333; Peck, 349; Leed, 330.

Hammond gives Grant 229 majority, and elects the rest of the Republican ticket by 239 majority.

Mercer goes Democratic for Governor, State Senator and Congressman by upward of 200 majority. Two members of the Assembly are elected. The others are in doubt. Maxwell Burlington is elected by 112 majority.

The following is the vote in Bloomfield: Grant, 368; Seymour, 256; John Hill, 468; Rafferty, 261; Blair, 461, Randolph, 263.

Linden, Union County, gives BLAIR, for Governor, 81 majority; CLARK, for Congress, Republican, 86; a Republican gain of 22.

New-Providence township, Union County, gives: For President—SEYMOUR, 160; GRANT, 144. For Governor—RANDOLPH, 167; BLAIR, 140.

Westfield gives SEYMOUR, 80 majority. A Republican gain of 5.

Middlesex gives GRANT 90 majority. A Republican gain of 20.

Hackettstown gives SEYMOUR 106 majority.

Westfield gives Seymour 272; Grant and Colfax 222. Republican gain, 5.

North Brunswick in Middlesex County, gives 90 majority for Grant—a gain of 20 over the highest Republican vote.

The total vote in Hackettstown, N. J., is as follows: Grant, 151; Seymour, 287; Randolph, 289; Blair, 145. For Assembly, the Democratic vote is 289; the Republican, 117. Congress is the same as for President.

Cumberland County gives a Republican majority of 1,300 for the whole ticket.

Newark gives GRANT 904 majority; BLAIR, the Republican candidate for Governor, 660; HALSEY (Rep.) for Congress, 1,166; TERR (Rep.) for Sheriff, 581.

Mercer County gives about 900 Democratic majority. The Democrats elect a State Senator and all their Assemblymen.

Essex County will give GRANT about 1,800 majority; BLAIR, for Governor, 1,200; HILL, for Congress, 600. The Republicans gain one Assemblyman.

The Township of Egg Harbor gives GRANT 66 majority; BLAIR, for Governor, 60; MOORE, for Congress, 55; ADAMS, for State Senate, 64, and KEEN, for the Assembly, 40 majority.

Newton Township gives SEYMOUR 245 majority, RANDOLPH, 261 majority; BAIRD for Congress, 279; MILFORD, for the Assembly, 115. A Republican gain of 90.

Atlantic County gives 300 majority for GRANT and JOHN I. BLAIR.

Salem gives 360 majority for GRANT and JOHN I. BLAIR.

Union Township gives SEYMOUR, 75; RANDOLPH, 79; BAIRD, 78; HAUGH, 91 majority.

Springfield Township gives GRANT, 6; BLAIR, 1; CLARK, 4, majority.

Atlantic City elects the whole Republican ticket by 65.

### Newark Republican by a Small Majority.

NEWARK, N. J., Tuesday, Nov. 3.

Returns from all the wards gives HALSEY, Republican, for Congress, 1,290 majority. The majority for GRANT for President and BLAIR for Governor is 900. We elect Sheriff and seven Assemblymen—a gain of one. The State close.

Cumberland gives Grant 1,800 majority. The whole Republican ticket is elected. Shepard, Republican, is elected to the Assembly in the First District by 281 majority—a Republican gain of 319. Atlantic County gives Grant 500 majority. Mercer County has gone Democratic, electing a Senator and one Representative of the county.

The State looks Democratic. Haight, in the Second District, is probably elected. Bird, Democrat, in the Third; Cleveland, Democrat, in the Fifth, are elected.

NEWARK, N. J., Wednesday, Nov. 4.

The Fifth District elects Cleveland, Democrat, to Congress over Halsey, Republican.

[illegible]

### The Vote in Hudson County.

[illegible]

## VERMONT.

### The Green Mountain State True to its Ancient Fame.

[illegible]

over the vote for Governor in the September election.

MONTPELIER, Tuesday, Nov. 3.

The vote to-day has not been a full one. It will fall somewhat below that of September last. The Republicans gain a little everywhere, and the Democrats lose everywhere. In forty-six towns, embracing over one-fourth of the State, the Republican gain is 410 and the Democratic loss 960; making a net Republican gain of 1,360 over the majority of September. It is believed the State has gone for GRANT by 31,000 majority.

Returns received up to midnight indicate a majority of 32,000 for Grant—an increase of 4,500 on the majority in September.

## PENNSYLVANIA.

### The Vote in Allegheny County—Large Republican Gain.

Special Dispatch to the New-York Times.

PITTSBURG, Tuesday, Nov. 3.

Returns from forty districts in Alleghany County show a Republican majority of 10,200. The majority for Grant will probably reach 11,000, a gain of over 2,000 over the October vote. Scattering returns from the western part of the State all show steady Republican gains.

Our majority in this (Allegheny) County will be fully 11,000. In the State it will certainly reach 20,000, and may exceed it. People here are jubilant over the result, and parading the streets with torches, banners, &c. Great enthusiasm, &c.

### The Keystone State Gives a Large Majority for Grant.

PHILADELPHIA, Tuesday, Nov. 3.

The polls in this city closed at 6 o'clock this evening. Partial returns indicate a Republican majority in the city of about 3,000. The street boys are already selling "SEYMOUR Salt River tickets," while the Republican clubs are making their preparations for a parade.

One hundred and six cities and towns in the State give 5,600 majority. Erie City gives a Republican majority of 460, a gain over the October election of 65. The majority in the county is about 3,500 for GRANT. In October the Republican majority was 3,171. A private dispatch from Pittsburg says, Allegheny County has given GRANT a majority of 11,000. In October the Republican majority was 9,257.

Adams County gives 260 Democratic majority; Indiana County, 1,018 Republican majority; Dauphin County, 2,160 Republican majority; Harrisburg City, 397 Republican majority; Lebanon County, 1,546 Republican majority; Chester County, 2,800 Republican majority; Lycoming County, 295 Democratic majority.

Chester County reports a majority of 2,400 for GRANT. Dauphin County complete is reported at 1,800 Republican majority, a Republican gain of 145. Eight districts in Schuylkill County show a Republican gain of 225. Fulton County, it is estimated, gives 300 majority for SEYMOUR. The City of Harrisburg gives GRANT a majority of 390, a Republican gain of 79.

Mr. GROW, the Chairman of the State Committee, says Pennsylvania has given a Republican majority of 15,000. Mr. WALLACE, the Chairman of the Democratic State Committee, concedes the State to Gen. GRANT by 15,000 majority.

Clinton County, 75 Democratic; Lebanon County, 1,500 Republican; Berks County, 6,000 Democratic; Montgomery County, 800 Democratic.

The estimated Republican majority in Bradford County is 4,000.

### Disturbance in the Fourth Ward of Philadelphia.

PHILADELPHIA, Penn., Tuesday, Nov. 3.

The only disturbance that has occurred here was in the Fourth Ward, and was trifling. A voter was challenged, and a rush was made, breaking in the window, when the Republican Inspector made his escape. The principal in the affair was arrested and held to bail.

Mr. WALLACE, Chairman of the Democratic Committee gives Pennsylvania to the Republicans by 15,000.

The Grant Invincibles are parading the streets with music and banners. Many of them are bearing new brooms instead of torches.

A Republican procession gathered in front of the *Press* office this evening, and Mr. FORNEY made a lengthy speech, announcing the election of GRANT and COLFAX by 169 electoral votes, without counting one of the original rebel States, and without counting New-York, New-Jersey, Connecticut, California, Nevada, Oregon, Delaware, Kentucky or Maryland.

### The Vote of Philadelphia.

| Wards. | Grant. | Seymour. | Rep. gain. | Dem. gain. |
|---|---|---|---|---|
| 1 | .... | .... | .... | .... |
| 2 | .... | 1051 maj. | .... | 55 |
| 3 | .... | 1544 maj. | 143 | .... |
| 4 | .... | .... | .... | .... |
| 5 | .... | 964 maj. | 123 | .... |
| 6 | 502 maj. | .... | 1067 | .... |
| 7 | 761 maj. | .... | 280 | .... |
| 8 | 246 maj. | .... | 180 | .... |
| 9 | .... | .... | .... | .... |
| 10 | .... | .... | .... | .... |
| 11 | .... | .... | .... | .... |
| 12 | 187 maj. | .... | 467 | .... |
| 13 | .... | .... | .... | .... |
| 14 | .... | .... | .... | .... |
| 15 | 1315 maj. | .... | 425 | .... |
| 16 | .... | .... | .... | .... |
| 17 | .... | 1373 maj. | .... | .... |
| 18 | .... | .... | .... | .... |
| 19 | .... | .... | .... | .... |
| 20 | .... | .... | .... | .... |
| 21 | 314 maj. | .... | .... | 46 |
| 22 | 789 maj. | .... | .... | 110 |
| 23 | 802 maj. | .... | .... | 5 |
| 24 | 260 maj. | .... | .... | .... |
| 25 | .... | 683 maj. | .... | 45 |
| 26 | 1169 maj. | .... | 207 | .... |
| 27 | 836 maj. | .... | .... | .... |
| 28 | 25 maj. | .... | .... | .... |

The Republican majority in the city is 1,441.

## NEW-ENGLAND.

### The Eastern States a Unit for Grant—Details of the Grand Triumph in the Several States.

Special Dispatch to the New-York Times.

BOSTON, Tuesday, Nov. 3—11:30 P. M.

Returns received up to this hour indicate that New-England will cast a unanimous vote for GRANT. In Massachusetts the total vote is estimated at 175,000, and the net Republican majorities at 70,000. Both branches of the Legislature will be almost unanimously Republican, thus securing the reëlection of Senator SUMNER. All the Republican candidates for Members of Congress are chosen, of course. The two Boston Representatives, Messrs. GINERY TWICHELL and SAMUEL HOOPER, are elected by majorities which will not vary greatly from 2,500 each.

The general result of the city election is peculiarly gratifying. The Republicans have reclaimed the city from the boasted Democrat sway, and the prestige which Copperheadism won here at the last municipal election has been lost. Four of the six State Senators have been elected, and we have gained in the number of Representatives; have chosen our Executive Councilor, all county officers, &c., &c.

In the Fifth District the vote is surprisingly large and surprisingly one-sided. Gen. BUTLER received 12,080 votes; DANA, 1,319, and LORD, 4,941. Even Mr. DANA's opponents were unprepared for such overwhelming success. But the work performed by Mr. DANA and his supporters has not been lost, as these Republicans, who are now firing guns and building bonfires in Salem and other Essex towns, may find out before the next term of their Representative expires.

In Maine the total vote is estimated at 106,000—a small vote; but the Republican majority is large, and there is a Republican gain in every town, so far as heard from, on the September election. GRANT's majority is put at 30,000, but it may fall a trifle under this figure.

In New-Hampshire and Vermont the vote is also a comparatively small one, but the Republicans gain everywhere. In Connecticut the battle has been splendidly fought, and the Republicans have won a glorious victory. The majority is computed at 2,000, or a gain over last year of nearly 4,500. In

(Continued on Eighth Page.)

ULYSSES S. GRANT

# The New-York Times.

VOL. XVIII.......NO. 5444. NEW-YORK, FRIDAY, MARCH 5, 1869.—TRIPLE SHEET. PRICE FOUR CENTS.


# INAUGURATION

## Commencement of the New Era of Peace and Prosperity.

## Ulysses S. Grant Formally Inducted Into Office as President.

## He Delivers a Brief and Characteristic Address.

## Speedy Payment of the Public Debt in Gold Insisted Upon.

## Economy and Faithful Collection of the Revenue Demanded.

## Installation of Schuyler Colfax as Vice-President.

## The Ceremonies Marked by Unprecedented Display and Enthusiasm.

## The National Capital Thronged with Visitors from All Sections.

## A Magnificent Reception and Ball in the Evening.

Special Dispatches to the New-York Times.

WASHINGTON, Thursday, March 4.

The ceremonies attending the inauguration of Gen. Ulysses S. Grant as the eighteenth President of the United States were to-day carried out, with a completeness and a degree of brilliant success which is a most auspicious augury for the success of the Government, now transferred to such earnest and patriotic hands. The attendance, the arrangements, the procession, the ceremonies, and, more than all, the spirit of the occasion, were admirable and perfect in all their parts. In the respect of weather the day was almost a *fac-simile* of the same day four years ago. The morning opened with a drizzling rain, and people mourned for the *ensemble* of the procession lost in advance. It was the shadow of one of your Northern snow-storms that was cast over the city, and the atmosphere was cold and chilly. The White House and Capitol were hidden from each other by a heavy mist, which enshrouded the prominent elevations, and which the croaking raven of the Democracy were fain to pronounce ominous. The promise was not good for a day of rejoicing, speaking meteorologically, but it was, nevertheless, a glad day for Washington, and a doubly glad day for all the nation.

The city was full to overflowing. No such crowd has been seen here on any previous and like occasion, and the numbers equaled the great military review of all the armies in 1865, with all their military and multitudinous *personnel*. But if the last hours of the expiring Administration were enshrouded in gloom, the first innocent moments of the new dominion were illuminated with the rays of brilliant sunshine which burst upon the scene just as the booming of the cannon and the ringing of the bells proclaimed the oath taken and a President inaugurated.

IN THE SENATE CHAMBER.

The great central point of interest to all spectators was the Capitol. Thither everybody bent their steps who could not be content alone with the procession. Every conveyance that could be procured was brought into requisition, and the possessor of a carriage and horses, willing to hire the same, was well nigh the possessor of a talisman to fortune. Every means of ingress to the Capitol was placed under the control of the Capitol Police, and it was only possible for certain persons armed with tickets or with some badge of distinction to obtain entrance through certain doors. Ten o'clock was the hour when the Senate galleries, the great central point of inside interest, were to be opened. An immense crowd of ticket-holders had gathered hours in advance at the northern and eastern entrances. When the doors were flung open, a frightful crush took place, in which many ladies were well squeezed, even if they suffered no greater damage. Then they mounted the stair cases on a gallop, and hurried into the front seats. In half an hour every place was filled, every aisle occupied, and forlorn late-comers frantically rushed through the halls in desperation over their misfortune. While the galleries were filling up the Senate was plodding on with its business, which gave the spectators not the least concern. Instinctively the mind reverts to the same scene four years ago. Then none but ladies were admitted to the galleries; and, notwithstanding the fact that intenser colors in ladies' toilets are the fashion of to-day, the audience is not as rich or brilliant in appearance as on that occasion, the sombre black of the American gentlemen reducing the effect by its dark contrast. It is composed of many familiar faces, to a large extent of the same faces that became so familiar during the days of impeachment, when tickets, as now, were coveted possessions, and when policemen's batons, as now, were the peace-makers.

While the occupants of the galleries are disposing themselves, the floor of the Senate begins to fill up with persons distinguished and otherwise. To the right of the presiding officer, in all the gilt array of full uniform sit Sherman, Thomas, Hancock, Terry and Farragut. To their left Ingalls, Ricketts, Dyer, Meigs and Van Vleit. To the left of the main door Howard, Sickles, Pleasanton and Dahlgren. Just in rear of the last circle of seats, where Roscoe Conkling usually rises to speak, sit a trio on whom many glasses are leveled—Senator Fenton, A. T. Stewart and Ex-Senator Creswell. To the right, here on a sofa in familiar chat with Sumner, is the renowned Spurgeon. Further to the right, several ex-members; to the left a score of other dignitaries; to the rear a dozen or more heads of bureaus. Now, at 11:30, the Senatorial seats on the Democratic side are vacated, and the Senators sit down familiarly and in close contact. Acrimony is at an end; good nature prevails, and congratulations are in order. Sumner is congratulated because to-day he enters upon a term which rounds out his Senatorial service to the full period of a quarter of a century; Fenton, because he succeeds Morgan; Pratt, because he places Indiana squarely on the Republican side in the Senate; Frelinghuysen and Morgan upon their relief from official cares; Schurz, because he is the first German statesman elected to the Senate; Thurman, because he succeeds Wade; Carpenter, because he succeeds Doolittle, and so on through the whole list, until all are satisfied with each other and every one with himself.

At 11:50 the Diplomatic Corps, led by Gerôlt, Berthemy and Thornton, enter the chamber from the marble room, and their brilliant court dress and decorations relieve the scene of the floor by their bright contrast with the Senatorial broadcloth. The ladies of the corps crowd their gallery, and are the subject of comment from the reporters who are their *vis-a-vis*.

ARRIVAL OF GEN. GRANT.

Precisely at 12 by the Senatorial clock, the President elect, escorted by Senator Cragin, of the Committee, and the Vice-President elect, escorted by Senator McCreery, enters the chamber from the room of Mr. Wade, by the rear corridor. Both officers are habited in plain black, the President with straw-colored gloves, and the Vice-President without gloves of any color. Grant takes a seat in front of the presiding officer, and Colfax another to the latter's right. Instantly a thousand glasses are leveled on the little man who sits so calmly and so compactly in his chair. His poise and demeanor are as calm as ever, his imperturbable expression as unchanged as ever. The scrutiny of the eyes of two thousand spectators are as devoid of effect as the thrusts of the politicians or guns of the enemy. There he sits, quiet "calm," self-possessed, as though he were at his own fireside, instead of being in the presence of the assembled wisdom, wealth, intelligence and power of the country, whose destinies have been confided to him. In the meantime the members of his staff, the Judges of the Supreme Court and the House of Representatives, headed by Speaker Pomeroy and Gen. Schenck, are announced and take the places assigned them.

VICE-PRESIDENT COLFAX.

At 12:05 o'clock Mr. Colfax is escorted into the Chamber, and, stepping up to Mr. Wade, he takes his hand warmly. The latter rises, and, with a rap of his gavel, calls the Senate to order. He then calls upon Mr. Colfax to step forward and be "inaugurated." He responds, and addresses the Senate in a brief and appropriate speech. Not a few are here who contrast this scene with that remarkable episode of four years ago this day and hour, when a thousand ears listened, first with eagerness, then with surprise, and at last with unutterable disgust; when the thousand radiant faces of the resplendent galleries were mantled with the crimson blush of shame at the spectacle before them; when the representatives of the Government who sat in that presence moved nervously in their seats, and whispered in alarm, "What if this man should be President?" and when the Diplomatic Corps who bore the brunt of the plebeian harangue of the plebeian before them smiled with a satisfaction that seemed to mean, "The end of the Republic is near." But, thanks to a patriotic and patient people, the fears of the one and the hopes of the other have alike been dissipated; and, as if to compensate for lack of decency then, the scene is invested with impressive dignity and deliberation to-day.

Colfax, the genial gentleman and practiced parliamentarian, accepts his new honors with a modest grace that makes the faces of Senators beam with satisfaction as they recall the parliamentary chaos whence they have just issued. So easy will be his task of presiding here, that he will forget that he was ever expert, and the chronic disorder of the Senate will be replaced by a sedate and steady gravity, the graceful equipoise of which will still further contribute to the reputation of the popular and new Vice-President. Rough and rugged and honest "Old Ben Wade" retired to a modest seat on the floor, profoundly thankful for his deliverance.

The new Senators are now called, and they advance in groups to be sworn. This proceeding occupies some little time, and while it lasts the impatient people in the galleries begin to move, in order to be in position for the scene on the platform, but a cordon of policemen keep the main Senate corridor clear for the procession, and the passages and stairways, &c., are at once choked up by the crowd which waits with not unnatural impatience. The passage to the Rotunda, and the Rotunda itself, are cleared of all occupants, and at 12:20 o'clock the Sergeant-at-Arms Brown, under whose sharp eye and exuberant energy these perfect arrangements are made and conducted, announces the order of the procession, and with Grant at the head of the column, the audience files out of the Senate Chamber, and proceeds to the platform on the east front of the Capitol.

THE INAUGURATION.

The east front of the Capitol was the grand centre of the events of the day. The platform on which the ceremonies of inauguration took place was erected in front of the main entrance of the main building, extending over half the steps and stretching out to the distance of perhaps fifty feet. Two or three feet of balustrade ran around it. The whole was covered with the national colors festooned with evergreens. A small table for the President, shortly to be a table for the Press, which was used as a standing point of vantage, and chairs for Senators, Representatives, Judges, Diplomats, &c., which were converted to similar purposes, were the only things on the platform either of adornment or utility. Two of the immense columns supporting the entablature which formed the pillars of a sort of doorway leading down to the stand were decorated with the everlasting Stars and Stripes. The platform was a mere speck in the centre of the 750 feet in length of the Capitol. Toward this speck thousands of faces were turned from an early hour in the morning. The square in front of the Capitol was kept clear of spectators until the procession arrived; at least that was the order, but it was not, like most other orders, carried out to the letter. A cordon of military was thrown around half the building, beginning on the south side, stretching across South A-street to the railings of the park opposite the east front, thence running along the railings the entire length of the building, until it reached North A-street, where the line ran down, so as to protect the Senate side of the building. Outside this line of military, as early as 9 o'clock in the morning, groups of twos and threes began to form here and there, and at 10 o'clock there was a dark fringe of people skirting the three sides of the rectangle, the Capitol building forming the fourth side. It was a sort of hollow rectangle, the vacant space being reserved for the procession. The morning was cold and rainy, and cheerless. The ground was muddy and soft, and full of puddles. There was not much prospect at this time that there would be any outside display. The unsatisfactory state of the weather rendered it more than probable that the inauguration of President Grant would take place in the Senate Chamber. But as the morning hours wore on and noon approached, there were rifts in the skies, a gleam of brightness broke forth once and again, and the hopes of sightseers were proportionately raised. At 11 o'clock the skies settled into an inky blackness, which might at any time pour down torrents of rain, but no rain came, and the procession moved from the other end of the avenue, near the President's house and the headquarters of the army. We at the Capitol could tell it by the sound of the signal gun.

Thousands of people now began to toil up the steep hills on either side of the Capitol, ranging themselves inside the railings of the park which contains that colossal abortion of a statue of Washington, with the motto—the only good thing about it—"First in war, first in peace, and first in the hearts of his countrymen." The throng surged away on one side down New-Jersey-avenue, leading toward those rising hills which skirt the Potomac, and on the other scattering over all that vacant space toward the railway depot. They massed themselves in solid ranks through the park, covering house-tops, filling windows, loading down trees, climbing lamp posts, placing and perching themselves in every place and on every point and eminence where a view could be obtained. At 11 o'clock at least ten thousand people were gathered in front of the Capitol.

At 11:55 o'clock, around on the crest of the hill, at the north side of the Capitol, there is a rush of people, and presently a ringing cheer, and then a clattering of horses hoofs and a shimmer of uniforms, and presently sounds of music and calling of bugles. President Grant has arrived on the plateau in front of the Capitol, preceded by a cavalry escort, his hat is in his hand, and he bows again and again his acknowledgements to the cheering thousands. Rawlins, known the earliest and beloved the most, his attendant and companion. The carriage drives along the whole length of the building to the Senate side, by which the General entered. In a few minutes the head of the procession comes along and the excitement commences. In they pour, with music and banners and brilliant and showy uniforms. All sections and almost all races are represented there. Colored companies of Zouaves march in and take up position near French Zouaves, flanked on one side by green banners, beneath which are marshaled Irish Republicans, few indeed in number. The masses of citizens become denser and denser. Half a dozen bands of brass are filling the air with martial and triumphant strains, at the same time causing strange but not unpleasing dissonance. The skies grow a little brighter, there is an occasional break in the heavy clouds, and a few rays of sunshine struggle out and light up the brilliant scene for a moment. Torn battle-flags are waving, fire-bells are ringing, cheers are going up, blue capes of Boys in Blue are moving in long line, bugles are sounding forth orders, marshals are riding hither and thither.

The acme of the excitement is reached at about seventeen minutes after 12; the main doors of the Capitol building are thrown open, and the procession marches out on the platform in the order in which it left the Senate Chamber. Senator Cragin escorts the President-elect down to the seat assigned him at the extreme front of the platform, which is soon filled to overflowing. The groups of statuary—representing on the one side the age of barbarism and its first contact with civilization, embodied by the sculptor in the ideal of an Indian arrested by the hand of a hunter as he raises the knife to slay an Indian woman—and on the other the age of discovery and science, Columbus holding in hand erect a globe, typical of the earth's rotundity—were taken possession of by dozens anxious not to miss a single incident in the historic scene beneath them. That platform, at that moment, contained nearly all that is great and distinguished in America.

It is 12:15 and cheers are making the very welkin ring. Hats are waving, and thousands upon thousands are boiling over with enthusiasm. All is silence for a few minutes as Chief Justice Chase administered the oath of office as follows:

"I do solemnly swear that I will faithfully execute the office of President of the United States, and will, to the best of my ability, preserve, protect and defend the Constitution of the United States."

Gen. Grant repeated the words, and at their conclusion kissed the Gospels. Twenty-one guns thunder out to the city and the country that the Administration of Andrew Johnson has passed away, and that the reign of Grant and loyalty, and truth and patriotism, has begun. The bugles break forth in triumphant anthems. Thousands of throats join in the acclaim, while the President sits quietly on the platform waiting the end of the salute. Chief-Justice Chase appeared very nervous. He fumbled with the paper on which the oath of office was written, and he was far more embarrassed than President Grant.

At 12:25 President Grant stood up, half a dozen sheets of paper in his hand, and began to read. There was no sign of embarrassment. His words were firm, his delivery was clear, though of course it could not be distinctly heard at a distance of more than thirty feet all around him. As he finished each page his thumb and forefinger went to his lips, and the manner in which he separated the paces was free from at least affectation. The inaugural address is as simple and pregnant and classic as that second one of Mr. Lincoln's, which is now regarded as one of the gems of the language.

The following is the Inaugural Address in full:

Citizens of the United States: Your suffrages having elected me to the office of President of the United States, I have, in conformity with the Constitution of our country, taken the oath of office prescribed therein. I have taken this oath without mental reservation, and with the determination to do, to the best of my ability, all that it requires of me.

The responsibilities of the position I feel, but accept them without fear. The office has come to me unsought; I commence its duties untrammelled. I bring to it a conscientious desire and determination to fill it, to the best of my ability, to the satisfaction of the people. On all leading questions agitating the public mind I will always express my views to Congress, and urge them according to my judgment, and, when I think it advisable, will exercise the constitutional privilege of interposing a veto to defeat measures which I oppose. But all laws will be faithfully executed whether they meet my approval or not.

I shall on all subjects have a policy to recommend—none to enforce against the will of the people. Laws are to govern all alike—those opposed to as well as those in favor of them. I know no method to secure the repeal of bad or obnoxious laws so effective as their stringent execution.

The country having just emerged from a great rebellion, many questions will come before it for settlement in the next four years, which preceding Administrations have never had to deal with. In meeting these it is desirable that they should be appreciated calmly, without prejudice, hate or sectional pride, remembering that the greatest good to the greatest number is the object to be attained. This requires security of person, property and for religious and political opinion in every part of our common country, without regard to local prejudice. All laws to secure this end will receive my best efforts for their enforcement.

A great debt has been contracted in securing to us and our posterity the Union. The payment of this, principal and interest, as well as the return to a specie basis as soon as it can be accomplished without material detriment to the debtor class, or to the country at large, must be provided for. To protect the national honor, every dollar of the Government indebtedness should be paid in gold, unless otherwise expressly stipulated in the contract. Let it be understood that no repudiator of one farthing of our public debt will be trusted in public places, and it will go far toward strengthening a credit which ought to be the best in the world, and will ultimately enable us to replace the debt with bonds bearing less interest than we now pay. To this shall be added a faithful collection of the revenue; a strict accountability to the Treasury for every dollar collected, and the greatest practicable retrenchment in expenditures in every department of government.

When we compare the paying capacity of the country now, with ten States still in poverty from the effects of the war, but soon to emerge, I trust, into greater prosperity than ever before, with its paying capacity twenty-five years ago, and calculate what it probably will be twenty-five years hence, who can doubt the feasibility of paying every dollar then with more ease than we now pay for useless luxuries? Why, it looks as though Providence had bestowed upon us a strong box, the precious metals locked up in the sterile mountains of the far West, which we are now forging the key to unlock, to meet the very contingency that is now upon us.

Ultimately it may be necessary to increase the facilities to reach these riches, and it may be necessary also that the General Government should give its aid to secure this access. But that should only be when a dollar of obligation to pay secures precisely the same sort of dollar in use now, and not before.

While the question of specie payments is in abeyance the prudent business man is careful about contracting debts payable in the distant future; the nation should follow the same rule. A prostrate commerce is to be rebuilt and all industries encouraged. The young men of the country—those who form this age and must be rulers twenty-five years hence—have a peculiar interest in maintaining the national honor. A moment's reflection upon what will be our commanding influence among the nations of the earth in their day, if they are only true to themselves, should inspire them with national pride. All divisions, geographical, political and religious, can join in the common sentiment.

How the public debt is to be paid, or specie payments resumed, is not so important as that a plan should be adopted and acquiesced in. A united determination to do is worth more than divided counsels upon the method of doing. Legislation on this subject may not be necessary now, nor even advisable; but it will be when the civil law is more fully restored in all parts of the country, and trade resumes its wonted channels. It will be my endeavor to execute all laws in good faith, to collect all revenues assessed, and to have them properly disbursed. I will, to the best of my ability, appoint to office only those who will carry out this design.

In regard to foreign policy, I would deal with nations as equitable law requires individuals to deal with each other, and I would protect the law-abiding citizen, whether of native or of foreign birth, wherever his rights are jeopardized, or the flag of our country floats. I would respect the rights of all nations, demanding equal respect for our own. If others depart from this rule in their dealings with us, we may be compelled to follow their precedent.

The proper treatment of the original occupants of this land—the Indians—is one deserving of careful consideration. I will favor any course toward them which tends to their civilization, christianization and ultimate citizenship.

The question of suffrage is one which is likely to agitate the public so long as a portion of the citizens of the nation are excluded from its privileges in any State. It seems to me very desirable that this question should be settled now, and I entertain the hope and express the desire that it may be by the ratification of the Fifteenth Amendment to the Constitution.

In conclusion, I ask patient forbearance one toward another, throughout the land, and a determined effort on the part of every citizen to do his share toward cementing a happy union, and I ask the prayers of the nation to Almighty God in behalf of this happy consummation.

The crowd cheer again and again; the policy of the new administration has been enunciated; nothing more needs be said; the platform is soon cleared of its distinguished occupants; the procession reforms, and Grant is already far on his way to the White House.

THE PROCESSION.

The procession was the grand feature of the outside ceremonies, and attracted by far the greater portion of spectators. Every available spot where a view could be had was occupied early in the morning by people with umbrellas, who clung to their position for many weary hours despite the falling rain. Pennsylvania-avenue was crowded with double lines of spectators its entire distance, and eligible positions for viewing the procession commanded fabulous prices. Windows and balconies were sold at from $5 to $50 each, and were all occupied to the fullest extent. The Avenue presented a most attractive sight, being profusely decorated by thousands of flags and streamers, and crowded with tens of thousands of spectators. Every window and housetop were occupied, while those who were not so fortunate as to have friends holding premises upon the Avenue had to content themselves upon the curbstone. The juveniles, as usual, climbed trees, awning posts, signs, &c., from whence they might obtain a desirable view of the procession as it passed to the Capitol.

The windows in the north wing of the Treasury building, where the Inauguration Ball is to be held to-night, presented a brilliant appearance, as they were crowded with ladies and children. The long colonnade on the east front of the building was also filled to its utmost capacity, the best places being yielded to the fair sex, who, in this case at least, did not scorn to avail themselves of the privileges accorded to them in consideration of their inability to hold their own in a general scramble for the good places with the pantalooned part of creation. The west front of the Capitol presented an animated scene, as all who were admitted to the building came out on the porticoes and balconies to get a bird's-eye view of the Avenue as the procession was coming down.

At 10:50 o'clock the President elect, Gen. Grant, came from his headquarters at the corner of Seventeenth and F streets, and, with Gen. Rawlings, entered his private carriage, which was open. Then followed all the members of his late staff. Next followed Vice-President elect Colfax, who entered a carriage with Admiral Bailey. The carriages then moved off, escorted by the Fifth Cavalry, which numbered seventy, men commanded by Col. J. M. Mason. Proceeding up Seventeenth-street the line of carriages containing the President and Vice-President elect and their sureties turned into Pennsylvania-avenue, when the military escort, commanded by Col. George W. Wallace, joined them. Brevet Major-Gen. A. S. Webb, Grand Marshal, in uniform, with committee badge and sash as officer of the day, with Major E. B. Russell, Capt. Eugene Welles, Wm. Kensen, Major R. M. Hill, Col. Knox, Col. Graves, Gen. H. H. Bingham, Capt. G. C. Plummer, Albert Delafield, Col. Thomas J. Hoyt, Capt. R. H. Montgomery, Capt. A. W. Preston, Willie A. Harlan, Lieut. Story, Lieut. Totten, Thomas M. Shepherd, Lieut. Metcalf, Lieut. Garrison, Major Gardner, Lieut. Gray, Mr. McBlair and Col. McNett, as aids in line.

First Division—Col. G. W. Wallace commanding. Twelfth Infantry, preceded by their band under the leadership of Prof. Reins, and numbering four companies of one hundred men each. Battalion of United States marines, preceded by the Marine Band under Prof. Schala, numbering 150 men and commanded by Major Charles Williams. Light Battery F, Fifth United States Artillery, four pieces, commanded by Col. H. A. Dupod.

Second Division—Chief Deputy Marshal Col. James A. Magruder, commanding. The Washington Grays Artillery of Philadelphia, mustering forty-five muskets and four officers. They presented a trim, soldier-like appearance, attired in gray uniforms with gold trimmings. McClung's cornet band of sixteen pieces accompanied the party. Philadelphia Fire Zouaves, 200 men; Gen. D. W. C. Baxter, Lieut.-Col. Sellers, Majors Mitchell and Costors, and Adjutant A. L. Murphy. There were 240 men in line, headed by a drum corps of twenty-two in the regular Zouave uniform—red pants, blue jacket, neat red cap, with gilt trimming, and red-and-white pompon. They also had overcoats and knapsacks, neatly put up, with the letters P. F. Z., and their appearance was highly complimented by all. This regiment is composed of many of those who served in the late war under their present commander, and they carried their battle-worn flag in line. Eagle Zouaves, of Buffalo, N. Y.; Capt. Richert and Lieuts. Bien and Wood, and Ensign Fuller. This company presented a very handsome appearance in their Zoozoo uniform, red pants, trimmed with yellow, white leggins and shirts, dark blue jackets trimmed with red, and cap wrapped with white and long yellow tassel. They had about fifty men in line, and were headed by the Union Cornet Band, led by Crimer, which they brought with them, numbering twenty-one pieces, uniformed in gray coat and cape, with red caps. Lincoln Zouaves, of Washington, numbering forty men, uniformed in red pants, with white leggins, blue jackets and caps trimmed with red, and commanded by Capt. Mirkland. Butler Zouaves, of Georgetown, numbering thirty men, with red pants, white leggings, blue jackets trimmed with red, and red caps, and commanded by Capt. Lenard. The Lincoln Zouaves, (colored,) of Baltimore, mustered forty-eight strong, commanded by Capt. Robert Burgess and Lieuts. Carroll and Shepherd. Their dress was of blue flannel, with yellow trimmings and white leggings, after the style of the French uniform. The Henry Winter Davis Guard, of Baltimore, colored, numbering between fifty and sixty men, arrived next in line with the Zouaves, and under the command of Capt. Fisher and Lieuts. Roberts and Young. They were uniformed with blue cloth and gold trimmings. Brig.-Gen. Martin, accompanied by his Aid, Capt. Hackett, was at the head of these companies—the latter officers having arrived here last night, to obtain one thousand of the muskets voted by Congress for the use of the Boys in Blue last Saturday night, but which were refused by President Johnson last night, who declined to permit either the small arms or artillery to be taken from the National Arsenal. National Guards of Philadelphia, numbering fifty men, and commanded by Capt. F. L. Gimber, preceded by a full drum corps, in regulation uniform, light blue pants and blue coat, with cap and white pompon. The Albany Burgesses Corps, regarded as one of the finest organizations in the State of New-York, formed a prominent feature in the procession. It mustered seventy-five rank and file, besides twelve honorary members in citizens' attire. The officers are Capt. Wm. H. Taylor, Lieuts. V. V. Wemple, Walter Dixon and N. H. Moore, Adjt. Kingley, Judge Advocate Parsons, Quartermaster Vosburg. Doring's Band of twenty pieces accompanied it in new and handsome uniform. The company also appeared in new uniform—red coats faced with buff and blue, sky blue pants with buff trimmings, and bear-skin shako. The Lancaster Fencibles mustered forty-five strong, under the command of Capt. Rockafeller. They were dressed in the regular army uniform of blue blouse and light blue pants, and were accompanied by Ermentrout's City Band of seventeen pieces. The Sheridan Grays, of Wilmington, Del., twenty-five men, Capt. A. Grimshaw. This company arrived at 2 o'clock this morning.

Third Division—Chief Deputy Marshal Gen. Gallaten Lawrence commanding. First came the Supreme Court of the United States and its officers, Court of Claims of the United States and its officers, Supreme Court of the District of Columbia and its officers, Senators and Senators elect and Ex-Senators, members of the House of Representatives, members elect and ex-members, foreign Ministers, Corps Deplomatique, the electors of the different States, about fifty in number in carriages, headed by the Committee—Whiting of Massachusetts, Brown of Tennessee, Young of Iowa, Barnes of Arkansas, and Bailey of Ohio, the City Councils of Georgetown and Washington, with the Mayor of Georgetown. Mayor Bowen was absent, because of illness. The surviving soldiers of the war of 1812, thirty in number, seated in one of Nailor's omnibuses, drawn by six white horses, the vehicle decorated with flags on top, and cards bearing the names of the States tacked around the sides; Veterans of the Mexican War, which organization embraced about sixty members, the most of whom were pensioned soldiers from the Soldiers' Home, attired in blue navy cap, blue coat and pants. Col. Kennedy was Commander-in-Chief of Corps, assisted, as Aids, by Cols. Kretsehmar and Schillem.

Fourth Division—Chief Deputy Marshal Major Church Howe commanding. Republican Invincibles, of Philadelphia, numbering about two hundred, marshaled by Geo. Trueman, Jr., headed by Van Dusen's Band. This association is composed altogether of young men dressed in black, with navy pattern cap. The Philadelphia Republican Executive Committee followed, after which came the Alabama delegation, one hundred strong, Executive Committee of the First Congressional District of New-York, Col. Bandy, thirty men, the Second Ward Republican Club, one hundred strong, Joseph Brooks, Marshal, German Republican Union Association of Balimore, Capt. H. Appel, Marshal, Spencer Legion of New-York City, numbering about fifty men, in citizens' dress, wearing a neat satin badge bearing "Spencer Legion Boys in Blue," headed by the President, Major J. Meeks, and field music.

Fifth Division—Chief Deputy Marshal Gen. Jas. A. Ekin, Malone's Band of thirteen pieces. The Grant Invincibles, of California, with three handsome flags and field music, numbering about seventy-five men, marshalled by Major Jack Stratman, each man wearing a satin badge with the name of the Association printed on them, as also the portrait of Gen. Grant. Montana Territorial Delegation, about forty members, headed by Gen. Lester S. Wilson, Col. N. F. Sanders and Capt. Fisk, editor of the Helena *Herald*. Montana was the most numerously represented of any of the Territories. German Soldiers' and Sailors' Union, George Brand, Marshal, with about sixty men in line, carrying German and American flags, Boys in Blue of Frederick, Md., numbering about 200, marshaled by Gen. Steiner, carrying the old American flag of the Club, headed by Moberly's Brass Band of fourteen pieces. Seven of this band are brothers. Grant and Colfax Printers' Club, with wagon handsomely decorated and motto, "Equal justice to all." On the wagon was a printing press in operation, impressions from which were thrown off to the crowd. Irish Republican Association, P. Cullinane, M. Murphy and T. Carraher, Marshals, 150 strong, carrying the Irish and American flags, followed by two ambulances.

Sixth Division.—Chief Marshal John Abendroth, commanding. Washington Schutzenverein, with their own band of twenty-two pieces and 120 men, in charge of Marshal Louis Beyer. The organization was headed by Bernard Henze, President, uniformed in Schuetzen dress of green, with white braided trimmings. This organization of German citizens presented a fine appearance. Columbia Turnverein, fifty men in citizen's clothes, with badges. "Columbia Turnverion of Washington." The Boys in Blue in the following order, Gen. A. Grant commanding, in full uniform, with staff in military dress: Engineer Corps of the Boys in Blue, in command of Col. L. P. Culter; uniform, black pants, red fire-shirts, blue military cap; fifty men. Carriage containing executive board of the organization. Company of artillery; five pieces of ordnance. First Regiment of Cavalry, Col. J. S. Crocker commanding. Col. A. M. Bland and staff. Brass band of Georgetown. Battalions from Second, Sixth and Seventh Regiments of the Boys in Blue. Each man in the ranks carried a flag attached to a long staff. The organization presented a fine appearance. Following the command of Col. Bland came a battalion composed of companies from the Fourth, Fifth and Eighth Regiments, under command of Col. A. C. Dyson. In this battalion were displayed a number of handsome regimental flags. The total number of men in this division was about 1,500.

In this division one of the most noticeable features was the miniature ship *Constitution*, which figured in the inauguration of Buchanan in 1857, and has been laid up in the ship-house of the navy-yard ever since, in charge of a company of the Sixth Ward Republican Club. She was full-rigged and equipped with stern and quarter boats and anchors and chains, arranged in regular man-of-war style. She also has a formidable looking battery and was manned by youths in sailor costume. The car was drawn by six richly caparisoned horses.

Seventh Division—Chief Deputy Marshal Gen. J. R. Obeirne, commanding. United States Fire Department with its visitors in order of date of institution; Hibernia Engine No. 1, Naval Academy Band, Government Fire Brigade, J. M. Callan, Foreman, eleven men; Washington Hose Company No. 5, of Reading, Penn., with thirty-five men; Meigs Engine No. 2, Government Fire Brigade, Thos. Thelsen, Foreman, engine decorated and drawn by four gray horses; Rucker Engine No. 3, Government Brigade, handsomely decorated and drawn by two fine bay horses; Engine Henry Addison, Samuel R. Swan, Foreman, eight men.

Eighth Division—Chief Deputy Marshal J. C. Clay, commanding. City of Washington Fire Department and visitors in order of institution; seven companies. The Good Will Engine Company No. 20, of Philadelphia, appeared to great advantage, having in line 102 men, in black overcoats, red shirts and belts with the name on red ground, and black New-York hats, with the name and number in gold. They were headed by four stalwart pioneers, four torchmen and four pipemen. A citizens' committee of twelve men were also with the company, and the splendid hose carriage with the frontispiece representing Peace and War, and five Zouaves on the side pieces, attracted much attention. They were headed by Beck's famous band of eighteen pieces. The engine was drawn by four splendid bay horses, with heavy collars, while the hose carriage was drawn by the firemen. In the procession of the Good Will Company were a number of beautiful flags, two of them being magnificent banners, which have been presented to them by the citizens of Philadelphia. Taylor Hose Company No. 35, of Philadelphia, numbered 82 men. They had with them the Frankfort Cornet Band, led by Butterfield, with sixteen pieces. Harmony Engine Company No. 6, of Philadelphia, with their beautiful steam fire-engine profusely decorated, and hose carriage handsomely set off. This company was headed by the Independent Band, led by McAllister. On the hose carriage was a wreath, with the word "Harmony" and Grant's portrait above it, with the Pennsylvania coat-of-arms on each side. A beautiful banner, bearing on the front a painting of Abraham Lincoln, presented by the citizens of the Twentieth Ward, was carried on a frame by four of the members. The Mount Vernon Hook and Ladder Company of Harrisburg, Penn., with Weber's Cornet Band of eighteen pieces, numbered forty-five men. The Fire Departments closed the procession, and being the chief feature of the display for the spectators, kept up the interest until the end. It occupied about twenty minutes in passing a given point, and was over a mile in length.

Arriving at the Capitol grounds, the column wheeled to the right and ascended Capitol Hill on the south side, and moved into the place on the east front, which had been kept clear for that purpose. The military then faced toward the Capitol, and Gen. Grant and staff, with the Committee, were escorted to the marble room of the Senate.

On the conclusion of the inaugural ceremonies the procession formed in the same order, and followed by the same route to the Executive Mansion. This was a most triumphal march. The mass of spectators was everywhere increased by the lifting of the clouds and brilliant sunshine, and cheer upon cheer rose upon the air as the President passed the enthusiastic assemblage.

THE PRESIDENT'S ARRIVAL AT THE WHITE HOUSE.

The gates of the inclosure of the White House grounds were promptly and carefully closed as soon as Mr. Johnson and the Cabinet had retired, at 12:30 o'clock, from the occupancy of the building, and policemen were stationed at every gate, with orders to admit only the privileged persons before the arrival of the new President. When the head of the procession reached the front of the White House, the carriage of the President and that of his staff were admitted, but no others, and they were quickly rolled amid the loud plaudits of the immense crowd to the door of the White House. Senator Cragin, Mr. Colfax, A. T. Stewart, Gens. Parker and Badeau accompanied the President. Senator Cragin and Mr. Colfax descended first from the carriage, Gen. Grant following. He had ascended two or three of the steps leading to the main entrance when he noticed that he had left the door of the carriage open, and hastily retracing his steps he carefully closed it and nodded to the driver, who immediately drove off. Gen. Schofield had been left by the retiring President in charge of the White House as the only non-retiring member of the Cabinet, and he had been joined by Gen. Rawlings, Gen. Porter, Gen. Babcock, Gen. Gibbon, Gen. Pitcher, Col. Taylor and Gen. Michler. The latter was constituted, as the officer in charge of public buildings, master of ceremonies, and on Gen. Grant's appearance at the door of the White House, Gen. Michler advanced, with that peculiar ease and grace and dignity which is always noticeable in him, and welcomed the new occupant to his temporary home. The President shook hands with him, and very warmly with Rawlings and the others, who had advanced, and then turned to speak a few words to those who had accompanied him from the Capitol. He then advanced, under the guidance of Gen. Michler, to the door of the Blue Room. In the hall the steward of the house, a colored man, was presented by Gen. Michler, who remarked:

"This gentleman will be glad to provide a dinner for you.

"Thank you," said the General.

"And this gentleman," said Michler, in his quiet, humorous way, presenting Mr. Johnson's late body servant, a perfect specimen of animate ebony, "will be happy to brush your clothes."

The President repeated his thanks, and then, turning about and looking in every direction, he said to Michler, in a half despairing tone, "Well, what am I to do next?"

Mr. Colfax suggested to him to retire to his room on the floor above, and after a few words the President did so. He was soon after followed by Mr. Colfax.

The procession meanwhile continued to pass in front of the White House, but outside of the inclosure.

An immense crowd was gathered on the sidewalks, and a great deal of confusion prevailed, but it was confined wholly to the Avenue. After remaining at the White House about an hour Gen. Grant departed for his residence on I-street to prepare for the reception this evening at the ball. The intended public reception in the East Room, for which preparation had been made, is postponed for the present.

EUROPEAN CONGRATULATIONS.

Directly after Gen. Grant reached his headquarters this morning, the following cable telegrams were placed in his hands:

BERLIN, March 4.

*President Gen. Grant, White House, Washington, D. C.:*

My cordial congratulations on this solemn day.

(Signed) BISMARCK.

MARCH 4, 1869.

*To President Grant, Washington:*

In honor of the man and the day, three cheers for the President.

Members of the Berlin Exchange.

FRITZ MAYER.

THE INAUGURATION BALL.

Before proceeding to give a description of the festal features of the ceremonies on Inauguration Day, it may be proper to narrate the perplexities preceding such interesting events as tending to show that some at least who dance make exorbitant remuneration to the violinists. For six weeks past the Inauguration Ball has evenly divided the daily Washington gossip with the question respecting the incoming Cabinet. "Who will compose the Cabinet?"—"Are we to have a ball?" were questions fraught with weighty moment, and however insignificant the latter question may seem to the nation at large, it was, to your true Washington small-talker, a matter of serious consequence. Next to bestriding a steed and figuring in an inaugural procession as Assistant Marshal, with profuse decorations, badges and formidable baton, the opportunity of appearing as a manager in the festivities to be proffered to a new President is the great object to be attained by members of a certain class, whose cares and pleasure it is to look after and protect the interests of each successive coming man. Rival local factions watch each other with jealous eyes, and bestir themselves early, lest they be left behind in the work of distributing honors. The occupants of comfortable Federal offices, in the fullness of their unselfish devotion, eagerly step forward to monopolize the management of the event. Those who do not hold good offices, but who anxiously await for such good luck to befall them, in a self-sacrificing spirit cheerfully consent to allow their names to be used in association with the homage to be bestowed on the rising sun. The stationers and other tradespeople, with an eye to business, join the disinterested throng, and generously offer their own names to serve on contracting committees, and even a parson has been known to act on such occasions, after solacing his conscience by calling the *fête* a reception.

This is the general history of Inauguration Balls in Washington, and the history of the present one is no exception. After the rival factions and associations had been disposed of, and the management of the ceremonies had fallen into discreet and trusty hands, it seemed as though the affair was half accomplished, but a very formidable obstacle met them in the very outstart. No room of sufficient capacity could be found outside of the Government buildings. To erect a temporary building, as was done at Mr. Lincoln's first inauguration, would cost a large sum, and at best would be a shabby edifice. And here let me say that, owing to the prevailing reticence respecting future political favors it has been a hard matter to find men to advance money with much liberality. The theatres were badly arranged for such gatherings, and besides were not to be obtained. While those casting about for an eligible place, and after having been driven to their wits' end, in a propitious moment, the Committee were struck with an idea, grand and practical. Like the lusty first and second citizens in the tragedy, they with one voice shouted, "To the Capitol!" and to the Capitol they went, with a well-worded petition to Congress, asking for the use of the famous rotunda for the night of March 4, in order that the light-hearted and light-footed disciples of terpsichore might give vent to their hilarity in the mazes of the dance. Many were the arguments presented in advocacy of this petition, not omitting the facetious one that the frescoed can-can in the eye of the dome would find itself surpassed by the real beauty and chivalry on the stony floor beneath it. Here the question became a matter of record, and for all time the preliminary history of the Inauguration Ball of 1869 will in part command a place in the recorded annals of the Republic. The House, in the exuberance of their joy at the prospect of having a jolly good time, promptly voted to grant the request, and even among the members of the Senate the proposition met with favor, to the extent at least of drawing forth a speech in favor of the graceful amusements from a Senator, who, despite the rough touches of age and increased accumulation of adipose matter, still delights in shaking the gravity of his ponderous person in an old-fashioned double-shuffle. The measure failed, however, and though the attempt was repeated with vigor, it was again defeated. For the time matters looked as though the "ball was up," as skaters have it. To relieve the Committee of a little unpleasantness, for, indeed, they were awkwardly fixed, the proposed recipient of the honors wrote a note to the Committee substantially stating that the custom, so far as he was concerned, would be as honored in the breach as in the observance. Just then, to the amazement of the aforesaid committee, a new committee sprung into existence, composed of men opposed to the Republican Party, and who, in a mock spirit of offended justice, insisted that the customary honor should be observed, even though the political enemies of the President-elect had to provide for it. It was at last determined that the ball should be held, that it should be technically known as a reception, and that the unfinished north wing of the Treasury building should be the place.

Here the tribulation of the Committee ceased, with the exception of disposing of two incidental questions: first, as to the admission of colored people, which was solved by the colored people themselves, who declined to attend in any event. The other question was one involving nice points of etiquette should the retiring President be invited. It was argued that the ball was no part of the inaugural ceremonies proper, but simply a reception extended to Gen. Grant—an affair intended as complimentary to him, but in no way indorsing his predecessor. The well-known personal estrangement between them would make an invitation a mere mockery, and, therefore, be it resolved, that Andrew Johnson be not invited. I leave it for others to decide upon the nice points in this case, simply contenting myself as a faithful chronicler in giving the facts. If the words of an English humorist be true there is wrath in the heart of the late President to-night beyond the power of political differences to produce. For after all that is said and done, the malice and spite of political party are poor to the malice and spite of "a party next door, to a party not invited."

It is to be regretted that events of this kind, commemorating as they do important political epochs, are not honored with more respectable *souvenirs* than the flashy overgrown cards which are invariably issued on such occasions. On the present, as on previous similar occasions, the brief time allotted to the engraver has not been sufficient to enable him to produce a work of art in which he can take a great amount of professional pride. The cards for to-night are lithographs of extravagant size, and at first glance look like an illuminated counting-house almanac. By a happy stroke of genius the artist surmounted the whole design with an heroic bust, combining in the one face the features of both Grant and Colfax. At least, it resembles one of those popular worthies as much as it does the other.

As previously agreed upon, the affair is christened a reception, but for the encouragement of the lovers of the dance, it is whispered with plain type in parenthesis (Dancing.) For the paltry sum of $10 any one can become the proprietor of one of these art gems, receiving in addition thereto a ticket of admission for himself and two ladies, with an equitable right to supper, if he can get it, and permit to dance if he understands the art.

The north wing of the Treasury building stands on the spot familiar to Washington visitors in times past as the location of the State Department. That venerable old building, in which for so many years diplomacy was concocted and put into execution, was at last forced to give way to the growing demands of the financial Department, and the ancient walls, within whose confines the Tallyrandic whisperings of successive Ministers of State had so long been uttered, were leveled as remorselessly as though the cement uniting them were as fragile as the great seal of a treaty. The *débris* of the fallen ruins was carted away by unlettered Celts, and like the rubbish of decayed and dismembered nations, was lost sight of and forgotten in the glories of the new structure which arose in its place. The celerity with which this part of the Treasury building has been erected and brought very nearly to completion, is a matter of just pride to the supervising architect, Mr. Mullett, and I may add that his energy in pushing forward the construction of the building is fully equaled by the good taste displayed in all cases wherein good taste was required. The massive building, as a whole, would be unsurpassed in symmetrical grandeur if it had been originally projected in the style in which it is to be completed; but, unfortunately, like the greater number of public buildings in the Federal City, it was commenced on one plan and continued on another. Like a faded patch in a new ground, these old features of architecture thrust their unwelcome ugliness forth to mar the beauties of the remainder of the edifice.

But we have lingered too long on the outside, so joining the constantly increasing throng which pushes its way up the spacious steps of the east front of the Treasury, we persuade our way through the rabble of curious bipeds who have come to see those who go to see, and passing undetected through the lines of scrutinizing policemen, we enter the temple dedicated to figures and measures, to witness and participate in figures and measures heretofore unknown within its strongly-built walls. Under any circumstances, the efforts of the Committee in preparing and adorning the rooms might well be called a success, but when it is taken into consideration that the time in which they were to perform this duty was very limited, and that the mass of rubbish incident to the work of the construction of the building had to be removed, and at the same time painters, carpenters, plasterers and upholsterers were simultaneously employed in finishing the rooms, their success is remarkable, as the first glance at the brilliantly-lighted rooms assures us. The work of decorating was commenced, we are told, on the 2d, and the energy with which it has been prosecuted is well attested by the display which brings ejaculations of admiration from each group of guests as they enter. On the outside of the building the massive columns were gracefully wreathed, and across the entire portico an arrangement of gas jets produced the talismanic words of the hour, "Peace." In the interior, each of the rooms used for the occasion was flooded with light and beautifully decorated with festoons and wreaths of flowers and evergreen, or draped with a profusion of national bunting. In the large Cash Room, as it is called, was placed the fine allegorical painting of "Peace," which for a time had its place in the Rotunda of the Capitol. In this room the highly-polished Carrara, Sienna and Tennessee marble, the airy balcony, which encircles the entire room, and the tastefully-finished ceiling, would of themselves, without further decorations, have been sufficient to challenge admiration.

In many respects this reception has been unlike any previous one, and the very necessities of the Committee, in driving them to these rooms, have served to add to the charm of the occasion. Instead of dazzling your eyes in a concentrated display of beauty and gayety, grouped together in one extensive room, and presenting throughout the night the one single view, you could wander from one room to another, taking in the gorgeousness of the affair by piecemeal, and contrasting each room's display with the others

(Continued on Tenth Page.)

# The New-York Times.

VOL. XXI......NO. 6435. NEW-YORK, SATURDAY, MAY 4, 1872. PRICE FOUR CENTS.


## GREELEY NOMINATED!

### How the Blair Family Manipulated the Convention.

### Gratz Brown Sells Out His Friends for the Second Place.

### Schurz Declares Greeley the Weakest Man They Could Take.

### The German Vote Irretrievably Lost to the Liberals.

### Mr. Greeley Hurriedly Telegraphs His Acceptance and Thanks.

Special Dispatch to the New-York Times.

CINCINNATI, May 3.—There were moments during the brief career of the Convention when it seemed to have symptoms of protracted and vigorous life, but the charlatans who brought it into existence attended it with too great solicitude, and it has died on their hands. The history of its last few hours is strikingly illustrative of the fact that a political movement matured by fraudulent practices cannot hope to survive. Since Sunday the Convention has been literally stolen by political knaves. First came the corrupt cohorts of Judge Davis, headed by John Defrees, who manufactured a tremendous outside pressure that would have resulted on Monday in the nomination of Davis. The moral sense of the Convention was all the time with Adams, as was all its political honesty and all its sincerity and intelligence. In these early stages of the struggle Davis was pushed by Messrs. Ward H. Lamon, David Dudley Field, Leonard Swett, Henry S. Cake and Gen. Gridley, of Bloomington, Ill., who was once arrested for frauds upon the Revenue. On the other hand, the advocates of Adams were Edward Atkinson, David A. Wells, Horace White, Samuel Bowles, Stanley Matthews, Judge Hoadley and many others, who possessed all the sincerity and honesty of the concern. On Thursday night the Philistines sneaked into their camp and out-manœuvred them. Late at night it was rumored that Frank Blair and Montgomery Blair had reached the city, and soon afterward it was ascertained that Gratz Brown was in their company. Such a combination could mean nothing but mischief, and the Adams forces were instantly on the alert, but did not succeed in learning the moves of the conspirators until it was too late to counteract them.

THE GAME REVEALED.

About 2 o'clock it was discovered that these men had been in consultation, in Covington and this city, with the corruptionists in the Convention, and that it had been determined that Brown should withdraw in favor of Greeley, and take the second place on the ticket. This made the combination a powerful one, and the Adams men, who believed its success would be the death of the movement, yet were aware of the danger of its being forced through the Convention. As shameless a political bargain as was ever made naturally enticed to its support such patriots as Gen. Cochrane, Waldo Hutchins, Alex. McClure, Gratz Brown, and some conscienceless political adventurers from the South, and the sort of influences which would be used by such men as these was naturally dreaded.

IN THE CONVENTION.

When the Convention assembled there was no signs of the conspiracy for some time in the proceedings, but its existence was generally known, and bitter comments upon it could be heard in every quarter by the friends of Adams, Davis and Trumbull. Having got safely through the platform, with manifestations of intense delight that a transparent cheat on the tariff question had been devised, the Convention proceeded to ballot for a candidate for President. The roll of States was called, and yet there was no sign of the conspiracy. But no sooner had the result been announced, showing that Adams had developed the full strength claimed for him in the special dispatches of the Times, than the bargain was sprung upon the Convention. Gratz Brown for the first time appeared on the floor. Raising his voice, it was recognized by his friend in the chair, and he then went, without invitation, to the platform, where his appearance did not evoke any considerable enthusiasm. He then proceeded to make that remarkable speech declaring for Greeley, when the explosion instantly came. Missouri changed her vote from Brown to Trumbull, and the Chairman of the Kentucky delegation, Hon. C. M. Clay, arose and cast the five votes given Brown for his "old and honored friend, Horace Greeley." whereupon a hot blood in the delegation claimed that this was a vote of the Chairman, and that the delegation had not been consulted. Whereupon Cassius appealed to his delegation for the vote, and remarked that he had lived too long in public life to notice the insinuations of the gentleman reflecting on his honor. Cassius evidently meant business, both in his voice and the look which flashed from his eyes, and his opponent sank down into the oblivion of the stunned mass. There were several other changes of votes, and then Missouri asked leave to retire for consultation. There was considerable commotion in the delegation, which happened to be seated immediately under your correspondent, who was thereby enabled to witness the sudden disintegration and hear the violent expletives with which several members greeted the exposure of the conspiracy. Finally the delegation got out of the hall without any actual physical collision, and then the second phase of the bargain appeared. Alex. McClure withdrew the name of Gov. Curtin, and asked leave for Pennsylvania to retire for consultation, by which he meant that he might have an opportunity to whet that knife which on the previous evening he had threatened to put into the free-traders.

SCHURZ OPPOSES THE BARGAIN.

The session of the Missourians was stormy in the extreme. Senator Schurz relinquished the chair to Mr. Julian, and, appearing before the delegation of his State, proceeded to make a brief but vigorous speech against the consummation of the bargain by the nomination of Greeley. He said that he yielded to no one in admiration of the high character of Mr. Greeley, or in appreciation of his great services to humanity, but, unfortunately, Mr. Greeley had idiosyncracies which made him the weakest candidate the Convention could select. He had been one of the most prominent and persistent advocates of temperance by legislation, so that it was idle to suppose that the German vote would be cast for him. Besides it was indispensable to the success of the movement that the candidate should carry Ohio. It was nonsense to say that Mr. Greeley could do that.

SOLD, BUT NOT DELIVERED.

Those arguments of Schurz, with the disgust of the Missourians at their transfer like sheep, caused both Brown and his bargain to be repudiated. Presently the delegates returned, and the balloting again began. The success of the conspiracy was even then far from assured. Alabama and Arkansas, two of the rotten borough States, which had before divided, led off solid for Greeley. California gave him half, and Georgia all, while before she had none for him. But there were no other breaks of consequence before Missouri was called, and that State gave Greeley only ten, while she gave Trumbull sixteen and Adams four. The announcement of the vote by Gen. McNeil, the Chairman, being instantly followed by one of the delegates shouting, "We've been sold, but not delivered." When it came to Pennsylvania it was found that McClure had been equally unable to fulfill his contract, as that State had only 18 for Greeley, with 26 for Adams and 11 for Trumbull. When the result of the ballot showed Adams 243, Greeley 245, Trumbull 148 and Davis 75, the conspiracy seemed a failure. The Adams men became radiant, and for a time delighted in the delusion that the days of political purity had come again, and that their candidate for whom no questionable means had been used, was to triumph by the mere force of merit over the chicanoery of professional politicians.

PROGRESS OF THE FIGHT.

At the conclusion of the ballot there was unusual uproar caused by the meeting of delegations. The emissaries of the corrupt Greeley-Brown ring were at work, and the Adams men became uneasy, but the roll-call of the third ballot soon began, and being completed showed Adams 264, Greeley 258, Trumbull 146, and Davis 44. Virtue was still triumphant against intrigue. Adams on the fourth ballot had 279, Greeley 251, Trumbull 141. Not only had Adams gained, but Greeley had actually lost, and it was generally supposed that the Trumbull vote, which was the balance of power, would, when it left him, go to Adams and nominate him. Those who were ignorant of the depth of iniquity into which the Greeley managers had descended, supposed the nomination of Adams certain, and telegrams to that effect were flashed over the country.

THE BREAK.

On the next ballot the break began, Trumbull going down to 91, Adams rising to 309, and Greeley to 256. The latter had gained only 5, but Adams had gained 30, and there was no longer any doubt in many mind, but that Adams would be nominated on the next ballot. The Trumbull men were going over to him. It was thought there was no longer any danger of a stampede to Greeley, and there was a general conclusion that the Blairs, Gratz Brown, Cochrane, Hutchins, McClure and the other intriguers had gained nothing by their labors. But they had not been given credit for the astuteness they possessed, for all this time they had been merely playing with the victim they were now prepared to crush. At this juncture, the Illinois delegation asked leave to retire, and in the confusion following their exit, the calling of the sixth ballot begun. Alabama and Arkansas voted solid for Greeley. Georgia next went solid the same way, and then the critical moment had come. John Cochrane jumped to his feet and set up a yell, in which all the plotters joined. It was minutes before the roll could be called further, Indiana followed almost solid for Greeley, and the yells were renewed with more volume and intensity than before. It was evident that Greeley was to be shouted down the throat of the Convention, and in vain Schurz pounded for order. There was no order in the crowd of political tricksters below him, and as gains for Greeley were announced in Iowa, Kansas, Kentucky, Mississippi, Louisiana, Missouri, which finally voted Greeley, with Adams 10 and Trumbull 2, it was evident that the *Tribune* philosopher was stamped into the nomination. But McClure had to make a proper showing, and Pennsylvania, before the changes commenced stood Adams 32, Greeley 18.

A SHOUTING MOB.

At the close of the call the Convention degenerated into a mob of yelling madmen. Private tallies had shown that the plot had succeeded, and everywhere chairmen of delegations were on their feet demanding to change the vote of their States, which was done, and finally the vote was announced—Greeley 482, and Adams 187, and Horace Greeley had been nominated as the Reform candidate for President. The scene at this point was simply indescribable, a motion for a recess had been made but had been defeated—yet there was an actual recess, because nothing could be done pending the return of the Illinois delegation. The fact that Greeley was actually nominated, as the figures stood, seemed incomprehensible, and, to many, impossible. The Convention awoke to the situation by degrees, as if stung by the shock of an awful calamity. On the New-York side there was uproarious confusion, and the red neck-ties of Tammany Republicans were actively at work trying to induce delegates to change their votes.

DISMAY.

But on all other hands the realization of the situation settled like a pall. The Southern States, which had been scattering their votes on Chase, Brown and Trumbull, hurried to change them to the winning man, and the announcements were made amid loud cheers and storms of hisses from the floor and the galleries. Cries of "shame" and yells of delight were mingled in the common discord. Every man's face was a study. Hundreds of delegates stamped their feet and swore. Judge Hoadley, of the Ohio delegation, shook with rage.. Stanley Matthews swelled until it seemed as if he would burst. The pig-iron arrow which he shot at McClure last night had been turned, and now pierced his own heart. The faces of the "independent journalists" which had just been all aglow with joyful hope at the splendid vote of Adams, now grew black under the overspreading clouds of disappointment and disgust. The face of Schurz was a fresh study for the facile pencil of Nast. The audience seemed to become enraged and delighted by turns. Hats flew wildly and anathemas were hurled at the heads of the bargainers.

ANNOUNCING THE RESULT.

It was a long time before the ballot was announced, and when it was it was mere guess work, for the changes had been accomplished in such a turmoil that the secretaries were unable to correct them, but it came at last in a voice trembling with visible emotion. Senator Schurz said: "The result of the sixth ballot is as follows: Whole number of votes cast, 714; necessary to a choice, 358, of which Charles Francis Adams has 187, and Horace Greeley has 482. You have, therefore, nominated Horace Greeley as your candidate for President." Both the enthusiasm of the New-Yorkers and the rage of the Adams men had nearly spent its physical force by this time, and the announcement served rather to quiet than to promote the disorder.

NO UNANIMITY EVEN YET.

In a moment more, however, three or four motions to make the nomination unanimous were launched at the Chair, but were met by stentorian cries of "No, no no," from all parts of the floor. The motion being put, it was met with wild cries of "Aye" from the Greeley men, mingled with scorning hisses, and when the negative was called for an angry shout of "No, no," went up from scores of the benches. But the deed was done, and a recess of ten minutes followed, against the protestations of the Greeley champions, who wanted to rush the Gratz Brown bargain right through.

A CHANGE.

During the intermission the scene was changed from the appalling to the ludicrous. The men at first stunned at the result began to realize the length and breadth of the farce, and then to laugh immoderately. Among the journalists the comments were various, as they telegraphed reserved comments or instructions to their papers. Samuel Bowles was asked what he was going to do about it, and replied that he was "going to think about it." Halstead, the Murat of "independent journalists" swore with an emphatic oath, while Watterson, of the Louisville *Courier-Journal*, surveyed his wrecked hopes with a sickening sensation, while Bromley, of the Hartford *Post*, at once bought a ticket for the Mammoth Cave, remarking, with that characteristic severity which never permits him to spoil a joke, even at the expense of his friends, that having seen one "mammoth cave," he desired to see the other in Kentucky. During this brief recess the complexion of the audience changed almost entirely. Scores of delegates left in utter disgust and rage, and the galleries emptied with great rapidity. The spirit of the Convention was broken and the interest was gone. The whole affair had collapsed like a bubble, and it required quite an effort to nerve the body up to the exertion of completing the remainder of the bargain by the renomination of Gratz Brown for Vice-President. The roll-call began, and amid the cheers of the Brown body-guard from St. Louis, and Greeley's strikers from New-York, and Greeley's States wheeled into line for Brown. The Adams men made a frantic effort to stem the tide of disaster, and, when Connecticut was reached, she cast ten votes for George W. Julian, and only one for Brown. Illinois, Indiana and Massachusetts followed suit, and it seemed for a moment as if that degree of respectability which pertains to Mr. Julian might be saved to the ticket, but it was only for a moment. Other States which might have nominated Julian, and thus restore a partial spirit to the despondent mass, fritted away, the vote on Trumbull and Cox and Walker and even Tipton and Scovell received eight and twelve votes respectively.

So that on the total result Brown was nearly ahead of all competitors, thus: Brown, 237; Trumbull, 156; Julian, 134½; Walker, 84½; Clay, 44; Cox, 25; Scovel, 12; Pipton, 8. At this point Gov. Koerner, of Illinois, withdrew Trumbull's name, saying that he had absolutely declined to take that nomination, and the name of Gov. Cox was also withdrawn by his authority. At this point, also, the announcement was made that the Ohio delegation would withdraw from the Convention for consultation at College Hall. The second ballot was then taken and the bargain no longer encountered any resistance. It went all one way, the farce being kept up by those who remained casting the full vote of the delegation, many members of which had departed until the result was announced: Brown, 435; Julian, 175; Walker, 75; Palmer, 8; Tipton, 2.

This was the sickening end.

THE ADJOURNMENT.

Mr. Schurz announced the result and reminded the delegates that they must select from each State a representative on the National Committee. But there was no heart for such work as this, and it wat quickly disposed of. Then Mr. Schurz nerved himself up to say a few parting words, and his heart and his eloquence failed him, and with a brief and ironical adjuration to elect the ticket, he adjourned what was left of the Convention *sine die*.

THE PARTY OF "BRAINS AND CONVICTIONS."

But of all the men who are literally "hoist with their own petard," the party of brains and convictions, the Free-trade Revenue Reformers, are the worst sold set that can be found. These men were very properly the leaders of the Convention. They embodied all of principle and convictions there was in it. They were honest men, and they came here first for principle and second for success. They sought to combine the two, according to their notions, in Adams as a candidate and the Missouri resolution as a platform; but they were not skilled in the ways of the politicians, and when they undertook to temporize and make concessions for the sake of success, they planned their own defeat. They insisted that they were not yielding anything, yet yielded the very key of the position. The New-Yorkers, under the telegraphic advice of Greeley, dictated step by step the terms of the tariff resolution, until what was asserted to be a square principle at the outset was transformed into a meaningless, ambiguous and absurd proposition. Having thus for the sake of conciliation surrendered their principles, the defeat of their candidate followed naturally at the hands of the bargainers, who knew that Adams was no sort of man for their purposes. Probably no men in the Convention are in a worse position than they are to-day, and when one of them was asked what was his purpose for the Summer campaign, he despondently replied that he thought he should go a fishing. E. C.

## THE FINAL ACT.

### Detailed Report of the Third and Last Day's Proceedings of the Convention.

CINCINNATI, Ohio, May 3.—The Convention was called to order at 10:10 o'clock. The reading of the journal was dispensed with.

The Chair stated that the statement in a morning paper pretending to give a dispatch from him (Schurz) to a candidate was utterly untrue.

Mr. Gilmore, of Missouri, offered a resolution that when the Convention reaches the point of balloting for candidates, there shall be no formal presentation of candidates, but that the Convention proceed to vote.

Mr. Dexter, of Illinois, sustained the proposition. He said he wanted to proceed to business, and avoid mere personal eulogies.

The resolution was carried.

THE ADDRESS AND RESOLUTIONS.

Mr. Horace White, from the Committee on Platform, reported a set of resolutions which had been unanimously adopted by the Committee.

*Address of the Committee on Resolutions.*

The Administration now in power has rendered itself guilty of wanton disregard of the laws of the land and of powers not granted by the Constitution. It has acted as if the laws had binding force only for those who are governed, and not for those who govern. It has thus struck a blow at the fundamental principles of constitutional government, and the liberties of the citizen. The President of the United States has openly used the powers and opportunities of his high office for the promotion of personal ends. He has kept notoriously corrupt and unworthy men in places of power and responsibility to the detriment of the public interest. He has used the public service of the Government as a machinery of partisan and personal influence, and interfered with tyrannical arrogance in the political affairs of States and municipalities. He has rewarded with influential and lucrative offices men who had acquired his favor by valuable presents, thus stimulating demoralization of our political life by his conspicuous example. He has shown himself deplorably unequal to the tasks imposed upon him by the necessities of the country, and culpably careless of the responsibilities of his high office. The partisans of the Administration, assuming to be the Republican Party and controlling its organization, have attempted to justify such wrongs and palliate such abuses, to the end of maintaining partisan ascendancy. They have stood in the way of necessary investigations and indispensable reforms, pretending that no serious fault could be found with the present administration of public affairs, thus seeking to blind the eyes of the people. They have kept alive the passions and resentments of the late civil war to use them for their own advantage. They have resorted to arbitrary measures in direct conflict with the organic law instead of appealing to the better instincts and latent patriotism of the Southern people by restoring to them those rights, the enjoyment of which is indispensable for a successful administration of their local affairs, and would tend to move a patriotic and hopeful national feeling. They have degraded themselves, and the name of their party, once justly entitled to the confidence of the nation, by a base sycophancy to the dispenser of executive power and patronage unworthy of Republican freemen, they have sought to stifle the voice of just criticism, to stifle the moral sense of the people and to subjugate public opinion by tyrannical party discipline. They are striving to maintain themselves in authority for selfish ends by an unscrupulous use of the power which rightfully belongs to the people, and should be employed only in the service of the country. Believing that an organization thus led and controlled can no longer be of service to the best interests of the Republic, we have resolved to make an independent appeal to the sober judgment, conscience and patriotism of the American people.

We, the Liberal Republicans of the United States, in National Convention assembled at Cincinnati, proclaim the following principles as essential to just government:

*First*—We recognize the equality of all men before the law, and hold that it is the duty of government in its dealings with the people to mete out equal and exact justice to all, of whatever nativity, race, color or persuasion, religious or political.

*Second*—We pledge ourselves to maintain the union of the States, emancipation and enfranchisement, and to oppose any reopening of the questions settled by the Thirteenth, Fourteenth and Fifteenth Amendments to the Constitution.

*Third*—We demand the immediate and absolute removal of all disabilities imposed on account of the rebellion which was finally subdued seven years ago, believing that universal amnesty will result in complete pacification in all sections of the country.

*Fourth*—Local self-government with impartial suffrage will guard the rights of all citizens more securely than any centralized power. The public welfare requires the supremacy of the civil over the military authority, and freedom of person under the protection of the *habeas corpus*. We demand for the individual the largest liberty consistent with public order, for the State self-government, and for the nation a return to the methods of peace and the constitutional limitation of power.

*Fifth*—The civil service of the Government has become a mere instrument of partisan tyranny and personal ambition, and an object of selfish greed. It is a scandal and reproach upon free institutions, and breeds a demoralization dangerous to the perpetuity of republican government. We therefore regard such thorough reforms of the civil service as one of the most pressing necessities of the hour; that honesty, capacity and fidelity, constitute the only valid claims to public employment; That the offices of the Government cease to be a matter of arbitrary favoritism and patronage, and that public station become again a post of honor. To this end it is imperatively required that no President shall be a candidate for re-election.

*Sixth*—We demand a system of Federal taxation which shall not unnecessarily interfere with the industry of the people, and which shall provide the means necessary to pay the expenses of the Government economically administered, the pensions, the interest on the public debt, and a moderate reduction annually of the principal thereof; and, recognizing that there are in our midst honest but irreconcilable differences of opinion with regard to the respective systems of protection and free trade, we remit the discussion of the subject to the people in their Congressional districts and to the decision of Congress thereon, wholly free of Executive interference or dictation.

*Seventh*—The public credit must be sacredly maintained, and we denounce repudiation in every form and guise.

*Eighth*—A speedy return to specie payment is demanded alike by highest considerations of commercial morality and honest government.

*Ninth*—We remember with gratitude the heroism and sacrifices of the soldiers and sailors of the Republic, and no act of ours shall ever detract from their justly earned fame or the full reward of their patriotism.

*Tenth*—We are opposed to all further grants of land to railroads or other corporations. The public domain should be held sacred to actual settlers.

*Eleventh*—We hold that it is the duty of the Government, in its intercourse with foreign nations, to cultivate the friendship of peace by treating with all on fair and equal terms, regarding it alike dishonorable either to demand what is not right or to submit to what is wrong.

*Twelfth*—For the promotion and success of these vital principles, and the support of the candidates nominated by this Convention, we invite and cordially welcome the co-operation of all patriotic citizens, without regard to previous affiliations.

(Signed,) HORACE WHITE,
Chairman of Committee on Resolutions.
G. P. THURSTON, Secretary.

The platform was adopted unanimously.

BALLOTING OF CANDIDATES.

The next order of business was stated by the Chair to be the nomination of candidates for the Presidency, without the formal presentation of candidates.

Before the result of the first ballot was announced, Gratz Brown, by unanimous consent, took the stand and thanked his friends for their support of him, but withdrew his name and asked his friends to support Horace Greeley. [Great cheers with many persistent hisses.]

Considerable confusion ensued, various delegations asking to change their votes, contention arising in some of them—notably Kentucky—as to what the changes among themselves really were, after which the Chair announced the following result:

*First Ballot.*

Whole number of votes......714
Necessary to a choice......358

| | | | |
|---|---|---|---|
| Adams | 203 | Greeley | 147 |
| Trumbull | 110 | Brown | 95 |
| Davis | 92½ | Curtin | 62 |
| Chase | 2½ | Sumner | 1 |

Missouri asked leave to retire for consultation. Mr. McClure withdrew Gov. Curtin's name, and asked leave for the Pennsylvania delegation to retire, which request was granted. The proceedings were suspended until the return of the absent delegations.

*Second Ballot.*

| | | | |
|---|---|---|---|
| Greeley | 245 | Adams | 243 |
| Trumbull | 148 | Davis | 75 |
| Brown | 2 | Chase | 1 |

*Third Ballot.*

| | | | |
|---|---|---|---|
| Adams | 264 | Greeley | 258 |
| Trumbull | 156 | Davis | 44 |

*Fourth Ballot.*

| | | | |
|---|---|---|---|
| Adams | 279 | Greeley | 251 |
| Trumbull | 141 | Davis | 51 |

*Fifth Ballot.*

| | | | |
|---|---|---|---|
| Adams | 309 | Greeley | 258 |
| Trumbull | 91 | Davis | 30 |
| Chase | 24 | Chase | 2 |

The announcement of Adams' vote was received with great cheers. The sixth ballot was ordered, amid a scene of great confusion. Missouri asked leave to retire for consultation. After an interval of twenty minutes, the call of the roll was proceeded with.

*Sixth Ballot.*

| | | | |
|---|---|---|---|
| Greeley | 332 | Adams | 324 |
| Chase | 32 | Trumbull | 19 |
| Davis | 6 | Palmer | 1 |

Before the vote was formally announced, Minnesota changed 9 from Trumbull to Greeley. Various States changed their votes. A scene of great confusion and noise followed. Mr. McClure changed Pennsylvania to 50 for Greeley and 6 for Davis. Indiana changed to 27 for Adams. A stampede of changes to Greeley here occurred, and the noise and confusion that followed was very great. Illinois changed solid to Greeley, except one delegate, who insisted that his vote should stand for Trumbull.

The Chair finally announced the whole vote as 714; necessary to a choice, 358. Adams had 187; Greeley 482.

Mr. Casement moved to make the nomination unanimous, but it was declared lost, as there were many nays before the vote was announced.

The Chair then announced that Mr. Greeley was nominated as the candidate for the Presidency by the Convention.

NOMINATING THE VICE-PRESIDENT.

On motion, it was ordered to proceed to the nomination of a Vice-President immediately, and Gratz Brown was nominated on the second ballot. During the balloting Gov. Koerner, of Illinois, stated that he had received a telegram from Mr. Trumbull positively declining to be a candidate for Vice-President under any circumstances. Several States offered their votes to Cassius M. Clay, but he declined to be considered a candidate, advising them to vote for Mr. Brown. Mr. Cox, of Ohio, also declined to be considered a candidate. Gov. Palmer, of Illinois, would not accept a nomination under any circumstances. Mr. Brown's nomination was then made unanimous, and the President and Vice-President of the Convention were appointed a Committee to announce the nominations to the candidates.

After resolutions of thanks to Cincinnati for her hospitality and to the officers of the Convention were adopted, the roll of the States was called for members of the National Executive Committee.

ILL-CONCEALED DISGUST OF SCHURZ.

In response to vehement calls for a speech, Senator Schurz said: My fellow-citizens—This Convention has overwhelmed me with kindness, and I have especially to thank them for the indulgence with which they have borne with me while I was endeavoring, to the best of my ability, to conduct with fairness and impartiality the deliberations of this large, and let us confess, a little unruly, body. [Laughter.] We have now accomplished our work. Our duty it will be now to proclaim to all the land the principles we have embodied in our platform, and go forward and solicit, with all entreaties which our minds and hearts are capable of making, the support of the people of the United States for the candidates we have nominated. I have already done so much speaking in this Convention, and, may be, I may have to do so much during the impending campaign, that you will certainly bear with me if I close my speech in the same manner in which I closed my first—then by seconding the motion to adjourn, and now by declaring the Liberal Republican Convention adjourned *sine di*.

## THE NOMINATION ACCEPTED.

### Mr. Greeley Gratefully Acknowledges the Compliment and Says Yes.

CINCINNATI, May 3.—The following telegram from Mr. Greeley was received here after he had been informed of his nomination:

NEW-YORK, May 3, 1872.

WHITELAW REID: Please tender my grateful acknowledgements to the members of the Convention for the generous confidence they have shown me, and assure them I shall endeavor to deserve it. HORACE GREELEY.

## THE DEMOCRATIC PROGRAMME.

### Meeting of the National Committee in New-York Next Week.

WASHINGTON, May 3.—The *Patriot* of to-morrow will have a leader on the Convention, of which the following is the closing portion:

The Democratic National Committee will meet in New-York on Wednesday next, to determine upon the time and place of holding the National Democratic Convention. This Committee will be composed of the wisest, ablest, best and most patriotic men of the party from all States and sections of the country, and will authoritatively speak the wish of the great Democratic heart. Its first duty will be to present to the people such candidates as will command the respect and secure the support of the good and true men of the country, and rally to the standard they bear. The great body of those who regard the promotion of the best interest of the nation as the paramount duty of the patriotic citizen

PHILADELPHIA, May 3.—The *Age* to-morrow will have an article, which concludes as follows: "We have not cherished a doubt that the Democratic Convention would, in due time, place a candidate in the field. Let him be one to meet the requirements of the times."

## THE RESULT IN WASHINGTON.

### A General Laugh—Gen. Butler's Opinion—Mr. Trumbull Modest, or Overpowered by His Feelings—What the Democrats Say.

Special Dispatch to the New-York Times.

WASHINGTON, May 3.—To-day, for the first time this week, the Cincinnati Convention has made impression enough in Washington to attract attention, and for an hour there was some excitement to hear returns of the ballots as they came over the wires. It was evident from the first that Greeley and Brown had been trading. Soon there came rumors of combination between Trumbull and Adams, and when the break on the fifth ballot from Trumbull to Adams was announced there was a general impression that he would win. Doubts, however, were still entertained of that result on the theory that whoever was ahead in the beginning, unless nominated the first time, would be beaten in the end. Gen. Logan put full trust in this theory, to which he remembered no exception. The sixth ballot was awaited with much interest. Returns came slowly, preceded by the simple announcement that Greeley was nominated. An indescribable scene took place in the House when this was announced. During the balloting large and noisy groups of members were discussing the latest news in all parts of the House, and tariff speeches fell unheeded. Democrats acted uneasy for an hour before the final ballot, it being clear from the first that either Adams or Greeley would be the man, and New-Yorkers like Wood, Cox and Potter did not hesitate to say that one would be as hard to swallow as the other. Mr. Schofield was in the chair, and when in response to demands for information, as it appeared in distant parts of the house that information had been received, he announced that Greeley was nominated, a loud and general guffaw broke out all over the floor. "It's a sell;" "Don't believe it," were the first words that came up from the excited throng of Congressmen through their laughter. "Sold out," accompanied by expletives, was the comment of Democrats, and among the Republicans the broad burlesque of the whole thing kept up a diversion which has not yet subsided. Some of the remarks of prominent and demoralized Democrats were amusing. Eldridge, of Wisconsin, said, "It's none of our funeral," and protested that the Democrats had had nothing whatever to do with the thing, never intended to from the first, and never would. Mr. Cox and others openly boasted that it was fixed as they wanted it; that Greeley was put up as a "decoy duck" to draw off Republican votes, and that the regular Democratic candidate was now certain to be elected. Mr. Kelley, meeting Dan Voorhees, said that it was a strange spectacle to see him (Kelley, the protectionist,) opposed to Greeley, and Voorhees, the free-trader, for him. "That is something you will never see," replied Voorhees. A prominent Illinois Republican, who has been reputed as hostile to Grant, said that the result was all that was necessary to give Illinois to Grant. "She went into that Convention with three candidates, and was kicked out," he added in explanation. A prominent Kentucky Democrat upbraided Greeley. He was "the cause of all their woes." Gen. Butler said it was the weakest nomination that could possibly have been made. "Greeley has at last got a nomination," he said, "on the same principle that an auctioneer up in my district accepted the bid of a man who was always bidding one cent, in order to get rid of him."

In the Senate, there were groups of Senators scattered about discussing the news. His emotions or modesty—nobody can tell which—kept Mr. Trumbull outside the Chamber during this time. He had not the fortitude to sit in his seat and feel the gaze of even the few in the galleries. When the brief agony—but still long to him—was over, he came back and smiled with the rest over the ludicrous finale of the performance. It was observed on several sides that he looked very white, and a copy of the *Globe*, which he attempted to read, seemed to share his emotions, and trembled so that he did not long continue to read. He went over on a sofa, and received sympathy from his colleague. Then he went and canvassed the situation with Mr. Fenton. The Democrats held small caucuses in the corners of the chamber. Mr. Trumbull is credited with saying that when the first wave of laughter subsided he did not know what would become of the ticket. The nomination was a complete surprise. Greeley had not been looked upon as one of the possibilities. He had been patted on the back by the rest of the candidates in order to secure the *Tribune*. But they none of them considered him seriously in the light of a rival. They are as far as has been heard from here much chagrined. The only unanimity in the reception of the nomination is the ridicule with which it is greeted. The first effect of the news on everybody was to excite laughter, and certainly Washington has never been in more excellent humor than to-night.

The prospects of the political effect of the nomination are discussed considerably. From the Democrats only one voice is heard. They will have their regular National Convention and their own nominees. They profess to believe that Greeley will have sufficient strength to draw off votes in the closer States from the Republican nominee and give them to the Democrats, while Greeley himself is not conceded anywhere to have strength enough to carry a single State for himself. Among the friends of the President there is no desire to have the action of the Cincinnati Convention changed in any particular. They laugh with the rest. Indeed, the city is so much filled with laughter, that sober reflection upon consequences is almost impossible.

## FEELING IN THE CITY.

### The Nomination Regarded as a Joke by All Except the Democrats, Who Like It.

To say that the citizens of New-York were surprised by the action of the Cincinnati Convention would be but a tame way of expressing their feelings. Indeed, the first thought of the matter was that a telegraphic joke had been practiced on the public by some wag. But when the truth actually was forced home to the minds of the people, New-York might have been said to smile audibly. The guns in the City Hall Park, which, by the way, are said to have been paid for by the *Tribune* office, seemed to be regarded in their blank cartridge explosions as typical of the harmless result of the Liberal movement. No one could be prevailed upon to consider seriously for a moment Mr. Greeley as a President. The majority of the Democrats, however, who long for Republican disintegration at any cost, were jubilant, and metaphorically patted the nominee on the back. As soon as he made his appearance in Printing-house-square he was surrounded by a large crowd of news-boys and young men, who followed him to the cars. One urchin hung to his coat tails and said, "Do make us a speech, Mr. Greeley! Hooray! for the President!" He was requited with a gentle pat on the shoulder, and Mr. Greeley went up to the Union League Club.

FEELING DOWN TOWN.

At the business centres—in Wall-street, at the Stock Exchange, the Gold-room, the Merchants' News-rooms and at the Cotton and Produce Exchanges—the news of the unexpected result of the Cincinnati Convention was received in an entirely different manner from that in which the tidings of Presidential nominations are usually greeted. Men spoke of Greeley's candidature as a huge joke, and some were even irreverent enough to couple the name of the agricultural philosopher of Chappaqua as a Presidential aspirant with that of George Francis Train or Daniel Pratt. With a sad look of appreciation of the gravity of the matter every one seemed to speak of the nomination with a quiet but expressive smile, or with a derisive laugh. The question asked, "What do you think of the nomination of Mr. Greeley?" was met by a questioning smile, as though doubtful of the interrogator's intent to have the matter considered seriously. For once the "interviewer" was baffled; scarcely any one seemed willing to express a serious opinion on the matter.

At the Stock Exchange, where the business in securities was rather brisk, the prices fluctuating very much during the day, the usual hubbub was checked for a time when the news was received, and Greeley's prospects hurriedly discussed. Men wondered how many Democratic votes he would poll; whether the Democrats will nominate Adams to take advantage of his very apparent popularity among many "Liberals;" whether the nomination was made with a view of drawing Democratic votes, ("anything to beat Grant;") and so on, *ad libitum*. Conjectures were indulged in, not as to whether Greeley would be elected, (that seeming to be deemed not worth consideration,) but as to what was behind the farce.

AT THE UNION LEAGUE CLUB.

Mr. Greeley called at the Union League Club, as usual, last evening, and took his bundle of letters from his box and proceeded into the reading-room to peruse them. At the time there were several members of the Club in the room, engaged in conversation on the nomination at Cincinnati, but on Mr. Greeley's entrance the conversation was hushed, and he was left completely alone. These quarters not seeming very agreeable, Mr. Greeley soon left. Later in the evening the Club-house was crowded with the members, who seemed to regard the nomination as a very good joke. No one except Mr. Greeley's friends for a moment thinks he will run. Among the opinions advanced was that the nomination of Mr. Greeley was unexpected, and, it is believed, will lead to the nomination of a Democratic candidate, which will leave Mr. Greeley without any followers at all. This Club will abide by the nomination of the Philadelphia Convention. One of the members said a Democratic Sachem of Tammany Hall told him that the Democrats would now put in a candidate, as Mr. Greeley does not suit them; but if they did not, he would vote for Grant, and in saying this he thought he might speak for the sensible men of the Democratic Party. But the great question is, "Who is going to furnish the money to canvass Mr. Greeley?" It will cost $1,000,000 to canvass the Union; New-York State alone cannot be canvassed under $150,000, and where is this money to come from? Not from the Democrats, surely. Thanks to the Committee of Seventy, they have not much spare money or "loose cash" about. They are short of money and cannot help, so where is Mr. Greeley to get the "necessary?" Another rumor current during the evening was that Greeley and Brown are sure of the State of Missouri, but they could carry no State without the Democratic indorsement.

THE MANHATTAN CLUB.

Early in the evening, as the members of the Club dropped in to obtain the latest news from the Convention, it was evident that the nominations of Greeley and Brown gave considerable satisfaction. The result of the ballots was discussed in the groups of members which formed in the corridor and parlors, and at times the quiet mirth of the gentlemen enlivened the more serious conversation on the political issue. Two well-known and prominent politicians entered, and shaking hands with those around them, jubilantly cheered for the nominees. "Why, said one of them, "I would rather cast my vote for his satanic majesty than give my voice for the re-election of Ulysses S. Grant. His re-election means the utter rout of the Democratic Party in this country for years. But in the present condition of the Democracy we cannot hope to put forward a prominent man who will carry strength enough to sweep Grant from the field, and it seems that the effect of Greeley's nomination will be to draw from the Radical Republicans the votes of all the disaffected, and then, if we please to unite with them, we have some hope of success." One of the group of gentlemen then took up the conversation, and said, "There is but little probability that the Democratic Party can elect its candidate, no matter whom it selects. It is divided in this State, and the effect of the division is almost universally felt. If we cast the whole strength of the party with the Reform Republicans, there is some assurance that the conflict will result in substantial benefit to the Democratic cause. What we may think of the candidates personally is another thing." Moving along the hall and through the rooms another group was met. "Around this section, and through New-England," said one, "we may regret that Adams was not chosen, but we should consider that the other parts of the country may prefer somebody else." "Ah, Mister, I suppose you are a Greeley man?" "No, Sir, I am not; although I may vote the ticket as a matter of necessity, where is his strength? Throughout the rural districts, where the poorer classes swear by 'What I know about potatoes,' he will probably pull a strong vote. His nomination is a well-arranged movement against the Grant Republicans, and if we cannot select a thorough and favorite Democrat, we will have to vote for the Philosopher." "Well," said another wealthy member, "if a split takes place in the Grant party, Greeley may go ahead of his ticket, but I doubt it. His mental qualifications for the position are somewhat deteriorated by his well-known and characteristic dignity of person." [Smiles.]

THE FIFTH-AVENUE HOTEL.

The Fifth-avenue Hotel was last night singularly free from political discussion. Senator O'Brien, in speaking to a fellow-Democrat, said that he considered the nomination of Mr. Greeley a good one, for the object for which it was made, and he rather thought, though speaking only for himself when giving expression to the thought, that there was an understood willingness on the part of the Democrats of the country to favor the running of any one against Grant.

It was, perhaps, a trifle too early yet to give positive expression to an opinion as to what may really be done. He felt, however, that the Democrats would be willing to do anything in reason to secure the defeat of Grant, and that they would be likely to speak well of Mr. Greeley's nomination, whatever might come of it in the end.

In another portion of the main hallway were ex-Collector Thomas Murphy, Hugh Hastings, Mr. Sellover and others prominent in the Republican ranks. Mr. Hastings, whose opinion was seemingly in entire accord with the friends around him, felt that it was difficult for any well informed politician to speak of the Convention's work with a serious face. The idea of the Democratic Party going over to the support of Mr. Greeley, who, so far as his mere declarations could go, had been its life-long enemy, was felt to be too absurd for a moment's credence. And so of the Republican Party; it was felt that to expect Republicans to support Mr. Greeley, beyond a few who might hope for subsequent favors through the columns of his journal, was equally absurd, for, as it must appear clear to every intelligent Republican, the only effect of throwing away a vote for him, however much they might incline to please him, would be simply doing so much in aid of the Democratic effort to weaken the Republican organization and lessen its power for good. It was held that Mr. Greeley's present position as a candidate would, if persisted in, simply show that he was willing to gratify his personal spite to the utmost, even while believing that he was endangering Republican success by so doing; and to expect any considerable portion of a party composed, in the main, of intelligent men to encourage him in so doing was expecting too much.

WHAT THE GERMANS THINK.

The news from Cincinnati was the subject of general discussion in all places of public resort for our German fellow-citizens, and in all their clubs and political organizations, the impression was one of mingled surprise and doubt. The adherents of the "Liberal" movement of course indorse the nomination, believing Mr. Greeley would make an honest President; but many even among these classes, doubt his qualifications for the office, and seriously question his statesmanship, notwithstanding his acknowledged ability as a politician. Some argue that his nomination will considerably weaken the "Liberal" movement, as it was well known that Senator Schurz's choice was Mr. Adams; and it is thought that those who have taken part in the movement with the German Senator will not give a candidate any very active support who was so unexpectedly foisted on them.

## LATEST CABLE TELEGRAMS.

### Contradictory Reports as to the Carlist Insurrection.

### The Priests Endeavoring to Create a Religious War.

### Debate on Home Rule in the English Parliament.

### Cessation of the Eruption of Mount Vesuvius.

### Loss of Life by a Cyclone in the East Indies.

THE CARLIST REVOLT.

**The Priests Endeavoring to Foment a Religious War—Flight of Carlists into France—Contradictory Reports as to the Progress of the Insurrection—Movements of Marshal Serrano.**

LONDON, May 3.—Advices received in this city by mail from Spain state that the priests are endeavoring to make the insurrection in that country a religious war. The Government has called upon the inhabitants of Barcelona to deliver up all the arms they have in their possession.

PARIS, May 3.—A dispatch from Bayonne confirms the report that the Carlist leader, Rada, with his command, has fled into France, having been closely pursued by the Spanish Government forces.

The French troops stationed on the Spanish frontier disarm and *intern* all Carlists. The men escape into France.

LATER.—Advices have been received here from Spain which contradict most positively the dispatches sent from Madrid in regard to the Carlist insurrection. *L'Union* announces, on what it terms official authority, that Don Carlos is in Spain at the head of his "volunteers," and Don Alphonso, his brother, is with him. The proclamation signed by him which was circulating in Madrid was genuine. There is deep uneasiness in Madrid. The fidelity of the troops even in the capital is doubted, and the precaution is taken to keep some regiments in their barracks. The Carlists, meanwhile, hold the field in respectable force, and are able to disconcert the Government troops.

Señor Castellar, the eminent Republican, writes to *Le Rappel* that the Republican Deputies in the Cortes will resign in a few days.

A special dispatch to *Le Temps* reports that the railway between Cordova and Madrid has been cut at the Des Pragnaperros defile, in the Sierra Moreña, by Republican insurgents, who are fortifying that important position, and it was rumored that two companies of infantry had joined them.

MADRID, May 3.—A conspiracy against the Government has been discovered at Linares, a town of Andalusia, on the Madrid and Cordova Railroad.

Marshal Serrano was, yesterday, at Huerta de Letonia and Ysurun, in the Sierra de Arater, on the northern boundary of Navarre.

The Carlists in Biscay have burned the railway bridge at Areta, near Bilbao.

GREAT BRITAIN.

**The London Times Advises that Canada be Absolved from Her Allegiance—Proceedings in Parliament—Death of a Brother of Tom Hughes.**

LONDON, May 3.—The *Times* of this morning, in discussing the attitude of Canada with regard to the Treaty of Washington, somewhat censures the conduct of the Home Government in its treatment of the Dominion, and hints that it might be beneficial to the world if England were to absolve Canada from her allegiance to the mother country.

The debate in the House of Commons last night, on the bill to repeal the Unlawful Assemblies act, was protracted to a late hour, and was a very exciting one. The motion was for the second reading of the bill. Several Irish members took occasion to make speeches in defense of "home rule." What they wanted was to have the laws of Ireland assimilated with those of England. The Marquis of Hartington, Secretary for Ireland, opposed and denounced "home rule" as synonymous with Fenianism. He explained the present law, showing that it in effect prohibited the assembling of an Irish Parliament.

Dr. Isaac Butt, member for Limerick, declared himself a "Home Ruler," but indignantly denied that he was a Fenian, as intimated by the Marquis of Hartington, of whom he demanded a retraction. He protested against such expressions coming from a Minister, who received his information of the country he sought to rule over through detectives and spies, the real ruling powers in Ireland. If it was true that Home Rulers were Fenians, it spoke well for Home Rule, which had been able to win back to peace men driven into rebellion by shameless legislation. Until Irishmen obtain the right to manage Irish affairs in an Irish Parliament, peace, content and prosperity were impossible. He warned the Commons that if the act was not repealed Ireland would endanger the safety of the Empire. He wanted for Ireland a local Government like that of an American State, and for the Kingdom a National Legislature similar to the American Congress.

Mr. Gladstone said the latter scheme was impracticable. Even American statesmen were divided in opinion as to its wisdom. The recent civil war in the United States grew out of the collisions the system involved. He vindicated home rule; if it converted Fenians, so much the better; but he could not but oppose the bill before the House.

The motion for a second reading was then rejected by a vote of 27 to 145.

In the House of Commons to-night, Lord Lennox, member for Chichester, gave notice that he would make a motion for the appointment of a select Committee to inquire into the practicability of reducing the existing rates for telegrams to India, the Colonies and the United States, and of purchasing the existing cables.

Dr. Parish, of Philadelphia, was examined to-day on the treatment of drunkards before a Select Committee of the House of Commons.

The strike of the Liverpool cartmen is ended. The masters conceded the demands of their men.

George Hughes, brother of Tom Hughes, died to-day.

ITALY.

**Vesuvius Quiet—The Devastated Country Swept by a Hurricane.**

NAPLES, May 3.—The eruption of Mount Vesuvius has entirely ceased, and the inhabitants of the villages which were threatened with destruction by the running lava have returned to their homes. Additional troubles, however, have fallen upon them. A hurricane of terrible violence has swept over the devastated country, greatly damaging the villages and remaining crops.

THE EAST INDIES.

**Terrible Cyclone at Madras—Disasters Among the Shipping, and Loss of Life.**

BOMBAY, May 3, via LONDON.—Intelligence has just reached here that the City of Madras and vicinity was visited by a terrible cyclone on Wednesday last, which caused a serious loss of life. A number of vessels at anchor in the roadstead, which were unable to put to sea owing to the sudden approach of the cyclone, were wrecked, and most of their crews perished. The immense pier leading out into the water was breached, and the city and suburbs were greatly damaged.

# The New-York Times.

VOL. XXI......NO. 6468. NEW-YORK, TUESDAY, JUNE 11, 1872. PRICE FOUR CENTS.


## CONGRESS ADJOURNED

### Hot and Protracted Contest Over Enforcement.

### Democratic Filibustering to Kill the Original Bill.

### They Accept as a Compromise a Clause of the Existing Law.

### Senator Chandler Exposes the Secret of the Reform Movement.

### A Conspiracy Between Sore-Heads and Democrats.

Special Dispatch to the New-York Times.

WASHINGTON, June 10.—The session of Congress today has been of extraordinary interest and much excitement. Both branches have been in constant turmoil since early this morning. An unusually large number of members were present in their seats, notwithstanding the increased ratio of absentees. The President and Cabinet came to the Capitol soon after 9 o'clock and occupied the President's Room, as usual, on the Senate side. At 1 o'clock they retired for luncheon, but returned at 3 and remained until adjournment. The proclamation convening an extra session at 12½ was ready to be issued, but the extension of the session until 6 o'clock, which occurred a few minutes before noon, caused it to be withheld.

SCENES IN THE HOUSE.

The House met at 8 o'clock this morning and received the report of the Conference Committee on the disagreeing votes of the two Houses on the Sundry Civil bill, and especially of the enforcement amendment of the Senate. The conference adopted the Enforcement bill as a part of the report, but amended it in several important particulars. These modifications did not pacify either party to the House dead-lock. They emasculated the bill to such an extent as to render it practically useless so far as its original purpose was concerned. while the Democrats objected to retaining any portion or semblance whatsoever. So the latter immediately began to filibuster as upon Saturday afternoon. Several dilatory motions were entertained, when Mr. KELLEY to the general surprise, moved to recommit the conference report. He then rather dramatically charged that the Enforcement bill was as portion of conference report under false pretenses, such as would have made a penal offense on the part of those responsible for it under the laws of his native State. Mr. KELLEY explained that he understood the Democrats to have accepted a conference on Saturday evening, only because one of the Senate conferers had come upon the floor and promised that the conference would recede from the objectionable Senate amendment, and because Mr. GARFIELD had intimated that he would favor such receding. Mr. KELLEY further confessed that he had himself pledged the other side of the House, if not that the conference would recede, at least that he would use his influence to make the majority of the House recede. What his object was in doing this he did not state, although he subsequently dropped remarks which indicated that he was opposed to the Enforcement bill itself, as well as to the manner in which it had been brought before the House. Mr. KELLEY'S motion was therefore made in redemption of a pledge, and, as he said, to vindicate his self-respect.

Mr. GARFIELD urged that the question was before the House in a perfectly legitimate and proper manner. There had been only five parliamentary methods of bringing the Appropriation bill before the House; and he, as Chairman of the Committee, had proposed each one of these methods in turn. The minority had filibustered against each, thus indicating plainly that they proposed to prevent any action whatever being taken. Mr. GARFIELD considered such a course equivalent to a parliamentary revolution utterly unprecedented and unjustiable on the part of the minority. It was simply preventing all action one way or the other.

Mr. BINGHAM took the same view. The eleventh hour talk of the Democrats about the constitutional restrictions was wholly irrelevant, because there was nothing in the amendment which had not been for two years on the statute-books, and ten days ago he had offered the other side every opportunity to debate the bill at length, and their solid vote had declined. Judge BINGHAM said he had no doubt on the score of unconstitutionality, but he did think that the attempt of the Democrats to prevent such legislation as the majority was ready to take the responsibility for, was the inauguration of a treason as disreputable, as dishonorable, and as disgraceful as that other treason on the same floor twelve years ago.

DISORDERLY CONDUCT.

Several Democrats called Judge BINGHAM to order for this language. He repeated it, not to be misunderstood, with even greater emphasis, and Gen. MORGAN, of Ohio, in his peculiar braggadocio and loud-mouthed manner, pronounced the statement "a damnable, disgraceful lie," and several other things equally obnoxious, but whose exact tenor was lost in the rattle of the gavel and the indescribable confusion which ensued upon the floor. A dozen gentlemen demanded that the language be taken down and ruled upon by the Speaker, and several motions were made to arrest both BINGHAM and MORGAN. Both gentlemen took it very coolly, considering the tempest of excitement and ill-temper which surged around them. MORGAN was ruled out of order at once, he having no claim to the floor, and the Speaker also decided that BINGHAM'S language was unparliamentary.

SENATORIAL ENCROACHMENTS.

After this episode, Mr. BINGHAM finished his speech in order, and Mr. KELLEY took the floor to close the debate. In calling the previous question on his motion to recommit, he made some remarks of grave import. He condemned without reservation the principle involved in attaching this character of legislation to an Appropriation bill, and he warned the House and country against the gradual tendency of the Senate to encroachments of power. He cited the cases of the Revenue bills of the past Winter, sent to the House by the Senate, as evidence of that tendency; he comforted the Democrats by citing Republican resistance sixteen years ago by the same means to a pro-slavery rider to the Army Appropriation bill which resulted in an extra session. The motion to recommit was then carried—yeas 99, nays 79. Among those favoring a recommittal, which was equivalent to instructions to recede from the enforcement resolution, were eighteen Republicans. Anxiety to prevent an extra session seemed to be the prevailing object of these eighteen gentlemen in receding, although it was clear that some of them voted because of objection to the bill itself.

EXTENSION OF THE SESSION.

By this time it was nearly 11 o'clock, and very clear that the hour of final adjournment would arrive before it would be possible to make and adopt a conference report which dropped the Enforcement amendment. Judge KELLEY, therefore, introduced a resolution extending the time of adjournment until 6 this evening. This passed by the very large vote of 131 to 31, which indicated the relative anxiety of the members to avoid an extra session, if possible. The minority was led by Gen. BUTLER, and was composed chiefly of Southern Republicans and some others who have made up their minds to pass the three political bills now pending if it takes all Summer.

A COMPROMISE.

While they were filibustering on a motion to reconsider, the Senate had acted upon the resolution, and returned it just twenty minutes before 12. Shortly afterward, the House took a recess until 2½ o'clock, to await the second conference report. At that hour the Committee again reported an utter disagreement, when the House resolved to adhere to the disagreement and ask a new conference, reappointing, however, the same Committee as before, viz.: GARFIELD, PALMER, and NIBLACK. When the Senate received this request, it immediately reappointed its old Committee. In the mean time, Gen. GARFIELD had been over among the Democrats in the House to see if there were any terms which they would accept. Finally, Mr. KERR, of Indiana, took the bill, and made a modification of one portion, providing that the supervisors should have no power to make any arrests or interfere in any other way with the regular officers of election except to remain at the polls and watch the voting and the making up of the returns. This, he said, if agreed to, would induce the Democrats to cease factious opposition, though they could not be expected to vote for it. Gen. GARFIELD submitted this to EDMUNDS and BUTLER privately, who said it was all right. EDMUNDS resisted the modification in Committee, but finally yielded reluctantly, laughing in his sleeve at what the Democracy had asked for, the same limitations as to power being already in the existing bill. But at 5 o'clock the report was made to the Senate, and, almost without debate, it was agreed to—yeas 39, nays 17.

INEFFECTUAL FILIBUSTERING.

In the mean time the House had extended the session until 9 o'clock, and at 5:40 the Senate concurred. Then Gen. GARFIELD brought the report before the House, and explanations followed from himself, from Mr. KERR, and Mr. NIBLACK, of Indiana, and from Mr. POTTER, of New-York. The Democrats disclaimed all idea of consenting to the bill, but declared they would filibuster no longer. The Republicans kept quiet, except Mr. GOODRICH, of New-York, who is opposed to the bill, and who thought he saw that the concession was a sham. ELDRIDGE and HOLMAN refused to be bound by the promise not to filibuster, and started a raid on their own account, which was speedily stamped out, as there were but twenty members at their back. The rules were then suspended, and the conference report was then agreed to—yeas 102, nays 79. That ended the contest, and rendered the final adjournment certain at 9 o'clock, so that at 7¼ the House ordered a recess until 8¼.

THE EXTRA SESSION PROCLAMATION.

One strong impelling force which induced the Democrats to yield the fight was the fact, not publicly admitted, that the President stood ready with a proclamation to reconvene Congress within a half hour after the session if the Appropriation bill failed. He first prepared the proclamation for 12½, and when the time was extended he changed it to 6½ o'clock, so that members would scarcely have gotten out of their seats before they would be back in them again under the Presidential mandate. The Democracy would not confess to any dread of this, but they felt it strongly nevertheless.

A HARD HIT.

One of the hardest hits received by any member this session was given by Gen. GARFIELD, this afternoon, to Gen. FARNSWORTH, during the discussion of the Sundry Civil Appropriation bill. FARNSWORTH was evidently provoked because the Conference Committee had cut out all the legislation with which he had attempted to hedge in MULLETT, the Supervising Architect of the Treasury. He took up the item of $15,000 for introducing shad and salmon into the waters of the United States, which has been secured through the joint efforts of Prof. BAIRD and Mr. GEORGE SHEPARD PAGE, of the American Fish Culturists' Association. This FARNSWORTH made fun of, and suggested that next there should be a commission on bull heads, to which FOSTER of Ohio added for FARNSWORTH'S benefit, suckers. Here GARFIELD gravely observed that FARNSWORTH'S discomfort all came from the fact that there was too much appropriated for mulletts, which set the House in a roar, and FARNSWORTH subsided. Mr. FARNSWORTH today introduced the bill abolishing the franking privilege, which was defeated early in the session. He expressed an anxiety to discover whether there was any sincerity in the professions of the Philadelphia platform. He was enlightened to the entire satisfaction of everybody, the vote standing 126 in favor, to 29 against. Of the latter, only twelve were Republican votes.

THE DAY IN THE SENATE.

The Senate met today at 8 o'clock. The day was practically spent waiting for the House to propose some action on the Sundry Civil Appropriation bill. But in the meantime a great many private bills and other bills of minor importance were taken up and disposed of in some manner, and many of them were passed. There were some sharp passages of debate and some funny scenes. Mr. CHANDLER at one time having the seeming purpose to talk against time to force an adjournment at noon, gave an account of the conference at the New-York Hotel, at which it was agreed by certain Democratic Senators and Republicans that a new party should be organized, and a Republican should be nominated by it for President. FENTON pressed him to name the Republican Senator alluded to, and several Democrats professed ignorance of any such transaction, and desired to know what Democratic Senator he meant. Gen. BLAIR said nothing but smiled in a mysterious way, which might mean much or little. Senators MORTON, EDMUNDS, FRELINGHUYSEN, MORRILL of Maine, and others, persuaded CHANDLER, POOL and FLANNAGAN in turn to drop the debate and let the time of adjournment be extended, which was done only in the minute of time to save an extra session. The Senate having got the Apportionment bill off its hands, by agreeing to the conference report, took a recess from 6 till 8 o'clock, adjournment having once more been extended till 9 o'clock, the hour from 8 to 9 was spent as the last hour of sessions is usually spent, and the appropriate formalities having been observed, the presiding officer, Mr. ANTHONY, at 9 o'clock, declared adjournment without date. Among the items of the Appropriation bill passed today was one authorizing the Joint Committee on the Library to purchase of Mr. THOMAS MORAN his painting of the "Grand Canon of the Yellowstone," at a cost of $10,000. It will be placed permanently in the Capitol.

EXECUTIVE BUSINESS.

The President occupied the whole day, save three hours, at the Capitol, in the room where he transacts Executive business, accompanied by his Cabinet, Gen. BABCOCK, Mr. LUCKEY, Assistant Private Secretary, and Mr. SNIFFEN, Executive Clerk. The proclamation convening Congress in extra session at 12½ o'clock, in case of the failure of the Appropriation bill, was ready for delivery, but the extension of the time at 11:40 until 6 o'clock required a change in the proclamation. The President quietly directed that 6½ o'clock should be inserted, and this fact had much to do with bringing the recalcitrant filibusters to terms. They became satisfied that the President would call an extra session, and hence became much more tractable. At 5½ the time was again extended until 9 o'clock, but the proclamation was not again changed, as it had become evident by that time that an agreement would be reached during the day.

HOW THE LETTER OF ACCEPTANCE WAS WRITTEN.

At 1 o'clock the President returned to the Executive Mansion, where he met Judge SETTLE and the Committee appointed to inform him of his nomination. As an instance of the remarkable nerve and readiness with which the President meets every exigency of his public or official life, it may be stated that, soon after he had returned to his room at the Senate, surrounded as he was by Cabinet officers, Secretaries and Senators running in and out, he sat down and wrote the letter of acceptance, and which contains, as a prominent Senator expressed it, a platform in every sentence. It was supposed that he would have waited for a quieter moment, but that could have yielded no more terse or pregnant utterances than did the moment of confusion in which the letter was so happily written.

## THE REFORMED SYNOD.

### The New-Brunswick Seminary Once More—Acrimonious Debate and Bitter Personalities—Dr. Anderson's Speech.

The General Synod of the Reformed Church in America resumed its sessions yesterday morning in the Harrison-street Church, Brooklyn. Dr. ELMENDORFF presided. After the religious services the report of the Committee on the Professorate, concerning the New-Brunswick Theological Seminary, which has been the cause of so much rather acrimonious debate, was again called up.

Dr. ANDERSON, of the Professorate Committee, opened the debate on the much-vexed seminary question. He charged Dr. VERMILYE with making false charges against the Committee, and having further befogged the subject by attacking their motives. He again denied the statement that the Committee had asked for the professors' resignations, and said that Dr. VERMILYE'S whole speech was ungentlemanly, and he did not mean to submit to it. It was insulting for him to say that the resolutions were written by the hand of Joab, who was a traitor and murderer, implying that the writer was a murderer of reputations and a conspirator against character. He characterized the doctor's speech as senseless rigmarole, and said that the gentleman who made it would have been more congenially employed defending the New-York Ring. "But," said the speaker, "enough of this rubbish; I will leave the low insinuations and the mean insinuator in order to consider the merits of the case." Dr. ANDERSON then proceeded to criticise the conduct of the seminary, and read several letters from students and others of a very personal nature, announcing that they were some of those which had been read before the Committee. Some of them accused the professors of utter incompetency, and one of them spoke of a certain professor as writing like "a cold, stupid-headed icicle."

Here some one rose and asked the speaker for the names of the writers, but he refused positively, and on the request being repeated, told the gentleman to "wait till he got it."

A delegate said that as the report of the Committee had been printed, and most of the members can read, the doctor was exercising himself unnecessarily. The doctor continued his reading, however, saying that one correspondent had stated that the present professors are sinking the ship, that new men are needed, and that the institution is become a "theological ice-house." Another says that these students for the Christian ministry are surrounded by teachers who do not live together in peace, and that the lectures are fitted for soft-headed infants. One communication vouches for the fact that a student was so dissatisfied that he went to a seminary of another denomination, where he was kindly received. The speaker urged the members to do all they can to improve the "factory," (so he called it,) saying that an entirely new factory should be placed in charge, the present one having failed, and not having shown themselves deserving of confidence. The speaker concluded by denouncing the author of an anonymous circular on the subject, that had been circulated, he said, for electioneering purposes and to create a false impression. The time for adjournment having come the meeting dispersed.

Last evening, Rev. RUFUS W. CLARKE, D. D., of Albany, preached the annual sermon before the Convention, on the subject of "Benevolence." The attendance in the Middle Reformed Church, where the services were held, was quite large.

## MURDERED AT MIDNIGHT.

### A German Citizen Killed by a Gang of Ruffians in Division-Street.

The terrible murder of Mr. AUGUST BROWN, the German gentleman, who, while returning to his residence, No. 78 Lewis-street, with his wife, from the theatre, on Saturday night, was stricken down and killed by a gang of roughs at the corner of Division and Lewis streets, is being investigated by the Police and Coroner YOUNG. The facts of the murder are few and simple. In Division-street Mr. BROWN and his wife were approached by a gang of young thieves and ruffians. One of them rudely pushed against Mrs. BROWN, at the same time making use of a most vile epithet. BROWN, turning round, began pulling off his coat with a view of punishing the ruffian. While doing so, one of the fellows struck him a terrible blow from behind. He staggered and fell on his back to the sidewalk. The back of his head struck the sidewalk, and the base of his skull was fractured. Mrs. BROWN seeing her husband unconscious, and, as she thought, dead, shouted, "Murder; help." To quiet her outcry, some other roughs who had arrived at the scene proposed to help her to carry the inanimate body of her husband to her residence. They did, and left her. The Thirteenth Precinct Police learned of the affair, and an ambulance being sent for, Mr. Brown was removed to Bellevue Hospital. He never regained consciousness, but gradually sinking, died at 3 o'clock on Sunday morning, a short time after his admission to the hospital. In this respect the conduct of the officials at the hospital is reprehensible and extremely unaccountable. Although Mr. BROWN died at 3 o'clock A. M. on Sunday morning, no notification was sent from the hospital to the Coroner's office until late yesterday afternoon.

The fullest investigation will be made. Capt. MCDONNELL, of the Thirteenth Precinct, with his detectives arrested three noted roughs—JOHN SMITH, who a few months ago stabbed a man in Water-street, and two brothers, named RICHARD and JOHN ALLISON. SMITH was brought before Mrs. BROWN, and she partially identified him as the man who had struck her husband. The ALLISONS admitted being present when the murder was committed, but denied being concerned in its perpetration. In order to give Capt. MCDONNELL time to secure positive evidence, which he is engaged in collecting, Coroner YOUNG has not as yet fixed a day on which the inquest will be held.

## THE CUSTOM-HOUSE.

### Report of the Minority of the Investigating Committee.

WASHINGTON, D. C. June 10.—The views of Senators BAYARD and CASSERLY, constituting a minority of the Committee appointed to investigate alleged abuses in the New-York Custom-house, are set forth at length in a paper submitted by them to the Senate today, which comprises about 180 pages of manuscript, besides a large amount of printed testimony incorporated therewith. They state that any incompleteness which may be found in their review of the extended investigation and of the two thousand two hundred printed pages of testimony relating to varied and important objects, may be accounted for by the circumstances attending the submission of the report of the majority, which, they allege, was, to their surprise, prepared and presented without consultation with the minority, who have, therefore, they state, had no reasonable opportunity to examine and sift the report, but only to obtain a summary view of its conclusions, from which they are, in the main, compelled entirely to dissent. The minority adduce the testimony of great numbers of leading merchants of New-York, the depositions of various importers, the statements of LEET & STOCKING themselves, and find that the statements of all these parties prove that the excessive extortions under the General Order business, after it had become a monopoly in the hands of LEET & STOCKING, were intensified so that there could be no doubt whatever, from the proof submitted that the system, as conducted by LEET & STOCKING, under the privilege of Collector MURPHY, was a monstrous abuse and a scandalous system of robbery. The report proceeds at great length in an endeavor to connect the President with Custom-house abuses. The tenure of good behavior is strongly recommended and argued, and the minority report closes with the statement that the evils so wide-spread and thorough, which have been discovered, show that no department of the public service in the Custom-house inquired into by the Committee, is free from the taint of demoralization and corruption which the rule of MURPHY has necessarily entailed upon them. The evil is not so much in bad laws, although the repeal of the law of seizures is recommended, but in the maladministration of laws growing out of the utter unfitness and incompetency of those who have been placed in high places of civil government.

### Fire in the Caisson.

A fire broke out yesterday in the caisson of the East River Bridge, on the New-York side. As soon as the fact was discovered a stream of water was let on into the chamber where the flame existed, and the danger is now deemed to be over. The origin of the fire is a mystery, as the interior of the caisson is lighted with gas. It is supposed that some of the gas-pipes leaked—hence the flame. The amount of damage done is unknown, as the men in charge were very reticent.

## THE REPUBLICAN CANDIDATES

### Gen. Grant Officially Notified of His Renomination.

### His Letter of Acceptance—A Characteristic Document—Interesting Report of the Interviews with the President and Gen. Wilson—Speech of the Latter—His Relations with Mr. Colfax.

WASHINGTON, June 10.—The following is a copy of the official letter notifying President GRANT of his nomination, which was handed him by the President of the Philadelphia Convention:

WASHINGTON, June 10.

*To the President:*

SIR: In pursuance of our instructions we, the undersigned President and Vice-Presidents of the National Republican Convention held in Philadelphia on the 5th and 6th inst., have the honor to inform you of your nomination for re-election to the office of President of the United States. As it is impossible to give an adequate idea of the enthusiasm which prevailed, or the unanimity which hailed you as the choice of the people, we can only add that you received the entire vote of every State and Territory.

Regarding your re-election as necessary to the peace and continued prosperity of the country, we ask your acceptance of the nomination.

THOMAS SETTLE,
President of the National Republican Convention.

Paul Strabach, of Alabama; Elisha Baxter, of Arkansas; C. A. Sargent, of California; Sabin L. Sage, of Connecticut; Isaac Jump, of Delaware; Benj. Conley, of Georgia, Vice Presidents. Emory A. Storrs, of Illinois; Gen. Solomon D. Meredith, of Indiana; W. H. Seeves, of Iowa; John C. Carpenter, of Kansas; R. M. Kelley, of Kentucky; Lewis Frasier, of Louisiana; F. F. Rohey, of Maine; Thomas Kelso, of Maryland; A. H. Rice, of Massachusetts; Eber B. Ward, of Michigan; C. T. Benedict, of Minnesota; R. W. Flannery, of Mississippi; J. F. Benjamin, of Missouri; John S. Bowen, of Nebraska; W. H. Y. Hackett, New-Hampshire; Dudley S. Gregory, New-Jersey; H. B. Claflin, New-York; Edward Cantwell, North Carolina; Jacob C. Muehler, Ohio; John F. Booth, Oregon; H. W. Oliver, Pennsylvania; Gen. A. E. Burnside, Rhode Island; A. J. Ramsier, South Carolina; Wm. H. Wisner, Tennessee; A. B. Norton, Texas; J. Fairbanks, Vermont; Charles J. Malord, Virginia; Charles Horton, West Virginia; Gen. Lucius Fairchild, Wisconsin; Dennis Egan, Florida; George M. Chilcott, Colorado; John F. Cook, District of Columbia; John R. McBride, Idaho; John W. Donnellon, Wyoming; J. F. Hollister, Utah; F. Breeden, New-Mexico; L. B. Church, Montana.

EXECUTIVE MANSION, WASHINGTON, D. C., June 10, 1872.

*Hon. Thomas Settle, President National Republican Convention; Paul Strabach, Elisha Baxter, C. A. Sargeant, and others, Vice-Presidents:*

GENTLEMEN: Your letter of this date, advising me of the action of the Convention held in Philadelphia, Penn., on the 5th and 6th of this month, and of my unanimous nomination for the Presidency by it, is received.

I accept the nomination, and through you return my heartfelt thanks to your constituents for this mark of their confidence and support.

If elected in November, and protected by a kind Providence in health and strength to perform the duties of the high trust conferred, I promise the same zeal and devotion to the good of the whole people for the future of my official life as shown in the past. Past experience may guide me in avoiding mistakes inevitable with novices in all professions and in all occupations.

When relieved from the responsibilities of my present trust, by the election of a successor, whether it be at the end of this term or next, I hope to leave to him as Executive a country at peace within its own borders, at peace with outside nations, with a credit at home and abroad, and without embarrassing questions to threaten its future prosperity.

With the expression of a desire to see a speedy healing of all bitterness of feeling between sections, parties or races of citizens, and the time when the title of citizen carries with it all the protection and privileges to the humblest that it does to the most exalted,

I subscribe myself, very respectfully, your obedient servant, U. S. GRANT.

### Details of the Interview with President Grant and Senator Wilson.

WASHINGTON, June 10.—Pursuant to a notice, Judge SETTLE, of North Carolina, President of the National Republican Convention, and the Vice-Presidents for the several States and Territories, met at the Ebbitt House at noon today, to take action in regard to officially notifying President GRANT and Senator WILSON of their nominations at Philadelphia. Judge SETTLE and most of the Vice-Presidents were present. An arrangement had been previously made with the President to meet him at 8 o'clock this evening, but as many of the gentlemen residing in distant States desired to take the evening train for home, Judge SETTLE and several of the Vice-Presidents waited on the President at the Capitol, and requested that he would fix an earlier hour. He accordingly fixed 1 o'clock P. M., and at that hour was at the White House, awaiting the arrival of the officers of the Convention. The latter arrived at about 1½, and were shown into the President's private office. The President came in a moment later, when each of the delegates was introduced by Judge SETTLE. After the ceremony of introduction had been performed, Judge SETTLE said:

MR. PRESIDENT: We are before you to perform a very agreeable duty. We are here to officially inform you of your unanimous nomination for the Presidency by the National Republican Convention, assembled in Philadelphia on the 6th inst. Beyond this I do not know that we have anything to say.

Here Judge SETTLE handed the President the letter officially notifying him of his nomination.

The President said:

GENTLEMEN: I am not now ready to respond to your letter, but will take an early opportunity to do so in writing.

Judge SETTLE—Yes, sir, your answer, I presume, should be addressed to me.

Mr. STORRS, of Illinois—I wish the President of the Convention would tell President GRANT what a superb convention we had. I have never seen anything to equal it.

Judge SETTLE—I confess I am unequal to the task and consequently I must decline. Suppose you do it.

The PRESIDENT—That is a speech to which I could appropriately respond. It is short and to the point.

Judge SETTLE—I am quite sure I should fail if I attempted anything like a description of the Convention. It cannot be described. The enthusiasm, the unanimity, the solid vote of every State cannot be adequately described, even in the public prints. The President himself must have been present to fully appreciate the Convention. What we now want to do especially is to tell the President what we intend to do in November.

PAUL STROBACH—Mr. President, as a Vice-President of the National Convention, and as a representative of the Germans of America, I pledge Alabama for you in November, with as handsome a majority as in 1868, and the overwhelming vote of the 800,000 German voters in the United States.

The PRESIDENT—It is certainly gratifying to me to learn that, after holding office for three years—never having before held a political office, and never having been a candidate for nomination—I have been indorsed by my former supporters. This is something I cannot forget. I am, of course, very grateful.

Gen. SOLOMON D. MEREDITH said: The nomination of President GRANT is unprecedented in the history of the United States. In the Philadelphia Convention every Congressional District was represented and every delegate cast his vote for you, Mr. President. I have been present at other Republican Conventions. I was present when you, Mr. President, were first nominated, and I can say unhesitatingly that I never before saw such an overwhelming unanimity as was exhibited at Philadelphia. It is very flattering to you, Mr. And now let me say for Indiana that she will give you fifteen electoral votes. I will not say anything about the precise majority, but I am sure of fifteen electoral votes.

The PRESIDENT—At any rate don't let your people vote more than once. [Laughter.]

Gen. MEREDITH—No, we propose to give you the State by a handsome majority by allowing each voter in the State to vote once only.

B. F. CONLEY, the Georgia Vice-President, said: We will do the best we can for you.

The PRESIDENT—That is as much as Georgia can do. [Laughter.]

Gen. JOHN F. BENJAMIN, of Missouri—You know, as well as I do, Mr. President, that disaffection has existed in the ranks of the Republican Party in Missouri, but let me assure you that the disaffection is very slight. We propose to do now as we did in 1868, and will do our duty at the polls.

Gov. FAIRCHILD, on behalf of Wisconsin, pledged the President a handsome majority, as did the Vice-President, from Michigan, and CHARLES J. MELORD, (colored,) of Virginia. The latter put down Virginia for 50,000 for GRANT.

Mr. A. D. NORTON, of Texas, said—If Mr. GREELEY should be indorsed in Baltimore, Texas will give you her electoral vote. Every loyal man will support you, inasmuch as they have already surrendered to you.

Mr. WILLIAM H. WISNER, of Tennessee—I promise you, Mr. President, that we will make a gallant fight in Tennessee. There are a good many of the Southern Democracy in my State, who, if they are called upon to give up their organization to GREELEY and BROWN, would prefer to surrender to you as they did in 1865.

A CALL ON SENATOR WILSON.

The delegation then took their leave and proceeded to the Capitol to wait on Senator WILSON. They met him in the room of the Senate Committee on Military Affairs.

Judge SETTLE, addressing Senator WILSON, said he had a very grateful duty to perform, under instructions of the Philadelphia National Convention, and handed him a letter informing him of his nomination for the Vice-Presidency, and added he was sure he could not, even if he attempted, give an idea of the enthusiasm which prevailed at the Convention.

Senator WILSON made the following impromptu reply:

I will, in a day or two, give you an answer in writing to this communication. I take this occasion, however, to thank you and the members of the Convention you represent for this manifestation of confidence. As I neither asked nor wrote to any member of the Convention to give me a vote, I am all the more grateful for their generous support. I am gratified, too, for the friendly tone of the Republican Press of the country. For thirty-six years, in public life and in private life, I have striven to maintain the distinguishing ideas of the Republican Party—the freedom and equality of all men. I have striven ever to be true to my country and to the rights of our common humanity, to know no sectional interest, nor race, nor color. In the future, as in the past, I shall unfalteringly adhere to those principles which are the convictions of my judgment, heart and conscience. I am clearly of the opinion that the great soldier, who rendered such illustrious services to the country in the great civil war, will be re-elected President of the United States. His humanity to the vanquished, his firmness to vindicate the rights of the humble and defenceless, and his devotion to the leading ideas of the Republican Party cannot be questioned. I esteem it a high honor to be associated with him in the coming contest. While I am grateful to the friends who gave me such generous support, I honor those who adhered with such devotion to Mr. COLFAX. We have been personal and political friends for nearly twenty years, and it is a source of profound satisfaction to me that our personal relations have not been disturbed by the recent contest. While I shall never cease to feel grateful to friends who honored me by their support, I shall ever entertain sincere respect for those who deemed it to be their duty to give their support to others. I hope we shall all strive to win to our support every honest and patriotic man in the country, every man true to the rights of humanity, every man who would elevate the condition of the toiling millions, and have our Republic become a great Christian nation, an example to the world. Let it be understood that our ranks are wide open to receive all devoted to the country, and who would advance the happiness and general well-being of all sections of the land and all conditions of the people. We, Republicans, should offer the hand of reconciliation to all fair-minded and honorable men and use all legitimate means to achieve success, for the honor and salvation of the country, as well as for that of the party which saved the Union and established freedom in every part of the land.

## THE BUELL RECORDS.

### Report of the Committee on Military Affairs—No Evidence that the Missing Documents Ever Reached the Adjutant-General's Office.

WASHINGTON, D. C., June 10.—The House Committee on Military Affairs today made a report, saying the object of the resolution was twofold: First—To investigate as to the loss of the papers in the matter of the Buell Court of Inquiry, and who is responsible therefor. Second—To inquire generally as to the preservation of the records of the War Department. The Committee have examined a large number of witnesses as to the first point, who might have a knowledge of those papers and their loss or abstraction, and find no trace as to where the papers of the Court of Inquiry are or may be. The evidence shows that they came into the possession of the War Department on the 15th of May, 1867, and for a time to have remained in the office of the Judge-Advocate-General; and also, to have been taken in part at one time to the office of the Adjutant-General. But they were at the time of deposit in the office of the Judge-Advocate-General not a proper part of the records of that office. The evidence shows they were brought to this city in a trunk, and were left while in the latter offices in the trunk until taken out to be carried to the office of the Adjutant-General. There seems to have begun the obscurity as to the care and keeping and the subsequent loss. Judge HOLT, on this point, says: The first error with regard to these records was in their being sent to this office at all. They did not pertain to the Judge-Advocate-General's office, and it should have been returned without delay. The only explanation is the amount of business. There is no evidence that they all ever reached the office of the Adjutant-General, and the weight of evidence is that they have never been put on file there. The Adjutant-General testifies that his official records show only the receipt of the opinion of the Court of Inquiry, and nothing more. Nothing appears as to the testimony of the proceedings of the Court. There is some evidence going to show that the papers were sent over from the office of the Judge Advocate-General, but it is obscure. The papers in the office of the Adjutant General are kept with scrupulous care. Complete memoranda and indexes are provided, and whatever is filed there is so noted, marked and arranged as to be easily found, or if taken away its absence can be accounted for. The only papers remaining on file in connection with the matter, is the finding or opinion of the Court. This document is found on file in the office of the Secretary of War. There is nothing in any office to show the presence or absence of any other paper in connection with the case. No blame seems to attach to any particular officer, person or employe for the loss. Gen. WALLACK, the President of the Court of Inquiry, and Gen. BUELL himself were examined as to the point whether any one who may have had possession of these papers was interested or influenced by any motive to destroy them, and especially whether the President or Gen. SHERMAN could have such an inducement, and both exonerated those officers from such a charge or suspicion. The Committee found that BEN PITTMAN, Esq., of Cincinnati, has his full notes in good preservation, and recommended unanimously the passage of a bill, which became a law, authorizing a transcript to be filed in the War Department so as to supply the loss of the original papers. The Committee have also found that Gen. BUELL has complete letter-press copies of the testimony. The other branch of the inquiry relates to the case generally of papers and records in the War Department. In this matter the Committee find that the letter-books of the army, and particularly the letter-book of Gen. HALLECK, have been mutilated. Leaves have been torn out, and in some places the stubs are marked as private or personal, and in the blank back leaves of some others there is a memorandum signed by an officer of Gen. HALLECK'S staff, ROBERT N. SCOTT, that they were torn out for the reason that they were personal and confidential letters, and taken out by order of Gen. HALLECK. The Committee have examined the indexes which are not full, to ascertain whether the last letters were, as stated, private, and find that in some instances they were, but cannot at present express an opinion as to what were the contents of these letters, since many of them were not indexed, and many others have but a slight memorandum indicating their character. A large number of them seem to have been on official business of the [illegible] importance, and necessarily of value as public historical documents. The testimony concurs in showing that these mutilations were made by order or by permission of Gen. HALLECK, and before they came into the hands of the [illegible] of the War Department. The Committee will hope to be able to procure additional facts from the testimony of the staff officers of Gen. HALLECK.

A complete list of these letters has been made out by the Adjutant-General, and is embodied in the testimony.

The Committee also ascertained that, by order of Gen. RAWLINS, late Secretary of War, a number of letters and documents were taken from the files of the War Department, and delivered to Gen. ADAM BADEAU, who was at the time writing a history of the war. An exact list of these is made out by the Adjutant-General. These letters were all of an official character and important in their nature, and are about 207 in number. As nearly as can be ascertained they appear to have been merely letters, and not reports of army operations and results. These latter were formal and lengthy documents, and are now all on file in the office of the Adjutant-General, there being no testimony of the loss or abstraction of any regular reports of army operations. The lost letters have been proven to have been sent to England, but whether they were returned to this country or not by Gen. BADEAU does not appear. They have not been returned to the files of the War Department. They are known perfectly by the notes, indexes and memoranda in the office of the Adjutant-General. The Committee have examined, as to the care, preservation and method of keeping the various records of the War Department, the Secretary of War, his chief clerk, the Adjutant-General, the Judge-Advocate-General, the Quartermaster-General, the Commissary-General, the Acting Chief of the Ordnance, the Paymaster-General, the Chief of the Engineers, the Surgeon-General, and a large number of clerks, and find that the records under their charge are in good order and well preserved; that the papers on file are noted with proper numbers and indorsements and are kept in regular files, with accurate memoranda and indexes by which they can, with facility, be found and identified, and that there are no papers lost, mislaid or missing, except such as have been mutilated.

The Committee are satisfied that the records and papers of the War Department are kept and preserved faithfully and carefully. The Committee ask further time to investigate the matter of the loss of the papers and documents, believing that further light may be thrown upon the subject by the examination of witnesses, who cannot be reached at this session of Congress.

## A TRIPLE TRAGEDY.

### An Italian Shoots His Wife and Her Brother—The Latter Wounds the Assassin in the Eleventh Ward Station-House—The Woman and Her Spouse Dangerously Wounded.

The quiet of that usually sober and respectable portion of the City, the Eleventh Ward, was broken last night by a shooting affray of a most desperate and horrifying character, the occasion being intense jealousy on the part of an injured husband, who sought revenge for his wrongs by shooting his wife.

CAROLINE MARGRAF, a German girl eighteen years of age, in January formed the acquaintance of CARLO J. MAGGIORI, an Italian painter. He paid his addresses to her, and, it seems, represented that he was worth some $2,000. Miss MARGRAF after marrying MAGGIORI about the middle of January, left him in disgust, a month ago, and refused to be reconciled to him. This was owing to the fact soon discovered after her marriage, that he was not only poor but a confirmed drunkard, and wife-beater. During the brief term of her wedded life she was compelled to support both her husband and herself by needle-work. On leaving MAGGIORI a month ago, she went back to her mother's house, and remained there. MAGGIORI yesterday morning sent a note to her mother's house, asking the girl to meet him at the rooms they had occupied while living together as man and wife, and which are on the second floor of No. 415 East Houston-street, within a few yards of the Eleventh Precinct Station-house, when they would arrange matters so that a divorce could be procured by mutual agreement. The girl went, taking her brother LOUIS MARGRAF, who is twenty-one years old, that he might protect her from insult and be a witness to any proposition which MAGGIORI would make. Before leaving the house the brother took a small Smith & Wesson revolver from the mantel-piece and put it in his pocket. She had an audience with MAGGIORI in her brother's presence in the rooms. The conference was not a pleasant one, and harsh language was used by both parties. At length MAGGIORI saw that the results to be attained were not what be desired, and said to his wife: "Let us go downstairs, CAROLINE, into the cool air, and we can fix this affair." She left the room with him, and the brother, fearing foul play, crept down the stairs after them. He stopped in the door-way, and MAGGIORI, putting his right arm around the girl's neck, with his left hand drew from a side-pocket a Lefaucheux self-cocking revolver, and fired at her. The ball entered her left breast in an oblique direction, passing toward the centre of the sternum. She fell in the hallway, saying, "Dear God, I am murdered." The brother sprang from the stairway, through the hall, and was in the act of seizing MAGGIORI, when the latter turned and fired upon him twice. One ball smashed the fingers of his left hand, but the other passed through his left jaw, fracturing the molar bone and lodging in his head. The brother staggered for a moment, and MAGGIORI, seeing that he had wounded him, turned and ran up Houston-street. MARGRAF in an instant recovered his nerve, and chased him, drawing his own revolver, and firing at the flying assassin as he ran. The chase continued but a few seconds, the firing going on all the while. MAGGIORI, finding that he was being rapidly overtaken and likely to be shot down, turned quickly round the corner of Union Market and dashed up the steps leading into the Eleventh Precinct Station-house. Young MARGRAF was close upon him, and as MAGGIORI ran up the stairway, fired on him twice. The last shot entered MAGGIORI'S right loin, just at the line of the kidneys. By this time the noise of the firing had awakened a Police Sergeant, named MILLER, who was on duty in the Station-house, and some officers were sent out to convey the wounded persons to the Station-house. Police Surgeon SAVILLE seeing that the case was a bad one, directed the nervous Sergeant to telegraph at once to Bellevue Hospital for ambulances. In a few minutes Warden BRENNAN and two ambulance surgeons with ambulances were at the Station-house. The wounds of MAGGIORI, his wife and her brother were not probed, it being deemed injudicious to defer all inquiry by means of instruments until the patients had reached the hospital. Enough was learned, however, to enable the statement to be made that MAGGIORI and his wife are in all probability fatally wounded, while the brother of the unfortunate girl is shot dangerously, but not in a necessarily fatal manner. The Police were singularly negligent in furnishing the facts in their possession, and were quite impudent when asked for them. Sergt. MILLER, who was in charge, delegated his duties to a special officer named BENNETT. It was noticeable that Capt. MURPHY, the Tammany appointee, had not been in his Station-house up to 10 o'clock last night, although the tragedy occurred two hours before.

## BY MAIL AND TELEGRAPH.

The President will leave Washington today, with his family, for Long Branch.

The Great Western steam-ship *Arragon* arrived at Bristol, England, on Sunday, from this port.

The steam-ship *Pereire*, Capt. DEURE, from New-York, June 1, arrived at Brest, France, last evening.

The United States steamer *Wachusett*, Commander C. H. CUSHMAN, arrived at Gibraltar on the 3d inst.

The Cunard steam-ship *Abyssinia*, from New-York, arrived at Queenstown at 12½ P. M. today, and sailed for Liverpool.

The Quincy (Ill.) *Whig* urges Hon. SCHUYLER COLFAX for a place in President GRANT'S Cabinet during his second term.

Hon. E. D. STANDIFORD is a leading candidate for the Democratic nomination for Congress in the Louisville, Ky., District.

The Montgomery correspondent of the Cincinnati *Commercial* writes that the negroes of Alabama present a solid front for GRANT.

Hon. JOHN H. GILMER, of Virginia, has written a strong letter giving his reasons why he will advocate the re-election of President GRANT.

Gen. BURNSIDE had a most cordial welcome to Norristown, Penn., on Saturday, by the old members of the *Fifty-first* Pennsylvania Regiment.

The Continental Hotel at Long Branch has been sold for $150,000 cash, which is one-third of its value, to Mr. BENNETT, for the LELANDS. It will open June 15.

Gov. HOFFMAN, yesterday, pardoned DAVID SILVERNAIL, who was convicted at Syracuse for burglary, and sentenced to three years imprisonment at Auburn.

Ten Democratic County Conventions thus far have been held in Georgia. Six unequivocally opposed indorsing GREELEY at Baltimore, and three were non-committal; only one indorsed GREELEY.

## TELEGRAPHIC NEWS.

### Earl Granville Promises Another Treaty Statement Today.

### Proposed Joint Note in Behalf of Roumanian Jews.

### Successes Claimed for the Revolutionists in Mexico.

### Sailing of a Supposed Cuban Privateer from Baltimore.

### Mr. Hendricks, of Indiana, Declines the Nomination for Governor.

GREAT BRITAIN.

*Another Treaty Statement in Parliament—The Ballot Bill in the House of Lords.*

LONDON, June 10.—Earl GRANVILLE will make a statement tomorrow in the House of Lords with regard to the negotiations for the amendment of the Treaty of Washington.

The Ballot bill passed to a second reading in the House of Lords to-night by a vote of 86 against 56, after a long debate.

THE JEWS IN ROUMANIA.

*An Effort for Joint European Action to Protect the Persecuted People.*

LONDON, June 10.—Earl GRANVILLE, seconded by the Italian Government, has proposed a conference of the European Powers to consider the course to be adopted in view of a constant recurrence of the barbarous outbursts against the Jews in Roumania, and the propriety of exerting a direct pressure on the Roumanian Government to compel preventive measures. Prince GORTSCHAKOFF in reply to Earl GRANVILLE'S proposal, sympathizes with the persecuted Jews, but apprehends that the course proposed would only excite agitation on the Eastern question, and that, therefore, he is not willing to enter into such a conference. He proposes a joint note to the Roumanian Government as to its intentions, and guarantees that it can afford protection to the Jews, and thinks that this would awaken it to some sense of its responsibilities. Should the reply to his proposal be unsatisfactory, he would suggest a settlement on the basis of the treaty of 1856. Prussia takes the same ground. The answers of the other Powers are not yet known, but it is probable that the suggestion of GORTSCHAKOFF will be adopted.

MEXICO.

*Monterey Recaptured by the Revolutionists.*

MATAMORAS, June 8.—The revolutionists, under QUIROGA, having recaptured Monterey on the 4th inst., before Gen. CEBALLOS could reach there with reinforcements, QUIROGA turned upon CEBALLOS with the whole of his force and compelled him to retreat to Mier, where he remained yesterday. It is believed today that CEBALLOS cannot remain in the field against the insurgents with his present force, and that he is retreating on Matamoras, to shelter himself behind the forts and the National Guards. Several of Gen. CEBALLOS' heavy guns have reached Reynosa, having been sent in advance, to prevent their retarding his retreat. Gen. QUIROGA'S force is estimated at 5,000, he having impressed into his service 1,500 prisoners captured from Gen. CORELLA in the engagement at Monterey. Gen. CEBALLOS issued a proclamation at Mier, yesterday, acknowledging the disaster at Monterey and the reoccupation of that place by the revolutionists, their advance upon his force, and indicating the probability of his retreat to this place, which is now being executed. Another siege of Matamoras is imminent, with the prestige of recent success in favor of the revolutionists.

*Remains of Corella's Force at Brownsville.*

BROWNSVILLE, Texas, June 10.—The steamer *San Juan* arrived here to-night from Camargo, which place she left yesterday afternoon, bringing Gen. CORELLA'S staff and twenty men, who are all of the Government force that escaped from the disaster at Monterey out of 4,000. Gen. CEVALLOS met the advance of QUIROGA'S army at Cevallo, on the 7th, and, after a slight engagement, retreated to Mier, and thence upon Camargo, closely pursued by the Revolutionists, which place he abandoned yesterday, and is in full retreat for Matamoras, with less than 2,000 men, while QUIROGA'S revolutionists are said to exceed 4,000. A small party of insurgents appeared today near Matamoras, and unless CEVALLOS reaches that place within one or two days, fears are entertained that the National Guard will pronounce.

Business is entirely suspended again in Matamoras, and the greatest anxiety prevails as to the result of the present defeat of the Government forces.

A CUBAN PRIVATEER.

*Departure of a Suspicious Steamer from Baltimore.*

BALTIMORE, Md., June 10.—The steamer, *Fannie*, which cleared from this port for Turks Island on Thursday last, had on board 200 tons of coal. The *Fannie* had been recently sold to the owner of the notorious steam-ship *Hornet*, and the crew of the latter vessel having been shipped on the *Fannie*, excited the suspicion of the Custom-house authorities here, and the ship was thoroughly searched before sailing. Nothing irregular was found on board. The *Fannie* was escorted by the revenue steamer *Northerner* from Baltimore, down the bay and outside the capes to a point seventy-five miles south-east of Cape Henry, and thirty-five miles from land. From the time of her leaving Baltimore, until parted with by the *Northerner*, the *Fannie* had no communication with any vessel or with the shore.

*The Fannie Takes on a Cargo.*

PROVIDENCE, R. I., June 10.—The steamer *Wilmington*, Capt. BROWN, at this port from Philadelphia, reports that on Sunday noon, off Barnegat, west by south thirty miles, saw the steamer *Fannie*, of New-York, taking cargo from an unknown schooner alongside. Afterward saw her move to another schooner and commence taking on board cargo from her. The steamer seemed to have many persons on board, both black and white.

INDIANA.

*The Coming Democratic State Convention.*

INDIANAPOLIS, Ind., June 10.—The hotels are already crowded with delegates to the Democratic State Convention, which will meet on Wednesday. It is authoritatively announced that Ex-Senator HENDRICKS declines the use of his name for the nomination for Governor. Hon. J. T. NIBLACK and Hon. M. C. KERR will be prominent candidates.

THE WEATHER.

*Synopsis and Probabilities.*

WASHINGTON, D. C., June 11—1 A. M.—The barometer is lower over New-England. It is higher over the Southern States. Clear and clearing weather is prevailing over the former, with light winds; clear weather very generally from the Middle and South Atlantic and Gulf coasts to the lakes, with light to fresh winds.

PROBABILITIES.

Clear weather will prevail on Tuesday over the New-England and Middle States, with light to fresh westerly winds, and over the Southern States, with light winds, and north and east of the Ohio Valley, with southerly winds, veering to westerly, except over the upper lake region, where partially cloudy weather prevails. Dangerous winds are not anticipated.

# The New-York Times.

VOL. XXI.......NO. 6470. NEW-YORK, FRIDAY, JUNE 14, 1872. PRICE FOUR CENTS.

## POLITICAL.

### Gen. Wilson's Letter Accepting the Philadelphia Nomination.

### Republican Prospects in Alabama, Arkansas and Tennessee.

### Secret Circular of the Bolters from Cincinnati.

### Action of the New-Hampshire Republican Legislative Caucus.

### Republican Nominations for Congress in Indiana.

#### THE VICE-PRESIDENCY.

**Senator Wilson Officially Informed of His Nomination at Philadelphia—His Letter of Acceptance.**

WASHINGTON, June 13—The following is the correspondence between THOMAS SETTLE, President of the National Republican Convention, and Hon. HENRY WILSON:

WASHINGTON, June 10, 1872.

Hon. HENRY WILSON: In accordance with a resolution passed by the National Republican Convention, held at Philadelphia on the 5th and 6th inst., we, the President and Vice-Presidents of that body, have the honor to inform you of your unanimous selection as the candidate of the Republican Party for the position of Vice-President of the United States. The enthusiasm and unanimity which prevailed among so many leading men, from every State and Territory, point unmistakably to the triumphant election of our ticket. As there is no one more worthy of the position, or whose election would give more universal satisfaction, we beg your acceptance of the nomination.

Your obedient servants,

(Signed,) THOMAS SETTLE,
President National Republican Convention, and the Vice-Presidents.

MR. WILSON'S REPLY.

WASHINGTON, June 14, 1872.

*To Hon. Thos. Settle and others, President and Vice-Presidents of the National Republican Convention, held at Philadelphia on the 5th and 6th of the present month:*

GENTLEMEN: Your note of the 10th inst., conveying to me the action of the Convention in placing my name in nomination for the office of Vice-President of the United States, is before me. I need not give you the assurance of my grateful appreciation of the high honor conferred upon me by this action of the fifth National Convention of the Republican Party. Sixteen years ago, in the same city, was held the first meeting of the men who, amid the darkness and doubts of that hour of slave-holding ascendancy and aggression, had assembled in National Convention to confer with each other on the exigencies to which that fearful domination had brought their country. After full conference, the highest point of resolve they could reach, the most they dared to recommend, was the avowed purpose to prohibit the existence of slavery in the Territories. Last week the same party met by its representatives from thirty-seven States and ten Territories, at the same great centre of wealth, intelligence and power, to review the past, take note of the present, and indicate its line of action for the future. As typical facts, hundreds of the nation's recent history, there sat on its platform, taking prominent and honorable part in its proceedings, admitted on terms of perfect equality to the leading hotels of the city, not only the colored representatives of the race which were ten years before in abject slavery, but one of the oldest and most prominent of the once despised abolitionists, to whom was accorded as to no other the warmest demonstrations of popular regard and esteem, and ovation. Not to him alone, but to the cause he had so ably and for so many years represented, and to the men and women, living and dead, who had toiled through long years of obloquy and self-sacrifice for the glorious fruition of that hour. It hardly needed the brilliant summary of its platform to set forth its illustrious achievements. The very presence of those men was alone significant of the victories already achieved, the progress already made, and the great distance which the nation had traveled between the years 1856 and 1872. But grand as has been its record, the Republican Party rests not on its past alone. It looks to the future, and grapples with its problems of duty and of danger. It proposes as objects of its immediate accomplishment "Complete liberty and exact equality for all; the enforcement of the recent amendments to the National Constitution; reform in the civil service; the national domain to be set apart for homes to the people; the adjustment of duties on imports so as to secure remunerative wages to labor; the extension of bounties to all soldiers and sailors, who, in the line of duty, became disabled; the continual and careful encouragement and protection of voluntary immigration, and the guarding with zealous care the rights of adopted citizens; the abolition of the franking privilege and the speedy reduction of the rates of postage; the reduction of the national debt and the rates of interest, and the resumption of specie payment; the encouragement of American commerce and of ship-building; the suppression of violence and the protection of the ballot-box." It also placed on record the opinions and purposes of the party, in favor of amnesty against all forms of repudiation, and indorsed the humane and peaceful policy of the Administration in regard to the Indians. But while clearly defining and distinctly announcing the policy of the Republican Party on these questions of practical legislation and administration, the Convention did not ignore the great social problems which are pressing their claims for solution, and which demand the most careful study and wise consideration. Foremost stands the labor question. Concerning the relations of capital and labor, the Republican Party accepts the duty of so shaping legislation as to secure the full protection and the amplest field for capital, and for labor, the creation of capital, the largest opportunities, and a just share of the mutual profits of these two great servants of civilization. To woman, too, and her new demands, it extends the hand of grateful recognition, and proffers its most respectful inquiry. It recognises her noble devotion to country and freedom, welcomes her admission to wider fields of usefulness, and commends her demands for additional rights, to the calm and careful consideration of the nation.

To guard well what has already been secured, to work out faithfully and wisely what is now in hand, and to consider the questions which are looming up to view but a little way before us, the Republican Party is today what it was in the gloomy years of slavery, rebellion and reconstruction—a national necessity. It appeals, therefore, for support to the patriotic and liberty-loving, to the just and humane, to all who would dignify labor, to all who would educate, elevate and lighten the burdens of the sons and daughters of toil. With its great record, the work still to be done under the great soldier whose historic renown and whose successful Administration for the last three years begat such popular confidence, the Republican Party may confidently—in the language of the Convention you represent, start on a new march to victory.

Having accepted, thirty-six years ago, the distinguishing doctrines of the Republican Party of today—having during years of that period for their advancement subordinated all other issues, acting in and co-operating with political organizations with whose leading doctrines I sometimes had neither sympathy nor belief. Having labored incessantly for many years to found and build up the Republican Party, and having, during its existence, taken an humble part in its grand work, I gratefully accept the nomination thus tendered, and shall endeavor, if it shall be ratified by the people, faithfully to perform the duties it imposes.

Respectfully yours,

(Signed,) HENRY WILSON.

#### THE SITUATION SOUTH.

**Alabama and Mississippi Republican in any Event—Effect of Greeleyism in Tennessee.**

Special Dispatch to the New-York Times.

WASHINGTON, June 13.—Information is received that the political prospects in Alabama and Mississippi are favorable to a Republican success in November, without reference to any action by the Baltimore Convention, whether indorsing GREELEY or taking a new man. There is an undoubted Republican majority in both those States, if it can be brought out, and there is every prospect that it will be. Greeleyism has had no effect whatever to detract from the Republican strength. In Tennessee there is no doubt, so far as can be learned, that GREELEY'S nomination by the Democrats will add strength to the Democratic ranks. There are many progressive Democrats in that State who, it is represented, if an old Bourbon were nominated, would leave the party and vote for GRANT, but the nomination of GREELEY will retain them. The old Bourbon Democracy of that State would vote for the Prince of Darkness if the Baltimore Convention should nominate him, and they will take GREELEY just as easy, but there is no contingency in which well-informed Republicans expect to carry that State.

The State election in North Carolina is held early in August. It gave a Republican majority in the last election, and there is no reason to expect any reversal of votes this year. Proper attention by the campaigners will, however, be given, to place such a desirable result beyond doubt.

#### A NEW MOVEMENT.

**Call for a Meeting of Dissatisfied Liberals.**

CINCINNATI, May 13.—The following circular has been sent to about 200 prominent gentlemen, who favored the original Cincinnati movement:

NEW-YORK, June 6, 1872.

The undersigned desire to have a conference of gentlemen who are opposed to the present Administration and its continuance in office, and deem it necessary that all the elements of the opposition should be united for a common effort at the coming Presidential election.

They respectfully invite you to meet a number of gentlemen belonging to the different branches of the opposition at the Fifth-avenue Hotel, New-York, on June 20, at 2 P. M., for the purpose of consultation, and to take such action as the situation of things may require.

Your attention is respectfully drawn to the fact that this invitation is strictly personal to yourself, and a prompt reply is earnestly requested, addressed to HENRY D. LLOYD, Secretary of the Committee, Post-office Box No. 2,206.

CARL SCHURZ,
JACOB D. COX,
WM. CULLEN BRYANT,
OSWALD OTTENDORFER,
DAVID A. WELLS,
JACOB BRINKERHOFF.

#### NEW-HAMPSHIRE.

**Nomination of Bainbridge Wadleigh for United States Senator at the Republican Caucus.**

Special Dispatch to the New-York Times.

CONCORD, N. H., June 13.—The Republican members of the Legislature met in Phœnix Hall this evening, at 8 o'clock, for the purpose of nominating a candidate for United States Senator. Great excitement has prevailed during the day. Senator PATTERSON lead on the first three ballots, having received 109 votes for his highest number. E. H. Rollins, Esq., Gov. Stearns, M. W. Tappan, Gilman Marston and Bainbridge Wadleigh were the other candidates on the fifth ballot. BAINBRIDGE WADLEIGH, of Milford, a member of the present House of Representatives, received the nomination. He had on the first ballot 3 votes, on the second 8, on the third 18, on the fourth 39 and on the fifth 152, and was declared nominated. Mr. WADLEIGH, the nominee, is a young man of marked ability and one of the first lawyers in the State.

**The Republican State Ticket Elected by the Legislature**

CONCORD, N. H., June 13.—Both Houses met in convention, and proceeded to the election of State officers, with the following result:

| | |
|---|---|
| For Secretary of State: | |
| Whole number of votes cast | 337 |
| Necessary for a choice | 169 |
| Benj. F. Prescott, of Concord, received | 216 |
| John H. Goodall, of Nashua | 121 |
| For State Treasurer: | |
| Whole number of votes cast | 333 |
| Necessary for a choice | 167 |
| Solon A. Carter, of Keene, received | 206 |
| Geo. B. Chandler, of Manchester, received | 125 |
| Horace Greeley | 1 |
| L. W. Cogswell | 1 |

Owen C. Moore, of Nashua, was then elected State Printer, and Charles F. Montgomery, of Strafford, Commissary-General.

#### INDIANA.

**Republican Congressional Conventions—Gen. M. C. Hunter Nominated in the Sixth and Gen. John Coburn in the Fifth District.**

Special Dispatch to the New-York Times.

INDIANAPOLIS, June 13.—Gen. MORTON C. HUNTER, of Bloomington, was today nominated unanimously as candidate for Congress by the Republican Congressional Convention of the Sixth District at Brazil. Gen. HUNTER was member for the Third District in 1867 and 1868, and during the war was one of Gen. SHERMAN'S ablest brigade commanders. In accepting the nomination, he took decided ground in favor of revenue tariff and against direct taxation, which was loudly applauded. D. W. VOORHEES is the present representative of the district, but Republicans are sanguine of Gen. HUNTER'S election. The Fifth District, in convention at Danville, unanimously nominated Gen. JOHN COBURN for re-election. Speeches were made by Gen. COBURN and Hon. G. S. ORTH. The greatest harmony prevailed. Gen. COBURN will be elected.

#### MAINE.

**Republican State Convention—Gov. Perham Renominated—A Large and Spirited Assemblage—A Strong and Honest Platform.**

Special Dispatch to the New-York Times.

PORTLAND, Me., June 13.—The Republicans of Maine held their State Convention today at Lewiston. It was a harmonious and enthusiastic gathering of more than a thousand delegates from all parts of the State. The Convention was called to order at 11 o'clock by Hon. FREDERIC ROBIE, of the State Committee, who nominated Hon. JOSEPH M. PORTER, of Burlington, for temporary President, and Z. A. SMITH, of Portland; H. S. OSGOOD, of Augusta, and H. MITCHELL, of Bangor, temporary Secretaries. Mr. PORTER made an able and appropriate speech of acceptance. Committees on Credentials and Permanent Organization were appointed, consisting of one from each county, after which Hon. W. P. FRYE, Congressman from the Second District, made a brilliant and eloquent speech, which was received with great enthusiasm.

The temporary organization was made permanent, and the permanent committees of the Convention were then appointed. The Committee on Resolutions is as follows:

Androscoggin, H. Dingley, Jr.; Aroostook, C. H. Powers; Cumberland, Clarence Hale; Franklin, Charles J. Talbot; Hancock, N. K. Sawyer; Kennebec, George E. Week; Knox, Hiram Bliss; Lincoln, C. R. Haraden; Oxford, John J. Perry; Penobscot, Hon. S. F. Humphrey; Piscataquis, James E. Rowell; Somerset, S. S. Brown; Sagadahoc, S. M. Hayes; Waldo, F. G. Mansar; Washington, S. H. Talbot; York, Nathaniel Hobb.

The State Committee is as follows:

Androscoggin, Wm. P. Frye; Aroostook, Eben Woodbury; Cumberland, S. T. Pullen; Franklin, F. C. Perkins; Hancock, John D. Hopkins; Kennebec, Jas. G. Blaine; Knox, E. R. Spear; Lincoln, S. S. Marble; Oxford, F. E. Shaw; Penobscot, John H. Lynde; Piscataquis, E. A. Thomson; Somerset, L. E. Prescott; Sagadahoc, F. D. Sewall; Waldo, Fred. Atwood; Washington, Nelson S. Allen; York, Leonard Andrews.

Hon. SIDNEY PERHAM was then renominated by acclamation for his third term as Governor, and Hon. S. E. SPRING and Hon. ALEXANDER CAMPBELL as electors at large. Gen. HERSEY declined a nomination as elector. At the afternoon session NELSON DINGLEY Jr., of Lewiston, from the Committee on Resolutions, reported the following which were adopted:

*Resolved*, That the Republicans of Maine assembled by delegates in State Convention, reaffirm the declaration of principles made by the National Republican Convention at Philadelphia, and point with pride to their past record in war and in peace as the best and only political organization, because of its ability and disposition to wisely and successfully deal with whatever question may arise in the future.

*Resolved*, That the Republicans of Maine most cordially and unitedly indorse the nomination of Gen. U. S. GRANT as President, and of Hon. HENRY WILSON as Vice-President, and pledge to the great soldier and patriot and to the eminent Senator and friend of the working men, the electoral vote of Maine by a majority even greater than was given the Republican ticket in 1868.

*Resolved*, That the thanks of the people of the State are due to Congress and to our delegation in that body, through whose able and earnest advocacy the measure was secured for the recent legislation to promote the interests of ship-building and to revive commerce, and we accept what has been accomplished as an assurance that their efforts in this direction will continue until that great interest is placed upon an equitable basis.

*Resolved*, That we reaffirm our faith in the principle of Prohibition and its impartial enforcement, and we view with satisfaction the popular movement in favor of the Temperance Reform recently inaugurated in this State.

*Resolved*, That the presentation of the name of Hon. SIDNEY PERHAM for Governor of the State, for the third time, is justly due to him for his fidelity to the interests of the State and for the prudence and care with which he has performed all his public duties.

Gen. JAMES A. HALL, of Damariscotta, made an eloquent and effective speech. The Convention was earnest and hearty for GRANT and WILSON. The enthusiasm it displayed in its reception of Congressman FRYE, and the vigorous cheers when he spoke of what Congress and the Administration had done, showed the party believe in its leaders, and that every Republican is in good hearty working trim.

This is the first time the Republicans of Maine have been in council since the Cincinnati Convention, and upon consultation of the leading men from all parts of the State, it is found that very few GREELEY men can be found in the Republican ranks, and that even these few are growing ashamed of the Democratic Company and coming back to our lines. The Democrats are very generally for GREELEY.

#### LOUISIANA.

**Republican Fusion in Support of Grant and Wilson Probable—Warmoth Disgusted.**

NEW-ORLEANS, June 13.—The Pinchback Republican Convention, which recently assembled here and adjourned to reassemble at Baton Rouge,* June 19, having passed a resolution declaring for Gov. WARMOTH, the latter has written a letter declining his proposed nomination to the Baton Rouge Convention. This action is taken because of the proposed fusion of the two wings of the Republican party in support of President GRANT, which the Governor opposes. He still declares his allegiance to the Cincinnati nominees.

#### WISCONSIN.

**The Democratic State Convention Indorse Cincinnati, and Appoint Delegates to Baltimore.**

MILWAUKEE, Wis., June 13.—The Democratic State Convention today elected the following delegates to Baltimore at large: JAMES R. DOOLITTLE, EDWARD S. BRAGG, GABRIEL BOUCK, JOHN W. CAREY.

*First District*—John Hackett, D. W. Small.
*Second*—A. G. Cook, G. W. Bird.
*Third*—Nelson Dewey, H. H. Gray.
*Fourth*—Geo. H. Paul, B. S. Weil.
*Fifth*—E. C. Loomis, James Vilas.
*Sixth*—A. C. Wesbrod, John P. Hume.
*Seventh*—L. P. Weatherby, Fred. Rudolph.
*Eighth*—W. T. Galloway, S. A. Pease.

The delegates were instructed to vote as a unit, and the following resolutions were adopted:

*Resolved*, That the address and resolutions of the Liberal Republican Convention, held at Cincinnati on the 1st day of May, embody the fundamental principles which the Democratic electors of the State of Wisconsin cordially indorse, and that they cheerfully acquiesce in the delegation to the people of the several States the political question upon which that Convention expressed no opinion that the exposition and elucidation of the platform of the Cincinnati Convention by HORACE GREELEY in his letter of acceptance of the nomination for President, furnish a satisfactory assurance to the American people that he will, if elected, administer the Government upon the principles in that platform. Therefore, in devotion to principles, waiving our preference for men and believing that the approval of the nominees of the Cincinnati Convention is a sure mode of obtaining the triumph and ascendancy of those principles, we approve the same and recommend that our delegates to the Baltimore Convention do ratify the action of the Cincinnati Convention.

The nomination of electors was postponed for the purpose of fusing with the Liberal Republicans.

#### POLITICS ON THE PACIFIC.

**Grant and Wilson Indorsed at San Francisco—Republican Majority in Oregon, 1,000.**

SAN FRANCISCO, June 12.—A large meeting ratifying the nomination of GRANT and WILSON was held last night. It was addressed by Gov. BOOTH and other prominent officials and politicians. The utmost confidence was expressed in the success of the Philadelphia ticket. The majority of the meeting favored WILSON.

The Republicans in Oregon have a majority of about one thousand. They have also a majority on a joint ballot in the Legislature.

#### POLITICAL NOTES.

JUBAL A. EARLY refuses to support GREELEY.

Efforts have been made to establish a Greeley organ in Connecticut, but the funds could not be raised.

The Republicans of the Third (Richmond) District of Virginia will nominate a candidate for Congress on the 7th of August.

"Admiral" RAPHAEL SEMMES supports GREELEY. It will be pretty safe for patriots to vote against the man he wishes elected.

Gen. GEORGE B. McCLELLAN is credited with having expressed a decided disapproval to the indorsement of GREELEY and BROWN at Baltimore.

BEAUREGARD, BRAGG, HOOD, D. H. HILL, GORDON and MAHONE, all of rebel notoriety, come forward to announce that the Greeley ticket is satisfactory to them.

The Delaware Democrats did not call for a straight-out nomination at Baltimore. The Wilmington *Commercial* says they are against GREELEY, but afraid to say so.

It has been finally decided to hold the National Democratic Convention in Ford's Opera-house, in Baltimore. With proposed alterations it is expected to admit about 6,000 persons.

The Terre Haute (Ind.) *Express* believes that Mr. COLFAX will not accept any offices hereafter, but will carry out his original determination to retire to private life at the end of his present term as Vice-President.

CASSIUS M. CLAY has written a long letter in the vain attempt to persuade the negroes of Kentucky that GREELEY is their best friend. The negroes can reply that they never know where to find him.

In the Delaware Democratic State Convention, SAM. TOWNSEND energetically declared that if the Declaration of Independence meant that all men were created equal, it was a living lie—that it was only true of white men.

One member of the Delaware Democratic State Convention loudly asserted that he would be a Democrat as long as he had a tongue to wag, an arm to lift, or a dollar to spend, but that if GREELEY was nominated at Baltimore, his head should be taken from his body before he would vote for him.

Speaking of GREELEY, the Portland (Maine) *Press* says that there is no escaping the conviction that no good cause has anything to hope from a character so weakly constituted; and that it has been often shown that his mental and moral defects develop in exact proportion to the responsibilities he assumes.

#### THE WEATHER.

**Synopsis and Probabilities.**

WASHINGTON, June 14—1 A. M.—An area of low barometer has moved north-eastward over Iowa, Missouri, Lower Michigan and Ohio, to probably north-eastern New-York, accompanied by fresh to brisk southerly winds, veering to northwesterly, and rain. Clear weather is now prevailing from Alabama westward, with light to fresh southerly winds; partially cloudy weather over the South and Middle Atlantic States, with light to fresh southerly winds and areas of light rain; cloudy weather over the northern portion of the Middle States, with light to fresh westerly winds; clear weather over the upper lake region, with fresh westerly winds.

PROBABILITIES.

Westerly winds and clear and clearing weather for the Middle States on Friday, and for New-England on Friday afternoon and night, and from the Ohio Valley northward and westward; cloudy weather and areas of rain for the South Atlantic States, but thence to the Ohio and Lower Mississippi Valleys clear and clearing weather and westerly winds.

**St. Louis Saengerfest.**

ST. LOUIS, June 13.—Notwithstanding a very heavy and continuous rain, the Saengerfest Hall was densely packed to-night with a brilliant audience of fully 15,000 people. This unexpected turnout indicates the great interest felt in the Saengerfest, and insures its success beyond question.

## THE STORM.

### Details of the Ravages of Wednesday's Tornado.

**Buildings Unroofed and Blown Down from the Delaware to Maine—Destruction of Stock, Trees, Fences, and Crops—Several Persons Injured and One Killed by Lightning.**

From Our Own Correspondent.

MILFORD, Pike County, Penn., Thursday, June 13, 1872.

About 6 o'clock last night a terrible tornado passed over this village, leaving great destruction in its wake. About 5 o'clock, what was supposed to be a thunder-storm was seen coming up in the south-west, but just before it broke forth the sky became overcast with clouds of peculiar shade, and amid the most terrific thunder and lightning the hurricane came upon the village. Rain and hail fell in such volume that objects could not be seen twenty-five feet away. In the midst of this blinding storm, and the roar of the wind, the crash of falling trees, roofs of buildings, fences, and other things which were unable to withstand the force of the storm, told of the work of destruction that was going on. The tornado lasted for about ten minutes, and when it had passed over, a scene of destruction was presented in all parts of the village. Large trees were stretched across the streets, fences were gone, buildings unroofed, and *débris* of all kinds piled in every nook and corner. The fine Mansard residence of Mr. A. D. BROWN, on Broad-street, was almost completely ruined, the roof had been lifted bodily from it, and carried 400 feet into a vacant lot and dashed to pieces. The building itself was shattered from top to bottom.

Mr. and Mrs. JOHN ROSENCRANSE were returning home in a carriage, and had just reached the door when the storm came down. Their horse became frightened and unmanageable. Mrs. ROSENCRANSE was thrown beneath its feet, and narrowly escaped being trampled to death. She escaped with a broken arm and other injuries. A tree carried on the wind came down with a crash along side of the carriage, just missing Mr. ROSENCRANSE, and increasing the terror of the horse, which broke loose and ran wildly away, and disappeared in the storm. Huge trees were twisted off and carried some distance. Valuable fruit-trees were leveled to the ground, E. B. ELDRED, Esq., losing twenty-five in one orchard. Not a yard or garden escaped damage.

When the storm commenced, the doors of ARMSTRONG'S drug-store were open, and before they could be closed the wind and water rushed in, and counters, bottles, boxes and other articles were blown down and broken. On the farms of WM. BRODHEAD and SIMEON CUDDEBACK, just out of the village, fences and trees were thrown down and fields destroyed. Trees two feet in diameter were torn up by the roots and carried as far as thirty feet in the air. A barn belonging to GEORGE OLMSTEAD, and one to GEORGE QUINN, near the village, were unroofed. One on the farm of S. V. DRAKE was blown down, causing a loss of $500.

There is a freshet in the Delaware River, and at the time of the storm the stream was thick with rafts. Several that were tied along the shores were broken from their fastenings, and were carried down the river. Raftmen were obliged to lie flat on their rafts, and secure themselves to prevent being blown into the water.

The storm proceeded in a north-easterly direction, and crossed the river into Sussex County, New-Jersey, where buildings were blown down, and still greater damage done to vegetation, as the fall of hail was much heavier. A barn and other out-buildings on the farm of DANIEL NEARPASS were blown down, and in two fine orchards, of two acres in extent each, not a tree is left standing. At SANFORD NEARPASS', the most damage was done by hail, although a large amount of fence was prostrated. A maple-tree, three feet in diameter, was torn up by the roots, leaving an excavation as large as a cellar. At DANIEL HOUSE'S, every tree in a long row of large maples was twisted down like a reed.

The storm must have done great damage before reaching Milford, but no particulars have as yet been received. The damage done in the small extent of territory described will amount to thousands of dollars.

**A School-House at Pawlenville Struck by Lightning and a Little Girl Killed.**

KINGSTON, N. Y., June 13.—During the storm yesterday afternoon a school-house at Pawlenville, in this county, was struck by lightning and a little girl named MERRITT was instantly killed. Several other children were stunned. The storm caused great damage throughout the county. In this city the lightning struck in several places, but no serious damage was done. Near Stone Ridge and High Falls a tornado, accompanied by terrific thunder and lightning, swept over a narrow strip of country, causing great destruction. Two barns, owned by ISAAC HOSBROUCK, were blown down and totally destroyed. Two men and a team of horses in one of the buildings destroyed narrowly escaped being crushed in the ruins. Much damage was done by the hail to the fruit trees and grape-vines, and the general damage to buildings, fences and other property was very heavy.

**Effect in Binghamton—A Circus-Tent Blown Down—Many Buildings Struck by Lightning—Damage in Pike County, Penn.**

BINGHAMTON, N. Y., June 13.—A terrific gale, accompanied by torrents of rain and hail, passed over the city between 3 and 4 o'clock yesterday afternoon. The menagerie and aquarium tents of JOHN ROBINSON'S circus were blown down, and the wagons upset, while the tents were full of people. Several persons were injured, but not very seriously. The crowd of terribly-frightened people in the drenching, pelting storm and amid the upturned cages of roaring, shrieking animals, presented a wild and almost appalling scene. During the storm the lightning struck the spire of the Congregational Church, the Fourth Ward school-house, the smoke-stack of BLANCHARD & BARTLETT'S sash and door factory, the residence of Mr. VINCENT WHITNEY, a slaughter-house and several trees within the corporate limits. A number of frames of unfinished buildings and many trees were blown down.

PORT JERVIS, N. Y., June 13.—A terrific gale of wind passed over Milford, Pike County, Penn., about 5 o'clock yesterday afternoon. During the storm of rain and hail a large house, belonging to Mr. BROWN, was badly wrecked, the roof taken off and carried by the wind 200 yards. Over 200 trees were torn up by the roots. One woman had an arm broken by a falling tree. Several barns near Milford were blown down and a number of horses injured, but no lives were lost.

**The Storm in Maine—Great Damage Done.**

BANGOR, Me., June 13.—A severe tornado, accompanied with thunder and lightning, passed over portions of Penobscot and Piscataquis Counties yesterday, doing much damage. In Parkman, the barn of Mr. DRAPER was demolished and several head of cattle were killed. The barn of Mr. STARBIRD, of Dover, one of Mr. WILSON, at Bradford, and a new house owned by FREDERICK WILSON, of North Bradford, were demolished. No injury to persons is reported. In Dexter a large amount of glass was broken by hail.

**Damage by the Storm in Other Localities.**

ALBANY, N. Y., June 13.—A violent rain-storm, yesterday, did a vast amount of damage to vegetation along the Albany and Susquehanna Railroad. It was accompanied by a strong wind, which unroofed many buildings, leveled fences, &c.

**Shocking Accidents in Pittsburg, Penn.**

PITTSBURG, Penn., June 13.—FRED. KRAMER and RICHARD D. MAXWELL, machinists employed in the Diamond Still Works, were crushed to death this morning by the fall of an immense bed plate which they were lifting on jack-screws and had neglected to properly secure.

JACOB SNYDER, an engineer of the brick-works in Allegheny, was torn to pieces by a fly-wheel this morning.

#### WASHINGTON NEWS.

**Comparative Statement of Collections—Results of Honest Administration—Gen. Howard and the Indians.**

Special Dispatch to the New-York Times.

WASHINGTON, June 13.—A statement was recently made out showing a comparison of collections from the various general sources of revenue from internal taxation, for the period from September, 1870, to April, 1871, with collections from September, 1871, to April, 1872. The increase during the latter period from spirits was 10 per cent., amounting to over $3,000,000; from fermented liquors 11 per cent., or $450,000; from banks and bankers 25 per cent., or $596,000; from gas 18 per cent., or $233,000; from adhesive stamps 11 per cent., or $1,000,000; from incomes 25 per cent., or $1,449,000; from tobacco, $265,000. The above are in round numbers. The total increase was $7,094,794. There was a total decrease during the same period from penalties remitted by law, and from articles and occupations then taxed, but exempt from taxation during the last period, of $7,834,814. Thus it will be seen that while Congress struck off above $7,000,000 of internal taxes for the period named, the increase of business, partly and chiefly the efficiency, honesty and vigor of collection under Commissioner DOUGLASS, almost made up the decrease by collecting all the taxes upon those articles on which taxes were levied.

MISSION OF GEN. HOWARD.

Gen. HOWARD has finished his mission to the Apaches, and is now on his return. He is expected about the 20th of the present month. He is bringing with him four Apache Indian chiefs, two Pimas, one Papago, and two Apache Mohaves. Besides there is an interpreter, and Capt. WILKINSON and Superintendent BENDELL is also with him. Gen. HOWARD'S reports are indicative of the success of his efforts to preserve peace. The Apaches are all now peaceable on reservations.

THE WASHINGTON COMMITTEE.

The resident Republican Committee will have all the Committee-rooms on the north side of the Senate Chamber, on the floor that gives entrance to the galleries, set apart for use during the coming canvass. In these large and airy quarters the usual business of this Committee will soon be vigorously begun.

Dispatch to the Associated Press.

ARREST OF AN INSANE MARYLANDER.

This morning a tall, wild-looking man was noticed walking about the lower rooms of the Executive mansion, and Officer KEARNEY, regarding him as a suspicious character, questioned him. He stated that his name was RICHARD F. JONES, from Prince George's County, Maryland, and demanded to see the President. Upon being told that President GRANT was absent from the city he demanded that he should be telegraphed for at once, as he (JONES) had whipped the world and could not rest satisfied until he had whipped the President, who ought to be ousted and the Pope of Rome put in his place. Officer KEARNEY took the world's champion into custody, and started with him to Police Head-quarters. After proceeding quietly for some distance, the prisoner suddenly turned on the officer and attempted to break away, tearing his coat in the effort. Officers DUVALL and SHELTON came to the rescue, and the prisoner was safely taken to head-quarters and locked up, a large crowd following him to the door.

THE AMNESTY ACT.

The following circular has been issued from the Pension Office:

The Amnesty act, approved May 22, 1872, provides as follows:

"That all political disabilities imposed by the third section of amendments of the Constitution of the United States are hereby removed from all persons whomsoever, except Senators and Representatives of the Thirty-sixth and Thirty-seventh Congresses, and officers in the Judicial, Military, and Naval service of the United States.

The only disability imposed by said third section of the fourteenth article of amendments of the Constitution was that of exclusion from holding office under the United States, or any of the States thereof. The Amnesty act restores the right to hold office, as above stated, to those not excepted, but does not in any other respect relieve those who have been disloyal from any of the legal penalties, restrictions, or requirements consequent upon their disloyalty, or the presumption thereof, nor have any other effect whatever.

(Signed,) C. W. SEATON, Acting Commissioner.

NAVAL INTELLIGENCE.

Capt. THOS. PATTERSON is ordered to command the receiving-ship *Ohio*, relieving Capt. R. B. LOWRY, who is placed on waiting orders. The United States steamer *Juniata* is daily expected home from the Mediterranean Squadron, having left Gibraltar about the middle of May for Boston. The second-class steamers *Omaha* and *Richmond* are now fitting out at the Philadelphia Navy-yard, and will be ready to go to sea in a month or six weeks. Rear-Admiral JOSEPH R. LANMAN, recently relieved from the command of the South Atlantic fleet, will be placed on the retired list on the 18th of July, on account of long and faithful service. His retirement will promote Commodore A. M. PENNOCK, now in command of the Portsmouth Navy-yard, to the grade of Rear-Admiral, and Capt. R. H. WYMAN, now in charge of the Hydrographic Office, to the grade of Commodore, and Commander S. R. FRANKLIN to Captain. The steamer *Victor*, from New-York, heavily laden with ordnance and other supplies for Ports Taylor and Jefferson, has arrived safely at Key West. The War Department has taken the precaution to reinforce all the forts on the Southern and Gulf coasts with the newest pattern and largest calibre of ordnance, while the Navy Department has accumulated large supplies of naval stores at all the naval stations on the Southern and Gulf coasts, in accordance with the desire of the Government to be prepared for all emergencies.

#### FROM ANNAPOLIS.

**Changes at the Naval Academy.**

Special Dispatch to the New-York Times.

ANNAPOLIS, Md., June 13.—EUGENE CRUGER, of Red Hook, N. Y., has passed the examination, and is a cadet midshipman. Capt. and Brevet Major B. R. FENDALL has been detached from the command of the marines at the Naval Academy, and ordered to command the marines at Portsmouth, N. H., Navy-yard.

#### THE SOLDIERS' HOME.

**Meeting of the Trustees at Albany—Drawing Lots for Terms of Office.**

ALBANY, N. Y., June 13.—The Trustees of the New-York Soldiers' Home, created by an act of the last Legislature, met today at the office of the Secretary of State and drew lots for terms of service, resulting as follows: For one year, Gens. H. A. Barnum, J. C. Robinson and C. D. McDougal; for two years, Col. Wm. Johnson, State Senator, Gens. John Hammond and N. M. Curtis; for three years, Gen. J. B. Kiddo and Col. Timothy Sullivan; for four years, Gens. James McQuade, James Jourdan, and John H. Martindale; for five years, Gens. John B. Murray, James E. Jones, and Major E. L. Cole; for six years, Gens. H. W. Slocum, W. T. Rogers, and Col. J. C. Carmichael; for seven years, Gen. Wm. M. Gregg, Major D. C. Stoddard, and Capt. Adolphe Nolte. The Governor, Controller and Attorney-General are *ex-officio* trustees. The trustees then adjourned to meet in Albany July 19, for organization, after which they will take active measures to establish a home for disabled soldiers and sailors.

#### THE TROTTING TURF.

**The Eastern Dutchess Association Meeting.**

AMENIA, N. Y., June 13.—The Eastern Dutchess Association Races were well attended today. Part of the track was soft. The *American Girl* and *Wm. H. Allen* trotted in the free for all race, the *American Girl* winning in three straight heats. Time—2:35, 2:29½, 2:27½.

The purse for 2:50 double teams was won by *Cloudman* and *Black George*, trotting six heats. The winning time was 3:13, 3:05½, 3:04, 3:12, 3:10, 3:02¼.

#### THE INDIANS.

**Gen. Howard's Movements—The Commission to Visit the Warriors Threatening the Union Pacific Railroad.**

WASHINGTON, D. C., June 13.—A dispatch received at the Indian Office today from Gen. HOWARD, dated Santa Fé, New-Mexico, 11th inst., says: "I have with me four Apache chiefs, two Pimos, one Papago, and two representatives of the Apache Mohaves, with an interpreter. The Indians had not left Camp Grant nor White Mountain Reservation. They are at peace, and wish to keep it. The story that the Apaches had killed an interpreter at Camp Grant proves to be untrue. Superintendent BENDELL and Capt. WILKINSON are with me. Expect us about the 20th."

The Secretary of the Interior today appointed the following Commission to visit the hostile tribes of Indians, demonstrating against the Union Pacific Railroad. Gen. B. R. COWAN, JOHN S. DELANO, and J. W. WHAM. The Commission will leave this city for the Yellowstone country about the 20th inst.

#### BY MAIL AND TELEGRAPH.

On their return from Niagara Falls, the Japanese Embassy will stop at Saratoga.

The World's Fair, in Copenhagen, Denmark, was opened yesterday by His Majesty King CHRISTIAN.

The sixth annual Convention of the American Car-builders' Association convened in St. Louis yesterday.

The American Railway Master Mechanics' Association have selected Baltimore for the place of next annual meeting.

The Central Pacific Railroad Company now receive and discharge freight at their new depot, at San Francisco.

The Commissioner of Patents yesterday extended the patent of STUART PERRY, of New-York, for his combination lock.

A dispatch from Bremen announces that the Austrian Poland Expedition has sailed from that port for the Arctic Ocean.

The marriage bond of DAVID CROCKETT is to be presented to the State Library of Tennessee. It bears DAVY'S signature.

The Japanese Embassy arrived at Niagara Falls last evening, and will be the guests of the International Hotel for a few days.

The Bridgeport (N. J.) *Independent* says that 187,562 boxes of strawberries have been shipped from that place and vicinity this season.

Judge HAWLEY has closed his Court at Beaver City, Utah, having cleared his docket, and is now in Salt Lake to attend the Supreme Court, which meets on Monday.

A New-Hampshire man of seventy-two years, lately married a widow of fifty-five, with a ready-made family of thirteen. A band serenade was given the happy fifteen.

A grand ball was given on board the German war steamer *Bertha*, at San Francisco, last evening. At the termination of the ball the *Bertha* sailed for Europe.

A new company of the late National Guard has been organized at Trenton, composed of fifty-four men, and known as the Freese Guard. It will be placed in the Second Brigade.

The steam-ship *France*, in going out of Montreal Harbor, yesterday morning, struck on Isle Ronde twice, and had to be run ashore. One man was killed by the machinery.

During a heavy shower on Wednesday evening the pencil factory of LEWIS BALL, in Acton, Mass., was struck by lightning, and Mr. BALL, the proprietor, was instantly killed.

Twenty-three Kuklux prisoners from South Carolina arrived at the Albany Penitentiary on Tuesday, in charge of United States Marshal WALLACE and a military guard.

TYLER BARKER, who committed suicide a fortnight ago, left his entire property, valued at $75,000, to the town of Boxford, Mass., for the establishment and maintenance of a high school.

JAMES E. BAUDERN, from Baltimore, a student in Lehigh University, was instantly killed by a shifting engine, on the Lehigh and Susquehanna Railroad, yesterday, at Bethlehem, Penn.

The Augusta (Ga.) Exchange, now working successfully, is intended to facilitate transactions in cotton, grain and produce, and especially for the purchase and sale of Southern securities.

The Maine Hotel at Berwick, Me., took fire at an early hour yesterday morning, and was damaged to the extent of $6,000. Several of the guests were injured by jumping from the windows.

The body of a boy of fourteen was found floating in the Hudson, near Newburg, last evening. It was identified as that of GEORGE TOMKIN, who was drowned in February last while skating.

Yesterday afternoon the foundation stone of the New Union Railroad station, designed to accommodate all the railroads running into Toronto, was laid by the Grand Master of the Grand Lodge of Freemasons of Canada.

Massachusetts arborists express the opinion that nearly all the juniper, arbor-vitæ, spruce, hemlock and other evergreens which at present appear to be Winter-killed will soon be as thrifty and beautiful as ever.

Loud complaints have been made in Cambridge, Mass., of the number of birds killed for "scientific purposes," and the cruel methods employed, and the Board of Aldermen has revoked the licenses permitting such slaughter.

The Democrats of the Fifth Massachusetts District in Convention at Salem yesterday, elected CHARLES P. THOMPSON, of Gloucester, and C. O. MORSE, of Newburyport, delegates to Baltimore. No instructions were given to the delegates.

Deacon JAMES FRANCIS, of Fittsfield, Mass., has deposited in the Berkshire Athenæum the front of Gov. WINSLOW'S chest, brought over in the *Mayflower*, and preserved by Capt. JOHN CHURCHILL, and now presented to the Athenæum in behalf of his family.

About 2 o'clock yesterday morning an unsuccessful attempt was made by three men to rob the Hingham, Mass., Bank. The noise made in driving the chisel under the bank vault awoke a citizen, upon whose appearance the burglars fled.

A large delegation of singers arrived at Boston from the West yesterday. The car which brought them from Albany was decorated with flags and banners, and bore the inscription "Wisconsin's World's Jubilee Chorus."

Reports from all parts of East Tennessee, the Knoxville *Herald* of the 11th inst. says, agree in representing the present harvest of wheat to be one of the largest that has been gathered in that section of the State, and the quality as fine as was ever grown on the soil.

President GRANT has appointed Hon. WM. BARNES, of Albany, one of the three American delegates to the International Statistical Congress, which is to assemble at St. Petersburg in August. His associates are EDWARD YOUNG, the able chief of the National Bureau of Statistics, and Dr. E. M. SNOW, of Providence, a scholar and statistician of fine reputation.

The thunder-storm in Massachusetts on Wednesday eve was sadly destructive of life. A daughter of HUGH GRAHAM was killed in Lexington. In Waltham, two women—Mrs. MARGARET FLAHERTY and Mrs. O'BRIEN—were killed. LEWIS F. BALL was killed in Acton. Several buildings were damaged and trees shivered.

Commissioner DOUGLASS and Superintendent MCCARTER have made arrangements to keep up the supply of revenue stamps by using the old ones with the surface imprint thereon of the changes made by the recent act of Congress. A large force is at work upon the stamps, and there is now a sufficient quantity to supply the demand.

THOMAS FOLEY has been indicted by the Grand Jury of Orange County for arson. It is charged that he fired his paint-store, in Cornwall, a few weeks ago, causing the destruction of several buildings, the total loss being about $12,000. It is said that the evidence against him is not very direct or strong. He has been admitted to bail.

**Killed by the Fall of Telegraph Wires—A Singular Accident near Bergen, N. J.**

A singular and fatal accident occurred on the Erie Railway, on the meadows, at the western end of the Bergen Tunnel, on Wednesday night. The wind-storm during the evening had blown down some of the telegraph poles and wires, delaying trains and throwing one locomotive off the track. Three men were sent out to put up the line, and had placed most of the wires in position, but had not secured them, when the whole fell with a crash. The wires struck EDWARD VAN NESS, one of the workmen, and threw him to the ground with such force as to break his neck. A man named O'CONNORS, another one of the workmen, was also caught in the wires and had his leg broken.

Dr. BIRD, Police Surgeon, dressed O'CONNORS' limb, and found that VAN NESS had been instantly killed. County Physician Dr. BUCK was notified, and the body of the dead man given in his charge.

**How Boston is to Receive its Visiting Bands.**

BOSTON, June 13.—The English and Germans of Boston are making extensive preparations to welcome the bands representing their respective nationalities now daily expected to arrive here. The First Regiment, Col. JOHNSTON, with the various German societies will receive the German band and escort the visitors to the Warwick House. The reception of the Grenadier Guard Band will also include a parade, in which all the British and Scottish societies will be represented. A request will be made that the entrance of the bands into Boston be made in full parade uniform.

## EUROPEAN NEWS.

### Important Statements on the Treaty by Mr. Gladstone.

### The United States Refuse to Apply for Postponement.

### Failure of the Alabama Case not to Affect the San Juan Case.

### Appalling Loss of Life by the Floods in Bohemia.

### [K]ing Amadeus, of Spain, at Loggerheads with His Cabinet.

#### THE TREATY.

**Mr. Gladstone's Replies to Questions Regarding the Treaty—A Statement by Earl Granville to be Made To-day.**

LONDON, June 13.—At the session of the House of Commons to-night, Mr. GLADSTONE, in reply to a question of Mr. CORRANCE, said nothing official had been received by the Government in relation to the San Juan boundary boundary question, now before the Emperor WILLIAM of Germany for his decision.

In answer to an inquiry from Sir HENRY IRBETSON, Mr. GLADSTONE said the Government of the United States declined to become a party to the application for the adjournment of the meeting of the Board of Arbitration at Geneva, as was proposed by Her Majesty's Government.

Mr. OTWAY asked the Premier if, in case the arbitration of the *Alabama* claims failed, (and no sane man could doubt that it would,) the Convention for the settlement of the San Juan boundary question, which was provided for by the Treaty of Washington, would be maintained.

Mr. GLADSTONE replied in the affirmative.

Viscount BURY asked if it was true that the American Government would oppose to the utmost any effort by the British Government to submit its argument at Geneva, on the 15th inst., under protest; and if this was true, how it was proposed to reserve the rights of Great Britain. The questions were not answered by Mr. GLADSTONE, who said that he would require notice to be given before doing so.

Another statement from Earl GRANVILLE is expected in the House of Lords to-morrow.

**Mr. Gladstone Again to be Called on to Answer Questions.**

LONDON, June 13.—In the House of Commons, this afternoon, Mr. HORSMAN gave notice that he would soon ask Mr. GLADSTONE whether the document to be presented to Parliament relative to the *Alabama* claims would explain why no record was kept of the proceedings of the sessions of the Joint High Commission, and also if they would contain any communications wherein the American Government asserted that the withdrawal of the indirect claims was only a matter of understanding and not of agreement.

#### THE BOHEMIAN FLOODS.

**Appalling Loss of Life—A Number of Villages Swept Away.**

LONDON, June 13.—Details of the floods near Prague, caused by heavy rains, of which brief mention was made by telegraph on the 27th ult., show that the destruction of life and property was far greater than at first supposed. The water poured over the country, sweeping everything before it. Fertile districts were devasted, and a number of villages swept away. The loss of life is appalling, the number of persons who perished being estimated at 700.

#### SPAIN.

**Another Cabinet Crisis—Amadeus at Variance With His Own Ministers—Internationals and Carlists.**

MADRID, June 13.—It is stated that the Ministry are not in harmony with the King on certain measures adopted by the Cortes.

The difficulty was caused by King AMADEUS disapproving measures which were adopted by the Cortes and supported by the Cabinet. The Ministry, as was anticipated, have tendered their resignations.

The journals of this city assert that a plan is in contemplation to unite the Carlists with the Internationale organizations in Spain, when an effort will be made by the combination to create disaffection in the army.

MADRID, June 13—Midnight.—The Cortes has adjourned. The Ministerial crisis continues.

#### RUSSIA.

**Cholera in the South—Vessels from Russian Ports Quarantined at Constantinople.**

CONSTANTINOPLE, June 13.—The cholera has appeared in the southern part of Russia. All vessels arriving here from Russian ports on the Black Sea are placed in quarantine.

#### GEN. SHERMAN.

**Count Audrassy Entertains the General in Vienna—Future Movements.**

VIENNA, June 13.—Gen. WM. T. SHERMAN, who is now in this city, will dine to-night with Count AUDRASSY, Minister of Foreign Affairs. Gen. SHERMAN will soon depart for Paris, where he will be joined by Lieut. FREDERICK D. GRANT.

Gen. SHERMAN and Col. J. C. AUDENRIED were presented to the Emperor FRANCIS JOSEPH today by Hon. JOHN JAY, the American Minister.

#### ASCOT RACES.

**The Gold Cup Won by M. Lefevre's "Henry"—"Favonius" Second.**

LONDON, June 13.—At the Ascot meeting today the race for the Gold Cup, value 500 sovereigns, was won by M. LEFEVRE'S *Henry*. The weather was pleasant, and there was a large attendance of spectators, including their Royal Highnesses the Prince and Princess of WALES.

The following is a summary of the race:

The Gold Cup, value 500 sovereigns, given from the fund, and added to a subscription of 200 sovereigns each; the second horse to receive 50 sovereigns out of the stake; three years old, 7 stone 5 pounds; four, 8 stone 10 pounds; five, 9 stone 3 pounds; six, and aged, 9 stone 5 pounds; mares and geldings allowed 3 pounds; about two miles and a half; twenty-two subscribers.

| | |
|---|---|
| M. Lefevre's Henry, four years | 1 |
| Baron Rothschild's Favonius, four years | 2 |
| Baron Rothschild's Hannah, four years | 3 |

The betting just previous to the start was seven to one against *Henry*; five to four against *Favonius*, and five to four against *Hannah*. Five horses ran. FORDHAM, the well-known jockey, rode *Henry*, the winner.

**Base Ball—Atlantics, of Brooklyn, vs. Baltimore.**

BALTIMORE, June 13.—The following is the score of the game between the Atlantics, of Brooklyn, and Baltimore Club:

| | | | | | | | | | | |
|---|---|---|---|---|---|---|---|---|---|---|
| Atlantic | 0 | 1 | 0 | 0 | 2 | 3 | 0 | 1 | 1 | —7 |
| Baltimore | 1 | 2 | 3 | 0 | 3 | 2 | 2 | 0 | 4 | —17 |

**The Japanese Embassy in Albany.**

ALBANY, N. Y., June 13.—Hon. CHAS. E. PERRY, United States Consul at Aspinwall, met the Embassy at the depot, and invited them to visit him at his residence, Effenhall, on the Troy road, on their return from the Falls. The invitation was received with much pleasure, and Mr. PERRY was assured that, if possible, it would be accepted. The Embassy cannot accept of any public receptions as yet; but as Mr. PERRY is connected with the State Department, this one may be accepted, when the Japanese will have an opportunity to visit the city, county and State institutions here.

# The New-York Times.

VOL. XXI.......NO. 6493. | NEW-YORK, THURSDAY, JULY 11, 1872. | PRICE FOUR CENTS.


## "MIDSUMMER MADNESS."

### Last Act of the Democratic Bedlamites.

### Confession of the Utter Hopelessness of their Cause.

### Gagged and Bound they Gulph Down Greeley and Brown.

### Tammany, in Ecstasy, Fires One Hundred Guns.

### Tweed and Pals Respond to the Nomination of their Apologist.

Special Dispatch to the New-York Times.

BALTIMORE, July 10.—At last the agony is over. With many expressions of extreme disgust, with some weak and vain attempts to hide the dose, the Democracy have swallowed Greeley, Brown and the Cincinnati platform. From first to last this affair has been the ghastliest of political shows. From beginning to end there has hardly been an endeavor to disguise the truth that only because of the delusion that through Greeley lies the only way to repeat at Washington the achievements of the Tammany gang in New-York, Greeley has been taken. Already it is apparent, the Democracy have abandoned the plan of trying to rush their puppet through by a burst of popular enthusiasm, and that their sole reliance is upon the discipline of the party which has so often carried the organization into absurdities and political crimes.

THE DISMAL SCENE OPENS.

When the Convention assembled at 10 o'clock this morning, it was evident that the session was to be more intolerable than that of the previous day. The day was much warmer, and although the building was no more crowded than on the prior occasion, the session being held in the middle of the day, the heat was dangerously intense. There was a manifest desire to get through as soon as possible, and Doolittle calling to order promptly, the report of the Committee on Resolutions, which was the Cincinnati platform *verbatim*, was read at once. It was greeted with a few shouts from the delegates and with applause from the galleries, but the portion which met with most enthusiasm was that which declared that no President should be re-elected, the Democracy evidently being delighted that they were not to have two doses of Greeley. At the conclusion of the reading a score of men jumped up and yelled, and there were cheers from about half the delegates.

THE GAG APPLIED.

Mr. Burr, of Connecticut, Chairman of the Committee, then announced that this platform had been adopted with only the dissenting votes of Delaware, Georgia and Mississippi, and moved the previous question on its adoption by the Convention. Instantly there was a scene of great confusion, and all attempts to keep the disintegrating influences which are at work in the Democratic ranks out of sight were futile. Senator Bayard, of Delaware, rose to a question of order, and bitterly protested against the gag law being enforced upon the Democracy, but he was ruled down by Doolittle. A dozen other members sprung up in different parts of the house to join in the protest, but Doolittle ruled all debate out of order, and after some minutes of wild confusion, the roll-call of the States on sustaining the previous question was proceeded with. There was some disorder during the call, but it was finally concluded and the result announced as 553 yeas to 176 nays.

DISSENSION READY TO BREAK OUT.

The previous question being sustained, Burr had an hour under the rules to close the debate, which had not been allowed, and he gave ten minutes to Mr. Bayard. That gentleman spoke from the platform, making a strong argument for the true Democracy, and against the surrender to Greeley, which was greeted with cheers and hisses. At this moment, it was observable that the Convention had so little of heartiness in its work that if a strong, magnetic speaker like Voorhees, of Indiana, had been in the place of Bayard, the Greeley conspiracy might have been defeated. Bayard had his time extended, so that he spoke altogether twenty minutes, but without much effect, as his voice was not powerful enough to fill the house. After him O'Connor, of South Carolina, made a stirring appeal for the surrender, in which he managed to show that the Democracy had been totally wrong on every political issue for the last twenty years. After him Reagan, of Texas, who was Jeff. Davis' Postmaster-General, made an appeal in behalf of the bailor of his rebel master, after which many of the delegates, remembering former sports began to call "time." There was then a demand that the resolutions should be voted upon separately, which was met with cries of "No," "No," from the venal majority. The call of States then commenced, but the Alabama delegation, the first, wanting to explain, an objection being made, refused to vote. The call proceeded, and during its progress showed the following negative votes: Delaware, 6; Georgia, 19; Mississippi, 9; Missouri, 2; New-Jersey, 9; Oregon, 6; Pennsylvania, 7, and West Virginia, 2, with nine in Tennessee which were not allowed to be counted in consequence of the whole vote being cast at the dicatition of the majority. There was great confusion during the call, the votes of the several States being greeted with cheers and hisses, and the result was at last announced as—Yeas 670, nays 62.

HOFFMAN'S LITTLE DODGE.

There was then a motion made and adopted to go into the nomination of President, whereupon Gov. Hoffman made a desperate attempt to manufacture some Greeley enthusiasm, by handing up a roll of a paper which he said was signed by 15,000 Germans of the City of New-York who would support Greeley and Brown. But those who were upon the platform were inconsiderate enough to allow this document for the sake of effect to be unrolled and stretched through the house. Thereby everybody could see that it was about 100 feet long, and those who were near enough to scan the thing, saw that the names were half an inch apart. This raised grave doubts of the veracity of the Governor of New-York, as a slight calculation showed that there could not be more than 2,500 names appended to the resolution praying for Greeley.

THE NEXT THING ON THE PROGRAMME.

After this [illegible]—which was a [illegible] greeted with only a few [illegible] of States began upon the [illegible] for President. Alabama, [illegible] to vote and, of course, led [illegible]. There was a desperate [illegible] surrender with *éclat*. [illegible] to their feet and [illegible]. There was a general idea that [illegible] there were loud [illegible] Sunset Cox was [illegible] pulling up the New-Yorkers, but without much success. The start was a failure, and the nomination was destined to prove a failure to the end. Presently Delaware showed the latent disaffection by giving her six votes to James A. Bayard. Florida cast 2 blank and Georgia 4 blank. There was an attempt to get up a scene over the 42 of Illinois for Greeley, which was a failure, and a like result attended a like effort when Iowa was called and voted solid for the "Sage."

THE CLIMAX OF DULLNESS.

Here the pivotal-point of this scene of prepared enthusiasm, which it was expected would be unparalleled, was reached. John T. Hoffman was the man of most renown in this Convention. Of national reputation, impressive presence and great power in rousing large masses of men, it was expected that his speech, when New-York was called, would at least stir this Convention into something approaching the grand display at Philadelphia. Through all the roll-call down to this point, it had been whispered through the house, "Wait for New-York. Wait until Hoffman speaks, then let us all get up and yell." But it was beyond Hoffman's power to revive a corpse. The man who had so often roused living assemblages to the highest point saw his words fall without power upon this mass before him. Twice or thrice a few feeble cheers greeted him, and when he concluded, and announced seventy votes for Horace Greeley, not more than 200 of all that body of delegates rose to their feet and cheered. There was nothing approaching even a general outburst of applause. After this failure the ballot went on with even less of life. Presently Pennsylvania was reached, and unexpectedly to all, its vote was announced as only 35 for Greeley, 21 for Jeremiah S. Black, and two blank. This was a damper, and from this point out the Convention never revived from the shock. True, all the votes except two given by West Virginia for Groesbeck were given to Greeley, and it was evident he was the nominee of the Democratic Party for President of the United States by more than the two-thirds required by the long-established usages of the party; but there was no joy in that fact, or if there was it was concealed with most consummate art. Here let me say distinctly, without any intention to color the truth in the least degree, that I watched this scene down to this point closely; I watched it for the purpose of stating plainly the facts as I could see them, and that having so watched I must say that, although occasionally there had been cheers, and that one or two occasions perhaps a third of the Convention had risen and yelled with some degree of vigor, and although from the start there was an evident straining for enthusiasm that never appeared, yet from first to last there was nothing that with a strict regard to truth could be called a general outburst of applause.

NOT UNANIMOUS.

The vote was announced, 687 for Greeley, 18 for Bayard, 2 for Groesbeck, and the remainder blank, and then there were general cries through the house for Pennsylvania, as it was expected that with this State wheeling solid into line for Greeley, the long desired display of popular enthusiasm would be had. Wallace, of the Keystone State, went to the platform, and commencing in his best style, which is always good, sought to revivify the dead mass before him. He spoke of the power and the majority of the State; he spoke of the certainty of its deliverance from Republican rule, and he closed by moving to make the nomination of Greeley unanimous. There were shouts again from a third of the house, but there were none of those unequivocal marks that this nomination sprung from the popular heart which were manifest to the dullest and most prejudiced observer of that glorious scene at the Academy of Music in Philadelphia. It was noticeable that the negative of this question was not put, and that Delaware and the nine votes of New-Jersey were never recounted. They went out from that Convention as they went into it, with an unalterable opposition to Greeley, his works and his ways.

COMIC CLOSE OF THE TRAGEDY.

The management had one card left. At this juncture there was a feeble imitation of Philadelphia. Those who witnessed that magnificent spectacle will remember that after the nomination of Grant a scene was let down at the back of the stage representing the nation's savior upon horseback, and will remember how that vast audience rose as if mad, and how mighty cheers shook the walls of that vast edifice. Here the imitation was so feeble as to be jocose. There was a scene dropped down at the back of the stage, it was an old property of the theatre, which was supposed to represent the White House, and the audience was required by a violent stretch of the imagination to suppose that "honest old Horace," with the Tammany gang behind him, was inside it. Nothing could have been more absurd than this. Instead of cheers there was a general laugh, and this last card also was a total failure.

THE CAUDAL APPENDAGE.

Having swallowed Greeley, the Convention proceeded to bolt B. Gratz Brown with something more of ease. On the call of the States he had 713 votes. Delaware, steadfast to principle, gave her six votes to Stevenson, of Kentucky, and the remainder were blank. Glad to get rid of this unpleasant task, prostrated by the herculean undertaking of transforming Horace Greeley into a Democratic candidate, and with much delight that it had succeeded in the effort, this Convention of the Democracy streamed perspiring into the hot sun of the noonday, and thus this farcial Convention of 1872 came to an end.

THE HONEST MEN OF THE PARTY.

During these expiring agonies of the Democratic Party at the Opera-house, the handful of the faithful had been waiting at the Maryland Institute for the result which every one knew was certain. As soon as it was positively ascertained the meeting was formally called to order by the temporary Chairman, Joseph R. Flanders, the Committee on Permanent Organization presented the following report: For President, Hon. Samuel J. Bayard, of New-Jersey; for Vice-Presidents, Ed. F. Stokes, of South Carolina; James Sweeny, of Pennsylvania; Ezra Kiser, of Texas, and Jesse Miller, of West Virginia.

For Secretaries, James Sherwood, of Connecticut, and T. J. Clute, of New-York. The report was unanimously adopted, and a committee was appointed to conduct Mr. Bayard to the chair. The Chairman, who was received with cheers, said: We are assembled here in obedience to the wishes of a very respectable portion of the Democratic Party in our respective States, to resist the attempt that has been made to destroy Democracy. A conspiracy now culminating in the accomplishment of one of its chief objects—a conspiracy for the dissolution of our party—has been formed and in operation for months, and to resist and defeat that conspiracy we are here today. [Applause.] We consider ourselves as representing vast masses of the Democratic Party whose voices have not been heard in this contest, who have not had an opportunity to express their opinions respecting this foul conspiracy to which I refer. These masses are imperfectly represented in that great Convention at the Opera-house, which is accomplishing these purposes of the conspirators. You have heard from these conspirators again and again that Democracy was a standing menace to the country, and you have heard them say that it must cease to exist. For that purpose it was called upon to indorse the platform and the nominees of Cincinnati. We are here to defeat all nefarious purposes of that sort. We desire to lift aloft the old flag and fling back defiance upon those who would heap so many indignities upon us. But a political coalition of this nature cannot succeed. It never did. When Greeley was nominated at Cincinnati it was received with contempt all over the country, but gradually these manipulations took place, and now they call upon us to indorse his nomination. He concluded by expressing his firm conviction that the honest Democrats of the nation would never permit their party to be destroyed in this way. [Applause.]

ADDRESS TO THE DEMOCRACY.

The Committee on Address reported the following, which was unanimously adopted:

In view of the action which has this day been taken by the Democratic National Convention, sitting in this City at the Opera-house, in the adoption of a platform, in its main features distinctively Republican, and the nomination as a candidate for the Presidency of a man, who for years has been the most bitter and implacable enemy of the Democratic Party, this conference of Democrats from different States of the Union has been convened, to take such action as the honor and safety of the Democratic cause and the interest of the country demand, and as a preliminary to and a justification of our proper action, we hereby declare:

That the aforesaid proceedings of the said National Convention are a virtual dissolution of the hitherto existing organization of the Democratic Party. That they are an unconditional abandonment of the principles of the Democratic Party and the acceptance of such as are conflicting and irreconcilable with them. That by this action the said Convention as claiming to represent the Democratic Party, has been false to its obligation of duty, to principles, to regard for consistence, and to every sentiment of political honor; and as it can represent the Democratic Party only by adhering to its principles, and can make nominations which Democrats are bound to support only by naming candidates who are known and recognized Democrats, therefore the action which it has taken, so far from being binding as the action of the Democratic Party, should be spurned by all true Democrats and resisted with unyielding tenacity and to the utmost extremity. Denying that Democracy is dead or that it can ever die while the principles of our fathers are cherished by even a few devoted hearts, we seize and again fling to the breeze for all true Democrats to rally around the banner so faithlessly lowered, and pledge our undying devotion to the principles which it represents, deeming those principles to involve living and enduring issues.

That the system of Government established by our fathers was a Federal Union of coequal States. That we hold to the doctrines of State Rights and of a strict construction of the Federal Constitution, as defined by Thomas Jefferson, believing their effective recognition to be indispensable to the maintenance of free political institutions and the perpetuation of popular liberty in this country, and to those essential principles of government enumerated by him in his first inaugural address, specially applicable to our time and condition, consisting of the admirable and ever-important propositions—"Equal and exact justice to all men, of whatever State or persuasion, religious or politics;" "peace, commerce and honest friendship with all nations, entangling alliances with none;" "a well-disciplined militia our best reliance in peace and for the first moments of war till regulars may relieve them;" "the supremacy of the civil over the military authority;" "freedom of religion;" "freedom of the Press;" "freedom of the person under the protection of the habeas corpus;" "trial by juries impartially selected;" to which should be added what Mr. Jefferson defined as "the sum of good government," "a wise and frugal Government, which shall restrain men from injuring one another; which shall leave them otherwise free to regulate their own pursuits of industry and improvement, and shall not take from the mouth of labor the bread it has earned."

We recommend our Democratic fellow-citizens in the several States to form Democratic State organizations, and do all in their power to check the growing defection from true Democratic principles; and we further suggest and recommend that a Convention be held at Louisville, Ky., on Saturday, the 3d of September, 1872, to take such steps as may be deemed prudent and essential.

Mr. Bitley made a proposition to proceed to the nomination of a candidate for President and Vice President of the United States, but by consent it was laid upon the table. Mr. Pickmore moved that the following be incorporated in the platform:

1st.—An act of universal amnesty and the restoration of political rights.

2d.—The repeal of all acts injuriously affecting the Southern States.

3d.—The extension of the Franchise laws to the soldiers of the South.

4th.—Payment for the liberated slaves from the National Treasury.

5th.—A change in the national flag to make it acceptable to the people of the whole country.

Mr. Flanders said this was not the place to entertain the motion just then, and it was withdrawn. The meeting then adjourned.

A WRETCHED CREW.

Without faith in the present, without encouragement for the future, ashamed of what they have done, fearful that they will have no recompense for the sacrifice which they have made, the Democratic delegates this evening are scattering to their homes. Horace Greeley has been bolted, swallowed without question, but he sits uneasy upon the Democratic stomach, and with the call for the Louisville Convention staring them in the face as they departed they went to their homes with a fear that their abandonment of principle, their acceptance of their greatest enemy for their candidate, had been without avail. E. C.

## SCENES AND INCIDENTS.

### Applying the Gag—Vigorous but Ineffectual Kicking During the Operation.

A. E. Burr, Chairman of the Committee on Resolutions, announced that the Committee were ready to report, and asked the clerk to read in the first place the introductory paragraph of the report, which is all of the report written by the Committee, and has already been printed. Mr. Burr continued after the rest of the report had been read: Mr. Chairman, these resolutions embrace the Cincinnati platform, word for word; nothing taken from it, nothing added, except the short preamble. The resolutions were adopted by every State in this Union except four, viz.: Delaware, Mississippi, Georgia and Oregon. Having been adopted with that unusual degree of unanimity, Mr. President, I move the adoption of the resolutions as a whole, and on that motion I move the previous question.

THE PRESIDENT—Mr. Burr, of the Committee on Resolutions, reports from that Committee a platform and moves its adoption, and on that motion he asks the previous question.

Senator BAYARD, of Delaware—I rise to a question of order. Has the previous question—another name for gag-law—become the law of a Democratic Convention, without notice to the delegates? [Loud cries of "No," and cheers and hisses.]

The PRESIDENT—The Chair overrules the point of order. The pending question is not debatable, but the Chair deems it proper to state that the Convention has adopted, by unanimous vote, as the rules to govern its proceedings, the rules of the House of Representatives. The motion for the previous question is in order under one of those rules, which are essential to the transaction of business in large bodies of men.

Senator BAYARD, of Delaware—I ask that the Chairman withdraw his call for the previous question for the period of at least ten minutes, that the minority may be heard. [Cries of "No," and much confusion.]

The PRESIDENT—The appeal is made by the gentleman from Delaware to the Chairman of the Committee on Resolutions, and not to anybody else.

Mr. BAILEY, of Pennsylvania—I second the appeal in behalf of the delegation from Pennsylvania. [Cries of "Question."]

Mr. BURR—I would concede what the gentleman asks with the greatest pleasure, but I am under instructions from the Committee and cannot yield the point, and must insist upon the motion I make.

Senator BAYARD—I wish to appeal to the sense of manhood of the Democratic Party, and appeal to the self-respect. Are you deaf to the voice of reason? [Confusion.]

The PRESIDENT—The gentleman from Delaware will come to order.

Hon. G. SAULSBURY, of Delaware—I say this proceeding is unfair. It is unjust to the Democracy of this country.

The PRESIDENT—The question is, Will the House sustain the previous question? [Cries of "Yes" and "No."]

A DELEGATE—Call the roll of States.

The PRESIDENT—The Secretary will call the roll. The roll call resulted in 573 yeas, 169 nays, as follows:

YEAS—Alabama, 10; Arkansas, 12; California, 12; Connecticut, 12; Florida, 5; Georgia, 1; Illinois, 42; Indiana, 30; Iowa, 22; Kansas, 10; Kentucky, 24; Louisiana, 6; Maine, 14; Maryland, 14; Massachusetts, 26; Michigan, 22; Minnesota, 10; Missouri, 26; Nebraska, 6; New-Hampshire, 10; New-York, 74; North Carolina, 20; Ohio, 44; Pennsylvania, 37; Rhode Island, 8; South Carolina, 3; Tennessee, 24; Texas, 16; Vermont, 10; Virginia, 22; West Virginia, 6; Wisconsin, 20.

NAYS—Alabama, 10; Delaware, 6. [When Delaware was called, Mr. Saulsbury said: "We vote no, Sir, now and forever."] Florida, 2; Georgia, 21; Louisiana, 10; Maryland, 2; Mississippi, 16; Missouri, 4; Nevada, 6; New-Jersey, 18; Oregon 6; Pennsylvania, 21; South Carolina, 11; West Virginia, 4.

THE SCREWS TIGHTENED.

Before the question on adopting the resolutions was taken, Mr. McRae, of Tennessee said: I rise to a question of privilege. I insist upon being heard. It is a question of privilege. [Cries of "Sit down." "Shut up."]

The PRESIDENT—What is the gentleman's question of privilege?

Mr. MCRAE—When I was in the last Democratic Convention, in 1860—[Cries of "Sit down."] this: I want to offer my protest against the centralization through the instrumentality of a Committee, by which free thought and free utterance in a Democratic assembly composed of representatives from all parts of the country——

Mr. FAULKNER, of New York, (interposing,) said—I arise to a point of order. It is not a question of privilege for a gentleman to enter a protest, under the form of debating a question that is closed.

The PRESIDENT—The gentleman from Tennessee is out of order.

Mr. MCRAE—I want to say another word on the question of privilege. [Loud cries of "No, no."]

The PRESIDENT—The Secretary will call the roll.

The Secretary then called the roll of States, upon motion for the adoption of the report of the Committee on Resolutions, with the following result—yeas, 670; nays, 62.

THE VOTES ON PRESIDENTIAL CANDIDATES.

The roll call being concluded, the President directed the clerk to read the result of the vote, which was as follows:

| | |
|---|---|
| Whole number of votes cast | 732 |
| Horace Greeley received | 686 |
| (Great applause.) | |
| James A. Bayard, of Delaware | 15 |
| Jeremiah Black, of Pennsylvania | 21 |
| William S. Groesbeck, of Ohio | 2 |
| Blank | 8 |

A motion to make the vote unanimous, failed.

The result of the vote for Vice-President was as follows:

| | |
|---|---|
| For Vice-President, whole number of votes | 732 |
| For B. Gratz Brown | 713 |
| For John W. Stevenson, of Kentucky | 6 |
| Blank votes | 13 |

Mr. Chalmers, of Mississippi, moved that the nomination be made unanimous, which was agreed to without a dissenting voice.

ADJOURNMENT SINE DIE.

The Reading Clerk announced that there would be in the evening at 8 o'clock a grand ratification-meeting at Monument-square, and then, on motion, the Convention, at 1½, adjourned *sine die*.

A DIFFICULT TASK.

Immediately after the adjournment of the Convention, the Committee appointed to notify Mr. Greeley and Mr. Brown of their nomination by the Convention held a meeting, Hon. J. R. Doolittle, Chairman, and L. P. Fenlon, Secretary, and appointed the following Subcommittee to prepare a letter to the nominees, to be submitted to the full Committee this P. M., viz: James S. Thayer, of New-York; Judge J. C. Abbott, of Massachusetts; James Chesnut, of South Carolina, John C. Burch, of Tennessee; A. M. Miller, of Illinois.

On motion of Judge Abbott, it was resolved that the Committee proceed in a body to New-York and present the letter to Mr. Greeley. Should Mr. Brown be in New-York at the time, the Committee will also wait on him.

### The Woman Suffragists Repelled With Scorn.

BALTIMORE, Md., July 10.—Isabella Beecher Hooker, of Connecticut; Susan B. Anthony, of New-York, and Laura De Force Gordon, of California, who have been in attendance on the Convention, hoping to obtain from the Democratic Party a broader recognition of their right to vote than was given by the Republican Convention at Philadelphia, are very much disappointed by the utter rejection of their claims by the Baltimore Convention, and declare their intention of working for the Philadelphia platform and its nominees.

## THE NATIONAL COMMITTEE.

### Augustus Schell Chosen Chairman—Meeting of the Committee Last Night.

BALTIMORE, July 10.—At a meeting of the National Democratic Committee this afternoon, all the members being present except from the States of Delaware and Florida, Hon. Augustus Schell, of New-York, was elected permanent Chairman, and Hon. F. O. Prince, of Massachusetts, was re-elected permanent Secretary and Treasurer. The following gentlemen were elected members of the Executive Committee: Theodore F. Randolph, of New-Jersey; Cyrus H. McCormick, of Illinois; Wm. A. Moore, of Michigan; Isaac E. Eaton, of Kansas; Frederick O. Prince, of Massachusetts; John G. Thompson, of Ohio; James P. Barr, of Pennsylvania; Wm H. Barnum, of Connecticut; Mathew W. Ransom, of North Carolina; Daniel W. L. Bate, of Tennessee.

The Chairman of the National Executive Committee was made a member of the committee *ex-officio*.

The following gentlemen compose the resident Democratic Committee at Washington: Samuel J. Randall, of Pennsylvania; W. W. Corcoran, of Washington; Allen G. Thurman, of Ohio; James Brooks, of New-York; and Montgomery Blair, of Maryland.

## IN THIS CITY.

### Reception of the News—Tammany Responds to the Nomination of the Baltimore Convention.

About ten minutes after the news of Greeley and Brown's nomination at Baltimore reached the City, the guns of Tammany Hall belched out a hundred guns in the City Hall Park. "Tammany responds to the nomination of the Baltimore Convention" was painted upon a canvas banner planted near the scene of the firing. Flags were hoisted upon the City Hall by Tammany's orders, upon the *Tribune* buildings and by the newspapers notorious for a partial and total suppression of the Tammany frauds. The noise of the cannon attracted the crowds usually drawn to the Park upon the occasion of the firing of a salute, and among them were many loud-mouthed champions of the man once honored by the Republican Party, when he was believed to be swayed by principle, and not a selfish desire of his own personal advancement, as is now so palpable to every one.

There were many readers of the newspaper bulletins, and the comments made upon the news were curious.

"What do you think about it?" said one man to his friend.

"Well, I suppose I'll have to vote for him, as he is the nominee of my party; but all that I have to say about is, that there is nothing in his favor but his availability."

Another gentleman, a Democrat, read the announcement again and again, as though there might be something wrong about it, and then walked slowly away, shaking his head mournfully.

Said one gentleman to another, in front of the TIMES bulletin, "How can we, as honest men, support this man? Why, there is not a thief in the City but who is in favor of his election."

"A worse representative of the Democratic sentiment of the country could not have been selected," said the other. These sentiments were seemingly reciprocated by every Democrat of acknowledged standing and probity encountered during the day.

A rush was made by a promiscuous crowd, while the guns were firing, for the *Tribune* office. It was soon flooded by the rough and ready gathering, who evidently anticipated the fun of a speech from Horace. They were not gratified, however, and they amused themselves by poking fun at the Tammany candidate. "Here's Horace. Hello! Horace. How do you do?" some of them would say to attract the attention of the others. There would then be a pushing and turning of heads, and finally a general guffaw at the joke. Several attempts were made to raise a cheer for the "Chappaquack" philosopher in the office, but each time it was a failure. It was impossible to raise anything but a laugh, and there was a broad grin upon the faces of everybody.

The gentlemen employed behind the counter looked upon these proceedings as though they were not relished, and to judge from the expression of their faces, seemed to think that their chief was in some way making himself ridiculous. A man with a shocking bad hat made a rambling speech to the rabble in the Park, and was cheered. This was the only cheering heard during the Tammany explosion. The officials in the City Hall, however, were wild with delight. Several of them were seen dancing an extravagant can-can in the lobby. The employes in Mayor Hall's office were prepared, they said, to bet fabulous amounts on Greeley's election. The same enthusiasm prevailed among the Tammany office-holders in the Sheriff's office, the County Clerk's and in the various Courts. These officials look on Greeley as their savior and have a mistaken idea that he is to be elected and they are to secure a new lease of office. Every Tammany [illegible] friends over the realization of their fondest wishes—a realization which their leaders had planned and worked for a year ago.

Broken, crushed and driven to hide themselves from the public gaze and probable punishment, the Tammany Ring exulted yesterday in a hopeful anticipation of a change of fortune, and their tribe of dependents were ready to shout hallelujahs to the man they have always despised, who has turned his back upon honest men.

Leaving the City Hall yesterday, and plunging into the slums of the City, everywhere the news was heard, and it spread rapidly. Tammany was found to respond to the nomination of the Baltimore Convention through the gin-selling Tammany mouth-pieces of these localities, who, while they debauch the miserable people of their neighborhoods, at the same time use them to corrupt our City politics.

The rum-sellers of Mackerelville, the Five Points, Water-street, Greene-street, the Fourth Ward Murderers' Row, Houston-street, and Bleecker-street, with some remarkable exceptions, "responded to the nomination of the Baltimore Convention." The inhabitants of Battle-row also responded.

Every gaming hell in the City responded, and so did Tweed, Sweeny, Hall, Norton, Genet, Bradley, Billy Cooke, Corson and the long list of Tammany plunderers whose names were made notorious in the TIMES. All of these men indorsed the nomination of the Baltimore Convention yesterday.

While the Tammany guns were thundering out their salute and the Tammany gang were "responding to the Baltimore nominations," and congratulating each other upon the choice of candidates, the Philosopher of many ideas was up town, surrounded by a small body of soreheads, waiting for the telegram announcing the anticipated action of the Convention. He was at the Glenham Hotel head-quarters in the morning, and then retired to the Lincoln Club, where the news reached him. He smiled, and was pleased over it, and appeared to feel no regretful pangs at the thought that he was now the standard-bearer of that corrupt Tammany Hall which he once professed to be opposed to, but with whom it would now appear he has been secretly in friendship.

At Greeley head-quarters, yesterday, only two men were present when the news of the Baltimore nomination was received. These two were asleep, and the noise of the firing of cannon in City Hall Park broke their slumbers but for a moment. They rolled over lazily, and soon the sound of their snoring was the only interruption to the prevailing quiet.

## THE NEUTRAL GROUND.

### Sentiments of the Chicago Times on the Present Political Situation.

CHICAGO, July 10.—The *Times* of this morning, in a leader based on the assumption that the Baltimore Convention will today nominate Greeley and Brown, announces adherence to its views heretofore expressed in regard to Greeley, and says it cannot and will not espouse his cause or labor for his election. It says Greeley is now the candidate of the Democratic Party, so far as he can be made such, a fact which it regards as a hard one, but which cannot be ignored. It is also a fact that the choice of the people must be either for Greeley or Grant. The question as to how Democrats shall vote in this contingency, the *Times* says, is one to be decided by individual voters themselves, inasmuch as the action of the Baltimore Convention has not placed Democrats under the slightest obligation to vote for Greeley, one of the worst embodiments of radicalism the country has ever known. At the same time it is clearly the duty of every Democrat to give himself with renewed devotion to the work of rescuing local Governments and the legislative branch of the General Government from the grasp of Radicals.

The article concludes as follows: "Holding these opinions respecting the duty of Democrats, in view of the hard alternative now presented, the *Times*, while it cannot and will not give to Mr. Greeley any positive support, even as the lesser evil, while it washes its hands of all responsibility for his election, if he shall be elected, will support with redoubled zeal and vigor all Reform candidates for State offices and for Congress—all whom it regards as fitted by their principles, abilities and characters to exert a wholesome conservative influence upon the next Administration, whether it be Grant or Greeley. More could not be accomplished under different auspices, but that fact only strengthens the motive to do everything it is still possible to do to arrest bad and dangerous tendencies of the times, and cleanse the policy and measures of the Government."

## LONG BRANCH.

### How the News of the Nomination was Received—Feeling of the Democrats.

Special Dispatch to the New-York Times.

LONG BRANCH, July 10.—The nomination of Mr. Greeley at Baltimore has failed to elicit any enthusiasm whatever, with one exception. Mr. Frank Leslie, of *Day's Doings'* notoriety, fired a salute of one hundred Chinese bombs, in honor of the event, in front of the Ocean Hotel, much to the annoyance of the dancers inside. He succeeded in nearly overturning several carriages and stages, but did not succeed in raising a single cheer. On the appearance of the police he hurriedly retired. A few Democrats are trying to look and feel easy, but their jollification is far too much like a funeral feast. They seem to feel that, let them try as they may to wash down their unsavory and indigestable meal, they cannot keep off political dyspepsia in November.

## ILLINOIS.

### Desperate Attempt at Enthusiasm Among the Democrats.

Special Dispatch to the New-York Times.

SPRINGFIELD, Ill., July 10.—The Democrats had a ratification meeting this evening, indorsing the action of the Baltimore Convention. A salute was fired from a very small gun, and $10 worth of fire-works were burned. Judge Trumbull was the principal speaker at the meeting. His speech consisted of a tirade against Grant and the Civil Service Reform bill, and in laudations of Horace Greeley. A very noticeable feature of the meeting was the absence of those Republicans who had heretofore gone off after strange gods. The laborers in this State have almost entirely repudiated the attempted coalition. The meeting was a very small affair.

## VIRGINIA.

### Gloomy Attempt at a Ratification Meeting—Coldness with Which the Nomination of the Tammany Candidate is Received.

Special Dispatch to the New-York Times.

RICHMOND, Va., July 10.—The news of the nomination of Greeley and Brown was received here today by the Greeleyites according to a matured programme. A piece of infant artillery was promptly carried to Capitol-square, where a number of rounds were fired, which were quite audible to all who were in the square, or who were not very far off. A mass meeting in front of Virginia Hall, tonight, was the best of the programme, but it was a most ridiculous failure, despite the music made by two dilapidated drums, the noise of the cannon and the burning of a scant supply of indifferent fire-works. The crowd that gathered was laughably small, and was chiefly composed of boys of both colors, and of curious persons on their way home who paused to see what the hideous noise was about. At length after waiting for the multitude that didn't loome there were three separate distinct efforts to make a speech by as many persons with as many separate and distinct failures as to the result. I will mention the names of these orators, whom I'll wager neither you nor your readers ever heard of before. They were Messrs. F. W. Mahood, W. W. Cosby and A. Q. Holliday. The whole thing was so lame, impotent and farcical that at an early hour it was announced by Mr. K. Mahood that this was a mere spontaneous running together of the people to manifest their abounding joy at the nomination of Greeley, and that the grand ratification meeting would take place Friday night. He concluded the melancholy services by calling for nine cheers for Greeley and Brown, when, to there was a deep silence in response. [illegible] and others then gloomily dispersed. This and other failures past and to come, are the consequences of counting upon a popular enthusiasm for Greeley that has no real existence.

## WASHINGTON NEWS.

### Preparations for the Campaign—Tricks of the Tribune—Naval Appropriation.

Special Dispatch to the New-York Times.

WASHINGTON, July 10.—Political advices received here from Indiana within the past few days are very encouraging for the Republicans. There is a well-grounded belief among the best judges that the State will elect the Republican ticket in October next. This belief is only entertained because of the known facts in regard to the thorough organization of the canvass thus early in the campaign, and because of the vigilant and untiring efforts of the State Committee and its accessions in the counties, towns and districts. An organization by school districts throughout the State is now being perfected, by which concert in action can be secured nearly as perfect as in New-Hampshire. No roseate views of the campaign prevail in Indiana. The Republican workers too well know that nothing but hard work will win the victory. The men of coolest judgment here, among whom are several members of the Administration, view the general situation somewhat as the Indiana Representatives view the situation in that State. They are confident of victory, but expect that it will be achieved only by hard work. What they look to especially for effective aid is local organization, initiated first in the State Committees and running down through to townships and school districts. They look to see this done with unusual energy in the States of New-York and Pennsylvania. They do not mean to be deceived or allow anybody to be deceived by false estimates of Republican strength any more than they mean to be bluffed by the extravagant game of brag which the Greeleyites are now playing. They expect to see hard work done, and know that only will secure victory over a desperate and unscrupulous enemy.

SHARP PRACTICE BY THE REFORM PARTY.

Every now and then the Reform preachers are caught in some contemptible trick which puts to shame all their professions. This time it is two liberal organs, the New-York *Tribune* and the St. Paul *Dispatch*. The *Tribune* prints Sumner's speech as a supplement, and sends it to its feeble country confreres for circulation in their editions, without paying postage. In this case the St. Paul *Dispatch* sought to change the *Tribune* supplement into a *Dispatch* supplement, by printing two turned rules, and the words, "Supplement to the St. Paul *Dispatch*" over the *Tribune* title, leaving the rest of the sheet, *Tribune*, prospectus column, title lines and all just as printed at the *Tribune* office. A copy of this document having been forwarded to the First Assistant Postmaster-General, it is found to be in direct violation of section 142 of the postal Code, which subjects the entire edition to letter postage, and the proprietor who attempts to circulate it to $5 fine for each document so inclosed and sent through the mails. The Postmaster at St. Paul has been instructed accordingly.

A NAVAL CLAIM.

Yesterday, W. E. Leroy, Earl English and Robert G. F. Lewis, the officers of the Navy appointed by the Judge of the District Court to appraise the value of the rebel ram Albemarle, which was sunk in Wilmington harbor during the war, submitted their report that $282,856 90 is a just and equitable appraisement. The Court made an order that $202,912 be deposited with the Assistant-Treasurer, 79,934 having been previously deposited for distribution.

THE POSTAL CARDS.

Numerous inquiries have been received by the Post-office Department in relation as to when postal cards will be supplied to the public, and if they are at present ready for distribution. As the clerks would have all of their time occupied by answering letters of this kind, the general statement is authoritatively made that the postal cards will not be ready for distribution for at least one month yet. They will be furnished by contract, and advertisements for proposals will be issued by the Department next week.

SEIZURE OF CUBAN PRIVATEERS.

The Secretary of the Treasury expects a full report by mail of all the circumstances attending the seizure of the alleged Cuban privateer Pioneer by the revenue-cutter Mocassin. No additional particulars have reached the Department today.

## BY MAIL AND TELEGRAPH.

Lieut. J. F. Meiggs has been detached from torpedo duty at League Island.

The New-York State Temperance Society is called to meet at Saratoga Springs on July 23.

The weather throughout England yesterday was fair, and favorable to the growing crops.

Lieut. R. D. Hitchcock has been detached from Newport on Aug. 1, and ordered to duty at the Hydrographic Office.

Continued and heavy rains, which have been very damaging to the crops, are reported in South Carolina.

Cotton caterpillars have appeared in many counties of Alabama, and cause much depression among the planters.

Pay-master C. P. Thompson has been detached from the Plymouth, and ordered to duty in the Bureau of Provisions and Clothing.

First Assistant Engineer E. A. Magee has been detached from the Canonicus, and ordered to special duty at the Treasury Department.

A company of wealthy Bostonians have purchased the furnaces, plant and lease of the iron-mines at Clementsport, N. S., and will commence work at once.

John H. Warland, for many years editor of the Lowell *Courier*, and widely known as a vigorous political writer, died in the Asylum on Sunday last, aged sixty-five.

The boat race at Digby, N. S., between Fulton and Browne, has been postponed for smooth water. Great crowds were present to witness the race. The accommodations are poor.

Last evening a severe storm, accompanied by thunder and lightning, passed over Philadelphia, Penn. Several culverts caved in. Trees were uprooted and telegraph-wires torn down.

David Smith, the youngest son of Joseph Smith, the Mormon prophet, lectured at Salt Lake City last night against polygamy. His presence excited the present Church authorities out a little.

The report that the time for the Saratoga races has been changed is not true. The races will begin on Saturday, the 13th, and continue every day, Sunday excepted, for six days. Longfellow and Bassett are both there.

A grand banquet was given Tuesday evening at Peterboro', Ontario, to Sir John A. Macdonald, the Premier of the Dominion. About 1,500 persons were present, including a large number of ladies. The town was handsomely decorated and brilliantly illuminated.

Tuesday afternoon Judge Steele addressed the Phi Beta Kappa Society of the University of Vermont, at Burlington, and the Junior exhibition occurred in the evening. Yesterday was the Commencement Day. Twenty-five have already applied for admission next year, of whom five are girls.

A Committee of the Board of Trade and of the Workmen's Benevolent Association met yesterday at Potteville, Penn., to average the prices of coal from the June returns, and found the same to be $1 99. In accordance with the agreement made in January, 1868, the wages for July will be paid on the basis then established.

Gen. St. John B. L. Skinner died yesterday morning, at Wilmington, of paralysis, aged seventy-five years. Gen. Skinner was a native of Washington County, New-York. He served in the war of 1812, and during the administration of President Pierce was made First Assistant Postmaster-General—a position which he retained under Presidents Buchanan, Lincoln and Johnson.

### Jubilee Finances—A Deficit of $150,000.

*From the Boston Post, July 8.*

The balancing of accounts by the Jubilee Committee reveals the unwelcome fact that there is a deficit of $150,000, which will have to be made up from the guarantee fund, unless some method of swelling the receipts is hit upon. The building and fixtures still remain, but even these will hardly make up the loss. Mr. Gilmore, who has worked night and day for many months in bringing his great conception into shape, finds no return for his exhaustive labors, and the proceeds of his benefit were generously donated by him to the association. The Executive Committee would doubtless find, if they chose to experiment, that the sentiment of the business community of Boston is heartily favorable to any scheme which can be devised for [illegible]

## FOREIGN AND DOMESTIC NEWS

### The American System of Representation in England.

### Efforts to Secure it for the House of Commons.

### Two Men Killed in Pope County, Arkansas.

### Release of Dr. Houard by the Spanish Government.

### Conclusion of the Commencement Exercises at Bowdoin.

GREAT BRITAIN.

Attempt to Introduce the American Elective System into England.

LONDON, July 10.—In the House of Commons today Mr. Morrison moved the second reading of the Proportional Representation bill, which adopts the American system of representation proportioned to population, readjusted according to each successive census.

Mr. Morrison explained the operation of the bill at great length. He demonstrated that under this system Birmingham would be entitled to seven and Liverpool to eleven representatives in Parliament, instead of three each as at present, and that London would be represented by sixty-two members instead of twenty as now.

Tom Hughes seconded the motion of Mr. Morrison.

Sir Charles Dilke opposed the motion, on the ground that Ireland and Scotland were not included in the operation of the bill.

Right Hon. Sir Alexander Cockburn, arbitrator on the part of England on the Geneva Tribunal, is to be created an Earl in recognition of his eminent services as Lord Chief Justice of England and in connection with the arbitration.

Lord Tenterden and Sir Roundell Palmer, agent and counsel for Great Britain before the Tribunal of Arbitration, will leave to-morrow for Geneva, whither Sir Alexander Cockburn went on Monday.

ARKANSAS.

The Troubles in the State—Two More Men Killed.

LITTLE ROCK, June 10.—Parties from Pope County this evening report that the militia to the number of sixty were near Dover last night. It is reported they intended to make an attack on that place today; also that two more citizens were killed last night at Dover. The Governor will send Major-General Upham, of the militia, to the scene of the troubles to-morrow to investigate the matter.

The counterfeiters were brought before Chief-Justice McClure this evening on a writ of habeas corpus, and the bail of each was fixed at $10,000. The party was remanded to prison in default of bail.

SPAIN.

Dr. Houard Released by the Spanish Authorities.

MADRID, July 10.—Houard is free. An order from Madrid offered his release as an act of pardon, to which Mr. Houard demurred, as his acceptance of it might appear an acknowledgement of guilt and a waiver of his right to compensation. He was then turned or forced out. He called yesterday on a Cadiz correspondent immediately after his release.

BOWDOIN COLLEGE.

Inauguration of New Scholarships—A Military Drill to be Introduced.

BRUNSWICK, Me., July 10.—At a meeting of the Boards of Trustees and Overseers of Bowdoin College today the following new scholarships were accepted: One thousand dollars from Rev. W. T. Savage, of Franklin, N. H.; $300 from Miss Mary Cleves, of Hallowell; $1,000 from Marshall Cram, of Brunswick, the scholarship to be called the "Cram Memorial Scholarship," in honor of his son, the late N. H. P. Cram, of the Class of '61; also, $1,000 from Mrs. Maria M. Sewall, of Kennebunk.

It was voted to repair Massachusetts Hall and fit up the upper rooms for a museum of natural science, to be called the "Cleveland Museum of Natural Science." The Department of Military Tactics was put on a footing with other departments, as regards authority and discipline, and all the students who are able will be forced to drill. The honorary degrees of LL. D. were conferred on James W. Bradbury and E. E. Bourne.

NATIONAL BANKS.

Condition of the Banks Throughout the Country.

WASHINGTON, D. C., July 8.—Abstract of reports made to the Controller of the Currency, showing the condition of the National Banks in the United States at the close of business on Monday, the 10th day of June, 1872:

RESOURCES.

| | |
|---|---|
| Loans and discounts | $847,[illegible] |
| Overdrafts | 4,097,851 |
| United States Bonds to secure circulation | 377,0[illegible] |
| United States Bonds and securities on hand | [illegible] |
| Other stocks, bonds and mortgages | [illegible] |
| Due from redeeming and reserve agents | [illegible] |
| Due from other National Banks | [illegible] |
| Due from State Banks and bankers | [illegible] |
| Real estate, furniture and fixtures | [illegible] |
| Current expenses | 6,719,794 |
| Premiums | [illegible] |
| Checks and other cash items | [illegible] |
| Exchanges for Clearing-house | [illegible] |
| Bills of other National Banks | [illegible] |
| Bills of State Banks | [illegible] |
| Fractional currency | [illegible] |
| Specie | [illegible] |
| Legal-tender notes | [illegible] |
| Clearing-house certificates | [illegible] |
| Three Per Cent. certificates | [illegible] |
| Aggregate | $1,770,[illegible] |
| Number of banks, 1,853. | |

LIABILITIES.

| | |
|---|---|
| Capital stock | $470,543,301 |
| Surplus fund | [illegible] |
| Undivided profits | [illegible] |
| National Bank notes outstanding | [illegible] |
| State Bank notes outstanding | [illegible] |
| Dividends unpaid | [illegible] |
| Individual deposits | [illegible] |
| United States deposits | [illegible] |
| Deposits of United States disbursing officers | [illegible] |
| Due to National Banks | [illegible] |
| Due to State Banks and bankers | [illegible] |
| Notes and bills rediscounted | [illegible] |
| Bills payable | [illegible] |
| Aggregate | $1,770,[illegible] |

(Signed,) JOHN JAY KNOX, Controller of the Currency.

THE WEATHER.

Events and Probabilities.

WASHINGTON, July 11—1 A. M.—The barometer has continued falling over New-England, Middle and Western Gulf States. It is highest over the South Atlantic States. Cloudy weather and areas of rain with fresh to brisk southerly to westerly winds have prevailed during the day from Ohio, eastward and northward, and over the Gulf States with fresh to brisk easterly winds. Telegraphic reports for Wednesday evening have not yet been received from stations in the Ohio Valley, and from Mississippi to Lake Michigan and westward, and for midnight reports have been received from Pennsylvania and south-eastern New-York to Georgia only.

PROBABILITIES.

Cloudy weather, areas of rain and easterly winds [illegible] partially cloudy weather and southerly to easterly winds [illegible] South Atlantic States [illegible] the Middle States; westerly winds for New-England.

# The New-York Times.

VOL. XXI.......NO. 6567. NEW-YORK, SATURDAY, JULY 27, 1872. PRICE FOUR CENTS.

## THE INFAMOUS ALLIANCE

### "Tammany Responds to Greeley."

### Hands Clasped Across Tammany Hall.

### Tammany Clubs Formed Again for "Honest Horace."

### The City and State to be Plundered.

### Tweed and Sweeny Preparing to Return to Power.

### Hoffman to be Re-elected and Andrew H. Green to be Kicked Out.

### Every Rascal in the State is For Greeley.

### Facts which Cannot be Answered.

### Let us all Vote for Greeley and More Tammany Robbery.

**"Tammany Does Support Greeley—Tammany is for Greeley."**—*New-York Tribune, July 18, 1872.*

Anybody who walks through our streets, or who takes the trouble to make a few inquiries among Democrats, may see or find out that Horace Greeley is supported by the entire gang of Tammany Democrats.

From Tammany Hall his flag is flying.

The Tammany which supports Greeley is the same as that which robbed the people. Respectable Democrats are everywhere holding aloof from him. Mr. Augustus Schell avows that he only supports Greeley as a means of bringing utter and final ruin upon the Republican Party.

But the Tammany which "is for Greeley" today is identically the same body which so abominably plundered New-York, and which was defended and advocated by the very newspapers now engaged in defending and advocating Greeley.

When the announcement of his nomination at Baltimore reached New-York, Tammany ordered a salute of 100 guns to be fired in his honor. The *Tribune* itself, on the following day, made the following boasts in its most prominent columns:

"In the City Hall Park was displayed a large banner bearing the inscription: TAMMANY RESPONDS TO THE NOMINATION OF THE NATIONAL CONVENTION AT BALTIMORE.' Directly in front of this banner was a four-pounder, from which 100 salutes in honor of the nomination were fired in quick succession. Soon after this small gun began to make itself heard, two ten-pounders were put in position a little to the left of it, each of which added fifty reverberating roars," &c. &c. "Upon the receipt of a dispatch from Baltimore announcing the nomination of the Cincinnati candidates, *a large flag was raised over Tammany Hall.*"

Tweed is working actively for Greeley. So is Sweeny. So is A. Oakey Hall. So is Matthew T. Brennan, who continues to cheat the City yearly out of thousands of dollars. There is not a rascal connected with the Ring which so wickedly plundered New-York who is not vitally concerned in Greeley's success. This is a matter of fact, which no respectable Democrat denies.

All these knaves are well aware that the election for Governor, and that for Mayor and other local officers, take place on the same day as the Presidential election.

Greeley's "Republican" friends must vote the entire Democratic ticket, and in return the Tammany gang will vote for Greeley.

Thus a Tammany Mayor will be secured, and Controller Green will instantly be turned out. The *Herald* is already suggesting Mr. John Kane as a candidate for Mayor. Mr. Kane is merely another edition of Mayor Hall. He is Hall's nominee. He worked hard to prevent Hall's expulsion from the Union Club, and Hall would be scarcely less powerful than he now is if Kane were elected. The City of New-York would once more be handed over to a rule of Thieves, and the Tammany system of government would be carried to Washington.

At a great meeting of citizens at Cooper Institute, on the 23d July, 1872, Mr. Jackson S. Schultz addressed a few words of grave warning to the people of New-York. He said: "The City and State of New-York must be saved as well as the nation. You cannot conceive, though you have read the papers as I have, how much corruption there is in the City of New-York. I do hope and expect that the good people of New-York will not forget their own City." Citizens who value the good name and prosperity of the City will do well to pay timely heed to this warning. The gang of plunderers, routed last Fall, are again in full cry after their prey. Everywhere the Tammany clubs and organizations are at work for Greeley. Do they love him? Not a bit of it—they only expect to sneak back to power under his mantle. Shall they be allowed to do it?

Brennan's part in this conspiracy is an active one. See the following quotations from the *Tribune*, Greeley's organ:

"The Boulevard Club, of which Sheriff Matthew B. Brennan is President, fired 100 guns in honor of the nominations."

"An impromptu ratification meeting of the Tenth Ward M. T. Brennan Association was held last night at the hall No. 161 Hester-street. Several addresses were delivered."

"A large number of the members of the *Manhattan Club* were at the club-house in Fifth-avenue, last night, waiting for intelligence from Baltimore, and canvassing the probabilities of Mr. Greeley's nomination on the first ballot. Considerable anxiety was manifested to obtain the latest news. Among the visitors at the Club during the evening were C. B. Hall, Judge Waterbury, Surrogate Hutchings, Edward Schell, Mayor Hall, Judson Jarvis and others.

The members of the *Blossom Club* assembled in large numbers and discussed the work of the Convention, commending the speech of August Belmont, and expressing the hope that no sudden caprice would prevent the nomination of Mr. Greeley."—*Tribune, July 10.*

"In the evening *Judson Jarvis and the blooded colts of the Sheriff's office* came in hilariously, and informed the head-quarters that the Twenty-first Ward was going for Greeley."—*Herald, July 18.*

Some of the same gang are compelled to keep a little more in the background, owing to circumstances "over which they have no control." They are afraid that the Police may be after them. The character of many of these men may be gathered from the following list of

#### GREELEY'S CHIEF SUPPORTERS.

**Under Criminal Indictments.**

PETER B. SWEENY, for conspiracy to defraud. Defended by Greeley in the *Tribune*, though he has offered hundreds of thousands to "settle" and be relieved of the fear of prosecution.

A. OAKEY HALL, for misdemeanor in office. Repeatedly defended by the *Tribune*.

JAMES H. INGERSOLL, felony and conspiracy to defraud.

WM. H. COOKE, forgery. Notorious ballot-box stuffer and repeater.

BENJAMIN B. MALLORY, twice indicted for attempt to kill, known as a "Kurfist."

WILLIAM JOHNSON, alias Jackson, alias "the Kid;" a Tammany voter, hailing from Fourth Ward; half a dozen indictments found against him for larcenies and burglaries; judgment always suspended.

NATHANIEL SANDS, Tax Commissioner, for misdemeanors. Cheated the City out of $75,000. The Controller now refuses to pay his salary, and he dare not sue for it.

TOM FIELDS, who played a confidence game in collecting money for the Volunteer Fire Department, and appropriating it himself. Indicted by the Grand Jury for misdemeanor.

JAKE DEPEW, arrested for a minor crime against the United States Government, and after being lodged in jail for some time, was pardoned by Andrew Johnson. President Grant, for good reasons, revoked the pardon, and Jake served out his term of two years. He is now an enthusiastic supporter of "Old Honesty," and shakes hands with him across the "bloody chasm."

**Gamblers.**

"BIG MURRAY, the bond-smasher," keeper of a keno-hell in Eighth-street.

HARVEY YOUNG, keeper of faro-bank corner of Bleecker-street and Broadway.

DAN KERRIGAN, of Bowery; nine indictments ordered against him for election frauds.

**Disturbers of the Public Peace.**

JOHN CONNERS, alias Jakey, a prize-fighter; ordered indicted for election frauds.

JIM CUSICK, "the man-eater," pugilist.

JOE COBURN, pugilist.

TIMOTHY alias TAD DONOVAN, the Nineteenth Ward ex-pugilist and wealthy retired gin-seller. He playfully bit off the ear of the late lamented Alderman Thomas Conner when Fernando Wood was Mayor. "Tad" has made nearly $60,000 in politics, and hopes to double it if Greeley is elected.

FRANK DUFFY, retired pugilist, who gets up the kind of balls and picnics the newspapers condemn so often.

MICKEY FAY, who held four sinecures under Tammany, fights dogs and cats, and used to kill rats with his teeth.

DENNIS SULLIVAN, keeper of a low groggery in the Sixth Ward.

JOHN U. ANDREWS, a leader of the rioters in 1863; was convicted and sent to Sing Sing; is now making stump-speeches for Greeley, just as he made speeches to incite the mob to burn down negro asylums and private dwellings in 1863.

ROCKY MOORE, pugilist.

MARK LANIGAN, keeper of a "bucket-shop" in James-street. Held at one time, if he does not now, a place under Police Board.

BILLY DONNELLY and his Twelfth Ward gang pledge Battle-row for Greeley and his Grats.

EDWARD L. CAREY, who incited the Hibernians to massacre the Orangemen last 12th of July; promised them arms and deserted his dupes on that day. His incendiary speeches are on file in this office.

STEPHEN JOSEPH MEANEY, figured as the self-constituted prosecutor of the military and Police authorities, who saved the City from a bloody riot on the 12th of last July.

**Men of Notoriously Bad Character.**

REUBEN E. FENTON: started in life as a dishonest clerk; has been intimately associated with Fisk and Gould; is known to have extorted large sums of money from the Central Railroad; connected with every dirty or corrupt job in New-York politics ever since he has been in public life; repeatedly charged with taking bribes for signing bills while Governor; is now compelling a Senate Committee clerk to forge his name to Greeley campaign documents.

M. P. BEMUS, of Chautauqua; boasted that he made $70,000 in one session.

ORANGE S. WINANS, of Chautauqua; sold himself to the Erie Ring; Greeley's "political leper."

JAMES NELSON, of Rockland, leader of Black Horse Cavalry in Legislature.

Dr. LOUGHRAN, of Ulster, leader of Black Horse Cavalry in Legislature.

ABNER C. MATTOON, of Oswego, Ex-Senator. Denounced by *Tribune* as corrupt.

HORACE BEMUS, of Steuben; Black Horse Cavalry.

MOSES S. SUMMERS; headed *Tribune's* "black list" of members of Assembly.

GEO. C. ELLISON, cheated soldiers.

JOHN CASHOW, of Kings County.

C. A. LAMONT, bounty broker.

**Other States.**

JUDSON KILPATRICK, New Jersey, formerly Minister to Chili; tried to force an abandoned woman into Chilian society, and was recalled. Has long been a reproach to the Republican Party, and has now happily gone over to the Democrats.

WM. M. GROSVENOR, of Missouri, of whom Horace Greeley said that he had "evinced the radical knavery of his character." Dismissed from the army for improper conduct.

JAMES M. SCOVEL, New Jersey, a notorious political trickster.

Gen. J. B. STEEDMAN, Defaulting Revenue Officer.

JOHN F. DRIGGS, of Michigan, Ex-Member of Congress and Cadet Broker.

Gov. WARMOTH, of Louisiana.

**Tammany Office-holders and Sinecurists, Mostly Tammany Republicans.**

JOHN COCHRANE, a faithful henchman of Tammany, under the disguise of a Republican. President of the Tammany Board of Aldermen. Man-of-all-work for Tweed. Greeley said of him, in 1865, that *"hell from beneath was stirred to demoniac joy"* by his treacherous course. On Jan. 7, 1860, Mr. Greeley denounced John Cochrane as a "double-dyed" apostate, and asked if there was "on the wide earth one man who believes that he would have so turned his back on himself, had he not found this his readiest road to office and power?" Cochrane was Greeley's chief manager at Cincinnati and Baltimore and is now Chairman of his Committee.

MATT. T. BRENNAN, Sheriff, guilty of defrauding the City, but defended by the *Tribune* and Greeley, because he is getting up "Brennan Clubs."

WALDO HUTCHINS, chief promoter of the "West Washington Market swindle" in 1860; Hutchins is said to have received over $100,000 for that job; a partner of Augustus Schell; Fenton's "right bower;" Hutchins' name constantly appears in the Tax Levies; is a great friend of Tweed's, and is now Greeley's cordial ally.

ANTHONY HARTMAN, Tweed's Police Justice; leader of black horse cavalry in the Legislature; ordered to be indicted by the Grand Jury for election frauds.

MICHAEL J. SHANDLEY.

J. SOLIS RITTERBAND, Counsel to Tax Commissioners, $10,000.

GEORGE H. VAN CLEFT, City Surveyor.

HENRY A. BARNUM, Deputy Tax Commissioner and corrupt Ex-State Prison Inspector; has long been in the pay of Tammany.

EDWARD J. SHANDLEY, Tweed's Police Justice.

PHILIP FRANKENHEIMER, removed for black-mailing poor Germans five dollars each.

WM. H. DE CAMP, Deputy Fire Marshal.

JAMES L. HASTIE. Has been the benchman of Police Commissioner Manierre, and has always acted as the latter wanted him. Hastie is termed the "Champion Skedaddler," because he was one of the first to run away from the battle of Bull Run, in which his Regiment, the Seventy-ninth New-York, was engaged.

Col. BOGUE, a chronic applicant for place. He was turned out of the Clerk's office in the Fire Department by the Republican Commissioners for inattention to his duties. He has now got some office under the Tammany Republicans, and is employed as a Greeley skirmisher in the Fifth Ward.

MICHAEL MADIGAN, who recently responded for the Democratic Greeley Association in the First District, is an Ex-Assemblyman. At present he keeps a rum-shop down-town. He is an active member of the Tammany fold.

"DENNY" McLOUGHLIN was a United States Gauger under Collector Pleasonton, but lost his position on account of inattention to his duties. He is a Second Ward rough, and now serves as President of the Greeley Campaign Club in the Second District.

HUGH NESBITT, President of the Greeley faction in the Sixth District, wants to get back in the Custom-house, which he prefers to his pleasant office in the Street-cleaning Department.

FREDERICK ENGEL, President of the Eighth District Club, was a sinecurist under Ex-Controller Connolly. When Mr. Green took charge of the City finances he was told he could not get his salary, because he had not done any work for it.

JOHN MULLALY, the Tammany Health Commissioner, who is notorious only for his activity in opposing improvements. The *Evening Post* thus describes a paper of which he is editor: "The *Record* was always notorious as a leading pro-slavery, secession, Tammany organ." Mullaly has an enormous claim against the City for advertising. He hopes to get it if Greeley is elected, and will certainly not get it until then.

**Sample Traitors.**

J. F. REGAN, Confederate Postmaster-General.

D. R. ATCHISON, Missouri "border ruffian."

J. Q. C. LAMAR, slave-trader, &c.

JAKE THOMPSON, Ex-Secretary of Interior; director of plan to burn Northern cities.

Col. E. M. YERGER, who murdered Union officer at Jackson.

Ex-Gov. WESTCOTT, of Florida, "because it kills the Republican Party."

GEORGE N. SANDERS, Greeley peace negotiator; aider and abettor of the St. Albans raid. See *Tribune* for description of his character. Now a guest of Greeley's, at Chappaqua, and a constant visitor at the Greeley Head-quarters.

Col. JOLLY, of Alabama, Grand Cyclops of Kuklux.

Gen. FOREST, Chief of Kuklux and author of the atrocious Fort Pillow massacre.

Ex-Senator GWIN, of whom Mr. Greeley insinuated (Nov. 18, 1861,) that he was "cowardly," that he had an "unscrupulous nature," and "that while in the Senate he was not so much the counselor and confident of Davis as his confederate and tool." Recently a guest at the Chappaqua revels.

**Soreheads Turned Out of Office.**

GEO. W. PALMER, late Appraiser.

E. A. MERRITT, late Naval Officer.

R. W. DE GRUSHE, late in Custom-house.

GEO. H. VAN CLEFT, late Engineer at Navy-yard.

HENRY M. WILLIAMS, late Deputy Collector.

P. FRANKENHEIMER, late Assistant Assessor.

THOS. F. RIGHTMIRE, late in Custom-house.

ROBERT MURRAY, late United States Marshal.

B. F. MUDGETT, late Appraiser, man whom jury didn't believe under oath.

GEO. F. COACHMAN, late in Navy-yard.

MORGAN L. FILKINS, late Postmaster at Albany.

HENRY C. LAKE, late weigher in Custom-house.

J. R. ALLABEN, late Assessor.

J. W. HASBROUCK, of Ulster.

J. S. GILMORE, who attended the Council from the Eleventh District, was a Gauger in the Custom-house, but was removed for cause. He was also elected by Republican votes to the Common Council, but sold out to the Democrats on taking his seat, and boasted that they trusted him. He now holds, or has very recently held a place under the City Government.

CHAS. W. GODDARD, Fenton's Captain of the Port.

WILLIAM CASEY, of Saratoga, removed as weigher in Custom-house, for good reasons.

JOHN DUKE, President of the Twelfth District Club, is another sorehead. He was displaced as United States Weigher by Collector Murphy, and subsequently joined the malcontents. After his removal, he got a profitable contract from the Board of Education.

V. HEIMBERGER, Secretary of the German Greeley Club, in the same district, got discharged from the internal revenue service, and has since been opposed to the Administration.

WILLIAM ATKINSON, President of the Sixteenth District Association, held a position in the Navy-yard some time ago, but was discharged by the President for cause.

MICHAEL BERNHARDT, Secretary of the German faction in the Sixteenth District, got an appointment as United States Census Marshal, but had to relinquish it because he was unfit to perform the duties.

**Disappointed Applicants for Office.**

WILLIAM DORSHEIMER, applicant for Minister to Berlin, Agent under Alabama Treaty, and various other positions.

ETHAN ALLEN, applicant for United States District Attorney, and for Attorney-General of State.

BURT VAN HORN, applicant for Weigher in Custom-house and Postmaster at Lockport.

ALANSON WELSH, applicant for Canal Commissioner.

CHARLES CARRICK, applicant for Custom-house.

FRANCIS SNYDER, applicant for Custom-house.

MOSES S. SUMMERS, applicant for Syracuse Post-office.

This catalogue might be indefinitely extended—but we have quoted enough for one day. EVERY MAN in the above list is actively at work for Greeley. Everywhere in the City they are forming clubs for his election. The following are samples of the news which daily fill the papers. Read them, and form your own conclusions:

**Tammany "Indorses" Greeley.**

"The Tammany Committee of Thirteen on Organization met last evening at Tammany Hall, *Henry W. Genet* in the chair. Among those present were Judge *Shandley*, Judge *Ledwith*, Judge *Dodge* and *John Morrissey*. Mr. *Morrissey*, in conversation with Judge *Ledwith* and others, said that *Horace Greeley* ought to receive the support of the Democracy, and in that event he will not only be elected, but the Democracy would be able to carry a majority of the Congressional districts of this State, and would probably secure a majority of the next House of Representatives."

"The Tammany Society met last night, and Ex-Gov. *Horatio Seymour* was installed as Sachem. In a speech which he subsequently made he indorsed the policy of the Cincinnati platform, and favored the adoption of his 'old friend,' *Greeley*, as the Democratic candidate for the Presidency."

Greeley's leading champions among the Republican papers cannot and do not deny his associations with Tammany. They are too notorious to be disputed.

The pretense of Greeley is that respectable Democrats support him. It is not true. Hoffman is the most "respectable" man among them in this State, and Hoffman signed fraudulent warrants for the Tammany Ring; signed the Erie bill; and vetoed Mr. Tilden's measure for bringing the Tammany thieves to justice. He also vetoed every Reform measure passed by the Legislature last session.

The oldest and best Democrats in the City and State are opposed to Greeley, because they look upon the bargain he has made as an immoral and detestable one, and because they know that he is surrounded by the most unscrupulous and disreputable men in the country.

Greeley's success next November, if it could be accomplished, would send down the prices of real estate in New-York City from twenty-five to fifty per cent., because it would mean the return of the Tammany thieves to power. If Greeley's cause were not identified with that of the Ring Thieves, *would A. Oakey Hall, "Pete" Sweeny and Matt Brennan support him so earnestly?*

We invite citizens of all shades of politics to consider these facts. They are of momentous importance to every honest tax-payer. The Reform fight must be renewed at the polls next November. Will you, *can* you expect Reform from Sweeny, Hall, Brennan & Co.?

Will you deliberately and with your eyes open, throw away all that you gained last year, and surrender the City to the gang which plundered it so remorselessly? GREELEY cannot control his present supporters. They will manage *him*. It is for that purpose they have entered into a bargain with him now.

Shall it be progress or reaction next November? We ask every tax-payer to inquire into the facts of the present canvass, and upon those facts to make up his mind.

**Did Fisk Own Two Governors?**

A curious story is current concerning Ex-Gov. Randolph, of New-Jersey, who is now Chairman of the Democratic National Executive Committee. It is alleged that Fisk, Gould & Co. gave him $30,000 as a consideration for his services in removing taxation from the Erie Railroad in Jersey City, and that afterward he was compelled by the precious rascals to sign bills of any nature, as they demanded. It is also said that the proofs of his connection with the Fisk-Gould party, and of his receiving money from it, are in the hands of the Attorney-General of the State of New-Jersey, and that he is about to publish them, to force Ex-Gov. Randolph out of his position as Chairman of the Democratic Executive Committee. It is also alleged that when the Erie Road was sending such immense numbers of cattle to New York, passengers wishing to pass through the Bergen tunnel were frequently compelled to wait for a number of hours until the cattle-trains had finished running, and that Gov. Randolph prepared a message to the Legislature in which he urged the passage of a law forbidding the use of the tunnel for cattle-trains to the exclusion of passenger traffic. In this message he is reported to have said that the people of New-Jersey were compelled to wait for half a day until all of the Western hogs had been accommodated with a sight of Bergen tunnel. This message coming to the knowledge of Fisk, he ordered Gov. Randolph to suppress it, which he did, under threats of the disclosure of the previous bribery.

## JUDGE BARNARD'S TRIAL.

### Curiosity at Saratoga to See the Modern Jeffreys.

### Evidence of His Undying Devotion to the Erie Cabal—He Rushes from Poughkeepsie to Put a Railroad in Their Hands.

Special Dispatch to the New-York Times.

SARATOGA, N. Y., July 26.—Judge Barnard's arrival here last night created considerable excitement. Although the hour was late, the news spread rapidly through the hotel, bringing numbers curious to see the man whose arbitrary abuse of his great office has made him the most conspicuous among the judicial tyrants of New-York, whose sceptre of power has been wrenched from their grasp by an indignant public. And this morning, in spite of the drenching rain, a large number of ladies and gentlemen repaired to the Court-room in expectation of his appearance. Owing, however, to the nature of his illness, rheumatic gout, and the state of the weather, he did not come, and the general desire to observe what effect the repetition of his own misdeeds and the revelation of the motives which prompted them would have on him, had to be deferred till another occasion. It is said, however, that he will be present to-morrow.

A great deal of evidence was submitted today, and all of the same inculpatory nature as that of the previous day. Indeed, it seems difficult amid such a mass of criminality to select any particular instance as more glaring than common, the only subject for wonder being that such a course of extreme wickedness could be pursued with success for so long a period, and that, to compare great things with small, this petty Cæsar has not long since met his Brutus. In regard to the trial itself, it is worthy of note that nearly all the witnesses produced by the prosecution have been from personal motives hostile thereto. What evidence they have given has been wrung from them on the direct by efforts more severe than are ordinarily called for on cross examination, because every word they uttered was an incrimination of themselves; and yet as case after case is unfolded, dispassionately and unostentatiously, one cannot help feeling that the language of the charges describes but feebly the villainy portrayed by the evidence. It is also somewhat amusing to observe with what extreme care these witnesses are handled by the defense on cross-examination, and how readily they respond to the suggestive questions of Mr. Beach. For instance, after detailing, in answer to the prosecution, arbitrary and illegal acts on the part of the accused, which carry one back in fancy to the revolutionary times of James II., they are remitted to the really tender mercies of Mr. Beach, who usually concludes with the question, "had you any knowledge of any conspiracy between Judge Barnard and James Fisk, Jr.?" How cordially they answer "No," sometimes improving upon the suggestion by adding that they neither knew nor suspected such a thing. Such charming innocence in men of the world would make one think better of his kind if pity for their dullness of comprehension left room for any other feeling. How unfortunate for the accused that men who have had no complicity with him, or others of his kidney, cannot view the transactions unfolded to their gaze with the same lenient eyes; that when they learn of his constant intimacy with Fisk and Gould and Fields and their tribe, and of his granting orders on their groundless applications at out-of-the-way places, and indeed everywhere but at the Court-room, whereby the control of powerful corporations was put in their hands; of his leaving the bedside of a dying mother to meet a gigantic rogue at the house of the latter's mistress, for the purpose of aiding him in the robbery of an important railroad, without at least suspecting that the conspiracy charged really existed. And this was the nature, chiefly, of the evidence adduced today.

It appeared from the testimony of John W. Sterling, who was recalled, and the papers in the case of Azro Chase against the Albany and Susquehanna Railroad Company, that the orders and writs issued by Barnard were all dated at the Court-house in the City of New-York; but the witness admitted that one of them at least was obtained from Barnard at Poughkeepsie. The order appointing Fisk and Courter receivers was granted *ex parte*, as usual, and was never entered on the records of the Court, and it was not shown that the Company was even in danger of insolvency or dissolution, nor was there any other or proper legal ground stated which could give the Judge jurisdiction or authorize the granting of said order. The witness said he met Fisk at the train that night, after he got the order from Barnard, and went with him to Albany. What passed between them did not appear, but it was made perfectly clear that the plaintiff was the mere representative of Fisk.

In the case of Pruyn against Parr, Sheriff of Albany County, and others, wherein an injunction had been granted to restrain the defendants from executing certain writs of assistance issued by Barnard to the Sheriffs of the various counties, authorizing the receivers, Fisk and Courter, to employ force to take possession of any property owned by the Albany and Susquehanna Railroad Company in the suit of Chase against them, it appeared that Barnard issued an order *ex parte* to show cause why the injunction should not be dissolved, and directing the writs of assistance to be executed immediately. There was no proper ground shown for the said order, which was an unwarrantable interference with the action of another Judge in another case. His order also required cause to be shown why Fisk and Courter should not be made defendants in the Pruyn action, his purpose, of course, being to aid the Fisk party in the Chase suit.

The evidence in the case of Bush against the Albany and Susquehanna Railroad Company showed that the respondent had corruptly appointed Wm. J. W. Fuller receiver of 3,000 shares of that Company's stock, and had issued writs of assistance to the Sheriff commanding him to put said Fuller in possession of the same; that the receivership order was granted *ex parte*, it actually appearing by the papers that the plaintiff had no right or interest in said shares, and that the writ of assistance was issued before final judgment in said action, and even before any summons had been served on any of the defendants or any demand made for the property. And Groesbeck's testimony showed that though Barnard's first order was granted on the ground that the shares were not legally issued, his subsequent order compelled the Company to accept the receiver's vote on those very shares. Comment is unnecessary.

Thomas R. Fox, telegraph operator at Poughkeepsie, testified that he saw the respondent at that place on the 6th of August, 1869; that about that time he made copies of telegrams sent by him to and from the respondent. He identified the copies spoken of, now shown him, and Mr. Stickney offered to read the same, when Mr. Beach objected to the introduction of secondary evidence. But the President, with that clearness and promptness which have distinguished him throughout, decided that notice to produce the originals having been given, secondary evidence was admissible. One of the telegrams reads:

NEW-YORK, 6th, 1869.

Come to New-York without fail to-night. Answer care No. 358 West Twenty-third-street.

JAMES H. COLEMAN.

15 D. H. Fisk's Pass, 505.

The answer was:

I will be there. If sent by you, answer.

G. G. BARNARD.

The witness explained that the words at the bottom of the first telegram meant that the message was free, on Fisk's pass.

James H. Coleman, being still detained by illness in his family, Mr. Stickney read, by consent, a portion of the testimony given by him before the Assembly Judiciary Committee, wherein he testified that he had not sent nor read either of the above dispatches, and had not consulted with Fisk, or Gould, or any one else, and felt greatly outraged that his name had been used, without his knowledge or consent. There was much more in his testimony which furnished conclusive proof that the telegram was sent by Fisk, and was but a step in the conspiracy alleged between him and his Erie *confrères* and the accused. Barnard had also telegraphed, in reply to Coleman, that night, that his mother was very low, and the sending and receiving of these four telegrams was admitted by him before the Judiciary Committee, the stenographers notes which were brought to him afterward by Mr. Prince, the Chairman, being corrected by him. He actually went to New-York that night, first to Mansfield's house, and at 10½ was waiting in Fisk's house, N... 313 West Twenty-third-street, to sign the order appointing Fisk and Courter receivers of the Albany and Susquehanna Railroad Company.

Joseph Bush, John F. Cole, Harris and Parr gave testimony corroborative of the previous witnesses. Thomas D. Sherwood, who was arrested for contempt on an order of Barnard's, in the case of F. A. Lane against the New-York Pier and Warehouse Company, and immediately discharged by him, Barnard admitting that no contempt had been committed, was called just before the adjournment of the Court. The important part of his testimony will be given to-morrow.

## WASHINGTON NOTES.

### Trials of Office-Seekers—A Whine of Disappointment from Greeley in 1861—Ex-Postmaster-General Randall—Repudiating Greeley—Unbuttered Water-melons.

Special Dispatch to the New-York Times.

WASHINGTON, July 26.—Mr. Greeley wanted a "share" of the patronage during Mr. Lincoln's Administration, and when he did not have all he sought he was not slow to make complaint. Below is one of his complaining letters to Mr. Chase:

OFFICE OF THE TRIBUNE,
NEW-YORK, Sept. 19, 1861.

DEAR SIR: I again trouble you in behalf of Mr. C. A. Perkins, candidate for Collector of Customs at Oswego, in this State. I will not use many words. The Weed-Littlejohn faction as yet have everything in that quarter. Mr. Littlejohn's old partner, Fitzhugh, is Postmaster, Mr. Littlejohn is Consul to Liverpool. Nobody who does not belong to them is ever allowed to hope for anything from the Republican Party. We of the contrary party ask a share. Mr. Perkins has been slandered. He is worthy and capable. I trust he will be appointed.

Yours, HORACE GREELEY.

Hon. S. P. CHASE, Secretary Treasury, Washington.

DEATH OF EX-POSTMASTER-GENERAL RANDALL.

The Postmaster-General will issue an official order announcing the death of Ex-Postmaster-General Randall and directing the draping of the Department, as usual on the death of any former head of the Department.

COUNTING GREELEYITE CHICKENS BEFORE HATCHING.

Senator Kellogg arrived here to-night. He came from New-Orleans by way of the West. At Chicago he met the Postmaster of the House of Representatives, Mr. King, of Minnesota, who, it has been reported, had become a Greeleyite. Mr. King denied the charge, and said he was not only working for Grant and Wilson, but was sure the State would go for Grant by several thousand majority.

SPOTTED TAIL'S BAND GIVEN TO WATER-MELONS WITHOUT BUTTER.

Spotted Tail and his band had a council at the Interior Department today with Commissioner Walker. They are growing impatient to return; and in concluding the interview Spotted Tail complained of the heat, and said some of his braves were not feeling well, and he feared they would be sick. The interpreter added an explanation of his own to the effect that water-melons were a novelty to the Indians, and they were eating too freely of them, but unlike Gratz Brown, they never eat them with butter.

BLAIR, OF MICHIGAN, TO BE ANSWERED.

Postmaster-General Creswell and Senator Chandler will speak at Lansing, Mich., Wednesday evening next, at Jackson Thursday, and at Detroit on Friday. Lansing and Jackson are in Gov. Blair's district, where his ranting speeches against the Navy Department will receive attention.

## FRANCE.

### The Mining Disturbances—Cavalry in Pursuit of Rioters—The Tariff—Stanley in Paris.

PARIS, July 26.—President Thiers has sent a dispatch to the Prefects of the Northern Departments, where the miners are on strike, praising those officials for the energetic measures they have taken to prevent disorder and excesses. He tells them they can have 100,000 men, if necessary, to repress disturbances, especially where they are produced by foreign instigators.

It is reported that an International agent from Chicago is among the fomenters of disorder, and that he seeks to induce the miners to emigrate to America.

Cavalry pursued and dispersed a large body of rioters near Denain, taking 100 prisoners.

Strong military cordons have been drawn around the disaffected districts, and the aspect of affairs is improving.

VERSAILLES, July 26.—The Assembly this afternoon passed the entire Tariff bill by a vote of 265 yeas to 34 nays.

Mr. Stanley, the discoverer of Dr. Livingstone, has arrived in Paris, and dines to-morrow with Mr. Washburne, the American Minister.

## SPAIN.

### Withdrawal of Gen. Sickles' Resignation—Policy Toward the Colored People of Cuba—Don Carlos.

PARIS, July 26.—The *Memorial Diplomatique* publishes a rumor that Gen. Sickles, the Minister of the United States at Madrid, has withdrawn his resignation, the differences between him and Señor Sagasta having been settled, through the intervention of Señor Zorilla; and that the Spanish Cabinet undertakes to carry into effect the liberal measures promised long ago, in favor of the colored race in Cuba.

GENEVA, July 26.—Don Carlos has arrived in Lausanne.

## GREAT BRITAIN.

### The Galway Contested Election in the House of Commons.

LONDON, July 26.—There was some debate in the House of Commons last night on the contested Galway election and Judge Keogh's disposition of the case, but without action on the subject the debate was adjourned. The House was well filled, as an exciting discussion of Irish topics was anticipated.

## THE BOARD OF ARBITRATION.

### No Session at Geneva Yesterday—Counsel on an Excursion.

GENEVA, July 26—P. M.—No session of the Board of Arbitration was held today.

Sir Roundell Palmer and family have gone on an excursion to the other end of the lake.

### Grant and Wilson in Watertown—Jefferson County All Right.

Special Dispatch to the New-York Times.

WATERTOWN, July 26.—The organization of a Grant and Wilson Club last evening, in this city, proved an impromptu mass-meeting, and was earnest and enthusiastic. The largest hall in the city was filled. Alexander Campbell was elected President. Watertown and Jefferson County are all right. A grand mass-meeting is to be held on Monday evening, to be addressed by Congressman Roberts, of Utica.

### Suit Against a Railroad.

KINGSTON, N. Y., July 26.—The Farmers' Loan and Trust Company, of New-York, have commenced proceedings looking to a foreclosure of a mortgage against the Rondout and Oswego Railroad, now known as the New-York, Kingston and Syracuse Railroad, under first mortgage bonds, the Company having failed to meet its interest.

### Heavy Storm in the North-West—Apprehended Damage to Crops.

CHICAGO, Ill., July 26.—Heavy rains have prevailed throughout the entire North-west for the greater part of the past two days, and telegraphic advices from various points indicate that some damage has been done to wheat and oats by being blown down and "lodged." The corn in many localities is also prostrated, but will suffer no damage where the crop is already cut. Altogether, the damage to the crop is not likely to prove serious.

### Over Niagara Falls.

NIAGARA FALLS, N. Y., July 26.—A boy and a girl, children of a fisherman named Lecor, were on the river in a boat today, and the high wind drove the boat into the rapids, and both children were carried over the Falls.

CLIFTON, Ontario, July 26.—A boat, containing an old fisherman named Ramey and his friend, whose name is unknown, was capsized in crossing the river near Chippewa, this afternoon. They were carried by the current over the Falls, and no traces of their bodies can be found.

## GREELEY AND THE SOUTH.

### Letter of an Intensely-Indignant Virginia Gentleman.

### The Choice Between a Renowned Warrior and a Renowned Fool.

### Catalogue of Greeley's Follies and Lack of Principle.

### Should the South Vote for the Vilifier of its Women?

### What Greeley Said of the Virtue of Southern Ladies.

Special Dispatch to the New-York Times.

RICHMOND, Va., July 26.—Hon. James Lyons, of this city, having been invited by a committee to address a Grant and Wilson ratification meeting, to take place at Fredericksburg on the 8th of August, has written the following letter in reply:

RICHMOND, July 23, 1872.

*To M. J. Griffith, Esq., Chairman, &c.:*

DEAR SIR: I have the pleasure to acknowledge your letter of the 20th on behalf of the Republican Committee of Fredericksburg, inviting me to address a Republican meeting at that place on the 8th prox. I am compelled to decline the invitation, as I have done others, although duly sensible of the honor done me. I have a business engagement in Richmond on that day which will prevent me from accepting, if there was no other impediment. But nothing would tempt me to take the stump this Summer except the conviction that by that means only can Horace Greeley be beaten, and as that cannot be, because he will be beaten certainly without it, and if not any speech from me would be of little avail, I must beg to be excused. To be candid as well as serious, however, I must say I am not prepared at present to take the stump for Gen. Grant. I am a Democrat (by which I mean a Constitutional Republican) on principle, and not without hope that the Louisville Convention will nominate a straight-out Democrat in September, qualified by character and ability to fill the high office of President. If it does, I shall vote for him. If it does not, I shall vote for Gen. Grant, and will then do anything which I can with honor to promote his election, because I think him a far better man in all respects than Horace Greeley, and far more fit to be President of the nation.

GRANT A MAN THE SOUTH MAY HONOR.

One is a renowned warrior of whom the South may well say: "Great let me call him, for he conquered me;" who enjoys the respect of the civilized nations of the world, except the conservative nation of Baltimore; whose great error has been that he followed too much the devices and desires of such men as Greeley and Sumner and Trumbull and Schurz and Brown, until they have nearly undone him, and now betray him for a price.

GREELEY RENOWNED ONLY FOR FOLLIES.

The other is a renowned lunatic, famous for nothing but his follies, his farming and wood-chopping, his political venom and vices, and his total want of principle. A Fourierite, a free-lover of the Macfarland order, and a woman's rights man, must be either fool or knave. If he sincerely believes in those dogmas in a state of organized society, he is a fool. If he does not, then he pretends to believe (for a consideration) what he does not, and is a knave. If the Almighty Maker of us all had intended that the world should be without government, and man without property, He would not have inculcated obedience to "the powers that be," or denounced the man who fails to provide for his own family as worse than an infidel; would have said charity begins abroad and not at home, and would not have said, "Thou shalt not steal," as man can steal property only. If he had intended to tolerate free-love, he would not have instituted marriage and denounced adultery. If he had intended man and woman to be equal, and woman to ride like Mrs. "Squatting Bear," he would not have given Eve as a helpmate to Adam; would have made Adam bear children as well as Eve, and would not have allowed side saddles to be made.

WORSE THAN ALL.

But great as these defects and vices are, Horace Greeley is stained by another, which is far more detestable to me, which makes it as impossible for me to vote for him as to denounce my wife and daughter. If there ever lived on earth, in Sparta or in Paradise, a race of pure, spotless, heroic women, the women of the South are such. They gave their husbands and sons, their homes and altars, and almost every hope of earthly happiness, to their country and their cause, and because they did so this demon of the *Tribune* uttered and published in his paper, as I am credibly informed, and the proof of it will be exhibited, the following false and infamous libel upon them:

"The women of the South, nursed by blacks, filled with animal passion, imbibe it from their nurses, and, on arriving at the age of puberty, immediately manifest a desire to gratify sensuality."

Was ever before, by any mortal or immortal demon, such a hateful thought expressed; such concentrated venom poured out? In the recollection of the great deeds of our noble dead, in the presence of their surviving mothers, widows, and daughters, will Southern men—can they, by their votes, say to this monstrous slanderer, "Well done, thou good and faithful citizen; receive the reward prepared for you by your suppliant victims since the overthrow of the hated Confederacy?" Spirits of Lee and Jackson, it was a merciful God who would not allow your last hours to be agonized, and your final repose disturbed by beholding such an offering. When it is made, but one thing will remain to be done to complete the shame and disgrace of the South, and that will be to burst the cerements of the graves in southern cemeteries and carry the sacred ashes to the Chappaqua farm, to manure its barren hill-sides. Women of the South forbid it! Women of the North forbid it! Sisters in sorrow, sisters in fame, the virtue of woman is your common property! Unite to defend it against its vilest traducer! Men of the North, have you no humanity, no brotherly love, that you would thus degrade us by electing our greatest reviler to rule over us? If you have any, do you think such a course will strengthen it with us?

But I must stop. My feelings run away with my pen. The sight of our poor, bleeding, suffering South, God bless her, lying at the feet of her worst foe, begging for favors, is unendurable to me.

Most respectfully, your obedient servant,

JAMES LYONS

P. S.—In proof of what I have said of European opinion, I subjoin several extracts from English newspapers which I have cut from the New-York *World*, just received. J. L.

## DESTRUCTIVE STORM.

### The Town of Van Wert, Ohio, Visited by a Hurricane—Two Lives Lost.

CINCINNATI, Ohio, July 26.—A terrible storm, accompanied with torrents of rain, passed over Van Wert, Ohio, last evening, carrying along in its pathway buildings, chimneys and fences. A house owned by J. L. Rumsey, near the town, was blown down and completely demolished. His wife and young boy were instantly killed, and other inmates were seriously injured. Mr. Rumsey lies in an unconscious condition from the effects of injuries received. The destruction of property was very great, but, so far as ascertained, no other lives have been lost.

The New-York Times.

VOL. XXII.......NO. 6594. | NEW-YORK, WEDNESDAY, NOVEMBER 6, 1872. | PRICE FOUR CENTS.

# VICTORY!

## A Sweeping Republican Triumph.

## Gen. Grant Carries Thirty States.

## The New-England and Middle States Republican.

## Overwhelming Majorities for Grant in the West.

## Pennsylvania in Line with 100,000 Majority.

## New-York Takes Her Place in the Column.

## New-Jersey Redeemed from Democratic Misrule.

## Large Gains in the Congressional Delegations.

### THE ELECTORAL COLLEGE.

The following table shows the majorities for President as far as heard from. They are simply overwhelmingly for Grant in every State but seven in the Union:

| State. | Grant. | Greeley. | Electoral Vote. | Electoral Vote. |
|---|---|---|---|---|
| Alabama | 16000 | .... | 10 | .. |
| Arkansas | 5000 | .... | 6 | .. |
| California | 5000 | .... | 6 | .. |
| Connecticut | 6000 | .... | 6 | .. |
| Delaware | 1500 | .... | 3 | .. |
| Florida | 2000 | .... | 4 | .. |
| Georgia | .... | 20000 | .. | 11 |
| Illinois | 25000 | .... | 21 | .. |
| Indiana | 20000 | .... | 15 | .. |
| Iowa | 50000 | .... | 11 | .. |
| Kansas | 15000 | .... | 5 | .. |
| Kentucky | .... | 30000 | .. | 12 |
| Louisiana | 15000 | .... | 8 | .. |
| Maine | 25000 | .... | 7 | .. |
| Maryland | .... | 20000 | .. | 8 |
| Massachusetts | 75000 | .... | 13 | .. |
| Michigan | 30000 | .... | 11 | .. |
| Minnesota | 20000 | .... | 5 | .. |
| Mississippi | 20000 | .... | 8 | .. |
| Missouri* | .... | .... | .. | .. |
| Nebraska | 10000 | .... | 3 | .. |
| Nevada | 1200 | .... | 3 | .. |
| New Hampshire | 6000 | .... | 5 | .. |
| New-Jersey | 5000 | .... | 9 | .. |
| New-York | 35000 | .... | 35 | .. |
| North Carolina | 10000 | .... | 10 | .. |
| Ohio | 40000 | .... | 22 | .. |
| Oregon | 1000 | .... | 3 | .. |
| Pennsylvania | 105000 | .... | 29 | .. |
| Rhode Island | 8000 | .... | 4 | .. |
| South Carolina | 25000 | .... | 7 | .. |
| Tennessee | .... | 15000 | .. | 12 |
| Texas | .... | .... | .. | .. |
| Vermont | 32000 | .... | 5 | .. |
| Virginia | .... | .... | 11 | .. |
| West Virginia | 3000 | .... | 5 | .. |
| Wisconsin | 15000 | .... | 10 | .. |
| | | | 300 | 43 |

*Doubtful.

### NEW-YORK.

**Grant's Majority in the State 25,000—Dix's Fully as Great—The Assembly 79 Republicans to 49 Democrats.**

Rarely in all her history, and never in her later years, has the Empire State done more nobly than yesterday, when she rolled up a majority for Grant and Wilson which can hardly be precisely stated, but it does not seem that it can possibly fall below 25,000, while all the indications are that it will double that figure. We have hardly a doubt that when all the figures are finally in and counted Grant will have a majority that will exceed rather than fall below 50,000.

Gen. Dix and the whole State ticket runs nearly up to the Presidential ticket throughout the State, and, while the majority may be somewhat less, it is elected by a majority that cannot be precisely stated to-night, but which greatly exceed any estimates which we have made.

While we regret that we have lost Hon. Charles St. John in the Orange District, and of Hon. John H. Ketcham in the Duchess District, both of whom are reported defeated, we yet have a certainty of having carried six districts now represented by Democrats, so that with the addition of the Congressman at large, the delegation from the State in the next Congress will stand 23 Republicans to 10 Democrats, whereas in the present it is 15 Republicans to 16 Democrats. While it is possible we may may not have carried two districts put down for the Republicans, we can scarcely credit the defeat of Mr. Ketchum, and the result as to the Congressional Districts will be about as stated.

The Assembly at the worst will be 79 Republicans to 49 Democrats, making a large Republican majority on joint ballot, and and securing a Republican successor to Hon. Roscoe Conkling in the United States Senate.

In many portions of the State the Republicans have accomplished wonders. Erie County rolls up a grand majority of 4,600 for Grant, and claims the banner, but her right is disputed by Albany, which is redeemed and gives Grant 200 majority, by Chemung, also redeemed, and giving Grant 400 majority. From every portion of the State comes the same grand story of unprecedented triumph. The news gets better and better every hour.

### THE VOTE IN THIS CITY.

The following table gives the complete vote, in all the twenty-one Assembly Districts, on the Presidential ticket. The vote for Governor is given as far as heard from up to the hour of going to press.

FIRST ASSEMBLY DISTRICT.

| Districts. | Grant. | Greeley. | Dix. | Kernan. |
|---|---|---|---|---|
| 1 | 107 | 187 | 46 | 260 |
| 2 | 57 | 164 | 38 | 167 |
| 3 | 52 | 209 | 18 | 249 |
| 4 | 55 | 211 | 8 | 269 |
| 5 | 52 | 167 | 10 | 214 |
| 6 | 74 | 321 | 29 | 317 |
| 7 | 56 | 286 | 25 | 325 |
| 8 | 141 | 141 | 119 | 168 |
| 9 | 57 | 64 | 55 | 55 |
| 10 | 118 | 117 | 106 | 133 |
| 11 | 87 | 186 | 57 | 206 |
| 12 | 85 | 111 | 84 | 110 |
| 13 | 94 | 154 | 88 | 164 |
| 14 | 64 | 116 | 125 | 105 |
| 15 | 125 | 112 | 102 | 137 |
| 16 | 53 | 105 | 43 | 117 |
| 17 | 95 | 170 | 90 | 178 |
| 18 | 137 | 163 | 110 | 203 |
| 19 | 96 | 120 | 87 | 117 |
| 20 | 112 | 202 | 74 | 248 |
| 21 | 172 | 171 | 162 | 180 |
| 22 | 180 | 90 | 65 | 217 |
| 23 | 70 | 216 | 57 | 232 |
| Total | 2120 | 3754 | 1646 | 4196 |

SECOND ASSEMBLY DISTRICT.

| District. | Grant. | Greeley. | Dix. | Kernan. |
|---|---|---|---|---|
| 1 | 71 | 199 | .... | .... |
| 2 | 70 | 117 | .... | .... |
| 3 | 41 | 183 | .... | .... |
| 4 | 36 | 148 | 21 | 162 |
| 5 | 35 | 245 | .... | .... |
| 6 | 8 | 155 | 6 | 155 |
| 7 | 29 | 255 | 24 | 261 |
| 8 | 38 | 181 | .... | .... |
| 9 | 8 | 150 | 4 | 156 |
| 10 | 51 | 200 | .... | .... |
| 11 | 15 | 141 | .... | .... |
| [illegible] | [illegible] | [illegible] | [illegible] | [illegible] |
| Total | 1007 | 2835 | [illegible] | [illegible] |

THIRD ASSEMBLY DISTRICT. [illegible] Total 1133, 3213, 861, 3498.

FOURTH ASSEMBLY DISTRICT. [illegible] Total 1476, 5070.

FIFTH ASSEMBLY DISTRICT. [illegible] Total 2988, 3539, 2156, 3367.

SIXTH ASSEMBLY DISTRICT. [illegible] Total 1590, 3131.

SEVENTH ASSEMBLY DISTRICT. [illegible] Total 3018, 2811, 2306, 2300.

EIGHTH ASSEMBLY DISTRICT. [illegible] Total 2030, 4537, 3415, 4373.

NINTH ASSEMBLY DISTRICT. [illegible] Total 2690, 2102, 4214, 2853.

TENTH ASSEMBLY DISTRICT. [illegible] Total 2417, 3250.

ELEVENTH ASSEMBLY DISTRICT. [illegible] Total 4059, 2863.

TWELFTH ASSEMBLY DISTRICT. [illegible] Total 1872, 3686, 2136, 3301.

THIRTEENTH ASSEMBLY DISTRICT. [illegible] Total 2300, 2797, 2382, 2880.

FOURTEENTH ASSEMBLY DISTRICT. [illegible] Total 1487, 2963.

FIFTEENTH ASSEMBLY DISTRICT. [illegible] Total 2871, 4407.

SIXTEENTH ASSEMBLY DISTRICT. [illegible] Total 2139, 4669.

SEVENTEENTH ASSEMBLY DISTRICT. [illegible] Total 4078, 4787.

EIGHTEENTH ASSEMBLY DISTRICT. [illegible] Total 2901, 3452.

NINETEENTH ASSEMBLY DISTRICT. [illegible] Total 1866, 2315, 1846, 2423.

TWENTIETH ASSEMBLY DISTRICT. [illegible] Total 4047, 5353.

TWENTY-FIRST ASSEMBLY DISTRICT.

| District. | Grant. | Greeley. | Dix. | Kernan. |
|---|---|---|---|---|
| [illegible] | [illegible] | [illegible] | [illegible] | [illegible] |
| 22 | 88 | 145 | .... | .... |
| 23 | 75 | 54 | .... | .... |
| 24 | 66 | 104 | .... | .... |
| 25 | 128 | 12 | .... | .... |
| 26 | 136 | 135 | .... | .... |
| 27 | 107 | 151 | .... | .... |
| 28 | 148 | 130 | .... | .... |
| 29 | 44 | 45 | .... | .... |
| 30 | 222 | 238 | .... | .... |
| 31 | 163 | 122 | .... | .... |
| 32 | 107 | 65 | .... | .... |
| 33 | 94 | 88 | .... | .... |
| 34 | 301 | 208 | .... | .... |
| 35 | 81 | 90 | .... | .... |
| 36 | 206 | 134 | .... | .... |
| 37 | 83 | 125 | .... | .... |
| Total | 4097 | 4853 | .... | .... |

The following is a summary of the vote by Wards for President;

| Ward. | Grant. | Greeley. | Ward. | Grant. | Greeley. |
|---|---|---|---|---|---|
| 1 | 594 | 1666 | 12 | 3411 | 4240 |
| 2 | 175 | 171 | 13 | 1530 | 3131 |
| 3 | 266 | 451 | 14 | 996 | 2730 |
| 4 | 542 | 2426 | 15 | 2479 | 1897 |
| 5 | 1094 | 1466 | 16 | 3745 | 3349 |
| 6 | 594 | 1891 | 17 | 4387 | 6783 |
| 7 | 1476 | 5070 | 18 | 3390 | 5203 |
| 8 | 2383 | 2920 | 19 | 5368 | 7115 |
| 9 | 4498 | 3583 | 20 | 4435 | 5957 |
| 10 | 1849 | 2645 | 21 | 4199 | 3960 |
| 11 | 2570 | 5097 | 22 | 4806 | 5825 |
| Total | | | | 54787 | 77546 |

### THE MAYORALTY.

The election of Havemeyer is assured by at least from 6,000 to 7,000 majority.

**Mr. Havemeyer Out of Town.**

Many inquiries were made for Mr. Havemeyer, the successful candidate for Mayor, last evening, but he could not be found. It was ascertained that he had left the City before the election, and was stoppoing in the country at the home of his son.

### STATE VOTE BY TOWNS.

**The Votes by Towns.**

The following table gives the majorities on the Presidential ticket by towns, as far as heard from up to the hour of going to press. The Republican gains and losses, as compared with the vote of 1868, are also given.

| Towns. | Grant maj. | Greeley maj. | Repub'n gain. | Repub'n loss. |
|---|---|---|---|---|
| Barton | 165 | .... | 34 | .... |
| Troy, First Ward | 30 | .... | 114 | .... |
| Third Ward | 210 | .... | .... | 2 |
| Eleventh Ward | .... | 245 | .... | .... |
| Thirteenth Ward | 196 | .... | .... | .... |
| Lansingburg | 595 | .... | 271 | .... |
| Greenwich—1st Dist. | 240 | .... | .... | 34 |
| 3d District | 13 | .... | 42 | .... |
| Courtlandsville—1st | 192 | .... | .... | 127 |
| 2d District | 93 | .... | 5 | .... |
| Skaneateles | 9 | .... | .... | 159 |
| Astoria—Fourth Ward | 78 | .... | .... | .... |
| Fifth Ward | 104 | .... | .... | .... |
| Haverstraw—2d Dist. | .... | 69 | 127 | .... |
| Mount Hope | 17 | .... | 11 | .... |
| Berlin | 177 | .... | 70 | .... |
| Lyons—1st District | 25 | .... | 115 | .... |
| 2d District | 29 | .... | 63 | .... |
| 3d District | 46 | .... | 64 | .... |
| Norwich | .... | 36 | 67 | .... |
| Oxford | 160 | .... | 72 | .... |
| L. Bridge—2d Dist. | 12 | .... | 16 | .... |
| Ledyard | 263 | .... | 160 | .... |
| Berkshire | 85 | .... | .... | 2 |
| White Creek, 1st Dist. | 153 | .... | .... | 8 |
| Warrensburg | .... | 44 | 96 | .... |
| Sherburne | 249 | .... | .... | 18 |
| Mentz | .... | 57 | .... | 167 |
| Brutus | 249 | .... | 76 | .... |
| Addison | 29 | .... | 58 | .... |
| Ossinging | 10 | .... | 68 | .... |
| Munroe—1st District | 113 | .... | 68 | .... |
| Washington | 152 | .... | .... | 101 |
| [illegible] | [illegible] | [illegible] | [illegible] | [illegible] |
| Phelps, (complete) | .... | 112 | .... | 124 |
| Conocton—2d Dist. | 29 | .... | .... | 26 |
| Springwater, (comp.) | 220 | .... | .... | 64 |
| Canadice | 106 | .... | 4 | .... |
| Seneca Falls | 19 | .... | 132 | .... |
| Little Falls | .... | 98 | .... | 48 |
| Manheim | .... | 87 | 99 | .... |
| Chatham—1st Dist | 167 | .... | 193 | .... |
| Austerlitz | 26 | .... | .... | 30 |
| Jackson | 117 | .... | .... | 1 |
| Canandaigua—1st Dis | 59 | 1 | 18 | .... |
| 2d Dis. | 80 | .... | 4 | .... |
| 3d Dis. | 106 | .... | .... | 34 |
| Bristol | 60 | .... | 8 | .... |
| Richmond | 165 | .... | .... | 6 |

**Congressmen Probably Elected.**

At large. Lyman Tremain, Rep.

Dist.
1. James W. Covert Dem.
2. John G. Schumaker, Dem.
3. Stewart L. Woodford, Rep.
4. Philip S. Crooke, Rep.
5. William R. Roberts, Dem.
6. James Brooks, Dem.
7. Thomas J. Creamer, Dem.
8. John D. Lawson, Rep.
9. David B. Mellish, (doubtful,) Rep.
10. Fernando Wood, Dem.
11. Clarkson N. Potter, Dem.
12. Charles H. Horton, Dem.
13. John H. Ketcham, Rep.
14. John Maxwell, (doubtful,) Rep.
15. Eli Perry, Dem.
16. James S. Smart, Rep.
17. Robt. S. Hale, Rep.
18. Wm. A. Wheeler, Rep.
19. Henry H. Hathorne, Rep.
20. David Wilber, Rep.
21. Clinton L. Merriam, Rep.
22. Ellis H. Roberts, Rep.
23. Wm, E. Lansing, Rep.
24. R. Holland Duell, Rep.
25. Clinton D. MacDougall, Rep.
26. Wm. H. Lamport, Rep.
27. Thos. C. Platt, Rep.
28. H. Boardman Smith, Rep.
29. Freeman Clarke, Rep.
30. Geo. G. Hoskins, Rep.
31. Lyman K. Bass, Rep.
32. Walter L. Sessions, Rep.

This shows twenty-four Republicans to nine Democrats, being a Republican gain of nine members, three of which are from additions by the new apportionment, leaving a net gain to the Republicans of six members.

**Assemblymen Elected.**

The following candidates have been elected:

| Dist. | | Dist. | |
|---|---|---|---|
| 1. | James Healy. | 12. | Wm H Cooke. |
| 2. | Denis Burns. | 13. | C Fine.j |
| 3. | James Hayes. | 14. | C G Cornel. |
| 4. | John Galvin. | 15. | J Bluementhal. |
| 5. | Michael Norton. | 16. | Peter Wood. |
| 6. | Timo'y J Campbell. | 17. | Wm J Graff, (Rep.) |
| 7. | Geo W Clarke, (Rep.) | 18. | B Biglin, (Rep.) |
| 8. | S B Smith, (Rep.) | 19. | J O'Callaghan. |
| 9. | Stephen Pell, (Rep.) | 20. | W S Opdyke. |
| 10. | J M Patterson, (Rep.) | 21. | C E Crary. |
| 11. | A B Cornell, (Rep.) | | |

**The Assembly Compared.**

In making up the following table only those are credited to the Republicans who are shown by the returns to be elected. The fuller returns will decrease rather than augment the Democratic strength in the Assembly.

The Republicans elect the following members: Albany, 1; Allegany, 1; Broome, 1; Cattaraugus, 2; Cayuga, 2; Chatauqua, 2; Chemung, 1; Chenango, 1; Columbia, 2; Courtland 1; Delaware, 2; Dutchess, 2; Erie, 3; Essex, 1; Franklin, 1; Fulton, 1; Genessee, 1; Herkimer, 1; Jefferson, 2; Kings, 4; Lewis, 1; Livingston, 1; Madison, 2; Monroe, 2; Montgomery, 1; New-York, 4; Niagara, 2; Oneida, 3; Onondaga, 3; Ontario, 2; Orange, 1; Orleans, 1; Oswego, 3; Queens, 1; Renaslaer, 1; Saratoga, 2; Schenectady, 1; Schuyler, 1; St. Lawrence, 3; Steuben, 2; Suffolk, 1; Tioga, 1; Tompkins, 1; Warren, 1; Washington, 2; Wayne, 2; Westchester, 1; Wyoming, 1; Yates, 1. Total, 80.

The Democrats have elected the following: Albany, 3; Columbia, 2; Erie, 2; Greene, 1; Kings, 5; Monroe, 2; New-York, 17; Oneida, 1; Orange, 1; Otsego, 1; Putnam, 1; Queens, 1; Rensselaer, 2; Richmond, 1; Rockland, 1; Schoharie, 1; Seneca, 1; Sullivan, 1; Ulster, 2; Westchester, 2. This makes a total Democratic strength of forty-eight, and it can hardly be increased beyond this, although it is possible there are four or five of the close districts they have carried. In any event, the Assembly is certainly Republican by a large majority.

### CONGRESS.

**Immense Republican Gains.**

The following is a table of Congressmen elected yesterday and in the October elections. It shows a Republican majority, according to present return, of

| | Republican. | Democratic. |
|---|---|---|
| Alabama | 3 | 5 |
| Arkansas | 2 | 2 |
| California | 3 | 1 |
| Connecticut | 3 | 1 |
| Delaware | .... | 1 |
| Florida | 2 | .... |
| Georgia | 3 | 6 |
| Illinois | 13 | 6 |
| Indiana | 9 | 4 |
| Iowa | 9 | .... |
| Kansas | 3 | .... |
| Kentucky | 2 | 8 |
| Louisiana | 3 | 3 |
| Maine | 5 | .... |
| Maryland | 5 | 4 |
| Massachusetts | 11 | .... |
| Mississippi | 5 | 1 |
| Michigan | 9 | .... |
| Minnesota | 3 | .... |
| Missouri | 7 | 6 |
| Nevada | 1 | .... |
| Nebraska | 1 | .... |
| New-Hampshire | .... | 3 |
| New-Jersey | 5 | 2 |
| New-York | 22 | 11 |
| North Carolina | 3 | 5 |
| Ohio | 13 | 7 |
| Oregon | 1 | .... |
| Pennsylvania | 22 | 5 |
| Rhode Island | 2 | .... |
| South Carolina | 5 | .... |
| Texas | 2 | 4 |
| Tennessee | 4 | 6 |
| Vermont | 3 | .... |
| Virginia | 4 | 5 |
| West Virginia | 1 | 2 |
| Wisconsin | 6 | 2 |
| Total | 182 | 109 |

### REPORTS FROM OTHER STATES.

#### MAINE.

**Gains for Grant Over the September Election—His Majority Probably Over 25,000.**

*Special Dispatch to the New-York Times.*

PORTLAND, Me., Nov. 5.—Portland and six towns in Cumberland County show a net Republican gain of 1,185 over the September election. Six other cities and towns give a gain over September of 862, making in ten cities and towns over September 2,047.

Grant's majority in Maine will exceed 25,000.

**Grant's Gains Over the Vote of September.**

*Special Dispatch to the New-York Times.*

PORTLAND, Me., Nov. 5.—The following towns and cities have been received: Portland gives a Republican gain over the September vote of 963; Pownal a gain of 22; Cape Elizabeth a gain of 98; Freeport a gain of 22; North Yarmouth, 13; Yarmouth, 31; Falmouth, 41; Farmington, 87; Rockland, 104; Bangor, 611; Deering, gain, 114; Lewiston, 772; Bath, a gain of 204.

#### CONNECTICUT.

**Splendid Work by the Republicans—New-Haven Close.**

*Special Dispatch to the New-York Times.*

NEW-HAVEN, Conn., Nov. 5.—The Republicans turned out and voted splendidly today. The vote of the First Ward is just in, and gives Grant 602 majority, which is a gain of 350 since 1868.

The Second Ward gives Grant 147 majority. The Fourth 235 majority. The Sixth 242 majority. The Seventh Ward 66 majority. This gives 1,292 majority, with the Eighth Ward to hear from, which will give about 35 majority.

The Third Ward gives 472 Greeley majority.

NEW-HAVEN, Conn., Nov. 5.—The vote of New-Haven is all in. Greeley carried it by 9 majority, a Republican gain of 1,000. O'Conor gets 42 votes, and Black, Temperance, 4.

Thirty towns in the lower and western half of the State show a gain of 8,456 for Grant over the vote of 1868, when the State went 3,000 for Grant.

**Gen. Hawley's Prospects—Greeley Runs Behind his Ticket.**

HARTFORD, Conn., Nov. 5.—Hartford gives Eaton, for Congress, about 500 majority. Hawley gets 350 in New-Britain, and 213 in Rockville, both large gains. It is thought Hawley is elected sure.

Greeley falls away behind Eaton in this Congressional District. The State looks sure for Grant by 2,000 majority.

LATEST.—The total gains so far reported for Hawley are 753, and the total losses 552. We look for his election by at least 500 majority.

The great excitement over the Congressional election has diverted attention for the time from the Presidential election, as everybody concedes the utter rout of Greeley in the State.

**Grant's Majority Probably Four Thousand—Hawley Certainly Elected.**

*Special Dispatch to the New-York Times.*

HARTFORD, Conn., Nov. 5.—Connecticut is sure for Grant by from 2,500 to 4,000 majority.

Gen Hawley is sure of his election by 300 to 500 majority.

Gov. Jewell has just sent a congratulatory dispatch to President Grant.

The Hartford *Times*, Democratic, gives up the State and this district.

**Hawley's Probable Majority.**

*Special Dispatch to the New York Times.*

HARTFORD, Conn., Nov. 5.—Hawley, in the First Congressional District complete, estimating seven towns on the vote of 1872, has 498 majority.

B. BENT, Chairman State Republican Committee.

**Grant's Majority 6,000—Greeley Only a Plurality in New-Haven.**

*Special Dispatch to the New-York Times.*

NEW-HAVEN, Conn., Nov. 5.—New-Haven County, with a few towns to hear from, gives Grant 137 majority, a gain of 1,607 over 1868. Sixty-two towns give a gain of 1,362 over 1868, for Grant.

Returns from ninety-one towns have been received, and they show a net Republican gain of 1,729 over the vote of 1868. This gives us the State by 6,000.

Official returns in New-Haven show that Greeley has no majority here. His plurality over Grant is only 60.

HARTFORD, Conn., Nov. 5.—One hundred and twenty-four towns give a Republican gain over the vote of last Spring of 4,062. B. BENT, Chairman Republican State Committee.

**The Contest in the First Congressional District—Hawley's Majority 624.**

*Special Dispatch to the New-York Times.*

HARTFORD, Conn., Nov. 5.—The First Congressional District complete gives Hawley (Rep.) 13,090; Eaton, 12,466, a Republican majority of 624. The majority for Grant in the State, with five unimportant towns to hear from, shows a Republican gain of 5,007 over the vote of last Spring. The Democrats are disgusted, and lay the defeat to the Liberal managers.

**The State Republican by 5,000 and Over—Hawley's Majority 700—Rejoicing in Hartford.**

*Special Dispatch to the New-York Times.*

NEW-HAVEN, Conn., Nov. 5.—Returns have now been received from 118 towns, and show a Republican gain over the vote of 1868 of 1,600. The remaining forty-nine towns are small, and cannot affect the general result. The State has gone Republican by 5,000 and over.

HARTFORD, Conn., Nov. 5.—This city is ablaze with excitement. An immense meeting is being held in Allyn Hall. Stirring speeches have been made by Gen. Hawley, Gov. Jewell, Judge Carpenter, Henry Clay Trumbull, and other leading Republicans. The Boys in Blue have turned out without uniforms, wearing on their caps the Republican ticket. They have an extemporized band of more than a hundred men, with a chorus of 1,000 cow-horns, and are marching the streets. Bonfires are blazing, and the scene is one which partially illustrates the unbounded enthusiasm of the Republicans over the great victory. The Democrats and their allies are advised on every hand to "go West."

Hawley, for Congress, has nearly 700 majority already, with several towns to hear from. There have been gains everywhere except in Hartford.

New-Haven did so well for Grant that Gov. Jewell telegraphed to Mr. Beers, of the State Committee:

"Oh, you are a bully lot of boys. Let's shake hands across the bloody chasm.

MARSHALL JEWELL."

**Grant Carries the State by 6,000—Sweeping Republican Victories.**

*Special Dispatch to the New-York Times.*

NEW-HAVEN, Nov. 5.—Returns from 125 towns show a gain of 1,647 over 1868, and give a Republican majority in the State, with 42 towns to hear from, of 4,890. The additional towns gave a Republican majority of 1,160 over 1868. If the gains go on we shall have in 6,000 majority for Grant.

Continued on Fifth Page.

# The New-York Times.

VOL. XXII......NO. 6694. | NEW-YORK, MONDAY, MARCH 3, 1873. | PRICE FOUR CENTS.

## THE INAUGURATION.

### Crowds Arriving in Washington Hourly—The Order of the Procession—Arrangements and Decorations.

*Special Dispatch to the New-York Times.*

WASHINGTON, March 2.—The second inauguration of President Grant promises to excel, in point of attendance, military display, the ball feature, and general excellence and fullness of detail, any like occasion here. Thirteen hundred passengers arrived by the train from New-York and Philadelphia last evening, the regular New-York express coming through in two sections. Upward of 1,000 more arrived this morning, and extra trains have been coming in all day. The city is already more crowded than at any previous time two days in advance of the day of inauguration. But Washington can accommodate more people in proportion to its size than any other city in the Union, because it has more people devoted to that particular kind of business.

THE PROCESSION.

The detail for the procession, the ceremony, the ball, and the display of fire-works will be fully completed by to-morrow night. The procession of the visiting military with the other associations through Pennsylvania-avenue, will be the great feature of the day, as the ball will be that of the evening. The Committee on Procession last night agreed upon a general programme as follows:

Posse of police.
FIRST DIVISION.
United States Heavy Artillery.
West Point Cadets.
Naval Cadets.
Marine Corps.
Light Artillery.
SECOND DIVISION.
District of Columbia troops.
THIRD DIVISION.
Cavalry acting as an escort to President Grant and the Governor of the District of Columbia.
The Fourth, Fifth, and Sixth Divisions will consist of infantry, and Seventh, Eighth, Ninth, Tenth, and Eleventh Divisions of civic bodies.

Major Richards, of the Metropolitan Police was also present, and arrangements were completed with him. The avenue will be cleared of all vehicles at 10 A. M. on the 4th, and the procession will move at 10 o'clock precisely. It will form west of and in the vicinity of the Executive Mansion, with the right resting on Seventeenth-street. The committee have decided to have a review of the procession in front of the Executive Mansion, at the conclusion of the inaugural ceremonies. A stand will be erected exclusively for the President and family. The Grand Marshal, Gen. Barry, arrived in town yesterday morning at 11 o'clock, and immediately appointed Gen. Whipple Deputy Grand Marshal.

OUT-OF-TOWN MILITARY CORPS.

The Sumner corps of Syracuse, N. Y., arrived this morning at 6 o'clock, and repaired at once to their quarters in Judiciary-square. This is the first command to arrive, and is in fine condition. The Boston Lancers arrived to-night at 10 o'clock, and are quartered at the National Hotel. The Albany Burgesses Corps, the finest military organization that will participate in the inauguration, will arrive here to-morrow morning, and will quarter at the Kirkwood House until the evening of the 5th. The other troops to arrive, and their quarters while in this city, are as follows: The Second Regiment, Connecticut National Guard of New-Haven, at Willard's; the Washington Grays, of Philadelphia, at Willard's; the State Fencibles of Philadelphia, the Fifth Maryland Regiment, and the New-York Fifth Regiment, National Guard, in Judiciary-square; the Old Guard, of New-York, at Willards; the Duquesne Grays, of Pittsburg, at Baltimore and Philadelphia Depot; the Third New-Jersey National Guard of Elizabeth, N. J., at the armory; the city troops of Philadelphia, at Willard's; the Monumental Greys, of Baltimore, in Judiciary-square; the Attuck Guards and Richmond Zouaves, of that city, and Company F, Tenth and Twelfth Regiments, National Guard of Pennsylvania, will arrive on Monday.

CLUBS.

Among the distinguished organizations already in the city for participation in the inaugural ceremonies is the Columbus Glee Club, over fifty strong. This club did good service in the last political campaign in Ohio, and it is meet that they should be here to enjoy some of the fruits of their labors. They are quartered at the St. James.

CLEANING AND DECORATING.

The work of cleaning the streets on the line of march of the procession commenced yesterday. The work of erecting the large platform on the east front, on which the oath will be administered, is progressing rapidly, under direction of the Congressional Convention, and will be suitably festooned. The workmen at the Washington Arsenal are busy preparing the fire-works to be furnished by the Government. The workmen of the artist who has charge of the avenue decorations are busily engaged in getting their flags and decorations in condition to be put in position on Monday morning.

FIRE-WORKS AND ILLUMINATION.

It is also probable that there will be a general illumination by the citizens on the night of the 4th. The display of fire-works will be the most elaborate and complete ever exhibited in this city. The fountains between the Executive Mansion and the Treasury building, at the north front of the Treasury, at Ninth-street, and the one at the Botanical Garden will be illuminated during the entire evening. Twelve hundred rockets will be fired from various points along the Mall extending from the Monument grounds to the Capitol. Bengal lights, Roman candles, and torches will be displayed along the Avenue, from First to Seventeenth street. Should the weather be unfavorable or doubtful, the exhibition will be deferred to the first clear evening. Prof. Gardner, Electrician at the Capitol, has his electric light, which is to be placed on the dome of the Capitol, put in perfect order, and will make immediate preparation for its assignment to position. The fire-works from New-York have arrived. They occupied three cars. Mr. Wilson, of the firm of Wilson & Caffrey, has arrived, with thirty-five calcium lights.

THE BALL-ROOM.

The ball building is the great centre of attraction, and is very nearly ready. It will be fully so by Tuesday afternoon. It has been specially erected for its purpose, and is 350 feet long, with its decorations, and, including the supper, it will cost $40,000. Workmen are busy in arranging the interior decorations, the gas fixtures are nearly completed, except the gold and crimson ornaments which will be hung at the last moment. The upper edges of these ornaments are attached to hoops, and the sides are pendant, the gas-jets being seen through them. The bases of the arches that span the building, about thirty in number, are covered with a frame-work which runs up about twenty feet and comes to a point at the top. The wood-work is painted so as to resemble columns, the colors used being light brown and yellow. On the space at the tops of these are the arms of the States. The President's platform is about completed. The front is covered with white muslin, and will be hung with evergreens and embellished with rosettes. At the rear of the platform is being placed the immense radius, which promises to be the most imposing decoration of the room. Separate supper, dressing, and retiring rooms will be provided for the President, the members of the Cabinet, and the ladies of the families. The committee having in charge the management of the floor have made very complete arrangements for the satisfactory performance of their duties. The Chairman, Mr. Solmons, is having a slightly-raised platform erected on the west side of the room, from which a view of the entire assemblage may be obtained. The ball room is to be divided into six sections, each to be under the control of six assistant floor managers, who are to report to Mr. Solmons by a system of signals. The latter gentleman will have telegraphic communication with the leaders of the different bands, so that he can communicate with them as to when the music is to begin or to cease. The sections are to be designated by flags hung from the sides of the room with the number of the different sections plainly marked thereon. By this means a gentleman making an engagement with a lady for any particular dance can designate the section where he will meet her at the given time, and then be able to find her as per engagement. The two balconies for the bands are nearly ready. That situated over the main entrance, on Fourth-street, is being covered with red, white, and blue canvas. That located at the south end of the building will not be finished until Monday. On the first-mentioned balcony will be placed the Annapolis Naval Academy Band. This will supply the music for dancing, while the West Point and Marine Bands will play alternate marches.

GAY UNIFORMS.

Secretary Fish has addressed communications to the members of the diplomatic corps requesting them to appear in full court-dress at the ball, and in conjunction with the glittering uniforms of our army and naval officers they will present a scene of brilliancy rarely witnessed.

THE SUPPER-ROOM AND TABLE.

The supper-room is nearly completed. The sides have been festooned the entire length with laurel; at short distances are placed rosettes of red, white, and blue muslin, the whole combined with a canopy of the same colors, rendering the effect most pleasing. The front of the table is also being covered with white muslin. The room will be brilliantly lighted with gas, and, viewed from the ball-room, will present a very pretty appearance. The kitchen is a model in its way. The catering is in charge of the famous cook, Mr. J. G. Torrilhon, of New-York, and twelve assistants, all experienced cooks. All the meats, hams, poultry, game, and oysters were shipped from New-York; and in order that there should be no danger of the supply falling short on the night of the ball, the committee have greatly exceeded the estimate of the quantity judged sufficient. The large joints of beef and mutton, and the game patés and the pies and pastry, were cooked in New-York, and shipped here by express. The rest of the cooking will be done here, and also the garnishing. The tea and coffee is prepared by steam in large copper boilers placed in the butler's pantries, adjoining the dining-hall, and conveyed to urns on the table—so, good hot tea and coffee will be supplied, a luxury seldom obtained at a ball supper. The kitchen and supper are under the superintendence of Mr. W. D. Colt, assisted by Mr. Wm. Wilkinson, of the Metropolitan Hotel, New-York.

*Dispatch to the Associated Press.*

WASHINGTON, March 2.—The First Troop of the Philadelphia Cavalry have been assigned to the right of the personal escort of the President in the inaugural procession. The troop is the oldest military organization, with a continuous history, in the United States. It participated in the battles of Trenton and Princeton, and was the body-guard of Washington during the Revolution. It has taken part in all the struggles through which the country has passed, and furnished over seventy officers during the last war, besides serving three terms of service as an organization. The troop will be under the command of Capt. M. E. Rogers and Lieut. A. L. Snowden.

INAUGURATION DECORATIONS.

The hotels and boarding-houses are fast filling with visitors. Several military companies have already arrived, and others will be here to-morrow by different trains. Many of the houses on Pennsylvania-avenue, the line of the inaugural procession, are decorated with flags, evergreens, and transparencies, and others will be similarly adorned to-morrow.

### The Departure for the Inauguration.

The scene at the Jersey City Railroad depot, last evening, was unusually lively in consequence of the general rush for Washington. Three trains left between 8 and 11 o'clock P. M. The first contained the West Point cadets and the Albany Burgess Corps, and started about 8:10 o'clock. For a long time previously the ticket-office was besieged by a long string of anxious travelers, whose patience was sorely tried by the long delay. The regular train, which should have started at 9 from the New-York side did not start until nearly 10 o'clock from the other side. It was followed soon after by another extra or special train, carrying large numbers of those who could not obtain berths on the regular train. Political organizations of New-York and neighboring cities were represented by delegations.

The Republican General Committee of this City appointed a few days ago a committee of twenty-one, one from each Assembly District, to be present at the inauguration. A few members of this committee went on Saturday, and some on last evening; but there were not many prominent New-Yorkers among the travelers of last night. Up to the last moment all was haste and bustle. The platforms were crowded and the cars besieged. The gathering was good natured, however, and put up without complaint with the inconvenience and delay occasioned by the great rush. Besides long trains of ordinary and drawing-room cars, about a dozen sleeping-cars were filled by the patriotic sight-seers thronging to the national capital.

The Hon. Simon Cameron Association, of New-York, John Heckler, President, will leave this evening for Washington to attend the inauguration of President Grant. They are the guests of the Cameron Club, of Philadelphia, of which Senator James B. Alexander is President. Major Downing's Ninth Regiment Band accompanies them.

### The West Point Cadets.

The West Point cadets arrived yesterday at the Thirtieth-street Depot of the Hudson River Railroad, by a special train from Garrison's, on the Hudson, en route for Washington. The corps numbers 218 cadets, under the charge of Lieut.-Col. E. Upton, First Artillery, U. S. A., and Commandant of the Academy, and his staff. The cadets are commanded by their own officers, and are accompanied by the Military Academic Band. A Government transport conveyed them across the river to Jersey City, and they were provided with supper at Taylor's Hotel. They left the city, in company with the Albany Burgesses, by a special train of ten cars. The young soldiers look forward to much enjoyment on their excursion, and expect to make a favorable impression in the grand spectacle at the inauguration. They have been making careful preparations for days past, and their uniform and equipments are remarkably neat, bright, and fresh looking. The corps will probably act at the inaugural as a body guard for the President, and will march at the head of the military column. They will be received by President Grant at 11 o'clock to-day. Col. Webster, who has made the arrangements for their reception in Washington, has hired a hall for their quarters. They will attend the ball and supper on the night of the inauguration, and will return to West Point on Thursday next.

The corps attends the inauguration by the express desire of the Secretary of War. His order on the subject is addressed to Col. Thomas H. Ruger, Superintendent U. S. M. A. The Secretary says that he believes the presence of the cadets will add to the character of the ceremony, and expresses himself gratified with the conduct and recent marked improvement in their discipline and bearing. The trip, he believes, will afford necessary and deserved relaxation, and he also desires to show to the people assembled at the capital from all parts of the country "a body of young military men, which, he believes, in discipline, drill, soldierly appearance and the qualities which make a military cadet cannot be surpassed." The order concludes with a wish that the cadets will endeavor to add to their high reputation in the presence of critical friends and foes who will be assembled in Washington at the inauguration. The following order was then issued:

HEAD-QUARTERS UNITED STATES MILITARY ACADEMY, WEST POINT, N. Y., Feb. 28, 1873.

GENERAL ORDERS, NO. 9.—In compliance with instructions from the honorable Secretary of War, Lieut.-Col. E. Upton, First Artillery, with the Battalion of cadets and its officers, such members of the academic staff as may be authorized to accompany the command, and the Military Academy Band, will, on the 2d proximo, proceed to Washington, D. C.

The Quartermaster's Department will provide the necessary transportation.

By command of Col. Ruger.

ROBERT H. HALL,
Captain Tenth Infantry, Adjutant.

The Seventh Regiment will receive the cadets on their return from Washington on Thursday morning. They will land at the foot of Canal-street or Battery, and will march from thence to and up Broadway to the Thirtieth-street depot of the Hudson River Railroad.

### The Fifth Regiment and the Old Guard.

The Fifth Regiment, under the command of Col. Charles S. Spencer, will form in line at the armory of the regiment, in Hester-street, at 3½ P. M. to-day. On Saturday, knapsacks and other equipments were distributed, and yesterday all horse equipments and officers' baggage were dispatched to Washington in the hands of the Quartermaster. The regiment is 800 strong, but only 600 will go on to the capital. The route from the armory will be up Hester-street to the Bowery, and through Fourth-avenue to Union square, where the regiment will await the arrival of the Second Connecticut Regiment, expected at 5.25 P. M. The officers and staff of the Seventy-first Regiment will parade at their armory, Thirty-fifth-street and Broadway, at 2¾ P. M., and will proceed to the Grand Central Depot to meet the Second Connecticut Regiment, whom they will escort to their armory, where they will partake of a collation. The Connecticut regiment will then march, with its escort, to Union-square, to meet the Fifth Regiment. After saluting, the Fifth will take up the rear, and the two regiments, led by the officers of the Seventy-first Regiment, will proceed down Broadway to Cortlandt-street, thence to the ferry, the Fifth taking the 7 o'clock train south, and the Connecticut the 7½ train.

The Old Guard, under the command of Major Geo. W. McLean, will leave the armory of the Twenty-second Regiment at 11 A. M. They will parade eighty men, and will be accompanied by Dodworth's full band. The line of march will be from Fourteenth-street to Broadway, to Canal-street, and Desbrosses-street to Jersey City Ferry. These veterans are to act as a special escort to the President.

### The Albany Burgess Corps.

The Albany Burgess Corps, composed of four line officers, nine staff officers, and fifty-eight men, and accompanied by Doring's Band of twenty-five pieces, under the command of Capt. Henry B. Beecher, passed through the City yesterday en route for Washington, to take part in the inauguration ceremonies on Tuesday next. On their arrival at the Grand Central Depot the corps was formed into line, for the purpose of marching to the Metropolitan Hotel, where, according to orders previously forwarded, they were to be furnished with dinner, but they were forbidden by the Police, under direct orders from Supt. Kelso, from parading through the streets at all, and were compelled to make the journey to the hotel on some of the Fourth-avenue cars, which appeared to have been expressly set aside for the purpose. On their arrival at the Metropolitan the members of the corps were greeted by a numerous assemblage of friends and acquaintances, who had been awaiting their coming for several hours. The corps was accompanied by about twenty invited guests, who were distinguished by the badges they wore, composed of a blue ribbon with silver fringe and surmounted by a handsome monogram, composed of the letters A. B. C., wrought in silver. This corps, which was organized on the 8th of October, 1833, by John O. Cole, who was the first commandant, and who yet lives, is particularly noticeable for the quietness of the uniform they wear, it being of dark-blue cloth, with scarlet cloth facings. That of the officers is a dark-blue cloth jacket, braided with black braid, pantaloons of the same, with a narrow band of gold braid at the side. On this occasion each of the officers wore on the left breast a badge displaying the initial letters of the corps in gold. After partaking of dinner the corps, headed by the band, marched down Broadway to Canal-street, to the Desbrosses-street Ferry, and were conveyed across the river to Jersey City, where they embarked on the special train provided for them and the West Point Cadets, leaving the station for Washington at 7½ P. M. On their arrival in Washington they will proceed to the Kirkwood House, where quarters have been specially secured. They will be received by the President to-day, and will afterward visit Senators Conkling and Fenton at their respective residences. The corps will leave Washington on Wednesday morning by the 8 o'clock train for Philadelphia, where they will remain until Friday morning, returning to New-York by the 10½ train. On their arrival in this City they will be the guests of the Metropolitan Hotel until Saturday, when they return to Albany.

### The Boston Lancers.

The Boston Lancers arrived here at 6 A. M., yesterday, by the Providence and Stonington steamer. They were landed in Jersey City, breakfasted at Taylor's Hotel, and left by a special train for Washington, at 11¼ A. M. The Lancers numbered 150, including a staff of twelve honorary members. They were accompanied by Edmonds' Boston Band, and among the honorary members were ex-Capts. Guild, Jinsen, Wilmarth, Fellows, and Hull, and Adjt.-Gen. Cunningham, of the Massachusetts State Militia. The latter gentleman makes the excursion by special invitation. Quartermaster Smith is now in Washington, having been dispatched ahead of the troop, to complete the necessary arrangements for their sojourn in that city during the inauguration ceremonies.

The Lancers will be received by the President to-day, and be entertained by their Washington friends this evening. To-morrow they will take part in the inauguration parade, and, in the evening, will attend the inauguration ball, be feasted at a sumptuous supper, and will return to Boston on Wednesday. The Lancers are a cavalry troop, and in their gay uniform of red and dark blue colors, and carrying lances, they will, undoubtedly, form one of the most attractive portions of the inauguration display. The troop is one of the oldest military organizations of the Modern Athens, and some of its wealthiest and most influential citizens appear on its roster. An escort will probably be furnished the Lancers on their return passage through New-York.

### The Trains to Washington—The Exodus from New-York.

The Pennsylvania Railroad Company has made arrangements to accommodate the extra Washington travel to-day and to-night, though, as the traveling capacity of the road is crowded to its utmost, it has not been deemed advisable to issue excursion tickets, or offer extra inducements in the way of a reduction of fare. In order so far as possible to accommodate the increased travel, the company has secured a large number of additional cars from the New-Jersey Southern Railroad Company, which requires a much larger rolling stock for its Summer travel than at any other time, and has placed them on the local trains, putting their own cars on the through trains. Last night two extra Washington trains were dispatched, one following the 7 P. M. Western express, and the other the regular Washington train. The two trains comprised fourteen cars, and contained 286 West Point cadets, and 150 members of the Burgess Corps from Albany. The cadets, according to a prearranged plan, dined at Taylor's Hotel. To-day several Eastern regiments, delegations from the New-York National Guard, the Third New-Jersey Regiment, the Colored Wilson Guard, of Jersey City, and other organizations will leave, fifty-four specially-chartered cars going out, besides the regular trains and others, to accommodate the expected increased travel. Chief McWilliams, Detective Watson, and others from Jersey City, who are familiar with New-York thieves, have gone to Washington at the especial desire of the authorities there.

### Arrival of the Tybee—List of Passengers, &c.

The steamer Tybee, plying between this City and the Santo Domingo ports, arrived off Pier No. 4 North River at 8 o'clock last evening, where she remained anchored for the night. As the Custom-house officer did not board her until after 10 o'clock, none of the passengers came ashore, and the mails were not brought off until this morning, when the vessel was docked at 6 o'clock. The Tybee left San Domingo City Feb. 20, Samana Bay Feb. 21, and Puerto Platta on the 22d, having had a fair passage. She brings merchandise to Spofford Brothers & Co., and the following passengers: W. H. Seaman, J. G. Adams, F. H. Soillet, A. F. Masino, Capt. Samuel Samuels, of the newly-formed Samana Bay Company, J. D. Ward, and Francisco Oliva, C. J. Grone, and Gus. Muller.

## WASHINGTON.

### Speaker Blaine and the Increase of Salary—The Congressional Globe—Business in the Senate.

*Special Dispatch to the New-York Times.*

WASHINGTON, March 2.—Speaker Blaine yesterday executed a piece of political strategy, in connection with the salary amendment, which is characteristic of his shrewdness as a politician and his executive capacity as a presiding officer. He called the attention of the House to the fact that the Speaker's salary had always been adjusted in the same clause and on the same basis as that of the Vice-President and the members of the Cabinet. He desired that it should so remain. The clause in the amendment under consideration did not make the salaries of the Vice-President and members of the Cabinet retroactive, but the Speaker being a member, would be entitled to the back pay; he therefore asked unanimous consent to insert the word "hereafter," so that it would read: "And the Speaker of the House shall hereafter receive," &c. Randall at first objected, but on the Speaker's appeal withdrew his objection, and the Speaker remarked he would interline the amendment himself, which he did, amid the laughter of the House. He had barely laid his pen down when Farnsworth, who had said that if that was permitted to be done it would forever be impossible to throw the fact back into a man's face, sprang to his feet and objected. "Too late!" cried the Speaker, amid roars of laughter. Farnsworth grew black with anger, and vociferated that he was not too late. He took an appeal, and the vote sustaining the decision of the Chair was an overwhelming "aye," mingled with great merriment, while Farnsworth alone voted "no." The whole affair occupied less than a minute, and was cleverly and thoroughly done.

OBSCENE LITERATURE.

About 1 o'clock this morning the House took up and passed, under suspension of the rules, the bill prohibiting the circulation of obscene literature through the mails, and importation of articles for purposes of abortion, &c. It was amended in an important respect, viz., by a proviso that the change of the penalty for these offenses should not operate to invalidate indictments already found or proceedings already begun. But for this, every man now under indictment for these offences would have been let loose, the Supreme Court having held that to be the effect of a change of the penalty in a statute pending proceedings. The Senate will concur in the amendment.

PUT RIGHT ON THE RECORD.

The report of yeas and nays in the salary amendment, as printed in some of the papers on to-day, omits the name of Mr. Sessions, of New-York, who voted against the increase.

THE CONGRESSIONAL GLOBE.

The Senate amendment to the Sundry Civil bill, which sends the printing of the *Globe* to the Government printing-house, was concurred in by the House last night by a very large majority. This is believed to be the final action of Congress on this matter. The amendment provides that the work shall be done at the Government office till a contract shall be entered into, and no contract is authorized, and all attempts to have the contracts given to Mr. Murtagh seem to have been exhausted. After the Congressional Printer shall have completed arrangements to do the work, it is hardly probable that any effort to get the work into the hands of private parties can succeed.

RIVERS AND HARBORS.

The Senate, last night, took up the River and Harbor Appropriation bill, and passed it late in the night. A large number of amendments were made, but they were for the most part small in amounts. The aggregate of increase of the bill, as reported to the Senate, will be considerable, but not like the increase made in the Sundry Civil bill. The bill will be ready for the House as soon as it meets to-morrow morning, and will probably be sent at once to a conference committee and will be disposed of without much difficulty.

BUSINESS IN THE SENATE.

The bill of the House making appropriation for the payment of awards found by the Southern Claims Commission was taken up in the Senate about 3½ o'clock this morning, and its reading was begun. As this would occupy about an hour there began to be some uneasiness, and a discussion in the nature of a free conference was had as to the time necessary to finish the business pending, and the best hours of meeting. It was finally determined that the Senate should meet this evening at 7 o'clock in order to act upon any conference reports that might be ready to submit. In order to expedite the Southern Claims bill, it was unanimously agreed that it should be read before the recess was taken, and that, when its reading was finished, no business but to vote the recess agreed on should be in order. This gave all but the Clerk and President, Mr. Anthony, an opportunity to retire at once, and compelled them to a dreary task an hour long, which at 4 o'clock they immediately began. Some amendments were made by the committee, which, if agreed to, will send the bill back to the House; but its passage seems probable, though till yesterday it was supposed it would have to go over to the next session, the injustice and bad policy of which was almost unanimously admitted.

PERSONAL.

Several Senators, elected to the next Congress, were on the floor of the Senate yesterday, including Messrs. Oglesby, of Illinois; Patterson, of South Carolina; Bogy, of Missouri; McCreary, of Kentucky; Merrimon, of North Carolina; Gordon, of Georgia, and Ingalls, the successor of Pomeroy. Ingalls was the subject of much curious attention. In person he is tall, slightly built, and erect in bearing. His complexion is dark, and he wears a rather long and heavy black mustache, and his hair is thick and black, giving him rather a striking appearance.

It is reported that Jos. B. Stewart, the recusant witness, will bring suit against Speaker Blaine and Sergeant-at-Arms Ordway for false imprisonment.

The Representatives of Illinois and Ohio, who have been urging the passage of the Two Per Cent. bill all Winter, leave to-morrow, having abandoned the contest for this Winter. They attribute their defeat to the persistent opposition of Senator Edmunds.

THE APPROPRIATION BILLS.

The Conference Committee on the Army Appropriation bill is ready to report. It makes no very important change in the bill as agreed upon in the Senate, except in respect to the appropriation for new uniforms for the army. This the committee has agreed to let stand as in the original House bill, at $1,500,000.

The Post-office appropriation bill has been agreed to by the Conference Committee. It recommends concurrence in the Senate amendment excluding all free matter from the mails, including newspaper exchanges.

The Conference Committee on the Legislative bill has not yet been able to agree to any report on the salaries amendment, and have adjourned till morning.

The Sundry Civil bill is nearly completed in conference, and will be ready early to-morrow.

The Deficiency bill has been read through in the Senate, and the printing of the Senate Committee's amendments has been ordered.

The Senate will meet to-morrow morning, at 10 o'clock, with ample time to finish all business which is necessary to avoid an extra session.

THE SUNDAY SESSION OF THE SENATE.

The unusual spectacle of a Sunday session of the Senate attracted a great crowd of people to the Capitol to-night, and the galleries were filled soon after the hour of meeting, at 7 o'clock. Among the audience were a very large number of ladies and gentlemen from other parts of the country, who have come to witness or take part in the inauguration ceremonies and festivities. Edmund Yates, the novelist, and J. M. Bellew, the English reader, were present in the gallery, and Frederick Douglass on the floor. The Boston Lancers, in their bright scarlet uniforms, were conspicuous in the gallery for an hour or more. When the Senate proceeded to the consideration of unobjected cases on the calendar a large part of the audience dispersed to wander about the Capitol, but the galleries remained quite well filled till nearly midnight.

*Dispatch to the Associated Press.*

CONFIRMATIONS.

The Senate, in Executive Session, to-night, confirmed the following nominations:

*Registers—Land Offices*—M. J. Taylor, Tallahassee, Fla.; J. S. Banks, East Florida Land District.

*Receivers of Public Moneys*—D. B. McGinnis, Tallahassee, Fla.; S. F. Halliday, East Florida District; D. C. Tuttle, Camden, Fla.

*Revenue Marine Service*.—Second Lieutenants F. S. Smith and Thomas Mason to be First Lieutenants; Thomas G. Walker and John Wyckoff to be Third Lieutenants.

*Postmasters*—Edward A. Scott, at Newbury, S. C.; H. Taylor, Corpus Christi, Texas; Wm. McPherson, Effingham, Ill.; Wm. Crawford, Wamego, Kansas; E. W. Ringgold, New-Orleans, La.

*Collectors of Customs*—George Hubbard, Stonington, Conn.; Henry Hazen, Fernandina.

*Surveyor-General*—J. W. Gilbert, for Florida.

F. E. Upton, Master of the Navy.

*Second Lieutenants*—Peter Leary, Jr., and George Duff, to be First Lieutenants in the Army.

First Lieut. O. W. Pollock, to be Captain.

THE MONEY BURNT IN BOSTON.

The number of cases of burnt money received from Boston after the great fire in that city was eighty-nine. The nominal amount of money contained in these cases was supposed by the parties remitting them, to be $88,812 90. The money that was identified, and for which returns were made, was as follows:

| | |
|---|---|
| Legal-tender notes and fractional currency.. | $4,332 05 |
| National bank notes | 4,172 00 |
| United States bonds (principally five-twenties) | 73,050 00 |
| Railroad bonds | 5,000 00 |
| Coupons of United States bonds | 1,629 00 |
| Certificate of bank stock | 100 00 |
| State bank notes | 7 00 |
| Counterfeit | 75 |
| Total | $88,290 80 |
| Total amount of "shorts" ... $1 672 35 | |
| Total amount of "overs" ... 1,150 25 | |
| Net short | 522 10 |
| Total | $88,812 90 |

In addition, a large amount of checks, promissory notes, and other valuable business paper, were either wholly or partially identified, and returned to their owners. The money was generally very badly burnt, and it was with the greatest difficulty that it could be separated and identified. The identification and restoration occupied the constant labor of three ladies for a period of four months.

THE NESBITT STAMPED ENVELOPE CONTRACT.

The Postmaster-General denies the telegraphed report that the files of his department show that Colfax was the attorney or lobbyist of Nesbitt. He says that, finding the Nesbitt contract for stamped envelopes had been extended by his predecessor without advertising for competition, he referred the question of its legality to the Attorney-General, who decided it to be without sanction of law, and that the department should terminate the same on reasonable notice, and issue proposals for a new contract, which was done. In the meantime a question arose as to the temporary supply until the new supply of the new contract should commence, and it was to this temporary supply that Mr. Colfax urged that the heirs of Nesbitt, who died in 1869, having the necessary buildings, machinery, and materials, and not having forfeited the contract by any malfeasance, should have an opportunity to work up the same until the new contract was let, or that they be allowed to present an argument as to the validity of their contract as extended. These views as to the temporary supply seemed so just and reasonable that they were adopted by the department, and the heirs of Nesbitt were employed to furnish the temporary supply, though at a reduced cost of fifteen per cent. upon old prices. The extension had been pronounced illegal by the Attorney-General, and no argument upon that point would have availed against his decision, no matter from whom it came. The Postmaster-General further says that he never supposed for a moment that Mr. Colfax designed or attempted to influence him in his official action in any improper manner whatever, and that similar suggestions as to the interests of constituents are frequently made by members of Congress without comment or intimation of their impropriety.

CONGRESSIONAL BUSINESS.

Committees of conference were in session to-day, at the Capitol, on disagreeing amendments to several of the general appropriations and the Geneva Award bills. The Senate has yet to act on the House Deficiency bill. The business is in such a state of forwardness that no one now seems to anticipate the necessity for an extra session of Congress, for legislative purposes. The Senate has more business than the House to act upon, but will make much progress by the long session of to-night. The Senate Utah bill has yet to be acted on by the House.

THE PENSION CODE.

The bill recently passed by both Houses codifying the Pension laws provides for the appointment of a Deputy Commissioner of Pensions, at an annual salary of $2,500. The opinion of numerous members of Congress is that this office will be filled by appointment from the old and experienced bureau clerks, in the spirit of civil service reform, the object being to afford the Commissioner a competent assistant, aside from the mere claims of politicians.

THE PRESIDENT AND CABINET IN CHURCH.

The Metropolitan Methodist Church was densely crowded this morning, President Grant, Vice-President elect Wilson, and nearly all the Cabinet officers, together with the Sumner Guard, of Syracuse, N. Y., in uniform, being among the auditors. Rev. Dr. Tiffany delivered a discourse on the relations of religion to the State, in the conclusion of which he incidentally made a complimentary allusion to President Grant, remarking, in that connection, that "peace hath her victories, no less renowned than war."

BOND PURCHASES AND GOLD SALES.

The Secretary of the Treasury has directed the Assistant Treasurer at New-York to purchase $1,000,000 of bonds on the first and third Wednesdays, and $500,000 on the second and fourth Wednesdays, and to sell $1,500,000 of coin on each Thursday during the current month of March.

DIPLOMATIC PROBABILITIES.

It is reported that Senator Cole will, shortly after the expiration of his term on the 4th inst., be nominated by the President as Minister to either Portugal or Holland; also, that Senator Nye will probably be nominated Minister to China, though his friends deny this, and he is understood to desire the appointment as Minister to Austria.

### The Indian Troubles—Fatal Epidemic in the Northern Park.

SAN FRANCISCO, March 2.—Gen. Crook arrived at the head-quarters at Prescott, Arizona, on the 17th ult., and then went to Camp Date Creek. The army is in excellent condition. Gen. Crook considers the backbone of the Indian war broken, but has no faith in Cochise's promises to keep the peace.

Thirteen deaths have occurred from the new fatal epidemic at Deer Creek, in the Northern Park. There is no danger of the disease spreading, it being confined to the locality where it first appeared. The schools are still kept closed as a precautionary measure.

## POMEROY AND PATTERSON.

### Aspect of the Cases—Conjectures as to the Action of the Senate.

*Special Dispatch to the New-York Times.*

WASHINGTON, March 2.—The report of the committee to investigate the charges against Senator Pomeroy, will be made to-morrow. The committee has attempted to keep its deliberations and intentions with great secrecy, and has succeeded unusually well, but still some things will leak out. There are some rumors afloat, too, which may or may not have a foundation, in fact which will be confirmed or disproved by the report itself. The report will be the unanimous conclusion of the committee, and will probably declare that the charges are not proven. This is quite different from an acquittal. It does not say that Mr. Pomeroy's defense is valid. It simply means that, in the opinion of the committee, the evidence weighed together is not sufficiently clear as to his guilt to warrant an absolute judgment against him. The explanation of the conclusion of the committee, which will be made in the report may, however, modify considerably the meaning that the verdict itself would have if made without comment by the committee. Mr. Pomeroy is, naturally enough, looking after his interests, and is anxious to have a point made in the report against the election of Ingalls. He is regarded quite as anxious to have a foundation laid in the report for challenging the qualification of Ingalls when the new Senate organizes, and the reference of his credentials to the Committee on Privileges and Elections, as to secure his own direct acquittal. This would give him a new chance to break up the election and get himself once more before the Kansas Legislature.

SENATOR PATTERSON.

There was some talk of having the Senate meet at 2 o'clock this afternoon, for the purpose of taking up the resolution against Senator Patterson, but it appears to be impossible that any full and proper hearing should be given to the matter, and, though no decision was made, it is not likely that any action can be undertaken. There is, however, a rumor of some *coup d'état* to be executed in Mr. Patterson's behalf, and there have been rumors, conferences, and private councils. If any action should be taken before adjournment in his case, it is likely that a proposition will be made to substitute for the resolution of expulsion one of censure, as in the case of Ames and Brooks in the House. Mr. Patterson's friends would be glad to have such a resolution passed rather than that the matter should be left by adjournment when it is in such shape that it may hereafter be said by any of his enemies that he would have been expelled if action had been taken. Mr. Patterson has many friends in the Senate who think expulsion too great a punishment, and who are attempting to prepare the way for some such action as that noted above. The committee will probably take the ground that it will not oppose any action which the Senate, assuming responsibility, shall see fit to take.

## THE WEATHER.

### Synopsis and Probabilities.

WASHINGTON, March 3—1 A. M.—The barometer has very generally fallen since Saturday night throughout the Atlantic States, but is now again rising from the lower lakes and South Atlantic States, westward; partly cloudy weather and light snow in New-York and Pennsylvania; cloudy and clearing weather in the Southern States; the low barometer which was in Louisiana has moved eastward over South Carolina and beyond our stations. Heavy rains have prevailed in the Southern and Gulf States during Sunday, and are now followed by fresh and brisk north and north-west winds and clearing weather, an area of high barometer, with very low temperature; north-west winds and clear weather has extended from Dakota eastward to the upper lakes, and southward to Texas.

PROBABILITIES.

For Monday, in New-England, northerly winds and partly cloudy weather; in the Middle States, north-west winds and generally clear weather by Monday afternoon, with local cloudy areas in New-York; for the South Atlantic and Gulf States generally clear weather with cold north-west winds; from the Ohio Valley to the Upper Lakes and the North-west, diminishing northerly winds and clear cold weather. Cautionary signals continue at Savannah, Charleston, and Wilmington, and are ordered for Norfolk and Cape May. Reports are generally missing from the upper lakes, Gulf States, and Western Territories.

### The Sandwich Islands and the United States—Proposed Revival of Reciprocity.

SAN FRANCISCO, March 2.—The steamer Moses Taylor arrived to-night from Honolulu, bringing dates till Feb. 15.

The *Hawaiian Gazette* of Feb. 15 says that strong efforts are being made to revive the project of the Reciprocity Treaty with the United States. At the present time a large portion of the sugar crop, which would otherwise go to California, goes to New-Zealand and British Columbia, breaking up the trade with San Francisco. There is a report that the Hawaiian Government is willing to cede a large section of land near Pearl Bay to the United States on condition that we establish a coaling station at that point.

The sugar market is depressed on account of the low prices in the United States, particularly in California. It has not been as greatly depressed since 1868.

The *Commercial Advertiser*, of Jan. 15, discusses the question of annexation with the United States. It strongly opposes the proposition.

At a meeting of the Chamber of Commerce of Honolulu held Feb. 12, a resolution was adopted appointing a committee of conference with the Government to see if a treaty of reciprocity can be entered into with the United States. A committee of five was appointed.

Mr. Rappiee, Director of the Government Press, died on Feb. 15.

His Majesty visited Hilo in the United States steamer Benecia.

### Murder and Robbery in California.

SAN FRANCISCO, March 2.—On Saturday last two Spaniards entered Willard's store, near Horsetown, in Shasta County, and shot and instantly killed a Chinaman, knocked down the clerk with a revolver, robbed the store of money and all the valuables they could carry away, and went toward Cottonwood. On the road they met a man named Simons, and robbed him and escaped. They are said to be a remnant of the famous Joaquin Murietta's band of highwaymen.

## BY MAIL AND TELEGRAPH.

A. B. Johnson, Chief Clerk of the Light-house Board, has resigned.

The first number of the Sharon Springs (N. Y.) *Gazette* appeared on Saturday.

A new line of ten first-class propellers is to be engaged this year in the lake-traffic between Montreal and Chicago.

Rev. Hugh Smith, from Belfast, Ireland, commenced his ministerial labors in the Seventh Presbyterian Church, in Cincinnati, last night.

The steam-ship Hansa, Brickenstein, from Bremen, Feb. 15, via Southampton, Feb. 18, arrived at this port yesterday.

A fire at Montague, Mich., on Tuesday last, destroyed the Dowling block, Montague Hotel, and several other buildings. The loss is quite heavy.

John H. Ring, keeper of a fancy-goods store in Worcester, Mass., committed suicide by poison on Saturday night. The act was the result of intemperance.

The boarding-house, in connection with the Social Manufacturing Company, at Woonsocket, R. I., was burned yesterday morning. The inmates, eighty in number, escaped safely.

## FOREIGN NEWS.

### The Carlist Insurrection in Spain—Condition of Affairs in the Insurrectionary Districts—Debates in the Assembly.

MADRID, March 1, via LONDON, March 2.—The *Gaceta* publishes an official dispatch announcing a defeat of the Carlists at Veramanos, with a loss of six killed and many wounded; also, the defeat and total rout of Ferrer's band, which lost thirty killed, including its leader.

The troops are in close pursuit of the insurgents under the curé of Santa Cruz. The latter is reported to have shot a woman.

Madrazo's band in Arragon has been defeated. Madrazo was badly wounded.

The Carlist bands in Old Castile have all been dispersed.

Gen. Contreras, commanding the national forces in Catalonia, has sent a telegram to the Minister of War demanding reinforcements. The General, on assuming his command, made a speech, in which he promised that the army of Catalonia would be disbanded as soon as the Carlist insurrection was suppressed.

BAYONNE, March 2.—The Carlists in Catalonia, Alicante, and Murcia are increasing in numbers and becoming more daring in action.

The Infante Alfonso and wife, with a large staff and a body guard of 200 young men, spent the whole day on Monday last at San Quirce. The Prince and Princess held receptions, during which the bells rang and the bands played. The peasants flocked into the town from the neighborhood to pay their respects to the Infante.

The national army in Catalonia is represented to be sadly disorganized, and the garrison at Barcelona is reported to have shown signs of insubordination.

The towns of Rich, Roda, and Centellas, having refused to pay taxes imposed by the Carlists, have been proclaimed by the latter in a state of blockade.

The Carlists have destroyed by fire the railway stations at Areta, Llodio, Lezama, and Amurrio.

MADRID, March 2.—In the Assembly yesterday the Government presented a bill to provide means for crushing the Carlist insurrection. It authorizes the immediate organization of fifty new battalions of 900 men each, and grants a supply of 100,000,000 pesetas.

Señor Sicilia advocated economical reforms in the administration, and, among other measures, urged the abolition of the Council of State and the Ministries of Justice, Public Works, and the Marine.

The majority of the Assembly is determined to carry through the bill for the abolition of slavery before the prorogation. The Conservatives are pressing their amendments, but it is believed that they will withdraw them when they see defeat is certain.

Gen. Cordoba, late Minister of War, and Señor Rivero, President of the last Congress, are ill.

### The Parisian Journals on M. Dufaure's Speech.

PARIS, March 2.—The Republican and Radical journals bitterly attack Mr. Dufaure for his recent speech in the Assembly, and warn President Thiers against carrying strategy to an excess. The Moderate Left have resolved to oppose certain clauses of the constitutional project, unless the Government consent to modify them.

### Another Terrible Disaster—Two Vessels Sunk—Twenty-four Lives Lost.

LONDON, March 3—6 A. M.—The ship Chacabuco, from San Francisco for Liverpool, ran into the ship Torch in the Irish Channel.

The Chacabuco sank a few minutes after the collision, and twenty-four of the ship's company were drowned. The Torch also went down, but all on board were saved.

### Extensive Frauds on the Bank of England.

LONDON, March 3—6 A. M.—The discovery has just been made of frauds, on a gigantic scale, on the Bank of England, committed by one Warren, alias Horton, an American, through a series of skillful forgeries of the names of the Rothschilds and other great financial houses. A reward of £1,000 has been offered for his apprehension, and the police are searching for him with hopes of success.

### Destructive Fire in Dublin, Ireland.

DUBLIN, March 2.—A large tar manufactory in this city was destroyed by fire to-day. The loss is estimated at $250,000.

## VENEZUELA.

### Affairs in the Republic Improving—Progress of Events.

The Atlas Steam-ship Company's mail steamer St. Thomas, Capt. Drakeford, the first vessel of the company's new line of steamers intended to run monthly between New-York and Venezuela, arrived on her maiden voyage yesterday. The St. Thomas has a large cargo, principally coffee, and complement of passengers. Among the latter is Mr. A. Forwood, one of the owners, who has been organizing the arrangements for the new enterprise.

Venezuela advices by the St. Thomas furnish us with items of interest from that Republic. The President, Guzman Blanco, was rigorously exercising the powers he had assumed and enacting many new and generally satisfactory laws. Among these is the abrogation of all local road dues, a very great relief to the poorer classes at the expense of the men who were generally the fomenters of rebellion. Another act is the institution of compulsory civil marriage, and, as an example, the President, although five years years married, according to the rites of the Church, was married civilly the day prior to the departure of the steamer. This measure was instigated in consequence of the action of the Roman Catholic Archbishop of Caracas in political affairs. For this interference this prelate had been banished to Trinidad. Much commotion had been caused by this expulsion, but on the 14th of February it was announced to Caracas, amidst the firing of rockets and ringing of bells, that the Papal Nuncio at San Domingo had so far supported the President as to appoint a supporter of his Government, Bishop Barralt, as Provisoire of the Diocese.

Steps were being taken about the construction of the railway to the coast from Caracas, and much was being done toward the improvement of that city, one of the most delightful as regards climate in the world. As an evidence of the vigor of the President it may be mentioned that his first Congress would assemble in a large, new Capitol, built within 100 days from the demolition of the walls of a convent garden from which the land had been taken. The coffee crop was arriving freely and realizing high prices.

### Anxiety in Utah as to Frelinghuysen's Bill.

SALT LAKE CITY, March 1.—Increased anxiety is felt as to the fate of Senator Frelinghuysen's bill. Nothing else is talked about. Both sides are doubtful of the result. The Mormons say that if the bill finally passes the question of its constitutionality will then come forward.

The *Journal* (Gentile) expresses the belief that Brigham Young has determined to resist the laws no longer.

All the railroads, except the Utah Northern, are now clear of snow. Trains from the East and West are now on time.

An immense amount of ore and base bullion is accumulating for the Union and Central Pacific Railroads.

# The New-York Times.

VOL. XXV.......NO. 7700. NEW-YORK, FRIDAY, MAY 19, 1876. PRICE FOUR CENTS.


## THE POLITICAL CAMPAIGN.

### ANOTHER DAY'S CONVENTIONS.

THE KENTUCKY REPUBLICANS ENTHUSIASTIC FOR BRISTOW—DELAWARE GOES FOR BLAINE — THE GREENBACKERS NOMINATE PETER COOPER FOR PRESIDENT —MISCELLANEOUS POLITICAL NEWS.

Three State Conventions were held yesterday, and the Greenback Party concluded the farce of their National Convention. The Republicans of Kentucky assembled at Louisville. It was the largest Republican Convention ever held in the State, Mr. Bristow's name being the spell which gathered it. Possibly the majority of the delegates present were personal friends, acquaintances, and neighbors of his; and mention of his name was received with unbounded enthusiasm. The delegation elected to Cincinnati was, of course, for Mr. Bristow solid.

The Republican Convention of Delaware was held at Dover. A delegation from Wilmington numbering forty votes, controlled the convention, and would hear of no other name than Blaine as the nominee for the Presidency. They carried their point, and elected a delegation solid for Mr. Blaine, and instructed it to vote for him.

The Greenback Party wound up their "National" Convention at Indianapolis yesterday, by nominating Peter Cooper for the Presidency, who declined to accept the nomination, and Hon. Newton Booth, of California, for Vice President, who, it is stated, would refuse to take the proffered honor at any price. About one hundred and fifty delegates were present at this farce, and they manfully cast 478 votes for the whole country.

### THE KENTUCKY REPUBLICANS.

THE LARGEST STATE CONVENTION EVER HELD—NOTHING BUT BRISTOW TALKED OF—A DELEGATION SOLID FOR HIM.

*Special Dispatch to the New-York Times.*

LOUISVILLE, May 18.—The Republican State Convention to-day surpassed in size the most sanguine expectations of the Republican Party of Kentucky. It was the largest and most respectable convention ever held in the State, and the enthusiasm at the mention of the name of Bristow was unbounded. It was a convention of those who know him best, his neighbors and friends, citizens who have watched his every step from a gallant and unflinching Union soldier to the present exalted position which he occupies. Gen. John Finnell, of Covington, was temporary Chairman, and on assuming the position he said, that when slavery threatened the life of the nation, Kentucky offered a compromise through Clay. When war threatened the existence of the Government Kentucky gave the great leader of the Union hosts, Abraham Lincoln, and now again when corruption threatens the life of the Union, Kentucky comes to the front and points with pride to the nation's new savior, Benjamin H. Bristow. Words fail to express the scene in the convention after this brief but brilliant speech, prefaced as it was by the remark that "one hundred years ago our forefathers affirmed that all men were born and created equal, and now we, the Republicans of Kentucky, have come together to reaffirm the truth of that assertion."

Ex-Attorney General Speed was permanent Chairman. He was introduced as the trusted friend of President Lincoln, and his appearance on the stage was cause for an earnest cheer. After alluding to the history of the party and its victories in war and peace, he said: Our work is not finished. The currency is yet debased, and by reason of that debasement the business of the country is deranged and morals are tainted. This must not be. Our party, in obedience to duty and honor, and the teachings of its past history, will grapple the question and correct the evil. Gold and silver must again become the standard of value. The war has left a legacy of spendthrift and dissolute habits in private and public life. When the nation was struggling for its life, such things could not and did not engage public attention, and immediately following the war the other great questions which have been happily settled, so absorbed the public mind that the bad habits engendered by the war were, in a measure, unnoticed and became fastened on the nation. It is now the duty of our party to protect the body politic against this evil, and just as surely as the rebellion was suppressed by the power and patriotism of the Republican Party, so surely will corruption disappear before its reawakened might. Let us in common—not for party purposes, not to accomplish party ends—but for the good of our country and love of honor and justice, proclaim it in all towns and cities, upon the hill tops and in the valleys, that no guilty official shall escape. Such a proclamation from the people will give courage, trust, and hope to the faithful, and terrify the guilty. Abraham Lincoln, a son of Kentucky, led the hosts that cleansed the country of slavery. May it not be that another son of Kentucky will lead in healing the wounds and purifying the field after the battle!

Mr. Speed was frequently applauded, especially when he mentioned the name of Lincoln and the triumphs of the party. Committees of the usual character were appointed, and after a short recess the convention was called to order to receive their reports. The platform reaffirms the adherence of the Republicans of Kentucky to the principles of the party. The declaration of principles speaks, first, for the fulfillment of all promises by the nation to the soldiers and sailors who fought for the Union; second, for thorough retrenchment and most rigid economy in all departments of the public service; third, for such reform in the civil service as will prevent the prostitution of public station to selfish ends and make honesty and capacity indispensable qualifications for all offices; fourth favors men in office who are honest and have the courage to fight corruption; fifth, repudiation in all its forms is a national crime, sixth, payment of the public indebtedness according to the letter and spirit of the contract; seventh, speedy return to the money of the Constitution—gold and silver; eighth, opposition to any postponement of a return to specie payment beyond the time now fixed; ninth, reduction of taxation as rapidly as the public faith will permit; tenth, opposition to all schemes which tend to place our common schools under other than popular control; eleventh, equal rights before the law of all citizens.

The following section was read amid great applause, handshaking, and hat throwing:

"As Kentucky gave Abraham Lincoln to his country and to mankind for the great work performed by him, she now presents Benjamin H. Bristow to complete the correction of the ills ever incident to war. His past conduct in office is an earnest evidence of his future course. He has been true to Republican principles in war and peace, manly, firm, and courageous, and ever faithful in the discharge of his duty. His persistent and successful warfare against corruption deserves the thanks of all the friends of honest government. In thus presenting and commending our fellow-citizen to the Republican National Convention we are not unmindful of the distinguished services and worth of other Republicans. We trust the Cincinnati Convention will present as candidates such men whose allegiance to the party has been proved, and who have the moral courage to enforce the laws."

The Committee on Resolutions recommended and the convention elected the following delegates:

*For the State at Large.*—Gen. John M. Harlan, of Louisville; Hon. W. H. Wadsworth, of Maysville; Hon. W. C. Goodloe, of Lexington, and Hon. Robert Boyd, of Laurel County.

*First District.*—R. R. Ratliffe.
*Second District.*—E. H. Murray.
*Third District.*—E. L. Motley.
*Fourth District.*—W. H. Hays.
*Fifth District.*—James Speed.
*Sixth District.*—J. J. Landrum.
*Seventh District.*—T. O. Rackerford.
*Eighth District.*—A. R. Burnam.
*Ninth District.*—C. B. Farris.
*Tenth District.*—W. W. Culbertson.

The Electors for State at Large are Col. Thomas Morrow, of Pulaski, and Hon. John Feland, of Christian, with one from each district.

The reports being read, loud calls were made for Gen. Harlan, Col. W. C. Goodloe, and others, who responded in brief speeches. The convention was in session over three hours, and, in consequence of the entire harmony prevailing, its conclusions were as quiet and happy as its entire proceedings. Delegates from all parts of the State are confident that Kentucky would give Bristow a handsome majority were he the nominee of the Cincinnati Convention, some of them, indeed, giving Kentucky to him by 20,000 majority.

9:05 A. M.—The delegates appointed by the Republican State Convention to-day held a meeting to-night, and upon a free expression of opinion it appeared that every delegate and every alternate was enthusiastically for Bristow.

### DELAWARE REPUBLICANS.

THE STATE CONVENTION YESTERDAY—A DELEGATION TO CINCINNATI SOLID FOR BLAINE AND INSTRUCTED FOR HIM.

*Special Dispatch to the New-York Times.*

DOVER, Del., May 18.—The Republican State Convention met here to-day. Manlove Hayes, of Kent, was chosen permanent President. It became evident from the first that the Blaine men were largely in the majority, and would bear the mention of no other name. From Wilmington there were forty delegates, elected by a solid colored vote; and this delegation assumed immediate control of the convention and ruled it with some severity. It had been thought that the Bristow men would have had some chance of giving expression to their preferences, but the Blaine men were not inclined to have any division in the State delegation. The delegation elected was solid for Blaine, and it was instructed to vote in his favor.

The resolutions adopted declare that the Republicans of Delaware pledge their unalterable devotion to the cardinal principles of the party, including the payment of the Government obligations in coin or its equivalent; and to honest administration, and that James G. Blaine meets the requirements of the Centennial year as the exponent of these principles. A number of Bristow men, from Newcastle County did not vote on this resolution, having left the convention. A sharp contest then took place over another resolution declaring that no Federal officeholder should be a delegate, the object being to exclude Dr. Prettyman, United States Collector, who had been named as a delegate by a majority of the Sussex County caucus, but who was suspected of being less friendly to Blaine than to Bristow. After a warm debate, the resolution prevailed, but Dr. Prettyman's friends insisted on their rights, and the caucus named a satisfactory substitute. The following are the delegates: James Scott, Richard E. Smith, John H. Hoffecker, James R. Lofland, Eli R. Sharp, David W. Moore. Under the instructions, all will vote for Blaine.

### THE NATIONAL GREENBACKERS.

THEY CONCLUDE THEIR FARCE—PETER COOPER NOMINATED FOR THE PRESIDENCY WITH NEWTON BOOTH SECOND—A VERY INFLATED VOTE.

INDIANAPOLIS, May 18.—It was a smaller and more discouraged crowd which assembled in the Opera-house this morning. The people who composed this National Independent Convention had been rid of one load, however, for they all knew that the committee, after long search, had found some principles for them, which had been embodied in a set of resolutions. But the greater trouble of finding a candidate still weighed upon them, and was the cause of their great sorrow. During yesterday they had, by means of the telegraph, ransacked the Union from end to end to find some one who would say plumply that would accept their nomination, and no one was found, the answer in every case being "Declined, with thanks," unless that of Gov. Allen be excepted. He was curt—even contemptuous—in his reply, saying he would accept of no nomination except from the St. Louis Convention. Peter Cooper was polite in his declination, for he placed it solely on the ground of his advanced age. But in one way or another all refused, and so the convention met this morning not only without a constituency, but without a ghost of a show of candidates to present, unless it seized them by main force and thrust them upon the ticket, which in the end was precisely what was done.

Shortly after 9 o'clock Mr. Durant rapped for order, and announced that the first business in order was the report of the Committee on Platform. The resolutions were read by the Secretary, and although a dozen men were on the floor to talk about them, Durant put the question, and declared them adopted in less than a minute. This was significant, and to tired journalists consoling, for it showed that the leaders had at last determined to shut off the stream of talk. But the irrepressible Vorhis, of Illinois, was not altogether conquered, for he bellowed until he forced recognition; then he was proceeding to explain how the resolutions were wrong in some way, when he was silenced by calls to order. Then he thought he could get at the thing by moving a reconsideration, and did it, but his motion was voted down, and by free exercise of lung power the delegates finally whooped him down. Troup, of Connecticut, made the next sensation by trying to introduce a resolution against railroad subsidies. Vorhis and others yelled for order, saying that all resolutions must go to the committee without debate, but Troup howled them down, and not only read his resolution but had it passed. Another delegate, encouraged by his success, wanted to pass a resolution in favor of the silver dollar, but failed.

At this point Durant neatly choked everybody off by calling for nominations for President of the United States. They were quickly named in succession. Peter Cooper, of New-York; William Allen, of Ohio; David Davis, of Illinois; J. W. Singleton, of Illinois; Newton Booth, of California; Andrew G. Curtin, of Pennsylvania, and Joseph F. Wingate, of Missouri. Messrs. Singleton and Wingate, who were present as delegates, both promptly withdrew their names, and then ensued a long and disorderly wrangle as to whether Allen or Davis would accept. Mr. Stevenson, a member of Congress from Illinois, although not a delegate, was permitted to make a statement, and said that, under no circumstances, would Judge Davis accept, and suggested that his name be withdrawn. Hinchcliffe, of Illinois, wanted to know how the gentleman knew it, the gentleman laconically saying he knew it and refusing to say any more. Happily, Hinchcliffe got so angry he was unable to talk for ten minutes. Several speeches were then made in favor of Allen, the first being by Rice, of Arkansas, who said they must have a man of prominence as they had no money, and never would have any until more greenbacks are printed. Then two delegates from Ohio announced that Allen would not accept, and that was the end of him. Troup, of Connecticut, next made a savage attack on Judge Davis, saying he had used their nomination in 1872 as a stepping-stone to that at Cincinnati, and failing in the latter, had repudiated them. That was the end of Davis, but there was a vast deal more of talk about Allen and Davis, and a succession of scenes of great confusion both ludicrous and disgusting. At last a grain of sense appeared in a home-spun gentleman from Indiana, who declared that there had been "enough of this yere tomfoolery," and demanded the call of the roll, but neither he nor the Chair were respected in the turmoil, and just here the tide turned and the convention began to have a glimmering of what it wanted. Gen. Singleton declared for Peter Cooper. State after State did likewise, among them Wisconsin, through Mr. Aldrich, who has a short memory, for he began by declaring that he had not yet had a chance to address the convention, when he made at least a dozen speeches yesterday. Singleton, seizing the opportunity given by this enthusiasm, rushed through a motion that Cooper be nominated by acclamation, but a few growlers got it reconsidered, and the roll of States was called, with the result of Mr. Cooper receiving all the votes except the fifty-eight of Pennsylvania and the twenty-eight of Kentucky. In every case the entire vote of the State was cast, which presented the curious spectacle of less than one hundred delegates casting 478 votes. New-York refused to vote until the close of the ballot, and then the four gentlemen representing the State gallantly fell into line and voted for Cooper.

The result being announced the nomination was made unanimous, and there was an attempt, which partially succeeded, to get up a show of enthusiasm. This subsiding, Hon. Newton Booth, of California, was almost unanimously nominated for Vice President, in the face of declarations, many times repeated, that he would not accept. The National Committee being appointed the work was done, and the convention adjourned.

It is hardly possible to seriously review such a thing as this convention has been. There were in it a few sensible, honest men, but they proved to be in a small minority. It was their programme to adjourn until after the St. Louis convention, but they were overpowered by the blatherskites. In all essentials, during the critical stages of its progress, the convention was under the control of such men as Richard Trevillick, the noted demagogue of Michigan, and John Siney, President of the Miners' Union of Pennsylvania. This being known, it is hardly necessary to analyze it further or to know whether the members were chiefly Democrats or Republicans. Yet it may be added that they came in about equal portions from the two parties, although it is not of the least consequence where they came from. There was not among them a single man of present influence or former good repute. There were some of a little prominence, like Singleton, Donnelly, and Durant. That the doings of the convention will have the slightest influence on the campaign not even the brassiest of the delegates are audacious enough to declare. The whole thing may, therefore, be relegated without further ado to the absurdities of the past.

### THE TENNESSEE DELEGATION.

PREFERENCES OF THE DELEGATES TO CINCINNATI—CLAIMS OF MR. MORTON'S FRIENDS.

*Special Dispatch to the New-York Times.*

WASHINGTON, May 18.—The friends of Gov. Morton claim that the press dispatches from Tennessee are untrue and unjust to him in their representation of the delegation to the Cincinnati Convention. This claim seems to be reasonable in view of the large number of dispatches received by Gov. Morton and his friends from some Tennessee people very well known, and whose statement ought to be worthy of confidence. According to these dispatches, the smallest number of delegates who are in favor of Mr. Morton is fifteen. The largest number is stated to be twenty, and this statement comes from a very trustworthy gentleman. The dispatch which credits Mr. Morton with having fifteen delegates gives all but two of the remaining number to Bristow. The information received here concurs in dividing the delegation substantially between Morton and Bristow, and the claim of Morton's friends that at least eighteen of the delegates are for him seems, from evidence here, to be entirely justifiable.

### NEW-ENGLAND DELEGATES.

THE SEVENTH MASSACHUSETTS DISTRICT REPUBLICAN CONVENTION—THE DELEGATES FROM MR. BLAINE'S DISTRICT.

LOWELL, May 18.—The Seventh District Republican Convention to-day elected William A. Russell, of Lawrence, and C. H. Waters, of Groton, delegates to the Cincinnati Convention. The delegates are unpledged, but are counted on as one for Blaine and the other for Bristow.

AUGUSTA, May 18.—The Third District Republican Convention in this city to-day elected R. B. Sheppard, of Skowhegan, and E. Flye, of Newcastle, delegates to the Cincinnati Convention.

BOSTON, May 18.—The Republican Convention of the Third Maine District (Mr. Blaine's) to-day was marked by strong resolutions indorsing Mr. Blaine, and also by the speech of Hon. Mr. Stevens, in which, as a fellow-townsman for the past twenty-two years, he reviewed his business career, and particularly defended him from the charge of having become suddenly rich since entering Congress, claiming that in 1863, when elected to Congress, Mr. Blaine in business had accumulated a fortune of $75,000, and that his gains since that time have been greatly exaggerated, and were far less than many other men of ordinary business capacity had acquired by legitimate investment.

### THE KANSAS DEMOCRATS.

A GREENBACK PLATFORM AND INSTRUCTIONS TO VOTE FOR HENDRICKS—THE CONVENTION IN SESSION AT MIDNIGHT.

TOPEKA, May 18.—The Democratic State Convention is the largest ever convened in this State. Amos Harris was made President. The Committee on Resolutions reported a set in favor of no bank issue to be authorized by the United States or State authorities; that the Government supply the paper money needed in the shape of greenbacks, demanded the immediate repeal of the act providing for the resumption of specie payment, and instructing the delegates to vote for Hendricks. No subject whatever is touched upon in the platform but the financial. At this time (11 P. M.) a few members, headed by Tom Fenton, are making a vigorous fight against the platform and the instructions to delegates to vote for Hendricks, but they will be carried by over a three-fourths vote. The delegates have not yet been appointed, but it is the intention to transact all business and adjourn sine die some time during the night.

### BOILER EXPLOSION ON THE OHIO.

A STEAM-BOAT BLOWS UP—FIVE PERSONS SUPPOSED TO BE KILLED AND TEN INJURED.

EVANSVILLE, May 18.—The steamer Pat Cleburne exploded her boilers at 11 o'clock last night, six miles below Shawneetown, while lying alongside the Arkansas Belle. The Belle was tied to the bank and disabled by the line of a coal-flat, which fouled her starboard wheel, preventing her from rendering assistance. The Cleburne floated down about a mile and burned. Capt. Fowler was caught in the timbers and burned to death; Dick Partridge, express agent, was lost; Walter McElhenny, engineer, was blown into the river and was badly hurt, but will recover; D. C. Moore, Mail Agent, was blown overboard, but saved; John McGune, pilot, was at the wheel, and fell through to the boiler deck, and was cut and scalded; Alex. Porter, second clerk, feet scalded and cut; Arthur Brown, freight clerk, hands and face scalded and head cut; all the cabin crew are supposed to be saved; Urnback, a musician, could not extricate himself from the timbers, and was burned. Albert Smith, barber, hand scalded; Charley Colton, second mate, supposed to be lost; passengers G. W. Smith, of Evansville, slightly scalded; G. W. Nichols, of Terre Haute, hands and feet scalded; John Harvey, of Cincinnati, scalded and face cut; will recover. An unknown passenger was blown to the roof of the Belle and killed. In the great confusion, and the officers being all disabled, it cannot be learned what other passengers are lost. The Belle is badly wrecked—her chimneys blown overboard, her state-rooms shattered, and she was on fire in many places. The first and second engineers are badly scalded. Charles Smith, of Cincinnati, a passenger, had a leg broken. Capt. Howard was knocked down and slightly hurt. Possibly ten persons on the Belle were injured. Arthur Peter and J. Gillies, of Evansville, were blown and fell down the front stairs, but are uninjured.

ADDITIONAL NAMES OF THOSE SUPPOSED TO BE LOST.

CINCINNATI, May 18.—A special to the *Gazette* gives the following additional names of persons lost by the explosion of the boilers of the steam-boat Pat Cleburne on Wednesday night:

A. Mattison, Paducah.

Walter McElhenny, engineer.

Man unknown, supposed by some to be G. G. Berry, of Louisville, and by others to be Harris, of St. Louis.

Sid Humphrey, first clerk.

The following were injured:

James Weston, second engineer, badly burned.
John Lamson, porter, slightly burned.
James Hay, violinist, slightly burned.
Frank Redden, striker, fatally burned.
Jordan Field, Scott Bower, Neal Hancock, Dan Lewis, and George Mansfield, roustabouts, were hurt, four of them slightly and one seriously.
Thomas McKim, striker, slightly scalded.

The Cleburne had nineteen roustabouts, five of whom, mentioned above, were saved, but injured, and the other fourteen are missing.

### CHICAGO MUNICIPAL TROUBLES.

CHICAGO, May 18.—Mayor Colvin to-day answered Mayor Hoyne's recent note demanding possession of the Mayor's Office; he, however, merely acknowledged the receipt of the demand without complying with it. Mayor Hoyne presided at the Council this afternoon for the first time, and submitted his message, which was an exhaustive review of the municipal abuses which have existed. The new City Council has passed, by 26 to 3, the following resolution, prepared by Controller Hayes and offered by the Finance Committee:

*Resolved*, That the Controller be and he is hereby authorized and directed to make such arrangements as may be practicable and legal to pay continually at maturity all certificates of indebtedness of the City of Chicago issued for actual loans of money to the city, or for other liabilities for which an appropriation and tax levy has been made.

The city is paying all its paper at maturity, and will continue so to do.

### KILLED IN THE BLACK HILLS.

ST. LOUIS, May 18.—A special dispatch to the *Globe-Democrat* from Leavenworth says: A private dispatch from Custer City states that three men, named Williams, Harrison, and Brown, the two former from Cleveland, and the latter from St. Louis, while returning from the Black Hills, were tomahawked and scalped by Indians near that city on the night of the 16th, and their entire outfit carried off. The bodies were found about twelve hours after the massacre, and taken to Custer City for burial.

### ESCAPE OF EIGHT CONVICTS.

ST. LOUIS, May 18.—Eight convicts in the Military Prison at Leavenworth escaped from the guards yesterday, and another, named William B. Callahan, was shot and killed while attempting to escape.

## LATEST NEWS BY CABLE.

### THE TROUBLES IN EASTERN EUROPE.

THE EXCITEMENT IN CONSTANTINOPLE—SOFTAS AND CHRISTIANS ARMING—PERIL OF THE FOREIGN RESIDENTS—PUNISHMENT OF THE SALONICA RIOTERS—MEN-OF-WAR IN THE BOSPHORUS—THE BERLIN CONFERENCE.

LONDON, May 18.—A letter from Constantinople to the *News* under date of the 12th inst., says the excitement during the last three days has amounted to a panic. The demand for weapons both by Softas and Christians is so great that most of the shops in Stamboul have sold out all their stock. The Softas, that is, all persons attached to the mosques in any capacity whatever, are practically masters of the situation. They number about 10,000 persons, and their influence over the proletariat is supreme. They utter threats against the Sultan and his Ministers, and sometimes against the Christians, although just now they profess to be friends to the latter. Yesterday a great number of them went to the palace and demanded the dismissals of the Grand Vizier, Mahmoud Nedim Pasha, the Cheikh-ul-Islam, and the Minister of War. The Sultan resisted for an hour, but the clamor of the mob finally induced him to demand the resignation of Mahmoud Nedim Pasha, the Grand Vizier. The scene was most riotous and disorderly. Constantinople contains only 1,600 regular soldiers, the remainder being redifs and recruits. The Turkish officers openly admit their inability to control the latter in case of an outbreak, and it is generally believed they would obey the Softas. Mobs of Softas have been parading the streets during the last three days, demanding the dismissal of Mahmoud Nedim Pasha, whom they accused of being under Russian influence. Threats have been made against Christians generally, and two or three murders have occurred, which the Police are doing their utmost to hush up. Constantinople, in fact, is in revolution. The Softas are not satisfied with the appointment of Mehmet Rushdi as Grand Vizier, and clamor for Midhat Pasha. They want Mehemet Rushdi as President of a national Parliament. Yesterday a large number of Softas at the Bajazet Mosque would not allow the prayer for the Sultan to be read. On the 10th inst. Prof. Bonamy Price and wife narrowly escaped violence of the mob while visiting a mosque. If a struggle should take place, as everybody is dreading, between the native Christians and the Mussulmans the Christians would prove victorious provided the troops did not aid the mob. But in a general rising of Mohammedans the large colonies of European subjects in Constantinople and along the Bosphorus would be in greater danger than the native Christians, because their comparative wealth would constitute an additional stimulus to the religious zeal of the Turkish rabble. This danger the respective Ambassadors provided against as far as the means at their disposal allowed. Last night all the dispatch boats were kept under steam. During the day a plan of joint action had been agreed upon. The foreign Consuls met to devise means for the mutual defense of their subjects. All foreign steamers in port had steam up. The streets of Pera were patrolled by a band of Austrian Croats. A deputation of Englishmen called Minister Elliot's attention to the exceptional danger of the English colony, and asked his assistance. The latter admitted the danger to all Christains, and that the English was the least protected colony. He invited the whole community in case of any outbreak, to seek shelter at the Embassy. He also promised to telegraph the British Foreign Office what had occurred, and to represent the urgency of the position.

A letter to the *Times* from Pera, dated the 11th inst., says the excitement caused by the Salonica affair has not abated. A party of Softas yesterday paraded the streets of Stamboul crying "Down with the Grand Vizier!" The dedication of the new English church, which had been arranged for, has been indefinitely postponed at the request of Right Hon. H. G. Elliot, the British Ambassador, who had consulted the Minister of Police on the possible consequences of the ceremony. The Softas have been dissatisfied with the Government since the *irade* of January and the acceptance of Count Andrassy's note, which evinced a disposition to place all religious denominations on an equal footing. The first alarm felt here was occasioned by a well founded report that Softas and Mussulman roughs who are ruled by them, were buying revolvers, daggers, and other weapons. The Christians have resorted to similar precautions. There is no doubt, meanwhile, that all our speculations on the peril that threatens us and of the various means by which we may attempt to avert it contribute largely to foster and increase our uneasiness and become in themselves our greatest and most real danger.

A *Times* dispatch from Constantinople, by way of Odessa, says an outrageous article, which appeared in the *Levant Herald* on Tuesday, has caused great indignation among the diplomatic body and the public at large. As the *Herald* is generally temperate and cautious, the invective is supposed to have been inspired by Midhat Pasha, or the anti-Russian party. The *Herald* has been suspended.

In the House of Commons to-day, Right Hon. George Ward Hunt, First Lord of the Admiralty, stated that the British fleet in the Mediterranean had been ordered to Salonica and a gun-boat to Constantinople.

In the House of Lords to-night the Earl of Derby stated that Turkey had left nothing undone to secure the punishment of the Salonica murderers. He said it was true that a British squadron had been ordered to Bessika Bay in consequence of a communication from the British Ambassador at Constantinople. According to the latest accounts the excitement which undoubtedly existed among the Mohammedans in Constantinople was much allayed. Lord Derby hoped the precautions which had been taken would prove unnecessary.

Several additional French and Austrian men-of-war have arrived in the Bosphorus. A Berlin dispatch to the *Pall Mall Gazette* says the measures taken by Turkey for the punishment of the Salonica assassins have given satisfaction here. The news from Salonica is somewhat reassuring. The burial of the murdered French and German Consuls took place on Wednesday.

A dispatch to the Reuter Telegram Company from Berlin says the resolutions of the Imperial Chancellor's conference have been submitted to the powers. They provide for an eight weeks armistice, and for assistance in the restoration of the homes of refugees and insurgents. The Consuls resident in the various districts, assisted by special delegates, are to overlook the execution of the agreement. In all other respects the original text of Count Andrassy's note has been adhered to. Advices from Bulgaria in regard to the disturbances there are conflicting and unsatisfactory.

POSITION OF GREAT BRITAIN ON THE BERLIN CIRCULAR—THE INSURGENTS OPPOSED TO AN ARMISTICE.

LONDON, May 19.—The *Daily Telegraph's* correspondent at Berlin says he is in a position to state upon unquestionable authority that the German and Russian Ambassadors in London have telegraphed their Governments that England does not agree to the propositions which resulted from the Berlin conference.

The *Standard's* Vienna dispatch says the Herzegovinians have declared, through their representatives at Cettinje, that they will not accept the rumored armistice, because it would give the Turks an opportunity to bring up reinforcements.

The German squadron will not be ready to sail for Turkey until three weeks from to-day.

### GREAT BRITAIN.

THE DERBYSHIRE COLLIERS STRIKE—CABLE STEAMERS—THE STOCK MARKET.

LONDON, May 18.—The strike of the colliers in Derbyshire is breaking up. A considerable number of the strikers have already resumed work at ten to twelve and a half per cent. reduction in their wages.

The Anglo-American cable steamer Minia sailed from Brest to-day for Placentia. The Telegraph Construction and Maintenance Company's steamer Hiberuia, which has been secured for the repair of the French cable, is expected home on the 25th inst., and will be refitted and dispatched as soon as possible.

The *Standard's* financial article says stocks are generally flat, chiefly owing to a report that England has declined to agree to the resolutions of the Berlin Conference. Advices from Constantinople, and rumors of impending mercantile embarrassments here, also prejudice prices. Silver is quoted at 52⅞, and is very flat.

AN ELEMENTARY EDUCATION BILL IN THE HOUSE OF COMMONS.

LONDON, May 19.—In the House of Commons last night, Viscount Sandon, Vice President of the Committee of Council on Education, introduced the Elementary Education bill. The measure provides that no child shall be employed in agricultural or other labor before the age of ten years, or between ten and fourteen, unless it has a certificate that it has attended school 250 days of the year for five years, or has passed an examination showing a certain degree of education. Local authorities are empowered to enforce penalties on parents for neglecting to send their children to school. The application of the bill is to be gradual, the number of times which children must have attended school before their employment is permitted being gradually increased until 1881, when the bill attains full force. The bill was read a first time. Mr. Forster expressed regret that direct compulsion is not prescribed.

### FRANCE.

LARGE VOTE AGAINST AMNESTY IN THE ASSEMBLY—FUNERAL OF JULES MICHELET—DIPLOMATIC RELATIONS WITH PARAGUAY RESTORED.

VERSAILLES, May 18.—The Chamber of Deputies this afternoon rejected the motion of M. Raspail for complete amnesty by a vote of 394 to 52. M. Marcou, Radical, introduced a motion for amnesty for all common law offenses committed with a political object. Minister Dufaure opposed the motion. He declared that pardons would be granted in the proportion in which the Chamber refrained from insisting upon amnesty. The Government would show no leniency toward those who continued to display violence and hate in anonymous pamphlets and articles. M. Marcou's motion was rejected by a large majority.

PARIS, May 18.—Senhor E. Machain, the Paraguayan Minister, will present his credentials to President MacMahon to-morrow, thus restoring diplomatic relations between France and Paraguay, which have been suspended since 1872. Senhor José Machain, Paraguayan Minister to the United States, will sail from Havre by the steamer France on Saturday for New-York.

The remains of the late M. Jules Michelet, the historian, who died Feb. 9, 1874, were deposited in the Cemetery of Père-la-Chaise to-day in the presence of an immense assemblage. They were followed to the grave by 10,000 persons, and thousands of spectators lined the streets through which the procession passed. Perfect order prevailed, and the precautions of the Police were superfluous. MM. Laboulaye and Challemel-Lacour made speeches at the grave.

### MISCELLANEOUS FOREIGN TOPICS.

THE PLAGUE AT BAGDAD AND HILLAH—ILLNESS OF THE KING OF GREECE—THE UPPER ITALIAN RAILWAY—GERMANY AND PRUSSIA.

LONDON, May 18.—Advices from Bagdad state that from the 23d to the 29th of April inclusive the deaths from the plague numbered 339. At Hillah during the same period they were 148.

A special dispatch from Copenhagen to the *Pall Mall Gazette* says: The King of Greece, who is visiting here, has a severe attack of gastric fever.

The bark Ilmatar, Capt. Backerstein, from Pensacola, for Hull, is ashore at Dungeness and full of water. Three tugs unsuccessfully endeavored to tow her off at the last tide.

Advices from Dover state that the Russian bark Ilmatar, Capt. Backerstein, from Pensacola March 9, for Hull, (before reported ashore and full of water,) is a total wreck.

Advices from Callao state that the ship Sagamore, Capt. Knapp, from Independencia Bay March 8, for Europe, (before reported put in at Callao March 29, leaky,) has discharged her cargo.

ROME, May 18.—The *Bersagliere* (newspaper) states that the Chamber of Deputies will probably reject the Basle Convention for the acquirement by the Government of the Upper Italian railways.

BERLIN, May 18.—The differences of opinion on the relations of the Imperial and Prussian Governments, which threatened to involve the retirement of Minister Camphausen, have been satisfactorily settled. In the Prussian House of Peers to-day the Railway bill passed its first reading by a vote of 57 to 26.

COPENHAGEN, May 18.—In the Folkething to-day the President of the Council stated that the Government was making a last effort to arrive at an understanding with the majority of the Chamber on the fortifications question. If unsuccessful, it would allow the whole matter to drop, and would resign if others could be found to accomplish the necessary measures of defense.

MADRID, May 18.—The *Imparcial* says Queen Christina will arrive here next Monday.

Gen. Garibaldi recently resigned his seat in the Chamber of Deputies, but afterward withdrew his resignation.

LONDON, May 19.—A Madrid dispatch to the *Times* says the Congress has passed the article of the Constitution on elementary education. The article is of a distinctly retrogressive character. Under it education will be neither free nor compulsory.

### THE CONNECTICUT CONSTITUTION.

HARTFORD, May 18.—The House of Representatives adopted to-day, by the necessary two-thirds vote, three constitutional amendments, which will now go to the people for approval. One extends the term of office of Judges of Probate from one to two years; another, the term of Common Pleas and District Court Judges from one to four years, and the third provides that no new town hereafter incorporated shall have more than one Representative unless it has 2,500 inhabitants, and the part of the town from which it is taken at least the same number.

### A CALL FOR RECIPROCITY WITH CANADA.

BUFFALO, May 18.—The Board of Trade to-day unanimously approved a joint resolution, introduced by Elijah Ward, of the House of Representatives, authorizing the appointment of Commissioners to ascertain on what terms a mutually beneficial treaty of commerce with Canada can be arranged, and expressing a hope that the recommendation made that three Commissioners be appointed by the President to confer with three from Great Britain be carried out. The extension of commercial relations with Canada has long been desired by citizens here.

### CALIFORNIA MINING STOCKS.

SAN FRANCISCO, May 18.—The following are the closing official prices of mining stocks to-day: Consolidated Virginia, 73; California, 79¾; Segregated Belcher, 75; Ophir, 55¾; Chollar, 93¼; Savage, 19¾; Consolidated Imperial, 5¾; Mexican, 31¾; Gould & Curry, 17½; Best & Belcher, 57¾; Hale & Norcross, 65½; Crown Point, 16¾; Yellow Jacket, 36¼; Alpha, 61½; Belcher, 21½; Confidence, 21¾; Sierra Nevada, 16½; Exchequer, 20¾; Overman, 68½; Justice, 26½; Caledonia, 8½.

### DOM PEDRO AT ST. LOUIS.

ST. LOUIS, May 18.—Dom Pedro inspected the iron works at Carondelet to-day, and while in that suburb visited the Kindergarten under charge of Miss Blow, daughter of Hon. Henry T. Blow, formerly United States Minister to Brazil. He expressed great interest in the school. The after noon the party took a drive around the city, and between 5 and 6 o'clock embarked on board the Grand Republic, which soon steamed away for New-Orleans. A great crowd of citizens congregated on the levee to witness the departure of the imperial party.

### THE WHISKY CONSPIRATORS.

REMARKABLE TESTIMONY OF A. C. HESING IN CHICAGO—BLEEDING DISTILLERS AND POLITICIANS ALIKE—AN ASTOUNDING TALE OF CORRUPTION—THE LOUISIANA CASES.

*Special Dispatch to the New-York Times.*

CHICAGO, May 18.—When Jacob Rehm gave in his testimony in the case of D. W. Munn, ex-Supervisor of Internal Revenue, on trial here, a day or two since, it was considered to be a pretty free exposé of the corrupt operations of the Ring, which has so long controlled the manufacture of illicit spirits here. But Rehm was tame as compared with the evidence given by Anthony C. Hesing in the same case to-day. It exceeds for directness of implication in corruption anything heretofore adduced in the whisky trials in any city in the country. He is one of the proprietors of the *Illinois Staats Zeitung*, and is under indictment for revenue evasions in the distillery in which he was interested. After referring to the present trials Hesing took occasion to go somewhat into the details of the withdrawal of his son from the Congressional canvass a year and a half ago. It was Jake Rehm's desire that young Hesing should withdraw, and he promised the old man that he would do something handsome for him. Rehm told him [Hesing] that Commissioner Douglas would soon go on the Supreme Bench, that Superintendent of Police Beck, of Milwaukee, would take the Supervisor's place here, and Munn, the Supervisor, would step in Douglas' shoes. "Then," said Rehm, "we can make enough in twelve months to make us both independent, and I can run the country."

Hesing testified that he received money from H. B. Miller, a distiller, from September, 1872, to May, 1874, and paid portions to Jake Rehm; that the first payment was $300, half of which Rehm took, and gave Hesing the remainder as his share, saying that he wanted him [Hesing] to make a little out of it; this and all other amounts Hesing kept; the next month the payment was $1,200, and so on during the entire time, one-third of the blood-money finding its way into his [witness'] pocket; the entire amount he realized out of Miller was $9,000, and Rehm got $18,000 from the same source. The witness related with a bold face the fact that he received money from various other distilleries who were running "crooked," and that he turned portions of the same over to Rehm, who was manipulating all the establishments and "fixings" things generally.

Not only did Hesing lay open the manner in which payments were made to him and Rehm by illicit distilleries, but gave an inside view into political transactions, one of which was the appointment of Jussen, Carl Schurz's brother-in-law, to office as Collector of Internal Revenue in 1869. The witness testifies that he received $2,000 for the appointment of Jussen, and kept the money. Continuing his revelations, Mr. Hesing testified that while Miller, the distiller, was engaged in swindling the Government, he [Miller] was elected Treasurer of Cook County, and that Miller shared his salary with the witness for assistance in getting him elected to the office. During the time he held the place—two years—he paid Hesing about six hundred dollars per month. The evidence of Hesing further showed how he sold out his son who was running for Congress for $25,000, the same being paid him by Rehm for C. B. Farwell. While Hesing's testimony was in the main far from relevant to the case at issue, the opposing counsel and the court made no effort to check him, but let him tell his story of corruption. It creates considerable sensation here.

NEW-ORLEANS, May 18.—The jury in the Fehrenback cases have not yet agreed upon a verdict. They stand eleven for conviction and one for acquittal. A jury in the O'Brien distillery cases is being impaneled.

Edward Fehrenback, Otto Kerstandeck, John R. Beales, and William M. Todd were found guilty. The verdict was rendered at 11:30 P. M.

### THE TEXAS FRONTIER.

A BAND OF CATTLE-THIEVES STRUCK AND TWO KILLED BY THE RANGERS.

GALVESTON, May 18.—A special dispatch to the *News* from Brownsville, Texas, to-day, says that Capt. McNeely, who has been stationed for some time with his command of Texas Rangers at Santa Maria, about forty miles from here, broke camp yesterday morning and left, it is said, with orders to report at Laredo, Texas. Last night, while near Edinburg, he struck a band of cattle-thieves as they were in the act of crossing the Rio Grande with cattle. The Rangers killed two and wounded one of the thieves, and captured some horses and cattle.

THE REVOLUTIONISTS MOVING OUT OF MATAMOROS.

GALVESTON, May 18.—The *News'* Brownsville special says the revolutionists commenced moving out of Matamoros last night. Gen. Gonzales will leave this morning with the rear guard, it is thought, to join Diaz and attack Escobedo's forces, who are this side of Reynosa, advancing on Matamoros.

### LOSSES BY FIRE.

The barn of Mrs. A. S. Pratt, on Spring street, South Framingham, Mass., in which was stored 2,000 barrels of cement belonging to Ward & Clark, contractors, and $700 worth of hub-blocks, the property of A. M. Eames, hub-manufacturer, was, with the contents, destroyed by fire yesterday afternoon. The loss is estimated at $3,000; partly insured. The cause of the fire is unknown.

The schooner Delmont Locke, Pendleton, from Bangor for Philadelphia, with a cargo of lumber, was in collision Wednesday night in Vineyard Sound with the schooner Sunlight, of New-Haven, and lost her main-mast, and met with considerable damage to her hull. The Sunlight's damage was slight.

Six buildings, including two stores, a restaurant, bakery, photograph gallery, and a dwelling-house, were destroyed by fire at Acton, Quebec, yesterday morning, causing a loss of $6,000; partially insured.

The residence of John Storm, in Paradise, Monroe County, Penn., was burned on Tuesday last. The loss is $3,500.

### A LAWYER AND BROKER ARRESTED.

BOSTON, May 18.—Albert T. Butterworth, attorney, of this city, and Helen S. James, a woman of some note as a stock operator, of this city, were arrested to-day by State Detective Pintkam for conspiring with others to defraud Moses M. Allen of a house valued at $30,000, which they purchased from him with stolen, and, therefore, worthless United States registered bonds. They deeded the house to Moses S. Marshall, a co-conspirator, who is already in jail for perjury and forgery. In transferring the bonds, Butterworth represented himself on some as Thomas Murphy, ex-Collector of the port of New-York, and on others as Charles C. Fulton, ex-Collector of the port of Baltimore. The accused will have a hearing to-morrow.

### MARINE DISASTERS.

BALTIMORE, May 18.—The bark O. M. Hume, (in tow,) bound down, and the schooner John McDonnell, bound up, were in collision last night off Thomas' Point, Chesapeake Bay. The Hume had her bowsprit carried away and received some other damage to her head. The schooner lost her mainsail, mizzentopmast, foreboom, fore-gaff, fore and main rigging, and chain plates on both sides. Her port rail, bulwarks, and stanchions were stove nearly her whole length.

### SIX MEN DROWNED.

BUFFALO, May 18.—The schooner Thomas C. Street, bound up from the Welland Canal, was struck by a squall, six miles this side of Long Point, and capsized, about 7 o'clock yesterday morning, six of the crew being drowned. The accident was witnessed by Capt. Maytham, who with the tug H. G. Nolton was doing wrecking service at Long Point, and went to their assistance. Three of the crew were saved, including the Captain, and were brought to this city.

### BAD WEATHER IN NEW-BRUNSWICK.

ST. JOHN, N. B., May 18.—Owing to heavy rains, little farming has been done in the country. Brooks and rivers everywhere are overflowing, and mills have been obliged to stop sawing. The Gulf ports are blocked with ice, preventing the entry of schooners from Quebec and other points, and flour is very scarce in consequence at Buctouche, Richibucto, Chatham, and Newcastle. Floating ice in the Gulf is causing much trouble and anxiety.

## LOUISIANA MATTERS.

### THE NEW-ORLEANS CUSTOM-HOUSE.

TESTIMONY OF AN EMPLOYE BEFORE THE HOUSE SPECIAL COMMITTEE—SMUGGLING WITH THE CONNIVANCE OF OFFICIALS.

WASHINGTON, May 18.—The select committee on Federal Offices in Louisiana held a secret session last night, at which the resolution offered by Mr. Blackburn, directing the Chairman to ask the Attorney General for immunity to the witnesses, was adopted by a strict party vote. The committee had a secret session to-day, at which the Chairman reported that he had applied to the Attorney General as directed, and that officer had requested that the application be made in writing.

The committee then examined G. W. Ferguson, of New-Orleans, an employe in the Custom-house at that place, who testified that he was employed in the Custom-house when he left New-Orleans to come here. Mr. Ayre, of New-Orleans, had met witness in this city, and witness received the impression that Ayre was here to arrest some of the witnesses who might testify before this committee, as Ayre is Deputy Marshal and brother-in-law of Marshal Packard.

In reply to Mr. Conger, witness said he asked his brother to go to the Custom-house and tell the officials that he was sick and could not attend to his duties, and then came up here. The reason for deceiving the officials about coming here was that if they had known it he felt certain he would not have been allowed to leave the State alive.

By Mr. Hoskins—Have you not requested this committee to allow you to testify in New-Orleans instead of Washington? A.—Yes, Sir.

Q.—Then you are not so much afraid of New-Orleans people as you would have us believe, are you? A.—I wanted to testify in that place because I would have the data to substantiate what I said, and I knew I would be under the protection of the committee while I was testifying.

Witness said he was employed in the sugar-room in the Custom-house in 1873, when twelve cases purporting to contain guava jelly were received at the Custom-house, consigned to a man named Husard, and the cases were taken to the store of Mr. Mason. One big box only contained jelly and the other eleven contained cigars. The case containing jelly was opened in the presence of witness and other laborers, and they were then told that there was no more work to be done that day, and they went away. Witness secretly returned and saw the jelly box opened, but he privately opened some of the other boxes and found they contained cigars. The cases contained 11,000 cigars, and the fraud consisted in entering them as jelly. The duty on the cigars was $2 50 per pound, twenty-five per cent. ad valorem duty, and the internal revenue stamps. On the jelly the duty was ten per cent. The loss to the Government amounted to quite a sum, which the witness was not able to submit till to-morrow.

To Mr. Conger—The cases were all marked, "Escepcian brand," indicating them to be cigars; even the case of jelly was marked to represent cigars; the marks were all alike; all this occurred in March, 1873; witness told Mr. Darrall about this matter about three weeks ago, and told his brother of it when it occurred; had never notified any official of this fraud; was afraid he would lose his place, and did not think it would expose the fraud if he had done so, as they were all in the Ring together.

Q.—How do you know they were in a ring? A.—The importers had told witness that Thomas Ong, who collected the money from them, had kept all the money, and had not divided with the others—and hereafter they would divide the money themselves, and then pay it over to the different employes; the importer paid $50 per thousand on the cigars, and that sum was divided; witness gave the names of Dillingham, Naval Officer; Herwig, Deputy Collector; Crawford, entry clerk, and Thomas Ong.

Q.—Was Collector Casey a member of this ring? A.—Not that I am aware of.

By Mr. Hoskins—Were you present when any money was divided between these men? A.—I decline to answer.

Q.—What are your reasons? A.—It might criminate me, and it might not; I wish to consult counsel. [After some discussion among the committee the witness was told that he might answer yes or no without criminating himself, and he answered yes.] He saw $600 paid by Mr. Domingo; had never received a penny himself, nor any other valuable consideration; this took place in Domingo's store about February, 1875, and the money was paid to Mr. Ong; witness knew that this payment related to cigars, because Domingo said after Ong went out, "—— these fellows, they come after me before I can get the cigars out of the cases;" knew it did not relate to the duty, for this was paid in greenbacks and the duty is paid in gold, and Mr. Ong had no authority to collect the duty; that was the Cashier's duty. Witness had frequent conversations with Domingo about these payments, and Domingo had complained that these Custom-house men would come down and get a box or two of cigars besides taking his money, and he thought it was not fair. Witness said that the Entry Clerk, Appraiser, Deputy Collector, and Naval Officer were the officials through whose hands these cigars must pass, and it was necessary that these persons should collude together, and that was the reason why they formed this Ring spoken of.

Q.—Now give us another case of irregularity. Witness testified that in the Fall of 1873 Mr. Massoch went to Havana, and before going he told witness that he was going to import a lot of cigars, and the clerks in the Custom-house had told him to send all his cigars to warehouse No. 6 instead of the cigar-room, and they would be taken care of. A lot of thirteen cases of cigars arrived and were sent to a vinegar factory on Bienville street, and Mr. Kinsella's deputy got after them, and they were found in the charge of Mr. Massoch's clerk. Mr. Kinsella is a special agent of the Treasury Department, and his deputy went to the vinegar factory and told Massoch's clerk if he got them out in one hour, all right, if not, he would seize them. The clerk asked for three hours, which the Deputy would not allow, and they were seized, confiscated, and sold. Three of the cases seized had on Custom-house stamps, with Mr. Massoch's initials on them, showing they were his property and had passed through the Custom-house. The other ten cases witness thinks, from what he heard and saw, were taken out of warehouse No. 6 and carried to the vinegar factory. Mr. Botts was Storekeeper of warehouse No. 6, and Mr. Hill transacted the business.

By Mr. Conger—Then this was an attempt to smuggle which was frustrated, was it?

Answer—Yes, Sir. Witness said it was generally understood in the Custom-house that Mr. Herwig and his brother were the owners of warehouses No. 6 and No. 12, and received the storage profits arising from them.

The witness then made a statement that about one hundred and forty thousand cigars had been shipped to New-Orleans in March, 1875, which were invoiced as 70,000, and were delivered to Mr. McCarty on the payment of duty on 70,000 only. Mr. McCarty made the entry on these cigars at the Custom-house, but they were taken to Massoch's store. Witness said that Mr. Massoch was a large importer, and his fraudulent practices in importing cigars had broken down the small importers, some of whom have said that they could buy cigars of Massoch $10 per 1,000 cheaper than they could import them for.

### THE RECENT DISTURBANCES.

ALL QUIET REPORTED—THE STORIES OF THE TROUBLE SAID TO HAVE BEEN EXAGGERATED.

NEW-ORLEANS, May 18.—The latest dispatches report everything quiet at Bayou Sara, Laurel Hill, and Woodville. The reports of the trouble have been greatly exaggerated. One white man and two negroes killed and several negroes wounded cover the casualties so far as known. The military declined to interfere.

PARTICULARS OF THE SHOOTING OF STATE SENATOR TWITCHELL—A VERY DELIBERATE ASSASSIN.

CHICAGO, May 18.—The official report of the Twitchell shooting affair at Coushatta, La., has been received by Gen. Sheridan, and gives new and interesting particulars of the assassination.

The murderer was disguised. He wore goggles and was slightly painted. He strolled down from the Post Office, leading his horse to the river landing, where the shooting occurred, and as the boat approached commenced firing, killing a man named King, who was in the boat, and wounding the colored ferryman. Twitchell was badly wounded in both arms and in one leg. Those who attempted to approach the assassin from the shore were warned off and threatened with the rifle that he used. Two women remonstrated with him, but he said at each shot he was shooting a black alligator. He started off on his horse, but, seeing the negro attempting to save Twitchell, returned and ordered him to desist, and being disregarded, fired several more shots, wounding both the negro and Twitchell again. The murderer then escaped, despite all efforts to capture him. One of Twitchell's arms has been amputated, and the other is badly shattered, but he may still recover. The report is dated May 2.

### EX-GOV. BULLOCK ARRESTED.

ATLANTA, May 18.—Ex-Gov. Rufus B. Bullock was brought back to-day under a requisition from the Governor, after an absence of five years. The ex-Governor was arrested under old indictments, which were found soon after his flight. His bail was fixed at $12,500, which he promptly gave. Several wealthy citizens of both parties were on his bond. His arrival created a great deal of excitement, as it was not expected.

# The New-York Times.

VOL. XXV.......NO. 7725. NEW-YORK, SATURDAY, JUNE 17, 1876.--WITH SUPPLEMENT. PRICE FOUR CENTS.


## HAYES AND WHEELER.

### AN INVINCIBLE COMBINATION.

EXCELLENT WORK OF THE NATIONAL CONVENTION—NOMINATION OF RUTHERFORD BIRCHARD HAYES, OF OHIO, FOR PRESIDENT, AND WILLIAM A. WHEELER, OF NEW-YORK, FOR VICE PRESIDENT—ENTHUSIASTIC RECEPTION OF BOTH NAMES BY THE CONVENTION AND THE NATION.

The Republican National Convention completed its labors yesterday by nominating Gov. Rutherford B. Hayes, of Ohio, for the Presidency, and Hon. William A. Wheeler, of New-York, for the Vice Presidency. The balloting began as soon as the Convention met in the morning. Before the result of the first ballot was announced, Mississippi wished to correct her vote, which raised a question whether this could be done under the rules adopted the day before on this subject. After a brief explanation, the correction was allowed, and the result of the ballot was announced by the Secretary. There was no choice, the highest number of votes being given for Mr. Blaine, which was 285. Gov. Hayes had 61. The second ballot being taken, a protracted debate occurred on the right of four Pennsylvania delegates to vote independently, the rules under which the delegation acted requiring them to vote as a unit. In the end, the Convention sustained the decision of the Chair, allowing the delegates to vote as they pleased. The result of the ballot was then announced, which still showed no choice. The balloting still went on, until, on the sixth ballot, Blaine had 308 votes. The names of Morton and Bristow were then withdrawn, and the seventh and decisive ballot gave Gov. Hayes 384 and Mr. Blaine 351. Gov. Hayes was then declared the nominee of the Convention amid the wildest enthusiasm. For Vice President Hon. William A. Wheeler, of New-York; Stewart L. Woodford, of New-York; Joseph R. Hawley, of Connecticut; Theodore Frelinghuysen, of New-Jersey, and Marshall Jewell, of Connecticut, were successively nominated. The roll was called, and about half the States had responded, giving Mr. Wheeler 366 votes, when, on motion, his nomination was made unanimous. This completed its work, and the Sixth National Republican Convention adjourned with cheers for the ticket.

### CLOSING DAY OF THE CONVENTION.

NIGHT OF HARD WORK IN EFFORTS TO COMBINE—THE BALLOTING FOR PRESIDENT—WITHDRAWAL OF BRISTOW AND MORTON—NOMINATION OF GOV. HAYES ON THE SEVENTH BALLOT—WILD ENTHUSIASM—NOMINATION OF HON. WILLIAM A. WHEELER FOR VICE PRESIDENT BY ACCLAMATION.

*Special Dispatch to the New-York Times.*

CINCINNATI, June 16.—Daylight had hardly come before the city was astir, for every one was sure that to-day was to determine the fate of the Republican party. It came with anxieties and fears, for every one knowing of the inner workings of the Convention knew that all the night had been passed by the friends of Blaine and Bristow in trying to make combinations for their favorites among the other candidates. For Hayes no special efforts were being made, but his chances were as good as ever, for the reason that he still continued to be the compromise candidate upon whom all the elements opposed to Blaine must eventually unite. The friends of Blaine still claimed everything, and ended the night with the assertion, if not the belief, that not more than three ballots would be required to make their favorite the standard-bearer of the party. The adherents of Bristow had promises made them at a late hour which made them more confident. So things stood when, long before 10 o'clock all the cars going to the Convention hall were crowded to suffocation, and the sidewalks of all the streets leading in the same direction were filled with pedestrians. Within the hall both delegates and alternates made an early appearance. Those fortunate enough to hold tickets of admission crushed around the doors, and as they succeeded in gaining admission took the seats indicated by their tickets, and there they remained during the long hours of the session. Although both the Convention, and the audience were prompt, Mr. McPherson did not call to order until half an hour after the appointed hour of 10 A. M. At that time the hall was packed as it had never been before, and contained at least eight thousand people, among whom were hundreds of ladies. Every delegate and nearly every alternate was in his seat. The platform seats were filled with men distinguished in all the walks of life. It was a Convention worthy of the great work confided to it, and it was an audience worthy both of the Convention and the occasion. A dozen taps of the gavel and a few moments of suspense were sufficient to bring the Convention to perfect quiet. There was then a short prayer by a clergyman whose name was not heard three feet away, and then came the critical moment.

The Convention at once entered upon the regular order of business, and the roll was called upon the first ballot for a candidate for President of the United States. The ballot was neither dramatic nor interesting for it resulted almost without exception in the way that had been expected, and when the Chair announced as the result that Blaine had 285, Morton had 120, Bristow 113, Hayes 61, Conkling 99, Hartranft 58, Jewell 11, and Wheeler 3, there was little of sensation in the announcement. But after it came the usual whirr of conversation among the delegates in preparing for the second ballot, and it was some moments before order could be restored and the Convention made ready for the second ballot. There was even thus early a feeling of relief, for the various elements had stood firmly by their colors and Hayes had developed more strength than had been expected. The only incident of the ballot was a long delay caused by Mississippi trying to correct its vote by adding that of a delegate who was not present when the vote of the State was announced; but the rule was rigidly enforced and the vote was not allowed. The result being given, there was a hint of the coming Pennsylvania trouble in the motion of Mr. Bartholomew to take a recess for fifteen minutes for consultation. There did not appear to be more than a score of affirmative votes, and the Convention proceeded at once to the second ballot. [illegible] called, except by Alabama failing to answer promptly and asking for the time. Shouts of "Ballot!" were heard all over the hall, but McPherson said that the Chairman could not be expected to prevent delegates from consulting. This protracted the delay, but at last Alabama voted and substantially as before. The second ballot was fairly started when Connecticut, dropping Jewell, voted mainly for Bristow. There were mingled cheers and hisses in the galleries, and Mr. McPherson, as he did several times afterward, threatened to clear them. Florida's vote being inaudible, the President requested the Chairman of the State to hold up his head and speak louder, whereat there was a peal of laughter, and perfect good humor for the moment was restored. Then the ballot proceeded without incident and almost without change until Pennsylvania was reached. The State being called, Don Cameron answered 58 for Hartranft, and it was so repeated from the platform. At that moment a delegate standing on the edge of the platform rose to a question of privilege and plainly charged Cameron with incorrectly reporting the vote of the State, by saying that it should be only 52 for Hartranft, and 6 for Blaine. Thus was the Pennsylvania trouble, growing out of the adoption of the unit rule of Harrisburg, thrust upon the Convention, and it not only occupied much valuable time, but came very near causing much bad blood. McPherson arrayed himself with great promptitude against the unit rule by deciding that every delegate had the right to vote his own conviction. Cameron was not disposed to be put down in this style and was on his feet in an instant appealing from the decision of the Chair.

It was apparent from that moment that whatever the Cameron interest wanted it was not Blaine, nor, as subsequent events disclosed, was it Conkling; but at the time the purpose of Cameron was not generally known, and his appeal from the decision of the Chair produced intense excitement. In an instant McPherson, who was rather more devoted to the interests of Blaine than befitted the President of the Convention, put the question, and, on a second vote, which had an uncertain sound, declared it lost, and the Chair sustained. Then came one of the most exciting scenes ever witnessed in a convention. A delegate from Pennsylvania charged the Chair with putting the motion prematurely, and in refusing to recognize him because he did not wish to hear him. Mr. McPherson at once resented this attack and marched up and down the stage brandishing his gavel, making wild gestures, and doubtless uttering words of burning indignation, but they had little effect on an audience where at least 5,000 were shouting "order" with extraordinary vigor. For a time it was impossible to tell what was happening. John Cessna, of Pennsylvania, was on the plaform by the side of the President's table, bellowing to be heard, and he can bellow better than most men; but he might as well have talked Chinese for any enlightenment it afforded. At last there was a little lull, and Mr. Thornburgh, of Tennessee, jumping on a chair in the body of the hall, managed to get in a motion to reconsider the vote by which the decision of the Chair had been sustained. It was seconded, and the yeas were so plainly in a large majority that Mr. McPherson was compelled to declare it carried. This opened up the whole question of the unit rule, and the speeches were all made from the platform. The motion to reconsider was carried by 381 yeas to 359 nays, and then the debate began. Col. Ingersoll, of Illinois, was the first to speak and of course he sustained the decision for it involved four votes for Blaine. He based his argument on the right of every delegate to vote his own convictions and not those of any ring. Col. R. W. Thompson, of Indiana, known for thirty years as "the silvery tongued," then spoke strongly against the decision saying that the question was whether any delegate had the right to violate instructions. The delegates from Pennsylvania had been instructed by the convention which elected them to vote as a unit on all questions, and if any one of them could violate that instruction they could commit any breach of faith and refuse to support the nominees of the Convention. Hon. Giles W. Hotchkiss next spoke to the same effect, and said that the simple question was, whether there was any such thing as party discipline. If the delegates from Pennsylvania are not bound by the unit rule, then they are not bound by any resolution of any State or National Convention. Charles C. Van Zandt, of Rhode Island, spoke in the same strain, and was followed by Hon. Stewart L. Woodford, of New-York, on the other side, for he argued that every delegate should be at liberty to vote his own conviction. Dwight Thatcher, of Kansas, was on the same side, and got at the gist of the matter by asking whether the State of Pennsylvania could make the rules of this Convention. Eugene Hale, of Maine, made the mistake of participating in the debate, advocating the decision of the Chair with a warmth which showed his interest in it. When he concluded, the previous question was called and ordered, and Mr. McPherson put the question in the usual form: "Shall the judgment of the Chair stand as the judgment of the house?" Somebody wanted to know what was the judgment of the Chair, and in answering this inquiry, Mr. McPherson attempted, after the main question, to make a speech justifying his decision. He had not uttered a dozen words before he was interrupted by shouts of "Order" and "Question," and the rest of his speech was inaudible, and at last he was put down by Silas B. Dutcher, and the vote being taken the chair was sustained by the close vote of 395 yeas to 353 nays. There was for a moment much indignation at the course of Mr. McPherson, but it soon disappeared, and when the end which all the best elements of the party hoped for was reached nobody remembered or cared anything about the unpleasant episode. It being over, and the rule established that no matter what might be the instructions of a State, every delegation could do as it pleased, the ballot was proceeded with, and Pennsylvania was recorded as 55 for Hartranft and 3 for Blaine. It went to the close without incident, and the result was: Blaine, 296; Morton, 120; Bristow, 114; Conkling, 93; Hayes, 46; Hartranft, 63; Wheeler, 3; Washburne, 1.

With the conclusion of this ballot there was an interval of dullness, for the fourth ballot was utterly without interest, except at its conclusion, the vote as announced showing that Blaine was losing, as he had only 292, Bristow, 126; Conkling, 84; Hartranft, 71; Hayes, 68; Morton, 108; Wheeler, 2; and Washburne, 1. There were changes, to be sure, but they were not such changes as gave any surety of what the end would be. With the fifth ballot came a sign of promise. It proceeded without incident until the State of Michigan was called. Up to that time the State had steadily voted 6 for Blaine, 11 for Bristow, and 5 for Hayes. When it was called on this ballot that veteran Republican, Gov. William A. Howard, stepped into the aisle, leaning on his crutches, and with a voice as clear and resonant as it was twenty years ago, said, "Michigan, wishing to insure success in this contest, now desires to vote for some man who has in succession defeated three Democratic aspirants for the Presidency—George H. Pendleton, Allen G. Thurman, and William Allen. Michigan, wishing to give him one more chance to defeat a Democrat, now casts her twenty-two votes for Rutherford B. Hayes, of Ohio." The effect was electrical. Two-thirds of the convention and the audience were on their feet in an instant, shouting and yelling, waving hats, handkerchiefs, and conducting themselves generally as men do only when they have surpassingly glad tidings. Every one felt that the Rubicon was passed, that the next President was already named. Michigan was the pivotal point upon which the whole thing turned, and it was a matter of rejoicing that he who had attended at the birth of the Republican Party had named the third of its Presidents. When at last the enthusiasm of the galleries, the crowded floor, and the vast masses everywhere in the building had subsided, the roll proceeded without interruption until North Carolina was called, when there was another change of twelve in favor of Hayes. Then there was a repetition of the Michigan scene, and after it was over the ballot proceeded to the end without the occurrence of anything of moment, all the leading candidates about holding their own. The figures being given, Blaine had 286, Bristow 114, Conkling 76, Hartranft 63, Morton 74, Hayes 104.

Here was solid encouragement, and with it the sixth ballot began. It was fated to be the decisive ballot of the day and the one upon which the destiny of the Republican Party turned. Just before it began Mr. McPherson left the chair to Pomeroy, and went down to turn Pennsylvania over to Blaine. Long before the State was reached the bounce with which the friends of Blaine conducted his canvass had circulated all over the hall that Pennsylvania was to give him 30 votes. Before Pennsylvania was called North Carolina suddenly and unexpectedly deserted Hayes and cast 12 votes for Blaine. Pennsylvania came with 14 gain for him, and for a moment hopes of the opponents of Blaine were faint indeed. On the other hand his friends were jubilant in the extreme and were certain of his nomination. When the result was declared Blaine had risen to 308 votes, and the gravity of the crisis was sufficiently apparent to any one who was not too blind to see anything.

The roll-call was begun on the seventh ballot with the whole Convention and the vast audience in a tremor of excitement, for everybody except a few *dilettanti* in politics knew that the supreme moment was at hand. Connecticut was the first anti-Blaine State on the list, and efforts were made to have it stop its voting for Bristow—which at such a time was suicidal—and go solid for Hayes. But Hawley and Kellogg thought that there was yet a chance for Bristow, although it was known to many that Kentucky had already determined to withdraw his name when the State was called. Expostulations were in vain, and after keeping the Convention waiting several minutes, Connecticut cast its stereotyped vote apparently without the slightest suspicion that it had done something grotesquely absurd under the circumstances. There was nothing further of significance until Indiana was reached. There was the hush of suspense, the lull of expectation. When Hon. Will Cumback mounted the platform everybody knew he was there to withdraw Morton, but none knew how Indiana would go afterward. In a few well-chosen, earnest words Mr. Cumback thanked the friends of Morton for their support, paid a well-merited tribute to that eminent statesman, and cast the vote of Indiana, 25 for Hayes and 5 for Bristow. Although this by no means ended a struggle which was now keeping nearly ten thousand people on the utmost tension of excitement, the whole Convention and two-thirds of the audience rose and cheered so lustily and so long that it was some minutes before business could proceed. In the uproar New-York went out to consult, leaving a great gap in the Convention. Iowa and Kansas voted as before, but there was presently another grander scene when Kentucky was called and that splendid specimen of American manhood, that true, lion-hearted Republican, John M. Harlan, mounted the platform. It was some moments before he could be heard in the wild cheering which greeted him, but at last he got a hearing and never did a man facing such an audience say so much in so few words. He thanked the friends of Mr. Bristow for the cordial support they had given, and especially Massachusetts, Vermont, and Connecticut, because this support, coming from New-England, was a sufficient refutation of the slander that Bristow can not be trusted as a Republican because he lives in Kentucky. He withdrew the name of Bristow and cast 24 votes for Hayes. Then there was another outburst and a new step toward that salvation which was not yet reached, for the great States of New-York and Pennsylvania yet held the situation in their hands. Massachusetts was the next to advance reform by voting all but one for Hayes, and Mississippi next had the honor of keeping on the good work by casting 16 votes the same way. New-Jersey also added her delegation.

Then came New-York. For the first time, there was absolute silence in the hall as Hon. Theodore M. Pomeroy ascended the platform. If any one expected anything dramatic from New-York that one was disappointed, for New-York, through Mr. Pomeroy, simply announced the conclusion it had reached, which was 61 for Hayes and 9 for Blaine. The effect cannot be described. Thousands of people were on their feet shouting like Comanches, hats were swung and thrown in air and handkerchiefs waved. The end was almost reached, the long agony almost over, and that the welcome fact confronted the Republican Party was largely due to the large majority of the New-York delegation. The members from the State who voted for Blaine were: William H. Robertson, James W. Husted, Jacob Worth, John H. Ketchum, Jacob W. Hoysradt, James M. Marvin, Stephen Sanford, Amos V. Smiley, and James C. Foster.

After New-York there was a disappointment and a fear, for North Carolina did not answer expectations. Ohio and Oregon voted as usual, and then came the last moment. When Pennsylvania was called there was great confusion, and the voice of Don Cameron not being of the strongest, hardly any one twenty feet away heard the vote when he stated it. After a moment or two of great suspense the vote was shouted from the stage—28 for Hayes, 30 for Blaine. The battle was over. Everyone knew it, and every one except the immediate personal followers rejoiced at it. Hayes at this point, to be sure, was not yet nominated; but the example was contagious, and from here to the end he picked up sufficient votes to make it sure, among them being those of Montana, which, following the lead its neighbor Nevada had given long before, went over solid to Hayes. When the roll-call was ended there was a scene hardly ever witnessed before in any political body. Mental tension and excitement had been so great during the call that hardly any two tallies kept among the correspondents or on the floor agreed; but in three or four minutes, and long before the result was officially announced it was certain that Hayes had more than a majority of all the votes cast, and the telegraph office was deluged with dispatches sending the news all over the world. At last the clerks were ready, and Mr. McPherson, after pounding several minutes with his gavel, succeeded in getting such quiet that the result was heard as Hayes, 384; Blaine, 351; Bristow, 21.

Then the Chairman proceeded to officially declare Rutherford Birchard Hayes the candidate of the Republican Party for President of the United States, but hardly a score of people heard him; for before he commenced the whole Convention, the whole audience—Blaine men and all—were on their feet welcoming the nomination in a way which proved how hearty was the enthusiasm it evoked. Again hats were tossed, throats were cracked, men danced in glee upon their chairs and up and down the aisles, and embraced each other in a wild delirium of joy. All this time the band in the gallery, which had been mute for three days so long as the Convention was in session, was supposed to be playing "Hail to the Chief," but nobody knew, for its notes were lost in the roaring, surging sea of human voices, and only now and then a struggling note floating on the surface reached any ear. It is hard to say how long all this lasted. It seemed an hour, so thoroughly was every one exhausted when it was over. But it was probably not more than a quarter of that time. It may be that there have been scenes of greater enthusiasm, more evident thankfulness for a result achieved, more plainly a consciousness of safety in the future than was seen here to-day, but they have been very rare. Not when Seymour was nominated in 1868 was it even approached; not even when Grant was nominated in 1872 was it surpassed, and the demonstration when Greeley was nominated here was ridiculous in comparison. With these presages of victory, these plaudits of a confident party, Rutherford Birchard Hayes became the Centennial Presidential candidate of the Republicans. Faith in his ability, his purity, his fidelity to every trust, his perfect blamelessness in public and private life had marked him for the highest honor in the gift of any people. After such a nomination the Convention could not go astray, and what came after was a fit conclusion to what had gone before.

The Convention was left in utter and complete confusion by the enthusiasm and demonstration attending the announcement of the nomination of Hayes, so that it was only after long and wearisome efforts that the Chairman could make the delegates hear the announcement that the nomination of candidates for Vice President was in order. The New-York delegation withdrew to consult, and while they were out, in the midst of such wild disorder that it was impossible to hear a single connected sentence, several speeches of nomination were made. Mr. Wheeler was named from several sources, the number of delegates who desired to bring him forward having quite a rivalry. There seemed to be no question whether it would be acceptable to the New-York delegation. When that delegation came in from consultation it was learned that New-York, by a majority of the delegates, supported Mr. Wheeler's nomination. Gen. Woodford was nominated by several delegates, and a negro from Mississippi seconded him in a neat speech. Gov. Jewell, Senator Frelinghuysen, and Gen. Hawley were put in nomination, and the balloting began. It progressed slowly at first, owing to the confusion and difficulty of announcing the votes. As the call proceeded down the list of States it became apparent that the voting was a mere formality, and that Wheeler would receive a large majority. While the New-York delegation were making a tally to divide their vote between Wheeler and Woodford the latter took the stand, and in a brief, manly speech withdrew his name. He was loudly applauded, and New-York immediately cast her 70 votes for Wheeler. He had already received the unanimous vote of Illinois, Iowa, Louisiana, Massachusetts except one, Michigan, Minnesota, and other smaller States. North Carolina and Ohio followed with 64 votes, together making 340 for him to 68 for Woodford, 66 for Jewell, and 41 for Frelinghuysen. Judge Poland, in accordance with the spirit of the Convention, at this point cut the proceedings short with a motion to suspend the rules, stop the ballot, and nominate Hon. William A. Wheeler unanimously and by acclamation. There was not a word of dissent, and indeed if there had been it could not have been heard in the tremendous applause with which the proposition was greeted. The vote could hardly have been put for the cheering, and the Chairman had nothing to do but to declare as best he could in the midst of the din that Mr. Wheeler was nominated. The delegates did not wait to continue the applause, but rushed off in every direction for the hasty dinner, the car tickets, and the out-speeding trains.

[The detailed report of the proceedings will be found on the second page.]

### THE FORCES IN THE CONTEST.

THE UNAVAILABLE CHARACTER OF BLAINE AS A CANDIDATE FELT BY EVEN HIS SUPPORTERS—THE POSITION OF GOV. HAYES FROM THE FIRST—BRISTOW'S STRENGTH—HARLAN'S CHIVALROUS COURSE—SPONTANEITY OF THE NOMINATIONS.

*Special Dispatch to the New-York Times.*

CINCINNATI, June 16.—The result of to-day's balloting cannot have been a surprise to the readers of THE TIMES' dispatches from Cincinnati. While it is always madness to attempt to forecast with assurance or pretense of wisdom what any political convention will do, the signs of the last two days have pointed unerringly to a contest between Blaine and Hayes or Bristow and Hayes, with the chances in favor of the latter in either case. These signs have been given the prominence they deserved. The Bristow sentiment in the Convention was absolutely hostile to Blaine, as it was to Conkling, as long as he seemed to occupy any standing as a candidate. The Blaine men and the Conkling men, and particularly the political sentiments by which they were sustained, were in such hostility to Bristow that his nomination seemed hopeless. From the first Hayes was in such a position that he must have been taken up whichever way the chances drifted with respect to the other candidates. At the same time the elements of opposition to Blaine were so scattered and unorganized that it was by no means assured that they could be combined and Blaine be beaten. The caution with which his defeat was foreshadowed is now clearly shown to have been necessary. The Bristow men made a gallant fight and clung manfully to the brave, true man of Kentucky. Gen. Harlan made hosts of friends, and will go away from Cincinnati dear to the hearts of the many men who never knew him before. The labors directed by him to aid Mr. Bristow's nomination were above reproach. The sudden stroke with which Blaine was prostrated was a case of paralysis to the opposition against him as a candidate, and for forty-eight hours his friends had the work all to themselves. When he became well enough to be treated, like other candidates, to opposition and discussion, the arguments that could be legitimately used against him were effectively presented. There was clearly and unmistakably a majority that did not deem it prudent to enter a canvass with him as leader. This feeling was not by any means confined to those who were disposed to believe in the truth of any charges against his character. Some of those who had the utmost confidence in his ultimate vindication saw that his nomination meant a defensive campaign which must needs be hotly contested and doubtful. There was no reason to doubt last night nor the night before that this feeling governed a numerical majority of the delegates. The feeling strengthened every hour, and would have culminated in some positive arrangements before balloting began if there had been more time, as there would have been but for Mr. Blaine's unfortunate illness. As it was, no combination could be effected, and the Convention assembled to-day with no understanding among the opponents of Blaine except the tacit knowledge that they must unite in some manner or be beaten in the end. The Bristow men were hopeful that the others might come to them. Morton's friends had expressed willingness to do so if such action promised success. Mr. Cameron had expressed a personal willingness to accept Bristow, and stated that Blaine could not carry Pennsylvania if nominated. The earnest adherents of Bristow would not consent to any arrangement looking to his withdrawal as long as a hope of accretions from other candidates remained. The Hayes men from Ohio simply awaited in a receptive spirit the issue of events. The hope of beating Blaine by holding the separated forces of the other candidates grew dim. Alexander McClure, to revenge himself upon Cameron, was working assiduously in the Pennsylvania delegation to secure a break for Blaine, and was succeeding so that it became unsafe to depend upon the votes of that delegation being cast for a hopeless candidate. To leave Hartranft except for a winning man was to release forty votes to Blaine. New-York leaving Conkling would give Blaine sixteen votes, and all this increase would draw enough of the Morton and Conkling Southern vote to secure Blaine's nomination. It was the hope of rendering this situation effective that held several delegations to Blaine who were expected to desert him on the third ballot.

This was the condition of affairs when the Convention assembled. It lasted till the fact became evident that Blaine would beat all the forces fighting in detail, and that Conkling and Morton were useless candidates, and that the continuance of Bristow in the field would simply secure the triumph of Blaine. The moment chosen to withdraw these candidates and turn their votes to Hayes was opportune. The men who had been reluctant to leave Bristow for Hayes acknowledged that the extreme risk of delay had been taken. The reception of the manifestation for Hayes was so grand, and the response in the Convention as well as in the galleries was so prompt and demonstrative that ten to fifteen Blaine votes in the Pennsylvania delegation, eight in New-York and a few elsewhere were swept away from him, as well as some which had clung to him up to this point, and Hayes gained the nomination, with a reserve force of thirty or more votes which had been cast for other candidates before Indiana changed from Morton and Harlan withdrew Bristow. The movement was spontaneous, and in its method almost impromptu. It was the natural and rapid union of sympathetic interests to defeat what the majority felt to be an unsafe nomination, by that of a man acceptable to all. Even the Blaine men will support Hayes heartily. Not a Conkling man but will stand by the ticket. Pennsylvania is satisfied. Indianians say they can carry their State for Hayes and Wheeler. There would have been a coolness among the Liberal vote if they did not see that Bristow could not have taken the nomination. As it is, Schurz will take the stump in Ohio and Indiana, and the German vote is always sure for Hayes. The nomination of William A. Wheeler in the manner in which it was made was a great compliment to him, and while the writer knows that Mr. Wheeler will accept with some reluctance he will undoubtedly not decline, being obedient to such a direct demand from the party. He should be returned from his district to Congress, and in the event of Republican success would be without a rival for candidate for Speaker of the next House. He stands almost at the head of parliamentarians in this country, and perhaps is excelled by no one in power to control a legislative body and secure from it hard and orderly work. He never opposed or advocated a proposition unsuccessfully during his service in Congress, and no man has greater esteem and affection from those who enjoy his acquaintance. He had many friends in the Convention who desired him above all for the first place on the ticket. His presentation and nomination for the second place were greatly aided by friends from his own part of the State, W. S. Dickenson and H. R. James.

Like Hayes, Wheeler is a man perfectly spotless in reputation—a plain man of the people, who hates shams and frauds with a cordial hatred. Not a single slander can attach to him by a thread. The nomination was absolutely spontaneous. The candidacy of Hayes has not caused the expenditure of any political funds beyond what would have been used in the ordinary contest of the delegation attending the Convention. No man has been furnished with a dollar from any source to contribute to the success of Hayes. Not a banner has been painted nor a band employed. The delegation has paid its own expenses here and a has every man who has taken pains to [illegible] about for Hayes. He would not [illegible] any such means to be used, and would [illegible] pay a dollar, though having an [illegible] to advance his own interests in the Convention. The machine has not run for him, and he owes it nothing.

### TRUE REPUBLICAN MANLINESS.

SENATOR MORTON EXPRESSES HIS ENTIRE SATISFACTION WITH THE TICKET—EX-SPEAKER BLAINE'S CHEERING DISPATCH TO THE NEXT PRESIDENT.

*Special Dispatch to the New-York Times.*

WASHINGTON, June 16.—Senator Morton expresses great satisfaction with the nominations. He says both Mr. Hayes and Mr. Wheeler are men for whom all Republicans can work with a will, and that he will go into the canvass heartily and labor for their election. He says the contest for the nomination has engendered no bitterness in his breast, and that he will inaugurate the campaign for Hayes and Wheeler to-morrow night in a speech at the ratification meeting which will be held in this city. He is more than pleased with the platform, and expresses great gratification that it clearly recognizes the vital principles for which he has always contended, and for advocating which he has been denounced as the "bloody shirt" standard-bearer. He desires THE TIMES to inform the country that he is grateful for the devotion manifested toward him by Indiana, and for the generosity shown by other States in supporting him so earnestly, and that he will manifest his appreciation of this kindness by giving out no uncertain sound during the campaign which has this day been inaugurated at Cincinnati. He believes that the ticket is one that does credit to the Republican Party, and that it will be ratified by the people in a triumphant election.

Mr. Blaine seemed to take his defeat with an exceedingly good grace, and he saw the scores of friends who came to offer him their congratulations upon the gallant fight he had made, and to express their regrets that it had not been entirely successful. For all who called he had the same pleasant words and hearty thanks for their sympathy. He seemed to be in excellent health, considering his recent severe illness, and remarked pleasantly, when asked how he felt, "first rate; my pulse is as regular as a kitchen clock." He spoke freely of the events of the past few days, and said that he felt highly flattered at the efforts of his friends to make him the nominee of the Convention. "From first to last," said he, "the whole power of the Administration has been against me, and it has been with my friends entirely a labor of love, for I had no money to spend, and no patronage to bestow, yet who ever had such friends? Besides the power of the Administration I had the combined power of all the other candidates arrayed against me, and I had no right to expect success. I am very greatful for the efforts of my friends, and feel that they have made a gallant fight." He seemed considerably pleased at the insignificant showing Conkling had made in the Convention, who, he said, could only rally twenty-nine votes outside his own State, with all the influence of the Administration to help him. He seemed to think Conkling's candidacy had been from first to last little more than a farce. He did not go into details about the history of the Convention, but seemed to think the action of the Camerons, in the management of the Pennsylvania delegation, two-thirds of whom were for him, was one of the prime causes of his defeat, and was such as to lessen the influence of that State in national politics. He expressed himself as pleased with the work of the Convention, and said it was a very strong ticket. With Wheeler's nomination for the Vice Presidency he is especially pleased. "I know Wheeler well," said he. "It is a splendid nomination, and it is a good ticket to win with." To a Western Democrat, who called to pay his respects, and who expressed the hope that he would not come West during the campaign, Mr. Blaine said "Yes, I shall go West, or go wherever I can aid in the success of the ticket. In this campaign I shall have as much interest as if I were a candidate myself." Mr. Blaine will address the ratification meeting to-morrow night if his health will permit.

Secretary Bristow is pleased with the nominations. He says Hayes is a man of splendid abilities, of unimpeachable integrity, and one who as President will administer the Government with dignity, fairness, and honesty. All things considered, he thinks the nomination of Hayes is the best the Convention could have made. No man who ever was a Republican can consistently refuse to vote for him, and he is convinced that Carl Schurz, and those who have been acting with him, will give Hayes and Wheeler hearty support. He is as much pleased with the nomination of Wheeler as with that of Hayes. He says the ticket is just what it should be, impregnable at both ends, and that even if it were reversed it would command the confidence and suffrages of the people. Secretary Bristow will engage actively in the work of the campaign, and will cheerfully go to any part of the country where his services will contribute to the election of the ticket. The platform receives his hearty approval, and he will address the ratification meeting to-morrow night.

### CONGRATULATORY AND CHEERING DISPATCHES.

WASHINGTON, June 16.—Immediately upon hearing of Gov. Hayes' nomination the following dispatches were sent him:

WASHINGTON, June 16, 1876.

*To Gen. R. B. Hayes, Columbus, Ohio:*

I offer you my sincerest congratulations on your nomination. It will be alike my highest pleasure, as my first political duty to do the utmost in my power to promote your election. The earliest moments of my returning and confirmed health will be devoted to securing you as large a vote in Maine as she would have given for myself. J. G. BLAINE.

WASHINGTON, June 16, 1876.

*Gen. R. B. Hayes, Columbus, Ohio:*

I congratulate you upon your nomination for the Presidency, and shall labor earnestly for your success. O. P. MORTON.

*Gen. R. B. Hayes, Columbus, Ohio:*

I beg you to accept my earnest and hearty congratulations. Your nomination secures victory in November. B. H. BRISTOW.

WASHINGTON, June 16, 1876.

*Gov. Hayes, Columbus, Ohio:*

I heartily congratulate the country, the Republican Party, and you on your nomination. You need no assurance of the cordiality of my support. Sincerely yours, ROSCOE CONKLING.

HARRISBURG, June 16.—Immediately upon the receipt of the news announcing the nomination of Gen. Hayes, the following dispatch was sent:

HARRISBURG, June 16, 1876.

*To Gen. R. B. Hayes, Columbus, Ohio:*

I most sincerely congratulate you on your nomination. Pennsylvania will surely give you her vote in November. J. F. HARTRANFT.

COLUMBUS, June 16.

*To Hon. J. G. Blaine, Washington:*

Your kind dispatch has touched me most deeply, and I hardly know how to respond in fitting terms. The assurance of your sympathy and support nerves me for the contest on which we are about to enter. With your returning health and strength I see an omen of Republican success. I trust that all trace of your recent illness will speedily disappear, that you may speedily be restored to your family and country. I send you my first dispatch since the nomination.

"R. B. HAYES."

## RESPONSE OF THE COUNTRY

### CINCINNATI AFTER THE CONTEST.

A SUPERB DEMONSTRATION—ALL THE CONFLICTING ELEMENTS HARMONIZED AND WORKING WITH A WILL FOR THE NATIONAL TICKET—THE CONKLING CLUB SPORTING THE NEW BADGE AND PLEDGE NEW-YORK FOR 50,000 MAJORITY.

*Special Dispatch to the New-York Times.*

CINCINNATI, June 16.—The grand result of the deliberations of the National Republican Convention has taken Ohio, and particularly the City of Cincinnati, by storm. To-night the streets are thronged with people of all classes, and almost at every turn is heard the cry, "Hurrah for Hayes and Wheeler!" At the Grand Hotel a ratification meeting was held, which was principally remarkable because it was joined in by nearly all the prominent friends of Hayes, Conkling, and Morton. In one corner was Gen. Brady, the steadfast supporter of the "war Governor." In another was Major Bickham, of the Dayton *Journal*, who, more than any other one, has contributed to the glorious success of Rutherford B. Hayes. New-York was represented by Hon. Theodore M. Pomeroy, who has won golden opinions here because of his fair and impartial rulings in the Convention, and by Senator William B. Woodin and ex-Senator Madden, who were chiefly concerned in bringing the New-York delegation over to Hayes. Mr. Pomeroy made a short address, in which he congratulated the Republican Party upon the wonderful success which it had achieved, and predicted for it a glorious victory in November. Even the Conkling men are enthusiastic. They have all taken off their blue badges and covered them with the white one, which bears the inscription, Hayes and Wheeler, and to-night they are going through the streets crying with all their might that New-York will give Hayes 50,000 majority. Collector Arthur is one of Gov. Hayes' most enthusiastic supporters. He fought hard for Conkling, but he is now willing to accept the situation and glad to do every thing in his power for the next President, Rutherford B. Hayes. Even A. B. Cornell, who is perhaps the only disappointed man in Ohio to-night, is not altogether displeased with the result. His good humor was somewhat restored by the receipt of the following dispatch:

*Hon. A. B. Cornell:*

Have just heard of the nomination of Gov. Hayes, and deem it good and wise. I wish I could make you and all my other friends know how deeply grateful I am for the efforts in my behalf.

ROSCOE CONKLING.

At Pike's Opera-house a grand ratification meeting was held. Theodore M. Pomeroy, Gov. William A. Howard, of Michigan, and many other prominent speakers addressed the meeting.

There were not a few interesting incidents connected with the nomination. For instance, Gen. Arthur, of New-York, as he stepped off the platform of Exposition Hall, was met by the Chairman of the Hayes delegation. "How is New-York?" asked the Chairman. "All right," said Arthur, "all the time for Hayes." Upon this a Hayes badge was given to the General, and he now goes about wearing a ribbon marked "New-York." Aside from the formal meeting, there were many impromptu ones held all over the city.

In the lobby of the Grand Hotel Col. Tanner, Commander of the Grand Army of the Republic, addressed a large audience. He said, among other good things, that the success of the Republican Party was the first consideration and desire among all good citizens, and that the nomination which had been made to-day assured that success beyond all question.

The feeling among the Southern delegation is one of great joy. They feel that they have been saved from a great calamity, a calamity which would have made it necessary for them to seek new homes, and they are hardly able to restrain themselves for happiness. Never in the history of politics in this country has the nomination of a national ticket been greeted with so much enthusiasm. The whole town is wild with excitement. Bands are parading the streets, rockets are flying through the air, and on every hand is heard the cry, "Hayes and Wheeler." It is the generally expressed opinion among all classes of politicians that there never was so enthusiastic a political convention held in this country. As to the result of the coming canvass there is no doubt.

### EVERYBODY FOR HAYES IN MISSOURI

B. GRATZ BROWN SAYS IT IS A MAGNIFICENT NOMINATION—40,000 GERMANS READY TO VOTE THE STRAIGHT TICKET.

*Special Dispatch to the New-York Times.*

ST. LOUIS, June 16.—The nomination of Gov. Hayes for the Presidency was a genuine surprise to both parties in St. Louis. It was generally admitted that if nominated he would make a strong candidate, but that result was not anticipated. The St. Louis papers in this morning's issue had uniformly expressed the opinion that it would be Blaine or Grant, therefore the popular belief was that it would be one of these gentlemen. All the newspaper offices had out prominent bulletins, and each ballot in detail was announced as it came by telegraph. Immense crowds were on hand, and intense excitement prevailed. When the result of the seventh ballot was announced there was much enthusiasm, and a universal feeling that the nomination was the best that could have been made. "That's a magnificent nomination," said ex-Gov. B. Gratz Brown, who was near one of the bulletin boards, "and the Liberal element of Missouri will give Gen. Hayes a hearty support." Even many of the Blaine men were free to acknowledge that Hayes was more free from objections than their favorite, and that the nomination was doubtless wiser than the one for which they had ardently hoped. "They cannot throw dirt at him," was the general remark, and Blaine's vulnerability seemed to find a more general admission than it had ever had before. Your correspondent has talked with a number of representative persons concerning the fitness of the nomination, and finds that there is a general agreement among the various shades of Republicans as to its wisdom. Dr. Preetorius, editor of Carl Schurz's paper, the *Westliche Post*, says that unless the Democrats nominate a man thoroughly unexceptionable the German vote of the State will go solid for Hayes. There are 40,000 German votes in the State. Preetorius says the *Post* will wait for Hayes' letter of acceptance, and if it is sufficiently strong for reform it will espouse his cause without reference to what the Democrats may do at their convention. He says, the support of Hayes in his last gubernatorial race by Schurz will go far in rallying the German element of the entire country around him. Dr. Daenzer, editor of the *Anzeiger*, a leading Democratic German paper, says [illegible] of the German vote will go for Hayes if Tilden is not nominated. Ex-Congressman F. Boyd, who has just returned from Cincinnati—where he had been at work for Blaine, and left thinking his nomination assured—says Hayes is really the stronger of the two. A Hayes club was organized here [illegible]. The hotels and saloons are full of people discussing the situation. The Republicans are arranging for a grand ratification. The Globe-Democrat, which has been the most enthusiastic paper in the country for Blaine, will give a [illegible] support to Gov. Hayes, [illegible]

# The New-York Times.

VOL. XXV.......NO. 7735. | NEW-YORK, THURSDAY, JUNE 29, 1876.---WITH SUPPLEMENT. | PRICE FOUR CENTS.

## TILDEN NOMINATED.

### A RAILROAD LAWYER AND A REPUDIATION PLATFORM.

THE DEMOCRATIC MACHINE AND ITS WORK AT ST. LOUIS—THE REPUTABLE ELEMENT IN THE PARTY IGNORED AND INSULTED—DISGRACEFUL SCENES—DEMOCRATS GAGGED IN A DEMOCRATIC CONVENTION.

The Democratic National Convention reassembled yesterday morning at 11 o'clock. The first business in order was the report of the Committee on Resolutions, but the committee were not ready to report, and a variety of resolutions concerning the order of business and other matters were offered and disposed of. John Kelly offered a memorial from influential Democrats in New-York, protesting against the nomination of Tilden, but it was declared out of order. Much wrangling took place, but it was finally ended by the announcement that the Committee on Resolutions would be ready to report at 2 o'clock. A recess was taken until that hour. On reassembling the Committee made a majority and minority report, the point of difference being the financial plank of the platform. The majority report condemned the Republicans for their imbecility in not returning to specie payment, accused them of placing hindrances in the way of resumption, denounced these hindrances, and demanded the repeal of the Resumption act. The minority report declared that this act was injurious to the country and demanded its unconditional repeal. After great confusion on motions and counter-motions, the majority report was adopted by a decisive vote. The nomination of candidates then commenced. Thomas Francis Bayard, of Delaware, was the first nominee; Thomas A. Hendricks of Indiana, came next; Joel Parker, of New-Jersey, followed; then came Samuel J. Tilden, of New-York, who was followed by William Allen, of Ohio, and Gen. Winfield Scott Hancock, of Pennsylvania. This completed the list of nominees, and the balloting ensued. On the first ballot there was no choice; on the second Samuel J. Tilden received more than the necessary two-thirds of the votes, and was declared the candidate of the Democratic Party.

### SECOND DAY OF THE CONVENTION.

CONFUSION AND TURMOIL THROUGHOUT THE SESSION—COX SNAPPING POINTS OF ORDER AT THE IMBECILE CHAIRMAN—GAGGING DEBATE ON THE PLATFORM—POWERLESS DELEGATES HOWLING FOR RECOGNITION—THE NOMINATION—THE SECOND PLACE LEFT FOR TO-DAY.

*Special Dispatch to the New-York Times.*

ST. LOUIS, June 28.—When the Convention met this morning it was with a hotter temperature, angrier mood, and a more bitter feeling prevailing among the factions. By 11 o'clock, the hour named for the commencement of the session, the building was densely packed, and what little air was astir without was not felt within the hall, which more literally than yesterday was a bake-oven. Perhaps it was the universal discomfort, or even positive suffering, which led to the promptness on the part of the Chair in calling to order and to the brevity of the morning session. McClernand, who has been resurrected only to furnish further and wholly unnecessary proofs of his imbecility, was rapping with his gavel soon after 11 o'clock, and before anybody had any chance to be disorderly, was lecturing the delegates upon the necessity of keeping order. When he finished Father Brady made a short and sensible prayer, immediately after which the Convention proceeded to get itself by the ears, as has become its custom. The first move was by Young, of Georgia, who offered a resolution commending everything done by the House of Representatives during the present session. This was treading on dangerous ground, for Young also moved to suspend the rules and adopt the resolution. There was instantly a squabble, and a dozen delegates were on their feet at the same moment clamoring for recognition. But McClernand was equal to the occasion, and speedily ended the row by the novel but effective ruling that the motion to suspend the rules was out of order. So much time was consumed in this that Vilas, of Wisconsin, came to the rescue of the Convention with a resolution that each delegate's time for speaking be limited to five minutes, except in presenting candidates for the Presidency, when ten minutes will be allowed. It was adopted almost unanimously, and the Convention felt a sense of relief. Sunset Cox was the next attraction, but he only wanted to present the memorial of the working men. John Kelly, of New-York, then made a movement which was without precedent in a National Convention. In his place he said he desired to present a document which would show that the Democrats of New-York do not desire the nomination of Gov. Tilden, and sent to the platform a copy of the circular which has already been presented in THE TIMES. The Chair, of course, ruled it out of order, but Kelly gained his point in bringing thus formally to the notice of the Convention the fact that there is a strong opposition to Tilden in his own State. The feeling for and against Tilden was made more manifest than ever before by the mingled cheers and hisses with which Kelly's declaration and the ruling of the Chair were received. This episode over, Mr. McLane, of Maryland, who wished to push things, moved that the Convention proceed to nominate candidates, and no doubt made a strong speech in behalf of his motion, but few of the reporters heard what he said. Senator Kernan, of New-York, thought it best to first inquire of the Committee on Resolutions when they would be ready to report, and to postpone action until a reply was received. Gov. Morris, of Missouri, offered as a substitute for Mr. McLane's resolution that there be no ballot until after the platform is adopted. Judge Abbott, of Massachusetts, came next with another substitute that the Convention proceed to ballot, and the vote of each State, as announced by the Chairman, should not be called in question. This last proposition was received with derisive laughter, and the thing was becoming so grotesque that the patience of Senator Wallace was exhausted, and he moved to lay the whole subject on the table. But this did not happen until McClernand, at whom Cox had been flinging points of order for some time, had become so thoroughly bewildered that he had not sense enough to let the Convention know where it was or what it was doing. At last the question was put on Wallace's motion, and the call of States had just begun, when Judge Meredith, of Virginia, Chairman of the Committee on Resolutions, came to the rescue with the announcement that a platform was being verbally revised, and would be reported at 1 o'clock.

The Convention then adjourned until 2 P. M., and the band striking up "Dixie," the old rebellion air, it so stirred the Democratic heart that they had to repeat it. Thousands in the hall refused to leave during the recess, and were for a time amused, but hardly instructed, by speeches from Doolittle, Breckenridge, and others.

Promptly at 2 o'clock McClernand called the Convention to order, for that session which was to prove in four hours, whatever might be its ultimate result, that the Democratic Party had lost none of its skill and vigor in organizing defeat. Late in the day, when this result was apparent, a prominent Democrat of New-York said to me, "Can you see success for us in this?" and I was happily able to answer that I could not. When McClernand, at the opening, after many frantic efforts, finally succeeded in getting something like order, he announced that the first business was the report of the Committee on Resolutions, and thereupon the ponderous Dorsheimer, appearing on the platform, proceeded to read the long document, which is the Democratic Centennial declaration of political faith. Dorsheimer, it is known, has a good voice, and every delegate should have heard the resolutions as he read them, and perhaps they did, but they were so prolix and complex that hardly had he concluded when several, who were perhaps not sober enough to understand anything, were on their feet demanding that the coolie and financial resolution be read again. This it was necessary to do a dozen times before the obfusticated delegates could master them. But these calls were merely trivial incidents, for the real Democratic disquietude on the financial question did not appear until Gen. Ewing, who was greeted with rousing cheers, went upon the platform and read the minority report, which perhaps a little more than that of the majority, but only a little more, committed the Democratic Party to the nursing of the rag-baby. Ewing, having made his report, proceeded to make his speech in support of it, and a very vehement, outspoken speech it was. He said that the resolution of the majority, by fair inference, committed the Democrats to the support of the whole of the Resumption act except the date fixed for resumption, and proceeded to give his reasons for this belief. When his ten minutes had expired there was a scene of great and disgraceful confusion. One delegate moved that his time be extended fifteen minutes. There were stentorian cries of "No" from all parts of the hall, and after a quarter of an hour of yelling and hurrahing at him, Ewing yielded to the pressure and retired.

Dorsheimer got the floor next, against the angry protest of Cox, and proceeded to give the Convention the entirely original information that the reports of the majority and minority presented it with the square issue of hard or soft money, for up to that time nobody had supposed there was anything hard in either. But he soon qualified this by declaring that the majority report was a compromise, and that in accepting it the hard-money men had gone to the uttermost possible limit, which was probably true, for as there was nothing in the resolution there could be nothing beyond it. When Dorsheimer ended, Dan Voorhees appeared on the platform, and again there was an uproar, commenced and mainly kept up by Cox flinging points of order at the irascible Chair. Getting a hearing at last, Voorhees made his appeal for the rag baby, and as he stepped down Watterson stepped up to the recognition of the Chair, whereupon there was another angry scene between McClernand and Cox, the latter claiming he was entitled to the floor. The President, McClernand, retorted in kind, but in the end, after much turmoil and much shouting of "Mr. President" by excited delegates in all parts of the hall, Watterson was accorded the floor according to the prearranged programme, and at last succeeded in making himself heard. He made a pretense of supporting the majority report, but speedily showed his hand in cutting himself and everybody else off by moving the previous question, which the Chair, without giving anybody a chance to vote for or against it in decent fashion, declared to be carried.

Then followed a scene unparalleled in disgraceful turbulence in any deliberative body. A hundred men were on their feet yelling for recognition. McClernand was pounding with his gavel, but Gen. Morgan, springing upon his chair, shouted so loud and clear that he managed to make himself heard, and, shaking his fist at the platform, said: "I denounce this gag law. I denounce the man who moved it, and the Chairman who fastens it upon us." Watterson at the moment happened to be standing by the side of McClernand. The latter seemed on the point of throwing his gavel at the head of his contemner and said something which was inaudible, but Watterson, shaking his fist at Morgan, was heard to yell: "I mark you." Naturally, this episode added fuel to the flames of discord, and the Convention fell at once into, and for over half an hour afterward continued in, a state of total and inextricable confusion. McClernand, wild with rage, lost control of himself and also of the Convention. Cox, of New-York, was constantly barking around him with points of order, as a smart terrier would about an ox. Wallace, of Pennsylvania, added to the turmoil with other points of order. Doolittle had a financial resolution which the committee had refused to take, and was constantly on his feet, bellowing for recognition so as to get it in. Leon Abbett, of New-Jersey; George W. Morgan, of Ohio; a strong-lunged man from Oregon; George M. Beebe, of New-York; McLane, of Maryland, and many others were rivaling each other for many minutes, until finally McClernand was daft and the Convention released from all control. While the delegates were making all the uproar themselves, one of them managed to be heard, and tried to make a diversion by saying it was the audience who made the noise, and moving that they be turned out. McClernand clutched at the hint thus presented and threatened to do it, which threat he repeated at many subsequent times during the session. At many times during all this confusion the Clerk started the roll-call with shouting "Alabama" in a cracked voice, which produced peals of laughter.

It was during this time, and between the intervals of these laughs, that Wallace manufactured another, by asking consent for Pennsylvania to retire for consultation, it being well known that the delegation was pretty evenly divided between hard and soft money. Leave was not given or refused, but Pennsylvania went out, nevertheless, and after an hour of hubbub the Convention got to a direct vote on the substitution of the minority for the majority report, and the minority report was rejected by a vote of 211 yeas to 524 nays. There was more uproar, but after it was over the majority report was adopted, with all the delegates but eighty-three voting for it. That ended the long struggle over the platform, but it was enlivened at the end by Doolittle trying to get in his additional resolutions and Cox seeking to make a speech on a motion to reconsider. Both were squelched, and there was general delight when McLane moved that the Convention proceed to nominate candidates for President and Vice President, and the Chair declared it carried.

Under the order of the Convention, the roll of States was called by the Secretary with the blinking eyes, and there was of course no incident until a delegate mounted the platform and proceeded to name Senator Bayard. He was very eloquent and fervent in his praise of his candidate, but the candidate was not received in a very effusive manner by the Convention, and was not seconded by anybody. The next State to make a nomination was Indiana, when Col. Williams, of that State, mounted the platform to nominate Gov. Hendricks. When the State was called there were great cheers, and when the name of Hendricks was announced so tremendous was the applause that one would have supposed that Hendricks had the Convention. Williams, in his speech, was of course highly eulogistic of his candidate, but he was guilty of the grave mistake of trenching upon facts, for he hinted that Tilden would lose both Ohio and Indiana in the October election, whereupon Tilden's friends began hissing him with a vigor worthy of the first serpent. Williams, however, took it in good part. McClernand feebly attempted to preserve order, and as the matter seemed in the end to be of no consequence one way or the other, good humor was restored by the time Williams was ready to leave the rostrum. After Indiana should have come without any interruption New-Jersey and Joel Parker, but the blinking Clerk by mistake called New-York, whereupon the temper of the Convention was shown in such an uproar for Tilden that the heart was taken out of Littlejohn, who had been intending up to that moment to take the stand as soon as Tilden was named and nominate Sanford E. Church. As soon as the noise subsided, the mistake was corrected, and New-Jersey was called in its order, when Leon Abbett proceeded in the usual way to nominate Joel Parker. His speech was somewhat florid, and considering the chances of his candidate, unnecessarily prolix.

At last the formality was over, and then then came what every one knew was to be the dramatic scene and the pivot of the day. New-York was called, and Senator Kernan was already on the rostrum, as was also John Kelly. Mr. Kernan advanced to the side of the chair, and being given a respectful hearing had a fair opportunity to parade the supposititious virtues of Samuel before an admiring Convention. His only interruptions were those of applause, and long before he concluded it was plain to see that sham reform and fat railroad contracts were dear to the Democrat heart. When he concluded John Kelly stepped to the front, and then was the moment of most intense interest. Nobody knew what he intended to do or say, but everybody knew that he was there to speak and act for the New-York opposition to Tilden. It has not been often that there has been an opportunity to speak in praise of Kelly, but his conduct to-day when he stood up before the Democracy of the nation to protest against the disgrace and disaster of the nomination of Samuel J. Tilden entitles him to at least a brief mention of his exploit. As he appeared at McClernand's side he was greeted with a storm of mingled cheers and hisses before he had uttered his first sentence. Then came a scene of wild confusion. Groans, yells, cheers, and hisses came from every part of the vast crowded hall, and Kelly stood before it calmly, smilingly. After this had continued for some time the New-York Tildenites became ashamed of themselves and their cause, and Weed, Beebe, and others from their places asked that Kelly be given a hearing. Delegates from other States shouted for the same thing, but it was of no use, for the uproar continued. Finally Senator Kernan came down to Kelly's side, brushed past him, and waved his hand for silence. He got it, strange to say, out of all that turbulence, and demanded a hearing for his colleague. Thus indebted to the champion of Tilden for the chance to utter a word in a Democratic Convention, Kelly proceeded to make his speech which was in the matter and manner one which surprised even those who knew him best. It barely escaped being eloquent. It was like a sledge hammer in its dealing with facts. He told the Convention plumply that Indiana and Ohio are the States upon which the Presidential election would turn in October, and asserted his firm conviction that Tilden cannot carry either. He went on to say that a respectable minority of the New-York delegation were unalterably opposed to his nomination, because of their knowledge that he cannot carry New-York and cannot be elected. He did not say all this in many more words without being frequently interrupted by enthusiastic Tilden idiots, by calls to order and all that sort of thing, but these being delegates they could not be interfered with. At last an indiscreet lunatic in the audience, lately appointed by Tilden a Canal Collector, interrupted Kelly by jumping and calling for cheers for Tilden. Quick as a flash Littlejohn was on his feet to a point of order, and demanding the ejection of the offender from the hall. Littlejohn picked out the man. It was ordered that he be removed, and Dan Able, Tilden's Sergeant at Arms, was so ordered, but that accommodating official merely went up to the satellite of sham reform, smilingly talked a moment, and then went away, leaving him where he was. Meanwhile, however, Kelly had got the attention of the Convention, and no further notice was taken of the disgraceful interruption. In a moment or two, however, the uproar was recommenced among the delegates, and Kelly ended his speech in a storm that rendered his voice inaudible five feet away from him. He was not, however, in any way dismayed by all this. He stood his ground bravely, denounced Tilden roundly, and so put himself upon record that any subsequent admission that he should support Tilden seemed incomprehensible.

When Kelly sat down up rose gray-bearded Flournoy, of Virginia, who seconded the nomination of Tilden; but sensation was over, and thenceforward the proceedings were nothing more than formal.

After New-York the next candidate was the ancient William Allen. With fine irony at the farmer statesman when Pennsylvania was called, Heister Clymer made the best speech of the day, considered merely as a speech. In presenting the name of Gen. Hancock he spoke of him in such a way as not to wound the sensibilities of the Confederates, while doing justice to his splendid services in the Union cause. He spoke of him in the great war as a soldier, great in peace as a citizen, honored by the nation, and known throughout the world. Sexton, of Texas, and a delegate from Louisiana seconded the nomination, with eulogies of Hancock. With their speeches the nominations closed.

Then came the moment of utmost tension. A motion to adjourn came from Massachusetts and was voted down. Another came from New-York and was also voted down. A ballot was ordered, and for a time there was something approaching order and the roll was called. So far as Tilden was concerned, the States voted almost exactly as THE TIMES had foreshadowed they would, and at the close the result was pronounced as Tilden, 417; Hendricks, 149; Hancock, 75; Allen, 56; Bayard, 23; Parker, 18.

Amid intense excitement a second ballot was ordered, and it was plain to any one knowing anything of the temper of the Convention that the end was at hand. The roll-call was commenced, and it was evident from the beginning that the "favorite son" business was over and the real work began. Delegate after delegate went over to him, so that when Wisconsin voted he only wanted three votes to nominate him. Then followed the scenes usual on such occasions in Democratic Conventions. State after State, anxious to be on the winning side, went over to him, but the first was Missouri, which gave him six additional votes and nominated him. Then came nearly all the others pell mell, and Tilden in a few minutes was the unanimous nominee of the Democracy for President.

So far as surface and formal indications went there was the usual cheering in which about one-third of the Convention did not join, and the usual playing by the band. It was by no means that general enthusiasm which greeted the nomination of Hayes at Cincinnati. It could not compare with the popular response to the nomination of Seymour at New-York, and could only be justly likened to the reception of Greeley at Baltimore. What enthusiasm there was, it was plain to see, was forced except among his immediate retainers. Tammany in the Convention and among spectators sat grimly silent, not perhaps meditating revenge, but certainly not for the moment anxious to work heartily for the nominee.

After the nomination came a lull, and then the tired Convention adjourned until 10 o'clock to-morrow. As the delegates left the hall the general opinion outside the immediate partisans of Tilden was epitomized by Col. McClure, of Pennsylvania, who said: "United States must be reversed if it's possible to elect Tilden President."

### HOW THE THING WAS DONE.

EFFECTUAL WORK OF TILDEN'S SHOUTERS AND TILDEN'S MONEY—HOTEL PARLORS AND ENTERTAINMENTS FOR DELEGATIONS PAID FOR—REPUTABLE MEN BULLIED AND HOWLED DOWN—CHARACTER OF HIS MOST ACTIVE SUPPORTERS.

*Special Dispatch to the New-York Times.*

ST. LOUIS, June 28.—The nomination of Samuel J. Tilden as the Democratic candidate for President of the United States is a singularly good illustration of the power of the machine in the party named. The same influences which were brought to bear in favor of one or two of the prominent candidates at Cincinnati, but which failed so utterly, were the very influences which made Mr. Tilden successful at St. Louis. His friends may say what they will, but they cannot deny that the Governor was, in every sense of the word, the machine candidate. He was supported from the first by all the political wire-pullers and tricksters and by the railroad corporations and great monopolies of the country. They all recognized in him a kindred spirit, and consequently they made him their candidate. The feeling regarding this kind of support which was entertained by some of the more reputable delegates may be inferred from the remark of a well-known gentleman from New-Jersey, who warmly favored the nomination of Gov. Parker. This gentleman said last evening, in a spirit of prophecy: "There can be no doubt that Tilden will be nominated. Hancock, Parker, Hendricks, and Thurman are far more popular with the masses, but Sammy has all the politicians with him, all the money, all its brass bands, all the bunting, and all the gas." This was indeed the case. Tilden's friends fairly took St. Louis by storm. They showered "the 'great reformer's' money right and left. They engaged all the parlors in the hotels. Hired shop windows in which to place the portrait of their favorite; hung banners bearing his name from almost every house, and sounded his praises through nearly every Democratic newspaper for miles around. The power of a perfect organization, and above everything else the power of an endless purse was never before in the history of American politics so well exemplified as it has been here. The earnest, thoughtful men who came to St. Louis to present the name of Hendricks, Hancock, Bayard, and the other gentlemen who were sacrificed by the Convention to satisfy the ambition of a man who has been appropriately christened "the great American humbug," were allowed no hearing, at every turn were prevented from raising their voice or expressing their honest convictions. Sam. Tilden's paid shouters drowned everything that they could say, and with a "hip" and a "hurrah" the most unpopular candidate who could possibly have been chosen was carried through the Convention.

How such a nomination was received by the people can well be imagined. It fell dead, and left not a few of the more earnest and thoughtful of the delegates regretting the fatal action which had been taken by the ill-advised majority.

Of course Democratic St. Louis is doing her duty, and spending the people's money in doing honor to the man who was the choice of the Democratic wire-pullers. All the streets are brilliantly illuminated. Ten burners have been attached to the street lamps in the principal streets and avenues, and fireworks are being set off from the City Hall.

Tilden's managers have, during the evening, been in receipt of many congratulations upon their success, and as they stood in the parlors of the Lindell House and received these congratulations they must have suggested many strange things to the thoughtful American citizen. They were men who secured for him his empty victory, and they were men who would be his advisers and counselors should the people be mad enough to send him to the White House. Foremost among the throng who did most of the hand-shaking was Lieut. Gov. William Dorsheimer, who has been accused publicly of defrauding the State of New-York out of trust funds to the amount of $4,000. He has never successfully denied or explained that accusation. The men who stood around him had records ever worse than this. Near him on one side was Stephen H. Hammond, the bribe-taking State Senator, who, while in the Attorney General's office, was guilty of many frauds and improper practices. Not far from Hammond was his friend Charley Fairchild, the incompetent little Attorney General, whose father is charged with having attempted to steal the Canastota and Cazenovia Railroad. These were the men, together with several notorious members of the Brooklyn Ring, a number of ex-Confederate Generals and Colonels, and two or three cowardly Copperheads who congratulated themselves upon the nomination of Samuel J. Tilden.

There is an old saying that the more Democrats fight before a nomination the better friends they become after the nomination has been made. The adage may have been true in former years, but unfortunately for Mr. Tilden it seems now to have lost its force. The fight which preceded the Convention here, and which was indulged in by the Tilden and anti-Tilden men, not only from New-York, but from all parts of the country, was too bitter and protracted not to leave much bad blood and ill-feeling behind. It will be remembered that for days past Gov. Tilden's friends in St. Louis and in the South and West have declared that all those who opposed the candidate were thieves and rascals. They made no qualifications in such statements. They were bold, defiant, and public in their talk, and said in so many words openly, every day, "the men who oppose Gov. Tilden are all thieves or disreputable men." Now they are anxiously looking and seeking for the support of the very men whom they denounced in these terms, and it is a somewhat noteworthy fact that the Tammany Hall men are the very first to respond to their overtures and to declare in their own peculiar style that they will support the candidate through thick and thin. Indeed it has been the joke of the evening that one or two Tammany leaders said, just after the nomination, that Tilden was their man from the first, and that all their opposition to him was only in fun.

John Kelly says very little about the nomination, except that it is an exceedingly weak one. He will support it, however, declaring that Tammany Hall was never false to a regular candidate, and never bolted a regular ticket. So there is every prospect that honest John Morrissey will soon have an opportunity of shaking hands and walking side by side with John Fox and the "Boss."

While Tammany falls thus readily into the traces, however there is every prospect that the more formidable opposition which was made to Tilden by men like ex-Speaker Littlejohn and ex-Attorney General Pratt cannot and will not permit them to be reconciled to the action of the Convention. They acted here from no personal motives and with no desire for a petty revenge. They opposed the nomination of the sham reformer from conviction, and because they know how hollow and vain were all his pretences. They have placed themselves on record, and they are not men who can or will give up a position which they have once taken.

The opposition to Tilden which came from Ohio and Indiana, and from some parts of the South, is thought just as strong as it was a week ago, and the action of Connecticut today has placed the October States beyond all doubt. In the words of Major Bill Bickham, that man who first nominated Hayes, "they will go Republican by an overwhelming majority."

The platform adopted by the Convention met with even more opposition than does the candidates. The financial plank is particularly distasteful to many delegates from the South and West, and there are numbers of them who declare they will bolt the ticket. One well-known Louisiana Democrat is going about to-night loudly denouncing Tilden as a fraud and the platform as a sham, and declaring that old Peter Cooper is a good enough candidate for him and for 20,000 more of the voters of Louisiana. The Ohio men cannot, indeed they do not attempt to conceal their vexation at the turn affairs have taken, and many of them threaten to bolt the ticket altogether. Everything considered, there can be no doubt that Tilden was by long odds the weakest candidate who could have been nominated. He has more bitter enemies than any other man in the Democratic Party, and he has only lukewarm support in several of the most important States. The mass of the people and the German and Independent voters cannot be deceived by his sham reform, and there can be no doubt that in the words of Gen. Tom Ewing, "Hayes can beat him without sitting upright."

### CANDIDATE FOR THE SECOND PLACE.

TILDEN'S FRIENDS ANXIOUS TO SECURE THE SERVICES OF HENDRICKS FOR CANDIDATE FOR VICE PRESIDENT.

*Special Dispatch to the New-York Times.*

ST. LOUIS, June 28.—The question of who shall receive the nomination for Vice President has now become the prominent one here. It is being excitedly discussed by the crowds about the hotels and the leaders display peculiar interest in it because of the weak health of their principal candidate. Mr. Tilden's friends are particularly anxious to secure Mr. Hendrick's services in that position, but as such a combination would be very much like putting the cart before the horse they greatly fear that the shrewd gentleman from Indiana will not consent to it. However they have telegraphed him asking his acceptance of the place, and they are now anxiously awaiting his reply. While doing so they are casting about for some other candidate. Congressmen Payne, of Ohio, Thurman, and Col. Broadhead are named among the rest.

### CONSTERNATION IN CONGRESS.

EFFECT OF THE NOMINATION ON THE PROSPECTS FOR THE RE-ELECTION OF DEMOCRATS—VIEWS OF REPRESENTATIVES AND SENATORS ON THE STRENGTH OF TILDEN.

*Special Dispatch to the New-York Times.*

WASHINGTON, June 28.—The nomination of Tilden was announced here this evening by bulletins from the telegraph offices posted in the hotel lobbies, and was carried about town by word of mouth from one to another. The news, though not published in any paper, spread rapidly, and by 10 o'clock every person who had interest enough in the result of the Convention to inquire learned of the nomination. There cannot be said to be a very great appearance of enthusiasm or even of common interest in the result. There is no comparison whatever in the state of public interest now and during the balloting at Cincinnati. The hotels are not thronged, and about the telegraph offices there are very small numbers in waiting, though the evening is cool and people at leisure. It costs no more to fire a hundred guns for Tilden than for Hayes, and [illegible] of the enthusiasm, having been prepared in advance, was successfully presented. The truth is that the nomination has fallen pretty flat on the Democracy. The crowds who show most interest are Republicans, and they are generally well satisfied. It is agreed that the contest is to be made in New-York, New-Jersey, and Connecticut, all of which States Tilden must carry to win; and even with all these, neither Louisiana nor North Carolina could be spared by him. Republicans, while feeling no doubt about the election, seem to feel that Tilden's nomination gives the Democrats the only ground upon which they could have made a canvass. The West, which was to rule with the South, is thrown away in the hope of saving New-York, and a forlorn hope it is.

The Ohio Democrats are the worst demoralized people that have been seen for many a day. Payne thinks the nomination the strongest that could have been made. He says it was no use doing anything for Ohio, as no man could beat Hayes in that State. Strength must be sought elsewhere, and Tilden is the man to get it. Payne hopes the ticket will be completed by nominating Hendricks for the second place. McMahon, of Ohio, says: "Am I not in luck? I wrote a letter last week declining a nomination." McMahon, Sayler, Neal and Savage regard a nomination in their districts as of no value. They agree that the Democrats can only hope for four members of the House from Ohio next Fall. Neal, however, denies that he has said that he would take the stump for Hayes. Savage says the platform means that the Democrats indorse the Republican platform, and will run their candidates upon it. Landers, of Indiana, says the Democrats will not now be able to get more than two Congressmen out of his State. This is his way of expressing disgust with the nomination. Bright, of Tennessee, says the nomination is weak, and talks of a third ticket. Young, of Tennessee, also regards the nomination as weak in that State. Tucker, Cabell, and Hunton, of Virginia, say the candidate is fairly strong for that State, and will carry it in the election. Lane, of Oregon, says Tilden is strong in his State and will win. Yeates and Robbins, of North Carolina, say Tilden can carry that State, and is a strong candidate there. Wells, of Missouri, says Tilden will be strong there, and will draw largely on the German vote. Singleton thinks the nomination is strong for Mississippi, and so says Lamar, who hopes Hendricks will be put in the second place. Senator Booth says Tilden is a weak man on the Pacific Coast, and cannot carry California.

Senator Thurman is non-committal. He does not want to say much to-night, and professes a desire to see the financial plank in its full text. He promises to give Tilden such support as he can, but says of course nothing can be done in Ohio. The Ohio Democrats generally concede Hayes 50,000 majority in their State.

New-York Democrats do not like to say much. The Republicans from that State have been expressing a hope that Tilden would be nominated, and they say his war record, his connection with Tammany as long as Tweed held power, and his connivance with and aid of the election frauds, when Seymour was counted in, though never elected, will destroy his chances of carrying the State. The New-York Democrats who are pleased are not demonstrative, but simply indorse the nomination as wise.

The prospects of the nomination for Hendricks are discussed, and it is generally regarded as settled that he will be put up for Vice President. It is not doubted that he will accept. Senator Morton says Hendricks will accept anything in the way of office that has a Democratic indorsement. Hendricks' nomination, in the opinion of Tom Ewing, would insure a Republican triumph in Indiana, because, while Governor, he had mortally offended the Germans, who will not vote for him under any circumstances. It is known that Ewing himself will not do any work for the ticket of Tilden and Hendricks. Those who regard Hendricks as weak in his own State think that over night he will be disposed of, and that some other candidate will be made to run with Tilden.

### THE PROCEEDINGS IN DETAIL.

The President called the Convention to order at 11:05 o'clock this morning in the following words: "The Convention will please come to order; we wish to have order; if we would proceed with our business intelligently and satisfactorily, I say we must have order, and I will employ all the means and energies with which I am invested to secure it. [Applause.] Father Brady will open the proceedings of the day with prayer."

Rev. Father Brady then offered a prayer.

### MISCELLANEOUS RESOLUTIONS.

On motion of Gen. Campbell, of Tennessee, the reading of the minutes of yesterday's proceedings of the Convention were dispensed with.

A Delegate from Georgia—I desire to offer a resolution, and ask that the rules be suspended, and that it be placed upon its passage.

The President—Let me inquire of the gentleman if his resolution relates to the platform? It it does, it is not in order, but must go to the Committee on Resolutions without debate.

The Delegate from Georgia—Let the resolution be read, and the Convention can judge of its merits.

The Secretary read as follows:

*Resolved*, That this Convention indorses the work of reform and economy of Government being inaugurated by the House of Representatives of the United States, in their efforts to cut down the expenses of the Government, and we express ourselves gratified at the efforts of the House of Representatives to discover and bring to light the frauds long and outrageously practiced upon the people by the present Administration. We congratulate our country that the time has come when we may stop, at least, some of the criminals who have brought the country into disgrace at home and abroad; that they are to meet with the punishment due to their crimes.

Mr. Young, of Georgia—I move to suspend the rules and pass the resolution.

The President—Under the rule adopted the resolution must go to the Committee on Resolutions; the Chair so decides.

Mr. Cox, of New-York—I propose the following resolution, Sir, for reference.

The President—The resolution offered by the gentleman from New-York, will go to the Committee on Resolutions under the rules already adopted.

Mr. Cox—I ask to have it read, Sir, if it be in order.

The Secretary read the resolution as follows:

*Resolved*, That, in the opinion of this Convention, the will of the people for retrenchment, as expressed in the preparation of the bills passed by the Democratic House of Representatives, and now before the Senate, should not be thwarted; and that we will sustain the Congressmen who are faithful to their trust in diminishing extravagance and repelling Senatorial dictation on our Money bill.

By the President—The resolution goes to the Committee on Resolutions.

Mr. Vilas, of Wisconsin—I ask leave to offer the following resolution, and move its adoption:

*Resolved*, That, in speaking on any question, no debate be allowed over five minutes, and that in presenting candidates, no delegate be allowed over ten minutes.

The resolution was carried unanimously.

Mr. Cox, of New-York—I have to present to this Convention, on behalf of the Workingmen's Central Union of the State of New-York, a memorial expressing their views. They are men who [illegible] would not ask to have their memorial read, for we have not time. I ask that it may be made a part of our proceedings here to-day, and I send it to the clerk's desk for that purpose.

The memorial was not read, but referred to the Committee on Resolutions. It has already been published.

Mr. Kelly, of New-York—I have been requested by some of my colleagues on the New-York delegation to present to the Convention the names of some gentlemen in New-York who are opposed to the nomination of Gov. Tilden for the Presidency. [Hisses and cries of "Sit down!"] I ask that it be read, so that the Convention will understand the character of the men in that State who are opposed to Gov. Tilden's nomination. [Applause and hisses.]

The Chair decided the motion out of order.

Mr. McLane, of Maryland—I ask the Chair to entertain a motion that the Convention now proceed to ballot, [cheers,] which is a motion of privilege. I submit this motion as a matter of privilege, which is always in order, and I would submit to the Chair and the Convention, it being a debatable question, the reasons why I make that motion.

Senator Kernan, of New-York—Will the gentleman from Maryland yield to me for a question? I suggest, first, and I move that a committee be duly appointed by the Chair to visit the Committee on Resolutions and to inquire if they are likely soon to present their report, and if they are not, then the gentleman from Maryland can put his motion.

Mr. McLean—The only practical result of such a motion would be to involve this Convention in a discussion with the Committee on Resolutions. It is not in the power of this Convention to interfere in any degree with the committee already appointed on resolutions. They have the whole subject now before them. It cannot be the wish of any member of this Convention to hasten in any degree the deliberations of that committee, or to put any pressure upon the committee.

Mr. Woodson, of Missouri—Mr. Chairman, I have a resolution I desire to offer in connection with the motion of the gentleman from Maryland, and I ask that the resolution be read for the information of the Convention.

The resolution was read as follows:

*Resolved*, That this Convention will not ballot for a candidate for President or Vice President of the United States until action is had on the report from the Committee on Resolutions. [Loud applause.]

Mr. Woodson—I have but one word to say upon that resolution. It occurs to me, Sir, that we ought not to vote for a candidate until we know what the action of this Committee is to be. It is hardly probable, Mr. President, that there will be a unanimous report from that committee. I hope, however, that in this I am mistaken, because I suppose that every member of this Convention is anxious to see harmony, not only on the part of the Committee on Resolutions, but harmony in the action of this great body of delegates representing the Democracy of the United States. But, Sir, we must have harmony upon principle or we can have no harmony. I want them to see the report of the committee. If we can harmonize upon the report of the Committee on Resolutions, then, Sir, we can answer the question propounded by the distinguished gentleman from New-York [Mr. Cox] as to who will be the next President of the United States and the answer will be the man who is nominated by this Convention.

Mr. Abbott, of Massachusetts—I move to amend the motion of the gentleman from Missouri by striking out all after the word "resolved," and inserting the following, which the Secretary will read:

The Secretary read the amendment of Mr. Abbott as follows:

*Resolved*, That the roll of States be called in regular order, and that each State be allowed to present the name of any candidate for the Presidency, and that thereupon this Convention do proceed to vote by States for candidate for President of the United States, and a candidate for Vice President of the United States, and that in casting their vote for President and Vice President the Chairman of each delegation shall rise in his place and name how the delegation votes, and his statement alone shall be considered the vote of the State. [Applause and cries of "No, no."]

Mr. Abbott—I desire to state that my only motive in presenting the resolution was, that we do not close the day, but proceed immediately to vote for a candidate for President. I have no doubt that any man who is selected as candidate for President will stand upon the platform that is finally adopted by this Convention.

Mr. Wallace, of Pennsylvania—I move to lay the resolution and amendment on the table, and upon that move that the vote be taken by States.

Mr. McLean adopted the amendment offered by the gentleman from Massachusetts.

There being misapprehension of the question before the house the Secretary read the original resolution and the proposition of Mr. Abbott, of Massachusetts, now made in the following words:

*Resolved*, That the Convention do now proceed to vote by States for candidates for President and Vice President of the United States, and that in the cases of their vote for President and Vice President the Chairman of each delegation shall rise in his place and name how the delegation votes, and his statement alone shall be considered the vote of the State. [Cries of "No, no," and a hiss.]

The Secretary read the amendment of Gov. Woodson, of Missouri, and was then proceeding with the call, when the Chair announced that the Committee on Resolutions had agreed on a report, and asked if the roll call should proceed.

Mr. Abbott, of Massachusetts—I withdraw my motion to take the vote of the States, and agree upon the motion that the vote be taken viva voce.

Mr. Kernan, of New-York—I suggest, now, what I believe to be for the best interests of the country and our party, and ourselves, and that is that we hear from the Committee on Resolutions, and if, as I am informed they expect to be ready to report by 1 or 2 o'clock, I suggest that we wait until we do hear from them and let us get through with this wrangling at once.

Mr. Meredith, of Virginia—Mr. President and Gentlemen of the Convention: I am instructed by the Committee on Resolutions to inform the Convention that they have agreed upon a platform and resolutions; [cheers;] that the resolutions have been referred to a committee of revision, and that the committee will reassemble at 1 o'clock and hear the report from the Subcommittee on Resolutions. I am instructed to ask leave of the Convention for the committee to sit longer for that purpose.

Mr. Kernan, of New-York—In view of this report, by which I rejoice to hear that a platform has been agreed upon and referred to a Committee of Revision, I move that the Convention take a recess until 2 o'clock, to hear that report. [Cries of "No, no."]

The motion was carried and the Convention took a recess until 2 o'clock.

### RECESS—MISCELLANEOUS TALK.

During the recess the vast audience remained in the hall, and there were loud calls for Pryor, Doolittle, Ewing, and others. Meantime the band played the popular airs of "Dixie" and "Yankee Doodle" amid loud cheers. Finally, in response to repeated calls, ex-Senator Doolittle came forward to the platform and spoke at considerable length, and was followed by Col. Breckinridge of Kentucky; Hon. B. Gratz Brown, of Missouri, and Senator Wallace, of Pennsylvania. There was nothing significant in these speeches, they being made to keep the attention of the audience; they were patriotic and fraternal in spirit, as well as critical of the Republican Party.

### REPORTS ON RESOLUTIONS.

The Convention reassembled at 2:15 o'clock. The President—The Sergeant at Arms will clear the aisles and see that order is preserved. The Committee on Platform, I am informed, is ready to report.

Mr. Meredith, of Virginia—Mr. President and Gentlemen of the Convention: The Committee on Resolutions have finally agreed upon their report. It is due to them to state that a great many resolutions were laid before them upon subjects likely to engage the attention of the Convention, that those resolutions have been read, examined, considered, deliberated on and discussed, and they have finally agreed upon the following declaration of principles, which I am instructed to report. I will ask Lieut. Gov. Dorsheimer to read the resolutions.

THE MAJORITY REPORT.

Mr. Dorsheimer then read as follows:

We, the delegates of the Democratic Party of the United States, in national Convention assembled, do hereby declare the Administration of the Federal Government to be in urgent need of immediate reform; [illegible]

The New-York Times.

VOL. XXV.......NO. 7736. NEW-YORK, FRIDAY, JUNE 30, 1876. PRICE FOUR CENTS.

# THE REPUBLICAN CAMPAIGN

## MR. WHEELER AT HOME.

A HEARTY WELCOME BY HIS FRIENDS AND NEIGHBORS AT MALONE—THEY HAVE A PLEASANT TALK WITH HIM—THE SAD FEATURES OF THE OCCASION.

MALONE, June 29.—Hon. W. A. Wheeler returned to Malone this morning. He was welcomed at the depot by cheers of hundreds of his townsmen, by music and firing of cannon. A procession was formed, headed by a band, and escorted him to his home. He spoke briefly, under great excitement, with so much of pathos as to claim the attention of the vast crowd present, and to bring tears to every eye. He said the honor of the nomination belonged not to him, but to the people of Malone. He was chosen Town Clerk by them while yet in his minority, and when the emoluments of the place, $30 a year, were of more value to him than the thousands he has possessed since. He had retained the confidence of the people steadily since, and had been the recipient of repeated honors from them. He owed to their steadfast adherence, their warm support, and their efforts, whatever of success he had achieved. Personally, he would have preferred to remain where he is, for what was the honor to him, standing in the shadow of his desolate home? To the young men, so many of whom were present before him that he had the right to speak to them, he would say: He knew every phase of the struggle of the young man seeking to make his way and to make his mark in life; for, years ago, he had tramped through the storms and snows of Winter to his first district school in an adjoining town. In the log houses of the neighborhood, through the shrunken roofs of the humble farmers' houses, he had at night literally been a star-gazer; but in his wildest dreams and highest building of castles in the air so complete a success in life, so great an achievement, had never occurred to him. This result shows that in this beneficent country every man of character is the equal of every other man. He would make no political speech; his address would be but a family talk; but whatever might be the result in November all should accept it as good and loyal citizens. Political feeling would assert itself during the campaign, but he hoped the personal relations existing between them would remain unchanged, as his greatest desire was to retain the esteem and respect of his immediate friends and neighbors. Mr. Wheeler retired amid hearty applause. He was deeply affected as he referred to the desolation which had come upon his home, and in the sympathy shown by the audience might be read the esteem and love in which he is held.

## CALL FOR THE STATE CONVENTION.

MEETING OF THE REPUBLICAN STATE CENTRAL COMMITTEE—THE STATE CONVENTION TO MEET AT SARATOGA SPRINGS ON THE 23D OF AUGUST—DELEGATES FROM ALL PARTS OF THE STATE CONFIDENT OF VICTORY.

The Republican State Central Committee met at 11 o'clock yesterday morning in one of the large parlors of the Fifth Avenue Hotel for the purpose of fixing the time and place at which the State Convention for the nomination of State officers and Presidential electors is to be held. The meeting was the largest that has been held in years. Every portion of the State was represented. In the discussions on the political situation indulged in by members of the committee, both before and after the meeting, confidence in a grand victory next November was expressed by all, and an amount of enthusiasm exhibited that gives promise of splendid work during the coming campaign. Every gentleman present seemed to be animated by a desire to promote harmony among all sections of the party, and this feeling is reflected in the call for the State Convention. It was evident, too, that while victory is confidently expected, the fact that vigorous work will be required from every Republican during the next four months was fully appreciated. Among the gentlemen in attendance were many who at Cincinnati fought under different banners, and fought gallantly while a chance remained for their respective candidates, but during the discussions incidental to the meeting it was made abundantly apparent that not a scar remained behind after the battle, and that the Republicans of the Empire State will march to victory in one unbroken column under the banner of Hayes and Wheeler. It will be seen from the call that past differences will be forgotten, and that all who are willing to co-operate with the Republican Party in support of Hayes and Wheeler on the platform adopted at Cincinnati are invited to meet in their respective localities at the call of the local Republican committees and take part in the election of the delegates to the State Convention. It is the purpose and wish of the State Central Committee that the will of the people should be fully expressed at these primaries, so that the delegates elected to the convention may form a representative body in the fullest sense of the word. Among the gentlemen present were Messrs. John Birdsall, Elias B. Dutcher, David Williams, Benjamin W. Wilson, Jacob M. Patterson, Jr., Austin Leake, Gilbert Hunter, Henry G. Leake, ex-Gov. Edwin D. Morgan, Senator William H. Robertson, Lewis F. Payne, Gen. George H. Sharpe, John F. Smythe, Gilbert Robertson, W. C. Squire, Charles S. Symonds, George W. Crouse, John A. Place, Gen. John W. Knapp, James D. Warren, George Hyland, and W. W. Crandall.

The meeting was called to order by Hon. A. B. Cornell, and Mr. Henry A. Glidden acted as Secretary. After the transaction of some routine business the time at which the convention should be held came under discussion. Some of the gentlemen present were in favor of holding it in the early part of August, advancing as a reason that the real work of the campaign could not be opened too soon. A majority of the committee were in favor of a later day. Those in favor of holding the convention about the end of August urged that the work of the campaign would commence long before that date; that it had in fact already commenced, and that it would receive a magnificent impetus from the right kind of nominations for State officers made two months before election day. It was finally unanimously agreed that the convention should be held on the 23d of August. The matter of the date out of the way, the place at which the convention should be held was next considered. On this subject there was a slight difference of opinion, which, however, disappeared after a short discussion. The gentlemen who favored the holding of the convention at an early date were of opinion that it should be called together at Utica or Syracuse. A large majority of the committee favored Saratoga Springs, and when the vote was taken it was unanimous in favor of that place.

The following is the call agreed on by the State Central Committee:

THE CALL OF THE COMMITTEE.

A Republican State Convention will be held at Saratoga Springs on Wednesday, Aug. 23, at 11 o'clock A. M., for the purpose of nominating candidates for State officers and Presidential Electors, and the transaction of other appropriate business.

All Republican electors and all other voters, without regard to past political differences, who are willing to co-operate with the Republican Party in support of Hayes and Wheeler on the platform adopted by the Republican National Convention at Cincinnati, June 15, 1876, are cordially invited to meet in their respective localities at the call of the Republican local committees, and participate in the election of delegates to the said State Convention.

The representation of the several Assembly districts will be in accordance with the subjoined schedule, pursuant to the order of the Republican State Convention adopted July 8, 1868.

By order of the Republican State Committee.
Dated June 29, 1876.

ALONZO B. CORNELL, Chairman.
HENRY A. GLIDDEN, Secretary.

Following is the schedule of representation:

| District | | District | |
|---|---|---|---|
| Albany, 1st | 3 | New-York, 13th | 3 |
| Albany, 2d | 3 | New-York, 14th | 2 |
| Albany, 3d | 4 | New-York, 15th | 3 |
| Albany, 4th | 3 | New-York, 16th | 2 |
| Allegany | 5 | New-York, 17th | 4 |
| Broome | 5 | New-York, 18th | 3 |
| Cattaraugus, 1st | 3 | New-York, 19th | 2 |
| Cattaraugus, 2d | 3 | New-York, 20th | 4 |
| Cayuga, 1st | 4 | New-York, 21st | 3 |
| Cayuga, 2d | 4 | Niagara, 1st | 3 |
| Chautauqua, 1st | 3 | Niagara, 2d | 3 |
| Chautauqua, 2d | 4 | Oneida, 1st | 4 |
| Chemung | 4 | Oneida, 2d | 3 |
| Chenango | 5 | Oneida, 3d | 3 |
| Clinton | 4 | Oneida, 4th | 3 |
| Columbia, 1st | 3 | Onondaga, 1st | 4 |
| Columbia, 2d | 3 | Onondaga, 2d | 4 |
| Cortland | 3 | Onondaga, 3d | 3 |
| Delaware, 1st | 3 | Ontario, 1st | 3 |
| Delaware, 2d | 3 | Ontario, 2d | 3 |
| Dutchess, 1st | 4 | Orange, 1st | 4 |
| Dutchess, 2d | 4 | Orange, 2d | 4 |
| Erie, 1st | 3 | Orleans | 4 |
| Erie, 2d | 4 | Oswego, 1st | 3 |
| Erie, 3d | 4 | Oswego, 2d | 3 |
| Erie, 4th | 2 | Oswego, 3d | 3 |
| Erie, 5th | 3 | Otsego, 1st | 3 |
| Essex | 3 | Otsego, 2d | 3 |
| Franklin | 3 | Putnam | 2 |
| Fulton and Hamilton | 4 | Queens, 1st | 3 |
| Genesee | 4 | Queens, 2d | 3 |
| Greene | 4 | Rensselaer, 1st | 3 |
| Herkimer | 5 | Rensselaer, 2d | 3 |
| Jefferson, 1st | 4 | Rensselaer, 3d | 3 |
| Jefferson, 2d | 4 | Richmond | 3 |
| Kings, 1st | 2 | Rockland | 2 |
| Kings, 2d | 4 | St. Lawrence, 1st | 4 |
| Kings, 3d | 2 | St. Lawrence, 2d | 4 |
| Kings, 4th | 4 | St. Lawrence, 3d | 4 |
| Kings, 5th | 3 | Saratoga, 1st | 3 |
| Kings, 6th | 3 | Saratoga, 2d | 3 |
| Kings, 7th | 3 | Schenectady | 3 |
| Kings, 8th | 4 | Schoharie | 3 |
| Kings, 9th | 5 | Schuyler | 3 |
| Lewis | 3 | Seneca | 3 |
| Livingston | 4 | Steuben, 1st | 3 |
| Madison, 1st | 3 | Steuben, 2d | 5 |
| Madison, 2d | 3 | Suffolk | 4 |
| Monroe, 1st | 3 | Sullivan | 3 |
| Monroe, 2d | 6 | Tioga | 4 |
| Monroe, 3d | 3 | Tompkins | 4 |
| Montgomery | 4 | Ulster, 1st | 3 |
| New-York, 1st | 2 | Ulster, 2d | 3 |
| New-York, 2d | 2 | Ulster, 3d | 3 |
| New-York, 3d | 2 | Warren | 3 |
| New-York, 4th | 2 | Washington, 1st | 3 |
| New-York, 5th | 3 | Washington, 2d | 3 |
| New-York, 6th | 2 | Wayne, 1st | 3 |
| New-York, 7th | 3 | Wayne, 2d | 3 |
| New-York, 8th | 3 | Westchester, 1st | 3 |
| New-York, 9th | 4 | Westchester, 2d | 3 |
| New-York, 10th | 3 | Westchester, 3d | 3 |
| New-York, 11th | 4 | Wyoming | 4 |
| New-York, 12th | 2 | Yates | 3 |
| | | Total | 424 |

## RATIFYING THE NOMINATIONS.

OLD FANEUIL HALL GIVES NO UNCERTAIN SOUND—NORWICH REPUBLICANS IN FORCE—CAMPAIGN CLUB AT UTICA.

NORWICH, June 29.—An enthusiastic meeting to ratify the Republican nominations was held here last night. Among the speakers was Prof. Jones, (colored,) of Leland University, New-Orleans. He said the colored people of the South would give the ticket their cordial support.

UTICA, June 29.—A Young Men's Hayes and Wheeler Club was organized in this city last night, with Charles H. Searle as President and a membership of over five hundred. The meeting was the most enthusiastic Republican demonstration made in this city in several years. Speeches were made by gentlemen heretofore representing different factions of the Republican Party in this city, the most conspicuous feature of the meeting being its complete harmony and unity of purpose.

BOSTON, June 29. Pursuant to a call to ratify the Cincinnati nominations and welcome home the Massachusetts delegates, a large meeting of Republicans was held at Faneuil Hall tonight. In the galleries were many ladies, while the body of the hall was filled to its utmost capacity with an attentive, and at times enthusiastic, audience. Gov. Rice presided, and speeches were made by Hon. R. H. Dana, E. R. Hoar, William T. Davis, George B. Loring, Rev. James F. Clarke, and others. The Massachusetts delegates were defended against the statement that they had no influence at Cincinnati, and their action was justified. The Republicans of the State were pledged to support the ticket, and carry Massachusetts for the Cincinnati nominees.

## THE REPUBLICANS OF ALABAMA.

A LETTER FROM HON. JERE. HARALSON—A UNITED STATES ORGANIZATION ASKED FOR—SOME EXCELLENT ADVICE.

*Special Dispatch to the New-York Times.*

WASHINGTON, June 29.—The following letter has been addressed by Hon. Jere. Haralson to the Chairman of the Alabama State Republican Committee. Mr. Haralson requests that the olive branch be held out to the defeated Spencer organization, in order that there may be a united State Republican organization in the approaching canvass. He represents a district which contains about one-third the negro voters in Alabama, and his views are entitled to be respectfully considered, even by so great a statesman as Senator Spencer:

WASHINGTON, June 21, 1876.

*To Hon. William H. Smith, Chairman Republican State Executive Committee, Montgomery, Ala.:*

SIR: It is earnestly hoped that by the time of the meeting of the National Executive Committee at Philadelphia, July 8, the whole party in our State will be united. The success of the party in Alabama should be paramount to all other considerations, hence I am satisfied that all true Republicans in the State will aid in bringing about that unanimity so much desired. I would suggest that you call your committee, and at the same time invite the other side, headed by Mr. C. E. Mayer, and have an honorable settlement of the pending difficulties, so that we may have but one ticket, one committee, and one party without faction. With this we can reasonably expect the proper aid and success at the polls. It will not do to permit the success of another Democratic victory in the State, with such an administration as we have there now, by ourselves being divided. I hope that you will appeal to the party in all portions of the State to aid you and the committee in bringing about that harmony that it takes to carry any party to success, and which is the rock upon which Republican principles are founded. It must not be forgotten that the greater the achievements greater are the responsibilities that follow; hence some sacrifice must be made always by giving and taking. Trusting that you will consider my suggestions favorably, and that they may aid in leading to the harmony of the party, I am truly yours, &c.

JERE. HARALSON,
Member of the National Republican Executive Committee for the State of Alabama.

## GOV. HAYES AT KENYON COLLEGE.

WARM GREETING TO THE NEXT PRESIDENT OF THE UNITED STATES—SPEECH OF THE GOVERNOR.

*Special Dispatch to the New-York Times.*

COLUMBUS, June 29.—Gov. Hayes was in attendance to-day at the Commencement exercises of Kenyon College, at Gambier, where he himself graduated in 1842. There was an unusually large attendance, including many distinguished gentlemen connected with the institution officially and as members of the Alumni, and the exercises were of much more than ordinary interest. At the conclusion of the class orations Bishop Bedell, of the Episcopal Diocese of Ohio, introduced Gov. Hayes, remarking that Kenyon did not create great men, but inculcated principles which led them to be great. Gov. Hayes was received with much enthusiasm and responded as follows:

LADIES, GENTLEMEN, FRIENDS OF KENYON: I beg you to receive my very grateful acknowledgment for this hearty greeting. During the years from 1838 to 1842 I was a student of Kenyon College. Of those who were here then, teachers, students, and citizens, very few are here to-day, and the narrow circle of those who were then here grows rapidly and steadily smaller. But those of us who are here will never forget those who are gone, some of whom I will name. Bishop McIlvaine; what a figure, what a character he was! We shall never forget him. And Dr. William Sparrow, a giant in those days. And there came to us from the Army of the United States those two remarkable men, Prof. Rosse and Major Douglass. These and others who were our instructors are gone, and of our much-loved college comrades we look in vain for Fitch, Matthews, Ira French, Christopher Wolcott, Albert B. Butler, and so many others of my own classmates; George Mason, Douglass Case, and he whose name was first on the roll, and who was first in scholarship, first in talents and promise, Lorin Andrews, a President of Kenyon College, and who, at the head of an Ohio regiment, gave his life to his country's good cause. These and others are gone. With a memory thronging with recollections of these persons and scenes and the events of those years, I do not attempt to address you now. My wish is, my earnest prayer is that Kenyon College and Gambier, and all beneath their roofs, may enjoy the best blessings that belong to this stage of existence.

Large crowds gathered at several stations along the railroad as the Governor returned to Columbus this evening. At two points the train stopped long enough to allow him to shake hands and respond in a few words to the popular greetings.

## GRAND REPUBLICAN RALLY.

ROUSING MEETING IN THE TENTH ASSEMBLY DISTRICT—RESOLUTIONS AND SPEECHES IN FAVOR OF HAYES AND WHEELER.

The Republicans of the Tenth Assembly District met at their headquarters, Nos. 28 and 30 Avenue A, last evening and ratified the nominations of Hayes and Wheeler, and indorsed the platform of the Cincinnati Convention. The meeting was well attended, and one of the most earnest and interesting of the campaign. Mr. J. M. Patterson, Jr., President of the Hayes and Wheeler Club of the district, presided. Having stated the object of the meeting, he said that the Democratic Party had just nominated for President Samuel J. Tilden, under the title of the "Great Reformer." It seemed almost a sarcasm to call Sammy Tilden a reformer, and it was more than a sarcasm for the Democrats to pretend that as a party they were earnest for reform. All the reforming which had been done for the last sixteen years had been the reforming of the Democratic Party, and for that party to cry reform was like the horse thief crying "Stop thief." No party had ever ruled a country more honestly than the Republican Party. Prof. Seelye told the truth when he said that considering the little corruption that had been brought to light during the six months of drag-netting carried on by the Democratic Party, he was proud of his party and of the country. Whatever of corruption existed, whatever burdens of taxation had fallen upon the people, whatever suffering the people had been forced to undergo, was due to the Democratic Party.

The meeting being declared open for business a series of resolutions, offered by Mr. William H. Lockwood, was unanimously adopted. Mr. Lockwood prefacing them by a short and eloquent speech, in which he spoke in the highest terms of the nominees and of the platform. He said that the Republican Party had seen some dark days, but the sun was now coming out from behind the clouds and the writing was plainly visible on the walls in glowing letters, "Hayes, Wheeler, and Victory." Following are the resolutions:

*Resolved*, That we heartily approve and indorse the action of the National Republican Convention in nominating for the offices of President and Vice President of the United States Gov. Rutherford B. Hayes, of Ohio, and Hon. William A. Wheeler, of New-York.

*Resolved*, That we recognize in these nominations men of undoubted integrity and ability, and of long and honorable public services, such as entitle them to the confidence and esteem of the American people, and make them the proper leaders of the great Republican Party in the coming national contest.

*Resolved*, That the principles laid down in the platform of the party are such as commend them to the patriotism, intelligence, and progressive spirit of all the people of this country.

*Resolved*, That we hereby ratify the nominations of Hayes and Wheeler, and promise hearty support to the ticket and platform.

Major Willard Bullard was then introduced. He said that the nominees of that Convention were men who commanded the respect of the State of New York and of the country at large. The party which is led by Hayes and Wheeler needed no introduction to the people of the United States. It was a party of great and glorious men and of great and glorious deeds. And when charges were brought against the Republican party it should be remembered that it was only the dross of the party, only the clinkers, that were open to the charges. The party which the Republican party supplanted was a mass of corruption. Every man south of Mason and Dixon's line proved false to his trust, and most of the party north of that line were no better. It was an old, superannuated bachelor President that was superseded by Abraham Lincoln and now the Democratic Party had put forward another old bachelor President. As for himself, Major Bullard said that he wanted no man for President who had not courage to take a wife. He did not want half a man for President. New-York, he said, was a strong Republican State. This year the Republican Party of New-York was a unit. It had been harmonized and concentrated by the mention of the name of Rutherford B. Hayes and William A. Wheeler, and New-York was getting ready to roll up one of her old-fashioned Republican majorities. Eleven years had passed since the breaking out of the war, and in that time the Southern people had learned a lesson. It was that there were better men north of Mason and Dixon's line than south of it. So at their Convention at St. Louis they said, "Don't nominate a Southern man; give us a man from the North and we will give our solid vote for him." And by this they meant that once let them get control of the government of the United States and they would undo the good work that had been done by the Republican Party, and once more make the United States, instead of a free land, a white man's Government. They want a total disorganization of the Government, a thorough undoing of the reforms and beneficent works of sixteen years. Major Bullard closed by exhorting the Republicans of the Tenth District to do their part to secure the election of Hayes and Wheeler. They must not risk the Government of the United States in the hands of the Democratic Party if they desired honest administration and a return to prosperity and happiness. Major Bullard spoke with his accustomed earnestness, and his audience responded with frequent applause. The meeting broke up with three rousing cheers for Hayes and Wheeler.

## THE LOUISIANA REPUBLICANS.

THE CONVENTION NOT YET ORGANIZED—A PECULIAR SESSION—UNWORTHY ARGUMENTS PRODUCED—ADJOURNMENT.

NEW-ORLEANS, July 29.—The Republican Convention is not yet permanently organized. The majority report of the Committee on Credentials came up for adoption. A vote was taken, and amid tremendous applause the report was declared adopted. Then came a dead-lock. The report was adverse to the Packard faction, throwing out several delegations that favor Packard. Numerous calls were made for the minority report, but without success. Later in the afternoon Mr. Pinchback declared the Convention adjourned until to-morrow, which created great commotion and cries of "Stamps." An attempt was made to place Mr. Stamps, a Packard man, in the Chair. A struggle took place on the stage, Stamps being thrown into the orchestra. Several fights took place on the floor, pistols being drawn on all sides but not used.

Partial quiet having been restored, Col. Packard made a conciliatory speech, and the convention thereafter agreed to adjourn until 10 o'clock to-morrow. The convention met yesterday and to-day in the St. Charles Theatre.

## CAMPAIGN SIGNAL GUNS.

A Hayes and Wheeler banner was flung to the breeze by the Henry Knoblo Association, of the Fifth Assembly District, last evening, at No. 192 Bleecker street. Col. Charles S. Spencer and other speakers addressed the immense crowd. Music and fire-works enlivened the occasion.

A special meeting of the Twenty-fourth Ward Republican Association was held last evening at the Wigwam, corner of Atlantic and Kingsland avenues, Brooklyn, at which the association was organized as a Republican campaign club, and speeches made and resolutions passed thoroughly indorsing the nomination of Hayes and Wheeler, and pledging them the hearty support of the Republicans of the Twenty-fourth Ward.

The Fifteenth Assembly District Republican Association met last evening at head-quarters, No. 332 West Thirty-fifth street, Mr. Henry G. Leask presiding. A committee of twenty-six was appointed to arrange for the raising of their banner, which will take place next Thursday evening, at the corner of Thirty-third street and Eighth avenue. Preparations will be made for a large meeting, to be held in connection with this event.

A Hayes and Wheeler Campaign Club has been formed in the First District, Jersey City, with the following officers: President, J. O. B. Vredenberg; Vice Presidents—First Precinct, Edward Skinner; Second Precinct, B. G. Clarke; Third Precinct, James H. Love; Fourth Precinct, J. Owen Rouse; Fifth Precinct, John Edelstein; Sixth Precinct, Robert Bumstead; Seventh Precinct, Dr. J. J. Youlin; Secretary, Charles H. Weber; Assistant Secretary, John Creech; Treasurer, George H. Farrier; Executive Committee, R. B. Seymour, L. Schermerhorn, H. E. Farrier, John A. Parker, and H. A. Greene. A Hayes and Wheeler Club is being organized in Hoboken.

## COLORED VOTERS TO THE FRONT.

THE FIFTH ASSEMBLY DISTRICT INDORSING THE CINCINNATI NOMINEES.

The Fifth Assembly District Colored Republican Association held a meeting on Wednesday evening, at the Spring Street Hall, A. F. Potter, President, in the chair. After the transaction of the regular routine business and the admission of a number of persons to membership in the organization, the following resolutions were presented, and read by Mr. George W. Francis, and after remarks by several persons were unanimously adopted:

*Whereas*, We are on the eve of a great political struggle, and the colored citizens throughout the country are particularly interested and feel the importance of a united effort on the part of every true Republican; therefore, we, the members of the Fifth Assembly District, have organized in the interest of the same.

*Resolved*, That the colored citizens of the Fifth Assembly District and of the Eighth Ward do hereby fully assure the Republican Party of the country that from to-night we intend to buckle on the armor and declare our entire opposition to any party or faction not in the Republican ranks.

*Resolved*, That the convention held at Cincinnati on the 15th of June, 1876, showed patriotism, wisdom, forbearance, and political acumen such as is seldom seen in a body of men met for the purpose of nominating candidates for the Presidency and Vice Presidency of the United States.

*Resolved*, That in the nomination of Rutherford B. Hayes, of Ohio, and William A. Wheeler, of New-York, for President and Vice President, we have gentlemen of reputation, intelligence, statesmanship, and integrity; also impartial friends to the colored race.

*Resolved*, That we hereby pledge ourselves to support the Republican ticket and use every effort to elect the heroic men who have been selected as our standard-bearers.

A mass-meeting (colored) of the Hayes and Wheeler Unity Republican Campaign Club was held last evening at No. 185 Spring street, Mr. Washington Parker presiding. The hall was filled with an enthusiastic audience, who manifested their approval of the speaking by frequent applause. The meeting was addressed by Hon. Charles S. Spencer, Hon. John D. Lawson, Hon. Abraham Lent, Hon. Austin Leake, and Mr. H. A. Mathews. At the conclusion of the speaking resolutions were unanimously adopted indorsing the Republican platform and the nomination of Hayes and Wheeler. This club has now a membership of 200, and has just put in front of its hall a fine transparency inscribed with the names of the Republican candidates.

## LETTER FROM MR. MORTON.

A CORDIAL TRIBUTE TO THE CHARACTER OF OUR CANDIDATES, AND A PROMISE OF EFFICIENT SUPPORT.

Senator Morton has written the following reply to an invitation from the Republican State Committee of Indiana to assist in opening the campaign for Hayes and Wheeler:

UNITED STATES SENATE CHAMBER,
WASHINGTON, June 25.

*Hon. G. W. Friedley, Chairman of the Republican State Central Committee:*

DEAR SIR: I received your letter yesterday saying that the Republicans of Indiana desire to begin the campaign on the 15th or 20th of July, and inviting me to speak about that time. Fully appreciating the compliment, and desirous to do all in my power to secure the triumph of the Republican Party in Indiana in the coming elections, I accept the invitation, but am unable now to fix the time. The trial of the impeachment case will begin on the 6th of July, and may continue through the month, though I hope not. Should it be protracted, I shall endeavor to get away long enough to go to Indiana and comply with your request.

The Cincinnati Convention has given to the Republican Party candidates for President and Vice President who will rally the whole strength of the party, and unite in their support all who fear the ascendency of the Democracy in our National and State Governments. Gov. Hayes is a man of ability and character, against whom nothing can be said, and whose record, remarkably free from blemishes, will be a tower of strength in the approaching canvass. The danger to the country from permitting the Government to pass under the control of the Democratic Party has been so fully illustrated by the conduct of the present House of Representatives that the people are greatly awakened, and the prospects for the success of the Republican candidates are exceedingly bright. No campaign within my recollection has opened so auspiciously, and nothing is required but energy and industry in presenting the principles, history, and spirit of the Republican Party to insure success.

For the hearty support given to me by the Republicans of Indiana in the late Cincinnati Convention, and by Republicans from other States, I am deeply grateful. Though it was not successful, it is appreciated none the less. It will be remembered with gratitude through life, and I hope to prove to my friends in the future, according to the opportunities permitted, that their confidence and support were not unworthily bestowed. The vital part of the platform, and that upon which the victory will be won, I have stood upon and for years battled for, and the success of the ticket placed upon it will be the triumph of principles which I hold most dear.

O. P. MORTON.

## NOMINATIONS IN PHILADELPHIA.

PHILADELPHIA, June 29.—The Philadelphia County Republican Convention to-day nominated W. Ellwood Rowan as their candidate for the office of Sheriff of the City and County of Philadelphia; Henry P. Southworth, for City Treasurer, and Jesse W. Hall for Register of Wills.

## A STRONG NOMINATION FOR CONGRESS.

PORTLAND, June 29.—The First Maine District Republican Convention, after an exciting all day's session, nominated Thomas B. Reed, of Portland, for Congress, by a vote of 134 to 113 for John H. Burleigh, of South Berwick, the present incumbent.

CINCINNATI, June 29.—The Republicans of the Eighth Ohio District nominated Gen. J. W. Warren Keifer for Congress on the forty-fifth ballot.

# THE TICKET COMPLETED.

## END OF THE ST. LOUIS CONVENTION.

THOMAS A. HENDRICKS, OF INDIANA, NOMINATED CANDIDATE FOR VICE PRESIDENT—THE INDIANA DELEGATION RATHER INDIFFERENT ABOUT IT—TAMMANY BARKERS WHIPPED INTO LINE FOR TILDEN—THE DESPONDENT UNWASHED DISPERSING.

The Democratic National Convention reassembled yesterday morning, in St. Louis, and immediately proceeded to the nomination of a candidate for Vice President. When Indiana was called the delegates shouted for Hendricks, and a motion to suspend the rules and nominate him by acclamation was offered and ruled out of order. Senator Wallace, of Pennsylvania, then formally presented the name of Hendricks, and he was nominated by a vote of 730 yeas and 8 blanks—the latter from Ohio. The Convention then lost all interest in the later proceedings, and could hardly be held together long enough to appoint the National Committee and finish some routine business.

## LAST DAY OF THE CONVENTION.

GRADUAL DISINTEGRATION OF THE DEJECTED BODY—ANOTHER BRILLIANT RULING BY M'CLERNAND—HENDRICKS CHOSEN TO PLAY SECOND FIDDLE TO THE RAILROAD LAWYER—A LUCKY DAY FOR GOV. HAYES.

*Special Dispatch to the New-York Times.*

ST. LOUIS, June 29.—Dejected by the acrimonies of yesterday, depleted by the numerous departures after the great fight was ended, the Democratic Convention met this morning to complete its work. Whether it was due to exhaustion consequent upon the excitement of yesterday or whether it was the natural result of the nomination of the "Cheap John" reformer could not be surely determined, but it was certain that the Convention was out of sorts. Although the hall was tolerably well filled, there was not during the entire session anything which could possibly be mistaken for genuine, hearty enthusiasm. McClernand, in his absurd, testy way, called the Convention to order and had Bishop Robertson read a prayer. Then the Secretary read a large number of telegrams from more or less obscure persons congratulating the Convention on the nomination of Tilden, and promising Democratic majorities in localities where there never were and never will be any. The Convention was so thoroughly aware of this fact that the telegrams were received almost in dead silence, and were finally shut off by cries for the regular order. This was the nomination of Vice President, and McClernand ordered the roll of States to be called for the naming of candidates. It proceeded without incident until Indiana was reached, when there were shouts for Hendricks all over the hall. Silence being restored, Senator McDonald said that the mission of Indiana in behalf of Gov. Hendricks ended yesterday, and that if the Convention desired to use his name further it must take the responsibility. The hint was seized with avidity and given tangible form by Senator Wallace, of Pennsylvania, who moved that the rules be suspended, the roll-call dispensed with, and Hendricks be nominated by acclamation. There were a dozen seconds in all parts of the hall, including Gen. Steadman, of Ohio, who in the name of his State declined to name Henry B. Payne. Yet McClernand refused to entertain it, although perfectly parliamentary, and directed a call of the States on the nomination. The result was that every State voted solid for Hendricks except Ohio and Indiana, the latter being passed on request, and the former casting eight blanks.

The call concluded, Col. Williams said Indiana had no right to say that Hendricks would accept, but joining in the general wish, would vote for him. Thereupon the result was announced as 730 for Hendricks, and 8 blank, and Hendricks was declared the nominee. Then the hall began to empty, for nobody was interested in the appointment of the National Committee, and the other proceedings with which the Convention closed. There was a little breeze made by the attempt to abrogate the two-thirds rule, but it was speedily over, for the resolutions took the harmless form of recommendation to the States to consider the subject, and in that form was passed. The only other episode of the brief session was the abject surrender of John Kelly to the Tilden faction. He who appeared yesterday to be a hero, appeared to-day in the guise of slave. After having for four days declared to the Democracy of the Union that Tilden would not be supported by the Democracy of New-York, Kelly took occasion after the nomination of Hendricks to go upon the platform and, in a long speech, to pledge Tammany to an active, earnest support of the whole ticket. All the Tammany faction, both publicly and privately, returned with great alacrity to its wallowing in the mire, and those who were most fierce in denouncing Tilden two days ago are now his most earnest supporters. They are seeking to make amends for the past, and with the Convention ends their opposition to its action. Happily for the country, and as further proof of the good luck of Gov. Hayes, Tammany is to give Tilden a zealous support, and thus insure his defeat. With this weight upon them, in addition to all they had before, the Democrats hurried from the hall and the Convention of 1876 was a thing of the past, and it was labeled, like all those of the last twenty years, "another of our failures."

When the Convention had adjourned, and the passion which had dominated it had partially subsided, it was possible to review it and its action. The first fact that stood out in bold relief was the truth that it was in every sense a representative body. Everything that has been done during the present generation that was mean, dishonest, disloyal, turbulent, and tricky was faithfully photographed in its membership and proceedings. Like the Convention of 1868 at New-York, like that of 1872 at Baltimore, it was dominated by the ghost of the dead rebellion. Now, as then, the arrogant assumptions of the South prevailed over the weakness of the Northern Democrats. Now, as then, the party took pains to prove that it is controllable by the spirit of retrogression, of tacit disloyalty to the Union and liberty. A glance over the hall revealed such men as Eli S. Shorter, of Alabama; Col. Wood, of Arkansas; H. G. Turner, of Georgia; Bayless W. Hanna, of Indiana; R. H. Marr, of Louisiana; Silas Woodson, of Missouri; the Tammany gang from New-York; T. L. Clingman, of North Carolina; Wallace and Clymer, of Pennsylvania; D. W. Aiken, of South Carolina; John C. Brown, of Tennessee; Fitzhugh Lee, of Virginia. These were the types of a Convention which was largely composed of men who had borne arms against their country, or had sought to betray it in the North by covert action with its open enemies. That there were many good and true men in the Convention cannot be denied; but that the majority were men in whose control the Union would not be safe, is equally true. From such men as these, to whom should be added such tricky politicians as McClernand, Watterson, Morgan, Ewing, Abbott, McLean, and a score of others, could come only such dishonest declarations, such turbulence, and such candidates as the Convention has left as legacy to its party. Its platform perhaps more than anything else shows the dire distress of the party. It is before the country, and comment here upon its text is unnecessary; but it is not wholly useless to say that, feeble as it is, it was not feeble enough when reported to suit a large minority of the party, who made such a fight for the Ewing amendment as led to the most disgraceful scenes in the Convention itself ever witnessed in any body of the kind, and nearly resulted in personal encounters between "distinguished gentlemen." That the Democratic Party is not in favor of honest money the resolutions prove, but the discussion and turmoil which ended in its adoption proved that it is really devoted to rag money.

The incidents of this struggle on the platform are already so fully before the people that repetition of them is not needed. The whole situation was stated by Dorsheimer, and by Voorhees, and the result was the Democrats practically said that they dare not say anything upon the most momentous question now before the American people. In its candidates, as in its platform, the Convention was equally unfortunate. How or why Tilden was nominated nobody knows, and never will until the "Cheap John" reformer chooses to divulge his secrets. Two days before the balloting a distinguished New-Yorker said: "If Tilden is using money we cannot beat him, and I believe he is." Whether he used money or not is a question which cannot be answered certainly, but his vote has a curious aspect. It may have been money that did it, but his supporters fortified themselves with the cry of "reform." The agency of Bates & Locke had done such good work for the moderate means put at their disposal that "Cheap John" Tilden was really believed by many of the delegates to be a genuine reformer, and this conviction was really the cause of his nomination. All the Democrats wanted was a ticket they thought could win. The choice of Hendricks was put on the ground of availability only. There was no question of fitness or congruity in the choice. The real salient points of the Convention were its turbulence, its disregard of common decency, its flagrant violation of all parliamentary law to effect the nomination of Tilden. But these were so fully presented yesterday that repetition is not required. That the work of the Convention has left a bad effect behind it forever former dispatches fully show. The whole situation, as the delegates are departing by every train from the city of their disaster, can be best put in the words of a prominent Democrat when he said: "Hayes is a lucky man, and yesterday was the luckiest of all his lucky days."

## AFTER THE CONVENTION.

GLOOMY ANTICIPATIONS OF DISASTER—LITTLE SATISFACTION WITH THE FRENZIED WORK—THE TICKET CONSIDERED TO BE WEAK AT BOTH ENDS.

*Special Dispatch to the New-York Times.*

ST. LOUIS, June 29.—The opening of another day finds the Anti-Tilden element of the Democratic faithful now in St. Louis even more down-hearted and dejected than it was last night. It is true that the vehement expressions, the loud threats of the past few days are heard no more, but the very calmness and silence of the opposition is far more ominous than were the boisterous demonstrations of the past week. Almost without exception the men who opposed Tilden's nomination have followed John Kelly's example, and promised to do what they can for the ticket nominated. This means, of course, they will give it their support, but it means also that secretly they will rejoice at the Democratic defeat, which they feel and know is unavoidable. Naturally, the machine leaders, the men who made their living out of politics, no matter what their personal feelings may be, are now loud in their declaration of friendship for the very men who for a week past they have been denouncing as thieves and rascals. Of what advantage this kind of support will be to Mr. Tilden will be seen in November. Of course, the Governor's friends are doing everything in their power to stifle the voice of the opposition. To this end they still have brass bands parading through the streets and serenading the different delegations, and their followers are loud in their predictions of victory in November. An effort has even been made to hold a ratification meeting this evening, but the idea has been abandoned because a majority of the Western delegates have either gone or are going home by the afternoon trains. They go asserting their determination to do what they can for the ticket, but they do not deny that the work they have undertaken is exceeding difficult. Indeed, in the words of one sturdy representative from Indiana, they admit that they have a "hard row to hoe."

The nomination of Hendricks for the Vice Presidency has not tended to relieve or lessen the feeling of gloomy foreboding with which the announcement of Tilden was received by a large wing of the party. There is a general impression that whatever strength the one possesses is neutralized by the other. For instance it was claimed by Tilden's managers here that his hard-money principles would carry him in triumph through Connecticut, and possibly give him success in New-Hampshire and Massachusetts; but now they do not deny that the addition of Hendrick's name to the ticket takes from it whatsoever strength it might have had in that section, and all Hendricks' strength will not avail to overcome the bitter opposition to Tilden in the West. The ticket as a whole, in the opinion of one of the shrewdest politicians in the country, will be looked upon by the people as a piebald affair—the trick of a set of political wire-pullers, who hope to please all parties by placing a hard and soft money man on a platform which says and means nothing. Another claim made by the Tilden men was that a large majority of the German vote of the West and East would be cast for their candidate. Whatever there may have been in this claim, so far as it concerned Tilden, there can be no doubt that it loses all force now that the second place has been given to a soft money man. This fact will become all the more apparent when it is remembered that Gov. Tilden is a victim to a very serious paralytic affection, which might at any moment make it necessary for Hendricks to assume the duties of Chief Magistrate.

One serious result of the bitter Tilden and anti-Tilden war is worthy of mention. It will be remembered that McClernand, the incompetent and thick-headed President of yesterday's disorderly Convention, ordered the Sergeant at Arms to arrest and remove Hon. S. S. Cox, for the reason—as well as a disinterested spectator could judge—that he was not friendly to Tilden. This morning Mr. Cox met McClernand in the Lindell House, and, referring to his action of yesterday, denounced him as a sneak and a coward. This was too much for the great warrior of Vicksburg, and he was about to prove the truth of the assertion by striking his spirited little opponent, when friends interfered and prevented a general row. There is a strong impression here that such scenes as these will not tend to unite the ever-warring Democracy.

## HENDRICKS IN A STATE OF DOUBT.

HE REFUSES TO GIVE AN ANSWER UNTIL HE HAS CONFERRED WITH THE RETURNED DELEGATION—THE NOMINATION FALLS FLAT.

*Special Dispatch to the New-York Times.*

INDIANAPOLIS, June 29.—The nomination of Gov. Hendricks at St. Louis to the second place on the ticket has elicited quite as little enthusiasm as did that of Tilden yesterday. A few guns were fired two hours after the nomination was made, but no one seemed happy. The prominent representatives of the party are disinclined to talk about the situation, and although Mr. Hendricks receives all with his usual blandness, he manages to say nothing worth recording. At 10 o'clock this morning he was very positive that he would not accept the second place. At 1 o'clock he reiterated the same thing, with increased emphasis. From 9 last night until 4 this morning he was in constant receipt of telegrams begging him to accept the second place upon the ticket, which requests came from the delegate representatives of Tennessee, Pennsylvania, Kentucky, Missouri, New-York, Illinois, Massachusetts, Oregon, and Alabama, and were signed by such men as Birch. Clymer, and so on. The dispatch from Tennessee read, "We stood by you from first to last, and now ask you to stand by us;" a second one read, "Please accept. A Democrat must stand where put," and a third, "For God's sake, accept!" To all these a negative was returned; but this afternoon he began to weaken, and in reply to the question of acceptance he stated that he would take no action until after a conference with the Indiana delegation, which will arrive here in the morning. Later in the day a band was chartered for a serenade, and in a three minutes' reply he said he thought the nomination of Gov. Tilden would result successfully to the party. As for himself, he thanked his friends for the noble manner in which they had pressed his claims, but could not then say what he should do with the nomination given him. In an interview this evening he talked freely, but declined to commit himself until after a conference with his Indiana friends. It is very generally believed here, however, that he has no intention of doing anything else than accept. Hendricks never declines anything when his party demands acceptance. He has no other interest now than his party.

## THE PROCEEDINGS IN DETAIL.

The Convention was called to order at 10:20 A. M. The interest in the proceedings had evidently greatly abated, and many delegates had left, leaving their alternates. The galleries contained but few spectators. Prayer was offered by the Episcopal Bishop, Dr. Robertson.

NOMINATION OF HENDRICKS.

The Chair announced that the next business was the nomination of a Vice President. When Indiana was called for its nomination the State was greeted with much enthusiasm. Indiana failing to present a candidate some one from his seat in Illinois nominated Hendricks, when Mr. McDonald, of Indiana, rose and said:

MR. CHAIRMAN: Whenever we find ourselves brought face to face with a great responsibility I know no means of meeting it excepting we take counsel by our judgment and by our conscience. The mission of the delegation from Indiana to this Convention, so far at least as the name of Gov. Hendricks is concerned, was ended yesterday, when we had struggled from the time the canvass opened in this city until closed last evening to place him before the country for the office which, as much as any man in all the broad land, he was qualified to fill. The Convention saw proper to decide otherwise, and so far as that decision is concerned, we bow to the will of the Convention. The Democracy of Indiana has never yet suffered its flag to trail in the dust; has never lowered its standard to the common enemy. Whether we shall be able to comply with the wishes of the large and most respectable assemblage of Democrats in what we may be able to do in our State in the coming election is one of the questions of the future. I have already stated that the mission of the delegation of Indiana, so far as the name of Gov. Hendricks is concerned, ended on yesterday evening. We have no authority to say to this Convention that, if it sees proper to place his name upon the ticket, he will accept it; therefore, we do not propose to place ourselves in any false position upon that subject. When we say that, Mr. President, we do not say it because the office of Vice President is beneath him; it has been held by men more distinguished than he; more known to history, and whose patriotism has illuminated some of the brightest pages of history, and of the history of our own party. For myself, Mr. President, I can only say that upon that question the Convention must take the responsibility—[Loud and prolonged cheering, and cries of "Hendricks." All efforts on the part of the speaker to conclude his sentence were futile.]

Mr. Woodson, of Missouri—Mr. President, I feel extremely gratified on this occasion, that we are told by the delegate from Indiana that the responsibility of placing Gov. Hendricks in nomination for the second office in the gift of the American people has devolved upon this Convention. [Cheers.] The Missouri delegation have instructed me, as the representative of this great State, to say that Missouri is a unit, and we believe the entire Democratic Party of America will be a unit in support of Tilden and Hendricks. [Cheers.] Gov. Hendricks has no truer friend from his own native State, or one who was willing to stand by him longer than I. When his name was placed in nomination for the first office within the gift of this Convention I stood by him; but, gentlemen, if I was disappointed in the realization of my expectation, I this morning feel that I can rejoice when I remember that the distinguished reformer, the profound statesman, the honest man, Samuel J. Tilden has been nominated by this Convention. [Applause.] And now gentlemen, let me say this, place Samuel J. Tilden upon the ticket first, Thomas A. Hendricks next, [applause,] and then inscribe upon your banner under these names "retrenchment and reform and honest administration," and from Maine to California our flag will float in triumph next November. [Applause.] I second the nomination of Gov. Hendricks. [Applause.]

HENDRICKS NOMINATED BY ACCLAMATION.

Mr. Wallace, of Pennsylvania—The Pennsylvania delegation, in obedience to the willingness of Indiana that this Convention should take the responsibility of nominating Mr. Hendricks give their support to that gentleman. [Great applause.] With the Governor of New-York, Mr. Tilden, for President, and the Governor of Indiana, Mr. Hendricks, for Vice President, upon this ticket we will be triumphant in November. [Applause.] I arise, Sir, to move that this Convention by acclamation declare Thomas A. Hendricks the nominee for Vice President of the United States. [Great applause and waving of handkerchiefs and cheers.]

Mr. Steadman, of Ohio—The delegation from the State of Ohio had thought of offering the name of one of her distinguished sons for Vice President of the United States—Hon. Henry B. Payne. We, however, decline to present the name, and second the nomination of Thomas A. Hendricks. [Applause.]

Gov. Hardin, of Missouri—I send up a resolution to the Secretary, which I desire to have read.

The Secretary read it, as follows:

*Resolved*, That it is the duty of this Convention to select for Vice President one who is the peer of him who has been nominated for the Presidency—[cheers]—and believing that Hon. Thomas A. Hendricks, of Indiana, is the full measure of this position, and also that, in our judgment, it is his duty to serve his country and his party in this position, if nominated and elected, we therefore nominate him unanimously for that office.

Mr. Brown, of Tennessee, seconded Hendricks' nomination, which, he said, would [illegible]

# The New-York Times.

VOL. XXVI.......NO. 7858. NEW-YORK, MONDAY, NOVEMBER 20, 1876. PRICE FOUR CENTS.

## THE VICTORY IN THE NATION

### *NO DOUBT OF THE REPUBLICAN TRIUMPH.*

SOUTH CAROLINA VOTES FOR HAYES, NOTWITHSTANDING THE EFFORTS OF THE REBEL RIFLE CLUBS—AND THE REBEL SUPREME COURT AS WELL—FLORIDA SURE FOR THE REPUBLICANS—THE DEMOCRATS GIVING UP LOUISIANA.

The news from South Carolina this morning shows more clearly than before the extent of the Republican victory. Notwithstanding the efforts of the Tilden Democracy, and in the face of intimidation before and after the election, the Palmetto State, on the official count, gives Gov. HAYES a majority of nearly 1,000 votes. This result has been arrived at after the purely "ministerial" count demanded by the "shot-gun" Democracy and enforced by the Democratic majority of the Supreme Court. Not content with depriving the State Board of their judicial powers, the Democratic attorneys, when they found the result going against them, endeavored to exclude the members of the press from the sessions of the board, and otherwise prevent the fact of a Republican majority from becoming public. In Florida, where the same policy has been attempted, it is hourly becoming clearer that HAYES has a substantial majority in the total vote of the State. Additional returns from the Democratic counties in the backwoods districts reduce the Democratic claims to the most hopeless figures, and virtually give the State to HAYES. The Democratic leaders are despondent, and as a last resort are endeavoring to prevent the Governor from canvassing the electoral vote according to the law of the State. There is not the slightest chance for the success of the Democratic schemes, however, and Florida is as safe for Gov. HAYES as Vermont. In Louisiana the Democrats practically concede the State to the Republicans, and admit that, excluding the votes returned for them by the "bulldozing" process, they are hopelessly beaten. The visiting Republicans in New-Orleans replied on Saturday to the last letter of the Democratic delegation from the North, to the effect that they will be happy to confer at all times with the latter and to co-operate with them as individuals in whatever may seem right. They think, however, that the conference for purposes of joint action, proposed by the Democrats, is not only improper but is rendered unnecessary by the communication of the Returning Board inviting five representatives of each political party to be present at the counting of the vote. They conclude with reminding the Democrats that concerted action, on their part, with the view of influencing the action of the State authorities would be entirely unjustifiable and beyond their privilege. The reply is signed by Hon. John Sherman, Hon. Stanley Matthews, Hon. James A. Garfield, Hon. E. W. Stoughton, and seventeen others. The indications now are that the Tilden managers, finding themselves in a minority in the Electoral College, propose to try to buy their candidate into the Presidency. The effort will not succeed. RUTHERFORD B. HAYES has been elected President of the United States, and will undoubtedly be inaugurated on the 5th of March next.

### *THE SOUTH CAROLINA VICTORY.*

REVIEW OF THE SITUATION—THE MAJORITY OF THE REPUBLICAN STATE TICKET ELECTED ON THE FACE OF THE RETURNS—WHAT THE REPUBLICANS HOPE—THE SUPREME COURT AND ITS PROBABLE ACTION.

*By Telegraph from our Special Correspondent.*

COLUMBIA, Nov. 19.—Late last night the State Board of Canvassers completed the footing up of the returns for State officers, with the exception of Governor and Lieutenant Governor, and the result will be announced to-morrow. All the Republican ticket except J. R. Tolbert, for the office of Superintendent of Education, and T. C. Dunn, for the office of Controller General, is elected on the face of the returns, the majorities ranging from seven in the case of Mr. Elliott for Attorney General, to more than two hundred for the others. Tolbert and Dunn are defeated, if at all, by some of the returns giving wrong initials to their names, such as *F* for *T* in the case of Dunn, and *H* for *R* in the case of Tolbert. If the correction of these initials is permitted by the court, as always has been done heretofore, then the entire ticket is elected. As to the Governor and the Lieutenant Governor, the Board has heretofore been in the habit of aggregating the returns, no one objecting to it; but the Democrats insist that the Constitution of South Carolina requires the returns for these officers to be transmitted to the Legislature, and gives that body authority to declare who is elected. Not desiring to exercise any authority not clearly warranted by the law, the board will waive the count for these officers and send the returns to the Legislature, which meets on Tuesday week. It is known, however, and admitted by all, that the returns on their face will elect Wade Hampton Governor and R. H. Gleaves Lieutenant Governor, both Democrats.

As to the members of the Legislature, although the returns are not yet footed up, it is conceded that they will give the Democrats 64 Assemblymen, and the Republicans 60; and that the Senate will stand 18 Republicans to 15 Democrats, making a majority of one for the Democrats on joint ballot. The Board of Canvassers are required, however, to certify what Assemblymen and what Senators are elected, and they receive their certificates of election from the Secretary of State, on this certification by the board. Unless the decision of the Supreme Court, which is expected to-morrow, compels the board to abide by the returns as they appear on the face, they will not certify to the election of the five members of the Assembly from Edgefield County, where the election was so palpably fraudulent, and in that case the Democrats would not have a majority in either house of the Legislature.

It will, therefore, be seen that everything depends on the decision of the Court, and it is awaited with great anxiety by everybody. The Republicans hope, and many of them believe, that it will be favorable to those enlarged powers which the board has heretofore exercised without question; while the Democrats hope the contrary. Gov. Chamberlain considers that his only chance of retaining the office to which he has undoubtedly been elected, lies in a favorable decision of the court as to the powers of the Board of Canvassers. If such decision is rendered, the Republicans will undoubtedly get both branches of the Legislature, and will declare Gov. Chamberlain re-elected Governor, in which case Hampton can contest the seat, and every facility will be offered him to do so. If, however, the decision is the other way, Hampton will be declared Governor, and it remains to be seen whether Gov. Chamberlain will be permitted to contest.

A contest for the office of Governor can only be brought about by a joint resolution of both houses of the Legislature, and if the Democrats have the lower house it is not believed they will concur in such a resolution.

The Democrats of South Carolina, as Gov. Chamberlain remarked to-day—and he wished the fact to be noted by the people of the whole country—have placed themselves in the attitude of trying to prevent all investigation into the manner in which the late election was conducted in this State, while the Republicans have sought in every possible way, and will continue to seek, to throw light on the whole canvass. If by any means they can get an investigation, they say, they are willing to invite the whole North, of both parties, to witness it, and will gladly abide by the result. Gov. Chamberlain is confident that such an investigation would prove to every candid man that the entire Republican ticket, both electoral and State, was fairly elected by over eight thousand majority.

A good deal of nervousness and some apprehension exists among Republicans here as to what the decision of the court to-morrow will be. It is said that Chief Justice Moses is not friendly to Gov. Chamberlain, because of his refusal to issue a certificate of election to his son as Judge—a refusal for which he was highly complimented by the Democrats at the time. Should the decision be manifestly partisan and unfair, it is believed that the Board of Canvassers will refuse to obey the mandate of the court, and thus a new complication would arise. Many Republicans claim that any action in the premises by the Supreme Court was unwarranted by law, and that if they should render such a decision as the Democrats ask for, it would be a virtual usurpation of the powers of the Board of State Canvassers. Some apprehension exists also as to what will be the action of the Democrats in case Hampton is not declared Governor. Threats are reported to be frequently made that he shall be installed Governor at all hazards, or there will be another revolution here. It is not believed, however, that Hampton would sanction violent action. He has many Republican friends here who would like to see him Governor, but whose support he would lose if his Democratic supporters resorted to violence.

Ex-Attorney General Akerman, of Georgia, arrived here yesterday, and will give the Republicans the benefit of his legal advice in any action that it may be deemed proper to take as events transpire. There is need of legal talent here to assist the Republicans, as most of the eminent lawyers of the State are on the other side. Whatever difficulties may hereafter arise on the question of the Governorship, there is no longer doubt that South Carolina has given its electoral vote to Hayes and Wheeler.

THE STATE SHOWN TO BE REPUBLICAN BY NEARLY ONE THOUSAND MAJORITY ON THE FACE OF THE RETURNS—A COUNT WHICH NO ONE QUESTIONS.

*From Yesterday's Edition of the Times.*

COLUMBIA, Nov. 18.—It is definitely decided at last that the electoral vote of South Carolina was cast for Hayes and Wheeler in spite of shot-guns and barrels of money. The State Board of Canvassers completed the count of this vote at noon to-day, in the presence of eight chosen representatives of each party, admitted by resolution of the board at the suggestion of Judge Cartter and Congressman Tucker, and there is no complaint from any one that the count was not perfectly fair. After the count was completed, the board took a recess while the clerks were footing up the figures. On reassembling, the Chairman of the board, Mr. Hayne, directed the Clerk to announce the result, whereupon Haskell, Chairman of the Democratic Executive Committee of South Carolina, objected to reporters of the press being present to take the vote as declared. Gen. Conner, Democratic candidate for Attorney General also objected to the board announcing the result until the count of votes on the other tickets was completed and return made to the court. In reply, Mr. Hayne said this was not intended as an official announcement of the result, but merely for the information of the board. As to the reporters, they had been permitted to be present during the count, and he could see no reason why they should not hear the result. It could make no difference any way, as they were in possession of the figures, and could add them up for themselves. Gen. Connor took exception to the ruling of the Chairman. Mr. Hayne remarked that he was not aware that any of the parties who had been admitted on either side were here as counsel, but only as spectators or witnesses to the accuracy of the count. The result of the Electoral vote was then declared by the clerk as follows:

THE VOTE FOR ELECTORS.

| REPUBLICAN. | | DEMOCRATIC. | |
|---|---|---|---|
| *Electors at Large.* | | *Electors at Large.* | |
| C. C. Bowen | 91,786 | T. G. Barker | 90,896 |
| John Winsmith | 91,870 | Samuel McGowan | 90,7.7 |
| *District Electors.* | | *District Electors.* | |
| T. B. Johnson | 91,852 | J. W. Harrington | 90,895 |
| Timothy Hurley | 91,136 | J. I. Ingraham | 90,798 |
| W. B. Nash | 91,804 | William Wallace | 90,905 |
| Wilson Cook | 91,432 | J. B. Irwin | 90,9 6 |
| William F. Myers | 91,830 | Robert Aldrich | 90,860 |

The reason of Hurley running so much behind the other Electors is owing to a clerical error of the Inspectors of Election in Blackville, Barnwell County, who accidentally omitted his name in their return to the County Commissioners. Pending decision of the Supreme Court as to the power of the board to go behind the face of the returns, as forwarded by the County Commissioners, the board could not, of course, correct this clerical error, or any other; but if the decision shall be in their favor, they will be able to show beyond any question that the majority of the Republican electoral ticket, instead of averaging 900, is nearer 3,000. The Democrats residing here appear to be much better satisfied with the result as announced by the board than the men sent down from the North to count the State in for Tilden.

All the South Carolina Democrats here hoped for was the election of Hampton, and it is probable that this is secured, provided the board shall not be permitted to go back of the face of the returns. If Edgefield County, where 2,000 more votes were returned than there are voters, should be thrown out of the count, or the returns corrected in accordance with the facts, the whole Republican State ticket will be elected, with a Republican majority in the Legislature. The decision of the court on the powers of the board in this regard is expected on Monday.

### *REPUBLICAN FLORIDA.*

THE GOOD NEWS CONTINUED—DEMOCRATIC COUNTIES WITH SMALLER MAJORITIES THAN ESTIMATED—REPUBLICANS SECURING EVIDENCE OF FRAUDS ON THE BALLOT—LAST HOPE OF THE DESPERATE DEMOCRACY.

*Special Dispatch to the New-York Times.*

TALLAHASSEE, Nov. 19.—The general situation remains unchanged, and the intense excitement of the past week continues unabated. The official returns from four more counties, all Democratic, have been received, and the majorities fall below the previous estimates, showing conclusively that the Republican claim of a good majority has been well founded. As the Democrats gradually lose faith in their own estimates, and find the frauds committed by their tools in many counties being exposed, they grow more desperate and bitter. Hon. W. W. Hicks, a prominent leader of the Republican Party, and a member of Gov. Stearns' Cabinet, was publicly assaulted on the streets in Jacksonville to-day for his opinions and labors during the campaign, and the lives of other Republican leaders are threatened. Nothing but the presence of the United States troops preserves the public peace. Tallahassee is full of Democratic politicians from New-York, Philadelphia, and other Northern cities, in addition to many from Georgia and Alabama. Michael Bannon, a well-known Democratic politician of Baltimore, who has been here for several days under an assumed name, left for home yesterday, disgusted with the situation. It will be a week or more before all the returns are in. Meanwhile, the Republicans, assisted by Gen. Barlow, Judge Robertson, and Assistant District Attorney D. G. Rollins, of New-York, are hard at work securing evidence of fraud already committed, and preparing to defeat the frauds which may be attempted in the future. Ex-Gov. E. F. Noyes, of Ohio, Hon. John A. Kasson, of Iowa, and Gen. Lew Wallace, of Indiana, will arrive here to-morrow. Perry H. Smith, a notorious Democratic politician of Chicago, who went to Milwaukee before the election to place Tilden's money where it would do the most good, will arrive here to-morrow to reinforce John T. Coyle, Sam. Bard, and other notorious Democratic outsiders.

A question has arisen whether the Governor is to canvass the Presidential vote, under the act of 1847, or the State Canvassing Board, under the act of 1872. The Democrats have asked permission to submit an argument on the question, and the Governor has requested them to do so. The question is not very material, as the majority of the Canvassing Board, as well as the Governor, are Republicans.

It has leaked out that any amount of money is on hand from patriotic Democrats from abroad for the man or men who will dispose of the nation's hope and right in this supreme hour of peril. It is safe to notify the gambling fraternity of patriots that the Republican Party of Florida does not contain the man. Conceding the State to Hayes, certain knowing Democrats resort to significant winks and shrugs to give emphasis to their assurance that one man can be found in 185 Electors to whom a fortune will prove more valuable than a good name and a good conscience.

ANOTHER DEMOCRATIC MANIFESTO.

*Dispatch from the Democratic Agent of the Associated Press.*

TALLAHASSEE, Nov. 19.—There is reasonable ground for believing that Gov. Stearns, of this State, will assume that the State Board has no power to canvass the electoral vote, but that that power resides in the Governor. This assumption will permit the Governor to decide all issues pertaining to the canvass, and to issue his certificate to whichever set of Electors he decides are elected. His assumption is based upon the fact that the act creating the Returning Board does not use the word "Electors" in giving the list of officers whose vote the board shall canvass. The power to canvass this vote not being specifically conferred upon the board, the power, he contends, resides in him, as he is required by a United States law to issue the Electors' certificates, and must canvass the vote in order that he may decide who is entitled to certificates. The Democrats are very much astonished that this claim should have been set up, and contend that the word "Electors" is not used in the act referred to, simply because Electors are included under the head of State officers, which expression is used in the act. The Democratic committee waited on the Governor and notified him that if he contemplated such a step, they should ask permission to file a protest. He stated that they should have an opportunity to do so, and this morning informed them by letter that he should be pleased if they would forward in writing whatever they had to say upon the subject. This is considered an intimation that he intends to move in the matter without delay. Elaborate opinions are being prepared on both sides of this question.

There is some movement ordered in military circles to-night; precisely what it is cannot be ascertained. It is supposed that troops are going to some of the contested counties.

### *LOUISIANA CONCEDED TO HAYES.*

THE STATE GIVEN UP BY THE DEMOCRATS—DISGRACEFUL ACTION OF SOME OF TILDEN'S EMISSARIES—DECENT DEMOCRATS LEAVING IN DISGUST—A WARNING IN REGARD TO FLORIDA—THE DEMOCRACY'S LAST HOPE—FULL DETAILS OF THE SITUATION—LOUISIANA SURE FOR HAYES AND THE WHOLE REPUBLICAN TICKET.

*By Telegraph from Our Special Correspondent.*

NEW-ORLEANS, Nov. 19.—The prominent Northern Democrats who came to Louisiana at the request of Messrs. Tilden and Hewitt are going home disheartened and disgusted. They see that Gov. Hayes has undoubtedly carried the State, and many of them are unwilling to give countenance to any attempt which may be made to defraud the Republicans out of the fruits of their honest victory. In the meantime, the politicians who remain here are beginning to talk a great deal about a compromise, and this morning a number of them tried to make some kind of terms with Mr. Packard. Both he and Gov. Kellogg, however, positively refused to listen to any plan of adjustment other than that which can be based upon a fair count of the votes. The proposition to which I refer was not definitely made, still it was very plainly intimated to Packard that he could be Governor without trouble if he would agree to have Tilden counted in by the Returning Board. The ex-Marshal replied that he had no influence with the board; that it was composed of honorable gentlemen who would do their duty honestly and fairly, and that even if he could control them he would decline to do so. I am informed, upon the very best authority, that plans of compromise, similar to the above, were made last night to at least one member of the Returning Board. He indignantly refused to listen to them, and in the name of himself and his colleagues protested against any further attempts to influencing the action of the board. It is but justice to state that Gen. Nicholls, the Democratic candidate for Governor, is not a party to any of these schemes. They were all concocted by friends of Mr. Tilden, who were willing to sacrifice the claims of all the State offices in order to secure the triumph of the great "reformer." Failing in these efforts, however, and seeing that they can never hope to honestly secure Louisiana's vote for their chief, they have now virtually abandoned New-Orleans, and are preparing to devote all their attention to Florida. In three days there will be a score or more of prominent Democrats in Tallahassee, and they go prepared to use every means known to the lowest politician to capture a majority in that State.

The leaders of the Republican Party should be warned in time. They must not neglect Florida. The Democrats are concentrating all their forces there, and they mean to defeat the will of the majority in that State, no matter what it may cost to do so. Florida has undoubtedly gone Republican by a majority of several hundred, but the Republicans must not be secure in their victory. Their opponents are desperate, and they must be watched closely.

As to Louisiana, there is no doubt. There need be no anxiety. Upon a fair count the State will give Hayes a majority of at least 6,000, and a fair count will certainly be had.

The canvass before the State Board commences to-morrow, in the presence of five prominent members of the Republican Party, and five well-known Democrats. The committee to represent the latter party has already been announced. On the part of the Republicans, Senator Sherman, Mr. Stoughton, of New-York, and Gen. Garfield, of Ohio, will attend the meeting.

Of the fifty-seven parishes in the State, forty have been officially heard from. They show a Republican majority of from seven to eight thousand. There will be contests in regard to at least twelve and perhaps twenty parishes, but they will not come up until the districts in which there is no contest have been disposed of. This is in accordance with the State election laws. The count of the uncontested parishes will be finished in about three days, and then the disputed ones will be considered. It is thought that they can be gone through within seven days, and that by the 1st of December an official announcement of the vote for President and Vice President can be made.

Both sides are now busy preparing testimony which is to be submitted in regard to the contested parishes. Chief among these are East and West Feliciana. In both these districts the Republicans have a majority of at least 1,000 votes; yet at the last election, as has already been announced, there was only one Republican vote cast in East Feliciana, and only twenty in West Feliciana. In this connection it has been noted that the full voting strength of both of the parishes was polled on the last election day, and the Democrats pointed to this fact as an indication that they had allowed the negroes to vote peacefully, and that they had all voted the Democratic ticket. The Republicans will be able to show before the board that this story is entirely unworthy of credit, and they will prove, by the sworn testimony of dozens of trustworthy witnesses, that the negroes in the parishes named were forcibly prevented from voting; that they were violently drawn away from the polls, and that hundreds of armed white men rode across the border from Mississippi and voted the Democratic ticket in their places and on their names. Overwhelming proofs of similar practices in other parishes are now ready, and will be produced at the proper time.

Regarding the difference in the vote for the National and State tickets, it now seems that the Republicans have been somewhat in error. At first it was announced, as will be remembered, that Gov. Hayes had run at least twenty-five hundred votes ahead of the State ticket. It was definitely ascertained yesterday, however, that the difference would not be more than eight hundred. Some of the Presidential Electors fall several hundred votes behind the others. In West Baton Rouge, for instance, where the negro State Senator Allain was running an independent ticket, he failed to print the names of two of the Hayes Electors. In this way they lost at least one thousand votes. The Democrats are attempting to make capital out of this unfortunate circumstance, by declaring that no matter what might be the result of the canvass for electors at large, these two District Electors have been defeated. They might have been if they did not have a majority of eight thousand to draw upon.

To-night the Democratic Campaign Committee is circulating what purports to be a copy of the official returns from forty-eight parishes, with nine estimated. According to their figures, the majority for two of Mr. Tilden's electors is 9,249, and for the other three 9,036. Of course the Democrats know that this is an absurd one. Their circular was prepared to influence the public mind at the North, and for no other purpose.

A nice question regarding the legality of the Returning Board, which was raised here yesterday, is worthy of a passing notice. It will be remembered that the board was created by the same Legislature that elected Pinchback to the United States Senate. He was refused his seat on the ground that the Legislature was not properly and legally organized. Now he claims that if the Returning Board is recognized as a legal body, he should be seated. Of course, his claim is simply another bid for notoriety. It is laughed at by all the lawyers here. H. C.

*Dispatch to the Associated Press.*

The following named gentlemen have left the city: Oswald Ottendorfer and F. R. Coudert, of New-York; C. W. Woolsey, of Connecticut, Gen. J. E. McDonald and J. Coleman, of Indiana; ex-Gov. J. Lee Carroll and W. F. Hamilton, of Maryland; ex-Gov. A. G. Curtin, of Pennsylvania; W. Chapman, of Iowa; Charles Gibson, of Missouri; Hon. W. R. Morrison, of Illinois; J. B. Jeffreys and W. K. Sullivan, of Chicago.

The gentlemen who are here at the request of the President, and also those sent by the Republican organizations of States other than Louisiana, say that they have determined to secure a full stenographic report of all the proceedings of and evidence given before the Returning Board, so that an impartial statement may be given to the public and sent to the President. They have also determined to change their committee of five from time to time, in order that all of them may observe the mode of proceeding and the appearance and character of the witnesses examined.

### *A SOUTHERN POLITICAL DOCUMENT.*

THE SORT OF ARGUMENTS USED BY THE DEMOCRATS IN SOUTH CAROLINA—A CHEERFUL THING TO FIND ON ONE'S DOOR-STEP.

Peaceable and law-abiding people, accustomed only to the peaceful, if noisy, methods of conducting a political campaign in the North, have some difficulty in understanding the deadly violence and furious passion which mark nearly every heated campaign in some of the Southern States. The subjoined letter may do something to open their eyes. The "warning No. 2" referred to in this choice specimen of political literature, and found inclosed in it, is a loaded rifle cartridge of fifty calibre, which is a very ugly missile to have shot at one, as the experienced know. A slip of paper was wrapped around the copper shell, scribbled over with something which looks like "not be long in coming." This cheerful missive was intended for Gov. Chamberlain, of South Carolina, and was thrown into what the writer evidently thought was his front garden, but it happened to be the garden of his next-door neighbor. The package was picked up by one of the children. Such an incident at the North would indicate little more than that the writer of the letter was some crazy idiot; but down South, where the shot-gun policy rules, such messages are apt to mean something. The following is the letter:

[Leave S C or die.]

*To His Honor Gov D. H. Chamberlain*

Please find enclosed warning No. 2. No. 3 will be a winding sheet & befor thirty days after warning No. 3, will come warning No. 4. which will be an end of Daniel H. Chamberlain. As you cannot be Gov of S C & wants to be a Gov we had I will have compassion on you & make you Gov of Hell where you can practice all your hellish games without having to to transport you else where as I hate you so much. if you were to go to heaven, & I knew it, I would go to hell to get rid of the Damnedest Villan the Devil ever made. If you leave S C in thirteen days after No. 4, all good and well if not take the consequences. I do not wish to stain my hands with blood of the blackest villand I ever saw. That is my reasons for sending you this warning. [Leave S C or die.]

### *MOVEMENTS OF TROOPS.*

FOUR COMPANIES OF THE FOURTH ARTILLERY IN WASHINGTON—RETICENCE OF THE ARMY OFFICERS.

*Special Dispatch to the New-York Times.*

WASHINGTON, Nov. 19.—Four companies of the Fourth Artillery arrived here this morning, direct from South Carolina, and are now quartered at the Arsenal. They number two hundred and fifty men, are under the command of Capt. Loder, and come here in pursuance of orders from Gen. Sherman. None of the officers of Gen. Sherman's staff knew of their coming, and profess ignorance of their future movements. On Monday night last Gen. Sherman sent Col. Bacon, of his staff, to South Carolina with sealed orders for Capt. Loder to move his command to Washington without delay. Upon receiving his orders Capt. Loder put the four companies in immediate motion for Norfolk, at which point they were embarked on a steamer for this city, and landed at the arsenal to-day, where preparations for quartering them had already been made. The arrival of a detachment of United States soldiers has caused considerable excitement, or rather curiosity, since it has been denied for two days by many prominent officers of the Government that any troops had been ordered here or elsewhere, and a statement of that denial was telegraphed to all parts of the country yesterday. Two or three Cabinet officers spoken to this evening did not known that the soldiers were here, or were coming, and Secretary Cameron this evening, in company where there was no need of concealment, made no mention of the affair. So far as appears from information accessible to-night, no one but Gen. Sherman knew of the movement, but that is hardly possible. It is reported that arrangements have been made at the arsenal to receive two regiments of infantry, which would be seven or eight hundred men, and it is quite probable that a thousand men, or at least two regiments, are to be brought here. It may be, on the other hand, that the preparations and movements are merely casual and temporary, as one officer of the Cabinet expresses the opinion they are. But while no explanation is made by the President or Gen. Sherman of the purpose of the movement, which is doubtless very simple and usual, there will be an attempt to treat the affair as mysterious and strange. A report prevails to-night that the three companies now on the way East from Forts Riley and Fetterman are also to be quartered at Washington instead of New-York.

### *THE ELECTORAL COLLEGE.*

SENSATIONAL STORIES ABOUT MR. SOLLACE, OF VERMONT—THE REPORTED INELIGIBILITY OF A RHODE ISLAND ELECTOR DISPOSED OF.

*Special Dispatch to the New-York Times.*

BURLINGTON, Nov. 19.—The dispatches sent from Montpelier and Boston to yesterday's papers concerning the Sollace case were entirely sensational. Democratic letters do not claim that Aldrich, the Democratic Elector, is chosen instead of Sollace. No notice has been served upon the County Clerks claiming that votes cast for Sollace were illegal. Possibly Judge Smalley may issue an injunction restraining the County Clerks from declaring the election of more than four Electors; but this is mere surmise, and such action is not generally expected. B. B. Smalley, son of the Judge and Clerk of the United States Court, says, to-day, that no request has thus far been made to his father to issue an injunction:

PROVIDENCE, Nov. 19.—Gov. Lippitt, yesterday, received the following telegram from Gen. Sickles:

NEW-YORK, Nov. 18.

*To Gov. Lippitt:*

It is reported here, on the authority of William Beach Lawrence, that one of the Republican Electors of Rhode Island is ineligible, and that the law of your State gives the office to the person having the highest vote, who is qualified. Lawrence claims to be elected himself. D. E. SICKLES.

To this Gov. Lippitt replied:

Our State laws provide for all contingencies in the case of vacancies from any cause in the Electoral College. This State will give four votes for Hayes and Wheeler. H. LIPPITT.

The only occasion for this correspondence is the fact that Hon. George H. Corliss, Elector elect, is a Centennial Commissioner appointed by the President on the nomination of the Governor.

### *THE VOTE OF NEW-YORK.*

The following table gives the majorities for Hayes and Tilden and for Morgan and Robinson, respectively, in the several counties of the State:

| Counties. | Hayes. | Tilden. | Morgan. | Robinson. |
|---|---|---|---|---|
| Albany | .... | 1,179 | .... | 1,314 |
| Allegany | 2,993 | .... | 3,006 | .... |
| Broome | 1,343 | .... | 1,282 | .... |
| Cattaraugus | 1,604 | .... | 1,538 | .... |
| Cayuga | 2,856 | .... | 2,609 | .... |
| Chautauqua | 4,380 | .... | 4,339 | .... |
| Chemung | .... | 498 | .... | 881 |
| Chenango | 1,348 | .... | 1,265 | .... |
| Clinton | 706 | .... | 681 | .... |
| Columbia | .... | 510 | .... | 450 |
| Cortland | 1,386 | .... | 1,312 | .... |
| Delaware | 595 | .... | 534 | .... |
| Dutchess | 398 | .... | 520 | .... |
| Erie | 767 | .... | 686 | .... |
| Essex | 1,522 | .... | 1,451 | .... |
| Franklin | 1,158 | .... | 1,121 | .... |
| Fulton | 278 | .... | 255 | .... |
| Genesee | 1,001 | .... | 1,007 | .... |
| Greene | .... | 1,093 | .... | 1,176 |
| Hamilton | .... | 247 | .... | 245 |
| Herkimer | 753 | .... | 660 | .... |
| Jefferson | 2,133 | .... | 2,031 | .... |
| Kings | .... | 18,518 | .... | 15,817 |
| Lewis | .... | 98 | .... | 137 |
| Livingston | 1,023 | .... | 1,091 | .... |
| Madison | 1,922 | .... | 1,819 | .... |
| Monroe | 1,611 | .... | 1,477 | .... |
| Montgomery | .... | 301 | .... | 312 |
| New-York | .... | 53,155 | .... | 51,405 |
| Niagara | .... | 315 | .... | 340 |
| Oneida | 1,175 | .... | 1,071 | .... |
| Onondaga | 3,707 | .... | 3,483 | .... |
| Ontario | 805 | .... | 677 | .... |
| Orange | .... | 346 | .... | 345 |
| Orleans | 1,136 | .... | 1,089 | .... |
| Oswego | 2,812 | .... | 2,752 | .... |
| Otsego | .... | 168 | .... | 265 |
| Putnam | 144 | .... | 152 | .... |
| Queens | .... | 3,024 | .... | 2,843 |
| Rensselaer | .... | 877 | .... | 928 |
| Richmond | .... | 1,453 | .... | 1,285 |
| Rockland | .... | 1,137 | .... | 1,167 |
| St. Lawrence | 7,681 | .... | 7,615 | .... |
| Saratoga | 991 | .... | 876 | .... |
| Schenectady | .... | 238 | .... | 291 |
| Schoharie | .... | 1,776 | .... | 1,789 |
| Schuyler | 665 | .... | 512 | .... |
| Seneca | .... | 537 | .... | 685 |
| Steuben | 939 | .... | 835 | .... |
| Suffolk | .... | 215 | .... | 213 |
| Sullivan | .... | 1,134 | .... | 1,067 |
| Tioga | 160 | .... | 110 | .... |
| Tompkins | 1,004 | .... | 913 | .... |
| Ulster | .... | 1,722 | .... | 1,672 |
| Warren | 473 | .... | 449 | .... |
| Washington | 2,469 | .... | 2,363 | .... |
| Wayne | 1,682 | .... | 1,834 | .... |
| Westchester | .... | 2,460 | .... | 2,466 |
| Wyoming | 1,168 | .... | 1,127 | .... |
| Yates | 1,264 | .... | 1,183 | .... |
| Total | 28,870 | 60,861 | 36,134 | [illegible] |

Tilden's majority, 31,991. Robinson's majority, 30,843.

### *THE CENTENNIAL EXHIBITION.*

PHILADELPHIA, Nov. 19.—At a meeting of the Board of Directors of the Permanent Exhibition Company, held yesterday, a partial organization was effected by the appointment of Clement M. Biddle as President, and H. A. Rollins as Treasurer. The general features of the proposed rearrangement of space in the Main Building were discussed, and plans showing the portions to be occupied by the principal sections were presented and partly perfected. The cash admissions to the grounds on Saturday numbered 563. Lieut. Gen. Saigo Izoubamichi, Vice-President of the Japanese Centennial Commission, leaves for San Francisco to-morrow, en route to Japan.

## THE MISSISSIPPI TERROR.

### *WHAT MISSISSIPPIANS WRITE.*

SENATOR BRUCE AND POSTMASTER PEASE ON THE LATE ELECTION—THE TERROR IN AMITE, LOWNDES, YAZOO, AND MADISON COUNTIES—LETTER FROM A MISSISSIPPI WOMAN—THE MASSACRE OF OKTIBBEHA—APPEALS FROM MISSISSIPPI TO THROW OUT HER ELECTORAL VOTE.

*From an Occasional Correspondent.*

WASHINGTON, Saturday, Nov. 18.

I.

Senator Bruce and ex-Senator Pease, of Mississippi, are here. Both of them say that the recent "victory" of the Democracy in Mississippi was characterized by fraud and terrorism as universal and as unblushing as the infamous election of 1875. They say that an official investigation will show that there was no pretense of a free or fair election. They will be heard from again.

In the meantime, I desire to make extracts from three letters just received from Mississippi, and to explain some statements in them.

II.

A prominent and influential lawyer of Mississippi, under date of Nov. 14, thus writes in a private letter to a friend in Washington:

"The election in this State was a stupendous fraud and shame. It may be, and doubtless is true, that Rutherford B. Hayes is elected President, even counting this State for Tilden; and that, as far as the electoral result goes, the vote of Mississippi will make no difference. Yet aside from and above this fact, is a dangerous principle that is sought to be established by recognizing, even indirectly, the vote of Mississippi as a legitimate vote, by consenting to count it at all. Republicans here do protest, and the lovers of liberty everywhere should protest against this recognition of the right of an organized ruffianism to decide the destiny of a State or nation. Thus to sanction it is to offer a reward to those who, by force and by bloodshed, are seeking to crush out Republicanism in the South.

It is almost tragical to us here to read in the Northern papers that there was an election in this State, and about the Democratic majority here, and to think that a nation, proud of its liberty, should even think of counting the electoral votes of Mississippi, when we here know that the pretended result was the fruit of terrorism and intimidation and bloodshed: when we know that every honest and intelligent Democrat in Mississippi never pretends, *here*, to deny that if the election had been a fair one, Hayes and Wheeler would have received a majority of at least 30,000, instead of being 60,000 for Tilden.

It makes every thoughtful man say—especially those who must submit to the great wrong—that America is no longer a free Government if her loyal citizens cannot be better protected.

III.

You know that I was born, raised and educated in the South, and stood by her in her days of darkness and danger. But I cannot and I will not follow again her violent men of to-day, knowing them to be the same—knowing their purpose to be the same—which led, nay, *drove* the South to ruin in 1860. They are not leading, but driving the people in the same way now; and if the Government does not interpose, the people will be driven as in 1860.

Self-preservation will force even negroes to take up arms against the Government, against his will, just as it now does to put a Democratic ballot in the box *against his will*; nay, stronger, to save his life. Republicans South, especially the black men of the party, must be protected by the Government, else they will go with the men of 1860, who are again upon the rampage, and who protect all who go with them with the same earnestness that they persecute and murder those who oppose them. Who can blame them if, to save their lives, or to be able to sleep in their cabins in safety they go with the Democracy!

IV.

The election here was a medley of tragedy, comedy, and farce. When, in the canvass, and at the polls, in any part of the State, men were shot down like dogs; when they were taken from their homes, and flogged and hung for opinion's sake, it assumed the dignity of a tragedy. And the campaign was full of such tragedies.

It was a comedy when ignorant black men were given apparently regular Republican tickets, with the likenesses of our candidates and their names, and then the Democratic Electors at the bottom of the ticket, and these were counted Democratic.

It was a farce when Democratic roughs were intrusted all night with ballot boxes and the keys to the same 'to see that all was fair' and that 'there was no cheatings,' or when the boxes were not opened before 2 o'clock in the afternoon, and often as late as 4 P. M., and then there remained just time enough to vote Democrats—who took charge. And this election was made still more of a farce than any that are put on the stages of the Washington or New-York theatres when, at Democratic head-quarters, it was determined and carried out that no white Republican should be appointed a Judge at an election, and no black man *who could read or write*; and when, at heavy Republican voting precincts, clerks delayed the voting so that three-fourths of the Republicans did not and could not vote.

V.

Then again it was a combination of all three when we read the returns from Yazoo—with *two Republican votes*—a county which, at a fair election, would have given a Republican majority of 2,500; and when we read that Madison County gave seventeen Republican votes—which, at a free election, would have given 2,000 Republican majority. It was the same in Lowndes; while the chivalrous county of Amite bears the banner with *not one Republican vote*. From other counties come the same news.

VI.

Let us pause a minute here. Yazoo County contains a white population of 4,884, and a black population of 12,395. This gives a black majority of 7,511. It gave Grant in 1872, a vote of 2,433, and Greeley 922. In 1869 the same relative proportion was maintained. It gave Alcorn (Republican) 2,642 votes, and Dent (Democratic) 815. The lesser Democratic vote in 1869 was probably owing to the fact that at that time a considerable number of the whites were disqualified as voters from their participation in the rebellion. Dent, the Democratic candidate, was a brother-in-law of President Grant, and he was expressly imported into the State by the Democracy—although he had never lived there, and did not mean to live there, and did not own a foot of soil there—in order to defeat Alcorn, the Republican candidate, who had lived in the State from his boyhood, had always been a conspicuous politician, and was one of the largest slave and land-owners in Mississippi. When the Democracy denounce the carpet-baggers of Mississippi in the North, they always remember to forget the name of Dent. In 1873 Ames ran against Alcorn. Ames was the regular Republican candidate. Alcorn had made an excellent Governor, honestly enforced the rights of the blacks, and shown that he was entitled to their support by his honorable action. But he made war against Ames, and Ames made war against him, and Alcorn became not the Democratic but the opposition candidate. What was the result? Ames, in 1873, polled 2,469 votes, and Alcorn only 617. There was an honest and full vote. The falling off that Alcorn suffered from the previous Democratic vote was owing to the support of men like Gen. Chalmers, who advocated the claims of Ames—as the "Fort Pillow hero" has recently said—in order to consolidate the black vote and thereby ruin the Republican Party, which, in his judgment, Alcorn's policy would have permanently estab-

# The New-York Times.

VOL. XXVI.......NO. 7939. | NEW-YORK, WEDNESDAY, JANUARY 31, 1877. | PRICE FOUR CENTS.


## WASHINGTON.

### THE ORGANIZATION OF THE ELECTORAL TRIBUNAL.

MESSRS. PAYNE, HUNTON, ABBOTT, GARFIELD, AND HOAR CHOSEN TO REPRESENT THE HOUSE—MR. GARFIELD COMPLIMENTED BY RECEIVING THE SMALLEST NUMBER OF DEMOCRATIC VOTES—THE SENATE'S CHOICE—THE NAME OF THE FIFTH JUDGE NOT YET ANNOUNCED.

*Special Dispatch to the New-York Times.*

WASHINGTON, Jan. 30.—At 1 o'clock to-day the House proceeded formally to choose five of their number to serve on the Electoral Commission created by the act passed last week. Mr. Lamar nominated Messrs. Payne, Hunton, Abbott, Garfield, and Hoar, and in order to save time, moved that as each member's name was called he should vote for the five candidates named. This was opposed by those Democrats who desired to cut Mr. Garfield, and who wanted to have a separate vote for each candidate. Mr. Lamar's motion was carried on a division, the vote standing 220 to 20. Mr. Abbott's name is the first on the roll, and when called he voted for all the candidates except himself. Until Mr. Blackburn's name was called all voted for the five candidates named, but that gentleman led the break which gave Garfield the distinction of receiving 24 Democratic votes less than were given for Mr. Hoar. The following named Democrats dropped Garfield, voting only for four candidates: Blackburn, of Kentucky; Cate, of Wisconsin; Cochrane, of Pennsylvania; Ross, of New-Jersey; Davis, of North Carolina; Ellis, of Louisiana, and Hurd, Poppleton, Rice, Southard, Vance and Walling, of Ohio. Buckner, of Missouri; Candler, of Arkansas, and Smith, of Georgia, substituted McCrary for Garfield. Cooke and Hartridge, of Georgia; Hereford, of West Virginia; Roberts, of Maryland, and Hopkins, of Pennsylvania, substituted Foster. Rankin, of Maryland, and John Reilly, of Pennsylvania, substituted Willard. Terry, of Virginia, dropped Garfield for Townsend, of New-York, and Townsend returned the compliment by dropping Payne and naming Terry. On the Republican side Hoge created laughter by voting for Mills, Singleton, and Blackburn, all of whom opposed the Electoral bill. Magoon dropped Payne for Lynde, and Wells, of Mississippi, named Wood for Hunton. Mr. Hoar received the highest vote, 264; Payne, Hunton, and Abbott each received 263; Garfield, 240; Foster, 5; McCrary, 3; Willard, 2, and Wood and Townsend of New-York, Terry, Lynde, Mills, Singleton, and Blackburn, each, 1. After the first 30 names had been called little interest was manifested in the election, which occupied one and a half hours. The galleries were crowded during the proceedings. The number of Democrats who declined to vote for Garfield or substituted some other name was six, greater than the number of Democrats who voted against the bill in the House, and the six who voted against him were among those who voted against the bill. The spirit of the opposition in the caucus was carried into the House by a *set* of men and in a manner that made it extremely ridiculous, and a high compliment to Mr. Garfield.

The Senate elected its members of the Electoral Committee at 3:20 o'clock without any incident whatever. Senators Edmunds, Frelinghuysen, Morton, Thurman, and Bayard were unanimously elected, and all by the same vote. No one could have perceived in the voting, or by action of any Senator, that there had been the least disturbance of the serenity of Senators in the caucuses yesterday that made the choice of those voted for to-day.

The four Justices of the Supreme Court named in the Electoral bill—Justices Clifford, Miller, Field, and Strong—met to-day, as required by law, to select a fifth Justice to complete the full number required upon the commission. Strange to say, it is not positively known whom they selected, but the almost unanimous understanding and belief is that the choice fell upon Justice Bradley. There are certain persons who ought to know what the Justices did, if there has been any revelation from inside the consultation room, but they all say they have no positive information; but they all believe that the fifth Justice is Mr. Bradley. The reason that the fact is not positively revealed is, that by an understanding or agreement of the committee the Justices were not to let their action be known till both houses had selected their members of the commission. This was a wise precaution to prevent the choice of a Justice from influencing the voting in either house. A determination of secrecy means something in the Supreme Court; therefore, when the fifth Justice was chosen, a written and sealed communication was prepared, conveying [illegible]

[illegible]

deem fit another of the Associate Justices of said court, which five persons shall be members of said commission."

### THE WORK OF THE TRIBUNAL.

THE PREPARATIONS FOR COUNTING THE VOTES COMPLETE—STATES THAT WILL BE CONTESTED—THE QUESTION OF GOING BEHIND THE RETURNS THE ALL IMPORTANT ONE TO BE DECIDED.

*Special Dispatch to the New-York Times.*

WASHINGTON, Jan. 30.—The two houses having formally elected their members of the Electoral Commission and provided for appointing tellers, and the four Justices having chosen a fifth, the entire commission is now formed and the preparations for beginning the counting of the votes on the day after to-morrow are complete, so far as preparations are required by law. The two Houses will meet together at 1 o'clock on Thursday, and the President of the Senate will immediately begin the opening of the certificates. The first State from which returns will be presented, under the law requiring the States to be taken alphabetically, is Alabama. It is probable that an objection will be made to the counting of the vote from that State on the ground of the existence of fraud, violence, and intimidation in the canvass sufficient to prevent a free and fair expression of the popular will. This objection, signed by a member of the House and a Senator, will compel an immediate separation of the two houses. Of course, the House will vote to overrule the objection, and what the Senate will decide is uncertain and unimportant so far as the result is concerned, because both houses under the law have to concur to sustain an objection to counting a vote, and therefore Alabama will be counted for Tilden by the action of the House alone. Colorado is the fourth State on the list, but it is not now probable that any objection will be raised against its vote by the Democrats, because it is not known that any Senator would unite with a member of the House in objecting that Colorado is not a State. There are some members of the House willing to object, but it would be useless. The vote will then, on Thursday, be counted down through the list—Alabama, Arkansas, California, Colorado, Connecticut, and Delaware. The next State is Florida, and from this State there are two returns, and they will be sent at once to the commission, and the two houses will resume their usual course of business till the commission is ready to advise how Florida shall be counted. At this point there will undoubtedly be a delay till next week; at least a decision this week would be unexpected, and could only be reached by cutting short the hearing of counsel and the consideration of any evidence except such as the certificates show on their faces. The only returns which can come before the Commission are from the States of Florida, Louisiana, Oregon, and South Carolina, as these are the only States from which there are double returns in the hands of the President of the Senate. Alabama and Mississippi were expected to send returns of the Republican Electors, but it appears that none have been received. The next State to be referred after Florida is Louisiana.

The great question which the commission have first to decide, a question far greater and of vastly more importance than how Florida and Louisiana have cast their votes in the present election, is whether they will go behind the returns and enter upon an examination of the number of votes cast in the States for the Presidential Electors. This question should never have been submitted to any tribunal except the Supreme Court as a court. Indeed, it should never have been raised before any court. It suggests more peril to the Republic than any power ever claimed under the Constitution, save alone the claim of the right of a State to withdraw from the Union. If the commission should decide to count the votes in Florida and Louisiana, no election of an Elector could ever be pronounced conclusive till it had been counted by order of Congress. Elections of President hereafter would be practically and would soon drift actually under the control of Congress. The possibility of such a decision by the commission is not conceded by Republicans. In fact, there is reason to expect that the commission will be positive on this point and against any such power existing in the Constitution. In case of a determination to go behind the returns, which the Democracy will strive desperately to secure, then there can hardly be any choice of President before the 4th, for it is quite impossible for any tribunal to go anew into Louisiana, for instance, and make an investigation, and render a decision upon evidence which would be entitled to any weight, in less than 60 days. This great question, greater than all others, will be first met when Florida is presented to them, and when it is decided the decision will carry with it the choice of President, for if the commission follows the Constitution and the law nothing is more certain than the election of Hayes.

### THE UNITED STATES NAVY.

ADDITIONAL INFORMATION PRESENTED BY THE SECRETARY—THE MATERIAL OF THE NAVAL SERVICE—SEVERAL VESSELS THOROUGHLY REPAIRED—THE IRON-CLADS—39 SHIPS AND 422 GUNS IMMEDIATELY AVAILABLE FOR WAR.

*Special Dispatch to the New-York Times.*

WASHINGTON, Jan. 30.—The addenda to the report of the Secretary of the Navy, recently submitted to the President, is intended to show the actual condition of the material of the naval service at the present time. Referring to the fact that many of the vessels after years of constant repair finally drop out of the service from utter worthlessness, the Secretary attributes this cause to the fact that the Navy in 1869 consisted largely of ships hurriedly built of perishable material, and says its present state of efficiency reflects great credit upon the knowledge and ability of the officers of the Navy. The Niagara, one of the first-rate class of vessels, measuring 5,440 tons displacement, was furnished with steam power as an auxiliary. In 1870 repairs were begun upon her with a view to make her an efficient war vessel. It was ascertained that it would cost over $1,000,000, and that a new vessel could be built for less money, which would be in all respects superior to her when completed. The repairs were suspended, and she is now laid up in ordinary at Boston. The Susquehanna, now lying in ordinary at Brooklyn, was also put under repairs with a view to change her from a side-wheel to a screw ship. The repairs were abandoned for the same reasons as were those of the Niagara. [illegible]

of no further use to the Government, are the steam-sloops Severn, Worcester, and Kansas, and the sailing-vessels New-Orleans, Vermont, Ohio, Independence, Potomac, Cyane, Saratoga, St. Louis, and Pawnee. The Connecticut, Java, and Pennsylvania are white-oak vessels, but were never launched. At present they are somewhat rotten, but could be made serviceable for a year's cruise in six months, although at great cost. The New-York is on the stocks at the Brooklyn Navy-yard. Her frame is of live oak, of good design, and in good preservation. The Iowa, a white oak vessel, and the Florida, built of live oak, have both been tested and found to be very fast. The former is quite rotten, and both vessels would have to be repaired before going to sea. The Franklin, Minnesota, Wabash, Pensacola, Hartford, Richmond, Alaska, Plymouth, Lackawanna, Monongahela, Ossipee, Kearsarge, Tuscarora, Wyoming, Ashuelot, Monocacy, Shawmut, Frolic, Gettysburg, Tallapoosa, and Palos have been thoroughly repaired, and the repairs upon some of them have been very costly. These vessels are now on duty or are ready for service. The Colorado, at present in commission as receiving-ship at Brooklyn, requires repairs, but is in good condition for one year's service.

Since 1869 there have been added to the Navy the Trenton, (second rate,) Adams, Enterprise, Alliance, Alert, Essex, Huron, and Ranger, (third rates,) and the torpedo-boats Alarm and Intrepid. Of these the first five are built of live oak, and the others of iron, all furnished with full steam power. The Despatch and Rio Bravo are purchased vessels; the former for quick dispatch service, and the latter for special service on the Rio Bravo River. There are 13 sailing vessels included in the list of vessels of the United States Navy, but these are considered of no value of importance as fighting vessels. Of these five are only available as practice ships.

There are 24 monitors, or iron-clad vessels, carrying 70 guns—each carrying two or four guns, excepting the Colossus, which is to carry 10 guns, but is still on the stocks at the New-York Navy-yard. The Massachusetts and Oregon are also on the stocks at other yards. Twelve are on duty in the North Atlantic squadron; five are under repairs; three are laid up at League Island, and the Roanoke is in ordinary at New-York. Aside from the sailing-vessels, which are not considered available for war purposes, the monitors, the two torpedo-boats, and the tug-boats in use at the navy-yards and naval stations, there are 71 steam war-vessels on the Navy list, divided into first, second, and third rates, of an aggregate capacity of 90,592 tons, and carrying 854 guns. Of these there are only 39 vessels that are considered immediately available for war purposes, having a capacity of 41,446 tons, and carrying 422 guns. These vessels are divided into the three different classes as follows: three of the first rate, 11 of the second rate, and 25 of the third rate.

The 39 vessels quoted above are only nine in excess of the number required under the provisions of the bill introduced by Mr. Willis in the House of Representatives Dec. 21, which provides "that the fleet of the Navy in peace, and until the public safety demands an increase, shall consist of 30 sea-going vessels of war, to be distributed among the respective squadrons and divisions." "The question" says the report "of what should compose a sound, economical, but efficient naval force has presented during the past two years many different aspects; and the question constantly recurs whether it would be better to enter upon the expensive construction of armor-plated gun-bearing vessels, or continue the building of fast, wooden-built cruisers." Commodore Ammen, Chief of the Bureau of Navigation and Office of Detail of the Navy Department, is acknowledged to possess the best developed ideas of the wants of the naval service, and his proposition to add to the force a marine ram, constructed upon scientific principles, is accepted by experts in the naval service and also in other circles, to be a new element which will make the force complete in itself, and a weapon of most destructive warfare. It is conceded that the officers of the Navy, as a class, know best the practical needs of the service; and it is beginning to be the custom, where difficult and responsible duties connected with the wants of the naval service, either in the construction of the vessels or improvements in other departments, are required, to call in their assistance.

### RESUMPTION OF SPECIE PAYMENTS.

THE MESSAGE OF THE PRESIDENT TO BE SENT TO CONGRESS TO-DAY—INDIFFERENCE OF MEMBERS ON THE SUBJECT.

*Special Dispatch to the New-York Times.*

WASHINGTON, Jan. 30.—The President is expected to send to Congress, to-morrow, his Message concerning an immediate resumption of specie payments. He contemplated two or three days ago issuing an order to the Secretary of the Treasury to begin the redemption of legal-tender notes immediately, but an examination revealed legal difficulties which seemed insurmountable. Any effort to take advantage of the favorable condition of affairs for resumption must have the hearty support of Congress, and its immediate consideration. The proposition meets with little encouragement in Congress. It is not regarded with anything more nearly approaching approval than almost entire indifference by more than a dozen men. A few realize the importance of the opportunity; but, till the count of the Electoral votes is completed, the subject cannot secure a hearing. When it does come up, the old difficulty of getting those who have the same end in view to agree upon any one method of securing it will stand in the way. Any action by this Congress to aid in hastening specie payments cannot be hoped for, and the President is deprived of the support which ought to be earnestly given him by the law-making power, and must be content with making an official record of his views and opinions. He has most earnestly desired to see specie payments resumed during his administration, and it is a great misfortune that he will not be able by reason of the inefficacy of law to bring that end to pass.

### THE POWERS OF THE PRESIDENT.

A JOINT RESOLUTION PROMPTLY VETOED—HIS REASONS THEREFOR RELATED BY THE PRESIDENT—CORRESPONDENCE WITH FOREIGN COUNTRIES—THE "REPUBLIC OF PRETORIA."

WASHINGTON, Jan. 30.—The President sent to the House to-day a Message vetoing two joint resolutions of Congress, one directing the Secretary of State to communicate to the Republic of Pretoria the high appreciation by the Congress of the United States of the complimentary terms in which [illegible]

than one such agency would necessarily lead to confusion, and possibly to contradictory presentation of views and to internal complications. The Constitution of the United States, following the established usage of nations has indicated the President as the agent to represent the national sovereignty in its intercourse with foreign powers, and to receive all official communications from them. It gives him the power, by and with the advice and consent of the Senate, to make treaties and appoint Ambassadors, and other public ministers. It intrusts to him solely the reception of Ambassadors and other public ministers, thus vesting in him the origination of negotiations, and the reception and conduct of all correspondence with foreign States; making him, in the language of one of the most eminent writers on constitutional law, "the constitutional organ of communication with foreign States." No copy of the addresses which it is proposed to acknowledge is furnished. I have no knowledge of their tone, language, or purport. From the tenor of the two joint resolutions it is to be inferred that those communications are probably purely congratulatory. Friendly and kindly intended as they may be, the presentation by a foreign State of any communication to a branch of the Government not contemplated by the Constitution for the reception of communications from foreign States, might, if allowed to pass without notice, become a precedent for the address by foreign States of communications of a difficult nature and with wicked designs. If Congress can direct the correspondence of the Secretary of State with foreign Governments, a case very different from that under consideration might arise when that officer might be directed to present to some foreign Government entirely different and antagonistic views or statements.

By the act of Congress, establishing what is now the Department of State, then known as the Department of Foreign Affairs, the Secretary is to "perform and execute such duties as shall from time to time be enjoined or intrusted to him by the President of the United States, agreeable to the Constitution, relative to correspondence, commissions or instructions to, or with, public Ministers or Consuls from the United States, or to negotiations with public ministers from foreign States or princes, or to memorials or other applications from foreign public ministers or other foreigners, or to such other matters respecting foreign affairs as the President of the United States shall assign to such department, and furthermore, that the said principal officer, the Secretary of State, shall conduct the business of said department in such a manner as the President of the United States shall from time to time order or instruct." This law, which remains substantially unchanged, confirms the view that the whole correspondence of the Government with and from foreign States is intrusted to the President; that the Secretary of State conducts such correspondence exclusively under the orders and instructions of the President; and that no communication or correspondence from a foreign State can properly be addressed to any branch or department of the Government except that to which such correspondence has been committed by the Constitution and law. I therefore feel it my duty to return the two joint resolutions without my approval to the House of Representatives, in which they originated.

In addition to the reasons already stated for withholding my constitutional approval from these resolutions is the fact that no information is furnished as to the terms or purport of the communication to which acknowledgements are desired; no copy of the communications accompany the resolutions, nor is the name even of an officer or of a body to whom an acknowledgment could be addressed given. It is not known whether the congratulatory addresses proceed from the head of State or from legislative bodies, and as regards the resolution relating to the "Republic of Pretoria," I cannot learn that any State or Government of that name exists.

(Signed,) U. S. GRANT.

### THE ELECTORAL INVESTIGATIONS.

THE SENATE COMMITTEE AND THE OREGON CASE—THE DISQUALIFIED MICHIGAN ELECTOR.

WASHINGTON, Jan. 30.—The Oregon Electoral case was the subject of a long discussion in the Senate Committee on Privileges and Elections. The committee were unable to decide upon a report, as there are a large number of telegrams relative to this case which have not yet been offered in evidence, but which will be so offered to-day or to-morrow.

The committee continued the investigation of the Oregon Electoral case this evening.

William H. Hollister, Cashier of the banking-house of Kountze Brothers, of No. 12 Wall street, New-York, testified that he has known J. H. N. Patrick, of Omaha, Nebraska, for several years; he knows Erwin Davis; understands that he is a man of wealth and leisure; on the 1st of December last $8,000 was deposited with Kountze Brothers by a stranger, who represented the deposit to be made by E. Davis; the $8,000 was in large bills, and was placed to the credit of J. H. N. Patrick. Witness was asked if he knew E. Davis, and replied: "I know Erwin Davis;" this sum of $8,000 was not deposited for Erwin Davis; on the 16th of December $1,039, in gold, was deposited in Kountze Brothers' bank by Charles Dimond, of New-York, subject to the order of J. H. N. Patrick, and it is still there; the bank of Kountze Brothers paid a draft of $8,000 on the 15th or 16th of December, in favor of Wells, Fargo & Co.; the witness did not know whether the money was paid to Wells, Fargo & Co. over the counter of Kountze Brothers' Bank or by draft through the Clearing-house; the draft on which Wells, Fargo & Co. were paid the sum of $8,000 was dated San Francisco, Dec. 5 and was given by J. H. N. Patrick.

M. T. Patrick, of Omaha, Neb., was the next witness. He is a brother to J. H. N. Patrick.

Senator Mitchell asked the witness if the signature to a certain cipher dispatch directed to W. T. Pelton, of New-York, was in the handwriting of his brother, J. H. N. Patrick.

Witness could not swear that it was or was not his brother's signature.

Major C. H. Hempstead, an acquaintance of J. H. N. Patrick was called, and asked to identify Mr. Patrick's handwriting, but he was unable to do so from the papers handed to him.

Senator Kelly was next called. He testified that he became acquainted with J. H. N. Patrick at Portland, Oregon, on the 27th of December last. A cipher dispatch directed to W. T. Pelton, New-York, signed by J. H. N. Patrick and indorsed by Senator Kelly, was produced by Senator Mitchell and handed to the witness, who stated that he could not translate the dispatch, but he could give the substance of it, which was that he [Mr. Kelly] indorsed a dispatch asking the Democratic National Committee to send $10,000 to Oregon to pay any legal expenses which might arise in connection with the Watts case, and it was also mentioned in the dispatch that any money not needed would be returned to the committee. An answer in cipher came to this dispatch, the substance of which was that there was "no money." Several telegrams passed between parties in Oregon and New-York in relation to paying any legal expenses in connection with the Watts case, and finally word was sent from New York to Oregon that $8,000 could be had. The cipher dispatches which passed between Senator Kelly and Patrick were in relation to transferring the $8,000 from New-York to Oregon; how it should be done, and through what bankers. The dispatches had no other meaning. The Senator further testified that this $8,000 was the only money used in connection with this case in Oregon to his knowledge; that the $3,200 which he drew on a check from the bank of Ladd & Bush was used for paying lawyers' fees and for sending a messenger to Mr. Laswell, who lives in the eastern part of the State. He never heard the unlawful use of money in connection with this case mentioned, and he never had an idea that any money would be used improperly in connection with it.

Senator Mitchell offered the following telegram, which he asked to have inserted in connection with the testimony of Mr. Hollister:

NEW-YORK, Nov. 27, 1876.

*J. H. N. Patrick, Salem, Oregon:*

Secure your points at all hazards. Communicate with me immediately, giving prospects. DAVIS.

At this point the committee adjourned until to-morrow evening.

The Committee on the Powers, Privileges, and Duties of the House in Counting the Electoral Vote to-day examined Benton Hanchett, of Michigan, who testified that at the late election he was a candidate for Presidential Elector on the Republican ticket in that State, and was elected; he did not vote in the Electoral College, and was not present. He explained his reasons for not voting by saying that in 1863 he was appointed a Commissioner of the United States in the prosecution of a case of violation of law, of which he had made [illegible]

L. Crosman, who was elected by the college to fill the vacancy caused by the absence of Hanchett, testified as to that fact.

### NOTES FROM THE CAPITAL.

WASHINGTON, Jan. 30.—The House Committee on Appropriations in the Legislative and Executive Appropriation bill only provide $25,000 for the salary of the President, and accompany it with a provision repealing the section of the revised statutes which increased the salary to $50,000. It will be remembered that the Senate, at this session, failed to pass over the veto of President Grant the bill restoring the salary to the old figure, and although it passed both houses by a majority, it is likely that the provision as it now stands in the Appropriation bill will be agreed to, and the next President will have to be content with $25,000 per annum.

Jeremiah M. Wilson, of counsel for the Louisiana Returning Board, denies the truth of the statement that he and Mr. Shellabarger had applied to the courts for a writ of habeas corpus in their behalf.

The Treasury to-day destroyed $1,070,272 in legal tender notes, that amount being 80 per cent. of the national bank circulation issued during the month.

Mr. Stephens became much worse during the evening, and at midnight was very low. Although his death is not apprehended immediately, it is feared he cannot recover.

Orders have been received at the arsenal directing four batteries of artillery, whose proper station is at Fortress Monroe, to return to that point by boat; but as the river is not entirely open, it is thought they will not embark before Monday next. The troops who will leave on Monday are those who arrived here on Sunday evening, Nov. 19, last, under the command of Col. Loder. The companies are Battery I, Fourth Artillery, Col. Loder commanding; Battery G, First Artillery, Col. Elder commanding; Battery C, Fifth, Major Randolph, and Battery A; Third, Col. Lorraine. They had been stationed at Fortress Monroe previous to the Presidential election, but were ordered to South Carolina to preserve the peace. The band of the Artillery School, which arrived here about Nov. 25, will return at the same time. It is thought that the other troops will leave for posts North and West shortly.

Mr. A. T. Britton has been appointed Metropolitan Police Commissioner in the place of Mr. Kimball, who was appointed to succeed Mr. Murtagh but declined to serve.

The Senate in executive session to-day confirmed the following nominations: G. A. Wetter, to be Register at Yankton, Dakota; Thomas Settle, to be Judge of the United States District Court for the Northern District of Florida; James H. Burdick, to be United States Marshal for Dakota Territory; Medical Director William Grier, to be Chief of the Bureau of Surgery, Navy Department.

The information has been received at the Department of State from the Vice Consul of the United States at Manila, respecting the port of Iolo, in the Sooloo Archipelago, which has been declared by the Spanish Government to be absolutely free from duties on foreign commerce from November 16, 1876, with the exception of arms, munitions of war, or such traffic as might prove injurious to morality or the public health. Vessels visiting the above port are required to present a full manifest of their cargo, stores, &c., within 48 hours after arrival.

Referring to the notice to mariners of Jan. 20, 1877, relative to the temporary discontinuance of the light on the shoal off Thomas' Point on the west side of the Chesapeake Bay, the Light-house Board gives notice that on and after this date the light will be again exhibited. It will be of the fourth order, showing a red flash every thirty seconds.

Commander George H. Perkins is ordered to command the Ashuelot, on the Asiatic station, relieving Commander E. O. Matthews, who is ordered home. Master James M. Wright is ordered to the Colorado. Civil Engineer U. S. G. White is ordered to temporary duty in the Bureau of Yards and Docks. Ensign W. C. Cowles is detached from the receiving ship Colorado, and placed on waiting orders.

Treasurer Wyman stated this afternoon that the Government has not lost any money through collections that have been made by parties claiming to represent others who have unclaimed interest due them on the books of the Treasurer's office where such claims are not correct. In all instances of this character the moneys so collected have been refunded. The department is solicitous that bondholders should not be made to pay too heavy fees to agents collecting interest for parties to whom it belongs.

The President sent the following nominations to the Senate to-day: A. T. Wickoff, to be Pension Agent at Columbus, Ohio; Joseph Grierson, to be Consul at Coquimbo; James D. Brady, to be Collector of Internal Revenue for the Second District of Virginia.

### TESTING OF IRON AND STEEL.

MESSAGE OF THE PRESIDENT RECOMMENDING FURTHER APPROPRIATION TO CONTINUE THE OPERATIONS OF THE TESTING COMMISSION.

WASHINGTON, Jan. 30.—The President sent the following Message to Congress to-day:

I desire to call the attention of Congress to the importance of providing for the continuance of the board for testing iron, steel, and other metals, which, by the Sundry Appropriation act of last year, was ordered to be discontinued at the end of the present fiscal year. This board, consisting of engineers and other scientific experts from the Army, the Navy, and from civil life—all of whom, except the Secretary, give their time and labors to this object without compensation—was organized by authority of Congress in the Spring of 1875, and immediately drafted a comprehensive plan for its investigations and contracted for a testing-machine of 400 tons capacity, which would enable it to properly conduct the experiments. Meanwhile the sub-committee of the board have devoted their time to such experiments as could be made with smaller testing-machines already available. This large machine is just now completed and ready for erection at the Watertown Arsenal, and the real labors of the board are therefore just about to be commenced. If the board is to be discontinued at the end of the present fiscal year the money already appropriated and the services of the gentlemen who have given so much time to the subject will be unproductive of any results.

The importance of these experiments can hardly be overestimated when we consider the almost endless variety of purposes for which iron and steel are employed in this country, and the many thousands of lives which daily depend on the soundness of iron structures. I need hardly refer to the recent disaster at the Ashtabula bridge, in Ohio, and the conflicting theories of experts as to the cause of it, as an instance of what might have been averted by a more thorough knowledge of the properties of iron and the best modes of construction. These experiments cannot properly be conducted by private firms, not only on account of the expense, but because the results must rest upon the authority of disinterested persons. They must therefore be undertaken under the sanction of the Government. Compared with their great value to the industrial interests of the country, the expense is very slight. The board recommend an appropriation of $40,000 for the next fiscal year, and I earnestly commend their request to the favorable consideration of Congress. I also recommend that the board be required to conduct their investigations under the direction of the Secretary of War, and to make full report of their progress to that officer in time to be incorporated in his annual report. U. S. GRANT.

EXECUTIVE MANSION, Jan. 30, 1877.

### THE POLICE BOARD INVESTIGATION.

WASHINGTON, Jan. 30.—The Special Committee of the House to inquire into the official acts of the late Board of Police Commissioners of the District of Columbia continued their investigation to-day. Secretary of the Navy Robeson was sworn and testified that he had read the report of the investigation of Mr. Murtagh as it was published in the newspapers. The Chairman read Mr. Murtagh's testimony regarding his interview with the witness in relation to Mr. Whitthorne. Witness did not remember that interview. He saw Murtagh frequently during the Whitthorne investigation, but had no conversation with him about Whitthorne. Murtagh did nothing about the Whitthorne affair at witness' request or with his knowledge. Witness talked about the Whitthorne business with various persons, as to Mr. Whitthorne's personal habits, but had nothing to do with the Police force; had understood that Whitthorne's habits were bad, and so may have smiled when Murtagh asked witness about him; thought that Whitthorne was opening himself to exposure, and, thinking some subordinate would take advantage of the opportunity, communicated with a member of Congress, who would use his influence in warning Mr. Whitthorne to be careful if there was any necessity; did this not for any feeling toward Mr. Whitthorne, [illegible]

none] had such a conversation with Murtagh as was given in his testimony, about not exposing Whitthorne while he was in office, but witness could recollect nothing of it.

### SUICIDE OF AN ENGINEER OFFICER.

THE RASH ACT OF A LIEUTENANT IN THE REGULAR ARMY—NO CAUSE GIVEN FOR THE DEED.

SAN FRANCISCO, Jan. 30.—Lieut. John H. Weeden, of the United States Engineer Corps, was found near midnight last night lying dead on a sofa in his room at No. 726 Bush street. Near the body were two empty bottles, which had evidently contained chloral hydrate. No one has been admitted except Gen. Barton S. Alexander, of the Engineers, physicians, a few friends of the deceased, and the Coroner. The cause of the act is as yet unknown, all parties being very reticent. Lieut. Weeden left a letter for a young lady, which contains but a few lines, and merely intimating that it was the last time he would address her.

[The military history of Lieut. Weeden is brief and uneventful. He was born in Rhode Island, from which State he was appointed to the Military Academy at West Point in 1862. He graduated number five in a class of 41, June 18, 1866, and the same day was promoted in the Army to be Second Lieutenant in the Corps of Engineers. He served for a while with the Engineer Battalion at Willet's Point, near this City. In March, 1867, he received his second promotion, and at the time of his death held the rank of First Lieutenant of Engineers.]

### CRONIN AT HOME IN OREGON.

*Special Dispatch to the New-York Times.*

PORTLAND, Jan. 30.—E. A. Cronin, the self-constituted Presidential Elector from Oregon, arrived home to-day from the East. His return fails to inspire the Democracy with the least enthusiasm. Cronin's ephemeral greatness is fast fading from the public view, and he is rapidly drifting into a well-merited obscurity from which no future political event can drag him forth to the gaze of an admiring world.

### A NEW PRESIDENT FOR DARTMOUTH.

CONCORD, Jan. 30.—The Trustees of Dartmouth College met to-day in this city to decide who should be Dr. Smith's successor in the Presidency of the institution. They easily fixed upon Rev. Prof. Samuel C. Bartlett, D. D., of Chicago, who, it is understood, will accept the responsible position. Dr. Bartlett is a graduate of Dartmouth, of the class of 1836, and was tutor in the college for a time. For several years he was Professor of Intellectual Philosophy and Rhetoric in Western Reserve College, Ohio, and then became Professor of Sacred Theology in the Chicago Theological Seminary, which position he has acceptably filled for the past 18 years. His advent to the Presidency of Dartmouth will be accepted as a guarantee of the continued prosperity of the institution, and will be satisfactory to the graduates generally. Resolutions were passed by the Trustees complimentary to retiring President Smith, whose 14 years of service have been full of progress to the college.

### THE ASHTABULA DISASTER.

CLEVELAND, Jan. 30.—The *Leader* has the following special from Ashtabula: "The Coroner's inquest was resumed to-day, and Job Abbot, civil engineer, of Canton, was sworn and testified: Is President of the Canton Bridge Company; has known of several bridges being built of wrought and cast iron on the Howe truss plan; he finds that the tension members had ample section, and, in fact, were considerably heavier than necessary for safety, and that the compression members were deficient in section; is of the opinion that the bridge had become gradually weakened by use, the form of construction being such that many of the compression members were strained over their safe working capacity. Copies of the testimony of Amasa Stone and the late Charles Collins were introduced, and will be used as evidence."

### MARINE DISASTERS.

LONDON, Jan. 30.—The American schooner W. L. Burroughs, Capt. Smith, which arrived at Liverpool Jan. 26 from New-York, was obliged to jettison 400 barrels of petroleum on the passage.

WASHINGTON, Jan. 30.—The Signal Service observer at Cape Henry reports to the Chief Signal Officer as follows: Wrecking tugs with the Italian bark Caspione in tow passed Cape Henry at 3:30 o'clock this afternoon, bound for Norfolk.

QUEENSTOWN, Jan. 30.—The steamer Somerset, from Bristol, which put in here Friday last with main steam-pipe broken, has repaired, and sailed for New-York to-day.

LONDON, Jan. 31.—The bark John E. Chase, for Savannah Jan. 2, has been towed into Liverpool. She lost her mainmast, and is otherwise damaged.

### OPERATING IN STOCKS.

SAN FRANCISCO, Jan. 30.—Financial men here scout the story that $20,000,000, or any large sum, has been transferred from here to New-York to operate in Western Union or any other stock. The Cashier of the Bank of California says D. O. Mills is in New-York on business of the bank, and states positively he has no connection with any such pool, nor has any other person connected with the bank. Henry Keene denies that his brother, James Keene, has any connection with the movement, or has had $6,000,000, or a tenth of that amount transferred to New-York, and characterizes the story, so far as he is concerned, as sheer nonsense.

### DEMOCRATIC IMPUDENCE.

SAN FRANCISCO, Jan. 30.—Congressman Piper, of this district, has written a letter to Horace Davis, Congressman elect, stating his intention of contesting the election on the ground that Mr. Davis received over 9,000 fraudulent votes, the votes having been cast on certificates of enrollment, and the names of the voters not having been entered on the great register. He also alleges that Mr. Davis received 4,000 votes which were cast by parties who were non-residents.

### OBSTRUCTIONS ON THE ERIE RAILWAY.

WAVERLY, Jan. 30.—The Erie Railway authorities promptly set to work to ascertain by whom the obstructions were placed on the track near Waverly, N. Y., on Sunday night, and after diligent investigation decided upon the arrest of two men, one of whom, named Samuel T. Bailey, of Rome, Penn., 18 years of age, confessed to having done the whole work alone, and claims to have had no object in view. He is in jail at Waverly. Fortunately the obstructions were discovered in time to prevent any accident.

### MANSLAUGHTER IN PHILADELPHIA.

PHILADELPHIA, Jan. 30.—This evening, as John Pye and John Keegan were returning from work, they encountered Samuel Ewing and James Keenan at the corner of Eighteenth and Wharton streets, both drunk. A dispute arose which ended in Pye drawing a chisel from his pocket, and stabbing Ewing with it above the eye, producing a wound which resulted in instant death. Keenan was also cut with the chisel, but his injuries were not dangerous. Pye and Keegan were arrested.

### CONVICTS SENT TO AUBURN.

AUBURN, Jan. 30.—A transfer of fifty convicts from Sing Sing arrived safely at Auburn Prison this morning. Among the gang were the four Astoria masked burglars, Eugene Christ, of New-York, Quimbo Appo, the Chinese murderer, and a number of other notorious criminals.

### THE WORK OF TRAIN ROBBERS.

BOSTON, Jan. 30.—Albert H. Prince and Joseph L. Palmer were detected yesterday in an attempt to commit a theft on a train of the Boston and Albany Railroad. They jumped off the moving train, and Palmer was fatally injured. Prince had an arm broken.

### A GUILTY BANK CASHIER.

POTTSVILLE, Jan. 30.—The jury in the case of Joseph F. Dengler, ex-Cashier of the Pennsylvania National Bank, at Pottsville, charged with embezzlement of $4,000, brought in a verdict of guilty this afternoon.

### MAN SHOT IN A QUARREL.

BOSTON, Jan. 30.—Thomas Mack was shot in the back of the head with a shot-gun in the hands of a man named Davis at Hovelling to-day. Mack's condition is critical. [illegible]

[illegible]

## THE LOUISIANA ELECTION

### RETURNING BOARD AND THE HOUSE.

UNSCRUPULOUS CONDUCT OF THE COMMITTEE ENGINEERED BY TILDEN'S ATTORNEY, FIELD—ARBITRARY TREATMENT OF THE IMPRISONED MEMBERS OF THE LOUISIANA BOARD OF CANVASSERS—COERCION OF WITNESSES—SELF-EVIDENT FALSEHOOD OF THE CLERK LITTLEFIELD'S TESTIMONY.

*Special Dispatch to the New-York Times.*

WASHINGTON, Jan. 30.—The White League and Kuklux leaders of the South have repeatedly accused ex-Gov. Wells, Gen. Anderson, and their associates of the Louisiana Returning Board of many crimes; but even if they were guilty of every corrupt act charged against them, because they are Republicans and have dared to do their duty in accordance with the laws of their State and the dictates of common justice, it is a question whether or not they deserve the extraordinary treatment which they are now receiving at the hands of the Democratic House. It will be remembered that the gentlemen named refused while in New-Orleans to produce certain papers demanded by Mr. Morrison's committee. For this they were called before the bar of the House, adjudged guilty of contempt of its privileges, and turned over to the tender mercies of Mr. Sergeant at Arms Thompson. This gentleman, supported no doubt by Watterson's *promised* army of 100,000 men, seems to have made up his mind that the unfortunate prisoners shall feel his greatness and have cause to remember his power. He has had them confined in separate rooms; they are watched day and night by Deputy Sergeants at Arms; are not allowed to consult together; are permitted to have no communication with their party friends, and are only allowed to see their counsel separately, and in the presence of one or more of the Democratic jailers. They have repeatedly protested against this remarkable treatment, but thus far their protests have had no effect. To-day Mr. Louis M. Kenner, one of the colored members of the board, was called before the Committee on the Privileges of the House. He was examined by Mr. David Dudley Field, whose overbearing, brow-beating manner would not for a moment have been permitted by any other tribunal than the one which Mr. Tilden sent him here to control. He demanded to-day, among other strange and unusual things, that Mr. Kenner should produce a private memorandum of the proceedings of the Returning Board which had been made by him. The witness said that the paper referred to was in his trunk in the room where he was confined, and that before producing it he would like to have an opportunity of consulting with his counsel, Judge Wilson. He was sent to his room in the custody of an Assistant Sergeant at Arms, and Mr. Wilson was allowed to accompany him, but was not permitted to speak with him in private. While the witness was in his room he took from his trunk the memorandum demanded by the committee, and also a bundle of papers which he was requested by the counsel of the board in New-Orleans to hand to ex-Gov. Wells, the President of the board. These papers he handed to Judge Wilson, with the request that he would give them to Wells. This request was, of course, overheard by the Deputy Sergeant at Arms, and the whole transaction was privately reported to Mr. Field. When Kenner returned to the committee-room he was again asked by Field if he would produce the memorandum, and he again replied that he could not do so until he had been allowed an opportunity of consulting with his legal adviser. A sharp debate followed, and in the course of it Mr. Field asked the witness what papers he handed to his counsel while in his own apartment. He replied that he had given him a bundle of papers which had been sent from New-Orleans to Gov. Wells. "Produce those papers," said Field. "I cannot," replied the witness, "they are now in the custody of my counsel." Tilden's man Dudley, seeing a mare's nest in this simple little transaction between a lawyer and his client, became more than ever anxious to secure the papers, and in the most angry tones protested against what he called a trick to gain time. "Well, what is the use of being in a hurry?" asked a Republican member of the committee. "What's the use of being in a hurry?" echoed Mr. Field; "what's the use of being in a hurry, when the Electoral count is to be commenced on Thursday, and we have only to-day and to-morrow to take testimony. I think there is every use of being in a hurry." "Oh, then you believe that the evidence we take will affect the action of the Joint Commission, do you?" asked the Republican member. "Most decidedly I do," replied Mr. Field, and then turning to a Deputy Sergeant at Arms who stood at his elbow, he whispered to him not to lose sight of Judge Wilson as long as he retained possession of the papers. Then, as Kenner still refused to produce his memorandum without first consulting with his counsel, he was allowed half an hour to do so.

During that time Gov. Kellogg was examined, and created some amusement by refusing to be "bull-dozed" by Mr. Field.

Then Mr. Kenner was again placed upon the stand and again requested to produce his private memorandum. He did so, after having been refused time for further consultation. The paper was pounced upon with the utmost eagerness by Tilden's man "Friday," but his face fell and he lost all interest in the document when he discovered that it contained nothing but an account of the acts of intimidation, violence, outrage, murder, and fraud, which had induced the board to throw out the votes of certain polls. Subsequently Mr. Kenner stated that in the bundle of papers held by his counsel for Gov. Wells was one belonging to him, the witness. This he produced, when it was discovered to be nothing more important than a printed report of the proceedings of the board. The bundle held by Judge Wilson contained nothing but similar pamphlets; still, as the gentleman named was about to leave the committee-room, he was stopped by Sergeant at Arms Thompson, who told him that he could not take the bundle with him. The committee finally allowed him to do so, however, with the understanding that he would return them to-morrow.

After Mr. Kenner's examination, the clerk, Littlefield, who produced the returns from Vernon Parish, was re-examined, and again swore that at the request of Gov. Wells, the President of the Board, he had altered the return by transferring 178 votes from the Democratic to the Republican column. This he did because, as he swears, Wells wanted to elect three friends of his named Andrews, Hunter, and Kelso, who were running for minor county offices. He swears, further, that the fraud perpetrated by him accomplished this end. Such is not the case, however. Kelso was defeated, and was so returned by the board.

To-night the Democrats are trying to make capital out of the story told by Littlefield, which is believed to be a deliberate falsehood by all those who know anything about the facts. According to the witness' own testimony, the Vernon return was the only one altered, as described by him. He is also obliged to state what all the world knows, that under the Election laws of Louisiana the Returning Board was authorized to throw out, and could legally throw out, the vote at any poll where there was evidence of violence or fraud. Such being the case, who will believe that they would use a weak instrument like Littlefield to change 178 votes which had no bearing upon and did not affect the Electoral canvass. The man's story is too ridiculous for serious consideration. It will be contradicted by Gov. Wells and a number of other competent witnesses.

[illegible]

# The New-York Times.

VOL. XXVI.......NO. 7931. NEW-YORK, TUESDAY, FEBRUARY 13, 1877. PRICE FOUR CENTS.

## THE COUNTING OF THE VOTE

### THE STATE OF LOUISIANA REACHED.

FLORIDA RECORDED FOR HAYES AND WHEELER—GEORGIA, INDIANA, AND KENTUCKY COUNTED FOR TILDEN, AND ILLINOIS AND KANSAS FOR HAYES—A LONG LIST OF OBJECTIONS TO THE COUNTING OF LOUISIANA FOR HAYES—ARGUMENT ON LOUISIANA TO BEGIN AT 11 A. M. TO-DAY.

*Special Dispatch to the New-York Times.*

WASHINGTON, Feb. 12.—The proceedings in the count of the Electoral vote were, to-day, exactly according to the programme explained last night. The count was continued down to Louisiana, and the double set of returns was sent to the Commission, which will meet at 11 o'clock to-morrow, to begin the examination of them. The debate in the House on the objections to the decision in the Florida case was much tamer than it would have been if it had taken place on Saturday. There were several wild speeches, temporarily suppressed on the consideration that abuse of the Commission would not improve the prospect of a decision favorable to Tilden in the Louisiana count. The speeches were, nevertheless, extremely partisan on the Democratic side. The day began with a notable attempt, headed by J. Proctor Knott, to have the decision referred back to the Commission to be revised. He pretended, with mock sincerity, to desire to give the Commission an opportunity to explain an inconsistency into which they had fallen. Mr. Hale made the absolutely sound point of order that the bill gave neither house the right to vote upon any such proposition, and Mr. Wilson, of Iowa, made the further objection that it was not in the power of the House, acting without the concurrence of the Senate, to refer anything to an outside Commission. Speaker Randall will not sustain a point of order made by Mr. Hale, no matter how plain the case may be, and so he overruled the point on Mr. Hale's objections, and sustained it on Mr. Wilson's, the effect being, of course, the same. The debate on the point of order lasted nearly an hour. The Democrats did not seem inclined to insist upon sustaining Knott, as that course was no part of the programme. The agreement was to go on and make a new fight over Louisiana, and that resolve having been taken the Democrats were no less anxious than the Republicans to have that State reached.

The debate on the Commission's decision was not marked by any able speeches against sustaining it, the burden of the Democratic complaint being that the country, as they say, expected the Commission to elect Tilden, and now it had already disappointed them and was likely to disappoint them to the end. Some speakers, indeed, endeavored to express hope of the future, but it was clearly hope without expectation. There was one remarkable speech on the Democratic side by Mr. Carr, of Indiana, the successor to the late Speaker, Mr. Kerr. He was one of those who voted against the bill when it was before the House, and to-day he gave the Democrats who voted for it a terrific scoring. He told them they must stand by the measure, and they could not get rid of the responsibility of passing the bill by abusing the Commission. They had abandoned all to their opponents when they voted for the bill, and their betrayed constituents would heap condemnation upon their treacherous heads. He made many points which produced applause and laughter. It was a speech which will deservedly give Mr. Carr much reputation.

On the Republican side the action of the Commission was sustained and supported with ability and candor. It was curious to see Robbins, of North Carolina, who is on record as having sold his vote in the State Legislature for $20, declaiming in favor of a decision of the Presidential dispute on the broad grounds of equity. The refusal to sustain the decision of the Commission was made by a strict party vote, no Democrat being honest or fair enough to break away from his party and vote according to justice and right.

The joint meeting assembled at 2:25 o'clock, and in an hour had counted through the list of States from Florida to Louisiana. The two houses not agreeing in overruling the Commission in the Florida case, the vote of that State was simply placed upon the tally sheets and announced without further formalities. The State of Illinois was passed without objection, Springer having been in some way suppressed, probably by the consideration stated last night that, counting Chaffee's vote, if he were proved ineligible, would be a strong precedent for the Republicans to carry before the Commission. Springer sat fidgety and self-conscious, and wore a simple smile, while all eyes were upon him expecting the objection which he did not make. The certificates from Louisiana were very long and occupied an hour in the reading. There was a return received by mail, without any duplicate by messenger, which was opened and read. It was the Republican certificate, but after it was mailed some real or fancied informality was remembered and a new set of certificates was made with the proper correction, and one was mailed and one sent by messenger. The Tilden certificates were read, and then the corrected Hayes certificates. The Vice President, to the surprise of everybody, opened a fourth envelope, received by mail, and indorsed as containing the Electoral vote of the State. It proved to be a burlesque document, and set forth that various John Smiths, numbered one, two, and so forth, had been chosen Electors and had cast the vote of Louisiana for Cooper and Cary. There were several suggestions to stop the reading but unanimous consent could not be obtained and it was read through, amid roars of laughter. It was finally suppressed from the record and destroyed, though it may be doubted whether this course was proper, since in reality the Cooper certificate was as good as that for Tilden. The brilliant and reckless author of it remains unknown.

The Commission was in session to receive the papers, and in a brief meeting the announcement was made that Representative Jencks and Senator McDonald would present the case as Democratic objectors, and Senator Howe and Representative Hurlbut will appear as Republican objectors to the counting the Tilden vote. Two hours on each side is alloted them for argument. The same time is granted to the counsel, and it is understood that Trumbull and Carpenter, lately professed Republicans are to represent the Democratic case, and Mr. Evarts and Stanley Mathews will probably speak for the Republicans. The arguments are now expected to be concluded in two days, but in any event will not extend beyond Thursday. The decision of the case may be hopefully expected this week. Republicans feel entirely confident of the result, and there is not so much hope on the part of the Democracy as is pretended.

### THE PROCEEDINGS IN THE HOUSE.

The House met at 10 A. M.

#### THE FLORIDA VOTES.

Mr. MCCRARY, of Iowa, rose for the purpose of opening the discussion upon the objection to the decision of the Electoral vote of Florida.

Mr. CLYMER, of Pennsylvania, raised the point of order that there was no quorum present, and unanimous consent was given that the debate on the question should not commence until 10:30, and that no business should be transacted until that time.

The House resumed its session at 10:30, when Mr. FIELD, of New-York, for the purpose of bringing the matter before the House in due form, offered the following order:

*Ordered*, That the counting of the Electoral votes from the State of Florida shall not proceed in conformity with the decision of the Electoral Commission, but that the votes of Messrs. Call, Yonge, Milton, and Bullock be counted as the votes from the State of Florida for President and Vice President of the United States.

Mr. HALE, of Maine, moved an amendment, as follows:

*Ordered*, That the counting of the Electoral votes from the State of Florida shall proceed in conformity with the decision of the Electoral Commission.

Mr. KNOTT, of Kentucky, offered as a substitute an order reciting the language of the Electoral act, that the Commission might take into view such petitions, depositions, and papers as shall, by the Constitution and now-existing law be competent; reciting also the fact that in the Florida case the Commission had decided and determined that no evidence should be received or considered which had not been submitted to the two houses in joint convention by the President of the Senate; that certificate No. 1 (that of the Hayes Electors) contained no evidence whatever, while certificates Nos. 2 and 3 (those of the Tilden Electors) did contain evidence fully and specifically showing the fact that the latter had been duly elected and appointed as Electors, and, therefore, ordering that the decision of the Commission and the grounds thereof be remanded and recommitted to the Commission, with the request that the same be so corrected or explained, and that the Commission be further requested to furnish in detail the true reason of its decision, so that the House may be enlightened as to the course it ought to pursue in the discharge of its duties, and that in the meantime the vote of the Hayes Electors be not counted.

Mr. HALE, of Maine, made the point of order that under the Electoral Commission law it was the imperative duty of the House, at the end of the two hours' debate, to vote on the main question, which was, whether the votes should be counted in conformity with the decision, and that nothing in the shape of delay, in whatever form presented, could now arrest the wheels of its decision.

Mr. WILSON, of Iowa, added to Mr. Hale's point of order, that this House could refer nothing to the Commission; that would require at least concurrent action.

Mr. WOOD, of New-York, declared that any intimation of a desire on the part of the Democratic side of the House to interpose any factious opposition to any decision of the Electoral Commission was entirely gratuitous, and unwarranted by anything that had taken place.

Mr. HALE, of Maine—Has anything been said this morning to indicate any charge of that kind?

Mr. WOOD—The gentleman has just spoken of delay, and has intimated that there is an intentional disposition on the part of the House to delay action. I can assure the gentleman that there is no such intention. While we are ready in good faith to carry out, in all respects, the Electoral Commission law, and the result that may be reached in pursuance of it, still, at the same time, we demand the right of free expression of opinion.

Mr. KNOTT, of Kentucky, contested the point of order, and thought there was nothing in the law which prevented the House, with the concurrence of the Senate, from remanding back to the Electoral Commission, for their further consideration, the decision which it had made in the Florida case, in order that it might have an opportunity to explain the glaring inconsistencies which existed in that decision.

Mr. BANKS, of Massachusetts, said that under the provisions of the Electoral act the House was compelled to give an affirmative or negative vote upon the decision of the Commission. It would not be respectful to the Commission to remand the decision to it.

The SPEAKER overruled the point of order made by Mr. Hale, but sustained that made by Mr. Wilson, holding that there was nothing in the Electoral Commission law that authorized a recommittal of the question back to the Commission, and also ruling that it was not competent for one house to refer a bill or any other matter to an outside Commission. The substitute offered by Mr. Knott was, therefore, not in order.

#### THE DEBATE—MR. M'CRARY'S ARGUMENT.

The House thereupon, at 11:15, proceeded to the discussion of the objection to the decision of the Electoral Commission.

Mr. MCCRARY, of Iowa, addressed the House in support of the Commission. He said that the decision of the Commission embraced several important propositions, upon the correctness of which the two houses were to decide; that these propositions were eminently sound and fully supported both by reason and authority seemed to him entirely clear. He said the first point decided was that the two houses of Congress, in the exercise of their powers to count the vote for President and Vice President, could not go into an inquiry as to the number of votes cast at the polls for the Electors in the several States. In other words, it was held that the decision of that question was left to the proper authority in the States, and that when that authority canvassed the votes, declared and adjudged the result, and certified the election of the Electors in due form, that is the appointment of Electors required by the Constitution. He claimed that this was in accordance with the precedent established by the bill of 1800, which passed both houses of Congress, and was only lost by a failure to agree upon the form of a single provision. That bill, he said, created a Grand Committee, to whom were to be referred questions arising upon the count of the Electoral votes of the States, but it was carefully provided both by the Senate and the House bill that no inquiry should be made as to the number of votes cast for the Electors at the polls; that being regarded by all the statesmen of that day as a matter within the exclusive control of the States. He said the House bill of 1800, drafted, reported, and advocated by John Marshall, afterward Chief Justice of the United States, embodied the views of that great constitutional lawyer upon this question. After providing for this Grand Committee, it defined their jurisdiction in these words: "And the persons thus chosen shall form a joint committee, and shall have power to examine into all disputes relative to the election of President and Vice President of the United States, other than such as might relate to the number of votes by which the Electors may have been appointed."

He held that the ruling of the Commission was also abundantly supported by most cogent reasons, and that to have ruled otherwise would have been to assert a jurisdiction to inquire into and overturn the action of all the States in the appointment of their Electors, and to institute proceedings in the nature of an action of *quo warranto* to try the titles of every one of the persons appointed as such. He argued that the power of the two houses, and, therefore, of the Commission, was conferred by these words of the Constitution: "And the votes shall then be counted," and that the Commission had decided upon the soundest reasons that these words confer no judicial power whatever, and that they describe, and very aptly describe ministerial duty only. The words of the Constitution, he maintained, would be the last words that would have been chosen by which to confer that immense power, that vast jurisdiction, which has lately for the first time been claimed for the two houses, and that the impossibility of exercising this power was a strong argument against its existence. How could the two houses of Congress, he asked, entertain and try a suit to determine the title of Electors to their offices? He claimed that if it could be done in one case it could be done in all, and that there might be brought 369 contests over elections for Electors, with witnesses numbered by hundreds in each, all to be determined within the brief interval between the meeting of Congress in December and the counting of the votes in February. He said it was plain that to establish this doctrine was to give the election of President and Vice President hereafter into the hands of Congress, and take it out of the hands of the State, where the Constitution placed it. The Commission had, therefore, very properly, he thought, decided that the record of the final canvass and decision and declaration of the result made by the proper State authority was final and conclusive, and that when this record was presented duly authenticated, and accompanied by the return required by law and the Constitution, there was but one thing that could be done, and that was to obey the mandate of the Constitution, which declares that "the votes shall be counted." The Commission, he said, decided one other point of importance, which was that the appointment of Electors made and certified in the manner prescribed by State law prior to the time when the Electors were to meet and vote for President and Vice President was final and could not be set aside by subsequent State action after the votes had been cast and the return thereof had been duly made to the President of the Senate. This decision rested upon the following among other grounds: First, for reasons of great public importance it was provided by the Constitution that the Electors should meet in the States upon the same day and cast their votes, and Congress was authorized by the Constitution to fix the day for such meeting. This power was exercised by the passage of the act of 1792, fixing the first Wednesday in December as the day on which Electors should meet and vote in all the States. The great wisdom of this provision of the Constitution was apparent, as its purpose was to prevent the very mischief which was attempted in the Florida case. It was to prevent a State from withholding its vote until it could be seen how it would affect the result. It was to prohibit a State from changing its vote after it had once been cast in order to change a result, and above all, it must be seen that the Constitution could not be so construed as to allow a new State administration, coming into power in January, to proceed to set aside and reverse the action of the State Government under a previous administration in the matter of appointing Presidential Electors, especially where it appeared that the Electors were chosen and returned as duly elected, and met and performed all their functions, including a return of their votes to the President of the Senate on or prior to Dec. 6, and nearly a month before such new administration came into power. Second, if proceedings, either by the State Legislature or the State courts, had in the latter part of January, could be allowed to set aside the constitutional action of the State in this respect, had in December, it must result not only in a violation of the constitutional requirement that the votes of all the States should be cast on the same day, but must also lead to the most serious consequences in the future. If a judgment in an inferior court in Florida, rendered on the 27th of January in an action of *quo warranto*, could annul the vote of that State cast on the 6th of December, it followed that similar judgments in any or all of the other States might be certified to the President of the Senate, and must govern the count. The vote of the great State of New-York would generally be decisive of the result of a Presidential election. In that State, he said, he believed there were more than 30 Judges possessing jurisdiction in *quo warranto*, and asked whether it should be decided that any one of those might, after the Presidential election was over, transfer the vote of that State from one candidate to the other. If so, how many of those Judges would hereafter enter the list and contend for the first chance to determine the Presidency? And what should be done if several of them, each claiming priority of jurisdiction, should render conflicting judgments? Who could fail to see that such a doctrine would result in confusion, disaster, and ruin? He wanted to know if, by an *ex post facto* judgment in one State one party should secure an advantage, why, by a similar movement in another State, a corresponding advantage might not be sought for by the other party? and claimed as a result of such policy that, instead of counting the votes under the Constitution and law at the time prescribed, it would become necessary to count the judgments in *quo warranto* rendered in the various States, and enter into an inquiry as to the regularity and conclusiveness of these judicial proceedings. There must be authority somewhere, and at some time, to decide who were appointed Electors, and that the only safe or sound or constitutional rule that could be found was that adopted by the Commission—to wit, that the decision made by the proper State authority, prior to the time fixed by the Constitution and law for electing the President and Vice President of the United States, was final, and not subject to be set aside by Congress. The power of Congress was to count, not to reject, duly certified votes of the States.

#### SPEECH OF MR. TUCKER.

Mr. TUCKER, of Virginia, followed on the opposite side of the question. He said he did not propose to criticise, much less to censure the action of any member of the Commission, but he did propose to criticise its judgment. The members of that Commission had taken an oath to render judgment according to the Constitution and law. The Commission in passing upon the eligibility of Humphreys had declined to pass upon the question of the validity of the vote of an incompetent Elector. Did the Commission mean to decide that the ineligibility of the Elector was to have no effect upon the validity of his vote? If a State appointed an ineligible Elector, was he, notwithstanding, to be declared by the Commission and by the two houses to be a competent Elector, and his vote to be counted a valid vote? If so, then the act of the Canvassing Board of a State was valid, and the Constitution, *quoad hoc*, was void. In regard to the main question, the decision of this Commission was to the effect that the only voice permitted to speak for a State in the matter of a Presidential election was the voice of a Canvassing Board, and of an Executive, and that the voice of the Judiciary and the Legislature must be hushed into silence before the omnipotent voice of a Canvassing Board and Executive. He contended that all the organism of a State must speak its voice, but the Commission had decided that the only organism to speak it was the organism of the Canvassing Board and the Executive.

Mr. Tucker's time expired before he had finished his argument.

#### MR. BANKS' ARGUMENT.

Mr. BANKS, of Massachusetts, said that it would be one of the highest privileges accorded to him to be able to cast his vote in support of the decision and report of the Electoral Commission. In regard to the question of the ineligibility of Humphreys, there was, according to the decision of the Commission and according to the facts of the case, no pretense of ineligibility. He had been a United States officer, but he had resigned his office. Unless the fact that a United States office had been once held incapacitated a man forever from being an Elector, this man was clear from any objection upon that ground. If people used due diligence in informing themselves of the eligibility or ineligibility of an Elector, and, notwithstanding the effort to gain that information, an Elector should be incapacitated, the people ought not to be deprived of their choice on that account. In regard to the main question he held that when an Elector had cast his vote he had fulfilled his duty and exhausted his functions, and no State court or United States Court could change that act. There was no court in Florida, nor any political party, nor any defeated candidate who had a right, or a shadow of a right, to reverse the decision of the Electoral College.

#### MR. SPRINGER'S SPEECH.

Mr. SPRINGER, of Illinois, opposed the decision because the Commission had adopted an order to receive and consider no evidence that had not been submitted to the Joint Convention, and because that order excluded evidence which would have showed conclusively that a majority of the legal votes actually cast and canvassed was in favor of the Tilden Electors. He quoted Mr. O'Conor's declaration that "There lives not a man, so far as I know, on the face of the earth, who, having the faculty of blushing, can look an honest man in the face and assert that the Hayes Electors were truly elected," and said that it being a conceded fact that the people of Florida had not voted for the Hayes Electors, and the Commission having adopted the procrustean rule which prohibited it from considering any question of fraud that might have arisen in the case, the House was brought face to face with a gigantic fraud, and the decision of the Commission rendered it utterly impossible to defeat the accomplishment of that fraud. He also opposed the decision because the Commission had held that it was incompetent to go into evidence *aliunde* of the papers opened by the President of the Senate. He held that that decision was not law, and quoted Cushing's Manual in support of his own view. He regretted that the decision had come with the significant vote of 8 to 7. He regretted it the more, because it was contrary to the spirit of the law, and disappointed the expectations of those who framed it that it would be carried out in a spirit of patriotism and justice, and not of partisanship. He quoted from Mr. Hoar's speech in support of the Electoral bill where it was asked whether there were not in all this Sodom 10 men who would obey any other mandate than that of party, and he [Mr. Springer] re-

## RESTLESS ENGINEERS.

### STRIKE OF LOCOMOTIVE DRIVERS.

THE ENGINEERS AND FIREMEN ON THE BOSTON AND MAINE ROAD STOP WORK—THEIR PLACES PARTLY SUPPLIED—THE COMPLAINTS OF THE STRIKERS—THE RAILROAD OFFICERS DETERMINED NOT TO MAKE THE DEMANDED CONCESSIONS.

*Special Dispatch to the New-York Times.*

BOSTON, Feb. 12.—The threatened strike of the locomotive engineers and firemen employed by the Boston and Maine Railroad Company, operated between this city and Portland, with several branches and tributaries, took place to-day. At 2 o'clock a committee representing the engineers waited on Superintendent Furber and presented the ultimatum of the dissatisfied operatives, and two hours were allowed for a final decision. The demands made were for a fixed schedule of rates of wages, the highest being $3 50 per day, with certain guaranteed rights, similar to those demanded by the Printers' Union. There was no discretion left with the employers in the matter of appointment or promotion, except so far as related to a decision of fitness or capability. The Superintendent promised to lay the matter before the Board of Directors at the next meeting, and had in the meantime agreed to make some advances in salaries, but could not guarantee any modifications of the existing rules and regulations of the corporation. The committee was told this substantially, and at 4 o'clock every engineer left his train just where he happened to be at the time. The management had been expecting this and had men scattered along the road, some of them on the trains, ready to take charge at once, and the regular trains came very near making time. The main cause of the dissatisfaction is said to be the tyranny of Master Mechanic Smith, who has charge of the train hands. The engineers say that he has made their lives as wretched and pinched as he could by arbitrary conduct and exacting demands, which the men could not comply with without great personal sacrifices. Their wages have been cut down, and the method of payment was such that they were perpetually annoyed. The regulations of train-time, the distance, &c., were so arranged as to produce inconvenience and trouble.

The excitement along the line of the road is intense. At Lawrence the President is in charge looking after the company's property and trying to direct the organized and vigorous movement made by the company against the strikers, which promises to be bitterly pushed to the end. Crowds surrounded the depot and watched for any developments that might arise. All the men who had left the trains in the vicinity came into town and, joined by their friends, formed little groups to discuss the wrongs of the Brotherhood. At Dover, N. H., the same state of affairs prevails. The trains which were due in the early evening had not come in, and the depot and the streets leading to it were lined with people. So far as heard from there have been no disturbances or disorder. The men are determined to "stick" and to force the company to come to their terms by peaceable means. The company, on the other hand, are equally earnest in their professions of ability to get along without the strikers. There were 63 engineers and the same number of firemen who left work, and about 20 of each class stepped in to take their places.

Mr. Furber, the Superintendent, had arranged a new time-table by which he could consolidate some trains and keep all his new men at work, but he has had so many offers of aid that he has determined to carry out the old schedule time on all through trains, at least. He has had promises of men from the Concord Railroad and other sections.

The Brotherhood here is a powerful organization with a large bank account, and it has voted to stand by the strikers. A public meeting will be held in Faneuil Hall to-morrow evening for the purpose of presenting to the people the true state of affairs, at least from the standpoint of the engineers. They assert that all the men who took trains to-day were discharged from the road or from other roads, for incompetency or drunkenness, and the people will not long patronize a road run by untrustworthy engineers. It is hard to predict which side will win, but one thing may be said—the road will suffer, owing to the trouble. Reports from all points along the road to-night state that the drawbridges are all guarded by policemen and special officers, and all the company's property is strictly watched. No demonstrations of hostility are reported, but trouble is apprehended to-morrow.

## RAILROAD FREIGHTS ON EXPORTS.

MEETING OF GENERAL FREIGHT AGENTS OF TRUNK LINES IN CHICAGO—RATES TO BRITISH AND EUROPEAN PORTS.

*Special Dispatch to the New-York Times.*

CHICAGO, Feb. 12.—A very important meeting of general freight agents of the trunk railroads was held at the office of the Lake Shore road in this city, to-day. There were representatives present from the Baltimore and Ohio, Michigan Central, Pittsburg and Fort Wayne, Pittsburg, Cincinnati, and St. Louis, and the Grand Trunk. The meeting was called to settle the schedule complications which have arisen regarding the rate on foreign freights, that is, to adopt a plan for insuring uniform rates upon competitive traffic destined to European ports. The following tariff was agreed upon: Chicago to Liverpool—Wheat, 52 cents; corn, 53 cents; provisions, 60 cents; flour, $1 24. Chicago to London—Provisions, 72 cents; flour, $1 39. Chicago to Glasgow—Wheat, 34 cents; corn, 56 cents; provisions, 72 cents; flour, $1 43. Chicago to Bremen—Provisions, 86 cents. Chicago to Antwerp—Wheat, 66 cents; corn, 69 cents; provisions, 83 cents; flour, $1 55. The rate from Milwaukee to the same points will be two cents higher in gold than the tariff from this city. Flour will be charged for by the barrel, and other freights by the 100 pounds. While the plan adopted admits of but one uniform rate on all export freights, the trunk lines are left free to make any inland rate they please, so long as it does not conflict with the agreed upon tariff to European points. This arrangement goes into effect to-morrow, and as an experiment, will remain in force during this week, at least, and for as much longer time as may be agreeable to all parties. It is a part of the agreement that the general freight agents shall meet every Saturday and revise, or if necessary, revoke, the new schedule, and at the meeting in New-York, on the 27th inst., the plan will be finally approved or disapproved by the Eastern and Western lines in convention.

## AN ENTERPRISING FARMER.

HE OFFERS $300 TO SECRETARY CHANDLER FOR A FAVORABLE DECISION IN A LAND CLAIM, AND IS PROMPTLY ARRESTED.

SAN FRANCISCO, Feb. 12.—United States Deputy Marshal Finnegan brought to the city from Marysville, last night, Tracey Stewart, a farmer in the vicinity of Wheatland, Yuba County, as a prisoner, on a charge of attempting to bribe Secretary of the Interior Chandler to render a decision in his favor in a contest over the title to a quarter section of United States land. He wrote to Secretary Chandler in October last, and again in November, offering him $300 for a prompt and favorable decision. Mr. Chandler referred the letters to the Attorney General, who transmitted them to District Attorney Coghlan with instructions to bring Stewart to justice. Stewart, when arrested, intimated that he thought the out-going administration would be ready to take advantage of an opportunity to make money. The Grand Jury of the United States Court found an indictment against Stewart on Friday last.

# The New-York Times.

VOL. XXVI.......NO. 7938. NEW-YORK, WEDNESDAY, FEBRUARY 21, 1877. PRICE FOUR CENTS.


## THE COUNTING OF THE VOTE

### NINE MORE STATES COUNTED.

TRIVIAL OBJECTIONS MADE TO ELECTORS FROM MICHIGAN AND NEVADA—SINGULAR ACTION OF THE SENATE ON THE MICHIGAN CASE—THE OBSTRUCTORS IN THE HOUSE REBUKED BY THE RESPECTABLE DEMOCRATS—THE OBJECTION TO THE NEVADA ELECTOR UNANIMOUSLY OVERRULED IN THE SENATE.

*Special Dispatch to the New-York Times.*

WASHINGTON, Feb. 20.—When the House met this morning at 10 o'clock, there were many members absent, and Vance, of Ohio, with several others, attempted to secure two hours' delay by moving a recess until noon. This effort resulted in nothing except a half hour's loss of time, and the debate on the objections to sustaining the decision of the Commission began at 10:30. About a dozen members spoke in the two hours allotted to debate, the first speech being by Mr. New, of Indiana, who proposed to stand by the consequences of the Electoral bill. Mr. Joyce, of Vermont; Mr. Townsend, of Pennsylvania; Mr. Crapo, of Massachusetts; Mr. Danford, of Ohio; Mr. Kelley, of Pennsylvania, and Mr. Pratt, of Iowa, made earnest speeches in defense of the action of the Commission. Of these perhaps Mr. Kelley's was the most forcible, since he met the charge of fraud by a vigorous protest and a strong declaration of the character of the crimes by which the Democrats had sought to carry the State of Louisiana. He quoted the recent opinion of Judge Church, of New-York, and was interrupted by Mr. Cox, who said that Judge Church meant that there was no way under the law of going behind the returns, a sentiment which Mr. Cox seemed to indorse, and which is precisely what the Commission decided and what the Republicans claim. Cox evidently had in mind that the Commission was a Democratic Returning Board instead of a body bound by existing law. Mr. Danford referred to the Oregon telegrams and Tilden's connection with the Oregon fraud, and expressed his gratification that Gov. Hayes had no such affair as that laid to his charge.

On the Democratic side, after Mr. New's speech, the decision was further attacked by Messrs. Levy, of Louisiana; McMahon, of Ohio; Rice, of Ohio; Watterson, Cox, Ellis, of Louisiana, and Fernando Wood. Their speeches were reinforced by Henry L. Pierce, of Massachusetts, and in some manner by Prof. Seelye. Mr. Watterson plainly expressed his purpose to accept the result of the Electoral Commission, and go home to his confiding constituents and tell them all about it. Mr. Cox mixed his speech in about equal parts with jokes, partisan recrimination, and profane allusions to Holy Writ. He declined to be held responsible for the result of the Commission's action, but seemed inclined to accept it without great opposition. Mr. Pierce concluded that the State of Louisiana had been carried by tremendous frauds, and he admitted the illegality of the action of the Returning Board, as he claimed it to be, and while he had a holy horror of Democratic rule, he could not endure the thought that the results of violence should be overcome, except in some manner to square exactly with his own judgment of what might be proper. Prof. Seelye concluded, on the whole, that the intimidation on one side and the fraud on the other were so great that, really, the State of Louisiana ought not to have any voice at all in the Presidential election. He approved the decision of the Commission in respect to its interpretation of law, but regarded this as a case where equity rises so much above the law as to compel the law to be set aside in behalf of the right. Both Seelye and Pierce voted with the Democrats against sustaining the decision. Both are men whose honest purposes can never be impeached, but they have been overcome by the popular delusion that what is not made right by law must be made right in some unlawful manner. Prof. Seelye's position on the general result would sustain the action of the Returning Board, if it had been as fraudulent as Mr. Pierce supposed it to have been, because the Returning Board in saving the State from being carried against the will of the people by murder and intimidation, would have preserved, according to Prof. Seelye's position, though in an unlawful manner, the exact equities of the election. Putting Mr. Pierce's allegations and Prof. Seelye's logic together, the Returning Board simply rose above the law to enforce the right. This demonstration by two such men is the remains of the sentimentalism by which a great many good people have been misled, because they seem to think there is some better way to right wrongs than the legal way. This was in the main the theory which Don Quixote pursued. The House sustained the objection to the decision of the Commission by a vote of 172 to 99.

The Senate was then notified that the House was ready to proceed with the count, and at 1 o'clock the Joint Convention assembled for the 11th time since Feb. 1. The eight votes of Louisiana were counted for Hayes, and the count proceeded, Maine, Massachusetts, Maryand, and Michigan being called in regular order. It was generally expected that the count would proceed until Oregon should be reached, that being the next State in alphabetical order from which there are two sets of Electors returned. It was a great surprise, therefore, when, in response to the inquiry of the Presiding Officer for objections to the vote of Michigan, Mr. Tucker, of Virginia, arose and presented formal objections to the counting of the vote of one of the Electors returned, on the ground that he was a Federal officer at the time of his appointment, and continued to be such officer, and there was, therefore, no election, and the vacancy was not legally filled. The objections having been read the Senate retired to its own Chamber. It was generally suspected that the objection to Michigan was made simply for delay, and when Mr. Southard, of Ohio, who has advocated every violent measure proposed in caucus, was awarded the floor to make a motion for a recess until 10 o'clock to-morrow, this suspicion was partly confirmed. It was subsequently pretended, however, that those who preferred the objection to the Michigan Elector were not acting in concert with the obstructionists. Mr. Tucker disclaimed all purpose of interposing unnecessary delay, and stated he was prepared to proceed with the argument in support of the objections. Fernando Wood also mildly opposed a recess, and the demonstration which followed on the Democratic side showed that the advocates of delay would be in a hopeless minority. The vote on Southard's motion for a recess was first taken *viva voce*, and the great volume of sound that rolled into "nay" left no doubt of the result. A division was demanded, when 86 arose for and 163 against recess. The filibusterers then demanded the yeas and nays, and they were ordered, resulting in a more sweeping defeat for them; only 57 were bold enough to record themselves for further delay, while 192 are recorded against it. The negative vote was furnished by the following States: Ohio, 10; Kentucky, 6; Pennsylvania, 4; Indiana, 4; Georgia, Maryland, and Tennessee, each 3; Alabama, Illinois, Louisiana, Mississippi, North Carolina, New-York, Virginia, and Wisconsin, each 2; Arkansas, California, Massachusetts, Missouri, New-Jersey, Oregon, Texas, and West Virginia each one. Meade and Odell were the New-York negative voters. It was 3 o'clock before debate began on the Michigan objections, and it continued until after 5, being marked by nothing of special interest. Some of the speeches delivered to-day were prepared for the Louisiana case, and were gravely read by their authors to listless auditors. Several times general impatience was manifested by some wearied members calling out, "Vote, vote," but the monotony was continued until the two hours devoted to debate had been exhausted. Then Mr. Jenks, one of the Democratic objectors in the Louisiana case, offered, as a substitute for Tucker's motion, a resolution providing that the vote of Michigan be counted, despite the objection, and much to the surprise of most of the spectators, this was carried by an overwhelming vote. After this, on motion of Mr. Hale, the Clerk was instructed to notify the Senate that the House was again ready to go into joint session.

When the Senate reached its own chamber, after the separation, Mr. Allison, of Iowa, offered a resolution to the effect that the vote of Michigan be counted for the Republican candidates, notwithstanding the objection made by the opposition. Upon this proposition Mr. Bayard surprised his non-partisan friends by making an exceedingly injudicious speech, in which he repudiated all the principles established by the decision of the Electoral Commission, of which he is a member. He declared, among other absurd things, that a vote for an Elector about whose eligibility there was a dispute was not a vote at all, or if it was a vote, it was only such a one as could be cast for a dead man. Messrs. McMillan and Christancy followed in strong speeches in favor of the resolution and against sustaining the objection made in the House. Then Mr. Hereford, of West Virginia, mustered up courage enough to open his mouth, and declared that although he did not desire to take up the time of the Senate, he thought it was his duty to his State to protest against the counting of the vote under discussion. Mr. Morton followed in support of the resolution, and he in turn was succeeded by Mr. Stevenson, of Kentucky, who, much to the surprise of his associates, supported the resolution and expressed a determination to vote for it.

At this point news was received that the conspiracy in the House to take a recess until to-morrow had been defeated by a vote of 192 to 57, and then Mr. Bayard, seeing that he had made a mistake in opposing the resolution, obtained the floor by unanimous consent, and declared that if he had had time to finish his speech he would have expressed the opinion that upon the testimony submitted in the Michigan case it would not be just nor legal to throw out the vote of the so-called ineligible Elector. This put an end to all partisan opposition to the counting of the vote. Messrs. Bogy and Kernan fell into line, making speeches in favor of the resolution. Senator Morrill, amid loud laughter, stated that for once he would be unpartisan and vote with his Democratic friend Mr. Kernan, and it seemed as if the resolution was going to be passed without further waste of time. This, however, was a mistake, for Mr. Whyte obtained the floor, and offered a substitute for the original motion, which greatly modified its language and scope. This gave rise to considerable debate, pending which Senator Norwood stated that when he signed the objection he was not aware of the insufficiency of the evidence upon which it was based. Then a vote was taken on Mr. Whyte's substitute, and it was lost by a majority of 10. The original resolution was then taken up, and Mr. McDonald made a motion to strike out the first clause, which set forth that the objection was not good in law. This was defeated by a vote of 38 to 26, and then the question recurring upon the first resolution, it was, at the suggestion of Mr. Cooper, voted upon separately. The first clause was adopted by a vote of 40 to 17. The last section, providing that the Michigan vote be counted, was carried by the unanimous voice of the Senate, Mr. Hereford voting with the rest.

Shortly after this a message was received stating that the House was ready to again meet in joint session, and the Senate proceeded to the Hall of Representatives. Then the vote of Michigan was declared for Hayes and Wheeler, and the count went on until Nevada was called, when Mr. Springer, one of the most prominently unscrupulous and dishonorable filibusters in Congress, objected to the count on the ground that one of the Electors from the State named was ineligible at the time of his appointment. This made it necessary for the two houses to separate again. The Senate returned to its own Chamber and by a unanimous vote declined to sustain the objection, and ordered that all the votes of Nevada be counted for the Republican candidates. Pending the discussion of the subject, the lower house took a recess until to-morrow morning. There was no roll call on the motion. Both sides were worn out with the labors of the day, and seeing that if the count proceeded the session would last until late at night, they were willing to let it be suspended for another day.

### SCHEMES OF THE REVOLUTIONISTS.

THE POLICY OF DELAY AND ITS WORK YESTERDAY—DUPLICITY AND UNSCRUPULOUSNESS OF THE EXTREMISTS—THE TRUMPED-UP OBJECTIONS REJECTED BY THE SENATE.

*Special Dispatch to the New-York Times.*

WASHINGTON, Feb. 20.—The new revolutionary policy of cheating the Democracy into an abandonment of the course marked out in the party caucus by offering plausible, well-appearing excuses for delay, met with a serious defeat to-day, which gives promise of a completion of the Electoral count without intentional procrastination. The Fabian policy of the handful of lunatics who propose to prevent an election, succeeded in securing the recess yesterday on a false pretense of wanting time to prepare for the Oregon case, and by a promise of contentment with one day only. Hurd, who was said to be sick and unable to go on with the Oregon case, was in the House to-day looking as well as ever. This would seem to give credence to the other story that Hurd had become disgusted, and had refused to claim the fraudulent vote of Cronin. The Louisiana case was permitted to be closed without delay, but when the Joint Convention met and had proceeded with the count as far as Michigan, it was found that a trumped up objection had been framed against the vote of one of the Electors chosen to fill a vacancy in the college. The disingenuousness of this objection is witnessed by the unanimous vote of the Senate against sustaining it. The motive of it was immediately revealed by the motion of Southard, of Ohio, that the House take a recess till to-morrow morning. The purpose to delay was scarcely attempted to be disguised. Southard could only say for himself that he did not have any intention of speaking, but this was a very important question, and he wanted a day for consideration. Some points of order were raised, but Randall ruled against them all, except one to the effect that if a recess was taken till evening, the question of sustaining the objection could not be set aside for legislative business. This was so plain a provision of law that any person who could read could not fail to understand it, though three or four members, including Sayler, of Ohio, endeavored to thrust a legislative evening session into the midst of the Electoral count. The motion of Southard was one for which no pretext could be presented in its support. The vote showed about the same number of revolutionists who had voted in caucus, while near a hundred Democrats voted with the Republicans against the proposed delay. This vote is regarded as a decisive defeat of the revolutionists, though it will by no means put a stop to their secret plots for delay.

The case made out against the Michigan Elector was similar in most respects, though much weaker than that which Springer had prepared against Chaffee, the Illinois Elector. Crossman, of Michigan, had been made a United States Commissioner for a special matter, and without ever coming into possession of a commission, had ceased to act 13 years ago, without any formal recognition. Chaffee, in Illinois, had been really a Commissioner, and had acted as such to the knowledge of his neighbors for some years. But the objection was not made in the case of Chaffee, lest the counting of his vote should prejudice the Louisiana case before the Commission. The objection in the case of Michigan was simply for delay, and shows in strong light the duplicity of the revolutionists in the party.

The objection trumped up to a Nevada Elector was of the same character and made for the same purpose, and the Senate, without even dividing, refused to sustain the objection, and, as in the case of the Michigan Elector, the House will probably refuse to reject the vote, though there may be the full two hours of debate, for many members have written speeches on the general situation which will fit this case as well as any other. There are, however, no more States which are known to afford opportunities for objection till Oregon is reached. After that the only State is the last on the list, (Wisconsin,) where there is some story about an ineligible Elector which may be taken advantage of. Of course, South Carolina must go to the Commission. The revolutionists may still consume considerable time, but cannot defeat the declaration of an election.

### HEWITT AND KENNER'S GAME.

A SCHEME TO SPRING KENNER'S STORY ON THE COMMISSION IN THE LOUISIANA CASE—HEWITT'S CONFIDENCES WITH A BABBLING JOURNALIST—FAILURE OF THE SCHEME THROUGH THE DECISION NOT TO TAKE TESTIMONY.

*Special Dispatch to the New-York Times.*

WASHINGTON, Feb. 20.—There is a history concerning Duncan Kenner's testimony as to his attempt to bribe the Louisiana Returning Board to vote to give the State to Tilden that is decidedly interesting. Wells was the first to allude to this attempt, and charged Kenner with an offer of $200,000 for the vote of the State. Kenner immediately came forward with his story that Wells had made the first proposition, and that Kenner had tried to raise the money, subscribing liberally himself, but had not succeeded. It was the purpose of the Democrats to reserve Mr. Kenner's testimony for the Commission, the expectation of some of them being that testimony would be received in the Louisiana case. It was noticed that Kenner was not called by the Field committee as soon as he arrived in town, and the explanation of the delay is as stated above. Mr. Hewitt imparted the story of Kenner to Sam Bowles, of the Springfield *Republican*, during a dinner at Mr. Hewitt's house, and also told Bowles of the very shrewd design of producing a tremendous effect on the Commission by springing this testimony unexpectedly upon them. Bowles promised to observe secrecy, but immediately wrote the whole story in a letter signed with his initials and printed in the Springfield *Republican*, before the decision of the Commission was announced. The intent which Mr. Hewitt at the same time expressed of submitting Kenner's testimony before Field's Committee if they should fail to secure his examination by the Commission, was afterward accomplished by his examination last Saturday. It is not generally supposed that Kenner's confession of his part in the transaction, supposing the story which he tells were uncontradicted, would have produced so great an effect upon the Commission in behalf of giving that State to Tilden as Mr. Hewitt expected; but at any rate the decision of the Commission not to take evidence defeated the theatrical exhibition which the great Democratic manager had prepared for the stage.

### DONN PIATT'S DEFIANT ATTITUDE.

HOW HE REGARDS HIS OWN INFAMOUS ADVICE—HIS EXPLANATION OF THE ARTICLE IN THE CAPITAL—AN ATTEMPT TO INCITE REVOLUTION.

*Special Dispatch to the New-York Times.*

WASHINGTON, Feb. 20.—Donn Piatt is said to have published the incendiary article in Sunday's *Capital* to secure for himself some gratuitous advertising, and he regarded the matter as a huge joke. Now that the case is in progress of examination in the courts it appears less funny to him than it did, and to-day he publishes a card in the *Star* in which he freely mingles explanation and defiance. He closes with the following Parthian shot:

"I only seek to protest the misconstruction put upon my words. None other than an insane man, or one desperately wicked, would ever think of assassination, let alone publicly advocate the commission of so horrible a crime. Beyond this I have nothing to say. I ask no odds of these people. They are playing with a dangerous element, when they openly innovate on right sanctioned by time and sanctified by the blood of the people. They will have enough to do in caring for themselves, without troubling me."

He incorporates in the card the incendiary paragraph from his former article, which he says he again repeats, and he explains that his appeal was to the people and not to the assassin. He means open attack instead of concealed murder, or, to give his words their most favorable construction, he incites to revolution instead of assassination. His interpretation of his own language is about on a plane with Kelly's explanation of the Oregon dispatches. The point which he makes is so fine that it will be necessarily determined by a jury in a public trial.

### NORTH CAROLINA DEMOCRATS.

THEIR ATTACK UPON A COMMISSION CREATED BY THEIR OWN PARTY—THE INAUGURATION OF THE PRESIDENT-ELECT BITTERLY OPPOSED—HOW 30,000 AMERICAN CITIZENS ARE TO BE DISFRANCHISED.

*Special Dispatch to the New-York Times.*

RALEIGH, Feb. 20.—The Senate having passed the resolutions telegraphed on Sunday last, a Democratic member on yesterday introduced the following in the lower house of the Legislature:

*Whereas*, The Joint Electoral Commission, by their action, deliberately sanctioned fraud and have violated the spirit and the letter of the act constituting said Commission; and *whereas*, The direct result of their action in refusing to inquire into the fraud of the Returning Boards is to place in the office of President a person who has no legal or moral right to hold said office, in defiance of the will of the people, and in opposition to a large majority of the Electoral vote legally cast; therefore,

*Resolved*, That the General Assembly of North Carolina do enter its solemn protest against the action of said Commission, and the Senators and Representatives of North Carolina in Congress are requested to use all lawful means, confining themselves within the terms of the act constituting the Commission, to prevent the inauguration of the person attempted to be illegally thrust upon the people of the United States.

An amendment was adopted making the resolution refer to a majority of the Commission. After considerable angry and excited talk, action was postponed until the night session to-morrow. The Georgia game is now on foot in the Legislature. A bill is now before the Senate to amend the Constitution so as to require each person who applies to vote to exhibit his receipt for poll-tax for the preceding year. The Democratic organs are pressing this bill upon the ground that it will virtually disfranchise 25,000 or 30,000 negroes, and thus make North Carolina as firmly Democratic as the State of Georgia.

### THE PHILADELPHIA ELECTION.

A SWEEPING REPUBLICAN VICTORY—MAYOR STOKLEY RE-ELECTED FOR A THIRD TERM BY A LARGE MAJORITY—DESPERATE EFFORT OF THE DEMOCRATS TO SECURE CONTROL OF THE CITY.

*Special Dispatch to the New-York Times.*

PHILADELPHIA, Feb. 20.—One of the hardest fought battles for municipal offices which has ever taken place in this city was that of to-day for Mayor, Receiver of Taxes, and City Solicitor. These three offices are very important, and the Democrats made strenuous efforts to capture all, but were not successful. Hon. William S. Stokley, the present incumbent, was re-elected Mayor by a good majority considering the opposition which was made against him. During his present term he incurred the displeasure of some of the Republicans who were ambitious for the office of Mayor, and failing to reach the prize themselves took up as their candidate Mr. Joseph L. Caven, an independent Republican. A combination was formed with the Democrats, and Mr. Caven foisted upon them as their candidate. To this the Bourbon minded, straight-out members of the party objected, and refused to support him, preferring Mayor Stokley again to a man whom they did not know, and who was crammed down their throats. In addition to this, the orderly citizens feared a Democratic Police force. Six years ago we had Democratic policemen, who bartered with thieves, and made life unsafe in the streets even in daytime. A complete reign of terror prevailed, but under Mayor Stokley the roughs were driven from the city and order has been preserved. The people took the matter in their own hands and re-elected Mayor Stokley to a third term.

The Democracy had a two-fold purpose in their desperate effort to secure control of the municipal offices, notably that of Mayor and Receiver of Taxes, because they could then use the latter office for the purpose of flooding the State with bogus tax receipts, and by fraud overcome the Republican majority in the city, and capture the State. This, in conjunction with a Democratic Police to club voters from the polls in the city, would have given them control of immense power. The majority for Mayor Stokley is estimated, at 1 o'clock A. M., from returns thus far received, at about 5,000. Nelson West, Republican, is elected City Solicitor, and Robert C. Roberts, Republican, Receiver of Taxes.

MUNICIPAL ELECTIONS IN PENNSYLVANIA.

READING, Feb. 20.—Charles F. Evans, Republican, was re-elected Mayor to-day.

YORK, Feb. 20.—The Democrats elected the Burgess to-day by 300 majority.

SUNBURY, Feb. 20.—The Republicans elected the Burgess to-day by 160 majority.

TYRONE, Feb. 20.—A Republican Mayor was elected to-day.

LEBANON, Feb. 20.—The Democratic candidate for Burgess was elected to-day. The Council is also Democratic.

LANCASTER, Feb. 20.—Macgonigle, Democrat, was elected Mayor to-day by 50 majority.

CHESTER, Feb. 20.—The whole Republican ticket was elected to-day by a majority averaging 400.

HARRISBURG, Feb. 20.—Metzgar, Republican, was elected Controller to-day. The Democrats gain in both branches of the Council.

PITTSBURG, Feb. 20.—Liddell, Dem., was elected Mayor to-day, and McCarthy, Dem., Controller. Kingore, Rep., was elected Treasurer over Cosgrove, Dem. Liddell's majority over Humphries, Rep., in 74 of the 101 precincts, is 1,414.

### THE MILITIA OF SOUTH CAROLINA.

THEIR PROPOSED PARADE ON WASHINGTON'S BIRTHDAY TO BE PREVENTED—THE PRESIDENT'S ORDER—COMPLIANCE OF GOV. HAMPTON.

COLUMBIA, Feb. 20.—Information having reached President Grant, through Republican channels here, that several white military companies, including the Washington Light Infantry, which attended the Bunker Hill and Centennial celebrations, intended celebrating Washington's Birthday by a parade, an order was issued to Col. Black, Eighteenth Infantry, commanding the post here, to prevent any such demonstration or parade on the part of such organizations. Gov. Hampton, upon hearing of it, issued a proclamation to-night calling upon the people to comply with the requirements of the President's order, but protesting in strong language against it and asking that the celebration be postponed until some more auspicious period. The order creates some excitement among the people and indignation among the citizen Militia.

### PETITIONS AND PRAYERS IN CANADA.

OTTAWA, Feb. 20.—On a motion to receive several petitions from boards of trade in the United States, the Speaker said he was of opinion that citizens of the United States or other aliens had no right whatever to petition this House, and ruled that they could not be received. The report of the committee on the form of prayer to be used at the opening of the House was presented. It recommends prayers for the Queen, Prince of Wales, and Parliament, ending with the Lord's Prayer. It was agreed that the Speaker should read prayers before the galleries were opened in his own language, and that the form of prayers should be printed with the votes and proceedings in French and English respectively, that all might understand them.

## LATEST NEWS BY CABLE.

### TURKEY AND HER ENEMIES.

ARRIVAL AT CONSTANTINOPLE OF MUNITIONS OF WAR—RUSSIA'S ARMY WELL ORGANIZED AND READY TO CROSS THE BORDER—THE CZAR'S NEGOTIATIONS WITH THE SHAH OF PERSIA.

BUCHAREST, Feb. 20.—The Turkish flotilla has returned to Sulina after an excursion to Rustchuk. It has just been reinforced by a second iron-clad corvette.

CONSTANTINOPLE, Feb. 20.—The Servian Plenipotentiaries had their first conference with Safvet Pasha to-day. The interview lasted three hours. The conciliatory impression continues. The Porte does not seem disposed to press its points relative to guarantees as a *sine qua non*. The British steamer Lotus, Capt. McNabb, which sailed from New-Haven Jan. 23, with a cargo of arms and ammunition for the Turkish Government valued at $1,750,000 has arrived here with boats and deck-house damaged, hatches and skylights washed away, and winches broken. The cargo is also reported to be damaged.

LONDON, Feb. 20.—The Vienna *Political Correspondence*, in its detailed account of the strength of the Russian Army, says: "In all Russia has 600,000 men, or two-fifths of her Army organized. Of these about half are ready on the frontiers, and only awaiting orders to begin operations."

The correspondent of the *Times* at Vienna says the statement of the *Political Correspondence* appears to be a tolerably correct one, when compared with information from other sources.

A special dispatch from Pera says: "Twenty more Bulgarians, charged with complicity in the May insurrection, have been sentenced each to 20 years' penal servitude. Chevket Pasha, of atrocities notoriety, has been appointed to command an army corps on the Danube."

LONDON, Feb. 21.—A dispatch from Vienna reports that the Roumanian representative has officially informed Count Andrassy that Roumania desires to remain neutral in any case, and the Roumanian Militia will be disbanded next week. A special dispatch from Pesth says it is rumored in Belgrade that Russia has informed Servia that she intends to cross the Pruth within 10 days. A correspondent at Pera telegraphs that peace with the principalities is considered certain. A dispatch says news has been received that the Russians are actively working in Persia to induce the Shah to join them in the event of war. The inducement held out to Persia is the possession of disputed frontier territory. The Shah does not appear to be altogether averse to the plan. The Turkish frontier is almost denuded of troops, and even with 20,000 soldiers whom the Shah can collect, something might be done. The chronic differences between Turkey and Persia would furnish a ready excuse for a declaration of war. The foregoing strengthens the impression that Russia, in the event of war, will make her chief effort on Turkey's Asiatic frontier.

### ENGLAND AND EASTERN AFFAIRS.

DEBATE ON THE EASTERN QUESTION IN THE HOUSE OF LORDS—SPEECHES OF THE DUKE OF ARGYLE, EARL DERBY, AND LORD SALISBURY.

LONDON, Feb. 20.—In the debate in the House of Lords to-day on the Eastern question the Duke of Argyle pointed out that the object of the Marquis of Salisbury's mission had been to secure peace in Europe and reform in Turkey. Neither of these objects had been attained. Turkey was not reformed, and there was no prospect of peace in Europe. He deprecated the unreasonable suspicion of Russia which actuated English policy up to August last. He admitted that England had a great interest in the neutrality of Egypt and in preventing Constantinople from falling into the hands of any great European power. But, except on these points, he could conceive of no injury to Great Britain by any transfer of power from the Turkish Empire. He pointed to the various instances where European powers, while professing to respect the independence guaranteed to Turkey by the Treaty of Paris, had interfered in Turkish affairs in a way that showed they regarded Turkish justice as utterly unworthy of confidence. It was necessary to carry this argument further in the sense indicated by the Marquis of Salisbury when he declared the independence of Turkey might at the present time be interpreted so as to be consistent with the joint military and diplomatic action of the guaranteeing powers. The speaker concluded with an eloquent appeal to the Earl of Beaconsfield to mark the close of his career by procuring some measure of liberty for Christians in Turkey.

The Earl of Derby asked if it was not premature to say the conference had failed. He could not yet say the peace of Europe was to be broken; and, relative to internal reforms it must be remembered that Turkey had lately introduced very comprehensive reforms. We were not justified in concluding because a particular mode of effecting reforms was not adopted, that Turkey, therefore, had a fixed purpose of rejecting all reforms. He pointed to the fact that the Government had never been willing to fight for Turkey, and had informed the Turks so as far back as last May. He admitted that although the Government had never changed its policy, they had in one respect changed their course of action; that is to say, that having to deal with the danger of a European war, which at one time appeared imminent, they had done and accepted many things which they would have thought impossible to do or accept if more had not been at stake than the suppression of a petty insurrection. The Government had said all along that the Turkish Government could be maintained only by the amelioration of their internal administration. He agreed with the Duke of Argyle that independence was a very elastic term. There were in all parts of the world States which by their weakness were exposed to measures on the part of stronger neighbors which those neighbors would not adopt toward more powerful States. In answer to the charge of undue suspicion of Russia, he said it was not his duty or wish to say anything of the Russian Government, but it was perfectly well known that official personages, personages connected with the Russian Government, were among the most active agents in stirring up the disturbance in Herzegovina. Lord Derby cited passages from former Blue Books, showing that in one case a Russian Consulate was the head-quarters of the insurgents. The Bulgarian outrages had only secondary influence on the change of the Government's course of action. The principal cause was that Servia entered a fight with an army of which the fighting element was almost entirely Russian. Russia was in the field in fact, though not in name. Russian feeling was so excited that there was very great fear of war. Lord Derby gave a detailed account of the efforts to procure an armistice. He was never so much surprised in his life as when Russia refused the five months' armistice. If the Duke of Argyll, or any other member of the Opposition, desired to raise the question of the advisability of coercion, he [the speaker] would undertake to show that coercion would be unreasonable unless it meant war, and war would be fraught with every possible danger to Europe. Since the conference the Government had been unremitting in pressing the expediency of peace on Servia, Montenegro, and Turkey—a few days would show with what success. If they were successful half the work of the conference would be done. There would, of course, remain the question of internal reform. He was not prepared to give a definite opinion on this subject, but he was much struck with the suggestion made by the Turkish representative at the conference that the Porte should be given a reasonable time to carry out reforms in its own way, and then if nothing was done the powers would have the right to demand guarantees. This was admitted by Midhat Pasha, and he [Lord Derby] thought the idea was a moderate and fair one.

The Marquis of Salisbury, replying to the Earl of Kimberly, who blamed the Government for having declared their intention not to coerce Turkey, said the present complications were traceable to the treaty concluded after the Crimean War. The idea of six European powers undertaking the tutelage of the subject populations of Turkey, was an impracticable chimera. Long and sad experience had proved that Turkey would not reform herself as the powers expected when they undertook the obligation to protect her Christian subjects. The Government, however, are bound by the acts of their predecessors. We, like all the Governments, since the Crimean war, are bound to respect the treaty by which that war was concluded. He pointed to the startling fact that the persons who signed that treaty guaranteeing the independence and integrity of Turkey are now attacking Lord Derby for not having fostered and encouraged the Herzegovinian insurrection when the hopelessness of Turkey's reform became evident. It is also plain that England's attitude toward Turkey could not remain the same as in 1856. Lord Salisbury asked, however, were we justified in immediately turning around on our ancient ally, who had long been encouraged to count upon our support. If the terrible events in Turkey were to alienate the undoubted affection which had been entertained by the English people for Turkey, surely it was our duty to struggle as long as possible against a change which forced us, at all events, to put a new and unexpected interpretation on words to which England was pledged. We have changed as far as force of circumstances have compelled us, but we have not dissolved our traditional alliance without sorrow, and we still cling to the hope that some change in counsels may restore that alliance. The refusal of the Turks to accept the recommendations of the conference is a mystery. Their infatuation seems tremendous. The assertions of the Porte's irresponsible advisers that the Russian Army was disorganized and diseased had much influence on its determination. In regard to England's not having used threats of coercion at the conference, Lord Salisbury thought it important to place upon record the fact that, as far as the proceedings of the conference went, no power had used such threats, and nothing had happened at the conference to pledge Russia as a matter of honor to take military action against the Porte. He energetically challenged the Opposition to bring forward a definite motion stating the policy which they advised. He showed that the only coercion England could threaten would be the destruction of Stamboul by a fleet. Turkey would probably disregard it. As the question of yielding is not in the hands of those who are most deeply interested in the prosperity of the country, the execution of the threat would destroy the only Government which now controls thirty millions of people. Our policy is to endeavor to secure some measure of liberty and safety for the subject populations. Of that we do not despair. Midhat Pasha was unquestionably the greatest opponent of the conference. It is fair to assume until we know otherwise, that his fall betokens a more conciliatory spirit. We hope that if the substance of the reforms be adopted, no power will consider itself bound or justified in trying to solve the question by the sword. If once the powers are assured that peace is hopeless, there is every reason to fear that the great energy which now induces them to strain every nerve to avert war will lead them in the future to say this question must be settled once for all. That is the terrible danger.

The Earl of Beaconsfield challenged the Opposition to propose a distinct motion. He deprecated the policy of coercion. The policy of Europe, and not merely of England, was to maintain the integrity and independence of the Ottoman Empire. That was the principle which has always been acted upon by all statesmen as affording the best security for the peace of Europe. Nothing had happened since the treaty of Paris to show that this principle was not wise and just.

### MISCELLANEOUS FOREIGN NOTES.

THE RINDERPEST IN ENGLAND—LONDON STOCK EXCHANGE—THE BANK QUESTION IN AUSTRIA—RADICALISM IN PARIS—SPANISH CONSPIRATORS ARRESTED.

LONDON, Feb. 20.—Much uneasiness is felt on account of an outbreak of rinderpest at Hull, which cannot be traced to any contact with infectious beast or matter. Stringent measures have been taken to isolate local outbreaks.

On the Stock Exchange to-day the foreign market was stagnant. Prices tend down, but there was no business doing. The suspense of the political situation flattens all international stocks. American railways are depressed.

VIENNA, Feb. 20.—The journals here report that an agreement has been reached on the bank question, and the Hungarian Ministers have started for Pesth.

PARIS, Feb. 20.—M. Duverdier, an extreme Radical, has been elected President of the Municipal Council.

LONDON, Feb. 21.—A dispatch from Barcelona says seven persons have been arrested there. It is said that they are charged with taking part in a Zorillist plot which was to have been carried into effect during the approaching sojourn of King Alfonso at Barcelona. The trial of the prisoners has already commenced.

LONDON, Feb. 21.—Mr. Hutchinson, Liberal, has been returned to the House of Commons from Halifax, receiving 5,750 votes against 3,624 thrown for Mr. Gamble, Conservative.

### BUSINESS FAILURE IN CHICAGO.

CHICAGO, Feb. 20.—The failure is announced of D. Kreigh, commission merchant in produce and provisions, and an extensive dealer on 'Change. The rapid decline in the price of provisions is assumed to be the cause of the failure. Mr. Kreigh says he cannot yet give any definite figures; but it is known the failure is for a very large amount. Among the secured liabilities are $100,000 in trust deed, to N. Corwith, of Chicago; $130,000 in warrantee deed to James L. Flint, of New-York, and a mortgage on real estate (amount unknown) to T. J. S. Flint of New-York. The unsecured liabilities are from $1,000 to $4,000 each, to numerous firms on 'Change. Mr. Kreigh is an old and highly respected citizen of Chicago, and his failure has caused great surprise to all except those who were informed of his late business transactions.

### THE ST. LOUIS MUTUAL LIFE.

ST. LOUIS, Feb. 20.—The Receivers of the St. Louis Mutual Life Insurance Company filed suit in the Circuit Court to-day against the Columbia Life Insurance Company for a settlement of accounts between the two companies. The petition sets forth that in December, 1873, the St. Louis Mutual Life Insurance Company executed a contract with defendant under which all its property and assets of every kind were transferred to the defendant, amounting to nearly $11,000,000, and that the contract was illegal and void, and judgment in the above amount is therefore prayed.

### MURDERER IDENTIFIED.

CINCINNATI, Feb. 20.—The proprietor of the hotel at Jefferson, Texas, at which Bessie Moore and her murderer stopped, while in that city, arrived here this morning and identified "Abe" Rothschild as the man who was last seen with Bessie Moore. While there he passed under the name of Monroe. It will be remembered these dispatches gave an account on Saturday last of an attempted suicide by Rothschild, supposed to have been caused by remorse for the murder of Miss Moore.

### THE ASHTABULA DISASTER.

CLEVELAND, Feb. 20.—A special dispatch to the *Leader* from Ashtabula says that the Coroner's jury to inquire into the cause of the disaster re-assembled to-day. Several brakemen were examined relative to the length of time it took to stop a train running at a given speed on which the patent brakes are used.

### MURDER IN THE SECOND DEGREE.

BALTIMORE, Feb. 20.—In the criminal court to-day George Waters, (colored,) who has been on trial for the past two days for the murder of William Giles (colored) in December last, was found guilty of murder in the second degree and sentenced to 15 years' imprisonment in the Penitentiary.

### AID FOR THE WAMSUTTA STRIKERS.

FALL RIVER, Feb. 20.—A mass meeting of mill operatives held here to-night resolved to aid the strikers of the Wamsutta Mills, New-Bedford, and voted an assessment for that purpose.

### THE MOBILE AND OHIO RAILROAD.

MOBILE, Feb. 20.—In the Mobile and Ohio Railroad case a rehearing of Judge Bruce's late decision in opposition to the former decision of Judge Woods will be heard in April.

### HOMICIDE IN KENTUCKY.

LOUISVILLE, Feb. 20.—E. D. Kennedy, Master Commissioner of the Garrard County Court, was killed to-day by his nephew, G. C. Kennedy, at Lancaster. They had a difficulty about a lawsuit. The murderer was arrested.

### THE RAILROAD STRIKE IN BOSTON.

ACCIDENTS AND APPREHENSION OF OTHERS MORE SERIOUS—THE STRIKERS TAMPERING WITH THE ENGINES—NARROW ESCAPES ALONG THE BOSTON AND MAINE ROAD.

*Special Dispatch to the New-York Times.*

BOSTON, Feb. 20.—The strike on the Boston and Maine Railroad does not change materially. Both parties are confident of success, and both are equally obstinate. Between them, the public has to suffer, if not from actual loss, at least from nervousness and inconvenience. There is a constant apprehension that some fearful catastrophe will happen. To-day, as a train from Medford was being pushed into the depot by the shifting engine "Lion," it left the rails in the yard, in consequence of a misplaced switch, and, went bounding over the sleepers for about 60 feet, striking a train standing upon the side-track. The collision raised both trains from the ground, and, as they crowded against each other, the seats were wrenched out of position, and the sill timbers sprung, one of them being broken. The panels of the front car of the incoming train were stove in half its length, and the timbers of one truck were smashed. The train was quickly stopped and all excitement allayed, but some of the women were badly frightened and screamed frantically. The damage done was not serious, but the escape from worse consequences was very fortunate. There was a danger of the cars upsetting and had this occurred the cars would undoubtedly have caught fire, when the worst results might have followed. It is said that the switchman had not had time to replace the switch.

A dispatch from Portland says an accident happened, at midnight, to the freight train, bound for Boston, and inquiry reveals the fact that the engine was burned at Wells, which is about 25 miles this side of Portland. The engine was the "Saco," the largest on the road. It is a most significant fact that workmen are changing the boiler plugs in all the locomotives, replacing the iron ones with lead ones. The "Granite State" arrived in this city burned so badly that with but little more heat she would have burst. Along the line several narrow escapes have been recorded, and people are getting extremely nervous. All the business that the other roads can do is being transferred from the Boston and Maine, and passengers who can get to their destination by any other route, however circuitous, much prefer delay to danger.

A general strike on the railroads leading out of this city is hinted at, but is neither denied nor confirmed by the officers of the Brotherhood. Chief Arthur says that due notice will be given to the public of such action. A movement is on foot among the stockholders to take advantage of the law which requires the company to open the books at the request of 15 stockholders, and if successful the public will probably know what the strike is costing the corporation. The Post Office authorities aver that the evening mail train from Portland is almost uniformly late since the strike began.

ONE OF THE LOCOMOTIVE ENGINEERS ARRESTED.

*Dispatch to the Associated Press.*

BOSTON, Feb. 20.—Charles Randall, one of the striking engineers of the Boston and Maine Railroad, was arrested to-day and held for examination, having been detected in the act of disabling the locomotive of the 9 P. M. outward-bound train.

### MARINE DISASTERS.

LONDON, Feb. 20.—The weather is now (7 P. M.) fair, but last night and this morning it was wet, cold and boisterous. A gale prevailed on the west coast, and great damage was done to shipping, but no loss of life is yet reported. The British ship Rowantree, Capt. Cunningham, from Liverpool Jan. 13, for Mobile, is on Penrhos beach, North Wales, full of water. Two coasting steamers and several sailing vessels are ashore near Holyhead, and several other vessels, in a damaged condition, have taken refuge in that harbor.

Last night's gale extended around the south coast and numerous shipping disasters are reported. A Liverpool dispatch states that the British ship Lizzie Burrill, Capt. Stuart, which arrived at that port from New-Orleans Jan. 29, and the Danish bark Tobasco, Capt. Klitgaard, which put back Jan. 29 from a voyage to Hampton Roads, are ashore. The American bark General Fairchild, Capt. Kedy, which arrived at Liverpool from Charleston yesterday, was damaged by collision in the Mersey.

HAVANA, Feb. 20.—The bark Kronprinsen, Capt. Caliborg, from New-Orleans Feb. 11, for Liverpool, with a cargo of cotton, was lost on the 17th on San Cayetano reefs. The crew was saved.

BOSTON, Feb. 20.—The schooner T. B. Pillsbury, New-Orleans for Boston, with a cargo of cotton, went ashore at Nausett at 2 o'clock this morning. She will probably get off.

### HOPEFUL FEELING AT FALL RIVER.

The Boston *Journal* of Monday says: "The Fall River manufacturers generally believe that their hardest experiences are over, and look for a lively Spring trade. Though the expense of running by steam and the large amount necessary to pay the yearly interest on costly and extensive mills have eaten up what little profit they have made during the past three years, the present business of nearly all the corporations is remunerative, and the prospect is of a steady increase. The drought during the past Winter has stopped many mills which are dependent entirely upon water, and the growing confidence in a satisfactory solution of the political situation has created a demand for cloths, which the Fall River manufacturers are prepared to take advantage of. The present production of all the Fall River mills amounts to 2,850,000 yards per week, on which there is a net profit of $58,500, and prices show signs of improving. It is a noteworthy fact that, though Fall River manufacturers made the first export of goods to England, and can compete with her in foreign countries, the home demand is so great that they cannot at present follow up the advantage, and this branch of the trade is practically monopolised, as far as New-England is concerned, by Rhode Island makers. Every indication points to the fact that the hard times in the dry goods trade are over, and it is fair to suppose that this new and encouraging state of things will extend to other lines of manufacture also."

### QUARRELS OF MUSICIANS.

The Springfield (Mass.) *Republican* of Tuesday says: "Charles E. Pratt and Emil Seifert of the Abbott concert troupe indulged in a few hard words at the depot, yesterday afternoon, just after their arrival on the fast train from the south, which ended in Pratt's giving Seifert a blow across the mouth. A policeman interfered just in time to prevent a fight, and, putting the combatants in separate hacks, sent them to their hotel. Seifert immediately set out to procure a warrant for Pratt's arrest for assault, and, after he had been refused by Judge Wells and M. P. Knowlton, finally obtained one of E. P. Bartholomew. None of the regular Policemen would serve the warrant, but Special Officer Tileston did so, and Mr. Pratt was arrested about sundown. His wife, with another member of the troupe, furnished bail in a few minutes, planking $100 in gold as security, and the two combatants appeared on the stage together last evening as if nothing had happened. As Judge Wells refused to give a warrant, he will doubtless dismiss the case when it comes before him this morning. The trouble is understood to have arisen over a criticism of Pratt's playing written by Seifert, and which appeared in a New-York paper."

### THE RICHEST MAN IN THE WORLD.

*From the London Spectator.*

The American accounts all agree in reporting that Mr. Vanderbilt was the richest American, and probably the richest man in the world. His heirs will, it is believed, pay legacy duty on £16,000,000 sterling, most of it invested to yield 7 per cent. per annum, and the whole of it made by a waterman's apprentice in one lifetime. Mr. Vanderbilt has left about a sixth of this property in legacies to his wife and younger children, and five-sixths to his eldest son, but absolutely nothing to any charity whatever, though it is said he asked his son before his death to make certain gifts. In America it is not considered quite right to make a will without charitable bequests, but in England nobody expects a great landlord to leave sixpence to anybody but his own people, and as a rule, he fulfills expectations.

# The New-York Times.

VOL. XXVI......NO. 7941. NEW-YORK, SATURDAY, FEBRUARY 24, 1877.—WITH SUPPLEMENT. PRICE FOUR CENTS.


## WASHINGTON.

### SUCCESSION TO THE PRESIDENCY.

CONSIDERABLE SPECULATION INDULGED IN—VARIOUS PROPOSITIONS ADVANCED—NO PROVISION WHATEVER MADE BY THE STATUTES FOR FILLING A VACANCY—WHAT MAY OCCUR IN CASE NO ONE IS DECLARED ELECTED—HOW PRESIDENT GRANT MAY CHECKMATE DEMOCRATIC REVOLUTIONISTS.

*Special Dispatch to the New-York Times.*

WASHINGTON, Feb. 23.—There is much talk about the succession to the Presidential office in case the Democrats should succeed in preventing, by filibustering, a declaration of the Electoral vote. It has been generally supposed that the course of the Republicans would be to stand by a continuation of the count by Mr. Ferry, the President of the Senate, and the declaration of the result on the last day of the session, in case no election had been declared under the operation of the Electoral bill before that time. It is argued in behalf of this course that the Commission has decided all the disputed questions, and that everybody in the country knows what the legal and equitable result would be if there were no revolution attempted on the part of the Democracy to defeat the formal announcement, which is all that would be left at the end of the session to make the operation of the law complete. The indignation of those Republicans who were opposed to Mr. Ferry counting the vote in the first place has been aroused to that extent that most of them are now willing to fully sustain him in such a contingency. It is admitted that this would have less foundation in law than the counting of the vote by him would have had if no legislation on the subject had taken place this session, but the excuse is found in the fact that the revolutionary proceeding of the House makes some extraordinary action necessary, and it is not improbable, if there were no other alternative, that this course would be pursued. There has been no definite plan agreed upon, and the views of Mr. Ferry on the subject are unknown. Various other propositions have been advanced, as for example, that Senator Sherman should resign from the Senate, allow Mr. Hayes to be elected by the Ohio Legislature to fill his place, and that the Senate choose Mr. Hayes President pro tem., and make him the President of the United States in case there were no election. This would be in direct violation of law in one respect, for the statutes make no provision whatever for filling a vacancy in the Presidency occurring by a failure to elect. Section 146 of the Revised Statutes is as follows:

> In case of removal, death, resignation, or inability of both the President and Vice President of the United States, the President of the Senate, or if there is none, then the Speaker of the House of Representatives for the time being, shall act as President until the disability is removed or a President elected.

It is provided in the sections following that a special election shall be held, which in this case would occur on the first Wednesday in next December. The only evidence required of a resignation of the office is the written instrument declaring the purpose signed by the President. Now, under this statute, the President of the Senate would not become President of the United States by reason of a failure to elect, and there would be no person having the authority after March 4 to hold the Presidential office, if the Electoral count should be left unfinished. President Grant, being in possession, it may fairly be supposed that he would continue to occupy the office until a new election could be had, in order that the nation might not be left without an official head. His only right to continue as President would be the right of possession, and that would be sufficient, doubtless, to maintain him in the office, as no other person would have the right to claim it from him. This is one of the conditions in which the country may possibly be plunged by Democratic obstinacy in the House, and they would not like to have President Grant hold the office under such circumstances. There is a way out under the statute to save the country from all difficulty in respect to the succession. In case President Grant should resign when it become evident that no declaration of Mr. Hayes' election could be made, even though it were within an hour of the end of the session, the President pro tem. of the Senate would immediately become President of the United States, and, under the law, would hold over until the new election provided for should be held. The President has it completely in his power, therefore, to checkmate, by his own action, any Democratic revolution, and it can hardly be doubted that he would take the necessary action. This last mentioned proceeding would be absolutely within the statute law, and would give the Republicans a vast advantage in the new election. The unlawful and revolutionary proceeding of the Democratic Party would destroy them before the people. Mr. Ferry, very probably, would become the President, and while it is very possible that if the office of President of the Senate were vacant some other person would be chosen to fill it, it is not believed that any effort will be made to displace him, and there is no reason to doubt he would be a just and strong executive officer during his incumbency.

### A MOUNTAIN OUT OF A MOLE HILL.

CONSIDERABLE EXCITEMENT CREATED BY AN OVER-ZEALOUS YOUNG MAN—HOW CERTAIN DEMOCRATS BECAME INTERESTED IN AN OHIO NEWSPAPER—THE MATTER FULLY EXPLAINED TO THE SATISFACTION OF EVERYBODY.

*Special Dispatch to the New-York Times.*

WASHINGTON, Feb. 23.—There was a good deal of excitement caused among the Southern Democrats to-day by the circulation of numerous copies of the *Ohio State Journal* of Feb. 22 containing a strong article in favor of the recognition of the Packard Government, which was claimed to have been written by Gen. Comley and inspired by Gov. Hayes. The article in that view was rather ominous, and had a decided effect upon the Southern men who have been known as being hostile to the filibustering policy to defeat the counting of the Electoral vote. This led to the holding of a conference to-night of many Southern members, and a desire was expressed to know whether the article was inspired by Gov. Hayes, as alleged. The following dispatches show what was the truth about the article. The paper containing it had been sent here in large quantities and by the revolutionists, and they attempted by an adroit use of it to force the agreement to filibuster upon the party:

WASHINGTON, Feb. 23, 1877.

*To J. M. Comley, Columbus, Ohio:*

The *Ohio State Journal* of yesterday was industriously circulated this morning among the Democratic members of the House, and soon after a motion was made to take a recess until to-morrow, supported by an almost solid Democratic vote, and carried. A caucus was called for immediately. The article on Louisiana is supposed by them to have been inspired by Gov. Hayes and to reflect his policy.

STANLEY MATHEWS,
CHARLES FOSTER,
WM. DENNISON.

*To Hons. Stanley Mathews, Charles Foster, and William Dennison, Washington:*

Gen. Comley has been very sick for a week past. He is not permitted to see or talk to any one, and your dispatch cannot be shown to him. He is not allowed even to read anything that appears in the *State Journal*. The article in the *Journal* of Thursday on Louisiana affairs was not written by him. Gov. Hayes neither inspired nor saw it, and did not hear of it until his attention was called to it by your dispatch from Washington.

A. W. FRANCISCO,
Associate Proprietor *State Journal*.

A further dispatch was received from Gen. C. H. Grosvenor, Speaker of the House of Representatives, of Ohio, stating that the article in question was originally a communication lying in the *Journal* office, and was used by a young man in charge in the absence and severe illness of Gen. Comley.

### DEMOCRATIC OBSTRUCTIONISTS.

CAUCUS OF THE DEMOCRATS OF THE HOUSE—A RESOLUTION TO TAKE A RECESS TILL MONDAY AGREED ON—THE REVOLUTIONISTS DRAGOONING THE RESPECTABLE MEMBERS OF THE PARTY—THE OBJECT TO DELAY THE COUNT.

*Special Dispatch to the New-York Times.*

WASHINGTON, Feb. 23.—The House adjourned at 4 o'clock this afternoon, in order to give the Democrats another opportunity to meet in caucus. Adjournment was carried by yeas 130, nays 109, 15 Democrats voting with the Republicans against the motion. It was supposed, but wrongly, in the House, that the report of the Commission was about to be received. The caucus was immediately assembled, and business was commenced at once by McMahon, of Ohio, who offered a resolution providing that when the two houses shall separate to-morrow to consider the decision of the Commission in the case of Oregon, a recess shall be immediately taken until 10 o'clock Monday. Mr. Kehr, of Missouri, and Neal, of Ohio, respectively offered substitutes providing that the business before the Joint Convention shall proceed to-morrow without delay. In the discussion which followed Messrs. Vance, Hurd, Southard, Knott, Lane, and Sparks advocated adjournment until Monday, and Messrs. Hill, of Georgia; Brown, of Kentucky; Wilshire, of Arkansas; House, of Tennessee, and Harrison, of Illinois, advocated proceeding with the count to-morrow. Randall spoke mildly in favor of moderation, in view of the great importance of the issues involved. Field also spoke, but devoted himself more to the explanation of two new bills which he has prepared, than to the pending resolution. One of these bills provides for a new election for President and Vice President, in May next, in case no President shall be declared to have been elected at the late election. The other bill provides that persons claiming to have been elected President may commence proceedings under *quo warranto* before the Supreme Court. The vote on the substitute offered to McMahon's resolution was defeated by yeas 44, nays 66, and the original resolution was then adopted without a division.

The vote for adjournment until Monday shows that those favoring delay in completing the Electoral count have received a considerable accession to their ranks since the last meeting of the caucus, but it is doubtful if these can be held together to ultimately defeat a final proclamation of the result of the Electoral count. A majority of those who voted against delay are outspoken in their determination to resist any action having for its purpose the defeat of the completion of the Electoral count, and while they may to-morrow go with their party for adjournment until Monday, they are determined to break with their associates, rather than follow them in any effort calculated to defeat the purposes of the Electoral act. No reasons were assigned for the delay until Monday, but it is apparent that the object is to prevent the completion of the Electoral count. The action of the caucus will bear no other interpretation, and those who desire to see the Electoral law carried out in good faith may as well recognize this fact now as next week. It is not believed the effort will succeed. Those who oppose delay are reluctant to take a step which will place them in antagonism to their party associates, but it is plain from the temper manifested that they are determined to do this rather than submit to the plans of the destructionists. If Hill, of Georgia, and Brown, of Kentucky, will make on the floor of the House the same earnest opposition to delay which they have uniformly made in caucus, they will be instrumental in breaking up the plotting of Randall and his followers.

*Dispatch to the Associated Press.*

It is reported that just before the adjournment of the caucus a resolution was adopted by a vote of 57 to 38 providing for another recess of the House from Monday until Tuesday. Prior to the introduction of this resolution a number of the members of the caucus had left the hall, saying they would not abide by the action which provided for a recess from to-morrow until Tuesday.

### MR. CONKLING AND THE DEMOCRATS

THE CONSULTATION WITH VOORHEES AND OTHER DEMOCRATIC LEADERS SAID TO HAVE BEEN ON BUSINESS ONLY.

*Special Dispatch to the New-York Times.*

WASHINGTON, Feb. 23.—The recent reports regarding Senator Conkling's interview with certain prominent members of the Democratic Party, which have been extensively published, have attracted a great deal of attention here to-day, and the Senator's friends are working hard to make excuse for him. They admit that he had consultations with Dan Voorhees and others of the same class, but say that these conferences related simply to business matters of a legal character, and had absolutely no connection with politics.

### THE APPROPRIATION BILLS.

THE NAVAL BILL PASSED BY THE SENATE—SEVERAL CLAUSES AMENDED—NO LESS THAN 544 CHANGES MADE IN THE LEGISLATIVE BILL.

*Special Dispatch to the New-York Times.*

WASHINGTON, Feb. 23.—The House continued the consideration of the Sundry Civil bill to-day, but took a recess until to-morrow without action. The Senate, which is further advanced with appropriation bills than it has been at the same period in the last session of any recent Congress, with commendable promptitude, passed the Naval Appropriation bill, thus disposing of the only business of this character now before it. The amount appropriated by the bill has been increased since it came from the House $4,321,500, and the clause providing for the establishment of a Naval Commission has been stricken out. The following are the principle clauses amended: The appropriation for pay of officers and men is increased $1,000,000; the appropriation for the Bureau of Equipment and Recruiting increased $270,000; the appropriation for the Bureau of Construction and Repairs increased $1,800,000, and the appropriation for the Bureau of Steam Engineering increased $1,200,000. Among other minor additions to the bill is one appropriating $1,500 to defray the expenses of observing the transit of Mercury on May 6, 1878. In the Legislative bill, passed by the Senate a few days ago, no less than 544 changes were made. There were 84 alterations in the Deficiency bill. Well-informed persons now believe that these discrepancies between the bills as passed by the two houses will render a short extra session unavoidable.

### CASHIER JORDAN MADE HAPPY.

A BANK OFFICIAL AT THE BAR OF THE SENATE—HIS AMUSING EFFORTS TO FREE HIMSELF FROM CONTEMPT—GRAVE SENATORS ENTERTAINED BY A NEW-YORKER—HE PROMISES TO ANSWER ALL QUESTIONS PUT TO HIM.

*Special Dispatch to the New-York Times.*

WASHINGTON, Feb. 23.—Quite a scene occurred in the Senate this afternoon when Mr. Conrad N. Jordan, Cashier of the Third National Bank of New-York, was called before the bar for contempt in refusing to produce the bank account of Messrs. Tilden, Hewitt, and Pelton, as called for by the Committee on Privileges and Elections. When asked why he had failed to comply with the order of the committee he produced a written answer which was read by the Clerk. In this paper the witness disowned all intention of being in contempt of the Senate. He said that he had failed to produce the books and papers called for because they were in the custody of the officers of the bank, and he had no control over them. He had refused to answer the questions asked him because he desired before doing so to consult with the counsel of the bank. In concluding, he begged that further time might be allowed him for this purpose.

The answer gave rise to a short but very lively debate, conducted by Senators Blaine, Conkling, Mitchell, Kernan, and others. Mr. Jordan was evidently very anxious to join in the discussion, and it was with the greatest difficulty that he could be prevented from doing so. Mr. Mitchell desired to have the witness adjuged in contempt, and treated accordingly. Mr. Blaine opposed this summary proceeding, and in doing so made one of his characteristic speeches. He said, among other things of the same kind, that he had a great deal of contempt for much that had been done by both sides in the recent investigations, but he knew that politicians did not differ materially from other men, and when they were struck they were very apt to strike back. The Democrats never liked that sort of policy, and evidently they had no taste for it in the present instance. Reference being made to the report that the members of the committee had agreed among themselves to stop the investigation into the financial operations of party managers, Mr. Kernan took the floor and disavowed all knowledge of such an agreement. The same disavowal was made by other members of the committee, and then a resolution was passed calling upon Jordan to state whether he was now willing to answer such questions as might be propounded.

In reply to this, the witness, a little gray-headed man, jumped to his feet with an assurance and readiness that would have done credit even to David Dudley Field himself, and created a marked sensation and considerable merriment by making a speech of some length. He said in substance that he had been badly treated by the committee; that he had been kept dancing attendance on them to no purpose, and that he desired to enter his protest against what he seemed to consider a curtailment of his rights as an American citizen. He concluded by stating that he was now ready to answer any questions which might be put to him, and upon this he was discharged. Before leaving the chamber he shook Senator Blaine by the hand with warm demonstrations of satisfaction, and then retired bowing and smiling to the Senators as he went. The scene was a very amusing one, and Mr. Jordan seemed to enjoy it quite as much as did the spectators.

### FRIENDLY RELATIONS WITH FRANCE

PRESENTATION TO THE PRESIDENT OF THE NEW FRENCH MINISTER—A FRANK EXCHANGE OF FRIENDLY GREETINGS.

WASHINGTON, Feb. 23.—M. Outrey, the newly accredited Minister of France to the United States, accompanied by the Secretary of State, presented his credentials to the President to-day, on which occasion he made the following remarks:

MR. PRESIDENT: I have the honor to present to you the letter of recall which terminates the diplomatic mission of Mr. Bartholdi in the United States. I also have the honor to place in your hands the letter whereby the President of the French Republic accredits me near your Excellency in the capacity of Envoy Extraordinary and Minister Plenipotentiary. All my efforts, Mr. President, shall be devoted to maintaining the cordial relations of France with the United States, and I can assure you that I shall fulfill the sincere wishes of my Government if I can aid in drawing still closer the bonds which have never ceased to unite the two countries. Permit me to solicit your personal good will and that of the Government of the United States to facilitate a mission which I am happy to be called to fulfill in a country to which I am attached by many pleasing recollections and by feelings of warm sympathy.

The President replied as follows:

M. OUTREY: I receive with entire satisfaction the letter by which the President of the French Republic accredits you as the diplomatic representative of that Government. The satisfaction arises in part from your having formerly been a sojourner with us in a diplomatic capacity upon which occasion you left an impression which could not fail to make you welcome on a return to this country. I am confident that you will discharge your official duty in a way which will be generally acceptable, and it is not to be doubted that in this you will always have the hearty co-operation of the President of the United States.

### NOTES FROM THE CAPITAL.

WASHINGTON, Feb. 23.—The borers of the shaft on the south side of the Washington Monument reached, a few days since, an immense gneiss rock, which is believed to extend under the base of the monument, and to form a rock foundation at a distance of 33 feet below the surface.

The Senate Sub-committee on Louisiana in secret session to-day continued their examination of the Returning Board records, which were brought here recently by the Louisiana Secretary of State. The investigation is now being carried on mainly with a view to the determination of contests expected to arise hereafter concerning the election of Senators from that State.

The Senate Committee on Privileges and Elections to-day discharged all the witnesses brought here to testify in regard to the Alabama election, and will to-morrow discharge the remaining witnesses from Mississippi.

Democrats who were present at the conference in Speaker Randall's room last evening, admit that they agreed to offer an amendment to the Army bill to fix the maximum of the Army at 17,000 men, and to provide that none of the troops shall be used to uphold either of the dual governments in Louisiana or South Carolina, but they deny that they have any filibustering intentions to defeat the counting of the Electoral vote.

## LATEST NEWS BY CABLE.

### THE EASTERN CAMPAIGN.

TORPEDOES BEING PLACED IN POSITION—MORE TURKISH OUTRAGES—THE FORTIFICATIONS AT WIDDIN—AUSTRIA'S NOTIFICATION TO RUSSIA—A LARGE FORCE OF TURKISH TROOPS ON THE BORDER—THE PEACE WITH SERVIA.

LONDON, Feb. 23.—A Lloyds dispatch from Constantinople says: "The Russian Consulate here warns shipping that torpedoes are being placed on the Black Sea coast between Sookgoom-Kalé and Fort Saint Nicholas. Guard-ships are stationed at Poti and Sookgoom-Kalé roadsteads to indicate the course. Balaklava must not be entered before communicating."

An evening paper, in a leading article, says: "Rightly or wrongly, there is a general impression that international complications are becoming easier, and war may be avoided for the time. This," it says, "is partly due to the prospect of peace between Turkey and Servia, which is as good as settled. Though this is no guarantee against a Russo-Turkish war, it will undoubtedly reduce to a minimum the chances of precipitate action by Russia."

A dispatch from Bucharest says a number of Turks, including soldiers, pillaged Guraumei Island in the Danube. A detachment of Roumanian troops captured 13 of the party, including a Turkish soldier. The leader of the marauders, who was a Turkish official from Rustchuk, and another Turk were killed.

LONDON, Feb. 24.—The Vienna *Presse* reports that the Russians have already finished seven pontoon bridges on the Pruth, each broad enough to allow eight men to march abreast. A dispatch from Vienna says 8,000 laborers are employed daily on the fortifications of Widdin. The Grand Vizier has sent an autograph letter to Prince Milan expressing a firm hope that the relations of Servia and Turkey will be amicable.

A telegram from Belgrade says of the 400 members of the Skupschtina, not 30 favor the continuance of war.

The Berlin correspondent of a morning paper says intelligence has been received from a trustworthy source that Austria has intimated to Russia that she will not consider the persistence of the Porte in its refusal to yield to the proposals of the powers as a *casus belli*, and that it will depend on each power to assume the attitude appropriate to the special occasion as circumstances are further developed.

A special dispatch from Berlin says the Porte has just received several hundred thousand Martini-Henry Rifles and 400,000,000 cartridges from America. A special from Widdin states that Osman Pasha's troops, quartered between Widdin and Saitschar, consist of 63 battalions of infantry, two regiments of cavalry, and 78 field pieces. Widdin alone has a garrison of 28,000. There are 30 battalions of Asiatics and the severity of the climate and the overcrowding at Widdin, have caused much sickness among the men. It is said that the rate of mortality is high. It is believed that the Turks will occupy Kalafat opposite Widdin in the event of war. They have already collected sufficient material for the construction of pontoon bridges.

The Belgrade correspondent of a morning paper says: The Servian Government has annulled the elections in Jagodina and Kragujevatz on account of disturbances during the polling. The authorities have ordered all volunteers not belonging to any regular corps to quit the country within three days. Fifty-six Russians accordingly left on Thursday; another detachment goes on Friday. The order is aimed at the crowd of military adventurers in Belgrade who are suspected of favoring intrigues against the dynasty. The Russian Consul entirely approved the action of the authorities. It is thought that this expression will cause a final breach with the Russian Slavonic societies, and the last external influence which is opposed to the conclusion of peace will thus be removed. The Pan-Slavists are apparently turning their attention to Montenegro.

The same paper's correspondent at Berlin says, in consequence of Austria's opposition to the cession of a harbor on the Adriatic to Montenegro the Montenegrins will content themselves with obtaining access to the sea through Lake Scutari and the Bajana River. They continue, however, to ask for more territory than the Porte will accord, and the latest intelligence renders it likely that the armistice must be prolonged. In the event of the Porte's making concessions the Montenegrin Commissioners are authorized to sign a preliminary treaty.

Gen. Tchernayeff publishes a denial of Lord Derby's statements relative to the number of Russians in the Servian Army. He says it never exceeded 3,000.

### MISCELLANEOUS FOREIGN NOTES.

REPUTED ELOPEMENT OF A DISTINGUISHED OPERA SINGER—CABLE RATES TO BE REDUCED—RESCUE OF SHIPWRECKED SAILORS.

PARIS, Feb. 23.—The *Figaro* names a distinguished prima donna whom it charges with having eloped from St. Petersburg with the tenor Nicolini. It states further that the Marquis of Caux followed them, and that judicial proceedings for a separation have been commenced.

LONDON, Feb. 23.—A statement is published here that a league has been formed by Ritualists for the purpose of agitating in favor of the disestablishment of the English Church.

Silver was quoted to-day at 56⅛ pence per ounce.

The Anglo-American Cable Company gives notice that on the 1st day of March the tariff on messages transmitted over its line will be reduced to 1 shilling sterling per word.

BERLIN, Feb. 23.—Herr von Forkenbeck has been elected President of the Reichstag, and Prince Hohenlohe Langenburg and Herr Stauffenberg Vice Presidents.

VIENNA, Feb. 23.—Prince Auersperg, the Austrian Prime Minister, has informed a conference of the Constitutional Party in the Reichsrath that the bank will agree to any arrangement effected between Austria and Hungary. A club of members of the Left have resolved to support the Government's project for the organization of the Board of Directors of the Bank, but reserve their decision on all other points of the compromise.

LONDON, Feb. 24.—A Vienna dispatch states that the members of the Upper House, at a private conference, declared in favor of accepting the bank compromise with Hungary.

A gun-boat has succeeded in reaching St. Kilda, and brought off the Captain, Captain's son, mate, boatswain, and five seamen of the bark Peti Dubrovacki, before reported wrecked on the island. It is officially denied that the Queen will go to Germany this year.

PARIS, Feb. 23.—M. De Stapland, Senator from the Department of the Nord, died to-day, aged 79 years. In the Chamber of Deputies this afternoon a motion was made on the part of the Government, that the Minister of the Interior be authorized to institute proceedings against Paul De Cassagnac for libels published in *Le Pays*.

### O'MAHONY'S REMAINS IN IRELAND.

QUEENSTOWN, Feb. 23.—On the arrival here this morning of the steamer Dakota from New-York, a local committee, appointed for the purpose, proceeded out in a tender and received the remains of John O'Mahony, and presented an address to the American deputation accompanying them. The coffin was conveyed to the Pro-Cathedral, where mass for the dead was celebrated at 8 o'clock. Owing to the early hour of landing there was no demonstration.

LONDON, Feb. 23.—A special dispatch from Queenstown to an evening paper says: "O'Mahony's remains will be taken to Cork at 6 o'clock this evening. The Nationalists there intend having a torch-light procession. The body will lie in the Democratic Club room until Sunday, when it will be taken to Dublin. The Fenians are indignant at Cardinal Cullen's refusal to allow the remains to lie in state in Dublin Cathedral, and say if they had anticipated it O'Mahony should have been buried in New-York.

CORK, Feb. 23.—The remains of John O'Mahony were taken from their temporary resting place in Queenstown this evening, and escorted by a large procession to a special steamer, which brought them to this city. On their arrival here they were quickly removed to the Mechanics' Institute, where they now lie.

LONDON, Feb. 24.—The reception of O'Mahoney's remains at Cork disappointed all expectations; only a few hundred people accompanied the corpse to the Democratic club. There was no torchlight procession and no political demonstrations were made. The delegates who accompanied the remains from New-York are indignant at the conduct of the Captain of the steamer Dakota, who refused to recognise them during the voyage or to supply them with an American flag to cover the coffin on landing because he would not countenance what he considered to be a disloyal demonstration.

### TWEED'S EFFORTS FOR RELEASE.

SUING HIS FORMER PARTNERS TO GET MONEY TO BUY HIS FREEDOM WITH—THE SECRET OF HIS POWER—CURIOUS DEFENSE TO A CLAIM—A SUGGESTION TO THE PEOPLE'S COUNSEL.

The statement published in THE TIMES recently concerning the proposed settlement of the litigations by the people against Tweed, and of the prosecution by the latter of his claims against various persons indebted to him, received additional corroboration yesterday, and there is, as has already been stated, no doubt that such is the fixed programme. Papers were drawn up by Tweed's counsel yesterday, in suits against the former partners of the "ex-Boss" in various business transactions. These papers will be served speedily, and the purpose of instituting the suits is to bring about a settlement so that Tweed may be enabled to pay back to the City a portion of the stolen money for his release from jail. Tweed's claims against his partners are claims in regard to real estate transactions, dealings in various classes of stocks and personal claims, such as money loans, &c. Many persons, it is said, who were benefited by Tweed's liberality in former times, have refused to surrender the property given to them in trust or loaned to them, and hence the litigations. There is no doubt that in these suits Tweed has the upper hand. Among his beneficiaries are men holding high positions in official and social life, and any exposure by him of transactions now shrouded from the public gaze would have a telling effect. There seems to be but little doubt but that Tweed is aware of his power to crush some persons. He seems, however, rather desirous of settling matters amicably, if this can be done. One of Tweed's claims is a rather peculiar one. The person against whom he makes the claim now holds a prominent position under the City Government. This man was rather inclined to "fight the tiger" a few years ago, and being once hard pushed borrowed $3,000 from Tweed to pay his proportion of a loss at faro. He neglected to pay up promptly, however, and when pressed for payment he pleaded the Gambling act; in other words, he contended that the money having been used for gambling purposes, he could not be compelled to return it, the money having been loaned to him with knowledge on Tweed's part of the purpose to which the money was to be put. Tweed, of course, by reason of certain "unpleasantnesses" which have taken place within the last six years, has not been, except, until very recently, in a position to demand his claims, and in the event of a refusal to pay his demands, to litigate concerning them. It may be said here that Tweed, in his usual conversation and in his letter written to Mr. Charles O'Conor, from Ludlow-street Jail, pretends to be very poor. As this is somewhat antagonistic to the general belief, it is rather singular that the counsel for the people have not availed themselves of their right to examine him under oath, in supplementary proceedings, in regard to his property. By this procedure he could be compelled under oath to disclose what property he now owns, what property he has disposed of during the past six years or more, and to whom each disposition has been made.

### REPORTED MARINE DISASTERS.

LONDON, Feb. 23.—A Lloyds dispatch from Buenos Ayres, dated Feb. 22, announces that the American ship Admiral, Capt. Blanchard, from New-York Dec. 14, for San Francisco, went ashore Feb. 8 at Patagones and has become a wreck. Part of her cargo will probably be saved. The Russian bark Matie August, Capt. Lammlin, from Ipswich Jan. 16, for Baltimore, has put into West Cowes, with port bow damaged by collision.

BLANKENBERGHE, Feb. 23.—The British bark Eliza McLaughlin, Capt. Phillips, from Lynn Jan. 5 for Baltimore or New-York, is ashore at Knocke, Holland, and likely to become a total wreck. The crew were saved.

HAMBURG, Feb. 23.—A telegram received here from St. Thomas says the steamer Franconia, reported wrecked at Cape San Blas, got off, and is safe at Aspinwall.

CHESTER, Feb. 23.—The steamer Ohio ran into the schooner George H. Turbill below Tinicum Island this afternoon, and cut her in two. The Ohio's boats picked up the schooner's crew.

### THE WEST INDIES.

HAVANA, Feb. 23.—Advices from Port au Prince to the 11th inst. report that peace continues. It is announced that President Canal is to be married to Miss Wilson on the 13th inst. Intelligence from Saint Domingo to the 9th represents that the opponents of President Baez continue to spread reports that he is endeavoring to secure the annexation of the Republic to the United States, with the object of acquiring assistance from the Haytians and promoting disturbances in the north.

St. Thomas dates to the 16th say Lamb & Co. advertise that the Spanish Government will probably indemnify shippers who lost their goods by the capture of the steamer Moctezuma, and request that shippers send their claims to Captain General Jovellar. The *Tidente* says several leaky American vessels are about to proceed to their destination with the aid of steam pumps, and that there is need of an American Plimsoll to look into this dangerous practice, which jeopardizes both lives and property.

### ARRESTED ON A CHARGE OF MURDER.

TERRE HAUTE, Feb. 23.—Light was thrown to-day upon the attempted train robbery and murder of Milo Eames, engineer, at Long Point, on the Vandalia Railroad, on July 8, 1875. The supposed murderers, Charles St. Clair, a hackman; Bud Shoemaker, a brakeman on the train at the time of the attack; Sam and Alexander Cauthorn, (colored;) Billy Carr, and Jennie Osgood, a prostitute, all of this city, were arrested to-day, on evidence which seems sure to convict them of the crime. St. Clair, the leader, is owner of a low house of prostitution here. The first clue to his guilt was obtained by women in his own house, who heard St. Clair talking to one of his associates about their failure in the Long Point business. The prisoners were taken to Prairie City, Ill., to-day for trial. The woman, Jennie Osgood, was dressed in men's clothes at the time of the attack on the train, and wore a false mustache. She was on the engine when Eames was killed. She has signified her intention to tell all she knows about the affair.

### THE LATE REAR ADMIRAL ALDEN.

PORTLAND, Feb. 23.—The remains of Rear Admiral Alden are lying in state in the Council Chamber, City Hall, guarded by a military escort. The floral donations are elaborate. The funeral will take place to-morrow at 11 o'clock, and all the military organizations will take part.

### COLUMBIA LIFE INSURANCE.

ST. LOUIS, Feb. 23.—The ground upon which Col. Celsus Price, State Superintendent of Insurance, asked the Circuit Court yesterday for the appointment of Receivers for the Columbia Life Insurance Company, is that by reason of the shrinkage of values the capital, assets, &c. of that company have become impaired to the extent of nearly $150,000, and that the company is not able to furnish the 5 per cent. reserve required by the State.

### A PAYING RAILROAD.

REPORT OF THE CHICAGO, BURLINGTON AND QUINCY RAILROAD—A LARGE SURPLUS BEYOND THE USUAL DIVIDEND REPORTED.

*Special Dispatch to the New-York Times.*

CHICAGO, Feb. 23.—The report of the Directors of the Chicago, Burlington and Quincy Railroad for the past year was submitted to-day. It shows the earnings for the year to have been $12,057,794, and the expenses, including taxes and also $136,808 of a disputed tax on capital stock, $6,868,545. The decrease of the funded debt has been $38,250. The construction and equipment account has been increased $379,363. The sales of lands amounted to 31,701 acres, and money received in this department $327,800. The road during the year has accumulated a surplus beyond its usual dividend of $339,623, which has been used for the sinking fund, and for new construction in Iowa.

### NORTHERN CENTRAL RAILROAD.

ANNUAL MEETING OF THE BOARD OF DIRECTORS—RECEIPTS AND EXPENDITURES—ELECTION OF OFFICERS.

BALTIMORE, Feb. 23.—At the annual meeting of the Directors of the Northern Central Railroad to-day, President Thomas A. Scott presiding, the report of the operations of the company for the year ending Dec. 31, 1876, was presented to the stockholders. The report gives the total revenue of the main line, with its leased and controlled roads, at $4,369,923 50, and the total operating expenses at $3,036,483 81, leaving as the net earnings $1,333,439 69. "In comparison with 1875 there was a decrease in the gross earnings of $556,322 22, equal to 11 29-100 per cent., and a decrease in the operating expenses of $325,637 87, equal to 9 69-100 per cent. The decrease in the net earnings was $230,681 35, or 14 75-100 per cent. The operating expenses were 69 48-100 per cent. of the gross earnings, which, in comparison with 1875, shows an increase of 1 23-100 per cent. In addition to the net earnings, as above stated, of $1,333,439 69, there was received from dividend and interest, $59,632, and contribution for operating the Elmira, Canandaigua and Canandaigua Division, from the Pennsylvania Railroad Company, $56,487 82, making a total $1,449,559 51, of which amount there has been applied to the payment of various indebtedness, interest on mortgages, &c., $1,260,133 54; leaving a balance for 1876 of $189,425 97. Notwithstanding the unexampled depression in business during the past year, the net earnings of the company have exceeded the interest charged upon its total mortgage, indebtedness, and leases.

The balance to the credit of the profit and loss Dec. 31, 1876, is stated at $176,546 77. While the above statement shows a balance of earnings equal to a dividend of 3 per cent. upon the capital stock, your board does not deem it wise to make a dividend, believing it to be more prudent to hold the existing balance in reserve. Although the expectations of your board have not been realized in the results of the past year, they are able to state to you that, notwithstanding the continued and increased depression in all departments of trade which prevailed during the entire year, especially in those branches upon which the traffic of your lines so largely depend—coal, iron, and lumber—all your property is greatly improved in its condition, in all branches of the service, in its earning capacity, and in its capability of more economical movement of the traffic."

Immediately following the Director's meeting, there was a meeting of the stockholders, and the following gentlemen were elected Directors for the ensuing year: Thomas A. Scott, Wistar Morris, S. M. Felton, A. M. Phillips, George B. Roberts, Edmund Smith, Jr., M. Hutchinson, Dell Abbott, Jr., all of Philadelphia; Wayne MacVeigh, Harrisburg, and George Small, S. M. Shoemaker, and N. B. Sellers, of Baltimore. The new Directors held a meeting, when Thomas A. Scott was re-elected President, A. J. Cassatt, Vice President, and S. R. Hollins, Secretary.

### THE MEXICAN VETERANS.

PROCEEDINGS OF THE NATIONAL ASSOCIATION—THE [illegible]—ESTIMATE OF THE SURVIVORS.

WASHINGTON, Feb. 23.—The second day's proceedings of the National Association of Mexican Veterans comprised a visit to the White House, where they were received by President Grant with a cordial greeting. The movement began four years ago. The veterans expressed the hope that the President would sign their pension bill before his term expired. Returning to Willard Hall Rev. Green Clay Smith was selected as orator of the day for the next annual meeting, which will take place at Baltimore on the 22d of February, 1878. The committee, consisting of one from each State, then organized, and proceeded to the Capitol to appear before the Committee on Pensions of the Senate, a special meeting having been called to hear the veterans. Senator Ingalls, of Kansas, presided. Besides the members of the committee Senators Logan, Burnside, and Maxey were present. Gen. Denver briefly stated the case, and called Secretary Kenady to read an extract from his annual report in regard to the probable number of survivors of the Mexican War. Mr. Kenaday informed the committee that extraordinary efforts had been made during the past four years to ascertain the whereabouts of every survivor. The number of names collected was 6,230, of which 4,629 were tabulated to show the regiments in which they served. From this compilation it was ascertained that 25 regular regiments show an average of 41 survivors, while 15 volunteer regiments from Indiana, Ohio, and Kentucky, average about 46 each. Assuming that 4,629 cover only one-half of the survivors there would not be over 80 or 90 men left of the full regiments that went to Mexico in 1846, less than 10 per cent. of the whole number mustered. These are vital statistics, based on facts susceptible of proof. Senator Ingalls, however, stated that an officer of the Pension Bureau had prepared an estimate which shows that the passage of the proposed bill will necessitate an appropriation of $7,000,000 or $8,000,000 a year. The Pension Committee have agreed to have a meeting to-morrow, to consider the matter.

The convention adjourned to meet again at 3 o'clock Saturday afternoon.

### THE WEATHER.

INDICATIONS.

WASHINGTON, Feb. 24—1 A. M.—*For the Middle States, rising barometer, north-east winds, cooler, cloudy and clearer weather.*

*For New-England stationary or falling, followed by rising barometer, north-east to north-west winds, partly cloudy and clear weather.*

### MORE INDIAN DEPREDATIONS.

DEADWOOD, Feb. 23.—On Wednesday evening, about 6:30 o'clock, a small band of Indians made an attack on Spearfish City, a small mining town near this place. About 100 shots were exchanged. None of the miners were injured, and owing to the darkness the damage done to the Indians is unknown. Last night Boughton's herd of cattle, which a party of armed citizens captured from the Indians a few days since, were again driven off by Indians from the False Bottom mining region.

### THE RAILROAD STRIKE IN THE EAST.

BOSTON, Feb. 23.—The Boston and Maine Railroad Company offer a reward of $100 for the detection of persons violating the State laws relative to obstructing the road or interfering with its rolling stock. There is no change in the situation, except that the road is daily increasing its facilities.

### NOVA SCOTIA AND NEW-BRUNSWICK.

HALIFAX, Feb. 23.—In the Assembly to-day the Provincial Secretary gave notice of a motion authorizing the Government to appoint a delegation to confer with delegates from New-Brunswick and Prince Edward's Island on the proposed union of the maritime provinces.

### THE PRESIDENCY OF MEXICO.

ST. LOUIS, Feb. 23.—José M. Iglesias, one of the Presidents of Mexico, accompanied by several of his staff, arrived here to-night, en route East.

### ARRIVAL OF THE BATAVIA.

The steam-ship Batavia, Capt. Moreland, of the Cunard line, which sailed from Liverpool for this port, via Queenstown, on the 10th inst., arrived here yesterday.

## OREGON VOTES FOR HAYES.

### DECISION OF THE COMMISSION.

UNANIMOUS REJECTION OF CRONIN AS AN ELECTOR—THE THREE REPUBLICAN ELECTORS DECIDED TO BE LEGAL BY A VOTE OF EIGHT TO SEVEN—POINTS OF THE ARGUMENT OF THE MEMBERS IN SECRET SESSION—CONSISTENCY OF THE REPUBLICAN POSITION THROUGHOUT—REPORT OF THE COMMISSIONERS.

*Special Dispatch to the New-York Times.*

WASHINGTON, Feb. 23.—The Commission met this morning, with Mr. Thurman absent by reason of sickness. Arguments were made on the Oregon case by Senator Bayard, Representatives Abbott and Hunton, and Justice Bradley, who spoke last. The two principal topics of discussion were the eligibility of Watts and the Governor's relation to the State canvass and his duty under the State law. There was no vote taken on Cronin's eligibility, but it was the unanimous opinion that he was not an Elector. No Democrat on the Commission went to the extent of claiming Cronin's vote for Tilden. It was developed that there would be eight Commissioners in favor of counting the votes for Gov. Hayes, and the six Democrats present were all in favor of a resolution that only two Electors were legally chosen in Oregon. It was rumored about the Capitol that the vote on counting the vote of Watts was nine to six, and it arose from a common impression that Senator Thurman would vote with the Republicans. About 4 o'clock, the resolutions and reports having been prepared, the Commission proceeded in carriages to Senator Thurman's house and the formal vote was taken, being eight to seven in favor of the resolution declaring that the votes of the three Republican Electors should be counted. As predicted last night, the Democratic Commissioners voted together to take advantage of the results of the Oregon fraud by throwing the election into the House. They repudiated Cronin, but sustained Grover in defeating the casting of three Republican votes in a regular and indisputable manner by issuing the certificate to Cronin.

The points of discussion in the Oregon case by the Commissioners, as above noted, were the election of Cronin, who received but a minority of the votes cast; the eligibility of Watts, to whom Gov. Grover refused a certificate, and the Oregon State law defining the method of the canvass and the Governor's duty. The claim that Judge Hoadley has advanced with so much ingenuity and pertinacity, that a minority candidate is elected when the candidate having the majority is ineligible or disqualified under the law to hold the office, was utterly repudiated by every member of the Commission. The doctrine is one entirely unwholesome to the American people, and one that has not been tolerated, as was pointed out in the Abbott case by Judge Thurman, by any respectable judicial opinion, save one in Indiana. The cases which Hoadley raked together with so much labor were all of inferior courts, and else had no bearing on the direct question at issue. This branch of the discussion occasioned no difficulty, therefore, and little time was spent upon it. The duty of Gov. Grover under the State law was carefully examined. The argument on the Republican side was that the Governor was no part of the canvassing machinery of the State—that the Secretary of State was given by the State statute exclusive and sole authority to canvass the vote cast. That law declares explicitly that it was his duty to report to the Governor the persons having the highest number of votes. This was the completion of the canvass. The duty of the Governor, as declared by the law, was to issue certificates of election to those persons reported to him by the Secretary of State as having the highest number of votes, and the Governor had no authority in law to examine into or question the eligibility of any candidate. His only duty was to issue the certificate as directed by law.

The Democratic argument, on the other hand, was that the Governor with the Secretary of State made the canvass of votes, because the canvass was made in the Governor's presence, as it were, as one of the counsel suggested, with the Governor looking over the Secretary's shoulder. The Democrats, claiming that the Secretary of State alone was not the canvassing officer, made the point that the Governor's certificate with his signature, certified to by the Secretary of State with the seal of the State attached was at once a certificate of the canvass, and that it therefore complied with the former rulings of the Commission, because the canvass and the certificate of election, according to their view, could not, under Oregon law, be separated.

Respecting the eligibility of Watts, the Republicans on the Commission held, as in the Louisiana case, that his holding an office of Postmaster at the time of the November election did not disqualify him for appointment as an Elector, and that the resignation of his office, and his ceasing to act before the meeting of the Electoral College was all that was necessary to remove his disqualification and make his vote as an Elector valid. They held that under the Oregon law the power of the College to fill a vacancy, no matter by what cause it might have been produced, was absolute, interpreting the language of the statute according to the argument of the Republicans' counsel, and disclaiming the argument of Judge Hoadley, that the word "otherwise" meant "in like manner." The Democrats on the Commission held that Watts was ineligible for appointment, and that his election was void, and that under the State law the failure to elect did not produce a vacancy which the Electoral College was authorized to fill. They therefore voted for the exclusion of the vote of Watts.

The report made to the two houses is in accord with the two reports made in the two previous cases, reiterating the reasons which were contained in them.

### PROCEEDINGS OF THE COMMISSION.

The Electoral Commission reassembled in secret session at 10:30 o'clock this morning, pursuant to last evening's adjournment, and remained in consultation on the Oregon case four and one-half hours. At 3 o'clock, the discussion being concluded, and Senator Thurman having been unable to attend the sitting owing to illness, a recess was taken in order to ascertain whether he would prefer coming to the Capitol or that the Commission should proceed to his residence, and there transact the business incident to taking a vote. A committee consisting of Senators Bayard and Frelinghuysen was appointed for this purpose, and reported in due time that Senator Thurman consented to receive the [illegible]

# The New-York Times

VOL. XXVI.......NO. 7941. | NEW-YORK, SUNDAY, FEBRUARY 25, 1877.—TRIPLE SHEET. | PRICE FIVE CENTS.


## THE PRESIDENTIAL COUNT.

### JOINT SESSION OF THE TWO HOUSES.

PRELIMINARY PROCEEDINGS IN THE HOUSE OF REPRESENTATIVES—FILLIBUSTERING EFFORTS BY THE DEMOCRATS—A REPUBLICAN'S POINT OF ORDER SUSTAINED BY SPEAKER RANDALL—NO DELAYS TO BE PERMITTED—THE VOTE OF OREGON COUNTED FOR HAYES—RECESS TILL MONDAY.

*Special Dispatch to the New-York Times.*

WASHINGTON, Feb. 24.—The vote of Oregon was counted in joint meeting of the two Houses to-day. This progress, though not great, was better than could reasonably be expected, considering the caucus action of yesterday afternoon, and the exhibition of Democratic spirit last night. The Senate and House reassembled at 10 o'clock this morning, and the Senate immediately sent to the House a message announcing their readiness to proceed with the count. In the House Mr. McMahon, of Ohio, offered the caucus resolution setting the hour of 1 o'clock for the joint meeting. Some points of order were made, and finally Mr. Randall admitted a substitute for McMahon's resolution, which Mr. Wilson, of Iowa, offered, declaring that the House was ready to meet the Senate forthwith. The yeas and nays were called on this substitute, and it was adopted by a vote of 145 to 87. This was an unexpected defeat to the filibustering faction, and the announcement of the vote was followed by great excitement in the House and an amusing display of activity on the part of David Dudley Field and his runners. Messrs. Springer and Vance were conspicuously active running about the House to get votes changed, or to secure pledges of votes for the next roll-call. Mr. Vance's activity is stimulated by his desire to secure the office of Public Printer, which it is understood has been promised to him substantially by the Tilden managers. He has earned this office by the defeat which he suffered as a candidate for re-election on account of a payment made by him, as Chairman of the Committee on Printing, to a country miller in Ohio, ostensibly as an expert in printing, but really to aid him to come to Washington on a pleasure trip. Mr. Vance as Public Printer has thus indicated his capacity to fill the office with millers, and, doubtless, grocers, and organ-grinders, without much regard to how the printing would be accomplished. The activity of the filibustering party was not fruitful, for on the next roll-call, being on a motion to lay on the table, a motion to reconsider the vote on Mr. Wilson's resolution, the yeas were 175, and the nays 74. This ended the attempt to delay the joint meeting, and a few minutes before 12 the Senate came into the House. The decision of the Commission was read and the objections presented, and the two houses separated again about 12:10.

After the Senate retired from the hall of the House, the first real test vote upon the policy of delay was taken, the motion being a recess until 10 o'clock Monday morning. Mr. Clymer offered this resolution, and undertook to say that it was proposed in entire good faith, and without any purpose to filibuster; but there were several objections to debate, and he was not permitted to go on. Mr. Hancock, of Texas, made the point of order which was made by Mr. Hale on the first occasion of the attempt to take a recess, to the effect that the law required the House to proceed at once to decide the objections without taking a recess. This point of order was again overruled by Mr. Randall, and the vote recurred directly upon Mr. Clymer's motion. In speaking on the point of order, Mr. Hancock took pains to say that he was disappointed at the defeat, but hoped he had manhood enough to continue to do his duty as a member of the House. Mr. Clymer replied to this that the question was not one of manhood, but of order, and afterward attempted to make some remarks, which were not heard in the gallery, owing to confusion on the floor. The vote was taken by yeas and nays, and the proposal for a recess was lost by a vote of 112 yeas to 158 nays. Mr. Lane, of Oregon, immediately attempted the scheme of filibustering by repeated roll-calls, and offered a motion to take a recess until 9:30 on Monday morning. Mr. Hale made the point of order that this was a dilatory motion, and not in order to be offered in the House under the provisions of the Electoral law. To the surprise of the floor and the galleries, Mr. Randall immediately sustained the point of order, saying that it was not in order when the Constitution of the United States and the law enacted under it required Congress to do a certain thing that any obstruction be offered to the performance of the act, and that Mr. Lane's motion was of the class of dilatory motions, and was not in order. The ruling was rather arbitrary, in the light of Mr. Randall's previous rulings in the same direction, for Mr. Lane's motion was no more designed for delay than was the motion of Mr. Clymer, which was admitted to be in order. But the distinction made by Mr. Randall that the House having by a decided vote refused to take the recess which, according to his ruling, was in order, it was very clearly indicated that their purpose to go on with the count and the calling of the roll for the sake of delay was a species of filibustering which the country would not tolerate. The decision was loudly and properly applauded on the Republican side of the house, for it was exactly in accordance with law and right, if not altogether consistent with the action of Mr. Randall a few days since, when he kept the Secretary of the Senate waiting nearly an hour with a message to the House, refusing to recognize him to deliver it. This ruling of Mr. Randall, if persisted in, defeats absolutely the power of the revolutionary element to prevent the conclusion of the count before next Saturday. They can cause considerable delay and trouble, and take up much time that ought to be devoted to legislation, but if a majority adhere to the refusal to take unnecessary recesses, and Mr. Randall refuses to permit motions intended to waste the time of the House in roll calls, there can be no method of delay which cannot be overcome by diligence in attending to the counting of the vote.

The defeat of McMahon's resolution was followed by the two hours' discussion on the resolution sustaining the decision of the Commission. The debate was for the most part dull and spiritless, except that it was enlivened by two or three interesting incidents. The fact is that the general subject of the Presidential contest has grown stale, and the ten-minute manuscript speeches which were prepared by nearly all the members have been used up in the previous debates, and nobody of much importance cares to speak. John Young Brown made one of his characteristic speeches, of which he made a few in the House, his speech to-day being the first of much importance since his famous attack on Ben Butler in the last Congress. He was full of Southern fire, and above all things repudiated the idea that there was any possibility of a coalition between any faction of the Southern Democrats and the Republican Administration of President Hayes. The Democratic Party was only divided on the question of the hour, and would be a unit on all questions of public policy after the Presidential contest had been decided. He stood manfully by the bill, and submitted to defeat.

Mr. Hewitt made his promised attack on Commissioner Hoar, charging him with bad faith, though in rather mild terms, which indicated that Hewitt was not quite certain of the ground on which he stood. He was cut off at the end of the 10 minutes with what he deemed the most important part of his manuscript unread. If his charge against Mr. Hoar had any point, it was simply that in his speech in the House, on the Electoral bill, Mr. Hoar had used the word "proof" in a way which Mr. Hewitt seemed to think required him to vote that evidence was to be considered by the Commission. Mr. Hoar replied in a sharp speech, first reading from a former speech of Mr. Bayard, in which he declared in the most absolute terms against Congress having any power to investigate an election for President, and claimed that bad faith could no more be imputed to himself than to Mr. Bayard, who had changed his opinion honestly, no doubt. Mr. Hoar stated that on this question of the admissibility of evidence himself and Mr. Hewitt had disputed two or three days in the committee, taking opposite sides, and it was absolutely understood that the question was to be submitted unconditionally to the Commission. Mr. Hoar's application to Hewitt of Webster's characterization of Ingersoll many years ago, that there was a screw loose in his mind, and not only one, but that the whole machinery was out of order and crazy, was loudly cheered by the House. Mr. Hewitt has become a kind of lunatic on the subject of the Presidency, and is incapable of forming any judgment or stating truthfully any fact.

When the Senate returned to its own Chamber after the division on Oregon, Mr. Sargent offered a resolution to the effect that the decision of the Commission be sustained. Mr. Kelly opposed this with much more vehemence than discretion. He was followed shortly after by his colleague, Senator Mitchell, who, in a very clear and forcible argument, proved, among other things, that Kelly was not quite so well informed regarding the statute law of Oregon as he should be. Senator Merrimon, who spoke next, made a long speech, which was principally devoted to a consideration of the Florida case. It was a very fine effort in its way, but came a little too late in the day to be effective. Mr. Morton, in his usual matter-of-fact style, clearly stated the question before the Senate, and then argued that not only right and justice, but every technicality of the law, demanded that the verdict of the Electoral tribunal should be approved and sustained. He contended further, that the duty of the Governor of Oregon, under the laws of that State, was purely a ministerial one. He was required to issue certificates of election to those persons who had received the highest number of votes. He was not a returning officer, and had no right to decide what persons had been chosen, or to determine who was eligible or ineligible.

Mr. Conkling took the floor after Senator Morton, and as he has not taken any part in the recent debate on the contested States, and is not on the record regarding them, his address was listened to with marked attention. He said that according to his understanding, the Joint Commission had sent two papers to the houses which required attention. One of them was the decision in the Oregon case, and the other the reasons upon which that decision was based. To avoid all misapprehension which might occur touching his position in the matter, he desired to say distinctly that he believed the vote of Oregon had been given to the Republican candidates, and he would vote to sustain the decision. He did not understand, however, that by such action he would be voting for or advocating the reasons assigned for the verdict. He said, in conclusion, that he was very anxous for the count to go on, and desiring to throw no obstacle in the way of its rapid progress, he would refrain from further remarks.

Mr. Saulsbury, who was the next speaker, had a great deal to say about Louisiana, and stated with considerable warmth that he did not believe there had been any intimidation or violence in that State. He was unable to show, however, why the vote of Oregon should be given to the distinguished correspondent of Gobble & Company. The next gentleman to address the Senate was Senator Bogy, who said in a blood-curdling tone, and with an air of high tragedy, that he wanted to enter his solemn protest against the counting of the vote of Oregon for Hayes and Wheeler. He warned the galleries that there were dark days coming, requested them to remember Augustus of Rome, and then sat down, evidently well pleased with his little effort.

Mr. Whyte, who was the next protesting Democrat, said he had been deceived by the men who had framed the bill preparing for the establishment of the Commission. He thought that a court, constituted as the Electoral tribunal was, would give a fair and impartial decision, but he was disappointed. Senator Kernan, who spoke soon after, referred to a casual remark which Mr. Mitchell had made regarding ex-Gov. Tilden, and said he thought it was very wrong for any one to say a word against that gentleman. Then little Mr. Eaton, of Connecticut, took the floor, and created quite a stir by announcing that at some future date he would discuss the Oregon case at length. Unfortunately for those who are obliged to attend the meetings of the Senate, there is good reason to believe that he was not joking. His speech to-day very forcibly reminded some of those present of the address he made in 1861, when he swore that the soldiers of Massachusetts should never march through Connecticut to the South, except over the dead bodies of all faithful Democrats. He declared to-day, among other things of the same sort, that if he had the power of the lower house of Congress he would, as God was his judge, prevent the count from going on. It will be remembered that Mr. Eaton was the only Democratic Senator who voted against the Electoral Count bill. When he concluded his oration this afternoon, Pulitzer, the German adventurer who tried to ruin his benefactor, Carl Schurz, rushed up to his seat, and, shaking his hand with a great display of satisfaction, warmly congratulated him. Shortly afterward, while Senator Jones, of Florida, was speaking, it [illegible] Pulitzer sat at his elbow, with a number of books of reference, and frequently prompted him. No one seems to know upon what authority this person makes himself so important in a chamber which is supposed to be reserved for Senators and a few high officials. It is suggested, however, that Senator Jones has retained him as his Private Secretary.

At the conclusion of the Jones-Pulitzer address a vote was taken on a substitute for Senator Sargent's resolution, and it was lost, yeas 24, nays 40. Then the original resolution, sustaining the action of the Commission, was adopted by a vote of 40 to 24. After the two houses had voted on the objections to sustaining the decision of the Commission in the Oregon case, there was a second joint meeting, and the vote of Oregon was counted for Hayes and Wheeler.

The next State on the list was Pennsylvania. When the returns were opened the demand was made by Mr. Tucker, of Virginia, and Mr. Springer, that they should be read in full. Meantime Mr. Cochrane went about the House getting signatures to a bogus objection to votes of certain Electors in that State; and having obtained a sufficient number, the document was presented, and the two houses were compelled to separate.

Immediately after the departure of the Senate, Mr. Vance, of Ohio, offered a resolution for a recess till Monday morning at 10 o'clock. The roll-call was watched with great interest, and the vote on both sides was nearly the same, till, finally, when the reading of the names of those voting began, the resolution was beaten by five or six votes. After the reading, several more votes were given, and five or six Democrats changed from nay to yea, and the motion was at last carried by 133 yeas to 121 nays. This was a small vote, but it was late, and many members neglectful of public duties had gone home to dinner. Only a few Democrats voted against a recess, and the excuse that some of them offer is that they felt they had forced the David Dudley-Springer filibusterers as far as was prudent for one day. The objections to the Pennsylvania count will be the first thing to be taken up on Monday morning.

After returning to its own chamber, the Senate at once took up the consideration of the Pennsylvania objections. It was supported by Mr. Wallace, while Senators Cameron and Morton in pointed address showed how utterly idle and ridiculous it was. In addition to this, Mr. Morton drew attention to the fact that in Virginia there was a Democratic Elector named Hardin, who was also a Centennial Commissioner, and he argued that if the vote of Morrill was illegal his [Hardin's] was no better. After some further discussion of no importance the objection was overruled by an almost unanimous vote, and then the Senate, having been informed of the action of the House, took a recess until Monday morning.

### AN IMPORTANT VOTE ANALYZED.

MR. CLYMER'S MOTION TO TAKE A RECESS—HOW AND BY WHOM IT WAS DEFEATED—ONE-THIRD OF THOSE WHO VOTED FOR DELAY REJECTED BY THEIR CONSTITUENTS AT THE LAST ELECTION.

*Special Dispatch to the New-York Times.*

WASHINGTON, Feb. 24.—The following is an analysis of the vote on Mr. Clymer's motion for a recess until Monday, which was taken prior to the assembling of the joint convention to receive the decision of the Commission in the case of Oregon. The vote stood for the recess, 112; against recess, 158. Of the votes against recess, 49 were Democrats, and of these 17 were Southern men. Five New-York Democrats voted for recess, namely: John H. Bagley, Bliss, Cox, Field, and Odell. Meade dodged, and Schumaker was absent. The New-York Democrats who voted against recess were Beebe, Hewitt, Lord, Metcalf, Walker, Ward, Whitehouse, Willis, and Wood. The vote for recess was distributed as follows: Alabama, 3; Arkansas, 3; California, 2; Connecticut, 2; Florida, 1; Georgia, 4; Illinois, 6; Indiana, 5; Iowa, 1; Kentucky, 5; Louisiana, 2; Maryland, 5; Massachusetts, 2; Mississippi, 4; Missouri, 8; New-Jersey, 2; New-York, 5; North Carolina, 6; Ohio, 10; Oregon, 1; Pennsylvania, 13; Tennessee, 9; Virginia, 6; West Virginia, 2; Wisconsin, 3; total, 112. Of the 10 representatives from Tennessee, one only is a Republican, and the nine Democrats voted solid for recess, this being the only State having more than one Democratic Representative where the delegation was solid. Of the six Democrats from Texas only one voted for recess. The Democracy of Pennsylvania and Ohio came near being solid; of the 18 from Pennsylvania, 13 voted yea, one was absent, and Randall did not assert his constitutional right to vote, as he did when the Electoral bill was passed by the House. Seven of the 13 who voted yea were defeated for re-election. Of the 13 Ohio Democrats, 10 voted yea, and of these, eight will not be on the rolls of the next Congress, and one of them, Banning, may be rubbed off. Of the entire number of those voting for recess, 38, or one-third, were defeated at the polls last year, and of the 38 thus defeated 26 are from Northern and Western States.

### ANOTHER DEMOCRATIC CAUCUS.

A PART OF THE MEMBERS IN CONSULTATION—DAVID DUDLEY FIELD'S FOLLOWERS—PREARRANGED PLANS AGREED UPON—GENERAL DISCUSSION INDULGED IN.

*Special Dispatch to the New-York Times.*

WASHINGTON, Feb. 24.—The Democrats, or a part of them, held another caucus to-night. There were, so far as can be learned, no more than 70 or 80 members present, and they were, with perhaps a half-dozen exceptions, the men who are operating under the command of David Dudley Field to defeat the count of the Electoral vote. David Dudley has secretly got the approval of his Committee on the Privileges and Powers of the House for the two bills which he explained in caucus last night. One is to provide for a President *ad interim*, and the other for a new election next Fall. These bills he presented to the caucus again to-night, and he was authorized to present them in the House. He will try to antagonize them to the continuation of the count on Monday; but Mr. Vance made a motion to-day to instruct Field's committee to find out what the House can do under the circumstances, and Mr. Randall ruled it out of order. Mr. Field's bills cannot be introduced except during a legislative session of the House, and that cannot be held till after the Commission takes up the case of South Carolina. The caucus was a fixed up affair, and the probability of the House following any action agreed upon to-night may be judged by the way in which the caucus action of last night, which was much better attended, was broken away from in the first vote. There was no opposition in the caucus, because only those were there who went to do the thing that was done. Many Democrats were about the hotels during the evening, who said they remained away from the caucus purposely. The prospect to-night is that the count will be finished in accordance with law, but not till near the end of next week.

*Dispatch to the Associated Press.*

After the House had to-day taken a recess until Monday, a Democratic caucus was announced for to-night at 7:30 o'clock. At that hour about 75 members were present. Some of those who favored dilatory proceedings in the Electoral count were absent, as they were dissatisfied with the action of the majority of their party to-day in voting to continue the count, while those who were in favor of continuing the count did not care to meet with those of opposite views. The object of the caucus, however, had no reference to the proceedings of the House regarding the count, but with regard to the law of 1792, which provides that, in case of removal, death, resignation, or inability of both the President and Vice President of the United States, the President of the Senate, or, if there is none, then the Speaker of the House of Representatives for the time being, shall act as President until the disability is removed or a President elected. It was contended in the caucus that, should there be no declaration before the 4th of March of the election of a President based on the Electoral returns, there would be no such vacancy as contemplated by the law, and therefore provision should be made for such a contingency.

Representative Field stated that he had prepared a bill to meet the contingency, which he explained. After some discussion, the caucus adopted a resolution instructing the Committee on the Powers, Privileges, and Duties of the House to report on Monday, or at the earliest practicable moment, Mr. Field's bill, providing that in case there be no election of President and Vice President under the count of the Electoral vote, the President of the Senate shall assume the functions of President, and a new election is to be held at a time to be fixed by the committee. The resolution further instructs the committee to report Mr. Fields' bill, providing for *quo warranto* proceedings before the United States Supreme Court with reference to the final settlement of the Presidential question, the Electoral bill containing no definite provision regarding the subject.

There was also some general discussion relative to the disposal of points of order that may arise during the further count of the Electoral vote, but no resolutions on this point were adopted, and the caucus, at 9:15 P. M., adjourned.

### WASHINGTON NOTES.

WASHINGTON, Feb. 24.—The House Committee on Appropriations this morning unanimously agreed to recommend non-concurrence in the Senate amendment to the Postal Appropriation bill, which proposes granting subsidies for the China mail service and for the line from New-Orleans to Brazil. Messrs. Holman, Blount, and Foster, who were subsequently appointed as the House members of the Conference Committee on this bill, are all understood to be opposed to the provision for subsidies, which are, therefore, not likely to be finally retained in the bill.

The President is giving his attention to-day to private business only, and has given audience to no visitors.

The receipts of national bank notes for the week ending Feb. 24, as compared with the corresponding week of last year, were as follows:

| | 1876. | 1877. |
|---|---|---|
| New-York | $1,264,000 | $784,000 |
| Boston | 1,483,000 | 1,240,000 |
| Philadelphia | 64,000 | 120,000 |
| Miscellaneous | 1,030,000 | 1,154,000 |
| Total | $3,843,000 | $3,251,000 |

The receipts for to-day were $410,000

The receipts from internal revenue to-day were $587,712, and from Customs $358,585.

National bank circulation outstanding this date $317,935,727, of which $1,42[illegible],920 is in national gold notes.

The President to-day sent the following nominations of Postmasters to the Senate: William H. Craig, at Albany, N. Y.; William Brujan, Hudson, N. Y.; W. D. Cooke, Southington, Conn.; Charles B. Loop, Belvidere, Ill.; Mrs. Priscilla Wilson, Braidwood, Ill.; William W. Freeman, Menasha, Wis.; Alonzo Shaw, Tipton, Iowa; N. C. Boles, Hutchinson, Kan.; W. H. Kennon, Columbus, Miss.

Hon. Daniel J. Morrill, of Jamestown, Penn., testified before the Committee on the Powers, Privileges, and Duties of the House to-day that he was appointed United States Centennial Commissioner, by the President, under the Act of March 3, 1871, and still held that office, which was one of honor and trust, but no profit. He said he did not attend the meeting of the Electoral College, because he had been informed of his ineligibility, and Mr. Henry A. Boggs was appointed by the college to fill the vacancy. Before the same committee to-day the examination of William K. Snearing, of New Orleans, was continued, and he testified in relation to the meetings of himself, Gifford, and Littlefield, corroborating the latter's testimony given yesterday in every essential particular. He also testified with reference to his, Littlefield's, and Murphy's trip to Springfield, Ill., and their interview there with Gov. Palmer, all of which has already been made public. He stated that he had no promise of money or any other reward for his trouble and services, and acted solely from a desire for and with a view to securing a good government for his State. Hon. E. J. Ellis, member of Congress from Louisiana, testified that Duncan F. Kenner's standing as a gentleman of character and social position was of the very highest, and whose reputation for integrity and truth was beyond all cavil; he did not believe that Mr. Kenner would offer a bribe to any one; as to J. Madison Wells his reputation was very bad, and witness would not believe him under oath in any matter in which his [Wells] pecuniary interest or his party interest should come into play. The committee then adjourned until Monday.

While sitting in the cloak-room of the Senate, smoking, to-day, Senator Hamlin was taken with what appeared to be a fainting fit, and had it not been for Senator McMillan, who sat by him, would have fallen into the fire. He soon recovered, but his friends thought it best that he be taken home. After arriving there he soon recovered, and this evening is in his usual good health.

About 11 o'clock this morning a rumor gained circulation that an attempt would be made when the Senate passed in procession through the rotunda, on its way to the House, to seize the two mahogany boxes containing Electoral returns, carried by Capt. Bassett, Assistant Doorkeeper of the Senate, in order to prevent any further count. But little credence was attached to the report; but Capt. Blackford, Chief of the Capitol Police, placed an additional number of policemen in the rotunda during the passage, both ways, of the Senatorial procession. No attempt was made, however, and probably none was intended.

The following were the balances in the Treasury at the close of business to-day: Currency, $9,055,792; special deposit of legal tenders for redemption of certificates of deposit, $38,590,000; coin, $90,153,663, including coin certificates, $54,748,400; outstanding legal tenders, $364,984,810.

Secretary Morrill continues to improve, and is able to sit up for a short time. The President called this morning and had an hour's conference with him.

To-day Judge Cartter, on the petition of Charles L. Steever and others, by Mr. Fullerton, directed a rule to issue on the Secretary of the Navy, returnable on Saturday next, to show cause why a mandamus should not be issued to compel him to pay them certain prize money. They state that under Lieut. William B. Cushing, on the 27th of October, 1864, they captured the rebel ram Albermarle; that, under the decree of the court of August 21, 1865, and Feb. 11, 1873, the petitioners were entitled to a share in the prize money ($273,135 00); their share being $44,886 49, and state that the amount was not fairly proportioned, and the sum of $23,925 has been paid; that this wrong was brought to the notice of the Secretary soon after its discovery, May 5, 1873.

### RAILROAD ACCIDENT IN KENTUCKY.

LOUISVILLE, Feb. 24.—At Beard's Station on the Louisville and Cincinnati Short Line Railroad, early this morning, a passenger train bound south was thrown from the track by a misplaced switch. The engineer saw the danger in time to avoid a serious disaster. Two passengers were slightly injured, W. H. Moore, of Memphis, had his shoulder partly dislocated, and a Mr. Cochran, of New-Orleans, had two ribs broken. No interruption to travel was occasioned by the accident.

## LATEST NEWS BY CABLE.

### THE EASTERN CAMPAIGN.

AN AGREEMENT BETWEEN TURKEY AND SERVIA—THE ASSEMBLING OF PERSIAN TROOPS EXPLAINED—RUSSIA'S ATTITUDE TOWARD ENGLAND—THE CZAR'S ARMY IN FINE CONDITION.

CONSTANTINOPLE, Feb. 24.—An agreement between the Porte and the Servian Envoys was concluded to-day. Prince Milan will address a letter to the Sultan accepting the Turkish conditions, except those claiming equality for the Jews in Servia and the right of the Porte to be diplomatically represented at Belgrade. The Sultan will grant Prince Milan a new *firman* determining the future relations of Servia and Turkey.

The Persian Minister has communicated to the Sultan a dispatch from the Shah explaining that the assemblages of troops on the Turkish frontier are solely meant to prevent the depredations of a nomadic tribe. These assemblages have been ordered to cease.

BRUSSELS, Feb. 24.—*Le Nord* to-day publishes a letter from St. Petersburg declaring that England will obtain no concession from Russia short of an agreement for the coercion of Turkey. In case the Porte persists in its refusal to execute reforms, England's present attitude might even precipitate Russia's decision to abandon a position which is neither peace nor war, yet imposes upon Russia all war's sacrifices.

LONDON, Feb. 24.—A special dispatch from Berlin says: "It is stated in well-informed circles that the Czar will certainly await the powers' replies to Prince Gortschakoff's circular before attacking Turkey." A Prussian officer just arrived from Kischeneff gives a highly favorable account of the Russian Army, but it is positively asserted that Russia in no case will commence hostilities before March 31.

### COMMERCIAL AND FINANCIAL.

LONDON, Feb. 24.—The depression in the Mincing-lane markets continues, and quotations have further given way. Plantation Ceylon and East India new crop coffee are about 4 shillings to 5 shillings per cwt. lower than last Friday's prices, owing to arrivals and full supplies expected. Pale descriptions have not varied much in price. Sugar, after receding 1 shilling per cwt. in many cases, closed steadier. The Glasgow market closes quiet, with prices barely supported, but the week's transactions show an advance of 1 shilling to 1 shilling 6 pence per cwt., the principal gain being on medium descriptions. A few cargoes of new Burmah rice sold, to arrive, at about last week's prices. There have been exceptionally heavy public sales of tea, prices in some cases favoring buyers. Lower grades of red-leaf Congou were most depressed. The private-contract market was dull as usual. The only feature in spices has been some inquiry for black and white pepper, to arrive.

Business on the Stock Exchange during the week has been very dull. Consols are ⅛ better on the week. A majority of foreign securities have declined. Russians, however, are in demand in consequence of repurchases by speculators for a fall who were alarmed by the pacific tone of the German Emperor's speech. Canadian railways are dull and lower. American Governments are steady, but some railways, including Erie, are flat at a reduction. Telegraphs have generally declined. Anglo-American are 3 and Direct United States ⅛ to ¾ worse in consequence of the announcement of the shilling tariff.

### MISCELLANEOUS FOREIGN NOTES.

VIENNA, Feb. 24.—A conference of the constitutional party of the Reichsrath to-day resolved that the Government plan for the formation of the bank's Board of Directors is not inadmissible, nevertheless the party reserves freedom of action upon the compromise proposals, especially regarding the appointment of Vice Governors of the bank as an open question.

BILBAO, Feb. 24.—Tempestuous weather has been prevalent here during the last few days, and still continues. One English and two French ships are reported to be lost at Santona with all hands.

LONDON, Feb. 24.—Seven of the seamen belonging to the bark Peti Dubrovacki, which was wrecked on St. Kilda Island, are supposed to have perished.

### SLAVERY IN CUBA.

HAVANA, Feb. 24.—The *Voz de Cuba*, referring to President Grant's Message and his statement that Cuba is the only land in which slavery now exists, says: "While slavery on a larger scale exists in Brazil, the Spanish law of gradual abolition will result in ending slavery in Cuba earlier than in Brazil. If foreign Governments insist that slavery be abolished in Brazil while it exists in Cuba, then let the Spanish law be exchanged for the Brazilian one, thus doing away with faultfinding and the pretexts of other nations, compelling them to blame Brazil when blaming Cuba. Whether under Spanish or Brazilian law, we shall have to pass through a transformation of the gravest importance. Nobody ignores this, yet nobody takes the provisory steps. We cannot understand this indifference, on the solution of which the future of the island largely depends. There is no other country where individual efforts are so strong, and where collective efforts are unknown. Let the initiative for a collective effort come from some prominent planter, acting in the preliminaries in concert with others and the authorities, and adopt in time the proper means looking toward the transformation of labor. Nothing outside of war, of equal of importance to the future of the island with this labor question exists."

### DEATH OF A BRIDE AT THE ALTAR.

*Special Dispatch to the New-York Times.*

RALEIGH, Feb. 24.—On Thursday night last, in the town of Thomasville, Davidson County, while William Thomas and a Miss Forney were before the altar for the purpose of being married, more than half of the ceremony having been performed, the bride dropped dead before the ceremony was concluded, a victim of heart disease.

### NO FEIGNED ISSUES ENTERTAINED.

*Special Dispatch to the New-York Times.*

RALEIGH, Feb. 24.—In the suit of Blake against Askew, involving the constitutionality of the special tax bonds, which has been before the Supreme Court of this State for nearly two years, the court filed an opinion yesterday, dismissing the action upon the ground that it was a feigned issue, which is forbidden by the Constitution; that it was not bona fide between the parties, and was gotten up expressly to procure the opinion of the court. In dismissing the case Justice Reade says: "The action is not fit to be entertained."

### COUNTERFEITERS ARRESTED.

*Special Dispatch to the New-York Times.*

RALEIGH, Feb. 24.—On Monday last 12 men were arrested at Sand Hill, Richmond County, while engaged in counterfeiting "nickels" and silver coin. A number of dies and a quantity of the counterfeit pieces were captured. Several of the gang escaped. Those arrested were taken before the United States Commissioner for commitment.

### ILLNESS OF A PHILADELPHIA OFFICIAL.

*Special Dispatch to the New-York Times.*

PHILADELPHIA, Feb. 24.—Capt. Terrance McCusker, formerly the Chief Engineer of the Philadelphia Fire Department, and at present Chief of the Insurance Patrol, is dangerously ill. The physicians have given up all hopes of his recovery. He is well known in New-York.

### A HORSE-THIEF LYNCHED.

ALEXANDRIA, La., Feb. 24.—Last night a man named Cage, hailing from Wilkinson County, Miss., was taken from jail by unknown parties and hanged. He had stolen Major Watts' horse the night before, and was pursued by Watts and captured, and when returning to town, turned and discharged a revolver twice at Watts, wounding him severely in the right breast, and escaped, but was recaptured and lodged in jail. Watts, who is seriously, though not dangerously wounded, was doing well this forenoon.

### THE PRESIDENT ELECT.

AT HIS HOME IN FREMONT—A GRAND FAREWELL RECEPTION TO BE GIVEN HIM IN COLUMBUS—ANXIOUS INQUIRIES MADE IN WASHINGTON ABOUT HIS COMING.

*Special Dispatch to the New-York Times.*

COLUMBUS, Feb. 24.—Gov. Hayes went to his home at Fremont to-day, accompanied by his family, and will remain until some time next week. Preparations are being made by the citizens here, regardless of party, to give him a farewell reception prior to his departure for Washington. It is expected that his resignation as Governor will be presented to the Legislature soon after his return from Fremont. Lieut. Gov. Young will thereupon immediately be installed as his successor.

WASHINGTON, Feb. 24.—Senator Sherman has returned from Ohio, and was in his place in the Senate to-day. He was anxiously questioned by many Republicans and a few Democrats, who desired to know if he had seen the President elect, and if he was soon coming to Washington. He was unable, however, to reply to these inquiries.

### THE SOUTH AND PRESIDENT HAYES.

*Special Dispatch to the New-York Times.*

RALEIGH, Feb. 24.—The *News* of this city, the accredited organ of Gov. Vance and the Democratic Party, speaking of the decision of the Electoral Commission in the Oregon case as making Hayes the next President, says: "The South will not suffer under Hayes' Administration. There is every assurance that he will be both liberal and just to our section."

### A PHILADELPHIA THEATRE BURNED.

FOX'S THEATRE DESTROYED—THE PLACE CAPABLE OF SEATING 3,000 PERSONS.

*Special Dispatch to the New-York Times.*

PHILADELPHIA, Feb. 25.—Fox's New American Theatre, at Tenth and Chestnut streets, was totally destroyed by fire at 1 o'clock this morning. The place had been closed at 11:45 last night, and no one was in the building except the watchman, Charles Charlton, who was overcome by the smoke, and dragged out of the rear portion. The fire commenced in the property-room, and in three-quarter of an hour the place was entirely destroyed. The players lost all their wardrobes, and the loss will be about $150,000, which is covered by insurance. The Mercantile Library building, and Carncross and Dixey's Theatre, in the rear, were damaged by water. A stiff wind was blowing, and for a while it was feared more of the large buildings in the neighborhood would be burned. The fire is still burning, but is under control.

*Dispatch to the Associated Press.*

PHILADELPHIA, Feb. 25.—At 12:50 this morning fire broke out on the stage of Fox's new American Theatre, and at this hour, 1 A. M., the whole place is in flames. Myriads of burning embers are flying in every direction, and the neighborhood is lighted up for squares. The fire spread with remarkable rapidity, and is communicating with Roger's wagon warehouse. The Mercantile Library Building is in danger, as is also the New-York Mutual's new building at the corner of Tenth and Chestnut streets. A general alarm has been sounded. Fortunately, all hands had left the theatre before the fire broke out. The building was a handsome one, and was erected about 1870.

LATER.—At 2 A. M. the fire is still burning at the Fox Theatre, but, owing to the confusion, no estimate of the loss can be made. The theatre was opened on the evening of Dec. 17, 1870. It occupied a lot 100 by 177 feet, with an entrance from Chestnut-street through an arcade 14 feet wide and had a seating capacity for 3,000 persons.

### CORTINA CAPTURED.

THE BORDER RAIDER IN PRISON AT MATAMOROS—GREAT EXCITEMENT THERE—EXPECTATION THAT HE WILL BE SPEEDILY SHOT.

BROWNSVILLE, Texas, Feb. 24.—Gen. John N. Cortina was arrested in Matamoros this afternoon at 5 o'clock, and placed in the military prison. It is believed that he will be court-martialed and shot for not obeying the order of President Diaz to present himself at the City of Mexico to answer for his conduct on the frontier for the past 10 months. Gen. Corales, Governor of the State, is outside of Matamoros with 1,500 men, and will aid Gen. Blanco in suppressing any attempt on the part of the friends of Cortina to rescue him. There is great excitement in Matamoros, and the partisans of Cortina are flying to the Texas side of the Rio Grande. The authorities express themselves thoroughly prepared to maintain order and execute the law in case of any attempt at violence.

### MR. KIDD IS AGAINST PAYING TAXES.

NEW-ORLEANS, Feb. 24.—In the Nicholls Legislature to-day Mr. Kidd, of Jackson Parish, offered the following:

*Declaration of the House of Representatives, State of Louisiana.*

We, the Representatives of the people of Louisiana, duly elected by and direct from the people, fully aware from positive knowledge of the feeling and determination that impel and control them, do declare that under no circumstances will the people of this State pay tribute to any other State Government than that at whose head stands the man of their choice, their endeared and truly elected Governor, Francis T. Nicholls; and do further declare the utter impossibility of gathering taxes by any other authority, and that any attempt to gather them by other authority than the Nicholls Government will not only prove abortive, but lead to lamentable civil strife, if not to bloodshed and actual war.

### ST. LOUIS LIFE INSURANCE COMPANY.

ST. LOUIS, Feb. 24.—The Grand Jury to-day returned to the Criminal Court indictments against Henry W. Haugh, President, and John L. Pierce, Secretary, of the Life Association of America, charging them with perjury in signing a statement, which they knew to be false, of the financial condition of the association on Dec. 1, 1875. The Directors of this association sent communications to the Grand Jury yesterday asking them to call for the production of the books and papers of the association, and to take the testimony of its officers respecting the statement upon which the indictments were founded; but the jury gave no heed to the request, and returned indictments against two of its signers. Both gentlemen entered into bonds of $1,500 to appear to answer to the charge.

### RETIREMENT OF DISABLED OFFICERS.

CHICAGO, Feb. 24.—A Board of Officers to retire disabled officers of the Army has been appointed by orders from Washington to convene in Chicago on Monday next. The following officers are detailed as members of the board: Cols. Sackett, Kiburn, and Dunn, and Lieut. Col. Sheridan as Recorder.

### THE "MOLLY MAGUIRES" CONVICTED.

POTTSVILLE, Feb. 24.—Hester, Tully, and Mullagh, the Molly Maguire prisoners on trial at Bloomsburg for the murder of Alexander Rea, near Centralia, were this afternoon found guilty of murder in the first degree.

### AN INSANE MOTHER KILLS HER CHILDREN.

ISLAND POND, Vt., Feb. 24.—Mrs. Hiram Young killed her two children, a boy and girl, at Newark to-day, horribly mangling them with an axe. Her husband had left her, and she is supposed to have become insane over her troubles.

## LEGISLATION FOR THE CITY.

### THE LINE OF POLICY PROPOSED.

REORGANIZATION AND PURIFICATION—REDUCTION OF SALARIES AND OF THE NUMBER OF OFFICES—SALARIES AND FEES—THE COURTS—MERGING DEPARTMENTS—THE POLICE AND FIRE DEPARTMENTS—STREET CLEANING.

*From Our Own Correspondent.*

ALBANY, Saturday, Feb. 24, 1877.

The most cursory examination of the mass of City bills which has been poured into the Legislature makes one fact clear above all others, viz., that no more are needed. The matter is becoming a little confusing. With all this mass of crude legislation in ferment, it is hard to keep clearly in mind the measures of purification and reorganization which are really necessary in the City Government. There is danger that these will be covered up and lost sight of in the confusion of schemes. In view of this circumstance, the present time seems a good one to briefly review the line of policy which the Republican majority appear to have marked out, and to indicate the means by which it is to be carried into effect, with the reasons therefor. For convenience, this may be arranged under the following heads:

I.—Single headed commissions for all departments except the Police.

II.—Reduction of salaries of officers and employes.

III.—Reduction of the number of employes, especially court attendants.

IV.—The offices of Register of Deeds, County Clerk, and Coroners to be made salaried offices.

V.—The Marine Court to be abolished.

VI.—The Dock Department to be merged in the Department of Public Works; that of Buildings to be merged in the Fire Department.

VII.—The street cleaning to be given to the Board of Health, or to a separate department created for the purpose.

VIII.—Street cleaning to be done by contract, the contracts to be for small districts.

IX.—The policemen and firemen to be graded in three classes, with salaries to correspond.

X.—A Police pension fund to be created, for the retirement of old policemen on half pay.

XI.—A question for further consideration is the merging of the Excise in the Police Department.

I. *Single headed commissions for all departments except the Police Department.*—Section 26, of article III., of the City charter provides that there shall be in the City Government the following departments: Finance, Law, Police, Public Works, Charities and Correction, Fire, Health, Docks, Parks, Taxes and Assessments, Buildings—11 in all. As these departments are now constituted, those of Finance, Law, Public Works, and Buildings have each one head; that of Health, two; Charities and Correction, Taxes and Assessments, Fire, and Docks have each three Commissioners; the Police and Park Departments have four each. So long as the Bureau of Elections is in the Police Department public opinion seems to require that the board shall consist of an equal number of men of both political parties; it is therefore proposed to reduce the commission from four to two—one Republican and one Democrat. This would save $12,000, the salary of the Commissioners to go out being $6,000 each. It may perhaps be considered reasonable that the salary of the two retained should be made equal. The President of the board now receives $8,000. It is the opinion of one of the best Police Commissioners the City ever had that a board of two is the best board to have. In the four departments having three Commissioners each, the salaries are as follows: Charities and Correction, President, $6,500; two Commissioners, $5,000 each; Fire, President, $7,500; two Commissioners, $5,000 each; Taxes and Assessments, President, $6,500; two Commissioners, $5,000 each; Docks, President, $6,500; two Commissioners, $3,000 each. The total saving by lopping off the extra Commissioners in these departments would be $36,000 per year. The President of the Park Department is paid $6,500; the other Commissioners receive no salary. The two Commissioners of Health are paid, respectively, $6,500 and $5,000 per year. The reasons urged for adopting the policy of single headed departments are economy and greater efficiency. Mayor Ely is warmly in favor of the plan.

II. *Reduction of salaries of officers and employes.*—The bill for this purpose now on the Assembly files, as reported from the Committee on Cities, will scale down salaries from 10 to 20 per cent. The reduction will be little loss to a very large number of City employes, since they do not receive more than from one-half to two-thirds of the salary placed opposite their names on the pay-rolls. Where the other portion goes it is needless to inquire now.

III. *Reduction of the number of employes, especially court attendants.*—This is not an easy matter for the Legislature to deal with directly, except as to the courts, where the evil to be remedied is flagrant and glaring. The *City Record* of Jan. 31 contains a carefully classified list of all persons drawing pay from the City, from the Mayor down. It is a most interesting document, which has been circulated among the members to some extent, and is deserving of all possible attention. The following list of court "attendants" is taken from it. Be it remembered that "attendant" does not mean clerk, but simply a person who "attends" court, hands up papers, keeps order, and sits about:

Court of General Sessions—36 attendants, at a salary of $1,200 each; total, $43,200. Many of these attendants are little more than the personal servants of the three Judges who preside over the court, viz., Recorder Hackett, Judge Sutherland, and Judge Gildersleeve. These gentlemen receive salaries liberal almost to extravagance, and, if it is not actually dishonest, it is certainly something very like meanness, to make the City pay for services they are well able to pay for themselves. There is no reason in the world why six, or at most eight, attendants could not do all the work for the supposed performance of which 36 have been appointed, and no one knows this better than the gentlemen who made the appointments. True, they have the technical right under the law to do this; that is to say, when the Ring was in its power laws were passed enormously swelling the number of court attendants, and these have not been repealed; but the Judges are not compelled to make all these unnecessary appointments. Do they consider it consistent with their sense of honor as gentlemen, and as repositories of a high public trust, to make their court such an example of gross extravagance as this official list shows it to be? It is not for them to plead their technical right to make the City pay thousands and thousands a year for which it gets no return. It is a matter which directly concerns their honor as gentlemen. Better things might have been expected of them than such a record of indefensible extravagance; and since the just expectations of those who desire to respect them have been disappointed, it is time for the Legislature to step in and apply the remedy. Six attendants are all that are necessary or should be allowed to this court.

Supreme Court—24 attendants, at $1,360 each; total, $28,[illegible]. The number of attendants in this court is not as large as in the Court of General Sessions, where extravagance reaches its climax, but still there are too many. Eight attendants is an ample number to do all the work which has to be done. The court should be limited to this number.

Court of Common Pleas—In this court the "attendants" appear on the pay-roll as "officers," of whom there are [illegible] at $1,[illegible] each—total, $24,[illegible]. There are also 14 "assistant clerks," which is more than the roll of any other court shows. Thirteen of these are paid $2,[illegible] each, the fourteenth receives $1,[illegible]; total for all $3[illegible]. Eight assistant clerks and six [illegible]

# The New-York Times.

VOL. XXVI.......NO. 7946. | NEW-YORK, FRIDAY, MARCH 2, 1877. | PRICE FOUR CENTS.


# EXTRA.

FRIDAY, MARCH 2, 6:30 A. M.

# HAYES PRESIDENT.

## The Great Contest in Congress Ended.

## Unparalleled Obstinacy of the Obstructors.

## The Final Joint Convention of the Houses.

### *Puerile Attempt of the Anarchists to Protest.*

After a night session, in which the obstructors of the Presidential count exhausted every pretext, fair and unfair, of delay in reaching a vote, the House, at 3:50 o'clock this morning, voted not to count the vote of the Elector from Wisconsin objected to by the Democrats. This terminated the long struggle to prevent the declaration of the election of the Republican candidate, the Senate having early in the night voted to count the State for Hayes, and notice was sent to that body to meet the House in joint convention to continue the count. The Senators appeared, the President of the Senate took the chair and the action of the two houses was announced. The ten votes of Wisconsin were then counted for Hayes and Wheeler, and these gentlemen were declared President and Vice President of the United States, having received a majority of all the Electoral votes.

### *THE LAST STATE COUNTED.*

SHAMELESS CONDUCT OF THE ANARCHISTS—TWELVE HOURS WASTED OVER VERMONT BY THE HOUSE—VIRGINIA AND WEST VIRGINIA COUNTED WITHOUT OPPOSITION—WISCONSIN OBJECTED TO—AN ALL-NIGHT SESSION—THE RESULT OF THE ELECTION ANNOUNCED.

*Special Dispatch to the New-York Times.*

WASHINGTON, March 1.—When the House met this morning at 10 o'clock, about 20 minutes were spent in the transaction of miscellaneous business, after which the regular order, which was the objections to counting the vote of Vermont, was demanded. The filibusters then began their movements for the day, and succeeded in defeating a joint meeting to count the vote of Vermont for nearly 12 hours. O'Brien, of Maryland, who is as near to being an idiot as any one of the crowd, raised the question whether there was a quorum, which Randall decided by counting the House and finding many more than a majority in attendance. Fernando Wood endeavored to offer a resolution concerning the objections, but Walling, of Ohio, insisted that he was entitled to have a call of the House, and made that motion. It should have been promptly rejected by Speaker Randall as a dilatory motion, but he hesitated and decided to submit it to the House. The yeas and nays were secured, and developed the fact that 237 members were present. Walling, of Ohio, then moved to reconsider the motion, and an attempt was made to have it ruled out of order, but Randall declined to decide a motion to reconsider, as belonging to the class of dilatory motions. The motion was made to lay the motion to reconsider on the table, and on this the yeas and nays were again called, and it was, of course, carried. The time was easily consumed till almost noon in calling the roll, and that hour the absurd ruling that a new day begins was foreseen to involve a chance for delay.

At 12 o'clock the legislative day of Thursday began, and the reading of the journal of yesterday was proceeded with. Springer occupied a seat in the front row, alternately studying the rules and consulting such light weights as O'Brien of Maryland, Walling and Vance of Ohio, and Lane of Oregon. Occasionally Sam. Cox, who was quietly aiding and abetting Springer, would be drawn into the consultation. Several times during the reading of the journal Springer bounded up and interrupted the Clerk by insisting that the journal was not being read. The point of Springer's objections was that the various papers and records of aye and nay votes, which are inserted in the journal, were not read in detail. The Speaker, however, overruled the objections and decided no point could be raised on the journal until the reading was completed. Springer objected to the journal, indicating wherein it was not correct. When Springer paused for breath, Fernando Wood cut him off the floor by moving that the rule requiring the journal to be read be suspended. Springer understands sufficient parliamentary law to know when he is caught in a trap. Throwing up his hands wildly, he demanded the yeas and nays on Wood's motion. O'Brien, Walling, and Poppleton echoed the demand, and the result of the call was yeas 175, nays 85, thus suspending the rule by the required two-thirds majority. As soon as the result was announced Springer again thrust himself forward, and propounded a foolish inquiry touching the journal, which the Speaker decided was no point of order, and which a member declared, in a voice audible to the galleries, was "a point of imbecility."

The decisions against the filibusters irritated, and for a brief period disconcerted, them. While they were in consultation Fernando Wood succeeded in getting the Speaker to declare that nothing would be in order but the consideration of the resolution with reference to the Vermont objections. Barney Caulfield, of Illinois, now came forward to relieve Springer and throw up points of order. He claimed that the paper which the President of the Senate refused to receive yesterday had been made a part of the Vermont objections, and until that paper was opened and laid before the House it would be impossible to discuss the objections. He wanted the Speaker to have the paper read. A rambling debate occurred on this point of Caulfield's, which was participated in by Fernando Wood, Hooker, and Reagan, with interlocutory interjections from Springer's bushwhackers, O'Brien, Walling, and Poppleton. This discussion should not have been permitted by the Speaker. Its effect—if not its purpose—was delay, and a prompt decision on Caulfield's question of order would have saved over an hour's time. Finally, the Speaker stated that the paper in dispute was not in the possession of the House, and that the question involved having been decided by the President of the Joint Convention, he nor the House had not power to revise it. He took occasion, however, to condemn the act of the President of the Joint Convention in not submitting the paper to the two houses.

At this point a scene of disorder began, which continued for three-quarters of an hour, and culminated in an exhibition of rowdyism which would have disgraced a Democratic ward convention. As soon as the Speaker had rendered his decision, a number of the filibusters sprang to their feet with questions of order. The shrill squeak of O'Brien was heard above the din, and being directly in front of the Speaker, he was recognized to propound some nonsense which the Speaker mildly pronounced a speculative inquiry, and not a question of order. To the numerous questions put to him, the Speaker replied that nothing would now be in order except the debate on objections. Proctor Knott succeeded in offering a substitute for the pending resolution and amendment, providing that the rejected package be opened by the Presiding Officer of the Senate, and that when the Senate adopted a similar resolution the House would be prepared to meet in joint convention. Knott's resolution further required that the paper purporting to be a certificate of the Electoral vote of Vermont should be referred to the Electoral Commission, with all other papers in the case.

It was now 1:30; all parliamentary obstacles to the inauguration of the two hours' debate on the objections had been removed, and Mr. Walling, of Ohio, who presented the objections, was assigned the floor to open the debate. Seeing their plans for delaying the debate were swept away, the filibusters became desperate. They were all on their feet at once, half of them addressing the Speaker while the rest were holding exciting arguments among themselves and with those who were expostulating with them for their folly. The Speaker overruled all points of order, holding that under the law nothing could be permitted to interfere at this stage of the proceedings with the consideration of the objections to the vote of Vermont. Caulfield appealed from this decision, but the Speaker declined to entertain the appeal. This action of the Speaker seemed to set the filibusters wild with excitement. The riotous demonstrations and threatening attitude of the filibusters caused the most intense excitement on the Republican side and in the galleries. The Republicans arose from their seats, many joining the Democrats in demanding the preservation of order. Many ladies, fearing that a free fight was about to take place on the Democratic side, left the galleries. All this time several of the filibusters were howling in concert at the Speaker about their rights and the rights of the people. Of this number was George M. Beebe, of New-York. Beebe occupies a seat in the rear on the Democratic side, and to the right of the Speaker. He worked himself up to a terrible pitch of excitement, and out-shouted the madmen who were howling all about him. The Speaker maintained a vigorous pounding with the gavel, while those desiring order were entreating members to preserve the dignity of the House. Finding the Speaker paid no attention to him, Beebe mounted his desk, and running over the tops of four desks in front of him, denounced the rulings of the Speaker as unlawful and unjust. At the same time a voice called out that the Speaker was a usurper. The noise and confusion which was caused by Beebe's disgraceful performance exceeded anything ever known in Congress. The Speaker called upon members to preserve order, while many members called back to the Speaker to enforce order. The filibusters clapped their hands and cheered Beebe as he stepped over the tops of desks. John Young Brown called upon the Speaker to instruct the officers of the House to enforce order. Springer and O'Brien made some remark to Brown, when that gentleman in an excited manner stepped toward the two filibusters and remarked in a voice loud enough to be heard in the galleries, "If I was an officer of the House I would enforce order; and enforce it upon such as you." The space in rear of the members' seats was crowded with outsiders who had been brought upon the floor in violation of the rules. Walling, of Ohio, demanded that the crowd should be cleared out. John Young Brown shouted at Walling: "It is not the crowd, but the disorderly members of the House who should be cleaned out." The pounding of the Speaker's gavel, cat-calls from the floor, hisses from the galleries, cheers and clapping of hands by some members, Beebe walking over the top of the desks like a skilled acrobat, made a scene never before equaled in Congress and seldom excelled in the most riotous of Democratic Conventions. For a few minutes it looked as if the House would be broken up in a free fight. The Sergeant at Arms was directed by the Speaker to remove every one from the floor not members of the House, and that officer, shouldering his mace, first walked up and down the Democratic aisles, seating the member, after which he drove the crowd into the cloak rooms. Attention being called to this fact, the crowd was expelled from the floor.

Order was finally restored. When Knott's substitute was read, Caulfield showed his ability to rank with Springer by demanding that the Speaker should have read the sealed package, which the Speaker had repeatedly stated was not in the possession of the House, and generally manifested a disposition to provoke another scene of disorder. Page, of California, asked Caulfield if he intended to occupy the floor all day? "I will, if necessary," said Caulfield, "to preserve the rights of the American people." The Speaker informed Caulfield there were others in the House who might be intrusted to look after the rights of the people, at which a general laugh was raised and Caulfield subsided. The Speaker, at this point, fearing another scene of disorder, showed a degree of firmness which would have been valuable if brought into requisition a half hour earlier. Pounding the desk with the gavel, and in a voice trembling with excitement, he said: "The Chair is determined to have order. In this he is resolute, and he now insists that officers of the House shall enforce order."

Walling was again awarded the floor to debate the objections, when questions were again started about the rejected package. During the discussion the manner of the disappearance of the package was talked over, some Democrats insisting that they saw Secretary Gorham put it in his pocket and take it away with him. It was finally ascertained that the package had not been taken away by Secretary Gorham, but had been left on the desk of the Clerk of the House. The package was subsequently brought in by a page, who sat with it in a chair in front of the Clerk's desk, flanked by O'Brien, and Harris, of Virginia. Walling opened the debate at 3:05. It was continued until 5:20, when a vote was taken on Knott's substitute, resulting—yeas 116, nays 148.

The debate was unimportant until near the close, when David Dudley Field, who was the last speaker, made a very adroit appeal to the Democrats to demand from the President of the Senate the reading of the paper which had been received by him, and which purported to be a second return from the State of Vermont. This, Mr. Field continued, would be necessary in order that the House might understand the question upon which it was voting. In his opinion the demand upon the Presiding Officer of the Senate was in strict accordance with law, and it was plainly the duty of the House to make it. At the conclusion of the address, Mr. Knott's resolution previously presented was read. It provided that the President of the Senate be required to open, in the presence of the two houses, the paper which was claimed to be a second return from Vermont, and that the progress of the Electoral count be stopped until this request be complied with. So well had Field impressed this view of the matter upon the minds of the Democrats that it was thought for a time that this motion would have carried, and had it done so there is but little doubt that the count would have been defeated. A number of honest Democrats, however, many of them Southern men, came to the rescue, and the motion was lost by a vote of 116 yeas to 148 nays. Messrs. Hewitt and Watterson were among those who voted in the negative, and as they answered to their names they were loudly applauded by the respectable men of both parties.

Pending the roll call Mr. Hopkins tried to make further delay by offering an amendment to the original resolution. Upon this Mr. Wood of New-York called the previous question, but the Speaker ruled that the amendment was in order. It was then read and found to be identical with the first resolution, except that the last clause was stricken out. It was defeated by the vote given on Knott's resolution, 116 to 148. After this, motion followed motion in quick succession, and nearly two hours were wasted. Then Wilson, of Iowa, in a forcible speech, which was listened to with attention, explained that under the provisions of the Electoral bill all dilatory motions were out of order. This brought Walling, the Corporal of the obstructionists, to his feet, and, amid shouts of laughter and loud cries for order, he declared that since fraud was law filibustering was patriotism.

The calling of rolls then began and proceeded almost without incident or intermission till about 10:40. From the end of the debate to the meeting of the two houses there must have been as many as 12 or 15 calls of the roll. At the end of each, there was a few minutes of disorder, and once or twice Caulfield, Springer, Lane of Oregon, Walling, Poppleton, or some one else of the filibusters who have only two days more of Congressional life would try to raise some new point of order. The seats were generally deserted, members managing to vote and then go outside the chamber, or into the cloak room, till the time come to answer to the call again. Randall was operating with the obstructionists all day. Consistency with his pronounced ruling against dilatory motions, when Oregon was presented, or even with his rulings of yesterday, would have brought the House to a vote on Vermont by 6 o'clock this evening at the latest. He is playing a double game—trying to gain the applause of one faction one day and of another the next. His desire to secure the Speakership of the next House explains his contradictory action. At 10:45 he sent word to the Senate that the House was ready to meet them, ruling at the same time that the law required him at this point to act ministerially. He refused to receive a motion ordering the Senate to be given notice, which would have permitted two more roll calls. He took pains to explain that he had allowed votes on every legitimate parliamentary question that could be raised, and he endeavored to show both factions that he aided both.

The Senate joined the House at 10:55, and at 11:25 Wisconsin, the last State to be counted, had been reached and objected to, and the houses separated.

After the Senate retired, Mills, of Texas, offered a long resolution, the substance of which was that the House proceed to the election of a President of the United States. There was considerable confusion before the reading of the resolution was obtained, a motion being made to take recess, and another, by Mr. Garfield, to suspend the rules and dispose at once of the objections. Mills' resolution was decided to be in order only as an amendment to some resolution touching the sustaining of the objections. Lynde was recognized to make a motion to take a recess, and it was voted down on a *viva voce* vote. While the yeas and nays were being demanded, the announcement came from the Senate that they had voted to count the Elector objected to. This was received with loud applause on the floor and in the galleries. The filibusters, who have all day insulted the American people, were greatly outraged, and demanded that the gallery be cleared. This was an attempt to gain a roll-call, but the motion was received with such dissent that no yeas and nays were demanded. Even Beebe soothed the rage of Caulfield on this question, saying, in his seat, "Wait a bit, Barney, it will be all right."

At 11:10 the House began to respond to a roll-call on a motion for a recess. The hall was full, scarcely a member being absent. The galleries, which had been well filled, were beginning to look vacant. On the Democratic side there were two or three groups in consultation. Mr. Wood was the centre of one, Field of another, and the great O'Brien, Springer, Mills, Walling and their gang were flying about in disorder. The vote against a recess was going strong as usual, and it became clear that the majority of the House intended to remain and finish the Electoral count before a recess.

At 12:10 A. M., in the House, the roll-call on the motion for a recess was not officially declared, and stood, subject to some unimportant corrections—Yeas 96, nays 132. This was very discouraging to the filibusters, and confidence increased among the reputable members that the end would be forced to-night.

After the motion for a recess was voted down Mr. Wood made a proposition for a recess till to-morrow, the vote to be taken without dilatory motions at 1 o'clock. Mills, of Texas, objected to such a left-handed whack at his proposition for an election by the House. O'Brien also objected: if the fraud was to be consummated it should be in the darkness of night. There was much confusion, but no bad temper shown. The usual resolutions were offered, and also that of Mills, and the reading of the testimony touching the Elector objected to was then demanded by Mr. Lynde.

12:55 A. M.—The objections to the Wisconsin Elector, with the evidence attached, when the reading was demanded were not to be found, and the House waited about 15 minutes while they were hunted up by the Clerk. They had probably been sent to the Senate. It was 20 minutes before 1 o'clock when the reading began. The House was then in order, and it seemed to be understood by the filibusters that they had exhausted all hopeful chances of defeating the count. Most of the obstructions had been insincere, and failure was expected, and by a few not undesired. The appearance of the House at this hour indicates that the debate will proceed in order; that when it is concluded, there will be very few roll-calls, and that the State of Wisconsin will be counted and Hayes declared elected before 6 o'clock in the morning. The reading of the objections and accompanying papers has been completed, and the two hours' debate has begun.

### *THE ELECTORAL VOTE DECLARED.*

LAST FUTILE EFFORT OF THE OBSTRUCTIONISTS—WITHDRAWAL OF A NUMBER OF THEM FROM THE FLOOR, BUT NOT FROM THE CHAMBER.

*Special Dispatch to the New-York Times.*

WASHINGTON, March 2—2:45 A. M.—Debate closed after discussion on the proposition that the House proceed to the election of a President, Mills, of Texas, who presented the resolution, trying to get a direct vote on his motion. Mr. Wood said, "If you press the resolution at this time we will vote it down." "If you do," replied Mills, "you will violate a solemn agreement, and I have been deceived and trifled with." John Young Brown and James B. Reilly, of Pennsylvania, both Democrats, protested against the consideration of the motion before the Wisconsin vote was counted.

Half a dozen points of order were raised, upon none of which the Speaker ruled. In answer to a question from Blackburn, Mr. Randall then stated that he had exhausted every power known to him to secure to the gentleman from Texas a vote on the proposition, but that he could see no way by which it could be had before action had been taken on the Wisconsin resolution, upon which the previous question had been called. Mills, with great excitement, replied that the Speaker had agreed some days ago, and again to day, to let him have a vote on his resolution.

Carter Harrison then made a strong speech against the consideration of the resolution. He was interrupted by Mr. Lane, who was so sleepy that he should have been removed to the cloak room, and for a time great confusion ensued. When quiet was restored John Young Brown spoke against the proposition. After wavering for a long time, the Speaker ruled that the motion could not be considered.

Then a vote was ordered by yeas and nays on the substituted resolution that the vote of all the Electors of Wisconsin be counted for the Republican candidate. This was lost by a vote of 79 to 134.

At 3:50 A. M. the resolution sustaining the objection was carried. Mr. Mills then demanded that a vote on his proposition be had. The Speaker refused to put the question, and the gentleman from Texas withdrew his resolution. Then, after delay, the Senate appeared.

As the Senators filed in, all but about 30 of the Democratic members left their seats, and stood outside the bar, thus protesting against the declaration of the election of Mr. Hayes, by refusing, as they supposed to be, a party to the action.

The joint session then convened. The 10 votes of Wisconsin were counted for Hayes and Wheeler.

Senator Allison, one of the Tellers, then handed a list of the votes and the result of the enumeration of the votes cast, and at 4:10 o'clock Rutherford B. Hayes, of Ohio, was declared to be elected President of the United States, and William A. Wheeler, of New-York, Vice President in the following words:

"The whole number of Electors appointed to vote for President and Vice President of the United States was 369, of which a majority is 185. The state of the vote for President, as delivered by the Tellers, and as determined under the act of Congress of Jan. 29, 1877, on this subject is:

For Rutherford B. Hayes........................185 votes
For Samuel J. Tilden...........................184 votes

The state of the vote for Vice President of the United States as delivered by the tellers, and as determined under the act of Congress approved Jan. 29, 1877, on this subject, is:

For William A. Wheeler........................185 votes
For Thomas A. Hendricks......................184 votes

Wherefore, I do announce that Rutherford B. Hayes, of the State of Ohio, having received a majority of the whole number of Electoral votes, is duly elected President of the United States for four years, commencing on the 4th day of March, 1877."

Then the two houses separated. The Senate retired to its own chamber and the House adjourned.

The President of the Senate signed the declaration of the result with the black eagle's quill, sent to him from the West for that purpose. There was no demonstration of any kind when the result was declared.

### *THE PRESIDENCY OF THE SENATE.*

SPECULATION REGARDING THE ACTION OF THE SENATE IF THE HOUSE PREVENTS THE DECLARATION OF THE VOTE—PROBABILITY THAT MR. MORTON WILL BE ELECTED PRESIDING OFFICER—SOUTHERN SENTIMENT IN HIS FAVOR.

*Special Dispatch to the New-York Times.*

WASHINGTON, March 1.—During the session of the House to-day the Republicans in the Senate had a great deal of private discussion upon the policy to be pursued with respect to a possible failure to finish the Electoral count in the House. There has been no formal caucus, but one has been called to meet to-morrow morning. The propositions to be considered are the choosing of a President pro tem. from among the number of Senators whose term does not expire on the 4th of March, and the proper action of the Senate in case the House delays, by filibustering or otherwise, the announcement of the vote for President, and also any specific propositions relating to these two general subjects, which may be brought forward. The general tone of expression is unmistakably in favor of Mr. Morton, as President of the Senate. There can be little doubt that he will be elected. Besides, the admiration which he has awakened among Republicans by his vigorous and straightforward course this Winter, there are many men in the Senate, including all the Republican Senators from the Southern States, who really prefer Mr. Morton for President to Mr. Hayes. This class is composed of those who are unfavorable to the moderate Southern policy which, it is generally understood, Mr Hayes will pursue, and which was pointed out in his letter of acceptance. It will be seen from this that there is a small number of Senators who would actually be pleased by a failure of the House to elect, in order that Mr. Morton might become President. In respect to the finishing of the Presidential count in the Senate Chamber, if the House does not conclude the work by Saturday, the feeling is not unanimous; but there is probably sufficient strength to carry out that proposition in the Senate. Mr. Conkling is the only Senator who is believed to be unalterably opposed to this course, and it is understood that he has impressed his views upon the President so far that the latter is unwilling to see this method adopted. In respect to the resignation of the President, which has been talked of, there has been much consultation as to the legal effect, and it is not altogether clear that even that action would satisfy the requirements of the Constitution. It is by no means clear that the President of the Senate holds his office beyond the end of the Congress for which he was elected. This has been a disputed question, and it has generally been held that the Senate being a continuous body, the office of President of the Senate did not expire until his successor was appointed. The question is of such importance, however, that it is not safe to depend upon past decisions in so grave a crisis as the present.

1:45 A. M.—The debate proceeded in a dull and quiet manner till a few minutes ago, when Blackburn, the Kentucky raider, began a profane and indecent speech. He called the Commission perjured miscreants. It was a fitting day, he said, for the fraud to be consummated. It was Friday—hangman's day. Mr. Williams, of Wisconsin, in reply said it was a good day for a pretender, who had kept the country in turmoil for months by a false claim to the Presidency, to be gibbeted on. Springer has been going about the House trying to have the Democrats withdraw when the declaration of the election is made. The obstructionists have apparently given up the contest.

### *BULL-DOZING IN SOUTH CAROLINA.*

A REPUBLICAN JUDGE FORCED BY THREATS OF VIOLENCE TO SIGN A DECREE SUSTAINING HAMPTON—HE SUBSEQUENTLY REVOKES HIS DECISION.

*Special Dispatch to the New-York Times.*

COLUMBIA, March 1.—The Supreme Court of South Carolina has had before it for two weeks the case of Tilda Norris, brought up on habeas corpus, to test the validity of a pardon from Hampton. It would have been decided a week ago, but for the sudden illness of Chief Justice Moses, who had a stroke of paralysis. This left the decision to Justices Willard and Wright, the latter a colored man. Willard has always been a violent partisan of Hampton, and announced his willingness to decide for him without the formality of hearing evidence. Wright was expected to decide against Hampton, and so there was apparently a divided court. Extraordinary efforts were made to win over Wright by Judge Willard, aided by frequent visits from Hampton and other leading Democrats. Tuesday morning last was set by the court for the decision, but Justice Willard appeared and announced that the court still was consulting on the case. To-day it was learned that on that morning Judge Wright was induced to sign an order discharging Tilda Norris, thus recognizing the validity of Hampton's pardon. He asserts that he did it while in fear for his life. He says that Judge Willard told him that the Democrats could no longer be restrained, and when it should be announced to the waiting crowd in the court room that nothing but his [Wright's] obduracy stood in the way of Hampton's recognition, their full fury would be visited upon him. He says, also, that Willard brought Gen. Conner, the leading Hampton counsel, into the consultation room, and Conner told him that if they did not get a favorable decision, many lives would be sacrificed. While laboring under great mental distress and fear, Judge Wright was induced to sign the order, but refused to sign the opinion of Willard, which sustained it, and he also exacted a promise that it should not be filed until Friday. Judge Wright concealed his action from his Republican friends until yesterday, when he informed them that he regretted it, that he signed under duress and fear, and that he intended to revoke his order. To-day he filed an opinion denying the validity of Hampton's pardon with the following indorsement:

"Having attached my name on the 27th ult. to an order discharging the petitioner in this case without due consultation, I do now, upon more mature deliberation, hereby recall, revoke, and cancel my signature to said order, and substitute the foregoing opinion in its place."

There will be a high degree of excitement to-morrow when all these facts are known.

### *NOTES FROM THE CAPITAL.*

WASHINGTON, March 1.—An intense commotion was created in the Treasury Department at about noon to-day by the appearance of a gentlemanly-appearing person, who called at the Treasurer's office, and, sending a card into the redemption division, upon which the name of Littleton was written, called out a lady employe, said to be named Storer, and immediately upon seeing her in the passage fired two shots at her, neither of which took effect, however, and, owing to prompt interference by Mr. Wilson, Chief of the Loan Division, who was attracted by the disturbance, he was seized. Upon releasing him, Littleton fired upon himself, though only inflicting a slight injury. The cause of the shooting appears to be a mystery, as neither party has given any explanation of the strange assault. The lady went immediately to her home, and her would-be murderer was promptly taken to the Police station. When Littleton was first arrested, he said he was anxious to complete the work he had begun, but on the way to the station-house exhibited some signs of anxiety for the condition of the woman. The halls and corridors of the Treasury where the shooting occurred were crowded with an excited and frightened throng of men and women immediately after the shooting, all of whom were unable to give any explanation of the event. Many were inclined to believe that another "Mary Harris" episode was being enacted. Some of the employes assert that the man declared that the woman he assaulted was his wife, but that she was employed here under a different name.

The President sent the following nominations to the Senate to-day: Silas B. Dutcher, to be Appraiser of Merchandise in New-York City; Albert C. Judson, to be Pension Agent at Albany, N. Y.; John Tyler, to be Collector of Customs for the district of Buffalo Creek, N. Y.; R. G. Pettibone, to be Postmaster at Ogdensburg, N. Y.; James Frankle, to be Postmaster at Haverhill, Mass.; Nathan F. Dixon, Jr., to be United States District Attorney for Rhode Island; F. Sevening [?], to be Pension Agent at Lexington, Ky.; Henry Esperson, of Wisconsin, to be Surveyor General for Dakota; Palmer G. Wood, to be Second Lieutenant of the [illegible] Infantry.

## MR. HAYES LEAVES OHIO.

### *ON THE WAY TO WASHINGTON.*

DEPARTURE OF THE PRESIDENTIAL PARTY FROM COLUMBUS—IMMENSE CROWDS OF PEOPLE AT ALL THE STOPPING PLACES—ONE SPEECH AND MANY HAND SHAKINGS—ENTHUSIASM ALL ALONG THE LINE.

*Special Dispatch to the New-York Times.*

PITTSBURG, en route to WASHINGTON, March 1.—Gov. Hayes and party left Columbus at 1:10 P. M. to-day for Washington via Pittsburg and Harrisburg. The Governor was escorted from the executive mansion to the depot, half a mile distant, by the Columbus cadets, preceded by a military band and followed by a large concourse of citizens. He rode to the depot in an open carriage and on his arrival was greeted with prolonged cheers by a crowd numbering many thousands, who had gathered to witness his departure. Two special cars had been provided for the Governor and family with their friends, and the intervening time between their arrival at the depot and the starting of the train was occupied in cheers for "Gov. Hayes," "President Hayes," "Our next President," &c., the band meantime playing "Auld Lang Syne." In response to repeated calls, the Governor finally stepped to the platform of the car and addressed the people as follows:

MY FELLOW-CITIZENS: I appear to say a few words in bidding good-bye to you. I understand very well the uncertainty of public affairs at Washington. I understand very well that possibly next week I may be with you again to resume my place in the Governor's Office, and as your fellow-citizen; but I also understand that it is my duty to be at Washington, prepared to assume another position, higher and more responsible, and with more difficult duties. I have thought, as I looked upon this great audience, and as to-day I gazed on the people who thronged our route to this depot, of a similar occurrence 16 years ago. A little less than 16 years ago I marched down High-street with 1,000 men, to pass to the East and to the South, to do what we could to restore the union of the States, and to re-establish the authority of the Constitution. [Cheers.] In that work we were eminently successful, so far as it was possible to be successful by force of arms. I am not here to say a word in disparagement of what was accomplished by the brave men who went out with me from different parts of the country. Of my comrades one-third and over never returned to their homes. They perished in the discharge of their duty that the Republic might live. But there was something force could not do. We would have our Union to be a union of hearts, and we would have our Constitution obeyed, not merely because of force that compels obedience, but obeyed because the people love the principles of the Constitution. [Long continued applause.] And to-day if I am called to the work to which Abraham Lincoln was called 16 years ago, it is under brighter skies and more favorable auspices. [Applause.] I do hope, I do fervently believe, that, by the aid of Divine Providence, we may do something in this day of peace, by works of peace, toward re-establishing in the hearts of our countrymen a real, a hearty attachment for the Constitution as it is, and to the Union as it is. [Long continued applause.]

At the close of the Governor's remarks, which were enthusiastically applauded, the band struck up "Hail to the Chief," and amid strains of music, whistling of steam engines, and wild cheering from the populace, the train started and Gov. Hayes took his departure from Columbus. Accompanying the Governor and his family, and occupying seats in the special cars, was a party of 15 or 20 ladies and gentlemen, mostly old and intimate friends of Governor and Mrs. Hayes, from Cincinnati, Columbus, and Fremont. Among the number were ex-Gov. Noyes, Col. L. C. Weir, of the Governor's staff; Gen. R. P. Buckland and wife, of Fremont; Dr. Webb, a brother of Mrs. Hayes, also of Fremont; Gen. John G. Mitchell and wife, and Miss Platt, of Columbus; George W. Jones, wife, and daughter; J. W. Herron and wife, and William Rodgers and wife, of Cincinnati; Thomas G. Nickell, a nephew of Gov. Hayes, from Chillicothe, and Mrs. Emma Foote. Col. H. C. Corbin, United States Army, stationed at Columbus; ex-Congressman McNulta, of Illinois; Attorney General William Hunt, of Louisiana, and Gen. Cyrus Bussey. President of the Board of Trade of New-Orleans, also joined the Governor's party, and on the same train were Speaker Grosvenor and 30 or 40 members of the Ohio Legislature.

The first stop was at Newark, a town of 5,000 or 6,000 inhabitants, a large share of whom where found waiting at the depot to give the Governor a farewell greeting. Without waiting to be called Gov. Hayes stepped out on the platform of the rear car and received the congratulations of the citizens. Among them he found many old friends and acquaintances, who insisted upon shaking hands with him, and occupied so much time in the process that Newark was cheated out of the speech it would otherwise have got. Just as Gov. Hayes was beginning his response to the demand for a speech, and had got as far as "Friends and fellow-citizens," the train started, and the Newarkers were left to finish the speech themselves; but they continued to cheer the Governor till he was out of sight.

At Coshocton, the next stopping place, a large crowd had also congregated at the depot, but the stop was too short for a speech, and the people had to be satisfied with a brief glance at the Governor's features, and the waving of the Gubernatorial hat, which they accepted with thanks and cheers. The same thing was repeated at a small station bearing the significant title of New-Comerstown, and again at Dennison, where the train stopped long enough to enable the Governor to shake hands with a few of his old acquaintances. At all the smaller towns and villages on the route where the cars did not stop, the people came out in force and cheered the train as it passed. If the new President succeeds in gaining the good will of the nation to the extent he has won the hearts of the people of Ohio, his administration will be among the most popular the country has ever known.

The last stop made in Ohio was at Steubenville, and there a crowd of 2,000 or 3,000 people had assembled to extend a parting greeting to the Governor as he passed out of the limits of the State. It was nearly dark when the train arrived, but the citizens had taken the precaution to provide a torchlight procession, in the glare of which they were enabled to get a good view of the incoming President as he stepped out on the platform. Mrs. Hayes accompanied him to the platform, which greatly increased the enthusiasm of the crowd, and it was impossible to stop the cheering long enough to give the Governor a chance to say a word. He shook hands, however, with all who came in reach, and after a 10-minutes' stop the train passed over the river, followed by the echo of a myriad of Buckeye voices.

ALTOONA, Penn., March 1.—Between Steubenville and Pittsburg there was no stop. On reaching the [illegible] Pittsburg an Agent of the Pennsylvania Railroad came aboard the train and informed the Governor's party that owing to the large crowd collected at the depot in the city, it would be impossible to run the train through it without great delay, and the Superintendent of the road had therefore directed the train to be run around the city by another route. These orders were given without consulting Gov. Hayes or any of his party and caused as much dissatisfaction to his friends as they probably did to the citizens of Pittsburg. Preparations had been made to give the President elect a grand reception at Pittsburg, worthy of the people of Allegheny County, which, for so many years has been steadfast in the maintenance of Republican principles. The order of the railroad officials prevented any demonstration whatever, and besides disappointing thousands of Republicans in that city, will afford the enemies of Gov. Hayes an opportunity to misconstrue and misrepresent the motive and object. Having thus dodged the crowd at the depot, the train ran around and stopped on the outskirts of the city long enough to have had a reception. [illegible] no one was there, and it was reported that railroad officials circulated the report that Gov. Hayes was not coming till to-morrow.

The trip from Pittsburg to Altoona was without incident. It was midnight when the train arrived here, and Gov. Hayes and family with most of the friends accompanying them, had already retired to their berths. The train is due in Washington about 9 o'clock to-morrow morning. Gov. Hayes and family, it is understood, will go to the residence of Sen. Sherman, of Ohio, immediately on their arrival, and stay there till the inaugural ceremonies are over. The President elect has not resigned his office as Governor of Ohio, and does not propose to do so until the final decision of the Electoral Commission. He is in excellent health and spirits and on the trip from Columbus has chatted freely with his friends on general topics, but no one has succeeded in getting an inkling of his Presidential policy or who are to be his Cabinet advisers.

### *THE OREGON INIQUITY.*

COL. PELTON PROFESSES IGNORANCE REGARDING THE PROPOSED PURCHASE OF AN ELECTOR—THE CIPHER DISPATCHES NEVER SEEN BY TILDEN.

WASHINGTON, March 1.—Col. W. T. Pelton, Secretary of the National Democratic Committee, was before the Senate Committee on Privileges and Elections, and read a written statement in relation to election dispatches. He testified in substance that all telegrams received by the Democratic Committee in New-York during the late election were delivered during the day at No. 59 Liberty-street, and during the night at the Everett House, in accordance with orders left at the telegraph offices; that none of the telegrams were received at No. 15 Gramercy Park, even when directed there, nor were the answers sent from there. The telegrams were opened by such members as were present at the time. None of the cipher telegrams were delivered at Gramercy Park, and Gov. Tilden never knew of any cipher telegrams received from or sent to Oregon. The famous "Gobble" dispatch was never seen by Gov. Tilden nor its contents known to him; Col. Pelton further stated that telegrams addressed to him [Pelton] were often opened and read and answered without his knowing of them, and some telegrams put in evidence, purporting to have come to him, he did not recognize as having come to his knowledge and were never received by him. The telegram from Portland, Oregon, dated Nov. 28, purporting to be signed by Mr. Patrick and Senator Kelly, was never translated or read by him, [Pelton,] and he never understood it to contain a proposition to purchase a Republican Elector or any other Elector. He never sanctioned the furnishing of money to purchase an Elector in Oregon, nor did any one else to his knowledge. His purpose was simply to furnish the Democratic Committee of Oregon with sufficient funds to meet their just and legitimate expenses and of maintaining their rights. He never heard it intimated by any one that Gov. Grover or any one else in office in Oregon was to be paid anything, or that Mr. Cronin was to be paid anything for loss of time, expenses, &c., and never heard that any money was [illegible] to be used for any purpose until he saw the evidence before the Senate Committee. After reading his statement, Col. Pelton was examined by Senator Kernan, but his testimony was simply corroborative of his written statement.

### *THE SOUTH AND THE DEMOCRATS.*

The Charleston (S. C.) *News and Courier* of the 27th inst. expresses itself thus emphatically: "South Carolina has not fallen so low that she can be kicked by the New-York *World* with impunity. The South, if she have not recovered her pristine power, is too strong to be safely reviled by the Metropolitan organ of the party to which the Southern vote gives its strength and national influence. [illegible]

### *THE NEW-JERSEY CENTRAL TROUBLES.*

EASTON, Penn., March 1.—Committees of the Firemen's and Brakemen's Union have called on Mr. Lathrop, Receiver of the Central Railroad of New-Jersey, for the purpose of learning something definite as to how soon they will receive their wages for December and January. [illegible]

### *THE DOMINION RIFLE ASSOCIATION.*

OTTAWA, March 1.—At the Dominion Rifle Association annual meeting yesterday, the report read showed that $13,000 were expended in rifle competition during the year. [illegible]

### *A SHIP STRUCK BY LIGHTNING.*

PORTLAND, March 1.—The bark [illegible], which arrived here to-day, reports that, while on her passage from St. John, she was struck by lightning. [illegible]

### *SPICE MILLS BURNED IN BALTIMORE.*

BALTIMORE, March 1.—[illegible]

RUTHERFORD B. HAYES

# The New-York Times.

VOL. XXVI.......NO. 7948. NEW-YORK, MONDAY, MARCH 5, 1877. PRICE FOUR CENTS.


## THE NEW ADMINISTRATION.

### THE INAUGURATION CEREMONIES.

PREPARING FOR TO-DAY'S EVENT—WASHINGTON CROWDED WITH STRANGERS—THOUSANDS OF SOUTHERN FRIENDS IN THE CAPITAL—A GRAND SIGHT TO BE WITNESSED ON THE AVENUE.

*Special Dispatch to the New-York Times.*

WASHINGTON, March 4.—The ordinary quiet of a Washington Sabbath has been disturbed to-day by the arrival of numerous military organizations and civil societies, which propose to participate in the inauguration ceremonies to take place to-morrow. To-night the city is crowded as it has seldom been, by representatives from all parts of the Union. It is a noteworthy fact that delegations from the South are particularly strong and particularly demonstrative of their regard for the new Administration. The often expressed hope that the two sections of the country might shortly be united in fraternal peace and good-fellowship seems now about to be realized. To this end the Southern portion of members of Congress now in Washington are striving with all the power which they have, and unless those who are best qualified to judge are very much mistaken, the country is destined, ere long, to enter upon a new era of general satisfaction, peace, fraternity, prosperity, and good will. It is remarkable that the inauguration ceremonies will be attended quite as extensively by Southern as by Northern and Eastern organizations, and it is equally remarkable that the Southern societies come here, not with a sectional, but with a national feeling. All through the day the hotels of Washington and the public places of the capital have been thronged by people who represent every State and almost every cross-road in the Union, and among all the crowd so assembled there has not been one man who is not ready to lift his hat to the new President, and to freely admit his title to the office upon which he is about to enter.

In signification of the general rejoicing over the end of a contest which at one time promised to be so disastrous the whole of Washington has put on a gala dress. The principal thoroughfares are decked with bunting, appropriate mottoes, flags, and emblems of rejoicing. Pennsylvania-avenue—the street through which the President-elect must pass to take the ceremonial oath of office—is one mass of flags. Private citizens have vied with proprietors of public places to do honor to the approaching event, and upon every hand there are indications that the citizen of Ohio who has been called upon to preside over the National Administration will be heartily welcomed to the city in which, for the next four years at least, he is to make his home. At the Capitol the preparations for the inauguration have been conducted with remarkable dispatch. Before the east portico a platform has been erected capable of seating all the Senators and Representatives, together with distinguished guests. The building has been appropriately decorated with flags and mottoes which fittingly responds to the gala appearance of the private buildings and residences in the city. There is now no doubt that the military and civil parade in honor of the inauguration will be an exceedingly imposing one. All through the day companies and unions have continued to arrive in Washington, and it is announced that many organizations may be expected during the night. President Hayes will have no reason to complain of the reception which he will receive at the hands of the American people now assembled in Washington. A more demonstrative crowd could not be desired. His name is upon every tongue; in every direction is echoed the toast, "Prosperity to our next President," and from almost every housetop flies a banner bearing the inscription, "Success to President Hayes."

### MOVEMENTS OF PRESIDENT HAYES.

HOW HE PASSED THE SABBATH—THE OATH OF OFFICE TAKEN ON SATURDAY.

*Special Dispatch to the New-York Times.*

WASHINGTON, March 4.—President Hayes has had a comparatively quiet day to-day. Only a few persons called upon him, and they were mostly old friends of the President's family from Ohio. Speaker Grosvenor and Assemblyman Wiltser, of the Ohio Legislature, called in the evening, when arrangements were made to receive the Ohio delegation in a body at the White House to-morrow afternoon, before their departure for home. The President and Mrs. Hayes attended morning service at the Church of the Epiphany, (Episcopal,) in company with Senator and Mrs. Sherman. Mrs. Hayes is a member and has been a regular attendant of the Methodist Episcopal Church in Columbus, and the family of the new President will, doubtless, attend a church of the same denomination here, probably the Metropolitan, the same that President Grant's family attended. President Hayes himself is said to be very liberal in his religious views, and was accustomed to attend churches of different denominations in Columbus.

The quidnuncs have been busy all day trying to find out whether President Hayes has taken the oath of office or not, and if not, whether he is President or not, or whether the country is to be without a President until to-morrow noon. Two or three Washington papers have issued extras to-day, devoted mainly to the solution of this important question, but differing widely as to the facts, some stating that the President had taken the oath, and others that he had not. The truth of the matter is this: President Hayes preferred not to take the oath of office on Sunday, unless it was absolutely necessary, and so stated to those who consulted him on the subject. It was not deemed essential by the Chief Justice of the Supreme Court, or by others who had investigated the law, that the oath should be subscribed at 12 M. to-day, rather than at any other hour. They were of the opinion that the requirements of the law would be fully met by taking the oath of office either before or after that date. In view of the disposition so prevalent in certain quarters to take advantage of every conceivable technicality, it was deemed advisable that President Hayes should take the oath in season to prevent an interregnum of a day. It was accordingly subscribed at the White House last evening, in the presence of Chief Justice Waite, who, with President Hayes, was a guest of Gen. Grant at the dinner at the Presidential Mansion. As the act was done merely to meet any technical objection that might be raised, and was not intended to supersede the regular formal administering of the oath in public at the inauguration ceremonies to-morrow, it was thought best not to give publicity to it, and hence the difficulty of the quidnuncs in getting at the facts.

A rumor was circulated about town to-day, which also brought out an extra, that Tilden had taken the Presidential oath in the Gramercy Park mansion at noon to-day, and was coming on to Washington to-night to take possession of the office. The rumor was very generally credited among Democrats, which shows that there is no limit to the absurd antics which they are still prepared to expect from their late candidate for the Presidency.

### PRESIDENT HAYES' CABINET.

THE INTERIOR BELIEVED TO HAVE BEEN GIVEN TO CARL SCHURZ—THE NAVY, WAR, AND POST OFFICE UNDISPOSED OF—THE NAVY TO GO PROBABLY TO NEW-ENGLAND.

*Special Dispatch to the New-York Times.*

WASHINGTON, March 4.—There is no positive addition to the stock of information about the composition of the Cabinet since last night. The report of the appointment of Carl Schurz to the Interior Department is generally credited and is no doubt true; and this leaves three places yet unsettled, so far as the public knows, and, very possibly, unsettled in the mind of President Hayes. There have been various reports to the effect that Gen. Joe Johnston had been offered a Cabinet position, but the statement is not true, and there is little reason to suppose he will be offered a position. The Post Office Department, the Navy Department, and the War Department are still unprovided for, with the prospect that one will be filled from the South and one from New-England. This leaves one position still undetermined, so far as locality is concerned, the desire being to recognize the State of Pennsylvania in the Cabinet. It is not probable that any name in the South has yet been fully determined upon. The representative from New-England will doubtless be assigned to the Navy Department, and there has been a report this afternoon that Mr. Forbes, of Boston, who was a member of the National Committee and a delegate to Cincinnati, would receive the appointment. The report is not entirely trustworthy. The position has been offered to a distinguished Senator from a New-England State, who has not yet signified his willingness to accept it, but whose appointment would give universal satisfaction.

*Dispatch to the Associated Press.*

It is confidently stated late to-night by a gentleman holding close political and personal relations with President Hayes that the Cabinet slate will be very certain to contain the names of Evarts, of New-York, for Secretary of State; Sherman, of Ohio, for Secretary of the Treasury; Schurz, of Missouri, for the Interior Department; McCrary, of Iowa, for Attorney General; and Key, of Tennessee, for Postmaster General. It is now probable that one of the other places will be given to Indiana. Who will represent New England has not yet been determined.

### PRAYERS FOR THE NEW ADMINISTRATION.

*Special Dispatch to the New-York Times.*

CHICAGO, March 4.—The President-elect was a special subject of prayer in nearly all the Chicago pulpits to-day. The clergy without exception invoked the richest blessings in his behalf, and prayed that his inauguration might be the inauguration of peace and harmony; that sectional strife might be allayed; that prosperity and happiness might abound, and wise counsel prevail at the national capital.

### GOVERNMENT OF LOUISIANA.

NO IMMEDIATE ATTACK UPON THE STATE-HOUSE ANTICIPATED—A STATEMENT BY GOV. PACKARD.

NEW-ORLEANS, March 4.—Gov. Packard made the following statement to-day to an Associated Press reporter: "I cannot say I anticipate any immediate attack upon the State-house, though in the excited condition of the public mind, fomented by constant sensational dispatches to the local press, such a thing is possible. I think it more likely that, under cover of a pretended process of law from courts not recognized, not having any legal standing, some effort will be made to arrest officers of the Government, or to serve process on them, and to enforce that service by a posse of the White League, or Nicholl's Militia and Police, as they are termed. I shall regard any such posse as a mob, and shall resist it accordingly. The State-house is amply provisioned and guarded, and cannot be successfully assaulted by any movement short of a general armed insurrection against the Government, which has been legally inaugurated under the State laws. I believe the ultimate recognition of the Republican State Government is assured. I attach no importance to the reported efforts of Pinchback, West, George Sheridan, Sloanaker, George Carter, and others, to prevent it. The unloading of these men is, in my judgment, a positive benefit to the Republican Party of the State. It enables us to attach firmly to its standard such old citizens as Attorney General Hunt, George Williamson, Minister to Central America; A. H. Leonard, Judges Taylor, Beattie, King, Bowman, Hunter, and others, who stand ready to join the party when thus purged, most of whom are Old Line Whigs, natives of the State, thoroughly identified with its every interest, and who are now acting with us, most of them for the first time. The people desire a good government. This can best be obtained by dividing the people other than on the color line. The accession of such men as I have named and others will equally divide the whites, intelligence, wealth, and influence. The sloughing off of the so-called Republicans who now have allied themselves to the opposition is a positive benefit to the State. Their only motive in adhering to the Republican Party heretofore has been a desire for the spoils of office. Their defection enables the party to purify itself. I entertain no doubt of my ability to maintain the Government when once recognized as the Constitution and laws of the United States require. Of 50,000 men in the City of New-Orleans capable of bearing arms, not more than 5,000 are in arms against the Government. Of the 57 parishes comprising the State only four (known as the bull-dozed parishes) are really in resistance, and they only in regard to local affairs. Of the 18 judicial districts in the State there is barely one outside of the City of New-Orleans where any mandate of the Nicholls Supreme Court could be enforced by officers of the court. President Grant himself, in the military orders, spoke of that court as entitled to no more respect than would be the decisions of any other five lawyers appointed by any other private citizens. Even in the city of New-Orleans not one Judge, Sheriff, or Clerk of Court, so far as I know, has had spread upon the minutes of the court his Nicholls' commission or qualifications in accordance with the custom heretofore prevailing. Gen. Nicholls' Government is bounded by the limits of White League authority and is nowhere enforced outside of their influence."

### A TOBACCO FACTORY BURNED.

ST. LOUIS, March 4.—The extensive tobacco factory of Leggatt, Hudson & Butler, Nos. 1,903 and 1,905 Buel-street, was totally destroyed by fire this morning. The loss is estimated at $60,000; insurance $2,500 in each of the following companies: Howard and Phœnix, of New-York; North America, Manhattan, Pennsylvania Fire, London Assurance, Continental Assurance, German-American, Imperial of London, Phœnix of Hartford, Lycoming, Merchants' of New-Jersey, Fire Association, Commercial, New-York, Westchester, Buffalo, German, St. Paul, and Scottish-American, and $700 in the Foreman's Fund, making a total of $45,700. The business of the firm will not be interrupted.

### FAILURE OF AN INSURANCE COMPANY.

BANGOR, March 4.—The Bangor Fire Insurance Company, having impaired its capital by unprofitable business, will close up its affairs, and is negotiating with the Hartford Company to reinsure its policies.

## ADJOURNMENT OF CONGRESS

### SCENES OF DISORDER IN THE HOUSE.

FITTING CLOSE OF A DISGRACEFUL AND HUMILIATING SESSION—LEGITIMATE BUSINESS NEGLECTED IN THE DEMOCRATIC CONTEST FOR PERSONAL OR PARTISAN ADVANTAGE—FAILURE OF THE BILL TO PROVIDE FOR THE EXPENSES OF THE ARMY—MEN WITHOUT CHARACTER OR A FUTURE ASSUMING THE RESPONSIBILITY FOR THE OUTRAGE.

*Special Dispatch to the New-York Times.*

WASHINGTON, March 4.—The Forty-fourth Congress expired at noon to-day. Its entire existence was marked by confusion and violence, and its expiring moments were spent in a struggle over the Army Appropriation bill which left its legitimate work incomplete. In this it was consistent with its record, and the lower branch of the late Congress has passed into history with a pre-eminence for turbulence and incompetency, and is distinguished more for those things which it left undone than for those things which it has done. The last 30 days of its existence was one continual struggle, unprecedented in legislative annals for the bitterness that marked its deliberations, and unequaled for the grave apprehensions with which it filled the public mind. Its last official act showed an utter disregard of duty, and its last official utterances were those of partisan malevolence, seeking to justify its shortcomings behind pretended patriotism and sham economy.

The closing session of the House will stand conspicuous for confusion and disorder. This was so marked that it was found impossible to transact business intelligently, and for the sake of common decency the House was compelled to take a recess from 2:30 o'clock this morning until 8 o'clock. Upon reassembling general confusion again prevailed. Those who were anxious to secure the passage of private bills and claims assembled in a crowd in front of the Speaker's desk and shouted themselves hoarse for recognition. Bills were read by the clerks and passed by the House of whose contents no one could be informed in consequence of the prevailing disorder. The confusion would cease for a few minutes when reports were presented by the several conferences on the appropriation bills, but as soon as those were disposed of disorder would again become supreme. By 10 o'clock all the appropriation bills except that for the Army were finally agreed upon, the last appropriation to receive approval being the sundry civil. The obstacle to agreement on this bill was the reduction of the President's salary, which was removed by the House conferees yielding and permitting the salary to remain at $50,000 per annum. At 10:30 the conferees on the Army bill reported their inability to agree. Mr. Atkins explained that there seemed to be no probability of an agreement being reached on the section forbidding the use of troops in the Southern States, but he recommended another conference to make a last effort. Some discussion followed, Mr. Field taking this opportunity to make a farewell speech, in which he urged Southern members to stand firm, and thereby secure their deliverance from fraud and violence practiced upon them by the use of the Army. A new conference was ordered, after which members rushed to the front again, shrieking for recognition to call up and pass private bills. Mr. Holman, who had been on the conference to reconcile the differences on the Sundry Civil Appropriation bill, appeared in his seat and at once protested against legislation proceeding amid the prevailing confusion. Most of the bills that were being called up were so many raids upon the Treasury, and Holman proposed that the House should know the full character of claims before ordering them to be paid. It was now after 11 o'clock. Less than one hour of the session remained, and Holman appreciated his advantage. Mr. House, of Texas, called up a private bill, and the vote to suspend the rules and pass it was declared carried. Mr. Holman insisted upon a division, and when the division was decided against him, demanded the yeas and nays. The confusion was so great that it was impossible for the Speaker to count the House on ordering the yeas and nays, and Mr. Holman demanded tellers. Tellers were ordered and the yeas and nays called, resulting in the passage of the bill. Mr. Holman's determined manner discouraged many who were struggling to have bills passed, and they retired anathematizing the "great objector."

At 11:35 the Conference Committee on the Army bill appeared and were recognized. The crowd about the Speaker's desk were driven back, and Mr. Morrison arose to explain the failure to agree. The importance of the issue, involving, as it doubtless does, an extra session of Congress, was recognized by the House, and order was speedily obtained. Mr. Morrison explained briefly that the Senate conferees would not agree to the bill unless the section preventing the use of troops in Louisiana and South Carolina was stricken out. He thought there was no use of further effort at reconciliation, and moved the House insist on its bill. This was met with a shout of approbation from the Democratic side. Mr. Foster, of the minority of the conference, was recognized, and proposed that a sum equal to one-half of the amount appropriated for the Army last year shall be appropriated for the coming year, in order to provide for the pay and maintenance of the Army until the appropriation can be regularly made. This proposition was bowled down with scorn by the Democrats. "Not a dollar," shouted Mills and Tucker in concert. "Then you must accept the responsibility," responded Foster, and Walling, who was defeated at the polls last October, yelled back, "We will accept the responsibility." A division on Morrison's motion resulted—yeas 150, nays 101. Mr. Garfield called for the yeas and nays, and was seconded by the Republican side in a body. It was 11:45 when the Clerk began the roll-call. All knew that the roll could not be completed, but both sides seemed satisfied to have the Forty-fourth Congress expire in an angry struggle over providing means for carrying on the proper functions of the Government. The Clerk called the names with unusual activity, and members on both sides responded with an emphasis that illustrated their determination. At 11:50 the Speaker interrupted the roll-call to announce the enrollment of the Sundry Civil Appropriation, and that bill was rapidly forwarded to the President, who was occupying his room in the Senate wing for approval. Resuming the call the Clerk went on for a minute, reaching the name of Jones, of Kentucky, when the Speaker again interrupted him, and announced that it was a physical impossibility to complete the roll-call. The Speaker then proceeded to glorify the Democracy in a stump speech, and upon its conclusion pronounced the Forty-fourth Congress adjourned without day.

### THE LAST FEW MOMENTS.

DIGNITY AND DECORUM IN THE SENATE—THE ARMY APPROPRIATION BILL—WAITING TO HEAR FROM THE HOUSE—THE CROWD OF SPECTATORS IN BOTH HOUSES.

*Special Dispatch to the New-York Times.*

WASHINGTON, March 4.—During the last night and day of the session in the Senate, business proceeded with the same degree of decorum and dignity that always mark the deliberations of that body. Nothing unusual occurred until 11:30 o'clock, when Mr. Blaine, from the conference on the Army Appropriation bill, reported that there was no hope of reaching an agreement on that bill. He explained the determination of the House conferees respecting the section of the bill which restricts the President's constitutional control of the Army in the Southern States. Mr. Blaine said there were not 1,000 troops from the Potomac to Texas, but if there were but a Corporal's guard he would not consent to such a restriction. This sentiment was applauded by the crowded galleries. At 11:55 the minute-hand of the Senate clock was pushed back five minutes, and a few minutes thereafter President pro tem. Ferry delivered a brief address, and pronounced the Senate adjourned without day.

During the morning both wings of the Capitol were crowded to overflowing, the large number of visitors to witness the inaugural ceremonies taking advantage of the opportunity to see the closing hours of this most remarkable session. In the House the numbers who crowded the floor were so great that it was with difficulty the officers could keep the spectators from pressing upon the outer row of seats. For hours after the adjournment the crowds lingered about the Capitol inspecting the building and the arrangements in progress on the east front for the inaugural ceremonies of to-morrow.

*Dispatch to the Associated Press.*

The galleries of both houses of Congress were crowded from 8 o'clock this morning until the closing hours at noon, and such visitors as could not obtain admission to the galleries gathered in front of the doors and thronged the vestibules, or moved in crowds from one house to another to consume time. When the final adjournment took place they rushed into the legislative halls and remained there until the officers cleared the chambers in order to give the employes, who had been on continuous duty for 24 hours, an opportunity to go to their respective homes for rest. All the general appropriation bills became law, with the exception of those making appropriation for the support of the Army and the improvement of rivers and harbors. The latter was reported from the Committee on Commerce, but was not considered. There is, however, a large surplus of money from last year, and therefore no improvement actually needed will suffer owing to the non-passage of the bill. With regard to the Army bill, the former appropriation leaves sufficient to support that establishment until the end of the present fiscal year, expiring on the 30th of June. When it became known that the bill was lost prominent members of Congress said this would necessitate an extra session of Congress, to convene about May 28. In this connection, it is said on the authority of an official of the War Department (likely to be well posted) that under some sections of an old law the War and Navy Departments can be carried on for two years without any special appropriation. This is, that the drafts of the Secretaries of War and the Navy will be honored by the Treasury Department. If that be so the calling of an extra session is not altogether a matter of certainty. The bill making appropriations for sundry civil expenses came very near failing. It was a long bill, and the fear being expressed that it would not be engrossed in time, the Secretary of the Senate tendered the services of five experienced clerks to assist, but this offer was not accepted of, as few clerks could work on the bill at the same time, owing to the somewhat confused state of the amendments. During the last five minutes of the session, however, the bill was signed by the presiding officers of both houses, respectively, and hurriedly presented to the President, who approved it without having time to read it. About 100 private bills were presented to the President too late for his approval. All of a public character presented became laws. The President was at his own room, in the Senate wing, from 9:30 in the morning until noon, accompanied by the members of his Cabinet and his clerks.

### THE ROCK ON WHICH THEY SPLIT.

FULL TEXT OF THE SECTION IN THE ARMY BILL—AN UNCONSTITUTIONAL PARAGRAPH PREPARED BY THE DEMOCRATS.

WASHINGTON, March 4.—The following is the full text of the section of the Army Appropriation bill which was the subject of irreconcilable difference between the House of Representatives and the Senate; and which being adhered to by the House, caused the failure of the bill:

SECTION 5. That no part of the money appropriated by this act, nor any money heretofore appropriated, shall be applied to the pay, subsistence or transportation of troops used, employed, or to be or employed, in support of the claim of Francis T. Nicholls or of S. B. Packard to be Governor of the State of Louisiana; nor shall any of the money be applied in support of the claim of the two bodies claiming to be the Legislature of said State, presided over respectively by L. A. Wiltz and Louis Bush; nor of the two bodies claiming to be the Legislature of said State, presided over respectively by C. C. Antoine and Michael Hahn; nor in support of the claim of Thomas C. Manning and associates to be the Supreme Court of said State; nor in support of the claim of John T. Ludeling and associates to be the Supreme Court of said State; nor in aid of the execution of any process in the hands of the United States Marshal in said State, issued in aid of and for the support of any such claims; nor shall the Army, or any portion of it, be used in support of the claims, or pretended claims, or claims of any State Government, or officer thereof, in any State, until such Government shall have been duly recognized by Congress.

Any person offending against any of the provisions of this act shall be deemed guilty of a misdemeanor, and upon conviction thereof shall be imprisoned at hard labor for not less than five nor more than 10 years.

### FIRE IN BALTIMORE.

BALTIMORE, March 4.—The Patapsco Guano Company's Works, on Philpot, near Dock street, were burned this afternoon. The Chesapeake main railroad, adjoining, was badly damaged. The loss to the Guano Company is estimated at from $75,000 to $100,000, and is covered by insurance, distributed as follows: Hartford, of Connecticut; Home, of New-York, and National of Baltimore, $7,000 each; Baltimore, Peabody, Howard Associated, and German, of this city, and the Lamar, German-American, and Glen Falls, of New-York; Traders', of Chicago; Royal, of London; National, of Hartford; St. Paul, of Minnesota, and British-American, of Toronto, $3,500 each; Western Assurance, of Toronto; Franklin, of West Virginia; Security, of Connecticut; Lycoming, of Pennsylvania; Atlantic and Manhattan, of New-York, and North British, of London, $2,500 each, and several other companies from $1,200 to $1,700 each.

### LEGISLATIVE FAILURE IN INDIANA.

INDIANAPOLIS, March 4.—Both Houses of the General Assembly continued in session until midnight on Saturday, it being the last day for the passage of bills. A large amount of important legislation failed for the want of time, including the General Appropriation bills. The final adjournment will take place to-morrow.

## LATEST NEWS BY CABLE.

### THE EASTERN QUESTION.

SAILING OF THE BRITISH FLEET FROM THE PIRÆUS—MOVEMENTS OF GEN. IGNATIEFF—RUSSIA AND TURKISH REFORMS.

ATHENS, March 4.—The British fleet sailed from the Piræus this morning for Malta.

BERLIN, March 4.—Gen. Ignatieff has arrived in this city.

LONDON, March 4.—Reuter's dispatch from Paris says Gen. Ignatieff goes to London and Paris. The Powers will delay their replies to Gortschakoff's circular until Ignatieff's mission is ended.

PARIS, March 4.—The *Journal des Debats* denies that Ignatieff will visit London.

LONDON, March 5.—The *Standard's* correspondent at Pesth telegraphs that there are good grounds for stating that Russia will not resist the proposition to grant the Porte a year's grace, but will require as a condition that the Sultan shall sign a protocol, accepted by the Great Powers, containing a collective guarantee to Europe for the execution of the reforms.

A Belgrade dispatch to the *Times* reports that 300 insurgents encountered the Turkish *redifs* in the Doutchaik Mountains, near Brod. The former lost 12 and the latter 41 men.

The *Times* publishes the following in an official form: "There is no foundation for the report that Gen. Ignatieff is coming to London either for health or on a mission. It is understood, however, that he will visit Paris, where he will meet Count Schouvaloff."

### FUNERAL OF JOHN O'MAHONY.

LARGE PROCESSION IN DUBLIN—A FENIAN DEMONSTRATION.

LONDON, March 4.—The funeral of John O'Mahony took place at Dublin to-day. Six thousand persons took part in the procession, which passed through the principal streets carrying mourning banners and accompanied by 30 bands of music. The coffin was placed upon a large funeral car, which was immediately followed by some 20 persons who had formerly been imprisoned for political offenses. About 100,000 people witnessed the demonstration, which was purely of a Fenian character. About 20 of the trade organizations of Dublin took part in the procession. Several delegations from the country attended. Mr. Charles J. Kickham, formerly a political prisoner, delivered the address, in the course of which he declared that Fenianism still existed. The remains were deposited in the grave of Terence Bellew MacManus. All the public houses in the city were closed during the day.

DUBLIN, March 5.—The procession began to move at 12:15 P. M., but large crowds were assembled in front of the Mechanics' Institute from early in the morning. Nearly all those who followed the funeral car wore mourning, and all had green badges. Many American flags were displayed. The flag of O'Mahony's regiment covered the coffin, and on it was a wreath of immortelles. The procession was headed by Mr. Roantree, an Irish-American, who acted as Grand Marshal. He was accompanied by mounted assistant marshals. The following was the order of the procession:

Grand Marshal and staff.
Band.
Funeral car.
Chief mourners.
American delegation.
Survivors of the rebellion of 1848 and of the Fenian rising.
Delegations from Bolton, Bradford, Liverpool, Newcastle, Preston, Sheffield, and other towns.
Trade organizations.
Other societies.
Citizens generally.

No clergyman took part in the demonstration. Mr. Kickham delivered his address outside of the cemetery. There was no disturbance. It is said a monument will be erected.

### MISCELLANEOUS FOREIGN NOTES.

LONDON, March 5.—A *Times* dispatch from Calcutta reports a decrease of 60,000 in the number of natives employed on the relief works in Madras during the past week, and a slight decrease in Bombay. A treaty has been concluded with Khelat, whereby Great Britain agrees to support the Khan against foreign and internal foes, pay him an annual subsidy of $50,000, and expend $12,000 yearly on public improvements. In return Great Britain will have the right to occupy the chief towns and construct railways, telegraphs, and forts. The news from Kohat Pass is more pacific. Only a small number of Afreedis continue in arms.

Mr. George Odger, the well-known agitator for the rights of the working classes, is dead. Charles Douglas Compton, Marquis of Northampton, died yesterday, aged 61 years.

The *Standard's* dispatch from Bilbao says the conscription in the Basque Provinces has been completed without disturbance. The Government shows a conciliatory disposition, and the republican agitation has entirely failed.

A dispatch from Alexandria says the Egyptian naval expedition to the Red Sea for the suppression of the slave trade, has sailed.

PARIS, March 5.—The Russian Telegraphic Agency has information from Japan that the Japanese troops have captured four insurgent vessels near Kumamoto.

### HEWITT'S FAREWELL.

HE RESIGNS HIS POSITION AS CHAIRMAN OF THE NATIONAL DEMOCRATIC COMMITTEE.

WASHINGTON, March 4.—Hon. Abram S. Hewitt this evening resigned his position as Chairman of the Democratic National Committee in a letter of considerable length, in which after reciting that the last official act of the Executive Committee was the announcement that Samuel J. Tilden was elected President, and Thomas A. Hendricks Vice President, and that this was followed by a scurrilous pronunciamento from the National Republican Committee, claiming the election of Hayes and Wheeler, he proceeds to assert that the result of the Electoral bill has disappointed the hopes of every lover of the country, and that the grievous wrong has been perpetrated of awarding the Presidency to a candidate who has no just title to its honors. Mr. Hewitt defends his action upon that bill, and, regarding his assent to the completion of the count, says as an honorable man no other course was open to him; but if honor had permitted otherwise, his judgment was that it was the wisest course for the country as well as for the Democratic Party to proceed in accordance with the law to the orderly completion of the count, although they knew that it would result in the installation of Hayes.

Continuing, he recites his opinion that disastrous consequences would have resulted in a defeat of the count, resulting eventually in civil war, and to him appeared on one side anarchy and civil war, and on the other peace and good order, and says in the conclusion of his letter: "Under the circumstances I could not hesitate as to my course. I felt that as a patriot and a trusted servant of the Democracy no other course was left open to me, and I feel sure that its wisdom will be vindicated by the early and triumphant success of the Democratic Party, standing as it does upon the rock of justice and patriotism, from which no amount of passion or provocation has been able to move it."

He continues: "For myself, I feel that I have now completed the duty which was assigned to me at St. Louis. The result of the campaign was the unquestionable election of our candidates. That they and the people have been defrauded of their rights is true, but for this result I do not hold myself any more responsible than any other member of Congress whose voted the duty of counting and declaring the votes. In the course of my very brief public experience I have already found that my usefulness as a Representative in Congress has been seriously impaired by my position as Chairman of this committee, and I had long since determined to ask to be permitted to retire from it as soon as the result of the election was definitely ascertained. The unforeseen complications which arose have necessarily compelled me to postpone the execution of this intention until the present time. Now, however, that all impediments to my retirement are removed, I beg to be relieved from future service as Chairman."

Senator Barnum, of Connecticut, was chosen the successor of Mr. Hewitt as Chairman of the National Committee.

### A CENTENNIAL MYSTERY.

TRACING A MURDER OF EXHIBITION TIMES—A TRAGEDY AT THE GRANGERS' ENCAMPMENT—PROBABLE CAUSE FOR THE BURNING OF THE HOTEL—THE MANGLED REMAINS OF A MAN FOUND.

*From Our Own Correspondent.*

PHILADELPHIA, Sunday, March 4, 1877.

A curious and, as yet, impenetrable mystery, involving the death of some unknown man, is engaging the attention of the residents in the western section of the city, and more especially those in the vicinity of the Centennial Grounds. The remains of a stranger, much decomposed, being, doubtless, all that is left of some Centennial visitor, have been found in a ravine near the ruins of the burned Grangers' Encampment at Elm Station, on the Pennsylvania Railroad, just over the Philadelphia County line. On Feb. 21 three small boys from the city were walking along the railroad, about 100 feet from the pile of ruins, when they observed the foot of a man sticking up through some weeds, and debris. The boys examined it and found the dead body of a man. Instead of making their discovery public, they kept the secret to themselves, and returned to the city. The next day, after having confided it to some young companions, they proceeded to the spot where the body lay. They then gave the alarm, and some of the neighbors came to the spot and dug the remains up. Coroner Pearce, of Ardmore, commenced an examination into the affair, and after a few days' search obtained such information as to lead to the belief that the man had been cruelly murdered at the Grangers' Hotel, and that the murderers had taken the body out of the building and buried it beneath the pile of rubbish where it was found. There seems no doubt whatever, from the further revelations, that the dead man was the victim of some scoundrels about the hotel. It was testified to at the inquest by some of the employes of the hotel, that about the 8th of November last, when there were at least 1,000 persons in the building, a room in corridor D had been found one morning in a terribly disordered condition, that the sheets on the bed were covered with blood, and that large pools were on the floor in the corridor. This information was kept quiet at the time, and the articles of bed-clothing were carried away, and cannot now be found. When the remains were found, the trunk of the body was detached from the head, the latter being blackened and terribly mutilated. There were marks on the skull, as if wounds had been inflicted with the sharp edge and also the pole of a hatchet. No other marks of violence were apparent. From the mangled condition of the head, it was evident that the blows inflicted were sufficient to cause death. The object of the murderers no doubt was robbery, and it is believed they attacked this unfortunate man in his room at the hotel, for the purpose of robbing him, and that he, offering resistance, was chopped to death. To get rid of the body and hide their bloody work was their next move, so it is thought the remains were taken out by the window, carried back of the hotel to the ravine, covered with rubbish, and there left to nature to carry on the remainder of the work of hiding the terrible crime. A few days after the hotel closed it was destroyed by fire, without doubt being the work of an incendiary, and the traces of the murder, which were so essential to establish the identity of the missing man, were thus obliterated. There were a number of people of bad reputation residing in the neighborhood of the hotel, and there are rumors that one night a guest from the hotel was badly beaten by a woman named Fury at a saloon kept by her. It is also reported that when the hotel building was destroyed she said, "I have had my revenge on the Grangers now," and that she had threatened different persons at various times with violence.

The deeper the matter is probed the greater the mystery becomes. About the time of the closing of the Centennial there were advertisements in the papers here of numbers of missing men, and the mystery attending their disappearance was as great as that of the celebrated East and North Rivers suicides or murders. Of course it cannot be told whether all of them have been returned to their friends by this time, but it is certain that some have not, and that this is one. The remains have the appearance of being those of a German, of about 25 or 30 years of age; weight about 140 pounds, five feet seven inches in height, light complexion, light hair, mustache and chin whiskers, excellent teeth; had on two shirts, outside shirt of muslin, with finely embroidered bosom; undershirt of linen, with old English letter H worked with red cotton on the skirt.

The stud-holes of the shirt appear torn, as if thieves in their eagerness to seize the studs had torn them out. The very indistinct marks "V. S." also appear on the clothing. The remains have been buried, and Coroner Pearce, at Ardmore, Montgomery County, is endeavoring to unravel this Centennial mystery.

### NOTES FROM THE CAPITAL.

WASHINGTON, March 4.—Justice Davis will appear with his associates of the Supreme Court at the inauguration ceremonies to-morrow, and will subsequently resign to President Hayes his office as Associate Justice.

There was quiet within the Executive Mansion during the day. The ex-President and Mrs. Grant, Col. Grant and Mrs. U. S. Grant, remain there, and will leave to-morrow morning. The mansion has been put in complete order for the reception of its new inmates. Floral decorations from the conservatory will be observable in the private part of the edifice, and every attention has been given to making a comfortable reception for the coming occupants. The library is ornamented with a colossal floral American eagle, sent here as a compliment to Mr. Hayes by a prominent Boston florist. This imposing decoration is manufactured from the choicest flowers. The body is of camellias, the head of violets, and the wings and other portions of the bird are made of the finest flowers, ferns, and evergreens that can be found in a conservatory. The entire bird, resting upon a bed of roses, forms one of the most attractive floral displays ever noticed at the White House.

The Senate in Executive session this morning confirmed the following nominations: Rev. John N. Jackson, to be Post Chaplain, and Alexis R. Paxton, to be a Second Lieutenant of infantry; Majors Frank E. Hunt and Henry Prince to be Deputy Paymaster Generals, with rank of Lieutenant Colonel vice Leonard, retired, and Fry, deceased; Culver C. Sniffen, of New-York, and James W. Wham, of Illinois, to be Paymasters with rank of Major, vice Hunt and Prince, promoted; and W. H. Cunningham to be Postmaster at Creston, Iowa. The nomination of A. K. Michler to be a Civil Engineer in the Navy was rejected.

The Legislative, Executive and Judicial Appropriation bill, as finally passed by both Houses and approved by the President, makes no changes in existing salaries, except as regards Assistant Treasurers and Territorial officers. The former are reduced $500 each, the salaries of all except the New-York Assistant Treasurer being fixed at $4,500 for the next fiscal year. Territorial Governors and Judges are reduced to $2,600, and Territorial Secretaries to $1,800 per annum. The amounts appropriated by the bill for wages and material at the mints and the New-York Assay Office are compromises between those first proposed by the House and Senate respectively, being for the Philadelphia Mint—wages of workmen and adjusters, $[illegible]; incidental expenses, $[illegible]; and for the New-York Assay Office—wages, $[illegible]; materials, $[illegible]. The bill also contains an item of $[illegible] for additional machinery for the mints and the New-York Assay Office.

## AFFAIRS IN ENGLAND.

### POLITICAL AND DIPLOMATIC.

THE OPENING OF PARLIAMENT—MR. GLADSTONE'S POSITION—HIS REPLY TO MR. CHAPLIN—THE EASTERN QUESTION—THE TRAP LAID BY PRINCE GORTSCHAKOFF—FINE WEATHER IN LONDON.

*From Our Own Correspondent.*

LONDON, Saturday, Feb. 17, 1877.

Parliament opened without a fight on the address. The Opposition waited until the Tory chiefs had spoken, and then took counsel together. Even then they arranged no positive programme. They, nevertheless, commenced the preliminaries which usually lead up to pitched battles. Independent members asked questions; Liberal leaders asked questions. They were questions which dwelt upon the supposed short-comings of the Government, questions which exposed the weak points in the Ministerial armor. The skirmishes were well conducted on both sides. Perhaps there was a touch of malice in the Opposition tactics, and a display of confidence on the part of the Government, which was mutually irritating. Then came notices in the paper; aggressive notices, placed there by men of distinction; not notices which should really challenge the strength and position of the Government, but notices that should stab it, possibly in vital places, leading it might be, during a kind of oratorical brawl, to that direct challenge which the Opposition were timid about making at the outset. Among these notices was one in the name of Mr. Gladstone, and the debate came on last night. It had reference to a particular dispatch of Lord Derby, but it opened up, of course, the whole question of the Government's action at Constantinople, and Mr. Gladstone, in bringing it before the House of Commons, hurled at the Ministry some ugly charges, but concluded in the elegant language of political courtiership. Nevertheless, the speech of Mr. Gladstone, which was not intended to provoke a party fight, speedily brought about the very chances of debate to which I have alluded. Mr. Chaplin, a young and wealthy member, representing the agriculture and obstinacy of Lincolnshire, leaped upon the veteran statesman with a vigor that astonished both his friends and his foes. The Chancellor of the Exchequer had vindicated the policy of the Government with the quiet dignity of officialism, and a desultory debate had ensued, in which one side says one thing and the other side says another with gentlemanly consideration and certain flashes of humor; when a simple "Knight of the Shire," (as Mr. Gladstone mockingly called him afterward,) rose and had the courage to say all he felt, and what a large share of the English people think, namely, that Mr. Gladstone, a statesman who understood all the responsibilities and difficulties of office in times of emergency, lowered statesmanship and was guilty of a certain meanness in stamping the country to embarrass the Ministry; that the so-called "National Conference" at St. James' Hall was a sham and an imposture; and that as a man of honor, if Mr. Gladstone believed as he declared, that the Government misrepresented the opinion of the country on the Eastern question, it was his duty to openly and honestly challenge Parliament upon it, and give both the Government and the Opposition an opportunity of vindicating their sentiments and their opinions. Mr. Gladstone, he said, had attacked members of her Majesty's Government at public meetings and Liberal assemblages, where he knew they could not be present to answer him, and he must now, "as a man of honor," either make them in the face of Parliament or withdraw them. When Mr. Chaplin spoke of the ex-Premier's duty "as a man of honor" there were cries of "Oh! oh!" from the Ministerial benches, and a lively scene thereupon ensued. "I rise to order," said Col. Mure; "this is a most painful personal attack on the right honorable gentleman." Mr. Gladstone also rose and said, "Mr. Speaker, is it competent for an honorable member to instruct me as to the course or courses which I, as a man of honor, ought to pursue?" The Opposition cheered. The dignified Speaker in his robes gave his usually prompt and sententious reply. "It is quite clear," he said, "that the honorable member has exceeded the limits of parliamentary discussion." Whereupon Mr. Chaplin withdrew the objectionable expression, and offered an humble apology, and immediately proceeded to put "the same old point" in another form, and presently Mr. Gladstone replied, and was cheered by his supporters at every sarcastic sneer which he flung at the youth and general insignificance of the member for Lincolnshire. But there was a little too much of contrasting his own position with that of the Knight of the Shire who had presumed to question him, and though Mr. Gladstone showed himself a supreme master of the English tongue and a polished debater, his dignity suffered somewhat under the rough, untrained oratory of Mr. Chaplin, who won a certain kind of victory in adjourning the debate on a challenge from the Government to Mr. Gladstone to make good his accusations. The ex-Premier accepted the adjournment, but declined to say what he meant to do, at the same time holding out an eloquent threat that Mr. Chaplin would not find him reticent when the proper time came. Lord Hartington, the leader of the Opposition, did not interfere, and the debate stands adjourned until next week. One almost feels that it is robbing us of a gladiatorial treat to think that all this time Mr. Disraeli was quietly asleep in bed, after having spoken a few prosaic formalities in the upper house as Lord Beaconsfield. But we shall have him on his legs next week, in answer to a notice on the paper of the Lords; and before many days are over the Eastern question will be discussed from every possible point of view in both houses.

In the meantime the news from Turkey is generally considered reassuring, but not by those who are behind the scenes of Russian diplomacy and intrigue. Has it ever struck you that the misunderstandings among relatives generally arise from brothers and others nearly akin expecting too much from each other. The thought occurs to me in connection with a paragraph in one of the papers to the effect that the United States Navy has emphasized its attentions and courtesies to Grand Duke Alexis. What nonsense. We are certainly as jealous of American sympathy and alliance of sentiment as if you were a great European power, within a day's sail of Dover. You ought to feel this as a compliment. Although our dailies do ill justice to your news, it is a common feeling to wonder what our American cousins think about us when we are wrapped up in some European or Eastern difficulty. How blessed are you to be anchored far away, beyond the ambitious passions of Kings, Generals, and statesmen.

It has been said that the powers will not be caught in the tree laid for them by Prince

# The New-York Times.

VOL. XXIX.......NO. 8921. NEW-YORK, TUESDAY, APRIL 13, 1880. PRICE FOUR CENTS.

## THE POLITICAL CAMPAIGN

### GRANT'S INCREASING POPULARITY IN THE SOUTH.

ELECTING GRANT DELEGATES TO THE SOUTH CAROLINA STATE CONVENTION—A VERY BITTER FEELING AGAINST SHERMAN—GRANT DELEGATES IN GEORGIA.

CHARLESTON, S. C., April 12.—The Republican Conventions held in Aiken and Darlington Counties, Saturday, instructed their delegates to exert themselves in nominating only such men in Columbia as favor Grant for first choice and Blaine second. The Executive Committee of York County, on the same day, appointed stalwart Grant men as delegates to the State Convention. Preparations for the approaching campaign are advancing with gratifying celerity. Primary meetings are well attended, and a noteworthy feature is the number and respectability of the white men who participate in the discussions. All County Conventions thus far held favor Grant's nomination. Next to Grant, they desire to see Blaine President. Col. Mackey confirms the previous reports of the intense bitterness of the anti-Sherman feeling all over the State, and expresses the belief that one-half of the Republicans would remain away from the polls should the Secretary be nominated.

SAVANNAH, Ga., April 12.—Six delegates from Chatham County for the Atlanta Convention were chosen here to-day and were instructed for Grant.

### TILDEN'S NEW-YORK INFLUENCE.

ELECTION OF MANY DELEGATES OPPOSED TO TO HIM—SOME OCCASIONAL SUCCESSES.

OSWEGO, N. Y., April 12.—The Democrats of the First Assembly District of Oswego County held two conventions here to-day. The anti-Tilden faction has control of the district organization and held the regular convention, which elected Clark Morrison, Michael O'Gorman, and E. H. Boyd, delegates to the State Convention. The convention adopted resolutions favoring Horatio Seymour as candidate for President, and requesting the State Convention to send delegates to the National Convention who will work for harmony. The Tilden faction adopted resolutions eulogizing Tilden and favoring him as a candidate for President. Charles N. Bulger, James Dowdle, and George Kellogg were chosen State delegates by this convention.

COOPERSTOWN, N. Y., April 12.—The Democrats of the First Otsego District elected to-day as delegates to Syracuse Hezekiah Sturges, George Merrill, and J. S. Browne, with instructions to oppose the unit rule and an instructed delegation to Cincinnati. They are anti-Tilden.

ROCHESTER, N. Y., April 12.—The Wyoming County Democratic Convention has elected the following delegates to the State Convention: C. W. G. Nobles, J. R. Howard, and J. H. Moore. They are anti-Tilden. Orleans sends E. Kirkehart, J. E. Didend, and William Jewett. They are requested to favor A. L. Warner as district delegate to Cincinnati, and are anti-Tilden. Livingston has elected L. B. Faulkner, H. P. Mills, Jr., and N. J. Ackley, Tilden men.

### LOUISIANA NEGLECTS TILDEN.

THE DEMOCRATIC DELEGATES INSTRUCTED FOR HANCOCK.

NEW-ORLEANS, April 12.—The Democratic State Convention met at noon to-day at Masonic Hall, with all parishes represented but six. Judge James Jeffries, of Rapides, was permanent Chairman. The Committee on Resolutions presented the name of Hancock as the unqualified choice of the Democracy of Louisiana, and instructed the delegates to vote as a unit and maintain the two-thirds rule. A motion that the delegates be not considered as instructed for Hancock was defeated by 305 to 152. John McEnery, Patrick Mealey, W. A. Strong, and Charles Parlange were elected at large. The districts elected delegates as follows: First, John Fitzpatrick and James D. Houston; Second, E. A. Burke and I. W. Patten; Third, J. L. Brent and John Clegg; Fourth, James Jeffries and Samuel Morrison; Fifth, G. W. McCrarie and G. C. Goldman; Sixth, M. D. Kavanagh and Thomas Duncan. The First District delegates renominated Randall L. Gibson for Congress. There were symptoms of a bolt, the dissatisfied men claiming that the delegates had no authority to make Congressional nominations. A resolution instructing the delegates not to support Tilden under any circumstances was laid on the table with only two dissenting votes. Pending a motion to reorganize the State Committee, the convention adjourned until noon to-morrow.

### TILDEN LOSING IN KENTUCKY.

SIGNS OF OPPOSITION MANIFESTED IN SEVERAL PARTS OF THE STATE.

LOUISVILLE, Ky., April 12.—Within several days signs of much opposition to Tilden have been manifested in several parts of Kentucky, particularly among the State editors. In Louisville, owing to a very bitter personal fight between the *Courier-Journal* and the present city Administration, there is some possibility that the delegation from here to the State Convention may be packed against Tilden. The present Mayor is encouraged by a strong "machine" backing, and declares he will fight Mr. Watterson "to the head-waters of Bitter Creek" if necessary to defeat him. His first move has been successful, and the blood thus tasted is moving the municipal head to follow up his victory, which was to take the city printing away from the *Courier-Journal* and *Anzeiger*, and give it to the *Commercial* and *Volksblatt*, the two former being Democratic and the two latter Republican papers. Mr. Watterson now accuses Mayor Baxter of allying himself with the Republicans and with Blanton Duncan.

It is reported from Washington that Senator Beck is coming to Kentucky to start a Hancock or Field boom. This seems absurd, however, as the only man who has any especial strength here besides Tilden is English, of Indiana, and he is for the old ticket of Tilden and Hendricks. If any large opposition is stirred up it will be in the line of any good Democrat except Tilden.

### VIRGINIA DELEGATES FOR GRANT.

WASHINGTON, April 12.—So far as heard from, the Grant men seem to have obtained a substantial victory in the recent election in Virginia for delegates to the State Convention. Each of the following-named counties have elected two prominent Grant men to the State Convention: Caroline, Chesterfield, Culpeper, Henrico, Hanover, Norfolk, Prince George, and Rockingham. Dinwiddie and Elizabeth City chose each one Grant delegate. This gives 18 Grant delegates out of a possible 20. It is believed that returns from the other counties will show that a large majority of Grant delegates have been chosen. A gentleman who arrived here to-day from Norfolk, and who has been actively engaged in the canvass of the State, said the Republicans are almost unanimous for the nomination of Gen. Grant at Chicago, and that many of the more conservative Democrats announce that they will support the ex-President if he is nominated.

### PROHIBITIONISTS AT WORK.

BOSTON, April 12.—A call is issued for a State Prohibitory Convention to meet in this city on April 20, to select delegates to the National Prohibition Reform Convention, to meet at Cleveland June 17. The call is issued to the citizens of Massachusetts, irrespective of sex.

### MASSACHUSETTS GREENBACKERS.

BOSTON, April 12.—A special meeting of the Greenback State Committee to select State delegates to the Greenback National Convention, was held here to-day, when it was decided to hold a State Convention at Worcester, on May 11, for that purpose. It was also voted that the State Committee meet at Worcester May 10 for the examination of credentials of the delegates to the State Convention.

### IOWA REPUBLICAN DELEGATES.

DES MOINES, Iowa, April 12.—The *State Register* has returns from 96 of the 99 Republican County Convention in Iowa. The counties not reported are Bremer, Cherokee, and Wright. The following are the Presidential preferences of the delegates from the 96 counties: For Blaine, 721; for Grant, 143; for Washburne, 2; for Sherman, 1. Few of the delegates to the State convention have arrived here.

### MISSOURI ADVOCATES GRANT.

ST. LOUIS, April 12.—The Republicans held their ward primary meetings to-night for the election of delegates to the State Convention to send delegates to Chicago. The indications are that of the 76 delegates chosen about 60 are Grant men, the remainder being for Blaine.

### A REPUBLICAN VICTORY.

HARTFORD, Conn., April 12.—The city election in New-Britain to-day resulted in the election of the full Republican ticket, with the exception of the City Clerk. Mayor Talcott's majority is 327.

### GRANT IN MASSACHUSETTS.

BOSTON, April 12.—Lowell sends to the Republican State Convention 13 Grant, 9 anti-Grant, and 5 unpledged delegates.

### FRIENDS OF GRANT IN CHICAGO.

CHICAGO, April 12.—Arrangements have been made for a monster Grant mass-meeting here on Thursday next at the Central Music Hall.

### TOPICS AT THE STATE CAPITAL.

MR. HUSTED AND THE SUPPLY BILL—THE UNIVERSAL LIFE'S DELAY IN REPORTING.

ALBANY, N. Y., April 12.—Mr. Husted is not disposed to communicate his plans about the Supply bill, and to-night declined to say what he would do about it. On Friday he had declared that he would do nothing, but that was immediately after the bill had been declared lost. To-night he moved a reconsideration of the vote by which the bill was lost, and that motion was laid on the table. Then he gave notice that at some future time he would move for the suspension of the forty-fourth rule. By suspending this rule he would be able to obtain a reconsideration of the vote on the Supply bill by a majority vote instead of a two-third vote. It is understood that he will then amend the bill by striking out all the gratuities, and endeavor to pass the bill by a majority vote, three-fifths of the members being present. This course is regarded by many members as being a hazardous one. Controller Wadsworth is reported to have said that he will not pay any of the items unless they are approved by a two-thirds vote of the Assembly. It may be that among the items which Mr. Husted will regard as gratuities will be included those for the Catholic protectories. Some of the members claim that these institutions, particularly the New-York Protectory, are provided for by their incorporating acts, and that the Legislature has no right to appropriate the money of the State for their maintenance if ample provision has already been made by constitutional enactments. The reports had gone around that Mr. Husted would amend the bill by striking out the objectionable items and a number of others interesting to members who voted against the bill on Friday. Mr. Husted says he will do no such thing, and that the notion of punishing his opponents has never entered his mind.

The opponents of the Supply bill are by no means disposed to submit to dictation, or to any attempt on the part of the majority to circumvent opposition by a suspension of the rules. Immediately after adjournment to-night a caucus of the opponents of the bill as it was voted on Friday was held in the Judiciary Committee room. About 40 members were present. Mr. Skinner presided and heard assurances from those present that they were determined to maintain their attitude of resistance so long as it appeared to be possible to compel a modification of the bill. No opposition will be offered to Mr. Husted's motion to reconsider the vote by which the bill was lost, but very positive resistance is to be made to his motion to suspend the forty-fourth rule. It was believed by many members that a sufficient number of votes could be obtained to prevent suspension, the opposition being confident of increasing the vote against Swift's claim. Some doubt was felt as to whether a two-third or majority vote was necessary to secure suspension. A committee consisting of Messrs. Skinner, Mitchell, Carpenter, Brennan, and Benedict, Democrat, was appointed to examine the rules and report to-morrow at a meeting to be held before the Assembly convenes.

The Assembly passed a resolution on April 8 calling upon the Insurance Department to furnish information as to why the Universal Life Insurance Company had not made its annual report for 1879, and also to show the condition of the company. Superintendent Smyth to-night sent to the Assembly several communications between the Insurance Department and James F. R. Hadden, Secretary pro tem. of the Universal Life. On March 6, Deputy Superintendent McCall telegraphed S. S. Herrick, President pro tem. of the company: "Your statement and valuation Register should be forwarded at once." On March 13 the Secretary of the company replied that the company had done no new business since 1877; that it had been reducing expenses, had a very small clerical force, and could not complete the report asked for in two weeks. He also stated that negotiations were in progress as to disputed claims, and were expected to be terminated in a few days. They were advised by counsel that their report should be delayed until the termination of the negotiations, and asked for an extension of time. Mr. McCall, on March 19, gave notice to Mr. Hadden that his statement was due on March 15, but recognizing the difficulty the company was laboring under, an extension was granted until March 31. Mr. Hadden sent word on March 31 that the negotiations were not yet completed, and requested a further extension of time of 10 days to file the annual report. This request was also granted. On April 7, Superintendent Smyth gave notice to President Herrick that Henry R. Pierson, Receiver of the North America Life Insurance Company, had informed him that the negotiations pending between the North America and the Universal Life, looking toward a settlement of Mr. Pierson's claim against the Universal, had been broken. The extension of time was, therefore, broken off, and a statement of the affairs of the company was requested at the earliest possible convenience of its officers. It seems to be an utter impossibility to obtain information concerning this company. All inquiries made at the office any time these three years have been answered in about as unsatisfactory a way as that in which the company now replies.

In the Senate, Mr. Forster moved to discharge the Committee of the Whole from the further consideration of the bill amending the act to authorize the formation of railroad corporations, which has relation to increasing the stock, and order the same to a third reading. Messrs. Sessions, Strahan, and Madden claimed that no great haste was necessary, and regretted that Mr. Forster seemed inclined to put Senators upon the record on a bill which they had not had time to consider. Mr. Forster, in reply, said that the press had given the Hepburn bills careful and thorough discussion, and he presumed every Senator was fully aware of the nature of this bill. Mr. Sessions moved to lay the motion upon the table, which was agreed to—yeas 14, nays 6.

### THE PROVIDENCE CONFERENCE.

NORWICH, Conn., April 12.—The Providence Methodist Episcopal Conference to-day adopted resolutions urging the General Conference to create a separate Connecticut Conference. The committee on the case of the Rev. Charles F. Walker, of Somerset, Mass., reported that the charges of unministerial and immoral conduct made against him had been sustained, and recommended his expulsion. Their report was adopted.

## AFFAIRS IN FOREIGN LANDS

### THE WHOLESALE SLAUGHTERS IN BURMAH.

SEVEN HUNDRED PEOPLE BURIED ALIVE AS A PROPITIATORY SACRIFICE—ANOTHER RUMOR OF KING THEEBAW'S DEATH.

LONDON, April 12.—The 700 men, boys, women, girls, priests, and foreigners sacrificed at Mandelay for the restoration of the King's health were buried alive—not "burned," as previously stated—under the towers of the city walls.

A dispatch from Rangoon says: "The following is an explanation of the massacres at Mandelay: When a city is built in Burmah human sacrifices are offered up. A new monarch usually has a new capital. The evil spirits are irritated that there has been no change of capital, and, the virtue of the old sacrifices being gone, to appease them the astrologers declared it was necessary to offer up 700 lives. The sacrifices were made by the order of King Theebaw."

A private telegram received at Liverpool, and dated to-day, announces the death of Theebaw, King of Burmah. This is possibly a revival of the former report of his death.

### GERMAN AND FRENCH QUESTIONS.

THE QUARRELS WITH THE CHURCH—REVERSAL OF THE VOTE WHICH CAUSED BISMARCK'S RESIGNATION.

BERLIN, April 12.—The *North-German Gazette* publishes a Ministerial resolution, which has been communicated to Mgr. Jacobini, stating that the German Government perceive in the Papal brief of Feb. 24 a fresh sign of pacific sentiments from the Vatican, and as soon as the Government have visible proof of these sentiments in acts, they will endeavor to obtain from the Legislature, powers which will allow them greater freedom in the application of the laws, thereby offering a possibility of mitigating or abolishing such regulations as are felt by the Vatican to be severe.

The Bundesrath has adopted a resolution proposed by a representative of Bavaria declaring that receipts for Post Office remittances shall be liable to stamp duty, thus reversing the vote of March 3, which led to the resignation of Prince Bismarck.

PARIS, April 12.—M. Clémenceau, Republican member of the Chamber of Deputies for the Department of the Seine, addressed his constituents yesterday (Sunday) amid great enthusiasm. M. Clémenceau attacked the Government's whole policy.

Prince Hohenlohe, the German Ambassador, will leave here on the 15th inst. on his return to Berlin to assume the functions of Secretary of Foreign Affairs.

The *Union* says Cardinal Nina, the Papal Secretary of State, has addressed to the French Government a protest against the decrees against unauthorized religious bodies. The *France* contradicts its own statement that the Government contemplated the repression of further manifestations on the part of the Bishops.

### THE ENGLISH POLITICAL CHANGES.

CABINET AND PEERAGE GOSSIP—THE INDIAN VICE-ROYALTY—THE POLLING YESTERDAY.

LONDON, April 12.—The *Morning Post* says: "As the Liberal leaders have not yet had any consultation, the rumors of appointments in the new Cabinet are founded only on mere possibilities."

The *Times*, in a leading editorial article this morning, says: "As a member of the Cabinet without a portfolio, Mr. Gladstone would occupy a dignified position."

In addition to the names heretofore mentioned, the following gentlemen will be raised to the peerage: The Right Hon. Viscount Barrington, member for Eye in the House of Commons; Sir Arthur Edward Guinness, member for Dublin City in the last House, and Sir Ivor Guest, an ex-member of Parliament.

The *Pall Mall Gazette* this afternoon says: "The resignation of Lord Lytton as Viceroy of India reached the India Office last week." If the Right Hon. Robert Lowe is raised to the Peerage, Sir John Lubbock will probably represent the London University in Parliament.

A Calcutta correspondent telegraphs as follows: "There is here a feeling of deep and general regret at the tendency lately shown at home the drag the Viceroy and Indian questions into party politics, and there is a consensus of opinion that it will be a most dangerous innovation if the Viceroy henceforth shall be liable to recall, or be expected to resign when the Government which appointed him goes out."

The following additional candidates for Parliament have been returned: The Right Hon. Col. Frederick A. Stanley, Secretary of State for War, and Major-Gen. Fielden, (Conservatives,) for Lancashire, North, the former re-elected; Patrick L. Martin and M. Marum, (Home Rulers,) for County Kilkenny, the former re-elected; R. H. Metge, (Advanced Home Ruler,) and Charles Stewart Parnell, (Home Ruler,) for County Meath, the latter re-elected; J. Barry and Mr. Byrne, (Home Rulers,) for County Wexford, receiving 3,075 and 2,879 votes respectively, and defeating Mr. Gibbon, (Conservative,) and Chevalier O'Clery, (Home Ruler,) who received 846 and 457 votes respectively; George Otto Trevelyan, (Liberal,) for the Harvick burghs, re-elected.

### EVENTS IN AFGHANISTAN.

NATIVE CHIEFS QUARRELING—GEN. STEWART'S ADVANCE—FIGHTING AT JANGDALAK.

LONDON, April 12.—A dispatch from Kabul says: "The Logar, Wardak, and Zurmut chiefs arrived here on the 10th inst. The chiefs having quarreled, they had no fixed programme when their demands for the recall of the ex-Ameer were refused at the durbar. On Monday, a brigade of 3,000 infantry and 600 cavalry, with 10 guns, will march to co-operate with Gen. Stewart, who will reach Ghazni on the 20th inst. The attacks on Jangdalak and its communications continue. Mohammed Jan has not yet arrived at Kabul, but he promises to come soon. Whether he comes or not is of small importance, as a great majority of his party have come in. He, being an adherent of Mustafi Habibulla Khan, will probably follow. A durbar will be held on the 12th inst., (to-day,) at which the insurgent chiefs, Sirdars, and people of Kabul will be invited to attend, when some definite reply will be given to the representations they propose to urge.

A dispatch from Kandahar says: "The appointment of Sirdar Shere Ali Khan as Wali of Southern Afghanistan gives general satisfaction."

### CURRENT FOREIGN TOPICS.

LONDON, April 12.—Prince Gortschakoff passed a quiet but sleepless night. His mental faculties are clear, but the action of his heart is weaker. No hopes of his recovery are entertained.

A dispatch from Portsmouth says: "Grave apprehensions are felt for the safety of the training ship Atalanta, which is now 73 days out from Bermuda. Had she put into the Azores, as was thought probable, the news should have been received by this time. Orders have been sent to Gibraltar directing the store-ship Wye to call at the Azores on her way home for possible tidings of the missing vessel. The Atalanta has 11 officers and more than 300 young seamen on board."

MADRID, April 12.—Otero, the condemned regicide, will be executed on Wednesday morning next. The prisoner, in accordance with a cruel custom still existing in Spain, will be placed in the Capilla for 24 hours previous to his execution.

CONSTANTINOPLE, April 12.—Many persons have perished in the floods near Ismid.

LONDON, April 13.—The agents of the Allan Steam-ship Line have received a telegram announcing that Prince Leopold has postponed his departure for Canada.

A fire broke out last night in the Creosote Works, near Victoria Docks, and one of the stills exploded. Eleven persons were killed, and several were wounded. Much damage was done.

### CRIMINALS AND THEIR DEEDS.

OFFENSES REPORTED YESTERDAY—PROCEEDINGS IN CRIMINAL CASES.

NEW-ORLEANS, April 12.—J. Tucker, colored, charged with the murder of Abe Frazer, in 1876, was taken from jail at Greensburg, St. Helena Parish, Sunday morning, by 15 men, and shot to death. It is stated that the people of the parish generally condemn this act of lawlessness.

CHICAGO, April 12.—A special dispatch from Anna, Ill., to the *Times* says that James M. McIntire, an old and respected citizen of the south-eastern portion of Union County, was found dead in a field, three-quarters of a mile from his house, with his gun by his side and his hunting-knife thrust through his throat. The body was so arranged as to give the impression that he had committed suicide, but on examination it was found that he had been shot through the back of the head. An old enemy McIntire was known to have was an uncle, with whom he had quarreled concerning the uncle's seduction of the murdered man's daughter.

NEENAH, Wis., April 12.—Early Sunday morning three masked burglars entered the residence of Mrs. J. L. Coates, and, pointing pistols at her head, demanded her money. On her refusing to give it up, they beat her into insensibility, ransacked the house, and fled with $4,000 worth of diamonds, watches, jewelry, &c. Mrs. Coates is in a critical condition. There were two other women in the house at the time.

NEWTON, N. J., April 12.—In the Sussex County Court to-day, Judge Magie presiding, Clarence Campbell, John Clark, and Peter Kane were arraigned on indictments charging them with the murder of Melancthon S. Walker, in Newton, Feb. 18 last. All pleaded not guilty. The trial is set down for May 24.

NEWTON, N. J., April 12.—Albert P. Fellows, a prominent druggist of Newton, was arraigned to-day on an indictment in the Sussex County Court charging him with perjury, in swearing to the correctness of an alleged fraudulent bill for goods furnished the Town of Newton. Five of his former clerks were subpoenaed before the Grand Jury. He pleaded not guilty. Within two years past Fellows has achieved much notoriety as a reformer.

### THE SOUTH AMERICAN TRADE.

ADVANTAGES WHICH ENGLISH COMPANIES ENJOY, TO THE EXCLUSION OF AMERICANS.

WASHINGTON, April 12.—Trenor W. Park, President of the Panama Railroad Company, was before the House Committee on Post Offices to-day. He addressed the committee particularly with reference to the difficulties under which American foreign commerce labors in competition with foreign steam-ship companies. He said that when he became President of the Panama Company he found the entire trade of the western coast of South America in the control of an English steam-ship company, but since then, by an arrangement with that company half of the trade from Callao, excepting that in cotton, wool, sugar, and coffee, was allowed to come by way of Panama, and consequently the tonnage of the railroad has increased enormously. The trade of that region is over $200,000,000 a year. Owing to the monopoly which the English steam-ship companies had, almost all the trade went to Europe, although the distance was much greater than to the United States. He spoke of the importance of this great trade and of the immense benefit it would be to American manufacturing and agricultural interests if a fair portion of it could be diverted to this country. He then showed why it was impossible for American steam-ship companies to compete with those of Europe. For instance, if the Panama Railroad Company should attempt to do this trade it would require at least eight vessels, and the cost of these would be at least $1,600,000 more than the cost of like steamers in the hands of the English companies. Besides that original difference in cost, the American company would have to pay 6 per cent. insurance on that difference and an annual depreciation of 10 per cent. on the same, so that if the two companies were to do exactly the same amount of business and at the same rates, the English company could pay a dividend to its stockholders while the American company would be losing money. In reference to the adverse laws under which American commerce labors, he cited the case of the Pacific Mail Steam-ship Company, which has had to pay in local taxes in New-York between $600,000 and $700,000 within the last 10 years, while it did not pay a single dollar in dividends. Such a state of things could not exist in England, where taxation is only upon net profits. He also alluded to the additional cost of running American steam-ship lines in he way of large pay to officers and crews, and in duties paid on all articles which enter into the construction of vessels, from which duties English steam-ship lines are free.

Mr. Park will continue his address before the committee to-morrow.

### ARMY AND NAVY INTELLIGENCE.

WASHINGTON, April 12.—Leave of absence for three months has been granted Major L. S. Babbitt, of the Ordnance Department. After his next re-enlistment, Commissary Sergt. James Davidson, of the Department of Texas, will be granted a furlough of four months, with permission to go beyond the sea. Six months' leave has been granted First Lieut. John L. Kane, Twenty-fourth Infantry. The leave granted First Lieut. S. K. Mahon, Sixteenth Infantry, has been further extended six months on account of sickness.

Capt. Lewis A. Kimberly has been ordered to the New-York Navy-yard, to be Captain of the yard; Commodore George H. Cooper has been detached from duty as President of the Board of Inspection on the 30th inst., and ordered to command the New-York Navy-yard on May 1; Commodore J. W. Nicholson has been detached from the New-York Navy-yard and placed on waiting orders; Cadet Midshipman Thomas O. Rodgers has reported his return home, having been detached from the Trenton, and has been placed on waiting orders.

First Lieut. A. C. Kelton, Marine Corps, at League Island, Pennsylvania, has been detached from the Marine Barracks at that station and ordered to proceed to Brooklyn, N. Y., and report for duty.

A bill was introduced by Mr. Ferry in the Senate to-day, regulating promotions in the Army. It provides that promotions of Lieutenants shall hereafter be made by seniority in the arm or corps, and not regimentally, as heretofore. It also provides that all Lieutenants who have been overslaughed and deprived of promotion in the order of their seniority, by the system heretofore prevailing, shall, upon promotion, take rank from the date on which they would have been promoted had promotion by seniority been recognized.

PANAMA, April 3.—The *Star and Herald* says: "The United States steamer Adams, it is reported, has formally established a coaling station at the Golfo Dulce, and as an earnest of the sincerity of the project, five tons of coal have been deposited on shore. There should be certain formalities attended to in the case, which appear to have been neglected. Such, for instance, as the consent of Colombia or Costa Rica, to one or other of which powers the territory belongs. There is a conflict between Colombia and Costa Rica as to the ownership of certain lands bordering upon the Golfo Dulce, and it is impossible to say at present upon whose soil the new coaling station is situated. That it is not the property of the United States is an indisputable proposition."

### DISASTERS TO VESSELS.

OSWEGO, N. Y., April 12.—The schooner David Andrews, which went ashore yesterday below Four-mile Point, is reported full of water. She is laden with 12,000 bushels of rye, and is bound from Bay Quinte to Toronto.

LONDON, April 12.—The Guion Line steamer Montana, Capt. Gadd, which was rescued from the rocks in Cook's Bay, has been towed to Liverpool.

The Norwegian bark Immanuel, Capt. Nielsen from New-York March 10, for Amsterdam, has arrived at Crookhaven with the loss of her fore-mast bowsprit, and boats. One of the crew was lost over board.

The Norwegian bark Frank, Capt. Arnsen, from London April 3, for Philadelphia, has put into Queenstown, leaking.

The Norwegian bark Staregrom, Capt. Olsen, from New-York March 17, for Cronstadt, has been spoken. She had lost her three top-masts and sustained injury to her main-mast.

The Spanish bark Flora, Capt. Asteyrina, before reported at Bordeaux, from Baltimore, is leaking badly and has lost rigging.

### TURNING A LOCOMOTIVE LOOSE.

ROCHESTER, N. Y., April 12.—James McInerney jumped on an unoccupied locomotive, about 6 o'clock this morning, pulled the throttle-valve, and jumped off. The locomotive dashed through the depot at the rate of 50 miles an hour, stopping six miles west, doing no damage. The man was seen, and secured after a desperate struggle. The penalty for the offense is 10 years in State Prison. Had the affair occurred an hour later, serious consequences must have followed, as there are usually many persons in the depot at that time.

### HIGH WIND AT MOUNT WASHINGTON.

MOUNT WASHINGTON, N. H., April 12.—The wind, this morning, was blowing at the rate of 114 miles per hour, and the thermometer stood 12° below zero.

## WOUNDED IN HONOR ONLY

### THE BLOODLESS DUEL OF TWO PHILADELPHIA MILITIAMEN.

PRIVATE ADAMS GRIEVOUSLY INSULTED BY SURGEON WHITE—A MEETING AT THE CORNER OF THREE STATES—ONE WILD SHOT AND ONE SHOT IN THE AIR—HONOR THEREBY SATISFIED.

PHILADELPHIA, April 12.—The *Press* of to-morrow will publish the following: "That exclusive military circle that goes to make up the First City Troop, of this city, has a sweet morsel of gossip to chew over just now—nothing less than a duel between two of its conspicuous members. If it were not that there is plenty of evidence that shots were actually exchanged between the principals, the circumstance that they, as well as their seconds, have been walking the streets to-day and smiling bland acknowledgments of the congratulations of friends, might go far to discredit their having tempted the law so far.

The principals are Robert H. Adams, Jr., of No. 124 South Sixteenth-street, and Dr. J. William White, of No. 220 South Sixteenth-street. Private Adams, of the City Troop, is tall, slender, freckled, and has $10,000 a year, left him by his grandfather. Surgeon "Billy" White, as he is known in the troop, is the nephew of Dr. S. S. White, of Dental Depot fame. He is also more recently known from an investigation of his methods of clinical instruction—when women physicians were present, at the Philadelphia Hospital ordered by President Chambers, of the Board of Guardians of the Poor. It is only just to say that Dr. White was more than vindicated by the investigation. The City Troop, which for almost a century has been the crack organization of the city, comprising, as it did, "the élite of its *jeunesse dorée*," has not kept up its reputation for a few years past, in the opinion of many old members. There has been an infusion of young blood into the organization, which, they say, has not improved the company's average of manhood. Its title to consideration latterly consists more in excellence in the german than in military exercises. Even the ring which was designed for a riding-school has been turned to instruction in street saddle-sitting, rather than a firm and confident seat in a McClellan tree. Snobbery has usurped the place of that thoroughly clubbable good-fellowship which went far toward raising the troop to its high rank among the military companies of the country. It will be sufficient to say that Mr. Adams is one of the newer acquisitions. He is tall, slender, addicted to parting his auburn whiskers at the chin, and his hair in the middle. A few years back he formed one of the Hayden exploring expedition, acting in the capacity of a civil engineer. Long since placed beyond the necessity of personal efforts to gain a livelihood, he has devoted his many leisure hours to the cultivation of club and female society. In the latter he especially shines. A reasonably regular attendant upon the Monday night drills of his troop, he had not succeeded in impressing upon his comrades in arms any profound persuasion of his personal prowess.

It has been an open secret that Surgeon White and Private Adams were not on exactly amicable terms. They had private grievances respecting campaigns in a totally different service than that of war. On last Monday night, after drill, there was the usual gathering into groups for social chat and convivial enjoyment, when Adams and White drifted toward each other. A private conference between them was not overheard, but an exclamation by Dr. White, that could only be construed into a deadly insult leveled at Private Adams, attracted the attention of all. For a moment it looked as though a much more vulgar method of settling the dispute than pistols was to be resorted to, but friends interfered, and the drill-room was soon deserted. Among the troopers generally it was regarded as a merely trivial matter, containing no possibilities of future hostilities. It proved, however, that correspondence looking to satisfaction in one shape or the other began the next morning. The chosen friends of the principals were discreet in more shapes than one. They wasted a great deal of time and paper in efforts to bring about some compromise that would avoid the necessity of a meeting, and at the same time they conducted the case with such secrecy that no one outside of themselves and principals suspected that anything of the sort was even contemplated. The event proved that something deeper than the apparent offense was the cause of the trouble, and all well-meant efforts at adjustment proved fruitless. It then became their duty to arrange for hostilities at some place that would reduce the possible legal consequences to a minimum.

On Saturday morning last, eight young gentlemen took a through Washington train at the West Philadelphia Depot. They traveled in fours, and did not fraternize, but singularly enough they all got out at Wilmington, and, hiring two carriages, they drove over the Walnut-street bridge of that city, and laid their course for Newark, Del. They told the drivers that they wanted to go to the spot at which the States of Delaware, Maryland, and Pennsylvania corner, which is about two miles beyond Newark. On arriving at that point, the party alighted and ordered the carriages to move back half a mile and there await them. The eight gentlemen then left the road, and were lost to sight behind a grove of trees. What followed is the report of the affair as rendered by the club and troop gossip. On arriving in a valley which hid them from the road and within a few yards of the stone which marks the corners of the three States, the parties halted. Mr. Adams's second again requested the retraction of the offensive expression, which was politely but firmly refused by Dr. White, although his second warmly urged some concession upon that point. All efforts at adjustment having failed, it only remained to measure the ground and place the men. Ten paces, stepped off by Dr. White's second, proved satisfactory, and, as the ground afforded no advantage to either, the men were placed without any question. The weapons were a pair of 9-inch rifled pistols of regulation dueling size, and were charged in the sight of all the participants.

Mr. Adams, having been the injured man, was adjudged entitled to the first shot. Dr. White's second gave the word, which was to be, "Fire, one, two," the shot to be fired between "one" and "two." He stood about five yards off the line between the principals, and, as it proved, in the most dangerous place, for Mr. Adams was fingering his weapon rather nervously and looking as if he had much rather be elsewhere. He fired correctly enough, as far as the order was concerned, but the direction of the line of smoke was much nearer the second commanding than the principal. The bullet, at all events, did not harm Dr. White. The latter, when his time came, fired in the air. Mr. Adams was asked whether he desired a second shot, but politely declined, saying that he was entirely satisfied. The seconds then held a consultation and decided unanimously that ample satisfaction had been given. The principals thereupon shook hands, and the party entered their carriages and returned to Wilmington, where they took a train for this city.

The dignity of the offended dueling law does not seem to have had any terrors for either of the principals. Mr. Adams was promenading Chestnut-street yesterday as coolly as if imprisonment and political disqualification were not the penalties to which he had exposed himself. He received friendly congratulations with a self-assured smile. In the afternoon he mounted his bay saddle-horse and took an hour's ride. It was when he returned that the reporter encountered him. Mr. Adams threw himself negligently from his horse, handed the bridle-reins over to a groom, and was adjusting his immaculate corduroys, when he noticed a very interesting bevy of ladies watching him eagerly from the steps across the street. He gallantly crossed over to them, swinging his ivory-handled riding-stick and striving to look unconcerned. They evidently congratulated him about something, for he blushed and bowed low as he took off his hat. This pleasing ceremony over, he recrossed the street and was overtaken by the reporter. "I know of no duel in Delaware, Sir," he said with truculence, which a paling face discounted. "I mean that little affair in which you and Dr. White exchanged shots on Saturday," the reporter persisted. "Really, you must excuse me. I intend nothing personal to you, of course, but I can tell you nothing. I must know nothing about it. Honor seals my lips." Wherewith he sought the seclusion of his house.

### THE PATERSON CITY ELECTIONS.

A REPUBLICAN VICTORY ALL ALONG THE LINE

The annual city election took place yesterday in Paterson. Two Tax Commissioners were chosen. The law provides that no voter shall vote for more than one, so that one was selected from each party. As both parties nominated two, however, leaving the individual citizen to make his own selection, the ballots polled by the candidates for this office are no criterion of the relative strength of the two parties. These were the only city officers chosen. In each ward there was one Alderman, one member of the Board of Education, and minor ward offices, to be voted for, and in the Second, Third, Sixth, and Eighth Wards there was a Chosen Freeholder to be elected. The Republican nominations for the various offices were unusually good, and the party was in excellent fighting trim in most of the wards where there was any chance of winning. Of the Chosen Freeholders, seven Republicans elected last year in the wards and townships hold over this year; one was elected in Manchester Township last month, and one—Assemblyman George W. Conkling—was re-elected yesterday in Passaic without opposition, thus securing a Republican majority next year, without regard to the result of the Paterson election. Republican Aldermen were elected in the First, Second, Third, Fourth, Fifth, and Sixth Wards; Democratic in the Seventh and Eigth Wards, and Republicans Chosen Freeholders in the Third, and Sixth Wards, and Democrats in the Second, Fifth, and Eighth Wards. Republican School Commissioners were elected in the First, Third, Fourth, and Fifth Wards, and Democrats in the Second, Sixth, Seventh, and Eighth Wards. The next Board of Aldermen will consist of 11 Republicans and 5 Democrats. The Board of Education will be a tie, and the Board of Chosen Freeholders will have 11 Republicans and 6 Democrats.

### THE RECORD OF ACCIDENTS.

RED BANK, N. J., April 12.—Mrs. Augustus Stillwell, in company with a colored woman, while driving home in a covered farm-wagon this afternoon, struck a match to light her pipe, when a spark ignited the canvas cover. The colored woman jumped out of the wagon, but Mrs. Stillwell remained until the entire cover was burned, when the frightened horses broke away, overturning the vehicle, and leaving the woman, who was enveloped in flames, lying in the road. Some farm hands noticing her peril, tried to stamp out the flames, but without success until, with their spades they buried her in the sand. Her injuries are of a frightful nature, and will probably prove fatal.

NEW-EGYPT, N. J., April 12.—William Chambers, 50 years old, drank a solution of corrosive sublimate on Saturday, supposing that it was something else. All efforts to neutralize the effects of the poison failed, and he died yesterday morning in the greatest agony. He leaves a large family.

BAYVILLE, N. J., April 12.—Philip Loomis was caught in the machinery of his ropewalk this morning, and instantly killed. His arm got entangled in a belt, and was torn from its socket, and part of his face was torn away.

NEW-ORLEANS, April 12.—David Crawford, an engineer on Morgan's Railroad, fell from his engine, was run over and killed to-day.

ST. PAUL, Minn., April 12.—Meagre accounts have reached here of a serious accident to a Canadian emigrant train bound for Winnipeg, near West Union, a station on the St. Paul and Winnipeg Railroad, which was caused by the breakage of a wheel on the fifth car. Several cars were wrecked, one man named Gould was killed, and his nephew severely injured. The train consisted of 11 cars of stock and emigrants' effects and 7 passenger coaches. A large number of cattle and small stock was killed. Gould and his nephew were in a car with stock. Gould's son and daughter, who were in a passenger car, are uninjured, and are now on their way back to Ontario, where the wife of the dead man remained.

### KEMBLE AGAIN IN CUSTODY.

HARRISBURG, Penn., April 12.—William H. Kemble, one of the bribery fugitives, arrived here from Philadelphia, accompanied by ex-Sheriff Kerns, of Philadelphia, and Detective Anderson, of this city, who has been following him since Tuesday last, and who took him into custody this morning in Philadelphia. Kemble was met at the depot by a few friends, who had been apprised of his intended visit, and was driven to the Dauphin County Jail, where it was expected that Judge Pearson would hear the application for new bail; but as the Judge did not appear, the party, after waiting a quarter of an hour, was driven to the residence of J. J. Clyde, where Kemble will remain until to-morrow at 9 o'clock, when, his counsel say, Judge Pearson will hear them. Judge Pearson is not entirely clear as to whether it is the proper thing to do to admit an arrested fugitive from justice to bail, and, unless Mr. Herr, who has been at his residence since 5 o'clock, succeeds in convincing him that Kemble came here voluntarily, the Judge will hardly hear the application until Judge Henderson, who lives in Carlisle, and who has been telegraphed for, arrives. Kemble says that he telegraphed his counsel that he would be in Philadelphia this morning, in time to take the 11:55 train. This will be an important part of the argument before the Judge. Detective Anderson came from Atlantic City this morning on the same train with Mr. Kemble, and arrested him in Fourth-street, Philadelphia, soon after his arrival. Kemble made no pretension of surprise, and told the detective he would not trouble him to read the warrant for his arrest.

### TELEGRAPH WAR IN THE WEST.

OMAHA, Neb., April 12.—The many injunction suits instituted in Nebraska, Kansas, Colorado and Missouri by the Western Union Telegraph and the Atlantic and Pacific Telegraph Companies to recover their lines on railroads in those States were all before Judge McCrary, of the United States Circuit Court, at St. Louis, last week. The great contest was in the suit by the Atlantic and Pacific Telegraph Company against the Union Pacific Railway Company and the American Union Telegraph Company. In his decision, filed yesterday, Judge McCrary says: "I am clearly of the opinion that the railway company cannot be permitted to oust the plaintiff from possession without process. The injunction heretofore granted will be so far modified as to make it clear that the railway company is at liberty to institute legal proceedings either by a cross bill in this case or otherwise to cancel and set aside the contracts upon a return of the consideration, and to settle and adjust upon principles of equity the account between the parties." The indications are that a very protracted litigation is to follow. Meanwhile the possession of the telegraph lines will be retained by the telegraph companies.

### ARCHBISHOP PURCELL'S COADJUTOR.

CINCINNATI, April 12.—A special to the *Commercial* from Natchez, Miss., says that on Saturday evening Bishop Elder received a telegram from Rome stating that his bulls of appointment had been sent to him by mail, and requesting him to proceed immediately to Cincinnati and assume the functions of the office of Coadjutor to Archbishop Purcell. On Sunday Bishop Elder preached a farewell sermon, and in the evening delivered his final lecture and benediction to his congregation in Natchez. During the latter there was scarcely a dry eye in the cathedral. To-day he received his congregation at his residence and bade them good-bye. Bishop Elder has no plans for the future, and says he knows not what a kind Providence has in store for him. He goes prepared to perform his duty at the bidding of those higher in power than himself. He will leave Natchez on Wednesday.

### HEAVY FROST IN THE WEST.

CINCINNATI, April 12.—Heavy frosts have fallen in Ohio, Indiana, and Kentucky during the past three nights. Peach, pear, quince, and plum trees were caught in full bloom, but high winds and the dryness of atmosphere, it is thought have saved those fruits from total destruction. There has been, however, much damage to peaches, and some fruit-growers claim that the early peaches, pears, and quinces are nearly all killed. Most reports agree that enough peach-buds are uninjured to insure a fair crop, if no further damage occurs. Wheat is looking splendidly all over Ohio, and the acreage is unprecedented.

### RELIEF FOR ARCTIC WHALERS.

SAN FRANCISCO, April 12.—The revenue cutter Thomas Corwin came down from Victoria Friday last, under telegraphic orders from the Treasury Department. It is presumed that, as she is the largest and strongest vessel in the revenue service of this coast, she will be loaded with supplies for the relief of the Arctic whalers and exploring yacht Jeannette.

## CADET WHITTAKER'S TRIAL

### SEEKING TO PROVE HIM GUILTY OF THE OUTRAGE.

A STRONG FEELING AMONG SPECTATORS AT WEST POINT THAT HE IS INNOCENT—SUPERINTENDENT GAYLER'S TESTIMONY FAVORABLE TO HIM—A STRAIGHTFORWARD STATEMENT FROM CADET HODGSON.

WEST POINT, April 12.—The result of to-day's investigation still further exposes the difficulties in the way of believing that the colored Cadet outraged himself. Superintendent Gayler, the expert from the New-York Post Office, after studying for several hours over 25 specimens of handwriting, one of which is understood to be Whittaker's, and comparing them with the anonymous letter, reports that he can find nothing among the batch corresponding with the letter. He has been since handed six other inclosures, "written," the Recorder says, "by a single Cadet," who is rumored to be Whittaker, and also another anonymous note, which he is to examine and report upon to-morrow. Whittaker's friends say that the "anonymous letter" charge has broken down completely. On Saturday and Sunday the colored boy's accusers claimed that the experts would readily pick out Whittaker's handwriting by comparison with the anonymous missive. A second Cadet, Hodgson, who was in Whittaker's room with Burnett, swears that the sheet found under the colored Cadet was wet with water, and the burned papers, hair, &c., were also wet, so that to the difficulty of believing the lad guilty of the whole of the complicated assault is added the necessity (on the theory of his accusers) of supposing that he deliberately, and with no possible motive, soaked his bedding and floor under it with water, in order to shiver as well as bleed until morning. The notion seems too preposterous to be entertained, but questions were asked by members of the court tending to bear it out. The Rev. Justin D. Fulton, of Brooklyn, who was present during the morning session, and has had an interview with the colored Cadet, can hardly keep his countenance in discussing the question of Whittaker's guilt or innocence. He says that the case sought to be established against the boy is so absurd, so inconsistent, and utterly without foundation as to border on the farcical. He is not the only spectator who holds to the same opinion.

There are some other things here which strike an impartial observer as peculiar, to say the least. The boy, while practically on trial on an infamous charge, is excluded from the sessions of the court, and has no opportunity of confronting the witnesses against him. He was excluded on Saturday during the remarkable tying scene by Cadet Burnett, and there are those who think that it would have been interesting had the dextrous and glib-tongued witness performed the feat under the eyes of the sufferer and given the latter the benefit of suggesting pertinent queries. Lieut. Knight is said to consent to this arrangement, but it is the first court of inquiry or court, as far as can be learned, in which the thing has been done. The Recorder seemed to feel that some explanation was necessary, and accordingly desired to have it entered on the minutes that the boy was detained by his studies. But it would seem as though he might be forgiven the time necessary to defend himself. A court of any kind with the person on trial excluded is certainly an anomaly. It is said that when the Congressional committee arrives it will not only have Whittaker confront his accusers, but let him have a lawyer as counsel. A gentleman from New-York, a friend of Whittaker, called on Gen. Schofield, the Recorder, and members of the court to-day, and said that the Hon. Stewart L. Woodford and A. W. Tenney, United States District Attorney in Brooklyn, would cheerfully look after the boy's interests if they would permit it. The officers politely replied that they preferred to have military men concerned. In the recent courts-martial and courts of inquiry in New-York the parties have invariably had civil counsel whenever they desired it.

In regard to Whittaker's standing in philosophy, which was alleged to be the moving cause of his committing the outrage, Prof. Michie says that the boy is doing well, and stands in no particular danger of being "plucked" on that account. There are white Cadets who stand lower in this study than Whittaker, but no one has suggested it as a cause for their slitting their ears. Prof. Greener, at the invitation of several of the Professors, visited the class-rooms to-day, and heard the class in philosophy—his protégé included—recite. This evening Gen. Schofield called at the hotel and left his card for the Professor. The great majority of Cadets and officers say they still think Whittaker had some sort of connection with the affair, but the view is not advocated as loudly as it was last week. Civilians and visitors not connected with the Point are almost unanimous in believing him innocent.

The court opened at 10 o'clock. The usual bevy of officers' ladies sat in one of the alcoves and watched the proceedings intently. Recorder Sears said that he had prepared a list of 25 sheets, each containing the handwriting of a different Cadet, which, with the anonymous letter found in Whittaker's room, he would submit to Superintendent Gayler, of the New-York Post Office, who had been especially summoned as an expert in handwriting. Mr. Gayler is an elderly gentleman, with pleasant features, gray whiskers, and spectacles. He was sworn and given the bundle of writing, and then he retired. Mr. Gayler was not told which one of the 25 specimens submitted along with the anonymous letter belonged to Whittaker. The specimens were pages from the Cadets' reports selected by the Recorder.

Cadet Burnett, whose tying feat was the sensation of Saturday, was recalled, and after making some corrections in his testimony, said that some of the burned pieces of paper on the floor of Whittaker's room had been taken charge of by Cadet Dickenson. He did not notice that Whittaker's legs were particularly stiff, or whether, in turning his head, his neck appeared stiff. He suspected that Whittaker was playing a part when he saw Dr. Alexander raise his eyelid. Whittaker showed only the white of his eye. In his [the witness's] judgment, Whittaker had control of the muscles of his eye. The witness told the Doctor he thought the whole thing was a hoax. At first they could see nothing but the white of the eye, but after shaking the boy two or three times he rolled down the pupil.

Q.—How do you know that this was not volition on his part?

Major Mordecai objected to the rather rigorous examination of the witness by the Recorder. He did not think Cadet Burnett was an expert. Lieut. Knight had no objection to the question, and the two other officers concurring, Major Mordecai withdrew his objection.

Burnett said he believed that when a person was unconscious he had no control whatever over his muscles. He did not know whether the boy's turning down his eye-ball was perfectly natural and due to the shaking administered by the Doctor or not. He did not think the shaking would have any affect. The Doctor attempted to open the left eye by raising the upper lid. The witness knew nothing about the normal position of the eye in a person lying on his right side and unconscious. He was not directed by any one to examine the condition of things. The drops on the knee looked as though made while Whittaker was standing up. On marching off the guard, the witness asked the commandant if he wanted him to make an official report of the state of things in Whittaker's room. The commandant said no. He made the remark about "shamming" five minutes after the Surgeon began his examination. He thought it strange that Whittaker's hands were not tied behind his back, and that he was not gagged. The hair seemed to have been cut while he was standing over the glass, and dropped on the floor around it, not scattered, as about a barber's chair. The blood spot on the wall looked as though put there intentionally. His opinion as to the club would be modified by knowing that Whittaker never claimed to have been struck by it. Col. Piper thought first that Whittaker must have been hit on the back of the head by the Indian club and knocked senseless, and that that was the reason he made no outcry.

At the afternoon session the Recorder asked to have it entered upon the record that Cadet

# The New-York Times.

VOL. XXIX.......NO. 8924. NEW-YORK, FRIDAY, APRIL 16, 1880. PRICE FOUR CENTS.

## VOICE OF MASSACHUSETTS

### BLAINE AND SHERMAN THROWN COMPLETELY ASIDE.

A HARMONIOUS CONVENTION ENDING IN THE CHOICE OF DELEGATES FOR EDMUNDS—A REMARKABLE BUT USELESS SHERMAN DOCUMENT—A PLATFORM WHICH IS A CONCESSION TO THE GRANT MEN.

WORCESTER, April 15.—The State Convention of Massachusetts Republicans, which met in Worcester to-day, was in every sense of the term a business-like gathering, and, as far as could be judged by outside appearances, all the delegates to it acted in the utmost harmony. It was composed of three distinct elements. The first, and, all things considered, the most important, was made up of a large number of thoroughly sincere, and in many cases distinguished, Republicans, who favored the nomination of Gen. Grant. The second was composed of the real friends of Senator Edmunds—and there are many of them in this State. The third element was composed of a class of office-holding and interested political wire-pullers who, for the most part, were working for Secretary Sherman, under cover of advocating Senator Edmunds, and all of whom came together with the rallying cry, peculiar to Massachusetts, of "Anything to beat Grant and Blaine." During last evening and this morning these Edmunds men, real and pretended, but particularly the latter, were loud in their professions of being able to secure the passage of a resolution denouncing the candidacy of Gen. Grant, and declaring that the election of any man for a third term was against the spirit of American institutions. The friends of Gen. Grant, though fully aware that by one reason or another they had been placed in a minority, were nevertheless convinced that they had influence enough to prevent the passage of any resolution which might injure their candidate, and, further, that they could defeat every proposition made to absolutely pledge the vote of the State to any particular candidate.

It was under these circumstances and with these feelings that the members of the convention came together. The meeting was called to order by Eben F. Stone, the Chairman of the State Central Committee, who briefly and in good taste asked the delegates to lay aside all personal feeling and to act only for the interests of the party in which the best interests of the country were bound up. While he was speaking, several gentlemen, who were doubtless ready on the slightest provocation to disclose themselves as ardently in favor of Mr. Edmunds, but who had about them an air of bustle and thrift very suggestive of the Customs Department of the Treasury, went about among the delegates distributing a circular which was headed by the following startling question: "Shall Massachusetts lead the Republican columns once more in battle and to victory?" This the body of the circular answered in the following truly remarkable fashion:

"Massachusetts holds the destiny of the National Convention of June next in her hands to-day, if she so wills. Let her recommend a name upon which many of her sister States of the West can unite, when the strength of Grant shall have become broken in the convention. Let her recommend a name that will carry New-York, Ohio, and Indiana in the coming contest. Let her recommend a name that will give us the solid vote of the German nationality. Let her recommend the name of one of the most distinguished statesmen of the Republic—a name known to every citizen of the Union as one of unsullied honor, a public servant whose long course of service is without a stain and without a blemish. Let her recommend the name of one to whom, over and above all others, the whole country is indebted for the recent restoration of our agricultural, commercial, manufacturing, and all other industrial pursuits to the high degree of health, vigor, and prosperity we now enjoy. Let her recommend the name of the man who has placed the finances of the nation on a firm and enduring basis, and who has rendered the restoration of commercial faith, confidence, and credit again a certainty. Let her recommend the name of the man who placed one of the largest and most popular loans of the Government in the hands of its citizens, remembering that every one of the bonds so placed is a guarantee of the honor and good faith of the Republican Party, and is a ballot for its candidate. Let Massachusetts, on this day, recommend the name of John Sherman, of Ohio, as her choice for the Presidency, and the sturdy sons of New-England will echo back the cry from Ohio, from Michigan, from Indiana, from Illinois and Wisconsin, for New-England's teaching of fidelity, faith, and religion are never lost. Let Massachusetts recommend John Sherman, and she presents a name upon which the Republican delegates of other States will unite with joy joy as soon as relieved from the instructions imposed by scheming and unscrupulous politicians. Her action will be the herald of another national triumph, and she will have presented to the people a President who will restore the Republic to something of its original integrity, purity, and grandeur."

In common justice to the Republicans of Massachusetts, it may be well to state that this document was prepared in Washington, and was distributed under the direction of gentlemen who are known to have a not inconsiderable pecuniary interest in the success of the gentleman who has made the Treasury Department of the nation very little better than an election bureau.

### THE ADDRESS OF SENATOR DAWES.

When the circular had been scattered all over the hall, the Chairman of the committee concluded his speech, and, in accordance with a previously-arranged programme, Senator Dawes was announced as permanent Chairman, and made a very long and somewhat tiresome speech. The most noteworthy portion of the address was substantially as follows:

For a moment let us consider, men of Massachusetts, what will be gained by triumph or lost by defeat in the great political campaign we are about to enter. This is the last Presidential election under the apportionment of political power based upon the present census. The 16 Southern States now hopelessly Democratic, have had, by the emancipation of their slaves, 15 at least, added to the number of their Representatives in Congress, and a like number in the Electoral College. This additional power, gained by making freemen of slaves, will be wielded in the Electoral College, not by the Republican freedmen, who are its basis, but by their masters, who are still masters of the ballot-box. This power, and much more, will forever pass out of their hands after the census of this year, and be lodged with the strong Republican States of the North-west, in obedience to that law of growth which is stronger than all human laws and human plans. Unless, therefore, the Democratic Party gain ascendency at the approaching election, it must yield to the inevitable and give up all hope of power in the future, based on its present support. Success, on the other hand, makes an indefinite lease of power possible with a party whose attempts to obtain place and perpetuate its own rule no scruple or law has as yet been able to restrain. Success is also a necessary condition to the maintenance of a "solid South." The forces which control Southern politics will not long adhere to the fortunes of a disheartened minority. Defeat will surely bring division, and with it dissolution. The Democratic Party will, therefore, enter the contest with the desperation of a last opportunity.

At the close of the permanent President's address, routine business of no importance was transacted, and then, with commendable promptitude, a ballot was called for and the resolution ordering it was adopted without debate. Then, knowing that the real business of the day had commenced, the delegates settled back into their seats, and, for the first time, gave entire attention to the proceedings. At this point, Col. Hopkins, who was at once recognized as one of the most prominent leaders of the Edmunds movement, took the floor and made a short speech in favor of the election as Delegates at Large of George F. Hoar, of Worcester; Julius H. Seelye, of Amherst; Charles R. Codman, of Boston, and John E. Sanford, of Taunton. This ticket was at once recognized as that which had this morning been agreed upon at the regular Edmunds caucus, and it was greeted with some applause. Following Col. Hopkins came Mr. P. C. Chandler, of Boston, who was the most prominent of the Sherman people, and who, knowing the weakness of his candidate in the convention, found it convenient to say that there was a natural alliance between the Edmunds and Sherman forces, and that he was glad to second the nomination of the Edmunds ticket. Such aid was just a little more than the disinterested friends of the able, upright, and justly-respected Senator from Vermont bargained for, but they were, of course, obliged to accept it with the best grace possible. Banks, who was known to represent the cause of Grant, rose to speak. It is no exaggeration to say that when he mentioned the name of his candidate he was cheered to the echo, receiving the first really enthusiastic applause of the day. Unfortunately, however, the cheers came from the galleries, not from the members of the convention. Gen. Banks presented the following ticket for delegates at large: Alexander H. Rice, of Boston; Enoch R. Mudge, of Swampscott; Charles A. Stoll, of Lowell, and L. L. Brown, of Adams. He urged its election with much force. He concluded by ridiculing the idea that anything but good to the country could come from the nomination of the distinguished ex-President, and by the statement that, under the circumstances in which the nation was now placed, Washington, Jefferson, Jackson, and Lincoln would have regarded it as their duty to accept a third term were they called upon to do so.

Ex-Secretary Boutwell followed Gen. Banks, in advocacy of the Grant ticket. He declared that in the present campaign the choice of the Republican Party must be either Blaine or Grant. ["Doubted! doubted!" cried a number of voices.] Then the speaker, after advancing many well-known facts in support of his statement, turned his attention to Mr. Dawes, and objected strongly to the assertion of that gentleman that all the Southern States were hopelessly Democratic. Under the lead of Gen. Grant, the speaker was assured, a number of them, perhaps five, could be carried by the Republicans. At this point the Chair announced that a telegraphic greeting, conveying the information that Iowa declared for Blaine, had been received from that State, but had been mislaid. Then the Rev. James Freeman Clarke made a well-turned speech against the Grant movement, and Mr. George L. Rufin, a colored man, who probably had more real interest in the matter than the distinguished clergyman, who is said to be never happy unless he is finding fault, spoke feelingly in favor of the hero of Appomattox.

By this time the delegates had grown weary of listening to speeches, and loudly demanded a ballot. This was had, and resulted in the election of the straight Edmunds ticket, by the following vote:

| | |
|---|---|
| Whole number of votes cast | 1,060 |
| Necessary to a choice | 531 |
| George F. Hoar | 779 |
| J. E. Sanford | 672 |
| C. R. Codman | 656 |
| J. H. Seelye | 581 |

Mr. Codman received the full support of the Edmunds men. Messrs. Hoar and Sanford were aided by others. Ex-Gov. Rice, who may be regarded as the leading Grant man, received 299 votes; another gentleman a smaller number.

### THE PLATFORM.

When the result had been announced, the following platform was read by the Chairman of the Committee on Resolutions:

I. We declare our steadfast adherence to the ideas and principles of government and policy which have made the Republican Party distinctively the party of freedom and equal rights, of patriotic devotion to the Union, of progress and reform.

II. We believe in an honest currency, with every dollar equal in value to every other dollar, and in a financial system which shall sacredly guard the national faith and credit, and assure the continuance of specie payments, and we congratulate the Administration and the country upon the conspicuous success with which resumption has been accomplished, commercial confidence restored, and the public debt refunded and reduced under the able management of the present Secretary of the Treasury.

III. We believe in the inviolable sovereignty of the National Union, as established by the Constitution, over all the States and all the people, and in the duty of the National Government, by wise laws efficiently executed, to protect the ballot in all national elections, and to maintain and vindicate the constitutional rights of all citizens of the United States, wherever and under whatever fiction of State sovereignty or other pretense such rights may be assailed.

IV. We hold that free and honest elections are essential to the stability and success of government by the people, and that any attempt to thwart the will of the majority, whether by preventing the lawful exercise of the right of suffrage by fraud in casting or in counting votes, or by unseating for partisan purposes, fairly-elected members of Congress or of State Legislatures, is a crime which will not be tolerated by a free people.

V. Grateful for what has been done during the Administration of President Hayes to improve the tone and methods of the civil service, we again invoke Congress to complete the work by necessary Legislative enactments, in order that there may be adequate and permanent security against the misuse of the public service as a machinery of party organization and personal influence; and so that, in the language of a distinguished Senator, "The holders of office may feel that they are the servants of the law, and not the personal tenants at will in their places of either heads of departments or Congressmen."

VI. We have our country and common interests as a nation; we deplore the existence of sectional strife and an animosity of parties bounded by territorial lines; we earnestly desire that the resources of the South, as well as of the North and West, may be developed under just and harmonious policies by the united energies of our whole people. To this end there must be an actual recognition of the equal rights of all by all. The privileges of citizenship must everywhere be respected. Results and settlements of past issues that have been reached at great cost, and once accepted, must not again be brought into question, and we hold that they who seek to reverse or set them aside or to revive past controversies for political effect are unwise statesmen and dangerous political leaders, justly responsible for disturbing the peace and obstructing the welfare of the country.

VII. The duty of all Republicans loyally to support the candidates of the party, and the duty of nominating conventions to present candidates who are acceptable to all Republicans, are reciprocal duties of equal force and obligation. Profoundly sensible of the importance of the impending election to the nation's safety, honor, and well-being, the Republicans of Massachusetts demand of their delegates to the National Convention that they use all proper efforts for the nomination of a candidate, who, having the requisite qualifications for the high office of President, will also have the confidence and approval of all who have hitherto acted with the Republican Party, who will invite the support of other patriotic citizens desiring good government more than party success, whose nomination will be most expedient, because most worthy and least objectionable, and whose triumphant election, to which we pledge our hearty and united efforts, will give assurance of the continuance of sound and beneficent policies of administration, and of uninterrupted and growing national prosperity. While we do not instruct our delegates, we commend to their consideration a Republican statesman who possesses in an eminent degree such qualities and requisites for the nomination—the Hon. George F. Edmunds, of Vermont.

The resolutions were unanimously adopted, upon motion of the Hon. George S. Boutwell. The convention adjourned sine die at 3:12 o'clock.

It will be noticed that in these resolutions there is no instruction for any candidate, and no slur upon the gentleman who is most likely to be the nominee of the Chicago Convention. The platform, as it was presented, was clearly a concession to the Grant men, and, on motion of ex-Secretary Boutwell, it was adopted without a dissenting voice. It may be well to state that the reference to Messrs. Hayes and Sherman was received with what may be called dignified applause.

Regarding the preference of the delegates, it is only necessary to say that they all profess to be strongly in favor of Senator Edmunds, and that Mr. Hoar's friends here declare his second choice to be Ulysses S. Grant.

### HONORING LINCOLN'S MEMORY.

SPRINGFIELD, Ill., April 15.—Services in commemoration of the death of President Lincoln were held at his monument to-day, under the direction of the Lincoln Guard of Honor. About 500 citizens were present. Services began at 7:22 o'clock this morning, the hour of his death, April 15, 1865. After prayer by the Rev. James A. Reed, there was singing by the choir of the Young Men's Christian Association, followed by the reading of Lincoln's farewell to the people of Springfield, (his letter to Eliza Gurney,) and his favorite poem, "Why should the Spirit of Mortal be Proud." Addresses were made by Gov. Cullom and the Rev. William B. Affleck, and a letter was read from Lieut.-Gov. Sherman.

## NATIONAL CAPITAL TALK

### AGAIN DISCUSSING THE GENEVA AWARD BILL.

SEVERAL LIVELY PASSAGES BETWEEN MESSRS. THURMAN, BLAINE, AND DAVID DAVIS—AN EXHIBITION FOR THE BENEFIT OF THE GALLERIES.

WASHINGTON, April 15.—When Mr. Thurman entered the Senate Chamber, late this afternoon, clad in a dress suit and wearing a rose in his buttonhole, it was announced that the debate upon the Geneva Award bill would be resumed, and the Senator, after giving notice that he would urge the bill to a vote on Saturday or Monday, sat down for the purpose of listening to speeches which had been prepared and which he expected to hear from the opponents of the bill. But no one manifested any inclination to speak, and after Mr. Eaton had introduced a substitute providing for the application of the unpaid money to the payment of the national debt, there was a call for a vote on Mr. Hoar's amendment. This amendment excludes the insurance companies, and its adoption would destroy the bill.

Mr. Thurman indignantly charged that certain Senators were withholding their speeches in order to force a vote on the amendment, and in this way disregard the courtesy of the Senate.

Mr. Blaine said that Mr. Thurman seemed to be angry because some one would not oppose him, and asserted that Senators who were ready to vote should not be subjected to such criticism.

Mr. Thurman then reproved Mr. Blaine for springing to his feet and interrupting him, and declared that such methods were not in use in the Senate until Mr. Blaine became a member. He urged that Mr. Hoar's amendment should be thoroughly discussed, and appealed to the high sense of honor which was supposed to prevail in the Senate.

Mr. Hamlin said that he was astonished that Mr. Thurman should solicit debate after so much had been said, and declared that too much talk was the bane and curse of the Senate.

Mr. Conkling maintained that arguments should be made before a vote and not afterward. A vote on the amendment would be the same as a vote on the bill, and it was well known that several speeches had been prepared.

At last Mr. Blaine took the floor and began an argument against admitting the insurance companies to the benefits of the award. In the course of his remarks he described the companies as gambling institutions, which, like those at Hombourg, were sure to win, and produced documents to show that their profits on war risks had been very great, and that some of the companies acknowledged that they would be ashamed to ask for part of the award. While referring to the slow progress of the bill in the Senate, he declared that the present Congress was a lazy and do nothing body, and the idlest Congress which had been known to this generation.

In a little passage with Mr. David Davis the latter was made to admit that he supported the bill because he must vote for something, although he believed that the remaining money should be returned to Great Britain. The corpulent Senator from Illinois, accustomed to cool deliberation and judicial exactness, was overwhelmed and routed by the impetuous Senator from Maine, at least in the opinion of the spectators in the galleries, but it is for the latter that Mr. Blaine's exhibitions are conducted. The committee-rooms know him not, and it is unkindly hinted that for this reason a criticism that Congress is lazy might come with better taste from some one else.

### TALKING ON TARIFF PROBLEMS.

THE OBSTRUCTIONISTS STILL DELAYING ACTION—A HOT-HEADED SOUTHERNER.

WASHINGTON, April 15.—The Committee on Ways and Means to-day resumed the consideration of the tariff question, but except upon the question of hoop-iron, nothing practical was accomplished. The question of modifying the existing rates of duty on band, hoop, and scroll iron was first considered. Mr. Tucker, of Virginia, moved that the rate of duty be fixed at 35 per cent. ad valorem. The present rate of duty on this class of iron is $1\frac{3}{4}$ cents per pound, which is equal to from 33 to 75 per cent. ad valorem. The vote on Mr. Tucker's motion resulted in a tie—Messrs. Carlisle, Tucker, Morrison, Mills, Felton, and Wood voting in the affirmative, and Messrs. Phelps, Garfield, Kelley, Frye, Conger, and Dunnell voting in the negative. Mr. Gibson was absent, but will be permitted to record his vote upon his return to Washington. It is believed that Mr. Gibson will vote in the affirmative, thus making a majority for the reduction.

The Chrome Iron or little tariff bill was next taken up and discussed. During the discussion it was proposed to substitute the Townshend bill for that portion of the bill under consideration which relates to placing on the free list printing-paper and the materials from which printing-paper is manufactured, but the tariff advocates argued that the Townshend bill was crude and impracticable. It provides, for instance, that all chemicals used in the manufacture of paper should be admitted free of duty. These same chemicals are used in the manufacture of articles other than paper, and it would be impossible to determine what preparations of the chemicals imported were used for making paper. To provide that the chemicals in question should be admitted free of duty would deprive the Treasury of revenue amounting to at least $750,000 annually. Finally, Mr. Carlisle offered a resolution, which was adopted, providing "That the several matters now pending before this committee relating to the tariff on imported goods, and all other matters pertaining to the tariff, be referred to a select committee of five members, with instructions to report, in whole or part, to this committee at its meeting next Thursday." In accordance with this resolution, the Chairman appointed Messrs. Carlisle, Tucker, Mills, Garfield, and Dunnell. The three gentlemen first named are pronounced tariff reformers; Mr. Garfield has acted persistently with Judge Kelley, and Mr. Dunnell is a revenue tariff man, with a decided disposition to act on tariff questions with his party associates.

It is very probable that the select committee will report a bill on Thursday next, but it does not follow that the measure which may be reported will meet with more success than has attended those heretofore considered by the full committee. The fact is that Messrs. Garfield, Kelley, Conger, and Frye are determined to use every effort to prevent any tariff bill being reported to the House for consideration, and this delay of one week, only to begin de novo with the entire question, is in the exact line of the programme of those gentlemen. The same tactics will be pursued next week which have been so successfully pursued thus far by the high tariff men, unless the majority will assert their strength to defeat filibustering in the committee, and force an issue on the proposition which may be reported on Thursday next by the Select Committee. Mr. Chairman Wood said to-day to THE TIMES's correspondent that he was convinced a tariff bill will be reported during the present session, and that the bill will include wood pulp, and other articles entering into the manufacture of paper, but the action of the committee thus far does not encourage a belief in Mr. Wood's prediction. There are sufficient votes in the committee to bring out a reasonable bill, but unfortunately the advocates of tariff reform do not seem to know how to use their strength.

During the discussion in the committee to-day, some sharp language passed between Messrs. Tucker and Kelley, growing out of a misunderstanding by the first-named gentleman of some remarks made by the latter. Mr. Tucker, during his remarks, said that the amendment to the Chrome Iron bill to put paper on the free list was offered by Judge Kelley. In correcting this statement, Judge Kelley said that he did not offer such an amendment because it would make him [illegible] public record. Mr. Tucker, understanding the statement made by him [Tucker] was false, he became very much excited, and rushed toward Mr. Kelley in a belligerent manner, exclaiming: "You shall not talk in that manner to me." Explanations and apologies followed.

### INTER-STATE TRANSPORTATION.

MR. CAMERON'S RESOLUTION FOR A COMMISSION FAVORABLY REPORTED TO THE SENATE.

WASHINGTON, April 15.—While the House Committee on Commerce has occupied a great deal of the present session in hearing the arguments of many persons who are opposed to the bill by which its Chairman, Mr. Reagan, has sought to solve the problem of inter-State transportation, and in an endeavor to agree upon some plan to be recommended to the House for consideration, the Senate has, through its Commerce Committee, approached the question in a different manner. Three weeks ago, Mr. Cameron, of Pennsylvania, introduced in the Senate a resolution providing for the creation of a commission of nine persons—three Senators, three Representatives, and three Commissioners to be appointed by the President—"to inquire generally into" the conditions that will most favorably affect the transportation of the commerce among the States carried by land and water routes, securing thereby to the people the required facilities at the lowest charges, with the greatest certainty and economy in time, and that will avoid and prevent any unjust discrimination, unnecessary burdens, or impediments in transportation, in order to ascertain whether these conditions can be secured by legislation by Congress." The resolution authorizes the commission to report its recommendations to Congress at its next session. In his address upon the resolution, Senator Cameron said that he had not much expectation of any favorable solution of the question, because he had some practical knowledge of the difficulties in the way; but he regarded the establishment of a commission as the first step toward any satisfactory result. The resolution was referred to the Committee on Commerce, and was favorably reported by that committee to-day. Objection was made to immediate action by Mr. Davis, of West Virginia, and the resolution was placed on the calendar.

### NOTES FROM WASHINGTON.

WASHINGTON, April 15, 1880.

The receipts from internal revenue to-day were $322,325 45, and from Customs, $612,307 62.

The President has recognized Yegawa Kinnihara as Consul of Japan at New-York.

Elias W. Thompson has been appointed Internal Revenue Storekeeper for the First District of New-York.

The Treasury Department purchased to-day 300,000 ounces of silver for the Philadelphia and San Francisco Mints.

The Senate Committee on Post Offices and Post Roads to-day appointed a sub-committee consisting of Messrs. Farley, Bailey, and Kirkwood, to examine into existing laws regulating the "star" service, its expedition and increase, and to report such revision of the same as may be needful to protect the interests of the Government.

### GEN. GRANT IN LITTLE ROCK.

LITTLE ROCK, Ark., April 15.—A procession was formed this morning and marched to the vacant block in Third-street, between Rings and Cross streets, where Messrs. Clayton, Root, Adams, and others of the Reception Committee presented Gen. Grant. Major Fletcher, and afterward Gov. Miller, welcomed him in brief terms, and the General responded as follows: "Citizens: On first landing on the soil of your State, and at every stopping-place on the road, in the crowds of people I met, and the greeting I received, I saw that the feelings of the past were gone. Nothing will advance your prospects so much as an entire absence of sectionalism. I have noticed in my travels that sectionalism is passing away, and the countries of the world are returning to that broad field of liberality which is progress. You have not enough people, but I have no doubt that the resources of your State will attract inhabitants. That all newcomers may be received as I have been to-day, and that they will make good citizens of Arkansas and aid in developing the country, is my ardent wish." From 15,000 to 20,000 persons were massed at the reception grounds. The enthusiasm was general and cordial. The column reformed, traversed the principal streets, occupying two hours in transit, and returned to the hotel, where the ex-President held a levee from 1 until 3 o'clock.

### A DEMOCRATIC NEGRO HUNT.

CINCINNATI, April 15.—The Democracy of Shelby County, Ind., enjoyed an exciting negro hunt to-day. The man who was pursued and shot was the same man who had the presumption to vote in the recent elections and, when set upon by a gang of Democratic ruffians, attempted to defend himself. This morning he had some words with a farmer named Wilson, who lives a few miles from Shelbyville. Wilson, who is a faithful Democrat, immediately went to town and swore out a warrant for the negro's arrest on a charge of carrying concealed weapons. A Democratic Justice of the Peace placed the warrant in the hands of the leader of the gang which assaulted the negro on election day. He immediately organized an armed posse and started in pursuit. The negro, apprehending trouble, secured a double-barreled shot-gun, and, taking his carpet-bag, started for a safer place. He was soon overtaken, however, by the posse, which fired a broadside at him from revolvers. At the first fire he threw up his hands, saying, "My God! I'm shot!" The brave pursuers fired several more shots at the man, and then secured him and brought him back to Shelbyville in triumph. A bullet had entered his thigh, inflicting a severe wound. He was locked up in jail on a charge of carrying concealed weapons with intent to commit murder.

### ON THE WAY TO FIGHT A DUEL.

PHILADELPHIA, April 15.—The story sent from Pittsburg, last evening, to the effect that two persons were in that city, on their way to Canada to fight a duel, receives some credence here. The story goes that the person known as Harry Joel Walden is a titled Frenchman from the Bordeaux district. His opponent is Martin F. Van Werth, a wealthy German of New-York. It seems that on Monday last Walden came here from the Metropolis in the company of a lady whom he left in the ladies' parlor of the Continental Hotel, where she was insulted by Van Werth. The insult was taken up, and Walden left word with a friend that he intended leaving the city for a few days, and that in case he should not return, to send his letters to an address in France. The party went to Washington, where the fight was originally to have taken place, but afterward agreed to go to Canada. The young lady is here yet awaiting news from Canada. The gentleman having charge of the letters says that the same gentleman had a bloodless duel some time ago over the same woman.

### A DEFAULTING CASHIER'S DEATH.

CINCINNATI, April 15.—About two years ago Matthew Weaver, the trusted and popular Cashier of the Citizens' National Bank of Urbana, Ohio, disappeared suddenly from his home, and the examination of his accounts which followed revealed a defalcation of $85,000. He had been speculating in grain on the Chicago Board of Trade, and, to cover his margins, had used the bank's funds. His surplus was exhausted, and [illegible] he fled to Canada, and in Montreal secured a position as a bookkeeper in a window glass and paint house, where he won the confidence of his employer. His wife and daughter remained behind until last Sunday night, when they started to join him. While on the way he took his life and killed himself. A dispatch from Mrs. Weaver to-day brings news of the death.

## AFFAIRS IN FOREIGN LANDS

### BRITISH ELECTION RESULTS.

PARNELL'S CANDIDATE IN CORK COUNTY DEFEATED—THE MINISTRY TO RESIGN ON THE QUEEN'S RETURN.

LONDON, April 15.—The vote for members of Parliament in Cork County has been declared as follows: William Shaw, (nominal Home Rule leader,) re-elected, 5,354; Col. David Colthorst, (Home Ruler,) re-elected, 3,584; Mr. Kettle, (Parnellite,) defeated, 3,430. The nomination of Mr. Kettle was made especially to contest the return of Col. Colthorst.

A correspondent for the Manchester *Guardian* says: "I have good reason for saying that the Ministers have decided to resign as soon as the Queen returns to England from the Continent." This accords with the statement of the *Daily News* that Lord Beaconsfield will have an interview with the Queen on Sunday, and that the Ministry will probably resign on Tuesday next.

J. C. Lawrence and Sir William E. Welby-Gregory, (Conservatives,) for Lincolnshire, South, have been returned, the latter re-elected.

Henry Bellingham, of Castle Bellingham, County Louth, Ireland, has announced his intention of becoming a candidate for the seat rendered vacant by the resignation of Mr. Alexander M. Sullivan, (Home Ruler,) who had just been re-elected for Louth County. Mr. Bellingham will address the constituency as a supporter of the measures advocated by the late members for this constituency in the last House.

The Queen has conferred the decoration of Knight Grand Cross of the Order of the Bath on Sir Stafford Northcote and on Lord John Manners. The Queen has appointed the Rev. John Charles Ryle Bishop of the newly-constituted See of Liverpool.

LONDON, April 16.—Mr. Kettle's defeat in Cork County was entirely the work of the clergy.

The *Daily News* says that the arrival of the Queen a day earlier than was expected will enable Lord Beaconsfield to have an audience on Saturday.

A dispatch from Dublin says one of the results of the impending change in the Government which will be regretted by all parties, and especially by the poor, is the retirement of the Duchess of Marlborough from the field of charity, in which she has labored with untiring zeal for so many months.

### AFFAIRS IN RUSSIA.

THOUSANDS OF FAMILIES STARVING—THE CHINESE TROUBLE—GORTSCHAKOFF'S CONDITION.

LONDON, April 15.—Regarding the famine in the Government of Ozenburg, Russia, the St. Petersburg *Golos* learns that thousands of families can neither obtain food nor the means to earn it, as there is a scarcity of work as well as of food.

A Berlin dispatch says: "The Russian press warns the Government against undervaluing the military power of the Chinese."

Prof. Martens lectured before the Navy Club at Cronstadt, Russia, on Tuesday. He declared that the idea of a Russian invasion of India was absurd, and strongly advocated an Anglo-Russian understanding in Central Asia, for the benefit of trade, progress, and humanity. These sentiments were loudly cheered.

A dispatch from Constantinople says: "The Russian representative here has sent a note to the Porte demanding that the proceedings in the case of the assassin of the Russian Colonel Commeroff be at once brought to a conclusion consistent with justice, and declaring that Russia will hold the Porte responsible if the assassin should escape or if further outrages should be committed."

ODESSA, April 15.—Nineteen persons, mostly students, have been tried by court-martial for various political offenses. Two of them were acquitted, and the others were sentenced to various terms at hard or military labor.

ST. PETERSBURG, April 15.—An official bulletin, issued this morning, reports that Prince Gortschakoff continues feeble and greatly agitated. He was delirious for half an hour in the morning. The *Vedomosti* states that, although his physician holds out hopes of recovery, Prince Gortschakoff is convinced he will die, and awaits the end calmly. His second son has arrived here.

LONDON, April 16.—A St. Petersburg dispatch states that the Empress's physician was specially summoned at 2 o'clock Thursday morning, and remained in the Palace all night. Prince Gortschakoff is better.

### FRENCH POLITICAL PROBLEMS.

THE BONAPARTISTS AND THE ANTI-JESUIT DECREES—A STUBBORN CONTEST TO BE MADE.

PARIS, April 15.—Prince Louis Lucien Bonaparte, a nephew of Napoleon I., has written from London to M. Jules Amigues, the French journalist, saying that he has read with the utmost satisfaction the protests of his nephews, the Cardinal Bonaparte and Prince Charles Napoleon, against the approbation given by Prince Jerome Napoleon to the decrees against religious congregations; that he is happy to associate himself with the protest, which he thinks will not be disapproved by the Princes Victor and Louis, nor by a great majority of the Bonapartists.

Cardinal Guibert, Archbishop of Paris, in his protest against the decrees respecting unauthorized religious congregations, says that the decrees at present are only a menace, but should they be executed, it is to be feared they will lead to painful conflicts between law and conscience, and that France may enter upon a period of internal troubles of which no man can foresee the end.

Baron von Radowitz, the new German Ambassador, has arrived here.

*La France* confidently asserts that the Government contemplates hastening the next elections, M. Gambetta having put forward reasons for such action. M. Dufaure, in an interview with his colleagues and political friends, deprecated as inopportune the idea of interpellating the Government relative to the decrees against unauthorized congregations. He pointed out that the congregations had only to have recourse to the legal tribunals.

The *Temps* states that a diplomatic circular is about to be issued by Premier De Freycinet, explaining in detail the foreign policy he has pursued since his accession to office.

LONDON, April 15.—A Paris correspondent says: "It is certain that the unauthorized religious congregations will defend themselves, at the proper moment, on the ground of individual liberty and the rights of property, and that the legal proceedings regarding the questions at issue between the Government and the congregations cannot last less than a year."

A dispatch from Paris says that 19 Socialist propagandists—Germans and others—have been required to leave France.

### CURRENT FOREIGN TOPICS.

BERLIN, April 15.—Prussia has proposed to the Bundesrath certain alterations in the imperial Constitution, whereby all Legislative business must be dealt with in a certain limited period, at sittings in which all the representatives of the Federal States will be required to participate, and has also proposed restrictions on the right of proxy representation generally. The proposals have been passed upon favorably and referred to the appropriate committee.

The Emperor William, the Princes, and several Generals went to Rathenow yesterday to witness the celebration by the famous Zieten Regiment of Hussars of the one hundred and fiftieth anniversary of Gen. Zieten's entrance into that regiment.

In the Reichstag to-day the first two clauses of the Army bill were read a third time.

MADRID, April 15.—In the Congress to-day, Gen. Martinez-Campos appealed to the Government in the Cuban budget of receipts, but Señor Armas, a Cuban Deputy, combated the proposal. He declared that the reforms suggested were impossible, considering the state of the Cuban Exchequer. Señor Labra, another Cuban Deputy, insisted on the necessity of reform in the administration of Cuba. The *Official Gazette* states that the floating debt of the Cuban Treasury, on March 1, was 107,000,000 pesetas. During March there was an increase in the debt of 51,000,000, which was afterward reduced to 45,000,000 pesetas. On April 1 the debt consequently amounted to 113,000,000.

LONDON, April 15.—Hamburg newspapers state that on Saturday last, the British steamer Alnwick Castle, bound for Venezuela, entered the River Elbe. The vessel, from the nature of her cargo, attracted the attention of the Peruvian Consul there. She had a large quantity of war material on board, and intended to take in 100 tons of powder at Hamburg, and then proceed to Valparaiso. While at anchor in the river she took fire and had to be scuttled to prevent an explosion. The ship and cargo, which included a number of Krupp guns, were insured in London and Hamburg for £137,000. The Peruvian Consul is about to proceed against the owners of the vessel.

The Channel squadron and the dispatch-vessel Salamis left Gibraltar yesterday to search for the missing training-ship Atalanta. The *Times*, in an editorial article this morning, says: "It is too probable that the Atalanta has met with some grave mishap, but there are many misadventures short of total destruction which might account for her disappearance. The Admiralty yesterday received 150 telegrams and 200 personal applications for information regarding the missing vessel. There was a report current that the steamer Tamar, from the West Indies, had passed a copper-bottomed ship capsized. Conjecture associated this report with the Atalanta, but the Captain of the Tamar contradicts the whole story, and says that he saw no such vessel."

The Commissioners for the Melbourne International Exhibition received a telegram yesterday announcing that a large additional area has recently been granted for exhibits from the United States.

A Paris correspondent says: "A political satire by an American ex-diplomatist, entitled 'The Political Comedy of Europe,' will soon be published here. Its object is the condemnation of excessive armaments. Its humorous and dramatic form is expected to give it a great run."

LONDON, April 16.—A dispatch from Rangoon confirms the denial of the Burmese Ambassador of the reports of massacres at Mandelay.

A dispatch from Kabul reports that Abdurrahman Khan is sending letters to all the chiefs, claiming the Ameership. There is a growing uneasiness among the Hindoos in Kabul.

### GRANT HONORED AT HOME.

GEN. LOGAN'S SPEECH AT A DEMONSTRATION IN CHICAGO.

CHICAGO, April 16.—A mass-meeting in the interest of Gen. Grant was held in Central Music Hall this evening. Nearly 3,000 persons were present, all available room being closely occupied. Several ladies were in the audience. Robert E. Lincoln was Chairman, and several prominent politicians occupied seats on the platform. The speakers of the evening were Emery A. Storrs, who made a humorous speech, which was heartily appreciated by the audience; Stephen A. Douglas, Jr., E. C. Larned, and others.

Gen. Logan, who had not known of the arrangements for the meeting until his arrival, being urgently requested to remain, spoke substantially as follows:

We meet to-night to ask ourselves why it is, when a nomination for President is tendered to a distinguished citizen of this State by the Republicans of other States, that we should hesitate. For myself, I answer that I do not. I am for Gen. Grant for President, and I will tell you my reasons: First, his personal integrity is not questioned by any man. Second, his qualifications are undisputed; they have been tested and found equal to all emergencies. He has always responded promptly to the calls of his country. He is a citizen of our own State, and one of whom all parties should be proud. Some object to his nomination. They say that when he was President he made mistakes in appointments. It is true; but you may search his unequaled career, and this is all the fault you can substantiate. In the general features of his Administration during eight years, his record will compare most favorably with that of his predecessors. Objection is made to the election of Gen. Grant for a third term because there is an unwritten law on the subject. We live under a written Constitution, based on the will of the people which prescribes no limitation on the subject of Presidential occupancy except the duration of a term. The people can always safely trust themselves under the forms of constitutional and statute law framed by and with their own authority. Certain so-called Republican journals in this city and other cities oppose a third term for Gen. Grant, but, if you well remember, these same journals, or the most prominent of them, opposed a second term for Gen. Grant as bitterly as they now oppose him. They even fought him after he was nominated, but if there was any betrayal of the Republican Party or the country during his Administration, the country has never yet been advised of it. Since Gen. Grant's retirement from the Presidency, has he done anything to forfeit your confidence in and admiration for him? For two years, in his travels around the globe, he has been fêted by the people of every civilized nation. He has spoken publicly to more audiences and intelligent ones than any other man now living. When and where in all these speeches did he do himself or his country discredit? What citizen of Illinois is not proud of the distinction thus durably won for his native State? The Federal Government, under the partial control of loyal men, is menaced by a solid South. We want to break that solidity. Who can so well lead in this movement as the great civil and military leader who has roused such intense enthusiasm in his recent passage through a portion of the Southern States? We are told we must have a plumed Knight for President this time. In the person of U. S. Grant we offer you the grandest knight who ever waved a plume or thrust a lance. He won his decoration on the field of battle. At the head of his brave Union legion he crushed the most audacious armies that ever waged war against their country. His plume is recognized as the symbol of constitutional liberty and equality by every man, woman, and child in the land. The orphans of Union soldiers recognize it; the widows of Union martyrs recognize it, and the blind Union veterans touch it that they may be thrilled by the patriotic memories associated with it.

It is claimed by some that Gen. Grant, after all his great services for his country in military and civil life, is ambitious. Cæsar, after he had led the Roman legions victoriously, in every hostile country, was assassinated by his friends because he was said to be ambitious. Wellington was stoned in the streets of London by a populace who had been defended and honored by his sword. Abraham Lincoln, toward the close of his first administration, was bitterly reviled and antagonized by professed political friends, on the assumption that he sought his second Presidential term. Gen. Grant, it seems, is not to have immunity from the malice of ingrates, for at the head of those attempting to organize an army of malcontents in this State is one who was treated most generously by him when he was in military and civil command. But in this instance, detraction and defamation will fail in their work, for the man whom the world has honored as man was never honored before, will not be deserted nor dishonored by the people of his own State of Illinois.

The meeting adopted a long series of resolutions favoring the nomination of Gen. Grant from motives of policy, prudence, public safety, and the preservation of law which protects all citizens in their political rights. In Illinois especially, considerations of gratitude, duty, and local pride should induce his nomination. There is too much talk of the unwritten law, when the other laws are disregarded. Grant is a man of victory and success. His election would mean stability of the Government and the finances, and the tranquillity of the country. It would be a step toward a plan of universal peace among the nations which his wise policy has encouraged. His nomination is the boon the dusky millions of the South have long hoped and prayed for. The turbulent element of the South will give way to that hero who has twice conquered them—once by arms and once by unequaled magnanimity. The resolutions close by stating that all Republicans are pledged to support the nominee of the National Convention.

### FARES TO THE CONVENTIONS.

CHICAGO, April 15.—The railway officers to-day held a meeting to fix special passenger fares for persons attending the national conventions at Chicago and Cincinnati, and the national gathering of the Knights Templar here in August. It was decided to make tickets from Nebraska to the Chicago Convention and return $20, and $26 to the Cincinnati Convention; from Sioux City to Chicago, $27 50, and a similar increase to Cincinnati. The rates by Eastern railway offices will be, it is presumed, will be equally low. To Knights Templar and their families attending the national gathering the rate to Chicago and return will be a single fare.

## GENERAL POLITICAL NEWS

### MR. TILDEN STILL IN THE FIELD.

HIS FRIENDS POSITIVELY DENY THAT HE HAS WITHDRAWN OR INTENDS TO DO SO.

WASHINGTON, April 15.—Democratic politicians who fear that the nomination of Mr. Tilden would place their party at a disadvantage which they could not hope to overcome, and who regard with alarm the indications of Mr. Tilden's strength, which are constantly appearing, have been laboring for some time to induce the public to believe that he has withdrawn from the canvass. Statements to this effect have been industriously circulated, and they frequently find their way into the newspapers as coming from persons who are on intimate terms with Mr. Tilden. But they are read only to be forgotten, until they are repeated in a different form. Such a statement appeared in a telegram sent to Philadelphia yesterday. In relation to it, Speaker Randall said to-day that Mr. Tilden undoubtedly was still a candidate, and it is universally believed that Speaker Randall can speak with authority on the subject, if any one in Washington can. It is said that Mr. Tilden did write a letter of withdrawal about two months ago, and that the Chairman of the Democratic State Committee of New-York, who was at the time in this city on important private business, was recalled to New-York very suddenly for the purpose of receiving the document. It is also said that the Chairman's influence was sufficient to induce Mr. Tilden to reconsider his determination. There are many persons, however, who do not believe that Mr. Tilden has ever had any intention of withdrawing his name, and so far as can be learned here from those who ought to know, he has no such intention at present. These gentlemen say that he will not relax his hold upon the party until compelled to do so; that if he does decide to withdraw it will be when the convention meets, and when he has his forces well in hand for delivery to some person of his own choice, and that he could not withdraw now without disgracefully deserting his many friends and supporters and leaving them in a very unenviable position.

### DEMOCRATIC STATE DELEGATES.

REPRESENTATIVES OF THE TILDEN, ANTI-TILDEN, AND SEYMOUR FACTIONS.

WHITE PLAINS, April 15.—The Democrats of the Third Assembly District in Westchester County this afternoon elected William Mabie, William E. Lawrence, and William R. Strong as delegates to the Syracuse Convention. They go to the convention instructed to vote for Tilden.

SING SING, N. Y., April 15.—At the Democratic Convention of the Third Assembly District of Westchester County, held at Merritt's Corners to-day, the following delegates were elected to the Anti-Tilden State Convention: Col. E. Payne, of Yorktown; Dr. Isaac G. Collins, of Sing Sing, and John Smith, of Cortland. Alternates—Charles R. Madden, William Reasoner, and Columbus W. Seely.

HUDSON, N. Y., April 15.—The Democratic Convention of Columbia County to-day elected Edward L. Gaul, Abram L. Schemmerhorn, and Walter Shults as delegates to the State Convention. They are all anti-Tilden.

RIVERHEAD, Long Island, April 15.—The following delegates were chosen to-day to attend the Syracuse Convention: Henry A. Reeve, Arthur Downing, and Henry C. Platt. The delegates are uninstructed.

JAMAICA, Long Island, April 15.—The Democrats of the Second Assembly District of Queens County met to-day and elected Francis McKenna, Alexander Moran, and A. N. Weller delegates to the Syracuse Convention. McKenna and Moran are, it is said, sympathizers with Tammany Hall, while Mr. Weller is a friend of Mr. Tilden.

MONTICELLO, N. Y., April 15.—The following delegates to the Syracuse Convention, from Sullivan County, were chosen to-day: G. M. Beebe, Frank Buckley, and B. W. Winner. The County Convention unanimously passed a resolution favoring Horatio Seymour for the Presidency.

WATERTOWN, N. Y., April 14.—The First Assembly District Convention of Jefferson County to-day nominated T. C. Chittenden, J. M. Cleveland, and J. C. Mather as delegates to the Syracuse Convention. Two are Tilden and one anti-Tilden.

The Anti-Tammany Convention of Lewis County to-day selected F. Garmon, George N. Whittaker, and James Doyle as delegates to the Syracuse Convention, and the Tammany Convention chose D. C. West, A. McVicker, and Anson Carter as delegates.

NEWBURG, N. Y., April 15.—In the First Assembly District of Orange County, the delegates to the Democratic State Convention are David M. Hollenbeck, Henry P. Clauson, and John P. Sears.

AMSTERDAM, N. Y., April 15.—The Montgomery County Democratic Convention, at Fonda, to-day, elected three delegates to the State Convention at Syracuse. Two of them are known to be strong Tilden men.

The Democratic Convention of Fulton County to-day elected three anti-Tilden delegates.

AUBURN, N. Y., April 15.—The following delegates have been elected in the First Assembly Democratic Convention, held at Weedsport: William T. Graves, Henry Stickle, and Edward Allanson. The Second Assembly Convention held at Moravia, has elected Michael Keeler, Henry O'Hara, and Frank W. Collins. The delegates are unpledged, but are all friends of Tilden.

MIDDLETOWN, N. Y., April 15.—The Democrats of the Second District of Orange County have elected W. H. Nearpass, John Wilken, and J. H. Murray as delegates to Syracuse. They are unpledged, but are opposed to Tilden.

SYRACUSE, N. Y., April 15.—The following are the delegates elected to-day from Onondaga County to the Kelly convention: First District—Gen. J. Dean Hawley, Col. James S. Crouse, and Major E. B. Griswold. Second District—Wilbur M. Brown, F. J. Torrington, and M. D. Higgins. Third District—P. P. Midler, W. W. Van Brocklin, and Daniel Pratt, Jr.

TROY, N. Y., April 15.—The Kelly Democrats, this evening, elected as delegates to the State Convention from the First District of Rensselaer Isaac McConihe, Edmund Fitzgerald, and John H. Colby. They are uninstructed, but are for Seymour. In the Third District, the Kelly Democrats elected Thomas Morton, James P. O'Shea, and Charles L. Fuller; uninstructed, but are for Seymour. The Democrats of the Second District elected Joseph Lord, Francis McCabe, and John McGalligan as delegates to the Syracuse Convention. They are uninstructed, but strong for Tilden.

ALBANY, April 15.—The Democrats to-day elected the following delegates to the Syracuse Convention: Second District—John McEwen, William D. Strevel, and John McNamara. Third District—Daniel Manning, Rufus W. Peckham, and T. J. Sullivan; Fourth District—Terence J. Hardin, John Mahoney, and Edward Kennar. They are uninstructed, but understood to be for Tilden.

### THE ILLINOIS REPUBLICANS.

CHICAGO, April 15.—A dispatch to the *Times* from Springfield, Ill., says that, in response to a request of the committee having charge of the arrangements for the National Republican Convention, a piece of swamp oak was to-day taken from one of the sills of the Lincoln mansion to be fashioned into a gavel for the use of the Chairman of the convention.

A Pontiac (Ill.) dispatch to the *Times* says: "At the Republican Convention for Livingston County nine delegates to the State Convention were elected. Of these, seven are for Blaine, and one each for Grant and Edmunds."

### SHERMAN NOT FORGOTTEN.

KEY WEST, Fla., April 15.—At the Monroe County Convention, held here this afternoon, Sherman delegates were elected, and E. L. Ware was nominated for Congress by an overwhelming majority.

ALBANY, April 15.—Erastus Uman, William W. MacFarland, Richard B. Whittemore, J. Frank Emmons, and others are named as Directors of the Staten Island Rapid Transit Railroad Company. The road is to be commenced in the Town of Southfield and terminate in the Village of Port Richmond. The capital is placed at $500,000.

# The New-York Times.

VOL. XXIX........NO. 8943. NEW-YORK, SUNDAY, MAY 9, 1880.---TRIPLE SHEET. PRICE FIVE CENTS.


## THE PRESIDENTIAL RACE

### *CHEERING NEWS FOR THE FRIENDS OF GEN. GRANT.*

ASSURANCES OF THE VOTE OF ILLINOIS IN THE NATIONAL CONVENTION—NO OTHER CANDIDATE HEARD OF IN ALABAMA—FLORIDA TAKING THE SAME PATH.

The reports of the action of county conventions in Illinois, yesterday, leave little doubt that that State will cast its vote in the Republican National Convention for Gen. U. S. Grant. Of the 439 delegates to the State Convention, 277 are credited to the ex-President. Chicago will send a delegation to its County Convention with a majority in favor of Grant. In Alabama, Montgomery County sends a solid delegation for Grant to the State Convention; all other counties yet heard from have spoken for him. In the First (Florida) District resolutions in his favor have been adopted.

### *GRANT SWEEPING ILLINOIS.*

THE EX-PRESIDENT HAS 277 OF THE 439 DELEGATES THUS FAR ELECTED—CHICAGO STRONG FOR HIM.

CHICAGO, May 8.—Eighteen out of nineteen wards in this city give Grant 61 delegates to the County Convention, Blaine 32, and Washburne 40. Two outside towns give Grant 6 and Washburne 2. Eleven counties outside the city, holding conventions to-day, give Grant 48 delegates to the State Convention, and Blaine 3. Of the delegates so far elected to the State Convention, 277 are for Grant, 153 for Blaine, and 9 for Washburne.

Reports from sources hostile to the Grant movement give the result of the Republican primaries in this city to-day as Washburne 63, Grant 58, and Blaine 25 delegates to the Cook County Convention. Returns from the outlying districts will not alter the complexion of the result. Evanston goes anti-Grant.

Special dispatches to the *Times* give the following results in 8 of the 19 Illinois County Conventions to-day: Winnebago instructs 11 delegates to the State Convention for Grant; Alexander, 3; Union, 2; Salem, 2; Jo Daviess, 7, and Cumberland, 3. Lake selects 6 for Blaine and 1 for Washburne, and Monroe 2 for Washburne. This makes a total of 28 for Grant, 6 for Blaine, and 3 for Washburne.

Dispatches to the *Tribune* state that the Piatt County Republican Convention to-day chose 5, Marion County 5, and Wabash County 2, Grant delegates to the State Convention.

### *GRANT LEADING IN ALABAMA.*

MONTGOMERY COUNTY SENDS A SOLID GRANT DELEGATION TO THE STATE CONVENTION.

MONTGOMERY, Ala., May 8.—The Republicans of Montgomery County met in convention to-day to elect delegates to the State Convention, which is to be held at Selma 10 days hence. The meeting was composed almost entirely of colored men. Resolutions in favor of Gen. Grant were passed, and a delegation solid for the ex-President was elected. The delegation is headed by Paul Strobach. Judge Rice and ex-Mayor Faber made a determined fight against the action of the convention in instructing its delegates to use every effort to secure a delegation from Alabama to the National Convention in favor of Grant, but were completely vanquished. This action is all the more significant because Montgomery County is the banner Republican county of the State, and has the largest representation in the State Convention. Every county that has yet spoken is for Grant.

### *TWO HONORABLE DELEGATES.*

SENATOR DENIS M'CARTHY AND JAMES BELDEN WILL ABIDE BY INSTRUCTIONS.

SYRACUSE, May 8.—There is no truth whatever in the statement that Senator Denis McCarthy and James Belden, delegates from the Twenty-fifth Congressional District to the Chicago Convention, have declared against Grant.

Senator McCarthy said to-day: "I see no reason why I should not abide by the instructions of the Republican State Convention. I feel honorably bound to do so."

Mr. Belden said: "I have not decided to disregard the instructions of the Republican State Convention, as has been alleged. I am in favor of the strongest man who can be nominated at Chicago, and, so far, no reasons have been advanced why I should not vote for Grant."

### *FLORIDA FOR GRANT.*

STRONG RESOLUTIONS IN HIS FAVOR PASSED WITHOUT OPPOSITION.

JACKSONVILLE, Fla., May 8.—The Republican Congressional Convention of the First District in this State has been in session two days, at Tallahassee, without making a nomination for Congress. Yesterday strong Grant and Settle resolutions were passed without opposition.

### *A BLAINE FALSEHOOD NAILED.*

GEN. KILPATRICK DENOUNCES THE STATEMENT THAT HE IS PLEDGED FOR "THE PLUMED KNIGHT."

Gen. Kilpatrick writes as follows to a morning paper which, with its usual inaccuracy, claims all the delegates from New-Jersey for Blaine:

In your leading editorial of to-day you inform the public that:

Of all the delegates chosen from New-Jersey, several frankly avowed that they would personally have preferred to vote for Secretary Sherman, but declared, as *Gen. Kilpatrick* did in the *convention*, in the meeting of the *Committee on Resolutions* and in *conversation with delegates*, that he had been *preferred as delegate because of his pledge to vote for Senator Blaine.*

Mr. Editor, this is not true. I made no pledge to vote for Mr. Blaine or any other candidate. In the Committee on Resolutions I opposed and prevented even a preference, couched in the mildest form, from being adopted for him, as well as for Mr. Washburne. I gave no pledge; I would not have done so for all the honors that New-Jersey could have conferred upon me. The convention selected me, above all others, as their first choice. I take it because its members preferred me, while the most pronounced friend of Mr. Blaine received the smallest number of votes of the Senatorial delegates chosen. Mr. Editor, I shall know three weeks hence better how to discharge my duties to my State and the Republican Party at Chicago than the united wisdom of the wisest leaders of our party can direct to-day. Yours truly,

JUDSON KILPATRICK.

### *BY NO MEANS A SHERMAN MAN.*

PATERSON, N. J., May 8.—Mr. Henry L. Butler, who is claimed by "Sherman's friends in New-York," to be a Sherman man, says Sherman is the last man he proposes to vote for, as he considers him a political trimmer. His first choice is Blaine, and his second is Washburne.

### *GREENBACKERS FROM CANADA.*

WASHINGTON, May 8.—William Wallace, member of the Canadian Parliament, and President of the Currency Reform League of Canada, has had the Secretary of that league address a communication to the leaders of the National Greenback Party, asking them whether the presence of a visiting Canadian delegation, representing a body thoroughly in accord with the views and aims of the National Greenback Party, would be agreeable to the National Greenback Convention, which will meet at Chicago June 9. In reply to this communication, Lee Crandall, Secretary of the Congressional Committee National Greenback Labor Party, after consulting the leaders of that party, wrote that the National Greenback Convention would feel themselves honored by receiving the Canadian delegation.

### *W. H. BARNUM AS A CANDIDATE.*

HIS FRIENDS CLAIMING THAT MR. TILDEN WILL SUPPORT HIM.

HARTFORD, April 8.—There have been occasional intimations that in case Mr. Tilden should not himself be a candidate for the Presidency, his influence might be exerted to bring prominently before the Cincinnati Convention the name of the Hon. William H. Barnum, of Connecticut. It has been strongly claimed by the supporters of the Hon. James E. English in this State that he would have, probably, the support of Mr. Tilden, but since the English movement was lost in the confusion of the late State Convention in this city the claim seems to have been abandoned. Many Democrats here have never entertained the opinion that there could be any possible chance for a Connecticut candidate, and they have generally believed that Mr. Tilden's favorite would be Judge Paine, of Ohio. But, from some recent movements, a strong basis is given to the belief that Mr. Barnum is really to have the support which so many have coveted. His relations to the party as Chairman of the National Committee, and his close personal affiliations with Mr. Tilden, give him certain advantages of position which none of the rival aspirants possess. That he enjoys the confidence of Mr. Tilden in an eminent degree is beyond question, and the relationship is entirely natural, because Mr. Tilden's political methods could not be more safely trusted to any man than to Mr. Barnum, who is bold and persistent, and, as an organizer, has few equals.

While the Republicans of Connecticut have made a warm fight against Barnum in many contests, it is admitted by all men that in point of executive ability there is no man in the State more capable, and when he was in Congress his Republican associates always found him in all matters of general State interest willing and useful, and always commanding an influence which many times surprised them. Not being a man of words, he is not so well known as many others, except as his position in his party brings him out occasionally; but he is, nevertheless, as hard a worker and as dangerous a man to fight as any Democrat in the country, and it is a question whether, if he should be taken as a candidate, it would not be Mr. Tilden's best judgment that he would be safer in New-York, Connecticut, and New-Jersey than any Western man who could be named. The assurances given of the possibilities of his being pushed at Cincinnati are such that they are worthy of consideration, and the supporters of other candidates will do well to ponder upon the elements of strength which he is liable to have working in his favor. The information received in confidential Democratic circles in this State is that his candidacy is extremely probable, and an open movement is predicted as soon as the Chicago Convention shall have finished its work.

### *POSTMASTER JAMES'S FRIENDS.*

A STRONG FEELING IN NEW-JERSEY IN FAVOR OF MR. JAMES AS POSTMASTER-GENERAL.

TRENTON, N. J., May 8.—The movement in this State in favor of the appointment of Postmaster James to the Postmaster-Generalship is hearty and active, and meets with cordial approval among all classes of citizens, Republicans, Independents, and Democrats, irrespective of party. A strong petition to the President has been signed by the Chairman, Secretary, and many of the leading members of the State Republican Committee, and will contain the names of the most prominent men in New-Jersey politics. The merchants and business men of New-York resident in this State, and they are many, are particularly active and earnest in their advocacy of Mr. James's elevation to the Cabinet, and it is understood that in a few days they will send a delegation to Washington to present their petition and views in the matter to President Hayes. Prominent business men of this city who have returned from Philadelphia say that among the best and most influential business men of that city, also, there is a strong feeling in Mr. James's favor.

### *DISCUSSING BAPTIST MISSIONS.*

LEXINGTON, Ky., May 8.—The morning session of the Southern Baptist Convention was mainly taken up in the consideration of reports of the Committees on Missions. Dr. Tieherson presented the report on Chinese missions, and made an eloquent address in its behalf. Mr. C. Lewis, of Kentucky, and Dr. Dodson followed in able addresses. Dr. B. Manley presented the report on African missions, and addressed the convention in their interest. He was followed by Dr. McDonald, of Richmond. The next convention will meet at Columbus, Miss. Dr. Landron, of Georgia, is to preach the opening sermon, and F. H. Kerfoot, of Baltimore, will be the alternate. The evening session was devoted mainly to woman's mission work. The motion to incorporate their report in the proceedings of the convention was carried. The night session was devoted to a mass-meeting on foreign missions.

### *TROOPS TO PUT DOWN RIOTERS.*

COLUMBUS, Ohio, May 8.—Gov. Foster to-day received a telegram from Sheriff Coulter, of Wayne County, asking for troops to keep down a riot which had been threatened by nearly 500 miners in case negroes employed in the mines were not discharged. The Governor has authorized the use of troops.

Col. Thomas, of Akron, has been ordered to hold his regiment of Militia in readiness to march to Wayne County. A company of Militia to-night left Wooster for Silver Creek Mine, where the trouble is, and the Massillon company is under orders. On Thursday night, about 12 o'clock, the proprietors of the Silver Creek Mine brought to their mine about 200 colored miners from Virginia, and sent them in the mines at 75 cents per ton. Anticipating trouble, they had a force of carpenters build a high fence around the mouth of the mine, and yesterday had a force of 25 special constables, under charge of Sheriff Coulter, to protect the colored miners. The white men held a meeting, and, it is said, voted to drive the colored miners away. To-day they stoned the barricade around the mines, and injured one of the constables. An attack is expected to be made to-morrow.

### *DEMOCRATIC ECONOMY.*

PORTSMOUTH, N. H., May 8.—The United States Marshal for New-Hampshire states that he has barely funds enough to pay the expenses of grand and petit jurors, and unless Congress makes an appropriation jury trials must cease.

### *GREENBACKERS FOR BUTLER.*

BOSTON, May 8.—The Greenback-Labor Party of the Fourth District last night elected delegates favoring Butler for first choice and David Davis for second.

### *HANGING HIMSELF IN HIS BARN.*

SCHENEVUS, N. Y., May 8.—A distressing suicide occurred at the village of Westford, near this place, yesterday morning. Amos Smith, an old and prominent citizen, arose about 5 o'clock and went to the barn, saying that he was going to fodder his stock. Not returning at the ringing of the breakfast-bell, a member of the family went to the barn to ascertain the cause of his staying so long. On entering the barn, the body of Mr. Smith was found suspended by a rope, which was fastened to a cross-beam. Mr. Smith was for several years a member of the Board of Supervisors of Otsego County. Severe losses in business transactions are believed to have led him to kill himself.

### *TWO BOYS BURNED TO DEATH.*

ROCHESTER, N. Y., May 8.—Roy McCrosan, 4 years old, and Thomas F. Garland, 5 years, were playing to-day in a barn in Francis-street. They made a bonfire, the barn caught fire, and the two boys were burned so as to have no semblance to human beings. They played with matches.

## MATTERS AT WASHINGTON

### *PERFECTING THE NEW TARIFF MEASURES.*

THE BILLS THAT ARE TO BE REPORTED—THE PROVISIONS AGREED TO YESTERDAY IN COMMITTEE—A SEPARATE MEASURE IN REGARD TO SUGAR.

WASHINGTON, May 8.—The Ways and Means Committee finally agreed upon Representative Tucker's Tariff bill this morning, and ordered it to be favorably reported to the House. The portion relating to sugar was agreed to as a separate measure, and will also be favorably reported to the House in a separate bill. The remaining provisions of the Tariff bill proper, which were agreed to to-day, are as follows: Salt is stricken from the bill entirely; the duty, therefore, remains, as at present, 12 cents per 100 pounds, in bags, and 8 cents per 100 pounds, in bulk. Upon screws of all descriptions, the duty is placed at 5 and 7 cents, instead of 5 and 8 cents per pound, as agreed upon yesterday. The duty upon wood-pulp is reduced from 20 to 10 per cent. ad valorem; jute butts from $6 to $3 per ton; manufactured flax, and all other fibres or fibrous material for the manufacture of paper, from $20 and $25 to the uniform rate of $10 per ton; sized or glued paper for printing, from 25 to 20 per cent.; unsized, for books and newspapers exclusively, from 20 to 15 per cent.; manufactures of paper or of which paper is a component part, not otherwise provided for, from 35 to 25 per cent.; plows, harrows, spades, shovels, hoes, and other like articles, of which iron or steel is a component material, used for agricultural, mining, or mechanical purposes, from 35 to 25 per cent. ad valorem.

The Sugar bill, as agreed to, is as follows: Upon tank-bottoms, syrup of sugar, cane juice, melado, concentrated melado, and concentrated molasses the duty is fixed at 1¾ cents per pound, instead of the present duty, which is equivalent to 62.48 per cent.; upon sugar not above No. 7, Dutch standard, 2 3-16 cents per pound, instead of the present duty, equivalent to 53.30 per cent. ad valorem; above No. 7 and not above No. 13, Dutch standard, the uniform duty is laid of 2¼ cents per pound, instead of the two rates, equivalent to 60.79 and 60.65 per cent., at present imposed; above No. 13 and not above No. 16, Dutch standard, 2 81-100 cents, instead of 64.80 per cent.; above No. 16 and not above No. 20, Dutch standard, 3 17-100 cents, instead of 70.82 per cent.; above No. 20, Dutch standard, 3 67-100 cents, instead of 64.01 per cent.; upon all sugar-candy and all confectionery made wholly or in part of sugar, sugar after being refined when tinctured, colored, or in any way adulterated, of all descriptions, the uniform duty of 50 per cent. ad valorem, instead of the three rates now imposed of 15 cents per pound, 10 cents per pound, and 50 per cent. ad valorem; provided, however, that upon all sugars not above No. 7, Dutch standard, which test above 85° the duty shall be 2¼ cents per pound; and the Secretary of the Treasury is authorized to employ, under regulations in conformity with law, such means, by chemical analysis, the polariscope, or otherwise, as shall be best adapted to adjust upon all sugars the rate of duty thereon imposed by this act.

The Sugar bill, it is understood, is not considered by a majority of the committee as the best measure which could have been adopted, but inasmuch as any system of ad valorem duties was deemed impracticable, the committee decided to report it to the House without recommendation, for the purpose of bringing the subject directly before the House for its consideration. At the meeting of the committee to-day, several propositions for an ad valorem tariff were presented, but all were voted down as impracticable. The amendment proposed on Tuesday last by Mr. Frye was renewed to-day by Mr. Carlisle, and failed by one vote of a majority. This measure, Mr. Carlisle gave notice, he should move as a substitute for the Tucker bill when the subject comes before the House. The Frye bill proposes a uniform tariff of 2 cents per pound on all raw sugars up to No. 13 Dutch standard, which is the dividing line between refining and grocery qualities; 2.25 from No. 13 to No. 16; 2.60 from No. 16 to No. 20, and 3.25 above No. 20. Melado is reduced to 1.50, and molasses to 5 cents per gallon. Mr. Frye's bill reduces the duties about 15 per cent., equal to $6,000,000, which he claims is in harmony with the prevailing sentiment for a reduction in the cost of food staples.

### *ARMY AND NAVY INTELLIGENCE.*

WASHINGTON, May 8.—The extension of the leave of absence granted to Surgeon William S. King, on account of sickness, has been extended six months. The leave granted to First Lieut. A. L. Morton, of the Fifth Artillery, has been extended to May 1, 1861. Leave of absence for one year, with permission to go beyond the sea when his services can be spared, has been granted to Second Lieut. H. W. Wheeler, of the Fifth Cavalry.

By direction of the President, and in conformity with section 1,229 of the Revised Statutes, Second Lieut. Horace B. Steele, of the Nineteenth Infantry, has been dropped from the rolls of the Army.

FORTRESS MONROE, Va., May 8.—The United States steamer Enterprise sailed for Washington to-day.

### *THE INDIAN TERRITORY INVASION.*

WASHINGTON, May 8.—The Secretary of the Interior has received telegraphic advices from Wichita, Kan., bearing the date of May 7, confirming the reported invasion of the Indian Territory by a number of white settlers under the lead of Capt. Payne. This dispatch was at once referred to the War Department, and necessary orders were issued to-day to officers in command of troops in that vicinity instructing them to drive out the invaders. In reply to inquiries on the subject, Secretary Ramsey said that he did not apprehend any trouble with the invaders; after they were once compelled to quit the Territory, they would not attempt to re-enter it.

### *NOTES FROM WASHINGTON.*

WASHINGTON, May 8, 1880.

A bill was introduced to-day by Mr. Hooker, of Mississippi, from the Committee on Indian Affairs, transferring the office of Indian Affairs from the Interior to the War Department. It was placed on the House calendar.

Mr. Singleton, of Mississippi, in the House, to-day, submitted the conference report on the Consular and Diplomatic Appropriation bill, and it was agreed to. The result of the agreement is to add $7,000 to the bill as it passed the House, $4,000 of which is for a Consul-General at Bucharest and $3,000 for an increase in the appropriation for the expenses of the commission appointed to act in conjunction with the Minister to China.

The House considered the contested election case of Curtin against Yocum, from the Twentieth District of Pennsylvania. The majority resolution declares the election to have been null and void, and the minority resolution that Yocum, the sitting member, is entitled to the seat. Mr. Beltzhoover, of Pennsylvania, spoke for over two hours in behalf of the majority report, stating his intention, however, of offering an amendment declaring Andrew J. Curtin entitled to the seat.

Mr. Seward, United States Minister to China, informs the department, under date of Feb. 21, 1880, that the education of the Chinese in Western knowledge is going forward in many ways. A hundred and twenty Chinese youths are receiving education at schools and colleges in the United States. There are several flourishing schools in China under the direction of American teachers. Through the Translation Department of the Empire, established in 1867, over 80,000 volumes of translated works have been sold, embracing publications on mathematics, engineering, geography, astronomy, science, medicine, law, arts, and manufactures.

### *FIGHTING VICTORIA'S INDIANS.*

SAN FRANCISCO, May 8.—A dispatch from Tucson, Arizona, says that Capt. Kramer, with 28 men of the Sixth Cavalry, attacked Victoria's band of Indians, 90 strong, near Rock Creek Cañon, yesterday. Blackman's command of 16 cavalrymen and 28 Indian scouts were momentarily expected to reinforce Kramer. When the courier came away several of Kramer's men had been wounded. Reinforcements are on the way from Camp Thomas and Camp Grant. A decisive engagement is expected to-morrow.

Another dispatch says: "Victoria, in yesterday's fight, killed George H. Stevens and about 20 families of Indians who were living on his ranch. Victoria is trying to reach the San Carlos Reservation to get the wives of his warriors and, if possible, reinforcements."

### *HANDEL AND HAYDN.*

SIGNOR CAMPANINI'S NEW TRIUMPH IN BOSTON—YESTERDAY'S CONCERT.

BOSTON, May 8.—This afternoon's concert of the Handel and Haydn festival was in many respects the crowning glory of the series. The receipts were $4,200, and at least 700 people were turned away, unable to get either seat or standing-place. The programme was of a miscellaneous character, arranged to present many of the soloists, including Campanini and Cary, prominently, and the excellently-trained orchestra was heard to the best advantage. The concert opened with Weber's overture, "Rubezahl." Then followed the Utrecht Jubilate, with the solos by Cary, Courtney, and Whitney. In this the work of the chorus was especially well done. Signor Campanini then appeared, and was received with the usual fervor. He sang the romance from Verdi's "La Forza del Destino" most exquisitely, and so moved his audience that the applause was something remarkable, worthy of audiences much warmer than those of Boston are credited with being. Miss Thursby next sang, very sweetly, a song, "La Calandrina," by Jommelli, and Mr. Courtney followed with the aria from "Il Duca d'Ebro," which he rendered with fine artistic skill, and was heartily applauded, as he deserved to be. Then came Campanini again in a duet with Whitney, the familiar but ever-fresh duet from "William Tell," and there was something like a repetition of his first reception, Mr. Whitney, whose fine voice was in admirable condition, sharing the honors. The numbers following included airs from Mozart's "Le Nozze di Figaro," ("Voi che sapete,") by Miss Cary; from Wagner's "Die Meistersinger," by Mr. Whitney; from Wagner's "Die Walküre," by Campanini; from Handel's "Julius Cæsar," by Miss Winant, and from Meyerbeer's "Star of the North," by Miss Thursby. The concert closed with the quartet and chorus from Bach's cantata, "Per ogni tempo," Miss Hubbell, Miss Winant, Mr. Courtney, and Mr. Whitney forming the quartet.

Signor Campanini's closing number, Siegmund's love song from "Die Walkure," was sung with Italian words. He retired from the platform amid a storm of cheers and cries of "bravo." He was in perfect voice and good spirits, and sang to-day with all the beauty, sweetness, and finish which have made him so famous. He returns to New-York with more friends and a still stronger hold on the best of the Boston musical public.

The festival closes to-morrow night with Handel's "Solomon." It has proved a success, not only musically, but financially as well.

### *TROUBLE CAUSED BY ONE WOMAN.*

TWO MEN DESERT THEIR FAMILIES FOR HER, AND THEN FIGHT ABOUT HER.

FLEMINGTON, N. J., May 8.—A curious case was tried before the Court of Quarter Sessions of this county during its present term. Reuben West and Ensign Decaurt are two well-known citizens of Lambertville, and well advanced in years. Each had a family, and each deserted his family some time since, and each fell in love with a woman named Rose Ellis, who occasionally kept house for West. One evening last November, Decatur and Rose went to West's house, about a mile from Lambertville. A quarrel soon arose between the two men. Decatur was seriously shot in the foot, and West was badly bruised in the face. West was indicted by the Grand Jury, and tried. The version of the affair, as told by the two men, was quite different. Decatur swore that West was lying in wait, and upon his approach shot at him, the bullet whistling past his ear; that he sprang at West, and struck down the gun just as it was being discharged the second time, and the charge lodged in his foot.

West swore that he was feeding his hogs, and saw Decatur and Rose go upon the porch and try the door. He also heard Decatur say that West was away, and as there was money in the house, it was their time to get it then. West swore that he went in the back entrance to the house, got his gun, came out and ordered Decatur to go away, at the same time firing his gun in the opposite direction, in order to frighten him; that Decatur sprang toward him, threw a club and some stones at him, one of the stones striking him in the eye and knocking him down. Rising upon his knees, he saw Decatur trying to get through the gate at him, and in that position he fired the other barrel. Afterward he swore that Decatur got to him and cut him with a knife, leaving him bruised and stunned upon the ground. He did not know how much injury his shot had done until the next day, and when he shot he was in fear of his life. He claimed that he fired in self-defense. The jury rendered a verdict of not guilty.

### *ARCHBISHOP PURCELL'S DEBT.*

DEPOSITIONS SHOWING HOW THE MONEY WAS EXPENDED—NOTHING USED FOR PERSONAL BENEFIT.

CINCINNATI, May 8.—Depositions of Archbishop Purcell and of Father Edward Purcell, his brother, have been taken, in a suit brought by one of the creditors of the Archbishop. Father Edward's deposition, which is very clear, is to the effect that he acted solely as a business and financial agent of the Archbishop, for the benefit of the diocese, and had done so since 1836. He stated that he did a sort of banking business, receiving money on deposit and paying interest. The money was not used for his or the Archbishop's personal benefit, but for building churches and orphan asylums, for charity, and to educate priests in Rome, France, and other places. The amount of indebtedness was over $3,000,000. With the exception of a few important creditors, who got mortgages, the debts were all unsecured, it being understood that the diocese was liable. The Archbishop has testified that none of the money received from depositors was applied to any personal use.

### *TRANSFERRING A SILK FACTORY.*

HAWLEY, Penn., May 8.—There is no longer any doubt as to the removing of the silk manufacturing business of Dexter, Lambert & Co. from Paterson, N. J., to this place. The contract for building the new manufactory here has been let, and work will begin at once, and it is the intention to have the building completed by Nov. 1, 1880. The building is to be of stone, 44 feet wide by 380 feet long, with a front addition of 23 by 80 feet, three stories high throughout, with a basement under the entire building. The factory is to be situated in the most prominent place along the Wollenpanpack Falls, just outside the village limit. This establishment will be a great help to the business of Hawley, and will give employment to from 400 to 500 hands. Since it has become an established fact that the new enterprise is going up, real estate in and about Hawley has advanced very rapidly, and landowners will realize large profits by their sales.

### *GEN. GRANT'S VISITS.*

MILWAUKEE, Wis., May 8.—Gens. Grant and Sheridan have informed a committee of the Wisconsin Soldiers' Reunion that they will attend the reunion on June 8, remaining during the 9th and 10th. Gen. Grant will be accompanied by his family.

## AFFAIRS IN FOREIGN LANDS

### *THE OPPOSITION TO PRINCE BISMARCK'S PROJECTS.*

THE ALTONA AND ST. PAULI QUESTION—A DISPATCH TO THE PRUSSIAN REPRESENTATIVES—BISMARCK'S SPEECH IN THE REICHSTAG UPON THE DISCUSSION OF THE MEASURE.

LONDON, May 8.—A Berlin dispatch says: "Amicable arrangements between Prussia and Hamburg are hoped for. Prince Bismarck, perceiving the impracticability of his projects, is evidently endeavoring to effect a compromise. It is stated that Baron Runhardt, the Bavarian Minister whom Prince Bismarck angrily reproved for opposing Prussia in the Bundesrath, will resign."

A dispatch from Berlin to Reuter's Telegram Company says: "The *Official Gazette* publishes a dispatch from Prince Bismarck to the Prussian representatives accredited to the Government of the Federal States, dealing with the Altona and St. Pauli question, in which he states that the committees of the Bundesrath have unanimously resolved to report to the Council only upon the technical side of the question, and to keep altogether out of consideration the constitutional aspect of the case. He lays stress on the necessity of avoiding, as far as possible, for the sake of concord, any interpretation of the constitutional rights involved. Prince Bismarck points out that it is the indisputable right of Prussia to divide any portion of her own territory from the Hamburg free port district, and he maintains that the proposed severance of St. Pauli has not been urged in the interest of Prussia, as it is an advantage to Altona that St. Pauli should remain outside of the Zollverein, but that it was rather in the interest of Hamburg that the new Customs line was proposed. The Bundesrath, he says, can decide upon the Customs line without entering into an examination of the constitutional bearing of the question, which would be likely to produce a conflict of opinion. These Governments which consider that, by the severance of St. Pauli from the Hamburg district, the Constitution of the Empire would be violated can vote against the proposal. But in that case Prince Bismarck would not advise the Emperor to renounce his right to uphold a demand which is undoubtedly no infraction of the Constitution. Prince Bismarck next urges the necessity of maintaining unimpaired the concord between the Governments, and expresses the hope that the respective proposals of Prussia and Hamburg may be settled by arrangement and without resorting to a decision by majorities and minorities. Prussia, he says, will willingly take into consideration any proposal which would, in its effects, be in accordance with the Constitution, provided that the Federal Government make a unanimous endeavor to oppose, with one accord, the attempts of certain members of the Reichstag to limit the authority of the Bundesrath."

A Berlin dispatch says: "In the Reichstag to-day the Anti-usury bill and the bill for preventing and extinguishing the rinderpest were read a third time. Legislation being disposed of thus rapidly, there is every appearance of the session coming to a close on Monday next. The House has refused permission to Herr Lasker to introduce a resolution declaring that the attitude of Prussia in the St. Pauli affair is unconstitutional. It now seems probable that the proposal for a declaration of opinion by the Reichstag on the subject will fall through."

BERLIN, May 8.—The Reichstag to-day discussed the second reading of the Elbe Navigation act, involving the question of the severance of Altona and St. Pauli from the free port territory of Hamburg. The committee moved that the House assent to the bill, with a proviso that a change of the Customs frontier stations on the Elbe shall only be enacted by a special law.

Prince Bismarck said this proviso was an attempt at pressure to which the Government could not submit. The Imperial Constitution was on the side of the Government and overrode provincial law, which established the Customs frontier on the Elbe. The free port rights of Hamburg could not be withdrawn without Hamburg's own consent, but the Federal Council had the right to fix the boundary of free port territory. Prince Bismarck regretted to say that particularism had reappeared with renewed strength. Constitutional disputes had been kindled for the first time in the Federal Council. He then referred to the opposition of the Catholic Centre. From them he had expected support; hence the concessions which were about to be submitted to the Prussian Diet. Opposition parties should beware of the consequences of their conduct. It was dangerous to sow discord between the Federal Governments. "Only one thing," he said, "retains me in office, namely, the will of the Emperor. When I see the obstacles I have to contend with I feel a strong desire for rest in retirement. If you consider the power of the Centre unconquerable, I should advise you, on my retirement, to select a Ministry representing both the Centre and Conservatives. I am tired—tired to death—when I see my efforts constantly thwarted by the Liberals, who will not yield on the smallest points when the continued existence of the Empire is at stake."

Herr Windhorst replied. He said the Centre did not oppose the Government from party motives. Prince Bismarck alone could restore peace to the Church. If he did it, he would obtain much which at present was unobtainable.

### *ENGLAND'S NEW GOVERNMENT.*

MR. GLADSTONE RE-ELECTED AND SIR VERNON-HARCOURT DEFEATED—THE REOPENING OF PARLIAMENT.

LONDON, May 8.—Prime Minister Gladstone has been re-elected for Mid-Lothian without opposition.

Sir William G. Vernon-Harcourt, who has taken office as Home Secretary in the new Ministry, has been defeated upon coming before his constituency in Oxford City for re-election to Parliament. The poll stood as follows: Mr. Hall, (Conservative,) 2,735; Sir William G. Vernon-Harcourt, 2,681.

A correspondent says: "It is believed that the Queen will reopen Parliament on the 20th inst. in person. Mr. William E. Forster, Chief Secretary for Ireland, is expected to arrive from Dublin, for the Cabinet council, on Wednesday next, to advise about measures connected with Ireland. The general supposition is that a bill will be introduced embodying the recommendations of the Select Committee appointed to consider the operation of the Bright clauses of the Irish Land act.

The *Standard*, in a leading editorial article this morning, says: "We decline to believe that a telegram was received from India relative to the budget deficit on the morning following the debate, in the last Parliament, on Mr. Henry Fawcett's motion in favor of England contributing a portion of the Afghan war expenses. When the House of Commons meets, the matter will have to be inquired into; but meanwhile it would be obviously most unfair to accept Mr. Fawcett's unsupported references to telegrams to the India Office."

The new evening paper, under the editorship of Mr. Frederick Greenwood, will appear in a few days. The preparations are being pushed as rapidly as possible, and only certain mechanical arrangements remain to be completed.

### *TURKEY'S EMBARRASSMENTS.*

A REVOLT AT BITLIS—SENTENCE OF THE RUSSIAN COLONEL'S ASSASSIN.

LONDON, May 8.—A dispatch from Constantinople says the inhabitants of Bitlis have revolted because the Governor had received orders to send all the available cereals to Van and Bashkaleh, as telegrams from Erzeroum stated that Van and Bashkaleh were hopelessly famine-stricken, and Bitlis was the nearest point whence assistance could be sent. It is believed here that the Governor of Bitlis connived at resistance with his people, and the English and Russian Embassies have complained to the Porte against him. The Porte is engrossed with military preparations. The Governors of the Provinces have been ordered to hold the Redifs ready for any emergency. Several thousand troops have arrived at Constantinople within the past week. There is great activity at the Government arsenals in Asia.

CONSTANTINOPLE, May 8.—The court-martial in the case of the assassin of the Russian Colonel, Commeraoff, passed sentence of death upon the prisoner on Thursday. M. Onou, chief interpreter to the Russian Legation here, wrote to the President of the court-martial demanding the execution of the condemned man within 24 hours. The President replied that diplomatic communications should be addressed to the Minister of Foreign Affairs.

### *TOPICS OF INTEREST ABROAD.*

LONDON, May 8.—The following appears among the marriage announcements in the *Times* this morning: "On the 6th inst., at St. George's, Hanover-square, John Walter Cross, of Weybridge, Surrey, to Mary Ann Evans, Lewes, of the Priory, North Bank, Regent's Park." Mr. Cross is, or was, a merchant in the city. A provincial correspondent says that Mr. Cross is the London representative of an American financial house.

A Berlin dispatch says: "Princess Pauline, of Wurtemburg was married at Carlsruhe, in Upper Silesia, a few days ago, to Dr. Wilm, a medical practitioner of Breslau. The King of Wurtemberg gave his assent to the marriage on condition of the lady abandoning her princely title."

The letter from Col. Prejevalsky, the Russian explorer, announcing the safety of his expedition, says: "The expedition left the Naushian Mountains in July, and entered Thibet through Shaidash. They were attacked by the Tanguts, of whom they killed four, and the remainder fled. The Thibetan troops stopped the expedition 250 versts from Lassa. A messenger from the Grand Llama brought his refusal to allow them to proceed. They returned with some difficulty through Northern Thibet, wintering 16,000 feet above the level of the sea. The expedition expects to reach Kiakhta, Siberia, in August, by the way of Alashanurgu."

A Paris dispatch says: "The irreconcilables have a project for organizing a large demonstration at Père la Chaise over the graves of the Communists who fell in May, 1871. Should any ill advised Communists persevere in the scheme the Government will take measures to preserve order."

A St. Petersburg correspondent says: "The beetle which ravaged the crops in Poltava and Ekaterinoslav in 1878 has been found in large numbers in a larval state, and the peasants fear to sow their Spring crops." The same correspondent says: "The greatest alarm prevails in Tiflis in consequence of the discovery of locust-eggs. Unless they are exterminated before their final development, a famine throughout the Caucasus will be inevitable."

A fire last night destroyed Nos. 80 to 84 Gray's Inn-road and No. 25 Partpool-lane. The Police state that 14 persons are missing.

A dispatch from Madrid to Reuter's Telegram Company, says that King Alfonso has signed a decree authorizing the laying of a telegraph cable between Cuba and Jamaica.

At the inquiry before the Board of Trade, yesterday, into the Tay bridge disaster, Mr. Edward Gilkes, one of the managing Directors and a member of the firm of contractors by which the bridge was erected, said that in his opinion none of the columns shifted from their base-plates previous to the accident, whom he believed was caused by the carriage of the guard's van leaving the line and coming in collision with the leeward girder. Counsel then addressed the court in behalf of Sir Thomas Bouch, the engineer of the structure.

ROME, May 8.—Signors Ricasoli and Peruzzi, formerly members of the Italian Ministry, have announced their withdrawal from political life.

MADRID, May 8.—In the Chamber of Deputies to-day, Señor Vivar called attention to the statement that an American steamer had been chartered for the purpose of conveying munitions of war to Cuba for the insurgents. The Minister of Justice replied that the representative of Spain at Washington possessed the confidence of the Government, and that he would do his duty to his country.

The Porto Rico budget proposes to abolish the 6 per cent. bounty on goods imported direct from producing countries, and to reduce the present import duties 50 per cent.

### *PRINCETON WORK AND PLAY.*

PREPARING FOR COMMENCEMENT—ATHLETIC AND LITERARY CONTESTS.

PRINCETON, N. J., May 8.—The last term of the collegiate year opens with every appearance of activity, both in doors and out. The Seniors enter upon their final examinations in a few days, and are, consequently, confined closely to their rooms and books. It is the custom to give the members of the graduating class two weeks rest between their examinations and Commencement, and, therefore, the Seniors will be through their finals the first week of June, and possibly on May 29. While they are making preparations for Class Day and Commencement, the other classes will be undergoing their annual examinations.

The crew returned this week from Philadelphia, where it has been in training for the intercollegiate race next month. The members feel quite confident of success, and Kennedy, the coach, speaks in the highest terms of the progress made by the boys. He says they pull in good form, a quality which Princeton crews have sadly lacked in former struggles. The men are in fine health and spirits, and give every indication of compelling their opponents to strain every energy if they would defeat them. Their practice on the canal every afternoon is watched with great interest by a large number of the students.

The base-ball nine also gives promise of successful work. It has succeeded in vanquishing several of the best professional nines so far this season, and shows, with the exception of Yale, the best collegiate record. Beginning with Brown to-day, it will play Amherst, Dartmouth, Yale, and Harvard between this time and Commencement, besides going on its New-England tour in the Senior vacation to play the return games.

The two halls for literary purposes—Whig and Clio—are great rivals, and have resorted for years to all laudable expedients in order to lead one another. It has been customary for the Seniors in the halls to leave those institutions a term or two before graduation, and to commemorate their departure by appropriate exercises. Last year Whig Hall varied the custom by introducing theatricals as the graduating feature. A drama, written by one of the members, caricaturing many of the college and hall usages, was performed, and a farce, also original, enlivened the programme. The innovation was so successful that it was repeated this year by the Seniors in Whig, who gave an original performance last Thursday night, to the entire satisfaction of the audience. Of course, only members and graduates of the hall were present, as the society is semi-secret. It is said that Clio is wild with jealousy, and is preparing something to offset the theatrical entertainment furnished by Whig Hall.

### *THEODORE THOMAS GOING ABROAD.*

CINCINNATI, May 8.—Theodore Thomas has secured passage on an ocean steamer that is to leave New-York for Germany on the first Wednesday after the Cincinnati May festival. He intends to make a long visit to his favorite modern composer, Richard Wagner, whose works he has done much to introduce in America. When Mr. Thomas returns, it is understood that he will reorganize his old orchestra, the members of which are anxious to be again under sway of his baton.

### *MAIL SERVICE CHANGES.*

WASHINGTON, May 8.—The Superintendent of Railway Mail Service has ordered through registered pouches between Utica, N. Y., and Cleveland, Ohio, to go into effect on Wednesday, May 12. The pouches are to leave Utica at 4:45 P. M. daily, except Sundays; leave Cleveland at 10:30 P. M. daily, except Saturdays and Sundays, and on Sundays to leave Cleveland at 7:35 A. M.

## THE DUTCH AND THEIR LAND

### *HOLLAND THROUGH A TELESCOPE.*

IN UTRECHT'S CATHEDRAL TOWER—THE WHOLE COUNTRY AT A GLANCE—THE INSPIRATIONS OF DUTCH ARTISTS—CLEVES AND ITS BATHS.

UTRECHT, April 23.—A calm, Spring day; the air soft and balmy as June. We are standing upon the platform of the cathedral tower of Utrecht. Above us play the silver chimes; higher still, in effigy, sits St. Martin on his horse, forming the weather-cock. He may have sat so 800 years ago, for the church was finished in 1015. It is certain that the sculptured saint was there 200 years back, and rode through one of the fiercest storms that ever swept over Holland. The nave of Utrecht Cathedral fell in during that historic hurricane, Aug. 1, 1674. It was never restored. Therefore the tower stands alone, a wide, open, unoccupied space still separating it from the remainder of the church. We have climbed 833 steps to reach the spot, from whence we gaze upon the splendid Gothic remnant of the famous cathedral.

Utrecht, the capital of the Dutch Province of that name, with its 61,000 inhabitants, is at my feet. The people moving here and there are pigmies in appearance. They are the representatives of men who were giants of intellect and courage. Utrecht itself, under this clear Spring sky, is a city of Old-World houses, with red pointed roofs, not the dull color of a mid-England town, but a bright, rich red, relieved here and there with a blue-slated Gothic gable. There are gardens planned like geometrical puzzles, variegated with patches of tulips, "a blaze of glory." Cherry-trees in full blossom give you contrasts of pure white flowers. A long, sparkling gleam of water cuts off one side of the town from the other. It is a bit of the old Rhine, now a canal crossed by many bridges. On its banks there are willows that droop to the margin of the silent highway. Also, there are houses that have their doors opening upon the water, as in Venice, with low arches that give out black shadows. Moored by them are two flat bulky barges. One has a gilded prow that shines and burns in the sun. Look beyond that gilded barge on the other side of the bank! You will see a gray, grim tower, from which clumps of ivy are hanging in green luxuriance. That is a relic of the Romans. They were here before Christ was born in Bethlehem. Many remains testify to their occupation of the site upon which these red houses below us are built. Motley will tell you how the Vreeburg, from which the square on our left takes its name, was destroyed in the war of independence 300 years ago. It was in this city that the celebrated Peace of Utrecht, which terminated the Spanish war of succession, was concluded, April 11, 1713. In the vaults beneath the church we are looking down upon are the hearts of the German Emperors Conrad II. and Henry V., who died here. To the east of the tower, upon which we are standing, still stands the house where Pope Adrian VI. was born in 1459, and close by is the famous Maliebaan, a triple avenue of lime-trees, which Louis IV. commanded his armies to spare when they raided this locality. The trees in Holland offer a perpetual topic of wonder to the stranger. There are miles and miles of green avenues in all directions. Most of the roads are planted, and nearly every road in Holland is of great length, stretching away over vast flats and appearing in each picture to end in a leafy cul de sac, though this is only an optical illusion. One is hardly in a position to realize the beauties of the great Dutch painters until one has seen the country itself, the characteristics of which are so exquisitely idealized by the Dutch artists, who have done as much as the Dutch sailors and soldiers of the past to make Holland famous. I wonder if those heroic men who have found a modern Homer in Motley allowed their women to till the soil and carry burdens. It is one of the painful sights of modern Holland and civilized Germany to see women carrying loads on their heads and shoulders while their husbands look on with pipes in their mouths; and it is nearly as sad a thing to meet on every highway dogs harnessed to carts and doing the work of horses and donkeys. But Europe is full of strange anomalies, and Holland has the one great virtue that is next to godliness so fully developed that we can afford to make allowances for her failings. The houses of the Dutch are the cleanest in the world. The old English City of Durham has been likened unto a gentleman who has been down a coal mine, and, coming back again, has forgotten to wash his face. Holland is a sturdy, broad shouldered fellow, who is always washing his face and cleaning his boots. There is no exception anywhere in Holland to this universal cleanliness. Every day is washing day in Dutchland, without, however, the smell of soap-suds in the houses. The linen is scoured and bleached out of doors; and the saying that a place is so clean that you might eat off the floor is literally applicable to Holland. And what artistic color there is in the dear sleepy old cities! Brown sails on the canals, green railings before the doors, shutters of blue and brown and green, old glass, quaint steps, bulging windows, women in russet gowns and quaint white head-dresses, men in jack-boots, and children with worsted caps; you can see in the people of to-day the men and women of the genre painters, the women and children of De Hooch in the houses of De Hooch, the Dutch models of Ostade and Teniers, and the splendid "effects" of Rembrandt. Truly a wonderful country, less changed, I should imagine, than any the sun looks down upon in this nineteenth century!

While I am making these notes the sacristan brings me a telescope, for the use of which I pay him 15 cents, the charge fixed by his ecclesiastical superiors. My "Baedeker's Guide," which, like its French rival, "Le Guide Conty," only gives me bare tantalizing facts, simply informs me that from this platform through a telescope I can see "almost the whole of Holland, and part of Guelders and N. Brabant." The sacristan is a polite and obliging person, and with his telescope and the aid of his experience I am enabled to pick out the chief landmarks of this wonderful "north-western corner of the vast plain which extends from the German Ocean to the Ural Mountains, occupied by the countries called the Netherlands," to quote the first lines of the best historical work of this century, "The Rise of the Dutch Republic," by John Lothrop Motley. To be great and powerful a nation need not occupy a vast territory. Russia, with its unwieldy empire, is a dwarf in history compared with Holland, nearly all of whose land and water can be seen through a telescope from the cathedral tower of Utrecht. It is not to be wondered at that England feels a tremor of anxious sympathy with the Dutch as often as there comes about a rumor of the desire of Germany to annex the land of the Hollanders, which is one of the links in the chain of human progress and liberty forged in the glorious revolutions which maintained the right in Holland, Zealand, England, and the United States of America during the sixteenth, seventeenth, and eighteenth centuries. And you may literally see nearly all this remarkable country of Holland through a telescope, standing on the tower of Utrecht Cathedral. The reader should not forget this the next time he finds himself in Europe. You can take a ticket from London to Harwich at 7 in the evening, step on board a steamer at 9, and be at Utrecht the following day. In the meantime take up your map of Holland, find Utrecht, draw an imaginary circle with a radius of about 30 miles from the centre, and follow the sacristan's telescope.

Yonder, away toward the south, is Hertogenbösch, the fortified capital of Brabant, with 25,000 inhabitants. It is situated on the Dommel, the Aa, and the Zuid-Willems Canal, and its railway crosses the River Maas, whose brown sails and broad Dutch beams have given inspiration to many a marine artist. At almost every important exhibition in London you will find reminiscences of the Maas. Cast your eyes eastwardly, and you will see the towers of Rotterdam, a city, in some parts, more artistic than Venice itself. Intersected with canals, Rotterdam has many points of view that suggest the Italian city of the sea. The water-ways are so deep that vessels of heavy tonnage discharge their cargoes in the very heart of the quaint, busy old town. Opposite the quarter called the Boompjes, (concerning which look up ...

# The New-York Times.

VOL. XXIX........NO. 8956. NEW-YORK, MONDAY, MAY 24, 1880. PRICE FOUR CENTS.

## THE TEXAS PACIFIC BRIBES

*PROOFS THAT MR. GEORGE'S CHARGES ARE TRUE.*

HOW COL. SCOTT'S CORRUPTION FUND WAS DISBURSED — EX-CONGRESSMAN PARSONS, OF CLEVELAND, ONE OF HIS AGENTS—MORTON C. HUNTER ALSO IMPLICATED—LETTERS FROM GEN. NEWELL, MR. PARSONS, AND OTHERS, TELLING A PART OF THE STORY OF SHAME.

WASHINGTON, May 23.—Just how guilty the Democratic portion of the House Pacific Railroads Committee has been in refusing to investigate the charges of corruption in the passage of the original Texas Pacific Railroad grant can be accurately determined, now that the facts submitted to Chairman McLane are sufficiently known. Only a portion of the facts submitted have been ascertained by THE TIMES's correspondent, but with what has been thus gathered, it is hard to understand how the Democratic majority of this committee should have decided that the subject was one that was beyond their jurisdiction without special authority from the House, and then take no steps to procure such authority. The question of extending the time of the grant to the Texas Pacific Company is one that is pending. If it can be shown that the original contract was obtained through fraud, the original contract surely falls. It is understood that a majority of this committee are already pledged to this extension, and for that reason will not go into anything likely to impair the prospects of their desired object.

It appears that Mr. George submitted to Mr. McLane evidence showing that R. C. Parsons—Dick Parsons—a former member of Congress from Ohio, and recently editor and proprietor of the Cleveland *Herald*, was the man who disbursed the land grant bonds among members to the amount of $1,000,000. This is shown in a letter from Parsons bearing as recent a date as April 20, 1880. It appears that Parsons had a contract with Col. Thomas A. Scott, upon which he was to be paid in land grant bonds 10 per cent. of the bonds disbursed by him. This would give him, if the contract had been carried out, as originally drawn up, 100 bonds of $1,000 each. Parsons, in the letter mentioned above, restates the terms of this contract, and further adds that Scott has not yet paid him, only $8,000 having been advanced on account. In the full letter shown to the committee, only an extract of which is given below, Mr. Parsons states what he did with the $8,000 advanced him. Three thousand dollars he placed in his own pockets and $5,000 he divided between two Government officers, one of whom at present holds a high position in this city. The $5,000 paid to these officers was for minor services connected with securing the passage of the subsidy. It appears that Col. Scott, in disbursing large sums in bonds among members and Senators, was not so careful about paying his agents. Although they had written contracts with him for a percentage of the bonds disbursed, yet these contracts were not of a nature that could be enforced in a court, and, as a part of the general system of dishonesty, refusal to pay the man who had done his work came as a matter of course.

Mr. McLane, when shown the letter of Parsons, asked: "Who is Parsons?" He was told that he was a former member of Congress from Ohio. Mr. McLane examined the Congressional records and found that Mr. Parsons was a member of the Congress succeeding that in which the subsidy was passed. Mr. McLane was also shown evidence criminating three Senators, one of whom is at present a member of the Senate. Mr. McLane took pains to ascertain this fact before deciding that no investigation should be had. The two officers who were paid $5,000 by Mr. Parsons performed the service of holding $62,000 in trust for the three Senators, among whom it was finally divided. This constitutes the entire amount of their services.

Gen. Newell, who is responsible for the George letter, has made answer to the statement made by Bond and recently published. He has prepared an interesting statement, covering some of the charges made against him by Bond. He gives first Parsons's letter, to show that Scott had made a similar contract with Parsons, and then quotes a letter from Col. Grafton, of the respectable legal firm of Grafton, Payne & Ladd, who witnessed the contract made between Scott and Newell. Gen. Newell's statement is as follows:

Mr. Bond, in his interview of the 21st, says: "The real agent in this scheme to black-mail us or prevent any legislation favorable to the Texas Pacific is one J. J. Newell." What Mr. Bond calls black-mailing on my part is this: I did call on him and other members of the board on the 11th and other days, and demanded of them the sum of $20,000, with interest for five years, not on a pretended contract with Morton, as stated by Bond, but on a contract with Col. Thomas A. Scott, in his capacity as President of the Texas Pacific Road. This I will show further on. I will now take up the matter as set forth in George's letter of the 17th. My connection with the parties began in May, 1870. The 3d of July, 1870, the Texas Pacific—not the El Paso, as stated by Bond—bill passed the Senate. I speak of the bill known as the Howard-Kellogg bill. By an amendment of Senator Nye, the Fremont incorporators were put in the Texas Pacific bill, which gave the Fremont interest control of the organization. Between the time of the passage of the bill in the Senate, viz., July 3, 1870, and the time it was acted on in the House, Fremont transferred his entire interest to Marshall O. Roberts, of New-York. Fears were entertained that the bill from the Senate could not pass the House, and arrangements were made to overcome the opposition. It was then that an arrangement was made between Roberts and R. C. Parsons for the distribution of $1,000,000 of land grant mortgage bonds of the Texas Pacific Road. Parsons was to have 10 per cent. for disbursing the bonds. The question is, did Parsons disburse the bonds? If he did, then there was due him $100,000 of said bonds. The following extract of a letter dated April 20, 1880, is good reading:

OFFICE OF THE CLEVELAND HERALD, EDITORIAL ROOMS, April 20, 1880.

Your letter received. I supposed you had long since received your fees and that I was the only one Mr. Scott had declined to pay. I had a written contract with the original parties for 100 bonds. I have it still. Mr. S. paid me $5,000 at one time, $3,000 at another, and I gave him a receipt for $8,000. R. C. PARSONS.

To J. J. NEWELL.

Is it true that I was trying to black-mail Col. Scott, or was I endeavoring to collect a debt due to me by him as per an agreement. Let the following letters and telegram speak for themselves:

WASHINGTON, D. C., Jan. 5, 1873.

*J. J. Newell, Adrian, Mich.:*

Come here. Want to see you. B. F. GRAFTON.

LANSING, Mich., Jan. 7, 1873.

*B. F. Grafton, Washington, D. C.:*

Senatorial caucus to-night. Can I get a settlement by coming to Washington? J. J. NEWELL.

WASHINGTON, D. C., Jan. 8, 1873.

*J. J. Newell, Lansing, Mich.:*

You can put claim in shape to secure it. B. F. GRAFTON.

WASHINGTON, April 12, 1880.

*Col. J. J. Newell, Washington, D. C.:*

COLONEL: In reply to your inquiry I have to say that I was present at an interview between you and Col. Thomas A. Scott at Willard's Hotel, in this city, in the month of January, 1873, and the matter of the indebtedness of the Texas Pacific Railroad for services rendered by you was there considered, and Col. Scott, in behalf of said company, agreed to pay you for such services $20,000 in the land grant bonds of said company. The payment was to be made after the adjournment of Congress, but was not conditional on obtaining any legislation. B. F. GRAFTON.

It was about this time that the Texas and Pacific was organizing their forces to make a raid on Congress for a moneyed subsidy, and were very profuse in promising to settle up for past work and work to be done in the future. What was Mr. Scott settling with me at that time? The following letter can throw some light on the subject:

WASHINGTON, D. C., April 21, 1880.

*J. J. Newell, Esq.:*

DEAR SIR: In answer to yours of the 15th inst., in regard to the old unsettled matters of the Texas and Pacific Railroad Company, and whether contracts were made with yourself and others, I have to state that contracts were made in 1870 and approved by Gen. Fremont, by which yourself and others and E. W. Rice and myself were to have in payment, for money expended and professional services rendered, $50,000 each in the bonds of the company, so soon as the company could reasonably issue the same. Mr. Roberts told me soon after, he had sold his interest in the road to Mr. Scott, that one of the conditions of the sale with Col. Scott was that those claims should be paid, and that Col. Scott would settle them as soon as he could get in working order. Yours truly, G. H. GIDDINGS.

Having now shown the right I have to make a claim on the Texas and Pacific, and shown the falsity of the charge of black-mail made by Mr. Bond, I will rest the case until I can get a committee of Congress to investigate, with power to send for persons and papers. Then I will show all that Mr. George claims in his letter to the committee will be made manifest. J. J. NEWELL.

Mr. G. H. Giddings is a brother of a present member of Congress. Upon the basis of percentages in the contract with Parsons, the gentlemen named in Giddings's letter must have disbursed another $1,500,000 in bonds. Bonds about that time must have been scattered about with royal profusion, for it appears that Gen. Morton C. Hunter, who also aided in working this grant through, received a large sum. Hunter was afterward a member of Congress from Indiana. The fact that he held $100,000 in these land grant bonds was brought out in a local court in Texas, where a suit was brought against Hunter by H. Clay Hynson. The attention of Congress will be invited to-morrow to Mr. Newell's statement. It is not proposed to importune any member to introduce a resolution of investigation, but to wait and see if there is any member who has no railroad interests to serve who will venture to ask for an investigation. Here is given the personal testimony of three gentlemen, backed by one of the most reputable lawyers in Washington, that Scott did contract, in large amounts, with agents, to influence legislation. Many investigations here have been started upon a smaller basis. The Crédit Mobilier investigation did not develop more than this promises.

## *CONGRESS AND THE UTE TREATY.*

THE PASSAGE OF THE RATIFICATION BILL AN IMPERATIVE NECESSITY—AN EXECUTIVE MESSAGE ON THE SUBJECT EXPECTED.

WASHINGTON, May 23.—From present indications, it is reasonably certain that the final adjournment of Congress will not take place until the Marshals bill, the Electoral Count bill, and the Ute Treaty Ratification bill have been passed. The Marshals and the Ute bills have passed the Senate, and are now on the calendar of the House, while the Electoral Count bill is pending in the Senate. The latter will undoubtedly lead to a protracted discussion, and if it be decided to pass it before adjournment the dissolution of Congress cannot occur on May 31. The other two bills mentioned can be readily passed this week if the House will take them up for consideration. Wednesday night next is fixed for the consideration of the Ute bill, and the importance which attaches to it should induce the House to dispose of it without unnecessary delay. It is known that the President regards the passage of this bill as essential to the preservation of peace with the Ute Indians, and it is intimated that he will send a message to the House to-morrow directing the attention of that body to the threatening attitude of the Indians in Colorado toward the whites, in consequence of the preparations being made to penetrate the Indian reservation, and urging the early passage of a measure to secure the ratification of the treaty negotiated some time ago between the Government and the head men of the several Ute bands. The failure to pass this bill will certainly result in hostilities with the Colorado Indians, which will cost many lives and the expenditure of several million dollars, the entire responsibility for which will be attributable to the criminal neglect of the House of Representatives. There is no serious opposition to the passage of the bill, and if a quorum of members will attend the session on Wednesday night it is possible that it will be passed. Should the passage of this bill fail in consequence of the absence of a quorum, the absentees should be held responsible by the country for the terrible consequences which are certain to follow.

## *A MUSICAL ROW IN CINCINNATI.*

MR. THOMAS LEAVES MUCH TROUBLE BEHIND HIM—AN OUTLOOK THAT IS NOT HOPEFUL FOR "THE MUSICAL CENTRE."

CINCINNATI, May 23.—Theodore Thomas took his final departure from Cincinnati last night, leaving behind a rich legacy of trouble in musical circles. His unexpected announcement, at the closing concert of the festival, that the festival chorus would hereafter be under the leadership of Michael Brand, took all by surprise. Brand is a young man, a violoncello-player in Thomas's orchestra, and has conducted one or two seasons of the orchestra concerts. He possesses none of the qualities required for a leader of a great chorus, and the friends of the college and festival are inquiring what it means. Otto Singer, who has held the post under Thomas for five years, has been summarily dismissed. He stood by the college in the recent trouble, and his friends say that Thomas's appointment of Brand was a blow aimed at the college. The matter promises to produce a great deal of discord. None of the projects to endow a permanent orchestra in Cincinnati, with Thomas at its head, are making headway. There is $25,000 in the festival treasury, and a citizen has offered to add $7,000 to it providing it is used to establish an orchestra; but as the income on this amount would not support such an orchestra as is proposed for more than a week in the year, the plan is not making hopeful progress. The festival receipts were $52,000; expenses, $38,000; profits about $14,000.

### *A CLERGYMAN EXONERATED.*

JAMESTOWN, N. Y., May 23.—After an exhaustive examination of the allegations of adultery against the Rev. Dr. Peltz, the principal testimony being sworn affidavits, his innocence has been thoroughly established. The committee of investigation and the church are unanimous. In the judgment of the church, however, he should abstain from preaching until he has recovered from the effect of the rumors.

### *NEW-YORK SPORTSMEN'S ASSOCIATION.*

SENECA FALLS, May 23.—The annual convention of the New-York State Sportsmen's Association for the Protection of Fish and Game will be held in this village to-morrow evening. The State shoot will begin on Tuesday morning. Thirteen thousand birds are now in the coops. The prize-list is the largest and most valuable ever offered by the association, and all the indications point to a large and successful meeting.

### *END OF A LONG DROUGHT.*

FREDERICKSBURG, Va., May 23.—General and plentiful rains throughout the Tide-water and Piedmont districts of Virginia for two days past have ended the drought that has prevailed for nearly two months. Corn-planting and other farming operations have been greatly delayed and the oat crop will be short.

## A DEMOCRATIC DARK HORSE

*SENATOR DAVID DAVIS PLACES HIS VIEWS ON PAPER.*

A LETTER PLAINLY INTENDED TO ADVANCE THE WRITER'S POLITICAL INTERESTS—THE THIRD TERM AND THE REPUBLICAN POSITION CONDEMNED—VARIOUS OTHER TOPICS OF THE DAY DISCUSSED.

WASHINGTON, May 23.—The Hon. David Davis, of Illinois, sometimes called an Independent in politics, but better known at present as a "dark horse" in the race for the Democratic Presidential nomination, has become alarmed at the support which ex-President Grant has received from the Republican Party, and at the many indications of the success of that party in the approaching election. He has, therefore, given to the public, in the form of a letter to the Hon. O. H. Browning, of Illinois, an attack upon the third term and "the Republican demand for a strong Government." He adds his opinions upon several other public questions, including civil service reform, the power of corporations, subsidies, the tariff, troops at the polls, and public economy. But these cannot obscure the main purpose of the document. Judge Davis, like some other Senators, who openly bear the name of Democrat, probably sees that the nomination of the ex-President is equivalent to the defeat of the Democratic Party. He may hereafter reach the conclusion expressed yesterday by a Democratic Senator from the South, who said that the ex-President would be nominated and elected, and that the Democratic Party could not prevent his election. The following is Judge Davis's letter, and the letter from Mr. Browning, to which it is a reply:

I.

QUINCY, Ill., May 6.

MY DEAR JUDGE: The approaching close of the present session of Congress will, it is to be feared, leave questions unsettled which are of large public interest, and which materially affect the peace and the prosperity of the Union. Many of your friends in this State and throughout the West had hoped, and indeed had expected, that an opportunity would have been offered in the Senate, by which your views on these matters could have been made known to the country. It unfortunately happens, amid the distractions of party and the strifes of rival ambitions, that the voice of statesmanship is hushed too often when wise counsel is most needed. This was never more true than at the present time. The country is just emerging from a long period of trial and suffering. The people seek rest from angry discords, and desire to avoid a repetition of the perils through which they have passed. They crave good government, stability, and perfect reconciliation between the sections. The statesman who can achieve these great objects will be blessed as a public benefactor. I have ventured to embody, in the form of inquiries, appended to this letter, some of the subjects upon which your opinions are desired, if it be agreeable to you to comply with the request of a large body of voters and friends, without distinction of party. Truly your friend,

O. H. BROWNING.

Hon. DAVID DAVIS, United States Senate.

II.

WASHINGTON, May 14, 1880.

MY DEAR SIR: I have had the pleasure to receive your letter of the 6th inst. As a constituent, a friend, and an honored citizen of Illinois, you have a perfect right to ask for my views on public questions, and I have no hesitation in expressing them, taking the inquiries in the order presented:

*Peace in the Union.*—Permanent prosperity and fraternal fellowship are only to be attained by silencing sectional strife. A faithful adherence to the Constitution and all the amendments, strict observance of the laws in conformity therewith, and equal rights and equal protection for every citizen in every part of the Republic, will soon end the discords that have too long vexed the country and injured its material welfare. The people are weary of agitation and want peace.

*Centralization.*—The Constitution wisely defines the respective limits of the Federal and State Governments, under a happy and harmonious system, wherein each is independent in its appropriate sphere, and both operate concurrently to protect the integrity and stability of the Union. Any encroachment of one on the distinctive domain of the other necessarily dislocates the machinery of the Constitution and involves danger to the whole body politic. In fact, every departure from the great charter of liberty and law is attended with peril. The demand made by adherents of one of the great parties for a strong Government means substantially a centralized Government, destructive of home rule in the States, and the very reverse of what Mr. Lincoln well described as a Government of the people, by the people, and for the people. Carried to its logical conclusion, such a change would finally overthrow the Republic.

*The Third Term.*—An innovation upon the sanctified traditions of the Presidency, first established by the example of Washington, is urgently demanded by a powerful interest in the Republican Party. If the limitation of two terms, heretofore universally accepted, be destroyed, the way to a self-perpetuating Presidency will be opened by the use and abuse of the enormous public patronage. Break down this barrier, and an end of the experiment of republican government looms up darkly as the cost of a fatal concession.

*Great Corporations.*—The rapid growth of corporate power and the malign influence which it exerts by combinations on the National and State Legislatures, is a well-grounded cause of alarm. A struggle is impending in the near future between this overgrown power, with its vast ramifications all over the Union and a hard grip on much of the political machinery on the one hand, and the people in an unorganized condition on the other, for control of the Government. It will be watched by every patriot with intense anxiety.

*Civil Service.*—Neither laws nor commissions created under them will effectually reform the many and glaring abuses of the civil service. The former have been constantly evaded, and the latter are powerless for good. An honest Executive, bent on real and not simulated reform, has abundant authority to make it effective everywhere, if he has the capacity to see his duty, and the courage to perform it.

*Subsidies.*—Experience has demonstrated that subsidies in any form are sources of corruption, and ought to be forbidden. Private enterprises that depend for success upon legislation procured by venal agencies do not deserve public favor.

*Public Lands.*—More than 150,000,000 acres of valuable lands, and more than $100,000,000, principal and interest, have been voted by Congress to railroad corporations. The remaining lands should be sacredly reserved for cultivators of the soil, so that the laboring man shall have a chance to improve his condition, and to open up a future for his children away from the seductions of the great cities.

*Revision of the Tariff.*—Tariff practically means taxation, and all taxation not equitably adjusted is odious. While the interest on an oppressive public debt, the pensions earned with the blood of soldiers and sailors who fought for the Union, and the regular expenses of carrying on the Government are to be met, duties on imports must continue to furnish one of the sources of revenue. So long as those duties are levied, manufacturers will be benefited according to the degree or the mode in which the duties may be distributed. The existing tariff is regarded as a confused mass of incongruities and monopolies, created by special legislation and open to constant fraud on the revenue. It taxes the consumer heavily on those articles especially that are most needed by the toiling masses. It taxes every newspaper, every school-book, every Bible, and the salt of the working man, with gross injustice, because the poor pretense of revenue does not exist to cover the wrong. A revision, therefore, which shall be at once searching and fair is demanded, and should be promptly and efficiently made.

*The Public Debt.*—The debt of the United States in round numbers is two thousand millions, deducting the hoarded coin in the Treasury. The interest upon it last year was over one hundred millions. These are appalling figures. The rapid extinction of this debt is to be desired, first, because it diminishes present burdens, and for the additional reason that one of the effects of a personal national debt is to create a preferred class to live on incomes and free from taxes under our laws. Having the protection of the Government at home and abroad, they would contribute nothing to its support.

*Economy.*—It is practicable by co-operation between the Executive and Congress to reduce the public expenditures many millions annually, without impairing the efficiency of the public service. Retrenchment is needed for the reduction of taxes, but it is also needed because, properly administered, it would become a potent factor in reforming the civil service.

*Elections.*—The ballot-box should be the safeguard of the Republic, for it is intended to express the free will of a free people. Therefore elections ought to be exempt from the presence of any menacing force, and to be free from the contamination of corrupt returning boards. No party deserves confidence that seeks ascendency by striking down honest suffrage, either by the use of troops, by fraud, or by intimidation. It would not be proper for me to express any opinion upon measures pending or proposed in Congress. My votes will speak for themselves at the fitting time.

Having thus freely answered your inquiries, I may add, in conclusion, that my support will be cheerfully given to any candidate for President who, in good faith, will strive to carry out this general line of policy, which, in my judgment, is of far more importance than the ambition of any man, or even the success of any party. As ever, your friend, DAVID DAVIS.

The Hon. O. H. BROWNING, Quincy, Ill.

## *RAILROAD THIEVES RUN DOWN.*

AN IMPORTANT CAPTURE NEAR SCRANTON—A DANGEROUS SYSTEM OF DISABLING RAILROAD CARS.

SCRANTON, Penn., May 22.—A desperate gang of railroad thieves, whose operations along the lines of the Delaware and Hudson Canal Company, and the Delaware, Lackawanna, and Western Railroad Company have been the cause of considerable alarm among officers and train hands during the past few months, have just been captured in this city. Their thieving consisted of stealing the brass seats and bearings from the cars, and then disposing of them as old brass in the junk-shops of New-York and Philadelphia. Within three months the Delaware and Hudson Company have lost from their cars in this valley 600 brass seats, valued at $2 each. These "seats" or bearings are constructed on the newest and most approved principle, and the brass of which they are made retails for 22 cents a pound in the city junk-shops. The loss of the Delaware, Lackawanna and Western Company has been even greater than that of the Delaware and Hudson Company. The former has lost more than 1,000 of these brass seats, and sustained greater damage from the robbery than the intrinsic worth of the property stolen. So frequent did the removal of car seats and bearings become that the train hands were actually afraid to undertake a trip lest some car in a long coal or freight train should develop some disabled part and culminate in a wreck, involving loss of life and limb. The Delaware and Hudson Company at length determined upon breaking up the system of robbery, and placed a number of detectives along its line. A short time before midnight, Friday night, one of the company's men, W. H. McDonald, while on duty near the Marvine Colliery, on the outskirts of this city, saw two men stealing out from the shubbery by the track. They adjusted a "jack" under a car-wheel and deliberately proceeded to remove its brass bearings. The detective immediately pounced upon the thieves, who fled, while the officer kept up a running fire in their trail, and threatened to take their lives unless they surrendered. One of the thieves, a junk-dealer named P. H. Coon, weakened after Detective McDonald had fired the third shot. The officer warned him that unless he halted the next shot would be fatal. Coon was brought before Alderman Roesler to-day. Several of the Delaware and Hudson Company's brass bearings were found in his possession and identified by Superintendent Manville, who appeared at the hearing. A check-book was found in Coon's possession, showing that he had paid his confederates large sums of money from time to time, and upon the information contained therein, an accomplice named W. H. Bond was arrested. Bond is a notorious bank-breaker, having been arrested for complicity in the Carbondale Bank robbery nearly five years ago, when Cashier Statt was bound and gagged and the vaults rifled of $20,000. The detectives are on the trail of the other members of the gang, who are supposed to be scattered all along the valley, and a number of arrests are expected soon.

### *GEN. GRANT WILL NOT WITHDRAW.*

CHICAGO, May 23.—A special dispatch to the *Tribune* from Galena, Ill., says: "The Galena *Gazette*, whose editor is a personal friend of Gen. Grant and knows whereof he asserts, will publish the following to-morrow: 'An item has been going the rounds of the press asserting that George W. Childs, of the Philadelphia *Ledger*, had stated that Gen. Grant would order his name withdrawn from the contest at the National Convention at Chicago. Neither George W. Childs nor any one else has authority for making such an assertion. Gen. Grant's name has never gone before the public as a candidate for the Presidency by any word or act of his own, and he most certainly will not order his name withdrawn. A very large class of American people have chosen to make him their candidate, and if the Republican National Convention at Chicago sees fit to tender him the nomination, he will not decline it. This we know to be a fact, and we publish it because it is well that the Republicans of the country should cease to hold the matter in doubt."

### *THE BANKRUPT CORPORATIONS.*

PHILADELPHIA, May 23.—There have been no new developments in the affairs of the Reading Railroad Company. President Gowen still declines to made any statement, and says that until matters are straightened out it will do no good to talk to the public. As far as can be ascertained, there have been no additional suspensions of brokers, and it is thought there will be no more. Well-informed men think if Trustees are appointed to take charge of the road the company will be able to clear itself in a few years.

### *FROM THE SAND LOTS.*

SAN FRANCISCO, May 23.—Resolutions were passed at the Sand Lots to-day indorsing the action of the Greenback wing of the State Convention. An attempt was made in the Board of Ward Presidents to condemn said action by resolutions, but after debate, the resolutions were ruled out of order.

### *THE MAINE DEMOCRACY.*

PORTLAND, May 23.—The Democrats of Portland have decided to urge the claims of Bion Bradbury for delegate at large to the Cincinnati Convention at the State Convention at Bangor. It is reported they will urge a local option plank in the platform.

### *THE MISSOURI DEMOCRACY.*

ST. LOUIS, May 23.—Well-informed Democrats to-night claim that the State Convention will contain a large majority of candidates favorable to Tilden.

### *END OF THE OMAHA STRIKE.*

OMAHA, May 23.—The strike at the smelting works ended to-day. A conference was held between Gov. Nance, the Smelting Works Company, and a committee from the strikers. The company had previously offered $1 50 for nine hours' work for common laborers. This afternoon the company offered $1 65 for 10 hours' work, and agreed to make no black lists. This was accepted by the strikers, who will all go to work to-morrow morning. The Government troops have been sent back to Fort Omaha and the Militia ordered to disperse immediately.

## GEN. GRANT FOR PRESIDENT

*THE CERTAINTY OF HIS CHOICE BY THE CHICAGO CONVENTION.*

DIVISION OF THE NATIONAL DELEGATES AS SHOWN BY THEMSELVES AND THE STATEMENTS OF TRUSTWORTHY CORRESPONDENTS—STRENGTH OF THE VARIOUS CANDIDATES IN CONVENTION—GEN. GRANT ASSURED OF 387 VOTES, A CLEAN MAJORITY, ON THE FIRST BALLOT—A CAREFUL ESTIMATE OF THE OUTCOME OF AN EXCITING CANVASS.

Republican conventions for the purpose of electing delegates to the National Convention, which will meet in Chicago next week (Wednesday) to nominate a candidate for the Presidency, have been held in all the States except Louisiana and Colorado. The convention in Louisiana begins to-day, that in Colorado on Tuesday of this week, and the Territory of Idaho has not yet been heard from. It will thus be seen that 732 out of the 756, or whole number of delegates who will compose the Chicago Convention, have already been chosen, and it is now possible, with something like accuracy, to make an estimate of the relative strength of the different candidates whose claims will be brought before the National body. Such an estimate is here presented.

This table has been prepared with great care from statements made by special correspondents of THE TIMES, and from advices received at this office directly from delegates to the National Convention themselves. In cases where there has been doubt, the benefit of that doubt has invariably been given to the weaker candidates. The column of remarks, which is a new feature in tables of this kind, will be found instructive, and accurately represents the position and action of the various States in their conventions.

The figures of this estimate divide the delegates as follows: Grant, 364; Blaine, 209; Sherman, 81; Edmunds, 37; Windom, 10; Washburne, 4; doubtful, 27; total—732.

It will be noticed that of the 70 delegates from New-York, 62 are put down for Grant, 2 for Sherman, and 6 for Blaine. In reference to this apportionment, while some days ago it seemed possible, or even probable, that there might have been as many as 10 or 13 delegates from this State who would have declined to vote for Gen. Grant, it has become known within the past week that not more than 6, and perhaps not more than 5, of them will now vote against him in the National Convention, but in order to avoid any possible charge of unfairness, 8 votes are given against him.

The Pennsylvania delegation is given solid to Gen. Grant. As for the reported break in that State, there never was any such disaffection there, as was represented for a very obvious purpose. It may be said briefly, as the truth of that matter, that the intention of the Blaine managers was to create an impression in New-York and other States that a large number of the Pennsylvania delegates would break away from Grant and for Blaine. It was hoped by this desperate scheme to induce New-York delegates to declare themselves for Blaine in defiance of their instructions in convention, to influence States which had not yet held conventions in their action, and by the reaction of the course of the New-York delegates upon Pennsylvania, to persuade the delegates there to really do what they had been falsely represented to have done long before. The plan worked successfully only so far as to lead astray Senators Robertson and Woodin and two or three other New-York delegates, who now doubtless deeply regret their ill-advised action. Further than that, it is needless to say, the scheme fell flatly through.

In Indiana no votes have been given in this table to Gen. Grant, though his friends claim no less than 10 on the first ballot, and our own advices from that State warrant the belief that he will receive from 4 to 6. But, in the absence of positive information from the delegates themselves, we decline to give him any.

There seems to be some question about Dakota's two delegates, but the preponderance of evidence goes to show that their votes will be cast for Gen. Grant.

In Minnesota, which instructed for Senator Windom, it is a significant fact that the second choice of the delegates is for Gen. Grant—a fact attested by citizens of that State who are personally anything but favorable to his nomination. It has already been pointed out in THE TIMES that of the other candidates themselves Senator Edmunds and Mr. Washburne are in favor of Gen. Grant, and that not only among their supporters, but even among those of Senator Blaine and Secretary Sherman, there is little evidence of an anti-Grant or anti-third-term sentiment except in so far as Gen. Grant is their rival for Presidential honors.

It remains to say that of the delegates who have been set down as doubtful, at a moderate estimate, at least one-half will vote for Gen. Grant. Nor is it at all unlikely that quite a number of the colored delegates whom the Sherman agents have succeeded in securing in the South will, when they get to Chicago, see the hopelessness of their cause before the Convention, and unite their fortunes with the winning side.

Advices from Colorado make it probable that Colorado's delegates will vote for Gen. Grant.

As for Louisiana, there seems little doubt that there will be two delegations sent from that State to Chicago, and, as the fight there is a bitter one, most likely it will not be possible to determine the character of the Louisiana delegation until the National body itself decides the contest. Without counting that delegation, after reviewing the entire ground and giving more than every reasonable claim to the opposition, we cannot see how Gen. Grant can fail to receive 387 votes on the first ballot at Chicago, or 8 more votes than are necessary to secure his nomination.

| States. | Remarks. | Grant. | Sherman. | Blaine. | Edmunds. | Washburne. | Windom. | Doubtful Del. against. | Total votes Del. |
|---|---|---|---|---|---|---|---|---|---|
| Alabama | Delegates pledged and instructed for Grant | 20 | .. | .. | .. | .. | .. | .. | 20 |
| Arkansas | Instructions for Grant | 12 | .. | .. | .. | .. | .. | .. | 12 |
| California | Instructions for Blaine | .. | .. | 12 | .. | .. | .. | .. | 12 |
| Connecticut | No instructions | .. | .. | 5 | 3 | 2 | .. | 2 | 12 |
| Delaware | No instructions | .. | .. | 6 | .. | .. | .. | .. | 6 |
| Florida | Instructions for Grant | 8 | .. | .. | .. | .. | .. | .. | 8 |
| Georgia | No instructions | 6 | 8 | 8 | .. | .. | .. | .. | 22 |
| Illinois | Instructions for Grant | 42 | .. | .. | .. | .. | .. | .. | 42 |
| Indiana | Anti-Grant delegates at large appointed by State Committee | .. | 2 | 24 | .. | .. | .. | 4 | 30 |
| Iowa | All delegates instructed, and pledged to Blaine | .. | .. | 22 | .. | .. | .. | .. | 22 |
| Kansas | No instructions; Blaine favorably mentioned; four contesting Grant delegates elected | .. | .. | ? 10 | .. | .. | .. | .. | 10 |
| Kentucky | Instructions for Grant | 24 | .. | .. | .. | .. | .. | .. | 24 |
| Maine | No State Convention | .. | .. | 14 | .. | .. | .. | .. | 14 |
| Maryland | Delegates "requested" to support Blaine by all honorable means | 10 | 2 | 2 | .. | .. | .. | 2 | 16 |
| Massachusetts | No instructions by Convention of the State; Edmunds supported | 2 | .. | .. | 24 | .. | .. | .. | 26 |
| Michigan | Delegates "requested" to support Blaine | 3 | .. | 19 | .. | .. | .. | 19 | 22 |
| Minnesota | Instructions for Senator Windom | .. | .. | .. | .. | .. | 10 | .. | 10 |
| Mississippi | No instructions | 8 | 4 | 2 | .. | .. | .. | 2 | 16 |
| Missouri | Instructions for Grant | 30 | .. | .. | .. | .. | .. | .. | 30 |
| Nebraska | Blaine strongly indorsed | .. | .. | 6 | .. | .. | .. | .. | 6 |
| Nevada | Instructions for Blaine and the unit rule | .. | .. | 6 | .. | .. | .. | .. | 6 |
| New-Hampshire | No instructions | .. | .. | 10 | .. | .. | .. | .. | 10 |
| New-Jersey | No instructions | 1 | 7 | 8 | .. | 2 | .. | .. | 18 |
| New-York | Instructions for Grant | 62 | 2 | 6 | .. | .. | .. | .. | 70 |
| North Carolina | No State Convention; delegates at large all for Sherman | 7 | 11 | .. | .. | .. | .. | 2 | 20 |
| Ohio | No instructions | .. | 44 | .. | .. | .. | .. | .. | 44 |
| Oregon | Instructions for Blaine | .. | .. | 6 | .. | .. | .. | .. | 6 |
| Pennsylvania | Instructions for Grant | 58 | .. | .. | .. | .. | .. | .. | 58 |
| Rhode Island | No instructions | .. | .. | 8 | .. | .. | .. | .. | 8 |
| South Carolina | Delegates pledged and instructed for Grant | 13 | 1 | .. | .. | .. | .. | .. | 14 |
| Tennessee | No instructions | 18 | .. | 6 | .. | .. | .. | .. | 24 |
| Texas | Unit rule recommended, but no candidate named | 14 | .. | .. | .. | .. | .. | 2 | 16 |
| Vermont | Instructions for G. F. Edmunds | .. | .. | .. | 10 | .. | .. | .. | 10 |
| Virginia | Instructions for Grant | 22 | .. | .. | .. | .. | .. | .. | 22 |
| West Virginia | Instructions for Blaine | .. | .. | 10 | .. | .. | .. | .. | 10 |
| Wisconsin | No instructions | .. | .. | 7 | .. | .. | .. | 13 | 20 |
| Arizona | | .. | .. | 2 | .. | .. | .. | .. | 2 |
| Dakota | No instructions | 2 | .. | .. | .. | .. | .. | .. | 2 |
| Dis. of Columbia | No instructions | 1 | .. | 1 | .. | .. | .. | .. | 2 |
| Montana | | .. | .. | 2 | .. | .. | .. | .. | 2 |
| New-Mexico | | .. | .. | 2 | .. | .. | .. | .. | 2 |
| Utah | Blaine delegates chosen, but not instructed by committee; contesting and uninstructed delegates chosen by a convention | .. | .. | 2 | .. | .. | .. | .. | 2 |
| Washington | | .. | .. | 2 | .. | .. | .. | .. | 2 |
| Wyoming | No instructions | 1 | .. | 1 | .. | .. | .. | .. | 2 |
| Total | | 364 | 81 | 209 | 37 | 4 | 10 | 27 | 732 |

## *THE CONTEST IN LOUISIANA.*

FAILURE OF THE SHERMAN AGENTS' COMPROMISE SCHEME—THE GRANT CAUCUS REFUSES TO JOIN IN TREACHERY.

NEW-ORLEANS, May 23.—The Sherman and Blaine men pushed their peculiar tactics here to-day, and made a desperate effort to win by a compromise what they knew they could not win in a contest. As the result of much manœuvring, a conference was arranged between the representatives of the three parties. Taylor Beattie, last Republican candidate for Governor of the State, Pardie, Pitkin, Pinchback, Morey, and Ludeling appeared for Gen. Grant, ex-Gov. Warmoth for Blaine, and Naval Officer Lewis, Collector Badger, Deputy Collector Dumont, and United States District Attorney Leonard for Sherman. The Sherman men evidently had some most effective arguments at command, which the Grant representatives could not withstand, since the latter entered into a conspiracy—compromise they called it—by which it was attempted to deliver over to Sherman and Blaine one half of the Louisiana delegation to Chicago.

The next thing, and the essential one, was to get the Grant party to ratify this compromise. A caucus was called at the head-quarters of the party, and the proposition was submitted for approval. Then the fun began, and the debate which followed was strong and stormy. Beattie, Phinchback, and Pardie urged with all their persuasive power the adoption of the Sherman scheme. Beattie's speech invited criticism, and the colored men who replied to it were not slow to expose its many weak points. Pinchback charged the delegates with having in their pockets Custom-house money to purchase their votes in convention to-morrow, and claimed that if the compromise was not ratified by the caucus, Grant would not get a vote from Louisiana in the National Convention. He said he had been sold out too often by Louisiana Republicans not to know how to avoid breakers in the future, and he proposed now to take the best terms he could get. He was warmly answered by Atwood, who declared that to accept the proposed disgraceful compromise would be an act of treachery toward the people who sent them there instructed to vote for Grant delegates. Robison, of Caldwell, an eloquent but uneducated full-blooded negro, said that his people knew no one but Grant. They had sent him to the convention to vote for the great soldier, and, although he was poor, and had been offered money and official place to vote for Sherman delegates, yet he would obey the unanimous wishes of his people, and vote for Grant, even though he had to work his passage back home on a steam-boat. The compromise was rejected decisively by the caucus, and it was made plain to the Sherman agents that they could not succeed by any such palpable trick in leading the Grant men from their just position. A committee of five was appointed to confer with the same number from the Custom-house party, and to demand 12 members of the delegation to Chicago for Gen. Grant. The evidence that money has been received from Washington was confirmed to-day by the free use of it among delegates by the Sherman officers. The effect was, indeed, only too apparent in the caucus to-day.

Another correspondent at New-Orleans says: A careful canvass of the delegates shows them to be about equally divided between Grant and Sherman and Blaine. A compromise will probably be made, giving Grant eight delegates and Sherman and Blaine the other eight.

### *NEW CHICAGO CHURCHES.*

CHICAGO, May 23.—A new and handsome Roman Catholic Church, erected at a cost of $100,000, on Wabash-avenue, between Twenty-ninth and Thirtieth streets, to be known as St. James's Church, was dedicated to-day with impressive ceremonies in the presence of an immense audience. Many prominent Catholic clergymen assisted in the dedicatory services, among whom were the Right Rev. Bishop Krauthauer and Bishop Duneger, of Fort Wayne. The sermon was preached by Bishop Spaulding.

The corner-stone of a large and costly Swedish Lutheran church, at the corner of May and Huron streets, was laid to-day by the Rev. Hurm Carlson.

### *THE MARYLAND JOCKEY CLUB.*

BALTIMORE, May 23.—The annual Spring meeting of the Maryland Jockey Club on the Pimlico Course will begin on Tuesday and continue four days. The track, improved by the rain of yesterday, was never in better condition for both safety and speed. Over 200 horses are reported in the stables at Pimlico, among which are the best-known racers, and representing all the noted stables of the country, including Belmont's, Lorillard's, Bowie's, Crouse's, Jennings's, Reed's, Frank Hall's, Barnes & West's, Brown & Lloyd's, and a number of others. The prizes given by the club at this meeting amount to over $10,000.

## THE VAGARIES OF JUSTICE

*AN UNFORTUNATE OLD FRENCH GENTLEMAN.*

THE INNOCENT TO BE MADE TO SUFFER IN PLACE OF THE GUILTY—WHAT THE JESUITS ARE GOING TO DO—THE ENEMIES OF CLERICALISM.

PARIS, May 10.—Prof. D—— is an eminent scientist, who lives in one of the most aristocratic hotels of the noble Faubourg, where the proud descendants of the Crusaders do not disdain to mark, by their presence at Mme. D——'s fortnightly receptions, their approval of his manly defense of the doctrine of a great First Cause. It requires a vast deal of moral courage to stand up for revelation, in these days of skepticism, to maintain that it is less humiliating to acknowledge Almighty God as the Creator of all things than to trace our origin back to a monkey or a mollusk. But Prof. D—— was brave, and so was rewarded by the patronage of the salt of the earth, which, as I have said, graciously noticed his existence by drinking his tea and eating his ices on alternate Thursday afternoons. Prof. D—— is oldish, while his wife is quite the other way; he is rising 65, she about 40 years his junior. It was the union of December with May, and, as the lady is skittish, there has been an unpleasant dénoument. Everybody predicted it, from the day when the wealthy old savant led his portionless bride to the fashionable altar of St. Clotilde, and everybody knew that there was a *ménage à trois*, so soon as the brilliant and fascinating Count de L——, who had been ever so attentive, suddenly ceased to do more than bow distantly to the lady when they met in public, although neither ever appeared in any *salon* to which both were not invited. Experts in such matters shrugged their shoulders and contemptuously pitied the the husband, months ago, but nobody cared to testify his disapproval, for, as the dowagers said, "they are so decorous with it all, and until the responsible editor finds out that he is a Georges Dandin and makes a row, what business of ours is it? we have no proofs!" Virtuous aristocracy is extremely lenient to peccadilloes of the heart, and shuts its eyes so long as the marital flag covers the merchandise; it is terrible, though, in its indignation, when the flag is lowered, and, however repentant may be the Magdalen, once the scandal is published, will never allow the slightest extenuating circumstances to the offender. How Prof. D—— discovered the infidelity of his spouse is not told; probably an anonymous letter from some disappointed suitor put him on the trail, which, following up, he soon acquired proof that he belonged to the category of horned cattle. I will be revenged, he said. I will take them *flagrante delicto*; he shall go to prison; she shall become an inmate of St. Lazare. Such, at least, were his sentiments, and to put them into execution he resorted to the old strategem—a pretended journey to the Provinces, an unexpected return, and a domiciliary visit in company with the Commissary of Police to establish the misdemeanor. Everything took place as he had planned it; Mme. D. accompanied her liege lord to the railway station, saw him safely in a first-class carriage labeled Bordeaux, kissed him good-bye, and incontinently went to console herself for his absence with the Count, who was in waiting at a little hotel in the Rue de Sèvres, where they were in the habit of flirting together. The Professor had left by the 8:30 P. M. express, but he only went as far as the first station on the line, where he got out, and whence he returned to the capital by the first train to Paris, making an irruption, flanked by the myrmidons of the law, upon Room No. 26, about midnight. First came a discreet knock at the door; no answer. Then there was a louder knock, equally ineffectual, and then that stern summons: *Au nom de la loi ouvrez!* to which none but most hardened malefactors venture on disobedience. The door was flung open, and there stood Count de L——, in a light costume, with his boots in hand, but of any woman there was not a sign. Where is the guilty wretch? howled the Professor, who requested somebody to hold him, lest he might do mischief. "Where is Mme. D.?" asked the magistrate, who was nonplussed. "What are you talking about," replied the Count; "you can see for yourselves that I am alone, and I should like an explanation of this unwarrantable intrusion." The Commissary was staggered by the gentleman's assurance; yet, as the husband insisted, a thorough search was made. They looked and they rummaged in the closets, under the chairs, under the bed—all in vain—and Dame Justice's incarnation was about to retire with an admonition to the Professor about credulity, when some one bethought him to try a door opening into an adjoining room, which the hotel-keeper affirmed was occupied by an old gentleman from the country, who had arrived by the 11 P. M. train, a good deal the worse for liquor. The door yielded, and, in a single bed, his head enveloped in a cotton night-cap, sure enough was the traveler, snoring peacefully, but, alas! on the other side of the bed, crouched down against the wall, was Mme. D. in the *simple attirail d'une beauté qu'on arrache au sommeil.* She had gotten away at the first alarm, had carried away her duds, but she had neglected to put them on; worse still, she had neglected to fasten the gate of salvation. The sleeper was aroused and told to dress himself and come along. "What for," he inquired, "I never saw this person before; I was ignorant of her presence; I have a wife and family at Amiens." It was no manner of use protesting his innocence; the French law is positive; in the matter of *crim. con.*, it recognizes none but incontestable evidence, and, as the woman was found in a situation which can leave no possible doubts of her infidelity, the commercial traveler from Picardy must be prosecuted, while the real delinquent, the Count de L——, will escape scot free. It is an extraordinary and unprecedented case, but there is no help for it, and the court, even with a moral conviction of the defendant's guiltlessness, cannot do otherwise than sentence him to imprisonment and damages.

The tribunals have plenty of business to dispose of; for the moment, suits for judicial separation motived on reciprocal infractions of marriage contracts, and suits for dissolution of marriages on the plea of the non-observance of legal formalities, take up all the leading barristers, but after the 29th of June questions of much more importance will be brought for examination and judgment, as at that date will commence the application of those "existing laws" against religious orders whose execution was decreed on the 29th of March. The Government has got an immense elephant to take care of, is at heart very sorry not to have left the congregations to their own devices, and regrets sincerely the advice given by some very genuine Republicans who said: Let the Jesuits alone; if they get away from lay schools too many young men, make the lay schools better, and French parents will not hesitate to give them their patronage. Unluckily, it was judged expedient to propitiate the mob, which needed a victim, and as the mob seemed more redoubtable than the clergy, this particular sop to Carberus was invented, it being supposed that the orders would jump at the chance of getting a license, and that the seculars would disavow all sympathy with the disciples of Loyola, who were represented to be regarded as parish dogs by the vast majority of nominal Catholics. All these considerations were taken for granted, without any careful reconnoissance of the position, and the result is just the contrary of what was anticipated. Not a single congregation has complied with the Government's invitation to send in its papers; not a single order, male or female, will deign to ask permission for the enjoyment of rights to which they consider themselves legally entitled, and every Bishop and priest in France has protested against the arbitrary dispossession and eviction of communities whose members have paid taxes and voted as unquestioned electors for more than half a century. With the dawn of the 30th of June will commence the struggle; how it will end, no man can foretell. The congregations will resist by every legal means at their command: they will not open their doors to the

# The New York Times.

VOL. XXIX........NO. 8968. | NEW-YORK, MONDAY, JUNE 7, 1880. | PRICE FOUR CENTS.

## WHO WILL BE NOMINATED

### A CLOSE AND EXCITING CONTEST PROBABLE TO-DAY.

THE FRIENDS OF GRANT AND BLAINE STILL EXPRESSING THE UTMOST CONFIDENCE—THE LATTER NOT SO SURE OF A LARGE VOTE ON THE FIRST BALLOT—THEIR EFFORTS TO BRIBE DELEGATES—INDICATIONS OF LARGE GAINS FOR GRANT—DISTRUST OF WASHBURNE'S SINCERITY.

CHICAGO, June 6.—It is now only certain in regard to the Chicago Convention, long destined to be remembered, that every one in attendance upon it heartily wishes that it may speedily come to an end. There are, of course, as there have been from the first, countless rumors in regard to its outcome, but they are only rumors, and must be taken for what they are worth, and with many grains of allowance. Still, there is a general impression that the fight is not at first to be between Blaine and Grant, and the leaders on each side continue, without giving their reasons, to express, even to their most intimate friends and supporters, the utmost confidence in the ultimate success of their favorites. On the one hand, Senator Cameron said today: "Grant is certain of the nomination. There can be no doubt about it. Our men will stick to the end, and the other side cannot possibly combine." Senator Conkling, who is, if possible, even more confident, will not admit even the possibility of defeat. On the other hand, William E. Chandler, together with Messrs. Frye and Hale, are almost at a loss for words to express their confidence in the nomination of Mr. Blaine. All of these leaders have every means of ascertaining the wishes of the various State delegations, and it is now known by those in whom they most confide that they never really felt the confidence which they profess. Such being the case, and the contest being, as is admitted on all sides, an exceedingly close one, it is obviously impossible, even for trained political observers, to hazard an opinion as to the outcome. Betting on the result has almost ceased, even among the most reckless gamblers, and, apparently by mutual consent, the advocates of all sides are waiting to see what a day may bring forth.

Meanwhile, there is much discussion as to the work of yesterday, and as to the changes which are likely to take place amon gthe different delegations in connection with the latter subject. The Blaine men are deeply regretting the choice of Mr. Joy as their candidate's spokesman in the Convention. "If our candidate can survive Joy's speech," said a prominent supporter of Blaine in the Maine head-quarters to-day, "he has great vitality. Why Joy was picked out to do the work, I cannot imagine." "Others lament the silence of "Bob" Ingersoll, and do not see the wisdom which induced the Blaine leaders to keep him in the background. The reason is, or ought to be, obvious. Eugene Hale and Mr. Frye were sharp enough to see that Ingersoll's advocacy of Blaine at this time would be worse than his opposition. Since 1876 this Blaine orator has revealed himself to the people of the country in his true colors, and the men who make up the strength of the Republican Party in New-England and the West and all over the land would be unwilling to be led into a great political contest under the command of a man whose life business is the ridicule, upon public platforms, of all the religious principles which they hold sacred, and which have guided them into the party which is denounced by Democrats as the party of a "God and morality."

On a tour of investigation to-day there were encountered some interesting estimates of Blaine's strength. At the Blaine head-quarters there was a marked difference of opinion. One prominent delegate placed the Blaine vote on the first ballot at 280, and said that the Grant vote would not exceed this by half a dozen votes. By some mysterious power of reasoning he had reached the conclusion that on the second or third ballot some of the Grant votes would be transferred to Blaine, but he could not predict a settlement of the great question until many ballots should be taken. Another Blaine man placed Blaine's vote on the first ballot at 334, but when his companions expressed astonishment at this estimate, he asserted that he wouldn't acknowledge defeat until every one knew he had been whipped. His figures were partly explained by his admission that he expected 40 votes out of the Pennsylvania delegation of 58.

The rooms which have usually been occupied by the Blaine men were almost deserted at 4 o'clock this afternoon, and those who were present manifested considerable anxiety about the Grant vote. Reckoning again on 18 votes by the admission of the 9 district delegates of Illinois, they agreed to offset these by losses caused by the action of the Convention when it endeavored to preserve its reputation for consistency after it had been endangered by a partisan Committee on Credentials. During a visit to the Rhode Island head-quarters, the delegates from that State being solid for Blaine, a recent statement of William E. Chandler was unearthed. "Chandler was in here a little while ago," said one of the delegates, before his companions could prevent the announcement, "and he was very conservative in his estimate. He said that Grant would lead Blaine on the first ballot by 10 or 15 votes." This was interesting, because other Blaine men had been claiming from 10 to 15 votes for Blaine over Grant, wherever they had been met in other places. It also suggested an explanation of something which THE TIMES's correspondent had overheard in the Blaine head-quarters. While passing through these head-quarters he saw three men in consultation, and heard one say with considerable emphasis, but in a low tone of voice: "We must buy 15 before to-morrow morning." This method of securing votes is a new way of getting "near to the people." There are no indications, however, that these men will find 15 votes which can be bought, although they will undoubtedly search high and low for them.

A rumor prevailed this afternoon that the missionary efforts of the Blaine men had secured three converts, two of them from Georgia, but an investigation showed that it had no foundation. "We are unchanged," said one of the Sherman delegates from Georgia. "We still stand eight for Blaine, eight for Sherman, and six for Grant; but there will be a break, and when it comes, some of the Sherman men, if satisfied that they can do the Secretary of the Treasury no further service, will vote for Grant." It was ascertained elsewhere, on excellent authority, that three of the Georgia delegates who came to the Convention as Blaine men, and who will vote for Blaine on the first ballot, will consider their obligations to Blaine discharged after that ballot, and will thereafter vote for Grant. Their action cannot fail to have its influence on the remaining 5 Blaine delegates from that State.

The Blaine men seem to have agreed to ignore Senator Conkling's remarkable speech, and to make their disregard for it more emphatic, they declare that the speech made by Elliott—Sherman's special agent—was the best which has been heard in the Convention.

Nothing could be more apparent to-day than the unshaken determination of the friends of Grant to vote for him first, last, and all the time. "We will stand by him," said one of the delegates from Missouri, "until we die in our tracks." In the Illinois head-quarters, a crowd of 150 persons had gathered around Senator Logan, who was quietly smoking a cigar as he sat in his chair. No anxiety could be seen on the face of any one in this party. Unalterable devotion to Grant was the sentiment expressed by all. "We need no gift of backbone," said a delegate in the Arkansas head-quarters. "Our determination cannot be shaken." The 20 delegates from Kentucky, who obey the most positive instructions of their State Convention, express great sorrow in speaking of the course taken by the four who glory in the shame of broken pledges. It is asserted that not one of the four could ever have been chosen a delegate if it had not been understood that he would carry out the wishes of his State. Very serious charges against one of the four, affecting his integrity as a man, were published in this city yesterday. The Grant men of the delegation have expressed to him their willingness to go with him to the place where they were published, and to punish the author of them, if he will show that they are false. At the same time, they say that he should resign his place as a delegate if they are true.

The Grant men in other delegations declare that their candidate will receive from 10 to 15 more votes on the first ballot than Blaine can muster, and there seems to be the greatest confidence, based upon good grounds, for expecting a large accession on the second ballot. It is said by some, who assert that they have the best of reasons for their claim, that among those who will come to Grant on the second ballot are seven of the ten delegates from Vermont. The Vermont delegates do not openly admit that they have any second choice, but they do not show any good reason for expecting any increase in the apparent strength of the Edmunds vote. This vote they make up as follows: Vermont 10; Massachusetts, 23; Tennessee, 1; Connecticut, 3. Edmunds will probably receive only 2 votes from Connecticut, and the great majority of the votes of Massachusetts will be transferred to Grant if there seems to be any chance for the nomination of Blaine. Seven of the Connecticut votes will probably be cast for Washburne on the first ballot, and, by the way, the events of to-day have not served to remove the feeling of distrust with which Mr. Washburne has for some time been regarded by the friends of the ex-President. It is publicly announced that he feels very much pleased at his nomination last evening, and his son has visited to-day, in his father's interest, at least one delegation which contains several Washburne men. It is not the first time in this canvass that this son has been active in a movement which is in direct contradiction to the published wishes of his father. Some of the Grant men remark that Mr. Washburne might not be able to control the actions of his friends, but ought certainly to exercise some influence in his own family, if his real sentiments are those which he has allowed to be published. The supporters of Washburne, as a nucleus, consists of seven in Connecticut, nine in Wisconsin, and nine in Illinois, and they hope to gain votes on the second ballot from Massachusetts and other States. Mr. Washburne, who has been in the East for some time, is now near at hand, and reports were received in this city to-day from him in Detroit repeating the assurances heretofore published—that he is not and will not be a candidate, and that he is anxious for the success of the ex-President.

During the day there have been various reports of combinations and arrangements entered or to be entered into by the various candidates, but a close investigation in each case has revealed the fact that there is little or no truth in any of them. For instance, it has been stated that Senator Conkling and Gen. Garfield have been in consultation during the day, and that as a result, it has been decided that the Grant forces were, under certain circumstances, to be transferred to Garfield. In this story there is absolutely no truth. Senator Conkling and Gen. Garfield did casually meet to-day, but they had no discussion about the Convention, and there certainly was no agreement as to any transfer of votes from Gen. Grant to any man. The idea could only have originated in the minds of some of Garfield's enthusiastic friends, some of whom think that he may be struck by lightning, and, in the end, carry off the nomination. It must be noted that, instead of there being any foundation for a fear that Gen. Grant's supporters will desert him, there is a prospect that by the very reason of their fidelity they may bring the nomination of some other candidate. Indeed, this is the one change which the Grant leaders have to fear and which, it cannot be concealed, they do not fully realize.

The present programme is to go into the Convention with the 285 to 300 votes which they control absolutely and hold them from one ballot after another until there is a break among the minor candidates, when they confidently expect that enough votes will come to them to nominate their man. The one defect in this plan, as it appears to cool observers, is that it does not provide for a combination of any of the friends of Sherman, Washburne, or Windom, with those who favor Blaine. Mr. Conkling, and those who are in his confidence, scout the idea that any such combination is possible. So far as the votes of Windom and the Southern votes of Sherman are concerned, there is every reason to believe that they are correct in this position. From Ohio, however, it is simply folly to suppose that Gen. Grant will receive as many votes when the Sherman break-up comes as Blaine will. By one means and another, which need not now be discussed, a good deal of sentiment against Grant has been manufactured among the Ohio politicians, while Blaine is very popular. Already that gentleman is assured of at least four votes from that State from delegates who will have the odium of breaking faith with Sherman by voting for the Maine Senator on the first ballot. It is known positively that at least 16 others will, at the earliest opportunity, follow their example, while up to the present time, only 10 of the Ohio men have been ready to admit that they could be induced, under any circumstances, to give their support to Grant. This is an important fact which, as far as can be discovered, the Grant leaders have sufficiently considered. It is just possible, however, that they are more watchful and have more consideration for all the chances than they are given credit for.

As to the outcome of the contest, it can only be said that the friends of both the leading candidates now depend for success upon accessions which they may get when the Sherman vote breaks. While they are thus calculating there are many here who still hold to the opinion that some such man as Edmunds will, in the end, carry off the prize. His friends profess to believe that Grant's votes will come to him while, on their part, the advocates of the ex-President are assured that the 10 votes from Vermont will, at an early stage in the proceedings, join in giving him the victory. H. C.

### SUNDAY AMONG THE DELEGATES.

TIRED-OUT MEMBERS GOING HOME—EVERYBODY ANXIOUS TO FOLLOW THEIR EXAMPLE.

CHICAGO, June 6.—If appearances and reports count for anything, the attendance of delegates and alternates will be somewhat reduced at to-morrow's meeting of the Convention. Tired out with the incessant wear and tear of the last six days, and anxious to go back to homes and neglected business, several delegates have left Chicago without having made provision for filling their places. New-Jersey will cast only 17 votes on the ballot for President, one delegate having gone home, his alternate being absent, and no provision having been made for filling the vacancy by substituting any stray Jerseyman who can be picked out of the contingent of visitors from that State. Another reason for the departure of delegates, and a very large number of persons who came here merely as visitors, is the fact that a great many of them came here unprepared to meet the heavy expenses, and what with high prices at the hotels, railway fares, $15 or $20 a day for tickets to the Convention, and incidental expenses inseparable from association with thirsty crowds, they are compelled to leave before being reduced to the necessity of living upon the charity of obliging friends. All of the reasons mentioned have had their effect upon the throng. Of the New-York visitors, who were to be found everywhere a day or two ago, the trains which left here to-day took away large numbers, and some of those who remain are extremely anxious about how they are to be provided for until after the Convention.

The day has been a very dull one about the hotels as compared with the preceding six days. Almost everybody has had enough of cheering and screaming. The extravagant performances in the Convention on Saturday morning and evening had worn out many who indulged in them, and the result was that the day of rest was welcomed and enjoyed to the fullest extent. The elements conspired to make out-door excursions about the city unpleasant. A "lake breeze," that amounted to a gale, howled through the streets, carrying dashes of rain which no umbrella could repel. The dampness of the open hotel halls made them unpleasant places for idlers, and the muddy streets prevented many persons who were making their first visit to Chicago from indulging in walks to the usual places which all strangers are urged to see. The churches were visited by many who were glad of the opportunity to listen to teachers who were not excited by the strife of politics. In and about the head-quarters of the State delegations, everything looked desolate until toward evening. The floors, covered with canvas protecting cloths, were dirty with the marks of the muddy feet that had tramped in and out upon them for a week. Here and there the decorations had become disarranged; pictures of Blaine or Sherman might have been seen hanging with the head reversed, swaying in the wind and held only by a tack. The few persons who peered in at the doors, as if seeking for acquaintances, went on from one place to another to find all very much alike and all uninviting.

Late in the afternoon, when the weather became brighter, the head-quarters assumed a more cheerful look, although they were not so crowded as they had been. At the Palmer House, in the rooms of the delegates from several of the Southern and Western States, there were little groups of men who quietly discussed things, past, present, and to come, dwelling principally on the discomforts attending so protracted a Convention. Some of these talkers still wore their State and candidate badges, very much soiled and crumpled, but yet held out as an indication that they were in the fight. The Indiana men listened to Col. Streight, the man whose name was once in everybody's mouth as the leader of the escape of Union prisoners from Libby Prison. He is not a delegate, but sympathizes with the Indiana men who intend to vote for Blaine on the first ballot, principally because he thinks, as the Indiana delegates do, that Blaine would be the best many to carry Indiana. Col. Streight is discreet and disposed to conciliation, as, perhaps, becomes a candidate for the office of Governor of Indiana. He counsels harmony, and would not be too tenacious of Blaine, if the sense of the Convention should indicate a preference for any other good Republican. He would not exclude Gen. Grant from the category of good Republicans, and his intimation to that effect has led many persons to suspect that one of the first Blaine States to go to the Grant side will be Indiana.

In the parlors of the Palmer House set apart for the friends of John Sherman there were visible very few of the white-hatted men who were there in such large numbers from Cincinnati on Friday and Saturday, the visitors consisting largely of hungry-looking delegates, decked with the conspicuous red badges which make the Sherman men easily known in the streets. At the Grand Pacific the halls and rooms occupied by the politicians presented no more attractive appearance than those of the Palmer and Sherman Houses. The air about them was heavy with stale tobacco-smoke, and floors and clothes were soiled and dingy to look at. One could not stop at any group of talkers for five minutes without discovering that next to the inevitable question: "Well, how does it stand now?" the inquiry would be: "What did you think of Conkling's speech?" Half a dozen of the Iowa men, who were heard talking on this subject, expressed surprise at the power of the man, having unquestionably been impressed with his oratorical effort of last night. In the hall of the Grand Pacific, Sheridan Shook broke in upon some friends who were talking about Conkling's speech. He was out of all patience with the bolters in the New-York delegation because they had not answered one of the Senator's statements, forgetting that it would have been hardly the proper thing to do. He was indignant because no one of the twenty anti-Grant men had not directed attention to Conkling's boast that Grant's friends could not be guilty of bolting, and told the Convention that several of them, including Mr. Shook himself, had gone into a Tammany Convention at Albany, when Hoffman was nominated against Fenton, and had afterward used their efforts to beat the Republican candidate at the polls. Mr. Shook somewhat vehemently spoke of the bolters as lacking grit, and insisted upon it that when Conkling asserted that Grant was the choice of New-York, Robertson, or Woodin, or Husted should have risen to deny it and declare their preference for Blaine.

The head-quarters of the gentlemen whom Mr Shook referred to, and who are not solid for Grant, as a banner sets forth which is hung opposite their rooms, were visited to-day by a number of the delegates from Pennsylvania with whom the rebellious New-York men have established a bond of fraternal sympathy. The bolters now boast that the break in the Virginia delegation was fomented by them in a series of missionary visits, and they seem to be very proud of having disturbed a delegation that was expected to be strong and unbroken for Grant.

There is no rush for tickets to the Convention to-morrow, although it is probable that before the Convention meets in the morning the interest felt in the voting will be as deep as it has been in any of the preliminary proceedings. Some reports were heard this afternoon to the effect that the Blaine men intended to produce some more speakers in behalf of their candidates but the Blaine leaders deny the report. The general desire is that there shall be some action—enough speech-making has been done. Sufficient time has been consumed in debate to fatigue even the most enthusiastic lover of political gatherings and disputes. The one demand that is heard above all others is, "Give us a vote; provide the party with a candidate and let us go home."

### THE EVENTS OF SATURDAY.

MR. CONKLING'S GREAT SPEECH CREATES MUCH DISCUSSION—GEN. GARFIELD'S IDEAL MAN.

CHICAGO, June —In reviewing the work of yesterday's meeting of the Convention, the delegates and others in Chicago join in the statement that no action was had and no vote taken which could be held clearly to indicate the outcome. Indeed, it has been impossible for either side to torture an appearance of advantage out of anything that was done, as was fully explained in these dispatches yesterday. Many of the delegates voted on every question which came up, entirely regardless of their choice for President. Such being the case, the most prominent topic of conversation has been the remarkable oration in which Senator Conkling nominated ex-President Grant. Although the speech has not failed to evoke some hostile criticism, the opinion is almost universal that it stands alone among the many addresses of the kind which American politics have called into being, peerless in adaptation to its purpose. There are some supporters of Senator Blaine who endeavor to ignore it, painfully aware of the inferiority of the addresses in which their candidate was presented. They bestow their praise upon the speech of R. B. Elliott, the special agent of Secretary Sherman. The friends of Grant who have come to the Convention from the South, find no limits to the enthusiasm with which they regard the oration of Conkling, and many of them have declared to-day that it alone has richly repaid them for their whole trip, and all its tribulations and expenses. There are some conservative men who are advocates of neither ex-President Grant nor Senator Blaine, who acknowledge the greatness of the oration, but who regard its reference to the means by which other candidates have sought to secure the nomination as impolitic and tending to repel delegates who have held the ex-President as a second choice. These men were not surprised because Senator Conkling included these references in what he said. They regard them as characteristic of an aggressive man, but they believe that they were also characteristic of a man who is not acquainted with the countless impulses which go to make up human nature. They point to Gen. Garfield as the type of a political conciliator, and assert that in such a Convention, conciliation is worth more than aggression. The treatment received by Senator Conkling while making this address has awakened no little indignation, which is by no means confined to the friends of the ex-President. It served to confirm the feeling which other similar manifestations had aroused, that the supporters of Blaine in the galleries are distinguished by their intolerance from the supporters of other candidates who have been given seats there. The friends of Blaine are not content with approval. They have lost no opportunity for the expression of their disapprobation, and their hoots and jeers and calls of "time," and other attempts to suppress speakers who were not of their way of thinking, will be the most disagreeable characteristics of this Convention, which will linger in the memory of those who have attended it.

The address made by Gen. Garfield received much praise as an oratorical effort from many who heard it, but curious remarks were made about it. Those who were utterly unable to recognise the Secretary of the Treasury in the ideal man whose portrait he drew, begin to think that the picture was Gen. Garfield's picture of himself. Suggestions to this effect have been frequently made to-day by men who are in no way hostile to Gen. Garfield, and who see in the course he has pursued during the Convention indications of an honest desire to advance his own fortunes.

### NOTES AND INCIDENTS.

CHICAGO, June 6.—An informal gathering of the newly-appointed National Committee was held this evening in the National Committee's head-quarters. It was called to order by Senator Cameron, and William E. Chandler acted as Secretary. It was decided that when the committee shall be organized it shall be officered by the members who are in sympathy with the candidate to be named by the Convention, whoever he may be. It was then resolved that the committee shall meet for organization immediately after the final adjournment of the Convention.

In consequence of the frequent and long interruptions of business caused by the unruly persons who throng the galleries, there has been some discussion to-day as to the propriety of clearimg them to-morrow if any further trouble is caused by the audience. As nominations are understood to be closed, nothing remains to be done but to proceed to a ballot. The Chairman has several times asked that a resolution should be passed ordering the galleries to be cleared, and the discussion was entirely in sympathy with his suggestions. So great is the desire on the part of delegates to get through with their business and leave the city that they will very readily adopt a resolution of the kind alluded to, as their impatience will brook no delay occasioned by a crowd who assemble to amuse themselves with their own noise.

Many delegates and visitors who were passing between the Palmer House and the Grand Pacific Hotel this afternoon, were attracted by the loud voice of a bare-headed speaker, who had gathered a little audience around him on the sidewalk near the new Custom-house. As soon as they could distinguish his words they went on their way, so that there was a continual stream to and from the spot. The man was not defending any of the candidates before the Convention, but was preaching the Gospel of Christ. One could have made an interesting study of the peculiar expressions seen on the faces of those who approached this roadside laborer. Some showed surprise when they found that this was not a political shouter; some went away thoughtfully, having discovered that it it was Sunday, and that there were other subjects than politics upon which something could be said in public; and others wondered as they listened, how this man had escaped the current of this great political maelstrom. But he and his appeals were soon forgotten in the business of the time and place.

John H. Starin, the well-known member of Congress from New-York, in commenting to-day upon the peculiarities of delegates, very justly remarked that the colored delegates had more conscience in the palms of their hands than any men he had ever seen.

"Bob" Ingersoll, who nominated Blaine in 1876, and whose absence from the platform last evening is so greatly deplored by many of Blaine's supporters, is in town. "Long" John Wentworth is a well known resident of Chicago and one of the Grant delegates who were deprived of their seats by the Convention. He is one of the tallest men in America, and has plenty of sound common sense. The two men met to-day. Ingersoll is large and tall, and he opened the conversation by saying: "Well, Mr. Wentworth, we are almost of a size." "Yes," replied Wentworth, "the only difference between us is that you are against God and Grant and I'm for both." "That's true," said Ingersoll, "and I'll bet a hundred dollars that they are both beaten."

Senators Conkling, Logan, and Cameron to-night made visits to all the head-quarters of the delegations friendly to Gen. Grant's nomination to ascertain the feeling among them and to counsel a firm stand for their candate. The result of this visit is said to be very satisfactory. The States which have heretofore been favorable to Grant were found as positive as ever in their determination to stand by him until he is nominated or defeated.

It is reported that when the State of New-York is called to-morrow on the ballot for candidates for President, that Senator Conkling, as Chairman of the delegation will, obedient to the instructions of the State Convention, deposit the 70 votes of New-York for Gen. Grant. If the men who have broken faith with the State Convention have objections to make to such a disposition of the votes of New-York, they will be forced to rise and make their protest individually. That this course has been decided upon it is difficult to ascertain, for Senator Conkling is mute about it, and his intimate friends here are equally reticent.

Ex-Gov. Pinchback, of Louisiana, although a colored man, is very light looking, and more like a sallow white man than a negro. He got into a discussion to-day in the corridor of the Palmer House with a rawboned Illinois cattle driver, who was not over pleased with the assurance by Pinchback that Gen. Grant would surely be nominated. The cattle-drover who did not know Pinchback, heard him out, drew a sigh of resignation, and said: "Well, I suppose we can swallow Grant if we've got to, but it makes me infernally mad to think that he's got to be nominated by these devilish Southern niggers."

### A JAPANESE OFFICER'S SUICIDE.

THE SECRETARY OF THE LEGATION IN WASHINGTON SHOOTS HIMSELF.

WASHINGTON, June 6.—Mr. Agee Takato, Secretary of the Japanese Legation, in this city, committed suicide this morning. He was found on the floor of his parlor, with a pistol in his hand, with which he had shot himself through the brain. He had received a first-class education in this country, and was a gentleman of unusual ability and of most agreeable manners. Before being assigned to a place on the legation here, he he held an important official position in Japan. The only clue to the cause of the suicide was a letter left by him, written in the Japanese language, in which he stated that he had been concerned in the insurrection of 1877 in Japan, and had forfeited his honor.

### PROGRESS IN MEXICO

HAVANA, June 6.—The English mail steamer from Vera Cruz brings dates from the City of Mexico to May 30. The leading politicians have held a caucus of all parties opposing Gen. Gonzalez for the Presidency. Señors Vallarte and Zamacona and Gen. Mejia were present. It is probable that this movement will unite all the opposition elements on Gen. Mejia.

The Simons, or Central, Railroad Company, having its concession secured by official action for the road to the City of Leon, has commenced work with 500 laborers. The privileges of branching to the Pacific and the Rio Grande will doubtless be granted before the end of the year.

Revolutionary indications appeared in the State of Colima on May 18. The Chamber of Deputies, formed as a Grand Jury to judge Gov. Teran, of Vera Cruz, for the hangings of June last, has declared itself to be without jurisdiction upon the question, Gov. Teran not having violated the Constitution, but having merely committed an ordinary offense.

Congress has authorized the Executive, during recess, to contract for the construction of railroads on the same basis as that of the railroad from Puebla to Matamoras.

### THE LONG-DELAYED UTE BILL.

WHY THE HOUSE SHOULD PASS IT TO-DAY UNDER A SUSPENSION OF THE RULES.

WASHINGTON, June 6.—To-morrow being the first Monday of the month, it will be in order in the House for any member, after the call of States, to move to suspend the rules and pass any measure which he may desire to present. The large number of absentees however, will enable 15 or 20 members, by withholding their votes and thus destroying a quorum, to prevent the passage of any obnoxious measures, should such measures be brought forward. The Speaker has promised to recognize Mr. Belford, of Colorado, to move to suspend the rules and fix a time for the consideration of the bill to ratify the treaty recently made with the Ute Indians, and it is likely that this motion will prevail. Mr. Belford proposes to fix Tuesday for the consideration of the bill, but in view of the urgent necessity for the speedy passage of this measure, it would be better if Mr. Belford would accept the bill as it passed the Senate and force a vote upon its passage to-morrow under a suspension of the rules. This would dispose of the question at once, whereas, if the bill be made a special order for Tuesday, it will be in the power of Mr. Hooker, of Mississippi, to defeat its consideration by captious opposition, as was done upon a previous occasion when it was fixed as a special order.

This bill was carefully considered by the Senate and passed by that body April 12, and is now on the House calendar with some unimportant amendments made by the Committee on Indian Affairs. It would be safer to accept the bill, either as it passed the Senate or as it now stands, with the amendments reported by the House committee, and take advantage of the opportunity to get a vote on its passage to-morrow, than to have a special time appointed for its consideration, when it may be successfully antagonized by a few members who desire, by such means, to force the House to take up their pet measures as the price of the withdrawal of their opposition to the Ute bill. A failure to pass this measure at an early day will certainly provoke hostilities with the Utes, who are becoming irritated under the long delay to fulfill the terms of a treaty which their head men signed three months ago, and who cannot be made to understand the methods and necessity for Congressional action. Several communications have been received by the Secretary of the Interior from Ouray, in which he speaks of the restlessness of the Indians with the inexcusable delay, and represents that immediate action is necessary to the successful fulfillment of the treaty and the preservation of the peace between the Indians and the people of Colorado.

### MAYOR KALLOCH'S CAREER.

ASKING A DISMISSAL OF THE NEILSON LIBEL CASE—THE PAMPHLET AGAINST KALLOCH.

SAN FRANCISCO, June 6.—In the Neilson libel case, Mayor Kalloch appeared in court yesterday afternoon, accompanied by counsel, who moved the dismissal of the case, upon an affidavit by Mayor Kalloch to the effect that the complaint in the case was not proffered at his instigation or request; that he did not know Kydd; that Kydd had not, to his knowledge, been requested to make complaint by any friends of the affiant or member of the church, and is an intruder in the matter; that all prosecution is collusive and formed upon the counter purpose of manufacturing an opportunity for the publication in private of obscene matter contained in the Neilson pamphlet, with a view of affecting the trial of the affiant's son on a charge of killing Charles De Young, and the trial of M. H. De Young on a charge of libeling the affiant. After some discussion on the part of the counsel the case was continued for the term.

The Neilson pamphlet, mentioned in Mayor Kalloch's affidavit, is said to be from the pen of William M. Neilson, a well-known journalist. There had been rumors of such a publication for several days before its appearance. These led Mr. Kalloch to write a letter to Mr. Neilson, under date of May 22, in which he says: "It is, of course, perfectly well understood that such unmanly and cowardly attempts to influence pending litigation and to gratify private vengeance, could only emanate from one quarter. I have now only to give you distinct notice that I do not intend to submit to such unmanly proceedings. I hope the Penal Code of this State will afford me adequate protection." Mr. Neilson's reply, addressed to the "Rev. Isaac S. Kalloch, Pastor of the Metropolitan Baptist Temple," was full of strong words. He says Mr. Kalloch's letter is an impertinence, is insulting, and is false. If he chose to write up the clergymen's career, regarding him as a public man, he should do so on his own motion. He continues, speaking of Kalloch's letter: "It is threatening. You say you don't intend to submit to such proceedings. Chief-Magistrate of the City * * * what are you going to do about it? Do you propose to send your second son on an errand of mercy? Don't. Come yourself. It is timid. You are fearful of a publication. Why? What's the matter with your conscience? Surely, a life-long minister of religion can have no objection to light being let in upon his career. It is prophetic. You are right: 'The Penal Code will afford you adequate protection' ere long. So, now, to quote a letter of yours, which is at my elbow, addressed to your boon companion, 'Charley,' you can 'pick up your flint and fire again, but you'll not fetch this old bird in that way.'"

### HEIRS WANTED TO AN ESTATE.

THE PROPERTY OF THE LATE LEONARD CASE, OF CLEVELAND, WORTH $15,000,000, TO BE DIVIDED.

PORT JERVIS, N. Y., June 5.—The Rev. William Case, of Kingston, N. Y., and Mr. William Case, of Hawley, Penn., have been in this village looking up the heirs of the late Leonard Case, who died in Cleveland, Ohio, on Jan. 6 last, leaving a property of $15,000,000. The heirs number about 600, and many of them live in Orange and Sullivan Counties, N. Y., and Pike and Wayne Counties, Penn. Leonard Case died leaving no will; consequently his estate will go to his legal heirs. Absalom Case was an Englishman. In 1816 he took a claim of 2,700 acres of land on the present site of the City of Cleveland. He became wealthy, and left his estate to three sons, Absalom, Leonard, and Steven. Leonard died leaving no heirs. Absalom and Steven left families, and the late Leonard Case was a grandson of one of them. His father, Leonard Case, Sr., married a Connecticut lady. The property that came from him to the late Leonard, Jr., was greatly increased in value by the building of the city, and at the time of his death it was estimated to be worth at least $15,000,000. One of the members of the family in Ohio, Levi Kerr, an uncle of the late Leonard, claims that Leonard had by will devised $7,000,000 for scientific purposes. The remaining $8,000,000 Kerr and three sisters proceeded to take possession of. Claims amounting to $420,000 were standing against the estate, and in order to settle the estate, Kerr, as Administrator, has advertised it for sale. Other heirs have secured a stoppage of the sale on the discovery that there is no will, either for the scientific or the family shares, and that, therefore, the entire estate of $15,000,000 is yet to be divided. The Rev. William Case is looking up the heirs, and securing power of attorney from them to push the matter of division among the heirs.

### KENTUCKY DEMOCRATS' CHOICE.

LOUISVILLE, Ky., June 6.—The election yesterday in this city of delegates to the State Democratic Convention at Lexington resulted in 9 Tilden delegates, 17 anti-Tilden, and 10 contested. Returns from county meetings are meagre. The indications are that the State Convention will send an uninstructed delegation to Cincinnati.

## AFFAIRS IN FOREIGN LANDS

### EUROPE'S PERPLEXING QUESTIONS OF STATE.

TURKEY AND THE GREEK FRONTIER—SUBJECTS OF HOME AND FOREIGN CONSIDERATION.

PERA, June 6.—Mr. Goschen, the British Ambassador, has promised the Sultan to submit to him a memorandum setting forth the English proposals regarding the administrative reforms.

ATHENS, June 6.—M. Brailas has started for Berlin for the purpose of explaining to the Ambassadors at the new conference the views of Greece on the frontier question.

LONDON, June 6.—The Irish residents of London gave a reception on Saturday to Mr. Parnell, in St. James's Hall, in recognition of his services in behalf of Ireland in America. The hall was crowded. Many ladies and representatives of various Irish organizations were present. Mr. Justin McCarthy presided, supported by 20 members of Parliament. Mr. Parnell was enthusiastically received. The Chairman presented an address of welcome, in which he highly eulogized Mr. Parnell's services. Mr. Parnell expressed his thanks to the meeting. On leaving the hall Mr. Parnell and many of those present at the meeting were escorted by a number of organizations, with bands and banners, to Trafalgar Square, where several hundred persons were waiting to receive them, but the demonstration was insignificant, owing to the rain. Mr. T. P. O'Connor moved the resolution welcoming Mr. Parnell.

ROME, June 6.—It is believed that negotiations between the Ministry and Signors Crispi and Nicotera have been broken off, the latter having demanded the immediate radical reconstruction of the Cabinet.

LYONS, June 6.—The second ballot to-day for member of the Chamber of Deputies resulted as follows: M. Ballue, 8,290; M. Blanqui, 5,947.

LONDON, June 7.—A Madrid correspondent reports that the business men and public officers are generally indifferent, but begin to feel anxious about the attacks on the Cabinet. The most serious feature of the present crisis is the presence in the ranks of the opposition of Gen. Martinez-Campos, Señor Sagasta, Marshal Serrano, Gen. Jovellar, and other famous Generals. Señor Canovas del Castillo being secure of a majority in both houses, has determined to prorogue the Cortes until November.

A Madrid correspondent telegraphs: "The political situation is getting cloudier daily. The mistakes of the Canovas del Castillo Cabinet are increasing."

A St. Petersburg dispatch says: "The *Golos* and *Bereg* publish articles agreeing that the Nihilist agitation is declining."

A dispatch from Kabul says: "It is believed that Abdurrahman Khan feels uncertain of his power in Turkistan, and also desires to understand exactly what will be required of him if he accepts the Ameership. He has not yet paid his troops, but they are well fled and content. Failing Abdurrahman Khan, the name of the ex-Ameer, Yakoob Khan, is mentioned as the most powerful in Afghanistan." A Candatar dispatch says: "The news from Herat is of continued anarchy and vacillation. Ayoole Rhan's troops are still encamped outside of the city, and disputing who should lead the van, the Cabulis or Heratis."

Correspondents at Pera agree in stating that Mr. Goschen's address to the Sultan was altered before being present, as it contained some passages impalatable to the Cabinet, but Mr. Goschen, in a private interview, placed the whole matter before the Sultan.

### FROM CHINA AND JAPAN.

THE WAR FEELING IN PEKIN—AMERICANS IN COREA—JAPANESE FINANCES.

HONG KONG, May 12.—The latest caprice of the Chinese Government respecting Chung How points to his respite and degradation to low rank with opportunities of a gradual rise to renewed power.

The anti-foreign leaders at Pekin continue their boistrous defiance of Russia, and threaten war soon in case of the failure of Tseng's negotiations for an unconditional rendition of Ili. The war party was never stronger than at this moment. The preparation is imperfect, the Chinese style is pursued everywhere. Careful observers, nevertheless, doubt the power of the minority Government faction to throw the country into war against the wish and judgment of statesmen like Prince Kung and Li Hung Chang. There is much activity in Russian ports for accommodation and supply. Minister Seward is unexpectedly visiting Shanghai.

YOKOHAMA, May 23.—The United States ship Ticonderoga will return presently to Corea. Her exact intentions have not been revealed, but she will probably renew the attempt to negotiate at some point nearer the capital of Zoul than Tusna, the port visited on May 4. The Japanese Government does not officially co-operate with Commodore Shufeldt's mission, though the agent in Corea has been informally instructed to show American visitors every attention. A bullion issue of Government bonds has been proposed to counteract the depreciation of paper currency, the bonds to be purchasable by paper at par, to bear interest at 4 per cent. in specie. The amount of the issue, and the period of redemption, is still undetermined, owing to diverse opinions of the Ministry, some of whom place much reliance on such an issue, while others regard it as unnecessary, the currency fluctuations being evidently the work of speculators and not due to a natural or legitimate cause.

### TOPICS OF INTEREST ABROAD.

PARIS, June 6.—M. Olivier Pain and M Lepelletier, of the *Mot d'Ordre*, have selected as their adversaries from the staff of the *Gaulois* MM. Weiss and Robert Mitchell. The seconds have been named, and have had a conference to arrange the meeting.

A duel was fought to-day (Sunday) at Angoulême, between the editor of the Bonapartist newspaper, *Le Suffrage Universel*, and the editor of a Republican provincial journal. The former was slightly wounded.

The *Telegraph* states that M. Rochefort's fever is increasing.

LONDON, June 6.—The *Observer's* financial article contains the following: "The Paris *Bourse* (newspaper) says it is enabled to state that all attempts at conciliation between the Anglo and French Cable Companies have been utterly defeated. A most ruinous tariff-war is being carried on, which, it is feared, will rather exhaust the means of the French than the Anglo Cable Company."

CARLSRUHE, June 6.—Charles Lessing, the German painter, is dead.

LONDON, June 7.—A Paris dispatch has the following: "The editor of the *Voltaire* fought a duel on Friday with a member of the Jockey Club, in which the former was wounded. The Prince de Santa Severina and M. De Fronsac fought a duel on Saturday on the Belgian frontier. The Prince was wounded."

A Dublin correspondent says: "Another week of most seasonable weather has made still brighter the prospects of the coming harvest."

A dispatch from Calcutta says: "It is believed that the Burmese rising has ended."

### A CHURCH BLOWN DOWN.

CINCINNATI, June 6.—A special to the *Commercial* from Lima, Ohio, says: "During a violent wind-storm to-day a church near Mount Carey, in Hancock County, was blown down, the roof falling on the congregation. Twenty persons were injured, three of them fatally. No particulars can be obtained to-night."

A later dispatch states that the fatally injured are the Rev. Mr. Strout, H. McKinley, and a man whose name is unknown. Among the most severely injured are George Greiser and daughter, A. Cartright, E. Nunemaker, two Arnold boys, and Laura Peebles.

# The New-York Times.

VOL. XXIX........NO. 8971. | NEW-YORK, THURSDAY, JUNE 10, 1880. | PRICE FOUR CENTS.


## THE REPUBLICAN TICKET

### *A RETROSPECTIVE VIEW OF THE CONVENTION.*

GEN. GRANT'S 300 FAITHFUL SUPPORTERS—BLAINE AND SHERMAN COMPELLED TO ABANDON THE FIELD—THE STAMPEDE TO GARFIELD—ONLY GRANT'S FRIENDS STAND FIRM.

CHICAGO, June 9.—The long Convention is ended. Through 36 successive ballots the defenders of the fame of America's greatest living citizen maintained their ranks unbroken, and repelled the assaults of 450 opponents. Deprived of the aid of those who ought to have been beside them, and with whom victory would have been assured, the faithful 300 stood by their colors to the end. There was something peculiarly impressive in the unfaltering allegiance of the colored delegates from the South. They were voting for the man who had led the armies which had overthrown their oppressors; for the man whose name is a household word in every lowly Southern cabin; for the man whose election would preserve the liberty which his victories in the field had gained for them. The name of Grant, the savior of a disorderly and divided Nation, meant to them safety, freedom, an honest ballot-box, and the complete discomfiture of their oppressors; and ignorance had no part in fastening this belief upon their minds, for the colored delegates from the South in this Convention have shown to the Northern Republicans an astonishing familiarity with the political history of what is now their country, and a common sense which has sometimes put white men to shame.

So these men, the white Republicans of the North who saw in Grant's nomination the second defeat of the party which was overthrown at Appomattox, and the emancipated slaves of the South, who saw in his name the safety of their race, joined hands and presented an unbroken front from morning until night. Confident in the excellence of their cause, they fought against the adjournment by which their opponents sought to gain time for a new combination, but they were defeated, and the Republicans who were crying "anybody to beat Grant" secured a dozen hours for consultation. They had discovered that the Senator from Maine had spent his strength, and could hope for nothing but the impossible. Under the cover of the night they might be able to find another leader. But great difficulties confronted them. The Blaine votes could not be delivered to Sherman, nor could the Sherman votes be transferred to Blaine. An attempt to unite the opposition upon Washburne or Edmunds would send a host of votes to Grant. The first transfer of a respectable body of votes to him would be the signal for a stampede, and his nomination would be effected in five minutes. The night was spent in vain efforts to shake the Southern supporters of the ex-President, and in making an agreement to test cautiously the strength of Sherman and Washburne. When the Convention reassembled, there was but little to raise hope in the breasts of the perplexed opposition. The first ballot disclosed no weakness in the column which had so firmly supported the silent soldier of Galena, but unveiled the plans of the opposition.

The strength of Sherman was first to be tested. Massachusetts was the instrument chosen for this purpose. The plan was a complete failure. The vote of Sherman rose t 120, and then began, slowly but surely, to fall. A little movement toward Washburne was no more successful. Where could the man be found? The leaders of the opposition were in close communication by wire with the Secretary of the Treasury and the Senator from Maine. The Secretary saw that his defeat was inevitable, and he directed his lieutenants to lead his supporters to the side of Garfield. The Senator from Maine would not release his men. He preferred to see them abandon him without permission. It became the lot of Wisconsin to turn the tide. She had made a diversion in favor of Washburne, and it had failed. On the thirty-fourth ballot, 16 members of her delegation cast their votes for Garfield, who until that time had been kept before the Convention by Grier, of Pennsylvania, who sometimes had had a companion. The galleries, weary of watching the long and monotonous contest, and caring comparatively little for the great principles involved in its settlement, cheered wildly as they saw an opening which might relieve their suspense. There were only the Territories to be called after the announcement of the vote of Wisconsin, and they sent no reinforcements to the Wisconsin skirmishing party. For the effect of the experiment, for such it was, the audience must look to the next ballot. Nine States were called, and 10,000 persons waited in silence for a response to Wisconsin's offer. The tenth was Indiana. In that State, 1 supporter of Grant, 12 followers of Blaine, 2 of Sherman, and 12 of Washburne hurriedly consulted, and then joined Wisconsin in her support of Garfield. Before the roll-call was ended, half a dozen more had forsaken their old leaders for the new one. The experiment would be successful, but the vote for Grant had risen to 313, and what was to be done by the opposition must be done quickly.

Then were Chairmen of delegations and agents of the Treasury seen running from one seat to another. The next ballot would decide the great question, but if the opponents of Grant should fail to transfer their forces at once, the tide might turn to the ex-President. A great deal of work was done in the five minutes which elapsed between the call of the last Territory on the thirty-fifth ballot and the beginning of the roll-call on the thirty-sixth. Plans which had been formed by the labor of four years were hastily thrown aside; sentiments which had been the motive force in a hard-fought campaign were ignored and forgotten. Considerations of all kinds were thrust into oblivion, for now had come the opportunity for the defeat of Grant.

Connecticut was the first to turn to what promised to be the winning side. Her delegates, with the exception of one of the three supporters of Blaine, cast their votes for Garfield. The most earnest solicitation had done its work with the representatives of the little State, where almost every man had seemed to have a separate candidate. Seven of the delegates from Illinois who had been created by the committee followed these men, and the transfer of the entire delegation of Iowa from Blaine to the coming man betokened a speedy nomination. The stampede had begun. Before the whirlwind of impulse, men who had so steadfastly defended their preference for Blaine, for Washburne, or for Edmunds were powerless. All their carefully-prepared arguments were forgotten, and they struggled only to see who should be first to salute the rising sun. Before the roll-call was ended, Gen. Garfield was the nominee of the Republican Party for President, and the great hall was the scene of a tumult which can hardly be described. Where were the friends of Grant? Through all this excitement they had remained fixed and immovable. They could not desert their best friend and the man by whom they felt that the safety of the Republic and the equality and security of all its inhabitants would be preserved beyond the shadow of a doubt. Like a solid phalanx they maintained their lines to the very end. On the first ballot they had given him 304; on the twenty-ninth, after 13 hours' work had been directed against them, 305, and on the thirty-sixth, and last, while delegates all around them were deserting their colors and urging them to come with them and conciliate the nominee, they responded with 306 votes for Grant. The pages of our political history contain no record of an act like this. If the votes of which they had been deprived had been restored to them on any one of the 36 ballots, their candidate would have been nominated. A glance at the last ballot shows that 20 of these votes were those of the New-York delegates, who repudiated their obligations; 31 were cast against them by seceders in Pennsylvania; 18 were the creation of the contested seats committee in the Illinois delegation, and 21 were those of men who disobeyed instructions in Alabama, Kentucky, Missouri, South Carolina, Texas, and Virginia. Here were 90 votes which would have raised the total Grant vote on the last ballot to 396, or 7 more than the number necessary for a choice.

There were some incidents in this Convention which can never be forgotten by those who carefully watched the course of the action. They were not the scenes of wild applause, when gray-haired men lost their heads, but among them were the quiet and sometimes pathetic indications of the mental strain caused by injustice, and the defeat of long-cherished hopes. The enforcement of the report of the committee in relation to the Illinois delegation was an act which brought Senator Logan in strong relief. The vote upon one district admitted two of the contestants, and, as the remaining contestants came in two by two, the black-haired Senator stood in his place and announced each time the vote of his delegation. Two by two his strength was slipping away, and each announcement which he made was given in a tone which showed how the injustice of the defeat was inwardly galling him. The eloquence of the Senator from New-York cannot be effaced from the mind of any person who heard his words. In print they express only a small part of the power which marked their delivery. The gloom which settled on the faces of Messrs. Hale, Frye, and Chandler when Blaine's defeat became certain, and their ineffectual attempts to conceal their emotion, were memorable and full of suggestion. But before these, and before all memories of things said and done within those walls, distinct and ineffaceable, will remain the impressions made by the grand and unparalleled support of Grant by his faithful body of delegates.

### DISCUSSING THE NOMINATIONS.

SOME DISAPPOINTMENT, BUT A GENERAL FEELING OF LOYALTY—THE BLAINE AND SHERMAN CONSULTATIONS OF MONDAY NIGHT.

CHICAGO, June 9.—The opinions expressed by politicians here to-day have, in the main, been most favorable to the ticket. Still, it is, perhaps, only natural that there should be a number of persons who are, for the moment, not altogether satisfied with the result. Under the circumstances, this is not to be wondered at. Two men of great national reputation entered the field. One of them bore a reputation which extended over the whole civilized world. Both these men were favored by a host of earnest Republicans, who are, and who since its birth have been, identified with the fortunes and defeats of the Republican Party. They were all most enthusiastic in the support of one or the other of the two great candidates. They had their hearts in their work, and they were defeated. A man who was not their choice was sprung upon them. He is a man of great ability and of great popularity, but he was not their man, and that they are, to a certain extent, disappointed is not to be wondered at. Still, they are Republicans, and through good report and evil report faithful to the fortunes of the Republican Party. Being so faithful, they are ready to give hearty support to the candidates of the Republican Party.

It may be stated that there continues to be a great deal of speculation here in regard to the manner in which the nomination of Gen. Garfield was brought about. When it becomes time to write the history of what has been done here within the past two days, much may be written on this subject. Meanwhile, the following account of the arrangement preceding the result, which can be relied upon as being its principal features, and correct, can be given to the public.

Late on Monday night and early on Tuesday morning, the Blaine men met in caucus and half-way decided that their candidate could not be nominated. Then it was asked, where can we find a man to beat Grant? and it was at last decided that either Washburne or Garfield was the man to secure that result. At this point, according to a well-authenticated statement current here, Congressman Frye went to ex-Gov. Dennison, of Ohio, and asked if the Sherman men would unite with the Blaine men upon Garfield. Gov. Dennison rejected the proposition, saying that they had come to Chicago to nominate Secretary Sherman, and proposed that the Blaine men should come over to him. To this Mr. Frye would not assent. He was then joined by several of the Blaine and Sherman leaders, and Mr. Frye insisted that another day would nominate Grant; that the delegates were tired, and would vote for Grant very soon, because they saw that his friends held the key to the situation, unless some new man could be proposed. Gen. Garfield was then consulted, and at his urgent request the proposition to make him a candidate was rejected. He felt keenly the delicacy of his position, and said that, if his name was proposed, he should himself rise in the Convention and withdraw. He insisted that the Ohio men should stand by Sherman, and that no negotiations for his own candidacy should be entered into, and his wish was respected. No further part was taken by Sherman's supporters in the consultation which followed. Congressman Aldrich, of Rhode Island; Mr. Cassidy, of Wisconsin; Senator Plumb, of Kansas; I. F. Mack, of Ohio; Gen. Harrison, of Indiana, and several other anti-Grant men continued the negotiations between the Blaine and anti-Blaine men. Blaine was informed, late Monday evening, that his nomination was improbable, and the private wire between his house in Washington and the Grand Pacific Hotel was kept busy for hours. After being informed of the situation, Mr. Blaine said that whenever it became apparent that he could not be nominated his friends were at liberty to make such combinations as were most advantageous to them. After this concession Senator Blaine's managers had a consultation, and determined that they would make another effort to nominate their man, and if it then seemed impossible, to make some nomination that they could control. The Blaine men in Ohio and Gov. Foster were taken into their confidence, and it was again proposed that Gen. Garfield should be voted for; but Gen. Garfield himself and the Sherman men in Ohio objected. It was then proposed that the Blaine men in the Ohio delegation cast their votes for Garfield, not earnestly, but as an experiment. After much consultation, this plan was abandoned, the fear being that Blaine might be beaten by a stampede. Then it was proposed that the movement in favor of Gen. Garfield should be made by a State which had not supported Blaine. This scheme was proposed to the Wisconsin men, who insisted upon giving Washburne a chance before a Garfield movement was attempted. So it was arranged that Wisconsin and Indiana should throw out a skirmish line for Washburne, to see how it would be received. This was done on the thirty-third and thirty-fourth ballots, but met with no success. The Wisconsin men then signified their willingness to experiment with Gen. Garfield's name, which they did on the thirty-fourth ballot, giving him 16 votes. Then, on the next ballot, the thirty-fifth, Indiana turned in for Gen. Garfield, giving him all but 3 of her votes, and raising his total to 50. From this point on, as the event proved, the nomination of Gen. Garfield was assured. When the time comes to discuss the matter in detail, however, it can be clearly proved that the break was made much earlier than was generally expected, and much to the disgust of many followers of Blaine.

As to the manner in which the Vice-President was nominated, it need only be said at this time that Gen. Arthur was accepted as the choice of New-York, and because of his great personal popularity among the delegates from other States. To-night, after the smoke of battle has cleared away, the general verdict is that the action taken was a wise one, and that with Garfield and Arthur the Republicans cannot fail to win in the coming election.

### WELCOMING GEN. GARFIELD.

ENTHUSIASTIC RECEPTIONS WHILE ON HIS WAY TO CLEVELAND—SPEECH-MAKING IN TOLEDO.

TOLEDO, Ohio, June 9.—The train with Gen. Garfield on board arrived here at 6 o'clock this evening. Crowds with flags, the firing of cannon, and bands of music greeted him at Laporte, South Bend, Elkhart, Ligonier, Kendallville, Butler, Edgerton, Bryan, Wauseon, and Swanton, and in response to the cheers and greetings Gov. Foster made brief remarks at all the above places, Gen. Garfield appearing on the rear platform and bowing to the people. It was the intention of the Republicans of this city to have met Gen. Garfield at Union Depot, on his way to Cleveland, at 5:30 o'clock this afternoon, and with a view of making an imposing demonstration a battery of artillery was stationed on the bluff overlooking the railroad grounds, to fire a salute of 100 guns on the approach of the train, and a band of music was stationed at the depot. A tremendous crowd had congregated at the depot to welcome Gen. Garfield, when it was announced that his car would be switched off about a mile up the railroad yards, and taken thence to Cleveland by a special engine. Several thousand people, headed by the band, then marched out and received Gen. Garfield with enthusiastic cheers. After the car was switched off, Gen. J. C. Lee, of this city, introduced Gen. Garfield to the crowd.

As the Presidential nominee stepped upon the front platform he was greeted with great enthusiasm, and when the applause subsided he spoke as follows:

GENTLEMEN: I am glad to meet my fellow-citizens of Ohio again, and I thank you for this cordial and enthusiastic welcome. I cannot make you a speech on this occasion, but I am glad to see the faces of Ohio men, and to receive such a welcome. Permit me to thank you. Our friend Gov. Foster is here, and he must do the talking." [Loud and continued cheering.] Gov. Foster said: "Fellow-citizens of Toledo, if I am asked what State he hails from, [a voice, 'Ohio!'] my sole reply shall be:

> 'He comes from old Ohio,
> And his name is General G.'

"The great Senator from New-York a few days ago said that nothing but the act of God would prevent the nomination of Gen. Grant. I accept Senator Conkling as a prophet. The act of God has come, and Gen. Garfield has become your candidate. [Cheers, and a voice, 'We'll elect him, too.'] But, my fellow-citizens, Providence is always on the side of the Republican Party." [A voice, "You bet!"] At this juncture the engine backed up and coupled with Gen. Garfield's coach. Speaking was given up, and as many as could rushed forward and shook hands with the General until he was literally dragged out of the crowd by the engine.

### THE NOMINATIONS ACCEPTED.

CHICAGO, June 9.—About midnight, the committee appointed to wait on Gens. Garfield and Arthur, and inform them of their nominations, found them in the club-room of the Grand Pacific Hotel, and Senator Hoar, as Chairman, made an appropriate speech. Gen. Garfield replied as follows:

MR. CHAIRMAN AND GENTLEMEN: I assure you that the information you have officially given to me brings the sense of very grave responsibility, and especially so in view of the fact that I was a member of your body, a fact that could not have existed with propriety, had I had the slightest expectation that my name would be connected with the nomination for the office. I have felt, with you, great solicitude concerning the situation of our party during the struggle; but, believing that you are correct in assuring me that substantial unity has been reached in the conclusion, it gives me a gratification far greater than any personal pleasure your announcement can bring. I accept the trust committed to my hands. As to the work of our party, and as to the character of the campaign to be entered upon, I will take an early occasion to reply more fully than I can properly do to-night. I thank you for the assurance of confidence and esteem you have presented to me, and hope we shall see our future as promising as are the indications to-night.

Senator Hoar, in the same manner, presented the nomination to Gen. Arthur, who accepted it in a brief and informal way.

### APPROVALS OF THE NOMINATION.

DENVER, Col., June 9.—The news of the nominations of Garfield and Arthur was received with great satisfaction by the Republicans throughout this State, and ratification meetings were held last night at Denver and other towns.

NEW-ORLEANS, June 9.—A Presidential salute of 21 guns was fired here this evening in honor of Gens. Garfield and Arthur.

KEY WEST, June 9.—The Republicans turned out in a torch-light procession and held a mass-meeting here last night, to ratify the nominations of Garfield and Arthur.

PITTSBURG, Penn., June 9.—The Allegheny County Republican Executive Committee, in session this afternoon, heartily indorsed the action of the Chicago Convention in nominating Gen. Garfield. To-night a large reception-meeting is in progress in Allegheny City.

WASHINGTON, June 9.—Arrangements are being made by the National Veteran Club and the Republican Club of Washington to serenade Gen. Garfield on his return to this city, where he is expected on Saturday next. Arrangements are also in progress for holding a grand ratification meeting in front of the City Hall, immediately after the final adjournment of Congress.

### A REMARKABLE COINCIDENCE.

HOW GENS. GARFIELD AND ARTHUR STARTED LIFE IN THE SAME ROOM.

WASHINGTON, June 9.—A correspondent of the *Evening Star* communicates to that journal the following interesting reminiscence of the early life of Gens. Garfield and Arthur, the Republican candidates for President and Vice-President: "North Pownal, Bennington County, Vt., formerly known as Whipple's Corners, is situated in the south-western corner of the State, and by the usually traveled road is an hour's ride from New-York, through the corner of Vermont, by way of North Pownal, into the State of Massachusetts. In 1851, Chester A. Arthur, fresh from Union College, came to North Pownal, and for one Summer taught the village school. About two years later James A. Garfield, then a young student at Williams College, several miles distant, in order to obtain the necessary means to defray his expenses while pursuing his studies, came also to North Pownal and established a writing-school in the same room formerly occupied by Mr. Arthur, and taught classes in penmanship during the long Winter evenings. Thus, from a common starting-point in early life, after a lapse of more than a quarter of a century, after years of manly toil, these distinguished men are, by the action of the Chicago Convention, brought into a close relationship before the Nation and before the civilized world."

### GEN. GRANT SATISFIED.

CHICAGO, June 9.—Gen. Grant passed through Chicago to-day en route for Milwaukee, where he will attend the soldiers' reunion. He took lunch with Senators Logan and Cameron, and in conversation with them expressed himself as not at all displeased with the result of the Convention. He said, among other things, that he would rather be assured, as he was, of the friendship of the 300 true men who stood by him to the last than be President of the United States.

### SENATOR WAGNER'S PARTY.

CHICAGO, June 9.—Senator Wagner's party left here this morning for New-York. Their car is decorated with flags, and the motto, "New-York solid for Gen. J. A. Garfield, of Ohio."

### *AN OREGON CONGRESSMAN GAINED*

M. C. GEORGE, A REPUBLICAN, RECEIVES 800 MAJORITY—LEGISLATURE PROBABLY REPUBLICAN.

SAN FRANCISCO, June 9.—A dispatch from Portland, Oregon, says M. C. George, Republican, for Congress, is elected by about 800 majority. Three Republican Supreme Court Judges have average majorities of over 1,000. The Legislature is doubtful, with the chances in favor of the Republicans.

### *ARMY AND NAVY NEWS.*

DETACHMENTS AND ORDERS TO OFFICERS AND MOVEMENTS OF VESSELS.

WASHINGTON, June 9.—Major Clifton Comly, Ordnance Department, has been ordered to return to his station, San Antonio, Texas, upon the completion of his examination for promotion. The recent order directing First Lieut. M. M. Macomb, Fourth Artillery, to report to the Commanding General, Department of West Point, for duty at the Military Academy, has been revoked, and Second Lieut. W. M. Medcalf, Fourth Artillery, has been ordered to report at that post, Aug. 28, for duty. First Lieut. William H. Law, Jr., Twentieth Infantry, has been detailed for duty with the Arctic expedition, and will report, accordingly, to the Chief Signal Officer of the Army; First Lieut. Gustavus C. Boon, Second Cavalry, has been formally assigned to duty as Acting Assistant Quartermaster and Acting Commissary of Subsistence in connection with the expedition to the Arctic seas, now organizing, and has been ordered to report accordingly.

Brig.-Gen. Benjamin Alvord, Paymaster-General, having served faithfully over 46 consecutive years as a commissioned officer, he has been, at his own request, and by direction of the President, retired, from active service, in conformity with section 1,243 of the Revised Statutes. Major T. C. H. Smith, Paymaster United States Army, having completed the business requiring his presence in this city, has been ordered to return to his proper station.

Commander Thomas O. Selfridge has been ordered to special duty in the Bureau of Navigation, Washington. The following detachments have been made: Commander Edward Terry, from the Pensacola, and granted leave of absence for one year; Lieut.-Commander Charles W. Schmitz, from the command of the Rio Bravo, and placed on waiting orders; Assistant Paymaster John R. Martin, from the Rio Bravo, and ordered to settle accounts; Lieut. Richard Mitchell, Mates Larkin T. Lee, Henry C. Fuller, and J. M. Creighton, Passed Assistant Surgeon Theodore C. Heyl, and Passed Assistant Engineer Charles F. Nagle, from the Rio Bravo, and placed on waiting orders; Paymaster John Fusey, from special duty at the New-York Navy-yard and placed on waiting orders; Paymaster R. P. Loch, from the receiving-ship St. Louis, and ordered to settle accounts; Passed Assistant Engineer D. P. McCartney from special duty connected with the Dispatch, and ordered to experimental duty at the Washington Navy-yard.

Commodore D. McN. Fairfax and Lieut.-Commander Frank Wilds have been ordered to examination for promotion; Paymaster George H. Griffing, to the receiving-ship St. Louis, League Island; Paymaster John F. Tarbell, to special duty at the inspection of provisions and clothing, New-York Navy-yard.

The Tuscarora has been placed out of commission at the Mare Island Navy-yard.

The Secretary of the Navy has received advices that the ship Portsmouth would sail from Georgetown, Bermuda, on the 3d inst. for Fayal, Azores. During the stay of the vessel at Hamilton, Bermuda, at the request of the British authorities, she participated in the celebration of the Queen's birthday by dressing the ship and firing the usual salute.

### *EXERCISING NAVAL CADETS.*

ANNAPOLIS, Md., June 9.—The Cadets at the Naval Academy were exercised to-day in a flotilla drill on the Severn, under Lieut. L. C. Logan. The flotilla performed a number of manœuvres, both under sail and under oars. In passing the Santee, off which, in launches, was the Board of Visitors, the flotilla lowered sail in salute of the Admiral's flag. The drill lasted about an hour and a half, and the manœuvres were excellently performed. Last night Admiral Balch entertained the graduating class.

The boat-races at the Naval Academy came off this afternoon, and were witnessed by a large throng of persons. The cutter race, three-quarters of a mile, was won by Capt. P. R. Alger, of the Fourth Division; time—5:38. There were four starters. The shell race was won by the University crew, beating the Academy crew 30 seconds. The latter had trained only two months. Secretary Thompson arrived at the Naval Academy this evening, and was received with a salute by the Santee and other naval honors.

### *THE MILLERS' EXHIBITION.*

CINCINNATI, June 9.—The Millers' International Exhibition is now in full and successful operation, the mills being all at work. The judges have made the following awards: On flour, Spring wheat, patent, gold medal to Washburne, Crosby & Co., Minneapolis; silver and bronze medals to the same firm. Spring wheat, straight, gold medal to Leonard Day & Co., Minneapolis; silver medal to Washburne, Crosby & Co., Minneapolis; bronze medal to the Iron Mountain Mills, St. Louis. Spring wheat, clear, gold medal to Hinkle Brothers, Minneapolis. Winter wheat, patent, gold medal to John Huegley, Nashville, Ill.; bronze medal to Wagons & Gates, Independence, Mo. Winter wheat, straight, gold medal to the Atlantic Milling Company, St. Louis; silver medal to James Gordon & Co., Sparta, Ill.; bronze medal to A. A. Taylor, Loudonville, Ohio.

### *ANOTHER PRINCETON STUDENT DEAD.*

ELMIRA, N. Y., June 9.—Bart Stanchfield, son of Dr. J. K. Stanchfield, a prominent physician, died this morning of malarial fever contracted at Princeton College.

## WORK OF THE CAMPAIGN.

### *INDIANA DEMOCRATS URGING HENDRICKS'S CLAIMS.*

PLATFORM ADOPTED BY THE STATE CONVENTION—THE CONTEST OVER THE GOVERNORSHIP WON BY EX-CONGRESSMAN LANDERS—MR. HENDRICKS'S SPEECH.

INDIANAPOLIS, Ind., June 9.—The State Democratic Convention, which met here to-day, was more like a ratification meeting than an organized deliberative body. There were three names mentioned for the nomination for Governor, although the fight was between ex-Congressman Franklin Landers and Lieut.-Gov. Isaac P. Gray. Landers was chosen for Governor on the second ballot, and Gray was renominated for Lieutenant Governor by acclamation. The contest between the two has been close and it will probably weaken the ticket in the field. Landers is backed by the soft-money Democrats, and is a man of the blue-jeans quality. While in Congress he opposed the election of Kerr as Speaker of the House, and Kerr's friends fought him desperately. The organ of the Democracy of Floyd County, the home of Kerr, and a Democratic stronghold, stubbornly refuses to support him. Landers is generally hated in the border counties, because he is pushed by an unpopular clique at Indianapolis.

Hendricks was chosen permanent Chairman of the convention because he has occupied his customary attitude on the fence in this controversy, and was, therefore, thought best qualified to preside impartially. His name was greeted with loud applause when the temporary Chairman alluded to him as the man "who can and will be the next President, and when we elect him, by the help of God, we will inaugurate him." The Democracy of this State will do all it can to nominate Hendricks at Cincinnati, but it has little hope of success, and a few men are candid enough to admit it. They claim only a few scattering and uncertain votes besides Indiana's 30 on the first ballot. Mr. William Henderson, Hendricks's brother-in-law, told THE TIMES's correspondent to-day that they count on a majority of the Missouri delegation, several votes from Alabama, and some from Texas to start with. A well-informed Hendricks man, who, too, has just returned from Washington, says that Senator Wallace, of Pennsylvania, thinks that Hancock's name will not come before the Cincinnati Convention, because the State is divided, and in that event Hendricks will get the entire Texas delegation, which is instructed for Hancock. He also said that Hendricks could carry New-York if Tilden does not use his influence against him, but if Tilden should express his determination to withhold his support from Hendricks, that would be sufficient to defeat his nomination. "Tilden can kill off Hendricks if he wants to."

The fraud issue was put forth as the key-note, and Garfield was denounced for being a member of the Electoral Commission. Gen. Arthur was referred to as "one whom even Hayes, polluted as he was by fraud, thought unworthy to stand in his presence." In his speech on taking the chair, Mr. Hendricks said: "Yesterday the Republican Party laid away forever the grim-visaged warrior and plumed knight together. To-day they lie in the obscurity of defeat. The Republican Party has said to the nations of the world, that did Gen. Grant uncommon honor, that he is no longer worthy of sitting at the head of national affairs, and it was no uncommon thing when that statement was made to mankind that Gen. Grant was no longer worthy of support in the National Republican Convention. I have heard Democrats, for the last two or three weeks, inquiring who is the weakest man at Chicago. I care not for that. I repeat it—I care not for that. The last election, when Tilden and Hendricks were elected, there was a majority on the Democratic side of the white voters of the United States of 1,000,000 men, and of the whites and blacks together there was a majority of more than 250,000. Now, when we meet in Cincinnati to respond to Chicago, we meet with the assurance upon our side that we have this strength, this power, this sentiment of the American people upon our side."

The following is a synopsis of the platform:

It congratulates the Democracy of the country upon the harmony prevailing within its organization, and upon its unanimity in purpose to cast behind it every occasion and sentiment of discord, and stand as a man for success in 1880, and pledges the acceptance of the platform that may be made at Cincinnati and the support of the candidates who may there be chosen. It declares that laws should be enacted, executed, and administrated only for the public good, and all class legislation and all favoritism in the affairs of the Government be made odious; demands rigid economy in public expenditures; that elections must be free from the control of the Army, so that they shall be fair and honest, as they once were; that the coin and paper money of the country should be of uniform value and readily convertible, and have as great purchasing power as the money of other first-class commercial countries of the world, and the paper money, like the coin, should be furnished by the United States, and should not be in excess of such quantity as will always remain at par with coin, and Treasury notes should be subject to taxation; announces gratification at the action of the Democratic members of Congress in reducing public expenditures, and in the cutting off of questionable and fraudulent claims, resulting in a saving to the Treasury of more than $100,000,000; opposes the aggression of the Republican leaders upon the rights of the States for the purpose of building up a strong central power; gives honorable mention of the legislation of 1879, for having redeemed the pledges of the Democratic Convention of 1876, to provide by law for the comfort and safety of laborers in the mines; declares pride in Indiana's system of free schools, but opposes the use of the school fund for sectarian or for any other purpose whatever, than the support of the common schools.

The party is gratified with the action of the Democrats in Congress in respect to bounties and pensions for soldiers. Other resolutions hold up to public detestation the conduct of the Republican Party in placing Hayes and Wheeler, by criminal practices, shocking to every honest sentiment, and damaging to our institutions, in the offices to which they were not elected; and also condemn the President for rewarding the guilty persons by conferring upon them high and lucrative offices; recognize the blessings of God upon our country in the return of business prosperity, and denounce it as false and blasphemous when partisan leaders claim that this is the work of their hands; denounce the coolie system which imports Chinese bondsmen; indorse the State Administration of Indiana; recognize the rights of colored citizens as well as whites who immigrate to Indiana, but denounce the action of the Republican Party in importing into the State pauper negroes for the sole purpose of using them as voters; and favors the continuance of the two-thirds rule in the National Convention and the nomination of Hendricks.

The delegates and nominations are as follows:

*Delegates at Large*—J. E. McDonald, D. W. Voorhees, W. E. Niblock, and J. R. Slack.
*For Governor*—FRANKLIN LANDERS.
*For Lieutenant-Governor*—ISAAC P. GRAY, renominated.

### *MR. SEYMOUR STILL DECLINES.*

SYRACUSE, N. Y., June 9.—It is firmly believed by the Democrats of this part of the State that ex-Gov. Seymour will be nominated at Cincinnati. In conversation with Judge Graham, of Utica, on Monday last, ex-Gov. Seymour said, "I see that one delegate at Chicago, Senator Conkling, says that Grant could carry New-York over any candidate. If I were nominated at Cincinnati I should carry New-York, but I am not a candidate, for I do not think the Democratic nomination belongs to New-York." Judge Graham took this statement down, and it may be relied upon as entirely authentic.

### *PREPARING FOR THE DEMOCRATS.*

CINCINNATI, June 9.—The resident committee of the Democratic National Committee, with Col. L. A. Harris, Chairman, has made considerable progress in preparing Music Hall for the use of the Democratic National Convention. The telegraph companies will have offices in the corridors on each side of the hall, in direct communication with the delegates, press representatives, and stage. The reporters' tables will be placed in two rows in front of the stage. Delegates will have the front portion of the hall. Ladies will be admitted to raised seats on the rear of the stage. The decorations will be simple, the grandeur of the interior of the hall itself forbidding any elaborate display. The committee is assured that railroads all over the country will give reduced rates to persons attending the Convention.

### *THE GREENBACK CONVENTION.*

A BEGGARLY ARRAY OF EMPTY BENCHES—A UNIQUE PRAYER—SQUABBLING OVER MINOR MATTERS.

CHICAGO, June 9.—It is said that a Greenback National Convention has its head-quarters in the Palmer House here, but persons who have become accustomed to the crowds that have occupied the immense building for more than a week scarcely notice the presence of the inflationists, and cannot find them unless they are sought for in their rooms. Now and then a man is seen with a green badge upon his breast, and if the corridors are searched roughly-drawn notices will indicate that the odd people within are Greenback delegates from Texas or Mississippi or some other State. There were conferences last night, and a great deal of talking was indulged in about everything but candidates. This morning one heard little gossip about who should be nominated.

The Convention met at noon in the hall recently occupied by the Republican Convention. As compared with their Republican predecessors, the Greenbackers presented a rather melancholy appearance. The delegates occupied only one-third of the space required for the delegates to the Republican Convention. There was a mere fringe of persons on the stage behind the desk, while the audience partly filled the galleries for about 100 feet on either side of the delegates. Beyond the audience and the platform on either side stretched acres of empty benches, among which the voices of speakers rattled loudly and mockingly. The decorations, including the portraits of the fathers of the Republican Party, remained where they were placed by the National Republican Committee, and the delegations from the different States appropriated the shields left by the Republicans, and bearing the names of the different States, to designate the dividing lines between delegations. Probably 1,500 persons were in the hall when F. P. Dewees, of Pennsylvania, called the Convention to order. The clergyman who was invited to make the opening prayer tickled the fancy of so many persons in the audience that they frequently interrupted him with laughter and applause, particularly when he thanked God that Jesus was a mechanic, and when he reminded the Creator that, while the Democrats and Republicans had been prayed for in many pulpits, not one prayer had ascended for the Greenback Party. "We come to Thee, O, Lord," he said, "on our own hook."

Gilbert De La Matyr, the Indianapolis parson-politician, was made temporary Chairman, apparently because he had more voice than the many talkers in the body, and under his guidance the Convention was in session until 2 o'clock. A great deal of time was spent in discussing a resolution offered by a delegate who was annoyed by the pictures of Republicans that hung about overhead. He wanted them removed, but a Mississippi delegate was of the opinion that they were portraits of men who had done a good work, and likened them to leaders in the Greenback Party who were to accomplish the task of "striking the shackles of capital from the hands of labor," he won a majority of the delegates to his opinion, and the pictures were ordered to be retained. Squabbles of a tiresome nature over a variety of details followed, and the Convention refused to adjourn, notwithstanding several of the delegates declared they were hungry and wanted to go to dinner. It was then decided to hear a delegation from the Woman Suffrage Association. These ladies, for whom Mrs. Lydia Jocelyn Gage was the chief spokeswoman, filled up so much of the remainder of the morning session as was not wasted by the performances of an excessively bad brass band stationed a quarter of a mile away at the end of the hall.

This evening the committees not being prepared to report the convention was addressed by the Hon. M. Wallace, M. P., of Canada, and A. W. Wright, of the Currency Reform League, of Canada, who urged the doctrine that a Government owes to its people the creation of a legal circulating currency, and on behalf of Canada extended sympathy and encouragement to the Greenbackers of the United States.

While awaiting the report of the Committee on Credentials, in answer to loud calls, Denis Kearney entertained the audience with one of his characteristic speeches. He thanked God that even the Republican Convention had the grace to reject imperialism in the candidacy of Grant. He prophesied that Garfield, in consequence of the weakness of the Republican platform on the subject, and his record on the Chinese Immigration bill, would not receive one-third of the vote of California, Nevada, and Oregon, while, James G. Blaine, whose record was rotten enough, would have polled two-thirds of the votes of those States had he been nominated, because of his fighting the battle against Chinese importation.

At the conclusion of Kearney's speech, a delegate offered a strong anti-Chinese resolution, which was referred to an appropriate committee without debate, and the convention adjourned until 10 o'clock to-morrow.

The Pomeroy-Hoyt, or club wing of the Greenback-Labor Party, calling itself the Union Greenback-Labor Party, also met to-day at Farwell Hall. Their candidates for President and Vice-President, nominated at St. Louis last March, are Stephen B. Dillaye, of New-Jersey, and B. J. Chambers, of Texas. This convention is held in the interest of party harmony, to emphasize the demand for a distinctively Greenback candidate, and to express hostility to any compromise or coalition with the Democratic Party managers, which they have feared would be attempted by the convention at the Exposition Building. Hugh Preyer called the meeting to order, and Ralph E. Hoyt took the chair. About 100 delegates were present.

At the evening session, Mr. Thomas, of Wisconsin, from the Committee on Conference, with the like committee of the National Greenback-Labor Party, reported that a plan by which the former should merge in the latter had been arranged. After a desultory debate, the convention decided to accept the arrangement, and abandon its organization as a convention, while continuing its present organization. The convention then adjourned sine die, and its members will take seats in the National Greenback-Labor Convention to-morrow.

### *THE DEMOCRACY IN GEORGIA.*

THE PARTY PREFERRING FIELD AS A CANDIDATE—DIVIDED ON STATE ISSUES.

ATLANTA, Ga., June 9.—The Democratic Convention here to-day was attended by 500 delegates from all parts of the State, and was composed of representative men. Recently the Field movement has been actively engineered in Georgia by special agents from Washington, who have met with singular success. In Georgia the sentiment two months ago pointed to Tilden as the most available candidate, but recent changes substituted Field, and when the convention met this morning it was evident that Field's friends had charge of it. The proceedings were brief, and marked by no special event except the hissing of Brown's name when one vote was announced for him for delegate at large. Gen. A. R. Lawton, of Chatham, will head the delegation. George T. Barnes, of Richmond; Evan P. Howell, of Fulton, and Gen. Pierce M. B. Young, of Bartow, are the other delegates at large. Barnes is for Bayard; the others favor Field, but are not inimical to Tilden. The State delegation is claimed to be almost solid by the Field men, but the Tilden men say that five or six of them are for Tilden, and that others will come to him in the event that Field should not be strong enough to secure the nomination. The convention adopted no platform, but recommended adhesion to the two-thirds rule. Several little incidents showed that discordant elements in State politics are actively at work, and the coming canvass will show the party hopelessly split on all State issues. Senator Hill was warmly pressed to lead the delegation, but there was opposition to him, and he telegraphed this morning, withdrawing his name from the contest. The general sentiment among the delegates shows that they regard the Republican ticket as very strong, and really have very little hope of beating it. The individual preferences of the delegates, taken by *Constitution* reporters, show that the majority prefer Field, while many are for Tilden, Thurman, and Bayard. The Independent faction was strong in the convention, and it is evident from several circumstances that the organized Democracy is in a bad way.

The delegates from the districts are as follows: W. A. Wilkin, J. M. Couper, J. R. Alexander, B. E. Russell, L. M. Felton, D. M. Roberts, T. W. Grimes, P. H. Brewster, John D. Stewart, C. C. Duncan, James G. Oakington, A. C. McCalla, J. C. Fain, A. H. Gray, Gen. D. M. Dubose, Patrick Walsh, editor of the Augusta *Chronicle;* W. P. Price, and T. M. Peeples.

### *FIELD FAVORED IN MARYLAND.*

PLATFORM ADOPTED BY THE DEMOCRATIC CONVENTION—DELEGATES AND ELECTORS.

BALTIMORE, June 9.—The Democratic Conservative State Convention, to select delegates to the National Democratic Convention at Cincinnati, and to nominate candidates for Electors for President and Vice-President, assembled in this City to-day. The proceedings were characterized by entire harmony. The resolutions declare adherence to the principles which have guided and controlled the policy of the National Democratic Party since the formation of the Federal Government. They repudiate the "great wrong by which the will of the people in the election of 1876 was reversed by fraudulent counts after the polls were closed, and, the Republican Party being in possession of the military power, the people had no choice except between civil war and such form of arbitration as the representatives of the Republican Party in Congress might see fit to devise. An offense was thus committed against a whole people, which ought never to be forgotten nor condoned. The Republican Party has used the public money and the public lands in fostering great monopolies; has filled the public Treasury by means of tariffs intended to promote the advantage of particular manufacturers at the expense of the producing States; has created a system of laws under which the National Executive may unduly and directly influence both State and Federal elections. It has increased the number of officers until they form an immense civil force, governed by and dependent upon its will, and it has used the Federal Army as a means of increasing its political power. More than once the people of the United States have been brought to the verge of bankruptcy by the legislation of the Republican Party, and they owe their returning prosperity only to the blessing of God and to their own increased economy and untiring labor."

The resolutions also declare the belief that the National Democratic Conservative Party will maintain the equality of all citizens before the law, and enforce and uphold their constitutional rights; that it will check the present extravagance in the expenditure of the public money; that it will reform the injustice and inequality of existing tariffs; that it will maintain absolutely the supremacy of the civil over the military power, and check the progress of centralization and keep the Executive and Congress within the limit of the powers confided to them by the Constitution. The resolutions decline to instruct the delegates, but express confidence in the distinguished ability of Thomas Francis Bayard, of Delaware. Adhesion to the two-thirds rule was recommended. The resolutions were unanimously adopted.

The following are the delegates and Electors:

*Delegates at Large*—William Pinkney Whyte, Philip F. Thomas, John Lee Carroll, and Bernard Carter.

*District Delegates*—First, Richard Hynson and E. E. Jackson; Second, Charles B. Roberts and Wilton Johnson; Third, George Colton and James Bond; Fourth, John W. Davis and William Keyser; Fifth, Barnes Compton and John T. Bond; Sixth, L. V. Baughman and L. Cass Smith.

*Electors at Large*—I. Nevitt Steele and J. Thomas C. Hopkins.

*District Electors*—First District, Levin L. Waters; Second, P. H. Walker; Third, John R. McNulty; Fourth, William H. Welsh; Fifth, Richard W. W. Bowie; Sixth, William M. Price.

### *CONGRESSIONAL NOMINATION.*

CHICAGO, June 9.—The Hon. William M. Springer was to-day renominated for Congress by acclamation by the Democratic Congressional Convention of the Twelfth Illinois District.

### *THE SEIZURE OF THE ATALAYA.*

QUEBEC, June 9.—The *Chronicle* this morning has the following: "The Atalaya is the first case of the kind in Canada. Under the Foreign Enlistment act of 1870 (imperial) it is provided that if any person within the limits of her Majesty's dominions prepares, with or without any naval or military expedition, to proceed against dominions of any friendly State, all ships and their equipments and all arms and munitions of war used or forming part of such expedition shall be forwarded to her Majesty. When the Governor-General is satisfied that there is reasonable and probable cause for believing that a ship is about to be dispatched contrary to the act, he may issue his warrant to seize and search the ship, and to detain the same until it has either been condemned or released by proof of law. The Governor-General must have issued his warrant, as the Atalaya is under detention. Subsequent proceedings in the case, as affecting imperial and foreign relations, have to be taken before the Court of Vice Admiralty at Quebec, which has exclusive jurisdiction in the matter."

### *THE RACING SEASON IN ENGLAND.*

LONDON, June 9.—The race for the Royal Hunt Cup took place to-day, at Ascot Heath, and was won by Mr. Foy's 4-year-old b. c. Strathern. The second place was secured by Sir G. Chetwynd's 5-year-old ch. h. Lord Clive, and the third place by Mr. H. Hall's 3-year-old Tertius. Thirty-one horses ran. The betting just before the race was twenty-five to one against Strathern, twenty to one against Lord Clive, and twenty to one against Tertius. Strathern won the race by three lengths, with one length between Lord Clive and Tertius. Mr. P. Lorillard's Parole, who started at seventeen to one against him, was never prominent in the race, and finished with the middle lot. Mr. J. H. Houldsworth's Ruperra came in among the last.

The *Sportsman* to-day says: "We understand that Fred Archer, the jockey, has abandoned his proposed trip to the United States."

### *THE SUNDAY-SCHOOL TEACHERS.*

OGDENSBURG, N. Y., June 9.—At the session of the New-York State Sunday-school Convention, a centennary jubilee service was held last evening, the house being crowded. James H. Kellogg, of Troy, delivered a historical address, and Charles F. Richardson, of Philadelphia, read a poem. This morning, J. W. Helmer, of Lockport, was chosen President; A. D. Mathews of Brooklyn, Ralph Wells, and ten others, Vice-Presidents; Thomas Dransfield, of Rochester, and four others, Secretaries. The various annual reports were read, and a discussion was had on the general work of the association. This afternoon, the Rev. Dr. John Hall, of New-York, delivered an address on "Efficiency in Sunday-school Work," and Ralph Wells spoke on "The Girded Teacher at Work." Dr. Hall was commissioned a special delegate to the London centenary meeting. The convention grows largely in number and interest, and is pronounced a very successful meeting.

### *CONTESTS ON THE TURF.*

POUGHKEEPSIE, N. Y., June 9.—At the Driving Park to-day, Uncle Dave won the first two heats in the 2:34 race, and Brookside Flora the next three. Time—2:34; 2:30¼; 2:29; 2:29; 2:30¼. Edwin Thorne won the 2:40 race. Time—2:33½; 2:35; 2:34¼.

ST. LOUIS, June 9.—This was the second day of the Jockey Club races. The first race, one and one-quarter miles, was won by L'Argentine, with Ilimyar second and Expectation third. Time—2:10¼. In the second race, three-quarter mile dash, Hindoo was first, Voltaigue second, and Storey third. Time—1:17¾. The third race, one and one-eight mile heats, was won by Ursilia in two heats, with Sam Ecker second and Genevieve third. Time—1:59; 2:01¼.

### *THE CHRISTIANCY DIVORCE CASE.*

WASHINGTON, June 9.—Minister Christiancy's counsel, Mr. E. C. Ingersoll, yesterday filed a formal replication to the answer of his wife to the suit for divorce instituted by him. This, it is thought, will be of no avail, as the order for payment of alimony and counsel fees stayed all proceedings on the part of the plaintiff until complied with. At the expiration of the time (15th inst.) given for the payment of the alimony, a motion will be made for an extension of time to enable Mr. Christiancy to be heard from.

# The New-York Times.

VOL. XXIX.......NO. 8980. NEW-YORK, MONDAY, JUNE 21, 1880. PRICE FOUR CENTS.


## MR. TILDEN WITHDRAWS

### HIS LETTER DECLINING THE BOURBON NOMINATION.

THE GREAT CLAIMANT ADDRESSES THE NEW-YORK DELEGATES, RECITING HIS GRIEVANCES AND RENOUNCING HIS CLAIM TO THE LEADERSHIP OF THE PARTY.

CINCINNATI, June 20.—Late this evening the long suspense in regard to Mr. Tilden's actual position, and the exact contents of his letter of withdrawal, which, as was announced in THE TIMES's dispatches yesterday, arrived here last night, was ended by the delivery to the public of the letter itself. This move was not made until the friends of Mr. Tilden from all parts of the country had been consulted, and they had decided that it was time for him to take some positive stand. Then it was determined that the New-York delegation should be called together. Mr. Manning, the temporary Chairman, at once set about this work, but found that it was no easy matter to bring together a number of gentlemen who had resolved upon amusing themselves in the beer palaces of Cincinnati, to the exclusion of the cares of politics. Another obstacle in the way of the meeting was the refusal of Senator Jacobs and a number of his friends to attend the meeting, which, as will be remembered, was adjourned last night until Monday morning. Still, Manning, as Chairman, insisted, and at last, after 9 o'clock, the meeting came together. Before it was called to order, Senator Jacobs was quietly approached by a number of the Tilden agents, and an effort made to induce him to present in the Convention a resolution to the effect that the ex-Governor was still the choice of the men of New-York. In order that he might be persuaded to do this more readily, it was represented to him that a letter positively withdrawing Mr. Tilden's name would be presented to the meeting. Still, Mr. Jacobs, knowing very well the people he had to deal with, declined to do this. Then Manning called the meeting to order and said that he did so for the purpose of presenting a letter in regard to the Presidency, which had been received from Mr. Tilden. Rufus Peckham, of Albany, was then called upon, and read the following will and testament of the great American claimant:

#### MR. TILDEN'S LETTER.

NEW-YORK, June 18, 1880.

*To the delegates from the State of New-York to the Democratic National Convention:*

Your first assembling is an occasion on which it is proper for me to state to you my relation to the nomination for the Presidency which you and your associates are commissioned to make in behalf of the Democratic Party of the United States. Having passed my early years in an atmosphere filled with traditions of the war which secured our national independence, and of the struggles which made our continental system a Government for the people, by the people, I learned to idolize the institutions of my country, and was educated to believe it the duty of a citizen of the Republic to take his fair allotment of care and trouble in public affairs. I fulfilled that duty to the best of my ability for 40 years as a private citizen. Although during all my life giving at least as much thought and effort to public affairs as to all other objects, I have never accepted official service except for a brief period for a special purpose, and only when the occasion seemed to require of me that sacrifice of private preferences to public interests, my life has been substantially that of a private citizen. It was, I presume, the success of efforts in which, as a private citizen, I had shared, to overthrow a corrupt combination then holding dominion in our Metropolis, and to purify the judiciary, which had become its tool, that induced the Democracy of the State, in 1874, to nominate me for Governor. This was done in spite of the protest of a minority that the part I had borne in those reforms had created antagonisms fatal to me as a candidate. I felt constrained to accept the nomination as the most certain means of putting the power of the Gubernatorial office on the side of reform, and of removing the impression, wherever it prevailed, that the faithful discharge of one's duty as a citizen is fatal to his usefulness as a public servant.

The breaking up of the Canal Ring, the better management of our public works, the large reduction of taxes, and other reforms accomplished during my Administration, doubtless occasioned my nomination for the Presidency by the Democracy of the Union, in the hope that similar processes would be applied to the Federal Government. From the responsibilities of such an undertaking, appalling as it seemed to me, I did not feel at liberty to shrink. In the canvass which ensued the Democratic Party represented reform in the administration of the Federal Government and a restoration of our complex political system to the pure ideas of its founders. Upon these issues the people of the United States, by a majority of more than a quarter of a million, chose a majority of the Electors to cast their votes for the Democratic candidates for President and Vice-President. It is my right and privilege here to say that I was nominated and elected to the Presidency, absolutely free from any engagement in respect to the exercise of its powers or the disposal of its patronage. Through the whole period of my relation to the Presidency I did everything in my power to elevate, and nothing to lower, moral standards in the competition of parties. By what nefarious means the basis for a false count was laid in several of the States I need not recite. These are now matters of history about which whatever diversity of opinion may have existed in either of the great parties of the country at the time of their consummation has since practically disappeared. I refused to ransom from the returning boards of Southern States the documentary evidence, by the suppression of which and by the substitution of fraudulent and forged papers, a pretext was made for the perpetration of a false count. The constitutional duty of the two houses of Congress to count the Electoral votes as cast, and to give effect to the will of the people, as expressed by their suffrages, was never fulfilled. An Electoral Commission, for the existence of which I have no responsibility, was formed, and to it the two houses of Congress abdicated their duty to make the count by a law enacting that the count of the commission should stand as final unless overruled by the concurrent action of the two Houses. Its false count was not overruled, owing to the complicity of a Republican Senate with the Republican majority of the commission. Controlled by its Republican majority of 8 to 7, the Electoral Commission counted out the men elected by the people, and counted in the men not elected by the people. That subversion of the election created a new issue for the decision of the people of the United States, transcending in importance all questions of administration. It involved the vital principle of self-government through elections by the people. The immense growth of the means of corrupt influence over the ballot-box, which is at the disposal of the party having possession of the executive administration, had already become a present evil and a great danger, tending to make elections irresponsible to public opinion, hampering the power of the people to change rulers, and enabling the men holding the machinery of government to continue and perpetuate their power. It was my opinion in 1876, that the opposition attempting to change the Administration, needed to include at least two-thirds of the voters at the opening of the canvass, in order to retain a majority at the election. If, after such obstacles had been overcome and a majority of the people had voted to change the administration of their Government, the men in office could still procure a false count founded upon fraud, perjury, and forgeries, furnishing a pretext of documentary evidence on which to base that false count, and if such a transaction were not only successful, but if, after allotments of its benefits were made to its contrivers, abettors, and apologists, by the chief beneficiary of the transactions, it were condoned by the people, a practical destruction of elections by the people would have been accomplished.

The failure to install the candidates chosen by the people—a contingency consequent upon no act or omission of mine, and beyond my control—has thus left me for the last three years and until now, when the Democratic Party, by its delegates in National Convention assembled, shall choose a new leader, the involuntary but necessary representative of this momentous issue; as such, denied the immunities of private life, without the powers conferred by public station, subject to unceasing falsehoods and calumnies from the partisans of an Administration laboring in vain to justify its existence, I have, nevertheless, steadfastly endeavored to preserve to the Democratic Party of the United States the supreme issue before the people for their decision next November, whether this shall be a Government by the sovereign people through elections, or a Government by discarded servants, holding over by force and fraud; and I have withheld no sacrifice, and neglected no opportunity to uphold, organize, and consolidate against the enemies of representative institutions, the great party which alone, under God, can effectually resist their overthrow.

Having now borne faithfully my full share of labor and care in the public service and wearing the marks of its burdens, I desire nothing so much as an honorable discharge. I wish to lay down the honors and toils of even quasi party leadership and to seek the repose of private life. In renouncing renomination for the Presidency I do so with no doubt in my mind as to the vote of the State of New-York, or of the United States, but because I believe it is a renunciation of re-election of the Presidency. To those who think my nomination and re-election indispensable to an effectual vindication of the right of the people to elect their rulers, violated in my person, I have accorded as long a reserve of my decision as possible, but I cannot overcome my repugnance to enter into a new engagement which involves four years of ceaseless toil. The dignity of the Presidential office is above a merely personal ambition, but it creates in me no illusion. Its value is as a great power for good to the country. I said, four years ago, in accepting the nomination:

> Knowing as I do, therefore, from fresh experience how great the difference is between gliding through an official routine and working out a reform of systems and policies, it is impossible for me to contemplate what needs to be done in the Federal Administration without an anxious sense of the difficulties of the undertaking. If summoned by the suffrages of my countrymen to attempt this work I shall endeavor with God's help to be the efficient instrument of their will.

Such a work of renovation after many years of misrule, such a reform of systems and policies to which I would cheerfully have sacrificed all that remained to me of health and life is now, I fear, beyond my strength. With unfeigned thanks for the honors bestowed upon me with a heart swelling with emotions of gratitude to the Democratic masses for the support which they have given to the cause I represented and their confidence in every emergency, I remain, your fellow-citizen,

SAMUEL J. TILDEN.

When the reading of the letter had been finished, Mr. Little, of Dutchess County, moved that, despite the communication, Mr. Tilden, because of his loyalty to the party, his self-denial, and all that sort of thing, should still be considered the most prominent candidate of the party. Mr. Jacobs was not to be caught by chaff of this kind, and on the ground that the delegates had not had time to consider the contents of the letter, moved that the meeting adjourn. This motion was carried.

Mr. Tilden's letter has had a singular effect upon the delegates from New-York, and also upon those from other States who came to this city determined to support him. Many of these delegates knew not how much weight to give to the rumors which have prevailed for two or three days concerning the existence of such a letter, and were awaiting some positive announcement before coming to a decision as to the course to be pursued. Others had already accustomed their minds to a contemplation of the old man's withdrawal, and had fixed upon the man to whom they would transfer their allegiance. It cannot be denied that the letter has caused a slight revulsion of feeling in Tilden's favor, but there is no reason to-night for saying that this revulsion will be sufficient to stem the strong current which has set against him. There are some who persist in regarding the letter as a subtle bid for renewed support. It is now too early, however, to say what the real effect of its publication will be. The local papers of to-morrow morning will lay it before every delegate, and nearly all of them will then see its contents for the first time.

The liveliest curiosity prevails in relation to the direction in which the strength of the New-York delegation will be exerted. Efforts had been made before the meeting of this evening to circulate the statement that at least two-thirds of the delegates were intending to vote for Payne, of Ohio, as the heir of Tilden's political fortunes. There are very good reasons for believing that this is not now the sentiment of the majority of the delegation, if, indeed, it ever has been. It is announced to-night by McLaughlin, of Brooklyn, that at an informal caucus of New-York delegates, held soon after the reading of the letter, 40 of them agreed that they would not support Payne. This agreement will probably render it impossible to cast the vote of New-York as a whole for any man. Those who did not enter into the agreement are understood to stand by Payne, while perhaps one-half of the anti-Payne men desire to vote for Calvin E. Pratt. Some of the remaining delegates like that of Connecticut, and the choice of others cannot be ascertained. This is the story that is told to-night, but the chaotic condition of the average delegate's mind, and the ease with which he has, within a few days, shifted from one Democratic statesman to another, make it impossible to predict that new agreements and most radical changes will not be made before the meeting of New-York delegates which will be held to-morrow. It is true, however, that the supporters of Payne have been seriously impressed by the opposition to his nomination which they have to-day encountered. The shrewdest of the Democrats declare that it will not do to take any man from Ohio.

So great a disturbance of the political atmosphere prevails, that many comparatively obscure representatives of the party are busy erecting lighting-rods around their persons, so as to attract the weakest current of electricity which may be wandering through the air. It is noticeable, in connection with the whole matter of the letter, that there are to-night scores of delegates in Cincinnati who cannot be brought to believe that any communication of withdrawal has been read from Tilden. "I won't believe it, till I see it," said one incredulous gentleman from Indiana. So, to the end, the members of his party doubt the sincerity of the able old trickster of Gramercy Park.

#### BEFORE THE LETTER WAS READ.

THE TALK DURING SUNDAY—EFFECT IT WAS EXPECTED THE LETTER WOULD PRODUCE.

CINCINNATI, June 20.—If any preacher of the Gospel could so far forget himself as to write a discourse in regard to a National Democratic Convention, he might, in reference to the meeting now in progress, take for his text the following sentence: "As to the general result no man dares to predict." All those who are delegates are waiting for the decision of New-York. Samuel J. Tilden is still feared by every one, and whether or not he can transfer his votes to some other candidate is a question yet to be decided. The announcement made last night, to the effect that Tilden, because of his knowledge of his inability, under existing circumstances, to secure the nomination, had decided at least to make a feint of withdrawing continued to-day to be the principal topic of conversation here. That such a letter has been written by Mr. Tilden, or at least that he has authorized acknowledged friends of his to state that he has written such a letter, no one here professes to deny. Such being the case, the one question everywhere asked by politicians is: "What does Tilden mean by this pretended withdrawal?" I say pretended withdrawal, for strangely enough there is no well-informed politician in Cincinnati to-night, who can be brought to believe that "the great claimant" is sincere in declining to be a candidate for the Presidency of the United States. The almost universal verdict in regard to the matter is, that from his friends here he received due warning of the fact that, as the situation now is, he could never secure the nomination. The men who gave him this information he knew he could trust: but instead of giving up the fight by their direction, as an ordinary man would have done the sage of Gramercy Park resolved upon a new effort and fresh endeavor. The result of this determination, as there now seems to be no doubt, has been the broadcast circulation of the report that Mr. Tilden, always and above everything else mindful of the welfare of his party, has determined to relinquish his claims upon the Democracy and resign his place to some man who will reconcile the conflict in the party which his candidacy has occasioned, and unite all the warring elements in one harmonious whole. That Mr. Tilden has written such a letter, and that it is in Cincinnati to-night, his confidants here freely admit, but whether or not such a letter will ever see the light, remains to be proved. It may perhaps be well to remember that no man who knows Samuel J. Tilden has any confidence in any of his professions. Still, under the circumstances, it is very safe to assume that he has written the letter described, and it will, in the judgment of his agents here, be in due time submitted to the delegates. It is the last expiring bid of Samuel J. Tilden for the Presidency of the United States. It is possible that it may prove successful. It is at least certain that already a number of those who were known to be most hostile to Mr. Tilden are now among the first to deplore what has been commented upon as his positive withdrawal from the contest.

It is significant that the closest friends of New-York's ex-Governor, and the men who have been most intimately associated with him, have been very frank in the statement that no letter of withdrawal which he might write would take him entirely out of the contest. In fact, their theory, openly expressed, has been that a letter from him, declining to be a candidate for the Presidency, would, 30 days after it has been received by the Democracy, make him the most popular man in the United States. I think it is very safe to assume that the revulsion of feeling in his favor, which might be produced by the publication of such a letter, was expected to occur very much before the expiration of the 30 days. There are one or two people here who have had long and intimate experience with the astute and wily Mr. Tilden. They unite in this view of the present situation. Their theory is as follows: Tilden saw that he was beaten for the Presidential nomination, as was hurriedly outlined in these dispatches last night. He became convinced that some new plan of action must be decided upon. As a result, he caused to be circulated the report that he had written a letter declining to be a candidate. Still further than this, he caused that letter to be read to his intimate associates of an honest character, who, knowing him well, might doubt his sincerity. All this he did, not with any real desire of withdrawing, but for the purpose of exciting a sympathy in his behalf which might bring to him the otherwise impossible Democratic nomination. This theory is not too far fetched. Mr. Tilden is equal to the most subtle of schemes, and to procedure the most mysterious. In fact, as far as can be ascertained to-night, the plan of his personal agents here is to continue the story that he positively declines to be a candidate. At the same time, and upon the ground that he does so decline, these gentlemen will continue to ask for him a much larger complimentary vote in the Convention than he would otherwise receive. This vote having been given, the letter of withdrawal, which is undoubtedly a masterpiece of pathos and rhetoric, will be presented, in the hope that through its agency such an enthusiasm may be created for Tilden as will secure his nomination by a popular hurrah. If this be, indeed, the theory upon which the Democratic "Old Man of the Sea" has caused to be announced that he would not accept the nomination, it must be admitted that he has builded almost better than he knew. In fact, as has been intimated, there are to-day in Cincinnati at least 50 delegates to the National Convention who have heretofore expressed themselves as strongly opposed to the candidacy of Mr. Tilden, but who, since the talk of his withdrawal, are loudly in his favor. How much sincerity there is in their profession remains to be seen.

In the meantime, it must be admitted that what seems to be the great majority of the delegates, are more than satisfied with the understanding that Tilden will no longer trouble them. This majority is now particularly exercised in regard to the direction in which their ancient incubus is likely to throw the strength which, by one means or another, he has been enabled to secure. As far as can be ascertained, ex-Congressman Payne, from the Cleveland (Ohio) District, is the gentleman upon whom he has decided as a last resort to cast his mantle. It can be positively stated that Mr. Tilden is not able to make this transfer of his strength. There is a strong and influential minority of delegates here who seem to be determined that the Democracy shall be no longer troubled by dark horses. They are fully determined that the party shall unite upon some man who has at least a reasonable chance of being elected. That they will ever be able to make such a union is perhaps out of the question, but that they will at least succeed in defeating Mr. Payne, there seems to be no doubt. It is sufficiently apparent to them, as well as to the most casual observer, that his nomination would be fatal to the Democratic Party. In the first place, he would have to encounter the antagonism and jealousy of Senator Thurman, who is the real choice of the Ohio Democracy, and who would, as there is scarcely a question, leave unturned no stone which might render Garfield's assured majority in this State all the greater. Further than this, Mr. Payne would have to combat the jealousy of ex-Gov. Hendricks, of Indiana, who could never forgive any Western man, other than himself, who might, by Mr. Tilden, be forced upon the party. To all these facts the average Democratic representative now in Cincinnati is not blind. Consequently, Mr. Tilden's friends find now, and will continue to find, the bitterest opposition to their scheme of transferring his votes to Payne.

In fact, it is almost out of the question that any Ohio man can receive the nomination. The Buckeye State must in advance be conceded to the Republicans, and, at the best, the most popular Democratic candidate could only succeed in cutting down Garfield's majority. On the other hand, and as far as concerns Indiana, there is a general and very just impression here that the nomination of Hendricks would be so distasteful to Tilden as to make New-York certainly Republican. So, both Hendricks and an Ohio man seem to be out of the race for the first place. Indeed, if any Western candidate secures the nomination, it is likely to be Senator McDonald, of Indiana. He does not oppose Tilden, and he has even greater strength in his own State than has Hendricks. Despite all this, however, there are not many well-informed politicians here who believe that his nomination is among the possibilities. The general impression seems to be that some Eastern man will secure the coveted prise. Ex-Gov. English, of Connecticut; Judge Pratt, of Brooklyn; Senator Randolph, of New-Jersey; Gen. Hancock, of Pennsylvania, and Speaker Randall, of the same State, are most frequently mentioned as among the possibilities. In regard to Gen. Hancock, it can be said that he will be warmly supported by a number of delegates from the South, who are of the opinion that the nomination of so distinguished a Union soldier would forever put a stop to the claim that the Democracy is desirous of elevating to the Presidency a rebel sympathiser. It is significant that Major Burke, of Louisiana, together with the 15 other delegates from that State, are most enthusiastic in their support of Hancock. Major Burke claims that the General's vote on the first ballot will not fall short of 85.

As to the general result of what is still a contest worse confounded, it can only be stated that the shrewdest and most experienced politician will express no opinion. The fight is still anybody's and the cry most frequently heard is "Every man for himself and his Satanic majesty take the hindmost."

#### CANVASSING AMONG DELEGATES.

A MAN NEEDED WHO CAN CARRY THE DOUBTFUL NORTHERN STATES—THE TWO ENGLISHES—MR. PAYNE'S FRIENDS AND OPPONENTS.

CINCINNATI, June 20.—A walk among the delegates to-day revealed the fact that many of them were either very drunk or willing to be so, and that a few were still engaged in the not very satisfactory employment of trying to make combinations. Prominent among these workers are some of the New-England delegates. The withdrawal of Tilden and Seymour seemed at first to transfer to some Western man the first place on the ticket, but the character of the struggle which followed these withdrawals has induced the New-England men to believe that the West can secure only one-half of the ticket, if the best interests of the party are consulted, and that the other half may be claimed with good reasons by New-England or the Middle States. These men describe the situation as follows, and their description is in accord with the views of many Western and Southern Democrats. The Southern vote is the inalienable property of the Democratic Party whoever may be the nominee, and Southern delegates have repeatedly declared that they desire nothing except the nomination of a man who will receive the most votes in the North, and wage the most effective campaign in the Northern States, which are, by common consent, to be the battle ground. Therefore, all preferences should be made to yield to the nomination of a ticket which will carry Indiana, New-York, New-Jersey, and Connecticut, whose 65 Electoral votes, added to the 138 votes of the solid South, will insure the success of the party. They admit, in the first place, that Indiana must be conciliated by bestowing upon her a part of the ticket, but they are by no means alone in making the assertion that this part cannot be first place. The Indiana delegates came to the Convention as a unit in support of Hendricks for President, and they refuse to consider any proposition to put him in the second place. The State contains two other candidates, Senator McDonald and William H. English, and the first named, while ostensibly working for Hendricks, is not forgetting his own interests. These New-England men say that if a part of the old ticket is thrown overboard the remainder must follow, and therefore they are unwilling to support Hendricks for even the second place. They refuse to admit the possibility of his securing the first place. Mr. Hendricks has frequently declared that he would not take a nomination for the Vice-Presidency, and they are willing to see him entirely ignored in the Convention. Assuming the ultimate failure of the movement in his favor, they regard McDonald as the man most available for their purposes and best fitted to awaken a local enthusiasm in Indiana. McDonald is also very ambitious, and is said to despise the Vice-Presidency and to aim, like Mr. Hendricks, at the first place on the ticket. But these men are confident that he will not refuse an opportunity to preside over the great legislative body in which he now holds a seat.

Having in this way disposed of Indiana, they yield Ohio to Garfield, and turn their attention to New-York, New-Jersey, and Connecticut, and seriously apply themselves to the task of finding a man who can carry these three States. New-York's two superannuated candidates having withdrawn, these men claim the State presents no man, for it is said that no New-Yorker could be found who could perfectly unite and harmonize the local Democratic factions. New-Jersey seems to press no one upon the Convention, although the names of McClellan and Senator Randolph were frequently mentioned yesterday. It is the general opinion that either one of these is out of the question. No one of the New-England States, except Connecticut, is presumptuous enough to suggest a Presidential candidate, but it is for Connecticut's man that these men have been laboring to-day. This Connecticut man is ex-Gov. and ex-Congressman James E. English, of New-Haven, and his supporters declare that with him at the head of the ticket the States of New-York, New-Jersey, and Connecticut would surely fall into line for the Democracy in November next. Mr. English is a wealthy man, and he has worked his way up from poverty by great industry and business ability. But his fortune by no means amounts to the $4,000,000 assigned to him by his supporters who are now in this city. His barrel is, however, very respectable in size, and the multiplication of it by three or four cannot fail to have some effect upon those who regret the loss of Tilden's money, and are anxiously looking for a big bank account to take its place. In their eager support of English, his friends have encountered a very big snag in the New-York delegation. It is understood that 50 of the 70 New-York delegates have followed the instructions of the dethroned old man of Gramercy Park, and have promised to vote for Payne, of Ohio. The remaining 20 are perhaps as friendly to English as they are to any candidate, but the supporters of Payne ask the Connecticut men to join them in a complimentary ballot for him. The friends of English are in a quandary. They fear that such a complimentary ballot will create a stampede for Payne and cause his nomination, and they do not wish to offend the New-Yorkers and thereby array them against English, by refusing to comply with their wishes. Two conferences have been held to-day for the purpose of considering this question. The friends of English were asked to-day why Bayard could not accomplish what is desired in New-York, New-Jersey, and Connecticut, after providing for Indiana in the manner desired above. The reply was that outside of a portion of the Massachusetts delegation there was a deep-seated opposition to Bayard in New-England, because of his speech in favor of secession in 1861, and because he was a Southern man. "It was true," said one of these men, "that Bayard's well-known hard-money principles would gain for him a strong support in New-York City, and he is quite popular in New-Jersey, but his nomination would make trouble for us in Connecticut, where, after a long struggle, we have at last conciliated the Greenbackers, who were a threatening factor in every election."

There is a serious division among the delegates who represent the New-England and the Middle States in relation to the proposed nomination of Payne. It will be noticed that in the plan described above Ohio is entirely ignored. The most absurd statements are made to-day by those who are working for Payne. His son, who asserts that he is merely a spectator, but who is really doing his best to secure his father's nomination, declared to-day that the Ohio delegation was solid for Payne. Fortunately for him, no friend of Thurman was near to question this remarkable assertion. "I tell you," said he, "that Thurman has not three of those delegates to-day, and Jewett will not be mentioned in the Convention." In answer to a question concerning the reported transfer of Tilden's influence to his father, he said that Tilden and his father had been on most friendly terms for many years, but that they had not seen each other, and had had no communication with each other during the canvass. He was then asked if it was not unwise to nominate a resident of a State which could not be carried by the party and if the prospect of reducing a Republican majority would do the party any good. The assumption that Ohio was a sure Republican State seemed to astonish this firm upholder of the prestige of the Payne family, and he declared that his father ought to be nominated, because he would carry Ohio beyond a doubt for the Democrats. When portions of this conversation were repeated to an intelligent Illinois Democrat, the latter was greatly amused. "Some of those fellows," said he, "were reasonable in their talk a day or two ago, but now they are as wild as lunatics. I have no objection to Payne as a man, but no Democrat of sense can believe for a moment in the possibility of a Democratic victory in Ohio." Young Mr. Payne is one of the men who are delighted to find an excuse for their opposition to Tilden in his physical incapacity. He eulogized the old candidate and declared that he had been a sort of Moses to the party which had been jumping from one issue to another, hoping to find somewhere a popular wave which would float it into power, and which had, for the first time since the war, been given a firm basis by him. But he was now too old and the party could not afford to support any man who was so superannuated and so weighed down by physical infirmities. Unfortunately for old Mr. Payne, there are many delegates who complain that he is not such a specimen of robust and magnetic manhood as they desire to support. "It looks now," said a delegate to-day, "as if we would not be able to nominate a man of brains. Seymour and Tilden have withdrawn, and other men of great mental ability are encountering serious opposition. If we can't have a man of brains, I am in favor of nominating a man who will be imposing physically, a man of good health and robust presence, whom we can look upon with some satisfaction. Now, Payne is an attenuated, dried up old fossil, whose activity was exerted in an era which is past and almost forgotten. I can compare him to nothing except an old umbrella. I won't vote for such a man."

#### NOTES AND INCIDENTS.

CINCINNATI, June 20.—A Democratic speaker addressed a crowd late last night in a beer garden near the spot where Cincinnati marksmen occasionally indulge in the bad habit of shooting Eph Holland. After the oration had proceeded for 10 minutes, two very bloody men were brought out of the audience and carried to the hospital. Democratic eloquence had been very effective.

Men appeared on the street corners to-day with large bundles of lithographed portraits of Hugh J. Jewett. These pictures were distributed with great liberality, and every beer saloon was provided with one.

A large flag was suspended over Fourth-street to-day, bearing the inscription, "For President, Thomas A. Hendricks." Displays of this sort are very rare in the city as yet, but will probably increase in number to-morrow, when the chariot which advertises Judge Field will resume its trips through the streets.

A large number of young men and boys walked the streets this afternoon wearing red badges, on which were the words, "Ohio solid for Thurman."

It is probable that Illinois will present the name of Cyrus H. McCormick, the manufacturer of reapers, for the Vice-Presidency.

There is in this city a letter from Horatio Seymour, in which he gives his reasons for declining a nomination. Very few persons have seen it, and these unanimously oppose its publication, for the reason that it would do the party no good. It is understood the old gentleman says in this letter that he would regard the announcement of his nomination as he would an invitation to attend a funeral. Delegates who have seen the letter hasten to explain that this remark is merely a reference to his age and infirmities and to the probability that the excitement of a campaign would bring his life suddenly to an end. At the same time they assert that Seymour is very indiscreet to make such a statement, because the Republicans will give to it a differ meaning and will maintain that it is the funeral of the Democratic Party to which he refers.

The Hon. John Kelly, of New-York, varied the monotony of the political canvass this evening by delivering a lecture in this city upon "The Sisters of Charity," for the benefit of a suburban Roman Catholic church.

Many of the delegates discovered the peculiarities of a Sunday in Cincinnati for the first time to-day. The variety theatres were all open for matinée and evening performances. Countless concert saloons and beer gardens were well patronized. Attractive programmes were advertised by many places of amusement in the suburbs, and at 3 o'clock the Brown Stockings and Buckeyes played a game of ball in the park.

Congressman Manning, of Mississippi, a supporter of Judge Field, says that he has taken that position because Field represents a sentiment or doctrine which no Democrat can oppose—the doctrine of State rights and decentralization. The currency and the tariff, on neither of which the party could agree, he would leave to Congress, and would make State rights the controlling issue of the campaign on the Democratic side, with Field as its exponent.

The managers of the Convention have been trying to find a Democratic clergymen in the city who will open the proceedings with prayer. For a time they sought in vain, and they were beginning to think that the only alternative lay between a Roman Catholic priest and no prayer at all, when it was discovered that the Rev. Dr. Pratt, who preaches in Music Hall, had the required political opinions. The committee may decide, however, to import a man for the purpose.

A large number of expert telegraphers from Washington, Philadelphia, and Chicago have been sent to reinforce the local office of the Western Union Company. It is, therefore, not at all likely that the trouble experienced by newspaper representatives in Chicago will be met with here.

Ex-State Auditor Henderson, of Indiana, says that the delegation from his State will stand by Hendricks for the first place, and will not support any Indiana man for Vice-President, even if he be proposed by other States.

The various delegations contain many of the most prominent men of the Democratic Party. Among them are United States Senators McDonald, Voorhees, Vest, Hampton, Butler, and Davis of West Virginia; David A. Wells, the well-known writer on economic subjects; ex-Senator W. H. Barnum; ex-Gov. Saulsbury, of Delaware; ex-Gov. McEnery, of Louisiana, Mayor Prince, of Boston; Frank Jones, of New-Hampshire; ex-Senator Stockton, of New-Jersey; ex-Gov. Robinson, Congressman Bliss, and a host of prominent New-Yorkers; Gen. Steedman, of Ohio, and William L. Scott, of Erie, Penn. Accompanying the delegates are United States Senators Wallace, Ben Hill, and Jonas.

The local Democratic paper makes the following suggestion to the party: "New-York is not absolutely essential to success. The Presidency can be stolen without that State."

The Ohio delegation has entered into a compact to vote as a unit from the beginning to the end of the Convention, and was instructed to vote for Thurman. The *Enquirer* of this city seems to fear that the delegates are going to do something dishonorable, and says to-day that they should not, with indecent haste or suspicious alacrity, abandon the name for which they were commanded to vote.

The Tammany delegation, 600 strong, reached here to-day and went to their hotel, with John Kelly and Augustus Schell at their head. Joe Harris, of the Atlanta *Constitution*, whose sketches, over the signature of "Uncle Remus," have attracted attention, went down to see the braves. When he had satisfied his curiosity, and had seen all the glory of their war-paint and feathers, a New York journalist said to him: "You have always been talking to me about Radical nigger thieves in the South. Now, did you ever see a band of Radicals that looked as bad as this gang?" Harris thoughtfully rubbed his chin for a moment to refresh his memory, and then replied: "Well, there's one gang of nigger gamblers in Atlanta who look almost as bad." At this point Spinola carried his four-story shirt-collar into the hotel, and the crowd of spectators dispersed.

An enthusiast, who has been amusing himself by making queer combinations for the Democratic ticket, and who desires to place Indiana and Connecticut in the front rank of Democratic States, wants to know how English and English would do.

The Jewett and Tilden head-quarters at the Grand Hotel are connected by special wire with the residences of those gentlemen in New-York. Mr. Hendricks has established similar means of communication with his friends at the Burnet House, and other candidates have made arrangements for private wires.

The Ohio delegation had two meetings to-day, at both of which great enthusiasm was manifested for Senator Thurman, and it was resolved to stand firm. It was stated that Jewett's candidacy was not to be considered so long as Thurman was in the field. Much bitterness was expressed against the supporters of Payne. It was decided that W. D. Hill should make the nominating speech, and that John McSweeney should second the nomination.

The public announcement of Mr. Tilden's position has induced some who have hitherto supported Mr. Hendricks to suggest in many places to-night that propriety and a regard for the success of the party require him to follow Mr. Tilden's example, so that the coast may be made clear for Senator McDonald, of Indiana.

Wade Hampton and Mr. Butler, of South Carolina, together with Senator Lamar, of Mississippi, and August Belmont, have been engaged during the day in seeking to gain support for the candidacy of Senator Bayard. Gen. Hampton has received another of those letters from ex-Gov. Seymour saying that he can under no circumstances be a candidate.

John Kelly and his Tammany Hall braves are going about to-night declaring that it was by their efforts that Tilden was induced to withdraw. This demonstration may help the expected revulsion of feeling in the old man's favor.

#### WHAT REBEL ARCHIVES PROVE.

MANY DEMOCRATIC STATESMEN IMPLICATED —THE CASE AGAINST SENATOR BAYARD.

WASHINGTON, June 20.—In a dispatch to last Saturday's TIMES mention was made of the material contained in rebel archives now in possession of the War Department. It appears that under the order for printing by Congress the War Department officers have carefully preserved all documents bearing upon the personal records of prominent men. So many Democratic statesmen are covered by these documents, it is believed here, that the Cincinnati Convention can hardly fail to put one man on the ticket whose loyalty cannot stand the test of these records. Adjt.-Gen. Townsend has made a specialty of gathering information of this character. He has been very anxious to get these records secured in some permanent form, so that no Democratic Administration could possibly make way with them.

THE TIMES's correspondent has learned to-day the particulars of the case against Senator Bayard, to be used should he be nominated. In the rebel records captured at Richmond was found a commission as Colonel in a rebel infantry regiment, made out in the name of Thomas F. Bayard, present Senator from Delaware. These is, of course, no pretense that this commission was ever offered Mr. Bayard, but it is inferred that a commission would not have been made out in his name if it had not been believed by the rebel authorities that Senator Bayard was in sympathy with them. At any rate, the Dover speech and this commission would make heavy handicaps. The same records that implicate Hendricks as a member of the Knights of the Golden Circle also include Daniel W. Voorhees.

#### BOUND FOR CINCINNATI.

JAMESTOWN DEPOT, N. Y., June 20.—The palace-car Warsaw, embellished with flags and mottoes and decorated with banners, passed through Jamestown to-day for Cincinnati. Among the passengers were leading Democrats of the Counties of Chemung, Steuben, and Allegany; ex-Congressman C. C. B. Walker and F. N. Drake, of Corning; the Hon. John McDougal, Judge C. E. Beard, and Mayor Near, of Hornellsville; Col. James E. Jones, of Addison; R. S. Armstrong, of Cuba; the Hon. F. C. Deming and S. C. Faber, of Elmira.

#### *POLITICS OF EUROPE AND ASIA.*

GREECE ARMING—THE MOROCCO CONFERENCE TO MEET AGAIN—FRENCH QUESTIONS.

ATHENS, June 20.—The Greek Government is taking measures to increase the Army from 12,300 to 40,000 men. A number of officers have gone to France, Italy, Hungary, Algiers, and Syria to purchase horses, ammunition, and clothing. The infantry are to be provided with 1,500 cartridges apiece.

BERLIN, June 20.—The Count de St. Vallier yesterday gave a banquet to the technical delegates connected with the conference and several Greek representatives.

PERA, June 20.—An attempt has been made to take the life of the new Grand Shereef of Mecca, but it failed, and the Shereef was not hurt.

There are disturbances in Diarbekir, Asiatic Turkey, owing to scarcity of food. The Governor has resigned.

MADRID, June 20.—There will be another sitting of the Morocco Conference Monday, when Señor Canovas del Castillo will make conciliatory proposals. Ministerial journals state that the Envoys have decided to maintain absolute secrecy hereafter with regard to their consultations.

PARIS, June 20.—In the election held to-day for Municipal Councilor for the Père la Chaise quarter, M. Trinquet, the Communist, now in New-Caledonia, received 2,338 votes, and his opponent 1,880.

M. Gambetta, speaking in Menilmontant, declared that the fête of July 14 would unite the people, the Army, and the public powers in one common brotherhood.

M. Langlois, a Deputy of the Left, has given notice of an amendment excluding murderers from the plenary amnesty to the Communists.

LONDON, June 21.—A dispatch from Madrid says the business of the conference will now proceed rapidly. Three meetings will be held this week. Señor Ludolf will introduce a memorandum in favor of religious liberty and the better treatment of the Hebrews, which the United States, Portugal, and Germany will support.

A Berlin dispatch says: There seems to be no doubt that the French propositions will be accepted, but it is questionable whether all the powers will support them, as Russia and Austria continue their attitude of reserve, but, as a majority is sufficient, this is of less importance.

A Kabul dispatch says the rising against the Russians in Central Asia is said to be rapidly increasing.

BERLIN, June 20.—The second clause of the Church Bill enacts that priests be deprived of the right of appealing to the ecclesiastical court against disciplinary decisions given by Bishops or Chapters, unless such appeal is especially sanctioned by the Government. It seems probable that the final result of the Church bill will be to effect but few changes in the existing laws and give only very moderate concessions to the Catholics.

#### *CURRENT FOREIGN TOPICS.*

LONDON, June 20.—The annual dinner of the Newspaper Press Fund took place last night. Mr. Edward Dicey, the well-known journalist and editor of the *Observer*, speaking as an old contributor to many journals in the Colonies and America, proposed "The Foreign, Colonial, and American Press." Sir Alexander T. Galt, the Canadian Commissioner, responded.

In the cricket match at Stockport on Friday the Canadians numbered 12 against the 12 of Stockport.

CAPE TOWN, June 20.—Letsea, the Basuto Chief, has issued a proclamation calling upon the Basutos to surrender their arms to the British.

DUSSELDORF, June 20.—The Emperor William has arrived here. He visited the Exhibition of Industry and Art, where he made a speech. He subsequently departed for Ems.

LONDON, June 21.—A dispatch from Pesth says the village of Homouna, in the County of Zemplen, has been destroyed by fire. Many inhabitants were burned, and others were injured. A famine having raged since the beginning of the Winter, the misery is indescribable. One thousand and eleven houses were burned in Hungary during May.

A dispatch from Berlin states that 63 persons were killed during the late terrible storm and waterspout near Dresden.

# The New-York Times.

VOL. XXIX.......NO. 8984. NEW-YORK, FRIDAY, JUNE 25, 1880. PRICE FOUR CENTS.

## THE BOURBONS STAMPEDED

### *THEY NOMINATE GEN. HANCOCK AND WILLIAM H. ENGLISH.*

THE CONVENTION TRANSFORMED INTO A HOWLING MOB—HANCOCK NOMINATED AFTER THE SECOND BALLOT BY A STAMPEDE—ENGLISH NAMED BY ACCLAMATION—A SHORT PLATFORM—SPEECHES BY SEVERAL DISAPPOINTED PARTISANS IN SUPPORT OF THE NOMINEES—THE OLD CHAIRMAN'S AMUSING BLUNDERS.

CINCINNATI, June 24.—The National Democratic Convention has done its work. By it, Gen. Hancock, who is politically from Pennsylvania, and in the Army Register from Missouri, has been nominated for President of the United States, and Mr. William H. English, of Indiana, for Vice-President. They owe their success, in the first place, to a wild and unreasonable stampede, which could not be controlled, and, secondly, to a union between the ex-rebel Brigadiers and Tammany Hall. During the whole of last night and this morning, the one cry heard on every side here was, "let us nominate a man who will satisfy John Kelly, and who will not be objectionable to the solid South." Such a man was found in the person of Hancock. Kelly favored him, for what reason nobody seems to know, and he was warmly pressed by the ex-Confederates of the South. Why they supported him it is hardly necessary to explain. They are determined to succeed in the present contest. They know it is the very last opportunity for success which they can ever hope for, and they have made a virtue of necessity, and aided by the men of Tammany Hall, have succeeded in nominating for President a man whom they have every reason to detest heartily, and about whose views on public questions they, in common with the rest of the world, know next to nothing. As to his record no man has spoken. If he has a record on any great public question in which the people of this country are now interested, no man here knows anything about it. Gen. Hancock is the candidate of sentiment. He has grown out of a dire Democratic dilemma. He is not the choice of the masses of the party to which he professes to belong; he is not known he has no personal following; he is the last man to attract independent votes; he can only hope for the support of the fraudulently-solid South, and of the political tricksters in the North, who will use him for their own purposes. Without further preface, the story of his nomination by the Convention may be soon told.

The national meeting resumed its work at 10:30 o'clock this morning. Immediately after the conclusion of the prayer, Rufus W. Peckham, of the New-York delegation, arose and said that the New-York delegates had heard with great sensibility the votes cast on the first ballot for Samuel J. Tilden. At this point he was interrupted by cheers and hisses, which came from all parts of the hall, and drowned his voice. As soon as he could resume his remarks, he said that Tilden had sent a letter of renunciation to the delegation, and that the delegation had accepted it as final and conclusive, and had agreed to vote for Speaker Randall. A motion that the letter should be read was lost.

After referring to the Committee on Resolutions a resolution declaring it unconstitutional to deprive any citizen of the United States of the right of suffrage, the convention proceeded to a second ballot for President.

HANCOCK'S GAINS ON THE SECOND BALLOT.

The call of the roll was closely watched by both delegates and spectators, for it was the belief of many that a third ballot would not be needed. In Alabama, Hancock had gained four, and in California five. Connecticut cast all except one of her votes for ex-Gov. English, who had been a promising dark horse until the opening of the Convention. Delaware and Florida would not desert Bayard. The changes in the Georgia delegation were unimportant, but when the Chairman of the delegation from Illinois arose and declared that his State had abandoned Morrison and decided to cast her 42 votes for Gen. Hancock, the excitement was intense, and the uncontrollable spectators made the hall a bedlam of noise. Indiana was true to Gov. Hendricks. Several changes were apparent in Iowa's vote. Hancock had gained two delegates, but 12 votes which had been cast on the first ballot for Morrison, Bayard, Payne, and McDonald, were combined and given to Randall. Kansas had turned from Ewing to Hancock. Seven Kentuckians had also forsaken their first choice for him, and there were only three left in the delegation to vote for Tilden. Louisiana, the original supporter of Hancock, remained unchanged, and the 14 votes of Maine were cast for him, as they had been on the preceding day. Maryland had not been induced to desert Bayard, but five votes had been gained in Massachusetts for Hancock and nine had come over to him in the Michigan delegation. Minnesota cast 10 for him as before, and the one Tilden man in Mississippi had joined his column. There had been a great change in Missouri. On the first ballot her votes had been distributed among five candidates and Hancock had received 12. Two men persisted in supporting Bayard now, but the remaining 28 had become supporters of Hancock. Nebraska changed her candidate from Payne to Randall, thus remaining in company with New-York. New-Hampshire gave Hancock 5 instead of 4, and transferred her remaining 5 votes from Bayard and Field to Randall. In New-Jersey there had been serious changes, and 7 new votes for Hancock appeared on her roll. When New-York was called, the solid vote of the State was cast for Randall, in accordance with the previous announcement. But this diversion could not stem the tide which was setting so heavily in another direction. North Carolina abandoned Bayard and her other candidates and increased her former vote of 9 for Hancock to the delegation's full 20. Ohio, after a consultation, remained true to Thurman, and Oregon to Field, but there were important developments in Pennsylvania. Thirty-two of her votes were cast for Hancock and 25 for Randall. Rhode Island had gathered her scattered votes, and turned 6 of them over to the coming man, but South Carolina still voted for Bayard. Hancock gained 3 in Tennessee, and 2 in Texas. Vermont repeated her original vote for him, and in Virginia he gained 4, while Bayard lost 2. West Virginia had turned to him from Thurman, and in Wisconsin his vote had been raised from 1 to 10. The ballot in detail was as follows:

| States. | Field | Bayard | Hendricks | Thurman | Hancock | Tilden | Randall | J. E. English | No. Delegates |
|---|---|---|---|---|---|---|---|---|---|
| Alabama | 4 | 5 | .. | .. | 11 | .. | .. | .. | 20 |
| Arkansas | 12 | .. | .. | .. | .. | .. | .. | .. | 12 |
| California | 5 | .. | 1 | .. | 5 | .. | .. | .. | 12 |
| Colorado | 6 | .. | .. | .. | .. | .. | .. | .. | 6 |
| Connecticut | .. | 1 | .. | .. | .. | .. | .. | 11 | 12 |
| Delaware | .. | 6 | .. | .. | .. | .. | .. | .. | 6 |
| Florida | .. | 8 | .. | .. | .. | .. | .. | .. | 8 |
| Georgia | 10 | 5 | .. | .. | 7 | .. | .. | .. | 22 |
| Illinois | .. | .. | .. | .. | 42 | .. | .. | .. | 42 |
| Indiana | .. | .. | 30 | .. | .. | .. | .. | .. | 30 |
| Iowa | .. | 1 | .. | .. | 9 | .. | 12 | .. | 22 |
| Kansas | .. | .. | .. | .. | 10 | .. | .. | .. | 10 |
| Kentucky | 4 | 7 | .. | 2 | 8 | 3 | .. | .. | 24 |
| Louisiana | .. | .. | .. | .. | 16 | .. | .. | .. | 16 |
| Maine | .. | .. | .. | .. | 14 | .. | .. | .. | 14 |
| Maryland | .. | 14 | .. | .. | .. | .. | .. | .. | 16 |
| Massachusetts | 1½ | 7 | .. | .. | 11 | 2 | 3½ | .. | 26 |
| Michigan | .. | 4 | .. | .. | 14 | 1 | 1 | 2 | 22 |
| Minnesota | .. | .. | .. | .. | 10 | .. | .. | .. | 10 |
| Mississippi | 2 | 8 | .. | .. | 6 | .. | .. | .. | 16 |
| Missouri | .. | 2 | .. | .. | 28 | .. | .. | .. | 30 |
| Nebraska | .. | .. | .. | .. | .. | .. | 6 | .. | 6 |
| Nevada | 4 | .. | .. | 1 | .. | .. | 1 | .. | 6 |
| New-Hampshire | .. | .. | .. | .. | 5 | .. | 5 | .. | 10 |
| New-Jersey | .. | 4 | .. | .. | 7 | .. | 4 | .. | *18 |
| New-York | .. | .. | .. | .. | .. | .. | 70 | .. | 70 |
| North Carolina | .. | .. | .. | .. | 20 | .. | .. | .. | 20 |
| Ohio | .. | .. | .. | 44 | .. | .. | .. | .. | 44 |
| Oregon | 6 | .. | .. | .. | .. | .. | .. | .. | 6 |
| Pennsylvania | .. | 1 | .. | .. | 32 | .. | 25 | .. | 58 |
| Rhode Island | .. | .. | .. | .. | 6 | .. | 1 | 1 | 8 |
| South Carolina | .. | 14 | .. | .. | .. | .. | .. | .. | 14 |
| Tennessee | 2 | 8 | .. | .. | 14 | .. | .. | .. | 24 |
| Texas | .. | 5 | .. | .. | 11 | .. | .. | .. | 16 |
| Vermont | .. | .. | .. | .. | 10 | .. | .. | .. | 10 |
| Virginia | 7 | 8 | .. | .. | 7 | .. | .. | .. | 22 |
| West Virginia | .. | 1 | .. | 2 | 7 | .. | .. | .. | 10 |
| Wisconsin | 2 | 2 | .. | 1 | 10 | .. | .. | 5 | 20 |
| Total | 65½ | 111 | 31 | 50 | 320 | 6 | 128½ | 19 | 738 |

*For Joel Parker, 2; for H. J. Jewett, 1.

THE STAMPEDE.

It was now plain that Bayard's nomination was out of the question, and that there was no hope for the man to whom the influence of New-York and Mr. Tilden had been transferred from Payne. The dark horses were forgotten in contemplation of the rapid growth of popularity which had almost doubled the original vote for Hancock. The mob howled and shrieked, so that for some time no business could be done. But while the disorder prevailed there were hurried consultations among the delegates and unmistakable signs of a stampede. The first delegation to yield to the pressure was that of Wisconsin, whose Chairman, after considerable difficulty, secured recognition from the Chair and asked permission to change the delegation's vote. The request was referred to the Convention and permission was granted. The Wisconsin Chairman thereupon announced that the State desired to cast her vote for Hancock. This was the spark which fired the train, and the explosion which followed was an exhibition of the noise and confusion which can be created by such a mass of people, confined by four walls, a floor, and a roof. The delegates were all on their feet, and the Chairmen, eager to get into the stream, were appealing to the Chair for recognition. The old presiding officer pounded his desk with the regularity and almost the force of a trip-hammer, and shouted until his ruddy face turned to a darker hue. The Pennsylvania Chairman stood upon a chair directly in front of the desk, and after some delay he was declared to have the floor. Having complimented both Randall and Hancock, he announced that the delegation now desired to cast all of its votes for Hancock. This was the signal for another outbreak in the galleries, and the temporary insanity which prevailed was increased by the exhibition at the Chairman's desk of a banner bearing Hancock's portrait. Other delegates endeavored to make announcements, but the confusion was so great that the band struck up a lively air in the hope of bringing the crowd back to their senses. Out of the multitude of noises arose the sharp crack of the big gavel as the Chairman brought it down upon the desk at the rate of about 48 strokes to the minute. The delegates crowded upon the platform and surged like a flood over telegraph messengers, clerks, and distinguished guests. In their hands they bore the banners which had marked their positions on the floor, and these they gathered in a group above the old Chairman's head, shrieking all the time. The Chairman stood firmly at his post, wielding the big gavel with precision and power. Occasionally a Chairman of a delegation would brandish his arms in the crowd below the desk and would announce his delegation's wishes. Messengers would convey his words to the Chair and the Secretaries. In this way New-York's vote was transferred from Randall to Hancock, and Ohio deserted Thurman and joined the majority. Preston, of Kentucky, desired to make an announcement not of the ordinary kind, and at last he succeeded in clearing away the noise from a small space around him and in telling the Chair that his State desired to cast 16 votes for Hancock, 5 for Bayard, and 1 for Thurman. Then Nebraska, Connecticut, and Virginia fell into line, and other delegations sought in vain for recognition. Their representatives crowded together in front of the desk, with the perspiration streaming from their faces, while the Sergeant-at-Arms ran about among them issuing hoarse commands, and the old Chairman continued his exercise with the gavel. The tumult could not always continue, and at last a New-Hampshire delegate got in a motion to call the roll again, so that a unanimous vote could be recorded. The motion was carried and something like quiet reigned for a few minutes. As State after State deserted their favorites the galleries cheered; but Indiana was true to the last. Two Maryland delegates voted for Bayard and John P. Irish, of Iowa, a devoted admirer of Tilden, refused to abandon the old man even on the last ballot. There was a look of anger and mortification and disappointment on his face, and he rudely thrust aside the friends who came to reason with him. There was no hilarity in the New-York delegation when it cast its vote. The Clerk announced that 705 votes had been cast for Hancock, 30 for Hendricks, 2 for Bayard, and 1 for Tilden. The full vote was as follows:

| States. | Hancock | Hendricks | Bayard | Tilden | No. of Delegates |
|---|---|---|---|---|---|
| Alabama | 20 | .. | .. | .. | 20 |
| Arkansas | 12 | .. | .. | .. | 12 |
| California | 12 | .. | .. | .. | 12 |
| Colorado | 6 | .. | .. | .. | 6 |
| Connecticut | 12 | .. | .. | .. | 12 |
| Delaware | 6 | .. | .. | .. | 6 |
| Florida | 8 | .. | .. | .. | 8 |
| Georgia | 22 | .. | .. | .. | 22 |
| Illinois | 42 | .. | .. | .. | 42 |
| Indiana | .. | 30 | .. | .. | 30 |
| Iowa | 21 | .. | .. | 1 | 22 |
| Kansas | 10 | .. | .. | .. | 10 |
| Kentucky | 24 | .. | .. | .. | 24 |
| Louisiana | 16 | .. | .. | .. | 16 |
| Maine | 14 | .. | .. | .. | 14 |
| Maryland | 14 | .. | 2 | .. | 16 |
| Massachusetts | 26 | .. | .. | .. | 26 |
| Michigan | 22 | .. | .. | .. | 22 |
| Minnesota | 10 | .. | .. | .. | 10 |
| Mississippi | 16 | .. | .. | .. | 16 |
| Missouri | 30 | .. | .. | .. | 30 |
| Nebraska | 6 | .. | .. | .. | 6 |
| Nevada | 6 | .. | .. | .. | 6 |
| New-Hampshire | 10 | .. | .. | .. | 10 |
| New-Jersey | 18 | .. | .. | .. | 18 |
| New-York | 70 | .. | .. | .. | 70 |
| North Carolina | 20 | .. | .. | .. | 20 |
| Ohio | 44 | .. | .. | .. | 44 |
| Oregon | 6 | .. | .. | .. | 6 |
| Pennsylvania | 58 | .. | .. | .. | 58 |
| Rhode Island | 8 | .. | .. | .. | 8 |
| South Carolina | 14 | .. | .. | .. | 14 |
| Tennessee | 24 | .. | .. | .. | 24 |
| Texas | 16 | .. | .. | .. | 16 |
| Vermont | 10 | .. | .. | .. | 10 |
| Virginia | 22 | .. | .. | .. | 22 |
| West Virginia | 10 | .. | .. | .. | 10 |
| Wisconsin | 20 | .. | .. | .. | 20 |
| Total | 705 | 30 | 2 | 1 | 738 |

THE SPEECH-MAKING.

The most important work of the Convention was done, and the crowd was allowed to strain their lungs to their hearts' content.

Mr. Niblack, of Indiana, was soon at the desk fighting for a hearing. There were hisses from many when his State was named. "I know no reason," he angrily exclaimed, "why Democrats should hiss at the name of the Hoosier State. I can't think that these hisses come from Democratic lips." "Never," shouted a delegate. Mr. Niblack then, in the name of Indiana, moved the unanimous nomination of Gen. Hancock. His delegation, he said, thought the man of their choice could be elected, and knew that he could carry Indiana, but, with Hancock as a leader, they promised to turn the right flank of the Republican Party, and they expected that New-York and Connecticut would turn the left, while the solid South would come up in the rear.

The next to appear was Speaker Randall, who calmly looked down from the desk upon the scene of his defeat. He seconded Mr. Niblack's motion, and then promised that Hancock would make Pennsylvania a Democratic State. Every energy of his own mind and body would be exerted in the support of the ticket. In conclusion he assured the Convention that he did not feel at all sore over his own overthrow.

Senator Wallace, the foe of Randall, who had been successful beyond his most sanguine hopes, then thanked the Convention in behalf of his State, and declared that Cincinnati had named the next Democratic President, as she had the last in 1856. The nomination of Hancock would enable the party to wage a campaign of aggression.

Wade Hampton, the Confederate Brigadier, then promised to the party the vote of the solid South, and declared that no man was held in greater respect by the South than Hancock. "On the field of battle," said he, "we met him, and knew him as a gallant soldier, who conducted war on civilized principles and who, at the end of the war, was one of the first to extend a knightly hand to the conquered. In behalf of South Carolina, once so overwhelmingly Republican that hardly any one dared to count a Democratic vote, I pledge that the State shall give as large a Democratic vote as any State in the Union." To those who remembered that the State was a small one, this seemed to be equivalent to a promise that the Democrats of South Carolina would make an unlimited use of the shot-gun and of tissue ballots, by which Republican voters have been deprived of their rights heretofore. The Senator's language was unhappily chosen.

Judge Hoadley, of this city, promised a Democratic victory in Ohio in October and a unanimous vote in November.

By this time the old Chairman had made so many amusing blunders that he had almost lost the power to surprise anybody by his remarks. Still, his crowning blunder was to come. "A motion has been made," said he, emphasizing each word by a stroke with the gavel, "that Winfield S. Scott be unanimously declared the Democratic President of the United States." Some of the delegates laughed, but no one suggested any correction, and the motion was actually passed in this form, so that the Democratic Party has nominated for President the dead General of the Mexican war, with an S, and has declared him to be President without the formality of an election.

After the passage of this motion, a Randall transparency, upon which the name of Hancock had been painted, was carried through the main aisle and placed behind the Chairman's desk. The band played "Hail Columbia" and "America," the great organ joining in both. Senator Voorhees then ascended the platform for the purpose of showing Northern Democrats how confidently they could rely upon the support of a solid South. Mr. Faulkner, of New-York, made a short speech, most of which was devoted to Tilden and his alleged wrongs, but at its close he promised the vote of New-York in November in a way which could not have been satisfactory to some of the enthusiastic delegates around him.

After the Chairman had again referred to the nominee, as Winfield S. Scott, he introduced Mr. Breckinridge, of Kentucky, who declared that the party has beaten the sword into a pruning-hook, with which it would reap a harvest in November. After thus displaying his knowledge of farming implements, he asserted that he had arisen from sectional patriotism to the higher plane of American citizenship, and, as a representative of the solid South, appealed to the States of the North. "New-York, can you carry this ticket?" A delegate remarked that New-York could. "Can you in Pennsylvania?" Another delegate hastened to answer in the affirmative. "What says the gallant McSweeny, of Ohio?" he continued. "We will tramp on them 400,000 strong," replied McSweeny. "What says Connecticut, with her Englishes and her Ingersolls?" Mr. Parsons, of New-Haven, rashly promised a majority of 10,000. To similar inquiries, New-Jersey and Indiana gave satisfactory replies, and the delegate from Kentucky closed by expressing a desire for the old days, when the party was in power, and by invoking the blessing of God upon the ticket.

Then came one of the most striking episodes of the day. The crowd had not had enough of speech-making, and a loud-mouthed fellow in the gallery cried out, "Kelly, Kelly, come up John Kelly and give us a talk." A number of the rebel Brigadiers, among them the gentleman known as the gallant Wade Hampton, gathered about the great Tammany brave, and by their persuasion he was induced to come to the platform. He did so amid loud shouts of applause and some hisses. He was accompanied by his ever faithful henchman, Spinola, of shirt-collar notoriety; by Grady, Holahan, and others of the chiefs. He looked well pleased at the frowns which he received from Smith Weed and the other disappointed gentlemen in the regular New-York delegation, and, bowing to those who cheered him, said, among other things of a general character, that New-York had been united by the nomination of Hancock.

John R. Fellows, the ex-Confederate, of New-York, who represents Mr. Tilden, followed with a sore throat, but to the same general effect, and amid the howls of the galleries he and Kelly shook hands, in fact, fell upon each other's necks and wept, as it were.

After this New-York matter had been disposed of Mr. Watterson, of Kentucky, attempted to read the platform reported by the Committee on Resolutions, but a solemn-faced woman pushed him aside, and thrust a document under the old Chairman's nose. This was Susan B. Anthony, and with a look over her spectacles, in which contempt, apprehension, and wonder seemed to be mingled, she glowered upon the old man's perspiring face, and compelled him to order the document to be read. It was the ordinary sort of thing with which the woman suffragists besiege political conventions, and after it had been read it was thrust aside with the woman who had brought it. No action whatever was taken in regard to it, and Miss Anthony vexed the Convention no more.

THE PLATFORM.

Mr. Watterson then read the following platform:

The Democrats of the United States in convention assembled declare:

I. We pledge ourselves anew to the constitutional doctrines and traditions of the Democratic Party, as illustrated by the teachings and example of a long line of Democratic statesmen and patriots, and embodied in the platform of the last National Convention of the party.

II. Opposition to centralizationism and to that dangerous spirit of encroachment which tends to consolidate the powers of all the departments in one, and thus to create, whatever be the form of Government, a real despotism; no sumptuary laws; separation of Church and State for the good of each; common schools fostered and protected.

III. Home rule, honest money, consisting of gold and silver, and paper convertible to coin on demand; the strict maintenance of the public faith, State and National, and a tariff for revenue only.

IV. The subordination of the military to the civil power, and a general and thorough reform of the civil service.

V. The right to a free ballot is the right preservative of all rights, and must and shall be maintained in every part of the United States.

VI. The existing Administration is the representative of conspiracy only, and its claim of right to surround the ballot-boxes with troops and Deputy Marshals, to intimidate and obstruct the electors, and the unprecedented use of the veto to maintain its corrupt and despotic power, insults the people and imperils their institutions.

VII. The great fraud of 1876–7, by which, upon a false count of the Electoral votes of two States, the candidate defeated at the polls was declared to be President, and, for the first time in American history, the will of the people was set aside under a threat of military violence, struck a deadly blow at our system of representative Government. The Democratic Party, to preserve the country from the horrors of a civil war, submitted for the time, in firm and patriotic faith that the people would punish this crime in 1880. This issue precedes and dwarfs every other. It imposes a more sacred duty upon the people of the Union than ever addressed the conscience of a nation of freemen.

VIII. We execrate the course of this Administration in making places in the civil service a reward for political crime, and demand a reform by statute which shall make it forever impossible for the defeated candidate to bribe his way to the seat of a usurper by billeting villains upon the people.

IX. The resolution of Samuel J. Tilden not again to be a candidate for the exalted place to which he was elected by a majority of his countrymen, and from which he was excluded by the leaders of the Republican Party, is received by the Democrats of the United States with sensibility, and they declare their confidence in his wisdom, patriotism, and integrity, unshaken by the assaults of a common enemy, and they further assure him that he is followed into the retirement he has chosen for himself by the sympathy and respect of his fellow-citizens, who regard him as one who, by elevating the standards of public morality, and adorning and purifying the public service, merits the lasting gratitude of his country and his party.

X. Free ships and a living chance for American commerce on the seas and on the land. No discrimination in favor of transportation lines, corporations or monopolies.

XI. Amendment of the Burlingame treaty. No more Chinese immigration except for travel, education, and foreign commerce, and therein carefully guarded.

XII. Public money and public credit for public purposes solely, and public land for actual settlers.

XIII. The Democratic Party is the friend of labor and the laboring man, and pledges itself to protect him alike against the cormorants and the Commune.

XIV. We congratulate the country upon the honesty and thrift of a Democratic Congress, which has reduced the public expenditure $40,000,000 a year; upon the continuation of prosperity at home and the national honor abroad, and above all upon the promise of such a change in the administration of the Government as shall insure us genuine and lasting reform in every department of the public service.

There was a little applause at the end of the currency plank, and again at the end of the tariff plank, and the references to the last election were quite satisfactory to some. But most of the delegates felt that by rejecting Tilden they had virtually repudiated the fraud issue, and the applause was very weak. The platform was then adopted.

Then three or four congratulatory telegrams were read. Mr. Collins, of Massachusetts, had been so impressed by the disgraceful performances of the spectators that he offered a resolution shutting them out from the next Convention. The galleries groaned, and Mr. Smalley, of Vermont, opposed the resolution, and moved to lay it on the table. Collins called for a vote by States, but no one seconded the call, and his resolution was submitted to the Convention and almost unanimously rejected.

THE VICE-PRESIDENCY.

The remaining work of the Convention was quickly done. Mr. Pulitzer, of Missouri, moved that a ballot for Vice-President be taken. There was no opposition. The roll of States was called. Mr. William H. English, of Indiana, and, all things considered, one of the most unpopular men in the State, was nominated by Mr. Pettis, of Alabama. By a bargain with Senator Voorhees, his name was seconded by every State until Iowa was reached. Then Mr. Irish, of that State, who, as was suggested, had an old grievance against English, moved the nomination of Mr. R. M. Bishop, of Ohio. The roll of States then went on, until it was clearly apparent that English was nominated. Then Bishop's name was withdrawn, and the nomination of English declared unanimous. Cheers followed, of course.

COMMITTEE TO WAIT ON THE NOMINEES.

The following committee was then appointed to inform the nominees of their selection:

John W. Stevenson, Chairman of the Convention; Alabama, A. H. Kelly, Arkansas, H. King White; California, Thomas L. Thompson; Colorado, B. M. Hughes; Connecticut, W. H. Barnum; Delaware, Gov. Saulsbury; Florida, P. B. Bishop; Georgia, D. M. Dubore; Illinois, William H. Green; Indiana, De Forest Shuman; Iowa, T. L. Bowman; Kansas, Richard B. Morris; Kentucky, C. M. Thomas; Louisiana, John Clegg; Maine, William G. Davis; Maryland, Barnes Compton; Massachusetts, Josiah G. Abbott; Michigan, Orlando M. Barnes; Minnesota, H. W. Lamberton; Mississippi, W. A. Persey; Missouri, Morrison Munford; Nebraska, F. A. Harman; Nevada, A. C. Ellis; New-Hampshire, Timothy B. Crowley; New-Jersey, John Stockton; New-York, Augustus Schoonmaker; North Carolina, Charles M. Stedman; Ohio, George Hoadley; Oregon, S. W. Wisdom; Pennsylvania, R. M. Speer; Rhode Island, Nicholas Van Slycke; South Carolina, J. R. Abney; Tennessee, S. A. Champion; Texas, Joseph E. Dwyer; Vermont, M. C. Haley; Virginia, John W. Daniel; Wisconsin, Anson Rodgers; West Virginia, Robert M. Delanney.

A resolution giving the District of Columbia and the Territories each a representative in future National Democratic Conventions was tabled, and then, when the new National Committee had been announced, the National Democratic Convention of 1880, which by this time had become a howling mob, adjourned without day.

THE NATIONAL COMMITTEE.

The new National Committee is as follows:

|  |  |
|---|---|
| Alabama | Levi W. Lawler. |
| Arkansas | John J. Sumpter. |
| California | James T. Farley. |
| Colorado | T. M. Patterson. |
| Connecticut | William H. Barnum. |
| Delaware | Ignatius C. Grubb. |
| Florida | Samuel Pasco. |
| Georgia | George T. Barnes. |
| Illinois | William C. Goudy. |
| Indiana | Austin H. Brown. |
| Iowa | M. M. Ham. |
| Kansas | Charles W. Blair. |
| Kentucky | Henry D. McHenry. |
| Louisiana | B. F. Jonas. |
| Maine | Edmund Wilson. |
| Maryland | Oaterbridge Horsey. |
| Massachusetts | Frederick O. Prince. |
| Michigan | Edward Canter. |
| Minnesota | P. H. Kelly. |
| Mississippi | Gen. W. T. Martin. |
| Missouri | John G. Prather. |
| Nebraska | J. Sterling Morton. |
| Nevada | J. C. Hagerman. |
| New-Hampshire | Alvah W. Sulloway. |
| New-Jersey | Orestes Cleveland. |
| New-York | Abram S. Hewitt. |
| North Carolina | M. W. Ransom. |
| Ohio | Not named. |
| Oregon | Not named. |
| Pennsylvania | Not named. |
| Rhode Island | Abner J. Barnaby. |
| South Carolina | F. W. Dawson. |
| Tennessee | Thomas O'Connor. |
| Texas | F. S. Stockdale. |
| Vermont | Bradley B. Smalley. |
| Virginia | Robert A. Coghill. |
| Wisconsin | William F. Vilas. |
| West Virginia | Alexander Campbell. |

## MR. TILDEN'S SECOND DECLINATION.

CINCINNATI, June 24.—Mr. Manning, Secretary of the New-York State Democratic Committee, sent a dispatch to Mr. Tilden late last night, urging him to permit his name to be used this morning as a candidate, and assuring him of success. Before the meeting of the Convention to-day Mr. Manning received the following reply:

Received your telegrams and many others containing like information. My action was well considered and is irrevocable. No friends must be allowed to cast a doubt on my motives or my sincerity. S. J. TILDEN.

Several other friends on the New-York delegation who had also telegraphed to Mr. Tilden urging him to withdraw his declination, received similar responses.

## DISSATISFIED WITH THE TICKET.

FIRM OLD DEMOCRATS DISAPPOINTED—STRAINED ENTHUSIASM IN CINCINNATI.

CINCINNATI, June 24.—To-night Cincinnati begins to assume its ordinary appearance. The delegates to the National Convention have, in many instances, left for their homes, and no longer make the streets noisy with their shouts. The ticket nominated to-day has been well received after a fashion. Brass bands have played in honor of it, and many would-be orators have sounded its praises. Under all the strained enthusiasm, however, there are many evidences of dissatisfaction among Democrats who in the past have had never a word to say in opposition to the only ticket nominated by their party. The friends of Garfield and Arthur regard the nomination of Hancock as the despairing appeal of the Democracy to the war sentiment. After having failed in every other direction, they say that if the American people are to be asked to look only at the military service of the two candidates, Garfield certainly has nothing to fear in the results of a comparison; but they add that Garfield was not nominated because of his military career, but because during his long and useful services in the National Legislature he has shown rare qualities of statesmanship. On the contrary, Hancock can show nothing of this kind and it is apparent that one strong reason for his nomination was the fact that he had never expressed an opinion upon any National question, and had never occupied a position where he could make a record, as having the qualities which the President of the United States ought to possess.

A crowd of men and boys, led by a dozen torch-bearers and a band, serenaded Wade Hampton and Henry Watterson this evening. Hampton, who served as the hero of the Convention, assured the crowd of the certainty of a solid South, and asserted that he knew Hancock was a good man because he had fought against him on the battle-field in the war of the rebellion. Watterson declared that he would support the ticket without reservation. Randall made a speech, abounding in sentiments of a general and diffuse political character, and "Baldy" Smith tried to say something, as a representative of the Union Army, but for lack of a voice and because of jeers in the audience, saw fit to retire at the conclusion of his third sentence.

## REBELS RUNNING THE PARTY.

THE NORTHERN DEMOCRACY OUTWITTED BY THEIR SOUTHERN ALLIES—KELLY AND THE WHITE LEAGUE STRIKE HANDS AND HANCOCK IS THE RESULT.

CINCINNATI, June 24.—Once more the Democracy appeals to the Nation for support. It makes a new plea in a new way, yet all the time loses in the concealment of its old methods and its old hopes. The Democracy is to-day what it was twenty years ago. It has changed its methods, not its aims, not its desires, not its policy. It wants power, and, by its nominations made to-day it has announced to the world that by hook or by crook, by fair means or foul, it will have power. In its struggle to regain the power which it lost in 1860, it has built its hopes on all sorts and conditions of men and on various issues. In 1872 it was reduced to the necessity of intrusting its fortunes to a Republican who had abandoned his own party in the last unfortunate days of his eventful life, and the experiment was the most ignominous failure in the series. The history of its unsuccessful contest with the great Republican Party in 1876 is well known to every one who takes an interest in American politics. The nomination of Tilden was an experiment which, by the aid of the most infamous attempts at bribery and the purchase of entire State votes, was almost successful. Throughout this long struggle its inherent sympathy with the South and opposition to the war, which was carried by its great opponent to a triumphant end, made it expedient and logically necessary for the Democratic Party to make its experiments with leaders taken from civil life. Civilians of all sorts have been tried and found wanting, and as the Democrats of the South gradually regained a place in the councils of the party, their views began to have an influence upon the choice of a leader. The revelations of baffled trickery in 1876 induced the Southern leaders to urge an experiment of an entirely different kind in the election which is to come. They saw the blunders of their Northern allies from the point of view of an outsider, and they came to this Cincinnati Convention with a determination to appeal to the people through a new kind of candidate. Without insisting upon the selection of any man from their own section, knowing that such a selection would inevitably result in overwhelming defeat, they have steadily applied the pressure of a solid Southern vote to their Northern friends, and aided by local quarrels in the North, have been able to dictate in an unobtrusive way, a nomination. Under this influence, the Democratic Party will now seek to regain power through the popularity of a soldier of the war which it so strongly opposed, and which doomed it to impotence for twenty years. This is the point which the party has reached in its zigzag course. For years it has bewailed the war and striven to nullify the benefits which it secured. It has denounced its heroes, and has, within three months, opposed the erection of statues to their memory in the capital of the Nation, and urged the substitution of those of civilians. Throughout the whole of the long struggle, it has fought the soldier because he was the representative of the rival party, and has magnified the civilian and sought success by his elevation. To-day, in half an hour, not only were the logical tendencies of the campaign of 1876 ignored, but the position of twenty years was abandoned, and the party goes into the coming contest under the command of a once Union General. His nomination was the result of as thoughtless a stampede as ever drove a flock of sheep over a stone wall; but this stampede was made possible by the superior sagacity of Southern Democrats, who now are in possession of the party, as they were at the outbreak of the war.

The Democracy of the North come out of this Convention in a pitiable condition. At any time within the last three days they could have named the nominee, but they stupidly threw away all the opportunities to do so. A more pitiful squandering of political power was never seen than has appeared in the action of the New-York delegation. Subservient to the will of the sage of Gramercy Park, this body of men wasted their strength upon candidates who were notoriously unavailable, and left the field open to the survivors of the Confederacy. At the end, when their votes were utterly worthless, they threw them at the feet of the successful man. The men who have nominated Hancock have fixed upon a candidate whose success would surely increase their own power in the Government. Assuming, upon their entrance into the Convention, the harmlessness of doves, they have exercised the wisdom of serpents against their Northern associates and have completely outwitted them. There are many disappointed men in Cincinnati to-night, but of them all the most utterly broken down and disappointed are the Tilden men from the State of New-York. They had it in their own hands to nominate the President of the United States, and they threw the opportunity away. They know that they did do so. They know that the Democratic Convention to-day, despite their influence, despite their plainly-expressed opposition, nominated a man who is not favored by Mr. Tilden, who is not favored by the interest in New-York, and who will, should he happen to be elected, give the patronage of his position to anti-Tilden men. The day has been an unfortunate one for the friends of "The Claimant." The Democratic "Old Man of the Sea" and his kitchen Cabinet have at last met their Waterloo. They do not attempt to disguise their bitterness of feeling or their disappointment. They can only console themselves by cursing their leaders, and by declaring that if better management had been displayed on the part of Tilden's most intimate advisers, the present result could never have been brought about. Their wail now is that Payne killed them and broke the influence of the Empire State. Their theory, and it is a most just one, is that, if Payne, who, in the light of recent events, appears to have been an impossibility, had never been presented as a Presidential candidate, and if, on the contrary, some other candidate who could get the support of his own State had been put forward, he might with ease have secured the strong support of the great majority of the Convention. It is suggested, for instance, and well suggested, that if on Monday night last Randall had been taken up by New-York and honestly pushed by her seventy delegates, he could without trouble have been nominated. There is no doubt that this is only the simple truth. Three days ago every delegate to the National Convention was ready to act in entire accord with New-York. The Empire State waited too long, lost its influence, and became of no account in the contest. It is noticeable that of the votes received by Hancock yesterday, 87 only were from the great North, while all the rest came from the South. To-day, in the first ballot, before Pennsylvania changed her vote, his vote from the South was 135, and afterward nearly all his strength came from the same locality. Gen. Hancock must be regarded as the candidate of the cotton States, the Democrats of which expect to serve him, and of Kelly and company, who were glad to agree upon him as the best man to give what politicians call a "black eye" to Tilden. Tammany and the White League are at last united under a respectable figure head. Whether or not they shall be allowed to succeed it remains with the country to decide. H. C.

## MR. ENGLISH'S UNPOPULARITY.

THE INDIANA MEN IN A BAD FIX—MURAT HALSTEAD DESCRIBES THE SECOND MAN ON THE TICKET.

CINCINNATI, June 24.—In regard to the second name on the ticket, Murat Halstead, who knows what he is talking about, said to-night: "Their ticket is obviously weak where it should have been, according to the great principle of winning at all events, especially strong. It is weak in the doubtful October State, Indiana. The nomination of Mr. English is not only not strong in itself, it is a blow at Hendricks, which strikes him in his tenderest part. Mr. English is the man who has been bepuffed for months by the Tilden organs, who have made it a point to hate and hurt Hendricks. English was put up for the annoyance of Hendricks and the whole Indiana delegation. After making it a merit to stick to their great man and wage a furious battle for him without hope, blaspheming Senator McDonald because he was thought of for the Presidency, and growing desperate over the suggestion that Indiana had any other favorite son than the one who was presented for the Presidency. After all this, to vote for English and make up the ticket by adding to the soldier, for the copperheads, an ex-banker for the Greenbackers, affords a spectacle that should be instructive. The brass-bound and copper-bottomed Indiana Democrat, who sympathized with the South when in trouble, and looked the other way when he heard the war drums, may consent to take his crow when it comes as gamecock dressed with the spurs on; but if he must take it seasoned with a banker and real estate speculator who has scraped the bones of the State, and joins to great wealth the reputation of a strict economist, he may, inspired by a superhuman sense of loyalty to his party, force the full dose into his stomach, but he will not hanker for it, and he will not, thus nourished, insist upon getting up in the morning at 2 o'clock to march upon the works of the enemy."

## NATIONAL COMMITTEE MEETING.

CINCINNATI, June 24.—The National Committee met in the evening and elected William H. Barnum temporary Chairman and Frederick O. Prince temporary Secretary. The permanent organization was postponed until the next meeting, in order to give time for consultation with the candidates. They adjourned to meet at the Fifth-Avenue Hotel, New-York, July 13.

## SPEECHES AFTER THE NOMINATION.

WILLIAM MACK SPEAKS FOR INDIANA.

I arise, in behalf of the brave Democracy of Indiana, [applause,] to move that the nomination of Gen. Hancock be unanimous [loud applause] in this convention. We came here instructed for Gov. Hendricks. We knew he was honest, capable, and faithful to the Constitutions—National and State—and we thought he could be elected, and we knew he could carry Indiana. The second choice of Indiana is Winfield Scott Hancock. [Applause.] And now, gentlemen of the Convention, when you hear from Indiana you will find that we have again turned the right flank of the Republican Party, [applause,] and when we do it this time, we will expect our friends in New-York and Connecticut to attend to the left flank while the solid South comes up behind, [applause;] and when we have driven them, as we did before, from the field of honorable competition and warfare behind the bulwarks and into the ditches of fraud and perjury, we do not propose to cease our labors, but drive them from power entirely. [Applause.]

SPEAKER RANDALL'S ADDRESS.

FELLOW-DEMOCRATS: I am here to second the nomination of Pennsylvania's son, Gen. Hancock. [Applause.] Your deliberations have been marked by the utmost harmony, and your act is an expression of the heart of every American Democrat in every State of the Union. [Applause.] Not only is your nomination strong, but it is one that will bring us victory, [applause,] and we will add another State to the Democratic column—the great Commonwealth of Pennsylvania—[applause,] the keystone of the Federal arch. Not only is this acceptable to every Democrat in the United States, but it is a nomination which will command the respect of the entire American people. [Applause.] I will not detain you longer than to say that you will find me in the front rank of this conflict, second to none, and that every energy of my mind and every energy of my brain will be given from now until we shall all rejoice in a common victory on the November Tuesday coming. [Applause.] There is a great mission ahead of the Democratic Party, and you have selected a standard-bearer whose very nomination means that if the people ratify your choice he will be inaugurated. [Applause.] I thank you for this cordial greeting, and I beg of you not to suppose for a moment that I am in the least discomfited, but, on the contrary, my whole heart goes forth with your voice, and I will yield to no man in the effort which shall be made in behalf of your ticket chosen this day. [Applause.] The Chair will have the honor to present to you Senator Wallace, of Pennsylvania, who desires to assure you that Pennsylvania is safe for Hancock.

MR. WALLACE'S SPEECH.

GENTLEMEN OF THE CONVENTION: On behalf of the great Keystone State of the Union, our delegation sends to you thanks and greetings. History repeats itself. In this great city of Cincinnati the Democrats of the Nation named their last President, and to-day they name their next. [Cheers.] History repeats itself. In those days they named a son of Pennsylvania, and to-day again they inscribe upon the banner of the Democracy the name of a gallant son of the Commonwealth of Pennsylvania. He will lead us to victory. His name is invincible. The word rings out, "Advance the column, move on the enemy's works!" Let there be no defense, but aggression, aggression, aggression, and victory is ours. [Cheers.] On behalf of that great Commonwealth, as one of her sons, I came here to assure you that I feel, as does every member of her delegation, that you have given us in this nomination the means once more of placing the Keystone in the column of Democratic States—[Cheers]—and when November shall have come, you will find that the energies of those who now clasp hands in behalf of this our standard-bearer, will have worked wonders in that Commonwealth. [Cheers, and howls for Voorhees.]

WADE HAMPTON'S SPEECH.

MR. PRESIDENT AND GENTLEMEN OF THE CONVENTION: On behalf of the solid South, that South which once was arrayed against the great soldier of Pennsylvania, I stand here to pledge you its solid vote. [Cheers.] We will prove no laggards in this great race for constitutional government, for home rule, and for freedom all over this great land. There is no name which is held in higher respect among the people of the South than that of the man whom you have given to us as our standard-bearer. We have met him on the field of battle. We knew then that he was a brave, a gallant, and an able soldier, one who always conducted war upon civilized principles, and when the war was ended he was among the first to extend his knightly hand to aid the people who had been fighting against him. [Cheers.] We recognize that, and, recognizing it, we will give him a cordial, a candid, a hearty, and an earnest support. And, in the name of South Carolina—that State which has so lately returned and come into the sisterhood of States—that State which was so overwhelmingly Republican that we scarcely dared to count the Democratic vote—in behalf of that State I here pledge myself, if work, if zeal, if energy can do anything, that the people of South Carolina will give as large a Democratic majority as any other State in this Union.

JUDGE HOADLEY SPEAKS FOR OHIO.

GENTLEMEN OF THE CONVENTION: Ohio sends me here to second the motion. Ohio is the right of the field of combat along the skirmish line, Ohio stands upon the right and Indiana upon the left. Victory in October in Ohio is a unanimous one in November, [applause,] and that we are going to have. Men of Ohio, fellow-delegates from Ohio, in the presence of this magnificent assembly of the Democrats of the Union, I wish to say for you these words: Sixty-seven years ago, in the darkness of the night and amid the thunderings of the great cataract, where the hosts of American soldiers met the embattled red coats at Lundy-lane, Gen. Brown said to John Miller, "See that battery; and take it." [Applause.] John Miller answered, "General, I will try," and did it. You have commanded us to take the Garfield battery; we will try. The good God with us, a holy cause of our own, the Democracy of other States sending their silver-tongued orators to our help, we will do it; [slight applause;] and when, on the 4th of March next, our gallant leader, Winfield Scott Hancock, shall have inscribed his name at the foot of the Inaugural Message, there will be recalled to every memory that other glorious Declaration of Independence signed by John Hancock. [Great applause and cheers.]

SENATOR VOORHEES'S SPEECH.

LADIES AND GENTLEMEN: This is no time for words or speech-making, and I arise simply to say that though somewhat soreheaded, the Democracy of Indiana knows its duty, and that duty will be performed in the coming contest under the gallant leadership of the nominee which has been [illegible]

# The New-York Times.

VOL. XXX........NO. 9096. NEW-YORK, WEDNESDAY, NOVEMBER 3, 1880. PRICE FOUR CENTS.

## THE GREAT TRUST RENEWED

*GARFIELD AND ARTHUR THE CHOICE OF THE NATION.*

FRAUD AND FORGERY REPUDIATED BY THE AMERICAN PEOPLE.

*NEW-YORK GIVES 25,000 REPUBLICAN MAJORITY.*

THE HOUSE OF REPRESENTATIVES ONCE MORE REPUBLICAN.

EVERY NORTHERN STATE EXCEPT NEW-JERSEY CARRIED FOR THE REPUBLICAN PRESIDENTIAL CANDIDATES—THE SUPERB SOLDIER AND THE SOLID SOUTH TAKE A BACK SEAT—A CLEAR REPUBLICAN MAJORITY IN THE NEXT HOUSE OF REPRESENTATIVES—A TREMENDOUS FALLING OFF IN THE DEMOCRATIC MAJORITIES IN NEW-YORK AND BROOKLYN.

The country speaks out again as it spoke in 1872. Every Northern State except New-Jersey has declared for Garfield and Arthur, giving them 222 of the 369 votes of the Electoral College, and an overwhelming majority of the popular vote. The Democratic Presidential candidates will receive but 147 Electoral votes. THE TIMES's dispatches tell of heavy Republican gains over the vote of 1876 everywhere except in New-Hampshire, where, however, the Garfield Electors and a Republican Governor have been chosen. The magnitude of the victory in this State surpasses all expectation. The Democratic majority in New-York City has been reduced to 41,000, and in Brooklyn it will not exceed 10,000. Maine redeems herself with a Republican majority of between 4,000 and 5,000. Connecticut gives Garfield 4,200 majority; Massachusetts more than 50,000; Pennsylvania, 45,000; Ohio, 40,000. Indiana fulfills the promise of her October election by giving a Republican majority of about 7,000. From all over the West comes news of increased Republican majorities; even in Kentucky there have been large gains. Nevada has chosen the Garfield Electors. At the hour of going to press it seems probable that the next House of Representatives will contain 157 Republicans, 181 Democrats, and 5 Greenbackers; but this estimate of the Republican strength covers 2 districts in North Carolina, 1 in Massachusetts, 1 in Nevada, and 1 in Pennsylvania which are, at least, doubtful. Conceding all these to the Democrats, however, the House would still have 152 Republicans to 186 Democrats, and 5 Greenbackers.

### *ELECTORS AND CONGRESSMEN.*

The Electoral College consists of 369 members, and the smallest number by which a candidate's election can be secured is 185, or a majority of the whole number. Each State is entitled to as many Electors as it has Senators and Representatives in Congress and therefore the number of each State's Electors exceeds the number of its Representatives in the House by two. The following table shows how the Electoral votes of each State will be cast for the opposing candidates, and also the result of the Congressional elections in each State:

| States. | Electoral Vote. | | Forty-Seventh Congress. | | |
|---|---|---|---|---|---|
| | Garfield. | Hancock. | Rep. | Dem. | Gr'b |
| Alabama | .. | 10 | .. | 7 | 1 |
| Arkansas | .. | 6 | .. | 4 | .. |
| California | 6 | .. | 4 | .. | .. |
| Colorado | 3 | .. | 1 | .. | .. |
| Connecticut | 6 | .. | 3 | 1 | .. |
| Delaware | .. | 3 | .. | 1 | .. |
| Florida | .. | 4 | 1 | 1 | .. |
| Georgia | .. | 11 | .. | 9 | .. |
| Illinois | 21 | .. | 14 | 5 | .. |
| Indiana | 15 | .. | 8 | 5 | .. |
| Iowa | 11 | .. | 9 | .. | .. |
| Kansas | 5 | .. | 3 | .. | .. |
| Kentucky | .. | 12 | 2 | 8 | .. |
| Louisiana | .. | 8 | 1 | 5 | .. |
| Maine | 7 | .. | 3 | .. | 2 |
| Maryland | .. | 8 | 1 | 5 | .. |
| Massachusetts | 13 | .. | 11 | .. | .. |
| Michigan | 11 | .. | 9 | .. | .. |
| Minnesota | 5 | .. | 3 | .. | .. |
| Mississippi | .. | 8 | .. | 6 | .. |
| Missouri | .. | 15 | 2 | 10 | 1 |
| Nebraska | 3 | .. | 1 | .. | .. |
| Nevada | 3 | .. | 1 | .. | .. |
| New-Hampshire | 5 | .. | 3 | .. | .. |
| New-Jersey | .. | 9 | 4 | 3 | .. |
| New-York | 35 | .. | 20 | 13 | .. |
| North Carolina | .. | 10 | 3 | 4 | 1 |
| Ohio | 22 | .. | 15 | 5 | .. |
| Oregon | 3 | .. | 1 | .. | .. |
| Pennsylvania | 29 | .. | 20 | 7 | |
| Rhode Island | 4 | .. | 2 | .. | .. |
| South Carolina | .. | 7 | .. | 5 | .. |
| Tennessee | .. | 12 | 3 | 7 | .. |
| Texas | .. | 8 | .. | 6 | .. |
| Vermont | 5 | .. | 3 | .. | .. |
| Virginia | .. | 11 | 2 | 7 | .. |
| West Virginia | .. | 5 | .. | 3 | .. |
| Wisconsin | 10 | .. | 6 | 2 | .. |
| Total | 222 | 147 | 159 | 129 | 5 |

The following table exhibits more plainly the division of the Electoral College:

| Garfield. | Votes. | Hancock. | Votes. |
|---|---|---|---|
| California | 6 | Alabama | 10 |
| Colorado | 3 | Arkansas | 6 |
| Connecticut | 6 | Delaware | 3 |
| Illinois | 21 | Florida | 4 |
| Indiana | 15 | Georgia | 11 |
| Iowa | 11 | Kentucky | 12 |
| Kansas | 5 | Louisiana | 8 |
| Maine | 7 | Maryland | 8 |
| Massachusetts | 13 | Mississippi | 8 |
| Michigan | 11 | Missouri | 15 |
| Minnesota | 5 | New-Jersey | 9 |
| Nebraska | 3 | North Carolina | 10 |
| Nevada | 3 | South Carolina | 7 |
| New-Hampshire | 5 | Tennessee | 12 |
| New-York | 35 | Texas | 8 |
| Ohio | 22 | Virginia | 11 |
| Oregon | 3 | West Virginia | 5 |
| Pennsylvania | 29 | Total | 147 |
| Rhode Island | 4 | | |
| Vermont | 5 | | |
| Wisconsin | 10 | | |
| Total | 222 | | |

### FORTY-SEVENTH CONGRESS.

LIST OF MEMBERS ELECTED—POLITICAL DIVISION OF THE HOUSE.

The names of the members of the House of Representatives who have been elected, so far as they can be ascertained at this time, appear below. The names of Republicans are printed in roman, those of Democrats in *italics*, and those of Greenbackers in SMALL CAPITALS; Independents and Readjusters are indicated by abbreviations:

ALABAMA.
1. *Thomas H. Herndon.* 2. *Hilary A. Herbert.* 3. *William C. Oates.* 4. *Charles M. Shelley.* 5. *Thomas Williams.* 6. *George W. Hewett.* 7. *William H. Forney*, I. 8. WILLIAM M. LOWE.

ARKANSAS.
1. *Poindexter Dunn.* 2. *James K. Jones.* 3. *Jordan E. Cravens.* 4. *Thomas M. Gunter.*

CALIFORNIA.
1. Horace Davis. 2. Horace F. Page. 3. George A. Knight. 4. Romualdo Pacheco.

COLORADO.
James B. Belford.

CONNECTICUT.
1. John R. Buck. 2. *James Phelps.* 3. John T. Wait. 4. Frederick Miles.

DELAWARE.
*Edward L. Martin.*

FLORIDA.
1. *R. H. M. Davidson.* 2. Horatio Bisbee, Jr.

GEORGIA.
1. *George R. Black.* 2. *Henry G. Turner.* 3. *Philip Cook.* 4. *Hugh Buchanan.* 5. *N. J. Hammond.* 6. *James H. Blount.* 7. *Judson C. Clements.* 8. *Alex. H. Stephens.* 9. *Emory Speer*, I.

ILLINOIS.
1. William Aldrich. 2. George R. Davis. 3. Charles B. Farwell. 4. John C. Sherwin. 5. Robert M. A. Hawk. 6. Thomas J. Henderson. 7. William Cullen. 8. Lewis E. Payson. 9. John H. Lewis. 10. Benjamin F. Marsh. 11. *James W. Singleton.* 12. *William M. Springer.* 13. Dietrich C. Smith. 14. Joseph G. Cannon. 15. A. P. Forsythe, I. G. 16. *William A. J. Sparks.* 17. *William R. Morrison.* 18. John R. Thomas. 19. *Richard W. Townshend.*

INDIANA.
1. William Heilman. 2. *Thomas R. Cobb.* 3. *S. M. Stockslager.* 4. *W. S. Holman.* 5. *C. C. Matson.* 6. Thomas M. Browne. 7. Stanton J. Peelle. 8. R. B. F. Pierce. 9. Godlove S. Orth. 10. Mark L. De Motte. 11. George W. Steele. 12. *W. G. Colerick.* 13. William H. Calkins.

IOWA.
1. Moses A. McCoid. 2. Sewall S. Farwell. 3. Thomas Updegraff. 4. Nathaniel C. Deering. 5. William G. Thompson. 6. Madison E. Cutts. 7. John A. Kasson. 8. W. P. Hepburn. 9. Cyrus C. Carpenter.

KANSAS.
1. John A. Anderson. 2. Dudley C. Haskell. 3. Thomas Ryan.

KENTUCKY.
1. *Oscar Turner.* 2. *James A. McKenzie.* 3. *John W. Caldwell.* 4. *J. Proctor Knott.* 5. *Albert S. Willis.* 6. *John G. Carlisle.* 7. *Joseph C. S. Blackburn.* 8. *P. B. Thompson, Jr.* 9. John D. White. 10. George M. Thomas.

LOUISIANA.
1. *Randall L. Gibson.* 2. *E. John Ellis.* 3. Chester B. Darrall. 4. *N. C. Blanchard.* 5. *J. Floyd King.* 6. *E. W. Robertson.*

MAINE.
1. Thomas B. Reed. 2. William P. Frye. 3. Stephen D. Lindsey. 4. GEORGE W. LADD. 5. THOMPSON H. MURCH.

MARYLAND.
1. *G. W. Covington.* 2. *J. F. C. Talbot.* 3. *F. S. Hoblitzell.* 4. *Robert M. McLane.* 5. *A. G. Chapman.* 6. Milton G. Urner.

MASSACHUSETTS.
1. William W. Crapo. 2. Benjamin W. Harris. 3. A. A. Ranney. 4. Francis B. Hayes. 5. Selwyn Z. Bowman. 6. Eben F. Stone. 7. William A. Russell. 8. John W. Candler. 9. William W. Rice. 10. Amasa Norcross. 11. George D. Robinson.

MICHIGAN.
1. Henry W. Lord. 2. Edwin Willits. 3. Edward S. Lacey. 4. Julius C. Burrows. 5. George W. Webber. 6. O. L. Spaulding. 7. Omar D. Conger. 8. Roswell G. Horr. 9. Jay A. Hubbell.

MINNESOTA.
1. Mark H. Dunnell. 2. Horace B. Strait. 3. Wm. D. Washburn.

MISSISSIPPI.
1. *Henry L. Muldrow.* 2. *Van H. Manning.* 3. *Hernando S. Money.* 4. *L. H. Davis.* 5. *Charles E. Hooker.* 6. *James R. Chalmers.*

MISSOURI.
1. *Martin L. Clardy.* 2. *Thomas Allen.* 3. G. Sessinghaus. 4. *Lowndes H. Davis.* 5. *Richard P. Bland.* 6. *James R. Waddill.* 7. *John F. Philips.* 8. R. T. Van Horn. 9. NICHOLAS FORD. 10. *Charles H. Mansur.* 11. *John B. Clark, Jr.* 12. *William H. Hatch.* 13. *Aylett H. Buckner.*

NEBRASKA.
Edward K. Valentine.

NEVADA.
Rollin M. Daggett.

NEW-HAMPSHIRE.
1. Joshua G. Hall. 2. James F. Briggs. 3. Evarts W. Farr.

NEW-JERSEY.
1. George M. Robeson. 2. John H. Brewer. 3. *Miles Ross.* 4. *Henry S. Harris.* 5. John Hill. 6. Phineas Jones. 7. *A. A. Hardenbergh.*

NEW-YORK.
1. *Perry Belmont.* 2. *William E. Robinson.* 3. *J. Hyatt Smith.* 4. *Archibald M. Bliss.* 5. *Benjamin Wood.* 6. *Samuel S. Cox.* 7. *Philip H. Dugro.* 8. Anson G. McCook. 9. *Fernando Wood.* 10. *Abram S. Hewitt.* 11. Levi P. Morton. 12. *Waldo Hutchins.* 13. John H. Ketcham. 14. *Lewis Beach.* 15. Thomas Cornell. 16. *Michael N. Nolan.* 17. Walter A. Wood. 18. John Hammond. 19. Abraham X. Parker. 20. George West. 21. Ferris Jacobs, Jr. 22. Warner Miller. 23. Cyrus D. Prescott. 24. Joseph Mason. 25. Frank Hiscock. 26. John H. Camp. 27. Elbridge G. Lapham. 28. Jeremiah W. Dwight. 29. D. P. Richardson. 30. John Van Voorhis. 31. Richard Crowley. 32. *Jonathan Scoville.* 33. Henry Van Aernam.

NORTH CAROLINA.
1. Cyrus W. Grandy. 2. Orlando Hubbs. 3. DANIEL L. RUSSELL. 4. Moses A. Bledsoe. 5. *Alfred M. Scales.* 6. *Clement Dowd.* 7. *Robert F. Armfield.* 8. *Robert B. Vance.*

OHIO.
1. Benj. Butterworth. 2. Thomas L. Young. 3. Henry L. Morey. 4. Emanuel Schultz. 5. *Benjamin Le Fevre.* 6. James M. Ritchie. 7. *John P. Leedom.* 8. J. Warren Keifer. 9. James S. Robinson. 10. John B. Rice. 11. Henry S. Neal. 12. *George L. Converse.* 13. *Gibson Atherton.* 14. *George W. Geddes.* 15. Rufus R. Dawes. 16. John D. Updegraff. 17. Wm. McKinley, Jr. 18. A. S. McClure. 19. Ezra B. Taylor. 20. Amos Townsend.

OREGON.
M. C. George.

PENNSYLVANIA.
1. Henry H. Bingham. 2. Charles O'Neill. 3. *Samuel J. Randall.* 4. William D. Kelley. 5. Alfred C. Harmer. 6. William Ward. 7. William Godshalk. 8. *Daniel Ermentrout.* 9. A. Herr Smith. 10. *William Mutchler.* 11. *Robert Klotz.* 12. Joseph A. Scranton. 13. Charles N. Brumm, G. 14. Samuel F. Barr. 15. Cornelius C. Jadwin. 16. Robert J. C. Walker. 17. Jacob M. Campbell. 18. Horatio G. Fisher. 19. *F. E. Beltzhoover.* 20. *Andrew G. Curtin.* 21. *Morgan R. Wise.* 22. Russell Errett. 23. Thomas M. Bayne. 24. W. S. Shallenberger. 25. Harry White. 26. Samuel H. Miller. 27. Lewis F. Watson.

RHODE ISLAND.
1. Nelson W. Aldrich. 2. Jonathan Chace.

SOUTH CAROLINA.
1. *John S. Richardson.* 2. *M. P. O'Connor.* 3. *D. Wyatt Aiken.* 4. *John H. Evins.* 5. *George D. Tillman.*

TENNESSEE.
1. A. H. Pettibone. 2. Leonidas C. Houk. 3. *George G. Dibrell.* 4. *Benton McMillin.* 5. *Richard Warner.* 6. *John F. House.* 7. *W. C. Whitthorne.* 8. *John D. C. Atkins.* 9. *Charles B. Simonton.* 10. William R. Moore.

TEXAS.
1. *John H. Reagan.* 2. *David B. Culberson.* 3. *Olin Wellborn.* 4. *Roger Q. Mills.* 5. *George W. Jones*, Ind. 6. *Columbus Upson.*

VERMONT.
1. Charles H. Joyce. 2. James M. Tyler. 3. William W. Grout.

VIRGINIA.
1. *John Critcher*, Readj. 2. John F. Dezendorf. 3. *George D. Wise.* 4. Joseph Jorgensen. 5. *John T. Stovall*, Readj. 6. *John R. Tucker.* 7. *John Paul*, Readj. 8. *John S. Barbour.* 9. *Conally F. Trigg.*

WEST VIRGINIA.
1. *Benjamin Wilson.* 2. *John Blair Hoge.* 3. *John E. Kenna.*

WISCONSIN.
1. Charles G. Williams. 2. Lucien B. Caswell. 3. George C. Hazelton. 4. *Peter V. Deuster.* 5. *Edward S. Bragg.* 6. Richard Guenther. 7. H. L. Humphrey. 8. Thaddeus C. Pound.

RECAPITULATION.

Following is a recapitulation showing the number of Representatives of the several parties in the Forty-seventh Congress, according to the list printed above, the Independents and Readjusters being included in the list of Democrats:

Whole number.......293 Democrats.........130
Republicans.........158 Greenbackers.........5

### *NEW-YORK.*

MAJORITIES BY COUNTIES.

The State of New York has been carried by the Republicans by 25,000 majority. The following table shows the majorities in the several counties, compared with those of 1876:

| Counties. | 1880. Garfield, Rep. | 1880. Hancock, Dem. | 1876. Hayes, Rep. | 1876. Tilden, Dem. |
|---|---|---|---|---|
| Albany | .... | 2,500 | .... | 1,178 |
| Allegany | 3,800 | .... | 2,908 | .... |
| Broome | 1,800 | .... | 1,343 | .... |
| Cattaraugus | 2,300 | .... | 1,664 | .... |
| Cayuga | 3,425 | .... | 2,859 | .... |
| Chautauqua | 5,250 | .... | 4,580 | .... |
| Chemung | .... | 100 | .... | 396 |
| Chenango | 1,200 | .... | 1,347 | .... |
| Clinton | 1,850 | .... | 706 | .... |
| Columbia | 351 | .... | .... | 512 |
| Cortland | 1,450 | .... | 1,396 | .... |
| Delaware | 800 | .... | 595 | .... |
| Dutchess | 2,700 | .... | 390 | .... |
| Erie | 3,000 | .... | 768 | .... |
| Essex | 1,900 | .... | 1,522 | .... |
| Franklin | 1,300 | .... | 1,158 | .... |
| Fulton & H'milton | 1,200 | .... | 31 | .... |
| Genesee | 1,335 | .... | 1,001 | .... |
| Greene | .... | 600 | .... | 1,093 |
| Herkimer | 1,275 | .... | 754 | .... |
| Jefferson | 2,400 | .... | 2,133 | .... |
| Kings | .... | 9,336 | .... | 18,492 |
| Lewis | 400 | .... | .... | 97 |
| Livingston | 1,274 | .... | 1,023 | .... |
| Madison | 2,200 | .... | 1,621 | .... |
| Monroe | 3,500 | .... | 1,611 | .... |
| Montgomery | 300 | .... | .... | 308 |
| New-York | .... | 42,000 | .... | 54,055 |
| Niagara | 500 | .... | .... | 315 |
| Oneida | 2,100 | .... | 1,176 | .... |
| Onondaga | 4,800 | .... | 3,705 | .... |
| Ontario | 1,200 | .... | 806 | .... |
| Orange | 200 | .... | .... | 346 |
| Orleans | 1,550 | .... | 1,136 | .... |
| Oswego | 3,500 | .... | 2,813 | .... |
| Otsego | 100 | .... | .... | 167 |
| Putnam | 625 | .... | 144 | .... |
| Queens | .... | 2,100 | .... | 3,024 |
| Rensselaer | 1,000 | .... | .... | 672 |
| Richmond | .... | 1,526 | .... | 1,455 |
| Rockland | .... | 723 | .... | 1,145 |
| St. Lawrence | 7,900 | .... | 7,681 | .... |
| Saratoga | 2,300 | .... | 903 | .... |
| Schenectady | 600 | .... | .... | 258 |
| Schoharie | .... | 1,400 | .... | 1,775 |
| Schuyler | 600 | .... | 606 | .... |
| Seneca | .... | 400 | .... | 537 |
| Steuben | 1,500 | .... | 959 | .... |
| Suffolk | 300 | .... | .... | 215 |
| Sullivan | .... | 200 | .... | 1,140 |
| Tioga | 1,142 | .... | 769 | .... |
| Tompkins | 1,000 | .... | 1,004 | .... |
| Ulster | .... | 100 | .... | 1,722 |
| Warren | 600 | .... | 472 | .... |
| Washington | 3,500 | .... | 2,488 | .... |
| Wayne | 2,400 | .... | 1,883 | .... |
| Westchester | .... | 500 | .... | 2,480 |
| Wyoming | 1,400 | .... | 1,162 | .... |
| Yates | 1,275 | .... | 1,282 | .... |
| Total | 85,102 | 61,490 | 58,664 | 91,482 |

Republican majority in 1880........23,612
Democratic plurality in 1876........32,818

### THE ASSEMBLY.

NAMES OF MEMBERS ELECTED—THE DIVISION BY POLITICAL PARTIES.

The names of the members of the Assembly of the State of New-York who have been elected are given in the following list. Those of Republicans are printed in roman, and those of Democrats in *italic*:

ALBANY. 1. *Miner Gallup.* 2. Andrew S. Draper. 3. *Aaron B. Pratt.* 4. George Campbell.
ALLEGANY. Samuel H. Morgan.
BROOME. L. Coe Young.
CATTARAUGUS. 1. Henry S. Bradley. 2. Joseph M. Congdon.
CAYUGA. 1. Thomas Hunter. 2. Hector H. Tuthill.
CHAUTAUQUA. 1. Albert B. Sheldon. 2. Milton M. Fenner.
CHEMUNG. *Henry C. Hoffman.*
CHENANGO. Solomon K. Bemiss.
CLINTON. Shepard P. Bowen.
COLUMBIA. John E. Gillette.
CORTLAND. Alburtis A. Carley.
DELAWARE. William Lewis.
DUTCHESS. 1. Isaac S. Carpenter. 2. James E. Dutcher.
ERIE. 1. *Jeremiah Higgins.* 2. Frank Sipp. 3. Arthur W. Hickman. 4. George Bingham. 5. Harvey J. Hurd.
ESSEX. James W. Sheehy.
FRANKLIN. William D. Brennan.
FULTON AND HAMILTON. David A. Wells.
GENESEE. J. W. Holmes.
GREENE. *O. L. Newton.*
HERKIMER. William D. Gorsline.
JEFFERSON. 1. Charles R. Skinner. 2. Henry Binninger.
KINGS. 1. *John Shanley.* 2. *John McTernan.* 3. *Lawrence J. Tormey.* 4. *James Coyne.* 5. *Thomas J. Sheridan.* 6. *Patrick J. Tully.* 7. John Reitz. 8. *Moses Engle.* 9. Charles H. Russell. 10. *Richard J. Newman.* 11. William H. Waring. 12. C. W. C. Dreher.
LEWIS. Charles A. Chickering.
LIVINGSTON. Kidder M. Scott.
MADISON. David A. Jackson.
MONROE. 1. Geo. Le Grand Seely. 2. John Cowles. 3. Frederick P. Root.
MONTGOMERY. Cornelius Van Buren.
NEW-YORK. 1. *Michael C. Murphy.* 2. *Constantine Donoho.* 3. *Thomas Smith, Jr.* 4. *John H. McCarthy.* 5. *Thomas Bogan.* 6. *Matthew Patten.* 7. Isaac I. Hayes. 8. John E. Brodsky. 9. *John W. Browning.* 10. Charles E. Brehm. 11. Robert Ray Hamilton. 12. *Louis Cohen.* 13. Arthur D. Williams. 14. *John Murphy.* 15. *M. J. Dougherty.* 16. *Francis B. Spinola.* 17. *James Fanning.* 18. *Joseph P. McDonough.* 19. *William H. Finley.* 20. *Fred'k Thilemann, Jr.* 21. Wm. J. Trimble. 22. *William S. Andrews.* 23. Donald McLean. 24. *William W. Niles.*
NIAGARA. 1. E. Adams Holt. 2. James Low.
ONEIDA. 1. James Armstrong. 2. David G. Evans. 3. Thomas D. Roberts.
ONONDAGA. 1. Thomas G. Alvord. 2. Albert Howland. 3. Henry L. Duguid.
ONTARIO. John Raines.
ORANGE. 1. Joseph M. Dickey. 2. *W. Harvey Clark.*
ORLEANS. Marcus H. Phillips.
OSWEGO. 1. Patrick W. Cullinan. 2. William H. Steele.
OTSEGO. 1. *J. Stanley Brown.* 2. David Russell.
PUTNAM. Samuel H. Everett.
QUEENS. 1. *Townsend D. Cock.* 2. *George E. Bulmer.*
RENSSELAER. 1. *Charles E. Patterson.* 2. Richard A. Derrick. 3. *Barnis C. Strait.*
RICHMOND. *Erastus Brooks.*
ROCKLAND. *John Cleary.*
ST. LAWRENCE. 1. Daniel Peck. 2. Worth Chamberlain. 3. Ebenezer S. Crapser.
SARATOGA. 1. Benjamin F. Baker. 2. Delcour S. Potter.
SCHENECTADY. George Lasher.
SCHOHARIE. *John J. Dominic.*
SCHUYLER. Lewis Beach.
SENECA. *S. R. Welles.*
STEUBEN. 1. *Charles S. Longwell.* 2. Russell M. Tuttle.
SUFFOLK. Everett A. Carpenter.
SULLIVAN. Alphcus Potts.
TIOGA. Edward G. Nowlan.
TOMPKINS. Truman Boardman.
ULSTER. 1. George H. Sharpe. 2. Marius Turck. 3. *Thomas E. Benedict.*
WARREN. B. C. Butler.
WASHINGTON. 1. Hiram Sisson. 2. James E. Goodman.
WAYNE. 1. Rowland Robinson. 2. Addison W. Gates.
WESTCHESTER. 1. *William F. Moller.* 2. *William H. Catlin.* 3. James W. Husted.
WYOMING. George M. Palmer.
YATES. Asa P. Fish.

RECAPITULATION.

A recapitulation shows that the Assembly is politically composed as follows:

Whole number........128
Republicans........84
Democrats........44

The Senate consists of 32 members, of whom 25 are Republicans and 7 Democrats, the Republican majority in the Senate being 18.

### GATHERING THE RETURNS.

RONDOUT, Nov. 2.—Garfield carries Kingston City by 6 majority, and probably carries the county. Major Cornell carries the city by 1,262, the county by over 2,000. He is making large gains in Greene as far as heard from, and the indications are that he is elected.

PORT JERVIS, Nov. 2.—The election to-day passed off quietly in comparison with what had been feared by the Republicans. In fact, the Democrats, seeing that their plans were being frustrated by the ever-active Republicans, who were forewarned as to the action of the Democracy, abandoned them and tried in other ways to carry the election. The polls were crowded early in the day, but in the afternoon few votes were cast. Only about one-half of those registered in the Fifth District voted, though many more attempted to do so and were prevented. In the other districts the vote was fully up to the average. Money as well as whisky flowed freely in the vicinity of the polls, and plenty of drunken men were to be seen. There were few disturbances, and these were speedily quelled. In one of these, in the Third District, Patrick Burns, one of the Inspectors and a Democrat, attempted to kick the ballot-box from the table where it was placed. For several minutes there was great excitement. An assault was made upon one of the Deputy Sheriffs, but when several arrests were made the disturbance ceased. The outlook at present is favorable for the Democratic Electoral ticket in five of the seven districts, but by a reduced majority from the vote of 1876. The Republican candidate for Congress, Charles T. Pierson, has made a strong run, and his opponent has run far behind his ticket. Two of the districts are for Pierson. The election is close in all of the districts, and the majority will be so small that neither party can boast of it.

POUGHKEEPSIE, Nov. 2.—The estimated majorities in Dutchess County are as follows: Dutcher, (Rep.,) for Assembly, 1,275; Carpenter, (Rep.,) for Assembly, 2,000; Ketcham, (Rep.,) for Congress, over 4,000; Garfield, 2,500.

ALBANY, Nov. 2.—Albany County will give Hancock over 2,000 majority. Nolan (Dem.) is elected to Congress by over 2,500. Of Assemblymen, Campbell is elected in the First District and Draper in the Second—both Republicans. The other two districts are Democratic, Gallup and Pratt being elected. This result is exactly as predicted in my dispatch of Sunday night.

NYACK, Nov. 2.—Rockland County gives Hancock a majority of about 720. In 1876 Tilden's majority was 1,157. John Cleary, Democratic candidate for the Assembly, is elected, and the Republican candidate for County Clerk is elected.

LYONS, Nov. 2.—Wayne County gives Garfield over 2,400 majority, Chief Judge and Congressman something more. Both Assemblymen are elected.

ROCHESTER, Nov. 2.—Monroe gives Garfield about 3,500 majority. Three Republican Assemblymen are elected. No gain. Van Voorhis, (Rep.,) for Congress, will have 4,500 majority. The Republicans are elated.

NEW-BRIGHTON, Staten Island, Nov. 2.—Erastus Brooks is elected to the Assembly. The whole Democratic ticket is elected in Richmond County.

CAMBRIDGE, Nov. 2.—Washington County's majority is estimated at 3,500 for Garfield. Both Republican members of the Assembly and Congressmen are elected.

CANANDAIGUA, Nov. 2.—From partial returns it is estimated that Ontario County gives the Republican Electoral ticket 1,000 majority. E. G. Lapham, Republican candidate for Congress in the Twenty-seventh District, is re-elected by an increased majority. John Raines, (Rep.,) is certainly elected to the Assembly.

SENECA FALLS, Nov. 2.—Seneca County complete gives 400 majority for Hancock, and about the same for Rapallo. Dr. S. R. Wells (Dem.) is elected to the Assembly by about 300 majority.

SARATOGA, Nov. 2.—Garfield gets 329 majority in Saratoga Springs.

CORTLAND, Nov. 2.—Cortland County complete gives the Republican Electors 1,325 majority. Folger has the same and Hiscock the same.

PLATTSBURG, Nov. 2.—Clinton County complete gives Garfield 1,840 majority, a Republican gain of 1,134 over 1876. Hammond for Congress, Bowen for Assembly, and the county ticket run about the same majority.

WARSAW, Nov. 2.—Wyoming County complete, with one town to hear from, gives a Republican majority of 1,400.

PENN YAN, Nov. 2.—Yates County gives 1,300 majority for Garfield.

NEWBURG, Nov. 2.—The Returns come in slowly. The indications are that a clean sweep has been made. It looks as though the county would give 800 majority for Garfield. Pierson is probably elected to Congress. Dickey, for Assembly, in the First District, will have nearly 1,000 majority.

TROY, Nov. 2.—The County of Rensselaer is Republican by about 1,000 majority. Murphy, (Dem.,) for Mayor, is re-elected by a reduced majority. Patterson, (Dem.,) in the First District, Derrick, (Rep.,) in the Second District, and Strait, (Dem.,) in the Third District, are probably elected to the Assembly. The local Police arrested several United States officers, who were subsequently released. The policemen will be brought before the United States court. In the Fourth Ward, which gave Garfield a majority of nearly 400, the Democratic Inspectors shamelessly counted out the Republican ward officers. There were various crimes committed in the city of Troy against the election laws.

BREWSTERS, Nov. 2.—Garfield's majority in Putnam County is about 625, and there is but a slight variation in the vote for Folger. Samuel H. Everett is elected member of Assembly.

BUFFALO, Nov. 2.—The Republicans carry Buffalo by 2,500, and Erie County by about 3,500 on the Electoral ticket. Folger, for Chief Judge, runs about even with the Electoral ticket, so far as counted. Bush, Republican, for Congress, runs nearly 2,500 behind in the city and slightly behind in the county, but is probably elected by a small majority. The Republicans have probably elected Assemblymen in all except the First District, which is conceded to the Democrats.

AUBURN, Nov. 2.—Cayuga, complete, gives Garfield 3,425 majority. The vote for Judge will not materially vary.

UTICA, Nov. 2.—The majority for Garfield in Oneida County will be about 2,100. The Congressmen and all three Assemblymen, Republicans, are elected by heavy majorities.

SYRACUSE, Nov. 2.—A Republican tidal wave swept over this city and county to-day. Garfield carries the city by 1,665, and the county by over 4,000. Hiscock (Rep.) is re-elected to Congress in the Twenty-fifth District by an increased majority. Alvord, (Rep.) in the First District, Howland, (Rep.) in the Second, and Duguid, (Rep.) in the Third, are elected to the Assembly.

PORT HENRY, Nov. 2.—Essex County gives 1,900 Republican majority on national and State tickets.

OGDENSBURG, Nov. 2.—Late and full returns show that Garfield's majority in St. Lawrence County will be 7,900. A few towns fall short of the estimate. The Judiciary ticket runs up to the Electors. The town of Potsdam gave 925 majority for Garfield.

WELLSVILLE, Nov. 2.—Returns from 11 towns of Allegany County give a net Republican gain of 268. If this continues throughout the county it will give Garfield 3,800 majority.

GENESEO, Nov. 2.—Livingston County, with three towns estimated, gives Garfield 1,250 majority.

AMSTERDAM, Nov. 2.—A largely increased vote was polled in Montgomery County. Returns indicate that the majority for the Republican Electoral ticket in the county will be 300, a Republican gain over 1876 of 609. Amsterdam gives 315 Republican majority. Cornelius Van Buren (Rep.) is elected member of Assembly, with the whole Republican county ticket. West, for member of Congress, runs ahead of his ticket and carries the county by 400 majority and his district by 2,500.

OWEGO, Nov. 2.—Tioga County gives Garfield 1,152, a Republican gain of 373 over the vote of 1876. Folger runs up with the Electoral ticket. Congressman Dwight's majority in the county is over 1,100. E. G. Nowlan is re-elected to the Assembly by over 900. Dwight, Congressman, is re-elected in the district by a largely increased majority.

JAMAICA, Nov. 2.—Perry Belmont, Democrat, candidate for Congress in the First District—Queens, Richmond, and Suffolk Counties—is elected by at least from 1,500 to 2,000 majority.

NEW-BRIGHTON, Nov. 2.—Richmond County gives Hancock 1,526 majority; Erastus Brooks, for Assembly, 1,546.

### REPORTS FROM THE COUNTIES.

WARSAW, Nov. 2.—Wyoming County and town gives an estimated majority of 1,400 for Garfield.
W. J. HUMPHREY,
Chairman Republican County Committee.

TROY, Nov. 2.—The Republican majority in Rensselaer County is about 700.
N. DAVENPORT,
Chairman Republican County Committee.

PLATTSBURG, Nov. 2.—Clinton County complete gives Garfield 1,850 majority. Bowen, (Rep.,) for Assembly, has over 2,200 majority.
W. J. MCCAFFREY,
Chairman Republican County Committee.

SCHENECTADY, Nov. 2.—Schenectady County gives Garfield 600 majority. West, for Congress, has 800 majority; Lasher, for Assembly, 400 majority.
JOHN W. VEEDER,
Chairman Republican County Committee.

CATSKILL, Nov. 2.—Greene County will not give over 700 Democratic majority.
THEODORE C. TEALE,
Chairman Republican County Committee.

NYACK, Nov. 2.—Rockland County gives Hancock 720 majority. Beach, for Congress, has 520 majority.
D. J. BLAUVELT,
Chairman Republican County Committee.

BINGHAMTON, Nov. 2.—Broome County gives a Republican majority of from 1,700 to 1,800, a Republican gain over 1876 of 400 or 500.
S. C. MILLARD,
Chairman Republican County Committee.

POUGHKEEPSIE, Nov. 2.—Garfield's majority in Dutchess County is 20,700; Ketcham, (Rep.,) for Congress, has 3,900; Carpenter, (Rep.,) for Assembly, First District, 800; Dutcher, (Rep.,) Second District, 1,200.
JAMES E. DUTCHER,
Chairman Republican County Committee.

JAMAICA, Long Island, Nov. 2.—Queens County gives Hancock a majority of 2,100. Cock and Bulmer are both elected; Belmont's majority is 1,500.
ISAAC H. COCKS,
Chairman Republican County Committee.

DANSVILLE, Nov. 2.—Livingston County gives the Republicans 13 majority. Twelve towns have been heard from, and five are estimated. K. M. Scott is elected member of Assembly. E. G. Lapham, for Congress, runs ahead of the Electoral ticket.
J. B. MOREY,
Chairman Republican County Committee.

ROCHESTER, Nov. 2.—Partial returns indicate a majority in Monroe County of from 3,000 to 3,500; Rochester City, 1,300.
H. F. VAN DAKE,
Chairman Republican County Committee.

LYONS, Nov. 2.—The returns indicate a Republican majority of 2,400 on the Electoral ticket in Wayne County. Both Republican Assemblymen are elected.
WILLIAM KREUTZER,
Chairman Republican County Committee.

AUBURN, Nov. 2.—Auburn City gives Garfield 1,045 majority. The county complete gives 3,425.
E. A. WOODIN,
Chairman Republican County Committee.

GLEN'S FALLS, Nov. 2.—Warren County gives 600 majority for Garfield and Arthur.
F. A. JOHNSON,
Chairman Republican County Committee.

ITHACA, Nov. 2.—The official majority in Tompkins County on the Electoral vote is 947.
T. J. MCELHENY,
Chairman Republican County Committee.

GOSHEN, Nov. 2.—Garfield carries Orange County by at least 500 majority. Pierson, for Congress, has about the same. Dickey, Republican, is elected to the Assembly in the First District; Clark, Democrat, elected in the Second.
W. E. MAPES,
Chairman Republican County Committee.

HAVANA, Nov. 2.—Schuyler County, partly estimated, gives a majority for Garfield of 600. Dwight, for Congress, has 600. Beach (Rep.) is elected member of Assembly.
J. C. BRODERICK,
Secretary Republican County Committee.

SYRACUSE, Nov. 2.—Onondaga County gives about 4,500 Republican majority.
FRANCIS HENDRICKS,
Chairman Republican County Committee.

OSWEGO, Nov. 2.—Returns from 28 election districts in this county out of 40 give a Republican majority of 2,800. The estimated majority in the county is 3,200.
CHARLES NORTH,
Chairman Republican County Committee.

ALBION, Nov. 2.—Orleans County gives a Republican majority of 1,550. C. D. KNAPP,
Chairman Republican County Committee.

ALBANY, Nov. 2.—Hancock will probably have 2,500 majority in this county. Nolan (Dem.) is elected to Congress. The Republicans elect Draper, Assemblyman, in the Second, and Campbell in the Fourth, District.
A. S. DRAPER,
Chairman Republican County Committee.

CENTRAL BRIDGE, Nov. 2.—Schoharie County, five towns complete, show net Republican gains over 1876 of 175. The indications are that Hancock will have about 1,500 majority in the county.
J. H. MEAD,
Chairman Republican County Committee.

CORNING, Nov. 2.—We have not received full returns from all the towns in this county. We estimate the majority for Garfield at 1,500.
T. S. PRITCHARD,
Chairman Republican County Committee.

CORTLAND, Nov. 2.—Returns from our county give 1,450 majority for the whole ticket.
J. C. CARMICHAEL,
Chairman Republican County Committee.

MORRISVILLE, Nov. 2.—The majority on Electors in Madison County, partly estimated, is 2,100.
A. M. HOLMES,
Chairman Republican County Committee.

FULTONVILLE, Nov. 2.—Montgomery County gives 200 majority for Garfield and elects Van Buren, Republican, to the Assembly.
T. R. HORTON,
Chairman Republican County Committee.

CANANDAIGUA, Nov. 2.—Ontario County gives about 1,200 majority for Garfield.
W. L. PARKHURST,
Chairman Republican County Committee.

BATAVIA, Nov. 2.—Genesee County complete gives Garfield 1,335 majority. Holmes, Republican Assemblyman, is elected.
H. F. TARBOX,
Chairman Republican County Committee.

RIVERHEAD, Long Island, Nov. 2.—Sixteen election districts in Suffolk County give Garfield 476 majority. The same district gave Hoskins last year 539 majority. The county will probably give 300 Republican majority.
G. F. STACKPOLE,
Secretary Republican County Committee.

WATERLOO, Nov. 2.—Jefferson County gives Garfield 2,400 majority; Miller, for Congress, runs up with the ticket; Skinner, for Assembly, has about 1,800 majority; Benninger, for Assembly, in the Second District, is elected by 200 majority.
C. R. SKINNER,
Chairman Republican County Committee.

JOHNSTOWN, N. Y., Nov. 2.—Fulton County gives Garfield and Arthur a Republican majority of 1,100, a gain over 1876 of 800.
A. J. THOMPSON,
Chairman Republican County Committee.

### THE ROLL OF CONGRESSMEN.

BALLSTON, Nov. 2.—My majority for Congress will be over 3,000. GEORGE WEST,
Republican candidate for Congress.

LYONS, Nov. 2.—My majority is about 5,000. Wayne County, about 2,400 for Garfield.
J. H. CAMP,
Republic canandidate for Congress.

CANANDAIGUA, Nov. 2.—My majority in the Twenty-seventh District is estimated at 3,500. Raines, for the Assembly, has 1,000.
E. G. LAPHAM,
Republican candidate for Congress.

ROCHESTER, Nov. 2.—My majority in this Congressional district, as near as I can now estimate, will reach 5,000.
JOHN VAN VOORHIS,
Republican candidate for Congress.

RONDOUT, Nov. 2.—We estimate my majority in this Congressional District at 800. Gen. Sharpe is elected in the First Assembly District of Ulster, Turck (Rep.) in the Second District, and Benedict (Dem.) in the Third.
THOMAS CORNELL,
Republican Candidate for Congress.

DRYDEN, Nov. 2.—The latest reports indicate that my majority will be 4,500, and perhaps more.
J. W. DWIGHT,
Republican candidate for Congress.

HAMILTON, Nov. 2.—My majority in this, the Twenty-fourth Congressional, district, is not less than 6,000. JOSEPH MASON,
Republican candidate for Congress.

DELHI, Nov. 2.—Returns already received, indicate that I am elected by about 2,000 majority. Lewis, (Rep.,) for Assembly, is also elected.
F. JACOBS, JR.,
Republican Candidate for Congress.

CROWN POINT, Nov. 2.—My majority will be about 5,000. J. HAMMOND,
Republican candidate for Congress.

HERKIMER, Nov. 2.—Herkimer County gives Garfield 1,360 majority. My majority in the Congressional district is over 4,000.
WARNER MILLER,
Republican candidate for Congress.

SYRACUSE, Nov. 2.—Majority in Syracuse is 1,800; in the County of Onondaga, 4,500. All three Republican members of the Assembly are elected. Cortland County gives about 1,300 Republican majority.
FRANK HISCOCK,
Republican candidate for Congress.

### THE ASSEMBLY MEN ELECTED.

CAMBRIDGE, Nov. 2.—I am elected to the Assembly by about 2,000 majority.
HIRAM SISSON.

SYRACUSE, Nov. 2.—The Republicans have about 5,000 majority: Hiscock, for Congress, has about 4,750 majority; Alvord, for Assembly, about 1,500 majority; Duguid, for Assembly, about 200 majority; Howland, for Assembly, about 1,500 majority. T. G. ALVORD.

ONEIDA, Nov. 2.—We estimate Garfield's majority in Madison County at about 2,500. My majority for Assembly is over 2,000.
D. A. JACKSON.

COMSTOCK, Nov. 2.—My majority in the Second District of Washington County is about 1,300. JAMES E. GOODMAN.

NEWBURG, Nov. 2.—I am elected by about 700 majority in the First Assembly District.
JOSEPH M. DICKEY.

ROME, Nov. 2.—My majority in the Third Assembly District of Oneida is from 600 to 800.
THOMAS D. ROBERTS.

RONDOUT, Nov. 2.—My majority in the Second District of Ulster, for the Assembly, is from 200 to 300. MARIUS TURCK.

BATAVIA, Nov. 2.—Genesee County gives a Republican Electoral majority of 1,360. For the Assembly I have 1,038, and two Republican towns to hear from. My estimated majority is 1,200. J. W. HOLMES.

MARATHON, Nov. 2.—The Republican majority in Cortland County is about 1,400; my majority for Assembly is about 1,500.
A. A. CARLEY.

UTICA, Nov. 2.—My majority in the First District of Oneida County is about 200.
JAMES ARMSTRONG.

SAG HARBOR, Long Island, Nov. 2.—I am re-elected to the Assembly from Suffolk County by at least 500 majority. E. A. CARPENTER.

ROCHESTER, Nov. 2.—I am elected by about 200 majority in the Second District of Monroe. JOHN COWLES.

### *THE EASTERN STATES.*

#### MAINE.

GARFIELD HAS A MAJORITY OF MORE THAN 4,000 OVER EVERYTHING.

AUGUSTA, Me., Nov. 2.—The election in Maine to-day was a very earnest one, both parties getting out their full vote. The Republicans have worked very hard, and Republican gains have been the rule throughout the State. The gains indicate a majority of from 4,000 to 5,000 for the Garfield Electors. The smaller towns yet to be heard from, however, did better in September relatively than the cities and large towns, and the gains in them will probably be lighter. The Prohibition vote having almost entirely disappeared, the straight Greenback vote will reach some 5,000, possibly more. The following is the latest summary: 180 towns give 2,848 Republican gain over the September vote. The total vote is estimated at 150,000.

PORTLAND, Me., Oct. 2.—One hundred and fifty-two towns give Garfield 44,426; Fusion, 36,642; Weaver and scattering, 1,288. The same towns in September gave Republicans 41,946; Fusion, 37,647; scattering, 338. Republican majority now 6,496, against 3,961 in September. Republican gain, 2,535. This is over half the vote of the State, and indicates a Republican Majority of between 4,000 and 5,000.

PORTLAND, Me., Nov. 2.—One hundred and ninety-three towns give Garfield 50,794; Fusion, 41,801; Weaver and others, 1,665. The same towns in September gave Republican, 43,932; Fusion, 44,174; scattering, 372. Republican majority now, 328, against 4,386; gain, 2,942. This indicates a little over 4,000 Republican majority in the State.

PORTLAND, Me., Nov. 2.—A careful estimate at this hour (midnight) indicates a majority for Garfield of 4,500 in the State. The Portland *Argus* concedes a majority of 4,000 and a plurality over the Hancock ticket of 5,000.

AUGUSTA, Me., Nov. 2.—The Republicans appear to have polled a larger vote than in September, but the Fusionists' vote has fallen off. There are Republican gains generally over the State. The largest gains are in the manufacturing and business centres. In Kennebec County there is a Republican gain of 800 over the September vote, and a majority for Garfield. This is Senator Blaine's county. It is estimated that Garfield will have 5,000 majority in the State. Meonian Hall is packed with the most delighted and enthusiastic crowd of men ever seen in this city, among them being Senator Blaine, whose presence in the hall was hailed with a perfect tempest of applause. The Weaver vote will be very small.

#### NEW-HAMPSHIRE.

THE GARFIELD ELECTORS AND A REPUBLICAN GOVERNOR ELECTED BY A SMALL MAJORITY.

BOSTON, Mass., Nov. 2.—Chairman Huse, of the New-Hampshire State Republican Committee, claims the election of Bell (Rep.) for Governor, and the Republican candidates for Congress in the Second and Third Districts. The First District is in doubt. One hundred towns give Garfield 15,783, Hancock, 14,[illegible]. The same towns in 1876 gave Hayes 14,947; Tilden, 14,822. Bell, (Rep.,) 15,685; Jones, (Dem.,) 14,595; scattering, 282. In 1878—Head, (Rep.,) 13,069; McKean, (Dem.,) 13,737; net Republican gain, 1,476.

MANCHESTER, N. H., Nov. 2.—Much excitement was caused by the discovery that about 200 Republican votes had been cast in five of the wards for Henry A. instead of Henry L. Tilton, one of their Presidential Electors. The error was immediately corrected.

CONCORD, N. H., Nov. 2.—The Republicans have made a clean sweep in the State, as in every Presidential election since 1860. Returns from two-thirds of the towns, covering all parts of the State, show handsome gains for Garfield on the Gubernatorial vote of 1878. The estimated majority at this writing is at least 2,000. The nomination of Jones for Governor by the Democrats, although his money has been liberally disbursed through the State, has proved entirely unavailing for his party. In some parts of the State he has been scratched by temperance Democrats who could not bring themselves to vote for a brewer. Hall, Briggs, and Farr, (Reps.,) are undoubtedly re-elected to Congress by increased majorities in every district except Hall's, where Sanborn, the Democratic candidate, has evidently been trading for votes for himself at Jones's expense. The Republicans here are jubilant, and a large meeting is now in progress at White's Opera-house, presided over by Gov. Head. Democrats are going home in disgust. The scattering vote will not reach 1,000, although the Prohibition ticket was assisted largely by Democrats who hoped to draw off support from the Republican local ticket. The Legislature and Council are largely Republican.

CONCORD, N. H., Nov. 2.—Returns up to midnight indicate that the State is Republican by 2,000 majority, and probably three Republican Congressmen elected. The State Senate will stand the same as last year—20 Republicans, 4 Democrats. The House is largely Republican. The delay in the returns of cities is owing to the extra labor in counting and sealing the votes as required by law. Vote of 145 towns: Garfield, 23,658; Hancock, 22,300. Same towns 1876: Hayes, 24,204; Tilden, 23,073; net Republican gain, 1,364. For Governor—Bell, 25,441; Jones, 23,086; scattering, 470. The same towns in 1878 gave Head, (Rep.,) 21,791; McKean, (Dem.,) 21,707; net Republican gain, 1,801.

THE GRANITE STATE REPUBLICANS.

CONCORD, N. H., Nov. 2.—One hundred and fifty towns give Garfield 27,184; Hancock, 24,909; scattering, 354. This would indicate a majority of 2,500 in the State, and the election of all our members of Congress. It has been the hardest struggle ever fought in this State on account of the immense amounts of money poured into the State on the eve of the election, with the intention of taking the Republicans by surprise. Thanks to the organization and pluck of the Republicans of the State, the efforts of the Bourbons have proved abortive. We have also carried both branches of the Legislature, the House by a larger majority than two years ago. Our victory is complete.
H. H. HUSE,
Chairman Republican State Committee.

#### VERMONT.

THE GREEN MOUNTAIN REPUBLICANS ROLL UP A MAJORITY OF 30,000.

RUTLAND, Nov. 2.—Thirty-six towns give Garfield 10,430 and Hancock 4,959, a net Republican gain of 815. This per cent. will give the State to Garfield by 30,000 majority.

WHITE RIVER JUNCTION, Vt., Nov. 2.—Ninety-two towns give Garfield 25,545, Hancock 10,408, Weaver 735. Garfield's majority, 14,400. In 1876 the same number of towns gave Hayes 24,418, Tilden 11,681, Hayes's majority, 12,737. Republican gain over 1876, 1,863, Democratic loss since 1876, 1,273.

MONTPELIER, Vt., Nov. 2.—The returns are coming in slowly. Sixty-one towns show a gain of 1,138 over the majority of September, which was 25,012. The indications are that Garfield will have a majority estimated at 28,000.

BURLINGTON, Vt., Nov. 2.—The election in Vermont was wholly without excitement. This city goes 118 Republican gain over September. Eleven towns in Chittenden County give Garfield 3,257; Hancock, 1,817; Weaver, 75; the same in September gave Farnham 3,530, Phelps, 2,123; Heath, 90. Scattering returns indicate a total vote of 65,000, a Republican plurality of 27,000 and a majority of 26,000.

WHITE RIVER JUNCTION, Vt., Nov. 2.—One hundred and eleven towns in Vermont give Garfield 30,346; Hancock, 12,518; Weaver, 871, scattering, 15; Garfield's majority, 16,942. The same towns in 1876 gave Hayes 28,830 Tilden, 13,832; scattering, 24; Hayes's majority, 14,974; increase in the Republican majority, 1,968.

#### MASSACHUSETTS.

A MAJORITY OF MORE THAN 50,000 FOR GARFIELD—ALL THE CONGRESSIONAL DISTRICTS REPUBLICAN EXCEPT ONE.

BOSTON, Nov. 2—11 *o'clock.*—The Republicans in Massachusetts have recovered their old-time majority. Returns from over half the State indicate that the Garfield Electors are chosen by a majority exceeding that of four years ago, which was about 40,000, and reaching toward the big majorities of 1872 and 1868. Long, Republican candidate for Governor, will have as decided a majority as the Republican Electors. The Republicans have swept all the Congressional Districts with one exception—the Fourth—which is the one Boston district held by the Democrats. In this district Leopold Morse is elected by a plurality of but 71 against a majority two years ago of nearly 4,000, and four years ago of something over a thousand. A. A. Ranney, Republican, is elected in the Third District by a majority of over 700, a gain on Field's majority of two years ago of 300. Stone, in the Sixth District, is elected over Boynton, Fusion, by a substantial majority. Bowman in the Fifth District has from 4,000 to 5,000 majority over his Democratic opponent, and Candler in the Eighth has made an unexpectedly good run. The Legislature shows an increased Republican majority.

Only three or four arrests were made here to-day for illegal voting. One hundred and fifty-two towns and wards give Garfield 82,684; Hancock, 58,859. The same towns in 1876 gave Hayes 75,116 and Tilden 62,269.

BOSTON, Nov. 2.—The complete vote of Boston is as follows: Garfield, 25,437; Hancock, 27,366; Weaver, 193; Dow, 50: Hancock's plurality, 1,929. For Governor—Long, 25,666 Thompson, 27,191; Sargent, 293; Almy, 84 Thompson's plurality, 1,527.

For Congressmen—Third District—Ranney, (Rep.,) 13,105; Dearborn, (Dem.,) 11,969; Fairbanks, (Grbk.,) 61; Cushing, (Proh.,) 16; Ranney's plurality, 1,136.

Fourth District—Morse, (Dem.,) 10,631; Hayes, (Rep.,) 10,560; Danforth, (Proh.,) 11; Phillips, (Grbk.,) 16. Morse's plurality, 71. This sets at rest the claim of Hayes's election, and leaves the Massachusetts delegation to Congress 10 Republicans and 1 Democrat.

The *Journal* claims a plurality in Massachusetts of from 40,000 to 50,000.

Returns from the Sixth Congressional District: Stone, (Rep.,) 14,119; Boynton, 11,959; Stone's majority, 2,160.

BOSTON, Nov. 2.—Midnight—It is now believed that Hayes (Rep.) is elected over Morse in the Congressional District, an official count showing 141 more votes for Hayes than at first reported, thus giving him a plurality of 26 votes. The district, at all events, is in doubt to-night, and a recount will probably be necessary. The Republicans claim Hayes's election, and thus a full Republican delegation in Congress. The full vote in the Third District gives Ranney a plurality of 1,136. Stone, in the Sixth District, has a plurality of about 2,000. Candler, in the Eighth, has 3,000 majority. Hancock, in Boston, has less than 2,000 majority, against 3,237 for Tilden in 1876. Long, for Governor, runs ahead of his ticket in Boston.

A CLEAN SWEEP IN MASSACHUSETTS.

BOSTON, Mass., Nov. 2.—The latest returns from all sections of our State indicate the election of the Garfield Electoral ticket and Gov. Long by a majority of 50,000 at least. We have carried, also, our full Republican Congressional delegation, although Morse claims an election. Clean sweep on the rest of our ticket.
EDW. H. HASKELL,
Chairman Republican State Committee.

#### CONNECTICUT.

THE STATE REPUBLICAN BY BETWEEN 2,000 AND 3,000 MAJORITY—THE LEGISLATURE LARGELY REPUBLICAN.

HARTFORD, Conn., Nov. 2.—One hundred and eleven towns give a Republican gain on President of 4,307 and Democratic gain of 400 net Republican gain, 3,807. Hartford gives English, Democratic candidate for Governor, but 89 majority, a loss of 1,100 since 1878. Hartford County gives Bigelow 892 majority, with two towns to hear from, a gain of 2,800. It is probable that the Republican majority in the State will not fall below 3,000. The Republican majority in the First Congressional District is about 1,000. Wait, (Rep.,) in Third District, has a large majority. The Second and Fourth Districts are uncertain. The Legislature is largely Republican.

NEW-HAVEN, Nov. 2.—New-Haven gives Garfield, 5,721; Hancock, 7,916. For Governor—Bigelow, 5,794; English, 7,811. For Congress—Wallace, 5,761; Phelps, 7,865.

HARTFORD, Nov. 2.—One hundred and twenty towns give Garfield 43,099; Hancock, 39,415; Republican majority, 3,684. The same towns in 1876 gave Hayes 38,098; Tilden, 38,960; Democratic majority, 862; Republican gain, 4,546.

The streets are crowded with people, and there is great rejoicing among Republicans over the result of the election. A large Republican meeting was held this evening, and addresses were made by Gen. J. R. Hawley, S. L. Clemens, (Mark Twain,) the Rev. J. H. Twitchell, the Hon. J. R. Buck, the Rev. Dr. Parker, and others.

HARTFORD, Conn., Nov. 2.—Garfield will have a plurality in the State of about 4,200. Bigelow (Rep.) and the whole State ticket is elected by from 2,000 to 2,500 majority. Buck, in the First District, Wait, in the Third, and Miles, in the Fourth, all Republicans, are elected to Congress, and Phelps (Dem.) in the Second, the same as the old [illegible]. The

JAMES A. GARFIELD

# The New-York Times.

VOL. XXX.......NO. 9301. NEW-YORK, SATURDAY, MARCH 5, 1881. PRICE FOUR CENTS.


## A NEW CHIEF MAGISTRATE

### GARFIELD AND ARTHUR REAP THE FRUITS OF VICTORY.

### IMPOSING CEREMONIES AT THE NATIONAL CAPITAL.

THE MOST MEMORABLE INAUGURATION DAY EVER KNOWN IN WASHINGTON—FIFTY THOUSAND PEOPLE WITNESS THE PROCEEDINGS—GEN. ARTHUR MADE VICE-PRESIDENT IN THE PRESENCE OF A DISTINGUISHED ASSEMBLAGE—GEN. GARFIELD'S INAUGURAL ADDRESS—A GRAND PROCESSION ESCORTS HIM TO THE WHITE HOUSE—THE INAUGURATION BALL.

WASHINGTON, March 4.—In conformity with the law and in the presence of fully 50,000 of his fellow-citizens, James A. Garfield to-day took the oath of office and became President of the United States. The scenes attending his inauguration were in many respects the most noteworthy, as they are destined to be the most memorable ever known in connection with a similar ceremony. The throng of visitors to the capital was unprecedented, the procession of military and civic organizations being the largest ever known to accompany an incoming chief magistrate of the Union. The enthusiasm was unparalleled, and the decorations more profuse than it is possible to describe. All the exercises were conducted punctually and with marked good order. During the morning the snow which had fallen during the night made the streets almost impassable, but an hour or so before the time set for the movement of the procession the sun came out brightly, and soon Pennsylvania-avenue was free from snow if not entirely of mud.

At 10 o'clock the Cleveland Mounted Troop, a magnificently uniformed body of men which accompanied Gen. Garfield here, and was known as his especial escort, drew up in front of the White House, which contained the President and Vice-President-elect with their attendants. The Governor's Guards of Columbus, Ohio, were also in front of the Presidential mansion. The grounds were clear of other troops, but all down the avenue as far as the eye could reach and upon every cross street, the sun glittered upon the bayonets of soldiers drawn up in line, awaiting the order to march. Gen. Sherman, Chief Marshal of the day, the very picture of an old soldier in his slouch hat and great coat, was stationed near the Cleveland Troop, and from time to time received communications from his orderlies, who dashed up to him on horseback from all directions. At last, when everything was in readiness, the Chief Marshal rode down the line of the First Division, receiving salutes from each organization as he passed, and the order of "Attention" and to make ready for the march was given.

Soon afterward two open carriages drove into the White House grounds. They were both drawn by magnificently caparisoned teams of four horses. Into the first of these carriages, which was driven by "Albert," the famous Presidential coachman, who acquired his knowledge of horses under Gen. Grant, stepped President-elect Garfield, who took his place on the left side of the back seat, and was immediately followed by President Hayes. Senators Thurman and Bayard, representing the Congressional committee, took seats opposite them, and the carriage moved out from under the portico. It was quickly followed by the Vice-Presidential carriage, in which were seated Vice-President-elect Arthur and Senator Pendleton. A detachment of Police led the way. Then the Cleveland troopers formed a hollow square about the Presidential party. A great shout of applause came from the immense crowd of people which thronged the sidewalks, and the procession moved down historical Pennsylvania-avenue to the Capitol of the United States. Upon every side both Garfield and Arthur were saluted with loud shouts of welcome, and from every window, hundreds of temporary balconies which had been erected for the purpose, house-tops, even from the trees, telegraph poles, and lamp-posts, flags, banners, and bunting, in a profusion which it is impossible to describe, waved in the damp morning air. At precisely 11:20 o'clock, the hour fixed upon, the head of the procession passed around the south wing and reached the eastern front of the Capitol, the Presidential carriage was driven to the lower entrance of the Senate side, and the President-elect, accompanied by President Hayes and the Senatorial committee, entered the building, and at once proceeded to the Vice-President's room, where they remained until noon. At that hour the impressive ceremonies in the Senate Chamber were begun.

### SCENES IN THE SENATE CHAMBER.

The scene in the chamber of the Senate at 9:30 o'clock this morning was not one of activity and there was nothing to betoken the impressive ceremonies which were to take place at noon, except the presence of a large number of cheap wooden chairs arranged in the open spaces for the accommodation of distinguished guests. At 5 o'clock in the morning the Senate, weary of filibustering, had taken a recess until 9:30, and now that hour had come, but the Senators had not come with it. Some had gone to their homes and were sleeping there; others had been confined in the Capitol by the horrible weather and were dozing in committee rooms and cloak-rooms. The Vice-President was in his place, soon to be occupied by him no more, and only four Senators met his eye in that wide space of empty chairs. These were Messrs. Eaton, Ferry, Garland, and Voorhees. Forty minutes passed before the Senate was called to order, and then there were less than 20 Senators in the chamber. At 10:30 the roll was called, and it revealed the presence of hardly more than a quorum, but the galleries were filled by those who had secured tickets. The careful selection of occupants, which was the result of the plan of admission, gave to these galleries an appearance far different from their appearance on other days.

Bright colors and costly clothing were to be seen everywhere, for the majority of the spectators were ladies from the families of Senators and other prominent persons. Opposite the Vice-President's chair and next to the little diplomatic gallery, about 40 seats had been reserved for the relatives and friends of the outgoing and incoming Presidents. The most prominent figure in this gallery was Mrs. Hayes, dressed in black and wearing a white bonnet. She held a large bouquet in which there were no colors except green and white. At her right hand sat a plain little woman with a careworn face, dressed unobtrusively in black and holding a bouquet of red [illegible] leaves. This was evidently the guardian genius of a household, a woman who had passed her life in the duties and pleasures of a quiet home and found them sufficient for her happiness. She quietly awaited the coming of her husband, who was to be made the chief magistrate of fifty millions of people. On the other side of Mrs. Hayes was seen the pleasant and wrinkled face of a very old woman, apparently happy because of the realization of some fond hope. Her eyes were not always on the chamber below and what was going on there, but had a look which accompanies meditation. This was the aged mother of James A. Garfield, happy in the elevation of her son, and thinking of the life which lay behind. She asked no questions. The scene was full of satisfaction to her, and she needed no explanation. Further along on this seat was a little daughter of Mrs. Garfield, sitting beside a daughter of Mrs. Hayes. Both were neatly but quietly dressed. Higher up in the same gallery sat the two sons of the President-elect, bright, manly, and healthy looking boys. The remainder of the reservation was occupied by friends of these two households. To this reservation were turned the questioning eyes of all in the chamber, and especially to the quiet group in the front row. The diplomatic gallery was the last to be filled. In it were several members of the Japanese Legation, the handsome daughter of the Chilian Minister, and several other ladies, among them a daughter of Secretary Evarts, who sat next to Gen. Garfield's aged mother. A part of the gallery was reserved for the heads of executive bureaus, and the remainder was devoted to the relatives and friends of Senators and members of Congress.

After 10:30 the chamber of the Senate was rapidly filled. The Senators, without regard to party, were closely massed on the Republican side and behind them were Governors of States, high officers of the Government, and other privileged persons. For some time the Democratic side remained empty and the rows of easy chairs between the Vice-President and the Senators' desks had no occupants. At 10:50 o'clock the western door opened to admit Senator Blaine, accompanied by a large and handsome man in the uniform of a Major-General of the United States Army. This was the man who had hoped to enter at another door to-day, escorted by a committe of the Senate, and to deliver an inaugural address at the east front of the Capitol. This was Maj.-Gen. Hancock, from Governor's Island, who had once received the thanks of Congress for his services in the late war, and was therefore entitled to one of the easy chairs. The spectators cheered him lustily as he advanced, accompanied by Col. Mitchell, his faithful aide. Mr. Conkling hastily arose from his seat, and was the first to greet the distinguished visitor. He was followed by Mr. Thurman, Judge Davis, Senators Hill and Brown of Georgia, and Wade Hampton. In a moment half the Senators in the chamber were standing around the General, and he was smiling an answer to many hearty welcomes. This was the defeated candidate coming to witness and take part in the inauguration of his successful rival. The scene was full of suggestion. Gen. Hancock was certainly the most imposing figure in the chamber. Favored by nature, his portly form was adorned by a uniform which was much more effective in appearance than the gaudy dress of some of the diplomats who came in later. He soon took his seat, and was then introduced to the Vice-President and others. The seats on the Democratic side were still vacant. Nearly all the Senators were in their places, and in one bunch were Mr. Conkling, Mr. David Davis, Mr. Thurman, Mr. Hamlin, and Mr. Blaine. Alone on the other side of the chamber were to be seen the bushy white hair and dark face of Frederick Douglass, who was talking with Secretary Ramsey. At 11 o'clock Mr. Saulsbury and Mr. Hoar were appointed a committee to inform the President that the Senate was ready to adjourn and was awaiting his pleasure. Mr. Ferry presented Mr. Conger's credentials.

At 11:10 o'clock the occupants of the galleries were again excited. The round head and furrowed face of Phil Sheridan appeared at the door at the left of the Chair. Throwing off his cloak, his uniform was revealed, and the audience applauded him loudly. To a person not versed in military matters the uniforms of the two Generals appeared to be exactly alike, but there was one more star on the Lieutenant-General's epaulets. Gen. Sheridan was accompanied by his brother, a member of his staff, and they sat down beside Gen. Hancock and Col. Mitchell. Until 11:20 o'clock the seats on the Democratic side were unoccupied, but at that time the central doors were thrown open and the diplomatic corps poured into the chamber, led by Sir Edward Thornton, the representative of Great Britain. Some who followed him wore uniforms heavy with gold lace and the jeweled badges of ancient orders. Others were clad in the ordinary evening dress of an American gentleman, but some appeared in strange costumes. The Turkish Minister wore the red skull cap and tassel of his nation, and the Chinese Minister, an old man, was clothed in the peculiar costume of his country, which was likened by some to a combination of silk petticoat and fur-lined silk cloak. There were about 40 of these representatives of foreign countries, and their varied uniforms and costumes made a bouquet of color on that side of the chamber. Among those in the front row were Sir Edward Thornton, Mr. Kurd von Schlozer, representing the German Empire; Mr. Preston, from Hayti, in evening dress; the Austrian Minister, Baron Mayr; the Turkish Minister, Aristarchi Bey; the Japanese Minister, Yoshida; the Envoy from Norway and Sweden, Count Lewenhaupt; M. Outrey, the French Minister; Chen Lan Pin, Minister from China; M. Bartholomei, Russian Minister; Señor Asta Buruage, Chilian Minister, and others. In the second row were most of the remaining prominent members of the corps, and in the third were young men connected with the legations. At one end of this row sat Mr. Victor Drummond, Secretary of the British legation; Lord George Montague, of the same legation, and other attachés. At the other end were half a dozen young men in Chinese costume from the Chinese legation, and one of them, who has a big, round, good-natured face, was continually finding something which excited his mirth. In this bunch of diplomats there were many strange contrasts. There were to be seen samples of the official dress of the nations of the world, gold lace laid on in every imaginable fashion, badges of orders without number, and types of many races. Across the aisle sat the representatives of 50,000,000 of people, clothed in plain black and white.

This many-colored assembly had hardly been seated when the Justices of the Supreme Court, in their black robes, came down the aisle and took the chairs in front of the diplomats. First came Chief-Justice Waite and then Justice Miller, Justice Field—who strove to get the nomination which the Major-General across the aisle secured and found to be worthless—Justice Bradley, Justice Harlan, and Justice Woods. Ex-Justices Swayne and Strong accompanied them, but wore no robes. The Senators, who had arisen in recognition of the arrival of the diplomats, again arose in honor of the Supreme Court, and among them Senator David Davis thus welcomed those with whom he once sat on the Bench.

At 11:40 o'clock the President's secretary, who has so often borne to the Senate the communications of the President, appeared with his last Message and was introduced by the old white-haired Door-keeper, who has served in that office so many years. The secretary bore a copy of the President's proclamation convening the special session of the Senate, and also the announcement that Senator-elect Benjamin Harrison, had resigned his office as member of the Mississippi Commission. A message was also received from the House declaring that a committee had been appointed to wait upon the President with the Senators chosen for that purpose.

### THE CEREMONIES IN THE SENATE.

At 11:55 the seats and nearly all the standing room in the chamber were occupied. One minute later it became evident that the chief actors in the drama would arrive a little late if something were not done to prevent it. The old Door-keeper was equal to the emergency. Seizing a staff, he deliberately turned back the minute hand of the Senate clock five minutes, and thus the march of time was stayed by act of Congress. Immediately thereafter the committee announced that the President had no further communication to make. At 11:55, by the corrected time, Mr. Pendleton, Mr. Bayard, and Mr. Anthony, the Senate's Inaugural Committee, entered the chamber. Behind them walked Rutherford B. Hayes and James A. Garfield, arm in arm, followed by President Hayes's Cabinet and his private secretary. The President and President-elect sat down in chairs in front of the Secretary's desk, facing the Senate, the occupants of the chamber arising as they passed down the aisle. The two families in the gallery were face to face with these two men. The old lady beside Mrs. Hayes smiled and spoke to her son's wife, who smiled in return.

Just before 12 o'clock Senator Anthony and Sergeant-at-Arms Bright entered at the central door, followed by Senator Pendleton and Vice-President-elect Arthur. Again the Senators and guests arose. Gen. Arthur passed on to a place beside Mr. Wheeler, and the latter briefly introduced him to the Senate as the Hon. Chester A. Arthur, Vice-President-elect of the United States. Gen. Arthur then addressed to the Senate a few well-chosen words, and then turned to Mr. Wheeler and raised his right hand. The outgoing Vice-President administered the oath of office to his successor, and immediately afterward bade farewell to the Senate in a brief address. Having adjourned the Senate, he stepped down from the chair and took a seat between Gen. Sheridan and Gen. Hancock. He was once more a private citizen.

At 12:04 Speaker Randall appeared at the central door, followed by nearly all the members of the House. Some members had come in a short time before. Again the Senate rose. For several minutes the members of the House were surging in, and some were still outside when the Chaplain offered prayer. During the prayer Mr. Conger crowded through his companions and took his place with the Senators, although at first the Sergeant-at-Arms held him back. Behind him were the ruddy-faced Robeson and the energetic Chittenden. After the prayer, the proclamation convening the Senate in special session was read by the Secretary and immediately afterward Vice-President Arthur called up the newly elected Senators and administered to them the oath. In the first group were Messrs. Bayard, Burnside, Conger, Dawes, Fair, and Gorman, each of whom was accompanied by his colleague. Mr. Gorman took the oath on the spot where he had once stood as a page. In the next group were Messrs. Camden, Cockrell, George, Jackson, Jones of Florida, and Maxey; and in the third were Messrs. Hale, Harrison, Hawley, McMillan, Miller, Mitchell, Platt, Sawyer, Sewell, John Sherman, and Van Wyck. Mr. Sherman stood by the side of Mr. Windom, who, it is supposed, will be his successor in the Treasury. Mr. Edmunds was absent. The roll was called, and for the first time the new Senators answered to their names. Mr. Allison was absent, because of indisposition, it was said. Mr. Sherman sat with his arms folded, and answered "Here" in a determined tone.

The scene was then changed. All prepared to enter the procession and go to the east front of the Capitol, to take part in the inaugural ceremonies. The occupants of the galleries hastened out to secure good places. The line was quickly formed. At its head were Marshal Douglass, of the District, and the Marshal of the Supreme Court. Then came the Justices of the Supreme Court, the Sergeant-at-Arms, the Senate's Inaugural Committee, President Hayes and President-elect Garfield, Vice-President Arthur and Secretary Burch, the Senators, the diplomats, President Hayes's Cabinet, members of the House, Governors and ex-Governors, and the officers of the two houses in the order named. While the line was being formed, Mr. Hayes and Mr. Garfield stood side by side trying to decide whether or not they would put on their overcoats. At last Mr. Hayes put on his, and soon his successor followed his example. The bright uniforms of the European diplomatists were hastily covered, and the scarlet and gold disappeared under thick ulsters. At the end of the procession were Gens. Hancock and Sheridan, followed by pages and clerks and negroes carrying chairs. These soon passed through the doors, and the Senate Chamber was deserted.

### THE CROWD OUTSIDE THE CAPITOL.

While the ceremonies described were going on inside the Capitol, the visiting regiments of military, the civic organizations, political clubs, and associations of all kinds, together with the naval Cadets from Annapolis and several detachments of Marines and regular troops, took up positions in front of the grand inaugural stand, which had been erected upon the east plaza, in front and still not immediately fronting the stand. The space nearest to that upon which the new chief magistrate was to take the oath of office was left free for the people, and it was filled by one of the most representative crowds ever assembled. On either side, as far as the eye could reach, the great space which has been the scene of so many similar ceremonies, but none so imposing as this, was densely packed with human beings. On the steps of the Capitol, far over to the colossal statue of Washington, which had been appropriately decorated for the occasion, every available inch of space was occupied, and even to the edges of the wide extending wings of either house of Congress people thronged in the endeavor to catch a glimpse of the grand stand. In the crowd were men and women, blacks and whites, people of high and low degree, millionaires and paupers. Still, it was a thoroughly good-humored crowd. Black men who had been slaves, and who still bore upon their persons the evidence of cruel lashings, had forgotten all that and jostled in the most friendly fashion typical Southern white men, who had grown poor during the war, but who seemed, nevertheless, to harbor no ill-feelings against their former chattels. There was a liberal representation of lank, earnest men from the East. Pennsylvania, in addition to thousands of magnificent soldiers, sent well-dressed and apparently well-fed civilians, almost without number. New-Yorkers of all sorts there were in abundance. The Pacific slope was represented by large companies of citizens. With the utmost patience this immense crowd waited while the proceedings in the Senate were in progress. It was particularly noticeable that the black men and women, many of whom had come from Virginia, Maryland, and other points on foot, to be present at the ceremony, were greatly impressed with its importance. Well they might be, for it was only 20 years ago, at the first inauguration of Abraham Lincoln, that they were still living in a state of slavery even in this District of Columbia, and were not permitted, at certain hours of the day, even to appear upon the streets of the Republic's capital. To-day, they stood side by side and shoulder to shoulder with the proudest of white men, clothed with all the powers and rights of citizenship. Until within 10 or 15 minutes before the appearance of the Presidential party the grand stand was left entirely vacant. Then representatives of the press, and here and there an odd Congressman, began to make their appearance upon it. Among the rest came Mr. Weaver, who enjoyed the somewhat doubtful honor of being the Greenback candidate in the recent campaign. He was recognized by some one in the crowd who spoke his name, and at once there came shouts of derisive, though good-natured, applause, from that portion of the throng which knew what was going on. It was only necessary, however, to start applause or laughter to have it taken up by the whole vast assemblage, and the cheer beginning in front passed along until it had died away at the outer edge of the great assemblage. Following the little knot of Congressmen who first appeared came a party of ladies and gentlemen, in which Mrs. James G. Blaine, wife of the distinguished Senator who is to be Secretary of State, was a conspicuous figure. She stepped for a moment to the front of the platform. A gentleman of more zeal than discretion announced her name, and again the crowd embraced the opportunity of cheering to the echo. The applause was nipped in the bud, for even while it was at its height, the Presidential procession was seen coming through the great bronze doors of the east front of the rotunda. At the same time the windows looking from the committee room of the Capitol down upon the stand began to fill up, and soon the roof tops of the portico, the wings, and every available inch of space about the building from which a view of the stand could be seen, were taken up.

At the head of the Presidential party came Frederick Douglass, the ex-slave, who is now the United States Marshal of the District of Columbia. He walked slowly down from the entrance to the stand to the front, followed immediately afterward by Col. Bright, Sergeant-at-Arms of the Senate, and his assistants, who are entitled to unstinted credit for the ample and adequate provision made for all those admitted to the ceremonies. Then came the Presidential party proper—James A. Garfield, the President-elect, arm in arm with Rutherford B. Hayes, whose official life was about to expire. Both gentlemen seemed in the best of health and spirits. Gen. Garfield gave no evidence of being dismayed by the great task before him, and President Hayes bore in his countenance every indication that he was rather gratified than otherwise at the near prospect of laying down the cares of office which he has borne during the past four years. Following the President and President-elect, came Mrs. Hayes—genial, smiling, and maturely handsome as ever. Near her was Mrs. Garfield, the slender and graceful wife of the President-elect, supporting his mother, a strong-faced and white-haired old woman, whose black eyes, keen despite her great age, sparkled with the pride of a mother at the wonderful success of her boy. As this party, with Chief-Justice Waite in the flowing robes of his office, upon one side, took position at the front of the platform, more than one of the spectators was heard to remark that it was in itself typical of the progress and station of the American Republic. Law reigned, the people were in front, the military behind, and James A. Garfield, sprung from the people—James A. Garfield, who had known all the hardships of abject poverty, in the presence of a mother who had worked with her own hands to keep him from want—was about to assume the highest civil office this world knows. As the party so stood for a moment, cheer after cheer, loud huzzas which could not be controlled or checked, echoed and re-echoed about the Capitol from the 50,000 men and women who stood upon the plaza or thronged the roofs and windows.

Immediately behind Gen. Garfield and Mr. Hayes came the Vice-President and Vice-President-elect—Mr. Wheeler, calm, smooth-faced, and earnest, as usual; Gen. Arthur strong, keen-eyed, and handsome as ever, and because of his commanding form and military bearing a central attraction. After them followed the Senators of the United States, Justices of the Supreme Court, members of the lower house, the diplomatic corps in glittering uniforms, which had already been displayed to full advantage in the Senate Chamber, and most of the ladies and gentlemen who had been admitted to the galleries during the ceremonies attending the induction into office of the Vice-President.

### THE INAUGURAL ADDRESS.

After he had taken his seat upon the front of the platform beside President Hayes, and with the Chief-Justice of the United States on his right, Gen. Garfield sat for several moments, until those behind him on the platform had settled into their places. At once there was a hush all about, and then, in clear, ringing tones, which penetrated to a great distance, and could be heard distinctly by several thousand persons, he delivered the following inaugural address:

FELLOW-CITIZENS: We stand to-day upon an eminence which overlooks a hundred years of national life—a century crowded with perils, but crowded with the triumphs of liberty and law. Before continuing the onward march let us pause on this height for a moment to strengthen our faith and renew our hope by a glance at the pathway along which our people have traveled.

It is now three days more than a hundred years since the adoption of the first written Constitution of the United States—the articles of confederation and perpetual union. The new Republic was then beset with danger on every hand. It had not conquered a place in the family of nations. The decisive battle of the war for independence, whose centennial anniversary will soon be gratefully celebrated at Yorktown, had not yet been fought. The colonists were struggling, not only against the armies of a great nation, but against the settled opinions of mankind, for the world did not believe that the supreme authority of government could be safely intrusted to the guardianship of the people themselves. We cannot overestimate the fervent love of liberty, the intelligent courage, and the saving common sense with which our fathers made the great experiment of self-government. When they found, after a short trial, that the confederacy of States was too weak to meet the necessities of a vigorous and expanding Republic they boldly set it aside, and in its stead established a national union, founded directly upon the will of the people, endowed with future powers of self-preservation and with ample authority for the accomplishment of its great objects. Under this Constitution the boundaries of freedom have been enlarged, the foundations of order and peace have been strengthened, and the growth in all the better elements of national life has vindicated the wisdom of the founders and given new hope to their descendants.

Under this Constitution our people long ago made themselves safe against danger from without, and secured for their mariners and flag equality of rights on all the seas. Under this Constitution 25 States have been added to the Union, with Constitutions and laws framed and enforced by their own citizens to secure the manifold blessings of local self-government. The jurisdiction of this Constitution now covers an area fifty times greater than that of the original 13 States, and a population twenty times greater than that of 1780. The supreme trial of the Constitution came at last under the tremendous pressure of civil war. We, ourselves, are witnesses that the Union emerged from the blood and fire of that conflict purified and made stronger for all the beneficent purposes of good government. And now, at the close of this first century of growth, with the inspirations of its history in their hearts, our people have lately reviewed the condition of the Nation, passed judgment upon the conduct and opinions of political parties, and have registered their will concerning the future administration of the Government. To interpret and to execute that will in accordance with the Constitution is the paramount duty of the Executive.

Even from this brief review it is manifest that the Nation is resolutely facing to the front, resolved to employ its best energies in developing the great possibilities of the future. Sacredly preserving whatever has been gained to liberty and good government during the century, our people are determined to leave behind them all those bitter controversies concerning things which have been irrevocably settled and the further discussion of which can only stir up strife and delay the onward march. The supremacy of the Nation and its laws should be no longer a subject of debate. That discussion which for half a century threatened the existence of the Union was closed at last in the high court of war by a decree from which there is no appeal, that the Constitution and the laws made in pursuance thereof are and shall continue to be the supreme law of the land, binding alike upon the States and the people. This decree does not disturb the autonomy of the States nor interfere with any of their necessary rules of local self-government, but it does fix and establish the permanent supremacy of the Union.

The will of the Nation speaking with the voice of battle and through the amended Constitution has fulfilled the great promise of 1776 by proclaiming "liberty throughout the land to all the inhabitants thereof." The elevation of the negro race from slavery to the full rights of citizenship is the most important political change we have known since the adoption of the Constitution of 1787. No thoughtful man can fail to appreciate its beneficent effect upon our institutions and people. It has freed us from the perpetual danger of war and dissolution. It has added immensely to the moral and industrial forces of our people. It has liberated the master as well as the slave from a relation which wronged and enfeebled both. It has surrendered to their own guardianship the manhood of more than five millions of people, and has opened to each one of them a career of freedom and usefulness. It has given new inspiration to the power of self-help in both races by making labor more honorable to the one and more necessary to the other. The influence of this force will grow greater and bear richer fruit with the coming years. No doubt the great change has caused serious disturbance to our Southern community. This is to be deplored, though it was unavoidable. But those who resisted the change should remember that under our institutions there was no middle ground for the negro race between slavery and equal citizenship. There can be no permanent disfranchised peasantry in the United States. Freedom can never yield its fullness of blessings so long as the law or its administration places the smallest obstacle in the pathway of any virtuous citizen. The emancipated race has already made remarkable progress. With unquestioning devotion to the Union, with a patience and gentleness not born of fear, they have "followed the light as God gave them to see the light." They are rapidly laying the material foundations of self-support, widening the circle of intelligence, and beginning to enjoy the blessings that gather around the homes of the industrious poor. They deserve the generous encouragement of all good men. So far as my authority can lawfully extend they shall enjoy the full and equal protection of the Constitution and the laws.

The free enjoyment of equal suffrage is still in question, and a frank statement of the issue may aid its solution. It is alleged that in many communities negro citizens are practically denied the freedom of the ballot. In so far as the truth of this allegation is admitted, it is answered that in many places honest local government is impossible if the mass of uneducated negroes are allowed to vote. These are grave allegations. So far as the latter is true, it is the only palliation that can be offered for opposing the freedom of the ballot. Bad local government is certainly a great evil which ought to be prevented; but to violate the freedom and sanctity of the suffrage is more than an evil—it is a crime which, if persisted in, will destroy the Government itself. Suicide is not a remedy. If in other lands it be high treason to compass the death of the King, it should be counted no less a crime here to strangle our sovereign power and stifle its voice. It has been said that unsettled questions have no pity for the repose of nations. It should be said with the utmost emphasis that this question of the suffrage will never give repose or safety to the States or to the Nation until each, within its own jurisdiction, makes and keeps the ballot free and pure by the strong sanctions of the law. But the danger which arises from ignorance in the voter cannot be denied. It covers a field far wider than that of negro suffrage and the present condition of that race. It is a danger that lurks and hides in the sources and fountains of power in every State. We have no standard by which to measure the disaster that may be brought upon us by ignorance and vice in the citizens when joined to corruption and fraud in the suffrage.

The voters of the Union who make and unmake Constitutions, and upon whose will hang the destinies of our Governments, can transmit their supreme authority to no successor save the coming generation of voters, who are the sole heirs of sovereign power. If that generation comes to its inheritance blinded by ignorance and corrupted by vice the fall of the Republic will be certain and remediless. The census has already sounded the alarm in the appalling figures which mark how dangerously high the tide of illiteracy has risen among our voters and their children. To the South this question is of supreme importance, but the responsibility for the existence of slavery did not rest upon the South alone. The Nation itself is responsible for the extension of the suffrage, and is under special obligations to aid in removing the illiteracy which it has added to the voting population. For the North and South alike there is but one remedy. All the constitutional power of the Nation and of the States and all the volunteer forces of the people should be summoned to meet this danger by the saving influence of universal education. It is the high privilege and sacred duty of those now living to educate their successors and fit them by intelligence and virtue for the inheritance which awaits them. In this beneficent work sections and races should be forgotten and partisanship should be unknown. Let our people find a new meaning in the divine oracle which declares that "A little child shall lead them," for our little children will soon control the destinies of the Republic.

My countrymen, we do not now differ in our judgment concerning the controversies of past generations, and 50 years hence our children will not be divided in their opinions concerning our controversies. They will surely bless their fathers and their father's God that the Union was preserved, that slavery was overthrown, and that both races were made equal before the law. We may hasten or we may retard, but we cannot prevent, the final reconciliation. Is it not possible for us now to make a truce with time by anticipating and accepting its inevitable verdict? Enterprises of the highest importance to our moral and material well-being invite us and offer ample scope for the employment of our best powers. Let all our people, leaving behind them the battle-fields of dead issues, move forward, and in the strength of liberty and the restored Union win the grandest victories of peace.

The prosperity which now prevails is without a parallel in our history. Fruitful seasons have done much to secure it, but they have not done all. The preservation of the public credit and the resumption of specie payments so successfully attained by the Administration of my predecessors has enabled our people to secure the blessings which the seasons brought. By the experience of commercial nations in all ages it has been found that gold and silver afford the only safe foundation for a monetary system. Confusion has recently been created by variations in the relative value of the two metals, but I confidently believe that arrangements can be made between the leading commercial nations which will secure the general use of both metals. Congress should provide that the compulsory coinage of silver, now required by law, may not disturb our monetary system by driving either metal out of circulation. If possible, such an adjustment should be made that the purchasing power of every coined dollar will be exactly equal to its debt-paying power in all the markets of the world. The chief duty of the national Government in connection with the currency of the country is to coin and declare its value. Grave doubts have been entertained whether Congress is authorized by the Constitution to make any form of paper money legal tender. The present issue of United States notes has been sustained by the necessities of war, but such paper should depend for its value and currency upon its convenience in use and its prompt redemption in coin at the will of the holder, and not upon its compulsory circulation. These notes are not money, but promises to pay money. If the holders demand it the promise should be kept.

The refunding of the national debt at a lower rate of interest should be accomplished without compelling the withdrawal of the national bank notes and thus disturbing the business of the country. I venture to refer to the position I have occupied on financial questions during a long service in Congress, and to say that time and experience have strengthened the opinions I have so often expressed on these subjects. The finances of the Government shall suffer no detriment which it may be possible for my Administration to prevent.

The interests of agriculture deserve more attention from the Government than they have yet received. The farms of the United States afford homes and employment for more than one-half our people, and furnish much the largest part of all our exports. As the Government lights our coasts for the protection of mariners and the benefit of commerce, so it should give to the tillers of the soil the lights of practical science and experience.

Our manufactures are rapidly making us industrially independent and are opening to capital and labor new and profitable fields of employment. This steady and healthy growth should still be maintained. Our facilities for transportation should be promoted by the continued improvement of our harbors and great interior waterways and by the increase of our tonnage on the ocean.

The development of the world's commerce has led to an urgent demand for shortening the great sea voyage around Cape Horn by constructing ship canals or railways across the isthmus which unites the two continents. Various plans to this end have been suggested, and will need consideration, but none of them has been sufficiently matured to warrant the United States in extending pecuniary aid. The subject, however, is one which will immediately engage the attention of the Government with a view to a thorough protection to American interests. We will urge no narrow policy, nor seek peculiar or exclusive privileges in any commercial route, but, in the language of my predecessor, I believe it to be "the right and duty of the United States to assert and maintain such supervision and authority over any interoceanic canal across the isthmus that connects North and South America as will protect our national interests."

The Constitution guarantees absolute religious freedom. Congress is prohibited from making any law respecting an establishment of religion or prohibiting the free exercise thereof. The Territories of the United States are subject to the direct legislative authority of Congress, and hence the general Government is responsible for any violation of the Constitution in any of them. It is, therefore, a reproach to the Government that in the most populous of the Territories the constitutional guarantee is not enjoyed by the people and the authority of Congress is set at naught. The Mormon Church not only offends the moral sense of mankind by sanctioning polygamy, but prevents the administration of justice through the ordinary instrumentalities of law. In my judgment it is the duty of Congress, while respecting to the uttermost the conscientious convictions and religious scruples of every citizen, to prohibit within its jurisdiction all criminal practices, especially of that class which destroy the family relations and endanger social order. Nor can any ecclesiastical organization be safely permitted to usurp in the smallest degree the functions and powers of the national Government.

The civil service can never be placed on a satisfactory basis until it is regulated by law. For the good of the service itself, for the protection of those who are intrusted with the appointing power against the waste of time and obstruction to the public business caused by the inordinate pressure for place, and for the protection of incumbents against intrigue and wrong, I shall, at the proper time, ask Congress to fix the tenure of the minor offices of the several executive departments and prescribe the grounds upon which removals shall be made during terms for which incumbents have been appointed.

Finally, acting always within the authority and limitations of the Constitution, invading neither the rights of the States nor the reserved rights of the people, it will be the purpose of my Administration to maintain the authority and in all places within its jurisdiction to enforce obedience to all the laws of the Union in the interests of the people; to demand rigid economy in all the expenditures of the Government, and to require the honest and faithful service of all executive officers, remembering that the offices were created not for the benefit of incumbents or their supporters, but for the service of the Government.

And now, fellow-citizens, I am about to assume the great trust which you have committed to my hands. I appeal to you for that earnest and thoughtful support which makes this Government in fact, as it is in law, a Government of the people. I shall greatly rely upon the wisdom and patriotism of Congress and of those who may share with me the responsibilities and duties of administration. And above all, upon our efforts to promote the welfare of this great people and their Government I reverently invoke the support and blessings of Almighty God.

### HOW THE ADDRESS WAS RECEIVED.

During the progress of the speech the scene was a truly remarkable one. Gen. Garfield's old mother, immediately behind him, listened with rapt attention to every word which fell from his lips. President Hayes, holding the hat of his successor, from time to time nodded approval. Senator Conkling, standing near at hand, listened throughout with careful attention, but gave no audible indication of either approval or dissent. Only when the President-elect referred to the civil service did he smile quietly at the hard task which Gen. Garfield had marked out for himself. In front of the great Senator from New-York was Senator Anthony, ruddy-faced, good-humored, and popular among those who know him. Near by was jovial, portly, and keen-eyed Ben Perley Poore. Senator Hawley, who had just assumed the position of representative from Connecticut in the upper house, was beside Mr. Conkling, and conspicuously applauded several portions of the address. Representative Hiscock, whose chances for the Speakership increase daily, was seen with his friend, John H. Camp, in the background. Mr. Randall, the Speaker of the House of Representatives that to-day passed into history, black-eyed and powerful, sat near Mrs. Hayes. Mr. Bayard, too, the Senator from little Delaware, was conspicuous. Mr. Pendleton, of Ohio, representing the Senate Committee on Arrangements, was in the forward row; while calm Edmunds, honest Hamlin, sturdy Thurman, Col. Burch, the Secretary of the Senate, Congressmen, and officers of lesser dignity almost without number thronged about.

The reception which the inaugural address received from the crowd must have been exceedingly gratifying to the President-elect. Many portions of it were loudly applauded, particularly the references to the colored people and their elevation to citizenship. The delivery of this and other portions was remarkably effective, so much so that in many instances old black men, who had been slaves, were seen weeping in the crowd. The close of the address was most impressive, and as the strong man who had won a great political fight stood with hands uplifted appealing to God for aid in the trial before him, there was the utmost silence upon the stand and plaza. When he had concluded his speech, the President-elect handed his manuscript to President Hayes and turned to the Chief-Justice, who arose to qualify him for the high office upon which he was about to enter. That officer administered the oath. James A. Garfield bent low, kissed the Bible, and was declared President of the United States. Three cheers for Garfield and Arthur were then shouted wildly by the crowd, and the throng upon the platform pressed about to greet the Nation's new chief magistrate. For a moment, however, President Garfield had no thought for congratulations. He had scarcely taken the oath when he turned and reverently kissed his mother and then his wife. Afterward he shook hands with the ex-President, Senator Bayard, who spoke a few pleasant words to him, Senator Anthony, Senator Hamlin, the Chief-Justice, the Hon. J. H. Starin—who to-day retired from Congress and who created much merriment by saying, "I was never so glad as I am to see you come in and myself go out"—Senator Pendleton, Speaker Randall, and scores of others. Toward every one the manner of the President was most affable. By his kindly presence and address it is undoubted that he won many new and sincere friends. It is noteworthy that the chair upon which he sat while on the grand stand was the same used by Washington in New-York at his inauguration as first President of the United States.

When the ceremonies at the east front were concluded, as described, the Presidential party separated; the President and ex-President took seats in their open carriage as before, accompanied by Senators Anthony and Bayard; a signal was given for the column to move, and the procession started for the White House by way of Pennsylvania-avenue, passing around the north, or Senate, wing of the Capitol.

### THE STREET DECORATIONS.

Pennsylvania-avenue has been the scene of many a memorable civil display, but to-night, with the much-talked-of inaugural procession over and its legions disbanded, old residents in the capital say that no President was ever so superbly escorted from the Capitol to the White House as President James A. Garfield. It was scarcely to have been expected at 7 o'clock this morning that the parade would be a success. The sky was gray and threatening, and a few dashes of snow promised to be followed by more snow or rain. The streets were in a deplorable condition. The snow that fell last night lay an inch and a half thick on road and sidewalk, and while it was white to look at, it was soaked with water and covered the feet of pedestrians at every step. Toward 8 o'clock, when the sun crept out furtively and began to send the snow in streams down the gutters, the marching men, wet and weary, following insufficient rest, took heart, and at 9 o'clock, when the wind became fresh and the sun shone out brightly, it seemed probable that the day would become a favorable one after all. And so it did, although when the sun shone brightest the air was chilly. The rain, wind, and snow had played havoc with the decorations, the red, white, and blue of the streamers that hung from the buildings having blended with the wetting they had undergone, while the high wind had disarranged many of the designs which had been so carefully constructed by enterprising Washingtonians and enthusiastic Government officers.

The most noteworthy general features of the decorations, by the way, were a series of 38 arches. These were of uniform size, and spanned the intersections of Pennsylvania-avenue, with all avenues crossing it, between Capitol Hill and the White House. Each arch, consisting of a light, graceful frame-work of iron, was covered with large flags, tastefully looped, and at the key was a shield bearing the coat of arms of one of the States of the Union. The Pension Office, a large and prominent brick building at Pennsylvania-avenue and Twelfth-street, fluttered with flags from top to bottom, and on the avenue front was a large picture of Columbia protecting a maimed soldier. The Census Office, on the south side of the avenue, was also decorated, but not so elaborately as the Pension Office. Further up toward the White House, at Fifteenth-street, the gray fronts of the Treasury Building were elaborately and gayly decked with flags. There were rows of flags flung out from poles on the roofs, streamers crossed the line of pillars, and the pillars were swathed with large ensigns. On Fifteenth-street, at the Treasury Building, a large and elaborate wooden arch, with a turreted tower at each end and painted glass windows staring out of its ugly brown sides, startled the visitor at first sight, from its remarkable resemblance to toy block buildings. Flags flew from every window of the old Freedman's Bank, now the Department of Justice, and just beyond, the White House and its grounds were almost hidden behind masses of flags stretched on ropes from the building to the ground, and from tree to tree in the park. All these efforts to give the city a gay appearance were noticed by the thousands upon thousands of people who swarmed Pennsylvania-avenue, sweeping in dense masses up and down from the White House to the Capitol. The sidewalks could not contain them. It was not long before the slush was trodden into water, and so much of it as did not run away by the gutters was dried up in the sunlight. The tiers of seats for spectators were carefully swept, and notwithstanding they were still uncomfortable to sit upon, they found many occupants who readily paid from 50 cents to $1 for places without cover and exposed to the full sweep of the keen west wind. The crowd

# The New-York Times.

VOL. XXX.......NO. 9303. | NEW-YORK, SUNDAY, JULY 3, 1881.---TRIPLE SHEET | PRICE FIVE CENTS.




## A GREAT NATION IN GRIEF

### *PRESIDENT GARFIELD SHOT BY AN ASSASSIN.*

### THOUGH SERIOUSLY WOUNDED HE STILL SURVIVES.

### *THE WOULD-BE MURDERER LODGED IN PRISON.*

THE PRESIDENT OF THE UNITED STATES ATTACKED AND TERRIBLY WOUNDED BY A FANATICAL OFFICE-SEEKER ON THE EVE OF INDEPENDENCE DAY—THE NATION HORRIFIED AND THE WHOLE CIVILIZED WORLD SHOCKED—THE PRESIDENT STILL ALIVE AND HIS RECOVERY POSSIBLE.

The appalling intelligence came from Washington yesterday morning that President Garfield had been assassinated and was dead. Later dispatches, however, modified this startling news by the announcement that the President, while dangerously wounded, was still living, and that there was a slight hope of his recovery.

Briefly told, the story of the tragedy is as follows: President Garfield and Secretary Blaine drove from the Executive Mansion, about 9 o'clock yesterday morning, to the depôt of the Baltimore and Potomac Railroad, where the President was to join other members of his Cabinet and proceed on a trip to New-York and New-England. As he was walking through the passenger rooms, arm in arm with Mr. Blaine, two pistol-shots were fired in quick succession from behind, and the President sank to the floor, bleeding profusely from two wounds. The assassin was instantly seized, and proved to be Charles J. Guiteau, a half-crazed, pettifogging lawyer, who has been an unsuccessful applicant for office under the Government, and who has led a precarious existence in several of the large cities of the country.

The wounded President was conveyed to the offices of the railroad on the second floor of the depot building. Several physicians were soon in attendance, and after an hour had elapsed it was decided to remove him to the Executive Mansion, where he was made as comfortable as possible. His mind remained perfectly clear all day, notwithstanding the desperate nature of his injuries, and when his wife, who had been summoned from Long Branch, arrived at his bedside, he was able to converse with and encourage her.

During the afternoon the physicians expressed little hope of the President's recovery, but late in the evening their bulletins were more favorable, and there is still hope of a favorable result.

#### THE TRAGEDY IN THE DEPOT.

GUITEAU FIRES HIS CRUEL SHOTS FROM BEHIND THE PRESIDENT—THE WOUNDED MAN'S REMOVAL TO THE WHITE HOUSE—AMAZEMENT AND HORROR OF THE POPULACE.

WASHINGTON, July 2.—The horrible report that the President had been shot and killed at the Baltimore and Potomac Depot was spread over the city about 9:30 o'clock this morning. The report was received at first by every one with a cry of unbelief, but soon after the announcement had been made the agitation on the streets leading from the depot, and the hurrying of carriages and mounted messengers in every direction filled the most incredulous with alarm. People of all conditions rushed wildly in the direction of the White House, and in about one hour after the shooting the terrible fact became generally known throughout the city.

The President, accompanied by Secretary Blaine, left the White House a few minutes after 9 o'clock in the carriage of the former, driven by the same faithful colored coachman who has continuously had charge of the President's carriage since the inauguration of President Grant. Secretaries Lincoln, Windom, and Hunt, and Postmaster-General James, accompanied by their wives, had preceded the President to the depot, and had taken seats in the special car that was to take the party on their journey to New-York and the East. The President reached the Sixth-street entrance to the depot at about 9:20. When the carriage stopped the President said to Officer Kearney, who stepped forward to open the carriage door: "How much time have we, officer?" to which Kearney replied: "About 10 minutes, Sir." The President lingered in the carriage for a few minutes as if to finish a conversation with Secretary Blaine, when he alighted, and, followed by the Secretary, proceeded to the ladies' entrance, the two gentlemen passing leisurely through the ladies' waiting-room arm in arm, the President being on the left of Mr. Blaine.

They had proceeded only a few feet into the general passenger room, when two pistol-shots were fired in rapid succession from the rear and to the right of Secretary Blaine. The first shot passed through the right coat-sleeve of the President, inflicting no injury, but the second shot entered his body above the third rib. When the President was struck he turned sharply to the right, but before he could take a step or make another motion he sank heavily to the floor, the blood spurting profusely from a jagged wound caused by a ball of the size known as calibre 42. Secretary Blaine turned toward the assassin, but discovering that he was in the custody of an officer, his attention was immediately given to the prostrate President, who was carried to a room in the second story of the depot building, where are situated the offices of the railroad company.

Secretaries Lincoln, Windom, and Hunt, and Postmaster-General James, having seen their respective wives seated in the special car, repaired to the long platform, where they walked up and down in front of the car, awaiting the President's arrival. While thus engaged, Col. Jameson, of the Postal Railway Service, rushed up to the Postmaster-General and informed him that the President had been shot, a statement which Mr. James and his companions would not believe until it had been repeated with intense earnestness by Col. Jameson, when they hurried out to the depot, and found the President prostrate and bleeding on the floor.

After remaining for about an hour in the depot, it was decided to remove the President to the White House. Accordingly, a Police ambulance was sent for and the wounded man, attended by Col. Rockwell, was driven home. The events above related were not generally known until some time after they had occurred.

Except the orderly crowd that assembled in front of the White House and Police Head-quarters, there was nothing to indicate that a national tragedy had been enacted that would startle the whole civilized world. The people first became convinced that something had happened out of the usual course by the rapid driving of a carriage through Pennsylvania-avenue, clearing the way for the ambulance which followed, carefully driven and attended by a guard of mounted Police. From mouth to mouth the intelligence spread, "The President is assassinated; was shot at the depot as he was going into the cars." There were no loud demonstrations, no disorderly language. The astonishment following the startling announcement deepened into unbelief, and the people seemed paralyzed with the horror of the moment. Still, the crowd followed the ambulance that entered the broad carriageway leading to the Executive Mansion. Policemen already guarded the gates and kept the crowd back, but through the fence and gateway the ambulance was seen to pause before the open door of the White House, while the large, fine form of the President was tenderly lifted from the vehicle, with the pallor of death stamped on his countenance. Glancing upward to the windows, he saw some familiar faces, and with a smile, which those who saw it will never forget, he raised his right hand and gave the military salute, which seemed to say: "Long live the Republic."

#### THE WOUNDED MAN AT THE WHITE HOUSE.

A few moments afterward carriages began to arrive, bringing the Presidential party from the special car where they had been seated only a few moments before in anticipation of a Summer's pleasure tour. Soon afterward Mrs. Hunt, Mrs. James, and Mrs. Windom were joined by Mrs. Blaine and Mrs. W. T. Sherman. Other friends of Mrs. Garfield quickly arrived, but were denied admittance, and soon the ponderous gates which lead to the Executive Mansion were closed, and armed military sentinels silently took their places about the house and grounds. These troops were ordered from the garrison at the arsenal in order to relieve the regular Police, whose services were needed in the city where the crowds were rapidly increasing in angry excitement. There was only one company of soldiers, but the glance of their bayonets flashing in the sunlight as they walked with measured tread the several paths to which they were assigned, recalled the last hours of President Lincoln, when the same astonishment and horror were reflected on the faces of the crowds that surged about the Executive Mansion.

The President was carefully lifted from the ambulance and carried to a sleeping-chamber in the south-east corner of the building, and was soon surrounded by the most eminent physicians in Washington. Owing to the nervous prostration which followed the shock, the surgeons did not deem it advisable to probe for the ball while the President was at the depot. Upon reaching the White House, this nervous prostration seemed to pass away and the President assumed his usual composed manner, greeting members of the Cabinet and other intimate friends who called with a warm pressure of the hand and with cheerful words. Before leaving the depot the President manifested some anxiety about the effect of the intelligence of his wound upon Mrs. Garfield, and, turning to Col. Rockwell, dictated to him the following dispatch to be sent to Mrs. Garfield at Long Branch:

> *Mrs. Garfield, Elberon, N. J.:*
> The President wishes me to say to you from him that he has been seriously hurt—how seriously he cannot yet say. He is himself and hopes you will come to him soon. He sends his love to you. A. F. ROCKWELL.

The cheerful manner of the President throughout the morning and the early hours of the afternoon excited the strongest hopes on the part of his surgeons and friends that the ball had not touched any vital part, and that when the wounded man had gained sufficient strength and composure an effort might be made to find the ball. Directions were given that the President should see as few persons as possible, and that he should be kept from conversation or making any particular effort whatever. After consultation, it was determined by the surgeons that at 3 o'clock, if the condition of the President would permit, they would probe for the ball. When this hour arrived it was found that the President was not in condition to undergo the operation, and from this time he began to show symptoms that were regarded as very unfavorable—internal hemorrhage having been distinctly recognized. From this time onward the bulletins issued by the physicians furnished little hope that the President would recover, and in conversations the members of the Cabinet and others expressed the greatest anxiety for the result.

During the afternoon, although suffering intensely from his wound, the President several times gave exhibition of his well-known good-nature and genial disposition. At one time, while Secretary Blaine was sitting at his bedside, the President, turning his head, said: "Blaine, what motive do you think that man could have had in trying to assassinate me?" To which Mr. Blaine replied: "I do not know Mr. President. He says he had no motive. He must be insane." To this the President smilingly answered: "I suppose he thought it would be a glorious thing to emulate the pirate chief." At another time, when one of his sons was sobbing at his bedside the President said: "Don't be alarmed, Jimmy, the upper story is all right, it is only the hull that is a little damaged." When Col. Rockwell announced to him that Mrs. Garfield had started on a special train from Long Branch he said, with evident feeling: "God bless the little woman; I hope the shock won't break her down."

#### ARREST OF THE ASSASSIN.

Immediately upon hearing the pistol-shot, Officer Kearney, who remained at his post of duty near the B-street entrance after the President entered the building, ran into the large reception-room, and was in time to see the assassin running toward the east door, which opens on Sixth-street. Before reaching this door the assassin turned back to make his way out of the north door, where he was met and arrested by Officer Kearney. The officer met the prisoner on the steps and said to him: "I must arrest you." "All right," said the the assassin, "I did it and will go to jail for it. I am a Stalwart, and Arthur will be President." Officer Kearney took his prisoner into the large waiting-room, where he was joined by one of the railroad officers and escorted to Police Head-quarters. On the way he gave Kearney a card on which was written: "Charles Guiteau, of Illinois," that being the prisoner's name. Guiteau is described on the books at Police Head-quarters as follows: "Charles Guiteau, arrested at 9:25, July 2, 1881, for shooting President Garfield; aged 36; white; born in the United States and a lawyer by profession; weight, 130 pounds; has dark-brown, thin whiskers and sallow complexion; dressed in a dark suit with black slouch hat."

Mrs. Sarah V. E. White, the lady in charge of the waiting-room at the depot, was the person who first reached the President after he was shot. She thus describes the shooting, and arrest of Guiteau: "I saw the whole thing. The man came in from the door, entering the ladies' room from the main waiting-room, just as the President entered the middle door from B-street. When he had approached within five feet of the President he fired, aiming, I thought, at the President's heart, and missed him. The President did not seem to notice him, but walked right on past the man. He fired again and the President fell. He fell right at the turn of the second row of seats. I was the first to reach him, and lifted up his head. The janitor rushed in and called the Police. I held him until some men came and lifted him up. He did not speak to me or to any one until a young man, who, I think, was his son, came. After he had vomited I think he said something to him. When he was lifted upon the mattress he spoke or groaned. The man who shot him said nothing; no words at all passed between them. The man walked deliberately out of the centre door, where somebody headed him off. He turned and started back the way he came and was seized at the door by the Police. I have seen the man once or twice before. One time in particular I noticed him, a few days ago. He promenaded up and down just as he did to-day, wiping his face and apparently excited. I thought he was waiting for some friends. This morning he waited here half an hour walking up and down. There were few people in the room when the shot was fired. All the passengers had gone out. I think there was a gentleman standing near the door."

The following letter was taken from the prisoner's pocket at Police Head-quarters, showing conclusively his intention to kill the President:

> JULY 2, 1881.
> *To the White House:*
> The President's tragic death was a sad necessity, but it will unite the Republican Party and save the Republic. Life is a flimsy dream, and it matters little when one goes. A human life is of small value. During the war thousands of brave boys went down without a tear. I presume the President was a Christian and that he will be happier in Paradise than here. It will be no worse for Mrs. Garfield, dear soul, to part with her husband this way than by natural death. He is liable to go at any time any way. I had no ill-will toward the President. His death was a political necessity. I am a lawyer, a theologian, and a politician. I am a Stalwart of the Stalwarts. I was with Gen. Grant and the rest of our men in New-York during the canvass. I have some papers for the press, which I shall leave with Byron Andrews and his co-journalists at No. 1,420 New-York-avenue, where the reporters can see them. I am going to the jail.
> CHARLES GUITEAU.

Mr. Andrews, to whom allusion is made in the foregoing letter, is the Washington correspondent of the Chicago *Inter-Ocean*. Upon learning of the shooting and the allusion made to him in the prisoner's papers, Mr. Andrews repaired to Police Head-quarters and made a sworn statement to the effect that he never heard of nor met Guiteau until he saw him under arrest to-day. The prisoner's statement, addressed to Mr. Andrews, was retained by the Police authorities and is a bulky package of manuscript written in a heavy, coarse hand, apparently covering 25 or 30 pages of letter paper. Among the papers was the following letter to Gen. Sherman:

> *To Gen. Sherman:*
> I have just shot the President. I shot him several times as I wished him to go as easily as possible. His death was a political necessity. I am a lawyer, a theologian, and politician. I am a Stalwart of the Stalwarts. I was with Gen. Grant and the rest of our men in New-York during the canvass. I am going to jail. Please order out your troops and take possession of the jail at once.
> Very respectfully, CHARLES GUITEAU.

The following address was upon the letter: "Please deliver at once to Gen. Sherman or his first assistant in charge of the War Department."

The Police authorities declined to make public the statements prepared by Guiteau. District Attorney Corkhill, who has them in his possession, produced them at the White House this afternoon, where they were read to members of the Cabinet. In addition to those above referred to there is a letter addressed to Vice-President Arthur, in which Guiteau informs him of the assassination of President Garfield and that he (Arthur) was by this act made President of the United States. Guiteau then proceeds to advise the Vice-President as to the selection of his Cabinet, and recommends Mr. Coulsburg for Secretary of State; Levi P. Morton for Secretary of the Treasury; Emory A. Storrs, of Chicago, for Attorney-General, and John A. Logan for Secretary of War. He further says in this letter that Postmaster-General James is doing so well in the Post Office Department that he might be retained; that the Departments of the Navy and Interior are not of much account, and it does not make much difference whether any change is made in them or not.

#### MRS. GARFIELD AND THE CABINET OFFICERS.

Secretary Lincoln, who, with his wife and little girl, remained in constant attendance at the White House from the time the President arrived, seemed to feel the blow more deeply, perhaps, than any one except Mr. Blaine. The memories of that terrible night, 16 years ago, when his father was assassinated, were evidently uppermost in his mind, and he referred to that sad event several times.

"My God," he exclaimed this afternoon when the news was brought out from the doctors that the case was well-nigh hopeless, "How many hours of sorrow I have passed in this town."

Postmaster-General James here interposed and said to Mr. Lincoln: "Do you remember how often Gen. Garfield has referred to your father during the past few days?"

"Yes," replied Mr. Lincoln, "and it was only night before last that I entered into a detailed recital of the events on that awful night."

Secretary Kirkwood said very little during the day except to refer to the remarkably good spirits of the President yesterday. "I never saw him so light-hearted as yesterday afternoon. We had a long Cabinet session, and the President was the life of the meeting. He interspersed the proceedings with anecdotes and jokes. He especially referred to the convalescence of Mrs. Garfield and the anticipated pleasures of his visit to his old Alma Mater, the meeting with his old school-mates, and his trip to New-England."

About 3 o'clock this afternoon his son, James, could not contain his pent-up grief any longer, and broke out into sobs. His father sadly said: "Jimmy, my son, hope for the best."

The President talked considerably during the day. According to Dr. Bliss he was at times jocular, and the vein of his conversation was of a light character and calculated to cheer up his friends and attendants. A short time after he was put to bed a messenger was dispatched to a neighboring establishment for one bottle of brandy. The man brought two, and the President, perceiving it, joked with Dr. Bliss about a double allowance. The President informed Dr. Bliss that he desired to be kept accurately informed about his condition. "Conceal nothing from me, Doctors," said he, "for remember that I am not afraid to die." Toward 4 o'clock, when the evidence of internal hemorrhage became unmistakable and all the indications pointed to his dissolution, the President asked Dr. Bliss what the prospects were. He said: "Are they bad, Doctor? Don't be afraid; tell me frankly. I am ready for the worst."

"Mr. President," replied Dr. Bliss, "your condition is extremely critical. I do not think you can live many hours."

"God's will be done, Doctor; I'm ready to go if my time has come," firmly responded the wounded man.

Of all the Cabinet, Secretary Blaine was, to all outward appearances, the most distressed. He was very pale, and evidently was making a strong effort to keep up his strength. When Mrs. Garfield alighted from her carriage, weeping, and followed by her daughter, Mr. Blaine broke completely down and wept for several minutes.

Mrs. Garfield was escorted by her son James up the stairs, the boy, a lad of 15, holding her tightly by the waist and constantly whispering words of comfort in her ear. Upon entering the apartment over which the shadow of death was beginning to hover, all present silently retired, and the dying President and his wife were left alone. This was at precisely 6:50. They remained together for 15 minutes. At the end of that time the Doctors were again admitted to the room. They found the President perfectly conscious, but much weaker, his pulse being 146. "There is no hope for him," said Dr. Bliss; "he will not probably live three hours, and may die in half an hour. The bullet has pierced the liver, and it is a fatal wound."

Col. Corbin, who came up with the President a few moments after he was shot, said he regarded his wound as mortal from the moment he saw him lying on the floor of the depot. "I had seen too many men die on the battle-field not to know death's mark. In my opinion, he was virtually a dead man from the moment he was shot."

Telegrams from all parts of the country and Europe kept pouring in at the White House all the afternoon. Great surprise was expressed that neither Gen. Grant, Conkling, Arthur, nor any of the leading Stalwarts had sent dispatches of sympathy up to a late hour in the afternoon. Many prominent Democrats, among them Senators Beck, Pugh, and Jones, of Florida, and Representatives Randolph, Tucker, of Virginia, spent several hours at the White House and were deeply concerned in the bulletins from the physicians. Senator Pugh said he regarded the death of the President as a great calamity and one that might tend to check the present posperity of the country and of his section.

The room to which Gen. Garfield was taken is on the south-eastern corner of the mansion. The one occupied by him when Mrs. Garfield is in the city adjoins this apartment. Besides the half-dozen attending physicians and three or four attendants, there was an average of five or six other persons in the room during the entire day. The library, the Cabinet room, and the private secretaries' rooms were filled with officers during the afternoon and evening. The correspondents of the press were given every facility to observe the progress of events by Private Secretary Brown, and were also given access to the doors of the sick room.

#### GUITEAU'S STORY AND HABITS.

The excitement and indignation became so great among the crowds that were rapidly assembling in all parts of the city that the authorities grew apprehensive for the safty of the prisoner, and in order that any attempt at lynching might be frustrated it was determined to remove him to the District Jail, and Gen. Sherman was applied to for the assistance of the military in case of an emergency. Gen. Sherman, after consulting Secretary Lincoln, ordered out three companies of United States artillery from the arsenal, one company being mounted as cavalry and two serving as infantry. One mounted and one foot company were stationed about the White House and grounds, and one was stationed at the jail. The District Militia were also ordered to hold themselves in readiness, and remained under arms at their armories all day. Guiteau was taken to jail in a carriage by Lieuts. Austin and Eckloff and Detective McElfresh, of the District Police. The last named officer reports the following conversation with the prisoner while being conducted to jail: "I asked him. Where are you from?" "I am a native-born American. Born in Chicago, and am a lawyer and a theologian."

"Why did you do this?"

"I did it to save the Republican Party."

"What are your politics?"

"I am a Stalwart among the Stalwarts. With Garfield out of the way, we can carry all the Northern States, and with him in the way we can't carry a single one."

Upon learning that McElfresh was a detective, Guiteau said: "You stick to me and have me put in the third story, front, at the jail. Gen. Sherman is coming down to take charge. Arthur and all those men are my friends, and I'll have you made Chief of Police. When you go back to the depot you will find that I left two bundles of papers at the news-stand which will explain all."

"Is there anybody else with you in this matter?"

"Not a living soul. I have contemplated the thing for the last six weeks, and would have shot him when he went away with Mrs. Garfield, but I looked at her, and she looked so bad that I changed my mind."

On reaching the jail the officers of the institution did not seem to know anything about the assassination, and when taken inside Mr. Russ, the Deputy Warden, said: "This man has been here before."

The detective then asked Guiteau, "Have you ever been here before?" He replied, "No, Sir."

"Well, the Deputy Warden seems to identify you."

"Yes, I was down here last Saturday morning and wanted them to let me look through, and they told me that I couldn't, but to come Monday."

"What was your object in looking through?"

"I wanted to see what sort of quarters I would have to occupy."

Continuing, the detective said: "I then searched him, and when I pulled off his shoes he said, 'Give me my shoes; I will catch cold on this stone pavement.' I told him he couldn't have them, and then he said, 'Give me a pair of pumps, then.'"

The pistol used by the prisoner is a bull-dog, 44 calibre, five-shooter, and there are three loads remaining in it. Guiteau did not throw it away, but had it in his hands when arrested. Guiteau has been noticed lounging about the White House and State Department since the 4th of March last. He was regarded as a harmless lunatic by the officers, and was frequently refused admission. When denied admission to the Executive Mansion he would linger about the grounds, and when told at the State


(Continued on Seventh Page.)


## THE NEWS IN THIS CITY

### *THRONGS OF EXCITED PEOPLE IN PUBLIC PLACES.*

THE STORY OF THE SHOOTING RECEIVED WITH HORROR AND SADNESS—SCENES ON THE STREETS AND IN HOTEL CORRIDORS—HOW THE PARTICULARS OF THE AFFAIR WERE GIVEN TO THE PUBLIC.

Not since the gloomy 15th of April, 186–, when the news of the death of the martyred President, Abraham Lincoln, was received, has this City been the scene of so much excitement, mingled with heartfelt mourning, as yesterday. At 10 o'clock in the morning, just when the active business of the day was beginning, and when the down-town streets were filled with merchants and business men, the first dispatch announcing that President Garfield had been shot in the depot at Washington was received. It was a somewhat indefinite message, but gave the impression that the President had been killed. In an incredibly short time the terrible news had spread throughout the business part of the community down town, and alarm and consternation were stamped on every face. The story seemed so preposterous at first that those who heard it refused to believe it and set it down as a canard. President Garfield's life had been of such a character that it seemed almost impossible for him to have made any personal enemies, and the notion that he had been murdered as a political measure could not be entertained for a moment. Scores of men hurried to the Western Union Telegraph office, hoping that the news would be found false. They were met there by a sad confirmation of the dispatch, although they learned that the President was not dead, and that hopes of his recovery were entertained by Surgeon-General Bliss and the other physicians in attendance upon him. These hopes were something to lean upon for a while, and men went about their business as usual, but faces were clouded with fear, and there were no smiles to be seen among the thousands of persons who thronged the lower part of Broadway.

Meantime, the news had spread with remarkable rapidity throughout the length and breadth of the City. The telegraph carried it to all the principal hotels, and from these common centres of information it radiated to the smallest side streets in the crowded tenement-house districts. Before noon there was scarcely a man, woman, or child on Manhattan Island who did not know that the chief magistrate of the Nation had been shot and probably killed. Groups formed on the sidewalks and discussed the terrible news excitedly. In the hotels and the clubs, in the parks and in the saloons, wherever there was room and opportunity for men to gather together, they assembled in crowds and talked over the tragedy which had been enacted at the capital of the Nation. But little of the details of the terrible crime were known at this time, and speculation had full swing, not only in debating upon the probable result of the attack on the President, but in seeking some plausible motive for the act of the assassin. If President Garfield should die, Vice-President Arthur would become the Executive of the Nation, and the effect of his accession to the power and patronage of the Executive office was the subject of grave discussion among the business men of the community. Merchants were alarmed at the possibilities involved in the death of President Garfield. On the whole, however, great confidence was displayed in the innate strength of our popular institutions. "It seems," said one prominent merchant, "that we are adopting the system of the Russian Nihilists in America, but it won't work here. If President Garfield dies we shall go on the same as before, only we shall mourn the loss of a pure and good patriot at the head of the State." This sentiment, after the first shock was passed, was echoed on all sides, and men went about their business with sad faces, but still hopeful that the worst to be feared might not be realized.

At 11 o'clock the news of the assault upon the President came slightly more in detail, and with the absolute knowledge that President Garfield was still living, and that Dr. Bliss gave great hopes of his recovery, men breathed more freely, but still there was a sad and subdued look upon the faces of all as they passed in the street or met in the public places. The newspapers were receiving dispatches every few minutes, and as fast as they came from Washington they were posted on the bulletin boards, so as to give the earliest possible information of any change in the President's condition to the anxious people. Park-row became the centre of attraction, and the sidewalks and streets in front of the different newspaper offices were soon crowded with men who stood in the broiling sun and forgot the heat in their eagerness to hear the latest news from Washington. The throngs became so great between 11 and 12 o'clock that six policemen were stationed at each office to keep the passageway clear for pedestrians. The men were very quiet and orderly, and talked in low tones of the tragedy and its probable and possible effects. The excitement was too deep to display itself in the ordinary noisy way, and the sadness of the people too genuine and heartfelt to expend itself in loud talk. There were men of all shades of political opinion in the crowds which surged around the bulletins, but they all had one sentiment in common upon the great crime which had been committed, and the invectives heaped upon the murderer were bitter and terrible. Broadway at its junction with Park-row was filled with a crowd so dense that a dozen policemen were required to furnish a passage for vehicles, and there was momentary danger of somebody being run over and killed. Drug stores and hotels also had their bulletins, and these, too, were crowded with men anxious to hear the latest news from the President.

At noon extras appeared, and the newsboys and girls pushed their way into the throngs around the bulletin boards, and flew up town as fast as the elevated trains could carry them. The demand for the papers was greater than the supply, and the boys sold out their stock as fast as they could peddle the papers out. Very little change was made, as people were too anxious to read the news to bother the boys for the change of a nickel or a dime. The papers were soon in everybody's hand, and the whole City was reading the meagre details of the tragedy which had been telegraphed up to noon. Nearly every passenger in the horse cars had a paper, and men edged their way through the crowds in the street reading the few lines which had come from Washington. The information given in these early dispatches was very brief, but it was of a reassuring nature. The President had been removed to the White House, was conscious, and the doctors thought that he might survive, while Guiteau, the assassin, was in jail under a strong guard. The house

# The New-York Times.

VOL. XXXI.......NO. 9371. NEW-YORK, TUESDAY, SEPTEMBER 20, 1881. PRICE FOUR CENTS.


## THE PRESIDENT DEAD

### *HE EXPIRES AT HALF-PAST TEN LAST NIGHT.*

### THE END COMES SUDDENLY AND WITHOUT WARNING.

### *GEN. ARTHUR TAKES THE OATH AS PRESIDENT.*

SYMPTOMS THAT WERE APPARENTLY FAVORABLE FOLLOWED BY SEVERE PAINS IN THE HEART—DEATH ENSUES IN FIFTEEN MINUTES—THE PRESIDENT UNCONSCIOUS—HIS WIFE AND DRS. AGNEW AND HAMILTON HASTILY CALLED—THE SUDDEN END CAUSES GREAT SURPRISE, EXCITEMENT, AND GRIEF—OFFICIAL NOTICE SENT TO VICE-PRESIDENT ARTHUR.

The sad announcement came at 11 o'clock last night that President GARFIELD had breathed his last at 10:35, thus putting an end to the long weeks of suffering he has endured. His condition yesterday, aside from a slight rigor in the early morning, was apparently more favorable than it had been on Sunday, and his surgeons and attendants, though realizing the fact that he was in an extremely critical state, were inclined to hope that he might grow better after all. At a few minutes after 10 o'clock last night, however, the sufferer complained of a severe pain in the region of the heart and almost immediately became unconscious. Dr. Bliss, who was hastily called, at once announced that he was dying, and Mrs. Garfield and the consulting surgeons were summoned. Within 15 minutes President Garfield had drawn his last breath and the sorrowful intelligence was being sent with lightning speed throughout the country. Everywhere, notwithstanding the lateness of the hour, the bells were tolled as a mark of respect and sorrow for the long-suffering, patient, and heroic President.

Vice-President Arthur took the oath as President of the United States at his residence, in Lexington-avenue, this morning at 2:10 o'clock. It was administered by Judge John R. Brady.

### THE PRESIDENT'S LAST MOMENTS.

A SUDDEN AND UNEXPECTED END—THE ANNOUNCEMENT A SURPRISE—THE CABINET SUMMONED AND VICE-PRESIDENT ARTHUR INFORMED—ATTORNEY-GENERAL MACVEAGH'S STATEMENT OF THE PRESIDENT'S DEATH.

LONG BRANCH, Sept. 19.—The President of the United States died to-night unexpectedly at 10:35 o'clock. Between 9 and 10 o'clock almost all the correspondents who had been closely watching the case left the Elberon and went to the West End to finish their dispatches and place them upon the wires there. The information that the President was sinking fast was sent to the West End Hotel at 10:45. At once the correspondents and others hastened to Elberon. When they reached that spot no particulars could be learned. At first Warren Young had brought the news across the lawn to the hotel. At 11:05 Attorney-General MacVeagh appeared in the hotel, took possession of the Western Union wire in the name of the Government and sent to Vice-President Arthur a dispatch informing him in the briefest manner that the President was dead, and saying that he would at once consult the other members of the Cabinet. The members of the Cabinet were at once summoned. In a few minutes, having started from the West End before the reception of the summons, they were at Elberon, and, arm in arm, they walked across the lawn in the darkness to the Francklyn cottage, where the dead President lay.

At 11:02 Attorney-General MacVeagh came to the Elberon Hotel and made the following statement: "I sent my dispatch to Minister Lowell about 10 o'clock. Just before that Dr. Bliss had seen the President, and had found that his pulse was 106, and that all his conditions promised a quiet night. He asked the President if he felt uncomfortable anywhere, and the President answered, 'Not at all.' Soon afterward the President fell asleep, and Dr. Bliss retired to his room across the hallway, while Gen. Swaim and Col. Rockwell remained with the President. About 10:15 o'clock the President said to Gen. Swaim that he was suffering great pain, laying his hand near his heart. Dr. Bliss was immediately called for across the hall, and when he entered the room he found the President unconscious and substantially without pulse, while the action of the heart was almost indistinguishable. He said at once that the President was dying, and directed them to send for Mrs. Garfield and Drs. Agnew and Hamilton. The President remained in a dying condition until 10:35 o'clock, when life was pronounced to be extinct. He died of some affection of the heart. It is supposed that neuralgia of the heart was the cause, but, of course, that is not certainly known as yet. I have notified the Vice-President and have endeavored to notify Secretaries Blaine and Lincoln, who are on the track from Boston to New-York." The other members of the Cabinet were called from West End and are now together in consultation.

The following persons were present when the President breathed his last: Drs. Bliss, Agnew, and Hamilton; Mrs. Garfield and her daughter Mollie; Col. Rockwell, O. C. Rockwell, Gen. Swaim, Dr. Boynton, Private Secretary J. Stanley Brown, Mrs. and Miss Rockwell, Executive Secretary Warren Young, H. L. Atchison, John Ricker, S. Lancaster, and Daniel Spriggs, attendants, the last-named colored.

Mrs. Garfield sat in a chair shaking convulsively, and with the tears pouring down her cheeks, but uttering no sound. After awhile she arose, and taking hold of her dead husband's arm, smoothed it up and down. Poor little Mollie threw herself upon her father's shoulder on the other side of the bed and sobbed as if her heart would break. Everybody else was weeping slightly. At midnight Mrs. Garfield was asked if she would like to have anything done, and whether she desired to have the body taken to Washington. She replied she could not decide until she became more composed. A dispatch was sent to W. H. Crump, the custodian of the White House, announcing the sad news.

Attorney-General MacVeagh was the first member of the Cabinet to get the news. He ran bareheaded through the darkness across the lawn from his cottage to the Franckly cottage, followed by his wife, and the first dispatch of sympathy received came from Gen. Arthur.

### THE FIRST NEWS OF THE EVENT.

HOW THE NEWSPAPER CORRESPONDENTS GOT THE ANNOUNCEMENT—FORTY CARRIAGES RACING BETWEEN THE WEST END AND ELBERON—THE SUMMONS TO THE CABINET.

LONG BRANCH, Sept. 19.—At 10:35 o'clock Dr. Boynton was sitting in the office of the Elberon Hotel talking with some newspaper men about the case. Suddenly a man's form appeared at the side-door and beckoned to the Doctor, who sprang to his feet and went outside. He returned in a minute and said: "The President is now sinking very rapidly," at the same time throwing up his hands with an expressive motion. A dispatch was instantly sent to the West End Hotel, and in less than a minute 40 carriages filled with newspaper correspondents were dashing through the darkness in the direction of the Elberon. Hardly had Dr. Boynton disappeared than Capt. Ingalls, the commander of the guard, ran across the lawn. He was asked whether the news was as bad as was supposed. "I think it is," was his reply; "I think the President has another rigor." "Why?" was asked. "Because," he answered, "the Sergeant on duty has ordered a soldier to mount and go for some mustard in haste." A moment later Messrs. Atchison and Ricker walked over from the cottage, and seated themselves upon the hotel porch. They were not aware of anything alarming. In another instant a bright light flashed from the President's window, showing that the gas had been suddenly turned on and they both ran toward it. In the meantime the newspaper men had swarmed into the hotel. For a short period they were compelled to remain in suspense. Then, at 10:53, Mr. Warren Young, the Executive Secretary, who has taken Miss Edson's place as nurse, appeared, carrying two dispatches. One was dispatched to the boys at Williams College and the other to Mrs. Eliza Garfield, the President's mother, and a formal warrant taking possession of the Elberon telegraph office in the name of the Government. He was surrounded by the eager crowd, whom he scattered like chaff by the announcement: "It's all over. He is dead!" Back at break-neck pace the carriages flew over the shockingly bad road, and in less than five minutes a hundred dispatches were flashing the news to all parts of the country and the world.

When the President died, the members of the Cabinet who were living at the West End—Secretaries Hunt, Windom, James, and Kirkwood—were retiring for the night. A dispatch announcing the news was sent up to the West End over the single wire which connects the two places. The news was proclaimed in the West End Hotel, and was heard by Assistant General Superintendent of the Railway Mail Service John Jameson, who verified it, and then ran across the street to the cottages where the members of the Cabinet and their families had rooms. He also hastily ordered carriages for them, and in a few minutes the members of the Cabinet were on their way to Elberon. As soon as they reached the cottage they sent the carriages back for Mrs. James and Mrs. Hunt, who came to the cottage and went to the room where Mrs. Garfield was.

### ALL THE DOCTORS SURPRISED.

THE PRESIDENT'S SUDDEN TAKING OFF TOTALLY UNEXPECTED—WHAT HIS ATTENDANTS SAID EARLY IN THE EVENING—ENCOURAGING SYMPTOMS WHICH DECEIVED EVERYBODY.

LONG BRANCH, Sept. 19.—The President's death was as complete a surprise to the doctors and attendants as to the outside public. As late as 10:15 o'clock THE TIMES's correspondent had a conversation with Dr. Hamilton in the porch of the Elberon Hotel, at the close of which he said: "You may quote me as saying that there is a little encouragement." Half an hour earlier I had a long talk with Gen. Swaim, who had then just left the sick-room. He said in substance that the President's symptoms were better; that he was weaker than he had been after the previous relapse, but that his mind was now clearer, he rested more quietly and breathed more easily, and his pulse had improved constantly since morning. "I believe," said Gen. Swaim, "that he has a firmer grip on life than he had. I can see evidence of a revitalizing of his blood, not only in his clearer brain but also in the better color of his skin. I was alarmed at the first rigors, because I saw in them a new attack of the enemy, but these more recent ones do not give me much concern, except for their weakening effect, because I regard them as mere incidents of his condition. I have formed my own judgment on his case throughout, without the aid of the surgeons or anybody else, and I have taken care not to be too much elated or too much depressed. I think there is good ground for encouragement, though, of course, the favorable conditions I have mentioned may be interfered with at any time."

At 9 o'clock Dr. Bliss strolled into Private Secretary Brown's cottage as usual to meet the representatives of the press. He found a package of letters, postal cards, and telegrams four inches thick awaiting him. "It is evident that the President has been worse for three or four days," he said, "from the number of suggestions that are sent to me. This is only the evening mail. I have had two others to-day. The first envelope he opened contained the following, scrawled on a scrap of foolscap: 'Don't give up the ship, oh, ye disheartened crew; Israel's God is at the helm and He'll pull him through.' "Well, we ain't disheartened," was the Doctor's comment. Many others contained prescriptions and hints more or less valuable, which he sarcastically said he would file away for study after the case had closed. One of them advised the administration of nutrition through the diseased lung.

Not ceasing his examination of the pile of documents, Dr. Bliss looked up and said: "The President is in many respects more comfortable and in better condition than he has been for two or three days."

"Why, in what respect has he improved?" was asked.

"I did not say he had improved," was the quick response; "I don't want to be credited with too much optimism. I say frankly that there is a better expression of all his symptoms, some than three or four days ago and others than 24 or 48 hours, respectively. He has coughed very much less. I can't ascertain that he has coughed more than twice this afternoon, and he then expectorated very easily; in fact, with no effort at all. We examined his lungs to-night and found the area of dullness diminishing in a slight degree. The respiratory murmur was heard over the entire field of dullness. The pulse ranged this afternoon from 102 to 106, and was a great deal fuller, rounder, and of better quality than for a few days past. Of course, his pulse is weak. It certainly is not that of a well man by any means."

"Doctor, have you noticed any sweetness of the President's breath?"

"There was some sweetness of breath, but I can't detect any this afternoon. That is not necessarily a pyæmia symptom. It may come from the muco-purulent secretions in the bronchia."

"What does the lessening of the field of dullness in the lung indicate?"

"It probably indicates resolution into a normal condition, or, in other words, a subsidence of the inflamation or congested condition of the lung."

"Did you discover any local cause for this morning's rigor?"

"No. We believe it was caused by the generally depraved condition of the blood. We have not been able to detect the presence of any pus cavity in the body."

"What do you now think to be the matter with the lung?"

"There are two or three possibilities. It is difficult to say, where there has been such a train of symptoms, whether small pus points have formed over the surface of the lung or whether the lung is free from pus entirely except so far as the bronchia and their ramifications are concerned. It is not settled whether pus points exist or not. It is possible that they do, but only the pathological progress of the case can determine. If there are more rigors and the temperature continues to alternate, as it has done, it would indicate a centre of irritation."

"Is it true that the trouble is extending to the other lobe?"

"It is not. The left lung is perfectly resolute over its entire region."

"How has his pulsation been to-day?"

"It has been very even since noon. After the rigor I recorded 135 or 130, and I think I got the highest, for I watched very closely."

"Have you made much effort to-day to keep up his temperature?"

"We have continued the b[illegible] applications and the stimulants."

All Dr. Agnew would say was that the case was very serious. Nothing, however, that can be written will describe the suddenness of the calamity better than the fact that at 10 o'clock, just before closing the cottage for the night, the family sent a dispatch to the Garfield boys at Williams's College countermanding a previous dispatch which summoned them hither.

Soon after dark a well-dressed man managed to pass the sentinels, and, walking up to the door of the private secretary's cottage, presented to the door-keeper a card on which was written: "From one sent by the Lord Jesus Christ to pray with the President." He was delivered into the custody of a village policeman.

A little more than one hour before Gen. Garfield died Dr. Boynton had talked for some time with THE TIMES's correspondent upon the aspect of the case. At that time (9 o'clock) he said the President was stronger than in the forenoon. He admitted that the sweet odor of the breath, long ago declared to be a symptom of pyæmia, was not only then very noticeable, but had been perceived even before the President's departure from Washington. He was clearly in a hopeless mood, and did not regard the amelioration of the symptoms during the afternoon as affording any ground for expecting recovery. He remarked that it would be several days before the result of the lung trouble would appear, and that a large amount of vitality would be needed to carry the President over that difficulty, just as a large stock had been required to overcome the deadly influence of the parotid abscess. It was plain, however, from the drift of his conversation, as also from the remarks made by the other surgeons, that a sudden death was not expected. It was believed that the President would die of exhaustion, and that there would be several hours' notice of approaching dissolution. Early in the case Dr. Bliss had explained the nature of embolism or blood-clot, and also the nature of similar fatal complications. THE TIMES's correspondent had frequently asked him about the possibility or probability of death by embolism. He had admitted before, as he did to-day, that such a death was possible, but not to be expected.

### THE LAST DAY OF LIFE.

FLUCTUATIONS IN THE PRESIDENT'S CONDITION DURING THE DAY—SYMPTOMS THAT WERE APPARENTLY FAVORABLE AND OTHERS THAT WERE UNFAVORABLE.

LONG BRANCH, Sept. 19.—A most gloomy and threatening morning was succeeded by an uneventful afternoon. A severe chill, which came without warning, indicated this morning that death must come in a short time. The great exhaustion which followed the chill seemed to leave no room for hope. At noon began a period of uncertainty. Six o'clock came, and yet it was feared that another chill would decrease the President's stock of vitality. Later on the continued evenness of the course of the case and the amelioration of some of the symptoms lifted the cloud a little from the surgeons and friends and the anxious people.

A night of anxiety and weary watching was followed this morning by the announcement of news that deepened the general despondency. Soon after midnight a rumor was in circulation that the President had had another chill, and visits were hastily made to Elberon for the purpose of verifying the statement. At 1 o'clock THE TIMES's correspondent could gain no information in regard to these latest rumors. The cottage was closed, and two dim lights were burning in the rooms of the attendants. Secretary Brown's cottage was closed. The Elberon was almost entirely in darkness. The sentries who paced in front of the President's cottage were not aware that there had been any serious change in the case. It was impossible to reach the door of the cottage or get a message to it. No foundation for the rumor was discovered beyond a statement that a little before midnight lights had been seen in the President's chamber and persons seemed to be busily engaged and moving to and fro for about 15 minutes. The correspondents returned to the West End, a mile and a half. In a few minutes some of them decided again to visit the Elberon. Knowing the President's critical condition, they feared that another chill might have occurred even since their last visit. At 2 o'clock this morning the President's cottage had the same appearance as at 1 o'clock. The sentries, pacing their beats in darkness, could give no additional information. The dim lights were still flickering in the rooms adjoining the President's chamber. None of the persons closely connected with the case were accessible. The night wore on, and darkness and quiet reigned around the Francklyn cottage. The weather remained perfect, as it had been throughout the day. Nothing could be heard except the long rollers breaking on the beach.

Day came with the promise of delightful weather. Signs of life were again seen around the Elberon. The President's condition at 7 o'clock seemed to be such, so far as accounts were received, as to promise a bulletin that would not be alarming. At 8 o'clock his temperature had fallen to normal, his pulse was 106, and very weak and fluttering, and his respiration was 22. It appears that the chill which soon afterward came on, was not expected, and that the premonitory symptoms were not so marked as to prevent its coming from being to some extent a surprise. At 8:30, just as the morning dressing was beginning, the President remarked that he felt cold. He at once turned his face aside and vomited two teaspoonfuls of milk porridge which he had recently eaten. Then the chill set in and racked him frightfully for 15 minutes. His body and limbs would become rigid, and then relax, and then become rigid again, these spasms being intermittent and very exhaustive to one already so greatly enfeebled. The subsidence of the chill left the President in a condition of great prostration, and the statements by the physicians an hour later were extremely discouraging. It was remarked that he rallied with great difficulty from this last attack. His stock of vitality seemed almost gone. The difficulty with which he rallied after the chill caused many telegrams to be sent and great anxiety to be expressed by the physicians and near friends. At 9:30 o'clock Dr. Bliss declared that at that time it was impossible to tell when or how the President would breathe his last. He might pass away during the next severe chill; he might endure it and survive for 48 hours or longer. It was apparent that it was feared there was not sufficient vitality remaining to carry him through the next attack.

At 10 o'clock the morning dressing, which had been postponed on account of the chill which had interrupted it, was accomplished. After the dressing the President called for a hand-glass, and scanned his features in it. "I can't understand how it is, feeling and looking so well as I do," said he, "that I am so weak." He was bathed, and then there was gentle perspiration. His pulse, which had risen during the chill to 143 and been almost imperceptible, fell to 126. Soon afterward he slept, occasionally waking. While awake his mind wandered.

At 11 o'clock Secretary Hunt described the situation in a telegram to Secretary Blaine. He was much depressed by the events of the morning. Last night, he said, the physicians had told him that if the President's condition should not improve he might not live through the week. The recurrence of the chill this morning had seemed to shorten this probable lease of life. At noon Dr. Bliss was seen coming from the President's cottage. In conversation with THE TIMES's correspondent he reviewed the main features of the situation, his statements varying but little, if any, from those made by him last night. He remarked, however, that there were indications that the lung trouble had become more serious. No question was asked concerning the appearance of signs of acute pyæmia, but the Doctor had said at an earlier hour that there was a peculiar sweetness of the breath—a "sweet hay flavor"—which indicated a septic condition of the blood. The appearance of this sweetness of the breath has for many weeks been feared, because it was acknowledged to be a well-known sign of pyæmia and not a symptom of the milder form of blood-poisoning known as septicæmia. The appearance of this sweet odor increased the probability that the lung trouble was caused by those gatherings of pus which accompany pyæmia. Dr. Bliss also remarked to THE TIMES's correspondent that upon coming out of each chill the President rested upon a lower plane than that which preceded the chill. The continuance of chills, therefore, would make his death only a question of time.

"Is it probable that he will die suddenly?" asked the correspondent.

"We can't predict," replied the Doctor, "how long he will live. We do not expect, however, that he will die without the appearance of symptoms that will give a warning of the end some hours before it comes. We can't be sure that he must die at all, but the pathological history of the case is now decidedly against his recovery."

"May he not be taken away suddenly by an embolism?"

"It is true," said the Doctor, "that death may be suddenly caused in that way. It is possible, but we do not expect it."

The bulletin issued at 12:30—the publication of noon bulletins having been resumed because of the President's very critical condition—declared that there had been no material change since the subsidence of the chill and the reaction which had followed it. The most noticeable announcement in this bulletin was in relation to the temperature, which had fallen to 98 2-10°, while the pulse had fallen to 104.

The early part of the afternoon passed quietly. The low temperature recorded at noon led the watchers around the Elberon to fear that another chill would occur late in the afternoon or early in the evening. At 4:10 P. M. Dr. Bliss came from the cottage to the Elberon Hotel. To THE TIMES's correspondent he said that the President was then sleeping. "His pulse," said he, "is now 102, his respiration 18, and his temperature about normal. It is not above normal." The Doctor expressed some anxiety lest the temperature should continue to fall.

At 4:50 P. M. Attorney-General MacVeagh came from the cottage, and reported that the President was resting quietly, and that there had been no material change in his condition. The bulletin issued at 6 o'clock admitted the gravity of the situation, but asserted that there had been no aggravation of the symptoms since noon. He had been sleeping, he had coughed little and with less difficulty. The temperature was normal, his pulse 102, and the respiration 18. There was fear among the anxious watchers outside of the little circle which surrounds the President lest the bulletin should be followed by a chill, but as time passed on hope, so often renewed and so often relinquished, began to revive again. Early in the evening it became known that the physicians were in better spirits. The evenness of the patient's condition throughout the afternoon had cheered them a little. Beyond all they were surprised by the President's remarkable fund of reserve force. It was asserted that he fully realized the critical nature of his condition and that he seemed to strive to aid his physicians in husbanding his vital resources.

At 9 o'clock there had appeared a very perceptible change in the feelings of the physicians and other attendants and friends. Ordinary words were too weak to express their admiration for his wonderful power in fighting disease. While it was not asserted that he had improved, it was said that he was more comfortable and in better condition than he had been for two or three days. The deep gloom and hopelessness of the morning had been succeeded by a more cheerful feeling, if not by hope itself, and the revelation of an unexpected stock of force in the patient, had shown the doctors that other unexpected events of a favorable sort might yet happen.

### PREPARATIONS FOR THE FUNERAL.

AN AUTOPSY TO BE HELD TO-DAY—PROBABILITY THAT THE BODY WILL LIE IN STATE AT WASHINGTON AND CLEVELAND.

LONG BRANCH, Sept. 19.—At 1:05 o'clock Attorney-General MacVeagh came from the cottage and said: "I have just received from Gen. Arthur the following telegram in answer to the first brief one which I sent him announcing the President's death. It is directed to me:"

I have your telegram, and the intelligence fills me with profound sorrow. Express to Mrs. Garfield my deepest sympathy.

C. A. ARTHUR.

Mr. MacVeagh then announced the arrangements which had been made. "Mr. Morris, the undertaker of the village of Long Branch," said he, "will be in charge of the body until an undertaker arrives from New-York. This undertaker and an embalmer have been telegraphed for and directed to come from New-York immediately. The body will then be embalmed and the autopsy will take place to-morrow afternoon. Dr. Curtis of Washington, has been asked to be present in company with the other surgeons who were so long in the case, Drs. Woodward, Barnes, and Reyburn. The arrangements for the funeral will of course be so made in all respects as to meet the wishes of Mrs. Garfield. Nothing has yet been definitely settled. It is now expected, however, that a special train will leave this place Wednesday morning for Washington, and that the President's body will lie in state in the Rotunda of the Capitol on Thursday and Friday. We expect that the body will be taken to Cleveland, Ohio, where it will lie in state during Sunday, and that the funeral will take place on Monday, and that the place of interment will be Lake View Cemetery, Cleveland, in accordance with the wish of President Garfield, frequently expressed. These arrangements are only suggestions, however, and will be subject to such modifications as may seem desirable."

The Attorney-General paused and reflected for a moment. He then resumed, with additional sorrow and sympathy in his face: "Mrs. Garfield," said he, "is bearing her affliction with the fortitude with which she has borne her trial for so long, and is as well as could be possibly expected." As he concluded this reference to a noble woman his voice faltered and he turned away. Before returning to the cottage he remarked that the first telegram sent after the President's death was directed to the President's sons in Williamstown.

"Has a telegram been sent to the President's mother?" asked one of the persons in the room.

"Telegrams have been sent," replied the Attorney-General, "to all the President's relatives."

James Jameson, Assistant General Superintendent of Railway Mail Service, who took the news of the President's death to the members of the Cabinet, was present in the Baltimore and Potomac depot in Washington when the President was shot, and also at that time was the messenger who informed the members of the Cabinet of that dreadful event. Mr. Van Wormer, the Chief Clerk of the Post Office Department, was present in the depot when the President was shot, and was here to-night aiding the arrangements for bringing the Cabinet together as he had done in Washington on July 2. To-day was the anniversary of the battle of Chicamauga, in which Gen. Garfield took such a prominent part.

### THE SUMMONS TO GEN. ARTHUR.

LONG BRANCH, Sept. 19.—The following dispatch was sent to Gen. Arthur at 11:30 o'clock:

*The Hon. Chester A. Arthur, No. 123 Lexington-avenue, New-York:*

It becomes our painful duty to inform you of the death of President Garfield and to advise you to take the oath of office as President of the United States without delay. If it concur with your judgment we will be very glad if you will come here on the earliest train to-morrow morning.

WILLIAM WINDOM, Secretary of the Treasury.
WILLIAM H. HUNT, Secretary of the Navy.
THOMAS L. JAMES, Postmaster-General.
WAYNE MACVEAGH, Attorney-General.
S. J. KIRKWOOD, Secretary of the Interior.

### THE OFFICIAL BULLETINS.

LONG BRANCH, Sept. 19.—The following official bulletins were issued to-day:

I.

9:15 *A. M.*—The condition of the President this morning continues unfavorable. Shortly after the issue of the evening bulletin he had a chill lasting 15 minutes. The febrile rise following continued until 12 midnight, during which time the pulse ranged from 112 to 130. The sweating that followed was quite profuse. The cough, which was troublesome during the chill, gave him but little annoyance the remainder of the night. This morning at 8 A. M. the temperature was 98.3°, the pulse 108 and feeble, the respiration 22. At 8:30 another chill came on, on account of which the dress-

(Continued on Fifth Page.)

## THE OATH ADMINISTERED

### *GEN. ARTHUR MADE PRESIDENT OF THE UNITED STATES.*

WITHIN THREE HOURS OF THE CABINET'S NOTIFICATION OF PRESIDENT GARFIELD'S DEATH—JUDGE JOHN R. BRADY, OF THE SUPREME COURT, ADMINISTERS THE OATH.

Gen. Arthur spent the day and evening in his house, No. 123 Lexington-avenue, where he received his first intelligence of the President's death. The news was brought by a messenger boy and was confirmed by a number of telegraphic messages which poured in from Elberon within the next half-hour. With Gen. Arthur at the time were Commissioner of Police Stephen B. French, District Attorney Daniel G. Rollins, Elihu Root, and John C. Reed, his private secretary. The colored door-keeper was asked if the General would give the press any information as to his probable movements. "I daren't ask him," was the reply; he is sitting alone in his room sobbing like a child, with his head on his desk and his face buried in his hands. I dare not disturb him." The General's son, who had heard the news came driving furiously up to the house in a coupé about midnight, and shortly afterward Barney Biglin and P. C. Van Wyck walked up the avenue. Mr. Biglin stood on the sidewalk and awaited the reappearance of his companion, who had been admitted to the house. Half a dozen uniformed messengers sped up the street within the next half-hour and disappeared for a moment within the vestibule door. At 12:25 came the formal notification of the President's death, dated Elberon, and signed by the members of the Cabinet.

Although declining to see members of the press, Gen. Arthur was not altogether oblivious of the anxiety which they manifested in his movements. He authorized the statement that he had received a number of dispatches in relation to the death of President Garfield, all of which, however, he considered confidential save the formal message from the Cabinet. A few minutes before 1 o'clock Gen. Arthur's friends retired, and soon after Commissioner French disappeared around the corner of Twenty-eighth-street, and a roundsman, accompanied by a patrolman, appeared and stationed themselves in front of No. 123.

Ten minutes before 2 o'clock District Attorney Rollins and Mr. Root returned accompanied by Judge John R. Brady, of the Supreme Court, and 20 minutes afterward Commissioner French appeared with Judge Donohue, also of the Supreme Court. The light which had been burning in the library on the second floor was suddenly turned low, and the gas in the front parlor was as suddenly lighted. The whole party repaired to this room and were joined by Gen. Arthur's oldest son. At 2:15 o'clock Judge Brady administered the oath which is prescribed in the Constitution. It was stated by Secretary Reed that requests to be present for the purpose of administering the oath had been sent to both Judge Brady and Judge Donahue; that Judge Brady, arriving first, was requested to perform this act, and that out of courtesy to Judge Donohue the party waited for him to appear. Both Judges Brady and Donohue are Democrats.

No. 123 Lexington-avenue, which becomes historic, is one of a row of plain brick dwellings, three stories in height, with a veneering of brown stone for its front. Save the presence of half a dozen carriages and a group of reporters, there was nothing unusual in the street outside that would indicate that an event of historical importance was occurring behind the closed green blinds of the Arthur residence.

Secretary Reed said, at the conclusion of the ceremony, that it was not probable that President Arthur would leave his house before this morning. A dispatch was received at the house during the evening from one of the Washington hotel-keepers saying that apartments would be reserved for him until such time as he chooses to occupy them.

### THE NEWS IN THE CITY.

TOLLING OF CHURCH BELLS—A FEELING OF SADNESS—POLICE ARRANGEMENTS.

The news of President Garfield's death was received in THE TIMES office at 11:05 o'clock last night, and soon afterward the bells of St. Paul's Church began to toll and continued tolling for nearly an hour. The bells of Trinity and other churches were also tolled, thus conveying the sad intelligence to the public. Telegrams announcing the President's death reached the principal hotels and clubs before 11:30 o'clock, and the sad news was generally known throughout the City before midnight.

The President, it will be observed, died on the 19th of September, the anniversary of the battle of Chickamauga. In proportion to the numbers engaged this was the bloodiest battle of the civil war. In that conflict the President, by his heroism, firmness, and calmness, undoubtedly laid the foundation of his future political success. The battle of Chickamauga was fought Sept. 19, 1863, and largely from the fame won in that action as Adjutant-General of the Army of the Cumberland, he owed almost his immediate election to Congress and his subsequent career, which has just closed in death.

When the news reached the Windsor Hotel the place was almost deserted. The brokers and bankers who frequent the hotel every evening had been discussing the subject of the President's sickness and the chances that he had for life. It was generally believed that he would die, but no one expected that he would pass away during the night. Mr. J. G. do Amaral Valente, Chargé d'Affaires of Brazil in the United States, is staying at the hotel, and when he heard the news of the President's death he seemed incredulous, and telegraphed to Long Branch inquiring whether the news was true. He said to a TIMES reporter that he had been instructed by his Government to make special inquiries about the President, and had gone on Saturday last to Elberon, where he had an interview with Private Secretary Brown. From Mr. Brown's remarks Mr. Valente inferred that President Garfield had not long to live, but he did not [illegible]

CHESTER A. ARTHUR

# The New-York Times.

VOL. XXXIII.....NO. 10,132. NEW-YORK, MONDAY, FEBRUARY 25, 1884. PRICE TWO CENTS.


## ARTHUR'S HOME HOSTILE

### HIS CANDIDACY NOT POPULAR IN HIS OWN STATE.

THE POWER OF THE MACHINE UNABLE TO AROUSE EVEN SYMPATHY WITH THE ADMINISTRATION.

ALBANY, Feb. 24.—"Can Mr. Arthur carry New-York State if he is nominated?" This is a question which has been heard many times during the past fortnight. Practical men are asking it. Why should sound, sensible Republicans pause to consider it if Mr. Arthur has so favorably impressed himself upon the party as his friends and office-holding advocates claim? Mr. Arthur is not popular as a Presidential candidate right here in his own State. This is becoming apparent, for the more his claims are pressed the more settled becomes the opposition to him.

The old machine has been broken. To that machine, and it was a wonderfully perfect one, was chiefly due the President's political successes. Without its power at his back, as a candidate, he is crippled. With the men who smash machines arrayed against him at the polls he is doomed. They will be against him in overwhelming numbers in those interior counties whose majorities have always been relied upon to sweep with irresistible force across the Harlem. All his political acts since the day he went to Albany in 1881 will return to plague him. The Garfield sentiment in whole districts will rise up against him. The stealing of delegates in 1882, the forcing of Folger, the forged telegram, the financial acts of Jay Gould's agents at that memorable Saratoga Convention, will all be charged up against him. Unredeemed pledges of one kind and another will swell the ranks of the disaffected. Hundreds of independent Republicans will accept his nomination as a direct challenge. Given some such Democratic candidate as Cleveland, and they will vote for him in preference to the candidate of their own National Convention. County Committees will labor in vain to bring hundreds of others to the polls. The bare intimation that schemes are on foot to procure Arthur delegates from counties in which no genuine Arthur sentiment exists creates bad feeling. It revives the unpleasant memories of the past. A year and a half in sackcloth and ashes is not a sufficiently strong argument that the penitent should be given another trial. With the rank and file in the country in active opposition, or totally indifferent to his fate, without the support of a machine worthy of the name, and with his old associates in party management secretly hostile to him, how could Mr. Arthur expect to carry this, the pivotal State, next November?

Of the 91 Republicans in this Legislature not more than 23 are Arthur men. This is a liberal allowance. It is doubtful if more than a score would, if polled, declare themselves as his followers. The other three-fourths regard Mr. Arthur's claims as having been fully liquidated by the party. They view with apprehension the possibility of his nomination. They know how sensitive is the feeling in their districts. They have passed through factional fights enough to realize their disastrous effects upon the party. They have seen the phenomenal growth of that sentiment which believes that party is good, but principle is better. It is impossible to create any sympathy with the President either in convention or at the polls, and these 58 Republican legislators only reflect the sentiment of their localities when they openly proclaim this to be the fact.

It has been averred that no efforts were being made to grind out Arthur delegates from unwilling districts. This is not true. The office-holders all over the State have received their cue. They are sounding their neighbors. Pliable half-breed leaders are the men through whom the objects sought are to be attained. Federal patronage is the bait with which they are to be tempted. There is much of it to be dispensed in this State. A suspicion prevails that it has been held in reserve for some such hour of need as this. Recent visits to New-York of the President's private secretary were intimately related to the general scheme for procuring delegates. From one point and another comes well authenticated stories of overtures to Republicans hitherto not only neglected but actually snubbed by the Administration. In some cases they have been declined. In others the result of betraying the sentiment of their localities are being considered quite as much as the temptations themselves. Political penetration is given to the masses more than formerly. Men who assume to represent them are more closely watched. Many political wrecks are scattered through the interior counties as the result of this vigilance during the last four years. There will be the closest scrutiny of the methods employed at the coming conventions and of their products.

Those who face the election figures of the last three years find conclusive arguments against the nomination of Mr. Arthur, or of any other man who has been identified with the factional fights in this State during that period. The plurality of Gen. Garfield was 21,000. Nobody, better than Mr. Arthur, knows the extraordinary efforts put forth in obtaining that result. How many of the strong Republican counties, where the Garfield vote reached high water-mark, would parallel their records with Mr. Arthur as a candidate? In how many counties where the Democratic majority was whittled down to the smallest point could this be repeated? A few of the counties where either indifference or downright hostility must be encountered—for already they are beginning to talk against the President's nomination—will serve as illustrations.

St. Lawrence gave Mr. Folger a plurality of 4,084. The Republican candidate for Secretary of State received a plurality of 8,164. Gen. Garfield's plurality in this stronghold was 7,913. St. Lawrence to-day is divided on the subject of a Presidential candidate. A strong Edmunds sentiment pervades the rank and file. A few of the leaders and the office-holders look favorably upon Mr. Arthur. Neither the leaders nor the office-holders could rally half of the Garfield vote for Mr. Arthur's candidate for Governor, Mr. Folger. The frank opinion of those who live in the county, and who know it thoroughly, is that little better could be done for Mr. Arthur than was done for Mr. Folger. Yet St. Lawrence would be good for 8,000 plurality for Edmunds. Any clean candidate who had never been identified with the factional quarrels in the county would receive close upon the same figures.

Jefferson County has no marked Presidential preferences. It can never, however, be drummed into line for Mr. Arthur. Should an Arthur delegate by any means be secured by the President's friends the whole county would be inflamed in consequence. Its factions have fought more bitter fights than those of any other county in the State. Its normal Republican majority is about 2,000. It gave the Republican ticket 2,080 in 1881. Twelve months later its voters left the polls after a hard day's labor for Mr. Cleveland. They gave him a plurality of 2,707. This was the extreme of bitterness. Gen. Garfield, however, had no difficulty in leaving the county with a plurality to his credit of 2,223. Can Mr. Arthur carry the county by any such figures, even by capturing its Congressman and compelling him to do duty alongside the triumvirate whose injudicious course has kept the county embroiled in all these years?

Oswego County, like Jefferson and St. Lawrence, has been the scene of fierce faction fights. Nobody disputed the argument that Mr. Folger was quite as good a man as Mr. Cleveland, or doubted that his experience better qualified him for the office of Governor. The county gave Mr. Cleveland 381 plurality, where the year before it united upon the Republican ticket and give a plurality of 3,014. To Gen. Garfield it gave 3,490 plurality. It was only by means of extraordinary pressure that the State Committee was enabled last Fall to bridge temporarily the breach between the factions. The old feeling still rankles. The candidate of the little clique of Stalwarts in Oswego City would become a target for the half-breeds.

In Orleans County there is not a spark of sympathy with this Administration. Republicans are content to pass along without criticising it. They will never vote to continue it. Orleans gave Cleveland 569 plurality. The Republican ticket received 1,135 plurality in 1881. To Gen. Garfield it gave 1,477 plurality.

Wayne is another example of the complete turning over of a county when a candidate is forced upon it. Ordinarily it will give the Republican ticket upward of 2,000 majority. Gen. Garfield carried the county by 2,393 plurality. Two years later it gave Cleveland 426 plurality.

There are counties which, in a Presidential year, will give a popular candidate a bare majority. Lewis is one. Gen. Garfield carried it by 362 plurality. The following year the Republican ticket got 85 plurality. Gov. Cleveland's plurality was 1,340.

Madison, Oneida, Herkimer, Delaware, Cortland, Columbia, Dutchess, Chenango, Tioga, Steuben, Saratoga, Tompkins, and Wyoming all give heavy Republican majorities to the right kind of candidate. They all repudiated Mr. Arthur's choice for Governor in 1882. No enthusiasm for Mr. Arthur himself prevails in them to-day and none can be aroused within the next eight months. Some of them have one choice for President, some another. The name of Mr. Arthur is not in the list. What can be the argument that will bring their support to him in November, when all that can be said for him is known and is unappreciated in February? A single Republican vote cast against him in every school district would mean a total loss in the State of 11,239 votes. The result of indifference would be equally as disastrous. Can the party afford to enter the race with a candidate so heavily handicapped as Mr. Arthur?

In the absence of any expressed preference on the part of Senator Miller, some of the influential Republicans in a number of the Congressional districts will endeavor to direct attention to some one candidate other than Mr. Arthur. It is intimated that a movement in behalf of Mr. Edmunds will soon be set on foot. Mr. Edmunds has positive strength along the northern tier. Franklin, Lewis, St. Lawrence, Wayne, Orleans, contain pronounced Edmunds men. So do Schenectady, Chenango, Tioga, Chemung, and Steuben. One argument in his favor is that he has a host of friends among the independent voters. Another is that he has never been obnoxious in his Republicanism. The third is that a long public career stands to-day untarnished. Mr. Edmunds would undoubtedly bring out a full Republican vote. Mr. Arthur might do the same thing. The night of election would show how much of it was registered against him.

It is not assumed that the State Committee which was elected at Richfield Springs will hold over another year. Perhaps it does not want to. How shall its successor be elected? By the Congressional district conventions at the same time they elect national delegates, or by the district delegations after these have reached the State Convention itself? If Mr. Arthur should not be nominated, but a committee as largely interested in him as the present committee should happen to be elected, the campaign of this Fall might prove exceedingly irksome to it. The Richfield Springs convention adopted a resolution urging the State Committee to take into consideration the idea of greater popular representation at party conventions and to devise some method of liberalizing the party policy in this respect. Of course the committee is prepared to make a full report.

The Twenty-third Congressional District, comprising Oneida and Lewis, is the first to agree upon a separate popular delegate convention and to arrange its details. The manner of procedure may prove instructive to other districts. Assembly Clerk Chickering, Chairman of the County Committee of Lewis, and Horace Bush, the Congressional delegate of the county under the old apportionment, met the Oneida Republicans in Utica yesterday. The latter were represented by James S. Sherman, Chairman of the County Committee, and by one member of each of the three district committees of the county. They formally organized a Congressional Committee, with Mr. Sherman as Chairman and Mr. Bush as Secretary. It was then resolved that a district convention, for the election of two delegates and two alternates to Chicago, should be held in Booneville, on a day to be fixed by the Chairman and Secretary after they have ascertained when the State Convention will be held. The idea of popular representation in that convention was elaborated to the fullest extent. Each town and each ward in the two counties will be entitled to one delegate. One additional delegate will be allowed in every town or ward casting 200 Republican votes or a fraction thereof equaling half. Under this appointment, the 26 towns of Oneida, the 5 wards of Rome, and the 12 wards of Utica will have 73 delegates. The 18 towns of Lewis will have 22 delegates. It is confidently predicted that in such a convention of 95 delegates, the national delegates will be selected who will determinedly represent the sentiments of a majority—not a minority—of the Republicans in the entire district. The primaries for the selection of delegates to this district convention will be called by the Chairmen of the two county committees. To the Assembly district conventions will be left the selection of the delegates to the State Convention, Oneida being entitled to 13 and Lewis to 4.

### SOUTHERN LIP SERVICE.

WASHINGTON, Feb. 24.—Senator Sherman's interest in the Danville and Mississippi investigations is strengthening him as a Presidential candidate among Southern Republicans. As a second choice, after the assumed coming break in the South from Arthur, Sherman is making steady progress. In Virginia, Gen. Logan has anxiously sought recently to create a following sufficient to give him at least a part of that delegation, but he has satisfied himself that, while he has the good wishes of the Coalition leaders, they will give him no help, at least to start with. The lip service to Arthur will continue in the South for weeks to come, but the drift toward Sherman, already visible in Virginia, will soon be seen in the States further South.

A Southern Congressman to-day compared Arthur's attitude to the coming National Convention to that of Andrew Johnson to the Democratic Convention of 1868. "Many surface indications," he said, "will be followed by few tokens of successful mining." Gen. Fitzgerald, of Mississippi, whose name will probably be sent to the Senate to-morrow for Associate Justice of Arizona, and who, Democratic Senators say, will be quickly confirmed, says Arthur will get the 18 votes of Mississippi, and that the support is meant in good faith and will be unwavering. District Attorney Speer promises an Arthur delegation from Georgia. Gen. Chalmers is actively working for Logan in Mississippi. In Louisiana Pinchbeck is the leader of the Administration forces and gives flattering assurances to the President's friends as to the prospect in that State and States adjacent. One of Mr. Blaine's closest and best known friends says that the policy of his following is to keep quiet while the struggle goes on among the leading candidates and await developments.

### REPUBLICANS IN NEW-JERSEY.

HOW THE NATIONAL CONVENTION DELEGATES WILL PROBABLY BE CHOSEN.

TRENTON, N. J., Feb. 24.—The New-Jersey Republican State Committee will meet to-morrow night to take into consideration the calling of the State Convention to elect delegates to the Republican National Convention. It is probable that the convention will be held in this city about the middle of April. There has been some canvassing of opinions as to the propriety of having the district delegates chosen by separate conventions held in the respective districts. There is undoubtedly a considerable sentiment in favor of that course, but it has taken little or no pains to make itself felt. On the other hand, it is argued that the same reasons for that plan do not exist in New-Jersey as in New-York, Pennsylvania, and other States. In this State no attempt has ever been made to enforce the "unit rule," and as a matter of fact, the delegations to the Republican National Conventions have very seldom cast their votes solidly for any particular candidate. The State Convention usually accepts as a matter of course the delegates agreed upon by the district caucuses. The delegates at large, however, are balloted for. It is claimed that the delegates in the past have been just as much the free and untrammeled choice of the people of their respective districts as if they had been chosen by separate conventions. Moreover, the plan takes but one day, while the holding of district conventions and the State Convention on different days would take two days, and time and railroad fares and hotel bills are matters of moment to the average Jerseyman. The expressions of opinion on the subject thus far have been in favor of adhering to the old plan—of electing State and district delegates at Trenton on the same day. The State Committee, accordingly, propose to recommend that district conventions, instead of caucuses, be called to meet at Trenton on the day of the State Convention for the selection of delegates to Chicago.

There has been a disposition all along on the part of the leaders to permit and encourage the freest choice in the selection of delegates to the National Convention on the assumption that individual preferences would be readily surrendered at Chicago in favor of the man who there should seem the strongest candidate for the country at large. But within the past few weeks there have been signs of a purpose to influence, if not control, the choice of delegates. There has been a mysterious activity in certain quarters. Influential Republicans who a short time since scouted the idea of taking up President Arthur are non-committal. Some indiscreet politicians declare that it would be an insult to the President and to his Secretary of State if New-Jersey should fail to show her gratitude for the placing of Mr. Frelinghuysen at the head of the Cabinet by choosing an Arthur delegation to Chicago. There are rumors of an Arthur-Blaine combination in New-Jersey. Mr. Blaine has always been the choice of the New-Jersey Republicans, who are disposed to support him at Chicago if it shall appear to be the proper thing to do; failing in this, they would be strongly inclined to throw their strength where he may indicate. A combination of Mr. Blaine's and Mr. Arthur's friends would be well-nigh irresistible in New-Jersey.

### SUING MESSRS. NEW AND WRIGHT.

ACCUSED OF MISREPRESENTING THE VALUE OF BANK STOCK.

INDIANAPOLIS, Feb. 24.—Considerable talk has been created in financial circles by a suit filed yesterday by John C. S. Harrison, Receiver of the Indiana Banking Company, against the Hon. John C. New and John C. Wright, leading capitalists here, to recover $200,000. It is alleged that in 1878, New and Wright sold to W. H. Morrison stock in the First National Bank amounting to $288,000 at the rate of $1 65. Part of this stock afterward became part of the assets of the Indiana Banking Company, of which Morrison was then President, and which has failed since his death. The allegation is made that the sale of the stock by the defendants at the rates named was brought about by their false representations regarding the bank's affairs, and that the stock was really not worth more than 90 cents on the dollar, inasmuch as the concern's assets were not then so large as claimed and its liabilities larger. Messrs. New and Wright say that Mr. Morrison bought the stock after carefully examining into the bank's condition and upon the recommendation of the Hon. A. D. Lynch, State Bank Examiner, who was necessarily conversant with the affairs and who afterward became the President of the bank. The defendants themselves paid $1 60 for the stock to the Hon. W. S. English, and sold it to Morrison at 5 cents advance. The latter lived three years after buying the stock, and during his life-time made no complaint about being defrauded in the transaction.

It is thought now that the suit was brought really for the purpose of shifting the responsibility for the disastrous failure of the Indiana Banking Company and the weakening of the First National, until it was again placed on a solid basis by the English and Depauw syndicate.

### THE FUNERAL OF MRS. PARAMORE.

HUNDREDS OF WOMEN CASTING FLOWERS ON HER COFFIN.

ST. LOUIS, Feb. 24.—The funeral of Mrs. Frederick W. Paramore, once known far and near as Nellie Hazeltine, the belle of St. Louis, took place this afternoon. Never in the history of St. Louis were so many women seen at a funeral before. Christ Church was crowded in all its parts, while women blockaded even the sidewalks and streets leading to the sacred edifice. If it had been a crowd of men the police would have beaten them back, but as it was the minions of the law stood powerless. It was a hard task getting the coffin into the church. Mrs. Paramore's body had been embalmed, and the glass above her face allowed all to take a look at one who in life had played such a prominent part in society circles. Crowds wended their way through the aisles of the church and looked at her face as they passed. Hundreds brought flowers to lay upon the coffin, and that part of the church lying near the altar soon resembled a bower of lilies and roses.

It was as hard work getting the coffin out of the church as it was getting it in, the women again blocking the sidewalks and street. The funeral cortége was a very long one, and just before the body was placed in the receiving vault at Bellefontaine Cemetery, there was another crowd of women, all eager to strew flowers over the bier. Dr. Boyd conducted the funeral ceremonies. The plate of the casket bore the name of the deceased and gave her age, 27 years, and the time of her death.

### A DAY OF TEMPERANCE SERMONS.

WILKESBARRE, Penn., Feb. 24.—At a meeting of prominent clergymen and church members in this city on Jan. 21 it was requested that Sunday, Feb. 24, be set apart by the clergy of all denominations to speak upon the necessity of having the existing laws against the sale of intoxicating liquors rigidly enforced. Accordingly nearly all the ministers of the city and county made the liquor question the subject of their discourses this morning. Large congregations were present. In most instances the general tenor of the remarks made was that the respectable portion of every community should be outspoken and positive in its opposition to evil deeds and evil men. The taxes, direct and indirect, which this evil traffic entailed upon a community, was spoken of as a great injury to its material interest and imposed most grevious burdens upon the sober, industrious classes of the community.

### DESPOILING NORTHERN VISITORS.

NEW-ORLEANS, La., Feb. 24.—The criminal classes have less to hinder them under the present imbecile municipal Government than ever before. Sand-bags and burglaries are of daily occurrence, and rarely an arrest is made, and then seldom by the police. They reaped a rich harvest Saturday night, carnival visitors from the North being the victims and several thousand dollars their spoil. Mayor Behan has taken all the places where these criminals resort under his protection by issuing gamblers' licenses and collecting a specified monthly fee. It is possible a resort will be had to hemp to rid the town of these outlaws.

### THE NEW RECTOR OF ST. IGNATIUS.

CHICAGO, Feb. 24.—The Rev. Arthur Ritchie, Pastor of the Church of the Ascension, gave notice on Saturday to the Wardens of his church that he had decided to accept the Rectorship of St. Ignatius's Church, in New-York, which was recently offered to him. His connection with the Church of the Ascension will end May 1. No reference was made to the subject at yesterday's services.

## AGAINST EL MAHDI'S ARMY

### AN ADVANCE OF THE BRITISH ORDERED FROM TRINKITAT.

OSMAN DIGNA EXPECTED TO ATTACK SUAKIN —THE ENGLISH TROOPS IN TRINKITAT— GEN. GORDON'S MANIFESTO.

SUAKIN, Feb. 24.—It is common talk in the Bazaar that Osman Digna will very soon make an attack on this place, in which event it is expected that the black inhabitants will declare for El Mahdi and massacre the European residents.

A number of Nubian troops were assembled at the wharf to-day to embark for Trinkitat. At the last moment, however, they refused to proceed, saying that their bullets would not penetrate the shields of the rebels, and asking why they were required, since British troops had been sent. It was then decided to employ the Nubians as camel drivers.

The whole British expedition, numbering 4,300 men, landed at Trinkitat to-day. Rebels could be seen on all sides. It is estimated that there are from 10,000 to 12,000 of them in the immediate vicinity of Trinkitat. The men-of-war Jumna, Hecla, Ranger, Carysfort, and Orontes are at Trinkitat, and the Euryalus, Decoy, and Sphinx at Suakin. Gen. Graham has sent forward from Trinkitat 200 cavalry, and more are following. A general advance will be made to-morrow. A fort has been erected 6,000 yards from Trinkitat.

CAIRO, Feb. 24.—Gen. Stephenson sent a telegram to London to-day strongly urging that an advance be made from Trinkitat. The Marquis of Hartington, Secretary of State for War, in reply, ordered an immediate advance. He also asked that the Europeans killed at Teb be buried in a fitting manner.

Gen. Graham, commander of the Tokar expedition, has telegraphed to Gen. Stephenson an urgent request for reinforcements of artillery, as he is armed only with camel guns against Osman Digna's artillery, which is now served by gunners from Tokar. The news of the surrender of Tokar has spread throughout the Soudan as an English defeat. The rebels are negotiating with the Kassala and other garrisons to induce them to join El Mahdi. The Government have ordered Admiral Hewett to send Commander Wolfe to King John, of Abyssinia, with instructions to offer to surrender part of the district of Sankeet, which is part of the territory taken from Abyssinia by Gen. Gordon, on the condition that the Abyssinians march to liberate the Egyptian garrisons in the Southern Soudan. The King demands an interview with Admiral Hewett and the concession of Massowah, without waiting to negotiate.

KHARTOUM, Feb. 24.—Gen. Gordon has published a manifesto in which he informs the insurgents that the Sultan, the Commander of the Faithful, intends to dispatch a great army to conquer their country. Gen. Gordon exhorts them to accept his offers of peace in order to preserve themselves from a Turkish invasion.

LONDON, Feb. 24.—A Khartoum dispatch says the effects of Gen. Gordon's proclamation are fading. It is reported that El Mahdi, with the main body of his army, has left Bara and is marching on Khartoum by way of Duem. Gen. Gordon has asked the Khédive to issue a decree confirming the independence of the Soudan. The Porte has warned the Khédive to maintain the integrity of the Soudan and to give no recognition whatever to El Mahdi. The Khédive's dilemma has given rise to fresh rumors of his abdication. The *Memorial Diplomatique* of Paris asserts that agents of the Khédive are preparing a hotel there for himself and family.

### ACTORS, AUTHORS, AND ARTISTS.

FEATURES IN LITERARY AND DRAMATIC MATTERS IN EUROPE.

LONDON, Feb. 24.—Mary Anderson has abandoned all intention of taking the Drury-Lane Theatre. She will make a tour of the provinces after finishing her engagement at the Lyceum. Mr. Belt, the sculptor, is engaged upon a bust of Miss Anderson for the Princess of Wales. Miss Anderson is earning additional popularity by arranging performances at the Drury-Lane Theatre in aid of the Stanley Institution for the Training of Nurses.

Minnie Palmer continues to crowd the Strand Theatre. She is doing the best business of the season, and has made a second extension of her engagement.

Miss Fortescue will appear at the Court Theatre as soon as her action for breach of promise against Lord Garmoyle is decided. The defense offers £10,000 to stop proceedings. It is probable that this sum will be accepted.

George Augustus Sala proposed Mr. Irving's election to the Reform Club. It is understood that Mr. Irving's motive in seeking the election was social and not political.

Lillian Russell is touring in France and Germany. She appeared in Havre last Thursday in "Billie Taylor." The audience was friendly and gave her a warm reception, though her company is poor. Mr. Solomon, the composer, is her manager.

Brander Matthews's new comedy, "Marjory's Lovers," is drawing half houses at the Court Theatre. It has received scant justice at the hands of the London critics.

Messrs. Jones and Herman, the authors of "The Silver King," have sold a three-act drama, entitled "Nora," to Manager Bruce, of the Prince's Theatre. Mr. Herman is recovering from a critical surgical operation upon both eyes.

Manager Harris, of the Drury-Lane Theatre, has invited the wives and children of the Bishop's and clergy of all denominations to see the pantomime gratis.

Genevieve Ward has begun a tour of Asia. She made her début at the Town Hall, in Calcutta, where she has been greeted by crowded audiences, made up of Government officials and fashionable English and native civilians.

An imitation of "Sarah Barnum" is the new sensation scandal just appearing in Paris. It is styled "Mana Judith," and it is intended as an attack upon Anna Judic, the diva of the Variétés.

Marie Colombier has organized a troupe to travel in Europe and America with Rochard's drama, the "Contes of Edgar Poe," which it is now rehearsing.

Ambigu Locutowski, a St. Petersburg manager, has been sent to prison for a hundred days for producing French pieces without the sanction of the authors. M. Michelet, representing the French authors, brought five other suits against Russian directors.

Johann Strauss has written a new comic opera for the Vienna Imperial Opera. The libretto is by Jokai, and is taken from a Hungarian legend of the time of Maria Theresa.

Tamberlik, the celebrated tenor, is singing in Paris at private concerts. His voice is nearly gone, but his declamation is fine.

Herr Millöcker, the composer of the "Beggar Student," is prostrated by a nervous disorder.

The company of English authors for aiding in securing English-American copyright law already counts 80 associates, including Blackmore, Wilkie Collins, George Augustus Sala, Charles Reade, Charlotte Yonge, Cardinal Manning, and Walter Besant.

Henry Blackburn, who has returned from America, writes to the *Athenæum*, giving a letter from Gen. Loring in which English artists are invited to exhibit works at the Boston Exhibition of 1885. Mr. Blackburn says that similar arrangements have been completed with the Metropolitan Museum at New-York and the Philadelphia Academy. The principals of the American museums and academies are united in their desire that the collections should be representative of English water-color art. It is proposed that the exhibition shall consist principally of the work of living artists, but include examples of Frederick Walker Mason, Pinwell, Rossetti, and others.

Dr. Schliemann gives, in a letter to the Academy, the results of his excavations in the mound upon the plain of Marathon, hitherto considered the tomb of the Athenians who were killed in the battle. The famous excavator found nothing in the tumulus except fragments of pre-historic pottery, probably belonging to the ninth century B.C., and rude arrow-heads of Obsidian glass. There were no traces of human skeletons or funeral trappings.

The forthcoming volume of the Encyclopædia Britannica is particularly strong in American articles. Among the contributors are Gen. McClellan, George W. Cable, and E. L. Godkin.

Nineteen autograph letters from Byron to his mother, bound in a volume, have been sold by Sotheby, the book auctioneer, for £283 10s. for the Boston Library.

Robert Louis Stevenson is dangerously ill at Nice.

Mr. Gladstone has offered Prof. Goldwin Smith the Professorship of History at Oxford. In case Prof. Smith declines the position will be offered to Prof. Edward Freeman.

Blanchard Jerrold is writing a biography of Gustave Doré. He has free access to the private papers of the Doré family. The biography contains the story of the boyish infatuation of Doré for Sarah Bernhardt.

The Frankfort *Gazette* declares that Dr. Busch's "Our Chancellor" is nothing but a reprint of the former Bismarck book. It shows that whole pages are a mere reproduction.

### THE LASKER RESOLUTION.

BERLIN, Feb. 24.—The *Deutsche Tageblatt*, commenting on the Lasker incident, says that the Americans themselves attributed no importance to the resolution of condolence that only about a dozen of the members of the House of Representatives were acquainted with the tenor of the resolution.

### TOPICS OF INTEREST ABROAD.

ST. PETERSBURG, Feb. 24.—The Czar has offered Gen. Ignatieff the Civil Governorship of Turkestan, with charge of the administration of all of the Central Asian Provinces.

PARIS, Feb. 24.—Gen. Millot, commander of the land forces in Tonquin, has left three battalions at Sontay and three at Haiphong, and is preparing to operate against Bac-Ninh with 9,000 men.

LONDON, Feb. 24.—The report of the sale of the Blenheim Palace pictures to the Berlin Museum was premature. Under the Heirlooms act it will be necessary to obtain the consent of the High Court of Chancery before a sale can be effected.

The German corvette Olga, which arrived at Plymouth a few days ago, from a cruise in the West Indies, with Prince Henry on board, sustained much damage in the recent gales and is now undergoing repairs at Devonport. Meanwhile the Prince is visiting Queen Victoria at Windsor.

DUBLIN, Feb. 24.—A pastoral letter from Bishop Carr was read in the Catholic churches in the Diocese of Galway to-day advising the people not to emigrate, and calling attention to a letter from the Archbishop of Toronto, in which he stated that there were in Toronto emigrants from Connaught who were actually starving.

ANZIN, Feb. 24.—The coal masters have agreed to advance the wages of the miners. The strikers, who appear to be satisfied with the terms, will meet at Denain to-morrow to decide whether to accept them.

VIENNA, Feb. 25.—Advices from the Province of Poltava, in South Russia, state that the Jews there who are unable to show that they are possessed of landed property are expelled from the Province. Many of them have been forced to cross the Austrain frontier. A petition presented to Count Tolstoi, Russian Minister of the Interior, begging for time to enable the Jews to purchase land remains unanswered.

### A HUSBAND IN THE WAY.

A SUDDEN DEATH FROM POISON AND A WIFE AND HER FRIEND UNDER ARREST.

SUNBURY, Penn., Feb. 24.—Frank Kleskeskis, a wealthy Polish citizen of Continental, Northumberland County, died suddenly on Friday night last. He was the proprietor of a large boarding-house, and was always known to enjoy unusual good health. His sudden taking off created great excitement, and it was openly asserted that he was the victim of foul play. His friends took the matter in hand, and determined to make an investigation. Continental is an isolated place, and many of the employes at the collieries boarded at Kleskeskis's. Among the number was a man named Kneppsky, who was suspected of being on too intimate terms with Mrs. Kleskeskis. Nothing, however, was said by the husband until several days ago. Mrs. Kleskeskis and Kneppsky were sitting together, indulging in a private conversation, when Mr. Kleskeskis walked into the room and accused Kneppsky of trying to ruin his home and family. The latter grew angry, and denied the charge. A long discussion ensued, which ended in a fight. They were soon separated, but Kleskeskis wanted revenge, and immediately had a warrant issued for the arrest of Kneppsky on a charge of assault and battery. Not being able to procure bail, he was lodged in prison at this place.

Mrs. Kleskeskis became indignant over what she called the cruel treatment of Kneppsky, and began immediately to negotiate for his freedom, which she obtained after the payment of all costs. She came to this place herself and returned home with the prisoner. Upon their arrival at Continental, they remained in each other's company, and invited Kleskeskis to share in their pleasure. A glass of beer or porter was handed to him, which he drank. Almost immediately afterward he was taken ill and died. Kneppsky's intimacy with Mrs. Kleskeskis was town gossip, and when the husband's death became known, sympathizing friends surrounded the house and much sorrow was expressed for the deceased man, who was well known, and who, by his industry, had placed himself in comfortable circumstances. A Coroner's jury was summoned and a post-mortem examination made, which revealed the fact that Kleskeskis's death was caused by poison. Mrs. Kleskeskis and Kneppsky were put under arrest and subsequently removed to Sunbury Jail. On their way to prison they both disclaimed any knowledge of the poisoning, and are apparently deeply affected over Kleskeskis's death, but past events strongly indicate that the old man was in the way. It is expected that either one of them will make a clean breast of the affair. Kneppsky is a miner and about 38 years of age. The woman is about 45 and not bad looking.

### A PATIENT SHOOTING HIS NURSE.

AN INSANE MAN FOLLOWING INTENDED MURDER BY SUICIDE.

ST. LOUIS, Feb. 24.—The sensation at Belleville, Ill., last night took place at St. Elizabeth's Hospital, just one block from the scene of the late convent fire. Jacob Barth, 21 years old, who was in the last stages of consumption, was a patient in the hospital. He went out yesterday afternoon and purchased a revolver. Upon his return he told several of his comrades that there was going to be a "picnic" in the hospital, and that he was going to attend it. Later a shot was fired, and those who followed the sound found that Barth had fired a bullet which pierced the head of Sister Liberia, and had then blown out his own brains. It was found that just as Barth had entered his own room Sister Liberia had followed him in, she intending to fix up the grate fire. While stooping over, heaping coals on the fire, Barth drew the revolver and fired. The bullet passed through her ear and into her head. The Sister screamed, and this attracted the attention of the inmates, and when they came to the door he fired the shot which put an end to his sufferings. It is not known what cause the young man had for attempting to kill the Sister, and it was ascribed simply to desperation. A physician was called, and upon examination of the Sister's wounds pronounced them not dangerous. Barth was past the physician's aid. The inmates of the hospital, Sisters of the Franciscan Order, took care of their wounded colaborer and laid out the would-be murderer and suicide. At the official investigation it was ascertained that Barth was insane, and that, from all accounts, the insanity was herodi-tary.

### YOUNG CASH SHOOTS TWO MEN.

CHARLESTON, S. C., Feb. 24.—A desperate shooting affray occurred at Cheraw yesterday afternoon, in which W. B. Cash, a son of Col. E. B. C. Cash, the notorious duelist, shot Richards, the Town Marshal, and James Coward, a by-stander. Both of them were shot through the lungs, and their wounds may prove fatal. Immediately after firing the shots Cash jumped on his horse, which was standing near, and made his escape. A posse of citizens was organized and started in pursuit of the fugitive, who had not been captured at last accounts. The shooting of the Town Marshal is supposed to have resulted from a difficulty which occurred on the previous Saturday, when Cash was roughly handled by the Marshal. On that occasion, he had gone to Cheraw, got gloriously drunk, and raised a disturbance. He was arrested by the Marshal, and in the struggle which ensued, was beaten over the head with a club. He succeeded in getting on top of the Marshal and stamping him in a horrible manner. Cash is very resentful and bears a bloodthirsty reputation. It is presumed that he went to Cheraw on Saturday to avenge his fancied wrongs, and shot the two men named. Cash is a giant in strength, and is regarded as a dangerous man. He has been engaged in several affairs of honor.

### THE INDIANA GOVERNORSHIP.

INDIANAPOLIS, Feb. 24.—The Republican convention of Wayne County, Commissioner Dudley's home, unanimously passed a resolution yesterday asking Col. Dudley, for the good of the party, to take the lead of the State ticket as candidate for Governor. This action was quite unexpected, in view of the Colonel's repeated declinations, and of the fact that in 1880, when a strong pressure was brought to bear upon certain quarters for Dudley's nomination, his own county was not unanimous in his support, and thereby put an end to any probability of his nomination. The action yesterday was taken with great enthusiasm, and may have great influence on this vexed question.

### THE YALE CREW AT WORK.

NEW-HAVEN, Conn., Feb. 24.—Louis K. Hull, last year's Captain of the Yale boat crew, is coaching the men in an eight-oared barge. Appleton will be the permanent stroke-oar. The crew's stroke this year is slower than last year, and all the power seems to be put in the beginning, causing the boat to jerk forward, which serious defect will be remedied under Bob Cook's supervision. The men are trying for positions and are in active training. They average less in weight than last year, and, on the whole, are regarded as good material.

### A JEWELER'S SAFE DESPOILED.

BURGLARS IN TROY SECURE DIAMONDS AND WATCHES WORTH ABOUT $50,000.

TROY, N. Y., Feb. 24.—One of the most daring and successful safe burglaries ever perpetrated in this city or its vicinity occurred at an early hour this morning at Emmanuel Marks's jewelry store, No. 282 River-street. When Mr. Marks entered his place of business this forenoon he saw at a glance that he had been robbed, and it required only a minute to satisfy him that his loss would not be less than $50,000. To the left of the door, as one enters the store, stood a Lillie safe, made in 1858. Immediately over it the gas was burning, and the safe could be plainly seen from the street. When Mr. Marks closed his store, at 10:30 o'clock last night, the safe contained securities, money, diamonds, watches, chains, bracelets, ear-rings, and other jewelry, worth in the aggregate over $100,000. This morning the greater portion is missing.

Mr. Marks immediately summoned the police and an investigation soon disclosed the manner in which the burglars, who are undoubtedly professionals, had done their work. The adjoining building on the south was formerly the National Exchange Bank, but when that institution went into liquidation, a few years ago, the premises were leased by McDonald & Van Alstyne, insurance agents. The burglars pried open a window in the insurance office and, having gained the inside, they fastened the window by forcing a gimlet through the sash into the casing. They then descended to the cellar and began work on the 12-inch wall between the two buildings. An aperture through which a steam pipe passed afforded an available starting point, and this opening was increased to a hole 32 by 18 inches. Then the burglars crawled through the hole in the wall into the cellar under Marks's store and, ascending a flight of stairs, forced a trap-door opening into the store. The latter place gained, it required only a short time to force off one of the safe-doors with steel wedges and despoil the safe of its contents. The burglars left behind them one tray of diamond jewelry. The property stolen consists of about 75 gold watches, a large amount of diamonds, diamond jewelry, including rings, studs, ear-rings and breastpins, gold chains, over $600 in currency, $1,700 in Citizens' Steam-boat Company stock, and several promissory notes. Mr. Marks's net loss will be in the neighborhood of $50,000.

Between 6 and 8 o'clock in the morning there are only two policemen on duty in the city, and the theory is advanced that the burglars remained in the cellar until after 6 o'clock, and after robbing the safe took their departure. They left their tools and a dark lantern behind them, and on a lot of silverware cards bearing the words "No good" were found. It is generally believed that the robbery was committed by non-residents, probably New-Yorkers, who had a confederate here. Great sympathy is expressed with Mr. Marks, who feels his loss very keenly. He was a self-made man, beginning business life about 35 years ago by peddling jewelry. By close attention to business and remarkable perseverance, he prospered rapidly and soon had a store, the stock in which was the best to be found in this city or its vicinity. The police are diligently at work, but thus far have not gained the slightest clue. Three safe robberies were committed in Waterford on Friday, but the methods of the burglars were different from those adopted in the Marks case. It is believed that the burglars who robbed Mr. Marks's store are the same who attempted to rob stores in Albany on Friday night by first gaining admission to a barber's shop over the stores. It was reported to-night that two men suspected of complicity in the burglary are under police surveliance in Amsterdam.

### MURDERERS CLOSELY GUARDED.

THE PEOPLE OF AVONDALE EXCITED TO FEVER HEAT AGAINST THE CRIMINALS.

CINCINNATI, Feb. 24.—The Avondale murderers have been closely guarded in the county jail to-day. It would be difficult for a mob to get at them there, and to that fact they owe whatever their lives are worth. Feeling is running so high that were they in the Avondale Jail, it would be stormed within an hour, and business and professional men, and even preachers, would lend a hand. Johnson said to-day that Ingalls's confession was all straight, except that he was the one who stood outside the cabin and Ingalls was the one who did the killing. He says Ingalls could make the doctor trouble if he had a mind to. To another interviewer, Johnson stated that Dr. Cilley, about a week ago, wanted to know why they did not bring in more bodies and said: "If you can't get them any other way, why don't you knock some one in the head?"

Ingalls was questioned in regard to his having been at one time in partnership with the murdered man, Taylor, in the business of resurrecting bodies. He laughed and replied that old Taylor had told him "lots of stories about stealing stiffs," but as to whether they had ever been out on such expeditions together, he would not say. It is the opinion of the community that Ingalls and Johnson are equally guilty and that the expressman and the medical college people have more responsibility in the matter than has yet been formally charged.

The funeral at the Avondale Town Hall this afternoon of Beverly Taylor and Elizabeth Taylor and Elizabeth Jane Lambert, their granddaughter, the victims of the prisoners, lasted over two hours. Over 1,000 persons were present, one-fourth of whom were the best citizens of Avondale. Several clergymen made remarks, all of them colored with the exception of the Rev. J. Emery, a city missionary, who was the first speaker. He said that these criminals by the law of God deserved no mercy. Theirs was a crime which merited summary punishment without resort to the courts by the citizens taking the law into their own hands. These remarks were greeted by shouts in which both whites and blacks joined. Elder R. W. Scott was the next speaker. He said the plea of insanity might be urged for these criminals, but he thought the best treatment for such men was a stout rope and the nearest lamp-post. "Do they deserve mercy?" he asked. "Did they show any? Did they show mercy when they knocked out Elizabeth Taylor's brains? Did they show mercy when they beat down that helpless little girl, or when they knocked old Beverly Taylor on the head as he pleaded for mercy?" To each of these questions the audience responded with a thunderous "No!" Resolutions were passed thanking the officers and denouncing the crime. One resolution read: "Resolved, That a searching and untiring investigation be continued, to develop if there be any complicity with the man who bought the bodies."

The bodies were viewed when the funeral services ended, and were afterward taken to the colored people's cemetery west of the city and locked in a vault.

### A COLORED MINISTER IN DISGRACE.

BALTIMORE, Feb. 24.—The Rev. William Wilson, a prominent colored preacher of the Methodist Protestant Church, and President of the district that includes Baltimore City and County, has been suspended from his pastorate and from his Presidency on the ground of immorality. The charge was preferred against him by the Trustees of his church, which is in Baltimore County, near Towson. The charge is that he took a woman, a member of his congregation, to a house of ill-repute. The trial was appointed for last Friday and on that day a committee of five colored clergymen went to the church but found it locked, and the Pastor was not about. They then returned to the city, heard the evidence of witnesses on both sides, declared the Pastor guilty of the charges, and officially suspended him. They declared his pulpit vacant, and appointed the Rev. W. H. Lee Pastor of the church. Wilson declares that the verdict is not justified by the facts and refuses to give up the church. It is likely that the case will go to the courts.

### THROUGH THE ICE TO POUGHKEEPSIE.

POUGHKEEPSIE, N. Y., Feb. 24.—The steamer John L. Hasbrouck, which left New-York at 7 o'clock last night, arrived off Magazine Point, north of West Point, at 4 o'clock this morning, where she encountered heavy masses of ice 10 inches thick. She had the barge Spear, of Newburg, in tow. Leaving the barge in the ice she returned to Cranston's Landing, where she coaled up, and she reached Magazine Point again about noon, when she fought the ice two hours and finally succeeded in getting through to Newburg with the barge, where she left it. She then came to Poughkeepsie, arriving here at 4 P. M. amid the blowing of whistles. Thus navigation to the city is opened for the season. Between here and Rhinebeck the ice is very weak. Rondout boats are expected to resume trips by next Saturday.

### CONFESSING THE PAWLING MURDER.

POUGHKEEPSIE, Feb. 24.—Although the authorities are very reticent, it is reported that George Mulkins and Seneca Miller, charged with murdering Samuel Groner with dynamite cartridges in Pawling last October, have made a full confession, in which they charge the crime on John B. Griffin. A gun, supposed to be the one with which Griffin shot Groner, has been found. Access to the confession cannot yet be had.

## KANSAS AND HER VOTERS

### ISSUES THAT WILL AFFECT THE PRESIDENTIAL CONTEST.

NO BOOM FOR ARTHUR—GEN. SHERMAN, EDMUNDS, AND LOGAN POPULAR—TARIFF, PROHIBITION, AND ANTI-MONOPOLY.

TOPEKA, Kan., Feb. 22.—The leading Republicans of Kansas say that the 18 delegates who will represent the State in the Chicago Convention will go to that Convention without instructions. "This will be something new for Kansas," said one of the most influential of these gentlemen, "for in 1860 our delegates were instructed for Seward, in 1864 for Lincoln, in 1868 for Grant, in 1872 for Grant, in 1876 for Blaine, and in 1880 for Blaine, although 4 of the 10 broke away in that year and persisted in voting for Grant. Our voters have their favorites, of course, and the delegates will have preferences, but all will be ready to join the majority in selecting the strongest candidate." The party in this State does not seem to be deeply interested at present in the Presidential problem. The tariff issue, as presented in the contest between Funston and Riggs, in the Second District; prohibition, and the State's attempt to bring the railroads to terms, absorb the attention of the people. I have not discovered a particle of evidence showing that any Republican candidate is at work here, or that the friends of any Republican candidate are trying to manufacture a "boom" or striving to get votes for him. "It would be easy, I think," said one prominent Republican, "to take an Arthur delegation out of Kansas, and I was asked, not long ago, to work in that direction, but it wouldn't pay. To get up a delegation for the President would do him more harm than good, and the men who made the suggestion now see this plainly. Kansas Republicans like Arthur, but if New-York isn't for him we don't want him." Another Republican, who has been a Blaine man, remarked that at one time the State's representatives at Washington thought of getting up an Arthur delegation, but had since changed their minds. "If there is a strong sentiment in favor of any one," said he, "it is for Gen. Sherman. I think he has more supporters here than Logan has, although there are many Illinois men and Illinois soldiers in Kansas, and no soldier would oppose Logan. Some talk about Edmunds, and my ticket would be Edmunds and Lincoln. Blaine's distribution plan hurt him in this State, where three-fourths of the Republicans are Prohibitionists, and although Kansas has been a Blaine State I don't think he will get much support in the delegation this time." Another said that Blaine could not get support unless he should come out boldly as a candidate. He added that the party would gladly vote for Arthur if he could get New-York, and that with a Grand Army Post at every cross-roads Logan had hosts of friends. An influential Republican who worked hard for Grant in 1880, said that several newspapers in the State were already supporting Gen. Sherman, and that if instructions should be given in any district they would probably be for Sherman. He declared, however, that no leader in the party had become committed to any one, and that no work had been done for any candidate by Federal office-holders or the rank and file. Senator Plumb had been a Blaine man, but no one in the State knew now whom either Plumb or Ingalls preferred.

"We must yield to the veteran soldiers," said a Republican who knows the State from one end to the other, "and they can control the selection of delegates. Yet I think they prefer Sherman to Logan. There is no pension bill that does not have their support. I think the arrears act was a great mistake, but I can't say so here. Ingalls fairly represents Kansas on that subject." In an article contributed recently by the Senator to a soldier's paper in Washington, he remarked, with reference to the arrears act: "The vociferous din and uproar of denunciation with which this beneficent statute has been assailed has no precedent in malign and indecorous calumny," and then asked that the act should be extended to all pensioners by a repeal of the limitation. "What better use," he wrote, "can be made of our surplus?"

The Republican delegates, except the four at large, will be chosen in the districts, and in two districts arrangements for direct representation have already been made. The State Convention to choose delegates at large will be held on April 29.

The Democrats are even further from a decision as to a candidate than the Republicans are. Many of them talk about "the old ticket," and it is probably stronger in the State at present than any new one. McDonald stands second in the list of favorites. One Democrat of influence, who finds no "crystallization of sentiment" in his party, predicts that Payne will be the nominee because he has money, is a resident of the only October State, and would not repel capitalists and business men. Seed has been sown in Kansas, however, that may yield fruit in the course of time. The Democrats of the State may discover in a few weeks that New-York has an ambitious "statesman" named Flower. A few days ago a mysterious visit was made to Atchison (and probably to other Kansas cities) by a politician of St. Louis, who was once known as one of Mr. Tilden's workers. "This man," said a gentleman who has a keen eye for political emissaries, "was H. Clay Conde. He spent some time in the office of at least one Democratic newspaper, and on the following day that paper contained an article in which the virtues and statesmanship and availability of Flower were eloquently set forth." Kansas Democrats haven't the least idea who Flower is, but they are willing to be enlightened if they can get their hands into the Flower barrel.

The contest in the Second Congressional District, where Haskell's successor is to be elected on March 1, is peculiarly interesting because the tariff is the main issue, presented as boldly on each side as the most unyielding protectionist or most radical free trader could desire. The late Mr. Haskell represented the majority of the Ways and Means Committee of the last Congress upon the floor of the House in the tariff debate with considerable energy, doing the greater part of the work which Mr. Kelley would have done if he had been a younger and stronger man. Funston, whom the Republicans have nominated to succeed Haskell, is stumping the district in support of protection for its own sake, while Riggs, his opponent, is a free trader without disguise. Reports of the speeches show that the tariff is almost the only subject discussed. Riggs's position is clearly defined in the following words taken from one of his speeches: "I would eliminate from the Customs law every vestige of protection. I will not define my position as to direct taxation. That question does not enter into this campaign. If my position loses me votes in the lead district, so be it; if it loses me the vote of the zinc interest, that does not matter. If my position on the wool tariff loses me the vote of any farmer who has an old ram, so be it." Riggs is a Greenbacker who was once a Republican, and 19,000 Democrats in the district allowed 5,000 Greenbackers to name the man for the sake of a fusion vote against Funston. The long published reports of Funston's tariff speeches show that he is using all the arguments of the ultra-protectionists which were used in the Congressional tariff debate, and trying to prove to his audiences that protection is the only thing that has kept them from starvation. It does not appear that

# The New-York Times.

VOL. XXXIII......NO. 10,142. NEW-YORK, FRIDAY, MARCH 7, 1884. PRICE TWO CENTS.


## THE REVISED TARIFF BILL

### IT IS ADOPTED BY THE WAYS AND MEANS COMMITTEE.

VOTES OF SEVEN TO FIVE AGAINST THE PROTECTIONISTS — THE BILL TO BE FAVORABLY REPORTED NEXT WEEK.

WASHINGTON, March 6.—In the Ways and Means Committee to-day Mr. Morrison pressed to a vote his revised bill to reduce the present tariff 20 per cent., and it was ordered to be favorably reported by a vote of 7 to 5. Mr. Hewitt was the only member of the committee absent. Had he been present the majority would have been one more. Before the final vote was taken Mr. Russell made the first move of the protectionist members of the committee, by asking that the lines referring to the proposed reduction of duties on cotton and cotton goods be stricken out. His request was denied by a vote of 7 to 5. Mr. McKinley, on behalf of the Ohio wool-growers and wool manufacturers, moved to strike out the paragraph reducing the duties on wool and woolen goods 20 per centum, and limiting all such goods to an ad valorem duty not greater than 60 per centum. This was rejected by the usual vote, as was the proposition made by the same gentleman to strike out the lines reducing the duty on metals. Mr. Hiscock, as the friend of the salt manufacturers of Onondaga, made an effort to have salt stricken from the free list and added to the dutiable list, but he was voted down —7 to 5. Before the revised bill was brought in Mr. Morrison had made an agreement that he would amend the line placing coal on the free list by inserting a provision that "this shall not apply to coal imported from the Dominion of Canada, until that Government shall have exempted from the payment of duty all coal imported into that country from the United States." Carrying out this promise, he moved to insert the provision and it was done. Then Mr. Kelley moved to strike out the whole clause and restore coal to the dutiable list. This was lost by the usual majority, and the rest of the revised bill was adopted as the form in which the committee will report its proposition to reduce taxes.

The bill will hardly be reported to the House before Monday next, and probably not until Tuesday. Mr. Morrison will draft the report of the majority, with the assistance, perhaps, of several of his associates. Mr. Hiscock and Mr. McKinley have been at work for some time preparing the report of the minority. The friends of tariff reform are disposed to criticise the form of Mr. Morrison's bill and to say that he has unnecessarily exposed himself to the danger of defeat by delay, by breaking up the measure into many paragraphs, instead of confining it to one paragraph to each section. In the first section there are 13 paragraphs, and if the bill is taken up by paragraphs the opportunities for delay in the House will be innumerable. The third section of the bill is broken up into many sentences, each of which may be considered alone, and upon each of which the debate may take a wide range, covering the whole subject. It appeared to be possible to avoid this breaking up by constructing the measure in three sections.

The vote in the committee on reporting the bill was east without any qualification or apology by the Democratic members, Mr. Hurd being one of the number. The exaggerated reports of Mr. Hurd's indignation because of his failure to obtain an opportunity to make a speech on the Converse wool resolution, and the unfounded statement that he proposed to resign from the Ways and Means Committee, are disposed of by this vote.

The revised bill provides that on and after July 1 duties shall be levied and collected at the following rates: On all the articles mentioned in schedule I, which includes all cotton and cotton goods; in schedule J, which includes all hemp, jute, and flax goods; in schedule K, which includes all wool and woolens; in schedule C, which includes all metals; in schedule M, which includes all books, papers, and other articles of this character; in schedule E, which covers sugar, molasses, and articles of like character; in schedule F, covering tobacco; in schedule D, which includes wood and wooden ware, (except as otherwise provided;) in schedule G, which includes provisions; in schedule N, which includes sundries, other than precious stones, salt, coal, and linseed or flax-seed, and in schedule H, which includes all chemical products, 85 per centum of the several duties and rates of duty now imposed on said articles severally. It provides, however, that none of the articles included in schedule I shall pay a higher rate of duty than 40 per centum ad valorem; in schedule K, higher than 60 per centum, and in schedule C higher than 50 per centum. It provides that the rate of duty on cast, polished plate glass, unsilvered, exceeding 24 by 60 inches square; on green and colored glass bottles, vials, demijohns, and carboys, (covered and uncovered,) pickle or preserve jars, and other plain, molded, or pressed green and colored bottle glass, not cut, engraved, or painted, and not specially enumerated or provided for in this act; and on all the articles subject to ad valorem duty in schedule B, which includes earthenware and glassware, shall be 80 per centum of the several duties and rates of duty now imposed on said articles severally. It provides, however, that nothing in this act shall operate to reduce the duty above imposed on any article below the rate at which said article was dutiable under "An act to provide for the payment of outstanding Treasury notes, to authorize a loan, to regulate and fix the duties on imports, and for other purposes," approved March 2, 1861, commonly called the "Morrill Tariff;" and that when, under existing law, any of said articles are grouped together and made dutiable at one rate, then nothing in this act shall operate to reduce the duty below the highest rate at which any article in such group was dutiable under said act of March 2, 1861. It provides that after July 1 the rate of duty to be paid on all unpolished cylinder, crown, and common window glass, on iron or steel sheets, or plates, or taggers' iron, coated with tin or lead, or with a mixture of which these metals is a compound part, by the dipping or any other process, and commercially known as tin plates, terne plates, and taggers' tin, and on linseed or flax seed, shall be 80 per centum of the several duties and rates of duty now imposed on said articles severally. It adds the following list of articles to the present free list: Salt in bags, sacks, barrels, or other packages, or in bulk; coal, slack or culm; coal, bituminous or shale; timber, hewn and sawed, and timber used for spars and in building wharves; timber squared or sided, not specially enumerated or provided for in this act; sawed boards, plank, deals, and other lumber of hemlock, whitewood, sycamore, and basswood, and all other articles of sawed lumber; hubs for wheels, posts, last blocks, wagon blocks, oar blocks, gun blocks, heading blocks, and all the blocks or sticks, rough, hewn, or sawed only; staves of wood of all kinds; pickets and palings, laths, shingles, pine clapboards, spruce clapboards; wood, manufactured, not specially enumerated or provided for in this act.

### THE SENATE'S DIGNITY OFFENDED.

With a charming display of spirit the Senate has resented what it considered a wanton attack by the House of Representatives upon its dignity and its privileges. Some time ago Mr. Sherman announced that the investigation of the riot at Danville, Va., would have to be suspended, because there was no money left in the Senate contingent fund to pay the expenses. The Senate promptly passed a bill appropriating $10,000 to be turned into the contingent fund, and sent the bill to the House for concurrence. The House deliberately tacked on an amendment providing that the money should be spent for investigations heretofore ordered by the Senate. Senator Sherman astonished his colleagues to-day by asking them to concur in this amendment. He followed up his motion with the explanation, in apologetic tones, that while the amendment seemed to be an attempt to interfere with the powers of the Senate, he understood that it was merely the expression of a desire on the part of the House that hereafter investigations should be paid for out of the general fund appropriated in the general law. Mr. Sherman's explanation was not at all satisfactory to the Senators, as he very soon learned. Mr. Allison protested against the making of such a precedent, and declared the House amendment a discourtesy to the Senate. Mr. Ingalls thought it was a plain interference with the independence of the Senate, and entirely in violation of the courtesy and comity which ought to prevail between the two houses. Mr. Sherman remarked that the older he got the less disposed he was to get into a quarrel. Mr. Allison protested against the amendment a second time, and Mr. Harris and Mr. Butler talked vigorously against the impertinence of the amendment. Mr. Call declared that the action of the House was a clear invasion of the constitutional rights of the Senate. As a result of the debate, Mr. Sherman retreated from his position, withdrew his motion to concur, and substituted for it a motion to disagree with the amendment. To make the Senate's expression of feeling more emphatic Mr. Wilson moved to agree to the amendment and called for the yeas and nays. There were 70 Senators present, and on the roll-call 50 negative votes were recorded. Mr. Sherman called for a committee of conference, which was appointed, and then the Senators settled down to routine business, satisfied that they had properly rebuked the impertinence of the legislative [illegible] of the Capitol.

### TROUBLE IN THE COAL MINES.

THE WAR AT CORNING LIKELY TO LEAD TO BLOODSHED.

COLUMBUS, Ohio, March 6.—There is a big strike of coal miners in the Hocking Valley, caused by the refusal of the coal operators to concede the demands of the haulers. On the 1st inst. the price of mining was reduced from 80 to 70 cents per ton, which was acceded to by the miners, but the haulers would not stand a reduction of 30 cents per day for hauling, which was insisted on. The Baird and Gore furnaces are now blowing out, and a large number of men will be thrown out of employment. These two furnaces were the only ones in blast in the valley. This morning the striking haulers arrived, demanding $2 05 instead of $1 75 per day. At New-Straitsville, about 1,106 miners have been forced to suspend work by the action of the haulers. It is not known how long this suspension of work will last, as the Hocking Valley syndicate which operate the mines at Straitsville do not seem at all disposed to accede to the demands of the teamsters, and the miners are quite as much inclined to stand by them. In the Sunday Creek Valley work is wholly suspended because of the religious war that has reigned at Corning during the past few days. The miners of W. P. Rend, at Rendville, where negro miners are largely employed, have also caught the prevailing contagion to stop work, and although they are no way interested, they prefer to watch events as they are developed among the excited men than to continue at work. The excitement still runs high and although all is quiet to-night there is no evidence that it can last long.

A dispatch from Corning to-night says: "The affair will without doubt end in bloodshed. The feeling between the factions here and at Rendville, added to the excitement caused by the arrest of the leaders of the mob which lynched Dick Hickey last month, will certainly cause war, and when it does start—and a feather's weight will start it—I predict that Corning will witness scenes of bloodshed and terrorism enough to last them for at least the next 10 years."

### OUTWITTED BY MRS. BROOKS.

THE WEALTHY NEW-YORK WIDOW ESCAPES FURTHER PERSECUTION.

CHICAGO, March 6.—Mrs. Jane A. Brooks, the wealthy New-York widow, who was held in custody at the Palmer House on a writ of ne exeat sworn out by Stanley B. Sexton, for whose guardian her husband was a bondsman, has outwitted her persecutors in a very clever manner and left the city with her portable fortune. The case came up before Judge Shephard to-day, and at 4 o'clock the Judge began reading a lengthy decision dismissing the writ on the ground of indefiniteness in describing the character and amount of the indebtedness, together with a failure to produce proof that Mrs. Brooks actually intended to leave the city. As soon as the decision was handed down the attorneys of the two parties ran in different directions. Mrs. Brooks's legal counselors ran to the Palmer House where the Deputy Sheriffs were keeping guard over their client. At 10 minutes of 5 o'clock the writ was produced, the deputies gracefully retired, and Mrs. Brooks was free for a moment. She had been reported sick in bed, but suddenly recovered sufficiently to take the train for the East, which left just 20 minutes after her guardians departed from the hotel. Meanwhile Sexton's attorneys had been pleading their case before Judge Tully. They obtained a new writ of ne exeat and hastened to the hotel only to find that the bird had flown, carrying off, it is said, nearly $300,000 in stocks, bonds, and personal property.

Sexton's attorneys are furious over the trick practiced upon them, but Mrs. Brooks's friends declared that she only met sharp pactice by equally acute tactics; that she is a persecuted woman, and that Sexton was trying to make her responsible for his own business incapacity in having invested his funds in his guardian's business.

### CHRYSLER'S THREE WIVES.

FREAKS OF A GEORGIA FARMER IN THE MATRIMONIAL MARKET.

ATLANTA, Ga., March 6.—James R. Chrysler, a well-to-do farmer of Jackson County, several years ago wooed and won Miss Josephine Webb, the daughter of a neighbor. For a while they lived in the neighborhood in which they were married, but later came to Atlanta and for two years lived happily. The husband, however, grew careless of his wife and finally neglected to support her. Then the wife started out to gain a living for herself and the husband returned to Jackson County. The wife sued for a divorce, and in 1881 a divorce was granted, but was set aside on account of irregularity in the proceedings. Meantime, six months before, Chrysler had married another Jackson County woman. In May, 1883, wife No. 2 deserted Chrysler. Chrysler then turned his face westward and settled in Ellis County, Texas, where he became acquainted with the family of Charles P. Bragg, a prosperous farmer. Mary E. Bragg was a beautiful girl of 20, and after a short courtship she promised to marry Chrysler, and on Jan. 6 last the ceremony was performed. She was ignorant of the true state of affairs and trustingly started with her husband for Atlanta, arriving here four days after her marriage. She went at once to the home of her sister in this city and was corially received, but when the husband was presented he was recognized as the man who had already married two wives.

The bride was shocked beyond description. Her husband claimed that he was legally divorced from the first wife, and that the second marriage was void because it occurred before the first divorce was granted. The records, however, show that no divorce was ever granted. The husband left town and the wife of four days began proceedings for divorce. Wife No. 1 is in Atlanta, wife No. 2 is in Jackson County, and wife No. 3 is also here.

### KILLED BY HER BROTHER.

NASHVILLE, Tenn., March 6.—Information of a homicide committed at Baker's Station, seven miles from Nashville, last night, was received here to-day. Jack Hirsch killed his sister, Rosa Hirsch, while the two were engaged in a quarrel. It is stated that Hirsch and his sister had not been on good terms for some time. Several nights ago the brother and sister got into a quarrel, when Rosa cut Jack severely with a pocket-knife. This affair was quieted down until last night, when they became involved in another fight, during which Jack injured his sister, from the effects of which she died shortly afterward. Hirsch went to the station, purchased a ticket for Texas, and left on the first train that passed.

### ANOTHER NIAGARA ATTRACTION.

TORONTO, March 6.—In the latter part of October, 1883, an old man choked to death while at dinner in one of the hotels at Niagara Falls. An undertaker of that place took charge of the body, and embalmed it with the expectation that some relatives would appear and claim the remains, compensating him for his work. No one has yet appeared to claim the body, and the undertaker is now exhibiting it as a specimen of his work. The case has created much interest, and people come from far and near to view the body of the unknown man. A number of physicians have been invited and will examine the body in a few days. It is now five months since he was embalmed.

### SOUTHERN IMMIGRATION.

NASHVILLE, Tenn., March 6.—Although invitations to attend the sessions of the Southern Immigration Association in this city next week have been sent ex-Senators Blaine and Thurman, they have not yet replied. The Commissioner of Agriculture has good reason, however, to believe they will be here and deliver addresses. The addresses by these two distinguished gentlemen are looked forward to with great interest, inasmuch as both are spoken of for the Presidency, and any utterances they might make about the South would necessarily be fraught with importance. The people of Nashville are making extensive arrangements for the entertainment of visitors.

### A GIRL'S SEVERE INJURIES.

PHILADELPHIA, March 6.—The blue ribbons dangling from the hair of Lizzie Diamond as she moved about her work this morning in L. W. Leiber's silk manufactory, on Garden-street, caught in a loom as she passed. Her braids rapidly followed the ribbons. The girl began to scream, and the machinery was stopped, but not until a portion of her scalp had been torn and a quantity of blood lost. Lizzie was removed to the Pennsylvania Hospital.

### VIRGINIA AND NEW-YORK SOLDIERS.

LOCKPORT, N. Y., March 6.—Last May, the Twenty-eighth New-York Volunteers entertained at Niagara Falls the Fifth Virginia (Confederate) Veterans. This year the New-York men are to be entertained at Staunton by the Virginia veterans on a day yet to be agreed upon.

## READY FOR ANOTHER FIGHT

### GEN. GRAHAM TO MAKE AN ADVANCE ON MONDAY.

THE REBELS DEFEATED BY A NATIVE TRIBE WHILE ADVANCING ON KHARTOUM—THE COST OF THE BRITISH EXPEDITION.

LONDON, March 6.—Earl Granville, Foreign Secretary of State, announced in the House of Lords this afternoon that he had just received Egyptian dispatches which reported that 1,000 men who were marching from El Obeid upon Khartoum had been defeated by tribes friendly to Gen. Gordon.

Gen. Graham, with 3,000 men, will advance from Suakin on Monday against Osman Digna. His force will consist of 126 artillerymen, with 6 7-pounders, 10 mountain and 4 Krupp guns; 62 sailors, with 2 9-pounders, 3 Gatling and 3 Gardner guns, and the Tenth and Nineteenth Hussars, the rest of the force being made up of infantry and marines. Osman Digna remains at Handoob, and is ready to do battle. Gen. Graham has been ordered to disperse the rebels within 10 miles of Suakin, but not to operate at a greater distance from that city. When these have been dispersed it is believed that the tribes will become friendly.

In the House of Commons to-day the Marquis of Hartington, Secretary of State for War, moved that an appropriation of £380,000 be voted to cover the cost of the Soudan expedition. The Right Hon. Frederick Stanley, Conservative, member for Lancashire, North, spoke upon the motion, and criticised severely the Government's Egyptian policy. Mr. Gladstone replied that the expedition to Assouan involved no change of policy. It was, he asserted, a necessary precaution to prevent the excitement from spreading. The Government would adhere to its determination to pay no heed to the remarks of foreign newspapers, and had no intention of assuming the government of Egypt. Such an act would be a gross breach of the public law of Europe. [Cheers.] The troops would be withdrawn at the earliest moment possible. Mr. Henry Labouchere, Radical, member for Northampton, moved to reduce the appropriation £100,000.

Earl Granville, Foreign Secretary, has assured France that England intends to maintain the existing conventions with the Soudan. It is necessary first, however, to restore the prestige of the English name in that quarter. The acts of Gen. Gordon are only partially approved.

The Sultan of Morocco has declared El Mahdi an impostor.

CAIRO, March 6.—Gen. Gordon telegraphs that Slatin Bey, an Austrian officer in the Egyptian service, has defeated an expedition sent by El Mahdi from Darfour, and that the Kabbabish tribe have defeated the rebels north of El Obeid.

### OPENING OF THE REICHSTAG.

THE PROGRAMME OF THE GOVERNMENT—A NEW POLITICAL PARTY.

BERLIN, March 6.—The Reichstag was opened to-day, with the usual formalities. The speech from the throne was read by Herr von Boetticher, Home Secretary of State and representative of the Chancellor. The speech asserts that the chief task of the Reichstag lies in the domain of social and political affairs, and says that the Emperor's wish, which has been solemnly and repeatedly expressed, for the improvement of the condition of workmen, has met with full appreciation on the part of the German people. Among the numerous bills announced is one providing for a scheme of accident insurance, after the adoption of which the Emperor recommends the formation of a system of insurance for the infirm and aged. "This," the speech says, "is intended to prevent any possible justification of attempts to overthrow the Divine and human order of things, and will pave the way for the abrogation of existing exceptional measures." A bill will be introduced providing that the anti-Socialist law shall remain in force for a further period. Another will propose an amendment to the present system of insurance against sickness. The control of joint stock companies will form the subject of another bill, and a convention with Belgium, protecting literary and artistic works, will be submitted for approval. "The foreign relations of Germany," the speech declares, "are in a highly satisfactory condition. Solidarity exists between the pacific sentiments of Germany and those of the neighboring friendly powers, which, so far as can be humanly foreseen, affords a guarantee of the security of peace both in Germany and the other countries." The speech concludes with these words: "The strengthening of the hereditary friendship of Germany with the neighboring imperial Courts and the cordial reception of the Crown Prince in Italy and Spain, prove that Germany's prestige is fortified by the confidence of foreign sovereigns and nations in the policy of Germany."

The National Liberals have decided not to raise a discussion of the Lasker incident in the Reichstag until the matter has been internationally disposed of. A fusion of the Secessionist and Progressist parties has been effected. The new combination will be called the German Liberal Party. Its programme embraces strict adherence to the Constitution, annual budgets, universal suffrage, secret voting, the payment of members of the Reichstag, the liberty of the press, of public meetings, and of association, equality before the law, religious liberty and perfect equality of all creeds, economic progress, the suppression of State Socialism, just assessment and taxation, with the exemption of articles of consumption. It will oppose any economic Customs policy which shall favor special interests, is against monopolies, and advocates unimpaired maintenance of the national defense, with universal military services of short period, and with an annual fixing of the peace contingent of the army. It further declares that progress must be based upon allegiance to the Emperor and to the Federal Constitution.

The report that the resignation of Herr von Gossler, the Prussian Minister of Ecclesiastical Affairs, was impending has no foundation.

A letter from Prince Bismarck was read in the Reichstag to-day informing that body that Herr Richter, Deputy for Muhradlitz, had been sentenced to six months' imprisonment and loss of his seat for insulting the throne.

### A LEAGUE AGAINST LAWLESSNESS.

LONDON, March 6.—Organized action between England and the Continental powers against anarchists and dynamiters has been agreed upon without any special treaty. The Police Departments of the powers have been instructed to co-operate with one another under this compact. The Swiss Government has ordered the arrest of a number of anarchists at Berne, and the search of the domiciles of suspected persons and the office of a working men's society at Berne. The Swiss police have arrested a German anarchist named Kennel. They sent information to Vienna which led to the seizure of Kammerer and other anarchists. The refugees at Geneva suspected a man named Penkert, a rampant anarchist speaker, to be a German spy. Penkert received warning and suddenly disappeared. The Vienna *Official Gazette* publishes an official order stating that letters opened by the police and afterward sent to their destination will bear an official seal, with mention of the fact that they have been opened at the office and distributed.

The clue mentioned in the *Standard's* Paris dispatch this morning, which leads the Paris police to believe that an assault is premeditated upon prominent officers in London on St. Patrick's Day, is afforded by a letter from America which has fallen into the hands of the police.

GENEVA, March 6.—It is believed that the police here hold clews to an extensive conspiracy, which would have sacrificed hundreds of lives.

LONDON, March 7.—A suspicious-looking bag has been found in the Chester Railway station.

The Paris police possess newspapers addressed to suspected dynamiters from America. It is supposed that the papers were used to transmit orders, as portions of them are punctured. The police are turning their attention to Bordeaux.

### THE GREELY SEARCH PARTY.

LONDON, March 6.—Capt. Nares, who commanded the British arctic expedition of 1875, assisted by Commander Markham, has drawn up a memorandum of great value in regard to the ice and navigation of Smith's Sound. This document has been sent to the American authorities. The *Times* says: "The Greely search expedition will be watched with as much interest and anxiety by Europe and America as that which went to the relief of Mr. Leigh Smith in 1882."

### CURRENT FOREIGN TOPICS.

LONDON, March 6.—Sir Henry James, Attorney-General, has served a writ upon Mr. Charles Bradlaugh for voting in the House of Commons on Feb. 11.

George Bubear, the English oarsman, and Wallace Ross, the New-Brunswick sculler, are practicing for their match of March 10. Betting is five to four in favor of Bubear.

Another suicide, due to losses at gambling, has occurred at Monte Carlo. This makes the nineteenth since Jan. 1. The newspapers are demanding that France shall suppress the scandal.

Advices from the far East report that a fresh Dutch expedition has been dispatched to Acheen, Sumatra, with the hope of securing the release of the crew of the wrecked British steamer Nisero, who are held captive by the Rajah of Tenom.

Two members of the firm of Messrs. Parker, solicitors, were supposed to have fled and it was alleged that the reason for their flight was that they had been misappropriating the title deeds of their clients and had borrowed £500,000 for various speculations. Solicitors for the firm have written to the newspapers, pronouncing the alleged cause of flight inaccurate and denying that any attempt had been made to secure a loan.

Earl Granville has instructed the Governor of Gibraltar to make a report concerning the boarding of the American ship Marianne Nottebohm by Spanish officials. A semi-official explanation of the affair has been received from Madrid, it being stated that although the ship paid the Gibraltar port dues she was not anchored in British waters.

The Court Theatre was filled to overflowing to-night with spectators eager to witness the rentrée of Miss Fortescue as Dorothy in "Dan'l Druce." The few lines which she has to speak were given with parrot-like care and mechanical delivery, but with no sign of dramatic power. The audience showed its sympathy with her position by giving her several warm recalls at the fall of the curtain.

Advices from Vienna and Berlin concur in contradicting the report that Germany, Austria, and Russia have entered into a formal alliance. It is reported that Prince Bismarck has informed the Italian Ambassador at Berlin that a friendly *entente* has been arranged with Russia, but no treaty, and that the recent pourparlers were limited to the restoration of cordial relations between Emperor William and the Czar.

A sacred white elephant consigned to a circus firm in America left Liverpool for Philadelphia to-day.

QUEENSTOWN, March 6.—On the arrival of the steamer City of Chicago this evening the bodies of Mr. Jerome J. Collins and his mother were received by the British Admiral, the American Consul, the Mayor and corporation of the city, relatives, and a large number of citizens. The bodies were conveyed to the cathedral on biers, followed by a long procession bearing torches and a band playing a dead march. The funeral will take place in Cork on Sunday. A guard of honor from her Majesty's ship Revenge will escort the bodies to Cork.

CONSTANTINOPLE, March 6.—The Porte has appointed Photiades Bey Governor of Crete.

DUBLIN, March 6.—The Justices of the Peace in Londonderry have asked the Government to proclaim the Orange and Nationalist meetings on St. Patrick's Day.

PARIS, March 6.—M. Charles Joseph Tissot, who was yesterday reported to be at the point of death, has partially recovered.

Workmen prompted by anarchists have published a manifesto, which urges a demonstration against the Government with a view to leading them to adopt measures for the amelioration of the condition of the unemployed.

The Committee of the Chamber of Deputies will report in favor of M. Paul Bert's proposal to settle the trichinosis question by the apportionment of a French board for the inspection of pork imported into France.

Mlle. Nevada, the American prima donna, received the rite of Catholic baptism at the English Passionist Church to-day. Mrs. Mackay acted as sponsor. The ceremony was private. Mlle. Nevada was dressed in white, with her hair flowing down her shoulders. Mr. Mackay sent a present of a bonbon box of massive oxidized silver, inlaid with gold.

The Director-General of Safety has asked the Prefects of Departments for details of the monarchical organization, especially in regard to the reconstitution of the old Legitimist committees.

ROME, March 6.—Mr. Errington, the unofficial English representative at the Vatican, has had an audience with Cardinal Jacobini, Papal Secretary of State, and Cardinal Simeoni, Prefect of the Propaganda, in which he imparted to them England's views regarding the nomination of Catholic Bishops in Ireland and the British colonies.

An affray occurred yesterday at Pressa, a small village near Aquila, between the laborers on the railway and the inhabitants of the village. The Carbineers interferred to suppress the disturbance and fired, killing 8 and wounding 14 of the villagers. The affair has caused a great sensation.

LONDON, March 7.—The commander of the Black Flags has offered a reward of £16 for each head of a French soldier and £32 for the head of an officer.

BERLIN, March 6.—Prince Bismarck had a narrow escape from a passing engine to-day while driving across a railway track.

### A MURDERER DEFIES THE LAW.

W. B. CASH STILL UNMOLESTED BY THE SHERIFF'S OFFICERS.

CHARLESTON, S. C., March 6.—It is nearly two weeks since W. B. Cash shot down two men in the streets of Cheraw, S. C., in broad daylight and without the slightest provocation. One of his victims is dead; the other can hardly recover. The murderer is still at large; no determined effort has been made to arrest him, and the entire community where the murder was committed has acted in a most cowardly manner. Sheriff Spofford, of Chesterfield County, went to Cash's house, took a drink with him, and left without attempting his arrest. All the other officers in the county are afraid of him. Gov. Thompson has offered $500 reward for his arrest. The law-abiding people of the State are indignant that Cash and his father should be allowed to bulldoze the whole State. It is reported that young Cash has fortified himself in his father's barn, and defies the officers to arrest him. He has been seen once since the murder with a rifle on his shoulder to intimidate the public. Col. Cash says his son will surrender quietly and give bail, but will not go to jail. United States District Attorney Melton and two other lawyers—editors and proprietors of the only newspaper in the county—have been retained for his defense.

The following from the *News and Courier* will show the temper of the people:

"There is an unmistakable issue between the Cashes, father and son, and the people of the State. The law is on trial; justice is defied; the officers of the law are mocked at, or are in collusion with the criminals. It must be determined now and here, once and forever, whether the law or the shot-gun is supreme in South Carolina; whether the law will punish malefactors or make heroes of them; whether the citizens must take the law into their own hands and protect and defend themselves in their own way, or can rely on the executive and judicial officers of the State for the arrest, detention, trial, and conviction of insolent and boastful assassins and their apologists and defenders. The public welfare demands that Col. Cash, as well as W. B. Cash, be arrested. It is sickening to read that he is parleyed with and conferred with as though he were a sovereign power, when he is merely a coarse and common criminal. Col. E. B. C. Cash is as guilty in morals as his son. It is an imperative duty to arrest and try him."

### DEFAULTING TREASURER VAN FLEET.

CLEVELAND, Ohio, March 6.—Further investigation of the affairs of M. O. Van Fleet, defaulting Treasurer of Huron County, shows that he had followed in the wake of many who have preceded him, in using other people's money to speculate with. New-York and Chicago bucket shops absorbed the money he stole from the county Treasury. The defalcation will not be less than $45,000, but the amount is amply secured by his bondsmen, 89 in number, who signed his bond for $150,000. To pay, however, will ruin many of them, as they are small farmers and not able to stand the loss. The defalcation has forced the firm of Van Fleet Brothers, at Wakeman, Huron County, of which M. O. Van Fleet was a member, into bankruptcy. Van Fleet has always borne a good reputation, and if he had desired $50,000 to help him out he could have got the indorsement of any number of his neighbors to secure it.

### THE CORRESPONDENCE PUBLISHED.

NEW-HAVEN, Conn., March 6.—The New-Haven *Palladium* to-morrow will publish a communication from D. C. Birdsall, in which he claims that the relations between himself and Gov. Waller were always intimate and friendly, but that duplicity shown by Gov. Waller leaves no other course open but for him to publish the correspondence between them. He gives copies of the correspondence between Gov. Waller and himself, in which campaign matters are referred to and plans broached and references made to the needs and work of the campaign, and also concerning the appointment of officials and arranging interviews. The correspondence indicates that Gov. Waller placed confidence in Birdsall. Mr. Birdsall concludes by saying that he leaves the public to judge who is in the wrong and who is guilty of duplicity.

### OUTRAGE BY UNION MEN.

TROY, N. Y., March 6.—At an early hour this morning three men fired pistol shots at a non-union boarding-house near the Malleable Iron-works. Policemen followed the men over the hills, firing at them. By the aid of lanterns blood was found on the snow where one of the men fell. The wounded man was carried off by his companions in a sleigh.

### FOR TAMPERING WITH A JURY.

PHILADELPHIA, March 6.—In the case of Dr. William S. McBride, charged with embracery, in connection with the Malone homicide cases, Judge Yerkes to-day delivered an opinion remanding the defendant for trial.

## O'BRIEN'S FORCE COUNTED

### HIS FRIENDS DROWNING THE WORDS OF WARNING.

A CAUCUS OF A BARE MAJORITY OF THE COUNTY COMMITTEE GIVES HIM 119 VOTES FOR PERMANENT CHAIRMAN.

The friends of John J. O'Brien who are determined to fasten that gentleman upon the Republican Party of this city held a caucus or conference last evening in Madison-Square Hall, No. 948 Broadway, and after a great deal of exciting debate, in which personalities were freely bandied, succeeded in having him declared the nominee of the meeting for permanent Chairman of the County Committee. The hall, which is not a large one, was packed with delegates to whom the call for the caucus had been sent, and by 8 o'clock there was scarcely standing room to be had.

The County Committee is composed of 273 members, and of this number 138, or 1 more than a majority, were present. The familiar faces of the politicians of the old machine were to be seen on all sides. Among the better known of those in attendance were Barney Biglin, Mike Cregan, Robert G. McCord, Frank Raymond, John E. Brodsky, William H. Townley, Col. Charles S. Spencer, Police Commissioner Joel W. Mason, George B. Deane, John H. Brady, John R. Lydecker, Col. Ethan Allen, John W. Marshall, Dennis Shea, Morris Friedsam, John H. Grimes, John McClave, Edmund Stephenson, George W. Blunt, and John J. O'Brien himself, around whom the delegates circled before the caucus was called to order. Every Assembly district in the city was represented, but the Eleventh and Twentieth were represented by only one member of the County Committee each, the former by Charles P. Miller and the latter by Henry C. Perley. From the First, Fourth, Sixth, and Eighth the full delegation was in attendance.

Mr. O'Brien called the meeting to order at a few minutes after 8 o'clock. He said that he had invited every member of the County Committee to participate in the proceedings, and he was glad to see so many present. For himself, he desired to say that he was ready and willing at all times to abide by any decision made by a majority of a Republican conference. "I hope," he said, "that every gentleman having friendship for me will refrain to-night, even though in doing so he may be obliged to allow unjust charges to go uncontradicted, from saying or doing anything which will tend to widen the breach in the Republican Party of this city. I would suggest that Col. Joel W. Mason be made Chairman of this meeting." Having made this little address in the interests of harmony, Mr. O'Brien modestly took a back seat at the side of the hall, and from that time until the close of the meeting opened not his mouth again.

Commissioner Mason was unanimously chosen Chairman, and George F. Hopper and John W. Marshall were selected as Secretaries. Mr. Mason, in taking the chair, said that he had been told that persons were present who intended to personate absent delegates. He did not know whether this was true or not, but he wished it distinctly understood that he should have all such men summarily ejected. He insisted that all persons standing in the hall should sit down, and when a number near the door failed to obey his order, he announced that no business would be done until all were seated. This threat had the desired result, and James Nodine was then appointed Sergeant-at-Arms to keep refractory delegates in their chairs. The roll-call of the County Committee was then ordered, and each man was required to rise and show himself when he answered to his name. Having thus satisfied himself that the caucus was not packed, the Chairman called for the pleasure of the meeting.

Leonard Hazletine, of the Twenty-first Assembly District, desired to know whether the meeting was a caucus by which the gentlemen who took part in it were to be bound. He should not feel that he had a right to sit there if that was the case, he said, without consulting a majority of the delegates of his district, who were not present. Mr. Mason answered that the meeting was a caucus, but whether those taking part in it should be bound by its action or not they must determine for themselves.

Col. Spencer, of the Thirteenth District, thought that all trouble could be obviated by a motion, which he made, that an informal vote be taken, in which each person present should name the man whom he preferred as permanent Chairman of the County Committee. That would bind nobody, and a formal vote could be taken afterward, which would be binding or not, according to the conscience of those who voted. "We are all brothers here," said the Colonel, looking about him with a beaming smile, "and we are bound to meet the Democratic Party. That's all we are bound to just now. Bless you, these quarrels of ours are very healthy things. [Laughter and applause.] Let us have the preference of each gentleman here first, and then those who don't want to be bound by our action can go out. If there is any man who calls himself a Republican, and who is not willing to join with the majority of his brethren in this Presidential year, why, let him go, that's all."

Henry L. Sprague, also of the Thirteenth District, insisted that the meeting should be called a conference instead of a caucus. "There is no means," he said, "of making us swallow any candidate whom we don't want. I shall stay here and vote for whom I please, and I shall go to the County Committee and do the same thing. I move an amendment that the vote be made formal, to save time, and that it shall bind nobody."

Mr. Miller—I came to this conference because I was invited, and I am the only delegate from my district present. I certainly had no idea that I was to be bound by any action of this meeting. I propose to vote in the County Committee just as I see fit.

Mr. Mason—This motion of Col. Spencer's binds nobody.

After some further discussion, in which a vain attempt was made to discover whether the meeting was a caucus or a simple conference, Col. Spencer's motion was put and carried.

The First District was called and four delegates gave O'Brien as their choice, while two named Marvelle W. Cooper. In the voting which followed the name of O'Brien was rapidly recorded amid the shouts, cheers, and stamping of his excited friends. In the Seventh District, Frederick W. Whitridge and Alfred R. Conkling voted for Cooper, and C. Volney King and John H. Dorn for O'Brien. When the Eleventh District was reached, Charles P. Miller, the only representative, named Marvelle W. Cooper, and the vote was signalized by very mild applause from the few Cooper men present.

The votes from the Thirteenth District were all recorded for O'Brien until the name of Henry L. Sprague was called. Mr. Sprague desired to be excused from voting. "Mr. O'Brien," he said, "has always acted like a gentleman to me, and if I consulted my own personal feelings I should not be compelled to vote against him. But, considering that a large majority of Republicans in this city are opposed to him—"

"That's not so!" shouted a voice.

"Considering," continued Mr. Sprague, without noticing the interruption, "that we are entering upon a Presidential campaign, I think that we should be committing suicide to place any man at the head of our organization around whom we cannot all gather. You know, as politicians, that we cannot afford to enter this campaign handicapped. A large number of the men who help you with their money and influence are not here to-night. Is this not a protest against the action which it was known in advance that you would take? Mr. O'Brien stands not as a representative of this committee in its entirety, but as the representative of a faction. The strong Republican districts are not fully represented here—"

A Voice—That's their fault!

"That may be, but—"

At this point the speaker was interrupted by hisses, shouts of "Oh, call the roll!" and "Sit down!" Mr. Mason pounded vigorously on the table and called for order; but it was a full minute before quiet was restored. "I have the floor and I'm going to keep it till I get through," shouted Mr. Sprague. "In 1880 we polled the largest vote we ever cast in the State; last year we polled the smallest. Are we going to do something here to-night to attract the wanderers back, or not? It is a very dangerous thing to enter this campaign weighted with Mr. O'Brien. I withdraw my excuse and vote for Mr. Cooper."

This conclusion was greeted with feeble cheers and loud hisses. The call proceeded, Mr. O'Brien getting nearly all the votes until the Seventeenth District was reached, when John McClave made a long speech in his favor, praising his energy and the untiring work that he had done for the party. If the majority of the delegates selected Mr. O'Brien for their leader, he said, it was unwise for any man to say, as Mr. Sprague had said, they did not represent the Republican sentiment of the county. "We don't want no theoretical politicians to run this campaign," he shouted, as the hall rang with the cheers and yells of O'Brien's friends. "What we want is a practical worker, and that practical worker is John J. O'Brien."

When the Twenty-first District was called Leonard Hazletine asked to be excused from voting. "I had hoped," he said, "that there would be a full representation of the County Committee at this conference, and that it might result in some compromise candidate."

"Oh, you did," suggested a voice in the rear of the hall, which evoked a roar of laughter.

"We have a bare majority of the committee here to-night, and the vote for Mr. O'Brien will be a minority of the committee. I admit that if we had a few men like O'Brien south of Twenty-third-street this city might be made Republican. I have no opposition to him personally, therefore, but I do hope that both he and Mr. Cooper will be magnanimous enough to step aside and allow us to select some man for Chairman of the County Committee on whom we can all agree. I shall vote for Mr. Cooper."

Emigration Commissioner Stephenson, of the Twenty-second District, was the next to give his reasons for voting against O'Brien. The 23,000 Republicans enrolled under the new organization, he said, did not represent 33 per cent. of the Republican vote of the city. "I know that the feeling of a large element of the party toward O'Brien is like that of men who are following a poor dog in the street and crying 'Mad dog!' The dog isn't mad, but the men are, and they will kill the dog. I can't remove the prejudices of these men and make them see Mr. O'Brien as I see him, and I honestly believe that if we elect him Chairman of the County Committe we shall be defeated at the polls. Many men have voted for Mr. O'Brien to-night who have told me that they wished he was out of the way. Many of them would have been ingrates if they had not supported him. Mr. Cooper was not my candidate at the Everett House. I wanted an old war horse, and I nominated John D. Lawson. I wish that both Mr. Cooper and Mr. O'Brien would withdraw, but as it is I shall vote for Cooper."

Mr. Tuttle, of the Twenty-third District, said that the elections of the last four years had shown that there was a great revulsion against boss rule, and he believed that the success of O'Brien in the County Committee would drive many Republican votes from the candidate for the Presidency. He asked to be excused from voting altogether.

This closed the vote, and the result was announced from the Chair. Of 138 votes, Mr. O'Brien had received 119, Marvelle W. Cooper 14, William Dowd 2, and George B. Deane 2. The announcement was greeted with a prolonged cheer, and the stamping of feet and clapping of hands.

When something like order had been restored Col. Spencer moved that John J. O'Brien be declared the candidate of the meeting for permanent Chairman of the County Committee. This motion resulted in another long discussion, which threatened at one time to result in trouble. J. L. N. Hunt insisted that the language of the call was so indefinite that many persons receiving it would not understand that a conference of the full County Committee was intended, and that 119 votes cast at the meeting could not be regarded as the sense of the County Committee. Henry C. Perley also protested against declaring O'Brien the candidate, when 154 delegates were either absent or had not voted for him. Mr. Stevenson saw no impropriety in the motion, but said that if it was proposed to bind him to vote for O'Brien he should leave, and at once put on his hat and coat and departed, followed by about 20 others.

Frederick W. Whitridge then stepped to the front and aroused a volcano. "O'Brien," he said, "does not command the confidence of a majority of the Republican voters of the city."

Col. Spencer—I deny that.

Mr. Whitridge—I will go further, and say that this want of confidence is justifiable. Mr. O'Brien represents the class of Republicans who are not regarded as respectable—"

A dozen men jumped to their feet at this remark and shook their fists at the speaker. "Put him out! Sit down! Out with him!" came from all quarters of the crowded hall.

"Who are you," shouted Col. Spencer, "that you come here to insult the friends of Mr. O'Brien!"

"Take your hands out of your pockets when you are speaking to gentlemen," shouted a man from the rear.

It was several minutes before Mr. Mason could restore order, and then Mr. Whitridge explained that he meant to say they were not considered respectable by the opponents of O'Brien. He thought that under the circumstances it was bad policy to nominate O'Brien, and worse policy to elect him.

"Oh, get out of here," screamed a voice as Mr. Whitridge sat down, and he took the advice very soon and disappeared.

Charles P. Miller gained the floor, and announced that he should remain until the vote was taken, but he should not consider himself bound to support Mr. O'Brien in the County Committee. "I don't suppose," he said, "I can have any influence here—"

A Voice—You can bet you can't.

"But," continued Mr. Miller, "I want to say that I believe it will be a great mistake to nominate Mr. O'Brien for Chairman of the County Committee. If you read the newspapers you know that he will not have the support of a single decent journal in this city. On every occasion when the Republican Party has had a chance to express its opinion of Mr. O'Brien it has snubbed him. By making him our leader now we defy the great body of voters upon whom we must rely for victory in the Presidential campaign."

This address was greeted with derisive shouts of laughter and hisses, in the midst of which Mr. Miller sat down.

Leonard Hazeltine entered a protest against the adoption of the resolution, and left the hall. The resolution was finally put and carried, a very small minority voting no in a very feeble voice. The caucus, after passing a resolution requesting Mr. Mason to nominate O'Brien in the County Committee, adjourned, and Mr. O'Brien was surrounded by his friends, who congratulated him on his victory over the "kid-glove element" of the party.

### ESCAPING BY FEIGNING DEATH.

MORGANTON, N. C., March 6.—Lucky Joe Wilson, the chief of a band of horse-thieves and outlaws, escaped from the jail of Wataugn County to-day by a sharp ruse. Wilson was sentenced to the State prison for 10 years for his outlawry. He took an appeal and was awaiting a decision of the Supreme Court in his case. For some weeks he has pretended to be ill. Last night he feigned death, was laid out by the prison officials, and prepared for burial. The coffin was ordered and all other preparations made for his burial. The body was placed in an outbuilding, where it was viewed by many of the prisoners and officers of the jail. The eyes were wide open and seemingly glazed in death. Blood had spurted from the mouth and ran down on the bed covering. A minister was sent for to preach the funeral of the notorious robber. The body was left alone until the time for burial. When everything became quiet about the prison Wilson suddenly resurrected himself, sprang up and dashed out of the room, and made his escape before any one was aware of what had occurred. He dashed down the mountain and fled toward Tennessee. The discoverers of the ruse played upon them by Wilson were so paralyzed that they permitted the prisoner to get two hours' start of them before they followed him. It is hardly probable that he will be captured.

### A YOUNG WIFE DESERTED.

CHICAGO, March 6.—Charles H. Bosworth, Superintendent of Mails in the St. Paul Post Office, disappeared Saturday evening. At the same time Belle Esterbrook, a hotel waitress, with whom, it is said, Bosworth has been very intimate, also disappeared, alleging that her sick mother required her presence in Illinois. Bosworth has been a member of the Minnesota Legislature and was very popular about town. Several years ago he married a German servant in a Red Wing hotel, who procured a divorce from him in Chicago on account of his relations with Belle Esterbrook, at the time employed in the Briggs House. He was in the mail service for a time at Chicago, and came to St. Paul in the Summer of 1882. The Esterbrook woman followed and obtained a position in the hotel at which he boarded. His relations with her became the subject of much talk. Jan. 14 he went to Chicago and married Miss Lotta Starles, who lived at No. 655 Walnut-street. They returned to St. Paul immediately. Since the marriage it is alleged that Belle Esterbrook made him promise to desert his wife for her. An examination of his Post Office accounts is now being made. Bosworth's bride of six weeks is visiting her people at No. 655 Walnut-street. She is a handsome woman and she keenly feels the situation in which she is placed.

### THE GROWTH OF FIFTY YEARS.

TORONTO, Ontario, March 6.—To-day being the fiftieth anniversary of the incorporation of the city, church bells were rung from 11 to 12 o'clock, and at noon a salute of 50 guns was fired by the Toronto Field Battery. This afternoon the new Free Library was formally opened by the Lieutenant-Governor, and to-night the Mayor held a reception in the City Hall. Two important points showing the growth of the city may be mentioned. In 1834 the city assessment was $934,000, and in 1884 $65,222,950. In 1834 the population was 9,200, and in 1884 95,000.

### A FATAL BOILER EXPLOSION.

LAWRENCE, Mass., March 6.—The boiler in J. T. Trees's dyeing establishment exploded this forenoon, killing John Trees, Jr., the engineer, and fatally injuring William Moreland and Michael Cronin, two employés. So great was the force of the explosion that the three buildings were shattered into splinters. Pieces of the boiler and débris were thrown 400 feet, crashing through roofs of dwellings, but fortunately injured no one. Cronin has since died.

### MURDERED AT A PRIMARY ELECTION.

SHREVEPORT, La., March 6.—Wash Wilson shot and killed a man named Taylor at Rocky Mount, Bossier Parish, Tuesday evening during a Democratic primary election. Wilson says that he acted in self defense.

### KILLED BY A FALL.

PITTSBURG, March 6.—Jury Commissioner Andrew Moreland slipped on an iron grating in Diamond-street, in this city, this morning, and, striking his head against the curbstone, was instantly killed.

## H. B. PAYNE FOR PRESIDENT

### THE OHIO MACHINE HARD AT WORK IN HIS INTEREST.

THE DIPLOMATIC ANSWER WHICH THE SENATOR-ELECT GIVES HIS FRIENDS WHEN ASKED ABOUT HIS CANDIDACY.

CLEVELAND, Ohio, March 6.—The full force of the Democratic Party machine in Ohio is at work in the endeavor to make Henry B. Payne the next Democratic Presidential nominee. The party management is in the hands of avowed and outspoken Payne men, and their efforts are supplemented by a great many who, although not Payne men at heart, would like to see him head the fight this year in order that all possible resources might be opened for the election of the State, Congressional, and local tickets. Mr. Payne is personally doing nothing, and on being questioned by newspaper men and private friends he has but one answer—that he is not a candidate, and does not desire to become one. There is safety as well as diplomacy in this attitude. It affords a safe refuge in case of failure, and at the same time adds to Mr. Payne's real strength among the great Democratic masses that are not privy to the efforts that are being quietly, but vigorously, made in his behalf.

There will be, at an early date, a formal and persistent demand that the Senator-elect shall allow the use of his name. The point has been already made by double-leaded emphasis in the Cincinnati *Enquirer*, that in accepting the Senatorship Mr. Payne knew of the extra demand upon him that it would inevitably involve, and that in this acceptance he had placed himself in the hands of his party and was estopped from retreat. All this preparation is undoubtedly a part of the programme, and if the Ohio Democrats place Mr. Payne's name before the National Convention there will be no injunction against such action issued from Cleveland. "If Mr. Payne finds within himself strength for six years of the Senate," says one of his friends, "there need be no fear of his not fulfilling four years of the White House." All the movements within the Democratic Party of the State are being made in accordance with this notion. There does not seem to be an idea extant anywhere that any other programme than that involving the presentation of Mr. Payne to the convention is to be thought of. And every mention that one hears of Senator Sherman as a candidate on the Republican side is followed by the declaration that in such a case Mr. Payne is the only Democrat who could stand up for a moment against him.

There are echoes of a Blaine movement all through the air in this part of the State. There may as yet be no organized effort, but the material for such effort is being put in shape. There are some who believe that the selection of Cleveland as the place for the coming Republican State Convention is part of a Blaine movement headed by ex-Gov. Foster. The idea put forth is that Cleveland stands in the centre of the Reserve, where Blaine is popular in his own right, and is also regarded as in some sense the political bier of Garfield, and that this sentiment will largely enter into the action of the State Convention.

### THE THIRTY-THIRD DISTRICT.

UNABLE TO AGREE UPON REPRESENTATION IN THE CONVENTION.

BUFFALO, N. Y., March 6.—The Republican conference of the Assembly Committees of the new Thirty-Third Congressional District to determine representation in the Congressional Convention, was in session in this city to-day. The new Congressional district includes Niagara County and the Fourth and Fifth Assembly Districts of Erie County. Each Assembly district was represented by three committeemen, so that Niagara County had six votes and the Erie districts six votes in the conference. The discussion began by an Erie committeeman moving that the Oneida-Lewis plan of representation be adopted, which provides for one delegate from each ward and town and one additional delegate for every 200 Republican votes cast in 1880, or parts thereof exceeding 100 votes. As the Erie part of the district has most towns and most votes this plan would give Erie a greater number of delegates than Niagara. A Niagara committeeman, therefore, moved as an amendment that each Assembly district have equal representation. This was lost by a tie vote of 6 to 6, and the Erie committeeman's motion was also lost by a tie. The discussion of the question took a very wide range, and many other propositions for settlement were made and rejected.

The Erie men offered to base representation on the Republican vote by election precincts, on the vote by towns, on the towns themselves, or to agree to any other entirely equitable basis which would give an Erie Republican as much voice in the convention as a Niagara Republican. The Niagara men replied with the single proposition that each Assembly district should have equal representation without regard to votes, and they would consent to nothing else. It was claimed by Niagara that wherever two or more counties were coupled together in a Congressional or Senatorial district it had always been the custom to give each county the same representation without regard to size. Niagara had been yoked with Genesee and Wyoming, and, being larger, had asked greater representation, but had never got it. Her representatives could not see, therefore, why they should yield to the portion of Erie with which they are now yoked what they had never got for themselves under similar circumstances. The Erie men replied that they only asked for justice and equality, and the fact that injustice had been suffered by Niagara was no reason for her inflicting it on Erie. The Erie men then offered to refer the whole matter to the State Committee, but the Niagara men declined the proposition. Finally an adjournment was taken for another week, when the conference will meet in Lockport.

### WILLING TO SWALLOW ARTHUR.

SCRANTON, Penn., March 6.—A conference of Luzerne and Lackawanna Republicans was held here to-day to decide a plan for electing delegates from the Twelfth Congressional District to the National Convention. The meeting was attended by Chairman Chase, of Luzerne, who is Revenue Collector for the district; Postmaster Shiffer, of Pittston; ex-Senator Hubbard B. Payne, of Kingston; Prothonotary Norris, of Wilkesbarre; Chairman Brooks, of Lackawanna; O. E. Vaughn, J. W. Seamans, and D. N. Green. The Lackawanna delegates strongly favored a popular convention, but it was opposed by Senator Payne and Chairman Chase, of Luzerne, on the grounds that it would be cumbersome and that there was no demand for it among their constituents. It was finally decided that the portion of the district lying in Luzerne should select one delegate in a manner to be announced by its own committee; that Lackawanna should do likewise, and that the delegates from the district to the State Convention should meet in Wilkesbarre on April 2 to ratify this choice, give the national delegates credentials, and name a Presidential Elector. Chairman Brooks told a reporter after the meeting that he was a Blaine man, but he could swallow Arthur very easily. This sentiment is in accordance with the action of the committee, which is looked upon as favorable to the Administration.

### OHIO PROHIBITIONISTS.

COLUMBUS, Ohio, March 6.—The Prohibition State Convention assembled here this morning, with a moderate attendance, to appoint 34 delegates to the National Convention at Pittsburg on May 21. J. W. Sharp was made Chairman and L. B. Logan Secretary. Speeches were made denouncing the Scott law and all sumptuary measures except prohibition. The usual committees were appointed. At the afternoon session delegates to the National Convention at Pittsburg on May 21 were selected, one for each district, and the following at large: G. T. Stewart, J. A. O'Dell, George P. Burwell, Ariel Cox, N. S. Caswell, J. S. Mouser, Thomas Evans, Jr., Miss Mattie McClelland Brown, Mother Stewart, F. Schumacher, F. C. Payne, J. W. Roseborough, and J. M. Myers. The delegation was instructed to use all honorable means to secure the nomination of G. T. Stewart, of Ohio, for President. A systematic plan for the organization of the State by counties was adopted.

### NOMINATED BY REPUBLICANS.

BANGOR, Me., March 6.—Judge Samuel F. Humphreys was to-night nominated as candidate for Mayor by the Republicans. He is in the same set of law offices as that of ex-Chief-Justice Appleton, and is considered a strong candidate. Ex-United States Senator Hannibal Hamlin made a speech especially defending the protective tariff in regard to lumber interests in Maine, and said that it was not necessary for a man with the character of Judge Humphreys to make pledges to the prohibitionist or any other interest.

### IN FAVOR OF RANDALL.

WILKESBARRE, Penn., March 6.—The *Union-Leader*, ex-Chairman Bogert's paper, and the leading Democratic daily in North-eastern Pennsylvania, to-night, in a leading editorial, nominates Randall as Pennsylvania's choice for the Presidency. It says no Democrat in the

# The New-York Times.

VOL. XXXIII.....NO. 10,154. NEW-YORK, FRIDAY, MARCH 21, 1884. PRICE TWO CENTS.

## THE BONDED WHISKY TAX

### *ANOTHER SUBJECT OF DEMOCRATIC DISSENSION.*

ONLY ONE REPUBLICAN ADVOCATES THE BILL—RANDALL'S TACTICS—FRIENDS OF THE BILL CLAIMING TOO MUCH.

WASHINGTON, March 20.—It is the policy of those who are opposed to the Bonded Whisky bill, as announced by Mr. Randall to-day, to interpose no further obstacle to its consideration, because, now that it has the right of way, the interests of the public business require that it should be allowed to come to a decisive vote as soon as possible. For this reason it was taken up this afternoon and the discussion upon the merits of the proposition was resumed, although two appropriation bills are waiting to be acted upon by the House. Representative Willis, whose district owns the greater part of the bonded whisky involved in the passage of the bill, made the most of the fact that the relief asked for was recommended by Secretary Folger, the Commissioner of Internal Revenue, and the Committee on Ways and Means, both in this Congress and in the last, but Mr. Randall interjected a few remarks that destroyed the intended effect of Mr. Willis's statement. Mr. Randall recalled the fact that a majority of the Committee on Ways and Means were not in favor of the bill, but had merely reported it for consideration as a matter of large importance and had reserved to themselves the right to oppose it on the floor. With reference to the favorable report to the last Congress Mr. Randall said that he, for one, had acted upon the advice of Commissioner Raum, but some things had happened since then to shake his confidence in Gen. Raum. Mr. Willis claimed that very little of the whisky that would be affected by the bill was owned by distillers, but by banks, that had lent money upon it, and men and women who had put their money in it as a safe investment. There had been an enormous shrinkage in value for two or three years, including $4,000,000 last year, and great distress and ruin would follow if the Government insisted on collecting the tax when it was due. He was opposed to removing the tax on whisky; but the main opposition to the bill came from the men who wanted whisky to be free of tax, and if the friends of the bill would yield to them it would pass with railroad speed. Strong objections to the proposition were made by Mr. Blount and Mr. Herbert, both members of the Committee on Ways and Means, and by Mr. Reese. Mr. Blount held that the proposition would only aggravate the evil complained of by the distillers, for they would go on over-producing as they had done year after year. Mr. Cox, of New-York, read a long speech in favor of a reduction of tariff taxation. It was generally listened to with interest, but the leaders of tariff reform were displeased that he should have thus prematurely begun the tariff discussion. Mr. Hiscock inquired whether this speech was to be taken as warranting further debate on the tariff bill while the whisky bill is pending. No reply was given, and Mr. Hiscock's remark is understood to be a notice that some of the Republicans will at once make tariff speeches.

Mr. Belford is thus far the only Republican who has advocated the Whisky bill. Having secured half an hour, he made one of his characteristic speeches about reducing the surplus in the Treasury by paying off the interest-bearing debt with the $140,000,000 of idle money which Secretary Folger was hoarding in the Treasury. He attacked the Democrats for what he called their "cheese-paring and peanutish policy" of cutting down the naval appropriations $8,000,000 and the Post Office Appropriation bill $4,000,000, and then insisting upon forcing the collection of $70,000,000 on whisky, to be hoarded in the Treasury. He wanted that money to go into the hands of the laboring classes. He wanted to help supply them with bread and butter. A voice on the Republican side added, "And whisky."

It is hoped by the friends of the bill that the debate will end in one more day, but the prospect is not very good, as many members of this talkative Congress want to speak on the subject. To-morrow is private bill day, and the whisky measure will be likely to go over until Saturday.

### A TARIFF CANVASS IN THE HOUSE.

The *Star* says to-night: "A committee of tariff reformers has been appointed to make a canvass of the House and ascertain the status of the Morrison bill. They made a preliminary canvass and found that the bill wanted the requisite number of supporters to secure its passage. They then held a consultation to see what modifications could be made, not materially affecting the principle of the bill, that would secure the few additional votes necessary to its passage. It was found that a few modifications in the clauses affecting the local interests in Pennsylvania, New-Jersey, and Ohio would make the bill acceptable to a sufficient number of those who oppose it to give it a majority. The committee, as a result of their canvass and conference, have decided to recommend these modifications, and have made out a list of the members who may be depended upon to support it. According to this list, the bill, with the proposed modifications, will have an assured majority of nine over the combined forces of the Republicans and Mr. Randall's followers. If this estimate proves correct, the passage of the bill will be assured, but a split will not be averted. The compromise upon this basis will be the subject of discussion in the caucus which it is proposed to call, and many not named in the list are expected to come over to the majority. But all will not come over. It is asserted that Randall and 10 or 12 of his followers refuse to be conciliated upon any but the basis of protection. These, it is understood, will vote with the Republicans, and the split will be violent and permanent. This result is looked upon as inevitable, and there is to-day more excitement over the tariff agitation than has been apparent since the question was first raised."

### A CHEESE-PARING POLICY.

The Indian Appropriation bill, as reported by the Committee on Appropriations of the House of Representatives, sets apart for the Indian Department $5,347,658 10 for use during the fiscal year ending June 30, 1885. The policy of slashing right and left into the estimates of the department has apparently been followed by the committee as in the case of the Postal bill, for the sum named in the bill is $3,119,156 81 less than the amount estimated as necessary by the department, and $13,002 81 less than the appropriation for the current year. For current and contingent expenses, the committee allows $198,900, when $313,300 was asked. The estimate of $3,681,828 for fulfilling treaties with and support of Indian tribes is cut down to $2,551,763, which is nearly $120,000 less than in 1884. For the support of schools $1,660,360 was asked, and $785,000 80 is allowed, which is an increase of nearly $135,000 over the current year. Among the items of the bill are $38,000 for salaries of 60 Indian Agents; $25,000 for interpreters; $17,500 for salaries and expenses of three Inspectors, and $1,117,000 for "miscellaneous support." The largest sum appropriated for a single tribe is $107,000 for the Crows, while the Sioux of different tribes are allowed $1,646,300. The tribe given the smallest appropriation is the Pottawatomies, of Huron, who are allowed $4,000. Five thousand dollars is appropriated for the detection and prosecution of persons furnishing liquor to the Indians, and the War Department is prohibited from introducing liquor into Indian reservations under any circumstances. The last paragraph of the bill provides that every Agent shall embody in his annual report a census of the Indians under his charge.

### A LIVERY STABLE KEEPER'S REVENGE.

Three agents of the Pension Office went to Knoxville, Tenn., a short time ago on business for the office. According to a report which has reached this city, the agents engaged a carriage at the livery establishment kept by a son of Congressman Houk, and when the bill was presented they declined to pay it on the ground that Mr. Houk had charged them an exorbitant price. Learning that one of the agents had expressed a preference for Mr. Blaine for the Presidential nomination, and that another had leanings toward Gen. Logan, the livery keeper wrote to the Secretary of the Interior, Mr. Teller, that agents in the employment of his department were engaged in working up Blaine and Logan sentiments in Tennessee. The Congressman's son named the two agents whose political preferences he had discovered, and it is stated that these gentlemen are now on their way back to Washington, in response to a summons from Mr. Teller, who is understood to be earnestly in favor of the renomination of Mr. Arthur.

### MR. RANDALL IN DEMAND.

Representative Randall has been invited by the Washington Society of the University of Virginia to deliver the principal address at the June Commencement of that institution, and he will go there if his duties in Congress will permit. A similar invitation has been given to Mr. Randall by the Washington and Lee University. Some of Mr. Randall's friends argue from this, that the South is disposed to take kindly to the ideas of this anti-tariff reform leader, and that he must be viewed with favor in the Old Dominion.

Postmaster Andrew S. Hunter, of Chicopee, Mass., died yesterday afternoon of pneumonia. He had been in Chicopee for nearly 20 years. He served all through the war in the First Massachusetts Cavalry Volunteers. He was in prison in Andersonville for a year in 1864.

### *A BAD RAILROAD ACCIDENT.*

AN ENGINEER AND FIREMAN KILLED AND SEVERAL PERSONS WOUNDED.

PITTSBURG, March 20.—This morning, shortly before daylight, the Chicago limited express met with an accident near Salem, Ohio, by which two persons lost their lives and nine others, six of them passengers, were injured. The train was running at the rate of 40 miles an hour, and when Franklin Hill was reached the engine left the tracks and went down an embankment 30 feet. The smoker and baggage car followed, but the rest of the train remained at a standstill. Almost immediately the boiler of the engine exploded, and James Richards, the engineer, and Charles Rhodes, the fireman, were hurled a distance of 400 yards and killed instantly. The wrecked cars took fire, but were extinguished without any difficulty. As soon as those in the other cars had recovered from the shock the search for the dead and wounded among the ruins was commenced. The bodies of Richards and Rhodes were found 400 yards away terribly mangled. The injured were: Mr. A. Rich, Chicago, badly bruised and cut on the head; Mrs. Dean, Chicago, right arm bruised; Mrs. Roch, also of Chicago, muscle of right arm cut; Mr. Newcombe, of Atchison, Kan., right foot badly bruised; E. G. Northam, of Philadelphia, slight wound on foot and face scratched; Fred Mather, also of Philadelphia, slightly bruised in the face; Charles Basiel, baggage-master, cut on the head; Conductor William Landis, brakeman, body bruised and several severe contusions on face; colored porter Pullman sleeper, name unknown, badly bruised and cut. Word was immediately sent to this city, and a train with physicians was quickly dispatched to the scene of the disaster. The train arrived at 11 o'clock, and the passengers were transferred to it and brought to this city, arriving here about 2:30 o'clock.

William Johnston, one of the passengers, said that the wreck was caused by the boiler exploding while the train was going at a very high rate of speed. It was a point known as Wells Junction, two miles east of Salem, Ohio. The engine was reduced to small sections of cast-iron, which were scattered for many hundred yards from the scene. Engineer Richards was blown quite a distance in the air, and while descending his body alighted on the net-work of telegraph wires suspended at the side of the track, where it hung for a few seconds, only to fall a bruised and mangled mass of human flesh by the side of the track. The fireman was found at the base of the hill bruised and mangled. Immediately after the boiler exploded the smoker and one sleeper left the rails, and, together with all that remained of the engine, rolled down the embankment at the side of the track, a distance of about 25 feet. The other four cars comprising the train remained on the track, but all were more or less damaged, the last car, which was a sleeper, being derailed and torn from its trucks by the shock.

Mr. Rich, of Chicago, who was among the injured, stated that at the time of the accident he was sleeping in the first sleeper. The first intimation of danger that he had was when he heard a loud report and found himself thrown out on the floor of the car. He then felt the car turning over and rolling, he could not imagine where, and when it finally stopped at the foot of the hill he got on his feet, and it was only after helping the injured out of the car, from some portions of which an exit had to be made through the windows, that he found himself to be injured.

### *THE BRIBERY IN CANADA.*

A CAUTIOUS NEWSPAPER EDITOR WHO TALKED TOO MUCH.

TORONTO, Ontario, March 20.—The Parliamentary committee continued its investigation into the charges of conspiracy to bribe members of the Provincial Legislature to vote against the Government to-day. The most important evidence was that of Mr. McKim, who received $1,000 from the accused, Wilkinson. He related in detail interviews with Mr. Bunting, editor of the *Mail*, Wilkinson, and Kirkland, showing that they were all three working in unison and cognizant of what was going on. Although Bunting refused to put his offer in writing, alleging as a reason his position on the *Mail* and in the Conservative Party, he went with the witness to the office of the defendant Meek, who is the solicitor and financial agent of the Conservative Party. Mr. Bunting at a subsequent interview, the witness said, told him he had been to Ottawa and had now power to defeat the Mowat Government, and that the witness would get all he had been promised. The witness told him about what Kirkland had promised him and Bunting told him to get all I could from the Yankee and he would help him to do so. He told witness that there would be no dissolution in case Mr. Mowat was defeated.

An application was made to Judge Galt to-day for bail for the prisoners Wilkinson and Kirkland, who filed affidavits denying in toto any attempt to bribe members. The application was opposed by the Crown, but Judge Galt made an order for their admission to bail in $8,000 each. They were accordingly admitted to bail to-day. The case will come up in the police court to-morrow.

### *A BOY POISONS HIS FAMILY.*

CAPE MAY COURT-HOUSE, N. J., March 20.—Gilbert Grace, the 18-year-old son of Mr. George Grace, was to-day arrested and put in jail on a charge of having poisoned his father, mother, and four brothers and sisters with ratsbane last Monday. The youngest child, an infant aged 9 months, is still at death's door as the result of her brother's murderous rage. It is now almost certain that the reason for the youth's fiendish act was a desire for revenge. Gilbert had been attentive for some time to a young woman, said to be named Maria Endicott, and had repeatedly defied his father's wishes in persisting in this intimacy. Last Sunday Mr. Grace positively refused to allow the affair to go on any longer, and on Monday Gilbert bought the ratsbane of the same druggist who afterward attended the family in their sickness. That evening he came near being left alone in the world. The warrant charges him with placing poison in the water or coffee of which the entire family, with the exception of his little sister, Bertha, partook, "with intent to kill them."

### *THE EXPORTATION OF WHISKY.*

CHICAGO, March 20.—The Executive Committee of the Western Export Association met to-day at the Grand Pacific Hotel, pursuant to a call of the President, to devise a ways and means for continuing the pool. The expenses of the pool are heavy, both on account of the large amount of spirits which has to be warehoused, owing to the excessive over-production, and the bonus paid to distillers who ship directly to Europe. To ease the market by exporting spirits to Europe, the pool enables distillers to sell abroad for the same price as at home by allowing them a bonus which is equivalent to the freight. To do this money is needed, and hence the meeting to-day. The committee voted funds sufficient to carry on the pool for April. The only jar came from Mr. Iler, of Omaha, who ships to California and wanted that market put on the same plane with Europe. The committee, however, would not agree to this.

### *A WELSH FESTIVAL.*

SCRANTON, March 20.—The Welsh people of this section held an Eisteddfod, or literary and musical festival, here to-day, which was largely attended. There were three sessions, at which competitions in solo singing and declamations took place, but the event of the gathering was a choral contest between six choirs of 100 voices each, for a prize of $100, in rendering Handel's "Then round about the starry throne." The competing choirs were the Wilkesbarre, Bellevue, Athens, Plymouth; Hyde Park, and Taylorville Choral Unions. Their singing was superb. The prize was awarded for general excellence to the Plymouth Choral Union. H. M. Edwards, of Hyde Park, was conductor of the exercises; Prof. E. Elmer Jones, of Utica, N. Y., adjudicator of music, and the Rev. J. G. Lewis, of Wilkesbarre, adjudicator of declamations.

### *A FATAL SHOOTING AFFRAY.*

MARTIN'S FERRY, Ohio, March 20.—A shooting affray occurred in Portland, seven miles north of this place, late last night. For a month or two past there has been bad blood between Charlie Pope and a man named Cochran. A disturbance took place about two weeks ago, but the matter died out and no one thought of a renewal of hostilities. Last night, however, Pope, who was drinking heavily, went to Cochran's house and began an assault with stones. Cochran being enraged by the proceeding of his enemy, appeared at the door in a few minutes with a revolver and fired several shots at Pope, two passing through his body inflicting fatal wounds.

### *GRAIN ELEVATOR CHARGES.*

BUFFALO, N. Y., March 20.—The canal boatmen here are greatly interested in the bill pending in Albany to reduce grain elevator charges. They have sent a man to Albany to represent them, and are co-operating with boatmen's associations elsewhere to secure votes for the bill. They feel especially ugly toward Senator Titus, who opposed and secured the defeat of the bill last year, and who is opposed to it now.

## OSMAN AND THE TRIBES

### *A COUNCIL OF WAR TO BE HELD AT SINKAT.*

THE REBEL CHIEF PREPARING FOR FRESH HOSTILITIES—GEN. GORDON'S MISSION A FAILURE—HIS PERILOUS POSITION.

SUAKIN, March 20.—Spies report that Osman Digna, with a few followers, has fled to the interior. His flight is attributed to the reward which was offered for his capture. The slaves are deserting him and fleeing to Suakin.

Admiral Hewitt has withdrawn his proclamation offering £1,000 for Osman Digna's head.

LONDON, March 20.—The dispatches received from the newspaper correspondents at Suakin are in serious conflict with one another. It is now reported that Osman Digna has summoned the sheiks of the tribes to a meeting at Sinkat to-morrow in order to arrange for a renewal of active warlike operations.

Col. Stewart, with the Gordon Highlanders and mounted infantry, has reconnoitred to a point one mile beyond Handoub, which is 20 miles from Suakin, on the road from Suakin to Berber. Sheikh Monisa, at the head of the Bisharis, numbering 8,000 men, is threatening Shendy. It is feared that the post-boat which left Berber yesterday to try to penetrate to Khartoum will be stopped at Shendy.

The French Consul at Cairo has received a dispatch from the French Consul at Khartoum saying that on March 4 Gen. Gordon held a conference with the Consuls of Austria, Greece, and France, when he declared that he would be unable to defend the town against the tribes advancing from the south, north, and west. In the meantime he committed the government of the town to three native Notables and Sheik Obeidullah.

It is stated in Cairo that Abd-el-Kader Pasha, Minister of War, will be sent to the rescue of Gen. Gordon.

The English troops going to Assouan have been ordered to Korosko, where the Arabs are reported to be restless.

DUBLIN, March 20.—The *United Ireland*, of which Mr. William O'Brien, member of Parliament, is editor, denounces the offering of a reward for Osman Digna's head, and says: "Irish people pray that Osman may escape British assassination and be spared to lead his gallant spearmen to victory."

CAIRO, March 20.—El Mahdi is organizing an artillery corps composed of Egyptian deserters. When the corps is completed he will set out on the march to Berber. He has with him 12 European and 60 Egyptian officers of Hicks Pasha's army.

LONDON, March 21.—Gen. Graham telegraphs from Suakin that three sheiks have come in from Handouk. Several slaves belonging to Osman Digna have arrived at Suakin.

The tribes have cut off retreat from Khartoum. They have environed the town except where it is protected by the river. Three tribes are advancing to capture the town.

### THE GERMAN ANTI-SOCIALIST LAW.

BISMARCK ASKS THE REICHSTAG TO EXTEND IT FOR TWO YEARS.

BERLIN, March 20.—In the debate on the Anti-Socialist law in the Reichstag to-day, Herren Hasenclever and Bebel protested against the identification of Anarchists with Socialists. They said that the law had not injured the Socialists; that its application only exasperated them. Dr. Marquardsen, in the name of the National Liberals, declared in favor of the bill. Herr von Puttkamer, Prussian Minister of the Interior, said he hoped that the social reform already begun would bring the masses to their senses; that the abrogation of the law was now less than ever advisable, as it protected Germany against the dangerous excesses with which most countries were afflicted. Referring to the aims of the Socialists as declared by Herren Liebknecht, Volmar, and Bebel, he said: "Who dares deny that there is danger or affirm that strong measures are unnecessary? The views which Herr Bebel expresses here are brutally taught elsewhere. Revolution is the final object. A weapon is demanded for a short time to defeat socialism, and must be furnished." Dr. Windthorst moved that the bill be referred to a committee. He hoped that the first result of the restored health of Prince Bismarck would be the complete return of Prussia to her former Christian manner of thought.

Prince Bismarck declared that the majority's want of confidence compelled the Government to ask that the law be prolonged for two years, not only as a regressive measure, but as a positive measure for the benefit of the working men, as proposed in the imperial message of 1881, to cure social evils. It was impossible to abandon the preventive measures. The Progressist press promoted the objects of the Socialistic press in rendering the aims of the Government odious by exciting the working men against the new social policy. The Reichstag then adjourned.

### THE EXPECTED CRISIS IN ENGLAND.

LONDON, March 20.—The *Daily News*, in an article discussing the possibility of a dissolution of Parliament and urging the Liberals to be ready to take action at a moment's notice, says: "Never since the days of Bolingbroke has England seen a great party so unscrupulous and unpatriotic as the Opposition, which takes every advantage of the difficulties of the Government and allies itself with any cause or party which promises to embarrass the Cabinet. Sir Stafford Northcote is not the originator of these tactics, but he winks at them."

Mr. Parnell is preparing for the anticipated dissolution of Parliament. He has already selected 60 parliamentary candidates. His party will contest 90 seats and expects to be able to carry 75.

### THE FRENCH CAMPAIGN IN TONQUIN

PARIS, March 20.—After the capture of Hung-Hoa the French will fix the western frontier of Tonquin at Tuan-Kwan, which is now in possession of the Black Flags. The Black Flags will be allowed to retain all the towns from Tuan-Kwan to Lao-Kai, on condition that they will guarantee the free navigation of the Upper Song-Koi. The northern frontier of Tonquin will extend from Phulang-huong to Tuan-Kwan by way of Phu-binh and Phu-doan-hong.

It has been decided that the French campaign in Tonquin will terminate with the capture of Hung-Hoa.

### CURRENT FOREIGN TOPICS.

ROME, March 20.—The Italian Ministry have resigned, owing to the smallness of the majority by which Signor Coppino was elected President of the Chamber of Deputies. Fifty-four blank ballots were cast.

DUBLIN, March 20.—The Land Commissioners have reduced the rental of the Limerick property of the Marquis of Lansdowne, Governor-General of Canada, from £2,400 to £1,800.

LONDON, March 20.—The Maori King will sail from Auckland for England, by way of San Francisco, on April 1.

The appointment of Crown Prince Gustaf as Viceroy of Norway is only during the temporary absence of the King.

A bill has been introduced in the House of Commons providing for the restriction of the sale of patented medicines until they have been officially analyzed and pronounced not poisonous.

The Marquis of Lorne has received from Canada half a million white-fish eggs, with which he will try the experiment of stocking English lakes.

Lieut.-Col. F. De Winton, who was military secretary to the Marquis of Lorne while the latter was Governor-General of Canada, has received from the King of the Belgians the appointment of Governor of the International Mission on the Congo River.

An election was held in Cambridgeshire to-day to fill the vacancy in the House of Commons caused by the retirement of Sir Henry Brand, (now Lord Hampden.) Mr. Thornhill, the Conservative candidate, received 3,815 votes, and Mr. Coote, Liberal, 2,912. Sir Henry Brand, the last representative, was elected as a Liberal.

ST. PETERSBURG, March 20.—Twenty-seven Nihilists have been arrested here to-day. Among them are four artillery officers.

The execution of the decree in the government of Poltava, expelling Jews devoid of real property, has been arrested in response to their petition, and an inquiry into the matter has been ordered.

PARIS, March 20.—Much attention has been excited by a letter from Rome which appears in the *Défense*, a clerical newspaper. The writer recounts the charges of the Papacy against Italy. The Pope believes that his independence is threatened, especially since the Court of Cassation rendered its decision that the real property of the Propaganda Fide should be converted into Italian rentes. The letter asserts that the Pope is again considering the advisability of leaving Rome. Malta is mentioned as the place of the Pope's future residence.

Mr. Bacon is represented at the Salon by two sea pieces, scenes off the coast of Normandy. This is the best work he has produced. Mr. Harrison has a moonlight sea piece and a shipwreck; Mr. Sargent, two portraits, and Mr. Donoho, who is represented for the first time at the Salon, a fine landscape.

Mlle. Nevada made her début to-night at the Théâtre des Italiens. The house was crowded, among the spectators being politicians, artists, and the principal American residents. Mr. Morton, the United States Minister, was greeted with cheers when he entered. Mlle. Nevada achieved a brilliant success. She was recalled many times and received a large number of bouquets.

### *A DRUNKEN COUNCILMAN.*

AN EXCITING SCENE IN THE PHILADELPHIA COUNCIL CHAMBER.

PHILADELPHIA, March 20.—There was a disgraceful scene in the Select Council Chamber this afternoon. Select Councilman O'Rourke from the Twenty-fifth Ward, came into the Chamber very drunk, and for a long time disturbed the deliberations of the body, without securing any more serious rebuke than the good-humored badgering of the members. Finally President Smith interrupted O'Rourke sternly and ordered him to sit down. O'Rourke stubbornly stood his ground and declared he had as much right on the floor as any one else. He had a right to speak and proposed to speak, and nobody could stop him. President Smith grew red and white by turns. Mr. Green suggested that the Chamber take a 10-minute recess. "There is no necessity for even a temporary adjournment," declared the President quickly. "I am perfectly able to preserve order. Besides, the gentleman is aware that he is disturbing the Chamber."

"No, I'm not," said O'Rourke, doggedly.

Without noticing the denial the President continued speaking quietly, but emphatically, and looking the refractory member in the face said: "If the gentleman cannot come to order, I shall order his removal from the Chamber." O'Rourke laughed derisively.

"Mr. President, I move that rule 25, declaring that any person acting in an unruly or indecent manner in this chamber shall be removed, be respected," said Mr. Matthews, excitedly springing to his feet. Then followed five minutes of comparative peace. But the discussion of the ordinance limiting the sale of meat by curbstone hucksters was too much for Mr. O'Rourke, and he took the floor again. "I want it adopted," he declared, after an incomprehensible speech. "I want it adopted."

"I move the gentleman sit down," yelled Mr. Hart.

"I'm just as good a man as you or anybody in the chamber," said Mr. O'Rourke.

"I am sorry," began Mr. Monroe, "to be compelled to ask for the enforcement of rule 25."

"Oh! go to hell," roared O'Rourke, "who cares?"

By this time the chamber was in a ferment. Councilmen were standing all over the room, and the excitement was intense. President Smith half rose from his chair. "The door-keeper and clerk will remove the gentleman from the Twenty-fifth Ward from the room," he said quietly. Rapidly crossing the floor Door-keeper Hamilton approached O'Rourke and caught him by the arm. Flinging the door-keeper aside with a blow in the face that made him stagger, O'Rourke sprang forward, yelling: "I won't submit. I leave it to a vote of the chamber whether I'm to be expelled." Then, turning to the President, "Do you mean this?" he asked.

"I mean it," was the answer, adding to the door-keeper, "I demand his removal." Reinforced by Clerk Johnson, the door-keeper caught O'Rourke again, and, with the aid of Messrs. Hart, Matthews, and Greene, and Mr. Hoffman, of the Common Council, they forced O'Rourke out of the aisle and into the centre of the room. O'Rourke struggled furiously. "Let me speak to the President," he entreated, wildly endeavoring to break away. "I appeal, Mr. President, I appeal," but the sentence was drowned in the scene of wild confusion that followed. Raised almost bodily from the floor, O'Rourke was forced, kicking and struggling, across the floor and into the hall-way. Still refractory, he insisted upon returning to the chamber, and it was only when the services of a policeman were suggested that he consented quietly to go away.

### *THE SOUTHERN FLOODS.*

RAILWAY TRAFFIC INTERRUPTED AND MUCH DAMAGE DONE.

NEW-ORLEANS, March 20.—Although the day has been clear and warm, the lower river continues to rise, and is to-day again at the high-water mark in front of the city. A gang of city employes have closed the Flathers crevasse, below the city. The work on the Davis crevasse has been abandoned and a torrent is running through without hindrance which floods the railroad tracks in the rear several feet. The trains on the Texas and Pacific have stopped running this side of Cheneyville, but the trains on the Morgan Road worked their way through to-day. No breaks have occurred so far on the east bank, and the trains of the Valley Road and Illinois Central are running as usual. A slight cave occurred on the Bonnet Carre levee, but the local guards mended the breach at once. The crevasse at Medville Point is being repaired, but the levees in Point Coupé and above are declared in great danger. There was a rise of 5 inches at St. Joseph, in Tensas, to-day, and 7 inches more will put the water over the high-water mark of 1882. The water is already running over the levees at Milliken's Bend, in Madison. Ships' Bayou and Hard Times levees still hold, but are slowly sinking, and will probably be washed away inside of the next 48 hours.

### *FOR ROBBING A POST OFFICE.*

BALTIMORE, Md., March 20.—William Lacey, a son of Major Lacey, of Indiana, was put on trial in the United States District Court on an indictment charging him with having robbed the Post Office at Suitland, Md., on Dec. 30, 1881. The robbery remained a mystery until August, 1883, when Arthur B. Suit, who was with Lacey on the night of the robbery, made the fact known to Postal Inspectors Henderson and Smith. Lacey confessed in the presence of the Inspectors that he was at the Post Office at the time of the robbery, but that Suit was the party who went through the window and procured the stamps, stamped envelopes, and postal cards. The trial will be continued to-morrow.

### *ON ADJOINING SLABS.*

PHILADELPHIA, Penn., March 20.—Archie Morris, colored, 60 years of age, disappeared about Jan. 19, and was not heard of until, by chance, his body was found on Tuesday last on the dissecting-table of a medical school in this city. Investigation disclosed the fact that Morris had died in the Bucks County Almshouse, and, as the body was unclaimed, it was sent to the medical school in accordance with an act of Assembly. The body of Albert Anderson, a friend of Morris's, who died on Jan. 10, was also found on an adjoining slab.

### *ACCIDENT TO A SOUND STEAMER.*

BRIDGEPORT, Conn., March 20.—The steamer Continental, of the New-York and New-Haven Line, broke her shaft in her up trip from New-York last night, and was compelled to anchor near the Bridgeport light, where she remained until 11 o'clock this morning. The steam tug Resolute was sent to her relief, and took her in tow for New-Haven. The passengers remained on board.

### *A CAR COMPANY IN TROUBLE.*

COLUMBUS, Ohio, March 20.—The Gill Car Manufacturing Company made an assignment this evening to George W. Gould, the book-keeper of the company. The assets are estimated at about $400,000 and the liabilities at about $260,000. The company became involved on account of the large quantity of material on hand during the panic of 1873 and has never recovered. An effort will be made to resume business.

### *ACCIDENT TO A PASSENGER COACH.*

SYRACUSE, N. Y., March 20.—A mixed train on the Utica, Ithaca and Elmira Railroad ran off the track near Perryville, Madison County, this morning, causing a passenger coach to roll over three times and land upside down against a tree. Half a dozen persons were injured, but none fatally.

### *ATTEMPTED MURDER AND SUICIDE.*

DAYTON, Ohio, March 20.—E. M. Eberhardt, of Arcanum, who left his wife last Summer, called on her yesterday and asked for a reconciliation. Upon his wife's refusing his request he drew a knife and attempted to kill her, but without success. He then went to the barn and hanged himself.

### *A LADY BURNED TO DEATH.*

KITTANNING, Penn., March 20.—Mrs. Mary J. Dunmire, wife of J. P. Dunmire, Esq., of Plum Creek Township, was burned to death yesterday by her clothing taking fire while standing before a fire in a grate. Mr. Dunmire was badly burned in his endeavors to save his wife.

## IS THIS THE DARK HORSE

### *GEN. SINGLETON NAMED AS THE DEMOCRATIC CANDIDATE.*

BELIEF THAT HE CAN CARRY ILLINOIS FOR HIS PARTY—WHERE HIS SUPPORT IS TO COME FROM.

CHICAGO, March 20.—A *Tribune* special from Quincy says: "The latest political sensation here is a report that Gen. James A. Singleton is a candidate for the Democratic nomination for the Presidency. The General has spent much of his time recently in Washington, has an intimate and extended acquaintance with leaders of the Democratic Party throughout the country, and is credited with the honor of securing the selection of Chicago as the place for holding the National Convention. It is claimed by his friends that with a popular candidate from any locality Illinois will be a doubtful State, and that if Gen. Singleton should get the Democratic nomination he could carry Illinois for the Democracy. It is believed here that the movement in behalf of his nomination will take definite shape at an early day in both Ohio and Indiana, and that it has already been inaugurated in some of the Southern States.

Tom Ochiltree, of Texas, and Hooper, of Mississippi, are known to be very intimate with Gens. Singleton, and are expected to espouse his cause for the national nomination. He has also warm friends in Maryland and Virginia who could be relied upon for support. Gen. Singleton has been a great admirer of McDonald, and regards him as probably foremost in the race for the Presidency. If he enters the canvass he will make it interesting for Mr. Morrison for the Illinois delegation."

### DAVID DAVIS AND LOGAN.

A PROPOSITION TO PLACE THE JUDGE AT THE HEAD OF THE ILLINOIS DELEGATION.

CHICAGO, Ill., March 20.—A *Tribune* special from Springfield says: "It is understood that Senator Cullom will, of course, be selected as delegate at large to the National Republican Convention if he desires it. But the project of new and special interest is to put ex-Vice-President David Davis on for one. Friends of Gen. Logan, it is known, have fully canvassed this scheme, and are satisfied that Judge Davis is so heartily friendly to the Senator that there will be a general push to place him on the delegation. It is known that Logan himself has the utmost confidence in Judge Davis's friendship and interest in his candidacy. It appears that when the suggestion of Judge Davis's name was first made the question arose whether he would not probably be so friendly to Secretary Lincoln as to render it questionable whether he ought to be urged for the place. His attachment to Lincoln is fully conceded, yet men in close relations to him—men whose names are sufficient voucher in this State—give assurance that the Judge's inclination to Logan for the Presidency is so strong that nothing would swerve him. They claim, as an additional reason for putting him on the delegation, that his national reputation and proverbial honor would strengthen the claim of the Illinois delegation as nothing else could.

The gentleman making these statements said: "I am certain of Davis's loyalty to Logan. And now suppose that in the outcome of the convention we should fail to secure the nomination for Logan, as I don't think we can fail, but suppose we did, and that the head of the ticket should be selected from the East. There we stand with a man whom we can urge for the second place, and whose name would prove a tower of strength. I tell you that the name of Judge Davis alone would give us Ohio and Indiana, and probably secure three of the Southern States. To my mind it is the wisest step that has been taken for some time."

### CINCINNATI REPUBLICANS.

SOME VERY FORCIBLE AND TIMELY REMARKS BY JUDGE FORAKER.

CINCINNATI, Ohio, March 20.—The Republican City Convention did a very good day's work, and it is the talk among Republicans to-night that the ticket nominated stands rather more than an even chance of being elected. The nominations were eagerly sought, which indicated faith on the part of candidates that the chances of the party are good. Judge Foraker presided over the convention during a part of the session and made a speech that did good. He characterized the election of Henry B. Payne to the United States Senate as the most absolutely corrupt transaction in American political annals, and on account of that sale and purchase and the disappointment that has been caused by Democratic legislation, State and national, he made the confident prediction that Ohio will in the coming campaign be given back to the Republican column with her old-time Republican majority.

The platform adopted by the convention denounces as dangerous to the existence of a republican form of government the repeated and notorious action of Democratic caucuses and conventions in this State in virtually selling places of trust to the highest bidder. A plank that is equally timely, and will meet with popular indorsement, declares against any measure that is calculated to increase the rate of taxation as injurious and prejudicial to the welfare of the city. The one well-defined policy the Democrats have had since coming into power in Cincinnati has been to increase taxation in order to make the spoils richer.

### ANY ONE RATHER THAN ARTHUR.

JAMESTOWN, N. Y., March 20.—The *Journal* this evening published a page of interviews with leading Republican manufacturers, business and professional men. In nearly every instance Blaine was personally preferred, but Edmonds was thought to be the most available candidate. Lincoln's name was the only one mentioned for second place. Little fault was found with Arthur's recent Administration, but his record previous to Garfield's death is remembered, and only four of those interviewed, including the Postmaster, were in favor of his nomination. In every instance the opinion was held that the Congressional district was strongly for Blaine or Edmunds. A prominent Cattaraugus County lawyer said that State Senator Vedder was strongly censured in his county for saying in a recent interview in an Eastern paper that that district was for Arthur. The lawyer said that not one in fifty in Cattaraugus County would choose Arthur. Nearly all of those whose views were sought expressed a willingness to support whatever candidate the Chicago Convention should nominate.

### ARRANGING FOR THE CONVENTION.

CHICAGO, Ill., March 20.—The sub-committee appointed by the National Republican Committee to make arrangements for the convention will meet in Chicago on Saturday morning. The members of the committee are John C. New, of Indiana, Chairman; W. C. Cooper, of Ohio; C. L. Magee, of Pittsburg; John A. Logan, of Chicago; Powell Clayton, of Arkansas, and the Treasurer, Lyman S. Gage, of Chicago. Chairman Sabin and Secretary Martin are ex officio members. It is likely that all the members will be on hand, except Senator Logan, who will be represented by proxy. The main duty of the National Sub-Committee will be to appoint a local committee which will have entire charge of the arrangements. As soon as this is done a consultation will be held with the managers of the May Music Festival, who are getting the exposition building ready for their concerts, and are anxious to make some arrangements by which both the Republican and Democratic Conventions will use the hall and bear part of the expense.

### JOHN F. SMYTH'S AMBITION.

ALBANY, March 20.—Although ex-Boss John F. Smyth was emphatically informed last Fall by three defeats that the Republicans of Albany County were tired of his misrule, he seems determined to appear as a disturbing element in local politics. He now aims to be chosen a district delegate to the National Convention, and wants to control the district delegates to the State Convention. At all the primaries thus far held a contest has been made. In the Fourth Assembly District the anti-Smyth men have been successful in four districts in West Troy, two in Cohoes, and one in Green Island, while the Smyth faction has won in one district of Green Island. Enough delegates have been elected in that Assembly district to insure anti-Smyth delegates to the State Convention. At the last meeting of the County Committee the divisions on disputed questions showed about 30 anti-Smyth and 20 Smyth men.

### REFORM AS AN ISSUE.

NORFOLK, Va., March 20.—The State Democratic Central Committee met at Alexandria to-day and decided to hold the State Convention in Richmond on May 14, the basis of representation to be one delegate and alternate to every 200 voters and fraction over 100 voters cast for the Electoral ticket for Hancock and English in 1880. A resolution was adopted deprecating agitation of the tariff question and urging concentration upon the one great issue of reform of the Government and its restoration to purity.

### JOHN KELLY ON PROHIBITION.

HIS OPINION OF PROHIBITORY LAWS AND HIGH LICENSE.

CHICAGO, March 20.—Joseph A. Connor, of Plattsmouth, Neb., sends to the Chicago *Tribune* a copy of a letter written him March 1 by John Kelly on the subject of the failure of the authorities in New-York to execute the excise laws. Referring to the recent trial of McGlory, the man whose brewer swore that the beer he sold was table beer and not intoxicating, Mr. Kelly says: Paid officers of the law, appointed to protect the lives and property of the people and to prevent the violation of the same, swore on the side of the person who kept the place that they had never seen intoxicating drinks sold on the premises that they were sent to watch. The plain inference from this testimony is that they were in some way interested by pecuniary gain, for no reasonable person can come to any other conclusion. The use of money in corrupting public officials seems to be incurable. I don't suppose that the people of New-York are worse off in this particular than those of other large cities in a comparative sense.

The abuse and immoderate use of intoxicating liquors have caused more demoralization and real injury to the welfare, morals, and prosperity of the people than any other temptation to which the human mind is subjected. The great question is: Can a remedy be provided that will overthrow and prevent the immoderate use of intoxicating liquors? This is an unsolved problem as yet. In my opinion, statute laws will not prevent people from indulging in intoxicating liquors and using them immoderately. The appetite once having been created, it is difficult to subdue. The moral law will have more effect in persuading people to control their appetites and to avoid the abuse which they entail than that made by Legislatures. The laws of prohibition can never be enforced. No better evidence of this can be demonstrated than its violation in the States of Nebraska and Maine and in cities in some of the States in the Union where option laws have been passed. And so we might go on and cite other circumstances, all of which, if properly considered, ought to convince any reasonable man that prohibitory laws and high licenses are not a success.

Very truly yours, JOHN KELLY.

### INSTRUCTED FOR RANDALL.

MEDIA, Penn., March 20.—The Democrats of Delaware County to-day elected Dr. J. L. Farwood delegate to the National Convention and instructed for Randall for President.

### *PARTING FROM HER CHILDREN.*

AN INSANE MOTHER SENT TO A LUNATIC ASYLUM.

JASPER, Ga., March 20.—A mother and seven children sat in the court-room to-day. The woman was about 35 years of age, with large, lustrous eyes, and hair falling wildly over her shoulders. Behind her stood her husband, Mr. Stephen Cowart. After sitting a while the woman cried out: "Don't take my children from me; please don't!" The husband vainly endeavored to soothe her, but she so raved and writhed in her sufferings as to draw tears from the eyes of the court attendants. At last, seeing her three-year-old child, she grasped it quickly, and, holding it closely to her breast, shrieked: "You shall not have him; I will not be parted from my child." For some time past Mrs. Cowart has acted in such a manner as to show unsoundness of mind, and she became so violent recently that, for her own safety as well as for the protection of those around her, it was deemed necessary to put her in an asylum.

With the sharp instinct which usually accompanies lunacy, she at once read the purpose of her friends and strongly resisted the effort to confine her. The only way in which she could be brought to town was by the whole family coming, avowedly to attend a meeting, but really to try the mother before a Court of Inquiry. When it was announced that she would have to go to the asylum her pleas not to be parted from her children were heartrending. She would press them to her bosom, between her paroxysms, and avow her purpose of dying rather than lose them, and when an officer took hold of her so that her family could return home, she cried loudly. While the family drove off in the wagon the mother was consigned to the County Jail to await transportation to Milledgeville.

### *THE CROUCH MURDER TRIAL.*

JACKSON, Mich., March 20.—The Crouch murder examination was continued to-day. Henry M. Eddy and Daniel S. Peterson, members of the Coroner's jury, testified to seeing Jud Crouch pick up two shells from the floor of his house on the morning after the murder. Neither of them saw any blood on the carpet. The prosecution placed Mrs. Galen Brown on the stand for cross-examination, and proceeded to sift her past history and character. Her answers consisted principally of denials of anything improper in her past conduct. The letter from her husband produced yesterday, was again produced, but was not read. It was filed with the stenographer. The defense then put Galen Brown on the stand, and he went through a similar examination. He refused to answer questions tending to injure his character regarding his actions previous to his connection with this case as a detective, and the court sustained him, which created a heated discussion between the attorneys. Gilbert H. Wilson testified that he noticed tracks near the house on the day after the murder. He said that Jud shed tears at the funeral. Several other witnesses testified to seeing the shells on the floor of the house, and to Dan Holcomb being at the house between 10 and 11 o'clock.

### *THE SHARON DIVORCE SUIT.*

SAN FRANCISCO, Cal., March 20.—In the Sharon divorce case to-day Miss Hill, the plaintiff, resumed her testimony. She denied that she instructed Neilson, her attorney, to have Sharon arrested for adultery, and stated that he did it on his own responsibility. She said she never stole the Belcher mine papers from Sharon's room. Mr. Barnes, counsel for defendants, said he could prove that she has stolen them. A letter from ex-Gov. Reichart, of Wisconsin, dated Beloit, Wis., March 25, 1883, to the plaintiff was introduced by the defense, in which Mr. Reichart says: "We have been waiting patiently for those cards. If the honorable Senator does not come to time pretty soon send for me and I will bring along my pet stuffed club and end the business." The plaintiff then continued. She believed that Gov. Reichart always thought that she was Sharon's wife, but she never told him about the secret marriage. After the trouble between herself and Sharon she sent two different persons to the latter, telling him that if he would permit her to obtain a divorce she would never again trouble him, but Sharon refused.

### *CONFESSING A DOUBLE MURDER.*

DANVILLE, Va., March 20.—The police arrested here to-day a man who, while drunk on a Midland train yesterday, confessed that he had killed two colored men named Sam and Henry Clark and wounded United States Bailiff Lee Jones. There was found on the prisoner what appears to be a part of an advertisement for the man who had committed such crimes, to the description of whom the prisoner answers. The crimes are stated to have been committed on the 17th of some month, but the name of the month, of the man advertised for, the place where the crimes were committed, and the name of the signer of the advertisement had been cut out. The prisoner has passed under the names of H. B. Ewing, John Smith, and Gideon Lamb. It is said that at one time he was a fugitive from justice, and was originally from Wake County, N. C. On his person was also found a check for $1,100, payable to H. B. Ewing, on the Planters' National Bank of Richmond, Va.

### *A PROFESSORSHIP ABOLISHED.*

BOSTON, March 20.—A special meeting of the Board of Overseers of Harvard College was held to-day. The meeting voted to concur in the vote to abolish the Professorship of Ancient, Patristic, and Modern Greek established in 1860. It was voted that the annual report of the President of the college be hereafter submitted to the Board before the printing, publication, and distribution thereof.

### *AN OLD CONDUCTOR KILLED.*

WHEELING, West Va., March 20.—Henry Cramer, aged 50 years, a conductor on the Baltimore and Ohio Railroad for the past 25 years, was instantly killed this morning at Grafton while making up a train. He was standing by some empty gondolas when an engine, unobserved by him, backed up against them throwing him under the cars, several of which passed over him.

### *WESTERN BEEF IN BALTIMORE.*

ANNAPOLIS, Md., March 20.—In the House of Delegates to-day the bill prohibiting the sale of Western slaughtered beef in Baltimore markets was effectually disposed of, being laid on the table by the decisive vote of 68 yeas to 11 nays.

## NO DISCORD IN THE PARTY

### *RHODE ISLAND REPUBLICANS AND THEIR OLD TICKET.*

NOMINATING THEIR FORMER STANDARD-BEARERS AND CHALLENGING ALL COMERS ON THE PARTY RECORD.

PROVIDENCE, R. I., March 20.—The Republicans held an enthusiastic State Convention here in Slade Hall to-day to nominate a Gubernatorial ticket. The attendance discounted that which marked the jubilee of the Democrats on the preceding day, but there was more order and less fighting over trivial matters. Major Pierce, the Chairman of the State Central Committee, presided as temporary Chairman. In calling the delegates to order he said:

"The Republican Party goes to the country the same as it has gone for the past 25 years and with a record that it can afford to hold up to all beholders. Our adversaries have no foothold, no platform, upon which they can stand. They have been struggling for the last 20 years, and every time that they have come to the front for recognition such recognition has been denied them. The last 25 years we have passed through are unequaled in the history of the past 100 years. The prospect never was better than at the present time. We are to-day only throwing out the skirmishing line for the fight later on. Whenever there has been a quarrel it has been in an off year. Last year when our adversaries captured four or five States we were gradually accomplishing what was necessary for the future, and last Fall all their brief success was swept away. The man deemed the best for a standard-bearer, no matter from what part of the country, should be selected, and this is the sentiment of the Stalwarts, half-breeds, and all other Republicans. Our measures can stand all the tests they are subjected to. The Democrats are generally 10 years behind us. If the Democrats shake the bloody shirt we are always prepared to meet them on this issue, and we need not go further than Virginia and Mississippi to find plenty of matter for comment. We know we have a walk-over this Spring, and yet we want no stragglers in our camp. When we look back only two days and see the exhibition that has been made, it is more than enough to call every man into our camp. Men worked 10 days in their shirt sleeves to get an independent Republican Convention together, and then not more than half the towns in the State were represented. It was a great fizzle. The Democratic Party, as usual, sold out for a mess of pottage. If the Democrats could swallow such a man as Horace Greeley, a man who had thrown more bombs into their camp than any other man in the country, they can swallow anything in Rhode Island, Massachusetts, and Maine."

When the roll of the convention was called every town in the State responded and every town sent in a full quota of delegates. The Hon. George A. Wilbour, of Woonsocket, was chosen temporary Chairman, and Eugene F. Warner and William R. Randall temporary Secretaries. One contest only was made, and that was on the Warwick delegation. This was quite laughable. There was a bolt at the caucus where the contesting delegation hailed from; the bolters held their caucus, elected delegates, and then had the audacity to choose a committee to wait upon the regular delegates and request them to withdraw. The contestants were not received, and the convention made the temporary organization permanent and proceeded to business. Ex-Lieut.-Gov. Fay, of Newport, offered the following resolution, which was passed and ordered communicated to Senator Anthony:

*Resolved*, By the representatives of the Republican Party in Rhode Island, in convention assembled, that, having in grateful remembrance the valuable services rendered to our State and Nation in the United States Senate during the last 24 years by our senior Senator, the Hon. Henry B. Anthony, we extend to him a most cordial greeting, congratulating him upon such restoration to health as enabled him to enter upon a fifth term of service, and uniting in the sincere desire that his life and strength may be spared and his able and faithful statesmanship continue to redound to the welfare and honor of his native State and country.

The following State ticket was nominated without opposition, being the ticket of last year in its entirety, as prophesied in to-day's TIMES: For Governor—The Hon. A. O. Bourn, of Bristol; for Secretary of State—Joshua M. Addeman, of Providence; for Attorney-General—Samuel P. Colt, of Bristol; for State Treasurer—Samuel Clark, of Lincoln.

The State Central Committee of 1883 was re-elected, and a committee was appointed to wait upon Gov. Bourn and escort him to the hall. The Governor, after being placed in the chair, said that the renewed expression of the confidence of the representatives of the Republican Party in Rhode Island was to him one of the most precious legacies to be handed down to his posterity. He accepted the nomination as coming from the Republican Party of the State, which was but a wing of the great national party of the United States which had held undisputed sway for nearly 24 years in the conduct of the affairs of government with success and wise judgment. He directed attention to the remarkable growth of the material interests of the country during this time in manufacturing and agricultural and mechanical industries, and added that the civil service had been placed on a solid basis so that the bulk of offices were held by men of merit. In a few months the people of the country would be called upon to say whether the Republican Party was to enter upon another four years of control of the policies of the country, or whether the Democrats should assume the reins of government with an uncertain hand. The election on the first Wednesday in April next should be conducted with reference to national issues. He believed that the State of Rhode Island would express itself in no uncertain manner, and that it would be a harbinger of a most glorious national victory in November.

A State Convention is to be held in a few days to nominate delegates to the National Republican Convention.

### *THE CATTLE DISEASE.*

CHICAGO, Ill., March 20.—Mr. Simon Beattie, representative of the *Breeder's Gazette*, of this city, telegraphs the Associated Press from Neosho Falls, Kan., where he has been investigating the reported cases of foot and mouth disease, as follows: "I visited the two herds most affected in this district to-day and found them much the same as those in Iowa and Illinois. I do not see any indication of contagious foot and mouth disease in them and am satisfied that there is not any. There are two Professors, two veterinarians, and two prominent cattle men here. I think that they are weakening some from their opinions as previously expressed."

ST. LOUIS, Mo., March 20.—Reports from Maries County, in South-west Missouri, say that the cattle disease has broken out in that county. Three herds are affected, but prompt action is being taken to prevent the spread of the disease.

TOPEKA, Kan., March 20.—The Senate this morning took no action regarding the cattle disease, but consumed all the session discussing the railroad bill. The House made the Cattle Disease bill, which was introduced yesterday, a special order of business for this afternoon. The bill for the appointment of a State Veterinary Surgeon was passed.

### *FITZ JOHN PORTER'S CASE.*

CHICAGO, March 20.—The *Tribune's* special from New-Hampton, Iowa, gives an interview with Gen. B. M. Prentiss, one of the members of the Fitz John Porter court-martial. Gen. Prentiss said the facts published in the *Tribune* of the 8th inst. in an interview with E. P. Brooks, in the main are true, but that all the findings of the court were unanimous except the sentence. "I have no objections to saying that there were votes for death." He intimated that Porter received the lightest punishment that any of the court thought he deserved, and that if Congress will pass the bill removing the bond of secrecy there never would be any doubt in the minds of the American people in the future of the correctness of the findings of the court. He also said that he went into that court Porter's friend, hoping and expecting to see him acquitted, and, of course, there must have been evidence to reverse that opinion.

### *FROM A SINKING BARK.*

SAVANNAH, Ga., March 20.—The Norwegian bark Stella, from Tarragona, arrived here to-day, having on board the Captain and crew of the Italian bark Adelaide Chiavari, from Leghorn, for New-York, with marble. The latter vessel was abandoned on Feb. 18, latitude 31° 54' north, longitude 19° 31' west, in a sinking condition, with six feet of water in the hold and the decks working open. The vessel was rapidly sinking when the crew went on board the Stella.

### *MURDERED BY HER HUSBAND.*

ALBANY, N. Y., March 20.—Information has been received here that Peter Edwards last night murdered his wife at Preston Hollow, a small and secluded settlement in the south-west corner of this county. No details have been received.

### *MOVEMENTS OF SECRETARY CHANDLER.*

NORFOLK, Va., March 20.—Secretary Chandler and party passed through the navy yard here to-day, and made an informal inspection of that institution. He went to Old Point in the afternoon on the Tallapoosa.

# The New-York Times.

VOL. XXXIII.....NO. 10,221. | NEW-YORK, SATURDAY, JUNE 7, 1884. | PRICE TWO CENTS.


## THE CONVENTION'S CHOICE

### BLAINE AND LOGAN TO BEAR THE REPUBLICAN STANDARD.

FOUR BALLOTS FOR PRESIDENT TAKEN AMID GREAT CONFUSION AND EXCITEMENT—BLAINE AT LAST GETS A MAJORITY OF 133—NO OPPOSITION MANIFESTED TO LOGAN FOR VICE-PRESIDENT.

FIRST BALLOT.

| | |
|---|---|
| JAMES G. BLAINE | 334½ |
| CHESTER A. ARTHUR | 278 |
| GEORGE F. EDMUNDS | 93 |
| JOHN A. LOGAN | 63½ |
| JOHN SHERMAN | 30 |
| JOSEPH R. HAWLEY | 13 |
| ROBERT T. LINCOLN | 4 |
| W. T. SHERMAN | 2 |

SECOND BALLOT.

| | |
|---|---|
| JAMES G. BLAINE | 349 |
| CHESTER A. ARTHUR | 276 |
| GEORGE F. EDMUNDS | 85 |
| JOHN A. LOGAN | 61 |
| JOHN SHERMAN | 28 |
| JOSEPH R. HAWLEY | 13 |
| ROBERT T. LINCOLN | 4 |
| W. T. SHERMAN | 2 |

THIRD BALLOT.

| | |
|---|---|
| JAMES G. BLAINE | 375 |
| CHESTER A. ARTHUR | 274 |
| GEORGE F. EDMUNDS | 69 |
| JOHN A. LOGAN | 53 |
| JOHN SHERMAN | 25 |
| JOSEPH R. HAWLEY | 13 |
| ROBERT T. LINCOLN | 8 |
| W. T. SHERMAN | 2 |

FOURTH BALLOT.

| | |
|---|---|
| JAMES G. BLAINE | 541 |
| CHESTER A. ARTHUR | 207 |
| GEORGE F. EDMUNDS | 41 |
| JOHN A. LOGAN | 7 |
| JOSEPH R. HAWLEY | 15 |
| ROBERT T. LINCOLN | 2 |

*From the Special Correspondent of the Times.*

CHICAGO, June 6.—The convention's work is done. On the fourth ballot James G. Blaine was nominated by the votes of 544 delegates to be President of the United States. Beginning on the first ballot with 334½ votes—a number which proves the substantial accuracy of the estimates sent from this city to THE TIMES—the Blaine men marched steadily and resistlessly forward to victory. The second roll-call revealed 349 Blaine votes, and the third 375. On the fourth, great States, whose delegations had been divided, closed their broken ranks and wheeled into line for the man from Maine. Favorite sons withdrew from the field and delivered their delegates to him, and the number of his supporters was increased by accessions, large and small, until he had received a majority and had 133 votes to spare.

Blaine's managers were unwilling yesterday that there should be any break in the course of the balloting. The first ballot would reveal their strength more accurately than it had been shown in the Lynch-Clayton contest, and if a night should intervene between the first ballot or the first two ballots and the succeeding ones they feared that their opponents would be able to outwit them by combining to support a new man, or in some other way. They were confident, but at the same time they remembered the defeat of their candidate in 1876 and 1880. They decided to guard their lines with the utmost care, and to enter the race under the most favorable circumstances if possible.

After all the speeches had been made last night, Judge Foraker, of Ohio, John Sherman's representative, surprised the Blaine men by moving that a ballot should be taken at once. Mr. Stewart, of Pennsylvania, sprang to his feet and moved that if a beginning was to be made the work of balloting should not be interrupted till at least five ballots had been taken. One ballot and an adjournment might ruin his candidate, but five, he believed, would give him the nomination. Mr. Thurston, prompted by Mr. Elkins, moved an adjournment. The Blaine and anti-Blaine men again locked horns on this motion, which was defeated by a vote of 391 to 410. The change of 15 votes, misplaced because the Alabama delegates did not understand the question, would have made the vote 376 to 425. Filibustering would have been continued through the remainder of the night if the Sherman men had not seen the folly of such a course and put an end to the contest. The Blaine men could have afforded to allow one ballot to be taken, for there could have been formed during the night no combination which would have beaten them to-day. But they wanted to be on the safe side.

When the convention reassembled this morning it was apparent that nothing could prevent a Blaine victory. Messrs. Roosevelt and Henry Cabot Lodge had been hard at work through the night trying to take the anti-Blaine vote to some candidate, new or old, whom Arthur men, Edmunds men, and the independents could heartily support. It had been a hopeless task, but these men had courageously undertaken to accomplish it. Even if the leading Arthur men had been willing to desert the President, and they were not, their votes could not be transferred. Nor would the Edmunds men go to Arthur for reasons that have been given in preceding dispatches. If a transfer of the Arthur vote could have been made, there was no man whom the combination could support against Blaine with the slightest hope of success. Lincoln was out of the question. His friends discovered that while he had seemed to be theoretically available, because of his character, record, and the universal acceptance of his name to be put in the second place on the ticket, he was practically unavailable in this convention for the first place.

When the session began the Arthur men had settled down into a condition of sullen indifference. From time to time they found cold comfort in cursing the Edmunds men and the independents because they would not vote for Arthur. "If Blaine is nominated," said they, "the independents will be responsible for the work. It is not probable that an Edmunds-Arthur alliance, with Arthur as the candidate, could now defeat Blaine, but if the Edmunds men had come to us some days ago we could have had some show. What could we do, and what can we do? We cannot go to any other man, for the moment we stir our block of delegates, that moment it will break into fragments." The active independents were despondent. They had done what they could to "stiffen up" the dark horses. If the Arthur men should stand firm, and if the minor candidates should retain their votes, the contest might be prolonged and delay might avert disaster. But could the anti-Blaine forces, which could not be united, withstand the Blaine attack? Knowing that many of the Logan and Sherman men were disguised allies of Blaine, that many of the Southern delegates were wavering and inclined to join the strongest battalion, and that in the convention the very air was full of Blaine, they could see no ground for hope.

The first ballot surprised no one except those who had been misled by the wild boasts of the Arthur men. It was plain to keen politicians that a few of the Blaine vote had been temporarily withheld. Edmunds's vote, which, unhappily, was doomed to a rapid decline, exceeded the number assigned to him by the average of careful estimates. Nineteen of these Edmunds men came from the North-western States Michigan, Wisconsin, and Minnesota. The instructed Pennsylvania delegates obeyed their instructions. New-Jersey yielded two Lincoln votes. On the second ballot Blaine drew 14 votes from his opponents, the majority of these coming from Arthur. On the third ballot it became plain that disintegrating forces were at work among the Arthur men and the weakest Edmunds men. Wavering delegates were going over to what seemed to them the winning side, and others would soon follow them, as panic-stricken sheep follow their companions over a fence. There was no force, no sentiment, no leader, to bind them to their original choice. Even in Pennsylvania Arthur's men were deserting him. The effect of the Clayton bargain could be seen in Missouri and Texas. Individual losses here and there in the South proved that old barriers had been broken down. Four of the Edmunds men in New-Jersey had gone to Lincoln, but this movement had no effect. Blaine was within 38 votes of a nomination, and had not yet been compelled to call upon the main body of the Logan men or the main body of the Sherman men for reinforcements.

With defeat and rout staring them in the face if another ballot should be immediately taken, the anti-Blaine men decided to fight for delay. Judge Foraker, who appeared to be honestly and earnestly devoted to the fortunes of John Sherman, and to hope that delay might serve his candidate, came to the assistance of the anti-Blaine men by moving for a recess, and his motion was seconded by Mr. Dutcher, of New-York. The convention at once became a mob. The incompetent Chairman made a ridiculous exhibition of his worthlessness, and became a mouth-piece for Stephen B. Elkins, ex-Senator Spencer, Chauncey I. Filley, and Warner Miller, who stood by his side or leaned over his chair prompting and guiding him and directing the reading clerks by nods and winks. Blaine's lieutenants were busy among the delegates. At last the vote was taken. It was the last desperate attempt of the anti-Blaine men to gain time, though none of them could have shown in what way delay could assist them. The motion was lost by a vote of 364 to 450. The contest was at an end. Nothing remained but to record the votes that were to nominate Blaine.

The roll was called. Large gains in Alabama, Kentucky, North Carolina, Tennessee, and Louisiana showed that the South had broken up. Kellogg voted for Blaine. Illinois withdrew Logan and Ohio withdrew Sherman, adding 56 to Blaine's pile. Indiana, Michigan, Minnesota, and Missouri cast all of their 102 votes at his feet. The clerks added the figures, the result was announced, and the great audience made the building ring with their shouts. Blaine's nomination was assured by the transfer of a majority of the Logan vote.

To-night the ticket was completed by giving Logan the second place on it. Robert T. Lincoln forbade his friends to present his name for this place.

The party's new candidate for President is deeply indebted to Powell Clayton, of Arkansas; Chauncey I. Filley, of Missouri; Stephen B. Elkins, of New-Mexico and New-York; Logan H. Roots, of Arkansas; ex-Senator Spencer, of Alabama; Richard C. Kerens, of Missouri, and Frank L. Money, of Louisiana, for political services rendered. Several of these have a practical knowledge of the operations and requirements of the United States Mail Service, and Republicans who regard the nomination as equivalent to an election are already indulging in some speculation as to which one of them will be made Postmaster-General.

The sessions of the convention have been marked by great disorder. Chairman Henderson was not only utterly incompetent to perform the duties of his office, but he was also weak enough to allow himself to be handled and directed by the gentlemen just mentioned, who surrounded his chair and did not conceal the exercise of their influence and authority. It is a curious fact that while these men were exhibiting to every body to-day their power behind the throne, and while many of their friends who are not well known were given the freedom of the Chairman's stage, Theodore Roosevelt of New-York, a most conspicuous figure in the New-York delegation, was unable to go upon the stage to ask a question until he had thrust aside several officious persons who were attempting forcibly to exclude him. Mr. Blaine has been unfortunate in the selection of some of his most active supporters. They have no use for Mr. Roosevelt and men of his kind. Mr. Blaine has many earnest supporters in the North-west and in the East who do not seem to affiliate with the South-western group or to enjoy heartily their companionship. It is impossible to ignore the existence of this South-western group or the very important, and in some respects effective, work done by its members for Mr. Blaine in the last two weeks. Their labors have been as conspicuous on one side as those of Mr. Roosevelt, Mr. Lodge, Mr. Curtis, and their friends have been on the other. They will undoubtedly play prominent parts in the coming campaign.

F. D. R.

## THE CONVENTION'S CLOSING WORK

WHY THE BLAINE MEN WORKED FOR AN ADJOURNMENT ON THURSDAY NIGHT—A SPIRITLESS CONVENTION ON FRIDAY MORNING—DISORDERLY PROCEEDINGS ON THE FLOOR—THE BALLOTING AND ITS RESULT.

*From Staff Correspondents of the Times.*

CHICAGO, June 6.—When the convention, by the vote of 410 to 391, agreed, at 1 o'clock this morning, not to adjourn, everybody supposed that at least one ballot for a nominee would be taken. The Blaine men, however, would not consent to that, and by hubbub and dilatory motions and suggestions showed their determination either to adjourn the convention or prevent it from transacting all business. Chairman Henderson acted like a man who was in a dream, so confused was he by the uproar and the yells for recognition from every direction that were hurled at him. "Wheelhorse" Dutcher, of New-York, moved to take a ballot, and on that moved the previous question. If the Chairman heard the motion he paid no heed to it, but stared blankly about him. The uproar was terrific. Senator Stewart, of Pennsylvania, moved to take a recess until 11 o'clock, and there was a dispute in the vicinity of the New-York and Pennsylvania delegations as to which motion was made first—that by Mr. Dutcher or that of Mr. Stewart. An idea struck the Chairman, and he pounded savagely with his gavel. "The Chair," he said, "will state to the convention that the order of business is a ballot, and there is no use of making a motion to that effect," when he settled back and declared he would entertain no motion until order was restored.

A convention which had been bullying its Chairman and paying no attention all along was not to be managed at this point, and for 10 minutes bedlam was let loose. Above it all, Mr. Bush, of California, demanded to know, "in the language of a distinguished gentleman, what are we here for?" Roars of laughter greeted the sally. Then a delegate asked what motion was before the house. The Chairman did not know himself, and he jumped at the answer that the motion was to adjourn. Finally he ordered a roll-call of the States upon this motion. Nine States had responded whose votes showed that 40 were recorded in favor of adjournment and 96 against. It was useless to attempt to do any business in this confusion, and by mutual agreement the Blaine and the Arthur leaders consented to an adjournment. Ex-Congressman McKinley, of Ohio, was recognized, and he said: "I move to dispense with the call of the States. I understand that the gentlemen all about me are willing that this motion to adjourn until 11 o'clock shall prevail, and in that spirit I make the motion." Congressman Burleigh seconded the motion on behalf of the anti-Blaine forces, and it was carried with a yell.

### THE LAST DAY'S WORK.

It is Friday, and the convention that was in session until nearly 2 o'clock this morning is again, at 10 o'clock, beginning to assemble. The great hall is already hardly filled, the delegates, looking weary after the tremendous excitement of the night before, coming in tardily. They find, as they come along Michigan-avenue, that the street vendors of refreshments are again in place, that carriages block the way, that the policemen have hard work to keep a passage open through the crowds to the doors. They learn that since 9 o'clock ticket-holders have been clamoring for admission, anxious to get the best seats, and when they get inside they discover that not only seats belonging to delegates but those assigned to alternates, the press, and special guests have been occupied. The assistants of the Sergeant-at-Arms are of no use whatever. They loaf about, very proud of their purple badges, but do nothing to keep the aisles clear, protect those who have rights on the floor, or restrain the disorder caused by the gathering crowds. Ticket speculators are selling a great many tickets, and those who buy them are conspicuously impudent when they have obtained admission. The chairs of newspaper writers are carried away against the feeble protests of the Sergeants, who, like Dogberry's men, know very well what the duty is of your average watchman. The hall shows the effects of the vandalism of Blaine's shouters. The flags and shields along the front of the galleries have all been stripped off, leaving a long line of tri-colored banner-cloths. The banners that hung over the platform have also disappeared. For one brief moment the guards in front of the stage become aware that they have authority, and they exercise it by hustling a small boy out of the passage with uncalled-for violence. Delegates who have come in a little early droop in their chairs, their eyes closed and their visages wan and weary in the bright morning light.

About 11 o'clock the Chairman comes in. He sees sitting near the edge of the platform Mr. Stephen B. Elkins, the Blaine manager. He has his tally lists all ready. Down on the floor at the edge of the seats for delegates he could see Tom Donaldson, another of the Blaine managers, who sits where he can get at the Chairman of the delegation. He looks as if he had not been in bed for a week, his coat-collar turned up, and his throat protected by a handkerchief tied about it. Behind the Chairman, who probably does not see them, are a group of Blaine's particular friends, among them Warner Miller. The Chairman hoarsely calls the convention to order. It is after 11 o'clock, and the crowd of Blaine's men, fretting for a vote, have become warmed up by the music of the band, the renewed bustle in the hall, and the assurances that are brought in that Blaine is surely to be nominated on the second or third ballot. The Rev. Dr. Scudder prays as the delegates are subsiding into a condition of order. Very few of those present can hear what he says, and few are as much interested as they might be.

### THE BALLOTING BEGUN.

The prayer over, a delegate from Alabama tries to offer a resolution. The Chair, very promptly for so dull and incompetent a Chair, decides that nothing is in order but the calling of States. An interruption is permitted, however, to States that wish to report the names of the National Committeemen.

The gavel is used once or twice, the delegates give attention, and the Chair commands the Secretary: "Call the roll." Alabama is called. The audience listens for the response. It is announced by the Chairman of the delegation: "Alabama—Blaine, 1; Logan, 1; Arthur, 17." One delegate is sick at his hotel and Arthur loses one vote. Arkansas responds with 4 for Arthur, 8 for Blaine, and 2 for Edmunds. There is applause, first from the Arthur men and then from the Blaine men. The noise of the cheers delays the clerks, who are singularly incompetent at best. Logan H. Roots, corpulent and puffy, gets upon a chair to challenge the correctness of the record. Shouts of approval follow his demand. "Call the roll," says the Chairman. The roll is called, but the result as announced is found to be correct. California and Colorado respond when called, both solid for Blaine, and both are cheered to the echo. Connecticut's 12 votes are cast by Chairman Brandegee for Joseph R. Hawley. A small volume of applause shows that Hawley's admirers are not numerous in the hall. When Florida is reached and it is announced as casting seven votes for Arthur and one for Blaine, the Blaine men, who have known that there was one vote there for them, indulge in more extravagant applause. There is a desire to hear the individual vote. The report is challenged, and John G. Long is smoked out as the Blaine man in the delegation. A delegate attempted to tell the convention that the State Convention had passed a resolution of instruction to vote as a unit for Arthur, but he was discouraged before he could finish his story. Georgia's 24 votes went solid for Arthur to the very warmly expressed satisfaction of the Arthur men. When Illinois was called the convention listened to learn the extent of the division in that State. Cheers went up from the galleries when it was announced by Senator Cullom that Illinois cast 40 votes for Logan, 3 for Blaine, and 1 for Arthur. Arthur's friends were poorer in this delegation than they had supposed. When Indiana was called the first vote for George F. Edmunds was reported. Blaine's men were almost uncontrollable at finding that Harrison's vote had nearly all been captured and that the State stood Arthur, 9; Blaine, 18; Edmunds, 1, and John Sherman, 2. Iowa's vote dropped solidly for Blaine. Kansas had doubters in her camp, and she cast 4 votes for Arthur, 12 for Blaine, 1 for Logan, and 1 for Hawley. Clisbee, the clerk who was so popular with the convention of 1880, and who has a powerful voice and rather more sense than several of the blundering clerks of the convention, makes the announcement. Kentucky, in spite of all the efforts of Internal Revenue Commissioner Evans to keep its delegates together, breaks up for Arthur, Blaine, Logan, John Sherman, and Robert T. Lincoln. Louisiana, after its usual fashion, concealed its bent for Blaine, giving 10 insincere votes for Arthur, 2 to Blaine, and 3 to Logan, one delegate being absent and not represented by the vote of an alternate. The vote was challenged, the roll called, and the Chairman, William Pitt Kellogg, expressed his gratitude to Chester A. Arthur for persecuting him with a star route indictment by voting for John A. Logan. The assertion made on Monday, that Powell Clayton had been nominated for temporary Chairman by an Arthur man was discovered to be false when Frank Morey voted for Logan as a step toward Blaine. Maine, of course, went solid for Blaine, and the hall shook with admiring applause. Massachusetts, through Senator Hoar, cast 25 votes for Edmunds, 2 for Arthur, and 1 for Blaine. Michigan, supposed to be nursing a large vote for Gen. Sherman, gave him only 2 of her 26, 2 going to Arthur, 15 to Blaine, and 7 to Edmunds. Minnesota's vote, cast by Senator Sabin, was 1 for Arthur, 7 for Blaine, and 6 for Edmunds. Senator Bruce, when Mississippi was called, reported 17 for Arthur and 1 for Blaine.

The crowd continued to express its approval at each announcement, every candidate having friends enough in the hall who appeared to enjoy indulging in loud demonstrations. Missouri was very much divided, giving 10 votes to Arthur, 5 to Blaine, 6 to Edmunds, 10 to Logan, and 1 to John Sherman, the Blaine men greeting their vote with more uproarious cheering and waving of handkerchiefs. With a pompousness that had made him ridiculous during the balloting last night, Mr. Thurston, of Nebraska, announced 8 of the votes of that State for Blaine and 2 for Arthur. New-Hampshire gave half her vote to Edmunds and half to Arthur. The boasted strength of Arthur in New-Jersey disappeared when that State was called and Senator Sewell cast 9 for Blaine, 6 for Edmunds, 1 for John Sherman, and 2 for Lincoln.

Everybody had his eye on George William Curtis when New-York was called. The Chairman of the delegation had polled the delegates, and he arose with a card in his hand to announce the vote. He began with the lowest vote, "Lincoln, 1;" he next announced, "Edmunds, 12," then called out, "Blaine, 28," and while the Blaine applause is still ringing through the hall he rolled out, "Arthur, 31." Great is the joy of the Arthur men when they find themselves in the lead. They are fearing the outcome of the day's work. They are keeping courage up, and would be glad to combine with anybody, if combination were possible. North Carolina, giving 19 votes to Arthur, as befits a delegation of office-holders, also gives Blaine 2 and Logan 1. Ohio divides her 46 between Blaine and Sherman, giving the Maine man 21 and her once "Honest John" 25.

Nothing for Arthur in the Buckeye State. Pennsylvania is called. There is a buzz in the convention, followed by silence, as Senator Stewart reads: "Arthur, 11; Blaine, 47; Edmunds, 1; Logan, 1." The Blaine men are richer by one vote than they had expected to be, and the Arthur men poorer by four votes. The Blaine men shouted as if they were mad, and the whole house seemed to rise to its feet to indulge again in the screams and cheers which had so frequently and thoroughly disturbed the proceedings late Thursday night and early this morning. Collector Robertson, carried away by the excitement by which he was surrounded, cheered, waved his hat and handkerchief, and then stepped across the aisle to shake the hand of Stewart. Blaine had broken into South Carolina and found 1 vote there, Arthur getting 17; and in Tennessee, which Chairman Houck had in vain tried to bring up in a solid column, Blaine got 7 votes, Logan 1, and Arthur 16. Vermont is solid for Edmunds, Virginia, not much broken, gave 21 for Arthur, 2 for Blaine. She is still "for Arthur," although Arthur cannot be much for her.

The Blaine vote is rolling up rapidly, and when West Virginia has given Blaine 12 votes, with the usual accompaniment of cheers, Wisconsin has added 10 more, while she gives 6 to Arthur and 6 to Edmunds. The Blaine men begin to predict a nomination on the second ballot. The Territories give no surprises. The District of Columbia excites laughter, because its delegates do not agree, and one will not allow the other to cast the 2 votes. Paymaster Cruger, of Washington, a dandy delegate, who has evinced a weakness for exhibiting himself with unnecessary frequency from the top of chairs and tables, announced 2 for Arthur, which Perry Carson, his associate, disputed, and a poll revealed one for Arthur and one for Blaine. The delegate from Alabama, who had been absent and reported sick, tried to get in his vote, which the Chair refused to accept.

When the clerks were getting the announcement of the vote ready delegates stood in the aisles, crowds of eager men rushed about to learn the figures, and listen when they were declared from the platform as follows:

FIRST BALLOT.

| States. | Full Vote. | Blaine. | Arthur. | Edmunds. | Logan. | John Sherman. | Hawley. | Lincoln. | W. T. Sherman. | Absent. |
|---|---|---|---|---|---|---|---|---|---|---|
| Alabama | 20 | 1 | 17 | | 1 | | | | | 1 |
| Arkansas | 14 | 8 | 4 | 2 | | | | | | |
| California | 16 | 16 | | | | | | | | |
| Colorado | 6 | 6 | | | | | | | | |
| Connecticut | 12 | | | | | | 12 | | | |
| Delaware | 6 | 5 | 1 | | | | | | | |
| Florida | 8 | 1 | 7 | | | | | | | |
| Georgia | 24 | | 24 | | | | | | | |
| Illinois | 44 | 3 | 1 | | 40 | | | | | |
| Indiana | 30 | 18 | 9 | 1 | | 2 | | | | |
| Iowa | 26 | 26 | | | | | | | | |
| Kansas | 18 | 12 | 4 | | 1 | | 1 | | | |
| Kentucky | 26 | 5½ | 16 | | 2½ | 1 | | 1 | | |
| Louisiana | 16 | 2 | 10 | | 3 | | | | | 1 |
| Maine | 12 | 12 | | | | | | | | |
| Maryland | 16 | 10 | 6 | | | | | | | |
| Massachusetts | 28 | 1 | 2 | 25 | | | | | | |
| Michigan | 26 | 15 | 2 | 7 | | | | | 2 | |
| Minnesota | 14 | 7 | 1 | 6 | | | | | | |
| Mississippi | 18 | 1 | 17 | | | | | | | |
| Missouri | 32 | 5 | 10 | 6 | 10 | 1 | | | | |
| Nebraska | 10 | 8 | 2 | | | | | | | |
| Nevada | 6 | 6 | | | | | | | | |
| New-Hampshire | 8 | | 4 | 4 | | | | | | |
| New-Jersey | 18 | 9 | | 6 | | 1 | | 2 | | |
| New-York | 72 | 28 | 31 | 12 | | | | 1 | | |
| North Carolina | 22 | 2 | 19 | | 1 | | | | | |
| Ohio | 46 | 21 | | | | 25 | | | | |
| Oregon | 6 | 6 | | | | | | | | |
| Pennsylvania | 60 | 47 | 11 | 1 | 1 | | | | | |
| Rhode Island | 8 | | | 8 | | | | | | |
| South Carolina | 18 | 1 | 17 | | | | | | | |
| Tennessee | 24 | 7 | 16 | | 1 | | | | | |
| Texas | 26 | 13 | 11 | | 2 | | | | | |
| Vermont | 8 | | | 8 | | | | | | |
| Virginia | 24 | 2 | 21 | | 1 | | | | | |
| West Virginia | 12 | 12 | | | | | | | | |
| Wisconsin | 22 | 10 | 6 | 6 | | | | | | |
| *Territories.* | | | | | | | | | | |
| Washington | 2 | 2 | | | | | | | | |
| Dakota | 2 | 2 | | | | | | | | |
| Arizona | 2 | 2 | | | | | | | | |
| Idaho | 2 | | 2 | | | | | | | |
| Montana | 2 | 1 | | 1 | | | | | | |
| Wyoming | 2 | | 2 | | | | | | | |
| New-Mexico | 2 | | 2 | | | | | | | |
| Utah | 2 | | 2 | | | | | | | |
| Dis. of Columbia | 2 | 1 | 1 | | | | | | | |
| Total | 820 | 334½ | 278 | 93 | 63½ | 30 | 13 | 4 | 2 | 2 |

Cheers were heard outside of the convention hall and the crowd inside responded with a prodigious demonstration of applause for Blaine. The hoarse and weak voice of the inefficient Chairman, addressing the boisterous throng, declared that it was not a vote, and that the roll must again be called.

### THE SECOND ROLL-CALL.

Alabama was again called. Arthur gained 1 vote, according to the announcement of the Chairman, but the State was polled to discover that the result was a gain of 1 for Blaine who got 2 votes. The Arkansas bargain was carried out for the 2 Arthur and Edmunds votes and 1 of Arthur's went to Blaine, who got 11 to Arthur's 3. California, Colorado, Connecticut, and Delaware did not budge. Florida insisted upon another roll call, but revealed no change. Georgia stood firm for Arthur. Illinois stood the test of a poll of the delegation without wavering. Indiana scattered its vote again between Arthur, Blaine, Edmunds, and Sherman, and polled so to show the individual preferences of the delegates. Kansas excited the most extraordinary feeling and noise among the Blaine men by taking one from Arthur and giving it to Blaine. In Kentucky, after the State had been polled, Arthur had gained only one vote, the half votes cast in the first ballot having disappeared. When Louisiana was reached, R. F. Guichard, who had voted for Arthur on the first ballot, changed to Blaine, and Blaine also got the vote of E. W. Wall, of the Fifth District, who had voted for Logan. Before the enthusiasm of the Blaine men over this gain had subsided, it was renewed to celebrate the gain of 2 votes in Maryland, leaving Arthur only 4. Missouri was polled upon a challenge, and showed Blaine a gainer by 1 vote from Edmunds and 2 from Logan. Dr. McLean, when he voted, excited shouts of derision from the Arthur men by voting for R. G. Blaine. Hoarse throats cheered the vote, but the Blaine men rested for a moment when New-Hampshire gave one of her Edmunds votes to Arthur. It was a very little gain, but was cheered by the New-York "boys" who were fighting for the President. New-Jersey polled no votes for Arthur on the second ballot.

The New-York vote was announced by Mr. Curtis, as Lincoln, 1; Edmunds, 12; Blaine, 28, and Arthur, 31. Delegate Connwell, of Penn Yan, who was exceedingly noisy for Blaine in the front row, demanded a poll, and the clerk, when he called the roll, after the Chairman had ordered the poll of the State, again bungled in his effort to get the name of John A. King, the delegate from the First District. The Edmunds band stood firm. It was made up of Messrs. Roosevelt, White, Gilbert, and Packard, the delegates at large; Curtis, King, Hobbs, Andrew D. Baird, who kept faith as he promised to do; Pease, Odell, Burritt, and Wadsworth. Alabama Claim Commission B. Platt Carpenter and Hamilton Fish, Jr., go to Arthur, along with "Wheel-horse" Dutcher and the "boys." Delegate Day, of the Fourth District, who had been fretting continually because the losing fight was not brought sooner to a close, displayed his ignorance of his candidate's name by voting for Chester F. Arthur. Some excitement was created by Mr. Burleigh, who had found ex-Senator Spencer sitting in the Alabama delegation, and had induced an Alabama delegate to call for his ejection lest he should do some mischief for Director Elkins. Ex-Attorney-General Russell was annoyed when the stupid clerk for the fourth time called him Leslie W. Proctor, although the roll had been distinctly corrected from the floor during the past day's proceedings. Mr. Platt was cheered and hissed when he voted for Blaine, and Mr. Warner was applauded when he was discovered to be the Lincoln man in the New-York delegation. The roll-call showed that the result as announced by Mr. Curtis was correct. Blaine gained 1 vote in North Carolina at Arthur's expense, and 2 in Ohio at the expense of Sherman. This change was heartily cheered. Pennsylvania stood as on the first ballot, and so did South Carolina, Tennessee, and Texas. The solid Blaine vote of West Virginia again excited the Blaine men to shout and wave their hats and handkerchiefs. Wisconsin let one of her Blaine men go to Edmunds, and the Blaine men were silent. There were no further changes, and after a delay and more excitement on the floor, which the Chairman did not attempt to restrain, the vote was announced as follows:

SECOND BALLOT.

| States. | Full Vote. | Blaine. | Arthur. | Edmunds. | Logan. | John Sherman. | Hawley. | Lincoln. | W. T. Sherman. | Absent. |
|---|---|---|---|---|---|---|---|---|---|---|
| Alabama | 20 | 2 | 17 | | 1 | | | | | |
| Arkansas | 14 | 11 | 3 | | | | | | | |
| California | 16 | 16 | | | | | | | | |
| Colorado | 6 | 6 | | | | | | | | |
| Connecticut | 12 | | | | | | 12 | | | |
| Delaware | 6 | 5 | 1 | | | | | | | |
| Florida | 8 | 1 | 7 | | | | | | | |
| Georgia | 24 | | 24 | | | | | | | |
| Illinois | 44 | 3 | 1 | | 40 | | | | | |
| Indiana | 30 | 18 | 9 | 1 | | 2 | | | | |
| Iowa | 26 | 26 | | | | | | | | |
| Kansas | 18 | 13 | 2 | | 2 | | 1 | | | |
| Kentucky | 26 | 5 | 17 | | 2 | 1 | | 1 | | |
| Louisiana | 16 | 4 | 9 | | 2 | | | | | 1 |
| Maine | 12 | 12 | | | | | | | | |
| Maryland | 16 | 12 | 4 | | | | | | | |
| Massachusetts | 28 | 1 | 3 | 24 | | | | | | |
| Michigan | 26 | 15 | 4 | 5 | | | | | 2 | |
| Minnesota | 14 | 7 | 1 | 6 | | | | | | |
| Mississippi | 18 | 1 | 17 | | | | | | | |
| Missouri | 32 | 7 | 10 | 5 | 8 | 1 | | | | 1 |
| Nebraska | 10 | 8 | 2 | | | | | | | |
| Nevada | 6 | 6 | | | | | | | | |
| New-Hampshire | 8 | | 5 | 3 | | | | | | |
| New-Jersey | 18 | 9 | | 6 | | 1 | | 2 | | |
| New-York | 72 | 28 | 31 | 12 | | | | 1 | | |
| North Carolina | 22 | 3 | 18 | | 1 | | | | | |
| Ohio | 46 | 23 | | | | 23 | | | | |
| Oregon | 6 | 6 | | | | | | | | |
| Pennsylvania | 60 | 47 | 11 | 1 | 1 | | | | | |
| Rhode Island | 8 | | | 8 | | | | | | |
| South Carolina | 18 | 1 | 17 | | | | | | | |
| Tennessee | 24 | 7 | 16 | | 1 | | | | | |
| Texas | 26 | 13 | 11 | | 2 | | | | | |
| Vermont | 8 | | | 8 | | | | | | |
| Virginia | 24 | 2 | 21 | | 1 | | | | | |
| West Virginia | 12 | 12 | | | | | | | | |
| Wisconsin | 22 | 11 | 6 | 5 | | | | | | |
| *Territories.* | | | | | | | | | | |
| Washington | 2 | 2 | | | | | | | | |
| Dakota | 2 | 2 | | | | | | | | |
| Arizona | 2 | 2 | | | | | | | | |
| Idaho | 2 | | 2 | | | | | | | |
| Montana | 2 | 1 | | 1 | | | | | | |
| Wyoming | 2 | | 2 | | | | | | | |
| New-Mexico | 2 | | 2 | | | | | | | |
| Utah | 2 | | 2 | | | | | | | |
| District of Columbia | 2 | 1 | 1 | | | | | | | |
| Total | 820 | 349 | 276 | 85 | 61 | 28 | 13 | 4 | 2 | 2 |

The Blaine vote was announced last, and as the declaration, "Blaine, 349," escaped from the clerk's lips the cheers that arose were deafening. As they cheered the Blaine men got up all over the floor, filled up the aisles, yelled and cheered and whistled in the galleries and waved their hats, handkerchiefs, and umbrellas. It took the crowd fully 10 minutes to get over their rejoicing. The Chairman looked through his glasses at the throng before him, but did not strike a blow with his gavel. He was plainly not the man for the place, but he had Elkins near at hand, and the Blaine manager did not intimate that the noise should be stopped.

### THE ROLL AGAIN CALLED.

At length the crowd was exhausted. "Call the roll," hoarsely shouted Gen. Henderson. The aisles were full of men. The Arthur "boys" were passing about packages of white muslin badges, upon which was printed in large black letters: "Arthur, if it takes all Summer." Poor "boys," the badges were to last only a brief part of one Summer's day. They already saw the trouble ahead while they pinned these little bits of muslin to their coats and hurried about to attach them to the whole Arthur line. Roosevelt, in his desperate effort to turn the tide to Lincoln, bustled back and forth between Massachusetts and New-York, went to several broken Western States, and conferred with Southern and Eastern men, all to little purpose. He could get a few votes for Lincoln in Alabama, but none elsewhere. He persuaded some of the Massachusetts men from attempting to swing the convention into line for Gen. W. T. Sherman. There was nothing in that, and he had the discernment to see it. Dutcher looked more cheerful than he felt. He would do anything to beat Blaine. He could do nothing but wait and go down with his colors. Again the roll was called. Again there were the scenes of confusion, now grown exceedingly tiresome. Alabama, Arkansas, California, Colorado, Connecticut, Delaware, Florida, Georgia, and Illinois voted as they did on the second ballot. Ex-Gov. Long took the Chair for a short time, and while he held it the convention was run from the Chair instead of acting as if there was no Chairman. The white-badged "all-Summer" Arthur men yelled with delight when the one Edmunds vote in Indiana was transferred to Arthur, but they suffered visible mortification when Arthur's vote in Kansas was wiped out and reappeared in Blaine's column. In Kentucky Blaine captured an Arthur man. There was no further change until Michigan was reached. When two of the Edmunds men went to Blaine the shouters shouted as if they had never shouted before, their liking for that sort of exercise appearing to grow. Arthur gained an Edmunds vote in Minnesota. It excited very feeble applause. It could do no good. Arthur gained one vote in Missouri, but Blaine gained four, probably Logan men. The howling Thurston, of Nebraska, attempted to make a hurrah speech in announcing that his State cast her 10 votes "solid for Blaine," and was hooted down and cut off by the Chair. At last New-Jersey found one vote for Arthur, but at the same time she increased Blaine's vote from 9 to 17 and transferred six votes from Edmunds to Lincoln. New-York cast her 71 votes—Edmunds 11, Blaine, 28, Arthur 31. In North Carolina Blaine gained one. Two of John Sherman's votes in Ohio go to Blaine, and the delegation was only kept back by Foraker, who was loyal to his candidate. The noise and confusion in the aisles was so great when Pennsylvania was reached that the Chair called upon the Sergeant-at-arms to clear them. Pennsylvania's vote was announced. The report was challenged and the State polled. Screams of victory went up when the call was ended, for the State gave Blaine 50, while Arthur's vote had dwindled to 8. The only Arthur men now left in Pennsylvania were Bingham, Pollock, Laws, Hunter, Thompson, Ruhl, Magee, and Flynn. Six of them are from Philadelphia and two from Pittsburg. The delegates at large, including the names of Disston and Emory, were welcomed with wild shouts as they cast their votes.

Mr. Dutcher, excited and warm, complained to the Chair that seats were occupied in the New-York delegation by persons who had no right in them, and Gen. McCook made the same complaint. The Chair, listening in a stupefied way, did nothing for the relief of the delegates, nor did he attempt to bear down the wild excitement without no perceptible cause, that suddenly seized upon the Blaine men, impelling to more frenzy of cheers. Blaine gained one vote in South Carolina. Arthur got one from Logan in Tennessee. Texas cut Logan's vote down and gave his loss of one to Blaine. The vote was challenged, and the roll call revealed nothing of interest except the fact that the historical Flanagan stuck to Arthur. Arthur lost a vote in Virginia, and Blaine got that and another from Logan, giving him 4 to Arthur's 20. It was small encouragement to the Arthur men that they gained 4 votes from Edmunds in Wisconsin, leaving the Vermont Senator with only one vote in the State. All was excitement again while the clerks were making up the report on the third ballot. The Arthur men desperately consulted together. Their "All Summer" badges did not appear to have done a perfect work. Blaine, of Maine, was appropriating Southern delegates, and unless a grand rally was made, all would be lost. A break appeared to be imminent. Everybody felt that and everybody thought he must stand up in the aisles on chairs, in the way of everybody else. There was a horrible report among the Arthur men that James D. Cullam had received a telegram from Senator Logan directing him to request the Logan men to give their votes to Blaine. The din was terrific. Clerk Clisbee came forward with the result of the third ballot. "Down!" "Down!" "Get down in front!" The Sergeant-at-arms who stood near the Ohio and New-York delegations in the very heart of the excitement, became conscious of the fact that there was confusion, and politely requested two or three messenger-boys to move along, while he overlooked the crowd of men who were the objects of the shouts to "get down." Judge Robertson gave himself up to the enthusiasm of the moment. Again and again he waved his white hat. Even "me too" Platt joined in the play, disregarding the Sergeant-at-Arms who stood on the stage and held his gilt-capped mace of authority over his head to command silence. Clerk Clisbee announced the result of the vote as follows:

THIRD BALLOT.

| States. | Full Vote. | Blaine. | Arthur. | Edmunds. | Logan. | John Sherman. | Hawley. | Lincoln. | W. T. Sherman. | Absent. |
|---|---|---|---|---|---|---|---|---|---|---|
| Alabama | 20 | 2 | 17 | | 1 | | | | | |
| Arkansas | 14 | 11 | 3 | | | | | | | |
| California | 16 | 16 | | | | | | | | |
| Colorado | 6 | 6 | | | | | | | | |
| Connecticut | 12 | | | | | | 12 | | | |
| Delaware | 6 | 5 | 1 | | | | | | | |
| Florida | 8 | 1 | 7 | | | | | | | |
| Georgia | 24 | | 24 | | | | | | | |
| Illinois | 44 | 3 | 1 | | 40 | | | | | |
| Indiana | 30 | 18 | 10 | | | 2 | | | | |
| Iowa | 26 | 26 | | | | | | | | |
| Kansas | 18 | 15 | | | 2 | | 1 | | | |
| Kentucky | 26 | 6 | 16 | | 2 | 2 | | 1 | | 1 |
| Louisiana | 16 | 4 | 9 | | 2 | | | | | |
| Maine | 12 | 12 | | | | | | | | |
| Maryland | 16 | 12 | 4 | | | | | | | |
| Massachusetts | 28 | 1 | 3 | 24 | | | | | | |
| Michigan | 26 | 18 | 4 | 3 | | 1 | | | | |
| Minnesota | 14 | 7 | 2 | 5 | | | | | | |
| Mississippi | 18 | 1 | 16 | | | | | | | 1 |
| Missouri | 32 | 12 | 11 | | | | | | | 1 |
| Nebraska | 10 | 10 | | | | | | | | |
| Nevada | 6 | 6 | | | | | | | | |
| New-Hampshire | 8 | | 5 | 3 | | | | | | |
| New-Jersey | 18 | 11 | 1 | | | 1 | | | | |
| New-York | 72 | 28 | 32 | 12 | | | | | | |
| North Carolina | 22 | 4 | 18 | | | | | | | |
| Ohio | 46 | 25 | | | | 21 | | | | |
| Oregon | 6 | 6 | | | | | | | | |
| Pennsylvania | 60 | 50 | 8 | 1 | 1 | | | 1 | | |
| Rhode Island | 8 | | | 8 | | | | | | |
| South Carolina | 18 | 2 | 16 | | | | | | | |
| Tennessee | 24 | 7 | 17 | | | | | | | |
| Texas | 26 | 14 | 11 | | 1 | | | | | |
| Vermont | 8 | | | 8 | | | | | | |
| Virginia | 24 | 4 | 20 | | | | | | | |
| West Virginia | 12 | 12 | | | | | | | | |
| Wisconsin | 22 | 11 | 10 | | | | | | 1 | |
| *Territories.* | | | | | | | | | | |
| Washington | 2 | 2 | | | | | | | | |
| Dakota | 2 | 2 | | | | | | | | |
| Arizona | 2 | 2 | | | | | | | | |
| Idaho | 2 | 1 | 1 | | | | | | | |
| Montana | 2 | 1 | | 1 | | | | | | |
| Wyoming | 2 | | 2 | | | | | | | |
| New-Mexico | 2 | | 2 | | | | | | | |
| Utah | 2 | | 2 | | | | | | | |
| District of Columbia | 2 | 1 | 1 | | | | | | | |
| Total | 820 | 375 | 274 | 69 | 53 | 25 | 13 | 7 | 1 | 4 |

Surpassing all the previous scenes of the session was that following the announcement that Blaine had received 375 votes. Up in the air fluttered thousands of handkerchiefs, waved by delegates who screamed as if they would go mad. Some one far down the hall stamped on the floor, and in an instant the cheering and hand-clapping was supplemented by a deep thunder roar that rolled back and forth beneath the wide-spreading roof. Whistles and cat-calls added to the noise. Again Collector Robertson waved his white hat, and ex-Speaker Sheard stood beside him indulging in violent vocal exercises. Gen. Husted, too, who had saved himself, got up briskly upon his chair and waved his handkerchief to the other wavers, and the cheers and stamping of feet and the cat-calls rose and fell, subsided and broke out again in an increasing volume.

### A MOTION TO ADJOURN.

Chairman Henderson's gavel was idle. He did not see Judge Foraker, who stood on a chair at the head of the Ohio delegation. He had been consulting with "Wheelhorse" Dutcher, and addressed the chair. He made a motion for a recess until 7:30. Dutcher had suggested the possibility of securing a combination of the Sherman and Arthur forces on Sherman. In this direction lay the only hope of defeating Blaine's nomination. Mr. Stewart, of Pennsylvania, standing in the midst of his excited colleagues shouted: "This convention has already passed beyond the skirmish line." When he was cut off by cries of "Regular order," "Oh no," and "Let down." Mr. Roosevelt, forcing the attention of the Chairman, made the point of order that the motion for a recess was not debatable or amendable. William Walter Phelps, standing just behind Mr. Roosevelt, flung his arms about and said something that pleased Stewart. He turned to the convention and addressed it. No one heard him at the front. Stewart and Roosevelt talked at each other vigorously. To the roaring crowd their conversation was but dumb show. The motion was put and a viva voce taken. The chair decided that the motion was lost, paying no attention to Roosevelt's demand, made before the decision that the roll of the States be called. The Chairman was heard to order the call of the roll for the fourth ballot, and now a strange state of things was seen upon the stage. About the Chairman stood Elkins, the Blaine captain, Warner Miller, ex-Senator Chaffee, Tom Donaldson, the clerks, and others, who were watching him industriously. The poor man's head was turned. Elkins was anxious and evidently determined that no small matter should prevent the Blaine men from marching straight to victory in the convention. He moved his head to the Convention as if to silence its noise. The turmoil ceased sufficiently to enable the Chairman's voice to be heard ordering the call of the roll for the fourth ballot. Ten hundred voices shouted in protest. Some one roared out: "The demand for a call on the motion to take a recess was not seconded." "Fair play, fair play," cried Draper out of the New-York delegation. "Let us have fair play in this convention."

The clerk called the State of Alabama. Mr. Titus Sheard climbed into a position under the eye of Manager Elkins and smartly made the point of order that as the State of Alabama had been called on the fourth ballot, no other business was in order. Elkins stood at the clerk's elbow and urged him to go on. Warner Miller braced the Chairman's back. Dutcher insists that Ohio and other States seconded the call for a vote by States. The situation was one threatening danger, perhaps the withdrawal of part of the delegates. Elkins was likely to have his way if some one did not interfere. The Chair sustained the point of order made by Mr. Sheard, and held that the fourth ballot should proceed. Gen. Husted made the point of order that the Chair had decided the motion for a recess lost. Elkins approved of this, and so did ex-Senator Spencer, who stood close behind the Chairman. But just then Major McKinley, speaking from the Ohio delegation, expressed the hope that no friend of James G. Blaine would raise any technical objection to taking the vote. The gentleman had the right to ask for a vote on the motion, and as a friend of Blaine's he hoped it would be taken. "Well said," shouted Mr. Roosevelt. The Chairman was allowed by Mr. Elkins and the other Blaine men who had usurped the powers of the Chair, to accord the rights for which Mr. McKinley had pleaded, and the roll was called.

The Blaine tide was now setting in with a rush. Gains were made in State after State. Many delegations were polled, New-York among the number. The vote was announced:

| | |
|---|---|
| Number of delegates | 820 |
| Whole number of votes cast | 814 |
| Yeas | 364 |
| Nays | 450 |

Victory was at hand for the Blaine men, and they cheered again and with redoubled energy. Roosevelt saw the chance of combination slip from him. There was nothing to be done but to await the next ballot. Judge Foraker, of Ohio, got the attention of the Chair, after he had waited for the hubbub to cease, and he brought it all on again by moving that the rules be suspended in order that the nomination of James G. Blaine might be made by acclamation. Mr. Roosevelt stood on his chair, and with a dozen others addressed the Chair. He demanded the call of the roll, while the crowds of Blaine men about him wanted Judge Foraker's motion adopted. Foraker, seeing that time would be wasted in carrying out his proposition, withdrew it.

### THE NOMINATION.

The Chair ordered the roll to be called, and the fourth ballot began while the convention was in terrible disorder. The Alabama delegates ran like sheep to Blaine. He gained six of them, and the gain was celebrated with noise indescribable. So absurd was it that Mr. J. C. Burrows, of Michigan, declared that if it was continued he would move that the convention adjourn to a hall by itself. Florida's vote went to Blaine. Georgia stuck to Arthur on a poll of the delegation. When Illinois was reached Blaine wanted only a handful of votes to be nominated. Senator Cullom rose with a telegram in his hand. Mr. Gilbert, Mr. Roosevelt, and others objected. Mr. Burrows, whose strong voice served him in good stead, made the point of order that it was not in order to read the dispatch. "Right!" "Roll-call!" "Go on!" was shouted by a hundred delegates. Cullom desisted, but he cast 34 votes for Blaine and he had a majority.

Once more the hall trembled with the cheering and the pounding of feet. Burrows rushed up through the reporters' chairs and demanded of the Chairman: "Stop this —— —— nonsense; use the gavel; pound away; stop this infernal racket!" The Chairman feebly tried to stop it and Indiana voted her 30 delegates for Blaine. Mr. Dutcher stopped to drink a glass of convention lemonade as the convention cheered Indiana. Kentucky was polled, and Commissioner Evans announced that he still voted for Chester A. Arthur. The sun had come out brightly and was shining in broad bands across the hall, slanting from the high clere-story windows down upon the thousands of faces and upon the decorated galleries. The crowd inside had been sending up cheer after cheer. When Louisiana was reached ex-Senator Kellogg made good the instructions he had given for months, that the delegates from his State would go to Blaine. He voted for the Plumed Knight on a poll of the State, and so did his colleague, Morey. Again New-York was polled upon the demand of John D. Lawson. The vote stood 31 for Arthur, 29 for Blaine, 9 for Edmunds, 2 for Hawley, and 1 for Lincoln. Wheelhorse Dutcher and "the boys" went down with their flags flying and put away their "all-Summer" badges for a more auspicious occasion.

Judge Foraker, when Ohio was reached, created an intense excitement by a brief speech. He said that he had from the first supported John Sherman, but would now withdraw his name and cast for James G. Blaine the 46 votes of the State of Ohio. In Tennessee, when it was polled, Delegates Watson and McElwee, who, with Delegate Pruitt, from the same State, applied to "Al Daggett" for $600 to assist them in standing by Arthur, went over to Blaine, and earned a title to assistance by Manager Elkins. "What are we here for?" Flanagan, of Texas, stuck to Arthur to the last. The clerks prepared their report. The convention went mad again with cheering, and returned to a condition of sanity to hear it read. It was as follows:

FOURTH BALLOT.

| States. | Full Vote. | Blaine. | Arthur. | Edmunds. | Logan. | Hawley. | Lincoln. |
|---|---|---|---|---|---|---|---|
| Alabama | 20 | 8 | 12 | | | | |
| Arkansas | 14 | 11 | 3 | | | | |
| California | 16 | 16 | | | | | |
| Colorado | 6 | 6 | | | | | |
| Connecticut | 12 | | | | | 12 | |
| Delaware | 6 | 5 | 1 | | | | |
| Florida | 8 | 3 | 5 | | | | |
| Georgia | 24 | | 24 | | | | |
| Illinois* | 44 | 34 | 3 | | 6 | | |
| Indiana | 30 | 30 | | | | | |
| Iowa | 26 | 24 | 2 | | | | |
| Kansas | 18 | 18 | | | | | |
| Kentucky | 26 | 9 | 15 | | 1 | | 1 |
| Louisiana | 16 | 9 | 7 | | | | |
| Maine | 12 | 12 | | | | | |
| Maryland | 16 | 15 | 1 | | | | |
| Massachusetts | 28 | 3 | 7 | 18 | | | |
| Michigan | 26 | 26 | | | | | |
| Minnesota | 14 | 14 | | | | | |
| Mississippi | 18 | 2 | 16 | | | | |
| Missouri | 32 | 32 | | | | | |
| Nebraska | 10 | 10 | | | | | |
| Nevada | 6 | 6 | | | | | |
| New-Hampshire | 8 | 3 | 2 | 3 | | | |
| New-Jersey | 18 | 17 | | 1 | | | |
| New-York | 72 | 29 | 30 | 9 | | 2 | 1 |
| North Carolina | 22 | 8 | 12 | | | 1 | |
| Ohio | 46 | 46 | | | | | |
| Oregon | 6 | 6 | | | | | |
| Pennsylvania | 60 | 51 | 8 | 1 | | | |
| Rhode Island | 8 | | 1 | | | | |
| South Carolina | 18 | 2 | 15 | 1 | | | |
| Tennessee | 24 | 11 | 12 | | | | |
| Texas | 26 | 15 | 8 | | | | |
| Vermont | 8 | | | 8 | | | |
| Virginia | 24 | 4 | 20 | | | | |
| West Virginia | 12 | 12 | | | | | |
| *Territories.* | | | | | | | |
| Wisconsin | 22 | 22 | | | | | |
| Arizona | 2 | 2 | | | | | |
| Dakota | 2 | 2 | | | | | |
| Idaho | 2 | 2 | | | | | |
| Montana | 2 | 2 | | | | | |
| New-Mexico | 2 | 2 | | | | | |
| Utah | 2 | | 2 | | | | |
| Washington | 2 | 2 | | | | | |
| Wyoming | 2 | 2 | | | | | |
| District of Columbia | 2 | 1 | 1 | | | | |
| Total | 820 | 541 | 207 | 41 | 7 | 15 | 2 |
| Necessary for choice, 441. | | | | | | | |

The victory was sure. All the noise that had gone before was but play to that which now arose. It seemed but a minute before the booming of a cannon was heard breaking the cheers of the crowds in the stand. The band played, but the cheers drowned its music. The Kansas delegates paraded the crowded aisles with a banner, carrying a portrait of Blaine and a promise of 75,000 majority for him for President, and at last landed it on the stage. The Colorado delegates carried about the great eagle swathed in flags which they had carried over the mountains to the convention.

### AFTER THE NOMINATION.

An excited throng clustered about the Chairman's desk. Senator Warner Miller loomed up behind the Chairman. Congressman Henry G. Burleigh, of New-York, took his position beside the New-York Senator and waited for the Chairman to quell the tumult. When it had somewhat subsided, the Chairman, whose voice was so hoarse that he could hardly be heard, nodded at Secretary McPherson. That gentleman inquired, "Shall the nomination be now made unanimous?" The boom of a gun sounded in the distance. Congressman Burleigh immediately stepped forward, and the audience grew silent. "In behalf of President Arthur and at his request," said Mr. Burleigh, "I move to make the nomination of James G. Blaine, of Maine, unanimous. I promise for the friends of Mr. Arthur, who always remain loyal to the ticket, [applause,] that James G. Blaine will receive 20,000 majority in Northern New-York. We will show you in November next that New-York is a Republican State. We elected Garfield and we will elect James G. Blaine, of Maine." [Applause.]

Then the hubbub began again, and above it all could be heard cries for a speech from George William Curtis. Congressman McKinley, of Ohio, pushed his way through the crowd in the aisles and reached the row of seats occupied by Mr. Curtis and Theodore Roosevelt. He first addressed himself to Mr. Roosevelt and asked him to make a speech. Mr. Roosevelt plumply declined. Then Mr. McKinley urged George William Curtis to respond. Mr. Curtis shook his head, and those who were watching his face knew that it was in sorrow and not in anger that he declined to say aught against the nomination or anything in its behalf. Senator D. M. Sabin, of Minnesota, got the eye of the Chairman, and in a brief speech seconded the nomination. Of course, he was cheered and applauded. He said:

MR. CHAIRMAN: Four years ago, in this very hall and as a delegate to the National Republican Convention, I was opposed to Chester A. Arthur and to the elements with which he then associated. Since then he has been called, under the most trying circumstances, to fill the first place in the gift of the people of this country. So well, so nobly, so faithfully, has he fulfilled this trust, and so happily has he disappointed not only those of his opponents but his friends, so fully has he filled the position of the scholar and the gentleman, that he is possessed of the great good common sense which has made his Administration a great and pronounced success, that he has grown upon me until to-day I honor and revere Chester A. Arthur. [Applause.] As a friend of his, I no less honor and revere that prince of gentlemen, that scholar, that gifted statesman, James G. Blaine, whose nomination it affords me the greatest pleasure to second, with the prediction that his name before this country in November will produce that same spontaneous enthusiasm which will make him President of the United States on the 4th of March next. [Loud and prolonged applause.]

Senator Plumb, of Kansas, suggested that as the convention was in good humor it should go on and complete the nominations. There were cries of "No," "No," "Recess," "Recess," and the Senator proceeded to second the nomination, concluding with the hope that there would not be a dissenting vote. Again there was a boisterous demonstration, which was with difficulty suppressed, even when Secretary McPherson came to the front of the platform and waved a telegraph dispatch over his head. "From the President," shouted he, and curiosity once awakened, something like quiet was again restored. Then he read its words, after first announcing that they had just been sent by President Arthur to Mr. Blaine at his home at Augusta. They were these: "As the candidate of the Republican Party, you will have my earnest and cordial support." Cheer after cheer followed the reading.

"Is the convention ready for the question?" demanded the Chairman.

"Question, question," was the response from all parts of the house.

"Those who are in favor of making the nomination of James G. Blaine unanimous will say Aye."

There was a long, loud shout, in which the galleries joined.

"Those who are opposed will say No."

There was no response.

William Walter Phelps, of New-Jersey, moved to take a recess until evening. The confusion was increasing again, and the Chairman blinked wildly and wondered what he ought to do. Gen. Husted, of New-York, shouted, "Mr. Chairman," in his sharp, penetrating voice, and the Chairman's wool-gathering wits once more reassembled. The General then moved to take a recess until 8 o'clock, and this was promptly carried. The spectators filed out in rare good humor to the booming of the guns planted on the green outside the convention hall. Those delegates who had been hurrahing for Blaine hurrahed again and again, and those who had contemplated with thoughtful faces his nomination were faces thoughtful still.

Efforts were made by the curious to wring some expression of opinion from George William Curtis and Mr. Roosevelt as to the attitude which the independents of New-York would probably assume. Neither of them cared to talk, and Mr. Curtis made his way to his hotel. "I was at the birth of the Republican Party, and I fear I am to witness its death," was a remark by Mr. Curtis before the balloting was ended, although it had proceeded far enough to demonstrate that Mr. Blaine was to be nominated.

"To say that I am satisfied with the nomination of Mr. Blaine," exclaimed Mr. Roosevelt, "would be false. I have participated in a Republican convention, and by all the usages of the party, I would be expected to support its nominee. I could have given an earnest and enthusiastic support to a ticket headed by such a man as George F. Edmunds, or Robert T. Lincoln, or Gen. Joseph R. Hawley, or Secretary Gresham. I should suppose, from what I have heard many independents say, that they would not give Mr. Blaine any support whatever; and I believe they will keep their promise. I have nothing further to say upon this subject at the present time."

## LOGAN FOR VICE-PRESIDENT.

THE EVENING AND LAST SESSION OF THE CONVENTION A TAME AFFAIR—NO OPPOSITION TO LOGAN—THE ADJOURNMENT.

*From a Staff Correspondent of the Times.*

CHICAGO, June 6.—There was no such crowd in the convention building in the evening as had attended all the previous sessions. Empty spaces were visible in the end gallery. The enthusiasm, which had been so marked a feature of the day's proceedings, was spent, and the delegates and audience once more acted like rational beings. It had got around that John A. Logan was to be nominated for the Vice-Presidency. A telegram from him to the effect that he was in the hands of his friends had been exhibited, and his friends were present in force.

The split in the District of Columbia delegation was the first thing to claim the convention's attention. It was indeed forced upon the convention by the irrepressible Conger, who demanded to know whether his colored colleague, Perry H. Carson, the coachman who drove Guiteau between the jail and his place of trial, appeared on the roll as the member of the National Committee from the District. The Chairman said it was, and that Mr. Conger's alternate had voted in favor of the selection of Mr. Carson. Mr. Conger was disposed to hold an argument with the Chairman, but the latter rapped him down. "Is the voice of the District of Columbia to be stilled in this way?" demanded Conger. "The Chair wishes he could so dispose of it," exclaimed the despairing Chairman. This, the only exhibition of brightness from the vicinity of the presiding officer's desk, caused peals of laughter, in which Conger himself had to join. Mr. Carson's name was on the roll to remain, and the convention, after an opening prayer by the Rev. Mr. Riley, of Detroit, again brushed the importunate Conger aside and proceeded to nominate a Vice-President.

Against the Chairman's desk leaned a stuffed black eagle, surmounting the standard of the Colorado delegation. Somebody yelled, "Take away that bird!" and the thing was removed. During the intermission there had been an active canvass around the hotels of candidates for Vice-President, Logan, Foraker, Lincoln, and Gresham being the leading names discussed. It was currently reported that Lincoln had telegraphed his friends that he would not take the nomination, and the drift of sentiment was toward Logan. The fact that he was the most conspicuous soldier among the list of candidates gave him the preference among a majority of delegates. The anti-Blaine men expressed their willingness to let Blaine's friends complete the ticket. The list of States which had not yet furnished candidates for the

The New-York Times.

VOL. XXXIII......NO. 10,225. NEW-YORK, THURSDAY, JUNE 12, 1884. PRICE TWO CENTS.

# MR. TILDEN WILL NOT RUN

## *HE ABSOLUTELY DECLINES THE NOMINATION AT CHICAGO.*

### HIS REASONS SET FORTH IN A LETTER TO MR. DANIEL MANNING—HE "SUBMITS TO THE WILL OF GOD" IN DEEMING HIS "PUBLIC CAREER FOREVER CLOSED."

**The publication of the subjoined letter from ex-Gov. Samuel J. Tilden to the Chairman of the Democratic State Committee has been foreshadowed in the political dispatches of THE TIMES. As it was expected he would, Mr. Tilden refuses to again enter the Presidential race:**

NEW-YORK, June 10, 1884.

*To Daniel Manning, Chairman of the Democratic State Committee of New-York:*

In my letter of June 18, 1880, addressed to the delegates from the State of New-York to the Democratic National Convention, I said:

"Having now borne faithfully my full share of labor and care in the public service, and wearing the marks of its burdens, I desire nothing so much as an honorable discharge. I wish to lay down the honors and toils of even *quasi* party leadership, and to seek the repose of private life.

"In renouncing renomination for the Presidency, I do so with no doubt in my mind as to the vote of the State of New-York, or of the United States, but because I believe that it is a renunciation of re-election to the Presidency.

"To those who think my renomination and re-election indispensable to an effectual vindication of the right of the people to elect their rulers—violated in my person—I have accorded as long a reserve of my decision as possible, but I cannot overcome my repugnance to enter into a new engagement which involves four years of ceaseless toil.

"The dignity of the Presidential office is above a merely personal ambition, but it creates in me no illusion. Its value is as a great power for good to the country. I said four years ago in accepting nomination:

"'Knowing as I do, therefore, from fresh experience, how great the difference is between gliding through an official routine and working out a reform of systems and policies, it is impossible for me to contemplate what needs to be done in the Federal Administration without an anxious sense of the difficulties of the undertaking. If summoned by the suffrages of my countrymen to attempt this work, I shall endeavor, with God's help, to be the efficient instrument of their will.'

"Such a work of renovation after many years of misrule, such a reform of systems and policies, to which I would cheerfully have sacrificed all that remained to me of health and life, is now, I fear, beyond my strength."

My purpose to withdraw from further public service and the grounds of it were at that time well known to you and to others; and when, at Cincinnati, though respecting my wishes yourself, you communicated to me an appeal from many valued friends to relinquish that purpose, I reiterated my determination unconditionally.

In the four years which have since elapsed nothing has occurred to weaken, but everything to strengthen, the considerations which induced my withdrawal from public life. To all who have addressed me on the subject my intention has been frankly communicated. Several of my most confidential friends, under the sanction of their own names, have publicly stated my determination to be irreversible. That I have occasion now to consider the question is an event for which I have no responsibility. The appeal made to me by the Democratic masses, with apparent unanimity, to serve them once more is entitled to the most deferential consideration, and would inspire a disposition to do anything desired of me if it were consistent with my judgment of duty.

I believe that there is no instrumentality in human society so potential in its influence upon mankind for good or evil as the governmental machinery for administering justice and for making and executing laws. Not all the eleemosynary institutions of private benevolence to which philanthropists may devote their lives are so fruitful in benefits as the rescue and preservation of this machinery from the perversions that make it the instrument of conspiracy, fraud and crime against the most sacred rights and interests of the people.

For fifty years, as a private citizen, never contemplating an official career, I have devoted at least as much thought and effort to the duty of influencing aright the action of the governmental institutions of my country as to all other objects. I have never accepted official service except for a brief period, for a special purpose, and only when the occasion seemed to require from me that sacrifice of private preferences to the public welfare.

I undertook the State administration of New-York because it was supposed that in that way only could the Executive power be arrayed on the side of the reforms to which, as a private citizen, I had given three years of my life.

I accepted the nomination for the Presidency in 1876 because of the general conviction that my candidacy would best present the issue of reform which the Democratic majority of the people desired to have worked out in the Federal Government as it had been in that of the State of New-York. I believed that I had strength enough then to renovate the administration of the Government of the United States, and at the close of my term to hand over the great trust to a successor faithful to the same policy.

Though anxious to seek the repose of private life, I nevertheless acted upon the idea that every power is a trust and involves a duty. In reply to the address of the committee communicating my nomination, I depicted the difficulties of the undertaking, and likened my feelings in engaging in it to those of a soldier entering battle, but I did not withhold the entire consecration of my powers to the public service.

Twenty years of continuous maladministration, under the demoralizing influences of intestine war and of bad finance, have infected the whole governmental system of the United States with the cancerous growths of false constructions and false practices. Powerful classes have acquired pecuniary interests in official abuses, and the moral standards of the people have been impaired. To redress these evils is a work of great difficulty and labor, and cannot be accomplished without the most energetic and efficient personal action on the part of the Chief Executive of the Republic.

The canvass and administration which it is desired that I should undertake would embrace a period of nearly five years. Nor can I admit any illusion as to their burdens. Three years of experience in the endeavor to reform the municipal government of the city of New-York and two years of experience in renovating the administration of the State of New-York have made me familiar with the requirements of such a work.

At the present time the considerations which induced my action in 1880 have become imperative. I ought not to assume a task which I have not the physical strength to carry through. To reform the administration of the Federal Government; to realize my own ideal, and to fulfill the just expectations of the people, would indeed warrant, as they could alone compensate, the sacrifices which the undertaking would involve. But, in my condition of advancing years and declining strength, I feel no assurance of my ability to accomplish those objects. I am, therefore, constrained to say, definitively, that I cannot now assume the labors of an administration or of a canvass.

Undervaluing in nowise that best gift of heaven, the occasion and the power sometimes bestowed upon a mere individual to communicate an impulse for good; grateful beyond all words to my fellow-countrymen who would assign such a beneficent function to me, I am consoled by the reflection that neither the Democratic Party, nor the Republic for whose future that party is the best guarantee, is now or ever can be dependent upon any one man for their successful progress in the path of a noble destiny.

Having given to their welfare whatever of health and strength I possessed, or could borrow from the future, and having reached the term of my capacity for such labors as their welfare now demands, I but submit to the will of God in deeming my public career forever closed.

SAMUEL J. TILDEN.

## CLEVELAND MEN REJOICING.

### AN ATTEMPT TO BE MADE TO SECURE THE FAVOR OF ALL STATE DEMOCRATS.

ALBANY, June 11.—There is great rejoicing here this evening among those Democrats who adhere to the fortunes of Gov. Cleveland and hope to see him installed in the Presidential chair. Daniel Manning returned this morning from a visit to Samuel J. Tilden, at Greystone, with the positive assurance that the Sage will not be a candidate before the Democratic National Convention. To make assurance doubly sure, Mr. Manning brought with him a letter to that effect from Mr. Tilden himself, which will be published in the *Argus* to-morrow morning, and will be sent out this evening for publication in the morning papers throughout the country. The *Argus* will print a double-leaded editorial commenting upon Tilden's declination, and presenting Grover Cleveland as the candidate of the New-York Democracy to take the place of the Sage of Gramercy.

From this date onward until the meeting of the Democratic Convention at Chicago the *Argus* will continue to boom Cleveland for the nomination. This is one cause of the rejoicing among the Cleveland Democrats here, for hitherto some doubt has existed as to the real position of Mr. Manning, and whether or not the Chairman of the State Committee was not secretly working in the interest of Flower, or of some man outside of the State, in case Tilden should refuse to be a candidate. There is nothing in Mr. Tilden's letter indicating that he wishes to make Gov. Cleveland his legatee, and Mr. Manning says that no such inference should be drawn from the fact that he has chosen to turn the *Argus* to the support of the Governor. Mr. Tilden, he says, will not attempt to influence the action of the National Convention in any way. The only thing that troubles the Governor's friends now is, whether they will be able to muster a majority of the delegates to the State Convention to be held next Wednesday. It has always been the custom for Democratic State Conventions to instruct the delegation to National Conventions to vote as a unit, and if, as the friends of Mr. Flower claim, they are sure to have upward of 200 of the 384 delegates to the State Convention, the delegation to Chicago will not vote for Cleveland unless there should be a compromise or unless Mr. Flower should withdraw from the field. Mr. Manning's efforts during the coming week will be devoted to bringing about such a compromise in order that the New-York Democracy may present a solid front for Cleveland at Chicago. A great many influential politicians in the party have got to be reconciled before this can be done.

After his visit to Mr. Tilden, Mr. Manning had an interview with "Boss" McLaughlin, of Brooklyn; Hubert O. Thompson, ex-Mayor Cooper, and others, and it was conceded that some pledge would have to be exacted from the Governor before he could get the united support of the Democracy of the State for the Presidency. McLaughlin was intending to send a solid delegation from Brooklyn for Tilden or Flower, but in no event for Cleveland. His orders will be modified, now that Tilden is out of the field, so as to include the Governor, provided the requisite assurances are given. Just where Tammany Hall is to "catch on" in the deal no one seems to know. It cannot be ascertained that John Kelly has been, or is to be, consulted by Mr. Manning or by any of the parties to the negotiations. The Governor has certainly not made any pledges to him, nor authorized his friends to make any. His pledges, if he makes any, will be to the "regular organization," and unless Tammany consents to disband as a separate organization, give up her identity, and join the regular army commanded by Chairman Manning, she is going to "get left." The Tammany Democrats here in Albany predict that John Kelly will not subscribe to any terms which require him to surrender his separate organization and leadership, and that, if pushed to the wall, he will find it more conducive to his "personal comfort" to enlist his brethren in the service of the "Plumed Knight," rather than fight in the ranks with Cleveland as a leader and Dan Manning as first lieutenant.

The following delegates were elected from this county to-day: First District—Erastus Corning, James W. Hutt, John H. Lynch; Second District—Samuel Hand, Charles Tracey, John D. Lendrum; Third District—Daniel Manning, A. Bleecker Banks, Edward A. Maher; Fourth District—George E. Simmons, John W. Hart, and James Stevens. Those in the Fourth District are claimed by the Flower men and the others are certainly for Cleveland. Two Cleveland National delegates will be chosen from this district. They will probably be Daniel Manning and Erastus Corning. If Mr. Manning goes as a delegate at large, it is likely that Judge Hand or Mayor Banks will be put in his place.

## WHAT LEADING DEMOCRATS SAY.

### A GENERAL TURNING TO CLEVELAND—FLOWER'S CANVASS THOUGHT TO BE ABSURD.

WASHINGTON, June 11.—Mr. Tilden's letter to Chairman Manning, of the Democratic State Committee, positively declining to become a candidate for President, has awakened a great deal of interest here to-night. Very few persons have read it, and Democratic members of Congress who have only learned that such a letter has been written and sent out are already discussing the probable result of the first trustworthy declaration from the sage of Greystone. After conversation with a number of Democrats, the conclusion is forced that the declination of Tilden has served to centre attention upon Gov. Cleveland as the candidate, at once available and strong, among all the Democrats who have been named for the place. Missouri, Kentucky, Louisiana, South Carolina, and other Southern States are strong for him. Joe McDonald has been here again, tramping about the halls of Congress and keeping himself before the Democratic Representatives and Senators, but there is no doubt that he has injured his chances of a nomination by this cheap way of bidding for it. The importance of taking the leading candidate from New-York is almost universally conceded. There is no doubt that Southern and Western Democrats are regarding with great concern the apparently increasing strength of Mr. Flower in his own State. The fact ought not to be concealed that Democrats look upon Mr. Flower as something to laugh at, while his ambition to be President is commented upon as good-natured presumption. Very sensible Democrats declare that if he should be nominated by some unfortunate accident they would look for Blaine's election by an enormous majority of Electoral votes. They see the reports from different New-York districts which are electing delegates to the State Convention for Flower, and comment upon them with alarm. It strikes them as absurd that any Democrat should be so blind to the condition of things as to offer a candidate who would become in the South and West a laughing-stock, whatever might be thought of him in New-York.

Senator Bayard's friends, in the belief that his chances for securing the Democratic nomination for the Presidency will be helped by the wide publication of his Dover speech in 1861, are disposed to circulate it, and copies of a paper containing it were given out to-day in large numbers. The Senator shows no desire to conceal it, and persons who enjoy his acquaintance and have heard him talk about it, say that he is of the opinion that a perusal will excite no hostility to him. But there are many Democrats who do not share this opinion. They are not unfriendly to Mr. Bayard, and the speech referred to would not deter them an instant from indorsing him as a candidate for President. The effect upon Democrats of the North and West, who were strong Union men in common with the Republicans of the same sections, would it is apprehended be seriously against the chances of a candidate who might be exposed to the charge of hesitation. Some of the New-York members—Mr. Dorsheimer, Mr. Belmont, and one or two others are among the number—are cordially in favor of the presentation of Mr. Bayard's name. They have not taken Tilden's chances into consideration, having been sure that he would not allow his name to go before the convention.

## A HOT FIGHT IN ST. LAWRENCE.

### DOUBLE DELEGATIONS CHOSEN IN THE SECOND AND THIRD DISTRICTS.

WATERTOWN, June 11.—This has been a busy day for the Flower and Cleveland Democrats of St. Lawrence County. Money flowed like water, and victory can hardly be reckoned to-night. In the Second Assembly District Convention at Canton, which was distinguished for disorder, a Cleveland delegate moved to proceed to perfect the temporary organization, but the Chairman refused to entertain the motion. The mover put the question and it was declared carried. The Cleveland faction then went on to organize the convention. They chose D. H. Carpenter, Atkins Foster, and Peter Martin as delegates to the State Convention and adjourned. The Flower minority then organized a convention and elected the Hon. W. H. Sawyer, C. V. Conkey, and J. R. Smith. In the Third District Convention, at Norwood, nearly the same tactics prevailed. Two delegations were chosen, Flower's being composed of V. H. Paddock, C. W. Peck, and Patrick Rennehan, and Cleveland's of John O. Bridges, Sumner Sweet, and John B. Whalen. The convention was divided from the beginning.

Later information from the Second District states that the Flower men held caucuses in the towns where they were defeated and admitted their delegates to their convention, thus gaining a quorum. The fight has developed into one of the hottest contests known to St. Lawrence County, and both sides claim the district. D. Magone telegraphs from Ogdensburg to-night to Cleveland's friends here that he has carried the three districts, but the matter will probably not be decided before reaching the Saratoga Convention. In case Magone's faction triumphs he, with D. D. Griffin, of this city, will be sent to Chicago in spite of the protestations of Flower's friends.

## A SET-BACK FOR CLEVELAND.

### THE HERKIMER COUNTY DEMOCRATS ELECT FLOWER DELEGATES TO SARATOGA.

UTICA, June 11.—Herkimer County Democrats, who have been claimed by ex-Assemblyman George W. Smith to be strongly for Cleveland, declared against him in emphatic terms in their County Convention to-day. Judge Smith wants the nomination for Congress in the Herkimer-Otsego-Schoharie district, which he helped to carve out with that purpose in view while in the Assembly. Clinton Beckwith, who was defeated in last Fall's Senatorial contest, has the same ambition. Both desired to go to the Saratoga Convention—Smith for Cleveland and Beckwith for Flower; both are left at home by the action of to-day's convention, and the friends of the Governor were further humiliated by a requirement that each candidate for State delegate make declaration against Cleveland. Five candidates were named from whom to choose three delegates, and four of these named Tilden for first choice and Flower for second. The fifth declared for Flower and no second choice. The latter was one of the three elected. A resolution declaring that the Democrats of Herkimer County are for Tilden first and Flower second for President, and directing the delegates to Saratoga so to vote, was declared adopted by a vote of 31 to 23. The announcement was challenged as fraudulent on the ground that 8 responses for Flower were counted as yeas in order, as is alleged, to embarrass Judge Smith in his Congressional canvass. A new County Committee was elected, though that business has heretofore been left to the second County Convention. The friends of Gov. Cleveland are thoroughly crestfallen over the fortunes of the day.

## DEMOCRATIC DELEGATES CHOSEN.

BUFFALO, June 11.—The Democratic caucuses to elect delegates to the conventions of the three Assembly districts in this city were held last evening. They were pretty generally contested, and it is not clear even yet what the contest was about. All the tickets were headed with Gov. Cleveland's name as a Presidential candidate, and no one confessed that he was not for Cleveland. It is said that the fight was over the question of who should be delegates to the National Convention from this district. Messrs. D. N. Lockwood and Solomon Scheu are mentioned as candidates on one side and Senator Titus and James Mooney on the other. Lockwood and Scheu have not been known as Cleveland men, but were supported by the Governor's friends, and are said to have carried nine of the 13 wards. There is an undercurrent of ill feeling to Cleveland here, coming chiefly from Democrats who have not received the offices or patronage they wanted, but it does not show itself openly.

JAMESTOWN, N. Y., June 11.—The Democrats of the Second Assembly District of Chautauqua County held their convention at Sinclairville to-day. The delegates elected to the State Convention are C. E. Weeks, Jamestown; C. D. Murray, Dunkirk, and Lorenzo Morris, Fredonia. They were not formally instructed, but a resolution favoring the nomination of Gov. Cleveland for President was passed.

ALBANY, N. Y., June 11.—The Delaware County Democratic delegates are Henry Davie, William H. Wilson, and George L. Gordon. They were instructed for Cleveland. F. R. Gilbert was named for delegate to the National Convention.

TROY, N. Y., June 11.—The Democratic District Convention held at Whitehall to-day for Washington County elected John C. Thomson, A. Gilligan, and James Donaldson delegates to the State Convention.

TROY, N. Y., June 11.—The delegates to the Democratic State Convention chosen at Westport, Essex County, are A. Ross, R. Trumbull, and W. W. Wyman.

SUSPENSION BRIDGE, N. Y., June 11.—The Second Assembly District Convention of Niagara County elected A. H. Lee, Walter Horne, and Stephen Mead delegates to the State Convention.

RIVERHEAD, Long Island, June 11.—The Suffolk County delegation will be Henry A. Reeves, Greenport; W. D. Woodend, Huntington; Brendley D. Sleight, Sag Harbor.

HERKIMER, N. Y., June 11.—A. W. Shephard, W. W. Moshier, and J. M. Dygert were elected delegates from this county to the Democratic State Convention.

OWEGO, N. Y., June 11.—Tioga County sends C. E. Holenbeck, S. W. Leach, and Patrick Malony as delegates to the Saratoga Convention.

CANANDAIGUA, N. Y., June 11.—Ontario sends John Flannigan, A. E. Spitz, and B. W. Freshour to the Democratic State Convention.

## MR. HENDRICKS NOT SURPRISED.

INDIANAPOLIS, June 11.—The Hon. Thomas A. Hendricks, in an interview concerning Tilden's letter of declination, said the news was not a surprise to him, for when he visited Tilden in August last that gentleman very firmly announced his intention to remain permanently out of politics. In his succeeding visit in April last the same determination had been expressed. Mr. Hendricks thought there was little doubt that the old ticket would have been unanimously nominated at the Chicago Convention if it had not been for his declination to-day. He said that the demand for it among the Democracy was almost universal and greater than any movement of the kind he had ever seen in politics. Personally he felt no great disappointment, as he did not want the office of Vice-President eight years ago and did not want it now. If the old ticket had remained in the field he should have considered an election to that place a great honor conferred by the people as a rebuke to what they consider a great wrong. It would have prevented the seating of Hayes in 1878 from becoming a precedent for future elections. Mr. Hendricks added that only as an expression of the indignation of the people would he have regarded his election to the Vice-Presidency as an honor to be sought.

## *THE DEMOCRATIC CONVENTION.*

### ROOMS ALREADY ENGAGED FOR THE LEADING DELEGATES.

CHICAGO, June 11.—July 7, the day before the Democratic Convention opens, will see over a dozen clubs representing strong Jeffersonian principles assembled here from all parts of the country. Each will be headed by a band of music, each will be dressed in uniform, and all will contribute more noise in a day than the entire Republican Convention did in a week. The Duckworth Club, of Cincinnati, numbering 150, will be at the Sherman House, and the Jefferson Club, of the same city, will come 200 strong. The Samuel J. Randall Club, of Philadelphia, will be quartered at the Commercial. The Americus Club, of Philadelphia, numbering over 100, have secured quarters at the Clifton. The clubs which will come from New-York and Brooklyn will doubtless outshine both the Cincinnati and Philadelphia boys. There will be numerous local organizations from both cities. The Tammany Hall organization will stop at the Palmer, with head-quarters in Parlor A. The Kings County Club will have Room No. 72 at the Leland, while the County Democracy of New-York will also hang up there. The leaders will be very generally scattered. Roswell P. Flower will have Rooms Nos. 17 and 19 in the Leland; Congressman Dorsheimer, Room No. 23, Leland; Gov. Ben Butler, Parlors J and K, in the Palmer House; John Kelly, Parlor G, Palmer, and Mayor Prince, of Boston, Parlor F, Palmer; Chairman Barnum, Parlor E, Palmer; S. P. Barbour, of Virginia, Room No. 61, Palmer; Committeeman Ham, of Iowa, Parlor H, Palmer; Brown, of Indiana, Parlor P, Palmer; Armstrong, of Ohio, Parlor Q, Palmer, and Kelly, of Minnesota, Parlor M, Palmer. At the Palmer also will be Alva Sulloway, of New-Hampshire; Orestes Cleveland, of New-Jersey; Abraham S. Hewitt, of New-York; Bradley P. Smalley, of Vermont; Alexander Campbell, of West Virginia; William F. Vilas and T. H. Sherley, of Kentucky.

## *A TREASURER'S ACCOUNTS SHORT.*

NEWARK, June 11.—At a meeting of the Common Council Committee on Finance to-night a resolution was adopted requesting the Council to instruct the City Counsel to commence suit against ex-City Treasurer Stout and his bondsmen to recover the $10,491 deficiency in his accounts in July, 1883. The Controller and City Counsel were instructed to confer with the Financial Committee of the Board of Freeholders in regard to the payment of $72,000 due the county by the city, and which the former threatens to have mandamused.

# LEGISLATING IN SECRET

## *THE SENATE VOTES TO BUY CONCESSIONS OF DOUBTFUL VALUE.*

### EXTRAORDINARY LEGISLATIVE METHODS ADOPTED — THE NICARAGUAN CANAL THE OBJECT IN VIEW.

WASHINGTON, June 11.—In its action upon the Consular and Diplomatic Appropriation bill to-day the Senate introduced an innovation in the methods of legislating upon important public measures. The bill was called up at the earliest moment it could be reached under the rules, and Mr. Allison repeated his tactics of yesterday by demanding a secret session, the only matter not having been acted upon being the mysterious Senate amendment, appropriating $250,000 to carry out the terms of the neutrality act. No sooner were the doors closed than the wrangle, which occupied most of yesterday afternoon, was renewed and kept up until its practical settlement several hours later. The appropriation is to be expended under the direction of the President, and this is the only definite information regarding the item which can be obtained from reading the bill.

The Senate had not been long in executive session yesterday before the fact was developed that a few members of the Foreign Relations and Appropriations Committees were the only Senators who knew just what was intended to be done with the $250,000, and that this little clique proposed to force the appropriation through without letting the other Senators know what it was for. Naturally, the uninformed Senators desired to know what they were voting for, and they tried to find out. The knowing ones pretended to answer, but spoke in such ambiguous terms that the more they explained the less able were the others to understand what it all meant. They gave up trying to find out late in the afternoon and took an adjournment until to-day. This afternoon they learned that the mysterious item really meant the payment of $250,000 by the United States Government for certain concessions from the Nicaraguan Government of such doubtful value that the present holders have been unable to dispose of them, and now seek to unload them upon the Government.

According to the understanding of some of the Senators, Secretary of State Frelinghuysen is in favor of the purchase by the Government, for the sum named, of the concessions made by the Nicaraguan Government, about four years ago, for the construction of an interoceanic canal in that country. These concessions were made to a number of American citizens, including Gen. Grant, the late Gov. Morgan, S. L. M. Barlow, and others, who were joined by certain influential Nicaraguans. An appeal was made to the Forty-sixth Congress by the promoters of the canal scheme to incorporate them, but the request was not granted. Later on an incorporation was effected under the laws of Colorado. Since then, it is asserted, efforts have been made in all parts of the world to find a purchaser for the concessions, but no country seemed to care to buy. By the terms of the concessions work must be begun on the canal before the 1st of October next, and at least $2,000,000 must be expended during the first year of construction. For this reason, it is claimed by the opponents of the proposed appropriation, the concessions at this late day are of no value to anybody, and least of all to the American Government, because, under treaties now in force, it would have just as many rights in case the Nicaragua Canal was built by citizens of any other country as it would if it constructed and paid for the canal itself. All this came out in the lively debate in the secret session to-day, together with the assertion that Secretary Frelinghuysen first induced a majority of the Foreign Relations Committee to favor the proposed purchase, and then, through these Senators, secured the insertion of the item by the Appropriations Committee. The debate showed, however, that a large majority of the Senators were willing to put the item through with no explanation in public.

After this had been settled the doors were opened, and the presiding officer announced that the bill was still open to amendment. Mr. Van Wyck, who is warmly opposed to star chamber proceedings, at once offered an amendment to the mysterious item providing that no part of the $250,000 shall be used, directly or indirectly, for the purchase of concessions for a canal in Nicaragua. This, of course, raised a breeze, and Mr. Allison insisted upon closing the doors again. Mr. Van Wyck protested vehemently against the proposition to act upon public measures in secret as setting a most dangerous precedent, but an overwhelming majority was against him, and the star chamber proceedings were resumed. Behind the locked doors the Senate voted upon and killed Mr. Van Wyck's amendment and then ordered the whole bill to its third reading. Having thus, by legislating in secret, got the bill beyond the stage where amendments can be offered, the Senators were willing the doors should be opened and the vote on the passage of the bill should be taken in public. The roll-call, however, showed that a quorum was not present, and the Senate then adjourned, leaving the final vote to be taken to-morrow.

It was said by a Senator to-night that the action of the Senate in voting upon the bill and amendments to it in secret session was without precedent. He considered it a most dangerous example to set for future Congresses, while in the present case the action was useless, because the whole matter would certainly be exposed and debated in the House, where the rules do not permit secret sessions.

## DEMOCRATIC NOTIONS OF ECONOMY.

The Democrats of the House have strange notions of economy. Yesterday, when Mr. Hewitt tried to show them that they must appropriate a sufficient sum to buy explosive material to blow up the sunken rocks at Hell Gate, they listened and then voted a less amount than that which Gen. Newton had declared to be absolutely necessary. The result will be that the explosion cannot take place until a larger appropriation is made, and in the meantime the Government will have to pay about $3,000 a month to pump the water out of the excavation and continue that great expense until Congress chooses to appropriate a sum which will enable the engineers to put explosive material into all of the chambers and break up the rocks which obstruct the channel of the East River. To-day, with delightful disregard of future economy, the House insisted upon appropriating $300,000 to begin the Hennepin Canal, notwithstanding that Mr. O. B. Potter protested most eloquently against it, and other members declared that the appropriation was only the committing of the Government to a work of doubtful utility, costing millions of dollars, which ought not to come out of the national Treasury. The House stubbornly refused to allow any amendments, good or bad, to be made to the bill, and to-morrow will probably endeavor to pass it just as it came from the River and Harbor Committee.

## DELAYING A CONTESTED CASE.

The Committee on Elections of the House of Representatives finished some time ago the hearings in the contested election case of Craig against Shelly, from the Fourth District of Alabama. No report has yet been made by the committee, and Judge Craig, the Republican contestant, does not like the delay. He claims to have proved before the committee, without contradictory evidence by the sitting member, that he was elected to Congress by more than 12,000 majority over Shelly, and he thinks it only fair that the committee, having all the facts before it, should make some kind of a report. Mr. Shelly has sought in every way to delay the investigation of the case, and is now trying to push off the report, although it is not at all certain that the committee will find that he ought to be ousted. Judge Craig is anxious to have the report made at this session, because he says he believes he can get the seat to which he is entitled if he can only get a hearing before the full House.

## THE VIEWS OF TWO STATESMEN.

Col. Michael Cregan and Mr. Michael J. Dady, of the New-York delegation to Chicago, have reached this city. Col. Cregan regards Blaine as a strong candidate, but says the "boys" in New-York will probably wait for some sort of a conference and need to be informed how they stand before they will take off their coats. Mr. Dady is extremely doubtful about Blaine carrying New-York, and says that the hope of the Republicans must lie in the blunders of the Democrats at Chicago. If they should select Cleveland as a candidate, he fancies that Blaine will acquire more respect for the Arthur business men, whom his followers characterized as "dudes" at Chicago, than they are now disposed to express.

## A "BRILLIANT FOREIGN POLICY."

The Republicans who hope for the election of Mr. Blaine and the adoption of a "brilliant foreign policy" found a spokesman yesterday in Mr. McCoid, of Iowa, who, in the course of a speech on the River and Harbor bill, pitched into the members who have presumed to criticise appropriations for river and harbor subsidies and other schemes for spending the public money. He advocated yesterday a broad and liberal policy. To-day, he said, if we had the right spirit, we would put a canal through Florida and make the terminus of the Mississippi practically on the east coast of Florida. We would construct the Hennepin Canal from the lake system of water to the Mississippi, the keystone of the water system of the country. By the Chesapeake and Ohio Canal we would give communication from the rivers to the Atlantic in another way, and then we would put a canal through the isthmus, under the American flag, and send our exports by water to the Pacific and to the islands of the sea, and then, with as much zeal as if he were a paid advertiser for Mr. Blaine's book, he quoted several pages of his recent work as furnishing cogent arguments for the position taken by Mr. McCoid. He quoted the *Pall Mall Gazette* as saying that "Blaine's nomination is the most notable event for England since Lincoln's assassination. Wherever Blaine can oust the British from the position they hold on the American continent, he will endeavor to replace the English influence and trade by American. His menacing intimation that he disregarded the Clayton-Bulwer treaty is an evil augury for the future relations of England and America. This intervention in Peru was most ominous. When he declared that he disliked England to win commercial triumphs in fields legitimately belonging to America." This Mr. McCoid hoped and believed to be true, and that "before long we may see our Government under the leadership of that great statesman, burning with commercial zeal, stimulated by a live, aggressive national policy."

## *YOUNG LADIES AS PEDESTRIANS.*

### ATLANTA ASHAMED OF A DISGRACEFUL EXHIBITION.

ATLANTA, Ga., June 11.—"I'll bet ten to one on the tall gal," said an excited sportsman in the armory of the Gate City Guards last night. Inside a singular sight was seen. The hall was fairly packed with the élite of Peach Tree and Decatur-street society. Fair belles, in all the profusion of extravagant dressing, and dudes wearing eye-glasses faintly cheered. A circle was clear around the outer edges of the hall, leaving open the course, 25 laps of which made a mile. "Thar she comes now," said the first speaker in glee, "don't she kiver the ground beautiful?" "But t'other one is a gainin' on her and will beat her on the next lap," said another speaker. Sure enough they came, Nos. 1, 2, 3, and 4, walking with all the determination of Madison Garden veterans. No. 1 cleared her first mile in 7 minutes, and, woman-like, fainted. Then the trainer made his appearance and the fainting pedestrian was properly sponged up, given a stimulant, and set upon the track again, but she never regained her lead.

The fair pedestrians, who belong to some of the most exclusive circles in the city, were arrayed in blue gingham Mother Hubbards, over which was thrown veiling of white tarletan. The dresses extended a little below the knees, from whence fancy colored stockings ran down into the daintiest of slippers, which bore striking red rosettes. The arms and bust were décolletée white, the hair fell over the shoulders, being caught together by red ribbon. Around their waists were ribbons of red, blue, green, and yellow, respectively.

For some time it had been announced by the Faculty of the Eclectic College that a walking-match of two hours would be engaged in by four young ladies—Misses Landell, Hutchins, Freeman, and Hammond—but no one foresaw what would actually happen. More than a thousand people, cheering and betting with all the abandon of the race course; pool-selling among professional gamblers, in which the names of the young ladies were offensively used, made such a scene as Atlanta is heartily ashamed of to-day. The pedestrians would now skip and dance, until finally, as the two hours had nearly expired, they grew exhausted, but were still cheered on by the gamblers whose money was at stake on the result. One of the girls gave way, and the trainer had to sponge her frequently to keep her on the track. So noisy became the audience that the sound of the band was entirely lost. Finally time was called, when the result was announced as follows: Miss Landell, 10 miles, 12 laps; Miss Freeman, 10 miles, 7 laps; Miss Hutchins, 10 miles, 4 laps; Miss Hammond, 9 miles, 8 laps. Much indignation is expressed to-day against the college Faculty, many of whom are fathers of families, for having brought about such a scene, which was unfortunate for the ladies named and discreditable to the men concerned in it.

## *LOSSES BY FIRE.*

### THE UNION RAILROAD STATION AT ST. PAUL DESTROYED.

ST. PAUL, Minn., June 11.—At 12:30 o'clock this morning the large Union Station was discovered in flames. The fire originated in the kitchen of the station restaurant, which is situated on the third floor, and spread so rapidly that 20 waiter girls and other employes escaped with only their night clothes. The building was owned by a stock company, in which the railroads centring here are the principal stockholders. The loss on the station is in the neighborhood of $200,000. It is impossible as yet to learn the insurance, but it is believed to be ample. Temporary sheds will be put up at the foot of Third-street for the accommodation of passengers. This having been the only station in the city, the inconvenience will be great. The building is a total ruin. At one time it was feared that the fire would spread to the large wholesale grocery houses which occupy the block above the station, but at 2 o'clock the fire was under control and all danger to adjoining property was passed. The principal stockholders in the Union Depot Company are the Chicago, St. Paul and Omaha; Chicago, Milwaukee and St. Paul; St. Paul, Minneapolis and Manitoba; Northern Pacific, and Minneapolis and St. Louis Railroad Companies. The building cost $150,000. Its contents were valued at $50,000, including $5,000 worth of property belonging to the Pullman Palace Car Company and a quantity of baggage. The insurance is placed in New-York companies.

Travelers to-day are compelled to find accommodations for themselves as best they can. Under the sheds back of the former station temporary accommodations will be fixed up until the station can be rebuilt, arrangements for which on a much larger scale are being made. A number of tickets having been stolen at the station fire this morning, all the roads are out this afternoon in a circular cautioning the public against buying tickets from other than the authorized agents.

A fire which occurred early yesterday morning in the building at No. 121 Liberty-street caused losses amounting to about $6,600, distributed as follows: Morris Livingstone, a liquor-dealer, on the first floor, lost $100; the New-York Land Company, on the second floor, $5,000; Joseph Hirsch, second, third, and fourth floors, $1,000, and the building was damaged about $500.

Fires in the woods between Setauket, Long Island, and Port Jefferson during the past three days have destroyed, besides a large area of timber, thousands of railroad ties which were becoming seasoned, causing a loss of from $10,000 to $12,000. The frequent recurrence of these fires has almost entirely driven out the game, formerly very plentiful in Central Long Island.

Goods on the third floor of No. 44 Mercer-street occupied by Philip Bernstein's Metropolitan Suspender Company, took fire at 7:15 o'clock last night, and $3,000 damage was done to the stock. The damage to the building can be repaired for $200.

The village of Grant Park, Kankakee County, Ill., was swept by fire Tuesday night which destroyed 20 of the principal buildings, including two hotels; insurance light.

A fire on Tuesday consumed several wooden and brick buildings near Market-square, in Winnipeg, Manitoba. The loss is 40,000; insurance, $16,000.

A fire in the lumber yards owned by Fowler, at Marion, Mich., Tuesday, destroyed property to the amount of $12,000; insurance, $8,000.

The dry goods house of J. M. Sprat & Co., at Galena, Ill., was damaged to the extent of $20,000 by fire yesterday. Insurance, $24,000.

Feurth & Sons' foundry, at Batesville, Ark., was burned yesterday morning. Loss, $13,000; insurance, $12,000.

## *IOWA FIREMEN'S TOURNAMENT.*

DES MOINES, Iowa, June 11.—The morning of the second day of the firemen's tournament dawned bright, and its promise was fulfilled in one of the finest days of the year. The decorations of the streets were gayer than ever. The grand parade took place in the forenoon. Not less than 30,000 people lined the principal streets, and as the brilliantly uniformed fire companies and bands and the shining engines were wheeled into line the scene was one to be long remembered. In the hose-car contest, 300 yards couple to hydrant and unharness, the Red Oak men scored 47¼ seconds, Newton, 49¾; Davenport, 46¼, and Cedar Rapids, 50. The Clinton men made an exceedingly fine run, but their time was not given, the judge saying his watch had stopped at the starting signal. They will be allowed to run to-morrow. Council Bluffs threw water first; time 5:23. Jennie Jewell, Waterloo, second, 5:56; J. J. Linehan, Dubuque, third, 6:30. The J. J. Linehan won on distance, 284¾ feet; Jennie Jewell second, 258 feet; Council Bluffs third.

## *NOMINATED FOR CONGRESS.*

CINCINNATI, Ohio, June 11.—The Republicans of the Fourteenth Ohio District, at Athens, yesterday, nominated Gen. Charles H. Grosvenor for Congress.

## *MRS. CHUBBICK'S TROUBLES.*

### SHE WANTS A DIVORCE BECAUSE HER HUSBAND ABUSES HER.

SYRACUSE, N. Y., June 11.—Five years ago Miss Butterfield, daughter of John Butterfield, once the proprietor of the hotel of that name in Utica, and a niece of Gen. Butterfield, of New-York, lost her heart to Lynhart Chubbick, a young and handsome clerk in a Utica store. Owing to the difference in their social positions, a union between the two was stoutly opposed by the girl's parents. Protestations, however, did not avail, and the couple were clandestinely married. Two children have been born to Mr. and Mrs. Chubbick, one of whom is 4 and other 1 year old. Some time ago they came to this city, Chubbick obtaining employment in a South Salina-street carpet store. Frequent quarrels and temporary separations are alleged to have taken place during their residence here. Their difficulties have now culminated in the engagement of counsel by both with a view to divorce, each charging the other with unfaithfulness. Mrs. Chubbick's friends assert that Chubbick recently pawned her five-hundred-dollar diamond ring and appropriated the proceeds. Mrs. Butterfield came here a few weeks ago to consult with her daughter, but was thrust out of doors by the husband. Then Mrs. Chubbick called in the police, but nothing was done. Last week Mrs. Butterfield returned and, after advising with a lawyer, drove to Chubbick's residence, and, taking her daughter and her two children, went with them to Utica. Counsel on either side had an interview to-day, and took steps to bring about amicable settlement. Mrs. Chubbick declares she still loves her husband, but says she cannot stand his bad conduct and cruel treatment.

## *BROUGHT TO BAY AT LAST.*

### CINCINNATI'S NOTORIOUS CRIMINAL LAWYER IN A TIGHT PLACE.

CINCINNATI, Ohio, June 11.—T. C. Campbell, the criminal lawyer, whose methods had much to do in precipitating the riot here, has been on trial since Monday before Judge Johnston, on a charge of attempting to bribe a juror who was summoned in the notorious Berner case. The case took an interesting turn this afternoon when the State's witnesses in rebuttal disproved statements which had been made by the defendant's witnesses as to a question of time, one of the two vital points in the case. Judge Foraker is defending Campbell. It is thought to-night that a disagreement of the jury is probable, and a conviction possible. A week ago nothing but an acquittal was thought of, it not being deemed possible that such a charge could be sustained against a man whose facilities for commanding any sort of evidence he wants here has long been the town talk. There has undoubtedly been false swearing in his behalf, but the State's attorneys are hoping to make it so palpable who it is that is telling the truth that a conviction may follow. The jury is made up of prominent business men. On Saturday proceedings to disbar Campbell will be instituted in the District Court.

## *THE SURFACE STILL SINKING.*

### SCENES AT THE SITE OF THE CAVE-IN NEAR WILKESBARRE.

WILKESBARRE, Penn., June 11.—The excitement at the scene of yesterday's cave-in continues. This morning the people living on the surface of the sunken earth made hurried preparations to leave for safer quarters, as it was not known at what moment another drop of the earth would take place, and thereby precipitate people, houses, and all into the mines below. In some spots, here and there, a further fall of several inches took place at noon, but where the dwellings were situated no further shrinkage was noticeable. The houses, 18 in number, affected by yesterday's cave-in, are in a very precarious condition, and ready to tumble over at any moment. The inmates have removed all their effects, including cows, pigs, &c. Large gaps in the earth's surface are plainly perceptible in the cellars of the wrecked houses. The foundations are completely torn from under the wood-work. All the wells in the vicinity have given up their water supply, the bottoms dropping out of them, and a water famine is inevitable. The distance from the earth's surface to the bottom of the mine is 600 feet. Operations at No. 4 colliery were suspended yesterday until the roof or portions of the caved-in part were propped.

## *ONLY THREE MEN DROWNED.*

THOMPSON, Montana, June 11.—The report that 11 men were drowned on Sunday night while crossing the river at Thompson's Falls, near this town, in a ferry-boat, was exaggerated. The loss of life is only three. John Stout, a young man, who started from the shore with a small boat to their rescue, fell a victim to his heroic action. The following were drowned: J. Stout, Paul Ducharme, and a Frenchman by the name of Denaut. The rescued are Perry M. Shuck, acting ferryman; S. S. McDermott, William Fisher, Mr. Finley, Mr. King, and two others unknown. The three drowned men were all single. Henry Blythe, owner of the pack animals, estimates his loss at $3,000. The total loss of property is estimated at $5,000. The accident was caused by the absence of an experienced ferryman. Thompson's Falls are in Bitter Root River, in North-western Montana, a short distance below the town of Thompson, on the Northern Pacific Railroad. Thompson is the first point, traveling west, at which miners bound for the Cœur de Lion region find a trail into the gold-fields. The river there is about one-quarter of a mile wide at this season of the year, and from 10 to 30 feet deep. The current is very rapid, and before reaching the falls the river becomes contracted to about one-third of the width which it has opposite the town, and at this point the current rushes over its stony bed in a perfect torrent. It is impossible to stem these rapids, and persons who have the misfortune to be drawn into them are hopelessly lost.

## *PURSUING AN ELOPING COUPLE.*

CLYDE, N. Y., June 11.—A scandal has been created here by the sudden disappearance of John York, Jr., the owner of a large grain ware house and malt establishment at North Rose, with the wife of one of his employes. Several years ago Mr. York married a well-educated, highly respectable, and wealthy young woman, whose parents lived near his place of business. Not long afterwards it is alleged, he became enamored of a village belle named Doremus, and did not desist from his attentions until Mrs. York threatened to invoke the law and make a public exposure. For some time after this their life was apparently happy. About two years ago the husband transferred his affections to Mrs. Dunham, the wife of a man in his employ. Last Saturday Dunham called on York and threatened to kill him on the spot unless he made immediate and satisfactory reparation. This York promised to do, and in the meantime visited a prominent lawyer in Clyde. Returning to North Rose, he secured several thousand dollars and left for Dakota. Immediately after York's departure Dunham discovered that his wife had deserted him. To-day he drove to Clyde and boarded a westward-bound train in search of her. Mr. York is a fine-looking man about 40 years of age, is Treasurer of the Sportsmen's Club at North Rose, and enjoys an excellent reputation for business capacity. He recently bought large quantities of grain on credit and disposed of it for cash. He has one child. Mrs. Dunham, who also leaves a child, is a fine-looking woman 28 years old.

## *NOT SO INDISPOSED AS SHE WAS.*

TROY, N. Y., June 11.—A few days ago Mrs. George Aldrich, of Lansingburg, a rather handsome and attractive young woman, who had been married but a few years, complained of being indisposed. She thought a change of air might do her good, and the husband decided to let her visit relatives in New-York. He furnished her with the money, and she took her best clothes and departed, promising to write. Not hearing from her, Mr. Aldrich telegraphed to the relatives in New-York, but the answer came that she had not been seen there. It then occurred to the husband that a former boarder who had always been very kind to Mrs. Aldrich was also out of town. He concluded the couple were together. Yesterday a letter was received from Mrs. Aldrich, dated in an Eastern town in Massachusetts, stating that she was living with their old boarder and that she was "happy as could be." The woman's sisters have started after her. The husband hardly knows what to do.

## *BURNED TO DEATH IN A BARN.*

CHICAGO, Ill., June 11.—Early this morning an unknown person entered the barn on the corner of Centre-avenue and Taylor-street with a lighted candle and ignited the hay. Fred Oeled, an expressman, aged 70 years, and a young man, whose name is unknown, who were sleeping in the barn, were burned to death.

# THE EGYPTIAN SITUATION

## *POSITION OF THE POWERS REGARDING THE CONFERENCE.*

### EARL GRANVILLE'S NOTE GIVING THE PROPOSED PROGRAMME—THE REPORTS OF THE BERBER MASSACRE DISCREDITED.

LONDON, June 11.—In the House of Commons to-day, Lord Edmund Fitzmaurice, Under Foreign Secretary, said that the report which reached London yesterday of an extensive massacre at Berber on June 1 was very difficult to believe. His reason for this attitude was the fact that a messenger who left Berber on June 3 reported that just before his departure he had seen Hussein Pasha Khalifa, the Governor, who was among those alleged to have been slain. The messenger had also said that steamers were working their way below Berber, and barges were passing to Khartoum, while the roads west of the Nile were fairly safe, and there was no unusual danger in that region. The news of the massacre, Lord Edmund thought, emanated from some emissary of the Mahdi.

Earl Granville, in his note to the powers giving the programme of the Egyptian conference, entirely ignores the agreement with France. The note is limited to a general statement of the financial condition of Egypt. It requires a revision of the law of liquidation and reiterates the desire of England to withdraw her troops from Egypt when order has been restored. The note avoids making definite proposals to the powers.

PARIS, June 11.—The *Gaulois* and *Figaro* concur in the belief that the English and French Cabinets have agreed to give a vague character to the note to the powers in relation to the Egyptian conference in order to aid in preventing Mr. Gladstone from being made subject to the formal disapproval of the English Parliament.

The *Journal des Débats* comments upon the agitation in England over the Egyptian question, and declares that the maintenance or rupture of relations between France and England is at stake.

CONSTANTINOPLE, June 11.—The Porte declines to appoint a delegate to the approaching Egyptian conference unless the whole Egyptian question shall be submitted to the conference or shall have been previously settled between England and Turkey.

SUAKIN, June 11.—The English Sergeants in the Egyptian Army here have tendered their resignations, owing to the cowardice of the Egyptian officers and men during the recent rebel attacks.

The rebels made another attack last evening. The men-of-war and the forts replied.

## BARTHOLDI'S STATUE COMPLETED.

PARIS, June 11.—Mr. Morton, the American Minister, gave a banquet to-night to the Franco-American Union on the occasion of the completion of Bartholdi's statue of Liberty. Among those present were Prime Minister Ferry, Vice-Admiral Peyron, Minister of Marine and of Colonies; M. Herisson, Minister of Commerce; M. Edmond de Lafayette, member of the Senate, and M. de Lesseps. At the conclusion of the banquet a number of toasts were given and responded to. Mr. Morton proposed a toast in honor of M. Bartholdi. M. de Lesseps, responding to the toast of "The Franco-American Union," said that the members of the union hoped the statue would be a symbol of attachment between the two countries. M. Ferry said that the construction of the statue was due entirely to the initiative taken by Frenchmen who were friends of America. Vice-Admiral Peyron said that the Government would send a vessel to convey the statue to America. M. Bartholdi thanked the Frenchmen and the Americans who had assisted him in effecting his design.

## AFFAIRS IN IRELAND.

DUBLIN, June 11.—The trial of the Westmeath murder conspirators, 24 in number, was brought to a conclusion to-day by the failure of the jury to agree. The prisoners were remanded to await a new trial, which will occur on the 18th inst.

Mr. Cornwall, the Secretary of the Dublin Post Office, brought action for libel a few days ago against Mr. William O'Brien, member of Parliament, editor of *United Ireland*. Meanwhile Mr. O'Brien has continued to publish in his paper cartoons and articles which impute disgusting offenses to Mr. Cornwall. The latter applied to the Court of Common Pleas for relief, and that court to-day granted him an attachment against Mr. O'Brien. The court, however, directed that the attachment should only be issued in case the offensive comments and cartoons continue to appear. The cost, it was ordered, should be paid by Mr. O'Brien.

The *Freeman's Journal* this morning publishes a letter from Mr. John O'Leary, who writes from Paris. He says that he proposes to visit Ireland in 1885. His opinions are the same as in 1848, but he has little faith in the party of action. He deprecates the "dynamite delusion," and says he would despair if he thought it anything but a passing craze. Other means must be used to save Ireland.

## CURRENT FOREIGN TOPICS.

LONDON, June 11.—A Zanzibar dispatch states that Mr. Thompson, the explorer, has returned in safety from the interior.

A large sleeper was fastened on the railway track leading to Brighton last night for the purpose of wrecking the Brighton mail train. The train, however, did not leave the rails.

Ugly rumors are afloat concerning the loss of torpedo apparatus worth £500 while in transit between London and Portsmouth.

The steam-ship owners of the North of England refuse to accede to any compromise in relation to the Merchant Shipping bill. They insist that the entire bill should be submitted to a select committee.

*Truth* asserts that Prince Bismarck has arranged the betrothal of Prince Frederick William, hereditary Grand Duke of Baden, and Princess Hilda, of Nassau, with a view to the reconciliation of the Duke of Nassau with Prussia and the establishment of the family of Nassau's succession to the Dutch throne, in case the Prince of Orange, Crown Prince of Holland, dies.

A game of lacrosse was played to-day at Wanstead between the American team and the Middlesex men. There was a very small attendance. The match resulted in a draw, neither side scoring a goal.

## *BUTLER'S PRESIDENTIAL BOOM.*

### THE GREENBACKERS FORMALLY TENDER HIM THEIR NOMINATION.

BOSTON, June 11.—Gen. Butler's campaign for the Presidency advanced a stage this afternoon. The committee appointed by the National Greenback-Labor Convention to notify him of his nomination by that party waited upon him and found him very civil. He received the committee at his Pemberton-square office in this city, and, after what they described as a pleasant conversation, intimated that he would accept the nomination. He will make public by Monday a letter setting forth at some length his views on the financial question, and discussing in his usual spicy manner other phases of the political situation. A dinner was given the committee before it met Gen. Butler. About 60 more or less prominent Greenbackers were present, and speeches were made by Charles H. Litchman, of Massachusetts; Gen. Innis, of Michigan; Ex-Gov. Sprague, of Rhode Island; E. M. Chamberlain, of Massachusetts, and others. A number of the speakers declared that Butler was the only man who could beat Blaine, and that next to Butler, Blaine was the popular choice. It was urged that the Democrats must nominate Butler if they hoped to win.

## *STAMPED INTO UNCONSCIOUSNESS.*

SYRACUSE, N. Y., June 11.—Last night several young men and women, among whom were Malachi, alias "Crick" Connelly, and James Dolan, met at the house of Mrs. Henry Fralech, widow of the man hanged in the Onondaga Penitentiary April 18, 1873, and spent several hours in carousing. The men continued their spree at various saloons until noon to-day. At about this hour they brought up in front of Dolan's house, and Connelly proposed that the party go in. To this the owner objected, and a fight ensued. Dolan struck Connelly in the breast with a stone, felled him to the ground, and then stamped him into unconsciousness. The exact extent of his injuries has not yet been ascertained, but there is a probability they will prove fatal. Two officers started after Dolan, who had run from the scene of the fight, and overtook him at his house, but succeeded in bringing him to-day only at the muzzle of their revolvers. Connelly is a cripple, one leg having been disabled by an accident. He has a bad police record. Dolan is a member of what is known as the "Fourth Ward Chain Gang," and has long been considered a dangerous character.

# The New-York Times.

VOL. XXXIII.....NO. 10,226. NEW-YORK, FRIDAY, JUNE 13, 1884. PRICE TWO CENTS.


## CLEVELAND THE FAVORITE

### THE EFFECT OF TILDEN'S LETTER AMONG DEMOCRATS.

CLEVELAND AND M'DONALD THE TICKET TALKED ABOUT AMONG CONGRESSMEN—DOUBTS OF MR. TILDEN'S SINCERITY.

WASHINGTON, June 12.—Everybody in Washington appears to have read Mr. Tilden's letter, and everywhere it is the subject of comment. It will not be unwelcome to Mr. Tilden to know that his literary style is almost universally approved. Many Democrats agree that he should have taken an opportunity to direct public attention to his skill as a letter-writer at the same time that he threw into confusion the Democrats who longed to see the old ticket nominated. Republicans of the shallow sort, who believe that any Republican can be elected next Fall, expose their shallowness by pretending to regret that Tilden has got out of the way because they considered him as the easiest man in the Democratic Party to beat. One interesting result of the declination of Mr. Tilden—if it is in fact a declination, about which there is still a lingering doubt in some minds—that of Senator Vest, for instance—is that it has set the Democrats chattering about the successor of Mr. Tilden in Democratic popularity. A hasty canvass of the House to-day revealed the fact that Gov. Cleveland leads all the other "favorite sons" in popularity, and that his availability is the controlling idea among those who advocate his nomination. It was Cleveland everywhere this afternoon, and the Democrats are becoming greatly concerned about the reports of Mr. Flower's growing boom. While Mr. Flower is spoken of with no ill-feeling or disrespect, those members of Congress who knew him as a member can recall nothing of great merit as having been done or said by him beside the delivering of a speech in favor of abolishing the internal revenue system of taxation. Gov. Cleveland's course at Albany has been watched by many Democrats with great solicitude, and it is flattering to him as a public officer and as an aspirant for the Presidency that his administration has commended him to men who have not always been guided by as high a sense of public responsibility as he has. This is regarded by those students of his work as embodying to a great extent that principle of reform for and of which Mr. Tilden delighted to be considered as the leading apostle and exponent.

Some of the Western Democrats still entertain a lingering hope that the ticket will be McDonald and Cleveland. One of these Democrats, a friend of both candidates, to-day defended Mr. McDonald from the charge of lobbying about Congress in his own behalf, and said that Mr. McDonald's visits have been upon legitimate business, entirely unconnected with politics, and that he has not spoken about his chances for nomination to any of the members whom he has met while here. That the ticket must be either McDonald and Cleveland or Cleveland and McDonald seems to be the opinion of nine-tenths of the Democrats in the House. The two doubtful States must have the candidates, and the preferences for the two men are not so old as to make it difficult to decide in favor of the one who shall be leader, upon the ground of the greater availability of the one or the other.

The talk in favor of Mr. Bayard is not so brisk or so hopeful as it was. While he is found to be acceptable to many Northern Democrats the Democrats from the South fear to press him. They see that pressure from the South in his behalf might hurt more than it would help. This feeling is entirely free from any distrust or reproach for the man. It is inspired by the reasonable doubt whether his Dover speech, now being passed about very freely, might not alienate a great many voters who could be induced to vote for a Democratic candidate who would be a man of integrity and free from any such drawback.

The Slocum talk heard in some quarters is not much more serious than that about Flower and Rosecrans. Gen. Slocum's claim for recognition appears to be based upon his majority for Congressman at Large, which certainly cannot bear comparison with that of Gov. Cleveland as a test of popularity.

The utterances of some of the Democrats who have talked to-day on the subject are worth publishing.

Judge Van Alstyne, of the Albany district, said he believed Tilden's letter would set the Cleveland boom going at once, while otherwise the boom would not have been started until after the State Convention. The Judge felt sure that Cleveland would be supported by his own State and would be nominated at Chicago, with a Western man for Vice-President. The Governor was strong among business men, and his veto of the Five-Cent Fare bill was now acknowledged by all to be just, while his veto message was one of the best State papers ever issued by a New-York Governor. His vetoes really added to his strength. Judge Van Alstyne declared that Tammany would not hesitate to support Cleveland, and that he would carry the State by 35,000 majority. The talk about Flower, the Judge remarked, was all nonsense, as would be seen when the State Convention met.

Mr. Abram S. Hewitt remarked that Cleveland was held in the highest esteem in New-York, and was a very superior man. Representative Spriggs, of the Utica district, thought New-York would decide the nomination, and that Cleveland had an excellent chance. Mr. S. S. Cox cracked a joke about the present situation among the New-York Democrats, saying it reminded him of the schoolgirl's definition of chaos—a big pile of nothing and no place to put it. Representative Murray, of Ohio, thought Tilden's declination was fortunate, as it left the field open and Cleveland, would be nominated. Like Judge Van Alstyne, Mr. Murray expected to see McDonald or some other Western man nominated for Vice-President. Mr. Morrison, whose name is occasionally heard as a possible dark horse, was ready to praise the Gramercy Park letter, but he did not care to talk about who would win the prize next month. Gen. Breckenridge, of Arkansas, expressed the opinion of some of the more thoughtful Democrats when he said he was sorry Tilden had sent out his letter at this time. Tilden ought, he thought, to have held it back until the convention met. As it was, there would be a continual uproar in the party until the nomination was made. Gen. Breckenridge believed no man could tell now who would be chosen at the convention. Congressmen Forney, of Alabama, and Culbertson, of Texas, had something to say in favor of Slocum and Voorhees, but when they had had more time to reflect, both admitted that Cleveland would make a strong candidate if the party in his own State would stand by him. Mr. Forney was not sure that Cleveland and Hoadly would not be the strongest ticket.

Among the Democratic Senators a variety of opinions were expressed. Senator Colquitt, of Georgia, who is a warm advocate of Bayard, declared that the Delaware Senator was the best man for the nomination in all that the adjective implied. He was a pure, upright, and able man, with whom the public interests could be safely trusted. "I think," said Mr. Colquitt, "the time has gone by when bloody-shirt arguments can sway any great number of our people. We hold and believe that Mr. Bayard was loyal to the Government. He wanted to keep our country together and to cement the Union upon terms of affection, not force. His kindly expressions toward the South were misconstrued and misrepresented as an overweening affection for that section. Now, my State is for Tilden, who was a war Democrat. He is out of the race and so we take Mr. Bayard. It is plain that we are not seeking to advance Mr. Bayard because of any belief that he is specially friendly to us. Then the contrast between Bayard and Blaine is more marked, more distinct, than it could be presented by any other man on our ticket. For 20 years, in round numbers, Mr. Bayard has been in public life, and throughout his entire service he has pursued a straightforward, honest, honorable, and patriotic course. His record is unspotted, his character unblemished."

Senator Vest regards Tilden's letter as such an excellent piece of work that he would not be surprised if it would nominate Tilden after all, if the Democrats should nominate him in spite of himself and insist upon his making the race. Representative Ermentrout echoed the same thought. "We'll nominate Tilden, of course," said Mr. Ermentrout, adding that he had read the famous letter. "Yes," said he, "I read the letter, but what of that. Tilden talks about the voice of God. The voice of the people is the voice of God, and Tilden cannot refuse to respond to the voice of the people, which will nominate him and put him in the White House."

### THE EFFECT OF TILDEN'S LETTER.

SOME DEMOCRATS REGRETFUL AND SOME REJOICING—A THURMAN BOOM STARTED.

CINCINNATI, June 12.—Tilden's letter fell like a wet blanket upon the Cincinnati Democracy. Had it not been written, he would undoubtedly have received the support of the delegates from this part of the State, and the party workers are loath to give him up. Of 67 Democratic office-holders and business men who submitted to interviews this afternoon, 22 were in favor of nominating the old ticket, notwithstanding Mr. Tilden's letter of declination. The others, accepting the letter as final, expressed their preferences as follows: Thurman, 15; Hoadly, 9; Cleveland, 13; Payne, 8; Bayard, 3; Hancock, 1, and McDonald, 1. Nearly all who expressed a preference for Cleveland suggested Hoadley for the second place on the ticket. McDonald was also frequently mentioned for second place. The Thurman men were the most enthusiastic. Until to-day there has seemed to be no chance for getting the old Roman on the ticket, but when it is realized that Tilden is really out of the race, a Thurman movement of considerable strength may be expected. It is proposed to-night to organize a young men's Thurman club with 1,000 members, and to send men to the interior towns to organize Thurman clubs. There is likely to be a Cleveland movement based upon the idea that he can carry New-York, and that impression may give him a portion of the State delegation.

CHARLESTON, S. C., June 12.—Mr. Tilden's letter formally declining to accept the Democratic nomination for President has removed the only serious cause of disagreement among the Democrats of South Carolina. There has been bitter opposition in this State to the old ticket, although Tilden has had some devoted supporters. The party will now unite on a better and stronger man. The leading favorites now are Cleveland and Carlisle for President and Vice-President. Bayard is also warmly supported, and McDonald is mentioned as a strong second to Cleveland. A leading local politician proposes Cleveland and Charles Francis Adams, Jr., as the very ticket to sweep the country. The delegates to Chicago will be pledged to no certain candidate, but will vote for the most available man, or for the candidate who will most effectually defeat Blaine. Although the campaign has not yet opened there is the thrill of new life in the Democracy of this State. The position of THE TIMES is most heartily applauded, and there is no doubt that the Republicans will meet a Waterloo here. They are without organization or leadership, and with the exception of a few office-holders, who are shouting for Blaine, the party has lost all of its elements of strength.

COLUMBUS, June 12.—Mr. Tilden's letter declining to allow the use of his name before the Democratic National Convention has been the theme of conversation in political circles during the day, and many are the expressions of regret that Mr. Tilden finds it a physical impossibility to accept the nomination. At the hotels the general opinion prevailed that New-York would be accorded the privilege of naming the candidate, Gov. Cleveland being regarded as stronger, especially at home, than any other candidate. The fact is fully recognized that the vote of the Empire State is necessary to achieve success. The name of Senator McDonald, of Indiana, is favorably mentioned, while Cleveland and McDonald would be regarded as a very strong ticket. Ex-Senator Thurman is strongly urged by many of the politicians who were strong advocates of Mr. Payne a few months ago.

WILKESBARRE, Penn., June 12.—Tilden's letter refusing the Democratic nomination for the Presidency is received here with regret by the Democrats and satisfaction by the Republicans. The *Leader* (Democratic) says: "While Tilden would have led his party to victory, there are a score of other Democrats equally fitted for the task."

STOCKTON, Cal., June 12.—A reporter this morning had interviews with a great number of prominent delegates to the Democratic State Convention, now in session here, on the effect Tilden's declination would have on their deliberations and on the party throughout the State. All expressed their surprise and regret, but unanimously declared that Thurman was now their man, as he represented the popular sentiment on the entire coast.

### CLEVELAND AND FLOWER FIGHTS.

THE GOVERNOR MEETING WITH MUCH OPPOSITION—HOW TILDEN'S LETTER IS REGARDED.

BUFFALO, June 12.—Conventions to elect delegates to the Democratic State Convention were held in the three Assembly districts of this city to-day. The result is as follows: First District—John C. Sheehan, John J. Griffin, Patrick Corridon; Second District—August Beck, Elijah Ambrose, Charles Lipp; Third District—Augustus Scheu, Frank Reynolds, the third man not yet elected. These conventions developed some of the ill-feeling which exists toward Gov. Cleveland among the worst class of Democrats here. The First District Convention was openly against Cleveland, and his personal friends here were denounced as bosses and tools of the Governor. The delegates chosen by this convention are understood to be for Senator Robert C. Titus for national delegate. Titus professes to be heartily for Cleveland for President, but the sincerity of his professions is questioned. The Second District convention was apparently friendly to the Governor and passed a resolution indorsing his Administration. The Third District convention elected two delegates without contest, but on the third delegate the convention was evenly divided and a great number of ballots were taken without breaking the tie. The two men voted for are Peter C. Doyle, a personal friend of the Governor, and John L. Crowley, who is understood to be unfriendly. The two men elected are said to be for Cleveland, but the contest over the third raises doubts as to their preference. The result of the contests cannot be said to be entirely favorable to Cleveland, but his opponents are men he could doubtless have conciliated had he chosen to use the patronage within his control, as many less scrupulous Governors have used it.

ROCHESTER, June 12.—The fight among the local Democrats over the delegation to the State Convention waxes hotter and hotter. It is conceded all around that Tom Brown is "knocked out" in the county districts, and that Mr. Purcell will have the majority of the delegation from this county, even if Mr. Raines secures representation. "The question now is," said a Raines man this morning, "shall the Democrats Mr. Raines represents have any voice at all at Saratoga? There has been a great deal of talk about the old ticket. Now, George Raines was always a friend of Tilden's, while Purcell was not. Had not Mr. Tilden signified his intention not to accept the nomination Mr. Raines would have supported the old ticket in earnest."

"Cleveland will be found to be Tilden's favorite in the race," said the Hon. William Purcell, this afternoon. "Mr. Tilden's declaration is a sore disappointment to the Democracy and the honest men of the country who desired to see the great wrong of 1876 righted in his person by a re-election to that Presidency. His influence, however, will be potent in the nomination at Chicago next month and in the election next November, and it will not be thrown for any man now holding an official public position. On that point I speak understandingly."

The Hon. George Raines expressed himself as follows: "The party expected such a letter from Mr. Tilden. It is well understood that he does not wish to re-enter public life. But the party will insist on his accepting this nomination, and in my judgment he will accept it. His letter is a much weaker declaration than I expected to see. I shall continue to hurrah for the old ticket."

The Hon. Henry L. Fish said: "I regret it exceedingly. I think Flower would stand a better show in this State than Cleveland. There are 100,000 anti-monopolists who would not vote for Cleveland. His run for Governor would help him outside of the State. We must nominate some such man as Bayard. Blaine's nomination is a strong one, and will not be beaten by being laughed at."

WATERTOWN, June 12.—Flower's friends here are jubilant to-night over the fact that he has so far secured 136 delegates in the State. To-day's developments in St. Lawrence County show quite plainly that the Magone proceedings in the Second and Third Districts yesterday were irregular. He placed gangs of heelers at Canton and Norwood, and Deputy Sheriffs were called on to guard the conventions in which the Flower men sat to choose delegates. It is evident that Magone's only hope lies in the organization of the State Convention. The Cleveland men feel confident that his contesting delegations will be admitted. The Flower delegation in the Second District is backed by the affidavits of 21 delegates—more than a majority—that they were regularly chosen. Much feeling exists. Both conventions were private, no one being admitted who had not secured a ticket of admission, and the facts are difficult to get at. Much feeling exists both here and in St. Lawrence County.

The Assembly District Convention of Lewis County, held at Lowville to-day, chose C. F. Moore, C. M. Allen, and William Hunt delegates to the State Convention. They are not instructed, but are in favor of Flower.

UTICA, June 12.—The Third Oneida District Democratic Convention elected Timothy Coughlin, Benjamin D. Stone, and H. Ray Barnes delegates to Saratoga. They are all for Flower, as are their alternates. The convention was virtually unanimous for Flower, in whose interest a large crowd of heelers was in attendance.

ALBANY, June 12.—The Warren County Democratic delegates elected to-day are Messrs. Brown, Cunningham, and Noble, all for Cleveland. This insures a Cleveland delegation from that Congressional district.

### TWO OHIO CONVENTIONS.

COLUMBUS, June 12.—The State Prohibition Convention will be held in this city on Wednesday next, while the Second Amendment or Voters' Convention will be held a week later. Last Fall the Prohibitionists polled 8,300 votes for Governor. The Second Amendment organization embraces all people who will vote for temperance men to hold public offices. The Hon. Mills Gardner is President of the Voters' Union, and expects to have nearly 100,000 names enrolled before the October election in the smaller towns and villages. Nearly the entire voting population are members of this organization.

### TEXAS DEMOCRATS CONFERRING.

THEY PRONOUNCE FLATLY FOR FREE TRADE AND RECEIVE MR. TILDEN'S LETTER.

FORT WORTH, Texas, June 12.—Ex-Lieut.-Gov. J. G. Sayers acted as Chairman of the State Convention to elect delegates to the Democratic National Convention, which began its sessions yesterday. He, ex-Gov. Hubbard, and others declared in their speeches that the tariff issue was to be the great one of the coming campaign. For the first time in the history of the Democracy of Texas the two-thirds rule in the selection of delegates at large was overruled, the vote being 303 to 145. Resolutions were adopted declaring that a tariff for protection is unconstitutional and unjust, and conflicts with the genius and spirit of free government. The present tariff is denounced as a scheme for the protection of monopolies and a masterpiece of injustice and false pretense. It has destroyed American commerce, diminished the profits and returns of American agriculture, and enslaved American labor. The resolutions say: "While we favor the education of the masses by every legitimate means, yet we regard the Educational bill pending in Congress as unconstitutional and a dangerous encroachment on the right of the States, and is another great step toward the centralization of all power in the Federal Government and the destruction of the Republic." Gov. Richard Hubbard was elected delegate at large by acclamation.

After midnight, in the midst of the balloting for delegates at large, Mr. Tilden's letter of declination, addressed to Mr. Manning, was read before the convention. Prior to this moment the convention had been wildly enthusiastic for Tilden and the "old ticket," and the letter chilled the convention, the delegates being unable to exhibit their usual enthusiasm after hearing the letter. It was after 1 o'clock this morning when the convention adjourned till 1 o'clock to-day.

When the convention reassembled this morning the delegates had not recovered from the depressing effect produced by Mr. Tilden's letter. A motion to reconsider yesterday's vote instructing delegates to vote for Tilden and Hendricks was tabled by a vote of 301 to 182. Notwithstanding the defeat of this motion a resolution was immediately adopted requesting and directing the delegates to use their own judgment in the selection of candidates for President and Vice-President, and leaving the delegation untrammeled with instructions. The following are the delegates to the National Convention: At Large—Ex-Gov. R. B. Hubbard, ex-Congressman D. C. Giddings, Judge T. J. Brown, and Peter Smith, Mayor of Fort Worth. District Delegates—First District, A. T. Holt and J. N. Henderson; Second, T. T. Gammage and D. A. Nunn; Third, H. Kretz and H. M. Cate; Fourth, J. B. Donahoe and J. M. Adams; Fifth, Silas Hare and G. B. Mead; Sixth, J. W. Ferris and W. P. McFarland; Seventh, N. Gussett and C. C. Sweeney; Eighth, W. H. Burgess and R. L. Foard; Ninth, L. C. Alexander and E. J. Simpkins; Tenth, Henry Exall and E. J. Dwyer; Eleventh, J. R. Fleming and C. K. Bell. The Democratic Senators and Representatives in Congress from Texas recently united in a request to their constituents that their names be not considered in the matter of selecting delegates to Chicago. The absence of Congressional names from the list is therefore explained.

The Democratic State Convention to nominate a Governor and other State officers will meet Aug. 19 at Austin.

### NOMINATED FOR CONGRESS.

CAIRO, Ill., June 12.—At the Democratic Congressional Convention held here this afternoon F. E. Albright, of Murphysborough, was nominated for Congress.

KANSAS CITY, Mo., June 12.—A dispatch to the *Times* from Downs, Kan., says: "The Democratic Convention in the Sixth District has nominated J. C. Uhl for Congress."

### DAMAGE DONE BY FLOODS.

PITTSBURG, Penn., June 12.—Points along the Allegheny Valley were visited yesterday by one of the heaviest rain-storms known in many years, causing the most destructive flood since 1865. At Brookville, Penn., a water-spout burst, and in less than two hours the creek rose 10 feet and became a roaring torrent. The rapid rise gave the mill men no chance whatever to save their property. The dams at the North Fork, Bryant & Wainright, and Litch mills gave way, carrying with them lumber valued at $70,000. Two bridges were washed away, many small buildings were demolished, and a number of families were compelled to seek shelter elsewhere for the night. At Pittsburg the Allegheny River rose very rapidly, and a number of coal barges were swept from their moorings, but were caught by tow-boats uninjured. The flood at Brookville brought down about 50,000 pieces of lumber, and almost every owner of a skiff is busy to-day catching drift wood. The water is subsiding, and no further damage is anticipated.

### ONE SWINDLER IN JAIL.

CHICAGO, June 12.—Frank L. Loring, the the partner of John Flemming in the swindling "fund" speculative scheme, was locked up in the County Jail to-day on his sentence of one year's imprisonment and $500 fine. Judge Blodgett's decision in the case was sustained by Justice Harlan on Wednesday, and Loring was in court. When he found what was coming he quietly skipped out, and a capias was issued for him. At 10 o'clock this morning he turned up in the District Attorney's office, looking as though he had passed a sleepless night, and said he merely had been bidding his sick wife good-bye. He was at once taken to the jail and locked up. Flemming, his partner, who received the same sentence, is in Dakota, and it is believed he will give himself up. Considering the magnitude of the steal, these two scapegoats of a powerful gang are getting off very easily.

### ELECTED PROFESSOR OF HEBREW.

DETROIT, Mich., June 12.—At the session of the General Synod of the Reformed Church in America at Grand Rapids, yesterday, an election was had to fill the newly established Gardner Sage Professorship of Hebrew in the seminary at New-Brunswick, N. J. Seven ballots were taken, with three leading candidates, the Rev. John M. Lansing, the Rev. Jacob Cooper, and Dr. Corwin. On the final ballot 154 votes were cast: necessary to a choice, 116. Lansing received 118, Cooper 30, and scattering 6. Mr. Lansing's election was then made unanimous. The newly chosen Professor is now Pastor of the Reformed Church at West Troy, N. Y., is about 30 years of age, and a scholar of high attainments.

### MR. BLAINE'S WESTERN FRIENDS.

NORTH CONWAY, N. H., June 12.—A party of Portland gentlemen and ladies accompanied the California Republican delegation up the Ogdensburg Railroad this morning. The day was overcast and a mist hung over the mountains, but there was no rain. The excursion party dined at Fabyan's and returned later in the evening. The Californians leave for Boston to-morrow morning. There they will separate, to meet in Chicago June 29. Their intention is to reach California by July 4. Senator McClure leaves the party to-morrow to go to Bangor, where he will probably deliver an address.

### GRADUATES FROM IOWA COLLEGES.

DES MOINES, Iowa, June 12.—Drake University held its second Commencement to-day. Four students received the degree of Bachelor of Arts and three that of Bachelor of Philosophy. One graduated in divinity, seven in medicine, and fourteen in law. In the latter class were W. G. Porter, of Thetford Centre, Vt., and Edward Merritt, of Lockport, N. Y. King Medical College, which seceded from Drake University nearly two years ago, graduated a class of six last night.

### POSTAL TELEGRAPH WIRES SEIZED.

PHILADELPHIA, June 12.—The Superintendent of Police and Fire Alarm Telegraph this morning took possession of the wires of the Postal Telegraph Company strung upon the city's poles, on account of the failure of the company to comply with the terms of the ordinance passed last February. This ordinance permitted the company to run two wires on the city poles upon condition that they should be placed under ground by May 1.

### SUNDAY-SCHOOL LESSONS.

LOUISVILLE, Ky., June 12.—The International Sunday-school Convention held its second day's session here to-day. Dr. E. W. Holly, of New-York, presented a memorial from the New-York Association asking that Christmas and Easter be recognized by the Lesson Committee; also a memorial from the Woman's Temperance Christian Union asking that temperance be recognized by the committee.

### A COLLEGE PRESIDENT RESIGNS.

DETROIT, Mich., June 12.—The Rev. Dr. D. W. C. Durgin, President of Hillsdale College, in this State, a Free-will Baptist institution, has resigned, the resignation to take effect at the close of the present calendar year.

## THE BOLT AGAINST BLAINE

### A GREAT MEETING TO BE HELD IN BOSTON TO-DAY.

THE CALL SIGNED BY HUNDREDS OF INFLUENTIAL REPUBLICANS OF THE OLD BAY STATE.

BOSTON, June 12.—The call for the meeting of Republicans and independents to protest against the Chicago nominations to be held in this city to morrow is published in the morning papers with the signatures of some of those in sympathy with it. The call is as follows:

"We, the undersigned Republican and independent voters of Massachusetts, believing that only men of high character should be elected to high office, and that the nominations just made at Chicago ought not to be supported in any contingency that now seems likely to arise, invite those who think with us on this point to meet in the old dining-room at Young's Hotel, Boston, on Friday, June 13, at 3:30 P. M., to consider what action to take in opposition to these nominations."

About 1,500 names are appended to the call. On the list are the names of many Republicans as well as pronounced independents and civil service reformers who are not intimately attached to either party, though leaning toward the Republican. Among the signers are the following: Henry L. Pierce, formerly Congressman from the leading Boston district, and several times Mayor of Boston; Col. Charles R. Codman, who presided at the Republican State Convention which nominated Gov. Robinson; William Endicott, Jr., Martin Brimmer, C. W. Eliot, Col. Henry Lee, James Freeman Clarke, Moorfield Story, Col. T. W. Higginson, Edward Atkinson, Phineas Pierce, Henry L. Higginson, Stanton Blake, George William Bond, Estes Howe, Moses Williams, Darwin E. Ware, Samuel Hoar, son of Judge E. R. Hoar; Hamilton A. Hill, Francis J. Child, C. W. Peabody, William H. Forbes, George S. Hale, William Lloyd Garrison. The meeting is expected to be one of consultation and delegates will be sent to the June 17 conference in New-York.

Among the letters received by the committee are the following, the first from the Rev. Rufus Ellis, Pastor of the first Church, Congregational-Unitarian, and the second from Judge Pitman, of the Superior Court:

I.

MY DEAR SIR: Platform and candidates are both utterly distasteful to me. It is time that we made a start, at least, upon an entirely different basis. The thing is rotten clear through. It was a mistake to go into a convention at all with such probabilities, or even possibilities, as to the outcome. I am ready to throw away my vote upon Independents, as I used to do in Free-soil days. Yours very truly, RUFUS ELLIS.

II.

MY DEAR SIR: I send you my name as that of a Republican voter, who in no contingency will support the nomination of James G. Blaine. I have voted for every Republican President from Fremont down. I should not lightly break with the grand old national party, but the time has come for Republicans when to defeat Blaine will be a far greater honor than success. Yours truly, ROBERT C. PITMAN.

### A SIGNIFICANT PROTEST.

SECRETARY LINCOLN'S LAW PARTNER OPPOSED TO BLAINE.

WASHINGTON, June 12.—Attention is directed by a Chicago gentleman to a letter from Chicago which appeared in THE TIMES of to-day, asking for the nomination by the Democrats of Grover Cleveland, and signed by Arthur Ryerson. The significance of the letter, it is suggested, is in the signature, which is that of the law partner of Secretary Robert T. Lincoln.

### BLAINE'S CHIEF SHOUTER IN MAINE.

BANGOR, June 12.—The first gun of the Blaine campaign was fired here to-night by Boutelle. This Congressman has so long shouted the name of Blaine, that he now considers himself the right hand man of that candidate, and is even now talked of for a Cabinet position. The occasion of his speech was a serenade given to him by about 200 admirers at his residence. Mayor Humphrey made the address of welcome. Boutelle gave the usual boastful eulogies of Blaine, and referred to the independent newspapers. "There are opposed to Blaine," he said, "THE NEW-YORK TIMES, the Boston *Advertiser*, and a few other journals. *Harper's Weekly* opposes him, but says what they all say, that Blaine is the choice of the people. In a very short time, however, those who oppose him will be too glad to join in the procession." The theory of the Blaine people is that after the Democratic nomination the independents will be glad to work their way back into the ranks. The campaign here promises to be bitter, and every effort will be made to frighten people by social means to support the ticket.

### THE OHIO REPUBLICANS.

COLUMBUS, Ohio, June 12.—The Republican State Central Committee met here to-night, and for the first time in 15 years every member was present. This clearly shows the great interest in the coming campaign which is manifested in every county and Congressional district. Gen. Robinson, candidate for Secretary of State, is in the city, and during the day has been in consultation with many of the prominent Republicans of the State relative to the conduct of the campaign. The State Committee met to-night and elected the Hon. J. W. O'Neall, of Warren County, Chairman, and Alexander Caine, of Perry County, Secretary. The committee were in session until midnight and were unable to agree on an Executive Committee, when they adjourned for one hour.

### BLAINE MANAGERS IN COUNCIL.

WASHINGTON, June 12.—A number of prominent Blaine leaders met to-day in the room of Secretary McCook, of the Senate. Mr. Steve Elkins was promptly on hand, as was William Walter Phelps and others, some of them delegates to the late convention. The conference lasted a considerable time, and was devoted mainly to a discussion of the Chairmanship of the National Committee and to a liberal interchange of mutual admiration, as well as to real views of campaign prospects. A general desire to make Mr. Elkins Chairman of the committee is entertained, a purpose which Mr. Elkins modestly puts away with the suggestion that the honor should go to one of the States, a view which precludes his own selection, as Mr. Elkins hails from New-Mexico.

### REPUBLICAN STATE COMMITTEE.

ALBANY, June 12.—The new Republican State Committee will probably be called to meet for organization in New-York on June 26, the day on which the National Committee assembles. The name most frequently mentioned for Chairman is that of Mr. John B. Dutcher. Secretary John W. Vrooman will undoubtedly be re-elected. Some of the Blaine managers are in favor of re-electing Mr. James D. Warren Chairman, if he will consent to take the place. They think such a move would have a good effect on the campaign.

### IOWA FIREMEN'S TOURNAMENT.

DES MOINES, Iowa, June 12.—At the State Firemen's tournament to-day the quickest ladder-climbing was by an Atlantic man in 5¾ seconds. The Storm Lake hand-engine threw water 196¾ feet, with Waterloo and Wilton close behind. Council Bluffs took the hose-coupling prize in 4.12 seconds. In the completed hand hose-cart race, 300 yards, attach to hydrant, unreel, and affix nozzle, Iowa City won in 42¼ seconds, Cedar Rapids second, Davenport third. Atlantic won the hook and ladder championship, making a run of 300 yards and getting a man on the ladder in 48¼ seconds. Waterloo took the hose-cart championship in 44 seconds, Council Bluffs second, and Cedar Rapids third.

### HE THOUGHT SHE WAS A GHOST.

CHESTERVILLE, Ontario, June 12.—Thomas Aggat was arrested to-day charged with murdering an old woman named Mrs. McCudden. It appears that late last night Aggat and his brother heard strange noises about the house and got up and went out with an axe. Seeing what they thought was a ghost, Aggat struck it two blows with the axe and then ran. They were notified of what they had done by neighbors, who found the old woman dead from loss of blood. The Coroner's jury this afternoon committed Aggat to the Cornwall Jail.

### A PHYSICIAN'S REMOVAL ASKED FOR.

DES MOINES, Iowa, June 12.—The State Eclectic Medical Society to-day had a hot debate over the recent reappointment of Dr. Hull to the State Board of Health. After considerable personality and ill-feeling had been worked off the society passed a resolution requesting the Governor to remove Dr. Hull and appoint Dr. McKiveen, of Chariton, in his place, as being more representative of the society's theories of medicine than the incumbent.

BOSTON, Mass., June 12.—The Harvard University boat crew took its last pull in Cambridge to-day, and will leave for its New-London quarters to-morrow. The university steam launch left for New-London yesterday, and the shell will be sent early to-morrow morning. The crew will leave Boston at 1 o'clock, arriving at its quarters early to-morrow evening.

### A LARGE FIRE IN BOSTON.

THE LOSS ABOUT $400,000—SEVERAL FIREMEN INJURED.

BOSTON, June 12.—A fire started this afternoon about 1 o'clock in the centre of the third floor of the building Nos. 152 to 158 Congress-street, occupied by Balderston & Daggett, agents for the New-Brunswick and National Rubber Companies. The flames spread with such rapidity, feeding on the large quantity of rubber which was stored upon all three floors, that the firemen were practically powerless to do a great deal in the way of saving property, and devoted their attention to staying the spread of the fire from the building in which it originated. Twenty minutes after the first alarm a second was sounded, which brought material assistance. District Engineer Cunningham entered the building, followed by a delegation from Engines Nos. 25 and 26, but no sooner had they got fairly to work than a heavy explosion occurred, and the flames were forced into their faces with such violence as to force them from their vantage point, from which grand execution was being done. They quickly returned to the battle, however, but had not been at work more than five minutes when a second and heavier explosion followed, literally blowing the gallant fellows down stairs, and seriously injuring many of them. The injured, as far as known, are: Assistant-Engineer Cunningham, slightly burned in the face; Hoseman Haley, of Steamer No. 25, seriously burned in the face and hands; Capt. Willett, of Steamer No. 26; Lieut. Grady, of Steamer No. 25; John McCarty, of Hook and Ladder No. 8; B. R. Barron, of Steamer No. 26, and Fireman Carlton, of Steamer No. 4, burned in the face; Thomas Boggs, of Steamer No. 26, badly burned in the face; Lieut. Neil, of Steamer No. 25, burned in the face and hands; Hoseman Patrick Kelly, of Steamer No. 25, burned in face; Thomas Strachan, of Hook and Ladder No. 1, Frank Turner, of Ladder No. 1, and Ladderman Hodgkiss, of No. 1, burned; Fireman Sweetzer, of Protective No. 1, cut in the hand; Capt. Frost, of Steamer No. 25, burned in face and hands; William Flavil, of Ladder No. 8, overcome by smoke. Laddermen Strachan, Turner, and Hodgkiss were so badly burned that they were taken to the City Hospital. Some of the other firemen were taken to their homes and the remainder were attended to on the spot.

The stock on the three upper floors was closely packed in wooden cases, which were piled up against the windows, a condition of affairs which materially hindered the firemen in the performance of their duty. At 2:15 the thick black smoke gradually gave way to that of a lighter shade, indicating that the flames were being got under control. But at 2:30 the flames rallied in the front of the building, on the third floor, and burst through the windows. Two or three fresh streams soon brought to bear again drove the flames inside the walls. The fire was then gradually subdued, although it burned fiercely inside the building for more than an hour.

At a late hour to-night engines are throwing water into the building, and the damaged stock is being cleared out. The agents had on hand an unusually heavy stock of goods. The loss by fire will be confined mainly to the two upper stories. These were closely packed with cases of goods, and, of course, all will be a total loss. The first floor was divided into office rooms, and was also used for storage purposes. The second floor was used for storing goods. Both these floors were deluged with water, and the loss upon the goods will be over $400,000. The total insurance on the stock is $565,000. The policies range from $5,000 to $30,000 each, and nearly all the leading companies are interested. The building is owned by Mrs. David Nevins. It is damaged to the extent of $10,000, and is insured for $15,000.

### MURDERED IN HER OWN HOUSE.

FACTS WHICH POINT TO THE HUSBAND AS THE GUILTY PERSON.

ATLANTA, Ga., June 12.—Intense excitement exists in the city to-day over an assassination which took place at 1 o'clock this morning. There lives on Ezzard-street the family of Mr. Charles Rose, Yard Master of the Atlanta and Charlotte Air Line Road. Last evening he left his family, consisting of his wife, baby, and cousin, Miss Nanny Frazer, all in good health. At 1 o'clock Miss Frazer awoke from her sleep and gave an alarm of murder. She heard a noise which she thought resembled that which would be made by the striking of a match. When she gave the alarm a masked man ran through her room, blew out the light, and jumped through the back window and escaped. Miss Frazer called to Mrs. Rose, but received no answer. Relighting the lamp she went into Mrs. Rose's room, where a horrifying sight met her gaze. There lay the child covered with blood beside the dying mother, who had a bullet hole through her brain. Miss Frazer caught the dying lady's hand, which gave a slight pressure, then fell nerveless on the bed. Soon the house was filled with officers, and later the husband made his appearance. It was ascertained that a box had been placed under the rear window, upon which the murderer stood while he cut away the putty and removed the pieces of glass, and through the aperture thus made entered the house. Mr. Rose's pistol lay on the mantel-piece. This the murderer secured on going into the lady's room. It was supposed he was rifling the trunk when Mrs. Rose, awakening, he placed the pistol to her temple, fired, and ran off.

When daylight appeared the mystery was increased by the discovery that there must have been two persons connected with the crime, a man and a woman. There were steps to and from the rear fence to the window as if a woman had been keeping watch while the man was doing his work inside. Bloodhounds were placed upon the trail, but the scent was cold, slight rain having fallen, and the hounds refused to follow. The Coroner summoned a jury of 12 leading citizens. While waiting for the meeting of that body opinion was freely expressed that the man who committed the crime must have been familiar with every detail of the arrangements of the house, and suspicion began to be directed against the husband. So strong did this feeling become that there were many who urged that a short shrift was the best remedy for him. A burglar would have went there armed, and would not have discovered so readily a weapon in the house he was entering. No one, it was argued, but an inmate could have opened the window in the manner in which it was done, and yet this theory would throw complicity upon Miss Frazer were it not for the woman's steps outside which led to the belief that it must have been some other woman.

The story told by Miss Frazer before the Coroner's jury mystified them, and yet there was no room to charge her with guilt. Finally it was ascertained that Rose was intimate with a female barber named Suggs, and that he spent most of his earnings with her. Late in the day while Rose was under surveillance, it was noticed that there was a piece of red putty stuck on the seat of his pantaloons, similar to that which had been removed from the window pane. This was considered clear proof, and it may be said that from that moment he was a prisoner. The whereabouts of the female barber then became a matter of interest, but she was nowhere to be found. After examining witnesses, taking a survey of the premises, &c., the Coroner's jury felt that there was a deeper design than burglary in the tragedy and ordered the imprisonment of the husband and the arrest of the two women. Investigation will be continued to-morrow.

### WILL CAMPBELL ESCAPE?

CINCINNATI, Ohio, June 12.—The trial of T. C. Campbell, the criminal lawyer, on a charge of attempting to bribe a juror, excited much interest to-day, because of the attempt of the State to break down the testimony of Charles H. Davis, a distiller of some prominence, who stated on the stand that he was with Mr. Campbell at the time it is alleged the bribe was offered, and that no such conversation as the prosecuting witness has related took place. Nothing had been heard of Mr. Davis as a witness in the case until he was placed upon the stand, and it was the talk last night and to-day that his statement was manufactured at Campbell's solicitation. This afternoon the State called reputable business men, who testified that they would not believe Mr. Davis under oath. The defense introduced witnesses who had never heard Mr. Davis's veracity called into question. As the case must stand or fall upon the statement of Davis, this line of testimony is likely to be followed through the greater part of another day. The State's case was strengthened by to-day's developments.

### BURNED BY A GAS EXPLOSION.

WHEELING, West Va., June 12.—By an explosion of gas in a ditch on Twelfth-street, this morning, David Thomas, Michael Burke, William Jerrold, August Wehoner, Cyrus Pryor, and Walter Pryor, laborers, were horribly burned. The men had just laid a section of 12-inch pipe, and had turned on the gas pressure to ascertain if a tight joint had been made, when the packing blew out, the gas igniting from a fire on the bank. Thomas may die.

### LIGHTNING INVADES A BEDCHAMBER.

FLANDREAU, Dakota, June 12.—The heaviest thunder-storm of the season occurred at 5 o'clock this morning. Lightning struck the house of S. Elbert Farris, nine miles from here, and passing down to the bed on which Mr. and Mrs. Farris were asleep, burned the pillows and rendered them insensible. It is thought they cannot recover. An infant only a few weeks old lying between them escaped uninjured.

### THE HON. HIESTER CLYMER DEAD.

STRICKEN DOWN WITH PARALYSIS HE DIES WITHOUT SPEAKING.

READING, Penn., June 12.—Ex-Congressman Hiester Clymer, who represented the Berks district four terms, died suddenly and unexpectedly shortly before 7 o'clock this morning from the effects of cerous apoplexy, aged 56. Up to 5:30 yesterday afternoon he was apparently in the enjoyment of excellent health. He was actively engaged in the iron business, and passed much time in superintending the repairs to his elegant residence on Perkiomen-avenue. At 5:30 yesterday afternoon he was sitting alone in his study, when suddenly, without any warning whatever, he was stricken unconscious by a sudden rush of blood to the brain. Medical aid was unable to rally him, and after lingering in a comatose state until 7 this morning, he died, without having uttered a word. Since the close of his Congressional career, some four years ago, he has been out of politics entirely, paying exclusive attention to his pig-iron furnaces, the greater portion of which he owns, together with a city residence worth about $40,000. Mr. Clymer has lost considerable money by keeping his furnaces going rather than discharge his men, to whom he was greatly attached. His two brothers, Edward and William, died of the same affliction. Mr. Clymer's first wife was Miss Brooke, of Birdsboro. His second wife was Mrs. Clemmen, *née* Von Schroeder, of St. Louis. There are no children. A Bar meeting will be held to-morrow night. The funeral will take place on Monday in this city.

Mr. Clymer was born in Berks County, Penn., Nov. 3, 1827. At the age of 20 he was graduated from Princeton College, New-Jersey, and after two years of study was admitted to the Reading Bar. In Pottsville, to which he moved after a brief practice in Reading, he pursued his profession for five years. In 1856 he returned to Reading, where he has since made his home, and at Temple, not far distant, he devoted his time to the management of his furnace after his retirement from politics. Originally Mr. Clymer was a Whig, and he early identified himself with the Democratic Party, serving as a delegate to the Charleston and Baltimore Conventions of 1860. That same Fall he was chosen to the Pennsylvania Senate to serve the unexpired term of Senator Muhlenberg, who had been elected to Congress. For six years this office was held by Mr. Clymer. Then he resigned to accept the Democratic nomination for Governor, and was pitted against Gov. Geary and defeated after a vigorous campaign, in which he stumped the entire State. Two years later he was a delegate to the Democratic Convention in this city. In 1872 he was elected to Congress. He was re-elected in 1874, 1876, and 1878. In Congress, as in the Senate of his own State, Mr. Clymer was recognized as one of the leaders of the Democrats. At one time he was a member of the State Boards of Revenue Commissioners and of Public Charities. At the time of his death he was Vice-President of the Union Trust Company, of Philadelphia.

### CUBAN DYNAMITER CAPTURED.

ARRESTED BY UNITED STATES OFFICIALS WHILE LANDING AT KEY WEST.

KEY WEST, Fla., June 12.—Upon the arrival of the Mallory Line steamer late last night from New-York, Federico Gil Marrero was arrested on a charge of having explosives in his possession upon an affidavit of the United States District Attorney. Since the quarantine season the Mallory steamers have not come to the wharf, but anchor at the quarantine ground, and the passengers and freight are brought ashore in boats. Upon Marrero's stepping into the boat he was arrested by the United States Marshal, under a warrant from United States Commissioner Locke, and lodged in jail. The information in the case was probably received from officials in New-York. Marrero is a resident of Key West. He went to New-York a few weeks ago, and his mission was evidently known through detectives. Upon searching his baggage the officials found fuse, detonating caps, and books of instruction upon the manufacture of dynamite. The articles were submitted to an expert, an officer of the United States frigate Galena, and the conclusions arrived at were that Marrero had the material and books of instruction for making dynamite and such other articles to be used in connection with it as could not be made here. Marrero was arraigned before Commissioner Locke to-day and held until to-morrow at 10 o'clock under $2,000 bail. Marrero is a Cuban and affected not to speak English until the officers commenced to search his baggage, when he exclaimed: "I did not think baggage was searched here coming from an American port." The vigilance of the officials has doubtless caused the dynamiters to pursue this course, to import materials separately and manufacture dynamite, &c., here.

### A QUARREL OVER A GIRL.

TRENTON, N. J., June 12.—John Murphy and Hyman Harris had a quarrel to-day which came near resulting fatally. The trouble between them arose over a girl named Maggie McDonald, who works for Harris, and who was engaged to be married to Murphy. The banns were published, the ring was bought, and the ceremony was to have been performed in St. John's Catholic Church. Suddenly the match was broken off, owing to a report circulated by Harris that Murphy was already a married man. It was said that he had a wife living in Philadelphia. Murphy denied this, but the girl nevertheless believed it, and Murphy took to drinking hard, and to-day it seems he made up his mind to kill Harris. He shot at him close at hand, but the latter ducked his head just as the trigger was pulled and so escaped. Murphy was arrested after a severe struggle with the police and locked up. He will have a hearing in the morning. Harris was but slightly injured in the cheek.

### ASSAULTED BY A NEGRO.

RED BANK, N. J., June 12.—The borough of Asbury Park has been thrown into a state of great excitement over a brutal assault that was committed on Mrs. John Ides, a lady residing just beyond Sunset Lake, on Tuesday evening. Mrs. Ides had been shopping, and on her way home she stopped a few moments at the residence of her brother, Dr. Wilcox. Then she proceeded alone up Broad-street on her way home. Near the bridge that spans Sunset Lake she was assailed by an unknown man, believed to be a negro, who struck her a blow from behind which felled her to the ground. He took her sachel, containing a considerable sum of money, and her gold watch and chain, leaving her senseless on the ground. As soon as she regained consciousness she proceeded to the residence of Mr. French, near by, who, with the assistance of some neighbors, conveyed her to her brother's house. Her injuries are mostly about the face and are not dangerous, but they will probably disfigure her for life.

### NO MORE OF THEODORE THOMAS.

CINCINNATI, Ohio, June 12.—It is proposed to make the Cincinnati Musical Festivals in the future more independent and distinctive than they have been for three or four years past. The partial failure this year is attributed mainly to the fact that the Cincinnati festival was only one of a concert series beginning in New-York and ending in Chicago, and all under the entire control of Theodore Thomas. There is a chorus here thought to be superior to that in other cities, and that is the only point in which the Cincinnati concerts surpassed those in other cities. It is proposed to organize a home orchestra as the first step toward independence. With two years of drill, it is claimed, the orchestral players resident here, if properly organized and directed, could be made a creditable feature of the next biennial festival.

### ANOTHER PENNSYLVANIA ELOPEMENT.

POTTSVILLE, Penn., June 12.—Peter McLane, 38 years of age, with a wife and four children, eloped with the wife of Michael Cuff, who is described as a very pretty woman, 20 years of age, and only recently married. Cuff and his wife boarded at the same house with McLane. Both men worked in the mines, but at different collieries and on different shifts. This fact gave McLane an opportunity to arrange all his plans for an elopement. He succeeded in winning the affections of the young bride, and on last Tuesday they left Deansville, in this county, drove to Shenandoah, and then came to Pottsville, and are now supposed to be either in Boston or on the sea. An officer left here to-day for Boston, where it is believed by the friends of the runaways they will be captured.

### FINE TROTTING STOCK SOLD.

ST. PAUL, Minn., June 12.—The inaugural sale of high-bred trotting stock was held yesterday at Commodore Kittson's Midway stables, between St. Paul and Minneapolis. It was an experiment made by several Minnesota breeders, and proved a success. There were 65 horses sold, the product of some of the best known and most cherished breeds and bloods. Col. Wilson, of Kentucky, secured a number of excellent youngsters and also purchased the trotter Silverton, Commodore Kittson's fine gelding, which has a record of 2:20¼. The sales aggregated $17,-780, an average of $273 50. The stock sold included yearlings, 2-year olds, brood mares, and stallions.

## RUNNING FROM HIS BRIDE

### A GLEN COVE WEDDING PARTY STARTLED.

THE DISAPPEARANCE OF ELWOOD D. LINCOLN ON THE DAY HE WAS TO BE MARRIED TO MISS IDA Z. MONTFORT.

GLEN COVE, Long Island, June 12.—The peace-loving little village of Glen Cove was much startled yesterday afternoon by the widely circulated report that Elwood D. Lincoln, one of the best-known young men of this part of Long Island, had deserted his bride at the altar, and had started for the South with a young lady who was reported to have deserted her groom a few days ago. Inquiry showed, however, that while young Lincoln had in reality run away from his own wedding he had gone alone. Up to a late hour to-night he had not returned.

For some time young Lincoln had been paying attention with youthful ardor to Miss Ida Z. Montfort, the young daughter of J. De Witt Montfort, who is employed in the office of the Glen Cove Planing Mill. Until recently he worked for his father in the office of the Glen Cove *Gazette*, and lived at home. He was greatly liked by the young people of the village and bore a thoroughly good reputation. He was a frequent visitor at the Montfort house, and in time became engaged to marry Miss Ida, whose parents sanctioned the arrangement and made preparations for the wedding. The wedding day was fixed for Wednesday. The clergyman was engaged, the guests were invited, and the house was made ready. On Monday young Lincoln went to Brooklyn with his sister, but returned and spent the evening with Miss Montfort. He seemed to be in a cheerful frame of mind and in no way out of spirits. Miss Montfort's vivacious younger sister, whom he sent to the drug store to make a small purchase, did not notice anything unusual in his manner. Yesterday morning he was seen to board a south-bound train on the Long Island Railway. The wedding ceremony was to be performed at 1 o'clock in the afternoon. At noon William Chapman, the groomsman, left the Montfort house to search for young Lincoln. He first visited the *Gazette* office.

"Where's Elwood?" he asked of the young man's father.

"I don't know," replied Mr. Lincoln. "What's up?"

"Why, don't you know Elwood's to be married at 1 o'clock?"

"Married! How's that?"

"Why, to Ida Montfort. Didn't you know?"

"Well," said Mr. Lincoln, complacently drawing out his watch, "if Elwood's going to be married at 1 o'clock he'll be there."

"But the last train's in, and he hasn't come," said Mr. Chapman, excitedly. He then made a hurried search of the village, but without result. The wedding guests were assembled, and the presents were ready for formal presentation, but young Mr. Lincoln came not. Miss Montfort felt the disappointment keenly, but bore up with more than usual bravery. She neither cried nor wrung her hands, nor did anything catalogued for disappointed brides to do. It was reported in the village that she was very sick and confined to her bed, but this is emphatically denied at the Montfort house. Mr. Montfort went to New-York this morning, and the rumor was industriously circulated that he was chasing young Lincoln with a horse-whip and other deadly weapons. Mr. Montfort went on a more peaceful errand. He consulted a doctor on the condition of his health.

It has been ascertained that young Mr. Lincoln went to an acquaintance in Printing-house-square on Tuesday and tried to borrow $500. He vainly sought to run his face for security. It is believed that he would have returned and carried out his engagement contract had he obtained the money. When spoken to on the matter this evening Mr. Eugene M. Lincoln, father of the young man, declared quite emphatically that he knew nothing whatever of the affair. "It's a lot of nonsense," said he. "If my son has engaged to marry Miss Montfort, why he'll marry her to be sure. Elwood went to Washington about three weeks ago. He has a situation there. I really don't know what it is. He came home some days ago, but went away again on Monday, with his sister. There was a report around that a neighbor and myself had raised him a large sum of money and had sent him away. That's all nonsense. Elwood was in no need of money. He told his brother Liss in New-York a few days ago, that he had plenty of money."

"Did you not know that your son was engaged to marry Miss Montfort?"

"I knew nothing whatever about it," said Mr. Lincoln. "Elwood kept his affairs to himself, and I had too much confidence in his uprightness of character to question him. He was a fine young man and liked to go out a great deal. I had every confidence in him. I do not know the Montfort people very well. I know Mr. Montfort only by sight. Further than that which I have already told you, I know nothing. If there is possible ground for action, I shall certainly sue some of the New-York evening papers for libel for what they published this forenoon."

In the Montfort House this evening a dozen or so of neighbors called to condole with the family, but seemingly very little condolence was needed. Mr. and Mrs. Montfort thought that, in running away, young Mr. Lincoln was influenced by financial difficulties. They do not doubt the sincerity of his affection for their daughter. They do not know whether or not the marriage will ever take place. Miss Montfort could not be seen. There is some question in the village as to the age of the young people. Well informed persons say that Miss Ida is only 16 years of age, and, in proof, hold to the fact that only last year she was in short dresses. Others claim, with much earnestness, that she is 20. Mr. and Mrs. Montfort say that she is somewhere between 16 and 20. The belief is general that she is not yet 17. Young Mr. Lincoln is 20 or 21.

Miss Carrie Hall, the young lady with whom the recreant bridegroom was first supposed to have eloped, was heard from this evening. She went away on the eve of her wedding day last week, pleading illness as an excuse. Charles Crabb, the deserted lover, started in pursuit, and to-night telegraphed from Lambertville, N. J., that Miss Carrie had been found, and that everything was all right. He and his bride will return to Glen Cove to-morrow. It is said that the young men of the village are preparing to give them a wholly informal and unquestionably enthusiastic reception.

### PANIC AT A THOMAS FESTIVAL.

CHICAGO, June 12.—A dispatch from Minneapolis, Minn., states that during the matinée at the Thomas Festival this afternoon a severe storm of wind and rain came up, in the midst of which one corner of the Coliseum Building was struck by lightning. Six hundred children were on the stage at the time, and the house was crowded, the majority of the audience being ladies. The darkened sky, howling wind, and terrific crash of thunder, with the tearing of timber and smashing of windows from the effect of the electric bolt, caused a frightful scare, that for a moment assumed the proportions of a panic. The children became frantic and literally stampeded, while many of the women fainted, others screaming and rushing out into the heavy rain. The building was fired by the lightning, but the prompt action of the firemen on the grounds and the descending rain extinguished the flames at the first start. It was fully half an hour before quiet was restored, and the concert proceeded. Besides a few bruises some received in the scramble no one was hurt.

### A LOVE-SICK YOUNG MAN.

POTTSVILLE, Penn., June 12.—Simon Smith, a resident of Mahanoy Plain, was committed to prison here to-day for safe keeping. He fell in love with a young lady named Eva Boltham. Everything went on smoothly for a while, when Eva's affection began to grow cold. This so enraged Smith that he resolved either to have the idol of his affection or do something desperate. Arming himself this morning with a pistol, a knife, and a rope he went to the residence of the young lady. He fastened one end of the rope around his neck and the other end to a hat peg, and then, with the pistol to his head and the knife to his throat, he asked if she would marry him. The words were hardly uttered before a brother of the young lady appeared and seized Smith, disarmed him, and brought him before a Justice, whence he was committed to prison. The young man says he only wanted to frighten Eva into giving her consent to marry him.

### KILLED BECAUSE OF A MULE.

NASHVILLE, Tenn., June 12.—Newton James was killed at Colesburg, a small town on the Nashville, Chattanooga and St. Louis Railway, two miles from Dickson, to-day, by Warren Bishop. The two had a dispute about a mule trade and were on bad terms. James attacked Bishop with a fence rail after the latter had endeavored to avoid a difficulty by running around a house several times. Bishop at last drew a knife and inflicted wounds which soon resulted in death. James is a nephew of Bishop.

### BISHOP SIMPSON FAILING RAPIDLY.

PHILADELPHIA, June 12.—Bishop Simpson's condition continued very alarming throughout to-day, and the attending physician, Dr. Harlow, and the consulting physician, Dr Agnew, were in constant attendance. A number of solicitous friends called during the day to inquire as to the Bishop's condition. Late to-night it was thought that he could not survive 24 hours longer, though hopes of a favorable change were entertained.

The New-York Times.

VOL. XXXIII.....NO. 10,250. | NEW-YORK, FRIDAY, JULY 11, 1884. | PRICE TWO CENTS.

# BALLOTING AT MIDNIGHT

## CLEVELAND RECEIVES 392 VOTES ON THE FIRST CALL.

### THE SPEECHES ALL MADE AND THE PLATFORM ADOPTED—GEN. BUTLER PRESENTS A MINORITY REPORT AND MAKES A SPEECH—A BALLOT ORDERED HALF AN HOUR AFTER MIDNIGHT.

FIRST BALLOT.

| | |
|---|---|
| CLEVELAND | 392 |
| BAYARD | 170 |
| M'DONALD | 56 |
| RANDALL | 78 |
| THURMAN | 88 |
| CARLISLE | 27 |
| HOADLY | 3 |
| HENDRICKS | 1 |
| TILDEN | 1 |
| FLOWER | 4 |

*From the Special Correspondent of the Times.*

CHICAGO, July 10.—The platform was not completed when the convention was called to order this morning. Ten orators made as many speeches in behalf of candidates, and then the convention was adjourned until 8 o'clock in the evening. Thurman was unfortunate in the selection of a champion from Missouri, who called the ex-Senator the Bismarck of America, and asserted that the independent Republicans of the East would vote for him because Roscoe Conkling had praised him. He also directed the attention of delegates to the division of the party in Ohio, and told them that Thurman had been promised the support of Tammany Hall. After he had taken his seat another Missouri delegate arose and declared that a majority of the delegation desired the nomination of Cleveland. Then McLean sent his spokesman up to the Chairman's desk to show the convention that Thurman's throat was to be cut in the house of his friends. This spokesman, on behalf of the majority of the delegation, named Gov. Hoadly. Those who expected that ex-Senator Wallace would serve his old rival, Randall, as Hendricks had served McDonald were disappointed, for the ex-Senator spoke earnestly in behalf of the leader of the Pennsylvania Democracy. Randall's nomination was also advocated by Gov. Abbett, of New-Jersey. Not content with eulogizing his candidate, he undertook to show that his brother Democratic Governor in an adjoining State did not deserve the support which so many Democrats had given him.

Butler and Kelly continued their war against Cleveland by sending to the Chairman's desk a Boston Democrat who would be one of Kelly's followers if he lived in New-York. This companion of Grady and Cockran secured the attention of the convention because he appeared in the guise of a Bayard man.

The best speeches of the session were those of Gen. Bragg and Gov. Waller. As soon as the hard and cynical face of Bragg appeared before the audience something sensational was expected. The young Democrats of Wisconsin loved Cleveland, he said, not only for his integrity, but most of all for the enemies he had made. This blow at Tammany struck a responsive chord in the vast audience, and delegates and spectators expressed their contempt for Kelly and his men by long and boisterous applause. Grady sprang up, shook his fist in Bragg's face, and tried to reply, but very few could hear what he said. This only encouraged Bragg, who relentlessly laid bare the motives of the Kelly men and likened them to the "vilest of the human species, who may defile a splendid statue and thereby only disgrace themselves." The professional "workingmen" were also scored by the General's sharp tongue.

The handsome and eloquent Governor of Connecticut poured oil upon the troubled waters. He had a good word for every candidate, and appeared as one who had carefully scanned the field before reaching a decision. He seconded the nomination of Cleveland.

After adjournment the delegates and hundreds of politicians swarmed again into the Palmer House beehive. The Cleveland men were in good humor. They had received satisfactory reports from several delegations. The events of the day, they believed, had increased the number of their votes. They had been assured of large reinforcements on the second ballot. Scores of red bandannas were seen in the corridors and on the streets, and the admirers of Thurman made more noise and show than the supporters of any other minority candidate. Here and there could be found a politician who predicted that Cleveland could never secure a two-thirds majority, and who regarded Hendricks as a possibility. Nearly all of the delegates were too weary to listen to missionaries or engage in missionary work. It was understood that the opponents of Cleveland, who were striving to postpone the balloting, expected that a debate upon the platform would consume the evening session. It was known that advocates of the platform that had been agreed upon were trying to induce a large majority of the convention to consent to an early application of the previous question.

Immediately after the reassembling of the delegates at 8 o'clock an unsuccessful attempt was made to bind the next convention to abrogate the two-thirds rule. Before Col. Morrison presented the platform adopted by a majority of the committee Gen. Butler climbed up to the Chairman's desk. He was to present a minority report. Both reports were read. Morrison gave notice that Butler, Converse, and Watterson should have three-quarters of an hour in which to say their say, and that he would then demand the previous question. Butler's speech was not well received. Ignoring all of the majority platform except the words "taxation shall be exclusively for public purposes," he held that there was no difference between this declaration and one favoring a "tariff for revenue only," which, he said, had broken Hancock's back. He wandered off to praise Greenbackism and to ridicule civil service reform. The weary audience urged him to sit down and at last he accepted their invitation.

Converse, the Ohio protectionist, assured the convention that Butler was the only member of the committee who was not satisfied, and then urged the importance of administrative reform. Watterson, the most radical of the low tariff men, joined Converse, the protectionist, in declaring that the majority platform was all right. It was good enough for him; he had never asked for more. The convention then began to realize that its committee had made a tariff plank upon which both Converse and Watterson could stand without inconvenience. The roll of States was called on a motion to strike out the tariff plank reported by the majority and to substitute Butler's resolutions. The motion was defeated by a vote of [illegible] to 1. The 97 affirmative votes were cast by delegates from California, Arkansas, Illinois, Indiana, Massachusetts, Michigan, Nevada, New-Hampshire, New-Jersey, Ohio, Pennsylvania, and Texas. New-York cast all her votes in the negative. The platform was then adopted by a viva voce vote, not more than a score of delegates dissenting.

At 11 o'clock it was decided to take a ballot for President. The anti-Cleveland men fought for delay and demanded a call of the States on a motion to adjourn. The motion was defeated by an overwhelming majority. A ballot was then ordered.

The anti-Cleveland men made another attempt after the first ballot to secure an adjournment. The roll of States was called and the convention refused to adjourn by a vote of 401 to 412. The filibustering opposition determined to take another trial, but before the clerk began to call the roll Mr. Manning, of New-York, arose and seconded the adjournment motion. The convention then adjourned till morning. F. D. R.

## WORK OF THE THIRD DAY.

*From Staff Correspondents of the Times.*

CHICAGO, July 10.—"We love him most for the enemies that he has made." This was the sentiment spoken of Grover Cleveland by Gen. Bragg, of Wisconsin, and greeted with wild screams of applause from floor and galleries, that most stirred the morning session of the Democratic National Convention. It struck a sympathetic chord. Already detested for its determined effort to protract the fight in the New-York delegation, Tammany's crowd of malcontents were everywhere regarded with unconcealed looks and expressions of aversion. To such an extent does this dislike and distrust prevail that the boys who line the streets shouting the Tammany organ in New-York for sale are frequently subjected to rude insults for boldly shouting that they have the "only Tammany paper" for sale and are advised to take them back to New-York or to throw them in the gutter. The Tammany delegates and the heelers who came with them have learned that they are not regarded with approving eyes, and many of them, in order to escape the unpleasant criticisms of bold and hostile delegates, have put away their gorgeous badges and roam in safety and obscurity about the streets. Mr. Maurice Hollahan and Mr. Kearney were of this prudent theory, and "Sid" Nichols and Justice Gorman put their badges in their pockets while about the Palmer House, to keep them there until they were in the convention and under the eye of Kelly, when they bravely put them on again.

Fine weather favored the convention to-day. The delegates and crowds of spectators wended their way to the convention hall to the sound of music from many bands. The streets were lined again with boys showering tally sheets and notebooks upon the moving throng, and overhead there was a bright, clear sky, that let the sunlight freely down upon the dirty streets. Boys were selling admission tickets at $4 each, the supply indicating that hard times had overtaken some of the people who had been attending the convention and had been so fortunate as to have something that they could sell. The weather was not so hot as it was when the Republican Convention was in operation, and there were few lemonade stands. This absence of mild beverages may have been accounted for by the traditional preference of the Democratic throat for stronger drinks, but that preference was not shown by any exhibitions of intemperance.

Half past ten was an early hour for meeting, but before that time the convention hall was occupied by many persons. As there was no reservation of front seats for privileged spectators, it was necessary for those who wished to obtain good places in the stations for which they had admission tickets to come early. The presence of many ladies in these front seats was only to be accounted for by early attendance. At all events there were many well-dressed women in the front, and they came prepared, with boxes of lunch in their hands, for a protracted session. Not with the procession of Tammany delegates, but obscurely and without music, John Kelly and Tommy Grady walked to the hall. They sat down side by side at the end of one of the rows allotted to the New-York men. No one cheered. They were not noticed and so escaped the hisses that would inevitably have been provoked by cheering or applause. The fine band provided to entertain the convention during its gathering once more played selections from Wagner and less ambitious composers, and when it played "Dixie" it excited the enthusiasm of the Southern delegates and the rest of the vast audience. Missouri's delegates came in, bringing the man of their number who yesterday indulged so freely in stimulants as to require frequent severe admonitions from the Chair and restraint from the Sergeants-at-Arms.

SETTLING DOWN TO BUSINESS.

Chairman Vilas was in his place. Behind Vilas sat ex-Chairman Hubbard, and by the Texas man's side was Speaker Carlisle. The platform was fully occupied with more or less distinguished guests. Eleven o'clock and the Chairman rapped once with his gavel. The sound of warning was heard all over the great hall, and the thousands of people who heard it settled down into an orderly condition. Three more raps and then order was commanded and the Rev. Mr. Lorimer was introduced as the Pastor of the Emanuel Baptist Church, to make the opening prayer. During the prayer there was much tramping of delegates along the aisles and a confused sound of brass bands playing conflicting tunes outside. Just after the prayer was ended, and during a wait, Mr. Hendricks, of Indiana, came in. He was received with a flattering burst of cheers and applause. So much of this noise came from the audience that the Chair appealed to it to refrain from such demonstrations.

Carter Harrison stood upon his chair, and, being recognized, spoke in defense of himself and the police to deny the charge made in a morning paper that he allowed some of his followers to cut their way through an engine house next to the convention hall and pack the building in behalf of his candidate. He happened to speak the name of Grover Cleveland during his statement, and the convention instantly broke into applause.

Chairman Vilas rapped sharply, and having discouraged the conversation that was humming all over the hall, directed Reading Clerk Bell to read a communication from the Committee on Resolutions, announcing that they would not be ready to report before 7 o'clock this evening and asking permission to be allowed to sit during the convention's proceedings. This request was granted. A resolution offered by a Maryland delegate making the preposterous request that all visiting delegations should be admitted to the hall upon their badges was received but not acted upon, and then the Chair sustained the point of order that the order of business was to be taken up at the point where it was suspended to take a recess. By consent a resolution authorizing the Committee on Resolutions to print 2,000 copies of their report for use by the delegates was adopted, one apprehensive delegate making the inquiry as to what was to be done if majority and minority reports were presented.

Gen. Charles H. Mansur, of Missouri, who had held the platform when the convention adjourned yesterday, made the opening speech. He was very hoarse and his remarks were not patiently listened to. His second of Thurman's nomination fell flat upon the convention, as it was known that a small minority of the delegates from his State were for Thurman. In the audience there was some cheering and waving of bandana handkerchiefs. Prolonged yells from one of the galleries provoked the Chair, and he commanded the Sergeants-at-Arms to remove offenders. The speaker's references to "the colossal Thurman" and "the superb Conkling," and his declaration that the party would exact of the Democrats that they should carry New-York or that the blood of the murdered Democracy would be upon them, were received with indifference.

Delegate B. F. Reavis, of Missouri, wiped out any effect that Gen. Mansur's speech might have had by rising to announce that a majority of the delegates from Missouri were for Cleveland. The Chair promptly told Mr. Reavis that the States could only be allowed to speak by the Chairmen of the delegations, to which Reavis checkily responded: "Well, we've got in our work, anyway."

GOV. HOADLY NOMINATED.

Ohio was called and Chairman John R. McLean rose to send up Col. Thomas E. Powell, who took the platform to nominate Gov. Hoadly. Col. Powell's account of the change of the vote of his State and his nomination of Hoadly caused scarce a ripple out of the Ohio delegation. When he referred to Gen. Hancock the convention showed its indifference to the late Democratic candidate by silence. There were calls for Thurman from the galleries, but the expectation that Thurman would rise to second Hoadly's nomination was not justified or gratified. Col. Powell's speech was as follows:

MR. CHAIRMAN AND GENTLEMEN OF THE CONVENTION: The auspicious omens with which we are to-day surrounded clearly indicate that the time which is to mark the final overthrow of the Republican Party is now at hand. [Applause.] If this convention shall be true to itself, faithful to its party, judicious in its platform, and wise in its candidates, our success in the coming struggle is already assured. As we enter upon such a contest, wisdom demands that he who is to be our leader shall be able to win the first great engagement of the campaign, and if possible settle it in October. In a few weeks this whole nation will be anxiously watching the vanguards of the party as they struggle for liberty and supremacy in [illegible]. He who doubts the courage, honor, patriotism, and the ultimate success of Democracy there has forgotten the brilliant record of that great State. At her admission Ohio ranked as the sixteenth State; to-day she stands the third State in this Union. In that great period in the great race of life in wealth and in population Ohio has already passed 17 of her sister States. Her progress in our cause has been still more marvelous. Within a few years she has overthrown and destroyed forever a Republican majority of upward of 100,000, [loud applause,] and in its stead, in two successive campaigns, she has recorded large majorities infavor of your candidates, and to the credit of her cause. At this hour her home government and all her destinies are in the keeping of your great party. The man who has been the acknowledged leader in the redemption of that State as well as one of the foremost citizens in all her borders is the candidate we now present to the thoughtful consideration of this convention Gov. George Hoadly, of Ohio. [Applause.] Our hope in him rests not upon faith, but upon recorded history and accomplished facts. As a candidate he has never been defeated at the polls. [Applause.] In the memorable contest of last year, upon a full vote, and when Ohio was fighting her first fight in this Presidential contest, he received the largest indorsement ever given to a Democrat in Ohio, [applause,] receiving 19,000 more votes than your great leader of the last Presidential contest, the soldier statesman, Winfield Scott Hancock. [Applause.] George Hoadly is known to the Nation as a great lawyer, as a wise statesman, as a fearless and aggressive leader. He is a man of acknowledged ability, of undoubted integrity: a man of courage as well as of wisdom. His whole public and private life is without a stain and without a scandal. Whenever and wherever he has been tried he has been found stronger than his party and as pure as his cause. He has been the chosen advocate of our party in denouncing and condemning the great fraud of 1876. [Applause.] Since that day, up to this hour, George Hoadly has been the friend and confidential adviser and to-day would make a worthy successor of that last and illustrious Democratic President, Samuel J. Tilden. [Applause.] Under his leadership, under his banner, we can save Ohio to ourselves in October and give it to you in November. Under his leadership Ohio can enter the race for the crowning glory at the polls. She can struggle with all her sisters to make her borders the hearthstone of free institutions and the central home of Democracy in this great Union. Under him, Ohio can strike the first successful blow in that victory, which, under the providence of God, will commit fifty millions of people to the protection of our great party. [Applause.]

EX-SENATOR WALLACE SPEAKS FOR RANDALL.

Pennsylvania sent to the platform as her spokesman ex-Senator Wallace. He walked to the front with a quick, nervous step and made his speech in a clear, penetrating voice. "Democrats," he said, with a sharp, ringing, even peremptory directness, "Democrats, the hour has struck for the nomination of a Democrat grounded in the faith." His words of praise for Randall were listened to with interest, and when he finished the Pennsylvania delegates rose to their feet and two rows of men were seen wildly waving their hats and canes and were heard shouting vociferously. That was all. The audience was not for Randall, the delegates refused to be aroused by appeals on Randall's behalf. Ex-Senator Wallace's speech follows:

MR. PRESIDENT AND GENTLEMEN OF THE CONVENTION: By direction of the Pennsylvania delegation I arise to present to the Democracy of the Republic here assembled the name of a candidate for the great office of President of the United States. The name I give you is found upon every page of your country's and your party's history in the last two decades. [Applause.] It is that of no untried tyro in political affairs. [Slight applause.] In the prime and vigor of his matured manhood, with every faculty trained in practical government, an official life of 20 years lies behind him, clear, luminous, and pure. No dishonest action, no corrupt practices, have ever stained his escutcheon. [Applause,] and while most of his contemporaries in official life have grown rich through devious and unknown ways, he is still a poor man, whose highest aim has been to fitly serve his people and the Republic. Democrats, the hour has struck for the nomination of a Democrat grounded in the faith [applause] and tried in the stern crucible of his party's service. [Applause.] The pathway of expediency lies behind us strewn with the wrecks of our failures; let us be honest now; let us stand by the record of our own pure public man; let us boldly appeal to the people upon that record and spurn the delusive promises of our erstwhile bitter foes. [Applause.] The name of such a man we bring you. His practiced hand, his experienced foresight, and his conversance with public affairs will lay the foundations of your return to power so broad, so high, so deep that they will be permanent. [Applause.] He has been practically the leader in the national House of Representatives for 12 years, [applause,] and his career there has been one of vast public benefit. Favoring a reduction of taxation and an economical administration of the Government, he has with skill and success resisted the lavish expenditure of the money of the people, the waste of the public domain, and the unconstitutional and tyrannical force bills. His iron will has put the knife to corrupting extravagance and has compelled a return to comparative purity of administration. Earnest in purpose, pure in life, a trained tribune of the people, and a thorough statesman, no favor sways him and no fear can awe. This man, her son, Pennsylvania presents to the Democracy of the Union here assembled in convention as her candidate for the mighty office of President of the United States in the person of Samuel J. Randall. [Cheers.]

An amusing incident occurred when Gov. Leon Abbett, of New-Jersey, took the platform to second Randall's nomination. He was well received, but, just as he was about to speak, a man far off in the gallery shouted, "Louder," with a long-drawn howl. Shouts of laughter followed. Gov. Abbett was annoyed, and when he could be heard he went on to say that when the great day of judgment had come and the angel Gabriel blew his trumpet some jackass would be heard shouting, "Louder!" The convention broke into a tremendous scream of laughter at this retort, and then listened while Mr. Abbett complimented Bayard, applauded when he referred somewhat reservedly to Cleveland, cried "Time!" when it felt that he had talked too long, and rewarded him with scattering applause when he finished.

The speech of Mr. John W. Cummings, of Massachusetts, in behalf of Bayard was delivered clearly and forcibly, but made slight impression. The speaker is a slight, dark man, with features indicating Irish antecedents. He met with approval when he pitched into New-York for fighting its State quarrels out on the floor, but awakened no sympathetic response to his attempts to belittle the New-York Governor.

Senator Wade Hampton stood up when South Carolina was called. "What name?" asked the Chairman, who did not recognize the man with the Burnside whiskers away off at the extreme right. The name was given, and South Carolina sent up Mr. Leroy F. Yarmans to second the nomination of Bayard. The only interesting part of Mr. Yarmans's speech was his mention of the name of Stephen J. Field. The name was received without notice. Mr. Grady, at this time, was prowling about the hall, trying to induce delegates from different States to stick to Bayard, and was finding that Cleveland was hopelessly intrenched everywhere.

Mr. U. M. Rose, of Arkansas, on behalf of the entire delegation of that State, seconded Cleveland's nomination.

AN OLD WAR HORSE GIVES TAMMANY A DRUBBING.

When Wisconsin was called Delegate A. K. Delaney asked that Gen. Edward S. Bragg, the Chairman of the delegation, be allowed to speak and second the nomination of the Governor of New-York. Screams of applause followed, continuing until after Gen. Bragg had reached the platform and made his bow and begun his speech. His first words, proclaiming that he had been delegated to voice the sentiment of the young men of his State, provoked new tumults of applause, and when, in measured tones, full of force and earnestness, he went on to say that the young men of Wisconsin not only admired Gov. Cleveland for his integrity, his iron will, and his honesty, but that they "love him most for the enemies that he has made," the convention could not restrain its delight. The speaker had said just what the convention wanted to hear, but not what Tammany and Grady were prepared to listen to without smarting. The delegates were cheering this reference to Kelly's men. Grady stood in the front aisle, and with a burning face and flushing eyes, his hand uplifted defiantly, he shouted: "I reciprocate that sentiment," and added something which the applause for Bragg cut off. Gen. Bragg spoke as follows:

GENTLEMEN OF THE CONVENTION: It is with feelings of no ordinary pride that I fill the post that has been assigned to me to-day. Grim and gray, personally fighting the battles of the Democratic Party, I stand to-day to voice the sentiment of the young men of my State when I speak for Grover Cleveland, of New-York. [Cheers.] His name is upon their lips, his name is in their hearts, and he is the choice not only of that band of young men, but he is the choice of all those who desire for the first time, as young men, to cast their votes in November for the candidate nominated by this convention. They love him, gentlemen, and respect him, not only for himself, for his character, for his integrity and judgment and iron will, but they love him most for the enemies he has made. [Loud applause, which lasted for several minutes, in the midst of which Mr. Grady, from New-York, arose in front of the Chairman's desk and interrupted the speaker as follows: "Mr. Chairman, on behalf of his enemies, I reciprocate that sentiment and we are proud of it." Loud hisses and great confusion, in the midst of which Mr. Grady retired to his seat.]

Gen. Bragg—I thank the emissary that represents a respectable name at least for calling himself again to my attention. [Loud applause.] This broad Nation witnessed the disgraceful spectacle of a Senator of the United States trading his proud possession for gain. [Applause.] Mahone and Riddleberger would scarcely be allowed to stand upon this platform to teach you gentlemen Democracy and whom you ought to nominate. [Loud applause.] Go to the Senate of the State of New-York since Gov. Cleveland has been Governor, [applause,] and there you find two worthy confreres playing in a small theatre Mahone and Riddleberger over again. [Loud applause.] And why? Because the Governor of the State of New-York had more nerve than the machine. [Applause.] They may speak of him, aye, the worst of the species may defile a splendid statue, but they only disgrace themselves. [Loud applause.] Wherever the thin disguise can be reached you will find it covering nothing but personal grievance, disappointed ambition, or a cutting off of the access to the fleshpots to those who desire to fatten on them. [Loud and long continued applause.] I do not assume here to speak for labor. The child of a man who always earned his daily bread by his steady labor, brought up for more than a quarter of a century from boyhood to manhood among laborers that have made the great Northwest what it is, I do not assume to speak for labor. Labor is not represented in political conventions by the political trickster. No matter where you find him, [loud applause,] the men who follow conventions and talk about the rights of labor are the Swiss contingent, who place their tent wherever the prospect of profit is greatest. [Loud applause and cries of "Bully for you."] while honest, intelligent, horny-handed labor will be found following the old Democratic flag, thanking God that its self-styled leaders have gone where they belong. They come here to talk of labor; yes, their labor has been upon the crank of the machine, [immense applause and laughter,] and their study has been political chicane in the midnight conclave. We are told the Democratic Party is suffering from fearful political disorders by these men. If we are to judge from past experience, those disorders, in the quarters where they are alleged to exist, can only be cured by a reapplication of Federal soap. [Laughter.] I have heard it said that the States of the Northwest ought to have no voice in this nomination. I have heard it said. "What boots it what their opinion may be?" What was it that placed the great States of the Northwest in the Republican column? It was because they followed blindly, implicitly, the old leaders, and they lead the party of union to defeat and they placed our States down under thousands and thousands of Republican majorities. We have fought our way steadily upward. We see through the water which has been so deep above our heads, now the glimmering again of sunlight, and we ask to breathe once more the air of victory. Our young men ask it, the religious sentiment of our country asks it, the intelligence of our people asks it. Our German, foreign born citizens [applause] say to us: "We come to you with Cleveland; the Old Guard will fight steadily and go down to death, shouting gloriously as they fall, under the lead of the chivalric Bayard." They will follow steadily and unflinchingly that sturdy old Democrat from Indiana, but with the same result, they fear. They will rally around that glorious old Senator from Ohio, [applause,] and they will accept that judicial-minded gentleman from Kentucky. But pardon me for saying there was a time when the 2:40 steeds stood first upon the list, but in these days something that has made 2:40 ought to be retired as stale, for it is of no account against 2:10¼. [Applause.] Let our old war horses be retired with honor. Let the records of their achievements be recorded and pointed at with pride and pleasure. But our people say, give us new life, give us new blood, give us something that has come to manhood and position since the war, that we may hear no more about what took place at, before, and during the war. Every breeze brings to us what would seem to be indications of victory, but we cannot accomplish victory without recruits. These recruits are at our bidding: young, middle-aged, and old, you see them, [applause,] in platoons and regiments, brigades and divisions. [Applause and calls of order from the Chair.] Every one of them bears upon its banner first, "Cleveland, of New-York." [Applause and loud yells from the galleries.] Let the countersign of the great Democratic camp in November be "Cleveland," and then men can make their way to it —[applause]—and recruited as we shall be, our Ides of November will not be a Waterloo, but will be a glorious sun of Austerlitz and Wisconsin. My own adopted State, I say to you, gives us every reason to believe that she will find herself once more in the Democratic column, and her 11 Electoral votes will be cast for the nominee of this convention. For that reason, on behalf of the majority representing my State, I second that nomination. [Applause.]

The excitement which prevailed during and at the conclusion of Gen. Bragg's speech was the most intense that had prevailed at any time during the convention.

MORE SECONDS FOR CLEVELAND.

Col. Henry O. Kent, of New-Hampshire, who followed Gen. Bragg, renewed the cheering and applause when he seconded Cleveland's nomination for his State, and cited Kernan, Seymour, and Tilden as Democrats who had given assurances that Cleveland can carry the State of New-York. There were loud and long cheers for Cleveland when Mr. Kent concluded his speech. The galleries took up the cry, and echoed it from one end of the vast building to the other. "Grapeshot" Bragg, of Wisconsin, again claimed the Chair's attention to say that another member of the Wisconsin delegation desired to second the nomination of Grover Cleveland. Ex-Senator Doolittle made his way to the platform, and in a husky voice which wearied the convention declared that a change of 10,000 votes would bring Wisconsin into the Democratic column, and that the change could be made if the convention would only nominate Grover Cleveland, [applause,] who more than any other Democrat, in the judgment of the Wisconsin delegation, was likely to carry his own State. The judgment of Seymour, of Kernan, and of Tilden, who knew their State thoroughly, was relied upon on this point. He begged the convention not to throw away this opportunity to make the election sure, and make no mistake. There were more cheers for Cleveland when the speaker left the stage.

Ex-Congressman John F. House arose to ask whether the convention had not agreed to take no ballot upon the nominations till after the report of the Committee on Platform. There were cries from the gallery of "Voorhees!" "Voorhees!" The Tall Sycamore of the Wabash sat in silence beside ex-Gov. Hendricks, of Indiana, and made no response to the clamor. Order having been restored, the Chairman replied to the Tennessean that the convention had so decided in the affirmative the point which he suggested. The ex-Congressman then moved to adjourn until 8 o'clock. The motion was declared out of order, the roll of States not having been completed. The Secretary was directed to announce the result of the roll call on nominations. He and his assistants were engaged in preparing it. A voice from the audience called for three cheers for Cleveland, and again the whole house responded.

Commotion was detected in the Connecticut delegation, to which the Chairman's attention was directed. A small man, with a mass of wavy hair, combed over the back of his head, was struggling to make himself heard. Far over on the other side of the building were heard the words: "Connecticut opposed to no one, not even to Tammany Hall." The speaker had by this time indicated to the convention that the voice of the Nutmeg State demanded to be heard. He was called to the platform, and a moment later the little giant, as Connecticut's Governor has been dubbed, stood before the convention. When the applause had subsided which greeted the suddenness of this movement, Gov. Waller, in a slow, steady tone, began a speech which, as he annouced, should be a very small one, for the State was a small one, in behalf of whose united delegation he spoke. "When the call of States was made," he said, "Connecticut named no one of her sons for the high office of President. Her delegates have sat in silence and listened to everything that has been said, and they have cheered almost everything which they have heard. [Laughter.] They have enjoyed, in common with you all, this magnificent convention, and they have felt proud with you, in realizing that no country on the face of God's earth could present such a scene as we have witnessed." The Governor had now the full attention of the delegates, and in his blandest tones he proceeded to compliment one after another the names that had been presented in nomination. The "old Roman" of Ohio was applauded when his name was mentioned, and so was the name of every other nominee. Then the speaker touched upon the harmony of the proceedings and announced that the utmost good fellowship existed between Col. Fellows on the one hand and John Kelly on the other. The time had come for them to shake hands. "They've got to do it," he exclaimed, with an emphasis that provoked laughter. Connecticut's delegation was now ready so far as their voice was concerned to give a verdict upon the nominees. "We may make a mistake," he said, "for human judgment is fallible, but our duty as delegates is done when we have listened to every consideration, when we have heard every argument, to give the result of our judgment in the vote we cast. Connecticut instructs me to say to you that with her every vote, and they will be cast as soon as you give the opportunity, and the sooner the better, she seconds the nomination of Grover Cleveland." The little giant slipped back to his seat on the floor, not, however, before the electrical effect of the mention of Cleveland's name had manifested itself in cheers which rang throughout the hall. The delegates themselves got up and cheered. Cleveland delegates were scattered through every delegation and they arose and added to the tumult. Democrats of the Northwest, of the South, of New-Jersey, Pennsylvania, and the New-England States united in a splendid ovation. They waved their hats and their canes, and even the red Thurman bandana was flung in the air. The audience caught the infection, and men and women waved their handkerchiefs. Three more cheers were called for and given, followed by the loudest of laughter, when a Cleveland man in the gallery yelled: "We've got 'em on the run, boys."

As the clerk announced the names of candidates placed in nomination each was applauded, though the applause for Cleveland led all the rest. The candidates, in the order in which they were called off by the clerk, were: Thomas F. Bayard, of Delaware; Joseph E. McDonald, of Indiana; John G. Carlisle, of Kentucky; Grover Cleveland, of New-York; Allen G. Thurman, of Ohio; Samuel J. Randall, of Pennsylvania, and George Hoadly, of Ohio.

Ex-Congressman House now moved to adjourn till 8 o'clock in the evening. The motion was amended by William H. Snowden, of Pennsylvania, so as to order the Platform Committee to report at that hour, and the convention adjourned in remarkably good humor.

## THE EVENING PROCEEDINGS.

*From Staff Correspondents of the Times.*

CONVENTION HALL, June 10.—As if music were the food of politicians instead of sustenance for a tenderer passion than that of politics, the delegates in the Democratic Convention to-night listened with unrestrained delight to the skillful performances of the cornet player in the gallery band, and while the great hall was filling up, applauded again and again and seemed to tire not a whit with the entertainment. Dense crowds of people surrounded the entrance to the convention. Enterprising boys were offering tickets for sale, and there were ready buyers. Policemen at all the doors examined passes, which were again scrutinized by doorkeepers. Efforts to get in on all sorts of pretexts were unavailing. Col. Bright having made careful preparations to keep out a miscellaneous mob like that which overwhelmed the Republican Convention. Tickets enough had been issued to quite fill the hall, and before 8 o'clock there were only a few seats, and those were at points distant from the stage, that were unoccupied. The hall was not brilliantly lighted. The hanging rings of gas jets overhead made it easy only to distinguish faces in the galleries and at a short distance on the floor. The faces of the spectators in the seats that sloped right and left from the delegates were only so many rows of dots, like the scene painter's representation of a crowded amphitheatre.

Among the incoming delegates there was a great buzz of conversation. Many inquiries were heard about the Committee on Resolutions, and as to the probability that the convention would adopt its platform, make nominations and get through before closing the evening session. Strangely enough, Tammany Hall began to talk about another candidate. The buglers of Kelly went about declaring that Cleveland could never get the nomination, and that Hendricks would be the man. This sort of talk and perhaps some industrious management by the Indiana men accounted for the very noisy reception given to Mr. Hendricks when he entered the hall and passed through the crowded aisle to the seats of the Indiana delegation.

It was nearly 8:30 before Chairman Vilas rapped upon his desk and called the convention to order. Delegate Henry, of Mississippi, offered a resolution expressing the admiration of the convention for the character and statesmanship of Samuel J. Tilden and the regret with which his letter declining the Presidency had been read. The convention did not express that great enthusiasm which might have been looked for. A delegate who objected to the reading of the resolution raised the point of order to refer it to the committee and was unceremoniously hooted down. The resolution was adopted and a call made for a committee to carry it to Mr. Tilden and Mr. Hendricks.

Mr. Orestes Cleveland had just offered a resolution, and it was about to be read when Ben Butler entered. The convention became boisterous, the delegates stood up, and the gallery audience screamed like mad as he walked down to the Massachusetts delegation. Mr. Cleveland's resolution was one to have a roll call of the States and Territories for nominations for members of the National Committee and the Committee of Notification of Candidates. It was promptly adopted, the roll was called, and the committees announced, as follows:

*Alabama*.—Henry C. Semple.
*Arkansas*.—S. W. Fordyce.
*California*.—M. F. Tarpey.
*Colorado*.—M. S. Waller.
*Connecticut*.—W. H. Barnum.
*Florida*.—Samuel Pasco.
*Georgia*.—Patrick Walsh.
*Illinois*.—S. Corning Judd.
*Indiana*.—Austin H. Brown.
*Iowa*.—M. M. Ham.
*Kansas*.—C. W. Blair.
*Kentucky*.—Henry V. McHenry.
*Louisiana*.—B. F. Jonas.
*Maine*.—Edmund Wilson.
*Maryland*.—A. P. Gorman.
*Michigan*.—Don M. Dickinson.
*Minnesota*.—H. H. Kelly.
*Missouri*.—John G. Prather.
*Mississippi*.—C. A. Johnson.
*Nebraska*.—James E. Boyd.
*Nevada*.—Dennis E. McCarthy.
*New-Hampshire*.—A. W. Sullaway.
*North Carolina*.—M. W. Ransom.
*Ohio*.—W. W. Armstrong.
*Rhode Island*.—J. B. Barnaby.
*South Carolina*.—Francis W. Lawson.
*Tennessee*.—Robert S. Looney.
*Texas*.—O. T. Holt.
*Vermont*.—B. B. Smally.
*Virginia*.—John A. Barber.
*West Virginia*.—Louis Baker.
*Wisconsin*.—William F. Vilas.
*Arizona*.—W. K. Meade.
*District of Columbia*.—William Dickinson.
*Idaho*.—John Haley.
*Dakota*.—M. H. Day.
*Utah*.—G. B. Roseborough.
*Montana*.—William McCormick.
*Washington*.—J. A. Kuhn.
*New-Mexico*.—Not announced.
*Wyoming*.—William E. Post.

The following members were reported to wait upon the Presidential and Vice-Presidential candidates when nominated:

*Alabama*.—Daniel P. Bestor.
*Arkansas*.—S. R. Cockrell.
*California*.—Miles Searles.
*Colorado*.—Not appointed.
*Connecticut*.—T. M. Waller.
*Florida*.—W. D. Shipley.
*Georgia*.—Milton P. Reese.
*Illinois*.—A. E. Stevenson.
*Indiana*.—E. D. Bannister.
*Iowa*.—L. G. Kinney.
*Kansas*.—C. C. Burns.
*Kentucky*.—Attilla Cox.
*Louisiana*.—James Jeffries.
*Maine*.—C. A. Osgood.
*Maryland*.—Dr. George Welles.
*Michigan*.—Daniel J. Campeau.
*Minnesota*.—Henry Poehler.
*Missouri*.—D. R. Francis.
*Mississippi*.—Charls E. Hooker.
*Nebraska*.—P. Fahey.
*Nevada*.—John H. Dennis.
*New-Hampshire*.—John F. Cloutman.
*North Carolina*.—W. G. Damb.
*Ohio*.—Not named.
*Rhode Island*.—D. S. Baker, Jr.
*South Carolina*.—Joseph H. Earle.
*Tennessee*.—William A. Quarles.
*Texas*.—Joseph E. Dwyer.
*Vermont*.—George L. Speer.
*Virginia*.—Robert Beverly.
*West Virginia*.—Not appointed.
*Wisconsin*.—William F. Vilas.
*Arizona*.—G. H. Oury.
*District of Columbia*.—E. D. Wright.
*Idaho*.—Not appointed.
*Dakota*.—M. S. McCormick.
*Utah*.—Rutherford Smith.
*Montana*.—S. T. Hauser.
*Washington*.—N. B. Dutro.
*New-Mexico*.—George W. Stevedore.
*Wyoming*.—William H. Holliday.

Mr. Malcolm Hay, of Pennsylvania, from the Committee on Resolutions, made a special report, recommending that owing to the great duties devolving upon the Chairman of the National Committee the committee be allowed to go outside the committee and select the Chairman from the whole party. This report and recommendation were approved.

Delegate Terry, of Arkansas, offered a resolution abolishing the two-thirds rule in future conventions of the party, in order that the will of the majority may prevail. Before the resolution was read Ben Butler left his seat. As he got up the audience cheered and delegates began to stand up, the word going about that he was leaving the convention. Instead of leaving, however, he went to the foot of the platform, and was helped up the steps by several stalwart guides, to the great merriment of the audience that watched the ascent. Some misunderstanding of the resolution prevailed, a few delegates having the impression that it was to apply to the present convention. A roll of the States was called for, but Gov. Abbett raised the point of order that this convention could not make the rules for the next convention. The Chair recognized the force of Mr. Abbett's argument, but overruled his point and ordered the call of the roll on a motion made to indefinitely postpone the resolution. The call had proceeded only as far as Delaware when it was suspended, and the motion to postpone was adopted.

THE PLATFORM OF PRINCIPLES.

Col. W. R. Morrison was then presented, to make the report of the Committee on Resolutions. The grizzled leader of the House, the head of the tariff reform party in Congress, was greeted with a cordial reception. His voice was not strong enough to be heard all over the hall and he very wisely called upon Bell, the prize reading clerk, who read the platform in a splendid manner. It was as follows:

The Democratic Party of the Union, through its representatives in national convention assembled, recognizes that, as the Nation grows older, new issues are born of time and progress, and old issues perish. But the fundamental principles of the Democracy, approved by the united voice of the people, remain and will ever remain as the best and only security for the continuance of free Government. The preservation of personal rights; the equality of all citizens before the law; the reserved rights of the States, and the supremacy of the Federal Government within the limits of the constitution will ever form the true basis of our liberties, and can never be surrendered without destroying that balance of rights and powers which enables a continent to be developed in peace, and social order to be maintained by means of local self-government. But it is indispensable for the practical application and enforcement of these fundamental principles that the Government should not always be controlled by one political party. Frequent change of administration is as necessary as constant recurrence to the popular will. Otherwise, abuses grow, and the Government, instead of being carried on for the general welfare, becomes an instrumentality for imposing heavy burdens on the many who are governed, for the benefit of the few who govern. Public servants thus become arbitrary rulers. This is now the condition of the country; hence a change is demanded.

The Republican Party, so far as principle is concerned, is a reminiscence. In practice it is an organization for enriching those who control its machinery. The frauds and jobbery which have been brought to light in every department of the Government are sufficient to have called for reform within the Republican Party, yet those in authority, made reckless by the long possession of power, have succumbed to its corrupting influence and have placed in nomination a ticket against which the independent portion of the party are in open revolt. Therefore, a change is demanded. Such a change was alike necessary in 1876, but the will of the people was then defeated by a fraud which can never be forgotten nor condoned. Again, in 1880, the change demanded by the people was defeated by the lavish use of money contributed by unscrupulous contractors and shameless jobbers, who had bargained for unlawful profits or high office. The Republican Party, during its legal, its stolen, and its bought tenures of power, has steadily decayed in moral character and political capacity. Its platform promises are now a list of its past failures. It demands the restoration of our navy—it has squandered hundreds of millions to create a navy that does not exist. It calls upon Congress to remove the burdens under which American shipping has been depressed—it imposed and has continued those burdens. It professes the policy of reserving the public lands for small holdings by actual settlers—it has given away the people's heritage till now a few railroads and non-resident aliens, individual and corporate, possess a larger area than that of all our farms between the two seas. It professes a preference for free institutions—it organized and tried to legalize a control of State elections by Federal troops. It professes a desire to elevate labor—it has subjected American workingmen to the competition of convict and imported contract labor. It professes gratitude to all who were disabled or died in the war, leaving widows and orphans—it left to a Democratic House of Representatives the first effort to equalize both bounties and pensions. It proffers a pledge to correct the irregularities of our tariff—it created and has continued them. Its own tariff commission confessed the need of more than 20 per cent. reduction—its Congress gave a reduction of less than 4 per cent. It professes the protection of American manufactures—it has subjected them to an increasing flood of manufactured goods and a hopeless competition with manufacturing nations, not one of which taxes raw materials. It professes to protect all American industries—it has impoverished many to subsidize a few. It professes the protection of American labor—it has depleted the returns of American agriculture, an industry followed by half our people. It professes the equality of all men before the law attempting to fix the status of colored citizens—the acts of its Congress were overset by the decisions of its courts. It "accepts anew the duty of leading in the work of progress and reform"—its caught criminals are permitted to escape through contrived delays or actual connivance in the prosecution. Honeycombed with corruption, outbreaking exposures no longer shock its moral sense. Its honest members, its independent journals, no longer maintain a successful contest for authority in its councils or a veto upon bad nominations. That change is necessary is proved by an existing surplus of more than $100,000,000, which has yearly been collected from a suffering people. Unnecessary taxation is unjust taxation. We denounce the Republican Party for having failed to relieve the people from crushing war taxes, which have paralyzed business, crippled industry, and deprived labor of employment and of just reward.

The Democracy pledges itself to purify the Administration from corruption, to restore economy, to revive respect for law, and to reduce taxation to the lowest limit consistent with due regard to the preservation of the faith of the Nation to its creditors and pensioners. Knowing full well, however, that legislation affecting the operations of the people should be cautious and conservative in method, not in advance of public opinion, but, responsive to its demands, the Democratic Party is pledged to revise the tariff in a spirit of fairness to all interests. But, in making reduction in taxes, it is not proposed to injure any domestic industries, but rather to promote their healthy growth. From the foundation of this Government taxes collected at the Custom House have been the chief source of Federal revenue. Such they must continue to be. Moreover many industries have come to rely upon legislation for successful continuance, so that any change of law must be at every step regardful of the labor and capital thus involved. The process of the reform must be subject in the execution to this plain dictate of justice. All taxation shall be limited to the requirements of economical government. The necessary reduction in taxation can and must be effected without depriving American labor of the ability to compete successfully with foreign labor, and without imposing lower rates of duty than will be ample to cover any increased cost of production which may exist in consequence of the higher rate of wages prevailing in this country. Sufficient revenue to pay all the expenses of the Federal Government economically administered, including pensions, interest, and principal of the public debt, can be got under our present system of taxation from Custom House taxes on fewer imported articles, bearing heaviest on articles of luxury and bearing lightest on articles of necessity. We, therefore, denounce the abuses of the existing tariff; and subject to the preceding limitations, we demand that Federal taxation shall be exclusively for public purposes, and shall not exceed the needs of the Government economically administered.

The system of direct taxation known as the "internal revenue" is a war tax, and so long as the law continues the money derived therefrom should be sacredly devoted to the relief of the people from the remaining burdens of the war, and be made a fund to defray the expense of the care and comfort of worthy soldiers disabled in line of duty in the wars of the Republic, and for the payment of such pensions as Congress may from time to time grant to such soldiers, a like fund for the sailors having been already provided, and any surplus should be paid into the Treasury.

We favor an American continental policy based upon more intimate commercial and political relations with the 15 sister republics of North, Central, and South America, but entangling alliances with none.

We believe in honest money, the gold and silver coinage of the Constitution, and a circulating medium convertible into such money without loss.

Asserting the equality of all men before the law, we hold that it is the duty of the Government in its dealings with the people to mete out equal and exact justice to all citizens of whatever nativity, race, color, or persuasion, religious or political.

We believe in a free ballot and a fair count, and we recall to the memory of the people the noble struggle of the Democrats in the Forty-fifth and Forty-sixth Congresses, by which a reluctant Republican opposition was compelled to assent to legislation making everywhere illegal the presence of troops at the polls as the conclusive proof that a Democratic Administration will preserve liberty with order.

The selection of Federal officers for the Territories should be restricted to citizens previously resident therein.

We oppose sumptuary laws which vex the citizen and interfere with individual liberty.

We favor honest civil service reform and the compensation of all United States officers by fixed salaries; the separation of Church and State and the diffusion of free education by common schools, so that every child in the land may be taught the rights and duties of citizenship.

While we favor all legislation which will tend to the equitable distribution of property, to the prevention of monopoly, and to the strict enforcement of individual rights against corporate abuses, we hold that the welfare of society depends upon a scrupulous regard for the rights of property as defined by law. We believe that labor is best rewarded where it is freest and most enlightened. It should therefore be fostered and cherished. We favor the repeal of all laws restricting the free action of labor and the enactment of laws by which labor organizations may be incorporated, and of all such legislation as will tend to enlighten the people as to the true relations of capital and labor.

We believe that the public land ought, as far as possible, to be kept as homesteads for actual settlers; that all unearned lands heretofore improvidently granted to railroad corporations by the action of the Republican Party should be restored to the public domain, and that no more grants of land shall be made to corporations or be allowed to fall into the ownership of alien absentees.

We are opposed to all propositions which, upon any pretext, would convert the General Government into a machine for collecting taxes to be distributed among the States or the citizens thereof.

In reaffirming the declaration of the Democratic platform of 1856 that the liberal principles embodied by Jefferson in the Declaration of Independence, and sanctioned in the Constitution, which make ours the land of liberty and the asylum of the oppressed of every nation, have ever been cardinal principles in the Democratic faith, we nevertheless do not sanction the importation of foreign labor or the admission of servile races, unfitted by habits, training, religion, or kindred, for absorption into the great body of our people, or for the citizenship which our laws confer. American civilization demands that against the immigration or importation of Mongolians to these shores our gates be closed.

The Democratic Party insists that it is the duty of this Government to protect with equal fidelity and vigilance the rights of its citizens, native and naturalized, at home and abroad, and to the end that this protection may be assured, United States papers of naturalization issued by courts of competent jurisdiction must be respected by the Executive and Legislative Departments of our own Government and by all foreign powers. It is an imperative duty of this Government to efficiently protect all the rights of persons and property of every American citizen in foreign lands, and demand and inforce full reparation for any invasion thereof. An American citizen is only responsible to his own Government for any act done in his own country or under her flag, and can only be tried therefor on her own soil and according to her laws; and no power exists in this Government to expatriate an American citizen to be tried in any foreign land for any such act.

This country has never had a well defined and executed foreign policy save under Democratic administration. That policy has ever been in regard to foreign nations, so long as they do no act detrimental to the interests of the country or hurtful to our citizens, to let them alone; that as a result of this policy we recall the acquisition of Louisiana, Florida, California, and of the adjacent Mexican territory by purchase alone, and contrast these grand acquisitions of Democratic statesmanship with the purchase of Alaska, the sole fruit of a Republican administration of nearly a quarter of a century.

The Federal Government should care for and improve the Mississippi River and other great waterways of the Republic, so as to secure for the interior States easy and cheap transportation to tide water.

Under a long period of Democratic rule and policy our merchant marine was fast overtaking; and on the point of outstripping that of Great Britain; under 20 years of Republican rule and policy our commerce has been left to British bottoms and the American flag has almost been swept off the high seas. Instead of the Republican Party's British policy, we demand for the people of the United States an American policy. Under Democratic rule and policy our merchants and sailors, flying the Stars and Stripes in every port, successfully searched out a market for the varied products of American industry; under a quarter century of Republican rule and policy, despite our manifest advantage over all other nations in high-paid labor, favorable climates and teeming soils; despite freedom of trade among all these United States; despite their population by the foremost races of men and an annual immigration of the young, thrifty, and adventurous of all nations; despite our freedom here from the inherited burdens of life and industry in Old World monarchies, their costly war navies, their vast tax-consuming, non-producing standing armies; despite 20 years of peace, that Republican rule and policy have managed to surrender to Great Britain, along with our commerce the control of the markets of the world. Instead of the Republican Party's British policy, we demand, in behalf of the American Democracy, an American policy. Instead of the Republican Party's discredited scheme and false pretense of friendship for American labor, expressed by imposing taxes, we demand, in behalf of the Democracy, freedom for American labor by reducing taxes, to the end that these United States may compete with unhindered powers for the primacy among nations in all the arts of peace and fruits of liberty.

With profound regret we have been apprised by the venerable statesman, through whose person was struck that blow at the vital principle of republics, acquiescence in the will of the majority, that he cannot permit us again to place in his hands the leadership of the Democratic hosts, for the reason that the achievement of reform in the administration of the Federal Government is an undertaking now too heavy for his age and failing strength. Rejoicing that his life has been prolonged until the general judgment of our fellow-countrymen is united in the wish that that wrong were righted in his person, for the Democracy of the United States we offer to him, in his withdrawal from public cares, not only our respectful sympathy and esteem, but also that best homage of freemen, the pledge of our devotion to the principles and the cause now inseparable in the history of this Republic from the labors and the name of Samuel J. Tilden.

With this statement of the hopes, principles, and purposes of the Democratic Party, the great issue of reform and change in administration is submitted to the people in calm confidence that the popular voice will pronounce in favor of new men and new and more favorable conditions for the growth of industry, the extension of trade, the employment and due reward of labor and of capital and the general welfare of the whole country.

The reading of the platform was listened to with strict attention. Two clerks were about used up in the task of imparting the Democratic declaration of principles to the convention. Not until the passages referring to the tariff, American shipping, and other such subjects had been passed and the passage had been reached regretting the inability of Tilden to become a candidate; was there prolonged applause. Col. Morrison announced that Gen. Butler would have 30 minutes in which to make a minority report and a speech. After that Converse, of Ohio, was to have five minutes. Ten minutes were to be taken up by Mr. Watterson, of Kentucky; then Col. Morrison would call for the previous question on the report.

GEN. BUTLER'S PLATFORM.

Gen. Butler came forward. He was greeted with tremendous applause by the audience as he stood bowing, with a long paper in his hand. To save his voice he asked the clerk to read the manuscript. The clerk began with the line "Gen. Butler's platform," when he was interrupted by applause. The delegates listened patiently to the reading of the report, the applause at occasional points coming from the distant seats outside the central part of the hall. The report was as follows:

[The planks of certain portions of a platform offered by Gen. Benjamin F. Butler, the Committee of Resolutions rejected. Other portions, such as the subject of the disposition of internal revenue taxes to a pension fund, the American foreign policy, and the appointment of Federal officers in Territories from the citizens thereof, were adopted by the committee.]

*Resolved*, That no taxes, direct or indirect, can be rightfully imposed upon the people except to meet the expenses of an economically administered Government; to bring taxation down to this point is true administrative revenue reform.

*Resolved*, That the people will tolerate direct taxation for the ordinary expenses of the Government only in case of dire necessity or war.

*Resolved*, Therefore, that the revenue necessary for such expenses should be raised by customs duties upon imports, after the manner of our fathers.

*Resolved*, That in levying such duties two principles should be carefully observed. First, that all materials used in the arts and manufactures and the necessaries of life not produced in this country shall come in free, and that all articles of luxury should be taxed as high as possible up to the collection point; second, that in imposing customs duties the law must be carefully adjusted to promote American enterprise and industries, not to create monopolies, and to cherish and foster American labor.

Faithful industry is the basis on which the whole fabric of civilization rests under our system. Toilers are producers. The mass of the people are the governing power. Being the true Democracy they demand the fullest consideration of measures for their education, their advancement, and their protection. Labor and capital are allies, not enemies. No contention can arise between them if each has done its duty to the other. Under the existing law, State and national, all such controversies can only be settled by brute force—capital starving labor and labor despoiling capital, the contention ending in the crippling or ruining of both. But capital is strong; labor is weak; therefore, labor has a right to demand of the Government to establish tribunals in which these great controversies, which may lead to revolution, may be judicially and justly determined with the fullest power to enforce their decrees; to provide by law that laboring men may combine and organize for their own protection as capital may be incorporated and combined for its protection, and that all devices, either by contract or terrorism or otherwise, to obstruct and set aside this right in laboring men are oppressive and in derogation of the rights of an American freeman and should be made penal by law.

All the great woes upon our country have come because of imported labor. Our fathers made this land the home of the free for all men appreciating our institutions, with energy enough to bring themselves here, and such we welcome. But our country ought never to be a bazaar house for the deportation of the pauper labor of other countries through governmental aid, or the importation of the same kind of labor as an instrument with which capital can debase American working men and women from the proud position they now occupy by competing with them by imported or convict labor, while at the same time capital asks and receives protection of its interests at the hands of the Government under guise of providing for American labor. This evil, like all others that finds birth in the cupidity and selfishness of men, labor demands should be redressed by law. Labor has a right to demand a just share of the profits of its own production.

The future of our country unites with the laboring men in the demand for the liberal support by the United States of the school system of the States for the common school education of all the children, the same affording a sufficient foundation for the coming generations to acquire due knowledge of their duties as citizens.

*Monopoly*.—That every species of monopoly engenders two classes, the very rich and the very poor, both of which are equally hurtful to a Republic which should give to its people equal rights and equal privileges under the law.

*Resolved*, That the public lands of the United States were the equal heritage of all its citizens, and should have been held open to the use of all in such quantities only as are needed for cultivation and improvement by all. Therefore, we view with alarm the absorption of those lands by corporations and individuals in large areas—some of them more than equal to princely domains—and demand of Congress to apply appropriate remedies with a stern hand, so that the lands of the people may be held by the many and not by the few.

*Resolved*, That the public lands of the Nation are held by the Government in trust for those who make their homes in the United States and who mean to become citizens of the Republic, and we protest against the purchase and monopolization of these lands by corporations and the alien aristocracy of Europe.

*Resolved*, That all corporate bodies created either in the States or Nation for the purpose of performing public duties are public servants, and to be regulated in all their actions by the same power that created them at its own will, and that it is within the power and is the duty of the creator to so govern its creature that by its acts it shall become neither a monopoly nor a burden upon the people, but be their servant and convenience, which is the true test of its usefulness. Therefore, we call upon Congress to exercise great constitutional power for regulating inter-State commerce: to provide that by no contrivance whatever under forms of law or otherwise shall discriminating rates and charges for the transportation of freight and travel be made in favor of the few against the many, or enhance the rates of transportation between the producer and the consumer.

*The civil service*.—The various offices of the Government belong to the people thereof and who rightfully demand to exercise and fill the same whenever they are fitted by capacity, integrity and energy, the last two qualifications never to be tested by any scholastic examination. We hold that frequent changes of federal officials are shown to be necessary, first to counteract the growing aristocratic tendencies to a caste of life offices; second, experience having shown that all investigation is useless while the incumbent and his associates hold their places. Frequent change of officers is necessary to the discovery and punishment of frauds, peculations, defalcations, and embezzlements of the public money.

*Resolved*, That we adhere to and affirm the doctrine enunciated and established by Jackson, that the Government alone has the power to establish and issue money for the people; that the issue of the legal-tender note, made by the Government as a method of borrowing money to carry on the war in the exercise of a constitutional power, has become the fixed currency of the United States, equal to coined gold and sil-

# The New-York Times.

VOL. XXXIII.....NO. 10,251. — NEW-YORK, SATURDAY, JULY 12, 1884. — PRICE TWO CENTS.


## A STRONG TICKET CHOSEN

### CLEVELAND AND HENDRICKS THE DEMOCRATIC NOMINEES.

AN OVERWHELMING VOTE FOR CLEVELAND ON THE SECOND BALLOT—HENDRICKS CHOSEN FOR VICE-PRESIDENT UNANIMOUSLY—KELLY'S LAST EFFORT—HIS HEELERS DEPART IN DISGUST.

THE SECOND AND LAST BALLOT.

| | |
|---|---|
| CLEVELAND | 683 |
| BAYARD | 81 1-2 |
| HENDRICKS | 45 1-2 |
| THURMAN | 4 |
| RANDALL | 4 |
| McDONALD | 2 |

*From the Special Correspondent of the Times.*

CHICAGO, July 11.—The Democratic Convention completed its work to-day by nominating Grover Cleveland, of New-York, to be President of the United States, and Thomas A. Hendricks, of Indiana, to be Vice-President. Cleveland won on the second ballot. On that ballot he received 475 votes. Before the result was announced opposing States threw aside their candidates and fought among themselves for the honor of being the first to get on the winning side. After all the changes had been made there were 683 votes for the Governor of New-York, and he was nominated by the unanimous voice of the convention.

After the tariff question had been disposed of last night by rejecting Butler's substitute and adopting the platform reported by the committee, the opponents of Cleveland, led by the Bayard men of Alabama, Mississippi, and Missouri, undertook to secure an adjournment. They were beaten by a vote of three to one. The most important work of the convention was at hand. The obstructionists had been overcome, and the delegates were to begin the task of making a national ticket. The first ballot was taken between midnight and 1 o'clock this morning. When the last Territory had been called Cleveland had only 369 votes. North Carolina had given her 22 votes to Bayard, and the Tammany quarrel had taken from Cleveland some other votes which his managers had at first counted in their list. He gained three votes by changes which were announced, and then McLean, of Cincinnati, who had received a telegram from Hoadly, arose and transferred nearly all of the anti-Thurman votes of Ohio to the New-York candidate. These reinforcements gave Cleveland a total of 392. Next on the list stood Bayard with 170. Thurman, rejected by a majority of the delegates of his own State, had gathered enough votes from other States to make a company of 88. Randall had lost 5 in Pennsylvania and had secured 23 elsewhere. McDonald lagged in the rear with only 56. Flower, who has an influential nephew in Wisconsin, had raked four votes out of that State. The tail of the "old ticket," who had thrust his knife between the ribs of McDonald, found Cullerton, of Illinois, voting for him, and hoped to become a second Garfield. In order that the convention might not lose sight of him, he arose and asked Cullerton to change his vote. Cullerton refused to do so. Immediately after the result had been announced the anti-Cleveland men moved an adjournment. Beaten once by a close vote, they returned to the assault, and Manning yielded because the delegates were weary and sleepy.

Until 4 o'clock this morning politicians were threading the mazes of the Palmer House. Kelly and Butler were again plotting in Butler's room. The Bayard men were striving to gain votes for their candidate, and they predicted that the Senator would have 250 on the second ballot. Young men and boys marched through the hotel corridors with red cotton handkerchiefs around their hats shouting for Thurman. Old politicians shook their heads and said that an adjournment after the first ballot could not fail to hurt the leading candidate. Cleveland's men were confident, however, for they knew that any attempt to consolidate the anti-Cleveland vote in support of a minority candidate or a dark horse would surely drive to them large blocks of delegates who were waiting to be released. There were no indications that the opposition votes could be bunched for Bayard, Thurman, or McDonald, but it was whispered that Hendricks was full of possibilities. Hendricks had been the subject of the mysterious conference between Butler and Kelly, and the result of that conference was to be seen later on.

When the convention reassembled this morning the plans of Butler, Kelly, and the intriguing politicians of Indiana had been completed. Cleveland lacked 155 votes of a two-thirds majority. Could he get them? The Governor's managers believed that the needed votes would be forthcoming on the second or the third ballot, and they had solid grounds for this belief. Butler and Kelly hoped to capture the convention for Hendricks by a carefully planned exhibition of sham enthusiasm. If their scheme should fail, the New-York Governor would quickly carry off the prize. There were new faces in the galleries and in the body of the great hall. These strangers had work to do.

Before the roll was called for the second ballot Pennsylvania withdrew Randall's name. This action indicated an early settlement of the contest. Eight States had been called, and Cleveland had gained nine votes, when Illinois again produced one vote for Hendricks. At once hundreds of spectators and many delegates sprang to their feet, cheering and yelling. The leaders on the floor were Butler's men, Kelly's men, and the Thurman men of California. Five minutes passed and the crowd was still yelling. Ten minutes passed, and the lungs of the shouters were not weary. "How long shall we holler?" asked a messenger, addressing some one on the platform. Politicians pushed their way through the crowded aisle and sought the white-faced representative of the "old ticket," who sat by the side of Dan Voorhees, with the Indiana delegation. Clunie, the California follower of Dana and Thurman, bowed down before him, and Dr. Munford, carrying the Field boom in his pocket, came with a smile on his boyish face.

Fifteen minutes passed. Yells rent the air and the band was playing. Blaine had been applauded for 17 minutes, and the Hendricks men were bound to distance him. "Hendricks and Slocum," cried the Butler men and the Kelly men in the galleries. Four years ago McDonald had been faithful to his trust and had supported his friend to the end. Would Hendricks be as faithful? No, for he yielded and allowed Voorhees to go to the Chairman's desk, withdraw McDonald, and place him in nomination. The Indiana delegation, unrestrained by the man who had nominated McDonald, had thrown over "Old Saddlebags" and were following the man who had yielded to temptation. Other delegations were hastily caucusing and deciding what they would do. Cleveland's men were hard at work, for they had become alarmed. There was danger that the convention would lose its head and nominate Hendricks.

But an antidote was to be served by the same delegation in which the poison had been found. Gen. Black, a friend and supporter of McDonald, angry because the ex-Senator had been robbed of the vote of his State, declared with bitter emphasis that Illinois cast 38 votes for Cleveland. This was a gain of 10. The crowd yelled for five minutes. The Butler men and the Kelly men hissed. Hendricks's column grew, as State after State was called, and so did Cleveland's. The Butler men in Massachusetts and Michigan and the Randall men in New-Jersey went over to Hendricks, but the danger point had been passed, and when the Pennsylvania men cast 42 votes for Cleveland the Hendricks boom perished. The New-York Governor had 475 votes. He had gained 83. Bayard had lost 20. McDonald had saved only 4 out of the wreck. Thurman had lost 28. Hendricks could show only 123. The last desperate attempt had been made to defeat Cleveland, and it had failed. Instead of causing the forces of the minority candidates to be bunched for a dark horse, the originators of the Hendricks movement had driven 83 outsiders into Cleveland's camp.

Seeing that the nomination of Cleveland was assured, the Chairmen of opposing delegations came with their votes in their hands, eager to join the majority. The stampede for Hancock at Cincinnati in 1880 was repeated at Chicago. Even California brought her tribute, a solid delegation. Menzies gave the 30 votes of Indiana to the winning candidate. When the result was announced it appeared that Cleveland had 683 votes; Bayard had 81½; McDonald, 2; Thurman, 4; Randall, 4, and 45½ votes—the majority of them from Massachusetts, New-Jersey, and Pennsylvania—were retained by Hendricks. While cannon were booming in the adjoining street the nomination was made unanimous upon Mr. Hendricks's motion.

There was substantially no opposition in the session this evening to the nomination of Hendricks for the second place on the ticket. Before this nomination was made it was suggested by many who were displeased by Hendricks's treatment of McDonald that it would be difficult to bring the friends of McDonald into line in Indiana. On the other hand, it was urged that the nomination of Hendricks would be good politics because he had been vigorously supported by the Kelly men and the Butler men for the first place on the ticket. Tammany, it was said, would not oppose a ticket bearing his name. Hendricks is very popular among the Democrats of Indiana, and those who urged his nomination hope that his popularity has not been affected by his course in the convention.

Kelly and his men packed their gripsacks and started for home before the evening session began. Cleveland had been successful and they took no interest in the subsequent proceedings.

There is some curiosity as to the course that will be taken by Butler. He declared to the convention that if his tariff resolutions should not be adopted the party would be forced to rely upon God and not upon Butler for help in the coming campaign. Some believe that the old General will strive to defeat the ticket. The great majority of the delegates, however, care no more for him than they do for Kelly and Tammany Hall. F. D. R.

### HOW CLEVELAND WAS NOMINATED.

*From Staff Correspondents of the Times.*

CHICAGO, July 11.—Grover Cleveland is nominated, and the streets are ringing with cheers from Northern and Western delegates and with yells of delight from the Southern men, who have seen Tammany once more brought to the dust. Congratulations are exchanged by excited men. Cleveland badges are put on in place of those hitherto worn for McDonald and Bayard and Thurman, and the bandanna handkerchiefs, which served for a time to arouse a degree of enthusiasm for the "old Roman" of Ohio, are fluttering in the air in celebration of the victory over Kelly and his men. Bitter indeed is the humiliation of Tammany. Bound and gagged by the operation of the unit rule, it has been compelled to sit still and have its vote for President cast over and over against its will. Nauseous as the performance was, it has been compelled to take its draught in a tin cup, to take it straight, and to admit by enforced silence that it was good.

The convention that nominated Cleveland was a remarkable one, particularly in its last two sessions. The session of Thursday night and this morning, with its sensational incident, when Butler was allowed to ridicule the platform in the presence of the delegated Democracy, is unique, and promises to become famous, if not mischievous, to the Democrats. It might have been prevented. The controllers of the convention could have kept Butler from the stage and compelled him to express his hostile criticisms elsewhere. But such was the disposition, particularly among the friends of Mr. Cleveland, to accord every opportunity for free discussion and to face even the most disagreeable circumstances, that Butler was given a hearing and treated courteously, while he vainly attempted to commit the majority to his personal platform.

When the convention adjourned last night, the opponents of Cleveland were encouraged to believe that they could beat him. They would not believe that Manning, in seconding the motion to adjourn, was inspired by any other feeling than one of fear, lest upon another ballot Cleveland would be so weakened by desertions as to make it apparent that his defeat was inevitable. The confidence that his friends had expressed, that Cleveland would be nominated on the first ballot, was laughed at by the Tammany men as they crowded into the Palmer House early in the morning. Gen. Frank Spinola, with well-affected glee, went industriously about telling everybody "We've licked this coon and sent Cleveland's chickens into their coop with their tails between their legs." Tommy Grady, strutting among his Tammany associates as a sort of hero, but aware of the aversion felt for him by the whole convention, added his own assurances to those of the man of the large shirt collar, promising a tremendous break in the morning for a candidate whom he wisely would not name. To give it out that Tammany was for any particular candidate would have been death to that candidate, and Tammany had learned the temper of the convention too well to do anything so palpably foolish. But they put their wits at work and spent the rest of the night in preparing a scheme which was made known later in the day.

#### THE WORK OF THE HEELERS.

The morning of the fourth day of the convention dawned clear and bright. The weary delegates, stimulated by excitement, came from their beds early. Tammany's braves were buoyant with confidence. Great things were to happen. Cleveland was beaten—utterly beaten—and had not a leg to stand on. It signified nothing to Tammany to know that Virginia's delegates had caucused, had decided to go to Cleveland if it was necessary for them to choose between Cleveland and other candidates, and that Colorado, Illinois, Maryland, Missouri, North Carolina, and Wisconsin were like-minded. Down to the convention hall at 10 o'clock the delegates walked in groups, most of them impressed by the talk with the belief that Tammany Hall was about to make a desperate effort to retrieve its losses. Major E. A. Burke, of New-Orleans, who was assured by a Tammany man that Cleveland was "knocked out," stroked his gray mustache, dropped a wink sidewise at his companion, and told the heeler of Kelly that he wished he was as sure of going to heaven as he was that Cleveland would be nominated on the next ballot. Tammany's crowd did not go in procession, as did the County Democracy, with their banner portrait of Cleveland at their head.

The weather was hot, for the first time since the convention met. Some misunderstanding prevailed as to the hour for meeting, and at 10 o'clock, to which time the adjournment had been taken, the seats of the delegates were but partly occupied. Curiously enough, the seats for spectators all over the hall were nearly crowded with an uneasy, restless audience. There were many boys and rough-coated men and a remarkable number of Indiana badges in the dense throng that held the best places on the floor and in the galleries. The band in the box over the platform entertained the audience with its usual preliminary concert. Kelly and Grady and Purcell came in. They were non-committal as to the programme to be carried out. They looked about the hall, and the appearance of the great audience evidently pleased them. Wade Hampton, coming in with the South Carolina delegates, was cheered. "Dixie" was also cheered, and when Mr. Hendricks, of Indiana, entered, the vast audience, as if impelled by an electric shock, rose to its feet, seemingly as one man, and sent forth a cheer that swept through the hall like a whirlwind. Ex-Minister Washburne, who had attended every sitting of the convention, sat among the distinguished persons on the platform, and looked and listened with amazement upon this strange spectacle. Gov. Cleveland's friends noted the exhibition, too. Manning, as calm and unmoved as ever, sat at the back of his lines of delegates, waiting for the tempest to pass over.

Chairman Vilas called the convention to order, and introduced the Rev. Mr. Locke, an Episcopalian clergyman. The brief prayer over, Mr. Munford, of Missouri, who had the Field boom concealed in a convenient place, ready to be sprung upon the convention, offered a resolution providing that on a roll-call of the States no vote should be changed after it was announced until the succeeding ballot. If the hope of the Field men depended for fruition upon the fate of this resolution it was doomed to be untimely sent to seek the society of the broken Flower. The resolution was put to vote. The responses came. "The nays have it," decided Chairman Vilas.

Orestes Cleveland introduced and secured the passage of a resolution providing for a report of the proceedings of the convention. There were rumblings of applause, apparently for nothing whatever. Sergeant-at-Arms Bright, standing on the stage, raised his hands and sent an aide or two out to stop the disorder. It soon ceased.

#### THE DECISIVE ROLL CALL.

While the catcalls and rumblings of feet were ceasing the roll call on nominations was ordered and begun. Delegate Eckley B. Coxe, of Pennsylvania, above the hum of conversation, was heard withdrawing the nomination of Samuel J. Randall. A burst of applause followed a repetition of this announcement from the Chair. The gallery crowd did not know whether to applaud or not. Amid some confusion Alabama was called and the announcement made that abundant time would be given to each State after it was called to collect its ballots. Alabama stood unchanged—5 for Cleveland, 14 for Bayard. California gave her 16 votes to Thurman. When Colorado was called and responded with 6 votes for Cleveland, all gained upon the vote of last night, there was applause from the delegates and from many parts of the hall. Florida gave Bayard 2 votes, which Cleveland lost, and the men and boys in the gallery and at the ends of the hall screamed and cheered and whistled with delight. Georgia increased her vote for Cleveland by 4 and it was the turn of the delegates to applaud.

#### TRYING TO STAMPEDE THE CONVENTION.

Illinois was called. The galleries applauded at once. Col. Bright's Illinois assistants were watching the delegation. Judge Black, standing upon a seat, waited for the confusion to cease. Dan Voorhees, in the Indiana delegation, just in front of Illinois, looked anxiously back and then toward the crowded galleries. "Illinois casts one vote for Hendricks," he began. Up went a mighty shout in an instant from every corner of the hall. From the midst of the sloping tiers of seats and from many of the delegations went up a deafening roar of shouts and clapping and shrill whistles. Col. Bright's aides, like so many leaders, waved their hands above their heads, facing the audience, and led in the din. The house had been packed. Any man could see that with half an eye. The Chairman could not stop it. As it continued it grew. Dan Voorhees got up. All the other Indiana delegates imitated his example. Presently other delegates got upon their feet and before an effort could be made to arrest the frenzy the whole convention was standing. Col. Bright sat near the Chairman, who was pounding with all his strength. Above the heads of the audience there fluttered a cloud of white handkerchiefs. Men endowed with phenomenal lungs were heard uttering prolonged howls that prevailed over the prodigious tumult. Indiana was all activity. One of her delegates tore the staff of the delegation from its place, giving no heed to the anxious protests of ex-Gov. Hendricks, who sat trembling in his place, evidently apprehending that their Presidential lightning was about to strike him. The staff, waved aloft, stirred the Indiana shouters to redoubled efforts. The cheering rose and fell; it never ceased altogether, but the cheerers tired, and when the Chairman rapped for order they tore their throats with frantic shrieks. When the long, slender staff was carried upon the stage and swung in the air the Chairman ordered the bearer off. Col. Bright's Indiana howlers applauded this repulse, and then John Kelly's secretary, Col. Mooney, was seen standing upon one of the desks in the press gallery, wildly waving his handkerchief. "Jimmy" Martin, in the rear of the platform, contributed his strong arms, throat, and handkerchief to the demonstration. Tammany's 11 delegates hung back a while in pretended doubt as to what part they should take. At last they got up with the rest, and flung their arms and tried their throats with lusty vigor.

It was in vain that Mr. Hendricks, surrounded by a crowd of friends, all imploring him to accept a nomination, tried to hold Mr. Voorhees down by the coat tails. The "Tall Sycamore of the Wabash" was determined to take advantage of what appeared to be an irresistible, overpowering demand for Hendricks. Mr. Hendricks, dumfounded at what appeared to be an inevitable nomination, made his way out of the hall unobserved. Mr. Voorhees, yielding to the solicitations of his brother delegates, and to the uneasy Californian, Clunie, the Charles A. Dana delegate, advanced to the platform. Chairman Vilas consulted with Bright, who did nothing to stop the shouting. The uproar had continued 10 minutes. One of Mr. Bright's able assistants in front of the press seats made a speaking trumpet of his hands and shouted across the heads of the correspondents to a superior officer: "How long have we got to holler?" There was no answer, and the "hollering" continued. By and by it stopped. Voorhees stepped out upon the table in front of the platform with his hands on his hips and his elbows sticking out at each side. He announced that at the request of the delegates from Indiana he withdrew the name of Joseph E. McDonald for the purpose of, at the proper time, casting the vote of Indiana for Thomas A. Hendricks.

#### THE HENDRICKS BOOM "BUSTS."

The excitement was renewed with redoubled intensity. It seemed to affect everybody. A great fear came over the friends of Cleveland. The men who came here to make a nomination in the hope of securing victory were trembling. The Arkansas delegates, who had just cast the solid vote of the delegation for Cleveland, watched the shouting delegates behind them with anxious eyes. Were the Democrats to repeat the scene of the last convention? Was there to be a stampede for Hendricks by which he was to be caught up and nominated with a whirl? "Give us the old ticket," screamed a man in the gallery over the Chairman's head. There was another burt of applause, more music from the bands, increasing the confusion, and at last, tired out, the weary audience came to comparative order.

Judge Black, of Illinois, was upon his feet claiming recognition. With the full expectation that he would cast a heavy vote for Hendricks, the Indiana shouters held their breath. "By direction of the delegates from the State of Illinois I cast 38 votes for Grover Cleveland." The thousands of listeners held their breath for a moment, and then the cheering broke forth afresh. It had seemed but a moment before as if everybody in the hall was shouting for Hendricks. Now it appeared as if the same throats were splitting for Cleveland. A look at the delegates, however, showed that they were nearly all joining in the last demonstration. The flagstaffs of a dozen States were snatched from their places, and that of Illinois, at one side of the hall, was waved toward the New-York staff at the opposite side.

The Illinois McDonald men were mad. They could not brook the desertion of McDonald in the interest of Hendricks, and they took an effective method of evincing their displeasure. Mr. Davis, of Manxville, spoiled the vote by insisting that his ballot should be taken for McDonald. After the Illinois vote had been cast, it only gave Hendricks 1, which he had secured last night. Indiana cast her 30 votes for Hendricks, and the gallery applause, now becoming tiresome, was repeated. Pennsylvania asked and received permission to withdraw for consultation. As they were going to an adjoining room, Kansas cast her vote, giving Cleveland 1 more than she did last night. Kentucky, at the request of Mr. Carlisle, withdrew his name and gave 1 vote to Thurman, 3 to Cleveland, 7 to Bayard, and 15 to Hendricks.

In spite of the clamor of the Hendricks men, the Cleveland column stood firm. Indeed, it grew constantly. Hendricks got 12½ votes from Massachusetts, 13 from Michigan, 2 from Mississippi, 8 from Missouri, 5 from Nevada, and 11 from New-Jersey, the latter cast by Gov. Abbett for "the man who got cheated in 1876." At the same time Cleveland had gained 2 votes in Louisiana, 4 in Maryland, 3 in Massachusetts, 1 in Mississippi, 8 in Missouri, 1 in Nebraska, and 1 in New-Jersey and had only lost 1 in Michigan.

The cheers made it impossible almost to hear Mr. Manning as, in response to the call for New-York, he cast 72 votes for Cleveland. One of the gagged minority in New-York endeavored to challenge the New-York vote "in the name of the disfranchised minority." He was howled down without mercy. North Carolina stuck to Bayard, although his line was melting away fast. A delegate stiffened the convention in upholding the unit rule by explaining that there were Cleveland votes in the delegation, but that the minority deferred to the unit rule and cast the whole vote for Bayard.

The Pennsylvania delegation were coming in. Henry Watterson, coming down to the press inclosure, sat down beside Murat Halstead and told him that Cleveland would be nominated before the ballot was concluded. The State was called, and Pennsylvania cast 1 vote for Thurman, 2 for Bayard, 4 for Randall, 11 for Hendricks, and 42 for Cleveland. Col. W. R. Morrison was delighted. "The Hendricks boom is busted," he said. "It came near closing us up, but we've scotched the snake," he added.

#### CLEVELAND VICTORIOUS.

The roll call was proceeded with as fast as the cheering and confusion would permit. Even before the Territories had fallen into the Cleveland line there were States clamoring for a chance to change. Polygamous Utah and Washington alone divided. Out of the distressing din that prevailed all over the hall, North Carolina was heard changing from Bayard to Cleveland. Wild excitement took possession of the audience. Congressman Barbour, of Virginia, abandoned Bayard, Thurman, and Hendricks, and gave 24 votes to Cleveland. Georgia followed suit. "Cleveland is nominated!" shouted a New-York Cleveland man, and in a moment a great floral design—a shield and anchor, capped by a young eagle with a streamer in its beak—bearing the name of Cleveland, was brought into the hall by "Jimmy" Oliver, who had paid $200 for it, and had it ready for production last night a little ahead of time. The boom of a cannon was heard as Texas secured recognition to change her vote. Florida got into line and so did Maryland and West Virginia, with the exception of two votes that stuck to Bayard. The band played "Hail to the chief," and the clerks could not hear the changes that were made until the music ceased. "Jimmy" Oliver's floral piece, with its nodding eagle, was put upon the table in front of the platform. Further changes were sent up, and again the audience gave itself up to the enjoyment of the violent exercise it had been taking for nearly an hour and a half.

While the excitement was highest a bustle was noticed on the platform. The guests who had seats there got out of the way as "Fatty" Walsh and three or four other stalwart County Democracy men climbed up the steps with the great portrait of Cleveland, which they had hastily torn from its place in the parlor hall at the Palmer, carried through the streets at a run, and brought into the convention to add something to the excitement. As the puffing and sweating men raised the big picture on the desk and held it by its broad gold frame, solid cheers arose, in which the Indiana boys were not required by Col. Bright to take an active part.

Exhausted, perspiring, satisfied, the convention at last stopped its noise. Mr. Menzies, of Indiana, attempted from the platform to make Cleveland's nomination unanimous. The Chairman informed him that this could not be done until the roll call was completed and the vote announced. California, which had been swinging about trying to boom Thurman and Hendricks, wanted to get in out of the rain, and Delegate Breckenridge cast her solid vote for Cleveland. The changes having all been announced, Reading Clerk Bell read the result as follows:

THE SECOND BALLOT.

| States. | Cleveland. | McDonald. | Bayard. | Thurman. | Hendricks. | Randall. | Total. |
|---|---|---|---|---|---|---|---|
| Alabama | 5 | 1 | 14 | | | | 20 |
| Arkansas | 14 | | | | | | 14 |
| California | 16 | | | | | | 16 |
| Colorado | 6 | | | | | | 6 |
| Connecticut | 12 | | | | | | 12 |
| Delaware | | | 6 | | | | 6 |
| Florida | 8 | | | | | | 8 |
| Georgia | 22 | | 2 | | | | 24 |
| Illinois | 43 | 1 | | | | | 44 |
| Indiana | 30 | | | | | | 30 |
| Iowa | 26 | | | | | | 26 |
| Kansas | 17 | | 1 | | | | 18 |
| Kentucky | 4 | | 21 | 1 | | | 26 |
| Louisiana | 15 | | | 1 | | | 16 |
| Maine | 12 | | | | | | 12 |
| Maryland | 16 | | | | | | 16 |
| Massachusetts | 8 | | 7½ | | 12½ | | 28 |
| Michigan | 23 | | | | 3 | | 26 |
| Minnesota | 14 | | | | | | 14 |
| Mississippi | 2 | | 14 | | 2 | | 18 |
| Missouri | 32 | | | | | | 32 |
| Nebraska | 9 | | 1 | | | | 10 |
| Nevada | | | | 1 | 5 | | 6 |
| New-Hampshire | 8 | | | | | | 8 |
| New-Jersey | 5 | | 2 | | 11 | | 18 |
| New-York | 72 | | | | | | 72 |
| North Carolina | 22 | | | | | | 22 |
| Ohio | 46 | | | | | | 46 |
| Oregon | 6 | | | | | | 6 |
| Pennsylvania | 42 | | 2 | 1 | 11 | 4 | 60 |
| Rhode Island | 7 | | 1 | | | | 8 |
| South Carolina | 10 | | 8 | | | | 18 |
| Tennessee | 24 | | | | | | 24 |
| Texas | 26 | | | | | | 26 |
| Vermont | 8 | | | | | | 8 |
| Virginia | 23 | | | | 1 | | 24 |
| West Virginia | 10 | | 2 | | | | 12 |
| Wisconsin | 22 | | | | | | 22 |
| *Territories.* | | | | | | | |
| Arizona | 2 | | | | | | 2 |
| Dakota | 2 | | | | | | 2 |
| Idaho | 2 | | | | | | 2 |
| Montana | 2 | | | | | | 2 |
| New-Mexico | 2 | | | | | | 2 |
| Utah | 2 | | | | | | 2 |
| Washington | 2 | | | | | | 2 |
| Wyoming | 2 | | | | | | 2 |
| District of Columbia | 2 | | | | | | 2 |
| Total | 683 | 2 | 81½ | 4 | 45½ | 4 | 820 |

Chairman Vilas now put the motion of Delegate Menzies, of Indiana, seconded by Missouri, that the nomination of Grover Cleveland be made unanimous. To the accompaniment of booming cannon and the cheers, yells, and screams of the audience, the motion was declared carried and Grover Cleveland announced as the candidate of the National Democracy for President of the United States. The band played "Hail to the Chief," there were more cheers, and then a gradual cessation of the tumult that had been so long kept up.

Ex-Senator William Wallace, of Pennsylvania, moved to take a recess until 5 o'clock, and this was seconded by Chairman Manning, of the New-York delegation. When the Chairman had quelled the tumult he announced that a dispatch had been received which was addressed to "The Convention." It was from Gov. George Hoadly, of Ohio, and was dated Columbus. It was as follows: "I congratulate the convention, the Democracy, and the country upon the wise work this day done. Ohio is the first battle ground. We are now firing 100 guns, and promise to salute you with cheers of victory in October and November." The dispatch was cheered, and the delegates broke away for their hotels.

As the crowd filed out of the building the smoking gun which had signaled the news to Chicago was being drawn past. Close behind it was the Albany Phalanx, 100 strong, marching to the music of "Cleveland and Victory." As the County Democrats, 500 in number, swept past the hall, cheering for their candidate, Tammany's two young braves, Cockran and Grady, came out arm in arm to cross the street. They halted at the curbstone, waiting for their ancient enemies to pass. As soon as they were spied by the procession, hat after hat was politely raised, and somebody cried "Take your medicine, gentlemen," and they did; they waited till the crowd passed by.

All of Flower's New-York friends—J. C. Truman, of Binghamton; L. B. Faulkner, John G. Sears, Elliot Danforth, and ex-Mayor Edward Murphy, of Troy—are shouting the Cleveland cry, and have pledged themselves to support the ticket and assist in giving the Governor the State they could not believe he could carry.

### THE NOMINATION OF HENDRICKS.

*From Staff Correspondents of the Times.*

CHICAGO, July 11.—The nomination of ex-Gov. Thomas A. Hendricks, of Indiana, the living tail of the old ticket of 1876, for the Vice-Presidency was notable for the remarkable demonstration made by the delegates and by the audience. His own State declined to present him or Joseph E. McDonald as a candidate, and the Chairman of the Indiana delegation, G. V. Menzies, in defiant tones, declared not only that Mr. Hendricks was not a candidate, but also that he would not accept the nomination, and that the convention would only have to do its work over again if it placed him in nomination. The convention declined to be impressed even with this emphatic declaration.

The roll was called on the order to present Vice-Presidential nominees soon after the convention reassembled at 5 o'clock, and had transacted some business of minor importance, such as the selection of the Chairman of the convention, Col. William F. Vilas, of Wisconsin, to be the chairman of the committee to inform the nominees. A dispatch was read from the merchants of the New-York Produce Exchange saying that Democrats and Republicans on the floor of the Exchange had just given three cheers for Grover Cleveland, and adding that the business men of New-York were solid for him. Editor E. A. Burke, of Louisiana, moved that the National Committee be authorized to fill any vacancies on the ticket, but this was received with so much disapproval that he withdrew his motion. A proposition to indorse the Morrison bill was made by a Georgian, but it was received with such dissatisfaction that the Chair referred it to the Committee on Resolutions. Speeches placing Vice-Presidential candidates in nomination were limited to five minutes, and the convention prepared to conclude its labors.

Gen. William S. Rosecrans, of California, was nominated by Niles Searles, of that State. Colorado presented the name of Joseph E. McDonald, of Indiana, through Mr. Branch. Georgia, through A. O. Bacon, offered the name of Gen. John C. Black, of Illinois. Gen. Black was a member of the Illinois delegation, and he promptly rose to reply that he was not a candidate and could not for a moment be considered as such. When Illinois was reached the solitary voter for McDonald for the Presidency in the entire delegation, J. B. Mann, arose and placed the Indianian in nomination for the second place. "Indiana has no candidate for Vice-President; neither will it present any," declared the Chairman of the delegation when the name of the State was called. Indiana was passed, and W. C. Perry, of Kansas, nominated Gov. George W. Glick, of Kansas. Missouri seconded McDonald's nomination, and Mississippi, through W. C. Faulkner, conferred a similar honor upon Rosecrans.

Ex-Senator William A. Wallace, of Pennsylvania, caught the Chairman's eye and was recognized. "I move," he said, "that the roll call be suspended and that Thomas A. Hendricks, of Indiana, be nominated by acclamation." The convention, as well as the audience, cheered lustily. Gov. Waller arose and in the name of Connecticut formally put Mr. Hendricks in nomination. Indiana's Chairman was on his feet to protest against the presentation of the name, but the Chair reminded him that Connecticut had the floor. The uproar in the building drowned whatever response Menzies made. Finally, however, he was recognized, and again he declared emphatically: "Mr. Hendricks is not a candidate and will not be a candidate. I am authorized to say this by Mr. Hendricks." He shook his head defiantly as he concluded, with: "And what the convention does in this matter will have to be done over again." The Georgian who had nominated Gen. Black demanded to know whether Mr. Menzies was authorized to say that Mr. Hendricks would not accept the unanimous nomination of Vice-President from the National Democratic Party. Menzies whispered to one of his colleagues, and immediately replied to the Georgian: "In Mr. Hendricks's own language, he is not and will not be a candidate for the Vice-Presidency."

In diplomatic language Connecticut's Governor continued his speech. Connecticut, he said, had no desire to force on Indiana a candidate against her will, but this was not an Indiana convention, [laughter and applause,] but one of the Democracy of the country, and the Democrats had the right to take any man that they saw fit for their ticket. If there was any Democrat who said he would not, under the circumstances here presented, take the nomination he would, of course withdraw his name, but Mr. Hendricks deserved it for the wrong that had been done in 1876. [Applause.] The party would have selected the same statesman from the East that it had eight years ago but for his lack of health. Mr. Hendricks was, thank God, in good health, and his selection was demanded by the party now.

Somebody asked that the rule be enforced requiring the call of States to proceed, and ex-Senator Wallace, declaring that Mr. Hendricks had once been elected Vice-President, and it was the party's demand now that he occupy his rightful seat again, moved that the rule be suspended and that the nomination be made by acclamation.

He was an Alabamian who now mildly suggested that a roll call be taken on the honorable names that had been presented. The convention, however, was set on having Hendricks, and no attention was paid to him. Judge John T. Harris, of Virginia, seconded Mr. Wallace's motion. The withdrawal of all names save that of Hendricks now began, amid the applause of the audience. Searles withdrew the name of Rosecrans and Colorado that of McDonald. Ex-Gov. Hubbard, of Texas, seconded Hendricks's nomination in a vigorous speech from the platform, in which he declared that the old ticket had been the desire of the Texas delegation when elected, and it still had a longing for it. "Gov. Hendricks will surely carry Indiana," said he, and again there was a shout. "He deserves it; give it to him, for God's sake." Black's name was withdrawn, and Smith M. Weed begged the convention not to give the nomination to Mr. Hendricks with a hurrah, but let the roll be called. Wallace withdrew his motion and substituted one that the nominations be closed, which was adopted with a hurrah, and the roll call began.

Down to Illinois the vote of each State was solid for Hendricks. Forty delegates voted for him and four refrained from voting. Menzies asked that Indiana be passed, as it was not authorized to vote under the circumstances. States and Territories cast their entire vote for the ex-Governor with the exception of Mississippi, which cast one vote for McDonald, and then Indiana was again called. Menzies asked that the delegates be excused from voting. Hisses were heard all over the hall. "I would like to ask," he said, "if the name of Joseph E. McDonald, of Indiana, is before the convention?" Mississippi had pulled its solitary McDonald voter into line, and the Chairman announced that Mississippi was solid for Hendricks.

"Then there is but one name before the convention?" asked Menzies.

"That is all," replied the Chairman.

"Then, Sir, Indiana casts 30 votes for Thomas A. Hendricks," was Mr. Menzies's announcement.

The uproar which followed this lasted nearly half an hour. The lances bearing the American colors were removed from their sockets, and State after State sent its representative, with its colors, down to the platform, where they were massed, and their flags were waved in the air. A procession was formed, and the color bearers marched to the music from the balcony and the cheers of the galleries around the floor. The orchestra played the "Star Spangled Banner," "Dixie," and "Yankee Doodle." When it struck up "Auld Lang Syne" and "Home, Sweet Home" and "My country, 'tis of thee" 5,000 voices caught up the refrain.

Order was restored, and Ransom, of Missouri, moved the appointment of a committee to wait on Mr. Hendricks, who was at the hotel, and bring him before the convention. No attention was paid to this, but the Chairman made the formal announcement that the 816 votes of the convention had been unanimously cast for Thomas A. Hendricks. Another five minutes was occupied in cheering, and the convention prepared to adjourn sine die.

B. Bradley Smalley, of Vermont, offered a resolution, which was adopted, directing the National Committee to make the call for the next convention upon the same basis of representation as that fixed by this convention. Then thanks were given everybody who had conferred the slightest favor upon the convention, Carter Harrison included, and even the press, for its impartial reports of the convention. The convention then adjourned.

### THURSDAY NIGHT'S BALLOT.

The following is the ballot by States taken by the convention late Thursday night:

| States. | Cleveland. | Bayard. | McDonald. | Thurman. | Randall. | Hoadly. | Carlisle. | Flower. | Tilden. | Hendricks. | Total. |
|---|---|---|---|---|---|---|---|---|---|---|---|
| Alabama | 4 | 14 | 1 | 1 | | | | | | | 20 |
| Arkansas | 14 | | | | | | | | | | 14 |
| California | | | | 16 | | | | | | | 16 |
| Colorado | | | 5 | 1 | | | | | | | 6 |
| Connecticut | 12 | | | | | | | | | | 12 |
| Delaware | | 6 | | | | | | | | | 6 |
| Florida | 8 | | | | | | | | | | 8 |
| Georgia | 10 | 12 | | | 2 | | | | | | 24 |
| Illinois | 28 | 2 | 11 | 1 | 1 | | | | | 1 | 44 |
| Indiana | | | 30 | | | | | | | | 30 |
| Iowa | 23 | 1 | 1 | 1 | | | | | | | 26 |
| Kansas | 11 | 5 | | 2 | | | | | | | 18 |
| Kentucky | | | | | | | 26 | | | | 26 |
| Louisiana | 13 | 1 | | 1 | | 1 | | | | | 16 |
| Maine | 12 | | | | | | | | | | 12 |
| Maryland | 6 | 10 | | | | | | | | | 16 |
| Massachusetts | 5 | 21 | | 2 | | | | | | | 28 |
| Michigan | 14 | 1 | | 11 | | | | | | | 26 |
| Minnesota | 14 | | | | | | | | | | 14 |
| Mississippi | 1 | 15 | | 1 | 1 | | | | | | 18 |
| Missouri | 15 | 10 | 1 | 3 | 3 | | | | | | 32 |
| Nebraska | 8 | 1 | | 1 | | | | | | | 10 |
| Nevada | | | | 6 | | | | | | | 6 |
| New-Hampshire | 8 | | | | | | | | | | 8 |
| New-Jersey | 4 | 3 | | | 11 | | | | | | 18 |
| New-York | 72 | | | | | | | | | | 72 |
| North Carolina | | 22 | | | | | | | | | 22 |
| Ohio | 21 | | | 23 | | 2 | | | | | 46 |
| Oregon | 2 | 4 | | | | | | | | | 6 |
| Pennsylvania | 5 | | | | 55 | | | | | | 60 |
| Rhode Island | 6 | 2 | | | | | | | | | 8 |
| South Carolina | 8 | 10 | | | | | | | | | 18 |
| Tennessee | 2 | 8 | 3 | 9 | 1 | | | | 1 | | 24 |
| Texas | 11 | 10 | 1 | 4 | | | | | | | 26 |
| Vermont | 8 | | | | | | | | | | 8 |
| Virginia | 13 | 9 | 1 | 1 | | | | | | | 24 |
| West Virginia | 7 | 2 | | 2 | 1 | | | | | | 12 |
| Wisconsin | 12 | 1 | 2 | 2 | | | 1 | 4 | | | 22 |
| *Territories.* | | | | | | | | | | | |
| Washington | 1 | | | | 1 | | | | | | 2 |
| Dakota | 2 | | | | | | | | | | 2 |
| Arizona | 2 | | | | | | | | | | 2 |
| Idaho | 2 | | | | | | | | | | 2 |
| Montana | 2 | | | | | | | | | | 2 |
| Wyoming | 2 | | | | | | | | | | 2 |
| New-Mexico | 2 | | | | | | | | | | 2 |
| Utah | 2 | | | | | | | | | | 2 |
| Dis. of Columbia | | | | | 2 | | | | | | 2 |
| Total | 392 | 170 | 56 | 88 | 78 | 3 | 27 | 4 | 1 | 1 | 820 |

### THE DISGUSTED TAMMANY MEN.

*From a Staff Correspondent of the Times.*

CHICAGO, July 11.—As soon as the convention adjourned the Tammany braves retired to their headquarters in the Palmer House in a sullen mood, and the leaders were admitted to the inner tent of the boss, in Parlor J. There was a wonderful change in their countenances from the time they entered the convention this morning, full of hope in anticipation of the Hendricks boom sweeping everything before it. Their only regret was that the boom had not been started in the convention last evening, in which case they feel confident that it would have gained such headway during the night as to have carried everything before it this morning. Mr. Kelly resolutely refused to be interviewed as to his future course toward Cleveland, but Democrats who have heard him make professions of loyalty will expect to see him do as well for Cleveland in 1884 as he did for Tilden in 1876. According to Mr. Cockran's statements, he will not have to exert himself very much to bring the Tammany organization into line. They are expected to cease their plea that they were disfranchised in the convention by the enforcement of the unit rule and to join hands with their brother Democrats of both the opposing halls, to elect Cleveland and Hendricks and avenge "the great crime of 1876." They were so disgusted with the result that they decided not to attend the evening session of the convention and participate in the nomination of Vice-President. Most of the party left for home between 6 and 7 o'clock this evening by the same route they arrived in a train of two sections. A few of them who remained were greatly mollified by the nomination of Hendricks for Vice-President, as they had been very persistent in asserting that the name Hendricks, as a Democratic candidate, would save to the party the straggling Irish and labor vote that has been represented as being attracted to Blaine.

### TALK ABOUT THE TARIFF PLANK.

*From a Staff Correspondent of the Times.*

CHICAGO, July 11.—Major E. A. Burke, a member of the Committee on Resolutions, a Southern man, who was interested in securing a tariff plank that would protect the sugar interests of Louisiana, says the whole matter was very frankly talked over, and while all were found to favor a revision of the tariff, no member of the committee was opposed to making a provision that would recognize the fact that Louisiana was compelled to compete with the slave labor of Cuba and the peon labor of Mexico. This fact was kept in mind in framing the clause which says that "The necessary reduction in taxation can and must be effected without depriving American labor of the ability to compete successfully with foreign labor and without imposing lower rates of duty than will be ample to cover any increased cost of production which may exist in consequence of the higher rate of wages prevailing in this country." Former Democratic platforms have denounced "the existing tariffs" without qualification. The platform just adopted denounces "the abuses of the existing tariff." The committee regarded the length of the platform objectionable, but the order of the convention that it be reported at a given time prevented the proposition to appoint a sub-committee of revision to reduce its formidable proportions.

### THE NATIONAL COMMITTEE.

CHICAGO, July 11.—The final session of the retiring Democratic National Committee was held to-night. After the consideration of financial matters and passing resolutions of thanks to Chairman Barnum and Secretary Prince, to the various local committees in connection with the late convention, and to the citizens of Chicago, the committee adjourned sine die. The new National Committee was then called to order by W. H. Barnum, as temporary Chairman, and without transacting any business the body adjourned to meet at the Fifth-Avenue Hotel, New-York, on July 24, when permanent organization will be effected. The members of the committee will accompany the Notification Committee in its call upon the candidates.

Gen. Butler was seen to-night, but declined to make any explicit statement in regard to what his course will be during the campaign.

### JAY-EYE-SEE AT CHICAGO.

HE TROTS WITHIN A SECOND OF THE BEST TIME ON RECORD.

CHICAGO, July 11.—For the sixth day of the Summer trotting meeting at the Chicago Driving Park the weather was warm, though cloudy, and the track fast. There were about 10,000 people present. The chief attraction of the day's programme was the special race, an attempt by J. I. Case's famous blk. g. Jay-Eye-See to beat the best trotting record—Maud S.'s 2:10¼. The conditions being so favorable it was generally supposed he would succeed, and before the second heat the betting was two to one that he would beat 2:11. He was first warmed up, going at an easy pace three-quarters of a mile, and coming home from the three-quarter pole in 0:31¾. In his trials he was accompanied by a running horse driven to a sulky to encourage him. The first heat, it was announced, would only be a good strong mile, with no attempt to beat the record. The time was as follows: Quarter, 0:38½; half, 1:12½; three-quarters, 1:47; mile, 2:19¼. For the second heat he was scored at a high rate of speed three times before his driver, Bithers, nodded for the word. The little black fellow went away from the wire at a wonderful speed. He reached the quarter post in 0:31¼, a 2:05 gait; the half in 1:03¼, a 2:06½ gait, and the three-quarters in 1:36¾, a rate of 2:09. After passing the seven-furlong post Jay-Eye-See slackened his speed perceptibly, and finished the mile in 2:11¼, making the last quarter at the rate of 2:16. The terrific speed to the half-mile pole was too much for him so early in the season, he not having had sufficient work to harden him for a bruising heat. Bithers attempted to take him back at the start, but the clattering hoofs of the runner were behind him and he stubbornly refused to check his speed. His driver feared to make him break by summarily taking hold of him. It was freely predicted by horsemen, in the light of his first half mile, that when the season had advanced enough to harden him so as to rate out a full mile he would beat 2:08. In the third heat no attempt was made to beat the record. The time of this heat was: Quarter, 0:32½; half, 1:14; three-quarters, 1:48¾, and mile, 2:21¾.

SECOND RACE.—The Ashland Stake; for 3-year-olds.

SUMMARY.

| | | | |
|---|---|---|---|
| C. W. Story's blk. g. Reference, by Referee | 1 | 1 | 1 |
| R. R. Terrill's blk. c. Gambetta, by George Wilkes | 2 | 2 | 2 |
| W. A. Sanborn's ch. c. Superior, by Egbert | 3 | 3 | 3 |
| J. W. Mackay's b. f. Aloise, by Sultan | 4 | 4 | 4 |

Time—2:32; 2:33¼; 2:33.

THIRD RACE.—The 2:35 class:

| | | | | | |
|---|---|---|---|---|---|
| Will Collender | 6 | 2 | 1 | 1 | 1 |
| Tom Rolf | 1 | 1 | 2 | 2 | 5 |
| Belle S. | 2 | 6 | 5 | 3 | 4 |
| Maud H. | 4 | 4 | 6 | 4 | 2 |
| Lady Wilkes | 3 | 5 | 0 | 6 | 3 |
| M. Y. D. colt | 5 | 3 | 0 | 5 | 6 |

Time—2:25; 2:22¼; 2:21¼; 2:23¼; 2:27.

The third heat was a dead heat between Lady Wilkes and the M. Y. D. colt for third place.

FOURTH RACE.—Chicago Stake, for 4-year-olds:

| | | | |
|---|---|---|---|
| John R. Graham's b. c. Don Carlos, by Cuyler Clay | 1 | 1 | 1 |
| H. C. McDowell's b. f. Fugue, by King Rene | 2 | 2 | 2 |
| O. A. Hickok's br. f. Ruby, by Sultan | 3 | 3 | 4 |
| Nat Bruen's br. c. Wildmont, by Egmont | 4 | 4 | 3 |

Time—2:23¾; 2:25; 2:23¼.

### THE PENALTY OF HIS CRIMES.

NASHVILLE, Tenn., July 11.—Shine Forrest was executed to-day near Paris, Henry County, for the murder of his mother and grandfather on Nov. 30, 1882. The hanging, which was public, notwithstanding that a law requires such an occurrence to be private, was witnessed by about 3,000 persons, most of whom were colored. Forrest made a brief speech, saying that he had committed an awful crime, but was prepared to die. He manifested a great deal of emotion, swaying to and fro. The drop fell at 2 o'clock, and after hanging about half an hour he was pronounced dead and his body was cut down. Forrest gave as his excuse for the crime that he wanted to get his victims out of his way, secure their property, and marry a girl who would not wed him while his mother lived. On the night of the murder he killed his mother with an axe while she was in bed. The noise awakened his grandfather, a paralytic, and Forrest told him he must die. The old man asked to be allowed to cover his head with a blanket, which he was permitted to do, after which Forrest murdered him to destroy evidence of his guilt. Forrest was poor, uneducated, and had led a vicious life.

### THREE OARSMEN DROWNED.

ST. LOUIS, Mo., July 11.—Just before dusk this evening the four-oared crew of the Modoc Rowing Club pulled out on the river. They had a boatswain with them, and he steered the boat across the bow of the ferryboat Mulligan. As a result the lighter craft was cut in two. Joseph J. Miller, one of the oarsmen, caught one of the ferry guards and then pulled M. G. Hazeltine on board the ferryboat with him. J. R. Rose, Harry Jasper, and Vincent Angelo, the three others, were carried in under the ferryboat and drowned. James A. St. John, the Modoc's President, witnessed the accident and exonerated the Captain of the ferry. All of the men who were drowned belong to old families in St. Louis, and were regular members of the Modoc Club, which is the oldest rowing club in the West.

### SHOT BY AN INJURED HUSBAND.

PIEDMONT, West Va., July 11.—A telephone message from Bayard, Md., 34 miles from here, on the West Virginia Central Railroad, says that a man named Glenn shot and instantly killed a man named Stevenson near that place this evening. The message says the tragedy grew out of bad feeling between the men on account of the intimacy of Stevenson with Glenn's wife. Stevenson was warned to stay away from Mrs. Glenn, but was caught in the house by the injured husband, who shot him through the heart.

### BALTIMORE'S HEAVY RAINSTORM.

BALTIMORE, July 11.—A heavy rainstorm passed over this city this afternoon, and was most severe in the western section. A few minutes after the rain began to fall the streets were flooded and hundreds of cellars filled with water. In some of the houses on West Baltimore, Fayette, and Stricker streets the first floors were covered with water. On Tremont-street a house was thrown down, and a block of buildings in course of construction on North Carey-street were wrecked.

## A PHENOMENON NO LONGER

### THE MUSCLE OF LULU HURST HER MYSTERIOUS FORCE.

HOW THE GEORGIA WONDER HAS BEEN FOOLING THE PUBLIC AND BREAKING UMBRELLAS REGARDLESS OF EXPENSE.

The fact that Miss Lulu Hurst, "the Georgia Wonder," or the "Phenomenon of the Nineteenth Century"—you pays your money and you takes your choice—is drawing tremendous houses and exciting the wonder of everybody who either does not see her at all, or else sees her from a distance through an opera glass darkly, only proves the statement of the philosopher who said that the public likes to be fooled. Miss Hurst had an audience last night that completely filled Wallack's Theatre from the hold to the hurricane deck. Galleries, balconies, orchestra chairs, boxes, and aisles were crowded, and the rest of the populace were jammed at the doors and climbing up each other's backs in frantic efforts to catch a glimpse of the stage. It was an audience for the most part that came to be amused and cared not how that object was accomplished or even if they helped to afford the amusement themselves, but some of them were Pickwickian scientists who were going to sift the mysterious force that enables a girl to break an umbrella or shove a man burdened with a heavy chair about a stage before a wondering world. The boxes were mostly occupied by ladies with their escorts. Major Benjamin Franklin Pond sat in the front row of orchestra chairs and pondered over his odic theory, but did not venture to ascend to the stage. Marcus Antonius Pastor occupied a chair well forward, and near him sat President of the Board of Education Walker. Billy Edwards modestly retired under the shadow of the gallery; Larry Jerome lolled indolently back in the left parquet circle with a number of gentlemen from the Union Club, and Jordan L. Mott contemplatively rested his chin upon the silver knob of his cane to the right of the centre aisle.

The curtain went up after half an hour of indiscriminate stamping, cheering, and cat-calling on the part of this audience, at about 9 o'clock, and disclosed Mr. Paul Atkinson, he of the perennial smile, smiling in the centre of the stage, while back against the scene sat the phenomenon, modestly self-possessed, attired in a suit of figured silk, her long brown curls hanging over her shoulders, and her irresistible bang shading her witching dark eyes. The other phenomena of the exhibition, Messrs. Bixby and Cohen, declared that the management had issued an edict of the Medes and Persian variety forbidding reporters to go upon the stage or behind the scenes, because there was no room for them, which did not seem very lucid in view of the fact that five men could not very well fill up a hundred square feet of space. Mr. Paul Atkinson permitted his smile to wax, and then he requested 12 gentlemen to come upon the stage to test the wonder. That number of good citizens complied with his invitation, and among them came a medium-sized man of powerful figure, who wore a scarlet neck scarf and carried a white high hat. He was Prof. D. L. Dowd, whom Dr. Sargeant, of Harvard College, alleges to possess the finest muscular development of any man he ever examined. Dowd has a record of lifting 1,442 pounds from the floor with his hands, and he gave exhibitions of strength with the Barnum circus, in Madison-Square Garden, last Spring. He took his seat quietly with the others and awaited developments. Mr. Paul Atkinson's smile having waned somewhat, he again permitted it to wax as he presented the "phenomenon of the nineteenth century," whom, he said, it was hardly necessary to introduce, since New-York already knew her so well.

"The exhibition to be given by Miss Hurst this evening," continued Mr. Paul Atkinson, his smile still operating, "is simply to illustrate a wonderful power she possesses to resist and baffle strength, by merely placing the palms of her hands against an object, thereby preventing the strongest man from keeping it under his control. She neither grips, holds, or pushes it, but simply keeps her open hand or hands as the case may be against it. She will first electrify an umbrella by her touch, thereby forcing strong men about the stage in their effort to hold it." [Applause.]

Miss Hurst came forward and Mr. Paul Atkinson operated his smile upon the audience, produced an umbrella from the wings, and asked the first candidate for honors to come forward. A short youth with a neck like a bullock and the shoulders and waist of a Hercules came up under the umbrella with a look of grim determination. Miss Hurst took hold of it and he grasped it lower down. Then there was a sudden contortion of the hands of both, and the frail umbrella came down on their heads and was wrecked as on previous nights. But the reason it was wrecked, as everybody on the stage saw, was because the fair Lula grasped it by the sliding shank and jerked it violently down on the lower catch, at the same time striking the slender ribs upon the devoted head of the youth who stood under it with her. When Mr. Paul Atkinson again permitted his facial muscles to relax and picked it up, he gave it a jab on the floor to break it more before he opened it and exposed its injuries to the audience. Another umbrella was brought out and treated similarly, and then they proceeded to demonstrate other wonderful things.

"Miss Hurst," Mr. Paul Atkinson announced with a smile, "will, by simply touching a walking cane with the palms of her hands, overcome the strength of the strongest man."

The volunteer for this test was a man of middle age, with poetically tangled hair, a drooping mustache, and a shabby frock suit, who apparently had about as much muscular development as a bladder. He took hold of the cane, and Miss Hurst put her hands against it and simply pushed him back. He made a desperate struggle, but was gradually forced back, amid the plaudits of the crowd, to the wings. So soon as this was effected he came forward and shouted to the laughing audience with a pronounced French accent:

"Ah, gentlemen, zis is very wonderful. I confess myself completely surprise. I came to find magnetism, but magnetism acts only with iron. Zere is a varry mysterious force here. I cannot explain what it is. I ——"

"Who asked you to?" shouted a voice, and the rest of the Frenchman's remarks were drowned in a universal shout of "Sit down," which he wisely obeyed.

A very tall, fine looking man, who occupied a seat on the stage arose and asked that Miss Hurst try the experiment with him, placing her hands over his. "I desire to ascertain," he said, "whether there is any power excited."

"Who are you?" asked a red-faced man in the second row. "Tell us your name," and everybody in the theatre echoed, "What's your name?"

"It doesn't make any difference what my name is," retorted the tall man. "I am trying this experiment for my own purposes."

"Give us somebody we know," shouted the red-faced man, and the entire throng echoed the shout. But the tall man paid them no attention. He only got Miss Hurst to put her hands over his, and then she pushed on the cane, but let her thumbs slip down to the stick. "Ah," said the tall man. "Please keep your hands over mine." She did so, and the two stood without a motion for two minutes. Then the tall man turned to the audience and said:

"I find no difficulty whatever in holding this stick perfectly rigid."

The audience shouted and hissed, and again demanded his name. To the men on the stage he said: "I have no objection to telling my name, but I won't give it to those fellows who demand it that way. My name is Gordon, and I am a relative of ex-Senator Gordon, of Georgia."

Dowd, who had been watching the girl's experiments, now asked to be allowed to take the cane. The girl put her hands against it and pushed, but Dowd pushed the harder, and with very little exertion shoved her back against the scene, while the spectators shouted and screamed and hooted. "It's only muscular force," said Dowd, as he sat down. "She puts her hand against the cane and pushes, that's all."

Miss Hurst next did the billiard-cue trick, and a light-waisted boy was unable to put the end to the floor because she had her arm under it and pressed upward with the palm of her hand, thus getting a tremendous purchase. Dowd, however, in spite of her advantage put the end of the cue on the floor with scarcely an effort, and again there was a pandemonium of cheers and hisses. A gentleman of disheveled exterior, who was afflicted with strabismus, attempted to put the cue down to the floor, and then tried to explain to the audience why he couldn't, but somebody squelched him with the remark, "Ah, sit down, Butler, Cleveland's got the nomination," which affected the audience to tumultuous mirth.

Mr. Paul Atkinson's smile had waned during Mr. Dowd's performance, but it now waxed once more, as he asked the 12 gentlemen on the stage to retire. Then there was an intermission of several minutes, during which Dowd explained to a throng of ladies and gentlemen that there was no wonder about the Georgia girl, except her muscle. He went upon the stage with the next batch of 12 and tried some more experiments. Mr. Paul Atkinson smiled as this second act began, and gave a stout youth a chair, which he told him to hold still while Miss Lulu exerted her mysterious power by placing her hands against it. The youth took the chair to his bosom and wound his arms around the rounds and the back. Then the phenomenon placed her hands against the chair, and the youth being burdened with the weight of it she pushed him about the stage. Dowd took the chair, braced himself, and she pushed against him in vain. Mr. Paul Atkinson

# The New York Times.

VOL. XXXIV......NO. 10,350. NEW-YORK, WEDNESDAY, NOVEMBER 5, 1884. PRICE TWO CENTS.


## GOV. CLEVELAND ELECTED

### A VERY DECIDED MAJORITY IN THE ELECTORAL COLLEGE.

### NEW-YORK GIVES CLEVELAND A PLURALITY OF 10,000.

### BOTH CONNECTICUT AND NEW-JERSEY DEMOCRATIC.

### WISCONSIN VOTES FOR CLEVELAND BY 5,000.

INDIANA DEMOCRATIC BY 5,000 MAJORITY—THE RETURNS FROM THE WEST COMING IN VERY SLOWLY—CLOSE VOTES IN MANY STATES—RETURNS FROM THE SOUTH SHOW NO BREAK IN THE DEMOCRATIC COLUMN.

The returns indicate that Grover Cleveland has been elected President of the United States. The State of New-York gives Cleveland a plurality of about 10,000. He has carried Connecticut by a plurality of from 1,500 to 2,500. Indiana is certainly Democratic by more than 5,000 majority. The latest estimates from Wisconsin are to the effect that Cleveland has carried that State by 5,000. Michigan is claimed by both parties, and the vote of the State is close. Both parties claim Virginia, but it is not probable that it has been taken from the Democratic column. The returns from New-Jersey are incomplete, but it is believed that Cleveland has carried the State by 6,000 plurality. The Republicans claim Essex County by only 2,500, which indicates a Democratic gain of 1,700.

There is no trustworthy indication that Cleveland has lost any of the 153 votes in the South hitherto assigned to him. If we add to those 153 votes the 36 votes of New-York, the 15 votes of Indiana, the 9 votes of New-Jersey, and the 6 votes of Connecticut, the total is 219, or 18 more than a majority of the entire number of Electoral votes. But there must be added to this total, according to late returns, the 11 votes of Wisconsin. The total may be therefore 230 instead of 219.

The Democrats will have a large majority in the House of Representatives of the Forty-ninth Congress.

The distinguishing feature of the election in the Southern States was the light vote polled in nearly all places where some local issue did not bring out the voters. Perfect quiet and freedom from all disturbance is generally reported. North Carolina shows large Democratic gains in nearly all localities. In Virginia the Republicans put in their heaviest work in the colored districts, and polled a large vote—so large that they claim the State. The Democrats, however, are confident that they have carried it by nearly 10,000 majority. Republican gains are reported in West Virginia, but the indications are that the State has gone Democratic. In Georgia the Republicans gained in the coal and iron districts.

Pennsylvania has, of course, been carried by the Republicans, but by a reduced majority. Of the 28 Congressmen the Republicans elect 20.

In this State the Democrats have elected 17 of the 34 Congressmen, while the Republicans have carried the Assembly, electing three more members than they had last year, when the number was 72. This insures a Republican United States Senator, to be elected next Winter.

### THE ELECTORAL COLLEGE.

The Electoral College consists of 401 members, and the smallest number by which a candidate's election can be secured is 201, or a majority of the whole number. Each State is entitled to as many Electors as it has Senators and Representatives in Congress, and therefore the number of each State's Electors exceeds the number of its Representatives in the House by two. The following table shows how the Electoral votes of each State will be cast for the opposing candidates, and also the plurality given by each State:

| States. | Cleveland, Dem. Plurality. | Cleveland, Dem. Electoral Vote. | Blaine, Rep. Plurality. | Blaine, Rep. Electoral Vote. |
|---|---|---|---|---|
| Alabama | 25,000 | 10 | ...... | .. |
| Arkansas | 42,000 | 7 | ...... | .. |
| California | ...... | .. | ...... | 8 |
| Colorado | ...... | .. | ...... | 3 |
| Connecticut | 1,000 | 6 | ...... | .. |
| Delaware | 8,000 | 3 | ...... | .. |
| Florida | 3,000 | 4 | ...... | .. |
| Georgia | 35,000 | 12 | ...... | .. |
| Illinois | ...... | 22 | 20,000 | .. |
| Indiana | 6,000 | 15 | ...... | .. |
| Iowa | ...... | .. | 20,000 | 13 |
| Kansas | ...... | .. | 60,000 | 9 |
| Kentucky | 45,000 | 13 | ...... | .. |
| Louisiana | 20,000 | 8 | ...... | .. |
| Maine | ...... | .. | 15,000 | 6 |
| Maryland | 10,000 | 8 | ...... | .. |
| Massachusetts | ...... | .. | 10,000 | 14 |
| Michigan | ...... | .. | ...... | 13 |
| Minnesota | ...... | .. | 40,000 | 7 |
| Mississippi | 40,000 | 9 | ...... | .. |
| Missouri | 70,000 | 16 | ...... | .. |
| Nebraska | ...... | .. | 15,000 | 5 |
| Nevada | ...... | .. | 1,000 | 3 |
| New-Hampshire | ...... | .. | 3,000 | 4 |
| New-Jersey | 6,000 | 9 | ...... | .. |
| New-York | 6,000 | 36 | ...... | .. |
| North Carolina | ...... | 11 | ...... | .. |
| Ohio | ...... | .. | 20,000 | 23* |
| Oregon | ...... | .. | ...... | 3 |
| Pennsylvania | ...... | .. | 85,000 | 30 |
| Rhode Island | ...... | .. | 5,000 | 4 |
| South Carolina | 30,000 | 9 | ...... | .. |
| Tennessee | 12,000 | 12 | ...... | .. |
| Texas | ...... | 13 | ...... | .. |
| Vermont | ...... | .. | 25,000 | 4 |
| Virginia | ...... | 12 | ...... | .. |
| West Virginia | 2,500 | 6 | ...... | .. |
| Wisconsin | 5,000 | 11 | ...... | .. |
| Total | ...... | 232 | ...... | 149 |
| Pluralities | ...... | .. | ...... | .. |

The following table exhibits more plainly the division of the Electoral College:

| CLEVELAND. States. | Votes. | BLAINE. States. | Votes. |
|---|---|---|---|
| Alabama | 10 | California | 8 |
| Arkansas | 7 | Colorado | 3 |
| Connecticut | 6 | Iowa | 13 |
| Delaware | 3 | Kansas | 9 |
| Florida | 4 | Maine | 6 |
| Georgia | 12 | Massachusetts | 14 |
| Illinois | 22 | Michigan | 13 |
| Indiana | 15 | Minnesota | 7 |
| Kentucky | 13 | Nebraska | 5 |
| Louisiana | 8 | Nevada | 3 |
| Maryland | 8 | New-Hampshire | 4 |
| Mississippi | 9 | Ohio | 23 |
| Missouri | 16 | Oregon | 3 |
| New-Jersey | 9 | Pennsylvania | 30 |
| New-York | 36 | Rhode Island | 4 |
| North Carolina | 11 | Vermont | 4 |
| South Carolina | 9 | | |
| Tennessee | 12 | Total | 149 |
| Texas | 13 | | |
| Virginia | 12 | | |
| West Virginia | 6 | | |
| Wisconsin | 11 | | |
| Total | 252 | | |

### FORTY-NINTH CONGRESS.

The following is a list of members elected to the House of Representatives of the Forty-ninth Congress, according to the latest returns The names of Democrats appear in roman, Republicans in *italics*, and Greenbackers and Independents are classed with the parties with which they will act and are further indicated by the abbreviations "Gr." or "Ind.:"

**ALABAMA.**
1. James T. Jones. 2. Hilary A. Herbert. 3. William C. Oates. 4. Alex. C. Davidson. 5. Thomas W. Sadler. 6. John M. Martin. 7. William H. Forney. 8. Joseph Wheeler.

**ARKANSAS.**
1. Poindexter Dunn. 2. C. R. Breckinridge. 3. James K. Jones. 4. John H. Rogers. 5. Samuel W. Peel.

**CALIFORNIA.**
1. Barclay Henley. 2. *J. A. Louttit.* 3. *Joseph McKenna.* 4. Robert P. Hastings. 5. Frank J. Sullivan. 6. R. F. Del Valle.

**COLORADO.**
1. *George G. Symes.*

**CONNECTICUT.**
1. *John R. Buck.* 2. Charles L. Mitchell. 3. *John T. Wait.* 4. Edward W. Seymour.

**DELAWARE.**
1. Charles B. Lore.

**FLORIDA.**
1. R. H. M. Davidson. 2. Charles Dougherty.

**GEORGIA.**
1. Thomas M. Norwood. 2. Henry G. Turner. 3. Charles F. Crisp. 4. Henry R. Harris. 5. N. J. Hammond. 6. James H. Blount. 7. Judson C. Clements. 8. Seaborn Reese. 9. Allen D. Candler. 10. George T. Barnes.

**ILLINOIS.**
1. *R. W. Dunham.* 2. *John F. Finerty.* 3. James H. Ward. 4. *George E. Adams.* 5. *Reuben Ellwood.* 6. *Robert R. Hitt.* 7. *Thos. J. Henderson.* 8. *Ralph Plumb.* 9. *Louis E. Payson.* 10. *Julius S. Starr.* 11. *Alexander P. Petrie.* 12. James M. Riggs. 13. William A. Springer. 14. *Jonathan H. Rowell.* 15. *Joseph G. Cannon.* 16. S. Z. Landes. 17. John R. Eden. 18. William R. Morrison. 19. R. W. Townshend. 20. *John R. Thomas.*

**INDIANA.**
1. John J. Kleiner. 2. Thomas R. Cobb. 3. Jonas G. Howard. 4. William S. Holman. 5. Courtland C. Matson. 6. *Thomas M. Browne.* 7. *Stanton J. Peelle.* 8. *James T. Johnston.* 9. *Charles T. Doxey.* 10. Thomas J. Weed. 11. *George W. Steele.* 12. Robert Lowry. 13. *Henry G. Thayer.*

**IOWA.**
1. Benton J. Hall. 2. Jeremiah H. Murphy. 3. *D. B. Henderson.* 4. Luman H. Weller, Gr. 5. *Milo P. Smith.* 6. James B. Weaver. 7. *Edwin H. Conger.** 8. *W. P. Hepburn.* 9. W. H. M. Pusey. 10. *A. J. Holmes.* 11. *Isaac S. Struble.*

*In the Seventh District Hiram Y. Smith is elected to fill the unexpired term of John A. Kasson, resigned.

**KANSAS.**
1. *E. N. Morrill.* 2. *E. H. Funston.* 3. *B. W. Perkins.* 4. *Thomas Ryan.* 5. *John A. Anderson.* 6. *Lewis Hanback.* 7. *Samuel R. Peters.*

**KENTUCKY.**
1. W. J. Stone. 2. Polk Laffoon. 3. J. E. Halsell. 4. Thos. A. Robertson. 5. Albert S. Willis. 6. John G. Carlisle. 7. W. C. P. Breckinridge. 8. James B. McCreary. 9. *Wm. H. Wadsworth.* 10. W. P. Taulbee. 11. Frank Wolford.

**LOUISIANA.**
1. Carleton Hunt. 2. William T. Houston. 3. *William P. Kellogg.* 4. N. C. Blanchard. 5. J. Floyd King. 6. Alfred B. Irvin.

**MAINE.**
1. *Thomas B. Reed.* 2. *Nelson Dingley.* 3. *Seth L. Milliken.* 4. *Charles A. Boutelle.*

**MARYLAND.**
1. Charles H. Gibson. 2. Frank T. Shaw. 3. William H. Cole. 4. J. V. L. Findlay. 5. Barnes Compton. 6. *Louis E. McComas.*

**MASSACHUSETTS.**
1. *Robert T. Davis.* 2. *John D. Long.* 3. *A. A. Ranney.* 4. Patrick A. Collins. 5. *Edward D. Hayden.* 6. Henry B. Lovering. 7. Richard S. Spofford. 8. *Charles H. Allen.* 9. *Frederick D. Ely.* 10. *William W. Rice.* 11. *William Whiting.* 12. *F. W. Rockwell.*

**MICHIGAN.**
1. William C. Maybury. 2. *Edward P. Allen.* 3. *James O'Donnell.* 4. *Julius C. Burrows.* 5. *John C. Fitzgerald.* 6. Edwin B. Winans. 7. Ezra C. Carleton. 8. *Roswell G. Horr.* 9. *B. M. Cutcheon.* 10. *Charles F. Gibson.* 11. *Seth C. Moffatt.*

**MINNESOTA.**
1. *Milo White.* 2. *J. B. Wakefield.* 3. *H. B. Strait.* 4. J. B. Gilfillan. 5. *Knute Nelson.*

**MISSISSIPPI.**
1. John M. Allen. 2. J. B. Morgan. 3. *A. G. Pierce.* 4. Frederick G. Barry. 5. Otho R. Singleton. 6. Henry S. Van Eaton. 7. Ethelbert Barksdale.

**MISSOURI.**
1. Wm. H. Hatch. 2. John B. Hale. 3. Alex. M. Dockery. 4. James N. Burns. 5. *William Warner.* 6. John T. Heard. 7. John E. Hutton. 8. John J. O'Neill. 9. John M. Glover. 10. Martin L. Clardy. 11. Richard P. Bland. 12. W. J. Stone. 13. A. L. Thomas. 14. William Dawson.

**NEBRASKA.**
1. *A. J. Weaver.* 2. *James Laird.* 3. *Geo. W. E. Dorsey.*

**NEVADA.**
1. *William Woodburn.*

**NEW-HAMPSHIRE.**
1. *Martin A. Haynes.* 2. *J. A. Gallinger.*

**NEW-JERSEY.**
1. *George Hires.* 2. *James Buchanan.* 3. Robert S. Green. 4. James W. Fidcock. 5. *Wm. Walter Phelps.* 6. *Herman Lehlbach.* 7. William McAdoo.

**NEW-YORK.**
1. Perry Belmont. 2. Felix Campbell. 3. *Darwin R. James.* 4. Peter P. Mahoney. 5. Archibald M. Bliss. 6. Nicholas Muller. 7. John J. Adams. 8. Samuel S. Cox. 9. Joseph Pulitzer. 10. Abram S. Hewitt. 11. T. A. Merriman. 12. Abraham Dowdney. 13. Egbert L. Viele. 14. W. G. Stahlnecker. 15. Lewis Beach. 16. *John H. Ketcham.* 17. *James E. Lindsley.* 18. *Henry G. Burleigh.* 19. *John Swinburne.* 20. *George West.* 21. *Frederick A. Johnson.* 22. *Abraham X. Parker.* 23. J. Thomas Spriggs. 24. John S. Pindar. 25. *Frank Hiscock.* 26. *Stephen C. Millard.* 27. *Sereno E. Payne.* 28. John Arnot. 29. *Ira Davenport.* 30. *Charles S. Baker.* 31. *John L. Sawyer.* 32. *John M. Farquhar.* 33. *John B. Weber.* 34. *Walter L. Sessions.*

**NORTH CAROLINA.**
1. Thomas G. Skinner. 2. *James E. O'Hara.* 3. Wharton J. Green. 4. William R. Cox. 5. James W. Reid. 6. R. T. Bennett. 7. John S. Henderson. 8. Thomas D. Johnston.

**OHIO.**
1. *Benj. Butterworth.* 2. *Charles E. Brown.* 3. James E. Campbell. 4. Charles M. Anderson. 5. Benjamin Lefevre. 6. William D. Hill. 7. George E. Seney. 8. *John Little.* 9. *William C. Cooper.* 10. *Jacob Romeis.* 11. Wm. W. Ellsbury. 12. *Albert C. Thompson.* 13. J. H. Outhwaite. 14. *Chas. H. Grosvenor.* 15. Beriah Wilkins. 16. George W. Geddes. 17. A. J. Warner. 18. *Isaac H. Taylor.* 19. *Ezra B. Taylor.* 20. *William McKinley.* 21. Martin A. Foran.

**OREGON.**
1. *Binger Hermann.*

**PENNSYLVANIA.**
At Large—E. S. Osborne. 1. *H. H. Bingham.* 2. *Charles O'Neill.* 3. Samuel J. Randall. 4. *William D. Kelley.* 5. *A. C. Harmer.* 6. *James B. Everhart.* 7. *I. Newton Evans.* 8. Daniel Ermentrout. 9. *John A. Hiestand.* 10. William H. Sowden. 11. John B. Storm. 12. *Joseph A. Scranton.* 13. *Chas. N. Brumm, Gr.* 14. *Franklin M. Bound.* 15. *F. C. Bunnell.* 16. *W. W. Brown.* 17. *Jacob M. Campbell.* 18. *Louis E. Atkinson.* 19. William A. Duncan. 20. Andrew G. Curtin. 21. Charles E. Boyle. 22. *James S. Negley.* 23. *Thomas M. Bayne.* 24. *Oscar L. Jackson.* 25. *A. C. White.* 26. *George W. Fleeger.* 27. *C. W. Mackey.*

**RHODE ISLAND.**
1. *Henry J. Spooner.* 2. *William A. Pirce.*

**SOUTH CAROLINA.**
1. Samuel Dibble. 2. George D. Tillman. 3. D. Wyatt Aiken. 4. W. H. Perry. 5. J. J. Hemphill. 6. J. W. Dargan. 7. *Robert Smalls.*

**TENNESSEE.**
1. *A. H. Pettibone.* 2. *Leonidas C. Houk.* 3. John R. Neal. 4. Benton McMillin. 5. J. D. Richardson. 6. A. J. Caldwell. 7. J. G. Ballentine. 8. John M. Taylor. 9. P. T. Glass. 10. *Zachary Taylor.*

**TEXAS.**
1. Charles Stewart. 2. John H. Reagan. 3. James H. Jones. 4. D. B. Culberson. 5. J. W. Throckmorton. 6. Olin Welborn. 7. William H. Crain. 8. James F. Miller. 9. Roger Q. Mills. 10. Joseph D. Sayers. 11. S. W. T. Lanham.

**VERMONT.**
1. *John W. Stewart.* 2. *William W. Grant.*

**VIRGINIA.**
1. *Robert M. Mayo.* 2. *H. H. Libbey.* 3. George D. Wise. 4. *James D. Brady.* 5. George C. Cabell. 6. J. Randolph Tucker. 7. C. T. O'Ferrall. 8. J. S. Barbour. 9. *D. S. Baily.* 10. John W. Daniel.

**WEST VIRGINIA.**
1. *Nathan Goff, Jr.* 2. W. L. Wilson. 3. C. P. Snyder. 4. Eustace Gibson.

**WISCONSIN.**
1. *L. B. Caswell.* 2. Edward S. Bragg. 3. *R. M. La Follette.* 4. P. V. Deuster. 5. Joseph Rankin. 6. *Richard Guenther.* 7. G. M. Woodward. 8. *William T. Price.* 9. James Meehan.

The representation of the different parties is as follows:

Whole number......325 Republicans..........143
Democrats......182

The Forty-ninth Congress will contain a slightly reduced Democratic majority, unless later returns should show further losses. California has several Republican representatives. She has none in the present Congress. Colorado sends a Republican member. In Connecticut the delegation is equally divided, the Democrats losing one by the defeat, in the First District, of ex-Senator Eaton. In Illinois the Democrats elect Springer and Morrison, and there is a probability that Finerty, the Blaine independent in the Second District, is elected. Massachusetts has three Democrats in the next Congress, electing Collins in the Fourth, Lovering over Lodge in the Sixth, and Spofford in the Seventh. The Republicans have not elected a single Representative in Missouri, which sends a solid Democratic delegation. Nevada, which is now represented by a Democrat, sends a Republican in his place. New-York has elected 17 Democrats and 17 Republicans. The present delegation is 21 Democrats and 13 Republicans. At this writing Pennsylvania has apparently elected seven Democrats and 21 Republicans, although several districts are in doubt, and the Democrats are claiming nine members elected.

| | Dem. | Rep. | | Dem. | Rep. |
|---|---|---|---|---|---|
| Alabama | 8 | .. | Mississippi | 6 | 1 |
| Arkansas | 5 | .. | Missouri | 12 | 2 |
| California | 4 | 2 | Nebraska | .. | 3 |
| Colorado | .. | 1 | Nevada | .. | 1 |
| Connecticut | 2 | 2 | New-Hampshire | .. | 2 |
| Delaware | 1 | .. | New-Jersey | 3 | 4 |
| Florida | 2 | .. | New-York | 17 | 17 |
| Georgia | 10 | .. | North Carolina | 7 | 1 |
| Illinois | 7 | 13 | Ohio | 11 | 10 |
| Indiana | 7 | 6 | Oregon | .. | 1 |
| Iowa | 5 | 6 | Pennsylvania | 7 | 21 |
| Kansas | .. | 7 | Rhode Island | .. | 2 |
| Kentucky | 10 | 1 | South Carolina | 6 | 1 |
| Louisiana | 5 | 1 | Tennessee | 7 | 3 |
| Maine | .. | 4 | Texas | 11 | .. |
| Maryland | 5 | 1 | Vermont | .. | 2 |
| Massachusetts | 1 | 11 | Virginia | 6 | 4 |
| Michigan | 3 | 8 | West Virginia | 3 | 1 |
| Minnesota | .. | 5 | Wisconsin | 4 | 5 |
| Total | | | | 182 | 143 |

### THE RESULT IN NEW-YORK STATE.

The following table shows the pluralities for the Presidential Electoral tickets in the various counties of this State, compared with the pluralities in 1880:

| Counties. | 1884 Cleveland, Dem. | 1884 Blaine, Rep. | 1880 Hancock, Dem. | 1880 Garfield, Rep. |
|---|---|---|---|---|
| Albany | 1500 | .... | 3060 | .... |
| Allegany | .... | 1500 | .... | 3345 |
| Broome | .... | 1397 | .... | 1723 |
| Cattaraugus | .... | 1000 | .... | 1935 |
| Cayuga | .... | 2500 | .... | 3396 |
| Chautauqua | .... | 4000 | .... | 4950 |
| Chemung | .... | 680 | 170 | .... |
| Chenango | .... | 900 | .... | 1210 |
| Clinton | .... | 687 | .... | 1930 |
| Columbia | .... | 556 | .... | 494 |
| Cortland | .... | 1200 | .... | 1375 |
| Delaware | .... | 237 | .... | 974 |
| Dutchess | .... | 1500 | .... | 2570 |
| Erie | .... | 1500 | .... | 3351 |
| Essex | .... | 1500 | .... | 2001 |
| Franklin | .... | 1716 | .... | 1386 |
| Fulton and Hamilton | .... | 1000 | .... | 1108 |
| Genesee | .... | 950 | .... | 1334 |
| Greene | 300 | .... | 626 | .... |
| Herkimer | .... | 837 | .... | 1361 |
| Jefferson | .... | 1994 | .... | 2323 |
| Kings | 15366 | .... | 9311 | .... |
| Lewis | .... | 60 | .... | 382 |
| Livingston | .... | 1000 | .... | 1280 |
| Madison | .... | 1400 | .... | 2110 |
| Monroe | .... | 4800 | .... | 3300 |
| Montgomery | 100 | .... | .... | 283 |
| New-York | 42786 | .... | 41285 | .... |
| Niagara | 300 | .... | .... | 541 |
| Oneida | .... | 150 | .... | 1946 |
| Onondaga | .... | 3400 | .... | 4421 |
| Ontario | .... | 600 | .... | 1007 |
| Orange | 200 | .... | .... | 416 |
| Orleans | .... | 1050 | .... | 1477 |
| Oswego | .... | 3100 | .... | 3460 |
| Otsego | 450 | .... | 23 | .... |
| Putnam | .... | 577 | .... | 406 |
| Queens | 1900 | .... | 2240 | .... |
| Rensselaer | .... | 250 | .... | 641 |
| Richmond | 1889 | .... | 1684 | .... |
| Rockland | 1300 | .... | 737 | .... |
| St. Lawrence | .... | 7225 | .... | 7813 |
| Saratoga | .... | 2000 | .... | 2306 |
| Schenectady | 200 | .... | .... | 622 |
| Schoharie | 1800 | .... | 1616 | .... |
| Schuyler | .... | 300 | .... | 497 |
| Seneca | 325 | .... | 403 | .... |
| Steuben | .... | 959 | .... | 1258 |
| Suffolk | 500 | .... | .... | 454 |
| Sullivan | 475 | .... | 379 | .... |
| Tioga | .... | 850 | .... | 1123 |
| Tompkins | .... | 300 | .... | 940 |
| Ulster | 200 | .... | .... | 124 |
| Warren | .... | 534 | .... | 712 |
| Washington | .... | 3113 | .... | 3634 |
| Wayne | .... | 2050 | .... | 2303 |
| Westchester | 2000 | .... | 491 | .... |
| Wyoming | .... | 1296 | .... | 1366 |
| Yates | .... | 1276 | .... | 1235 |
| Total | 71713 | 61716 | 61765 | 82798 |

Democratic plurality in 1884..........9,997
Republican plurality in 1880..........21,033

### THE ASSEMBLY.

The next Assembly will consist of 75 Republicans and 58 Democrats. The Senate, which holds over another year, contains 19 Republicans and 13 Democrats. The number of votes on joint ballot that will be required to elect the next United States Senator is 81. The names of the new Assemblymen so far as ascertained are as follows, Republicans being printed in roman, Democrats in *italics*, and those reelected with a *:

ALBANY COUNTY. Districts. 1. *Stephen H. Niles.* 2. H. M. L. Hotaling. 3. *Patrick Murray.* 4. *Terrence J. Hardin.*
ALLEGANY COUNTY. William R. McEwen.
BROOME COUNTY. William H. Olin.*
CATTARAUGUS COUNTY. 1. Fred W. Kruse.* 2. A. E. Nash.*
CAYUGA COUNTY. 1. W. B. Priddy.* 2. M. B. Van Buskirk.
CHAUTAUQUA COUNTY. 1. Dana P. Horton.* 2. Julian T. Williams.

NEW-YORK COUNTY. Districts. 15. *J. B. McGoldrick.* 16. *Edward P. Hagan.* 17. *John H. O'Hara.* 18. *John F. Kenny.* 19. *Eugene S. Ives.* 20. *James Haggerty.** 21. Henry A. Barnum. 22. [illegible] 23. *Jacob A. Cantor.* 24. *John B. Shea.*
NIAGARA COUNTY. 1. *Jacob A. Driess.** 2. W. J. Mackey.
ONEIDA COUNTY. 1. H. A. Steber. 2. *Lewis B. Sherman.* 3. T. J. Owens.*

CHEMUNG COUNTY. District. Jonas S. Van Duzer.*
CHENANGO COUNTY. George B. Whitmore.
CLINTON COUNTY. George W. Palmer.
COLUMBIA COUNTY. John T. Hogeboom.
CORTLAND COUNTY. H. P. Andrews.
DELAWARE COUNTY. S. S. Cartwright.*
DUTCHESS COUNTY. 1. Joseph H. Storm. 2. *Edward B. Osborne.**
ERIE COUNTY. 1. *William F. Sheehan.* 2. *Frank M. Giese.* 3. William M. Hawkins. 4. John Kraus. 5. Amos H. Baker.
ESSEX COUNTY. Wesley Barnes.
FRANKLIN COUNTY. William T. O'Neil.*
FULTON AND HAMILTON COUNTIES. A. W. Berry.
GENESEE COUNTY. Lucian R. Bailey.*
GREENE COUNTY. Stephen T. Hopkins.
HERKIMER COUNTY. John M. Budlong.
JEFFERSON COUNTY. 1. A. E. Kilby. 2. E. J. Seeber.*
KINGS COUNTY. 1. *Moses J. Wafer.* 2. *Richard Nagle.** 3. *Peter K. McCann.* 4. *Patrick Burns.** 5. *Michael J. Coffey.** 6. *Thomas F. Farrell.** 7. *George H. Lindsay.** 8. *Robert E. Connolly.* 9. Lewis A. Myers. 10. James Taylor.* 11. Henry Heath. 12. *Mortimer C. Earl.**
LEWIS COUNTY. *H. P. Gould.*
LIVINGSTON COUNTY. Kidder M. Scott.*
MADISON COUNTY. E. F. Haskell.*
MONROE COUNTY. 1. Walter S. Hubbell.* 2. *James P. Tumilty.* 3. Philip Garbutt.*
MONTGOMERY COUNTY. Thomas Liddle.
NEW-YORK COUNTY. 1. *Daniel E. Finn.* 2. *James Oliver.** 3. *Charles Eiseman.* 4. *Patrick H. Roche.** 5. *Michael Brennan.* 6. *Edward F. Reilly.* 7. Lucas L. Van Allen.* 8. Charles Smith.* 9. John P. Rockefeller. 10. *George F. Roesch.* 11. Walter Howe.* 12. *S. D. Rosenthal.* 13. J. P. Windolph. 14. *Jacob Kunzenman.*

ONONDAGA COUNTY. District. 1. Wallace Tappan. 2. Francis Hendricks.* 3. Conrad Shoemaker.*
ONTARIO COUNTY. John Raines.
ORANGE COUNTY. 1. Samuel L. Carlisle. 2. *George W. Greene.*
ORLEANS COUNTY. J. Marshall Dibble.*
OSWEGO COUNTY. 1. H. G. Howes. 2. G. M. Sweet.*
OTSEGO COUNTY. 1. *W. Caryl Ely.** 2. Frank B. Arnold.
PUTNAM COUNTY. R. A. Livingston.
QUEENS COUNTY. 1. *Louis K. Church.** 2. Thomas A. Smith.
RENSSELAER COUNTY. 1. *James P. Hooley.** 2. Eugene L. Demers. 3. *Charles C. Lodewick.*
RICHMOND COUNTY. M. S. Tynan.
ROCKLAND COUNTY. *John W. Felter.**
ST. LAWRENCE COUNTY. 1. Newton M. Curtis.* 2. Andrew Tuck. 3. George Z. Erwin.*
SARATOGA COUNTY. 1. Daniel C. Briggs.* 2. Bartlett B. Grippen.
SCHENECTADY COUNTY. *Edward D. Cutler.*
SCHOHARIE COUNTY. *Addison H. Bartley.*
SCHUYLER COUNTY. Fremont Cole.
SENECA COUNTY. *William B. Clark.*
STEUBEN COUNTY. 1. *Geo. E. Whiteman.** 2. Charles D. Baker.
SUFFOLK COUNTY. Simeon S. Hawkins.*
SULLIVAN COUNTY. *James D. Decker.*
TIOGA COUNTY. C. F. Barager.*
TOMPKINS COUNTY. Hiland K. Clark.
ULSTER COUNTY. 1. Robert A. Snyder. 2. G. D. B. Hasbrouck.* 3. *C. A. J. Hardenburgh.*
WARREN COUNTY. *Frank Byrne.*
WASHINGTON COUNTY. 1. George Scott. 2. C. K. Baker.*
WAYNE COUNTY. 1. A. S. Farnum.* 2. *E. K. Burnham.*
WESTCHESTER COUNTY. 1. *C. P. McClelland.* 2. *S. W. Johnson.** 3. James W. Husted.*
WYOMING COUNTY. John E. Lowing.
YATES COUNTY. Clark Smith.

### RETURNS FROM CONGRESSMEN.

BABYLON, Long Island, Nov. 4.—The Democratic majority for Congress in this district is about 4,000. PERRY BELMONT, Democratic Candidate for Congress.

SYRACUSE, N. Y., Nov. 4.—I have not heard from Cortland County definitely, but estimate my majority will be 5,500. FRANK HISCOCK, Republican Candidate for Congress.

BUFFALO, N. Y., Nov. 4.—I am elected Representative in Congress by nearly 1,000 majority. JOHN M. FARQUHAR, Republican Candidate for Congress.

WHITEHALL, N. Y., Nov. 4.—The Hon. H. G. Burleigh is re-elected to Congress from the Washington and Rensselaer district. The Republican majority for Blaine in Washington County is about 3,000. H. G. BURLEIGH, Republican Candidate for Congress.

BINGHAMTON, N. Y., Nov. 4.—It is impossible to estimate with any certainty the majority for the Presidential ticket. My majority in the district is nearly, if not quite, 5,000. S. C. MILLARD, Republican Candidate for Congress.

BUFFALO, N. Y., Nov. 4.—Erie County gives from 1,500 to 1,800 majority for Blaine. My majority is about 500. JOHN B. WEBER, Republican candidate for Congress.

RONDOUT, N. Y., Nov. 4.—My majority in the district is estimated at 600. JAMES G. LINDSLEY, Republican Candidate for Congress.

### FROM ASSEMBLY CANDIDATES.

STAPLETON, Staten Island, Nov. 4.—M. S. Tynan has carried Richmond County by 500. M. S. TYNAN, Republican Candidate for Assembly.

WELLSVILLE, N. Y., Nov. 4.—My majority for Assembly in Allegany County will be 2,800 to 3,000. Blaine's majority in the county is 2,500. WILLIAM R. M'EWEN, Republican Candidate for Assembly.

SCHENECTADY, N. Y., Nov. 4.—Schenectady County gives Blaine about 200 majority, a Democratic gain of over 400. I am elected to the Assembly by over 200 majority over Veeder, Republican. EDWARD D. CUTLER, Democratic Candidate for Assembly.

DOBBS FERRY, N. Y., Nov. 4.—I am elected to the Assembly in the First District of Westchester County by about 300 majority. C. P. M'CLELLAND, Democratic Candidate for Assembly.

SENECA FALLS, Seneca County, N. Y., Nov. 4.—No doubt of my election. The majority cannot be found out to-night. E. K. RUMSEY, Republican Candidate for Assembly.

POTSDAM, Nov. 4.—I am elected to the Assembly from St. Lawrence County, Third District, by about 1,600 majority. G. Z. ERWIN, Republican Candidate for Assembly.

OGDENSBURG, N. Y., Nov. 4.—For Assembly in the First District of St. Lawrence County Curtis (Rep.) receives 358; Wheeler, (Dem.) 294. WILLIAM WHEELER, Democratic Candidate for Assembly.

GAINESVILLE, N. Y., Nov. 4.—The vote in Gainesville, Wyoming County, stands: Blaine, 304; Cleveland, 135; St. John, 31; Butler, 4. Congress—Sawyer, (Rep.,) 297; Stevens, (Dem.) 169; Richmond, (Proh.) 27. Assembly—Lowing, (Rep.,) 316; Decot, 119; Cotton, 38. The county will probably give 1,200 majority for Blaine. J. E. LOWING, Republican Candidate for Assembly.

FISHKILL LANDING, N. Y., Nov. 4.—The majority for Blaine in the town of Fishkill, Dutchess County, is 222, with a probability of the election of Storms (Rep.) to the Assembly in the First District. J. M. DAVIES, Democratic Candidate for Assembly.

FULTON, N. Y., Nov. 4.—My majority is about 500. H. G. HOWE, Republican Candidate for Assembly.

BUFFALO, N. Y., Nov. 4.—The following is the result in the First Assembly District: Sheehan (Dem.) will have a majority of about 1,300. This district last year gave a majority to the Democratic candidate of 2,900, a Democratic loss of 1,600. T. P. DONOVAN, Republican Candidate for Assembly.

LOCKPORT, N. Y., Nov. 4.—I am elected by 100 majority in the First District, Niagara County. JACOB A. DRIESS, Democratic Candidate for Assembly.

BATAVIA, N. Y., Nov. 4.—My majority in Genesee County for the Assembly is about 800. Blaine's majority is about 1,000. L. R. BAILEY, Republican Candidate for Assembly.

CATSKILL, N. Y., Nov. 4.—I am elected by over 400 majority for the Assembly. STEPHEN T. HOPKINS, Democratic Candidate for Assembly.

GLOVERSVILLE, N. Y., Nov. 4.—My plurality will be about 800. A. W. BERRY, Republican Candidate for Assembly.

OLEAN, N. Y., Nov. 4.—I have been elected member of Assembly, First District, Cattaraugus County, by about 400 or 500 majority over Day, Democrat. FREDERICK W. KRUSE, Republican Candidate for Assembly.

YONKERS, Nov. 4.—The result in the First Westchester District was still in doubt at 2 A. M. N. P. OTIS, Republican Candidate for Assembly.

SAUGERTIES, N. Y., Nov. 4.—My majority in the First District of Ulster County is about 1,500. ROBERT A. SNYDER, Republican Candidate for Assembly.

WAYLAND, N. Y., Nov. 4.—I am elected without a doubt in the Second District of Steuben County. G. E. WHITEMAN, Democratic Candidate for Assembly.

ALBANY, N. Y., Nov. 4.—My majority is from 800 to 1,000 in Orleans County. J. MARSHALL DIBBLE, Republican Candidate for Assembly.

ROME, N. Y., Nov. 4.—My majority from 200 to 300 in the Second District, Oneida County. L. B. SHERMAN, Democratic Candidate for Assembly.

TROY, N. Y., Nov. 4.—J. P. Hooley, the Workingmen's and Democratic candidate, is elected to the Assembly over E. H. G. Clark, Republican, Independent Democrat, and Butlerite, by 1,000 majority. J. P. HOOLEY, Democratic Candidate for Assembly.

FAIRPORT, N. Y., Nov. 4.—There is no doubt but that I am elected by a handsome plurality in the First District, Monroe County. WALTER S. HUBBELL, Republican Candidate for Assembly.

DUNKIRK, N. Y., Nov. 4.—My majority for the Assembly is about 1,500 in the Second District of Chautauqua County. J. T. WILLIAMS, Republican Candidate for Assembly.

SYRACUSE, Nov. 4.—Wallace Tappan (Rep.) is elected to the Assembly from the First District of Onondaga. WILLIAM KIRKPATRICK, Democratic Candidate for Assembly.

BALDWINSVILLE, Nov. 4.—Wallace Tappan is elected Assemblyman for the First District of Onondaga by a large majority. W. TAPPAN, Republican Candidate for Assembly.

DUNDEE, Nov. 4.—My majority in the county is 1,320. CLARK SMITH, Republican candidate for Assembly.

RONDOUT, Nov. 4.—I am probably elected to the Assembly from the Second District of Ulster by a majority of 100. G. A. B. HASBROUCK, Republican Candidate for Assembly.

GENESEO, Nov. 4.—The returns indicate the election of the Republican Assemblyman. K. M. SCOTT, Republican Candidate for Assembly.

NEWARK, N. Y., Nov. 4.—In Wayne, Second District, I am elected by over 100 majority probably. E. K. BURNHAM, Democratic Candidate for Assembly.

NORTH GRANVILLE, Nov. 4.—My majority is about 1,000. CHARLES N. BAKER, Republican Candidate for Assembly.

### COUNTY COMMITTEE REPORTS.

BALLSTON, N. Y., Nov. 4.—Blaine's majority in Saratoga County is about 2,000. West (Rep.) is elected member of Assembly by about 1,700. Briggs, (Rep.,) Assembly, is probably elected. J. S. LAMOREAUX, Chairman Republican County Committee.

NORWICH, N. Y., Nov. 4.—The estimated majority of Chenango County for Blaine is 900. Whitmore, (Rep.,) for the Assembly, is elected. F. W. ROGERS, Chairman Democratic County Committee.

MALONE, N. Y., Nov. 4.—Franklin County gives Blaine a majority over Cleveland of 1,718—one election district being estimated. This is correct within a very few votes. CHARLES A. BURKE, Chairman Democratic County Committee.

KATONAH, N. Y., Nov. 4.—Cleveland's majority in Westchester County will be 1,500. W. H. ROBERTSON, Chairman Republican County Committee.

MALONE, N. Y., Nov. 4.—Returns to this hour, on a close estimate, show the Republican majority in Franklin County to be about 1,800. William T. O'Neil is elected to the Assembly by a majority of about the same amount. N. H. MUNSILL, Chairman Republican County Committee.

HAVANA, N. Y., Nov. 4.—Blaine and Logan carry Schuyler County by 700. It is estimated that Fremont Cole (Rep.) is elected member of the Assembly. B. T. SMELZER, Chairman Republican County Committee.

BELFAST, N. Y., Nov. 4.—Sixteen towns heard from make Blaine's majority in Allegany County over Cleveland about 1,500. For Assembly, McEwen is elected. Sessions, for Congress, has about 1,200 majority over Smith, Democrat. G. W. TIBBET, Chairman Democratic County Committee.

ALBION, N. Y., Nov. 4.—Blaine's majority in Orleans County is 1,100. Dibble (Rep.) is elected to the Assembly. R. TITUS COAN, Chairman Republican County Committee.

SCHENECTADY, Nov. 4.—Schenectady city, complete, gives Blaine 125 majority. The county will give Blaine over 300. Veeder is probably defeated for member of the Assembly. Wemple will get about 250 majority. J. W. VEEDER, Chairman Republican County Committee.

SALAMANCA, N. Y., Nov. 4.—Cattaraugus County gives 1,500 for Blaine. Both Republican Assemblymen and Congressmen are elected. The Prohibition vote is large. We lose there. J. S. WHIPPLE, Chairman Republican County Committee.

BATAVIA, Nov. 4.—Blaine's majority is about 950 in Genesee County. Sawyer, (Rep.,) for Congress and Bailey, (Rep.,) for Assembly, are elected. MYRON H. PECK, Jr., Chairman Democratic County Committee.

NYACK, Nov. 4.—Rockland County gives Cleveland a majority of about 1,000. Felter (Dem.) is re-elected to the Assembly. JOHN CHARLTON, Chairman Republican County Committee.

JOHNSTOWN, N. Y., Nov. 4.—Blaine's majority in Fulton County is 1,000. A Republican Assemblyman is elected. JAMES P. ARGERSINGER, Chairman Republican County Committee.

NYACK, N. Y., Nov. 4.—Rockland County gives Cleveland 1,300 majority; Beach, (Dem.,) Congress, 900; Felter, (Dem.,) for Assembly, probably elected. ORLANDO HUMPHREY, Chairman Democratic County Committee.

BINGHAMTON, N. Y., Nov. 4.—Binghamton, Broome County, is a tie, making a Democratic gain of 187. O. W. EARLE, Chairman Democratic County Committee.

ALBANY, N. Y., Nov. 4.—Murray (Dem.,) is elected in the Third District, Albany County by 1,800 plurality. PATRICK MURRAY, Democratic Candidate for Assembly.

PEEKSKILL, N. Y., Nov. 4.—My majority is about 500, probably more. J. W. HUSTED, Republican Candidate for Assembly.

PLATTSBURG, N. Y., Nov. 4.—The Republican majority for Assemblyman is about 500. G. W. PALMER, Republican Candidate for Assembly.

POUGHKEEPSIE, N. Y., Nov. 4.—Dutchess County, Second Assembly District, gives Osborne (Dem.) 300 majority. PETER HULME, Republican Candidate for Assembly.

ROME, N. Y., Nov. 4.—There is a reduced Democratic majority in Rome from 400 to 114. I think I will win by a small majority in the Second District. G. P. NOCK, Republican Candidate for Assembly.

EAST WORCESTER, N. Y., Nov. 4.—I am re-elected to the Assembly from the First Assembly District of Otsego County. W. C. ELY, Democratic Candidate for Assembly.

LOCKPORT, N. Y., Nov. 4.—The First Assembly District of Niagara County is probably Democratic. THOMAS SCOVILLE, Republican candidate for Assembly.

FORT EDWARD, N. Y., Nov. 4.—The probable majority for George Scott, First Assembly District, Washington County, is from 1,200 to 1,500. GEORGE SCOTT, Republican candidate for Assembly.

ELMIRA, N. Y., Nov. 4.—I am elected in Chemung County by about 300 majority. I. S. VAN DUZER, Republican candidate for Assembly.

GARRISONS, N. Y., Nov. 4.—My majority for Assembly is 600. The Blaine vote is similar in this (Putnam) county. ROBERT A. LIVINGSTON, Republican candidate for Assembly.

BUFFALO, N. Y., Nov. 4.—My majority in the First Assembly District is 1,600. WILLIAM F. SHEEHAN, Democratic candidate for Assembly.

ADAMS, N. Y., Nov. 4.—The indications are that Kilby (Rep.) is elected to the Assembly, First District, Jefferson County, by a decreased majority from the Republican vote of last year. A. W. INGRAHAM, Democratic candidate for Assembly.

SALAMANCA, N. Y., Nov. 4.—Cattaraugus County shows a gain for Cleveland over 1880 of over 1,000. Sessions, (Rep.,) for Congress, is elected. The Assembly is in doubt. Nearly every town in the county gives an increased Democratic majority. C. E. GALLAGHER, Chairman Democratic County Committee.

OWEGO, N. Y., Nov. 4.—Tioga County gives Blaine 950 plurality over Cleveland; same for Millard for Congress, Twenty-sixth District. Barager is elected member of the Assembly. E. W. STONE, Chairman Republican County Committee.

CAMBRIDGE, N. Y., Nov. 4.—Blaine receives 3,113 majority in Washington County. Scott and Baker, (Rep.,) are elected to the Assembly. JOHN LARMON, Chairman Republican County Committee.

ONEIDA, N. Y., Nov. 4.—Madison County gives 1,400 majority for Blaine. W. E. NORTHROP, Chairman Democratic County Committee.

BREWSTER, N. Y., Nov. 4.—Blaine's majority is probably 500 in Putnam County; Congressman Ketcham (Rep.) has 800 majority; Assemblyman Livingston (Rep.) 350 majority. E. C. HOWES, Chairman Democratic County Committee.

GOSHEN, N. Y., Nov. 4.—Orange County gives Cleveland 300 majority. George W. Green is elected to the Assembly from the Second District; Carlisle, probably, from the First. HENRY BACON, Chairman Democratic County Committee.

BATAVIA, N. Y., Nov. 4.—Genesee County gives a majority to J. G. Sawyer (Rep.) of 800; Bailey (Rep.) has 1,200; Blaine, 1,000. JOHN McKENZIE, Chairman Republican County Committee.

TOMPKINSVILLE, Staten Island, Nov. 4.—Richmond County gives Cleveland 2,000, Belmont 1,800. The county ticket is all elected by 1,800 majority. JOHN G. VAUGN, Chairman Democratic County Committee.

CANANDAIGUA, N. Y., Nov. 4.—Ontario County gives Blaine 800 majority. Raines (Rep.) is elected to the Assembly. F. H. HAMLIN, Chairman Republican County Committee.

JAMAICA, N. Y., Nov. 4.—Cleveland has carried Queens County by about 1,900 plurality. Butler received about 500 votes in the county and St. John 275. Louis K. Church, Democratic candidate for the Assembly in the First District, is re-elected by an overwhelming majority. In the Second Assembly District the contest was close. The indications are that Thomas A. Smith (Rep.) is elected by a small majority. Perry Belmont, (Dem.,) candidate for Congress from the First Congressional District, has about 1,800 majority in Queens County. J. H. SUTPHIN, Chairman Democratic County Committee.

MORRISVILLE, N. Y., Nov. 4.—Madison County gives Blaine 1,700 majority; Millard the same. J. W. LIPPITT, Chairman Republican County Committee.

HUDSON, N. Y., Nov. 5.—Columbia County is Republican probably by a majority of 500. Hogeboom is elected to the Assembly. Ketcham is elected to Congress. S. J. TILDEN, Jr.

CORTLAND, N. Y., Nov. 4.—Blaine's majority in Cortland County is 1,200. Andrews, Republican candidate for Assembly, is elected. Hiscock, Republican candidate for Congress in the Twenty-fifth District, is re-elected by an increased majority. R. H. DUELL, Chairman Republican County Committee.

CANANDAIGUA, N. Y., Nov. 4.—We estimate Blaine's majority in Ontario County at about 600. I. Davenport, Republican Congressman, and John Raines, Republican member of Assembly, have about the same majority. E. L. BEECHER, Chairman Democratic County Committee.

ROCHESTER, N. Y., Nov. 4.—Monroe County gives Blaine close on 5,000 majority. Charles S. Baker (Rep.) is elected to Congress by about 1,000 majority. W. S. Hubbell (Rep.) is re-elected in the First District. James P. Tumilty (Dem.) is elected in the Second District, and Philip Garbutt (Rep.) is re-elected in the Third District. R. H. SCHOOLEY, Chairman Democratic County Committee.

WATERTOWN, N. Y., Nov. 4.—The Republican majority in Jefferson County is estimated at 1,050. Forty-three election districts in this county show a net Democratic gain of 220. Kilby and Seeber (Rep.) have been elected in the First and Second Assembly Districts. The Second District is close. S. S. TROWBRIDGE, Chairman Democratic County Committee.

HAVANA, N. Y., Nov. 4.—Schuyler County gives Blaine 500 and elects a Republican member. S. J. BROWN, Chairman Democratic County Committee.

UTICA, Oneida County, N. Y., Nov. 4.—Spriggs (Dem.) is re-elected to Congress by 1,000 majority. CHARLES H. BALLOW, Chairman Democratic County Committee.

WATERTOWN, N. Y., Nov. 4.—Jefferson County gives Blaine 2,000 majority. Allen E. Kelby (Rep.) is elected to the Assembly in the First District, and Eli J. Seeber (Rep.) is re-elected in the Second District. CHARLES R. SKINNER, Chairman Republican County Committee.

ALBANY, N. Y., Nov. 4.—The majority in Albany County is probably 1,500 for Cleveland. Three Democratic members of Assembly and a Republican Congressman are probably elected. D. CADY HERRICK, Chairman Democratic County Committee.

PLATTSBURG, N. Y., Nov. 4.—Clinton County gives Blaine 800 majority, and Palmer, (Rep.,) for Assembly, 400 majority. J. H. MYERS, Chairman Republican County Committee.

BATH, N. Y., Nov. 4.—Steuben County gives 950 majority for Blaine. Witeman (Dem.) is elected to the Assembly in the First District; Baker (Dem.) is elected to the Assembly in the Second District. E. S. UNDERHILL, Chairman Democratic County Committee.

BALLSTON, N. Y., Nov. 4.—Saratoga County gives Blaine about 2,000. George West, for Congress, has about 1,800 probable majority in the Twentieth Congressional District. D. C. Briggs, (Rep.,) Assemblyman, First District, and Bartlett Griffin, Second District, (Rep.,) are both elected. SETH WHALEN, Chairman Democratic County Committee.

BINGHAMTON, Nov. 4.—The largest vote ever polled here has been cast to-day. The city is tied on Electors, the Democratic gain being 187; Butler's vote, 46; Prohibition, 111. Complete returns are not obtainable from the county to-night. Millard, Republican candidate for Congress, has a majority of about 1,800 in the county. Olin, Republican candidate for Assembly, is elected by about 800. Brown, Republican candidate for Sheriff, and Rider, Republican candidate for Treasurer, are elected. O. W. EARLE, Chairman Republican County Committee.

BUFFALO, N. Y., Nov. 4.—Erie County gives Blaine about 1,500 majority. A. F. SCHEU, Chairman Democratic County Committee.

UTICA, Nov. 4.—To Assembly in Oneida, Steber, (Rep.,) in the First, is elected by 100; Sherman, (Dem. and Wrk.,) in Second; Owens, (Rep.,) in Third. Spriggs, (Dem.,) for Congress, is elected over Cookingham by about 800. Oneida County goes 200 or 300 for Cleveland. JAMES SHERMAN, Chairman Republican County Committee.

ELMIRA, Nov. 4.—Blaine is estimated to have 500 majority. The Republican Assemblyman is probably elected. A Democratic Congressman is elected. E. B. YOUMANS, Chairman Democratic County Committee.

GREENPORT, N. Y., Nov. 4.—Suffolk County gives Cleveland a plurality probably over 500. Hawkins is probably elected Assemblyman. H. A. REEVES, Chairman Democratic County Committee.

OGDENSBURG, N. Y., Nov. 4.—St. Lawrence County gives Blaine 7,200 majority. A. A. SMITH, Chairman Republican County Committee.

OSWEGO, Nov. 4.—Blaine's plurality in Oswego County is 3,100, closely estimated, after hearing from 38 election districts out of 40. H. C. Howe (Rep.) is elected to the Assembly over Willard Johnson, (Dem.,) in the First District by about 800. For Congress, Payne, (Rep.,) in the Twenty-seventh District, is elected. J. K. STOCKWELL, Chairman Republican County Committee.

NORWICH, N. Y., Nov. 4.—Returns indicate a plurality for Blaine in Chenango County of over 1,000. The Republican member of Congress and member of Assembly are elected. J. E. NICKERSON, Chairman Democratic County Committee.

### REPORTING THE RESULTS.

GENERAL DEMOCRATIC GAINS REPORTED OUTSIDE NEW-YORK AND BROOKLYN.

PLATTSBURG, N. Y., Nov. 4.—Plattsburg complete, four districts, gives 249 for Cleveland, a Democratic gain of 363 over 1880; Beekmantown, 38 for Cleveland, a Democratic gain of 139; Saranac, 71 for Blaine, a Democratic gain of 173. Clinton County will probably give 800 Republican majority, a Democratic gain of about 1,000. The vote is very close on member of Assembly. SMITH M. WEED.

ELMIRA, N. Y., Nov. 4.—Corrected returns of Elmira, Chemung County, complete, give Blaine 2,854; Cleveland, 2,114; Butler, 278; St. John, 86. Five out of 16 country districts of Chemung County give Blaine 711; Cleveland, 729; Butler, 52; St. John, 40. John Arnot, Protectionist Democrat, is re-elected to Congress in the Twenty-eighth District. Ira Davenport (Rep.) is elected to Congress in the Twenty-ninth District. Hornellsville gives Cleveland 88 plurality.

NEWBURG, N. Y., Nov. 4.—Blaine carries Newburg, Orange County, by about 300, a Democratic gain of 50.

BALLSTON, N. Y., Nov. 4.—In Saratoga County 20 districts show a net Republican gain on Congress over 1882 of 444. The majority for Blaine will be 2,000. Shine (Dem.) is probably elected to the Assembly in the First District.

WATKINS, N. Y., Nov. 4.—Schuyler County gives Blaine a majority of 600. Fremont Cole, Assemblyman, (Rep.,) was elected by 300. John Arnot, (Dem.,) Congressman, indorsed by both Republican and Democratic tickets, has a majority.

CORNING, N. Y., Nov. 4.—Nineteen of the 32 towns of Steuben County show a net Democratic gain of 174. The Republican majority in the county will be 1,000.

WHITEHALL, N. Y., Nov. 4.—Whitehall, Washington County, complete, gives Cleveland 17 majority, a Democratic gain of 128 over 1880.

COMSTOCKS, N. Y., Nov. 4.—Charles K. Baker, Republican Assemblyman in the Second District of Washington County, is re-elected by nearly 1,500 majority—the largest ever given in this district.

LYONS, N. Y., Nov. 4.—Full returns from seven towns in Wayne County show a Republican gain of 150 over the vote of 1880.

PLATTSBURG, N. Y., Nov. 4.—Clinton County returns come in slowly. Those in indicate a Republican majority of 800. Palmer (Rep.) is probably elected to the Legislature.

COHOES, N. Y., Nov. 4.—Cohoes, Albany County, complete, gives Blaine 75 over Cleveland, a Democratic gain over Garfield of 66.

GLEN COVE, Nov. 4.—Incomplete returns show a slight Republican gain in Queens County, which will give Cleveland about 1,800 majority. Belmont, for Congress, is elected.

WAVERLY, Nov. 4.—Blaine's majority in Tioga County is probably 700. Stephen C. Millard, (Rep.,) for Congress, is surely elected. C. F. Barager, for member of Assembly, is elected by a rousing majority.

WHITE PLAINS, Nov. 4.—Returns from various parts of Westchester County give Cleveland about 2,000 majority. For Assembly, the returns indicate the election of Charles P. McClelland (Dem.) in the First District, Samuel W. Johnson (Dem.) in the Second District, and James W. Husted (Rep.) in the Third.

TROY, Nov. 4.—Blaine's plurality in Rensselaer County, from official and estimated returns, is about 250. Hooley and Lodewick (Dem.) are probably, and Demers (Rep.) is certainly, elected to the Assembly. Burleigh (Rep.) is elected to Congress.

MILLERTON, N. Y., Nov. 4.—The town of North East, Dutchess County, gives Blaine 15 majority, a gain of 8. Ketcham, for Congress, and Storm, for Assembly, are probably elected.

UTICA, N. Y., Nov. 4.—The Republicans elected Henry A. Steber to the Assembly in the First District and T. James Owen in the Third District of Oneida County. L. B. Sherman (Dem.) is elected in the Second District.

SARATOGA, N. Y., Nov. 4.—Returns from 24 of the 34 election districts of Saratoga County show a net gain for Blaine over Garfield's vote of 176. His majority in the county will be about 2,500. West (Rep.) has about 2,000 majority in the district for Congress.

OGDENSBURG, Nov. 4.—Reports from seven towns in the First District of St. Lawrence County, indicate the re-election of Gen. W. M. Curtis to the Assembly by 2,300 majority.

ALBION, N. Y., Nov. 4.—Fifteen out of 17 districts in Oneida County give Blaine 959 majority, a Democratic gain of 300. Sawyer, (Rep.,) for Congress, has 283 over Stevens, with four towns to hear from.

NYACK, N. Y., Nov. 4.—Cleveland has a majority of about 1,000 in Rockland County, which is a Democratic gain of about 275. John W. Felter, the Democratic Assemblyman from this district, is re-elected by a slightly increased majority over last year. The returns on the Congressional vote are so meagre that nothing definite can now be known. The Prohibition vote was much smaller than anticipated and will probably not exceed 100 in the county.

ROCHESTER, N. Y., Nov. 4.—In Monroe County, 38 out of 57 election districts give Blaine 10,951, Cleveland 7,833. When complete Blaine will have 4,000 majority. Baker, for Congress, (Rep.,) has 9,764 and Greenleaf 8,701. Baker's majority will be 2,000. Tumility (Dem.) beats Voshall for Assembly by a majority of 4,000.

FLUSHING, Long Island, Nov. 4.—Cleveland has 3,500 majority in Queens County. L. K. Church, Assemblyman, First District, has 1,300 majority; Belmont's majority, for Congressman, in Queens County is 3,500; in the district, 4,500.

ALBANY, N. Y., Nov. 4.—Albany County gives Cleveland about 1,500 majority. The Republicans made large gains in the Democratic wards, where the labor vote is heavy. Dr. John Swinburne (Rep.) is elected to Congress by several hundred majority. The Assemblymen probably elected are: First District—Stephen H. Niles, (Dem.;) Second District—Lansing Houtaling, (Rep.;) Third District—Patrick Murray, (Dem.;) Fourth District—Terence I. Hardin, (Dem.)

MEDINA, N. Y., Nov. 4.—Blaine's majority in Orleans County is between 1,000 and 1,200. The Prohibition vote is about 600. Dibble, (Rep.,) Assemblyman, is elected. Sawyer, for Congress, has about 500 majority in the county.

MALONE, N. Y., Nov. 4.—Franklin County complete, except two small districts, gives Blaine 1,668 plurality. Further returns are likely to increase this by 10 or 20. O'Neil (Rep.) is elected to the Assembly, and F. A. Johnson (Rep.) to Congress. The Butler and St. John vote will be about the same—say, 50 to 75 for each.

ELMIRA, Nov. 4.—John Arnot is elected to Congress by a large majority. M. H. ARNOT.

GLENS FALLS, N. Y., Nov. 4.—Byrnes, for Assembly, has 250 majority.

OSWEGO, N. Y., Nov. 4.—Tioga County gives Blaine 800. Charles A. Barager, (Rep.,) for Assembly, and S. C. Millard, (Rep.,) for Congress, in the Twenty-sixth District, are elected.

LOCKPORT, N. Y., Nov. 4.—Fifteen out of 25 election districts of Niagara County give Cleveland over Blaine 215, which is a gain of 446 over Garfield. An estimate of the balance give Cleveland 300 over Blaine in Niagara County, which figures may be much increased. Driess (Dem.) is probably elected to the Assembly in the First Niagara District. Reports as to Congressman are few, but such as are received favor the election of Payne, (Dem.)

BUFFALO, Nov. 4.—Returns indicate that Blaine has carried this city by about 1,100 and Erie County by about 1,800. John M. Farquhar (Rep.) seems to be elected to Congress in the Thirty-second District by a small majority. Meagre returns also indicate the election of John B. Weber (Rep.) in the Thirty-third District. The following Assemblymen in this county seem to be elected: First District, William F. Meehan, (Dem.;) Second District, Frank M. Giese, (Dem.;) Third District, William M. Hawkins, (Rep.;) Fourth District, John Kraus, (Rep.;) Fifth District in doubt, with chances in favor of Amos H. Baker, (Rep.) Cleveland gained largely in the upper wards of this city, but lost somewhat in the Irish wards. His total gain over Hancock's vote in the county is 1,300 to 1,500.

ALBION, N.Y., Nov. 4.—Orleans County gives Sawyer, (Rep.,) for Congress, 500 majority. The election of Stevens (Dem.) is considered probable.

MALONE, N. Y., Nov. 4.—Eleven towns give Blaine 1,545 plurality; six towns to hear from. The estimated majority in Franklin County is 1,800 for Blaine. The entire Republican ticket is elected in the county. Frederick A. Johnson is elected to Congress from the Twenty-first District; William T. O'Neil is re-elected to the Assembly from Franklin County. There is a large Republican gain throughout the county. The Butler and St. John vote is light.

SCHOHARIE, N. Y., Nov. 4.—Schoharie County gives Cleveland a majority of 1,800. Addison Bartlett, (Dem.,) for the Assembly, is elected. Congressman John Pindar, (Dem.,) has a majority in the county of about 1,700.

WHITE PLAINS, Nov. 4.—The returns have come in very slowly, and meagre at that, being in detached districts of various towns. The Democrats claim Westchester County by not less than 2,000 majority, while the Republicans say it is not over 1,100. The indications are that William G. Stahlnecker (Dem.) has 1,500 majority in the county over Edwin A. McAlpin, for member of Congress. The entire Democratic county ticket is probably elected, though David Cromwell (Rep.) may be elected Treasurer.

TOMPKINSVILLE, Staten Island, Nov. 4.—Twenty-three districts out of 30 in Richmond County show about 2,000 majority for Cleveland, or 400 more than Hancock received. This indicates exactly the independent Republican vote. Butler's vote is trifling, and is exceeded by that for St. John. The Assemblymen will be in doubt until the last district is in, the Democratic nomination having caused large defection. Perry Belmont gets 1,600 majority.

LONG ISLAND CITY, Nov. 4.—The election passed off very quietly. The city gives Blaine 1,263; Cleveland, 2,094; Butler, 10; St. John, 24. Democratic plurality, 831. Republican gain, 615. Cleveland's majority in Queens County is about 1,800, and he has probably carried Suffolk by a small majority. Congressman Belmont's majority is estimated here at 3,000.

ROCHESTER, N. Y., Nov. 4.—Philip Garbutt is elected by a good majority as Assemblyman, Third District, Monroe County. W. D. GARBUTT.

SANDY HILL, N. Y., Nov. 4.—Blaine carries Washington County by 3,300 a loss of about 350. Burleigh, (Rep.,) for Congress, is elected in the Eighteenth District. Scott (Rep.) is elected to the Assembly in the First District; Baker (Rep.) is elected to the Assembly in the Second District.

OSWEGO, N. Y., Nov. 4.—Oswego County gives Blaine 3,000 majority. Howe and Sweet (Rep.) are elected Assemblymen. Payne (Rep.) is elected to Congress.

WATKINS, N. Y., Nov. 4.—Blaine's plurality in Schuyler County is 575. Cole (Rep.) is elected to the Assembly. John Arnot, (Dem.,) for Congress, in the Twenty-sixth District, has no opposition.

BATH, N. Y., Nov. 4.—In Steuben County Blaine's majority is 950. The First Assembly District result is in doubt. Probably George E. Whiteman (Dem.) is re-elected. In the Twenty-ninth Congressional District Ira Davenport (Rep.) is elected.

COOPERSTOWN, N. Y., Nov. 5.—Otsego County gives Cleveland about 600 majority. Republicans elect F. B. Arnold in the Second District. Pindar, (Dem.,) for Congress, is elected in this district.

HORSEHEADS, N. Y., Nov. 4.—Chemung County gives Blaine 620 majority. Dexter, (Rep.,) for Judge, has 300; Van Duzer, (Rep.,) for Assembly, at least 300; Baxter, (Rep.,) for County Clerk, 378; School Commissioner doubtful, with chances in favor of Van Dewaker, (Rep.;) he is only voted for in the towns. The temperance vote is about 160 in the county; the Greenback from 1,000 to 1,600. Schuyler gives Blaine a majority of 672, and all the balance about the same.

ROME, N. Y., Nov. 4.—Cleveland carries Oneida County by 600 majority. Spriggs, (Dem.,) in the Oneida-Lewis District, is re-elected to Congress by 2,000 majority. Sherman (Dem.) is elected to the Assembly in the Second District.

WATERTOWN, N. Y., Nov. 4.—Forty-three towns and districts in Jefferson County give Blaine 7,084; Cleveland, 4,457; Butler, [illegible]; St. John, 685. Democratic gain, 125. [illegible]

GROVER CLEVELAND

The New York Times.

VOL. XXXIV......NO. 10,453. NEW-YORK, THURSDAY, MARCH 5, 1885. PRICE TWO CENTS.

# THE REFORM PRESIDENT

## GROVER CLEVELAND SWORN IN AS CHIEF MAGISTRATE.

### A MULTITUDE OF PEOPLE PRESENT AT THE CEREMONY.

THE GREATEST AND MOST ENTHUSIASTIC CROWD EVER SEEN IN WASHINGTON—THE MARCH TO THE CAPITOL—GEN. GRANT'S RETIREMENT—SCENES IN THE SENATE CHAMBER AND ON THE EAST FRONT—THE INAUGURAL ADDRESS—A GRAND PROCESSION AND A SUCCESSFUL BALL.

WASHINGTON, March 4.—Grover Cleveland is President. In the presence of an imposing multitude, the like of which has never before been seen in Washington, the chosen Chief Magistrate was sworn into office. The good fortune which had attended the man and his party in the hotly contested political battle attended both to-day. Surpassingly fair weather, a warm sun, an almost cloudless sky, little wind, and clean streets combined to make the day a comfortable one for an out-of-door celebration. The enormous crowds, swelled by rapidly incoming trains, which arrived long after the President-elect had become President and President Arthur had become ex-President, were good natured, and in the main orderly and tractable, and there was unbounded enthusiasm.

The closing hours of Congress were not without incident. In the House there was much fatigue and hurry and some impatience to be through in order that the members could get to the Senate Chamber. In the Senate an impressive gathering were witnesses of the most moving legislative and executive transaction when the passage of the Edmunds bill to retire Gen. Grant was announced, and was immediately followed by the nomination of Gen. Grant to be General on the retired list and his prompt confirmation by the Senate without the formality of closing the doors. The cheers for Mr. Cleveland in the Senate Chamber, on his appearance before the brilliant audience that filled it, were but as a whisper to a cyclone as compared to the roar that went up a little later from 50,000 of his fellow-citizens, gathered on the broad and sunlit eastern plaza.

The parade back to the White House was imposing, both in appearance and in numbers. The multitude of spectators along the streets was much greater than the throng that witnessed the procession of four years ago. The whole programme, including the escort to the Capitol, the parade back to the White House, the coming display of fireworks, and the great ball closing the day, has been carried out, thanks to the beneficent assistance of nature in furnishing good weather, with remarkable success. The greeting to the President has been spontaneously cordial. The new Administration comes in with every augury of success.

### THE MARCH TO THE CAPITOL.

Gen. Hazen, in charge of the Weather Bureau, had been doing his best to bury the tip end of a storm over the District, and many persons, who did not know that his predictions should be taken reversely, went to bed last night expecting clouds and rain this morning. His career as a weather manager had been stopped by military arrest, and when the time came for the sun to rise it rose to be visible, nothing but a slight haze obscuring it. A Spring-like breeze blew up the Potomac from the south, and sun and wind soon drove off the haze. The drummers and brass bands were moving. Rattle and blare were heard on every hand. Every street about the centre of the city was full of men, uniformed or badged. To crowds that had been rushing about until late the night before the morning movement seemed to follow closely upon the serenades and parades that had furnished them with preliminary enthusiasm. Flags were thrown to the breeze from hotels, house-tops, and windows. The capital had put on its best clothes, and men, women, and children, packed street cars, herdics, hansoms, and all sorts of conveyances bound for the avenue, while thousands who could not ride trudged along the asphalted avenues. There was general rejoicing that the weather was fine, for tradition says that inauguration day was never fine before. While there were many policemen they had not much to do. Eager and curious as the crowds were, they were not difficult to control.

The President-elect was up early, and long before the time appointed for him to leave the Arlington Hotel he had breakfasted with his brother, Col. Lamont, and the rest of his party, and, having looked out upon the great throng that had gathered about the Arlington Hotel, he leisurely made his toilet. The escorting soldiers, in the uniforms of the United States and the District of Columbia, were forming in the neighboring streets, their colors and arms flashing brightly in the sun. Back to the curbs on Fifteen and a Half-street the policemen pressed the crowds. At 10:30 o'clock carriages containing the personal friends of the President-elect were driven off to the Capitol. Up through the lane lined with crowds an open carriage drawn by four spanking bays with banged tails was driven by Albert Hawkins. It was the White House turnout, driven by the well-known White House driver appointed by Gen. Grant. In the carriage were Senators Sherman and Ransom, who entered the hotel for a moment and then reappeared in company with Mr. Cleveland. As a cheer went up the President-elect and escorting Senators took their seats in the carriage, and again the crowd cheered lustily as it was driven off toward the White House, only a square away.

It had just passed the iron gates and President Arthur was receiving Mr. Cleveland in the Blue Parlor when another barouche, drawn by four fine white horses, drove up under the porch. It contained Vice-President-elect Hendricks and Senator Hawley, who joined the group in the Blue Parlor. Everything was in readiness for a start when, precisely at 10:30 o'clock, a gorgeously attired aide drove to the White House door and announced that the escort was prepared to move. The President-elect took his seat in the barouche drawn by the spanking bays, with President Arthur on his right, Senator Ransom and Senator Sherman occupying the front seat. On the avenue the escort was in line, gleaming in the brilliant sun. It took only a moment, but that moment was filled with cheers. As the crowds on the stands in Lafayette-square were cheering and waving their handkerchiefs the two barouches drove into the avenue. The bands played, the glittering muskets of the soldiers flashed again as they were brought to a "shoulder arms," and the procession moved east past the gayly decked Treasury Building. Screams and yells and cheers rent the air as the crowds fell back in masses. As Gen. Slocum led his command between the swaying, surging crowd and passed out of Fifteenth-street upon Pennsylvania-avenue, where the white dome of the Capitol was in sight, a deafening roar of cheers, beginning at the Treasury, went up from the multitude, was taken up and passed along, and was repeated with increasing volume all along the avenue until the wave of sound reached the foot of Capitol Hill.

Mr. Cleveland and Mr. Hendricks were everywhere greeted with vociferous cheers and the characteristic yell by which men of the South express their enthusiasm. Mr. Cleveland acknowledged the applause and cheers by bowing, holding his hat in his hand, while Mr. Hendricks occasionally rose to respond to unusually fervent plaudits. There was no waste of time on the march to the Capitol, the horsemen, infantry, artillery, marshals, committeemen in carriages, and district militia proceeding without delay to the east end of the line of march.

As the first sounds of approaching music were heard by the crowds about the Capitol there was a rush of thousands toward the north end of the plaza. For a moment the police seemed unable to cope with the almost irresistible throng that massed itself in the way of the on-coming procession. Driving their horses against the swaying wall it was at last forced back. A way was opened to the vaulted entrance under the Senate porch, the carriages of the Presidential party and the Vice-President were driven up and all alighted. Escorted by the Senatorial Committee, they passed up stairs to the Senators' lobby by the private stairway and stopped at the room of the Vice-President. President Arthur went to the President's room to sign such bills as awaited Executive sanction, and Mr. Cleveland awaited the time for him to enter the Senate Chamber, chatting in the meantime with a few Senators and with Mr. Hendricks.

### CLOSING SCENES IN THE SENATE.

While Mr. Cleveland was waiting in the Vice-President's room for the Senate to announce its readiness to receive him, that body was closing up its business in a rather informal way. Between 300 and 400 persons saved the expense of a night's lodging by sleeping in the Senate galleries during the long hours of the night. They were not disturbed until 8 o'clock this morning, when a recess was taken until 9:30 o'clock and the doorkeepers were ordered to clear the galleries. During the night the conferrees had made reports on all the appropriation bills except the Sundry Civil and Legislative, Executive, and Judicial, and these two were all that remained to be acted upon when the recess was taken. Just before 8 o'clock Mr. Blair made a motion to take up some private pension bills. Mr. Conger protested vigorously, and while the two Senators were wrangling Mr. Edmunds succeeded in getting the recess ordered. The announcement of the recess had hardly been uttered before a force of laborers swarmed into the chamber with brooms and dusters, and hastily cleared away the odds and ends with which the floor was littered. Behind them was another lot of men carrying chairs. In less than half an hour several hundred of these had been placed between the Senators' desks in close rows wherever space could be found. Large easy chairs and sofas were then brought in and placed before the front circle of desks. While this was going on on the floor of the chamber, carpenters took possession of the gallery, just to the right of the diplomatic gallery, and in a few minutes a space was fenced off to be reserved for the families of President Cleveland, ex-President Arthur, Vice-President Hendricks, and ex-Presidents and ex-Vice-Presidents. Then the chamber was deserted for nearly an hour by all except two or three pages, who caught cat-naps on the sofas.

When Mr. Edmunds stepped into the chamber at 9:30 o'clock he saw only half a dozen Senators present, including Messrs. Cockrell, Ingalls, Gorman, Plumb, and Van Wyck. A moment after Mr. Edmunds had taken his seat Mr. Cockrell, who was standing just in front of him, presented the report of the conferrees on the Legislative, Executive, and Judicial bill. Mr. Edmunds made the formal announcement of what the document was, and then put the question on agreeing to the report. Mr. Cockrell and Mr. Gorman, who stood beside him, nodded their heads and the report was agreed to. The bill was grabbed by one of the clerks, who hurried with it to the engrossing clerks, and thus the last but one of the Appropriation bills was disposed of. All had been done in low tones, and none but the Senators mentioned were aware that they had been called to order and that business was being transacted.

After this matter had been got out of the way the Senators lounged about the chamber waiting for something to do, and half a dozen ladies, who had been passed by the policemen, ventured into the galleries. The first who gained entrance was the wife of Senator Ingalls, who was accompanied by the wife of ex-Gov. Glick, of Kansas. Ten minutes after the final sitting of the old Senate began, Mr. Edmunds called Mr. Garland to the chair, and five minutes later Clerk Clark appeared with a message from the House announcing its concurrence in a Senate Private Pension bill. Both the Clerk and the veteran Capt. Bassett, who announces all messages, showed the wear and tear of an all-night session, and although they advanced to within 10 feet of the presiding officer, they could hardly make themselves heard. The few Senators present again began strolling about, stopping occasionally to admire a beautiful ladder of roses and lilies, which some appreciative friend had sent in to be placed upon Mr. Garland's desk. Finally, Mr. Garland asked Mr. Cockrell to relieve him and took a look for himself at his floral gift. A few minutes later, Mr. Hale, who had wandered in with a dozen or more Senators, asked the Senate to consider the report received early in the morning from the conferrees on the Naval Appropriation bill. To his consternation, the clerks reported that they could not find the report. The Maine Senator danced anxiously about the chamber, and clerks were hurried off in every direction to search for the missing papers.

Meanwhile, 10 o'clock had arrived, and the doors of the Capitol and Senate galleries were opened to such persons as had tickets of admission. A crowd of ladies came pouring in, with here and there a gentleman, and in two minutes half the gallery seats were filled with visitors, who at once began a lively chattering and buzzing, which was rarely interrupted during the rest of the session. Mr. Ingalls brought ex-Gov. Glick, of his State, into the chamber, and Secretary of the Interior Teller, who was to become a Senator in two hours, walked in and hunted up his successor in the Cabinet, Mr. Lamar. The two held a long and seemingly earnest conversation on one of the sofas reserved for the Supreme Court Judges, and were, for the time being, oblivious to all that was going on around them. The first ladies to appear in the specially reserved gallery were two members of Mr. Edmunds's family, who were soon followed by John Tyler, son of President Tyler, who acted as escort to three ladies. At 10:08 o'clock Mr. Hale ran in, waving the just discovered report on the Naval bill, and on his motion it was read and agreed to, amid such a hum of conversation that the clerk's voice could not be heard.

While this was being done visitors continued to arrive and the floor assumed a spirited appearance. Secretary of the Navy Chandler chatted with Mr. Hale, and Postmaster-General Frank Hatton went from group to group as if too nervous to keep still. Secretary of the Treasury McCulloch shook hands with numerous friends, and Commissioner of Agriculture Loring took advantage of his right to the floor to exhibit himself in a dozen different parts of the room in as many minutes. Gov. Ordway, of Dakota; First Controller Lawrence, the Justices of the District Supreme Court, and several ex-Senators were scattered about the floor, while ex-Gov. Smith, of Virginia, was shaking hands with all the Democrats he could find. While Senator Garland, who would be a Senator only a few hours longer, was holding an animated consultation with Mr. Beck, Senator-elect William M. Evarts walked into the chamber, leaning on the arm of Senator Morgan. Both Democrats and Republicans hastened to greet him, and it was some time before Mr. Miller could get at him to take him in charge. Mr. Evarts paid a brief visit to the cloak room and then hunted up Mr. Lapham, whose seat he was to take two hours later. During the rest of the session the two New-Yorkers sat beside each other, with their tall hats resting together on the same desk.

While Mr. Evarts was receiving his friends Mr. Conger, who had a good deal to say during the night and was impervious to fatigue, raised a laugh by asking unanimous consent that the River and Harbor bill be considered, read a third time, and passed. Mr. Platt stopped that little scheme by an objection, and then Mr. Conger pleaded that the bill might at least be taken up for consideration. Instead of doing this the Senate, on the last roll call of the Forty-eighth Congress, voted to lay the bill upon the table, and the Michigan Senator sat down with fire in his eyes.

It was now 10:50 o'clock, and all the galleries were filled to repletion except that reserved for the Presidential parties and the families of foreign Ministers. The first couple to take seats in the diplomatic gallery were Mrs. Hugo Fritsch, wife of the Austrian Vice-Consul at New-York, and her sister, Miss Gilbert. Just after they had arrived Mrs. Hendricks and three other ladies took seats on the Vice-President's bench, in the third row from the front of the gallery. Five minutes later Mr. Cleveland's family and friends appeared at the door of the reserved gallery. The party included 12 persons—Miss Cleveland and Mrs. Hoyt, sisters of the President; his brother, the Rev. W. N. Cleveland, and Mrs. Cleveland; Mr. Hastings, the President's nephew; Miss Hastings and Misses Nellie and Anna Yeomans, nieces of Mr. Cleveland, Mr. and Mrs. Bacon, of Toledo, and Col. and Mrs. Daniel Lamont. As they stepped into the gallery all eyes and scores of opera glasses were turned upon them. There were too many in the party to find seats in the single row which had been reserved for them, and the usher placed them both in that row and in the front bench set apart for Mr. Arthur's family. After Mr. and Mrs. Cleveland and Mr. and Mrs. Bacon had been seated in the second row with Mrs. Hoyt and Miss Cleveland and the President's nieces and Col. and Mrs. Lamont in front of them, it was decided to change the order, and those in the front row exchanged seats with those in the second. Nearly half an hour later Mr. and Mrs. McElroy, Mr. Arthur's son, and Mrs. John Davis reached the gallery to find only single seats on the side of the aisle vacant. After some consultation Mr. Cleveland's sisters and nieces proposed to take the side seats, and the offer was accepted, the Arthur party taking the second row from the front.

The Senators watched the throng of ladies and gentlemen in the galleries until 11 o'clock, when Mr. Beck ran down the centre aisle with a document which he handed to the Clerk, at the same time calling to Mr. Allison. The latter jumped up and presented the document as the report of the conferrees on the Sundry Civil Appropriation bill. It was read and agreed to without delay, and this cleared away the last danger of an extra session of Congress.

While this was being done the Diplomatic Gallery became so crowded that the aisle steps were occupied. Conspicuous in this aisle were Miss Tillie Frelinghuysen and Mr. Charles E. Miller, Mr. Arthur's intimate friend. The floor of the chamber had also received a large accession of visitors, among them being Surgeon-General Gunnel, of the Navy, the first person in full uniform who appeared on the floor; Civil Service Commissioners Eaton and Thoman, George Bancroft, the historian; Mr. Bissell, the President's law partner, and Mr. George H. Sharpe, ex-Chairman of the South American Commission. Senator-elect Payne was surrounded by friends, and Representative Payson was making sure of as good a seat as any Congressman was permitted to have.

At 11:30 o'clock the first applause of the day was heard, when Gen. Sheridan and Gen. Hancock walked in from the lobby in full dress uniform. Gen. Sheridan was as happy as usual, and Gen. Hancock's face fairly beamed. He was the picture of ruddy health, and looked much better than in the Winter of 1880-81. The applause which greeted his entrance woke up Senator Blair, who had chosen his last hour in the Senate to fall into a deep sleep.

### GEN. GRANT'S RETIREMENT.

Twenty-five minutes before the hour when the Congress was to expire the most dramatic event of the day occurred. A message was received from the House announcing that that body had passed the Senate bill authorizing the President to nominate one person to go on the retired list of the army with the rank and full pay of General of the Army. Mr. Ingalls asked that the bill be read. As this was done the spectators realized that this was the famous Edmunds bill for the retirement of Gen. Grant. Instantly a great shout arose from both the floor and the galleries, and then everybody cheered. At the first break in the applause Mr. Ingalls asked that by unanimous consent, the usual reference to a committee be waived and the bill passed at once. Mr. Garland, who was then in the chair, informed the Kansas Senator that the measure had already passed the Senate and there was nothing more to be done about it. Then followed an outburst of such enthusiastic cheering that all who heard it were thrilled. It was a spontaneous tribute to the career of Gen. U. S. Grant, and was proof of the admiration and love with which all classes of citizens regard the old hero, now struggling with disease at his home in New-York. Cheer followed cheer, until it seemed as if the throng could never tire of praising Gen. Grant. Five minutes later Mr. Edmunds took the chair and announced that the bill had been signed. Then there was another cheer, which the Vermont Senator made no effort to stop. When quiet had finally been restored Mr. Morrill asked for the appointment of the usual committee to inform the President that the Senate had finished its work and was ready to adjourn. This had just been decided upon when the diplomatic corps made its appearance at the central door resplendent in full court dress. The distinguished foreigners were headed by the Portuguese Minister, Dean of the corps, by virtue of having served the greatest number of years in Washington. They filed into seats on the left of the chamber, and all uncovered their heads except the representatives of Turkey and China.

It was then 11:45 o'clock, and the minutes were slipping away so fast that Capt. Bassett stood upon a chair and pushed the hands of the Senate clock back six minutes, while everybody laughed at the cheating of time.

At 11:58 by the corrected time the President's private secretary hurried into the room bearing President Arthur's last message to the Senate. It proved to be the nomination of Gen. Grant to be placed on the retired list in accordance with the bill, the passage of which had excited such hearty applause a few minutes before. The Clerk read the communication, which was as follows:

I.

*To the Hon. George F. Edmunds, President pro tem. of the United States Senate:*

The accompanying communication, although an executive message, may be read in open session.

CHESTER A. ARTHUR.

II.

*To the Senate of the United States:*

I nominate Ulysses S. Grant, formerly General commanding the armies of the United States, to be General on the retired list of the army with the full pay of such rank.

CHESTER A. ARTHUR.

EXECUTIVE MANSION, March 4, 1885.

The President pro tem. then announced that the nomination would be considered in open session. "The question is: Will the Senate advise and consent to this appointment? All Senators in favor will say aye. [A storm of ayes.] All opposed no. [Dead silence.] The ayes have it unanimously.

The applause which followed was tremendous, and everybody agreed that Mr. Arthur's last official act was one of the most gratifying things that could have been done.

### SWEARING IN THE VICE-PRESIDENT.

Messrs. Morrill and Harris then reported that the President had no further communication to make to the Senate. A moment later, the Justices of the Supreme Court, wearing their silken robes, and led by Chief-Justice Waite, advanced to the easy chairs and sofas in front and to the right of the presiding officer's desk. They had barely time to take their seats when Mr. Arthur, with Senators Sherman and Ransom on either side, was announced; every person in the chamber rose and remained standing until the President had taken one of the big arm chairs in the space in front of the Vice-President's desk, in which he sat facing the audience. Mr. Arthur was received with a round of applause. Before it had ceased Mr. Hendricks stepped quietly in from the lobby and took a chair at the right of Mr. Edmunds, and Mr. Arthur's Cabinet officers filed in from the same lobby and were seated on the left of the President. At 10:52 by the Senate clock Messrs. Sherman and Ransom again appeared at the central door, acting as an escort to Mr. Cleveland. The President-elect held his hat in his hand, and as he crossed the threshold the entire audience rose and cheered. Bowing slightly, Mr. Cleveland walked firmly down the aisle, while the throngs continued to cheer as if trying to raise the roof. When the applause was subsiding some ardent Democrat in the gallery called for three more cheers for Grover Cleveland, and they were given despite Mr. Edmunds's pounding for quiet. The Vermont Senator angrily remarked that unless order was restored the galleries would be cleared, while Mr. Cleveland smiled and chatted with Mr. Arthur, by whose side he had taken a seat.

The moment silence had been secured Mr. Edmunds asked Mr. Hendricks if he was ready to take the oath of office as Vice-President. "I am," replied the Indiana Statesman, as he rose from his chair. With uplifted hand he listened to the reading of the oath and at 11:54 a pen was handed to him and he signed the oath he had just taken. He held the pen in an awkward way, between the first and second fingers of his right hand and wrote his name with great deliberation. After this act the Vice-President returned to his seat and Mr. Edmunds spread a few pages of manuscript before him and read a two-minute farewell address as President pro tem. of the Senate. It was as follows:

SENATORS: We now close another epoch in the course of the Republic under the Constitution. The brief period of our national existence has, by the exertion of the co-ordinated forces of national and State systems, brought the experiment of free social and political government to an established and secure triumph. I think I may safely say for us all that we believe that the long years to come in the future of the Republic will more and more increase the peace, liberty, order, and security of all the people of our country. But perhaps it may not be improper for me to say that, in view of our recent experience, it may be doubted whether Congress can congratulate itself on being the best example of a legislative body, conducting its business with that deliberate and timely diligence which is the inseparable handmaid of wisdom and justice, as well in the making as in the administration of laws. It is, I think, an evil of large and growing proportion that measures of the greatest importance, requiring much time for proper examination and discussion in detail, are brought to our consideration so late that it is not possible to deal with them intelligently, and which we are tempted—overtempted, I fear—to enact into laws, in the hope that fortune, rather than time, study, and reflection, will take care that the public suffer no detriment. The Chair has heard with deep sensibility of the resolution you have kindly adopted concerning the administration of his duties, and he begs to express sincerely his gratitude for it. If, in the course of the execution of his duties, he has (as he sometimes may have done) wounded the feelings of any Senator or officer of the Senate, he can truly say that he has not intentionally given offense to any one, and in closing the session of the Senate he assures every Senator, whether retiring or continuing in public duty, that he wishes for him every friendly good wish, and hopes that he may long enjoy all the happiness that can be realized by citizen or Senator. He now declares the Senate adjourned without day.

Mr. Hendricks at once stepped forward, and, as he did so Chaplain Huntley invoked Divine aid and guidance for the incoming and outgoing Presidents and all who have anything to do with the administration of the Government. The prayer was long, but all on the floor, including Mr. Arthur and Mr. Cleveland, remained standing until its close. While Dr. Huntley was praying the members of the House of Representatives, following Speaker Carlisle, reached the chamber, expecting to listen to the exercises. They were, of course, too late, and only such Congressmen as had wisely come in earlier saw the Vice-President sworn in. When the prayer was over Mr. Hendricks rapped for order and read a one-minute speech from notes written on chocolate colored paper. He was agitated more than he could conceal, but at the close he recovered his voice and declared the Senate in session by virtue of a proclamation issued by the President. Mr. Hendricks's speech was as follows:

SENATORS: In entering upon the duties of the office to which I have been chosen may I express the hope and the desire that our relations may at all times be harmonious and agreeable? I beg to assure you that in the discharge of my duties I will seek to observe the most absolute impartiality. It is some years since I was connected with the business of the Senate, and it may be that I shall find myself less familiar with its rules, usages, and modes of proceeding than formerly; and therefore I may have occasion to lean upon your indulgence and to ask your support. The Senate is now in session by virtue of the proclamation of the President of the United States, which the Secretary will read.

Mr. Arthur's call for an extra session of the Senate was read by the Clerk, and then Mr. Hendricks called upon the newly elected Senators present to step forward and take the oath of office. Messrs. Allison, Blackburn, of Kentucky; Brown, and Call comprised the first group sworn in by the Vice-President. The second included Messrs. Cameron, of Pennsylvania; Eustis, of Louisiana; Evarts, of New-York, and Hampton. In the third group were Messrs. Ingalls, Jones, of Arkansas; Jones, of Nevada, and Morrill. The fourth group contained Messrs. Payne, of Ohio; Platt, Pugh, and Spooner, of Wisconsin, the last of whom resembles Mr. Gorman in a marked degree. In the last lot were Messrs. Stanford, of California; Teller, of Colorado; Vance, Vest, Voorhees, and Wilson, of Iowa. The only new Senator absent was Mr. Wilson, of Maryland. After each of these had shaken hands with Mr. Hendricks the order of proceedings at the inauguration of Mr. Cleveland was read by Secretary McCook, and the procession was at once formed and proceeded to the platform on the east front of the Capitol.

### THE SCENE ON THE EAST FRONT.

Before the proceedings in the Senate Chamber were over there was a rush somewhat precipitate and eager from the galleries. It was checked in the Senate lobby, and none but the representatives of the press, provided with blue tickets, were allowed to pass the temporary gate that barred the way to the rotunda. It was nearly 12:30 when the procession of Senate officers, Justices, diplomatists, and Representatives filed out of the Senate Chamber and passed along the corridor. It was only a short march to the east front door. As President-elect Cleveland and President Arthur passed between the pillars that support the great pediment they saw a magnificent sight. Beyond a new and unpainted platform, about an acre square, and far out on the edge of the broad plaza, extended an unbroken sea of faces. An audience of thousands—some say 30,000, others 40,000, and many insist that it was more than 50,000—awaited the appearance of the future Chief Magistrate. It had been there for more than an hour, growing in dimensions until it filled up the area bounded by the flower beds on the east, while it reached north and south beyond the halls of the House and the Senate. The platform upon which the ceremony of inauguration took place was about 30 feet above this audience. Out of the sea of heads the white statue of Washington, seated and without his clothes, rose against a low-toned back ground. Determined boys and men clung about Washington's neck and arms to get a view of the platform. All the windows of all the houses around the square, although the houses are far away from the Capitol, were filled with spectators. Every window of the Capitol that commanded a view of the spot where Mr. Cleveland was to be sworn in was filled with sightseers, none of whom could bear a word that might be spoken. Boys and men clung about the statues that stand at each side of the great central stairway, entwining their arms about Columbus and the Indian who is his opposite in order to pull themselves up to a commanding position. Up on the pediment, upon the roof, out on the lofty courses of the dome, were black lines and groups of men. The crowd on the plaza, controlled by a mere handful of policemen, was packed closely together: black and white, rich and poor, huddled together as closely as sardines in a box. Now and then when pressure from the side or rear moved a part of the throng the whole body moved like an ocean. Over all the sun shone clear and bright, and in the distance its rays were reflected by the arms of the troops that stood in line on East Capitol-street, on Pennsylvania-avenue east, along the border of the Capitol grounds, and in every other direction as far as the eye could reach. Tall and conspicuous on the edges of the immense throng before the Capitol rose two stands, upon which enterprising photographers were preparing their cameras to make a picture of the President just as he took the oath of office.

The crowd had just been cheering and applauding some venturesome ladies who had gone to the front and looked down upon the area of gay drapery of flags that hid its timbers, when Mr. Cleveland and President Arthur appeared. In an instant a cheer began. It was strong at first as it echoed from the walls of the Capitol, and in an instant it swelled into a chorus that was like the roaring of Niagara. It was resonant, universal, deafening, and it continued while Mr. Cleveland walked by President Arthur's side down to the projecting platform at the front, when it swelled again. Mr. Cleveland was as calm and self-possessed as if he had been accustomed to such sights. He was not a bit disturbed, and on his way to the front nodded to ex-Commissioner Hubert O. Thompson, who had made his way to the front through a crush that threatened dire disaster to his robust figure. While the crowd was still cheering, and after Mr. Cleveland had acknowledged its greeting to him by bowing, he took his seat in the right-hand corner upon a red morocco covered chair, President Arthur taking another chair by his side. Opposite to him sat Chief-Justice Waite. At Mr. Arthur's side the historian Bancroft, bright and hale for all his venerable gray hairs and beard, took a place, after he had shaken hands with the President and the President so soon to be.

Down the stairs from the Capitol came the diplomatic corps, gay in their scarlet, gold, blue, and white, the steel-blue dress of the military attachés of the German Legation scarcely less conspicuous than the dark blue and gold on the coat of the Russian Minister, De Struve, or the picturesque turbans of the Chinese Ambassadors. They took seats just behind the Justices of the Supreme Court, who sat along the front, while the diplomats were arranged in a hedge-shaped group, reaching to the aisle. The Senators sat at the right, with the press correspondents uncomfortably close to and somewhat dangerously mixed up with them. The Representatives in Congress, including many who had voted that they did not want to see Mr. Cleveland inagurated, filled up the seats at the rear end on the side. The steps further back, from which a fine view of the entire grand crowd on and off the platform could be had, were densely thronged.

Mr. Cleveland chatted with President Arthur, smiling as he talked, and occasionally turning to look over the expectant throng before him, and even upon the awkward colored policeman who paced up and down in the cleared space before the staging. Gen. Sheridan, ruddy and vigorous, and gorgeous in blue and gold, sat only a few feet away, and at his shoulder were the handsome soldierly face and figure of Gen. Hancock. Gen. Terry, another brave soldier, tall, strong, and keen-eyed, his beard grayer than it was 20 years ago, sat at Gen. Hancock's right.

### THE INAUGURAL ADDRESS.

There was no music, no preliminary flourish to introduce Mr. Cleveland to the vast throng before him. It knew him already. It had seen a man entirely at his ease under very trying circumstances, had instinctively concluded that he would support himself with dignity and credit, and relations of confidence were established immediately. Rising from his chair and patting his head lightly with his hand where the breeze was scattering the thin locks upon it, he faced the multitude, and in a strong, clear, penetrating voice that was heard far out in the listening crowd he delivered his inaugural address. It was as follows:

FELLOW-CITIZENS: In the presence of this vast assemblage of my countrymen, I am about to supplement and seal by the oath which I shall take the manifestation of the will of a great and free people. In the exercise of their power and right of self-government they have committed to one of their fellow-citizens a supreme and sacred trust, and he here consecrates himself to their service. This impressive ceremony adds little to the solemn sense of responsibility with which I contemplate the duty I owe to all the people of the land; nothing can relieve me from anxiety lest by any act of mine their interests may suffer, and nothing is needed to strengthen my resolution to engage every faculty and effort in the promotion of their welfare.

Amid the din of party strife the people's choice was made; but its attendant circumstances have demonstrated anew the strength and safety of a Government by the people. In each succeeding year it more clearly appears that our democratic principle needs no apology, and that in its fearless and faithful application is to be found the surest guarantee of good government. But the best results in the operation of a Government wherein every citizen has a share largely depend upon a proper limitation of purely partisan zeal and effort and a correct appreciation of the time when the heat of the partisan should be merged in the patriotism of the citizen.

To-day the executive branch of the Government is transferred to new keeping. But this is still the Government of all the people, and it should be none the less an object of affectionate solicitude. At this hour the animosities of political strife, the bitterness of partisan defeat, and the exultation of partisan triumph should be supplanted by an ungrudging acquiescence in the popular will, and a sober, conscientious concern for the general weal. Moreover, if from this hour we cheerfully and honestly abandon all sectional prejudice and distrust and determine, with manly confidence in one another, to work out harmoniously the achievements of our national destiny, we shall deserve to realize all the benefits which our happy form of government can bestow.

On this auspicious occasion we may well renew the pledge of our devotion to the Constitution, which, launched by the founders of the Republic and consecrated by their prayers and patriotic devotion, has for almost a century borne the hopes and the aspirations of a great people through prosperity and peace and through the shock of foreign conflicts and the perils of domestic strife and vicissitudes. By the Father of his Country our Constitution was commended for adoption as "the result of a spirit of amity and mutual concession." In that same spirit it should be administered, in order to promote the lasting welfare of the country and to secure the full measure of its priceless benefits to us and to those who will succeed to the blessings of our national life. The large variety of diverse and competing interests subject to Federal control, persistently seeking the recognition of their claims, need give us no fear that the greatest good to the greatest number will fail to be accomplished if, in the halls of national legislation, that spirit of amity and mutual concession should prevail in which the Constitution had its birth. If this involves the surrender or postponement of private interests and the abandonment of local advantages, compensation will be found in the assurance that thus the common interest is subserved and the general welfare advanced.

In the discharge of my official duty I shall endeavor to be guided by a just and unstrained construction of the Constitution, a careful observance of the distinction between the powers granted to the Federal Government and those reserved to the States or to the people, and by a cautious appreciation of those functions which, by the Constitution and laws, have been especially assigned to the executive branch of the Government. But he who takes the oath to-day to preserve, protect, and defend the Constitution of the United States only assumes the solemn obligation which every patriotic citizen, on the farm, in the workshop, in the busy marts of trade, and everywhere, should share with him. The Constitution which prescribes his oath, my countrymen, is yours; the Government you have chosen him to administer for a time is yours; the suffrage which executes the will of freemen is yours; the laws and the entire scheme of our civil rule, from the town meeting to the State Capitol and the National Capitol, are yours. Your every voter, as surely as your Chief Magistrate, under the same high sanction, though in a different sphere, exercises a public trust. Nor is this all. Every citizen owes to the country a vigilant watch and close scrutiny of the public servants and a fair and reasonable estimate of their fidelity and usefulness. This is the people's will impressed upon the whole framework of our civil polity—municipal, State, and Federal—and this is the price of our liberty and the inspiration of our faith in the Republic.

It is the duty of those serving the people in public places to closely limit public expenditures to the actual needs of the Government economically administered, because this bounds the right of the Government to exact tribute from the earnings of labor or the property of the citizen, and because public extravagance begets extravagance among the people. We should never be ashamed of the simplicity and prudential economies which are best suited to the operation of a republican form of government and most compatible with the mission of the American people. Those who are selected for a limited time to manage public affairs are still of the people, and may do much by their example to encourage, consistently with the dignity of their official functions, that plain way of life which among their fellow-citizens aids integrity and promotes thrift and prosperity.

The genius of our institutions, the needs of our people in their home life, and the attention which is demanded for the settlement and development of the resources of our vast territory dictate the scrupulous avoidance of any departure from that foreign policy commended by the history, the traditions, and the prosperity of our Republic. It is the policy of independence, favored by our position and defended by our known love of justice and by our power. It is the policy of peace suitable to our interests. It is the policy of neutrality, rejecting any share in foreign broils and ambitions upon other continents and repelling their intrusion here. It is the policy of Monroe and of Washington and Jefferson—"Peace, commerce, and honest friendship with all nations, entangling alliances with none."

A due regard for the interests and prosperity of all the people demands that our finances shall be established upon such a sound and sensible basis as shall secure the safety and confidence of business interests and make the wage of labor sure and steady; and that our system of revenue shall be so adjusted as to relieve the people from unnecessary taxation, having a due regard to the interests of capital invested and workingmen employed in American industries, and preventing the accumulation of a surplus in the Treasury to tempt extravagance and waste. Care for the property of the Nation and for the needs of future settlers requires that the public domain should be protected from purloining schemes and unlawful occupation. The conscience of the people demands that the Indians within our boundaries shall be fairly and honestly treated as wards of the Government, and their education and civilization promoted with a view to their ultimate citizenship, and that polygamy in the Territories, destructive of the family relation and offensive to the moral sense of the civilized world, shall be repressed. The laws should be rigidly enforced which prohibit the immigration of a servile class to compete with American labor, with no intention of acquiring citizenship and bringing with them and retaining habits and customs repugnant to our civilization.

The people demand reform in the administration of the Government and the application of business principles to public affairs. As a means to this end civil service reform should be in good faith enforced. Our citizens have the right to protection from the incompetency of public employes who hold their places solely as the reward of partisan service and from the corrupting influence of those who promise and the vicious methods of those who expect such rewards. And those who worthily seek public employment have the right to insist that merit and competency shall be recognized instead of party subserviency or the surrender of honest political belief.

In the administration of a Government pledged to do equal and exact justice to all men there should be no pretext for anxiety touching the protection of the freedmen in their rights, or their security in the enjoyment of their privileges under the Constitution and its amendments. All discussion as to their fitness for the place accorded to them as American citizens is idle and unprofitable except as it suggests the necessity for their improvement. The fact that they are citizens entitles them to all the rights due to that relation and charges them with all its duties, obligations, and responsibilities.

These topics and the constant and ever-varying wants of an active and enterprising population may well receive the attention and the patriotic endeavor of all who make and execute the Federal law. Our duties are practical, and call for industrious application, an intelligent perception of the claims of public office, and, above all, a firm determination, by united action, to secure to all the people of the land the full benefits of the best form of government ever vouchsafed to man. And let us not trust to human effort alone, but humbly acknowledging the power and goodness of Almighty God, who presides over the destiny of nations, and who has

# The New-York Times.

VOL. XXXVII....NO. 11,434. NEW-YORK, MONDAY, APRIL 23, 1888. PRICE TWO CENTS.


## THE KAISER'S SUFFERINGS

### *HIS CONDITION SOMEWHAT IMPROVED.*

LESS FEVER AND A BETTER APPETITE—CHARLOTTENBURG CROWDED—QUEEN VICTORIA STARTS FOR BERLIN.

BERLIN, April 22.—The following bulletin was issued at 9 o'clock this morning: "The Emperor passed a more quiet night. His fever has moderated and his general condition is better."

The Emperor was disturbed by coughing until 3 A. M., but then slept well until 6 o'clock. His temperature was never above 102°. During the day it was 101°.

The *North German Gazette* says: "During the course of yesterday the Emperor's fever slightly abated. His appetite improved, and he expressed himself as feeling better. The discharge of pus was lessened and he suffered no pain. He swallowed freely and his respiration was unimpeded."

A special edition of the *North German Gazette* published at 1:35 this afternoon says: "Although the Emperor's rest last night was frequently broken by fits of coughing and expectoration, he enjoyed intervals of quiet sleep, which, taken in conjunction with a slight abatement of his fever, had a strengthening effect and put him in better spirits. Despite his small appetite he took this morning a fair quantity of nourishment, chiefly milk."

The bulletin issued at 9 P. M. said that the Emperor had passed a pretty good day, with less fever than on former days, but his temperature began to rise toward evening.

The doctors attending the Emperor declare that the published descriptions of the Emperor's sufferings, with the exception of the difficulty in breathing, are exaggerated. He suffers from no local pain whatever. To-day has been one of the best days he has had since the present illness began. Absolute rest is still imperative. It is impossible to predict whether or not the improvement will continue.

Charlottenburg was full of visitors to-day. An endless stream of carriages moved to and fro between Berlin and Charlottenburg all day.

On Saturday Prince Bismarck reported to the Emperor the arrangements made for the reception of Queen Victoria, and also discussed the question as to who shall represent the Emperor during the Queen's stay.

A large number of financiers and artists have been ennobled in commemoration of the Emperor's accession. Formerly the honor was conferred only upon officers and high Government officials. Among those honored are Bankers Schwabach and Hainauer.

Saturday was an anxious day in Berlin until evening, when better accounts of the Emperor's condition were made public. In the morning there were widespread rumors that the end was only a question of hours. The bulletins to-day inspired renewed hope that there is still a chance for the Emperor to get over the attack, but nobody is sanguine. The Emperor showed a keen interest in to-day's celebration of his daughter Margaret's birthday. He congratulated the Princess in writing.

The pus now discharging from the Emperor's throat is thicker than formerly. This is probably a symptom that the abscess is beginning to heal. During the day the patient had a refreshing sleep. The Grand Duchess of Baden asked him if he suffered any pain. He replied: "I only feel uncomfortable occasionally."

FLORENCE, April 22.—Queen Victoria, with Prince and Princess Henry of Battenberg, attended divine service this morning in the Villa Palmieri, the Dean of Windsor officiating. About the close of the service telegrams were received from Berlin giving better news of Emperor Frederick. At Innsbruck preparations are being made for the meeting of Emperor Francis Joseph and the Queen. The town is gayly decorated in honor of the occasion. The Austrian Court Chamberlain, Prince von Hohenlohe-Schillingsfurst, and the British Ambassador to Austria, Sir A. Paget, have arrived at Innsbruck, and will proceed to Franzensfeste to meet the Queen.

Queen Victoria, Princess Beatrice, and Prince Henry of Battenberg started for Berlin to-day. The streets were packed with enthusiastic crowds. The Queen informed the authorities, who bade her farewell at the station, that she had received another good report on the condition of Emperor Frederick.

### THE BOULANGIST AGITATION.

PARIS, April 22.—Premier Floquet was waited upon to-day by a deputation of students who came to complain of the action of the police during the political disturbance held on Friday last. The Premier informed them that he would repress all disorders with a firm hand, and at the same time would see that the police did not exceed their duties. He subsequently visited the principal police stations and assured the officers of the Government's support in the exercise of their duties. He reminded them that they owed fidelity to the Republic, and ought to be vigilant and firm in order to insure the security of the public and respect for the law.

*La Cocarde* says the nomination of Gen. Boulanger for the Chamber of Deputies in the Department of Isère is contrary to the wish of the General and his committee.

M. Ferroul, a Radical, was to-day elected member of the Chamber of Deputies for Carcassonne.

### LEAGUE MEETINGS IN IRELAND.

DUBLIN, April 22.—Mr. O'Brien spoke at Fermoy to-day. He was not molested. He declared that the meeting would have been held if it had been proclaimed.

Mr. John Dillon, member of Parliament, addressed a meeting at Kellystown to-day under the ausices of the National League. The police did not interfere with the meeting.

A crowd of 500 persons rescued a prisoner at Abbeyfeale to-day and stoned the police. Fifteen officers were injured, four of them severely. The police were subsequently reinforced and arrested five of their assailants.

### CURRENT FOREIGN TOPICS.

ROME, April 22.—The Pope to-day received the King of Sweden. The audience lasted for an hour.

LONDON, April 22.—Mrs. Birdie Grover, a rifle-woman in Col. Cody's company, had a disagreement with the Colonel last week and sailed from Liverpool for New-York on Saturday on the steamer Arizona. This morning, having relented, she landed at Queenstown with the intention of returning. There the police and customs officers, suspecting her to be a Fenian disguised as a woman, searched her baggage and seized three rifles. Mrs. Grover, who is indignant at the manner in which she has been treated, is trying to regain her rifles.

### *RATES BY THE "SOO" ROUTE.*

CHICAGO, April 22.—The time is now near at hand when the Minneapolis, Sault Ste. Marie and Atlantic Railroad will be open for passenger business, and the question of what the rates are to be is becoming an interesting one. The Canadian Pacific will make the west-bound rates from Canada points, and is already negotiating with lines running west from St. Paul for the purpose of ascertaining which will make the best rates for it to interior points. On these negotiations will also depend the extent of territory the line can enter on its west-bound business. The distance from St. Paul to Boston is practically the same by the "Soo" as via Chicago, the difference being only four miles, so that in that respect the new route affords no advantage. If the rate to St. Paul from New-England and Canadian points is made the same as that via Chicago the latter route will still hold the business in the territory west and southwest of St. Paul, to the exclusion of the "Soo" interests.

As passenger rates are at present adjusted the fare from Chicago to Kasota, on the Omaha Road, is less than from Chicago to St. Paul, and to any point on the Western Division of the Omaha the rate from Boston would be cheaper via Chicago. The same applies to points on all the roads running out of St. Paul westward, with the exception of the Northern Pacific, the Manitoba, and the Minneapolis and Pacific. It may be that the Canadian Pacific will aim for Omaha and insist on making the same rate from the East to that city via St. Paul as the one via Chicago.

### *WRECK OF A BRILLIANT MAN.*

ST. LOUIS, April 22.—The vehicle popularly known as the "Black Maria," which conveys prisoners from the public court to the Court House, contained an individual to-day whose fall is the talk of the town. His name is Jefferson D. Storts. Four years ago he was Prosecuting Attorney of Shannon County, and at that time was elected to the Legislature. He was only 28 years old, was a brilliant speaker, and was soon recognized as a leading member of the House. He fell into the hands of lobbyists, became dissipated, came here to practice law, and for a time had some success. Then his dissipation increased, clients left him, and to-day he went down to the workhouse, and is now wearing stripes.

### *TO DEFEAT MR. OUTHWAITE.*

THE TALLY-SHEET GANG COMBINING AGAINST HIM.

COLUMBUS, Ohio, April 22.—A very dirty fight is being made by the boodle crowd against the renomination of Congressman Outhwaite of this district. While Mr. Outhwaite is rather too much of a free trader to suit his constituents, he is a very able gentleman and well thought of by the better class of Democrats. The fact that he had no word of sympathy for the defendants in the tally-sheet trial has been quite sufficient to array the gang of leaders against him solidly, and no effort will be spared to defeat his renomination. Mr. J. C. L. Pugh, a young attorney, is the leading candidate against Outhwaite, and Pugh, to all appearances, stands solid with the gang, having gone on the bond of the notorious Fred Stenloe. Yesterday afternoon the County Committee held a meeting, and it had been expected that some steps would be taken in the direction of the choice of county candidates, but the subject was not mentioned, the entire attention of the convention being given to the arrangements for the Congressional and State Conventions. The question was sprung as to whether the primaries to choose delegates should be held under the new law, which extends to such elections, when the request is made for the protection of the Election Boards. Ex-Probate Judge J. M. Pugh, the father of John C. L. Pugh, the opponent of Mr. Outhwaite in the contest for the Congressional nomination, was present and opposed this plan urgently. After considerable debate the Pugh faction won, and it was decided not to call on the Election Board for help.

The incident is significant, as it showed the strength of Pugh's friends in the committee. The methods adopted by young Pugh are a surprise to his friends, and are very objectionable. In addition to identifying himself with the tally-sheet defendants he took a mortgage on a saloon in order to allow the proprietor to open up business, and in other ways has made himself solid with the Democratic strikers and heelers. Should he beat Outhwaite he would likely be repudiated by the people, as were the candidates on the tally-sheet ticket at the election three weeks ago. Hocking County yesterday instructed its delegates to support Outhwaite.

### *THE CHICAGO PLAYHOUSES.*

CHICAGO, April 22.—Another quiet, but remunerative, week has been added to the season's record at the Chicago playhouses. A feature of the week has been the public liking for music in one shape or another, for, besides both the opera companies which have been in town, concerts have been plenty, and have been successful enough to warrant a good many more before the close of the season. Financially, however, French opera has not proved a pecuniary success in Chicago. The company got away for the East early this morning, leaving part of its baggage with various hotel keepers. At different times during the week leading members of the company succeeded in securing part of the arrears due them by declining at the eleventh hour to sing in rôles for which they had been cast until some cold cash had been put into their hands. The money was got together by collections and loans, and so the second week's engagement was ended and the singers started for Washington in strong hopes of finding brighter fortunes there. Hard luck, the theatrical people say, has followed the company since it began its American experiment.

Outside of the revival of public interest in operatic matters the gossip of the last seven days has been enjoying another turn at the new theatre possibilities, with this time a novelty in the shape of a new place of amusement which is not only contracted for, but well under way toward completion. While there has been plenty of talk about a new south-side theatre, a west-side playhouse has been going up at the corner of Madison and Throop streets. It is to be known as the Waverly Theatre and it occupies the site of the old "Garden Theatre." Burr Robbins, who heretofore has confined his efforts to educate the public taste managing a circus, has the new enterprise in hand, and says he means to make it a "go." The opening of the new theatre is set for some time in May, either the 12th or the 19th, when the Dunlop light opera company will introduce the Waverly to the public. Mr. Robbins means to run his theatre during the hot weather. He says he is through with elephants and lions, and means to confine his future efforts to his playhouse.

The Chicago Press Club is to have a matinée at the Chicago Opera House on Thursday, when many professionals have volunteered to appear, including De Wolf Hopper, Digby Bell, Marion Manola, Annie Myers, and Hubert Wilke of the McCaull opera company; Mlle. Brambrilla, a première danseuse; Eddie Foy, Mabel Bert of the McKee Rankin company, and others. Kate Claxton and her company will give the last act of "The World Against Her," and Mr. and Mrs. George S. Knight with their company will appear in the second act of "Baron Rudolph."

The McCaull company has one more week at the Chicago Opera House, where it has been drawing crowded houses regularly. Last week the new version of "Boccaccio" was the attraction, and the coming week will be devoted to an old favorite, "Falka."

At McVicker's Theatre the racing melodrama, "A Run of Luck," has finished its four weeks' stay. It will be followed by "The Jilt," given by Dion Boucicault and his company, whose engagement is for two weeks.

Arthur Rehan's comedy company has played "Nancy & Co." and "Love in Harness" to good houses at the Grand Opera House. Mr. and Mrs. George S. Knight follow in the old "Baron Rudolph," rewritten and rechristened as "Rudolph."

The French Opera Company, which has given grand and light opera at the Columbia Theatre, has departed, and opera will give place to Kate Claxton, who will play in "The World Against Her," with the support of Charles A. Stevenson and her company.

Evans and Hoey have drawn good houses to the Haymarket Theatre to see "A Parlor Match." For the next seven days the attraction at this playhouse will be McKee Rankin and his support in "The Danites."

### *SENATOR CULLOM NOT A CANDIDATE.*

WASHINGTON, April 22.—Senator Cullom, whose attention was yesterday called to the frequent mention of his name in connection with the Presidential nomination, has authorized a reporter to say that he is not a candidate for the honor. "I feel," he said, "very hopeful of the success of the Republican Party in the coming campaign, but the fact cannot be disguised that the Democracy will enter upon the contest certain of the electoral votes of the solid South, no matter what may be the vote actually cast in that section, and that the whole power of the pretended 'reform' Administration will be exerted in the doubtful Northern States to secure the perpetuation of Democratic rule. I believe that the success of the Republican Party in the coming campaign is of vital importance to the party, and that the logic of the situation demands that personal ambition and personal preferences shall be subordinated absolutely to the success of Republican principles. It is the time above all others when the nominee should be the choice of the whole party as nearly as possible. So far as I am personally concerned, I am not a candidate for the Presidency, and have told my friends at home that I desire that Illinois shall send a delegation to the Chicago Convention prepared to support the most available candidate that can be found, the one who shall seem to be the most acceptable to the party, whoever he may be. If in the deliberations of the convention it should be thought that Illinois might again, as she has twice in her history, furnish a candidate who, all things considered, would best promote the success of the party, he should and would receive the loyal and hearty support of the delegation." In conclusion, the Senator said that what he desired most of all was the selection of the strongest possible candidate, and an aggressive, vigorous campaign. Under such circumstances he would feel confident of the triumph of Republican principles.

### *AFTER LITTLE ROCK'S TRAFFIC.*

CHICAGO, April 22.—There will be an important meeting of representatives of Southern roads in St. Louis to-morrow, when the Missouri Pacific, St. Louis and San Francisco, St. Louis, Arkansas and Texas, Memphis and Little Rock, and Kansas City, Fort Scott and Gulf will try to reorganize the Arkansas Traffic Association. There are now five practically parallel roads in the St. Louis-Texas trade, and, although so far they have all managed to do very well, trouble is looked upon as pretty certain to come sooner or later. As matters now stand, Little Rock is an open field, and all the roads are working hard for its business. To regulate matters the attempt will be made to revive the old association.

### *THE NORTHERN LIGHTS IN VIEW.*

KINGSTON, N. Y., April 22.—A brilliant display of northern lights was visible in localities in the Catskill Mountains this evening. This and previous auroras, with the fact that electric storms accompanied by thunder have occurred this Spring, is regarded as a sign by the wiseacres that the Summer of 1888 will be a cool one.

## AT THE NATIONAL CAPITAL

### *SHERMAN'S FRIENDS MAKING LARGE CLAIMS.*

BUT THEY DISTRUST FORAKER AND FEAR BLAINE—DURATION OF THE TARIFF DEBATE—ARMY CHANGES.

WASHINGTON, April 22.—The Sherman managers have started out with the announcement, just published in a dispatch that has reached Washington by way of Chicago, that Sherman's "approximate" vote in the National Convention will be 312. Upon what information this confident prediction is made is not learned here by the friends of Allison, Hawley, and Hiscock, to say nothing of the men who prefer Blaine, and they include nearly all of those who favor any of the others. The boldness and largeness of the claim, as well as the source from which it emanates, suggest to some of the politicians here that Sherman's interests are to be looked after and his canvass made for the newspapers, by some one who did the same work in behalf of Gen. Arthur when he was a candidate for renomination. The figures made up in Washington, however, for Gen. Arthur were excessively large, although they were based upon hopes that were better grounded than any present hope for Sherman. The Federal patronage was in the hands of the man who sought renomination, and a good deal of it constrained its holders to loyal support of the Administration that made it possible for the delegates to get to Chicago. Now there is no such constraint upon Southern Republicans who hope to get to Chicago as delegates. The only delegates of whom Sherman can be reasonably sure on the first ballot are the 46 from Ohio. A break for Blaine at an early stage of the proceedings would carry away two-thirds of the Ohio delegates at once. Sherman may have some delegates from Mississippi, North Carolina, Georgia, and Alabama, but not all of them together would give him 300 votes. Gen. Grosvenor of Ohio calculates that Sherman will stand in the convention with 300 votes. The Sherman men undoubtedly base their hope of a large vote upon the expectation that they will be able to control a large share of the New-York delegation. None of them at the Ohio Convention expressed any hope of obtaining votes from Connecticut, Massachusetts, or any of the other Eastern States. That they are fearful that Sherman will not succeed was indicated by some of the remarks of Sherman's friends. They thoroughly distrust Gov. Foraker, and they are aware that time must be taken by the forelock if his plans are to be successfully headed off. It is not at all unlikely that, if the Foraker men, when the assurrance that Blaine will not be a candidate, attempt to "break" the convention for Foraker for President, the Ohio delegation will divide, a part going to Foraker and the rest to William McKinley. The Foraker men are so thoroughly wrapped up in the Foraker idea that they are not able to see that the enthusiasm for him is strictly local, and that outside of the State he is regarded by Republicans as about as cheap a man as D. B. Hill is to the Democrats outside of New-York. Major McKinley, on the contrary, is a man of national reputation, one of the admitted leaders in the House, and a gentleman of attractive personal qualities. He is quite as brave as Foraker, but he does not go about Washington "with a chip on his shoulder," asking the President to knock it off. The proposition of McKinley as a candidate in opposition to Foraker would not only prove an embarrassing move to the "boys" who are meditating a dash for "Little Breeches," but it would bring on an extremely interesting fight, in which Foraker could scarcely expect to be a victor.

To-morrow morning the Democratic and Republican members of the Ways and Means Committee will try to reach some sort of a mutual understanding as to the time to be given to general debate on the Tariff bill, which is to be resumed on Tuesday. To-morrow evening the Democratic committeemen will report the result of the conference to a caucus of the whole party. While members of both parties hope that a satisfactory agreement will be made, not much surprise will be felt if the conference fails to accomplish its object. Democrats are naturally very anxious so to limit the tariff debate that a vote upon the bill may be taken before the 5th of June, when the National Convention will meet at St. Louis. This idea is not at all to the liking of Republicans, and their demands for time in which to present their objections to the tariff bill are likely to be based on the notion of staving off the final vote until a later date. Under the circumstances it will not be easy to devise a compromise to which all will agree. The majority members of the Ways and Means Committee declare that from ten days to two weeks should be ample time for both parties to define their positions in general debate, leaving an entire month for consideration of the bill in detail under the rule limiting speeches to five minutes each. The Republican committeemen assert that at least 10 days should be allowed for the general presentation of their side of the case, and they would be glad to see the same or even a much longer time allowed to the Democratic side. Both parties agree that a month is not too much time to allow for consideration of the measure item by item, and the contest will be over the length of general debate. The Democrats need only to stand together to enforce their views, and they declare with emphasis that the Tariff bill will be out of the way, so far as the House is concerned, before the St. Louis Convention is called to order.

The House Military Committee has received a number of petitions from army officers asking an amendment to the mileage law. Most of the petitioners favor a return to the law granting 4 cents per mile for incidental expenses and the payment for transportation exclusive of sleeping or parlor car accommodations. The objection to the present method of providing for traveling expenses is based on the delay experienced in securing transportation through the Quartermaster's department. Some of the petitioners strongly favor the old 8-cent mileage. The Paymaster-General favors the proposition of the majority.

The extensive movement of troops required by recent orders from the War Department will cost the Government fully $300,000. The transfer will begin early in June. The change was expected, although not until after the close of the fiscal year. The regiments concerned have been at their respective stations long enough to desire a change. The Eighth Cavalry, which goes from the Department of Texas to the Department of Dakota, has been in Texas since 1875. The Third and Twenty-fifth Infantries, which exchange within the Department of Dakota, went to their present stations in October, 1887, and May, 1880, respectively. The former had served for a considerable period in Mississippi and Louisiana, and the latter had had ten years' service in Texas. The Fifth Infantry, ordered to Texas, has been in Montana since 1876, having previously served five years in Kansas and Colorado. The Sixteenth Infantry had three years' service in Kansas and the Indian Territory before going to Texas, and has been there since 1880. The companies of the Sixth Infantry which are to be relieved in Utah by the Sixteenth Infantry have been in that Territory since 1881, and went there from Fort Snelling, Minnesoto, where they had been for eight years. The Twenty-second Infantry, ordered to Montana, has been in Colorado and New-Mexico since November, 1882. Previously it had served five years on the lakes and three in Texas. The Thirteenth Infantry, which is to exchange with the Twenty-fourth, has served in Colorado and New-Mexico since June, 1880, and prior thereto had seen seven years' service in the Southern States. The Twenty-fourth Infantry has been in the Indian Territory since 1880, and went there after eleven years in Texas. Battery G, First Artillery, ordered to exchange with Battery F, went to Fortress Monroe in 1867, and the latter to California in 1881. The Seventh Cavalry has had fourteen years' service in Dakota and Montana.

It is probable that the appropriation for naval supplies for the next fiscal year will be made in bulk. The Secretary of the Navy is convinced that a gross appropriation is necessary for the success of his consolidation scheme. He now has in course of preparation estimates for naval supplies without regard to bureaus, and will soon submit them to the House Naval Committee. The estimates will be based on those received from the various bureaus. The committee is understood to be favorable to the Secretary's plan. Should a gross appropriation be made the services of a representative officer for the bureaus at the many navy yards and their quota of clerks will be dispensed with.

### *A WEALTHY WELSHMAN'S DEATH.*

MILWAUKEE, Wis., April 22.—Uriah Dabies, a wealthy merchant of Columbus, in this State, whose princely gifts in behalf of Welsh religious works has made him known to his countrymen all over the United States, died this morning, aged 65. He leaves a fortune of $500,000. Dabies was the founder of the Society for the Support of Aged Welsh Ministers.



### *ON SECOND THOUGHTS.*

THE CHICAGO, BURLINGTON AND NORTHERN'S PROPOSED REDUCTION.

CHICAGO, April 22.—The proposed reduction of rates on the Chicago, Burlington and Northern is just now a fruitful theme for comment and speculation in railway circles. While at first there seemed to be a feeling that the refractory road should be taught a lesson once for all by the making of a rate war that would force it to sue for peace on any terms, this feeling has been modified to some extent by a faint suspicion that such an undertaking might not prove entirely successful. The question has presented itself to the competing lines whether they might not be the greatest sufferers in such a struggle.

It is remembered that during February the Burlington and Northern pursued a policy in regard to rates dictated solely with reference to its own interests, and the statement of February earnings showed a profit from operating of $41,000, the best showing made in any month of the year so far. The determination to lower rates again is just what might have been expected of it, for to agree to a complete restoration of rates would be a surrender of its advantages arising out of the manner of its construction and the devotion of the road to through traffic. It is beginning to be a serious question with the other roads whether it would not be the wisest plan to let the Chicago, Burlington and Northern alone, since a fight would not have the effect of robbing it of its advantage and would only injure the lines that engage in the fight. And that is the way many railroad men are looking at the situation.

ST. PAUL, Minn., April 22.—The notice sent to Chairman Faithorn by Vice-President and General Manager Harris of the Burlington and Northern that rates would again be reduced May 1 created no little excitement among railroad men. Mr. Harris's notice did not state what rates would be put in, and consequently every one is in doubt about the extent of the cut intended. Mr. Harris was asked about this point, but did not give the figures. He stated that the Burlington had consented to advance rates temporarily on April 9, but that it was understood then that the whole question would be reopened. He says the Burlington desires an arrangement for prorating or for some plan of making through rates as low as are made by any other line. It is the intention of the Burlington to meet competition by the Lake Superior line by lake and rail rates via Chicago and to establish as low all-rail rates as are made by any other line.

The question of prorating is again opened. While all lines prorate to St. Louis, Davenport, Rock Island, and Dubuque, they refuse to extend the same privilege to the Northwest, although no good reason has ever been given why St. Paul and Minneapolis are not as much entitled to the privilege as the other points.

### *ENFORCING THE SUNDAY LAW.*

VERY LITTLE LIQUOR TO BE OBTAINED YESTERDAY IN CLEVELAND.

CLEVELAND, Ohio, April 22.—The new Sunday closing law went into effect to-day. A city ordinance has been in force nominally some time, but it was successfully evaded. Although the ordinance imposed a penalty of imprisonment, the period was left to the discretion of the Judge, and in most cases it had come to be fixed at one hour, while the fine was placed at the minimum rate of $5. Saloon keepers do not mind a fine, and were ready to take the risk of arrest and one hour in prison. But the Owens law makes the lightest penalty $25 fine and 10 days in the workhouse, giving the Judge no discretion. It is the workhouse feature which strikes terror to the saloon keeper's heart, and as a consequence the closing to-day was almost universal.

In the very few places where liquor was to be obtained the customer had to be well known, and then thread labyrinthian passages to reach the bar. Contrary to expectation the Police Commissioners at their last meeting adopted a resolution directing the Superintendent to see that the law is strictly enforced, and to hold the Captains and Lieutenants responsible for their several districts. To-day policemen have been going about in civilian garb watching for violations, but up to evening no arrests had been made. The saloon keepers of one ward banded together to make the law obnoxious by an honest enforcement of it, thus depriving their customers of their beverages. They also appointed a committee to watch their brethren in business and agreed to boycott any brewers or others who sell beer or other liquor in small quantities to customers to help them over Sunday. It has been a dry Sunday in Cleveland, and many a one has been exercising his wits to discover a way to make this law inoperative.

### *A SUCCESSFUL STRIKE.*

CHICAGO, April 22.—Seventy-one boss bakers to-day yielded to the demands of the striking journeymen who are members of the Scandinavian, the Bohemian, and the two German unions, and to-night the strike is settled in favor of the men. The terms which they have succeeded in forcing upon their employers include a complete recognition of the organizations and its rules. None but union men are to be employed. They are to be hired through the union's intelligence office. Walking delegates are to have access to the shops at all times. The system of boarding employes on employers' premises is to be done away with. Six days' work is to constitute a week, 10 hours making a full day, except on Friday and Saturday, when the schedule allows 12 hours. The strike has succeeded because it did not concern the largest shops, and because it was so timed as to make resistance by the smaller boss bakers a pretty difficult task. Journeymen bakers to-night are rejoicing over the first successful strike that Chicago has seen this year.

### *WAS HE MURDERED?*

The police are trying to find out whether a murder was committed on Saturday evening in or near the saloon of P. B. Eagan, at University-place and Eighth-street. The victim is Robert O. Jolly, a man of 58, who had boarded for six years at James McAndrews's house at 45 Clinton-street, and who formerly was a well-to-do glove manufacturer, but had sunk into poverty through drink. A year back he reformed, however, and with the help of well-to-do and influential friends was regaining his old status; but about New Year's he had a relapse, and since then he had been on a prolonged spree. On Saturday afternoon he went into Eagan's saloon and drank heavily, but managed to get to his home in Clinton-street about 6:30. He returned to the saloon later, and about 7:45 he was found lying on the sidewalk opposite the saloon unconscious, with his nose broken, eyes blackened, and the base of his skull fractured. Three-quarters of an hour later he died. Eagan stated to Officer Cary, who first discovered the dying man, that he saw him shortly before in the company of a negro; but no one could be found to corroborate the story.

### *SMALLPOX IN NEW-HAVEN.*

NEW-HAVEN, Conn., April 22.—Mrs. Burreu Davis died to-day of smallpox at her house in this city. She was buried a few hours after death. The Board of Health superintended the funeral. Mrs. Davis contracted the disease in nursing a neighbor, who with her husband was ill with what the attending physician diagnosed as measles. Mrs. Davis's 5-year-old daughter is now lying ill with the dread disease and her death is expected. The house in which are confined all cases so far reported is under a strict quarantine, and everything will be done to avoid an epidemic. The physicians in attendance had reported the cases a mild type of varioloid, but the death of Mrs. Davis has created much apprehension.

### *A MANIAC'S MURDEROUS WORK.*

SPRINGFIELD, Mo., April 22.—News of a triple tragedy at Cabool, Texas County, was brought here to-day by Deputy United States Marshal Davis of this district. The hamlet of Cabool is situated among the Ozark Hills, away from all telegraph or railroad communication. Saturday morning a resident of the place named Linkens became violently insane, and locking his family in the house proceeded to kill every member. He brained two of his children, aged 9 and 11 years, with an axe. Meanwhile his wife, with two younger children, managed to escape through a window. The maniac then cut his own throat with a pocket knife and died beside his children.

### *THE FIRST "STRAW" OF THE YEAR.*

BUFFALO, N. Y., April 22.—A "straw" was taken on Saturday of the 32 delegates from Erie County to the Republican State Convention as to their preference for a Presidential candidate. For first choice 18 were for Depew, 5 for Blaine, and 5 for Sheridan; 2 were not seen, and 2 refused to express their opinions, but of these 3 at least are reported to be for Depew, making him 21 out of 32, with 1 doubtful. Some were for Depew first, last, and all the time. The delegates favor ex-Senator McMillan for delegate at large.

## GENERAL TELEGRAPH NEWS

### *WANTED, A NAVAL RESERVE.*

SECRETARY WHITNEY POINTS OUT THE IMPORTANCE OF THE PLAN.

WASHINGTON, April 22.—In a letter written to Representative Whitthorne, Chairman of the Naval Reserve Sub-committee of the House Committee on Naval Affairs, Secretary Whitney declares himself earnestly in favor of the proposed legislation for the establishment of a naval reserve. The necessity for the maintenance of a naval reserve the Secretary says is so universally recognized at the present day that an indorsement of the proposition is necessarily a matter of mere form. No nation maintains a standing army and navy adequate to its defense, or to the maintenance of its rights in war. All of them rely upon reserves and upon the preparation previously made for expanding quickly from a peace to a war basis. The maintenance of a naval reserve, he asserts, is a measure of economy. Under such a system a body of men supporting themselves by ordinary civil pursuits is enrolled and maintained by the Government sufficiently for its purpose in the event of war at comparatively small expense. England, he says, maintains, with an annual expenditure of less than $2,000,000, an auxiliary naval force twice as large as the entire American navy. The suggestion that a naval reserve should be established the Secretary continues, has awakened the greatest interest in all parts of the country, and already more than one State has indicated a determination to co-operate with the Government, and the department is in almost daily receipt of resolutions of representative bodies of citizens throughout the country expressing the greatest anxiety that the necessary steps to secure a reserve should be immediately taken. He adds:

"The necessity for a naval reserve has become more imperative with the changes which have come about in the art of war. In former times, when the implements of war were simple in construction and the ship was handled wholly or mainly by sail, the seafaring class were available for immediate incorporation into the naval force; now seamanship plays an unimportant part. The ship is handled below deck, and no man is fit to be ingrafted into the naval force who has not been previously trained to a knowledge of the modern implements of war and naval tactics. It may therefore be said that there is no longer any naval reserve in the merchant marine. More than this, preparation which has not been previously made cannot be extemporized. The speed and power of modern navies are such that a fortnight is sufficient for a European power to concentrate an absolutely overpowering force where months were formerly required, and hence the only time for preparation is now in a time of peace."

After indorsing in a general way one of the measures for the establishment of a naval reserve now before the committee and suggesting some amendments, the Secretary concludes his letter as follows:

"In the judgment of the department it is both necessary and economical that the Government should have in reserve a fleet of auxiliary merchant ships, previously prepared with the necessary fittings for instant conversion into cruisers, which would therefore be available upon a moment's notice for use by the Government in time of war."

### *THE COW SETTLED IT.*

A MOUTHFUL OF HAY WHICH DECIDED AN IMPORTANT CASE.

OLEAN, April 22.—In September, 1871, Griffith Jones, a farmer of Forestport, Oneida County, purchased at tax sale a tract of 360 acres of land in the town of Allegany, this county. The tract was wild and barren, and had been abandoned by it former owner. Jones, who was a man of small means, paid $150 for the lot, and on looking over the property made up his mind that it was not worth putting any more money in, and he paid no more attention to the purchase beyond securing his tax deed, which gave him a clear title to the land on the 23d of September, 1873, two years after the time of the purchase, according to the New-York law of tax sales.

In 1879 petroleum was discovered in Allegany, and the former owner of the tract Jones had purchased reassumed control of it and leased it to the Bradford Oil Company. Jones knew nothing about this transaction until 1880, when the tract had 10 large producing wells on it and had yielded many thousands of barrels of oil, which had been sold for the profit of the oil company. The territory was then valued at $300,000. Jones at once began proceedings in the Cattaraugus County Court to recover possession of his land and an accounting for the oil on the strength of his tax deed. The oil company disputed Jones's title to the property on the clause of the tax sale law which makes tax deeds invalid if the purchaser does not serve on the occupant of the premises bought at tax sales notice to redeem the same within two years. The oil company claimed that James Hill, the former owner of the tract, was occupying the premises when the deed passed to Jones, and received no redemption notice, and the occupancy was based on the novel point of law that although the owner was not living on the tract he had left a quantity of hay in a shanty on the place. This was the entire defense to the suit, and the Cattaraugus County Court decided that if the simple fact of there being hay on the place as claimed could be established it would be ample proof of legal occupancy and would destroy Jones's title to the property. The trial resulted in favor of the oil company in 1882.

A new trial was granted, and Jones proved by six witnesses that on the 22d of September, 1873, one day before he became entitled to the tax deed, Hill's cow had entered the shanty and eaten all the hay that Hill had left there, thus depriving him of legal domicile and leaving no one in occupancy on whom redemption notice could be served. By that act of Hill's cow, and by that alone, Jones's title to the valuable property was established, and he was given a verdict. The defendants obtained an order for a third trial on the alleged discovery of new evidence, but Jones was again successful. The oil company carried the case to the General Term, where the judgment was affirmed. The case was then taken to the Court of Appeals, where an effort was made to have the judgment reversed on the ground that the tax sale law was unconstitutional. The Court of Appeals has just handed down an opinion sustaining the decision of the lower courts, and Jones will receive nearly $500,000 for the oil that the property yielded during its possession by the Bradford Oil Company.

### *A PERSISTENT LITIGANT.*

CHICAGO, April 22.—In the Circuit Court to-day Henry Llewellin began suit to obtain possession of the suburban village of Wilmette, to which he claims title. It is worth many hundreds of thousands of dollars now, but when it was his father's farm of 270 acres, in 1856, it was valued at $16,000. When, after the father's death, the land was sold to John G. Westerfield, Llewellin claims that no notice was served upon him when his guardian disposed of the property. He is now suing a number of defendants, including the township Trustees, the Chicago, Milwaukee and St. Paul Railroad Company, and half a dozen property owners of the villages. Llewellin began a similar suit in 1871. The case came up for trial on Oct. 8, 1871. That night occurred the big fire, and all the papers in the case were destroyed. Then, in 1886, Llewellin began the suit again, but it was dismissed in 1887 for want of prosecution. He now takes advantage of his legal right to reinstate the suit within a year.

### *SUICIDE OF THE ENGINEER.*

BORDENTOWN, N. J., April 22.—William McCullough, who was a son of the late Capt. Amos McCullough of this place, and who was to have answered in May to the charge of having killed a coal passer in the steamer Comal, of which he was chief engineer, committed suicide by shooting himself early this morning. He was found in an old vacant barn near Blacks Creek. In his hand was a double-barreled pistol, one barrel empty, and the ball had entered his head just over the right ear. By his side lay an envelope on which was written, "I am a dead man." The crime which the suicide was to have answered for is said to have been a fiendish one. During the voyage of the Comal for Galveston he became angry with a coal passer and threw hot coals at him, causing his death. Coroner Naylor of Burlington will hold an inquest to-morrow.

### *THE CHEROKEE STRIP.*

LITTLE ROCK, Ark., April 22.—An Indian Territory special says: "It is probable that the Cherokee Legislature will be convened in extra session at Tahlequah early in May to determine the matter of leasing the Cherokee strip. The question was submitted to the Legislature at the regular session, but that body adjourned without definite action on it. The Cherokee Live Stock Association, who hold the present lease at $100,000 per year, desire to renew it for three or five years at an advance of $25,000 or $50,000. The land comprises over 5,000,000 acres. The lessees re-leased the larger portion of the tract at a profit of over $50,000."



### *A PARTY BOYCOTT FEARED.*

THE AUDITORIUM AND THE REPUBLICAN CONVENTION.

CHICAGO, April 22.—There is trouble in the Republican camp over holding the National Convention in the Auditorium Building. The Laborites have given it out that they will fight the men nominated under the Auditorium roof, for the reason that non-union labor was employed in putting up the building. The union men will thus have a chance to get even in a political way, by repudiating the nominees, and they are making the most of their opportunities. Some Republican leaders do not like to run the risk of antagonizing the Labor men, and a conference was held where the question was secretly and earnestly debated. The Conservatives urged a change of hall, pointing out as a reason for the change the probable situation when it became known that the Republicans refused to heed a request of the labor unions not to hold a nominating convention in a building upon which non-union men had been employed, when a similar request on the part of the same labor unions had caused the Democratic Committee to ignore Chicago and select St. Louis. It was claimed by this same element that the change from the Auditorium to the Exposition Building could be made on the ground that the former could not be placed in proper shape.

The opponents to the change belittled the idea of truckling to the tin bucket brigade and ridiculed the idea of following in the wake of the Democrats. A representative of the Auditorium Company, so it is said, represented that there was no question about having the convention hall in shape, although the rest of the building might not be so far advanced. He said that an arrangement had been entered into between the National Republican Committee and the Auditorium Company for the occupation of the hall, and he did not think any but the contracting parties had the authority to break the agreement. That nipped the plan for a change of hall in the bud.

James L. Brennock, Secretary of the United Carpenters' Council, to-day plainly outlined the union's views of the case when he said: "In voting at the Presidential election I can tell you that the carpenters will look upon the Auditorium Building as a non-union job, unless they employ union carpenters and union men all through on it, and any man who is nominated there will be treated as an enemy of organized labor. We have control over our branch of labor in Cook County. Whether the national organization, the Brotherhood of Carpenters and Joiners, the Amalgamated Carpenters, and the Knights of Labor carpenters, will take up the matter and extend it beyond this county and State, I don't know. But we can get the National Building Trades' Council to take it up, and that represents the building trades in many of the biggest cities."

The Auditorium Building first began to cut a figure in politics at the time of President Cleveland's visit to Chicago last Fall. The company invited him to lay the cornerstone of the building, and the Committee on Reception wanted the labor organizations to turn out and march in the procession. The organizations answered that the Auditorium was built by "scab" labor, and the "scabs" could march in the procession if they wanted to. A committee of the labor organizations waited on the committee and said that if President Cleveland laid the cornerstone it would be considered a slap at organized labor, and might have political consequences. They received no reply, but President Cleveland did not lay the cornerstone. When the Democratic National Committee was considering the location of the National Convention a committee was formed in Chicago, consisting mostly of Knights of Labor, and opened correspondence with Chairman Barnum of the Democratic National Committee, and even, it is said, wrote to the President himself, notifying them that if the convention was held in the Auditorium Building the candidates would be considered as enemies of organized labor, and the machinery of the labor organizations would be used against them. There is no doubt that the Auditorium will be finished in time for the convention, and work on it is going ahead at a great rate.

### *SAVED FROM THE MARIA.*

THE END OF PECK'S TREASURE-HUNTING EXPEDITION.

PROVIDENCE, R. I., April 22.—At noon to-day the lumber schooner Williamine came into this port from Apalachilo. She had on board besides her crew 11 storm-tossed seamen, the officers and crew of the schooner yacht Maria, whose mysterious sailing from New-York attracted considerable interest some time ago. It was subsequently learned, however, that the purpose of the fleet schooner's party was nothing more sinister than the discovery of buried treasure in the vicinity of Belize, and from this point an expedition was to have been set on foot to dig up the country around about. One John D. Peck headed the expedition, and his pretended knowledge of the treasures inspired it. The expedition died a natural death. Peck left his comrades and came North, and the rest of the ship's company headed the Maria's nose for home. They got away from Belize on the 31st of March, but had to anchor in Mauger Bay because the yacht was leaking a little. However, they got off the next day. On the 5th, when off the San Antonio Light, Cuba, the yacht was discovered to be making water badly, and despite the efforts of the crew at the pumps she settled down by the head, and threatened to take a plunge under water. That afternoon they sighted a Nova Scotia ship, and when signals were seen they were taken on board.

The Maria had five and a half feet of water in her, and they were glad to get off, and shortly after the yacht went down, and that was the last of Peck's treasure-hunting expedition. The Nova Scotian proved to be bound for Buenos Ayres, but they were lucky enough to get taken off by the Williamine bound north. They will go to New-York. C. J. Ward is the Captain. The mate's name is Barrett, R. A. Annet is the steward, and there are six seamen and two cabin boys.

### *BAD FOR WINTER WHEAT.*

CHICAGO, April 22.—The following crop summary will be printed in this week's issue of the *Farmer's Review:*

"Our reports of last week fail to show any better condition of the Winter wheat than previously reported. A considerable acreage has been plowed up and seeded to other crops in Ohio, Illinois, Indiana, Missouri, and Southern Michigan. From all sections comes the complaint that the season is cold and backward and Spring seeding much delayed. Meadows and pastures show considerable injury from the drought of last Summer, the severity of the Winter, and the long period of Spring freezing and thawing. The country is nearly bare of forage from last year's crops, and in many cases the farmers have been barely able to carry their stock through the grass.

"The prospects for fruit, especially small fruits, is reported fairly good. While the season might open more propitious, there is yet a chance for the making of a full crop in all farm products, Winter wheat alone excepted, which must fall considerably below an average crop."

### *A DRY SUNDAY IN NEWBURG.*

NEWBURG, N. Y., April 22.—Mayor Odell issued an order yesterday that hotel and saloon keepers in this city must obey the excise laws on Sundays, and it was intimated that policemen who failed to do their duty in making arrests would be investigated. To-day no arrests have been made, and there has been no excitement. There are people who allege that considerable side-door business was carried on this evening. The police deny this and say that Newburg has been a strictly temperate city today. It is understood that the Mayor means to enforce this order from now on, which may have a depressing effect on prospective Sunday excursionists bibulously inclined by boat from New-York.

### *FORGED HIS FATHER'S NAME.*

A well-dressed young man, who gave his name as Mall Barnicky and his address as 365 Hicks-street, Brooklyn, but whose real name is Al Barnicle, and his home 6 Willow-place, Brooklyn, was arraigned in the Jefferson Market Police Court yesterday charged with having passed a forged check for a small sum of money on the Bank of New-York. He was released on bail pending examination. The prisoner's father, Michael F. Barnicle, whose name was forged upon the check, is a well-to-do tea merchant of Brooklyn.

### *CAPSIZED AND DROWNED.*

SANDUSKY, Ohio, April 22.—While George Heaton and F. H. Henning, residents of Pelee Island, were out in a small boat last night, the sail became tangled, the boat capsized, and Heaton was drowned. Some fishermen rescued Henning.

### *ATTACKED WITH A PITCHFORK.*

Frederick Schmitt, a farmer, of Valley Stream, Long Island, and his wife, were injured in a quarrel with their neighbors, Joseph George and his son, on Saturday afternoon. The quarrel was the result of a long-standing feud. Schmitt's wounds, which were made with a pitchfork, are dangerous. A warrant for the arrest of the father and son has been issued by Justice Healo, of Far Rockaway.

## A PERSISTENT CANDIDATE

### *JOHN SHERMAN'S WORK TO GAIN THE PRESIDENCY.*

OHIO UNWILLINGLY FORCED TO SUPPORT HIM SEVERAL TIMES—HOW HE USED TREASURY PATRONAGE IN 1880 AND HIS GALLING DEFEAT—GARFIELD'S ELECTION AND ARTHUR'S DEFEAT—FORAKER'S FORCED SUBMISSION—HARD SLEDDING THIS YEAR FOR "HONEST" JOHN.

I.

OFTEN BEATEN BUT NOT DISCOURAGED.

WASHINGTON, April 21.—The Republicans of the Buckeye State have nominated, at Dayton, Ohio, delegates at large to the National Republican Convention that is to meet at Chicago on June 19, and have repeated the indorsement of John Sherman's candidacy that was declared in the State Convention at Toledo in July last. At that time the situation was an embarrassing one to the Ohio opponents of Sherman. Gov. Foraker, full of a sense of his own importance as a rising "favorite son," was inspired with a hope that circumstances might oblige him to become the candidate for President. But he desired to be a candidate for Governor and to be elected by an increased majority, so that he could go into the National Convention with all the prestige of accumulated victories. His friends and the friends of James G. Blaine met their match politically when they came face to face with Sherman in that convention. They found that Sherman had made a "still hunt" of the State, that he had a majority of the delegates, and that he was prepared to accept nothing short of unconditional surrender. Foraker's friends, who had been talking about a "Blaine and Foraker" ticket, gave up at once. Even so cantankerous and talkative a Blaine man as Judge West, who idolizes the Plumed Knight, was silenced. Fearful lest opposition by him should result in punishment from the Sherman men in the State campaign and a reduced majority or a defeat, Foraker permitted the resolution to pass committing the State to John Sherman. He has had his reward. The great majority was secured. Sherman himself, in his address to the convention, admitted that the expression of the body in his favor meant nothing unless ratified by the election of district delegates. Everybody present in the hall regarded that admission as significant, and as revealing a feeling of concern about what the outcome of the district conventions would be.

The disagreeable fact to the followers of Mr. Sherman and to Mr. Sherman himself is as plain now as it was eight years ago that the man who insists upon having the support of Ohio is not desired as a candidate by the Republicans of that State, and that there is not enough of State pride in him to make him acceptable. The Ohio Republicans have been committed to Sherman by main force. In their heart of hearts they are for Blaine—and Foraker. They expect to be for them for some purpose, and one has only to talk briefly with the younger Ohio men, the sort who have organized the zealous Blaine clubs all over the State, to find that they look to a repetition in the convention of 1888 of the scene in the convention of 1884, when Foraker, borne down by forces which Mr. Conkling would have described as "forbidden abhorrent," transferred the restless and impatient remnant of the Ohio delegation from Sherman to Blaine, and made the victory of the man from Maine as glorious as the defeat of Arthur was complete and overwhelming. If Mr. Sherman succeeds, however, in mustering the full vote of Ohio, he will probably not command as large a column of supporters in 1888 as he did in 1880. Not through any lack of effort on his part, however, but for the reason that in 1880 he was a part of the National Administration, the head of the chief executive department, with patronage at his command which he did not scruple to employ to accomplish his purposes, and with the power to punish those subordinates who shirked or faltered in his cause or betrayed greater interest in Blaine or Grant than they did in John Sherman. He was an exacting political taskmaster. Even the average Ohio political place hunter, who is not a supersensitive creature, finds his yoke a hard one to bear, and he takes at best but a feeble and perfunctory interest in the consuming desire of "Honest John" to be raised to the head of the Government—to an office in which, if the past be any guarantee of the future, he would devote the time, the money, and the power confided to his care to be used to demolish his opposers and to perpetuate his own domination. At his age a man changes little in eight years. To persons who are regarding his nomination for the Presidency as a desirable or a possible thing, it ought to be interesting to look back over some of the incidents of the preliminary campaigns of 1880 and 1884. Much of what he then did has been forgotten, although his desperate efforts to grasp the nomination evoked at the time the reprobation of the country. At a time when his nomination for the Presidency is being urged by a considerable number of his admirers and by himself, it will be interesting to look back over the record of his political exploits in two campaigns.

II.

THE CAMPAIGN OF 1880.

In 1879 the term of President Hayes was drawing to a close. The President had ceased to be talked of as a candidate for renomination. Sherman was the Secretary of the Treasury, and his management of that department, in every change of subordinate officers, had been conducted in a way that was destroying party harmony while it was building up a servile following for its chief. Arthur and Cornell had fallen under his withering touch, and the Republicans of the State of New-York, not with resentment, were divided in their allegiance between Grant and Blaine. Sherman had a few adherents. They were in the Custom House or expecting to be there, or they held places in the Internal Revenue Service at Sherman's discretion to continue them or cut them down. Like Richelieu, he first sought to conciliate the man whom he desired to capture. If conciliation did not conquer, he did not hesitate to crush. While he was attracting the attention of the unsuspicious public by his financial course he was cultivating his chances for a nomination in 1880. With system and diligence he reached out to the Custom House officers and officers of internal revenue, particularly in the Southern States. Scarce one of them failed to learn that retention in office depended upon the degree of zeal manifested in the ambition of the Secretary of the Treasury. Special agents, paid liberally by the Government for work that needed to be done, scoured the South as Sherman canvassers, teaching and preaching and menacing. Relying upon these mercenaries, who were ready to exchange masters at a moment's notice, Sherman was confident that he would be able to bring to the support of his candidacy the delegates from all the Southern States. That he failed was not because his protégés in office lacked boldness or because their master was too scrupulous.

The Sherman agents began early the work of directing conventions. In January, 1880, they made a dash for a control of the Republican organization in North Carolina. There was a strong attachment to Grant in the State, and the Chairman of the State Committee, Col. Thomas B. Keogh, was a pronounced admirer of the ex-President, and a cordial opponent of Sherman. The State Committee consisted of 10 men. Among them were Col. W. P. Canaday, Collector of Customs at Wilmington; J. J. Mott, Collector of Internal Revenue at Statesville; Pinckney Rollins, a clerk of the Loan Division of the Treasury; J. H. Harris, a colored man who held a clerkship in the Government service, and D. H. Starbuck, a man who was inclined to be for Grant, but who had a great hankering for place and salary. The committee met at Raleigh and without delay deposed Col. Keogh from the Chairmanship and elected C. W. Grandy, another Sherman man. Four of the committee remained steadfast to Grant. This pitched battle had been preceded by a reconnoitre of the State in force by troops of Special Agents of the Treasury and the Internal Revenue Office. Some time before the meeting of the State Committee W. J. Kilpatrick arrived in Greensborough, the home of Col. Keogh. He had been sent out by Special Agent Tingle to report to Gen. J. C. Abbott at Wilmington. Abbott was in the Government service and a Sherman man. To Col. Keogh, this man, Kilpatrick, showed a letter of introduction from Sherman to Internal Revenue Collector Young, at Raleigh, and one also to Col. Canaday at Wilmington. These letters bespoke the fullest confidence in Kilpatrick, who questioned Keogh about Sherman's chances for getting the delegation from North Carolina. Keogh promptly declared that he thought the chances were poor. "But you can change all that," suggested Kilpatrick, and he added, as if by way of inducement, "and you could get any place you

# The New-York Times.

VOL. XXXVII....NO. 11,464. NEW-YORK, MONDAY, MAY 28, 1888. PRICE TWO CENTS.


## SHERIDAN SLOWLY DYING

### *HE CANNOT LIVE MORE THAN TWENTY-FOUR HOURS.*

MORE ATTACKS OF HEART FAILURE FOLLOWED BY GREAT WEAKNESS—HIS DOCTORS ABANDON ALL HOPE.

WASHINGTON, May 27.—Lieut.-Gen. Sheridan's chances of living through the night are extremely slight. It is believed by his relatives and those most conversant with his real condition that at the best his death is a matter of hours only, rather than of days. Early this evening there was a recurrence of the dreaded heart failure, and it found the patient less able to withstand it than before any previous attack. The four doctors who are attending the General speak less hopefully to-night than ever before, and there is no longer any attempt to conceal the fact that their patient is almost beyond hope. His blood is rapidly thickening, and the use of oxygen has been resorted to by the physicians. This in itself tells the story of Gen. Sheridan's desperately critical condition.

The attack of heart failure which overtook the General at 5 o'clock yesterday afternoon was not overcome by the doctors until after 4 o'clock this morning. It was a grim struggle with death, and all through the long hours of the night the contest seemed likely to end at any moment in victory for death. But in the early morning the skill of the physicians prevailed once more, and their patient gained a respite, but he was left in a terribly weak condition, and the doctors knew that another attack was more than ever to be dreaded.

During the day Gen. Sheridan rallied somewhat. He caught occasional naps, which seemed to refresh him, and he was able to take such nourishment as the doctors prescribed; in the hope of helping him to build up his strength for the next attack of heart trouble, which they knew was sure to come. In the afternoon the improvement was encouraging enough to give color to the reply made to all inquiries that the General was much better, but as the day wore on the tendency of the fainting fits to return became more pronounced again, and to-night the sick man is again hovering between life and death, with much less strength to withstand the attacks than he had 24 hours before.

Gen. Sheridan's mother has been unable to come to Washington. It was expected that she would reach the city last night, but her health forbade her to undertake the the long journey from Ohio.

*Associated Press Dispatches.*

A call at Gen. Sheridan's house at 2 o'clock this afternoon elicited the information that there had been no particular change in the patient's condition since the last bulletin was issued. It was stated that the General had taken several short naps during the forenoon and was resting quietly at 2 o'clock.

At 3:30 o'clock it was stated that Gen. Sheridan was sleeping quietly and that his condition remained unchanged.

At 5:15 P. M. it was learned that all the physicians except Dr. O'Reilly had left Gen. Sheridan's house. Dr. O'Reilly could not leave the sick room, but sent out the following message: "The General is sleeping quietly, and his condition remains unchanged."

At 6:30 P. M. it was stated that Gen. Sheridan woke about 5 o'clock refreshed, but dozed off a few minutes later. At 6:30 he was sleeping quietly. He is able to take nourishment and retain it.

8:15 P. M.—Gen. Sheridan is not as strong nor as well this evening as he was earlier in the day. There has been no recurrence of the heart trouble, but all efforts of the physicians to rally him from the attack of last evening have proved unavailing. The doctors are less hopeful than at any time before.

10:30 P. M.—All hope has been abandoned and it is not believed that Gen. Sheridan can live another 24 hours. His condition is much worse than it was last night. He appears to be gradually sinking. His strength is gradually failing, and while there has been no recurrence of the heart failure there is a continued tendency in that direction, and his pulse has been growing weaker and his breathing more labored. The blood is thick and black. Ever since the attack last night the physicians have been doing everything in their power to stimulate the action of the heart, but without success, and its beating is feeble and uncertain despite the administration of digitalis and other powerful remedies. His strength has gradually failed during the day, and the hope that he would be able to rally has proved illusive.

Gen. Sheridan rested well during the early part of the evening. He had some trouble in breathing during the night, but he improved early in the day. He rested easily and was perfectly conscious and rational, recognizing those around him. Peptonized milk and chicken broth were given him and he took the latter with relish. His appetite was good and he retained all the food he took. The nourishment, however, did not seem to give him any strength, and he grew weaker and weaker. His interest in passing events did not seem so keen as on the previous day and he read no newspapers as formerly, not seeming to care for them. A few intimate friends were admitted to his room and to these he listened with attention. His respiration grew worse as the day wore on, and the lungs failed to properly purify the blood. Digitalis failed to have much effect on him, and about 2 o'clock it was found necessary to give him oxygen in order to prevent the blood from becoming poisoned. This gave him considerable relief. From 2 until 5 o'clock he slept for quite a while and since that time he has been dozing at frequent intervals. Bromide of potassium mixed with chloral has been given to induce sleep. Two physicians remained constantly at his side to give immediate attention in case of need, and all of the doctors attending the sick General were frequently there together. He did not leave his bed during the day, but remained there propped up with pillows. About 6 o'clock he desired to be lifted up higher, and two attendants, assisted by Mrs. Sheridan, endeavored to raise him. He was so heavy that they had some difficulty, and the General, noticing this, said jokingly: "I am pretty heavy, but I haven't got any paralysis," referring to a newspaper statement giving that as his malady. Gen. Sheridan fully recognizes that his end may come at any time, and it is said has made all arrangements he desires to have perfected prior to his demise. One of the physicians said this evening: "Gen. Sheridan has great vitality, but I do not think he will be alive 30 hours from now, and certainly not in two days, unless there is a great change. He has no pain, and I think he will sink away easily. A recurrence of the heart trouble may come, the heart will cease to beat, and all will be at an end."

There was a steady stream of callers at the residence during the day, and many telegrams were received asking for information as to his condition. The callers included many persons well known in Washington life, and a considerable number of them were ladies. The President sent a basket of flowers and a note of sympathy to Mrs. Sheridan in the morning. He asked to be informed of the General's condition and expressed a sincere hope that his life would be spared. Gen. Sheridan has always been a great favorite with the President, who admired his frank, open manner of expressing his opinion upon current topics and his peculiarly pleasing way of emphasizing the statements by little anecdotes. The General appeared to gradually grow weaker as night fell, and this change was noted in the doctors' bulletin, which was prepared at 8 o'clock and issued later. It was as follows:

8 P. M.—The repeated attacks of partial failure of the heart and its continued feeble action have induced a condition of the lungs which prevents the proper aeration of the blood. This condition has hitherto been measurably controlled, but shows such a tendency to recurrence as to justify the most serious apprehensions. It is critical. He is free from pain and distress, and so expresses himself.

M. O'REILLY,
CHARLES B. BYRNE,
H. C. YARROW,
W. MATTHEWS.

Two hours later another bulletin was issued. It simply said: "No change for the better has taken place in Gen. Sheridan's condition."

To an inquiry made at 11:30 P. M. the answer returned was: "He is hovering between life and death."

### *THE MERCY OF THE COURT.*

IT ADMITS A MAN CONVICTED OF MANSLAUGHTER TO BAIL.

PHILADELPHIA, May 27.—Henry E. Gettys, the Lambertville bridge builder who killed Charles T. Kitchen of New-Hope for intimacy with his wife, and who was convicted of voluntary manslaughter at Doylestown late last night and recommended to the mercy of the court, and whom the people of Bucks County suppose to be yet in the Doylestown Jail, was a somewhat conspicuous figure on Chestnut-street this morning. He was accompanied by Dr. H. T. Sharp of McCrory, Ark., and Gustav A. Tredder, a subordinate of Getty's in the service of the Phœnix Bridge Building Company. After the announcement of the verdict in the Bucks County Court House last night Senator George Ross, one of Gettys's lawyers, moved for an arrest of judgment on the ground that the indictment was found by the Grand Jury in January last in the absence of the prisoner. While the Senator was making his plea the crowd had made its way out of the court room and scattered to all portions of the county to spread the news of the verdict. After everybody had left the court room except Judge Yerkes and the lawyers in the case Mr. Ross moved that the prisoner be admitted to bail as he had a sister in Philadelphia in a dying condition, and he desired to see her.

Judge Yerkes said that as the jury had recommended Gettys to the mercy of the court he thought there was no danger of his running away. The Judge then admitted Gettys to $1,000 bail to appear for sentence on Tuesday. When he realized that for the first time in six months he was for the time being a free man, he was overjoyed. A great deal of his old energy and vigor returned, and as he said: "I feel like a boy just let out of school." With Dr. Sharp, Gustav Tredder and William Hudson of Thorle, Ontario, all of whom left their homes to come to Pennsylvania to testify in his behalf, Gettys took the first train this morning for this city. After visiting his sister he met his friends at the Windsor Hotel. They spent the afternoon visiting Fairmount Park and the Zoological Garden.

### *LOSING PART OF THEIR PAY.*

HOW THE ST. PAUL ROAD TREATED ITS STRIKERS.

MILWAUKEE, Wis., May 27.—There have been rumors afloat that the Chicago, Milwaukee and St. Paul Railroad had assessed its losses through the Burlington strike upon its employes throughout its system. The men are paid about the 23d of each month for the month preceding. They were paid last week for April, which was the month of the switchmen's sympathetic strike on the St. Paul, at which time an order was made cutting down the operating force of the road one-third and reducing the salaries of those remaining in its employ 33⅓ per cent. This order was revoked in six days. From the April pay of the employes the deduction was made of six days' pay for those suspended for that length of time. The others suffered a cut of 33⅓ per cent. in their pay for the same six days. Many had supposed that salaries would be untouched, and hence arose the rumor referred to.

President Miller of the St. Paul said to-night that the story of an attempt to make up from his employes for losses by the "Q" strike was utterly unfounded. The cause of the April order was the strike of the St. Paul's own switchmen. While they were on strike the other employes had little to do, and the order to curtail expenses was issued. The switchmen stood out for six days, and when they went back to work the old order of things was restored. In making out the pay roll for April the company simply deducted the time lost during the side strike, and paid its men exactly as their bills stood under the terms of the six days' order.

### *A WRONGED WIFE'S REVENGE.*

SHE COWHIDES THE WOMAN SHE BELIEVES HER RIVAL.

READING, Penn., May 27.—The talk of the city to-day was a sensational cowhiding case which took place at a late hour last night. The wife of John H. Derr, a well-known citizen, who conducts broker offices in this city, Lebanon, Tamaqua, and other places, visited the house occupied by Mrs. Agnes Townsend. She rang the bell, and Mrs. Townsend opened the door. Mrs. Derr cried out:

"You will make ribbons out of me, will you? I'll show you what law a wife has."

With these words she drew a cowhide, and laid it over the back and shoulders of Mrs. Townsend, who escaped further punishment by closing the door. Mr. and Mrs. Derr have been separated for the past year. Mr. Derr resides in this city, while his wife lives in Lebanon. To-morrow his application for a divorce will be heard in Lebanon. Mrs. Derr claims that Mrs. Townsend is responsible for all her family troubles.

### *THE IMPRISONED ANARCHISTS.*

CHICAGO, Ill., May 27.—Dr. Ernst Schmidt, Chairman of the Anarchist Defense Committee, said in an interview to-day: "The pardon of Neebe, Fielden, and Schwab will enter into the present Illinois political campaign. If a promise to grant Executive clemency were made by either candidate it would result in his defeat. I am not in favor of pushing the movement for a pardon at present, and believe that any attempt to secure one would compromise the chances of the men."

The Anarchist Defense Committee will go before the Circuit Court this Fall and make application for a writ of habeas corpus in the case of Oscar Neebe. It is claimed that errors have been discovered in the Supreme Court record. Gen. Butler is quoted as saying that Neebe has a fair chance of being released. At a recent meeting of the Pioneer Relief and Aid Society a demand was made on the old Defense Committee for the money in its possession, about $3,000. Frank Stauber refused, and explained that Neebe had a fair chance of being released, and that he was authorized to hold the money for the purpose of employing first-class legal talent. It is not claimed that any errors have been found in the cases of Fielden and Schwab. In fact, the more rabid Anarchists have gone back on Fielden and Schwab for neglecting to become "martyrs."

### *TO FIGHT THE LIQUOR EVIL.*

CHICAGO, May 27.—Central Music Hall was filled this afternoon by ministers and church members of all denominations, who had met to protest formally against the stand taken by the Mayor and the Aldermen on the liquor question. A petition which is to be presented to the Aldermen to-morrow night was read and indorsed. It asks the enactment of an ordinance forbidding the location of a saloon within 200 feet of any church or school, and for another to keep the saloons closed on Sunday. In support of the petition addresses were made by the Rev. Arthur Little, the Rev. Dr. Lawrence, the Rev. Dr. Bolter, Dr. E. P. Goodwin, Bishop Fallows, C. C. Bonney, the Rev. F. W. Gunsaulus, and others. All the speakers urged public agitation of the liquor question in order to offset the political pull of the saloon keepers, which just at present seems to be running things. The petition to the Aldermen will be presented by a committee of leading clergymen and laymen who were present at to-day's meeting.



## POPE LEO'S ACT DENOUNCED

### *MANY EXCITING MEETINGS IN IRELAND.*

THE BISHOPS WHO SUPPORT THE RESCRIPT ALSO ASSAILED BY THE LEADING PARNELLITES.

DUBLIN, May 27.—Mr. John Dillon, speaking at Kildare to-day, denounced the Bishops who support the Papal rescript regarding Ireland. He said the Nationalist Party was not afraid of any Bishop's threats nor of any mandate from the Vatican, and it was not going to abandon the plan of campaign or boycotting, with which weapons it had fought the battle until now.

Mr. Healy, in a speech at Waterford, twitted the Pope with working his own plan of campaign when the Sardinians grabbed his territory and with boycotting Victor Emmanuel.

Mr. William O'Brien addressed a large meeting at Limerick. He uttered bitter invectives against Bishop O'Dwyer, saying the threats contained in the Bishop's manifesto with reference to the rescript were the rashest and most unjust ever made. The Bishop, Mr. O'Brien said, left Limerick yesterday after supplying copies of his manifesto to every Orange newspaper, but he did not send a copy to the Mayor, to whom the manifesto was nominally addressed, and who discovered it in the journals. Mr. O'Brien declared that there never was anything falser than Bishop O'Dwyer's assertion that the Nationalists were agitating against the Pope. The audience, which was greatly excited, uttered groans for Bishop O'Dwyer. Twenty thousand persons attended the meeting. The better class of citizens and most of the local clergymen were absent. A dozen other Parnellites spoke at various places.

A copious rainfall in Southern Russia has saved the crops and an abundant harvest is insured.

A report comes from Egypt that Osman Digna's camp has been burned by incendiaries in order to compel him to retreat. Two thousand of his followers are said to have perished.

A dispatch from Tangier says that Maranee, a pretender to the throne, and several of his adherents have been killed.

Archbishop Walsh has received instructions to publish in the Dublin *Freeman* a letter which will rectify the erroneous views that have found expression with regard to the Papal rescript.

### THE SICK MONARCHS.

BERLIN, May 27.—The Emperor passed a fair night. He remained in bed until noon. Owing to chilly weather he did not go into the park to-day, but he appeared at the window several times this evening. He complains of a feeling of lassitude, which his physicians attribute to the warm weather.

The Crown Prince and the Empress to-day inspected the launch Alexandra, which is lying close to the Schloss in readiness to convey the Emperor to Potsdam. The Empress has postponed her visit to the scene of the Vistula floods until after the arrival of the imperial party at Potsdam.

Dr. Simion, who presided at a meeting of the Goethe Society of Weimar, in proposing a toast to the health of the Emperor, said: "It is idle to believe in the infallibility of doctors, German or English. Many heroes have been great in action; others have been great in endurance. The Emperor is equally great in both. We hope and desire that years equal to the number of drops in our glasses may be added to his life."

MILAN, May 27.—The Emperor of Brazil had a good night, but he does not gain strength. The hypodermic injections of caffeine and the administration of strychnine are continued. Massage is about to be tried for the purpose of promoting the Emperor's circulation. The physicians fear the worst on account of the patient's weakness.

The Emperor passed a good day. His appetite has improved. The doctors have decided that his journey to Aix-les-Bains must be deferred.

### RACING IN EUROPE.

THE PRIX DU JOCKEY CLUB.

PARIS, May 27.—The race for the Prix du Jockey Club was run at Chantilly to-day. The starters and their jockeys, with the last betting, were as follows: Stuart, (Lane,) 7 to 4 on; Saint Gall, (Bridgeland,) 12 to 1 against; Galaor, (Storr,) 16 to 1 against; Reyezuelo, (Hopkins,) 6 to 1 against; Dauphin, (Dodge,) 12 to 1 against; Saint Léon, (Rolfe,) 16 to 1 against; Walter Scott, (Madge,) 16 to 1 against; La Flandrie colt, (Ashman,) 30 to 1 against; Sapajou, (Harkey,) 40 to 1 against; Wolf, (Carney,) 40 to 1 against; Jeudi, (Bartholomew,) 100 to 1 against; Carlo, (Hunter,) 100 to 1 against. Jeudi made the running at the start, Galaor, La Flandrie, and Stuart following, and Saint Gall, Wolf, Sapajou, and Walter Scott bringing up the rear. Saint Gall and Galaor then drew up, and, Reyezuelo following, went to the front on the right side. Galaor drew away with Stuart, but the latter shook Galaor off and took the lead easily. Saint Gall now made a strong effort to capture Stuart, but was beaten off, Stuart winning by a length and a half, Saint Gall second, a length in front of Galaor, third. Time—2:39.

LONDON, May 27.—The Austrian Derby was run to-day. Apponyi's Rajtraita was first, Esterhazy's Ugod second, and Festeti's Hungaria third.

### A NEW AGREEMENT WITH SPAIN.

MADRID, May 27.—The *Official Gazette* publishes the text of an agreement between Spain and the United States prolonging the existing commercial arrangement pending the conclusion of a more ample treaty. The agreement may be terminated on two months' notice being given by either side.

### *A SNUB FOR THE POPE.*

CHICAGO, May 27.—Seventy-five societies were represented at the annual convention of the Irish Catholic societies of Chicago and Cook County this afternoon. A motion relating to the mass meeting of the Irish Catholics, to be held at Battery D on Thursday night, to act on the Pope's stand on the "plan of campaign" was carried unanimously. The motion in effect was that it is the sense of all Irish Catholics that they could manage their own affairs without the assistance of foreign powers, and that all the societies in the city should attend the meeting to lend their voice to this belief. "Unless all do what they can in this direction and assert themselves squarely on this proposition the meeting will have a calamitous effect on the cause in Ireland," said the President. "We are to come together to announce our political independence, and if the gathering is not a representative one the claim will be set up that the Irish Catholics in Chicago are not free in spirit and are yet controlled by foreigners in their home troubles."

### *MRS. CLEVELAND'S QUIET SUNDAY.*

PHILADELPHIA, May 27.—With to-day's blue skies and bright sun came the first pleasant weather that Mrs. Cleveland has had since she has been the guest of the Rev. Charles and Mrs. Wood in Germantown. She attended worship in the morning at the First Presbyterian Church, where the Rev. Mr. Wood is the Pastor. When the carriage drove up, Chelton-avenue was black with people, and the sidewalk was so crowded that it required the efforts of two stalwart policemen to keep a passageway open. Mrs. Cleveland occupied the Pastor's pew, near the front of the church, with Mrs. Wood and Miss Bessie Wood, and all through the service heads were turned and necks craned to get a glance at her pretty face. As the organ struck up a lively tune after the benediction she skipped quickly down the aisle, and behind her two friends tripped lightly across the sidewalk, and springing into the carriage was away before half of those who had only come to church to see her knew that she had gone. Mrs. Cleveland looked pale and tired, and kept her eyes down as if she were annoyed or embarrassed. She wore steel-gray velvet, trimmed with silver braid, and a walking hat to match, with white flowers.

She spent the rest of the day quietly at the Wood mansion, and attended the Sunday school celebration in the afternoon and the services in the evening.

### *AN UNEXPLAINED CRIME.*

WATERTOWN, N. Y., May 27.—In a small farmhouse in the village of Pierrepont Manor, Jefferson County, a terrible crime was committed last night. The victim, Julia E. Dewey, is slowly dying as the result of five large gashes on her head and face, evidently inflicted with an axe. The walls of the rooms and the bed clothing are covered with blood. The axe has been found in the sluiceway on the road passing the house, a short distance away. Mrs. Dewey is a widow and resides with her two young children. The Sheriff is making an investigation. Several persons are suspected, but as yet the clues are not clear. The woman may live two or three days. She is conscious, but does not disclose the name of her assailant, or whether she was able to recognize him. No motive is given for the crime.

### *ONE LINE FROM SEA TO SEA.*

THE PENNSYLVANIA SAID TO BE TRYING TO BUY THE BURLINGTON ROAD.

OMAHA, Neb., May 27.—An effort to effect a purchase of the Chicago, Burlington and Quincy Railroad is at present being made by General Manager McCrea of the Pennsylvania Company, which, if consummated, will prove one of the most stupendous of schemes that has been known for years. Since the Pennsylvania has no direct interests here it must naturally be inferred that it is looking for something big to capture. Since the Santa Fé opened its new line between Kansas City and Chicago rumors have been circulated purporting to expose a scheme hatched by this company to get control of the Erie Road and thus have a continuous line from New-York to San Francisco. With past actions of the great Boston corporation to judge from, business men in Chicago and New-York, especially capitalists, placed a great deal of confidence in the truthfulness of the rumor, and it seems to have already turned their attention to enterprises the success of which depends entirely upon the consummation of the Santa Fé scheme.

Evidently the Pennsylvania people, who would not be outdone by any concern on this continent if they can do anything to prevent it, also fear the Santa Fé's proposition and are stirring themselves to keep up with the procession. To do this they must get hold of some of the transcontinental lines, either by purchase or by lease, and be ready to compete with the great Southern route. Taking, therefore, this view of the situation there is but one suggestion to put forth. That suggestion involves the Burlington and points strongly toward a deal whereby the Pennsylvania Company will get possession of that road and thus have a line of its own from sea to sea. For a long time those two roads have been closely allied in the interchange of business and their terminal facilities at Chicago.

Furthermore, it is well known that the Burlington has assumed a defiant attitude toward the Santa Fé and stands ready to buck the interests of that corporation at any point and on all occasions. By paralleling the Burlington between Kansas City and Chicago, the Santa Fé gave it a black eye, and in retaliation for this movements were being made to get even. One most effective back-handed slap was given the obstreperous and encroaching concern when the Burlington dropped the Rio Grande and entered into an agreement with the Union Pacific for the transportation of transcontinental traffic.

It is also hinted rather loudly, too, that the Pennsylvania folks have their eye on the Union Pacific, and, in connection with the Burlington, would like to gobble it up. If they could do this the Santa Fé would then be small potatoes. The latter denies that it is trying to get hold of the Erie, but, since the Kansas City-Chicago extension was commenced, there is no dependence to be put on its denials of anything. In a word, all the Chicago roads are anxiously waiting just now to do something that will give Santa Fé a set back. Several of the Burlington and Union Pacific officials were asked for an expression of opinion as to the object of Messrs. McCrea and Ford's visit West, but they pretend to know nothing whatever about it. The men arrived here Saturday morning from the West, but only remained a few hours and proceeded on their journey East. Soon after they reached Chicago the story that they had been making a tour of inspection of the Burlington came back, and with it the report that their company is negotiating for a purchase of the system. Those Burlington officials who are at present in the city, while they will not deny that they have been approached, refuse to give any information whatever.

### *THE WISCONSIN BUTCHERY.*

FOUR PERSONS MURDERED IN COLD BLOOD FOR MONEY.

VIROQUA, Wis., May 27.—Further particulars of the quadruple murder in Vernon County serve but to increase its horrors. It is now known that the motive was to secure $1,400 which Mrs. Drake was to receive from an estate in Pennsylvania, and which it was commonly reported had already passed into her hands. Reuben Drake was probably the most prosperous farmer in the neighborhood, but he lived in a small house of three rooms, a sitting room, bedroom, and kitchen. The old couple were living alone, but two grandchildren from an adjoining county had come that day to visit them. Witnesses first on the scene describe it as a veritable slaughter pen. The body of Mrs. Drake lay near the door with a bullet hole through each breast. She had evidently gone to the door to open it in response to a knock and been shot from the threshold. Her husband lay in the centre of the room on his face with one bullet hole through the right eye and brain and another through the body near the breast.

In the bedroom was a most fearful sight. On one bed lay the two children, the girl in front on one side as if sleeping. The head was nearly severed from the body by one powerful knife-stroke. The boy had struggled all over the bed. His throat was partially cut and his heart was penetrated by a terrible knife-stab. Blood was spattered all over the room, on the floor, walls, and bedding. The bullets showed that the weapon was a 32-calibre revolver, and the knife tells its own story. It is the general opinion that the deed was done by some one in the neighborhood who was acquainted with the circumstances of the family. People of this vicinity would make short work of the murderer if in their hands.

### *LUM SMITH LOCKED UP.*

ANTHONY COMSTOCK'S ENEMY AGAIN IN TROUBLE.

PHILADELPHIA, May 27.—This afternoon a meeting was held in Horticultural Hall to discuss the "Moral Purity of Our Children and Youth." Anthony Comstock made the principal address, and in the course of his remarks he alluded to the National Defense Association as an organization that had been formed for the purpose of having the law prohibiting the passage of obscene literature through the mails repealed. The speaker paid particular attention to one man, whose name he did not mention as being at the head of the movement. While Mr. Comstock was speaking, Lum Smith, to whom the remarks were supposed to refer, was in the lower end of the hall distributing printed circulars which denounced the speaker as being very vile. Two policemen ordered Smith to stop, but he refused. He was handed over to other officers and given a chance to depart, but he again refused and created considerable excitement upon the sidewalk. A great crowd gathered, and when it was learned who the man was a rush was made for the prisoner with shouts of "Lynch him! hang him!" The officers were compelled to use their clubs, and a free fight ensued.

All the extra policemen in the Fifth District Station were sent for, and by their aid the prisoner was landed in the station, while the crowd yelled for vengeance on the outside of the building. Charges of inciting to riot were preferred against Smith, who will be given a hearing to-morrow. As the prisoner was being led away to a cell he begged the Sergeant with tears in his eyes to spare him the humiliation of being locked up, but his appeal was fruitless.

### *A SUSPECTED HAUNT OF ANARCHISTS.*

NEW-HAVEN, May 27.—Rudolph Koepke, his two nephews, wife and children, live in a little cottage under the Whitneyville Hills. He is employed in the Marlins Firearms Company factory. His mode of living has been a cause of remark among his neighbors, and the recent visit of Herr Most to New-Haven has led them to believe that his house is the haunt of a group of Anarchists. At all hours of the night and day mysterious explosions are heard, which expert gunmakers who are employed in the Whitney Arms Works in the vicinity pronounce to be similar to those produced by experimenters in explosives. Every Sunday long-bearded Germans assemble at the house, make speeches, and sing revolutionary songs. Herr Most made a speech at one of these gatherings while he was in this city about a fortnight ago. Since his visit the experiments with explosives have been more frequent. The house is in a retired spot just outside the city limits, and therefore comparatively free from police surveillance. The yard is littered with pieces of gas and lead pipe which seem to serve no useful purpose. A reporter visited the place this evening and found nothing suspicious in sight, but met with an extremely discourteous reception.

### *CALLED TO NEW FIELDS.*

WORCESTER, Mass., May 27.—The Rev. Charles Wadsworth, Jr., Pastor of Plymouth Church, resigned to-day, having accepted a call to San Francisco.

SPRINGFIELD, Mass., May 27.—The Rev. Orville Reed to-day resigned his position as associate Pastor of Hope Church. The resignation is to take effect on June 15, when he will accept the Pastorate of Trinity Presbyterian Church at Montclair, N. J.

## CLEVELAND AND THURMAN

### *THE LATEST TICKET FIXED FOR ST. LOUIS.*

OHIO'S EX-SENATOR SAID TO HAVE BEEN CONSULTED AND TO HAVE CONSENTED TO THE USE OF HIS NAME.

PHILADELPHIA, May 27.—The Philadelphia *Times* will say to-morrow:

"The Democratic ticket to be placed in nomination at the St. Louis Convention will be: For President—Grover Cleveland of New-York; for Vice-President—Allen G. Thurman of Ohio. Ex-United States Senator Thurman has been asked if he will accept the nomination for Vice-President, and he has given his consent to allow his name to be presented to the Convention, and will go on the ticket. The nomination has been tendered to the Ohio statesman with the full knowledge and approbation of the leading men of the party in all sections of the country, North, East, South, and West. For the past 10 days there has been a rapid concentration of opinion that Thurman was the one man among men to nominate for Vice-President. The Nestor of the Democratic Party; the sturdiest and acknowledged representative of Jackson Democratic principles; an advocate of half a century for honest and economical government and with an integrity above suspicion; loved by his friends and admired by his political opponents, the thinking Democrats of the States turned to the Ohio statesman as the best, the strongest, and in every way the most acceptable Democrat to make the great battle of 1888 with Grover Cleveland.

"In the few consultations which have been had on the subject it was conceded that the nomination of Thurman would keep the Republicans busy with preventing him from running away with Ohio; that the old men of the party who had grown up in the faith and had been fed upon its principles would give Thurman such support as they would accord no other Democrat, and that the young men would rally with unexcelled enthusiasm around the man they have been taught to accept as one of the purest, ablest, and grandest characters in the Democratic Party.

"Congressman Samuel J. Randall was in the city to-day, and when asked as to the probable composition of the national ticket replied: 'Senator Thurman will undoubtedly be the nominee for Vice-President. He is agreed upon by everybody, is willing to accept the nomination, and, in my judgment, is the best and strongest man in the country to place upon the ticket. I think it is a wise selection—the wisest that could have been made.'

"The mention of Thurman's name, it is believed, will lead to the result of there being but two ballots taken in the National Convention—the first to nominate Grover Cleveland, and the second to nominate Allen G. Thurman. The South has no candidate, and stands ready to do whatever New-York may ask for, and that will be Thurman. Pennsylvania will join hands with New-York, and there will be no differences of opinion in the Ohio delegation. That much would be enough to nominate, and the thought is that such candidates as have been mentioned will not further press their claims. In the light of recent events, the leading Democrats feel perfectly safe about Indiana, and the nomination of Thurman, they think, will sweep away all petty wars and troubles and cement the party for a vigorous and aggressive campaign."

### ST. LOUIS GETTING READY.

TO ENTERTAIN THE DELEGATES TO THE DEMOCRATIC CONVENTION.

ST. LOUIS, Mo., May 27.—Arrangements for the reception and entertainment of the delegates to the Democratic National Convention next week are almost completed. The big hall in the Exposition Building will be turned over to the decorators to-morrow and the most beautiful and elaborate decorations are promised. They will be of China silk, rich fabrics of national colors, and natural flowers and plants. Portraits in cathedral glass and oil of the fathers of the Republic will occupy prominent positions in the hall. The street illuminations will be magnificent. Most of the arches on Olive-street are up and covered with myriads of vari-colored globes. At Fourteenth-street an arch is surmounted with a cathedral glass portrait of George Washington. At the intersection of Twelfth and Olive streets are four arches, forming a square. In the centre is the American eagle in cathedral glass, and beneath, in small gas jets, the words "Public Office a Public Trust." The features of the entertainment will be a big Tuesday night parade by local societies, military and civic, a river excursion, and a grand pyrotechnic display.

The question of the proper way to distribute the tickets to the hall is still agitating the Executive Committee. It has finally been decided to submit the matter to the Executive Committee of the National Committee, who will arrive here this week.

### POETIC JUSTICE IN POLITICS.

HARTFORD, Conn., May 27.—The removal of two Republicans from the clerical force in the United States Government Envelope Agency here and the appointment of two Democrats in their places must be considered an infraction no doubt of the civil service reform policy of the Administration, but in the case of one of the appointments the change is an example of poetic justice. Joseph Mairson, one of the new clerks, is a Democratic ward politician, and his selection would not have been possible except on the ground of politics. Charles E. Pease, the second clerk, is also a Democrat, but has been charged with being a Republican. The Government agent here, William L. Eaton, son of ex-Senator Eaton, says in a public card: "Pease was recommended for the position in the envelope agency by influential and respected Democrats. He was appointed as a Democrat, and if it can be shown that he has been a Republican and voted their ticket I will recommend his dismissal."

The statement in point in connection with Pease is that four years ago he was discharged from a clerkship in a Republican manufacturing house here solely because he voted for President Cleveland. It is well authenticated that the Republican henchman who threatened him with dismissal from his place because he would not vote for Blaine is now an active manager of Republican politics and interests in this city. Partisan criticism of Agent Eaton's course in appointing Pease will react on the politicians who promote it when the real facts in the case are presented.

### PLENTY OF CANDIDATES.

LITTLE ROCK, Ark., May 27.—The contest for Governor before the Democratic State Convention which meets here on Thursday grows in interest. Gov. S. P. Hughes is a candidate for the third time and is opposed by J. G. Fletcher, J. P. Eagle, W. M. Fishback, and E. W. Rector. Yesterday 39 counties held conventions and elected and instructed delegates to the State Convention. The strength of the candidates as shown by returns so far in is: Fletcher, 142; Hughes, 103; Eagle, 80; Fishback, 78; Rector, 17. The contest in the convention promises to be very bitter. It requires 228 votes to nominate, there being 454 delegates.

### *IN MEMORY OF SECRETARY SEWARD.*

AUBURN, N. Y., May 27.—A memorial service attended by several hundred people was held at the grave of the late Secretary Seward, in Fort Hill Cemetery this afternoon. The Sons of Veterans and Seward Post, G. A. R., marched in a body to the Seward burial plot and placed a floral pillow at the head of the tomb of the statesman. Prayer was offered by the Rev. J. K. Dixon of the First Baptist Church, and an address was delivered by the Rev. F. H. Hinman of Calvary Presbyterian Church. General Seward with the ladies of his family were present in his carriage.

### *A FOREST FIRE IN VERMONT.*

ST. JOHNSBURY, Vt., May 27.—A forest fire is raging in the vicinity of Hazen's Mills, in Victory, threatening the destruction of the entire settlement. Yesterday afternoon about 20 families vacated their dwellings, and all live stock was driven out. Eighty or more men have been fighting the fire, and this morning it was thought the mills and houses would be saved. Quite a quantity of wood and bark has been burned, but the loss is covered by insurance.

### *STILL AFRAID OF THE POISON.*

William H. Gore, whose life was saved by liberal doses of whisky after being severely bitten by a rattlesnake recently, is, according to last accounts, still taking his medicine regularly. He was found drunk at Lexington-avenue and One Hundred and Twenty-fifth-street Saturday night and arrested. Yesterday in the Harlem Police Court he said that he was still drinking by order of his physicians, and Justice Gorman discharged him after admonishing him to take his antidotes at home hereafter.



### *GOV. LESLIE DENIES IT.*

SERIOUS CHARGES MADE BY A WYOMING SHERIFF.

HELENA, Montana, May 27.—Under Sheriff Thomas Farrell of Jackson County, Wyoming, who was recently in Montana with a requisition for Charlie Brown, charged by Wyoming authorities with larceny, makes a statement which contains some severe strictures upon Gov. Leslie of Montana. The latter is charged with using his official influence and knowledge to prevent the capture of the notorious prisoner wanted by the authorities of Wyoming. Farrell also asserts that the Governor sought to shield Brown because of the fact that his son was acting as attorney in the requisition case. Farrell claims that for some reason the Governor seemed inclined to dishonor his requisition papers and kept him waiting in Helena for more than a month. Three requisitions were sent for by the Sheriff before the Governor would honor the papers. When he finally honored them Farrell started for his man, who was at Great Falls.

Arriving at Sun River Crossing, where Brown's headquarters were, he found that the game had flown. Farrell says that when Brown was first arrested he hired as his counsel the son of Gov. Leslie. So confident was the latter of winning his case that he made a bargain with Brown that if he cleared him he was to receive $100, otherwise not a cent would be charged. Farrell also asserts that Attorney Leslie made his boast that the requisition papers would not be issued by the Governor. At Sun River Farrell says he discovered that a telephone message had arrived four hours ahead of him, dated Helena, addressed to Devine, which stated that "the warrant had been issued," and was signed "L." This put Brown on his guard and he rode away. Farrell alleges that a telegram was sent by Gov. Leslie himself.

Gov. Leslie says that Brown did have a civil suit some time ago in Cascade County, and the Governor's son was his lawyer in that case, and the Governor knew it, but he never heard until yesterday that his son had anything to do with the defense or management of Brown's case, on account of which a warrant was issued upon the requisition papers. The first two requisitions were not sufficient under the law to justify the Governor in issuing a warrant for the arrest and transportation asked for, and hence the refusal complained of. It is not true, the Governor says, that he telegraphed to "Devine" at Sun River or anywhere else, nor did he telegraph any one or write to any one with a view in any way to interfere with the arrest of Brown.

### *AMERICAN ART.*

THE EXHIBITION OF THE CHICAGO ART INSTITUTE.

CHICAGO, May 27.—The first Chicago Art Institute exhibition of American art was opened to the public last night. The exhibition is the first of the series under the double prize fund. J. W. Elsworth gives $300 for the best picture painted by an American in the country. The Art Institute gives $250 for the next best painting by all Americans anywhere. The prizes will be awarded in three weeks.

Over 300 pictures are on exhibition, including works by many well-known painters. Among them are canvases by Will H. Low of New-York, Charles C. Curran, F. S. Church, Thomas Dewing, George Inness, Percy Moran, William Chace, A. H. Thayer, J. Alden Weir, Theodore Wores, Kenyon Coxe, Alfred Kappes, Frederick Bridgman, Charles D. Welden, W. A. Coffin, Charles Platt, and Gilbert Gaul. The attendance at the opening was extremely good, about 2,000 people visiting the gallery. The exhibit is considered very good, especially for the first exhibition given by the institute. The present officers of the institute are C. L. Hutchinson, President; Eison Keith, Vice-President; L. J. Gage, Treasurer; N. H. Carpenter, Secretary, and W. M. R. French, Director. The Executive Committee consists of C. L. Hutchinson, Eison Keith, James H. Dole, Joseph M. Rogers, C. D. Hamil, John C. Black, and W. T. Baker.

### *THE BONANZA MEN SUED.*

A STOCKHOLDER OF CONSOLIDATED VIRGINIA HAS A GRIEVANCE.

SAN FRANCISCO, May 27.—John Nelson filed suit yesterday afternoon against the Nevada Bank, John W. Mackay, James C. Flood, J. P. Jones, the Comstock Mill and Mining Company, the Consolidated California and Virginia Mining Company, and others, wherein he alleges that Mackay, Flood, and Jones, who own a controlling interest in the Consolidated Virginia, entered into a combination and conspiracy to defraud the other stockholders, including complainant, in pursuance of which they allowed the Consolidated Virginia ore to be crushed at the mills of the Comstock Mining Company, organized by themselves. On this ore they charged from $2 to $3 per ton more for milling than other mill companies would have done, thereby defrauding the stockholders, it is claimed, out of fully $800,000. In addition to this, defendants, as Directors of the Nevada Bank, charged commissions for the sale of the bullion, whereby they again swindled the stockholders out of over $800,000. Other charges are made, and the complainant asks that the defendants be compelled to account for these sums; that all contracts between the Consolidated Virginia and the Comstock Company, and between those companies and the Nevada Bank, be declared void.

### *CHARGED WITH A TERRIBLE CRIME.*

PHILADELPHIA, May 27.—Joseph Gallen, aged 13 years, a son of Patrick Gallen of Somerville, a suburb of Germantown, died at the Germantown Hospital this afternoon from concussion of the brain caused by a fall from the third story of his father's house. The boy was found lying unconscious in the road at an early hour by some of the neighbors, and was sent to the hospital. There was a severe wound in the back of the head, the body was badly bruised, and one leg was broken. He died at 4 o'clock without having uttered a word. Officers Youngkin and Pollock were summoned, and on the strength of the story of a number of the neighbors that his father, while wild with drink, had thrown the boy out of the window, Gallen was taken to the Fourteenth District Police Station. He was too drunk to be given a hearing when Magistrate Diamond came to the station house to hold his Sunday morning hearing.

### *BELONGS TO A BAD GANG.*

ELMIRA, N. Y., May 27.—James, alias Bernard, Farley, who broke into the residence of Charles Smith at Horseheads on May 1, and who was arrested at Newburg last night, is implicated in other questionable transactions that will probably keep him behind the bars for some time. Farley is from the Bowery, New-York, and is reputed to be one of the toughest members of the several bad gangs that infest that thoroughfare. Detective John Hogan of Horseheads left this evening for Newburg to secure Farley, who will be brought here to answer for burglary, as well as for being the leader of the gang that recently robbed the Westlake residence at the Horseheads brick yard and the boarding houses there of several thousand dollars. There have been several other burglaries in this section that, no doubt, are traceable to this Bowery gang. Officers are on the track of Farley's accomplices, and their capture is confidently expected.

### *NOTES FROM NEWPORT.*

NEWPORT, R. I., May 27.—Five hundred and seventy-four barrels of fish, 337 for Philadelphia and 237 for New-York, representing Saturday's and to-day's catch, were shipped to-night. There are no shipments Saturday nights. In the lots shipped there were only about 40 barrels of scup.

Mr. Isaac Bell, Jr., ex-Minister to the Netherlands, left here for Washington to-night for the purpose of officially reporting his return and of settling his accounts. He will not return to join his family here until after the Democratic Convention, and he will meet the Rhode Island delegation, of which he is Chairman, in New-York.

### *DAMAGING WIND AND RAIN STORM.*

DAYTON, Ohio, May 27.—A rain and wind storm, which raged with some severity for several hours, visited this locality this morning. Numerous trees were blown over. Large damage to crops is reported. While the family of Jacob Stroble was at church, the residence was struck by lightning and partly destroyed.

BELFAST, May 27.—Searle, one of the men who was accused of being implicated in the Equitable Life Insurance frauds, has volunteered to give information covering the whole period of his connection with fraudulent insurance.

## MR. MAYNARD DEFENDED

### *SECRETARY FAIRCHILD APPROVES HIS COURSE.*

THE SUGAR FRAUDS UNDER INVESTIGATION FOR YEARS—MR. FAIRCHILD SHOULDERS ALL RESPONSIBILITY.

WASHINGTON, May 27.—The Secretary of the Treasury to-day expressed himself freely in regard to the removals which have been made in the New-York City Appraiser's Department in consequence of alleged frauds in the classification of sugars, and particularly as to the testimony thus far developed before the Senate committee upon that subject. Mr. Fairchild said that this matter had been under investigation for nearly two years; that the investigation was originally begun by the late Secretary Manning, who, some time in the Fall of 1886, called it to his attention, and that since Mr. Manning's retirement from the department the whole subject had been personally known to him (Mr. Fairchild) in all of its details; that nothing had been done about it by Judge Maynard, except by the direction and with the previous knowledge and approval of Secretary Fairchild; that Judge Maynard knew nothing of the matter until some time after he became Assistant Secretary, which was in April, 1887; that all of the removals which had been made because of the alleged sugar frauds were made by Mr. Fairchild's express direction, and solely with a view to the purification and improvement of the public service, and with no regard whatever to any personal or political consideration; that the same was true of the non-removals and the restoration after removal mentioned in said investigation; that he (Mr. Fairchild) was himself personally responsible for the same; that it was grossly unjust to censure Judge Maynard, but that if there was occasion for censure it should be directed against Mr. Fairchild himself. "Of one thing," he added, "I am sure, and that is that the Government has in its service no better, more conscientious man and none more faithful and devoted to the public interests than Judge Maynard."

Mr. Fairchild further said that the question of civil service reform, as such reform had heretofore been understood, was not at all involved; that if what had been done by the department in this matter was in violation of the principles of civil service reform, then this reform would itself be a greater evil than were the evils which it was designed to remedy; that the judgment and action of the responsible head of a department could not be hampered in the way indicated without serious danger to the integrity and efficiency of the public service, and that, if it was to be so hampered, whether by law or otherwise, then no self-respecting man could afford to take charge of any department. He added: "Examination and criticism of the actions of public officers are wholesome, but the habit of believing the tale of every subordinate whom his superior may have thought it well to remove, and of assuming that all officers who make removals are actuated therein by unworthy motives, is not wholesome, but on the contrary most pernicious to the public welfare."

Mr. Fairchild further said that the matter of the investigation of alleged sugar frauds was by no means at an end, and although the efforts of the department to learn the truth and to correct what he feared to be gross irregularities and wrongs of long standing might and probably would be seriously impeded by the uses to which certain men of fair repute in the community suffered themselves to be put, yet he had hope and confidence that in due time such efforts would be successful.

### *FOR THE BLACK REPUBLIC.*

THE YANTIC TO SAIL FOR PORT AU PRINCE AT ONCE.

PORT ROYAL, S. C., May 27.—The recent news of approaching troubles of a serious nature, which may to an important degree affect United States interests in the Black Republic, has been fully confirmed by Washington dispatches and has caused a partial change of programme as far as the disposition of the vessels of the North Atlantic squadron is concerned. The Yantic, Commander Heyerman, with 3 guns and 140 officers and men, the only vessel at present immediately available unless the new steel cruiser Boston might seize this occasion to make her maiden bow to old Neptune, will leave Beaufort to-morrow morning for Port Royal naval station, there to fill up with coal and take provisions from the other vessels at the anchorage. These preparations being completed, she will proceed with the utmost speed to Port au Prince, the seat of Government of President Salomon, the quasi King of the Haytien Republic. Should the present troubles develop into something of sufficient importance the other war vessels in commission in North Atlantic waters will no doubt quickly follow the Yantic.

### *SPECIAL LUTHERAN SERVICES.*

LANCASTER, Penn., May 27.—The Lutheran ministers in attendance at the Ministerium of Pennsylvania here filled a majority of the pulpits in this city to-day. At old Trinity, where the Synod is meeting, the Rev. Dr. Seiss of Philadelphia preached in the morning, and the Rev. J. M. Anspach of Easton in the evening. A festal service was held in the Sunday school this afternoon, at which addresses were made by the Rev. Dr. G. F. Krotel of New-York, Dr. Samuel Laird of Philadelphia, and D. H. Geissinger of Easton, former Pastors, and others.

At Zion's Lutheran Church the fifteenth anniversary of the consecration of the present building was celebrated with jubilee services, which attracted three large congregations. In the morning the Rev. Dr. A. Spaeth of Philadelphia preached the sermon; in the afternoon a children's service was held at 2 o'clock, consisting of responsive readings, music, and addresses by the Rev. Dr. W. J. Mann of Philadelphia, the Rev. F. Wischan of Philadelphia, and others. The Pastor, the Rev. F. P. Mayser, made a statement showing that the church and Sunday school were in a flourishing condition. In the evening the Rev. B. W. Schwank of Lebanon preached the sermon. The church was handsomely decorated, and special music was rendered at each service.

This evening the Rev. D. H. Geissinger of Easton preached the Memorial Day sermon to George H. Thomas Post, No. 84, and Admiral Reynolds Post, No. 405, G. A. R., in the Presbyterian Church.

### *WANT THE LAW ENFORCED.*

LONG BRANCH, N. J., May 27.—The new Law and Order League here is raising money for the prompt and thorough prosecution of all hotel men who violate the laws as well as all the gamblers. The league has raised a breeze by issuing a circular addressed to residents and others owning property here, signed by 70 well-known citizens, including the Pastors of the several churches. This circular alleges that the prosperity of Long Branch has waned because of "a total disregard of official oaths and neglect of duty by officers of the law," and says: "In fact, every citizen knows the law has been continually violated, and numerous disorderly places permitted to exist which could not exist unless under the protection of the legal authorities. A certain locality has hardly a building within 300 yards of it which has not either a barroom or gambling outlay in it. One can hardly step into the street without facing the flashily-dressed habitués of these places and their brazen-faced companions of the other sex.

"Three murders have been commited here within one year. One occurred in a place for a long time known to the police as a notoriously-disorderly house, and yet until a murder was committed there the authorities never took any steps to purify it. There is no Sunday here, and law is exceedingly scarce." The circular closes by saying: "This confession of the immorality of our town is reluctantly made, but we had better face and extirpate it rather than try to conceal it, for, like murder, it 'will out.'"

### *DROWNED IN SIGHT OF THOUSANDS.*

BRIDGEPORT, Conn., May 27.—Charles Mason and James Kelly were returning from Black Rock this afternoon. When off Sea Side Park their boat was overturned. Mason clung to the boat, but Kelly attempted to swim ashore. Thousands of spectators at the park rushed to the water's edge, but were unable to render succor to Kelly, who shouted for help. Women on the shore wept and fainted with excitement. Kelly soon sank and his body went out with the tide. Mason was afterward rescued.

# The New-York Times.

VOL. XXXVII.....NO. 11,473. NEW-YORK, THURSDAY, JUNE 7, 1888.—WITH SUPPLEMENT. PRICE TWO CENTS.




## CLEVELAND RENOMINATED

### AND HIS TARIFF REFORM POLICY INDORSED.

THE CONVENTION SPENDS HALF AN HOUR IN WILDLY CHEERING THE PRESIDENT—A PLATFORM TO BE REPORTED TO-DAY INDORSING THE MESSAGE AND THE MILLS BILL—THE FIGHT IN THE PLATFORM LONG AND CLOSE.

ST. LOUIS, June 6.—The long and tiresome struggle over the tariff between the opposing factions in the Committee on Resolutions came to an end to-night. The resolution which the committee will report to the convention renews the party's pledge of fidelity to Democratic principles, indorses the last annual message of President Cleveland, and declares that message to be a correct interpretation of the tariff platform of 1884, and approves and applauds the efforts of Democratic Representatives in Congress to secure reduced taxation. There will also be offered to the convention a supplementary resolution commending the Mills bill and urging Democrats to vote for it and pass it. Mr. Watterson says: "My original idea did not contemplate a recurrence to the resolution of 1884, and of course I opposed a repetition of that resolution when it was proposed, but as it is coupled with an authoritative interpretation of that ambiguous platform and with an indorsement of the work of our party in Congress, the resolution as finally adopted meets my most hearty approval."

It is announced that the committee will present a solid front in support of the tariff plank, and that ex-Gov. Abbett of New-Jersey will move the adoption of the report. Mr. Lehmann of Iowa declares that he will support the report. He regards it as "an advance," but it is not entirely satisfactory to him.

The sub-committee of eleven, to which the work of framing a platform had been referred, was busily engaged until 3 o'clock this morning, and at 9 o'clock that part of the work which related to the tariff was brought back into the whole committee. It is understood that the sub-committee had been unable to agree and that a majority of its members were not in accord with Mr. Watterson, although seven of the eleven had voted to make him Chairman. It is also stated that when the subject came back to the whole committee the sub-committee had taken no steps toward the indorsement of the President's message. The first vote in the whole committee was upon a preamble in which the tariff resolution of 1884 was reaffirmed. Mr. Watterson moved that this be stricken out, and was beaten by a vote of 25 to 21. Thereupon the committee adjourned, and the work was resumed at 6 o'clock this evening. Lawrence T. Neil of Ohio had voted to make Gorman Chairman because he admired the man, although his opinions concerning the tariff coincided with those of Watterson. After Watterson's motion to strike out had been lost Neil moved the adoption of additions which were substantially those relating to the message and the Mills bill, which were finally adopted.

Early in the day there was some probability that the contest would be taken into the convention. But the compromise that was reached this evening appears to have prevented any such outbreak. The real tariff reformers made great gains in the closing hours of the fight. As has been shown heretofore, their opponents were determined at first that neither the message nor the Mills bill should be mentioned. But considerable pressure was applied to the committee by means of telegrams from Congressmen and others. Several members who had betrayed their trust were placed under discipline, notably the Missouri member, O'Day, who had surrendered to Gorman, in the face of the strongest State resolutions and the most positive instructions. Early this evening some of the obstructionists were forced to admit that the message would be indorsed, but they declared that an "unqualified" indorsement was neither probable nor expedient. This was the attitude of ex-Senator Davis of West Virginia.

Mr. Morrison expresses satisfaction with the result. One of the reasons which kept him out of the committee was this, that it had become the duty of the Illinois member to urge the adoption of a resolution in support of the proposed Hennepin canal, and this project is not advocated in the southern part of the State, where Mr. Morrison lives. He prefered that the duty should be performed by some other man.

The history of this contest will show that owing to the neglect of leaders of the majority, a committee which ought to have fairly represented the party was at one time almost evenly divided upon the question whether it should indorse or even recognize the most prominent feature of the policy of a President whom a convention of the party had actually renominated unanimously for another term. And only in the last hours of the struggle was the influence of protected interests and mischief-makers overcome. The other work of the convention has been delayed by this struggle in committee. Nothing has been done beyond the nomination of Mr. Cleveland. A nomination for the second place will be made to-morrow.

"He has done his duty; let us do ours," said Mr. McKenzie to-day while seconding the nomination of Mr. Cleveland. If the differences of the Resolutions Committee on the tariff had been carried into the convention to-day the obstructionists would speedily have been routed.

The scene in the convention hall immediately after the closing words of Mr. Dougherty's speech, "I give you a name entwined with victory; I nominate Grover Cleveland of New-York," was one long to be remembered. For nearly 25 minutes the vast crowd applauded. The standard of all the States were taken from their stations and grouped around New-York's uplifted shield. The vote for adjournment appears to have had no special significance with regard to the nomination for second place.

F. D. R.

## TARIFF REFORM INDORSED.

THE PLATFORM WILL REAFFIRM THAT OF 1884 AND APPROVE PRESIDENT CLEVELAND'S TARIFF REFORM MESSAGE.

ST. LOUIS, June 6.—The Committee on Resolutions, at 8:30 to-night, have agreed upon the tariff plank of the platform by a unanimous vote. The plank is as follows:

"The Democratic Party of the United States in National Convention assembled renews the pledge of its fidelity to Democratic faith, reaffirms the platform adopted by its representatives in the convention of 1884, and indorses the views expressed by President Cleveland in his last annual message to Congress as the correct interpretation of that platform upon the question of tariff reduction, and also indorses the efforts of our Democratic Representatives in Congress to secure a reduction of excessive taxation."

This plank was the outcome of a long fight begun in the sub-committee last night and continued to-day in the meeting of the whole committee. The sub-committee, which was supposed to consist of seven men in accord with Mr. Watterson and four who were in accord with Mr. Gorman, turned out at an early stage of the proceedings to be opposed to Mr. Watterson, who would not consent to a reaffirmation of the tariff plank of 1884. The draft of a platform prepared by Mr. Scott, and which was understood to satisfy the Administration, did not at all meet Mr. Watterson's expectations. The sub-committee gave up its efforts to agree and the full committee took up the subject. Mr. Scott had taken the place of Mr. Mutchler as the member from Pennsylvania, and he appealed to the committee to give careful consideration to the platform offered, as one prepared with the hope of reasonably satisfying all sections of the party. It was not deemed necessary to reiterate the language of the platform of 1884, but to reiterate fidelity to its principles as understood and acted upon by the President and Congress.

Soon after the committee met Mr. Watterson's strength was tested. He made a motion to substitute for the plank offered by Mr. Scott a plank of his own of a more radical character, containing no references to the platform of 1884, but committing the party to tariff reform as the supreme issue. There were 46 members of the committee present. Of these 21 voted with Mr. Watterson and 25 voted against him. Having decided not to follow Mr. Watterson's advice the committee directed its attention to the verbal form of the leading resolution. The plank, as submitted by Mr. Scott, stopped at the words "tariff reduction." Upon the suggestion of Mr. Neal of Ohio the words beginning "We also indorse the efforts of our Democratic Representatives in Congress" were added, as he considered that the platform would be lame and imperfect if it did not directly approve the attempt being made in Congress to reduce taxation. Mr. Cooper of New-York was inclined to split hairs as usual. He contended a long time for a verbal change. It seemed important to him to say that the convention considered the President's message as "in accord with the platform of 1884" instead of characterizing it as "a correct interpretation of the language of the platform of 1884."

Mr. Scott is satisfied with the plank. So is Mr. Watterson, or at least he says it is satisfactory. Mr. Watterson likes it, of course, as he reported the platform of 1884, and his interpretation of it was always the interpretation that the President gave of it in his message to Congress. Mr. Barnum does not know whether he likes it or not. Mr. Kelly of Minnesota thinks that it rather squints both ways, but he does not grumble.

If the plank is not satisfactory to exacting tariff reformers, who had been led to believe that the Democratic Party was ready boldly to take hold of tariff reform in the convention, it will be because the party managers could not see their way to victory with a radical utterance. The representatives of protected industries—Democrats of Pennsylvania of prominence and influence, whose co-operation in the coming campaign was desired—undoubtedly intimated that a radical utterance would compel them to remain indifferent spectators during the coming struggle.

The action of the committee will probably be found to mean that Mr. W. H. Barnum will be at the head of the National Committee; that Mr. Gorman will also be an active worker in the campaign, and that Mr. Davis of West Virginia, Mr. Abbett, and other sensitive Democrats will be kept in the harness and help in the campaign for Cleveland and Thurman.

## THE CONVENTION AT WORK AGAIN.

MR. CLEVELAND'S RENOMINATION MADE AMID THE WILDEST EXCITEMENT—DANIEL DOUGHERTY'S NOMINATING SPEECH—GEN. COLLINS PRAISES THE INDEPENDENTS—TARIFF REFORM EXPRESSIONS.

ST. LOUIS, June 6.—Grover Cleveland is the candidate of the Democratic Party for President—renominated with a degree of enthusiasm remarkable in a period that has seen some of the most remarkable demonstrations of the popularity of public men. At high noon, under a fervid Summer sun, in the presence of a magnificent audience of spectators, in a hall radiant with the national colors, and without a suggestion of opposition to the spirit that moved the vast assemblage of delegates and spectators, the name of Cleveland was submitted as a candidate for renomination.

The half hour of cheering that followed the first mention of his name, the roar of shouts that rang against the high roof like the beating of a thousand cymbals, the gradual tearing from their places of decorations that were afterward waved in the air in the frenzy of enthusiasm, with the fluttering of flags, banners, and bandana handkerchiefs, the tumult that no Chairman could have controlled, are unmatched since the partisans of Grant and Blaine strove against each other in the Republican Convention of 1880.

From the moment of presentation to that of nomination, including the time consumed by those who made the speeches seconding the nomination, until the rules were suspended and Grover Cleveland declared to be the absolutely unanimous choice of the convention, was just one hour and a quarter. The task was one to which the convention addressed itself with pleasure, and it discharged it with celerity as well as impressive enthusiasm.

The convention had been called to meet at 10 o'clock. As the hour approached and it was known that the sub-Committee on Resolutions was still at work on the draft of the platform, the impression that the convention would be delayed to wait for the committee's report made the delegates slow about moving toward the hall. The weather was hot. The breeze that blew through the streets from the southwest was agreeable and the atmosphere was not so oppressive as it was yesterday noon. But the wear and tear of street and corridor life had begun to tell upon the delegates as well as the effort to survive St. Louis hospitality.

It was a motley throng that crowded along Olive-street. Delegates in uniform, with bandana handkerchiefs or gray bands about their hats, sweltered as they made their way and as they stopped in groups to quench their thirst at soda fountains or the stands of lemonade vendors. Some of them wore little roosters in their hats or upon their shoulders. Some were decorated with three or four gold and blue or gold and red badges. Those who marched in clubs to the hall carried bandana handkerchiefs tied at the knobs of canes and waved them overhead.

In the hall before 10 o'clock an audience even larger than that of yesterday had assembled. The long line of flags and loops of colors were as fresh and in as good order as when left by the decorators. The boxes were filled with ladies, and all along the front of the upper gallery and from seats on the platform fans of delicate make fluttered before the faces of the fair damsels of St. Louis. The band played at the end of the hall under Washington on horseback, but its music came faintly down over the buzzing of the conversation and the moving feet of the thousands who were making their way to their seats. The bandana handkerchiefs were again tied to the tops of banner staffs at the heads of delegations, making more cheers at each display of the old Roman's colors. Each delegate found on his chair an advertising fan, and when, long after 10, they had come in to the extent of two-thirds of the entire number there was a flutter of color all the way from the front to the last row of spectators.

### THE DAY'S BUSINESS BEGUN.

It was 10:20 when Chairman White, with his bandana flapping over his California badge and a rose in the lapel of his coat, rapped for order. There was a sudden scurrying of the crowds in front. Newspaper men who had come late, and whose places were not on the aisles, had to disturb whole rows of other newspaper men, as the meagre space allotted to them had compelled the packing of about 250 men as closely as sardines. A grant of three or four inches more to each row would have taken very little space in the aggregate, and would have deprived the convention of none of the space it needed.

While the people hurried to their seats confusion reigned. A pause of a few moments sufficed to bring order out of the confusion. Then the Chairman rapped again with his silver gavel, and he introduced the Rev. J. P. Green of Missouri, to make the opening prayer. Cries of "Down," "Silence," and "Sit down in front" went up from distant parts of the hall while the preacher was uttering the opening words of his prayer. Most of the delegates stood with bowed heads, but the aisles were thronged with pages and Sergeants-at-Arms who paid no heed to the platform exercises at any stage.

The prayer ended, the Chairman read a resolution offered by Secretary F. O. Prince of Massachusetts accepting with thanks the gift of the silver gavel by Colorado, and recommending that it be placed in care of the National Committee for use at future conventions. It was promptly approved.

Delegate T. J. Campbell of New-York sent up some resolutions which were read demanding an enforcement of the Monroe doctrine, and they were sent to the Committee on Resolutions.

A strong tariff expression was offered in the form of a resolution by S. R. Malloy of Florida, and its language, approving and indorsing the principle of tariff reform laid down by the President in his message, was heard and applauded. It went in due course to the Committee on Resolutions.

Through Chairman T. C. Webb of Alabama the Committee on Credentials reported that the only contest was that between the Church and the Day factions of the Dakota Democracy, and this had been settled by admitting by an almost unanimous vote the delegates of the Louis K. Church wing. The committee also reported in favor of admitting Arthur K. Delaney and A. H. Goddard as delegates from Alaska. The convention adopted the report, and thus for the first time in its history Alaska is admitted to the convention of a national political party.

William R. Cassidy of Pennsylvania reported that his Committee on Permanent Organization had unanimously selected Congressman Patrick A. Collins of Boston for permanent Chairman, and recommended that no State be allowed to change its vote during a roll call until the roll call is entirely finished. This proposition to prevent the stampeding of the convention was immediately approved by the convention, and so was the committee's selection of a permanent Chairman. Chairman White appointed William H. Barnum of Connecticut, Roswell P. Flower of New-York, and John O'Day of Missouri to escort the young Congressman to the chair. The Massachusetts delegates sent to the platform a handsome floral piece of roses and carnations artistically arranged to represent the seal of the old Bay State. Tennessee also contributed a floral gift, and both were conspicuously displayed upon the platform.

### GEN. COLLINS'S ADDRESS.

Gen. Collins was comfort and coolness personified. He wore a loose alpaca coat and carried a fan. He was cheered as he stepped forward and placed his manuscript upon the desk. His voice, though distinct and strong, was incapable of being heard by anybody in the seats beyond the section occupied by the delegates. But it was to the delegates that he addressed himself, and the applause that was frequently bestowed was sufficient to indicate that they understood him and appreciated his points. His tribute to the Administration of President Cleveland, and particularly his declaration that it compels the respect, confidence, and approval of the people of the United States, was received with demonstrations that were vigorous and at the same time sincere. Congressman Collins differs with some of his party in the estimation to be placed upon the services of the independent voters. He frankly asserted that "to the patriotic and independent citizens who came to our support the Democratic Party and the country owed a debt of gratitude," a sentiment which evoked only the most formal recognition.

"To stand by your favor in this place, so often filled by the foremost men in our great party, is a distinction of the highest character and an honor for which I am profoundly grateful. In performing the delicate and difficult service to which you have assigned me, I can scarcely hope to justify the wisdom of your choice. I shall at all times need a continuance of your indulgence and courtesy, as well as your full co-operation to promote order, decorum, and good will until these proceedings are brought to a happy close.

"We represent in this convention more than 30,000,000 of the American people; we bear the commission to act for them and their injunction to act with all the wisdom that God has given us, to protect and safeguard the institutions of the Republic as the fathers founded them.

"In a time when the world was king-ridden and pauperized by the privileged few, when men scarcely dared to breathe the word 'Liberty,' even if they understood its meaning, the people scattered along our eastern coast with a sublime heroism never equaled, broke from all traditions, rejected all known systems, and established, to the amazement of the world, the political wonder of the ages, the American Republic, the child of revolution nursed by philosophy. The hand that framed the immortal Declaration of Independence is the hand that guided the emancipated country to progress and glory. It is the hand that guides us still in our onward march as a free and progressive people. The principles upon which our Government can securely rest, upon which the peace, prosperity, and liberties of the people depend are the principles of the founder of our party, the apostle of Democracy, Thomas Jefferson.

"Our young men under 30 have heard more in their time of the clash of arms and the echoes of war than of the principles of government. It has been a period of passion, force, impulse, and emotional politics. So that we need not wonder that now and then we hear the question asked and scarcely answered, 'What difference is there between the two parties?' Every Democrat knows the difference. The Democratic creed was not penned by Jefferson for a section or a class of the people, but for all time. These principles conserved and expanded the Republic in all its better days. A strict adherence to them will preserve it to the end, so the Democracy of to-day as in the past believe with Jefferson in (1) equal and exact justice to all men of whatever state or persuasion, religious or political; (2) peace, commerce, and honest friendship with all nations, entangling alliances with none; (3) support of the State Governments in all their rights as the most competent administrators of our domestic concerns, and the surest bulwarks against anti-Republican tendencies; (4) the preservation of the general Government in its whole constitutional vigor, as the sheet anchor of our peace and safety abroad; (5) a jealous care of the right of election by the people, a mild and safe corrective of abuses, which are lopped off by the sword of revolution where peaceable means are unprovided; (6) absolute acquiescence in the decisions of the majority, the vital principle of republics, from which is no appeal but to force, the vital principle and immediate parent of despotism; (7) a well-disciplined militia, our best reliance in peace and for the first moments in war; (8) the supremacy of the civil over the military authority; (9) economy in the public expenses, that labor may be lightly burdened; (10) the honest payment of our debts and the preservation of our public faith; (11) encouragement of agriculture and of commerce as its handmaid; (12) the diffusion of information and arraignment of all abuses at the bar of public reason; (13) freedom of religion; (14) freedom of the press; (15) freedom of the person under the protection of the habeas corpus; (16) trial by juries impartially selected. Add to these the golden economic rule that no more taxes should be levied upon the people in any way than are necessary to meet the honest expenses of government, and you have a body of principles to sin against which has been political death to every party hitherto, to sin against which in the future will be political suicide.

"True to these principles the Democratic Party fought successfully our foreign wars, protected our citizens in every clime, compelled the respect of all nations for our flag, added imperial domain to our territory, and insured peace, prosperity, and happiness to all our people. False to these principles the great Federal, Whig, and Know-Nothing parties went down, never to rise, and we are here to-day, representatives of the party that has survived all others, the united, triumphant, invincible Democracy, prepared to strike down forever the last surviving foe in November.

"Our standard must be the rallying point now and in the future for all good citizens who love and cherish republican institutions, who love liberty regulated by the Constitution and law, who believe in a Government not for a class or for a few, but a Government of all the people, by all the people, and for all the people. This has been the asylum for all good men from over the earth who flee from want and oppression, and mean to become Americans. But we invite and welcome only 'friends to this ground and liegemen' to the Republic. Our institutions cannot change to meet hostile wishes, nor be so much as sensibly modified save by the peaceful and deliberate action of the mass of our people in accordance with the Constitution and the laws of the land. Whatever problems the present has or the future may present, so far as political action can effect them, will be dealt with by the American people within the law. And in the future, as in the past, the people will find security for their liberty and property, encouragement and protection for their industries, peace and prosperity in following the party of the American masses, which will ever shield them against the aggressions of power and monopoly on the one side, and on the other the surgings of chaos. While almost all the rest of the civilized world is darkened by armies, crushed by Kings, or nightmared by conspiracies, we alone enjoy a healthy peace, a rational liberty, a progressive prosperity. We owe it to our political institutions, to democratic teachings, at least as much as to the exuberant soil. The man is not a good American who, knowing what we are, by act or word, experiment or thought, in any way, will attempt to weaken the foundation of this splendid political structure—the Republic of the United States.

"We meet to-day under conditions new to the Democrats of this generation. How often we stood in conventions in the past when to others it seemed as if the shadows of death closed about us, when the day of victory seemed almost as far away as the day of general judgment. It could not then be said that we met for spoils or personal advantage. We met to keep the fires of Democratic liberty alive till the dawn of a better day. If we were a party of misfortune it must also be agreed that we were a party of undaunted courage and inflexible principles. Twenty-eight years ago the Democratic Party, rent in fragments, heated by feuds that only time could allay or punishment destroy, met, as it looks now, merely to settle in angry mood the terms upon which they should become exiled from power. By their mad dissensions they elected to go to defeat rather than wait for the sobering influence of time to close the breach. To the younger men of that day the act seemed suicide, initiated by insanity. Their madness transferred to a minority of the American people the political government of all. That party, whatever the honesty and respectability of its members, however patriotic its motives, was not broad or national at its base. It had almost but one central idea, and when that idea was set in the Constitution and crystallized into law it ran a career of riot that appalled all men. The history of that period of political debauchery is too sad and familiar to Americans to be recited anew. The Republican Party, sometimes peacefully and sometimes by force, sometimes fairly and sometimes by fraud, succeeded in holding power 24 years, till at last the American people, no longer condoning its faults or forgiving its sins, hurled it from power and again committed to the historic party of the Constitution and the whole Union the administration of our political affairs. We won by the well-earned confidence of the country in the rectitude of our purpose, by the aid of chivalrous and conscientious men who could no longer brook the corruptions of the Republican Party. It was a great, deserved, necessary victory.

"The day on which Grover Cleveland, the plain, straightforward, typical American citizen chosen at the election, took the oath of office in the presence of the multitude—a day so lovely and so perfect that all nature seemed exuberantly to sanction and to celebrate the victory—that day marked the close of an old era and the beginning of a new one. It closed the era of usurpation of power by the Federal authority, of illegal force, of general contempt for constitutional limitations and plain law, of glaring scandals, profligate waste and unspeakable corruption, of narrow sectionalism and class strife, of the reign of a party whose good work had long been done. It began the era of perfect peace and perfect union. The States fused in all, their sovereignty into a Federal Republic with limited but ample powers, of a public service conducted with absolute integrity and strict economy; of reforms pushed to their extreme limit; of comprehensive, sound, and safe financial policy; giving security and confidence to all enterprise and endeavor, a Democratic administration faithful to its mighty trust, loyal to its pledges, true to the Constitution, safeguarding the interests and liberties of the people. And now we stand on the edge of another era, perhaps a greater contest, with a relation to the electors that we have not held for a generation—that of responsibility for the great trust of government. We are no longer authors, but accountants; no longer critics, but the criticised. The responsibility is ours, and if we have not taken all the power necessary to make that responsibility good the fault is ours, not that of the people.

"We are confronted by a wily, unscrupulous, and desperate foe. There will be no speck on the record that they will not magnify into a blot; no circumstance that they will not torture and misrepresent; no disappointment that they will not exaggerate into a revolt; no class or creed that they will not seek to inflame; no passion that they will not attempt to rouse; no fraud that they will not willingly perpetrate. They fancy, indeed, that there is no imposture too monstrous for the popular credulity, no crime that will not be condoned. But we stand at guard, full armed at every point to meet them. Our appeal is not to passion nor to prejudice, to class or faction, to race or creed, but to the sound common sense, the interest, the intelligence, and patriotism of the American people.

"The Administration of President Cleveland has triumphantly justified his election. It compels the respect, confidence, and approval of the country. The prophets of evil and disaster are dumb. What the people see is the Government of the Union restored to its ancient footing of justice, peace, honesty, and impartial enforcement of law. They see the demands of labor and agriculture met so far as Government can meet them by the legislative enactments for their encouragement and protection. They see the veterans of the civil war granted pensions long due them to the amount of more than twice in number and nearly three times in value of those granted under any previous Administration. They see more than 32,000,000 acres of land recklessly and illegally held by the grantees of the corrupt Republican régime restored to the public domain for the benefit of honest settlers. They see the negro, whose fears of Democratic rule were played upon by demagogues four years ago, not only more fully protected than by his pretended friends, but honored as his race was never honored before. They see a financial policy under which reckless speculation has practically ceased and capital freed from distrust. They see for the first time an honest observance of the law governing the civil establishment, and the employes of the people rid at last of the political highwaymen with a demand for tribute in one hand and a letter of dismissal in the other. They see useless offices abolished and expenses of administration reduced, while improved methods have lifted the public service to high efficiency. They see tranquillity, order, security, and equal justice restored in the land; a watchful, steady, safe, and patriotic Administration—the solemn promises made by the Democracy faithfully kept. It is 'an honest Government by honest men.' If this record seems prosaic, if it lacks the blood-thrilling element, if it is not lit with lurid fires, if it cannot be illustrated by a pyrotechnic display, if it is merely the plain record of a constitutional party in a time of peace, engaged in administrative reforms, it is because the people of the country four years ago elected not to trust to sensation and experiment, however brilliant and alluring, but preferred to place the helm in a steady hand, with a fearless, trustworthy, patriotic man behind it. Upon that record and upon our earnest efforts, as yet incomplete, to reduce and equalize the burdens of taxation, we enter the canvass and go to the polls confident that the free and intelligent people of this great country will say, 'Well done, good and faithful servants.'

"To the patriotic, independent citizens who, four years ago, forsook their old allegiance and came to our support, and who since that time have nobly sustained the Administration, the Democratic Party owes a deep debt of gratitude. That they have been reviled and insulted by their former associates is not only a signal compliment to their character and influence, but another evidence of the decadence of the Republican Party. Blind worship of the machine—the political juggernaut—is exacted from every man who will take even standing room in that party. The Democratic temple is open to all, and if in council we cannot agree in all things our motto is: 'In essentials, unity; in non-essentials, liberty; in all things, charity.' To all good men we say: 'Come in.' 'Good will ne'er halted at the doorstone.' As four years ago you voted with us to reform the Administration, to conserve our institutions for the well-being of our common country, so join with us again in approval of the work so well accomplished to complete what remains undone. We ask you to remember that it is a 'fatal error to weaken the hands of a political organization by which great reforms have been achieved and risk them in the hands of their known adversaries.' Four years ago you trusted tentatively the Democratic Party, and supported with zeal and vigor its candidate for President. You thought him strong in all the sturdy qualities requisite for the great task of reform. Behold your splendid justification. No President in time of peace had so difficult and laborious a duty to perform. His party had been out of power for 24 years. Every member of it had been almost venomously excluded from the smallest post where administration could be studied. Every place was filled by men whose interest it was to thwart inquiry and belittle the new Administration; but the master hand came to the helm, and the true course has been kept from the beginning.

"We need not wait for time to do justice to the character and services of President Cleveland. Honest, clear-sighted, patient, grounded in respect for law and justice; with a thorough grasp of principles and situations; with marvelous and conscientious industry; the very incarnation of firmness—he has nobly fulfilled the promise of his party, nobly met the expectations of his country, and written his name high on the scroll where future Americans will read the names of men who have been supremely useful to the Republic.

"Fellow-Democrats: This is but the initial meeting in a political campaign destined to be memorable. It will be a clashing of nearly even forces. Let no man here or elsewhere belittle or underestimate the strength or resources of the opposition. But great as they are, the old Democratic Party, in conscious strength and perfect union, faces the issue fearlessly."

### MISSOURI DENOUNCES THE TARIFF.

T. D. Shewalter of Missouri was the first man to claim the new Chairman's attention. The Missourians were evidently not exactly satisfied with the action of Tom O'Day in voting for Senator Gorman for Chairman of the Committee on Resolutions. Mr. Shewalter sent to the desk a resolution defining the attitude of the delegation upon the tariff. It was the same resolution adopted by the Missourians at the same meeting at which O'Day was elected a member of the Platform Committee. O'Day had been instructed to submit it to his committee and labor for its insertion in the platform. It declares that the power vested in Congress by the Constitution to lay and collect taxes and duties on imports is a power to be exercised for public, not private purposes, that the authority to regulate commerce is an authority to pass rules respecting that subject having for their object the facilitation of commerce, and not destructive of the markets thereby secured for our surplus products in the interests of monopoly; that taxes including import duties should be levied for the purposes of raising the revenue required to meet the needs of the Government administered economically and with strict fidelity as a public trust; that the building up of one industry by a tax, or at the expense of another, is foreign to the true aims of a free Government, in which all the people as to their legal and industrial rights stand on an absolutely equal footing. It demanded that the revenue laws shall be put on a revenue basis as soon as possible, with such safeguards as shall not disturb unduly the business of the country in the transition from a high to a low tariff in such reduction. The luxuries rather than the necessaries of life should be made to bear the principal burden. The present tariff, "levied upon nearly 4,000 articles," is denounced as "a masterpiece of injustice, inequality, and false pretenses. It has impoverished many industries, subsidized a few. It prohibits imports that might purchase the products of American labor. It has degraded American commerce from the first to an inferior rank on the high seas. It has cut down the sales of American manufactures at home and abroad, and depleted the returns of American agriculture on industry followed by half our people. It costs the people five times more than it produces to the Treasury, obstructs the process of production and wastes the fruits of labor. It advocates falsely the claim that it enables the laborer to receive 25 per cent. more wages, while they carefully conceal the truth that it compels him to pay 50 per cent. more for all necessaries of life manufactured." Under the rules the resolution has to be referred to the Committee on Rules without debate.

### WOMAN'S RIGHTS AND SYMPATHY WITH SHERIDAN.

A communication was read asking that the convention listen to Virginia L. Minor and E. A. Merriwether, representatives of the Women's National Convention that met recently in Washington, and it was accompanied by a pledge that they would limit their addresses to 10 minutes each. The delegate in the New-York delegation who so gallantly solved this question by a motion to hear the women was Joseph J. O'Donohue of Tammany. The request seemed to stagger the convention, but the Chairman's sympathies were enlisted, and he pressed the motion through before there was time to object, if, indeed, objections were entertained by the delegates.

It was understood that some of the delegations who are outspoken for tariff reform were prepared to emphasize their views by submitting resolutions by them adopted before their arrival in this city. This was prevented by the adoption of a motion by C. E. Boyle of Pennsylvania that all future resolutions be referred to the Resolutions Committee without reading or debate.

Congressman T. J. Campbell of New-York was just a moment too late. He had a resolution expressive of regret at the illness of Gen. Phil Sheridan and the hope that he would speedily recover his health.

"I ask unanimous consent that it be read." A chorus of objections went up.

"But, gentlemen, I am satisfied you wouldn't object if you knew what it was," persisted Campbell. There was another roar of nays, in which the Virginians and the Wisconsin delegates were especially emphatic. Somebody whispered in Mr. Bird's ear, and that son of Wisconsin shouted:

"If it relates to the platform I object; if, however, it relates to another subject, as I am assured it does, I withdraw my objections."

"It ought to be read," put in Congressman Collins, and he read it. It was cheered lustily and applauded as well. At Chairman Collins's suggestion the resolution was adopted by a rising vote, and by him was declared unanimously adopted. The Virginians, who have the best reasons for remembering the cavalryman, were first on their feet. Some of the Louisianians, Georgians, and Mississippians managed to hold fast to their chairs during this formality. A copy of the resolution was ordered to be sent to the General.

Mrs. Merriwether now came upon the platform. She was very self-possessed, and acknowledged with a bow the applause which greeted her. She is the first woman, probably, who ever confronted a convention of a great political party, unless, indeed, that term can be applied to the Prohibition Convention, which listened to a speech from her in Indianapolis last week. She is perhaps 45 years of age, and lately her time has been almost wholly devoted to the work established by the Woman's Christian Temperance Union in the Southwest. She wore a dark-colored dress striped with gray and black, a black straw bonnet, and silk mits covering the arms to the elbows. Her text was the equal rights of the sexes. It was easy to see that she was interested in having the convention indorse it. It was impossible, however, to hear what she said, and in that respect she was upon an equality with some of the male speakers who addressed the convention during the day. Chairman Collins rapped several times for order, but the galleries were in confusion, and, crane their necks as they might, the delegates could catch only now and then a word. Some of them did hear her remark, "You are not often troubled with women and you ought to hear one once," and they applauded. Mrs. Merriwether was given a round of cheers as she retired. Mrs. Minor evidently shrank from a similar experience for she did not present herself.

There was a disposition to adjourn. Mr. Piggott of Connecticut declared that the Committee on Resolutions would not complete its labors in season to report to-night, and at its request offered a motion to adjourn until to-morrow morning at 10 o'clock.

W. U. Hensel of Pennsylvania caught the Chairman's eye. He caught the convention as well by his business-like proposition that the roll of States be called; that the speeches placing candidates in nomination be made, but that no ballot be taken until after the presentation of the platform. The convention hurrahed, and with a tremendous "No" voted down the motion of Brown of Tennessee to adjourn.

### THE RENOMINATION OF PRESIDENT CLEVELAND.

Speeches nominating a candidate for the Presidency were in order. Alabama announced that it tendered to New-York its privilege of placing a candidate in the field. All eyes were immediately focused on the New-York delegation and cries of "Dougherty! Dougherty!" filled the hall. A man of 55, perhaps 60, with a marked facial resemblance to ex-Senator Francis Kernan, made his way up the aisle. The delegates were on their feet and in his way, but he brushed them aside and, with a peculiar stride, suggestive of the burlesque imitation of Henry Irving's gait, he reached the platform steps and finally the platform itself. He nodded to Congressman Collins and placed upon the table the half of a lemon that had been his nourishment for the preceding half hour. The convention rose up to greet him, but he was quite prepared to receive its homage, let alone its attention. He said something to the Chairman and that gentleman seized hold of his table and meekly pulled it from its central position on the platform. A Secretary lent a generous hand, and in a jiffy a clear space six feet square was prepared. Colored boys were passing water around among the delegates and the clatter of their tin cups was an inharmonious sound. "Let those boys keep still," and again the Chairman regarded the mandate of the visitor, this time shaking his gavel fiercely in the direction of a group of dusky little scamps who had collected in front of the platform.

Not until these little preliminaries had been arranged could the procession move. Then, and not until then, did Philadelphia's distinguished loss and New-York's magnificent gain, the Hon. Daniel Dougherty, beam triumphant upon this mighty gathering, and by his manner indicate a readiness to be heard. Twelve thousand persons were in waiting and in wonder. Mr. Dougherty's fame as an orator is well known. His opening sentence was a disappointment: "I greet you, my countrymen, with fraternal regard." His "r's" had the burr of an up-country Scotchman. There was something so strikingly suggestive of the spread-eagle orator that some of the audience tittered. The next sentence was better and within two minutes he had his audience and was carrying it along in the happiest manner. He spoke just 10 minutes and his references to the President, his courageous message to Congress, the reclamation of lands belonging to the public domain, his discharge of duty, were each and every one most heartily applauded. When he spoke of sectional strife having been allayed the whole convention rose up and shouted. When he declared that New-York would pledge him her Electoral vote the New-Yorkers responded with cheer upon cheer. When he concluded with "I give you a name entwined with victory; I nominate Grover Cleveland," it was the signal for the nominating hurrah to begin. Mr. Dougherty tarried no longer upon the stage, but with the same odd strides picked his way back to his seat in the midst of the Tammany delegation. Mr. Dougherty's speech was as follows:

"I greet you, my countrymen, with fraternal regard. In your presence I bow to the majesty of the people! The sight itself is inspiring; the thought sublime! You come from every State and Territory, from every nook and corner of our ocean-bound, continent-covering country. You are about to discharge a more than imperial duty with simplest ceremonials. You, as representatives of the people, are to choose a magistrate with power mightier than a monarch, yet checked and controlled by the supreme law of a written Constitution.

"Thus impressed I ascend the rostrum to name the next President of the United States. New-York presents him to the convention and pledges her Electoral vote. Delegations from the 38 States and all the Territories are assembled without caucus or consultation, ready simultaneously to take up the cry and make the vote unanimous. We are here, not indeed to choose a candidate, but to name the one the people have already chosen. He is the man for the people! his career illustrates the glory of our institutions. Eight years ago, unknown save in his own locality, he for the last four has stood in the gaze of the world, discharging the most exalted duties that can be confided to a mortal. To-day determines that not of his own choice, but by the mandate of his countrymen, and with the sanction of Heaven, he shall fill the Presidency for four years more. He has met and mastered every question as if from youth trained to statesmanship. The promises of his letter of acceptance and inaugural address have been fulfilled. His fidelity in the past inspires faith in the future. He is not a hope. He is a realization.

"Scorning subterfuge, disdaining re-election by concealing convictions, mindful of his oath of office to defend the Constitution, he courageously declares to Congress, dropping minor matters, that the supreme issue is reform, revision, reduction of national taxation. That the Treasury of the United States, glutted with unneeded gold, oppresses industry, embarrasses business, endangers financial tranquillity, and breeds extravagance, centralization, and corruption. That high taxation, vital for the expenditures of an unparalleled war, is robbery in years of prosperous peace. That the millions that pour into the Treasury come from the hard-earned savings of the American people. That in violation of equality of rights the present tariff has created a privileged class, who, shaping legislation for their personal gain, levy by law contributions for the necessaries of life from every man, woman, and child in the land. That to lower the tariff is not free trade. It is to reduce the unjust profits of monopolists and boss manufacturers and allow consumers to retain the rest. The man who asserts that to lower the tariff means free trade insults intelligence. We brand him as a falsifier. It is furtherest from thought to imperil capital or disturb enterprises. The aim is to uphold wages and protect the rights of all.

"This Administration has rescued the public domain from would-be barons and cormorant corporations faithless to obligations and reserved it for free homes for this and coming generations.

"There is no pilfering. There are no jobs under this Administration. Public office is a public trust. Integrity stands guard at every post of our vast empire.

"While the President has been the medium through which has flowed the undying gratitude of the Republic for her soldiers, he has not hesitated to withhold approval from special legislation if strictest inquiry revealed a want of truth and justice.

"Above all, sectional strife as never before is at an end, and sixty millions of freemen in the ties of brotherhood are prosperous and happy.

"These are the achievements of this Administration. Under the same illustrious leader we are ready to meet our political opponents in high and honorable debate and stake our triumph on the intelligence, virtue, and patriotism of the people. Adhering to the Constitution, its every line and letter, ever remembering that powers not delegated to the United States by the Constitution nor prohibited by it to the States are reserved to the States respectively or to the people, by the authority of the Democracy of New-York, backed by the Democracy of the entire Union, I give you a name entwined with victory. I nominate Grover Cleveland of New-York."

### A DEAFENING UPROAR.

The delegates were now standing on their chairs waving their hats, handkerchiefs, and canes, and cheering like mad. Some of them opened their umbrellas and waved them. The uproar was deafening. Somebody pressed an electric button upon the platform and the band at the far end of the convention struck up. Just what the air was nobody could distinguish from the reporters' gallery. The spectators in the galleries were more wildly enthusiastic than the occupants of the floor. The bronzed eagles were torn from their fastenings and hoisted to view by eager hands. The delegates upon the floor below were bombarded with wads of morning newspapers. One of the Vice-Presidents crowned the bust of President Cleveland with a wreath of laurel. By means of an ingenious contrivance a life-size figure representing the President appeared upon the screen that covered the end of the hall and disappeared within the doors of the Capitol thereon depicted. The standards were snatched from their sockets, and the banners of the States and Territories were massed above the New-York delegation. Gilroy of Tammany had the New-York banner in his hand and was standing upon a chair waving it furiously. It was a demonstration that for wildness would have done credit to a Blaine gathering. It lasted 25 minutes, and then, as the din died away, the strains of "The Star-Spangled Banner" and "Yankee Doodle" filled the air.

### KENTUCKY SECONDS THE NOMINATION.

Not until delegates and spectators were thoroughly wearied by their exertions did Chairman Collins attempt to bring order out of chaos. He recognized James A. McKenzie, who asked that Kentucky be given the privilege of seconding the nomination. It was granted, and a tall, broad-shouldered Kentuckian with a full beard was introduced as the spokesman of the Blue Grass State. Mr. McKenzie enlisted the sympathies of his audience at the very opening of his remarks when he declared that there was only one other Democrat more popular than Grover Cleveland, and that was the queenly woman he has made his wife. It was now Mrs. Cleveland's turn to be applauded, and the great throng rose up and cheered again and again. "Now you are shouting," yelled somebody in the gallery in response to the ex-Congressman's sally. When the latter drew a picture of a racecourse and in the vernacular of the turf described the activity of their Presidential candidate in covering the course, every Democrat in the building laughed and joined in the applause. He made a ten strike when he spoke of the President's message as having all the "directness and force of a Kentucky rifle and the executive ability of a dynamite cartridge," and he contributed to the campaign vocabulary of the day by referring to Blaine as "the Florentine Mosaic of Maine." All in all his speech is worth reproducing. It was as follows:

GENTLEMEN OF THE NATIONAL CONVENTION: I bear the commission of the State of Kentucky to this National Convention, and in the name of the Commonwealth that has given to that State a Clay and a Crittenden I desire to second the nomination of Grover Cleveland for the office of the Presidency of the United States. [Great applause and wild cheering.] Within the broad limits of this great land there is but one more popular Democrat than he and that is the queenly woman he has made his wife. [Great applause.] It must be, Mr. Chairman, a matter of felicitation to every good citizen within the limits of our land that the historic White House, around which cluster so many memories that are dear to every patriotic heart, is presided over by a man who has the courage to inforce obedience to bad laws until they be repealed and recommend the enactment of good ones until they shall be enacted. [Applause.] At the same time its social destinies are guided by the fair hand of the uncrowned Queen of our American womanhood. I never intend to let Mrs. Cleveland out of this canvass. [Laughter and applause.] *In hoc signo vinces.* It was said, gentlemen of the jury, [laughter,] in our last National Convention, that Grover Cleveland was loved for the enemies he had made; still latter, it has been said that he was loved for the rascals he had turned out, [applause;] still later it has been said that he was loved for the message he had written. [Applause.] Kentucky loves him for the fight there is in him, [laughter and applause,] and for his splendid racing qualities. [Laughter.] He is as game as Lexington and as speedy as Ten Broeck. In his earlier form he won the Buffalo Mayoralty Stake hands down, and he won the New-York handicap. He was then entered against the Florentine Mosaic from Maine, [great applause and cheering,] and won the National Derby by a neck. It does not matter, gentlemen of the Democratic jury, it does not matter how this national sweepstakes shall be made up, whether it be filled out by hyperborean icicles, Florentine mosaics, or dark horses. When the race is run through the bulletin board will show Eclipse first, the balance not placed. [Laughter and applause.]

"The State of Kentucky loves Mr. Cleveland for the reason that he has had the courage to storm the entrenchments of subsidy and monopoly by recommending such a judicious revision of our tariff system as will secure equality in the distribution of the public burdens and lighten the exactions of labor. [Applause.] He has had the courage to inaugurate such a war on that horrible misnomer called trusts as that before this national campaign shall close it will cease to be a popular race for a dog. [Laughter and applause.] He has had the courage and patriotism to regard the Presidency of the United States not as a personal perquisite acquired by purchase, or discovery, or diplomacy, or escheat. But he has regarded the Presidency as a great public office conferred by the unbought suffrage of the people, to be administered wisely, fairly, judiciously, impartially, honestly, in the interests of everybody. [Cheers.] Well, the fact of the business is, he has got so much courage that it is unnecessary to enumerate. But there is one thing that I want to call special attention to. While others have wavered and others have written doubtful messages, he has written a message to the present American Congress that has about it the directness and force of a Kentucky rifle and the executive ability of a dynamite cartridge. [Applause and laughter.] In lawyer parlance it had about it the energy of a *capias profine* and the force and effect of a replevin bond. Now, gentlemen, this is the first instance in the history of American politics where we had a man who furnished in his own

# The New-York Times.

VOL. XXXVII......NO. 11,485. NEW-YORK, THURSDAY, JUNE 21, 1888.—WITH SUPPLEMENT. PRICE TWO CENTS.


## EXPELLED FROM BERLIN

### TWO FRENCH JOURNALISTS ORDERED TO LEAVE.

THEIR OFFENSE UNKNOWN, BUT SUPPOSED TO BE THE LIBELING OF THE IMPERIAL FAMILY.

BY COMMERCIAL CABLE FROM OUR OWN CORRESPONDENT.

*Copyright, 1888, by the New-York Times.*

BERLIN, June 20.—Two French journalists, representing the *Gaulois* and the *Matin*, were to-day expelled from Berlin by the police at two hours' notice. Their offense is believed to be libeling the royal family. The incident caused no sensation here, but was taken quite as a matter of course.

Prince Radolin, Lord Chamberlain in the Government of Frederick III., retires to his estates. This is probably the beginning of considerable changes in the personnel of the Government.

A rescript is published to-day ordering a eulogy of the late Emperor to be read next Sunday in all the Christian churches. Apparently the Jews may read it if agreeable.

The royal speech opening the Reichstag on Monday is looked for anxiously, but it is doubtful if it will be more important than the policy already declared. The course of appointments is a better indication of the imperial intentions than any guarded words can possibly be.

It is officially stated that all reports in regard to differences between the Emperor and the other members of his family are wholly untrue.

*Associated Press Dispatches.*

BERLIN, June 20.—The *Post* declares that there is no foundation for the idea that a change will be made in the German policy adverse to Russia. French fears, it says, are also baseless. "The moon is more likely to visit the earth than the German Emperor to dream of attacking France only to earn laurels. Germany wishes nothing from France but to be let alone. As soon as the French see this, conditions will exist for perpetual peace and friendship. At the same time the tone of the Emperor's proclamations may well serve to remind elements unfriendly to Germany, whether in the East or in the West, in a manner perhaps not agreeable to them, of the Hohenzollern way of waging war, and make clear to them that any unjust attack upon Germany will meet the fate of the French attack of 1870. The Emperor will wield his sword like his glorious ancestors, but only in defense of the Fatherland against unjust attacks."

The *Vossische Zeitung* states that the Emperor, in declaring amnesty, will adhere to the terms of his father's proclamation, remitting sentences in force at the date of his accession.

Emperor William has telegraphed to President Carnot of France thanking him for his message of condolence on the death of Emperor Frederick, and expressing the hope that the good relations now existing between France and Germany may continue.

The Prince and Princess of Wales paid another visit to the Dowager Empress Victoria at Potsdam to-day. Gen. Mischke has been sent to England to officially notify the Queen of Emperor William's accession to the German throne.

The Government has issued a circular regulating the sale of wheat on the Produce Exchange, and fixing the normal weight of rye at a scale of 72 kilos per hectoliter instead of 70 kilos, as at present. The circular refers to quality and weight for future delivery and comes into force on Oct. 1. Dealings are forbidden in Russian rye for future delivery. The circular has caused excitement on the Exchange.

The *Kreuz Zeitung* says that Empress Victoria under the will of Emperor Frederick inherits the Charlottenburg Castle and the palace in Berlin occupied by the late Emperor when he was Crown Prince.

It is reported that the Czar while en route to Copenhagen this Summer will land at Stettin and pay a visit to Emperor William.

Prince Bismarck is suffering from rheumatism and was unable to visit the Emperor to-day.

It is rumored that Count von Waldersee has had a difference with the Chancellor and will be transferred to a provincial command.

Prince Bismarck has notified the powers, including Russia and France, that it is Emperor William's most sincere desire to maintain friendly relations with them.

## ARCHBISHOP WALSH ON THE RESCRIPT.

DUBLIN, June 20.—The *Freeman's Journal* to-day publishes an interview with Archbishop Walsh. Regarding the Papal rescript, the Archbishop said that he had not consulted with the Bishops, and could, therefore, say nothing as to the manner in which the rescript would be enforced. He strongly insisted that whatever influences had been brought to bear upon the Pope, they had not had the slightest effect upon his view of Irish affairs. The disquieting conclusions, drawn from the fact that the rescript was first published in Unionist organs, were entirely erroneous. The Pope had graciously accorded him the amplest opportunity to state his views, and the result was that his Holiness was in full possession of the Irish Nationalist programme. Nothing was further from the Pope's thoughts than to put any obstacle in the way of the success of the Nationalist cause. On the contrary, it was the Pope's firm conviction that the rescript, by condemning those points of practical working which evoked hostile criticism, would be of most decided assistance in the advancement of the programme.

On the general situation the Archbishop spoke most hopefully. He said that the Irish cause was winning all along the line. Even if the present session of Parliament did not see a substantial act of justice done for the protection of the poor peasantry, the coming Winter would certainly be the last during which it would be possible for heartless landlords to oppress their tenants.

## THE MISSION CONFERENCE CLOSED.

LONDON, June 20.—Mr. Blackwood presided at the closing meeting of the Protestant Mission Conference to-day. In replying to the *Times's* criticism that the missionaries had met with too little success to expect further support, he denounced as the foremost obstacle in the way of missionary work the action of the Government in pushing the liquor and opium traffic and licensing vice. Resolutions in accordance with the sentiments of the Chairman were adopted. Mr. Taylor of New-York moved the resolution referring to the liquor traffic.

Mr. Murdoch of Boston paid an eloquent tribute to the King of the Belgians for his efforts to suppress the sale of liquor in the Congo State. A committee, including Mr. Murdoch, was appointed to present an appropriate address to King Leopold.

Mr. Pierson of Philadelphia made the concluding address. He testified to the deep impression that the Conference had made on the delegates.

## RACING IN ENGLAND.

LONDON, June 20.—This was the second day of the Newcastle and Gosforth Park Summer meeting. The race for the Northumberland plate of 1,000 sovereigns was won by Matin Bell. Tommy Tittlemouse was second, and Bellatrix third. The last betting was 12 to 1 against Matin Bell, 10 to 1 against Tommy Tittlemouse, and 14 to 1 against Bellatrix. There were 10 starters, with Castor, the favorite, at odds of 5 to 2 against.

This was also the second day of the Four Oaks Park Summer meeting. The race for the Shifnal Plate of 600 sovereigns for 2-year-olds was won by H. E. Tidy's b. c. Indian Prince. A. W. Merry's c. c., by The Miser, out of Lady Hester, second, and Mr. Abington's b. c. Isleworth third, and T. Jennings, Jr.'s c. f. Buvcuse fourth. The last betting was 6 to 1 against Indian Prince, 7 to 1 against the Lady Hester colt, 3 to 2 on Isleworth, and 7 to 1 against Buvcuse.

## JOHN DILLON IN PRISON.

DUBLIN, June 20.—The appeal of Mr. John Dillon from his sentence to six months' imprisonment for violation of the Crimes act was heard to-day and the sentence was confirmed.

Mr. Dillon was taken to Dundalk Jail and imprisoned. On the route to the prison he was heartily cheered. An address was presented to Mr. Dillon, signed by 150 members of the House of Commons, resenting the policy of sending him to unmerited imprisonment, and expressing the hope that his sojourn in prison would be made less bitter by the knowledge that sympathy for him is not confined to Ireland.

## REBELLION IN CHINA.

SHANGHAI, June 20.—An alarming rebellion has broken out among the people made destitute by the floods in Ho-Nan and Hon-Tung. It is reported that the troops have joined the rebels and murdered the Government officials.

## MR. BLAINE DECLINES TO SAY.

LONDON, June 20.—The Hon. James G. Blaine, in an interview at Newcastle to-day, declined to state whether or not he would accept the nomination for President.

## CURRENT FOREIGN TOPICS.

LONDON, June 20.—In the House of Commons this afternoon Mr. Balfour referred to the rumor that he was about to resign the Chief Secretaryship for Ireland as one of those ridiculous fictions which are periodically circulated by a section of the Irish press.

Detailed accounts of the gales which occurred on the coast of Iceland last month show that 400 French fishermen were drowned, 30 vessels having been wrecked.

Advices from Zanzibar state that no news has been received there in confirmation of the report of Henry M. Stanley's death. The report is discredited there.

ST. PETERSBURG, June 20.—The Russian Government will permit women to become pharmaceutists if they pass the same examination to which men are subjected. Apothecaries receiving female pupils will not be allowed to receive males.

DUBLIN, June 20.—Mr. Thomas Joseph Condon, member of the House of Commons, who was imprisoned in the Cork Jail for offenses under the Crimes act, was released to-day.

The persons arrested on the charge of swindling the Equitable Life Assurance Society of New-York City will be tried at the next Wicklow Assizes.

COPENHAGEN, June 20.—The centenary of the emancipation of the peasants was celebrated to-day. The town was appropriately decorated and was crowded with visitors. There was a procession in which 20,000 persons took part.

BERLIN, June 20.—Mr. Carl Schurz has returned to Berlin.

A Mr. Mullins was arrested at Carrick-on-Suir to-day on suspicion of being an agent of the Clan-na-Gael Society. The magistrate before whom he was brought dismissed the charge as frivolous and unsubstantiated. Mr. Mullins is a cousin of Canon Mullins of Thurles College.

BERNE, June 20.—The Swiss Bundesrath to-day rejected a proposal to enact special laws affecting agents provocateurs and regulating the expulsion of foreigners.

THE HAGUE, June 20.—Dr. Pynacker Hordyk has been appointed Governor of the Dutch East Indies.

PARIS, June 20.—M. Déroulède has decided not to be a candidate again in the election in the Charente district.

## *FLOODS IN MINNESOTA.*

### THE MISSISSIPPI RISING AGAIN UNDER HEAVY RAINS.

ST. PAUL, Minn., June 20.—Very heavy rains are reported in the northern part of the State, and the rivers are again on the rise. At Brainerd during last night the water in the river had risen to such a height that the fires of the water works engine were put out. The electric light works met a like fate and the fires were quenched. The river is rising to-day under the influence of the tremendous rains of last night, and by evening the city will doubtless be without fire protection as well as enveloped in darkness. The reports as to the coming of a heavy mass of water from the Government dams are to-day confirmed, and a two-foot rise is reported which should, however, not reach here for another day or two. The reports as to opening the dams are partially true, some of the gates being opened to relieve the stress of the immense storage, which is the greatest ever before experienced.

The rumor as to the Pokegama Dams having broken was false and arose from the overflow of the flat lands extending to Split Hard Lake, and the Pokegama waters are going out that way, thence reaching the Mississippi. Between Aiken and the mouth of the Big Willow no land is visible for 20 miles on either side of the Mississippi. People are living in wigwams alongside of their homes, with their stock living on rafts.

REDWING, June 20.—The second flood of the season visited this section yesterday. The water pursued its usual course. Coming down South Bush-street it scattered sidewalks, fences, &c., about promiscuously. The volume of water increased until it grew into a veritable torrent, dashing down Plum-street and submerging different parts of the eastern section of the city.

## *IT WAS AN IMPORTANT ARREST.*

BOSTON, June 20.—The arrest of a woman a few days ago by the Police Inspectors on suspicion of being a thief turned out to be quite an important capture. The woman was none other than Nellie Byron, alias Nellie Scott or "Scotty," well-known in New-York from her shrewd work. With her was a young fellow named James D. Grady, a New-Yorker, who is alleged to be a horse sharp. Scotty was the woman who three years ago stole a twelve-hundred-dollar diamond from Shreve, Crump & Low of this city. She was caught in New-York and served time for the offense. About a week ago, however, Messrs. Palmer & Batchelder, the well-known jewelers, reported that a pair of diamond earrings and a pair of turquoise earrings had been stolen from their store, they thought by a woman. "Scotty," who has been living in the city recently, was suspected, and she was arrested. At her house were found three solid gold chains, one diamond set, two pairs of diamond earrings, one pair of turquoise and pearl earrings, one pair of sapphire earrings, three pairs imitation diamond earrings, two pairs of gold ball earrings, one pair black enamel turquoise earrings, ten gold collar buttons, two gold-plated collar buttons, three gentlemen's scarf pins, one plated gold watch chain, one elegant French traveling clock, one piece of gold drapery, one and one-quarter yards of pearl and gold trimming, one blue and gilt lace tidy. Ever since her arrest prominent storekeepers have been calling at Police Headquarters identifying the goods and in many cases the woman.

## *AN UNEXPLAINED SUICIDE.*

PHILADELPHIA, June 20.—George Hemple, the 23-year-old son of the veteran actor, Samuel H. Hemple, blew out his brains this morning on Ridge-avenue, near Thirty-first-street, a few squares from his home at 2,404 Thompson-street. No cause is assigned for his suicide. Young Hemple was employed as a salesman by the Novelty Brass Company. He left his home this morning about 8 o'clock, after eating a hearty breakfast. He told his parents that he was going to New-York on some business connected with the firm, and would probably be gone a day or two. On his way to the cars the young man met a friend named Washington Henderson. With him he chatted gayly until he reached Twenty fourth-street and Ridge-avenue. There he boarded a car and rode out to the station. He walked down Ridge-avenue until he came to Thirty-first-street, where he was seen to draw a pistol from his pocket, place the barrel against his right temple, and pull the trigger. Death was instantaneous. The body was taken home. His father says he was bright and cheerful before leaving home, was always healthy, and he is at a loss to know why his son committed suicide.

## *SHERIDAN STEADILY IMPROVING.*

WASHINGTON, June 20.—The following bulletin was issued this evening by Gen. Sheridan's physicians:

"There is very little to be said about Gen. Sheridan's illness for the past 24 hours. No unfavorable symptoms have appeared, and he is apparently progressing by steady, though almost imperceptible degrees, toward convalescence."

R. M. O'REILLY,
W. MATTHEWS,
C. B. BYRNE,
H. C. YARROW.

## *LUMBER ON FIRE.*

OTTAWA, Ontario, June 20.—The lumbering firm of Perley & Pattee have been advised that a serious fire is raging on their limits on the Petawawa River. The information is brought by one of their employes and the particulars are very scanty. The conflagration is supposed to have originated with fires started by settlers for the purpose of clearing their land. The limits are the best in the lumbering districts of the Upper Ottawa.

## *A MOTHER'S FEARFUL CRIME.*

### SHE POISONS HER THREE CHILDREN AND THEN HERSELF.

PITTSBURG, Penn., June 20.—"It is horrible!" "Oh, how could she do it!" These were a few of the exclamations uttered wildly and with deep sobs by a dozen frantic women as they gazed upon the bodies of a woman and her two children. The dead woman was Mrs. Josephine Marek, who at 7:30 o'clock this morning murdered her two young children, Mary and Helena, by administering strychnine and then ending her own life by drinking the fatal draught. A third child was given some of the poison, and its life now hangs by a thread. The tragedy occurred on the second floor of a small tenement house, 26 Sycamore-street, a short distance from Ohio-street. As the three bodies lay peaceful in death no indications of their terrible sufferings a few minutes before could be discerned. The grief-stricken, half-crazed father of the children excited the deepest sympathy. He appeared oblivious of the wailings of the women and the crush and push of the hundred or more strangers whose curiosity led them to invade the house of the dead. He moaned and rocked himself in his agony, but no word of reproach upon the author of the crime escaped his lips.

Through all the hurry and excitement of the first hour little Emma, aged 4 years, the one child who had so far escaped the results of the poison administered to her, wandered through the three plainly furnished rooms unable to understand the cause of all the commotion. She gazed first at her mother, quiet and still, then she would wander to the bed where lay the still form of Mary, the eldest, and gaze at the inanimate form, gently lisp her name, and pass on to the baby, where the same action was repeated. In the great excitement little attention was paid to her. The maternal grandparents of the children, in their great grief, forgot the living until suddenly her little legs refused to obey the will of their owner and she fell with a cry into her grandmother's arms. Then, and not till then, was it evident that death was hovering near her. She was seized with convulsions and fresh terror reigned in the household.

The motive for the deed is believed to have been anger because her husband turned from the house a boarder whom he suspected of criminal intimacy with his wife. Every evidence indicates that the deed was the result of calm deliberation, and was not committed on the spur of the moment while under excessive excitement. Her intention was to kill her entire family—every member of it—and failed in one instance because her husband would not drink the cup of milk in which lurked his death. She purchased the poison at a drug store in the vicinity and placed it in the milk which the family was to drink for breakfast. All partook of the fatal draught but the husband, who refused because he did not care to drink milk. The little girl, Emma, is still living, and the physicians now have hopes of her recovery.

## *DICKINSON SAYS BLAINE.*

### THE POSTMASTER-GENERAL SURE OF A DEMOCRATIC VICTORY.

SPRINGFIELD, Mass., June 20.—Postmaster-General Dickinson, speaking of the political situation in Chicago to-day, said:

"The Chicago Convention, after airing its favorite sons, will rush like a tidal wave to Blaine, whom, I believe, will be the nominee. But first there must be an opportunity granted for letting off a vast quantity of pent-up eloquence in support of various insignificant booms. Blaine, I believe, is sure to be the candidate of his party, but he will never be President. Cleveland and Thurman will sweep all before them. Thurman will unite all factions in Indiana into a harmonious whole, and Cleveland will carry New-York by 50,000 majority. Depew has no chance. The red bandana will wave from the North to the South, and the Democrats will score a handsome victory. I feel just as sure of it as that I am alive. Cleveland's Administration has been a clean one, and Thurman will give the ticket strength that no Republican Convention can overthrow."

## *AN EX-BANK CASHIER IN JAIL.*

TROY, N. Y., June 20.—Asa W. Wickes, ex-Cashier of the Central National Bank, was arraigned before United States Commissioner Landon to-day on a charge of violating the United States bank statutes. The complaint is made by the Guarantee Company of Montreal, which issued a guarantee to the bank against any loss that might be sustained by defalcation or any other unlawful acts of the person guaranteed. Several witnesses were examined and the case was adjourned till July 6. Bail was fixed at $5,000. Mr. Wickes was taken to jail in default of bail. He is charged with appropriating to his own use about $9,000 of the funds of the bank, besides private funds intrusted to his charge. Recently he has been employed in his brother's hat factory.

## *MR. T. HARRISON GARRETT'S WILL.*

BALTIMORE, June 20.—The will of the late T. Harrison Garrett was admitted to probate at Towson yesterday. It is dated November, 1884, and there are two codicils dated Jan. 12, 1887, and April 23, 1888, respectively. In the second codicil the appointment of the testator's brother, Robert Garrett, as sole Executor and Trustee is revoked because of the likelihood of his continued absence abroad, and Mrs. T. Harrison Garrett, Charles F. Mayer, and Charles Nitze are appointed Executors and Trustees in his stead. The will directs that the clear sum of $40,000 per annum be paid to Mrs. Garrett during her widowhood and that she be given the use of the city and country residences belonging to the estate. The entire estate is to be divided in equal shares among the three sons of the deceased under certain conditions.

## *CLASS DAY AT HAMILTON COLLEGE.*

CLINTON, N. Y., June 20.—At the Alumni meeting of Hamilton College to-day Senator Joseph R. Hawley, '47, was re-elected Trustee by 270 votes out of a total of 280. President Peck of Rensselaer Polytechnic School of Troy was chosen orator for the college year, and the Rev. Dr. James Rood of Albany poet. The Rev. A. R. Evans, '82, was elected by the Trustees Assistant Professor of Greek. At 3:30 in the afternoon the usual Class Day exercises were held in the stone chapel. This evening the oration before the Alumni was delivered by Dr. E. G. Orton, '48, of the Ohio State University, on "The Progression Due to the Right Method of Scientific Study and the Effect of this Method on Other Studies." The poem was by the Rev. M. M. Woolsey Stryker, '72, Chicago, Ill.

## *A COTTON OIL TRUST.*

NEW-ORLEANS, La., June 20.—To-day in the State Senate at Baton Rouge Senator Cordill introduced a concurrent resolution instructing the Attorney-General to bring suit against the American Cotton Oil Trust. The object of the suit is to break up the combination and place the companies in the hands of Receivers. The resolution set forth that the trust is arbitrarily fixing the price of agricultural products, thereby injuring farmers and planters and destroying all competition by threatening to break up any new mills which may be built in the State. A bill to the same effect was presented in the House yesterday and will probably pass both bodies.

## *FATAL EXPLOSION OF GAS.*

SHAMOKIN, Penn., June 20.—An explosion of gas occurred in the Neilson shaft of the Red Ash Tunnel this afternoon, by which George Schmack was fatally injured and Michael Kelly and Kerin Kerins very seriously burned and injured. Three others, whose names are unknown, were also seriously burned. The cause of the explosion is a mystery, as the tunnel was supposed to be clear of gas. The force of the explosion was terrible, and great excitement prevailed until the extent of the explosion was made known. The mine is owned by Langdon & Co. The damage to it is not great.

## *FIVE PENNANT REGATTAS.*

NORWALK, Conn., June 20.—The second of a series of five pennant regattas by the Cedar Point Yacht Club will be sailed over its rectangular course of 15 miles on Thursday, the 28th inst. The club has a large membership, and some of the fastest boats between New-Rochelle and New-London will take part in the race. Should the day prove favorable one of the most exciting contests ever participated in by the club may be expected.

## *TENNESSEE WANTS A LOAN.*

NASHVILLE, Tenn., June 20.—State officials will leave to-morrow for New-York to negotiate a loan of $85,000, the balance required to pay the July interest on the debt of Tennessee. Of the $219,000 needed $134,000 is now in the State Treasury.

## HARRISON HAS THE LEAD

### *THE CONVENTION LAGGING IN ITS WORK.*

BUT THE PLATFORM COMMITTEE WILL REPORT TO-DAY—THE NOMINATING SPEECHES WILL FOLLOW AND A BALLOT MAY BE REACHED TO-NIGHT—MAHONE'S CLAIMS REJECTED IN CONVENTION—DEPEW STEADILY LOSING GROUND.

CHICAGO, June 20.—This convention promises to be a long one. At a short afternoon session to-day the permanent organization was completed, but the Committee on Credentials was not ready to report, and a recess until 8 o'clock in the evening was taken. It was stated after the first adjournment that the Committee on Platform could not report until to-morrow.

The permanent Chairman, Morris M. Estee, is the man whom the Californians offered for the temporary Chairmanship, and he appears to owe his election to the exertions of Mr. Stephen B. Elkins. Immediately after Estee had been defeated by Thurston Elkins sought out the members of the Committee on Permanent Organization and secured a number of pledges in behalf of Estee for his election to the more important office which he now holds. It was necessary that the Californians should be appeased. It was also expedient that they should be persuaded to forego their purpose to nominate Blaine and vote for him from the start. The defeat of Estee had not made them more tractable and Thurston's declaration that the nomination of Blaine in disobedience to his expressed will would be a political crime had made some of them angry. Even after the greater prize of the permanent Chairmanship had been awarded to them they remained steadfast in their purpose, but they were addressed in caucus before the meeting of the convention to-day by Mr. Elkins, and it is understood that he prevailed upon them to keep their hands off for a time.

Estee appears to have entered into bonds to keep the peace, for in his short address to the convention he made no mention of Blaine or any other candidate, saying only that he could not guess who the nominee would be. Estee is one of the leading lawyers of his State. He has been a candidate for Governor and for Senator. He was a member at large of the Constitutional Convention of 1879, and served in that body as Chairman of the Committee on Corporations.

Mr. Depew has gained no ground to-day. As the time for balloting draws near the selection of a railroad candidate is condemned more openly. The *Tribune* of this morning says:

"If the convention will accept this issue and really desires to test the question whether the Republican Party will commit itself to railroad Presidents and railroad policies it can find no stronger, abler, or more attractive candidate than Depew. The name of the issue would, of course, be monopoly and anti-monopoly. The Republicans would have to assume the title of railroad monopoly, while Cleveland would run as the anti-monopoly candidate, and on that lucky issue he would hold down the Executive chair for four years longer. In the West the people have only the use of the railroads and not their incomes. There are comparatively few who own railroad securities in the Granger States, and they remember Depew's bitter opposition to the Inter-State act, his predictions of 'ruin' that it would inflict, and his defense of the doctrine of charging 'all the traffic will bear.' These ideas may win doubtful Eastern States, where railroad stocks and bonds are largely held by multitudes of people, but they would make many Republican States worse than doubtful. The Democracy would pretty surely make a clean sweep west of Pittsburg to the Pacific Ocean. Then good-bye to the Republican Party."

It is noticeable that in the first two sessions there has been no call for Depew from the spectators or others in the convention. He has sat in a prominent place, but has received no more attention than the most obscure delegate in the hall. The candidate of the Empire State for the Presidency may well long for even such recognition as is accorded to Delegate Foraker and others who are not candidates.

The opinion is now expressed by influential Western delegates that if New-York shall support Depew for several ballots the men of the Upper Mississippi Valley may be driven to Sherman. But there are indications that such a result will not be caused by an alarming increase of the Depew vote. It is more probable that Depew's support will fall away and that Harrison will become a more formidable candidate than he is now. Mr. Elkins would not look with displeasure upon the growth of Harrison's following.

The impression prevails that there is no room for Blaine unless the convention should be unable after many ballots to nominate any one else, and that the chances are against such conditions as would open the door for him. But the temper of the convention is not so steadfast that any prediction as to Blaine can safely be made. The proceedings are marked by good humor and earnestness, and the delegates generally appear to be moved by a desire to do the best they can for the party.

At the evening session, before the report of the Committee on Credentials was brought in, speeches were made by W. O. Bradley of Kentucky and Gov. Foraker of Ohio. When the first of these speakers said, "We are here for victory, and it is for you to say who shall lead us," there were cries of "Blaine, Blaine," in all parts of the house, and when these cries had ceased one of the spectators yelled "Gresham."

The demand for Foraker was followed by a motion that he should be invited to speak, and when the young Governor came to the platform the applause was hearty and prolonged. Referring to the man to be nominated he remarked that he could not give the convention the fortunate candidate's name, whereupon a spectator expressed the opinion that it would be Foraker. This recalled to some the Garfield incident in the convention of eight years ago. Possibly that incident had not been forgotten by Foraker. Continuing, the speaker said that the nominee would have "a record as a Republican, without spot or blemish." It was inferred that he did not believe that any man who had gone out of the party in 1872 could be nominated.

The submission of the majority and minority reports concerning the dispute in Virginia caused debate. The contest in committee had been a bitter one and it was renewed before the convention.

While trying to dispose of the several motions made the convention became entangled in parliamentary difficulties, owing to the incompetency of the Chairman, and much time was wasted. The election of Estee has probably delayed final adjournment one or two days. At last a path out of the labyrinth was made by Senator Miller of New-York, and the roll was called on a motion to substitute the minority report. Ohio diplomatically cut her vote in two. The motion was lost, 2 to 1, although there was great confusion, and many could not have known just what the questions involved were. The impression prevailed that the vote indicated for Sherman a maximum strength of not more than 260 votes.

F. D. R.

## HARRISON'S FRIENDS CONFIDENT.

### GOOD WORK FOR THE INDIANA MAN—THE OTHER BOOMS ALL IN A STATE OF COLLAPSE—DEPEW'S CASE HOPELESS.

CHICAGO, June 20.—Among all the boomers none are as confident to-night as those who have been pushing so industriously the fortunes of Benjamin Harrison of Indiana. They have left no stone unturned for their candidate. They have visited every State delegation; they have talked with the friends of all the other candidates. Where they found some opposition, as they did in California, they have sought diligently to remove the opposition. Harrison's availability has been urged with eloquence. Some of the objections to Sherman have helped to make Harrison acceptable to men who would not otherwise have found him to their liking. Where some of the delegates were committed to favorite sons, they turned easily toward Harrison as a candidate who would be entitled to receive their votes on the second ballot. The result of the canvassing for Harrison is not yet announced by his friends, but an estimate of his strength made by one of them is interesting. Sherman, it is admitted, will lead on the first ballot with 257 votes. Harrison will have 138 votes on the first ballot. Gresham will come next with 92 votes, and Depew fourth with 84 votes. This is, of course, an approximate estimate. The Harrison men have been assured by California that this State will come to his assistance with a good vote. Other States, some of them without entreaty, have offered their votes. To prevent a break for any other candidate the Harrison men say they will not ask to have these States brought to their aid at first. Two or more ballots may be allowed to pass before an attempt is made to consolidate all the friends of Harrison.

While Harrison's friends are so hopeful those of Gresham are not quite cast down, although they can give no reason for confidence. They do not like the report of the Committee on Rules, which they fear was intended to carry out a Blaine plan to defeat anybody but a Blaine candidate or Blaine himself. They do not like the decision of the Committee on Credentials, by which Sherman is deprived of votes that might have come to Gresham if Sherman's friends discovered that Sherman could not be named. The remarks of a Gresham man who declared that the trouble with the Gresham movement was internal hemorrhages is probably true.

Allison's boom stands still. Alger's has perceptibly weakened, and cannot be saved even if a share of the New-York vote shall go to him. Depew's case is past salvation. The West will not be reconciled to him, and the Western men are encouraged in their opposition to him by the talk of New-York men. They fear to support him. They repeat the remark of Mr. Depew in the New-York caucus on Tuesday, that it was his opinion that he ought not, out of regard for the chances of the party, to be nominated.

It is probable that a good deal of doubt about the chances of all the candidates will be removed to-morrow. If the Committee on Resolutions reports the platform, as it is expected to to-morrow morning, the nominating speeches will be made during the afternoon and the first ballot reached as the first business of the night session.

Many of the New-Jersey people here no longer think there is any probability nor even a possibility that New-Jersey's favorite son has any chance of receiving the nomination for President, and they fear that even the presentation of his name for first place may endanger his chances for second place. This is certain. No man is so generally and so favorably spoken of for the Vice-Presidency as William Walter Phelps. The only thing that stands in his way of securing the nomination is the possibility that New-York may demand the Vice-Presidency on the plea that it is a doubtful State, and with a candidate on the ticket the chances will be more favorable for carrying the State. As an eminent and practical politician remarked to-night: "If William Walter Phelps lived on the New-York side of the Hudson nothing could prevent his nomination for the Presidency by this convention. If the New-York delegation would conclude to present no candidate for the Vice-Presidency Mr. Phelps's nomination for that office would be assured and he would be out of the race for the Presidency. Some of his friends urge him even now to insist that his name shall not be presented for first place, but he is reluctant to do this, for the action of the New-Jersey State Convention in urging him for the Presidency was entirely spontaneous by the Republicans of the State, and it might seem ungrateful were he now to refuse to let them have their way." There is unquestionably a very friendly feeling toward Mr. Phelps in the convention, but it has been mainly directed toward supporting him for the Vice-Presidency, which would go to him spontaneously by a three-fourths vote should New-York present no candidate. While it is possible that Phelps may be taken up for first place, it is not at all probable. He has spent no money in getting up "booms" such as have been indefatigably pushed for other candidates, and the only indication of his candidacy is a handsome lithographic portrait which quickly made its appearance last evening. The New-Jersey delegation is disposed to stand by Phelps as long as he has a chance, but it is evident that many are anxious to desert him at the first favorable chance to go toward the probable nominee of the convention.

## LABOR LOST FOR CHAUNCEY.

### THE NEW-YORK DELEGATES BEGINNING TO REALIZE THIS FACT.

CHICAGO, June 20.—The New-Yorkers are beginning to discover how difficult it is to push the canvass of a candidate who does not fit the situation. They have hung out of the windows of the Depew headquarters the transparencies procured by State Committeeman George Urban and illuminated with mottoes breathing defiance from the Buffalonians. James S. Stewart, H. H. Warner, and ex-Congressman Henry G. Burleigh have been perspiring all day over the Depew boom. O. G. Warren, Charlie Gould, ex-Senator McMillan, Senator John McLaughlin, and George Urban have all been tugging in the same traces. They all say that they have been encouraged by their labors.

Considered purely as a vote-getting day for Chauncey, it is a day's labor lost. Combinations have been made all along the line against the New-Yorkers, and no matter where these begin they all end somewhere in the West. The question which will have to be considered by the New-Yorkers at an early day is, when shall they withdraw their candidate, and for whom shall they vote after he is out of the race? At present they are sewn up in a bag, and when they are delivered they can be of no practical value to Mr. Depew, and certainly to nobody else. If the drift of the day means anything, it means that Mr. Depew is no more a factor in the present situation than the Gresham boom. The convention might lose its head and nominate one of these gentlemen, but under no other circumstances does it seem possible to nominate either of them.

Gresham is too poor a man to be exalted in a convention which, so far as Blaine's friends could do it, has been put up for Blaine. The Blaine men want neither Gresham nor Sherman, for these men are not "their kind." The man least offensive to them and most likely to secure the largest vote in the convention will satisfy them if they must accept as final Blaine's two letters withdrawing from the fight. The man who to-night seems most certain to become his legatee is Harrison of Indiana. He has gradually been picking up votes and pledges, and now he seems to have a solid backing of nearly one-fourth of the convention. More eyes in the New-York delegation are now turned toward him than to any man in the race or likely to be enrolled in the list of dark horses. Harrison has had a better organization and a better corps of workers than any other candidate. The politics of the situation favor him, from the fact that his is regarded as a doubtful State, and now the delegates of the three other doubtful States in the East, New-York, New-Jersey, and Connecticut, are deliberately revolving his candidacy in their minds. If his proves to be a waiting candidacy, if he can hold his forces and gradually add to them—and certainly the indications are all affirmative to-night—he stands the best choice of any man in the race.

Sherman will lead him a long length at the start, but it is the general expectation that his followers will desert him one by one, and every old campaigner knows what that means in a convention. Even Warner Miller's friends are forced to admit that Sherman seems to have a canvass far less substantial than the Indianian.

The New-Yorkers will soon be called upon to determine whether they will fritter away their power or not. If Mr. Depew fails to recognize the situation that will soon be presented to him by his friends, even if it has not already been, and persists in believing that he can be nominated, the point will be reached and passed at which the New-York delegation can effectively dispose of the whole or any portion of its vote. The New-Yorkers are in the main desirous of being on the winning side, and for a fact are booming Chauncey less and discussing Harrison more and more, and Sherman little at all. The friends of the four delegates at large would like to see them agree upon the policy to be pursued, if it becomes apparent that Mr. Depew's nomination is out of the question. One point has been gained by them, and that is an agreement on the part of all four to get together and endeavor to agree upon somebody. Whether this will result in any agreement is, of course, another question. The very fact, however, that even this little understanding has been reached is accepted as evidence of a desire to secure a second place on the ticket for a New-York man, even if they cannot get the first.

Less talk of Blaine has been heard to-day than on any day since the delegates began to gather. The convention proceedings seem to be moving unnecessarily slow, but the fact is not yet accepted as one of the parts of a programme to nominate Blaine. Shed Shook has got out his old Blaine fowling piece, and seems to be determined to go a-gunning along with John J. O'Brien, but then the weather is intensely hot, and naturally that affects Republicans like Mr. Shook, who are strongly magnetized.

The contest seems to be between Harrison, Sherman, and Blaine again to-night, just as it was last night and the night before. Harrison's canvass is improving. Sherman's is not. Blaine is the dark horse whose grooms are divided in opinion as to the advisability of running him at all. If Allison's candidacy has produced any effect upon anybody to-day, the New-Yorkers are not the ones.

## THE CONVENTION AT WORK.

### MR. ESTEE MADE PERMANENT CHAIRMAN—TWO VALUABLE GAVELS—THE REPORTS ON RULES AND CREDENTIALS.

CHICAGO, June 20.—The first session of the second day of the convention attracted a larger audience than the session of yesterday. There were few empty seats in the broad, sloping parquet, the greater balcony above it, and in the little ridge-pole gallery that runs straight across the house, so close to the roof that it seems possible for its occupants to reach it and touch the ceiling with their fans. The air was like that of an oven, and every man and woman waved a palmleaf or a pasteboard or a decorated fan with such energy as to keep up all over the theatre a constant rustle like the sighing of a soft breeze. Temporary Chairman Thurston was on time and found his small platform partly occupied by a lady, two or three "distinguished guests" of no distinction, and the space about the platform in front and at the sides filled up with acquaintances of Sergeant-at-Arms Fitzsimmons, whom that person, in a spirit of accommodation to his friends and with entire indifference to the newspaper men whom they interfere with, would not have removed. In this respect, lack of order on the platform, the Republican Convention is unlike that of the Democrats at St. Louis, where no intrusion upon the newspaper space was permitted, and no loafers tolerated about the aisles for a moment. The platform was uncomfortably crowded, first with chairs that are for show, with high backs that obstruct the view of four rows of reporters put where they can see the chair backs and nothing more except the extreme sides of the convention, and, second, by a half dozen gentlemen who stand up still further to exasperate the unfortunate writers who sit behind them.

The band in the gallery under the picture of Logan at Atlanta played for a time to the sweltering thousands below it and the time wore away until 12:30, when Chairman Thurston rapped with his gavel and called for order. The Rev. Stephen A. Northrop of Fort Wayne made the opening prayer. There was no applause to-day as there was yesterday after the prayer by the Rev. Mr. Gunsaulus. Off in the Colorado delegation Mr. Hamill, who saw no chance for a report from the Committee on Credentials, suggested an adjournment. Some one else called for the report of the Committee on Permanent Organization. Delegate J. A. Harris of North Carolina, who thought the convention could not proceed until the Committee on Credentials had established the status of the delegates, insisted that the report of that committee was the only thing in order. Chairman Thurston having looked the subject up beforehand stated that in the two last Republican Conventions the report of the Committee on Permanent Organization was received without waiting for the Credentials Committee. The convention could do as it pleased, therefore, about proceeding or deferring business until after the report of the Committee on Credentials, which would not be ready before 8 o'clock.

PERMANENT ORGANIZATION.

The report of the Committee on Permanent Organization was called for, and ex-Gov. Foster of Ohio came forward to the platform and was greeted by cordial applause as he faced the convention. He is a man of strong frame, dark haired, his beard and mustache a mixture of gray and black, glasses on his nose, an alpaca jacket fitting close up to a flaring standing collar, and an air of composure acquired by many public appearances. He read the report, recommending the selection of Mr. Morris M. Estee of California for permanent Chairman and the following persons as the other permanent officers of the convention:

Alabama—F. R. Baker. Arkansas—F. Havis. California—W. W. Byington. Colorado—J. W. Wingate. Connecticut—I. L. Spencer. Delaware—J. R. Whittaker. Florida—G. Wells. Georgia—W. J. White. Illinois—H. S. Clark. Indiana—W. A. Cullen. Iowa—H. Rood. Kansas—W. A. Johnson. Kentucky—E. M. Hobson. Louisiana—H. C. Minor. Maine—R. B. Shepherd. Maryland—W. B. Brooks. Massachusetts—J. H. Gould. Michigan—D. W. Crawford. Minnesota—M. S. Chandler. Mississippi—J. W. Lee. Missouri—S. R. Crawford. Nebraska—B. S. Baker. Nevada—W. F. Sharon. New-Hampshire—P. C. Cheney. New-Jersey—G. A. Halsey. New-York—Jesse Johnson. North Carolina—J. H. Harris. Ohio—Benjamin Butterworth. Oregon—Z. F. Moody. Pennsylvania—James McManes. Rhode Island—W. R. Walker. South Carolina—F. H. Deas. Tennessee—W. W. Woodruff. Vermont—S. D. Hobson. West Virginia—R. L. Berkshire. Wisconsin—H. O. Fairchild. Arizona—L. H. Goodrich. Dakota—J. B. Richardson. Idaho—George M. Black. Montana—T. C. Power. New-Mexico—J. F. Chavez. Utah—J. J. Daly. Washington—Thomas Hayes Minor. Wyoming—F. F. Warren.

And we would give authority to such States as have not yet named a candidate for Vice-President to hereafter name such officer. For Honorary Secretaries as follows:

Alabama—Albery Boyd. Arkansas—J. T. Trent. California—George T. De Golyer. Colorado—Irving Hobart. Connecticut—Henry R. Durand. Delaware—Charles H. Maull. Florida—E. R. Gunby. Georgia—J. H. Deveraux. Illinois—C. F. Snively. Indiana—John D. Cockrum. Iowa—The Hon. John W. Cockburn. Kansas—W. W. Scott. Kentucky—Charles Pendleton. Louisiana—George W. Wickham. Maine—Eben D. Haley. Maryland—L. F. P. Dennis. Massachusetts—George S. Merrill. Michigan—N. M. Richardson. Minnesota—George B. Edgerton. Mississippi—S. P. Hurst. Missouri—The Hon. R. G. Parker. Nebraska—E. D. Einsel. Nevada—E. Williams. New-Hampshire—A. G. Batchelder. New-Jersey—Henry S. White. New-York—Robert Ray Hamilton. North Carolina—George M. Fuller. Ohio—Henry C. Hedges. Oregon—J. R. Bean. Pennsylvania—L. C. Dart. Rhode Island—The Hon. Melvin Bull. South Carolina—T. T. Oliver. Tennessee—George W. Hill. Texas—E. H. Terrill. Vermont—B. J. Leroy. West Virginia—James J. J. Peterson. Wisconsin—G. A. Knapp. Arizona—L. F. Eggers. Dakota—J. M. Bailey. Idaho—Louis Sweet. Montana—T. C. Power. New-Mexico—M. S. Rovisso. Utah—John J. Daly. Washington—O. C. White. Wyoming—E. D. Clark.

The report was adopted and Chairman Thurston appointed ex-Gov. Foster of Ohio, Senator George B. Sloan of New-York, and M. D. Foley of Nevada to escort the permanent Chairman to the platform. The attorney of the Union Pacific, who had beaten Mr. Estee as a candidate for temporary Chairman in the National Committee, stepped out. His opponent, an anti-monopolist was to come in as a foil. The new Chairman was a man of agreeable presence, past 50 years of age, bronzed, bald well back to a line drawn over his head from ear to ear, with prominent eyebrows, a strong nose, beard full and of the Garfield cut. The convention listened for the first sound of his voice. It heard it, and it was satisfied with the sample. He could be heard. He spoke as follows:

GENTLEMEN OF THE CONVENTION: I thank you in the name of the States and Territories of the Pacific coast, as well as from my own heart, for the distinguished honor that you have seen fit to confer upon me. I appreciate to the fullest extent the grave responsibilities which devolve upon me, and it being a Republican Convention, I shall ask in all things its charitable judgment and its candid and earnest support.

Gentlemen of the convention: Following so illustrious a gentleman as your temporary Chairman, I shall not attempt to detain you by any lengthy speech. I only want to say to you that we live so far from the centre of the Republic over on the Pacific shore that I cannot even guess who your nominee is going to be. [Laughter.] I say further to you, my friends and gentlemen of the convention, that I am not able to say exactly what your platform will be, but the people of the country have echoed its sentiments and the rattle of the skirmish line was heard only two weeks ago from Oregon, [great applause,] and, God willing, next November you will hear from Cleveland's Appomattox all over this great Republic. [Cheers.] My friends and gentlemen of the convention, again thanking you for the very high honor you have conferred upon me, and impressing you. I hope and pray, with the belief that our duties are the gravest and most solemn in character, and trusting from the depth of my soul that every act may be done to promote the best interests of our common country and to advance the great Republican Party, I will call for the next order of business. [Applause.]

There was some applause, but not much. The speech was so short as to forbid the developing of enthusiasm, but the reference to the Republican victory in Oregon brought down the convention in scattered plaudits, and then with a regular "three cheers for Oregon."

Mayor Roche of Chicago went upon the platform a moment later. In his hand he carried a glistening gavel of gold, the head of which was attached to a twisted handle of silver. It is a beautiful piece of workmanship, 12 inches in length and weighing 33 ounces, 25 of which are of silver and 8 of gold. The handle is 9 inches in length, of solid twisted silver, at the top of which are two escutcheons of the United States in gold and enamel. Above this is the American eagle, bearing on its back the gavel proper, which is of silver, bearing upon it the names of the 38 States of the Union. At each end is a heavy gold plate, upon one of which is a three-carat diamond and the arms of the State of Illinois, and at the other end is engraved: "Presented to the Republican National Convention of 1888 by his Honor the Mayor, on behalf of the citizens of Chicago." Mr. Roche held this handsome object aloft as he presented it to the convention in the following words:

"MR. CHAIRMAN AND MEMBERS OF THE REPUBLICAN NATIONAL CONVENTION: As emblematical of the substantial character of the Republican Party and its identification with the interests of both capital and labor, I am instructed by my fellow-citizens, in their name and in their behalf, to present to this convention this gavel. [Here Mr. Roche waved the gavel aloft and was greeted with cheers.] It is not made of silver alone, but of gold and silver, [applause,] the bimetallic basis of our sound national currency, [applause,] a boon given by the Republican Party to the people of this country. [Applause.] The material dug from the bowels of the earth, the separating and refining processes, and the adornment of precious stones represent both crude and skilled labor [applause] and teach the lesson which the Republican Party by its legislation for a generation has taught of free homes, free schools, and a free ballot, [applause,] and not only this, but free labor, intelligent labor, shall have its just rewards, [cheers,] as it is the foundation of all wealth, individual and national prosperity. [Cheers.] Mr. Chairman, as gold and silver regulate our national currency and maintain the wheels of progress and industry in normal and healthy condition, may this emblem of authority in the hands of the Chairman of this convention enable him to conduct it to a successful issue and a happy result. [Loud and continued cheers.]

The convention now had two gavels. There was a third coming. Delegate Charles A. Works of Illinois produced it, and he also presented it in a speech in which he told that it was made out of a desk in Grant's old tannery at Galena, and expressed the hope that it would not only pound the life out of the Democracy, but would also "tan its hide."

THE REPORT ON RULES.

The Committee on Rules was now ready, and the Hon. T. M. Baynes of Pennsylvania made the report. The code of rules offered was as follows:

RULE 1.—This convention shall consist of a number of delegates from each State equal to double the number of its Senators and Representatives in Congress, 10 delegates from the Territory of Dakota, [cheers and applause,] 6 from Washington Territory, 2 from each one of the remaining Territories, and 2 from the District of Columbia.

RULE 2.—The rules of the House of Representatives shall be the rules of this convention so far as they are applicable and not inconsistent with the following rules.

RULE 3.—When the previous question shall be demanded by a majority of the delegates of any State and the demand seconded by two or more States, and the call sustained by a majority of the convention, the question shall then be proceeded with and disposed of according to the rules of the House of Representatives in similar cases.

RULE 4.—Upon all subjects before the convention the States shall be called in alphabetical order and next the Territories and next the District of Columbia.

RULE 5.—The report of the Committee on Credentials shall be disposed of before the report of the Committee on Resolutions is acted upon, and the report of the Committee on Resolutions shall be disposed of before the convention proceeds to the nomination of candidates for President and Vice-President.

RULE 6.—When a majority of the delegates of any two States shall demand that a vote be recorded, the same shall be taken by States, Territories, and the District of Columbia, the Secretary calling the roll of the States and Territories and the District of Columbia in the order hereinbefore stated.

RULE 7.—In making the nominations for President and Vice-President, in no case shall the calling of the roll be dispensed with. When it appears at the close of any roll call that any candidate has received a majority of all the votes to which the convention is entitled the President of the convention shall announce the question to be: "Shall the nomination [of the candidate] be made unanimous?" But if no candidate shall have received such majority the Chair shall direct a vote to be taken again, which shall be repeated until some candidate shall have received a majority of the votes, and when any State has announced its vote it shall so stand unless in case of clerical error.

RULE 8.—In the record of the votes by States, the vote of each State, Territory, and the District of Columbia shall be announced by the Chairman, and in case the vote of any State, Territory, or the District of Columbia shall be divided, the Chairman shall announce the number of votes cast for any candidate, or for or against any proposition, but if exception be taken by any delegate to the correctness of such announcement by the Chairman of his delegation, the President of the convention shall direct the roll of the members of such delegation to be called, and the result shall be recorded in accordance with the votes individually given.

RULE 9.—No member shall speak more than once upon the same question, and not longer than five minutes, unless by leave of the convention, except in the presentation of the names of candidates.

RULE 10.—The Republican National Committee shall be appointed to consist of one member from each State, Territory, and the District of Columbia. The roll shall be called and the delegation from each State, Territory, and the District of Columbia shall name, through its Chairman, a person who shall act as a member of such committee. Such committee shall issue the call for the meeting of the National Convention six months at least before the time fixed for said meeting, and each Congressional district in the United States shall elect its delegates to the National Convention in the same way as the nomination for a member of Congress is made in said district, and in the Territories the delegates to the convention shall be selected in the same way as the nomination of Delegates to Congress is made; and said National Committee shall prescribe the mode for selecting the delegates for the District of Columbia. An alternate delegate for each delegate to the National Convention, to act in case of the absence of the delegate, shall be elected in the same manner and at the same time as delegates are elected. Delegates at large for each State and their alternates shall be elected by State Conventions in their respective States.

RULE 11.—The Republican National Committee is authorized and empowered to select an Executive Committee, to consist of nine members, who may or may not be members of the National Committee.

RULE 12.—All resolutions relating to the platform shall be referred to the Committee on Resolutions without debate.

RULE 13.—No person except members of the several delegations and officers of the convention shall be admitted to the section of the hall apportioned to delegates.

RULE 14.—The convention shall proceed in the following order of business: 1. Report of the Committee on Credentials. 2. Report of the Committee on Resolutions. 3. Naming of members of the National Committee. 4. Presentation of candidates for President. 5. Balloting. 6. Presentation of candidates for Vice-President. 7. Balloting.

The rules, the Chairman explained in a brief speech, were substantially the rules of the last convention. They gave 10 instead of 2 votes to

# The New-York Times.

VOL. XXXVII.....NO. 11,486. NEW-YORK, FRIDAY, JUNE 22, 1888.—WITH SUPPLEMENT. PRICE TWO CENTS.


# POSTSCRIPT.

*Friday, June 22, 1888—3 A. M.*

## THE BLAINE MEN'S SCHEME

### THEY WILL TRY TO STAMPEDE THE CONVENTION.

ELKINS AND OTHERS WORKING FOR A BLAINE-FORAKER TICKET — THE SHERMAN AND HARRISON MEN COMBINE TO DEFEAT IT—A HARD BATTLE EXPECTED AT TO-DAY'S SESSION —LAST NIGHT'S CONFERENCE.

THE LIST OF CANDIDATES.

JOSEPH R. HAWLEY of Connecticut.
WALTER Q. GRESHAM of Illinois.
BENJAMIN HARRISON of Indiana.
WILLIAM B. ALLISON of Iowa.
RUSSELL A. ALGER of Michigan.
CHAUNCEY M. DEPEW of New-York.
JOHN SHERMAN of Ohio.
EDWIN H. FITLER of Pennsylvania.
JEREMIAH RUSK of Wisconsin.

CHICAGO, June 21.—As a result of two informal conferences to-night between the friends of Sherman and Harrison in one instance, and those of Blaine and Foraker in the other, it is evident that the Blaine and anti-Blaine battle will be fought out in the convention to-morrow. So far as the information obtained by the Blaine conferees was concerned, it was not so encouraging as the Blainiacs had hoped to find it.

Steve Elkins, Logan R. Roots, Powell Clayton, and others, 20 all told, met in Room 44 at the Grand Pacific to consider the advisibility of pushing the nomination of Blaine. Mr. Elkins was fresh from the convention and was full of the idea that Blaine had only to be named as a candidate to assure his nomination. In his enthusiasm he bubbled over. He declared that Blaine had 500 votes in the convention, and that they could be secured at any time. He was confident that Blaine would accept if nominated. His enthusiasm was not contagious. One of the delegates present considered it inadvisable to attempt Mr. Blaine's nomination. He had sounded the delegates supposed to be devoted to Blaine and he believed that there were not more than 100 upon whom Blaine's friends could rely for votes. A good deal of conversation followed, but no one had a plan to suggest. The conference broke up without having decided upon any plan to be followed in the convention.

While the Blaine men were knocking their heads together the Harrison and Sherman men were discussing ways and means to check the break for Blaine. The Pennsylvanians held a conference at their headquarters and it was found that Sherman would have 30 votes on the first ballot and 55 on the second. If, after that, it was found that he could not be nominated, the vote of the Pennsylvania delegates, including Senator Quay, was to go to Harrison rather than to Blaine.

At Harrison's headquarters there were visitors from Alger's camp and from the New-York headquarters until long after midnight. Senator Hiscock was one of the latest callers. There had been no decision reached as to any course to be pursued, but the Harrison and Sherman men are confident that none of the friends of either of those candidates will help the Blaine-Foraker stampede.

Foraker's speech this afternoon has angered the New-York men for its attack upon Depew, and the Michigan men for its implied contempt for Alger. The Harrison men say that it has helped them by provoking the hostility of the New-York and Michigan delegates. The Harrison men hope to force the fighting to a conclusion to-morrow.

## FORAKER'S MAGNETIC PLEA.

### THE GOVERNOR OF OHIO FIRES THE CONVENTION.

CHICAGO, June 21.—The greatest burst of enthusiasm seen thus far in this convention came this afternoon at the end of Foraker's speech for John Sherman. The young Governor touched the hearts of both delegates and spectators as no one before him had done. Their eyes had been upon him from the beginning of the first session. Many have seen in him a leader in campaigns of coming years, and some would be glad to follow him in the campaign so near at hand.

Before Ohio was called on the roll of States for presentation of candidates the applause had in most cases been perfunctory. In accordance with the understanding reached when Estee was made permanent Chairman, California had not presented the name of Blaine she gave up her cherished purpose and asked that the State should be passed. "Our position is well known," said the Chairman of the delegation. Frazer had made a good speech for Alger, appealing skillfully to the veteran soldiers, and especially to the friends of Logan. Gresham had been nominated in a matter-of-fact way by the old associate of Lincoln, Leonard Swett, and the nomination had been supported by Davis of Minnesota and by Lynch of Mississippi, who drew out as much applause for Harrison as for the man of his choice. Harrison's name had been presented by Porter of Indiana and Gallinger of New-Hampshire. Hiscock had praised and defended Depew. During the polished oration of Hastings in behalf of Sherman a Pennsylvania's "beloved son, James G. Blaine," had caused the audience to applaud heartily for three minutes, but the most impressive demonstration of the day was yet to be made.

Hastings sat down, and from all parts of the house came the cry, "Foraker!" "Foraker!" The speech which followed was a most effective appeal to party sentiment. No other speaker had seemed to be so much in earnest. No other had come so close to his audience and shown so much skill in gaining their entire sympathy. Apparently it was the address of a man with whom Republicanism had become an absorbing passion. There were in it none of the flowers of rhetoric, nor was the speaker a master of the grace of oratory, but he said just what the audience wanted to hear, and appeared to say it with great sincerity. Although actually upon the platform apart from and above the delegates, he seemed to have every one of them by the hand. When he cried: "I want a man who has been a Republican all his life," and declared that Sherman had never strayed away in bad company, New-Yorkers were carried with him, and for the moment forgot Depew. And when at last he predicted that the red bandana would give way to the American flag, in an instant, as if by magic, the great hall glowed with thousands of bright little flags, and all who had been hanging on his words were on their feet yelling and cheering.

For 10 minutes the little flags were flying, and the applause continued, while some one not unmindful of the young Governor's interests and ambition raised and displayed before the audience a great floral shield, which bore the words, "No rebel flags surrendered while I am Governor."

Although this seemed so natural there was art in it. Foraker is a great favorite in the convention, but the applause was not all for him and his candidate. He had shrewdly appealed to partisan feeling, and both the audience and the delegates were really shouting for the Republican Party, while Sherman gained the benefit of the display.

After a short and forcible address by John M. Langston, a colored orator of exceptional ability, and Mr. Charles Emory Smith's description of Mayor Filter's many excellent qualities, to an audience which was at first indulgent and then impatient, an adjournment until to-morrow morning was taken on the motion of ex-Senator Miller, by general consent.

After adjournment it was conceded that the effect of the Foraker-Sherman demonstration would be to hasten a concentration of the forces opposed to Sherman, and that some important work would be done during the night. No one could show that as a result of the demonstration Sherman had gained votes, but it was feared that gains would be made by the Ohio delegation before the balloting, rather on account of the popularity of his friends than because of any newborn admiration for the man himself. It was seen that these friends could at any time exert influence in the convention. Moreover, it was clearly seen that the nomination of Depew of New-York had not been well received, and it was believed that the movement in behalf of Depew might drive to Sherman many conservative Republicans who would, under other conditions, have continued for several ballots to vote for other candidates. It was not forgotten that the vote upon the motion to admit the Mahone delegates from Virginia had indicated that Sherman could not then count upon more than 269 delegates, but there was an impression that the situation had undergone some change.

In some quarters there was a tendency to swell the vote of Harrison. It was known that certain prominent Blaine men, among them Stephen B. Elkins, were at work for the Indiana candidate. "Blaine ought to be nominated," said Elkins this afternoon, "but I am for Harrison now." Connecticut, New-Hampshire, and Vermont had held a conference and agreed to vote for Harrison upon an early ballot. It was urged by some that it might not be possible to give Harrison a majority, and that after all it would be necessary to take up Blaine. Some of the local papers published this morning a dispatch from the town reached by the Blaine coaching party last night, and in this dispatch it was said, upon the authority of Mr. Carnegie, that Blaine, if nominated, "would not refuse." Accompanying this assertion was the following statement, said to have been written for publication by Mr. Carnegie after Blaine had read the latest telegrams from Chicago:

"If the Republican Party finds it cannot agree upon a man and then calls upon its former leader to lead it again, it goes without saying that it would be his duty to do so, more especially since it is now clear that the campaign is to be fought upon the issue of protection versus free trade, the former of which Mr. Blaine feels to be essential to his country's prosperity. It is not anticipated that this call will be made upon him, but if made it must be accepted."

By some this was regarded as authoritative because it came from Mr. Blaine's trusted friend and traveling companion, but to the majority it seemed improbable that the long-continued disagreement in the convention would bring about the conditions under which the nomination could be urged as the only satisfactory solution of the problem.

When Senator Hiscock told the convention to-day that the Republicans of New-York were now united in support of a candidate many delegates must have wondered why they could not have united for the presentation of a man who did not represent the wrong side of an issue which is of great importance to the party in the West. The Senator's argument that due attention should be paid to the recommendations of the great doubtful State, and that Mr. Depew would not only hold every Republican vote in New-York, but would also draw farmers and mechanics from the Democratic Party, would have more weight if the Western delegates had believed that the delegation was supporting Depew in dead earnest, and if they could have been convinced that with Depew on the ticket the party would not lose the whole Northwest. Unfortunately Mr. Hiscock's speech was, of necessity, a defense and an explanation.

The Minnesota delegate who urged the convention not to be alarmed about the Grangers, lives in the Congression district which covers the northern half of the State, and in which the Farmers' Alliance has thousands of members. It is this Farmers' Alliance which has waged war upon the railroads for years, and the railroad legislation of the State is the fruit of its labors.

The Blaine managers were not encouraged by the results of a conference held to-night, and the friends of the other candidates made some progress toward an agreement to prevent a stampede. F. D. R.

## THE DEPEW AND BLAINE MEN

### ATTEMPTS TO STAMPEDE THE CONVENTION IN FAVOR OF BLAINE TO BE RESISTED BY THE NEW-YORKERS.

CHICAGO, June 21.—The New-Yorkers held their second meeting as a delegation this morning. Their headquarters were crowded with delegates and alternates, at least 100 of whom were present. Col. Coggswell of Queens called the meeting to order, and Warner Miller was elected Chairman, a position which he will continue to hold in the convention so long as Mr. Depew is in the field. Mr. Miller made a speech, in which he took as his text the thought that New-York is the next battle ground, and that the New-Yorkers, having decided to present a candidate, were in honor bound to support him loyally, and to do all in their power to promote his candidacy. Senator Frank Hiscock made a similar speech, in which, however, he dwelt chiefly upon the importance of New-York in the coming campaign. Committees were then appointed to visit the delegations of every State and Territory and labor with increased energy for Candidate Depew. The delegation will hold another meeting to-morrow morning.

Warner Miller had two visitors to-night who tried to interest him in the scheme of the Blaine men to stampede the convention. They were Charles Emory Smith of Philadelphia and Steve Elkins. He told them both that he should oppose any such scheme upon the floor of the convention, and they need expect no assistance from him or his friends. The nomination now seemed, in his judgment, certain to go to the West, and he could not see how that could be prevented. He expressed the opinion to some of his friends this evening that certain failure would attend any attempt to create a stampede. Thomas C. Platt said the same thing.

The talk about a conference to-night to plan for the dramatic nomination of Blaine set the young New-Yorkers to pricking up their ears. There are some goslings in the delegation who know just about enough to tumble into any procession which the Californians may lead. That the latter will vote for Blaine when the balloting begins in the morning is now accepted as a fact. they expect to pick up enough votes in Connecticut, Massachusetts, Vermont, Alabama, Mississippi, and Kansas to infect the whole convention.

The Harrison and Sherman men have compared notes, and are satisfied that they can head off any stampede. The Sherman men among the New-Yorkers share the enthusiasm of Ohio Sherman men after to-day's nominating speeches. The Sherman boom has received a little boost, and that fact stimulates many of Blaine's friends to all the more effort to defeat him. The Allison men feel just a trifle more confident, but do not themselves know exactly why. The Harrison men have felt apprehensive all day about the Blaine business, but this evening they are in better spirits. The battle still seems to be between Harrison, Sherman, and Blaine.

## THE PROSPECT FOR TO-DAY.

### ONE OR TWO BALLOTS LIKELY TO BE FOLLOWED BY ADJOURNMENT—A FEVERISH ANXIETY TO TEST THE STRENGTH OF CANDIDATES — THE BLAINE OUTLOOK—SHERMAN'S PROBABLE VOTE.

CHICAGO, June 21.—The real battle of the Republican National Convention begins to-morrow. All of the comparatively wearisome routine rubbish and mere oratory that stood in the way of the balloting was cleared up in the two sessions of the convention to-day, and to-morrow morning, when the delegates reassemble in the Auditorium there will be nothing to do but to call the roll and vote. According to a desire that is common with the friends of nearly all the candidates, there will probably be an adjournment after the first or second ballot. A ballot is needed to develop the relative strength of the long list of aspirants for Presidential honors. After the first ballot there will be an opportunity for reaching conclusions. The impatience to reach the ballot is feverish. It has infected the crowds at the hotels and perceptibly increased the demand for tickets of admission. The audience of the afternoon was large. It is probable that it will be exceeded in size by the gallery to-morrow.

It begins to look as if the Republicans might nominate their candidate for President on Friday. The tendency of the business of the convention is toward a conclusion of the main contest to-morrow, although there may be enough left of the original "Blaine or Bust" scheme to prolong the fight over Sunday, in order to prove that no one else can be united upon. The Blaine boom faded almost out of sight on Wednesday. There may have been a purpose in suppressing it, and its suppression is believed to have had about everything to do with the nomination of Chairman Estee as presiding officer. It was nearly a clear Blaine vote by which John S. Wise was given a majority of the delegates from Virginia. There were enough votes against Mahone, or against Sherman, to nominate any man who could get them all. The 512 votes against substituting the minority report may not all be for any one of the candidates against Sherman, but very few of them are for him. The Sherman vote as shown in that roll call is as follows by States:

| State | Votes | State | Votes |
|---|---|---|---|
| Alabama | 10 | New-York | 22 |
| Florida | 4 | North Carolina | 18 |
| Georgia | 12½ | Ohio | 19 |
| Illinois | 2 | Pennsylvania | 56 |
| Kentucky | 1 | South Carolina | 18 |
| Louisiana | 9 | Tennessee | 6 |
| Maryland | 1 | Texas | 2 |
| Massachusetts | 6 | Virginia | 10 |
| Mississippi | 16 | West Virginia | 4 |
| Missouri | 4 | Wisconsin | 3 |
| Nebraska | 6 | Dakota | 10 |
| Nevada | 6 | Wyoming | 1 |
| New-Jersey | 4 | | |
| Total | | | 250½ |

It is known that not more than 35 or 40 of Pennsylvania's delegates will vote for Sherman. When the time comes he will lose more than half of Ohio's vote; perhaps all but seven. He counted upon the whole vote of Alabama and had claimed seven votes from Arkansas. The Sherman men also declared that they had 16 votes in Kentucky. They may get more than the one cast for his friends last night but it is doubtful. Louisiana had been relied on for 13 votes instead of 9. There were supposed to be votes in Maine, too; 5 in Maryland, 20 in Missouri, 12 in Tennessee, and some in Texas. Some of these may yet be recovered and probably will be after Alger has been shown to be a hopeless candidate and some of the Sherman men who were captured for Alger are released.

One thing that dashed the Harrison men to-day was inspired by something that was published in the Indianapolis *Journal*, free copies of which were in everybody's hands this morning. In their anxiety to advance Harrison's chances the publishers had allowed a paragraph to appear in that paper declaring that the Granger States would not consent to the nomination of Depew. It as true, but connected with the assertion that Alger's candidacy was imperilled by fear of "boodle" talk, it incensed many of the New-York men and the friends of Alger in other States than Michigan. It was a mistake to say anything of the kind just at the time when Harrison was being talked of so favorably and when it was being generally admitted that he was standing highest in general estimation as the candidate against whom the least objection could be made.

This backset of Harrison's popularity was observed by the Blaine men at once. It was just in their way. They helped it on. Stephen B. Elkins was at once quoted as having said that it did not seem probable that the nomination of any one except Blaine was possible. The latest dispatch from the European wanderer was quoted as again leaving the way open for the proffer of the nomination, and ex-Chairman Thurston, who had spoken so pointedly in his address to the convention about the impiety of disregarding the will of the great leader, was heard to say that he believed Blaine would take the nomination if it was found, after protracted balloting, that none of the candidates could get a majority of the convention.

Alger men, after the morning recess, had heard that the attempt to stampede for Blaine was yet to be made, and that the convention business was to be dragged along for several days in order to give the original Blaine delegates a chance to vote for the favorite son from Maine.

The New-York men, who had heard Elkins and his immediate friends talking favorably of Harrison and intimating that he would be a strong and acceptable candidate, at once detected the coolness of the prominent Blaine men for the Indiana candidate, and they began to question the sincerity of the expressions that they had been listening to for several days.

The Allison men also felt the cool breeze blow over the Harrison boom, which told them to be comforted by it. Was the popularity temporarily enjoyed by Harrison to be transferred under direction to Allison, and in such moderate quantities as to make it safe to accumulate a vote large enough to make the candidate appear without going the length of making him the nominee?

The hesitating friends of Gresham, Alger, and Depew asked these questions and others like them. They began to fear that delegates were being moved back and forth like pawns in a game of chess, or like soldiers marched and countermarched in feigned movements. The Allison talk was renewed with some show of spirit.

But the friends of Sherman and Harrison may bring all the calculations of the frantic Blaine men to naught. How the followers or managers of these two were brought together is not yet apparent, but that they have come together for conference is true. Last night's vote was an approximate test of Sherman's strength. The Harrison men knew their own strength and their chances of gain. It was plain to both sides that the Sherman and Harrison vote, if combined, was nearly, if not quite, enough to nominate. Before the convention had adjourned this afternoon it was evident that the movement to nominate Blaine had taken a grip, and that it had been stimulated by talk on the latest Blaine dispatch and by a large number of very young men who were shouting all over the city, "Blaine, Blaine, James G. Blaine," with an accompaniment of fish horns. More and more the impression deepened that after all Elkins and other Blaine men had determined to have the Plumed Knight as a candidate. The friends of those three other candidates who had accepted the alleged letters of declination as honest and who had been working sincerely and assiduously for other candidates began to grumble. Whatever luck the Blaine men might have it was evident that a Blaine rush to overthrow the smaller men would provoke ill-feeling and perhaps disgust, a sensation of having been deliberately fooled for Blaine's benefit. And so it is that the prospect of an attempt to stampede for Blaine may bring on a sharp fight between the men who will have nothing but Blaine and those who are convinced that it will be better to have anybody but Blaine.

The elaborate programme prepared for the New-York men, by which the delegation was to be divided into committees to do missionary work among the delegates from other States, was laughed at even in the New-York delegation. Some of the committeemen have gone about the work laid out for them. Others have taken their assignments and paid no further heed to them. While Mr. Louis F. Payn was wrestling with the Southern delegates, other delegates were looking around for comfortable resting places. Those who started out as missionaries soon found that while Mr. Depew was personally regarded with the kindest of sentiments, there was everywhere a conviction that Depew's nomination would be suicidal.

Here and there the Blaine boom was encountered, pushing itself into prominence as it has always done with much noise. Mr. Reid of the *Tribune*, who had appeared on the scene, was credited with having come here on purpose to insist that Blaine shall be nominated and that no time should be lost in getting the other small and cheap candidates off the track. The Blaine men soon became aware of the necessity for concerted action. They had kept the Californians down until the permanent Chairman had been chosen. They had refrained from wild and noisy demonstrations long after they would have enjoyed making the welkin ring with shouts for their champion and idol. But it was time to be heard. When Foraker made his speech for Sherman and exhibited himself in a halo of flags, the huzzas that broke forth were not for Sherman, but were for Blaine and Foraker. The conspiracy by which the friends of Harrison, Sherman, Gresham, Alger, and others had been led to advocate more or less sincerely the nomination of one or other of these men was about to be hatched while the boys were shouting "Blaine" and blowing their toot horns in hotels and streets. Blaine and Foraker got together to contrive a way of springing Blaine in the balloting. California was found to be a willing State to lead in the proposed stampede. Creed Hammond, a Blaine man "from way back," announced that having refrained, as he had promised, from placing Blaine in nomination he had complied with the request of Blaine that his name should not be mentioned in the convention. He did not understand that the injunction prevented him or any one else from voting for Blaine. At all events, he should do as he thought best and as he greatly preferred to do.

There was some surprise felt when New-Jersey made no response on the roll call of States this afternoon. It had been understood that State Senator Griggs was prepared to present as New-Jersey's candidate William Walter Phelps. His speech would have been less flowery than that of Davis of Minnesota, but it would have been no less a bit of finished oratory that would have been far above the average of the day's speeches. It is hoped that he may have a chance to deliver it yet in presenting Phelps as a candidate for the Vice-Presidency. It seems that Mr. Phelps personally requested Mr. Griggs not to present his name formally as a candidate for the Presidency. He said that if the New-Jersey delegates chose to cast their votes for him that was their affair, and he would greatly appreciate the unsolicited compliment; but if he were named in a set speech it would antagonize the other candidates against him, which he did not want. Of course, when New-Jersey casts her 18 votes for him it will be notice to the convention that in Phelps they have a possible dark horse that would need but little training to go upon the course ready to compete for the great November sweepstakes. He is well enough known to need no biographical sketch, and doubtless will receive as many votes as if he had been formally nominated.

The platform, although it was greeted in its references to the devotion of Republicans to protection with the most strikingly enthusiastic applause that has greeted any utterance in this convention, interests no one, and creates no conversation. It was inevitable that it should denounce the Democrats and find fault with the Congress for not reducing taxation when the Republicans in Congress have notoriously defeated every attempt at reduction by the Republican-Randall alliance. It was also inevitable that a bid should be made for popularity in the Territories following the Democratic example. It would have been safe to assume that it would avoid the liquor question, save by its reference to the whisky ring as an opposer of international revenue reduction. But it was not expected by Illinois or Iowa Republicans that the pet Illinois waterways scheme would be ignored. While it is satisfactory to the men who made it, and entirely so to Mr. McKinley, who was the author of the tariff points of the declaration of principles, it has already been spoken of slightingly by old Republicans, who say that it contains no new, progressive, or inspiring phrase, and that it is like the convention, which intends it merely as a reminder of the fact that there was once a party in the land that stood for progress and liberality, and that that party had lost its courage, with a good deal of its senses.

## BLAINE AND GRESHAM MEN FIGHTING.

CHICAGO, June 21.—There was a small riot in the main corridor of the Grand Pacific to-night, and all because a boy yelled "Hurrah for Blaine!" The corridor was comparatively quiet, but the boy's cry brought hundreds of men from every direction, the Blaine and Gresham factions quickly taking up the cry for their favorites. At the same time two processions, one of Blaine and one of Gresham men, entered the corridor at different entrances, each headed by a band and each bearing transparencies. The corridor was in a wild uproar in a moment—the wildest scene since the crowd began to gather here. Gresham men climbed up the pillars supporting the ceiling and Blaine men took other pillars, each side waving transparencies. For 10 minutes the din was kept up. Then a Gresham man slipped to the floor with his transparency. In an instant it was torn to shreds by the Blaine men. Then the Gresham men retaliated and tore the Blaine transparencies to tatters. Blows followed and canes were whirling in the air while several men were knocked down. The police tried to quell the disturbance, but it died out in a few minutes of its own accord. Nobody was seriously injured.

## THE SERIOUS WORK BEGUN.

### A LONG, HIGH PROTECTIVE PLATFORM ADOPTED AND A FLOOD OF ELOQUENCE HEARD IN THE PRESENTATION OF THE CANDIDATES.

CHICAGO, June 21.—When the convention hall was opened this morning the streets in the neighborhood of the Auditorium were not so crowded as on yesterday by the throngs moving toward the convention. It was still hot. The flags, wet with an early morning shower, flapped listlessly and heavily in the faint south wind. The water tanks were overflowing with ice, and about each one there stopped a crowd waiting in turn for a chance at the bright tin cups.

Just before 10 o'clock Chairman Estee, fan in hand, stepped upon the platform. The Sergeant-at-Arms, wearing a dress coat and carrying in his hand a mace with a gold eagle and a tuft of red, white, and blue at his head, had come in with his brigade of personal friends, who proceeded to get in the way and to add to the disorder by getting in the way instead of maintaining order by keeping other people out of the way. Nothing had been done to correct the errors in the arrangements for the press, the worst encountered in any National Convention for 12 years for discomfort and inconvenience.

The Chairman, not at all conscious, perhaps, that his blunderings of last night were still under discussion, was at least mindful of his promise to be punctual. He did not wait a minute after 10 o'clock, but rapped for order on the hour. The delegates were only about half in. The seats for spectators were sparsely occupied. It was evident that the punctuality of the Chairman would not hasten business much. The electric signal to the band brought no response. The band had not arrived. So the Rev. Thomas E. Green of Chicago, a dark-haired, dark-skinned, and slight man with a pointed black beard, made the opening prayer. When he had concluded the band was again rung for, but there was no music. A third ring brought a response. The seats filled up while the band was playing. Among those who came in through the main entrance and passed down the hall were Col. F. D. Grant and his wife, who were again applauded as they were last night.

With a sparse attendance there was something that could be done. The roll of States was called and the names of the new National Committeemen so far as chosen were announced. The Committee on Resolutions would be ready in 10 minutes Delegate Warner of Missouri announced. The audience called for Ingersoll, but the Chairman was evidently determined not to have him at that stage. The band filled up the gap.

### THE PLATFORM OF PRINCIPLES.

"Mr. McKinley of Ohio" announced the Chairman, as the Chairman of the Resolutions Committee was seen coming down the aisle. He was as cool and fresh to look at as a god new-risen instead of showing fatigue after a prolonged session over a declaration of principles. He never looked more like Napoleon. A frock coat, buttoned notwithstanding the heat, carried on its lapel a large fat rosette of red, white, and blue, and a Sherman badge. He stepped upon the Chairman's platform, and, facing the audience, he was given a rousing reception. He had been spoken of with much acceptance as a "dark horse," and his friends and many who would be his friends joined in the ringing applause that rolled down toward him from the floor and galleries. He unrolled his report, and, in a low voice that was as clear as a bell and presently rose musically strong until it was heard in the remotest corner of the hall, he read the declaration of principles, as follows:

"The Republicans of the United States, assembled by their delegates in national convention, pause on the threshold of their proceedings to honor the memory of their first great leader, the immortal champion of liberty and the rights of the people—Abraham Lincoln; and to cover, also, with wreaths of imperishable remembrance and gratitude the heroic names of our later leaders, who have more recently been called away from our councils—Grant, Garfield, Arthur, Logan, Conkling. May their memories be faithfully cherished. We also recall with our greetings and with prayer for his recovery the name of one of our living heroes, whose memory will be treasured in the history both of Republicans and of the Republic —the name of that noble soldier and favorite child of victory, Philip H. Sheridan.

"In the spirit of those great leaders, and of our own devotion to human liberty, and with that hostility to all forms of despotism and oppression which is the fundamental idea of the Republican Party, we send fraternal congratulation to our fellow-Americans of Brazil upon their great act of emancipation, which completed the abolition of slavery throughout the two American Continents.

"We earnestly hope that we may soon congratulate our fellow-citizens of Irish birth upon the peaceful recovery of home rule for Ireland.

"We reaffirm our unswerving devotion to the National Constitution and to the indissoluble union of the States; to the autonomy reserved to the States under the Constitution; to the personal rights and liberties of citizens in all the States and Territories in the Union, and especially to the supreme and sovereign right of every lawful citizen, rich or poor, native or foreign born, white or black, to cast one free ballot in public elections and to have that ballot duly counted. We hold the free and honest popular ballot and the just and equal representation of all the people to be the foundation of our republican government, and demand effective legislation to secure the integrity and purity of elections, which are the fountains of all public authority. We charge that the present Administration and the Democratic majority in Congress owe their existence to the suppression of the ballot by a criminal nullification of the Constitution and laws of the United States.

"We are uncompromisingly in favor of the American system of protection. We protest against its destruction as proposed by the President and his party. They serve the interests of Europe; we will support the interests of America. We accept the issue and confidently appeal to the people for their judgment. The protective system must be maintained. Its abandonment has always been followed by general disaster to all interests, except those of the usurer and the Sheriff. We denounce the Mills bill as destructive to the general business, the labor and the farming interests of the country, and we heartily indorse the consistent and patriotic action of the Republican Representatives in Congress in opposing its passage.

"We condemn the proposition of the Democratic Party to place wool on the free list, and we insist that the duties thereon shall be adjusted and maintained so as to furnish full and adequate protection to that industry.

"The Republican Party would effect all needed reduction of the national revenue by repealing the taxes upon tobacco, which are an annoyance and burden to agriculture, and the tax upon spirits used in the arts and for mechanical purposes; and by such revision of the tariff laws as will tend to check imports of such articles as are produced by our people, the production of which gives employment to our labor, and release from import duties those articles of foreign production (except luxuries) the like of which cannot be produced at home. If there shall still remain a larger revenue than is requisite for the wants of the Government we favor the entire repeal of internal taxes rather than the surrender of any part of our protective system, at the joint behest of the Whisky Trusts and the agents of foreign manufacturers.

"We declare our hostility to the introduction into this country of foreign contract labor, and of Chinese labor, alien to our civilization and our Constitution; and we demand the rigid enforcement of the existing laws against it, and favor such immediate legislation as will exclude such labor from our shores.

"We declare our opposition to all combinations of capital organized in trusts or otherwise, to control arbitrarily the condition of trade among our citizens, and we recommend to Congress and the State Legislatures in their respective jurisdictions such legislation as will prevent the execution of all schemes to oppress the people by undue charges on their supplies, or by unjust rates for the transportation of their products to market. We approve the legislation by Congress to prevent alike unjust burdens and unfair discriminations, between the States.

"We reaffirm the policy of appropriating the public lands of the United States to be homesteads for American citizens and settlers, not aliens, which the Republican Party established in 1862 against the persistent opposition of the Democrats in Congress, and which has brought our great Western domain into such magnificent development. The restoration of unearned railroad land grants to the public domain for the use of actual settlers, which was begun under the Administration of President Arthur, should be continued. We deny that the Democratic Party has ever restored one acre to the people, but declare that by the joint action of Republicans and Democrats about fifty millions of acres of unearned lands originally granted for the construction of railroads have been restored to the public domain in pursuance of the conditions inserted by the Republican Party in the original grants. We charge the Democratic Administration with failure to execute the laws securing to settlers title to their homesteads and with using appropriations made for that purpose to harass innocent settlers with spies and prosecution under the false pretense of exposing frauds and vindicating the law.

"The government by Congress of the Territories is based upon necessity only to the end that they may become States in the Union; therefore, whenever the conditions of population, material resources, public intelligence, and morality are such as to insure a stable local Government therein, the people of such Territories should be permitted, as a right inherent in them, the right to form for themselves Constitutions and State Governments and be admitted into the Union. Pending the preparation for Statehood all officers thereof should be selected from the bona fide residents and citizens of the Territory wherein they are to serve. South Dakota should of right be immediately admitted as a State in the Union, under the Constitution framed and adopted by her people, and we heartily indorse the action of the Republican Senate in twice passing bills for her admission. The refusal of the Democratic House of Representatives, for partisan purposes, to favorably consider these bills, is a willful violation of the sacred American principle of local self-government, and merits the condemnation of all just men. The pending bills in the Senate for acts to enable the people of Washington, North Dakota, and Montana Territories to form Constitutions and establish State Governments should be passed without unnecessary delay. The Republican Party pledges itself to do all in its power to facilitate the admission of the Territories of New-Mexico, Wyoming, Idaho, and Arizona to the enjoyment of self-government as States, such of them as are now qualified, as soon as possible, and the others as soon as they may become so.

"The political power of the Mormon Church in the Territories as exercised in the past is a menace to free institutions, a danger no longer to be suffered. Therefore we pledge the Republican Party to appropriate legislation asserting the sovereignty of the Nation in all Territories where the same is questioned, and in furtherance of that end to place upon the statute books legislation stringent enough to divorce the political from the ecclesiastical power, and thus stamp out the attendant wickedness of polygamy.

"The Republican Party is in favor of the use of both gold and silver as money, and condemns the policy of the Democratic Administration in its efforts to demonetize silver.

"We demand the reduction of letter postage to 1 cent per ounce.

"In a republic like ours, where the citizen is the sovereign and the official the servant, where no power is exercised except by the will of the people, it is important that the sovereign—the people—should possess intelligence. The free school is the promoter of that intelligence which is to preserve us a free nation, therefore the State or Nation, or both combined, should support free institutions of learning sufficient to afford to every child growing up in the land the opportunity of a good common school education.

"We earnestly recommend that prompt action be taken by Congress in the enactment of such legislation as will secure the rehabilitation of our American merchant marine, and we protest against the passage by Congress of a Free Ship bill as calculated to work injustice to labor by lessening the wages of those engaged in preparing materials as well as those directly employed in our shipyards.

"We demand appropriations for the early rebuilding of our navy; for the construction of coast fortifications and modern ordnance and other approved modern means of defense for the protection of our defenseless harbors and cities; for the payment of just pensions to our soldiers; for necessary works of national importance in the improvement of harbors and the channels of internal, coastwise, and foreign commerce; for the encouragement of the shipping interests of the Atlantic, Gulf, and Pacific States, as well as for the payment of the maturing public debt. This policy will give employment to our labor, activity to our various industries, increase the security of our country, promote trade, open new and direct markets for our produce, and cheapen the cost of transportation. We affirm this to be far better for our country than the Democratic policy of loaning the Government's money without interest to 'pet banks.'

"The conduct of foreign affairs by the present Administration has been distinguished by its inefficiency and its cowardice. Having withdrawn from the Senate all pending treaties effected by Republican Administrations for the removal of foreign burdens and restrictions upon our commerce and for its extension into better markets, it has neither effected nor proposed any others in their stead. Professing adherence to the Monroe doctrine, it has seen with idle complacency the extension of foreign influence in Central America and of foreign trade everywhere among our neighbors. It has refused to charter, sanction, or encourage any American organization for constructing the Nicaragua Canal, a work of vital importance to the maintenance of the Monroe doctrine and of our national influence in Central and South America, and necessary for the development of trade with our Pacific territory, with South America, and with the islands and further coasts of the Pacific Ocean.

"We arraign the present Democratic Administration for its weak and unpatriotic treatment of the fisheries question and its pusillanimous surrender of the essential privileges to which our fishing vessels are entitled in Canadian ports under the treaty of 1818, the reciprocal maritime legislation of 1830 and the comity of nations, and which Canadian fishing vessels receive in the ports of the United States. We condemn the policy of the present Administration and the Democratic majority in Congress toward our fisheries as unfriendly and conspicuously unpatriotic and as tending to destroy a valuable national industry and an indispensable resource of defense against a foreign enemy.

"The name of American applies alike to all citizens of the Republic and imposes upon all alike the same obligation of obedience to the laws. At the same time that citizenship is and must be the panoply and safeguard of him who wears it, and protect him, whether high or low, rich or poor, in all his civil rights. It should and must afford him protection at home and follow and protect him abroad in whatever land he may be on a lawful errand.

"The men who abandoned the Republican Party in 1884 and continue to adhere to the Democratic Party have deserted not only the cause of honest government, of sound finance, of freedom or purity of the ballot, but especially have deserted the cause of reform in the civil service. We will not fail to keep our pledges because they have broken theirs, or because their candidate has broken his. We therefore repeat our declaration of 1884, to wit: 'The reform of the civil service, auspiciously begun under the Republican Administration, should be completed by the further extension of the reform system already established by law to all the grades of the service to which it is applicable. The spirit and purpose of the reform should be observed in all Executive appointments and all laws at variance with the object of existing reform legislation should be repealed, to the end that the dangers to free institutions which lurk in the power of official patronage may be wisely and effectively avoided.'

"The gratitude of the Nation to the defenders of the Union cannot be measured by laws. The legislation of Congress should conform to the pledge made by a loyal people, and be so enlarged and extended as to provide against the possibility that any man who honorably wore the Federal uniform shall become an inmate of an almshouse or dependent upon private charity. In the presence of an overflowing Treasury it would be a public scandal to do less for those whose valorous service preserved the Government. We denounce the hostile spirit shown by President Cleveland in his numerous vetoes of measures for pension relief, and the action of the Democratic House of Representatives in refusing even a consideration of general pension legislation.

"In support of the principles herewith enunciated we invite the co-operation of patriotic men of all parties, and especially of all workingmen, whose prosperity is seriously threatened by the free trade policy of the present Administration."

### THE PLATFORM CHEERED AND ADOPTED.

There was more or less applause of a formal kind as the report touched upon the Irish question, the obstructionist policy of the Republicans in Congress, or the treatment of Democratic attempts to reduce the tariff, and the most tremendous and unanimous applause of the convention at the declaration of uncompromising adherence to the system of protection. The noise of voices was like the roar of a monster cataract rising and falling until the crowd grew faint with its exertions. It was, from beginning to end, a reversal of the Democratic platform at St. Louis, except where it made an effort to go further in the same direction for political effect. The shot at the Independents and Mugwumps of 1884 was applauded with such vigor as to indicate that the convention was disposed to thrust all "deserters" out of the ranks for good and all, but the indorsement of civil service reform as a Republican invention elicited only a slight wave of applause.

There was a speech from W. H. Marine of Maryland in support of the proposition to pass the platform by a rising vote. The speaker recalled the blind orator of Ohio, Judge William West, but he imparted a strong nasal tone to his utterances and became distressingly intense as he spoke his little speech. When he had concluded, the previous question was ordered, and under its operation the platform was adopted by a rising vote.

### THE PRESENTATION OF CANDIDATES.

There was now nothing in the way of the most interesting business of the convention. At 11:20 the Chairman announced that the next thing in order was the presentation of candidates. The Chairman directed the Secretary to call the roll of States, first, however, requiring him to read Rule 7, the rule regulating the vote upon nominations and tightening the method of procedure so as to avoid a stampede. Then the Chairman explained that the rules permitted any delegate to nominate a candidate of any other State than his own; and the calling of the roll was begun. Alabama and Arkansas announced that they had no name to present.

California was next on the list and the convention waited for the Californians to carry out their threat to nominate James G. Blaine, regardless of what the rest of the world might think of such asininity. Creed Hayward responded for his State and after speaking a moment threaded his way to the platform where he made this brief little speech: "California asks for the present to be passed." The request was granted.

Connecticut had a duty to discharge, and it did it perfunctorily. It was called twice before it responded. Then Samuel L. Warner arose and made this, the briefest speech that has been heard in the convention: "Connecticut presents the name of Joseph R. Hawley." The ripple of applause that greeted the Senator's name was not so marked as to prevent the clerk making himself heard distinctly when he called the name of the next State.

### LEONARD SWETT NOMINATES GRESHAM.

Illinois had a candidate and Leonard Swett, an elderly man, tall of figure, with heavy, bushy eyebrows came down the aisle to nominate him. "Judge Walter Q. Gresham of Indiana" was the candidate of the Illinoisians. The delegates cheered heartily at the mention of his name. The Illinois delegates waved their colors and joined in the applause. Every other State in the convention sat coolly by and fanned itself. Mr. Swett was a trifle tiresome in his speech, and the mob in the galleries, lacking that sense of propriety which regulates the actions of decent men, endeavored to cut him short. The Chairman would allow no interruption, however, and Mr. Swett concluded his speech. It was as follows:

MR. PRESIDENT AND GENTLEMEN OF THE CONVENTION: This presence recalls a scene enacted in this city 28 years ago. That was the second National Republican Convention, and the first nomination of Abraham Lincoln. At his inauguration the Republican Party first assumed the reins of governmental control. With unimportant interruptions the Democratic Party had controlled our national policy for 32 years. The country in 1861 stood upon the verge of political and financial ruin, and the sharpest and most deadly conflict of arms ever known succeeded. We have had of Republican rule since then, four years of war and 20 years of peace. The four years of war produced heroes, sacrifices, and suffering without parallel and a reunited country. The 20 years of peace increased the population, internal improvements, manufactories, useful inventions, comforts in homes, and the general development of all classes with a rapidity unequaled in the history of the world within the time named. In the language of Daniel Webster, we may say of this Republican rule, the suffering and the fruits of the war, and the unparalleled prosperity of this peace, "The past is at least secure."

We have assembled again to select a President for 60,000,000 of free people. Who most in character is the very essence of those people? Who of all the names suggested will draw support most largely from all classes? Who can best bring together and reunite the broken fragments of our party? Who by a personal courage and sublime confidence in his own convictions is an ideal leader of the American people? Who most strikingly stands for cosmopolitan American character? These are the questions of the hour addressed to us all.

"I suggest the name of Walter Q. Gresham of Indiana and Illinois, and invite a thoughtful consideration of some of the reasons why he should be nominated. He was born of sturdy and rugged parents, in Harrison County, Ind., fifty-seven years ago, and has spent one-third of his life in labor upon a farm. He acquired, by nature and education, a profound belief in the fundamental doctrines of government and the union of the States, "one and inseparable," as taught by the lives and examples of Washington and Hamilton, Clay and Webster, Lincoln and Thad. Stevens, and a disbelief in and aversion for the political heresies of John C. Calhoun, Breckinridge, Jefferson Davis, and Lamar—of property in man and the right of secession. He has always been an unwavering and inflexible Republican. One-third of a century ago he organized the party of Fremont and Dayton in his native county, which consisted, all told, of four people. In 1860, then at the age of 29, he was elected to the State Legislature at the same time Mr. Lincoln was elected President, from a strong Democratic county, and by the aid of German votes. There he originated and passed a law which authorized Oliver P. Morton, our greatest war Governor, to organize and arm at the expense of the State any regiment anywhere in the State. We owe the peace and loyalty of Indiana at this critical period to the admirable working of this law and the fact that she was not behind the call of the President one moment in furnishing her quota of men.

After performing this service, of great value to his State, he selected 1,000 young neighbors and friends and marched at their head into Kentucky with Gen. Sherman at the very beginning of the war. These forces aided the loyal element there in holding true to the Union the northern part of that State, while the southern part broke off and went with the rebellion. But for the presence of these troops the Ohio River would have probably been the dividing line and Southern Ohio, Indiana, and Illinois would have been the first battle ground. He served with Grant at Shiloh and Vicksburg, and was a distinguished figure with Sherman in his march upon Atlanta in 1864. He was frequently promoted for gallant conduct on the battlefield, and was called upon when sharp work was to be done, and finally fell, pierced by a Minié ball, while leading his division into the shot and shell of the enemy at the bloody fight of Leggett's Hill, in the suburbs of Atlanta. Carried to the rear he met Col. Richard S. Tuthill, whose presence now adorns the judicial bench of this State, and who was then a commander of batteries of artillery making their way to the front. The scene was one of confusion, of the tramping of horses' hoofs and the rattling of artillery and caissons dashing into battle. Col. Tuthill turned aside a moment to Gen. Gresham, then bleeding on a stretcher, and said, inquiringly: "Are you hurt badly?" The fight was not all out of him yet, and, turning his pale face to see who made the inquiry, he replied: "You had better hurry your batteries to the front; they are needed there." He was placed in a freight car and hurried to the North. The next day he awoke from a morphine sleep in a dazed condition and said to a soldier in attendance, "Whose body is that?" pointing to a coffin in the same car with him. "That is the dead body of your commander, Gen. McPherson." Thus the commander of the army and the division commander had mingled their blood upon the red field at Leggett's Hill. Wherever in all the war the battle's wreck lay thickest there was the manly form of Gen. Gresham, a type of enthusiastic heroism and an inspiration to the soldier who followed him.

But it is not in his military career, dashing and brilliant as that is, that we find the crowning reasons for his nomination. For him "Peace hath her victories, no less renowned than war." After his relations with the army were voluntarily severed, he was called by President Arthur into his Cabinet to the office of Postmaster-General. Here he greatly promoted the rapid expedition of the mails, shortening materially the time of their transit across the Continent. He also aided in reducing the letter, newspaper, and parcel postage, thereby saving millions to the people and encouraging the dissemination of literature and intelligence. He was also the first vigorously to enforce the United States statutes against the abuses of the mails by lottery vendors and other swindling schemes by which the the credulous and weak-minded were imposed upon, and their confidence betrayed. It is, however, in the discharge of his duties as United States Judge that the higher and crowning glories of his character appear. The image of justice among the Greeks was represented as blindfolded, holding the scales balanced in her hand, but unable to see the rank or standing of the parties before her. Judge Gresham has been the living ideal of this Grecian figure. Unmoved by the threatenings of power, he has gone straight on in the line of his duty to the integrity and right of the question under consideration, and has administered justice to the high and the low, the rich and the poor, with a steady but impartial hand. The contestants in one of the greatest railroad strikes that has arisen in our country have also been before him. By a wise and happy decision he administered exact justice to all, prevented the strike from becoming universal, public traffic from being paralyzed, the Nation from convulsion, and the most serious damage to an unknown number of individuals. Wherever in all his life he has touched anything, it has been improved, beautified, or adorned. He has always had the happy faculty of quietly doing the right thing at the right time, and he possesses in his own great character all the good qualities of the Republican Party. Under his leadership the campaign cry will be "Live and let live." There will be no attacks on capital and no attacks upon labor, but the country will march on with gigantic strides in settlement, development, and growth. The true leveling system will be adopted of making all men equal before the law and placing all men's feet on a level. Then the

# The New-York Times.

VOL. XXXVII.....NO. 11,489. NEW-YORK, TUESDAY, JUNE 26, 1888.---WITH SUPPLEMENT. PRICE TWO CENTS.


## GERMANY'S IMPERIAL SHOW

### EMPEROR WILLIAM'S SPEECH TO THE REICHSTAG.

**BISMARCK AND VON MOLTKE CENTRAL FIGURES IN THE IMPOSING PROCESSION—HISTORICAL SCENE IN THE GREAT WHITE HALL.**

BY COMMERCIAL CABLE FROM OUR OWN CORRESPONDENT.



BERLIN, June 25.—Only 126 people of the public and press were admitted to the opening of the Reichstag to-day. The gallery was full at 12 o'clock. Fortunately I secured the celebrated corner on the right side of the gallery whence the best view is had below. At 12 o'clock, save a few Court gentlemen in brilliant uniforms, the gorgeous white saloon was empty. Behind the throne the wall was draped with rich curtains of golden satin, embroidered with the Prussian eagle and crown. The other walls were festooned with gray and black crape, combined emblems of mourning for Emperors William and Frederick.

At 12 o'clock the procession of Court pages and Court officials entered. Then came the Emperor between the King of Saxony and the Regent of Bavaria. He was in the uniform of a Prussian Infantry General, with the massive gold chain of the Order of the Black Eagle. He carried a white plumed helmet.

With firm and measured step Bismarck ascends the steps of the throne, bowing low, and places the speech on white paper, with gold border, in the Emperor's hand. The Emperor begins reading in a firm, staccato voice, like a commanding officer. There is only one remarkable emphasis on the word "me," where he says: "I am resolved to preserve peace so far as it depends on me," when he pauses. He reads in very earnest tones the passage about the continued friendship of the Czar. He is dignified and resolute, but pale, and wears a tired look.

The speech was greeted with frequent bravos. The address ended, Bismarck advances and bends over the Emperor's hand to kiss it. The Emperor raises him, shaking hands cordially and gratefully smiling amid the ringing cheers. Then the Grand Duke of Baden calls for three cheers more for the Kaiser, and the procession re-forms, the Emperor, now in his royal mantle, between the King of Saxony and the Regent of Bavaria. Around him are borne 10 rich cushions with the insignia of the realm, the imperial standard banner, orb, and scepter, each with a General or high noble in charge.

Between the standard and the orb on the left, Von Moltke, his Field Marshal's staff in hand, looks feeble and aged. On the right is Bismarck, like an old lion. Around are Knights of the Black Eagle in their red velvet mantles, including the sailor Prince Henry, his sad face recalling his father's charm.

The Empress is in a red-draped box on the left. Her condition explains her wearied look. She is in deep mourning, and wears the heavy gold chain of the Black Eagle over her weeds. The little Crown Prince looks pale, but crosses his arms on the red-covered rail, tilts his head, and peers around. The President of the Reichstag shouts, "Long live the Emperor, King William of Prussia!" and three great cheers ring out on the air. The Court preachers, Koegel and Porsius, who ministered to the last hours of William and Frederick; the famous Catholic Socialist priest of Main, Deputy Mouffang, in a cassock of violet; the great political leader, Benningsen; National Liberals in the uniform of the land directors of old; little Windthorst of the Centre in evening dress, with his yellow ribbon orders, are in the diplomatic gallery with the Ambassadors and Ministers. Carl Schurz accompanies the American Minister.

The royal procession passes out. The deputies are ranged in a crowded semicircle in the space before the throne. Bismarck appears alone, in a gleaming white Magdeburg cuirassier uniform, erect, with a firm step, keen eyes, and thick snow-white eyebrows. He mounts the dais, gazes around, and retires to announce to the Emperor that the Reichstag waits. A detachment of the First Guards, with their famous mitre caps, enter, and pass out between the crowded Deputies and the throne, when the procession passes through in the same order as before, only the Bundesrath Council, 100 strong, precede the Emperor in double file. The solemn procession moves through the saloon to the chapel, whence arise the rich tones of the organ choristers, composed of manly voices, the whole assembly joining in the service, especially in the clear, sweet thanks hymn, which literally rendered reads: "Jesus, still lead on, till rest be come," and in the Te Deum with which the service ends, and the procession then returns through the hall.

Prince Henry wore an Admiral's uniform covered with orders. The red velvet mantle and black eagle were only assumed after the services in the chapel by the Grand Dukes of Ratibor and Baden and Crown Prince of Würtemberg. Many members of the Reichstag wore rich uniforms as Knights of St. John, in red coats and white facings, and military uniforms of all colors of the rainbow were to be seen. Several ecclesiastics wore vestments as rich as those of the famous Court Chaplain.

*Associated Press Dispatch.*

BERLIN, June 25.—At noon the Emperor, accompanied by the federal Princes and a host of officials, repaired to the Court chapel. The Emperor walked between the King of Saxony and the Prince Regent of Bavaria. Following them came the Grand Duke of Baden and Hesse, Prince William of Würtemberg, Princes Henry, Leopold, and Albrecht of Prussia, and the Grand Dukes of Saxe-Weimer and Mecklenburg-Schwerin.

Chaplain Koegel preached the sermon. At the conclusion of the service all proceeded to the White Hall, where the members of the Reichstag were assembled. At the stroke of 1 Prince Bismarck entered the hall at the head of the members of the Bundesrath. The Bavarian Minister walked at the Chancellor's side. After greeting the members Prince Bismarck withdrew to inform the Emperor that the Reichstag had assembled. His Majesty thereupon entered the hall, the federal Princes following in the prescribed order.

The Emperor and the Knights of the Black Eagle wore cloaks of purple velvet. Gen. von Moltke walked immediately behind the Emperor. In front of his Majesty was borne the imperial standard. The Emperor took his position on the dais between the standard and the imperial sword. The Empress, accompanied by ladies in waiting, occupied a seat on the right of the throne, the Crown Prince, attired in the black dress of a page, sitting by her side.

When all were assembled the President of the Reichstag proposed three cheers for the Emperor and his federal allies, which were enthusiastically given. The Emperor then read his speech in a clear voice. During the reading of the speech he was frequently interrupted by cheers. At the conclusion of the address the Emperor shook hands with Prince Bismarck, who then kissed his Majesty's hand. At the close of the proceedings Baron Lutz proposed three more cheers for the Emperor, and when the procession left the hall the members were still cheering loudly.

### EMPEROR WILLIAM'S SPEECH.

**HE WILL MAINTAIN PEACE SO FAR AS IT IS IN HIS POWER.**

BERLIN, June 25.—The Emperor's speech in full was as follows:

I greet you with deep sorrow in my heart. I know you mourn with me. The fresh remembrance of the heavy sufferings of my deceased father and the affecting fact that I have been called upon to ascend the throne three months after the death of his Majesty Emperor William I., will exercise a similar effect upon the hearts of all Germans. Our sorrow has evoked warm sympathy from all the countries of the world. Beneath the burden of these things I pray God to give me strength to accomplish the high duties to which His will has called me. Obeying this call, I have before my eyes the example of peaceful rule which Emperor William I., after bitter wars left to his successors, and to which my late father's rule corresponded, in so far as he was not prevented from executing his designs by his illness and death.

I have summoned you in order to declare in your presence that, as King and Emperor, I am resolved to pursue the same path by which my deceased grandfather secured the confidence of his allies, the love of the German people, and good-will abroad. I also, with God's help, will strive earnestly to accomplish the same end. The most important duties of the German Emperor lie within the province of assuring the military and political safety of the empire abroad and watching over the execution of the imperial laws at home. The chief of these laws regards the Imperial Constitution. To defend and guard it in all the rights which it guarantees to the two legislative bodies of the nation and to every German, and also in those which it assures to the Emperor and the confederated States and their sovereigns, appertains to the chief rights and duties of the Emperor.

In the legislation of the empire I have in accordance with the Constitution to co-operate more in my capacity as King of Prussia than as German Emperor, but in both capacities it will be my endeavor to proceed in the same spirit in which my grandfather began and especially will I appropriate to myself in its full significance his message of Nov. 17, 1881, and shall continue to strive in the spirit of that document so that imperial legislation may afford to the working people that further protection which in accordance with Christian morality is needed by the weak and oppressed in their struggle for existence. I hope that in this way it may be possible to arrive at an equalization of unhealthy social contrasts, and I cherish confidence in the belief that for the care of our domestic welfare I shall have the clear-sighted support of all true friends of the empire and of the allied Governments without division or party differences. I also hold myself bound to support our national and social development within the paths of legality and sternly to oppose all efforts the aim and tendency of which shall be to undermine public order.

In foreign politics I am resolved to maintain peace with every one, so far as it lies in my power. My love for the German Army and my position in it would never induce me to attempt to endanger for the country the benefits of peace, unless the necessity for war is forced upon us by a hostile attempt on the empire or one of its allies. Our army will assure us peace, or if peace be broken it will enable us to fight for it with honor. That, with God's help, will be possible for it to do by reason of the strength it has derived from the army laws you recently unanimously voted. To employ this strength for offensive wars is far from my heart. Germany needs neither new military renown nor any conquest, since she finally won for herself by fighting the right to exist as a united and independent nation.

Our alliance with Austria is publicly known. I shall hold fast to it with German fidelity, not only because it exists, but because I see in this defensive compact the foundation for the maintenance of the European equilibrium, and also a legacy from German history, the purport of which the public opinion of the whole German people sanctions, and which corresponds with European international law as it has undisputedly existed since 1866.

Similar historical relations and national needs now bind us to Italy. Both countries will maintain the blessings of peace and work out in the quiet security of new won unity the perfection of national institutions and the promotion of their welfare. Our existing agreements with Austria and Italy will permit me, to my satisfaction, to maintain my personal friendship with the Czar and the friendly relations existing for a century with Russia, which correspond with my own feelings and German interests.

In the conscientious care of peace I shall devote myself equally as readily to the service of the Fatherland as to the care of the army, and I rejoice in our traditional relations to foreign powers through which my endeavors in behalf of peace will be aided. Trusting in God and my people's ability for their defense, I entertain confidence that it will be permitted to us for an indefinite time to defend and assure by peaceful effort what my two predecessors, now resting in God, won by arms.

A committee of the Reichstag, composed of senior members, has directed the President of the Chamber and the two Vice-Presidents to compile the address in reply to the speech from the throne, and instructed them to avoid political allusions.

The Reichstag was formally opened at 3:30 o'clock. The President in his speech referred to the grief of the country at the death of Emperor Frederick. He said: "The late Emperor was the hope of the German people. On his knightly form we had gazed with pride and admiration for many years, ever mindful of what he had accomplished for Germany. The heroic way in which he bore his sufferings placed even his valor on the battlefield in the shade. The nation will pay its debt of gratitude to him by showing unwavering fidelity to his son, for whom the hearts of the people beat." The President concluded by invoking God's blessing on the new Emperor.

In response to the call of the President three cheers for Emperor William were heartily given. The President and Vice-Presidents were re-elected, and the House proceeded to draft an address in reply to the speech from the throne.

The Reichstag instructed the President to convey to the Dowager Empresses Victoria and Augusta an expression of his deepest sympathy.

### MR. MORLEY MOVES TO CENSURE.

**THE GOVERNMENT PLACED ON THE DEFENSIVE ON THE CRIMES ACT.**

LONDON, June 25.—In the House of Commons this evening Mr. Morley moved to censure the Government for its administration of the Irish Crimes act, as calculated to undermine respect for the law, estrange the people of Ireland, and prove injurious to the interests of the empire. He accused Mr. Balfour of refusing to give information as to how the Coercion act operated; of grave inaccuracy in statements regarding prosecutions; of injustice toward prisoners, both before trial and after conviction, and of balking their appeals and allowing them to be maltreated under prison rules. A crying instance of perversion of the law, he said, was the conviction of Mr. Dillon. The Government had contended that the Crimes act created no new offenses; but Mr. Dillon had been convicted of no offense against ordinary law, but simply of an imaginary offense created under the Crimes act. He instanced a number of other convictions as a burlesque of justice, and said that the proceedings of the courts resembled incidents in a comic opera. [Cheers.]

Mr. Goschen, Chancellor of the Exchequer, replied that it was the introduction of anarchical ideas regarding obedience to the law and a new and immoral interpretation of the duties of the citizen that had made Ireland what it was. The Government, conscious of a just administration of the Crimes act, and of the approval of law-abiding people, were ready to meet the motion with every respect.

Mr. Shaw-Lefevre warmly defended Mr. Dillon. After speeches by Major Saunderson and others the debate was adjourned. It is expected that the division on the motion will be taken on Wednesday.

### PANAMA CANAL STOCK TUMBLES.

PARIS, June 25.—Panama Canal shares have fallen 52f. The *Journal des Débats* attributes the decline to the operations of a ring, which, it says, is trying to affect the Panama Canal loan, which closes to-morrow. The *Temps* says the opponents of the loan are making desperate efforts to prevent its success, but that the issue is probably already covered.

### THE WERRA AFLOAT AGAIN.

LONDON, June 25.—The steamer Werra, which went ashore at Dungeness yesterday on her way from Bremen to New-York, has been hauled off. She will be placed in the dry dock at Southampton for examination. It is expected that she will proceed to-morrow, as she is thought to be undamaged.

### CLEANED OUT THE BANK.

**THE TELLER OF A PROVIDENCE BANK MAKES A BIG HAUL.**

PROVIDENCE, R. I., June 25.—Charles A. Pitcher left wife and home Saturday after dinner to go to the Union Bank, where he was Teller, and he said he might not be back at night, as he proposed to go to Boston and stay over Sunday. He has not been seen since, and this morning the bank officials discovered that the bank was entirely cleaned out of money, notes, bills receivable, securities, and bonds, including $20,000 in cash, and even the memoranda of notes. The popular fund for a memorial to the late Mayor Doyle, which amounted to $6,600, was included with the bank's missing cash. The defaulting Teller had left everything in perfect order, and detectives were put in charge of the case. Experts were summoned to overhaul the books, and the Directors promptly assembled. The bank suspended payment, but it was stated that if depositors would only keep their patience everything would be settled all right.

The bank people say that it would not be possible for Pitcher to negotiate the notes in his possession. Every bank in the country had been telegraphed to, and if they received them they would, of course, do it at their own cost. He might bother them for months, but he could not himself gain a profit from the paper. It consisted of trade notes entirely, including no bonds. He had taken probably fully $20,000 in currency, but this is all that can yield him a return. It is supposed that Pitcher took the notes and the securities so that he might hold them for a compromise. With the business of the bank pretty thoroughly blocked, as it is by the absence of every bit of paper it had, the defaulting Teller can bargain for exemption from prosecution and practically bring the bank to terms. It is said that the private fortunes of many of the Directors are involved.

Pitcher is 45 years old. He was born here and his past life is irreproachable. He is a member of the Central Baptist Church and has been its Treasurer. He entered the Union Bank in 1871 and his salary as Teller was $2,000. His wife has been long a sufferer from nervous diseases and he has been under heavy expenses for doctor's bills and attendance for some time. Mrs. Pitcher, who has been on the verge of insanity, may not get over the shock.

The Union Bank is one of the oldest banks in the city or State. It was founded as a State institution in 1814 and has a capital stock of $500,000. Its officials are: President—Henry G. Russell; Cashier—Joseph C. Johnson; Directors—Henry G. Russell, Elisha Dyer, Jr., John H. Congdon, William H. Dunnell, Joseph C. Johnson, William A. Tucker, and John W. Slater. The business of the bank has always been carried on after the best methods. The Directors said to-night that the bank would resume business as usual in the morning and publicly announce that $50,000 will cover the loss.

A description of the fugitive Teller was telegraphed to Inspector Byrnes and several of the detectives were detailed to search for him in this city. The Inspector is, however, of the opinion that Pitcher is in Canada.

### DIED FROM HEART DISEASE.

NEW-ORLEANS, June 25.—At about 8 o'clock last night a lodger at Vonderbank's Hotel was found dead in his room, seated in a chair and partially dressed. Coroner Lemonnier was sent for and declared death to have resulted from heart disease. There were no marks of violence, and no inquest was found necessary. An examination of his letters and papers showed that the deceased was John W. Benson of Paterson, N. J. He had a gold watch and chain and other valuables, also a metallic badge showing him to be an exempt member of the Paterson Fire Department. A bank deposit pass book from the First National Bank of Paterson showed that John W. Benson, Treasurer, had deposited at various dates, the last being April 21, 1888, a total sum of $3,335. The deceased was about 50 years of age, and had the appearance of being a very respectable man. He had been at Vonderbank's since the 19th of May. There was nothing suspicious in the entire affair, and it was doubtless a case of death from heart disease. The Coroner has the dead man's effects.

### A MOONSHINERS' RESORT BURNED.

NORWALK, Conn., June 25.—The old house on Cockenoes Island was totally destroyed by fire yesterday. It was a large two-story frame structure, erected nearly 50 years ago, and for a long time was used by the owner as a Summer resort. At his death some enterprising Yonkers man ran an illicit distillery there, and a large quantity of whisky was manufactured. This was carried away in the night, and found a ready sale in the different cities along the coast. The business continued uninterruptedly till about 17 years ago, when some revenue officers made a raid upon the place, but the wary moonshiners had fled. The whisky had been secreted on a neighboring island, and the apparatus in the building was never used again, as the place was constantly watched by the officers, and the island has since been untenanted except by occasional pleasure parties. It lies about three miles east of the Norwalk light, and contains 20 acres of land. The fire is supposed to be the work of an incendiary.

### A HYDROPHOBIA SCARE.

WICHITA, Kan., June 25.—A startling state of affairs exists in Greenwood County from the fear of rabid dogs. A gentleman who arrived from there last night says the whole country is terrorized. Nine persons have been bitten, and three have died from hydrophobia. A mad dog went through the county about a month ago and bit a number of dogs and cattle, and thus appeared to infect the whole country. Two weeks ago a dog came into the yard of William Jones and bit Mr. Jones and two of his children. Wednesday one of the children died in great agony, and the next day the father and the other child followed. A madstone was circulated among the persons who had been bitten, and it is hoped that no other deaths will occur, as these persons were all bitten before the Jones family. A wholesale slaughter of canines is now going on.

### SUICIDE ON THE TRACK.

LOCKPORT, N. Y., June 25.—Train No. 52 on the Grand Trunk Road, which is due at Suspension Bridge at 8:45 A. M., struck and instantly killed a farmer named George Hopkins, aged 74 years, at a small station just this side of Hamilton, Ontario, called Stony Creek. Charles Domville states that it was a clear case of suicide, as the old gentleman was lying alongside the track and just as the train came thundering along to make up a little lost time he raised himself up on his knees and deliberately thrust his head and shoulders in front of the engine, which threw him away to one side into the ditch. His son saw the accident from an adjacent field and took his father's remains to the house.

### CROPS DAMAGED BY RAIN.

LITTLE ROCK, Ark., June 25.—This afternoon the town was visited by a severe rainstorm, which did considerable damage. Apprehension is felt at the continued wet weather, rain having fallen at intervals for several days past. Reports coming in say that cotton is badly affected. The rainfall has been general, extending all over the State, and the growing crop cannot be cultivated. It is estimated that another week of wet weather will damage the cotton crop 50 per cent.

### THE CHEROKEE LEGISLATURE.

LITTLE ROCK, Ark., June 25.—An Indian Territory dispatch says the Cherokee Legislature convened at Tahlequah to-day, Chief Joe L. Mays having called an extra session to consider the question of leasing the Cherokee strip. Nearly all the members of both houses were present. It is probable the strip will be leased to the Cherokee Live Stock Association for three years at $150,000, an advance of $50,000 over last year.

### HANGED HIMSELF IN HIS CELL.

AUBURN, N. Y., June 25.—Jacob Merker, a convict from Rochester, committed suicide during the night by hanging himself to a hook with a strap and handkerchief. The latter broke, and he was found on the floor of his cell this morning. He had been in prison only since last April.

### PETERSON IS THE CHAMPION.

VICTORIA, British Columbia, June 25.—Henry Peterson of California and William Payne of this place rowed here, single scull, yesterday, for $1,000 and the championship of the Pacific slope. The race was three miles with a turn, and Peterson won, coming in 12 lengths ahead of his rival.

### SHE WAS ONLY SIXTEEN.

YARMOUTHPORT, Mass., June 25.—Miss Lillie Cash, a schoolgirl of Hyannis, aged 16 years, shot herself dead in her room this morning. Cause unknown.

## THE VERDICT OF CONGRESS

### SENATORS AND REPRESENTATIVES ON HARRISON.

**HOW THE NEWS OF THE NOMINATION WAS RECEIVED IN WASHINGTON AND THE COMMENTS IT AROUSED.**

WASHINGTON, June 25.—The seeker after Republican enthusiasm over the nomination of Harrison will find none in Washington. It is far wide of the truth to say that it has fallen flat. A half minute of Republican applause when the nomination was announced in the House of Representatives and the firing of a salute by local Republicans on the Monument grounds constituted all the enthusiasm thus far discovered here. Not a hurrah anywhere; not even from the crowds around the bulletin boards. Upon the Republican Senators, particularly, the news fell like a wet blanket. There were only three or four of them in the Senate Chamber when the pages began distributing the manifold bulletins of Harrison's selection, but the news was carried to the committee rooms as quickly as to the chamber.

To Mr. Allison, who read the dispatch in the room of the Appropriations Committee, it was not a surprise. He knew that his friends, with his concurrence, were going to turn their strength over to Harrison rather than to Sherman, and he had no fault to find with the result. No Senator has shown less concern than Mr. Allison since the convention began its work. His friends say he is the only candidate who comes out of the convention unscorched and without leaving some ill feeling behind.

Mr. Sherman was alone in the Foreign Relations Committee room when he received the announcement of his failure to win. It was some time before he permitted would-be callers to be admitted, and then he made little effort to conceal his disappointment. Up to the last moment he had not given up hope that he might attain the supreme object of his ambition, and it took all the grit in his make-up to enable him to keep a calm countenance while talking with his colleagues. Mr. Sherman had more or less sympathy among the Senators, but there was as little real sorrow over his defeat as real joy over Harrison's success. If the nomination had been made by the Republican Senators, the candidate would have been Allison.

Over in the House the result was read from the Clerk's desk. The Republicans jumped up and cheered and waved American flags and handkerchiefs, and sat down. The Democrats laughed derisively, and a moment later routine business was going on as drearily as if it was not a convention year. A good many Republicans hung on their desks little American flags bearing the legend "Protection to American Industries," and then sought the lobbies and cloak rooms to talk over the news.

The most-to-be-pitied people here are the Blaineites. Up to this morning they were perfectly sure their man was to be the nominee. Even the reports of the break-up at Chicago did not convince them that they were beaten, nor would they believe it until they heard of the Blaine Edinburgh dispatches read to the convention. Then they gave it up, and to-night they see no hope of Republican success in November.

Many inquiries were made to-night why the Allison forces went to Harrison in preference to Sherman. The explanation was given by a Western Senator. It was not that they loved Harrison more, but Sherman less. Iowa, Kansas, and some other Western States would not have Sherman because they did not like his record on certain financial measures. When they found that it must be Sherman or Harrison they chose the lesser of two evils and threw their votes for Harrison. This is the statement of a Republican Senator who will take the stump for Harrison during the campaign. The general feeling among the Republicans is that they will have an uphill campaign. It would have been the same, perhaps, with Sherman or Alger, but with Harrison the feeling is pronounced. No Republican will allow himself to be quoted as having any doubt of success, but very many are wondering how Harrison will run on the Pacific slope, and only his ardent supporters credit him with qualities which will draw support from beyond his party's lines. His nomination was not expected here, possibly because Washington was less well informed than other places, and the Harrison men were in a small minority. The latter admit the almost total lack of enthusiasm for the nominee, which old-timers compare to the days when Hayes and Garfield were nominated, but they say it is due to the disappointment of friends of other candidates, which will soon wear off. They look to see the nominee grow in popularity within his own party as the campaign goes on.

Among the Democrats no fault is found with Harrison's selection. They regard him as easy to beat in all the doubtful States except his own.

The nomination of Morton for Vice-President was received with little interest to-night. He was regarded as sure to be the man as soon as Harrison was placed at the head of the ticket. Both Republicans and Democrats think that Morton strengthens the ticket, the former in a general sense and the latter in a financial sense.

After Mr. Sherman had returned from a long drive late this evening he added a little to the statement made by him in the afternoon. "I know both the nominees very well," said the Ohio Senator. "They are both men of high standing. I served with Mr. Harrison during his term in the Senate. I sat beside him in that body. I have a very high opinion of his ability and character. Mr. Morton is known everywhere as an active and liberal Republican. The ticket was made to give strength to our party and to the two great doubtful States, if carried, will undoubtedly secure the election.

A large number of Republican Senators are in Chicago, and numerous Democratic Senators have taken advantage of the lull in Senatorial work to take trips out of town. Below will be found what most of those who were here when the announcement of Harrison's nomination was made have to say about it:

Senator Sherman of Ohio—I don't care to express any opinion now. It is all over, and there is really nothing for me to say. I have no regrets to express.

Senator Allison of Iowa—All very well. It is satisfactory to me. Harrison is a strong candidate. I predict a Republican success.

Senator Ingalls of Kansas—I have nothing to say.

Senator Edmunds of Vermont—It is a very good nomination. Mr. Harrison is a clean, honest, able, upright, clever, judicious man. Secondly, he will be elected, and will make a first-rate President.

Senator Butler of South Carolina—If we can't beat Harrison we can't beat anybody.

Senator Gorman of Maryland—I thought the Republicans would nominate Blaine. Harrison may poll the full strength of his party, but he will make no converts.

Senator Pugh of Alabama—Harrison is the weakest man in the Republican Party.

Senator Hawley of Connecticut—Mr. Harrison is a very able lawyer, an eloquent and effective speaker, and a wise legislator. In private and public life his character is above reproach. I can imagine nothing to prevent his receiving the vote of every man who believes in the Republican Party.

Senator Frye of Maine—It is a good nomination. Harrison is a pure and upright man. His career in the army and his service in the Senate are entirely creditable to him.

Senator Beck of Kentucky—If we can't beat Harrison we can't beat anybody.

Senator Chandler of New-Hampshire—It will help us to carry Indiana.

Senator Turpie of Indiana—I think we [the Democrats] can carry Indiana. Harrison is no stronger there than any other man of his party. Yes, we shall carry Indiana.

Senator Faulkner of West Virginia—It is a very weak nomination.

Senator Plumb of Kansas—The enthusiasm that flares up at first is not always the best; I think Harrison is a candidate who will grow as the campaign progresses. He is, perhaps, a little weak in California, but he is all right in the West.

Senator Whitthorne of Mississippi—I am glad it wasn't McKinley.

Senator McPherson of New-Jersey—The nomination of Harrison has fallen flat here in the Senate. It leaves many disgruntled men. Harrison cannot carry his own State, nor can he carry New-York. New-Jersey is sure for Cleveland.

Senator Blair of New-Hampshire—Harrison is as strong as any man that could have been nominated. With Harrison and a platform for the protection of American industries, the Republicans cannot lose.

Senator Berry of Arkansas—I would rather see any other Republican than Harrison in the White House, because he has more bitterness in his heart toward the South than any other man. I'm glad he can't be elected.

Senator Reagan of Texas—He is simply a man of straw put up for Cleveland to knock down.

Senator Hampton of South Carolina—We will beat Harrison just as we would have beaten anybody else.

Senator Colquitt of Georgia—If the Democrats had selected the candidate they could not have done better. He has not one element of popularity about him to attract the people.

Senator Blodgett of New-Jersey—Harrison is a weak nomination. It doesn't make any difference who is on the ticket as far as New-Jersey is concerned. Cleveland is bound to carry my State.

One of the Southern Senators—Harrison had the most winning way of making men cordially hate him I ever knew. When he left the Senate there wasn't a wet eye in the chamber.

Senator Platt of Connecticut—I like the nomination.

Members of the other branch of Congress were quite as free as the Senators in expressing their views. This is what some of them said of the nomination:

Mr. Reed (Republican) of Maine—It is entirely satisfactory. It will call out the full strength, not only of the Republican party, but also of the protection sentiment of the country, and will give full play to the rising feeling against President Cleveland, his message, and the Democratic Convention. I think Harrison will carry all the industrial States, the West, and the Pacific slope.

Mr. Farquhar (Republican) of New-York—Entirely satisfactory to all Republicans in the western part of New-York.

Mr. Spinola (Democrat) of New-York—Harrison is a gentleman with no positive points about him, and has never shown any special advantage with the people, having been defeated in nearly every contest when he had to go before the people. If the Republicans had the power to put 10 tails to their kite they could not carry New-York.

Mr. Buchanan (Republican) of New-Jersey—Harrison will be very strong in our State. McKinley had a strong following, but Sherman knocked him out. We will carry New-Jersey if the Democrats do not shift their cut on the tariff question.

Mr. Morrill (Republican) of Kansas—It's as good a nomination as could have been made.

Mr. Burrows (Republican) of Michigan—The convention has made the strongest possible ticket to carry the doubtful States. Harrison can carry every State that Blaine carried in 1884 and he will surely, in addition thereto, sweep Indiana. This will elect him, for the issue of free trade tendered by the Democracy will lose them New-Jersey and Connecticut without regard to the candidate, thus leaving New-York out of the calculation.

Mr. Anderson (Democrat) of Illinois—I think Harrison is weaker than several of the other candidates who were spoken of. He cannot be elected; that is certain.

Mr. Wilson (Democrat) of West Virginia—I do not consider him a strong man at all, and I don't think his record on the Chinese question will help him at all. We will beat him sure.

Mr. Bynum (Democrat) of Indiana—Harrison is a clean man and of good ability, and his nomination will prove satisfactory to the people of Indiana, but I don't think it will add any extra strength to the ticket there. He (Harrison) will produce activity and great demonstrations by Republicans, but it will be overbalanced by the Democracy uniting and carrying the State.

Mr. Breckinridge (Democrat) of Kentucky—It is a very good nomination, and yet is is a very easy ticket to beat.

Mr. Tim Campbell (Democrat) of New-York—It is a charming nomination; I think it a very clever ticket for Cleveland to beat. He will beat Harrison in a walk, and any person that does not think so can step up to my office, and I will bet any amount to back my convictions.

Mr. Randall (Democrat) of Pennsylvania—I have nothing to say. I did not say anything, did I?

Mr. Burnes (Democrat) of Missouri—The Republicans have blundered. Harrison is not their strongest man.

Mr. Allen (Republican) of Massachusetts—It is a very strong nomination. Any man against whom no charges can be made is strong.

Mr. Ermentrout (Democrat) of Pennsylvania—I think it a very weak ticket, and an easy one to beat.

Mr. Wilkins, Democrat, of Ohio—It is the strongest nomination the Republicans could have made. Mr. Harrison is a good organizer and comes from a pivotal State, and in my opinion the Republicans will nominate Porter again for the Governorship, and with both of these gentlemen running in the same campaign it is very likely they will be successful. The result in Indiana will depend upon the best organized party.

Mr. Henderson, Republican, of Illinois—I think the nomination is very good. His great grandfather was one of the signers of the Declaration of Independence.

Mr. Parker, Republican, of New-York—It will be accepted with general commendation and will grow stronger steadily until November.

Mr. E. B. Taylor, Republican, of Ohio—Harrison was my choice after Sherman, and you may whisper it around that he will be elected.

Mr. Morrow, Republican, of California—California will go for Harrison, in my opinion. I have looked up his record on the Chinese question, and I find it entirely satisfactory.

Mr. Biggs, Democrat, of California—It is the weakest nomination that could have been made for the Pacific coast. The Democrats can raise more money there to beat Harrison than any other man.

Mr. Yoder, Democrat, of Ohio—It is a fair nomination, but can easily be beaten. It makes Ohio a doubtful State.

Mr. Hines, Republican, of New-Jersey—It is the best that could have been done under the circumstances.

Mr. Browne, Republican, of Indiana—If we can't carry Indiana with Harrison, Indiana can't be carried by anybody. With Harrison for President and Porter for Governor the story is told.

Mr. McKenna, Republican, of California—There is no danger from disappointed Blaine men in my State, although we would rather have Blaine. Harrison is an honorable man, and his party has progressed to be an absolute exclusion party on the Chinese question.

Mr. Allen, Democrat, of Mississippi—I really don't believe Harrison can carry a single Southern State. You see the niggers down there are prejudiced against Harrison, and of course that beats him.

Mr. Lawler, Democrat, of Illinois—It is the weakest nomination that could possibly have been made. We will carry Illinois against him.

Mr. Lodge, Republican, of Massachusetts—It is a first-rate nomination personally, politically, and every otherwise.

Mr. Allen, Republican, of Massachusetts—It is a good, clean nomination, and with combinations which will be made the success of the Republican ticket is assured.

Mr. Goff, Republican, of Virginia—I am very much delighted. It suits my people, suits the Southern soldiers, and gives us Indiana.

Mr. Wilson, Democrat, of Minnesota—I don't see how he can add any strength to the Republican vote in Minnesota with the Republican platform.

Mr. MacDonald, Democrat, of Minnesota—I think Harrison is as weak a candidate as could possibly have been selected.

* *

President Cleveland received the news from Chicago over the regular White House wire, and soon afterward drove out to Oak View to spend the night, as he has done since the advent of the warm weather. The announcement of Morton's nomination for Vice-President was sent to him by messenger this evening. Temporary Chairman White of the St. Louis Convention, National Committeeman Tarpey of California, and the Democratic representatives from the Pacific States are holding a quiet conference to-night. It is understood that they are making a careful examination of Mr. Harrison's record on the Chinese question, and will see to it that the voters of the far West are kept well-informed on that point from the start.

* *

Members of the Democratic National Committee and the committee which is to formally notify President Cleveland of his renomination have been coming in on every train to-day, and to-night nearly all the members of the two committees are in town. The National Committee will meet to-morrow morning to organize for the Fall campaign. In the afternoon the Notification Committee will meet at the White House, where the President will receive them in the east room. After the formal speech-making, which is not likely to be very long, the President will entertain the committee at lunch. Then the visitors will be taken in charge by the local Democrats who have prepared an attractive programme for their entertainment. Some disappointment is felt because Mr. Thurman has decided not to visit Washington at this time, as was originally intended.

### THEY WANT A CANDIDATE.

DETROIT, Mich., June 25.—The Prohibition State Convention meets in this city to-morrow and will put the first State ticket in the field. There has been no preliminary talk on candidates except for Governor. Three months ago the Rev. John Russell, a prominent Methodist minister, Prohibition editor, speaker, and leader, was formally put up as a candidate and the announcement of his name was received with every token of favor by the party, and the suggestion was hailed as a deserved recognition of one who had spent more time and made more sacrifices than any other 10 men in the party. But within the past two or three weeks such determined opposition has suddenly arisen that it seems to be conceded that he is already out of the question. What it is that has been discovered that makes him all at once so unavailable is not quite discernible to outsiders, but the fact remains that his nomination is now considered impolitic.

Last week several attempts were made to get the consent to run of J. L. Hudson, the popular clothing merchant of this city, but he positively declines on the score of business, while promising moral and financial support. A. B. Cheney of Kent County, who has also been named, refuses to go on the ticket. The head of the ticket, therefore, goes begging and the rest follows suit.

### A FORGER SENTENCED.

ROCHESTER, N. Y., June 25.—In the Court of Sessions this morning Judge Morgan pronounced sentence upon Frederick V. Murray, against whom eight indictments were found by the last Grand Jury, for forgery. Murray is a well-known character who has heretofore escaped the clutches of the law owing to good luck and influence. He is of a good family. His wife secured a divorce from him some months ago. His counsel pleaded for the lightest sentence that could be imposed in view of the fact that Murray had pleaded guilty. Murray with an effrontery scarcely paralleled signed the District Attorney's name as indorser on one of the forged checks. In sentencing the self-confessed forger, Judge Morgan said: "In all these years that I have been engaged in this Court, Murray, now almost 10 years, I don't know of a case where a man has so persistently and with apparent determination endeavored to get into prison as you have. You are intelligent and had a good start in life. The sentence of the Court is that you be committed to the Auburn State Prison for seven years and six months."

### WILLIAMS COLLEGE.

WILLIAMSTOWN, Mass., June 25.—Williamstown is rapidly filling up with visiting Alumni and friends of Williams College. To-day's programme was short, an address by Prof. Safford at the fiftieth anniversary of the founding of the observatory in the evening being the only thing of note. Prof. Safford reviewed the growth of study of astronomy from the earliest times and proposed some changes in the usual manner of study of all branches taught in preparing for college and some of those taught in college. The two society events of the day were the reception given at the Alpha Delta Phi and Kappa Alpha houses in the evening. Dr. John Allen of Sheffield, Mass., presented the college with $40,000 to found a John Leland Allen Professorship of American History, Literature, and Eloquence, on condition that $1,600 be paid him yearly, or to his wife in case she survived him, and that the balance of interest be added to the sum until it reached $50,000, unless he himself shall make up that sum. The Trustees to-day elected E. B. Parsons as Register. They did not accept the resignation of Dr. Denison, the college Pastor. James White was elected a Trustee in place of the late Judge Dewey of Worcester.

### SHERIDAN TO GO TO NONQUITT.

WASHINGTON, June 25.—Gen. Sheridan's physicians to-night issued the following bulletin:

There is no substantial change to be noted in Gen. Sheridan's condition since the last report. He passed a comfortable night, and his condition to-day is fairly good notwithstanding the heat.

R. M. O'REILLY,
CHARLES B. BYRNE,
HENRY C. YARROW,
WASHINGTON MATTHEWS.

It has been determined to remove Gen. Sheridan to his cottage at Nonquitt, Mass., the latter part of the present week, but neither the exact time nor whether by water or rail has been definitely settled upon.

### DEATHS FROM SUNSTROKE.

PHILADELPHIA, June 25.—The heat in this city for the past five days has been unprecedented for the month of June. The thermometer has ranged between 92° and 98° during the day at the Signal Office, and about four or five degrees higher than that on the street. Inquests were held to-day in eight cases of death from sunstroke which occurred Saturday and Sunday. To-day two more deaths were reported, and seven cases of prostration occurred. At midnight the mercury stood at 82°, and to-night it is at the same figure. All kinds of animals, and street car horses in particular, are suffering terribly, and the mortality among them is great. The mortality among young children is also very large.

### JUDGE THURMAN WON'T WITHDRAW.

COLUMBUS, Ohio, June 25.—The case of Allen O. Myers, indicted for the famous tally-sheet forgeries of 1885, was called in Common Pleas Court to-day and postponed until to-morrow. Judge Thurman, the Democratic candidate for Vice-President, who participated in the first trial of Montgomery for the crime, was expected to withdraw. The prosecuting attorney, however, announced that Mr. Thurman would continue in the case, acting as advisory counsel.

### STEVE BRODIE'S LONG SWIM.

ALBANY, N. Y., June 25.—Steve Brodie reached Tivoli in his swim to New-York from here at 4:45 o'clock this afternoon. Peter Green, one of the men who accompanied him in the small boat, was overcome by the heat and taken ashore. Tivoli is 43 miles distant from here, and the feat of covering it in two days is considered excellent and favorable to Brodie reaching New-York within seven days as contemplated.

### BRIDGES SWEPT AWAY.

CHESTER, Vt., June 25.—Heavy thunder showers last night changed the river and brooks into mighty torrents, which overflowed the meadows and highways and in some places cut gulleys in the roads 10 or 15 feet deep. A large number of bridges and the dams at the chair stock factory of J. Powers were carried away and the factory was badly damaged. The damage to crops will go into the thousands.

### BOTH WERE KILLED.

MONTGOMERY, Ala., June 25.—Melvin Lites, a young white man, and a negro, Wash Haralson, fought with pistols yesterday near Richmond, Ala., and both were killed. They were living on the plantation of A. T. Jones, Lites as an overseer and the negro as a laborer. The negro had been ordered to leave the place, but refused to do so, and when Lites went with Jones to the negro's house he fired on them. Lites was shot twice and died within 15 minutes. Haralson was also fatally shot and died in a few hours.

## HARRISON AND MORTON

### THE REPUBLICAN TICKET AT LAST NOMINATED.

**THE BLAINE CONSPIRATORS LOSE THEIR GRIP ENTIRELY AND RETIRE FROM THE FIGHT—HOW HARRISON'S VOTE INCREASED UNTIL HE WAS NOMINATED—LEVI P. MORTON PREFERRED TO PHELPS FOR VICE-PRESIDENT—THE CONVENTION ADJOURNS.**

**THE FINAL BALLOT.**

| | |
|---|---|
| BENJAMIN HARRISON of Indiana | 544 |
| JOHN SHERMAN of Ohio | 118 |
| RUSSELL A. ALGER of Michigan | 100 |
| WALTER Q. GRESHAM of Indiana | 59 |
| JAMES G. BLAINE of Maine | 5 |
| WILLIAM McKINLEY of Ohio | 4 |
| WHOLE NUMBER OF VOTES | 830 |
| NECESSARY TO A CHOICE | 416 |

CHICAGO, June 25.—The Blaine conspirators discovered last night that they had lost their hold upon the convention. The revolt against them had become so formidable that they were forced to withdraw from the field. Having thrust them aside, the delegates this morning took up the problem, and in three ballots solved it by yielding to the judgment of the doubtful States. On the sixth ballot the votes of the great States of New-York and Indiana, that of one delegate excepted, were cast for Harrison, and with these were 14 of New-Jersey's 18 votes. On the eighth ballot the convention acknowledged the force of this recommendation by giving Harrison a majority of 128 votes to spare.

This result had not been foreseen, although it had generally been admitted that it might be reached. The impression prevailed up to last night and even this morning that Sherman's chances were better than Harrison's. New-York had decided that her votes should be cast for Harrison on the first of to-day's ballots, and should not be transferred to another candidate until it should appear that Harrison could not win. But it was the general opinion that Harrison had had his day and could not be nominated. With the aid of New-York his vote had been raised to 217 on the fourth ballot, and in spite of the support of that great State it had fallen away on the fifth. It was believed that the test of Harrison's strength was to be prolonged, not with an expectation that he would gain a majority, but to satisfy Harrison's men, who were heartily cursing the Blaine jugglers and crying out that they had been misled and cheated. It was well known, moreover, that the New-York delegates were looking forward to a test of Sherman, and had decided that their votes should be cast for Sherman after Harrison's inability to gain a majority should have been shown.

The Sherman men had been greatly encouraged by this and by other developments favorable to their cause. They were predicting with great confidence that Sherman would be nominated on the second or third ballot of to-day's first session. For several reasons, however, it was more probable that Harrison would secure a majority than that he would fail and that the convention would afterward take up Sherman. In the first place, the grip of the Blaine ring had been loosened, and the delegates were acting with more independence. Although the telegrams from Blaine, which were read before the roll was called, were not so explicit and emphatic as they might have been, yet when joined to the general belief that the Blaine tricksters had given up all hope, they cleared the air. The delegates ceased to look to Scotland for light, and confined their attention to work in the convention hall. Again, the candidacy of Harrison represented the interests of the doubtful States. He was the choice of Indiana and had been supported earnestly and powerfully by earnest men. He was the choice of New-York. He was acceptably to New-Jersey. This was to be the convention's last opportunity to give this candidate of the doubtful States a majority. If the delegates of other States should withhold their votes from him for two or three ballots, the votes of New-York would be cast for John Sherman. They would then be called upon to vote for Sherman. He was not the choice of the doubtful States. The Pacific coasters early opposed him. Would it not be better to take Harrison than to pass him by and take Sherman?

Such were the doubts of many delegates after Boutelle had read the two dispatches from Blaine. On the sixth ballot, Harrison gained 18 votes and Sherman 20, while Blaine lost 8. Harrison's gains for the most part were from New-York, New-Jersey, Colorado, and Dakota. He lost one vote on each of nine States and five in Massachusetts. His loss in the last named State was Sherman's gain. Blaine still held the vote of California.

On the seventh ballot Harrison held the solid vote of New-York, and made small gains in 18 States. This was encouraging. His total was raised from 231 to 278. New-York would not desert him so long as his vote grew in this way. On this ballot California, the most persistent advocate of Blaine, turned over to Harrison all of her votes but one.

At the beginning of the eighth ballot Henderson of Iowa withdrew Allison and the Pennsylvania delegation went out of the hall for consultation. It was seen that the end was near at hand. When Iowa was reached Harrison fell heir to nearly all of Allison's votes from that State. The drift was clearly toward Harrison. State after State saw this and fell into line. Massachusetts gave him 25, Minnesota, 13; Nebraska, 9; New Jersey, 18. Illinois stood by Gresham and Ohio would not desert Sherman. When Pennsylvania's Chairman announced that Sherman retained only 1 of the votes of that State, while 59 were cast for Harrison, the contest was ended. The Indiana ex-Senator had 399 votes, and in a few moments Tennessee raised the total to a clear majority. The following table shows the figures, beginning with the ballot on which New-York gave up Depew and came over to Harrison:

| | Fourth. | Fifth. | Sixth. | Seventh. | Eighth. |
|---|---|---|---|---|---|
| Harrison | 217 | 213 | 231 | 278 | 544 |
| Sherman | 235 | 224 | 244 | 231 | 118 |
| Alger | 135 | 142 | 137 | 120 | 100 |
| Gresham | 98 | 87 | 91 | 91 | 59 |
| Allison | 88 | 99 | 73 | 76 | .. |
| Blaine | 42 | 48 | 40 | 15 | 5 |
| McKinley | 11 | 14 | 12 | 16 | 4 |

There was scarcely any applause when the majority was reached, and even at the end of the call, when everybody knew that

# The New-York Times.

VOL. XXXVIII.....NO. 11,605. NEW-YORK, THURSDAY, NOVEMBER 8, 1888. PRICE TWO CENTS.




## TARIFF REFORM DEFERRED

### THE REPUBLICAN NATIONAL TICKET VICTORIOUS.

CONGRESS DEMOCRATIC BY A SMALL MAJORITY—RE-ELECTION OF GOV. HILL—THE STATE LEGISLATURE REPUBLICAN.

Harrison and Morton have been elected President and Vice-President of the United States. The majority for the Republican candidates in the Electoral College will be fourteen more than that cast in 1884 for Cleveland and Hendricks. Harrison has carried New-York, Indiana, California, Michigan, and Colorado, all of which had been regarded as debatable States. The majority in this State for Harrison will not be far from 11,000. In Indiana it will be very small, but in Minnesota, Iowa, and Michigan, where the interest manifested in the tariff question was relied upon to effect a considerable change in the vote, the Republicans have developed their full strength, and obtained pluralities for the national ticket much larger than those cast for Blaine in 1884.

Connecticut gives a small majority for Cleveland, and shows marked Democratic gains in the manufacturing towns, where the question of tariff taxation was constantly and thoroughly discussed during the long campaign. New-Jersey, a State greatly interested in manufacturing, not only more than doubled its Democratic majority of 1884, but choses a Legislature that will elect a Democratic United States Senator to succeed McPherson.

The returns from the Western States are still very imperfect, but it is apparent that Merriam, (Rep.) has been elected Governor of Minnesota, Hoard (Rep.) in Wisconsin, and Luce (Rep.) in Michigan, and that the legislative contests in those States have resulted to the advantage of the Republicans.

The Congressional elections have been hotly contested, and the outcome of the battles in many districts is surprising. By the latest reports it appears that the Fifty-first Congress will be controlled by the Democrats by an extremely small majority, which may be wiped out altogether by the corrected returns from Virginia, Arkansas, North Carolina, and Michigan, in all of which States there are disputed results. The Democrats secure a solid delegation from West Virginia, including Mr. William L. Wilson, a member of the Ways and Means Committee, who was re-elected by an increased lead. The defeat of Mr. Clifton R. Breckinridge, another member of the Ways and Means Committee, in the Second Arkansas District, is claimed by the allied Wheelers and Republicans, but is not admitted by the Democrats.

Gov. Hill has been re-elected in his State by a majority of about 19,000, and there seems to be no doubt that Lieut.-Gov. Jones has also been re-elected, and that Justice Gray has been retained as a member of the Court of Appeals.

The Republicans will have 79 members of the next Assembly and the Democrats 49. Full returns show that there are only a few changes to be made in the tables printed in THE TIMES of yesterday. They are as follows: Peter Schaaf, (Dem.,) in place of John Reitz, Seventh Kings; James P. Graham, (Dem.,) in place of D. W. Tallmadge, Twelfth Kings; Moses Dinkelspiel, (Dem.,) in place of Sol D. Rosenthal, Twelfth New-York; William Murray, (Dem.,) in place of T. Irving Burns, First Westchester; Bradford Rhodes, (Rep.,) re-elected, Second Westchester.

A revision of the vote in this city gives Cleveland a plurality of 57,213 and to Hill, for Governor, a plurality of 58,353. The vote cast for Governor was also larger by several thousands than that cast for President, which is unusual. Warner Miller, the Republican candidate for Governor, received 3,198 more votes than Harrison, and Hill 4,238 more than Cleveland.

### THE ELECTORAL COLLEGE.

| States. | Cleveland (Dem.) Plurality. | Cleveland (Dem.) Electoral Vote. | Harrison (Rep.) Plurality. | Harrison (Rep.) Electoral Vote. |
|---|---|---|---|---|
| Alabama | 50,000 | 10 | .... | .. |
| Arkansas | 20,000 | 7 | .... | .. |
| California | .... | .. | .... | 8 |
| Colorado | .... | .. | 10,000 | 3 |
| Connecticut | 385 | 6 | .... | .. |
| Delaware | 2,500 | 3 | .... | .. |
| Florida | 3,000 | 4 | .... | .. |
| Georgia | 40,000 | 12 | .... | .. |
| Illinois | .... | .. | 18,000 | 22 |
| Indiana | .... | .. | 1,000 | 15 |
| Iowa | .... | .. | 30,000 | 13 |
| Kansas | .... | .. | 70,000 | 9 |
| Kentucky | 40,000 | 13 | .... | .. |
| Louisiana | 30,000 | 8 | .... | .. |
| Maine | .... | .. | 23,000 | 6 |
| Maryland | 5,982 | 8 | .... | .. |
| Massachusetts | .... | .. | 31,457 | 14 |
| Michigan | .... | .. | 28,000 | 13 |
| Minnesota | .... | .. | 20,000 | 7 |
| Mississippi | 40,000 | 9 | .... | .. |
| Missouri | 8,000 | 16 | .... | .. |
| Nebraska | .... | .. | 35,000 | 5 |
| Nevada | .... | .. | .... | 3 |
| New-Hampshire | .... | .. | 2,500 | 4 |
| New Jersey | 8,200 | 9 | .... | .. |
| New-York | .... | .. | 11,805 | 36 |
| North Carolina | 25,000 | 11 | .... | .. |
| Ohio | .... | .. | 20,222 | 23 |
| Oregon | .... | .. | 7,000 | 3 |
| Pennsylvania | .... | .. | 71,000 | 30 |
| Rhode Island | .... | .. | 4,427 | 4 |
| South Carolina | 40,000 | 9 | .... | .. |
| Tennessee | 20,000 | 12 | .... | .. |
| Texas | 140,000 | 13 | .... | .. |
| Vermont | .... | .. | 24,469 | 4 |
| Virginia | 6,000 | 12 | .... | .. |
| West Virginia | 5,000 | 6 | .... | .. |
| Wisconsin | .... | .. | 25,000 | 11 |
| Total | .... | 168 | .... | 233 |

The following table exhibits more plainly the division of the Electoral College:

| Cleveland. States. | Votes. | Harrison. States. | Votes. |
|---|---|---|---|
| Alabama | 10 | California | 8 |
| Arkansas | 7 | Colorado | 3 |
| Connecticut | 6 | Illinois | 22 |
| Delaware | 3 | Indiana | 15 |
| Florida | 4 | Iowa | 13 |
| Georgia | 12 | Kansas | 9 |
| Kentucky | 13 | Maine | 6 |
| Louisiana | 8 | Massachusetts | 14 |
| Maryland | 8 | Michigan | 13 |
| Mississippi | 9 | Minnesota | 7 |
| Missouri | 16 | Nebraska | 5 |
| New-Jersey | 9 | Nevada | 3 |
| North Carolina | 11 | New-Hampshire | 4 |
| South Carolina | 9 | New-York | 36 |
| Tennessee | 12 | Ohio | 23 |
| Texas | 13 | Oregon | 3 |
| Virginia | 12 | Pennsylvania | 30 |
| West Virginia | 6 | Rhode Island | 4 |
| | | Vermont | 4 |
| Total | 168 | Wisconsin | 11 |
| | | Total | 233 |

### WEST VIRGINIA.

WHEELING, West Va., Nov. 7.—West Virginia has certainly been carried by Cleveland, but by a majority somewhat reduced from 1884. The tendency of strong Republican counties, except Kanawha, has been to increase their majorities, while the average of the Democratic counties shows that they about hold their own or show a very moderate increase. Ex-Senator Camden, Senator Kenna, Gov. Wilson, and other prominent Democrats, place the majority in the State for Cleveland in the neighborhood of 5,000, but the returns are not holding it up that high. This county complete, including Wheeling City, gives Cleveland 7 majority, a Democratic loss of 118. Hancock gives Harrison 312, a Republican gain of 200. Brooke gives Harrison 30 majority, a Republican gain of 83. Marshall is claimed at 950 for Harrison, a Republican gain of 330. Preston is stated at 1,500 for Harrison and Monongalia 800, both gains. Kanawha shows a heavy Republican loss, more than 1,000, and is the notable exception. Hubbard, (Rep.,) for Attorney-General, runs ahead of his ticket, going out of Ohio County with 500 majority. He will push Caldwell (Dem.) rather close.

Twenty-two counties, casting one-half the vote of the State, show Republican gains of 2,454. Cleveland's majority in 1884 was 4,221. The same relative gain through the rest of the State would make it Republican by 700. This is from the Chairman of the State Republican Committee.



### THE VOTE OF NEW-YORK STATE.

The following table shows the pluralities in the several counties of this State for President compared with the pluralities of four years ago:

| Counties. | 1888 Cleveland, Dem. | 1888 Harrison, Rep. | 1884 Cleveland, Dem. | 1884 Blaine, Rep. |
|---|---|---|---|---|
| Albany | 2,467 | .... | 746 | .... |
| Allegany | .... | 3,440 | .... | 2,782 |
| Broome | .... | 1,068 | .... | 1,462 |
| Cattaraugus | .... | 2,414 | .... | 1,398 |
| Cayuga | .... | 3,304 | .... | 3,164 |
| Chautauqua | .... | 5,930 | .... | 4,809 |
| Chemung | 573 | .... | .... | 479 |
| Chenango | .... | 1,158 | .... | 1,052 |
| Clinton | .... | 1,545 | .... | 825 |
| Columbia | .... | 380 | .... | 570 |
| Cortland | .... | 1,478 | .... | 1,268 |
| Delaware | .... | 1,276 | .... | 978 |
| Dutchess | .... | 996 | .... | 1,024 |
| Erie | .... | 2,042 | .... | 1,490 |
| Essex | .... | 2,113 | .... | 1,775 |
| Franklin | .... | 2,728 | .... | 1,690 |
| Fulton and Hamilton | .... | 1,175 | .... | 1,147 |
| Genesee | .... | 1,317 | .... | 988 |
| Greene | 34 | .... | .... | 15 |
| Herkimer | .... | 1,072 | .... | 810 |
| Jefferson | .... | 2,313 | .... | 1,954 |
| Kings | 12,034 | .... | 15,729 | .... |
| Lewis | .... | 570 | .... | 77 |
| Livingston | .... | 1,517 | .... | 1,153 |
| Madison | .... | 2,560 | .... | 1,743 |
| Monroe | .... | 4,981 | .... | 5,080 |
| Montgomery | .... | 698 | .... | 92 |
| New-York | 57,213 | .... | 43,064 | .... |
| Niagara | .... | 459 | 318 | .... |
| Oneida | .... | 2,066 | 30 | .... |
| Onondaga | .... | 6,125 | .... | 3,727 |
| Ontario | .... | 1,206 | .... | 739 |
| Orange | .... | 409 | .... | 128 |
| Orleans | .... | 1,063 | .... | 1,090 |
| Oswego | .... | 3,869 | .... | 2,542 |
| Otsego | .... | 938 | 436 | .... |
| Putnam | .... | 583 | .... | 577 |
| Queens | 1,682 | .... | 1,922 | .... |
| Rensselaer | 510 | .... | .... | 345 |
| Richmond | 1,666 | .... | 1,970 | .... |
| Rockland | 927 | .... | 1,104 | .... |
| St. Lawrence | .... | 8,001 | .... | 7,406 |
| Saratoga | .... | 2,025 | .... | 2,344 |
| Schenectady | .... | 305 | .... | 283 |
| Schoharie | 1,310 | .... | 1,867 | .... |
| Schuyler | .... | 729 | .... | 577 |
| Seneca | 75 | .... | 318 | .... |
| Steuben | .... | 2,523 | .... | 988 |
| Suffolk | .... | 660 | 553 | .... |
| Sullivan | .... | 90 | 275 | .... |
| Tioga | .... | 1,238 | .... | 988 |
| Tompkins | .... | 1,175 | .... | 428 |
| Ulster | .... | 346 | .... | 59 |
| Warren | .... | 1,252 | .... | 784 |
| Washington | .... | 3,718 | .... | 3,115 |
| Wayne | .... | 2,729 | .... | 2,113 |
| Westchester | 1,179 | .... | 1,238 | .... |
| Wyoming | .... | 1,732 | .... | 1,252 |
| Yates | .... | 1,269 | .... | 1,273 |
| Total | 79,670 | 91,485 | 69,570 | 68,523 |

Cleveland's plurality, 1884....1,047
Harrison's plurality, 1888....11,815

### FIFTY-FIRST CONGRESS.

The following is a list of members elected to the House of Representatives of the Fifty-first Congress, according to the latest returns. The names of Republicans are in roman, Democrats in italics, and Independents in SMALL CAPS:

ALABAMA.
Dist.
1. Richard H. Clark.
2. Hilary A. Herbert.*
3. William C. Oates.*
4. Louis W. Turpin.
5. James E. Cobb.*
6. John H. Bankhead.*
7. William H. Forney.*
8. Joseph Wheeler.*

ARKANSAS.
1. W. H. Cate.
2. C. R. Breckinridge.*
3. Thomas C. McRae.*
4. John H. Rogers.*
5. Samuel W. Peel.*

CALIFORNIA.
1. John J. De Haven.
2. Marion Biggs.*
3. Joseph McKenna.*
4. Robert Ferral.
5. Thomas J. Clunie.
6. William Vandever.*

COLORADO.
1. Hosea Townsend.

CONNECTICUT.
1. W. E. Simonds.
2. W. F. Willcox.
3. Charles A. Russell.*
4. R. W. Seymour.*

DELAWARE.
1. John B. Penington.*

FLORIDA.
1. R. H. M. Davidson.*
2. R. W. Bullock.

GEORGIA.
1. Rufus E. Lester.
2. Henry G. Turner.*
3. Charles F. Crisp.*
4. Thomas W. Grimes.*
5. John D. Stewart.*
6. James H. Blount.*
7. Judson C. Clements.*
8. Henry H. Carlton.*
9. Allen D. Candler.*
10. George T. Barnes.*

ILLINOIS.
1. Abner Taylor.
2. Frank Lawler.*
3. William E. Mason.*
4. George E. Adams.*
5. Albert J. Hopkins.*
6. Robert R. Hitt.*
7. T. J. Henderson.*
8. Charles A. Hill.
9. Lewis E Payson.*
10. Philip S. Post.*
11. William H. Gest.*
12. Scott Wike.
13. Wm. M. Springer.*
14. J. H. Rowell.*
15. Joseph G. Cannon.*
16. George W. Fithian.
17. Edward Lane.*
18. Jehu Baker.*
19. R. W. Townshend.*
20. George W. Smith.

INDIANA.
1. William F. Parrett.
2. John H. O'Neall.*
3. Jason B. Brown.
4. William S. Holman.*
5. George W. Cooper.
6. Thomas M. Browne.*
7. William D. Bynum.*
8. E. V. Brookshire.
9. Joseph B. Cheadle.*
10. William D. Owen.*
11. A. N. Martin.
12. C. O. McClellan.
13. B. F. Shively.*

IOWA.
1. John H. Gear.*
2. Walter I. Hayes.*
3. D. B. Henderson.*
4. J. H. Sweeney.
5. Daniel Kerr.*
6. John F. Lacey.
7. Edwin H. Conger.*
8. James P. Flick.
9. Joseph R. Reed.
10. J. P. Dolliver.
11. Isaac S. Struble.*

KANSAS.
1. Edmund N. Morrill.*
2. Edwd. H. Funston.*
3. Bishop W. Perkins.*
4. Thomas Ryan.*
5. John A. Anderson.*
6. Erastus J. Turner.*
7. Samuel R. Peters.*

KENTUCKY.
1. William J. Stone.*
2. William T. Ellis.
3. J. H. Goodnight.
4. A. B. Montgomery.*
5. Asher G. Caruth.*
6. John G. Carlisle.*
7. W. C. P. Breckinridge.*
8. James B. McCreary.*
9. Thomas H. Paynter.
10. J. H. Wilson.
11. Frank Finley.

LOUISIANA.
1. Theo. S. Wilkinson.*
2. H. Dudley Coleman.
3. Edward J. Gay.*
4. N. C. Blanchard.*
5. Charles J. Boatner.
6. S. M. Robertson.*

MAINE.
1. Thomas B. Reed.*
2. Nelson Dingley, Jr.*
3. Seth L. Milliken.*
4. C. A. Boutelle.*

MARYLAND.
1. Charles H. Gibson.*
2. Herman Stump.
3. Harry W. Rusk.*
4. H. Stockbridge, Jr.
5. Sidney E. Mudd.
6. Louis E. McComas.*

MASSACHUSETTS.
1. Charles S. Randall.
2. Elijah A. Morse.
3. A. W. Beard.
4. Joseph H. O'Neil.
5. N. P. Banks.
6. Henry C. Lodge.*
7. William Cogswell.*
8. F. T. Greenhalge.
9. John W. Candler.
10. Joseph H. Walker.
11. Rodney Wallace.
12. F. W. Rockwell.*

MICHIGAN.
1. J. Logan Chipman.*
2. Edward P. Allen.*
3. James O'Donnell.*
4. Julius C. Burrows.*
5. C. E. Belknap.
6. Mark S. Brewer.*
7. Justin R. Whiting.*
8. Aaron T. Bliss.
9. Byron M. Cutcheon.*
10. S. O. Fisher.*
11. S. M. Stephenson.

MINNESOTA.
1. Mark H. Dunnell.
2. John Lind.*
3. Darius S. Hall.
4. S. P. Snider.
5. S. G. Comstock.

MISSISSIPPI.
1. John M. Allen.*
2. James B. Morgan.*
3. T. C. Catchings.*
4. Clarke Lewis.
5. C. L. Anderson.*
6. T. R. Stockdale.*
7. Charles E. Hooker.*

MISSOURI.
1. William H. Hatch.*
2. Charles H. Mansur.*
3. Alex. M. Dockery.*
4. James N. Burnes.*
5. John C. Tarsney.
6. John T. Heard.*
7. Richard H. Norton.
8. H. Niedringhaus.
9. Nathan Frank.
10. W. M. Kinsey.
11. Richard P. Bland.*
12. William J. Stone.*
13. William H. Wade.*
14. James P. Walker.*

NEBRASKA.
1. W. J. Connell.
2. James Laird.*
3. Geo. W. E. Dorsey.*

NEVADA.
1. H. F. Bartine.

NEW-HAMPSHIRE.
1. Alonzo Nute.
2. Orren C. Moore.

NEW-JERSEY.
1. Chris. A. Bergen.
2. James Buchanan.*
3. J. A. Geissenhainer.
4. Samuel Fowler.
5. Chas. D. Beckwith.
6. Herman Lehlbach.*
7. William McAdoo.*

NEW-YORK.
1. James W. Covert.
2. Felix Campbell.*
3. W. C. Wallace.
4. John M. Clancy.
5. Thomas F. Magner.
6. F. T. Fitzgerald.
7. E. J. Dunphy.
8. John H. McCarthy.
9. Samuel S. Cox.*
10. Francis B. Spinola.*
11. John Quinn.
12. Roswell P. Flower.
13. Ashbel P. Fitch.*
14. W. G. Stahlnecker.*
15. Moses D. Stivers.
16. John H. Ketcham.*
17. Charles F. Knapp.
18. J. A. Quackenbush.
19. Charles Tracey.*
20. John Sanford.
21. John H. Moffitt.*
22. Frederick Lansing.
23. James S. Sherman.*
24. David Wilber.*
25. James J. Belden.*
26. Milton De Lano.*
27. Newton W. Nutting.*
28. Thomas S. Flood.*
29. John Raines.
30. Charles S. Baker.*
31. John G. Sawyer.*
32. John M. Farquhar.*
33. John M. Wiley.
34. William G. Laidlaw.*

NORTH CAROLINA.
1. Thomas G. Skinner.
2. H. P. Cheatham.
3. C. W. McClammy.*
4. B. H. Bunn.
5. John M. Brower.*
6. Alfred Rowland.
7. John S. Henderson.*
8. W. H. H. Cowles.*
9. Thomas D. Johnston.*

OHIO.
1. Benj. Butterworth.*
2. John H. Caldwell.
3. Elihu S. Williams.*
4. S. S. Yoder.*
5. George E. Seney.*
6. M. M. Saltzgaber.
7. Henry L. Morey.
8. R. P. Kennedy.*
9. William C. Cooper.*
10. W. E. Haynes.
11. A. C. Thompson.*
12. Jacob J. Pugsley.*
13. J. H. Outhwaite.*
14. C. P. Wickham.*
15. C. H. Grosvenor.*
16. James W. Owens.
17. Joseph D. Taylor.
18. Wm. McKinley, Jr.*
19. Ezra B. Taylor.*
20. Martin L. Smyser.
21. Theo. E. Burton.

OREGON.
1. Binger Hermann.*

PENNSYLVANIA.
1. H. H. Bingham.*
2. Charles O'Neill.*
3. Samuel J. Randall.*
4. William D. Kelley.*
5. Alfred C. Harmer.*
6. S. Darlington.*
7. Robert M. Yardley.*
8. William Mutchler.
9. David B. Brunner.
10. Marriott Brosius.
11. Joseph Scranton.
12. E. S. Osborne.*
13. James B. Reilly.
14. John W. Rife.
15. Myron B. Wright.
16. H. C. McCormick.*
17. Chas. R. Buckalew.*
18. Louis E. Atkinson.*
19. Levi Maish.*
20. Edward Scull.*
21. S. A. Craig.
22. John Dalzell.*
23. Thomas M. Bayne.*
24. Joseph W. Ray.
25. C. C. Townshend.
26. W. C. Culbertson.
27. Louis F. Watson.
28. James Kerr.

RHODE ISLAND.
1. Henry J. Spooner.*
2. Warren O. Arnold.*

SOUTH CAROLINA.
1. Samuel Dibble.*
2. George D. Tillman.*
3. James S. Cothran.*
4. William H. Perry.*
5. John J. Hemphill.*
6. George W. Dargan.*
7. William Elliott.*

TENNESSEE.
1. Alfred A. Taylor.
2. Leonidas C. Houk.*
3. H. C. Evans.
4. Benton McMillin.*
5. J. D. Richardson.*
6. J. E. Washington.*
7. W. C. Whitthorne.*
8. E. A. Enloe.*
9. Rice A. Pierce.
10. James Phelan.*

VERMONT.
1. John W. Stewart.*
2. William W. Grout.*

TEXAS.
1. Charles Stewart.*
2. William H. Martin.*
3. C. B. Kilgore.*
4. D. B. Culberson.*
5. Silas Hare.*
6. Jo Abbott.*
7. William H. Crain.*
8. L. W. Moore.*
9. Roger Q. Mills.*
10. Joseph D. Sayers.*
11. S. W. T. Lanham.*

VIRGINIA.
1. Gilmore S. Kendall.
2. George E. Bowden.*
3. George D. Wise.*
4. E. C. Venable.
5. Posey Lester.
6. Henry St. G. Tucker.
7. Charles T. O'Ferrall.*
8. W. H. F. Lee.*
9. John A. Buchanan.
10. Paul C. Edmunds.

WEST VIRGINIA.
1. J. O. Pendleton.
2. William L. Wilson.*
3. John D. Alderson.
4. J. Monroe Jackson.

WISCONSIN.
1. Lucien B. Caswell.*
2. Charles Barwig.
3. R. M. La Follette.*
4. I. W. Van Schaick.
5. George H. Brickner.
6. Charles B. Clark.*
7. Ormsby B. Thomas*.
8. Nils P. Haugen.*
9. Myron H. McCord..

Whole number of members....328
Democrats....164
Republicans....161
Democratic majority....3



### THE STATES IN CONGRESS.

| States. | Fiftieth. Dem. | Fiftieth. Rep. | Fifty-first. Dem. | Fifty-first. Rep. | Dem. loss. | Rep. Loss. |
|---|---|---|---|---|---|---|
| Alabama | 8 | .. | 8 | .. | .. | .. |
| Arkansas | 5 | .. | 5 | .. | .. | .. |
| California | 2 | 4 | 3 | 3 | .. | 1 |
| Colorado | .. | 1 | .. | 1 | .. | .. |
| Connecticut | 3 | 1 | 2 | 2 | 1 | .. |
| Delaware | 1 | .. | 1 | .. | .. | .. |
| Florida | 2 | .. | 2 | .. | .. | .. |
| Georgia | 10 | .. | 10 | .. | .. | .. |
| Illinois | 6 | 14 | 6 | 14 | .. | .. |
| Indiana | 6 | 7 | 10 | 3 | .. | 4 |
| Iowa | 2 | 9 | 2 | 9 | .. | .. |
| Kansas | .. | 7 | .. | 7 | .. | .. |
| Kentucky | 8 | 3 | 9 | 2 | .. | 1 |
| Louisiana | 6 | .. | 5 | 1 | 1 | .. |
| Maine | .. | 4 | .. | 4 | .. | .. |
| Maryland | 5 | 1 | 3 | 3 | 2 | .. |
| Massachusetts | 4 | 8 | 1 | 11 | 3 | .. |
| Michigan | 5 | 6 | 3 | 8 | 2 | .. |
| Minnesota | 3 | 2 | .. | 5 | 3 | .. |
| Mississippi | 7 | .. | 7 | .. | .. | .. |
| Missouri | 12 | 2 | 10 | 4 | 2 | .. |
| Nebraska | 1 | 2 | .. | 3 | 1 | .. |
| Nevada | .. | 1 | .. | 1 | .. | .. |
| New-Hampshire | 1 | 1 | .. | 2 | 1 | .. |
| New-Jersey | 2 | 5 | 3 | 4 | .. | 1 |
| New-York | 15 | 19 | 15 | 19 | .. | .. |
| North Carolina | 7 | 2 | 7 | 2 | .. | 1 |
| Ohio | 6 | 15 | 6 | 15 | .. | .. |
| Oregon | .. | 1 | .. | 1 | .. | .. |
| Pennsylvania | 8 | 20 | 7 | 21 | 1 | .. |
| Rhode Island | .. | 2 | .. | 2 | .. | .. |
| South Carolina | 7 | .. | 7 | .. | .. | .. |
| Tennessee | 8 | 2 | 7 | 3 | 1 | .. |
| Texas | 11 | .. | 11 | .. | .. | .. |
| Vermont | .. | 2 | .. | 2 | .. | .. |
| Virginia | 4 | 6 | 9 | 1 | .. | 5 |
| West Virginia | 3 | 1 | 4 | .. | .. | 1 |
| Wisconsin | 2 | 7 | 2 | 7 | .. | .. |
| Total | 170 | 155 | 164 | 161 | 18 | 14 |

### THE GUBERNATORIAL VOTE.

The following table shows the pluralities in the several counties of this State for Governor, compared with the pluralities given for Governor in 1885:

| Counties. | 1888 Miller, Rep. | 1888 Hill, Dem. | 1885 Davenport, Rep. | 1885 Hill, Dem. |
|---|---|---|---|---|
| Albany | .... | 2,840 | .... | 1,977 |
| Allegany | 3,346 | .... | 2,501 | .... |
| Broome | 1,884 | .... | 1,381 | .... |
| Cattaraugus | 2,183 | .... | 1,598 | .... |
| Cayuga | 2,727 | .... | 2,050 | .... |
| Chautauqua | 5,828 | .... | 4,222 | .... |
| Chemung | .... | 1,000 | .... | 1,335 |
| Chenango | 1,145 | .... | 889 | .... |
| Clinton | 1,463 | .... | 1,706 | .... |
| Columbia | 336 | .... | 195 | .... |
| Cortland | 1,200 | .... | 1,089 | .... |
| Delaware | 1,463 | .... | 1,136 | .... |
| Dutchess | 990 | .... | 201 | .... |
| Erie | .... | 4,830 | 2,225 | .... |
| Essex | 1,975 | .... | 1,658 | .... |
| Franklin | 2,516 | .... | 1,721 | .... |
| Fulton & Hamilton | 1,200 | .... | 814 | .... |
| Genesee | 1,146 | .... | 679 | .... |
| Greene | 75 | .... | 224 | .... |
| Herkimer | 1,037 | .... | 809 | .... |
| Jefferson | 2,080 | .... | 1,721 | .... |
| Kings | .... | 13,569 | .... | 9,479 |
| Lewis | 460 | .... | 400 | .... |
| Livingston | 1,280 | .... | 952 | .... |
| Madison | 2,180 | .... | 1,943 | .... |
| Monroe | 2,940 | .... | 2,642 | .... |
| Montgomery | 447 | .... | .... | 190 |
| New-York | .... | 68,353 | .... | 48,239 |
| Niagara | 35 | .... | .... | 244 |
| Oneida | 1,669 | .... | .... | 30 |
| Onondaga | 5,000 | .... | 3,518 | .... |
| Ontario | 1,072 | .... | 756 | .... |
| Orange | 424 | .... | 242 | .... |
| Orleans | 997 | .... | 626 | .... |
| Oswego | 3,610 | .... | 2,835 | .... |
| Otsego | 675 | .... | .... | 72 |
| Putnam | 646 | .... | 517 | .... |
| Queens | .... | 1,716 | .... | 1,680 |
| Rensselaer | .... | 569 | .... | 1,087 |
| Richmond | .... | 1,900 | .... | 1,376 |
| Rockland | .... | 740 | .... | 536 |
| St. Lawrence | 7,526 | .... | 6,234 | .... |
| Saratoga | 1,815 | .... | 581 | .... |
| Schenectady | 258 | .... | .... | 239 |
| Schoharie | .... | 1,300 | .... | 1,387 |
| Schuyler | 587 | .... | 27 | .... |
| Seneca | .... | 100 | .... | 378 |
| Steuben | 1,938 | .... | 1,379 | .... |
| Suffolk | 600 | .... | 369 | .... |
| Sullivan | .... | 60 | .... | 188 |
| Tioga | 1,214 | .... | 437 | .... |
| Tompkins | 1,351 | .... | 680 | .... |
| Ulster | 219 | .... | .... | 112 |
| Warren | 1,113 | .... | 717 | .... |
| Washington | 3,713 | .... | 2,930 | .... |
| Wayne | 2,416 | .... | 1,151 | .... |
| Westchester | .... | 1,213 | .... | 1,477 |
| Wyoming | 1,420 | .... | 1,173 | .... |
| Yates | 1,120 | .... | 1,031 | .... |
| Total | 79,119 | 98,190 | 58,862 | 69,996 |

Hill's plurality, 1885....11,134
Hill's plurality, 1888....19,071

### ILLINOIS.

CHICAGO, Nov. 7.—No returns have yet been received which would indicate that Harrison's plurality in Illinois would fall below 15,000. From the interior of the State the returns are very slow in coming in, but those received to-day go to show that the Republicans have the State safely enough for the national ticket. Their committee claims that Harrison's plurality will run up to 20,000 votes, with from 10,000 to 14,000 plurality for Fifer, their candidate for Governor, who ran behind the national ticket. Chicago Republican afternoon papers are claiming from 20,000 to 25,000 plurality for Harrison.

Secretary Mize of the Democratic State Committee says the returns received by the committee are too meagre to base a claim on, but that they are favorable, being fully up to the figures claimed in the poll made before the election, and that if they continue on the same basis Palmer will be found to be elected Governor by about 5,000 plurality. He is unable to make any estimate on the vote on the Presidential ticket. Cleveland ran exceedingly well in Chicago. He received 63,943 votes in this city, while Harrison was given 60,399; Fisk, 1,223; Streator, 558; Cowdrey, 175, and Mrs. Belva Lockwood, 3, Cleveland's plurality over Harrison in the city being 3,544.

The Prohibition vote generally does not appear to have reached the figures expected, and the Labor vote was also light. It was small Republican gains in the country which kept the State in the Republican column.

As closely as it can now be figured the result of the election in Illinois gives Harrison about 18,000 plurality. All the returns are not yet in, but the missing precincts are not expected to change the figures to any great extent. While the Democrats made substantial gains in some counties the Republican strongholds have not been captured.

A dispatch from Springfield says that friends of Gen. Palmer, the Democratic candidate for Governor, admit his defeat by Fifer (Rep.) by 4,000. Gen. Palmer himself no longer claims to have carried the State, but insists that there is a faint hope that he has beaten Fifer. He made a vigorous canvass and had great hopes of being elected. If he is beaten he says his defeat is due to a failure of the southern counties to give gains proportionate to those in the rest of the State.

### FLORIDA.

JACKSONVILLE, Fla., Nov 7.—State reports come in very slowly, but from best data at hand Cleveland and Fleming, the Democratic candidate for Governor, carry the State by 3,000.



### NEW-JERSEY.

CLEVELAND'S PLURALITY IN THE STATE PROBABLY OVER EIGHT THOUSAND.

The latest returns from New-Jersey place Cleveland's plurality in the State at no less than 7,500, while it may reach 8,500. The Democrats gain a Congressman, Geissenhainer, who defeats Kean by from 2,000 to 2,500 majority. The Legislature will be Democratic in both branches and will choose a successor to Senator McPherson, whose term expires next March. The Senators and Assemblymen elected were correctly printed in THE TIMES yesterday with these exceptions: Albert Hansell, (Rep.,) is chosen to the Assembly in the Second District of Burlington; John Schrott, (Dem.,) in the Third District of Mercer, and Ephraim Cutter, (Dem.,) in the First District of Middlesex. The name of James West, chosen to the Assembly from Gloucester, was omitted in yesterday's account. These changes make the lower house stand: Democrats, 32; Republicans, 28. The Democratic majority on joint ballot will be 5.

Evidences are abundant of the interest taken by the liquor men and brewers in the contests. They worked against the high-license men to some purpose. They seek the modification or repeal of the new law. It is doubtful whether they can succeed in repealing it, but changes in the law will be insisted on.

Essex County gives Harrison a majority of 140. The city of Elizabeth had the closest Mayoralty contest in years. Grier, (Dem.,) who had 700 last year, has this year only 150 plurality. At Asbury Park last evening there was a general jubilation over the result of the national election, Democrats and Republicans joining in a parade. The Democrats marched with draped bandanas and cheered as lustily as their former opponents.

The result of the Presidential contest is as follows:

THE PLURALITIES BY COUNTIES.

| Counties. | 1888 Cleveland, Dem. | 1888 Harrison, Rep. | 1884 Cleveland, Dem. | 1884 Blaine, Rep. |
|---|---|---|---|---|
| Atlantic | .... | 469 | .... | 585 |
| Bergen | 703 | .... | 639 | .... |
| Burlington | .... | 360 | .... | 378 |
| Camden | .... | 2,600 | .... | 1,993 |
| Cape May | .... | 300 | .... | 231 |
| Cumberland | .... | 1,200 | .... | 1,021 |
| Essex | .... | 140 | .... | 1,215 |
| Gloucester | .... | 886 | .... | 626 |
| Hudson | 8,100 | .... | 8,325 | .... |
| Hunterdon | 1,700 | .... | 2,007 | .... |
| Mercer | .... | 600 | .... | 613 |
| Middlesex | 856 | .... | 587 | .... |
| Monmouth | 1,500 | .... | 1,106 | .... |
| Morris | .... | 260 | .... | 377 |
| Ocean | .... | 500 | .... | 496 |
| Passaic | .... | 1,011 | .... | 1,887 |
| Salem | .... | 300 | .... | 158 |
| Somerset | 200 | .... | .... | 189 |
| Sussex | 1,200 | .... | 1,240 | .... |
| Union | 951 | .... | 736 | .... |
| Warren | 1,700 | .... | 2,149 | .... |
| Total | 16,910 | 8,626 | 13,799 | 9,769 |

Democratic plurality in 1884....4,412
Democratic plurality in 1888....8,284

### OHIO.

HARRISON RUNS BEHIND THE STATE TICKET—NO FREE-TRADE SCARE.

COLUMBUS, Ohio, Nov. 7.—Unofficial returns received indicate that the candidates on the State ticket have been elected by a plurality of 25,000, while the plurality for Harrison is only 20,222. It is found that in Cleveland and Cincinnati the labor vote went to Cleveland, but that the Republican State officers received the bulk of the vote. In Cleveland alone Ryan's plurality exceeds that of Harrison by 1,000. While the official figures will not materially change the above estimate, no figures are obtainable to-night to give an estimate by Congressional districts. The Ohio delegation will stand 16 Republicans and 5 Democrats, there being no change in the standing during the day.

CLEVELAND, Nov. 7.—The count of votes in this city and county was slow, and not finished until this morning. The Republicans carried the county by greatly reduced pluralities on a much larger vote for all the candidates, except one. The Democrats elect E. D. Sawyer Sheriff by 500. The county gives a plurality of 2,000 for Harrison, a Republican loss of 1,000 over last Fall.

Burton is elected to Congress by 500 over Tom L. Johnson. This is a Republican gain in that Burton will succeed Foran, a Democrat, who was elected by votes of workingmen three times in a nominally Republican district. But the result is significant in another way. When the Democrats nominated Tom L. Johnson it was known that he had radical ideas on the tariff, and in his letter of acceptance he declared himself a free trader in opinion, although aware that "free trade is not in the present issue." The Republicans and a formidably-organized protective tariff league made the most of this, while manufacturers who employ large numbers of men electioneered against him with great earnestness, not a few going so far as to undertake to coerce their men as much as they dared to vote against him. This is preeminently an iron manufacturing district, and last Fall gave Foraker a plurality of 2,300. Furthermore, nearly all of the manufactories, the iron ore interests, &c., are in this city, and Johnson carried the city precincts of the district by 3,000. The tariff was constantly discussed during the campaign, and under the circumstances the tariff reformers feel highly elated over the Republican losses of 1,600 in the city precincts and 1,800 in the district. The Republicans exhausted every means at their command to achieve a sweeping victory. The total vote of the county is 51,000, an increase of 14,500 in one year. The Democratic vote increased 8,500, the Republican vote increased 7,500, the Prohibition and Labor totals falling off. The net Democratic gain in this county is 1,000.

### DELAWARE.

WILMINGTON, Del., Nov. 7.—A canvass of yesterday's vote in this State gives the Democratic Electoral ticket a majority of about 2,000. Sussex County is Republican by an average of 85 majority on the Legislative ticket, and Kent County gives a majority of 145 on the same branch of the ticket. The Republicans have elected 14 Representatives and two State Senators and the Democrats elect seven Representatives, one Senator, and have six holding-over Senators. This gives the Democrats a majority of seven in the Senate of nine members, and the Republicans a majority of seven in the House of 21 members. On a joint ballot the Republicans will have a majority of two in the General Assembly. Upon this vote the Republicans will elect a United States Senator in December to succeed Eli Saulsbury who is closing his third term.

This is the first time the Delaware Legislature has been Republican, and frequently it has been unanimously Democratic, as was the case last session. The tickets and party platform were entirely acceptable to every Democrat, and the Republican success is the outcome of Saulsbury's treachery. The Prohibition vote is probably 200 in the State.

The Every Evening bulletin says: "Kent County has gone Democratic and the legislative ticket is elected by 169 plurality. This insures the election of a Democratic Senator to succeed Saulsbury."

Advices received by the Morning News show that Kent and Sussex Counties have both given safe Republican majorities on the Legislative and county tickets, the first time in the history of the party. This insures a Republican majority of two votes in the next Legislature on joint ballot, which will elect a Republican United States Senator to succeed Senator Saulsbury (Dem.) New-Castle County Democratic ticket is elected and the Electoral vote of the State will be for Cleveland. Congressman Pennington (Dem.) is returned by 2,000 majority.

### CONNECTICUT.

DEMOCRATIC BY A NARROW MAJORITY—A REPUBLICAN LEGISLATURE.

HARTFORD, Conn., Nov. 7.—The summary of the Presidential vote in Connecticut by counties is:

| Counties. | Cleveland. | Harrison. | Fisk. |
|---|---|---|---|
| Hartford | 14,955 | 13,561 | 781 |
| New-Haven | 22,150 | 18,011 | 830 |
| New-London | 7,583 | 7,726 | 633 |
| Fairfield | 15,242 | 14,920 | 605 |
| Windham | 3,185 | 4,194 | 276 |
| Litchfield | 5,843 | 6,014 | 813 |
| Middlesex | 3,514 | 4,369 | 273 |
| Tolland | 2,402 | 2,734 | 240 |
| Total | 74,904 | 74,519 | 4,151 |

The total Labor vote was 130. The plurality for the Democratic national ticket in the State is 385. Morgan G. Bulkeley, the Republican candidate for Governor, ran upward of 1,500 behind Luzon B. Morris, the Democratic nominee. His total vote lacks 5,901 of a majority, so that the election will go into the Legislature, giving it to the Republicans. The Republicans have a majority of 53 in the House of Representatives and 10 in the Senate. The candidates for Speaker will be William B. Glover and John H. Perry, both of Fairfield. Ex-Speaker Hoyt of Greenwich will not probably again be a candidate for the place.

NEW-HAVEN, Conn., Nov. 7.—The story current throughout the State to-day that an error had been discovered in the count of one of the wards in this city altering the result proved to be without foundation.

The vote for Congressmen is as follows: First District, Simonds, (Rep.,) 18,252; Vance, (Dem.,) 17,441. Second District—Wilcox, (Dem.,) 25,040; Lines, (Rep.,) 24,155. Third District—Russell, (Rep.,) 11,534; Hall, (Dem.,) 10,854. Fourth District—Seymour (Dem.) has 293 plurality over Miles (Rep.) The returns last night gave the election in the Fourth District to Miles, but an error in the vote as sent from Newtown was discovered to-day.



### MISSOURI.

THE GOVERNORSHIP SAID TO BE STILL IN DOUBT.

ST. LOUIS, Mo., Nov. 7.—The most sensational feature of the great campaign in the West is the enormous gain of the Republican ticket in Missouri. Although the Electoral ticket is for Cleveland and Thurman by a small plurality, the Governorship is still doubtful. That E. E. Kimball, an unknown country lawyer from Vernon County, should come to this city and beat the Democratic Mayor, D. R. Francis, by 10,000 votes, was something so unlooked for that it could scarcely be believed. The St. Louis vote on the Governorship was: Francis, (Dem.,) 23,567; Kimball, (Rep.,) 33,636. The entire city Republican ticket was elected. Going out of the city with 10,000 plurality, Kimball made gains in the southwestern and northwestern parts of the State, and basing estimates on these returns, Secretary Beach of the Republican State Committee and his associates claim the election of Kimball for Governor by 3,000. Not more than half the precincts in the State have yet been heard from, and it will require two or three days to determine the actual result. The Democratic State Committee, which has good sources of information, say that Francis is surely elected by about 8,000 plurality. The Republicans concede the election of the rest of the Democratic State ticket. The returns show that Francis was scratched by 4,000 Democrats in St. Louis, for that is the number of votes he ran behind his ticket, and by an enormous number throughout the State. The cause of this was the recent Chicago wheat corner and the rise in flour. Francis is a heavy dealer in grain, and he was bitterly attacked on this issue.

The Republicans have gained three Congressmen in this city. The returns to-day show that Clardy (Dem.) has been defeated in the Tenth district by Kinsey. (Rep.) This was the result of the Republican landslide in the city. The three St. Louis Congressional districts which were filled by Democrats are now in possession of the Republicans. The correct list of the new Congressmen elected, based on the returns in and estimated is: First District—W. H. Hatch, (Dem.;) Second—Charles H. Mansur, (Dem.;) Third—A. M. Dockery, (Dem.;) Fourth—James Burnes, (Dem.;) Fifth—John C. Tarsney, (Dem.;) Sixth—John T. Heard, (Dem.;) Seventh—R. H. Norton, (Dem.;) Eighth—F. G. Niedringhaus, (Rep.;) Ninth—Nathan Frank, (Rep.;) Tenth—William M. Kinsey, (Rep.;) Eleventh—R. P. Bland, (Dem.;) Twelfth—W. J. Stone, (Dem.;) Thirteenth—W. H. Wade, (Rep.;) Fourteenth—James P. Walker, (Dem.)

The Republicans celebrated their victory today by a mass meeting on 'Change, in which the party individually and collectively congratulated itself.

### MICHIGAN.

HARRISON HAS A PLURALITY OF ABOUT 28,000.

DETROIT, Nov. 7.—Returns from the State are so slow and conflicting that it is impossible to give precise returns. No Congressional district in the State has yet returned all precincts, and many that have been reported are disputed. The new law regulating the manner of counting has created much confusion, and many boards have not yet finished the count. Also in many cases the returns have been sealed in the ballot boxes, and are not accessible. This has caused to a great extent a variance of the figures of the two parties. Michigan has given Harrison 28,000 plurality and has elected a Republican State ticket by about the same plurality, with the exception of the Governor, who is elected by about 11,000. The Democratic nominee, Wellington R. Burt, runs about 9,000 ahead of his ticket. There is no question that the Republicans have elected all but three Congressmen. The Democrats claim the election of Fisher by 300, and the Republicans make a counter-claim for their candidate. Whiting, (Dem.,) is elected by 600, and Chipman, from the Detroit district, by 2,000 plurality. Ford, the Grand Rapids Congressman, is beaten, although he ran ahead of his ticket. Brewer, (Rep.,) defeats Barnes, (Dem.,) by 200 plurality in the Sixth District. The delegation in the next Congress stands 8 Republicans and 3 Democrats. The Democratic vote is heavier than ever before, but there have been greater Republican gains. The Prohibition vote shows a great falling off in the State, and the Republican has increased accordingly. The cities generally show heavy Democratic gains, and the country greater Republican gains. Detroit City, the home of Postmaster-General Dickinson, gave the largest Democratic majority for President ever polled in its history, being 2,000 greater than four years ago.

### OREGON.

REPUBLICAN BY A PROBABLE MAJORITY OF ABOUT 7,000.

PORTLAND, Oregon, Nov. 7.—Returns from the more remote sections of this State are coming in very slowly. Sufficient have already been received, however, to place Harrison's majority much larger than Hermann's, (Congressman.) At the election last June Hermann's majority was 7,407 over Gearing. The very latest and most authentic news justifies the estimate of between 7,000 and 8,000. Some sanguine Republicans place Harrison's majority even higher. Returns show a very large vote polled everywhere. By to-morrow early complete returns will be received from all portions of the State.

The latest and best estimates from Washington Territory place the election of John B. Allen (Dem.) to Congress over Charles S. Voorhees by a majority of from 2,500 to 3,000.

### RHODE ISLAND.

A FALLING OFF IN THE REPUBLICAN VOTE IN THE STATE.

PROVIDENCE, R. I., Nov. 7.—The complete vote of the State gives Harrison 21,960, Cleveland, 17,533; Fisk, 1,281, giving Harrison a plurality of 4,427. Both Republican Congressmen, Spooner and Arnold, ran several hundred votes ahead of the Presidential ticket. The Republican gain over the election of 1884, in round numbers, is 2,000. The Democratic gain was 5,000, showing a net Democratic gain of 3,000. Though it is not possible to exactly account for all the elements, this gain, or a fair proportion of it, is due to the tariff reform movement and the local reform organizations, which drew its strength largely from the Republican ranks.

### COLORADO.

DENVER, Col., Nov. 7.—Returns from Colorado, both State and Arapahoe County, (Denver,) are unusually slow coming in. Only partial returns have yet been received. These indicate the election of the Republican ticket by majorities ranging from 8,000 to 12,000. The next General Assembly will probably be as follows: Senate—6 Democrats, 19 Republicans. House—10 Democrats, 39 Republicans.

Partial returns from 23 counties give Cleveland 5,044; Harrison, 7,664. Complete returns from 25 precincts in this city and county out of 73, give the following vote: Harrison, 4,765; Cleveland, 3,527; Townsend, 4,691; Macon, 2,398; Cooper, 4,370; Patterson, 3,589.

The official vote will not be in for a week, owing to the remoteness and inaccessibility of a dozen counties.

### MASSACHUSETTS.

BOSTON, Nov. 7.—All but two towns in the State have been heard from and they give Harrison 183,447; Cleveland, 151,990, and Fisk, 8,641. The same towns in 1884 gave Blaine 146,613; Cleveland, 132,294; Butler, 24,376, and St. John, 9,916; Harrison's plurality, 31,457. The Gubernatorial vote is: Ames, 180,439; Russell, 152,846; Earle, 9,170; Republican plurality, 37,593. The two missing towns will probably increase the Republican plurality by about 30 votes.

### MARYLAND.

BALTIMORE, Md., Nov. 7.—The total vote in Maryland is 212,423, divided as follows: Cleveland, 106,788; Harrison, 100,896; Fisk, 4,741. The vote in 1884 was 186,019, divided as follows: Cleveland, 96,866; Blaine, 85,748; scattering, 3,405. Cleveland's plurality is 5,982, against 11,118 in 1884. Cleveland's plurality in Baltimore City is 4,915. The defeat of Morris A. Thomas for Clerk of the new court in this city is overwhelming. He has been a notorious figure in machine politics. He was slaughtered so extensively that he runs 6,119 behind his ticket, and Capt. Suter, the Republican candidate, is elected by a plurality of 3,386. There is much rejoicing over Thomas's defeat. Daniel Giraud Wright is elected Judge by a plurality of 4,260. The Republicans have tied the Baltimore City Council for the first time on record. The vote of the State was about 88 per cent. of the registered vote. It was the heaviest vote ever polled in Maryland.



### INDIANA.

THE STATE GOES REPUBLICAN BY 1,000 PLURALITY.

INDIANAPOLIS, Nov. 7.—If the Democratic Party is beaten the Democrats in Indiana do not know it or will not believe it. They were confident yesterday that they would win, and confident to-night that they have won. The Journal this morning said that it looked as if Harrison had been elected, and the Sentinel admitted that the figures indicated that result. Conflicting reports of what New-York papers were conceding and were not conceding, and uncertainty as to the result in this State buoyed the Democrats up, and in the afternoon a rumor that Senator Gorman had declared that errors discovered in returns from Kings County, that when corrected would give the State to Cleveland, roused a great deal of enthusiasm. Bets of $60 to $100 were made that Cleveland would pull through after all.

The rain fell heavily all day, but great crowds surrounded the bulletin boards, and smaller ones paraded through the streets, cheering themselves hoarse for Cleveland or for Harrison. Returns from the State came in very slowly all day. The Democrats had no confidence in those put out by the Western Union, and relied solely on those reaching the State Committee. These were necessarily slow in coming in, but early in the day and until early evening they indicated that the Democrats had carried the State. Then the situation changed, and the returns showed unexpected Republican gains and Democratic losses. It became apparent that the State was, at the best, dangerously close.

At a late hour to-night there seems to be no good reason to doubt that boodle and bulldozing have carried this State for Harrison and Morton. The Democratic State Committee has received returns from nearly every county in the State, and though some of these are probably based on estimates, they show a plurality of at least 1,000 for Harrison. Up to 9 o'clock this evening there was good reason for believing that the plurality would be the other way, but returns which for the first time began to come in rapidly, dispelled the hope that Cleveland had carried the State. The Democratic State Committee is naturally averse to giving up the State, but on its own returns can do nothing else. It is impossible on the imperfect returns now in to make any satisfactory analysis of the vote, but one significant fact appears on the surface, and that is that where the country is afflicted with Republican protectionist manufacturers the Republicans have made their largest gains, while in those where workingmen were left free to express their honest choice the Democrats have made gains.

In Allen County, for instance, where the manufacturers in the city of Fort Wayne are mainly Democrats, the Democrats have made a gain of nearly 500. In this county—Gen. Harrison's own home—he has not only not equaled the Blaine vote of four years ago, but has run behind it nearly 500, the Democratic Electoral ticket carrying the county by about 250. Hopeful Democrats say that the counties yet to be heard from may bring the vote down so close that an official count will be necessary to decide that result, but there is nothing in the returns to warrant any such belief. Some little hope is built upon the fact that four of the Democratic Electors are also upon the Union Labor ticket, but the returns as far as received upon that ticket give no ground for the belief that these Electors will fare any better than their fellow Electors.

The present Indiana delegation in the House of Representatives is composed of seven Democrats and six Republicans. Returns thus far received at the Democratic Headquarters make it certain that the new delegation will have at least 10, and possibly 11, Democrats. In the Eighth District Brookshire (Dem.) has defeated Johnston, the present member. Martin, has defeated Steele, the present Republican member in the Eleventh, and McClelland, the Democratic candidate in the Twelfth, has defeated White, the present Republican member. It is probable that in the First District Judge Parrott, the Democratic candidate, is elected. The State ticket is in doubt and will very likely require an official count. Several of the Democratic candidates are also on the Labor Union ticket, and in that way may possibly pull through. In the State Senate the Democrats will have a majority of 6 and will also have a good majority in the lower house.

### NEW-HAMPSHIRE.

CONCORD, N. H., Nov. 7.—Harrison's plurality in New-Hampshire is a trifle under 2,500 Nute (Rep.) is elected in the First Congressional District by from 300 to 500 plurality, and Moore (Rep.) in the Second, by about 1,000. The Legislature is surely Republican by about 25 majority in the House, the Senate having 12 Republican members and 8 Democratic members, with no choice in three districts. The plurality of Goodell (Rep.) for Governor is but 750, so that there is no choice, he lacking a majority over all. Mr. Goodell will be elected by the Legislature. The vote was the largest ever cast in the State, aggregating nearly 90,000.

### IOWA.

DES MOINES, Iowa, Nov. 7.—The plurality on the Republican State ticket will probably not fall below 30,000 and may exceed that considerably. The Republicans made gains everywhere and particularly in Polk County, where their plurality tops 1,900—the largest since 1880. The Railroad Commissioners on both tickets were badly scratched, but the Republican candidates are elected by even a heavier vote than the rest of the ticket.

### WISCONSIN.

MILWAUKEE, Wis., Nov. 7.—There is no doubt that Wisconsin has gone heavily Republican. Estimates vary from 16,000 to 20,000. The Democratic State Committee concedes that the State has undoubtedly gone for Harrison, but is not willing to allow more than 12,000 to 14,000, which would mean a net Democratic gain of several thousand. The Republican candidate for Governor two years ago received over 18,000 plurality. The returns are not half in yet, however, and it will be several days before the actual figures are known.

### SOUTH CAROLINA.

CHARLESTON, S. C., Nov. 7.—All returns from Presidential Electors and Congressmen will not be in for several days, but the official returns so far received assure the election of the Democratic State ticket and Electoral ticket by majorities of 40,000. The entire vote of the State will not exceed 80,000, and outside Republican estimates do not give Harrison and Morton more than 20,000.

### TENNESSEE.

NASHVILLE, Tenn., Nov. 7.—The Presidential and Gubernatorial returns come in slowly. It is now believed by the Democratic managers that Cleveland will have a majority of 20,000, and Taylor, candidate for Governor, a majority of from 14,000 to 17,000.

### MISSISSIPPI.

JACKSON, Miss., Nov. 7.—Advices to-day do not change the estimate of last night on Cleveland's majority in the State. It will be between 30,000 and 45,000. There is a large Democratic increase in all portions of the State except the river district.

### VIRGINIA.

RICHMOND, Va., Nov. 7.—Sixty-two counties and all the cities, or about two-thirds of the State, indicate a Democratic gain over 1884 of 744. At this ratio of gain the State will give over 6,000 for Cleveland. Many of these returns received are not official.

### NORTH CAROLINA.

RALEIGH, N. C., Nov. 7.—Returns received and estimate of the rest of the vote give Cleveland a majority of about 17,000. The indications are that he received about 153,000 to Harrison's 137,000.

### KANSAS.

TOPEKA, Kan., Nov. 7.—Returns have been received from every county in Kansas. An estimate by Chairman Booth from the reports received gives Harrison 70,000 majority over Cleveland and 65,000 for the entire Republican State ticket.

### CALIFORNIA.

SAN FRANCISCO, Cal., Nov. 7.—Cleveland's majority in this city will be 4,600, while the Democrats claim that the majority of Cleveland will approximate 8,000 to 9,000 in the city, and that the Republicans will ...

BENJAMIN HARRISON

# The New York Times

VOL. XXXVIII.....NO. 11,705. NEW-YORK, TUESDAY, MARCH 5, 1889.----WITH SUPPLEMENT. PRICE TWO CENTS.




# UNDER A NEW PRESIDENT

## *HARRISON ASSUMES THE REINS OF OFFICE.*

### TAKING THE OATH IN A STORM OF WIND AND RAIN.

### *CLEVELAND'S DIGNIFIED EXIT FROM HIGH POSITION.*

A WET, BEDRAGGLED CROWD, HUGE IN ITS PROPORTIONS, WATCHING THE CEREMONIES AND PROCESSIONS—A BRILLIANT SCENE IN THE SENATE CHAMBER—COURTESIES BETWEEN THE OUTGOING AND INCOMING EXECUTIVES—THE GRAND BALL WHICH WOUND UP THE INAUGURATION FESTIVITIES.

WASHINGTON, March 4.—Grover Cleveland to-day vacated the office of President of the United States and Benjamin Harrison took his place.

According to custom the incoming President took the oath of office before the east front of the Capitol in the presence of a large and enthusiastic concourse of people. The weather was thoroughly unpropitious. The rain fell steadily from early morning until night, destroying the beauty of the elaborate decorations along the streets and drenching the thousands of men who participated in the parade.

President Cleveland laid aside his work early and joined the President-elect at the White House, whence they were escorted in an open carriage to the Capitol by a division composed entirely of military. Along Pennsylvania-avenue, going east, the President and his successor were vehemently cheered by an immense throng, and again on their return, after the President had been sworn in and Mr. Cleveland had become an ex-President, they were greeted by continuous applause and cheers as they led the whole parade westward, still in a pelting storm.

The review of the procession by President Harrison was a long and fatiguing task. It has been, indeed, a day's test of the endurance of all who have taken part in it rather than an occasion of pleasure.

The fireworks exhibition, proposed to be given in the White lot to-night, had to be abandoned in consequence of the execrable weather, and the competitive contest of campaign flambeau clubs was spoiled by the persistent storm.

The ball, which closed the day, was a success. The hall was tastefully and effectively decorated. The President and Vice-President and the ladies of their families attended. The President was gracious, the costumes were varied and elegant, and there was such a crowd that most of the dance music was wasted because there was no room to dance. The crush was not by any means too great, however, as it was at the Inaugural Ball in 1885.

The city is still oversupplied with drunken men. It is worthy of mention that none of the drunken ruffians who last night resorted to the front of the White House to insult the President of yesterday has been so drunk as to feel it incumbent upon him to offer insults to the President of to-day.

## PREPARING FOR THE CHANGE.

### EARLY HOURS OF THE OUTGOING AND INCOMING PRESIDENTS.

The first thought of Mrs. Cleveland, and doubtless of almost every one else in Washington this morning, was of the weather, and her bright and lovely face clouded slightly when she discovered that rain and wind had formed a partnership that promised to interfere seriously with the day's ceremonies. President Cleveland—for at 8 o'clock in the morning he still possessed that official title—also expressed regret that his successor was not to be greeted by a clear sky and a blazing sun. The White House grounds looked as cheerless in the early morning as leafless trees, withered grass, and a rain that seemed never ending could make them. The White House looked as if it were in perfect accord with its surroundings.

But, if there was nothing enlivening about its exterior, there was no lack of cheer and cheerfulness within the White House walls. President Cleveland, always self-contained, gave no indications in manner or speech that his equanimity was at all disturbed by the close approach of the greatest change but one an American citizen can experience. Mrs. Cleveland's spirits seemed perhaps a trifle higher than usual. Their last breakfast at the White House was a pleasant, if not a long, meal. The outgoing President pleaded business as an excuse for shortening it, and left the table for his office.

There he found a number of bills waiting for his signature. While he dashed off his autograph, unconscious of the wanderings of the distinguished personages who were in charge of the Executive Committee of the body that had full charge of the inaugural ceremonies. Mrs. Cleveland and her mother gazed through one of the windows in the north front of the White House at the scurrying crowds on Pennsylvania-avenue.

As they looked, at 9:30 o'clock, the first organization to appear in the avenue came in sight from the east. It was a club, gorgeous in silk hats and drab-colored topcoats. Every man carried a cane. They had not calculated upon rain when they decided upon their uniform, and they refused to permit the rain to interfere with their programme. The club was headed with a white-coated band that played "Marching Through Georgia." Stray bars of the music drifted to the ears of the watchers of the White House. The club marched like veterans; so much Mrs. Cleveland could see, and that they were veterans she was certain, for they paid no more attention to the rain that trickled from their hats down their necks than if they had been accustomed to nothing but rain all their lives.

Rain has no effect upon Father Time. That inexorable personage swallowed 15 minutes. Just as Mrs. Cleveland thought of turning away, the big iron gates of the northeastern entrance to the White House grounds were swung open. A dashing-looking horseman rode through. This was Col. Samuel Merrill. He was accompanied by two mounted aides, and was followed by all that was left of the Seventieth Indiana Regiment, of which Gen. Harrison was a member during the war of the rebellion. The veterans were 150 strong. Sturdy old men they were. They formed company front on the driveway, midway between the entrance to the grounds and the White House. The inevitable man and his camera appeared; the regiment was photographed—not once, but four times, each time in a different position. All was in readiness for the appearance at the White House of the President-elect.

Even the darkest, rainiest, most disagreeable night must have an ending, and inauguration morning came at last. It rained harder and harder as the day advanced. Gen. Harrison and his family met in their parlor at about 7:30 o'clock, and, on this eventful morning, he preceded, as ever, the labors of the day with prayer. He and his son Russell were dressed from head to foot in clothes of American make; not a foreign thing was upon them. Their suits were of cloth given to them by John F. Plummer, who had it manufactured in one of his Connecticut mills. Their coats were double-breasted frocks and their trousers were striped with neutral tints.

It is easy to believe that breakfast was quickly eaten. Hearts were beating too quickly for sharp appetites. Even young Master Benjamin Harrison McKee was excited and Baby McKee was restless. At 9 o'clock Gen. Joseph K. McCammon and Gen. George B. Williams of the Reception Committee appeared and announced that the carriages would be ready at 10. Everybody said "All right," and proceeded to array themselves in their wraps. There was a large family party, larger, probably, than ever before attended or accompanied a President to his inauguration. There were Gen. and Mrs. Harrison, Mr. and Mrs. J. R. McKee and their two children, Mr. and Mrs. Russell Harrison, Dr. Scott, Mrs. Harrison's father, a vigorous nonogenarian; Senator and Mrs. Saunders, Mrs. Scott Lord, Mrs. Harrison's sister, and her daughter; Mrs. Parker, Mrs. R. S. McKee, J. R. McKee's mother, and J. S. Harrison of Kansas City, a brother of the General.

Presently came Mr. and Mrs. Morton and their family and Mr. Morton's partner, Mr. Bliss, and his wife. Mr. Morton wore a large fur-lined and trimmed overcoat, so big that he wrapped himself in it as if it were a cloak. His hat was an old brown derby in deference to the rain. Gen. Harrison and Russell sported brand-new silk hats and defied the rain to do its worst. Not yet, even, was the Presidential party fully made up. Mr. and Mrs. Halford and Miss Halford and Miss Sanger, the private stenographer, were to be added. Mrs. Britton and Mrs. Williams, wives of members of the Inauguration Committee, also joined it. It took 12 carriages to accommodate them all.

At last 10 o'clock came, and with it the carriages. By some strange neglect no awning had been extended from the door of the Johnson annex to the curbstone, although the distance was 30 feet or more, and the ladies grumbled in spite of the protection of their water-proofs. Mrs. Harrison, Mrs. Morton, and Mrs. McKee carried handsome bouquets. Gen. Harrison smiled and, escorted by Gen. McCammon, walked serenely to his carriage. Notwithstanding the heavy rain, a large crowd had gathered around, many of them soldiers, and they cheered the new President lustily. He smiled again and lifted his hat. Mr. McKee carried his daughter, and Russell Harrison carried Master Benjamin Harrison McKee. The crowd cheered them, too.

They started off to Willard's, whereat the crowd cheered again. This Willard business is a curious job. Somebody had been giving out in certain newspapers that Willard's would be the meeting ground of Mr. Cleveland and Gen. Harrison, whence they would be driven to the Capitol. The reason given for this was custom, the assertion being made that it had been the meeting ground at several previous inaugurations. This was not the case, and the whole affair looked very much like an advertisement for somebody. Mr. Cleveland knew nothing about it, and staid at the White House, waiting for Gen. Harrison to come. Senator Hoar, Senator Cullom and Senator Cockrell, the Senate Committee on Inauguration, were at Willard's, and received the party.

After some consultation and delay, the handsome barouches, each drawn by four horses, which were to take the old and the new Administration to the Capitol and back, were driven up to the ladies' entrance of Willard's and Gen. Harrison, Senator Hoar, and Senator Cockrell got into the first and Mr. Morton and Senator Cullom into the second. An immense crowd was jammed together around Willard's and lined Pennsylvania-avenue to the White House. It cheered and cheered as Gen. Harrison drove by, to which he frequently responded by lifting his hat. Meanwhile the rest of the party, which left the Arlington with Gen. Harrison and Mr. Morton, was driven to the Capitol to witness the inauguration ceremonies.

The veterans of the Seventieth Indiana were posing for a fourth time when once more the gates at the northeastern entrance to the White House grounds were swung open and a carriage, drawn by four bays, was whirled up the driveway and under the portico that covers the entrance to the White House on its north front. Another carriage, drawn by four dapple grays, rapidly approached. From it stepped Deputy Sergeant-at-Arms Lewis of the Senate. A man much below the average height, with a pale face, the lower part hidden by a bushy beard, next emerged from it. This was President-elect Harrison. He waited a moment on the marble platform and was joined by a smooth, chubby-faced man, who wore glasses and was instantly recognized as Senator Hoar. In their wake, as they approached the entrance, stalked a man who towered almost a foot above them. The giant with the long, gray hair and immense slouch hat was Senator Cockrell of Missouri. He and Senator Hoar had been deputed by the Senate to accompany the President-elect until he had been made President.

Once inside the White House, Senator Hoar, whose right arm held the left arm of Gen. Harrison, turned to the left and hesitated, as if he was not sure of his way. Gen. Harrison partook of this hesitation. They were at once directed toward a stained-glass door that almost faced the entrance. Through this they passed, and were in a few moments ushered into the Blue Room, where they met President Cleveland and the members of his Cabinet. The latter reached the White House just before 10 o'clock, and had spent the intervening time with the President. The occupants of the carriage drawn by the four bays were Vice-President-elect Levi P. Morton and Senator Cullom of Illinois. The latter was one of the Senate Committee. They, too, went to the Blue Room and met President Cleveland and the other gentlemen there assembled.

As they conversed, President Cleveland's landau, drawn by four seal-brown horses—splendid-looking animals—was driven up to the north entrance. It was open. The seats were hidden from the rain by an immense white bearskin. On the box sat the White House colored Jehu, Albert Hawkins. At his side sat another colored coachman, Beverly Lemos. Police Officer West, mounted on a spirited bay, was stationed a few feet in advance of the landau. It was 10:45 o'clock.

A doorkeeper cried: "Make way, gentlemen," and the little knot of correspondents, who stood near the entrance looking out upon the gathering crowds, moved to one side. In a moment the glass doors were thrown open. President Cleveland and Senator Cockrell appeared. The President looked well, and he bowed in return for a general salute. Following him came President-elect Harrison and Senator Hoar. Then came Vice-President-elect Morton and Senator Cullom. Secretaries Fairchild and Whitney and other members of President Cleveland's Cabinet formed the rest of the procession.

As President Cleveland reached his carriage, he stood to one side and begged Gen. Harrison to enter it. The latter did so, taking a position to the left on the back seat. President Cleveland took the seat next to him and opened an umbrella, smilingly remarking that it might be necessary. Senator Hoar sat with his back to the horses, and Senator Cockrell followed his example. Senator Hoar tried to open an umbrella. One of the ribs broke and rendered the umbrella useless. President Cleveland smiled, turned to Secretary Fairchild, and calmly borrowed his umbrella, remarking that the party was an honest one and would probably return it. Secretary Fairchild sighed and handed over his umbrella. Vice-President-Elect Morton and Senator Cullom entered a carriage drawn by four grays.

Secretary Fairchild followed the President's glance. The latter was directed at a window that overlooked the entrance. The Secretary smiled and lifted his hat. Every one else looked up, and every one else immediately followed Mr. Fairchild's example and received a smile from a beautiful woman who stood at the window. It was Mrs. Cleveland, and she continued to bow and smile to all who looked up until the carriages disappeared in the distance, and the men who remained behind became absolutely ashamed of glancing in her direction. At Mrs. Cleveland's side, while she remained in sight, stood her mother, Mrs. Folsom.

Secretary Bayard and Assistant Secretary Moore entered the third carriage. Secretary Whitney captured Secretary Endicott and carried him off in his carriage. Secretary Fairchild had a carriage to himself. Secretary Vilas and Postmaster-General Dickinson paired off and left Attorney-General Garland and Secretary of Agriculture Coleman to enter the last carriage, which, by the way, was of a variety widely known as the "night lines."

The carriages proceeded at a slow gait toward the entrance. The veterans were divided. One company preceded the carriage containing their old comrade and commander and the second company brought up the rear. Behind the second company of veterans the other carriages fell in, the next to the veterans being that in which sat Vice-President-elect Morton and Senator Cullom. At 11:15 the cavalcade was in Pennsylvania-avenue and the yell that issued from a thousand throats told that the President-elect was recognized.

## MARCHING TO THE CAPITOL.

### THE CROWDS WHICH CHEERED THE NEW PRESIDENT ON HIS WAY.

The great thoroughfare of the city, Pennsylvania-avenue, at 8 o'clock this morning presented a novel sight. Had the sun been shining, it would have presented a gorgeous spectacle. But the sun was not shining. There was no indication that the sun would ever shine again. How it rained. Jupiter Pluvius had a large dash of bitterness in his disposition this morning, and he seemed to have formed a close alliance during the night with King Boreas, for at unpleasantly frequent intervals gusts of wind rushed through the broad avenue, and dashed the rain in faces that even would looked pleased.

The national colors in the decorations had evidently come to stay. The rain had undoubtedly taken the stiffening out of them. They did not wear a defiant air, but stuck close to the buildings or to whatever they were attached to.

But the colors were still red, white, and blue, and not a malarial mixture of all three. The avenue looked as its looks only once in four years. There were other decorations on it besides flags and bunting and shields. Every vacant spot on both sides was occupied by a structure that wore a circus air. One half expected to see the ringmaster appear. With its face toward the north side of the White House grounds was a tall structure closed at the back, furnished with a roof and open in front. In it were 800 chairs. At 8 o'clock it was vacant. There were two men on the roof covering it with waterproof cloth. In this stand it was intended that President Harrison should review the inaugural parade. The entrance to this stand was through the White House gates. At these gates stood guards. Admission to the stand was to be gained by ticket.

Opposite this stand was another. It was a giant in size. It was about 300 yards long. In portions it was two stories high. The chairs in it were countless. Ten dollars each was asked for them. On the north and east sides of the Treasury building were thousands of seats. They were uncovered and wet. They did not cost $10. They looked provocative of pneumonia and other ills. These stands were samples of perhaps 50 others that could be found on the avenue. There were thousands of other stands. They looked intensely cramped and uncomfortable. Their ugliness was relieved by a generous covering of bunting, that would have looked comfortable if it had only been dry.

It was early, but there were thousands abroad. It seemed as if the entire population must have been on or drifting toward Pennsylvania-avenue. Every man and every woman sightseer carried an umbrella. To stand at Fifteenth-street and look toward the Capitol gave one the impression that the rain had given birth to an enormous crop of umbrellas. The sidewalks were covered with them. There were patches of them at short intervals in the middle of the thoroughfare. At 9 o'clock the avenue was a trifle crowded. It seemed narrower than usual. There were few people in the seats yet. It was expected that the President-elect would begin his triumphal progress to the Capitol at 11 o'clock, and few desired to sit in the rain that might last for hours before it was absolutely necessary.

At 10 o'clock a new scene was presented. The crowd on the sidewalks was so dense that it was difficult to make headway through it. The avenue was roped off on both sides. The ropes were of wire, and were too taut to stretch any more. Mounted policemen trotted up and down the avenue. Policemen on foot were stationed at points not more than 50 yards apart. The policemen warned people not to cross the avenue. The centre of the avenue was closed to all but paraders. Mounted aides began to dash hither and thither. Bodies of soldiery were marching toward the White House at a double-quick. A battery of United States artillery rumbled through the avenue. Its appearance elicited a cheer. A few minutes later a battalion of blue jackets swaggered past, their caps well set on the backs of their heads. They were greeted with a hoarse roar of approval. Their indifference to the deluge met with general approval and people told each other that no sort of weather could hurt those fellows.

It was almost 11 o'clock. Once more the avenue put on a new dress. Solid ranks, 10 to 15 deep, faced the avenue on both sides. No one entertained the thought of crossing that thoroughfare. As far as a man with unimpaired sight could see both sides of the avenue were packed with people. The umbrellas had disappeared, trampled out of sight, for those in the rear ranks could not be induced to permit those in front to hoist a covering. The windows of every building were wide open and filled with faces. The vacant chairs were no longer visible. An anxious public stood or sat upon them, and calmly accepted the rain as something that could be spared, but must be endured. Some of the stands, built to a height of 50 feet, looked as if they would tumble forward on small provocation. They were frightfully overloaded. None of them fell, however. Enthusiasm began to wage war with discomfort.

At the head of Fifteenth-street the people hushed their clamor for a moment. The sound of a hoarse cheer had been borne to their ears. They knew intuitively that Gen. Harrison had left the White House, in company with President Cleveland, and that the old and new ruler of sixty-odd millions of American sovereigns would soon be within sight. The cheer on Pennsylvania-avenue signaled aright. At 11:15 o'clock the veterans of the Seventieth Indiana Regiment filed out of the White House gates and turned their faces toward the Capitol. The rain seemed to gather renewed vigor. The veterans smiled as they listened to the cheer that greeted their old commander. Gen. Harrison lifted his hat to the multitude that lined his pathway. President Cleveland sat, as sturdy as an oak, holding an umbrella over the head of the man who was to succeed him as President of the United States.

The escort of the Presidential party on its march from the White House to the Capitol consisted of about 4,000 men. It was under the command of Gen. James A. Beaver, the one-legged soldier Governor of Pennsylvania, who acted as Chief Marshal of the inaugural parade of 1889, just as he did that of 1885. Gov. Beaver rode a black stallion, and rode him well, looking every inch a commander. Almost at his side, but slightly in the rear, was his chief of staff, Brig.-Gen. Daniel S. Hastings of the Keystone State, a giant in stature. Fifty aides-de-camp followed in his train.

The escort comprised the first division of the grand parade, Brig.-Gen. H. G. Gibson, commanding, and composed of the Indiana Veterans, the Third Regiment Artillery, United States Army; four batteries of the First Artillery, United States Army; a battalion of United States Cavalry, Col. L. H. Carpenter of the Fifth Cavalry commanding: Troops B, Sixth Cavalry, and B, Fourth Cavalry; the National Guard of the District of Columbia, Brig.-Gen. Albert Ordway commanding, and the Second Pennsylvania, National Guard, Col. R. P. Dechert; a battalion of United States Marines, and a battalion of United States sailors. The gallant appearance of the escort called out hearty cheers from crowds that were glad of an excuse for being noisy. The music of the Marine Band, too, had an inspiriting effect.

The sight of two Presidents was not likely to dull the edge of enthusiasm. Truth to say, though, there was not that continuous cheering to which the American populace is given on provocation not always of the strongest. It might be the weather; that certainly was bad enough to engender the blues, but, at any rate, the cheering was spasmodic. There were ominous gaps in the enthusiasm. The people understood full well that the cheers were intended for President-elect Harrison, and not for President Cleveland. They all showed curiosity to see the new occupant of the White House, but only those who were jammed against the wire ropes could see even his head and shoulders. The umbrella was held high enough not to hide him from those on the pavements, but not much of President-elect Harrison could be seen by those who had the best opportunity, for, apparently, much to their surprise, he seemed, as he is, a much smaller man than Cleveland, and seemed so even in a sitting posture. But when the bands played their loudest and the Presidential carriage arrived in front of one of the huge stands its occupants gave play to their lungs and shook the raindrops from their head coverings.

The mile between the White House and the Capitol was finally covered. On the east front of the Capitol was gathered a crowd that, in comparison with the multitude that lined the route of the parade, seemed strangely small. The people had evidently concluded that there was nothing there for them to see until the Presidential party emerged from the Capitol, in order to allow the incoming President to deliver his inaugural address. With an absolute lack of inconvenience the party was transferred from the outer world to the interior of the Capitol, and Mr. Cleveland went to the President's room, while Gen. Harrison was shown to the Vice-President's room, there to remain until ready to enter the Senate Chamber.

## AMONG DISTINGUISHED MEN.

### THE CROWD WHICH WATCHED THE ASSEMBLAGE IN THE SENATE CHAMBER.

As the hands on the big clock in the Senate Chamber pointed to 9:30 o'clock President Pro Tem Ingalls rose for order for the last time before yielding up his gavel and the authority it represents to the Vice-President of the United States and the constitutional presiding officer of the Senate.

The Senate had been in recess for about six hours. All those who left the chamber at 3 o'clock this morning hardly recognized it now. A small army of laborers had been at work. All the litter and débris of two all-night sessions had been swept up, the 76 desks had been cleared of all the bills, documents, and other papers that usually cover them, and the whole place had been made to look as fresh and bright as if it had never before been occupied. About 300 brand-new camp chairs had been placed in every available space on the floor. Two capacious easy chairs, gaudily upholstered in red, stood squarely in front of the presiding officer's desk. They were later on to be occupied by the President and President-elect. On either side were lounges and easy chairs to be used by ex-Vice President Hamlin and the Senate Committee on Inauguration Ceremonies. Just in front, on the left of the semi-circular space, were eight dark-red armchairs for the members of the Cabinet, and a sofa for the head of the army and his staff. Opposite were ranged sofas and chairs for the Justices of the Supreme Court.

On the right of the desk, just below the top platform, was a plain red chair marked "reserved," which was kept for Levi P. Morton. In all the other spaces, and sandwiched between the Senators' desks, were the camp chairs for the use of the diplomatic corps and all other distinguished persons allowed on the floor. During the recess the galleries had been cleared of the hundreds of visitors who were there at 3 o'clock, and every entrance to the building was guarded by policemen.

When Mr. Ingalls's rap resounded through the chamber less than a dozen Senators were present. Among them were Messrs. Plumb, Edmunds, Walthall, Harris, Berry, Teller, Chace, Hale, McPherson, and Chandler. A half dozen ladies, who had been admitted early through the courtesy of individual Senators, looked lost in the empty galleries. The less fortunate spectators could not get in the building until 10 o'clock. Nothing was done for a quarter hour. Mr. Plumb presented a conference report on an unimportant bill, and it was agreed to by the few Senators present. Mr. Walthall had a little correction made in the record, and the credentials of Senator-elect McMillan of Michigan were read and put on file. A few enrolled bills received from the House were signed by Mr. Ingalls, and that was all.

At 10 o'clock the doors were opened for the admission of fortunate holders of tickets. Among the first ladies to reach the chamber was the wife of ex-Representative J. V. L. Findlay of Baltimore. She is a cousin of Mrs. Harrison, and was therefore shown into the gallery just west of the diplomatic gallery, and to a seat in a pew marked "Family of the President-elect." The pew in front of Mrs. Findlay was labeled "Family of the Vice-President." In front of this was another pew, reserved for members of Gen. Harrison's family. Opposite this was the pew reserved for President Cleveland's family, and behind the latter was one marked "Family of the President pro tem. of the Senate."

The galleries filled up slowly at first. A party of Gen. Harrison's friends from Indiana filled up one of the pews in the Presidential gallery. People were coming in faster now, and during the next 15 minutes the galleries east and west were rapidly filled. Assistant Secretary of State Rives and a party of ladies reached the diplomatic gallery in time to get a front pew. Mr. Voorhees escorted a number of ladies to seats in the Democratic gallery, and Warner Miller secured a poor seat in the rear of the Republican gallery. Mrs. Findlay was joined by her husband, and the two sat alone in the Harrison pew.

The floor of the chamber was also gradually filling up. The venerable Gilman Marston, tall and portly, who is to succeed Mr. Chandler as a Senator from New-Hampshire, walked in with Mr. Blair, and the two stopped to chat with ex-Senator Cheney, who was mistaken by many New-Yorkers for ex-Mayor Edson. Near them was Senator-elect Wolcott of Colorado, who was taken in charge by Mr. Teller and looked much younger than his predecessor, Mr. Bowen. Representative Hiestand was the first member of the House who appeared, and he selected a choice seat on the Democratic side, all the Senators having taken seats on the Republican side. The Rev. Dr. Bullock, ex-Chaplain of the Senate, greeted old friends on the floor, and ex-Senator Windom dropped into a seat on Mr. Sherman's right. A moment later Hannibal Hamlin, looking 20 years younger than his years, sat down on Mr. Sherman's left, and the three enjoyed an animated conversation. Ex-Senator Jones of Iowa, whose bushy gray beard and hair attracted attention, sat alone behind the Sherman group.

There was no stir in the Presidential gallery until 10:30 o'clock, when Mrs. John J. Ingalls and seven of her children took places in the pew reserved for them and watched their husband and father as he directed the closing acts of the Senate. Ex-Senator Cattell of New-Jersey, clad in a heavy overcoat, shook hands with many friends, and ex-Postmaster-General J. A. J. Creswell's shining bald head bobbed up here and there as he greeted those around them. Long-bearded ex-Senator Ferry of Michigan was another familiar figure who spent much time in greeting old friends.

Senator-elect Washburn of Minnesota, with his close-cropped Burnside whiskers, was chatting with Mr. Sabin, whose place he will take, when, at 10:50 o'clock, there was another stir in the Presidential gallery, and Mr. John Harrison of Kansas City, a brother of the President-elect, and his wife and family, were shown into one of the reserved pews. Behind them walked Judge John Scott, Mrs. Harrison's brother, accompanied by his family, and the party found room in the same pew. They were followed by a small crowd of ladies and gentlemen holding tickets for the Presidential gallery, and in a moment there were but three vacant pews in the gallery. There were no other vacant seats in any gallery. Even the aisles were crowded and the doorways thronged by late comers.

The hum and buzz of hundreds of voices which filled the place were suddenly hushed as Mr. Ingalls rapped and rose to receive a message from the House of Representatives. It turned out to be a notice that the lower house had directed its Sergeant-at-Arms to see that its members were allowed free access to the corridors of the Capitol. Senators smiled as they heard this little "dig" at the work of the Committee of Arrangements, but they took the reprimand gracefully, and, on Mr. Edmunds's motion, they voted to formally accede to the resolution. Amid the laughter which followed, Mr. Edgarton, who hopes to be South Dakota's first United States Senator, found a seat on the floor. Just as he was seated the venerable assistant doorkeeper, Isaac Bassett, stepped over to ex-Vice-President Hamlin, and, giving him his arm, led him to an easy chair beside the one reserved for President Cleveland. As he took this seat Mr. Hamlin was greeted with a round of hearty applause from galleries and floor, and acknowledged the compliment with a slight bow and a genial smile. Two highly-privileged colored men, whom nobody knew, took seats in the rear of those reserved for Representatives.

President Ingalls's gavel fell again, and again the great crowd became quiet. Assistant Private Secretary Pruden stepped into the centre aisle and delivered to the Senate Grover Cleveland's last official message. It was an announcement of the Executive approval of "Sundry Senate bills."

Capt. Bassett had just handed the bills to a clerk when the gallery spectators suddenly broke out with loud applause. They saw Mr. James G. Blaine slipping into the chamber from the private corridor door on the left of the chair, and they were bound to greet the Premier of the new Administration. With his black frock coat buttoned tightly about his body and his hands encased in dark brown kid gloves, Mr. Blaine dropped into a chair beside Mr. Wilson of Iowa, leaned over that Senator to shake hands with Mr. Evarts, and began to talk at a lively rate.

Mr. Ingalls thought it was time to reprove the spectators for profaning the Senate Chamber with applause, and he did so in a little speech which he had made very familiar since he has presided over that body. The crowd was evidently disposed to laugh at the dignified Kansas Senator, but the applause ceased, and the visitors noted how quickly Mr. Hale ran round to take Mr. Blaine's hand and to lead him to a better seat, where he could see and be seen, while he chatted with Mr. Hale and his next neighbor, Mr. Stewart.

## THE SENATE CEREMONIES.

### BRILLIANT SCENES AMID WHICH MR. MORTON TOOK THE OATH OF OFFICE.

It lacked now only a short hour of the time for the chief ceremony which had brought the throng of spectators to the Senate Chamber, but there were still vacant the rows of chairs reserved for the Cabinet, the Justices of the Supreme Court, the diplomatic corps, and the members of Congress. Representatives were constantly straggling in, however, anxious to secure good places, and it was apparent that when those who waited for the House to adjourn should come over they would find all their best seats pre-empted by their more enterprising colleagues.

It was 11:08 o'clock when the next to the last formal message was received from the House. It was the formal notice that the House had completed its business and was prepared to appoint a committee to join a Senate committee in informing the President that both houses were ready to adjourn sine die if he had no further communication to make to them. As soon as this message was received Mr. Sherman rose and offered the last resolution to be passed by the Senate. It provided for a committee of two to join the House committee of notification. Mr. Ingalls put the question, on its adoption declared it carried, and immediately named Mr. Sherman and Mr. Saulsbury as the representatives of the Senate. It was Mr. Saulsbury's last duty as a Senator from Delaware, for his successor, smooth-faced Anthony Higgins, was in the chamber waiting to be sworn into office.

Gen. Schofield, the head of the army, in full uniform, accompanied by his staff, stepped inside the chamber through the eastern door. A page hurried over and told the General he had come the wrong way. The military party backed out, and in a moment they appeared in the private corridor and entered the chamber at Mr. Ingalls's left, taking seats on a big red sofa. Beside Gen. Schofield sat hale and hearty old W. T. Sherman, the retired General of the army, who looked as if he would greatly prefer a less conspicuous place in the gallery. The General was dressed in plain broadcloth, and wore on the left breast of his coat the badge of the Grand Army of the Republic.

Gen. Schofield had just taken his seat when the doors at the head of the central aisle were thrown open and the members of the diplomatic corps stepped proudly into the chamber, which seemed instantly to take on new life and color from the glitter of the gorgeous Court uniforms worn by the diplomats. At the head of the corps was Baron de Fava, the Italian Minister, who acts as dean of the corps in the absence of Minister Preston, the Haytian representative. Behind him came Señor Romero, the Mexican Minister; Señor Muruaga, the Spanish Minister; Mr. Chan Yen Hoon, the Chinese Minister; Mavroyeni Bey, the Turkish Minister; Mr. Pak Chung Yang, the Corean Minister; Count von Arco-Valley, the German Minister; Mr. Munemitsu Mutsu, the Japanese Minister, and nearly every other representative of a foreign Government accredited to the United States Government. There were also a score or more of the Secretaries and attachés of the various legations, all resplendent in bright and showy Court costumes and covered with the insignia of the orders conferred upon them by their sovereigns.

Perhaps the most conspicuous of the uniforms were those worn by Count von Arco Valley, covered with gold lace, bright ribbons, and medals; Baron Sternberg of the German Legation, in the bright hues of the Lancers, and Baron Eckartstein, also of the German Legation, in the clear white of the Cuirassiers. Almost in the centre of the diplomats were seated the Chinese Minister and his suite, in flowing silk costumes, forming an attractive bit of coloring in the general picture. As the Minister slowly moved his fan a large jade ring was noticed on his left thumb. Over to the right of the corps sat the Corean Minister, wearing his tall, broad-brimmed hat of horsehair, and displaying a native dress of many colors, red predominating. In marked contrast were the plain American dress suits of the Japanese Minister's suite, the Minister himself wearing black, with moderate trimmings of gold lace. All in all, the diplomatic corps form a gay relief to the sombre black of the gentlemen around them, and for a time they monopolize the attention of the galleries.

While the foreign representatives were taking their places Marshal A. A. Wilson found a seat on the floor, and 15 or 20 more Congressmen glided into the chamber by a side door and seized upon the best chairs left in their section of the floor. One Harrison pew, the Morton pew, and the Cleveland pew are the only vacant spots to be seen in the galleries at 11:35 o'clock, when the final message came from the House announcing the selection of Messrs. Breckinridge of Arkansas, McMillin, and Kelley as its representatives on the joint notification committee. The three Congressmen, who were already on hand, were joined by Messrs. Sherman and Saulsbury, and they passed through the Democratic cloakroom to the west corridor and thence to the President's room, where they found Mr. Cleveland waiting to receive them.

While they were away Capt. Bassett announced the presence of the Justices of the Supreme Court. The great throng rose and stood while the learned jurists, clad in their official robes, entered and passed down to their easy chairs on the right of the space in front of the President's desk. Chief-Justice Fuller was at their head, and they were marshaled by the Clerk and Marshal of the court. With them was ex-Justice Strong and Official Court Reporter Davis. Clerk McKenney carried with him the Bible on which Gen. Harrison was to take his oath of office less than an hour later. When the Justices sat down the spectators followed their example. Mr. Hamlin had been rather lonely until now, and he welcomed the presence of the Justices who sat near enough to engage him in conversation.

Ex-Senator Pomeroy of Kansas and District Commissioner Webb, whose renomination was to fall with the end of the session, were squeezing their way into the chamber, when a movement in the Presidential gallery turned all eyes in that direction. It lacked only 15 minutes of high noon and the spectators saw the narrow aisles of the Presidential gallery suddenly filled to overflowing with 40 or 50 gentlemen and ladies, who found only two pews open to them. They were the families and relatives of Gen. Harrison and Mr. Morton. Not more than half of them could be accommodated with seats, and there was a deal of confusion while the ushers tried to straighten the matter out.

Mrs. Harrison, wearing a street dress of dark-green material and carrying a very large bouquet of lilies of the valley, was crowded down to the end of the aisle and forced to stand with her back to the Senate. Mrs. Morton, also wearing a walking costume of green cloth, was finally crowded into her pew with her two daughters. Ex-Assistant Attorney-General McCammon accompanied her, and the little room left in the pew was filled by members of the Harrison party. After much confusion and more pushing and crowding than was at all pleasant, Mrs. Harrison was provided with a seat in the front pew, and the audience had an opportunity to see her face. With her in the pew were her son Russell, wearing an immense white campaign badge, upon which was stamped a picture of his father; her father, the venerable Rev. Dr. Scott; Mrs. Russell Harrison, Mr. and Mrs. McKee, her son-in-law and daughter, the latter holding a big bouquet of red roses, and Mrs. Scott Lord, her sister.

The rest of the party found seats on the aisle steps and wherever else they could be crowded in. Among them were Mr. and Mrs. Saunders, parents of Russell Harrison's wife; Mr. and Mrs. Devon and Mrs. Eaton, the ladies being half sisters of Gen. Harrison; Mr. William and Mrs. Bettie Harrison, the latter a sister of Gen. Harrison; Lieut. and Mrs. J. Parker, his nephew and niece; Judge John Scott, Mrs. Harrison's brother, and Mrs. Britton, wife of the Chairman of the local Inauguration Committee.

It was 11:52 and these distinguished visitors had been crowded into seats, when Mr. Sherman formally announced to the Senate that President Cleveland had no further communication to make to Congress. The time was growing very short, but Gen. Harrison, President Cleveland, and the Congressmen were still absent. Old Capt. Bassett therefore went up to the clock and with a long stick deliberately turned the minute hand back 10 minutes. A storm of laughter greeted this time-honored method of cheating old Father Time, and before it died out, official programmes of the proceedings were distributed in the Presidential gallery. It was 11:49 o'clock by the Senate time when the members of the House of Representatives came in in a body, and instantly filled every vacant nook and cranny left. They even filled up all of the cloak rooms from which a view of the chamber could be had, and the place was a solid mass of humanity.

Still the President and President-elect were missing, and, as the clock hands again approached the noon mark, Capt. Bassett again set them back, this time six minutes. While the crowd was laughing a crash was heard in the chamber, and Gen. Grosvenor of Ohio picked himself up from the wreckage of the camp chair he had been occupying. A new chair was passed to him over the heads of the throng.

It was 11:53 by the twice-corrected clock when the central doors swung open, the audience rose, and President Cleveland, leaning on the arm of Senator Cockrell, walked down the aisle and took one of the two conspicuous easy chairs facing the throng in front of the presiding officer's desk. Behind him marched the members of his Cabinet, led by Secretaries Bayard and Fairchild, and including Secretaries Endicott, Whitney, Vilas, and Colman, Postmaster-General Dickinson, and Attorney-General Garland. President Cleveland's pew, in the reserved gallery, was still vacant, and it remained unoccupied to the end of the ceremonies. Once more the hour and minute hands got very close together on the clock dial, and for the last time the minute hand was put back, thus saving five minutes more.

Having been corrected three times the clock pointed to four minutes of 12 when the audience stood up again, and President-elect Harrison, escorted by Senator Hoar, hurried down to the easy chair on Mr. Cleveland's left. While the audience was on its feet Vice-President-elect Morton appeared on the arm of Senator Cullom, and walked down to a chair on the right of Mr. Ingalls.

Touching the desk lightly with his gavel, Mr. Ingalls announced that Mr. Morton would now be sworn into office. The vast audiences became perfectly silent, as Mr. Morton rose, and, with uplifted right hand, took the oath of office, read in clear tones by Mr. Ingalls. As he dropped back into his seat Mr. Ingalls faced the Senate and briefly said farewell, declaring the Senate adjourned:

SENATORS: Conscious of a serious desire to deserve your approval, and aware that that would be secured only by constant devotion to your service, the Chair assumed with diffidence the great trust conferred by your suffrage which to-day he relinquishes with the profoundest gratitude for the honor of your resolution of commendation; and declares that the Senate now stands adjourned sine die.

As he spoke the last word, Mr. Ingalls turned, handed the gavel to the new President of the Senate and the latter rapped for order. Chaplain Butler made a fervid prayer, and, with just a trifle of embarrassment, Mr. Morton, glancing at his notes, made this little speech:

SENATORS: I shall enter on the discharge of the delicate and (at times) important duty of the position to which I have been called by the people of the United States without experience as a presiding officer, and therefore bespeak in advance the indulgent consideration which you have been always ready to extend to the occupant of the chair. As presiding officer of the Senate it will be my effort to administer the rules of procedure with entire fairness and to treat every Senator with the courtesy and consideration due at all times to the representatives of great States in a legislative body. I hope that our official and personal relations will prove mutually agreeable, and that our duties will be discharged in a manner to maintain the dignity of the Senate and to add to the prosperity and happiness of this great Nation.

Applause followed, and the President directed Secretary McCook to read the proclamation convening the Senate in extraordinary session. "The names of new Senators whose credentials have been filed will be called," said Mr. Morton, "and they will step forward and take the oath." The first name called was that of Mr. Barbour, Mr. Riddleberger's successor from Virginia. Mr. Beck, to everybody's regret, was un-

10 Pages

# The New-York Times.

10 Pages

VOL. XLI....NO. 12,620. NEW-YORK, FRIDAY, FEBRUARY 5, 1892. PRICE THREE CENTS.



## NEW-YORK'S BONE HUNTERS

*A RATHER CHILLY RECEPTION BY THE PRESIDENT.*

COMMISSIONER ROOSEVELT A STUMBLING BLOCK FOR THE PLACE HUNTERS—NOBLE REPUBLICANS LOOKING FOR DEMOCRATIC SALARIES.

WASHINGTON, Feb. 4.—Patronage, spelled with capital letters, has been an engrossing topic in Washington to-day. How could it be otherwise, with ten stalwart patronage hunters from New-York City in town?

Mr. Jacob M. Patterson mustered his braves quite early this morning. The number had been increased by several New-Yorkers who did not get here with the main body last night, and comprised representatives of ten out of the twenty-four Assembly districts in New-York City. This is the way the delegation lined up at the Arlington Hotel previous to the opening of hostilities:

J. M. PATTERSON, Tenth District.
M. J. HEALY, First District.
CHARLES F. MURRAY, Third District.
JOHN SIMPSON, Sixth District.
JOHN R. NUGENT, Fourteenth District.
R. A. GREACEN, Fifteenth District.
GEORGE W. WANMAKER, (not Wanamaker,) Seventeenth District.
BERNARD BIGLIN, Eighteenth District.
MICHAEL GOODE, Twentieth District.

All these men had come to Washington to further a preconcerted plan to ask the Administration for more patronage for Republicans in the City of New-York. They made no secret of their mission, and most of them appeared to think that they would be successful. Some of them had private axes to grind, and these were decidedly foxy in answering the queries of newspaper men.

About 11 o'clock the procession started for the White House. The President had been warned of the coming invasion and was fully prepared to receive the place seekers. They were ushered into his presence without delay, and in about fifteen minutes he was made fully acquainted with the object of their call. Mr. Patterson acted as spokesman and introduced the gentlemen to the President. Mr. Harrison was already acquainted with Mr. Biglin and one or two others of the party. They had been to see him before on similar errands.

The position of the New-York Republicans was fully set forth by Patterson and Biglin. The party, they said, was on the eve of a great struggle. They believed that victory could be won in the State of New-York if the Republicans adopted the right tactics. The Democrats were torn by dissensions, and the recent acts of David B. Hill had done much to make Republican success possible. In the city it was hard to contend against Tammany and its enormous resources in the shape of party patronage. Patronage was necessary to party organization, and party organization was necessary if victory was to be had at the polls. There were in the employment of the Government in New-York City many Democrats who were appointed by the last Administration. Their places ought to be filled by Republicans. The sight of Democrats holding office under a Republican Administration was repugnant to old-time Republicans, who believed that victory should carry with it all the spoils consistent with good government. While the delegation believed in the civil-service law, (everybody looked solemn at this juncture,) there were many places which this law did not cover, and these were the ones the Republicans coveted.

Mr. Harrison was requested to examine the subject carefully, and the remark was added that the delegation believed that if he did so he would act in accordance with their desires. The President was very diplomatic in his reply, if the utterances of some of his hearers are to be believed. He alluded to the civil service law, and said that it had been his aim to follow the spirit of the law to the best of his ability. It was possible that an injustice had been done to Republicans in New-York, but it was not intended that such should be the case.

"He talked quite a little, but it didn't strike me that he met our proposition even half way," said one Republican this evening. "For one, I came away with the impression that our prayer for more patronage would meet with the same kind of reply the President has vouchsafed ever since the crusade was begun by the Republicans."

The interview came to an end at last, and the delegation marched from the White House to the Treasury Department. Secretary Foster had been apprised of its coming and was "in." For fifteen minutes he listened to the tale of woe. However much he may have sympathized with the object of the visit, he was exceedingly circumspect, and no man in the party could say afterward that he had promised to do anything definite. "He talked about the outlook for the party and even discussed the subject of turning the Democrats out, but he didn't say positively that anything would be done," said the Republican who is quoted above. "He promised to talk the matter over with the President, and we had to be content with that."

The delegation went back to the Arlington, and spent the remainder of the day there comparing notes. Theodore Roosevelt of the Civil Service Commission is the man whose scalp they deem necessary to the furtherance of their plan. Nothing about Mr. Roosevelt was said to the President or to Secretary Foster, but some very broad hints were let fall. On this subject one of the delegation, who has exercised a controlling voice in its movements, said to-night:

"Mr. Roosevelt alone stands in the way of Republican occupancy of the offices we have come to Washington to see about. The Civil Service Commissioners, it is well known, have the power to make many rules which can be used to the detriment of the party in power if they so elect. Mr. Harrison could meet all our demands and strengthen himself with the party if he would remove Roosevelt and put in a man who would be willing to change the rules to suit the occasion. These are plain words, but they express our feelings exactly. Mr. Harrison needs only to look between the lines of our argument to-day to recognize our position as regards the Civil Service Commission. If he does this, and acts as we would like to have him do, he will be more favorably regarded by the members of the party at large."

The Republican who made this utterance was certainly in earnest, and there can be no question that he stands high in the ranks of the New-York City members of the party. Perhaps the President did not "look between the lines." If not, this will be sufficient notice to him to do so.

The offices which the delegation is after are greater in number than the general public imagines. To begin with, Mr. Patterson wants to be one of the Commissioners provided for in the law controling the construction of the new Custom House in New-York. There are five of these Commissioners to be appointed by the Secretary of the Treasury, and they are to superintend the construction of the proposed new building. They are to be known as United States Building Commissioners and are to receive "a fair and reasonable compensation," to be fixed by the Secretary. Ex-Governor McCormick of Arizona, now of Long Island, is another candidate for one of these Commissionerships. There are many chief clerkships at $2,500 a year, which the Republicans regard with covetous eyes. These are now filled by Democrats, who are protected by the civil service law. It is claimed that they were placed on the classified list of the service some time before Mr. Cleveland retired from the Presidency.

Other places which are demanded are those of the Paymaster, the Superintendent of Weighers, Superintendent of Laborers in the Public Stores, and Superintendent of Warehouses. Then there are any number of Deputy Collectorships, which the Democrats now hold, carrying salaries which would handsomely support Republican families. Many of the "hold-overs," it is said by the delegation to-night, are not protected by the civil service rules, and might just as well be put out to make room for Republicans and thus strengthen the hands of the Administration.

The leaders of the delegation professed to feel confident, after their visits to the President and Secretary of the Treasury, that their mission would prove successful. Barney Biglin said he believed that the Administration was disposed to do "what was right," and he believed that in good time the rank and file would have no cause to complain of its action in regard to the offices at its disposal. He expressed the opinion that the Republicans would win in New-York State and the Nation next Fall. "You may say for me that I believe that Mr. Harrison will be the Republican nominee, and that he will be elected." He added: "The Republicans of the State were never in better heart. Hill's antics since the last election have given them a first-class chance to win, and you will see that they will improve it."

Some of the district leaders who came to Washington to express the Republican demand for more patronage are not so sanguine this evening of final success. They say that the President "did not enthuse worth a cent" over their proposition. "The fact remains," said one, "that if we are to win in the coming fight we must be furnished with some of the stimulus which patronage is supposed to afford. The Republicans of the city have stood loyally by their standard, as the figures will show, and they ought to be rewarded for it. Some of these positions which we are asking for are of the kind calculated to do a party lots of good. They carry much minor patronage and have great weight with the men in the ranks. In New-York it is necessary to fight fire with fire. Tammany has plenty [illegible] of office holders. We ought to be better intrenched than we are. I believe the President and the Secretary are good Republicans, and that, if it is permissible under the law to give us relief, they will do so. Of course, being good Republicans, they will enforce the law. We wouldn't have the President violate the law under any circumstances."

The tone in which this last remark was made was thoroughly significant of the gentleman's state of mind. To-night the members of the delegation have haunted the lobby of the Arlington and discussed the situation. William M. Ivins, who came to the city last night with the first detachment, has been constant in his attentions to the gentlemen. He did not go with them to the White House or the Treasury, but he called upon the President. The leaders say he has no connection with their mission. For a man who is not in this movement for pap, Mr. Ivins has been remarkably active. Gen. Knapp and Lou Payn have had their heads together all day, and occasionally Mr. Ivins has been with them. Payn is after the general stores carting contract. He is backed by Thomas C. Platt, but there are several other influential Republicans who do not wish to see him get it. These believe that much more good would result to the party if the carting were done by the day, and only good Republicans were allowed to perform the work.

Collector Hendricks and Surveyor of the Port Lyon have kept away from the crowd of avowed patronage hunters to-day, but they have, nevertheless, put in some quiet "licks" calculated to help along the work of turning out Democrats from the Custom House and other Government places of employment. There is a number of weighers and assistant weighers in New-York who are accused of conniving at the underweighing of invoices. On the Surveyor's staff there are persons who are charged with having committed gross frauds. These charges have been investigated, and the documents were presented to the Secretary of the Treasury to-day, it is said. It is thought likely that they will be heard from in a short time.

In all their talk to-day the Republicans were a unit in declaring that the prospect of Republican success in the coming fight was first-class.

## CUSTOM HOUSE CHANGES.

A NEW ASSISTANT APPRAISER—SIX INSPECTORS REMOVED.

News was received at the Appraiser's Stores yesterday from Washington that John J. Lydecker had been appointed Assistant Appraiser to fill the vacancy in the tenth division caused by the death of David C. Sturges. Mr. Lydecker is a Custom House broker. Under the Administration of Chester A. Arthur as Collector of the Port he was Special Deputy Collector. The tenth division, to which he will be assigned, at least temporarily, is the one in which groceries, wines, liquors, and tobacco are classified and appraised. The salary of the office is $3,000 a year.

Six customs Inspectors have left the service by act of the Collector. They are William H. Allabon, appointed July 22, 1880; William Banham, appointed June 10, 1879; Bartholomew G. Buckley, appointed Oct. 10, 1887; James T. Cosgrove, appointed June 17, 1884; Noble W. Cook, appointed Oct. 27, 1886, and John J. Cauldwell, appointed June 18, 1888. Buckley, Cook, and Cauldwell are classed as Democrats, the others as Republicans. The official announcement of their removal says that it is due to inefficiency.

It will be noticed that the unlucky half dozen have names beginning with letters at the head of the alphabet. The fact is that the higher officials are going to peruse the whole list of Inspectors, and when they get down to X, Y, and Z's they will probably create about twenty-five more vacancies in the force. Those to take their places will come, it is said, from the civil service eligible list.

There is talk at the Custom House that before the shake-up of the Inspectors is over other charges than inefficiency may be made.

### *A BOOM FOR BOIES.*

IOWA'S DEMOCRATIC COMMITTEE TO URGE HIS NOMINATION.

DES MOINES, Iowa, Feb. 4.—The Democratic State Central Committee had a meeting here to-day and without any formal action, which was in the nature of the case impossible, steps were taken to organize and prosecute a movement in favor of Gov. Boies for President.

This is a new departure in Iowa, for it is a fact that while Gov. Boies has been largely discussed for President outside of Iowa, in this State he has been regarded as an available candidate for the second place with Cleveland. As matters are now shaping themselves the Iowa leaders have come to recognize the chance of the nomination of a Western man, and are determined to begin an active canvass for Boies.

His strength as an effective advocate of tariff reform and his conservative character as a public man are to be urged in support of his nomination, and the claim is to be strongly made that his two successful campaigns in the State mark him as the most available man for the conquest of the Northwest. These views were strongly expressed by such leaders as Charles D. Fullen, Edward L. Hunter, S. T. Pusey, John C. Kelley, and others, and the course of the Iowa Democrats in Congress in their support of Mills for Speaker was warmly commended.

Arrangements are to be made for headquarters at Chicago for the accommodation of Iowa Democrats in support of the Boies boom.

The convention to elect delegates to Chicago will be held in Council Bluffs on May 11.

### *THE INFLUENZA IN EUROPE.*

FEMALE PATIENTS IN A PRISON MADE DELIRIOUS BY THE DISEASE.

VIENNA, Feb. 4.—Twenty women who were stricken with influenza in the prison at Agram became delirious and extremely violent, so that male assistance had to be summoned from the outside to keep order. Many of the patients had visions and hallucinations.

COPENHAGEN, Feb. 4.—The influenza in this city is abating. There were reported during the past week 462 new cases of the disease and 19 deaths as resulting from it.

### *NO INDIAN OUTBREAK FEARED.*

CHICAGO, Feb. 4.—Capt. Eli L. Huggins, aide de camp to Gen. Miles, returned this morning from an extensive trip in the Indian Territory. He was sent there to investigate and report on the rumors of ghost dancing among the Indians there.

"The Arapahoe, Cheyenne, and Osage Indians still cling to the belief that the Messiah will some day appear to save them," said Capt. Huggins, "and they are not at all disappointed in the failure of the Messiah to come among them last year. They do not pretend to know the date of his coming. The former frenzy among them and their excited dances have given way to a quiet belief, which has almost become a religion with them, that the whites are to be destroyed and the Messiah will come. No outbreak is feared."

### *COL. WITHERS'S FUNERAL.*

SAN ANTONIO, Texas, Feb. 4.—The body of Col. John Withers, cashier of the San Antonio National Bank, who committed suicide yesterday, was buried this afternoon in consecrated ground. The funeral mass was sung at 4 o'clock at St. Mary's Catholic Church, of which Col. Withers was a devout member for many years. The interment took place with military honors, as Col. Withers was a West Pointer. The pall bearers were Gen. David S. Stanley, commanding the Department of Texas; Dr. F. Herff, Major C. C. Dutton, Col. C. C. Coppinger, Col. L. N. Waltham, John A. Frazer, Judge J. H. McLeary, P. M. Sullivan, Col. J. P. Simpson, F. Groos, F. Herff, Jr., and Jesse Prossnoll.

### *TROUBLE OVER A KIRMESS.*

KINGSTON, N. Y., Feb. 4.—Preparations for the kirmess for the benefit of the new public hospital, which will open next Monday, are stirring up this place. One result of them is a quarrel between two social leaders, in which one said things to the other which may cause a suit for slander. The ministers are still talking against the kirmess, and three revivals of religion are in progress in as many churches. The ministers, when they visit the large villages near this city where the kirmess is advertised, speak in condemnation of the affair.

### *HEDSPETH IN A NEW RÔLE.*

CHICAGO, Feb. 4.—A dispatch from Jackson, Mich., says: "A few days ago a man giving his name as J. F. Beeby of Jackson, Mich., reported that he had been robbed at Niles. Investigation was made here, and it was ascertained that Beeby had never been heard of in Jackson. It now turns out that Beeby is Marion C. Hedspeth of Cooper County, Mo., who is wanted for robbing the Adams Express Company's messenger on the St. Louis and San Francisco train at Glendale of a large amount of currency and other property on the night of Nov. 30, 1891.

### *PARIS BANKERS ARRESTED.*

RUMORS THAT A GREAT FINANCIAL CRISIS IS IMPENDING.

PARIS, Feb. 4.—The afternoon papers confirm rumors that have been in circulation here regarding the financial troubles of a large banking house in this city. Two of the members of the firm, it is announced, were arrested last night and were subjected to a searching examination which lasted throughout the night. The names of several houses are mentioned as being in trouble, but there is no certainty as yet as to which one it is that is involved.

Shares of the Bank of Paris have dropped 40f. since Tuesday, and shares of the Crédit Foncier fell 25f. to-day.

The police refuse to say anything in regard to the reported arrests. Many diverse rumors with reference to the firm's affairs are in circulation. The *Temps* says it hears that the arrested culprits will be released in order to protect a high political personage who is implicated in the financial trouble and to avoid a financial crisis, which would involve 6,250,000f.

LONDON, Feb. 5.—The *Times's* Paris correspondent says: "What originated the panic was the suspension of the negotiations of the Ottoman Bank with a Swiss banking syndicate for the creation of an Eastern Stock Trust. Then came the rumor of the arrest of a banker, an affair which turned out to be merely a matter of deficit in an industrial enterprise guaranteed by the family of the inculpated manager. The Bourse is extremely susceptible, owing to the difficult and often uncertain position of one of its most enterprising financiers, who has been struggling for years, and whose eventual collapse is expected."

### *NO UNITARIANS WANTED.*

THEY WILL NOT BE INVITED TO ATTEND MR. SPURGEON'S FUNERAL.

LONDON, Feb. 4.—Mr. James Spurgeon declares that while the heads of every religious denomination will be invited to attend the funeral of his brother, the Rev. Mr. Spurgeon, which will be held on Thursday next in the Metropolitan Tabernacle, no Unitarians will be asked to be present.

MENTON, Feb. 4.—The coffin containing the remains of the Rev. Mr. Spurgeon has been taken to the Scotch church in this place, and to-day impressive services were held over the body. The church was decorated with palm branches and a few floral wreaths. A large number of the relatives, friends, and admirers of the deceased were present, and the church was not large enough to hold all who were desirous of gaining admission.

The services commenced at 10 o'clock. After the delivery of the addresses and the offering up of prayers there were read the telegram of condolence from the Prince of Wales and the message from Mr. Moody, the American evangelist, quoting the twenty-fifth and twenty-sixth verses of the eleventh chapter of St. John.

Upon the conclusion of the services the coffin was conveyed to a hearse beautifully decorated with flowers, and was taken to the railway station for conveyance to London. The hearse was followed by a number of carriages containing the mourners, and by many persons on foot. A large crowd gathered along the route from the church to the station and reverently watched the procession.

### *MRS. OSBORNE UNDER ARREST.*

SHE VOLUNTARILY SURRENDERS TO BE TRIED FOR PERJURY.

DOVER, Feb. 4.—Upon the arrival here to-day of the channel steamer from Calais, Florence Ethel Osborne came ashore. She was in charge of a detective. The detective and the lady were met by several policemen, who escorted them to the railway station, where they took the 4:25 P. M. train for London. There was much excitement on the pier when the story spread that the much-talked-of Mrs. Osborne had returned to England, and a large crowd of idlers followed the party on their way to the station.

Mrs. Osborne, for whose arrest on a charge of perjury a warrant is in the hands of the police, returned from Irun, in Spain, to surrender to the authorities of her own volition. She says she does not want to inflict any further ruin on her husband, Capt. Osborne, who, unless she came back and answered the charge against her, would be compelled to leave the army.

Capt. Osborne married the lady after Mrs. Hargreave had charged her with the theft of her jewels, and he was a firm believer in her innocence until indisputable proof of her guilt was placed before him. He has stood by her in all her troubles, and after she arrived at Irun he expressed to her his willingness to join her and accompany her in a flight to a more remote region if she so desired.

### *GREAT BRITAIN AT THE FAIR.*

HER APPROPRIATION SMALLER THAN THAT OF FRANCE, MEXICO, OR BRAZIL.

LONDON, Feb. 4.—The papers of this city to-day devote much attention to the report on the Chicago Columbian Exhibition made by Col. J. H. Sadler, British Vice Consul in that city.

The *Standard* says that the trading nations of all the world will compete at the fair and expresses the hope that British manufacturers and business men will realize this, adding that it hardly looks as if the British Government did, while France is giving £80,000, Brazil and Mexico each over £100,000, and England only £25,000. It will be a serious misfortune, the *Standard* says, if Great Britain is not adequately represented at the exhibition.

It concludes its article by expressing the hope that the Government will not sacrifice the interests of commerce by applying for smaller space than is likely to be required by the large number of British exhibitors.

### *THE EIDER'S PASSENGERS.*

BREMEN, Feb. 4.—The North German Lloyd steamer Havel, Capt. Jungst, from New-York Jan. 26, via Southampton, which arrived here this morning, had on board a large number of the passengers and a part of the crew of the North German Lloyd steamer Eider, which stranded on Atherfield Ledge, off the southwest coast of the Isle of Wight, during a fog on Monday night.

They had traveled overland from Atherfield to Cowes, whence they proceeded by steamer to Southampton. At this port they awaited the coming of the Havel, and upon her arrival there yesterday morning they were transferred to her.

### *CARDINAL MANNING'S POVERTY.*

LONDON, Feb. 4.—The will of the late Cardinal Manning was opened to-day. It showed that he possessed less than £100, which was in consols, and a collection of books. This fact speaks louder than words in showing the benevolence of the Cardinal. The will contains no statement of public interest.

### *JUSTICE BRADLEY'S WILL.*

NEWARK, Feb. 4.—The will of the late Justice Bradley of the United States Supreme Court was offered for probate yesterday. It was drawn at Litchfield, Conn., last September, with Sydney Dillon as one of the witnesses. It bequeaths all of his estate to his widow for life, and at her death to his children.

### *SAN FRANCISCO EXCHANGE.*

SAN FRANCISCO, Feb. 4.—Drafts—Sight, 20; telegraphic, 27½.



## VOTERS FAVOR CLEVELAND

*THE FEELING EXISTING AMONG INDIANA DEMOCRATS.*

GRAY'S STRENGTH LARGELY FOR THE SECOND PLACE ON THE TICKET, ALTHOUGH HE MAY GET A COMPLIMENTARY VOTE FOR THE FIRST.

INDIANAPOLIS, Ind., Feb. 4.—Inquiry among the members of the Democratic Editorial Association, which held its midwinter meeting in this city to-day, developed the fact that Gov. Gray is not the first choice of all the Democratic editors of the State. Upon the positive promise that no names would be published in connection therewith, a poll of undoubted reliability was secured. Gov. Gray led the procession slightly, but it is plain that Cleveland has a powerful hold upon the people. Some of the Gray men and others of the Cleveland men refused to name a second choice, and for this reason the totals show a slight discrepancy.

The following is the vote as polled according to the preference of each member:

| | |
|---|---|
| Gray—first choice | 20 |
| Gray—second choice | 18 |
| Cleveland—first choice | 16 |
| Cleveland—second choice | 8 |
| Hill—first choice | 3 |
| Hill—second choice | 8 |

The main support of Gray seems to come from the fact that he is an Indiana man, and the only Indiana man who has been directly mentioned in connection with the Democratic nomination. Not long ago a leading Democrat of the State made the statement that Indiana had no Presidential candidate, and this is taken to mean that, while Gray's support is of considerable extent, it is rather of the perfunctory kind, as far as the first place is concerned.

Gray will undoubtedly, however, have a strong following for the Vice Presidential nomination, arising out of the agreement which is believed to exist as a result of the last Senatorial election, when Mr. Voorhees was returned to the Senate. When this election was pending in the Legislature of 1889 Gray became for a time a rather powerful opponent to the Tall Sycamore of the Wabash. This brought about the agreement before mentioned. A conference was had between the supporters of Senator Voorhees and Gov. Gray, and it was agreed by the former that if Gray would keep out of the Senatorial contest no obstacles would be placed in the way by the Indiana Democrats of his securing the Democratic Vice Presidential nomination in 1892. The fruit of this agreement is now maturing, and while Gov. Gray will probably receive the complimentary vote of the Indiana delegation at the Chicago Convention for first place, the real work and real support will be for his nomination for the Vice Presidency.

Though there is practically no active campaigning going on throughout the State in behalf of any of the leading Presidential aspirants, there is no question that Cleveland is the favorite of the masses, who favor him largely because of his unequivocal position on the tariff. The silver question is entirely secondary to the tariff in Indiana, and the ex-President seems to be the logical representative of the Hoosier citizens on this issue. Probably 95 per cent. of the Indiana Democrats, especially of that portion not directly connected with politics, favor him, and there is no question that if the selection was made at this time the voice of Indiana's Democratic masses would be almost unanimous for his election.

Hill's supporters are not numerous, but they are very noisy in their support of New-York's new Senator. They point to his "strength" in New-York and what they believe to be his popularity with large numbers of the people throughout the country as reasons for his nomination. The astute politician, however, is chary about expressing his preferences at this time, saying that there is no telling what may develop between now and June 21 to alter the situation. All agree that Gov. Gray is Indiana's candidate, because he is the only candidate that Indiana has, and the Democratic phase of that State pride which did so much for Harrison in 1888 is now showing itself. There seems to be hardly a question, though, at this time, that Indiana will have him nominated for second place if she can.

ST. PAUL, Feb. 4.—There is about no Hill sentiment in Minnesota. The Democratic National Committeeman, Michael Doran, is uncompromisingly for Cleveland and unsparingly denounces Hill. Chairman Campbell, and almost every other member of the State Central Committee, are for Cleveland, and interviews with Democrats in all the large cities of the State show that more than 90 per cent. of the voters are for Cleveland.

They also manifest a great deal of irritation when discussing Hill, and if the latter were nominated it is thought that at least 15 per cent. of them would refuse to vote for him.

### *FOR THE CHINA STATION.*

THE BALTIMORE LIKELY TO JOIN ADMIRAL HARMONY'S SQUADRON.

WASHINGTON, Feb. 4.—Capt. Schley has asked Secretary Tracy to allow him to remain in command of the cruiser Baltimore, and has intimated that he would like to go to the China station in her. His wishes will probably be gratified, as there is need for more ships on that station, where they may be wanted at any moment on account of the anti-missionary riots that are liable to break out. If it had not been for the Chilean trouble, there would have been an increase of the Asiatic squadron some time ago. In fact, the Charleston was sent over, but was almost immediately recalled so as to be on hand for service against Chile if necessary.

If the Baltimore is sent to China, her first cruise will have been remarkable, in the fact that she will have served on every naval station during its progress. She was first the flagship of the North Atlantic and was then sent to Europe to carry the body of John Ericsson to Sweden. She was in the Mediterranean when she was ordered to Chile, and she went to the South Pacific by way of the South Atlantic. She is now in the North Pacific, and a trip to China will complete the circuit. The Baltimore will be quite an addition to Admiral Harmony's squadron, and it is probable that he will transfer his flag to her from the Lancaster, his present flagship, though the latter vessel has rather the larger cabins and is very comfortable.

It is understood that one or two more vessels besides the Baltimore will be sent to China soon, and it is probable that the Yorktown and the Bennington will be selected for this duty, as most of the trouble there is in the river towns, where vessels of the Baltimore's size cannot go, and where the smaller vessels have to be depended upon altogether.

### *THE BOSTON MUSEUM COMPANY.*

ITS MEMBERS NOT DISSATISFIED AND FEW CHANGES EXPECTED.

BOSTON, Feb. 4.—A somewhat sensational article was published here this afternoon, in which a member of the Boston Museum company was quoted as saying that his associates were greatly discontented, and that several of them were to leave at the end of the present season.

There seems to be but the slightest foundation for such a story. For years it has been the custom of the management of the Museum to engage its actors for the coming season during the months of February and March, and no exception has been made to that rule this year. Only one old member has been re-engaged thus far, and that is Mr. Wilson. Of the three actors who were mentioned as being about to leave, Mr. Davenport has already advertised in a New-York dramatic paper for a situation, Mr. Booth has made an application for a re-engagement, and Miss Burress's contract is such that her presence in the Museum company next season is a certainty.

So far as is known, there will be no marked changes in the organization next year. John E. Kellard, the leading man of the "Lost Paradise" company, has been spoken of as being engaged for a similar position in the Museum company next year. That is not the case. Mr. Field has not even made him an offer.

### *THE POPE IS A SOVEREIGN.*

PARIS, Feb. 4.—In the case of the disputed right of the late Marquise Plessis to make the Pope her universal legatee, the court to-day decided that, in spite of the events of 1870 and the abolition of temporal power, the Pope is a sovereign, and is entitled to inherit property in France like other sovereigns.

### *NEW HONOR FOR AMERICANS.*

PHILADELPHIA, Feb. 4.—Prof. Henry W. Rolfe of the University of Pennsylvania and Edward T. Devine, staff lecturer of the American Society for the extension of university teaching, have been invited to deliver each a course of lectures at the Oxford Summer meeting in the month of August. This is the first time that such an honor has been conferred upon Americans.

### *THE NEBRASKA GOVERNORSHIP.*

ANOTHER SCHEME TO KEEP BOYD FROM THE EXECUTIVE CHAIR.

OMAHA, Neb., Feb. 4.—Another scheme developed to-day whereby Gov. Boyd will be indefinitely deprived of the chief executive chair of Nebraska. It is reported on the undisputed authority of a prominent Republican State official that Lieut. Gov. Majors will assume the duties and responsibilities of Governor next week. Gov. Thayer has announced that he will then start South, to remain permanently. The official quoted says:

"Majors will call a special session of the Legislature, and he will enumerate specifically the matters that the Legislature shall take into consideration. An additional appropriation for the World's Fair will be one, and there will be a lot of minor improvements suggested for the Australian ballot system adopted at the last session. But the railroad and freight rate question will be studiously avoided. This is attributed to a plan of the railroad managers, who fear that if Boyd gets into office now he will convene the Legislature and transact some disastrous railroad legislation. If Majors can get in and convene the Legislature, the expenses incurred will prevent Boyd calling another special session when he gets in, and thus no railroad legislation will take place."

The gentleman said further: "Majors is aching all over to get in to office any way, and this is about the best chance, possibly, that he will ever have. Then it will be a very nice way to get around the question of legality as to the action of the present incumbent. Thayer is afraid to exercise the full power of a Governor as matters now stand, because he is afraid his action might be illegal, but he wants to keep Boyd out of the office just as long as possible. If he can get Majors in the chair and block up the way for Gov. Boyd for another sixty days he will do it."

### *CRAZED BY HIS LOSSES.*

JUDGE RITTER OF GLASGOW, KY., A DEFAULTER AND INSANE.

LOUISVILLE, Ky., Feb. 4.—Judge John Ritter, cashier of the Deposit Bank of Glasgow, which failed a few days ago, is a defaulter and insane. He was found to be in debt to the bank for $25,000.

Judge Ritter, besides being one of the representative citizens of Barren County, is one of the most widely-known men in that part of the State. When the failure of the Deposit Bank was announced as imminent, Judge Ritter took prompt measures to turn over to the bank all of his property, worth about $10,000. Yesterday morning the Judge arose at 7 o'clock, ate his breakfast, and walked into the bank, which is now in the hands of a receiver. About 9:30 o'clock the Judge went to his home.

In the rear of Judge Ritter's house is a large field in which several farm hands were working. At 10 o'clock their attention was attracted toward the house by loud cries for help, and they saw running across the field a man perfectly nude, gesticulating like a maniac. He was recognized as Judge Ritter, their employer, and they all started in pursuit.

After a long chase he was captured and overpowered and removed to the house. Dr. Grinstead, the family physician, pronounced the affliction a case of acute insanity brought on by great mental strain. Judge Ritter's financial trouble is assigned to injudicious speculations.

### *JACKSON IS SORE.*

HE THINKS HE WAS NOT TREATED RIGHT IN THE SENATORIAL CONTEST.

BALTIMORE, Feb. 4.—Ex-Gov. Jackson is still very sore over his defeat for the United States Senatorship. In an interview published to-night he says that it was due to misrepresentation of his responsibility in the Archer case.

"In regard to Mr. Gibson," he continued, speaking with more emphasis, "I have this to say: If I had been in his place and he in mine, there is not money enough, there is not power enough, and there are not offices enough to have made me accept the place without first going to him.

"Mr. Gibson has said that he had made no pledges. There was no occasion for any. It was I who sent him to Congress three out of four times. After his appointment by me he was very profuse in his thanks. He said he was for me for the place, and that he had made three or four speeches in his county in my favor.

"Within twenty-four hours afterward, however, he was a candidate working for the place, and, I am informed, sent some of his former colleagues in the National House of Representatives to Gorman to urge the latter to use his influence in Gibson's favor for the Senatorship.

"The fact is, Mr. Gibson wanted the office so badly that he could not help working for it."

### *DR. MACKENZIE'S SOUVENIRS.*

GIFTS FROM THE ROYAL PATIENTS SIR MORELL HAD TREATED.

LONDON, Feb. 4.—The house occupied by Sir Morell Mackenzie, the celebrated English physician who died last night, contains a large number of gifts from celebrated people whom he had attended in sickness.

A photograph of the picture of Empress Frederick of Germany, (eldest daughter of Queen Victoria,) painted by Angeli, with her signature, hangs in the place of honor in one of the rooms. A framed letter from the late Emperor Frederick hangs over the mantel beside a letter from Queen Victoria to Emperor Frederick. The Queen's letter reads:

DEAR FRITZ: I shall take pleasure in conferring Knighthood on the physician who has rendered you and us such great services, for Dr. Mackenzie has indeed treated you with the greatest skill. VICTORIA, R. I.

### *AN EXCHANGE AS A NUISANCE.*

BOSTON, Feb. 4.—Robert Codman, who owns the property in Exchange Place between the Boston Exchange Building and Kilby Street, was reported to-day to have sued Mr. Cotting, as representative of the Exchange Building, for maintaining a nuisance in the shape of the Stock Exchange. Mr. Codman said this afternoon, however, that the report that he had begun suit was untrue.

"I suffer considerably from the noises issuing from the floor of the Exchange," he said. "My tenants complain bitterly of the yelling and screeching, which is annoying and irritating. Some of the tenants threaten to move out unless something is done to remedy the matter. We are going to settle the question amicably without going to law, however."

### *IT WAS PADLEWSKI.*

SAN ANTONIO, Texas, Feb. 4.—It has now been established beyond doubt that Otto Hauser, who was found dead in a park on Oct. 28, was the Nihilist, Stanislaus Padlewski, who assassinated Gen. Michael de Seliverskoff in Paris, Nov. 18, 1890. Dr. Louis Schroeder of Buffalo, N. Y., who knew him in Warsaw, Poland, writes here that Hauser was Padlewski, and that to avoid detection he traveled under different names—in Posen being known as Otto Hoffman, in New-York as Otto Heller, and in Buffalo and Texas as Otto Hauser.

Padlewski wrote Shroeder that he feared he would be delivered up to the Russian Government, but declared that he would never be taken alive.

### *PUBLISHER BANKS MUST PAY.*

ALBANY, N. Y., Feb. 4.—Charles W. Little, a law bookseller, brought action against A. Bleecker Banks to recover damages for the nonperformance of a contract between the defendant and the State for the publication of the New-York law reports. Mr. Banks had the contract for publishing the reports, which he agreed in the contract to sell to the public at a certain rate. Mr. Little tried to buy some of the volumes at the price named, but Mr. Banks would not sell any to him, hence the suit. A judgment for the one-thousand-dollar penalty was given for Little in the Circuit Court to-day.

### *THE FLORIDA'S CREW SAFE.*

LONDON, Feb. 4.—The White Star Line steamer Britannic, Capt. Smith, from New York Jan. 27 for Liverpool, arrived at Queenstown to-day. She reported that on Feb. 2 she signaled the British steamer Victoria, Capt. Gray, from Philadelphia Jan. 19 for Hamburg. The latter vessel reported that she had on board the crew of the Norwegian bark Florida, Capt. Ellefsen, from Pascagoula Dec. 21 for Dordrecht, abandoned at sea.

## NEITHER SIDE WILL YIELD

*LOUISIANA'S CAMPAIGN LIVELY WITHOUT THE LOTTERY.*

RIFLES BOUGHT BY THE CASE—MANY EVIDENCES OF BITTER FEELING—DISTRUST OF THE LOTTERY'S INTENTIONS.

NEW-ORLEANS, La., Feb. 4.—The withdrawal of the lottery proposition from the politics of the State greatly relieves the situation. Political excitement had been growing every day, until the feeling on both sides had grown so bitter that it was almost impossible for the campaign to have closed without some terrible disaster.

But although the chief disturbing element is gone, there are still two Democratic tickets in the field, and neither will surrender. The Foster faction maintains that it is the true Democratic Party and therefore entitled to possession of the State, while the McEnery people are as determined as ever to maintain their position. All rests with Gov. Nicholls, who conducts the election. The Antis are determined to give no recognition to the other faction. Gov. Nicholls is shaping all matters to the end that the McEnery ticket shall not be represented inside the polling booths. Several Anti parishes, notably Natchitoches, have already declared to that effect.

Both sides continue to anticipate a hard struggle, and even a bloody one, notwithstanding the retirement of the lottery issue. Gov. Nicholls is making the militia available by mustering out commands he cannot depend upon and deposing chiefs to be succeeded by men of his own liking. Semi-military commands of Foster men have been organized in all parts of the city, and are being armed from the State Armory.

The McEnery faction has not been idle along this line either, and is organizing and preparing for the struggle. Yesterday the steamer El Paso, from New-York, brought a consignment of forty-four cases, containing 444 rifles and 3 cases of ammunition, to A. W. Crandall, Chairman of the McEnery Campaign Committee.

The withdrawal of the lottery proposition was made in all sincerity, it is believed. Yet there is no small number of Antis who refuse to believe that the action was taken in good faith, and say that the McEnery tickets will contain the amendment just as before, since the matter rests with the Secretary of State.

The *New Delta*, the organ of the Anti-Lottery Party in this State, will to-morrow contain an interview with E. B. Kruttschnitt, the Chairman of the Anti-Lottery Democratic State Executive Committee, who uses the following language:

"The letter published by Mr. John A. Morris in the morning papers, withdrawing his lottery proposition, does not make the slightest change in the campaign or in the programme of our party. We are all convinced that the withdrawal of the lottery proposition is not sincere; that is made merely in order to enable Mr. Morris and his associates to renew their scheme in a more insidious form.

"The proposition heretofore made by the lottery is no longer acceptable to its advocates by reason of the curtailment of its revenues through the late decision of the Supreme Court of the United States; but should their attempt to capture the State Government succeed, they may yet strive to call a constitutional convention under the pretext of regulating suffrage, as was done in the State of Mississippi.

"Then they may obtain another grant for the lottery in the new Constitution upon terms more favorable to its advocates than the amendment now before the people, or adopt some other means of achieving their object.

"All former experience with the lottery has taught us that it is fertile in occult schemes to effect its purposes. We intend to see that the amendment is voted down in April by such a majority as to preclude all possibility of further agitation of the question, and to make sure that none but anti-lottery men be placed on guard.

"We are perfectly satisfied with the present condition of the canvas, and with our prospects of success."

The action of the lottery company in refusing an extension of its charter is due to the fact that the anti-lottery postal law passed by Congress in 1890, and declared constitutional by the Supreme Court last week, has made it impossible for the company to do business and pay the State the annual license of $1,250,000.

The scheme of the lottery calls for 312 daily and 12 monthly drawings each year as follows: Two grand extraordinary semi-annual drawings with 100,000 tickets at $40 each, yielding, if all the tickets are sold, $8,000,000; ten monthly drawings with 100,000 tickets, each $20, 312 daily drawings with about 75,000 tickets at $1 each, only a small proportion of which are sold, besides policy tickets unlimited.

The total in the scheme is $31,322,000, if all the tickets are disposed of. The daily drawings, however, cut but a small figure, the tickets being sold only in Louisiana and mainly in New-Orleans. The monthly drawings have been the principal source of revenue, and for the success of these the use of the mails is indispensable.

From the moment the law was passed the business began to shrink. The first month it shrank nearly one-half. The company tested various schemes for getting rid of the law, and did a great deal of business through the express companies.

The company before the law had been paying dividends of 100 per cent. Its State charter had still four years to run.

BOSTON, Feb. 4.—Gen. G. D. Johnston, who is in this city, received a telegram from New-Orleans to-day, which stated that the anti-lottery people in that city look with great distrust upon the statements made yesterday by John A. Morris, announcing that the Louisiana State Lottery would not accept the proposed new charter if granted. The anti-lottery people, he says, are disposed to regard the card as a scheme to draw the attention of the public from some plan for future action which the lottery managers are concocting.

### *RESIN AND TURPENTINE CHEAP.*

PRICES BELOW THE RECORD MADE LAST YEAR.

SAVANNAH, Ga., Feb. 4.—In the last few days the price of resin has dropped 15 cents a barrel on lower grades. At present E and below are quoted at $1. One year ago they were quoted at $1.30.

On higher grades prices are correspondingly low, water white, the highest grade, being quoted at $3.90 against $4.25 last year. The price of spirits of turpentine is also down. On this date last year the quotation was 38 cents per gallon. To-day it is 31 cents. The difference means a decrease in value per cask of $3.12.

Statistics show that every year the demand grows, but the output from the Savannah district will be larger than ever before. In the Wilmington and Charleston district there will be a decrease. The world's supply as a result will not be increased to meet the increased demand, and good prices will result.

Exporters attribute the low prices of resin to the temporary cutting off of the demand from the Baltic provinces. Last year it was announced that the Russian Government intended to increase the import duty. The dealers there at once stocked up and accumulated a large supply sufficient to carry them over this season.

Last year in January, February, and March 5,000 barrels were shipped from Savannah to the Baltic ports. This year nothing has been sent there.

### *BANKER DILL DISCHARGED.*

PITTSBURG, Feb. 4.—A special from Clearfield, Penn., says: "The embezzlement case against Banker Dill here ended to-day.

"Judge Mayer took the case from the jury. He said that the prosecution against Dill could not stand. He, therefore, ordered that a verdict of 'not guilty, but pay the costs,' be recorded, and Dill was discharged."

### *FORTY PERSONS DROWNED.*

BERLIN, Feb. 4.—Thirty barges were torn from their moorings by drift ice at Breslau to-day. Several of the barges sank, and it is reported that forty persons were drowned, including many women and children. The fate of the occupants of the barges was the cause of many heartrending scenes.

### *RESULT OF THE NEW FRENCH TARIFF.*

PARIS, Feb. 4.—Prices are rising rapidly as a result of the new tariff. Pork and mutton have advanced 2d. per pound. Italian and Dutch cheese has risen 100 per cent., and foreign soap 200 per cent. The extra cost to workmen for necessaries of life is estimated at 1f. daily.

The Danube has overflowed its banks in the Pesth district, causing much distress.

10 Pages

# The New-York Times.

10 Pages

VOL. XLI....NO. 12,631. NEW-YORK, THURSDAY, FEBRUARY 18, 1892. PRICE THREE CENTS.



## WHERE CLEVELAND LEADS

### THE CHOICE OF MOST OF THE MISSOURI DEMOCRATS.

ONE FRIEND OF HILL SHOWN BY A POLL OF THE LEGISLATURE—FRIENDS OF BOIES—TARIFF THE ISSUE.

JEFFERSON CITY, Mo., Feb. 17.—The members of the thirty-sixth General Assembly of Missouri have manifested the greatest interest in the coming National Conventions, and are daily and hourly discussing national candidates. A partial poll of the House and Senate to-day shows the members still largely for Cleveland. But one Hill vote was found, that one being by Representative Mayo of Greene County.

The next strongest Democrat, in the estimation of the Legislature, is Gov. Boies of Iowa. It was a peculiar fact that not one of the members suggested Cleveland as second choice, those who are for him being for him first, last, and all the time. Following is the recapitulation of the vote by the members present at the time the poll was taken:

First Choice—Cleveland, 30; Hill, 1; Boies, 12; Palmer, 5; Flower, 3; Carlisle, 2; Morrison, 2.
Second Choice—Boies, 27; Morrison, 8; Palmer, 6; Carlisle, 6; Flower, 3; Gray, 2; Gorman, 1; Vest, 1.

The Republican members rallied largely to Blaine, with an evident leaning toward Harrison in the event Blaine persists in remaining out of the race. Following are the Republican preferences:

First choice—Blaine, 9; Harrison, 6; McKinley, 1; Weaver, 1.
Second choice—Lincoln, 11; Harrison, 6; McKinley, 4; Gresham, 1; Blaine, 1.

Following are the expressions of some of the leaders of the Democratic Party of the State:

E. P. Stone—First choice, Grover Cleveland; second choice, the strongest Western man, to be determined by the National Convention for the welfare of the people; the issue of greater interest than the man. The issue is tariff reform. Grover Cleveland has proved that he thoroughly comprehends the issue and possesses the moral courage to declare and enforce it. I believe the wisdom, honesty, intelligence, and true Democracy of the country approve his record, and will support him if nominated.

J. F. Davidson—First choice, Grover Cleveland; second choice, William R. Morrison. If New-York will not support Cleveland, then we had better risk defeat under the leadership of some other honest tariff-reform Democrat than court success under the banner of a Republican parading under the mask of a Democrat.

Robert O. McLin—First choice, Grover Cleveland; second choice, some Western man. If New-York will not concede to the West the New-York nominee they want, then let the West select some Western man.

C. B. Baird—First choice, Cleveland; second choice, Carlisle. If Hill beats Cleveland in New-York State I favor Carlisle as first choice; as second choice, the Western field.

James F. Kinney—First choice, Boies; second choice, Carlisle. We want free silver and free trade, do away with banks, elect all officers by direct vote of the people.

C. C. Fogle—First choice, Boies; second choice, Carlisle. I am of the opinion that the tariff reform question will be the leading question in the next campaign.

Thomas F. Dookery—First choice, Flower; second choice, Gray; Boies of Iowa for Vice President.

## GEORGIA FOR CLEVELAND.

SHOWING OF A POLL OF PROMINENT DEMOCRATS OF THE STATE.

ATLANTA, Ga., Feb. 17.—The State Central Democratic Committee will not meet until the 2d of March, and consequently no official form has as yet been given to the Presidential campaign in this State. Notwithstanding this, the Atlanta *Journal*, as the advocate of Mr. Cleveland, and the Atlanta *Constitution*, as the defender of Mr. Hill, have been carrying on a preliminary campaign which has grown interesting.

The *Journal* to-day announces as the latest phase of the poll it is making of the State the following preferences:

Total prominent Georgians polled, 1,460; for Grover Cleveland, 1,022; David Bennett Hill, 808; no choice, 84. The nominee, 24; Alliance man, 4; New-York man, 11; Gray, (of Indiana,) 13; Arthur P. Gorman, 26; free-coinage man, 2; Western man, 1; Holman, 1; Polk, 2; Crisp, 1; Morrison, 1; Hill or Gorman, 1; J. C. C. Black, 1; Roswell P. Flower, 1; Roger Q. Mills, 1; anti-tariff man, 1; Tom Watson, 1.

Among the prominent citizens who to-day announce their preference for Mr. Cleveland are ex-Senator Johnson of Muscogee, Judge Alexander McArthur of Montgomery County, and Col. J. B. Wilson of Crawford County. Senator Johnson, who is strong in West Georgia, says:

"Mr. Cleveland is unquestionably the greatest living exponent of pure and undefiled Democratic doctrines. The mantle of Samuel J. Tilden, the greatest Democratic leader since the days of Thomas Jefferson, has undoubtedly fallen upon his shoulders, and he wears it well. To compare Hill to Cleveland is to compare a pigmy to a giant, a political trickster to a statesman, and a vulture to an eagle. Mr. Cleveland is an advocate of principles, while Mr. Hill is the tool of political and financial intriguers.

"The only objection that I have heard urged against Mr. Cleveland by Democrats was that during his Administration he adhered too closely to the enforcement of the civil service law. I have felt the same way, but I must confess the fact that he only did his duty and enforced the law as he was sworn to do. The attempt to impress the country with the idea that Mr. Hill is a better friend to the people than Mr. Cleveland—a better and a purer Democrat—will in my opinion fall flat. The free coinage of silver is certainly an insignificant question in comparison with tariff reform, and the people will not be misled by the effort to rush it to the front.

"It is evident that the political wireworkers will do all in their power to thrust Mr. Hill upon the country as the Democratic nominee for President, but defeat for the party would be inevitable if they should succeed. Let every good citizen see that the delegation from Georgia is for Grover Cleveland and good government."

The citizens of Rome will probably organize a Cleveland Club next Monday night.

## THE VOICE OF MARYLAND.

BALTIMORE, Feb. 17.—A canvass of Presidential preferences in the various counties is being taken in this State. So far, the expressions are practically unanimous for Cleveland. There is not a single vote for Hill. The legislative correspondent of the *News* to-night telegraphed as follows from Annapolis:

"Not a representative citizen comes here who, if he is a Democrat, does not express himself—and voice the sentiment of his county—for Cleveland. The strength of the ex-President with the masses seems to have more significance than ever, for nowhere is doubt expressed concerning him, even in quarters where his availability as a candidate was questioned not long ago. In view of this fact, it appears as if Senator Hill's snap-convention scheme is strengthening Cleveland's chances, as well as weakening his own."

## *MR. BRETT'S GOLDEN WEDDING.*

NEWARK, N. J., Feb. 17.—The golden wedding of Mr. and Mrs. Charles H. Brett was celebrated at the home of their son, Everett J. Brett, 50 South Street, this city, to-night. The couple were married in Matteawan, Dutchess County, N. Y., on Feb. 17, 1842, by the Rev. James M. Pease. Mr. Brett will be seventy-five years of age in July next. His wife is two years his junior. There are three children—C. Howard Brett of Lawrence, Kan.; Mrs. Oliver M. Jenks of Philadelphia, and Everett J. Brett, for many years with Tiffany & Co., New-York. There are five grandchildren—one a son of C. Howard Brett, a daughter and son of Mrs. Jenks, and a daughter and son of Everett J. Brett. The bridesmaid, Mrs. Barkley, is still living, and resides in One Hundred and Nineteenth Street, New-York City. Many letters of congratulation and gifts from friends were received, the presentation of the children being in the form of a joint gift in gold.

## *GOT RID OF THREE WIVES BY DIVORCES.*

NEWARK, Feb. 17.—Goetzel Leser Cohn, a Russian Hebrew, called upon Justice Doctor to-day and asked that the Justice take steps to compel his four children to pay him 50 cents a week each for his support. When Fischel Cohn, one of his sons, appeared in court in response to its summons, he admitted that the old man was his father.

"But," he said, "at 25 Broome Street lives my mother, an old woman, who was a true wife to this man for thirty-eight years. He obtained a divorce from her through a rabbi and put her out of the house. He was without money to pay the fee, and gave the rabbi an old overcoat in settlement of it. My mother came to Newark, and my brothers and I take care of her. This man has married twice since getting the divorce, and each time has got rid of his wives by divorces gotten from a rabbi."

The Justice denounced the old man as an old rascal and cleared him out of his court.

## *RIVALS FOR THE UNIVERSITY.*

A NEW QUESTION FOR THE MISSOURI LEGISLATORS.

JEFFERSON CITY, Mo., Feb. 17.—A remarkable contest is to be carried on throughout the entire extra session of the Missouri Legislature, which began here to-day. The immediate occasion for calling the Legislature in extra session was the destruction of the State University Building at Columbia by fire about six weeks ago.

There were reasons, including the Congressional redistricting of the State, why the extra session should have been called, but the Governor had refused to call it until after the university fire had made an immediate appropriation for rebuilding necessary. It has been understood that $250,000 is to be appropriated for the purpose, but it has also been understood that the question of a site for the building of a new university was also to be considered.

Eight or ten of the most enterprising cities of the State have been competing to secure the location with offers of lands, and some of them with propositions to erect buildings costing $250,000. Columbia, the old site, has made no proposition whatever.

In his message to-day Gov. Francis called the attention of legislators to the fact that they were to be restricted to work indicated in the call for the extra session. This is understood to mean that only an appropriation without change of location is to be considered. Representatives from districts in the competition are in ugly mood thereat.

The Governor says, with emphasis, that the Assembly must confine its operations to the subjects mentioned in the proclamation. Nothing whatever is said about the movement to take the university from Columbia. The Assembly can do nothing now but appropriate the $400,000 to be expended in Columbia or refuse to appropriate a penny.

## *SOCIETY IN THE ORANGES.*

THE CLOSING ASSEMBLY WAS A VERY SUCCESSFUL AFFAIR.

ORANGE, Feb. 17.—The closing Orange Assembly, held in Musical Hall this evening, was one of the most brilliant of this season's events in Orange society. The main hall was used for dancing, the parquet being floored over for the occasion. A palace scene was set on the stage, and a profuse display of ferns, palms, and roses constituted the decorations. The balcony was literally covered with a robe of roses. Supper was served in the upper hall. The affair was commenced at an early hour with a cotillion. Among those present were:

W. D. Osborn, Mrs. T. S. Kingman, Miss Webb, Frank Q. Barstow, I. Day Flack, Richard S. Storrs, Mr. and Mrs. A. J. Woodworth, Miss Bowen, John Wiley, Mr. and Mrs. William Barr, A. C. Zimmermann, Mr. and Mrs. J. V. Bacot, Miss Roundery, Miss Richey, Frank Richey, John N. Robins, J. Wood Wentworth, Mrs. A. D. Smith, Douglass Schneider, Norman McElliott, James Marshall, George Richards, Mrs. L. C. Fairchild, George C. Fairchild, S. Bayard Dodd, George L. Wall, Henry A. Potter, Alden Freeman, Miss Smith, Edward B. Aymar, Mr. and Mrs. W. H. Aymar, Stephen M. Smith, Bertha Fuller, George N. Gill, William E. Quimby, Miss Cynthia Quimby, Frank Childs, Edward H. Graves, J. H. Hyde, Farnham Yardley, Miss Carter, W. R. Stephenson, E. N. Fay, Mr. and Mrs. William M. Vanderkieft, F. Bird Dixey, Miss May Jennings, Miss Ward, Miss Helen Stocking, Miss Beckwith, Walter Osborn, Mr. and Mrs. Arthur Colby, Harry Burdick, Winthrop Burdick, Graham Brewer, Robert M. Miles, Lewis H. Hyde, Allerton D. Hitch, Miss Hitch, S. B. Wiley, Mrs. S. H. Howe, Newell B. Woodworth, Miss Martin, Mr. and Mrs. A. W. Vanderhof, Mrs. C. A. Sterling, Miss Sterling, John Rafferty, R. W. Speir, Miss Wallis, Col. A. H. Ryan, B. T. Kissam, Roland S. Pettitt, Mr. and Mrs. Cyrus Leutrell, Mr. and Mrs. John Pettitt.

## *THE GERMANS IN EAST AFRICA.*

CORRESPONDENT WOLFF MAKES SOME VERY SERIOUS CHARGES.

BERLIN, Feb. 17.—Eugen Wolff, the newspaper correspondent, whose reports to the *Tageblatt* on the disaster to the Zelewski expedition and other matters caused Chancellor von Caprivi to order his expulsion from German East Africa in November last, has published an amplified attack on Baron Soden's administration of the Governorship of the East African colony.

It will be remembered that about the middle of September last word was received that in the then recent fight between the German corps under Capt. Zelewski and a body of natives 300 of Capt. Zelewski's blacks were killed and all the guns and ammunition were lost. Besides Capt. Zelewski, Officers Zitewitz and Pieroh, Dr. Dunschow, and four non-commissioned officers were reported missing.

Wolff now declares that no reports on the actual losses in the last two fights with the natives have ever been published. Nor, he adds, has the fact ever been announced that an English caravan had been plundered. Wolff says that all the officers of experience in East Africa have either been dismissed from the service or have resigned in disgust, and that the Soden régime has destroyed public confidence and stopped progress, and is bound to end in disaster.

Wolff's article will form the subject of an interpellation in the Reichstag.

## *TARIFF THE RIGHT ISSUE.*

CONGRESSMAN BRECKINRIDGE ON THE DUTY OF DEMOCRATS.

BOSTON, Feb. 17.—"It is my belief that the move of the Ways and Means Committee in placing three bills before Congress affords at least some promise that we are going to do something with the tariff question," said Congressman W. C. P. Breckinridge of Kentucky at the Parker House this afternoon. He is here to deliver an address on "Southern Problems" before the Young Men's Catholic Union in the hall of Boston College.

"If the Democratic Party will back that move," he added, "by demanding that the bills passed by the House shall be a substantial repeal of the McKinley bill, it may furnish an opportunity for the Democrats to make a platform which the people will believe in, and then there will be some hope of electing a Democratic President, if the right man is selected, next Fall. In my judgment, the only hope of electing a Democratic President is to nominate a candidate who will in himself and his past political life afford a sufficient platform for the party, so that the country will understand that his nomination and election means in good faith not only a pledge, but a promise that the pledge will be kept if he is elected. Any form of an ambiguous or uncertain platform simply means Democratic defeat."

Among the prominent men who called on Gen. Breckinridge to-day was ex-Congressman John E. Russell. They are very warm personal friends.

## *LONDON-MADE CLOTHING SEIZED.*

TWO MORE OF KENDRICK'S TRUNKS CAPTURED IN BOSTON.

BOSTON, Feb. 17.—Converse J. Smith, Special Agent of the Treasury Department, to-day seized a lot of clothing from the London house of F. Poole & Co., imported principally for students and professors of Harvard College. For several months the Special Agents in this city have been looking for clothing from England, it being the impression that, if duties were paid, the clothing was greatly undervalued. The present seizure substantiates the belief.

The person bringing in the merchandise is Henry B. Kendrick, a resident of this city, who arrived in New-York last week on the Teutonic with three large trunks, two of which came to this city in bond. The third was seized in New-York.

In the trunks arriving at this port are sixteen suits of clothes, one of which is a dress suit, rich overcoats, extra trousers, a white vest, samples, &c., all intended for Spring or Summer service. The declared value of the contents of the two trunks is £55, while the invoices found more than double the value.

## *HELD ON A SERIOUS CHARGE.*

NEWARK, Feb. 17.—Charles Dexheimer of East Orange is held by Police Justice Hayes to answer a serious charge. He had been till yesterday morning employed in the leather factory of Joshua Weil at 15 New-York Avenue, this city. Yesterday he was discharged. It is alleged that, with the knowledge that he was to be dismissed, he closed the steam gauge on the boiler, and unscrewed the nuts and bolts on the steam chest. But for the discovery of the disarrangements there would have been an explosion and many lives would have been imperilled.

## *MAKING PEACE WITH HARRISON.*

QUAY AND CAMERON SAID TO BE READY FOR A DEAL.

PHILADELPHIA, Feb. 17.—A special dispatch to the *Times* from Washington says: "It is an open secret within limited political circles in this city that a movement for a reconciliation between the President and Senators Cameron and Quay has been in progress for some days, and it is confidently asserted that it will be effected before Senator Quay's return from Florida. By this our Pennsylvania Senators will resume their control of Pennsylvania patronage and Harrison will be given the vote of Pennsylvania for renomination.

"This is not a mere rumor, and I speak advisedly when I say that the effort to reconcile these parties has taken positive shape and has been steadily progressing since Quay left on his Southern journey. Strange as it may seem, negotiations are actually conducted by Dudley, although he is not brought into personal relation with Harrison. Dudley has been very fortunate during the present Administration in building up a profitable practice in the different departments, and while Harrison and Dudley have had no personal intercourse, the President has not in any way interfered with or hindered Dudley's professional success. Dudley now regards it as his interest to have the present Administration continue for another four years. While the President is personally distasteful to him, he is not only in the deal to aid in Harrison's renomination, but he is really the master spirit in conducting the negotiations.

"I have every reason to believe that these negotiations will be successfully concluded by the time that Senator Quay returns from Florida next week. He did not choose to appear in them at all, but that they have been conducted in his absence, with his knowledge and with the assurance that if satisfactorily concluded he would give his assent, there is no reason whatever to doubt. I have reason to believe that the President confidently expects within a few weeks to have the support of Quay and Cameron in Pennsylvania and thus practically control the delegation of the State, and to have the active co-operation of Dudley in Indiana, which would disarm the opposition to Harrison in his own State. If so, the renomination of Harrison will be absolutely assured, and, with the announcement of such a combination in the interest of Harrison, no opposition candidate could take the field with any reasonable hope of success.

"It is safe to say that this movement would not have been made had it not been for the apprehension on the part of Quay and Dudley that Harrison may be renominated in spite of all their efforts to defeat him."

## *BOUND TO RETIRE QUAY.*

ADDRESS ISSUED BY THE PENNSYLVANIA REPUBLICAN ASSOCIATION.

PHILADELPHIA, Feb. 17.—The Pennsylvania Republican Association, through its Executive Committee, to-day issued the following address to Republican voters:

"Believing that the best interests of the Republican Party demand the retirement of M. S. Quay from the United States Senate at the expiration of his present term, and that he should be succeeded by a Republican possessed of the qualities necessary to perform the duties of that high and responsible position, we hereby appeal to you for your support in our effort to accomplish this result.

"We, and those in whose behalf and by whose direction this declaration is made, have no other purpose in view than the advancement of the true principles of the Republican Party and the highest interest of our Commonwealth and country. This declaration comes from the Pennsylvania Republican Association, whose members have always believed that the remedy for evils of leadership is to be found by timely and well-directed action within party lines, such as we propose to pursue in this instance. But as American citizens we can remain no longer silent and see a man continued in place and power whose influence is constantly working to the detriment of our party, our State, and our Nation, and we therefore are impelled to make the positive declaration contained in our sentiments and are prepared to make it effective by giving our time and our means to that end.

"A point has been reached where, unless prompt action is taken within the Republican Party to deprive Mr. Quay of further capacity for disastrous leadership, the party in this State will utterly fail to achieve its true mission, and will, sooner or later, meet with final overthrow. We have no personal feelings or grievance against Mr. Quay. We regret that his conduct as a party leader and United States Senator has rendered it impossible for us to longer support him. We do not forget the services which he has rendered the party, and, while giving full credit therefor, cannot but feel that he has not only been amply rewarded by the bestowal of its abundant official and pecuniary favors, but that the scale has been turned against him by the evils and defeats he has brought upon the party."

After reviewing Quay's record and giving reasons why he should not be supported, the address concludes:

"We issue this address by the authority of the Pennsylvania Republican Association, whose Executive Committee we are, which organization has its representatives in every Republican county of the State, and which was born of the necessity for concerted action to oppose the banded officialism which has been at the beck and call of Mr. Quay. It is the purpose of our organization to carry on the contest strictly within party lines, and to secure the election of a majority of Republican members of the next Legislature who will unalterably oppose the re-election of M. S. Quay to the United States Senate, and who will favor the choice of any honest Republican as his successor, whose personal character, intellectual and forensic ability, statesman-like qualities and loyalty to the Republican Party shall stamp him as a fitting representative of the great Keystone State in the upper House of Congress."

## *THE NORTH STAR CLUB INCIDENT.*

IT IS THE TALK OF THE POLITICIANS OF MINNESOTA.

ST. PAUL, Feb. 17.—The snub given to the North Star Democratic Club by the Democratic State Central Committee yesterday has been the talk of the State to-day.

The North Star Club is a State organization formed last June, and has a membership of nearly 8,000. Although nothing was said openly in regard to the real objects of the club, it soon became known everywhere that it had been launched into State politics to unhorse Kelly and Doran, the Minnesota dispensers of patronage under the last Administration.

In yesterday's State Committee meeting the Cleveland men, who stand by Messrs. Kelly and Doran, took occasion to rebuke the North Star men, who seem to be fighting Cleveland merely to get even with Kelly and Doran for a fancied slight. The Executive Committee of the North Star Club met in Minneapolis this afternoon and adopted the following resolution:

*Whereas*, The Democratic State Central Committee at its meeting held in St. Paul on the afternoon of Tuesday, Feb. 16, refused to recognize the North Star Democratic Club as an organization or as an adjunct of the State Central Committee, and, moreover resolved, that this club's pathway to prestige was conditioned upon its becoming a tail of the Minnesota Democratic Association's kite, therefore, be it

*Resolved*, That the North Star Association of Democratic Clubs in executive session assembled this day, declares that despite the evident attempt of the Democratic State Central Committee to control the possible patronage of the State to the exclusion of the party interests, the North Star Democratic Club will support the nominees of the Democratic Party, and will do so without expectation of reward or hope of being the sole arbiter of the distribution of the spoils in Minnesota.

## *SEVEN PERSONS HURT.*

A STREET CAR STRUCK BY A RAILROAD TRAIN IN NEWARK.

NEWARK, N. J., Feb. 17.—Horse Car No. 18 of the Broad Street line drove through the gates of the Morris and Essex Road here to-night and was struck by the 11:20 P. M. train from Morristown. The car was wrecked and seven persons were injured. Ten feet of the gate were broken off.

John Calligan, the driver of the car, of 99 Howard Street, Newark, was mortally injured. The injuries of the others are slight. The horses escaped.

The injured are:

JOHN CALLIGAN, driver.
JOHN KETCHAM, conductor; slightly.
ERNEST HERST, 56 Spring Street; back and head hurt.
FRANK GOULD, 216 Parkhurst Street; legs cut.
GEORGE W. JORALEMON, 23 Crane Street; legs and back cut with glass.
ANNIE BARCLAY, 84 Ogden Street; bruised and hurt internally.
SILAS MATTHEWS, Pompton Plains; cut by glass.

The blame for the accident is placed upon the driver.

## *COUNCILMEN'S GOLD BADGES STOLEN.*

BOSTON, Feb. 17.—Thieves have broken the hearts of the members of the Boston Common Council. The beautiful golden badges of office, which the members of the lower branch voted to themselves at the rate of $67.75 apiece, were ruthlessly taken from the express team that was conveying them to Boston and by this time the gold in them has no doubt been melted and transformed to some other design. The members expected to have an opportunity to pin the badges to their manly bosoms at the meeting of the Council to-morrow evening.

## TO PROBE THE COAL DEAL

### *THE NEW-JERSEY LEGISLATURE APPOINTS TWO COMMITTEES.*

INDICATIONS THAT GOV. ABBETT WILL WORK THE INVESTIGATION FOR POLITICAL EFFECT—HIS MEN CONTROL THE COMMITTEES.

TRENTON, Feb. 17.—The Senate took its little turn at the railroad coal combination this morning. Senator Hinchcliffe of Passaic started the ball a-rolling with a resolution directing the appointment of a special committee to investigate, report, &c. The Senators saw no objection to this harmless little diversion, and the special committee was appointed.

Courtesy required that, having offered the resolution, Mr. Hinchcliffe should be Chairman of the special committee, and, of course, when President Adrain came to make the selection, the Paterson mover was accorded the customary recognition, even though he is not a very earnest and enthusiastic Abbett man. But the Chairman gave him two cast-iron Abbett men in Senators Barrett and Keyes to keep him company. Mr. Barrett is one of the Governor's gilt-adorned military staff and Keyes is the most obsequious Abbett man in the Senate.

The tendencies of these gentlemen are noted because it is assumed here that the inquiry will not be prosecuted without its political bearing. Everybody takes it for granted that the Governor will mold the inquiry in such a way as to shape its results to the advancement of his Senatorial boom. President Adrain, to whose hands the resolution committed the selection of the committeemen, happens just now to be Gov. Abbett's choice for the Democratic Gubernatorial nomination, and he has won the Governor's gratitude by availing himself of the opportunity to appoint men on the committee a majority of whom the Governor can wind around his finger.

President Adrain happens also to stand in the Senate and in the approaching Gubernatorial contest as the particular ward of Boss Miles Ross of New-Brunswick. It is to please Mr. Ross that the Governor is disposed to look kindly upon Adrain's Gubernatorial aspirations. Mr. Miles Ross, in his turn, has some close and intimate relations to the problems the special committee is to consider. He has made his fortune as an agent in the handling of the coal output of the Lehigh Valley Railroad Company. Whether the new combine means for him the disaster of the loss of his job and promotion to a new prominence in the new system is one of the things no one seems to know just now. It can be easily seen, however, that, whichever it may mean for him, he is not an entirely disinterested watcher of results.

There is apt to be friction in the House between the two committees to which the subject was referred by Mr. Lane's resolution of last Monday night. The regular standing Committee on Railroads and Canals was directed by the resolution to find out what the nature of the deal between the contracting railroad companies was, and whether it is an invasion of public interest or a violation of law. The special committee was directed to find out how the combination can be defeated, if it should be defeated, and to devise a bill to that end. It seemed odd that one committee was given power to find out what was to be remedied without the power to apply the remedy and another was given the power to find out the remedy without knowing what it was that needed the remedy, and Lane's resolution, offered to-day, that the special committee be authorized to send for persons and papers was not unexpected.

The general idea was that the special committee was to send for only such persons and papers as it required for the formulation of its bill; but a member of the standing committee said to your correspondent to-day that the resolution of to-day is so sweeping in its character as to place the whole matter within the purview of the special committee, leaving nothing for his committee to do. Railroad men in the lobby regard the point as well taken, and the special committee will be the decisive factor in the solution of the problem.

The committee consists of Lane of Union, Daley of Middlesex, and Heaney of Hudson. Perhaps, if Speaker Bergen had not felt compelled by courtesy to name Mr. Lane, as the mover of the resolution, to the chairmanship of the committee, he might have preferred some one else. Lane is a Summit editor, with only faint leaning toward Abbett, and a man of general independence of action. He was charged on the floor of the House the other evening with having offered the resolution in the interest of the Pennsylvania Railroad; but railroad men say that he has no corporation affiliations. Daley is the creature of Boss Miles Ross. Heaney is known to have very close relations with Gov. Abbett. Through Daley and Heaney the Governor can probably give the inquiry whatever twist his interests may prompt.

A notable thing about the two committees—that in the Senate and that in the House—is that no Republican is on either. The misfortune that gave the chairmanship of each committee to legislators who do not wear the Abbett collar probably explains this legislative phenomenon. The other two places on the committee were needed for tractable men to outvote the Chairmen.

PHILADELPHIA, Feb. 17.—A special to the *Evening Telegraph* from Harrisburg says: "After the conference at the Executive Mansion last night between Gov. Pattison, Secretary Harrity, and Attorney General Hensel, the last named left for Lancaster. Mr. Harrity left for Philadelphia this morning.

"It cannot be learned what was done, but it is understood that the Reading deal was up for discussion, and that the matter has been placed in the hands of the Attorney General, not that he shall bring suit to prevent the consummation of the deal, but to prepare reasons for showing that the State cannot interfere in the matter.

"This statement will be given out for publication in the course of time, and the newspaper correspondents have been waiting in the antechamber of the Executive Department all day in expectancy. Private Secretary Tate professed not to know the character of the statement which he will in due time give out for publication, and everybody else in authority professed profound ignorance."

## GOV. PATTISON'S ATTITUDE.

A BRIEF STATEMENT FROM PENNSYLVANIA'S CHIEF MAGISTRATE.

HARRISBURG, Penn., Feb. 17.—Gov. Pattison, having had his attention directed to-day to various newspaper reports purporting to represent his attitude toward the railroad consolidation of last week and the contemplated action or non-action of the Law Department, said: "The first information, direct or indirect, I had of the mergers, leases, or consolidation of the coal-carrying companies was the newspaper reports of the same. Since their publication the bearing of the State Constitution upon the transaction and its effect upon the public interest and the welfare of the Commonwealth have been the subject of attention. I have conferred with the Attorney General on the subject, which is one that relates to his department exclusively, and I have entire confidence that he will dispose of it with due regard to the requirements of the law and the public interests involved.

"The published reports I have seen purporting to give his views or mine have been unauthorized and untrue."

Attorney General Hensel, upon having the above statement of Gov. Pattison shown to him, and upon being asked what truth there was in the published report that he had considered the railroad deal before it was announced and had determined then or since to take no action in the premises, said: "With regard to the particular statement printed, I believe, first in Philadelphia and amplified elsewhere, that I had information of the leases ten days ago and had decided the State would not interfere. I have just sent a dispatch to the Philadelphia *Record* saying its statement is utterly incorrect and that I never had any information of the arrangements between those railroads other than such as was conveyed to the public through the newspapers. I have neither come to any determination nor decided upon any course of action further than I have made known the same to the public, and any statement heretofore made or hereafter made to the contrary is untrue. This department is not responsible in any way for the somewhat misleading reports sent out from day to day purporting to represent conclusions reached and action determined upon."

## *OKLAHOMA REPUBLICAN CLUBS.*

OKLAHOMA CITY, Oklahoma, Feb. 17.—The Territorial Convention of Republican Clubs met here yesterday, with 240 delegates present, representing a membership of 10,000. Lodan Guthrie was made Chairman and C. E. Horton Secretary. T. G. Risley was elected President of the league and E. T. Sadler Secretary. Delegates were elected to the National Convention, and resolutions were adopted indorsing the Administration of President Harrison and particularly commending the appointment of Gov. Seay.

## *HOWARD MURDER CASE.*

PETER E. BLOW GOES TO ROLLA TO VINDICATE HIS HONOR.

ROLLA, Mo., Feb. 17.—The Hudson case has taken the additional sensational turn predicted for it. Peter E. Blow is now in Rolla to refute the statement made by witnesses that Hudson told them he had been paid a sum of money by Blow to assassinate Louis G. Howard. He stated in open court that he came from Knoxville, Tenn., for the sole purpose of vindicating his good name and that of his family, and that he stood prepared to surrender himself if an indictment was found against him.

When Peter Blow suddenly appeared in the Rolla courtroom and lifted his right hand to be sworn as a witness for the defense in the Hudson murder case, the scene marked the most dramatic moment yet recorded in that trial. With the exception of the lawyers for the defense, not a soul present until that moment knew that Blow was in Rolla. He had arrived on the 1 o'clock train from St. Louis, and had been at once taken charge of by Hudson's lawyers.

As Judge Bland administered to Blow the usual witness's oath it was felt that a great and unexpected crisis had arrived in the Hudson case. Peter E. Blow immediately took the stand as a witness and for nearly two hours he was subjected to examination and cross-examination by the attorneys. In many respects his testimony was a remarkable addition to the history of the case. In some respects it was as pathetic a story as has ever been told from the witness stand, and when it was ended a great change had manifested itself in the aspect of the case.

Taken in connection with to-day's further developments, it means that from now on to the close the trial of George Hudson for the murder of Dr. Louis G. Howard is going to be the most bitterly-contested criminal case ever known in Missouri. There are certain unusually remarkable plans for its being so contested.

The testimony of Mr. Blow was drawn out more by the cross-examination of the State than by the direct examination of the defense. At one point, when cross-questioned as to his motive in coming to Rolla and to his present family relations, the witness broke down completely and sobbed like a child.

"As to my coming here," said he, "I came to vindicate my character. I have been charged," here the prisoner's voice broke and he burst into tears, "with having hired that man to kill Dr. Howard. None of the lawyers for either side knew I was coming."

"Mr. Blow," said Lawyer Benton, "are you still living with your wife and children?"

The prisoner broke down completely at this question, but amid his sobs managed to say in a low voice, "I am, and, gentlemen, I am not ashamed to say that she is still my wife."

"Have you ever received any communication from the prosecution in this case promising you immunity if you would come down to Rolla?"

"No, Sir."

There is loud talk of the indictment of Tanish and Barbee, who swore to Blow's complicity in the crime, for perjury. The defense is now trying to prove an alibi for Hudson.

## *WARMOTH FACTION CONVENTION.*

A STATE TICKET NOMINATED — DELEGATES FOR HARRISON.

NEW-ORLEANS, Feb. 17.—The Warmoth faction of the Republican Party met in convention at Odd Fellows' Hall to-day. T. B. Stamps was chosen as temporary and Gen. W. L. McMillen as permanent Chairman. The convention was a very harmonious one, no opportunity being given for wrangling. The following ticket was nominated:

*For Governor*—JOHN C. BREAUX of Pointe Coupee.
*For Lieutenant Governor*—JAMES C. WEARS of Ouachita.
*For Attorney General*—JAMES M. EDWARDS of Avoyelles.
*For Auditor*—STEPHEN B. GAY of Iberia.
*For Treasurer*—Col. JAMES LEWIS of Orleans.
*For Secretary of State*—JOHN E. STAES of Orleans.
*For Superintendent of Public Education*—EDWARD J. BARNETT of Rapides.

The Presidential Electors' names are: At Large—John T. White, Iberia, and Solomon T. Clanton, Orleans. The district delegates are: First—John W. Brooks, Plaquemines; Second—McCamp Field, Orleans; Third—Claudius Mayo; Fourth—Isaac H. Bell, Caddo; Fifth—Benjamin F. Ludeling, Ouachita; Sixth—Benjamin A. Guidrey, St. Landry.

The two representatives from Orleans are the only colored men on the ticket. The delegates to the National Convention are: At Large—Pearl Wright, Orleans; James W. Barnett, St. Mary; John W. Cook, East Carroll, and Edward Butler, Plaquemines. Alternates—John O'Connor, East Baton Rouge; George W. Whitworth, Iberia; T. B. Stamps, Orleans, and Robert J. Brooks, St. Mary.

Collector Warmoth made a speech predicting a victory that could only be rendered futile by the counting-out process. The delegates to the National Convention were instructed for Harrison first, last, and all the time.

## *FIVE THOUSAND DOLLARS ENOUGH.*

EX-GOV. LONG ON THE PAY OF MASSACHUSETTS'S GOVERNORS.

BOSTON, Feb. 17.—Gov. Russell having indorsed the proposition to increase the salary of future Governors from $5,000 to $10,000, ex-Gov. Long comes out squarely in opposition.

"I cannot help thinking," says he, "that on second thought Gov. Russell and the Legislature will not favor such an increase. The Governor's is the very last salary that should be raised. It is already enough. It is equal to that of a member of Congress, and the office is much less expensive. A rich man does not want more than $5,000. To a poor man $5,000 is a fortunate plum. A young man, especially a lawyer, could well afford to take the place for two or three years without pay, looking at it even as a business investment. The prestige of having been Governor insures him a largely increased revenue when he returns to his business or profession.

"I fancy, too, that if the Governor's salary is raised to the large sum of $10,000, every other salary must follow. Every other official may just as justly demand an increase of 100 per cent. I do not care whether New-York pays $10,000 or $15,000. I prefer the Massachusetts system to the New-York system. Five thousand dollars is enough. Increase the pay above that reasonable figure, and you decrease the honor and dignity."

## *DECLARED DEAD BY A COURT.*

THE CASE OF R. J. BARTON, MISSING FOR OVER SEVEN YEARS.

BOSTON, Feb. 17.—Robert J. Barton is dead. Nobody knows when or where he died, but the Suffolk County Probate Court has judicially determined that he is dead, and has granted administration on his estate.

In 1880 Barton, who lived in Boston, enlisted in the United States Army and went West. When his relatives next heard from him he was in Detroit. That was about nine years ago and at that time he wrote to his sister in Boston that he was sick and feared he would die of consumption, although he had not given up hope. He also wrote that whatever he did or wherever he went he would always notify his sister.

From that time on nobody heard from him. Two years ago his mother died, leaving considerable property, but no will. In settling Mrs. Barton's estate a share was deposited for Robert in a bank, where it now lies, and in order that it may be distributed among his heirs it becomes necessary to take out administration on his estate. The Probate Court has appointed William A. Barton of New York administrator, it being assumed that as Robert has not been heard from for more than seven years he is dead.

## *MILLIONS INVOLVED.*

BOSTON, Feb. 17.—It is said that several million dollars are involved in the decision of a case which was presented to Judge Barker, in the Supreme Court, this morning. It concerns the proper distribution of a French spoliation claim, and is that of F. V. Balch, administrator of Henry Hatch, against H. W. Blagge and Susan B. Samuels.

Henry Hatch died several years ago in Roxbury. The defendants are the administrators of the estate of Crowell Hatch, who died in 1850. The case was reserved for the full court upon the agreed statement of facts, and it will be heard, it is expected, in March.

## *TOBACCO CULTURE IN GEORGIA.*

HOMER, Ga., Feb. 17.—Considerable interest is being manifested among the Bank County farmers in the subject of tobacco as a money crop. J. E. Strange, one of the leading farmers, is preparing to plant twenty acres of tobacco. He will erect barns for curing and employ experts to assist in the process. The soil of the county is especially adapted to tobacco culture.



## THE PARTY'S GREAT DANGER

### *DEFEAT THREATENED THROUGH THE SILVER BILL.*

THE MAJORITY IN CONGRESS IN SAD NEED OF SALVATION FROM ITSELF—THE ADVOCATES OF FREE SILVER MORE CONFIDENT THAN EVER.

WASHINGTON, Feb. 17.—It is not a hopeful sign for the Democratic Party that the opposition yesterday by Mr. Tracey (Dem.) of New-York to approaching the Silver bill is reported to have strengthened the silver men and rendered it more certain than ever that a free-silver bill will be passed during this session. Every man who can be called a Conservative is convinced that there is nothing but danger to the party in the bill, and none except those who are not conservative are supposed to push silver legislation at all hazards. Yet it is asserted to-day with some heat by silver men who were exasperated at what they regarded as uncalled-for interference on Mr. Tracey's part that the anxiety exhibited by the opponents of free silver converted to the silver side many members who were inclined to set aside the silver question until a more favorable season.

The truth shines through such assertions as this, that there is at least a suspicion abroad that the silver question cannot be trifled with without bringing evil consequences. It is admitted, on what appears to be undoubted authority, that the Committee on Rules would, if it had its own way and could by failure to report a rule for the Coinage Committee avert the silver discussion, decline to give the committee a day; yet, with that implied confession of the inadvisability of following Bland's silver flag, it is the general opinion that the Silver bill will be taken up by permission of the Rules Committee, and that it will be passed at an early day.

It is many years since the majority in the House found itself powerless to save itself from itself. In the same breath that the admission is made that a Free Silver bill means the defeat of the party that passes it the prediction is made that the bill will pass and by a stronger vote than it would have had if Mr. Tracey had not made his parliamentary fight to prevent the bill from being taken up. Mr. Tracey was simply trying to save his party from itself. It needs many such friends just now, and it will need them more before it elects its President.

There is just a chance that the Appropriations Committee may keep the Democrats of the House out of this silver mischief for a week or two. The Indian Appropriation bill, which was taken up to-day, will be followed promptly by the Pension bill, and Mr. Sayers of Texas says that other bills will be ready right along after the Pension bill, except the Deficiency bill, which must necessarily be made up at the latest possible moment. If anybody is impatient to make a speech on silver he can easily get in the speech, as Mr. Watson of Georgia to-day spoke on the dreams of the Farmers' Alliance in a fashion that recalled Dickens's descriptions of the oratorical manner and tones of Pogram or J. J. Brick, Esq. If he is the sort of man who is the ideal of the people of Georgia, it is evident that the people who are so devoted to free silver are also addicted to the encouragement of "smart Aleck" orators, possessed principally of presence of mind and vocal endurance. Arguments of his sort may do in the Empire State of the South; in the Empire State of the North they would excite inquiry as to the antecedents of the man, and perhaps a telephone message to Bloomingdale to ascertain whether that institution had lost any of its inmates.

It is easy to understand that the people who would demand free silver would be easily led away by such a glib and fallacious arguefier as Tom Watson. There is no doubt that there is a Democratic conviction that the less the party has to do with silver legislation the better it will be for the party. But still the party goes on heading for free silver, as if it were its fate to be wrecked on silver. The mine owners, who probably know better, see them on in the wrong way for what there is in it for the producers of silver. Men who have something to sell for which they can get $1 for every 80 cents' worth, and who get silver out of the ground at a cost of from 15 to 50 cents an ounce will of course demand free coinage, and will demand of the party in power that they legislate for free coinage "for the people." A leader with brains and convictions that he could make known would be cheap to the Democrats in the Fifty-second Congress just now at any price.

BERING SEA PROCLAMATION.

The regular annual proclamation by the President, warning all persons against illegal sealing in Bering Sea, has been prepared and will probably be issued in a few days. The proclamation, it is understood, is couched in the usual terms. It contains, first, a recital of the law forbidding the killing of seals except as authorized and requiring the President to issue his proclamation forbidding such killing. Then follows the warning against poaching in the waters of Alaska within the dominion of the United States. The question of continuing the modus vivendi for the protection of seal life in Bering Sea, which was in operation last Summer, had not been agreed upon up to a day or two ago.

## *IRISH BILLS DISCUSSED.*

A LIVELY TIME PROMISED IN THE HOUSE OF COMMONS TO-NIGHT.

LONDON, Feb. 17.—In the House of Commons to-day the bill introduced by Mr. Thomas J. Condon, member for East Tipperary, extending the municipal franchise in Ireland so that municipal authorities in that country will have powers similar to the same class of officials in England, passed its second reading. The Government did not oppose the measure.

Mr. Thomas Sexton, member for West Belfast, in expressing regret for the absence of Mr. W. L. Jackson, Chief Secretary for Ireland, during the discussion of the first Irish bill of the session, said that Mr. Balfour's Irish Local Government bill would not be received without contest when it is introduced to-morrow. He promised the Government a lively fight.

Mr. John P. Nolan, member for North Galway, moved the second reading of the bill to enlarge Irish laborers' allotments and to empower local authorities to purchase land for the erection of laborers' houses. In making the motion Mr. Nolan said the bill would enable the laborers to improve their position as they had done in the colonies and the United States.

Mr. Balfour, the Government leader in the House, opposed Mr. Nolan's motion. He said the bill would take the money provided by his own (Mr. Balfour's) [illegible] Land Purchase act for the creation of small holdings in order to purchase cottages a very little cheaper than they could otherwise be obtained. Mr. Balfour denied that his Land act was a failure, and declared that it was yet too soon to judge of its operations.

Mr. Sexton said he did not see why a small portion of the Land act funds should not be devoted to the present scheme.

Mr. John E. Redmond, member for Waterford City, demanded the application of the cloture, but the Speaker refused to close the debate.

## *A BILL WHICH NEEDS WATCHING.*

NEWARK, Feb. 17.—Lawyers of this city are preparing to make an argument against the passage of Assembly bill No. 49, which is now pending at Trenton. It has been commonly referred to as a bill in the interest of sugar trusts, but it is now believed to have been introduced for the defeat of Chancery proceedings designed to restrain the Chicago Junction Railway and Union Stock Yards Company, commonly known as the New-Jersey Company, from entering into a certain trust agreement with Armour & Co., Swift & Co., and Nelson Morris & Co. This combination is one described in THE TIMES two or three months ago to crowd out the smaller meat packers in the interest of the firms named. The bill which meets this case is also expected to defeat any contemplated proceeding for the defeat of the railroad coal combination, and it is believed that the Sugar Trust, which will be benefited by it, is also helping to secure its passage.

## *VIRGINIA STATE DEBT.*

RICHMOND, Va., Feb. 17.—The Senate to-day unanimously passed the bill providing for the settlement of the State debt. The bill was also discussed in the House. The House Committee on Finance agreed to report favorably a bill appropriating $35,000 for Virginia's exhibit at the World's Fair.

10 Pages

# The New-York Times.

10 Pages

VOL. XLI....NO. 12,704. NEW-YORK, FRIDAY, MAY 13, 1892. PRICE THREE CENTS.



## HARRISON FEARS SHERMAN

*ALARMED AT THE OHIO SENATOR'S GROWING BOOM.*

THE ADMINISTRATION SERVES NOTICE ON HIM THAT HE IS EXPECTED TO AID THE PRESIDENT—A PRETTY LITTLE PARTY FIGHT PROMISED.

WASHINGTON, May 12.—The Administration has served notice on Senator Sherman that it expects from him some substantial return for its vigorous assistance in his re-election to the United States Senate.

When Senator Sherman's name was first mentioned in connection with Platt's effort to defeat President Harrison, the latter expected a prompt repudiation of Platt and his colleagues by the Ohio Senator. But now President Harrison and his friends have become convinced that Senator Sherman is not only pleased with the manner in which his name is being used, but that he really encourages it. Mr. W. D. Brickell, the editor of the Columbus *Dispatch*, has been spending several days in Washington, and has had several consultations with Secretary Foster and other Ohio office holders, and to-night quite a sensation was created in the Ohio colony by the appearance of the *Dispatch* containing a Washington special severely denouncing Senator Sherman and accusing him of ingratitude toward President Harrison.

The *Dispatch* special not only denounces Sherman, but alleges that the President, through Secretary Foster and other Ohio officials, used every Federal office holder in the State of Ohio and drew on the office holding contingent from outside States in order to secure Senator Sherman's re-election and the downfall of Foraker. This, it is said, was done with the understanding that President Harrison was to have the loyal support of Mr. Sherman in his effort to be renominated at Minneapolis. Now the office holders charge that Sherman has broken faith and is allowing his name to be used by the President's enemies for the purpose of bringing about his defeat.

Secretary Foster and his friends have waited a sufficient length of time for Sherman to repudiate the efforts now being made in his behalf, but he has neglected to do so, and they now propose to strike from the shoulder and fight Sherman as hard as they fought Foraker. From now on, the Administration forces will take advantage of every opportunity to discourage the Sherman boom, and all the friends of the Administration in Ohio will be asked to assist.

Congressman E. B. Taylor is one of the President's strongest friends in the Ohio delegation. He is out in an interview to-night in which he gives the Sherman boom a dash of ice water. Said Mr. Taylor:

"Mr. Harrison is absolutely sure of the nomination, unless Mr. Blaine permits the use of his name in the convention. If Mr. Blaine appears as a candidate when the convention meets, Mr. Harrison's name will not go before the convention at all. But I do not believe that Mr. Blaine will be a candidate. I do not see how he can be, and if he is not, Mr. Harrison will be nominated on the first ballot. That opposition which is merely looking for a candidate with which to defeat some one, simply to gratify resentment for personal disappointment, cannot accomplish anything. They can do nothing with Sherman, McKinley, or Alger as a candidate, and they are dependent entirely upon Blaine."

"I believe that the people in this country want Mr. Harrison renominated. Since Lincoln, I think there has been no man in the White House whose renomination has been desired and expected by the people as is that of Mr. Harrison. He will have the Ohio, Indiana, Illinois, and Pennsylvania delegations solid behind him in the convention. Quay will not oppose him after the convention meets, and, in spite of Platt, he will have many New-York delegates."

This sudden onslaught of the Administration forces and the bold determination to fight the Sherman boom with bare knuckles has amazed Senator Sherman's friends and his new allies, the Foraker people. It is freely predicted that this strange state of affairs will lead to a combination between Sherman and Foraker on one side, and Harrison and Foster and McKinley on the other, and that from now on the fight for the Ohio delegates will be fast and furious. In case Sherman should be nominated for the Presidency he will be expected to use his influence to secure the election of Mr. Foraker to the United States Senate, and this is a slate Foster and McKinley will try to break.

A well-known Kentucky Republican said to-day, in talking about the disposition of the delegation from that State to the Minneapolis Convention: "It is nominally for Harrison, but it contains no man who is attached to Harrison, and there are many men in it who believe that a new man, who has not made a crowd of disappointed office seekers, would be much stronger. From what I know of the men in the delegation and the feeling behind them, I would say that they would be glad to take up a man who would interest all the party instead of interesting only those members of it who are in office and are only working for a sure thing. Should Blaine have a strong following, and other candidates secure enough votes on the first ballot to keep Harrison from being nominated at once, he will never get through that convention. It must be a nomination for him on the first ballot or not at all. While there has not been much said about it, there are many Republicans in Kentucky who believe that the nomination of Sherman would be more popular, as it certainly would be in Indiana, than that of Harrison. For myself, I would regard the nomination of Judge Gresham as a miraculously popular one for the Republicans at this time, and should he be nominated by the Republicans and anybody except Cleveland nominated by the Democrats, I think that we would have a victory greater than any since Grant was elected over Greeley."

### *DIAZ'S STUDENT FOES.*

THEY WANT TO NOMINATE EX-CHIEF JUSTICE VALLARTA.

CITY OF MEXICO, May 12.—A group of students in opposition to the re-election of President Diaz propose to place in nomination as the Radical Liberal candidate ex-Chief Justice Vallarta, a famous lawyer of this city, but he does not desire to allow his name to be used, as it is his firm intention to remain outside of politics and he is unwilling to antagonize the administration of Gen. Diaz.

The students will probably have to secure some other candidate. The general opinion of business men and bankers is that President Diaz will be re-elected without strong opposition, there being a remarkable unanimity of opinion in his favor all over the country.

The campaign is going on quietly. The National Liberal Party's platform of retrenchment, taxation reform, and educational progress is favorably received.

#### Robert C. Winthrop's Birthday.

BOSTON, May 12.—Robert C. Winthrop, the oldest ex-Speaker of Congress, is eighty-three years old to-day and is receiving many congratulations.

Last night he returned from Washington, where he was received by the President and other distinguished leaders of political and social circles.

Mr. Winthrop enjoys the distinction of having known personally every President of the United States except Washington and Jefferson. In 1832 he saw Charles Carroll, the last surviving signer of the Declaration of Independence, at his own house in Baltimore, and in 1836 visited at Stratham, N. H., Paine Wingate, then ninety-nine years of age, the last surviving member of the first Senate of the United States, who had dined with Washington on the day of his first inauguration. Mr. Winthrop is in excellent health.

#### The University Convocation.

ALBANY, May 12.—This year the sessions of the University Convocation will begin at 9:30 o'clock, and will be continued afternoon and evening. They are to be held July 5, 6, and 7.

Prof. B. I. Wheeler of Cornell University is to read a paper on, "Should Greek be Studied Before Entering College?" On the sixth a paper is to be discussed on the question, "The Seminar Method; to What Extent Should it be Used in University, College, or Academy?"

The morning session of the concluding day will be given over to discussing practical workings of university extension. Then a prize of $100 will be awarded to the members of the library school for the best essay on "Relation of University Extension to Local Libraries." Prof. Nicholas Murray Butler, Dean of School of Philosophy, Columbia College, will read a report on "World's Progress in Higher Education During the Past Academic Year."

Chancellor Curtis's reception will be held in the State library July 5.

### *O'BRIEN'S FRIEND KEATING.*

ARREST OF A MAN WITH A NOTABLE CRIMINAL RECORD.

UTICA, N. Y., May 12.—Edward C. Keating, one of the men indicted for aiding O'Brien to escape, was brought here in charge of a Deputy Sheriff this evening. He was arrested in Schenectady.

Keating has a record. May 6, 1879, he was indicted in Herkimer County on the charge of burglary. He was tried and found guilty, but before sentence was pronounced he was indicted for body snatching. He then went under the name of William Van Alstyne.

In company with two men named Kane and Lewis, Van Alstyne broke open a vault in the cemetery at Little Falls and removed therefrom the body of Harry Burrell. The body was secreted and held for a reward. The men were all indicted and finally confessed the crime. Kane and Lewis were sent to Auburn for ten years each. Van Alstyne, alias Keating, was sentenced to ten years for body snatching and five years for burglary.

When he left Auburn he went to Rome and started a saloon, which he conducted with much success till recently. It was a headquarters for the Dishler politicians in Rome, Keating being one of the lieutenants and close friends of John D. McMahon, who is now Second Deputy Attorney General of this State. His connection with the O'Brien escape is said to be the procuring of a horse and the piloting of O'Brien to Norwich.

Dishler's escape is occasioning about as much talk as did O'Brien's. Dishler was in this city before the Grand Jury met. Before leaving for New-York he is known to have said to a friend who advised him to remain here that he would be safer down where "the boys" were. He was indicted late on May 5. Early on May 6 the Sheriff telegraphed Inspector Steers to that effect, and asked that he be arrested. The warrants followed by mail. May 7 a telegram was received here by the Chief of Police from New-York and signed by Dishler. It read:

"I see by the papers I am wanted in Utica. Will be home some time Sunday."

Dishler's friends here say that he has too many friends among New-York politicians to be arrested there, and as soon as he found out that District Attorney Jones was after him he started for New-York, where his and O'Brien's friends were.

### *HUSBAND'S PROMISE BINDING.*

MRS. BARBOUR GETS A HOUSE AND LOT AND PERHAPS A DIVORCE.

TRENTON, N. J., May 12.—Vice Chancellor Bird to-day filed an opinion in the case of Margaret Barbour against her husband, John Barbour, of New-Brunswick. On Sept. 14, 1891, Mrs. Barbour began a suit for divorce, naming Nellie Ayres co-respondent. Her husband told her that if she would dismiss the suit, return to his home and live with him again, he would be a faithful husband and would give her a house and lot.

Mrs. Barbour agreed, returned to her home, and after a few days asked for the promised property.

Her husband made some excuse, and after few days more had elapsed Mrs. Barbour asked again for the house and lot.

They were not forthcoming, and Mrs. Barbour, seeing that she had been swindled, renewed the suit for divorce, and is now likely to get both the house and lot and the divorce.

The Vice Chancellor said that after a husband and wife had been separated and had entered into contracts which were reasonable to become reconciled and to continue their conjugal relations, it is not against public policy to enforce such contracts.

He ordered that the deed for the property be passed from the husband to the wife.

Mrs. Barbour will continue the suit for divorce.

### *LARGE POTTERY BURNED.*

CRITICISM OF THE NEW TRENTON FIRE DEPARTMENT.

TRENTON, N. J., May 12.—The pottery of Thomas A. Maddock & Sons, the largest sanitary ware manufacturers in this city, was totally destroyed by fire early this morning. The buildings destroyed occupied a square and were filled with valuable molds and green ware.

The fire was not discovered until after it had gained a good headway, and by the time the Fire Department arrived it was raging with great fury.

The buildings were four stories high, built of brick, and nothing remains but one corner of the walls. Several firemen narrowly escaped injury.

The loss will reach $175,000, partially insured.

One hundred and fifty men are thrown out of work.

This is the first large fire since the establishment of the paid Fire Department, and there is more or less adverse criticism on the efficiency of the department, many believing that the new department is not large enough to cope with fires in large buildings, such as many factory buildings here.

The matter will be investigated by the Fire Commissioners at once.

### *CONSISTENT SECRETARY TRACY.*

HE WILL CONFORM TO THE LETTER OF THE CIVIL SERVICE LAW.

WASHINGTON, May 12.—Secretary Tracy will soon issue a special order announcing an examination of applicants, to be held at the Portsmouth (N. H.) Navy Yard on the 23d inst., for filling the position of foreman mason.

There has never been such a position at this yard since the new regulations went into effect, and its establishment now is only temporary. For a time the Secretary questioned the expediency of holding a formal examination to fill the place, and if he had followed the recommendation of the commanding officer of the navy yard the place would have been filled during the short time needed for the services of a foreman mason by the selection of a man at the yard who formerly occupied a similar place.

The Secretary's attention was called to the expense of filling the position in the way prescribed by the new regulations, but he preferred to adhere to the requirements he had laid down, and with that end in view has directed the Board of Examiners to meet at Portsmouth on May 23.

#### Cuban Importers Bar Silver.

HAVANA, May 7.—The dry goods importers have passed a resolution to the effect that all their sales will be made on a gold basis only, and that they will refuse to accept silver (which, owing to the heavy importation from Spain, is already quoted at from 4½ to 5 per cent. discount against gold) in any quantity above $5.

The process of a French chemist, consisting of the mixing of molasses with the cane juice, for manufacturing sugars seems to have proved a complete success, if the recent reports from Cienfuegos are true. It is said to yield 11½ per cent. of first-class sugar, polarizing 98.30° on an average.

#### Threw Red Pepper in His Eyes.

PATERSON, N. J., May 12.—Albert Ross, a cigarmaker hailing from Boston, Mass., was arrested this afternoon in this city for throwing red pepper into the eyes of Joseph Wade of Montclair.

Ross was engaged at the same place until a few days ago, when he was discharged. He claimed that Wade was the cause of his dismissal.

Ross was committed to jail in default of bail. Wade's eyes are in a frightful condition, but it is believed that he will recover the use of both.

#### For Mrs. Harrison's Health.

WASHINGTON, May 12.—The President and Mrs. Harrison will probably leave here Saturday on the lighthouse tender Jessamine on a short cruise in Chesapeake Bay, touching at Fort Monroe. The trip is to be made for the benefit of Mrs. Harrison's health. They will be accompanied by Mrs. Dimmick and Lieut. Parker, United States Navy. The President expects to return by Monday.

#### The Day of Fales's Trial Set.

NEWARK, N. J., May 12.—Robert Aldan Fales, the boy who confessed to the murder of Thomas Hayden on April 30, was brought into court this morning to plead to the indictment of murder.

The boy was pale and nervous, and for the first time showed signs of worry.

Judge Depew remanded him to jail and fixed May 23 as the day for the trial.

### *SWINDLER, THIEF, AND WOOER.*

THE MANY MATRIMONIAL SCHEMES OF MR. THOMAS LA CROIX.

PROVIDENCE, R. I., May 12.—Thomas La Croix was taken to Lowell yesterday from Bowenville, Mass., to serve out a sentence for obtaining money under false pretenses. La Croix's career in Bowenville is something startling, and before he serves his term in Lowell a dozen other charges will doubtless have been brought against him by the Grand Jury.

La Croix is a Frenchman and comes from Sherbrooke, Canada. He began his career by watching at the bedside of a sick friend. While the patient was sleeping La Croix helped himself to a gold watch and a silver watch. Then he took a horse and buggy and started for the States. He was captured before he crossed the line. After that he served two months in prison, "did time" in several Canadian jails, and moved to Lowell.

In that city he was convicted of obtaining money on false pretenses and was sentenced to twelve months on two counts. He made friends with his keeper, took advantage of certain privileges, and at the end of two months emigrated to Fall River with a stolen watch, which the police recovered yesterday.

Although he left a wife and family behind him in Canada, he did not let a responsibility of that kind weigh on him, and at once devoted himself to arranging plans for marrying in quick succession a good many young women. Officers who have been making inquiries say that if they had not interfered with him he would probably have been pronounced a husband by six or seven different clergymen this week.

He began by courting a Globe Village girl, whose mother loaned him $25 to settle up an imaginary estate. This girl was to meet him at the Ferry Street Station and they were to marry en route for the north. She did meet him, but he had a fit and could not start. The girl never saw him again, and the mother is still looking for her $25.

La Croix then became engaged to a damsel in Flint Village. She loaned him a ring, which he presented to a maiden in Globe Village, and the latter consented to become his wife. A young woman in Border City next lost her heart to him, and from her he obtained another ring, which he gave to an Assonet girl.

In the meantime La Croix agreed to marry two girls in Bowenville. They didn't have any rings, but his Western ranch needed fixing and they each loaned him money to make the necessary repairs. He also persuaded a married woman, who lives in Seventh Street, to elope with him, and insisted on mending a clock which belonged to her. He forgot to elope, but did not forget to raise $3 on the clock.

The end came when he went to St. Anne's Church to be married in earnest. He informed the priest that references concerning him could be obtained at his home in Canada, and he was taken at his word. The priest learned that La Croix was a hard case, and his arrest followed. Detective Hayes took him to Lowell yesterday to serve out his sentence, and the Bowenville authorities will prefer charges against him to the Grand Jury.

### *TROUBLE ALONG THE LEVEES.*

DANGER IN MANY PLACES FROM THE MISSISSIPPI FLOODS.

NEW-ORLEANS, La., May 12.—The general flood situation to-day is practically unchanged, although two new crevasses are reported on the lower coast, both too far down the river and in too thinly planted a vicinity to do any but local harm. Of the two breaks reported yesterday, one was closed last night, and the workers expect to stop the other by 2 o'clock to-morrow afternoon.

Latest advices show that the authorities in the upper part of the State are without funds to continue the fight against the water, and efforts to borrow have proved futile, owing to uncertainty as to whom the new Governor will appoint to the Levee Board in charge. Levee Contractor S. L. James, the convict lessee, to-day went to the rescue, placing 600 convicts under the orders of the board, payment to be accepted in warrants.

With the present stage of the river, which is higher than ever before in many localities, the danger daily increases, and is the greater, perhaps, in that it is not marked at any one point. The utmost vigilance is required along the whole line, and levee men are kept very busy.

At this point the river maintains its height, varying from 16 8-10 to 17 1-10 feet above low water, occasionally slopping over the approaches to the wharves in the centre of the business front.

There is no danger of even an extensive flooding of the streets, but some of the wharves are much lower than the banks back of them, and inconvenience to commerce results. This is especially true at the wharf of the Harrison Steamship Line. The inner edge of the wharf is lower than the outside, and about one-third its width is four inches under water. Three inches more will compel its abandonment, and a six-inch rise would cover it. It is only with difficulty that cotton and other freight is now loaded on the vessels of this line.

### *JOHN BARDSLEY'S DUEBILLS.*

A VERDICT RENDERED AGAINST THE KEYSTONE NATIONAL BANK.

PHILADELPHIA, May 12.—Ex-City Treasurer John Bardsley was to-day brought from the Eastern Penitentiary, where he is serving his fifteen-year sentence, to appear as a witness in the suit of Edward W. Magill, his assignee, against the Keystone National Bank, which was placed on trial this morning. The action was brought to recover of the Keystone National Bank $945,000, the amount of the now famous duebills given to Bardsley.

After the bills had been identified by ex-Paying Teller Edward L. Maguire, expert testimony was taken to show how the State's money had been traced through Bardsley's hands into the bank, and that duebills of the bank had been issued in exchange and loaned again by Bardsley to the bank.

Bardsley, when placed on the stand, repeated the story which he has always told, and admitted that he had received interest on the State's money deposited in the bank. No denial was attempted on the part of the receivers of the bank, but the question was raised whether $15,865 paid to Bardsley as interest should not be deducted. Judge Willson instructed the jury to give a verdict for the full amount claimed, and the question of interest could be subsequently determined on a motion for a new trial.

The statement of claim as submitted to the jury was: "Amount of fourteen duebills, $945,000; deduct bonus on amount not paid in, $25,000, leaving $920,000; add interest from Nov. 1, 1890, to date, $84,640, making a total of $1,004,640."

Under the instruction of the court a verdict for that amount was rendered.

#### Englishmen Buy Site for Carpet Factory.

ELIZABETH, N. J., May 12.—An acre of ground has been purchased from the executors of the Trumbull estate here by the representatives of an English firm for the manufacture of Axminster and Wilton carpets and rugs. The firm has been in operation over 200 years, and has branch factories at Wilton, Southampton, and Manchester, England.

The plans have been prepared for its Elizabeth plant, which will consist of two brick buildings each 150 by 50 and three stories high. One will contain the looms, weaving room, and storehouse, and the other the dyehouse, shearing room, engine room, and office.

Ground will be broken for the buildings in a few weeks, and it is intended to have them ready for occupation by next Fall.

Employment will be given to a large number of persons, chiefly women and girls.

#### To Keep Naval Accounts Straight.

WASHINGTON, May 12.—The regulation circular appears to-day from the Navy Department, directing that hereafter disbursing officers of the navy and Marine Corps making requisitions for funds for the payment of salaries or for labor will state what period the payments are to cover, and when they have balances on hand will, in addition to stating the amount of such balances, explain the purpose to which they are to be applied.

#### Would Not Meet a Colored Debater.

NEW-HAVEN, May 12.—An attempt to draw the color line in the Yale Law School is being frowned upon by the large majority of the students in that department. S. R. Willey of Mexico, Mo., a high-stand man, who was chosen as one of eight to participate in a prize debate, has withdrawn from the contest because, as his friends allege, another of the eight is a colored man, J. B. Spurgeon of Richmond, Va.

Spurgeon is a bright fellow, and has been prominent in Law school debates. He has the sympathy of nearly the entire school, and will take part in the debate. A substitute for Willey has been chosen.

## LEAGUED WITH CRIMINALS

*DR. PARKHURST DENOUNCES THE POLICE OF NEW-YORK.*

THEY CANNOT EXECUTE THE LAW IMPARTIALLY EXCEPT ON THE RUINS OF TAMMANY HALL—WHAT MUST BE DONE TO SAVE THE CITY.

The Rev. Dr. Parkhurst last night at Scottish Rite Hall addressed a large audience of young men representing the various church guilds and societies of New-York and Brooklyn upon the subject, "What Can We, as Young Men, Do to Make New-York a Better City?"

Mr. Lewis L. Delafield was Chairman of the meeting. Besides himself and Dr. Parkhurst, those on the platform were Chancellor McCracken, David J. Whitney, Edward A. Newell, James H. Seymour, Frank Moss, William H. Wiley, and Dr. J. N. Hallock. Dr. Parkhurst said, among other things:

"I love my city, and so do you. To me the great, inspiring element in this labor upon which we verge is the singularly commanding position New-York holds in this great country of ours. I have happened lately to enjoy a large correspondence from all over the country, and what has amazed me—yes, and helped me to keep going through some days and nights that were dark to me—was the passionate sympathy taken in the progress I was making by people 3,000 miles away. I tell you, we can work nowhere to more advantage than right here. Our country's heart throbs here on Manhattan Island. Whatever problem is solved here is solved for all the country. Whatever purification is accomplished here has its good effect in every municipality throughout the country. That is the inspiring element, and it should set every young, earnest man in flame.

"I have a profound admiration, in one way, for Tammany Hall. Now, let me explain. I know and admit that there are men in Tammany Hall that we can all admire. Men who are bright exceptions to the almost universally disreputable character of the institution. It is a fact that Tammany has richly earned the position of influence and administrative power she holds. She has been unflinching and faithful and consecutive in her devotion, year after year, to her own ends. Her fidelity never takes a recess. She is what she is, and she wields an almost inexpugnable power in this unhappy island.

"And there is the lesson for us to learn and take to heart—single-eyed devotion to the object in view. We want that same kind of fidelity. You and I have not labored so steadfastly and earnestly to our end, and that is why we stand where we do. We have allowed ourselves to forget our civic obligations, and to live regardless of them. There is but one way to get out, but one way to solve this difficult problem, and that is for you and me to turn on our path, face the other way, and say: 'As for me, I will devote myself in conscientious loyalty to our town.' We must recognize the fact that, as men with brains and hearts and consciences, we have no right to sublet our obligations toward the city we live in.

"And there springs up machine politics, and Tammany has not a monopoly of it, either. There is the weakness of men in their readiness to let a coterie or committee of men exercise for them those obligations from which they should never part. We shall never get over this, never be safe in city or country, till we secure release from this damnable machine politics.

"I tell you that during the past month there has not been a move made in our municipal checker board that I have not watched with jealous, anxious regard. I have tried to believe that things were opening out into a better and brighter future. A while ago Superintendent Murray resigned his position, and was succeeded by Superintendent Byrnes. Now, I am going to speak carefully, but frankly. There is nothing gained by beating around the bush. I have honestly tried to believe the best possible with regard to Mr. Byrnes—and I am not going to speak an unkind word of him. But whatever his disposition may be to keep the promise he made so earnestly to execute the law impartially, he cannot do it, except on the ruins of Tammany Hall.

"I wonder if you have watched some things that have transpired recently. I am going to say a little about them, so that you may see how evident it is that our municipal authorities—I am speaking now of the Police Department—stand in a league with the criminal classes.

"There is no question of it. You can't bore down into the heart of things for weeks as I have and not know it. The Police Department is in league with the criminal classes, and Tammany's exchequer is filled as the result of that league. Destroy the excise sham, nail up the gambling hells and the brothels, and Tammany's exchequer would be empty.

"A while ago I was visiting a house in the course of some nocturnal explorations. We came to the foot of the stairs leading to a temple of Venus. A policeman stood near the door. We went in, and while there the door bell rang. One of my friends was in a room nearer the door than that in which I was, and he heard the talk between the girl who answered the ring and the person who rang. It was the policeman taking care of the house.

"Well, that's the kind of police you've got. And there is a concrete demonstration that the police and the criminals understand each other.

"A few nights ago there was a raid—four disorderly houses in a certain street were raided. It had the air of thoroughness, but twenty-one other houses are close to those four and they were not molested.

"Saturday night there was a raid upon gambling houses in the Tenderloin precinct—and there's a good deal that's funny about it if you know what's back of it. Superintendent Byrnes issued eighteen warrants, supposed to include all the houses in that district. It was going to be a clean sweep. The raid took place, and the papers have told you how clean each place was found—like the house in Scripture that was swept and garnished.

"Well, one of these warrants was for Daly's place. There was a gentleman at my house about the time the raid was going on. He had been out to gamble a little and went to Daly's, but they wouldn't let him in. They said: 'We know you and would like to let you in, but we are doing nothing now. In fact, we have received instructions from the authorities to keep very quiet till the storm blows over.'

"But they told him of a place where they were temporarily accommodating their customers, and this man went there and lost all he had. That place was in the same precinct and it was not touched by the raid. There is some comedy in that.

"Well, now, what kind of a municipal administration do you call that? It is abominable hypocrisy. It's a lie straight through. Don't you let them pull wool into your eyes. The changing of a few Captains from the Fourth Precinct to Goatville does not change the genius of the administration. It is intrinsically corrupt, and will remain so until the devil of Tammany is cast out and the spirit of purity has been borne in upon it."

Dr. Parkhurst picked up from the table a big bundle of letters. "Here are 170 letters," he said, "from different parts of the town calling my attention to one or twenty disreputable spots on Manhattan Island, written by mothers, fathers, anxious citizens, imploring me, from my connection with the Society for the Suppression of Crime, to do something toward washing out the black spots. And we have a police force of 4,000, to which we pay $5,000,000 yearly, to do it.

"Then the community comes to me, a minister of the Gospel and the law, and asks me to do the duty of the Police Department. I try to, and then Tammany Hall and the *Sun* take hold and damn me.

"We don't for a moment think it possible to stamp out all crime. But it is one thing to let crime exist tacitly, within defined limits, and another to let her stalk forth day and night, flaunting her corrupt colors. As Tammany estimates it, criminality does not consist in committing crime. It consists in exposing it, and the man who honestly tries to do it is bound to be blackguarded. If you let me refer to myself—in the Court of General Sessions you would not have thought it was the keepers of those disorderly houses who were on trial. You would have thought it was I and my good friend Erving.

"I have taken this up for a long season and I'm sure you're with me. We are not working for next November. We look for nothing short of a purified municipality, and that means time and hard work. In some form we must study the principles and conditions of city government and disseminate an interest in them among young men."

At the close of the meeting pledge cards were handed around and were numerously signed. The cards read:

"I hereby pledge myself to study the municipal interests of the city, and to do everything in my power to promote the purity and honesty of its Government."

Steps will be taken to form a league of young men to study the subjects and to further more rapidly the object of the work.

#### The Bering Sea Patrol.

VICTORIA, B. C., May 12.—The British Bering Sea patrol leaves about June 1 with orders to seize all vessels found sealing, whether they had been notified or not. The patrol consists of the Melpomene, Nymphe, and Daphne.

### *SECRETARY BLAINE'S FALL.*

AN ACCIDENT THAT MIGHT HAVE HAD SERIOUS RESULTS.

WASHINGTON, May 12.—Secretary Blaine attended the garden fête given this afternoon in aid of the Fresh Air Fund, and came near having a serious accident.

While approaching the large pavilion in which the greater number of the guests were gathered, he stopped on the narrow board walk running along the driveway to greet some friends. Among the young ladies was Miss Leiter, who, selecting a lovely red rosebud from a cluster at her belt, fastened it in the lapel of his coat. Raising his hat in acknowledgment of the pretty act, the Secretary of State made a misstep, and before he could regain his balance his foot slipped off the board, and his length was measured on the ground, after turning over several times in the effort to break the fall.

He was at once helped to his feet, and declared himself wholly unhurt. After mounting the short flight of steps Secretary Blaine rested for about five minutes in the little reception room and then insisted upon joining the company outside, with whom he remained for some time.

As though to convince every one that the fall was of no moment the Secretary walked about from one booth to another talking to the groups of pretty girls, and leaving the cashier in each instance the richer by his stay.

### *TEN OF GARZA'S MEN KILLED.*

MEXICAN TROOPS HAVE A FIGHT WITH REVOLUTIONISTS.

SAN ANTONIO, Texas, May 12.—The Garza revolution has broken out afresh, and this time the outlook is more serious than during the disturbances along the Lower Rio Grande border a few months ago. The state of things is indicated by the following telegram received to-day by Dr. Plutaro Ornelias, Mexican Consul at this place, from Gen. Lorenza Garcia, commander of the troops in the field in the northern zone of Mexico, with headquarters at Mier, in the State of Tamaulipas:

"Lieut. Invalecio Sada, commanding a detachment of cavalry, yesterday morning met and had an engagement with a party of Garza's revolutionists at a place called La Meca, in this State. After a hard-fought battle the Government troops won a victory over the invaders, killing ten of the latter.

"Among those killed were Julian Flores and Abelardo Diminguez, alias Cuarteron. On the Government side one soldier and three horses were killed. The troops are in close pursuit of the remnants of the band."

This band crossed the Rio Grande to Mexican territory on May 10, at 7 o'clock, at the Ramireno Crossing. Julian Flores, one of the revolutionists killed, was a First Lieutenant in Garza's so-called army, and was under indictment in the Federal court here on several charges of violating the United States neutrality laws. He had been next to Garza in leading this revolutionary movement, and, in fact, it has been generally believed that he really did the most of the planning for the movement. He had been a political refugee from Mexico for several years and was a daring and brave man. He owned a ranch of several thousand acres in Starr County, where he made his home prior to the time of the outbreak. After that he had lived in the saddle. He had been badly wanted, but was successful in evading the numerous United States scouting parties.

It is estimated that he was surrounded by about 175 desperate men. Dr. Ornelias is of the opinion that this fight will end the so-called revolution, and that those who were not killed in battle will be captured and summarily dealt with by the Government.

### *SOLDIER SPEER'S WOODEN LEG.*

IT INVOLVES A DECISION OF THE THIRD AUDITOR AND CONTROLLER.

WASHINGTON, May 12.—Abram C. Speer traveled from Woodville to Portland, Oregon, and back to procure an artificial limb, under the law which provides that every soldier who in the line of duty in the military service lost a limb shall receive once every five years an artificial limb. It is also provided that the Quartermaster General of the army shall furnish transportation to limbless pensioners to have their artificial appliances fitted.

The Oregon and California Railroad carried Mr. Speer on his journey, and sent in a bill for the fare, which is $24.50. The Third Auditor disallowed the claim, insisting that when to the railroad lands were granted by the Government it agreed to transport "troops" of the United States free, and, to the mind of the Auditor, Mr. Speer, if there were enough of him, would be "troops" within the letter of the law, and must be carried without charge. The report which came over with the case from the War Department failed to give Mr. Speer's military record, and the Second Controller assumes that the pensioner was a volunteer in the war, or at least a soldier long since discharged. The action of the Third Auditor, according to the Controller's notion of the law, was justifiable only on the ground that the former soldiers to whom the Government has obligated itself for artificial limbs are included under the term "troops."

"This," says the Controller, "I cannot hold, as such a construction seems entirely unwarranted. The claimant company should be paid for its services."

#### Suicide in a New Way.

MONTREAL, Quebec, May 12.—In the Village of St. Antoine L'Abbe in Chautauguay County, twenty-two miles from here, a farmer's son, named Prevost, had some trouble with his family over property. He left his house to go plowing, but, as he did not come home for supper, search was made for him. He was found dead in the field, having committed suicide.

He first tied a rope around his feet and fastened the other end to a tree. With another piece of rope he made a noose, which he slipped over his head, and then he tied the other end to the plow handles. After doing this he struck his horse with the whip. He was thrown down and his head was nearly torn from his shoulders.

#### Cheyennes on the War Path.

KANSAS CITY, Mo., May 11.—A special to the *Journal* from Guthrie, says: "Gov. Seay to-day had delivered to him the dispatches by a courier from the Cheyenne and Arapahoe Reservations, stating that 100 Cheyennes were off their allotments and were driving white settlers off their claims.

"The Indians claim that they never signed the treaty for sale of their lands, and that if the white settlers do not leave the country within ten days they will be driven out. The Indians are all armed. At the town of Cheyenne a line of guards surrounds the town day and night, and the citizens request that troops be sent at once for protection."

#### The Will of George A. Camp.

MINNEAPOLIS, Minn., May 12.—The will of George A. Camp, which was filed for admission to probate to-day, contained a surprise for the heirs-at-law. The estate amounts to over half a million, and the will bequeaths half of it to Mrs. Jessie D. Carr-Seale of Salina City, Cal., the other half to Mrs. Henry Von Wadelstaadt of St. Paul, his only daughter, and her son, Henry Von Wadelstaadt, Jr. Mrs. Carr-Seale, it is learned, was the fiancée of the late Major Camp, and was to have married him early next month had not death prevented. She is said to be wealthy in her own right already.

#### Gov. Flower Back from Watertown.

ALBANY, May 12.—Gov. Flower returned late this afternoon from Watertown and went at once to the Executive Chamber. He realizes that he has a hard ten days before him if he hopes to take any action upon the large number of bills which still remain for his consideration, and said that he should start in to-night and early to-morrow morning to make a hole in the big pile.

#### The Mercier Case Closed.

QUEBEC, May 12.—This morning, after G. G. Stuart for the Crown and F. X. Lemieux for the defense had addressed the court, the Mercier alleged conspiracy case was declared closed. Judge Chauveau took the case en délibéré.

#### Union League Club.

Vice President Horace Porter presided over the monthly meeting of the Union League Club last night at which the following new resident members were elected: John W. Griggs of Paterson, N. J.; H. Edwards Rowland and Aaron S. Thomas of this city, and the Rev. F. L. Humphreys of Garden City, L. I.

## MARRIED FIVE YEARS AGO

*WARD M'ALLISTER'S YOUNGER SON HAS A WIFE.*

THE FATHER GREATLY SURPRISED AND DISPLEASED BY THE NEWS—MISS JANIE GARMANY OF SAVANNAH THE BRIDE—A WELL-KEPT SECRET.

The marriage notice printed in THE TIMES this morning stating that Heyward Hall McAllister and Miss Janie Champion Garmany of Savannah were married in this city on Aug. 22, 1887, will doubtless be read with surprise by a great many people.

Heyward Hall McAllister is the younger son of Ward McAllister, and Mrs. McAllister is the daughter of the late George W. Garmany, a prominent lawyer of Savannah, who died in the Spring of 1888, having no suspicion that his daughter Janie was married. The secret has been kept absolutely.

Mrs. Garmany has, since her husband's death, lived in Savannah in the family home with her son Howard, who is a lawyer; her daughter, and her three younger sons, who have been absent from home part of the year studying at Princeton. The fact of the daughter's marriage was known to nobody in the family except to the daughter herself.

Mr. McAllister became engaged to Miss Garmany immediately after her graduation from Mrs. Cary's girls' school in Baltimore, with the approval of the entire Garmany family. Miss Garmany was scarcely eighteen years old at the time.

Ward McAllister opposed his son's engagement on the ground that the young man ought not to enter into such a condition of life until he should have so established himself in a profession as to be able properly to support a wife. The young people became engaged in the Autumn of 1886, and this fact was known in the families. It now transpires that the marriage followed in August of the next year.

The reason now given by the husband and wife for marrying was that they wished to make sure of each other beyond force of separating accident, and the reason for keeping such strict secrecy was the opposition of Ward McAllister to the match.

During all the years since the engagement Mr. McAllister was a frequent visitor at Mrs. Garmany's house, where he held the footing of a prospective son-in-law. Mrs. McAllister passing none of her time in the society of Mr. McAllister except in the presence of her mother or some other chaperon. The news of the marriage has come as a complete surprise to the family of the bride, and Mrs. Garmany, it is said, is much distressed at the sensational features of her daughter's marriage.

Ward McAllister when seen last night declared that he had nothing whatever to say upon the subject of his son Heyward's marriage. He finally stated, however, that the first announcement of the fact had come to him on Sunday from Albert Gallup, his son's lawyer. Mr. McAllister said that he had always opposed his son's marriage with anybody, not specially with this young lady, whom he had not the honor to know, but with anybody, because his son was not able to support a wife.

He said that he did not know where his son was at present. The last time he had seen his son was last Saturday. He said he knew absolutely nothing of his son's wife, and had never known her family in Savannah, although he lived there years ago, and had often visited in the city since then.

When asked if his son would still be a welcome visitor at his home, Mr. McAllister said that he could not answer that question.

Dr. Jasper J. Garmony, a brother of Mrs. Heyward McAllister, now lives at 40 West Fortieth Street. He said last night that the announcement of the marriage had come to him as a complete surprise within a very short time. He said that Mr. and Mrs. McAllister had determined to make the matter public, but he could not say why they had come to this conclusion.

He said that the secret marriage was a matter of great regret in the family, and that it was possible that his brother Howard, as the present head of the house, might have something to say in the course of a week or two. He declined to make public any details of the affair, saying, however, that his actual knowledge was very limited. He said that he saw his sister last Wednesday, when she called at the house, but that she and her husband had not remained as guests in his house while they were in town together.

Where they had staid he did not know, nor could he say where they were at present, beyond the fact that they were not in town. He said his sister was in high health and spirits, and that he could form no idea why she had elected to disclose her marriage at the present time after waiting so long, beyond the conjecture that she happened to take a fancy to do so.

### *TO GO BEHIND THE RETURNS.*

NEW PHASES OF LITIGATION IN THE PHELAN-WALSH CASE.

NEW-HAVEN, May 12.—The Republican expectation that Judge Hall's ruling might delay the Phelan quo warranto, to test the title to the office of the State Secretary, beyond the period when it could be taken to the June sitting of the Supreme Court, may not be realized.

The Judge's ruling was that the best evidence as to the actual result of the State election of November, 1890, was not the returns made to the State Canvassing Board, which the Democrats offered, but the certificates lodged with the Town Clerks, the presentation of which should be accompanied by the evidence of at least one of the counters at each polling place.

That required the summoning of over 300 witnesses. The Democratic State Committee authorized the expense, and sheriffs have been scouring the State yesterday and to-day for witnesses.

The Democratic counsel and the sheriffs worked like beavers, and as a result about 120 witnesses were in court here to-day, and the Judge obligingly continued the court session long after the usual hour in order to accommodate the witnesses.

The testimony thus far taken shows no change in the announced result, which was a majority of over 500 for Mr. Phelan.

The interesting part of the trial will come when the Republicans go behind the returns. But the counsel for Mr. Phelan are positive that Mr. Phelan's majority cannot be wiped out. Their main effort is to get before the Supreme Court in June.

The Republicans will try to prevent that in order to postpone the final decision if possible beyond the November election, and to retain for themselves a majority on the State Canvassing Board, which they would lose if Hold-Over Secretary Walsh should be displaced by Secretary Phelan.

### *FOUR BOILERS EXPLODED.*

THREE MEN WERE KILLED AND SEVERAL FATALLY INJURED.

SAGINAW, Mich., May 12.—About 2 o'clock this afternoon the little City of Midland, twenty miles west of Saginaw, was shaken by the explosion of a battery of four boilers that furnished steam for operating the sawmill of the Midland Salt and Lumber Company. The boiler house was detached from the mill and was completely wrecked, and considerable damage was also done to the sawmill.

Three employes were killed. They were:

JOHN ALLEN, fireman, thrown 200 feet from the mill.
EUGENE VALKENBURG.
DICK STEARS.

THE INJURED.

GUS MALCOLM, fireman, fatally.
ARTHUR ROBINSON.
E. P. ELTON.
CHARLES BLYNN.
CHARLES BURT.
ALBERT MALL.
SANFORD WALTON.

Elton was blown some distance from the mill, receiving a severe scalp wound.

The cause of the accident has not been definitely ascertained, but it is charged to a defect in one of the boilers. The damage to the property will not exceed $7,000.

#### A Large Artificial Reservoir.

PHOENIX, Arizona, May 12.—A company was organized to-day for the construction of one of the largest artificial reservoirs in the world. The site taken is the Box Canyon, 400 yards below the junction of Tonto Creek and Salt River.

The height of the dam is to be 200 feet, and the backwater will extend sixteen miles to Sierra Anch Mountains, making a capacity, according to reports of the County Surveyor, of 103,038,040,800 cubic feet of water. Owing to the abundance of limerock, timber, and other building material on the ground, the cost of the building is not expected to exceed $1,500,000.

The new reservoir will have a capacity to irrigate all lands of the Gila, Verde, and Salt Valleys from the point where the water is taken out to the Colorado River at Yuma. The enterprise is backed by New-York capitalists.

12 Pages

# The New York Times

12 Pages

VOL. XLI...NO. 12,728. NEW-YORK, FRIDAY, JUNE 10, 1892. PRICE THREE CENTS.



## HARRISON'S GREAT DAY

*HE CAPTURED A MAJORITY OF THE CREDENTIALS COMMITTEE,*

AND, ON A TEST VOTE, A MAJORITY OF THE CONVENTION ALSO—476 DELEGATES SUPPORTED THE REPORT IN FAVOR OF SEATING CONTESTING HARRISON MEN—ONLY 365 DELEGATES FOLLOWED THE BLAINE LEADERS—THE CONVENTION ADJOURNS TILL TO-DAY, AFTER THE READING OF THE PLATFORM—VICTORY WITHIN SIGHT OF THE HARRISON COLUMN.

MINNEAPOLIS, June 9.—The great event in the Convention proceedings to-day was at to-night's session.

The Committee on Credentials presented a majority report, which gave Mr. Harrison a net gain of twelve votes over the number of his advocates seated by the National Committee in the temporary organization.

A minority report, changing this in a great measure and giving Blaine the advantage, was submitted by the anti-Harrison men.

The fight began on a motion to substitute the minority for the majority report, and, as this was a test vote of the strength of the two divisions of the convention, much interest was manifested.

A vexatious delay was caused when the vote of Texas was reached by the electric lights going out, and at midnight a panic was very narrowly averted.

In this first test vote, the Harrison men were the victors by a vote of 462 to 423.

In the second, which was a motion to adopt the majority report in the Alabama case, the Harrison men were again victors by a vote of 476 to 365.

### BLAINE'S GROWING WEAKNESS.

THE ANTI-HARRISON MEN UNABLE TO CONCEAL THEIR SOLICITUDE.

MINNEAPOLIS, June 9.—Hottest of all the days of the convention was this, that dawned upon the host of Harrison auspiciously, while the bright sunlight was a mocking of the fading Blaine boom. The clouds that had hovered overhead for many days were dispersed by a fresh southeast wind, which fluttered banners gayly.

But the crowds of delegates and visitors, while glad of the good weather, were more interested in the convention. The reports from the Credentials Committee that has been at work all night was not altogether assuring to the Blaine men. The Harrison men did not care anything about them. They were so confident of their strength independent of the result of contests that they were ready and even anxious for a chance to show their strength on a roll call with that of the Blaine men who had been offering wagers as the last indication of their desire that the apparently impossible should happen.

Very significant was the silence of the Blaine leaders, who had last night conferred, and after their conference had admitted, for the first time, that Blaine really lacked sixty votes of a majority. They did, in fact, lack more, and every moment of delay, contrived for the purpose of helping Blaine, was only increasing Harrison's strength. It was impossible to keep down the conclusions reached in the conference. Blaine was not only in a fair way of being beaten, but the prospect indicated that he might be beaten more severely than he ever was before in a Republican convention.

It was impossible for the Blaine men to conceal their changed feelings. Among the managers, the "touters" and "boomers," including the plume-carrying clubs and headquarters howlers, there was still a disposition to keep up the noise. But it was merely what a subsidence is after an earthquake. The power of the name of the magnetic Blaine to stick had been tried. It was found to have gone, probably forever.

One sensible and wise thing was done last night, to stop the conflict of noisy partisans in the rotunda of the West Hotel. This area had become the battle ground of partisans, who fought each other with staffs and banners and marched to the time of bands and drum corps in never-ending circles, with plumes, portraits, and flags high in the air, while there was an increasing and unintelligible cheering. Many of the more sane persons who forced their way across the floor to the hotel desk noticed that the floor swung with the weight and the tramp of hundreds of noise makers angrily shouting Blaine and Harrison. There seemed imminent danger that the floor would give way and large numbers of active and vociferous Republicans would be precipitated into the basement.

The Mayor of Minneapolis had his attention directed to the situation. As he had the power to avert danger and to suppress public nuisances, he issued an order to the police force, directing a body of officers to clear out all marching organizations, to disperse the circulating boomers, and see to it that none of them were permitted to congregate in the rotunda. He also included in his direction an order against mass meetings in the hall that would be apt to draw crowds.

It was a sore blow to the pulverizing Blaine boom. The last display of it in the hall had been interesting and the shouters took to the streets in squads or went home to bed.

With the apprehended collapse of the Blaine boom was revived the effort to organize in favor of a third man. It did not promise well. The Blaine men were full of hatred for Harrison, and the matter was and is simply "anybody to beat Harrison." But they had made the fatal error of relying too much on old-time affection for Blaine to accomplish their purpose.

The absence of would-be enthusiasm on the part of men who heard, with disgust, the "boom-de-ay" songs for Blaine, the assurances that he would not veto a free silver bill if it were passed, and who feared to face the country with a candidate who became available through an act of unparalleled treachery and infidelity to a Republican Administration, impressed other delegates that the safe course seemed to be to take the President after all, even if Quay, Clarkson, Payn, Platt, and Fassett, to say nothing of Warner Miller, were opposed to him.

Alas for Warner Miller! He has been a very unfortunate man in his political ventures. He has repeatedly sold himself very cheaply, to be very soon betrayed by his purchasers, but he has never before made an error which everybody has so quickly discovered as that of choosing between Harrison and Blaine. Years ago, when he would have been glad to have Platt's assistance in nominating Blaine, and when Platt was allowing Conkling's hatred of Blaine to control him, he would have died rather than go into Platt's camp just to be victor in a struggle in which he sympathized with the side to which Platt was opposed.

A personal dislike of Harrison, returned no doubt by the President, who is not above resentment, has led him to surrender to Platt, almost in the moment when victory seemed assured to the President and in the face, too, of the protests of the leading business men of his State against the cause that promised, a day or two ago, to result in the selection of a man whose nomination strikes the entire business community as dangerous to both party and country.

After the day session was over and the delegates had withdrawn from the convention hall, the Blaine men resorted to Quay's room in the West Hotel, for news and comfort. They did not get much.

### THE HARRISON MEN'S ROLL.

AT A CONFERENCE THEY HAVE 520 DELEGATES—QUAY'S COLORED VISITORS.

MINNEAPOLIS, June 9.—After the day session the Harrison men had business on hand. While the convention was in progress several of John C. New's men went about from State to State, inviting Harrison men in each State to a meeting, to be held immediately after recess was ordered. So, as soon as they were free, they flocked to Market Hall, near the bridge over the Mississippi. There was a great crowd of them, including Gen. New, Col. Michener, Col. Hall, and other supporters of the President.

They were regularly organized, and Mr. Depew told the delegates what the meeting had been called for. It was to make sure of the President's strength, and to verify the canvasses that had already been made. It was like one of the gatherings in 1880 of the old guard of Grant's 306, or of the "all Summer" friends of Arthur in 1884, excepting it was larger.

State by State the roll was called, and when it was made up it was found that Harrison had 520 votes in the gathering.

This report went over the bridge and into the Blaine headquarters with the usual rapidity of movement of bad news. It was received with marks of incredulity. "Our Own" Burleigh would not believe it at all at first, and then, remembering his other unfortunate experience with Arthur, when he had 370 men in a conference, and who had expected, "with the Edmunds men," to get more than a majority, but turned up next day with only 278 votes, he affected to sweep aside this incident as one of very small political consequence. He prepared to talk about a "dark horse" and the prodigious gains of McKinley.

At Matt Quay's room, or the room of the National Committee, a strange sight was witnessed. Quay did not attend the convention, but kept his room all through it. He had many visitors, white and black. They came in with the badges of North Carolina, Texas, Tennessee, South Carolina, and Georgia on their coats. They were let in separately and left by another door than that by which they were admitted.

To those who remembered Quay's reputation it was suggestive. The colored men are beginning to feel expenses already. They are apt to be solicitous about such matters. Does anybody doubt what business Quay had with these men in the private room of the Blaine headquarters? The roll call will tell. If the negroes nominate Blaine, it will be because the balance of power in this tenth convention of the Grand Old Party was purchaseable and purchased.

There was hope of a ballot at night, but no assurances that it would be reached.

The Harrison and Blaine camps were again canvassed by THE TIMES's correspondent. The inquiries developed smaller strength for Harrison than the reports of the meeting at Market Hall, but quite enough, from a safe standpoint, to nominate Harrison on the first ballot. The canvass was as follows:

| *States.* | *Harrison.* | *Blaine.* |
|---|---|---|
| Alabama | 15 | 9 |
| Arkansas | 15 | 1 |
| California | 4 | 14 |
| Colorado | .. | 8 |
| Connecticut | 4 | 8 |
| Delaware | 4 | 2 |
| Florida | 8 | .. |
| Georgia | 26 | .. |
| Idaho | .. | 6 |
| Illinois | 31 | 17 |
| Indiana | 30 | .. |
| Iowa | 22 | 4 |
| Kansas | 13 | 7 |
| Kentucky | 22 | 4 |
| Louisiana | 16 | .. |
| Maine | .. | 12 |
| Maryland | 16 | 10 |
| Massachusetts | 16 | 10 |
| Michigan | 4 | 24 |
| Minnesota | 8 | 10 |
| Mississippi | 9 | 9 |
| Missouri | 20 | 14 |
| Montana | 5 | .. |
| Nebraska | 10 | 8 |
| Nevada | .. | 6 |
| New-Hampshire | 4 | 2 |
| New-Jersey | 17 | 3 |
| New-York | 30 | 38 |
| North Carolina | 20 | 2 |
| North Dakota | 3 | 3 |
| Ohio | 26 | 15 |
| Oregon | 2 | 6 |
| Pennsylvania | 12 | 50 |
| Rhode Island | 2 | 4 |
| South Carolina | 9 | 9 |
| South Dakota | 6 | 2 |
| Tennessee | 14 | 2 |
| Texas | 22 | 8 |
| Vermont | 4 | 4 |
| Virginia | 14 | 10 |
| Washington | .. | 8 |
| West Virginia | 8 | .. |
| Wisconsin | 17 | 4 |
| Wyoming | 4 | 2 |
| Arizona | .. | 2 |
| New-Mexico | .. | 2 |
| Oklahoma | 2 | .. |
| Utah | .. | 2 |
| District of Columbia | .. | 2 |
| Total | 512 | 364 |

McKinley has 3 in Wisconsin, 4 in Massachusetts, 1 in Montana, 2 in New-Hampshire, 3 in New-York, 5 in Ohio, 2 in Rhode Island, 1 in Texas, and 2 in Pennsylvania—24.

Sherman has 1 in New-York.

### DEPEW'S JOYFUL STORY.

TALE OF THE ROUND-UP OF 463 HARRISON DELEGATES.

MINNEAPOLIS, June 9.—The severest blow yet administered to the Blaine canvass occurred immediately after the adjournment of the convention to-day, when 463 Harrison delegates were rounded up in the Market Hall, under the skillful direction of Chauncey M. Depew, Frank Hiscock, Gen. John C. New, Gen. Sewell of New-Jersey, ex-Senator Spooner of Wisconsin, and Delegate Massey of Delaware.

An enthusiastic meeting took place. At its conclusion the word was passed that these 463 delegates represented 520 copper-fastened, steel-riveted, iron-bound, bed-rock Harrison men, who would vote for the President on the first ballot. As only 450 votes are necessary to nominate, the margin of safety was so great and inspired the leaders with so much confidence, that Mr. Depew announced publicly that "it mattered not what course the Committee on Credentials might take, no contest would be made in the convention. Even if every Blaine contestant is admitted, you will find that we will accept the decision with meekness and without objection."

The meeting was called under these circumstances: Last night Mr. Depew and Senator Hiscock made a tour of the different delegations. They were at this work until 2 A. M., and, at a conference of the Harrison managers held later, the reports and votes, with figures they received, were so encouraging that the perilous experiment was suggested of bringing together all the Harrison delegates under one roof and ascertaining to a certainty the exact situation. Mr. Depew's description, in his own picturesque language, is this:

"The whole story, in plain English, is a simple one. Senator Hiscock and I, after our tour last night, went into a conference with the Harrison managers. They had made up and were verifying a canvass, and were confident of Gen. Harrison's renomination. Naturally, we were all very much elated, and after this discovery we felt we were strong enough to undertake the hazardous risk of calling the Harrison delegates together to stand up and be counted. Every man present fully realized that unless we had an absolute majority the experiment might prove, if not fatal, at least injurious to the President's chances.

"We therefore concluded to keep silent until this morning, when some one suggested that we summon all our friends immediately after the convention adjourned. I do not know who it was who made this suggestion; it was an inspiration, a mental flash of lightning, a composite political photograph. The convention adjourned so quickly that many delegates who were late in arriving and who had been detained failed to get there because we had no time to notify them all. I, myself, failed to reach the convention hall, but went direct from the hotel to Market Hall, where the conference, if we may so call it, took place.

"After we had assembled, the delegates were good enough to elect me Chairman and our friend Chris Magee of Pennsylvania Secretary. They called upon me for a speech, and I talked to them twenty minutes, congratulating the brethren that none were on the anxious seat and that all were counted among the saints. The Chairman of each delegation was then asked to come upon the platform, and, where the State Chairman was not present, the delegates elected one of their own for the time being. All the States and Territories were represented except those in which Gen. Harrison had no votes.

"The roll was called and the Chairman came forward, stated the number of delegates in all, then the number that were open and avowed Harrison men, the number who were doubtful, and the number who might come over to us. This statement was then submitted to the assemblage for any question as to its accuracy. The bed-rock statement was then accepted and the other statements were dismissed. The Chairman of each delegation thereupon announced how many Harrison men were in the hall and accounted for those who were not present.

"From these statements by the different Chairmen, it was found that 462 delegates were in the hall. The roll call of those pledged footed up 511, and before we left we were informed by a messenger that the Committee on Credentials had admitted nine of our friends in Alabama, so that, when we separated, 520 immovable, steadfast, and loyal delegates stood for Benjamin Harrison. As only 450 are necessary to nominate, the subsequent proceedings interested him no more."

The Blaine managers heard of this round-up with mixed feelings of anger, skepticism, and indignation. They refused to believe it. Thomas C. Platt scoffed at it. Matthew C. Quay ridiculed it, and Henry G. Burleigh was willing to bet $500 to $250 that Harrison would not be nominated on the first ballot.

But one way was left for the Blaine people to meet this news, and, of course, they were equal to the emergency. The word was passed that 463 delegates attended the meeting. They said that over a hundred of their friends attended it, and when shown the ridiculousness of such a statement they answered: "Well, if they were not our friends, they were office holders."

They were plainly distressed and embarrassed by the great showing made by the Harrison men.

Facts and figures were the best arguments made to-day, and on this basis the Harrison men have certainly had the best of it. Brag and bluster have been the only ammunition possessed by the Blaine people, and this was not a good day for Blaine ammunition. Their powder was wet and the projectiles were too large for the muzzles of their guns. Mr. Platt and Mr. Quay were most assiduous in disseminating denials of the Harrison round-up, but the Harrison managers and delegates were neither disturbed nor upset by the false and malicious statements.

The policy of Gen. Harrison's managers has been sagacious and conciliatory from the first. The Blaine men have boasted much because they happened to control the National Committee. They blustered because the Harrison delegates refused to contest the selection of Mr. Fassett as temporary Chairman, when they knew that Chauncey M. Depew and Frank Hiscock joined Mr. Platt and Mr. Miller in written application to the National Committee for Mr. Fassett's selection. Then the Blaine men wanted to know why, if friends of Mr. Harrison controlled the convention, a contest was not made over the failure of the Committee on Credentials to make a more expeditious effort.

Carroll E. Smith, editor of the Syracuse *Journal*, explained the policy of the Harrison forces to-day as follows:

"If there is a fight in this convention, the Harrison men will not be found in it. We don't propose to make a contest on anything but the nomination, and we have that to a certainty. Nor do we propose to allow the impression to be spread broadcast over the country, for effective use in the doubtful States, that the Republican Party is split beyond redemption. It is our policy to conciliate and not to antagonize the members of our own party. If the Blaine forces desire to fight, I trust they will fight among themselves. They can't involve us. We can afford to be magnanimous."

A little man who has been doing considerable missionary work for Gen. Harrison in a quiet way and unobtrusive but nevertheless effective manner was Mr. William Leary of the Twenty-first New-York Assembly District. Scarcely a day has passed that Mr. Leary has not had an interview in the local papers from the standpoint of the business man of New-York, in favor of Gen. Harrison's nomination. He very shrewdly engaged quarters on the fifth floor of the West Hotel, adjoining those of the Blaine headquarters, and spent the greater part of his time beguiling Blaine delegates into his room, to talk the situation over from the standpoint of a business man.

The reports submitted at Mr. Depew's mass meeting of delegates, at Market Hall this afternoon, give the total number of delegates for Gen. Harrison, excluding the nine allowed him by the Committee on Credentials from Alabama, to be as follows:

| | | | |
|---|---|---|---|
| Alabama | 7 | Nevada | .. |
| Arkansas | 15 | New-Mexico | 5 |
| California | 8 | New-Hampshire | 8 |
| Colorado | .. | New-Jersey | 18 |
| Connecticut | 3 | New-York | 28 |
| Delaware | 3 | North Carolina | 16 |
| Florida | 8 | North Dakota | 2 |
| Georgia | 26 | Ohio | 27 |
| Idaho | .. | Oregon | 4 |
| Illinois | 36 | Pennsylvania | 13 |
| Indiana | 30 | Oklahoma | 2 |
| Iowa | 21 | Rhode Island | .. |
| Kansas | 13 | South Carolina | 15 |
| Kentucky | 20 | South Dakota | 4 |
| Louisiana | 8 | Tennessee | 16 |
| Maine | .. | Texas | 18 |
| Maryland | 18 | Utah | 1 |
| Massachusetts | 16 | Vermont | 6 |
| Michigan | 5 | Virginia | 9 |
| Minnesota | 7 | Washington | .. |
| Mississippi | 12 | West Virginia | 10 |
| Missouri | 24 | Wisconsin | 19 |
| Montana | 1 | Wyoming | 4 |
| Nebraska | 4 | | |

### THE SHORT DAY SESSION.

DELEGATES KEPT WAITING FOR THE CREDENTIAL COMMITTEE'S REPORT.

MINNEAPOLIS, June 9.—The sun beat down merrily this morning through the ventilating shafts of Convention Hall. The brown flags, the brown pillars, the gold stars upon the brown decorations, the sheaves of grain set against the shields, and the cornices of the columns stood out in stronger colors than at any time since the delegates began to occupy their seats.

Good weather and good music drew the audience together early. While the strains of "Poet and Peasant" floated down from the roof balcony the tramp of feet increased below, as the holders of tickets climbed the stairways and then clambered down again into their places. The chill of yesterday had given way to a soft Summer air. Fans were already fluttering in the seats where ladies were sitting, and men came in mopping their heads with their handkerchiefs.

There was not much cheering to-day. The cheer had all gone out of the Blaine men. The Harrison men were resting their lungs for a more appropriate season. They were sure that they would nominate their man, and the Indianians were so confident that they had posted a notice in their headquarters that read:

"In consequence of the night session, parade is postponed until after the nomination of Harrison."

This was too strong a bluff for the Blaine stomachs.

The great men were allowed to come in almost without notice, the exception being in favor of Ingalls, whose bright red tie and light overcoat made him conspicuous and led to his recognition, and who met with a few plaudits.

It was 11:20 o'clock when Gov. McKinley stepped out of the crowd of officers on the platform and rapped, over and over again, for order. There was a subsidence of the disorder on the floor, groups breaking up and melting away, delegates finding their seats, and deputies of the Sergeant at Arms hurrying to their proper places. Presently there was complete order and no noise except the heavy rumbling tramp of feet in the corridors outside, as late comers made their way into the immense building.

The audience was not quite as large as that of yesterday, but it was large enough to be impressive. It rose majestically as Chairman McKinley introduced the Chaplain who had officiated Tuesday at the opening.

When the opening prayer had been made Mr. Cogswell of Massachusetts, the Chairman of the Committee on Credentials, was upon his feet. Everybody listened attentively. He announced, in a deliberate way, with wide intervals of time between his words, that the Committee on Credentials was still in session. It had made diligent work and achieved reasonable progress. It hoped to be able to report in full to-night at 8 o'clock, and asked for further time.

Gen. Sewell, the leading Harrison man in New-Jersey, promptly rose. As it would be impossible to go on until the report of the committee was made he moved that the convention take a recess until 8 o'clock.

Senator Cullom of Illinois offered a resolution for reference, which was read, in regard to the World's Columbian Exposition. It was as follows, and was referred to the Committee on Resolutions:

*Resolved*, That the World's Columbian Exposition, to be inaugurated in the City of Chicago in 1893, is rightfully considered by all classes of our citizens, regardless of their political affiliations, as a "great national undertaking," and that, in recognition of its character and importance, Congress ought promptly to provide by appropriate legislation such reasonable appropriation in aid thereof as will enable the Government fully to discharge its express and implied obligations incident thereto, and as will insure the attainment of such results therefrom as will be commensurate with the dignity, progress, culture, and development of a free and enlightened people.

Another resolution authorizing members of the Grand Army of the Republic to occupy seats not claimed by other visitors, was also referred, after which the convention was called upon to consider Gen. Sewell's motion for recess. Mr. John D. Lawson called for a division on the motion. There was a rising vote. Chairman McKinley counted heads and announced the result to be yeas, 407; nays, 260. The negatives were largely Blaine men. The convention was declared in recess until 8 o'clock.

### THE PLATFORM.

PLANKS FOR PROTECTION, RECIPROCITY, AND THE SILVER QUESTION.

MINNEAPOLIS, Minn., June 9.—The following is the full text of the platform as completed by the Committee on Resolutions:

The representatives of the Republicans of the United States, assembled in general convention on the shores of the Mississippi River, the everlasting bond of an indestructible Republic, whose most glorious chapter of history is the record of the Republican Party, congratulate their countrymen on the majestic march of the Nation under the banners inscribed with the principles of our platform of 1888, vindicated by victory at the polls and prosperity in our fields, workshops, and mines, and make the following declaration of principles:

I. We reaffirm the American doctrine of protection. We call attention to its growth abroad. We maintain that the prosperous condition of our country is largely due to the wise revenue legislation of the Republican Congress. We believe that all articles which cannot be produced in the United States, except luxuries, should be admitted free of

(Continued on Page 2.)

## D. B. HILL WILL WITHDRAW

*THE SENATOR HAS WRITTEN A LETTER TO THAT EFFECT.*

IT IS IN EDWARD MURPHY'S SAFE—CROKER, M'LAUGHLIN, AND SHEEHAN HAVE SEEN IT—THE BIG FOUR AUTHORIZED TO TAKE DOWN HIS PRESIDENTIAL SIGN WHENEVER IN THEIR DISCRETION THEY SEE FIT.

TROY, June 9.—There is in existence a letter signed by Senator David B. Hill, authorizing the withdrawal of his name from all further consideration by the Democracy, State and National, whenever, in the opinion and discretion of Richard Croker, Hugh McLaughlin, and Edward Murphy, Jr., and W. F. Sheehan such a step should be taken.

That letter is in this city at this moment. It is in the safe of Edward Murphy, Jr., Chairman of the Democratic State Committee.

There will be hasty and perhaps angry denials of the above statements, but they are based upon information which THE TIMES has taken pains to verify, and which is believed to be absolutely reliable.

True, Mr. Hill was never "in" the Presidential race to an extent appreciable by unbiased minds.

His friends, of course, have believed differently, but for reasons not remotely connected with the holding of sundry Democratic Conventions throughout the country, even they may be excused for having of late had misgivings.

The delegates who were elected in February were not all "friends" of Mr. Hill, and they have had something more than misgivings about "their candidate." Notably those from New-York and Kings have declared that they couldn't see how he could possibly be nominated.

There is ground for the belief that a "letter of withdrawal" has for some weeks been considered by the more astute leaders as essential for their own protection, if for no other purpose.

The letter was brought to New-York by Lieut. Gov. William F. Sheehan on Sunday night from Washington in the same pocket in which Mr. Sheehan also brought the resolution, a part of which only was adopted at the delegates' meeting on Monday night last.

The knowledge of the letter was supposed to be confined to Messrs. Murphy, Sheehan, Croker, and McLaughlin, and its existence will be vigorously and emphatically denied by the parties in interest for the next few days.

It will be remembered that Edward Murphy, Jr., announced as soon as the delegates' meeting adjourned (as stated in THE TIMES on Tuesday morning) that no one need be afraid of the action taken on Monday night; that Mr. Hill would not allow his name to be used if it was indicated after the balloting began that it was not for the best interest of the Democratic Party.

The letter throws a good deal of light on the Monday night's meeting of the delegates. It fits in exactly with the resolution that was adopted—to vote for Hill until he was nominated or "until he withdraws his name."

It is understood in political circles that that meeting was called at the request of Mr. Hill. Men like Mr. Croker and Mr. McLaughlin did not quite like the idea of this extraordinary meeting. They were anxious to know where it was going to leave them. They had been watching the course of political events closely. They could not see any Hill strength to amount to anything outside of New-York. They had no desire to be placed in a position where they would be dragged down with Hill. They didn't want all loopholes of escape closed to them.

Mr. Hill has been known to throw his friends overboard. They wanted some assurance that he would not do it on this occasion. They wanted a guarantee from him that would leave them in a position to make other combinations if a fitting time came. Consequently they insisted that Senator Hill send them just such a letter as he did.

With this in their possession they were perfectly willing that the bluff resolution which was adopted by the delegates should be passed, so long as that clause relating to the withdrawal of his name should be included.

Why was it that when William C. De Witt of Brooklyn tried to get that clause stricken out in the executive session of the delegates, that W. Bourke Cockran said that if that was done the delegates might be voting for Mr. Hill until 1896?

It is known here that Messrs. Murphy, Croker, and McLaughlin had a long talk at the Hoffman House late on Monday afternoon.

It was at that time that Croker and McLaughlin read the letter and were satisfied with its contents.

The conference at which Gov. Flower and other State officers and leaders were present came later, and whether the matter was discussed at this meeting or not is not known here. But it was at this latter meeting that the resolution stating that Mr. Cleveland was "unavailable," was squelched, and Messrs. Croker and McLaughlin displayed the same kind of independence of Hill as they did in the Saratoga Convention of 1891, when Mr. Sheehan was nominated for Lieutenant Governor against Hill's will and when Mr. Maynard, Hill's candidate for Attorney General, was "turned down" and Simon W. Rosendale was nominated in his stead.

That "unavailable" resolution was treated in much the same manner as Mr. Hill's silver plank was treated when the leaders were considering the Saratoga platform, and which plank, Mr. Croker said, was "thrown out of the window."

The Hill letter now in the possession of Mr. Murphy is the clearest possible explanation of the action taken by the delegates Monday night in proclaiming themselves to the world as solid for Hill. The "Big Four" were preparing the way to get in out of the wet. With that letter comfortably stowed away the leaders could direct their followers in the delegation to vote "Aye" enthusiastically on the resolution to vote for Mr. Hill "until his name is withdrawn."

When the news of Mr. Hill's letter reached this city there were a number of politicians who were enlightened. Ever since the delegates' meeting it has been rumored that there was more to the preliminary conferences than was indicated in the published reports of the delegates' meeting itself.

There has been an air of mystery about the whole matter, especially when it is considered that the talk about Gov. Flower as a compromise candidate was started almost simultaneously with the adjournment of the delegates' meeting.

This talk of Flower has been somewhat popular with certain of the Tammany men ever since. It has been passed from mouth to mouth, and, while the leaders themselves would say nothing for publication about it, there have been many hints that Flower would make a good candidate for the Presidency.

There is something in this talk beyond the bare idea of securing the nomination and election of Mr. Flower. His election would mean that William T. Sheehan, one of their own kind, would be Governor. Although Mr. Flower has done very well by them so far, there is no telling when he will get tired, but with Mr. Sheehan in the chair there would be a long and uninterrupted vista of plums that could be had just for the picking.

It will be recalled that the Tammany delegates had made all their arrangements to leave this city for Chicago with the other Tammany braves on Saturday, June 18, but at the delegates' meeting they determined to start on Thursday, June 16.

The reason for this is very clear. They want to be on the ground early, so as to get an early and accurate idea of the precise situation among delegations from other States. Having obtained this they will know which way to turn when the turning time comes.

Richard Croker is at Richfield Springs.

Commissioner of Public Works Thomas F. Gilroy, when asked last night what he thought of the letter, declared with marked rapidity that he did not believe such a letter existed. "If there is such a letter," said he, "I do not know of its existence."

Mr. Gilroy was not at the conference which preceded the delegates' meeting on Monday night. He was in the lobby of the Hoffman House while the conference was going on up-stairs, and his absence from the conference was a source of much comment in the lobby.

Benjamin Wood, the only delegate to Chicago who voted against the resolution to vote for Mr. Hill "until he withdraws," said last night that the report about the letter was untrue, but in view of Mr. Wood's vote he would probably be the last man in the delegation who would be informed as to the letter.

### DAVID WON'T TALK.

WASHINGTON, June 9.—Senator Hill sent word from his room in the Arlington Hotel to-night that he would not see the TIMES's correspondent, who called to ask him as to his letter withdrawing from the race for the Presidential nomination. He remained concealed all the evening.

Senator Calvin S. Brice was asked if he knew anything about it.

"I have not heard that such a letter is in existence," he said.

"I have not had any communication with Hill on that subject for a month.

"If he has sent any word to the delegates from the Albany Convention I know nothing about it."

Senator Brice, however, made this remark when asked what, in his opinion, was the object of the delegates in passing a resolution to stand by Hill until he withdraws his name.

"I do not know all the proceedings of the delegates at the Hoffman House meeting. Some of their proceedings were not made public. I know nothing further than what I have learned from the published reports."

## *ADVISED TO WITHDRAW HIS SUIT.*

GREGORY'S EVIDENCE AGAINST HIS WIFE INSUFFICIENT.

TRENTON, N. J., June 9.—The Gregory divorce case was continued to-day before Vice Chancellor Bird. Mrs. Gregory, the defendant, resumed her testimony. She testified that she and her husband separated in June last by mutual arrangement, at the husband's solicitation. No articles of separation were signed, although the plaintiff said he would meet her at the Astor House to sign them.

Mrs. Gregory swore that her husband had seemed anxious for a separation for about a year, and that he had expressed happiness when they parted, and he escorted her to the station, paying her marked attentions.

Mrs. Gregory, when asked by her counsel as to her husband's treatment, said that he had handled her cruelly on different occasions. Nevertheless she said: "I loved him then and I love him yet."

One time, she said, he threw her down stairs, and another time placed his knee on her breast and injured her so that she had to get a physician. She assigned no reason for his wanting a divorce, and said: "I think he always had the greatest faith in me."

She corroborated the testimony of Mr. and Mrs. Thomas Letson, who swore that Mrs. Gregory spent the nights of Dec. 31, 1891, and Jan. 1, 1892, (when her husband alleges she was with Samuel Sickel of New-York,) at their house, 44 Jayne Street, New-York. Mr. Letson is a brother of Mrs. Gregory's.

Mrs. Gregory related her connection with Samuel Sickel of New-York as a reader. She swore she secured the position with him through answering an advertisement, and that she received $5 a week for reading to him two or three hours a day. Sickel, she swore, was blind. Her employment by him ceased about Christmas, 1891.

She testified to receiving four or five anonymous letters seeking interviews and naming places of meeting. One of the letters she produced. The others had been lost.

Mrs. Gregory denied her husband's charges in his petition.

She testified that her husband, in a fit of unjustifiable passion, had cut a silk dress into shreds.

When asked why she repeatedly followed her testimony with the statement, "This is the truth," she burst into tears, saying: "If my name is gone I might as well be dead."

Mrs. Deborah Brady of Long Branch, Mrs. Gregory's sister, testified to several conversations with Mr. Gregory, in which he said he wanted to be divorced from his wife because of her extravagance. He assigned no other cause. She chided him, but he was determined, and said that he had been told by Detective Faller that if he sent his wife to New-York he could get evidence enough in six months to secure a divorce.

In rebuttal the plaintiff's counsel called Charles Neal, one of the detectives, to identify Mrs. Gregory as the woman whom he had seen in company with Sickel. Mr. Barton objected to such testimony and was sustained by the court.

Mr. Gregory was called to the stand in rebuttal and denied ever having struck or ill treated his wife. He swore that only when she struck him would he take hold of her, and then only to prevent further assaults.

Vice Chancellor Bird, after the counsel had finished their argument, advised that the suit be discontinued for the want of evidence to sustain the charges made against Mrs. Gregory.

He commented severely on the work of the detectives, and said that they had hoodwinked Mr. Gregory when he saw his wife as often as he did. It was his duty to have met her face to face when the detectives alleged she was with Sickel and not taken chances of having another woman palmed off on him.

He censured the complainant for implicating six co-respondents and not substantiating the charges.

### What a Tennessee Delegate Says.

"I have been a delegate from Tennessee to every Democratic Convention since 1876," remarked ex-State Senator Thomas O. Morris of Nashville at the Hoffman House last night, "but this is the first time I have ever been instructed how to vote.

"Every one of us twenty-four is to vote for Cleveland, and these instructions fairly reflect the sentiment of the Democrats, not only of the South, but throughout the country, and in saying that I wish to include New-York State, for the people made their declaration at Syracuse, and not at Albany."

### Col. Polk Better.

WASHINGTON, June 9.—The condition of Col. L. L. Polk, President of the Farmer's Alliance, is somewhat improved.



## AN INDIAN PASSION PLAY

*GIVEN AT ST. MARY'S MISSION IN BRITISH COLUMBIA.*

IN HONOR OF A VISIT OF CATHOLIC PRELATES FROM THE EAST—IT SHOWED WHAT COULD BE DONE IN OBJECT TEACHING.

OTTAWA, Ontario, June 9.—Archbishop Duhamel of Ottawa says that the Passion Play performed at St. Mary's Mission, British Columbia, ten days ago by the Indians proved a great success. The strange spectacular production was given in honor of the visit of Catholic prelates from the East.

St. Mary's Mission presented an unusual and picturesque sight. Pitched in regular lines along the base of the hill which leads up to the mission buildings were the hundreds of snow-white tents of the Indian visitors. The camping ground was slightly contracted in limit, so that the tents were close together. Crowning the eminence were the convent, the chapel, and the boys' school, with the few other buildings in connection.

Almost west from the boys' school a large tent, made into a temporary chapel, had been erected, while along the walk in front of the grounds were several steps of plank, from which the bands would play for the torchlight procession. The Indians, including the boys and girls from the mission, were assembled at the station to receive the incoming clergymen. Brass bands were present and played several times.

Greetings were exchanged and the people were addressed through an interpreter. The visiting clergymen were taken to the convent, where a luncheon had been prepared for them. Some idea of the extensive work being done by the Roman Catholic missionaries in British Columbia may be had from the number of Indians assembled. Each tribe had its own tenting ground, and above each division floated a banner inscribed with some device of religious signification.

It had been first intended to hold this monster gathering in Kamloops, but on account of the trouble in Tillicoet over the arrest and imprisonment of Father Cherouse, it was thought advisable to select another place, and St. Mary's Mission was chosen. Had the first arrangement been carried out, it was expected that from 10,000 to 12,000 natives would have been present. As it was, the crowd numbered about 1,200 people.

The Roman Catholic Church has adopted a plan of teaching the Indians the events of the Bible almost similar to that adopted in England in the sixteenth and seventeenth centuries, that of tableaus, as their language is not well adapted to copious and graphic description. It is hoped by this means to bring the events of Biblical history so vividly before the minds of the natives that they will never forget them.

After prayer in the impoverished chapel the procession was formed at the bottom of the hill, each priest from the various settlements accompanying his people. The passion hymn was kept up as the procession wended its way by a circuitous route up the hill and passed the walk in front of the grounds where the representation of the crucifixion was.

On the route the procession had to pass representations of various scenes a few hours preceding the crucifixion of the Saviour. First came the agony in the garden. Four Indians, in the habits the disciples are supposed to have worn, represented the characters in that event. Then came the taking of Jesus by Judas and the soldiers. The third scene was Christ before Pilate, and then the scourging.

Next came the crowning of the Saviour with thorns, and then the holy women meeting Jesus, and last the crucifixion. All of these were very realistic representations, the garments and the accoutrements being representative of the time of the Saviour. The Indians assumed the various characters of the tableaus with an accuracy of representation that it would have been hard to excel, all the scenes being very impressive and such as could not but be understood and remembered by all who had learned the story.

This long procession took almost an hour to assemble around the crucifixion, which was the last tableau, and formed the rallying point for the whole assembly. They still continued to chant the passion hymn, which called on all to express contrition for their sins. The representation of the crucifixion was very full and complete.

The figure of the Saviour had been brought from the chapel and elevated on a cross from the platform by a mechanical contrivance. What represented blood was made to trickle from the wounds in the hands, head, and the side. One soldier stood ready with hyssop upon a staff, and on the other side stood another soldier with a spear, while at the feet was the Virgin Mary, whose grief seemed inconsolable as she threw herself in despair against the cross.

In the background stood the soldiers and the executioners. The whole scene formed a weird spectacle, which by the beholders will never be forgotten.

## *MORGAN MAKES ANOTHER ATTACK.*

AN EFFORT TO SMOKE THE SILVER DEMOCRATS OUT OF THEIR HOLE.

WASHINGTON, June 9.—Senator Morgan (Dem., Ala.,) gave Senator Hill (Dem., N. Y.,) another prod this morning for his silence on the silver question. In the course of some remarks on this subject he characterized the Ocala platform as an unsound one. Speaking of the silver question he said:

"Why cannot we have statesmen in this Chamber calling themselves Democrats come up and say what they are going to do about it? At any rate give the people so much interested some sort of an idea as to how they stand."

Hill was sitting near Senator Brice (Dem., Ohio,) in the rear row of seats, holding a whispered conference with Senators Gorman and Brice. All three had raised their eyes toward Senator Morgan as if slightly startled, but they soon went on with their conference. This was toward the end of a speech on the silver question which Mr. Morgan began shortly after the opening of the Senate. He went over about the usual ground of the free-coinage side. Alluding to Senator Sherman and his little Presidential boom, Mr. Morgan said it might be that the Minneapolis Convention would put Mr. Sherman up as a target for the slings and arrows of all Democratic advocates of free coinage. If that were not done, he assured the Senator that he himself would shoot a few arrows at him, as he stood in the position taken last week on this question.

### Ballot-Reform Law Upheld.

TRENTON, N. J., June 9.—The Supreme Court rendered a decision to-day upholding all the features of the ballot-reform law. The decision was in the case of Ransom V. Black, brought in the interest of the Prohibition Party, which wanted the law declared unconstitutional because of the provision requiring parties polling less than 5 per cent. of the total vote to present a numerously-signed petition in order to have their candidates' names printed on the official ballots.

The Prohibitionists had less than 5 per cent. of the total vote in many sections, and contended that the petition's provision exposes a voter's politics and violates the secrecy of the ballot.

### Plume Has Amended His Order.

NEWARK, N. J., June 9.—Major Gen. Plume has amended his order disorganizing the First Brigade of the State Militia, in some respects affecting the reorganization of the regiments in the brigade.

One of the local newspapers says that Plume amended his order before it was submitted to Attorney General Stockton, and that it was on the amended order that the Attorney General's decision sustaining its legality and validity is based.

### Shannon and Robertson Reappointed.

ALBANY, June 9.—Under the new insurance law Superintendent Pierce is allowed several deputies in the Insurance Department. To-day he reappointed Michael Shannon as his first deputy and Chief Clerk Matthew H. Robertson as his second deputy. The latter has been Chief Clerk of the department since it was established in 1860.

### Getting the Wigwam Ready.

CHICAGO, June 9.—The canvas roof was to-day put on the Wigwam, in which the National Democratic Convention is to be held. Sergeant at Arms Bright says that everything will be in readiness by the close of the week.

10 Pages

# The New York Times.

10 Pages

VOL. XLI...NO. 12,729. NEW-YORK, SATURDAY, JUNE 11, 1892. PRICE THREE CENTS.

## HARRISON WINS THE PRIZE

### *BLAINE BEATEN AS HE NEVER WAS BEATEN BEFORE.*

THE PRESIDENT RENOMINATED BY A PLURALITY OF 166—WHITELAW REID THE CANDIDATE FOR VICE PRESIDENT—BLAINE FORCES DIVIDED IN THE BALLOT, ABOUT HALF GOING TO M'KINLEY.

*For President*—BENJAMIN HARRISON of Indiana.

*For Vice President*—WHITELAW REID of New-York.

MINNEAPOLIS, June 10.—The Republican ticket for 1892 is made up.

After three days of preliminary work, and in the first session of the fourth day, Benjamin Harrison of Indiana was nominated on the first ballot, receiving 535 1-6 votes to 182 1-6 for William McKinley of Ohio, and 182 votes for James G. Blaine of Maine, with 4 votes for Thomas B. Reed of Maine and 1 for Robert T. Lincoln of Illinois.

At the second session, Whitelaw Reid of New-York was nominated for Vice President by acclamation.

The omen of last night, when the lights went out on the initial conflict between the Harrison and Blaine men, was as true of the beginning of his search for the Presidential nomination as it was of the close of it, for everybody now assumes that Blaine will never again become or allow his friends to cause him to be considered a candidate for President.

Harrison's friends refrained from harsh references to Mr. Blaine, while Mr. Blaine's supporters have indulged in coarse, bitter, vindictive epithets about the President. The Harrison men, with a candidate absolutely without a personal friend or any magnetic qualities of attraction, demoralized the adherents of the Plumed Knight, and have left the once brilliant leader crushed and beaten, after desertion in battle by half of his noisy and vengeance-breathing supporters.

Blaine has been beaten before, but never under such humiliating conditions, or in a way from which so little satisfaction can be gleaned. His supporters in the convention, in placing him in nomination, lauded him as little less than a god, and then, with their laudations still ringing in the ears of the thousands to whom they had been addressed, they fled away from the advancing Harrison hosts in a divided body that would have lacked, if united, almost a hundred votes to make a majority.

Blaine's men flung in the faces of the Harrison men the taunt that Harrison was to be nominated by the Solid South, which has no Republican votes, yet in the States of New-York and Pennsylvania he secured more votes from Northern States than either Blaine or McKinley.

Harrison's nomination has seemed inevitable from the beginning of the contest, as the readers of these dispatches have had reason to conclude, if they have followed the accounts sent to THE TIMES. The only day upon which there appeared to be a possibility that Blaine might regain the old following upon which he has always been able to rely for handsome support, and for demonstrations of admiration, wonderful by illustration of physical and emotional endurance, was on the day of the reception of the news of his resignation from the President's Cabinet. Even then it was not discoverable among the delegates.

The Harrison line of official supporters, the 200 or more who were delegates and the 400 others who were volunteer supporters of the Harrison people, were alarmed. The delegates stood the shock extremely well.

Quay's surrender to the Credentials Committee was not a surprise. He and Platt and Clarkson had looked over the vote of this morning, and they saw no encouragement for a renewal of the contest. They knew they were beaten, and that Harrison would be nominated when they entered the convention hall this morning. They leaned but lightly upon the shift to McKinley. They had found out, in their canvassing, that Harrison held his forces by a strong hand. It was not office holding, but party fidelity, tempered and regulated by the infidelity of Blaine.

Blaine may not be able now to appreciate the full extent to which he has suffered in this convention in the withdrawal of admiration for his supposed knightly qualities. He has lost thousands of friends, who held him as a hero and who are now only deterred from condemning him as an ingrate and a foe of his party because they believe that he cannot be held to the same responsibility for his course that would have been imposed upon him four years ago.

It was not a convention of remarkable speeches. Excepting the effort of Mr. Depew, which was one of his very best, although it was destitute of the graceful wit for which he has become famous, and the effusion of Senator Wolcott, that was tinged with the ill-concealed bitterness of hate, they were all ordinary. Those of the renominators of Harrison were in unvarying good temper, studiously free from expressions of a resentment against Mr. Blaine that was felt if not uttered. They were much more argumentative and rational than any of the Blaine speeches, which were all appeals to the old idolatry of the now decrepit leader and the obsolete campaign cries that were effective coupled with the name of Blaine four, eight, and twelve years ago.

Senator Wolcott's fustian for Blaine would have been admissible, if he ever considered it advisable, if it had not been coupled with criticisms of Federal office holders that were provoked rather because they were friendly to Harrison than from any aversion to having them change their allegiance to Blaine.

The convention was not as impressing as a spectacle of men gone mad with zeal on behalf of a candidate as any one of the conventions, Republican or Democratic, in the last twelve years. The Blaine noise exceeded the racket made by the friends of Harrison, but it was palpably as mechanical as the production of theatrical thunder. It had no plausible producing or exciting cause, except the inadvisable women behind the presiding officer. They permitted themselves to be so zealous and active as to excite fears for their bodily health.

The crowd cheered the women and the flags they waved, and then perhaps as much to express their amazement as for any better reason, cheered on beholding the corpulent person of Thomas B. Reed as he wrought himself into a perspiration, cheering and waving his hat for his life-long enemy and despiser, James G. Blaine.

Warner Miller's speech was a wail, heavy, pleading, apologetic, lacking in applause-getting quality. The audience rested, while Miller perspired with perfunctory zeal in the name of "a majority" of New-York delegates "for James G. Blaine." He spoke as if the recollection of last night's melancholy exhibition of demoralization oppressed him.

Mr. Miller did not begin to exert as much enthusiasm for Blaine as Representative Cheatham of North Carolina, a colored man and a natural orator, aroused for Harrison, or a tithe of the uproar that another colored man, Boyd of Tennessee, called forth for Blaine, although Mr. Boyd was impolitic in suggesting that he would be for Harrison if Blaine were out of the race.

Miller, like Blaine, has injured himself needlessly, foolishly, perhaps irreparably, for the lack of judgment that led him into a camp of his enemies just on the eve of a defeat that must have appeared inevitable to any observer with as much experience as Mr. Miller has had might properly excite distrust in him as a leader of New-York Republicans.

## BEGINNING THE DAY'S WORK.

### CONTESTS QUICKLY SETTLED—ALASKA AND INDIAN TERRITORY GIVEN VOTES.

MINNEAPOLIS, June 10.—It was only the lucky few who caught more than one or two winks of sleep in this town last night. The events of the late session had put everybody at odds with the idea of bed, and, in consequence, probably more men here saw the eastern sky streak with gray and then brighten into a new day than ever before since Father Hennepin made his famous voyage up the Mississippi.

The Harrison men were celebrating. The Blaine boomers, in despair at their defeat, were seeking to discover some new doll which they could stuff with sawdust and foist upon the convention as a better man than the President, and the newspaper men were, most of them, hard at work.

The morning opened with a storm of wind and rain, which played havoc with the decorations and made everybody fearful that there was to be a return of the disgraceful weather of the early part of the week. The Pillsbury arch of barrels, near the convention hall, was almost demolished, so, in order to prevent its falling down upon the crowd, the remains had to be removed.

By 10 o'clock, just as the first few stragglers began their march to the hall, the sun came out warm and bright—a propitious omen for Mr. Harrison, so his friends thought. The delegates were rather slow in getting to their places, owing, perhaps, to the late hours which they had kept. The most noticeable thing about the gathering in its early stage was the scarcity of Blaine badges. There were almost none to be seen. Not a single man in the Pennsylvania delegation wore one, and Henry G. Burleigh was the only New-York delegate who still flaunted the little crimson ribbon bearing the "Plumed Knight's" name in letters of gold.

The air of the hall seemed charged with expectation and excitement, and the rumors of conferences among the Blaine leaders and what they proposed to do to prevent the nomination of President Harrison were many. It was at first generally conceded among the delegates that Harrison would be nominated on the first ballot. But when the Ohio delegation came in, it was learned that Clarkson, Platt, Quay & Co. had persuaded its members to cast a solid vote for Mr. McKinley on the first ballot. This was the result of the night's conferences, and the anti-Administration men seemed to feel certain that this, their latest scheme, would be crowned with success.

The Harrison leaders said nothing, but were smilingly sure that the game was in their hands.

H. O. Armour was among the first of the New-York delegates to take his seat. A moment after in came Senator O'Connor and Frank S. Witherbee, the new member of the National Committee. They were without Blaine badges and looked decidedly crestfallen. Senator O'Connor, who has the reputation of being a most rabid Republican, said:

"You can put me down hereafter as a Mugwump. I have been thoroughly won over to the doctrines of George William Curtis. I think, with him, that the sooner the office-holding element is obliterated from conventions the better it will be for the Republican Party."

Senators Wolcott and Teller of Colorado, who have been busy for the last ten days pumping wind into the Blaine boom, acknowledged that the fight was practically over.

"We were sent as delegates by our State," said the latter, "to defeat, if possible, the nomination of Harrison on account of his silver views. We have made the best fight we knew and I am afraid that we must confess ourselves beaten."

The massive figure of Senator Hiscock loomed up. He looked as happy "as a basket of chips," quite as if he were personally responsible for last night's defeat of the Blaine men.

Platt hastened up the aisle a moment after, with his hair rumpled and his cravat awry. He walked over to the seats of the Pennsylvania delegation, evidently in search of his side partner, Quay, but that gentleman had not yet appeared. Platt was finally buttonholed by Senators Washburn and Wolcott, and the three stood together, with their heads bent toward a common centre, in animated conversation for five minutes. Platt's face brightened, and as he walked over to his seat he said over his shoulder to Senator Wolcott, "We will beat them yet."

The aisles were crowded with delegates, asking each other as to the results of the many rumored conferences, and the opinion seemed to be gaining ground with them that the Harrison haters might still succeed in stampeding the convention to another. There was a rumor that the Blaine crowd had lost four of its supporters to Harrison in the New-York delegation, but Fred Gibbs, who was said to be one of the four, denied that there was any truth in the report.

As Senator Quay took his seat, the band struck up the "Lost Chord." The Senator smiled. Warner Miller slipped quietly to his place, wearing a blue ribbon, indicative, perhaps, of his feelings. He looked as if he were rather ashamed of the exhibition that he made of himself last night. Lou Payn was particularly down at the mouth and even refused to say good morning to his friends.

Mr. Depew was the last man to appear, and, as usual, was recognized by the crowd and applauded. He was evidently well pleased with himself and the world, for he smiled, bowed suavely to the right and left, and then sat down to listen to the prayer which had just begun.

It was 11:33 when Gov. McKinley called the convention to order. Minnesota, belated in making its selection, presented the name of R. G. Evans as its National Committeeman, and Pennsylvania that of David Martin, as the successor of Quay, the "Judas" of Bob Kennedy.

The Chairman then announced that the next thing on the programme was the consideration of the report of the Committee on Contested Seats in the Ninth Alabama case. Senator Quay created a very decided breeze when he arose and, in his usual small voice, said that there would be no further opposition to the adoption of the majority report. His announcement was greeted with great applause and, when McKinley put the question upon the adoption of the report, there was a chorus of "Ayes," almost sufficient to crack the glass of the blue-domed hall.

Motions to admit the two delegates from Alaska and the Indian Territory were adopted.

Gov. Seay of Oklahoma made a demand that his Territory be allowed six delegates. The audience, however, had come for business. They wanted the nominations. Throughout the vast hall there was much disorder, confusion, and nervousness displayed, and, although a dozen delegates claimed recognition from the Chair, and got it, not more than ten persons could hear what they said or what it was about. A messenger walked down the aisle and presented Chairman McKinley with a basket of cut flowers. The audience applauded.

Warner Miller, who sat in the first row directly under the Chairman's eye, arose and said something about patriotic ladies, but the rest of his remarks were buried in the confusion and disorder. He handed to the Chair a petition, which was read by John S. Kenyon, formerly Clerk of the Senate at Albany, and who made a robust impression by his clear-cut tones compared with the mouthing and indistinguishable reading of the other wretched clerks.

It was a petition from the National Women's Rights Association, and after Mr. Kenyon had finished reading it Chairman McKinley, at the request of Mr. Miller, introduced Mrs. J. Ellen Foster, who, without removing her bonnet or wrap, harangued the convention for twenty minutes or more. Mrs. Foster declared that a woman who loved her country should love the grand old party, which was the party of great moral ideas. She believed that moral reforms should be carried on outside of party lines. She praised the Republican as the party of action and of progress.

The Alabama delegates, who, by their frequent quarrelsome interruptions, were rapidly degenerating into a nuisance, created another disturbance by attempting to elect their National Committeeman in the convention against the protest of a number of the delegates. At Chairman McKinley's suggestion the delegation was given more time in which to select their man.

## THE NOMINATIONS MADE.

MINNEAPOLIS, June 10.—It was past noon when the preliminary work of the convention was finished, and the nervousness among the vast audience was only too apparent, so that, when Chairman McKinley announced "the regular order of business is the presentation of candidates," the spectators displayed unmistakable manifestations of satisfaction.

"It is in order," said the Chairman, "to call the roll of States. Is that the desire of the convention?"

"Yes, yes!" was the response from all parts of the hall. The decks were cleared for action, sawdust, metaphorically speaking, was sprinkled over the arena, and the butchery of Blaine began.

It was preceded by the customary bombardment of eloquence. Clerk Raney began the call of States. The great assemblage sat subdued, quiet, and expectant. He reached Colorado, and Senator Wolcott, with a quick, businesslike gait, started for the platform. From all parts of the hall arose murmurs and cries of "Sit down!" The Chairman directed the Sergeant at Arms to clear the aisles, while Wolcott made his bow. He was perfectly at home, and during the delivery of his speech he walked up and down the platform with the ease of a man in his own drawing room. His dark three-buttoned cutaway coat and striped trousers were cut by a scientific tailor, and fitted his well-knit form to perfection.

Almost at the opening of the speech he announced that he was there to nominate James G. Blaine. The demonstration that followed must have been disappointing to him. It lasted not more than thirty seconds. Burleigh of New-York led the applause. Jumping on his seat, he waved a handkerchief as big as a small sheet, while "Tom" Platt languidly arose and beckoned the faithful to their feet with a tired and hopeless motion of his hands. Fassett was also in the front row with the shouters, and Col. Quay's infantile treble was heard exhorting his Pennsylvania slaves to arise and make themselves heard in the good cause.

As Wolcott warmed to his work his face grew paler. He was interrupted here and there by zephyrs of applause from the Blaine zealots in the audience. The prize idiot appeared with an American flag, with a colored parasol and umbrella, a plume, and a foghorn, and he gave expression to his feelings by waving the one and raising the other. He was the most vociferous nuisance in Minneapolis. He was well sprinkled through the audience, and he was sometimes accompanied by a woman, who assisted him in the noisy and wearisome demonstrations. When Wolcott concluded his speech the idiot let himself loose all over the convention hall for the exact period of twenty-five seconds by the watch.

MR. CHAIRMAN AND GENTLEMEN OF THE CONVENTION: The Republicans of the West sometimes differ with the Republicans of the East as to what is wanted. On this occasion there is remarkable unanimity between genuine Republicans of the West and genuine Republicans of the East as to who is needed, and his name is Blaine.

It is to us a matter of comparative indifference who shall lead the Democratic hosts, but we trust they will once more renominate their prophet of tariff reform in order that we may demonstrate how short a life have slander and calumny, that a chastened country may repair the wrong of 1884 and stamp with the seal of final disapproval a policy which could only lead to impoverishment at home and which brought only contempt and dishonor abroad.

There is practical agreement among the delegates at this convention, certainly among the representatives of the Republican States, as to whom our leader should be, and its expression would find unanimous voice were there not a mistaken feeling among certain of our associates that the bestowal of offices is a personal gift. The welfare of our beloved party, Mr. Chairman, is of infinitely greater importance than the vindication or nomination of any man within its ranks, and when the roll of States is called I believe it will be remembered that the obligations of office are repaid solely by faithful performance of its duties, and that manhood and independence are never bartered among good men for the emoluments and honors of public station.

Our candidate, Mr. Chairman, has never been President of the United States. He will be; but if he has not yet occupied that office, he has, by his devotion to the party, made Republican Presidents possible, and he has enriched and guided two Administrations with his sagacity and statesmanship. We are honored and respected abroad. We owe that to his statecraft. We are gathering the republics of all America together in bonds of closest friendship. It is because he devised the plan and has shaped the policy. We are protecting our own people on the farm and in the workshop, and by wise concessions are inducing the nations of the world to open their gates to our products. His far-seeing and discriminating vision saw the possibilities of reciprocity and induced us to foster it.

There is no public measure since the days of reconstruction which hastened the advancement of our country with which he is not identified, and when the history of this generation of our Republic shall be written his name will stand foremost among its statesmen. No official title or station can add to or detract from the lustre of his fame, but we may at least let history record that such as we had to give we gave with loyal and loving hearts.

The best gifts in this world are not for those who seek them. Our votes are to be cast for one who is almost every Republican's candidate except his own. For my own part, I rejoice that the opportunity is given me of casting my vote for a nominee who seeks nothing for himself, but everything for his country. And the same devotion to the Nation's welfare which has guided him in his public life for nearly a generation insures his acceptance of any duty which this convention may impose upon him.

For many months there has been apprehension in the public mind respecting his health and strength. It is gratifying to be able to state that the fears which have moved us are groundless. For our country's sake and his own, we could wish that he were again the young and ardent leader who has guided his party through countless battles and that his youth could be renewed like the eagle's. Experience, however, Mr. Chairman, comes only with ripening years. The same unconquerable will and lofty patriotism still dominate his being, and, though time has tinged his hair with white and the years of struggle in his country's service have left their impress, he still stands, for us who love him, the embodiment of all that is brightest and the best in American statesmanship, and, mellowed and broadened by the creeping hours of time, we thank God that he is still amply able and equipped to give to the people of these States an administration which shall protect our own citizens, and, looking beyond the confines of our border, embrace the well-being of all America.

And so, Mr. Chairman, we turn, in the hour when victory is at hand, to the intrepid leader who shaped for his party the policy which has lifted it above the danger of further defeat.

To those of us who belong to the younger element of the party, who are content to follow and not to lead, but who only ask to bear their share of the burden and heat of the day, he stands as our idol, our inspiration. His name is engraved in all our hearts in loving letters that can never fade. Brave, true-hearted, and great, there is no true Republican who will but follow when he leads, and with loving faith and trust that a kind Providence may long spare him to a people whose grateful homage he has earned, and whose affectionate devotion he possesses, we pledge our unfaltering and loyal support to James G. Blaine.

After the insensate cheering had subsided, the call of the roll of States was resumed and peace ensued until Indiana, the home of the President, was reached, when the "Ancient Mariner of the Wabash" walked down the aisle, stopping on his way to whisper to Mr. Depew, amid a generous roar. He took the platform, made a brief businesslike address informing the audience that while he was simply there to nominate Gen. Harrison, the real speech would be made by an orator who had no equal either in this or any other country. The audience cheered lustily and Mr. Depew blushed like a schoolgirl. Mr. Thompson said:

MR. CHAIRMAN AND GENTLEMEN OF THE CONVENTION: I do not intend to make a speech. I propose to make a nomination for the Presidency which shall strike a cord of sympathy in every true Republican heart. I propose to nominate for the Presidency a man who does not seek elevation by detraction of any other great Republican in the Republican Party. [Applause.]

I do not propose, however, to defend the history of his life before this convention, because that will be done in words of burning and breathing eloquence which cannot be surpassed in this or any other country in the world. [Applause.] Therefore, with these simple words of praise, I nominate to this convention for the Presidency of the United States, the warrior-statesman Benjamin Harrison of Indiana.

When it was found that "Col. Dick" had finished his speech, the hall shook with applause, and for four minutes there was one unceasing cheer from the thousands of throats. A very stout man in the Illinois delegation, Mr. Roberts, jumped on his chair, opened his umbrella, and yelled like a Comanche who had captured his first scalp. The same Roberts four years ago was one of the most enthusiastic Blaine men in the National Convention.

The State of Maine was passed in silence.

Michigan was reached and some one in the gallery called, "What's the matter with Alger?" There was no answer, even of applause.

As Minnesota was mentioned, William Henry Eustis bobbed up on the platform and wearied the audience for fifteen minutes by the dreariest speech of the day. He made numerous references to Father Hennepin, Père Nicollet, Christopher Columbus, and the discovery of America, and the spectators were in some doubt as to whether Mr. Eustis realized where he was or whether he had got lost in the labyrinth of ancient American history.

His closing sentence, however, which had nothing whatever to do with any other part of his speech, let them into the reason for his being there, by his saying, in a matter-of-fact tone: "I arise to second the nomination of James G. Blaine."

While this speech was the most insignificant and uninspiring of the day, the proceedings that followed it were of the most flamboyant character and impressed the greenhorns with the fear that a deliberately-laid plot had been made to stampede the convention for Blaine. After Eustis concluded very little applause was heard until three ladies, who sat immediately behind Tom Reed and directly in the rear of the Chairman, rose. One was stout and middle-aged. She had in her hand an American flag of service size, which she waved mechanically. The second was a comparatively young woman, who shook aloft a dark umbrella.

The third was the wife of a newspaper man, and she at once became a conspicuous mark for the audience, especially those interested in Mr. Blaine. She wore a tailor-made gown of light woolen material, and waved aloft a white silk parasol in a commanding way that attracted general attention. From cheering Blaine, the audience began to cheer her and to wave their arms frantically and yell hoarsely, and proceed on the lines usually laid down by Blaine persons in conventions. Men jumped on chairs and whooped. Ladies produced flags and cried "Blaine!" till they were red in the face and hoarse of voice.

Then some one yelled, "Blaine, Blaine, James G. Blaine." The band played, but it might as well have blown its music into Bedlam for all that the audience heard of it. Tin horns and shrill whistles and cymbals broke in when the general din began to subside. Still the three ladies continued their gymnastic performances. They waved and shrieked. The whole audience, irrespective of factional feelings, was on its feet, and several of the Blaine leaders, who had evidently passed their time at some period of their lives in leading an orchestra, succeeded in reducing the "Blaine, Blaine, James G. Blaine" war whoop to a rhythmical chorus, which shook the entire building.

At one side Mrs. Thurston and Kate Field, each with a white silk parasol with "Blaine" in the largest and blackest letters, contributed to the general uproar. As each wave of applause began to diminish the New-York woman, who was artfully supplied at different times with an American flag and a red, white, and blue star with Blaine's photograph in the centre, waved the audience to its feet again, and the cheering and yelling went on with increased vigor.

"Tom" Reed, fat and sleek, caught the infection, and it was a sight for the gods to see his burly figure shaking with the spirit of the occasion, and his No. 10 hand waving an American flag for Blaine, the man whom he has hated until now. The crowd saw him, and what had been a tempest of applause before was now a cyclone. The audience called for him, and gave cheers for him and yelled for him.

At the height of the tumult Henry G. Burleigh jumped upon the platform, forced his way through the crowd, and besought Reed to come to the front and make his speech for Blaine. Reed was willing to put himself on exhibition for what there was in it, but he was not there to do any talking for James G. Blaine, and he shook his head negatively.

The Chairman rapped for order, but the sound of his gavel was not heard twenty feet away. The band played again, and again its strains were smothered. The tumult lasted twenty-five minutes. One idiot, who was surrounded by ladies on all sides, took off his coat and vest and waved his arms and shrieked like a madman, and, when an Assistant Sergeant at Arms directed him to resume his garments, in his frenzy he ripped his coat in two parts from its collar to the waist.

Col. Swords, Sergeant at Arms of the National Committee, who had been prompting the three energetic women behind the Chairman, now suggested, as there was evidence that the applause was dying out, that the little woman in white should carry her Blaine star down to the platform. She had proceeded as far as the Secretary's chair, when her husband, in a gentle but firm tone, very sensibly suggested to her that it was more becoming for her to return to her seat, which, with a crestfallen and dejected air, she proceeded to do, and it was noticed subsequently that, in all her ebullitions of ecstacy when Blaine's name was mentioned, she first cast a lingering and inquiring look in the direction of her husband before giving way to her patriotic impulses.

Quiet restored, William E. Mollison, a colored gentleman from Mississippi, in a few well-selected and dignified phrases, let the audience into his friendship and admiration for Mr. Blaine. The colored gentleman's jaw dropped when the audience allowed him to leave the platform without even a departing cheer.

Peace, quiet, and harmony now prevailed until the Secretary called the great State of New-York, when "Our Own" Chauncey, in his easiest and most matter-of-fact way, ascended the platform even while the crowd was bawling for him to take it. The reception he received was certainly one to touch the heart of any man, no matter how great or famous. He was rather pale, and his double-breasted frock coat was buttoned almost to his chin. His modest, cool looking cravat carried a small scarfpin.

The audience expected a treat, and they got it. The speech was one of the best Mr. Depew has ever delivered. It had evidently been prepared more carefully than his speeches usually are. He built his argument in a manner at once skilled and artistic, and he convinced the great body of his auditors that whatever good the Administration had accomplished had been done, not by Mr. Blaine or by any other individual member of the Cabinet, but by the President himself.

At the very opening of his speech he bestowed a complimentary allusion upon Mr. McKinley, which was received by the convention in a rapturous manner. The restless Burleigh was on his feet, beckoning his colleagues to join him in paying tribute to the so-called dark horse of the convention. And it was observed that the delegates who acknowledged this testimonial most vociferously were of the Blaine persuasion. When Mr. Depew spoke of Wolcott's superiority to him as an orator, the crowd repudiated the compliment by cries of "No!" "No!" from all parts of the hall, and when he proved conclusively that President Harrison was the only Republican who had carried the State of New-York in twelve years, a most amazing exhibition took place.

MR. PRESIDENT AND GENTLEMEN OF THE CONVENTION: It is the peculiarity of Republican National Conventions that each one of them has a distinct and interesting history. We are here to meet conditions and solve problems which make this gathering not only no exception to the rule, but substantially a new departure. That there should be strong convictions and their earnest expression as to preferences and politics is characteristic of the right of individual judgment, which is the fundamental principle of Republicanism. There have been occasions when the result was so sure that the delegates could freely indulge in the charming privilege of favoritism and friendship.

But the situation which now confronts us demands the exercise of dispassionate judgment and our best thought and experience. We cannot venture on uncertain ground or encounter obstacles placed in the pathway of success by ourselves. The Democratic Party is now divided, but the hope of the possession of power once more will make it in the final battle more aggressive, determined, and unscrupulous than ever. It starts with fifteen States secure without an effort, by processes which are a travesty upon popular government, and, if continued long enough, will paralyze institutions founded upon popular suffrage. It has to win four more States in a fair fight—States which in the vocabulary of politics are denominated doubtful.

The Republican Party must appeal to the conscience and the judgment of the individual voter in every State in the Union. This is in accordance with the principles upon which it was founded and the objects for which it contends. It has accepted this issue before and fought it out with an extraordinary continuance of success.

The conditions of Republican victory from 1860 to 1880 were created by Abraham Lincoln and U. S. Grant. They were that the saved Republic should be run by its saviors, the emancipation of the slaves, the reconstruction of the States; the reception of those who had fought to destroy the Republic back into the fold, without penalties or punishments, and to an equal share with those who had fought and saved the Nation in the solemn obligation and inestimable privilege of American citizenship. They were the embodiment into the Constitution of the principles for which two millions of men had fought and a half million had died. They were the restoration of public credit, the resumption of specie payments, and the prosperous condition of solvent business for twenty-five years. They were names with which to conjure and events fresh in the public mind which were eloquent with popular enthusiasm. It needed little else than a recital of the glorious story of its heroes and a statement of the achievements of the Republican Party to retain the confidence of the people.

But, from the desire for a change which is characteristic of free governments, there came a reversal; there came a check to the progress of the Republican Party and four years of Democratic Administration. Those four years largely relegated to the realm of history past issues, and brought us face to face with what Democracy, its professions, and its practices, mean to-day.

The great names which have adorned the roll of the Republican statesmen and soldiers are potent and popular. The great measures of the Republican Party are still the best part of the history of the century. The unequaled and unexampled story of Republicanism in its progress and its achievements stands unique in the record of parties in Governments which are free.

But we live in practical times, facing practical issues which affect the business, the wages, the labor, and the prosperity of to-day. The campaign will be won or lost not upon the bad record of James K. Polk, or of Franklin Pierce, or of James Buchanan; not upon the good record of Lincoln or of Grant, or of Arthur, or of Hayes, or of Garfield. It will be won or lost upon the policy, foreign and domestic, the industrial measures, and the administrative acts of the Administration of Benjamin Harrison. Whoever receives the nomination of this convention will run upon the judgment of the people as to whether they have been more prosperous and more happy, whether the country has been in a better condition at home, and stood more honorably abroad under these last four years of Harrison and Republican administration than during the preceding four years of Cleveland and Democratic government.

Not since Thomas Jefferson has any Administration been called upon to face and solve so many or such difficult problems as those which have been exigent in our conditions. No Administration since the organization of the Government has ever met difficulties better or more to the satisfaction of the American people. Chile has been taught that, no matter how small the antagonist, no community can, with safety, insult the flag or murder American sailors. Germany and England have learned, in Samoa, that the United States has become one of the powers of the world, and, no matter how mighty the adversary, at every sacrifice American honor will be maintained. The Bering Sea question, which was the insurmountable obstacle in the diplomacy of Cleveland and of Bayard, has been settled upon a basis which sustains the American position until arbitration shall have determined our right.

The dollar of the country has been placed and kept on the standard of commercial nations, and a convention has been agreed upon with foreign Governments, which, by making bimetallism the policy of all nations, may successfully solve all our financial problems.

The tariff, tinkered with and trifled with to the serious disturbance of trade and disaster to business since the days of Washington, has been courageously embodied into a code which has preserved the principle of the protection of American industries. To it has been added a beneficent policy, supplemented by beneficial treaties and wise diplomacy, which has opened to our farmers and manufacturers the markets of other countries.

The navy has been builded upon lines which will protect American citizens and American interests and the American flag all over the world. The public debt has been reduced, the maturing bonds have been paid off. The public credit has been maintained. The burdens of taxation have been lightened. Two hundred millions of currency have been added to the people's money without disturbance of the exchanges. Unexampled prosperity has crowned wise laws and their wise administration.

The main question which divides us is, to whom does the credit of all this belong. Orators may stand upon this platform, more able and more eloquent than I, who will paint in more brilliant colors, but they cannot put in more earnest thought, the affection and admiration of Republicans for our distinguished Secretary of State.

I yield to no Republican, no matter from what State he hails, in admiration and respect for John Sherman, for Gov. McKinley, for Thomas B. Reed, for Iowa's great son, for the favorites of Illinois, Wisconsin, and Michigan, but when I am told that the credit for the brilliant diplomacy of this Administration belongs exclusively to the Secretary of State, for the administration of its finances to the Secretary of the Treasury, for the construction of its ships to the Secretary of the Navy, for the introduction of American pork in Europe to the Secretary of Agriculture, for the settlement, so far as it is settled, of the currency question to Senator John Sherman, for the formulation of the tariff laws to Gov. McKinley, for the removal of the restrictions placed by foreign nations upon the introduction of American pork to our Ministers at Paris and Berlin, I am tempted to seriously inquire, who, during the last four years, has been President of the United States, anyhow.

Cæsar, when he wrote those commentaries which were the history of the conquests of Europe under his leadership, modestly took the position of Æneas when he said, "They are the narrative of events the whole of which I saw and a part of which I was." Gen. Thomas, as the rock of Chickamauga, occupies a place in our history with Leonidas among the Greeks, except that he succeeded where Leonidas failed. The fight of Joe Hooker above the clouds was the poetry of battle. The resistless rush of Sheridan and his steed down the Valley of the Shenandoah is the epic of our civil war. The march of Sherman from Atlanta to the sea is the supreme triumph of gallantry and strategy. It detracts nothing from the splendor or the merits of the deeds of his lieutenants to say that, having selected them with marvelous sagacity and discretion, Grant still remained the supreme commander of the National Army.

All the proposed acts of any Administration before they are formulated are passed upon in Cabinet council, and the measures and suggestions of the ablest Secretaries would have failed with a lesser President; but for the great good of the country and the benefit of the Republican Party they have succeeded because of the suggestive mind, the indomitable courage, the intelligent appreciation of situations, and the grand magnanimity of Benjamin Harrison.

'Tis an undisputed fact that during the few months when both the Secretary of State and the Secretary of the Treasury were ill, the President personally assumed the duties of the State Department and of the Treasury Department, and both with equal success. The Secretary of State, in accepting his portfolio under President Garfield, wrote: "Your Administration must be made brilliantly successful and strong in the confidence and pride of the people, not at all diverting its energies for re-election and yet compelling that result by the logic of events and by the imperious necessities of the situation."

Garfield fell before the bullet of the assassin and Mr. Blaine retired to private life. Gen. Harrison invited him to take up that unfinished diplomatic career where its threads had been so tragically broken. He entered the Cabinet. He resumed his work and has won a higher place in our history. The prophecy he made for Garfield has been superbly fulfilled by President Harrison. In the language of Mr. Blaine, "the President has compelled a re-election by the logic of events and the imperious necessities of the situation."

The man who is nominated here to-day, to win, must carry a certain well-known number of the doubtful States. Patrick Henry, in the convention which started rolling the ball of the independence of the colonies from Great Britain, said: "I have but one lamp by which my feet are guided, and that is the lamp of experience. I know of no way of judging of the future but by the past."

New-York was carried in 1880 by Gen. Garfield and in every important election since that time we have done our best. We have put forward our ablest, our most popular, our most brilliant leaders for Governor and State officers, to suffer constant defeat. The only light which illumines with the sun of hope the dark record of those twelve years is the fact that, in 1888, the State of New-York was triumphantly carried by President Harrison. He carried it then as a gallant soldier, a wise Senator, a statesman who inspired confidence by his public utterances in daily speech from the commencement of the canvass to its close. He still has all these claims, and, in addition, an Administration beyond criticism and rich with the elements of popularity with which to carry New-York again.

Ancestry helps in the Old World, and handicaps in the new. There is but one distinguished example of a son first overcoming the limitations imposed by the pre-eminent fame of his father, and then rising above it, and that was when the younger Pitt became greater than Chatham. With an ancestor a signer of the Declaration of Independence and another who saved the Northwest from savagery and gave it to civilization and empire, and who was also President of the United States, a poor and unknown lawyer of Indiana has risen by his unaided efforts to such distinction as lawyer, orator, soldier, statesman, and President that he reflects more credit on his ancestors than they have devolved upon him, and presents in American history the parallel of the younger Pitt.

By the grand record of a wise and popular Administration, by the strength gained in frequent contact of the people, in wonderfully versatile and felicitous speech, by the claims of a pure life in public, and in the simplicity of a typical American home, I nominate Benjamin Harrison.

When Mr. Depew finished, the scene that ensued was very much like the demonstration for Blaine. But, where the applause for Blaine had come mostly from the galleries, the applause for Harrison was certainly controlled by the delegates themselves. The band struck up "Carry the News to Mary," while a handsome young girl of seventeen in the gallery to the rear of the Chairman unfurled a large American flag which she waved back and forth, while the spectators sprang to their feet, and the mad scene of a half hour before was renewed. Three men lugged in a large crayon of the President, decorated with red, white, and blue bunting, while from an opposite door two men appeared bearing the beautiful banner of the Chicago Blaine Club. This was carried to the stage, where the roaring was still under way, and placed alongside of Gen. Harrison's crayon.

One of the delightful episodes of this tumultuous occasion was the appearance of the woman delegate from Wyoming, arrayed in a gown of buff serge. She mounted a chair, waved her handkerchief with frantic zeal and chewed gum industriously. Off in one corner the American tin-plate fool made himself a nuisance by pounding a tin wash basin and tin dishpan with drum sticks contributed, it was reported, by Nathaniel Delap.

A beautiful young woman in a light-gray suit, who was coached by "Long" Jones of Chicago, was the most enthusiastic person in the hall at this time. She shook a flag in one hand and a fan in the other, and imitated the war whoop of an Indian by slapping the fan repeatedly against her mouth. Thrice her voice broke, but she recovered it quickly by drinking a glass of water, and started in again with renewed vigor. When the audience grew tired of cheering Harrison, they cheered the attractive young creature in light gray, who seemed to enjoy the compliment as much as she enjoyed her own interest in the President's cause.

A touching sight was Col. Elliott F. Shepard, standing on a chair, waving an American flag energetically in one hand and wiping the perspiration with a handkerchief from a wilted collar with the other.

Warner Miller had been slated by the Blaine crowd to second the nomination of Blaine. Mr. Miller's performance last evening in seeking to scare the convention into adjourning when the electric lights went out had weakened him immeasurably with the convention, and there was very little applause when he stood up to play his part.

He spoke only about ten minutes, but managed to lug in plenty of ancient clap-trap about the man from Maine in the course of his remarks. When he declared that he represented a majority of the delegates from New-York State and that they desired the nomination of Blaine, the Blaine shouters in the gallery sought to bring about a repetition of the scene of the previous hour, but they failed. The women on the platform, who had figured so conspicuously in that outburst, swung Blaine's portrait attached to a new broom, but the desired effect was not produced. The Blaine enthusiasm had reached its limit.

MR. PRESIDENT AND GENTLEMEN OF THE CONVENTION: You have no longer time to listen to the records of our great statesmen of the past. You have come now to the supreme hour of this convention. Thus far, it has been a convention in which kindly spirit has prevailed upon all sides, and I have no doubt, Sir, that it is to prevail to the end, and that whatever may be the outcome of this convention it will be ratified by the whole Republican Party of this country and by a majority of the votes of the people. [Applause.]

We have a portion of the New-York delegation that I represent, which does not come here to make any detraction from the worth or character of any man who has been in high authority, or from the President of the United States. [Cries of "Good, good!"] We indulge in nothing of that kind. We upheld the hands of the men whom we put in power by our votes in New-York four years ago, but we come here believing that the candidate I name or shall second can do much more for us in the great State of New-York in enabling us to achieve a victory in November than any other candidate that can be named. [Applause.]

The Republican majority in the State of New-York are found in the great interior counties north of the city. Since I have been in Minneapolis I have received hundreds of dispatches from leading citizens in the great Counties of St. Lawrence and Chautauqua that I might mention and they all tell me that the idol of their people in the East is the idol that we have held for twenty years. [Applause.] If I did not believe that this candidate, who has already been named here, would give us greater assurances of success than any other, I should not give him my voice nor my vote. [Cries of "Good!"]

Nothing that I can say or do and nothing that any one can say or do here will add anything to the honor or fame of the idol of the Republican Party of this country. [Applause.] Nothing can be said here that can detract anything from the honor and merit that belong to him as a statesman. [Applause.] I would not weary your patience by any recital of his history or of his achievements, because they are known to every one in this audience. They are known to the whole people of America, aye, they are known to the whole world. [Applause.]

The prince of all statesmen, he has been at the front since 1860. For more than thirty years he has led in every combat and has loyally supported every ticket that has been put before the American people. Time and again his admirers have sought to make him President of the United States, but for one reason or the other, either in convention or in election, they have failed thus far to do it, but it is a remarkable fact that, notwithstanding all the variations of American politics, the ups and downs which come to our public men and the changes which come to our party, our candidate, or the one that I should name here, has lost nothing of the love and affection of the great masses of the Republican Party. [Applause.]

It is the common people, if I may so express myself, who have always followed his banner with devotion, with energy, and with courage, and to-day, speaking for a majority of the delegates from New-York, [applause,] speaking for what I know to be a vast majority of the loyal Republicans of the State of New-York, [applause,] I stand here to say to you that if our candidate shall be given to us we shall go into the canvass with the highest expectations and belief of success. [Applause.]

Thus, finally giving you my assurance of what I know to be the sentiments of the people in the interior of the State of New-York, and of the delegates who represent to a large extent those constituencies, I, in behalf of a majority of the delegation of the State of New-York, second the nomination of James G. Blaine. [Applause.]

When North Carolina was reached on the roll, Representative Cheatham, from that State, who is a colored man, made a vigorous speech seconding Harrison's nomination. Mr. Cheatham has a light complexion and hair that is fast turning gray. When he referred to Harrison as a great soldier and statesman, the Harrison delegates cheered lustily.

There were shouts for Foraker when Ohio was called. Foraker, who sat with the Ohio delegation, shook his head. The call was continued until it became evident that Mr. Foraker had nothing to say.

There was laughter when G. Q. Boyd, colored, arose in response to the call of Tennessee. He has a bright face and close-cropped hair, and wore a blue coat, with red, white, and blue badge. He mounted the platform with the greatest assurance, and proceeded to second Blaine's nomination. Mr. Boyd has a penetrating voice and an evident idea that he is an orator. When the convention cheered him he placed his hands on his hips and stood with his head thrown back, waiting until the noise subsided. He referred to Blaine's fame as of the kind which needed "no pyramid, whose towering heights would pierce the storm clouds."

"Whew!" said a voice in the rear of the hall when this metaphor was unloaded. This was the signal for another outburst on the part of the delegates.

"Spooner!" some one cried when the clerk called the name of Wisconsin. In response to it, a man bearing a close resemblance to Senator Gorman walked rapidly to the platform. He was ex-Senator John C. Spooner, one of the best fighters and organizers in the Harrison force. He wore a brown Prince Albert coat, and his sandy hair was brushed carelessly back from his forehead.

He made a forceful speech in favor of the nomination of Mr. Harrison, and it was enthusiastically received. He spoke as follows:

MR. PRESIDENT AND GENTLEMEN OF THE CONVENTION: The preliminaries are settled, and it is a relief that we are at last face to face with the great duty which we came hither to perform. That the action of this body, composed of representative men who love the Republican Party and seek to promote its success for its record and its principles, will be deliberate, thoughtful, and patriotic, and such as to secure for it the approval of those who sent us here, cannot well be doubted.

National Republican Conventions have not been accustomed to make mistakes. That which met at Chicago in 1888 made no mistake when it intrusted the power and responsibility and leadership to Ben Harrison of Indiana, and Ben Harrison made no mistakes.

He quickly proved himself an ideal candidate and a leader who led. Millions of hostile and eager eyes searched his whole life in vain for spot or blemish. On the march and in the battle, no man rode before him. Calm, dignified, and wise, every day brought from his lips a deliverance in itself a perfect platform, unexcelled for grace of diction, power of epigrammatic statements, and the spirit of true eloquence. He imbued the party with renewed vigor and strength, and intrepidly led it to victory.

His friends bring his name into this convention, proudly conscious that the record which he has made needs not to be supplemented by words of advocacy. He has been from the day of his inauguration what the people elected him to be—the President of the United States. He has given to the country an Administration which for ability, efficiency, purity, and patriotism challenges admiration without fear of comparison with any which has preceded since the foundation of the Government.

He has been free from "variableness or shadow of turning" in his devotion to the principles of the Republican Party and to the redemption of the pledges made by it to the people. He has stood for the protection of American industries and the interests of American wage workers, and placed with alacrity the seal of approval upon the great tariff bill of the Fifty-first Congress, which has outridden the flood of misrepresentation which swept over it as did the ark in the deluge of old, and now rests upon a foundation as solid as Mount Ararat.

He championed and promoted, by every means in harmony with the dignity of his great office, the adoption of the scheme of reciprocity, which, as enacted, has found favor with our people, not limited to the South American republics or bartering the interests of one industry for the benefit of another by the free admission of competitive products, but compelling fair treatment by all Governments of all our people and our productions under penalty of commercial retaliation.

Openly friendly to the use of silver as one of the coin metals of the country, under conditions which shall surely maintain it at a parity with gold, and striving to secure by international agreement the existence of those conditions, he stands, nevertheless, as firm as the granite which underlies the continent against a policy which would debase the currency of the people, and must drive the coin of either metal out of circulation.

Nor did he forget or disregard the solemn pledge of the Republican Party that "every citizen, rich or poor, native or foreign-born, white or black," is entitled at every public election to cast one free ballot, and to have that ballot honestly counted and faithfully returned.

With a skill, dignity, and courage which has compelled the admiration of political friend and foe alike, he has caused it to be understood throughout the world that the American flag represents a Government which has the power and the will to protect the American uniform and American interests at all hazards everywhere, whether assailed by peppery neighbors to the southward of us or by the diplomacy or power of Great Britain.

Every interest of the people has had his best care and his best thought, and he stands before the country to-day well approved and universally acknowledged to be a man of transcendent ability, of extraordinary capacity for the discharge of executive duty, of exalted patriotism and lofty purpose, who would not for a unanimous renomination by this convention and a re-election by the people swerve one hair's breadth in any matter of duty, great or small, from what he believes to be just and right.

It is said against him that he has made enemies, and it is evidently thus. So did Washington, so did Jackson, so did Lincoln, so did Grant, so did Garfield, so did Arthur. But this convention will not mistake the lamentations of the disappointed for the voices of the "plain people." This judgment against him overestimates the importance of individuals and underestimates the intelligence and patriotism of the masses. They will not be gulled into the belief that the object of government is the bestowal of office.

Parties care little for the ambition of leaders, and whether John Smith secures an office this month, next month, or not at all. They do not demand of a President that he shall be able to please every one. They want good government; they demand honesty and ability and industry and purity in public and private life, and all this they have had in Ben Harrison—and they know it.

We place him before this convention as one who can bear and will bear, whether nominated or not, (for he is a Republican,) his full share in the great contest which to-day is to begin. The Republicans of every State, save one, in convention assembled, have indorsed with enthusiasm his Administration. Upon that Administration and its record of efficiency and achievement the Republican Party is to invite the coming campaign. There is nothing persuasive in the assertion that the people who officially approve an Administration will withhold their approval from the man who is responsible for it, and who has largely made it.

Put him again at the head of the column. Place in his hand the banner of Republicanism and he will carry it aggressively all the time at the front, and he will lead us again to victory. There will be irresistible power and inspiration in the knowledge which pervades the people that, so long as he is President, there is one at the helm who, whatever betides us at home or abroad, will bring to the solution of every question, to the execution of every policy, and to the performance of every duty a splendid and disciplined intellect, absolute rectitude of purpose, and unfaltering desire to conserve every interest of every section, a self-poise which is a sure safeguard against hasty or mistaken judgment and a patriotism which never has wavered, either in war or in peace.

The convention was getting weary, but this did not prevent Bruno Fink of Wisconsin from making a long speech in support of the President's renomination. It took the convention some time to ascertain whom Mr. Fink favored. When the fact was learned, those Harrison men who had indulged in cat-calls and calls of "time" at Mr. Fink's expense, felt a little ashamed of themselves.

Wyoming was finally reached, and the crowd breathed more freely. A groan of despair was heard when a tall man, with a face which looked like that of the gentleman with the portraits of his three daughters in his whiskers, rushed down the aisle toward the platform. He turned out to be S. W. Downey of Wyoming. His first utterance set the convention wild.

"I come from the far-off State, which is many miles from here," he yelled, and the delegates immediately began to wish he was back in that far-off land. He had a loud voice and loud manners, and would not be suppressed until he had had his say. Such a hubbub was raised by the crowd that the Chairman was obliged to intercede in his behalf. In return for his favor Mr. Downey asked the convention to make no pledges, "but, when four years reel around, nominate him," pointing to Mr. McKinley. The Chairman did not seem to relish this sudden disposition of his little boom, but the convention did.

Mr. Downey was finally disposed of and then the clerk called the name of Utah. A hearty cheer was heard. The Chairman announced that representatives of five or six States, who had missed the opportunity to speak when their States were called, now desired to be heard. A roar of dissent greeted this announcement.

Gen. Sewell of New-Jersey caused satisfaction by moving that the convention proceed to ballot for Presidential candidates. The motion was carried, although a faint vote in the negative was heard from Boss Quay's people.

## THE PRESIDENT'S EASY VICTORY.

MINNEAPOLIS, June 10.—The roll of States for nominations was ended without trapping any more orators, and the Chairman announced that the convention would proceed to ballot. This was not agreeable to a few men, who remarked that it was Friday and they did not care to disregard the popular superstition.

But the delegates were thrown into a great state of excitement by the call. They abandoned their seats and took to the aisles in groups. Platt's men were closed up about his manly form. Quay, with his most obedient machine, started a little caucus, but presently began to talk so loud and with so much emphasis that they concluded to withdraw. They went out in a body for consultation. Pennsylvania is always going out for consultations in conventions. It is a practice not exclusively indulged in by either party.

Very hot was it now, and some of the audience, who had overheated themselves with yelling and flinging their arms for Blaine and Harrison, were uncomfortable. The historical

10 Pages

# The New-York Times.

10 Pages

VOL. XLI...NO. 12,740. NEW-YORK, FRIDAY, JUNE 24, 1892. PRICE THREE CENTS.



## MR. GLADSTONE'S APPEAL

*ELECTION ADDRESS OF THE HOME RULE LEADER.*

HE CALLS ON GREAT BRITAIN IN HONOR AND JUSTICE TO GRANT IRELAND LOCAL SELF-GOVERNMENT—PROBABLY HIS LAST APPEAL.

LONDON, June 23.—Mr. Gladstone's election address is as follows:

"Great Britain will now decide whether three countries shall henceforth constitute in reality as well as in statute name the United Kingdom.

"Ireland was never so loyal to the Crown or united in heart as in the years following 1782, when she enjoyed local government, until the concord was disturbed in 1795 by wicked machinations. For a generation after the union Ireland slept a deadly sleep of physical misery and political servitude. The reforms of 1829-32 gave her consciousness and a voice. From then her heavy grievances in battling for her aspirations have constituted a great standing burden in Parliament, and the chief impediment to the fulfillment of its duties.

"The proposal for which the Liberals have for the last six years contended will set Ireland free to manage her domestic affairs by a local legislature in close sympathy with Irish life, and will set Parliament free to overtake vast arrears of business and supply the legislative wants of England and Wales.

"The constant growth of sound opinion testified to by the result of a multitude of bye-elections, has shown that the British people now thoroughly comprehend how irresistible are the claims of Ireland on our honor and justice, and how a settlement will open a direct road to the satisfaction of British interests long held in suspense.

"The government of Ireland by the past Parliament has utterly failed in every respect except that of enabling the Irish agriculturist to improve his condition by the act of 1887, the main provisions of which the Ministry denounced in 1886 as immoral and dishonorable and thereby drove the people to the plan of campaign and became the true author of whatever dangers and hardships were thus produced.

"Ireland, indignant at the broken pledges of the Tory-Dissident coalition, is more than ever hostile to the methods of government of Dublin Castle, but calm and peaceful in reliance on the electors of Great Britain. The sentiments already prevailing between the British and the Irish supply a happy omen of the reciprocal affection which must follow a frank concession of home rule, sheltered by imperial supremacy. Even in the two counties in the north, where alone alarm prevails over calm reason, I have no doubt experience will quickly bring the population back to that sense of brotherhood with the rest of Ireland, which before the union so honorably distinguished their fathers."

Mr. Gladstone here reviews the Government's legislation, dwelling upon the imperfections in the English Local Government bill and Small Holdings bill, which he says the majority, especially the ex-Liberals, prevented the Liberals from bringing to a tolerable standard of efficiency. He then proceeds to enumerate the chief items of the Newcastle programme. He says that the proposed payment of labor members of Parliament and similar measures will render labor the greatest possible service by placing it in a condition to help itself.

Regarding shorter hours of labor, he says that much has already been done by legislation, and voluntary arrangement constitutes a guarantee of future progress, but he impresses upon workers that what is achieved is due to popular government, which is founded upon a just appreciation of personal liberty, with which the true strength of the working classes is essentially allied.

In conclusion, he says he feels that this must surely be the last general election in which he shall solicit the suffrage of his constituents, and that he can only expect to execute a small special share of the work he has sketched out.

## EVIDENCE AGAINST NEILL.

HIS BLACKMAILING LIKELY TO CONVICT HIM OF MURDER.

LONDON, June 23.—The web that the police are weaving about Thomas Neill, now in custody on the charge of attempted blackmail, threatens to so entangle him that he will have to answer a charge of murder.

The case is a peculiar one, and the Scotland Yard authorities deserve much credit for the manner in which they have followed up every thread of evidence that leads to the prisoner as the poisoner of the unfortunate girls whose deaths were for a time such deep mysteries, and which probably would have remained mysteries so far as the guilty person was concerned had not the prisoner attempted to blackmail Dr. Harper by writing him that he had in his possession evidence showing that Dr. Harper's son, who is now a practicing physician, had poisoned the two girls Alice Marsh and Emma Shrivell.

An inquest was held to-day on the body of the girl Matilda Clover, who died in October last. The authorities had reason to suspect that she had met her death in a manner similar to that of the Marsh and Shrivell girls, and the body was exhumed for examination.

Dr. T. Stevenson, Lecturer at Guy's Hospital and Analyst to the Home Office, examined the stomach and viscera and obtained positive evidence that death was caused by strychnine. The fact was also revealed that just prior to her death she was seized with spasms, which are the usual accompaniment of strychnine poisoning.

Among the witnesses who testified at the inquest that was held on the body to-day was Mr. Kirkley, a chemist, who identified Neill as a man who had purchased from him a quantity of nux vomica, a drug from which strychnine could be extracted. He also purchased 100 capsules.

It is pretty clearly established by the evidence in the hands of the police that the strychnine was administered to the girls in capsules, and the testimony of the chemist therefore has a most important bearing on the case.

## ENGLAND'S EMPIRE TRADE LEAGUE.

CANADA WANTS PREFERENTIAL DUTIES LAID ON AMERICAN GOODS.

LONDON, June 23.—The Empire Trade League held a conference to-day. The Right Hon. James Lowther, who represents the Isle of Thanet division of Kent in the House of Commons, presided.

He said that Lord Salisbury sympathized with the desire of the league that preferential rates be established, but he wanted the constituencies educated before undertaking to legislate on the matter. Mr. Lowther said that in his Hastings speech Lord Salisbury had shown that he no longer ignored the essential elements of the commercial situation in Great Britain. Though Lord Salisbury did not precisely indorse the fair-trade principles the league advocated, he said in his Hastings speech enough to show that he did not entertain the narrow prejudices with which the subject was too frequently surrounded in Ministerial utterances.

Sir Charles Tupper, Canadian High Commissioner to England, urged that the Government should place a duty of 5s. per quarter on American grain, and that Canadian wheat should be admitted free.

The Agents General of the Australian Colonies, New-Zealand, and the Cape of Good Hope spoke in favor of the establishment of preferential duties.

## A FATAL DUEL IN PARIS.

CAPT. MAYER KILLED BY THE MARQUIS DE MORES.

PARIS, June 23.—A duel was fought to-day between the Marquis de Mores and Capt. Mayer, in which the latter was so severely wounded that he died this evening.

The duel grew out of the anti-Semite campaign that has been carried on in the *Libre Parole*, the Anarchist paper of which Edouard Drumont is the editor. The weapons used in the duel were swords.

The Marquis de Mores is a close friend of Drumont and was one of the witnesses in his favor in the recent libel suit brought against him by M. Burdeau, Vice President of the Chamber of Deputies. Drumont, in this case, was sentenced to three months' imprisonment and to pay a fine of 1,000f.

A warrant has been issued for the arrest of the Marquis de Mores, and orders have been given to prosecute the seconds of both the contestants.

## THE REVOLT IN AFGHANISTAN.

SIMLA, June 23.—Advices received here from Afghanistan show that the rebellion among the Urgaghan Hazaras against the Ameer is assuming formidable proportions. Of the 5,000 regular troops and the 5,000 irregulars sent against the rebels 250 of the regulars and 1,250 of the irregulars have been killed in the various engagements that have been fought. The Ameer's soldiers have become dispirited, and many of them are deserting.

## BISMARCK LOUDLY CHEERED.

THE PRINCE ADDRESSED A CROWD IN A VIENNA BEER HALL.

VIENNA, June 23.—Toward midnight last night Prince Bismarck visited the Munich Beer Hall in this city. The place was crowded, and as the Prince entered he was at once recognized. The people sitting about the tables rose to their feet and everybody cheered the ex-Chancellor lustily. Cries for a speech were heard, and these were taken up and repeated until Prince Bismarck raised his hand to secure silence so that his voice might be heard.

At once everything became quiet, and Prince Bismarck addressed the crowd. He said that now he was bound to Vienna by ties of relationship, and in view also of the fact that he was a free and independent man he hoped to make more frequent visits to the hospitable Austrian capital.

When the Prince had finished his short speech the crowd again broke forth in cheers and gave other tokens of their enthusiastic appreciation of him.

The *Neue Freie Presse* of this city states that the Czar has telegraphed to Count von Schouvaloff, the Prussian Ambassador at Berlin, who was one of the guests at Count Herbert Bismarck's wedding, to tender his Majesty's congratulations to Prince Bismarck and Count Herbert upon the latter's marriage.

Prince Bismarck and party left this city to-day. Few people assembled at the railway station to witness the departure. The Prince was in excellent health. The party was accompanied by the Hoyos family. No speeches were made at the station, but there were repeated shouts of "Hoch, hoch" and "Auf wiedersehen."

At the station at St. Poelten, a deputation of students presented Prince Bismarck with a bouquet with gold and green streamers. The Prince thanked the students from the carriage, adding that he himself was once a happy student. This was received with loud cheering, and as the train departed the Prince shouted, "I'll return soon."

ST. PETERSBURG, June 23.—Count Schouvaloff received formal permission from the Czar to attend the Bismarck marriage and fêtes.

## THE GERMANS DEFEATED.

BARON VON BÜLOW AND MANY OF HIS OFFICERS AND MEN KILLED.

BERLIN, June 23.—Official advices received here from Dar-es-Salaam, on the east coast of Africa, confirm the reports of the disaster that befell the German force under the command of Baron von Bülow in the Moshi territory, near Kilima-Njaro. The advices received to-day add that Baron von Bülow, Lieutenant Wolfram, and twenty of the Soudanese soldiers attached to the expedition were killed.

The non-commissioned officers, Wutzer and Wittstock, hold Kilima-Njaro with sixty-four men. A detachment of 180 men has been sent to their relief from Dar-es-Salaam.

It is said that Baron von Bülow recently ordered all the English missionaries to leave the Moshi territory in East Africa, as he intended to attack and, if necessary, exterminate the Moshi tribe. The attempt to enforce this policy resulted disastrously to the German force, for the Moshis have practically exterminated the whites.

## MANY IRONS IN THE FIRE.

MORE ABOUT THE FAILURE OF G. BARKER & CO. OF LONDON.

LONDON, June 23.—The failure of G. Barker & Co., bankers of 52 Mark Lane, which was announced yesterday, affects a host of thrifty poor persons throughout the country, who were induced to deposit money with the firm by the exceptionally high interest offered. The average rate of interest that the firm promised to pay was 7 per cent.

Aside from its banking business, the firm indulged in outside speculations. Among these were three papers, the *Daily Oracle*, the *Weekly Oracle*, and the *Weekly Trade and Finance*. None of these papers nor any of the firm's other recent speculations was successful. The firm also ran a money-lending concern, a grocery, and a public house.

It is expected that the assets will cover the liabilities, which, as stated yesterday, amount to £650,000. The firm had no bills, nor is its estate mortgaged.

## MISS HARJES WEDDED.

THE BRIDE OF M. CHARLES WADDINGTON OF PARIS.

PARIS, June 23.—An interesting wedding occurred this afternoon in the French Protestant Church near the Arc de Triomphe, when Miss Bertha Harjes, daughter of Mr. Harjes, the American banker here, was married to M. Charles Waddington, son of M. Richard Waddington, a member of the French Senate, and a nephew of M. Waddington, the French Ambassador to England.

There were many Americans present. The bride's witness was T. Jefferson Coolidge, the American Minister to France.

A large reception at the residence of Mr. Harjes followed the ceremony.

## CONCOCTED BOGUS PLOTS.

A RUSSIAN'S SCHEME TO SECURE A LARGE REWARD.

CRACOW, June 23.—A Russian *agent provocateur* named Hengery has been arrested here on the charge of concocting a bogus dynamite conspiracy in Poland, entailing the banishment to Siberia of hundreds of Poles whom he had enticed into making incautious statements and then denounced to the police.

Hengery's object was to obtain 250,000 rubles that had been promised from the St. Petersburg police for revealing the so-called conspiracy.

The Austrian police discovered Hengery through his buying dynamite for an alleged Polish plot against the Czar and Gen. Gourko.

KING HUMBERT IS PLEASED.

BERLIN, June 23.—The King of Italy received a deputation from the Italian colony to-day. Replying to the address presented to him, the King said he hoped that the Italian wine trade in Germany would prosper. He expressed himself as highly pleased with the warm welcome extended to him in Berlin.

MILITARY TELEGRAPH OPERATORS.

MADRID, June 23.—The Government has decided, in view of the confusion and delay in official and private business arising from the strike of telegraph operators, to dismiss all the civilians belonging to the telegraph staff. Henceforth all the telegraphing in Spain will be done by military operators.

CONDENSED CABLEGRAMS.

—Director Lequay, arrested on a charge of misappropriating funds of ex-Deputy Barbe's dynamite company, was released by a Paris magistrate yesterday.

—Cholera is spreading to the Caspian provinces of Persia. Several cases have appeared at Baku on the Russian shore.

—The Brazilian Minister of Foreign Affairs takes the place of the Minister of Husbandry, who has resigned.

—Several miners and a girl were killed by an accident at the Amercoeur Colliery in Belgium yesterday.

—The Prussian Landtag was prorogued yesterday.

### Workingmen Pleased.

Matthew Barr, walking delegate of the Tin and Sheet-Iron Union, is a Republican, but will vote for Cleveland, as he believes in the ex-President's tariff-reform ideas.

John Ballantine, Secretary of the Amalgamated Carpenters' Union, hopes Cleveland will be elected, as he is frank in his convictions and a manly man.

Mr. Pratt, Secretary of the Building Trades Section, is heartily pleased with Cleveland's nomination. Aside from his admiration of the man himself, Mr. Pratt indorses Mr. Cleveland's views on the silver question and on tariff reform.

George Coleman of the Operative Painters has been in favor of Cleveland all along, and will vote for him.

### Hurt at a Fire.

Fire broke out at an early hour this morning on the seventh floor of the Edison Building in Broad Street. It was extinguished, but not until considerable damage had been caused by flames and water.

A plate of glass fell on Fireman John O'Neill of Truck 10 and cut his hand badly. He was taken to Chambers Street Hospital.

## *HAZARD TURNS CATHOLIC.*

THIS FOLLOWS HIS GIFT OF THE HAZARD MEMORIAL SCHOOL.

NEWPORT, R. I., June 23.—Twelve months ago a sensation was caused here when it became known that George Babcock Hazard had paid the whole cost of the land and palatial school buildings for the Roman Catholic parish. St. Joseph's Schools are now known as the Hazard Memorial Schools.

Hazard came to Newport in the twenties, before Andrew Jackson was President, a comparatively poor boy, with practically no education. But by close application and strict economy, even to parsimony, he amassed an immense fortune. Up to a year ago he was looked upon as an avaricious money grabber of very eccentric mind, always in hot water with the owners of land adjoining his properties, and several times he has been brought up in police court for assaults and on other charges.

The school buildings are the finest in Rhode Island, with splendid halls, well furnished rooms, and good acoustic properties. Until the day of its consecration the secret was so well kept that when public announcement was made that Hazard was the donor people were incredulous.

This afternoon the first graduation exercises were held. On the platform were Bishop Harkins of Providence and prominent citizens of Newport. The bishop made an eloquent address on the munificence of Hazard, but not a word escaped him of the denouement to follow. After diplomas, with gold and silver medals as the principal prizes, had been awarded, and all the exercises concluded, the rector, the Rev. Father Coyle, called on his assistant, Father Downing, to read the written statement, signed by George Babcock Hazard, giving a resume of his life and winding up with the statement that he, George Babcock Hazard, gave the school as a Protestant, but now had been received into the Roman Catholic Church, and promising to erect a building suitable to the parish. This means a new stone church.

The gold and silver medals and the diplomas were announced as Hazard gifts. When it becomes known to-morrow, this will create profound surprise. The schools cost nearly $100,000.

## *HARRISON AND REID CONFER.*

STILL SEEKING THE RIGHT CHAIRMAN OF THE NATIONAL COMMITTEE.

WASHINGTON, June 23.—Mr. Whitelaw Reid's visit to Washington to-day has been generally accredited to the desire on the part both of the President and himself to discuss the make-up of the National Committee.

Mr. Reid has persistently declined to be interviewed. His conference with the President lasted for several hours. The President is desirous of learning as accurately as he can the situation in New-York, Connecticut, and New-Jersey, and his choice for Chairman is likely to be the man who, in his judgment, can best handle the problems arising in those States. It was this particular point that was supposed to be under consideration to-day.

While Indiana is equally important, the President is disposed to let his own crowd, which is experienced in the intricacies of Hoosier politics, look after his interests there without much interference from the national organization. He believes that Mr. Reid can give him valuable information as to the three States near by, and he desired to compare his ideas with those of Mr. Depew and Gen. Horace Porter, with whom he has already consulted.

The National Chairmanship is, according to the present announcement, to be determined next Monday, and so, while it is publicly stated that the object of Mr. Reid's visit was to pay his respects to the Vice President, according to a custom of long standing, the absence from the city just now of Mr. Morton has led to the belief that it was largely for the purpose of conferring with the President before the arrival of Mr. Clarkson, who is expected to be here Saturday.

During the afternoon Mr. Reid took a drive with the President, and in the evening dined with Secretary Elkins and Representative Hitt at the latter's residence. At 11:30 P. M., accompanied by his secretary, he left the city for New-York via the Baltimore and Ohio Railroad.

## *COMMENCEMENT AT BOWDOIN.*

MR. SEARLES'S GIFT ANNOUNCED AT THE ALUMNI MEETING.

BRUNSWICK, Me., June 23.—Bowdoin commencement exercises took place in the Congregational Church at 10 o'clock this morning. The Cadet Band from Salem, Mass., furnished music. Prayer was offered by the Rev. C. L. Nichols of Princeton.

Four men, Emery, Fobes, Linscott, and Wood, were by rank entitled to the salutatory. The honor fell by lot to Wood. The addresses were as follows: "The Revelation of God," with Latin salutatory, Earl Boynton Wood, Bangor; "Restriction of Immigration," Roy Fairfield Bartlett, Caribou; "Loyalty to Principle, the True Element of Reform," John Carpenter Hull, Woodfords; "Russian Advance into Central Asia," Charles Selyn Rich, Portland; "Should Young Men Go into Politics?" Henry Crosby Emery, Ellsworth; "The Christ in History," Harry Woods Kimball, Woodfords; "The Electric Railway," Leon Melcher Fobes, Portland; "Some Aspects of American Journalism," Percy Bartlett, Ellsworth; "Preservation of the New-England Towns," Fred Vincent Gammer, Brunswick; "Qualifications Essential to Success," Charles Melvin Pennell, North Harpswell; "Conservative and Radical," Thomas Flint Nichols, Brunswick; "The Spirit of American Scholarship," Harry Farrar Linscott, Chicago.

Honors in French were awarded to Leon Melcher Fobes, honors in Latin to Percy Bartlett, Fred Vincent Gammer, and Earl Boyton Wood; honors in English literature to Harry Woods Kimball.

The Goodwin Commencement Prize was awarded to Charles Selwyn Rich.

The alumni dinner was served in Sargent Gymnasium to 400 alumni. Among the speakers were the Rev. E. C. Smyth of Andover, Gen. Thomas Hubbard and James McKeen of New-York, Charles F. Libby of Portland, Lincoln Bodge of Minneapolis, and Prof. Robinson.

The announcement of another gift to the college, a sixty-thousand-dollar laboratory, by Mr. Searles of Boston was hailed with great applause. President Hyde presided as toastmaster.

Edgar Myrick Simpson, '94, was awarded the mathematical prize of $300. Simpson also received the Sewall Latin prize. The Sewall Greek prize was awarded to Frank George Farrington.

## *MASONIC APPOINTMENTS.*

GRAND MASTER TONEY ANNOUNCES HIS CHOICE OF OFFICERS.

ALBANY, N. Y., June 23.—Most Worshipful James Toney, Grand Master of Masons in the State of New York, has made the following appointments:

Grand Chaplains—Orrin Root, Clinton; Warren C. Hubbard, Rochester; William I. Chalmers, Riverhead. Grand Marshal—Rollin M. Morgan, New-York. Grand Standard Bearer—James K. Stockwell, Oswego. Grand Sword Bearer—Loftin Love, Brooklyn. Grand Stewards—Solomon Strasser, Albany; Charles E. Ide, Syracuse; C. Witwer, Rochester; Charles E. Palmer, Schenectady. Senior Grand Deacon—E. C. McDonald, Tonawanda; Junior Grand Deacon—L. Russell, New-York; Grand Lecturer—George H. Raymond, New-York; Grand Librarian—Herman H. Carter, New-York; Grand Pursuivant—George Skinner, New-York; Grand Tiler—John Hoole, New-York.

District Deputy Grand Masters.—First District—Townsend Scudder, Glencove; Second—Elberta Crandall, Brooklyn; Third—James Huggings, Brooklyn; Fourth—Charles M. Frost, New-York; Fifth—John Little, New-York; Sixth—Charles W. Jackson, New-York; Seventh—David Kay, New-York; Eighth—George W. Hamilton, New-York; Ninth—R. Frank Palmer, Larchmont; Tenth—E. D. Woodhull, Munroe; Eleventh—Marshall D. Bice, Schoharie; Twelfth—C. Maulss, Greenbush; Thirteenth—Loyal L. Davis, Glens Falls; Fourteenth—I. T. Burney, Little Falls; Fifteenth—John Webb, Jr., Gouveneur; Sixteenth—William H. Rees, Clayton; Seventeenth—E. Trevette, Utica; Eighteenth—Oscar F. Lane, Schenevus; Nineteenth—Herbert W. Greenland, Syracuse; Twentieth—C. Scott, Oswego; Twenty-first—J. E. Batesford, Waterloo; Twenty-second—H. F. Falkner, Le Roy; Twenty-third—G. A. Greene, Belmont; Twenty-fourth—Edward J. Taylor, Lockport; Twenty-fifth—Charles W. Cashman, Buffalo; Twenty-sixth—William G. Martin, Mayville; Twenty-seventh—Harvey B. Rich, New-Brighton; Twenty-eighth—Henry Braunch, New-York; Twenty-ninth—Auguste Poret, New-York; Thirtieth—Andrew Tromble, Fort Henry.

### The Canadian Canals.

OTTAWA, June 23.—In the House of Commons to-night Sir Richard Cartwright inquired for information respecting canal tolls in the dispute with the United States. Sir John Thompson said the Government had no intimation of the President's message to Congress except from the newspapers. Negotiations had been going on and in pursuance of an understanding effected by Canadian Ministers Bowell and Foster on their recent visit to Washington, a communication reached Washington for transmission to the President on the very day that the message was issued.

### Platt—Innis.

POUGHKEEPSIE, N. Y., June 23.—This evening Mr. Edmund Platt, son of the Hon. J. I. Platt of the *Eagle*, himself one of the editors of the paper, was married to Miss Adèle Innis, daughter of Arron Innis of this city. The wedding was attended by about 100 guests, and was one of the most brilliant affairs ever seen here.

## CLEVELAND AND STEVENSON

*TWO STRONG LEADERS FOR ALL DEMOCRATS TO FOLLOW.*

THE CONVENTION COMPLETES THE TICKET BY ADDING ADLAI E. STEVENSON OF ILLINOIS—BOTH CANDIDATES WERE SELECTED ON THE FIRST BALLOT—END OF A CONTEST CHARACTERIZED BY MUCH EARNESTNESS AND SOME BITTERNESS.

*For President*—GROVER CLEVELAND of New-York.

*For Vice President*—ADLAI E. STEVENSON of Illinois.

CHICAGO, June 23.—Grover Cleveland will again lead the Democracy of the United States as candidate for President.

At daybreak to-day, in the presence of the greatest audience that ever witnessed such an event, after a contest characterized by intense earnestness and patriotism, and by bitterness on the side of the opposition, the confidence in the great leader of the Democracy as the fittest candidate was expressed in the nomination of Grover Cleveland on the first ballot and before the roll call of States was fully completed.

Gen. Adlai E. Stevenson of Illinois was chosen for Vice President this afternoon, and also upon the first ballot. His most formidable opponent in the contest was ex-Gov. Isaac P. Gray of Indiana.

Cleveland and Stevenson present a very strong ticket to the country.

The candidate for President, already held in high esteem by every citizen who is capable of feeling pride, is a grand type of Americanism. He is admitted by candid Republicans to be so popular in Illinois as to justify the expectation that his record for personal integrity and executive bravery and efficiency may prove so great an attraction to the voters of this State as to take its Electoral vote out of the Republican column in November.

Gen. Stevenson is in many respects an admirable candidate to strengthen the ticket and to encourage the hope of the Democrats of the country that Illinois may be won upon a low-tariff and sound-money platform. A soldier of the Union, a gentleman of education, with affable manners and possessing decided executive ability, he has, through his administration of a branch of the Postal Service under President Cleveland, become known, by name at least, in every hamlet in the land. This acquaintance has been widened by his recent official connection with the World's Columbian Exposition, so that it will be unnecessary to introduce him to the country. His record is one that offers no mark to the most unscrupulous foe.

## ADLAI E. STEVENSON CHOSEN.

THE CONTEST FOR THE NOMINATION FOR VICE PRESIDENT.

CHICAGO, June 23.—For the last time the delegates to the Democratic National Convention of 1892 assembled this afternoon in one of the worst halls ever provided for the accommodation of human beings to finish up their business by nominating a candidate for the Vice Presidency.

The hour to which adjournment was taken after the nomination of Mr. Cleveland this morning was 2, but it was some time after that hour when the weary delegates began to take their seats. Every one of them looked the worse for having seen the sun rise, but there seemed to be general satisfaction over what had been accomplished, and there was a vast deal of handshaking and congratulating.

Gov. Flower, Murphy, and Sheehan were among the first of the New-Yorkers to appear, looking decidedly glum over their defeat. Every seat in the convention-hall was water-soaked, and sizable puddles were seen at intervals all over the floor as the result of the rain in the early part of the day. Not the slightest effort had been made by the Sergeant at Arms and his assistants to make the old icehouse even comfortable.

The hall was not so full as yesterday, although there could not have been less than 16,000 people present when the convention was called to order.

The gossip about the hall before the work of the afternoon was begun had it that Isaac P. Gray of Indiana was certain of the nomination, and no one expected that the session would last longer than an hour or two; but there was a surprise in store for the oversanguine.

At 2:30 o'clock the Young Men's Gray Club of Indianapolis and the famous Hendricks Club of the same place marched in and around the hall, bearing aloft white pampas plumes tied with blue ribbons. At their head was a band, which pounded out "Yankee Doodle" in very vigorous fashion. This procession created tremendous applause and cheering, and it looked more than ever as if the lightning would strike Gov. Gray, if shouting could attract it.

The hall had been gradually growing darker and darker, the darkness being a forerunner of another of Chicago's innumerable and terrific thunderstorms, and it was necessary to turn on the electric light.

It was just 2:50 o'clock when Chairman Wilson's gavel fell and he stepped back to make way for a very self-possessed parson from Iowa, who said in a loud voice that the delegates would much oblige him if they would take their seats and keep quiet in order that he might offer the opening prayer. After this appeal had been repeated the necessary quiet was secured and the Iowan began a very long and a very instructive address to the Deity. He managed to work in Mr. Cleveland's famous remark to the effect that a "public office is a public trust," which resulted in a most unbecoming and promptly-rebuked display of enthusiasm by the audience.

Chairman Wilson announced that the first business in order was the presentation of a candidate for the office of Vice President of the United States. Ex-Gov. Porter of Tennessee then offered a resolution limiting nominating speeches to five minutes and seconding speeches to two. There was some little objection to this when the question was put, but the Chairman had evidently picked up a little sand since last night, and declared the motion carried.

When the roll of States was begun, Alabama declared that she had no candidate, and Arkansas, the next on the list, waived her right in favor of Indiana.

John E. Lamb of the latter State then put in nomination Isaac P. Gray. His reference to Cleveland and to the fact that, no matter what differences of opinion existed yesterday, the ex-President was now the unanimous choice of the Democratic Party, brought forth loud and repeated cheering. He paid a pretty compliment to Bourke Cockran by referring to his statement of last night, when Tammany's orator declared that New-York was as rock-ribbed as Texas for any Democrat. A reference to Hendricks resulted in very general applause.

He said:

MR. CHAIRMAN AND GENTLEMEN OF THE CONVENTION: When I was elected as a delegate to this convention from my district I hoped to have the honor as well as the pleasure of casting my vote for an honored son of Indiana for the Presidency of the United States, [cheers,] but when I arrived at this convention we found that the majority had already decided that another than an Indianian should lead the contest in the coming campaign. [Cheers.] We bowed our heads to their judgment and united with the Cleveland Democracy. [Great applause.]

Yesterday Grover Cleveland was the choice of a majority of the Democratic Party. To-day he is the unanimous nominee of the Democratic Party. [Applause.] And the question which confronts this convention is, Who shall it be that will have the honor to hold up the hands and the arms of the candidate who carries the banner of Democracy in this campaign? [Tremendous cheering, and cries of "Gray, Gray."] Where shall he come from? [Cries of "Indiana, Indiana."]

New-Jersey, God bless her, is always Democratic. Connecticut is surely safe, and when dawn broke upon us this morning, after a night of struggle and of toil, the eloquent tongue of the distinguished gentleman from New-York, the Hon. Bourke Cockran, [applause,] whose name I love to honor, told this convention that New-York was as rock-ribbed as Texas for any Democrat that could be nominated by this convention. [Applause.] That being true, the 36 Electoral votes of New-York are solid for that prince of Democrats, Grover Cleveland. [Applause.]

I come from a State which is the centre of the political battle field of the great West, a State which has given to the history of American politics the immortal name of Thomas A. Hendricks. [Loud applause.] Whenever the Democratic Party has listened to its advice, whenever you have honored the State of Indiana with a place upon your ticket, whether it was in the grand battle of 1876, the fruits of which victory were stolen from us, or in the grand battle of 1884, when you had Indiana on your ticket, you had Democratic victory. [Enthusiastic applause.]

And now, in behalf of that State which has never faltered, which has never sulked, which has fought every inch of ground, I desire, upon behalf of the united delegation from Indiana, to ask this convention to make fifteen votes in the Electoral College certain by placing upon your ticket the name of that honored leader who never lost a battle, the Hon. Isaac P. Gray. [Cheers long and loud.]

As for our candidate, he has been tried in the balance and never found wanting. [Applause.] In the great contest of 1884 he carried the State of Indiana for Governor by a thousand more votes than Cleveland and Hendricks. What more can I say for him? The tongue of slander has never been able to pierce his Democratic armor. For twenty years he has fought the battles of Democracy. He will fight them again, whether upon the ticket or not. [Applause.] But, my friends, if there is a certainty of 15 Electoral votes for Grover Cleveland and Isaac P. Gray in the State of Indiana, nominate that ticket and we will deliver the votes. [Great applause.]

The expected rain had begun to come down in torrents, and the edifying spectacle of Murphy and Croker huddling under the same umbrella in a vain attempt to get in out of the wet amused the inconsiderate.

THE SUCCESSFUL CANDIDATE.

Colorado, when her name was called, gave way to Illinois, in order that "Nick" Worthington might nominate Gen. Adlai E. Stevenson. There was a great shout when Mr. Worthington declared the purpose for which he had taken the platform. He said:

MR. CHAIRMAN AND FELLOW-DELEGATES: Illinois has presented no Presidential candidate to this convention. It has within its borders more than one favorite son whom it would have delighted to honor, and who is worthy of all the political honors that could be conferred upon him. But here in this great City of Chicago, in this great commonwealth of Illinois, bordering upon the lake and the Mississippi, in the centre of this great Republic of the Democracy, catching the vibrations of the ground swell that came from the South and the East and the West, we put aside our favorite sons, for the time buried our State pride, and with Texas, Connecticut, and California, with 48 votes, shouted the name of Grover Cleveland.

"But for the Vice Presidency, for the second highest place in the gift of the people, it has a candidate so fully equipped by nature and education that it feels that it would be a political fault to fail to urge his name for nomination before you. I stand here, then, gentlemen, to name as a candidate for that position a man who is known by every woman and child and voter that ever licked a postage stamp in any village or hamlet of the land. [Applause.]

"He is a big-bodied, big-hearted, big-brained man; a man of commanding presence, of dignified mien; a man whose courtesy in his every-day manners is rarely equaled and never excelled; a man who in the administration of his duties in the last Democratic Administration was the beau ideal of an honest, honorable, useful, and efficient Democratic office holder, like his great leader who bears your banner.

"He believes that a 'public office is a public trust,' but he believes, also, that the Democrats are the best trustees of this public trust. [Cheers.] Nor can the pride of office make him proud or haughty. I appeal to every Senator and Congressman who is here if ever he found the haughtiness of office, the chilling indifference of a little brief authority, in the atmosphere of the room of the Assistant Postmaster General during Cleveland's Administration.

"Gentlemen, we have nailed our banner to the mast. A Democrat never surrenders. We propose to make true what our Republican friends say of us, that we do our quarreling before the convention, and our fighting against our enemies afterward. [Cheers.] We believe that every Democrat will put on his armor. We of the West have been making a magnificent campaign of late years. We have been educating the people, and the proud results are seen in Boyd of Nebraska, Boies of Iowa, and Peck of Wisconsin. [Applause.]

"They are seen in that grand old man who represents Illinois in the United States Senate. [Cheers.] They are seen in the reduction of the Republican majority from 60,000 to 13,000 in Illinois. They are seen in the election of a Democratic Treasurer and Superintendent of Public Instruction in this State. We propose in this campaign to attack the last citadel. We have a Governor that we are going to elect.

"Will you help us give the twenty-four Electoral votes to Grover Cleveland? If you will vote for the man whose name I now present, a man who does not have to get a certificate from a labor organization to prove that he is a friend of the people, [applause,] a man that we all love—give us Adlai E. Stevenson of Illinois." [Prolonged applause.]

Chairman Davis, one of the Nutmeg delegation, seconded the nomination of Gray when the name of Connecticut was called. He was followed by a Florida man who did the same thing.

Iowa created a little furor by declaring, through her Chairman, that "Iowa has no candidate for the Vice Presidency. It is the wish of Gov. Boies and of the united delegation that his name be not presented to this convention for nomination."

The Gray men seemed to be having it all their own way, so far as talking was concerned, Kansas next seconding the Indiana man.

John S. Rhea took the platform to declare that Kentucky had no candidate, and wished to second the nomination of Gen. Stevenson. He made a long reference to the part that his State has taken in the fight for tariff reform. In seconding Mr. Stevenson he declared that he did so because he understood that the General believed in the old-time Democratic doctrine that "To the victors belong the spoils." He wound up his remarks by the taking statement that "Kentucky takes her Democracy as she does her whisky—straight."

Edward S. Uhl next trotted forth Michigan's favorite son, Gen. Allen B. Morse, "the one-armed hero of Missionary Ridge." He promised, among many other things, that if the convention would accept Gen. Morse, Michigan would give her Electoral vote to the Democratic ticket.

The rubicund countenance of Gov. Flower appeared a moment later in the centre aisle. In a very still, small voice, which was hardly audible fifty feet away, he said that New-York had no candidate. North Carolina seconded Gen. Stevenson; Tennessee, Gray; Virginia, Stevenson, and Washington, Gray.

There were shouts for Campbell when Ohio's name was called, but the ex-Governor was not forthcoming, and the Chairman of the State delegation passed.

Gen. Edward S. Bragg tried to put in nomination Congressman John L. Mitchell of Wisconsin, but rain pattering upon the Wigwam's tarred roof made it impossible for him to be heard, and he finally sat down in despair to wait until the storm had somewhat abated in its violence.

When Gen. Bragg stopped, his voice lost in the rattle of the rain on the roof, the band played. The air produced by the musicians was the familiar "baby song" from "Wang." It played the air over two or three times. Upon the desks and chairs had been scattered dodgers, upon which were printed a few lines arranged by some zealous Democrat for a campaign ditty. A natural-born conductor in the convention took the hint of the bandmaster in the gallery. He started the refrain, and presently half the delegates and the audience were singing the chorus:

"Grover, Grover,
Four more years of Grover;
In he goes,
Out they go,
Then we will be in clover."

It was just as well that the crowd found something to amuse itself with, else it might have been stampeded by the dreadful storm which was raging. It was almost as black as night outside, and there was a constant roll of thunder, preceded by vivid flashes of lightning. "Grover, Grover," was sung over and over again until the band tired of the monotony and struck up "Dixie" and "My Old Kentucky Home," which sent the Southerners into paroxysms of enthusiasm.

Gen. Bragg finally decided to try his luck again, and succeeded in delivering his speech of nomination, although it was almost impossible for anybody to hear any part of it except the few dignitaries on the platform.

New-Mexico seconded Gray, and then the orator of the Alabama delegation told the audience all over again about "the one-armed hero of Missionary Ridge, Gen. Morse of Michigan."

THE BALLOT TAKEN.

This ended the speechifying. The roll of States for the first ballot was begun. Everything went along smoothly and without excitement until Iowa was reached, when it was announced that Gov. Boies's State would cast her 26 votes for Col. Henry Watterson. Col. Watterson looked pleased at the compliment, but shook his head in declination of the honor.

Minnesota's Chairman declared his delegation was divided, but as the majority of the votes were for Gray, and since the delegation was acting under the unit rule, the Indiana man would be given the State's solid vote.

Montana distinguished herself by casting five votes for Bourke Cockran, quite forgetful of the fact that he was born in Ireland and was therefore not eligible to the office of Vice President, and also that he was a resident of the same State as the head of the ticket. The sixth vote from Montana went to Judge Lambert Tree of Chicago.

New-York turned the tide for Gen. Stevenson by casting her solid 72 votes for him, thus putting him 42 ahead of Gray, but Pennsylvania evened matters by giving her 64 votes to the Indianian.

As the contest became closer and closer, the cheering became general and the excitement increased. It looked very much as if another ballot would have to be taken, but after the roll call had been finished the Chairman of the Iowa delegation got upon a chair and, with difficulty making himself heard above the hubbub, shouted that, at the request of Col. Watterson, Iowa withdrew her 26 votes from him and gave them to Gen. Stevenson.

This began the scramble to get into the band wagon. Montana abandoned Cockran and gave her 6 votes to Stevenson. Nebraska, Idaho, Minnesota, and Kansas followed suit in quick succession. It was very evident that the end had come. Delegate Bohl of the Twelfth Ohio District, after several minutes of wild gesticulation, finally attracted the attention of the Chairman, and moved that Gen. Stevenson be nominated by acclamation. Mr. Wilson put the motion, and it was carried with a yell.

The Illinois men were prepared for the result. They had a banner all ready, and immediately hoisted it into prominence. Two-thirds of the delegates had left their seats and were clustered about in the space just before the platform.

Gen. Patrick A. Collins of Massachusetts climbed to the side of the Chairman and finally succeeded in quieting the crowd sufficiently to offer a resolution which he said he had sent to the Committee on Rules, but which had not appeared therefrom, to the effect that the National Committee be instructed to provide for future conventions sufficient quarters only for the delegates, alternates, the press, and the National Committee. In support of this resolution, he said that the time had come when a National Convention should be a deliberative body and in nowise affected or influenced by the vast throng of spectators which had of late years, and particularly at this convention, made themselves prominent.

GENTLEMEN OF THE CONVENTION: I propose to address myself to the common sense, good judgment, and experience of the 900 men selected by the Democratic Party as delegates to this convention. Twelve years ago I sent to the Chair a resolution instructing the National Committee to provide accommodations in the next convention for the delegates, the alternates, the National Committee, the members of the press, and none others. [Cries of "That is right."]

The time was not then ripe for the adoption of that resolution, and, without disparagement to our National Committee, I feel free to say in the presence of a small fraction of the great American public outside of ourselves, the delegates, that a mistake has been made here, and that the time has now come when a Democratic Convention should be a deliberative body and not governed by outside influences. [Cries of "Good, good."]

If we could be on exhibition in the view of 65,000,000 of people and 7,000,000 of Democrats who will vote the Democratic ticket, well and good; but what is the use? what is the sense in having 15,000 people who can hardly see and cannot hear, prolonging the proceedings of a Democratic Convention and preventing them from being deliberative? [Cries of "Good, good."]

It is not the discomfort, it is not the inconvenience but it is the danger of wrecking the good work of a convention that we are face to face with to-day; and I feel confident that we have reached the climax of absurdity. I therefore venture to ask my fellow-delegates to pass the following resolution:

*Resolved*, That the Democratic National Committee be instructed to provide in the next National Convention the accommodations necessary for the delegates, the alternates, the press, the National Committee, and none others.

While Mr. Collins was speaking there came the best argument which he could possibly ask for in favor of his very sensible demand. One of the ropes which held the big electric lights in place over the centre of the auditorium broke and let a lamp down on the heads of the New-York delegates, who seemed to have been peculiarly unfortunate in the situation of their seats.

For a moment it seemed as if all the other lamps might meet with the same fate, and there was a general panicky rush toward the exits by both delegates and spectators. But there were shouts of "Keep quiet!" "It's all right!" and with the aid of the band something like quiet was soon restored.

Gen. Collins's resolution was then referred to the National Committee with the recommendation that it be adopted.

The usual resolutions thanking the Chairman and the officers of the convention, the Citizens' Committee of Chicago, and providing for the printing of the proceedings of the week, were adopted, and then Chairman Wilson declared the convention adjourned, without date.

## THE RESULT OF THE WORK.

BOTH TICKET AND PLATFORM PLEASE THE PARTY.

CHICAGO, June 23.—The ticket is Cleveland and Stevenson, instead of Cleveland and Gray, as was expected this morning, when the convention adjourned after selection of the head of the ticket.

To the Indianians, who contributed so much, and at an important moment in the preliminary work, to the nomination of Cleveland, the failure of ex-Gov. Gray to get second place was a keen disappointment. It was also regretted by those friends of the leading candidate who had been influential in securing the co-operation of Indiana.

But it could not be helped. The New-York delegation was perhaps responsible for the result. It had sought for aid from Indiana for Hill, or for any opponent of Cleveland, and had only succeeded in driving the Indiana thirty to Cleveland. It was only natural, perhaps, that it should find out, after that, what Indiana did not want, and to endeavor to make the choice of Indiana's opponent certain. It was about the only triumph of New-York in the whole convention, and the Tammany people, in need of some such consolation prize, appreciated it fully.

Already there is a rush to the favor of men who desire to be known as the persons to whom particular credit shall be given for rendering the success of Cleveland sure. They lose sight, in their zeal to be identified with a result that is only an expression of party will, of the significance of platform and candidates, and seek to make of themselves political factors of extraordinary importance.

In this throng there do not yet appear any of the throng of United States Senators who have been so conspicuously and stupidly opposed to Mr. Cleveland's nomination. Senator Daniel of Virginia who has been an offensive, and needlessly offensive, opponent of the ex-President, and an extravagant adulator of Senator Hill, managed to exhibit himself in the closing moments of the convention this morning, when he scrambled, with unconcealed haste, over the tailboard of the band wagon to make the nomination of Cleveland unanimous.

The ticket is yet too new, as to its second candidate, for one in Chicago to make a fair estimate of its national strength. The nomination of Gov. Gray would have made the task of carrying Indiana a very difficult one to the Republicans. He is a politician of skill, a good organizer, an industrious campaigner, and a Democrat almost as popular as Mr. Holman, whom he in many respects resembles. His friends say that his record, by some Democrats regarded as vulnerable, has stood all tests in Indiana and proved no obstruction to him in carrying the State.

Gen. Stevenson, however, is as truly as Gov. Gray a "practical politician." He is also a good organizer and campaigner, and it is not at all to his disadvantage that he possesses some personal qualities that may make him quite as popular in general estimation.

There was an intimation this morning before the convention met that an effort would be made to reconsider the vote by which the platform was adopted, and to secure the substitution of the plank on the tariff rejected last night.

If such an attempt had been made it would have failed. The convention was for a clear expression against Republican protection. The overwhelming vote of last night was a correct expression of the feeling of the convention. The Eastern delegates as well as those from Southern States, where protection has found qualified friends, preferred a conservative plank. But these conservatives became convinced that they were

10 Pages

# The New-York Times.

10 Pages

VOL. XLI...NO. 12,803. NEW-YORK, TUESDAY, SEPTEMBER 6, 1892. PRICE THREE CENTS.

## ADDING TO THE DEATH LIST

*CHOLERA CLAIMS NEW VICTIMS AT QUARANTINE.*

ONE DEATH ON THE NORMANNIA, ONE ON THE RUGIA, AND ONE IN THE HOSPITAL—SIX NEW PATIENTS—A NURSE STRICKEN DOWN—ANXIETY AMONG DETAINED PASSENGERS.

Dread cholera's havoc among the quarantined steamships in the lower bay yesterday was of a startling character. Not only were there deaths and new cases aboard the Normannia and the Rugia, but one of the Normannia's steerage passengers, all of whom were ashore on Hoffman Island, was stricken while he was being bathed and cleaned and his baggage disinfected. There were deaths, too, among the sick on Swinburne Island, and one of the female nurses there fell a victim to the scourge while ministering to the sufferings of others.

The developments were indeed discouraging. Having transferred the steerage passengers of the Normannia to Hoffman Island, it had been hoped that with the fumigation of the vessel the disease there would be stopped. The sick on the steamer having been isolated, it was thought that, with the steerage passengers all removed, the cabin passengers would be safe from further outbreak.

Yet one of the stokers was stricken, and died before he could be taken off to the hospitals on Swinburne Island. Soon afterward two more stokers had to be lowered down into the hospital boat, exhibiting violent symptoms of the plague.

This fresh outbreak caused renewed panic among the cabin passengers and caused them to so urgently demand that they be taken off the Normannia, if only to be put on another vessel, that an effort will be made in that direction. The same may be done with the Rugia's cabin passengers.

The death list yesterday was as follows:

ENGEL, OTTO, twenty years of age, stoker on Normannia; died on board after an hour's sickness.

BUSS, JOHANNA, fifty-four years old, steerage passenger on Rugia; died on board after a very short sickness.

CHILD, five months old, name not reported; died on Swinburne Island.

The list of new cases was as follows:

QUERNF, WILLIAM, nineteen years old, stoker on Normannia.

SINNIZEK, THEODORE, twenty-three years old, stoker on Normannia.

STERR, HENDRIK, five years old, steerage passenger on Rugia.

PJEKOSKA, JOSEPHO, thirty years old, steerage passenger on Rugia.

FEMALE NURSE, name not reported, on Swinburne Island.

ADULT MALE, steerage passenger from Normannia, name not reported; on Hoffman Island.

The three deaths of yesterday brings the total number among the three quarantined ships now in the lower bay up to forty-one. Ten of these deaths have been in port. Of the forty-one deaths twenty-three have been among the Moravia's passengers, eleven among the Normannia's passengers and crew, and five among the Rugia's passengers.

All of the passengers have been from the steerage except Jacob Hynemann, a first cabin passenger on the Normannia. While his death is counted in the list of those resulting from cholera, the ship's physician diagnosed his disease as diabetes, and the prevailing opinion is that that diagnosis was right. If it was, then it can be said that the disease has not shown itself as yet among the cabin passengers.

Its attack on the crew of the Normannia is, however, a most discouraging matter. The health authorities had been congratulating themselves that the scourge only seemed to be working among those who came in immediate contact with the isolated patients. It was pointed out that nearly all those who had been attacked had been relatives of those who had died. They, it was urged, caught the disease while attending their sick relatives during the early stages of their illness before they were isolated in the sick bay. The stokers did not attend the sick steerage passengers.

The effect of the attack of the disease on the steerage passenger while he was going through the cleansing and disinfecting process with the rest of the steerage passengers of the Normannia was to create the wildest excitement among them. The being put on Hoffman Island they had looked upon as delivery, for anything was better to their mind than the steerage compartments in which death had run riot among their fellows.

Terror returned when soon after putting their feet on shore they saw one of their number—a strong man who had looked as healthy as any of them a few minutes before—carried away exhibiting the symptoms which all knew so well. So horror-stricken were they that the shrunk back from the sufferer, and refused to go anywhere near where he was lying and he was carried off to Swinburne Island.

It was a little different on the Rugia. Her passengers were not shocked by the death and new cases among them as were the passengers of the Normannia, for their hopes of riddance from the plague had not been so stimulated. Their dead had been removed from the ship as they had died, but the sick had remained on board instead of being transferred to Swinburne Island.

With the scourge thus in the vessel they did not so keenly feel the gravity of another death on board and of the addition of two patients to their sick list. Last evening the Rugia's sick were removed, and all patients will hereafter be taken off as they are attacked.

The succumbing of the female nurse on Swinburne Island was one of the saddest things of the day. The woman was one of three who went there to risk life in the work of stamping out the cholera. That she had fallen ill had a most depressing effect upon all the other employes on the island.

It is believed that the nurse neglected some one of the precautions which those who are around the patients are warned to exercise. She may recover. Every possible effort will be made by the doctors to save her life, and she will get special care. Should the disease refuse to yield to the efforts of the doctors to suppress it more nurses must be found who will go to Swinburne Island.

The one bright spot in the dark story of the day's doings around the quarantined ships was that the disease did not reappear on the Moravia, which was the first ship to bring the cholera to this port. Her passenger list had already been depleted by the deaths of twenty-four immigrants, but her two convalescents had been taken to Swinburne Island and were doing well; her surviving passengers had all been taken to Hoffman Island for baths and the disinfection of their baggage, the ship had been fumigated, and now, after being on board again for thirty-six hours, the physicians were able to report "All well." This does not mean that the disease has been certainly stamped out on that ship, but it warrants that hope.

Startlingly contrasted were the general conditions down the bay and the gruesome scenes within the quarantine circle. Under a warm sun the water, tossed into white caps by a strong southeast wind, sparkled and seemed to reflect all the colors of the rainbow. It being Labor Day, hundreds of excursion steamers could be counted carrying crowds of merry-makers to beach resorts. Now and then the music of a brass band, toned down to tuneful harmony by distance, would salute the ear. Now and again the singing of excursionists could be heard. There were a half dozen yacht races being sailed over as many courses, and the small, white sails of the catboats appeared almost as numerous as the white caps themselves.

Like blots in this picture of happy, merry, moving life were the anchored Normannia, Rugia, and Moravia, objects of beauty in themselves, yet the saddest things which could be conceived—pest-ridden ships, laden with human beings, forbidden to leave their prisons for fear of the taint of the scourge they might carry with them. On their decks the passengers could be seen, leaning over the rails with eyes fixed on the green shores only a few miles away, or else stolidly watching the passing craft. There seemed to be little excitement on the decks, except when a heavy body, lowered by a canvass swing into the tug Crystal Water alongside, told that another had died from or been stricken with cholera.

The pest ships were given a wide berth by nearly all craft. A few vessels now and then would sail or steam up to within perhaps 100 yards or so, but that was as near as most of them cared to go to cholera's quarters. In the morning the tugs of some newspapers went so close that they could hail the passengers on the decks, in spite of the fact that they had been informed that doing so was committing a penal offense.

The detail of New-York policemen, with two tugs, saw these tugs in their wrong-doing just after noon and gave them a lively chase, but without result.

As these policemen will hereafter patrol day and night to keep all craft at a proper distance from the pest ships, it is not likely that the public will again be submitted to danger through the matter which the news gatherers of sensational newspapers have been bringing ashore.

Hoffman Island and Swinburne Island were also given a pretty wide berth by the steam and sailing craft. They went only so near that with marine glasses they could see the Normannia's steerage passengers on Hoffman Island and could see the buildings in which the immigrants were getting their cleansing baths and in which their baggage was being disenfected in 220° of steam, but none cared to go nearer.

Swinburne Island was given a still wider berth, although many glasses were leveled at the hospital buildings, in which it was known that men, women, and children were struggling against cholera's violence. All could see a thin cloud of vaporous smoke circling up from the centre of the island, but probably few knew that it came from the furnaces of the crematory in which the bodies of those who died were finding their end.

Panicky as was the general feeling among the passengers on the detained ships, there was not the terror that might have been expected. There was more of that to be noticed on Sunday. This was largely due to a trip that Health Officer Jenkins took among the ships on Sunday night. On the Normannia and the Rugia he called the cabin passengers together and delivered a brief lecture.

Dr. Jenkins told the passengers that in trying to communicate with the shore, as they had been doing, they were simply injuring themselves and making more remote the time when they could be put ashore. In plain language he explained the precise condition of cholera in the port and the part they were playing in the fight of the authorities to bring the scourge to an end. He impressed particularly upon them that for their own good they must do precisely as they were told to do.

The passengers all gave him their promise to this end. He advised them not to let fear run away with them, and without exaggeration spoke to them of how little chance they ran of falling victims to cholera if all precautions were observed and all instructions obeyed.

The passengers of the Normannia, speaking through United States Senator McPherson, personally thanked the Health Officer for the encouragement he had given them. They said, however, that their great desire was to get off the ship. They believed that without danger to anybody they might be transferred to some other vessel which might be anchored near by. The expense of getting such a vessel they would cheerfully meet by subscription.

In impressing this idea upon the Health Officer the passengers said they were satisfied that the one death among their number, that of Jacob Hynemann, was not the result of an attack of cholera. They further argued that it was a fearful hardship for them to have to stay on the ship because of the scourge among the immigrants. Most of them had taken passage on the Normannia under a guarantee from the Hamburg-American Packet Company that there would be no immigrants aboard.

Dr. Jenkins promised that he would consider the matter of transferring them to another vessel. The breaking out of the cholera among the stokers of the Normannia seemed to settle his mind on that matter. He at once ordered that all hands on board the Normannia, except deck hands, stewards, officers, and cabin passengers, be put ashore with the steerage passengers on Hoffman Island.

Last night Dr. Jenkins sent a telegram to the agents of the Hamburg-American Packet Company asking them if they could not secure two of the Sound steamers now moored at New-London for the transfer of the Normannia's cabin passengers and the Rugia's cabin passengers.

Application has been made to Dr. Jenkins for permission to run a cable telephone out to the quarantined ships which have cabin passengers aboard, and especially the Normannia. The friends of the passengers are said to be behind the application. It is suggested that the health officers can have supervision over both ends of the line. Dr. Jenkins has not said whether he will grant the application or not. It is not believed that he will, as he is very much opposed to any news getting off the steamers that he does not personally give.

All the physicians and experts now seem to be agreed that there is no longer any question that Asiatic cholera, pure and simple, is the scourge in the bay. They do not consider that it is necessary to longer wait for the results of bacteriological examinations to assert this.

At the same time the prevailing opinion seems to be that there is no reason why the public should become alarmed. Opinions agree that the plague has been handled in the best possible manner here, and if the same good work is kept up and the same good results obtained, it is believed the life of the epidemic will be short.

No fear is expressed that incoming steamers will bring so much cholera that the health authorities will be unable to cope with it. General acceptance is given to the assertion that the prompt and vigorous quarantine methods here will practically stop the shipping of immigrants from infected ports, the steamship companies not being able to stand the expenses of quarantine, and that in this way the authorities will be able to quickly stamp out the plague.

The ships in the lower bay and off Hoffman and Swinburne Islands were visited yesterday not only by nearly all the local health officials, but by State officials, Secretary of the Treasury Foster, Collector Hendricks, members of the Conference Committee of the State Board of Health, and many well-known physicians. There was no indication of anything but harmony among all the officials and a general intent to exert every effort for the general good.

### NO NEW CHOLERA SHIPS.

BUT THERE WAS ENOUGH WORK FOR HEALTH OFFICERS AT QUARANTINE.

No vessels arrived at the upper Quarantine station yesterday with cholera on board, yet the day was a busy one there. La Bourgogne of the French Line, carrying a thousand persons, was anchored out in the stream, as were the North German Lloyd steamships Fulda and Darmstadt, the Italian steamer Garigliano, with the statue of Christopher Columbus on board, and the Hamburg steamer Stubbenhuk, sent up from the lower bay Sunday.

During the day a number of freight steamers and coasters anchored until the fleet became one of the largest seen there since the cholera came into port. All of the arrivals of the day before except the three ocean liners, were given permission to go to their wharves during the early morning, there being no sickness on them and the orders in regard to fumigation having been complied with.

Soon after sunrise there arrived the Morgan Line boat El Sol, from New-Orleans; the Atlas Line mail steamer Alene, from Haitian ports; the Clyde Line steamship Iroquois, from Jacksonville, and the Miranda, from Liverpool. All these were released after examination.

Then Dr. Tallmadge started to make the rounds of the ships which had been in Quarantine over night. The oil tank Brilliant, from Hamburg, he found to be in the same good condition of health as on her arrival, and she may be released at any time. On the Darmstadt, from Bremen, the orders in regard to disinfection had been thoroughly carried out. He ordered her fumigated again, however, as she is from an infected port. There has been no sickness on the Darmstadt, but she will probably have to undergo a few days' more quarantine for safety's sake. She has 39 cabin passengers and 284 in her steerage.

Then the doctor went to La Bourgogne, which came in Sunday morning with practically a clean bill of health, but being from Havre, the taint was upon her and her passengers had to suffer. They fairly besieged Dr. Tallmadge for permission to go ashore, but, of course, in vain. He found that the steamer had been fumigated as ordered, and directed that the process be repeated.

Later in the morning Health Officer Jenkins ordered the agents to provision the steamer for a five-day quarantine. When this news got among the passengers there was considerable of a panic, in which Mrs. Hicks-Lord is said to have played a very heroic part in soothing the troubled feelings of the ladies aboard.

The passengers of La Bourgogne have little call for sympathy, however, as compared with those on the pest ships. Their ship is as clean as a whistle. Every passenger on her was personally examined before the ship sailed from Havre by experts. She has had no cholera and is not likely to have any. Therefore her passengers have little to worry about except the delay.

The Fulda and Stubbenhuk were visited and no sickness found. The orders in regard to fumigation had been carefully carried out. They, too, were directed to repeat the fumigation. The Fulda will probably be at her pier this morning, as she comes from Italian ports in which there is no cholera. The Stubbenhuk will likely have to remain for several days.

The only other arrival of consequence during the afternoon was the big White Star Line freighter Bovic. She came from Liverpool. She had no sickness among her crew, and will probably make only a short stay at Quarantine. She was ordered to be thoroughly fumigated.

There was much speculation around Quarantine as to the condition in which the Elbe and the Scandia will arrive. The former is from infected Bremen and the latter from infected Hamburg. Both have large lists of cabin and immigrant passengers. Both sailed after cholera broke out in Bremen and Hamburg. Great anxiety is especially felt in regard to the Scandia. She was originally booked to enter Baltimore, but will come here instead. Both vessels are expected to-day.

There were hundreds of anxious persons around the station during the day making inquiries for relatives and friends on the quarantined steamers. They made no concealment of attempts to bribe employes of the station to row them off to the boats anchored at the upper station, but such efforts were wasted.

The fact that proper mail service had been established between the ships and the shore was a great comfort to all. The mails were especially heavy between the shore and La Bourgogne and the Normannia. Those which come to shore are thoroughly disinfected before they are placed in the hands of the Post Office authorities.

The many officials, doctors, and Commissioners who went down to inspect the work in the lower bay returned to the Quarantine station at 6 o'clock last evening. They arrived on the tug State of New-York and the revenue cutter Chandler. They went to Dr. Jenkins's house, and had a short conference. In the party were Dr. Jenkins, Quarantine Commissioner Allen, Secretary of the Treasury Foster, Collector Hendricks, Surgeon General Hamilton, Dr. Bryant of the Health Board, Dr. S. McCormack, Secretary of the Board of Health of Kentucky; Dr. Baker, Chairman of the State Board of Health of Michigan; Dr. Watson, Secretary of the State Board of Health of New-Hampshire; Dr. Lindsay, Secretary of the State Board of Health of Connecticut; Dr. Balch, Secretary of the State Board of Health of New-York, and Dr. Bryce, Provincial Health Officer of Ontario. They returned to the city before 7 o'clock. Drs. McCormack, Watson, Baker, and Bryce are the Quarantine Inspection Commission of the International Conference of State Boards of Health.

Secretary Foster had very little to say. He said he had been on the pest ships, but not on the Quarantine islands, as Dr. Jenkins did not think it was worth while to so far expose the party to the disease. So far as his investigation had gone, he was very much pleased with the work done by the health officers.

"Is there any likelihood that there will be any further discord between the Federal and the local authorities as to the release of vessels?" Mr. Foster was asked.

"Oh, no," he answered. "There has been no discord, but perhaps just a little confusion. We have thorough confidence in Dr. Jenkins, and all of us will work in harmony now."

Surgeon General Hamilton said he had only taken a general survey of the work at Quarantine and did not care to speak upon it then, further than to say that everything seemed to be working admirably as far as he could see.

"I shall begin on a thorough inspection to-day, through the courtesy of the local authorities," said Dr. Hamilton.

Dr. Jenkins said: "As matters look now I feel very much encouraged. The disease seems to be pretty well in hand, and unless some unforeseen circumstances arise I do not see that we are at all in danger of an invasion.

"This must not be taken to mean, however, that any degree of care should be abridged. At Quarantine we shall be as vigilant as ever, and no ship with the least suspicion of sickness on board will be passed without due inspection.

"However, I cannot but feel very much encouraged. We are in excellent shape to handle any new cases that may come up, and if any of the ships which are now at sea bring any number of passengers afflicted with the disease our arrangements are such that we can care for them without trouble."

Quarantine Commissioner Allen said a mistake had been made in the statement that the bodies of the dead were immediately cremated. "We must keep the bodies twenty-four hours," he said. "For that purpose we have a mortuary in connection with the crematory that holds thirty-six bodies. If relatives ask that the bodies be not cremated, we hold them for burial, or, if the dying person asks that they be not cremated, we give them burial."

All the patients on the pest ships, and on Hoffman Island, Mr. Allen added, were being fed by the Hamburg-American Packet Company. The company had sent down its own cooks, too. It had also sent two doctors to work on the Normannia and Rugia. There were five tug boats now in the service of the Health officers, and hereafter there would be no delay in removing the sick and the dead from the pest ships.

### POLICE PATROL PROVIDED.

OFFICERS OF THE STEAMBOAT SQUAD GUARDING THE PEST SHIPS.

The Police Commissioners met informally yesterday to give Superintendent Byrnes power to establish a sub-precinct to watch the plague ships in the lower bay on the hospital ship Carlton, with steam tugs and launches for patrolling around them to keep away all craft and arrest any one attempting to get on board the steamer or to take anything from the passengers. Mr. Byrnes, when notified that he had full power to act, started for Quarantine with Inspector McAvoy.

Superintendent Byrnes did not return to his office until 8 P. M., when he told how he policed the lower bay. "After obtaining the authorization of the Board of Police," said he, "I sent out to hire two tugs, to report immediately at Pier A North River, and at 2 P. M. the Golden Rod and the H. B. Rawson were there. I went to the office of the steamboat Patrol, which is not in commission, with President Martin, mustered the command, and after telling them that a force was needed to watch the plague ships and the duties which those sent down the bay would have to perform, I called for volunteers, and the entire squad was at my disposition. In fact, all of them were anxious to go. I selected seven men for each tug and put Sergt. Ivory in command of one and Sergt. Halpin of the Eleventh Precinct in command of the other, and ran up the State and police flags on each tug and told the Sergeants to report at Quarantine.

"I, Health Commissioner Bryant, President Martin, Dock Commissioner Cram, and Detective Sergeant Heidelberg were taken on a Dock Department tug to Quarantine to see Health Officer Jenkins. He was not there, and we went to the lower bay for him, leaving the police fleet at Quarantine. We went round the Rugia, Normannia, and Moravia to find four tugs cruising round them. I'm not going to say if they were newspaper tugs, because I take no cognizance of newspaper quarrels or rivalry. But we ordered the tugs away and threatened the men who commanded them with revocation of their licenses if they didn't clear out, and the way they left the steamer fleet was refreshing.

"We did not find Dr. Jenkins until we got to Hoffman Island. Asked what he desired the police patrol to do, he said he wanted all but authorized craft to keep half a mile from the quarantined steamers. Intruders were to be warned first and threatened with a report for revocation of license, and then, if they persisted in keeping within the cordon, the duty of the police would be to arrest all hands and take them to Quarantine for arraignment before a Staten Island magistrate.

"Then we picked up the police boats and started for the lower bay again. On the way the force under Sergts. Ivory and Halpin were told of Dr. Jenkins's wishes, and received full instructions, which were repeated when we mustered them on the hospital hulk Carlton, which will be their headquarters. Then all the details of this police water service were arranged, and it was planned that one tug at a time should do patrol duty, with the other in reserve, but within hail. The service must be done by tugs. Rowboats couldn't live on this water.

"Complete arrangements were made in regard to the commissariat, sleeping, watches, and means for communicating with the Carlton. After the precautions taken by the Boards of Health and Police there will be no chance for any unauthorized person to board the cholera vessels after to-day."

On the receipt of Mayor Grant's communication urging special vigilance on the part of the Police Department in detecting nuisances and enforcing sanitary and city ordinances, the gist of it was sent to every precinct by general alarm, and every precinct commander was notified later in the evening to at the Central Office at 10 A. M. to-day to receive instructions from President Martin in aiding the Health Department to make the city ready for a visitation of cholera.

### RUGIA'S FIREMEN REFRACTORY.

The Dock Department tug Manhattan, which brought Dr. Jenkins to the city last night and which has been engaged in transporting various health officials around the quarantine establishment, tied up at the Barge Office last night to await Dr. Jenkins's return.

In conversation with a TIMES reporter some members of the crew said they had heard positively that several of the Rugia's firemen had become refractory and had been placed in irons. Some of the men, it was said, tried to escape from the cholera-stricken ship by swimming ashore.

### ACCUSED OF DECEPTION.

NORMANNIA PASSENGERS WHO UNDERSTOOD THERE WERE NO EMIGRANTS.

Among the passengers imprisoned on the Normannia are Miss Mary Sanborn, Mrs. Henry Howard and her son John, and Mrs. Ballantyne of Michigan. Miss Sanborn is the daughter of Gen. John P. Sanborn of Detroit, who was formerly a member of the National Republican Committee. Accompanied by Mr. Howard, he is in this city. Mr. Howard is a wealthy banker tug owner, and lumberman of Port Huron.

Both Mr. Sanborn and Mr. Roberts received letters from the members of their families yesterday which contained statements on which Gen. Sanborn severely criticised the agents of the Hamburg-American Packet Company abroad.

"The letter received to-day was written Saturday," said Gen. Sanborn last evening. "My daughter said that she was well, as were the others of the party. The letter from John Howard was written to-day, and in it he said that the reports of the situation aboard the vessel had been greatly exaggerated by the newspapers. There was no panic aboard, he said, and the passengers were enjoying themselves as well as they could in the circumstances.

"The Michigan party said that they had gone aboard the Normannia under the impression that there were no emigrants on the ship," said Gen. Sanborn. "They are all persons of good sense and they knew of the presence of cholera in Hamburg before they sailed. They boarded the vessel at Southampton. The agents of the Hamburg-American Packet Company assured them there were no emigrants on the ship. The vessel did not pass quarantine at Southampton, and our people went out to board her in a tug.

"It was not until they were aboard and it was too late to go ashore that they learned that the steerage was filled with emigrants taken on at Hamburg. Had they known this they would not have come on the Normannia. They all had tickets good on any of the Hamburg-American Packet Company's boats, and all had letters of credit from Morten, Bliss & Co. They were advised by cable to take every precaution, and were fully prepared to have waited an indefinite period had it been necessary to avoid any chance of coming in contact with the contagion.

"They had seen the statements that one of the vessels of that line had discharged her freight at Southampton and were careful to make inquiries as to the passengers before they decided to come on the Normannia.

"I consider the misrepresentation an outrage, and it seems to me the company should be held responsible for all damage. The fumigation of the baggage of the Normannia's passengers will practically ruin it.

"My daughter wrote that there had been no especial alarm on the part of the passengers when it became known that there was cholera aboard. On the way over it was impossible to get the best of food. So many of the passengers had objected to drinking plain water that the supply of Apollinaris was exhausted, and wine and beer had been the regular drink. It was expected that the food would be of a better quality now that the vessel was in port."

Last night Mr. Howard received the following telegram from his son on board the Normannia:

"Send 200 cigarettes and one-half pound Oolong tea immediately."

In regard to the statement that some of the cabin passengers of the Normannia had secured passage with the understanding that no steerage passengers were to be carried, Mr. Boas, agent of the Hamburg Line, was of the opinion that the arrangement had been misunderstood by the purchasers of the tickets. He was certain that no such information ever emanated from the New-York office, and said he did not know what classes of passengers would be carried by the Normannia until advised by cable on the day of her departure.

### DISINFECTANTS AND THEIR USE.

RECOMMENDATIONS IN A NEW BOARD OF HEALTH CIRCULAR.

The Health Board decided yesterday to issue the following, which annuls any circular that has been distributed to give directions in regard to disinfectants and their use:

HEALTH DEPARTMENT, NEW YORK, Sept. 5, 1892.

The Board of Health has approved the following (prepared by one of its consulting pathologists, Dr. Hermann M. Biggs,) in respect to disinfection and disinfectants, and directs that the disinfectants described and the methods of their use be employed in the hospitals for contagious diseases in charge of this department, and recommends the same to the public in all cases of contagious disease:

DISINFECTION AND DISINFECTANTS.

The contagious diseases are caused by minute living germs. The object of disinfection is to destroy these. In order that as few articles as possible shall be exposed to infection by the disease germs at the very beginning of the illness all unnecessary furniture (especially upholstered furniture and curtains) and other unnecessary articles should be removed from the sick room.

The following are the best-known disinfectants:

1. *Heat.*—Continued high temperatures destroy all forms of life. Boiling for at least one-half hour will destroy all disease germs.

2. *Carbolic Acid.*—Standard solution No. 1 is composed of six ounces of carbolic acid dissolved in an equal quantity of glycerine, and then added to one gallon of hot water. This makes, approximately, a 5 per cent. solution (one-twentieth) of carbolic acid. The commercial colored impure carbolic acid will not answer for this purpose. Great care must be taken that the pure acid does not come in contact with the skin. When practicable, the carbolic solution should be used as hot as possible.

3. *Corrosive Sublimate,* (Bichloride of Mercury.)—Standard solution No. 2 is composed of sixty grains of pulverized corrosive sublimate and sixty grains of chloride of ammonia, dissolved in one gallon of water. This solution must be kept in glass, earthen, or wooden vessels, (not in metal vessels.)

The above solutions are very poisonous when taken by mouth, but are harmless when used externally.

The proprietary disinfectants, often widely advertised, and whose composition is kept secret, are relatively expensive and often unreliable and inefficient. It is important to remember that substances which destroy bad odors are not necessarily disinfectants.

METHODS OF DISINFECTION.

1. *Hands and Person.*—Standard Solution No. 1 should be diluted with an equal amount of water. Hands soiled in caring for persons suffering from contagious diseases, or soiled portions of the patient's person, should be immediately and thoroughly washed in this solution, and then washed in soap and water. The nails should be kept perfectly clean, and the hands should always be carefully disinfected before eating.

2. *Soiled Clothing, Towels, Napkins, Bedding, &c.,* should be immediately immersed in Standard Solution No. 1 and soaked for twelve hours, being occasionally moved about in the fluid so as to bring the disinfectant in contact with all parts. They should then be wrung out and boiled in soapsuds for one hour. Articles such as beds, &c., that cannot be washed, should be burned.

3. *Food and Drink.*—Food thoroughly cooked and drinks that have been boiled are free from disease germs. In presence of an epidemic of cholera or typhoid fever, milk and the water used for drinking, cooking, washing dishes, &c., should be boiled just before using, and all persons should avoid eating fruit, fresh vegetables, and ice. Ice may, however, be used when ordered for the sick by a physician.

4. *Discharges* of all kinds from patients suffering from contagious diseases should be received into earthen vessels containing standard solution No. 1. Special care should be observed to disinfect at once the vomited matter and the intestinal discharges from cholera patients, as these alone contain the dangerous germs. The volume of the disinfecting solution used should be at least five times as great as that of the discharge. After standing for at least one hour in the disinfecting solution, these discharges may be thrown into the water closet. Bedding or clothing soiled by the discharges must be at once placed in solution No. 1 and the hands of the attendants disinfected as described above.

5. *Closets, Sinks, &c.*—Each time the closet is used for infected material, at least one quart of solution No. 1 should be poured into the emptied pan and allowed to remain there. All discharges should be disinfected before being thrown into the closet. Sinks should be flushed at least once daily with the same solution.

6. *Dishes, spoons, &c.* used by the patient should be kept for his exclusive use, should not be removed from the room, but should be washed there, first in solution No. 1, and then in hot soapsuds. These washing fluids should afterward be thrown into the water closet.

7. *Soiled woodwork, floors, plain furniture, &c.,* should be thoroughly washed with solution No. 2. Upholstered furniture, curtains, or carpets which have been soiled by the discharges should be referred to the Health Department for disinfection or destruction.

It is important to remember that an abundance of fresh air, sunlight, and absolute cleanliness not only help protect the attendant from infection, but also aid in the recovery of the sick.

*Note.* The cost of the carbolic solution is much greater than that of the bichloride solution, but generally is to be much preferred. When the cost is an important element, the bichloride solution may be substituted for all purposes for which the carbolic is recommended, excepting for the disinfection of discharges, eating utensils or articles made of metal, and of clothing, bedding, &c., which is very much soiled. Its poisonous character when taken internally must be kept constantly in mind.

By order of the board.

CHARLES G. WILSON, President.

EMMONS CLARK, Secretary.

### LETTERS MAY BE SENT.

The passengers detained on vessels at Quarantine will not be entirely shut off from communication with the rest of the world. The Post Office authorities will forward letters addressed

(Continued on Page 5.)



## SOME RELIEF IN EUROPE

*THE CHOLERA SAID TO BE ABATING IN HAMBURG.*

CITIZENS MORE HOPEFUL OF THE EARLY DISAPPEARANCE OF THE SCOURGE—THE STEAMSHIP COMPANIES REJECTING STEERAGE PASSENGERS—THE DISEASE IN HOLLAND.

HAMBURG, Sept. 5.—The ambulances took to the hospitals yesterday 280 cholera patients, of which number 158 died. This was 45 fewer patients than were conveyed to the hospitals Saturday, while the deaths were 38 less in number.

The city yesterday presented quite an animated scene compared with its appearance on the preceding Sunday. The promenades and public resorts were largely patronized, and altogether there was displayed a more confident feeling, which still prevails this morning, as it is believed that the decrease in new cases and deaths will continue.

LONDON, Sept. 5.—The steamer Elbe, from Hamburg, arrived in the Tyne last evening with one of her officers down with the cholera. He was removed to the floating hospital that has been provided for cholera patients, where he died this morning. The steamer has been placed in quarantine.

The Elbe is a British steamer hailing from London. She was bound from Hamburg for Oporto when she put into the Tyne.

The Guion Line officials announce that in consequence of the twenty-days' quarantine imposed in the United States against steamers carrying steerage passengers, the steamer Wisconsin, sailing from Liverpool on Sept. 10; the Arizona, sailing Sept. 17; the Wyoming, sailing Sept. 24, and the Alaska, sailing Oct. 1, will carry only first and second class passengers. The Nevada, which will sail Sept. 14, will take steerage passengers.

A newspaper correspondent in Hamburg denies the statement that the Senate concealed the first outbreak of cholera in that city. He declares that on Aug. 22, immediately after a bacteriological examination had been made in the first case reported in the city, the medical authorities notified the Imperial Sanitary Bureau and took measures to prevent a spread of the disease.

The correspondent says that on Saturday there were in the hospitals in Hamburg 2,083 cholera patients. The removal of the bodies of cholera victims to cemeteries outside the limits of Hamburg has been prohibited. The public relief fund now amounts to £9,250.

It having been reported in Berlin that the Hamburg-American Line steamers, although at present sailing from Southampton, were receiving their provisions from Hamburg, thus incurring great risk of infection, the representative of the Associated Press to-day waited upon the agents of the company at Southampton and made inquiries regarding the matter. He was informed that the reports were untrue. The agents declared that all the meat and other provisions taken on board the steamer Columbia for use during her present voyage to New-York had been supplied by Southampton tradesmen, and that the steamer First Bismarck would obtain her supplies for her next trip from the same source.

LIVERPOOL, Sept. 5.—The steamer Clement has arrived in the Mersey from Hamburg, where two of her crew died from cholera. On the voyage seven others were attacked with the disease. Three of them were landed at Falmouth. The other four are still on board the steamer. They are recovering. The vessel was placed in quarantine.

BREMEN, Sept. 5.—There has been one new case of cholera reported here since noon yesterday. No deaths have been reported.

BERLIN, Sept. 5.—Two new cases of cholera are reported to-day in Lubeck. No deaths from the disease have occurred in that city.

At Niendorf, a bathing resort near Lubeck, two cases and one death from the disease are reported.

Eighty-six persons suffering from cholera were to-day admitted to to the Moabit Hospital in this city. Among the cases which occurred here to-day were two of the true Asiatic type.

Eleven persons who slept in the same house with a workman who died from cholera on Friday have been detained for observation. One of them is already suffering from a choleraic disorder, and it is feared that some of the others may have caught the infection.

A girls' school, situated in the Thurmstrasse, has been closed, owing to one of the pupils being taken sick with choleraic trouble.

The soldiers stationed at Potsdam and Lichterfelde are not allowed to visit Berlin, this action being taken by the authorities for fear that they might contract the prevailing disease.

ST. PETERSBURG, Sept. 5.—There were reported throughout Russia on Friday 3,812 new cases of cholera, and 1,791 deaths from the disease.

In the City of St. Petersburg 103 new cases and 40 deaths were reported yesterday. It should again be pointed out, however, that these figures include only the patients who are taken to the hospitals and who die in them.

Lectures are delivered daily at the Town Hall on the best methods of disinfection. Some 400 ladies have volunteered their services as sisters of charity. Some of these, as well as those who have attended the disinfection classes, will give their services gratuitously, while others will be paid at the rate of 1 ruble a day.

Compared with the official figures of Thursday, the returns of Friday for all Russia show a decrease of 2,881 new cases and 923 deaths.

Compared with the new cases and deaths reported in St. Petersburg on Saturday, Sunday's figures show a decrease of 17 cases and an increase of 9 deaths.

HAVRE, Sept. 5.—Seven new cases of cholera and nine deaths from the disease were reported in this city yesterday.

ROTTERDAM, Sept. 5.—The child of a man who died here of cholerine on Friday died of the same ailment to-day, and the widowed mother and another child in the family have been attacked with cholerine.

A man was seized with Asiatic cholera at Groningen on Sunday.

### The Police Justice Was His Match.

A number of men returning from a picnic early Sunday morning created a disturbance before the house of Police Justice Edmund M. Beldenlinden of College Point, L. I. He came out and all fled, but the Justice caught one of the gang, Hugo Freggang.

Freggang struck the Justice in the face several times, but the Justice finally threw him to the ground and pounded his head until he begged for mercy. One side of the Justice's moustache was torn out by the roots.

In May last Justice Beldenlinden held Freggang for the Grand Jury on a charge of assault in the second degree on a man named John Becker. The Grand Jury found an indictment for the crime charged. Justice Beldenlinden will lay the facts of the attempted assault on him before County Judge Garretson.

### Shot and Fatally Wounded.

MERIDEN, Conn., Sept. 5.—Daniel J. Singleton, night operator at the Consolidated Railroad freight depot, shot Joseph Casey, a former employe of the road, in the temple at 7 o'clock this evening and inflicted a fatal wound. Casey is thirty years old, and has a wife and three children. He laid his discharge to Singleton and had threatened the latter. Singleton says Casey, who is a powerfully-built man, attacked him and he warned him to keep away. He then fired a blank cartridge and followed that with a ball. He then went to Police Headquarters and surrendered himself. Singleton came from Springfield, Mass., and has always borne a good reputation.

### Harry Marchbank Disappears.

NEWARK, N. J., Sept. 5. Nothing has been heard of Harry Marchbank, the agent of the Brooklyn Supply Company in this city, who was arrested on two charges of fraud on Saturday, but who went to look for bail in company with Constable Hale, who was a former neighbor of Marchbank in Ironia, in Morris County.

It is feared he gave Hale the slip and escaped, as it threatened to go hard with him. He had served a term in prison for complicity in the Mechanic's Bank failure. Everything is in his wife's name, and he fled to New-York when he was threatened with arrest before.

—A big fire raged in East Haven, Conn., Sunday. Barns and outhouses belonging to Sidney Smith, a farmer, were destroyed. In one of the buildings ten horses were burned to death. The origin of the fire is not known. The loss is estimated at $3,000.

### *ELECTION IN ARKANSAS.*

DEMOCRATIC LEADERS CLAIM THE STATE BY AT LEAST 30,000.

LITTLE ROCK, Ark., Sept. 5.—Returns from the election for State officers held to-day are beginning to come in. They show a uniformly light vote. Two years ago the total vote reached 192,000. Belief is expressed that it will hardly reach 180,000 at to-day's election.

The cause assigned is the new election law, which is similar to the Australian system, and which has kept from the polls the bulk of illiterate electors. The negroes largely voted the straight Democratic ticket. This is true of them in Pulaski, Jefferson, Lee, St. Francis, and other largely-populated negro counties.

The Republican vote shows on the face of the returns a decided decrease as compared with former elections, while the People's Party have evidently made large gains. The Chairman of the Executive Committee claims that their total vote will reach 40,000 in spite of the election law, which he bitterly denounces.

The Democrats have had no fear of losing the State unless through indifference. The Democratic leaders claim the State to-night by a majority of at least 30,000.

The coalition between the People's Party and the Republicans was not effected. Whipple, it is said, flatly declining to withdraw in favor of Carnahan. Whipple did not expect to be elected, making the race simply to put himself in line for a Federal appointment in event of the re-election of Harrison.

Nothing in the way of official returns has as yet been received, nor will be until to-morrow. The great length of the ticket makes the count exceedingly laborious, and while some larger towns have reported, the county districts for the most part have not been heard from.

### *RABBI SONNESCHEIN'S SUIT.*

HIS WIFE WILL NOT BEGIN ANY CROSS ACTION FOR DIVORCE.

ST. LOUIS, Sept. 5.—Nathan Frank, ex-member of Congress from St. Louis, has been retained by Mrs. Rosa Sonneschein to look after her interests in the divorce proceedings about to be instituted by her husband, the distinguished rabbi. It was first reported that Rabbi Sonneschein would come to St. Louis to enter his suit, and that he would again take up his residence here, but friends here who are in a position to know say that Dr. Sonneschein has settled in New-York, and will in future reside there.

Mr. Frank said to-day that Mrs. Sonneschein greatly regrets the notoriety of a divorce suit, but that she will not file a counter-suit, as has been reported, either in Chicago or elsewhere. He admitted that Mrs. Sonneschein had refused to accompany the doctor on his European trip, and practically said that if the suit is based on desertion, he would have to admit that Mrs. Sonneschein had, refused to live with the doctor.

Mrs. Sonneschein returned to St. Louis from Chicago this morning, but declined to make a statement for publication. She is engaged in literary work.

### *ORDERED TO VENEZUELA.*

NAVAL VESSELS TO PROTECT THE INTERESTS OF AMERICANS.

WASHINGTON, Sept. 5.—Information received at the State Department from the United States Minister at Caracas as to the condition of affairs in Venezuela has led the President to direct that another naval vessel be sent to La Guayra.

The United States steamship Kearsarge, now in the West Indies, having lately been investigating matters at Navassa Island, has been ordered to proceed to Venezuela immediately, and it is expected that by the last of this week both the Kearsarge and the Concord (which was ordered to La Guayra about a week ago) will be in communication with Minister Scruggs and prepared to protect American interests in those waters.

Mr. Foster, the Secretary of State, said the reports from Venezuela showed a very disturbed state of affairs in that country. Anarchy seemed to exist, there being three or four contending parties. The two vessels will look out for American interests, and it may be that protection will be rendered to citizens of other countries which have no vessels in Venezuelan waters.

### *BISHOP HURST MARRIED.*

NUPTIALS POSTPONED ON ACCOUNT OF SICKNESS SUDDENLY SOLEMNIZED.

BUFFALO, N. Y., Sept. 5.—The wedding of John F. Hurst, a leading Bishop of the Methodist Church and the promoter of the proposed Methodist university at Washington, to Miss Ella Root, was to have taken place next Thursday. Invitations had been issued in profusion, and a ceremony in consonance with the high standing of both parties was planned.

But all this was changed by the sudden illness of Mr. Root. The wedding was announced yesterday as postponed indefinitely, but was solemnized at the Root family mansion, on Main Street, this afternoon by the Rev. Willis P. O'Dell, pastor of the Delaware Avenue Methodist Church.

This second change in plan was at the earnest desire of Mr. Root, whose heart was set on this union of two families so high in Methodism. Mr Root has long been a liberal supporter of the Church in all branches of its work, and is Vice President of the Chautauqua Assembly.

The bride, who has been assiduous in the care of her father since his unexpected illness, will not leave his side now, and so the wedding trip and not the wedding is postponed indefinitely.

### Affairs in Mexico.

CITY OF MEXICO, Sept. 5.—The new Congress held its first preparatory meeting this afternoon. The House of Representatives elected Señor Trinidad Garcia President and appointed a Committee on Credentials.

A young man who had been gambling and had lost all his money became desperate, and, obtaining possession of a dynamite cartridge, threatened to blow up the place where he had been playing. A number of bystanders seized him, however, before he could carry his threats into execution, and after a struggle the cartridge was taken from him.

A waterspout occurred to-day at Patzquaro, a town in the State of Michoacan. Considerable damage was done to property by the rushing water.

### Eleven Persons Capsized and Rescued.

ATLANTIC HIGHLANDS, N. J., Sept. 5.—The yacht Edna D., owned by Charles Burd, while returning to Red Bank from the Fort Hamilton yacht race with seven ladies and four men aboard, capsized in a squall two miles off Sandy Hook to-day. Capt. T. H. Patterson of the life-saving station manned a boat and went to the rescue, and the launch of the steam yacht Stranger and a big sailboat from Fair Haven did the same. All were saved, and the yacht was righted and towed home by the steam launch Leon Abbett.

### Another Sealer Seized.

WASHINGTON, Sept. 5.—Third Lieut. F. G. Dodge, attached to the revenue steamer Rush, reports to the Treasury Department, under date of Sitka, Alaska, Aug. 17, that he arrived at that port Aug. 17 with the American bark Lydia, which had been seized near Ounalaska for violating the modus vivendi, and that he had turned her over to the Collector of Customs, together with her cargo and equipment.

### Receiver for Iron Hall in Delaware.

WILMINGTON, Del., Sept. 5.—In pursuance of a bill in equity filed before him, praying for such action, Chancellor Wolcott has granted an injunction against the continuation of business by the local branches of the Iron Hall, and appointed Frank D. Carpenter of this city receiver for the same, who will now proceed to take charge of the property and funds of the order in this State.

### Judge Hilton's Sheep.

SARATOGA, N. Y., Sept. 5.—Judge Henry Hilton will exhibit his large flock of imported Southdown sheep, from Woodlawn Farm, at the Saratoga County Fair this week in charge of an English shepherd and two imported shepherd dogs, in a pen 40 by 80 feet in size.



## THE REPUBLICAN ISSUES

*STATED IN MR. HARRISON'S LETTER OF ACCEPTANCE.*

A LONG ARGUMENT TO SUSTAIN THE POLICY OF A HIGH PROTECTIVE TARIFF—LIBERAL SUBSIDIES TO AMERICAN STEAMSHIP LINES ADVOCATED—THE PRESIDENT'S ELABORATE DEFENSE OF HIS ADMINISTRATION.

WASHINGTON, Sept. 5.—The following is the President's letter of acceptance:

WASHINGTON, Sept. 5, 1892.

*Hon. William McKinley, Jr., and Others, Committee, &c.:*

GENTLEMEN: I now avail myself of the first period of relief from public duties to respond to the notification which you brought to me on June 20 of my nomination for the office of President of the United States by the Republican National Convention recently held at Minneapolis.

I accept the nomination and am grateful for the approval expressed by the convention of the acts of the Administration. I have endeavored, without wavering or weariness, so far as the direction of public affairs was committed to me, to carry out the pledges made to the people in 1888. If the policies of the Administration have not been distinctively and progressively American and Republican policies, the fault has not been in the purpose, but in the execution.

I shall speak frankly of the legislation of Congress and of the work of the Executive departments, for the credit of any successes that have been attained is in such measure due to others—Senators and Representatives and to the efficient heads of the several Executive departments—that I may do so without impropriety. A vote of want of confidence is asked by your adversaries; and this challenge to a review of what has been done we promptly and gladly accept.

The great work of the Fifty-first Congress has been subjected to the revision of a Democratic House of Representatives, and the acts of the Executive Department to its scrutiny and investigation. A Democratic National Administration was succeeded by a Republican Administration, and the freshness of the events gives unusual facilities for fair comparison and judgment. There has seldom been a time, I think, when a change from the declared policies of the Republican to the declared policies of the Democratic Party involved such serious results to the business interests of the country. A brief review of what has been done, and of what the Democratic Party proposes to undo, will justify this opinion.

NATIONAL BANK POLICY.

The Republican Party during the civil war devised a national currency, consisting of United States notes, issued and redeemable by the Government, and of national bank notes, based upon the security of United States bonds. A tax was levied upon the issues of State banks and the intended result, that all such issues should be withdrawn, was realized. There are men among us now who never saw a State bank note. The notes furnished directly or indirectly by the United States have been the only and the safe and acceptable paper currency of the people. Bank failures have brought no fright, delay, or loss to the bill holders. The note of an insolvent bank is as good and as current as a Treasury note—for the credit of the United States is behind it. Our money is all national money—I might almost say international, for these bills are not only equally and indiscriminately accepted at par in all the States, but in some foreign countries.

The Democratic Party, if intrusted with the control of the Government, is now pledged to repeal the tax on State bank issues, with a view to putting into circulation again, under such diverse legislation as the States may adopt, a flood of local bank issues. Only those who, in the years before the war, experienced the inconvenience and losses attendant upon the use of such money can appreciate what a return to that system involves. The denomination of a bill was then often no indication of its value. The bank detector of yesterday was not a safe guide to-day as to credit or values. Merchants deposited several times during the day, lest the hour of bank closing should show a depreciation of the money taken in the morning. The traveler could not use in a journey to the East the issues of the most solvent banks of the West, and in consequence a money changer's office was the familiar neighbor of the ticket office and the lunch counter.

[illegible]

IN FAVOR OF SUBSIDIES.

[illegible]

PROTECTION AND RECIPROCITY.

[illegible]

10 Pages

# The New-York Times.

10 Pages

VOL. XLII....NO. 12,859. NEW-YORK, THURSDAY, NOVEMBER 10, 1892. PRICE THREE CENTS.

## MR. CLEVELAND'S VICTORY

*LATER RETURNS ONLY CONFIRM FIRST REPORTS.*

THE DEMOCRATIC MAJORITY IN THE ELECTORAL COLLEGE WILL BE AT LEAST ONE HUNDRED AND FIFTY-SIX—REPUBLICANS AND THIRD-PARTY MEN WELCOME TO THE STATES YET IN DISPUTE—THE "DOUBTFUL" STATES FIRMLY FIXED IN THE DEMOCRATIC COLUMN.

Later reports of Tuesday's election extend the lines of the Democratic conquest. Mr. Cleveland's majority in the Electoral College will be at least 156 votes, and it is possible that it may be still greater.

The official count weakens the Republican column. Colorado, which was admitted to the Union under a Republican Administration, has cast its votes for Weaver Electors. Of the five States the Republicans created in the Northwest in order to preserve their majority in the United States Senate they have assuredly carried three—Washington, Wyoming, and Montana. North Dakota is placed in the Republican column, but the chances are that the People's Party has won it. Kansas and Nebraska, which have voted the Republican Electoral ticket since they were admitted to Statehood, have cast their votes for Weaver. California has been carried by the Democrats for the second time in nine Presidential elections. In Illinois the Republican majority of over 20,000 in 1888 has given place to a Democratic plurality nearly, if not quite, as large, and the State has for the first time since before the war chosen Democratic Electors.

Michigan for the first time in more than thirty years divides its vote and gives at least six Electors to the Democrats, and Wisconsin breaks a line of Republican victories stretching back for a life time by choosing the Democratic Electoral ticket by a plurality of 11,000 or more.

Illinois furnished the surprise of the first news from the West, but it is equaled this morning by that from Ohio. It is reported on what seems to be good authority that McKinley's own State has cast its vote for the Cleveland Electors. Harrison carried the State by nearly 20,000 in 1888, and McKinley, when he ran for Governor, by over 21,000. The State has never before gone Democratic in a Presidential year.

The so-called doubtful States are Democratic. In this State Mr. Cleveland's plurality is over 41,000, in New-Jersey 12,000, in Connecticut over 5,000, in Indiana nearly 10,000, and in West Virginia 7,000. Whatever States are still in doubt are to be divided between the Republicans and the third party. Any changes that may be disclosed by the official figures will not lessen Mr. Cleveland's total vote. On the contrary, it is more likely to be increased.

Yesterday reports of the elections for Representatives in Congress have made several individual changes in the list as presented in THE TIMES of Wednesday, but have not materially affected the strength of the Democrats, who will have more than 80 majority over Republicans and People's Party members combined. These returns make the ante-election predictions of ex-Clerk McPherson and ex-Journal Clerk H. H. Smith appear to have been about as ill considered as the predictions of Clarkson and *Platt* before the Minneapolis Convention.

California has done better than the Democrats expected it would do. The delegation was increased one member by the apportionment of 1891, and the Democrats have elected all of the seven members to which the State is entitled. Olin Welborn, who formerly represented a Texas district in Congress, has been elected from the Seventh District. Connecticut has made an admirable record, the Democrats holding the three districts now represented by that party.

Iowa has not kept up with the record it made in 1890, having lost all of the districts it holds in the present Congress except the Second. Ex-Gov. Gear, who was one of the Ways and Means Committee when the fatal McKinley bill was made, has been sent back from the First District, and ex-Representative Updegraff has been chosen in the Fourth. John F. Lacey, recently Comptroller of the Currency, and W. P. Hepburn, Solicitor of the Treasury, have been elected in the Sixth and Eighth Districts.

The Democrats have but three Representatives from Massachusetts instead of seven, as now. Mr. John F. Andrews and Mr. George Fred Williams are both unfortunately defeated—and "Steve Polish" Morse is unfortunately re-elected. The New-York delegation is divided exactly as in the present Congress, 23 to 11, but there have been changes from one party to the other in several of the districts.

Illinois sends Gen. J. C. Black to Congress as a Representative at Large, and it also sends Joseph G. Cannon, who may turn out to be an inadvisable person to set "at large" for his district, as he has developed a tendency to bad language in his campaign that may prove to be troublesome in a Democratic Congress. The Republicans made a great effort to defeat all of the Democrats in what were formerly Republican districts in Illinois, but they only succeeded in a few districts. The Democrats still have a majority of the delegation.

According to the latest advices the Democratic plurality in the next Legislature will amount to 9, and perhaps more. The Republicans will control 55 votes and the Democrats 72. On joint ballot the Democratic majority will be at least 16, more than sufficient to elect a Democratic United States Senator from this State.

A number of changes have occurred in the Assembly districts since the official vote came in. In the Sixteenth Kings Arnold H. Wagner (Rep.) is defeated by Walter L. Durack (Dem.) Charles W. Scudder, the Republican candidate in Montgomery County, succumbs before Howard J. Hand, his Democratic competitor. In the First Onondaga David A. Munro, Jr., retires before Duncan W. Peck, his Democratic rival, and in the Second Ulster the well-known features of George H. Bush have disappeared for a number of years to be succeeded by a Republican—James Lounsberry. The Democrats have lost their strongest men in this election, and will be forced to rely upon representatives of mediocre ability.

### POPULISTS CARRY NEBRASKA.

OMAHA, Nov. 9.—But five counties complete had been heard from up to 8 o'clock this evening. Less than 250 precincts out of 1,320 in the State have been heard from. If the ratio of the vote holds out, the Weaver Electors will carry the State by about 3,000.

The Republican State ticket will no doubt be successful. In the First District Bryan (Dem.) is about 200 ahead, with several precincts to hear from. He claims 270 plurality. The Republicans concede 75. In the Second, Mercer (Rep.) is elected by less than 800. In the Third, Meiklejohn (Rep.) is running away ahead of his ticket and is doubtless elected. In the Fourth, Hainer (Rep.) is elected by a good plurality. In the Fifth, McKeighan (Populist and Dem.) is elected by about 2,000 majority. Two years ago McKeighan had 14,800 majority. In the Sixth, Kem (Populist) is slightly ahead of Whitehead, (Rep.,) but the result is in doubt.

The Legislature will be anti-Republican, the Populists having the most members, the Democrats the least.

It will be two days more before complete returns are in, many voting precincts being from thirty to fifty miles from a telegraph station.

### THE ELECTORAL VOTE.

The following table shows how the votes in the Electoral College will be cast, as shown by the returns thus far received:

| | *Cleveland.* | *Harrison.* | *Weaver.* |
|---|---|---|---|
| Alabama | 11 | | |
| Arkansas | 8 | | |
| California | 9 | | |
| Colorado | | | 4 |
| Connecticut | 6 | | |
| Delaware | 3 | | |
| Florida | 4 | | |
| Georgia | 13 | | |
| Idaho | | | 3 |
| Illinois | 24 | | |
| Indiana | 15 | | |
| Iowa | | 13 | |
| Kansas | | | 10 |
| Kentucky | 13 | | |
| Louisiana | 8 | | |
| Maine | | 6 | |
| Maryland | 8 | | |
| Massachusetts | | 15 | |
| Michigan | 6 | 8 | |
| Minnesota | | 9 | |
| Mississippi | 9 | | |
| Missouri | 17 | | |
| Montana | | 3 | |
| Nebraska | | | 8 |
| Nevada | | | 3 |
| New-Hampshire | | 4 | |
| New-Jersey | 10 | | |
| New-York | 36 | | |
| North Carolina | 11 | | |
| North Dakota | | 3 | |
| Ohio | 23 | | |
| Oregon | | 4 | |
| Pennsylvania | | 32 | |
| Rhode Island | | 4 | |
| South Carolina | 9 | | |
| South Dakota | | | 4 |
| Tennessee | 12 | | |
| Texas | 15 | | |
| Vermont | | 4 | |
| Virginia | 12 | | |
| Washington | | 4 | |
| West Virginia | 6 | | |
| Wisconsin | 12 | | |
| Wyoming | | 3 | |
| Total | 300 | 112 | 32 |

Total number of votes....444
Necessary for a choice....223
Cleveland's majority....156

### VOTE OF NEW-YORK STATE.

The following table shows the pluralities in the several counties of the State of the Republican and Democratic candidates for President this year, and also the pluralities of the candidates for President in 1888:

| *Counties.* | 1888 Cleveland. | 1888 Harrison. | 1892 Cleveland. | 1892 Harrison. |
|---|---|---|---|---|
| Albany | 1,675 | | 483 | |
| Allegany | | 3,442 | | 2,580 |
| Broome | | 1,959 | | 2,197 |
| Cattaraugus | | 2,418 | | 2,200 |
| Cayuga | | 3,266 | | 2,341 |
| Chautauqua | | 5,930 | | 5,297 |
| Chemung | 570 | | | 739 |
| Chenango | | 1,158 | | 1,020 |
| Clinton | | 1,547 | | 362 |
| Columbia | | 410 | 524 | |
| Cortland | | 1,569 | | 1,225 |
| Delaware | | 1,270 | | 1,714 |
| Dutchess | | 1,016 | | 380 |
| Erie | | 2,069 | 205 | |
| Essex | | 2,113 | | 1,868 |
| Franklin | | 2,729 | | 2,490 |
| Ful.&Hamilton | | 1,257 | | 1,150 |
| Genesee | | 1,319 | | 1,046 |
| Greene | 34 | | | 141 |
| Herkimer | | 1,072 | | 694 |
| Jefferson | | 2,299 | | 2,646 |
| Kings | 12,457 | | 29,412 | |
| Lewis | | 562 | | 596 |
| Livingston | | 1,517 | | 1,200 |
| Madison | | 2,560 | | 2,479 |
| Monroe | | 4,973 | | 3,606 |
| Montgomery | | 688 | | 400 |
| New-York | 55,813 | | 73,159 | |
| Niagara | | 457 | 184 | |
| Oneida | | 1,965 | | 853 |
| Onondaga | | 6,115 | | 4,109 |
| Ontario | | 1,204 | | 940 |
| Orange | | 409 | | 660 |
| Orleans | | 1,063 | | 957 |
| Oswego | | 3,867 | | 3,317 |
| Otsego | | 857 | | 714 |
| Putnam | | 583 | | 301 |
| Queens | 1,666 | | 2,500 | |
| Rensselaer | | 309 | 1,205 | |
| Richmond | 1,664 | | 2,034 | |
| Rockland | 927 | | 885 | |
| St. Lawrence | | 8,101 | | 7,150 |
| Saratoga | | 2,024 | | 1,628 |
| Schenectady | | 304 | 608 | |
| Schoharie | 1,310 | | 1,366 | |
| Schuyler | | 729 | | 925 |
| Seneca | 129 | | 88 | |
| Steuben | | 2,483 | | 2,269 |
| Suffolk | | 567 | | 712 |
| Sullivan | | 103 | | 200 |
| Tioga | | 1,243 | | 1,299 |
| Tompkins | | 1,164 | | 1,321 |
| Ulster | | 838 | 418 | |
| Warren | | 1,252 | | 1,100 |
| Washington | | 3,789 | | 2,983 |
| Wayne | | 2,729 | | 2,229 |
| Westchester | 1,147 | | 2,632 | |
| Wyoming | | 1,733 | | 1,472 |
| Yates | | 1,271 | | 1,302 |
| Total | 77,392 | 91,747 | 115,703 | 74,812 |

Harrison's plurality 1888, 14,355.
Cleveland's plurality 1892, 40,891.

### IDAHO FOR WEAVER.

DOUBT ABOUT THE RESULT ON THE STATE TICKET.

BOISÉ CITY, Nov. 9.—The count in this city was not completed until a late hour this morning. There is a Democratic gain in the three precincts of 84 over the vote of two years ago. The Populists have captured Alturas and other strongholds of the Republicans. The Weaver Electors have probably received 500 majority. Sweet (Rep.) is elected to Congress by about 800.

The Republican State ticket is elected. In the Legislature it is not at all improbable that the Populists may hold the balance of power. It elects a United States Senator.

Phil Tillinghast, Chairman of the Democratic Central Committee, says only forty-three precincts in the State have been heard from. They indicate that the Weaver Electoral ticket has carried the State by 500.

The State ticket has been lost, with the exception of Secretary of State and Attorney General.

The Republicans will probably have control in the Legislature, although it is not certain, and Democrats strenuously fight the proposition. As a summing up it is probable the State has gone for Weaver on the Electoral ticket, and that the Republican candidate for Governor has been elected, as well as the member for Congress.

### WEAVER CAPTURES NEVADA.

CARSON, Nov. 9.—The Weaver silver Electoral ticket has been elected by a safe plurality. Francis G. Newlands, silver Democrat, is elected to Congress by a plurality of 2,000. The only Republicans in the State Legislature will be the Senators holding over from the last Legislature. United States Senator Stewart will be re-elected by the Legislature, as the silver party has only been organized about six months. The result is in the nature of a revolution.

### THE FIFTY-THIRD CONGRESS.

The House of Representatives of the Fifty-third Congress will consist of 356 members, the membership having been increased by the apportionment of 1891. The Fifty-second Congress consists of 232 Democrats, 86 Republicans, and 9 Farmers' Alliance men, who do not affiliate with either party. Of the Fifty-third Congress there will be 220 Democrats, 121 Republicans, and 13 members representing only the People's Party. The Democratic majority will be 87; Democrats over Republicans, 109. There will be but 354 members until a second election in Rhode Island, in which State there has not been an election in either of the two districts.

In the following list of members-elect the names of Democrats are in *italics*, those of Republicans in roman, and those of the People's Party in SMALL CAPS. Names followed by a star (*) are those of members re-elected.

ALABAMA.
1. *R. H. Clarke.**
2. FRANK BALTZELL.
3. *William C. Oates.**
4. *Gaston A. Robbins.*
5. *James E. Cobb.**
6. *J. H. Bankhead.**
7. *W. H. Denson.*
8. *Joseph Wheeler.**
9. *Lewis W. Turpin.**

ARKANSAS.
1. *P. D. McCulloch, Jr.*
2. *C. R. Breckinridge.**
3. *Thomas C. McRae.**
4. *William L. Terry.**
5. *H. A. Dinsmore.*
6. *Robert Neil.*

CALIFORNIA.
1. *Thomas J. Geary.**
2. *A. Caminetti.**
3. *W. B. English.*
4. *James J. Maguire.*
5. *L. R. Ryland.*
6. *Marion Cannon.*
7. *Olin Welborn.*

COLORADO.
1. LAFE PENCE.
2. JOHN C. BELL.

CONNECTICUT.
1. *Lewis Sperry.**
2. *James P. Pigott.*
3. Charles A. Russell.*
4. *R. E. De Forest.**

DELAWARE.
1. *John W. Causey.**

FLORIDA.
1. *S. R. Mallory.**
2. *C. M. Cooper.*

GEORGIA.
1. *Rufus E. Lester.**
2. *Benj. E. Russell.*
3. *Charles F. Crisp.**
4. *Charles L. Moses.**
5. *L. F. Livingston.**
6. *Thos. B. Cabaniss.*
7. *J. W. Maddox.*
8. *Thomas G. Lawson.**
9. *F. C. Tate.*
10. *J. C. C. Black.*
11. *H. G. Turner.*

IDAHO.
1. Willis Sweet.*

ILLINOIS.
*J. C. Black*, *A. Hunter*, At large.
1. J. Frank Aldrich.
2. *L. E. McGann.**
3. *A. C. Durborow.**
4. *Julius Goldzier.*
5. A. J. Hopkins.*
6. Robert R. Hitt.*
7. T. J. Henderson.*
8. *Lewis Steward.**
9. H. K. Wheeler.
10. P. S. Post.*
11. Benj. F. Marsh.
12. *J. J. McDannold.*
13. *Wm. M. Springer.**
14. *Owen Scott.**
15. Joseph G. Cannon.
16. *G. W. Fithian.**
17. *Edward Lane.**
18. *W. S. Forman.**
19. *James R. Williams.**
20. George W. Smith.*

INDIANA.
1. *A. H. Taylor.*
2. *John L. Bretz.**
3. *Jason B. Brown.**
4. *W. S. Holman.**
5. *George W. Cooper.**
6. H. U. Johnson.*
7. *W. D. Bynum.**
8. *E. V. Brookshire.**
9. Daniel Waugh.*
10. *Thomas Hammond.*
11. *A. N. Martin.**
12. *W. F. McNagney.*
13. *Charles G. Conn.*

IOWA.
1. John H. Gear.
2. *Walter I. Hayes.**
3. D. B. Henderson.
4. Thomas Updegraff.
5. R. G. Cousins.
6. John F. Lacey.
7. J. A. T. Hull.*
8. W. P. Hepburn.
9. W. L. Hager.
10. J. P. Dolliver.*
11. George D. Perkins.*

KANSAS.
W. A. HARRIS, At large.
1. Case Broderick.*
2. H. L. MOORE.
3. *Thomas J. Hudson.*
4. Charles E. Curtis.
5. JOHN DAVIS.
6. WILLIAM BAKER.*
7. JERRY SIMPSON.

KENTUCKY.
1. *W. J. Stone.**
2. *W. T. Ellis.**
3. *J. H. Goodnight.**
4. *A. B. Montgomery.**
5. *Asher G. Caruth.**
6. *A. S. Berry.*
7. *W. C. P. Breckinridge.**
8. *Jas. B. McCreary.**
9. *T. H. Paynter.**
10. *Marcus Lisle.*
11. Silas Adams.

LOUISIANA.
1. *Adolph Meyer.**
2. *R. C. Davy.*
3. *Andrew Price.**
4. *N. C. Blanchard.**
5. *C. J. Boatner.**
6. *S. M. Robertson.**

MAINE.
1. T. B. Reed.*
2. N. Dingley, Jr.*
3. S. L. Milliken.*
4. C. A. Boutelle.*

MARYLAND.
1. *R. F. Brattan.*
2. *J. F. C. Talbott.*
3. *H. W. Rusk.**
4. *Isidor Rayner.**
5. *Barnes Compton.**
6. *Wm. M. McKaig.**

MASSACHUSETTS.
1. A. B. Wright.
2. Fred H. Gillett.
3. Joseph H. Walker.*
4. L. D. Apsley.
5. *M. T. Stevens.**
6. William Cogswell.*
7. H. C. Lodge.*
8. S. W. McCall.
9. *Joseph H. O'Neil.**
10. *M. J. McEttrick.*
11. William F. Draper.
12. Elijah A. Morse.*
13. C. S. Randall.*

MICHIGAN.
1. *J. Logan Chipman.**
2. *James S. Gorman.**
3. J. C. Burrows.*
4. H. F. Thomas.
5. *G. F. Richardson.*
6. D. D. Aitken.
7. *J. R. Whiting.**
8. Wm. S. Linton.
9. John W. Moon.
10. *T. A. E. Weadock.**
11. John Avery.
12. S. M. Stephenson.*

MINNESOTA.
1. James A. Tawney.
2. J. T. McCleary.
3. *O. M. Hall.**
4. A. R. Kiefer.
5. Loren Fletcher.
6. D. B. Searle.
7. Henry Feig.

MISSISSIPPI.
1. *John M. Allen.**
2. *J. C. Kyle.**
3. *T. C. Catchings.**
4. *H. D. Money.*
5. *John S. Williams.*
6. *T. R. Stockdale.**
7. *C. E. Hooker.**

MISSOURI.
1. *W. H. Hatch.**
2. *U. S. Hall.*
3. *A. M. Dockery.**
4. *D. D. Burnes.*
5. *J. C. Tarsney.**
6. *D. A. De Armond.**
7. *J. T. Heard.**
8. *R. P. Bland.**
9. *Beauchamp Clark.*
10. Richard Bartholdt.
11. Charles F. Joy.
12. *Seth W. Cobb.**
13. *R. W. Fyan.**
14. *Marshall Arnold.**
15. *C. H. Morgan.*

MONTANA.
1. C. S. Hartman.

NEBRASKA.
1. *Wm. J. Bryan.**
2. D. H. Mercer.
3. G. W. Meiklejohn.
4. E. J. Hainer.
5. W. A. McKEIGHAN.*
6. O. M. KEM.*

NEVADA.
1. F. G. NEWLANDS.

NEW-HAMPSHIRE.
1. H. W. Blair.
2. *H. W. Parker.*

NEW-JERSEY.
1. H. C. Loudenslager.
2. John J. Gardner.
3. *J. A. Geissenhainer.**
4. *Johnston Cornish.*
5. *C. A. Cadmus.**
6. *Thomas D. English.**
7. *George B. Fielder.*
8. *John T. Dunn.*

NEW-YORK.
1. *James W. Covert.**
2. *John M. Clancy.**
3. *Joseph C. Hendrix.*
4. *William J. Coombs.*
5. *John H. Graham.*
6. *Thomas F. Magner.**
7. *Franklin Bartlett.*
8. *Edward J. Dunphy.**
9. *T. J. Campbell.**
10. *Daniel E. Sickles.*
11. *Amos J. Cummings.**
12. *W. Bourke Cockran.**
13. *J. De Witt Warner.**
14. *John R. Fellows.**
15. *Ashbel P. Fitch.**
16. *William Ryan.*
17. Francis Marvin.
18. Jacob Le Fever.
19. *Chas. D. Haines.*
20. *Charles Tracey.**
21. *S. J. Schermerhorn.*
22. N. M. Curtis.*
23. John M. Wever.*
24. C. A. Chickering.
25. *H. W. Bentley.**
26. George W. Ray.*
27. James J. Belden.*
28. Sereno E. Payne.*
29. Charles W. Gillet.
30. J. W. Wadsworth.*
31. John Van Voorhis.
32. *D. N. Lockwood.**
33. Charles Daniels.
34. Warren B. Hooker.*

NORTH CAROLINA.
1. *Wm. A. B. Branch.**
2. *F. A. Woodard.*
3. *Benj. F. Grady.**
4. *Benj. F. Bunn.**
5. *A. A. H. Williams.**
6. *S. B. Alexander.**
7. *J. S. Henderson.**
8. *Wm. H. Bower.*
9. *W. T. Crawford.**

NORTH DAKOTA.
1. M. N. Johnson.*

OHIO.
1. Bellamy Storer.*
2. J. A. Caldwell.*
3. *Geo. W. Houk.**
4. *F. C. Layton.**
5. *D. D. Donovan.**
6. Geo. W. Hulick.
7. Geo. W. Wilson.
8. L. M. Strong.
9. *Byron Ritchie.*
10. W. H. Enochs.*
11. C. H. Grosvenor.
12. *J. H. Outhwaite.**
13. *D. D. Hare.**
14. *M. D. Harter.**
15. H. C. Van Voorhis.
16. *A. J. Pearson.**
17. *J. A. D. Richards.*
18. *Geo. P. Ikert.*
19. S. A. Northway.
20. Wm. J. White.
21. *Tom L. Johnson.**

OREGON.
B. Hermann,* W. R. Ellis, At large.

PENNSYLVANIA.
Alex McDowell, William Lilly, At large.
1. H. H. Bingham.*
2. Charles O'Neill.*
3. *William McAleer.**
4. J. E. Reyburn.*
5. A. C. Harmer.*
6. J. B. Robinson.*
7. *Edwin Hallowell.**
8. *William Mutchler.**
9. *C. J. Erdman.*
10. Marriott Brosius.*
11. Joseph Scranton.
12. *W. H. Hines.*
13. *James B. Reilly.**
14. E. M. Woomer.
15. M. B. Wright.*
16. A. C. Hopkins.*
17. *S. P. Wolverton.**
18. T. M. Mahon.
19. *F. E. Beltzhoover.**
20. J. D. Hicks.
21. D. B. Heiner.
22. John Dalzell.*
23. William A. Stone.*
24. *William A. Sipe.*
25. T. W. Phillips.
26. *J. C. Sibley.*
27. C. W. Stone.
28. *George F. Kribbs.**

RHODE ISLAND.
1. No election.
2. No election.

SOUTH CAROLINA.
1. *W. H. Brawley.**
2. *W. J. Talbert.*
3. *G. W. Shell.**
4. *A. C. Latimer.*
5. *T. F. Strait.*
6. *J. L. McLaurin.*
7. George W. Murray.

SOUTH DAKOTA.
W. V. Lucas, J. A. Pickler,* At large.

TENNESSEE.
1. A. A. Taylor.*
2. J. C. Houk.*
3. *H. C. Snodgrass.**
4. *Benton McMillin.**
5. *J. D. Richardson.**
6. *J. E. Washington.**
7. *N. N. Cox.**
8. *Benj. A. Enloe.**
9. *J. C. McDearman.*
10. *Josiah Patterson.**

TEXAS.
1. *J. C. Hutchinson.*
2. *S. B. Cooper.*
3. *C. B. Kilgore.**
4. *D. B. Culberson.**
5. *Joseph W. Bailey.**
6. J. C. KIRBY.
7. J. N. BARBER.
8. *C. K. Bell.*
9. *Joseph D. Sayers.**
10. *Walter Gresham.*
11. *W. H. Crain.**
12. *George N. Paschal.*
13. *J. V. Cockrill.*

VERMONT.
1. H. H. Powers.*
2. William W. Grout.*

VIRGINIA.
1. *W. A. Jones.**
2. *D. G. Tyler.*
3. *George D. Wise.**
4. *James F. Epes.**
5. *C. A. Swanson.*
6. *P. C. Edmunds.**
7. *C. T. O'Ferrall.**
8. *E. E. Meredith.**
9. *James W. Marshall.*
10. *H. St. G. Tucker.**

WASHINGTON.
J. L. Wilson,* W. H. Doolittle, At large.

WEST VIRGINIA.
1. *J. O. Pendleton.**
2. *W. L. Wilson.**
3. *J. D. Alderson.**
4. *James Capehart.**

WISCONSIN.
1. H. A. Cooper.
2. *Charles Barwig.**
3. J. W. Babcock.
4. *John L. Mitchell.**
5. *G. H. Brickner.**
6. *Owen E. Wells.*
7. George B. Shaw.
8. *L. E. Barnes.*
9. *Thomas Lynch.**
10. N. P. Haugen.*

WYOMING.
1. C. D. Clark.*

### THE RESULT IN SOUTH CAROLINA.

COLUMBIA, S. C., Nov. 9.—Incomplete returns from the State show Cleveland's majority to be 35,510. Only two counties in the State show majorities for Harrison. Complete returns will probably run Cleveland's majority up to 37,500. The total vote for Weaver in the State will not be over 3,200. In a number of the counties there was not a single third-party vote cast.

The indications are decidedly unfavorable to Moise, (Dem.,) candidate from the Seventh or Black District. The total vote so far reported is: Murray, 3,450, and Moise, 1,649, with Williamsburg and Colleton Counties to hear from. These counties will hardly counterbalance Murray's lead. There is not a suspicion of doubt of the election of six Democratic Congressmen. Five of them were indorsed by the Alliance in the State primary, but consider themselves Democrats first.

CHARLESTON, S. C., Nov. 10—2:30 A. M.—The wide extent of the Seventh Congressional District, consisting of nine counties and parts of counties, with precincts in the backwoods, accounts for the slowness of election returns. Sumter, Gen. Moise's home county, gives him 939 majority over the colored Republican, Murray. Orangeburg gives Moise 800 majority. Colleton, Berkeley, Beaufort, and Georgetown, the blackest counties in the black belt, have yet to be heard from.

At the densest Republican poll in the black district, the historical haute gap in Berkeley, where there are only 36 whites to 1,000 colored voters, there was no election at all. Ostendorff, white Republican candidate, in primaries evidently tried to knife Murray, and there was great apathy in the black belt.

In Edisto Island, where 960 are registered, only 106 voted, and in St. Stephen's only 66 out of 600 Republicans voted at all. Democrats of both factions used every effort to elect Moise and he will probably get there.

### THE UNITED STATES SENATE.

THE REPUBLICAN MAJORITY HAS DISAPPEARED.

There is no doubt that the Administration of President Cleveland will be supported by a Senate having a majority of his own political friends. According to the latest returns the Republicans have lost the Legislatures in the States of California, Kansas, Montana, Nebraska, Nevada, New-York, and Wisconsin, and those States, now represented by Republicans, will send Democrats and other opponents of the Republicans to fill the places of the Republican incumbents. The Legislature of Connecticut turns out to be Republican, but the loss of that State will not deprive the Democrats of a majority. Montana, New-York, and Wisconsin are secure, and will choose Democratic Senators. Kansas, which has elected a Legislature with a majority of People's Party members, will choose a colleague for Peffer of the same sort. In all probability Nebraska will elect a Senator by combination of Democrats and Alliance members of the Legislature, and he may be a Weaverite or a Democrat, but the place is given to the People's Party in calculating the probable division of the next Senate. Senator Stewart will undoubtedly be re-elected from Nevada, and may act with both political parties, according to circumstances, but always against the Republicans on silver-coinage propositions.

The present Senate stands 47 Republicans, 39 Democrats, and 2 People's Party, a Republican majority of 6. The Senate, after March 4, 1893, will be divided as follows:

| | *D.* | *R.* | *P.* | | *D.* | *R.* | *P.* |
|---|---|---|---|---|---|---|---|
| Alabama | 2 | | | Montana | 1 | 1 | |
| Arkansas | 2 | | | Nebraska | | 1 | 1 |
| California | 1 | 1 | | Nevada | | 1 | 1 |
| Colorado | | 2 | | N. Hampsh'e | | 2 | |
| Connecticut | | 2 | | New-Jersey | 2 | | |
| Delaware | 1 | 1 | | New-York | 2 | | |
| Florida | 2 | | | N. Carolina | 2 | | |
| Georgia | 2 | | | N. Dakota | | 2 | |
| Idaho | | 2 | | Ohio | 1 | 1 | |
| Illinois | 1 | 1 | | Oregon | | 2 | |
| Indiana | 2 | | | Pennsylvania | | 2 | |
| Iowa | | 2 | | Rhode Island | | 2 | |
| Kansas | | | 2 | S. Carolina | 2 | | |
| Kentucky | 2 | | | South Dakota | | 1 | 1 |
| Louisiana | 2 | | | Tennessee | 2 | | |
| Maine | | 2 | | Texas | 2 | | |
| Maryland | 2 | | | Vermont | | 2 | |
| Massachu'ts | | 2 | | Virginia | 2 | | |
| Michigan | | 2 | | Washington | | 2 | |
| Minnesota | | 2 | | West Virginia | 2 | | |
| Mississippi | 2 | | | Wisconsin | 2 | | |
| Missouri | 2 | | | Wyoming | | 2 | |
| Total | | | | | 43 | 40 | 5 |

### REPRESENTATIVES IN CONGRESS.

[Vacancies were caused in the Fifty-second Congress in the Third California District by resignation of Joseph McKenna, (Rep.,) Twenty-fourth Pennsylvania by death of A. K. Craig, (Dem.,) Sixth South Carolina by death of E. T. Stackhouse, (Dem.,) Seventh New-Jersey by death of E. F. McDonald, (Dem.,) Sixteenth Ohio by death of J. G. Warwick, (Dem.)

| *States.* | Fifty-second Congress. Dem. | Rep. | F. A. | Fifty-third Congress. Dem. | Rep. | Peo. |
|---|---|---|---|---|---|---|
| Alabama | 8 | | | 8 | | 1 |
| Arkansas | 5 | | | 6 | | |
| California | 2 | 3 | | 6 | 1 | |
| Colorado | | 1 | | | | 2 |
| Connecticut | 3 | 1 | | 3 | 1 | |
| Delaware | 1 | | | 1 | | |
| Florida | 2 | | | 2 | | |
| Georgia | 9 | | 1 | 11 | | |
| Idaho | | 1 | | | 1 | |
| Illinois | 14 | 6 | | 13 | 9 | |
| Indiana | 11 | 2 | | 11 | 2 | |
| Iowa | 6 | 5 | | 1 | 10 | |
| Kansas | | 2 | 5 | 1 | 2 | 5 |
| Kentucky | 10 | 1 | | 10 | 1 | |
| Louisiana | 6 | | | 6 | | |
| Maine | | 4 | | | 4 | |
| Maryland | 6 | | | 6 | | |
| Massachusetts | 7 | 5 | | 3 | 10 | |
| Michigan | 7 | 4 | | 5 | 7 | |
| Minnesota | 3 | 1 | 1 | 1 | 5 | 1 |
| Mississippi | 7 | | | 7 | | |
| Missouri | 14 | | | 13 | 2 | |
| Montana | 1 | | | | 1 | |
| Nebraska | 1 | | 2 | 1 | 3 | 2 |
| Nevada | | 1 | | | | 1 |
| New-Hampshire | 2 | | | 1 | 1 | |
| New-Jersey | 4 | 3 | | 6 | 2 | |
| New-York | 23 | 11 | | 21 | 13 | |
| North Carolina | 8 | 1 | | 9 | | |
| North Dakota | | 1 | | | 1 | |
| Ohio | 13 | 7 | | 11 | 10 | |
| Oregon | | 1 | | | 2 | |
| Pennsylvania | 10 | 17 | | 11 | 19 | |
| Rhode Island | 2 | | | No election. | | |
| South Carolina | 6 | | | 6 | 1 | |
| South Dakota | | 2 | | | 2 | |
| Tennessee | 8 | 2 | | 8 | 2 | |
| Texas | 11 | | | 11 | | 2 |
| Vermont | | 2 | | | 2 | |
| Virginia | 10 | | | 10 | | |
| Washington | | 1 | | | 2 | |
| West Virginia | 4 | | | 4 | | |
| Wisconsin | 8 | 1 | | 6 | 4 | |
| Wyoming | | 1 | | | 1 | |
| Total | 232 | 86 | 9 | 220 | 121 | 13 |

Whole number of members....354
Democrats....220
Republicans....121
People's Party....13
Democratic majority....87

### WISCONSIN DEMOCRATIC.

A MAJORITY OF 11,000 FOR THE CLEVELAND ELECTORS.

MILWAUKEE, Nov. 9.—Wisconsin has given a majority for both the Democratic national and State tickets, and it has elected a majority of Democrats to the Legislature, which insures a Democratic United States Senator to succeed Senator Sawyer. The early returns last night were favorable to the Republicans, who did not believe Harrison's majority of 21,000 of four years ago would be wiped out, but the later returns showed steadily-increasing Democratic gains.

The Democrats have carried the State by about 11,000. Ex-Senator Spooner, the Republican candidate for Governor, to-day admits his defeat by 5,000, and the majority is likely to be twice that.

Chairman Wall of the Democratic National Committee says the returns show that the Lutherans who left the Republican Party two years ago on the compulsory school law issue, have staid with the Democrats, and to them he attributes the victory which the Democrats have won.

The next contest will be for the United States Senatorship. It will be a three-cornered fight between John H. Knight, a millionaire lumberman of Ashland; John L. Mitchell, a Milwaukee Congressman, and Gen. Bragg, with the probability that the real fight will be between Knight and Mitchell.

Democrats elect Congressmen as follows: Mitchell in the Fourth District, Barwig in the Second, Brickner in the Fifth, Lynch in the Ninth, Barnes in the Eighth, and Wells in the Sixth. The Republicans elect Cooper in the First, Babcock in the Third, and Haugen in the Tenth. In the Seventh, Coburn (Dem.) is probably elected.

### OLD-FASHIONED NEW-HAMPSHIRE.

CONCORD, N. H., Nov. 9.—One hundred and seventy-one towns and wards give Smith, (Rep.,) for Governor, 26,071; McKinney, (Dem.,) 24,757; Carr, (Proh.,) 981; Noyes, (People's,) 115. Same places in 1890 gave Tuttle, (Rep.,) 25,453; Amsden, (Dem.,) 24,808; scattering, 820.

These returns indicate that Harrison will have a plurality of 23,500 in the State. Baker's unexpectedly large vote for Congress indicates not only his own election, but that Smith (Rep.) will be elected Governor by the people.

The latest returns show that the Republicans have from 40 to 50 majority in the Legislature.

### OHIO IN THE SWIM.

PROBABLE SELECTION OF DEMOCRATIC ELECTORS IN THE STATE.

COLUMBUS, Nov. 9.—The Democrats are jubilant here to-night over the hopeful prospect of carrying Ohio for Mr. Cleveland and the State ticket. Ohio is in the doubtful column, with the returns coming in favorably to the election of the Cleveland Electors and the State ticket. This result was not dreamed of last night, as the Republicans claimed the State by 20,000, and the Democrats were not anticipating a material change from the figures held by the Republicans, owing to the remarkable tardy manner in which the returns came.

The result in almost every other State was practically known before the Ohio returns began to be telegraphed to the capital. This was partly owing to the fact that the polls are open till 6 o'clock, and there are numerous districts away from telegraphic centres. It was known this morning and commented upon as significant that there was a Democratic gain of 700 over the vote of 1888 in Mansfield, the home of Senator Sherman, while there was a gain of about 1,500 in McKinley's county of Stark and in Mahoning County, in the same Congressional district.

The Democrats now claim the State by from 1,000 to 5,000, and insist that the following twelve Democrats are elected to Congress: Houk, Third District; Laylin, Fourth; Donovan, Fifth; Ritchie, Ninth; Outhwaite, Twelfth; Hare, Thirteenth; Harter, Fourteenth; Pearson, Sixteenth; Richards, Seventeenth; J. Kert, Eighteenth; Ellen, Twentieth, and Johnson, Twenty-first, leaving the Republicans nine districts, when they had expected to capture sixteen.

Reports from fifty-four of the eighty-eight counties show a net Democratic gain over McKinley's majority of last year of 20,159, and with thirty-four counties to hear from it would require a gain of but 45 votes to a county to elect the Democratic ticket, while the lowest average gain has been 245.

The Democrats claim that Col. Poorman, Secretary of State, is defeated in the Sixteenth District, in which he was a candidate, while Col. Poorman telegraphs the Republican Committee that he is elected by 60 votes.

Col. W. A. Taylor, Democratic candidate for Secretary of State, sent the following:

COLUMBUS, Ohio, Nov. 9.

*To Grover Cleveland, Commander in Chief, New-York City, N. Y.:*

I have the honor to report that the Buckeye Brigade moved in force at 6 A. M. on the 8th inst. upon the McKinley Heights and succeeded in storming them after twelve hours of continuous fighting. Our troops rested on their arms during the night. This morning the enemy had retreated, leaving the following spoils: 23 Electors, 12 Congressmen, 1 Secretary of State, 2 Supreme Judges, 1 Clerk of the Supreme Court, 1 member of the Board of Public Works, and a full complement of baggage, supply, and ammunition trains. I have the honor to be,

W. A. TAYLOR,
Commanding Brigade.

The Republicans claim to have reports from the Chairmen of sixty-one counties which show a Democratic gain of 14,785, based upon McKinley's majority last year, which was 21,511, and is an average gain of 234 to a county, and not sufficient to elect the Democratic ticket. They claim that the Republican State ticket is elected by 4,000, and that S. M. Taylor, for Secretary of State, will have about 1,500 less than Mr. Harrison. They concede the defeat of Hodge, E. G. Johnson, and Morgan, and others are admitted to be in doubt.

Ohio Republicans are disgusted and thoroughly angry, and freely attribute their defeat in the Nation and Ohio to the McKinley tariff. The Governor has absolutely refused, upon solicitation, to say a word about the election, but it is known that he feels very keenly Mr. Harrison's defeat, which is the defeat of high protection.

W. M. Hahn, the National Republican Committeeman from Ohio, has called down upon his devoted head the dire wrath of several Republicans who are lighter in purse because of his rainbow messages. Mr. Hahn telegraphed to Ohio last night that it was only a question of plurality in New-York, and his Republican friends went out to find some bets. They lost their money, and to-day Mr. Hahn received in New-York several caustic messages, of which the following are samples:

DEAR WILLIE: Come home and help us figure out New-York's plurality. We are busted.

"Many Republicans congratulate you upon your magnificent work. A few more like you would have it unanimous."

It is a surprising result for Ohio, but Ohio is nothing if not "in the swim."

CLEVELAND, Nov. 9.—Surprising news comes from Columbus. The outlook for the Ohio vote has steadily become more Democratic since early this morning. At 10 o'clock this morning the Democrats began to take courage sufficient to claim that Ohio would probable be Democratic. These claims were based on scattering returns showing material gains for the party. Telegrams were sent to County Chairmen, and returns soon began to come showing steady Democratic gains. Then the claim went out that Ohio would be Democratic, and there was a panic at the Republican Headquarters. Republicans also telegraphed to counties for the latest returns. Both committees got down to earnest figuring. The Republicans became more discouraged as the hours passed. At 9 o'clock to-night they were claiming the State on Electors by only 3,000 or 4,000. This was after the Democrats had received official figures from sixty-five of the eighty-eight counties, showing a net Democratic gain of 20,420, leaving only 1,091 of McKinley's 21,511 to overcome in the remaining twenty-three counties. Excitement became intense, and at 10 o'clock the Democratic State Committee made the emphatic claim that the Cleveland Electors and Democratic State ticket had carried the State. The heaviest Democratic gain is in this (Cuyahoga) county, where Cleveland gains about 5,000, and Tom L. Johnson is elected to Congress by 3,200.

CINCINNATI, Nov. 10—2:30 A. M.—The *Commercial Gazette*, (Rep.,) on the basis of complete returns from fifty-four counties and estimates on the remaining thirty-four counties in the State, estimates that Cleveland Electors are chosen by 353 plurality, and that S. M. Taylor (Rep.) for Secretary of State has been elected. It also figures ten Republican and eleven Democratic Congressmen.

### NO DOUBT NOW OF CALIFORNIA.

ALMOST COMPLETE RETURNS ASSURE DEMOCRATIC VICTORY.

SAN FRANCISCO, Cal., Nov. 9.—Almost complete returns from the entire State have been received, and careful estimates can now be made on the result in California.

There was a general falling off in the Republican vote in Southern California, and Cleveland swept San Francisco City by 7,500 plurality. Best estimates obtainable to-night on almost complete returns place Cleveland's majority in California at 6,000, with a possibility of 8,000 or 10,000. The State Legislature will be Democratic in both Houses and will have a good working majority on joint ballot. This insures the election of a Democrat to the United States Senate, and at this writing Stephen M. White has the best chances of election.

The following Congressmen are elected by handsome majorities: Grey (Dem.) in First District, Caminos (Dem.) in Second District, Maguire (Dem.) in Seventh District, Cannon (Dem. and Populist) in Sixth District. Ryland (Dem.) is elected in the Fifth District by 200 majority and English (Dem.) in the Third District, and Wellbonrne (Dem.) in the Seventh District are in all probability elected by small majorities. This gives a solid Democratic delegation of seven from California.

The result in this State, which was an overwhelming surprise to Democrats as well as Republicans, was due to two causes: First, to dissatisfaction of wholesale merchants in San Francisco with the McKinley bill which has caused the wholesale trade with the Sandwich Islands and Australia to be ruined. Merchants almost to a man voted for Cleveland and worked for him at the polls. This accounts for large Democratic majority in San Francisco. Second, the efforts of M. H. De Young to foist himself upon the people as Republican Senator from California. Republicans all over the State waged war on De Young and rebuked him at the polls.

### THE VOTE IN OREGON.

PORTLAND, Oregon, Nov. 9.—The election of three Harrison Electors is conceded by the Chairman of the Democratic State Central Committee by pluralities ranging from 2,500 to 3,000. One Weaver Elector, who was indorsed by the Democrats, is claimed by that party.

### INDIANA GIVES 8,000.

A COMPLETE DEMOCRATIC TRIUMPH IN MR. HARRISON'S STATE.

INDIANAPOLIS, Nov. 9.—The Democrats have carried Indiana for Cleveland by a majority exceeding 8,000, have elected the entire State and Judicial tickets, eleven of the thirteen Representatives to Congress, and two-thirds of the Legislature in each house.

Chairman Taggart of the Democratic State Committee attributes this grand victory to several causes: First, to the popularity of Grover Cleveland; second, to the sound tariff platform; third, to the Australian ballot law; and, fourth, to the Force bill. "'The tariff is robbery,' and 'Down with the Force bill' were the mottoes inscribed upon our banners," said Mr. Taggart to a TIMES representative. "Indiana," he continued, "is an original reform State, and, therefore, a Democratic State. The Australian ballot law enacted by the Democratic Legislature in 1889 makes it possible for workmen to cast their ballots without the interference of employers. It makes it impossible for the Republicans to purchase 'floaters.' With our present system Indiana would have been carried by Cleveland four years ago. Republican employers bulldozed enough of their men then to carry the State. Indiana is permanently Democratic. It has always been Democratic except during the war period and when purchased in 1880 and 1888."

S. E. Morse, editor of the Indianapolis *Sentinel*, the author of the Indiana ballot law, who led the fight in this State for the nomination of Cleveland, says: "Without the Australian system the Republicans would have carried the State by fraud and bulldozing. I do not believe there would have been such a tidal wave if Cleveland had not been the nominee, for the tariff issue would not have been so strongly defined. The people, too, believed that Cleveland was cheated out of a second term four years ago by the plutocrats. They demanded his nomination, that they might have an opportunity to avenge the wrong. Their desire was gratified and they emphasized their condemnation of the tariff barons in no uncertain tone. The management of the State campaign was most admirable. Chairman Thomas Taggart as an organizer and leader of men I believe has no equal in this State. His name inspired confidence among the rank and file of the party, and yet he is but thirty-six years old."

To-night the streets are crowded with men, women, and boys tooting tin horns and parading. Business is suspended.

Marion County, Harrison's home, gives Cleveland 1,300 plurality, a net Democratic gain of 750.

INDIANAPOLIS, Nov. 10—1 A. M.—Chairman Gowdy still claims the State for Harrison, but Chairman Taggart sends out these figures over his signature: "Seventy-five counties out of ninety-three report Democratic gains of 3,859 over 1888, giving Cleveland 6,511 plurality." Conservative men say that Cleveland will surely have from 3,500 to 4,000 plurality. The People's Party claim to have cast a vote of 4,000, but have received returns from only three counties.

### RUSSELL ELECTED GOVERNOR.

BUT HARRISON WILL CARRY MASSACHUSETTS BY 20,000.

BOSTON, Mass., Nov. 9.—All day the result of the Gubernatorial contest hung in the balance. Both sides claimed a victory. The Republicans up to 3 o'clock insisted that they had a plurality of about 1,300 for Haile, while the Democrats held to 1,700 plurality for Russell as their lowest estimate. About that hour, however, a telegram from Haile to the Governor was given out in which the former congratulated the latter on his election. Even then the *Journal* and *Advertiser* refused to concede the election.

The returns kept coming in slowly during the afternoon, and the percentages were carefully figured by expert accountants. At this hour (midnight) all the cities have been heard from, including Boston, and all the towns except five.

The result may be stated definitely as follows: Boston gives Russell 43,133; Haile, 28,937. The cities outside of Boston give Russell 75,905; Haile, 73,591. The towns outside give Russell 68,533; Haile, 82,209, a total of 187,571 for Russell and 184,737 for Haile.

This gives a plurality to the Governor of 2,834 in a total vote of 372,308. The five towns to be heard from are small and may give Haile 200 plurality, reducing the figures down to about 2,500. In that vicinity they will permanently remain. Gov. Russell is re-elected, while Harrison will carry the State by perhaps 20,000.

This triumph is due to the Governor's personal popularity and to the respect in which he is held by the people. The Republicans have elected nine Congressmen and the Democrats three. There is doubt about the result in the First District. Crosby still claims to be elected, and a recount may be necessary to determine the result. A good working majority in both branches of the Legislature has been secured by the Republicans, insuring a Republican Senator to secure Mr. Dawes. The Lieutenant Governor, Treasurer, Secretary of State, Auditor, and Attorney General have also been elected by the Republicans. The Governor will also have a hostile Executive Council, only one Democrat being elected to that effete body.

Police Commissioner Osborn may begin to pack up his traps. He will not be reappointed. The Boston liquor dealers are apt to hear from the voters in the city in December on the question of license. They stabbed the Governor in the back and they will get their pay in statutory prohibition unless the temper of the Democrats changes.

### THE VICTORY IN ILLINOIS.

CLEVELAND'S PLURALITY WILL REACH 17,000—THE STATE TICKET.

CHICAGO, Nov. 9.—Returns from all over the State, although incomplete, indicate that Cleveland's plurality will approximate 17,000. He runs ahead of Altgeld for Governor 3,000 votes, and the Democrats elect the rest of the State ticket by about the same plurality, as follows: Governor—John P. Altgeld; Lieutenant Governor—Joseph B. Gill; Secretary of State—William H. Henrichsen; Treasurer—Rufus O. Ramsay; Auditor—David Gore; Attorney General—Maurice D. Maloney; University Trustees—James E. Armstrong, Napoleon B. Morrison, and Isaac S. Raymond.

This great Democratic victory was brought about by the enormous vote in Chicago, where Cleveland received a plurality in round numbers of 27,000 and Altgeld of 25,000. The German Lutherans claim the honor of the victory. They say that their strength in the State is 35,000, two-thirds of which was transferred from the Republican Party to the Democratic Party, owing to the dissatisfaction of the Germans with the school law passed by the Republican Legislature.

Gov. Fifer in his campaign for re-election promised to see that the obnoxious law was repealed by the next Legislature, but the Germans preferred to take the responsibility off the hands of the Republicans and intrust it to the Democrats, who fought the bill in the Legislature. Cleveland's strength over Altgeld came from votes given to him by men who did not like Altgeld's Socialistic tendencies. The Lutherans as a rule voted straight tickets. The colored voters of the State also had a bone to pick with Hertz, the Republican candidate for Treasurer, and knifed the entire ticket so as to be sure to beat him. Their leaders instructed the ignorant colored men to vote straight Democratic tickets, fearing to leave to them the difficult operation of picking out Hertz's name on the blanket ballot.

The State Legislature is surely Democratic in both branches, which will insure a reapportionment of the State and the repeal of the obnoxious school law. The Republicans had compromised their position on the school question by promising to enact a new law, after repealing the present one, which was to be made satisfactory to the German Lutherans. The Germans do not want any such law.

Fifteen Democrats and nine Republicans who were elected to the State Senate, will hold over into the next session of the Legislature, two years hence, which will elect a successor to United States Senator Cullom. The Democrats have elected a majority of the delegation to Congress. In Chicago the Democrats have elected the entire city and Cook County ticket.

### COLORADO FOR WEAVER.

DENVER, Col., Nov. 9.—The Republicans concede Colorado to Weaver by from 3,000 to 5,000. J. C. Bell (fusionists) is elected to Congress in the Second District by a large vote. Lafe Pence is elected to Congress in the First District by a close vote. The entire Weaver State ticket is elected, with the possible exception of Harry Mulnix, (Rep.,) for State Treasurer.

The fusionists will have a majority in the Legislature. A United States Senator, however,

(Continued on Page 2.)

## THE DUKE OF MARLBOROUGH

*FOUND DEAD IN HIS BED IN THE BLENHEIM PALACE.*

ROMANCE OF A DISSIPATED ENGLISH NOBLEMAN AND AN AMERICAN BELLE—MARRIAGE OF THE DUKE TO MRS. HAMERSLEY, AND THE HARD WORK OF THE DUCHESS TO SECURE SOCIAL RECOGNITION.

LONDON, Nov. 9.—A dispatch from Blenheim Palace, the seat of the Duke of Marlborough at Woodstock, Oxfordshire, announces that the Duke was found dead in bed there this morning.

On Saturday last the Duke was in London, and then appeared to be enjoying good health.

The Duke was out driving yesterday and was in good spirits. He showed no symptoms of illness. Upon his return from his drive he took dinner and ate well. He passed the evening in reading and writing, and retired at midnight, still seemingly in good health. His conversation was cheerful.

When his valet entered the Duke's bedroom this morning he found his master lying on his back in bed. One of his arms was thrown over his chest, and his hand was clenched above his heart. His face was serene, and he appeared to be asleep. The valet made no attempt to arouse him until he noticed the growing pallor of the face. Then he made an attempt to wake him, but found he was dead.

It is supposed that death resulted from heart disease.

It was evident when the body was found that life had been extinct several hours, and that death was painless. Rigor mortis was then well developed. In view of the suddenness of the Duke's death, while he was apparently enjoying good health, a post-mortem examination of the remains will be made to-morrow.

The Marquis of Blandford, the Duke's son, and Lord Randolph Churchill, his brother, arrived at Blenheim this afternoon. They found the Duchess prostrate with grief.

George Charles Spencer-Churchill, the eighth Duke of Marlborough, Marquis of Blandford, Prince of the Holy Roman Empire, and Prince of Mindelheim in Suabia, was born in England May 13, 1844. He served as a Lieutenant in the Royal Horse Guards. As Marquis of Blandford he married Lady Albertha Hamilton, the daughter of the Duke of Abercorn, in 1869. By her he had a son, Charles Richard Spencer-Churchill, who was born in 1871 and who succeeds him, and three daughters, Ladies Frances, Lilian Maude, and Norah Beatrice.

The Duke succeeded his father in 1883, and at that time his wife obtained a divorce from him on account of marital infidelity and cruelty. The charges brought against him by the Duchess, who was related to half the old ducal houses in England, were such as to exclude him from society. He continued to live in a most profligate manner, and shortly after succeeding to his title and estates, in 1883, he was forced to despoil his ancestral seat of Blenheim of its choicest artistic and literary treasures to meet the most pressing demands of his creditors.

The Duke of Marlborough was a man of much force of intellect, and was remarkably gifted. In politics he was a Liberal, and attempted, without success, to prevent his brother, Lord Randolph Churchill, from being elected as Conservative member for Woodstock, his own borough. He opposed him bitterly. He contributed to a number of magazines and reviews, and his papers were well written and the subjects treated, principally dealing with social economics, were well and skillfully handled.

He was a frequent visitor to America, and shared social popularity with two other English Dukes—Sutherland and Manchester—then known as Lord Mandeville, who were profligates like himself, and who have both died within the past three months.

In the Summer of 1887 he was at Newport, the guest of Mrs. Paran Stevens, and was generally received by society. That Winter he met the widow Hamersley, one of the wealthiest and most beautiful women in New-York society. As Miss Lillian Price of Troy, N. Y., she had been a great belle, and she was one of the eight beautiful girls entertained by the late Mr. Corcoran of Washington at his cottage at the Virginia White Sulphur Springs early in the eighties. She married Louis C. Hamersley, who died a few years afterward, leaving no issue, and with the income of a fortune estimated at $6,000,000.

Mrs. Hamersley and the Duke were married in June, 1888, by Mayor Hewitt at the City Hall in this city, and afterward by a Baptist clergyman. Arthur Leary was the best man, and the Duke and Duchess sailed immediately for England. For some time, the new Duchess occupied a very equivocal social position in England, on account of Queen Victoria's disapproval of divorced people remarrying, and refusing to receive the American wife of Marlborough at Court. Then again, the first Duchess's family connections were such as to preclude her successor from being invited to any of the great houses in England.

The first Duchess was the daughter, as has been already stated, of the Duke of Abercorn and Marquis of Hamilton. Her mother was the daughter of the Duke of Bedford. One of her sisters is the Marquise of Lansdowne, another is the Countess of Litchfield, and another is the Duchess of Buccleuch and Lady in Waiting to the Queen. Her brother, Lord John Hamilton, is Aide de Camp to the Queen, and a younger brother, Lord George Francis Hamilton, is a Lord of the Admiralty. The first few years of the new Duchess's married life were spent in frequent trips to this country and tours on the Continent. At last she was received at Court, but not able for a long time to take the same social position as her rank either in England or in this country would justify. Her own delightful personality has, however, won her a position. From the income of the Hamersley fortune the Duchess succeeded in restoring Blenheim House, the ducal seat, and in fitting up a handsome London town house. During a part of the Autumn she entertained large parties of her New-York friends at Blenheim.

The will of Louis Hamersley left the estate in trust with power of reversion to the male heirs of his cousin, J. Hooker Hamersley, who married a Miss Chisholm several years ago. A little girl was born to the Hooker-Hamersleys and it died in 1891. A second girl was born two weeks after the death of the first, and last Summer J. Hooker Hamersley was made at Newport the proud father of a male heir, which has been facetiously called the six-million-dollar baby. This child will inherit the Hamersley fortune, the income of which the widowed Duchess now enjoys.

The Duke of Marlborough had for the head of his house the famous John Churchill, first Duke of his name and the hero of England's army in the days of Queen Anne. His wife was the famous Sarah Jennings, known in the correspondence of Queen Anne as "Dear Mrs. Freeman." The military achievements of the great Churchill at Blenheim and in the various Continental wars of the period are still preserved by his enemies, the French, in the children's game, with the refrain "Marlbro va t'en guerre" sung to the old tune of "We Won't Go Home Til Morning."

The Duke of Marlborough had invested heavily in Tennessee lands since his marriage, and had an interest in steel and iron works in the Tennessee mountains. His younger brother is the famous English politician, Lord Randolph Churchill, who also married an American, Miss Jennie Jerome, the daughter of the late Leonard Jerome of this city. One of his sisters is Lady Wimborne, another Lady Ramsay, and a third the wife of the Duke of Roxburgh.

### Congressman McDonald's Funeral.

NEWARK, Nov. 9.—The funeral of Congressman Edward F. McDonald took place this morning from his late residence, at Davis Avenue and Crooss Street, Harrison. Zabriskie Post, G. A. R., of which the Congressman was a member, acted as guard of honor.

The pall bearers were George B. Fielder, Peter Hauck, James Smith, Jr., John W. Strahan, Dennis McLoughlin, Michael T. Bret, William J. Tirney, Marion Lawless, Bryan Smith, and Allan McDermott. Among those in the procession were Gov. Abbett, Mayor Haines of this city, Mayor Stanton of Hoboken, James O'Neil, Surrogate of Hudson County, and county officials of other places in New-Jersey. The Common Council of Harrison and the Township Committees of Kearney were also present.

The services were conducted by the Rev. Father O'Connor, assisted by the Rev. Dr. Brogan and the Rev. Father Morris.

### Heavy Snowfall in Missouri.

DEXTER, Mo., Nov. 9.—Eight inches of snow have fallen here since this morning and the storm is still raging. Such a fall is unprecedented, the midwinter depth seldom exceeding four inches.

CHARLESTON, Mo., Nov. 9.—A severe snowstorm began here this morning and is still raging furiously. The ground is covered to a depth of six inches.

# The New-York Times.

VOL. XLII...NO. 12,957. NEW-YORK, SUNDAY, MARCH 5, 1893.—TWENTY PAGES. PRICE FIVE CENTS.




## PRESIDENT ONCE AGAIN

*MR. CLEVELAND IN THE HIGHEST OFFICE A SECOND TIME.*

LARGE THRONGS VIEW THE IMPRESSIVE CEREMONIES.

*STURDY DEMOCRACY NOT DETERRED BY BAD WEATHER.*

THE CLOSING COURTESIES BETWEEN THE OUTGOING AND INCOMING ADMINISTRATIONS—THE NEW RÉGIME BEGUN IN THE SENATE CHAMBER WITH VICE PRESIDENT STEVENSON'S INDUCTION INTO POWER—WARM RECEPTION OF MR. CLEVELAND BY THE WAITING CROWDS—HE READS HIS INAUGURAL ADDRESS BARE-HEADED IN A COLD, DRIVING WIND—THE PARADE OF THE ENTHUSIASTIC DEMOCRACY—THE WHITE HOUSE IN NEW HANDS—SCENES AT THE INAUGURATION BALL.

### THE INAUGURAL ADDRESS.

MY FELLOW-CITIZENS: In obedience to the mandate of my countrymen, I am about to dedicate myself to their service under the sanction of a solemn oath. Deeply moved by the expression of confidence and personal attachment which has called me to this service, I am sure my gratitude can make no better return than the pledge I now give before God and these witnesses of unreserved and complete devotion to the interests and welfare of those who have honored me.

I deem it fitting on this occasion, while indicating the opinions I hold concerning public questions of present importance, to also briefly refer to the existence of certain conditions and tendencies among our people which seem to menace the integrity and usefulness of their Government.

While every American citizen must contemplate with the utmost pride and enthusiasm the growth and expansion of our country, the sufficiency of our institutions to stand against the rudest shocks of violence, the wonderful thrift and enterprise of our people, and the demonstrated superiority of our free Government, it behooves us to constantly watch for every symptom of insidious infirmity that threatens our national vigor.

The strong man who, in the confidence of sturdy health, courts the sternest activities of life and rejoices in the hardihood of constant labor may still have lurking near his vitals the unheeded disease that dooms him to sudden collapse.

It cannot be doubted that our stupendous achievements as a people and our country's robust strength have given rise to a heedlessness of those laws governing our national health which we can no more evade than human life can escape the laws of God and nature.

Manifestly nothing is more vital to our supremacy as a nation and to the beneficent purposes of our Government than a sound and stable currency. Its exposure to degradation should at once arouse to activity the most enlightened statesmanship, and the danger of depreciation in the purchasing power of the wages paid to toil should furnish the strongest incentive to prompt and conservative precaution.

In dealing with our present embarrassing situation as related to this subject, we will be wise if we temper our confidence and faith in our national strength and resources with the frank concession that even these will not permit us to defy with impunity the inexorable laws of finance and trade. At the same time, in our efforts to adjust differences of opinion we should be free from intolerance or passion, and our judgments should be unmoved by alluring phrases and unvexed by selfish interests.

I am confident that such an approach to the subject will result in prudent and effective remedial legislation. In the meantime, so far as the executive branch of the Government can intervene, none of the powers with which it is invested will be withheld when their exercise is deemed necessary to maintain our national credit or avert financial disaster.

Closely related to the exaggerated confidence in our country's greatness which tends to a disregard of the rules of national safety, another danger confronts us not less serious. I refer to the prevalence of a popular disposition to expect from the operation of the Government especial and direct individual advantages.

The verdict of our voters, which condemned the injustice of maintaining protection for protection's sake, enjoins upon the people's servants the duty of exposing and destroying the brood of kindred evils which are the unwholesome progeny of paternalism. This is the bane of republican institutions and the constant peril of our government by the people. It degrades to the purposes of wily craft the plan of rule our fathers established and bequeathed to us as an object of our love and veneration. It perverts the patriotic sentiment of our countrymen, and tempts them to a pitiful calculation of the sordid gain to be derived from their Government's maintenance. It undermines the self-reliance of our people and substitutes in its place dependence upon Governmental favoritism. It stifles the spirit of true Americanism and stupefies every ennobling trait of American citizenship.

The lessons of paternalism ought to be unlearned and the better lesson taught that, while the people should patriotically and cheerfully support their Government, its functions do not include the support of the people.

The acceptance of this principle leads to a refusal of bounties and subsidies, which burden the labor and thrift of a portion of our citizens, to aid ill-advised or languishing enterprises in which they have no concern. It leads also to a challenge of wild and reckless pension expenditure, which overleaps the bounds of grateful recognition of patriotic service and prostitutes to vicious uses the people's prompt and generous impulse to aid those disabled in their country's defense.

Every thoughtful American must realize the importance of checking at its beginning any tendency in public or private station to regard frugality and economy as virtues which we may safely outgrow. The toleration of this idea results in the waste of the people's money by their chosen servants, and encourages prodigality and extravagance in the home life of our countrymen.

Under our scheme of government the waste of public money is a crime against the citizen, and the contempt of our people for economy and frugality in their personal affairs deplorably saps the strength and sturdiness of our national character.

It is a plain dictate of honesty and good government that public expenditures should be limited by public necessity, and that this should be measured by the rules of strict economy; and it is equally clear that frugality among the people is the best guarantee of a contented and strong support of free institutions.

One mode of the misappropriation of public funds is avoided when appointments to office, instead of being the rewards of partisan activity, are awarded to those whose efficiency promises a fair return of work for the compensation paid to them. To secure the fitness and competency of appointees to office, and to remove from political action the demoralizing madness for spoils, civil service reform has found a place in our public policy and laws. The benefits already gained through this instrumentality and the further usefulness it promises entitle it to the hearty support and encouragement of all who desire to see our public service well performed, or who hope for the elevation of political sentiment and the purification of political methods.

The existence of immense aggregations of kindred enterprises and combinations of business interests, formed for the purpose of limiting production and fixing prices, is inconsistent with the fair field which ought to be open to every independent activity. Legitimate strife in business should not be superseded by an enforced concession to the demands of combinations that have the power to destroy, nor should the people to be served lose the benefit of cheapness which usually results from wholesome competition. These aggregations and combinations frequently constitute conspiracies against the interests of the people, and in all their phases they are unnatural and opposed to our American sense of fairness. To the extent that they can be reached and restrained by Federal power, the General Government should relieve our citizens from their interference and exactions.

Loyalty to the principles upon which our Government rests positively demands that the equality before the law which it guarantees to every citizen should be justly and in good faith conceded in all parts of the land. The enjoyment of this right follows the badge of citizenship wherever found, and, unimpaired by race or color, it appeals for recognition to American manliness and fairness.

Our relations with the Indians located within our borders impose upon us responsibilities we cannot escape. Humanity and consistency require us to treat them with forbearance, and in our dealings with them to honestly and considerately regard their rights and interests. Every effort should be made to lead them, through the paths of civilization and education, to self-supporting and independent citizenship. In the meantime, as the Nation's wards, they should be promptly defended against the cupidity of designing men and shielded from every influence or temptation that retards their advancement.

The people of the United States have decreed that on this day the control of their Government in its legislative and executive branches shall be given to a political party pledged in the most positive terms to the accomplishment of tariff reform. They have thus determined in favor of a more just and equitable system of Federal taxation. The agents they have chosen to carry out their purposes are bound by their promises, not less than by the command of their masters, to devote themselves unremittingly to this service.

While there should be no surrender of principle, our task must be undertaken wisely and without vindictiveness. Our mission is not punishment, but the rectification of wrongs. If, in lifting burdens from the daily life of our people, we reduce inordinate and unequal advantages too long enjoyed, this is but a necessary incident of our return to right and justice.

If we exact from unwilling minds acquiescence in the theory of an honest distribution of the fund of Governmental beneficence treasured up for all, we but insist upon a principle which underlies our free institutions. When we tear aside the delusions and misconceptions which have blinded our countrymen to their condition under vicious tariff laws, we but show them how far they have been led away from the paths of contentment and prosperity. When we proclaim that the necessity for revenue to support the Government furnishes the only justification for taxing the people, we announce a truth so plain that its denial would seem to indicate the extent to which judgment may be influenced by familiarity with perversions of the taxing power, and when we seek to reinstate the self-confidence and business enterprise of our citizens by discrediting an abject dependence upon Governmental favor we strive to stimulate those elements of American character which support the hope of American achievement.

Anxiety for the redemption of the pledges which my party has made, and solicitude for the complete justification of the trust the people have reposed in us, constrain me to remind those with whom I am to cooperate that we can succeed in doing the work which has been especially set before us only by the most sincere, harmonious, and disinterested effort. Even if insuperable obstacles and opposition prevent the consummation of our task, we shall hardly be excused, and if failure can be traced to our fault or neglect, we may be sure the people will hold us to a swift and exacting accountability.

The oath I now take to preserve, protect, and defend the Constitution of the United States not only impressively defines the great responsibility I assume, but suggests obedience to constitutional commands as the rule by which my official conduct must be guided. I shall, to the best of my ability and within my sphere of duty, preserve the Constitution by loyally protecting every grant of Federal power it contains, by defending all its restraints when attacked by impatience and restlessness, and by enforcing its limitations and reservations in favor of the States and the people.

Fully impressed with the gravity of the duties that confront me, and mindful of my weakness, I should be appalled if it were my lot to bear unaided the responsibilities which await me. I am, however, saved from discouragement when I remember that I shall have the support and the counsel and co-operation of wise and patriotic men, who will stand at my side in Cabinet places, or will represent the people in their legislative halls. I find also much comfort in remembering that my countrymen are just and generous, and in the assurance that they will not condemn those who, by sincere devotion to their service, deserve their forbearance and approval.

Above all, I know there is a Supreme Being who rules the affairs of men, and whose goodness and mercy have always followed the American people; and I know He will not turn from us now if we humbly and reverently seek His powerful aid.

### A NEW ADMINISTRATION BEGUN.

INSTALLED IN POWER WITH DIGNIFIED CEREMONY AND GREAT ENTHUSIASM.

WASHINGTON, March 4.—Grover Cleveland is twenty-fourth President of the United States. With impressive ceremonies in the Chamber of the Senate and upon the exposed platform thrown out from the eastern portico of the Capitol, the new Administration was formally installed in power.

Like the day of the inauguration of Garfield, twelve years ago, there was a morning's snowstorm and a cold, searching northwest wind, making outdoor existence uncomfortable, when President Harrison and President-elect Cleveland rode to the Capitol. The escort of troops had been exposed to the storm for hours and were damp with snow. The spectators along the line were enthusiastic in spite of the storm, which unquestionably diminished the crowd along Pennsylvania Avenue and naturally detracted from the enjoyment of the pageant. The audience that assembled four years ago in the Senate Chamber, when Benjamin Harrison was to be inaugurated, was large and impressive. It is doubtful whether the chamber has ever contained a more brilliant, interested, expectant throng than that which saw, soon after the real hour of noon, but before noon of the Senate clock, Benjamin Harrison enter as the outgoing President and Grover Cleveland as the President that was soon to be.

The historical interest of the circumstances, that are not likely to be soon or ever again paralleled, occurred to hundreds of those who saw the ceremonies. The sturdy Democracy of Grover Cleveland was understood by the 10,000 men who stood for more than an hour in the storm and wind, before the east front, to await his coming and to hear his inaugural address. Those who dreaded the storm and who trusted that the inauguration would take place in the Senate did not know the man who was about to take the oath of office. If Benjamin Harrison could stand for an hour in a plain rainstorm to read his inaugural address, it was but a slight thing to exact of a Democrat that he should face a blizzard which was not feared by thousands of his fellow-citizens. It did not rain or snow, but it only lacked one thing or the other to make an outdoor inauguration a cruelty.

The throng was not disappointed. They saw the choice of the election of 1892 stand before his audience with head bared to a blizzard and heard him briefly, but very impressively, indicate the principles that would control him in his Administration.

Near him, in full view of the throng, sat his wife, whose appearance had moved the great throng to vociferous applause. Beside her, in several rows of seats, were friends and acquaintances, and when, after he had kissed the old family Bible that was extended to him by Chief Justice Fuller, he turned toward the Capitol as if to go, Mrs. Cleveland stopped his way with a kiss, the cheer that went up from the crowd was a impressive as any applause of the day. The audience applauded as if it felt that the prize was fairly won.

The parade to the White House was successful in the display of numbers in line, spectators, and of enthusiasm for the new President. But it fell upon a day so bad that the proposition to change the day of inauguration to April 30, the day upon which Washington was first inaugurated, ought to have gained many advocates, among them Senators and Representatives of the Fifty-third Congress, who shivered in the blizzard upon the east front of the Capitol, and the spectators, who huddled, in heavy wraps, in the half-occupied stands along Pennsylvania Avenue.

Catching the spirit of their leader, the Democratic hosts in that part of the parade made up of campaign clubs and party organizations braved the inclement weather in full force. They kept their silk hats and badges and new overcoats in presentable condition, and were brought past the White House reviewing stand by Grand Marshal McMahon in orderly enthusiasm.

The Tammany legions were the favorites of the procession. They bore themselves with dignity, were received with cordiality all along the line, and enjoyed the day in spite of the cold wind and bad weather.

President and Mrs. Cleveland and their little daughter are once more the occupants of the White House, to which they were courteously welcomed by ex-President Harrison and Mrs. McKee. The ex-President soon afterward left the city on his way to his home in Indiana.

### MR. HARRISON'S WORK ENDED.

LAST HOURS OF THE OUTGOING PRESIDENT IN THE WHITE HOUSE.

WASHINGTON, March 3.—President Harrison closed his Administration, so far as the Executive Mansion is concerned, in a modest, quiet way that impressed upon all visitors that it is a simple thing for our Chief Magistrate to retire and welcome his successor to office.

A cloud of snow, compared with which the walls of the White House looked dingy, had been spread over the spacious grounds about the Executive Mansion during the night, and it was still falling in large flakes when the President arose from his last night's sleep as President. It promised to interfere with the splendor of the inauguration pageant, and Mr. Harrison expressed regret at that.

But the snow made the White House grounds a beautiful scene, and gave to the place a delicate arctic setting, which has never before been seen on Inauguration Day. Mr. Harrison contrasted the weather with that of the day when he entered the White House four years ago, when it rained furiously, and he remarked that, however much the snow might interfere with the proceedings, the day was fairer and the place place more beautiful when he left it than when he came.

President Harrison arose at 6 o'clock, after a rest of only six hours, and, after dressing and looking after a few personal preparations for the day, went to his office and gave his attention to the bills which had been passed by Congress during the small hours of the night, after the last batch had been brought to him in the evening.

He had passed judgment on all that had gone through the legislative mill up to midnight before he went to bed. He signed the remainder before breakfast, and had completed his work at 7:45 o'clock.

Mrs. McKee, the mistress of the White House, watched the snowflakes carried through the trees, and she, too, commented on the weather. In fact, the weather was talked of by the Presidential family with as much interest as any topic of the day. Young Benjamin McKee was delighted. He danced up and down in the nursery and asked the nurse if he might go out and make snowballs.

Breakfast in the White House was served at 8 o'clock, and it was in nowise different from the usual breakfast. After it was over the President conducted prayers and then went to his office, where he looked over a few letters and received a few callers. From time to time there came through the cloud of snowflakes the straggling notes of the bands as they formed out on Pennsylvania Avenue and gave warning that the ceremonies of the day were approaching.

The preparations for the family departure were completed by 10 o'clock, and a dozen trunks were loaded upon an express wagon at about that time. One of these was young Benjamin's. The child had been packing it himself, and, among other things, had put into it some small models of engines and other pieces of machinery which have been his playthings during the last year or two. He said to some of the callers that he was glad he was going back to Indianapolis.

All of the members of Mr. Harrison's Cabinet came to the White House nearly an hour before it was time to start for the inauguration ceremonies. "Uncle Jerry" Rusk came first. His white beard was filled with snowflakes and his shoulders were sprinkled with them as he stood for a few minutes on the portico in front of the White House entrance. His coat collar was turned up. He wore a delicately-shaded pair of light gloves that were useless, except for ornament, on such a day.

Secretary Noble was the second of the Cabinet, and following him came Secretary Tracy of the navy. His successor, Mr. Herbert, was with him, and the two went together to the President's office. Mr. Herbert remained for about ten minutes and then was escorted to his carriage by Mr. Tracy and driven away.

Just then four dark bay horses, in silver-mounted harness and drawing an open barouche, came at a lively trot up the White House drive. William Willis, who came to the White House with President Garfield, was on the box, and he sat as proudly as if he were to drive for a King. He was to drive the Presidential party. Black fur robes covered the seats, and the attendants at the door at once began to shake the snowflakes out of them. The crowd on the avenue looked toward this team and there was a little cheering as it halted.

While it waited Secretary of the Treasury Foster and Assistant Secretary of State Wharton came and joined the others of the Cabinet up stairs. Attorney General Miller arrived in a few minutes. A few good-byes were being said upstairs. Mr. Tibbott, the stenographer, Miss Sanger, and the others of the executive force met in the waiting room, just outside the President's office. Mrs. McKee, the children, and Lieut. Parker came in and all shook hands and gave each other good wishes and expressions of regret at parting.

### THE FIRST CEREMONY.

RECEPTION OF THE PRESIDENT-ELECT BY MR. HARRISON.

WASHINGTON, March 4.—Mr. Cleveland was up and at breakfast with Mrs. Cleveland and other members of the Presidential party at 8:30 o'clock. Like every one else here at the capital, the first thing the President-elect did was to look out and see what sort of a day it was. At that time the snow was pelting down and putting a fine white carpet on the town, but, as there was no use in complaining, the Cleveland party hoped that it would clear up as the day wore on, and went to breakfast. After the morning meal was over the stream of callers began.

The forenoon scenes around the Arlington were interesting in the way that all such inauguration scenes are interesting. At every turn in the hotel was some man great in his own section, if not in the Nation. There were all sorts of great men about the Arlington and no end of men who may be great sometime, if they live long enough and the world does not wind its affairs up and go out of business. The Tammany chieftains were all at the hotel, wearing their big badges and looking glum over the weather, for the Tiger had dressed himself in his best and was groomed up in wonderful shape for the parade. A rumor went flying about that, because it was so wet, Tammany would not parade, but Mr. Croker said that the braves would be in line if the weather gave them half a chance.

Meanwhile matters were lively in the suite of rooms on the first floor which were occupied by the Cleveland party. Several distinguished callers were received before 10 o'clock. Many others would have liked to visit the incoming President, but his time was necessarily very limited and he had important business ahead of him. The little doorway in the portion that shut off the hallway of the Cleveland suite from the other portion of the hallway was carefully guarded by Philip Bray, the trusty attaché of ex-Secretary William C. Whitney. Mr. Bray knows all the big public men and when any of those presented themselves this forenoon they were slipped through the doorway without delay.

Don M. Dickinson was in and out all the morning. Henry Villard was one of the early callers, as was also President James T. Woodward of the Hanover Bank of New-York. Col. Daniel G. Lamont was with the President-elect a goodly portion of the morning, and Private Secretary Thurber was in and out, getting his first day of real official business. Several members of the new Cabinet saw Mr. Cleveland during the morning and had pleasant chats with him.

Mr. Cleveland took the important occurrences of the day quite as matters of course. He was not at all disturbed or made nervous by the preparations for departure that the company about him was making, getting ready for the inauguration ceremonies. He had been through this thing once before, and was used to it. Military aides hurried in with their swords clanking and their overcoats buttoned tightly up. They brought messages of one sort or other, delivered them, and then their swords went clanking out again. Josiah Quincy, the member of the Democratic National Committee from Massachusetts; Richard Watson Gilder, and J. Sterling Morton, Hoke Smith, and other members of the new Cabinet were also among the callers upon the President-elect. Messages were coming in hurriedly from various quarters.

At just 10:07 o'clock Richard Watson Gilder led the Vice President's party into Mr. Cleveland's apartments. It was made up of Vice President-elect Stevenson, Mrs. Stevenson, and one or two others. The President-elect received the Vice President-elect in the reception room, and Mrs. Cleveland took charge of Mrs. Stevenson. All the ladies and gentlemen in the apartments gave great attention to Baby Ruth, and that child had a very jolly morning of it.

At 10:30 two gentlemen of military appearance presented themselves at the door and asked permission to enter. They proved to be Lieut. Patterson of the First Battery, from Fort Washington, and Col. Dickinson of New-York. They were two of the aides appointed by the Grand Marshal to ride alongside the President's carriage. They saw Mr. Cleveland and asked when he was going to start. Mr. Cleveland explained that he could not start until the White House carriage arrived. The aides went out with the impression that Mr. Cleveland expected Mr. Harrison to call at the hotel for him, and, for some reason or other, a great many people about the hotel had this impression, but of course it was not correct.

Senator Ransom of the Committee of Escort, from the Senate, was the first member to arrive of that committee. Senator Teller came next, and soon afterward Senator McPherson. It was now 10:15. Senator McPherson had evidently brought the final information as to the arrangements, for within a very few moments after his arrival the start from the Arlington was made. The carriages and escort were in waiting at the ladies' entrance on Vermont Avenue.

Senator McPherson led the little procession out of Mr. Cleveland's apartments. He was followed immediately by Mr. Cleveland, and then came Senators Teller and Ransom with Vice President-elect Stevenson. The elevator was waiting for the party and it took only a few seconds for it to reach the hallway on the floor below. Here there was a dense crowd of young women waiting to see the incoming Executive and the party passed through a lane of pretty faces to the door leading to the carriages. It was from this group of young women that the first applause of the day came.

President Harrison's carriage was waiting for Mr. Cleveland, and he and Senators Teller and Ransom got in and were driven at once to the White House. Mr. Stevenson and Senator McPherson took the next carriage. After Mr. Cleveland's departure, the members of the Democratic National Committee marched out of the Arlington in a body and took carriages. James Oliver, Sergeant at Arms of the National Committee, showed them into their carriages. Into the first he handed Chairman Harrity, Secretary Sheerin, Treasurer Robert B. Roosevelt, and Lieut. Gov. Sheehan. Bradley B. Smalley, Josiah Quincy, Daniel Campau, and E. C. Wall took the second, and Mr. Oliver dispatched other members as rapidly as possible.

No sooner had the National Committeemen departed for the Capitol than James L. Norris, Chairman of the Executive Committee of the Inaugural Committee, came down with Mrs. Cleveland and Mrs. Stevenson. Mr. Oliver handed the party into their carriage and they started for the Capitol at a lively pace. Mr. and Mrs. Don M. Dickinson, Mr. and Mrs. E. C. Benedict, and Mrs. Lamont and a party of her friends followed in carriages. Daniel S. Lamont, Hilary A. Herbert, and Wilson S. Bissell remained in the Cleveland apartments.

Presently the first sign that a ceremony of any sort was to take place was noted by those who were at the White House windows. A rider on a spirited horse came dashing up from the west entrance to the grounds and halted in front of the entrance. It was Myron M. Parker, the new District Commissioner, who was one of the Marshals for the day.

Behind him was a closed carriage which bowled up to the entrance and was halted with a sharp crack of the driver's whip. The door was opened and Gen. Schofield, the gentleman commanding the army, in uniform, stepped out, and with dignity passed through the entrance to the Executive Mansion. In the black plume which arched over his chapeau snowflakes were glistening and his heavy cape coat was sprinkled with them. Lieut. Schofield, his aide, followed him, and after him came Admiral Gherardi, in full uniform, and Lieut. Ridgley Hunt, flag officer of the Admiral's squadron. These representatives of the military and naval branches of the Government stood in a group in the White House lobby for a time and then passed up stairs.

Presently there came up the walk from the east gate the figure of a man bent forward and hurrying to get away from the snow that sifted in behind his umbrella. His collar was turned up. He stepped quickly as if he had important business. As he drew near it turned out that the visitor was Mr. Carlisle, the new Secretary of the Treasury. He went inside and up stairs, remaining until the distinguished party started for the Capitol. He then rode with Secretary Foster, whom he succeeds.

At length two carriages, each drawn by four horses, came up the east walk. Four of the horses were black and four were white, with white harness. In the first was Mr. Cleveland and the committee of Senators. They alighted, and Mr. Cleveland hurried through the doors. He stopped to exchange greetings with some whom he knew, and then came out to meet Mr. Harrison. They shook hands cordially, though with the dignity becoming the occasion. Mr. Stevenson, escorted by Senator McPherson, was in the second carriage. They alighted and followed Mr. Cleveland to the corridor.

The party was then made up for the drive to the Capitol. It had stopped snowing, except for a few fine flakes, and there were signs that the sky would clear. Mr. Cleveland and Mr. Harrison entered the carriage drawn by the four blacks. It was open, and they turned up their coat collars. The committee escort followed. Mr. Stevenson and Senator McPherson entered the third carriage and Secretary Foster and Mr. Carlisle the fourth. After them, each in a coupé, came Secretaries Tracy, Noble, and Rusk, Attorney General Miller, and Secretary Wharton. Gen. Schofield and the other officers entered the last carriage.

The horses drawing the President-elect and the retiring President danced down the road leading to the west gate. The thousands about caught sight of the occupants and a mighty cheer went up. Mrs. McKee, from the White House window, waved her handkerchief, and, as the carriage reached the broad avenue, and Mr. Harrison for the last time as President passed out from the Executive Mansion grounds to which, in two hours, he was to return bringing the man who sat beside him as the President, a band of a hundred pieces, just outside the gate, began to play. It could be heard inside the White House. The air was "See the Conquering Hero Comes."

As the Presidential party came upon the avenue the military companies stepped into the parade in front and rear. The crowds at the Treasury stands and along the avenue greeted the President and President-elect with cheers. Once or twice Mr. Cleveland raised his hat in response. He was powdered with snow. At Ninth Street a band saluted the Presidential carriage with "Hail to the Chief." In front of the Metropolitan Hotel the Duckworth Club of Brooklyn waved its banners and cheered so wildly that Mr. Cleveland raised his hat and smiled. Crowds whose ardor was not entirely dampened by the snow lined the avenue all the way as the carriages wound their way by the hill to the Senate wing of the Capitol.

### SIGHTSEERS DEFY THE STORM.

WASHINGTON CROWDED WITH VISITORS FROM ALL OVER THE COUNTRY.

WASHINGTON, March 4.—Washington went to bed last night with nervous forebodings about to-day's weather. In the course of the evening a rainstorm, which had begun before 9 o'clock, had grown, until by midnight it was of the dignity of the steady downpour. That was bad enough, and this morning dawned with very little improvement.

There had been a very decided change, however. The edge of a cold wave had arrived in time for the inauguration and the rain had formed into snow. It had fallen to the depth of one inch by the hour visitors and townsmen were astir, and it had wrought a great transformation in the appearance of the city.

All the trees were snow-trimmed, for the flakes, once touching a surface, either staid there or melted. The black branches and their white trimmings formed as sharp a contrast as any artist could wish, but unfortunately the populace was not devoting itself entirely to the picturesque. It was far more concerned with the strictly material question of personal physical comfort. The snow was evidently more than many of the visitors had bargained for. To the New-Yorkers it was familiar enough, for the storm was like two or three their city has experienced this Winter, but for the people from the States of milder climate it was great discouragement. The thermometer was just low enough to keep the flakes from turning to drops, but there was a damp chilliness in the air which made midwinter wrappings none too heavy. There was a keen breeze, too, which appeared to gain an icy edge from the snow.

In the streets the snow melted almost as it fell. Asphalt, brick paving stones, and concrete were covered, not with a white carpet, but with a choice combination of slush and water. Luckily for the paraders, the slope from the middle of the street to the gutters served to keep Pennsylvania Avenue in fair condition. The pavement was wet and gave treacherous footing, of course, but its general condition was far better than could be shown in any New-York avenue in similar circumstances.

Many visitors were early abroad, but even the earliest of them found the snow in possession of the city. Besides the crowds which reached town yesterday were thousands brought in by trains arriving, some of them before daybreak. These people had little to do but to wander about until the ceremonies of the day began, and on their travels up and down Pennsylvania Avenue they were joined by others, who, arriving here last evening, had failed to secure accommodations, and had passed the night as best they could in chairs in hotel offices and similar sheltering places. From these two sources of supply the early crowds were principally drawn.

By 9 o'clock the streets grew more lively. The holders of tickets for seats in the stands along the line of march began to appear, many of the militia men started for a stroll before their labors of the day began, bodies of regulars hove in sight on their way to the White House neighborhood, and a few political organizations braved the storm to the extent of marching from one hotel to another. At this hour, though, the majority of the visitors were still under cover. They had little reason to venture out before they had to.

The storm effectually prevented the eleventh-hour additions to the decorations of the city, and consequently the route over which the parade was to move was left as it was yesterday, with the adornments of the buildings almost entirely confined to national flags and red, white, and blue bunting. Luckily, most of the decorations were able to stand moisture. Had the colors run, there would have been a curious looking lot of structures. As it was, the flags simply flattened out and the loops of bunting exhibited a tendency to shrink into colored ropes.

Between 9 and 10 o'clock the crowd in the streets increased considerably. Persons anxious to avoid a rush went to the stands or searched the avenue for promising places along the curb line. The wind had increased in strength and had fallen into a habit of coming in biting gusts. In these flurries it blew the flakes almost on a level with the sidewalks. It was moist snow, and wherever it struck it stuck. The round flat tops of the militiamen's caps gathered little banks of snow; overcoats took on a white veneer; whiskers and mustaches collected a coating which hid the color of the hair.

The women had a hard time of it, although they pinned up the hems of their skirts and pluckily faced the storm. But it had no mercy for them. The wind whirled the flakes under umbrellas and through the openings of waterproofs. In all the half-sheltered nooks afforded by the supports of the stands, in doorways, in spots about which fragmentary awnings were spread, the women collected in little groups. They turned their backs to the wind and it retaliated by filling their hair with snow and doing its best to freeze the combination into a solid mass. Frequently it succeeded.

To add to these woes, very little better conditions were to be found even on the covered stands. There, too, the snow had driven in and had covered the seats to the depth of a couple of inches, freezing to the wood, and resisting all efforts to brush it away. It was not a difficult matter to get seats on these stands. The proprietors had given up all hope of fancy prices. A dollar a seat was a common rate, even for the best of the structures along Pennsylvania Avenue, while plenty of less pretentious stands were to be entered for 50 cents.

Seats commanding a view of the avenue from windows of buildings along that thoroughfare, and possessed, of course, of the great advantage of complete shelter, were to be obtained at reasonable rates. "A comfortable chair, a warm fire, and a good view, all for a dollar," shouted a man with a bunch of tickets in his hands, but he found few takers for his offer. The weather was dead against the speculators, and the people understood the fact thoroughly. Fancy prices were entirely out of fashion, except for particularly choice spots in very desirable buildings.

Along the avenue the throng gained in numbers steadily. National Guardsmen were seeking the headquarters of their organizations. Among them were seen the trimly-uniformed men of the New-York Seventh, by long odds the nattiest soldier boys in Washington. The Pennsylvania Guardsmen were everywhere, a few of them showing signs of prolonged rejoicing, but the great majority intent simply on the business of the day.

All along the avenue the city police kept an eye on them, but, as a rule, the officers had no cause for trouble. There were two mounted patrolmen at each corner along the line of march, while their brethren on foot abounded. To reinforce the uniformed police, scores of specials were on duty. Each of them wore a badge which shone in spite of the storm, and twirled a whitewood club about half the size of New-York's abandoned night sticks.

As the bodies of regulars moved along the avenue toward their assembly point near the White House, it was made clear that all who marched were bound to have an unpleasant time. The infantry trudged along without great difficulty, although the snow drove into their faces with more or less viciousness. The mounted men had fully as much trouble. They were saved the annoyance of tramping through puddles, but the horses were restive and the streets slippery. Several civilian organizations tried the experiment of marching along the sidewalks, but they found not much better traveling there, and in addition had to force their way through a crowd.

As late as 11 o'clock the stands were still sparsely occupied, but the sidewalks were full of people. Washington residents, on their way to places they had secured to see the parade, were beginning to appear in force and practically all the visitors were moving about. The Southern delegations found the weather particularly disagreeable, and many of them underwent positive suffering in their determination to see all they could of the ceremonies marking the inauguration of a Democratic President. In the driving snowstorm it was almost impossible to keep comfortably warm, no matter how heavy the wraps, for the wind cut like a knife and the thickest of ulsters hardly served to turn its edge.

By noon the snow fall was lighter, but the breeze still blew. It was beginning to loosen the white covering of the roofs, and everywhere avalanches were frequent. People were huddled against the buildings, and the lumps of snow found the groups a fair target. Many a man, bending over to lessen the force of the wind, was straightened out instantly by a cold, wet mass plunging down the back of his neck.

Those who had gone early to the stands to avoid the danger of a crush were thoroughly chilled by this time. Their faces were blue and their feet like ice. Such relief as could be had by running about their cramped quarters was not great, but everybody availed himself of it. It was curious to note how many family parties were among the early birds in all the stands. Little children were to be seen huddled up against their elders for warmth, and looking as if they found very little of it. Babies in arms were by no means a rarity in this crowd of storm-defying sightseers.

The snow-covered benches of the great open stands near the Treasury Building offered few attractions to anybody not possessed of the constitution and likings of a polar bear. The open space near them gave the wind a particularly effective sweep. As late as noon the people on these tiers of seats numbered only scores, where there was room for thousands, and at no time were the structures fully occupied. In fact, the weather resulted in cutting down the crowd everywhere, and the streets showed this as well as the stands.

But, with all the weather conditions so greatly against them, the people were good-natured. They laughed and joked at every opportunity and sought to amuse themselves during their long wait in the manner characteristic of an American crowd on pleasure bent and determined to get as much fun as possible out of the situation. The merriment was not continuous, of course, and in the intervals the thousands lining Pennsylvania Avenue looked uncomfortable. Being human, they couldn't help it.

They chaffed the vendors of campaign badges, but bought liberally as well, although the emblems generally had to be saved from destruction by the storm by being hidden under an overcoat. A few roosters and tigers were kept in view on the hats of enthusiasts, but a good deal of the picturesqueness to be found in a great street crowd making holiday in fair weather was lost in a monotony of overcoats and umbrellas.

Almost the only available offsets to the cold and dampness were in liquid form. They were used extensively, for it was a day of the kind that keeps down the Prohibition Party. Places of refreshment all along the route were as busy as beehives, in spite of their signs, "No mixed drinks," while thousands of far-seeing and provident spectators, for whom such asylums were out of the question, brought a stock of bottled comfort with them. Pocket flasks abounded on all the stands. A good many women carried dainty little silver affairs, which were displayed as frankly as were those which caused so much newspaper talk after the frigid afternoon last Fall when Yale beat Princeton at football on Manhattan Field.

The business of sightseeing for those who were content with nothing short of all of the day's spectacles was a very long one. It meant going without anything to eat, unless luncheons

Two Parts
12 Pages

# The New-York Times.

Part One
Pages 1-8

VOL. XLV....NO. 13,972. NEW-YORK, MONDAY, JUNE 1, 1896.—TWO PARTS—TWELVE PAGES — COPYRIGHTED, 1896, BY THE NEW-YORK TIMES PUBLISHING CO. PRICE THREE CENTS.

## FIELD STREWN WITH DEAD

### Ditches Filled With Victims of the Moscow Disaster.

### THE FATALITIES NUMBERED 1,138

**Servants Increased the Danger by Hurling Liquids Among the Frenzied Populace.**

**SEARCHING FOR MISSING RELATIVES.**

**People Grateful for the Czar's Promise of 1,000 Rubles to Each Bereaved Family.**

MOSCOW, May 31.—The city has not yet recovered from the shock occasioned by the frightful calamity on the Hodynsky Plain yesterday during the progress of the great free feast and entertainment in connection with the coronation ceremonies given at the expense of the Czar to whomsoever desired to partake.

The extent of the disaster was not exaggerated in the first reports. As stated in these dispatches yesterday, the representative of The United Press was an eye witness of the stampede of the great multitude of people gathered on the plain, estimated to have numbered fully 500,000, and the sight was one never to be forgotten for its horror. After the crowd had been dispersed by the police and military, the field was strewn with the dead, who had been killed by being crushed, trampled upon, or by suffocation.

A great number of children were among the victims. In the wild rush of the frenzied crowd they were swept away from their parents or others having charge of them, and their puny strength availed them naught when pitted against the irresistible force of the surging mob. The instant they stumbled and fell life was crushed out of them. But this was also the case with many adults. No human strength could withstand the mad onrush of the crowd, and safety could alone be found in allowing oneself to be carried forward and back in the pulsating crowd, devoting every energy to keeping upon the feet.

When a body was recognized by a relative—more frequently a mother whose little one had been torn away from her and its young life crushed out—the scene was heartrending. The stolid demeanor of the Russian peasant would vanish, and the low, plaintive wailing and floods of tears would bear witness to the bitter grief experienced.

Far into the night ambulances, fire trucks, and other vehicles were busily engaged in conveying the dead and injured into the city.

The representative of The United Press went again to the plain to-day, and saw one of the effects of the mad rush. The ditches of the abandoned earthworks on the plain had been filled to the level with the bodies of those who had been driven into them by the awful pressure from behind. Here those who were not crushed to death were suffocated by the dead and dying above them.

In the passages between the booths from which the food was distributed there were still lying the bodies of hundreds of men, women, and children—women and children predominating. Some of the corpses were frightfully distorted, and on the faces still in death there were looks of fear and horror. The sight was altogether a most gruesome one.

The assertion is repeated to-day that the police were not on the scene in sufficiently strong numbers at an early hour to handle the crowd. It is a fact that there were only comparatively few of them present at 6 o'clock in the morning, at which time the disaster occurred. There were then about a thousand attendants engaged in distributing the gifts of the Czar to the importunate mob, and to them the calamity is indirectly attributable.

When the thousands of persons in the rear began to press forward upon those in front and a number of the latter were crushed against the barriers, the shrieks of the injured and the groans of the dying caused the attendants to become stricken with terror, they dreading what afterward actually occurred—the breaking down of the barriers by the enormous human pressure upon them.

In fear of their lives, they threw thousands of the memorial cups, filled with mead, beer, &c., at the struggling mass of humanity in attempts to drive them back. This led to a wild scramble in the crowd. The immense quantity of liquids thus thrown formed a sort of pond in front of the long line of booths and rendered the ground slippery and treacherous, making a foothold very precarious. A great number of persons who might otherwise have escaped fell to the ground, where life was soon crushed out of them by the howling, frenzied mob.

The officials made every effort and offered every facility for the identification of the dead, but the bodies in hundreds of instances are utterly unrecognizable, the faces having been literally crushed out of all semblance to humanity. A careful search is made of each body for papers to establish its identity, and a record is made of the clothing on each corpse for the same purpose.

It was officially announced this morning that the total number of victims was 1,138. Most of them were moujiks from the provinces, a poor class of people, but among the number were many of the poverty-stricken residents of Moscow and villages in the neighborhood of the city. The fête was particularly for the benefit of this class of the population, and the middle class generally held aloof from the entertainment or else visited the plain in the capacity of spectators.

The scene in the city last night and to-day has been a most painful one. The injured and large numbers of the dead were taken to the hospitals and other charitable institutions, and thither have gone thousands of persons seeking relatives or friends, hoping that the missing ones would be found among those who were only hurt, but dreading the worst. Many affecting scenes were witnessed when it was found that those who were thought to be dead were still alive, though often terribly injured.

Thirty bodies were found to-day in an old disused well in the middle of the plain. The well had been covered with planks, which had collapsed when the crowd passed over them. Some of the victims had in their hands, clutched with a death clasp, the memorial cups which had been presented to them at the booths before the rush began.

Among the bodies in the well were two living persons, who had been made insane by the horror of their position. Their ravings when rescued were terrible to hear.

In some parts of the plain the ground looks as though it had been newly plowed. This is where it was torn up by the heavy wooden shoes of the peasants.

The dead were placed in long lines upon the ground. There were very few coffins to be seen. In fact, the supply of coffins and caskets was exhausted early yesterday, and to-day it is impossible to procure one in the city at any price.

So great has been the rush of visitors at the hospitals to-day in search of missing relatives and friends that the work of the doctors and physicians was seriously interrupted. This afternoon, therefore, the authorities gave orders for the transfer of the unclaimed bodies to the Vogankoffsky Cemetery, where they will remain for a time to enable them to be identified if possible.

The feeling of the Moujiks was very bitter against the authorities, who, they declare, did not take sufficient precautions to guard against an affair such as occurred. As a matter of fact, however, the authorities were in nowise to blame. It was impossible for them to foresee that such a great multitude would be present at such an early hour, but, at any rate, the precautionary measures adopted would have been sufficient had not the people become so frenzied. After the disaster the large force of military and police had the greatest difficulty in restoring even a semblance of order.

The Czar's promise to help the bereaved families, coupled with the published expression of his intense grief and deep sympathy, has allayed the bitter feeling, and the people are warmly grateful to him for his action.

As was stated in yesterday's dispatches, his Majesty has ordered that the sum of 1,000 rubles be paid to each family that has lost a member through the catastrophe. In addition, the State will pay the expenses of burying the dead, while the physicians at the hospitals and elsewhere have been instructed to spare nothing to alleviate the sufferings of the injured.

At the request of the Czar, there will be a solemn requiem mass in the chapel of the palace in the Kremlin to-morrow morning. All the members of the imperial family will attend.

The Bishop of Peterborough, who is in Moscow as the representative of the Established Church of England, preached a sermon in the English church here to-day. Among those who were present were the Duke of Connaught, who represents his mother, Queen Victoria, the Duchess of Connaught, and their suite. A collection was taken up for the benefit of the sufferers, and a goodly sum was raised.

The statement that the disaster would bring the coronation festivities to a close has not the slightest basis in truth. The functions have not been stopped. A ball was given at the French Embassy last evening. It was attended by the members of the imperial family, the foreign Princes, diplomats, and the highest Russian and visiting aristocracy. The function was one of the most brilliant that has taken place in connection with the coronation ceremonies.

### POLICE CHIEF IN DESPAIR.

**The Moscow Official Tried to Kill Himself, It Is Reported**

LONDON, May 31.—The Daily News will to-morrow publish a dispatch from Moscow saying that the Chief of Police is reported to be in utter despair over the terrible catastrophe, and that he has attempted to commit suicide.

The dispatch adds that many of the attendants at the booths are among the dead. Some of the booths were broken into splinters by the resistless rush of the crowd.

It further says that the great ball given by the French Ambassador was, owing to political reasons, not cancelled. It was also determined that it should be held, lest the disaster be supposed to have been even greater than it actually was.

## HIS WIFE'S DEATH MADE HIM MAD.

**Police Justice Schwarting of Long Branch Under Restraint.**

LONG BRANCH, N. J., May 31.—Judge August Schwarting, who is serving his second term as Justice of the Peace, was placed under restraint at 6 o'clock this morning, suffering from an attack of acute mania, and confined in the corridor of the Police Headquarters.

Judge Schwarting, since the death of his wife a month ago, has given indications of mental disorder. Besides dispensing law, the Judge deals in cigars. Persons who passed his place of business late last night noticed the Judge at work with scrubbing implements cleaning the interior of the store. He was still at work this morning, having kept at it all night. When questioned as to the reason for his work he said he was preparing to decorate his store in white and gold. He had ruined his stock with water, and smoking implements and cigars were piled in heaps about the place.

While apparently rational at times, the Judge occasionally displays unmistakable signs of dementia.

## A FLEMING JUROR INJURED.

**R. M. Montgomery and His Wife Thrown Out of a Carriage.**

Richard M. Montgomery, Juror No. 6 in the trial of Mrs. Fleming, and his wife met with an accident yesterday. They were at Babylon, L. I., and went out driving in a carriage. The horse got frightened, became unmanagable, and ran away. Finally the carriage was upset, and Mr. and Mrs. Montgomery rolled out.

Fortunately, their injuries were slight. Mrs. Montgomery's face was somewhat scratched. Mr. Montgomery was unhurt, though both were somewhat shaken up. Both returned to this city in the evening, and went to their home, at 317 West Seventy-fourth Street.

Late in the evening they were resting quietly, and it was said that Mr. Montgomery will be in his place in the jury box to-day, and that Mrs. Montgomery will also be able to be about.

## SCHOONER LOST OFF POINT JUDITH.

**The Willie D. of Parrsborough, N. S., Capsized in a Squall.**

VINEYARD HAVEN, Mass., May 31.—The schooner Willie D., Capt. Bullerwell, from Stamford, Conn., of Parrsborough, N. S., was capsized at 6 o'clock this morning, about three miles west of Point Judith, in a westerly squall.

The Captain and two seamen clung to the capsized vessel's spars, and were nearly exhausted when they were rescued by the steamer Pentagoet, from New-York, for Eastport, Me. William Spinney, a seaman, aged thirty years, a resident of Parrsborough, was drowned. The survivors were landed here this evening by the Pentagoet. They saved nothing.

The schooner registered ninety tons, and was launched at Parrsborough, N. S., April 1, of this year. She was returning home from her first trip. Steam tug Joshua Lovett left here this evening to look for the schooner.

**Dropped an Iron Pot on Her Enemy.**

Mrs. Mary Doyle lives on the third floor and Mrs. Rachel Kittrick lives on the second floor of the tenement at 128 West Fifty-first Street. They got into a quarrel last Monday, and at the time failed to settle it. Mrs. Doyle felt that she had still in store one unanswerable argument, and later in the evening, while Mrs. Kittrick was enjoying the air on the steps, Mrs. Doyle dropped an iron pot down on her. Mrs. Kittrick was taken to the hospital, while Mrs. Doyle was taken to the police station. She was arraigned in the Yorkville Police Court the next day, and held to await the result of Mrs. Kittrick's injuries. She was rearraigned yesterday, and discharged, on the representation of a lawyer, who said that Mrs. Kittrick had abandoned criminal proceedings, and begun a suit for $2,000 damages.

**Drank Himself to Death.**

WATERBURY, Conn., May 31.—George Eczmay, thirty-five years old, in a Polish saloon on Bank Street last night drank three pints of beer and three glasses of whisky in five minutes on a wager. He was taken to his home, 86 South Riverside Street, where he died fifteen minutes later.

## THUNDER DROVE HIM MAD

**FEAR-CRAZED WILLIAM SCARLET TRIED TO KILL HIS CHILD.**

**Attempted to Murder with a Hatchet the Policeman Who Had Been Called to Arrest Him—Ran Naked to the Roof and Was for a Time Calmed, Only to Break Out Again in Ravings Against His Daughter's Approaching Marriage.**

Driven insane by fear of the thunderstorm early yesterday morning William Scarlet, a coachman, attempted to kill his eight-year-old daughter by throwing her down stairs, and when a policeman was called, did his best to brain him with a hatchet. For four hours he kept the neighborhood awake with his cries and the crash of furniture broken in his struggles.

Scarlet drives for Miss Mary T. Cockcroft, the Treasurer of the Young Woman's Christian Association, who lives at 147 Madison Avenue. He himself lives over his employer's stable, at 30 East Thirty-second Street.

He has always been more or less afraid of thunder and lightning, and at the approach of a heavy storm always sought shelter. His paroxysms of fear yesterday morning were extremely violent, and about 2:30 o'clock he ran through his apartments stark naked, yelling that the electricity had entered his body and increased his strength.

He woke his children to show them his new-found strength, and battered the walls of the apartment with his fist, leaving the marks of his knuckles in the plaster.

Tiring of this, he began to hurl cups and saucers at his children, who fled to the kitchen and locked themselves in. He broke in the door, seized the youngest girl, Annie, carried her to the head of the stairs, and was about to hurl her to the floor below when his eldest daughter, Maggie, who has acted as housekeeper since the death of her mother, five years ago, caught his arm.

She soothed him, and he promised to return to bed. She went to look for him a short time after, but found him on the roof, in the same nude condition in which he had been for several hours.

She induced him to come down, and then he raved about a hair dye that he said Miss Cockcroft compelled him to use to keep the color of his hair. He has been using the dye for years. He insisted that he had always feared that it would affect his brain.

When he finished raving about the hair dye, he discussed the approaching marriage of his daughter Maggie. She is to be married Wednesday, and her father had until yesterday morning been pleased with the arrangements. His mind suddenly changed during his raving, and he demanded her engagement ring. When she gave it to him he threw it in the refuse on the stable floor and declared that she should never be married.

It was then after 6 o'clock, and she sent her fourteen-year-old sister Sarah for the family physician, Dr. W. C. Kennedy of 65 West Thirty-sixth Street. The father accused his daughters of sending for a policeman, and started to strike Maggie with a hatchet, but changed his mind when he had the weapon poised above her head.

The girls then ran screaming into the street and into the Opera Stables, where they told Mr. Search, the proprietor, their story. He summoned Policeman Stephenson of the West Thirtieth Street Station, and just at that moment Dr. Kennedy, who keeps his horses at the Opera Stables, came along. The three, accompanied by a colored stable hand, went to Scarlet's stable and found Scarlet prepared for them.

In one hand he held a whiffletree and in the other the hatchet. Miss Scarlet, who had accompanied the men back, managed to get the hatchet from her father after he had made two or three ineffectual attempts to use it.

The men then closed in on him. They got him on the floor, but not before he had hit each of them at least once. Even when they got him down he managed to strike Policeman Stephenson on the head.

At the policeman's request a call was then sent for an ambulance, and for a patrol wagon. The patrol wagon arrived first, and when they had succeeded in getting a part of Scarlet's clothes on he was bundled in and taken to the West Thirtieth Street Police Station. From there he was transferred to the insane pavilion of Bellevue Hospital.

No one was seriously hurt by the crazed coachman in all his raving. Scarlet is known in the neighborhood as a steady, sober man, but his daughter says that a brother, Henry, has been confined in an insane asylum in Canada for the past three years.

## MR. JACKSON BET HIS LIFE.

**Tried to Drown Himself When the Cuban Giants Lost a Game.**

HACKENSACK, N. J., May 31.—The Cuban Giant baseball team came here yesterday and played a game with the Oritani Club. Samuel Jackson, a colored resident, had been waiting for the coming of the Giants for a week, and expected great things of them.

He said if they did not beat the local team he would drown himself in the Hackensack. Some one said he would not do it, and Sam made a bet of a dollar that he would. The Giants came and lost, and at the close of the game Jackson went to the river and jumped in.

Thus far he had carried out the terms of his bet, and when an attempt was made to rescue him he tried to fulfill the terms to the letter. He was rescued with difficulty and sent to the hospital, where he is recovering.

## FATAL PANIC IN ST. LOUIS.

**Girl Killed, Another Mortally Injured, by a Live Trolley Wire.**

ST. LOUIS, May 31.—One person was killed, one fatally injured, and two were seriously injured yesterday afternoon in a panic on an electric car on the Carondelet Line. The trolley wire broke and fell on the car, frightening the passengers, who rushed out.

Miss Veronica Pavelock, seventeen years old, came in contact with the wire and was instantly killed; Miss Lillie Cloquette, seventeen years old, sustained a compound fracture of the skull and will die; Miss Blanche Cloquette, her sister received a scalp wound, and Oswald Vatt, a butcher, has his right shoulder dislocated.

**Descendant of Gen. Stark Dead.**

MANCHESTER, N. H., May 31.—Miss Elizabeth B. Stark, granddaughter of Gen. John Stark, died to-day, aged sixty-nine years. She was born in the house in which she died, on the old Stark place. She was a daughter of John Stark, third, and Sarah Fletcher Pollard. She was a member of Grace Episcopal Church, the New-Hampshire Historical Society, and the Colonial Dames, and Vice President of the Daughters of the American Revolution. She leaves a brother, Augustus H. Stark.

**Hotel Employes and $500 Gone.**

NEWARK, N. J., May 31.—George Perkins, a clerk at the Continental Hotel, and Benjamin Loltimer, a bellboy, have disappeared, and so has a package containing $500 belonging to Louis E. Cooke, one of the proprietors of the hotel. The pair were missing a couple of hours after Perkins had signed the express receipt for the package. Mr. Cooke will not prosecute, as Perkins's mother has promised to make restitution out of money held in trust for her son.

## CONVERTS TO CATHOLICISM.

**Some Well-Known Persons Who Have Changed to the Roman Faith.**

In connection with the missions to non-Catholics by the Paulist Fathers, a partial record is kept of those who have been won over to the Roman Catholic communion from other denominations. Some of the converts of note during the past three months in the United States and Europe, as published in The Missionary, the official organ of the community, are:

Robert James, a brother of Prof. James of Harvard University, and Henry James, the novelist. He was received from the Protestant Episcopal Church in Arlington, Mass., a suburb of Boston; Miss Alice English, daughter of the poet, Thomas Dunn English, Newark, N. J.; A. F. Du Pont Coleman, a clergyman in the Protestant Episcopal Church, and son of the Right Rev. Leighton Coleman, D. D., Bishop of Delaware; the Rev. F. W. Pelley, the rector of an Episcopal church at Norwich, Conn.; William Low, formerly the English Consul at Mentone; Mrs. Royal Phelps Carroll of Yonkers, N. Y.; Mr. and Mrs. George D. Mackay, the former having been President of the Christian Industrial Alliance; the Rev. Frederick Sherman, Chaplain in the United States Navy; M. Zola, Grand Master of Masons, who followed his predecessor in office by renouncing Masonry and entering the Catholic Church. His predecessor was the Marquis of Ripon. Others referred to are the Countess Nelson, wife of a prominent member of the English Church Union; Constance Fletcher, niece of Dr. Pusey; Miss Bayliss, and two members of an Anglican sisterhood in Exeter, England.

## THIEF CHASE ON A BICYCLE.

**Knocked His Man Down with His Wheel, Then with a Pair of Shoes.**

Policeman Gillis of the bicycle squad attached to the West Sixty-eighth Street Station, arraigned in Jefferson Market Police Court yesterday Patrick Falvey, a plumber of 263 West Thirtieth Street, on a charge of petit larceny preferred by Louis Gutterman, proprietor of a second-hand shoe store at 584 Seventh Avenue.

Gillis was riding down Eighth Avenue at 7 o'clock Saturday night, when he saw a crowd running through Fortieth Street after Falvey, who had stolen a pair of shoes. Gillis chased the fleeing man and caught up with him at Ninth Avenue.

To escape running into an elevated railroad pillar Gillis ran against Falvey and knocked him down. A friend of the thief kicked Gillis in the left leg so severely that he was knocked down. Falvey tried to escape, but Gillis hit him over the head with the shoes he had taken from Falvey. Falvey was knocked down and was easily recaptured, but on the way to the station the fight was renewed several times and Gillis had to get help before he locked up his prisoner in the West Thirty-seventh Street Station.

In court yesterday Falvey did not deny the charge of having stolen the shoes, which were valued at $1.50, and Magistrate Simms held him in $500 for trial.

## JERSEY CONVICTS CONFIRMED.

**Bishop McFaul of Trenton Anoints Thirty-seven Men.**

TRENTON, N. J., May 31.—Thirty-seven male convicts, including four negroes, were confirmed at the State Prison this afternoon, the rite being administered by Bishop James A. McFaul, who was assisted in the ceremonies by the Rev. Fathers Aloysius and Henry.

Three of the convicts, one a wife murderer serving a twenty years' term, are converts to the Roman Catholic faith, and were baptized at the prison yesterday morning. The confirmation took place in the north wing of the prison, where an altar had been erected. Two hundred and fifty Catholic prisoners were present, and formed the congregation. All were in prison garb. Those confirmed wore white shirts, however.

Before their anointment there was singing by a quartet from St. Mary's Cathedral and an address by Bishop McFaul, who criticised the city officials of Trenton for denying the Catholic clergymen the privilege of administering the sacraments of the Church to Catholic inmates of the city almshouse.

## LIGHTNING KILLS A POLICEMAN.

**A Child That Was Clinging to His Side Was Not Injured.**

NEWPORT, R. I., May 31.—A severe, but brief tempest, which had been threatening all day, visited Newport about 5 o'clock this afternoon.

Policeman William Henry Dewick was struck by lightning and killed. A three-year old child clinging to his side escaped injury. Dewick was standing before a mirror, and the bolt came through the southeast corner of the house, connecting with his body at the forehead. Dewick leaves a wife and six children.

What resembles two bullet holes are the only marks on the house. Rain fell in torrents, intermingled with hail.

## FOX HUNT IN CENTRAL PARK.

**Lost Pet Keeps a Policeman Busy for an Hour.**

A resident of West Ninetieth Street lost a pet fox about a week ago, and advertised for its recovery. Last night a Park policeman while on the West Drive, in the neighborhood of Ninety-sixth Street, saw the animal among the shrubbery. He approached the fox, thinking he could make an easy capture, but the fox darted across the lawn and took refuge behind a heap of rocks. The policeman gave chase, and then the animal made a dash for another clump of shrubbery. For more than an hour Reynard led his pursuer a merry chase, and then, becoming winded, was caught. The animal spent last night at the Menagerie, and will be returned to its owner to-day.

## THEIR CRIES FRIGHTENED HIM.

**Lunneys and Meltzer Attacked by an Unknown Man with a Club.**

A man armed with a club attacked Adam Meltzer of 245 Eldridge Street and William Lunneys of 208 Sixth Street early yesterday morning, at Stanton and Allen Streets.

Their assailant, having broken Lunneys's nose and given Meltzer a scalp wound, attempted to rob them, but the two men set up such a shouting that he was frightened and ran away.

An ambulance surgeon from Gouverneur Hospital dressed the men's wounds, and they went home.

**Toomey Worked for the Tramp.**

RAHWAY, N. J., May 31.—John Toomey, son of Section Superintendent Patrick Toomey of the Pennsylvania Railroad, reached here yesterday in custody of his father, from Downingtown, Penn. John left home two months ago, being enticed away, it is claimed, by a tramp named Carroll or Daly. The tramp uses two names, as it suits him. He is now under arrest at Downingtown. Toomey says he supported Carroll while with him by working and begging.

**Wife Murderer and Suicide.**

MARYSVILLE, Kan., May 31.—While the two were working in a field yesterday, George Mock killed his wife with a hoe after a quarrel and fled. A crowd started in pursuit of him. Seeing that he was about to be overtaken he cut his throat with a knife and then jumped into a river. His body was recovered.

## SAFETY IN TWO-THIRDS

**SOUND-MONEY DELEGATES WILL STOUTLY OPPOSE ANY CHANGE.**

**Precedent Established at Democratic National Conventions Should Be Adhered To, It Is Maintained—Abrogation of the Rule "Would Be a Calamity the Consequences of Which Cannot Be Foreseen," Mr. Scott Says.**

If an attempt, warning of which was given in THE NEW-YORK TIMES Sunday, shall be made by the free-silver delegates to the Democratic National Convention at Chicago to abolish the two-thirds rule, under which all Democratic Presidential nominations have been made, it will be stoutly resisted by the sound-money delegates. The free-silver men, of course, cannot accomplish such a result unless they constitute a majority in the convention, and their purpose would be to bring about the nomination of Presidential and Vice Presidential candidates favorable to their views on the currency question.

"The abrogation of the two-thirds rule would be a calamity the consequences of which cannot be foreseen," said Corporation Counsel Francis M. Scott to a reporter for THE NEW-YORK TIMES yesterday. "It would have to be repealed by a majority, and in that case the minority would be justified in taking independent action. Every sound-money delegate elected to the Chicago Convention will go there with the expectation that the two-thirds rule will prevail as it has always done, and if it should be abrogated it would be a complete change of expectations and plans, and the minority would be relieved of any obligation to abide by the decision of the majority.

"The two-thirds rule is the safeguard of the Democratic Party. It necessitates deliberation and the exercise of the best judgment in the selection of candidates. It prevents stampedes, and its wisdom has been demonstrated in every Democratic National Convention. I do not know whether the silver men will be in the majority, but I trust the sound-money men will control the convention."

Ex-Gov. Flower is heartily opposed to any proposition for doing away with the two-thirds rule.

"I do not think the silver men will be in the majority at Chicago," he said, "and I do not think the two-thirds rule will be repealed. It should not be abrogated, and I never will vote to have it abolished. The abrogation of the two-thirds rule is more apt to come up for discussion when there is a scramble for the Democratic nomination. The Democratic Party will have to draft a candidate this year, because there will be no candidate for the nomination unless things change before the convention is held.

"I do not believe the Southern delegates will antagonize the Northern Democrats on the silver question. It is a minor question to them. If they desire the platform for free coinage adopted they will know that that means the Democrats cannot carry a single Northern State, and that McKinley will be nominated and elected probably on a gold platform, as at least twenty-five States with Republican majorities will have delegates at St. Louis in favor of a gold platform, and they will be States that control a majority of the Electoral votes. The Southern men will be told that they can have the silver platform if they desire, with all its consequences, or we can make the platform on the currency question and try to carry New-York, New-Jersey, Connecticut, and Indiana. They will be told, as they know now, that the McKinley tariff law had a hundred force bills in it; what can they expect when McKinley himself is President?

"Personally, I believe most of the Southern delegates fear negro domination and force bills from the Republican Party, and that this issue of the home they will place above the question of currency, as they have in the past joined together and placed it in the front without regard to their particular ideas of the tariff. There are just as good protectionists as tariff-for-revenue-only men in the Democratic Party, and in many States protectionists are in the majority. Still, they never have failed, when their homes were in danger, of joining together and voting the Democratic ticket solid since 1865. The duty of every Democrat who has any influence should be to exert it at Chicago and in the convention so that the Government will not issue one dollar in currency that will not be redeemed in the best money that is issued; in other words, that the present gold standard should be sustained."

## SUICIDE OF A YOUNG WOMAN.

**No Reason Known for Ellen Mahony's Killing Herself.**

Ellen Mahony, a young woman who kept house for her father, James Mahony, at 319 East Twenty-fourth Street, committed suicide yesterday morning by taking a dose of carbolic acid. She died fifteen minutes after her admission to Bellevue Hospital.

The suicide was evidently discovered by her father. He notified a policeman, who summoned an ambulance. Any information about the girl or her motive in taking her life was refused at the house of her father. He said that he was out when the attempt was made, and came home to find his daughter dying in her room. There are several other children in the family, and one of them said that no one was home when Ellen took the poison. The policeman, however, says that when he came to the house he found several persons there, some of them being members of the family.

**Arrested for Selling Peanuts.**

Lena Pinney, who gave her age as ten years, was arrested by Agents King and Pissara of the Gerry society, at 1 o'clock yesterday morning, in the Staten Island Ferryhouse, where she was selling peanuts. She said she lived at 94 Willett Street, where her father and mother were both ill, and that she was trying to earn money to support the family. In the Centre Street Court, Magistrate Flammer committed her to the care of the Gerry society.

**Gen. Harrison Going to Wisconsin.**

DARTFORD, Wis., May 31.—Ex-President and Mrs. Harrison, it is said, will spend part of the Summer here with Gen. John C. New, who has had a cottage here for many years. The Harrisons will arrive next week. Gen. Harrison will get his news of the St. Louis Convention while a guest of Gen. New.

**TELEGRAPHIC BREVITIES.**

—The will of Mrs. Julia C. Van Arsdale of Newark contains these charitable bequests: Society for the Relief of Respectable Aged Women, $5,000; American Bible Society, $3,000; Home Missionary Society of America, $3,000; Newark Female Charitable Society, $3,000; Woman's Missionary Society of America for Heathen Lands, $1,000. There also is a bequest of $1,000 to the Rev. B. C. Young, a warm personal friend of Mrs. Van Arsdale.

—The schooner Hathaway of Jonesport, Me., loaded with 150,000 feet of lumber, caught fire yesterday from the signal lights while lying at anchor near Millbridge, Me., and was burned to the water's edge. The vessel was owned by James Murchie & Son of Calais. Part of the lumber will be saved.

—John G. Nazro, who was cashier of the American Biscuit and Manufacturing Company at Chicago, is under arrest on the charge of embezzling $2,500 of the company's funds. He may escape prosecution by making good the shortage.

—Scott Jackson, murderer of Pearl Bryant, has been removed to the jail at Covington, Ky., for safe keeping by order of Judge Helm, who considers the jail at Newport, Ky., unsafe.

—About $40,000 worth of property was destroyed by fire yesterday at Afton, Iowa. S. Richard's general store and other business buildings were burned.

## DEMOCRATS THINK MONEY IS THE GREAT ISSUE

### In Every State All Other Issues Have Been Made Subordinate to the Financial Question.

### COMPROMISE AT CHICAGO IS HARDLY POSSIBLE

### Only Florida and Louisiana Show a Disposition to Send Delegations Not Pledged to Either Side.

### CONTESTING DELEGATIONS WILL HOLD THE BALANCE OF POWER

### Gold Men from Illinois, Texas, and Nebraska Will Contest Ninety-four Seats, and Silver Men from South Dakota Eight.

**Strong Sentiment Among Democrats in the Eastern, Middle, and Southern States for a Sound Money Democratic Candidate if the Chicago Convention Declares for Silver.**

Are the Democrats of your State in favor of the gold standard, or of free coinage of silver and gold at the ratio of 16 to 1?

What action will they take through their delegation in the National Convention?

Will the Populists of your State fuse with the Democrats on a free silver Presidential candidate? Would this combination carry your State?

Do the gold Democrats of your State favor a separate gold Democratic candidate if the Chicago Convention declares for free silver?

In order to gain an intelligent idea of the feeling among Democrats and the probable outcome of the National Democratic Convention and coming Presidential campaign, the above questions were telegraphed by THE NEW-YORK TIMES to its correspondents in the various doubtful States. The correspondents were in close touch with the party sentiment in their States, and their replies have been sent after consultation with Democratic leaders.

The replies show that the result of the contests that are now assured will determine the complexion of the Chicago Convention. The gold men will contest ninety-four silver seats, in Illinois, Nebraska, and Texas, while the silver men will contest the eight seats of South Dakota. In these contests will be found the balance of power. Neither the gold nor the silver men can secure two-thirds of the delegates. A majority of 200 would be the limit.

It may be safely predicted that the Democratic Convention will not straddle the financial issue. Everything indicates that it will declare unmistakably for either silver or gold. In almost every State the issue has been made between the silver men and gold men. Moreover, the Democrats will recognize the financial issue as paramount in the coming campaign. With them tariff has become of secondary importance.

It is doubtful if there will be a bolt of any considerable dimensions from the National Democratic Convention. The organization leaders in both gold and silver States have shown an inclination to accept the judgment of the convention, no matter what it may be. They will not be able, however, to control the Democrats of their States, and it is not impossible that a separate gold Democratic candidate might be nominated if the Chicago Convention declares for silver and the St. Louis Convention does not unequivocally indorse the gold standard. As to the silver men, they have announced their determination to nominate an independent candidate if neither party nominates a silver man.

## THE EASTERN STATES

### Strong Sentiment for a Separate Gold Candidate if Free Silver Controls at Chicago.

Do the sound-money Democrats of your State favor the nomination of a separate gold-standard Democratic candidate if the Chicago Convention declares for free silver?

The above inquiry was telegraphed to the correspondents of THE NEW-YORK TIMES in that group of great Eastern States in which there is no doubt of the financial attitude of the Democracy. In these States the Populists are inconsiderable, and therefore their attitude cuts no figure. A fusion with them would bring no strength to the free-silver Democrats.

The replies to the question indicate that there is a strong feeling among such Democratic leaders as are strongly identified with the organization against any independent gold movement. Though they are fighting the silver craze, these leaders will support the nominee of the Chicago Convention and hold the organization of the party, hoping that the lapse of a few years will bring the party back to sound principles.

Among the more independent Democrats, however, there is a strong feeling against any truce with the silver men. Should the Republican Convention declare for gold and place a gold man in nomination and the Democratic Convention declare for silver, these men will swell the Republican majorities in the great Eastern States either by voting the Republican ticket or declining to vote. They will recognize that the financial issue is paramount in the coming campaign.

If the Republican National Convention straddles the financial issue and places McKinley in nomination, or even if it declares for gold, with McKinley as a candidate, it is probable that there will be a general movement in favor of a separate gold candidate.

**WOULD REPUDIATE SILVER.**

**New-York Democrats Might Favor a Separate Candidate.**

The Democrats of New-York State are emphatically in favor of a gold standard. They will send a delegation to the Chicago Convention prepared to make the hardest kind of a fight for a platform which recognizes gold as the money standard.

The leaders profess to believe that there is sense enough in the party all over the country to give the gold standard a majority of the convention, although they are fully aware of the possibility that silver men may control.

It is impossible to say whether the party in New-York would repudiate the candidate of the Chicago Convention and inaugurate or join in a movement to nominate a man who represents their views on the currency, but it is certain that they would repudiate any platform which declared in favor of the free coinage of silver at the ratio of 16 to 1.

If the Chicago Convention shall be in control of the silver men, and an out-and-out free-coinage advocate shall be nominated, and a silver plank be put into the platform, a considerable element of the party will be in favor of a bolt. They will favor a separate gold candidate and a platform that will set forth the principles of the business men who favor honest money. They will have none of the silver delusion. They believe they would be doing a great service for the Democratic Party and the country by repudiating the work of the Chicago Convention.

If the Republican National Convention shall adopt any currency plank short of a flat declaration in favor of a gold standard and against the free coinage of silver, and if the Democrats shall declare for free silver, then the likelihood that the New-York Democrats will insist upon a gold candidate upon a gold platform will be increased.

**FOR A STRAIGHT GOLD PLANK.**

**New-Jersey Delegates Will Not Compromise with Silver Men.**

TRENTON, May 31.—The New-Jersey delegation to Chicago is pledged to stanch support of the strong gold plank in the Democratic State platform. The delegates will be controlled by the prevailing sentiment among the Democrats. They have expressed themselves as a unit for sound money and would resist the adoption of a silver plank most forcibly, and they would be likely to favor the nomination of a gold-standard man. The Democrats of New-Jersey are almost unanimous on the subject of sound money. A few Democrats in Warren and Hunterdon Counties are talking silver, but they were formerly members of the People's Party and Farmers' Alliance.

**BATTLE IS NOT OVER.**

**Mr. Harrity Says Courage Will Bring Success for Sound Money.**

PHILADELPHIA, May 31.—According to National Chairman Harrity, there is no need of considering whether or not the sound-money men of Pennsylvania will favor the nomination of a separate gold Democrat if the Chicago Convention declares for free silver. He said to-night to the correspondent of THE NEW-YORK TIMES:

"Speaking for myself, I expect to support the candidates of the Chicago Convention, and I believe they will be sound-money men on a sound-money platform. I shall certainly continue to aid in the effort to bring about that result.

"Allow me to say," he continued, "that the sound-money cause has been materially prejudiced of late by those sound-money men who are so ready to take counsel of their fears and either to abandon their colors before the battle is fought or to retreat even before the enemy is in sight. I believe the contest against free silver will

Two Parts
16 Pages

# The New-York Times.

Part One
Pages 1-8

VOL. XLV....NO. 13,988. NEW-YORK, FRIDAY, JUNE 19, 1896.—TWO PARTS—SIXTEEN PAGES.—COPYRIGHTED, 1896, BY THE NEW-YORK TIMES PUBLISHING CO. PRICE THREE CENTS.

## SILVER MEN WALK OUT

### Dramatic Scene in the Republican Convention.

### SENATORS LEAD THE BOLT

Twenty-one Delegates Join in the Procession from the Hall.

A FORMAL PROTEST PUT ON RECORD.

Free-Coinage Men Say They Cannot Support a Candidate on a Gold Platform.

FINANCIAL VIEWS SHOWN BY BALLOTS.

Half the Utah Delegation Remains with the Party—New Experience for Republicans.

ST. LOUIS, June 18.—A bolt from a Republican Convention is a new thing. Democratic Conventions have furnished sensational spectacles of this sort, attended by tumult and all the customary demonstrations provoked by the delegates who thus approve or disapprove of such a course of procedure. Republicans have sometimes threatened, but they have not actually walked out. It was reserved for the Republican Convention of 1896 to furnish the exhibition of the first bolt from that party.

The silver men until last night had persisted in refusing to declare their intention to bolt. The early menaces of Dubois were not repeated, the counsel of Senator Teller prevailing to suppress threats and to let the intentions of the silver men be made known by acts. The conference of silver men held last night, after Senator Teller's emotional parting from his party friends in the Committee on Resolutions, made it plain that there was to be a bolt, but that it would be but a fragmentary one—dramatic, but not imposing in numbers.

Before the convention met to-day "Boss" Hanna was of the opinion that the report of the Committee on Resolutions could be disposed of in an hour after it was taken up. He was mistaken in that opinion, as he has been in some other opinions he has expressed concerning the details of the convention. It required four hours to receive and dispose of the platform presented. In that time there were several roll calls, each showing that the gold standard was sustained by a prodigious majority. This was expected, but the determination of the question, as between acceptance of the gold plank of the committee and the silver substitute of the minority, provoked a degree of enthusiasm at once gratifying and splendid, the very best of the convention.

The majority had no apology or defense to offer in response to the silver opposition, and ex-Gov. Foraker was satisfied to let the silver men do the talking; his side would do the voting.

Senator Teller was accorded respectful attention when he spoke in remonstrance against the gold plank of the platform. There was no doubt in the mind of any man who heard him that he was distressed; that he was touched by his own reflections on the seriousness of the step he was taking. But the delegates from twenty-nine States had just voted solidly for a gold plank, and they were not to be moved by the pleadings of the leading silver advocate, even though his appeal to them was made in broken tones and while the tears rolled from his eyes and streamed down his face. A few brutal invitations, not from delegates, but from spectators, to "Get out" were hurled at him from the gallery as he finally left the platform, shaking hands in parting with ex-Senator Washburn of Minnesota and others with all the impressiveness that could have been given if he had been on his way to the block.

The speeches that by grace were allowed to be made by Senator Cannon and Senator Mantle, the one in justification of the bolt and the other merely in protest against the gold plank, and with an implied menace of a Montana bolt later on, were heard with indifferent courtesy and interest.

There has never been in any recent convention, or in any convention, perhaps, another such a scene as that at the time of the withdrawal of Teller and his handful of fellow-bolters. There were cheers, but they were not for Teller, and presently, when the band struck up "The Red, White, and Blue," the defiance of the convention was expressed in a grand chorus, sung with such intrepidity and zeal that it was continued after the band had ceased its accompaniment and the deserters had disappeared from the hall.

## A TEARFUL FAREWELL

### Silver Men Leave the Convention When the Gold Plank Is Adopted —Their Reasons Given.

ST. LOUIS, June 18.—Chairman Thurston found it impossible to call the convention to order at 10 o'clock to-day. There were thousands of empty seats. Not more than half of the delegates were on the floor. It was with the best intentions that Mr. Thurston called upon a singing quartet to entertain the crowd while the seats were filling. The four handsome young men who lined up at the front of the platform doubtless sang well, but nobody heard them. Their mustaches wagged and their bosoms heaved, but this was the only sign that they were singing. They tried only one number and then retired in confusion.

The gavel fell at 10:40, and Mr. Thurston introduced a colored preacher, who invoked the Divine blessing. The convention applauded vigorously when he concluded. Then the business of the day was entered upon with a rush. The report of the Committee on Rules was called for, and Senator Foraker, the Chairman of the committee, arose to respond. Immediately the convention was in an uproar. The Ohio delegates jumped to their seats and cheered, and their example was followed by others. The galleries echoed the cry, and Mr. Foraker was obliged to wait a minute or more before opportunity was offered for him to be heard. He read the platform in clear, ringing tones, which penetrated to every part of the immense hall.

The crowd failed to show enthusiasm when the paragraph relating to protection was reached. A few delegates clapped their hands, and a man in the gallery gave a weak imitation of a war whoop. There was quite a demonstration when Foraker read the clause which sets the seal of disapproval upon the re-enactment of an out-and-out McKinley law. The reference to American shipping met with a hearty reception.

Apparently the convention was reserving its energies for the sound-money plank. When it was read flags were waved, fans were flourished, hats were thrown into the air. The scene from the platform was inspiring. Every sound-money delegate was on his feet attesting to his appreciation of the declaration. For three minutes the immense pit looked kaleidoscopic. The sound of 10,000 voices filled the vast chamber. The Chairman was powerless to control the storm. It ceased when the delegates resumed their places, only to break out afresh when the specific declaration against free coinage was read.

"Hurrah for Tom Platt!" shouted a New-Yorker in the rear of the platform, and the cry was repeated by others. Mr. Platt, sitting with the New-York delegation, smiled and looked satisfied.

The other satisfactory features of the plank also were applauded. There were a few scattering cheers when Senator Foraker read the reference to Hawaii and the Nicaragua Canal. The paragraph about Cuba did not excite the convention, although Col. Fred Grant, from the rear of the platform, waved a flag and invited a demonstration.

Not a sound was heard in response to the utterance about civil service reform. Since the last sweeping order of President Cleveland relating to the civil service the average Republican has not yearned for this kind of reform.

Mr. Foraker required twenty minutes in which to read the platform. When he finished the convention again expressed its satisfaction.

(The full text of the platform will be found on the first page of THE NEW-YORK TIMES.)

### TELLER'S VALEDICTORY.

An Address Which Convinced All of the Senator's Earnestness.

ST. LOUIS, June 18.—Senator Teller had occupied a seat on the platform up to the time when Mr. Foraker had finished reading the platform. To him had been assigned the task of presenting the views of the silver men. It was generally understood that Mr. Teller intended to make use of the occasion to deliver his valedictory, and there was the hush of expectancy when the Chairman announced that the Colorado Senator would submit a minority report. This report was read by the Secretary as follows:

We, the undersigned members of the Committee on Resolutions, being unable to agree with that part of the majority report which treats of the subjects of coinage and finance, respectfully submit the following paragraph as a substitute therefor:

"The Republican Party favors the use of both gold and silver as equal standard money, and pledges its power to secure the free, unrestricted, and independent coinage of gold and silver at our mints at the ratio of 16 parts of silver to 1 of gold."

**Teller Gives His Reasons.**

Mr. Teller advanced to the desk and stood calmly surveying the scene, while the convention was cheering. Certainly he has not reason to complain of his treatment by the men with whose views his own are at such variance. He was attired as usual in black broadcloth. His opening sentences were not distinctly understood, and there were cries of "Louder!" Mr. Teller's voice soon reached sufficient volume. He spoke in his most impressive style. He said:

Gentlemen of the Convention: I will not attempt to inflict upon you a discussion of the great financial question which is dividing not only the people of this country, but of the whole world. The few moments allowed to me will not enable me to do more than state, in the briefest possible manner, our objection to the financial plank proposed for your consideration. I am a practical man, and I recognize the conditions existing in this convention, foreshadowed as they have been by the action of the Committee on Resolutions, to whom this proposition was presented, and by whom it was rejected. Loyalty to my own opinion compels me, in the face of unusual difficulties, to present this substitute for your consideration, not with that abiding hope nor with that courage to which I have presented the same in other bodies with greater measure of success than I have hoped for here. The great and supreme importance of this question is alone my excuse for the few words which I have to say to you. I have dealt with this subject in a public capacity for now twenty years. I represent a State which produces silver, but I want to say to you here now that my advocacy of the proposition is not in the slightest degree influenced or controlled by that fact.

I contend for it because I believe there can be no sound financial system in any country in the world that does not recognize this principle. I contend for it because, since 1873, when it was ruthlessly stricken from our statutes, there has been continued depreciation of all the products of human nature and human energy. I contend for it because, in this year 1896, the American people are in greater distress than they ever were in their history. I contend for it because this, in my judgment, is the great weight, the great incubus, which has weighed down enterprise and destroyed progress in this favored land of ours. I contend for it because I believe that the progress of my country is dependent upon it. I contend for it because I believe that the civilization of the world is to be determined by the rightful or wrongful solution of this financial question.

**Tolerant of Others' Views.**

I am tolerant of those who differ with me. I act from my judgment, enlightened as well as I have been enabled to enlighten it by many years of study and many years of thought. In my judgment the American people, in the whole line of their history, have never been called upon to settle a question so great to them as this. The great contest, in which many of you participated, whether we should have two flags or one, was not more important to the American people than the question of a proper solution of what shall be the money system of the land.

I have said enough to show you that I think that this is not a question of politics, but a question of principle. It is not a mere idle thing, but one on which hang the happiness, the prosperity, the morality, and independence of American laborers. For the first time in the history of this great country we are confronted with the danger of a financial system, which, in my judgment, will be destructive of all the great interests of this land. We are called upon to give this provision of our platform our adhesion, or to reject it. Mr. President, I do not care to say any unkind or unfriendly thing, but I will state in a moment why I object to this provision in the platform.

The Republican Party has never been the party of a single standard. [Applause.] It was a bimetallic party in its origin, and in all its history. In 1888 it declared for bimetallism. In 1892 it declared for bimetallism. In 1896 it declares for the single gold platform. Mr. President, in 1888 we carried the State which I here represent for the Republican nominee. We carried it on a bimetallic platform. We carried it with a majority which was equal, considering our votes, to that of any State in the Union. Colorado has been a Republican State from the hour of its admission. It has kept in the Senate Republican Senators, and in the House Republican members. But I promised not to discuss the silver question, and I will not, except to say that this platform is such a distinct departure from everything heretofore held to by this party that it challenges our Republicanism to accept it. The platform contains some platitudes about an international conference. It provides that we will maintain the gold standard in this country, until the principal nations of the world shall agree that we may do otherwise.

Mr. President, this is the first great gathering of the Republicans since the party was organized that has declared the inability of the American people to control their own affairs. And to my horror this declaration comes from the great political party of Abraham Lincoln and Ulysses S. Grant. [Cheers.] Do you believe that the American people are either too weak or too cowardly to maintain a financial system commensurate with the greatness of the country, and to do that of their own will?

**No General Agreement Possible.**

Gentlemen of the convention, you will have no bimetallic agreement with all the great commercial nations of the world. It cannot be obtained. And so this is a declaration that the gold standard is to be put upon this country, and to be kept here for all time. Do you believe that Great Britain, the principal commercial nation of the world, our powerful competitor in trade and commerce, will ever agree to open her mints to the free coinage of silver, or consent that we shall open ours so long as she gets the advantage of the low prices and of depreciating values brought about by the adoption of the gold standard in 1873? In a partial degree only are we the great debtor nation of the world. Great Britain is the great creditor nation. We pay her every year millions and hundreds of millions in income upon her investments in this country or upon her loans. The gold standard, in my judgment, lowers prices and decreases values, and she buys of us millions and millions more than she sells. She buys upon the gold standard, which is a lowering and depreciating standard. How long do you think it will be before she will agree to a system of finance that raises the prices of our foreign products or of the products of our mines.

This proposed financial plank is a declaration that the Republican Party intends to maintain low prices and stagnant business for all time.

Mr. President, there is a beautiful provision in this platform about the tariff. I subscribe to it. I believe in a protective tariff, and have advocated it for forty years. But it is my solemn conviction that a protective tariff cannot be maintained upon a gold standard. The tariff protection principle is for the raising of the price of human toil. The gold standard of the country, everywhere that it is in force, is for the purpose of reducing values. Gentlemen of the convention, I am going to make this simple objection, as the protective system is, I think, endangered by the proposed platform, and I will simply call your attention to it and leave the matter to your judgment as to whether this platform shall be adopteted or whether it shall be rejected. Under existing conditions we undoubtedly have the gold standard. I do not deny that. What you have sought for twenty years is to change it into a bimetallic system. I have believed, and I now believe, that when the Almighty created these twin metals of coin He intended that the world should use them for the purposes for which they were created. And when He blessed this land of ours with more gold and more silver than any other country in the world, He meant that we should use them for the purposes for which they were intended, to wit, as money for the people.

**Not the Popular View.**

We to-day reverse the traditions of our country and declare that we will use only one of these two metals. If the American people are in favor of that, I have nothing to say. I must submit to the majority vote and majority voice in this country of ours. I do not believe it. I do not believe that the people are in favor of a single gold standard. I believe that 90 per cent. of the American people are in favor of bimetallism in the old-fashioned meaning of the word up till 1873.

I want to say two things which may seem to you to be personal, and that ought not to be introduced in an audience like this. But I must beg your indulgence if I seem to transcend the proprieties of this occasion in saying something personal to myself. I have formed my convictions of this great question after twenty years of study, after twenty years of careful thought and careful reading. I have been trained in a school which, it seems to me, ought to fit me fairly well for reaching just conclusions from established facts. I have formed my conclusions to such an extent that they have become binding on my conscience. I believe that the adoption of the gold standard in the United States will work great hardships; that it will increase the distress, and that no legislation touching the tariff can relieve the difficulties which, all now admit, prevail in this land. I believe that the whole welfare of my race is dependent upon a rightful solution of the question; that the morality, the civilization, nay, the religion, of my country are at stake in this country. I know, and you know, that men in distress are never patriotic or brave. You and I know that hunger and distress will destroy patriotism and love of country. If you are to have love of country, patriotic fervor, and independence, you must have your citizens comfortably fed and comortably clothed.

That is what made me a Republican in 1858. That is what made me a Republican during all these years. It was because I believed that the Republican Party stood for the great mass of men, and that its legislation was intended to lift up and elevate and hold up and sustain the unfortunate and the distressed and to give to all American citizens equal opportunities before the law. I do not believe that that will be had with the gold standard. You may doubt my judgment. Many of you will, but why should I doubt it. I must act on my own judgment and not on yours. I must answer to my conscience and not to that of my neighbor. I must do my duty as it is presented to me, and not as presented to you.

**Must Leave the Party.**

I say to you now that, with the solemn conviction upon me that this plank means disaster to my fellow-men, I cannot subscribe to it, and I must, as an honest man, sever my connection with a political organization which makes that one of the main articles of its faith. I repeat here what I said yesterday to the committee—I wouldn't, on my own judgment, carefully as I have attempted to prepare it, take this step alone. But, my friends, I am sustained in my views of the danger that is coming to us and coming to the world by the adoption of the gold standard. I am sustained in it by the intelligence of the entire world. The best thought of Europe—the best thought of the world—is with the advocates of bimetallism. All of the great political speakers of Europe, except five or six, are the pronounced advocates of unrestricted and unrestrained bimetallism; and all of the great teachers of political philosophy in European colleges, without a single exception, are in favor of bimetallism. My own judgment, arrived at, as I have said to you, with careful preparation and careful study for twenty years, bears me out and puts me in accordance with them. And I would be recreant to my trust given to me by the people of my State if I came here to protest and I failed when the Republican Party makes the single gold standard one of the tenets of its faith, to sever my connection with that party. [Cries of "No," "No," "No," all over the hall.]

Do you suppose that myself and my associates, who hold with me and who take the same view of it that I take—do you suppose that we can take this step without distress? Do you suppose that we can take it for any personal advantage or for any honors that can be conferred upon us? With us it is a question of duty. You may nominate in this convention any man you choose; if you put him on the right kind of a platform, I will vote for him. You may take any method to nominate him which you think proper. I will defer to your judgment and will support him if your platform is the right one. But when you ask me to surrender my conscience, as an honest man I cannot do it. [Applause.]

I realize what it will cost me. I realize the gibes and sneers and contumely that will be heaped upon us. But, Oh, my fellow-citizens, I have been there before. [Cheers.] I have been there before the political party to which you belong had a being. I advocated a cause more unpopular than the silver cause. I stood for the doctrine of free men, free homes, and free speech. I am used to detraction. I am used to abuse, and I heed it not, when my judgment is with me.

When the Republican Party was organized I was there. It has never had a National candidate since it was organized that my voice was not raised in his support. It has never had a great principle announced in its platform that had not my approbation until now. With its distinguished leaders and its distinguished men for forty years I have been in close communication and close friendship. I have shared in its honors and in its few defeats and disasters. Do you think that we can sever our connection with a party like this unless it be a matter of duty —a duty not to our State alone, but a duty to all the people of this great land?

**A Tearful Farewell.**

Mr. President, there are few men in the Republican Party that have been more honored than I have been. There are few men in this convention, or anywhere else, who have been longer connected with this organization than I. There are few men in it—no, not one—that are more attached to the great principles of the party than I have been. And I cannot go out of it without heartburnings and feelings that no man can appreciate unless he has endured them. And yet I cannot, before my country and my God, agree to this provision that will put upon this country a gold standard, and I will not. [Loud applause.]

I don't care what will be to me the result. If it takes me out of political life, I will go out with the feeling that my conscience is clear, and that my countrymen have no right to find fault with me. [Applause.]

I beg your pardon for saying so much that is personal, but I think in justice to myself and

Continued on Page 7.

## THE REPUBLICAN PLATFORM.

The Republicans of the United States, assembled by their representatives in National convention, appealing for the popular and historical justification of their claims to the matchless achievements of thirty years of Republican rule, earnestly and confidently address themselves to the awakened intelligence, experience, and conscience of their countrymen in the following declaration of facts and principles:

For the first time since the civil war the American people have witnessed the calamitous consequences of full and unrestricted Democratic control of the Government. It has been a record of unparalleled incapacity, dishonor, and disaster. In administrative management it has ruthlessly sacrificed indispensable revenue, entailed an unceasing deficit, eked out ordinary current expenses with borrowed money, piled up the public debt by $262,000,000 in time of peace, forced an adverse balance of trade, kept a perpetual menace hanging over the redemption fund, pawned American credit to alien syndicates, and reversed all the measures and results of successful Republican rule. In the broad effect of its policy it has precipitated panic, blighted industry and trade with prolonged depression, closed factories, reduced work and wages, halted enterprise, and crippled American production while stimulating foreign production for the American market. Every consideration of public safety and individual interest demands that the Government shall be rescued from the hands of those who have shown themselves incapable of conducting it without disaster at home and dishonor abroad, and shall be restored to the party which for thirty years administered it with unequaled success and prosperity. And in this connection we heartily indorse the wisdom, the patriotism, and the success of the Administration of President Harrison.

**Higher Tariff Rates.**—We renew and emphasise our allegiance to the policy of protection as the bulwark of American industrial independence and the foundation of American development and prosperity. This true American policy taxes foreign products and encourages home industry; it puts the burden of revenue on foreign goods; it secures the American market for the American producer; it upholds the American standard of wages for the American workingman; it puts the factory by the side of the farm and makes the American farmer less dependent on foreign demand and price; it diffuses general thrift and founds the strength of all on the strength of each. In its reasonable application it is just, fair, and impartial, equally opposed to foreign control and domestic monopoly, to sectional discrimination and individual favoritism.

We denounce the present Democratic tariff as sectional, injurious to the public credit, and destructive to business enterprise. We demand such an equitable tariff on foreign imports which come into competition with American products as will not only furnish adequate revenue for the necessary expenses of the Government, but will protect American labor from degradation to the wage level of other lands. We are not pledged to any particular schedules. The question of rates is a practical question, to be governed by the conditions of the time and of production; the ruling and uncompromising principle is the protection and development of American labor and industry. The country demands a right settlement, and then it wants rest.

**Reciprocity and Protection, Twins.**—We believe the repeal of the reciprocity arrangements negotiated by the last Republican Administration was a National calamity, and we demand their renewal and extension on such terms as will equalize our trade with other nations, remove the restrictions which now obstruct the sale of American products in the ports of other countries, and secure enlarged markets for the products of our farms, forests, and factories.

Protection and reciprocity are twin measures of Republican policy, and go hand in hand. Democratic rule has recklessly struck down both, and both must be re-established. Protection for what we produce; free admission for the necessaries of life which we do not produce; reciprocal agreements of mutual interest which gain open markets for us in return for our open market to others. Protection builds up domestic industry and trade and secures our own market for ourselves; reciprocity builds up foreign trade and finds an outlet for our surplus.

**Protection for Sugar Growers.**—We condemn the present Administration for not keeping faith with the sugar producers of this country. The Republican Party favors such protection as will lead to the production on American soil of all the sugar which the American people use, and for which they pay other countries more than $100,000,000 annually.

**Wool and Woolens.**—To all our products—to those of the mine and the field as well as those of the shop and factory—to hemp, to wool, the product of the great industry of sheep husbandry, as well as to the finished woolens of the mill, we promise the most ample protection.

**Merchant Marine.**—We favor restoring the early American policy of discriminating duties for the upbuilding of our merchant marine and the protection of our shipping in the foreign carrying trade, so that American ships—the product of American labor employed in American shipyards, sailing under the Stars and Stripes, and manned, officered, and owned by Americans—may regain the carrying of our foreign commerce.

**Financial Declaration.**—The Republican Party is unreservedly for sound money. It caused the enactment of the law providing for the resumption of specie payments in 1879; since then every dollar has been as good as gold.

We are unalterably opposed to every measure calculated to debase our currency or impair the credit of our country. We are therefore opposed to the free coinage of silver except by international agreement with the leading commercial nations of the world, which we pledge ourselves to promote, and until such agreement can be obtained the existing gold standard must be preserved. All our silver and paper currency must be maintained at parity with gold, and we favor all measures designed to maintain inviolably the obligations of the United States, and all our money, whether coin or paper, at the present standard, the standard of the most enlightened nations of the earth.

**Favor Liberal Pensions.**—The veterans of the Union armies deserve and should receive fair treatment and generous recognition. Whenever practicable they should be given the preference in the matter of employment, and they are entitled to the enactment of such laws as are best calculated to secure the fulfillment of the pledges made to them in the dark days of the country's peril. We denounce the practice in the Pension Bureau, so recklessly and unjustly carried on by the present Administration, of reducing pensions and arbitrarily dropping names from the rolls, as deserving the severest condemnation of the American people.

**Foreign Relations.**—Our foreign policy should be at all times firm, vigorous, and dignified, and all our interests in the Western Hemisphere carefully watched and guarded. The Hawaiian Islands should be controlled by the United States, and no foreign power should be permitted to interfere with them; the Nicaragua Canal should be built, owned, and operated by the United States, and by the purchase of the Danish Islands we should secure a proper and much-needed naval station in the West Indies.

**Armenian Massacres.**—The massacres in Armenia have aroused the deep sympathy and just indignation of the American people, and we believe that the United States should exercise all the influence it can properly exert to bring these atrocities to an end. In Turkey American residents have been exposed to the gravest dangers and American property destroyed. There and everywhere American citizens and American property must be absolutely protected at all hazards and at any cost.

**The Monroe Doctrine.**—We reassert the Monroe Doctrine in its full extent, and we reaffirm the right of the United States to give the doctrine effect by responding to the appeals of any American State for friendly intervention in case of European encroachment. We have not interfered, and shall not interfere, with the existing possessions of any European power in this hemisphere, but those possessions must not, on any pretext, be extended. We hopefully look forward to the eventual withdrawal of the European powers from this hemisphere, to the ultimate union of all of the English-speaking part of the continent by the free consent of its inhabitants.

**Sympathy for Cuba.**—From the hour of achieving their own independence the people of the United States have regarded with sympathy the struggles of other American peoples to free themselves from European domination. We watch with deep and abiding interest the heroic battle of the Cuban patriots against cruelty and oppression, and our best hopes go out for the full success of their determined contest for liberty.

The Government of Spain, having lost control of Cuba, and being unable to protect the property or lives of resident American citizens, or to comply with its treaty obligations, we believe that the Government of the United States should actively use its influence and good offices to restore peace and give independence to the island.

**Navy Should Be Enlarged.**—The peace and security of the Republic and the maintenance of its rightful influence among the nations of the earth demand a naval power commensurate with its position and responsibility. We therefore favor the continued enlargement of the navy and a complete system of harbor and seacoast defenses.

**Foreign Immigration.**—For the protection of the equality of our American citizenship, and of the wages of our workingmen against the fatal competition of low-priced labor, we demand that the immigration laws be thoroughly enforced, and so extended as to exclude from entrance to the United States those who can neither read nor write.

**Civil Service Reform.**—The civil service law was placed on the statute book by the Republican Party, which has always sustained it, and we renew our repeated declarations that it shall be thoroughly and honestly enforced and extended wherever practicable.

**Free and Unrestricted Ballot.**—We demand that every citizen of the United States shall be allowed to cast one free and unrestricted ballot, and that such ballot shall be counted and returned as cast.

**Condemn Lynchings.**—We proclaim our unqualified condemnation of the uncivilized and barbarous practices, well known as lynching or killing of human beings, suspected or charged with crime, without process of law.

**National Arbitration.**—We favor the creation of a National Board of Arbitration to settle and adjust differences which may arise between employers and employed engaged in inter-State commerce.

**Free Homesteads.**—We believe in an immediate return to the free-homestead policy of the Republican Party, and urge the passage by Congress of the satisfactory free-homestead measure which has already passed the House and is now pending in the Senate.

**Admission of Territories.**—We favor the admission of the remaining Territories at the earliest practicable date, having due regard to the interests of the people of the Territories and of the United States. All the Federal officers appointed for the Territories should be selected from bona fide residents thereof, and the right of self-government should be accorded as far as practicable.

**Alaska in Congress.**—We believe the citizens of Alaska should have representation in the Congress of the United States, to the end that needful legislation may be intelligently enacted.

**A Temperance Plank.**—We sympathize with all wise and legitimate efforts to lessen and prevent the evils of intemperance and promote morality.

**Rights of Women.**—The Republican Party is mindful of the rights and interests of women. Protection of American industries includes equal opportunities, equal pay for equal work, and protection to the home. We favor the admission of women to wider spheres of usefulness, and welcome their co-operation in rescuing the country from Democratic and Populistic mismanagement and misrule.

Such are the principles and policies of the Republican Party. By these principles we will abide, and these policies we will put into execution. We ask for them the considerate judgment of the American people. Confident alike in the history of our great party and in the justice of our cause, we present our platform and our candidates in the full assurance that the election will bring victory to the Republican Party and prosperity to the people of the United States.

## McKINLEY AND HOBART OF NEW-JERSEY

### Nominated at St. Louis by the Republican Party for President and Vice President.

### VOTE FOR THE GOLD PLATFORM 812 1-2 TO 110 1-2

Twenty-one Silver Men Bolt the Convention, Led by Teller, Who Weeps Copiously as He Leaves the Hall.

FOUR SENATORS AND TWO REPRESENTATIVES WALK OUT

They Are Going to Chicago to Make an Attempt to Capture the Democratic Nomination for Teller—Chairman Carter Decides to Stick to His Party—Convention Adjourns Sine Die and Delegates Start for Home.

FIRST BALLOT.

|  |  |
|---|---|
| McKinley | 661 1-2 |
| Reed | 84 1-2 |
| Quay | 61 1-2 |
| Morton | 58 |
| Allison | 35 1-2 |
| Blank | 4 |
| Cameron | 1 |
| Total | 906 |

FIRST BALLOT.

|  |  |
|---|---|
| Hobart | 533 1-2 |
| Evans | 277 1-2 |
| Bulkeley | 39 |
| Walker | 24 |
| Lippitt | 8 |
| Reed | 3 |
| Depew | 3 |
| Grant | 2 |
| Thurston | 2 |
| Morton | 1 |
| Total | 893 |

ST. LOUIS, June 18.—William McKinley of Ohio was nominated this afternoon as the candidate of the Republican Party for President, and Garret A. Hobart of New-Jersey was named for Vice President.

This outcome, secured in one prolonged session of the convention, the fourth sitting since it was called to order on Tuesday, was more than half expected last night. Gov. Morton's chances were then very doubtful, partly owing to his reiterated disinclination to accept the nomination for Vice President "under any circumstances," and partly because of the bitter opposition to Gov. Morton in his own State—an opposition that was cultivated with complete disregard of the tarnish that it was putting upon the State and its Chief Executive, and which provoked the contempt of Gov. Morton's opponents in other States.

Hanna came to St. Louis, as has been repeatedly stated in these dispatches, determined to make Hobart the candidate with McKinley. He resented the fight made to put "gold" in the financial plank, and he was alarmed when he found that his resentment was not only futile to keep "gold" out, but that the men who were for the use of the word "gold" were disposed to express their thanks to Mr. Platt and the gold people of New-York by voting for Morton for Vice President if he would present him. Morton's dispatch of declination to Mr. Depew helped Hanna. It assisted the protesting anti-Platt men to fix the impression that Morton could not get the unanimous indorsement of his own State.

Battered though his influence was after the fight for a straddle, Hanna was still influential, and his power was fully restored when Mr. Morton to-day telegraphed Mr. Depew that he could only take the Vice Presidency if nominated unanimously. Hanna, Warner Miller, and Bliss had made that impossible.

The ticket is Hanna's. The platform is the work of the convention. At Hanna's request the declaration on the tariff was allowed to come first. Mr. Lodge had promised that, and Foraker was not enough concerned about the order of the paragraphs to assert his contempt for Hanna by insisting that the most important policy should be asserted in the first paragraph of the platform.

To the people the ticket is not likely to be as interesting as the platform. If the Republicans shall be successful in November it will be the money plank, not the tariff plank nor the names of McKinley and Hobart, that will win the victory.

The thoughtful and well-informed Republicans here know that in the bolt of Teller and his following of silver men to-day lies the menace of a serious breaking of party lines. To such Republicans it is known that the silver fever is higher than generally supposed, and that it is prostrating victims heretofore regarded as sound with the suddenness and completeness with which grip overcomes the subjects of its attacks. The wide distribution of the silver bacilli, as suggested by Teller's elaborate farewell, was ominous and threatening.

The platform makers were alive to the condition of the country and to the general indifference to talk about McKinley duties; otherwise it would not have been possible to secure from a Republican convention a practical denunciation of McKinleyism on the same day that McKinley, for making his unpopular bill, was honored with the nomination for the highest office in the land. It was a tub to a whale, a bait to catch those Republicans who are not so zealous for protection as they were in 1890.

Teller's desertion of his party may make him the candidate of the silver party and the Populists, and if the Chicago Convention, affected to conservative action by the gold stand of the Republicans, shall take the middle course indicated by Hanna, as the one to be followed by the Republicans and shall name a doubtful man, rejecting Bland and Boies, it would not be at all astonishing to see another St. Louis ticket, with Teller and Bland, or Teller and some silver Democrat at its head.

This will not help the Republicans. It will make the selection of McKinley depend very largely upon the nomination of a gold Democrat of character and capacity, the division of the Democratic vote in several States in which the Republican vote is large, but not a majority, and the prevention of a silver success by a reference of the contest to the House of Representatives.

The convention presented no incident so thrilling as that of the bolt of Teller and his silver associates. The noisy demonstrations for candidates were evidently contrived with the properties and music prepared in advance by a political theatrical manager. It was a disorderly convention, badly officered with perhaps the least efficient Sergeant at Arms and the most utterly useless corps of assistants ever collected for a similar purpose. The presiding officer, Senator John M. Thurston, really presided, commanding the noisy body well, speaking briefly when occasion required, and inspiring confidence in the audience by his own composure and by an easy assumption of the authority conferred upon him.

## MAKING THE TICKET.

### Merits of the Several Candidates for President Presented to the Convention.

ST. LOUIS, June 18.—The nomination of the Presidential and Vice Presidential candidates by the Republican National Convention followed the exciting incidents in connection with the adoption of the platform. The only intervening business was the call of the roll for members of the National Committee. While the committee was in process of formation a good deal of applause followed the announcement of names.

When Missouri was called and R. C. Kerens's name was reported there was a storm of cheers from the Missouri shouters of the Kerens faction. Some one in the Missouri delegation challenged the selection of Mr. Kerens. Chairman Thurston ruled that Missouri must settle its own troubles, as the convention could not pass upon challenges on this question. Perry Cason and Andrew Gleeson of the District of Columbia could not agree as to which should serve on the National Committee. The District was passed, and when the list had been called, the committee was authorized to fill vacancies.

**Iowa Nominates Allison**

The call of States for candidates for the Presidential nomination came next, and the crowd, which had been waiting for this, cheered. The first State to respond was Iowa. John N. Baldwin of Council Bluffs, a smooth-faced, fat man, who resembles Wilson S. Bissell of Buffalo, made the speech. His speech was almost unique in that it could be heard. Before he spoke the name of Allison he baited the convention with the name of Blaine, and the crowd rose to it like a trout to a fly. But the enthusiasm quickly died and did not return. When a minute later Allison's name was spoken the response was faint in comparison. Mr. Baldwin, in the course of his speech, said:

Mr. Chairman and Gentlemen of the Convention: There is one, but only one, of those whose names will be presented to this convention who can claim that there has been placed for him in history's golden urn an estimate of his character and worth made by him on whom nature stamped her royal seal; God exhibited as his greatest design of American manhood, genius, statesmanship, and patriotism; who, now in heaven, wears a crown of deathless praise, and whose great soul is a portion of eternity itself, James G. Blaine.

Blaine, writing to Garfield, said: "Then comes Allison. He is true, kind, reasonable, fair, honest, and good. He is methodical, industrious, and intelligent, and would be a splendid man to sail along with smoothly and successfully."

Complying with the request of the Iowa delegation, I rise to propose to this convention the nomination of him to whom this heritage was bequeathed—William B. Allison, and to ask you to make it on the Old and New Testament of Republicanism.

That which this country has lost, is that which it now seeks, "Protection." To get it the people have worked hard, prayed fast, paid high, and now let them have it. Allison does not believe in a tariff for revenue only, but in a tariff for protection and revenue jointly. He has always insisted that the protective system is the [illegible]

"All the News That's Fit to Print"

# The New York Times

LATE CITY EDITION

Weather: Cloudy, windy today; cold tonight. Fair, seasonable tomorrow. Temperature range: today 28-37; Tuesday 36-43. Details on page 8?.

VOL. XLV....NO. 14,003. NEW-YORK, TUESDAY, JULY 7, 1896.—TWO PARTS—TWELVE PAGES.—COPYRIGHTED, 1896, BY THE NEW-YORK TIMES PUBLISHING CO. PRICE THREE CENTS.

## GOLD GAINS A POINT

### Silverites a Minority in the Committee.

### HILL NAMED FOR CHAIRMAN

### Free-Coinage Men Give Notice that They Will Contest.

### DANIEL WILL BE THEIR CANDIDATE

### The Fight Between the Factions Will Begin When the Convention Is Called to Order.

### MICHIGAN'S GOLD MEN SEATED

### Stevenson's Gold Delegation Is Placed on the Roll—The Texas Contest Withdrawn.

CHICAGO, July 6.—The situation on the eve of the convention is by no means satisfactory to the silver leaders. The day has but added to their difficulties. In a preliminary encounter with the sound-money Democrats of the National Committee, they were worsted. That committee this afternoon decided that Senator Hill should be named as temporary Chairman of the convention. The silver men had begged Mr. Hill not to enter the contest for this honor, but his Democracy is not of that kind that yields to Populistic clamor, and he refused.

The test of strength in the committee had come a short time before, when the proposition to seat the contesting delegates from Nebraska was made. The vote stood 27 to 23, and the figures were the same in the Hill case. Some of the votes in opposition to Mr. Hill were cast by silverites acting as proxies for sound-money members of the committee.

The proceedings up to this point were not free from unpleasant incidents. The silver men lost their heads completely when they saw that they were outvoted and insisted upon a settlement of the Michigan contest, which is to be the vital one of this convention. If, as they assert, they intend that the convention shall unseat the sound-money delegates from Michigan, their proper course to-day was to permit the case to go over for action by the convention. Instead, they brought it before the committee, sitting as a jury, and it was decided in favor of the sound-money men.

There can be no question of the regularity of the credentials of these delegates. Now that they have been approved by the committee, they can be rejected only by the convention. Their rejection by that body undoubtedly would lead to a bolt by the sound-money men, the excuse for which would be strengthened by the palpable injustice of the convention's action.

The sound-money leaders are quite well satisfied with the existing conditions. Their opponents have placed weapons in their hands.

There does not appear to be any doubt that the silverites will refuse to accept Senator Hill as temporary Chairman. Senator Daniel of Virginia is their candidate. If they follow the advice of the hotheads, there will be war immediately upon the presentation by Chairman Harrity of Mr. Hill's name.

There is a probability that the Committee on Credentials will throw out the Michigan sound-money delegates and that the convention will indorse this action. The likelihood of such action would be lessened if the sentiment for the abrogation of the two-thirds rule were stronger. A canvass made to-day showed that there was a majority of about 100 of the delegates in favor of the retention of the time-honored rule. This being the case, there is nothing for the majority to do but seat the silver contestants from Michigan, if a free-coinage man is to be nominated. The attempt to adopt this programme would bring on the most sensational fight of the convention.

#### AN EXCITING MEETING.

##### Factional Strength Early Shown—Proxies Aid the Silverites.

CHICAGO, July 6.—The National Committee, beginning its meeting at noon to-day, transacted its business at a single session, disposing of all the contests for seats and voting, 27 to 23, to report the name of Senator David B. Hill of New-York for temporary Chairman of the National Convention. The first test vote in the committee was on this proposition, and it showed the relative gold and silver strength of the organization. The silver showing was made by the presence of several proxies for members of the committee who would have voted for Mr. Hill had they been present. There were also one or two members of the committee who within the last few days had announced the transfer of their allegiance from gold to silver, notably J. L. Norris of the District of Columbia and Arthur Sewall of Maine.

The first business in order was the calling of the roll of Secretary Sheerin, which showed the following present:

Alabama—HENRY D. CLAYTON.
Arkansas—T. V. McRAE, proxy.
California—M. F. TARPEY.
Colorado—CHARLES S. THOMAS.
Connecticut—CARLOS FRENCH.
Delaware—LEWIS C. VANDERGRIFT.
Florida—SAMUEL PASCO.
Georgia—CLARK HOWELL, Jr.
Idaho—BERRY N. HILLIARD, proxy.
Illinois—BEN T. CABLE.
Indiana—SIMON P. SHEERIN.
Iowa—J. J. RICHARDSON.
Kansas—CHARLES W. BLAIR.
Kentucky—THOMAS H. SHERLEY.
Louisiana—JAMES JEFFRIES.
Maine—ARTHUR SEWALL.
Maryland—L. V. BAUGHMAN, proxy.
Massachusetts—JOSIAH QUINCY.
Michigan—DANIEL J. CAMPAU.
Minnesota—D. W. LAWLOR, proxy.
Mississippi—CHARLES B. HOWRY.
Missouri—JOHN G. PRATHER.
Montana—A. J. DAVIDSON.
Nebraska—TOBIAS CASTOR.
Nevada—R. P. KEATING.
New-Hampshire—A. W. SULLOWAY.
New-Jersey—MILES ROSS, Senator J. J. Smith, proxy.
New-York—WILLIAM F. SHEEHAN.
North Carolina—F. H. BUSBEE.
North Dakota—WILLIAM C. LEISTIKOW.
Ohio—GEORGE F. GILLILAND, proxy.
Oregon—FREDERICK V. HOLMAN, proxy.
Pennsylvania—W. F. HARRITY.
Rhode Island—RICHARD B. COMSTOCK, proxy.
South Carolina—M. L. DONALDSON.
South Dakota—JAMES M. WOODS.
Tennessee—HOLMES CUMMINS.
Texas—O. T. HOLT.
Vermont—BRADLEY B. SMALLEY.
Virginia—J. TAYLOR ELLYSON.
Washington—HUGH C. WALLACE.
West Virginia—JOHN SHERIDAN.
Wisconsin—Senator W. F. VILAS, proxy.
Wyoming—W. L. KUYKENDALL.
Alaska—A. L. DELANEY.
Arizona—CHARLES M. SHANNON.
District of Columbia—JAMES L. NORRIS.
New-Mexico—H. B. FERGUSON.
Oklahoma—T. M. RICHARDSON.
Utah—SAMUEL A. MERRITT.
Indian Territory—ROBERT L. OWEN.

##### Why Texas Withdrew.

Secretary Sheerin stated that the Clark contestants from Texas, known as gold men, had withdrawn from the further contest for seats in the convention. The withdrawal was accompanied by a statement of the reasons which impelled them to enter upon the contest and now to voluntarily abandon it. This statement was read by the Secretary, and made a part of the records of the committee.

Senator Jones of Arkansas, representing the "steering" committee of the Bimetallic League, was given an opportunity to address the committee. He stated that the silver men had no candidate to present for temporary Chairman. The selection of any one who was in accord with the idea of the silver men would be acceptable to them, and he urged, in the interest of harmony, that the wishes of the majority of the convention be not antagonized in the choice. He was heard with respectful attention, but no answer was given to him, and he withdrew.

The committee decided to proceed with the consideration and settlement of the contested cases first, and that from Nevada was settled in favor of Gen. Keating and his associates, silver men, without a vote.

In the cases over which a contest was made fifteen minutes were given to each side for argument. The first case of that kind called was that of John P. Frenzel (gold) against Charles M. Cooper, (silver,) from the Seventh (Indianapolis) District of Indiana. Mr. Cooper made his own argument, while ex-Attorney General Green Smith spoke for Mr. Frenzel. Cooper had been recognized by the State Convention of Indiana, and he was placed on the temporary roll by a vote of 47 to 1, the negative vote being cast by Mr. Campau of Michigan.

##### The Michigan Contest.

A contest brought by the silver men for seats for three districts in Michigan was argued for the contesting gold men by Elliott G. Stevenson, Chairman of the gold delegation, and for the silver men by Daniel J. Campau, the Michigan member of the National Committee. On motion of Charles S. Thomas of Colorado the gold men were placed on the temporary roll, Mr. Campau's being the only vote cast for the contestants.

D. J. Mahony spoke for the contesting gold delegates from Nebraska, headed by Tobias Castor, and he warned the Democratic Party, through the National Committee, of the danger there was before it of defeat at the polls should it nominate a Populist rather than a Democrat. C. J. Smythe replied for the Bryan silver delegation, and by the first test vote of the afternoon—27 to 23—it was decided to place the Castor delegation on the temporary roll.

Next came the Ohio contest—that from the Eighteenth District—wherein John H. Clark and A. M. Raff, gold men, sought the places of Conrad Schweitzer and W. S. Potts, silver men. The gold men had been recognized by their District Convention and the silver men by the State Convention, and their cases were presented to the committee by Mr. Clark in person for himself and Mr. Raff, and by John C. Welty for the silver men. The committee voted—24 to 17—to sustain the decision of the State Convention, and gave the silver men a place on the roll.

A rather unexpected contest came up from South Dakota, where a delegation of silver men, headed by Dr. Ross, sought to secure the seats certified by the State Convention to the delegation headed by Delegate F. M. Stover. It was a clear case of silver against gold, but the committee decided, without the formality of a ballot and practically by a unanimous vote, to seat the Stover or gold delegation.

##### Bryan Is Surprised.

This ended the contests for seats in the convention, as far as the National Committee was concerned. Mr. Bryan was somewhat surprised at the action in the Nebraska case, having been firmly of the opinion that the gold men had no show. When the result was announced, he said to a reporter:

"Well, we received more than the silver votes of the committee anyhow, and will be seated by the Committee on Credentials without question, because we have as clear a right to a place in the convention as the delegation of any State."

Ex-Postmaster General Don M. Dickinson was more than usually smiling and complacent when the vote upon the Michigan contest was announced to him. "You will notice," he remarked, "that Mr. Campau's motion to seat the silver delegates received only his own vote, and that the motion to give the gold delegates their seats was made by Charles S. Thomas, one of the leading silver members of the National Committee."

"What will be done in the convention about the matter?" Mr. Dickinson was asked.

"Oh, that's immaterial, quite immaterial," he replied airily, as he walked away.

##### Senator Hill Selected.

The committee then decided to recommend a temporary Chairman of the convention, and Mr. Clayton, the delegate from Alabama, nominated for that place Senator John W. Daniel of Virginia. He spoke briefly in support of his nomination, urging the committee to recognize the overwhelming majority in favor of free silver that was known to exist among the delegates to the convention, and at the close of his remarks he was loudly applauded.

Ex-Lieut. Gov. Sheehan of New-York presented the name of Senator David B. Hill, setting forth his capabilities as a presiding officer and his merits as a Democrat.

No other candidates being named, the committee proceeded to ballot, and Mr. Hill was chosen by a vote of 27 to 23.

Mr. Hill received the votes of the committeemen from the following States and Territories:

Connecticut, Delaware, Illinois, Indiana, Iowa, Kentucky, Maryland, Massachusetts, Minnesota, Mississippi, Missouri, Nebraska, New-Hampshire, New-Jersey, New-York, Ohio, Oregon, Pennsylvania, Rhode Island, South Dakota, Tennessee, Texas, Vermont, Washington, West Virginia, Wisconsin, and Alaska—27.

Committeemen from the following States and Territories voted for Senator Daniel: Alabama, Arkansas, California, Colorado, Florida, Georgia, Idaho, Kansas, Maine, Michigan, Montana, Nevada, North Carolina, North Dakota, South Carolina, Virginia, Wyoming, Arizona, New-Mexico, Oklahoma, Utah, Indian Territory, and the District of Columbia—23.

James Jeffries, the committeeman from Louisiana, was not recorded as voting. His support had been expected by the friends of Senator Hill.

##### The Silver "Bluff."

After the result of the vote had been announced, the only exciting incident of the afternoon occurred. Mr. Thomas of Colorado rose and stated that he had been assigned to the unpleasant task of notifying the committee that in case the Senator from New-York was selected as the choice of the majority, that a minority report would be made, and the name of John W. Daniel of Virginia would be presented to the convention as a substitute. Mr. Thomas said:

The views of the Senator from New-York on the currency question are at variance with these of a majority of delegates to the convention. He stands as the representative of the Eastern gold men. We have been informed by the press that these men have sent delegations here to influence the action of the convention, and statements have been made by these men in the press, and at public meetings which they have held in this city that they will agree to no compromise, and will spare no effort to accomplish their end. We would say to them that the majority will accept no compromise, and also will spare no effort to secure their purpose, which is to name a man in accord with their views. They do not desire to work in secret, but to fight in the open, and therefore notify the committee that a minority report will be presented with John W. Daniel named for temporary Chairman of the convention, and they will ask that this deliberative body be permitted to select a presiding officer who is in accord with the views of the majority.

In conclusion, Mr. Thomas asked Chairman Harrity, in view of the statement that had been made, what kind of reception the silver men might expect to be accorded to a motion to substitute the minority for the majority report.

Mr. Harrity responded with promptness and some feeling that such a reflection upon the Chairman as was implied in the question was not justified. He was only the organ of the committee, and should endeavor to discharge the duties that were incumbent upon him with absolute impartiality and a strict regard for the rights of the members.

##### Sheehan Makes a Speech.

Mr. Thomas disclaimed any intention to reflect in the slightest degree upon the Chairman of the committee.

Lieut. Gov. Sheehan followed Mr. Thomas in an impassioned speech, which evoked applause at intervals from the gold men on the committee. He said:

I recall that four years ago, sitting in this very room, then, as now, members of the Democratic National Committee, Mr. Thomas and I labored and voted side by side to secure the nomination as temporary Chairman of the convention, about to assemble, of William C. Owens of Kentucky. Mr. Owens, it is well known, was opposed to the nomination of the man who, as developments afterward proved, was the choice of an overwhelming majority of that convention. We were successful then, as I remember, by about the same vote as that by which the committee to-day has determined to recommend the selection of the Senator from New-York. But, as I also remember, there was on that occasion no Democrat so disloyal to the only existing National Democratic organization as to even suggest to the convention that it repudiate the judgment and overturn the decision of the National Committee. On the eve of the gathering of the next National Convention, such action as that outlined in the declaration of Mr. Thomas will establish a most dangerous precedent, and those who support him in the attitude that he has assumed must be responsible for whatever may occur, for which their acts may be taken as an example.

Mr. Sheerin, Secretary of the committee, was named as temporary Secretary of the convention and John I. Martin as Sergeant at Arms.

This completed the business before the committee, and at 5:45 P. M. it adjourned, subject to the call of the Chairman.

##### Mr. Hill Unmoved.

The moment the vote on the temporary Chairmanship was announced, Don M. Dickinson, who was in the committee room, rushed out, and, tearing down the corridor to Senator Hill's room, which was at the extreme end of the hall, announced the result. Mr. Hill received the news in his usual impassive way. Gathered in the room at the time were ex-Secretary Whitney, ex-Gov. Flower, Smith M. Weed, and others. All congratulated the Senator on his selection. Mr. Whitney and the other gentlemen had been waiting to hear from the National Committee on the temporary Chairmanship question, and on the announcement of the result left the Senator's room. Mr. Hill was asked if he was satisfied with the result of the vote.

"Oh," said the Senator, with a shrug of his shoulders, "I don't care anything about it; it makes no difference to me one way or the other."

"Will you prepare a speech as temporary Chairman?" was asked.

"Well, now," said Mr. Hill, "I don't think I will, for divers reasons. What's the use of preparing a speech I may not have a chance to deliver?"

"Do you think the convention will refuse to accept the National Committee's recommendation?"

"I don't know. It's hard to tell what the enemy will do under the circumstances. I am prepared for anything that is possible to happen."

#### SOUND-MONEY MEN PLEASED.

##### Action of Committee in Naming Mr. Hill Satisfies Them.

CHICAGO, July 6.—The action of the National Committee in selecting Senator Hill for temporary Chairman and in seating the Michigan and Nebraska gold delegates was applauded by every sound-money man here. Perry Belmont, who arrived to-day and who is at the Palmer House, and Don M. Dickinson expressed great gratification at the result.

"If we had a few more days we might do much more," said Mr. Dickinson.

John D. Crimmins said: "The work of the National Committee to-day was a victory for sound money at every point. The selection of Senator Hill is a most excellent one and it is good politics. It will put the silver men in the position of being the first to bolt from party customs if they override the recommendation of the committee. Sound money did well to-day, but to-morrow—oh, to-morrow!"

"There is a great deal of satisfaction on all sides among the sound-money men over the selection of Senator Hill for temporary Chairman," said ex-Mayor Thomas F. Gilroy to-night. "If he is not elected, and if the silver men offer to affront so prominent a party leader and so able a Democratic leader as Senator Hill, the silver men will injure their cause distinctly among the sensible conservative Democrats of the country. I have heard that the silver men propose to defeat Senator Hill. I cannot understand that kind of politics."

#### TRAMP CHASED WITH AN ENGINE.

##### He and His Confederates Had Tried to Hold Up a Train.

ELIZABETH, N. J., July 6.—A gang of tramps undertook to hold up a west-bound Pennsylvania Railroad freight train to-night as it was running from Waverly to Elizabeth.

They assaulted a brakeman and drew a revolver on the engineer. The police here were notified, and the train stopped when it reached this city. Detectives McGrail and Decker and Officer Bishop grappled with some of the gang, and, after a sharp scrimmage, overpowered two of them.

Another fellow ran along the high railroad trestle. Detective Decker gave chase, but the tramp would have escaped had not the engineer, cutting loose from the train, joined in the pursuit. The detective, who had fired twice at the fugitive without effect, boarded the engine when it reached him, and was rapidly overhauling the tramp. He then plunged from the trestle down the high embankment and fled into the heart of the city. A crowd joined in the pursuit, and he was finally cornered. He showed fight, and tried to draw a pistol on the detective, who stunned him with a blow that broke the butt of the officer's revolver.

#### LAY TOGETHER WITH THROATS CUT

##### Triple Murder or a Double Murder and Suicide in Marion.

PALMYRA, N. Y., July 6.—The little village of Marion, four miles north of this place, is excited over what may prove to be a triple murder or a case of murder and suicide.

This morning the neighbors, noticing no stir around the residence of Frank O. Murdoff, broke open the door and found Mr. and Mrs. Murdoff stretched out upon a bed with their throats cut. Life was not extinct, but they are both unconscious. Search being made for their daughter, she was found in bed, unconscious from some drug, supposed to be chloroform.

Nothing had been stolen, apparently, from the house, so the robbery and murder theory does not seem plausible. Mr. Murdoff seemed to be contented, and had no financial troubles.

The three persons were still alive, though insensible, to-night.

##### Menagerie Gets a Cinnamon Bear.

Director Smith of the Central Park Menagerie yesterday received a cinnamon bear cub named Knuttsford, from Primrose & West's Minstrels. The cub is now about two months old, and was captured about ten miles from Salt Lake City by George W. Holmes, who was compelled to kill the mother. It was presented to Primrose & West by Holmes while the minstrels were in Salt Lake City in April, and traveled with the company to California.

##### George Law Very Ill.

George Law is seriously ill at his home, 259 Fifth Avenue, and is not expected to live. He was taken ill three weeks ago and acute meningitis developed. For the past three days he has been unconscious. He has been attended by Drs. Bourke and Gouley, who, yesterday, called in Dr. Janeway for consultation. At an early hour this morning it was said that Mr. Law's death was a question of only a few hours.

##### The July Grand Jury.

The July Grand July was sworn in yesterday in Part I., General Sessions, by Recorder Goff, who charged it, without mentioning any specific matter requiring investigation.

Frederick Wagner, 8 Union Square, was made foreman.

## NEW-YORKERS ARE FIRM

### WILL MAKE THE BEST FIGHT POSSIBLE TO SAVE THE PARTY.

### Mr. Whitney Will Take a Seat in the Convention—Preparation Made for a Hasty Meeting to Decide on Bolting—Mr. Sheehan Again Chosen as National Committeeman—Ex-Gov. Flower Will Be Chairman of the Delegation.

CHICAGO, July 6.—Ex-Secretary Whitney will sit as a delegate in the convention after all. At a meeting of the New-York delegation to-night at the Auditorium Hotel he was substituted in place of Ashbel P. Fitch of New-York City. Mr. Whitney was present at the delegation meeting and made no objection to the proceeding.

The meeting of the New-Yorkers was held at 8 o'clock, and while it did not settle any question of the attitude which the State will take, it listened to reports of the work of the sound-money men since they came here, and had a tone which was decidedly in favor of maintaining the fight as long as possible.

On the question of a bolt or of a refusal to take part in the proceedings after a silver candidate has been nominated, the only reply to be had is the one which Senator Hill made at the first meeting of the gold men last week:

"We will cross that bridge when we come to it."

The Tammany delegates have had some advice to-day from the leaders who are not of that organization to consider if it were not their duty to the party to withhold any support from the free-silver heresy. But the disposition of the Tammany man is to bolt nothing that has the stamp of regularity upon it.

The meeting of the New-Yorkers attracted a crowd that filled the Auditorium parlors. The session was executive, and continued for about three hours, in which time a great deal of routine work was transacted.

William F. Sheehan, the member of the Democratic National Committee, was chosen as his own successor. It has been reported that he did not want another term. But after consultation, the delegation asked him to serve. He was re-elected without opposition.

Ex-Gov. Flower was made Chairman of the delegation. He took the chair at once, presiding over the subsequent deliberations of the meeting. Representative George B. McClellan was made Secretary. The following were selected to serve on the Convention Committees:

Smith M. Weed—Credentials.
Senator Hill—Resolutions.
Frederic R. Coudert—Organization.
Elliot Danforth—To notify the Presidential candidate of his nomination.
Clinton D. Beckwith—To notify the Vice Presidential candidate.
J. D. Bell—Honorary Vice President.

Ex-Lieut. Gov. Sheehan gave a detailed account of the action of the National Committee during the day with reference to the contests from Michigan, Indiana, and Ohio, and in selecting Senator Hill as the candidate of the gold men for temporary Chairman.

"Is there any precedent for a convention's refusal to ratify the selection made by a National Committee?" asked De Lancey Nicoll.

"No, there is none, so far as I know, and this was admitted by silver men in the room of the National Committee to-day," replied Mr. Sheehan.

Smith M. Weed then gave a review of the work done by the gold men since their arrival here, and among other things he attributed the action of the National Committee in making Senator Hill the Chairman of the temporary organization to their influence.

"What will be done?" was asked, "if the convention decides to overturn the action of the National Committee?"

Gov. Flower replied that the delegates were commissioned by the State to represent the State as Democrats, and it would be proper for the delegation to stand by the party so long as Democratic principles prevailed.

Senator Grady presented a resolution, worded in sarcastic terms, expressing the thanks of the delegation to the National Committee for its action in selecting Senator Hill for temporary Chairman, and not overriding the wishes of the New-York delegates. The resolution was adopted.

There was considerable informal discussion of the action the sound-money men should take if the silverites attempted to carry through any of the extreme measures which have been discussed as a part of the programme. No formal action was taken further than the implication contained in an announcement, which evidently contemplates a quick conference during a recess of the convention to determine a line of policy. This was that arrangements had been made to hold a conference to-morrow at the Washington Park Clubhouse, which is but a short distance from the convention hall, "in case a conference is needed."

#### TAMMANY MEN ARRIVE.

##### Braves Are Few and Remarkably Undemonstrative—for Them.

CHICAGO, July 6.—Tammany's special train arrived in two sections at 10:30 o'clock this morning, and the Tigers made their entry on the convention scene as quietly as so many lambs. There was no hurry about their coming. There were fewer than 200 of them, the smallest number of braves that have attended a National Convention in the last twenty years.

The special train traveled as one section of ten cars until Buffalo was reached, when two sections of five cars each were made of the train. One section came over the Lake Shore and the other over the Michigan Central. They arrived here within a few moments of each other, and by 11 o'clock all the braves were in the lobby of the Auditorium, having their rooms assigned to them. "Wiskinskie" Daniel M. Donegan was invited behind the desk by the clerks and he assigned the rooms.

Tammany had not been in town ten minutes when there was a great demand for its badge. This is the neatest badge here. From a gold-rimmed bar, which is inscribed "Tammany," depends a miniature American flag, to which is attached a portrait of Tammany, the Indian chief from whom the organization derives its name. On the reverse of this is a star, the Democratic State emblem, surrounded by the words, "Chicago, July 7, 1896." "Wiskinskie" Donegan could not immediately supply the demand for the badges, because he had lost his trunk temporarily. Later in the day he found it, and several hundred badges were distributed.

The braves had some sport on their way here. Those in the first section concluded that they ought to bring a candidate with them to Chicago who could not be accused of being crazy on the silver question, so they posted this sign upon the car windows:

For President—Tom Dunn.
For Vice President—Tim Sullivan.
Platform: Don't sell bonds. Give them away.

Mr. Dunn is the leader of the Twenty-sixth Assembly District. He took the joke good naturedly, and when he arrived here he was hailed as "President Tom."

A New-Yorker who met Mr. Dunn, said, as he shook hands with him: "Well, Tom, mighty glad there is one sane candidate for President here anyway."

"I'll tell you what I'll do when I'm President," said Mr. Dunn, "I'll annex Ireland."

Most of the Tammany leaders came in on the special train. The party included John C. Sheehan, Senator Jacob A. Cantor, Congressman George B. McClellan, Congressmen Sulzer and Walsh, Aldermen Kennefick, Campbell, and Brown, Assemblyman Andrews, ex-Sheriff John B. Sexton, ex-Police Justices Daniel F. McMahon and Patrick Divver, William Pitt Mitchell, Register Sohmer, and County Clerk Purroy.

Three Tammany men who were conspicuous here four years ago are absentees this year. Richard Croker and W. Bourke Cockran have long since fallen out with each other. They are both now in Europe. The other absentee is William H. Clark, the ex-Corporation Counsel, who was one of the advisers the Wigwam had in 1892. He remained in New-York City this year. There is some coolness between him and some of the present leaders of Tammany, which prevents one of the best of Tammany's advisers from taking an active part in its affairs at present.

#### STALWART JERSEYMEN.

##### They Stand Like a Rock for Sound Money—All Good Fighters.

CHICAGO, July 6.—The New-Jersey delegates met in their headquarters at the Auditorium Annex this morning, and were serenaded. They did not know whether to take this as a compliment or not, for when the big bass drum was turned so that the inscription could be read it was learned that the music was by Hobart's Band, a musical organization from one of the Western States.

The Jerseymen remarked that they could not be alarmed by music by any Hobart band in existence, and then they held a meeting to determine on committee members and officers for the convention.

Senator James Smith, Jr., was selected as a member of the National Committee to succeed Miles Ross. This was by unanimous action and without a struggle. Allan L. McDermott was made Chairman of the delegation and W. D. Edwards Secretary. Henry D. Winton was selected for the Committee on Rules, E. P. Meaney for Credentials, George A. Helme for Permanent Organization, J. J. Bergen for honorary Vice President of the convention, and G. K. Krueger to act on the Committee of Notification. The delegation then had a brief discussion as to candidates, and adjourned until the afternoon.

The Jerseymen were positive on two or three questions. They expressed themselves as in favor of the two-thirds rule in making nominations, and on any proposition from the silverites to abrogate that rule they profess to be ready to make a prolonged fight. They also are in favor of a protracted fight for a sound-money platform. With these two propositions before them, they went out to ascertain what was to be the programme of the sound-money men.

They met again in caucus at 4 o'clock, and for two hours were in session, preserving the utmost secrecy as to what was going on. While they were there they received a delegation from Pennsylvania, headed by John J. Curley of Philadelphia, who came to urge the claims of ex-Gov. Robert Pattison.

The Jerseymen assured the Pennsylvanians that they had come here without a candidate, and that they were opposed to each and every one who was being boomed by the free-silverites, and with this encouraging information Mr. Curley went away fairly well satisfied.

The Jerseymen then discussed whether or not they should declare for any candidate until the programme of the sound-money men should be known fully, and, so far as they committed themselves after the meeting, no absolute action was taken.

One of the delegates said that the delegation was not prepared to announce any choice, because it did not know what it would do if a silver platform should be adopted. If the time should come when the delegates should feel that they could participate in the nomination of a candidate they would prefer Pattison to any one yet in the field.

The delegation considered for some time the Michigan contest, and after learning the merits of the case passed a resolution instructing Mr. Meaney, its member of the Committee on Credentials, to favor the regular delegation as against the contestants, whom the silverites were proposing to bring into the field, expressing the opinion that on all the facts in the case the regulars were entitled beyond question to sit in the convention.

The delegation also expressed itself as in favor—first, last, and all the time—of maintaining the two-thirds rule. The delegation is thus formally in line with the programme of the sound-money men.

#### CONNECTICUT ALL RIGHT.

##### Her Delegation Wants No Nonsense as to the Money Question.

CHICAGO, July 6.—The Connecticut delegation met at its headquarters, in the Palmer House, this morning and perfected its organization. Ex-Gov. Thomas M. Waller is Chairman and ex-Judge Lynde Harrison will serve on the Committee on Resolutions. Mr. Harrison will have several suggestions to make to that committee, and he will make it clear that Connecticut wants no nonsense on the money question. The delegation will cast its vote every time and on all propositions for sound money.

Ex-Congressman Carlos French has been re-elected as National Committeeman.

Ex-Gov. Waller is co-operating with the gold men in every way possible. If the conditions here were different and there was any chance of nominating a sound-money man, Connecticut would push Mr. Waller for the Presidency. The Connecticut delegation is made up as follows:

Delegates at Large—Miles B. Preston of Hartford, Lynde Harrison of New-Haven, Thomas M. Waller of New-London, and James Aldiss of Torrington.

District Delegates—E. D. Coogan, William Kennedy, Cyrus G. Beckwith, M. J. Houlihan, F. A. Morrell, C. P. Lyman, H. R. Butler, and L. Tinger.

Charles H. Fowler of New-Haven is one of the alternates.

The Connecticut men wear blue badges with the State coat-of-arms at the top, and over the coat-of-arms a nutmeg.

Alexander Troup of New-Haven, a free-silver advocate who ran for delegate and was defeated, is here working with the silver men. He favors Senator Daniel for President. Mr. Troup is editor of The New-Haven Union, and was Collector of Internal Revenue in President Cleveland's first Administration.

#### TELEGRAPHIC BREVITIES.

—Mrs. Adolf Menard and her daughter, Eva, were terribly burned by an explosion of a gasoline stove at their home, Northampton, Mass., yesterday. The daughter, who was eighteen years of age, died from the effects of her injuries. She had attempted to replenish the fluid without extinguishing the jets which were burning. The flames ignited the clothing of the girl. Her mother ran to her assistance, and her clothing also became ignited. Their screams brought neighbors to the house, and both were found on the floor with their clothing burned off, their faces blackened, and their hands and lower limbs badly burned. Mrs. Menard's condition is critical.

—The trial of Samuel C. Carpenter, accused of murdering his paramour, Mrs. Rachel Blackwell, in Phillipsburg, N. J., will be begun to-day in Belvidere, N. J. Carpenter is a wealthy man, and has been the most prominent citizen in Asbury, Warren County, N. J.

—The safe in the office of the Nelson Morris Beef Company, Hudson, N. Y., was blown open, with powerful explosives early Sunday morning by burglars and about $75 taken.

## THE SILVER FANATICS ARE INVINCIBLE

### Wild, Raging, Irresistible Mob Which Nothing Can Turn from Its Abominable Foolishness.

### SOUND-MONEY MEN SURELY DOOMED TO DEFEAT

### They, However, Have Won in the Encounter Before the National Committee—Hill Named for Temporary Chairman.

### ALL THE CONTESTS ALSO DECIDED IN THEIR FAVOR

### Improbable, However, that They Will Enjoy Their Triumph Long—Silverites Say Mr. Hill Shall Not Take the Gavel—No Doubt They Are Strong Enough To Make Their Word Good.

CHICAGO, July 6.—The fight between the opposition of free silver and the infatuated devotees of a debased coinage began this afternoon with a skirmish in the National Committee, out of which the sound-money men came victors.

Upon the eve of the convention the sound-money forces are standing shoulder to shoulder, calm, resolute, knowing their rights and prepared to assert and defend them. The silver men are united in a demand for a free-silver plank and candidate. Upon the make-up of the ticket they are scattered widely. Bland leads, with less than 300 votes that he can call his own; Boies comes next with less than 200 delegates committed and doubtful. After these come McLean, Matthews, Stevenson, Pennoyer, Bryan, White, and Teller, all silver candidates, and Pattison, the sound-money candidate, who will be worked for, unless all the sound-money men shall be forced, out of self-respect and a sense of obligation to their constituents, to abandon the convention.

Two features of to-day's work were interesting. One was the adoption by the Bland men of the old Blaine tactics of throwing their man into prominence. This was in the face of a strong and openly expressed Southern hostility to Bland, upon the reasonable ground that he is not fitted by natural ability and training for the office of President. The Southern opposition was supported by furious but unworthy attacks upon Bland by Democrats who had discovered an objection to him in the fact that his wife and daughter were Roman Catholics. This attack did not appear to do Bland as much harm as the more reasonable and justifiable objection offered by the Southern men, who coupled their opposition to Bland with advocacy of the nomination of Teller.

A most remarkable effort is that being made here for Teller. It is directed by the Democratic and Republican associates of Teller in the Senate, and by a throng of Populists who marshal most enticing arrays of figure to show that Teller, a Republican and protectionist, would be a much more available opponent of McKinley than any Democrat in all the forty-five States.

With more than 300 delegates still in doubt as to whom they will vote for, even on the first ballot, it is plain enough that it is anybody's race. Any one of the men mentioned to-day, or none of them, may be nominated. The controlling Democrats of the convention are in such confusion and so absorbed by the one prevailing sentiment, that it would not be surprising if a whirl should be created for Teller and the convention stampeded to him after a brief struggle by the Bland and Boies men to prevent a repetition of the unfortunate experiences of 1872.

The Democratic sound-money and "slush-money" forces will have their first great encounter to-morrow, soon after the National Convention shall have been called to order by Chairman Harrity. It will come on the very first motion, before the prayer of the Chaplain has ceased echoing through the vast hall. Following an old custom, rarely departed from in National or State Conventions, the National Committee selected Senator David B. Hill as temporary Chairman. With a confidence that was not justified, it was assumed that the committee would be affected by the noisy and dictatorial silver crowd, and that a majority would be obtained for Senator John W. Daniel, chosen to be the leader of the free-silver forces. By a majority vote—slender, it is true, but sufficient—the National Committee named Hill instead of Daniel.

This action was the last and most interesting one of a long session of the committee, during which the silver men were beaten in every contention in which the sound-money men were interested. With a fatuity that seems to characterize all the attempts of the silver men, they insisted upon submitting the Michigan contests on the merits, and expressed their willingness to abide by the decision of the committee. So clearly did the Stevenson or gold delegation establish its right to seats that the committee voted to seat it, thus taking the ground from under the Michigan silverites, and furnishing the gold-standard men with the very opportunity they sought for.

The silver men may undertake to undo the work that has been done. Resort to unusual or harsh methods will give the minority an excuse for resenting a high-handed course, and may increase the excitement that promises to be an inevitable condition of to-morrow's session.

Vice President Stevenson's friends made an effort last night to sneak their favorite into the circus "under the canvas." As a forlorn hope, it was not conducted with conspicuous brilliancy, and it does not promise to be followed by success. It was not to much purpose that he had waited until July 5, 1896, to assert, very timidly, that he owed an election to Congress in 1878 to his advocacy of free coinage, when silver hardly was an issue before the country. Stevenson might be nominated; but the chances for him are not as good as they were four years ago. His own State, under the control of Altgeld, has not a word for him; Teller would be preferred to Stevenson by the Altgeld crowd.

With about 300 votes with which to meet about 600, it is inevitable that the sound-money men must be beaten. Whether they shall be beaten or be successful, they already have accomplished a great part of the task undertaken for the party. Mr. Whitney expressed the general opinion of all the sound-money men when he said to-night: "We came here to enter a protest against the adoption of a course that must, if persisted in, inflict incalculable harm to the Democratic Party. We have protested. We shall protest until we are no longer entitled to be heard. That is all there is in it."

Not exactly all, perhaps, because Mr. Whitney shares with most of his resolute friends the conviction that in a convention that resorts to all methods short of personal violence to suppress a minority because it represents a part of the country that cannot understand or accept the free-coinage lunacy, the time may come when it may be necessary for the Eastern delegates to withdraw, to report their action to their constituents and to trust to them for the justification that they are convinced they will have won.

The non-participation plan among the Eastern delegates does not promise to be adhered to by all the sound-money delegates. Pennsylvania has a candidate in ex-Gov. Pattison. If the State should determine to present him and vote for him the delegates would be regarded as bound to abide by the action in which they should participate, although Mr. Pattison should not be nominated. Should the other Eastern delegates remain in the convention, it is probable that their votes would be cast for Pattison.

It is expected that an animated debate will follow the motion by Chairman Harrity that Senator Hill be the temporary Chairman and the proposition from the minority of the National Committee that Senator Daniel's name be substituted. Such a debate took place in the Republican National Convention of 1884 here in Chicago. The National Committee then offered Powell Clayton of Arkansas as temporary Chairman, as representing the Blaine men. Henry Cabot Lodge, for the Arthur and Edmunds opposition, moved to substitute the name of John R. Lynch of Mississippi. There was a long debate then, and Lynch was chosen by forty majority, the National Committee being beaten.

To-morrow's debate will afford the sound-money men the opportunity they have contended for, in the preliminary struggle, to set forth the grounds of their opposition to the course indicated by the Populistic Democrats. There is no lack here of men of ability as speakers to express the convictions of the Eastern men, with whom the West is anxious to part company. Some of the most vigorous and convincing of the sound-money men are Western men who do not share the insane aversion of the East that has been cultivated until it has produced a new sectionalism quite as intense as any that ever has affected the country or menaced the integrity and success of a party.

The statement is made late to-night that the silver men have concluded not to try to unseat the sound-money delegates from Michigan. Committeeman Thomas of Colorado and other rabid silver men say they will have votes enough without trying to steal any. The sound-money leaders are puzzled to know where the votes are to come from. To many here it is clear that if the sound-money men should stand together they could dictate the nomination of any one not connected with the sound-money movement.

The silver men would like to know whether the sound-money men will take this responsibility. The question adds to the worriment of silver leaders. Senator Hill is not bothered by the declaration

"All the News That's Fit to Print."

# The New York Times.

LATE CITY EDITION
U. S. Weather Bureau Report (Page 54) forecasts:
Mostly sunny, chance of showers.
Clear tonight. Cloudy tomorrow.
Temp. range: 88—68; yesterday: 90—69.

VOL. XLV....NO. 14,007. NEW-YORK, SATURDAY, JULY 11, 1896.—TWO PARTS—TWELVE PAGES.— COPYRIGHTED, 1896, BY THE NEW-YORK TIMES PUBLISHING CO. PRICE THREE CENTS.

## BOLT OF NEW-YORKERS

### Announce They Will Not Support the Ticket.

### NO FREE SILVER FOR THEM

#### Outspoken and Vigorous Denunciation of the Chicago Platform.

#### NOTHING OF DEMOCRACY IN IT.

#### Ex-Mayor Grant, ex-Gov. Flower, ex-Lieut. Gov. Sheehan, De Lancey Nicoll Among the Bolters.

#### REVOLTS ALL OVER THE COUNTRY

#### Democratic Leaders and Influential Democratic Newspapers Repudiate Bryan and Populism.

CHICAGO, July 10.—Several of the New-York delegates have bolted the ticket. They will have none of it. They repudiate it absolutely.

As a rule, the Tammany delegates simply say they will not decide on a course of action until they shall consult their constituents. Some of them, however, are so disgusted that they openly announce their opposition to the ticket.

While no official announcement of Tammany's policy has been made, there are many indications that the leaders of the Wigwam have decided that their Congressional, Assembly and local candidates shall be nominated on strong sound-money platforms. This probably will be done, no matter what action the State organization may take. Mr. Sheehan and the other Tammany managers are now undoubtedly awaiting a communication from Richard Croker before announcing a line of policy.

Following are declarations made to-day by prominent New-York Democrats:

EX-MAYOR GRANT—I will not support the ticket, and I will not take any part in any conference looking to its support. The platform is repudiation. There is no Democracy in it. It is absolutely dishonest.

EX-LIEUT. GOV. SHEEHAN, New-York's Member of the National Committee—In my opinion, the action of this convention in the construction of the platform will wreck the Democratic Party.

FREDERIC R. COUDERT, Delegate at Large—Have we not condemned ourselves to silence? There is a parable in this: "Silence is golden; speech is silver."

CONGRESSMAN GEORGE B. McCLELLAN, District Delegate—The work of the convention has resulted in an immoral and dishonest platform. It departed absolutely from the real spirit of the Democratic Party. It is not Democracy. It is my firm conviction that within sixty days most of those who were instrumental in the wicked work of this convention will be heartily ashamed of it.

COMMISSIONER GEORGE WALTON GREEN, District Delegate—I certainly shall not support this ticket. How can any honest man support it? When I came out here I felt that the ticket nominated here on a silver platform might be elected. I felt that the country stood in that grave danger; but now I feel immensely relieved, for I believe that other outrageous planks in the platform will so astound and disgust the people of the country that the silver craze will be checked and the ticket will go down to ignominious defeat. From the standpoint of the safety of the country, the conditions are very much better now than they were before the convention completed its miserable business.

Anarchy, Socialism, and Tillmanism have held full riot, and thereby have called the people to their own defense. All the revolting "isms" of the day have been put into this hodge-podge platform, and true Democratic doctrines have been left out.

EX-SECRETARY WHITNEY—I have nothing to say now. Personally, I may express my views at another time. The New-York delegates have not taken the responsibility of deciding upon what is to be done in the future. That will be decided by the constituents of the delegates.

EX-DISTRICT ATTORNEY DE LANCEY NICOLL—New-York State will go Republican by at least 200,000 plurality, and I believe that Indiana, Illinois, and Ohio will give heavy Republican pluralities. I am of the opinion that nothing can stop the formation of a third party, into which sound-money Democrats will go. It is doubtful whether the sound-money Democrats will nominate Electoral tickets in all of the States, for it might not be expedient to do so; but they will be nominated in those States in which it is necessary to have a ticket for Democrats to rally around who otherwise might be tempted to vote for the silver ticket. I don't think that any one has yet decided what States the third Electoral tickets should be nominated in. That will be decided after a comparison of views has been had. We have an organization already perfected, as a result of the sound-money conferences here in Chicago.

I would rather cut my right hand off than vote for this ticket. I would not vote it if Senator Hill was running on such a platform. I would not vote for it if I was the only man in New-York to vote against it.

CONGRESSMAN FRANKLIN BARTLETT, District Delegate—In a platform that is so full of wicked and pernicious things it is somewhat difficult to pick out at once the worst feature, but the thing that impresses me as the worst feature is that which assails the Supreme Court of the United States.

This section of the platform proposes to reverse the judgment of the Court of Last Resort by the action of Congress. Of course, if the Federal Legislature, by majority vote, can destroy the Supreme Court of the United States, it follows that the Legislatures of the various States can destroy the supreme tribunals in their States

This means Anarchy.

It not only means the taking from us of our property, but the destruction of every safeguard, whether of life, liberty, or property.

Another base feature of the platform is that which attacks the executive power of preserving property and life by calling out the troops in case of riot and insurrection. Of course, in connection with the attack upon the Supreme Court, we must consider the declaration in favor of class legislation as provided for in the income-tax plank.

No nation can ever thrive by dishonesty and the attempt to repudiate 50 per cent. of the debts of the country at large is dishonest. I refer now, of course, to the silver coinage plank.

It strikes at the interest of every wage-earner in the country, because it seeks to reduce the purchasing power of the dollar one-half, and when the mechanics and laborers understand, as they will, that it will bring them no increase of wages and will lessen the purchasing power of their money to such an extent that their wages will buy but one-half the amount of the commodities they need they will rise up against this craze.

The people at large do not sympathize with any plot that strikes at property. I shall certainly not support the ticket.

ASSISTANT DISTRICT ATTORNEY JOHN F. M'INTYRE—The policy of New-York Democrats in the coming campaign should in my judgment be the nomination of hard-money candidates for Congress, so that all our energies could be bent in the direction of their election alone. With their aid in Congress, silver legislation might be defeated and the faith and credit of the Nation preserved.

DANIEL S. LOCKWOOD of Buffalo—I want to be quoted as saying that I don't propose to vote for or to support this ticket in any way.

EX-GOV. FLOWER—The nominee fits the platform. There can be no doubt what the one or the other means. Both go well together, and neither is better nor worse than the other.

CHAIRMAN HINKLEY of the Democratic State Committee of New-York—It is our policy to wait until we reach New-York before we come to conclusions. When we we reach home and have a little time for consideration, we will act.

GEN. TRACY of Albany left yesterday in disgust. He will not support the ticket.

PERRY BELMONT will not support the ticket.

#### MUST HAVE A NEW TICKET.

##### Ex-Gov. Waller Reviews the Proceedings at Chicago.

CHICAGO, July 10.—Ex-Gov. Waller of Connecticut to-day said:

"The action of this convention has left only one course for the sound-money men to pursue. They must, if they desire to hold the Democratic Party together in the East, call a convention and nominate a man upon the gold platform. The convention assembled here has sounded the death knell of free silver. Their high-handed method of procedure will be resented by Democrats generally. The silver men here have overridden themselves and left the way open for the gold men to bolt their nominees."

#### NEW-HAVEN PAPERS BOLT.

##### The News Urges Democrats to Nominate an Honest Ticket.

NEW-HAVEN, Conn., July 10.—It was announced by the editor of The Register tonight that the paper would not, under any circumstances, support the nominee or the platform of the Chicago Convention. The Morning News (Dem.) of this city will say to-morrow morning, editorially:

"Sound Democracy must repudiate the Populistic Chicago platform as anti-Democratic. We call upon the Democrats of this State to indorse the action of the ten Connecticut delegates who, acting with Hill and Whitney, declined to vote for any candidate to stand upon a platform of dishonesty and Socialism, and we exhort Democracy to all efforts to bring about the provision of a new ticket and a platform that honest Democrats can support."

#### WASHINGTON HESING WILL BOLT.

##### His Newspaper, the Staats-Zeitung, Represents Western Germans.

CHICAGO, July 10.—The Staats-Zeitung of Chicago, the leading German paper of the West, which has been an important aid to the Democratic Party of recent years, will bolt the ticket and the platform.

Washington Hesing, the editor and proprietor, said: "The Staats-Zeitung will bolt this ticket, but not until Saturday morning. We intend to let them nominate their candidates first, so that we can give the better reason for leaving the party.

"The Germans of the West, whom The Staats-Zeitung represents, have no sympathy with such a platform as was adopted to-day, and the paper speaking for them cannot honestly indorse it."

#### ALABAMA GOLD MEN DISGUSTED.

##### The Nomination of Bryan Is Not Favorably Received.

BIRMINGHAM, Ala., July 10.—The nomination of Bryan for President has not pleased Democrats at this place. Shortly after Bryan's speech at Jackson, Miss., last year, when he declared he would not support a gold-standard man for President, a remark which he reiterated at Mobile, he spoke in the Winnie Davis Wigwam in this city and for the third time in a week publicly stated that he would not vote for a gold candidate on a gold platform.

The business men of the community express the gravest apprehension of the results of placing such an arch silverite in the Executive chair, and many of them have asked the question, "Does the man who would not vote for a gold Democrat expect gold Democrats to vote for him?"

On the other hand, Populist State leaders express the greatest satisfaction at the result, saying Bryan is just such a man as they want. Silver Democrats say little.

#### LOUISVILLE PAPERS BOLT.

##### The Courier-Journal Wants Another Democratic Ticket.

LOUISVILLE, Ky., July 10.—The Courier-Journal will publish to-morrow morning an editorial article written by its acting editor in chief, Mr. Harrison Robertson, repudiating the action of the Chicago Convention. The Courier-Journal will say:

Such foolhardy and bastard leadership and such a radical revolution of the life principles of Democracy will be disowned by those Democrats whose subserviency to party form is not dictated by their desire to share in the official spoils of party success, and whose fealty to party organization means fidelity to the views for the advancement of which party is only the instrument.

Speaking of these Democrats, The Courier-Journal, whose whole existence has been spent in battle for Democracy, rejects the new faith of fiatism, repudiation, and Anarchy which the Chicago Convention has proclaimed as the Democratic creed, refuses to support the nominees, who have been in unprecedented convulsion of frenzy ordained the apostles of that faith, and calls upon true Democrats everywhere, sick at heart though they may be but undaunted and resolute, to stand forth for their cause and put out a ticket planted on a platform that shall embody alike the undying purpose and the immortal record of the Democratic Party, and shall, in these evil days of storm and wreck, shine a beacon and lower a bulwark for the salvation now and in the future of the party which was born with the birth throes of the Republic and which must live as long as the spirit of the Republic shall survive.

Let a Democratic convention be called; let a Democratic organization be perfected; let a Democratic ticket be nominated on a Democratic platform, and let a Democratic campaign, thorough, zealous, unflagging, be made in every State in the Union until the November polls shall have closed.

We shall not elect that ticket, but we shall save many a sound-money Democrat to Congress; we shall prove the right of the Democratic Party to continue in existence, and with the crash of the impious fabric which the fever-brained insurgents at Chicago have erected under the Democratic flag we shall survive with a compact, intelligent, and vigorous organization—the nucleus, the instrument, and the guarantor of a regenerated and reinvigorated Democracy, chastened, strengthened, and in the end dominant for the Nation's good in the century to come as it has been in the century that is history.

The Evening Post, also an important Democratic newspaper, will bolt to-morrow, repudiating the nomination of Bryan and the platform of the Chicago Convention.

#### FOR CAUTIOUS DELIBERATION.

##### Albany Argus Advises Democrats to Wait for the State Convention.

ALBANY, July 10.—The Argus to-morrow will say editorially:

Stand firm; this is a time that tries men's souls. Be not splenitive and rash. The Saratoga Convention which elected delegates to the Democratic National Convention at Chicago defined the views of the Democracy of the Empire State upon the great monetary question which is now agitating the people of the United States. The Democracy of New-York stand upon the Saratoga platform, and their delegates, acting as a unit under the instructions of the State Convention, have refused to accept the new declaration of principles formulated at Chicago and have refused to participate in nominating candidates to be the standard bearers of the new doctrine.

Our delegation has not bolted from the National Convention, but has maintained an attitude of reserve, and will report to the coming Democratic State Convention, which alone has authority to determine what shall be the course of the Democracy of the State of New-York. Individuals may act for themselves; independent journals may say what they please, but nobody has any authority to speak conclusively for the Democratic Party of the State except its duly elected representatives assembled in convention. Fortunately, a few weeks must elapse before that convention can be held, and there will be abundant time for calm deliberation and cool reflection.

We regret to see that several of our newspaper contemporaries, as well as a number of individual Democrats, are inclined to manifest their displeasure with the proceedings at Chicago by rashly threatening to bolt their party ties and even to co-operate with the traditional enemies of Democracy. Let them pause and reflect, as has been well said, "aside from the National contest, the Democracy of New-York have their State to redeem and have in their hands the weapons with which to make a successful fight. To this end they must keep their organization intact and their ranks unbroken. Democrats can, in the election of representatives to Congress, assert their convictions on the coinage question if not in the appointment of Presidential Electors."

The New-York delegation at Chicago have appointed a committee to prepare a statement for the public after the adjournment of the National Convention, setting forth the reasons for their attitude. An early State Convention will be held, and that convention will decide what the Democrats of this State shall do. Until then let every loyal Democrat be patient. Stand by the Democratic organization of New-York and abide by the decision of the coming State Convention, which will be composed of delegates freshly elected by the people, in full view of all the facts and circumstances, and authorized to express their will. That is the only wise, prudent, and safe course for every New-York Democrat to take.

##### A Watertown Dissenter.

WATERTOWN, N. Y., July 10.—B. G. Griffin, who was Chairman of the Executive Committee of the New-York State Democratic Committee in the Flower Gubernatorial campaign, announces that he will not vote for the nominee of the Chicago Convention. In an interview, he characterizes Tillman and Altgeld as "wretches," and says the platform is a mass of heresies and undemocratic theories. He hopes the Democrats will so vote as to effectually rebuke those who have brought about the present situation and purge the party of its obnoxious elements.

##### Syracuse Courier Objects.

SYRACUSE, N. Y., July 10.—The Syracuse Courier in an editorial to-morrow will decline to support Bryan on a platform so undemocratic as that of Chicago.

##### Will Go to McKinley.

BOSTON, July 10.—Collector Winslow Warren of the Port of Boston announced to-day that he would vote for McKinley. The action of the Chicago Convention has, he said, disgusted the Democrats of this State, two-thirds of whom, he said, will vote for McKinley and the other third will refrain from voting.

##### A Vermonter Protests.

CHICAGO, July 10.—William H. Creamer, one of the delegates from the Second Congressional District of Vermont, said: "Under no circumstances will I support this ticket. I am going home and bolt it. I hope that a new Democratic sound-money party will be formed without delay. I want none of this."

##### Put His Flag at Half Mast.

ELIZABETH, N. J., July 10.—When the news of the nomination of William J. Bryan at Chicago was received here this afternoon, the flag over the building occupied by The New-Jersey Herald, the only Democratic paper here, was lowered to half mast, and it continued to flutter there for the rest of the day. Dr. Reiner, the editor, when asked what his views on the nomination were, said the position of the flag indicated them.

##### Mississippi Democrats Cold.

JACKSON, Miss., July 10.—Bryan's nomination was received with no enthusiasm here. Even conservative free-silver Democrats express humiliation and chagrin, and some of them repudiate the platform. The gold standard advocates think a real National Democratic ticket should be put in the field, and business men, in the absence of such a ticket, will vote for McKinley. It will be remembered that it was in this city that Bryan stated, in response to a question, that he "would not vote the Democratic ticket, so help me God, if a gold standard plank" should be contained in the platform.

##### Connecticut Cannot Accept.

CHICAGO, July 10.—Lynde Harrison of Connecticut said to-night: "I cannot support the ticket on that platform. That is the position of the majority of Connecticut delegates. I do not believe that any man could be elected in this country on such a platform as that. Every sound-money man I met here was individually in favor of a Democratic sound-money party."

##### Repudiated by The Mobile Register.

MOBILE, Ala., July 10.—The Mobile Register, for seventy-five years a Democratic newspaper, has repudiated the nomination of the Chicago Convention.

##### Heavy Bail for Bicyclist Beggs.

David W. Beggs of 306 West Twenty-ninth Street was arraigned in Jefferson Market Court yesterday on a charge of assault. The complainant, Mrs. Mary Murphy, of 255 West Fifteenth Street, was not able to appear.

Mrs. Murphy was run down by Beggs, who was on a bicycle, at Eighth Avenue and Fifteenth Street. Her left ankle was fractured. Beggs told Magistrate Flammer that the collision was not due to his negligence. He was held in $1,000 for examination.

## TRIED TO KILL A WOMAN

### THEN JOHN GOLDEN THREW HIMSELF UNDER A TRAIN.

#### Death Came Instantly to Would-Be Murderer, While Catherine Havnor, Whom He Shot in the Head and Hand, May Recover—Tragedy Takes Place at One Hundred and Thirty-fifth Street Elevated Station in Eighth Avenue.

After a day's debauch and enraged by the action of Mrs. Catherine Havnor, John Golden, a conductor on the Sixth Avenue elevated road, fired three shots at the woman last night, and then, finding escape impossible, threw himself in front of a moving train. His body was ground to pieces.

The tragedy occurred about 8:30 o'clock at the One Hundred and Thirty-fifth Street elevated station, in Eighth Avenue. Golden had a holiday, and it was said that he had spent the greater part of the afternoon with Mrs. Havnor in a saloon near the station.

When they left the saloon in the evening, they walked to the down-town station. After they had deposited the tickets in the box, they walked to the south end of the platform, and it was noticed that they were engaged in earnest conversation. The couple was evidently quarreling about some matter, and when the woman, with an angry toss of her head, started to leave her companion, he was heard to say, "Katie, I want to speak to you."

Mrs. Havnor paid no attention to Golden's remark, but continued to walk toward the steps leading to the street. Golden, enraged by her refusal to listen to him, pursued her, leveled a revolver at her head, and fired. The bullet, true to its aim, struck the victim in the head, and she fell senseless to the floor of the platform.

Golden stood over the body and fired two more shots, but his aim was poor, and the bullets inflicted only slight wounds in the left hand.

Edward M. Kirk, the ticket taker, was standing with his back to the couple when the shots were fired. When he turned he saw the woman lying on the platform and Golden, with his weapon clutched in his right hand, standing over the prostrate form. Kirk attempted to seize Golden, and for a moment the two were engaged in a struggle while several others on the platform looked on horror-stricken.

Finally Golden freed himself from the grasp of his captor, and with a wild dash fell in front of Engine No. 332, which was just being brought to a stop at the station. The engine was moving slowly, but before it could be stopped Golden's body was beneath the wheels and his life had been crushed out.

After the third shot the woman had struggled to her feet, and while Kirk was engaged in the struggle with her would-be slayer she staggered into the women's waiting room and sank on one of the seats. At first she refused to give the police any information concerning her identity or her relations with Golden, but when threatened with arrest she told, amid her sobs, that her name was Catherine Havnor, and that she was the wife of Harvey Havnor, a barber who has two shops in the city, and lives at 460 West Thirty-fourth Street.

An ambulance was summoned and Mrs. Havnor was taken to the Manhattan Hospital. She was suffering greatly from shock, but the physicians announced late last night that her wounds were not serious, and that she would probably recover. She is thirty-one years old, while the would-be murderer was forty.

Golden was instantly killed. His body was frightfully mangled, and it was after nearly an hour's work and with the aid of jackscrews that it was taken from beneath the wheels. It was removed first to the One Hundred and Twenty-fifth Street Police Station, and afterward taken to undertaking rooms at 175 East Ninety-sixth Street.

The news of the tragedy spread rapidly, and within a few minutes a crowd of 1,000 people had congregated. Golden lived at 2,120 Eighth Avenue. He leaves a wife and a young son. Three weeks ago he buried his father, and a short time before that his youngest child died.

The scene at the station when Golden's wife arrived was most pathetic. When she saw the body of her husband she wept bitterly and finally became hysterical.

Coroner Dobbs, who had been summoned, took the statement of Kirk and then went to the hospital to take Mrs. Havnor's statement. The physicians said she was suffering too much from shock, and her testimony will be taken at the inquest.

The police were inclined to believe that Golden jumped on the tracks with the intention of making his escape, but those who saw the leap believe that it was made with suicidal intent.

Golden had been in the employ of the elevated railroad company about ten years. Some of his acquaintances among the employes said they had frequently seen him in the company of the woman whose life he sought to take.

## CHILDREN SAVED FROM DROWNING.

#### Two Rescued from the East River and One in Central Park.

While smoking his pipe on the pier at the foot of East Seventy-eighth Street at 7:30 o'clock last night, Joseph Larkin, a plasterer living at 1,357 Avenue A, heard a splash in the water and the screams of two small children. He threw his pipe overboard and his coat on the pier, and after seeing where the children were, dived into the water. He reached the children as they were sinking for the second time. He returned to the shore with them quickly, a great crowd cheering him, and they were taken to their home, at 451 East Eightieth Street.

Mrs. Mary Lebendig of 137 Pearl Street took her daughter Annie, twelve years old, to Central Park yesterday, and while there on the edge of the lake at a point near Eighth Avenue and Seventy-seventh Street at 6 o'clock P. M., the child fell into the water. Mrs. Lebendig sprang into the water at once to save her child, and Park Policeman John H. Kelly followed her. The policeman soon had mother and child safe on shore. They were taken to the Presbyterian Hospital and afterward went to their home.

##### A Summernight's Festival.

An event in the amusement world of the week will be the first Summernight's festival given at the Grand Central Palace Roof Garden, Lexington Avenue and Forty-third Street, this evening. In addition to the long and attractive regular bill of high-class vaudeville and the promenade concerts, there will be a special musical programme, rendered by twelve of Gotham's leading singing societies, numbering between 500 and 600 members. The final feature of the evening will be the closing choral, sung by the united societies from the two-tiered observatory tower. Engel's Band will assist the two regular bands. In anticipation of the popular success of these novel innovations, Manager Amberg is planning an "Italian night," which will be an elaborate festival, with fireworks effects, after an order quite the rage on the Continent.

##### Boy Dies from a Mate's Kick.

TARRYTOWN, N. Y., July 10.—Thomas E. Bergh, the six-year-old son of Axell Bergh, a baker, died this morning at his parents' home from the effects of a kick received upon the back of his head while playing leapfrog with some other boys a short time ago.

## DECLINE IN THE GOLD RESERVE.

#### Drop of Nearly $1,000,000—Net Reserve $99,171,518.

WASHINGTON, July 10.—A loss of nearly $1,000,000 and a decline below the old customary limit of $100,000,000 was the response of the gold reserve to-day to the victory of the silver extremists at Chicago. The decline below $100,000,000 was in some measure a mere coincidence, as the reserve has been hovering about that point for the last two weeks. The significant and less favorable features of the situation were the announcement early in the morning of the loss of $500,000 in gold coin for export and $120,000 for domestic purposes.

There had been no exports of any magnitude for some weeks, and the reserve, according to the official figures, not including the losses of to-day, declined only from $102,418,002 June 30 to $100,293,688 this morning. The loss reported in the morning was followed by the withdrawal of $200,000 for export and an additional withdrawal for domestic purposes, which carried the total up to $218,400 in gold coinage, and $16,300 in gold bars. The gross losses for the day were $934,700, and the net reserve at the close of business was $99,171,518.

The loss was principally in coin, because the present charge for gold bars makes coin more profitable in certain cases. The supply of coin is now ample, being reported to-day at $112,263,728, against bullion to the amount of $32,481,533. The sum of $42,327,259 in coin is set aside against outstanding gold certificates, leaving the amount available for general uses about $70,000,000.

No special alarm is felt at the Treasury regarding the immediate future of the gold reserve. It is believed that the effect of the declaration for free silver at Chicago has been discounted by the stock market, and that confidence prevails abroad that the United States intends to adhere to the gold standard. This is not the season of heavy gold losses under normal conditions, and they have amounted to only about $8,500,000 during the last six weeks. The gross losses have been somewhat larger, but have been offset by some considerable deposits of gold at the mints and assay offices and exchanges of gold for other currency at the Sub-Treasuries. A deposit of $500 in gold certificates was made at Philadelphia a day or two ago in exchange for silver certificates, and the gold thus released was carried to the net reserve.

The season has hardly begun for large demands for small notes, which usually come in the late Summer and early Autumn, but the present is usually the period when the tide of gold turns toward the United States. There may be some doubt whether there will be actual gold imports of any moment during the next four or five months, but it is hoped that the offerings of bills of exchange against exports of American merchandise will be sufficient to prevent heavy exports of gold.

##### Gold to be Sent to Europe.

Heidelbach, Ickelheimer & Co. withdrew $500,000 in gold from the Sub-Treasury yesterday for shipment to Europe to-day. The Merchants' Bank of Canada withdrew $100,000 for shipment to Canada.

Zimmerman & Forshay have been taking gold out of the Sub-Treasury nearly every day this week for counter use. They withdrew $120,000 yesterday. Mr. Zimmerman said that some of the firm's customers wanted gold and were willing to pay a small commission for it. The firm has withdrawn altogether this week about $800,000 in gold for counter use. It is understood that a large proportion of this gold is being locked up in safe-deposit vaults by individuals.

The steamship Etruria, departing for Europe to-day, will take out 728,000 ounces of silver, shipped by the following houses: Zimmerman & Forshay, 250,000 ounces; Handy & Harman, 150,000 ounces; J. & W. Seligman, 150,000 ounces; M. Guggenheim's Sons, 126,000 ounces, and Fuller & Wilson, 50,000 ounces. The La Touraine will take out to-day 300,000 ounces of silver, shipped by J. & W. Seligman.

## NINETY-FIVE DEGREES IN CAMP.

#### Twenty-five Unseasoned Amateur Soldiers Overcome by Heat.

PEEKSKILL, N. Y., July 10.—The sudden change from cloudy weather to clear skies and a hot sun had a rather disastrous effect upon the Thirteenth Regiment and the provisional battalion this morning. The ambulance and medical departments were kept pretty busy during guard mount, which began at 8:30 o'clock.

Several of the new guards were overcome by the heat, and later, at the regimental drills, so many cases occurred that the recall was sounded at 10:45 o'clock, three-quarters of an hour earlier than is usual.

Twenty-five cases were reported, but the larger part of them were slight, and the sufferers soon recovered. The thermometer at its highest registered 95 degrees at the hospital tent.

Private Krebs of the Thirteenth Regiment is in the hospital suffering from appendicitis. Private Wallace of Company K was one of those who fell during the morning drill. After being taken to the hospital he became hysterical, but was brought around. He is resting easily, and will be able to march out of camp on Saturday, it is thought.

The excursion of Company E, Thirteenth Regiment, came up to-day from Brooklyn, bringing 2,500 persons. The Twenty-third Regiment and the Third Provisional Battalion will arrive on Saturday.

## WOMAN ATTACKED BY A DOG.

#### The Animal Seized a Leg and Shook Her Viciously.

NEWARK, N. J., July 10.—Mrs. Theresa Crenucacia, sixty years old, of 37 Adams Street, while walking along Passaic Avenue to-day sat down to rest on the stoop of a house. She had been seated but a few moments when a large Newfoundland dog owned by Patrick Murphy attacked her.

The dog sank its teeth in the woman's leg and began to shake her vigorously. She screamed for help, and several persons in the neighborhood responded, but in the meantime the dog had thrown Mrs. Crenucacia to the ground and was dragging her about.

The dog was finally driven away, but not before he had terribly lacerated the woman's limbs.

The woman was then carried into a neighboring house and a doctor cauterized her wounds. He said they were very severe and that she was suffering from shock.

##### To Ratify Chicago Nominations.

A meeting to ratify the nominations made at Chicago will be held this evening at the Democratic Club of the Twenty-first Assembly District, 64 West Ninety-seventh Street. The meeting will be addressed by Edwin T. Taliaferro, John Connolly, James E. Kelly, and others.

##### An Exchange Out of Business.

The Mining and Industrial Exchange, which was started in this city recently as the American Stock Exchange, has sublet its office at 45 New Street and practically gone out of business. The corporation will be kept up, with its headquarters in the office of the President, Dr. Stephen H. Emmens, at 1 Broadway.

##### A Runaway on Broadway.

A pair of horses attached to a truck, owned by John Stanley, cloak dealer, of 646 West Thirtieth Street, ran away while in front of 31 Broadway, yesterday afternoon. They came into collision with a cable car in front of 18 Broadway, and were stopped. The horses received bruises, but no other damage was done.

#### TELEGRAPHIC BREVITIES.

Michael F. O'Brien, twenty-six years old, head bookkeeper for Louis J. Miller & Co., liquor dealers on Hanover Street, Boston, was arrested yesterday for embezzlement. According to the statement of the firm, O'Brien's shortage is $8,154, all of which was taken between January and March 24 of the present year. He has a wife and two children.

—George R. Jenkins, Deputy Postmaster at Short Hills, N. J., where James R. Pitcher is Postmaster, is under arrest on a charge of defalcation. Jenkins had a salary of $10 a week, and was in sole control of the office for Mr. Pitcher. What the basis of the charge of defalcation is is not known, even by Mr. Pitcher.

## BRYAN, FREE SILVER, AND REPUDIATION

### Chicago Convention Chooses a Fit Candidate to Stand on Its Populistic Platform.

### HE IS NOMINATED ON THE FIFTH BALLOT

#### Tremendous Stampede in His Favor, in Which Practically All Join Except the Sound-Money Delegations.

#### SELECTION OF MAN FOR SECOND PLACE POSTPONED

#### Silverites Take an Adjournment Over Night So that They May Have Time to Deliberate—Afraid of Spoiling Their Ticket by Giving It a Weak Tail—Plenty of Candidates.

CHICAGO, July 10.—The Populist Democrats of the United States have chosen William Jennings Bryan as their candidate for President on the fifth ballot, with 162 votes in the convention refusing to consent by participation in the nominations to the revolutionary platform previously adopted or to bind themselves to support the man who was placed upon it. Bryan's nomination was made with a whirl, in the same impetuous manner in which the platform was constructed and put through.

Worn out with excitement the convention took a recess until to-night at 8 o'clock, with the expectation that the ticket would be completed then. At the night session the delegates who had named a Presidential candidate with a rush, paused for reflection. "In order that no mistakes might be made," it was decided to adjourn until Saturday at 10 o'clock to complete the ticket that will be repudiated by all Democrats who have not lost all sense of National honor and credit.

Bryan's nomination was not a surprise to anybody who was in the convention Thursday when Bryan made the speech that stirred the convention so mightily. When Garfield in 1880 rose to name Sherman as the choice of the Buckeye State his eloquence and his presence were a greater recommendation for the speaker than for the man for whom he spoke. So it was with Bryan. But Bryan sways men of the emotional sort more readily and profoundly than Garfield did. Indeed, Garfield never was so superficial, dramatic, sophistical, as Bryan is whenever he speaks. Bryan's bearing is graceful; his face is handsome; his utterance is clear and strong, with something of the McKinley sing-song, and his style is free, bold, picturesque, and brilliant.

No wonder that his oration moved the emotional and enthusiastic silverites, and at once turned the delegates in several Southern States who had declined to pick a man, to the "Boy Orator of the Platte." But the Bland forces, represented by delegates who had insisted that Bland more fitly represented the silver cause than any other man, because he had been identified with it longer and more prominently, hung back. They had built up a boom with great care for the Missouri "Commoner," as they called him when they did not call him "Silver Dick" or "Honest Dick" Bland, and they expected Bland to win as the result of great expenditure for headquarters, bands, uniforms, and singing clubs.

When the convention met to-day the Bryan boom was the popular one. The Bland shouters were on hand, as vociferous as ever. Missouri reinforced its lines by consultation with other States, and was prepared to sweep away Bryan, if possible, by a prodigious lead at the start.

On the very first roll call the zealous silver men once more were reminded that the Democratic Party had been divided. In the States of Connecticut, Delaware, Maine, Maryland, Massachusetts, Michigan, Minnesota, New-Hampshire, New-Jersey, New-York, Rhode Island, and Wisconsin there were refusals to vote; no votes whatever were cast by New-York and New-Jersey. One gold man in Ohio refused to sit still, and he voted under the unit rule.

Gen. Bragg of Wisconsin, a fighter still, and evidently proud of it, insisted upon applying the unite rule in Wisconsin, but was prevented by the ruling of Permanent Chairman White. The ruling was forced. Wisconsin instructed her delegation to vote as a unit "when and how" the majority should decide. Senator White ruled that this should not prohibit delegates from voting in spite of the will of the majority to the contrary, and according to this decision five of Wisconsin's votes were cast for silver candidates. It was not difficult for a convention that had overturned so many Democratic doctrines and practices to add this violation of the unit rule to its list of offenses.

Bland's strength never was more than 300, as ascertained by recent canvasses, and the result of the first ballot showed that the canvasses had been inflated or that Bryan had weakened Bland's line.

Boies gathered 86 votes, a ridiculously small number considering the expenditures for lithographs and the boastful confidence of the candidate's friends.

Pattison, who ought not to have been in the race, according to the opinion of some of his friends, ran up to 95, and Blackburn, with 83 votes, was closer to Boies than any Iowa boomer would have believed he could be.

The boasted strength of Teller, which was almost exclusively in the minds of a few silver Senators, Republican and Democratic, amounted to merely a handful of votes, a beggarly eight.

The stampede to Bryan was looked for at the beginning of the second ballot. All that that ballot showed, however, was that the men who secretly had objected to Bland, but who were committed to him, had put Bryan to good use in introducing him for exhibition. Alabama went over from Boies to Bland, and "Silver Dick" picked up 58 votes. Boies dropped 49 votes and Bryan gained 92. Pattison had 100 votes. Blackburn dropped half of his string. McLean, who had 53 to start with, picked up 1. Teller increased to 17. Marsden of Louisiana, who made a ridiculous attempt to drown himself the night before while making a nominating speech, boisterously attempted to have the two-thirds rule abolished offhand. Representative Richardson, who was presiding, took advantage of the house rules to send the motion to the Committee on Rules, which disposed of it and Marsden, but did not shelter Marsden from merciless ridicule.

Again the Bryan stampede was not brought on.

The third ballot began auspiciously for Bland, but it soon turned Bryan's way. Bland's gains were 10, but Bryan increased his vote 22. Teller disappeared. Stevenson lost one of his 10 votes, and Blackburn had only Kentucky and one vote added.

When the fourth ballot began with the shifting of Alabama's 22 votes from Bland to Bryan, and California, Idaho, and Kansas gave their votes to Bryan, the end was in sight.

Bryan's friends gave themselves up to celebrating with a zeal that prevented business from proceeding rapidly, and at times stopped it altogether.

Illinois went out while the vote was being completed—everybody knew what that meant. The announcement of the fourth ballot, with Bryan leading with 280 votes and Bland next with 241, was the signal for a rumpus. It was stopped with difficulty, and after much delay the fifth and final ballot was begun.

As the roll call proceeded for the fifth ballot an exciting scene developed. Alabama, California, Colorado, Georgia, Idaho, Kansas, Kentucky, Louisiana, Michigan, Mississippi, Nebraska, North Carolina, South Carolina, South Dakota, Tennessee, Virginia, and most of the Territories enrolled their votes for Bryan.

When the fifth call was completed he still needed votes. To recruit the line a common convention expedient was adopted. Amid cheers and frantic demonstrations of delight, the Bryan men made a collection of State banners about Nebraska, organized a march about the body of delegates, and under the inspiration or infection of excitement presently were able to collect near a majority of two-thirds.

Illinois came in to swell the list with her forty-eight votes.

The stampede had come. Bulletins began to fly out of the hall announcing Bryan's nomination. Illinois did not nominate him. It was not until Gov. Stone, speaking for Missouri, hauled down the Bland standard and cast 34 votes for Bryan that the gifted blatherskite was selected as the Presidential candidate of the Democratic-Populist Convention.

Not a gold State had budged.

The gold standard States that had refused to participate in the nomination, refusing to be disgraced by committing themselves to a Populistic declaration and its revolutionary methods, did not object to the motion to make the nomination of Bryan unanimous. Pennsylvania, however, that had offered a candidate and voted for him, voted against the motion.

This action provoked some manifestations of resentment. Chairman Richardson did not notice them, and declared that the motion was carried.

The night session was brief and disorderly. The presiding officer was used up. The Secretaries were not all in precisely the condition to conduct business decorously, and there were aspirants for the second place who had not been able to complete arrangements they desired to make during the recess of five hours. Many delegates did not return to the hall at night. All of the Tammany men except Mr. Cummings had gone home. The Pennsylvania seats were mostly unoccupied.

Chicago turned out in vast numbers to

"All the News That's Fit to Print."

# The New York Times.

THE WEATHER.
Fair, slightly warmer Thursday; Friday, fair, warmer; moderate winds, becoming south.
For full weather report see Page 12.

VOL. XLV...NO. 14,053. NEW-YORK, THURSDAY, SEPTEMBER 3, 1896.—COPYRIGHTED, 1896, BY THE NEW-YORK TIMES PUBLISHING CO. PRICE THREE CENTS.

## BURGLARS READY TO KILL

### SHOTS FIRED AND CHLOROFORM USED IN GLENVILLE, CONN.

**Thomas F. Burke, Whose House Was Visited, Overpowered After a Desperate Struggle and Rendered Unconscious—One of the Thieves Wounded—Got Nothing for All Their Pains—Thought a Large Sum of Money Was in the House.**

It will be a long time before the people of Glenville, Conn., will get through talking about a visit which burglars paid that village Tuesday night. They went there prepared to kill as well as to rob. Eight pistol shots, a wounded burglar, a fierce struggle in the dark, a dose of chloroform, and the screams of a terrified family were the incidents crowded into the few exciting moments when the presence of the intruders was known. Help came an hour after they had vanished. It included, before daylight, nearly everybody within call.

The burglars took nothing away. A general upset of furniture in two of the lower rooms and four bullets driven into the interior walls and woodwork bore evidence of the difficulty that attended their departure.

The house they visited is occupied by Thomas F. Burke, Superintendent of the Hawthorne Woolen Mills. It belongs to J. H. Hunt, President of the company which owns the mill, and it is conspicuously attractive in a neighborhood of comfortable homes. Mr. Hunt resided there until a death in his family impelled him to move. If burglars strange to that section were out exploring they would probably choose this house as the most promising in Glenville. It is probable, however, that the inviting appearance of the house had nothing to do with this visit, which is to be explained by the presence there Tuesday evening of David C. Broderick, Mr. Burke's brother-in-law, with a large roll of bills. Burglars could have no object in calling on Mr. Burke, as they might easily have learned by the most casual inquiry anywhere between Port Chester and Greenwich.

**Man with the Money Not There.**

Mr. Broderick resides in Greenwich. He follows the races, and is known as a man who usually carries a full wallet. He displayed a bunch of money at Greenwich late on Tuesday afternoon, and drove over to Glenville with his wife and child in time for supper at Mr. Burke's. Probably he was followed. Doors are usually ajar or unlocked until bedtime in that region. Any one might have entered Mr. Burke's house without knocking or being seen or heard, as easily as Mr. Broderick did. While Mr. Broderick was preparing for supper in an up-stairs bedroom he heard a door close softly. It startled him for the moment, because the sound did not seem like that which would be made either by the wind or by any one walking freely about. Since there were nearly a dozen persons in the house he concluded that there could be no reason for uneasiness, and when he went to supper he said nothing of the incident. At about 9 o'clock in the evening he drove back to Greenwich, leaving his wife and child at Mr. Burke's.

The Burke family, in which there are Mrs. Burke and five children, Mrs. Broderick and her child, Miss Humphrey, a teacher, who had begun her services that day in the village school, and had taken board with the Burkes, and Mr. Burke were all stirring about the house, which was lighted throughout, when Mr. Broderick went away. A man concealed in the house could not know that Mr. Broderick had gone.

**Mr. Burke Seeks the Burglars.**

Before 10 o'clock the doors were locked and the household retired. One door opens on a porch in front and the other is at the rear. At about midnight Mr. Burke was awakened by a noise which sounded as if some one were on the porch. He thought it might be his St. Bernard dog until he recalled that when the doors were locked the dog lay on a rug in the sitting room, where it usually slept at night. The noise continuing, Mr. Burke took his revolver and started forth to learn the cause of the noise.

He became informed of it in startling fashion. As he stepped from his bedroom into a hallway which runs the length of the house, and in which gas is burned all night, he saw a tall, slender man with a mask over his face, fumbling at the door of the bedroom to which Mr. Broderick had gone to prepare for supper. The man looked around at Mr. Burke and then started swiftly down the hall. Before he had taken half a dozen steps Mr. Burke fired. The man cried out as if hit.

Mr. Burke stepped into his doorway to escape the smoke of his revolver. He had barely done so when a shot was heard and a bullet from the burglar's pistol buried itself in the window frame at Mr. Burke's end of the hall. The hallway is only wide enough for two persons to pass each other, and a duel in it at such close range could not fail to be effective. Mr. Burke, his excitement increased by the burglar's return fire, stepped quickly into the hall and fired again, as the burglar plunged down a back stairway at his end of the hall. The bullet plowed into the framework of the window there, at about the height of a man's shoulders.

Then Mr. Burke gave chase. The back stairway is narrow and winding, and beyond the first turn it was dark. Mr. Burke heard the man descending it by jumps, but did not see him until he dashed out of the kitchen door at the bottom. The door was open. Mr. Burke sent a shot after the fugitive, and then turned from the kitchen, intending to pass through the dining room and sitting room, on the lower floor, to a hallway in the front of the house, where the main stairs are built. He had emptied his revolver of three shots, and wished to go back to his bedroom for a shotgun.

**Grapples with One of the Thieves.**

In the dining room, which was wholly dark, he ran into a man, who grasped him around the body and tried to throw him. Although the meeting completely surprised him, Mr. Burke recovered himself, and, still grappling his assailant, fired. The two men tumbled into the sitting room adjoining. They knocked over a centre table at the beginning of the encounter. Chairs were banged about as they fought. Both were strong, plucky, and nerved to a high pitch.

The encounter had proceeded only a minute or so when Mr. Burke felt himself overpowered. He was too much excited to know whether his antagonist outmatched him or whether help had reached the assailant. He was forced to the floor. Strong hands pinioned him there. In a moment he felt a sponge pressed over his mouth and nostrils. He tore himself loose and pitched over a chair into the dining room. Then he heard a pistol shot. One of the burglars, supposing him in the sitting room, had fired into a corner there. The bullet entered the wall. Another shot quickly followed, this time into the dining room wall near where he lay. Then Mr. Burke lost consciousness, but his household of women and children, who were screaming up stairs, heard two additional shots.

**Women and Children Behind Barricade.**

It was a little after midnight when Mr. Burke became unconscious. His wife and Mrs. Broderick had assembled the six children in one of the up-stairs bedrooms, barricaded the door with the bed and other furniture, and were calling for help from the window at the top of their voices. They did not dare go below, fearing that the armed burglars were still there, and, hearing nothing from Mr. Burke, they thought he had been killed.

The side of the house from which they called overlooks a gulch through which the Byron River flows. That part of the river is dammed to supply power for the woolen mill near by. The noise of water flowing over the dam drowned their cries, except when they were at their highest pitch, and then the sound was misleading.

Frantic with terror, they screamed continuously for a full hour before response came. It was after 1 o'clock before a sign of life appeared in the neighborhood. Exhausted and despairing, they were about to cease screaming when a light moved up the river bank from the mill. It was the lantern of John Burleigh, the mill watchman. He had heard the cries all the time, but had only then been able to locate them.

"Hurry, John, for God's sake!" Mrs. Burke implored. "I think Tom is dead."

**Mr. Burke Found Unconscious.**

Burleigh ran to the house. The front door was wide open. Jumbo, the St. Bernard, met him on the bank, rejoiced apparently over the late call, until he spied the watchman's dog, when a fight began. Both dogs were monsters, and their racket woke the neighborhood. Burleigh gave up trying to part them, and ran into the house. He stumbled over Mr. Burke's body in the dinging room. The women and children emerged from the up-stairs room in which they had imprisoned themselves. Neighbors, awakened by the fighting of the dogs, were called in. They carried Mr. Burke to his bedroom, and while some disrobed him others went out for a physician. His face was cut under one of the eyes, as if from a blow with brass knuckles. One of his temples had swollen in a broad lump. There were red marks at his throat, and his lips were inflamed.

The fall over the dining-room chair when he released himself from his assailant had torn the flesh on one of his knees. Dr. Dalbeck of Port Chester arrived at about 3 o'clock and said that chloroform had doubtless been administered. Signs of nausea confirmed this diagnosis.

Mr. Burke kept his bed all day yesterday, but was able to be up last night. He said he still felt the effect of the chloroform, but expected it to pass off in a day or so. He spoke with some respect of the man who got the better of him in the sitting room, saying that he must be a good man, "because I am slick myself at a rastle." His theory was that one man had entered the house before the doors were locked, perhaps following Mr. Broderick in. When the household had retired the first intruder had opened the doors for his associates, and Jumbo, the St. Bernard, had walked quietly out. There were no marks anywhere of forcible entry into the house.

David C. Broderick said that when he was in Greenwich yesterday Deputy Sheriff Fitzroy had informed him that three men, one tall and two short and stout, had alighted from a train there Monday night. He accosted them and they hurried away with their collars upturned and their faces averted. Fitzroy suspected that these men were Mr. Burke's visitors, and that Mr. Burke was overcome in the sitting room, because the stout man who first attacked him had been joined by a second stout man, the tall burglar having gone off to attend to his wound. It is not supposed that it was serious, for he left no blood trail, and trace of the men had disappeared before daylight yesterday.

A curious circumstance in the affair was that Miss Humphrey, the school teacher, slept through it all, although the first three shots were fired in a hallway on which her room opens. She offered in explanation of her sound slumber that at Wilkesbarre, where she last taught school, shooting was so common that she had learned to sleep through it.

Attempts at burglary are not common in Glenville. Last Winter, however, at two visits the Post Office was robbed of $35 and some stamps, and a fuse was laid to blow open the safe at the woolen mill, but the men were frightened off before the fuse could be lighted.

## JUMPED IN WATER FOR $20.

**Four Men Could Not Swim and a Stranger Got the Bill.**

CONEY ISLAND, Sept. 2.—A picnic was held in Feltman's Pavilion to-day by the Belgian Benevolent and Protective Association. During the afternoon the picnickers visited Henderson's swimming pool. Most of them were content to stand on the platform and view the others as they sported in the water.

Daniel Albriguer, one of the party, stood on the edge of the pool with a twenty-dollar bill in his hand. A gust of wind blew it into the water. Immediately he and three of his friends, without disrobing, jumped into the pool in search of the bill. None of them could swim, so while they were spluttering about in the water one of the bathers got possession of the bill. The Belgians found that the bather had the bill, and made a disturbance.

They were all arrested. When taken to the police station they gave their names as Daniel Albriguer, aged thirty years, of 285 Fifth Avenue, Brooklyn; Bernard Peters of 441 Seventh Avenue, Brooklyn; Edgar Ingelberger, aged twenty-nine years, of 191 Eighth Street, Brooklyn, and John Frebau of 281 Seventh Street, Brooklyn.

Justice Van Nostrand fined each $5, in default of which they were sent to jail. What became of the twenty-dollar bill does not appear.

**Alabama Congressional Fights.**

BIRMINGHAM, Ala., Sept. 2.—G. W. Taylor of Marengo, the only sound-money man in the Democratic Congressional party fight, was nominated at Thomasville in the First District to-day. The dead-lock in the Fifth continues, with the chances of ex-Congressman Cobb's defeat. In the eighth, the result will be decided on Sept. 26, by a primary in Colbert County, which was contested. The candidates are Congressman Wheeler and Judge William Richardson of Huntsville. The race is close.

## THE VICTORY IS GROWING

### REPUBLICAN PLURALITY IN VERMONT WILL EXCEED 38,000.

**Grand Triumph of Sound Money over Free Silver and Repudiation—The "Common People" of the Green Mountain State Have Set a Magnificent Example for the Country to Follow—No Doubt as to Their Opinion of Bryan's Policies.**

ST. ALBANS, Vt., Sept. 2.—According to the returns gathered here by the Chairman of the Republican Committee, with six towns to hear from, Grout, the Republican candidate for Governor, has a plurality of 38,757.

The missing towns in 1892 gave a Republican plurality of 161, and in 1894 a Republican plurality of 225.

WHITE RIVER JUNCTION, Vt., Sept. 2.—Returns from 235 cities and towns in the State, including all the towns in Addison, Caledonia, Essex, Franklin, Grand Isle, Orange, Washington, and Windsor Counties give Grout, (Rep.,) for Governor, 52,565; Jackson, (Dem.,) 14,627; Battelle, (Pop.,) 616; Whittemore, (Proh.,) 511. According to these figures Grout's plurality is 37,938; majority, 36,811.

The same towns and cities in 1892 gave Fuller (Rep.) 35,239; Smalley (Dem.) 18,203. All others, 1,721. Fuller's plurality was 19,336 and his majority was 17,615. The scattering vote, or all in opposition to the two leading parties, is 594 less this year than in 1892. The percentage of gain in the Republican majority this year over that of 1892 is still maintained at 110. The remaining towns will not change, to a great extent, the majority estimates, based upon returns of the large majority of towns that have reported, but it is expected the final figures will show a plurality for Grout of a little over 38,000.

### AN IMPORTANT VICTORY.

**Result in Vermont a Great Gain for Sound Money.**

WASHINGTON, Sept. 2.—The day before the election in Vermont the silverites declared that a Republican majority of less than 20,000 would be construed as a distinct gain by the advocates of free coinage. Now that the majority approaches 40,000 the white-metal leaders say that no significance whatever attaches to the election.

Chairman Faulkner of the Democratic Congressional Committee said to-day that he did not believe a single Democratic meeting had been held in the State.

"I did not get an application for literature from that State until last Wednesday," said he, "and I am certain that not fifty letters have passed between here and that State. We made no attempt to carry the State, while the Republicans have spent lots of money and have exerted every energy to win. I am told that a house-to-house canvass was made by prominent Republicans. The only wonder to me is that the Democrats had the heart to vote at all."

Mr. Faulkner and his associates choose to ignore the fact that the voters of Vermont had full knowledge of the issue. The silver question was the chief one in the minds of the Vermonters. It is the opinion of unprejudiced persons here that the overwhelming Republican victory is a distinct disaster to the silver cause which will have its effect in the campaign.

Chairman Babcock of the Republican Congressional Committee expressed himself to-day as follows: "The election is a fair expression of the sentiment of the people. It points strongly and plainly to what the balance of the country will do in November. It is a repudiation of the wild fallacies expounded at the Chicago Convention, and is a ringing notice served that the people of the country do not propose to have their country dishonored.

"Vermont is a thermometer to the rest of the country. Two years ago, after the elections held in Vermont, Maine, and Oregon, I predicted the result that followed. I now make the prediction that the balance of the country will follow Vermont's lead. Silver has received a serious blow.

"Too much stress cannot be laid on the fact that the Democrats claimed that the silver sentiment had reached the farmers of New-England and would make itself felt in the elections in those States. It now can be seen whether the farmers were affected by the craze. The enormous Republican gain and the enormous Democratic loss cannot fail to make an impression on the balance of the country."

Senator Warren of Wyoming, who reached Washington to-day, says the silver tide in the West is receding, and that it will be checked in enough States to prevent the Democrats from realizing their hope of capturing a solid West.

"We will carry Wyoming, South Dakota, and Nebraska," said Senator Warren; "we also will get some of the coast States. I am free to admit that the Presidential race is nobody's yet, but I am confident that the work the Republicans are doing will be so effective that McKinley will be elected by a large majority."

Wyoming is surrounded by the wildest of the silver States, but most of the prominent Republicans there have stood firm, and will not "buck." Senator Clark and Representative Mondell are doing hard work for the Republican nominees, and it is said that not more than a half dozen Republicans of State reputation have bolted the ticket.

Senator Pritchard of North Carolina said to-day that McKinley would carry the "old North State" against all combinations. The two North Carolina Senators are on opposite sides of the political fence this year, each working earnestly for success. Pritchard says the silver sentiment in the State is subsiding.

### E. J. PHELPS ON THE RESULT.

**Thinks Vermont Will Be Followed by Maine Next Week.**

BURLINGTON, Vt., Sept. 2.—In an interview on the results of the election, E. J. Phelps, who voted for Major Grout, instead of the Democratic candidate, said: "I regard the magnificent result of the election yesterday as an event of the highest consequence. It was the emphatic response of the people of Vermont to the proposals of repudiation, dishonor, and debased public currency that have been so insidiously, and, at the same time, so vigorously pressed upon us. It is all the more interesting because it is the first response that any State has as yet had the opportunity to make, and it is therefore the unprompted and natural sentiment of Vermont. The eye of many a distant Vermonter will kindle when he reads it, and sees that it is not the voice of a party, but of a people courageous enough not to wait for an example, but to set it.

"It cannot fail, in my opinion, to exert a strong and possibly a decisive influence upon the National election. The crisis is so novel and so dangerous that grave apprehensions have been felt everywhere as to the effect of the new and untried element that it introduces into political controversies, which hitherto, however sharply defined, attacked the foundations of society; but it is now fair to expect that, as it has utterly failed among the plain people of Vermont, it will equally fail among their countrymen generally; and, if there are any, as there usually are, who are waiting to see which way the current sets before determining their own course, the report of the Vermont election will convey to them no uncertain sound.

"We may reasonably look to see its indications strongly corroborated by the voice of Maine next week, and to find that throughout the country party lines will be loosened, and party considerations laid aside for this time, in the presence of so great a danger as menaces us."

### VERMONT AND WALL STREET.

**Decided Effect of the Republican Sound-Money Victory.**

The news of the sound-money victory in Vermont had a very favorable effect on the stock market yesterday. The day was the most cheerful one that has been experienced in several months.

Wall Street and all business centres in the city recognized that the victory meant a great deal more than the election of a Republican Governor in Vermont. The overwhelming victory of the Republicans and the defection in the ranks of the Democracy which Bryan had hoped to control for himself are interpreted as indications of certain victory for sound money throughout the entire country in November. The issue had been fully presented in Vermont, and the result was the largest Republican majority obtained in recent years.

Business revived at once. The stock market grew stronger hourly, as fuller returns came in. Some of the net advances above Tuesday's quotations were as follows: American Sugar Refining, 3¼; Chicago Gas, 2⅛; Colorado Fuel and Iron, 2⅛; Consolidated Gas, 4; Delaware and Hudson, 3⅝; New-Jersey Central, 3¼; New-York Central, 1⅜; St. Paul preferred, 5; Western Union, ⅞.

The prospects of further gold news appeared in Wall Street yesterday, when rates for sterling exchange, which had lately reacted, become easy again. This indicated that the supply of commercial bills has exceeded even the recent large demand for them, and that the gold movement may proceed on the substantial basis which has already resulted in the arrival or engagement of about $20,000,000 from Europe. There arrived yesterday by the Teutonic $750,000 of gold, engaged last week.

Another encouraging feature of the situation was the low rate of call loans in the money market. This was construed to mean that the stringency under which the banks have labored is already relieved, so that money that had been used last week in loans to banks seems to be free again for general market purposes.

## BARBAROUS FIRE SUFFERERS.

**Michigan Militia Sent to Protect the Weak from the Strong.**

CALUMET, Mich., Sept. 2.—So distressing has become the condition of the fire sufferers in Ontonagon that they have nearly reached a condition of barbarism. The food contributed is away below the demand, and the strong and able-bodied fight back the weak and take the sustenance for themselves, leaving the weaker to starve. The authorities there have been unable to meet the condition, and yesterday a squad of Company D, Fifth Regiment, left for the fire district to protect the supplies against the raids of the half-crazed sufferers.

Gov. Rich was appealed to, and will send the entire State militia in the upper peninsula to guard the food if necessary. Every soldier is supplied with twenty rounds of ball cartridges and goes equipped for active war. Thieves and pillagers will be shot down if necessary to protect the weak.

## THE PRESIDENT INTERESTED.

**Receiving News of the Indianapolis Convention by a Special Wire.**

BUZZARD'S BAY, Mass., Sept. 2.—The President is receiving over a special wire the proceedings of the Indianapolis Convention as he did those at St. Louis and Chicago.

The wire is run from the main line over to Gray Gables, a special operator being sent from Boston.

**Burned to Death in a Hotel.**

VAN KLEEK HILL, Ontario, Sept. 2.—The Commercial Hotel, owned by George Constantineau, was partially destroyed by fire last night, and five persons burned to death. They were Mary Louise Yandeau, Christy Villaneuve, Joseph Deschamps, Mrs. T. Finn, and Miss K. McLeod. The fire started in the kitchen, and spread so quickly that it was impossible to make any attempt at rescue. Loss on the hotel is $10,000; insurance, $4,500.

**Two Men Struck by a Train.**

PEEKSKILL, N. Y., Sept. 2.—Michael Hennesy of Mount Vernon and John Roach were walking on the Hudson River Railroad tracks this evening. They were run down by a train. Hennesy was killed. Roach was struck as he was getting out of the way, but escaped death, although injured. He was brought to the hospital.

**Baron Fava Not Recalled.**

BAR HARBOR, Me., Sept. 2.—Baron Fava, who has been here for a few days, has left town. Baroness Fava was seen, and shown the dispatch stating that Baron Fava had been recalled, and she completely denied the report. Baroness Fava leaves here to-morrow, probably for Washington.

**Severe Frost in Connecticut.**

ROCKVILLE, Conn., Sept. 2.—There was a severe frost in various parts of Tolland County last night, especially in Tolland and Coventry.



## CYCLIST DIES IN COLLISION

### ROBERT WHITTEMORE DASHES HEADLONG INTO A BUGGY.

**Strikes the Shaft Sidewise and Is Instantly Killed in Ninth Avenue, Brooklyln, at the Third Street Crossing—The Youth's Family Waiting Dinner Two Blocks Away and He Hurrying Home—The Wheel Unhurt.**

Henry Whittemore, a publisher, and one of the editors of the National Encyclopedia of American Biography, and several members of his family were awaiting dinner last night in 487 Third Street, Brooklyn. Robert, the eighteen-year-old son, had gone bicycle riding and was due any minute. A neighbor came in and said that he was dead, that he had been killed at Third Street and Ninth Avenue, two blocks away. The body was brought to the house a few minutes afterward.

Charles M. Creamer, a liquor dealer, living at 154 Hewes Street, Brooklyn, E. D., and a woman friend had been driving slowly up Third Street toward Prospect Park. The pavement is asphalt, and very smooth. Just as the carriage was in the centre of Ninth Avenue, young Whittemore, in a hurry to get home for dinner—it was then past 7 o'clock—came dashing down Ninth Avenue toward Third Street.

He was going so fast that he could not stop his wheel, and before Mr. Creamer could realize what was going to happen the bicycle crashed into the right side of the carriage. Mr. Creamer pulled the horse up so tightly that he was thrown. Mr. Creamer and the woman were thrown out of the carriage into the street. They both escaped injury.

The wagon was upset and the right-hand shaft was snapped asunder. Whittemore lay on the pavement. Dr. Otis of Seney Hospital came and he said the young man was dead and that death had been instantaneous. Mr. Creamer was in great grief.

The bicycle did not appear to have been damaged a particle. A small drop of blood was on the rubber tire of the front wheel.

Mr. Creamer was arrested by Patrolman McVeagh of the Prospect Park police and was taken to the Litchfield Mansian, where the nature of the accident was stated to Capt. McNamara. As the accident took place outside the park, the policeman was instructed to take Mr. Creamer to the Sixth Avenue Station, where Capt. Campbell was notified of the accident.

He caused Mr. Creamer to be detained on the charge of homicide and word was sent to his friends and also to Justice Teele of the Myrtle Avenue Police Court in order that Mr. Creamer could be admitted to bail. The woman who had been with him went home during the excitement. He did not give her name.

Not the slightest bruise was on the body of the young man. A little blood had run from the nose.

The Whittemore family is well known in the neighborhood and much sympathy was expressed by the neighbors.

Coroner Coombs will hold a thorough investigation and it is said may make some recommendations as to fast riding within the city limits.

## WAS SAVED FROM DROWNING.

**W. H. Lowery Rescued from the North River by Thomas McKeon.**

William H. Lowery of 31 Bowery was rescued from drowning at Pier A North River yesterday afternoon by Thomas McKeon of 37 Monroe Street.

Lowery had been sitting on the Battery sea wall and was seized with an attack of vertigo. He fell unconscious into the river. The tide was high and the water was running swiftly up stream.

Without removing any of his clothing McKeon jumped into the water and reached Lowery as he was sinking for the second time. Lowery struggled so fiercely that the two men were swept under the stone arches of Pier A before assistance reached them.

As they floated to the north side of the pier, Sergt. Mangin and Patrolman Nolan of the harbor police threw to them a life preserver, with a line attached. McKeon grasped the life preserver and bore the drowning man to the bulkhead, where he was taken up a ladder.

An ambulance call had been sent to the Hudson Street Hospital, where Lowery was taken after Surgeon L'Abbé had partially resuscitated him. He will recover. He is forty years old and is a compositor. McKeon is a bookbinder, and is thirty-five years old. He was not much the worse for his plunge, though he had a severe struggle to prevent being drowned with Lowery.

**Stumbled with a Lamp on a Stair.**

Mary O'Brien, sixty years old, employed as a servant by Mrs. O'Neill of 213 Warren Street, Jersey City, was going down stairs last night with a lighted lamp in her hand, when she tripped and fell. The lamp exploded, setting fire to Mrs. O'Brien's dress and the stairway. Several persons ran to Mrs. O'Brien's aid and wrapped her in a piece of carpet torn from the floor. The flames were extinguished, but the woman was so badly injured that her recovery is doubtful. She was taken to the City Hospital.

**Wanted No Runaway Notoriety.**

A team of bay cobs attached to a road wagon took fright at a steam derrick at One Hundred and Forty-fifth Street and Seventh Avenue yesterday afternoon and ran away. The horses fell at One Hundred and Fortieth Street. They were taken to a near-by livery stable.

A fashionably dressed man and a handsome young woman, who were in the carriage, were thrown out and sustained slight injuries. They hired a cab and went home, after refusing to give their names.

**Fire Might Have Been Serious.**

A fire which demonstrated the fire-proof character of the unfinished sixteen-story Manhattan Hotel, at Madison Avenue and Forty-second Street, was discovered last evening on its roof. It was due to sparks which settled on bags of coke used in plumbers' furnaces. Firemen found a difficult task before them. This was not the matter of extinguishing the blaze, but of reaching the roof. Men climbed to it, however, and with buckets of water extinguished the blaze. The damage will not exceed $100. It is covered by a builder's risk.

## IN A SHOWER OF GLASS.

**Visitors to the County Courthouse Injured by a Falling Skylight.**

A piece of heavy glass, four feet square and an inch thick, fell from the skylight in the County Courthouse at 3:30 o'clock P. M. yesterday and half a dozen persons narrowly escaped being killed.

The glass, which formed part of the skylight in the dome, fell with a fearful crash to the floor below, where it was dashed to a thousand pieces on the marble floor. A spray of powdered glass flew into the air after the crash, and a large piece struck S. H. Taylor, the assignment clerk of the Supreme Court, in the knee, and hurt him badly.

Another piece knocked off an attorney's hat, and several of the flying pieces cut his face. He said that had he not instinctively closed his eyes after the crash he would have been blinded. The glass missed by a few inches a knot of lawyers who were standing in the rotunda.

The rest of the skylight on the side from which the glass fell will be taken down, and the whole skylight will be strengthened. Had the accident happened in the morning hours, when there are hundreds of persons in the corridor, there would probably have been some fatal results.

## REPUBLICAN LOCAL NOMINEES.

**The Candidates Thus Far Named for the Assembly.**

The complete list of the Republican candidates for Assembly nominated at the Assembly District conventions Tuesday night is as follows:

| Dist. | | Dist. | |
|---|---|---|---|
| 1. | Arthur Pezold. | 21. | George C. Austin. |
| 2. | William H. Kilboy. | 23. | Richard Gilleland. |
| 3. | L. J. Hoenninger. | 25. | P. H. Murphy. |
| 5. | Richard Van Cott. | 27. | Francis H. Laimbeer. |
| 8. | Charles S. Adler. | 29. | Lawrence E. Brown. |
| 9. | John D. Blackburn. | 30. | Theodore W. Brickner. |
| 12. | Rudolph Maas. | 31. | H. T. Andrews. |
| 17. | D. Frank Lloyd. | 32. | Frederick Horn. |
| 19. | Robert Mazet. | 33. | James P. Degnan. |
| 20. | Charles H. Edlich. | 34. | P. W. Reinhard, Jr. |

The nomination of Mr. Brown in the Twenty-ninth District is disputed by Samuel G. French, the other candidate, and the contest made by him will have to be settled by the County Committee. It is understood that the nomination will be awarded to Mr. Brown.

The conventions in the Fourth, Sixth, Seventh, Tenth, Eleventh, Thirteenth, Fourteenth, Fifteenth, Sixteenth, Eighteenth, Twenty-second, Twenty-fourth, Twenty-sixth, Twenty-eighth, and Thirty-fifth were adjourned.

Messrs. Adler of the Eighth District, Austin of the Twenty-first, Murphy of the Twenty-fifth, Laimbeer of the Twenty-seventh, and Andrews of the Thirty-first were elected to the Assembly last year.

## GIRL SWIMMERS IN A PANIC.

**A Lighter Smashes a Twelve-Foot Hole in Bathhouse No. 1.**

Free Bathhouse No. 1 is moored at the foot of East Ninety-first Street. It was ladies' day yesterday. About 150 persons, mostly young girls, were in the water.

The thirty-foot lighter, Jane Mora, heavily laden with glucose, attempted to land at the dock. She came in at such a speed that her skipper could not make the end of the dock. She passed it, and her heavy twelve-foot bowsprit and several feet of her blunt bow smashed through the thin side of the bathouse, but not through any occupied dressing room.

The sprit and bow knocked a hole about twelve feet square in the side of the house, broke down the partitions and fronts of three dressing rooms, and toppled them into the water in the swimming pool. The bathers scrambled in safety to the opposite side of the inclosure.

The lighter was pulled away without injury to her hull.

## RAIDED A PARK ROW PLACE.

**Three Men and $305 Captured in an Alleged Poolroom.**

A raid upon an alleged poolroom on the second floor of 33 Park Row was made yesterday afternoon by Police Inspector O'Keefe and a squad of eight men. Frederick Wallace of 176 Sixth Street, John C. Dudley of 33 Park Row, and John Molan of 324 Broome Street were arrested. A ticker and $305 were seized.

The men were arraigned in the Centre Street Police Court, where Molan was discharged. The other two prisoners waived examination, and were held in $1,000 bail each, which was furnished.

The evidence against the place was secured by Detectives Schulke and Hughes, who assert that they played certain horses that lost. The police allege that Peter De Lacy is the owner of the establishment.

## THE WEATHER.

**The indications for to-day are for increasing cloudiness, probably showers, southwesterly winds.**

The indications for to-day are for increasing cloudiness, probably showers, southwesterly winds.

The barometer last night had fallen in the lake regions, the Ohio and Central Mississippi Valleys, and Middle Atlantic States, and had risen in the regions from Texas and the Indian Territory northward over the eastern slope of the Rocky Mountains. The barometer was highest over the Dakotas. It also continued high over the Atlantic coast. The depression which was central over Lake Superior yesterday morning covered the lake regions and was central over Lake Huron.

It was warmer generally over the Northern States east of the Mississippi, and in Tennessee, North Carolina, Kentucky, and Virginia, and cooler in the Northwest and warmer west of the Rocky Mountains.

Heavy local rains were reported from the Gulf coast, and light showers from the lake region and the Northwest. The weather continued generally clear from the Gulf States northeastward to New-England.

Local rains are indicated for the lake region and fair weather, followed by local rains, from New-England and the Middle Atlantic States westward to the Mississippi Valley. Warmer, southwesterly winds are indicated for the Atlantic coast north of Hatteras, and cooler northerly winds for the Central Mississippi Valley.

The record of temperature for the twenty-four hours ended at midnight, taken from THE NEW-YORK TIMES's thermometer and from the thermometer of the Weather Bureau, is as follows:

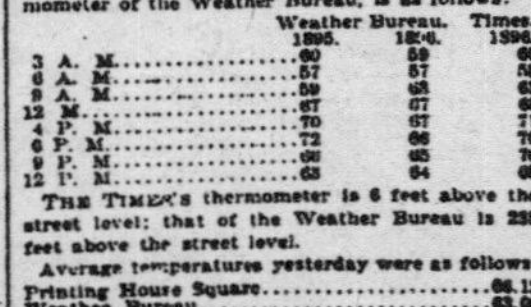

| | Weather Bureau. 1895. | Weather Bureau. 1896. | Times. 1896. |
|---|---|---|---|
| 3 A. M. | 60 | 59 | 60 |
| 6 A. M. | 57 | 57 | 58 |
| 9 A. M. | 59 | 63 | 63 |
| 12 M. | 67 | 67 | 68 |
| 3 P. M. | 70 | 67 | 71 |
| 6 P. M. | 72 | 66 | 70 |
| 9 P. M. | 66 | 65 | 70 |
| 12 P. M. | 65 | 64 | 69 |

THE TIMES's thermometer is 6 feet above the street level; that of the Weather Bureau is 235 feet above the street level.

Average temperatures yesterday were as follows:

| | |
|---|---|
| Printing House Square | 66.12 |
| Weather Bureau | 63.00 |
| Corresponding date 1895 | 64.00 |
| Corresponding date for last twenty years | 70.00 |

Complete "Weather Forecast," Page 10, Column 1.

## PALMER AND BUCKNER

### Probable Nominees of the True Democrats.

### NO STAMPEDE TO BE MADE

**Candidates Will Be Selected After Mature Consideration.**

### PLATFORM MAKERS ARE AT WORK

**Declarations Will Be Strictly in Line with the Traditions of the National Party.**

**TWO SESSIONS OF THE CONVENTION**

**Ex-Gov. Flower and Senator Caffery Make Speeches Which Arouse Enthusiasm.**

INDIANAPOLIS, Ind., Sept. 2.—A ticket composed of Palmer and Buckner, or Black and Buckner, upon a platform for sound money, the strictest regard for the public credit and National honor, respect for all the co-ordinate branches of the Government, devotion to law and order, and loyalty to all Democrats who have upheld the Democratic faith inviolate, promises to be the outcome of the convention of the National Democratic Party.

John M. Palmer,
Will Be Nominated for President if He Will Consent.

Two sessions of the convention—a convention never equalled in its personal quality, and never surpassed in earnestness and enthusiasm—have cleared the way for the adoption of the platform and the nomination of candidates. In the meantime careful consideration of the availability of the men whose names have been considered has led to the setting aside of some and the concentration of attention upon others. The favor extended to Gen. Bragg yesterday, coming over from the conference of Aug. 7, reluctantly was withdrawn to some extent, when it was suggested that he has a silver record to answer, although his denial of the criticism has largely relieved him of the odium of the charge. But a sort of controversy as to whether Senator Vilas or Gen. Gragg, both from the same State, should be preferred, has helped to send the delegates in search of another candidate.

A conference this afternoon took steps to secure from Senator Palmer his consent to be named, with the expectation that he would respond to-night or to-morrow morning. He is aware that the convention would promptly name him should he consent. It is said the conference will be prepared to offer the name of Gen. Black in case of Senator Palmer's final refusal.

Roswell P. Flower.
Temporary Chairman of the Indianapolis Convention.

As the Florida men are still determined to name Grover Cleveland, and this determination does not, in the absence of information from the President as to his feelings in the matter, commend itself to sound judgment, it has been arranged that, in the event of concentration by a number of States upon a candidate, his name shall be presented from the State of Alabama when that State is called, and that the nominating speech shall assure the convention that the man named will receive the votes of all the States that have agreed to adopt the choice of the Middle West, and South. This [illegible] will stop the stampede for Cleveland which

"All the News That's Fit to Print"

# The New York Times

LATE CITY EDITION

Weather: Fair, very cold today and tonight. Chance of snow tomorrow. Temp. range: today 24-14; Sunday 33-26. Full U.S. report on Page 30.

VOL. XLV...NO. 14,054. NEW-YORK, FRIDAY, SEPTEMBER 4, 1896.—COPYRIGHTED, 1896, BY THE NEW-YORK TIMES PUBLISHING CO. PRICE THREE CENTS.

## EXCITING THUNDERSTORM

### AN ELECTRICAL DISPLAY OF UNCOMMON BRILLIANCY.

**High Winds and a Heavy Rainfall—An Hour and a Half of Stirring Incidents—Fall of a Ball of Fire in Broadway—Not Much Harm Done in This City—Considerable Damage in Brooklyn—Trolley Wires Affected.**

The thunderstorm which broke over New-York about 6:30 o'clock last evening, while of comparatively short duration, was one of the most severe of the season, and no other storm of the year has been accompanied by such a brilliant electrical display.

Lowering clouds appeared in the west shortly before 6 o'clock, and people on their way home from work hastened their steps to catch the New-York cars or the bridge trains. The wind freshened up to a perceptible degree, and for a time it looked as if the storm might blow around. But at 6:33 o'clock the rain began to fall, and for nearly an hour it came down in torrents.

Almost simultaneously with the rain came the electrical disturbance. There were comparatively few sharp bolts of lightning, and the thunder was not particularly terrifying, but the whole atmosphere seemed surcharged with the electrical fluid. Beginning with a faint shimmer on the horizon, the sheets of lightning expanded into one broad sheet, until the whole heavens were lighted up with a beautiful electric blue. This display continued almost uninterruptedly for nearly an hour, with intermittant flashes of sharp lightning.

During the storm the wind attained a high velocity, driving the rain before it in sheets. The records at the Weather Bureau show that the storm began at 6:33 o'clock, and was practically over at 8:06 o'clock. During that time .48 of an inch of rain fell. When the storm was at its height the wind attained a velocity of 36 miles an hour, blowing from the southwest. After the storm passed the velocity of the wind decreased to 12 miles, but at 10:30 it increased again.

At the Weather Bureau the storm was considered an ordinary Summer thunderstorm. The rainfall was not considered extraordinary; neither was the velocity of the wind. There is no apparatus for measuring up electrical disturbances, so the weather man could tell no more about it than any other person.

**Fall of a Ball of Fire.**

Following a sharp peal of thunder, a huge ball of fire was seen to descend from the west, in a slanting direction, and when directly over the old Victoria Hotel, at Fifth Avenue, Broadway, and Twenty-seventh Street, it took a zigzag course, and passed within a few feet of the top of the flagstaff, which is on the Broadway corner of the building.

Policeman Fitzgerald of the West Thirtieth Street Station was about a block away, and saw the ball of fire as it descended. In describing it, he said that it came down with great velocity, and appeared to him to be about 18 inches in circumference. When about thirty feet above the pavement, directly in the centre of the Broadway cable track, it burst with a report like a huge torpedo. Sparks of fire flew in every direction, illuminating the street for half a block.

The fall and explosion of the ball of fire caused a large crowd of people to assemble in that locality. When the policeman reaching the scene, he found that portions of the flagstaff of the Victoria were distributed about the street, but no other damage was done. Some of the people in the crowd picked up the fragments of the pole as souvenirs.

During the storm a large tree in front of 31 West Thirty-fifth Street was blown down, and five manhole covers between Sixty-sixth and Sixty-seventh Streets on First Avenue were blown out of their places. A team of horses attached to a wagon ran away at Seventy-ninth Street and Park Avenue and was caught at Seventy-second treet. No damage was done.

**No Serious Damage in This City.**

So far as known there was no serious damage from the storm in this city. While the storm was at its height signs creaked ominously, chimneys trembled, and the sewers were overtaxed by the sudden downpour of rain, and some cellars were flooded, but the damage was trifling. The dark clouds which presaged the coming storm gave everybody sufficient warning and plenty of time to seek shelter. The elevated trains were crowded, and the passengers were treated to a panoramic display of light effects such as they seldom had seen before.

The damage to the telegraph companies was, strange to say, very slight. Night Manager E. S. Cummings of the Western Union said that his company had fared remarkably well considering the severity of the storm. About one-third of the wires were out of working order for nearly two hours, but there was no interference with the transaction of business, as there were plenty of reserve wires. The greatest trouble was experienced on the New-Jersey and Long Island wires. The Postal Telegraph wires held up under the strain, and business in all directions was carried on without interruption.

In connection with the storm it might be remarked that New-York had a taste of Summer weather yesterday, which brought a disagreeable recollection of the sizzling, sticky weather of a month ago. At 8 o'clock yesterday morning the mercury registered 66° above. At noon it had risen to 76°, and refused to stop at that mark. The highest point reached was 83° above at 3 o'clock. Just before the storm the temperature was 77°, and at 8 o'clock it had dropped 10°. The humidity was also particularly noticeable. At 8 o'clock yesterday morning there was 86 per cent. of humidity, and the highest registered was 100 per cent.

**Republican Banner Blown Down.**

While the storm was at its height last evening the Republican banner which is stretched across East Twenty-third Street, at the Metropolitan Building, was caught by a gust of wind, and torn from its fastenings. The banner fell on a team of dray horses, which was passing at the time, completely enveloping it. The horses were badly frightened, but the driver managed to keep them under control. One corner of the banner was fastened to a sash in one of the windows of the Republican Headquarters, and when the emblem went down the sash and glass went with it, causing a crash that was heard for blocks.

The lightning played a curious freak in a saloon on Eighth Avenue, near Thirty-fourth Street. One of the bolts ran into the saloon on the ticker wire, and the instrument was burned out with a report that resembled an explosion of giant powder. The people in the place made a wild dash for the doors, but no one was injured, and there was no damage aside from the destruction of the telegraph instrument.

**Bridge Traffic Suspended.**

Traffic on the Brooklyn Bridge was suspended for about ten minutes shortly after 7 o'clock last night. It was while the storm was at its height, and at once people surmised that a serious accident had occurred on the structure. The rush hour was nearly over, but the outgoing platform on the New-York end was jammed by the time traffic was resumed.

The delay was caused by the inability to unload passengers and switch the cars fast enough on the Brooklyn end, and it became necessary to flag trains on the Brooklyn incline. The signal was sent back, and one train was caught on the level in the middle of the span. The trains on the New-York incline ran back and took the cable again at the New-York terminus, but traffic could not be resumed until the train in the middle had been pulled off the level by a switch engine.

### DAMAGE IN BROOKLYN.

**An Explosion Caused by Lightning—Trolley Cars Interfered With.**

The residents of Brooklyn witnessed last evening one of the finest electrical displays that has ever been seen in that city. Beginning about 6:30 o'clock, the heavens were illuminated for over an hour. It was true that some of the people were not pleased with the display, as they were of a nervous temperament, and the heavy artillery of thunder made them more nervous than usual. This, however, did not prevent others gazing at the heavens and enjoying the sight.

The telephone drops at Police Headquarters kept falling during the storm, and the operators with fear answered what they believed were calls from the various stations. It was found that the rain and wind brought the telephone and the trolley wires into constant touch, but the wires were not injured. Neither were the batteries at Headquarters, as the lightning arrester there prevented the batteries burning out.

**Explosion in a Subway.**

There was an explosion at 7:30 o'clock which sounded to the residents of East New-York as if a large cannon had been fired. The explosion took place in the electric subway at the northeast corner of Atlantic and Alabama Avenues. A hole ten feet square was torn up, and the rocks were thrown some distance, but, fortunately, no person was injured. The firemen were sent for, but they found on their arrival that their services were not required. It is believed that the explosion was caused by a collection of sewer gas in the subway, and when the heavy rush of water began through the sewers last night it caused the gas to be forced into the subway, and

Continued on Page 5.

SIMON B. BUCKNER,

The National Democratic Party's Choice for Vice President.

## MR. FRANCIS TAKES THE OATH.

**He Will Assume Charge as Secretary of the Interior To-day.**

WASHINGTON, Sept. 3.—Ex-Gov. David R. Francis of Missouri took the oath of office as Secretary of the Interior at 12:35 to-day. The oath was administered by Associate Justice Harlan of the United States Supreme Court in the private room of Secretary Carlisle, in the Treasury Department. There were present Secretaries Lamont and Carlisle, besides several newspaper reporters.

David R. Francis.

The New Secretary of the Interior.

The new Secretary of the Interior reached the department in the afternoon and met Assistant Secretary Reynolds, and, after a brief conversation, the doors of his office were thrown open to receive the heads of bureaus, who introduced their chiefs of divisions. The new Cabinet official gave all a hearty handshake, which was accompanied by a pleasant word.

To-morrow morning the clerks and other employes will be presented, after which Secretary Francis will begin active duties at the head of the Department of the Interior.

## KATE FIELD'S WILL FOUND.

**It Provides, as Expected, for the Cremation of Her Body.**

WASHINGTON, Sept. 3.—The will of Kate Field, who died recently in Hawaii, was found to-day under peculiar circumstances. Miss Field was in the habit of stopping at the Shoreham while in the city, and on one of her visits some time ago she left a tin box. Mr. Devine, the proprietor, took charge of the box, intending to return it to her when she came again.

After her death he waited for the appointment of an executor, so he could turn over the box. To-day Mr. George Riddle of Boston, Mass., came to the city to qualify as administrator until a will should be found. Mr. Riddle is a cousin of Miss Field, and came as next of kin. By chance he also put up at the Shoreham, and there he fell into conversation with Mr. Devine, and the latter mentioned the box and his suspicions that it contained private papers. Mr. Riddle wished to open it, and sent for J. Nota McGill, Register of Wills, and an attorney. In their presence a locksmith broke open the box, and at the bottom was found the will.

It appointed as executors Mr. H. H. Kohlsaat of Chicago, proprietor of the Times-Herald, and her employer at the time of her death, and Mr. T. Sanford Beatty, secretary to Senator Brice. As anticipated, it provided for the cremation of her body, and directed that the ashes be interred at Mount Auburn, Mass. Mr. Beatty was appointed her literary executor. The disposal of her estate could not be learned.

## AN ENGINEER DROWNED.

**His Fate a Subject of a Good Deal of Mystery.**

SOUTH AMBOY, N. J., Sept. 3.—William Scully, a licensed engineer and a cousin of Councilman John Scully of this place, was drowned in Raritan Bay, between Perth Amboy and this place last evening. Councilman Scully is the owner of the tug Mary Ann, which has not been regularly in commission this Summer. Yesterday he asked Pilot Bell to take the Mary Ann to Perth Amboy so that her tanks could be filled. The pilot consented, and as there was no crew or engineer, William Scully was asked to take charge of the engine room.

He did so, and the boat reached Perth Amboy all right. After the tanks had been filled, the pilot headed the Mary Ann for this place. After she had been out some time Pilot Bell gave the engineer the bell to slow down, but the speed of the boat continued. He rang his bell again, thinking the engineer had not understood the signal, and when the Mary Ann did not slow down, went down into the engine room to find out what was the matter.

Scully was not there, but Pilot Bell saw him struggling in the water. The Mary Ann was put about and Pilot Bell tried to reach him. He also signaled to the tug Clara, Capt. Ford, and the latter tried to get to Scully, but he had disappeared. A search was made for his body, without success. It is believed that Scully accidentally fell over the side of the boat.

**Money in the United States.**

WASHINGTON, Sept. 3.—The Treasury circulation statement shows that Sept. 1 all kinds of money in the United States, outside of what is held in the Treasury, aggregated $1,539,169,634, or $21.48 per capita on an estimated population of 71,645,000. As compared with Sept. 1, 1895, the circulation shows a decrease of $64,413,394. During the month of August the circulation shows an increase of $24,266,492, made up largely from the Treasury's loss of gold.

**Commander John Clark Newell Dying.**

SEATTLE, Washington, Sept. 3.—Commander John Clark Newell of the United States cruiser Detroit, at present on the China station, is dying in this city. Capt. Newell arrived here five weeks ago on his way to Washington to make a report on the Central China missionary massacres, and was taken ill a few days after his arrival. He has been unconscious for twenty-four hours.

**A Small Boy Smothered at Play.**

WHITE PLAINS, Sept. 3.—Felix Weisbrad, ten years old, was smothered to death this afternoon by the caving in of a sandbank beneath which he was playing. Arthur Ohlsen, a playmate, was buried to the neck, but was unhurt.

## PLATFORM OF THE NATIONAL DEMOCRATIC PARTY.

This convention has assembled to uphold the principles upon which depend the honor and welfare of the American people, in order that Democrats throughout the Union may unite their patriotic efforts to avert disaster from their country and ruin from their party.

The Democratic Party is pledged to equal and exact justice to all men of every creed and condition; to the largest freedom of the individual consistent with good government; to the preservation of the Federal Government in its Constitutional vigor and to the support of the States in all their just rights; to economy in the public expenditures; to the maintenance of the public faith and sound money; and it is opposed to paternalism and all class legislation.

The declarations of the Chicago Convention attack individual freedom, the right of private contract, the independence of the judiciary, and the authority of the President to enforce Federal laws. They advocate a reckless attempt to increase the price of silver by legislation, to the debasement of our monetary standard, and threaten unlimited issues of paper money by the Government. They abandon for Republican allies the Democratic cause of tariff reform to court the favor of protectionists to their fiscal heresy.

In view of these and other grave departures from Democratic principles, we cannot support the candidates of that convention nor be bound by its acts. The Democratic Party has survived many defeats, but could not survive a victory won in behalf of the doctrine and policy proclaimed in its name at Chicago.

The conditions, however, which make possible such utterances from a National Convention are the direct result of class legislation by the Republican Party. It still proclaims, as it has for years, the power and duty of Government to raise and maintain prices by law, and it proposes no remedy for existing evils except oppressive and unjust taxation.

**Taxation for Revenue Only.**

The National Democracy here convened therefore renews its declaration of faith in Democratic principles, especially as applicable to the conditions of the times. Taxation tariff, excise or direct, is rightfully imposed only for public purposes and not for private gain. Its amount is justly measured by public expenditures, which should be limited by scrupulous economy. The sum derived by the Treasury from tariff and excise levies is affected by the state of trade and volume of consumption. The amount required by the Treasury is determined by the appropriations made by Congress.

The demand of the Republican Party for an increase in tariff taxation has its pretext in the deficiency of revenue, which has its causes in the stagnation of trade and reduced consumption, due entirely to the loss of confidence that has followed the Populist threat of free coinage and depreciation of our money and the Republican practice of extravagant appropriations beyond the needs of good government.

We arraign and condemn the Populistic Conventions of Chicago and St. Louis for their co-operation with the Republican Party in creating these conditions, which are pleaded in justification of a heavy increase of the burdens of the people, by a further resort to protection.

We therefore denounce protection and its ally, free coinage of silver, as schemes for the personal profit of a few at the expense of the masses, and oppose the two parties which stand for these schemes as hostile to the people of the Republic whose food and shelter, comfort and prosperity, are attacked by higher taxes and depreciated money. In fine, we reaffirm the historic Democratic doctrine of tariff for revenue only.

**Relief for Shipping.**

We demand that henceforth modern and liberal policies toward American shipping shall take the place of our imitation of the restrictive statutes of the eighteenth century, which have been abandoned by every maritime power but the United States, and which, to the Nation's humiliation, have driven American capital and enterprise to the use of alien flags and alien crews, have made the Stars and Stripes an almost unknown emblem in foreign ports, and have virtually extinguished the race of American seamen.

We oppose the pretense that discriminating duties will promote shipping; that scheme is an invitation to commercial warfare upon the United States, un-American in the light of our great commercial treaties, offering no gain whatever to American shipping, while greatly increasing ocean freights on our agricultural and manufactured products.

**Gold the Necessary Money.**

The experience of mankind has shown that by reason of their natural qualities, gold is the necessary money of the large affairs of commerce and business, while silver is conveniently adapted to minor transactions, and the most beneficial use of both together can be insured only by the adoption of the former as a standard of monetary measure, and the maintenance of silver at a parity with gold by its limited coinage under suitable safeguards of law. Thus the largest possible enjoyment of both metals is gained, with a value universally accepted throughout the world, which constitutes the only practical bimetallic currency, assuring the most stable standard, and especially the best and safest money for all who earn their livelihood by labor or the produce of husbandry. They cannot suffer when paid in the best money known to man, but are the peculiar and most defenseless victims of a debased and fluctuating currency, which offers continual profits to the money changer at their cost.

Realizing these truths, demonstrated by long and public inconvenience and loss, the Democratic Party, in the interests of the masses and of equal justice to all, practically established by the legislation of 1834 and 1853 the gold standard of monetary measurement and likewise entirely divorced the Government from banking and currency issues. To this long-established Democratic policy we adhere and insist upon the maintenance of the gold standard and of the parity therewith of every dollar issued by the Government, and are firmly opposed to the free and unlimited coinage of silver and to the compulsory purchase of silver bullion. But we denounce also the further maintenance of the present costly patchwork system of National paper currency as a constant source of injury and peril.

**Currency Reform Demanded.**

We assert the necessity of such intelligent currency reform as will confine the Government to its legitimate functions, completely separated from the banking business, and afford to all sections of our country a uniform, safe, and elastic bank currency, under Governmental supervision, measured in volume by the needs of business.

**President Cleveland Indorsed.**

The fidelity, patriotism, and courage with which President Cleveland has fulfilled his great public trust, the high character of his Administration, its wisdom and energy in the maintenance of civil order and the enforcement of the laws, its equal regard for the rights of every class and every section, its firm and dignified conduct of foreign affairs, and its sturdy persistence in upholding the credit and honor of the Nation are fully recognized by the Democratic Party and will secure to him a place in history beside the fathers of the Republic.

**Civil Service Reform.**

We also commend the Administration for the great progress made in the reform of the civil service, and we indorse its effort to extend the merit system still further.

We demand that no backward step be taken, but that the reform be supported and advanced until the un-Democratic spoils system of appointments shall be eradicated.

We demand strict economy in the appropriations and in the administration of the Government.

We favor arbitration for the settlement of international disputes.

We favor a liberal policy of pensions to deserving soldiers and sailors of the United States.

**The Supreme Court.**

The Supreme Court of the United States was wisely established by the framers of our Constitution as one of the three co-ordinate branches of the Government. Its independence and authority to interpret the law of the land without fear or favor must be maintained.

We condemn all efforts to degrade that tribunal or impair the confidence and respect which it has deservedly held.

The Democratic Party ever has maintained and ever will maintain the supremacy of law, the independence of its judicial administration, the inviolability of contract, and the obligations of all good citizens to resist every illegal trust, combination, or attempt against the just rights of property and the good order of society, in which are bound up the peace and happiness of our people.

Believing these principles to be essential to the well-being of the Republic, we submit them to the consideration of the American people.

Adopted at Indianapolis Sept. 3.

## WHEELMAN BADLY HURT.

**Louis B. Wolfe Loses Control of His Machine and Is Injured.**

Louis B. Wolfe, a clerk living at 50 East Eighty-ninth Street, was riding rapidly on a bicycle at the Fifty-ninth Street and Fifth Avenue entrance to Central Park yesterday forenoon when he lost control of his wheel, colliding with a small cart used by the Park employes to gather up refuse on the lawns. He was thrown violently to the ground, sustaining several severe contusions of the head and knees, with a possible fracture of the skull.

Park Policeman Henry summoned an ambulance from the Presbyterian Hospital, where Wolfe was removed. As Wolfe was riding faster than the law allows, it is the intention of the officer to charge him with violating a city ordinance.

Wolfe will probably be confined to the hospital for a week or more.

## SUNK WITH ALL SAILS SET.

**The Fruit Sloop Jaquette Brought in by the Tug Bouker.**

The tug J. A. Bouker, Capt. Day, returning from sea yesterday morning, fell in with the sloop Jaquette, laden with melons, sunk. All sails were set. No one was on board. The tug took her in tow. She capsized, spilling her cargo, off Owl's Head, Lower Bay.

The tug brought her up to the foot of Jackson Street, East River, where she now lies. The Jaquette was built at Keyport, N. J., in 1869, and is thirty-two feet long.

It is not known what has become of her crew, but it is supposed they took to their boat.

## STABBED FOR A CIGAR PUFF.

**Patrick Doolan Near Death as the Result of a Request.**

Patrick Doolan, a laborer, of 340 East Sixty-first Street, while slightly intoxicated, was standing in front of his house at about 11 o'clock last night. Anthony Frank of 330 East Sixty-third Street and Frederick Danneckar, thirty-eight years old, a shoemaker of 243 East Ninety-third Street, passed by. Frank was smoking a cigar and Doolan asked him for a puff. Frank replied that if Doolan walked down to the corner he, Frank, would give him a cigar.

Both men passed on and Doolan followed, using insulting language. They turned and Doolan ran, and they followed him to the stoop of 338 East Sixty-first Street, where, it is alleged, Frank stabbed Doolan in both shoulders and in the back, inflicting severe, if not fatal injuries. Two of the wounds penetrated the lungs.

Doolan, after being stabbed, ran to the rooms of his uncle, Patrick Doolan, at 336 East Sixty-first Street. By this time a crowd had collected in the street, and some one shouted for the police. Policeman McCarthy saw a man running away from the place and arrested him. This man proved to be Frank. Doolan identified him as the man who did the stabbing.

Danneckar was discovered creeping out of the hallway of 340 East Sixty-first Street a half hour later, and he was also arrested. A large pocketknife, the biggest blade of which was covered with blood, was found lying in the gutter opposite 343 East Sixty-first Street. The men both denied the ownership of the knife.

Doolan was in a very critical condition at a late hour, and his chances of recovery were pronounced very slight.

## THE DEMOCRATIC TICKET

### Palmer and Buckner Nominated at Indianapolis.

### GOOD MEN TO LEAD A GOOD FIGHT

**Platform Sound in Its Financial Declarations and Strong in Denunciation of Populism.**

**A VIGOROUS CAMPAIGN IS PROPOSED**

**Fighting to Begin at Once in All Parts of the Country Against Bryan and His Doctrines.**

President—JOHN McAULEY PALMER of Illinois.

Vice President — SIMON BOLIVAR BUCKNER of Kentucky.

INDIANAPOLIS, Sept. 3.—Gen. John M. Palmer of Illinois and Gen. Simon B. Buckner of Kentucky were named this afternoon as the candidates for President and Vice President of the United States by the National Democratic Party. Gen. Palmer's nomination, which was made on one roll call, Gen. Edward S. Bragg receiving about 130 votes, was the acceptance of the first intention of the party. Nothing except his unwillingness to stand, expressed positively—and, it was feared, irrevocably—at the time of the conference of Aug. 7, ever made his nomination seem doubtful.

If he had been out of the contest, the warm admiration for Gen. Bragg in many States would have made him a formidable candidate, and it is probable he would have commanded so much support as to deprive Illinois of the honor of selecting Gen. John C. Black as an alternative candidate.

**A Business-Like Convention.**

The convention has more than satisfied those who organized the movement that brought it here, and it has surprised those who knew only of the strength of this Democratic impulse by observation in their own States. The men who made up the body of delegates were of the best type, devoted to business, not devoid of some boisterous zeal, but never carried away by their own emotions nor disposed to devote time to excessive cheering and banner carrying in procession. All the work of the convention was done with reasonable promptness.

When it came to making the nominations the disposition to unite made it easy to concentrate upon men. Nearly everybody wanted Gen. Palmer for President; absolutely everybody favored Gen. Buckner's nomination for second place. Both candidates were nominated within the same hour. From the first session of the convention Wednesday to the close of proceedings to-day the temper of the body was of the best. The enthusiasm increased as the business proceeded. The mass meeting last night, which was as large a gathering as Tomlinson Hall could contain comfortably, not only was remarkable in size, but it was one of the most thoroughly interesting, appreciative, and encouraging gatherings of enthusiastic Democrats that ever assembled in Indianapolis. Delegates were still praising the speeches of Col. Fellows and Charlton T. Lewis and Mr. Ehrich of Colorado when they took their places in the hall this morning to complete the business that brought them here.

**No Nostrums in the Platform.**

Diverting as was the speechmaking to-day, the convention began to be somewhat impatient before the Committee on Resolutions was ready to report the platform. When at last Senator Vilas reached the stage with the declaration of Democratic doctrines he was received with a glad shout

JOHN M. PALMER,

Nominated by the National Democratic Party for President.

## THE WEATHER.

**The indications for to-day are for cooler and generally fair weather, with northerly winds.**

The barometer had fallen last night along the Atlantic and Gulf coast, and in the Northwest, and had risen over the lake region, and thence southwestward to Texas. It was highest over the upper lake region, and the depression which was in the St. Lawrence valley yesterday morning was central on the northeast New-England coast.

It was decidedly cooler in the lake region and generally throughout the central valleys, and warmer on the Atlantic and Gulf coast, and in the Northwest.

Showers and thunderstorms prevailed in New-England and Middle Atlantic States, Tennessee, and the Ohio Valley, and Gulf coast yesterday. The weather was fair in the upper lake region, the Upper Mississippi and Missouri Valleys.

Cooler and fair weather is predicted from Southern New-England southwestward to Virginia, and generally fair weather over the lake region, the Ohio, Upper Mississippi, and Missouri Valleys. Local thunderstorms are likely to occur in the Gulf and South Atlantic States.

The record of temperature for the twenty-four hours ended at midnight, taken from THE NEW-YORK TIMES's thermometer and from the thermometer of the Weather Bureau is as follows:

| | —Weather Bureau— 1895. | 1896. | TIMES. 1896. |
|---|---|---|---|
| 3 A. M. | 61 | 59 | 69 |
| 6 A. M. | 58 | 60 | 70 |
| 9 A. M. | 66 | 68 | 73 |
| 12 M. | 74 | 76 | 78 |
| 4 P. M. | 73 | 82 | 81 |
| 6 P. M. | 71 | 77 | 79 |
| 9 P. M. | 70 | 69 | 73 |
| 12 P. M. | 66 | 60 | 70 |

THE TIMES's thermometer is 6 feet above the street level; that of the Weather Bureau 285 feet above the street level.

Average temperatures yesterday were as follows:

Printing House Square....74.12
Weather Bureau....73.00
Corresponding date 1895....67.00
Corresponding date for last twenty years....70.00

Complete "Weather Forecast," Page 10, Column 7.

**Mr. Hill Dies in a Hospital.**

Henry G. Hill, a wholesale dry goods merchant of 65 Worth Street, who was taken to Gouverneur Hospital from the Bowery, near Canal Street, Wednesday night, died in the hospital last night without having recovered consciousness. It was supposed that death was caused by the bursting of a blood vessel in his brain. Mr. Hill was taken suddenly ill in a car on the Bowery and was removed to the hospital in an ambulance.

## TELEGRAPHIC BREVITIES.

—Cosimo Oliva, sentenced a year ago to ten years in Massachusetts State prison for assault with intent to kill upon James O'Brien of Chelsea, was pardoned yesterday, later evidence showing conclusively that Oliva was innocent.

—The Manufacturers' Bank of West Duluth, Minn., has been placed in the hands of a receiver by order of the State Bank Examiner. Deposits amount to $40,000. The failure was due to inability to realize quickly on assets.

—George Chesterman of New-York was arrested yesterday morning at Narragansett Pier for alleged larceny. Thomas Cronan, a New-York dramatist, claims that Chesterman has in his possession notes belonging to him valued at $1,000.

Two Parts
16 Pages

# The New-York Times.

SECOND EDITION

VOL. XLVI...NO. 14,106. NEW-YORK, WEDNESDAY, NOVEMBER 4, 1896.—COPYRIGHTED, 1896, BY THE NEW-YORK TIMES COMPANY. PRICE THREE CENTS.

## McKINLEY

## ELECTED

### PRESIDENT UNITED STATES

| State. | Electoral Vote. | McKinley & Hobart. | Bryan..... | Sewall..... | Watson.... |
|---|---|---|---|---|---|
| Alabama | 11 | .. | 11 | .. | .. |
| Arkansas | 8 | .. | 8 | 5 | 3 |
| California | 9 | 9 | .. | .. | .. |
| Colorado | 4 | .. | 4 | 3 | 1 |
| Connecticut | 6 | 6 | .. | .. | .. |
| Delaware | 3 | 3 | .. | .. | .. |
| Florida | 4 | .. | 4 | 4 | .. |
| Georgia | 13 | .. | 13 | 13 | .. |
| Idaho | 3 | .. | 3 | 2 | 1 |
| Illinois | 24 | 24 | .. | .. | .. |
| Indiana | 15 | 15 | .. | .. | .. |
| Iowa | 13 | 13 | .. | .. | .. |
| Kansas | 10 | 10 | .. | .. | .. |
| Kentucky | 13 | 13 | .. | .. | .. |
| Louisiana | 8 | .. | 8 | 4 | 4 |
| Maine | 6 | 6 | .. | .. | .. |
| Maryland | 8 | 8 | .. | .. | .. |
| Massachusetts | 15 | 15 | .. | .. | .. |
| Michigan | 14 | 14 | .. | .. | .. |
| Minnesota | 9 | 9 | .. | .. | .. |
| Mississippi | 9 | .. | 9 | 9 | .. |
| Missouri | 17 | .. | 17 | 13 | 4 |
| Montana | 3 | .. | 3 | 2 | 1 |
| Nebraska | 8 | 8 | .. | .. | .. |
| Nevada | 3 | .. | 3 | 3 | .. |
| New-Hampshire | 4 | 4 | .. | .. | .. |
| New-Jersey | 10 | 10 | .. | .. | .. |
| New-York | 36 | 36 | .. | .. | .. |
| North Carolina | 11 | 11 | .. | 6 | 5 |
| North Dakota | 3 | 3 | .. | .. | .. |
| Ohio | 23 | 23 | .. | .. | .. |
| Oregon | 4 | 4 | .. | .. | .. |
| Pennsylvania | 32 | 32 | .. | .. | .. |
| Rhode Island | 4 | 4 | .. | .. | .. |
| South Carolina | 9 | .. | 9 | 9 | .. |
| South Dakota | 4 | 4 | .. | .. | .. |
| Tennessee | 12 | .. | 12 | 12 | .. |
| Texas | 15 | .. | 15 | 15 | .. |
| Utah | 3 | .. | 3 | 2 | 1 |
| Vermont | 4 | 4 | .. | .. | .. |
| Virginia | 12 | .. | .. | .. | .. |
| Washington | 4 | 4 | .. | .. | .. |
| West Virginia | 6 | 6 | .. | .. | .. |
| Wisconsin | 12 | 12 | .. | .. | .. |
| Wyoming | 3 | 3 | .. | .. | .. |
| Total | 447 | 313 | 122 | 102 | 20 |

PLURALITIES.

| State. | McKinley. | Bryan. |
|---|---|---|
| Alabama | | 30,000 |
| Arkansas | | 45,000 |
| California | | ...... |
| Colorado | | 75,000 |
| Connecticut | 50,000 | ..... |
| Delaware | 2,000 | ..... |
| Florida | | 10,000 |
| Georgia | | 30,000 |
| Idaho | | 9,000 |
| Illinois | 100,000 | ..... |
| Indiana | 20,000 | ..... |
| Iowa | 50,000 | ..... |
| Kansas | 50,000 | ..... |
| Kentucky | 20,000 | ..... |
| Louisiana | | 25,000 |
| Maine | 50,000 | ..... |
| Maryland | 30,000 | ..... |
| Massachusetts | 165,000 | ..... |
| Michigan | 30,000 | ..... |
| Minnesota | 40,000 | ..... |
| Mississippi | | 50,000 |
| Missouri | | ..... |
| Montana | | 5,000 |
| Nebraska | | ..... |
| Nevada | | 5,000 |
| New-Hampshire | 25,000 | ..... |
| New-Jersey | 67,000 | ..... |
| New-York | 300,000 | ..... |
| North Carolina | | ..... |
| North Dakota | 2,000 | ..... |
| Ohio | 75,000 | ..... |
| Oregon | 3,000 | ..... |
| Pennsylvania | 300,000 | ..... |
| Rhode Island | 20,000 | ..... |
| South Carolina | | 9,000 |
| South Dakota | 5,000 | ..... |
| Tennessee | | ..... |
| Texas | | ..... |
| Utah | | 40,000 |
| Vermont | 30,000 | ..... |
| Virginia | | ..... |
| Washington | | ..... |
| West Virginia | | ..... |
| Wisconsin | 100,000 | ..... |
| Wyoming | 1,000 | ..... |

TIMES OFFICE, Nov. 4.—3 A. M.

William McKinley and Garret A. Hobart, the Republican candidates for President and Vice President of the United States, have been elected by a tremendous majority in the Electoral College and by an enormous plurality of the popular vote.

Out of the 447 Electoral votes, the Democratic-Populist combination of Bryan, Sewall, and Watson was only able to secure 122, as against 313 for their Republican competitors, with one State in doubt.

The victory for sound money is even more strikingly shown in the popular vote. In this, the pluralities from the most trustworthy data make it appear that McKinley and Hobart lead the opposition by more than 1,000,000 ballots.

In the analysis by States, as shown in the adjoining column, the fact is made clear that the attempted coalition of the South and West has been an absolute and thorough failure.

The boasted "Solid South" has been broken. Of the States which formerly made up this mass that was regarded as Democratic under all circumstances, the Republican candidates for the Presidency have carried Delaware, Maryland, West Virginia, North Carolina, and Kentucky. In nearly all cases, moreover, the pluralities were large.

In the Middle West, which was by common consent made the principal fighting ground, the Republicans have made a clean sweep. Illinois, the pivotal State, has gone Republican by an immense pluralities. Ohio, Indiana, Michigan, Wisconsin, Iowa, the Dakotas, Kansas, and Nebraska have followed.

The three Pacific coast States and Wyoming are also to be placed in the Republican list.

In the East, every State from Maine to North Carolina, inclusive, has gone for McKinley and Hobart, with the exception of Virginia, which is in doubt.

Thirty States went Republican and fourteen Democratic and Populist.

Every record for large pluralities in the history of the country has been broken by New-York and Pennsylvania, each of which gives the Republican candidates about 300,000. Of other States in the same column, Illinois gives 150,000, Massachusetts 110,000, and Wisconsin 100,000.

The landslide for honest money came according to prediction.

## CONGRESS

## GOLD

### HOUSE AND SENATE

House of Representatives.

| | Fifty-fourth Congress. Rep. | Dem. | Pop. | Fifty-fifth Congress. Rep. | Dem. | Pop. |
|---|---|---|---|---|---|---|
| Alabama | 2 | 6 | 1 | .. | 8 | 1 |
| Arkansas | .. | 6 | .. | .. | 6 | .. |
| California | 6 | 1 | .. | 4 | 2 | 1 |
| Colorado | 1 | .. | 1 | 1 | .. | 1 |
| Connecticut | 4 | .. | .. | 4 | .. | .. |
| Delaware | 1 | .. | .. | .. | 1 | .. |
| Florida | .. | 2 | .. | .. | 2 | .. |
| Georgia | .. | 11 | .. | .. | 11 | .. |
| Idaho | 1 | .. | .. | .. | .. | 1 |
| Illinois | 22 | .. | .. | 19 | 3 | .. |
| Indiana | 13 | .. | .. | 11 | 2 | .. |
| Iowa | 11 | .. | .. | 11 | .. | .. |
| Kansas | 7 | .. | 1 | 8 | .. | .. |
| Kentucky | 5 | 6 | .. | 8 | 3 | .. |
| Louisiana | .. | 6 | .. | .. | 6 | .. |
| Maine | 4 | .. | .. | 4 | .. | .. |
| Maryland | 3 | 3 | .. | 6 | .. | .. |
| Massachusetts | 12 | 1 | .. | 12 | 1 | .. |
| Michigan | 12 | .. | .. | 12 | .. | .. |
| Minnesota | 7 | .. | .. | 7 | .. | .. |
| Mississippi | .. | 7 | .. | .. | 7 | .. |
| Missouri | 11 | 4 | .. | 7 | 8 | .. |
| Montana | 1 | .. | .. | 1 | .. | .. |
| Nebraska | 5 | .. | 1 | 4 | 1 | 1 |
| Nevada | .. | .. | 1 | .. | .. | 1 |
| New-Hampshire | 2 | .. | .. | 2 | .. | .. |
| New-Jersey | 8 | .. | .. | 8 | .. | .. |
| New-York | 29 | 5 | .. | 29 | 5 | .. |
| North Carolina | 3 | 3 | 3 | 4 | .. | 5 |
| North Dakota | 1 | .. | .. | 1 | .. | .. |
| Ohio | 19 | 2 | .. | 16 | 5 | .. |
| Oregon | 2 | .. | .. | 2 | .. | .. |
| Pennsylvania | 28 | 2 | .. | 24 | 6 | .. |
| Rhode Island | 2 | .. | .. | 2 | .. | .. |
| South Carolina | .. | 7 | .. | .. | 7 | .. |
| South Dakota | 2 | .. | .. | 2 | .. | .. |
| Tennessee | 4 | 6 | .. | 3 | 7 | .. |
| Texas | 1 | 12 | .. | 2 | 7 | 4 |
| Utah | 1 | .. | .. | .. | 1 | .. |
| Vermont | 2 | .. | .. | 2 | .. | .. |
| Virginia | 1 | 9 | .. | 2 | 8 | .. |
| Washington | 2 | .. | .. | .. | 2 | .. |
| West Virginia | 4 | .. | .. | 4 | .. | .. |
| Wisconsin | 10 | .. | .. | 9 | .. | 1 |
| Wyoming | 1 | .. | .. | 1 | .. | .. |
| Total | 250 | 99 | 8 | 242 | 99 | 16 |

Whole number of members....357
Republican majority, Fifty-fourth Congress...143
Republican majority, Fifty-fifth Congress....115
Populist increase over Fifty-fourth Congress.. 8

The New Senate.

| | 54th Congress. Rep. | Dem. | Pop. | 55th Congress. Rep. | Dem. | Pop. |
|---|---|---|---|---|---|---|
| Alabama | .. | 2 | .. | .. | 2 | .. |
| Arkansas | .. | 2 | .. | .. | 2 | .. |
| California | 1 | 1 | . | 1 | 1 | .. |
| Colorado | 2 | .. | .. | 2 | .. | .. |
| Connecticut | 2 | .. | .. | 2 | .. | .. |
| Delaware | .. | 1 | .. | 1 | 1 | .. |
| Florida | .. | 2 | .. | .. | 2 | .. |
| Georgia | .. | 2 | .. | .. | 2 | .. |
| Idaho | 2 | .. | .. | 1 | .. | 1 |
| Illinois | 1 | 1 | .. | 2 | .. | .. |
| Indiana | .. | 2 | .. | 2 | .. | .. |
| Iowa | 2 | .. | .. | 2 | .. | .. |
| Kansas | 1 | .. | 1 | 2 | .. | .. |
| Kentucky | .. | 2 | .. | 1 | 1 | .. |
| Louisiana | .. | 2 | .. | .. | 2 | .. |
| Maine | 2 | .. | .. | 2 | .. | .. |
| Maryland | .. | 2 | .. | 1 | 1 | .. |
| Massachusetts | 2 | .. | .. | 2 | .. | .. |
| Michigan | 2 | .. | .. | 2 | .. | .. |
| Minnesota | 2 | .. | .. | 2 | .. | .. |
| Mississippi | .. | 2 | .. | .. | 2 | .. |
| Missouri | .. | 2 | .. | 1 | 1 | .. |
| Montana | 2 | .. | .. | 2 | .. | .. |
| Nebraska | 1 | .. | 1 | 1 | .. | 1 |
| Nevada | .. | .. | 2 | .. | .. | 2 |
| New-Hampshire | 2 | .. | .. | 2 | .. | .. |
| New-Jersey | 1 | 1 | .. | 1 | 1 | .. |
| New-York | .. | 2 | .. | 1 | 1 | .. |
| North Carolina | 1 | .. | 1 | .. | .. | 2 |
| North Dakota | 1 | 1 | .. | 1 | 1 | .. |
| Ohio | 1 | 1 | .. | 2 | .. | .. |
| Oregon | 2 | .. | .. | 2 | .. | .. |
| Pennsylvania | 2 | .. | .. | 2 | .. | .. |
| Rhode Island | 2 | .. | .. | 2 | .. | .. |
| South Carolina | .. | 2 | .. | .. | 2 | .. |
| South Dakota | 1 | .. | 1 | 2 | .. | .. |
| Tennessee | .. | 2 | .. | .. | 2 | .. |
| Texas | .. | 2 | .. | .. | 2 | .. |
| Utah | 2 | .. | .. | 1 | 1 | .. |
| Vermont | 2 | .. | .. | 2 | .. | .. |
| Virginia | .. | 2 | .. | .. | 2 | .. |
| Washington | 2 | .. | .. | 2 | .. | .. |
| West Virginia | 1 | 1 | .. | 1 | 1 | .. |
| Wisconsin | .. | 2 | .. | 1 | 1 | .. |
| Wyoming | 2 | .. | .. | 2 | .. | .. |
| Total | 44 | 39 | 6 | 53 | 31 | 6 |

THE CONGRESS.

The Republicans have secured control of both branches of the Fifty-fifth Congress.

In the Senate the Republicans gain Senators from Kentucky, Illinois, Indiana, Kansas, New-York, South Dakota, and Wisconsin.

Free silver has now 49 votes in the Senate. It will have but 42 after March 4, 1897.

Vest may be doomed to retirement from Missouri; Voorhees will be beaten in Indiana; Ingalls may return from Kansas; Hill will be followed by a Republican from the State of New-York.

With the majority secured by the Republicans, that party will be able to carry any political legislation it desires through the Senate.

The House of Representatives will be Republican by nearly, if not quite, 130 majority, the indications promising to give to the Republicans most of the districts reported as doubtful.

The Democrats come out of the election with very few solid delegations to the next House. Arkansas, Florida, Georgia, Louisiana, Mississippi, South Carolina, form the short line of "solid" States.

The majority in the House for sound money will be approximately the Republican majority. A Republican in Colorado is for free silver; one Democrat in Kentucky is for the gold standard and was indorsed by the Republicans; the Silver Party elects the Nevada Representative, who is unwilling to be classed with either of the other parties.

"Silver Dick" Bland is probably beaten in Missouri, but "Objector" Holman has been once more elected from Indiana.

New-York sends but five Democratic Representatives to the next Congress, and they are about as inconspicuous and unworthy a group as ever managed to secure election to such responsible positions.

The Populists have certainly doubled their strength in the present Congress, and it is possible they may increase by contests in close districts.

## NEW-YORK

## 270,000

### REPUBLICAN PLURALITY

VOTE BY COUNTIES.

The following table shows the pluralities in the several counties of New-York of the Republican and Democratic candidates for President. The figures in the last column give votes cast for the National Democratic candidate:

| Counties. | McKinley, Rep. | Bryan, Dem. | Palmer, Nat. Dem. |
|---|---|---|---|
| Albany | 4,755 | ...... | 600 |
| Allegany | 3,200 | ...... | ..... |
| Broome | 5,080 | ...... | ..... |
| Cattaraugus | 3,500 | ...... | ..... |
| Cayuga | 4,214 | ...... | ..... |
| Chautauqua | 7,935 | ...... | ..... |
| Chemung | 2,837 | ...... | 108 |
| Chenango | 2,600 | ...... | ..... |
| Clinton | 3,020 | ...... | ..... |
| Columbia | 2,425 | ...... | 200 |
| Cortland | 2,308 | ...... | 40 |
| Delaware | 3,000 | ...... | 200 |
| Dutchess | 5,200 | ...... | 220 |
| Erie | 15,240 | ...... | ..... |
| Essex | 3,506 | ...... | ..... |
| Franklin | 3,511 | ...... | ..... |
| Fulton & Hamilton | 3,700 | ...... | 250 |
| Genesee | 2,208 | ...... | ..... |
| Greene | 840 | ...... | ..... |
| Herkimer | 3,000 | ...... | 146 |
| Jefferson | 4,620 | ...... | 126 |
| Kings | 30,000 | ...... | ..... |
| Lewis | 1,300 | ...... | ..... |
| Livingston | 1,350 | ...... | ..... |
| Madison | 4,164 | ...... | ..... |
| Monroe | 9,500 | ...... | ..... |
| Montgomery | 2,438 | ...... | 300 |
| New-York | ...... | ...... | ..... |
| Niagara | 2,400 | ...... | ..... |
| Oneida | 4,800 | ...... | 850 |
| Onondaga | 10,905 | ...... | ..... |
| Ontario | 2,032 | ...... | ..... |
| Orange | 4,800 | ...... | ..... |
| Orleans | 1,792 | ...... | ..... |
| Oswego | 3,500 | ...... | ..... |
| Otsego | 2,800 | ...... | ..... |
| Putnam | 1,290 | ...... | 40 |
| Queens | 9,274 | ...... | ..... |
| Rensselaer | 4,500 | ...... | 300 |
| Richmond | 1,923 | ...... | ..... |
| Rockland | 1,331 | ...... | ..... |
| St. Lawrence | 9,500 | ...... | 400 |
| Saratoga | 6,500 | ...... | ..... |
| Schenectady | 920 | ...... | ..... |
| Schoharie | ...... | 500 | ..... |
| Schuyler | 1,025 | ...... | ..... |
| Seneca | 800 | ...... | 50 |
| Steuben | 4,801 | ...... | ..... |
| Suffolk | 4,800 | ...... | ..... |
| Sullivan | 1,000 | ...... | ..... |
| Tioga | 4,500 | ...... | ..... |
| Tompkins | 1,800 | ...... | 112 |
| Ulster | 1,700 | ...... | ..... |
| Warren | 2,522 | ...... | ..... |
| Washington | 4,958 | ...... | 123 |
| Wayne | 3,797 | ...... | 50 |
| Westchester | 8,7[illegible] | ...... | ..... |
| Wyoming | 2,195 | ...... | ..... |
| Yates | 1,250 | ...... | ..... |
| Total | 208,002 | 500 | ..... |

McKinley's net plurality.........207,502

TIMES OFFICE, Nov. 4.—4 A. M.

McKinley carried New-York State by a plurality that broke all previous records. It is about 270,000.

The sound-money wave took everything before it.

The greatest plurality ever given to a candidate of either party before this year was 192,854. That was the Democratic plurality given to Grover Cleveland for Governor in 1882. For the first time a Republican candidate for President has carried New-York County.

The heretofore Democratic stronghold, which has figured in all the calculations, to overcome the majority up the State with which the Republicans "come down to Harlem," led the procession in its Republican plurality.

Kings County gave a plurality for McKinley which was not far from that of New-York, and Erie, Monroe, Onandaga, and Albany showed large gains over their usual figures.

In many parts of the State the National Democrats voted for McKinley, and the Palmer and Buckner vote in those places was far less than the number of men enrolled by that organization.

The total vote in the State was large, and reports are uniform that it was polled early. Such interest has rarely been manifested.

Schoharie County held to its record of always going Democratic. That was the only county in the State which gave a plurality for Bryan. The Democratic plurality in that county four years ago was about 1,300, and two years ago it was about 400. This year it was about 300.

Chemung County, which was one of the two counties north of the Harlem to give a plurality for Hill for Governor two years ago, gave a plurality of more than 2,000 for McKinley.

The town of Red Hook, in which Mr. Bryan spent a week on his first campaigning trip to what be called "the enemy's country" gave McKinley 247 votes more than it gave to Gov. Morton two years ago.

## B L A C K

## ELECTED

### GOVERNOR STATE NEW-YORK

VOTE BY COUNTIES.

The following table shows the pluralities in the several counties of New-York of the Republican and Democratic candidates for Governor. The figures in the last column give votes cast for the National Democratic candidate:

| Counties. | Black. Rep. | Porter. Dem. | Griffin. N't.D'm. |
|---|---|---|---|
| Albany | 4,500 | ..... | 600 |
| Allegany | 3,000 | ..... | ..... |
| Broome | 4,830 | ...... | ..... |
| Cattaraugus | 3,200 | ..... | ..... |
| Cayuga | 3,800 | ..... | ..... |
| Chautauqua | 7,707 | ..... | ..... |
| Chemung | 2,520 | ...... | 108 |
| Chenango | 2,750 | ..... | ..... |
| Clinton | 2,450 | ..... | ..... |
| Columbia | 1,850 | ..... | 200 |
| Cortland | 2,268 | ...... | 46 |
| Delaware | 2,700 | ..... | 200 |
| Dutchess | 5,0[illegible] | ..... | 226 |
| Erie | 10,200 | ...... | ..... |
| Essex | 3,450 | ..... | ..... |
| Franklin | 3,399 | ..... | ..... |
| Fulton and Hamilton | 3,300 | ..... | 250 |
| Genesee | 2,150 | ...... | ..... |
| Greene | 700 | ..... | ..... |
| Herkimer | 2,700 | ...... | 146 |
| Jefferson | 4,220 | ...... | 198 |
| Kings | 22,506 | ...... | 5,399 |
| Lewis | 1,276 | ...... | ..... |
| Livingston | 1,200 | ..... | ..... |
| Madison | 3,616 | ...... | ..... |
| Monroe | 6,000 | ..... | ..... |
| Montgomery | 2,300 | ..... | 300 |
| New-York | .... | ..... | ..... |
| Niagara | 1,900 | ..... | ..... |
| Ontario | 1,950 | ...... | ..... |
| Onondaga | 6,500 | ..... | ..... |
| Ontario | 2,200 | ..... | ..... |
| Orange | 4,500 | ..... | ..... |
| Orleans | 1,792 | ..... | ..... |
| Oswego | 3,390 | ..... | ..... |
| Otsego | 2,000 | ..... | ..... |
| Putnam | 1,253 | ..... | 46 |
| Queens | 4,000 | ..... | ..... |
| Rensselaer | 4,000 | ..... | 300 |
| Richmond | 1,265 | ..... | 473 |
| Rockland | 1,100 | ..... | ..... |
| St. Lawrence | 9,000 | ..... | 420 |
| Saratoga | 6,137 | ..... | ..... |
| Schenectady | 685 | ...... | ..... |
| Schoharie | ...... | 475 | ..... |
| Schuyler | 900 | ..... | ..... |
| Seneca | 730 | ..... | 50 |
| Steuben | 4,500 | ..... | ..... |
| Suffolk | 4,800 | ..... | ..... |
| Sullivan | 950 | ..... | ..... |
| Tioga | 4,200 | ..... | ..... |
| Tompkins | 1,500 | ..... | 112 |
| Ulster | [illegible],800 | ..... | 200 |
| Warren | 2,239 | ...... | ..... |
| Washington | 4,650 | ..... | 122 |
| Wayne | 3,772 | ..... | 53 |
| Westchester | 8,400 | ..... | ..... |
| Wyoming | 2,100 | ..... | ..... |
| Yates | 1,275 | ..... | ..... |
| Total | 222,205 | 475 | ..... |

Black's net plurality, 221,730.

A MAP SHOWING HOW ALL THE STATES IN THE UNION HAVE CAST THEIR ELECTORAL VOTES, THOSE WHICH HAVE GONE FOR M'KINLEY BEING IN WHITE AND THOSE FOR BRYAN IN BLACK

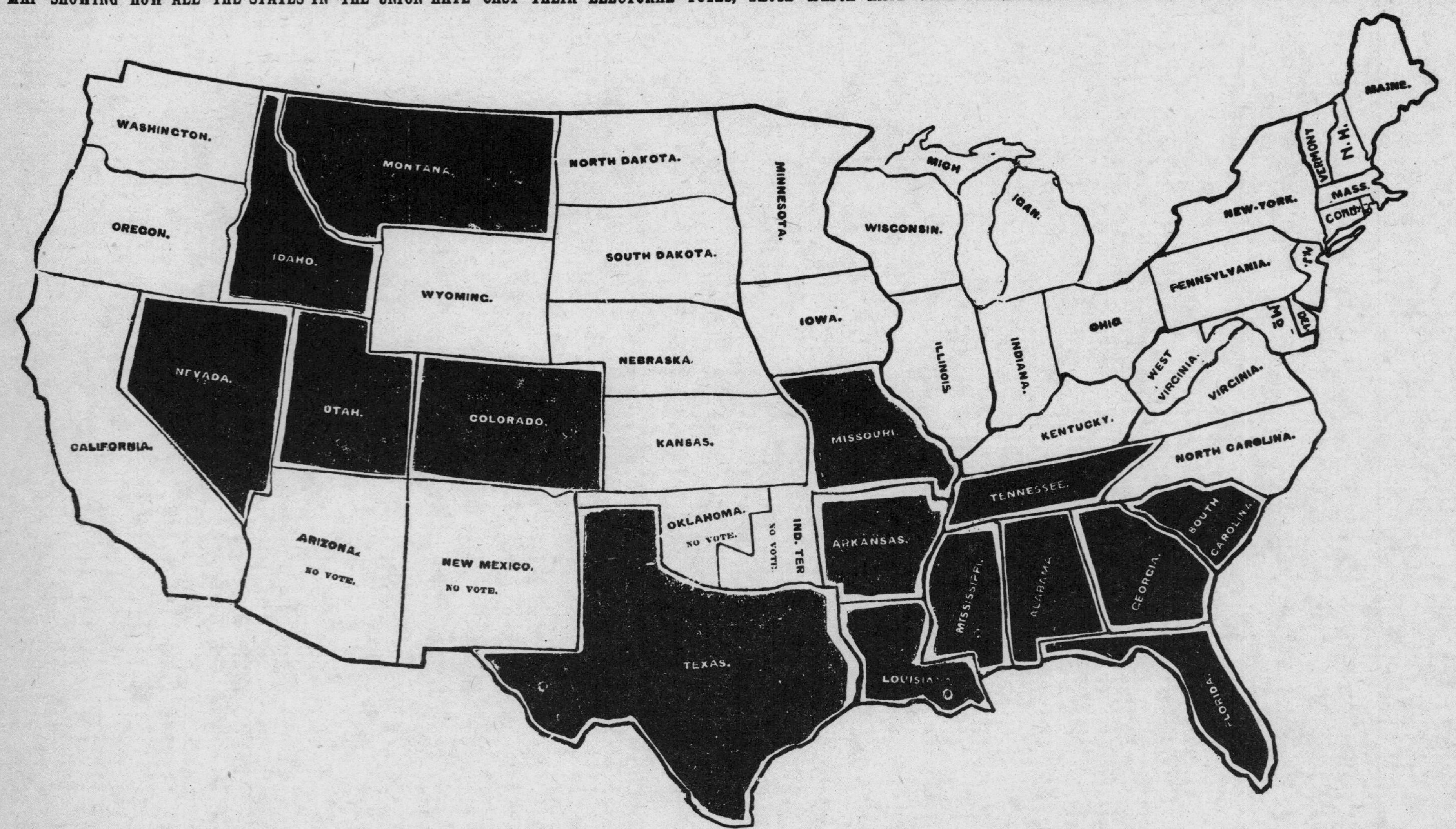

WILLIAM McKINLEY

"All the News That's Fit to Print"

# The New York Times

LATE CITY EDITION

Weather: Fair, very cold today and tonight. Chance of snow tomorrow. Temp. range: today 24-14; Sunday 33-26. Full U.S. report on Page 30.

VOL. XLVI...NO. 14,210. NEW YORK, FRIDAY, MARCH 5, 1897.—FOURTEEN PAGES. PRICE THREE CENTS

## THE NEWS CONDENSED.

Stock Market—Buoyancy succeeded by weakness.

Wheat, 85¼; corn, 27; cotton, 7 3-16.

CONGRESS.—Five of the appropriation bills reached President Cleveland at so late an hour that he refused to sign them. This included the General Deficiency bill, and prompt action will be taken in the extra session to prevent inconvenience to the public. The House unanimously passed a resolution of thanks to Speaker Reed, the Democrats leading with evident sincerity and pleasure.—Page 6.

FOREIGN.—The great gale which has been raging off the coast of Europe has caused much damage to property and the loss of the lives of many sailors. Guillermo Prieto, Mexico's most famous poet, died in the City of Mexico, on Wednesday. The Queen's drawing room in Buckingham Palace was held by the Princess of Wales yesterday. The Wilson Line steamer Cambrian is adrift on the Atlantic. She has been towed by two vessels, both of which have lost her.—Pages 1 and 9.

**Page 1.**

Cecilia Paget of London has brought suit for $8,725 against Mrs. Lewis Baker, Jr., of St. Paul, as the result of an unsettled real estate deal.

A Baltimore and Ohio work train jumped the track near Zanesville, and as a result, three men were killed and several others injured.

Under a code forbidding the appearance of unclean persons on highways, Mrs. Belledina of West Mount Vernon was yesterday sent to the penitentiary for three months for not keeping her children clean.

**Page 2.**

President McKinley will to-day issue his proclamation for an extra session of Congress on the 15th inst.

**Page 3.**

The brokers at the Stock Exchange and at the Custom House observed the change of Administrations by singing patriotic songs and cheering.

Expressions of approval of the main points of President McKinley's inaugural address were general among New York business men, though some had expected a stronger declaration in regard to the tariff. His words about financial reform, the arbitration treaty, and civil service were warmly commended.

**Page 4.**

Mrs. Margaret P. Buchanan, widow of Dr. Alexander Buchanan, accuses Mrs. Kate M. Foster of alienating her husband's affections, and begins suit against her for $50,000.

Capt. Gen. Weyler returned to Havana yesterday. There was no popular demonstration to greet him, and he walked to his palace unescorted. It is said that he fears the McKinley Administration will take more vigorous means to protect Americans in Cuba than have hitherto been adopted.

The typographical unions are taking an active interest in bills pending in the Legislature relating to public printing in the State prisons. A circular has been issued in favor of the Hughes bill, providing that a penal institution shall do only such printing as is required by its own necessities.

**Page 6.**

A young man at Paterson, N. J., who was made crazy by observing hypnotic tests, tried to kill his mother and aunt.

The second anniversary of Grammar School No. 96 was celebrated yesterday with pleasing exercises by the pupils of all departments.

Mr. and Mrs. William H. Acklan of Washington have separated, and the lady is petitioning the Delaware Legislature for a divorce.

Mrs. E. A. Stevens, widow of the founder of the Stevens Institute, Hoboken, yesterday added a $30,000 gift to those previously received by the institute.

Ex-Alderman Charles Parks of New York, who was convicted three years ago at Asbury Park of operating a gambling house, is to have a new trial.

The East Baptist Church, at Madison and Gouverneur Streets, has been sold. It will be torn down and a building for business purposes erected on its site.

George H. Richmond and his son, the publishers, were accused by Anthony Comstock of selling an improper book, and were held for examination next Monday.

Edward J. Russell, who has been on trial in Brooklyn, charged with attempting to blackmail former Corporation Counsel A. F. Jenks, was yesterday declared guilty.

Southern California fruit growers gave a carload of oranges to provide funds for an orphanage at Harpoot, Armenia. About $1,000 was received from the sale of the fruit at auction.

After two years of tedious and intricate litigation the minority stockholders won their fight against a bond issue by the Interior Conduit and Insolation Company. Justice Russell promised them an injunction.

The New York Commissioners of the Tennessee Centennial met and decided to issue an appeal for exhibits and funds, so that the State may be worthily represented at the exposition. The apathy so far shown was deprecated.

The wedding was announced of Caspar Whitney to Cora Adele Chase of Chicago. This was the last chapter in a story of marital infelicity in which besides Mr. Whitney and his first wife, Charles A. Baudouine figured.

The Rev. E. J. O. Millington, pastor of the Fairmount Baptist Church, of Newark, N. J., came to this city last Monday, and has not been seen since. The police of Newark and New York are hunting for the missing clergyman.

Opponents of the Finn bill to legalize sidewalk obstruction express the opinion that the measure will be beaten in the Senate. Effective arguments and appeals have been addressed by the New York Board of Trade and Transportation to individual Senators, and the influence of the Administration, it is believed, favors the policy of weeding out such measures of doubtful Constitutionality.

**Page 7.**

Simon Scharlin and his son, Simon H., were indicted for fraud in the sale of 2 cents' worth of snuff which, it is said, was adulterated.

The death of Mrs. Emma K. Mouton last Monday, in Louisiana, has taken away a woman who once took a very prominent part in the social life of the Capital and in the South.

Sheriff Tamsen has asked the Civil Service Board to find him a Warden for Ludlow Street Jail. The indictments against the Wardens and Keepers who were in charge when the Post Office robbers escaped have been dismissed.

By an explosion of gas which had leaked from two mains at the corner of Tremont and Boylston Streets, Boston, six persons were killed outright and fifty others were injured. Street cars and stores were wrecked.

**Page 14.**

The Rev. Dr. Charles Frederick Hoffman, rector of All Angels' Protestant Episcopal Church, West End Avenue and Eighty-first Street, died yesterday morning at Jekyl Island, Ga.

The harness and saddle makers have sent a petition to Congress asking for an ad valorem duty of 60 per cent., and have given their reasons for the request.

Senator Edward O. Wolcott of Colorado who went abroad early in January on a mission to the bimetallists of Europe, returned on the Majestic, which reached this port yesterday. Mr. Wolcott said his mission had proved successful.

The Chamber of Commerce at its meeting departed from its usual routine to do honor to the outgoing and to the incoming President. A letter was read from Mr. Cleveland declining a proffered banquet. A communication has been sent to Mr. McKinley urging the necessity of a special session of Congress to consider the financial question. Resolutions were adopted requesting the prompt ratification of the arbitration treaty, and speeches on the subject were made by Abram S. Hewitt and William E. Dodge.


Arrivals at Hotels and Out-of-Town Buyers.—Page 5.
Post Office Notice—Foreign Mails.—Page 13.
Marine Intelligence.—Page 5.
Business Troubles.—Page 12.
Yesterday's Fires.—Page 5.
Court Calendars.—Page 12.
Losses by Fire.—Page 5.
Legal Notes.—Page 14.
Real Estate.—Page 12.
Railroads.—Page 7.


## TROUBLE IN OLD SERVIA.

**Christians Attacked by Rioting Arnauts and Turks.**

VIENNA, March 4.—Reports have been received here of outrages upon Christians in Old Servia, by Arnauts and Turks.

A wedding procession was set upon near Tetovo, and twenty-one of the party killed or wounded, and an attack was made upon a priest and two peasants near the Town of Prilip, all three of whom were killed.

## MORE TROUBLE IN SAMOA.

**King Malietoa Menaced with War by His Enemies.**

LONDON, March 4.—A dispatch from Auckland, New Zealand, says that advices from Samoa under the date of Feb. 23 report that King Malietoa was being menaced at Apia by a strong force of natives led by ex-King Tamasese, who was taking advantage of the absence of foreign warships to attack the capital.

Fighting was imminent, and the foreign Consuls could do nothing to avert disorder without the presence of warships.

## NEWFOUNDLAND WILL ACT.

**She Will Enforce the Bait Act Against French Fishermen.**

ST. JOHN'S, N. F., March 4.—The Newfoundland Government intends to enforce the Bait act against French fishermen next month, though such enforcement is strongly opposed by the British Cabinet on the ground that it will interfere with the friendly relations between England and France.

The colony maintains that the proceeding is necessary to prevent her being driven out of the foreign markets.

## TWO VESSELS FOUNDERED.

**The Crews of Both Supposed to Have Been Drowned.**

LONDON, March 4.—A steamer supposed to be the Siracusa, a German vessel, which was last reported as having sailed from Hamburg, has foundered off New Quay, Cornwall. Her masts show above the water. Nothing has been heard of her crew, and it is supposed that it has been lost.

The ketch Engineer has foundered off Padstow, Cornwall, and all her crew were drowned.

## LAW AGAINST THE UNWASHED.

**Imprisoned Because She Did Not Keep Her Children Clean.**

MOUNT VERNON, N. Y., March 4.—In the Court of Special Sessions in this city to-day, Mrs. Marie Belledina of West Mount Vernon was sentenced to three months in the Kings County Penitentiary because she did not keep her children clean.

She was sentenced under Section 434 of the Penal Code, which forbids the appearance of an unclean person on the highways. She is the first woman to be sentenced on that charge in this city.

## PAGET-BAKER SUIT IN ST. PAUL.

**Action Against the Late Commodore Kittson's Daughter.**

ST. PAUL, Minn., March 4.—Cecilia Paget of London, a relative of Almeric Hugh Paget of this city, who married the daughter of William C. Whitney, has brought a suit in the District Court of St. Paul against Mrs. Lewis Baker, Jr., daughter of the late millionaire Commodore Kittson.

Miss Paget asks for the appointment of a receiver for Mrs. Baker to collect the latter's income until she is paid $8,725, the balance of a judgment obtained as the result of real estate transactions. Mrs. Baker is the daughter-in-law of Lewis Baker, now United States Minister to Nicaragua.

## COLLAPSE OF A VIADUCT.

**Narrow Escape of Street Car Passengers in Cincinnati.**

CINCINNATI, Ohio, March 4.—At a late hour last night 200 feet of the west end of the immense Eighth Street viaduct gave way and crashed into Mill Creek. All the electric lights on the elevated thoroughfares were at once extinguished.

So far as known no lives were lost. A street car had crossed the viaduct but a minute or two before, and another car was stopped just on the brink of the chasm. Both cars were filled with passengers. The cause of the accident was the high waters that have undermined and generally weakened the foundation. To repair the damage will cost $20,000.

## FATAL RAILROAD ACCIDENT.

**A Baltimore and Ohio Work Train Jumps the Track Near Zanesville.**

ZANESVILLE, Ohio, March 4.—A Baltimore and Ohio work train jumped the track at Deep Cut, about three miles east of this city, shortly after 12 o'clock to-day, rolling down a twenty-four-foot embankment, killing three men instantly, and fatally injuring two others. The killed are:

DUTTON, GUS, Newark, Ohio; married; engineer.

JOHNS, E. P., Newark, Ohio; married; fireman.

TOWY, JOHN, Newark, Ohio; married.

The injured are:

DUBOIS, BILL, Newark; front brakeman; body crushed, leg broken.

SMART, J. H., assistant foreman of work train; badly crushed.

Six or seven others were more or less seriously injured.

The dead and injured were brought to this city this afternoon



# THE INAUGURAL ADDRESS.

### President McKinley Outlines the Policy of His Administration of National Affairs.

### STRICT ECONOMY IS NECESSARY

### A Stronger Protective Tariff Recommended as Surest Remedy for Our National Troubles.

### APPROVAL OF THE ARBITRATION TREATY IS ADVISED.

**Favors Bimetallism and a Commission to Revise Financial Laws and Policy.**

### A SHARP RAP AT THE TRUSTS

**Reasons for the Extra Session of Congress Which He Announces Will Convene March 15.**

WASHINGTON, March 4.—Following is the text of President McKinley's inaugural address:

Fellow-citizens: In obedience to the will of the people, and in their presence by the authority vested in me by this oath, I assume the arduous and responsible duties of President of the United States, relying on the support of my countrymen and invoking the guidance of Almighty God. Our faith teaches that there is no safer reliance than upon the God of our fathers, who has so singularly favored the American people in every National trial, and who will not forsake us so long as we obey His commandments and walk humbly in His footsteps.

The responsibilities of the high trust to which I have been called—always of grave importance—are augmented by the prevailing business conditions, entailing idleness upon willing labor and loss to useful enterprises. The country is suffering from industrial disturbances from which speedy relief must be had.

**FOR A FINANCIAL COMMISSION.**

Our financial system needs some revision. Our money is all good now, but its value must not further be threatened. It should all be put upon an enduring basis, not subject to easy attack, nor its stability to doubt or dispute. Our currency should continue under the supervision of the Government. The several forms of our paper money offer, in my judgment, a constant embarrassment to the Government and a safe balance in the Treasury. Therefore I believe it necessary to devise a system which, without diminishing the circulating medium, or offering a premium for its contraction, will present a remedy for those arrangements, which, temporary in their nature, might well in the years of our prosperity have been displaced by wiser provisions. With adequate revenue secured, but not until then, we can enter upon such changes in our fiscal laws as will, while insuring safety and volume to our money, no longer impose upon the Government the necessity of maintaining so large a gold reserve, with its attendant and inevitable temptations to speculation. Most of our financial laws are the outgrowth of experience and trial, and should not be amended without investigation, and demonstration of the wisdom of the proposed changes. We must be both "sure we are right," and "make haste slowly." If, therefore, Congress in its wisdom shall deem it expedient to create a commission to take under early consideration the revision of our coinage, banking, and currency laws, and give them that exhaustive, careful, and dispassionate examination that their importance demands, I shall cordially concur in such action. If such power is vested in the President, it is my purpose to appoint a commission of prominent, well-informed citizens of different parties, who will command public confidence both on account of their ability and special fitness for the work. Business experience and public training may thus be combined, and the patriotic zeal of the friends of the country be so directed that such a report will be made as to receive the support of all parties, and our finances cease to be the subject of mere partisan contention. The experiment is, at all events, worth a trial, and, in my opinion, it can but prove beneficial to the entire country.

**PARITY OF METALS.**

The question of international bimetallism will have early and earnest attention. It will be my constant endeavor to secure it by co-operation with the other great commercial powers of the world. Until that condition is realized, when the parity between our gold and silver money springs from and is supported by the relative value of the two metals, the value of the silver already coined, and of that which may hereafter be coined, must be kept constantly at par with gold by every resource at our command. The credit of the Government, the integrity of its currency, and the inviolability of its obligations must be preserved. This was the commanding verdict of the people, and it will not be unheeded.

**STRICT ECONOMY NEEDED.**

Economy is demanded in every branch of the Government at all times, but especially in periods, like the present, of depression in business and distress among the people. The severest economy must be observed in all public expenditures and extravagance stopped wherever it is found and prevented wherever in the future it may be developed. If the revenues are to remain as now, the only relief that can come must be from decreased expenditures. But the present must not become the permanent condition of the Government. It has been our uniform practice to retire, not increase, our outstanding obligations, and this policy must again be resumed and vigorously enforced. Our revenues should always be large enough to meet with ease and promptness, not only our current needs and the principal and interest of the public debt, but to make proper and liberal provision for that most deserving body of public creditors, the soldiers and sailors and the widows and orphans who are the pensioners of the United States.

**MORE REVENUE REQUIRED.**

The Government should not be permitted to run behind or increase its debt in times like the present. Suitably to provide against this is the mandate of duty; the certain and easy remedy for most of our financial difficulties. A deficiency is inevitable so long as the expenditures of the Government exceed its receipts. It can only be met by loans or an increased revenue. While a large annual surplus of revenue may invite waste and extravagance, inadequate revenue creates distrust and undermines public and private credit. Neither should be encouraged. Between more loans and more revenue there ought to be but one opinion. We should have more revenue, and that without delay, hindrance, or postponement. A surplus in the Treasury created by loans is not a permanent or safe reliance. It will suffice while it lasts, but it cannot last long while the outlays of the Government are greater than its receipts, as has been the case during the past two years. Nor must it be forgotten that, however much such loans may temporarily relieve the situation, the Government is still indebted for the amount of the surplus thus accrued, which it must ultimately pay, while its ability to pay is not strengthened, but weakened, by a continued deficit. Loans are imperative in great emergencies to preserve the Government or its credit, but a failure to supply needed revenue in time of peace for its maintenance of either has no justification.

**A PROTECTIVE TARIFF.**

The best way for the Government to maintain its credit is to pay as it goes—not by resorting to loans, but by keeping out of debt—through an adequate income secured by a system of taxation, external or internal, or both. It is the settled policy of the Government, pursued from the beginning and practiced by all parties and Administrations, to raise the bulk of our revenue from taxes upon foreign productions entering the United States for sale and consumption, and avoiding, for the most part, every form of direct taxation except in time of war. The country is clearly opposed to any needless additions to the subjects of internal taxation and is committed by its latest popular utterance to the system of tariff taxation. There can be no misunderstanding, either, about the principle upon which this tariff taxation shall be levied. Nothing has ever been made plainer at a general election than that the controlling principle in the raising of revenue from duties on imports is zealous care for American interests and American labor. The people have declared that such legislation should be had as will give ample protection and encouragement to the industries and the development of our country.

It is, therefore, earnestly hoped and expected that Congress will at the earliest practicable moment, enact revenue legislation that shall be fair, reasonable, conservative, and just, and which, while supplying sufficient revenue for public purposes, will still be signally beneficial and helpful to every section, and every enterprise of the people. To this policy we are all, of whatever party, firmly bound by the voice of the people—a power vastly more potential than the expression of any political platform. The paramount duty of Congress is to stop deficiencies by the restoration of that protective legislation which has always been the firmest prop of the Treasury. The passage of such a law, or laws, would strengthen the credit of the Government both at home and abroad, and go far toward stopping the drain upon the gold reserve held for the redemption of our currency, which has been heavy and well nigh constant for several years.

**RECIPROCITY APPROVED.**

In the revision of the tariff, especial attention should be given to the re-enactment and extension of the reciprocity principle of the Law of 1890, under which so great a stimulus was given to our foreign trade in new and advantageous markets, for our surplus agricultural and manufactured products. The brief trial given this legislation amply justifies a further experiment and additional discretionary power in the making of commercial treaties, the end in view always to be the opening up of new markets for the products of our country, by granting concessions to the products of other lands that we need and cannot produce ourselves, and which do not involve any loss of labor to our own people, but tend to increase their employment.

**FOR A BUSINESS REVIVAL.**

The depression of the past four years has fallen with especial severity upon the great body of toilers of the country, and upon none more than the holders of small farms. Agriculture has languished and labor suffered. The revival of manufacturing will be a relief to both. No portion of our population is more devoted to the institutions of free Government nor more loyal in their support, while none bears more cheerfully or fully its proper share in the maintenance of the Government or is better entitled to its wise and liberal care and protection. Legislation helpful to producers is beneficial to all. The depressed condition of industry on the farm and in the mine and factory has lessened the ability of the people to meet the demands upon them, and they rightfully expect that not only a system of revenue shall be established that will secure the largest income with the least burden, but that every means will be taken to decrease, rather than increase, our public expenditures. Business conditions are not the most promising. It will take time to restore the prosperity of former years. If we cannot promptly attain it, we can resolutely turn our faces in that direction and aid its return by friendly legislation. However troublesome the situation may appear, Congress will not, I am sure, be found lacking in disposition or ability to relieve it, as far as legislation can do so.

The restoration of confidence and the revival of business, which men of all parties so much desire, depend more largely upon the prompt, energetic, and intelligent action of Congress than upon any other single agency affecting the situation.

**TO PRESERVE ORDER.**

It is inspiring, too, to remember that no great emergency in the 108 years of our eventful National life has ever arisen that has not been met with wisdom and courage by the American people, with fidelity to their best interests and highest destiny, and to the honor of the American name. Those years of glorious history have exalted mankind and advanced the cause of freedom throughout the world, and immeasurably strengthened the precious free institutions which we enjoy. The people love and will sustain these institutions. The great essential to our happiness and prosperity is that we adhere to the principles upon which the Government was established and insist upon their faithful observance. Equality of rights must prevail and our laws be always and everywhere respected and obeyed. We may have failed in the discharge of our full duty as citizens of the great Republic, but it is consoling and encouraging to realize that free speech, a free press, free thought, free schools, the free and unmolested right of religious liberty and worship, and free and fair elections are dearer and more universally enjoyed to-day than ever before. These guarantees must be sacredly preserved and wisely strengthened. The constituted authorities must be cheerfully and vigorously upheld. Lynchings must not be tolerated in a great and civilized country like the United States; courts—not mobs—must execute the penalty of the law. The preservation of public order, the right of discussion, the integrity of courts, and the orderly administration of justice must continue forever the rock of safety upon which our Government securely rests.

**TRUSTS AND COMBINATIONS.**

One of the lessons taught by the late election, which all can rejoice in, is that the citizens of the United States are both law-respecting and law-abiding people, not easily swerved from the path of patriotism and honor. This is in entire accord with the genius of our institutions, and but emphasizes the advantages of inculcating even a greater love for law and order in the future. Immunity should be granted to none who violate the laws, whether individuals, corporations, or communities; and as the Constitution imposes upon the President the duty of both its own execution, and of the statutes enacted in pursuance of its provisions, I shall endeavor carefully to carry them into effect. The declaration of the party now restored to power has been in the past that of "opposition to all combinations of capital organized in trusts, or otherwise, to control arbitrarily the condition of trade among our citizens," and it has supported "such legislation as will prevent the execution of all schemes to oppress the people by undue charges on their supplies or by unjust rates for the transportation of their products to market." This purpose will be steadily pursued, both by the enforcement of the laws now in existence and the recommendation and support of such new statutes as may be necessary to carry it into effect.

**BETTER IMMIGRATION LAWS.**

Our naturalization and immigration laws should be further improved, to the constant promotion of a safer, a better, and a higher citizenship. A grave peril to the Republic would be a citizenship too ignorant to understand, or too vicious to appreciate, the great value and beneficence of our institutions and laws—and against all who come here to make war upon them our gates must be promptly and tightly closed. Nor must we be unmindful of the need of improvement among our own citizens, but with the zeal of our forefathers encourage the spread of knowledge and free institutions. Illiteracy must be banished from the land, if we shall attain that high destiny as the foremost of the enlightened nations of the world, which, under Providence, we ought to achieve.

**CIVIL SERVICE REFORM.**

Reforms in the civil service must go on. But the changes should be real and genuine, not perfunctory, or prompted by a zeal in behalf of any party, simply because it happens to be in power. As a member of Congress, I voted and spoke in favor of the present law, and I shall attempt its enforcement in the spirit in which it was enacted. The purpose in view was to secure the most efficient service of the best men who would accept appointment under the Government, retaining faithful and devoted public servants in office, but shielding none, under the authority of any rule or custom, who are inefficient, incompetent, or unworthy. The best interests of the country demand this, and the people heartily approve the law wherever and whenever it has been thus administered.

**FOSTER MERCHANT MARINE.**

Congress should give prompt attention to the restoration of our American merchant marine, once the pride of the seas in all the great ocean highways of commerce. To my mind, few more important subjects so imperatively demand its intelligent consideration. The United States has progressed with marvelous rapidity in every field of enterprise and endeavor, until we have become foremost in nearly all the great lines of inland trade, commerce, and industry. Yet, while this is true, our American merchant marine has been steadily declining, until it is now lower, both in the percentage of tonnage and the number of vessels employed, than it was prior to the civil war. Commendable progress has been made of late years in the upbuilding of the American navy, but we must supplement those efforts by providing as a proper consort for it a merchant marine amply sufficient for our own carrying trade to foreign countries. The question is one that appeals both to our business necessities and the patriotic aspirations of a great people.

**DIGNIFIED FOREIGN POLICY.**

It has been the policy of the United States since the foundation of the Government to cultivate relations of peace and amity with all the nations of the world, and this accords with my conception of our duty now. We have cherished the policy of non-interference with the affairs of foreign Governments, wisely inaugurated by Washington, keeping ourselves free from entanglement, either as allies or foes, content to leave undisturbed with them the settlement of their own domestic concerns. It will be our aim to pursue a firm and dignified foreign policy, which shall be just, impartial, ever watchful of our National honor, and always insisting upon the enforcement of the lawful rights of American citizens everywhere. We want no wars of conquest; we must avoid the temptation of territorial aggression. War should never be entered upon until every agency of peace has failed; peace is preferable to war in almost every contingency.

**FAVORS ARBITRATION.**

Arbitration is the true method of settlement of international as well as local or individual differences. It was recognized as the best means of adjustment of differences between employers and employes by the Forty-ninth Congress in 1886, and its application was extended to our diplomatic relations by the unanimous concurrence of the Senate and House of the Fifty-first Congress in 1890. The latter resolution was accepted as the basis of negotiations with us by the British House of Commons in 1893, and upon our invitation a treaty of arbitration between the United States and Great Britain was signed at Washington and transmitted to the Senate for its ratification in January last. Since this treaty is clearly the result of our own initiative; since it has been recognized as the leading feature of our foreign policy throughout our entire National history—the adjustment of difficulties by judicial methods, rather than force of arms—and since it presents to the world the glorious example of reason and peace, not passion and war, controlling the relations between two of the greatest nations of the world, an example certain to be followed by others, I respectfully urge the early action of the Senate thereon, not merely as a matter of policy, but as a duty to mankind. The importance and moral influence of the ratification of such a treaty can hardly be over-estimated in the cause of advancing civilization. It may well engage the best thought of the statesmen and people of every country, and I cannot but consider it fortunate that it was reserved to the United States to have the leadership in so grand a work.

**NEED OF EXTRA SESSION.**

It has been the uniform practice of each President to avoid, as far as possible, the convening of Congress in extraordinary session. It is an example which, under ordinary circumstances and in the absence of a public necessity, is to be commended. But a failure to convene the representatives of the people in Congress in extra session when it involves neglect of a public duty places the responsibility of such neglect upon the Executive himself. The condition of the public Treasury, as has been indicated, demands the immediate consideration of Congress. It alone has the power to provide revenues for the Government. Not to convene it under such circumstances I can view in no other sense than the neglect of a plain duty.

I do not sympathize with the sentiment that Congress in session is dangerous to our general business interests. Its members are the agents of the people, and their presence at the seat of Government in the execution of the sovereign will should not operate as an injury, but a benefit. There could be no better time to put the Government upon a sound financial and economic basis than now. The people have only recently voted that this should be done, and nothing is more binding upon the agents of their will than the obligation of immediate action. It has always seemed to me that the postponement of the meeting of Congress until more than a year after it has been chosen deprived Congress too often of the inspiration of the popular will, and the country of the corresponding benefits.

It is evident, therefore, that to postpone action in the presence of so great a necessity would be unwise on the part of the Executive, because unjust to the interests of the people. Our actions now will be freer from mere partisan consideration than if the question of tariff revision was postponed until the regular session of Congress. We are nearly two years from a Congressional election, and politics cannot so greatly distract us as if such contest was immediately pending. We can approach the problem calmly and patriotically, without fearing its effect upon an early election. Our fellow-citizens who may disagree with us upon the character of this legislation prefer to have the question settled now, even against their preconceived views, and perhaps settled so reasonably, and I trust and believe it will be, as to insure great permanence, than to have further uncertainty menacing the vast and varied business interests of the United States.

Again, whatever action Congress may take will be given a fair opportunity for trial before the people are called to pass judgment upon it, and this I consider a great essential to the rightful and lasting settlement of the question. In view of these considerations, I shall deem it my duty as President to convene Congress in extraordinary session on Monday, the 15th day of March, 1897.

**NO MORE SECTIONALISM.**

In conclusion, I congratulate the country upon the fraternal spirit of the people and the manifestations of good will everywhere so apparent. The recent election not only most fortunately demonstrated the obliteration of sectional or geographical lines, but to some extent also the prejudices which for years have distracted our councils and marred our true greatness as a Nation. The triumph of the people, whose verdict is carried into effect to-day, is not the triumph of one section, nor wholly of one party, but of all sections and all the people. The North and the South no longer divide on the old lines, but upon principles and policies, and in this fact surely every lover of the country can find cause for true felicitation. Let us rejoice in and cultivate this spirit; it is ennobling, and will be both a gain and blessing to our beloved country. It will be my constant aim to do nothing, and permit nothing to be done, that will arrest or disturb this growing sentiment of unity and co-operation, this revival of esteem and affiliation which now animates so many thousands in both the old antagonistic sections, but I shall cheerfully do everything possible to promote and increase it.

Let me again repeat the words of the oath administered by the Chief Justice, which, in their respective spheres, so far as applicable, I would have all my countrymen observe: "I will faithfully execute the office of President of the United States, and will, to the best of my ability, preserve, protect, and defend the Constitution of the United States." This is the obligation I have reverently taken before the Lord Most High. To keep it will be my single purpose; my constant prayer—and I shall confidently rely upon the forbearance and assistance of all the people in the discharge of my solemn responsibilities.

## THE WEATHER.

The storm has moved from Maine to Newfoundland. The second storm has moved from the north of Montana to South Dakota. A third storm appears to be developing off the North Pacific coast.

The area of high pressure has moved from Illinois to the Middle Atlantic coast, and a second high area has developed to the north of Montana, causing steep barometrical gradients, with winds of 30 miles at Winnipeg and 26 at Havre.

Rain has fallen in New England, the lake regions, the Ohio, Mississippi, and Lower Missouri Valleys.

The temperature has fallen in the Atlantic States, in the extreme Northwest, and has generally risen elsewhere.

The record of temperature for the twenty-four hours ended at midnight, taken from THE NEW YORK TIMES's thermometer and from the thermometer of the Weather Bureau, is as follows:

| | —Weather Bureau.— 1896. | 1897. | TIMES. 1897. |
|---|---|---|---|
| 3 A. M. | 18 | 30 | 35 |
| 6 A. M. | 17 | 29 | 32 |
| 9 A. M. | 21 | 31 | 34 |
| 12 M. | 28 | 32 | 36 |
| 4 P. M. | 26 | 35 | 38 |
| 6 P. M. | 21 | 34 | 37 |
| 9 P. M. | 17 | 33 | 35 |
| 12 P. M. | 18 | 32 | 34 |

THE TIMES's thermometer is 6 feet above the street level; that of the Weather Bureau is 285 feet above the street level

Average temperatures yesterday were as follows:

| | |
|---|---|
| Printing House Square | 35¼ |
| Weather Bureau | 33 |
| Corresponding date 1896 | 20.9 |
| Corresponding date for last 20 years | 34 |

# M'KINLEY IS NOW THE PRESIDENT

### He Took the Oath of Office as Chief Magistrate at the East Portico of the Capitol Yesterday.

### A BIG CROWD IN ATTENDANCE

### The President and His Predecessor Greeted with Profuse Cheers on Their Appearance.

### MRS. M'KINLEY SUPPORTED AS SHE COMES TO THE PLATFORM.

**The New Executive Delivers His Address in a Voice Which Reaches Nearly All His Auditors.**

### A VERY IMPRESSIVE CEREMONIAL

**The Chief Justice Swears in the President—Procession from the Senate Chamber.**

WASHINGTON, March 4.—William McKinley is President. Under a cloudless sky, in the presence of 40,000 of his applauding fellow-citizens, a citizen of Ohio, a State that has furnished four Presidents, to-day took the oath of office and succeeded Grover Cleveland of New York.

If good weather for so important an event may be accepted as a favorable augury, President McKinley has begun an administrative career that should be full of sunshine, good order, good humor, and general satisfaction. Not a cloud cast its shadow over any part of the inaugural proceedings.

For the fourth time Grover Cleveland occupied a place as one of the principal persons concerned in an inauguration ceremony. Twice has he ridden to the Capitol to be sworn into office, and twice has he been the companion in the spectacular journey from and to the White House of men who represented a party antagonistic to that which chose him for Chief Magistrate. No other American has ever enjoyed that honor and distinction.

Very fortunately, Mr. Cleveland's persistent lameness did not prevent him from participating in all the proceedings requiring his presence. He greeted the President-elect cordially and with sincere satisfaction on his arrival at the White House. He rode with him to the Capitol between unbroken throngs of people, who did not spare their throats.

President McKinley, thoughtful of his afflicted companion, who was in some physical distress, never did a kinder thing more gracefully than in the Senate Chamber, when he tactfully turned Mr. Cleveland from the chair at the left, that was most convenient, to the chair at the right, in front of the desk of the Vice President, because it was most honorable and appropriate.

President McKinley's address at the east front of the Capitol was heard by perhaps 40,000 persons, as nearly as can be estimated. His reception was cordial but not tumultuous. He read from printed sheets, but effectively and impressively. The utterance that provoked the most comment was his warm approval of the treaty of arbitration recently submitted by President Cleveland.

The parade back to the White House of about 20,000 soldiery and civilians was admirably marshaled by Gen. Horace Porter, and, while smaller than had been expected, was creditable in numbers, excellent in its military features, and the civic organizations were enthusiastic enough to meet the expectations of the most intense partisan

For those who did not go to the inaugural ball there was a display of fireworks on the "White Lot." President McKinley and Mrs. McKinley attended the inaugural ball, remaining an hour or more in the splendid ballroom.

## PRESIDENT TAKES THE OATH.

**SWORN IN AT THE EAST FRONT OF THE CAPITOL.**

**An Immense Crowd Witnesses the Ceremony and Cheers the Utterances in the Inaugural Message.**

WASHINGTON, March 4.—William McKinley took the oath of office as President with the sun shining full upon his face, to show 30,000 or 40,000 of his fellow-citizens what sort of man they had chosen to sit in the White House for four years. Long before he had left the White House on his way to the Capitol, the wide plaza in front of the building had been occupied by persons who arrived early to be near the platform. By 11 o'clock an area equal to Madison Square had been packed solidly with spectators. So dense became this throng that it would sway and surge like a great body of water under pressure from one quarter or another. There were many wo-

"All the News That's Fit to Print."

# The New York Times.

THE WEATHER.
Fair, slightly warmer Thursday; Friday, fair, warmer; moderate winds, becoming south.
For full weather report see Page 12.

VOL. XLIX...NO. 15,683. NEW YORK, SATURDAY, APRIL 14, 1900.—FOURTEEN PAGES. ONE CENT In Greater New York and Jersey City. Elsewhere, TWO CENTS.

TO-DAY:
FOURTEEN PAGES
WITH
REVIEW OF BOOKS AND ART.

THE NEWS CONDENSED.

CONGRESS.—In the House yesterday Mr. [illegible] blocked Mr. Hepburn's effort to get the Nicaragua Canal bill up for consideration May 1. The House passed a resolution providing that the Constitution be so amended that Senators be elected by popular vote. The House also passed fifty-three pension bills.—Page 5.

FOREIGN.—The Boers have apparently changed their tactics. Their transports, it is said, can now move almost as quickly as cavalry. Large forces of burghers are moving west of Glencoe and south of Bloemfontein. It is asserted that the Boer peace envoys have documents showing that the Kaiser originally urged them to war. The reports that Capt. Reichmann, the American Military Attaché, took part in the fighting are officially denied. Kimberley fears an attack by the Boers, and is preparing for it. The Boers were repulsed at Wepener, but renewed the attack. The Paris Exposition will be formally inaugurated to-day by President Loubet. The gates will then be closed, to be reopened to the public Monday. The buildings are in an unfinished state, and few exhibits are installed. It is said that several German rulers will visit Vienna.—Pages 6 and 7.

Page 1.

A Colorado jury awarded $50,000 damages against Samuel Strong for breach of promise. A similar suit is to be brought by another plaintiff.

Lieut. J. L. Donovan of the regular army disappeared from Louisville, Ky., a week ago.

Admiral Dewey will not issue his promised statement of his political views for several days. He was visited by friends and politicians at Beauvoir, in the suburbs of Washington, yesterday.

Mayor Van Wyck yesterday signed the bills enlarging the power of the Rapid Transit Board and extending certain bonded indebtedness, the latter making available $8,000,000 for the extension of rapid transit to Brooklyn Borough.

The Populist-Silver element expects to dominate completely the Democratic Convention at Kansas City July 4, believing they have the "goldbugs" where they can dictate terms to them.

Minnesota is making on a scheme to form an international Farmers' Trust by reducing the wheat output 20 per cent. and holding the price at $1.

Page 2.

Nearly a hundred deputies of the Sheriff of Westchester were held at bay yesterday by Italian laborers employed on the Cornell dam at Croton-on-Hudson and now on strike.

Miss Heffman, who was employed as May's maid by Mrs. H. S. Rubens, asserts that she and her husband conspired to put her in an Havana insane asylum, although sane. Mrs. Rubens declared the charges false, saying that Gen. Ludlow and others are trying to injure her husband politically.

Page 3.

Samuel Ely Quigg confirms the report that he is to be the successor of John Reisenweber as a member of the Republican State Committee.

Page 5.

It is said to be certain that Senator Clark of Montana will not resign.

Secretary Gage decided that the Puerto Rico tariff goes into effect May 1.

Democrats and Populists nominated a ticket in Oregon and the Silver Republicans indorsed them.

J. A. Porter, the President's private secretary, resigned, and is succeeded by George B. Cortelyou.

Residents of Puerto Rico have brought suit to recover duties paid on imports from the United States since the signing of the protocol.

The Navy Department has bought the Holland and made a contract looking to the purchase of other submarine boats of the same type.

Page 8.

Arguments for and against the Davis School Teachers' Salary bill were presented to Gov. Roosevelt at a hearing in Albany.

Page 14.

The hearing for the prosecution in the charges brought against the District Attorney by members of the City Club was resumed yesterday.

In a decision ruling on demurrers in two prevailing rate of wages suits Justice Bischoff disagrees with Justice McAdam as to the preservation of rights of plaintiffs.

Two persons were probably fatally burned in an east side tenement house fire, while in another 200 women and children were in imminent danger of suffocation until rescued by policemen.

Amusements.—Page 7.
Arrivals at Hotels and Out-of-Town Buyers.—Page 8.
Business Troubles.—Page 12.
Court Calendars.—Page 12.
Insurance Notes.—Page 12.
Legal Notes.—Page 9.
Losses by Fire.—Page 3.
Marine Intelligence and Foreign Mails.—Page 8.
Markets.—Page 11.
New Corporations.—Page 11.
Railroads.—Page 8.
Real Estate.—Page 12.
Society.—Page 7.
United Service.—Page 5.
Weather Report.—Page 3.
Yesterday's Fires.—Page 3.

## BEAU HICKMAN'S SISTER DEAD.

### Was the Last Survivor of the Family Made Famous by Her Brother.

*Special to The New York Times.*

CHARLOTTE, N. C., April 13.—Miss Mary Jane Hickman, the sister of Beau Hickman, the wealthy North Carolinian, who made a brilliant appearance in Washington, New York, and London society, between 1845 and 1855, is dead at the family home in Warren County. Her brother was called "Beau" after Brummell, whose style he imitated, and his life resembled in many points that of Beau Brummell.

Hickman, after a splendid and brilliant appearance in society, found himself without money, and from that time he became one of the most famous "dead beats" ever known. But he still obtained means to live; in fact, one of his sayings was, "Let the dull work; I live by my wits." A remarkable instance of his ingenuity occurred while Hickman was in New York City. After spending several weeks at a fashionable hotel there, the proprietor one day asked Hickman to settle his bill. In answer to Hickman's excuses the proprietor said, "No, it must be settled at once." Asking if there were witnesses present, Beau said, with tearful eyes, "Would you take the last cent a man has?" "Yes, Sir," said the proprietor. "I call you to witness, gentlemen," said Beau, and reaching into his pocket he produced one cent. "That's my last cent," said he. "Please give me my bill receipted." The proprietor saw the joke and laughed with the rest, but said to Hickman: "If you will go over to the Astor House and play that trick on the proprietor, I'll give you $50."

"Why," replied Beau, "he gave me $100 to play the trick on you."

### Social Science Association Meeting.

*Special to The New York Times.*

WASHINGTON, April 13.—The general meeting for 1900 of the American Social Science Association will be held in the Columbian University here from May 7 to 11, inclusive. The address of welcome will be made by President Whitman of the Columbian University and the annual address by Charles Dudley Warner, the President of the association. Among the other speakers will be Dr. William A. Hall and Adele M. Rickey of New York, Surgeon General Wyman, Frank B. Seaborn of Concord, Mass.; Julia Ward Howe, Miss Kate Sanborn, Prof. S. M. Lindsay, Col. Jacob L. Greene of Hartford, Conn.; Prof. Joseph F. Johnson of the University of Pennsylvania, Prof. C. G. Tiedemann, and John Brooks Dill of New York, William Wirt Howe of Louisiana, and Miss Isabella M. Petters of the New York University.



## POPULISTS' PLANS AT KANSAS CITY

### Expect to Dominate the Democratic Convention.

### GOLD MEN AT THEIR MERCY

### It Is Proposed to Demonstrate that the East Is Not the "Whole Thing"—Sectional Feeling Strong.

*Special to The New York Times.*

KANSAS CITY, April 13.—A few years ago a Topeka official received this inquiry from an Eastern State: "Where is the town called Kansas City?" This was the reply: "Kansas City is a Kansas town, but for convenience and for prudential reasons it is located just across the line in Missouri."

More and more since Kansas City began to work for the National Democratic Convention have her citizens realized that what the Topeka man said was true. The newspapers here have their principal circulation in Kansas, and the hotels find their guests and the jobbing houses their customers in that State. Nearly all the trade of this city comes not from the State in which it is situated, but from that for which it was named. Many of the city's business men have their homes in Kansas, and in various other ways the place is really the metropolis of a State in which it is not located. The politicians of Kansas nearly always come here to fix up their slates; the country accounts of Kansas City banks are largely in the banks of Kansas; in recent years the Populists of Kansas have been a sort of continuation of the Missouri Democratic Party, or rather the Missouri Democracy has been a sort of propagandist of Kansas's political heresies; the committee on "How to Capture the Democratic Convention for Kansas City" got its orders from Kansas Populists, and on July 4 Kansas will turn the crank of the convention machinery and present Mr. Bryan as the product of the grinding.

SECTIONALISM IN THE CAMPAIGN.

This political element has now the upper hand in the West and it believes that the time has come to show the East—they always speak of that portion of the country as though it were a foreign nation—that it is not the "whole thing." The ultra-silver people believe that they have the "goldbugs," as they call them, where they can dictate terms to them. There is a good deal of feeling here over this attitude of the silver partisans, and the conservative element decries the effort to make sectionalism an issue during the convention. But the silver people have the bit in mouth and they threaten to run away and smash the carriage.

It is only justice to the members of the local committees to say that they are emphatic in their denunciation of the sectional policy of the campaign. They realize that they have taken a mighty big contract to entertain the convention, even if there was no friction. They understand now that their town was no place in which to hold the great gathering, and they fear that even should everything be harmonious from a political standpoint, it will take great tact and manoeuvring to send the guests away with a good opinion of the place. They despair of getting the "Pops" to modify their feelings toward the Eastern delegates, and so they are now bending all their energies to make the best of a bad bargain, and to see that accommodations suitable to a civilized people are furnished to the visitors. This task alone is enough to make the most sanguine hesitate. The three hotels which are counted as places of the first class are really very creditable hostelries. They are modern in appointments, well managed, and pleasantly situated. There are three others, which size up as fairly good second-class hotels. Below these are a few others, which cannot be classified, or, as the want "ad" man would say, they are "too late to classify." When you get beyond these you are in the vast and dangerous field of lodging houses and restaurants, where the three-legged stool predominates. Of course, there are besides many clean furnished rooms, with or without board, near the business district, as well as near the site of Convention Hall. This is always the case in Western towns the size of this. Many people who are coming to the convention have already spoken for such places as these, where they were able to secure them with the understanding that the apartments were not to be crowded with cots for strangers. Even then high prices are demanded, and, of course, they will not have the conveniences of the hotels in giving their occupants the closest touch with the night meetings and caucuses.

SIX IN A ROOM THE PROSPECT.

The local committee already has had the hotel men on the carpet for their alleged intention to "hog it." This meeting took place last week, and the managers were given to understand that the rates must be kept within reasonable bounds, and that any attempt to charge exorbitant prices would be followed by reprisals after the convention. The hotel men replied that they did not intend to take advantage of the visitors; that the rates would be put little, if any, higher than usual, but that the ancient and inalienable right to "double up" was reserved. If it were only doubling up it might not be so bad, but it threatens to be sextupling up, considering the small number of good hotels in the city. This process will not be confined to the hotels, but will also extend to the boarding houses and lodging places as well. Every one with a vacant room, be it in a business block, or a private house, already has placarded it. The newspapers are advertising many more such rooms than is usual, and office buildings down town which have wanted for tenants in whole or part are plastered with signs, and are being subjected to the unwonted companionship of soap and brooms.

It is plain that the city expects to reap a rich harvest from the convention. The idea in the West is that the coming of such a concourse to a town means the expenditure of vast sums of money by the visitors. Under some circumstances it does. It all depends upon the nature of the crowd and the reason for its coming together. A county or State fair in a country town brings cash to the place. The World's Fair helped Chicago, and any great gathering of people for over a week leaves cash behind. The amount depends upon whether the object for which they came together is one of pleasure or business. An exposition or a fair belongs to the former class. People come there to spend money and have a good time. The women come, and they buy many things from the merchants which they could procure cheaper and of better quality at home. They call for extra things at restaurants and hotels.

But a political convention is not a pleasure excursion. It is clear business, and not always agreeable business at that. The women do not come to conventions in large numbers. The men who come as delegates have little time to spend money unless it is in buying up a delegation. The political hangers-on have their time fully taken up trying to secure seats in the hall. The other visitors under such circumstances are merely those who are attracted by the low rates and who come to see the sights. In this case they say there will be no special rates on the railways. And there are no sights! Kansas City is about the most uninteresting place on the face of the earth. In July it is one of the hottest places in the whole country. There is no thermometer, Fahrenheit, Ramaur, or Centigrade, which pretends to do justice to the temperature of Kansas City in that month. The prospect of spending four days here in July in a convention hall improvised with wooden walls and roof is not an alluring one to any one unaccustomed to Kansas weather.

RAILROAD PROTESTS WITHDRAWN.

The railways have withdrawn their attempt to have the date of the convention changed. Their objection was that they could not handle the business. Their objection was well taken, and it still holds good. The natural flow of passenger traffic toward the nearest town on July 4 is always large, and gives the roads about all they can do. When to this is added the extra crowds which will attend a National Convention on that date, and especially a town so poorly equipped as is Kansas City, the railway managers easily saw that they would be swamped. But the Populists were not to be dissuaded from their patriotic intent of making the National holiday coincident with the nomination of Bryan, and they refused to listen to reason. They said that the railways were controlled by the money power of the East, and that the objections of the roads were dictated by influence inimical to the candidate. In placing the estimate of prospective visitors at 100,000 there have been included those who are merely Fourth-of-July tourists, but they will come, and they will have to be accommodated. They must have rooms in which to sleep and places in which to eat.

The local committee is depending largely on the transient character of the visits. They presume that for the most part the visitors will be of the sort who are said to come to town with $2 and a shirt, and who do not change either. Such people will not complain of the lack of accommodations. They will sleep in tents or in vacant lots or any old place, and will bring their luncheons with them. In that case the delegates who expect something better will find no trouble in getting it at the hotels. As a matter of fact, there is only one direct road from the East to Kansas City—the Alton. There are many roads running there, but they are not so direct. It was this fact which made the Alton protest against the date of the convention. Undoubtedly, all the lines will be uncomfortably crowded during the first week of the month.

## CONTROL OF JAMAICA BANK.

### New Yorkers Purchase the Majority Interest.

A syndicate represented by John Alvin Young, Secretary of the Atlantic Trust Company, and including his brother, President George W. Young of the United States Mortgage and Trust Company; A. C. Bedford, Treasurer of the Long Island Railroad Company, and other New Yorkers, has purchased the Jamaica Bank of Jamaica, L. I. The new interests will be represented in the Directorate of the bank after the annual meeting of the stockholders, which takes place on April 24.

The Jamaica Bank was started in 1889, and had a capital of $50,000, a surplus of $50,000, and some $6,000 or $7,000 of undivided profits. Its stock sells at about 2.0. The syndicate has acquired 251 of the 500 shares, it is said. While nothing definite has been decided in the matter, it is possible that the people who now control the bank may later establish branches of the institution at Richmond Hill and Elmhurst.

### National Union Bank Liquidating.

The business of the National Union Bank is rapidly being liquidated, and the merger of the institution with the National Bank of Commerce may be accomplished next week. It is currently reported that Vice President E. O. Leech of the National Union will be First Vice President of the future Bank of Commerce. Mr. Leech is now at Mount Sinai Hospital recovering from the effects of an operation for appendicitis.

## WORLD-WIDE FARMERS' TRUST.

### Scheme to Reduce Wheat Output 20 Per Cent. and Hold Price at $1.

MINNEAPOLIS, April 13.—The Journal says:

"All the farmers in the world, in a sort of international trust to restrict the production of wheat and raise prices," is the plan which it is hoped to carry into effect at the International Agricultural Conference in Paris July 9-16. It is proposed to ask the farmers of the world to reduce their wheat output by 20 per cent. and not to sell a bushel for less than $1.

J. C. Hanley of St. Paul, executive agent of the Farmers' Alliance and Industrial Union, the National Cotton Growers' Association, the Farmers' Federation of the Mississippi Valley, and the National Grain Growers' Association, is the chief promoter of the International Agricultural Trust in America. Prof. G. Ruhland of the University of Fribourg, Switzerland, is the chief promoter of the plan in Europe.

The idea was conceived by these two men independently. Mr. Hanley has been interested in many "hold-your-wheat" schemes and is prominently associated with the farmers' elevator and various co-operative undertakings. He has long believed that if the farmers would only come to an understanding as to limiting production and agree to sell only when their price could be obtained, they could easily master the situation.

As a professor of economics Prof. Ruhland had come to the same conclusion. His study of the agrarian problems of different countries led him to believe that the only cure for the widespread troubles of farmers, which are much more severe in the Old than in the New World, is to restrict production. Both were hard at work getting the idea into practice when they encountered each other through correspondence. Since then they have been working with a common idea, namely, to persuade the International Agricultural Congress to indorse the plan and recommend it to the various national associations present for application next year.

While 20 per cent. reduction in acreage is desired, Mr. Hanley points out that if only 5 per cent. can be secured the world's wheat crop will be reduced about 125,000,000 bushels, which is, he says, enough to bring the price at Liverpool up to $1. To help out the effect of restricted production the farmers are to hold their wheat for ninety days, and are to market it at not less than $1 a bushel.

"Almost everything the farmer buys," Mr. Hanley said, "is regulated in price by some trust. On the other hand, all that the farmer sells has its price determined by the competition of all the rest of the farmers of the world. The farmers propose to unite, stop ruinous competition among themselves, and make the world pay a fair price for their product."

Following the Paris conference, it is hoped to have established a permanent international grain growers' association.

## ARMY OFFICER DISAPPEARS.

### Lieut. J. L. Donovan, Recruiting Officer, Left Louisville a Week Ago.

*Special to The New York Times.*

LOUISVILLE, Ky., April 13.—Lieut. J. L. Donovan of the regular army, and who was Lieutenant Colonel of the Sixty-ninth New York during the Spanish war, has disappeared from the local recruiting office of which he has been in charge. He left about a week ago, and to-day a friend of Mrs. Donovan reported the case to the police.

At the recruiting office it was stated that Lieut. Donovan was supposed to be opening a new recruiting office in Somerset, as he was last reported there. Though nothing has been heard from him, it is thought he will return.

Lieut. Donovan was severely wounded in the Philippine campaign, and, being incapacitated for active service, was assigned to Louisville as recruiting officer.

### New Yorkers to Make Glazed Paper.

*Special to The New York Times.*

FITCHBURG, Mass., April 13.—Louis Dejonge & Co. of New York have purchased the Mitchell mill property and will convert it into a glazed paper mill. The work of disposing of the present machinery in the mills and of preparing for the new plant will commence at an early date. The property all told extends over ten acres, and it is the intention of the purchasers to make extended alterations in the buildings, after which they will be equipped with the latest improved machinery for the manufacture of the finest grades of glazed paper.



## SEEKING TO FILL THE REPUBLICAN TICKET

### One Faction Wants New York Man for Vice President.

### WEST DEMANDS RECOGNITION

### Politicians Claim That Section Is Entitled to the Place—Mention Mercer of Nebraska.

*Special to The New York Times.*

WASHINGTON, April 13.—With the apparent certainty that the Republican candidate for Vice President will not be either Gov. Roosevelt, Lieut. Gov. Woodruff, or Cornelius N. Bliss, the rapid flight of time admonishes the leaders here that they must concentrate attention upon some other candidates. Secretary Long, it is asserted, would be an acceptable candidate, but his desire to retire from public life is so strong that nothing except the desire of the President that he shall remain will keep him at the head of the Navy Department until next March.

Very positive assertions are made of the determination of the President to use all his influence to dissuade the admirers of Major Gen. Wood from urging his nomination as a Massachusetts candidate. The Administration relies upon his admirable executive ability to bring about the establishment of that liberal government for Cuba, with stability that was aimed at when the war ended. Gen. Wood is therefore counted out.

There is a lingering line of gossip about Representative Sherman of New York, who has been frequently prominent as an aspirant for some other place than that of a member of the House. He enjoys a large popularity in the House and also at home. It is understood that he did not approve of the Puerto Rican Tariff bill, and at one time it was thought that he might vote against the motion of the Ways and Means Committee to concur in the Senate amendments. Had he so voted, he would not be in the running for the Vice Presidency. He voted with his party, however, and made no open protest.

The Republicans have no actual fear of not being able to carry New York at the Presidential election this Fall, but, realizing the importance of doing so, they are disposed to make assurance doubly sure by putting a popular New York man on the ticket if one who is available can be found. Sherman seems to be less involved in complications than others in the State whose names have been discussed, but there is a decided opposition in Administration circles to the selection of Woodruff.

Mr. Cannon of Illinois has been put forward as the possible candidate of the Middle West.

The latest addition the political gossips have made to the list of availables is Mr. Mercer of Nebraska. The main argument in his behalf is the possibility of his carrying Nebraska against Bryan. Mr. Mercer is very popular in his State, and has been elected to Congress four times, twice in the face of a powerful fusion of Democrats, Populists, and Silver Republicans. He is an original sound-money man, and voted for the repeal of the Sherman act when some other distinguished Nebraska Republicans were seeking cover on the financial question.

There is a well-defined movement on foot among Republicans to go to the West for a running mate for Mr. McKinley. The spirit shown in the election of Mr. Henderson as Speaker in compliance with a demand from the West for recognition is being manifested again. The claim is frequently put forward that the centre of population in the Republican Party has moved west of the Alleghanies and that the Western Republicans must be considered. So, while Mr. Platt and the Eastern Republicans are gravely discussing the available men in the East, the Western politicians are seeking at home a candidate to take the second place on the National ticket.

The Westerners are as strenuous in this affair as they were in the Speakership contest, when, in their breezy Western fashion they so rudely upset the plans of a number of calculating politicians of the East.

## PLATT DESTROYS A BOOM.

### Sherman, He Declares, Is Not a Vice Presidential Candidate.

Senator Thomas C. Platt returned from Washington yesterday, and the first thing he did after reaching the Fifth Avenue Hotel was to destroy the James S. Sherman Vice Presidential boom.

"Not a word of truth in that report," said the Senator. "Congressman Sherman will be permanent Chairman of the convention next week, but he is in no sense considered for the Vice Presidential nomination. I have not committed myself to the candidacy of any man for the place.

"I can say, too, that the convention will not by resolution or otherwise indorse any man for Vice President, Governor, or any other office."

Asked whether he expected to see Gov. Roosevelt to-day, the Senator replied:

"I don't know that the Governor is coming to town to-morrow. If he does I shall certainly see him."

Chairman Odell said yesterday that he did not expect Gov. Roosevelt in the city to-day, nor did he believe he would come to the State Convention.

HESS NAMES GEN. GREENE.

**Not a Vice Presidential Candidate, the General Intimates.**

The opinion was expressed by Charles A. Hess last night that Gen. F. V. Greene would be a formidable dark horse in connection with the Republican Vice Presidential nomination.

When a TIMES reporter called Gen. Greene's attention to the report last night, he said:

"Really, this is news to me, and I do not think it should be taken seriously. I did see some reference to myself in connection with the Vice Presidency in a newspaper several months ago, but I paid little or no attention to it. I suppose that New York can have the Vice Presidential nomination if the party is agreed on any one man, but I doubt that I could rally the party to me.

"A statesman, not a soldier, is needed for the place. It is a very honorable position, to which anybody might reasonably aspire, but I know nothing of politics.

"I am satisfied that neither Gov. Roosevelt nor Mr. Bliss will accept a nomination. I know that their final decision has been made, and is irrevocable.

"In my opinion, some one west of the Mississippi River will be named.

"I have heard fifty names suggested. I suppose I am the fifty-first. But, in my case, it is only a fleeting fancy, and will be forgotten to-morrow."

### Launches Boom for Wolcott.

COLORADO SPRINGS, Col., April 13.—In its leading editorial of to-morrow morning The Colorado Springs Gazette will strongly indorse Senator Wolcott for the Vice Presidency. The Gazette is the only daily paper in Colorado that supported Mr. McKinley in 1896, and it urges upon the Republicans the wisdom of taking a man from the Far West for Vice President, as the East is already numerously represented in the Cabinet, and says that Wolcott is one of the most consistent and brilliant Republicans in the West. It suggests that he would take away from Bryan the vote of the real bimetallists of the country.

### For McKinley and Woodruff.

COLUMBIA, Tenn., April 13.—The Republicans of the Seventh Congressional District to-day elected delegates to the National Convention instructed for Congressman Brownlow for National Committeeman, for McKinley for President, and for Timothy L. Woodruff of New York for Vice President.



## ADMIRAL DEWEY IS NOT DISCOURAGED

### Adverse Criticism of His Candidacy Fails to Disturb Him.

### STATEMENT NOT YET READY

### Waiting for an Opportune Moment to Set Forth His Views on Political Questions.

*Special to The New York Times.*

WASHINGTON, April 13.—Admiral Dewey is not yet ready to make the announcement of his views on political questions that he intimated he would submit after due consideration, and it is learned that he does not contemplate putting them out for some days. This, he frankly admits to his friends, is not to increase the mystery about his candidacy, but merely to defer until the proper occasion arises an expression from him.

The Admiral spent to-day at Beauvoir, in the suburbs, where he was called upon by a number of personal friends and political admirers. The visitors found the Admiral interested in the newspaper references to himself, and not at all distressed by the utterances of those papers which have treated his ambition lightly or rudely.

A very warm friend of the navy and of Admiral Dewey said to-night in regard to the Admiral's offer of himself as a candidate: "Every naval officer must see in Dewey's possible nomination the sincerest flattery of the service and of the qualifications for general public service developed by naval training. It is absurd to suggest that Dewey did only what any other naval officer would have done at Manila, with the idea of showing that he was merely an average naval officer. It is praise to say that, for it is in a measure true, and it shows just what long service prepares naval officers for.

"Then there is his tact and firmness after the fight, displayed so constantly that Secretary Long was as enthusiastic about his diplomatic ability as was Secretary Hay, and both had to rely upon him for months to maintain the prestige and supremacy of the United States while troops and reinforcements in the way of vessels were going forward. These things all go to make up the executive officer.

"The people know that the man who in time of peace commands a battleship directs a little community of his own, dependent for its good order and comfort upon the training, firmness, and thoughtfulness of the Captain. A man may be ever so fine an orator and political theorist, and yet turn out to be a failure as an executive."

## DEWEY SENTIMENT GROWING.

### Congressman Driggs Talks on the Feeling in Washington.

Congressman Edmund H. Driggs of Brooklyn came up from Washington Thursday night, and was at Democratic Headquarters, in Willoughby Street, yesterday. In discussing Admiral Dewey's candidacy, he said that there was a reaction at Washington in favor of the Admiral.

"When Admiral Dewey announced his candidacy," said the Congressman, "the general opinion at Washington was that that would be the last of it. In the last week, however, a different state of affairs has developed. Even among conservative men the sentiment as to the Admiral's candidacy is changing. It is nearly three months to the time of the Kansas City Convention, and much can happen in that time.

"Many Bryan men have been surprised at the sentiment that has sprung up for the Admiral. Many good Democrats in Washington are saying that in the next two or three months such a sentiment may develop to such an extent to make the nomination of the Admiral advisable and necessary.

"There is no doubt that Admiral Dewey is a good diplomatist and a great man. There appears to be no good reason why he should not make a good President. It seems to me that with the right candidates we should have a walkover."

## WANTS BRYAN TO WITHDRAW.

### Representative Levy Sees Admiral Dewey Who, He Says, Would Sweep the Country.

*Special to The New York Times.*

WASHINGTON, April 13.—Among those who called on the Admiral this afternoon was Representative Jefferson M. Levy of New York City, who went to Beauvoir to offer Admiral Dewey assurances of his support in his candidacy for the Presidency. On his return Mr. Levy made a statement in regard to his call.

"I have long been an ardent admirer of Admiral Dewey," said Mr. Levy, "and advocated his nomination by the Democratic Party long before he announced his candidacy. I believe his nomination would be the wisest the Democrats could make. I called on the Admiral this afternoon to express my personal admiration and to offer him my warmest support for the Presidency. The Admiral received me very pleasantly, and our conversation was principally devoted to the navy, in which I take great interest, owing to the fact that my uncle was a Commodore. Admiral Dewey recalled the fact that he was a midshipman on the Mediterranean fleet when it was commanded by my uncle, with whom he was personally acquainted.

"I do not feel at liberty to discuss anything that was said with regard to Admiral Dewey's candidacy, except that I told him I thought the drift of sentiment in his favor was growing every day. I said that I favored an uninstructed delegation to Kansas City, and I felt that if the Democrats nominated Admiral Dewey instead of Mr. Bryan they would win.

"Admiral Dewey I believe to be a Jeffersonian Democrat of the old school, and I believe the qualities that he displayed at Manila when he stood between his country and half of Europe indicate his undeniable fitness for the Presidency. Had he shown the slightest sign of weakness there were half a dozen nations ready and willing to jump in and take possession of the Philippines. His coolness saved the United States an empire, the value of which is indisputable. The American people want a President who has just such qualities.

"Although America has won many naval victories and has had many naval heroes, such as Jones, Decatur, Perry, Goldsborough, and Farragut, there has never been one who has acquired one-tenth the prominence and world-wide renown as the hero of Manila Bay. The people have always been willing to bestow the highest gifts in their power on successful Generals, and it is now an opportune time to recognize the navy, in which Admiral Dewey stands supreme.

"With McKinley and Dewey as opponents, business men will be assured that whomsoever is elected, the business interests of the country will be protected and the prosperity which has existed under the present Administration will be continued without interruption.

"Mr. Bryan should realize the fact that with Dewey as their candidate the Democrats will sweep the country, whereas with Bryan and the free-silver platform they cannot win. This being the case, I hope Mr. Bryan will withdraw in favor of Admiral Dewey. I believe that a majority, if not all, of the Eastern States will go for Dewey, and I have been assured that some of the most influential Democrats of the country are ready to take up his cause.

"Within a short time Admiral Dewey will have sufficient backing to give him a large support in the convention, if not, indeed, to assure him of the nomination. I know Admiral Dewey feels very much encouraged by the assurances of support which he has received, and within a short time the country may hear more of his candidacy."

## DEWEY AND BRYAN TO MEET.

### Both Candidates to be Guests of Chicago's Lakeside Club May 1.

CHICAGO, April 13.—Admiral Dewey and William Jennings Bryan will meet Tuesday evening, May 1, for the first time since the hero of Manila announced that he was a Presidential candidate.

All doubt as to Mr. Bryan's presence was dispelled to-day when Max J. Risse of the Lakeside Club received a telegram from him saying that he would cancel previous engagements in order to be present at that organization's celebration, which is a part of the general programme.

Both the distinguished guests are aware of the prospective meeting. The officials of the club did not arrange that they should be present at the same event until each had been consulted. In reply Mr. Bryan and the Admiral replied that, so far from being objectionable, the meeting would give them great pleasure.

## ALTGELD AGAINST PATTISON.

### Ex-Governor Says Candidate Must Be the Counterpart of the Head of the Ticket.

*Special to The New York Times.*

CHICAGO, April 13.—The Democratic leaders are having great difficulty in finding a candidate for the Vice Presidency who will please all factions of their party. Judge Tarvin of Kentucky and Congressman Sulzer of New York have been suggested, but they did not appear to fill the long-felt want. Then some of the National leaders brought out ex-Gov. Pattison of Pennsylvania, and for a time Mr. Pattison's bark floated smoothly down the political stream. Now the radicals are rebelling against Pattison.

Yesterday Mr. Altgeld was asked what he thought of Pattison as a candidate, and his reply was not encouraging to the Pennsylvania man's ambition. Said Mr. Altgeld: "Personally I believe that the nomination of Mr. Pattison for the Vice Presidency would be as great a misfortune as the nomination we made in 1896 for that place. Mr. Pattison has not been with us on any proposition, and it is safe to say that at least 85 per cent. of the Democrats of America would be disappointed at such a nomination.

"Our people are in earnest all over the country, and they demand not only the enunciation of definite and progressive principles, but they demand the nomination of men whom they know to be intense in their support to those principles. The Republican Party is catering to every influence that is controlled by concentrated and corrupt wealth, and the Democratic Party cannot hope to gain anything by entering into competition with the Republican Party in that line.

"The hope of the Democracy to-day depends not on money and not on politics, but depends on the dynamic force of ideas, and on the conquering power of justice. The Democratic Party must name a man for Vice President who possesses the same character, the same convictions, and the same aggressive force as the man at the head of the ticket."

## DELEGATES FROM NEW MEXICO.

### Democratic Convention Instructs for Bryan, Who Is at Albuquerque.

ALBUQUERQUE, N. M., April 13.—The Territorial Democratic Convention to-day elected six delegates to the National Convention, and instructed them to vote for William J. Bryan for President. Ex-Delegate Fergusson was chosen as National Committeeman.

Mr. Bryan arrived here to-night, and will speak to-morrow twice. The Santa Fé shops will be closed to-morrow to permit the employes to hear Mr. Bryan.

## $50,000 FOR BREACH OF PROMISE.

### Colorado Jury's Verdict Against Samuel Strong—Another Suit.

*Special to The New York Times.*

COLORADO SPRINGS, Col., April 13.—In the breach of promise suit brought by Miss Nellie M. Lewis against Samuel Strong, a reputed millionaire, the jury to-day returned a verdict in favor of the plaintiff, awarding her $50,000 out of $200,000, for which the suit was brought. The jury was divided only on the extent of the damages.

Throughout the proceedings much interest was manifested in the trial, Miss Lewis winning much sympathy, while the feeling against the defendant became quite bitter.

Strong must soon face a similar suit brought by a Miss Vance.

## J. D. SARVEN'S WILL FILED.

### Many Liberal Bequests Made to Charitable Institutions.

WHITE PLAINS, N. Y., April 13.—The will of the late James D. Sarven of Tarrytown has been filed with Surrogate Silkman. It is dated Sept. 18, 1899. The value of the estate is unknown. It contains the following bequests:

John H. Sarven, $20,000; George H. Sarven, $20,000; Iona Nichols, $20,000; Helen Content, $1,000; Trustees Sleepy Hollow Cemetery, $500; Howard Williams, $3,000; James S. Williams, $6,000; in trust for, Sarah M. Trowbridge, $10,000, of which the income to be paid her annually for life; Mollie Williams, $2,000; Nellie Williams Foster, $4,000; Sadie Williams Carter, $4,000; George F. Carter, in trust, $600 for Ruth Williams and Mary Williams, until they are twenty-one years of age; Sarah H. Hawes, $2,000; Anna Hawes, $5,000; Catharine Stephens, Charles F. Hawes, William P. Hawes, Edward Hawes, each $1,000; James D. Sarven of Pulaski, Penn., $8,000, and Tarrytown Hospital, $5,000 to endow "Sarven free bed."

Harriet L. Burgess, nurse in Tarrytown Hospital, 200 shares Northern Pacific first preferred stock, "for her constant attendance while I was under treatment for my eyes at hospital, and great advantage to me in keeping my books." Young Men's Lyceum, Tarrytown, $1,000; John McShay, coachman, $1,000.

The residue and remainder of the estate is to be divided into four equal parts and distributed as follows: Presbyterian Hospital, New York City; American Bible Society; St. Luke's Hospital, and American Tract Society. The executors are Richard Coutant, Frank V. Millard, and William D. Humphreys.

### Western Terminal Road Absorbed.

*Special to The New York Times.*

CHICAGO, April 13.—The Chicago Terminal Transfer Company has absorbed the Chicago, West Pullman and Southern Road, and Monday it will take possession of the property. The Chicago, West Pullman and Southern Road is a terminal property, uniting all the industries of West Pullman. It will be an important addition to the Terminal Transfer Company's system, placing it in absolute control of the traffic of all the manufacturing industries at West Pullman and connecting it with the only manufacturing centre around Chicago not previously reached by it.

### 20,000 Cots for G. A. R. Men.

*Special to The New York Times.*

CHICAGO, April 13.—One of the largest contracts to be awarded in connection with the coming Grand Army encampment is that given to Marshall Field & Co. It calls for 20,000 canvas cots at 77 cents each. These are to be used in the schoolhouses and armories throughout the city, under the direction of the Committee on Free Quarters.



## THE MAYOR'S WORK FOR RAPID TRANSIT

### Signs Bills Enlarging the Board's Power and Giving Millions.

### ASSURE BROOKLYN EXTENSION

### West Side Residents Appeal to the Commission to Save the Boulevard Parkway.

Mayor Van Wyck yesterday signed the bill extending the powers of the Rapid Transit Commission to all boroughs in the city, and at once informed the commission of his approval of the measure. The bill gives the commission exclusive control over all avenue franchises in the city, and will permit the extension of the underground rapid transit line to South Brooklyn.

In approving this measure, the Mayor denied practically the request of the Municipal Assembly, which on Tuesday adopted a resolution asking him to veto the bill because it deprives that body of all power over tunnel franchises. Every application for a tunnel franchise that has come before the Municipal Assembly since consolidation has been held up for from one month to two years, and in one instance, that of the Long Island Terminal Railroad Company, it was asserted that an effort had been made to force the purchase of votes. There are before the Municipal Assembly about ten such applications.

The Mayor also signed the bill introduced by Senator Featherson extending certain bonded indebtedness to the counties within the City of New York.

The bill will make available $8,000,000 for the extension of the rapid transit system to Brooklyn. The extension of these bonds is practically a refunding of them at a lower rate of interest.

The Mayor notified the Rapid Transit Board that the State Railroad Commission had arranged for a hearing to be given to the New York and Brooklyn Union Transportation Company and to the New York and Brooklyn and Jersey City Rapid Transit Company. The commission will have its engineer and counsel at the hearing in order to make sure that the plans of these companies, if carried out, shall not conflict with rapid transit plans. The hearing will probably be at the Fifth Avenue Hotel at 11 A. M., April 17.

RAPID TRANSIT BOARD MEETS.

The Rapid Transit Commissioners met and granted a hearing to a delegation of the West Side Association on the question of a change of plans for the Broadway or Boulevard construction, by which the trees of the Central Parkway may be preserved. All of the Commissioners except Mr. Rives were present, as were Chief Engineer Parsons and Edward F. Shepard of counsel. A score of members of the West Side Association were present.

President Alexander E. Orr explained that any change of route would have to be approved not only by the commission, but by the Mayor, the contractor, the Council, and by the Supreme Court.

Cyrus Clark, President of the West Side Association said that the association had been so wrapped up in securing rapid transit that the possible damage to the parkway of the Boulevard had been overlooked at the time the plans were approved. Between Fifty-ninth Street and One Hundred and Twenty-fifth Street, west of Central Park, he said, there was now a population of 400,000. These people were all interested in preserving the Parkway, and, further, the question was one of moment to the entire city.

A change in the plans, by which the construction could go on without injury to the central parkway, Mr. Clark thought, might be made without great expense to the contractor, and if there was some extra expense, he thought the contractor should consider it counterbalanced by the fact, not known to him when the contract was signed, by which he would be enabled to get rid of excavated earth at very much less expense than he must have expected, since the proposed widening of the Riverside drive 400 feet, into the river, would give a near-by dumping ground, which would offer a great saving.

WANTS PARKWAY PRESERVED.

John C. Coleman reviewed the history of the Boulevard, and said that he considered that the parkway should be preserved at any cost; that the engineers could devise a scheme by which the parkway might escape injury, and that the contractor should be willing to agree to a change of plans.

John McDonald, another member of the association, who next spoke, said that he had taken the pains to measure the trees on the Boulevard and had found that they varied from 15 to 25 inches in circumference. It would take many years, he said, to replace trees of that size, even if all those removed were replaced by the contractor with new trees. He further did not think that, with the shallow depth of earth between the ceiling of the tunnel and the surface, trees would thrive, and the proposed airholes would detract materially from the beauty of the parkway.

Cassius M. Wicker said that instead of one tunnel in the centre, which would necessitate the destruction of the parkway and its replacing by the contractor and the building of supports for the underground trolley, it would be cheaper to build two tunnels for two tracks each between the electric roads and the curb on either side.

The hearing ended with a statement by Engineer Parsons which was regarded as throwing a great deal of light on the whole situation and evidently was quite satisfactory to the west siders. Mr. Parsons said that the work of construction, as at present planned, with the four tracks in the centre of the Boulevard in one tunnel, would undoubtedly destroy all of the trees in the central parkway, though they must all be replaced under the specifications. It would, however, set the parkway back, so far as the tree growth was concerned, at least ten years, and it would also involve the building of temporary supports for the electric tracks of the surface roads. There was, however, ample room, he said, for a two-tunnel road, one tunnel on either side, between the surface tracks and the curbs, but two tunnels would require four side walls, where one tunnel would require only two side walls, and these two extra side walls would require extra excavations amounting to 6 feet in width and 25 feet in depth. The extra expense for this, he said, might be offset by the saving in the avoidance of the renewing of the parkway, and the difficulties to be overcome in the building under the electric subway.

WATER MAINS IN THE WAY.

Another difficulty presented itself, however, in the disposition of water mains which were now under the Boulevard, and another section of water main, now being built. If these were placed under sidewalks, there would be trouble with owners, and if they were placed under the tunnel, there would be trouble in getting at them.

The contractor, he said, had agreed that if he could build two tunnels as cheaply as one he would do so, and further consideration was necessary to determine that point.

The matter ended here, without action by the commission.

Engineer Parsons submitted to the commission a plan showing a cross section of the rapid-transit tunnel, including pipe galleries, at the intersection of Canal Street and Elm. It was not acted upon.

No sub-contracts were let by Contractor McDonald yesterday. It was announced at the office of the construction company, however, that some of the sub-contracts for the building of the tunnel would be awarded Monday.

"All the News That's Fit to Print."

# The New York Times.

THE WEATHER. Fair and warmer; winds variable.

COPYRIGHT, 1900, BY THE NEW YORK TIMES COMPANY.

VOL. XLIX...NO. 15,706. NEW YORK, FRIDAY, MAY 11, 1900.—FOURTEEN PAGES. ONE CENT In Greater New York and Jersey City. Elsewhere, TWO CENTS.

## THE NEWS CONDENSED.

Stocks irregular.

Wheat, No. 2 red, 79¾c; corn, No. 2 mixed, 44¼c; cotton, middling, 9¾c.

CONGRESS.—The House yesterday by a vote of 129 to 127 unseated Mr. Crawford, Democrat, Ninth North Carolina District, and seated Richmond Pearson, the Republican contestant. Notice was given in the Senate that the Clark case would be called up Tuesday. It is asserted that it will be pushed to final disposition.—Page 6.

FOREIGN.—The whole of Lord Roberts's army yesterday crossed the Zand River, and after an engagement of which particulars have not yet been received, the Boers fled. It is now confidently expected in London that Lord Roberts will be in Kroonstad next Monday, and bets were made in the House of Commons last evening that he would be in Pretoria in two months. It is stated that the Boers intend ultimately to retire to Lydenburg, leaving the defense of Pretoria and Johannesburg in the hands of the foreign mercenaries. The Free Staters are reported to have held a meeting, at which the advisability of submission was approved. The Cape Argus publishes a report saying that well-informed foreigners in Pretoria now consider the Johannesburg mines safe. Neither the United States nor Germany participated in the joint note said to have been presented to President Krueger by the representatives of the foreign powers, holding him personally responsible for the preservation of the mines. Mr. Krueger has received an offer from a Boer woman to form a corps of women volunteers to assist in the defense of the Transvaal. There is a ministerial crisis in Spain owing to the opposition to the Government's taxation scheme. The sale of the Peel heirlooms was begun in London yesterday.—Pages 6 and 7.

**Page 1.**

The Populist Convention at Sioux Falls yesterday nominated W. J. Bryan for President and Charles A. Towne of Minnesota for Vice President.

W. Bourke Cockran said yesterday he would only support Bryan if militarism, imperialism, and trusts were made the main issues in the Democratic platform.

Citizens of Brooklyn and Staten Island appeared before the Rapid Transit Commissioners yesterday and argued for the extension of the tunnel along Hamilton Avenue, Brooklyn, and thence to Staten Island.

Edward Lauterbach, at the meeting of the Citizens' Committee last evening, declared that the Republican Party must adopt a plank in favor of the South African republics in advance of the Democrats or it would be certainly defeated.

**Page 2**

The Middle-of-the-Road Populist Convention at Cincinnati nominated Wharton Barker for President and Ignatius Donnelly for Vice President.

**Page 3.**

Robert Herbst, a messenger boy, was decapitated by an elevator at 154 Mercer Street yesterday.

Clara Barton Hunter, the actress, has brought suit for breach of promise, placing her damages at $50,000, against Frederick H. Man, the well-known lawyer.

The President of the Police Board yesterday received from Inspectors Cross and Thompson reports asked for by the board in regard to alleged poolrooms running in their district.

**Page 5.**

The National Board of Fire Underwriters yesterday elected officers. The fire losses in 1899 were reported the greatest since 1883, and exclusive National supervision was desired because of inimical legislation.

John W. Gates left the country on the Kaiser Friedrich yesterday. He has resigned from the Chairmanship of the American Steel and Wire Directorate, and his fellow-Directors have approved his course.

**Page 6.**

At the conference on charities yesterday at the United Charities Building, Dr. Frederick R. Sturgis attacked the whole system of public aid for private charitable institutions.

**Page 11.**

The American Cotton Company, to be organised to-day with a capital of $1,000,000, will have on its Board of Directors several officers of labor unions.

**Page 14.**

Evidence against the Ice Trust is furnished by a suit under a factor agreement of 1898. Detectives are seeking copies of the agreement with ice peddlers to take ice at a rebate.

Dr. Parkhurst, testifying at the Gardiner hearing yesterday, admitted that he consulted Foreman Putnam and Recorder Goff as to the exclusion of the District Attorney from the Grand Jury room.

Arrivals at Hotels and Out-of-Town Buyers.—Page 5.
Business Troubles.—Page 9.
Court Calendars.—Page 12.
Insurance Notes.—Page 11.
Legal Notes.—Page 11.
Losses by Fire.—Page 5.
Marine Intelligence and Foreign Mails.—Page 3.
Markets.—Page 13.
New Corporations.—Page 11.
Railroads.—Page 11.
Real Estate.—Page 12.
Society.—Page 7.
United Service.—Page 6.
Weather Report.—Page 5.
Yesterday's Fires.—Page 5.

## RECEPTION TO MR. COLER.

### Says He Will Remain City Official—Attack on Gov. Roosevelt.

At a reception tendered to him last night by the National Civic Club in Brooklyn, Controller Coler again made the unequivocal statement that he intended while his term lasted to remain an official of the City of New York. While there was no attempt to put Mr. Coler forward as a candidate for any office, yet it was stated that a man who had made the record he had made could not refuse such honor as the people at some time might insist upon bestowing upon him.

Edward M. Shepard, the President of the club, led the speechmaking in an address of welcome. Mr. Shepard said it was a common thing in this country to criticise men in public life. There was, therefore, great danger in underrating the mental and moral strength of men who represented in season and out of season great public interests. Mr. Shepard then called on Mr. Coler to speak.

In replying, the Controller spoke of the relation of the city to the State. "I speak," he said, "as an official of the City of New York, and as one who intends to remain an official of the city." He spoke of the equalization laws, of the Davis law which he again denounced, and advocated the principle of allowing each municipality to take care of its own financial affairs. He urged a campaign of education all through the State, that should have for its object the bringing to the minds of the people the principle that the prosperity of the one meant the prosperity of all.

Charles J. Patterson made an address which developed an attack on Gov. Roosevelt for the Governor's alleged failure to live up to what had been expected of him in the line of independent action. He contrasted the positions of Gov. Roosevelt and Controller Coler, in favor of the latter. When it came to supporting measures that were supposed to be vote getters, the speaker said, there were political breakfasts and lunches and dinners and nothing was done without the most "debasing recognition" of the "power of the monarch of the Republican Party."

"Such an exhibition of alleged independence," said Mr. Patterson, "I sincerely hope we will not find in our next Governor."

Addresses were also made by F. W. Hinrichs, Richard Young, Col. James P. Bell of the East River Bridge Commission, and Dr. Cruikshank, Principal of School No. 12.



## DEMANDS BOER PLANK FROM REPUBLICANS

### Edward Lauterbach Declares That Otherwise the Party Is Lost.

### MUST ACT BEFORE DEMOCRATS

#### Asserts at Citizens' Committee Meeting that Judgment Has Gone by Default Against England.

Edward Lauterbach created a sensation at the meeting of the Citizens' Committee last night at the Manhattan Hotel by advocating a Boer plank in the Republican platform. The committee met for the purpose of arranging for the entertainment of the Boer envoys, who are expected on the Maasdam next Tuesday. Addressing the meeting Mr. Lauterbach said:

"Neither of the two great political parties has taken any definite action on the position of this Government with respect to the Boer war. My own party has not seen fit to define its position. It is equally true that no other nation has done so. But judgment has gone by default against England in all civilised countries because of her action in South Africa.

"In our own country and in my own party I believe there is a latent fire that will require but a small amount of fanning to cause it to break into a vast and powerful flame that will inspire the people who love justice, freedom, and all that tends to a higher civilization and right.

"I believe the Republican Party is irretrievably lost if it leave to the Democratic Party the first opportunity to insert in its National platform a plank that will declare for the South African Republic. In Michigan the Republicans take the same stand with regard to the National party. I am unalterably opposed to leaving such action to the Democrats.

"I am a delegate to the convention, and I shall struggle and work harder there for a Boer plank in the platform than I worked and struggled for a gold plank in the platform that was made up at St. Louis."

Mr. Lauterbach's remarks were greeted with great applause.

The Rev. Father Ducey, who preceded Mr. Lauterbach, said:

"This country cannot afford to go to war over this question. We can talk now and arbitrate later. What the Boers want is sympathy and arbitration."

The following officers were elected: Chairman—Killaen Van Rensselaer; Treasurer—Theodore M. Banta; Secretary—T. A. Moynahan.

The following were appointed as the Entertainment Committee: Judge George M. Van Hoesen, Alderman R. J. Kennedy, Thomas L. Feitner, Major E. T. McCrystal, George M. Van Siclen, Edward Van Ness, John E. Milholland, Prof. Adolffe Cohn, W. F. Jennings, Edward Lauterbach, John D. L. Payn, Coroner Zucca, Patrick Egan, E. C. Sheehy, H. H. De Vos, Denis Spellissy, and John J. Rooney.

This committee will engage tugs and go down the bay to meet the envoys. They will conduct them to the City Hall and introduce them to the Mayor. It is intended that a mass meeting shall be held in the City Hall Park and that the envoys will address the people from the steps of the City Hall.

The committee received $285 in contributions last night. Edward Lauterbach contributed a check for $20, George M. Van Siclen another for $50, Theodore M. Banta, $50, and John E. Milholland, $50

## THE PROSPECT IN THE WEST.

### Editor Rosewater of Omaha Predicts Sweeping Republican Victory—Hard Fight in Nebraska.

*Special to The New York Times.*

WASHINGTON, May 10.—Edward Rosewater, editor of The Omaha Bee and a prominent Republican of the West, who was recently elected a delegate at large to the Philadelphia Convention, in conversation to-day said that the Republican Party in the West was in excellent shape, and he predicted a sweeping victory in November. He looks for a hot fight in Nebraska, perhaps the most hotly contested campaign the State has ever known, as not only the Presidential ticket, but the entire Legislative, Congressional, and State elections come off at the same time. The Democrats would undoubtedly make a great fight for the control of the Legislature, but he thought the Republican Party would surely win.

When asked whom the West favored for Vice President, Mr. Rosewater said that the Postmaster General would be the most acceptable if an Eastern man were selected, and if the nomination went West his people were for Senator Fairbanks. He did not believe that the Democrats would make free silver a prominent issue in the campaign, although he had no doubt a free silver plank would be in the platform. The farmers of the West, he said, were pretty well convinced that there was nothing in free silver, and the only interest they took in the financial question was in the abolishment of National banks and the issuance by the Government direct of greenbacks. People in the West were all opposed to trusts.

Along the Pacific Coast everybody was in favor of the retention of the Philippines. In fact, it might be said that the entire West believed it was the duty of the Administration to hold the Philippines. As to their future, why, of course, coming events must settle the question. There was no doubt in his mind or in the minds of the people with whom he had talked, of the right of Congress to legislate for their government. No one questioned the right of Congress to legislate for the District of Columbia, and he cited this as a case in point.

### SILVER-REPUBLICAN VIEWS.

#### Ex-Senator Dubois Sees Little Change in Western Silver Sentiment.

*Special to The New York Times.*

WASHINGTON, May 10.—Ex-Senator Dubois of Idaho is visiting Representative Wilson of his State for a few days. He declares that there is no change to speak of in the silver sentiment in the silver-producing States, and that Bryan will carry them by substantially as great majorities as in 1896.

He says that the Democrats may carry Vermont, the Republicans may carry Texas, but the chances are that the Republicans will carry Vermont and the Democrats will carry Texas. The chances for the Republicans to carry Colorado, Utah, Idaho, or Montana are less than they are to carry Arkansas. The fight will be hard in Oregon, California, Washington, and Wyoming and the result doubtful. No one is considered as a possible nominee for President in the States west of the Missouri River excepting McKinley by the Republicans and Bryan by the reform parties.

Mr. Dubois is Chairman of the Executive Committee of the Silver-Republican Party and says that assurances make it certain that there will be a convention of silver Republicans of at least 1,500, at Kansas City July 4.

### Inventor of Grain Drills Insane.

LYONS, N. Y., May 10.—Lyman Bickeford of Macedon has been declared insane by a Sheriff's jury. When nearly eighty years old he invented grain drills, founding the Bickeford & Huffman Company at Macedon, the largest manufacturers of grain drills in the United States. Mr. Bickeford has been prominent in Democratic politics.



## CUBAN POSTAL DEFICIT.

### Definite Information Concerning the Operations of C. F. W. Neely Not Yet in Hand.

*Special to The New York Times.*

WASHINGTON, May 10.—If the War Department and the Post Office Department are in possession of full and definite information as to the extent and character of the offense of C. F. W. Neely, recently Financial Agent of Posts in Cuba, they are not willing to communicate that information to the public.

That the officers of those departments believe that crime has been committed there is no doubt; indeed, a prominent officer of the army who is acquainted with information not yet given to the newspapers said to-day that there was not the slightest doubt that the Government had discovered a bad case of embezzlement.

The anxiety of the Administration to have the matter probed to the bottom is manifested by the earnest efforts being made to secure early and thorough investigation of postal affairs in Cuba, and to-day the President consulted with the Attorney General, Secretary of War Root, and Postmaster General Smith about the course to be pursued to ascertain precisely the extent of the irregularities.

Great confidence has hitherto been reposed in Director Rathbone, who was credited with having performed a good work admirably, yet some circumstances coming to the knowledge of the War Department make it appear almost impossible that gigantic losses could have been possible under his eyes if he had exercised the diligence that experience should have suggested to protect the Government from loss and scandal.

The authorities will not state how the investigations are to be pushed in Cuba. Inspectors Lawshe and Nettleton of the office of the Auditor for the Post Office Department, who have been ordered to Cuba to begin a thorough investigation, have had large experience in the service and know exactly how to proceed to ascertain discrepancies in accounts.

John Douglass Lindsay of Nicoll, Anable & Lindsay, New York, who is here as Neely's counsel to secure the trial of his client in New York rather than in Cuba, attempted to see Secretary Root to-day, but had not succeeded at a late hour. Secretary Root had informed him that the whole matter so far as he was concerned was in the hands of Attorney General Griggs. Mr. Lindsay contends that as the papers charge Neely with having brought to the country property of the United States obtained in Cuba, Neely ought to be tried where he was arrested, and not in Cuba. The President is understood to be firm in his determination that the crime shall be revealed where it was committed, and the penalty inflicted, if the offense charged was committed, where it was discovered.

With the arrival here to-morrow of Col. Burton, the War Department expects to obtain information to enable it to judge better of the extent of the defalcations than it has been able to do yet. Postmaster General Smith is deeply disappointed and humiliated by the discovery that the service is not sound and secure, as he believed it to be, and is determined that the decayed spots shall be cut out regardless of who is hurt.

### A CONFESSION AT HAVANA.

#### One of the Men Implicated Makes a Complete Disclosure.

HAVANA, May 10.—The investigation of the postal frauds has now reached a point that within the next few hours further arrests will probably be made, and it is believed that a considerable sum will be recovered at the same time. One of the culprits has made a complete confession, conditional upon being accepted as State's evidence. What he says proves conclusively what was known before, that several others besides Charles F. W. Neely, late Financial Agent of Posts at Havana, are more or less implicated.

The exact dates have been obtained by the authorities. The latter refuse to give the name of the man who has confessed, but, though shocked at the nature of the cold-blooded swindle and conspiracy, they are still glad that they have evidence to completely justify their actions regarding Neely.

### CARRIES RELIEF TO INDIA.

#### The Quito Starts with Her Cargo of 200,000 Bushels of Corn.

The steamship Quito, carrying 200,000 bushels of corn for the famine sufferers in India, sailed yesterday from Pier No. 1, North River. The sailing of the Quito was marked by impressive ceremonies, which were attended by several hundred people. Among those who delivered brief addresses were the Countess Schimmelman and Commander Booth-Tucker of the Salvation Army.

It is expected that the Quito will reach Bombay in forty days, and on the way there she will stop at the Azores, Port Said, and Aden. The Quito was chartered by the United States Government at a cost of $40,000, and her cargo is valued at $100,000. She is commanded by Capt. Baird.

### FROSTS INJURE CROPS.

#### Peaches and Strawberries in This State Badly Damaged.

RHINECLIFF, May 10.—There was a heavy frost in the upper Hudson Valley last night and in some locations back from the river ice formed. The peach and strawberry crop is badly damaged, if not a total loss. Apples, it is thought, have escaped, as the blossoms were not far enough out to be injured.

NYACK, May 10.—The mercury was down to freezing point in Rockland County last night and thick ice formed in some parts of the county. Grave fears are felt that if the cold continues the fruit will be injured.

ROCKVILLE, Conn., May 10.—The lowlands of this city and throughout Tolland County were covered with frost and serious damage to fruit trees and early crops was done. It is thought the peach crop will prove an entire failure as a result.

#### Early Vegetables Frostbitten.

EAST MORICHES, L. I., May 10.—Ice formed in exposed places this morning throughout this section, and it is feared that fruit buds have been injured.

LYNBROOK, L. I., May 10.—Frost last night injured all kinds of tender vegetables which were planted on low ground. Sweet corn and melons are killed and will have to be replanted. It is not yet known whether the fruit buds are injured.

#### Ice on Ponds in Jersey.

HILLSDALE, N. J., May 10.—A heavy frost prevailed throughout Northern New Jersey last night and did a great deal of damage. The fruit crops suffered heavily, apple, cherry, strawberry, and other blossoms being destroyed. The temperature fell so low here that a thin layer of ice formed on the water in the ponds.



## CHINESE WOMAN PLAINTIFF

### Sues American Citizen to Recover Interest in a House.

#### Court Interpreter Did Not Understand Her Language, and the Clerk Could Not Swear Her.

San Toy Fong, a young Chinese woman, appeared in Part V., Special Term, of the Supreme Court yesterday as the plaintiff in an action to recover from Robert Kerr, an American citizen, a half interest in some property in the Chinese quarter. She was accompanied by her husband, Chu Fong, and her baby, Ting Fong. All were gorgeously attired in native costume.

Mrs. Fong was the first witness called. She handed the baby over to her husband and walked toward the witness chair as fast as her bandaged feet would permit her. The baby began to cry as soon as Mrs. Fong left it. As a result the father, Chu Fong, spent the remainder of the time his wife was in court walking up and down in the corridor with Ting in his arms.

When Mrs. Fong had taken the stand Justice Lawrence ordered the clerk to administer the regular oath to her. Then came the first hitch in the proceedings. She did not understand English, and the clerk did not know how to swear a person in Chinese. The official interpreter was called in, and while he can talk in many different tongues, he had to confess that he was not up in Chinese.

Randolph Parmly, counsel for the defendant, then offered to provide an interpreter. This was objected to by counsel for the plaintiff. Finally after much arguing the case was adjourned until this morning with the understanding that the Chinese Consul would be appealed to to furnish a reliable man.

"But who will pay his expenses?" asked the counsel for San Toy Fong.

"That is a matter you will have to adjust among yourselves. The court has a regular interpreter, but he cannot be expected to know the languages of all the tribes of Asia."

It was finally agreed that the plaintiff should pay the costs of an interpreter providing he was acceptable.

The case itself offers some peculiar features. This is the first case on record in the Supreme Court where a Chinese woman appears as plaintiff and makes an American citizen the defendant in an action to recover real property. San Toy Fong claims a half interest in the property at 20, 22, and 24 Pell Street, and is suing Robert Kerr, the owner, to have her rights established as well as for an accounting for the rents for two years.

It appears that in 1897 John G. Ritter purchased the property and erected a Chinese tenement house on it. He gave a mortgage to Mr. Kerr for money loaned. Eventually the mortgage was foreclosed, and Mr. Kerr purchased the property. Mrs. San Toy Fong now produces a certificate of trust, showing that Mr. Ritter had transferred to her a one-half interest in the property. This certificate was not placed on record until two years after it was executed. She claims that she invested in the property $10,000, which she had received as a dowry. She asks the court to order Mr. Kerr to execute a new certificate of trust.

## MR. COCKRAN'S ATTITUDE.

### Says He Will Only Support Bryan if Militarism, Imperialism, and Trusts Are the Main Issues.

MONTGOMERY, Ala., May 10.—"It has been said that I shall support Bryan if he is the Democratic nominee for President," said W. Bourke Cockran to-night.

"That depends, I say frankly, upon the Kansas City platform and the spirit in which it is submitted to the American people. If that platform is only a reiteration of the platform of 1896, I shall not support it or the nominee.

"I am unalterably opposed to the McKinley policy toward our new possessions. I oppose militarism. I oppose imperialism. I oppose trusts. If the platform takes a decided stand in opposing these things, and the spirit is in favor of making these questions predominant, I shall support it, and do all I can in my State for the ticket. Otherwise I shall not. I consider these questions the issues of the campaign.

"The money plank, if it must, can remain the same as in 1896, because it is impossible to make it effective, and the other issues are graver and far more important from the standpoint of present conditions. As to New York State, I can say nothing, for I am there only a private citizen."

## METHODISTS DISCUSS WOMAN.

### Proposition to Change "Layman" to "Lay Member" Brings on a Lively Debate.

*Special to The New York Times.*

CHICAGO, May 10.—The question of the admission of women as delegates was reached in the Methodist Conference to-day, and the discussion was precipitated by the proposition to substitute the expression "lay member" wherever the word "layman" occurred. It was Dr. Moore of Cincinnati who proposed this, and a contest ensued. Presiding Bishop Mallalieu kept Dr. Buckley off the floor as long as he could. While the New Yorker was shouting to be heard, Dr. Brown of Columbia River raised a laugh at Buckley's expense by saying:

"It was said at one time there was a great gathering, which may be spoken of as the first General Conference, and a certain dignitary came also, who was the chief speaker on the floor. So it is not to be wondered at that this individual should appear here." When Buckley, who had been thus characterized as Satan, got the floor he replied:

"A limited knowledge of the Holy Scriptures has betrayed many a man. The personage referred to by the distinguished gentleman preceding me first appeared in the Garden of Eden, and he spoke so plausibly that the woman desired to go out of her proper place." This remark turned the laugh against the women's advocates.

Dr. Buckley argued that the proposed change would be unconstitutional. Dr. Potts declared that what was needed was a constitution good for a century, and that women representation should be embodied in it. T. N. Boyle of Pittsburg said that this conference should not be bound by the Cleveland action. Dr. Oldham said the 800 ministers who voted four years ago that a woman was not a layman belonged to the generation that is passing off the stage.

Dr. Jacob Grow of New Jersey created great amusement in speaking against the women. He declared with emphasis that there was not a scintilla of evidence in the Word of God for the argument favoring the election of women to the annual conferences of the ministry.

It was decided to make the subject the first order for to-morrow.

Much interest was manifested in the quadrennial reports of the missionary Bishops, Hartzell of Africa, and Thoburn of India. These reports, set by special order for 11 o'clock, were eagerly awaited by the 700 delegates present. Bishop Thoburn, it was announced just before the presentation of his report, has decided to withdraw from the missionary field for at least a year owing to enfeebled health, caused by the climate in India.

In discussing the outlook in India, Bishop Thoburn said the famine in Central Northern India and the pestilence in Bombay and Western India had been detrimental to missionary work, but in spite of these drawbacks there was an increase in the strength of the work over five years ago, the missionary community now numbering 111,000 souls.

It would be absolutely impossible, however, he claimed, to hold the present ground, much less to make a further progress, unless the resources were largely increased within a few years. In speaking of the Church's invasion of the Philippines, he said that arrangements for permanent religious services had been made in Manila.



## THE TUNNEL EXTENSIONS

### Routes in Brooklyn Discussed Before Rapid Transit Board.

#### Arguments Advanced in Favor of a Hamilton Avenue Line—Joralemon Street Plan Defended.

The Rapid Transit Commissioners yesterday gave a hearing to residents of South Brooklyn and Richmond Borough who seek the construction of a tunnel under the East River from the foot of Whitehall Street to Hamilton Avenue, Brooklyn, and thence along Hamilton Avenue to Fourth Avenue, with connections ultimately to South Brooklyn and under the Narrows to Staten Island.

The Committee of Fifty which appeared at the last hearing favored a route from the Battery to Joralemon Street, connecting with the Long Island Railroad Station at Flatbush Avenue.

E. J. Tysen, speaking for Staten Island citizens, said that the plan would aid both the southern portion of Brooklyn and Staten Island.

W. A. Short, also of Richmond Borough, argued for the Hamilton Avenue route that the opening up of the districts to the south would give an opportunity for those crowded in tenements to have homes in the suburbs.

Erastus Wiman wanted a tunnel which would not only extend to South Brooklyn and Staten Island, but through the island itself to connect with a bridge across the Kill von Kull, to Elizabeth, so that railroad freight and passengers might be carried through to Brooklyn. Such a scheme, he said, would conduce to the restoration of the commercial supremacy of the port and would give to Brooklyn a close connection with the trunk lines to the West. This, he said, would benefit Manhattan as well, for 90 per cent. of the people needed access to cheap property.

When Mr. Wiman added that, unless something of this sort was done, Brooklyn was doomed, Controller Coler spoke up, saying, "No, it isn't; no quitters come from Brooklyn."

Frederick Cocheu produced a map of Brooklyn showing the wards and cited statistics to show that 468,000 people would be reached by the Hamilton Avenue route. He suggested that the road should be carried up Hamilton Avenue or a parallel Street to Fourth or Fifth Avenue, the Hamilton Avenue route.

Another member of the delegation said that the Joralemon Street route would increase the present congestion.

William McCarroll of the Committee of Fifty said that he was not opposed to any tunnel scheme, but that he advocated the Joralemon Street route because it would give relief where it was needed immediately, rather than open up new districts for the benefit of unimproved real estate. Most of the South Brooklyn population, he said, was contiguous to the section reached by the Joralemon Street route.

The Rev. Dr. McConnell, rector of Holy Trinity Church of Brooklyn, said that the South Brooklyn tunnel would take care only of the traffic now accommodated by the South Ferry, and would not relieve the crowding at the bridge.

Ludwig Nissen of the Manufacturers' Association of Brooklyn, said that the Committee of Fifty represented over 90 per cent. of the people of Brooklyn, and that the will of the majority should prevail.

Engineer Theodore L. Frothingham gave figures to show that to pay the route should reach the most populous centres.

Stephen Moye, who said that he represented the New York, New Jersey and Staten Island Junction Railroad, which held necessary franchises, sought a hearing, but was told that he would have to appear at the next meeting, when residents of Queens and the Bronx will also be heard.

The Rapid Transit Commissioners yesterday announced the following appointments: Division engineer, W. L. Value, salary $4,000; Inspector of Designs, St. John Clark, $3,600; assistant engineer, Robert Ridgeway, $2,200; George H. Clark, $2,200; John Myers, Jr., $1,800; Justin Burns, $1,800; Ralph N. Wheeler, $1,800; transit men, Henry L. Oestreich, Jr., $1,500; Joshua Binion, $1,500; Edwin H. Thomas, $1,500; John B. Griffiths, $1,500; draughtsman, Daniel E. Baxter, $1,500; stenographer, William Guilfoyle, $1,200; rodman, Robert L. Jacobs, $960; axemen, Otto Claussner, $720, and Joseph Goldberg, $720.

Herman A. D. Holman was appointed auditor to the commission at a salary of $2,500.

## MR. SAGE CAUSES TROUBLE.

### Raises Freight Transportation Rates for Hudson River Hospital.

*Special to The New York Times.*

POUGHKEEPSIE, N. Y., May 10.—The Board of Managers of the Hudson River State Hospital have been "put in the hole" by Russell Sage, the New York financier, who among his other enterprises owns and conducts the Poughkeepsie and Eastern Railway, one end of which connects with the hospital, and is in demand by the hospital officials for the transportation of supplies.

The railroad was extended to the hospital through the efforts of the managers. The extension cost the State about $40,000, and it was supposed that the money expended would be turned back through the reduction in the cost of handling supplies. Last year the railroad hauled coal to the hospital for 20 cents a ton less than the teamsters charged, but this year the rate was made the same, and when the managers protested they were reminded that the railroad could charge any rate it pleased, as the managers neglected to make a contract or enter into any agreement on this subject when the extension was built.

The hospital officals have applied to the State Railroad Commission for relief. They ask the commission to compel Mr. Sage's road to fix lower rates.

## FIELD WORK FOR WOMEN.

### Illinois Farmers Employ Them for Plowing and Similar Labor.

*Special to The New York Times.*

CHICAGO, May 10.—Gustave Schwartz, a farmer, who lives ten miles northwest of Ravenwood, has hired Mary Phennig to work on his farm. He has found in Mary a woman who will go into the fields in the morning and guide a plow through the rocky ground until nightfall.

This is the third woman within a month who has accepted work on farms in Illinois. Inquiry at the State Employment Agencies shows that there have been many applications from women of foreign birth who desire to take service in the country districts as assistants on farms, not to do housework, but to labor in the fields.

## ADMIRAL DEWEY AT NASHVILLE.

### He Visits Various Points of Interest in and About the City.

NASHVILLE, Tenn., May 10.—Admiral and Mrs. Dewey were entertained by the citizens of this city to-day under sunny skies. Thousands of visitors were here.

Mrs. Dewey was entertained at breakfast by Mrs. McMillin, wife of Gov. McMillin, and the members of the committee in charge of the flower parade, which was given during the afternoon.

Admiral Dewey, escorted by a committee representing the citizens and the commercial organizations, visited various points of interest in and about the city.



## KILLED BY AN AUTOMOBILE.

### A Doctor's Page Meets Death While Taking a Ride on His Bicycle.

In a head-on collision at Central Park West and Seventy-fifth Street last night between an automobile and a bicycle, the rider of the bicycle, M. Alexander, sixteen years old, employed as a page by Dr. Judd of 225 Central Park West, was thrown from his wheel and his skull fractured. He died at Roosevelt Hospital a few hours after the accident.

The young man, who had finished his work and had started out for a spin, was riding south on the avenue. The electric automobile belonging to the General Electric Carriage Company of 66 West Forty-third Street was in charge of George M. Schaeffer of 353 West Forty-fourth Street, and was going in a northerly direction. The car tracks on the avenue are alongside the Park sidewalk and other vehicles keep to the asphalt outside.

There was a maze of vehicles between Seventy-fourth and Seventy-fifth Streets, and the bicyclist was caught as he tried to thread his way through them. He came suddenly out from behind one vehicle to meet the automobile, and he was struck and thrown off with great force. He landed twenty-five feet away from where the collision took place, and struck on his head.

The boy was carried, unconscious, into the San Remo Hotel, whence he was taken to the hospital. Schaeffer was arrested and locked up in the West Sixty-eighth Street Station.

## LORD SALISBURY'S SPEECH.

### His Alarmist Words Ascribed to Nationalist Successes in France.

LONDON, May 11.—The alarmist tone of Lord Salisbury's Primrose League speech on Wednesday has been much discussed in the lobbies of Parliament; and the impression is that the apprehensions of the Premier are even more serious than those he gave expression to.

His utterances are ascribed to the recent successes of the Nationalists in France, hatred of Great Britain being one of the weapons of the campaign. The revival of military glory, one of the ideals set up in France, is regarded as dangerous to Great Britain.

## RACE PROBLEM CONFERENCE.

### Speakers at Montgomery Discuss Lynching—Extermination of Blacks Said to be Inevitable.

MONTGOMERY, Ala., May 10.—At the morning session of the Race Conference the discussion centred about the negro in relation to religion.

Prof. John Roachstraton of Mercer University, Macon; the Rev. D. Clay Lilley of Tuscaloosa, Secretary of the Southern Presbyterian Board of Negro Evangelization, and W. A. Guerry, Chaplain of the University of the South, took part in the discussion. The Rev. C. C. Brown of Clinton, S. C., and the Very Rev. J. R. Slattery of Baltimore, spoke for the advisability of raising the standard of ordination.

Bishop Rennick of Baltimore declared that from five to eight negroes in the North under Northern conditions committed crimes to one in the South. Prof. W. F. Willcox, Statistician in the Census Bureau, declared that the ultimate extermination of the black race was inevitable. "There will be a rapid decrease of the birth rate and a slow increase of the death rate until the negro race will stand as the American Indian stands to-day," said Prof. Willcox.

Prof. Willcox was followed by Secretary Herbert Welsh of the Indian Rights Association. At the afternoon session Alex. C. King of Atlanta opened the discussion of the lynching question. He spoke on "The Punishment of Crimes Against Women—Existing Legal Remedies and Their Sufficiency."

Mr. King said it was in those communities where the dominance of the white race was the least secure and the menace of the black criminal the greatest that lynch law is most likely to prevail. He called attention to the fact that with the passage of time since the abolition of slavery the crime seems to grow in importance. Mr. King also noted the apparently inherent prejudice existing between the lower class of white people and the negro, who, in being educated and by imitation, was menacing the social status of this class of white people. He said that this prejudice is resented by the negro and produces strong racial animosity.

Mr. King gave two reasons why extra judicial means are resorted to, namely, the delay of legal punishment and the protection of the victim of the assault from the ordeal of the witness chair. He suggested two remedies for mob violence. He thought that when a party begins a hunt for a fugitive each member should be sworn in as a Deputy Sheriff by the Sheriff of the county and a memorandum of his name taken. In case violence came to the prisoner, those committing it could be detected. He also suggested that for every county where a lynching occurred a tax should be levied by the State authorities of not less than $5,000 and the amount appropriated to the School Fund of the State. He closed with a plea for the domination of law.

He was followed by Clifton R. Breckinridge of Arkansas, who discussed the advisability of lynching.

W. Bourke Cockran of New York boldly advocated the repeal of the Fifteenth Amendment to the Federal Constitution. He argued that it was a bad limb on the tree; that it had been nullified by the States; that it had been lynched, so to speak, by the people of the South.

He declared that the reconciliation of the theoretical status of the negro under the Constitution should be reconciliation with his actual status in the public opinion of the country. He maintained that this repeal was best for the negro as well as for the white man, since both races had to live together, to prosper together, or go down together. Every source of irritation between the two should be removed, and the Fifteenth Amendment was the greatest.

Mr. Cockran asserted that the path of the negro to political and social rights lay through the development of the unit, the individual, and that the only means was by industrial education.

## GOV. ROOSEVELT IS FIRM.

### Confers with Senator Hanna—He Will Not, It Is Said, Be Asked to Stand for Vice Presidency.

WASHINGTON, May 10.—The Post to-morrow will say that at quite a long conference with Senator Hanna, Gov. Roosevelt reiterated his statement that he did not want a Vice Presidential nomination, and that he believed he could add to his party's strength more by running again for Governor than for the National office. The Post adds:

"Senator Hanna offered no counter arguments, and the conference closed with the understanding that for the present at least Gov. Roosevelt's name would not be considered. No decision has been reached as to the man to whom the nomination shall be given, but Secretary Long's chances are considered excellent."

Gov. Roosevelt, in company with Senator Lodge of Massachusetts, paid a visit to the Capitol to-day. He arrived there at about 11 o'clock in the morning, and spent a brief time in greeting his friends among the Senators, leaving the building before the Senate convened.

In the afternoon Gov. Roosevelt drove over to Fort Myer to witness one of the famous cavalry drills at that army post. President and Mrs. McKinley, Secretaries Hay and Root, and many other well-known people were present, and witnessed a remarkable exhibition of horseback riding by the troopers.

Gov. Roosevelt was the guest of honor this evening at a dinner given by Capt. and Mrs. Cowles at their home on N Street. Among others present were the Secretary of War and Mrs. Root, the Secretary of the Navy, Mr. and Mrs. Arnold Hague, Mr. and Mrs. Thomas Nelson Page, and Mrs. Tuckerman.



## BRYAN AND TOWNE POPULISTS' CHOICE

### National Ticket Nominated at Sioux Falls by Acclamation.

### UPROAR IN THE CONVENTION

#### Delegates Pull Off Their Coats, Ready to Fight.

#### Platform Adopted Demands Silver at 16 to 1, Condemns Trusts, and Declares Sympathy for the Boers.

President—WILLIAM JENNINGS BRYAN of Nebraska.
Vice President—CHARLES A. TOWNE of Minnesota.

SIOUX FALLS, South Dakota, May 10.—The Populist National Convention has nominated William Jennings Bryan of Nebraska for President and Charles A. Towne of Minnesota for Vice President.

The nomination of Mr. Bryan was made by acclamation as soon as the platform had been adopted.

The nomination of Mr. Towne also was made by acclamation, but not until the convention had fought for hours over the question whether any nomination for the Vice Presidency should be made. As soon as it was determined to nominate, several candidates were named, but one after another withdrew, until J. J. Lentz of Ohio alone remained to contest against Mr. Towne. A motion to nominate Mr. Towne by acclamation was made and prevailed, only a few Montana men voting in the negative.

The convention met at 9:45 o'clock this morning and permanently organized with Thomas M. Patterson of Colorado as Chairman and T. H. Curran of Kansas, Leo Vincent of Colorado, and E. M. Deicher as Secretaries.

The Committee on Credentials presented its report, declaring that there were no contesting delegations, and recommending that the vote of Missouri be increased by two votes, that of Ohio by two votes, and that of South Dakota by three votes.

The report, which was read by Gov. Poynter of Nebraska, was adopted without a dissenting vote. The minority report threatened last night by Committeeman Madden of Colorado did not materialize.

Aside from listening to the address of the permanent Chairman and a number of short speeches the convention transacted no business in the morning session. Early in the afternoon the Committee on Platform reported, and the resolutions then presented were adopted by a unanimous vote.

The long financial plank of the platform, including the denunciation of the recent banking law and especially the demand for the free coinage of silver at the ratio of 16 to 1, was received with wild cheering. The demand for an inheritance tax also received a round of applause. Vigorous cheering was also accorded the reading of the plank on transportation, the demand for the abolition of all tariffs on "trust" goods, and the indorsement of the initiative and referendum. Cries of "Good!" "Good!" greeted the denunciation of the Administration's Philippine policy and the Porto Rican tax.

When that portion of the plank extending sympathy to the South African republics and denouncing any alliance with foreign powers was read the convention broke into wild applause. Indorsement of the municipal ownership of public utilities received but faint applause, but vigorous handclapping ensued when direct election of United States Senators was demanded.

#### NOMINATION OF BRYAN.

Then came the nomination of Bryan.

"The next thing before the convention," said Chairman Patterson, "is the presentation of the names of candidates for the nomination for the office of President of the United States." Then, without pausing or calling for any call of States, he went on: "I have the pleasure of introducing Senator Allen of Nebraska."

This could mean but one man, and that was Bryan. Before Senator Allen could come to the front of the platform the convention was on its feet, cheering frantically, waving flags, hats, and handkerchiefs. The speech of Senator Allen was brief and to the point. He spoke as follows:

"He embodies in his political convictions, in his life, all that is good in an American citizen; all that is pure and loyal; all the most exacting could desire; a statesman of ripe experience, a philosopher, a patriot without a peer on this or any other continent. Peerless, bold, determined, thoroughly united to the interests of the great mass of his countrymen, who would make and will make an ideal candidate for the exalted office of President of these United States.

"Since the result of the election in 1896 was known to the American people, among the fusion forces of the United States there has been but one name connected with the office and with the nomination at this time. He is the embodiment of all that opposes plutocracy, that opposes greed, that opposes the exercise of [illegible] power in public life. He is, in my judgment, the most American citizen of the age. I think he is an orator, a statesman, the equal of Webster and Clay, if not their superior. He was a Nebraskan, but belongs now to the world.

"Without further discussion, without further description of this magnificent man, I present to this convention, this hero, statesman, and orator, William Jennings Bryan."

The announcement of Mr. Bryan's name was the signal for another enthusiastic outburst. The Minnesota delegation hoisted a large star having the portrait of Mr. Bryan in the centre, and the convention cheered again, more vigorously than before. When his voice could be heard, Chairman Patterson introduced Gen. James B. Weaver of Iowa. Another round of cheers rang out as the veteran from Iowa came forward to second the nomination of Mr. Bryan. He spoke in part as follows:

"I had the honor to present at St. Louis the name of the distinguished gentleman who has just been mentioned. I am glad that I can say here to-day that there has never been a moment from that day to this that I have regretted or any Populist in America has regretted that he was the choice of that convention. The century past has produced but three great civic names—Thomas Jefferson, Abraham Lincoln, and William Jennings Bryan. The delegates in this convention are disciples of the first, many of them helped put the second in the chair, and we are followers of the third."

#### BRYAN BY ACCLAMATION.

"Cyclone" Davis of Texas announced that in former conventions he had been a political opponent of Mr. Bryan, but had now come over to the ranks of the elect. Continuing, he said: "McKinley has been called the Napoleon of Republican politics, and perhaps the title is not inappropriate, for we all know that Napoleon made a dash into the Orient, and it did not pan out very well."

Senator Butler of North Carolina and W. J. Thomas of Colorado made brief second speeches, and Mr. Olds of Pennsylvania, eighty-six years old, was introduced. Mr. Olds, bent and white-bearded, said that

"All the News That's Fit to Print."

# The New York Times.

THE WEATHER. Showers and cooler; southerly winds.



VOL. XLIX...NO. 15,742. NEW YORK, FRIDAY, JUNE 22, 1900.—FOURTEEN PAGES. ONE CENT In Greater New York and Jersey City. Elsewhere, TWO CENTS.

## THE NEWS CONDENSED.

Stocks irregular.

Cash wheat, No. 2 red, 82¼c; corn, No. 2 mixed, 48½c; oats, No. 2 mixed, 28½c; cotton, middling, 9 3-16c; iron, No. 1 foundry, $19; butter, extra creamery, 19½c.

FOREIGN.—A dispatch from Admiral Kempff, received at the Navy Department in Washington yesterday, stated that the bombardment of Tien-Tsin had been begun, and that the United States Consulate and a large part of the foreign concessions in that city were being destroyed. No intelligence has been received as to the fate of the envoys and foreigners in Peking, and no confirmation is obtainable of the reported arrival of Admiral Seymour's column at the capital. One rumor, which is not credited in London, is that Admiral Seymour is dead. Minister Wu, at Washington, received a message yesterday from the Viceroy of the three great provinces of the Yang-tse-Kiang District saying that there was no danger to foreigners in that part of the empire. Li Hung Chang has, at the request of the Consuls at Canton, decided not to go to Peking. Gen. Buller is pushing on fast in the Southern Transvaal, and it is expected that he will be able to help in cutting off the Boers in the Orange River Colony, or, at any rate, in preventing their communicating with Gen. Botha in the South African Republic. Commissioner General Peck was fifteen minutes late yesterday, and so was unable to welcome President Loubet to the United States section of the exposition. Lady Randolph Churchill announces that she will wed Lieut. West in July. The Khedive of Egypt is ill from diphtheria on board the royal yacht Osborne. Count Muravieff, the Russian Minister of Foreign Affairs, died suddenly in St. Petersburg yesterday. The event is said to be fraught with great moment for France, and it is said that the Russian-French alliance may be abandoned for an alliance between England and Russia. The text of President McKinley's decree of amnesty to the Filipinos was made public by the War Department. Kumassi is completely invested.—Pages 1, 6, and 7.

**Page 5.**

M. Rothstein, the Russian financier, said in this city last night that the Empress Dowager will restore order in China, and he blamed the powers for procrastination.

**Page 7.**

A deed filed in the Register's office yesterday transfers a child for a consideration of $100. The mother, a sweatshop worker, was compelled by poverty to sell her baby.

H. C. Banham, who was sentenced to death Sept. 11, 1897, for wife murder, was acquitted yesterday as the result of a retrial of his case at Canandaigua.

**Page 14.**

Degrees were conferred upon 134 young men at the City College commencement last night.

Judge Aspinall, in Brooklyn, yesterday described Coney Island as a "sink of infamy" and made a sarcastic reference to the detectives.

At the Normal College Commencement yesterday diplomas were given to 468 graduates, prizes were awarded, and degrees were conferred.

Aaron Halle, the murderer of Mamie Branigan, was found guilty of murder in the first degree yesterday, just thirty-five days after his crime.

Arrivals at Hotels and Out-of-Town Buyers.—Page 2.
Business Troubles.—Page 9.
Court Calendars.—Page 12.
Insurance Notes.—Page 11.
Legal Notes.—Page 14.
Losses by Fire.—Page 5.
Marine Intelligence and Foreign mails.—Page 9.
[illegible]—Page 9.
[illegible]—Page 2.
Real Estate.—Page 12.
Society.—Page 7.
[illegible] Service.—Page 5.
Weather Report.—Page 5.
Yesterday's Fires.—Page 5.

## WOODRUFF FOR SENATOR.

### He Does Not Want to be Governor, He Says—May Try for Platt's Place.

*Special to The New York Times.*

PHILADELPHIA, June 21.—Lieut. Gov. Woodruff, whose friends yesterday started to boom him as a candidate for the Republican nomination for Governor in New York, to-night said that he was not a candidate and would not seek the nomination.

"I have never authorized anybody to say that I was seeking the nomination for Governor," said Mr. Woodruff. "I am going to serve out my term as Lieutenant Governor, and shall then go back to my business, although I have no intention of retiring from politics."

The hotel gossip to-day attributed to Mr. Woodruff an ambition to succeed Thomas C. Platt as United States Senator. Mr. Platt has said that he will not seek a re-election to the Senate.

New York Republicans who are here look forward to an interesting struggle in the party before the candidate for Governor is finally agreed upon. "Odell can have it if he wants it," is heard from every organization man, but the State Chairman says he does not want it, and that he does want to remain at the head of the State Committee.

## SOUTHERN CROPS IN DANGER.

### Incessant Rains Threaten Cotton, Corn, and Fruit with Ruin.

*Special to The New York Times.*

BIRMINGHAM, Ala., June 21.—The incessant rains which have fallen almost every day this month and were heavy in April and May have so seriously menaced crops that there is unfeigned alarm. All over Alabama, especially in the central and northern portion, the grass has grown thick and high over the cotton. In some places the grass is from two to three feet high in rows, while the cotton, held back by cold nights and mornings is but ten inches or so high. There has been too much rain even for corn, and it, too, is overgrown with grass.

The peach crop, which was just about to ripen, has commenced to rot, and it is the same with other fruits. While vegetables are also rotting from a similar cause. The rainfall from April 1 to date has been twenty-two inches, and seven inches have fallen already this month. The nights are extremely cool and injurious to cotton.

## Dr. Goodchild Called to Baltimore.

*Special to The New York Times.*

BALTIMORE, June 21.—The Rev. Dr. F. M. Goodchild of the Central Baptist Church, New York City, has been called to the Franklin Square Baptist Church of Baltimore, to succeed the Rev. Sparks W. Melton, who resigned last April to become pastor of the First Baptist Church of Augusta, Ga. It is understood that Dr. Goodchild will accept the call.

The Rev. Dr. Frank M. Goodchild was called to the pastorate of the Central Baptist Church in 1893. Before that time he had been pastor of the Spruce Street Church, in Philadelphia. He was born in that city Dec. 26, 1860.

## Iowa Railroads Elect Officers.

*Special to The New York Times.*

BURLINGTON, Iowa, June 21.—The annual election of the Burlington and Western Railroad and the Burlington and Northwestern Railway officers took place this afternoon. The following were named for the Burlington and Northwestern: Directors—T. W. Barhydt, W. W. Baldwin, J. T. Remey, W. F. McFarland, J. W. Blythe, H. B. Scott, C. P. Squires, H. S. Rand, and William Carson. Officers: President T. W. Barhydt; Vice President—J. T. Remey; Secretary and Treasurer—R. M. Green. T. W. Barhydt was elected President of the Burlington and Western, and C. P. Squires was made Vice President. R. M. Green was elected Secretary and Treasurer.



# BOMBARDMENT OF TIEN-TSIN BEGUN

## Admiral Kempff Reports that Attack on the City Is in Progress.

## NO NEWS ABOUT ENVOYS

### Rumor of Death of Admiral Seymour Is Not Credited.

### The Monocacy Said to Have Been Shot Through the Bows—Japan May Send an Army Division to China.

WASHINGTON, June 21.—Acting Secretary of the Navy Hackett received a cable message this afternoon from Admiral Kempff, dated Che-Foo, June 21, saying that Tien-Tsin is being bombarded and that the American Consulate as well as much of the foreign concessions are being destroyed.

A relief party is en route to Tien-Tsin. It includes 130 American marines under Major Waller.

LONDON, June 22.—The scantiness of authentic news with reference to the situation in China continues. Admiral Kempff's dispatch to the United States Navy Department announcing that Tien-Tsin is being bombarded was prominently used by the London papers and commented upon as indicating a change for the worse.

The British Admiralty does not believe the report of the death of Admiral Seymour, commander of the international relief column, and semi-official assurances are given that there seems to be not the slightest evidence to back up such a report. It is pointed out that Admiral Seymour had sufficient supplies to enable him to get to Peking or to get back. "We are hopeful," says the semi-official announcement, "that, since he has not done the latter, he has done the former."

A dispatch from Shanghai, dated yesterday, says:

"The Consuls met to-day to consider the situation, which, in the absence of news from Peking, is looked upon as particularly threatening. Grave fears still exist as to the safety of the Europeans in Peking. It was agreed to wire to the senior Consul at Che-Foo to communicate with the senior officers at Taku, asking for immediate assistance in communicating direct with Peking, which they believe can be brought about through Sheng, Director of Telegraphs. They wish that Sheng be asked to explain the interruption of communications."

Special dispatches from Shanghai continue to recount wholesale slaughter at Peking. The soldiers and Boxers are said to be massacring each other, and the Chinese and Manchus are also reported to be engaged in mutual slaughter.

Prince Tuan is alleged to have sacked and burned the palace, the Emperor is reported to have been killed, the Dowager Empress is represented as missing, and in some quarters it is believed she has committed suicide.

All this purports to have been contained in a letter from Peking received by a high official Chinaman at Shanghai, where it is hoped the desperate struggle between the leaders of the different mobs, allegedly for possession of the vast treasures of the Dowager Empress, will continue and prevent the various sects from combining against the Europeans.

All the Englishwomen at Tien-Tsin left there on Saturday by train for Taku. Shanghai wires that they had some exciting experiences, and would not have gotten through except for the assistance of the Chinese troops. The Boxers made several desperate attempts to attack the train.

The Shanghai correspondent of The Times says:

"Great destruction was caused by the Boxers in the native quarter of Tien-Tsin on June 15, but the presence of the foreign troops in the foreign settlement protected that.

"The native press asserts that there are bitter dissensions in the Manchu party."

Taking advantage of the political disorders, bands of robbers are pillaging in the vicinity of Sam-Chung. The Chinese authorities are powerless.

The United States gunboat Monocacy was two miles up the Pei-Ho River when the international fleet began the bombardment of the Taku forts. According to the Shanghai correspondent of The Daily Express, she was shot through the bows. The correspondent says that Chinese riflemen on both sides of the river attacked her, but unsuccessfully.

BERLIN, June 21.—A semi-official dispatch from Tokio, dated June 21, says the Japanese Consul at Shanghai confirms the reports that Vice Admiral Seymour has arrived at Peking and that the members of the Diplomatic Corps are safe.

According to an official Japanese report from Che-Foo the foreign settlement at Tien-Tsin was reduced to ashes on June 18.

SHANGHAI, June 21.—The British destroyer Whiting at Che-Foo reports that nothing has been heard from Admiral Seymour's force for six days.

The French Consul wires that the British Mission at Tsang-Chow has been looted and the missionaries conveyed to an unknown place by a Chinese General.

YOKOHAMA, June 21.—The reports of the murder of foreign Ministers at Peking and the death of Admiral Seymour, although viewed with suspicion, have created a profound sensation. The press expresses the opinion that Japan must, with or without the consent of the powers, adopt active measures. The naval and military officers are very busy.

Probably the whole Hiroshima Division, under the command of Gen. Hiroshima, will be afloat within a few days.

The Russian cruiser Rurik has arrived here with the new Russian Minister to Japan and leaves here for Taku to-day.

## RUSSIA BEHIND THE BOXERS?

LONDON, June 22.—The Singapore correspondent of The Daily Express, telegraphing yesterday, says:

"Kang-Yu-Wei, the reformer, asserts that Russian agents precipitated, if they did not entirely organize, the present disturbances, for purely Russian purposes."

## LI NOT GOING TO PEKING.

HONGKONG, June 21.—Reports have been received here from Canton that owing to the representations of the Foreign Consuls Li Hung Chang has consented to remain in Canton.

LONDON, June 21.—The statement that Li Hung Chang has canceled his passage to Peking is regarded here as interesting. How he manages to disobey the Dowager Empress's urgent command is not clear, but, evidently, fear of a revolution at Canton in the event of his departure, induced the Consuls to bring strong pressure to bear on him.

The explanation given at Hongkong of the failure of Li to go to Peking is that there is a rising on the border of the Kow-Loon Hinterland.



## MESSAGE TO MINISTER WU.

### Viceroy Tells Him that There Is No Danger to Foreigners in the Yang-tse-Kiang Provinces.

WASHINGTON, June 21.—Minister Wu was seen to-day after a visit to the State Department. He said that Secretary Hay had expressed his gratification at news the Minister had brought from Viceroy Liu of the three great Yang-tse-Kiang provinces—Kiang-Su, Kiang-Si, and Anhui.

The Viceroy said that he, in conjunction with his colleague, Viceroy Chan of the provinces of Hu-Nan and Hu-Peh, were fully competent to maintain order and insure protection to all foreigners within their jurisdiction. He also asked that no foreign forces be landed within the provinces.

Mr. Wu said he would reply to Viceroy Liu and repeat Secretary Hay's assurances that no foreign troops, or, more specifically, no United States forces, would invade his territory so long as peace and order are preserved therein. The appearance of alien forces in these provinces, said Minister Wu, far from having a subduing effect on any disorder that might be brewing under cover, would only bring the flame, if the spark were there.

The Minister was very much incensed at a suggestion published this morning that he be held as hostage by this Government for the safety of Minister Conger and the legation at Peking. He characterized the writer as a narrow-minded pedant, and a person wholly incompetent to speak upon international affairs. "If a state of war existed in China," the Minister said, "I should ask for my passports, or they would be handed to me. That is the only course that would be followed if such were the case."

The Minister reiterated his former statements scouting the suggestion of a state of war between China and the United States.

"Was your Government at Washington responsible," he queried, "for the Italian lynchings at Tallulah? No. Neither is the Chinese Government responsible for the depredations of lawless natives over whose movements it has no control. Does not the action of the Empress Dowager in degrading the commandant of the Taku forts for firing upon the foreign fleet prove that the Imperial Government had no part in it?"

The Minister was surprised and sorry to hear of the report that Li Hung Chang had reconsidered his intention and would not go to Peking. He said he had great faith in his (Li Hung Chang's) ability to relieve the situation. He also expressed his belief that Admiral Seymour's column has arrived at Peking and that the legations there are safe.

Mr. Wu has received no news from the north, but as the troubles which the French Consuls have been experiencing have been in the south, the reassurance as to the ability of the Chinese Government to maintain order in that section is gratifying to the officials here.

## NO STATE OF WAR YET.

WASHINGTON, June 21.—The State Department still holds to the view that no state of war exists in China, basing its position on the absence of any authentic information showing that the Chinese Government has directed or been a party to any of the overt acts so far committed against the foreign interests in China. Therefore, it has not only been careful to refrain from any act that might prevent a peaceful and honorable settlement with the Chinese Government of the issues raised by the Boxer trouble, if it shall appear conclusively that that Government was blameless in the matter, but it has also used its moral force with other powers to the same end.

The developments of the day, apart from those at Tien-Tsin, greatly encouraged the officials in their hope that the worst is past in China, and that the difficulty can now be settled without any very serious change of the political status of the country, at least in its relations with the outer world.

The State Department is much gratified with the attitude of the powers. So far as it is informed, there is no difference of opinion or intention among the different powers respecting the situation. Their object is simply to restore peace, protect life and property, and leave all further questions for future settlement. So far as can be gathered there is not a dissenting voice among the powers in regard to the proposition made by the United States to limit the operations of the foreign armies and navies in China to that simple programme. If there is a different intention entertained anywhere the power holding it has not signified that fact.

The prompt and voluntary assurance given by Russia yesterday that her troops were to be limited in their activity strictly to the succor of Russian and other foreign subjects in China may be regarded as a direct outcome of the course adopted by the State Department at the beginning of the trouble.

## REPORT FROM ADMIRAL BRUCE.

LONDON, June 21.—The Admiralty has received the following dispatch from Rear Admiral Bruce:

"Taku, via Che-Foo, June 21.

"No communication from the Commander in Chief in seven days, and from Tien-Tsin in five days.

"The allies hold the Taku forts and Tong-Ku securely, and they will advance to the relief of Tien-Tsin when in sufficient strength. Troops are expected from Hongkong to-morrow, and 300 from Wei-Hai-Wei the following day.

"It is believed that fighting is constantly proceeding around Tien-Tsin. Our garrison there should be about 3,000 men.

"The following proclamation was agreed upon this morning, to be issued forthwith:

"'The Admirals and senior naval officers of the allied powers in China desire to make known to all Viceroys and authorities along the coasts and rivers, and in the cities and provinces of China that they intend to use armed force only against the Boxers and people that oppose them on their march to Peking for the rescue of their fellow-countrymen.'"

The date at which the above dispatch was sent off from Taku is not given, but it was probably June 19.

## SAIL FROM MANILA FOR CHINA.

WASHINGTON, June 21.—A cablegram received at the Navy Department to-day from Admiral Remey at Manila, states that the Zafiro sailed yesterday from Cavite for Hongkong. She is a supply ship, and may proceed to Taku after communicating with Capt. Wilde of the Oregon at Hongkong.

It is said at the Navigation Bureau that the Zafiro has aboard 150 sailors in addition to her crew. These men may go on the Oregon at Hongkong to round out her complement, or be dispatched on the Zafiro directly north to Taku, in the discretion of Admiral Kempff, who will have communicated with Admiral Remey before the Zafiro can get to Hongkong.

Admiral Remey supplemented his brief dispatch relative to the sailing of the Zafiro by one later in the day announcing the departure of the Iris from Manila for Taku.

The Iris is a water boat, but on this trip she carries a quantity of supplies for Admiral Kempff's little squadron, as well as a cargo of good coal, of which a supply is badly needed.

## The Buffalo Sails for Manila.

SOUTHAMPTON, June 21.—The United States training ship Buffalo, formerly the Brazilian dynamite-gun cruiser Nictheroy, sailed at 2 P. M. to-day for Manila.

## Bluejackets Landed at Woo-Sung.

SHANGHAI, June 21.—Bluejackets have been landed at Woo-Sung to protect the telegraph station.

Woo-Sung is a small maritime town at the mouth of the Woo-Sung River, and ten

Continued on Page 2.



# ROOSEVELT GETS BACK FROM THE CONVENTION

## Cheered on His Way to the Union League Club.

## FEW PLANS FOR THE FUTURE

### Refuses to Discuss His Nomination Until Formally Notified of It—His Experiences in Philadelphia.

Gov. Theodore Roosevelt, the Republican nominee for Vice President, arrived in New York a few minutes after 8 o'clock last night, from the National Convention in Philadelphia. The Governor traveled in a special car from Philadelphia and came across the North River from Jersey City to West Twenty-third Street. From the ferry he was driven to the Union League Club, where he spent the night. He said that he would go to his home in Oyster Bay this morning, but he had not decided how long he would remain there. He will leave New York a week from to-day for Oklahoma Territory, where he will be the guest of honor at the annual reunion of his old regiment, the First United States Volunteer Cavalry, better known as the Rough Riders.

Gov. Roosevelt declined to discuss his nomination, and to a reporter for THE NEW YORK TIMES, who saw him just before he boarded the train at Philadelphia, he said:

"I do not care to be quoted at this time. I shall reserve what I may have to say until I am formally notified of my nomination by the committee appointed for that purpose."

"What are your plans for the future?"

"I shall go to New York this evening, and will spend the night at the Union League Club. To-morrow I am going to Oyster Bay. I do not know how long I shall remain there, and I have made no plans further than that. There is one thing that I wish you would say for me, and that is that while I am down in the country I will see nobody unless by appointment. I am going down there for a rest and do not wish to be bothered."

"Then you will not make any statement regarding your nomination?"

"No, Sir. And anything you see that purports to be an interview with me until I am waited upon by the Committee of Notification, put it down as a pure fake."

The Governor arose at an early hour yesterday morning. He had spent the night at a private house, where Mrs. Roosevelt has been a guest during her stay in Philadelphia. After breakfast he went to the Walton, where he found a crowd of reporters awaiting him. While it was known that he had at last consented to accept the Vice Presidential nomination, he refused to say a word on the subject to anybody except the leaders. One persistent correspondent asked:

"If you are nominated to-day, will you accept?"

"On that point I cannot talk," said the Governor, and then he added: "As yet I have made no statement that I would accept."

The Governor was driven to the convention hall in company with Benjamin B. Odell, Jr., Chairman of the Republican State Committee, and Gen. Francis V. Greene, one of his advisers and close personal friends.

HIS RECEPTION AT THE HALL.

When they reached the grounds the Governor was greeted with a cheer by the crowd which surrounded the main entrance, but this reception was trivial compared with the outburst of enthusiasm when the Rough Rider entered the hall and started down the centre aisle to his seat among the delegates from the Empire State. Apparently he desired to avoid recognition, as he had removed his broad-brimmed slouch hat, which had become so well known to the convention crowds. He had not gone a dozen steps when a voice called out:

"Roosevelt! Roosevelt!"

All eyes were turned toward the entrance, and the first genuine cheer of the convention filled the vast auditorium. At first the Governor appeared not to notice the enthusiasm of delegates and spectators alike, but it swelled to such proportions that he bowed to the right and left, which only increased the cheering of the thousands. Delegates left their seats and forced him to shake hands, while they promised him their support. At length, with the help of Mr. Odell, the Governor succeeded in reaching his seat, where he was forced to hold a reception, delegates from all parts of the country crowding around him. Senator Sewall of New Jersey was the first prominent man to reach his side. He said:

"Roosevelt, I knew this would come around. I am one of your happiest friends. Accept my heart's best wishes."

"Senator," was the reply, "I stood out as long as I could. I had to fall into line and here I am."

The Governor smiled as he espied a delegate whom he knew personally and said:

"Hello, John, I know you told me so. Well, the fact is I couldn't help it."

"Hurrah for Roosevelt!" came from a woman in the gallery, and it was taken up with a will by those who were in the big hall.

HANNA GREETS ROOSEVELT.

A few minutes later Chairman Hanna entered the hall and started down the aisle to the familiar strains of "The Star-Spangled Banner." Mr. Hanna made his way to Mr. Roosevelt's side and shook his hand warmly as he whispered something in his ear. Both men smiled and the National Chairman started for his seat on the platform.

After the convention adjourned, the Governor went to the home of a friend for luncheon. An hour later he went to his headquarters in the Walton where he found Sheriff Sherman Bell of Cripple Creek awaiting him.

The Sheriff was a member of the Rough Riders regiment and had called to ascertain if the Governor would attend the annual reunion of the members of that body. Secretary William J. Youngs urged the Governor not to make the long trip to Oklahoma in view of the fact that he would have to participate in a hard campaign. To this the former commander of that famous regiment replied:

"No! no! I must go. I have promised the boys I would be present and they would be disappointed if I failed to keep my promise. I will sacrifice everything to be there, but I trust this will be the last annual reunion, as I do not think I will be able to be on hand next year. I have given up all my engagements, including the reunion of my class at Harvard, but I cannot give up the regiment. Tell the boys I will be there."

"You are still our Colonel," said Sheriff Bell, "and while I know that the boys would be greatly disappointed if you were not on hand, still if you say that you cannot go because of the additional duties imposed upon you by your nomination for Vice President, I know that they will understand it."

"You can telegraph to the boys that I will be present, no matter what happens. I will leave New York on June 29."

The Vice Presidential nominee was then driven to the Pennsylvania station, where a special car was attached to the regular 5:50 express. In the party with the Governor were Chairman Odell and his son, Senator Depew and his son, Attorney General John C. Davies, Gen. Francis V. Greene, Nicholas Murray Butler, Reuben L. Fox, W. Loeb, Jr., and Amos Knapp of the Governor's office staff. The Governor was in good spirits on the way to New York and chatted pleasantly with his companions.

When the train arrived at Jersey City a carriage and two detectives from the Central Office were on hand to meet the nominee. The passengers on the train gathered and gave him a hearty cheer as he made his way to the waiting carriage. When the New York shore was reached a mounted police escort was on hand and accompanied the Governor to the Union League Club house. A crowd had assembled outside the ferryhouse, and as the Governor was recognized a cheer went up, in which the policemen detailed to handle the crowd joined.

Before leaving Philadelphia the Governor received the following telegram from the President:

Executive Mansion,
Washington, D. C., June 21.

Your nomination is a high, deserved honor. I extend my heartiest congratulations. WILLIAM McKINLEY.

The first letter of congratulation received by the nominee was handed to him twenty minutes after he had left the convention hall. It was from Secretary Youngs and the assistants in the Executive Chamber at Albany. It read:

"Theodore Roosevelt, Governor of New York:

"Sir: We who have been most close to you personally and officially from the beginning of your administration as Governor, and who know better than anybody else the patience and fortitude with which you have endured the many impediments which have surrounded you in the efficient and virtuous administration of your office, and who also know the human sympathy which you have evinced to all those under you, wish to be the first to tender you our congratulations upon your nomination to the Vice Presidency. We know that this nomination was neither sought nor desired by you. We know from expressions of opinion given to us from every county in the State of New York that the hope of the people of the State was that they could retain your services for two years more. We know that to the young men of the State and to all in the State who have sought unselfishly to improve conditions, you were an inspiration, and your work in the executive department has been an earnest of the greater work which it had been hoped you would be able to achieve. Speaking as we know we do for every man in the Executive Department at Albany, our departments are tempered with sincere and unalloyed regret. In whatever position you may hereafter occupy, whether in private or public station, it is unnecessary to assure you that you will carry with you not only the respect and admiration, but to a still higher degree the love of your subordinates."

Mrs. Roosevelt did not return to New York. She remained in Philadelphia to visit some friends with Secretary and Mrs. Youngs.



## CAUSE OF HANNA'S DEFEAT.

### He Realized at Last that Gov. Roosevelt's Nomination Was Inevitable.

*Special to The New York Times.*

PHILADELPHIA, June 21.—Everybody in the Republican Convention knew to-day, while Gov. Roosevelt was making his speech to second the nomination of McKinley, why Hanna had decided not to defer capitulation to the friends of Roosevelt until after McKinley had been presented.

When the Governor stood rigidly before the applauding convention, calmly awaiting a cessation of the torrent of applause from the delegates and the tiers of spectators, the explanation of Hanna's course in choosing surrender rather than rout flashed through thousands of minds. Hitherto Roosevelt had been heard only by the delegates who could see him in his room, where he had persistently appealed to his friends not to take him from the State of New York. His protests had been helped, as far as Hanna could sustain them, by the exertion of party organization in behalf of Long, in whom there was almost no interest, and Dolliver, in whom there would have been greater interest if he had not become, without fault on his part, a tool for Hanna to accomplish the defeat of Roosevelt.

The vast convention audience saw plainly, after Roosevelt had begun his speech—the most aggressive, intense, and characteristic speech of the convention—what would have happened if at dawn on Wednesday morning Hanna had not decided to quit fighting and find a way to get out of the contest with his baggage intact. Washington may not have seen the inevitable earlier than Hanna, but Washington admitted it more promptly.

SENTIMENT OF DELEGATES.

If the President waited until Wednesday to telephone Hanna to let the delegates have their way, he waited a day longer than was necessary. A canvass of the delegates would have advised Mr. Hanna of the futility of his objection to Roosevelt's nomination. With the delegates it was largely sentiment, effective, absolute faith in the honesty, energy, and right-mindedness of Roosevelt, that kept his friends quiet in spite of suggestions about his erratic, dramatic, and combative propensities. For the weaknesses of the Governor have been as freely discussed here as his strength, his own State delegates contributing in large measure to the general store of knowledge about his restlessness, his impatience of machine restraints, his reluctance to compromise with scheming and selfish politicians, and the apprehensiveness with which his every official act has been watched.

When Mr. Hanna's advice was asked, as he says it was, during the twelve hours preceding the publication of his statement, he could properly have spoken of the situation as one in which he was permitted to say whether he would fight to a calamitous defeat or choose to jump upon the band wagon and become a part of the triumphal procession. His consultation with delegates showed him that upward of 600 of them were determined to vote for Roosevelt if they had a chance. He kept them off longer than they were willing to be reported as favoring other candidates. His decision to release them was not a dictation of terms of surrender; it was unconditional acceptance of the inevitable.

## QUAY MEN CLAIM VICTORY.

*Special to The New York Times.*

PHILADELPHIA, June 21.—Almost before the convention was over the admirers of Senator Quay began to boast of the victory they had won over Mr. Hanna. The Quay papers, disregarding the talk of yesterday that all reference to a Quay-Platt fight on Hanna was to be dropped and never again alluded to, are now renewing the boast, and even go into particulars to prove their assertions.

According to the Quay men the success of the Roosevelt cause was assured when Pennsylvania declared, by a vote of its delegation, to vote for Roosevelt. This determination, made at an early stage, was followed by the active mustering of Roosevelt forces in many of the States by Senator Platt, Senator Wolcott, and H. C. Payne. To those who kept in touch with all the delegations the boast that Quay led them to support Roosevelt does not appear to be justified.

It is certain that on Tuesday night, when the Roosevelt boom was threatened with interference from Washington, Kansas strengthened the Roosevelt line by demanding that he accept and promising to present and vote for him. But the Quay men claim the credit for giving Roosevelt's boom a start, and also for scoring Hanna at the last moment yesterday by offering a rule to establish convention representation on a basis of votes cast in each State.

Quay discovered that he could muster votes enough to pass his resolution if he chose to press it. To permit a fight would have alligned the Southern delegates against the Administration, and perhaps make possible the nomination of Roosevelt for President. Mr. Hanna was already convinced that he must permit the nomination of Roosevelt, and he very quickly became a helper to the Roosevelt men when he was promised that Quay's resolution should be withdrawn.

Col. Quay, before the convention met, in speaking of his intention to withdraw his resolution regarding representation on the National Committee, said it had served its purpose; that last night the Southern delegates flocked to Roosevelt, and made the nomination of the New York Governor a sure thing.



# M'KINLEY AND ROOSEVELT

## Ticket Nominated by the Republican Convention.

## TUMULT OVER THE GOVERNOR

### Great Enthusiasm in the Republican Convention.

### The President's Renomination Unanimous—Gov. Roosevelt Received Full Vote of the Convention, Minus His Own.

*Special to The New York Times.*

PHILADELPHIA, June 21.—The twelfth Republican National Convention to-day completed its work by the nomination of William McKinley for President and Theodore Roosevelt for Vice President.

President McKinley's nomination was made with enthusiasm, the customary tumult of shouts, the frantic fluttering of banners, hats, handkerchiefs, plumes, and flags.

The demonstrations were not as prolonged, however, as they have been in conventions where nomination has been preceded by conflict.

Gov. Roosevelt was the idol of the convention, but the idolatry was not frenzied. His speech was a model of directness and conciseness, his bearing was soldierly, dignified, and satisfactory to his most anxious friend.

The tumult over him was manifestly spontaneous, universal, and sincere. It was not overdone. His conduct plainly strengthened him in the estimation of the convention.

The work of the convention was closed up in a session less than five hours long. This was made possible by the abandonment by Senator Quay of his amendment to the rules proposing to fix future representation.

McKinley and Roosevelt were nominated upon a call of the roll, as provided by the rules. McKinley received every vote in the convention. Roosevelt received 929, one delegate not voting. The delegate who did not vote was Theodore Roosevelt.

The temper of the convention was admirable. Its balance was maintained, although the hall was overcrowded, and many incapable speakers tried the forbearance of the vast, sweltering audience as well as the nerves of Senator Lodge, the presiding officer.

All the States except New York are cordially glad of the nomination of Roosevelt with McKinley. The West is sure that Roosevelt will help the party. A few Republicans are anxious about the State of New York, but they are not many.

Senator Hanna accepted the outcome not only with cheerfulness, but with enthusiasm. He waved a triple plume to spur on the cheers, and afterward consented to be re-elected Chairman of the National Committee.

## WIND-UP OF THE CONVENTION.

### Delegates Give Vent to Their Pent-Up Enthusiasm—No Hitch in the Proceedings.

*Special to The New York Times.*

PHILADELPHIA, June 21.—Fully 20,000 persons gathered in a convention hall which had but 16,000 seats, but which, all things considered, is the finest convention hall in this country, took part to-day in the proceedings of the Republican National Convention. As a spectacle the convention was one of the greatest witnessed in the country. The great mass of people, and the great majority of the delegates held in suspense here for three days while the party leaders selected their candidates for President and Vice President, and prepared the platform upon which they were to run, were longing for an opportunity to give vent to the pent-up enthusiasm. When the opportunity came, as it did at to-day's session of the convention, it was made the most of.

The result was that the convention, which until to-day was positively stupid, closed in a blaze of glory, a mighty uproar of delight, and the delegates have scattered to the States and Territories from which they came with hearts filled with confidence for the coming campaign. Great, however, as was the enthusiasm in the convention to-day, there was lacking in the uproar that electric force and spontaneity that make the cheering of a great multitude of people so impressive. There was no note of triumph in it all. There could not be in a convention such as this has been, where the candidates were practically decided upon before the body met, and where "the Administration" was the controlling force. Viewed merely as a monster ratification meeting, however, the session of the convention to-day was a magnificent success.

AUDIENCE PREPARED TO SHOUT.

The day was warm, very warm, but Convention Hall is so splendidly lighted and ventilated that those who thronged it were able to make themselves comfortable. They came prepared to shout and approve. There was scarcely a man, woman, or child there who did not carry a flag, a bunch of pampas plumes, or something to be waved overhead when occasion required, so that the scene could suddenly be transformed from an eager listening multitude into a sea of waving red, white, and blue.

The impatience of the convention to finish up the business which has been dragging along so monotonously for two days past was shown by the fact that while the hour set for the session was 10 A. M., the delegates were all in their seats five minutes ahead of time and the spectators were impatient for the fall of the gavel. This in spite of the fact that for a half hour previous the people had been "letting off steam" by singing the airs which the band played and howling with delight whenever a popular leader entered.

Gov. Roosevelt got a splendid reception and a leather-lunged man from Arizona threw the convention into a spasm of mirth by shouting "Teddy, you're it." Senator Hanna was bustling around the stage with Senator Henry Cabot Lodge and others who were to be chief actors in the great drama that was soon to be enacted. Ex-Senator Quay received an ovation almost as great as that accorded to Gov. Roosevelt. In fact, all through the convention his Pennsylvania friends have kept his name to the front.

Ex-Gov. Taylor of Kentucky has been another popular idol of the convention, and there has been an evident effort to put him forward as a martyr.

Senator Depew has not been very conspicuous until to-day, but this afternoon, the people insisted on a speech from him and honored him as he has seldom been honored before.

NO HITCH IN THE PROGRAMME.

The proceedings moved with perfect precision. If there was a man in that convention whose ideas were at all at variance with the programme laid down by the party leaders he swallowed his grievances and joined in the harmonious chorus. Lieut. Gov. Tim Woodruff sat among the spectators and cheered the nomination of Gov. Roosevelt as heartily as though he had never wanted the nomination himself, and so did Congressman Dolliver and all others whose names had been mentioned for the honor.

Mr. Quay was recognized by Chairman Lodge and promptly proceeded to join the harmony chorus by withdrawing the motion he made before the convention adjourned last night for a change in the rules, a motion which threatened to precipitate a contest. Thereupon Mr. Lodge announced that nominations for President were in order. The Chairman of the Alabama delegation gave way so that Senator Foraker might take the stage and place William McKinley's name before the convention.

Mr. Foraker is an orator of fine presence and much force, but his speech was necessarily a disappointment. It was the speech of Temporary Chairman Wolcott and Permanent Chairman Lodge over again. The throng who listened to him quickly tired. Foraker saw it, realized that his effort was a failure, and from that time on there was little in his manner or his speech to arouse enthusiasm.

CHEERS FOR THE PRESIDENT.

Cutting short his speech, he unexpectedly sprang the name of William McKinley upon the convention. For a few seconds over ten minutes then there was the wildest tumult. Every person in that great hall seemed to be making as much noise as possible and waving everything available. At the very height of tumult Mark Hanna jumped upon a table with a bunch of pampas grass in his hand and began to shout at the top of his voice as he waved the red, white, and blue flag over his head. Twenty thousand voices shouted and screamed at top pitch. When the people tired of cheering they joined with the band and sang "America." When that was over they cheered again.

It was a peculiar fact, though, that not once during that ten minutes of pandemonium, and, in fact, not once during the entire convention, did any individual call directly for "Three cheers for William McKinley." Many times there were individual calls for cheers for Roosevelt and for other convention and party favorites, in which the convention heartily joined, but not once were cheers for the President brought out in this way.

GOV. ROOSEVELT'S RECEPTION.

Chairman Lodge finally managed to shout to Gov. Roosevelt to take the stage and second the nomination of William McKinley. His appearance started the uproar again, and for another ten minutes all was shouting, screaming, and banner waving. Gov. Roosevelt's strong personality seemed to inspire the people. He stood with jaws set, eyes glistening, and shoulders squared as though facing a hostile host, instead of an army of worshippers. He beckoned for silence, but it did no good.

There came a lull and Roosevelt took quick advantage of it. With a bound forward he launched his speech. He carried the crowd before him as no other speaker had. He scored a triumph, and when he went back to his seat all realized that the convention had acted wisely in compelling Roosevelt to take the standard of the party through a campaign in which just such resistless energy as he possesses is needed.

Senator Thurston of Nebraska followed with a speech that was brief, commonplace and vociferous. He was followed by Yerkes of Kentucky, George W. Knight of California, and Gov. Mount of Indiana. The crowd listened patiently to all of them except the Governor of Indiana; his voice was so feeble that the convention guyed him and there was a laugh all around when an irreverant Republican back among the spectators shouted: "They've made a Mount out of a molehill."

THE NOMINATIONS.

The tedious process of balloting began, and of course every vote in the convention was cast for McKinley. There was an outbreak when Hawaii cast two votes, the first votes of that new possession in a National convention. When it was all over there was another general hurrah.

Chairman Lodge called for a nomination for Vice President. Again Alabama, the first State on the list, yielded to Iowa, the State from which Congressman Dolliver hails. Col. Young, a rough rider himself, made the nominating speech. Col. Roosevelt stood in his place on the floor and seemed to enjoy the scene immensely. Delegates from all over the hall flocked toward him, shook his hand, slapped him on the back, and told him that all talk of other men than himself for the nomination had been absurd. The Chairmen of the State delegations again began to parade around the hall with their standards, but this time Mr. Hanna did not get up on a table and wave his bunch of pampas plumes. The uproar, however, was quite equal to that which followed the nomination of McKinley.

Michael J. Murray of Massachusetts, and James Ashton of Washington made speeches that were brief, and when they had finished, Chairman Lodge called for other nominations, but the crowd yelled "No, no," and then they yelled for Chauncey M. Depew. They insisted on hearing from the New York Senator, and Mr. Depew, who was as pleased as a man could be at the honor, went to the platform and made a speech that delighted his hearers.

The roll call began again, and Theodore Roosevelt received 929 of the 930 votes of the convention, he refraining from voting. While he was shaking hands with all who could get near him, and while the crowd was cheering as it poured out of the building, a few formal resolutions expressing thanks to the people of Philadelphia and the National Committee were passed, and the convention adjourned.

[A detailed report of the proceedings of the convention will be found on Page 3.]

## CASE OF TOO MUCH SENATOR.

### Practically All the Business of the Convention Was Monopolized by Them.

*Special to The New York Times.*

PHILADELPHIA, June 21.—Every Senator of the United States who has figured conspicuously in the convention is aware of the fact that the convention has resented the extent to which the business of the convention has been monopolized by the Senate.

A Senator, Mr. Hanna, called the convention to order. A Senator was made temporary Chairman. A Senator presided over the Committee on Permanent Organization and reported a permanent Chairman who was a Senator. A Senator guided as Chairman the deliberations of the Committee on Resolutions and reported the platform. Senators were recognized to make all the motions offered until to-day, excepting a few trivial motions of order. It was a convention in which the honors were accumulated by the Senate up to the moment that Roosevelt was to be nominated.

RESPONSIBLE FOR THE PLATFORM.

To the fact that Senators had so much to do with the running of the convention is attributed the fact that the proceedings lacked interest, and that the platform was a disappointment. The members of the

"All the News That's Fit to Print."

# The New York Times.

THE WEATHER.
Partly cloudy; southwesterly winds.



VOL. XLIX...NO. 15,754. NEW YORK, FRIDAY, JULY 6, 1900.-FOURTEEN PAGES. ONE CENT In Greater New York and Jersey City. Elsewhere, TWO CENTS.

## THE NEWS CONDENSED.

Stocks strong.

Cash wheat, No. 2 red, 87½c; corn, No. 2 mixed, 49⅝c; oats, No. 2, 28½c; cotton, middling, 10c; butter, Western creamery, 19½c; iron, No. 1 foundry, $18.

FOREIGN.—Much alarm is now felt for the 12,000 allied troops in Tien-Tsin. A dispatch to Berlin says their retreat has been cut off, and that they are surrounded. Emperor Kwang-Su is said to have been poisoned by Prince Tuan. The Dowager Empress also took poison by order, but is still living. Details of the massacre of foreigners in Peking leave little room for doubts of the truth of the reports. There are many indications that the outbreak is spreading to the South. The Chinese commanders are preparing for a long and arduous campaign. The Oregon is now on her way to Japan. She is said to be in no danger. President Krüger, through Secretary Reitz, has again stated to a correspondent that the war will be continued until there are no more than 500 burghers left in the Transvaal. Sipido, who tried to assassinate the Prince of Wales, was found guilty of attempted murder in Brussels yesterday. His punishment was set down as incarceration in a reformatory until he becomes of age. The three men who instigated the crime were acquitted, because the Court said they evidently thought the attempt was a joke. In the French Senate yesterday the Premier obtained a vote of confidence in the Ministry.—Pages 1 and 6.

**Page 5.**

Gen. Francis V. Greene was last night elected President of the Republican County Committee, in place of Lemuel E. Quigg, who resigned, and made a speech on the campaign.

**Page 6.**

The Saengerfest in Brooklyn came to a close yesterday. A charge was made that considerable of the money received had mysteriously disappeared.

**Page 11.**

Representatives of the iron and steel industry, in conference here yesterday, considered a proposed readjustment of prices. The stocks were strong.

**Page 14.**

Eighty-two victims of Saturday's fire on the North German Lloyd piers in Hoboken were buried yesterday. Three more bodies were found yesterday, making a total of 128 recovered.

Arrivals at Hotels and Out-of-Town Buyers.—Page 3.
Business Troubles.—Page 9.
Court Calendars.—Page 9.
Insurance Notes.—Page 11.
Legal Notes.—Page 14.
Marine Intelligence and Foreign Mails.—Page 5.
Markets.—Page 12.
Real Estate.—Page 12.
Society.—Page 7.
United Service.—Page 14.
Weather Report.—Page 3.
Yesterday's Fires.—Page 5.

## SIPIDO FOUND GUILTY.

### Tried to Kill the Prince of Wales, and is Sent to a Reformatory—Instigators Thought It a Joke.

BRUSSELS, July 5.—The Assize Court to-day returned a verdict of guilty of attempt to kill the Prince of Wales against Jean Baptiste Sipido, who fired at the Prince on April 4 as the train bearing his Royal Highness was leaving the Northern Station in this city for Copenhagen.

The Court considered that Sipido acted without discernment, and sentenced him to a reformatory until he shall have attained his majority.

Meert, Penchot, and Meire, the instigators of the attack upon the Prince, were acquitted on the ground that they considered the plot a joke.

LONDON, July 6.—The morning papers generally publish editorials commenting upon the verdict in the case of Sipido, the would-be assassin of the Prince of Wales. The Daily Telegraph says the result of the trial is "monstrous." The Daily Chronicle declares that it is "an outrage on humanity," and The Daily Mail characterizes it as "a reproach on Belgium."

## KRUEGER STILL AGGRESSIVE.

### Declares that Fight Will Go On as Long as 500 Burghers Survive—British Reports Vague.

LONDON, July 6.—The cordon around Gen. De Wet appears still to be wide; at least, he has not yet been cornered. Dispatches from the front, except official ones, deal with trifles or vague probabilities.

The Daily Telegraph's Lorenzo Marques correspondent attempted on July 4 to interview President Krüger at Watervalonder. Herr Krüger was there, but he deputed State Secretary Reitz to talk. The Secretary said:

"We do not need to discuss peace. President Krüger wishes, through me, to repeat what he has said over and over again. The South African Republic will fight for independence as long as 500 burghers remain alive, and even then will continue to fight. Such is our decision."

Lord Roberts reports from Pretoria, under date of July 5, that Lieut. Rundle of the Carbineers and a patrol were captured by the Boers near Pretoria July 4.

## THE RESULT OF MIXED SEEDS.

*Special to The New York Times.*

CINCINNATI, July 5.—Superintendent of Parks Critchell has been somewhat mystified by the presence, in large quantities, in the most prominent flower beds of Eden Park, of an apparently new species of flora. Upon a close inspection on Wednesday, when the flowers had matured to some extent, the mystery was explained. In planting the beds, under ex-Superintendent Warder's administration, other seeds were carelessly mixed in, and, as a result, onions, peppers, cabbages, and tobacco plants are scattered among the flowers.

Nearly every bunch of pinks and roses has as its neighbor a large cabbage or tobacco plant, and the sight is anything but beautiful. Under orders from Superintendent Critchell to-day workmen went all through the park beds and removed the alien plants and vegetables.

## THE GREAT DANE AND THE OTTER.

*Special to The New York Times.*

CINCINNATI, July 5.—The sale to a New York visitor at the Zoological Gardens of a Great Dane dog nearly precipitated a fierce fight at that place to-day. In the cage with the dog was a small fish otter, which had grown very fond of its giant companion. When the dog was taken from the cage the little animal set up a mournful cry and began dashing itself against the bars of the cage.

This excited the dog, and he was preparing to jump at his new master, when the Superintendent of the garden suggested that the sale be declared off. To this the visitor agreed, and the two animals are again sharing their big outdoor cage.

## TRAVERS FAMILY IN RUNAWAY.

OYSTER BAY, L. I., July 5.—Four members of the Travers family, which has a country seat here, had a narrow escape from being seriously injured while driving on Main Street to-night.

Kittie, May, Gertrude, and Mrs. Vincent Paul Travers left the homestead shortly after 7 o'clock this evening for a drive through the village. In Main Street their horse shied at F. H. Benedict's double motor vehicle, which was standing in the roadway, and run away. After running for a block the front wheels of the carriage struck the curb, upsetting the vehicle and throwing the occupants to the ground. None received serious injuries, although they were pretty well shaken up.

F. H. Benedict, who was out riding in his single motor vehicle, happening to come along, had the Travers family removed to their home in both his vehicles. Dr. Hall of Oyster Bay was summoned and attended the Travers family.



# ALLIED TROOPS AT TIEN-TSIN CUT OFF

## 12,000 Men There Surrounded by 100,000 Chinese.

## EMPEROR REPORTED DEAD

### Tuan Gave Poison to Him and the Dowager Empress.

## THE MASSACRE AT PEKING

### Detailed Accounts Leave Hardly Any Room for Doubt that All Foreigners Are Dead—Rising Spreads to South.

Great alarm is now felt for the allied forces in Tien-Tsin. A dispatch to Berlin says their retreat to Taku has been cut off and that they are surrounded, the Chinese artillery dominating the foreign concessions.

There are 12,000 foreign troops at Tien-Tsin. The Chinese operating against them now probably number at least 100,000.

It is reported, from supposedly reliable sources, that Prince Tuan offered to Emperor Kwang-Su and the Dowager Empress Tsze-Hsi An the alternative of death by poison or the sword. Both are said to have chosen the former.

The Emperor is declared to have died within an hour. The Empress is said to be still alive, though according to one account she is insane.

If the reports that a new Government has been formed in Peking are true, the attitude of the powers that no state of war exists will no longer be tenable.

Details of the massacre of all foreigners in Peking leave hardly any room for doubt that the reports printed yesterday are true. One Shanghai correspondent says all that can be hoped is that the men of the legations had time to kill the women and children before the Chinese entered the British Legation.

There are many indications that the outbreak is about to spread to the South. Consul General Goodnow wired to the State Department yesterday that this would be the case unless the international forces were increased.

Bishop Anzer, one of the greatest European authorities on Chinese affairs, says if the rebellion spreads throughout China, the powers will be unable to quell it.

The Chinese commanders are preparing for a long and arduous campaign. They are putting into operation plans prepared by German officers last year, when an invasion by Russia was feared.

## EMPEROR KWANG-SU DEAD?

Copyright, 1900, The Associated Press.

SHANGHAI, July 5.—Emperor Kwang-Su committed suicide by taking opium under compulsion of Prince Tuan on June 19.

The Empress Dowager, Tsze-Hsi An, also took poison, but is still alive, though reported to be insane from the effects of the drug.

The foregoing has been officially reported to the German Consular staff.

LONDON, July 6.—Two Manchus who have arrived at Shanghai certify to the truth of the statement that Prince Tuan visited the palace and offered the Emperor and the Dowager Empress the alternative of poison or the sword.

The Emperor, they say, took poison, and died within an hour.

The Dowager Empress also chose poison, but craftily swallowed only a portion of what was offered to her, and survived.

On the same day the Chinese Customs Bureau was destroyed, Sir Robert Hart, the Inspector of Customs, and his staff escaping to the British Legation.

Kwang-Su, Emperor of China, was born in 1871, and was the son of Prince Chung, seventh brother of the Emperor Hien-Feng. He succeeded to the throne by proclamation at the death of Emperor Tung-Che, in 1875. He was the ninth Emperor of China of the Manchu dynasty of Tsing, which overthrew the native dynasty of Ming in 1644.

There exists in China no law of hereditary succession to the throne, it being left to each sovereign to appoint his successor from among the members of his family of a younger generation. In cases where the Emperor has failed to nominate a successor, the omission is remedied by the family, who, in solemn conclave, proceed to choose a successor likely to uphold the traditions of the dynasty.

Kwang-Su achieved his greatness by this means. He did not possess the slightest claim to ascend the throne. The position within the "purple forbidden city" was, however, something peculiar in the early sixties. The Emperor Tung-Che had succeeded Hien-Tung, the last of the great Chinese rulers, and as the former was but five years old at the time of his succession, it became necessary to appoint a regency.

The management of affairs was accordingly placed in the hands of two women, the Dowager Empress Tsi-Thsi, widow of Hien-Lung, and the Empress by courtesy, Tsze-Hsi An, who had been favorite concubine of that monarch and who is now known to all the world as the Dowager Empress.

All went well for a while, but after fourteen years, on Tung-Che coming of age, he evinced a decided desire to manage his own affairs without assistance from his guardians, and even chose a wife on his own initiative. Such revolutionary procedure could not be tolerated, and accordingly Tung-Che was quietly disposed of, bulletins as to the state of his health being regularly issued by his relatives for many weeks after he had been put out of the way.

All danger to the State being thus averted, the Dowager Empress Tsze-Hsi An, who had taken things into her own hands, proceeded to select a new Emperor. The evident heir to succeed Tung-Che was Uin, the grandson of Prince Kung. But the heir presumptive was passed over and the Empress chose Tsai-Tien, who was named Kwang-Su, signifying "illustrious succession." He entered upon his nominal reign on Feb. 4, 1875.

The Emperor, always a weakling, remained a mere puppet in the hands of his advisers until 1898, when his attention happened to be directed to the emissaries of the reform party. Chang-Yin-Han and Kang-Yu-Wei, pronounced supporters of Western ideas, obtained considerable influence over him, and various edicts were promulgated, startling to the Chinese, but seeming hopefully progressive to the outside world.

Tsze-Hsi An refused to allow such an upsetting of traditions, and accordingly a proclamation was suddenly issued in the name of the Emperor, in which he resigned the Government into the hands of the Empress Dowager. Since then he has been several times reported as having been killed or having committed suicide.

## THE TRAGEDY AT PEKING.

LONDON, July 6.—The correspondent of The Daily Express at Shanghai has gathered together from Chinese sources details of the massacre of the foreigners at the British Legation in Peking.

When the foreigners' ammunition was exhausted the Boxers and imperial troops rushed the legation and poured into the courtyard with fanatical fury. The foreign troops were so hopelessly outnumbered that their fate was certain. The moment the mob broke into it, the courtyard was converted into a shambles. Others of the invaders spread into the interior of the building. The correspondent adds:

"It is only left to hope that in the final rush of the murderous hordes the men of the legations had time to slay with their own hands their womenkind and children. The Chinese are whispering the terrible story under their breath. Their attitude toward foreigners in the streets has undergone a strange change. The demeanor of the better class of Chinese is one of pity rather than of triumph. Even the rabble in the native quarter are silent.

"Something of this culminating tragedy in the ghastly history of recent events in Peking seems to pervade the very atmosphere here, and to compel belief against all our hopes. The Consuls fear that the report is too true, and the Chinese officials do not attempt to seek reasons for a denial."

The story that all the foreigners in Peking were murdered on June 30 or July 1 appears to be circulating simultaneously at Che-Foo, Shanghai, and Tien-Tsin.

The correspondent of The Daily Mail at Shanghai, telegraphing under date of July 5, says he believes that when official information comes regarding Peking it may include news of the outraging of foreign women and the torture of children.

It may almost be taken for granted, the correspondent asserts, that all the foreigners in Peking have been wiped out. These are the whisperings of startling rumors in the native quarters, and it must not be forgotten that the telegraph lines over which alone the news can come are solely in the hands of the Chinese. The native rumors are likely to have their source in a solid basis, and the native officials are believed to be preparing the way for the reception of news of the greatest crime of the century.

Taoti Yu admitted to the correspondent that the case of the Europeans in Peking was utterly hopeless in his opinion. He believed that if they had not yet been massacred it was only a matter of hours before they would be.

The Shanghai correspondent of The Daily Telegraph wires, under date of July 4:

"Yuan-Shi-Kai telegraphs the French Consul here that Prince Tuan is preparing an edict ordering the extermination of all foreigners. This is probably intended to prepare the public for the worst news.

"Chinese cumulative reports, which are generally believed here, declare that all the foreigners in Peking have been massacred.

A dispatch received yesterday by a news agency of this city from Shanghai, under date of July 4, announced that the British Legation at Peking, with 1,600 refugees, was still safe when the message was sent.

The dispatch, however, does not give the Peking date. It adds:

"With the last reinforcements the force investing the Legation numbers 80,000 men. But for the opportune arrival of the Japanese troops the place would have been captured long since. The heavy fighting resulted in filling the Legation with wounded."

In the House of Commons yesterday the Right Hon. W. S. John Brodrick, Parliamentary Secretary for the Foreign Office, said the Chinese Minister in London had been informed that the authorities at Peking would be held personally guilty of any injuries sustained by the Europeans, and he had been requested to convey this information in such a way as to have it reach without fail the authorities at Peking.

The purport of this message, said Mr. Brodrick, would be communicated to the various Viceroys.

The Government, he also said, had no confirmation of the reported massacres at Peking.

PARIS, July 5.—The French Consul at Che-Foo telegraphs that a Chinaman who left Peking on June 25 reports that all the Ministers and residents were then assembled at the British Legation, the French, German, and Japanese Legations were guarded by their own detachments, and M. Pichon, the French Minister, and his wife were well.

The other legations, the Custom House, and the missions, had been burned. The foreign troops had lost six men killed and had six men wounded, including the commander of the British detachment.

SHANGHAI, July 5.—A messenger with official advices who left Peking on June 27 says that over 100,000 Chinese soldiers and rioters surrounded the legations, but, in spite of the fierce attacks, they had not then succeeded in breaking through the walls.

The messenger also said that all persons connected with the Palace were pro-Boxer, even the Princes and Dukes worshipping the god of the Boxers.

The gates of the inner city, it was added, were open for half a day.

BERLIN, July 5.—The German Consul at Tien-Tsin, reporting the contents of the letters of Sir Robert Hart and a French lady, dated Peking, June 24, already known, adds:

"Owing to the destruction of the railroad, the beginning of the rainy season, and the necessity of protecting Tien-Tsin, the commanders of the international forces are unable to send troops to Peking.

"The Chinese have pierced the Grand Canal and flooded the country in order to prevent the advance of the international forces toward Peking.

"Messengers from Peking say that after the German marines burned the Tsung-li-Yamen they occupied the city gate in front of the Palace with four guns, two of which were captured from the Chinese. All the other gates are held by the Chinese.

"Prince Ching's troops are said to be fighting against the Boxers."

## THE FOREIGNERS IN PEKING.

Following is a list of the members of legations in Peking at the beginning of the present year.

UNITED STATES.—Envoy Extraordinary and Minister Plenipotentiary—Edwin H. Conger.
Secretary of Legation—H. G. Squiers.
Second Secretary—W. E. Bainbridge.
Interpreter—F. D. Cheshire.
Naval Attaché—Lieut. Albert L. Key, (now in Tokio, Japan.)

GREAT BRITAIN.—Envoy Extraordinary and Minister Plenipotentiary—Sir Claude Maxwell MacDonald, K. C. B., K. C. M. G.
Second Secretary of Legation—H. G. N. Dering.
Acting Chinese Secretary—H. E. Fulford.
Assistant Chinese Secretary—W. P. Ker.
Honorary Attaché—C. C. Bingham.
Accountant—B. G. Tours.
Assistants—B. Twyman, S. Barton, and D. Oliphant.
Officiating Chaplain—The Right Rev. C. P. Scott, Bishop of North China.
A physician.
Student Interpreters—W. P. Thomas, R. F. Tebbitt, J. T. Pratt, L. G. Graham, G. W. Pearson, W. P. Russell, H. Phillips, C. C. Kirke, A. J. Flaherty, W. M. Hewlett, H. H. Bristow, H. Porter, C. A. Rose, G. P. Peachey, J. G. Hancock, R. D. Drury, L. H. R. Barr, H. Warren, L. Giles, and M. E. Townsend.
Sergeant of Escort—M. H. Bourne.

FRANCE.—Envoy Extraordinary and Minister Plenipotentiary—H. Pichon.
First Secretary of Legation—M. d'Anthouard.
First Interpreter—H. Leduc.
Second Interpreter—M. Morisse.
Military Attaché—Commandant Vidal.
Physician—Dr. Dètheve.
Chancellor—M. Berteaux.

GERMANY.—Envoy Extraordinary and Minister Plenipotentiary—Baron von Ketteler, (killed June 18.)
Secretary of Legation—Dr. von Prittwitz und Gaffron.
Second Secretary of Legation—Dr. von Bergen.
Physician—Dr. Velde.
Secretary and Interpreter—Baron von der Goltz.
Second Interpreter—H. Cordes.
Chancellor—O. Fenselau.

RUSSIA.—Envoy Extraordinary and Minister Plenipotentiary—Michael de Giers.
First Secretary—B. Kroupensky.
Second Secretary—B. Evréinow.
First Interpreter and Consul—P. Popow.
Second Interpreter—N. Kolessow.
Military Agent—Col. Dessinow.
Physician—Dr. Korsakow.

AUSTRIA-HUNGARY.—Envoy Extraordinary and Minister Plenipotentiary—Baron Czikann von Wahlborn.
Secretary of Legation—Dr. A. von Rosthorn.
Vice Consul—R. Natiesta.

ITALY.—Resident Minister—Marquis Salvago Raggi.
Attachés—Livio Caetani and Baron Vitale di Pontaggio.

JAPAN.—Envoy Extraordinary and Minister Plenipotentiary—Baron Nishii.
First Secretary of Legation—Mr. Kikoujiro.
Second Secretary of Legation—Nakashima Takeshi.
Third Secretary of Legation—Marumo Naotosi.
Military Attaché—Major Aoki Nobousumi.
Naval Attaché—Capt. Takikawa Tomokasu.
Physician—Dr. Nakagawa.
Interpreters—Tei Nagakuni and Fokoumarou Sakouzo.
Chancellor—Sugiyama Akira, (killed at beginning of outbreak.)

SPAIN.—Envoy Extraordinary and Minister Plenipotentiary—B. J. de Cologan.
First Secretary of Legation—F. Soliveres.

BELGIUM.—Resident Minister—Baron de Vinck de deux Orp.
First Secretary of Legation—E. de Cartier de Marchienne.
Attaché—M. de Melotte.
Student-Interpreter—A. Splingaerd.

HOLLAND.—Resident Minister and Consul General—F. M. Knobel.
Secretary and Interpreter—W. J. Van Duysberg.

PORTUGAL.—Envoy Extraordinary and Minister Plenipotentiary—F. H. Galhardo.
Secretary of Legation—M. P. M. Baudeira de Lima.
Interpreter—C. A. R. de Paes Assumpçao.

There were a number of student interpreters attached to various legations.

The diplomatic representative of Denmark was the Russian Minister.

The following were the principal officials of the Chinese Imperial Maritime Customs Department:

Inspector General—Sir Robert Hart, Bart.
Assistant Inspector General—R. E. Bredon.
Secretary in Peking—J. R. Brazier.
Assistant Secretary—P. von Rautenfeld.
Assistant Chinese Secretary—C. H. Brewitt-Taylor.
Auditor—F. W. Maze.
Secretary of Posts—J. van Aalst.
Assistant Secretary of Posts—C. E. Tennant.

No idea can be obtained of the number of missionaries who remained in Peking, as many of them had reached places of safety soon after the Boxer troubles began. The largest staff was that of the French Roman Catholic mission. Other societies well represented were the American Board of Commissioners for Foreign Missions, the American Presbyterian Mission, the London Missionary Society, the Christian and Missionary Alliance, the Church of England Mission, and the Methodist Episcopal Mission.

One of the leading educational institutions in Peking was the Peking University, the staff of which was as follows:

H. H. Lowry, M. A., D. D., President and Professor of Practical Theology.
F. D. Gamewell, M. A., Professor of Chemistry and Physics.
M. L. Taft, M. A., D. D., Professor of Exegetical and Historical Theology.
I. T. Headland, M. A., Professor of Mental and Moral Science.
G. N. Lowry, M. A., M. D., Professor of Histology and Pathology.
E. K. Lowry, B. A., Director of Industrial Department.
H. E. King, M. A., Professor of History and Political Science.
N. S. Hopkins, Lecturer on Diseases of Eye and Ear.
Miss Alice Terrel, M. A., Professor of Mathematics.
Mrs. H. E. King, M. A., Professor of English.

The Imperial College was also manned by foreign professors of different nationalities.

## AMERICAN OFFICERS IN PEKING.

WASHINGTON, July 5.—The Navy Department has received the following cablegram:

"Che-Foo.

"Myers of the Oregon commands force Peking. Capt. Hall and Dr. Lippitt also there.

KEMPFF."

Capt. John T. Myers, or "Jack" Myers as he is known, who, according to Admiral Kempff's dispatch was assigned to command the legation defenders at Peking, was born in Germany and was appointed from the State of Georgia, entering the Marine Corps in September, 1887. He is the reputed author of the famous satirical poem, "Hoch der Kaiser," which involved Capt. Coghlan in so much difficulty. He was attached to the flagship Baltimore, and was afterward assigned to duty with the marines aboard the Oregon.

Capt. Newt H. Hall, United States Marine Corps, was born in and appointed from Texas. He was graduated from the Naval Academy in 1895 with Ensign Bagley and Lieut. Breckinridge, both of whom lost their lives in the war with Spain. He was stationed at the Naval Station at Cavite, Philippine Islands, before being detailed for duty with the first marine detachment that went to China.

Dr. Thomas M. Lippitt, Assistant Surgeon, was born in Berryville, Va., in 1873. He was commissioned an Assistant Surgeon in the Navy on June 27, 1898, and served on the hospital ship Solace during the Spanish war. After the war he was attached to the flagship Baltimore on the Asiatic Station, and has since served on the Oregon, and then on the Newark, going to Taku with the marine detachment.

### Miss M. C. Smith with the Congers.

The private secretary of Cyrus Field Judson said yesterday afternoon that Mr. Judson had called up the State Department for the purpose of getting news of his sister-in-law, Miss Mary C. Smith, who had been for some time a guest of Minister Conger at Peking. The department could give no hope that any of the foreigners had escaped. One of Miss Smith's sisters is the wife of Gov. Gen. Wood of Cuba. Another sister is the wife of Lieut. Key, now at Tokio.

## MINISTER CONGER'S CAREER.

Edwin Hurd Conger, the United States Minister to China, was born in Knox County, Ill., on March 7, 1848. He was educated at Lombard University, whence he was graduated in 1862, and, like many another young American of those days, left the university to join the army. He enlisted as a private in the One Hundred and Second Illinois Volunteer Infantry, and served throughout the war.

Mr. Conger's military record was a brilliant one. He was only nineteen years old when he became a soldier, but before the end of the war he had obtained the rank of Captain and the brevet rank of Major. When peace was restored he began the study of law, and was graduated from Albany Law School in 1866. He was admitted to the bar in Illinois, and began the practice of his profession at Galesburg. In 1868 he removed to Dallas County, Iowa, where he became engaged in stock raising, farming, and banking.

Mr. Conger became interested in politics almost immediately after he became a resident of Iowa. In 1877 he was elected Treasurer of Dallas County, and a year afterward he was chosen as State Treasurer, in which capacity he served two terms. Subsequently he served three terms as a Republican member of Congress from Iowa, acting during that period as Chairman of the Committee on Coinage and Weights and Measures.

In 1890 Mr. Conger was appointed Minister to Brazil by President Harrison, and served until President Cleveland named his successor. He was very popular in Rio de Janeiro, and was himself so well satisfied with his experience there that he promptly accepted the same post when asked to do so by President McKinley, with whom he had served in Congress.

When, in 1898, Charles Page Bryan was suggested as Minister to China there was some disposition to question the suitability of the appointment on account of Mr. Bryan's youth and inexperience as a diplomat. President McKinley solved the difficulty by appointing Mr. Bryan to Brazil and transferring Mr. Conger to Peking. The appointment met with the approval of every one. Until the present outbreak began Mr. Conger had maintained the friendliest relations with the Tsung-li-Yamen and other officials in the Chinese capital.

## THE WORK OF SIR ROBERT HART.

The most famous foreigner in Peking in recent years has been Sir Robert Hart, Bart., G. C., M. G., the Inspector General of Chinese Imperial Maritime Customs. His career has been almost as remarkable a one as that of Rajah Brooke. He was born in Ireland in 1835, and in 1854 entered the Chinese Consular service. He made himself master of the language, and succeeded in gaining the confidence of the Chinese authorities.

At that time China lost millions of dollars a year through the incompetency and dishonest of the customs officials. Mr., afterward Sir Thomas, Wade suggested to the imperial authorities the advisability of placing the whole system on a business-like basis. His suggestion was accepted, and he was appointed Inspector General, with full power to appoint his own assistants and to conduct the various offices as he saw best. He was succeeded by Mr. Lay, and in 1885 the post was given to Robert Hart.

The customs receipts of China have grown in the last few years from about 4,000,000 taels (about $2,600,000) a year to an average of over 13,000,000 taels, after paying all costs of collection. Besides this a further sum, estimated at 5,000,000 taels yearly, has been collected at native maritime and inland Custom Houses.

The total number of foreign employes of the imperial maritime customs service is now about 1,000, of various nationalities. A considerable number of these have been serving in Peking, in the great house in which Sir Robert resided, and which was the headquarters of the service.

The British Government has on various occasions shown the confidence it possessed in Sir Robert. Once he was appointed Ambassador to China, but declined to serve in that capacity. He was made a Grand Commander of the Order of St. Michael and St. George, and in 1893 a Baronetcy was conferred upon him. The Chinese Government also honored him in many ways, and it is doubtful if any foreigner, with the exception of "Chinese" Gordon, was ever equally trusted by the Chinese. The decorations of the Red Button, the Double Dragon, and the Peacock's Feather were among those conferred by the Emperor on Sir Robert.

## RISING IN SOUTH IMMINENT.

WASHINGTON, July 5.—A cablegram has been received by the State Department from Consul Gen. Goodnow at Shanghai declaring that there is imminent danger of an extension of the Boxer rebellion to the southern Chinese provinces, unless the international forces are maintained and increased.

LONDON, July 6.—The situation in Quang-Tung Province grows worse. Li-Hung-Chang is said to be trying to raise a force of 200 militia.

Anarchy is widespread in the Province of Shan-Tung, in spite of the efforts of Yuan, the Governor, to control the revolt. Happily, a band of thirty-five American and other missionaries reached Tsin-Tau safely on July 3.

Viceroy Liu is reported to be freely executing disturbers of the peace at Nanking.

The Chinese Minister has received replies from the Viceroys of Nanking and Sze-Chuen saying they will be responsible for the lives and property of the foreigners in their provinces, as requested by the British Foreign Office.

Dispatches from Hongkong say the "Triods," a secret society, are assuming a threatening demeanor on the mainland.

## OUTBREAK AT CHE-FOO FEARED.

BERLIN, July 5.—A telegram from Che-Foo says that, owing to the threatening situation, the American Admiral is preparing for the departure of those under his protection.

It is added that the peaceful relations heretofore existing between the foreign residents and natives were so endangered by the influx of agitators and the threatening attitude of the Chinese soldiery that special steps were considered necessary to safeguard the foreigners.

The German Consul recirculated the Admiral's proclamation intended to counteract the Peking edict ordering war on foreigners.

## POWERS IN A QUANDARY.

### The Fiction of "No War" Can No Longer Be Maintained If There Is a New Chinese Government.

*Special to The New York Times.*

WASHINGTON, July 5.—The report that Emperor Kwang-Su and the Empress Dowager Tsze-Esi-An of China are dead may not be true, but it is sufficiently probable to call for serious consideration on the part of the American Government. If the present Government of China is replaced by a new one, some very serious considerations will be presented, and the State Department is already preparing for them. If the expected happens, and the Government, headed by the Empress Dowager, is succeeded by an entirely new Government, headed by Prince Tuan or his son, it will become extremely difficult to avoid a declaration, or at least a recognition, of war.

Our Government has been straining every nerve to avoid such a catastrophe. Secretary Hay's contention that the trouble in China is as much a rebellion against the Empress Dowager as it is an anti-foreign movement, and that therefore no act of the rebels can be construed as an act of war, has been supported to his complete satisfaction by events. Everything that has occurred has tended to assure the Government of the truth of Minister Wu's assertions that the Empress Dowager is trying to the best of her ability to protect the foreigners, and that the rebellion is aimed at her as well as at them.

As long as that remains the case it is perfectly easy for the State Department to maintain its position that not even the murder of Minister Conger can be taken as an act of war. The State Department believes that this position is not only technically correct, but is correct in the broadest sense, and that the Empress has done what she could for the protection of the legations.

The latest news from China indicates that this state of things will not long continue, if it is not already swept away. It has been reported that Prince Tuan has deposed the Emperor and the Empress Dowager, and has proclaimed a new Emperor, and now it is reported that the late rulers of China are dead, either by assassination or suicide.

The problem that now confronts the Administration is this: If Prince Tuan's usurpation has extended so far that the old Government has passed out of existence, and if a new Government has been installed, it is with the new Government that we shall have to reckon, and it is doubtful if it can be maintained for any length of time; that the acts of the new Government are not acts of war. In other words, as soon as it is officially learned that there is a new Emperor on the throne, who is employing his army to make war on Americans, an open and recognized state of war between the United States and China is likely to ensue. The same would, of course, be true as between China and the European nations, as well as Japan.

It is needless to say that the Administration will do everything it can to avoid such a state of things. Only official assurances that a new Government has been installed at Peking will be accepted as true, and all possible leeway will be given to the theory that even the new Government is not making war. But even the most optimistic officials are not able to deny that the installation of a new Government, headed by an Emperor under the influence of Prince Tuan, would almost certainly be followed by open war.

Minister Wu-Ting-Fang would then be no longer the representative here of the Chinese Government, for the Government which sent him here would have passed out of existence. As long as the Empress remains alive, even after the establish-

Continued on Page 9.

# BRYAN NOMINATED; 16 TO 1 PLATFORM

### Resolutions Committee Votes for Silver After Long Contest.

## NO FIGHT IN THE CONVENTION

### Hill Accepts the Platform and Says the East Will Approve.

### Remarkable Demonstration Follows Presentation of Bryan's Name to the Convention—Nomination Was Unanimous.

*Special to The New York Times.*

KANSAS CITY, July 5.—William Jennings Bryan was nominated to-night for President by the Democratic National Committee Convention on a 16 to 1 platform.

The nomination was made by acclamation, after a presentation followed by scenes of delirious excitement. For more than half an hour the vast audience of 20,000 persons gave themselves up to demonstrations of delight, cheering wildly while the delegates marched about the hall with flags, State standards, and extemporised banners with inscriptions upon them, borne high in the air.

The platform was reported by Senator Tillman of South Carolina, and was read by him with excellent effect. Its references to imperialism provoked one of the tumultuous demonstrations that have been so frequent in the convention for two days, the interest in that issue, which was declared to be paramount in the campaign, being evidently greater than the concern about trusts, militarism, and the reduction of war taxes. The free-silver plank was rapturously applauded for twenty minutes.

The platform was adopted as reported, the opponents of free silver abandoning their determination to dispute its adoption in the interest of party harmony.

Mr. Bryan is expected to be in Kansas City to-morrow and to attend the convention to accept at one time the nominations of the Democrats, Populists, and Silver Republicans, the latter to be completed as soon as the Democrats have chosen a Vice Presidential candidate.

The choice for Vice President appears to-night to lie between Towne, Stevenson, and Hill, with the chances favoring the elimination of Hill. New York will stick to Keller, its candidate, until it is apparent that he cannot be nominated. It then will probably go to Stevenson. Should Bryan indicate a preference for Towne it may bring about his nomination.

Ex-Senator Hill received a great ovation when he seconded the nomination of Bryan. He accepted the platform without criticism, and spoke hopefully of Democratic success.

It is expected that the work of the convention will be completed to-morrow in one session.

## CONVENTION'S SECOND DAY.

### Chairman Richardson Has a Hard Time Keeping Down Enthusiasm for Ex-Senator Hill.

*Special to The New York Times.*

KANSAS CITY, July 5.—This was the great day of the convention, the day of the adoption of the platform which the leaders had prepared, the day of the nomination of William Jennings Bryan for President, the day when the star orators of the party had the opportunity of their lives to charm with words an audience of 20,000 persons who were responsive to any suggestion which would give them a chance to shout and cheer.

From early morning until late to-night the convention hall has been in an uproar, except during a midday recess. Whatever may be the division among the delegates over the platform and the candidates, certain it is that no convention crowd has ever been imbued with a spirit of patriotic enthusiasm to a greater degree than is the crowd which is here. The sight of the flag or the sound of a patriotic air is all that is needed to throw the crowd into a tumult.

Twice to-day the enthusiasm became a perfect frenzy, and the crowd simply took the convention out of the hands of its controlling officers. The first occasion was just after 4 P. M., when Senator Tillman, who was reading the platform with great effect, made a declaration against imperialism and declared that it was the paramount issue in this campaign. The other occasion was when an hour or so later the name of William Jennings Bryan was put in nomination for the Presidency.

On both of these occasions there was much of what might be called "manufactured enthusiasm," produced according to prearranged programme, but at the same time it is only fair to say that the crowd was more than ready for the opportunity to break loose which the committee had so carefully prepared for. Hence the demonstrations were genuine, far surpassing in this respect any of the outbreaks at the Philadelphia Convention.

THE FEELING FOR HILL.

At such times to-day as the convention was not engaged with the adoption of the platform and the nomination of Mr. Bryan, ex-Senator Hill of New York was its critical figure when present, and the crowd wanted to shout his name even when he was not here. This remarkable feeling on the part of the convention toward Senator Hill, as shown yesterday and to-day, is not taken entirely as being a mark of personal admiration for him. Unquestionably it is largely promoted by the feeling of indignation which has been engendered against the Croker-Murphy-Van Wyck combination, because they dared to bring their dirty political linen out here to wash instead of attending to it before their State Convention. Their humiliation of Mr. Hill here at the National Convention has made them immensely unpopular.

Although the convention hall will only seat 12,000 persons, those in authority permitted 20,000 to jam their way in, crowding the aisles and all standing room, and even standing between the rows of seats. Ticket speculators were hawking tickets around the streets at almost any old price, and consequently matters were made very uncomfortable in the hall. The temperature was high, and there was more humidity than is common in this part of the country. The only thing to do was to dress down as close to the skin as possible and sweat and bear it.

The morning session was decidedly breezy. It was a case of wind and endurance from start to finish. The audience furnished the endurance, speakers provided some wind, the band the rest.

TO CHECK DEMONSTRATIONS.

David B. Hill of New York did not put in an appearance. There was apparent a deliberate and carefully prepared plan to check any ovation to the New York ex-Senator. But Chairman Richardson had a very difficult task to stem the manifestations in favor of Mr. Hill. The Committee on Resolutions not being ready to report something had to be done to entertain the Kansas City people, who had given up their money to get the convention and the thousands of visitors.

Chairman Richardson first presented ex-Gov. Hogg of Texas, who made a very acceptable speech and awakened as much enthusiasm for Bryan as he did at the Tammany Hall meeting in New York on July 4, 1899. The fact that ex-Gov. Hogg was refused an election as a delegate has not reduced his avoirdupois or dampened his ardor. He was for Bryan and free silver from A to Z, but Mr. Hogg had no sooner taken his seat than there were cries of "Hill, Hill, Hill." It was but a murmur at first, but it rapidly increased in volume and 70 per cent. of the delegates and audience were shouting for the New Yorker.

Then Chairman Richardson signaled to the band to play and hustled for another speaker. He found one in ex-Congressman Dockery of Missouri, who is the Democratic nominee for Governor, but when Dockery closed the cries for Hill revived, and again the band played, and it played on because Mr. Richardson had some trouble in securing another speaker in the person of Mayor Rose of Milwaukee. Rose spoke well, and when he retired the roar for Hill was taken up in all parts of the hall. Chairman Richardson signaled the band, which played desperately, but, stopping to catch a breath, the Hill enthusiasm at once was demonstrated, and the tired musicians had to play a cakewalk and a lively rag-time march.

Mr. McCullough was the next time consumer presented by Chairman Richardson, but before he had resumed his seat there were roars for Hill all over the hall. Then the band played on while ex-Senator Murphy and Mr. Croker, both wearing a very tired look, walked out of the building. The musicians were in distress when George Fred Williams of Massachusetts came to their relief with a resolution calling for a conference with the silver Republicans.

This was so promptly adopted that the band had little rest. It was "Hill! Hill!" everywhere on the floor, on the platform, and in the galleries. Chairman Richardson found a victim in Congressman Williams of Illinois, a Representative seldom heard of in the halls of Congress. He spoke for a few minutes. Then there was another outbreak for Hill, and after the band had played, Gov. Beckham of Kentucky was called. Chairman Richardson introduced him as the Lieutenant Governor of the Blue Grass State. Beckham is young and delicate, and after promising Kentucky's Electoral vote to Bryan, retired, despite Richardson's exhortation for him to continue.

The band had to play again, as almost everybody was shouting for Hill, and music, strong and loud, alone could charm the audience into silence. Chairman Richardson next introduced J. W. Miles of Maryland, who made an excellent speech in a loud and distinct voice, but when he concluded and the Hill sentiment again immediately became manifest, the band being tired and Richardson having no more speakers, he ordered a recess until 3:30 P. M.

Through the two long hours of recess fully one-half of those who had seats remained in them, fearful that if they left they would not be able to get back. They had sat through a morning session that was somewhat wearisome, owing to the fact that so few of those who had made political speeches had been able to make themselves heard.

The crowd did not know whether to expect a fight upon the floor over the platform or not, but certain it was that, fight or no fight, there would be a scene that it was worth while suffering inconvenience and discomfort to witness.

The Committee on Platform did not arrive at 3:30 o'clock, as expected, so there was nothing to do but wait. Word reached the convention hall, however, that only one report would be made by the committee, that the platform would stand for 16 to 1 specifically, but that it would not be put forward as the paramount issue. This was soon known to all, and it seemed to please everybody. It meant that the convention was all over but the shouting, and the people were anxious to shout.

THE PLATFORM PRESENTED.

At 3:45 o'clock ex-Senator Hill, who had been absent at the morning session, strolled down the aisle. As soon as he took his hat off and was recognized—for Mr. Hill generally has to remove his hat to be recognized in convention—the convention greeted him as it had on every occasion. Thousands shouted his name, and all cheered and waved their hats, handkerchiefs, and flags. The demonstration lasted five minutes.

The Platform Committee, headed by burly Senator Jones, who walked with Augustus Van Wyck, and Senator Tillman, walking with dapper George Fred Williams, started toward the stage. At last the real business of the convention was to be done. Mr. Jones merely announced that his committee had unanimously agreed upon a report, and then called on Senator Tillman to read the platform.

Tillman, one-eyed and leather-lunged, began to read. The hall was more nearly quiet than it had been at any time during the convention, for everybody was intensely interested in the contents of the document which Tillman held in his hand. He had proceeded but a moment or two when a delegate from California jumped to his feet.

"Mr. Chairman," he shouted, "this is the vital moment in this convention. As a delegate here I must hear that platform read. I demand that the aisles be cleared and that complete order be restored."

"Sit down, sit down," roared Tillman. "You keep quiet, all keep quiet and I will see that every man and woman in this hall hears my voice."

He made his word good. His voice was loud and clear, and he read with tremendous earnestness. In fact, his reading of the platform was the most eloquent half hour of the convention, for he had carefully studied each plank, and knew just how to put stress upon it. When he came to any heroic declaration he threw all the energy of his aggressive nature into it.

Consequently the reading was interspersed by cheers from start to finish, and when he declared that no Nation could long last as a republic and have empire, the cheering continued for several minutes. The same was true when he denounced the keeping of an army in Cuba, and when he declared that Democracy stood for protection and independence for the Filipino. Then he read this sentence: "The importance of other questions before the American people is in no wise diminished, and the Democratic Party takes no backward steps from its position on them, but the burning issue of imperialism growing out of the Spanish war involves the very existence of the Republic and the destiny of our free institutions. We regard it as the paramount issue of the campaign."

A GREAT DEMONSTRATION.

This sentence was the signal for one of the most dramatic and impressive spectacles of the convention. As the speaker was speaking the words hundreds began to put in the hands of every person long-handled flags about 2 by 1½ feet in size, bearing the inscription: "The Constitution and the flag are one and inseparable now and forever. The flag of a Republic forever, of an empire never."

The cheering started among the delegates, but in a few seconds it had spread over the entire hall; but Tillman silenced it with a terrific appeal for silence and repeated the paragraph from the platform, fairly screaming forth the words, "We regard it (imperialism) as the paramount issue in this campaign."

It was the signal the audience had been waiting for. It was the news that the large majority in the convention which was opposed to shoving free silver to the front among the issues had been hoping for. The words acted like an electric shock upon the multitude. Up the people stood, until the small flags were frantically waved until the vast hall was a stormy sea of color, while underneath the flood of color and almost buried from sight by it were 20,000 persons, standing on chairs and jumping

"All the News That's Fit to Print."

# The New York Times.

THE WEATHER. Showers and thunderstorms; southwest winds.

COPYRIGHT, 1900, BY THE NEW YORK TIMES COMPANY.

VOL. XLIX...NO. 15,755. NEW YORK, SATURDAY, JULY 7, 1900.—FOURTEEN PAGES. ONE CENT In Greater New York and Jersey City. Elsewhere, TWO CENTS.

TO-DAY:
FOURTEEN PAGES.
WITH
REVIEW OF BOOKS AND ART.

THE NEWS CONDENSED.

Stocks irregular.

Wheat, No. 2 red, 88c.; corn, No. 2 mixed, 50½c.; oats, No. 2 mixed, 28¼c.; cotton, middling, 10¼c.; iron, No. 1 foundry, $18; butter, Western creamery, 19½c.

FOREIGN.—It is announced that neither Russia nor any other of the powers will restrain Japan from sending as many troops into China as she is able to do. It is unlikely, however, that Japan will be the mandatory of the powers to quell the Chinese disturbances. The proposal that this be the case is said to have come from Great Britain, and Russia fears that Japan would simply be acting as Great Britain's representative. No further news has been received as to the foreigners in Peking. It is announced that thousands of native Christians in the city have been massacred. The position of the allied troops at Tien-Tsin is becoming increasingly difficult. A body of 1,000 Russian troops that started from Tien-Tsin for Peking many days ago has not been heard of since, and it is feared that it has been annihilated. The outbreak is still spreading, and it is now considered likely that it will affect the great southern provinces. In the French Chamber yesterday a row was brought about through M. Lasies, a Nationalist Deputy, insulting the Government in regard to the recent verdict favoring Lieut. Col. Picquart. Lasies refused to be silenced by the President of the Chamber, who thereupon left the building. A free fight ensued, and many Deputies were roughly handled.—Pages 1, 6, and 7.

Arrivals at Hotels and Out-of-Town Buyers.—Page 14.
Business Troubles.—Page 12.
Court Calendars.—Page 12.
Insurance Notes.—Page 11.
Legal Notes.—Page 5.
Marine Intelligence and Foreign Mails.—Page 9.
Markets.—Page 12.
New Corporation.—Page 11.
Real Estate.—Page 12.
Society.—Page 7.
United Service.—Page 14.
Weather Report.—Page 14.
Yesterday's Fires.—Page 14.

## ANDREW FREEDMAN ARRESTED.

### Croker's Friend Assaults a Reporter, Is Pummeled, Apologizes, and Is Then Discharged.

*Special to The New York Times.*

KANSAS CITY, July 6.—Andrew Freedman, the bosom friend of Richard Croker, was arrested here this afternoon on a charge of disorderly conduct. The arrest caused little or no indignation among the members of Tammany Hall, while the Kings County and up-State delegates seemed rather to enjoy the discomfiture of the baseball magnate. The Kansas City Star has made frequent references to Tammany's representatives, and in at least one of these Freedman was referred to in a somewhat uncomplimentary manner. Freedman credited Paul Tieman with the authorship of the paragraphs.

After the convention adjourned to-day Mr. Tieman went to Mr. Croker's rooms to obtain an expression of opinion on its work. He was met at the door by Freedman, who said angrily: "You cannot come in here; you are nothing but a dirty bum." Mr. Tieman insisted that he had a right to be admitted, as other reporters had passed in. "Well, you can't go in," said Freedman, pushing Tieman aside. Not desiring to create a scene, Tieman retired, and, going to the hotel office, wrote a polite note to Mr. Croker, in which he asked for his opinion and also made allusions to Mr. Freedman's acts. Whether Croker said anything to Freedman or not is known only to themselves. Neither would say a word on that point, but a few minutes later Freedman appeared at the Seventh Street entrance to the Midland.

Mr. Tieman was near by when Freedman saw him and made a pass at him. Tieman dodged the blow and landed his right on Freedman's face, drawing blood. There was an immediate clinch, and while both Freedman and Tieman were getting in good short blows Policeman William H. Young put in an appearance and hit both combatants with his club to separate them. Then he placed them under arrest.

"You must not arrest that man," shouted an excited Tammanyite. "He's got to leave here at 5 o'clock."

"I can't help that," responded Young; "just now he goes to the station house."

Young took his prisoners to the Central Station, where they were arraigned before Lieut. Webber. Tieman charged Freedman with assault. The Lieutenant placed both under bonds for appearance to-morrow, but a few minutes later, Mr. Freedman having made an humble apology to Mr. Tieman, the latter at the suggestion of his employer, Col. Nelson, withdrew his charge and Freedman was able to leave with the Tammany contingent.

Many delegates expressed to Mr. Tieman their regrets that he had been attacked. In defense of his act Freedman said Tieman had enjoyed the hospitality of the Tammany delegates and had then abused them generally, and him particularly, with no just cause. Tieman's reply is that no sensible politician would have taken umbrage at the remarks Freedman complained of.

## IMPROVED PORTO RICAN TRADE.

### Both Imports and Exports in May Show a Remarkable Increase.

*Special to The New York Times.*

WASHINGTON, July 6.—The Bureau of Statistics of the Treasury Department to-day issued the following statement to show the good results of the Payne-Foraker Porto Rico bill:

"The effect of the new Porto Rican tariff act is plainly perceptible in the commerce between the United States and that island during the month of May. The monthly summary of commerce and finance, just issued by the Treasury Bureau of Statistics, shows that exports to Porto Rico have more than doubled as compared with the preceding May, and imports from the island have nearly doubled. Exports to the island from the United States in May 1899, were $305,564, and in May, 1900, $696,479. The imports into the United States from the island in May, 1899, were $647,179, and in May, 1900, $1,103,867. This increase is the more remarkable because it has been understood that the people of Porto Rico had little to sell and little with which to buy, since the hurricane of last August had gone far to impoverish the people of that island.

"It is also interesting to observe that the May commerce with Porto Rico shows a much greater increase than is the case with any of the other islands. With Cuba the commerce of May differed little from that of May, 1899, and this was also the case with the Hawaiian Islands; while in the Philippine Islands the imports show no increase, though the exports show a remarkable gain."

## Prof. Cornwell of Princeton Hurt.

*Special to The New York Times.*

PRINCETON, N. J., July 6.—Prof. Henry B. Cornwell of the Princeton University Faculty was seriously hurt while wheeling yesterday. Prof. Cornwell was going down Rocky Hill, just beyond Princeton, and his machine caught in a rut while whirling at a swift clip. It struck a stone, throwing Mr. Cornwell heavily, fracturing his elbow and severely shaking him up. He is confined to his home.



# JAPAN CAN SEND ARMY INTO CHINA

## But It Is Doubtful If She Will Act as Powers' Mandatory.

## THE ATTITUDE OF RUSSIA

### Afraid That Japan Would Only Be Great Britain's Catspaw.

### Native Christians Massacred in Peking—Kaiser Offers Big Reward for Every Foreigner Saved.

LONDON, July 7.—The Russian Government announces that it will give Japan a free hand to apply military force in China. The terms of this consent are summarized in the subjoined dispatch from St. Petersburg, under date of July 6:

"In reply to an inquiry from the Japanese Cabinet regarding the dispatch of Japanese troops to China to render aid to the foreigners in Peking the Russian Government declared that it left the Japanese Government full liberty of action in this connection, as the Tokio Cabinet expressed its readiness to act in full agreement with the other powers."

It is in consequence of this, no doubt, that Japan is preparing to embark 20,000 more troops.

Political considerations that were thought to have been numbing the action of the powers are thus laid aside, for a moment at least, by the Government supposed to have the clearest purposes respecting China's future. Japan's sending of troops now can, however, have little bearing on the fate of the foreigners in Peking.

Baron Hayashi, the new Japanese Minister, who arrived in London on Friday, said that ten days would probably be required for the carrying of troops to China. His dictated statements contained these sentences:

"If all the conditions Japan asked were conceded, I see no reason why Japan should not undertake the task of suppressing the trouble. The powers are all agreed in wishing to put down the rebels, but it does not seem that they are agreed on the means."

From these authoritative utterances it is inferred that Japan does nominate conditions, and that the concert of the powers is a little jangled.

In the House of Commons yesterday the Parliamentary Secretary of the Foreign Office, the Right Hon. William St. John Brodrick, announced that the Government of Japan had received assurances that the prompt dispatch of a large force to Taku would be welcomed by her Majesty's Government.

No objection Mr Brodrick added, had been raised by any European power. As the negotiations were being continued he was unable to say more, but he assured the House that the Government was fully alive to the exigencies of the situation.

The British Cabinet had a long meeting yesterday morning, under the Presidency of Lord Salisbury, and fully considered the crisis.

The Tien-Tsin correspondent of The Times, in a dispatch dated July 3, says:

"Twenty-two hundred Japanese troops, with fourteen guns, have arrived at Taku, and 800 more are expected to-night."

*Special to The New York Times.*

WASHINGTON, July 6.—The State Department has been unable to understand the declarations so vehemently made in London newspapers that Russia is preventing Japan from rescuing the Peking legations by withholding her consent to Japan's offer to send troops. The department was officially informed four days ago that both Russia and France had granted Japan's request, and not a word has come to it since to indicate that there was any reservation about this consent. The furious denunciations of Russia as responsible for the Peking massacre have therefore been utterly unintelligible here.

Things are gradually leaking out which afford some explanation of the mystery. It is now suspected that the proposition which, according to the English newspapers, has been rejected by Russia, is not the proposition made by Japan at all. Japan's request was that she be permitted to land a large force, exceeding her quota of the international army. No other proposition has been made by Japan, so far as can be learned here. The request was at once acceded to by the United States, and immediately after we had given our consent we were officially informed that Great Britain, France, and Russia had done the same. This is all the backing Japan needs, since Germany will offer no objection to anything of this sort which is regarded as necessary by the other powers.

It is now believed, however, that the proposition which Russia has rejected is one made, not by Japan, but by Great Britain. This is borne out by the statement made semi-officially in Berlin that Germany has declined Great Britain's request that she use her influence with Russia to have Japan "undertake the work of pacification in China." This sounds like a very different proposition from Japan's simple request that she be allowed to furnish the major part of the foreign army. Besides this, there are press dispatches from Europe saying that Russia objects to granting to Japan the sole mandate in China, because she regards it "as a British intrigue." With this comes a denial that Russia has any objection to Japan's sending an army of any size whatever.

This furnishes the explanation of the violent tone taken toward Russia by the English press. It is believed here that all the requests Japan has made have been readily granted, but that Great Britain has complicated the situation by proffering a request of her own that the sole mandate in China be granted to Japan, and that she be intrusted alone with the pacification of the rebellious provinces. The interests of Great Britain and Japan are so nearly identical that such a request is almost equivalent to asking that the former be intrusted with the sole mandate. There is no surprise here that Russia has declined such a request, or that Germany feels that it would be unfriendly to Russia to act as intermediary in proffering it.

There is in Washington a growing suspicion that if any power is endangering the harmony with which the nations are acting by dragging politics into the question, it is not Russia, but Great Britain. The American Government does not share the feeling which is manifested toward Russia in England. The State Department has from the first discouraged the tendency of some Americans to take the popular British view that Russia is not to be trusted in anything. Every move Russia takes is regarded in England as a manifestation of her mysterious and subterranean diplomacy, and no matter how much Russia may protest her good faith, all such protestations are met in England with a sneer.

The State Department has from the first seen reason to believe that Russia is acting honestly and fairly, and is actuated, for the present, at least, by the desire to put a stop to the anarchy in China. When the settlement comes Russia is expected to play politics, but her actions now are believed in Washington to be as sincere as those of Great Britain. Russia was the first power to declare to the United States that she would act simply for the preservation of life and property and the restoration of order. This assurance, it is understood, was not asked by the United States, but was volunteered.

An official dispatch received by the Japanese Legation here this afternoon from Tokio announces that the Japanese Government has decided to send to China a mixed division of troops to reinforce the Japanese force already there.

This will make an aggregate of 22,000 Japanese troops in China.



## PEKING A CITY OF BLOOD.

LONDON, July 7.—Recitals of further horrors in Peking are gathered by correspondents at Shanghai from Chinese sources, especially of the slaughter in the Chinese and Tartar city of thousands of native Christians, so that the capital reeks with carnage.

The ruthless thirst for blood is spreading in all the northern provinces, and wherever there are native Christians the scenes enacted in the capital are reproduced.

Nothing further comes regarding the legation forces, except a repetition of the reports that they are all dead. The correspondents aver that if the Chinese officials in Shanghai wished to throw light on the real state of affairs in the capital they could do so, and, therefore, the worst reports are accepted as true.

In response to inquiries cabled to Shanghai in regard to the situation at Peking, the following cablegram has been received from an authoritative quarter:

"SHANGHAI, Thursday, July 5.—Prepare to hear the worst."

Other Shanghai dispatches tell of executions and unnamable tortures inflicted on captured foreigners.

Henry W. Lucy, manager of the Parliamentary corps of The Daily News, says that Lady Bigham, wife of Justice Bigham, received a cablegram on Friday announcing the safety of her son, who was last heard of as shut up in Peking. Mr. Lucy says that if one can have escaped there is some hope for the others.

Mr. Bigham is attached to the British Embassy at Constantinople, and was visiting China.

BERLIN, July 6.—The firm of Melchers & Co. of Shanghai, telegraphed to Bremen under date of July 6:

"We have reason to believe that all the foreigners in Peking have perished."

The German Consul at Tien-Tsin wires, under date of July 1, that an authentic letter from the British Minister at Peking, Sir Claude M. MacDonald, to the British Consul here, dated Peking, June 25, had just arrived. The Consul adds that it confirmed the statements that Baron von Ketteler, the German Minister, was shot dead on June 20 by Chinese soldiers while on his way to the Tsung-li-Yamen. His body had not been found. His companion, an interpreter named Cordes, was dangerously wounded.

Sir Claude feared an immediate attack on the British Legation.

WASHINGTON, July 6.—The State Department is waiting with almost an agony of expectation for news from Peking, but none comes. Heart-rending appeals are being received from the relatives and friends of the persons supposed to have been in the United States Legation, praying for information as to the fate of their people, but the department is unable to give them any satisfaction.

Copyright, 1900, The Associated Press.

TIEN-TSIN, June 29.—Gen. Tung-Fu-Siang, with 10,000 of the best-disciplined troops in the Chinese Army, Mohammedans, is marching from the southwest toward Peking. The army thereabouts numbers 50,000 men.

The Empress has fled to the Summer palace. The Mohammedans and Boxers are fighting in Peking. Ten regiments of Gen. Nieh's command, north of Tien-Tsin, are reported to have deserted and to be pillaging the country.

## EMPEROR WILLIAM'S OFFER.

BERLIN, July 6.—Emperor William has telegraphed to the commander of the German squadron in Chinese waters, to the Governor General of Shan-Tung, to the Viceroys, and to others offering a thousand taels (about $650) to any one accomplishing the deliverance of any foreigner of any nationality whatever now shut up in Peking, who is handed over to any German Magistrate.

The Emperor also offers to pay the expenses of the publication of this offer in Peking.

## TUAN'S COUP D'ETAT.

LONDON, July 6.—Prince Tuan's seizure of power is described by the Shanghai correspondent of The Daily Mail as a sequence to the Grand Council of Ministers, at which Yung-Lu advocated the suppression of the Boxers promptly. The Dowager Empress gave her whole support to Yung-Lu, and a scene of disorder ensued.

Prince Tuan passionately intervened, backed by Kang-Yi. They rushed from the council, and their partisans raised the cry, "Down with the foreigners."

The effect was electrical. The palace officials of all sorts and most of the populace took up the cause of Tuan and his agents and immediately put the Emperor and the Dowager Empress under restraint.

## PEKING CONGREGATIONALISTS.

The Rev. Dr. C. C. Creegan, the New York representative of the American Board of Commissioners of Foreign Missions, the Congregationalist Foreign Missionary Society of this country, prepared a list of Congregational ministers yesterday who so far as is known were in Peking at the time of the reported massacre there. According to latest reports there were twenty-eight American missionaries in Peking, eleven of them being women. Only eight of these missionaries are stationed at Peking, but the rest of them started for Peking at the commencement of the trouble, hoping to find protection with the legations there.

"Of course," said Mr. Creegan yesterday, "some of the ministers on the list I have prepared may not be in Peking, but, according to the latest reports from China, they were all either there or on their way there. To the best of my belief, almost all of our missionaries in North China were in Peking at the time of the massacre. They probably thought that the safest place in the country would be at the capital, where the legations were, and with that idea they went into a trap. We have heard nothing from China from our missionaries for some time, and are dependent entirely upon the papers for news. Needless to say, we have the gravest fears for our missionaries."

The list of Congregationalist ministers supposed to be in the affected district is as follows:

The Rev. WILLIAM S. AMENT, D. D. Dr. Ament was born in Owosso, Mich., in 1851. He was graduated at Oberlin College in 1873, and at the Theological Seminary, Andover, Mass., in 1877. He was pastor of the Congregational Church at Calumet, Mich., for three years, and of the church at Hancock, Mich., for eight months. He sailed for China from San Francisco in 1877. He is stationed regularly at Peking. His wife is now in Owosso, Mich.

The Rev. CHARLES E. EWING of Massachusetts, and his wife, Mrs. BESSIE GOODYEAR EWING of Connecticut. Mr. Ewing is a son of the Rev. E. C. Ewing of 77 Cedar Street, Roxbury, Mass. He was born in Enfield, Mass., in 1890, and was graduated at Amherst College in 1890. He was also graduated from the Yale Theological Seminary in 1893. He was ordained at Danvers, Mass., in 1893, and sailed for China on Aug. 28, 1894. Mrs. Ewing was born in North Haven, Conn., in 1870, and educated at the Hillhouse High School and Welch Training School. Mr. and Mrs. Ewing had two children with them at Peking, Helen, aged five, and Ellen, aged two.

Miss ADA HAVEN of Brookline, Mass. Miss Haven was born at Brookline in 1850. Her father was the Rev. Joseph Haven, D. D. She

Continued on Page 7.

# GOLD DEMOCRATS TO OPPOSE MR. BRYAN

## National Party May Place Candidates in the Field.

## SILVER PLANK IS CONDEMNED

### Defeat of Bryan Assured, Say Messrs. Hewitt and Wheeler—Ex-Gov. Hoadly's View.

The National Committee of the National Democratic Party, or Gold Democrats, will meet in Indianapolis on Wednesday, July 25, to consider what action will be taken by the party as an organization in the Presidential campaign. George Foster Peabody, Chairman of the committee, has received letters from Democrats all over the country who four years ago followed the standard of Palmer and Buckner, in which the writers give their opinions as to what stand should be taken this year.

These opinions widely differ. Some say that they will support the Republican candidates, because of the position taken by the Republicans regarding the currency; others believe that there should again be a third ticket placed in the field for those who are opposed to free silver, and who cannot bring themselves to vote for McKinley. A third view is that the currency question in this campaign is overshadowed by other issues, and that Democrats should support Bryan.

MR. PEABODY'S STAND.

Mr. Peabody was not in the city yesterday, but he has all along declined to give expression to his personal views on the ground that it would not be proper for him, as Chairman of the committee, to say what should be done until the committee meets.

Edward M. Shepard, who in the campaign of 1896 was opposed to Bryan and took a prominent part in the campaign for Palmer and Buckner, was also out of the city, and none of his friends could say what his position would be in this fight.

Charles Jerome Edwards, one of Mr. Shepard's most trusted lieutenants in past campaigns, said:

"I am not authorized to speak for Mr. Shepard, and I do not know what attitude he will assume now. There is a possibility that the fact that it is impossible for Mr. Bryan or any one else to change the character of our currency in four years, even if elected, may influence some of the old Gold Democrats to give him their support on the anti-imperialism plank.

"Personally, I do not know what I shall do, or what my friends will do. Perhaps McKinley is the lesser evil of the two, but only the lesser evil. It may be we may have to vote for a Governor and local candidates only."

MR. WHEELER TALKS.

Everett P. Wheeler said yesterday:

"I do not know whether the sound money Democrats will decide to nominate a third candidate or to support McKinley. Nothing, I imagine, has been settled on this point. Very few, if any, Gold Democrats will support Bryan. The Gold Democrats had a National Committee four years ago. Its existence was continued. George Foster Peabody is the New York member. I cannot say what this committee has done, but I understand that the question of putting up a sound money candidate has been discussed.

"If there is no third ticket my impression is that the majority of the Gold Democrats will vote for McKinley. Some might abstain from voting. As to the Kansas City platform, I don't consider it a Democratic platform. It is not in accord with the principles of the party, as they were understood down to 1896. The whole idea, for instance, of Government money is entirely opposed to the old Democratic principle. As I read it, the Bryan element advocates the issue of money entirely by the United States.

"It seems to me that the Bryan-Stevenson ticket will be defeated by a larger Electoral majority than that of four years ago. Some of the Western States will go into the Republican column. I have every reason to believe that Wyoming will be carried by McKinley. Most of the old Republican States carried by Bryan in 1896 will this Fall be for the Republican candidate. It may be that no action at all will be taken by the Gold Democrats. It is our general hope that Bryan will be so badly beaten that he will be extinguished as a factor in American politics, and so an opportunity to build up the Democratic Party will be presented."

EX-GOV. HOADLY'S ADVICE.

"Support the Republican nominees" is the advice given by ex-Gov. George Hoadly to all Democrats dissatisfied with the Kansas City candidates and platform. Lying upon a bed of pain at the Hotel Castleton, Staten Island, yesterday afternoon, the ex-Governor uttered these words:

"If I thought it was as certain as it was four years ago that the State of New York would vote for McKinley, it would be very gratifying to my feelings to throw away my vote.

"I then voted for Palmer and Buckner because I proved my principles, and I thought it was perfectly safe to vote for them. Although Mr. McKinley represents views, principles, and courses of action that Gold Democrats do not approve, he is so much better than Bryan that it can hardly be said to be a choice of evils.

"Mr. Bryan, if elected, will endeavor to pay the National debt or the interest on it in silver, which would introduce a series of appalling calamities greater than any that are to be dreaded from any other cause. Therefore, my advice to Gold Democrats and the action I shall take myself will be to vote the Republican ticket at the Presidential election.

"I do not believe the objections to what is called 'imperialism' amount to anything. I do not say that no President or no Government under any circumstances could conscientiously treat the Philippines differently from the way in which Mr. McKinley is treating them.

"If I supposed that the Republican Party were committed to the permanent ownership of the islands as colonies or satrapies I should feel very hostile to such a course and share in the fears of Mr. Schurz and Gov. Boutwell.

BRYAN AND THE TREATY.

"The treaty which made the islands ours and by which the large sum of $20,000,000 was paid for them was advocated by William J. Bryan. It certainly does not lie in his mouth to object to the possession of the islands now. To Mr. Bryan I would say: 'You personally went to Washington and by the ratification of the treaty helped to bring the United States into control. Now you are responsible. What will you do with them if you are elected President? Will you give them back to the Tagalog tribe or nation? The war was begun by the Tagalogs and not by us.'

"'Mr. McKinley says, restore order, educate the people, and after order has been restored and when a reasonable time has passed to enable the people to pass upon what they shall do, then ask the people what they wish.' It would take the whole of Mr. McKinley's second Administration to accomplish this. That is one of the great questions of the future for the United States.

"'We agree, you and I, that Mr. McKinley's attitude on the Dingley tariff was offensive. Possibly, if you had had the making of the tariff you would have made it better than it is, but we must have a tariff, and no one proposed a new one except the men who in making it would debase the currency.

"'It is far more important to secure a gold currency than to reduce the tariff to which our people are accustomed, or to

Continued on Page 3.



# GOV. ROOSEVELT IN CANTON

## First Meeting with the President Since the Convention.

## WARM WELCOME GIVEN HIM

### He and the President Make Short Addresses—Left for New York Last Night.

CANTON, Ohio, July 6.—The home city of the President to-day accorded to his colleague on the Republican National ticket an ovation almost unprecedented even in Canton. It would be hard to say whether the citizens of Canton voiced a louder welcome to President McKinley or to Gov. Roosevelt, yet it may be said that Canton did not discriminate in to-day's demonstration, the first occasion on which the Republican candidates for President and Vice President have personally met since the Philadelphia convention.

Gov. Roosevelt arrived in Canton over the Valley Railroad at 5:30. As the Governor alighted from the train whistles blew and cannons boomed, and an immense crowd gathered about the station gave him a mighty cheer of welcome. The President's secretary, George B. Cortelyou, was the first person to greet him as he stepped off the platform. Carriages were in waiting and the march to the President's home was at once taken up. All along the line from the station to the McKinley residence, nearly a mile, the streets were lined with people, and Gov. Roosevelt was kept busy bowing his acknowledgments to the acclaims of the people of Canton.

The carriage in which Gov. Roosevelt rode was surrounded by small boys, shouting at the top of their voices, and by bicyclists, who seemed anxious to feast their eyes on the Rough Rider. The yard of the McKinley residence and the streets adjacent were packed with people when the Governor alighted from his carriage and walked briskly toward the house. Then a tremendous cheer burst forth from the assembled multitude. President McKinley was standing on the porch waiting with outstretched hands to greet his associate on the National ticket. The assemblage was clamorous for speeches, and when something like quiet was restored the President introduced Gov. Roosevelt in the following words:

"I cannot express the pleasure it has given me to see the generous welcome my fellow-citizens have given to Gov. Roosevelt, and I now have the pleasure of presenting him to you."

"My fellow-citizens," said the Governor, "I thank you most cordially for the way you have come forward to greet me. I know that none of you, least of all my old comrades here, will grudge my saying that I thank particularly those who wear the buttons that show they fought in the late war.

"I cannot say how I appreciate this reception, coming as it does from the townsmen of the President, who is now in a peculiar sense my leader, and whom I shall follow and support with every ounce of strength that there is in me. And, at least there is to be said for our side that we know what we believe. In Kansas City they have had a little difficulty in finding out what they believe. I see by the papers that they had some difficulty, extending finally to a vote of 27 to 25 in putting in free silver.

"Now, we believe with our faith in a dollar worth a hundred cents. Apparently, they have 52 per cent. of faith in a forty-eight-cent dollar. I do not intend to do more this afternoon than again thank you most cordially and to say that I appreciate what this greeting means, coming, as it does, from the home of the President. I shall try to show myself not wholly unworthy of the way in which you have met me this afternoon."

The President and Governor then retired into the house, but the crowd was not satisfied. The demand for McKinley was so persistent that at length the President stepped out again upon the porch. A great cheer went up, which he silenced with a wave of his hand.

"I only appear," said the President, "that I may say to you that I am going to be with you most of the Summer." Cheers and laughter followed this remark of the President, and the crowd soon afterward broke up. At dinner the only guests at the McKinley residence besides the regular household were Gov. Roosevelt and Judge and Mrs. Day.

President McKinley and Gov. Roosevelt were in conference most of the evening, but nothing could be learned as to the matters discussed. The Governor left for New York at 10:50 o'clock. "I am going direct to Oyster Bay to-morrow afternoon," he said, "and we are going to have some fireworks—a sort of belated Fourth of July for the children."

Gov. Roosevelt refused to discuss the Kansas City platform or the candidates.

ROOSEVELT SEES HANNA.

CLEVELAND, Ohio, July 6.—Gov. Roosevelt spent eight hours in Cleveland to-day. The most part of the Governor's stay was taken up by a consultation with Senator Hanna. Just before leaving for Canton Gov. Roosevelt said:

"I have been conferring with the Senator about the itinerary that we shall follow out this Fall. It has been determined that if possible I shall visit all the Rocky Mountain States."

## ROBERTS REPORTS FIGHTING.

LONDON, July 7.—Gen. Paget is moving toward the heart of the country held by De Wet.

Lord Roberts telegraphed to the War Office, under date of Pretoria, July 6, 2:25 P. M., as follows:

"Paget engaged the enemy on July 3 successfully at Pleisirfontein. He drove them out of a very strong position across Leeuwkop to Bronerifontein, where he bivouacked for the night. He followed up the enemy, and on the afternoon of July 4 was at Blaauwkopje, fifteen miles northwest of Bethlehem.

"He reports that all of Steyn's Government officials, except the Treasurer General, who has gone to Vrede, are at Bethlehem, which has been proclaimed the capital. Stein himself is reported to have taken flight to the mountains.

"Buller reports the line to Heidelberg restored, thus completing railway communication between Pretoria and Natal."

Lorenzo Marques on Friday learned that the Boers were showing fresh activity. A British force is reported within forty miles of Koomatipoort.

## LOUISIANA CIVIL SERVICE.

*Special to The New York Times.*

NEW ORLEANS, July 6.—Civil service in New Orleans was annihilated by the Louisiana Legislature to-day, when the lower house passed favorably on the Senate civil service "modifier," which throws the bars down again to the spoilsman and boodler, by whom New Orleans has suffered so heavily in the past.

In explaining his vote, Mr. Vincent of Calcasieu Parish said that he had changed from an anti-civil service to a civil service adherent because "the shield of civil service reform must be thrown around the drainage fund of the city and around the City of New Orleans in order to protect them from the political rapacity of men who in this chamber have exhibited so little consideration for the rights of the people."

The fund referred to is the money to be derived from the sale of $14,000,000 of bonds soon to be sold for municipal improvement in New Orleans.



# ADLAI E. STEVENSON FOR VICE PRESIDENT

## The Illinois Candidate Nominated on the First Ballot.

## MR. HILL REFUSES THE HONOR

### Takes the Platform to Stop Movement Started by Tammany.

### After His Refusal 200 Votes Were Cast for Him—Four Other Candidates Presented—J. Hamilton Lewis Withdraws.

*Special to The New York Times.*

KANSAS CITY, July 6.—Bryan and Stevenson is the Democratic ticket for 1900. The nominations were completed this afternoon, on the third day of the convention, after some exciting and remarkable scenes.

Stevenson, Towne, and four other candidates were formally presented, Stevenson's name being received with many marks of approval, while the greeting accorded to Towne was confined to the audience, the delegates in large part remaining passive.

When Thomas F. Grady presented the name of David B. Hill the ovation extended to Hill was prodigious. Mr. Hill indignantly protested against his own nomination in a speech, and declared that he would not take it if offered, for personal and valid reasons.

The New York delegation could not force the nomination of Hill, which was to be had by him if he had kept silent, partly owing to the refusal of Hill to accept the honor, and somewhat to the active work of the friends of Bryan, who sent messages to the friends of Towne in the convention to vote for Stevenson to defeat Hill.

Stevenson was nominated on the first ballot, and almost on the first roll call. The votes cast for other candidates were transferred to Stevenson before the result of the first ballot was announced, Stevenson's nomination being made unanimous.

The Silver Republicans are grievously chagrined at the failure to indorse Towne. They say that Stevenson's nomination will cost the Democratic ticket 400,000 votes in the Northwest next November, and the loss of every silver State except in the South. Hartmann of Montana says that it will be impossible in his State to support Stevenson, for the reason that the convention that named him seated the Clark delegation, representing the wrong side of a moral issue.

The Free Silver Republicans will finish their own ticket through their National Committee, as the convention had adjourned without completing its business.

The Democrats do not look upon their ticket with an excess of confidence. They went away from the convention disappointed at not hearing W. J. Bryan, whose appearance had been promised by some of his intimate friends. Mr. Bryan changed his mind about coming at a late hour last night or early this morning.

Kansas City to-night has resumed almost its normal condition. The crowds have disappeared from the streets, only a few tardy brass bands are heard as they go to the station, and the town folk rest from a week of very hospitable entertainment of its visitors. The weather, which has not been as hot as that reported from other parts of the country, has become comfortably cool.

## A DAY OF MANY SPEECHES.

### Delegates Have Much to Say About the Candidates for the Vice Presidential Nomination.

KANSAS CITY, July 6.—At 10:45 o'clock Chairman Richardson advanced to the front of the platform, a great bouquet of sweet peas in his hand, and with a sweep of the gavel cut off the strains of the band, slowly stilled the confusion, and brought the convention to order for its third day's work. But it was some minutes before there was sufficient quiet for the opening invocation, and then the great audience arose while Rabbi Harry H. Mayer of Kansas City delivered a prayer breathing the sense of responsibility resting upon the convention. He said, in part:

O, our Heavenly Father, Father, too, of all mankind, Thou who art nigh unto all who call upon Thee in truth, we invoke Thy name to-day with the thrill of stirring scenes and strong emotions upon us that we may profess before Thee the conviction of our hearts that unless Thou art with us we labor in vain. We thank Thee for the many worthy men Thou hast raised in leadership over us. Bless them and all those who labor for the establishment of wise government and just laws.

Make us to rejoice not so much in the largeness of our domain as in the spread of truth and justice. Make us to perceive more and more clearly our duties toward those who stretch forth unto us their helpless hands in piteous appeal for that succor which we as common children of Thee, our Father, dare not deny them. May we be free from bitterness and bigotry toward those who hold opinions that clash with ours.

Thou, O Lord, hast lifted up an ensign to the nations from afar and hast called for one of them from the end of the earth. May it come with speed, swiftly, not to blight but to bless, that the partition walls of party affiliation and racial affinities dividing men against themselves may be leveled and Thy spirit of kindness rule everywhere and always.

Oh, may there be none weary nor stumbling among its men. We ask it for the sake of Thy name. Amen.

CALL OF THE STATES.

Immediately following the prayer the call of States began for the purpose of making nominations for the Vice Presidency. Great confusion prevailed, and very few of the delegates were aware of what was going on until Alabama and Arkansas had been passed, and California was called.

Then Senator White emerged from the California division, and in stentorian tones he demanded to know what was going on, and that the aisles be cleared of the disorderly intruders. When the Chairman responded that California was being called for nominations, Senator White announced that California yielded to Arkansas.

"And Arkansas yields to Illinois, to place in nomination Adlai Stevenson of Illinois," shouted Jeff Davis, the Democratic candidate for Governor of Arkansas, standing on a chair and receiving a cheer for his mention of Stevenson.

Now all business was suspended, as the confusion had become so overpowering that the call of the Secretary was inaudible above the roar. The police and the Sergeant at Arms struggled vainly to dispossess the mob, which was now well-nigh in control of the floor. Men fought to retain their places, and there were many exciting encounters, which at times threatened to precipitate a fight under the eyes of the multitude.

STEVENSON'S NAME PRESENTED.

It took fifteen minutes to restore some semblance of order, and then the spokesman for Illinois, Representative James Williams, presented the name of Stevenson. He spoke as follows:

Illinois is grateful to Arkansas for this evidence of her regard. The united Democracy of Illinois desires to present to this convention for the next Vice President of the United States a Democrat—one who drew his first breath from the pure, Democratic atmosphere of old Kentucky, [cheers;] one baptized in the great and growing Democracy of Illinois; one who has stood squarely on every Democratic platform since he became a voter; one who has twice represented in Congress a district overwhelmingly Republican; one who is not a rough rider, but a swift rider, [cheers;] not a warrior, but a statesman.

A man who stands for civil government against military rule; a man who believes that a President of the United States who ignores the Constitution, as the present President has done, must be one who loves his own glory far more than he loves the Republic; a man who believes American despotism is no better than any other despotism; a man who places human blood above human greed; a man who will not trade away the precious life of an American soldier for a nugget of gold in the Philippine Islands, [cheers;] a man who would not give the 3,000 or 3,500 brave American soldiers whom McKinley has sacrificed in that hotbed of disease and destruction for all the islands in the seas. [Applause.]

A man who, during four years of faithful administration as First Assistant Postmaster General of the United States, demonstrated that he knows a Republican when he sees him in an office that belongs to a Democrat. [Applause.] Nominate our man and you will not have to explain any speech made against Democracy, for he has never made that kind. [Applause.] A man in the full strength of his manhood, able to canvass any State in this Union.

Gentlemen of the convention, Illinois makes no exaggeration when she tells you that in that great State the conditions are far better, the prospects are much brighter for Democracy than in 1892, when our candidate for Vice President carried it by 30,000 majority. [Applause.] We have a State ticket stronger than we ever had before. We have but one Democracy in Illinois.

We voice the sincere sentiment of the Democracy of Illinois when we ask you to nominate a man whose name we will present; a man who has been tried, gone through the contest, and developed no weak spots found in his armor; a man whose high character and ability recommend him to the people in every part of this Republic; a man who possesses all the noble attributes of a nobleman, great enough and good enough to be President of the United States, with a platform that reads like a Bible, and with these two faithful Democrats standing together, shoulder to shoulder, we can sweep criminal aggression and McKinley hypocrisy off the face of the earth.

Gentlemen, we now present to you as the choice of our State that distinguished statesman, that splendid, vigorous, reliable Democrat, ex-Vice President Adlai E. Stevenson of Illinois.

Mr. Williams spoke rapidly and briefly, and at his mention of Adlai E. Stevenson Illinois was on its feet cheering wildly. Kansas was up, as was Alabama, Arkansas, Minnesota, and a large number of delegates in different parts of the hall. The applause, while vigorous, was short, not lasting above a minute.

MINNESOTA PRESENTS TOWNE.

When the roll call reached Connecticut that State gave way to Minnesota amid cheers and cries of "Towne." T. A. Rosing of Minnesota then took the platform to present the name of Charles A. Towne. His speech in part was as follows:

The Democracy of the North Star State has a candidate for the nomination of Vice President to submit to the right judgment of this convention. We come to you to present the name of a man worthy of the high honor of being placed upon the same ticket with the splendid champion of equal rights whom you have nominated for President.

The veterans of the campaigns of 1896 and 1898 now stand shoulder to shoulder, determined that this year the Electoral vote of Minnesota shall be cast for the nominees of this convention. This condition was made possible because of the brilliancy, courage, and fidelity to principle of the men who in the memorable campaign of '96 patriotically put country above party and severed their relations with the Republican Party, casting aside personal ambition, prejudices, and self-interest.

The man of this type, who, perhaps, sacrificed more than any one else, who more than any other was called upon to lay upon the sacrificial altar a brilliant future, filled with promise enough to satisfy vaulting ambition, who had the courage to sever the ties of personal friendship that he might be true to his ideas of Americanism, is the man whom Minnesota to-day proposes to this convention as its candidate for Vice President.

We ask your support of him because he is a Democrat of Jeffersonian principles; a Democrat of the stern school of Andrew Jackson; a Democrat of the broad philosophy and humanity of Abraham Lincoln; a Democrat defending the flag of the Union, and in believing that to whatever land that flag be carried there the people over whom it floats are under the protection of the Constitution.

We present him to you not because he is rich in this world's goods; not because his nomination would mean contributions, but because a beneficent God has endowed him with an eloquent tongue, a brilliant mind, a splendid courage, a big heart, and all the qualities of American manhood. We ask your support for Minnesota's able statesman, orator, and patriot, whom I have the honor to place in formal nomination as the unanimous choice of the Minnesota Democracy, a leader of the people, Charles A. Towne.

LITTLE ENTHUSIASM FOR TOWNE.

Mr. Rosing is a tall, powerful man with a voice befitting his stalwart frame. He could be heard in every direction. His first applause was gained when he spoke of Mr. Towne as a man who embodied the best characteristics of American manhood. When he pronounced the name of Towne there was cheering from the Minnesota delegation, which rose to its feet, waving flags in frantic fashion. The galleries joined in the applause with fervor, but there was less enthusiasm among the men on the floor who had the votes.

A stout woman in the northwest corner of the first gallery climbed upon a chair, holding in her left hand a colored lithograph of Bryan and Towne, while with her right she waved a handkerchief vigorously. Congressman Shafroth of Colorado, a zealous supporter of the candidacy of Towne, climbed into the gallery in an effort to get the woman forward to the platform, but she declined to come.

By degrees the enthusiasm spread throughout the delegations, and in a short time men were up in the States of Washington, Wyoming, Montana, and South Dakota, but their number was much less than that which had risen to the name of Stevenson.

NEW YORK PRESENTS HILL.

While the galleries were enthusing over Towne there was an excited little group about the chair of ex-Senator Hill. In it was Croker.

"You must take the nomination and save the day," said Edward Murphy, excitedly.

"I cannot, I cannot," replied Hill, his face white and set. "I do not want it."

"You must take it," said Croker.

Croker leaned over him, while Norman E. Mack and Frank Campbell held Hill, one on each side, and urged him to accept. An excited man from New Jersey, shaking his fingers under Mr. Hill's nose, shouted: "You can't refuse; you can't. The party must have you to save the East."

"I don't want it. You can name Stevenson. He's as good as I am," said Hill, and then turning to Murphy and Croker and gripping his hands he said: "Please don't force this; please don't."

Mr. Murphy then gave an indication of a prearranged scheme to nominate by saying to the excited Jerseyman: "You keep quiet and it will be all right. We have it fixed."

When the State of Delaware was called the announcement was made that the State would yield to New York. Then the result of the Hill conference was apparent.

A tremendous shout of applause swept through the hall. Delegate Grady, one of the leaders of Tammany Hall, had already ascended the platform, and as he stepped to the front to address the convention the applause and cheering increased.

His first sentence rang through the great building in trumpet tones:

"On behalf of the Democracy of New York I present to the convention for the nomination of Vice President the name of David Bennett Hill."

A TEMPESTUOUS SCENE.

It was dramatic in the extreme. The effect was electrical. His words set the convention in a frenzy of enthusiasm. The scene which followed was by far the most tempestuous of the session, and the name of Hill echoed and re-echoed through the hall. State standards were seized and held aloft, and the convention was canopied with fluttering flags and handkerchiefs. Delegates and spectators cheered, and the great structure fairly shook with the noise, when the galleries became infected with enthusiasm.

Mr. Hill, meantime, has worked his way through the surging multitude to the platform. As he ascended it his hands were eagerly grasped, and he was escorted to the seat of the permanent Chairman. He asked Mr. Grady to yield to him that he might make a statement, but Grady declined.

Judge Van Wyck of the New York delegation hurried to Mr. Hill and began an earnest conversation with him, urging him not to decline the nomination, which evidently seemed to be within his grasp. Hill only shook his head. It was a pretty, even a dramatic, sideplay. All the convention was pulsating with enthusiasm and cheers.

Finally Mr. Grady was permitted to proceed, and said Hill might decline, but decline or not, he shouted, New York's united

"All the News That's Fit to Print."

# The New York Times.

THE WEATHER. Fair and cooler; winds fresh, becoming northwesterly.

COPYRIGHT, 1900, BY THE NEW YORK TIMES COMPANY.

VOL. XLIX...NO. 15,816. NEW YORK, MONDAY, SEPTEMBER 17, 1900.—Twelve Pages and Supplement. ONE CENT In Greater New York and Jersey City. Elsewhere, TWO CENTS.

## MINERS PASS A QUIET DAY

### No Disorder in the Coal District, but Many Mass Meetings.

### MINES TO BE OPENED AS USUAL

**Operators, However, Do Not Expect Men to Report—A Final Effort for Arbitration.**

PHILADELPHIA, Sept. 16.—That the strike of the mine workers in the anthracite coal regions of Pennsylvania, which President Mitchell of the United Mine Workers of America has officially ordered to begin to-morrow morning, will be one of considerable magnitude seems certain to-night from reports received from the regions affected. It seems equally certain that a number of operators will make an effort to run their collieries, even though they may be shorthanded, but whether they will be successful only can be determined when the breaker whistles sound the call to work. The operators generally will have their collieries in condition to begin operations, and the whistles will blow as usual, but a large number of the employers admit that there is but little hope of being able to start.

To-day was one of quiet throughout the entire coal district. The mine workers were orderly, and their leaders were busy addressing meetings to encourage and enthuse the members of the union and to win over such of the non-union men as they could. Many of these latter, although not favoring a strike, will, it is the general opinion, remain away from the mines rather than bear the criticism and reproaches of their fellow-workmen.

An effort is being made to-night to have Archbishop Ryan of Philadelphia act as arbitrator. Father Phillips of Hazleton, who has been laboring hard to effect a peaceful settlement of the labor troubles, was in conference at a late hour with President Mitchell of the United Mine Workers, urging him to delay the strike until Archbishop Ryan shall have exhausted his efforts.

### EFFORT TO ARBITRATE.

**President Mitchell to be Asked to Withdraw and Allow Archbishop Ryan to Act for the Men.**

HAZLETON, Penn., Sept. 16.—A last desperate attempt is being made to-night to bring about peace between the coal operators and their men. Father Phillips, who has worked hard for a settlement of the differences between the employers and the mine workers, has again entered the field, with the proposition that Archbishop Ryan of Philadelphia be accepted as arbitrator. Father Phillips held a conference with President Mitchell of the United Mine Workers to-night and asked that the organization he represents stand aside and allow Archbishop Ryan to approach the operators on behalf of the men and the public generally. To-day Father Phillips sent to the prelate the following telegram:

To the Most Rev. P. J. Ryan, D. D., Bishop of Philadelphia—I thank you for offer of assistance and sentiments expressed in to-day's papers. I had retired from the field, believing that all my resources had been exhausted, but now, encouraged by you, will resume efforts. Will see Mitchell to-night on his arrival, and suggest further appeal by miners to operators through you as mediator, acting for the public in general. This telegram made public will also suggest to operators a way out of the difficulties that will not include any direct recognition of the union, the chief obstacle to settlement. Even this step may fail, but the situation now desperate demands prompt action on our part. Will advise you to-morrow of progress.

E. S. PHILLIPS.

At 10:30 o'clock to-night Father Phillips held a secret conference with President Mitchell and National Committeeman Benjamin James, at which Father Phillips laid before them his latest proposition to have Archbishop Ryan act as arbitrator. After the conference Mr. James stated that President Mitchell would issue a statement on the matter. Shortly after midnight Mr. Mitchell left the conference room and informed the waiting reporters that he would issue no statement, and that he would not discuss the subject to-night. He might have something to say to-morrow. Mr. James to-night wired the three district Presidents that engineers, firemen, and pump runners can continue at work, but that all others must strike until a conference is called.

### MARKLE MEN WILL STRIKE.

HAZLETON, Sept. 16.—Officials of the United Mine Workers' Union to-night brought all their resources to bear upon the Markle men at Jeddo, Highland, Oakdale, and Elbervale to obey the strike order. The union leaders want them to strike to-morrow, and a big meeting was held at Jeddo for the purpose of inducing them to do so.

President Mitchell went to Jeddo to address the meeting. He called on the Markle men to reconsider their action and said if they failed to respond to the call to strike it would work great injury to the cause of the men. After he had concluded, a viva voce vote was taken, which resulted in the Markle miners deciding to strike.

On his return from Jeddo President Mitchell said he was satisfied with the situation. He had reports from the three anthracite districts, which, he said, indicate that 125,000 men will not start to work to-morrow. He said the First and Ninth Districts would be tied up tight, while the Seventh will be almost so.

Earlier in the day Father Phillips called on John Markle, at Jeddo, the manager of G. B. Markle & Co., who control the Jeddo, Highland, Oakdale, and Elberdale collieries, employing about 2,500 men, for a conference regarding his arbitration proposition. General Superintendent Smith and Alvin Markle, a partner, were present. John Markle, whose firm has an agreement with its men to settle all differences by arbitration, accepted the proposition of Father Phillips. The firm is willing to accept Archbishop Ryan as a third party.

Father Phillips stated to-night that he thought G. B. Markle & Co. could offer no fairer proposition to their men than arbitration, and said their proposal was just. He added that if all the other operators followed this example and submitted their case to arbitration, the whole labor trouble would be settled next week or maybe within three days.

This firm in its agreement with its men stipulates that no differences shall be settled through the medium of labor leaders or labor organizations, so the acceptance of Archbishop Ryan, in accordance with the proposition of Father Phillips, on the part of the mine workers would leave the labor leaders out entirely and place the whole matter in the hands of the operators and their men, involving no recognition of the union.

John Markle said to-night: "Our men will work to-morrow, and every colliery of this firm will be in operation. So the whole situation is up to the mine workers, whether they are in favor of arbitration or want to strike."

Officials of the United Mine Workers' Union to-night brought all their resources to bear upon the Markle men at Jeddo, Highland, Oakdale, and Ebervale to obey the strike order. The union leaders want them to strike to-morrow, and a big meeting was held at Jeddo for the purpose of inducing them to strike.

### MITCHELL AT HAZLETON.

HAZLETON, Penn., Sept. 16.—With the exception of President Mitchell's arrival, there was little evidence shown here to-day that Hazleton was the storm centre of the present coal war between labor and capital. Nothing occurred to disturb the serenity of the Sabbath. Quite a large number of miners came to town, but soon left when they found that there was no news. With the exception of the engineers, firemen, pump runners, and repair men, no one was around any of the mines in this vicinity.

Public meetings of miners were held during the day at Harley, Ebervale and Freeland, on the north side; Shepton and Harwood on the west side, and at Coleraine, south of here. The largest gathering was that at Freeland, twelve miles north, where the union men are not so strong as the organizers would like to have them. This meeting was held in the open air and was addressed by National Committeeman Benjamin James and a number of other labor leaders well known in these regions. There were 2,000 persons in the crowd. When Mr. James asked all those to raise their hands who were against a strike, not an arm went up. All the meetings were held for the purpose of encouraging the men to stand firm in the present conflict, and also to strengthen the union by recruiting new members.

All sorts of guesses are still being made as to the number of men who will remain from work to-morrow morning. The foreign-speaking miners are in the majority in the Hazleton district, and most of them are not in favor of the strike. The English-speaking workmen, who are in favor of striking, are not so numerous. It seems to those who are in close touch with the situation that all depends on the foreigners. If they conclude to stay away from their work, the mines will be so crippled that operations will have to cease. The territory south of Hazleton is well organized, and there is some apprehension here to-night that disturbances might occur among the foreigners in that locality. Some of them have made threats of bodily harm against any one who starts work in the morning. The United Mine Workers' officials are doing their best to prevent any outbreaks.

Mr. James to-night authorized a denial of a story telegraphed from here that the Italians at Bunker Hill, seven miles south of here, are manufacturing "bomb balls" for use in case trouble with the police should arise. He also denied the printed statement that committees had been sent to Altoona, Penn., and other places in the bituminous coal fields of this State for the purpose of agitating a sympathetic strike. Mr. James said that no such move is contemplated, and no steps will be taken in that direction while the anthracite strike is on, unless the bituminous fuel is sent into the hard coal regions. In that event President Mitchell would call out the soft coal miners within forty-eight hours.

Contrary to expectations, only three or four clergymen in the Lehigh Valley preached on the labor troubles, and only one, the Rev. Carl Houses, took a decided stand against the strike. He is the preacher of three Lithuanian churches, one at Eckley, another at Harwood, and the third at Freeland. He preached in all three to-day, and pleaded with his people to go to work to-morrow.

### WYOMING VALLEY MEETINGS.

WILKESBARRE, Penn., Sept. 16.—The United Mine Workers spent the Sabbath in strengthening their lines where they were weak. Organizer James came up from Hazleton and addressed a large mass meeting at Hudson, a mining town five miles north of this city. In the course of his address Mr. James was loudly applauded. There were many women in the audience, and they seemed to be as enthusiastic as the men. At Plains, Organizer Nicholls addressed a large meeting. He, too, aroused much enthusiasm.

In one of the suburbs of this city a big meeting of union and non-union men was held. A man named Edwards was the first speaker. He advised the men that if they knew their best interests they would go to work to-morrow. This remark caused the union men to leave the meeting. After Edwards had concluded several other speakers addressed the meeting. The upshot of it was that the meeting resolved itself into a union gathering, and a resolution was adopted requesting all men to keep away from the mines to-morrow. Meetings were also held in many other places in the county, and all were largely attended.

The coal companies will attempt to keep some of the mines going. All the men that can possibly be secured will be sent to one mine, it is immaterial which colliery, and in this way it is hoped to be able to mine some coal and make a showing. The operators realize that the quickest way to break the strike is to show the strikers that some mines are in operation. But no operator or miner can make a prediction as to what is to come to-morrow. There may be surprises in store for both sides.

Vice Grand Master Fitzpatrick of the Brotherhood of Railway Trainmen addressed a secret meeting of railroaders at Parsons this afternoon. After the address a lodge of trainmen was organized. Mr. Fitzpatrick will organize other lodges in the district in the next few days. The leaders of the Miners' Union are confident that if the coal-carrying roads attempt to carry bituminous coal into the anthracite region during the strike the railroaders will stand by them.

### LACKAWANNA DISTRICT QUIET.

SCRANTON, Penn., Sept. 16.—To-day was devoid of any excitement in connection with the strike. At the Mine Workers' headquarters Organizer Dilcher sat during the greater part of the day chatting with the other officers. As far as could be learned the mine officials were absolutely idle. One prominent mine Superintendent who has charge of half a dozen collieries frankly said that he had an interview with his foremen Saturday night and from what they reported he was thoroughly satisfied that not one of his 3,500 men would offer to go to work to-morrow.

Superintendent E. E. Loomis of the Delaware, Lackawanna and Western and Superintendent C. C. Rose of the Delaware and Hudson Mining Departments, held similar views as to the possibilities of to-morrow. Each was confident, however, that a great many of the men want to go to work and that it is even possible a goodly number of them will be on hand at each colliery. Every colliery of the two companies will be started up and as many men as present themselves will be put to work. The officers of the Mine Workers' Union say there will not be a mine in the whole Lackawanna region that will have enough men on hand to-morrow to make even a pretense of operating.

Organizer Dilcher said to-night that there will be no pickets posted to dissuade men from going to work. They will be altogether unnecessary, he said, for the reason that there will be no men going to work. The union officers, Mr. Dilcher says, have not only advised, but practically commanded the men to keep away from the companies' properties altogether.

Scranton dealers have had their store of small firearms completely exhausted by the demands of the past few days from the small storekeepers up and down the valley. The larger-sized expensive revolvers are almost exclusively specified in the order, and from this is gathered that it is not the miners, but the bosses and company clerks, storekeepers and the like, who are doing the buying.

A mass meeting of miners was held at Throop this afternoon. It was attended by 3,000 men, and was addressed by Organizer Fred Dilcher. He assured the men that they had the strike as good as won, and that all they had to do now was to keep away from the companies' properties, discuss their grievances in their halls, and not on the street, and avoid the saloons.

It looks to-night as if the Lackawanna region would be completely tied up to-morrow, and that not a single colliery would be operated. No trouble is likely to occur. The men seem to have great reliance on the judgment of the officers, and will obey the order to keep away from the companies' properties.

### SITUATION AT SHAMOKIN.

SHAMOKIN, Penn., Sept. 16.—At 7:30 o'clock this evening the United Mine Workers' leaders said that from reports at hand from Dauphin, Columbia, Schuylkill, and Northumberland Counties, indications pointed to at least 50 per cent. of the men, principally between here and Centralia, going on strike to-morrow, in which event the collieries cannot be operated. Before the close of the week the United Mine Workers expect to have most of the operations in the district at a standstill. The leaders say the operators and coal companies underrate the strength of the union.

The officials of the Philadelphia and Reading Coal and Iron Company in this district announced this evening that when the colliery whistles are blown to-morrow 60 per cent. of the employes will be at the mines. The officials also stated that if men staid away from the mine in sufficient numbers to compel the Henry Clay shaft to shut down, the mules will be hoisted, after which the colliery will be abandoned.

The United Mine Workers assert that the company will not permit the shaft to be flooded.

Everything was quiet at the collieries between Treverton, this place, and Centralia to-day. No miners were at work, and no one was in the mines excepting the pumpmen and fire bosses. A mass meeting was held here this afternoon, which was attended by between 4,000 and 5,000 miners. They were very enthusiastic over speeches by Samuel Gompers, President of the National Federation of Labor, and John Fahy, President of the Ninth Anthracite District. Mr. Fahy advised the men to stay away from the mines and not indulge in intoxicating drinks and to avoid quarrels which would tend to injure the cause of the miners. President Gompers informed his hearers that by reason of their great patience in seeking to induce operators and coal carrying companies to grant them a conference, and by the operators refusing to meet them, the sympathy of the American public was with the men.

**PENNSYLVANIA RAILROAD'S MINES.**

HARRISBURG, Penn., Sept. 16.—The miners in the Lykens region are divided on the strike question, and it is expected that at least half of them will go to work to-morrow. A meeting of the union men at Lykens was held this afternoon, at which it was decided not to work, but it is thought enough will stand by the company to operate the mine.

Reports from Wiconisco are that the men there will obey the strike order as long as there is any hope of a compromise with the operators. A secret session of the Lykens and Wiconisco miners was held to-night at Lykens to invite the mine employes at Williamstown to join the strike. The men there do not belong to the union and are opposed to a strike because of the refusal of the miners at Lykens and Wiconisco to support them in the strike of 1886.

The collieries in the Lykens region are controlled by the Pennsylvania Railroad and employ in the aggregate about 2,300 men and boys, 1,200 of whom live at Lykens.

**No Trouble Expected in Schuylkill.**

POTTSVILLE, Penn., Sept. 16.—The strike situation remains very quiet in Schuylkill County. Only the Lehigh Company's collieries at Mahanoy City and Lost Creek will be affected by the strike order in the Schuylkill district.

**SYMPATHY OF UNIONS HERE.**

The Central Labor Union, at its meeting yesterday in Central Hall, 147 West Thirty-second Street, took up the question of the strike of the coal miners in the anthracite regions. It was held that, though the trouble was not a local one, the principle involved made it the business of every member of a labor organization. Delegate Farrell of the National Association of Steam Fitters and Helpers, who brought the matter up, said:

"The grievances of the strikers ought to have the sympathy of every true Knight of Labor. They never know what the use of money is; they have to buy everything in the company's stores, and have checks on the stores to represent their wages."

Farrell went on to say that the child labor at the mines ought to be abolished. It was against the sentiment of every working man and woman.

On the motion of Delegate Farrell a resolution was then passed to extend the sympathy of the Central Labor Union to the miners, and to assure them of any support it was able to give, financially or otherwise.

Delegate Wilson of the Safety Engineers' Union brought the subject up at yesterday's meeting of the Central Federated Union. He said he had been informed on good authority that the first batch of immigrants to replace the strikers had been sent to the coal regions on Saturday by the Delaware, Lackawanna and Western Railroad. They were bound for Scranton and other towns in the mining district, he said, and were mostly Slavs and Italians. A committee was appointed the see the immigration authorities about this complaint to-day.

### FATHER DUCEY ON THE STRIKE.

Father Ducey, in his sermon at St. Leo's Roman Catholic Church yesterday morning, fiercely criticised the action of the coal-mine owners in Pennsylvania. The great monied interests, he declared, are quickly converting this country, which used to be "the land of the free and the home of the brave," into a "land of the rich and a home of the slave."

"Men sit from Sunday to Sunday in fashionable churches listening to essays which leave their consciences practically untouched," said he. "This with them is religion, but as for exercising such virtues as religion demands—the chief of which is charity and love to your fellowmen—you can count on your finger ends the men who give these serious thought.

"I know men who sit in the chief places of the churches right under the pulpits, and their hands are as red with the blood of their fellow-men as were those of Cain. And these men will go out and find fault with their fellow men for trying to protect themselves and put up a fight for the right of gaining a livelihood for themselves and their families.

"We need only to look at the struggle now beginning in the Pennsylvania coal regions. It is the greatest crime of modern society which compels children of only eight years of age to work for 35 cents a day in these dark mines. Their education is entirely neglected until their intellect becomes as clouded as their faces. And all this in order that their taskmasters may live lives of luxury and refined ease.

"A few days ago I read in the morning papers that the operators had threatened to flood the mines should their oppressed slaves dare to lay down their picks. These mines have to be pumped every day, and to flood them would mean they would be rendered useless for all time. It would be a crime and a calamity as great as the pumping out of the ocean.

"I am glad that a Catholic Bishop of Pennsylvania has insisted that justice must be done to these men and their claims be settled by arbitration. But what do the wealthy mine owners say? When the priest from Pennsylvania came down to New York last week to discuss the matter with them the answer he received was that they had a perfect right to manage their own property as they saw fit. This is a lie. No man has a right to use the gifts of God according to his own pleasure or for satisfying his desires for luxury or his sensuality.

"And any man who raises his voice against these wrongs will be proclaimed a demagogue. Jesus Christ in his day was called a demagogue and an impostor because he was the friend of sinners and consorted with the common people. But the Anarchists are not the men who protest. The real Anarchists in this case are the mine owners—the men of this class constitute the greatest danger to modern society."

## KRUEGER ALLOWED TO SAIL

### Portuguese Government Will Permit Him to Leave for Europe.

**Holland Offers a Warship to Convey Him to That Country—Mrs. Krueger Joins Her Husband.**

LISBON, Sept. 16.—The Portuguese Government has telegraphed to the Governor of Mozambique authorizing the departure of Mr. Krüger for Europe. The Governor, however, must satisfy himself that Mr. Krüger is really going to Europe.

Meanwhile he is instructed to take all precautions to safeguard his personal security.

The newspapers here say that Mr. Krüger will take the German steamer Herzog at Lorenzo Marques, his destination being Holland by way of Marseilles.

THE HAGUE, Sept. 16.—The Government of the Netherlands has telegraphed to Lorenzo Marques offering a Dutch warship to bring Mr. Krüger to Holland.

LONDON, Sept. 17.—Mrs. Krüger, according to a dispatch to The Daily Express, has arrived in Lorenzo Marques.

**NETHERLANDS RAILWAY SEIZED.**

**MacDonald Routs Boers and Captures Wagons and Ammunition.**

CAPE TOWN, Sept. 16.—The military authorities have taken over the Netherlands Railway.

Gen. MacDonald, operating in the northeastern corner of Orange Colony, compelled the Boers to make a hasty flight from the Vet River. He captured thirty-one wagons, a quantity of cattle, and stores and 65,000 rounds of rifle ammunition.

### FEMALE FAGIN IN NEW YORK.

**Child Found Picking Pockets in Washington Tells Remarkable Story.**

*Special to The New York Times.*

WASHINGTON, Sept. 16.—A female Fagin keeps a school of pickpockets in a street near the Bowery, New York, and is turning out graduates in crime, some of whom are turned loose on other cities. This is the story told by little Rebecca Rosenberg, a pretty Jewish child of fourteen years, with sparkling eyes and short, curly hair, who plied the pickpocket trade like an expert in the markets of Washington until she was caught.

Complaints of pocket picking have been coming in from customers at the markets in Pennsylvania Avenue. One of the victims, Miss Nora Callahan, remembered that a little girl of striking appearance, whom she described, had been among those near her at the time. She did not suspect her of the crime, but when asked to describe the people near her she remembered that the beauty of this child had attracted her attention.

Detectives were put on the case, and yesterday afternoon they found a little girl, whom they recognized from the description, in the markets. They watched her until they caught her in the act of picking Miss Annie Wright's pocket, and then placed her under arrest.

The child said that her father, Max Rosenberg, a shoemaker, had a small shop on Norfolk Street, New York City. The number was in the neighborhood of 2[illegible], but she cannot remember exactly what it is. There she became acquainted with a bigger girl named Annie Russell. Two weeks before last Labor Day, Annie took Rebecca to a tenement building near the Bowery, in the basement of which a woman was instructing children in thieving. A pair of scissors was given to her and she was taught how to cut the straps by which women's pocketbooks are hung from their arms, until after a week or two she had become an expert.

On Labor Day Annie Russell took Rebecca out on her first pocketpicking expedition, which proved an unqualified success. She always gave the purses to Annie, who paid her $2 for a day's work. This didn't last long, for a few days afterward Rebecca's family moved to Germantown, Penn. She determined to run away and go to Washington, there to resume pocketpicking on her own account.

There is no 200 Norfolk Street, the numbers on that thoroughfare only running as high as 188. Inquiry in the vicinity of the northern terminus of the street last night failed to discover any trace of a shoemaker named Max Rosenberg or of a family named Russell.

### CARS RUNNING IN HACKENSACK.

**Company Must Fight for Strip of Land to Complete the Line.**

HACKENSACK, N. J., Sept. 16.—After years of effort and many failures of companies to enter the town, the cars of the Newark and Hackensack trolley line are at last running into Hackensack.

The final work began on Friday night, when the company evaded a restraining order forbidding it to erect poles on the Gott farm, near Hasbrouck Heights, by erecting a high pole on either side of the property and then stringing a feed wire. A trolley car was then dragged beyond the Gott farm and the work of getting the tracks into Hackensack was begun. It was finished to-day, and the car is now running from Hackensack to the Gott farm. There there is a break of 500 feet, but beyond that the cars are now running.

The possession of the strip of 500 feet is now to be fought out in the courts. President Giles of the Newark and Hackensack declares that the opposition to his road using the strip is instigated by the North Jersey Street Railway Company, which is to aproach Hackensack from the other direction.

### PRINCE HENRY OF HESSE DEAD.

**Was Brother of the Father of the Grand Duke of Hesse.**

MUNICH, Sept. 16.—Prince Henry of Hesse died here to-day.

Prince Henry Louis Gillaume, Adelbert Waldemar Alexander of Hesse was born at Bessinger Nov. 28, 1838. He was a brother of the father of the present Grand Duke of Hesse. He became a General of the Prussian cavalry, and was attached to the suite of the King.

He was married morganatically to Caroline, Baroness de Nidda, at Darmstadt Feb. 28, 1878. The Baroness's title was conferred upon her on the day of her marriage by the Grand Duke of Hesse. The Baroness's maiden name was Willech. She was born Nov. 5, 1848, of humble parentage. Jan. 6, 1879, at Darmstadt, the Prince was married to Emilie Mathilde Hedvige of the house of Sopaska, who was born at Karlstadt May 6, 1868. Three days after the marriage the title of Baroness de Dornberg was conferred upon Emilie Mathilde, and by letters patent, issued at Darmstadt Oct. 4, 1893, the Baronial title was conferred upon her descendants as well as herself.

The Prince leaves two sons, one by the first wife, and one by the second. They are the Comte de Nidda and Baron de Dornberg.

### LIGHTNING STRIKES A FOOT.

SYRACUSE, N. Y., Sept. 16.—While the Rev. Matthew Gaffney pastor of the Presbyterian Church at Jordan, was asleep in a passenger coach of a New York Central train coming from New York his foot, which was resting on the window ledge, is supposed to have been struck by lightning, the train passing through an electrical storm at the time.

The boot was burned, and the minister is confined to his home.

## CAPT. M'QUISTON KILLED BY A PRIVATE

### The Captain, Temporarily Insane, Attacked His Soldiers.

### WOUNDED ONE OR MORE

**Man Who Shot Him Acted in Self-Defense—Death Reported by Gen. MacArthur.**

WASHINGTON, Sept. 16.—The War Department to-day received information from Gen. MacArthur of the tragic death in the Philippines of Capt. Charles McQuiston of the Fourth Regiment of United States Infantry, the result of a wound by a private soldier. Gen. MacArthur's dispatch is as follows:

"Charles McQuiston, Captain of the Fourth United States Infantry, died yesterday at Manganone, Bacoor, Cavite Province, at 8:30 in the evening, from a gunshot wound caused by a private soldier.

"Capt. McQuiston, in a fit of temporary insanity, attacked men of his company. Shot one or more, and was shot himself in self-defense.

"Further particulars when received."

Capt. McQuiston was appointed a cadet at West Point July 1, 1879. On graduation he became a Second Lieutenant in the Fourth Infantry. He became a First Lieutenant Feb. 24, 1891, and was assigned to the Nineteenth Infantry. July of that year he was transferred to the Fifteenth Infantry; November of the same year he was transferred to the First Infantry, and the following December was attached to the Fourth Infantry. He became a Captain July 23, 1898. He was born in Indiana and appointed to the Military Academy from that State.

### SCHOONER ASHORE IN STORM.

**Crew of the Willie Rescued by Life-Saving Patrolmen—Atlantic City Suffers.**

*Special to The New York Times.*

ATLANTIC CITY, N. J., Sept. 16.—In the heavy wind and rain storm which set in on the coast last evening the schooner Willie went ashore on the southerly end of Egg Harbor shoals, north of Brigantine Inlet. On board were Capt. Orluf Anderson, John Farrell, John Olsen, and Gustav Anderson. They left New York Friday on a fishing cruise.

The schooner drove hard on the shoals before the heavy northeast blow, and efforts to get her off proved fruitless. A high sea was running, and steadily grew more dangerous toward morning, when the wind veered and blew a gale from the southeast. The schooner was pounding heavily and the seas were breaking over her when daylight discovered her to the Little Beach United States Life-Saving Station. The crew put off, and with great difficulty brought the men ashore in an exhausted condition. The life-saving crew returned to the vessel when, by 9 o'clock, the storm had abated and they succeeded in floating her.

The storm is the worst on the coast here this season. The beach has been badly cut up in many places, and porches, trees, and flagpoles were blown down. Some merchants on the board walk have suffered much damage. There was great alarm among visitors.

### BANK TELLER A SUICIDE.

**Confessed Theft, but Officials Cannot Discover Where It Was.**

*Special to The New York Times.*

CHICAGO, Sept. 16.—George S. Forbes, a teller in the First National Bank, killed himself at a hotel in South Chicago to-day. In a note to his parents he said he preferred death to disgrace. His self-confessed theft is still hidden. Officers of the old Union National, of which Forbes was a teller until its consolidation with the First National a week ago, cannot conceive, if Forbes had tampered with any of their funds, how it had been covered up to escape discovery during the transfer to the First National, while officials of the latter aver that the young man was not in a position in the consolidated institution that would enable him to manipulate any of the money.

In his letter Forbes wrote that he had loaned money and being unable to get it back he feared disgrace. He had been in the consolidated institution only a week, and this is considered too short a time for the sequence of events that ended with the suicide. Forbes spent the morning reading, and before dinner wrote the letter which was found after his death.

He registered at 3:30 o'clock in the South Chicago Hotel, asked for a room, saying he wanted to rest, and told the porter to call him in an hour. An hour later the landlord went up to arouse the guest, but found him dead on the floor. Near one hand lay a revolver. The letter addressed to the parents was on the bureau. Officials of both banks say Forbes was considered an exemplary young man.

### TAKES A WAYFARER TO HIS HOME.

**The Man Robs His Benefactor and Is Caught After a Chase.**

NEWARK, N. J., Sept. 16.—Frederick B. McKee, who says he is a traveling salesman of 103 Merrimac Street, Boston, Mass., was held for the Grand Jury to-day. Martin Albright of 210 Broome Street charged McKee with having taken his pocketbook containing $78 from his pocket.

According to Albright's story, he met McKee last night on the street, and the latter told him he was hungry and without any place to go. As he appeared to be respectable, Albright took him to his home to have a meal. After supper they sat in the parlor talking. Albright's daughter joined them. Albright, who was tired, fell asleep, and Miss Albright stepped into another room for a moment.

When she returned McKee had disappeared. Becoming suspicious, she awakened her father, who at once felt for his wallet, which had been in a pocket in his vest. It was gone. He ran to the Fourth Precinct Station, and Detectives Koerber and Remise jumped on a trolley car with him to go to Market Street Station to try to intercept McKee, who they suspected would go to New York.

Just as they boarded the car McKee jumped off, and Albright saw him. He shouted to the detectives and they followed. After a long chase Koerber pulled his revolver and was about to fire, when McKee tripped and fell. He was captured before he could regain his feet.

When searched $62 of the stolen money was found in one of his socks. He had thrown away the pocketbook, which contained Albright's railroad pass. He could not tell what had become of the balance of the money, but supposed he must have overlooked it in the pocketbook.

## LINEMAN SAVED BY HIS BELT.

**Unconscious from Electric Shock, He Dangles at the Top of a Pole.**

NEWARK, N. J., Sept. 16.—John W. Warner, a lineman of the New York and New Jersey Telephone Company, had a narrow escape from death on the top of a high pole in Belleville yesterday afternoon, and is in a serious condition at his home in this city.

Warner, with a fellow-lineman named Spiker, was stringing wires in Washington Avenue, near Rutgers Street, when Warner screamed and fell apparently lifeless against the pole. A strap around his waist which was hooked to a cross-arm, prevented him from falling to the ground.

Spiker saw that Warner's clothing was burning. He beat out the flames, and, descending to the ground, summoned several other linemen, who were working a couple of blocks away.

When they reached the pole Warner was still dangling at the top, but the belt which held him had slipped from his waist to his arm pits. Two of the workmen quickly climbed the pole, and, slipping a rope over a cross-arm, secured it around Warner's waist. He was then lowered to the ground, where a physician was already in waiting and succeeded in reviving Warner. It was found that his right arm had been burned to the bone where the wire had touched him, and his back was badly scorched where his clothing had been on fire. Warner was removed to his home. The wire which Warner was stringing had sagged and come in contact with a trolley feed wire.

### HURT IN DOUBLE COLLISION.

**Wheelman Runs Down a Laborer, and Both Are Struck by a Car.**

A double collision occurred at Fifty-sixth Street and Third Avenue last night, in which a trolley car struck and badly injured two men, one of whom, a wheelman, had run down the other, who had just alighted from a car going in the opposite direction.

The men are John Clark, a laborer, of 244 East Fifty-ninth Street, and Charles Adamtz, a clerk, of 919 Third Avenue. Clark, who was on a north-bound car, had alighted and was crossing the tracks. As he stepped from behind the car, Adamtz, going very fast, came along in front of the south-bound car. The bicycle struck Clark and both he and the rider rolled between the tracks, the wheel going to one side. Adamtz fell at the edge of the west track, his head striking an elevated railroad post and his feet, according to witnesses, resting along the edge of the rail.

Motorman Freemeyer saw the two men and made strenuous efforts to stop his car, but had succeeded only in reducing its speed when it struck them. Adamtz was pushed out of the way, but Clark, who had been stunned by the force of contact with the wheel, was pushed in front of the fender for several feet, and then lifted by it before the car was stopped.

A Flower Hospital ambulance surgeon found that both men were badly cut about the head and besides were considerably bruised. They were taken to the hospital.

### DOWIEITES ROUGHLY TREATED.

**People of Mansfield, Ohio, Break Up Service—Elder Rescued by Police.**

*Special to The New York Times.*

MANSFIELD, Ohio, Sept. 16.—While twenty-five members of the Christian Catholic Church were holding a meeting this morning at the home of E. H. Leiby, a crowd surrounded the house, threw stones, and threatened Elder Bassinger of Bluffton, who was conducting the service.

For three successive Sundays Bassinger has been sent out of the city by the police to avoid trouble. Officers again succeeded in rescuing him to-day. The mob tried to get him from the police, who accompanied him to the Union Station, where 500 persons quickly gathered. The police kept the crowd back, and the baffled mob, which had greatly increased, proceeded to the Leiby home, where two doors were broken open. The crowd rushed in and secured Leiby and F. D. Calver, another Dowieite, whom they took to the station. When the mob arrived with the Christian Catholics fully 1,500 people were at the station. The police placed the two men in the waiting room with Bassinger, and the three were sent to Crestline this afternoon.

Only the fact that it was broad daylight prevented the mob from tarring and feathering the Dowieites.

### $25,000,000 FROM KLONDIKE.

**Encouraging Reports from Stewart and Little Salmon Rivers.**

VANCOUVER, Sept. 16.—W. A. Baer, a mining engineer of this city, just returned from Dawson, says that according to the latest information in the possession of the Gold Commissioner's Office at Dawson, royalty will be paid this season on $16,000,000. The actual clean-up will be $9,000,000 more.

Just before Baer left Dawson encouraging reports had come from Stewart River placers, 200 miles distant, and it was stated that another exodus to that river had taken place. Good reports have also come from the Little Salmon, and great results there are confidently anticipated.

### EXPRESS COMPANY TO PAY LOSS.

**Will Make Good Theft of $20,000 in Transit to Burlington Bank.**

*Special to The New York Times.*

CHICAGO, Sept. 16.—Early this week the Treasurer of the Adams Express Company here will hand the cashier of the Commercial National Bank a check for $20,000, in payment of the loss sustained by the bank by the theft of a package in transit to the National State Bank of Burlington.

When the officers of the bank were apprised of the robbery they sent $20,000 more to the National State Bank of Burlington, Iowa, and have carried the loss on their books since that time. A month has elapsed now without the discovery of the culprit or the recovery of the money. Papers have been drawn up at the New York office of the express company and are now on the way to Chicago, binding the Chicago and Burlington banks to reimburse the express company should it be proved that the loss of the package occurred in either bank, and Tuesday the amount will be paid to the Commercial Bank.

**Author of "Mr. Dooley" to Live Here.**

*Special to The New York Times.*

CHICAGO, Sept. 16.—Finley P. Dunne, author of the "Mr. Dooley" papers, has resigned as managing editor of The Chicago Evening Journal, and, it is said, will remove permanently to New York City.

Mr. Dunne has been connected with various Chicago newspapers for about fifteen years.

**Condition of Marcus Daly.**

Marcus Daly, the Montana silver mine owner, who has been ill in the Hotel Netherland since the 8th of this month, is improving. He is said to be suffering from heart trouble. He is able to be about his room.

**Two of the Yantic's Sailors Drowned.**

DETROIT, Sept. 16.—Paul E. Dodt of this city, a fireman on the United States steamer Yantic, and his cousin, Paul Salonsky, were drowned in the river this afternoon, the result of their boat capsizing. The boat was one of the yawls of the Yantic, with a sail rigged in her. There were six men in the party, but the other four clung to the capsized craft and were picked up. Dodt and Salonsky tried to swim to the shore, and were drowned in full view of several hundred people.

## GOV. ROOSEVELT FORMALLY ACCEPTS

### His Letter to the Vice Presidential Committee's Chairman.

### NATION'S WELFARE AT STAKE

**To Put Into Practice the Principles of the Kansas City Platform, He Says, Would Mean Grave Disaster.**

Gov. Roosevelt has addressed the following letter of acceptance to Senator Edward O. Wolcott, Chairman of the Committee on Notification of Vice President:

Oyster Bay, N. Y., Sept. 15, 1900.

Sir: I accept the nomination as Vice President of the United States, tendered me by the Republican National Convention, with a very deep sense of the honor conferred upon me and with an infinitely deeper sense of the vital importance to the whole country of securing the re-election of President McKinley.

The Nation's welfare is at stake. We must continue the work which has been so well begun during the present Administration. We must show in fashion incapable of being misunderstood that the American people, at the beginning of the twentieth century, face their duties in a calm and serious spirit that they have no intention of permitting folly or lawlessness to mar the extraordinary material well-being which they have attained at home, nor yet of permitting their flag to be dishonored abroad.

I feel that this contest is by no means one merely between Republicans and Democrats. We have a right to appeal to all good citizens who are far-sighted enough to see what the honor and the interest of the Nation demand. To put into practice the principles embodied in the Kansas City platform would mean grave disaster to the Nation; for that platform stands for reaction and disorder; for an upsetting of our financial system which would mean not only great suffering but the abandonment of the Nation's good faith; and for a policy abroad which would imply the dishonor of the flag and an unworthy surrender of our National rights.

Its success would mean unspeakable humiliation to men proud of their country, jealous of their country's good name, and desirous of securing the welfare of their fellow-citizens. Therefore we have a right to appeal to all good men, North and South, East and West, whatever their politics may have been in the past, to stand with us, because we stand for the prosperity of the country and for the renown of the American flag.

The most important of all problems is, of course, that of securing good government and moral and material well-being within our own borders. Great though the need is that the Nation should do its work well abroad, even this comes second to the thorough performance of duty at home. Under the Administration of President McKinley this country has been blessed with a degree of prosperity absolutely unparalleled even in its previous prosperous history.

While it is, of course, true that no legislation and no Administration can bring success to those who are not stout of heart, cool of head, and ready of hand, yet it is no less true that the individual capacity of each man to get good results for himself can be absolutely destroyed by bad legislation or bad administration, while under the reverse conditions the power of the individual to do good work is assured and stimulated.

This is what has been done under the Administration of President McKinley. Thanks to his actions and to the wise legislation of Congress on the tariff and finance, the conditions of our industrial life have been rendered more favorable than ever before, and they have been taken advantage of to the full by American thrift, industry, and enterprise. Order has been observed, the courts upheld, and the fullest liberty secured to all citizens. The merchant and manufacturer, but above all the farmer and the wageworker, have profited by this state of things.

**FREE SILVER DANGER.**

Fundamentally and primarily the present contest is a contest for the continuance of the conditions which have told in favor of our material welfare and of our civil and political integrity. If this Nation is to retain either its well-being or its self-respect, it cannot afford to plunge into financial and economic chaos; it cannot afford to indorse Governmental theories which would unsettle the standard of National honesty and destroy the integrity of our system of justice. The policy of the free coinage of silver at a ratio of 16 to 1 is a policy fraught with destruction to every home in the land. It means untold misery to the head of every household, and, above all, to the women and children of every home.

When our opponents champion free silver at 16 to 1, they are either insincere or sincere in their attitude. If insincere in their championship, they, of course, forfeit all right to belief or support on any ground. If sincere, then they are a menace to the welfare of the country. Whether they shout their sinister purpose or merely whisper it makes but little difference, save as it reflects their own honesty. No issue can be paramount to the issue they thus make, for the paramountcy of such an issue is to be determined, not by the dictum of any man or body of men, but by the fact that it vitally affects the well-being of every home in the land.

The financial question is always of such far-reaching and tremendous importance to the National welfare that it can never be raised in good faith unless this tremendous importance is not merely conceded but insisted on. Men who are not willing to make such an issue paramount have no possible justification for raising it at all, for under such circumstances their act cannot under any conceivable circumstances do aught but grave harm.

The success of the party representing the principles embodied in the Kansas City platform would bring about the destruction of all the conditions necessary to the continuance of our prosperity. It would also unsettle our whole governmental system, and would therefore disarrange all the vast and delicate machinery of our complex industrial life. Above all, the effect would be ruinous to our finances. If we are to prosper, the currency of this country must be based upon the gold dollar worth 100 cents.

The stability of our currency has been greatly increased by the excellent financial act passed by the last Congress. But no law can secure our finances against the effect of unwise and disastrous management in the hands of unfriendly administrators. No party can safely be intrusted with the management of our National affairs unless it accepts as axiomatic the truths recognized in all progressive countries as essential to a sound and proper system of finance. In their essence these must be the same for all great civilized peoples. In different stages of development, different countries face varying economic conditions, but at every stage and under all circumstances the most important element in securing their economic well-being is sound finance, honest money. So intimate is the connection between industrial prosperity and a sound currency that the former is jeopardized, not merely by unsound finance, but by the very threat of unsound finance.

The business man and the farmer are vitally interested in this question; but no man's interest is so great as that of the wage workers. A depreciated currency means loss and disaster to the business man; but it means grim suffering to the wage worker. The capitalist will lose much of his capital and will suffer wearing anxiety and the loss of many comforts; but the wage worker who loses his wages must suffer, and see his wife and children suffer, for the actual necessities of life. The one absolutely vital need of our whole industrial system is sound money.

**THE TRUST PROBLEM.**

One of the serious problems with which we are confronted under the conditions of our modern industrial civilization is that



INDEX TO DEPARTMENTS.

Arrivals at Hotels and Out-of-Town Buyers.—Page 5.
Court Calendars.—Page 11.
Losses by Fire.—Page 5.
Marine Intelligence and Foreign Mails.—Page 5.
Real Estate.—Page 10.
Weather Report.—Page 5.
Yesterday's Fires.—Page 5.

"All the News That's Fit to Print."

# The New York Times.

THE WEATHER. Partly cloudy; fresh southerly winds.

COPYRIGHT, 1900, BY THE NEW YORK TIMES COMPANY.

VOL. L...NO. 15,860. NEW YORK, WEDNESDAY, NOVEMBER 7, 1900.—SIXTEEN PAGES. ONE CENT In Greater New York, Elsewhere, and Jersey City. TWO CENTS

# M'KINLEY RE-ELECTED

## McKinley 284 Bryan 155

## REPUBLICANS CARRY

NEW YORK,
INDIANA,
WEST VIRGINIA,
DELAWARE,
MARYLAND,
KANSAS,
NORTH DAKOTA,
SOUTH DAKOTA,
CALIFORNIA,
WYOMING,

## DEMOCRATS CARRY

NEVADA,
KENTUCKY,

## DOUBTFUL

NEBRASKA.

| | |
|---|---|
| Total Electoral Vote . | 447 |
| Necessary to a choice . | 224 |
| William McKinley . . | 284 |
| William J. Bryan . . | 155 |
| McKinley over Bryan . | 121 |

The expected has happened. The Republican Presidential ticket has swept the country.

William McKinley of Ohio, the Republican candidate for President of the United States, has been re-elected to that office, and Theodore Roosevelt of New York has been chosen Vice President.

The Republicans carried twenty-seven States and the Democrats eighteen.

In 1896 the Republicans carried twenty-three States, including California and Kentucky, in each of which the Democrats secured one Electoral vote. The Democrats carried twenty-two States.

The Republicans have regained the States of Kansas, South Dakota, Washington, Utah, and Wyoming.

The Democrats have recovered the State of Kentucky.

Kentucky has given her entire Electoral vote to Bryan.

While victorious in Kentucky in securing the Electors for Bryan, the Democrats have suffered a great defeat in the election of John W. Yerkes, Republican, as Governor, over Beckham, the successor to Gov. Goebel.

Colorado's Electoral vote will be cast for Bryan.

A fusion Legislature has been elected in Colorado. It will elect an opposition Senator to succeed Edward O. Wolcott, Republican, whose term will expire March 3, 1901.

Delaware has chosen Electors favorable to McKinley and Roosevelt.

The election in Delaware of a Democratic Legislature assures the election of two Democratic Senators, one to fill a vacancy and another to succeed Senator Richard R. Kenney, Democrat, whose term will expire March 3, 1901.

Idaho's Electoral vote will go to Bryan and Stevenson.

The victory in Idaho for the fusion legislative ticket assures the election of an opposition Senator to succeed George L. Shoup, Republican, whose term will expire next March.

Kansas has decided to cast her Electoral vote for McKinley.

The election in Kansas of a Republican Legislature will give to that State a Republican Senator to succeed Lucien Baker, Republican, whose term will expire March 3, 1901.

Montana persists in its allegiance to free silver and to Bryan and will give him its Electoral vote.

Although Montana has chosen a Democratic Legislature, it is not yet certain that the partisans of William A. Clark can command votes enough to elect him. The Daly Democrats and Republicans may combine to choose Senator Thomas H. Carter, Republican, to succeed himself, and a Democrat of the Daly faction for the short term.

South Dakota has returned to the Republican column and will cast her Electoral vote for McKinley and Roosevelt. Senator Richard F. Pettigrew, who calls himself a silver man, the most active and bitter opponent of the Administration in the United States Senate, will be succeeded by a Republican, South Dakota having chosen a Republican Legislature.

Utah has reversed the position occupied by that State four years ago, and will give its three Electoral votes to McKinley.

Having elected a Republican Legislature, Utah will choose a Republican Senator to fill the vacancy created in that State by failure to elect.

West Virginia adheres to the Republican Party, and will give its Electoral vote to McKinley.

The election in West Virginia of a Republican Legislature will be followed by the return to the United States Senate of Stephen B. Elkins, whose term will expire March 3, 1901.

McKinley's plurality of the popular vote is about 550,000.

This is smaller than his plurality of 603,514 in 1896, which was exceeded only by Grant's plurality over Greeley, in 1872, of 762,991.

### REPUBLICAN.

| State | Votes |
|---|---|
| California | 9 |
| Connecticut | 6 |
| Delaware | 3 |
| Illinois | 24 |
| Indiana | 15 |
| Iowa | 13 |
| Kansas | 10 |
| Maine | 6 |
| Maryland | 8 |
| Massachusetts | 15 |
| Michigan | 14 |
| Minnesota | 9 |
| New Hampshire | 4 |
| New Jersey | 10 |
| New York | 36 |
| North Dakota | 3 |
| Ohio | 23 |
| Oregon | 4 |
| Pennsylvania | 32 |
| Rhode Island | 4 |
| South Dakota | 4 |
| Utah | 3 |
| Vermont | 4 |
| Washington | 4 |
| West Virginia | 6 |
| Wisconsin | 12 |
| Wyoming | 3 |
| Total | 284 |

### DEMOCRATIC.

| State | Votes |
|---|---|
| Alabama | 11 |
| Arkansas | 8 |
| Colorado | 4 |
| Florida | 4 |
| Georgia | 13 |
| Idaho | 3 |
| Kentucky | 13 |
| Louisiana | 8 |
| Mississippi | 9 |
| Missouri | 17 |
| Montana | 3 |
| Nevada | 3 |
| North Carolina | 11 |
| South Carolina | 9 |
| Tennessee | 12 |
| Texas | 15 |
| Virginia | 12 |
| Total | 155 |

### DOUBTFUL.

| State | Votes |
|---|---|
| Nebraska | 8 |

McKinley's majority 121

## FIERCE RIOT ON BROADWAY.

### Police Commissioner Hess Buffeted by the Crowd.

The sidewalk in front of the Rossmore Hotel was the scene of a fierce riot shortly before 2:30 o'clock this morning. It was precipitated by a number of Columbia students.

Before peace was restored by the reserves from the Tenderloin Station Police Commissioner Hess had been buffeted by the crowd and Samuel B. Harry, a hunchback, of 506 East Sixth Street, had been trampled underfoot on the pavement and so badly injured that he had to be removed in a carriage by some friends who witnessed the affray.

About 300 of the college boys, all of whom were shouting for Bryan, started the trouble by lining up on the sidewalk and striking at every passer-by who came between their lines.

On some they used their canes and on others fists and gloves, and nobody attempted to interfere with them until a band of hilarious young Republicans, each man of whom bore an American flag, came between the lines.

One of the students cried: "Why should they have a monopoly of the flag?" and seized it. Several others supported him, and in an instant there were a dozen free fights in progress along the street.

Commissioner Hess ran out of the hotel and shouted:

"Stop this disorder."

The rioters then turned on him, and, after beating him, threw him back into the hotel and held the doors so that he could not again come out.

He sent an alarm to Police Headquarters over the hotel telephone, and a few moments later two Sergeants with forty of the reserves were being hurried up Broadway in the patrol wagon.

The police did not try to make arrests, but used their clubs freely, and before long the fighters had broken and run, and a guard of policemen was stationed about the hotel to prevent the young men from again assembling there.

Only one prisoner was taken, Frank Butler, a newspaper man, who was pointed out by Rufus Silberman of 306 West Forty-seventh Street, as being the instigator of the riot.

Butler had many friends who protested that he had nothing to do with it, but Silberman, who was one of the McKinley paraders, insisted that he be locked up.

Harry, the cripple, when picked up from where he had fallen, was bleeding profusely. The police wanted him to go to a hospital, but he declined to do so.

Before the fighting was over many who were not students had been drawn into it.

# CONGRESS BOTH HOUSES REPUBLICAN

## About 24 Majority in Senate.

## About 47 Majority in House.

## REPUBLICAN GAINS IN MANY STATES.

### Clean Sweep in Maryland—General Overturn in Nebraska—Increased Republican Majority in Both Houses.

The Fifty-seventh Congress will be Republican in both branches.

In the Senate the Republicans will have a majority of sixteen on a straight party vote.

There will be a Republican majority in the House of Representatives of 47.

In the Fifty-sixth Congress the Republicans have majorities in both houses. The Senate, with 86 members, consists of 51 Republicans and 35 in the opposition, giving a majority of 16. There are four vacancies.

The House of Representatives, consisting of 357 members when full, consists of 185 Republicans and 167 Democrats and others, showing a Republican majority of 18. There are five vacancies to be filled at this election.

The Republican majority in the House, 18 in the present House, will be 47 in the next.

Maryland elects a solid Republican delegation.

The Republicans succeeded in breaking into the North Carolina delegation. James M. Moody, Republican, is elected in the Ninth District.

In all probability Spencer Blackburn (Rep.) is also elected in the Eighth District by 500 plurality.

One of the most surprising results was the defeat of William McAleer in the rock-ribbed Democratic Third District of Pennsylvania. His successor is Henry Burke, a Republican.

The Democrats reclaimed the district in Texas now represented by Hawley and made the delegation solid.

Bryan's own State overturned her Congressional delegation. In the present House she is represented by two Republicans and four Fusionists and Democrats. In the next she will be represented by five Republicans and one Fusionist.

One of the biggest changes is in New York. In the Fifty-sixth Congress she is represented by 15 Republicans and 18 Democrats. In the Fifty-seventh Congress New York will have 20 Republicans and 14 Democrats.

"Billy" Lorimer, the Republican boss in Chicago, is defeated by John J. Feeley.

Two districts are in doubt. One is Congressman Lentz's district in Ohio. The Republicans made strenuous efforts to defeat Lentz because of his violent attacks on the Administration in the last session. Tompkins, his opponent, is probably elected, but not by more than 100 majority.

The Third Massachusetts is claimed by Washburn, (Rep.,) by 300 majority, and by Thayer, (Dem.,) by 200. Thayer is probably elected.

### UNITED STATES SENATE.

| | |
|---|---|
| Next Senate—Republicans | 57 |
| Opposition | 33 |
| Republican majority | 24 |
| Present Senate—Republicans | 51 |
| Opposition | 35 |
| Republican majority | 16 |

### HOUSE OF REPRESENTATIVES.

| | |
|---|---|
| Fifty-seventh Congress— | |
| Republicans | 202 |
| Opposition | 155 |
| Republican majority | 47 |
| Fifty-sixth Congress— | |
| Republican | 185 |
| Opposition | 167 |
| Republican majority | 18 |

## CLOSE IN KANSAS.

### One-third of a Number of Precincts Show a Gain for Bryan.

*Special to The New York Times.*

TOPEKA, Kan., Nov. 6.—Seventeen Kansas precincts, one-third counted, show a gain for Bryan over 1896 of 15 per cent. The result in the State is close and cannot be known before to-morrow.

Election day dawned clear and pleasant throughout the State. The polls in this city opened at 8 o'clock. The vote was extraordinarily heavy during the morning, due to splendid weather.

The heaviest vote in years has been polled in Southern Kansas. Democratic hopes lie in the country districts. The fair weather caused nearly all the farmers to go to the polls.

Wichita will probably go Republican.

Fusion Headquarters claim the State for Bryan and the Fusion ticket. W. E. Stanley, Republican candidate for Governor, predicts his own election.

## DEMOCRATS CONCEDE NEBRASKA.

CHICAGO, Nov. 6.—Henry C. Payne has received the following message from the Assistant Secretary of War, Meiklejohn, at his home in Fullerton, Neb.: "The Democrats concede Nebraska to McKinley by 7,000.

## CLOSE IN NEBRASKA.

*Special to The New York Times.*

OMAHA, Neb., Nov. 6.—The returns from the State are coming in very slowly, but the Republicans are showing gains on an average of ten to a precinct. There are 1,250 precincts in the State. At this rate the State will give a Republican majority for the electoral ticket of at least 10,000.

At 10 o'clock this evening Vice Chairman Edmiston of the Populists' National Committee and also Chairman of the Populist State Committee, said:

"The returns received by us indicate that Bryan has carried Nebraska by 15,000 votes. I do not care to comment on National returns. They show for themselves."

The State Journal claims Nebraska by a small majority for the Republicans, if the present ratio of gain holds out.

The Republican State Committee claims the State by 10,000.

The State ticket will be close, but the indications now are that the Republicans will elect the full State ticket and the Legislature.

A dispatch from Lincoln says the Congressional ticket is very favorable to the Republicans. G. J. Burkett is elected in the First District, David H. Mercer in the Second, and John R. Hays in the Third, all Republicans.

McKinley in Lincoln has a majority of 1,602, a gain of 555 over 1896.

In the Fourth the returns indicate the election of John D. Pope, (Rep.,) and the Fifth and Sixth are in doubt, but will probably be carried by the Fusionists A. C. Shallenberger and William Neville.

Nine precincts outside of Omaha and Douglass give McKinley 1,338; Bryan, 849. The same precincts in 1896 gave McKinley, 1,997; Bryan, 815.

Fourteen precincts out of twenty in Lincoln give McKinley a gain of 562 over 1896.

The Fusion managers are very much disconcerted, and the State news, together with information of overwhelming majorities for McKinley received from the East, has caused considerable depression among the Fusionists.

As the news is received here on the street the scenes beggar description, the excitement being intense. Many thousands of dollars were wagered on the last moment on Nebraska by Republicans, and it is estimated that $100,000 changed hands in Omaha on the result at odds in favor of Bryan of from 1 to 3.

The weather throughout Nebraska today could not be improved on, being far above the average of November temperature, with the skies clear throughout the State. In Omaha the polls were open at 8 o'clock. The early voting was unusually heavy. The leaders were out early, getting their men in line, and conditions were favorable for the full vote being polled.

The number of votes registered at noon broke the record.

At Kearney, where there was no registration this year, several challenges were made and some arrests threatened for illegal voting.

## GOV. ROOSEVELT'S COMMENT.

### He Hears the News at Oyster Bay and Sends Message to the President.

OYSTER BAY, L. I., Nov. 6.—Gov. Roosevelt, surrounded by his family, to-night received the returns at his home on Sagamore Hill. The Governor at no time during the evening seemed anxious about the result. He did not make any special arrangements to receive the news, and depended on messages to be brought from the telegraph office in the railroad station, nearly three miles away.

The first definite information of the Republican victory was conveyed to the Governor at about 10 o'clock. He was in the reception room with his wife and daughter. When he appeared at the door to meet a newspaper correspondent he was in evening dress. He invited his visitor into the parlor and closely scrutinized the returns and briefly commented on the result. After reading the message, he said:

"Isn't that fine. It shows what the American people are. It shows that they want the good times to continue, and are in favor of honest money and are for the flag."

The Governor at once dictated the following dispatch to President McKinley:

To President William McKinley, Canton, Ohio:
I congratulate you and far more the Nation. You have my heartfelt gratitude over the result.
THEODORE ROOSEVELT.

Gov. Roosevelt also sent messages of congratulations to Senator Hanna and Mr. Odell.

## MR. ODELL JUBILANT.

### Says the General Result of the Election Far Exceeds His Expectations.

Governor-elect Odell, talking to THE NEW YORK TIMES over the telephone from his home in Newburg at 11 o'clock last night, said:

"The general result of the election far exceeds my expectations. President McKinley appears to have carried every doubtful State. The story is one of increased majorities everywhere. The people have not only given a grand indorsement of President McKinley's Administration, but they have administered a rebuke to Mr. Bryan and his party leaders which will retire them from the councils of the Democratic Party, and which will put an end to the theories which they have been advocating.

"To the Republican Party has been given a full measure of power in the National Government, and the country is safe.

"So far as this State is concerned, it seems now that the Republican ticket has won by 150,000 majority. My estimate of 100,000 for the party was given out as conservative, and the vote justifies the prediction. I scarcely looked for so sweeping a victory.

"Mr. Croker has carried New York County for Mr. Bryan as he said he would, and Greater New York appears to have given Mr. Bryan a majority, but while Mr. Croker has done this he has heard from the 'men from cornfields' for whom he has expressed such contempt. The result in the State demonstrates his unfitness for State leadership.

"Of course I regard my own election with great satisfaction. It proves that the people are not afraid to elect a Governor simply because he has been able to serve his party as a practical politician. As Governor I shall try to bring into use the same practical, businesslike methods as I have tried to apply as a party leader."

## CROKER'S MESSAGE TO BRYAN.

Richard Croker said just before leaving Tammany Hall at 11:15 last evening that he would give out only one statement about the election returns received by him. Here is the statement:

"I can't say what caused the defeat of Mr. Bryan, if he has been defeated, and I don't admit that he has been. I cannot attribute it to anybody, but I can say that we in New York have done everything in our power to elect Mr. Bryan, and we have made a splendid showing."

"This ends Mr. Bryan's political career so far as the Presidency is concerned," said a reporter.

"Not by any means," replied Mr. Croker. "Mr. Bryan is a natural leader of the people, and he will be heard from again."

Before leaving Tammany Hall Richard Croker caused the following telegram to be sent to William J. Bryan at Lincoln, Neb.:

As you no doubt already know, this State has gone heavily against us, but whereas this county in 1896 gave McKinley 23,000, it gives you to-day 32,000, a gain of 55,000.
We are defeated but not discouraged.
RICHARD CROKER.

Mr. Croker announced again that he would make no further statement under any circumstances about the election, and he left Tammany Hall to go to the Democratic Club. He was accompanied by John F. Carroll.

# ODELL ELECTED GOVERNOR

## 110,559 PLURALITY

## LEGISLATURE REPUBLICAN

### 16 Maj. in Senate. 58 Maj. in House.

### McKINLEY RUNS ABOUT 3,000 AHEAD OF ODELL.

The State of New York has given a plurality of over 140,000 to William McKinley, Republican candidate for President, and a plurality of 110,559 to Benjamin B. Odell, Jr., Republican candidate for Governor.

Both Bryan and Stanchfield have carried the counties of New York, Queens, Richmond, and Schoharie. Mr. Stanchfield also has carried the County of Chemung by 584, although the county gave McKinley a plurality of about 403. In 1896 McKinley carried every county in the State except Schoharie, and Black, the Republican candidate for Governor, did the same.

Mr. Odell had a narrow escape from losing Greene County, where his plurality is only 6 votes. Mr. McKinley's plurality in Greene County is 107, which is 19 above his plurality in 1896.

Elmira, Mr. Stanchfield's home, supported him handsomely. While Mr. Bryan's plurality in that city was 172, Mr. Stanchfield's was over 800.

### STATE VOTE FOR PRESIDENT.

| County. | Pluralities. McKinley. Rep. | Bryan Dem. |
|---|---|---|
| Albany | 4,080 | ...... |
| Allegany | 3,475 | ...... |
| Broome | 3,300 | ...... |
| Cattaraugus | 3,750 | ...... |
| Cayuga | 3,950 | ...... |
| Chautauqua | 8,618 | ...... |
| Chemung | 403 | ...... |
| Chenango | 1,894 | ...... |
| Clinton | 2,087 | ...... |
| Columbia | 1,459 | ...... |
| Cortland | 2,075 | ...... |
| Delaware | 3,200 | ...... |
| Dutchess | 4,203 | ...... |
| Erie | 5,500 | ...... |
| Essex | 3,155 | ...... |
| Franklin | 3,700 | ...... |
| Fulton & Ham | 3,522 | ...... |
| Genesee | 2,148 | ...... |
| Greene | 107 | ...... |
| Herkimer | 2,900 | ...... |
| Jefferson | 4,800 | ...... |
| Kings | 3,492 | ...... |
| Lewis | 1,509 | ...... |
| Livingston | 1,725 | ...... |
| Madison | 3,290 | ...... |
| Monroe | 7,000 | ...... |
| Montgomery | 2,135 | ...... |
| New York | ...... | 27,230 |
| Nassau | 2,000 | ...... |
| Niagara | 1,974 | ...... |
| Oneida | 6,326 | ...... |
| Onondaga | 9,842 | ...... |
| Ontario | 2,055 | ...... |
| Orange | 4,500 | ...... |
| Orleans | 1,810 | ...... |
| Oswego | 4,669 | ...... |
| Otsego | 1,700 | ...... |
| Putnam | 851 | ...... |
| Queens | ...... | 1,094 |
| Rensselaer | 3,000 | ...... |
| Richmond | ...... | 695 |
| Rockland | 166 | ...... |
| St. Lawrence | 8,700 | ...... |
| Saratoga | 2,900 | ...... |
| Schenectady | 1,800 | ...... |
| Schoharie | ...... | 875 |
| Schuyler | 600 | ...... |
| Seneca | 337 | ...... |
| Steuben | 1,500 | ...... |
| Suffolk | 4,152 | ...... |
| Sullivan | 900 | ...... |
| Tioga | 1,704 | ...... |
| Tompkins | 1,559 | ...... |
| Ulster | 2,000 | ...... |
| Warren | 2,302 | ...... |
| Washington | 4,860 | ...... |
| Wayne | 3,478 | ...... |
| Westchester | 2,989 | ...... |
| Wyoming | 2,131 | ...... |
| Yates | 1,200 | ...... |
| Total | ...... | ...... |
| plurality, 1896 | ...... | ...... |
| plurality, 1898 | ...... | ...... |

### STATE VOTE FOR GOVERNOR.

| County. | Pluralities. Odell Rep. | Stanchfield Dem. |
|---|---|---|
| Albany | 1,264 | ...... |
| Allegany | 3,325 | ...... |
| Broome | 3,750 | ...... |
| Cattaraugus | 3,249 | ...... |
| Cayuga | 3,800 | ...... |
| Chautauqua | 8,126 | ...... |
| Chemung | ...... | 584 |
| Chenango | 1,730 | ...... |
| Clinton | 1,746 | ...... |
| Columbia | 1,374 | ...... |
| Cortland | 1,362 | ...... |
| Delaware | 3,000 | ...... |
| Dutchess | 2,970 | ...... |
| Erie | 6,049 | ...... |
| Essex | 3,137 | ...... |
| Franklin | 3,650 | ...... |
| Fulton and Hamilton | 3,350 | ...... |
| Genesee | 2,121 | ...... |
| Greene | 6 | ...... |
| Herkimer | 2,800 | ...... |
| Jefferson | 4,500 | ...... |
| Kings | 1,202 | ...... |
| Lewis | 1,490 | ...... |
| Livingston | 1,475 | ...... |
| Madison | 3,182 | ...... |
| Monroe | 5,000 | ...... |
| Montgomery | 1,722 | ...... |
| New York | ...... | 34,963 |
| Nassau | 2,000 | ...... |
| Niagara | 1,000 | ...... |
| Oneida | 5,151 | ...... |
| Onondaga | 8,500 | ...... |
| Ontario | 2,000 | ...... |
| Orange | 4,200 | ...... |
| Orleans | 1,734 | ...... |
| Oswego | 4,599 | ...... |
| Otsego | 1,700 | ...... |
| Putnam | 803 | ...... |
| Queens | ...... | 1,989 |
| Rensselaer | 2,800 | ...... |
| Richmond | ...... | 993 |
| Rockland | 42 | ...... |
| St. Lawrence | 8,500 | ...... |
| Saratoga | 3,000 | ...... |
| Schenectady | 1,300 | ...... |
| Schoharie | ...... | 330 |
| Schuyler | 450 | ...... |
| Seneca | 160 | ...... |
| Steuben | 3,300 | ...... |
| Suffolk | 3,885 | ...... |
| Sullivan | 800 | ...... |
| Tioga | 1,670 | ...... |
| Tompkins | 1,376 | ...... |
| Ulster | 1,500 | ...... |
| Warren | 2,200 | ...... |
| Washington | 4,700 | ...... |
| Wayne | 3,351 | ...... |
| Westchester | 1,949 | ...... |
| Wyoming | 1,975 | ...... |
| Yates | 1,100 | ...... |
| Total | 149,468 | 38,909 |
| Odell's plurality | | 110,559 |

### THE NEXT LEGISLATURE.

The Senate.

| | |
|---|---|
| Republicans | 33 |
| Democrats | 17 |
| Republican majority | 16 |

The Assembly.

| | |
|---|---|
| Republicans | 104 |
| Democrats | 46 |
| Republican majority | 58 |

Yesterday's election gives the Republicans a safe working majority of 16 in the Senate and 58 in the Assembly. The present Senate is made up of 27 Republicans and 23 Democrats, and the Assembly of 93 Republicans, 56 Democrats, and 1 Independent Democrat. This gives the Republicans a gain of 12 in the Senate and 21 in the Assembly and a majority of 74 on joint ballot.

Republicans marked R; Democrats, D; re-elected, *.

## SPEECH BY MR. M'KINLEY

### Addresses a Few Words to Canton Crowd, in Response to a Tremendous Ovation—How He Received the News.

CANTON, Ohio, Nov. 7.—At midnight Canton was in a frenzy of enthusiasm which knew no bounds. The crowds which had been burning red fire down town marched en masse to the McKinley residence with bands playing, rockets sending lurid streaks across the sky, and tumultuous cheers mingling with the din of horns and steam whistles.

The crowd was stilled for a time with some of the cheering news received. This included dispatches from the Kansas Chairman, claiming that State by 40,000; from Secretary Heath of the Republican National Committee, saying Indiana gave McKinley 29,000 plurality; from the Iowa Chairman, saying Iowa's Republican plurality was 100,000, and from the Union League Club, Chicago, giving the President glowing congratulations on the triumphant indorsement given him by the American people. But the crowd soon clamored for the President, and he appeared, waving his acknowledgment of the deafening cheers. Mr. McKinley said:

"Fellow Citizens: I thank you for the very great compliment of this call on this inclement night, and at this late hour. Of the many gratifying reports from every part of the country, none have given me more genuine and sincere gratitude than those from my own city and my own county of Stark. And I appear now only to do as I have done on so many former occasions, to thank you once more for the warm and hearty indorsement which you have to-day given my public acts."

President McKinley received the election returns to-night at his home, surrounded by a large number of his old friends and neighbors, including many women who came as the guests of Mrs. McKinley.

Direct wires connected the house with the Republican National Headquarters at New York and Chicago, with Senator Hanna at the Union Club in Cleveland, and with the home of Gov. Roosevelt, at Oyster Bay, so that the President was in constant telegraphic touch with his associate on the ticket and with the campaign leaders.

The President made his headquarters in his library, where most of the men guests congregated, while Mrs. McKinley entertained the women in another room.

Secretary Cortelyou read most of the dispatches, some of the more cheering announcements being heartily applauded by the guests. Most of the early advices were fragmentary, and inconclusive, but the strong indications that New York and probably Illinois had gone for McKinley were received with great satisfaction.

The President's first congratulations from headquarters came from J. H. Manley, at New York, as follows:

"Praise God, from whom all blessings flow. Your triumphant re-election is conceded by Democratic managers. I tender my earnest congratulations. We are very happy at headquarters."

Even at 11 o'clock the President had given no intimation to those nearest to him as to his own opinion of the results, although it was the general view of those at the house that his re-election was assured beyond a doubt. The advices from headquarters had been uniformly favorable. The announcement that Croker conceded New York and Illinois to McKinley was greeted with applause. There was another outburst when strong assurances were received that Missouri and Indiana would be in the McKinley column. The Kentucky headquarters sent word that the contest was very close.

## SECRETARY GAGE'S VIEWS.

### He Says the Result of the Election Will Be New Confidence and Courage Everywhere.

WASHINGTON, Nov. 6.—The jubilation here over President McKinley's re-election broke all bounds. Never, except at inauguration times, did such crowds surge up and down Pennsylvania Avenue, cheering, singing, and blowing horns.

In the absence of the President there was no gathering at the White House, and such advices as were received there were conveyed by telephone to the members of the Cabinet now in Washington. Only three are here—Secretaries Hay, Gage, and Root—the last-named reaching the city this evening after casting his ballot in New York. Secretary Hay was feeling indisposed, and remained at his home during the evening, but Secretary Gage was at the Treasury Department and with a number of friends heard the results there. Mr. Gage said:

"The result will bring a sense of gratification and triumph to the rank and file, as well as to the leaders of the Republican Party.

"If this were all which the result involved one could look on it with a sense of comparative indifference. To my mind, however, this is but the most minor consideration. It is to the broad industrial and commercial interests that the result must bring a feeling of profound thankfulness. It is not necessary to descant upon the propositions of the opposition.

"These propositions have been rejected, and we have the assurance that no serious interruption to the on-going of business affairs is to occur. The country, that portion of it at least which carries the burdens and risks of enterprise and industry, will give a sigh of relief that we have been delivered from dangers which could not be measured. Thus relieved, new confidence and courage will everywhere be felt, and the good conditions in finance, trade, and industrial activity, now so observable on every hand, ought to and undoubtedly will be strengthened and advanced.

"It is to be hoped that the victorious party will realize that its triumph only serves to increase its responsibility; not to its adherents merely, but to all the people. The protests and criticisms of the minority, when made in good faith, may justly demand honest and patient consideration from the party invested with legislative and administrative power.

"Protests and criticism have filled the air with clamorous tongue. Intensified by partisan heat though they have been, the elements of truth they may carry are educational, and may bring light to National councils.

"My own deep conviction—freed as far as possible from political bias—is that every right-minded man and woman in our land is to be congratulated upon the result. I know, if I know anything, that in the President-elect the country may impose its trust with full sense of security. He is superior to mere party advantages. He loves his country better than his party, and his highest aim is to secure it, as a whole, conditions of domestic peace and economic well-being. This opinion is, I believe, fully shared by those of the opposing party, whether from the North or South, who, representing their constituents in the halls of the National Legislature, have come into contact with his spirit and motives during the four years of Administration now drawing to a close."

# NEW YORK CITY

## Bryan Carries It By About 28,000.

## BELMONT ELECTED

## RUPPERT WINS

### McClellan and Cummings Re-elected.

## DOUGLAS DEFEATS HILL

### Manhattan Gives Bryan Over 28,000 Plurality.

### Kings County for McKinley By Small Margin.

### JACOB WORTH DEFEATED IN BROOKLYN.

### VAN COTT-CREAMER CONTEST

Mr. Bryan carried the City of New York by a plurality of about 31,000 over Mr. McKinley. The total vote cast for the Presidential candidates in the five boroughs of New York was about 600,000. The total registration was 642,034.

The latest returns from the entire city, with forty-one election districts missing out of a total of 1,522, show that Mr. McKinley received 273,179 votes and Mr. Bryan 301,309, a plurality of 28,130.

The Boroughs of Manhattan and the Bronx, with 33 districts missing out of 822, give Mr. Bryan a plurality of 28,639.

Richard Croker sent a telegram to Mr. Bryan saying that New York County had gone for him by 32,000, an increase of 55,000 over the vote of 1896, and he wrote, "We are defeated, but not discouraged."

The vote in Brooklyn was very close, but the plurality for Mr. McKinley is about 2,000. With fifty-two districts the vote for Mr. McKinley was 97,951 and for Mr. Bryan 94,459.

In the Borough of Queens, with twelve missing election districts, Mr. Bryan carries the county by 1,994. The vote was as follows: McKinley, 10,069; Bryan, 12,063.

The complete returns from the Borough of Richmond show that this district was closely contested. Mr. McKinley received 6,038 and Mr. Bryan received 6,733, a plurality on the latest returns of 695 for the Democratic ticket.

The registration was: Brooklyn, 230,459; Queens, 29,318, and Richmond, 13,982.

Tammany has probably elected eight Congressmen. There was some doubt expressed as to whether Richard Van Cott had defeated Assistant Corporation Counsel Thomas Creamer in the Eighth District.

The latest news received by Richard Croker from the Assembly District leaders last evening at Tammany Hall showed that if Creamer was elected it would be by a small majority.

The young candidate, J. Sprunt Hill, whom Mr. Richard Croker put up in the Fourteenth District, was defeated by the Republican candidate, William H. Douglass.

George B. McClellan defeated Herbert Parsons in the Twelfth District by about 4,500, according to Congressman McClellan's report to Mr. Croker at Tammany Hall.

O. H. P. Belmont was elected over William R. Willcox in the Thirteenth District.

Jacob Ruppert, Jr., succeeded in defeating Elias Goodman, Republican, in the Fifteenth District.

In the other Congressional districts the contests resulted as follows:

Nicholas Muller, Democrat, defeated Gen. J. R. O'Beirne in the Seventh District.

Henry M. Goldfogle, Democrat, defeated Theodore Cox in the Ninth District.

Amos J. Cummings, Democrat, defeated John Glass, Jr., in the Tenth.

William Sulzer, Democrat, defeated Charles Schwick in the Eleventh.

There were some surprises in the contests in New York and Brooklyn.

In the Eighth Assembly District Charles Adler has always succeeded in being elected to the Assembly when nominated on the Republican ticket, although the district is strongly Democratic.

In Brooklyn the Republican and Democratic politicians alike were surprised at the defeat of Jacob Worth for Congress.

Mr. Worth has also been one of the Republicans who always able to win in a Democratic district. The Democratic leaders in Kings County conceded the election of Jacob Worth by about 1,000 votes a few days before election.

There are two election contests in New York in which the vote is so evenly divided that the result may not be accurately known until the official canvass is made.

In the Eighth Congressional District the returns wavered from Thomas Creamer, Democrat, to Richard Van Cott, Republican, several times before 1 o'clock A. M. The news Mr. Croker received at Tammany Hall was that Mr. Van Cott had been defeated.

The police returns given out at 1 A. M. showed that Mr. Van Cott was elected by a very small plurality. Later the vote on

"All the News That's Fit to Print."

# The New York Times.

THE WEATHER.
Rain, turning to snow; northeasterly winds.

COPYRIGHT, 1901, BY THE NEW YORK TIMES COMPANY.

VOL. L...NO. 15,961. NEW YORK, TUESDAY, MARCH 5, 1901.—SIXTEEN PAGES. ONE CENT In Greater New York, Jersey City, and Newark. | Elsewhere, TWO CENTS.

## M'CULLAGH RAIDS "THE" ALLEN'S CLUB

### Capt. Chapman Performs a Gymnastic Tour de Force.

#### Climbs Out on a Ledge and Breaks Through a Window—Three Men Arrested and Locked Up.

"The" Allen's "West Side Club," at 80 Sixth Avenue, was raided in a spectacular manner for the second time within a week by Capt. Chapman of the Mercer Street Station late yesterday afternoon, in the presence of a large crowd.

This raid was conducted by the Committee of Fifteen, and was under the personal supervision of Robert Grier Monroe and State Superintendent of Elections John McCullagh. There was no "tipping off," and the poolroom department of the club was in full operation when Capt. Chapman gained access to the place by a daring climb along a narrow coping, smashing a front window in his progress.

Consternation reigned in the room when the Captain burst in, and the excitement among the crowd which stretched across Sixth Avenue was intense. News that a raid was in progress spread through the Jefferson Market Court district rapidly, and the numbers of the spectators was constantly augmented. Sixth Avenue cars passed with difficulty, and each added its quota to the mob of curious lookers-on. The Eighth Street elevated road station offered a splendid point of vantage for a hundred or more.

Five of Capt. Chapman's officers had been stationed in front of the place all day. "Nothing doing" was their report, and to emphasize this three members of the club who attempted to enter were arrested and taken to the Jefferson Market Court by the zealous sleuths only to be immediately discharged by Magistrate Pool.

Superintendent McCullagh's detective, George P. Hammond of Mazet fame, entered the place during the afternoon, and when about seventy-five of the members had gathered, Superintendent McCullagh was notified at 5 o'clock that the "club" was in full blast. Superintendent McCullagh communicated with Robert Grier Monroe and Justice Jerome, who had issued warrants for the arrest of three men, said to be the managers and employes of the place, and together Mr. Monroe and Superintendent McCullagh went to the Mercer Street Station. The warrants were placed in Capt. Chapman's hands, and he was asked to serve them.

"Why, I've got five men in front of that place now!" said the surprised Captain. "They arrested three men and Magistrate Pool discharged them."

"Well, I guess the men you've got there will be enough," said Superintendent McCullagh grimly.

The front door to the "West Side Club," although its members say it is simply a social organization, was locked, barred, and chained. Efforts to gain an entrance this way were futile. The entrance from the restaurant beneath was also closed tight. Capt. Chapman, in full uniform, went through the cigar store next door to the first floor front windows, climbed out on the narrow ledge, and reached for the windows of No. 80.

Capt. Chapman's whiskers were immediately recognized by the crowd as he appeared on the ledge. The Captain got a good grip with his feet on the window sill and grabbed for the next window. He nearly missed, and the crowd thought he was going to fall to the sidewalk. His fingers just fastened on the shutters of the clubroom, and with his right hand he wrenched them open and smashed the glass. Superintendent McCullagh and Mr. Monroe surveyed the gymnastic feat from the sidewalk. In the room the Captain entered there was a stampede and much confusion. The seventy-five persons who had taken alarm at the pounding on the front door rushed for the roof and the rear windows.

Some escaped, but, as the raiders were not after players, all were allowed to go except three men identified by Detective Hammond as the men he wanted. These three were arrested and taken to the Mercer Street Station, together with a large number of race cards and betting slips. There the men gave their names as Arthur Moore, William Lewis, and William Campbell. They were charged with aiding and abetting pool selling and bookmaking, in violation of Section 351 of the Penal Code. Justice Jerome was on hand at the station house to accept bail, but up to a late hour the three were still locked up.

Supt. McCullough, speaking of the raid last night, said:

"We got just what we went after. My men obtained the evidence against the place several days ago, being allowed to enter the room and place bets without question. I was notified late yesterday afternoon that the place was in full operation, despite the fact that policemen were stationed in front of the door. We decided to raid the place."

Capt. Chapman's version of the raid differed slightly from his ex-Chief's.

"I raided that place Friday," said he, "and the men were discharged in the Police Court. I stationed five men in front of it to-day and three arrests were made of people who tried to go in. They were also discharged. The players went in through the rear and over back yards, despite my men in front, and I heard about it and telephoned Deputy Commissioner Devery.

"He instructed me to break into the place if I had to, and I had just started, taking Detectives Hall and McGuire with me, when I met Superintendent McCullagh and Mr. Monroe. They gave me the warrants. They must have been expecting us inside for there wasn't much doing."

Chairman W. H. Baldwin, Jr., of the Committee of Fifteen refused to comment on the raid. Austen G. Fox was equally reticent.

## MR. CLEVELAND'S WARNING.

### Tells a Young Men's Democratic Club to Beware of Temptation.

Grover Cleveland has written a personal letter to Arthur De Vere Storey, President of the Young Men's Democratic Club of the Twenty-first Assembly District, the pioneer club in the movement to organize the young Democrats of the city in a political association to give supplementary work to the regular Democratic organizations in each Assembly District. The letter says in part:

What I have written concerning young men in politics is based very largely upon my own personal experience; and I know that a body of young Democrats associated for the purpose of disinterested work and whose object is to make better known and stimulate devotion to intelligent Democracy, will not be long ignored by party managers, and that when once recognized their influence for political good will easily follow. But it is of vital importance that their efforts should be patriotic, untrammeled, and intelligent. As soon as an association of this kind becomes effective and strong, temptations will be put in its way that must be shunned or resisted if it would retain its usefulness and influence in the attempt to attain the best political results.

## INDEX TO DEPARTMENTS.

Stocks Strong. Financial Affairs.—Pages 12 and 13.
Wheat, No. 2 red, 80¾c; Corn, No. 2 mixed, 45¾c; oats, No. 2 mixed, 31c; iron, Northern, No. 1 foundry, $16.00; butter, Western creamery, 22c. Commercial World.—Page 14.
Amusements.—Page 8.
Arrivals at Hotels and Out-of-Town Buyers.—Page 10.
Business Troubles.—Page 6.
Court Calendars.—Page 11.
Legal Notes.—Page 10.
Losses by Fire.—Page 5.
Marine Intelligence and Foreign Mails.—Page 5.
New Corporations.—Page 12.
Railroads.—Page 10.
Real Estate.—Page 14.
Society.—Page 9.
Weather Report.—Page 5.
Yesterday's Fires.—Page 5.



## LOOK FOR "COMING MAN."

### Political Astrologers Talk of Mr. McKinley's Successor.

*Special to The New York Times.*

WASHINGTON, March 4.—There was one class of people who viewed the brilliant inaugural pageant to-day to whom President McKinley was not the figure of greatest interest. They were the politicians, and to their view the President was second in importance to "the coming man." The politicians were certain "the coming man" was in the parade, but the uncertainty of his position in the line and the air of mystery which hung about him made him the object of absorbing speculation to the political horoscopists.

Eagerly did these seers scan the leaders of the moving hosts for a sight of the new star of 1904. And when they discovered him, or thought they did, they were delighted with their prophetic vision. Unfortunately for the exactness of political prophecy, the conclusions of the political horoscopists as to the identity of "the coming man" did not agree, but these differences add to rather than detract from the interest in their astrological observances.

There were some who were certain that in Vice President Roosevelt they beheld "the coming man." So certain were they as to the accuracy of their forecast that they resented the casting of doubts upon it. It was to be remarked, however, that the political astrologers who saw "the coming man" in the dashing Rough Rider were nearly all of the class who rely upon popular signs. Whenever a question was raised as to the reliability of their horoscope they pointed to the crowds for verification. And the verification, such as it was, seemed ample enough.

The Rough Rider is the popular idol of the hour. There can be no doubt about that. Everywhere along the line he was received with vociferous acclaims. In their outbursts of admiration and affection for him the people cast all thought of the dignity of the Vice President to the winds. He was still "Teddy" to them, and evidence which was given to him of how near he was to the hearts of the people, despite the new and oppressive dignity thrust upon him, was manifestly a keen delight to Mr. Roosevelt. He bowed and smiled, and showed his teeth, and, in the language of one of his youthful curbstone admirers, he was voted "the greatest ever."

But while the political horoscopists who saw "the coming man" in the San Juan hero, watched with overflowing pleasure the reception their idol received, it was not so much with the scene to-day that their minds were occupied as it was with the vision which they had of the avenue four years hence, when their hero would ride to the Capitol to have conferred upon him the greatest honor in the gift of his own or any other people.

There were other political seers of more sober and calculating mien, who smiled sardonically at the enthusiasm of those who proclaimed Roosevelt as "the coming man," and when the Roosevelt admirers said to them indignantly, "Well, if Roosevelt is not 'the coming man,' then you point the coming man out to us," they replied: "Wait, and we will show him to you."

And, strangely enough, it was when the banners of New York came in sight that those who ridiculed the claims of Roosevelt pointed out a man of athletic build and determined mien, seated upon a spirited steed which he held under perfect control, and said:

"There he is."

It was Gov. Benjamin B. Odell, Jr.

"In four years from now Roosevelt will be politically dead," said the Odell prophets. "You have put him into a political tomb. Odell is the rising man. He will keep growing, and four years from now the New York delegation will go to the convention for him, and not for Roosevelt."

There were still others who thought those who picked Odell as "the coming man" were as far wrong as those who selected Roosevelt. Their contention was that the ambitions of Odell and Roosevelt running counter to each other would destroy New York's chances of naming the candidate.

"The rivalry between those two," they said, "will be so intense that it will be political wisdom to look elsewhere than in New York for a Republican candidate."

When asked for their view of where "the coming man" would be found, they said:

"Why, he was seated alongside the man who is now the whole thing in the parade to-day. It is Hanna."

The people of the country, they said, attributed the present prosperity of the country to Hanna, as well as to McKinley. It was Hanna's resourcefulness as a leader, they said, which made McKinley twice President, and, to a large extent, had guided his Administration over dangerous ground. The people, they asserted, had confidence in Hanna as a business man, and now that we were reaching out for the world's trade, it was a business man who was wanted at the head of the Nation's affairs.

But there was a little band of political astrologers who could not "see" Hanna any more than they could see Roosevelt or Odell. They agreed with the Ohio soothsayers, that Odell and Roosevelt would kill each other off in the contest of 1904, but they said the country would not be willing to have President McKinley succeeded by an Ohio man. They were confident they saw "the coming man" in Gov. Leslie M. Shaw of Iowa.

Gov. Shaw is now regarded as probably the strongest man in the Republican Party west of the Mississippi, and the theory upon which his probable nomination is based is that four years from now the Republican Party will find it to its advantage to go west of the Mississippi for its candidate. Gov. Shaw enjoys the reputation of being "a safe man," and as such his admirers believe he would be entirely acceptable to the East.

## ITALIAN ACTRESS MURDERED.

### Minnie Cralla, Shot and Killed by Rejected Suitor at Mulberry and Bayard Streets.

Antonio Friolli, twenty years old, living at 55 Oliver Street, shot and killed Minnie Cralla, sixteen years old, of 40 Madison Street, at Mulberry and Bayard Streets at midnight last night. Friolli was arrested and locked up in the Elizabeth Street Station.

The girl was a member of an Italian company playing at the Italian Theatre, 109 Mulberry Street, this week. When in the city she lived at 40 Madison Street with her mother, Santina Malgareus.

Friolli, it is said, had asked the girl to marry him several times, and she had repeatedly refused. He attended the theatre last night, and after the show was over walked to Bayard Street and waited several minutes for the girl to leave the playhouse. She soon appeared, accompanied by her mother and William Sorrentina.

Friolli then it is alleged, pulled a revolver and fired five shots. One took effect in the girl's temple and the other struck her in the back. The other went wild. The girl was carried into 83 Bayard Street, but died in a few minutes. Friolli ran through the coffee house, at 83 Bayard Street, out the rear door and into the cellar of 79 Bayard Street where he was caught by Policeman Rogers, and locked up.

## FORMER NEW YORKER MISSING.

### H. H. Pieper, While Ill, Disappears from His Home in Monsey.

*Special to The New York Times.*

SPRING VALLEY, N. Y., March 4.—Last Thursday Herman H. Pieper of the firm of Ester Sherwood & Co. of Monsey village complained of feeling ill. He shortly thereafter left the home of his brother-in-law, where he lived, and has not been seen since, excepting on Thursday afternoon, when a workman on the Sprague farm near Monsey saw him wandering about in the woods. Searching parties were out with hounds yesterday, but found no trace of the missing man.

Pieper is twenty-eight years old, a bachelor, and popular in this locality. He came from New York several years ago, and became a partner in business with Ester Sherwood, a prominent Rockland County politician. No reason can be assigned for Pieper's disappearance.



## OPERA COMIQUE TRIP OF VENEZUELA'S NAVY

### Rich Fittings of Jay Gould's Old Yacht Burned for Fuel.

#### Gorgeously Uniformed American Officers Run Her Aground and Are "Turned Down" by an Agent—How the Skipper's Pride Was Humbled.

The ship's company that left this port on Jan. 24 in Jay Gould's old yacht Atalanta, transformed into the gunboat Restaurador, under Venezuelan colors, and equipped with gaudy naval uniforms and a certain picturesque hope of attaining to a man Venezuelan commissions, got back home yesterday on the Red D liner Philadelphia. Men who have been at sea for years describe the trip as the most grotesque of their lives. They were gone a little over a month, when they expected to deliver the boat to the Venezuelan Government in ten days.

The yacht was sold to the Venezuelan Government early in January, and constitutes the entire Venezuelan Navy. She received her armament, consisting of four six-pounder Hotchkiss guns, a three-pounder, and two two-pounders, and was loaded with ammunition speedily. Then a ship's company was gotten together, under the direction of the Venezuelan Consul, and the ship went out to sea to try her guns. She saluted the Alabama off Tompkinsville, who didn't notice her efforts at international dignity. Then she came in again, completed her crew, and, having been transferred to the South American Government, put to sea under the flag of Venezuela.

Capt. Jeremiah Merithew was in command. Under him were forty-six men. Signor Kebrum went along as the representative of the South American republic. The men shipped under a contract stipulating that a month's wages would be paid in any event, and their passage back. They were given to understand, however, that the trip would take but ten days, and all that would be required of them was to deliver the boat over to the Government at La Guayra. Then they could return or take service in the cause of the republic. The men, most of whom were sailing on private yachts in the Summer, decided to stay. The Captain and his crew bought uniforms modeled after those of American naval officers.

The first night at sea trouble began. The ship ran into a storm that, increasing in the morning, raged for four days. Two of the boats were carried away, the force of the waves smashed in the galley door and put out the fires three times in one day. The bowsprit was snapped off. When the storm abated the ship was found to be short of fuel. This seemed very mysterious to the men, as they thought they were outfitted for a direct run to La Guayra.

Rigging and things on the deck were in such shape that it was decided to run into San Juan, but the coal had given completely out before that port was reached. The cabin furnishings, rich articles of furniture that had been in the yacht since the days of Jay Gould, were dumped into the furnaces. The fancy wood paneling of the staterooms, then portières, carpets, and tables followed. Finally the provisions—such of them as would burn readily—fed the fires under the boilers.

AS THE SHIP'S POET PUT IT.

The ship's poet, who was also the ship's baker, thus refers to their straits in verse in his log:

All on board were very glad when the storm was done;
You should have seen them smile and grab their tack when we reached San Juan,
And each one kicked himself full hard that he had left New York,
For none dreamed that on that trip we'd burn up all the pork.

In San Juan the Restaurador lay from Jan. 3 to Feb. 6, being repaired and refitted. Here she was joined by another agent of the Government, who had been waiting for her, proving to the men that it had never been intended that she should proceed straight to her ultimate destination. What followed after leaving San Juan is told in the words of the ship's poet and the chef, George Casbay, long a steward for the Cunard Line. This is what they related yesterday:

"We left San Juan on the 6th of February, under some sort of secret orders. It leaked out that we were to be ordered to bombard a town held by the insurgents then making war on the Government. This comforted us a little—we had been grumbling hard before over our deception—for we thought we'd have a little fun, anyway, out of the trip. But about this time the skipper and most of the officers began to get high and mighty. They regarded themselves as commissioned officers in the Venezuelan Navy. They brought out the uniforms they had bought in New York and put on swords and pistols. The language that was used on the quarter deck, so to speak, would have made a pirate blush.

"Finally, we came within sight of the coast town of Carupano, supposed to be held by the rebels. All of our officers came on deck in their New York uniforms, with their swords and pistols. The crew were armed with pistols, rifles, and knives, and at every gun of the yacht men were stationed. As we got nearer to the town the guns were trained on its walls. The signal for firing was about to be given when a yellow flag was raised from shore. Our officers in turn ran up a yellow flag. The signal from the shore meant that the Government had recaptured the town, which wasn't anything more than a collection of mud huts.

"After that we lay off shore with all guns loaded and aimed and the deck covered with ammunition, waiting, for we suspected a trick. In a few hours boats began to put off for us, and we learned that everything was all right. That was the 8th of February. We lay off the town there until 3 o'clock of the next afternoon. In that time we were made to receive a lot of prisoners, rebels, and soldiers. These last were a filthy lot. We had some sixty of them.

"Among the prisoners, all of whom seemed to us to be far superior to their captors, was the rebel General commanding in that part of the country. He had been sentenced to be shot on the morning of our arrival, but when they sighted us it was decided to send him to La Guayra and thence to Caracas, where the sentence was to be carried out. He was a fine-looking old fellow, resembling in general appearance the Cuban Gen. Gomez.

"They let the old General stay on deck as long as the town was in sight. He was hopelessly crushed and spoke to nobody. As long as the boat was visible from the town his wife and daughters stood upon a high peak of rocks gazing after him.

SKIPPER DECLINES TO BE DEPOSED.

"Just after we got under way there was a grand row between the skipper and the Venezuelan agent, Caprillas, who had joined us at San Juan. The skipper had understood all the time that he was to remain in command right along, even after the yacht had been taken to La Guayra. But at Carupano the agent shipped a Venezuelan skipper and a pilot. Our skipper got up on the bridge, sword and uniform and all.

"'I am in command of this man-of-war,' he roared. 'That pilot and that greaser can come along as passengers if they want to, but I, the commanding officer, forbid them the bridge.'

"Caprillas expostulated and tried to smooth things over, but it wouldn't go.

"'I'll shoot the first passenger that sets foot on this bridge,' was the skipper's decision.

"What might be expected to happen did happen. We ran hard and fast aground that night at 7:30 on the Island of Coche, in the Straits of Margarita. There was a pretty stiff sea on, and when we turned in that night we expected to wake up somewhere else. The next day the imitation soldiers, who were of Indian blood, got off in boats and sent for tugs. We staid there hard and fast from the 9th of February until early in the morning of the 12th. We were pulled off by a tug and a German and a Dutch steamer that happened along.

"On the same day that we got afloat again we touched at three other small ports, two of which were Waunda and Cumana, at which we got 270 more prisoners and soldiers. With this motley, dirty crowd of soldiers and fair-looking prisoners we set out finally for La Guayra.

"After our accident in running aground there was another big row between our skipper and Caprillas. Caprillas went up to the bridge.

"'I want you to take that pilot up here at once,' he told the old man.

"'Not in a million years,' the skipper yelled.

"Caprillas stepped to one side quickly, just as the old man was reaching for his sword. Then he pulled a gun and stuck it just back of the skipper's ear.

"'A pilot or hell,' Caprillas said in a quiet tone of voice.

"Then the skipper took the pilot on the bridge. There was more gunplay between the two before the old man would let the yacht touch at the little ports we visited last. Caprillas got the drop on him again and the old man gave in.

"Well, we got into La Guayra at last, on Feb. 13. The ship was no sooner in port and the prisoners and soldiers discharged than the Government put the skipper, his officers, and most of the men ashore. Their New York uniforms didn't seem to go down there. Then there was a time in that town. The skipper and his men stormed for their commissions, but to no use. Three or four of the men who had been quiet during the voyage were allowed to remain on board, but we decided that we had had enough of that sort of thing, and held the Government to its contract.

"'We've had enough of Yankee skippers and Yankee crews,' Caprillas told the old man was the reason that he didn't want us; 'besides, our Government mistrusts you.'

"The last straw that ruined our skipper was this. While he was still on board in the harbor it was Washington's Birthday. The United States gunboat Scorpion saluted us in honor of Washington. Our skipper, who happened to be aboard in spite of the fact that he had been suspended, ordered that we return the salute with all our guns. That we did with a will. The skipper hadn't asked the yellow boy's permission. Caprillas said that he didn't object to Washington, but he did to our skipper's Yankee assumption. Then they made him stay on shore.

"They tried to pay us off in Venezuelan silver. For a number of days we went around loaded down to the gunnels, to speak that way, with their bags of coin. But after we made a big kick they exchanged it, paying eighty cents on the dollar into American gold."



## CONVICTED BY A PHOTOGRAPH.

### Picture of Sunday Scene in His Saloon Leads to Plea of Guilty by Naugatuck (Conn.) Man.

*Special to The New York Times.*

DERBY, Conn., March 4.—A camera plate was the only evidence needed this morning in the town court of Naugatuck to convict Henry Fox, a saloonkeeper, of violation of the Sunday liquor law.

In a raid on Fox's barroom on Sunday the police entered just as a group of five men were posing before the camera of Thomas Foy, an amateur photographer. Both camera and men were locked up. It developed that Foy, who is a friend of Fox, had promised to photograph the interior of the latter's newly furnished barroom. As he worked in a factory on week days, he went to take the pictures on Sunday. The proprietor invited the five men to include themselves in the pictures. One view had already been taken, and the men were posing for another when the police arrived.

In court this morning the State failed to make out a case against the prisoners after an hour's examination, when Prosecuting Attorney Sweeney, as a last resort, asked that the plate of the first picture be developed. Judge Hungerford consented, and a recess was taken while the plate was hurried to a photographer.

When returned to court the plate showed one of the men in the act of drinking a glass of beer. Before this evidence Fox broke down, and changed his plea to guilty. He was fined $25 and costs. Foy was released, and the others got off with $10 fine each.

## BUFFALO-DETROIT TROLLEY.

### A Continuous Line to be Completed This Summer.

*Special to The New York Times.*

PHILADELPHIA, March 4.—C. D. Barney & Co., brokers, of this city, associated with the Moore-Everett syndicate of Cleveland, Ohio, have just consummated a big trolley deal, perfecting the consolidation of the Lorain and Cleveland, Interurban, and Sandusky, Norwalk and Southern lines, including both local Sandusky railways. The name of the new organization is the Lake Shore Electrical Railway Company; capital, $4,000,000 stock and $4,000,000 bonds.

By this deal a chain of electric roads will extend from Buffalo to Detroit, paralleling the Michigan and Lake Shore Railroad. The entire line will be completed this Summer. The equipment of the road will be of the highest standard, and the cars will have a speed of fifty miles an hour over a seventy-pound rail. It is said that none of the stock will be put on the market.

## THE RESULT OF A NIGHTMARE.

*Special to The New York Times.*

PITTSBURG, March 4.—E. W. Stewittinus of Chicago, Vice President of the Sterling Manufacturing Company of that city, is at the West Penn Hospital suffering from an injury of a peculiar nature.

While struggling in a nightmare in a sleeping car early yesterday morning he pushed his foot through a window. The jagged glass severed an artery, and before medical aid could be secured there was the gravest danger of Mr. Stewittinus bleeding to death.

Mr. Stewittinus had been East and was on his way home. As the train was rushing by Cresson he was rolling around in a lower berth on the Pennsylvania, St. Louis and Chicago Express. Finally one of Mr. Stewittinus's feet went through the window. Blood spurted from his injured foot.

His danger was so apparent that word was telegraphed to Johnstown. Dr. W. B. Lowman met the train there and accompanied the injured man to Pittsburg, all the time endeavoring to stop the flow of blood. He finally succeeded, but the Chicago man was so weak that he was sent to the hospital.

## TO SELL MANCHESTER CORSETS.

*Special to The New York Times.*

CINCINNATI, March 4.—Next Wednesday the women of Cincinnati who have a hobby to wear or possess anything that is connected with the nobility will have an excellent opportunity to gratify it. There are three pairs of corsets stored away in the Government Building basement here, which will figure as a drawing card for dozens of women at the sale on March 6 of abandoned goods.

The corsets were intended for her Grace the Duchess of Manchester, who, with her husband, is now en route to Europe. They were made to fit by a fashionable corsetmaker in Paris, France. They are of the finest texture and most delicate tints, while the lace work and embroidery all go to make up what fair women would call "dreams of delight."

For some reason the corsets were not accepted nor the duty paid by the Duchess. The duty was upward of $12. Notices that the stays had arrived were sent repeatedly to the Mount Auburn home of Eugene Zimmerman, but no attention was paid to them, and now the Federal authorities will sell them to the highest bidder. Although there are in the collection numerous articles of value, it is safe to say the corsets of the Duchess will be the articles to command the women's attention.

### Clarence Coles Burned to Death.

While delirious, suffering from an attack of pneumonia, Clarence Coles, a blackboard manufacturer of 68 Vesey Street, Manhattan, rose from his bed in the back parlor of the boarding house, 47 Hoyt Street, Brooklyn, struck a light in the room and in some way the furniture of the room caught fire. The blaze had been going for fifteen minutes before it was discovered, and in their panic the people in the house forgot Coles. He was burned to death.



## MR. M'KINLEY BEGINS HIS SECOND TERM

### Rain Fails to Mar Inauguration Ceremonies

### CROWDS IN THE STREETS

### Col. Roosevelt Shares in the Cheers of the Multitudes.

*Special to The New York Times.*

WASHINGTON, March 4.—William McKinley of Ohio, the first President to be elected to succeed himself since Gen. U. S. Grant, was to-day inaugurated with a renewal, in great measure, of the enthusiasm with which his installation in office was accomplished four years ago, and Theodore Roosevelt of New York, sworn into office in the presence of the retiring President, who was soon to be the new President, shared with the Chief Executive in receiving the acclaims of many thousands.

The cheers came from spectators, many of whom had stood for more than an hour in a drenching rain, that took all the life out of the gay decorations, soaked the men in line to the very skin, and marred the satisfaction of the committeemen who had been for weeks making the preparations, of which in the early morning they were so proud.

Yet the day was not all wet and dreary. The morning was dull, with streaks of sunlight now and then through the heavy clouds that were drifting up from the southeast to overwhelm Weather Prophet Moore and his predictions. Those who had observed yesterday's beginning and ending hoped that it would be repeated to-day.

While soldiers afoot and mounted were hurrying here and there to reach assembling points, and crowds of people were pushing into the already packed street cars going toward the Capitol in great numbers, but not in such great numbers as four years ago, or at the time of Mr. Cleveland's first inauguration, the Vice President-elect made his way, with Squadron A as an escort, to the Senate. He got a foretaste, along Massachusetts Avenue on the march, of the enthusiasm that his later appearance was to create.

GREETING OF THE MULTITUDE.

The warmth of the greeting accorded to him disposed of the ill-natured suggestion that the inauguration was one to be made impressive by military under orders. The crowd was not under orders, and it welcomed Col. Roosevelt with obviously spontaneous admiration.

The progress of the President down Pennsylvania Avenue to the Capitol, riding in his own carriage with Senator Hanna, was a continuous ovation from throats that defied all restraint. The military did not have anything to do with that cheering. It came from the plain spectators, massed along the streets and filling every available window, and to the last row and seat the stands at the reservations. Senator Hanna could have taken as much of this applause to himself as he liked, but he did not appear to claim any of it, for he sat with his head covered, while the President almost constantly raised his hat and bowed from side to side.

The Senate Chamber proceedings seemed a bit dull, owing, possibly, to the nature of the business attending the closing of work. While the distinguished guests, the diplomatic representatives, and the fortunate civilians who could secure tickets, were entering and endeavoring to find seats, Senator Carter was singing the requiem over the River and Harbor bill. Only a few of the visitors knew the significance of the fight he was making, and only a few cared whether there was a fight or not.

There was impatience for the arrival of the Vice President-elect, and after the Ambassadors had come in to be given seats in the front row and next the aisle, thus giving them precedence over the Cabinet, the curiosity that had been temporarily arrested was gratified by the appearance of Col. Roosevelt, introduced from the main door as he was led to his seat down to the front to be sworn in, a superb picture of health, the suggestion of prodigious energy.

ENTHUSIASM UNDAMPED.

Every east front crowd that attends inauguration ceremonies knows how to cheer. The throng that met the eyes of President McKinley and Vice President Roosevelt when they took their places under the dripping canopy at the front of the platform was a vast one, extending well out over the plaza.

The pitiless rain may have been accountable in a measure for the reduction of the crowd that had come unprepared for rain, but the rain had not washed out the enthusiasm of the American citizen. As the President smilingly made his way from the porch of the Capitol to the canopied platform wisely erected to shelter him against the unpredicted shower or blizzard, the multitude sent up a roar of cheers that rose and fell like the pounding of a line of surf in a storm. It rose and fell and rose and fell again, until it was seen that the President was ready to take the oath of office.

Four years ago, when he succeeded to the office made vacant by Grover Cleveland, there sat in the front row of spectators a venerable woman, the mother of the new President, to whom the President turned affectionately when he had finished his inaugural address and kissed reverently before the great throng. This act was remembered by many who were present to-day, and who had shared with "Mother" McKinley the pride in the choice of the people for President.

While there were perhaps fewer people in the plaza before the Capitol than there had been on some former occasions, a greater number of spectators was seated. On the central platform, of which the President's canopied stage was a part, there were seats for the 3,000 privileged persons who had witnessed the events in the Senate Chamber. At each side of this platform were lesser platforms accommodating 2,000 persons each, the occupants of the stands being supplied with seats by Senators or Representatives.

All these platforms were uncovered, except a space some 20 feet square for the use of the President and Mrs. McKinley and some immediate friends. When the rain descended many of the occupants of the platform imitated the example of the diplomats in their fine clothes and feathers and fled to shelter. The crowd fled from the edges, but the men who had but a few moments before made a line of red, yellow, and white off on the edges of the multitude suddenly became uniformly blue and stood where they had been ordered to stand until the order to march was given.

CHEERS FOR COL. ROOSEVELT.

To avoid an interruption of the parade it had been arranged to provide the President with a luncheon before he left the Capitol to go back to the White House. While he and the Vice President lunched, the crowds along Pennsylvania Avenue, the military awaiting in the side streets the signal to fall into line, and the spectators who were so unfortunate as to be without cover or umbrellas fretted and speculated and bought umbrellas, in which a sudden and brisk trade was developed.

As soon as the President appeared at the head of the line returning to the White House that roar as of prodigious waves beating on a beach that had been heard at the east front began as the President's carriage came in sight, and advanced without interruption or rest ahead of the procession all the way to the White House. It was no hireling cheer, no perfunctory shouting, that greeted President McKinley reinstalled, and it gained a little in force as Vice President Roosevelt came in sight. If the crowd cheered twice in that way in one day for McKinley it did not begrudge a lifting of the cheer for the soldier who had shared with him in the receipt of the greatest of political victories.

For a mile and more this double wall of shouting spectators stretched, at first defying the pelting storm and then rejoicing because the rain had ceased and umbrellas were no longer necessary.

FIGHTING MEN NOT FORGOTTEN.

Not until after 3 o'clock did the head of the line arrive at the President's stand in the Court of Honor. The throng that occupied places in this court, although it may have paid bigger prices for seats within sight of the President's stand, was quite as profuse in its demonstrations of joy and satisfaction as the multitudes nearer the Capitol, but not more so. It was especially demonstrative, however, over Admiral Dewey and Lieut. Gen. Miles, not without cause, for two finer military figures never occupied the rear seat in a barouche at any inauguration. There was no room for jealousy, either. The applause for the two officers was as cordial as that for McKinley and Roosevelt, and there was honor enough for both.

## AROUND HANNA'S "THRONE"

### Scenes Near the Balcony Occupied by the Ohio Senator.

*Special to The New York Times.*

WASHINGTON, March 4.—The point of greatest attraction along the route of the parade next to the President's reviewing stand in the Court of Honor was at the corner of Fourteenth Street and Pennsylvania Avenue, where Hanna's "throne" was situated. The so-called "throne" was a covered balcony of fair design commanding a sweeping view of the avenue. Senator Hanna had this stand built for the members of his family to view the parade.

Several hours before the head of the line reached this point the crowd had congested there. "Hurrah for Hanna and the trusts!" shouted one individual who had more than his share of "wet goods." There was no response. The rain, which by this time had developed into a downpour, had taken all the spirit out of the crowd. They did not seem disposed to hurrah much for anything. Hundreds became discouraged at the prospect and started up the side streets for home. But there were thousands left who seemed determined to brave it out. The amount of millinery which was destroyed by the rain is beyond computation. Around Hanna's "throne" there were many fashionably attired women, whose bedraggled appearance by the time the parade reached Fourteenth Street was laughable. It was a good-natured crowd withal. A number of those who had purchased soap boxes on which to stand caused merriment by putting the boxes over their heads to protect them from the rain.

Before the parade started, negroes several times created excitement by engaging in fights, but later they gave much amusement to Senator Hanna and his guests by doing the cakewalk to the music of the bands.

The number of drunken men along the line of march was probably never surpassed. As there are many saloons in the vicinity of the corner upon which Senator Hanna's stand was erected, the number of intoxicated individuals in that vicinity seemed to be greater than elsewhere. At least half a dozen men at this point became so helplessly drunk that they fell in the street. They were men who were well dressed. One veteran lurched against a crowd and sent three others sprawling in the dirt. It was incidents such as this, principally, which kept the crowd amused.

It was a half-intoxicated man who, when engaged in an argument with a friend about imperialism, pointed to a sign above Hanna's "throne" as conclusive evidence that an empire was to be established. The sign bore the word "Empire" in large letters, but under it in characters which were smaller were the words "Fire-Proofing Company."

When the rain was coming down in torrents a number of speculative white and colored men went to the furnishing goods stores and bought up all the umbrellas they could obtain. They went among the line and sold them. They had no difficulty in disposing of their stock at advanced prices. In the trees and on telegraph poles in the neighborhood of the Hanna stand there were a number of human sparrows, who amused themselves by dropping pieces of bark or anything they could spare upon the raised umbrellas. The indignant protests of the owners were greeted with derision.

When the President's carriage approached the corner of Fourteenth Street and the avenue, Mr. McKinley raised his eyes to the Hanna balcony and bowed a number of times to the ladies on the stand, who were waving their handkerchiefs wildly. Senator Hanna, who was seated beside the President, looked straight ahead.



## PRESIDENT'S ADDRESS

### Mr. McKinley Reviews Events of the Past Four Years.

### CUBA AND THE PHILIPPINES

#### Says Promises Made to Cubans Must Be Made Good—Filipinos to Have Self-Government When Ready for It.

*Special to The New York Times.*

WASHINGTON, March 4.—In a steady, drizzling, noiseless rain that beat down on thousands of heads and on very few umbrellas President McKinley for the second time took the oath of office as Chief Executive of the United States. For hours before the time for his appearance on the east front of the Capitol the crowd had been steadily gathering, and when he did come out it was to face a mass so densely packed that it seemed as if one could walk from the Capitol to the Library grounds upon their heads. It was not, however, so large a crowd as that of 1897, for it did not stretch very far back into the Library grounds.

Good management was shown in the filling of the east ground, and the seats were taken in an orderly and gradual manner. It was 12:40 o'clock when the spectators of Vice President Roosevelt's inauguration, leaving the Senate Chamber, began to appear on the platform, to face the solid crowd, from the centre of which rose two immense batteries of cameras.

The sky was already overcast, and long before the advance guard of the distinguished guests had appeared the rain had begun, at first with a few scattered drops, but growing heavier every minute. Relying on the promises of Chief Moore of the Weather Bureau, who had staked his reputation that the day would be fair, very few had brought umbrellas.

After a while Representative McClellan of New York appeared, and after that a stream of prominent men began to trickle from the doors down on the platform, until at last the Senators and Representatives came down in a body. After the Justices of the Supreme Court—all except Chief Justice Fuller—they moved with slow and dignified step down the long stairs, and were followed by the Cabinet.

MRS. McKINLEY APPEARS.

All this time the vast crowd had been watching intently, but manifesting no enthusiasm. There were faint bursts of handclapping here and there when prominent men were recognised, but for the most part there was a complete though interested silence. But at last the doors were seen to swing open and some Capitol employes to step down and push aside the crowd lining the steps, and then a stalwart, handsome man in a Major General's uniform was seen to step down, supporting and almost carrying a sweet-faced woman.

Then the apathy of the crowd melted. A shrill cheer broke forth from those nearest the platform, which swelled into a roar as the lady and her escort came into full view, until the cheer was ringing and echoing far back into the Library grounds, and those too far away to see were being told by their neighbors the cause of the cheering, and were joining in as madly and devotedly as if they could see. And in this great cheer there was more than enthusiasm; there was a note of respect and admiration. For the sweet-faced woman, coming down the steps on Adjt. Gen. Corbin's arm, was Mrs. McKinley.

In such a heavy downpour of rain that many of the would-be spectators refused to come out and face it at all, and many of those who did fled before the ceremonies began, the gentle invalid was coming, at the risk of her health, to see her husband take the oath. It was a risky proceeding, in her state of health, and she could not stay long enough to hear the inaugural address; she had to go back as soon as the President had been sworn in, but she could not be dissuaded from coming down to the platform long enough to see it.

After Mrs. McKinley had taken her place there was no more cheering until at last the Vice President came rapidly down the steps, talking earnestly to Secretary Bennett of the Senate. Then there was some cheering, but in the big crowd Mr. Roosevelt was not seen by the majority. He took his place at the foot of the President's stand, where his wife and children joined him, and waited for the President.

PRESIDENT TAKES THE OATH.

At last the President appeared with Chief Justice Fuller, and then there was a tremendous cheer and a great waving of hats and flags. Mrs. McKinley turned and watched him eagerly as he came up the step of the little stand, followed by Vice President Roosevelt. The President was in an unusually happy frame of mind. He walked jubilantly and jauntily, with a quick, elastic step, and as he appeared on the stand and faced the crowd, his eyes gleamed and he smiled with pleasure. Hat in hand, he bowed briskly in every direction with a cheerful smile. Mr. Roosevelt, on the other hand, looked profoundly serious, and walked with a measured tread. He did not smile at all.

As the Chief Justice repeated the form of the oath, the President, with his right hand raised, looked at him earnestly and repeated each phrase after him. This was in contradistinction to Mr. Roosevelt's way of taking the oath, which was simply to listen to the whole form and then, at the conclusion, say, "I do."

The President's voice was clear and ringing, and he spoke loudly, so that the audience on the platform heard the whole oath, not from the lips of the Chief Justice, but from those of the President. At the conclusion of the oath, the President bowed his head and kissed the Bible, and another great cheer broke forth from the crowd, for with this act the ceremony was complete, and William McKinley had again become President of the United States.

Clerk McKenny had opened the Bible at random, and before closing it noticed that President McKinley's lips had touched the following verses of Proverbs, xvi.:

"He that handleth a matter wisely shall find good, and whosoever trusteth in the Lord happy is he."

"The wise in heart shall be called prudent; and the sweetness of the lips increaseth learning."

The ceremony completed, Gen. Corbin assisted Mrs. McKinley down from the stand and up the steps, amid another cheer.

THE INAUGURAL ADDRESS.

Then the President, facing the crowd, delivered his inaugural address. He was never in better voice. His clear, penetrating tones rang out above the crowd, and a cheer after each of his principal points showed that he was heard for some distance. He held his notes in his hand, but did not often refer to them. He spoke as follows:

"My Fellow-Citizens: When we assembled here on the 4th of March, 1897, there was great anxiety with regard to our currency and credit. None exists now. Then our Treasury receipts were inadequate to meet the current obligations of the Government. Now they are sufficient for all public needs, and we have a surplus instead of a deficit. Then I felt constrained to convene the Congress in extraordinary session to devise revenues to pay the ordinary expenses of the Government. Now I have the satisfaction to announce that the Congress just closed has reduced taxation in the sum of forty-one millions of dollars. Then there was deep solicitude because of the long depression in our manufacturing, mining,

"All the News That's Fit to Print."

# The New York Times.

THE WEATHER.
Fair, with variable winds mostly east to south.



VOL. L...NO. 16,121. NEW YORK. SATURDAY. SEPTEMBER 7. 1901.—SIXTEEN PAGES. ONE CENT In Greater New York, Jersey City, and Newark. | Elsewhere, TWO CENTS.

# PRESIDENT SHOT AT BUFFALO FAIR

## Wounded in the Breast and Abdomen.

## HE IS RESTING EASILY

### One Bullet Extracted, Other Cannot Be Found.

### Assassin Is Leon Czolgosz of Cleveland, Who Says He Is an Anarchist and Follower of Emma Goldman.

BUFFALO, Sept. 6.—President McKinley, while holding a reception in the Temple of Music at the Pan-American Exposition at 4 o'clock this afternoon, was shot and twice wounded by Leon Czolgosz, an Anarchist, who lives in Cleveland.

One bullet entered the President's breast struck the breast bone, glanced and was later easily extracted. The other bullet entered the abdomen, penetrated the stomach, and has not been found, although the wounds have been closed.

The physicians in attendance upon the President at 10:40 o'clock to-night issued the following bulletin:

"The President is rallying satisfactorily and is resting comfortably. 10:15 P. M., temperature, 100.4 degrees; pulse, 124; respiration, 24.

"P. M. RIXEY,
"M. B. MANN,
"R. E. PARKE,
"H. MYNTER,
"EUGENE WANBIN.

Signed by George B. Cortelyou, Secretary to the President."

This condition was maintained until 1 o'clock A. M., when the physicians issued the following bulletin:

"The President is free from pain and resting well. Temperature, 100.2; pulse, 120; respiration, 24."

The assassin was immediately overpowered and taken to a police station on the Exposition grounds, but not before a number of the throng had tried to lynch him. Later he was taken to Police Headquarters.

The exact nature of the President's injuries is described in the following bulletin issued by Secretary Cortelyou for the physicians who were called:

"The President was shot about 4 o'clock. One bullet struck him on the upper portion of the breast bone, glancing and not penetrating; the second bullet penetrated the abdomen five inches below the left nipple and one and one-half inches to the left of the median line. The abdomen was opened through the line of the bullet wound. It was found that the bullet had penetrated the stomach.

"The opening in the front wall of the stomach was carefully closed with silk sutures; after which a search was made for a hole in the back wall of the stomach. This was found and also closed in the same way. The further course of the bullet could not be discovered, although careful search was made. The abdominal wound was closed without drainage. No injury to the intestines or other abdominal organs was discovered.

"The patient stood the operation well, pulse of good quality, rate of 130, and his condition at the conclusion of operation was gratifying. The result cannot be foretold. His condition at present justifies hope of recovery."

Leon Czolgosz, the assassin, has signed a confession, covering six pages of foolscap, in which he states that he is an Anarchist and that he became an enthusiastic member of that body through the influence of Emma Goldman, whose writings he had read and whose lectures he had listened to. He denies having any confederate, and says he decided on the act three days ago and bought the revolver with which the act was committed in Buffalo.

He has seven brothers and sisters in Cleveland, and the Cleveland Directory has the names of about that number living in Hosmer Street and Ackland Avenue, which adjoin. Some of them are butchers and others are in other trades.

Czolgosz is now detained at Police Headquarters, pending the result of the President's injuries. He does not appear in the least degree uneasy or penitent for his action. He says he was induced by his attention to Emma Goldman's lectures and writings to decide that the present form of government in this country was all wrong, and he thought the best way to end it was by the killing of the President. He shows no sign of insanity, but is very reticent about much of his career.

While acknowledging himself an Anarchist, he does not state to what branch of the organization he belongs.

## TO-DAY: SIXTEEN PAGES

### INDEX TO DEPARTMENTS.

Stocks irregular. Financial Affairs.—Pages 12 and 13.
Wheat, No. 2 red, 76¾c; corn, No. 2 mixed, 60c; oats, No. 2 mixed, 38c; cotton, middling, 8 15-16c; iron, Northern, No. 1 foundry, $15.25; butter, Western creamery, 20c. Commercial World.—Page 13.
Amusements.—Page 9.
Arrivals at Hotels and Out-of-Town Buyers.—Page 6.
Business Troubles.—Page 10.
Court Calendars.—Page 13.
Legal Notes.—Page 16.
Marine Intelligence and Foreign Mails.—Page 13.
New Corporations.—Page 13.
Railroads.—Page 6.
Real Estate.—Page 14.
Religious.—Page 10.
Society.—Page 9.
Weather Report.—Page 6.



## HOW THE DEED WAS DONE.

### Assassin Came with the Crowd to Greet the President and Shot When Two Feet from Him.

BUFFALO, Sept. 6.—Czolgosz's attempt on the life of the President was made at about 4 o'clock in the Temple of Music, where Mr. McKinley had gone to hold a reception at that hour. He had spent the day at Niagara with about 100 invited guests, and arrived at the exposition grounds at 3:30. Mrs. McKinley proceeded to the Mission Building and the President went directly to the Temple of Music.

A vast crowd had assembled long before the arrival of Mr. McKinley. The daily organ recital was nearing its end as the President entered and went to the slightly raised dais at one end of the hall.

The President, though well guarded by United States Secret Service detectives, was fully exposed to such an attack as occurred. He stood at the edge of the raised dais, and throngs of people crowded in at the various entrances to see their Chief Executive, perchance to clasp his hand, and then fight their way out in the good-natured mob that every minute swelled and multiplied at the points of ingress and egress to the building.

The President was in a cheerful mood and was enjoying the hearty evidences of good-will which everywhere met his gaze. Upon his right stood John G. Milburn of Buffalo, President of the Pan-American Exposition, chatting with the President, and introducing to him persons of note who approached. Upon the President's left stood Mr. Cortelyou.

THE ASSASSIN APPEARS.

It was shortly after 4 o'clock when one of the throng which surrounded the Presidential party, a medium-sized man of ordinary appearance and plainly dressed in black, approached as if to greet the President. Both Secretary Cortelyou and President Milburn noticed that the man's hand was swathed in a bandage or handkerchief. Reports of bystanders differ as to which hand. He worked his way with the stream of people up to the edge of the dais, until he was within two feet of the President.

President McKinley smiled, bowed, and extended his hand in that spirit of geniality the American people so well know, when suddenly the man raised his hand and two sharp reports of a revolver rang out loud and clear above the hum of voices and the shuffling of myriad feet. The assassin had fired through the handkerchief which concealed the revolver.

There was an instant of almost complete silence, like the hush that follows a clap of thunder. The President stood stock still, a look of hesitancy, almost of bewilderment, on his face. Then he retreated a step while a pallor began to steal over his features. The multitude seemed only partially aware that something serious had happened.

Then came a commotion. With the leap of a tiger three men threw themselves forward as with one impulse and sprang toward the would-be assassin. Two of them were United States Secret Service men, who were on the lookout and whose duty it was to guard against just such a calamity as had here befallen the President and the Nation. The third was a bystander, a negro, who had only an instant before grasped the hand of the President. In a twinkling the assassin was borne to the ground, his weapon was wrested from his grasp, and strong arms pinioned him down.

Then the vast multitude which thronged the edifice began to come to a realizing sense of the awfulness of the scene of which they had been witnesses. A murmur arose, spread, and swelled to a hum of confusion, then grew to a babel of sounds, and later to a pandemonium of noises.

The crowds that a moment before had stood mute and motionless in bewildered ignorance of the enormity of the deed, now with a single impulse surged forward, while a hoarse cry welled up from a thousand throats, and a thousand men charged forward to lay hands upon the perpetrator of the dastardly crime.

CONFUSION REIGNS.

For a moment the confusion was terrible. The crowd surged forward regardless of consequences. Men shouted and fought, women screamed and children cried. Some of those nearest the doors fled from the edifice in fear of a stampede, while hundreds of others from the outside struggled blindly forward in the effort to enter the crowded building and solve the mystery of excitement and panic which every moment grew and swelled within the congested interior of the palatial edifice.

Inside on the slightly raised dais was enacted within those few feverish moments a tragedy, so dramatic in character, so thrilling in its intensity, that few who looked on will ever be able to give a succinct account of what really did transpire. Even the actors who were playing the principal rôles came out of it with blanched faces, trembling limbs, and beating hearts, while their brains throbbed with a tumult of conflicting emotions which left behind only a chaotic jumble of impressions which could not be clarified into a lucid narrative of the events as they really transpired.

But of the multitude which witnessed or bore a part in the scene there was but one mind which seemed to retain its equilibrium, one hand which remained steady, one eye which gazed with unflinching calmness, and one voice which retained its even tenor and faltered not at the most critical juncture.

They were the mind and the hand and the eye and the voice of President McKinley.

After the first shock of the assassin's shots, he retreated a step, then, as the detectives leaped upon his assailant, he turned, walked steadily to a chair and seated himself, at the same time removing his hat and bowing his head in his hands.

In an instant Secretary Cortelyou and President Milburn were at his side. His waistcoat was hurriedly opened, the President meanwhile admonishing those about him to remain calm and telling them not to be alarmed.

"But you are wounded," cried his secretary; "let me examine."

"No, I think not," answered the President. "I am not badly hurt, I assure you."

Nevertheless his outer garments were hastily loosened, and when a trickling stream of crimson was seen to wind its way down his breast spreading its stain over the white surface of the linen their worst fears were confirmed.

A force of Exposition guards were on the scene by this time, and an effort was made to clear the building. The crush was terrific. Spectators crowded down the stairways from the galleries, the crowd on the floor surged forward toward the rostrum, while despite the strenuous efforts of police and guards the throng without struggled madly to obtain admission.

IN THE HOSPITAL.

The President's assailant in the meantime had been hustled to the rear of the building by Exposition Guards McCauley and James, where he was held while the building was cleared, and later turned over to Superintendent Bull of the Buffalo Police Department, who took the prisoner to No. 13 Police Station, and later to Police Headquarters.

As soon as the crowd in the Temple of Music had been dispersed sufficiently the President was removed in the automobile ambulance and taken to the Exposition Hospital, where an examination was made.

The best medical skill was summoned and within a brief period several of Buffalo's best-known practitioners were at the patient's side. The President retained the full exercise of his faculties until placed on the operating table and subjected to an anaesthetic.

Upon the first examination it was ascertained that one bullet had taken effect in the right breast just below the nipple, causing a comparatively harmless wound. The other took effect in the abdomen, about five inches below the left nipple, two inches to the left of the navel, and about on a level with it.

Upon arriving at the Exposition Hospital the second bullet was probed for. The walls of the abdomen were opened, but teh ball was not located. The incision was hastily closed and after a hasty consultation it was decided to the remove the patient to the home of President Milburn. This was done, the automobile-ambulance being used for the purpose.

Arrived at the Milburn residence, all persons outside the medical attendants, nurses, and the officials immediately concerned were excluded and the task of probing for the bullet, which had lodged in the abdomen, was begun by Dr. Roswell Park.

When it was decided to remove the President from the Exposition Hospital to the Milburn residence, the news was broken to Mrs. McKinley as gently as might be, by the members of the Milburn family. She bore the shock remarkably well, and displayed the utmost fortitude.

CROWD READY TO LYNCH.

While the wounded President was being borne from the Exposition to the Milburn residence between rows of onlookers with bared heads, a far different spectacle was being witnessed along the route of his assailant's journey from the scene of his crime to Police Headquarters. The trip was made so quickly that the prisoner was safely landed within the wide portals of the police station and the doors closed before any one was aware of his presence.

The news of the attempted assassination had in the meanwhile been spread broadcast by the newspapers. Like wildfire it spread from mouth to mouth. Then bulletins began to appear on the boards along "Newspaper Row," and when the announcement was made that the prisoner had been taken to Police Headquarters, only two blocks distant from the newspaper section, the crowds surged down toward the terrace, eager for a glimpse of the prisoner. At Police Headquarters they were met by a strong cordon of police, drawn up across the pavement on Pearl Street, who denied admittance to any but officials authorized to take part in the examination of the prisoner.

In a few minutes the crowd had grown from tens to hundreds, and these in turn quickly swelled to thousands, until the street was completely blocked by a surging mass of eager humanity. It was at this juncture that some one raised the cry of "Lynch him!" Like a flash the cry was taken up, and the whole crowd re-echoed the cry, "Lynch him!" "Hang him!" Closer the crowd surged forward.

Denser the throng became as new arrivals each moment swelled the swaying multitude. The situation was becoming critical when suddenly the big doors were flung open and a squad of reserves advanced with solid front, drove the crowd back from the curb, then across the street, and gradually succeeded in dispersing them from about the entrance to the station.

By this time there were probably 30,000 people assembled in the vicinity of Pearl, Seneca, Erie Streets, and the Terrace. The crowd was so great that it became necessary to rope off the entire street in front of Police Headquarters, and at a late hour to-night the police were still patrolling in the streets in the neighborhood, in squads of three or four. Inside the station house were assembled District Attorney Penny, Superintendent of Police Bull, Capt. Reagan of the First Precinct, and other officials.

The prisoner at first proved quite communicative, so much so in fact, that little dependence could be placed on what he said. He first gave his name as Fred Nieman, said his home was in Detroit, and that he had been in Buffalo about a week. He said he had been boarding at a place in Broadway. Later this place was located as John Nowak's saloon, a Raines-law hotel, 1,078 Broadway. Here the prisoner occupied Room 8.

THE PRISONER'S STORY.

Nowak, the proprietor, said he knew very little about his guest. He came there, he declared, last Saturday, saying he had come to see the Pan-American, and that his home was in Toledo. He had been alone at all times about Nowak's place, and had no visitors. In his room was found a small traveling bag of cheap make. It contained an empty cartridge box and a few articles of clothing.

With these facts in hand the police went at the prisoner with renewed vigor in the effort to obtain either a full confession or a straight account of his identity and movements prior to his arrival in Buffalo. He at first admitted that he was an Anarchist in sympathy at least, but denied strenuously that the attempt on the life of the President was a result of a preconcerted plot on the part of any Anarchist society.

At times he was defiant and again indifferent. But at no time did he betray the remotest sign of remorse. He declared the deed was not premeditated, but in the same breath refused to say why he perpetrated it. When charged by District Attorney Penny with being the instrument of an organized band of conspirators, he protested vehemently that he never even thought of perpetrating the crime until this morning.

After long and persistent questioning it was announced at Police Headquarters that the prisoner had made a confession, which he signed.



## MRS. McKINLEY COURAGEOUS.

### Bears Up Well When She Hears of the Attempt on Mr. McKinley's Life.

BUFFALO, N. Y., Sept. 6.—After the President was cared for at the Exposition grounds, Director General W. I. Buchanan started for the Milburn residence to forestall any information that might reach Mrs. McKinley there by telephone or otherwise. Very luckily, he was first to arrive with the information. The Niagara Falls trip had tired Mrs. McKinley, and on returning to the Milburn residence she went to her room to rest.

Mr. Buchanan broke the news as gently as possible to the nieces of Mr. and Mrs. McKinley, and consulted with them, and Mrs. Milburn as to the best course to pursue in breaking the news to Mrs. McKinley. It was finally decided that on her awaking, or shortly thereafter, Mr. Buchanan should break the news to her, if, in the meantime her physician, Dr. Rixey, had not yet arrived.

Mrs. McKinley awoke from her sleep at about 5:30 o'clock. She was feeling splendidly, she said, and at once took up her crocheting, which, as is well known, is one of her favorite diversions.

Immediately on Mr. Buchanan's arrival at the Milburn home he had telephonic communication therewith cut off, for already there had been several calls, and he decided on this as the wisest course to pursue lest Mrs. McKinley, hearing the continued ringing of the bells, might inquire what it meant.

While the light of day remained, Mrs. McKinley continued with her crocheting, keeping to her room. When the day began to wane and the President had not arrived, she began to feel anxious concerning him. "I wonder why he does not come?" she asked one of her nieces. There was no clock in Mrs. McKinley's room, and when it was 7 o'clock she had no idea it was so late, and this is when she began to feel anxious concerning her husband, for he was due to return to Mr. Milburn's house about 6 o'clock.

At 7 o'clock Dr. Rixey arrived at the Milburn residence. He had been driven hurriedly down Delaware Avenue in an open carriage, and at once entered the house. At 7:20 o'clock Dr. Rixey came out of the house accompanied by Col. Webb Hayes, a son of the late ex-President Hayes, who is a friend of President McKinley. They entered a carriage and returned to the Exposition hospital.

After Dr. Rixey had gone, Mr. Buchanan said that the doctor had broken the news in a most gentle way to Mrs. McKinley. He said she stood it bravely, though considerably affected. If it was possible to bring him to her, she wanted it done. Dr. Rixey assured her that the President could be brought with safety from the Exposition grounds, and when he left the Milburn house it was to complete all arrangements for the removal of the President.

A big force of regular patrolmen were assigned to the Milburn residence.

## "CAUGHT THE ASSASSIN."

### Capt. Wiser of Coast Artillery Says His Men Did So.

WASHINGTON, Sept. 6.—The War Department to-night received the following telegram from Capt. John B. Wiser, commanding the Seventy-third Company of Coast Artillery at Buffalo:

"BUFFALO, N. Y., Sept. 6, 1901.—Adjutant General, U. S. A., Washington: President shot at reception in Temple of Music about 4 P. M. Corporal Bertschey and detail of men of my company caught the assassin at once and held him down till the secret service men overpowered him and took the prisoner out of their hands, my men being unarmed. Condition of President not known. Revolver in my possession.

"WISER, Commanding."

## OPINIONS OF SURGEONS.

### Injury to Stomach Serious for a Man of the President's Age—Danger of Peritonitis.

According to well-known surgeons, there are in New York four or five persons each year who, through various causes, suffer from injuries similar to those received yesterday by President McKinley at Buffalo. Operations similar to those performed on the President have been successful and the patients have recovered. The prominent surgeons interviewed last evening said that the chances of recovery would be much greater if President McKinley were a younger man.

Dr. John B. Walker of 33 West Thirty-third Street said:

"Any injury to the stomach similar to that which has been inflicted on President McKinley is serious. There have been cases of stomach perforation where the patients have recovered. The diagnosis of any perforated wound of the stomach in an adult is very serious. The trouble is that inflammation following such an injury is more acute to an older person than to one more youthful. The fear is that the contents of the stomach will ooze into the intestines and peritonitis set in."

"Do you recall any recent cases similar to that of President McKinley," was asked.

"Dr. Bull performed an operation on a young man a short time ago. The intestines were perforated and an operation similar to that performed on President McKinley resulted in complete recovery. If President McKinley were a man between thirty-five and forty years of age the chances would be more in his favor. I cannot recall at this time a case of a man of the age of the President recovering from similar wounds. There is one advantage the President had, and that is the prompt assistance of a surgeon. Dr. Roswell Park is one of the most eminent surgeons in the United States."

"What other cases do you recall?"

"The case of the football player in Princeton who was shot by a negro is one of the latest. In that case the young man was of powerful physique. He did not receive the attention of a surgeon for twelve hours, and the result was that peritonitis set in and death occurred in a few days."



## MR. ROOSEVELT EN ROUTE.

### One Receipt of News the Vice President Leaves for Buffalo.

BURLINGTON, Vt., Sept. 6.—The first news of the attempted assassination of President McKinley reached Vice President Roosevelt at Isle La Motte at 5:30 o'clock this afternoon, when the Vice President was informed over the telephone that there was a rumor that the President had been shot. It was confirmed by another message a moment later.

The Vice President seemed stunned by the news, and put his hands to his head, then exclaimed, "My God!" Those around him were immediately informed of the tragedy, and it was decided to announce it to the company of a thousand persons who had gathered to hear Col. Roosevelt speak at the annual outing of the Vermont Fish and Game League. Senator Proctor made the announcement, and men, women, and children wept.

A later bulletin was received, stating that the President was resting quietly and that the chances were favorable for his recovery. "Good!" exclaimed the Vice President, and his face lighted up. He showed his pleasure by eagerly announcing the good news to the assembly.

The Vice President then left immediately on the yacht Elfrida, owned by W. Seward Webb, and came to this city as quickly as possible, having directed that all messages should be held for him here. The yacht was to have gone to Arrow Point, where a special train was waiting for the Vice President, but the train was sent on to Burlington, and was there when the yacht came into the harbor, at 8:15.

President Clement of the Rutland Railroad placed the train at the disposal of the Vice President, and made arrangements to take him on it to Buffalo. Col. Roosevelt was asked at the wharf for a statement for publication, and said:

"I am so inexpressibly grieved, shocked, and horrified that I can say nothing."

He boarded the train at once and left for Buffalo.

## CABINET WILL ASSEMBLE.

### Postmaster General Smith and Secretaries Root and Gage Off for Buffalo.

PHILADELPHIA, Sept. 6. — Postmaster General Charles Emory Smith was greatly affected by the news of the shooting of President McKinley, and expressed himself as shocked beyond measure. He immediately telegraphed to Washington and Buffalo, asking for further particulars than the early news dispatches contained. Mr. Smith said he hoped the President's injuries might not prove so serious as was at first intimated.

Mr. Smith left here on a late train tonight for Buffalo. He expects to be at the President's bedside by 9 o'clock to-morrow morning.

NEWBURY, N. H., Sept. 6.—A message containing information from Buffalo was received here early this evening and forwarded by messenger to the home of Secretary Hay. No reply came to it, and up to a late hour Secretary Hay could not be reached.

BUCKFIELD, Me., Sept. 6.—John D. Long, secretary of the Navy, who has been passing his vacation at the Long homestead, two miles from this place, learned to-night of the shooting of President McKinley. He was deeply affected, and proceeded to his home at once, declaring that he was undecided about future plans. The Secretary positively refused to say anything for publication.

PITTSBURG, Sept. 6.—When informed of the shooting of President McKinley, Attorney General Knox said: "I cannot imagine how any living creature could harbor such a thought as to take the life of the President. I am so shocked at the awful news that I cannot talk further."

Mr. Knox left at 11 P. M. for Buffalo. Just before leaving he said:

"I can only express the common sentiment of horror at the cruelty of the dastardly blow inflicted upon the lovable and beloved man who has stood for all that is best for the people, who have so implicitly trusted him. His bodily wounds, grievous as they are, will cause him less pain than the thought that any human heart could have harbored against him the malice that inspired the deed."

DUBLIN, N. H., Sept. 6.—Secretary of the Interior Hitchcock, who has been at Mount Monadnock, when informed to-night of the tragic incident at Buffalo, said:

"I am too horrified to make any expression whatever." He immediately prepared to leave for Buffalo.

Secretary of War Elihu Root left the Grand Central Station at 11:10 last night for Buffalo in a special train. He was accompanied by a Dr. Dixon, a specialist, with whom he is hastening to the bedside of the President. The train was made up of a single coach and locomotive, and all possible speed will be made to reach Buffalo on record-breaking time.

When Secretary Root was asked to express an opinion of the President's injury, he said:

"What is there to say? I do not know how seriously injured President McKinley is, but I hope his condition is not so serious as reported. I am almost overcome by the terrible news."

Secretary Root came up from Southampton, L. I., in a special train. With Dr. Dixon and a valet, he rode in a cab to the Grand Central Station. The special train had already been made up, and in less than three minutes after their arrival at the station they were speeding on their way to Buffalo.

*Special to The New York Times.*

CHICAGO, Sept. 6.—Secretary of the Treasury Gage, who was visiting his son, Eli Gage, in Evanston, seemed dazed by the news, and with bowed head walked slowly into the house. Preparations were made at once for the Secretary to go to Buffalo, accompanied by his son. Before he took the train for Buffalo, an hour later, Secretary Gage said:

"I am too shocked to speak. The news of such a happening is simply overwhelming to me. The President was always confident that no harm would ever come to him. He is a man who is honored by all. I received no official message that he had been assassinated. The first things were brought me by friends."



## WASHINGTON STUNNED BY THE TRAGEDY

### No Member of Cabinet Is at the Capital City.

### MILITARY GUARD DETAILED

### Under the Law Vice President Roosevelt Will Discharge the Purely Routine Duties of the President.

*Special to The New York Times.*

WASHINGTON, Sept. 6.—For the third time in thirty-seven years Washington has been stunned by the shooting of a President of the United States. Like lightning out of the fair September sky the report from Buffalo arrested attention here about 5 o'clock, and in a few moments anxious crowds were hurrying from all parts of the city to the offices of the newspapers seeking additional information. People stopped in their hurry to ask of every one met whether the President had been killed, and there was the utmost impatience because of the brevity and indefiniteness of the bulletins and the failure of assurance that the wounds inflicted upon Mr. McKinley were not fatal. To-night the street in front of the newspaper offices is crowded with women and men hungering with anxiety and waiting to catch the announcements that come at long intervals through a megaphone operated by a man in an upper window of a newspaper office.

Grief has not checked a torrent of indignation at the crime committed against humanity and a President who has always trusted himself implicity to the protection of his fellows, venturing from day to day to walk the streets without guard. The rage against the assassin was immediate and outspoken with men of all parties, for Mr. McKinley has no personal enemies here or elsewhere.

The disability of the President occurred at a moment when the Administration was entirely unrepresented at Washington by a Cabinet officer. When the information of the shooting reached the White House by a telephone message from Buffalo, Col. Montgomery and a few clerks were the only members of the President's official family present, Col. Pruden getting the news while he was dining at home. From the moment he heard the news, Col. Montgomery began making efforts to reach the members of the Cabinet except Secretary of Agriculture Wilson, who is in Buffalo. There was a stream of visitors to the White House from the moment the news of the shooting was received until late to-night, but few of the visitors were persons high in official life.

HOW THE NEWS WAS RECEIVED.

The force at the White House since the President's departure has been in constant communication with him, and while he has conducted most of the business of his office at his home, in Canton, Ohio, the majority of the papers with which he has had to deal have been prepared in Washington and forwarded through the White House clerical force. All reports received from him by officials here were cheerful and high-spirited.

The work of the official day was done when the news of the calamity arrived here and the executive departments had generally emptied themselves of their workmen, and very few of the officials were to be found at their desks.

Mr. Adee, the acting head of the State Department, was met at the station as he was leaving for his country home near Laurel, Md., and returned at once to the State Department. He waited for official confirmation of the news, and it was not until he received a copy of the bulletin issued by the physicians through Secretary Cortelyou that he undertook to acquaint officially the Governments of all the nations of the world with the facts of the shooting. He then drew up a message, which will be sent to every United States Embassy, Legation, and Consulate throughout the civilized world directing them to acquaint the Governments to which they are accredited of the facts. With these he embodied a condensation of the physicians' bulletin with Mr. Cortelyou's statement.

In the Navy Department Mr. Hackett, the acting Secretary, who had also quitted the building, was speedily recalled by Capt. Cowles, the acting head of the Navigation Bureau, and he immediately put himself in readiness to take any official action that might be necessary to meet the emergency. At Buffalo in the Exposition grounds the navy had a splendid representation in the shape of the marine battalion under Capt. Leonard, and this force will be immediately available if it is decided by the persons about the President that a guard is necessary near his person.

At the War Department Gen. Gillespie, Chief Engineer of the army, was acting Secretary in the absence of Secretary Root, and Assistant Secretary Sanger, who is away on leave. He also had quitted the building, but he had not been gone half an hour before word reached him and he hastily returned to his desk. He immediately sent messages to the Secretary of war and to Gen. Brooke, commanding the Department of the East, giving such unofficial information as was available.

Gen. Gillespie finally got into communication with Secretary Root and Assistant Secretary Sanger, and as a result of the telephonic talk he proceeded to use some of the forces at his disposal. He telegraphed an order to Fort Foster, N. H., to have an officer, a physician, and a squad of men proceed immediately to the house where the President is lying to act as a guard.

PROVIDING FOR EMERGENCIES.

Steps were next taken to provide for the future of the Executive branch of the Government. It was realized that even under the most favorable conditions the President's injuries are of such a character as to make it almost certain that he cannot undertake for a long time to discharge the duties of Chief Executive, even in the most formal way. Every member of the Cabinet able to travel is expected to at once go to Buffalo, and there a Cabinet council will be held to decide upon the course to be followed by the Executive branch. Vice President Roosevelt is in readiness to do whatever is necessary and to meet the obligations imposed upon the Vice President by the Constitution of the United States. These are contained in Paragraph 6, Section 1, Article II., in the following words:

6. In case of the removal of the President from office, or of his death, resignation, or inability to discharge the powers and duties of the said office, the same shall devolve on the Vice President, &c.

Under the terms of this article, as soon as Mr. Roosevelt is assured by proper authority, probably in this case by the senior member of the Cabinet, Secretary Hay, who will doubtless be in Buffalo by to-morrow evening, he will undertake at once in a provisional way to discharge such duties as may devolve on him. Much will depend upon the report of the physicians on the character of the President's injuries as to the extent to which Mr. Roosevelt will discharge the Presidential duties, if he undertakes them at all, and it is almost certain that in the absence of great emergency in public affairs, even if called to assume these obligations, the Vice President will confine himself in the exercise of his powers to the discharge of the most routine and indispensable functions.

Such public men as were in the city called at the White House during the evening. They included Assistant Secretary Spaulding of the Treasury Department, Assistant Secretary Hackett of the Navy Department, ex-United States Senator H. W. Blair, Controller Dawes, and Register Lyons of the Treasury, and Capt. Towner, Assistant Commissioner of Indian Affairs. There were also calls from representatives of several foreign legations.

No official confirmation of the shooting came to the White House for three hours after its occurrence, when Col. Montgomery, the chief operator at the White House, was informed at 7:20 o'clock by Secretary Cortelyou at Buffalo that a surgical operation upon the President was in progress, and that "so far everything is favorable." Later he gave information of the completion of the operation, and followed that statement with other messages giving private information as to the President's condition and his removal to Mr. Milburn's residence.

STRONG MILITARY GUARD.

During the early evening a conference was held at the War Department of such of the prominent army officers as could be gathered at short notice by Gen. Gillespie. He informed them that he had communicated with Gen. Brooke at Governors Island and that the General had replied that he would start immediately for Buffalo, where he expected in the early morning to take personal charge of all arrangements made for the guarding of the President.

Meanwhile he had directed that the troops which had been placed as a guard around the hospital in the Exposition grounds be transferred to the Milburn home, where the President lies, to serve as a guard and keep back the public and preserve quiet. Gen. Brooke has at Buffalo at his disposal a company of coast artillery, stationed in the Exposition grounds; a company of the Fifteenth Infantry, also stationed at Fort Porter, within the limits of the Exposition preserves, and other troops at Fort Niagara.

The conference decided that there was little more that the War Department could undertake at this time. Surgeon General Van Reypen of the navy, who came down to the Navy Department, called at Gen. Gillespie's office, and, discussing the case from a medical point of view, took occasion to mention Dr. Nicholas Senn of Chicago as an expert of high grade in such cases of injury, and the suggestion was promptly telegraphed to Buffalo that his services be secured.

Assistant Secretary Ailes of the Treasury Department received a message to-night from Secretary Gage at Chicago stating that he was about to leave at once for Buffalo, where he will arrive to-morrow morning.

Admiral Dewey arrived in Washington early in the afternoon. He proceeded at once to his suburban home and was occupied with the details of the approaching Schley court of inquiry when the news reached him by the telephone. He at once sought all the particulars and placed himself in readiness for any service that might be required of him, informing Acting Secretary Hackett of that fact.

The Admiral found himself unable to express his feelings at the news, and all that could be extracted from him was that he was plunged in grief too deep for utterance at this time. He said that he could not now express an opinion as to the effect that the calamity might have on the court of inquiry, or even whether it would result in the postponement of the approaching sitting.

DIPLOMATS' CONDOLENCES.

Owing to the absence of many of the Diplomatic Corps at Buffalo and of many others at the various Summer resorts there were only two representatives of this body of rank in Washington to-day. Minister Wu was one of these, and when seen tonight he was a picture of distress. He said he realised keenly the tremendous indebtedness of China to President McKinley's kindly impulses in her great trials in the past year, and was shocked at the great calamity that had befallen him. He said he could not conceive of any sort of motive for such an inexcusable deed as that of Nieman's, and he was severe in his denunciation of Anarchists. He asked why they were permitted to hatch such plots as this in a Republic where the people could readily change their President if they were in the slightest degree dissatisfied with his official conduct or his private personality. In conclusion, he expressed the hope that the President would shortly recover.

Another diplomatic representative in Washington was Señor Herran, representing the Government of the United States of Colombia. He also was greatly distressed and he affirmed that his whole country would sympathise with the President in this moment of pain. He also could not understand, he said, why such a benevolent character as President McKinley should be thus assaulted by one of the people, and he declared it is time that the Anarchists should be suppressed.

It was somewhat gratifying to the officials here that the very first expression of official sympathy should come from the Island of Cuba, in the shape of the following telegram:

Sept. 6, 1901.
(Received at War Department, 7:45 P. M.) Havana.
Adjutant General, Washington:
Mayor and City Council of Havana have called, expressing sorrow and solicitude for the President, and desire that his family be advised of these expressions.
SCOTT, Adjutant General.

Mr. H. T. Scott of the Union Iron Works at San Francisco, at whose house the President staid while visiting that city, telegraphed the Navy Department as follows:

"So shocked with news, words fail to express our feelings."

Messages of sympathy and of inquiry already have begun to arrive at the State Department.

"All the News That's Fit to Print."

# The New York Times.

THE WEATHER.

Fair; light to fresh winds, mostly westerly.



VOL. L...NO. 16,127. NEW YORK, SATURDAY, SEPTEMBER 14, 1901.—FOURTEEN PAGES. ONE CENT In Greater New York, Jersey City, and Newark. | Elsewhere TWO CENTS.

# MR. M'KINLEY DIES AFTER A BRAVE FIGHT

## End Comes at 2:15 o'Clock This Morning.

## MR. ROOSEVELT SUMMONED.

### President's Touching Farewell to Stricken Wife.

### "God's Will Be Done" Were His Last Words—A Remarkable Display of Vitality Marks the Final Hours of Suffering.

*Special to The New York Times.*

BUFFALO, Sept. 14.—President McKinley died at 2:15 o'clock this morning. He had been unconscious since 7:50 o'clock last night. His last conscious hour on earth was spent with the wife to whom he devoted a lifetime of care. He died unattended by a minister of the Gospel, but his last words were a humble submission to the will of the God in whom he believed. He was reconciled to the cruel fate to which an assassin's bullet had condemned him, and faced death in the same spirit of calmness and poise which had marked his long and honorable career.

For three hours before his death the President apparently suffered no pain. He uttered no connected sentences. Those at his bedside say that the words of the hymn "Nearer, My God, to Thee" were running in his mind, and that occasionally he would murmur a few of the words.

Senator Hanna left the house with Harry Hamlin at 2:25 o'clock. As he walked to the corner his head was bowed and shoulders stooped. When he entered the runabout tears were streaming from his eyes. He bowed his head upon the head of his cane, sobs that were audible shook his frame, he had not a word to say. Abner McKinley and his wife left five minutes after Senator Hanna.

His last conscious words reduced to writing by Dr. Mann, who stood at his bedside, when they were uttered, were as follows:

"GOD'S WILL BE DONE."

"Good bye. All good bye. It is God's way. His will be done, not our."

The announcement to the members of the Cabinet of the President's death was made by Webb Hayes, who said: "It is all over."

Mrs. McKinley last saw her husband between 11 and 12. At that time she sat by the bedside holding the hand of her dying husband. The members of the Cabinet were admitted to the sickroom singly at that time.

Death probably occurred about 2 o'clock, it being understood that Dr. Rixey delayed the announcement until 2:15 to assure himself.

THE DEATH SCENE.

From authoritative officials the following details of the final scenes in and about the death chamber were secured:

The President had continued in an unconscious state since 8:30 P. M. Dr. Rixey remained with him at all times, and until death came. The other doctors were in the room at times, and then repaired to the front room where their consultations had been held.

About 2 o'clock Dr. Rixey noted the unmistakable signs of dissolution, and the immediate members of the family were summoned to the bedside. Mrs. McKinley was asleep, and it was deemed desirable not to awaken her for the last moments of anguish.

Silently and sadly the members of the family entered the room. They stood about the foot and sides of the bed where the great man's life was ebbing away.

Five minutes passed, then six, seven, eight—

Now Dr. Rixey bent forward, and then one of his hands was raised as if in warning. The fluttering heart was just going to rest. A moment more and Dr. Rixey straightened up, and, with choking voice, said: "The President is dead."

The announcement of the news to those waiting below was postponed until the members of the family had withdrawn. Through Secretary Cortelyou the waiting newspaper men received the notification. There was the keenest excitement on the broad avenue, but there was no semblance of disorder.

Those present at the time of the President's death were Secretary Cortelyou, Dr. Rixey, Mrs. and Miss Barber, and Miss Duncan, William M. Duncan, a nephew; Charles G. Dawes, the Controller of the Currency; F. M. Osborne, a cousin; Col. Webb C. Hays, John Barber, a nephew; Secretary George B. Cortelyou, Col. W. C. Brown, the business partner of Abner McKinley; Dr. P. M. Rixey, the family physician, and six nurses and attendants. In an adjoining room sat the physicians, including Drs. McBurney, Wasdin, Park, Stockton, and Mynter.

With the momentary excitement incident upon the announcement at an end, the entire scene became one of unmistakable and deep mourning. As if nature lent its aid to the grieving crowds a dense fog settled like a pall over the city. The Milburn house became a tomb of silence. Lights—not extinguished—were dimmed; visitors were denied admittance, and the mourning family and their more intimate friends were speedily left alone with their distinguished dead.

GUARD INCREASED.

The military guard was augmented immediately upon the announcement. The waiting crowds melted away rapidly, giving expression in unmistakable terms to the great sorrow they felt. Within a brief space of time the newspaper men, the police, the sentries of the guard, and those whose duties kept them abroad were the only persons in evidence within the immediate vicinity.

Within 30 minutes after the President's death a private of the United States Army Hospital Corps was detailed for duty, and took his position by the body.

The immediate cause of the President's death is undetermined. His physicians disagree, and it will possibly require an autopsy to finally fix the exact cause. The President's body will be taken to Washington, and there will be a state funeral. The interment will be in Canton.

At 3:23 Drullard and Koch, the undertakers, arrived at the Milburn house and will take charge of the body of the President.

# CLOSING HOURS AT PRESIDENT'S BEDSIDE.

### Mr. McKinley's Farewell to His Wife—Cabinet Officers Take Leave of Chief Executive—Story of a Weary Vigil.

*Special to The New York Times.*

BUFFALO, Sept. 14.—Before 6 o'clock last evening it was clear to those at the President's bedside that he was dying, and preparations were made for the last sad offices of farewell from those who were nearest and dearest to him. Oxygen had been administered steadily, but with little effect in keeping back the approach of death. The President came out of one period of unconsciousness only to relapse into another.

But in this period, when his mind was partially clear, occurred a series of events of profoundly touching character. Down stairs, with strained and tear-stained faces, members of the Cabinet were grouped in anxious waiting. They knew the end was near and that the time had come when they must see him for the last time on earth. This was about 6 o'clock. One by one they ascended the stairway—Secretary Root, Secretary Hitchcock, and Attorney General Knox. Secretary Wilson also was there, but he held back, not wishing to see the President in his last agony. There was only a momentary stay of the Cabinet officers at the threshold of the death chamber. Then they withdrew, the tears streaming down their faces and the words of intense grief choking in their throats.

"NEARER, MY GOD, TO THEE."

About 7:45 o'clock the President awakened from the stupor in which he had lain and faintly murmured the name of his wife and indicated that he wished to see her. She came to the room strong in her weakness compared with the weakness of the strong man whose life was so fast ebbing. The physicians and all but one of the nurses left the room, and for ten minutes husband and wife sat alone. Mrs. McKinley came from the room and was escorted back to her own. This was the second time last evening she had been by the side of the dying President. When she left Mr. McKinley murmured words from the hymn, "Nearer, My God, to Thee."

From the Milburn house came State Senator Martin Dodge of Cleveland, an old friend of the President and a fellow-worker with him in years gone by. He was not permitted to enter the room, but stood in the hall trying to catch one last glimpse of the face of his early companion. As he reached the barrier in the street he stopped, looked about, and, while weeping, said, "Gentlemen, the Nation's chief is dying. There is absolutely no hope, no chance."

At 9:30 Secretary Cortelyou sent out word: "The President is dying." There were no bulletins; there was necessity for none. Every one knew the end was near, and far down the streets leading to the house thousands were crushing up to the barrier, waiting for the moment that would end their agony of suspense and deprive the Nation of its President. The minutes grew into an hour, and then came the announcement from Secretary Cortelyou that the President's hold on life would last about an hour more.

MRS. MCKINLEY'S COURAGE.

Through all the despair and gloom Mrs. McKinley has been even more courageous and stronger than in the first days of the President's sufferings. She was not allowed to see him, as usual, this morning, and until late this afternoon knew nothing of the change in her condition. When the news was broken to her there was not even a sob, not an outbreak, just a clenching of the hand, a compression of the lips, and she was ready to watch with the man who had so often watched beside her bed of sickness.

The announcement from Secretary Cortelyou that the President had but an hour to live was supplemented by one made by Senator Depew, who came from the house shortly after 10:40 o'clock. He, while realizing there was no hope, felt that death was still some hours away.

FRIENDS ASSEMBLE.

All the evening those who had hastened here fast as steel and steam could carry them continued to arrive. They drove up in carriages at a gallop or were whisked up in automobiles, all intent upon getting here before death came. One of the last to arrive was Attorney General Knox, who reached the house at 9:30. He was permitted to go up stairs to look for the last time upon the face of his chief.

The Rev. C. D. Wilson, a Methodist clergyman of Tonawanda, N. Y., who was the President's pastor for three years at Canton, called at the residence to inquire whether his services were needed, but did not enter the house. Another Methodist clergyman, who has a church near by, remained at the Milburn residence for two hours in the belief that his services might be desired.

NO NEED OF BULLETINS.

There was no need for official bulletins after this. Those who came from the house at intervals told the same story—that the President was dying and that the end might come at any time. His tremendous vitality was the only remaining factor in the result, and this gave hope only of brief postponement of the end. Dr. Mynter thought he might last until 2 A. M. Dr. Mann said at 11 o'clock that the President was still alive and probably would live an hour. Midnight came, with the President still battling against death.

At this hour the Milburn house was the centre of a scene as animated as though it were midday, although a solemn hush hung over the great crowd of watchers. The entire lower part of the house was aglow with light, and the many attendants, friends, and relatives could be seen within, moving about and occasionally coming in groups to the front doorway for a breath of air. In the upper front chambers the lights were low, and around on the north side, where the chamber of death is located, there were fitful lights, sometimes burning brightly and then turned low.

AWAITING THE END.

Secretary Root and Secretary Wilson came from the house about midnight, and paced up and down the sidewalk. All that Secretary Root said was: "The end has not come yet."

Despite the fact that vitality continued to ebb as midnight approached no efforts were spared to keep the spark of life glowing. Dr. Janeway of New York City arrived at the Buffalo station at 11:40 o'clock. George Urban was waiting for him and they drove at a breakneck pace to the Milburn house. He was shown to the President's room at once and began an examination of the almost inanimate form.

Secretary of the Navy Long arrived at the Milburn house at 12:06, in time to see the President alive, though unconscious.

Coroner Wilson reached the house about 12:28 A. M. This led to startling reports, but at 12:30 Frank Baird announced from Secretary Cortelyou that the President was still alive and his condition practicaly as it had been for an hour.

The arrival of Coroner Wilson is explained by the statement that he was ordered by the District Attorney to go to the Milburn house because he had heard a report that the President was dead. Coroner Wilson's arrival was followed immediately by his departure, his presence not being necessary, as the President still lived.

Shortly after midnight the President's breathing was barely perceptible. His extremities were cold. It was recognised that nothing remained but the last struggle, and some of the friends of the family who had remained through the day began to leave the house, not caring to be present at the final scene.

RUMORS OF DEATH.

Such an intense state of anxiety existed among the watchers that rumors gained frequent circulation that death had already occurred, and a flood of dispatches were sent saying that the end had come. These were speedily set at rest by an official statement from within the house that the reports of death were groundless and that the President still lived.

Coroner Wilson said that he had been ordered by the District Attorney of the county to go to the Milburn residence as soon as possible after the announcement of death. He had seen a reputable local paper issued, with the announcement that the President died at 11:06 P. M., and had hurried up so that there would be no delay in removing the body.

Dr. Mann met him at the door and told him that his services were not required and that he would be notified when he was wanted. Dr. Mann said that the President was still alive and that Dr. Janeway was examining the heart action. There was really no hope, but they did not desire gruesome anticipation.

In the Milburn house at midnight awaiting the end were Senator Hanna, Mrs. Hanna, Abner McKinley, Mrs. Abner McKinley, Miss Mabel McKinley, Mrs. Baer, Secretary Root, Secretary Wilson, Secretary Long, Secretary Hitchcock, Mrs. McWilliams, and Drs. Park, Janeway, Johnson, Mynter, Mann, McBurney, Rixey, and Wasdin; Senator Burroughs, Senator Fairbanks, Russell B. Harrison, Gen. Otis, Attorney General Knox, and Ainsley Wilcox.

RAGE AGAINST CZOLGOSZ.

The people of Buffalo are wildly excited. At all points of interest are crowds of many thousands. In the streets leading to the county jail the crowds are thickest, and are threatening all sorts of violence. The authorities are prepared to meet this, the police, the militia, and Federal troops being on guard. Within the last ten minutes a crowd of 10,000 men rushed toward the jail, shouting, "We'll break into the jail," "We want Czolgosz."

The situation was very ugly, but the police authorities acted promptly. Policemen and militiamen charged the crowd and drove it back two blocks in each direction. In order to prevent anything like a successful onslaught on the jail, orders were issued to strengthen the military guard and the Seventy-fourth and Seventy-sixth Regiments were ordered on reserve in their armories.

WAITING FOR ROOSEVELT.

Everybody here is anxiously awaiting the arrival of Vice President Roosevelt. He is being brought here on a special train from the Adirondacks, which should arrive between 6 and 7 o'clock this morning.

The situation which will confront the Vice President is so serious that arrangements will be made to administer the oath of office as President to him immediately upon his arrival, if the President has passed away. During the meantime, pending the arrival of the Vice President, Secretary of War Root appears to have taken up the reins of government by the common consent of the Cabinet officers here.

Mrs. McKinley's condition is such that the doctors have grave fears lest her life too shall pay the forfeit to Czolgosz's bullet. She has scarcely been in her right mind since 9:10 o'clock last night, when the President had a short period of consciousness, during which she was led to his bedside and he uttered his last farewell.

# MR. McKINLEY'S LAST DAY OF SUFFERING.

### Following the Sinking Spell in Early Morning There Were Occasional Periods of Hopefulness.

*Special to The New York Times.*

BUFFALO, Sept. 13.—Since early this morning, when the first bulletin was issued telling of the unfavorable condition of the President, an indefinable fear filled the hearts of all in Buffalo. People in the streets, in hotels, and at the fair discussed it in low tones and one pitiful prophecy gave the President but a few hours to live.

In the Milburn residence there was more than an inclination to hope. There was an almost positive assertion that the President, with his wonderful strength and determination, would overcome this last weakness and again be on the road to recovery. There seemed to be little chance of this, though, when it was announced that it had become necessary to administer powerful stimulants and later resort to the use of oxygen.

The President began to sink shortly after 2 o'clock this morning after a critical period of 12 hours. Trouble began on Thursday afternoon through the failure of the digestive organs to perform their functions. The necessity for nourishment had been pressing for several days, and the partial failure of artificial means had led to the adoption of natural means. The rectum, through which nourishment had been injected previously to Wednesday, became irritated and rejected the enemas. This forced the physicians to try to feed the patient through the mouth, probably before the stomach was prepared. The first administration of beef juice through the mouth, however, seemed to agree with the patient, and the physicians were highly gratified at the way the stomach seemed to receive the food.

Dr. McBurney was especially jubilant over the action of the stomach, and yesterday morning, before his departure for New York, dwelt upon the fact that the stomach seemed to have resumed its normal functions. The breakfast of chicken broth, toast, and coffee given yesterday morning was spoken of by all the physicians as strong evidence of the President's marked improvement. It was only when it became apparent late in the morning that this food had not agreed with the President that the first genuine anxiety appeared.

FIRST NOTE OF ALARM.

The first note of alarm was sounded in the official bulletin Thursday afternoon, which spoke of the President's fatigue. President McKinley complained of an increasing feeling of fatigue. He had theretofore been so buoyant and cheerful that his complaints were seriously regarded. The pulse was then also abnormally high, 128 beats to the minute. With a temperature of 100.2 it should have been 80 beats lower. The weakness of the heart began to arouse serious concern. Instead of growing better the President's condition after that grew steadily worse.

The staff of physicians, augmented by Dr. Stockton, who had temporarily taken the place of Dr. McBurney, was summoned early in the evening, and there was a conference. At 8:30 o'clock Thursday evening the physicians announced officially that the President's condition was not so good. The problem of disposing of the food in the stomach was becoming a serious one, and the danger of heart failure increased. As midnight approached the situation was growing critical. Calomel and oil were given to flush the bowels and digitalis to quiet the heart. However, just before midnight the President had two operations of the bowels, which relieved him very much, and the midnight bulletin was more favorable. It stated that all the conditions had improved since the last bulletin.

It was believed then that the opening of the bowels would have the effect of allaying the wild pulsations of the heart. His pulse did drop to 120, and the prospect was slightly brighter. But owing to the President's extreme weakness and his fatigue no attempt was made to conceal the serious apprehension which was felt.

Secretary Cortelyou insisted that the truth should be made public by the doctors, and the bulletins themselves were telling their unfortunate story all too plainly. There was still hope that the patient would be better in the morning, and at midnight Secretary Cortelyou said it was not probable that another bulletin would be issued until morning.

Hope came once more to the breasts of those who had waited for hours in anxiety. The physicians parted for the night, and every sign was a cheering one. There had been disquieting pulse action for several hours, but practically all of the unfavorable symptoms had been linked to the stomach trouble, and it was thought that they would probably disappear with the removal of the cause which was supposed to have created them. The unofficial reports at 1 o'clock and 1:30 o'clock were both of a satisfactory nature, and the watchers gathered about the house prepared for an uninterrupted night.

SIGNS OF COLLAPSE.

Shortly after 2 o'clock the physicians and nurses detected a weakening of the heart action. The pulse fluttered and weakened, and the President sank toward collapse. The end appeared to be at hand. Restoratives were speedily applied. Action was immediate and decisive. Digitalis and strychnia were administered, and as a last resort saline solution was injected into the veins.

A general alarm was sent to the consulting physicians and trained nurses. The restoratives did not at once prove effective, and it was realized that the President was in an extremely critical condition. That realization led to a summons to the Cabinet, relatives, and close personal friends of the President. Soon the word was passed out that the President had partially collapsed. Dr. Mynter was the first of the consulting physicians to arrive. Dr. Mann came directly afterward. After them came Abner McKinley, pale and agitated. He had left the house scarcely two hours before with the assurance that the tide had turned in the case of his distinguished brother. Secretary Wilson and Secretary Hitchcock arrived within a few moments. Another hurrying visitor was Dr. Wasdin, whose arrival completed the circle of physicians.

Secretaries Hitchcock and Wilson and Mr. Milburn came out of the house shortly after 6 o'clock. Secretary Hitchcock declared that "the President is rallying slowly, and we still think that he has more than an even chance of recovery."

THE RELAPSE A SURPRISE.

The sudden attack of depression of the early morning came in the nature of a great surprise to the President's friends and physicians. They were prepared to hear that he might not be so well in the morning, but felt confident that the change would not be as severe as it proved to be.

"We are more surprised at the depression than at the fact of his rallying," said one member of the Cabinet.

The physicians, after their consultation and the examination of the patient, could offer little encouragement. He was very weak and his heart was so feeble that they feared his life might go out at any time. The bulletin they issued at 2:50 A. M. told of the very critical condition of the President.

"It gives rise," they said, "to the gravest apprehensions."

The movement of the bowels had occurred, but the heart did not respond to stimulations. At 4 o'clock the President rallied slightly. The saline solution which saved Mrs. McKinley's life in San Francisco had proved in a measure effective. Dr. Mann and Dr. Mynter left for their homes. Their only reassuring word was that they had not given up hope. During the night Mrs. McKinley knew nothing of the sudden change that had come. In her feeble condition it was considered best not to inform her of the President's critical condition, and she slept peacefully in her room through it all.

The bulletin usually issued at 6:30 A. M. was omitted. Dr. Rixey at 7:30 said that he felt slightly encouraged.

"The President has rallied somewhat," said he, "but then, you know," he added, "the President is usually better in the morning."

THE CITY AROUSED.

The Buffalo papers all had extras on the street at daylight, with the sad intelligence of the President's relapse. One paper announced that the President was dying. The result was that the whole city was thoroughly aroused and alarmed early, and before 7 o'clock crowds of people flocked in the direction of Ferry Street and Delaware Avenue. They stood at the ropes far down the intersecting streets and waited patiently for the appearance of the morning bulletin.

The first physician to arrive for the morning consultation was Dr. Wasdin, who drove up at 8:15. "I have been absent for a couple of hours," said he, "and I do not know the condition of the President. I hope he is better." Two minutes later Abner McKinley walked down to the corner to tell his coachman, who had been waiting for him with a carriage for an hour, that he would not go to his hotel for breakfast. The new detail of soldiers for guard duty arrived from Fort Porter a few minutes later. The guard was changed and the sentries posted for the day. Lieut. Charles N. Murphy was the first to arrive. He arrived at 8:23. "I saw the President at 5 o'clock," said he. "His condition was then very grave."

Dr. Mann came up in an automobile two minutes later. "I have nothing to say now," he said. Dr. Park did not reach the house until 8:46 o'clock, being the last of the physicians to arrive for the morning consultation.

At 8:50, while the consultation was going on inside, an old woman approached the inner rope and insisted upon being admitted. She said she desired to see Mrs. McKinley. "I have something important to say to her," she said. One of the Secret Service men kindly led her aside and listened to her long story of how she proposed to cure the President by means of herbs and prayers.

PHYSICIANS GROW SERIOUS.

The doctors finished their consultation at 9:40. They left the house together and stopped for a few minutes on the lawn to convey their verdict first to the President's brother. Dr. Mann and Dr. Mynter came away together. "We are very anxious," said Dr. Mann, "very anxious," he repeated as he entered the carriage in waiting.

"Have you given up hope?"

"By no means," replied the doctor.

"Is he better than when you saw him last?"

"He is better than he was in the early hours of the morning," he responded.

Dr. Mynter had little encouragement to offer. "I am not absolutely without hope," said he. "The President has a fighting chance, but I would be more hopeful if the day was passed and he had gained a little strength. He has improved some since early this morning, but the improvement is very slight. The trouble lies with his heart. We are stimulating it and our treatment has been fairly successful."

Dr. Mynter admitted that saline solution and other means to keep up the action of the heart were being administered.

At a time when the surgeons imagined him to be asleep, about 9:30 o'clock, Dr. Mynter gave the patient a hypodermic injection of strychnine. The President was conscious and asked, feebly:

"What is that, doctor?"

"A heart stimulant," was the reply.

"Is the necessity great?" continued the President.

"Yes, your Excellency," answered the doctor. "You are a brave and very sick man."

"I realize it," said the President, resignedly and cheerfully.

The bulletin when issued was slightly reassuring, and indicated that the crisis might be prolonged, stating definitely that the President's condition had somewhat improved during the past few hours, and that there was better response to stimulation. But his pulse was up to 128, and the conviction grew that it was almost a forlorn hope.

Shortly after 10 o'clock the intimate friends and relatives of the President who were telegraphed for early this morning began to arrive, and soon after 10 o'clock there were assembled in the down-stairs rooms of the Milburn house Senators Hanna and Fairbanks, ex-Secretary of State Day, Secretary Wilson, and Secretary Hitchcock, Mr. and Mrs. Hermann Baer, Abner McKinley, Miss Helen McKinley, a sister of the President; Mrs. J. T. Duncan, another sister, and Mrs. Lafayette McWilliams, Mr. John G. Milburn, Postmaster General Bissell, John N. Scatcherd of Buffalo, and Representative Alexander of Buffalo.

SENATOR HANNA ARRIVES.

Senator Hanna came on a special train from Cleveland, making the run in the remarkably fast time of three hours. He was accompanied by Mrs. Hanna, Col. Myron T. Herrick, Miss Barber, and a few other friends of the President. He had received the news at 4 o'clock this morning, and immediately ordered a special train.

The President was perfectly conscious despite his extreme weakness. This morning, when the nurses sought to adjust the pillows so as to shut out the light of the

(Continued on Page 2.)

# HUNT OVER MOUNTAINS FOR MR. ROOSEVELT

## The Vice President Is Found on Mount Marcy.

### Special Train in Waiting to Take Him from the Adirondacks—Will Be in Albany This Morning.

NORTH CREEK, N. Y., Sept. 14.—Vice President Roosevelt started at 6 o'clock yesterday morning from the Tahawus Club with guides on a hunting trip through the forests. On receipt of the dispatches stating that President McKinley's condition was critical men were immediately started in search of him. Up to 5 o'clock last evening it was impossible to locate him, but he was finally found on the top of Mount Marcy, at which place the dispatches from Buffalo were delivered to him.

These dispatches gave but few details of the President's condition and did not inform Mr. Roosevelt that there was no hope for Mr. McKinley. At 8:30 o'clock last evening a team was dispatched to the lower clubhouse, ten miles from the upper clubhouse, with the latest bulletins, stating that the President could not live. These reached the Vice President, and at 1:15 A. M. he started for this village. He is obliged to drive or ride thirty-five miles over dark roads before North Creek is reached, and will probably arrive here at about 5 A. M.

Immediately upon his arrival here Mr. Roosevelt will take the special train which is waiting to carry him to Albany. He should get there at about 7 A. M. At Albany he will enter another special train, which will convey him to Buffalo over the New York Central Road.

SARATOGA, Sept. 13.—Vice President Roosevelt, when he passed through Saratoga last Wednesday, en route to the Tahawus Club, ninety-five miles distant in the Adirondacks wilderness, said that he expected to leave there to-day for his Oyster Bay home. The Vice President, it is understood, yesterday changed his plans, as he desired to remain with his family at the club until next Monday morning. The Tahawus Club is thirty-five miles north of railway and telegraphic facilities and ten miles beyond a private telephone line. Messages informing him of the dangerous condition of the President were this forenoon rushed into the Adirondacks as far as possible, and were then transferred to mounted messengers, with instructions to reach Mr. Roosevelt at the Tahawus Club as rapidly as possible. A dozen mounted mountaineers are now fleeing over the mountain roads.

When the Vice President receives the news he will move south as rapidly as possible to North Creek, where a Delaware and Hudson Railroad special fast train has been ordered to meet him. A fast run will be made from North Creek via Saratoga to Albany, where a special train will convey him to Buffalo. How soon he can make the thirty-five-mile mountain drive from the Tahawus Club to North Creek cannot be learned at this time, as recent rains have rendered the roads very heavy.

Superintendent C. D. Hammond of the Delaware and Hudson Railroad, has personal charge of the special train intended for the use of Mr. Roosevelt. It now lies at North Creek, awaiting the arrival there of the Vice President. The locomotive, No. 882, is the fastest on the system, and the coach, No. 200, is the one used by Second Vice President H. G. Young of the Delaware and Hudson Road.

The Adirondack Stage Company has established relays of horses between Tahawus Club and North Creek, in order to expedite Vice President Roosevelt's movements as soon as he gets out of the wilderness.

ALBANY, Sept. 13.—Supt. H. H. Farrington of the New York Central and Hudson River Railroad Company late to-night received a telegram from Supt. Hammond of the Delaware and Hudson Railroad Company, who is at North Creek with a special train to convey Vice President Roosevelt to this city, stating that the Vice President will not reach North Creek before 5 or 6 o'clock to-morrow morning, and cannot be brought to Albany before 7 or 8 o'clock.

# EX-PRESIDENT CLEVELAND EXPRESSES HIS SORROW.

### Hard, He Declares, to Await the Unfolding of the Purpose of God.

PRINCETON, N. J., Sept. 14.—When interviewed by The Associated Press correspondent, who conveyed to him the first news of President McKinley's death, ex-President Grover Cleveland, at his home on Bayard Lane, made the following statement on this sad event:

"This is dreadful news and the more cruel because it strikes down the confident and comforting expectation which all our people were encouraged to entertain that their President would be saved from death.

"In the afflictive gloom surrounding this third Presidential murder within the memory of men not yet old, we can scarcely keep out of mind a feeling of stunning amazement that in free America, blessed with a Government consecrated to popular welfare and contentment, the danger of assassination should ever encompass the faithful discharge of the highest official duty. It is hard at such a time as this to calmly and patiently await the unfolding of the purpose of God."

The bell on historic Nassau Hall was tolled for upward of an hour upon the receipt of the sad news. The flag of this building has been placed at halfmast.

## GOV. ODELL TO GO TO BUFFALO.

NEWBURG, N. Y., Sept. 13.—Gov. Odell is here to-night. He has kept in close communication with Buffalo by telephone, and has been greatly shocked and depressed by the change for the worse in the President's condition. He will leave for Buffalo to-morrow morning by the Empire State Express, which will stop for him at Fishkill Landing.

TO-DAY:

FOURTEEN PAGES,

WITH

REVIEW OF BOOKS AND ART.

INDEX TO DEPARTMENTS.

Stocks break sharply.—Financial Affairs.—Pages 10 and 11.
Wheat, No. 2 red, 76¾; corn, No. 2 mixed, 62¼c; oats: No. 2 mixed, 38¼c; cotton, middling, 8¾c; iron, Northern, No. 1 foundry, $15.25; butter, Western creamery, 20½c.—Commercial World.—Page 11.
Business Troubles.—Page 8.
Court Calendars.—Page 11.
Insurance Notes.—Page 10.
Losses by Fire.—Page 10.
Marine Intelligence and Foreign Mails.—Page 11.
New Corporations.—Page 10.
Real Estate.—Page 12.
Religious.—Page 9.
Society.—Page 7.
United Service.—Page 7.
Weather Report.—Page 9.
Yesterday's Fires.—Page 10.

THEODORE ROOSEVELT

"All the News That's Fit to Print."

# The New York Times.

THE WEATHER. Partly cloudy; light to fresh south to southeast winds.



VOL. L...NO. 16,127 NEW YORK, SUNDAY, SEPTEMBER 15, 1901.—Twenty Pages and Magazine Supplements. PRICE THREE CENTS.

## NATION GRIEVES AT LOSS OF PRESIDENT

### Funeral Service Arranged for Thursday.

### MR. ROOSEVELT SWORN IN

### He Promises to Follow the Policy Mr. McKinley.

**Autopsy Shows that Death Was Due to Gangrene Poisoning—Czolgosz to be Indicted To-morrow.**

While the Nation took on the habiliments of mourning yesterday, the body of the assassinated President, William McKinley, rested in the Milburn home in Buffalo.

Mr. Roosevelt, after looking upon the face of the dead President, went to the home of Ansley Wilcox, where the oath was administered to him as President of the United States by Judge John R. Hazel. The ceremony was simple but impressive. President Roosevelt promised to continue unbroken the policy of Mr. McKinley, and asked the members of the Cabinet to retain their portfolios, to which they all assented.

Grave fears are expressed for the condition of Mrs. McKinley. While it is asserted that she is doing as well as could be expected, a note of apprehension is evident.

The autopsy on the body of President McKinley showed that death was due to gangrene poisoning, the entire track of the bullet being contaminated. One of the physicians expressed the belief that the bullet with which the President was wounded had been poisoned.

Arrangements for the funeral have been made. A brief service will be held in the Milburn house to-day. To-morrow the funeral train, accompanied by President Roosevelt and the members of the Cabinet, will leave for Washington, where the body will lie in state in the Capitol Building until Wednesday. The body will then be taken to Canton, where the interment will take place on Thursday.

President Roosevelt's first official act was the appointing of Thursday as a day of mourning.

Czolgosz, the assassin, is to be indicted to-morrow, and will probably be sentenced in about twelve days.

The Governors in every State and the Mayors of the principal cities of the country have taken action to have the funeral day observed appropriately.

## THE DAY'S HAPPENINGS AT THE MILBURN HOUSE.

**Officials and Friends Call and Many Telegrams of Condolence Are Received.**

BUFFALO, Sept. 14.—Absolute quiet prevailed in the neighborhood of the Milburn house through the early hours of the day. The police maintained the lines on Delaware Avenue and the streets which intersect it, and double picket lines patrolled by Fourteenth Infantrymen protected the house from any intrusion. Many persons came to the outer police lines and gazed in silence at the house. The deepest sorrow was manifest.

Many of the Grand Army men in the throng pleaded with the police for admission to the lines, declaring that it was their right and privilege to guard the body of the man who had fought in their ranks and was their comrade. The police, however, enforced the order.

A heavy, damp fog hung over the city and gave the air a chill that was penetrating. At 8 o'clock a company of the Fourteenth Infantry, commanded by Lieut. James Ware, came to relieve their comrades, who had been on guard for twenty-four hours, and new guards were posted. None who came to show their sorrow for the dead President failed to ask solicitously for Mrs. McKinley.

The large American flag which has hung from the front of the Milburn home almost continuously since the exposition began was not removed. There was no means of half-masting it, and it was left where it draped across the front of the veranda. It was the only bit of color in a gray and cheerless scene.

Mr. Cortelyou, despite the strain of the last few days, was up again early, seeing to all of the arrangements. Col. Bingham, Superintendent of Public Buildings and Grounds in Washington, arrived early in the morning to assist Secretary Cortelyou in every way that he can.

Mrs. Barber and Miss McKinley drove to the Milburn house at 9:30.

The gates of the Pan-American Exposition will be closed and will remain shut until Monday. The city is crowded with Exposition visitors, but they, like all others, are in deep mourning. Flags fly mid-mast and preparations are in progress to give the public buildings a draping of sombre black.

At all the city churches to-morrow there will be services and prayers for the martyred President. Plans for formal civic action and for a large escort of military and civic organisations, when the body is removed to the train that will carry it to Washington, are under consideration.

Abner McKinley, brother of President McKinley, drove to the Milburn house at 10 o'clock, accompanied by Lieut. James McKinley, Col. Brown, and Mr. Meek of Canton. The police removed the rope lines, and the carriage rolled slowly up to the entrance of the house. Mr. McKinley bent forward in his seat in the carriage and shaded his eyes with his hands. When he alighted, he walked slowly up to the door of the house with his eyes downcast and head bent. His face plainly showed the strain and grief of the night.

Efforts were made to obtain an authentic statement from the physicians giving a technical history of the case. Drs. Mynter, Stockton, Park, and Mann asked to be excused from discussing the subject at this time. They explained that copious notes of the developments in the case had been taken by each of them, and these will be used in the preparation of a general statement of the case that will be published. Dr. McBurney declined to be seen this morning, pleading fatigue from last night's ordeal.

While crowds of people occupied every street of prominence in the city this morning, near the jail where Czolgosz is confined there was hardly a handful of people, and there was no particular display of police. In fact, the assassin seemed to be forgotten in the general grief.

At 10 o'clock the Milburn house showed its first stir. The relatives of President McKinley began arriving, and the waiting attendants stood at the open door to receive them. Mr. Milburn joined the party at 10 o'clock, and for a time stood at the door with bared head with some of the friends of the McKinley family. By that time great crowds were banked at either end of the rope inclosure, but perfect order was observed.

CORONER VIEWS THE BODY.

The Coroner of Buffalo, James Wilson, arrived at the residence at 10 o'clock and officially viewed the body. He stated that it had been his intention to impanel a jury, but he had been officially advised by the District Attorney that such a proceeding would be unnecessary. After the autopsy he said that he would issue a certificate of death and a permit for the removal of the body.

Senator Hanna came to the house at 10:40, accompanied by Controller Dawes and Elmer Dover, his private secretary. The Senator walked slowly and haltingly and bowed his head as he approached the house. Exaggerated reports of his illness had previously been sent out. His appearance on the streets completely dispelled them.

An affecting incident of the morning was the coming of Mrs. Garret A. Hobart, wife of the former Vice President of the United States, and young Mr. Hobart, her son. Mrs. Hobart was in deepest mourning.

ASSEMBLING OF THE CABINET.

The members of the Cabinet began assembling at 10:30 o'clock. Secretary Root was the first to arrive, and after him came Secretaries Long, Wilson, and Hitchcock; Attorney General Knox, and Postmaster General Smith. They went to a rear parlor of the Milburn home, and there began their conference. The only absentees were Secretaries Gage and Hay, who had not yet reached the city.

At the same time the surgeons selected to perform the autopsy had assembled with their assistants in the room up stairs where the President had died and where his body still rested.

Gen. Charles F. Roe presented himself informally at the house. He said that, until the funeral arrangements had been completed, he could say nothing about the New York troops that would be assigned as escort.

Senator Chauncey M. Depew and his son, C. M. Depew, Jr., came to the Milburn house shortly before noon. Mr. Depew said that Railroad Day at the Exposition had been indefinitely postponed.

Dr. McBurney was asked later in the day for a general statement as to treatment by the physicians. He said: "You really must excuse me from any comment bearing on the treatment of the case at this time. I want to be obliging, if possible, and feel that the public has a right to be informed on the subject. Dr. Mann, who was the chief surgeon in the case, should be given the opportunity to make his report before I can say anything. After that is published I may feel at liberty to discuss the matter somewhat, but I cannot do so now."

Dr. Munson reached the house at 11:45 and the autopsy then proceeded.

MANY MESSAGES OF CONDOLENCE.

The expressions of condolence began to arrive almost simultaneously with the announcement of the President's death, showing that the people everywhere had waited on through the weary watches of the night for the news that the end had come. After daylight the telegrams began arriving in a steady stream, thousands reaching the house before noon. Those for Mrs. McKinley were laid aside, it not being deemed safe to intrude upon her in her feeble condition.

MEXICAN COMMISSIONERS CALL.

Carlos Sellerier, Jesus M. Nuncio, and J. D. Fleury, Mexican Commissioners to the Pan-American Exposition, called to express their sympathy and that of the Government they represent. Representatives of other South American countries also called and left their cards to express their regret at the death of the President and the loss sustained by the people of the United States.

## PRESIDENT ROOSEVELT ISSUES A PROCLAMATION.

**Appoints Thursday as a Day of Mourning and of Prayer.**

BUFFALO, Sept. 14.—President Roosevelt to-night issued the following proclamation:

BY THE PRESIDENT OF THE UNITED STATES OF AMERICA.

A PROCLAMATION.

A terrible bereavement has befallen our people. The President of the United States has been struck down; a crime committed not only against the Chief Magistrate, but against every law-abiding and liberty-loving citizen.

President McKinley crowned a life of largest love for his fellow-men, of most earnest endeavor for their welfare, by a death of Christian fortitude; and both the way in which he lived his life and the way in which, in the supreme hour of trial, he met his death, will remain forever a precious heritage of our people.

It is meet that we as a Nation express our abiding love and reverence for his life; our deep sorrow for his untimely death.

Now, therefore, I, Theodore Roosevelt, President of the United States of America, do appoint Thursday next, September Nineteenth, the day in which the body of the dead President will be laid in its last earthly resting place, as a day of mourning and prayer throughout the United States.

I earnestly recommend all the people to assemble on that day in their respective places of divine worship, there to bow down in submission to the will of Almighty God and to pay out of full hearts their homage of love and reverence to the great and good President whose death has smitten the Nation with bitter grief.

In witness whereof I have hereunto set my hand and caused the seal of the United States to be affixed.

Done at the City of Washington, the 14th day of September, A. D. one thousand nine hundred and one, and of the independence of the United States the one hundred and twenty-sixth.

[Seal.] THEODORE ROOSEVELT.

By the President.

JOHN HAY, Secretary of State.

## THE EFFECT ON EUROPE.

PARIS, Sept. 15.—The morning papers all publish appreciations of the late President McKinley and of President Roosevelt. The Gaulois says:

"The death of President McKinley will have a greater reverberation throughout Europe than had the disappearance of Garfield, Lincoln, or Carnot. He played a bigger part on the world's stage than any of his predecessors. Bolder than they, he threw down the gauntlet to one of the nations of the Old World and inaugurated at the expense of Spain a policy of expansion and conquest. He installed himself in the Philippines, joined uninvited in the European concert in China, and finally took up a determined and very American attitude in regard to the Panama question.

"Now this great perturber of our quietude reposes in his coffin. Will his imperialist policy disappear with him? Logically, Mr. Roosevelt is heir to the views and ambitions of Mr. McKinley, and hence nothing will be changed in the United States. So much the worse for Europe!"

The Figaro, after expressing condolences over the death of President McKinley, says:

"We also salute President Roosevelt, whose chivalrous mind is known to all, and who undoubtedly will continue, especially in the relations with France, the traditions of his predecessor. There is not another man who better responds to the ideal of his countrymen. He has been long prepared for the supreme rank, and he will occupy this high station with ease and success. He is supported by public sentiment, and will know how to use this strength."

The Matin says:

"There is something grandly tragic in the death of this man (Mr. McKinley) who fell shaking hands with his assassin in the presence of a crowd. But in the midst of this terrible mourning the Americans may consider themselves fortunate. They lose their chief of State, but find a man in Roosevelt."

## MRS. M'KINLEY'S STATE AROUSES GRAVE FEARS

### Utterly Grief-Stricken and Much Broken Down.

**Friends Express Grave Apprehensions as to her Condition—Dazed at Final Parting She Did Not Shed a Tear.**

*Special to The New York Times.*

BUFFALO, Sept. 14.—Mrs. McKinley's condition, her health, her general bearing, and the direct effect the death of Mr. McKinley will have upon her are the matters in which the thousands of visitors who came here for pleasure and remained to mourn are most concerned.

From the Milburn house it is announced, and that repeatedly, that she is "bearing up well," but behind this there seems to be a note of doubt, an indication of fear that all is not as well with the stricken widow as her friends would gladly believe. In fact, the statement made last night by Frank B. Baird, a friend of the McKinley family and of Senator Hanna, that if President McKinley should die there would be a double funeral from the Milburn home, finds many reluctant believers, who, having loved the martyred President, have now transferred their affection to her to whom the murdered husband gave his life's love. Mr. Baird's statement was repeated this morning by the Rev. Dr. Charles B. Locke of the Delaware Avenue Methodist Episcopal Church, who will conduct the funeral services to-morrow. He is the son of Mr. McKinley's former pastor in Canton, and will officiate at the special request of the family. As Dr. Locke left the Milburn home he was asked as to the condition of Mrs. McKinley, and said:

DOUBLE TRAGEDY FEARED.

"All great ideals have been consecrated in blood. Mrs. McKinley's nobleness and piety are her own. She is keeping up wonderfully well, although there may be a double tragedy."

The next intelligence concerning Mrs. McKinley was furnished by Col. Brown, who came out of the Milburn home about 11:15 o'clock.

"Mrs. McKinley does not seem to fully realise the awful blow," said he. "She is in a sort of dazed condition, and acts mechanically. We expect her to collapse during the day, but we do not anticipate any fatal results."

At 11:35 o'clock John G. Milburn was asked as to the condition of Mrs. McKinley. "Although I have not seen her this morning," said Mr. Milburn, "I understand that she is bearing the terrible misfortune better than was anticipated. Dr. Rixey, Miss Barber, and Mrs. Lafayette McWilliams are with her almost constantly."

Before the end came last night Dr. Rixey administered an opiate to Mrs. McKinley. Her condition made it necessary. She slept through the night, knowing nothing of what had passed in the chamber on the other side of the house.

Slowly the incidents touching the death of President McKinley are coming to light. The occupants of the Milburn home, now that suspense is ended, are recalling the scenes which have now so much to do with the well-being of Mrs. McKinley. Col. Brown, the partner of Abner McKinley, tells of the last meeting of the devoted pair. He agrees with others in saying that when Mrs. McKinley realized, in some intuitive manner, that Mr. McKinley was dead, while appearing to bear up well, she wandered from room to room, uttering no word, broken, stricken, dazed.

The awful suddenness of the President's relapse, when everything seemed to point to an early recovery, was that which the physicians dreaded would prove such a blow to Mrs. McKinley that she would be unable to bear up under it. They expressed fear openly that immediate collapse would follow the knowledge of the President's true condition.

The physicians met in consultation for the last time at about 11 o'clock last night, with what hope, or with what object in view so far as relief of the dying President was concerned, none can tell. They had announced that there was no longer any hope, had said the President was dying, and the awful intelligence had been given to an anxious, waiting world. At this meeting they discussed the propriety of imparting the bad news to Mrs. McKinley. They agreed they could no longer keep it from her. She was wandering from one room to the other, and, though no whisper of the truth reached her, the drawn faces and tear-filled eyes of those about her told her the story. Then Mrs. McKinley spoke of her fears for the first time.

DR. RIXEY BREAKS THE NEWS.

In a calm, unnatural voice she said:

"The President is dying. You can't deceive me. I must see him."

The physicians then felt that they could no longer keep her in ignorance. Dr. Rixey, the President's private physician, was the one to whom was assigned the task. He went to Mrs. McKinley's room. With her at the time was the President's niece, Miss Barber. Mrs. McKinley's first question made it easier for Dr. Rixey. As he entered, Mrs. McKinley quietly remarked:

"I understand the President is sleeping, doctor."

"He is sleeping," replied Dr. Rixey; "he is sleeping that sleep that knows no awakening."

There was no reply. There were no tears.

Mrs. McKinley had previously insisted on seeing the President. None dared deny her. Others in the house turned away their heads, choked their sobs, and gave way to their grief. Past these persons Mrs. McKinley was escorted to the chamber.

There she gazed her last upon the features of the dying President, to her ever a support and comfort, a lover in his early days, and no less so on that, the last day of his life.

THE LAST FAREWELL.

There she took her last farewell of the man who for years had given her his tenderest care, but who at this time failed to recognize the features of the wife whose devotion to him, and his to her, had been the admiration of the entire Nation.

Mrs. McKinley was led into the death chamber by Dr. Rixey. She went immediately to the bedside, sat upon the edge, took the dying President's hands in both her own, gazed fondly, tearlessly, at the changing features, then smoothed back the hair from his brow, half arose, placed both arms around his neck, held them so for an instant or two, then arose and turned, ready to be led from the chamber. She walked from the room, through the halls, attended by Dr. Rixey, just as one in a dream. Her gaze was fixed, her grief evident, but still there were no tears.

On returning to her room, Dr. Rixey administered a stimulant. Then she gave way to bitter sobs and heartbreaking lamentations. Dr. Rixey and Miss Barber did their utmost to console her. Their efforts were unavailing. She was wrapped in her grief and had ears for none.

This morning Mrs. McKinley awoke early. She was pale and wan. It was plain that her rest had been disturbed. When those in the house glanced at her sweet, wan, pale face and realized the great load she was so heroically bearing they turned away to hide their tears. No words can tell of the suffering that this devoted woman was undergoing. It was oppressive and pervaded the entire household. Few cared to stay long. All who had left the house had but one word. A greater part of the morning she kept to her room, with Miss Barber as her sole confidante and companion.

She had not yet asked to see the dead President. This afternoon John G. Milburn came from his home, and the first question addressed to him was regarding Mrs. McKinley's condition. There was some perturbation in his countenance, some tremor in his voice, as he said:

"Mrs. McKinley, all things considered, is bearing up wonderfully well—the doctors say as well as can be expected. I think medicines and stimulants are being administered, but I do not know whether she is under the influence of opiates. Miss Barber is with her all the time; Dr. Rixey the greater part of it."

UTTERLY GRIEFSTRICKEN.

Yet a moment later, in response to a question as to her actual physical condition, Mr. Milburn declared seriously and gravely: "Mrs. McKinley is deeply bereaved, utterly griefstricken, and very, very much broken down."

These words, from the man in whose home the body of Mr. McKinley lies, have tended more to confirm the feeling that Mrs. McKinley is in danger than anything else of which the public has learned.

At the Milburn home late to-night it was said that Mrs. McKinley's condition of mind is the same as yesterday. She hardly seems to realize what has happened, and appears to be wholly dazed.

It is stated that Mrs. McKinley will not be taken to Canton, as originally planned. Her desire is to go to Washington. She has signifed this to President Roosevelt. It is stated that she asked to go with the funeral train to Washington, to remain in the White House while the body is lying in state, and then to go with the funeral train to Canton. It is understood that President Roosevelt has said that her request will be granted.

## PRESIDENT ROOSEVELT'S FAMILY.

*Special to The New York Times.*

SARATOGA, N. Y., Sept. 14.—Mrs. Theodore Roosevelt and family will arrive in New York City to-morrow morning. They left Tohawus Club early this morning, proceeded to Albany via Saratoga, and took the Hudson River night boat Adirondack for New York City, where they are due Sunday morning.

## SOLDIER CURSED THE PRESIDENT.

WILKESBARRE, Penn., Sept. 14.—Company F, Ninth Regiment, N. G. P., had arranged to hold a banquet in the armory in this city last night; but owing to the serious illness of President McKinley it was decided yesterday to postpone the event.

Corp. Hiram Wentz was highly indignant at the fact that the banquet was postponed, and he cursed the dying President. He was immediately set upon by other members of the company and so badly beaten that he is in a serious condition. If he recovers from his injuries he will be court-martialed.



## MR. ROOSEVELT IS NOW THE PRESIDENT

### Will Continue Unbroken the Policy of Mr. McKinley.

### OATH SOLEMNLY SPOKEN

### Simple Ceremony at the Home of Ansley Wilcox.

**Members of the Cabinet Asked to Serve in Present Capacities and They Agreed to Do So—Senator Hanna Offered His Services.**

*Special to The New York Times.*

BUFFALO, Sept. 14.—Theodore Roosevelt to-day became President of the United States, with a solemn promise that he would follow out the policy laid down by President McKinley.

His exact words, which produced a most profound impression upon the small company of people to whom he spoke, were: "I wish to say that it shall be my aim to continue absolutely unbroken the policy of President McKinley for the peace and prosperity and the honor of our beloved country."

A more solemn scene would be hard to conceive than was the swearing in of Mr. Roosevelt as President. It occurred in the library of the home of his personal friend, ex-State Senator Ansley Wilcox, which home is a little, old-fashioned Colonial mansion on Delaware Avenue, within a mile of the residence of Mr. Milburn, where the body of the assassinated President is lying.

There was nothing of pomp in the ceremony. It was as simple and as sanctified as a family religious service, such as a wedding. It was hard to realise that it was an event of world-wide import.

Mr. Roosevelt, as Vice President, arrived here at 1:30 o'clock this afternoon. He had been brought on, as fast as the best of horses and the swiftest of special trains could bring him, from his retreat in the Adirondacks, where he went last week, fully satisfied that President McKinley would recover.

AVOIDS WAITING CROWDS.

It was Mr. Roosevelt's particular desire that there should be no demonstration from the crowds here in Buffalo. Many thousands of persons were waiting to greet him at the Exchange Street station. To avoid this crowd the train ran on to the Terrace Station. An escort of twelve mounted patrolmen and several detectives waited there. The authorities felt that they could not take too much care in guarding the man who was to take the place of the martyred McKinley.

Jumping from the train, Mr. Roosevelt got into a closed carriage with Mr. Milburn and was at once driven to the home of Ansley Wilcox, where a light lunch was served, and where he became acquainted with the developments of the day. He was told that it was desired to administer the oath to him very soon, and he agreed with the suggestion. Mr. Roosevelt expressed a desire to be taken to the Milburn house, in order that he might gaze upon the face of President McKinley. The Fourth Signal Corps and two platoons of mounted police had been stationed before the Wilcox house as a further escort for the Vice President.

OBJECTS TO MILITARY ESCORT.

It had been intended to swear Mr. Roosevelt in at the Wilcox house immediately upon his arrival, but his request to be first permitted to go to the Milburn house was respected. When he came out of the Wilcox house, at 2:30 o'clock, to go to the Milburn house and saw the soldiers and police, he appeared to be displeased.

"I do not want such an escort as that," he said. "It is not necessary. A couple of mounted policemen will be quite enough."

Three mounted policemen were put on either side of his carriage as he drove to the Milburn house. With him were William Loeb, his private secretary, and George L. Williams. The carriage was closed, but the crowds along Delaware Avenue knew that it contained the man who is to be President for the next three years and a half, and could not restrain its applause, although this never took on the character of an ovation. The people seemed to be fully impressed with the solemnity of the time.

President Roosevelt was dressed in a long frock coat, which fitted his athletic figure to perfection. The waistcoat was buttoned high, revealing very little of the black silk four-in-hand tie, which was knotted under a turn-down collar. He had a very thin gold watch chain across his waistcoat. His trousers were almost a solid gray. His patent leather shoes were heavy soled and square toed. He had come on without a high hat, and, not having time to buy one, had borrowed one of his friend John N. Scatcherd. It did not fit him.

The Vice President jumped from the carriage when it stopped at the Milburn house, and advanced, with bowed head, across the broad lawn. Mr. Cortelyou, the dead President's private secretary, came out to meet him.

Mr. Roosevelt inquired anxiously after Mrs. McKinley. He breathed a sigh of relief when told that there had been a marked improvement in her condition since yesterday. Learning that she was resting, he left a message of sympathy for her, and Secretary Cortelyou then took him to the up-stairs room in which the body of President McKinley rested.

OVERCOME WITH GRIEF.

Mr. Roosevelt gazed upon the features of the Chief Executive, by whose assassination he had been placed at the head of the United States Government. He did not speak a word. He stood silent with bowed head, for several minutes, and then walked from the room, tears streaming from his eyes and his strong frame shaking with convulsive sobs. It was several minutes before he had sufficiently recovered himself to meet the members of the Cabinet who were in the Milburn house.

Vice President Roosevelt was driven back to the Wilcox house, a quaint old vine-covered home, with big Colonial pillars extending to the roof along the front. It stands back under the shade of big trees, and is the last place in the world that one would pick out as the scene for such a ceremony as the swearing in of a President of the United States. Mr. Roosevelt got back there shortly after 3 o'clock this afternoon.

All of the members of the Cabinet except Secretaries Hay and Gage, who are in Washington, were awaiting the arrival of the Vice President. There were also present many other men who have played a conspicuous part in the events connected with the National tragedy which has been enacted here during the past week. There were a few women in the house, but they kept mostly in the background.

There were a score of men with cameras standing about waiting to take pictures of Mr. Roosevelt, but at his request they were ordered to desist.

The library of Mr. Wilcox's house had been chosen as the place in which the oath should be administered. It is a room not more than 18 by 25 feet, with a low ceiling. There is a bay window in it, in which some potted palms are effectively arranged, and which is canopied over by green draperies. The general color of the room is green, although its walls are almost entirely covered by well-filled bookcases. There was no furniture in the room other than the bookcases, a library table, and a few chairs.

PRESENT AT THE CEREMONY.

Vice President Roosevelt advanced into the bay window alcove, where he shook hands with Judge John R. Hasel, United States District Judge, who was to administer the oath to him. On his right stood Secretary Long, Secretary Hitchcock, Secretary Wilson, Secretary Smith, Secretary Root, and Secretary Knox. On his left stood Ansley Wilcox, Private Secretary Loeb, George Urban, Dr. Mann, and Dr. Stockton. Around the sides of the room were Secretary Cortelyou, whom Col. Roosevelt had asked to continue to serve him as he had served President McKinley; Mr. Milburn, Clerk George B. Keating of the United States District Court, Judge A. R. Haight of the Court of Appeals, Senator Depew, John N. Scatcherd, George L. Williams, and about a score of reporters. Back in the doorway stood Mrs. Ansley Wilcox, Miss Wilcox, Mrs. John G. Milburn, Mrs. Carleton Sprague, Mrs. Mann, and Mrs. Charles Carey. The entire company present numbered forty-three persons:

The silence in the room was painfully oppressive when Secretary Root advanced to Vice President Roosevelt and Judge Hasel and said:

"Mr. Vice President, I have been requested by all of the members of the Cabinet of the late President McKinley who are present in the City of Buffalo—"

When Mr. Root mentioned the name of the assassinated President there was an audible sigh from the company standing about, and he himself had to stop speak-

"All the News That's Fit to Print."

# The New York Times.

THE WEATHER.
Fair, slightly warmer Thursday; Friday, fair, warmer: moderate winds, becoming south.
For full weather report see Page 22.

VOL. LIII....NO. 16,996. NEW YORK, FRIDAY, JUNE 24, 1904.--SIXTEEN PAGES. ONE CENT In Greater New York, Jersey City and Newark. | Elsewhere, TWO CENTS.

## JAPANESE CLOSING IN ON A 60-MILE FRONT

### Russian Outposts Give Way Before Two Great Armies.

### NIU-CHWANG IS MENACED

### Mikado's Soldiers Approaching Tashi-Chao and a Battle Either There or at Kai-Chow Expected.

ST. PETERSBURG, June 23.—The General Staff has received the following dispatch from Lieut. Gen. Sakharoff under date of June 22:

"At 8 o'clock on the morning of June 21 the Japanese vanguard resumed its advance against our outposts, four miles south of Senuchen. The outposts retired slowly toward Senuchen, and further on in the direction of Kai-Chow.

"At noon a Japanese column consisting of nine squadrons of cavalry, a battery of artillery, and a considerable number of infantry were observed advancing in the direction of Senuchen. Other strong columns of the enemy appeared, and the Japanese occupied Senuchen toward evening with over a division of infantry, a brigade of cavalry, and thirty-two guns.

"According to information received from our scouts and the inhabitants the enemy over a division strong is concentrated southward of Chapan Pass, near Chang-Tia-Tien and Long-Tia-Tien.

"The Japanese did not advance beyond Chapan Pass, in the direction of Tanchi, fifteen miles southeast of Tashi-Chao.

#### Japanese Advance from Siu-Yen.

"Our scouts report that a large detachment of all arms advanced from Siu-Yen to Khranza on the morning of June 22. A battalion of the enemy, taking advantage of a thick fog, tried to surprise our vanguard near Vandiapudze, on the Siu-Yen—Hai-Cheng Road.

"The movement was discovered in time and the Japanese received volleys from five companies of Russians. The enemy retired with some losses toward Siu-Yen. One Russian sharpshooter was wounded.

"The Japanese occupied Wafang-Tien, on the main road to Liao-Yang, on the evening of June 19, with a battalion of infantry and a squadron of cavalry. A detachment of the same strength occupied Chanlin-Ju, in the Valley of the Tsuo River, seven miles north of Feng-Wang-Cheng."

Emperor Nicholas has received the following dispatch from Gen. Kuropatkin under date of June 21:

"A Japanese army from Kai-Chow is gradually advancing northward.

"Gen. Kuroki's advance from Siu-Yen has been suspended, evidently to effect an alignment of the two armies.

#### Strong Japanese Vanguard.

"The strength of the enemy's vanguard is approximately a division and several squadrons of cavalry, and the Siu-Yen force of nine squadrons is supported by a strong column of infantry toward the south.

"The enemy's position on June 19 and June 21 extended within seven miles southward of Senu-Chen along a line from the sea to the mountainous and difficult district east of the railway.

"The enemy's advance lines are being strongly held by cavalry and a screen of infantry. The passes and defiles in the mountains east of the railway are also vigilantly guarded.

"A movement of strong Japanese mounted patrols with infantry supports was noted June 20 from 5 in the afternoon onward. We had no losses in the firing which ensued, while the Japanese had several killed and wounded.

"An increase in the Japanese forces has been noticed south of Vandiapudze, and near the villages of Manziapudze, Takiapudze, and Khakahei. Reinforcements are also reaching the Japanese at the furthest point of the road between Siu-Yen and Tanchi via Paiahanlou and Siakhotan.

"The Japanese are erecting field fortifications on the road from Siu-Yen to Kai-Chow."

Gen. Kuropatkin's report also says the Japanese have seized more passes on the northern road and they have occupied the village of Sapenhai, twenty-five miles northeast of Sai-ma-Tsze, where they are firmly intrenched.

(The foregoing reports indicate that the Japanese are closing in on a sixty-mile front from Chapan Pass on the north to Senuchen on the south. Kai-Chow, where Stakelberg's corps retreated, is about midway between these points. Tashi-Chao, threatened by the Japanese, is where the railway to Niu-Chwang joins the main line from Port Arthur to the north.)

#### To Prevent Russian Counter-Move.

The Japanese movement north of Feng-wang-Cheng is interpreted both as a threat to detain as many Russians as possible in the northern part of the Liao-Tung Peninsula, and as a protection of the Japanese flank against a counter move on the part of Gen. Kuropatkin in case the opposing armies should become seriously engaged in the vicinity of Hai-Cheng.

The occupation of Siung-Yue-Cheng (twenty-five miles southeast of Kai-Chow) by a Japanese detachment indicates that the connection between the enemy's armies is practically assured. Siung-Yue-Cheng is half way between Gen. Oku's and Gen. Kuroki's positions, at Senuchen and Siu-Yen, respectively. In the opinion of the General Staff, the Siung-Yue-Cheng detachment is an outpost of the Siu-Yen army, or of another force, recently landed at Ching-Tai-Tse, (fifteen miles southwest of Taku-Shan.) The roads from Siu-Yen and Ching-Tai-Tse pass Siung-Yue-Cheng, whence they proceeded respectively to Senuchen and Kai-Chow.

The information of the War Office accounts for the positions of twelve Japanese divisions. The whereabouts of two others is unknown. These are the Sixth and Seventh, which probably were the last to arrive, as they come from Hakodate. One or both may have just landed, furnishing a link between the armies of Kuroki and Oku.

#### Expectation of Great Battle.

The expectation of a great battle has been intensified by Gen. Kuropatkin's speech to Gen. Stakelberg's corps on Monday at Kai-Chow, when the Commander in Chief said he would see the troops again soon; that they must settle the Japanese promptly, and that they were not going home until this had been done. The General is understood to have meant that he would return from Liao-Yang with a large force and give battle.

LIAO-YANG, June 22.—According to reports received at the Russian Headquarters the Japanese intend to attack either Kai-Chow or Tashi-Chao (on the railroad about midway between Kai-Chow and Hai-Cheng) from two sides. Their armies continue to advance from the south and east.

Gen. Kuroki's army has appeared on the road leading westward from Siu-Yen and in the neighboring valleys.

The success of the Japanese plan would mean that Korea would lose its value as a base, Niu-Chwang then being available for this purpose. The movements of the Japanese troops are facilitated by the cessation of the rains and by the fact that hot weather has set in, which has dried the roads.

#### Cossacks Fall Into Ambush.

Another Cossack detachment has fallen into an ambush of Japanese infantry, losing a number of men wounded.

GEN. KUROKI'S HEADQUARTERS IN THE FIELD, via Fu-San, June 23.—Russians from Samimak attacked the Japanese outposts in force yesterday, apparently for the purpose of testing their strength. The Russian force consisted of two regiments of cavalry, one of infantry, and one battery of artillery.

The enemy were defeated and retired toward Shin-tai-Ling. They are supposed to have sustained considerable loss. On the Japanese side Major Kubota was killed and nine men were wounded.

A party of foreign Military Attachés on a visit to the outposts probably witnessed the fighting.

The Russians are still occupying the towns on the main road in front of Gen. Kuroki's army with considerable forces.

Major Gen. Mistchenko is in command of the Russian forces in the vicinity of Siu-Yen. Small parties of Cossacks hover about the Japanese lines of communication, but the damage they have inflicted amounts to little.

## OYAMA TO LEAD JAPANESE.

### Famous Field Marshal Appointed Commander in Chief in Manchuria.

LONDON TIMES—NEW YORK TIMES Special Cablegram.
Copyright, 1904. THE NEW YORK TIMES.

TOKIO, June 23.—Field Marshal Oyama is going to Manchuria as Commander in Chief, with Lieut. Gen. Kodama as Chief of Staff.

Their places on the General Staff in Tokio will be taken by Field Marshal Yamagata and Major Gen. Nagaoka.

It was Field Marshal Marquis Oyama who captured Port Arthur from China in the war of 1894-95, when he led the famous Japanese "Second Army." This army also, among other notable exploits, captured Ta-lien-Wan and Wei-hai-Wei. Oyama and Yamagata are the only Field Marshals of the Japanese Army. Oyama is sixty-one years old.

Lieut. Gen. Baron Kodama has recently been Chief of the General Staff. He is regarded as one of the finest tacticians of Japan.

## A BATTLE PROBABLE.

### Reinforcements Arriving for Russians on the Peninsula.

LONDON TIMES—NEW YORK TIMES Special Cablegrams.
Copyright, 1904. THE NEW YORK TIMES.

PARIS, June 23.—A dispatch from Niu-Chwang says that reinforcements are arriving for the Russian troops south of Kai-Chow and that a battle appears probable.

Convoys with wounded are being sent northward.

The Chinese are once more evacuating Niu-Chwang.

TOKIO, June 23.—The London rumors of a battle at Hai-Cheng are not credited in Japan.

## FEUD MURDER IN KENTUCKY.

### Mack White, Sole Eye Witness of Salyer Killing, Shot from Ambush.

*Special to The New York Times.*

LEXINGTON, Ky., June 23.—Sheriff Edward Callahan of Breathitt County and a posse of forty men and three bloodhounds are searching the mountains to-night for the slayer of Mack White, who was shot from ambush at his home, three miles from Jackson, late this afternoon.

White was the only eye-witness to the killing of Chad Salyer by Bob Chaney last Fall, and since then threats have been made that he would not live to give his testimony in open court. The White faction is one of the strongest in Breathitt County. White was a member of the Hargis faction in the Hargis-Cockrill feud, and if his murderer is caught, it is likely the feud of two years ago will be reopened.

## POLICE STOP TICKET SELLING.

### Power Off on Third Avenue Elevated Caused Delay and Danger.

Trouble in the power house of the Interborough Rapid Transit Company, at Seventy-fourth Street and the East River, yesterday afternoon caused the shutting off of the electricity on the Third Avenue elevated line for forty minutes, just at the height of the rush of down-town workers to their homes in Harlem and the Bronx. Trains were stalled and many of them left powerless between stations.

Passengers, impatient of the delay, left the cars and climbed along the structure to the nearest stations, whence they sought surface cars. At several stations there was much complaint because the ticket sellers continued to take fares. Many passengers demanded transfers to the surface lines, or insisted upon the return of their money, but the ticket sellers ignored them.

At the City Hall station the power failed at 5:30 o'clock, just as a crowded train had been dispatched and was half way up to the Chatham Square station.

The crowd on the platforms of the City Hall stations increased to an uncomfortable extent by the failure to stop selling tickets. Capt. Murtha of the Bridge Police Station sent Roundsman Tighe and ten reserves there to care for the passengers. Tighe ordered the ticket sellers to close their windows until traffic was resumed. At 6:10 o'clock, as suddenly as it had failed, the power was supplied again and trains were able to move.

## INDEX TO DEPARTMENTS.


Commercial World.—Page 13.
Amusements.—Page 9.
Arrivals at Hotels and Out-of-Town Buyers.—Page 6.
Business Troubles.—Page 10.
Court Calendars.—Page 10.
Losses by Fire.—Page 6.
Marine Intelligence and Foreign Mails.—Page 15.
New Corporations.—Page 12.
Real Estate.—Page 15.
Society.—Page 9.
United Service.—Page 15.
Weather Report.—Page 9.
Yesterday's Fires.—Page 6.


## NEW PRINCE ARTHUR HAS TUSSLE WITH MONMOUTH

### Both Vessels Claim Victory in Red Hot Harbor Race.

### MANY BAY CRAFT LOOK ON

### New Munson Liner Was on Her Trial Trip and Many Guests Aboard Saw Her Fine Race.

The passengers aboard the steamboat Monmouth of the Central Railroad of New Jersey's Sandy Hook route, on the 1 o'clock run down the bay, had a treat yesterday when the smart little steamship Prince Arthur of the Munson Line, fresh from the builders' hands and on her trial trip down the bay, tried to wrest the laurels from the fleet bay steamboat.

Both contestants claimed the victory, the Prince Arthur officers because they were ahead when the West Bank Light was reached, and the steamship slowed down, and the Monmouth Captain because he was ahead when, he said, the Prince Arthur crowded him on to the right bank of the channel.

Among those who are familiar with the races the Monmouth has had with other craft, it was said yesterday that nothing of the size of the Prince Arthur had ever before held the Monmouth so well.

The Prince Arthur is the latest addition to the Munson Line service. She has two stacks, both of which are painted red and give her the appearance of a small French liner, and twin screws.

General Manager Gifkins of the Dominion Atlantic Railway and Steamship Service, gave a luncheon on board the Prince Arthur yesterday, during which the vessel left her pier and started down the bay. As she approached the Narrows the Monmouth was sighted coming down the bay at a great rate of speed. The Prince Arthur was slowed up to await the Monmouth, and all of the guests were called from the dining room to watch the coming test.

The Monmouth's white hulk was not more than a few lengths behind the Prince Arthur when the latter sounded three whistles as a challenge, and at the same time coal was heaped on her furnaces until the smoke came in clouds from her funnel. The Monmouth replied with three toots, her pilot rang for full speed, and the two vessels were off with a bound.

The pilots in the wheel house of the Monmouth knew nothing of the Prince Arthur, and when they saw her sudden burst of speed they were so surprised that they brought the engineer, James Whitehead, into consultation to make sure that the steamboat should do her best.

A moment later Whitehead was in the Monmouth's engine room himself, directing matters. Draughts were opened and coal heaved on until the flyer was pouring forth a column of smoke that covered her wake with darkness.

Gradually she pulled up on the Prince Arthur. Other craft cleared the channel and gave room to the two fleet ones. Slowly, almost imperceptibly, the Prince Albert fell back, and when the race had been under way for about two miles, their bows were nearly even. Then the officers of the Prince Arthur crowded on more steam, and she once more began to shove her black bows ahead of the Monmouth, but not for long, for the old harbor vessel again overhauled her.

It was nip and tuck all the way down the Swash Channel. At length the Monmouth pulled away, until the Prince Arthur hung on her quarter. Then the steamship began to work in; closer the two came until finally a person could almost jump from one to the other. Then the Monmouth, feeling the danger of running aground called it off.

Some time later the Monmouth started back up the bay, and the engineer, discussing the contest with the Prince Arthur, remarked that it was no race at all. "Why, man, dear," he said, "we were not racing. This vessel is only a harbor craft of moderate speed, and we do not try to beat."

A knock came at his door and one of the officers shouted, "She's coming up the Swash, Chief; get ready for her!" The engineer jumped to his post, and in a moment all was again ready for another trial, but the Prince Arthur only followed a short distance.

## DARED TO DIVE, DID AND DIED.

### Boys Who Challenged Comrade at Last Moment Took It Back, but Too Late.

Arnoldt Thiessen, twelve years old, of 49 Thorne Street, Jersey City, lost his life on Wednesday afternoon because he would not take a dare from his playmates. He and three other boys went to swim in the Hackensack River near the Lackawanna Railroad bridge. At one end of the bridge is a dump of piles thirty feet high.

The other boys dared young Thiessen to dive into the river from one of the piles. He accepted the challenge. Climbing to the top he made a moment's pause, his companions shouting to him not to dive, and that they would rather withdraw the dare. He laughed, and as he started to dive his foot slipped, so that instead of going head foremost, he struck the water on his stomach. His body floated down stream, while his companions, frightened, ran away. Later they told of what had happened. Searchers failed to find the body.

## DUEL BEHIND BARRICADES.

### Southerners Begin with Revolvers, Change to Rifles, Shoot All Day.

*Special to The New York Times.*

MEMPHIS, Tenn., June 23.—Barricaded behind barrels and boxes in front of their respective places of business at Sarah, Miss., Asa Moon and L. A. Johnson, merchants and plantation supply dealers, engaged in the worst duel in the history of Sarah to-day.

A dispute arose yesterday over the possession of several head of cattle. It resulted in the merchants formally declaring war.

Early this morning citizens were startled by the report of a revolver. Investigation showed that Moon and Johnson had opened fire on each other from behind impromptu forts.

Samuel Moon, brother of Asa, arrived on the scene at about 9:30 o'clock, armed with two shotguns. Together they drove Johnson to cover, inside his store. They kept firing into Johnson's store until he sent a colored boy for a Winchester rifle.

The boy returned after being fired on by the Moon brothers. With the rifle Johnson held his own until an officer, summoned from Clarksdale, arrived on the scene and put a stop to the duel.

About one hundred shots in all were exchanged. Asa Moon is thought to be mortally wounded. Johnson was brought to Memphis to-night and placed in St. Joseph's Hospital with buckshot wounds in his side and arm.



## BRITISH PRIMATE COMING.

### Archbishop of Canterbury to Attend Episcopal Convention in Boston.

LONDON TIMES—NEW YORK TIMES Special Cablegram.
Copyright, 1904. THE NEW YORK TIMES.

LONDON, June 24.—The Archbishop of Canterbury (the Most Rev. Dr. Randall Thomas Davidson) has definitely accepted the invitation of the Protestant Episcopal Church of the United States to be present at the General Convention at Boston in October.

His Grace hopes to leave England before the end of August and to visit some of the chief centres of the United States and Canada, but final arrangements have not been made.

The Archbishop hopes to return to England about the middle of October.

## MRS. FAIRBANKS PLEASED.

### Would "A Little Rather" Prefer Her Son in Senate, Though.

*Special to The New York Times.*

SPRINGFIELD, Ohio, June 23.—Mrs. Mary A. Fairbanks, the aged mother of Senator Charles W. Fairbanks, is pleased over the nomination of her son as Vice President.

"Of course I am proud that the Senator should be nominated for Vice President, but I would just a little rather he should stay in the Senate," said she.

"While I was in Washington many men came to see the Senator and asked him to be a candidate for Vice President. He told them, as he has told them since, that he did not want it.

"I think now that he really doesn't want it at all, and that he would rather stay where he is. I think the position he now has is one of the most honorable a man can get in politics. There is a great deal of influence in it and dignity, and a good many opportunities to do good. I am proud that he was nominated as he was, that everybody seemed to demand it, and it certainly is a great compliment to him."

Mrs. Fairbanks received an affectionate message from her son this afternoon within a short time after the convention adjourned.

Senator Fairbanks has extensive manufacturing interests in Springfield, and owns much real estate. He frequently comes here to visit his mother.

## DRESSMAKER SUES ACTRESS.

### New York Woman Says She Loaned Annie Ward Tiffany $2,863.

*Special to The New York Times.*

BOSTON, June 23.—Annie Ward Tiffany, the actress, was defendant in a suit tried before Chief Justice Mason of the Superior Court to-day, the plaintiff being Sarah A. Miles of New York, who seeks to recover $2,868, with interest from September, 1890.

Mrs. Miles, who was formerly engaged in the dressmaking and lodging house business in New York, asserted that the money was loaned by her to assist in the staging and production of the plays "Lady Blarney" and "The Stepdaughter." At that time the actress was the wife of C. H. Greene, who acted as her manager, and the money was paid over to Greene.

The defense says the money was not loaned, but was invested in the production of the plays as a speculation. Decision was reserved.

## SIGNS OF A HONEYMOON.

### They Were on the House and Trees and Told a Lucid Tale.

*Special to The New York Times.*

ST. LOUIS, June 23.—Passers-by on Washington Street Thursday morning were treated to an unusual sight. From the top of a house was suspended a large paper sign, some 15 feet long and 6 feet wide, and on it was painted:

"We have just been married. Will answer all questions after July 1. Please do not disturb us—we are busy."

Below this was a smaller one, which read: "Just married. Signed, Al. C. Dette, 2,608 Washington Street, up stairs. At home from 9 A. M. to 9 P. M."

From the roof the house and the corners of the sign were strings of old shoes swaying in the breeze.

Dette is a salesman at a book and stationery store, and his wife was formerly a nurse at the Lutheran Hospital.

## BRIDAL PAIR IN RUNAWAY.

### J. J. Hill's Son Wanted to Drive Them to Station—Horses Balked.

*Special to The New York Times.*

ST. PAUL, Minn., June 23.—Walter L. Lindke and his bride of half an hour were unwilling participants in a wild runaway this evening, in which neither was hurt, but which came near ending in a tragedy.

Mr. Lindke and Miss Ethel Mae Xanten were married this evening at the residence of Dr. and Mrs. Xanten, on Congress Street. As the bridal party was about to leave for the station Walter Hill, son of J. J. Hill, President of the Great Northern Railway, persuaded the driver of the carriage the bride and bridegroom were to use to lend him his coat and hat, as he desired to drive them to the station.

The driver reluctantly made the change, saying one of his horses was balky and required careful handling. The runaway began as soon as young Hill took the reins.

## FATAL FIGHT AT PICNIC.

### Game of Craps at Staten Island Leads to Murder at Colored Outing.

"Funny" Gibbs, fifty years of age, a colored man well known on the middle west side, was shot and killed last night at Sea Breeze, S. I. Isaac Stedman, also colored, who is alleged to have shot him, is in the S. R. Smith Infirmary, at New Brighton, with several stab wounds in the left side, and he is not likely to live. Several negroes are held at the Eightieth Precinct Station House, in Stapleton, as witnesses.

Gibbs lived at Minetta Lane. Stedman lives at 16 Fleet Street, Brooklyn. They went to Sea Breeze yesterday on an outing of the Central Pleasure Club, composed mainly of colored men from the vicinity of West Thirty-sixth Street.

There was a crap game during the afternoon. Stedman lost. He and Gibbs quarreled, but were pulled apart by members of the club, and the affair was supposed to be ended. The men met when the party was preparing to start to the railroad depot. In the fight Gibbs was killed. Stedman was mortally wounded. The police arrested several of the witnesses.



## ROOSEVELT AND FAIRBANKS NAMED

### Republicans Cheer Roosevelt Twenty-one Minutes

### NEW YORKERS LEAD OFF

### Gov. Odell Provides Delegates with Flags to Wave.

### CHEERS FOR FAIRBANKS, TOO

### All Other Candidates for Vice President Withdrawn and the Nomination is Made Unanimous.

**For President — THEODORE ROOSEVELT of New York.**

**For Vice President—CHARLES WARREN FAIRBANKS of Indiana.**

**For Chairman of the Republican National Committee—GEORGE B. CORTELYOU of New York.**

*Special to The New York Times.*

CHICAGO, June 23.—With a mighty roar of human voices that swelled through Chicago's great Coliseum like the rumblings of an avalanche for a full twenty-one minutes and accompanied by a demonstration of enthusiasm delirious and picturesque, the Republican National Convention to-day proclaimed Theodore Roosevelt of New York as the party's choice for President of the United States. The nomination of Senator Charles Warren Fairbanks of Indiana for Vice President, which followed by acclamation, also called forth a wild outburst.

The scene witnessed in the convention to-day when ex-Gov. Black of New York closed his speech submitting the name of President Roosevelt to the convention seemed proof positive that the lack of enthusiasm on the part of the delegates which has been so much remarked here since last Monday was not indicative of indifferent regard for the man who was to be the party's candidate. It suggested the idea that all that was needed to dispel the sobriety of demeanor which has marked the gathering was a drink from some fountain of real eloquence.

Obtaining that drink to-day, the convention at once livened up, and, as it relaxed more and more under the influence of the rhetorical spirits which were served up to it by ex-Gov. Black, Senator Beveridge, and George A. Knight, the brilliant orator from the Pacific Coast, it cast off all reserve and gave itself over to the delight of its intoxication. It subsided only when it was exhausted.

#### Delegates Slow in Gathering.

The hour set for the meeting of the convention was 10 o'clock, but many of the delegates had been up late the night before, and they were slow in gathering. The notables were not cheered on their arrival, as on the two previous days. The delegates seemed to realize that there would be a tax upon their power for creating enthusiasm later on, and were disposed to conserve their energy.

It was noticed that when the New York delegation came in all of its members carried folded flags. Col. Reuben Fox had purchased these last evening under instructions from Gov. Odell, who had begun to be a little disturbed over the general criticism of New York's apparent lukewarmness toward its candidate, and who was determined that there should be no ground for complaint against the delegation when the great moment arrived to-day.

All the seats left at the disposal of the National Committee and of the local committee after those entitled to get into the hall had been cared for were sold to-day. It was said that the National Committee realized $14,000 from the sale of tickets for to-day's session. There were a great many more ladies in the hall at to-day's session than there were in the two previous days, and their costumes and hats gave the needed touch of color to the audience.

Permanent Chairman Cannon was on hand at the appointed hour, but as the delegates and spectators were filing into the hall in swarms he did not attempt to call the convention to order. While he was standing on the platform waiting for the crowd to be seated, Mrs. Margaret Plummer of the American Flag Association advanced and presented him with a bunch of calla lilies. The incident was witnessed by all who were in their seats, and Mr. Cannon and Mrs. Plummer were cheered.

When the Indiana delegation filed in it was noticed that Senator Fairbanks was not with it. His nomination for Vice President being assured, he had remained away from a sense of propriety, giving his alternate instructions that, in the event that there should be a roll call on the Vice Presidency he was not to vote for him.

#### Cannon Calls Convention to Order.

At 10:25 Chairman Cannon's gavel fell for order, but, as there was still a good deal of confusion in the hall, consequent upon the people taking their seats, he did not insist upon order until five minutes later when he walked to the front of the platform, and waving his huge gavel aloft shouted his demand for attention.

When silence had been obtained, the Rev. Thaddeus A. Snively was introduced to offer prayer. Mr. Snively read his prayer from manuscript, the vast audience maintaining such strict silence that the twittering of sparrows in the rafters was the only other sound which came into competition with the preacher's voice. The prayer lasted six minutes.

Then Chairman Cannon advanced to the front of the platform again and announced that the clerk would begin the roll call of States for nominations for the office of President.

"Alabama!" shouted the clerk, and Oscar R. Huntley, the Chairman of Alabama's delegation, mounted a chair and said:

"It is Alabama's proud and pleasurable privilege to yield to the State of New York."

#### Cheers for ex-Gov. Black.

This declaration was greeted with cheers, which became tumultuous as ex-Gov. Black arose and started for the platform. The cheering was mingled with the music of the band as New York's orator threaded his way through the crowd. As he emerged from the group at the back of the platform, Chairman Cannon met him, and hand in hand they walked to the front while applause rang through the hall.

"Three cheers for the young Abraham Lincoln!" shouted an enthusiast in the gallery. They were given vociferously.

In introducing ex-Gov. Black to the convention Chairman Cannon remarked that the New Yorker was a Republican "by nature as well as by name."

As Gov. Black stood facing his audience, clutching a handkerchief which he held behind his back, the suggestion undoubtedly came to many that his being there to place in nomination Theodore Roosevelt was one of those curious turns of politics which excite both interest and wonder.

It was Theodore Roosevelt who was chosen by Senator T. C. Platt in 1898 to bring about the defeat of Black for a renomination for Governor of New York and who accomplished it. And yet there stood Black, proud and pleased to perform the office of nominating for President the man who had once checked his cherished ambition.

Gov. Black has not a particularly strong voice. It was not of a volume to penetrate to all parts of the hall, but all of the delegates and those in the gallery immediately in front of him, could hear him, and followed him with the closest of attention. His brilliant epigrams were as draughts of wine to the delegates. They fairly drank them in, and the pleasure which they gave was evident on the sea of upturned faces, strained lest a word should be lost.

#### Wild Outburst of Enthusiasm.

The statement is made, to be taken almost literally, that Gov. Black's speech was punctuated with applause. When he concluded by nominating President Roosevelt, the New York delegation arose as one man and started a demonstration which will never fade from the memories of those who witnessed it. The flags which the delegates had were unfurled and waved while a great wave of applause swept over the vast edifice.

All of the delegates with the exception of those from Illinois, who were seated right across the aisle from the New Yorkers, were soon on their feet shouting, waving flags and banners and making noise in any fashion that occurred to them. The galleries up to this time had remained unmoved for the most part, and, indeed, it was not until some time later, that they appeared to catch the infection of the enthusiasm.

Those who occupied seats above looked down upon the demonstration below as people in the theatre look upon a performance on the stage. Apparently the idea had not occurred to many of them that they were expected to take part in the show. If it did they did not evince more than a slight disposition to contribute. But this was only for a while.

#### Old Man Waves Big Flag.

From the beginning, however, there was one exception to the general apathy displayed by the galleries. That exception was a white-haired old man, who wore a lot of decorations on his coat and looked as if he might be a civil war veteran. This individual, as soon as the demonstration started on the floor, unfurled a large American flag, which he had been holding, and swung it out over the heads of the delegates immediately below him, he having a front seat in the gallery which faced the platform.

The pole was so heavy that every time he waved the flag his body swayed from the exertion, but nevertheless he kept up the good work, with only momentary rests, until the twenty minutes demonstration was at an end.

The Alaskans added to the joy of the occasion by bringing their bald-headed eagle totem poles over into the New York delegation's territory, and when the outburst called forth by that action had spent itself the men from Massachusetts gave a fresh start to the enthusiasm by opening red, white, and blue umbrellas bearing the pictures of Roosevelt and Fairbanks. Evidently they either never had heard of the superstition that to open an umbrella in the house is bad luck, or if they had they were not disturbed by it.

#### Cannon Brings Out Historic Flag.

To give further impetus to the demonstration, "Uncle Joe" Cannon advanced to the front of the platform, holding an American flag, faded with age and having a number of holes in it. It was not until later that explanation was made that the flag, which is the property of the Lincoln-McKinley Association of Missouri, was first shown at the Republican Convention held in Chicago in 1860, and was waved at the moment that Lincoln was nominated, and that it had been waved in every Republican Convention since that time at the moment that the nominee for President had been announced.

But the crowd knew from the condition of the flag that it had some history—a battle-flag probably most of them thought—and when Chairman Cannon waved it aloft they went wild.

When the demonstration over the Lincoln flag had spent itself, an immense crayon portrait of President Roosevelt was brought up on the stage, and again the vast crowd worked itself up into a frenzy. Three of the sergeants at arms held the big picture aloft, turning it so that the people in all parts of the hall might draw what inspiration they could from its exhibition.

With the subsidence of the storm of applause evoked by the display of the President's picture, the New York delegation aroused the vast throng anew by starting a parade. Gov. Odell led the parade, carrying one of Alaska's bald-headed eagle totem poles. As the New Yorkers went around the hall the band struck up the "Star-Spangled Banner," and every man and woman not already up arose, while cheer upon cheer resounded through the hall.

When the New Yorkers had returned to their seats the band struck up "There will be a hot time in the old town to-night," and hundreds of the delegates and spectators began to sing the words of the song. While the singing was going on, J. Henry Smythe of Philadelphia, a member of the Pennsylvania delegation, ran up on to the platform with a megaphone in his hand. Waving a small flag with one hand, he held the megaphone to his mouth with the other, and shouted through it:

"Rosey," "Rosey," "Rosey."

The New Yorkers and others took up the cry, a man in the gallery adding to the hilarity by shouting:

"Rosey, you are my posey."

#### Rallied Once More by Cannon.

At 11:12 by the Coliseum clock, just twelve minutes after the first demonstration had started—for in reality it was a series of demonstrations linked together with cheers—the megaphone man was down and out. He was led to the rear exhausted, but revived later and gave a sort of a side show in the Pennsylvania delegation. Chairman Cannon again charged to the front with the Lincoln flag to rally the hesitating forces. They responded nobly.

Then California's delegation started out on a parade, carrying aloft the State banner. They were lustily cheered all along their route, Gov. Odell leading the cheering for New York.

No sooner had the California parade ended than the Massachusetts delegation began to march, carrying the red, white, and blue umbrellas.

As the Massachusetts men returned to their seats a terrific uproar was raised by members of the different delegations seizing the standards of the States and waving them wildly as they stood on chairs.

The standard bearers of the States having exhausted themselves by their efforts to outshout each other, Chairman Cannon once more brought the Lincoln flag into service, this time handing it down to Gov. Odell.

#### Cannon and Odell Cheered.

In view of the impression which had gotten abroad that there was some feeling between Speaker Cannon and Gov. Odell because of an interview afterward pronounced a fake, in which Mr. Cannon was made to say some harsh and ugly things about New York's chief executive, Mr. Cannon's graceful act in passing the historic flag to Gov. Odell made a big hit. Gov. Odell stood in the aisle and waved the flag, receiving a big ovation.

A small colored boy, James Blaine Caslun of Georgia, was hoisted on to the platform and he waved a small flag, while the delegates and spectators renewed the cheering.

A moment later one of the delegates from California carried a little girl in white to the stage. She was Naomi Da Foe of Alpen, Mich. As she advanced to the front of the platform, waving the National emblem, the demonstration was given renewed inspiration, and when a man on the platform seized her and lifted her on to his shoulder, where all could see her, there was a wild shout.

A look at the faces of the delegates was sufficient to disclose what was in their minds as they deliriously manifested their delight over the spectacle which the child made as she sat securely on the shoulder of the great, big, manly-looking chap who had picked her up. To them she symbolized the purity of the American home and stirred the deepest emotions of their souls.

When the little girl was let down by her supporter, after the demonstration over her had been going on for fully two minutes, the band struck up "The Red, White, and Blue," and the audience began to sing it. President Roosevelt's picture was carried on to the floor. It provoked an ovation wherever it went.

#### Cheering Lasted Twenty-one Minutes.

At 11:25 Chairman Cannon rapped for order. The sound of his gavel caused a fresh outburst of the cheering and the standards of the States and the totem poles of the Alaskans were carried to the front of the platform and stands, and with one last mighty cheer the great demonstration was brought to an end. It had lasted just exactly twenty-one minutes.

When order had been restored one of the secretaries read the history of the Lincoln flag, and Chairman Cannon made a short speech about it. Waving it over his head, he said:

"It prophesied victory in 1860; its life has been baptized on many a battlefield since, and it is safe in the hands of Theodore Roosevelt."

#### Ovation for Beveridge.

Chairman Cannon then recognized Senator Beveridge of Indiana. When the handsome young Senator walked out on to the platform, proud and confident of bearing, he was given a great ovation. As he stood before the cheering multitude, his face alight with the pleasure his reception gave him, he evidently was not troubled by the thought that the assemblage in a vast Coliseum might ever cry "Thumbs down" at him.

He looked the incarnation of ambition and confidence, and when his opening words rang out through the hall, so firm and strong that they were caught by all, there was a fresh outbreak of cheers which prevented him from going on for a moment.

The heat in the convention hall was intense, to-day's weather being an exception to that which has prevailed since the convention opened, and as the young Indiana Senator warmed up to his theme beads of perspiration rolled from his face and wilted his collar.

#### Veiled Hit at Parker.

His greatest hit was when he said:

"No mystery was ever elected President of the United States, and none ever will be."

The vast audience vigorously cheered this patent reference to New York's silent candidate for the Democratic nomination for fully fifteen seconds.

When Senator Beveridge had concluded his oration his collar was a complete wreck and his countenance, which had been pale almost to whiteness when he began, was covered with a red glow. He was warmly congratulated on his effort by his friends on the platform, and Congressmen Hemenway, Overstreet, and Landis of Indiana, and Murat Halstead reached over the railing of the gallery in the rear of the platform to shake hands with him. When he got back to his seat in the Indiana delegation, all of the members of the delegation crowded about him to express their admiration for his effort.

#### Orator from Pacific Coast.

George A. Knight, the eloquent Pacific coast orator, was the next delegate recognized by Chairman Cannon for a seconding speech. He was escorted to the platform by members of the California delegation, bearing aloft the State banner, and accompanied by a colored boy who scattered flowers right and left.

Mr. Knight was an instantaneous hit with the convention, because of his voice. It is a voice which would carry from California to Maine.

"Geography counts but little," he began in clarion tones which penetrated the remotest corner of the furthest gallery. Delighted to find that they were to have a speaker whose every word could be heard by them, the occupants of the galleries broke in with an enthusiastic cheer before Mr. Knight could complete his sentence. He repeated it.

"Not so loud," shouted a man who was standing up against the wall of the north gallery over half a block away from the platform. This sally brought forth a gen-

"All the News That's Fit to Print."

# The New York Times

THE WEATHER.
Thunderstorms; light variable winds.

VOL. LIII....NO. 17,008. NEW YORK, FRIDAY, JULY 8, 1904.--SIXTEEN PAGES. ONE CENT In Greater New York, Jersey City and Newark. [illegible]

## JUDGE PARKER'S LIFE THREATENED BY CRANKS

### Safe and Sane Democracy Denounced by One "Lunatic."

### [illegible] WARNINGS RECEIVED

**The Judge Sits for His Portrait and for Photographer—Esopus to Have New Station and to Experience a Boom.**

*Special to The New York Times.*

ESOPUS, N. Y., July 7.—In striking contrast to the peaceful quiet of Judge Alton B. Parker's life here in this little village is the information made public to-day that the candidate for the Presidency has been the recipient of several letters from cranks threatening his life.

These communications have been arriving daily and the utmost secrecy regarding them has been maintained by Judge Parker. The one which came to-day, however, transcended in audacity and in detail of expression any which he has yet received. It was deemed best to make them public.

[illegible] came from a man in the West and [illegible] of a warning than of a threatening nature. In great detail the writer told of a plot planned by his political enemies, and warned him not to travel. The letter urged the Judge to stay at home; that he must not under any circumstance move away from it if he wished to become and remain the President of the United States, which the writer takes for granted. This letter, however, was the only one which merely warned the Judge.

A writer, who is as skilful at drawing as he is in coining sentences, and evidently a man of education, has been sending a series of postal cards numbered consecutively every day for some time. He signs himself "A Lunatic." Each communication is more virulent in its attacks than the last.

At the top of each card there is a drawing of a crescent moon. Above this appear the words "Safe and Sane Democracy." The writer damns safe and sane Democracy and tells the Judge what dire consequences will befall him and his party if the motto with which he heads his frank [illegible] is perused.

The cards are all postmarked from a town in Virginia.

The Judge kept in touch with what was going on at St. Louis to-day. He was informed of the progress which was being made in the convention very much as any private citizen might be who has the interest of his country or his party at heart. Mr. McCausland, his secretary, took the telephone messages down in short hand and read them to the Judge when he was at [illegible]. Even when these messages were read to him in the presence of visitors the Judge refrained from comment. He did not depart from his customary silence even when one was read to him containing the information that Mr. Bryan was addressing the [illegible] delegation of Illinois.

The Judge seemed well pleased with the way things were going.

Judge Parker is sitting for his portrait, which is being painted by a celebrated artist. His identity is a secret. According to rumor the portrait is to be slightly smaller than life size. It was begun before the name of Judge Parker began to be prominently mentioned for the Presidency. It is being completed now principally because it has been contracted for. Whether the painting is to be used for campaign purposes or not, the Judge will not say.

A New York photographer was about the grounds to-day, taking photographs of the Parker household. It is believed that the Judge was compelled by confident friends who believe his photographs will be needed for the coming campaign to sit for several pictures.

The West Shore Railroad is evidently confident also of the Judge's nomination and possible election. A new station for Esopus has been begun.

An observation car arrived here to-day, to which were attached two full carloads of lumber. The men in charge of the work freely admit that Judge Parker's candidacy is the cause of the work. The building is to be erected on a plot which is now a millpond. Not only is it to be erected more quickly, but it is also to be much more elaborate than was at first intended.

Superintendent Thompson, in charge of the work, explained that the nomination even, but surely the election, of Judge Parker would boom the town so as to make a larger station a necessity. The structure is already being built at Kingston, and is to be moved to Esopus in sections. A new hotel near the site of the station is also to be erected soon.

Preparations for the parade by the citizens of Esopus and adjacent places are going ahead swimmingly. There is talk to-night of the women of Esopus also joining in the festivities in some appropriate way.

The Judge's routine to-day was materially the same as usual. He took several drives, and cantered a short distance on his saddle horse. On one of these trips Mrs. Parker and the grandchildren were with him.

There were few visitors at Rosemont to-day, those who called being mostly women friends of Mrs. Parker.

Something of a sensation was created at Kingston to-night by the arrival of John D. Rockefeller, Jr., and Mrs. Rockefeller at the Eagle Hotel. The rumor got abroad that he had come to see Judge Parker, but there was nothing to indicate any such intention on his part. Judge Parker's secretary pronounced the story preposterous.

Mr. Rockefeller declined to see callers, and it is believed he is going into the Catskills by an early train.

### Driven Insane by the Heat.

James Kenny, fifty years old, a deckhand on the lighter Tiger, the property of the Singer Sewing Machine Company, and living at 62½ Fourth Street, Jersey City, went insane from the heat last night and jumped into the East River from Pier 10. Peter Mattson, the foreman of a gang of longshoremen jumped in after the drowning man and kept him above water until they were pulled out by ropes thrown them by the other longshoremen. He was taken to the Hudson Street Hospital.

## INDEX TO DEPARTMENTS.

Commercial World.—Page 13.
Amusements.—Page 9.
Arrivals at Hotels and Out-of-Town Buyers.—Page 10.
Business Troubles.—Page 10.
Court Calendars.—Page 13.
Losses by Fire.—Page 7.
Marine Intelligence and Foreign Mails.—Page 13.
New Corporations.—Page 13.
Real Estate.—Page 15.
Society.—Page 9.
United Service.—Page 12.
Weather Report.—Page 9.
Yesterday's Fires.—Page 7.

## NINE LIVES LOST IN FLOOD.

**Kansas City Inundated When Kaw River Breaks Its Banks.**

KANSAS CITY, Mo., July 7.—Nine persons are known to have lost their lives in the flood throughout this section. One-half of Armourdale, in the suburbs on the Kansas side, is under water, on account of the overflow of the Kaw River. The water is still rising at a rapid rate, and conditions approaching the great flood of 1903 are feared.

The stage of the river is higher than at any time since then. The lowlands of Argentine and Rosedale, other suburbs, also are flooded, and hundreds of laboring people have left their homes.

Grain men here received to-day many telegrams placing the damage at from 10 to 50 per cent., and in a few localities it was claimed that no wheat at all would be saved.

On July Kansas had a wheat crop apparently assured of 85,000,000 bushels. Probably 20 to 25 per cent. of the wheat is in shock. The rest is dead ripe, and should have been cut a week to two weeks ago. Incessant rains for a week have beaten the wheat flat on hundreds of acres, and some thousand acres have been flooded in the valleys, but the greatest loss will be from the wheat shattering and falling out of the heads before it can finally be delivered to the threshers.

West of Kansas City, along the Kaw, great damage has been done at North Topeka, Lawrence, and at other points, and its tributaries are rising. There has been almost incessant rain in this part of the Southwest for five days, and for a month past heavy rains have fallen intermittently. All last night a steady downpour of rain fell here and in many parts of Kansas, and to-day it continued.

The first break in the Kaw came at Armourdale at midnight, when water began running through a large dike built across a new channel made by the flood last year. To-day the water reached the Live Stock Exchange, and drove the occupants from the basement floor.

The damage to crops will be enormous. In the vicinity of Abilene alone it is estimated that the damage will amount to $250,00. The Kaw has made a new channel at North Lawrence, cutting the west portion off from the rest of the town.

The market in cash grains was suspended owing to the nonarrival of trains from the Southwest.

The water in Kansas Avenue in the low-lying portion on the outskirts of the town, is three feet deep this afternoon. Armourdale was practically deserted. At 3 o'clock this afternoon 5,000 persons had left their homes.

Reports from other towns show the flood to be still rising. Wichita is flooded worse than ever before in its history. The dikes at several places along the Little River gave way before the rush of water which poured down Waco Avenue, one of the principal residence streets, in a raging torrent, becoming waist deep. People living within seven blocks of the Little River have been forced to vacate their homes.

The Kaw River gauge at Topeka shows the water is above the twenty-two-foot mark and rising slowly. In North Topeka the water is running through the principal streets knee deep, and the town is deserted.

The Stine pottery warehouse, at White Cottage, has been washed away and manufactured goods have been dumped into Kent's Run at Zanesville, Ohio.

The house of Cass Woods, a park policeman in Riverside Park, at Wichita, was washed away and Mrs. Woods and her two children were drowned.

OKLAHOMA CITY, O. T., July 7.—A waterspout, accompanied by terrific wind, passed through Clinton, Oklahoma, and vicinity at midnight last night, in which six persons were killed and several injured.

Reports from Araphie, Wetherford, Geary, Cordell, Anadarko, and other points in Western Oklahoma tell of great damage by flood.

## LIGHTNING WRECKS HOUSE.

**Ten Occupants of Flushing Home Hurt—Two May Die.**

Lightning struck the two-and-a-half-story frame house, 244 Couldon Avenue, Flushing, the home of Charles Jacobson, a boss cabinet maker, yesterday afternoon, tearing out the whole of the east wall of the structure and injuring everybody who was in the house. Four of them were taken to Flushing Hospital, where it was said last night that two would probably die. The bolt was accompanied by a terrific explosion, and set fire to the wrecked house. Neighbors rushed into the ruins and carried out the senseless forms of those who had been stunned. Those in the hospital are:

JACOBSON, CHARLES, Jr., 13 years old; burns on left leg; sole and half of left shoe torn off.

JACOBSON, WALTER, 8 years old; both eyes destroyed, burns on face and body, right shoe and most of his clothing torn off. Will probably die.

WILHELMSON, Mrs. HELEN, 43 years old, 420 West Forty-fourth Street, Manhattan; burns on body. May die.

WILHELMSON, MARIE, 16 years old, daughter of Mrs. Wilhelmson; severe shock and burns on back.

Others not taken to the hospital were Mrs. Jacobson, John Jacobson, ten years old, and Mrs. Margaret Wise of 624 Tenth Avenue, Manhattan.

All these were in the basement dining room. The lightning, which those who saw it describe as a large globe of fire, struck a tree in front of the house, and running down a limb, darted in an open window on the second floor front. It went through several romos, tearing out the partitions, and then shot down the stairs.

At the back of the parlor floor were Annie Jacobson, six years old; Nellie Wilhelmson, ten years old, and Bertha Wilhelmson, five years old. They were hurled through the back door of the house and down the stoop, being picked up in the yard outside stunned and bruised. George Hulst, twenty-four years old, of 40 Larch Street, saw the havoc played by the lightning, and ran to the Flushing Police Station, where Sergt. Walsh turned in a fire alarm. Neighbors found most of the victims lying pinned down by the wreckage, which was blazing fiercely, but they got them all out before the firemen arrived. The fire was quickly extinguished.

## PREACHER WOULD REJOIN WIFE

**Cordova, Who Ran Away with Miss Bowne, Seeks Forgiveness.**

NEW BRUNSWICK, N. J., July 7.—The Rev. J. B. Cordova, who in May last ran away with Miss Julia Bowne, is anxious to return to his wife, it is said. Mrs. Cordova has received letters and telegrams from her husband making overtures for a reconciliation. Cordova is at present in El Paso, Texas, where he has a brother. The whereabouts of Miss Bowne is not known.

The official disciplining of Cordova by the Church authorities will be taken up next week. Four charges have been brought against him by the Rev. J. B. Sawn of this city.

The committee which will hear the charges consists of the Rev. James Moore, Long Branch; the Rev. E. B. Harris, Westville; the Rev. S. K. Hickman, Keyport, and the Rev. J. N. Ogden, South Amboy. It will meet at South River.

## BISHOP POTTER'S WIFE LOSES $50,000 JEWELS

### Thief Ransacks Clark Estate's Office at Cooperstown.

### $1,000 REWARD IS OFFERED

**Bishop Potter Was Absent, the Clerks Went Out to Luncheon, and Forgot to Lock the Safe.**

*Special to The New York Times.*

COOPERSTOWN, N. Y., July 7.—The office of the Clark estate was visited by a thief to-day while the employes were out at luncheon. The safe was ransacked and jewels valued at $50,000, the property of Mrs. Elisabeth Potter, wife of Bishop Henry C. Potter of New York, were stolen.

It is believed that the thief entered the office in the morning, secreted himself, remained in hiding until the force went out for luncheon, and then went through the safe.

A reward of $1,000 has been offered for the arrest of the thief and the recovery of the jewels, which include a pearl necklace, several diamond brooches, and a number of solitaire diamond and ruby rings.

The robbery was not discovered until 6 o'clock this evening, when the boxes in which the jewels had been kept were found in the cellar, empty. That the thief had found difficulty in forcing them open was shown by numerous blood stains upon them.

The police were called into the case as soon as the loss of the jewels was discovered. So far not the slightest clue as to the identity of the thief has been gained. The detectives believe, however, that he was well informed as to the conduct of the office.

When Bishop Potter is in Cooperstown he spends a large portion of his time in the office looking after his wife's affairs. Generally he remains through the lunch hour. This morning he left early, and when noon time came the clerks went out, neglecting the precaution of locking the safe.

Not content with taking the jewels the thief also carried away several insurance policies. He overlooked several valuable documents in his haste.

Mrs. Potter had been a resident of Cooperstown for a number of years prior to her marriage to the Bishop. She was the widow of Alfred Corning Clark, from whom she inherited a fortune variously estimated at from $1,000,000 to $2,000,000. Mr. Clark was for a number of years President of the Singer Sewing Machine Company, in which he was one of the largest stockholders.

Although never a devotee of society, even before the death of her first husband, Mrs. Potter has long been noted for the possession of a collection of jewels of singular beauty and value. In recent years she has worn them very little, keeping them in the safe at the office of the Clark estate. It is entirely probable that the loss of the jewels would have remained undiscovered for days had not the thief left the boxes behind.

Besides calling in the Cooperstown police, Bishop Potter has wired to New York for the best detective talent, and every effort will be made to run down the thief and regain the gems.

## RUN OUT OF VICTOR.

**Six Agitators Taken by Masked Men from Custody of Deputy Sheriffs.**

*Special to The New York Times.*

CANON CITY, Col., July 7.—Six agitators recently deported, and who returned to the gold camp, were run out of Victor last night by masked men, and were ordered never to return to Teller County.

They were escorted several miles before being released. The men are J. C. Frazier, David O'Neill, William Haney, C. M. Tully, Fred Warburton, and Patrick McCarvel.

All except McCarvel arrived in Canon City this morning and boarded a train for Denver, where they will lodge a complaint with Gov. Peabody. The men say they were brutally treated by their captors, and were robbed of $300.

The men were picked up in Victor yesterday afternoon, and held under guard at the Baltimore Hotel until 10:30 o'clock last night, when they were secretly removed by Deputy Sheriffs. It was the intention of the deputies to take the prisoners to Cripple Creek, but they were intercepted by the masked men, and forced to surrender the captives.

## TRAIN RUSHED DOWN MOUNTAIN

**Passengers Saved from Death by Recently Installed Safety Switch.**

*Special to The New York Times.*

ASHEVILLE, N. C., July 7.—A dispatch from Spartanburg says the night express from Asheville, while going down Saluda Mountain, became beyond control and ran wild down the mountain at fearful speed.

The train was heavily loaded, and every passenger would have been dashed to pieces but for a safety switch which had only recently been placed on the mountain. The airbrake refused to work, and as the cars descended the momentum of the train increased every second. The crew were appalled, and the wildest panic reigned among the passengers, who expected every minute would be their last. Many women fainted.

After a few minutes' suspense a safety switch was passed and the train ran up an incline and came to a standstill. No one was hurt.

The distance down the mountain is six miles, and the grade is one of the steepest railroad grades in the world. There have been a large number of accidents on this mountain, and in order to stop wild trains the Southern Railway lately installed three safety switches.

## THE GOULDS WILL FIGHT.

**Resist Attempt to Throw Virginia Power Company Into Receiver's Hands.**

*Special to The New York Times.*

RICHMOND, Va., July 7.—In the individual reply of Frank Jay Gould to the complaint of George E. Fisher, who seeks to throw the Virginia Passenger and Power Company into the hands of a receiver, it is declared that Gould and his sister, Miss Helen Miller Gould, first became interested in the company through Dr. J. H. Munn, a friend of the family, upon whose representations they were induced to advance nearly $800,000 to meet maturing obligations of the company while Fisher was the majority stockholder. Dr. Munn is closely allied with Fisher.

It is said the Goulds have nearly $5,000,000 invested in the company at the present time, and they have employed the ablest counsel in the State to defend the suit.



## ANGELSEY'S JEWELS PASTE.

**Even Experts Deceived at First, and Overvalued Them $650,000.**

LONDON, July 7.—The jewels of the Marquis of Anglesey, one of the chief assets relied upon by his many creditors, have been discovered to be made mainly of paste.

The workmanship is so exquisite that experts on making a first examination were deceived, and valued the famous jewel collection at $850,000.

It is now found to be worth $200,000.

## NEWPORT STEAMER AGROUND.

**New York Passengers Carried Across Bay in Little Launch.**

*Special to The New York Times.*

NEWPORT, R. I., July 7.—On the early evening trip yesterday the steamer General, which connects with the New York train and brings the passengers across the bay from Wickford, ran on a ledge at the entrance to Wickford Landing and remained there all night.

The New York passengers were landed at Wickford. There was no other craft able to take them to Newport. It was very foggy and the steamboat landing afforded little shelter.

A naphtha launch was finally secured to make the trip. The little boat with its canvas hood was anything but a comfortable craft in the dense fog, but many preferred to make the trip rather than to remain on the landing.

Among the passengers on the fifteen-mile run were Mr. and Mrs. John R. Drexel, Mr. Egerton L. Winthrop, and Miss Gerry. It was after 1 o'clock this morning when the boat reached Newport.

## PARDON FOR MURDERESS.

**Freed as She Stands at Prison Gate with Babe in Her Arms.**

*Special to The New York Times.*

FRANKFORT, Ky., July 7.—Mrs. Nancy May, sentenced to ten years' imprisonment for the murder of Alice Smith, who she thought was her rival for her husband's affections, was pardoned at the prison gate to-day as she stood waiting to enter with a three-months-old babe clasped to her breast.

In his written reason for granting the pardon, Acting Governor William P. Thorne said: "There is a certain sentiment in Kentucky called unwritten law, which has prevailed in many cases under my observation as a practicing lawyer when men have been acquitted by Judges and juries in similar cases which met with applause."

The killing of Miss Smith was a typical mountain murder. The Mays and Smiths lived two miles apart in Leslie County. Mrs. May, hearing that Miss Smith was going to elope with her husband, walked to the Smith home with a rifle and fired two shots at the girl as she sat alone by a window sewing. When the family returned they found her dead on the floor.

At the trial of Mrs. May ten of the jurors were for life imprisonment.

## CONEY ISLAND BOATS CRASH.

**Passengers in Panic When the Grand Republic Hits the Dreamland.**

The steamboats Dreamland and Grand Republic were in collision last evening off Coney Island. The passengers aboard both vessels were thrown into a panic, but soon were reassured. A portion of the planking of the Dreamland's port paddle box was shaved off, but there was no other damage done. Nobody was hurt.

The collision occurred just about dusk. The Dreamland was carrying a big load of passengers from Manhattan to the Coney Island resort from which the vessel takes its name, and the Grand Republic was on its way from the island to the city. There was a heavy fog, and the vessels were feeling their way along the channel. The foghorns were being kept busy, but the atmospheric conditions were such that the sound did not carry.

Capt. Giffen of the Dreamland and Capt. Carmen of the Grand Republic were unaware that danger was threatening, when suddenly the vessels crashed. The Grand Republic's bow struck the Dreamland's port paddle box, and there was a sound of splintering timbers. Fortunately, the blow was glancing. The shock of the collision was plainly felt on both boats, and there was a rush for life preservers, but the feeling of alarm was soon quelled, and the vessels proceeded to their destinations.

## MRS. SMITH SEEKS WORK.

**Sister of Nan Patterson Tries to Get Old Position in War Department.**

*Special to The New York Times.*

WASHINGTON, July 7.—The hunt for J. Morgan Smith, wanted as a witness in the trial of Mrs. Nan Patterson for the shooting of Caesar Young in a cab in New York City, has been renewed. Mrs. Smith, sister of Miss Patterson, is here at the home of her mother, although at the Franklin apartment house, where the Patterson family live, the presence of Mrs. Smith is denied.

It is certain, however, that she is in the city, for she has made an effort to secure an appointment as a clerk in the War Department, and has had an interview within the last few days with F. E. Rittman of the War Department to see if she could be reinstated in her old place which she had before she was married. Mrs. Smith was a good clerk and her record would commend her for reinstatement.

Last Spring she took a two months' vacation to travel with the Florodora Company, and before the two months were up met and married Smith. She then resigned.

In asking for her old place Mrs. Smith said frankly that she knew of no other way to support herself.

A year has not passed since her resignation took effect, and according to the civil service rules she is entitled to have her name placed on the eligible list, subject to appointment to any vacancy. There is no vacancy at present in her former office.

These regulations were explained to Mrs. Smith, and she was sent to the Civil Service Commission to place her application for reinstatement on file.

No one here seems to know where J. Morgan Smith is.

## CHOLERA EPIDEMIC IN PERSIA.

**Three Hundred Deaths Daily in Teheran—Precautions by Russia.**

LONDON, Friday, July 8.—A dispatch to The Standard from Odessa says that the Government is establishing with all haste a medical and military cordon in Trans-Caucasia against the importation of cholera from Persia.

A dispatch from Tiflis to The Standard says there are 300 deaths daily in Teheran and that the cholera epidemic is rapidly spreading throughout Northern Persia.



## COMMITTEE ADOPTS BRYAN TARIFF PLANK

### Doubt Whether Gold Resolution Will Stand Unmodified.

### TILLMAN IS FIGHTING IT

**Bryan Less Prominent in the Discussion—Showed Conciliatory Attitude in Sub-Committe.**

*Special to The New York Times.*

ST. LOUIS, July 8.—At a late hour to-night some doubt was expressed by the gold Democrats over being able to hold their plank before the full Committee on Resolutions.

The plank agreed upon by the sub-committee was as follows:

The discoveries of gold within the past few years and the great increase in the production thereof, adding two thousand millions of dollars to the world's supply, of which seven hundred millions falls to the share of the United States, has contributed to the maintenance of a money standard of value no longer open to question, removing that issue from the field of political contention.

After considerable discussion the full committee adopted Bryan's tariff plank in lieu of the declaration submitted by the sub-committee. The plank drafted by the sub-committee reads as follows:

We favor the reduction of tariff taxation on trust-produced articles to the point where foreign competition may enter the American market whenever trusts and combines, seeking monopoly, raise their prices to the American consumer above a reasonable and just profit, by such reduction depriving trusts and monopolies of the power to extort from the American people, under shelter of American law, prices higher than those charged foreigners for identical articles.

The Bryan plank is shorter and more direct than that of the sub-committee. It declares in effect that al tariff for protection is robbery, and advocates a gradual reduction along lines that will not disturb business interests.

The Resolutions Committee took up the report of the sub-committee which was submitted with a favorable recommendation immediately when the full committee assembled at 8 o'clock.

One of the most persistent and vociferous opponents of the report was Senator Tillman, who directed his opposition mainly to the currency plank. Mr. Newlands, who voted against this plank in the sub-committee, also occupied considerable time opposing it to-night.

Mr. Bryan has been less prominent in the discussion to-night than some others of the opposition. It is the desire of the majority that the report may go to the convention with practically a unanimous recommendation, and that an agreement shall be reached in the committee, by which the platform may be submitted to the convention and disposed of without protracted debate.

To this end it has been suggested that all the members unite in a favorable recommendation, and that Mr. Bryan and two or three others representing the minority shall have the privilege of explaining on the floor their reasons for not being able to concur in some of the features of the platform.

In the event that an agreement of this kind shall not be reached, it is believed that the majority, when submitting the report, will move to limit the debate to a time to be agreed upon, not to exceed two hours, to be divided equally between the two sides and on that motion will move the previous question.

### Sub-Committee's Work.

The real battle on the platform began this morning with the meeting of the sub-committee of the Resolutions Committee. The labors of last night were mainly over what may be called the non-essentials, and the main features, which include the currency, the tariff, and the trusts, were reserved for to-day.

At yesterday's meeting there were informal conferences and exchanges on the three questions named, but these were in the nature of inquiries to ascertain the views of members, and this preliminary quizzing served an excellent purpose and was the means of enabling the sub-committee to save time and friction to-day when the several matters are taken up.

The earnest disposition of the members to reach a unanimous agreement was shown by the fact that several of them sat up all of last night in discussion over the currency and tariff planks. When the sub-committee assembled to-day, the members were fully acquainted with each other's views and were prepared to act with a degree of fairness and liberality that gave assurance of an agreement that would be approximately unanimous and in which all could unite in making a final report to the full committee.

As was anticipated, the most troublesome question was involved in the formulation of the currency plank. Mr. Bryan advocated a recognition of former declarations of the party in regard to the quantity of money needed for the conduct of business, with a tacit acknowledgment of the correctness of the Kansas City and Chicago platforms, but at no time indicated a disposition to dictate to his associates, on the contrary, suggesting that he was willing to surrender at least a portion of his faith so far as he could consistently in order that a declaration might be secured on which the entire party could stand.

The resolution presented for adoption was substantially the financial plank of the Mississippi platform.

The resolution is so carefully and skilfully drawn that even those members of the sub-committee who have been classified as free coinage men admit that its effect will be to practically remove the currency question from partisan disputation, and although they recorded their votes against it, they did not ask for a division when the platform came to be voted on as an entirety.

One of those gentlemen remarked after the meeting that he believed the declaration was wise and politic, but that he would have to place himself on record against it for the reason that his constituents had not quite reached that stage when they would regard the question as having been virtually settled by the infusion into the currency of the country of hundreds of millions of gold.

Mr. Bryan was not present at the afternoon session of the committee, having been required to attend the session of the convention, and Mr. Williams was absent for like reasons.

### Vote on Coinage Plank.

The vote on adoption of the resolution was 7 to 3. The affirmative vote was composed of Daniel of Virginia, Hill of New York, Davis of West Virginia, Pattison of Pennsylvania, Poe of Maryland, Hampton of Massachusetts, and Cable of Illinois. Those who voted in the negative were Dubois of Idaho, Newlands of Nevada, and Shively of Indiana. Bryan would probably have recorded himself in the negative, but as the resolution is substantially that incorporated in the Mississippi platform, of which Mr. Williams is the author, it is fair to assume he would have voted for it.

Mr. Daniel was one of the most ardent of the free coinage men during the Bryan campaigns of 1896 and 1900, and one of the most enthusiastic adherents of Mr. Bryan. His support of the resolution therefore was the more gratifying to its advocates. Senator Daniels not only gave his vote in the affirmative, but his advocacy of the resolution and his pleading with the opposition for united and harmonious action had a very salutory influence, both in the sub and in the General Committee.

The resolution on the tariff was regarded next in importance to that on the currency. There was not, however, so much discussion on this resolution, nor was there at any time during the process of its consideration a division taken. Action on this was unanimous.

There was considerable discussion on the trust resolution, in which Mr. Bryan took a leading part. Mr. Bryan desired that a form of remedy should be declared and inserted, and in this he had the support of several members of the committee. In reply to this demand it was pointed out that it would neither be wise nor practicable to insert a form of remedy in a declaration of principles. Such a proceeding could have no practical value, and would be entirely futile.

The application of remedies was for the legislative power, which power alone could correct the evil complained of and prescribe the punishment. When Mr. Bryan was asked to frame the form of remedy he would have expressed and made part of the resolution, he yielded the point and gracefully acknowledge that the application of remedies should be left to the legislative power.

## RUSSIAN TROOPS SURPRISED.

**Two Companies Cut Up—Chinese Guides Led Japanese.**

LIAO-YANG, July 7.—The Japanese, led by Chinese guides, have badly cut up two companies of Russian troops near the village of Afatoy.

During a thick fog the Japanese surrounded and destroyed the Russian outposts.

The rest of the Russians at the post, after a desperate struggle, cut their way through the Japanese lines, losing eighty of their men.

The Japanese also lost heavily.

## CHINAMAN ROUTS ITALIAN.

**With Hot Iron and Water He Resents Attack on His Queue.**

MOUNT VERNON, N. Y., July 7.—John Trepori, an Italian, of 48 North Fourth Avenue, this morning went to the laundry kept by Lang Ung at 36 North Fourth Avenue and started to make fun of the Chinaman, who was busily engaged in ironing shirts. The Chinaman paid no attention to his tormentor till the Italian reached for his queue and with a stiletto attempted to cut a piece of it off.

Then the Chinaman woke up with a vengeance. He threw a hot iron at the Italian, striking him full in the face. Then he picked up a kettle of boiling water and flung the contents over Trepori, scalding him severely. All the time he was engaged in doing this he was screaming for help and using many strange terms.

Trepori was not silent during the encounter, and when the shower of scalding water fell on his shoulders his shouts drew many of his countrymen to the scene.

Trepori managed to quiet his comrades, and then he drew a revolver, walked cautiously to the door of the laundry, and fired point blank at the chattering Chinaman. The bullet failed to do any damage, but it frightened Ung, and he redoubled his previous efforts in the vocal line.

The noise of the revolver and the shouts of the crowd attracted Detective Atwell and he with some difficulty managed to make his way through the crowd. He arrested both men.

## CHASED BY BROADWAY CROWD.

**Woman Who Told of Robbery Started Pursuit of Express Wagon.**

Policeman John A. Brady of the Broadway Squad was at Fortieth Street and Broadway last evening when a well-dressed woman ran up and pointing to an express wagon, which was being rapidly driven down the street, said that she had been knocked down at Forty-second Street and Eighth Avenue and robbed of a purse containing $15.

Brady chased the man as far as Thirty-second Street and Broadway, calling "stop thief," before he overhauled him. A large crowd joined in the chase and there was considerable excitement for a while.

The driver was taken to the West Thirtieth Street Station where he gave his name as Harry Russell of 754 Seventh Avenue, but absolutely denied all knowledge of any robbery. When questioned by the Sergeant the woman, who gave her name as Mrs. Mary Danielson of 308 West Forty-third Street, said her husband had robbed her and jumped into Russell's wagon, and that he was trying to help her husband escape. She thought he should be arrested. The Sergeant refused to hold Russell, but detailed a detective to look for the woman's husband.



## BRYAN CRUSHED IN TEST OF STRENGTH

### His Report on Illinois Fight Rejected by 647 to 299

### PLOT TO STAMPEDE FOILED

**Pre-Arranged Ovation Cheered Down by the Parker Forces.**

### PARKER ON FIRST BALLOT SURE

**Money Question Taken Out of Politics in Platform—Belmont May Be National Committee Chairman.**

*Special to The New York Times.*

ST. LOUIS, July 7.—William Jennings Bryan made one desperate effort in the convention to-day to bolster up his lost cause and met with ignominious defeat, the delegates voting him down in his attempt to overthrow the report of the Committee on Credentials by a vote of 647 to 299, Illinois not voting because its contest was the issue.

To-morrow's sessions of the convention will witness the final and complete departure of the Nebraskan from the scene of political power. Against his pleadings, protests, and threats, which it is expected will be varied with the full measure of the oratorical ability for which he is noted, the leaders of the new democracy will nominate Judge Alton Brooks Parker for President upon a platform that will be devoid of any suggestion of the teachings that have come to be known as Bryanism.

What Bryan will do, then, is problematical, but it can be said that it seems to be beyond his power to do any particular harm, and for that reason he probably will not do anything. It is said that in the Committee on Resolutions he has been showing a desire to "harmonize." Some of the leaders therefore think that Bryan not only will not bolt, but will give active support to the ticket. He has called upon his few remaining supporters to confer with him after the convention adjourns.

### Parker's Real Strength.

This test vote on which Bryan met with defeat by a vote of 647 to 299, does not by any means indicate Judge Parker's strength in the convention on the first ballot. To the 647 must be added the 54 votes of Illinois. The 26 votes of Kentucky and the 18 votes of South Carolina were cast with Bryan in this instance as a compliment to him because the delegations from those States understood that he had decided not to bolt the convention under any circumstances. They will go to Parker on the first ballot. So probably will the 21 votes of Ohio.

That will give Parker 766 votes on the first ballot, if Ohio votes for him, and 745 if Ohio does not. It only requires 667 votes to nominate.

To-day's session of the Convention was not especially interesting, the proceedings being delayed by the failure of the Committee on Resolutions to hand in its report, as expected. The perspiring, sweltering, and impatient crowd had to be entertained much by the band just to fill in time. The actual business disposed of in two sessions might just as well have been transacted in one session of two hours.

Left to amuse itself, to a very large extent, the crowd naturally became rather boisterous, making demonstrations over very trivial matters.

### Big Bryan Demonstration.

Altogether the day was rather featureless until a demonstration was started for Bryan at the opening of the afternoon session. That demonstration was really a magnificent one in volume and in duration but a careful analysis of it disclosed that it was very largely based on a sentimental and sympathetic feeling for the leader, who everybody knew was going to be dethroned, as he was by the vote two hours later.

It pleased Bryan mightily, but he must have been conscious of the fact, as everybody else was, that the great crowd was animated by an entirely different spirit from that which moved other great crowds which similarly honored him at the previous two National conventions.

The Vice Presidential nomination seems to be anybody's plum. Hill, Sheehan, Belmont, and the other political big guns declare that they have no candidate for the office, and want to leave the selection entirely to the convention.

It has been generally stated to-day that the chance of Senator Turner of Washington, which was so bright four days ago, has practically gone because of the criticism of his political predilections in the past. The names of Marshall Field of Illinois, John C. Black of Illinois, John R. Williams of Illinois, Joseph W. Kern of Indiana, Edward C. Wall of Wisconsin, David A. Rose of Wisconsin, John Sharp Williams of Mississippi, Gov. Dockery of Missouri, and Ja-

"All the News That's Fit to Print."

# The New York Times

THE WEATHER
Fair and warmer, with showers in afternoon; fresh south winds.

VOL. LIII....NO. 17,009. NEW YORK, SUNDAY, JULY 10, 1904.—THIRTY-SIX PAGES. PRICE FIVE CENTS

## PARKER NOMINATED ON FIRST BALLOT

### Received 667 Votes to 204 Cast for Hearst.

### WEIRD ALL-NIGHT SESSION

### Thousands of Women Eager Spectators to the End.

### GREAT CROWD IN FIERCE MOOD

### Roused to Fury by Speakers Attempting to Nominate Presidential Candidates—Melted by Bryan's Plea.

*Special to The New York Times.*

ST. LOUIS, July 9.—Memorable in the history of National Conventions will be the record-breaking all-night session at which Alton B. Parker was nominated on the first ballot by 667 votes to 204 cast for William R. Hearst, who received the next highest total. When Cleveland was nominated in 1892, daylight was streaming in, but when Parker was nominated the convention hall had long been illuminated by the light of day, and the delegates went out into busy streets. It was five minutes to six.

The session was not a record breaker in dramatic scenes, but it had as many as most conventions. It was a session of thrills, turbulence and wild excitement; a session that had less of the humorous side than most, but more of the pathetic, and as much of the stirring.

The story of its earlier hours has been fully told, but no one who was not there can appreciate the scenes which took place from one to six o'clock in the morning, assigned to bulletins in the morning newspapers.

The daylight, looking into the blazing hot hall which had been a furnace of emotion for hours, lighted a seething multitude howling like maniacs at every sentiment and every name, roaring down even good speakers and blowing tedious ones off the platform in gales of rage.

#### Thousands of Enthusiastic Women.

It lighted galleries thronged with people who, though they were merely onlookers and did not have to stay, had clung to their seats all night, and would see it through. Among them were thousands of daintily dressed women, who had come to see a show and who missed the night's sleep no more than the hardiest men there. Their little handkerchiefs were wet, their palm leaf fans were brokn into splinters from too much participation in wild demonstrations, and they were eating thick ham sandwiches brought in from neighboring places with as much gusto as they ever ate the most tempting of breakfasts at home.

As for the men, a coat was as rare as a petticoat with them. Their hair was disheveled, their voices hoarse and broken, their tempers ruffled. They were drinking ginger ale out of bottles because there were no glasses to be had. All over the hall was a perpetual roar of sound, lifted into violent gusts whenever occasion arose. Everywhere exhausted delegates who had been up for two nights and had given way to the strain were fast asleep in their chairs.

In at the doors were crowding hundreds of men, although the hall had been taxed to its capacity hours before. Discipline and organization were at an end, tickets were no longer good, and the strongest man had the best chance.

It was 5 o'clock when Senator Martin of Virginia, rushing like a madman down the aisle, his face distorted with rage, shouted to Chairman Bailey:

"Bailey, stop the proceedings and put a stop to this infernal outrage. The doorkeepers are letting everybody in. They are jamming the aisles so that we cannot move around. Stop it, I say."

#### Crowd Wroth with Speakers.

The delegates were tired by the time midnight arrived, and their tempers were short. The same was true of the galleries, and it was little chance a speaker had in that maelstrom. "Tom" Grady's impassioned speech had beaten the proposition to limit seconding speeches to one minute, but they were limited to four, and this did not satisfy the crowd. The best of speakers had but little chance unless they were men like Tillman, whose appearance arrested the rush because they really wanted to hear him.

The saddest fate was that of poor little Fitzgerald of Rhode Island, who tried to second Hearst in a voice that did not reach the middle of the hall. He knew the temper of the crowd, and he wore a fixed smile of good nature to disarm its wrath as he took the platform, but the smile only maddened them. He had not uttered a single sentence before thousands were shouting "Sit down!" Fitzgerald talked bravely, and at last Bailey asked him what he was going to do.

"Oh, I'm not going to sit down, you can bet on that," answered Fitzgerald, pluckily, but he had to.

In the midst of the shrieks, with his original idea of disarming wrath by good nature, he called out:

"Give me half a minute, men; I won't keep you, I just want to say a word."

This touching plea might have had its effect had any one heard it, but the galleries were singing then, and it failed.

David Overmeyer is a good speaker, but he was so maltreated by the multitude that he hardly got the chance to bring out the name of Gen. Miles.

When Mayor Rose of Milwaukee, took the stand, it was comparatively early in the morning, and his clear voice won attention, but he frittered away his opportunity by making attacks upon other candidates, and the galleries and delegates became enraged.

"You are trying to stir up something."

"Cut out the alley talk and give us your candidate." "Back to Sherwood Forest for yours," were some of the yells that greeted him, and Rose made it worse by talking back to the galleries.

When South Carolina was called and the great rough head and fierce face of old Ben Tillman upreared themselves above the crowd, its temper changed on the instand and fifteen thousand voices yelled "platform." The fierce face disappeared in the waves of humanity beneath, and a few seconds later the burly figure was seen climbing the platform.

It was a remarkable speech that Tillman delivered. It was unusual for him; it was an appeal and a reproach. Rose's attacks upon other candidates had grieved him. This was a time for Democrats to get together. He pleaded earnestly with them to forget their differences, to stop squabbling among themselves, and end the old unhappy days of the past ten years. There was a yearning note in it, and it melted the crowd as no other speech had done.

#### Melted Guffey to Tears.

He is not an orator, but there is something in downright earnestness and manly sincerity that is as captivating as any oratory. One who was not there can hardly realize the spell of his manner. As he talked tears rolled down the cheeks of Col. Guffey of Pennsylvania—not a little moisture of the eyes, but big tears. He was not the only one who wept.

Had the convention been less steel-riveted than it was the Cockrell demonstration would have swept it off its feet. Bryan himself never had a greater tribute to the mere power of oratory than had Champ Clark. The Cockrell demonstration was largely prearranged—that is, Cockrell's friends had distributed flags through the hall and were ready to wave them and yell. But no prearrangement could have brought about the madness that seized upon the convention when ever man and woman in it went wild at Clark's words, and even the friends of other candidates shrieked and pounded the furniture.

#### Billows of Beautiful Flags.

It was the most beautiful demonstration ever seen in a convention, thanks to the flags. The Cockrell boomers probably hoped that a considerable number of the flags would be waved, but they could not have expected that everybody there would seize a flag and wave it. The vast arena, covering a city block, was a vibrating, undulating, changing sea of red, white, and blue, and for once the old toast which tells how gold never made a more beautiful thing than the American flag was literally true.

And with it all was the wild cheering of genuine and frantic enthusiasm, not forced or pumped up in any degree, as had been, to some extent, the demonstrations for all the other candidates.

So great was the demonstration that Champ Clark did not finish his speech. He had only begun to mention the qualifications of his candidate. All that had gone before was merely the introduction. He had been laying down general propositions to the effect that the time for the South's long self-abnegation had ended and that she should no longer be ostracized.

He had spoken of John Sharp Williams and Senator Bailey as men of full Presidential size; he had pointed out old Judge Reagan of Texas, who has served in high station under three flags, those of the Republic of Texas, the Confederacy, and the United States; he had struck Benton McMillan upon the shoulder and almost pushed him off the platform as he mentioned the Tennesseean's ability. This was all by way of preliminary.

Then he said he came to nominate a Southern man for the Presidency, and that this man measured up in every way to the qualifications of any other candidate. Letting out that gigantic voice of his in a roar that rang and echoed and vibrated in every corner of that city block, he cried:

"They talk of Roosevelt's bravery. Old Cockrell is braver than he."

At these words the crowd went mad, the delegates and all. It was really only the beginning of Clark's speech. He waited for fifteen or twenty minutes for it to die down, and then, realizing that it was only half over, and that he had done his work, he left the platform.

#### Bryan Checks Demonstration.

But the most remarkable scene of the whole convention was when, at 4 o'clock in the morning, William J. Bryan, in a black alpaca jacket, mounted the platform. The crowd cheered for nine minutes, and it was Bryan himself who stopped it. He scowled at the shouters, and imperiously motioned them to stop shouting and sit down. After a minute or two they realized that he meant it, and they did so.

It was in many ways the most remarkable speech Bryan ever delivered. It was as near to harmony talk as a man of his pugnacity could make. Also, it was a plea for mercy as he could make it. It was dignified and manly in tone, but the undercurrent was this, and everybody realized it as well as if it had been put in words instead of being deftly and subtly suggested by inunendo and inference.

"I led you twice, and you once followed me and believed in me. Now you have overruled me and cast me out. I accept it because I am a loyal Democrat. But be merciful to your former leader. You have got plenty of good men; take one—any one—whether he is a free-silver man or not, but don't force me to take this candidate of yours, for he represents the money interests, and to take him would be too bitter a dish of crow."

Over and over again this was suggested in sentences that came as near to the blunt and plain ones above as Bryan could in self-respect make them. In manner and in matter it was a wonderful speech. It was such a speech as that which he made in Chicago in 1896, but with the tawdriness gone and in its place a development of the larger dignity that has come to Bryan with years and experience. Again this was a speech which would have swept a convention less steel riveted.

#### Evoked Audiences's Sympathy.

Of course, it had no effect as far as votes were concerned, but it did have a good effect for Bryan's cause, for it led to a great feeling of sympathy and even admiration for a good fighter who was battling heroically against unconquerable odds.

Wherever one looked men who have had no use for Bryan and are not supporting him, and are glad of his defeat, were looking at each other and nodding their heads and saying softly, "This is a great speech, the greatest he ever made." He was hoarse when he took the stand, and he apologized for it. "It's too bad that in this hour of extremity his voice should fail him," whispered many a man who though against him admired the fight he was making.

But in a few moments the old inspiration came to him; his eyes lighted up and his voice rang out firm, loud, and clear. To see Bryan pleading, pleading pathetically and desperately with the party whose idol he had been in two campaigns, pleading not for the nomination of a man of his own faith, but for the nomination of anybody at all not connected with what he called "the god of gold," was as dramatic, strange, and sad a sight as has ever been seen in a great gathering. Certainly it is without precedent in a National Convention.

His declaration that there was not so much in geographical considerations as politicians supposed, and that a good man on the ticket from a Democratic State would get more votes than a weak man from a doubtful State, struck a responsive chord and has had a great deal to do with the talk to-day of a Southern man for Vice President, coupled as it is with Champ Clark's ferocious ridicule of the idea that Southern men could be barred.

#### Seized His Last Chance.

When, after saying that even a gold-standard man like Pattison would be satisfactory to him, he suddenly announced that he had come to second the nomination of Cockrell, the crowd went wild. It was a case of desperate clutching after a straw. Bryan had seen the demonstration for Cockrell and had seized upon it as his last chance.

It shows the extent to which Hill and his friends had the convention nailed down and sealed up that not even such a combination as the speeches of Clark and Bryan and the Cockrell demonstration could sweep it off its feet.

The balloting went ahead smoothly and rapidly. The only delay for a roll call was in the case of Ohio, which was demanded for the sake of starting a McClellan boom. Here it was noticeable that Tom L. Johnson voted for Cockrell.

When the result was announced, Parker was nine votes short of the requisite number, and the rush for first place on the band wagon began. The delegations were wild with excitement. In every direction men were jumping on chairs and shrieking themselves hoarse, and gesticulating like lunatics in an effort to catch the Chairman's eye. The hall was in an uproar, men running to and fro in every direction, and climbing over each other.

Bailey saw all the men who were trying to get recognition, but could not give the floor to any because none of them could be heard in that tempest. Idaho was the first State which shouted out a change in its vote. Nobody heard it outside the delegation, but the news was carried to Bailey. Then came a pandemonium of sound. "Nevada changes"—"West Virginia changes her vote"—"Washington—" and so on.

It was all perfectly futile. Bailey stood leaning on his gavel, while the clerks shouted through megaphones that it was useless for any State to attempt to change its vote until the noise subsided. Some of the State Chairmen plunged through the shrieking masses of humanity in the aisles, climbed over backs and shoulders, got down in front of Bailey, and shrieked their changes of vote at him. The massive, imperturbable figure in the chair never moved a muscle; Bailey simply stood there leaning on his gavel. The changes of votes never were announced, and Parker got no more votes than those on record, which were nine short of the requisite number.

#### Motion of Unanimity Put.

Before it was possible for any change to be announced, Gov. Dockery of Missouri climbed a chair and in the first interval in which it was possible to make his voice heard, bawled something at the Chair. Nobody could hear his words, but he had sent a messenger to Bailey apprising him of what he was going to do, and the clerk immediately shouted through a megaphone:

"The gentleman from Missouri moves to make the nomination of Alton B. Parker unanimous."

The motion was put and carried in a bedlam of sound. The New York State banner was marching around the hall, followed by Georgia's, and then by the banners of all the other States. Every man in the convention, except a few defeated and glum delegates, was standing on the top of a table, a desk, or a chair, screeching and yelling and waving things.

But nature was worn out. It was impossible to keep such things up for ever. It was bedlam for a few minutes, and then collapse. The delegates and the crowd would have liked to keep it up longer, but the voices refused to work—even that of August Belmont, who was mounted on a chair with a straw hat going like a teetotum. Ex-Lieut. Gov. Sheehan was not shouting, he was handshaking and receiving congratulations from frantic delegates.

The uproar was short-lived. Home, breakfast, and sleep for such as could get it were calling loudly to everybody. The crowd was streaming out into the street to meet the morning sun.

## PARKER FAVORS DAVIS.

### Nomination for Vice Presidency Delayed by Rumors of Parker's Gold Telegram.

ST. LOUIS, July 9.—When the time approached for the reconvening of the Democrats at 2 o'clock in the afternoon signs were not wanting to show that it was the fag-end of a great show. Empty benches appeared all through the galleries and in plenty on the main floor, while great gaps also appeared in the delegates' seats, many having left the city, and the others still being in their beds trying to catch some sleep after the long all-night session which had broken up only after sunrise.

From 1:30 o'clock until nearly 3 the band played almost continuously, but Chairman Clark, who was on the platform, failed to call the convention to order for more than an hour after the time set, much to the surprise of the waiting guests.

#### Delay Starts Rumors.

To the delegates on the floor it soon became apparent that there was another "scrap" on that would cause still more delay and wrangling. All along the line the word was passed that the leaders had failed to agree on the Vice Presidency.

First came reports that Marshall Field had been appealed to to take the nomination, but that no favorable answer had been received. Then it was definitely learned that many of the Parker leaders had practically determined on the nomination of Judson Harmon of Ohio for Parker's running mate, but that the plan was being bitterly opposed by Senator Tillman of South Carolina. The one-eyed "Pitchfork Senator" had taken a sudden notion, after his short and fitful sleep, that a Southerner should go on the ticket, and a Southerner he would have, so he took up the name of Senator John W. Daniel of Virginia and boomed him, although he said he would be willing to support any good Southerner.

#### Called to Order at Last.

Finally at 3 o'clock, because there was nothing else to do, Chairman Clark called the convention to order, but there was no business to transact. Gov. Dockery of Missouri read a telegram from Senator Cockrell thanking the delegates who had voted for him for President and congratulating the convention on having nominated Judge Parker. Following this John P. Hopkins of Illinois said that A. M. Lawrence of that State had a telegram which he wanted to read to the convention. It was from W. R. Hearst, and thanked the delegates who had voted for his name.

During this time the friends of the various Vice Presidential candidates were scurrying around the floor, and it developed that the delegations from Pennsylvania, Massachusetts, Tennessee, Indiana, and Michigan were urging Harmon as the candidate. Senator Hill, William F. Sheehan, and [illegible] Sheehan immediately, and quickly left the [illegible].

A motion for a recess was made, the recess being taken from 3:20 to 5:20 o'clock.

At this time the seats occupied by the Tammany contingent were almost empty, most of the delegates having returned on the special trains that left in the morning. The only Tammany men in town during the afternoon were Charles F. Murphy, Senator Grady, ex-Senator Towne, ex-Controller Bird S. Coler, ex-Senator John Fox, Lewis Nixon, and M. Warley Platzek.

The intermission disappointed the crowd, which, although small, evidently was there to get action. As soon as the recess was taken, however, there was a gathering of the leaders at Mr. Sheehan's rooms in the Southern Hotel. Senator Hill, Senator Murphy, Col. James M. Guffey of Pennsylvania, National Committeeman Daniel J. Campau of Michigan, Thomas F. Bryan, and August Belmont gathered there to see Mr. Sheehan and go over the situation.

#### Names Submitted to Parker.

Soon after the conferrees had got together it was learned that Mr. Sheehan had dispatched a telegram to Judge Parker at Esopus submitting the names of four men as Vice Presidential material, requesting his preference. The names submitted were those of Senator John W. Daniel of Virginia, Judson Harmon of Ohio, Congressman Williams of Illinois, and ex-Senator Henry Davis of West Virginia, one of the leading Gorman men.

Right on top of this telegram young Arthur Pue Gorman was summoned to the conference, as were Senator Bailey of Texas, Senator Carmack of Tennessee, and National Committeeman James H. Head of the same State. For nearly two hours the conferrees were busy, some leaving the meeting place and later returning, but pulling very strong to get together.

Finally, word was received from Judge Parker, which, it was said, favored Senator Davis. On this the conferrees immediately agreed, and the conference broke up to allow them to return to the convention hall.

The delegates had been waiting some time, but had been called to order a few minutes before the parties to the conference returned.

After the convention had been called to order Representative John Sharp Williams of Mississippi was recognized and moved that nomination speeches be limited to fifteen minutes and seconding speeches to five minutes, and that not more than four second speeches be allowed for any nomination.

T. H. Ball of Texas offered a substitute limiting the nominating speeches to ten minutes, leaving the time of the seconding speeches at five minutes and limiting the number to three.

#### Work of Nomination Begins.

Mr. Williams at once withdrew his motion in favor of the substitute, which was adopted without dissent.

The roll of States was then called for the presentation of candidates for Vice President. At this time the galleries were less than half filled, and great areas of vacant seats were visible.

Alabama was called several times, with no response, but finally Mr. Russell of that State announced that Alabama would give way to Illinois.

Samuel Alschuler of Illinois arose and announced that Freeman B. Morris would speak for that State. Mr. Morris took the platform to name James R. Williams of Illinois. Cheers greeted the mention of Mr. Williams's name, but they did not come in great volume from the delegates.

Colorado yielded to Washington, and Chairman Clark recognized Frederick C. Robertson of that State, who spoke for ex-Senator George Turner.

There was considerable confusion in the aisles by this time, and Mr. Robertson was not able to begin his address for about two minutes.

The report that a telegram had been received from Judge Parker, declaring his position on the financial question, had become general. A crowd of delegates hurriedly gathered around Sheehan of New York and Tillman of South Carolina. Little conferences began to occur, and the orators did not receive much attention, except from the galleries and the small fry, who did not know that a probable sensation was ripening all about them.

Delaware gave her place in the call to West Virginia, and the Chair recognized John D. Alderson of that State, who placed in nomination Henry G. Davis of West Virginia. A vigorous round of applause came from the delegates when Mr. Davis's name was mentioned, but little from the galleries.

Senator Dubois of Idaho was the next speaker, and he rose to second the nomination of George Turner of Washington.

David Overmeyer of Kansas placed ex-Senator William A. Harris of that State in nomination in a brief speech from the floor.

The roll call of States proceeded until Maryland was reached without response. For Maryland, John Prentice Poe took the platform and seconded the nomination of Davis of West Virginia. Applause punctuated his speech.

Senator William E. Clark of Montana was the next to speak. He first paid a high tribute to the West and then seconded the Turner nomination. He was listened to with marked attention.

Nebraska's response was a statement that she waited with interest the choice of New York. New York requested to be passed when called on the roll.

"Ohio has no candidate," was announced when the Buckeye State was reached.

H. G. Davis's nomination was seconded from the District of Columbia delegation.

The first rumble of the approaching storm was heard at just 7 o'clock. Senator Smith of Arkansas broke in on the roll call with a motion, that in view of the rumors that were disturbing the convention a recess be taken until 8 o'clock. His motion did not prevail.

The convention was in such an uproar because of the Parker telegram rumors that the latter part of the roll call for the presentation of candidates for Vice President was inaudible.

Chairman Clark directed that the roll be called for the announcement of the votes.

Senator Culberson of Texas received recognition, and addressing the Chair said:

"For reasons which are obvious to all the delegates here, it seems to me that we ought not to proceed at this time to nominate a candidate for Vice President, and I therefore move that the convention—"

Here cries of "Why? Why?" interrupted him.

"I think that the delegates understand what I mean," he proceeded.

"Proceed," interjected Chairman Clark.

#### Demands an Adjournment.

"And I repeat," concluded Senator Culberson, "that in the present exigencies which confront the convention it ought not to proceed to the nomination of a Vice President."

"Right!" "Right!" greeted the statesman. "We want to know before a candidate for the Vice Presidency is nominated, who is the candidate for President."

Applause and cries of approval again interrupted the Senator. When he continued he made a motion for a recess until 8:30. The din and excitement increased, and "Keep on" and "Sit down." His motion was put by the Chairman. The vote was, in the opinion of most people, a tie, but the Chair loudly banged his desk, declared it carried, and quickly left the platform before the convention recovered from its amazement.

## Judge Parker's Ringing Message to the Democratic Convention.

ESOPUS, N. Y., JULY, 9, 1904.

HONORABLE W. F. SHEEHAN,
HOTEL JEFFERSON, ST. LOUIS, MO.:

I REGARD THE GOLD STANDARD AS FIRMLY AND IRREVOCABLY ESTABLISHED AND SHALL ACT ACCORDINGLY IF THE ACTION OF THE CONVENTION TO-DAY SHALL BE RATIFIED BY THE PEOPLE.

AS THE PLATFORM IS SILENT ON THE SUBJECT MY VIEW SHOULD BE MADE KNOWN TO THE CONVENTION, AND IF IT IS PROVED TO BE UNSATISFACTORY TO THE MAJORITY I REQUEST YOU TO DECLINE THE NOMINATION FOR ME AT ONCE, SO THAT ANOTHER MAY BE NOMINATED BEFORE ADJOURNMENT.

ALTON B. PARKER.

## The Convention's Reply Accepting His Position.

THE PLATFORM ADOPTED BY THIS CONVENTION IS SILENT ON THE QUESTION OF THE MONETARY STANDARD BECAUSE IT IS NOT REGARDED BY US AS A POSSIBLE ISSUE IN THIS CAMPAIGN, AND ONLY CAMPAIGN ISSUES WERE MENTIONED IN THE PLATFORM. THEREFORE THERE IS NOTHING IN THE VIEWS EXPRESSED BY YOU IN THE TELEGRAM JUST RECEIVED WHICH WOULD PRECLUDE A MAN ENTERTAINING THEM FROM ACCEPTING A NOMINATION ON SAID PLATFORM.

## JUDGE PARKER SAYS IT MUST BE GOLD OR HE WILL NOT RUN

### His Stand Approved by the Delegates After a Long Wait.

### DAVIS FOR VICE PRESIDENT

### Former United States Senator from West Virginia Nominated by Acclamation.

### DEBATE OVER PARKER MESSAGE

### Bryan Rises From Sick Bed to Discuss the Demand of the Nominee Before the Convention.

*Special to The New York Times.*

ST. LOUIS, Sunday, July 10.—The Democratic National Convention adjourned sine die at 1:30 o'clock this morning.

It completed the ticket at 1:10 o'clock by nominating ex-Senator Henry G. Davis of West Virginia for Vice President by acclamation.

But that event was completely overshadowed by the remarkable action of Judge Alton B. Parker, candidate for President, in declaring that he would not accept the nomination except upon the understanding that he was uncompromisingly for the gold standard. The Convention, after an exciting conference and strong debate, indorsed the position of Judge Parker by a vote of 785 to 190.

Judge Parker announced his position in a telegram to the Hon. W. F. Sheehan of the New York delegation. This telegram was received while the convention was in session late yesterday afternoon. It's text follows:

**Hon. W. F. Sheehan, Hotel Jefferson, St. Louis:**

**I regard the gold standard as firmly and irrevocably established, and shall act accordingly if the action of the Convention to-day shall be ratified by the people. As the platform is silent on the subject, my view should be made known to the Convention, and, if it is proved to be unsatisfactory to the majority, I request you to decline the nomination for me at once, so that another may be nominated before adjournment.**

**A. B. PARKER.**

The convention was adjourned yesterday afternoon just as it was ready to ballot for the Vice Presidency. A conference of the leaders who had brought about the nomination of Judge Parker was called immediately. After discussion it was agreed to ask the convention to send this telegram to Judge Parker:

**"The platform adopted by this convention is silent on the question of the monetary standard because it is not regarded by us as a possible issue in this campaign, and only campaign issues were mentioned in the platform. Therefore there is nothing in the views expressed by you in the telegram just received which would preclude a man entertaining them from accepting a nomination on said platform."**

The motion to send this telegram was made by John Sharp Williams after the convention had reconvened at 9:10 o'clock in the evening.

Mr. Williams, Senator Tillman, Senator Daniel, and Senator Carmack spoke in favor of the agreement. William J. Bryan, who had risen from a sick bed, spoke twice in opposition.

## TELEGRAM HALTS CONVENTION.

### Sensation Among Delegates When Parker's Ultimatum Comes.

*Special to The New York Times.*

ST. LOUIS, July 9.—Chief Judge Alton B. Parker's long silence on the subject of his views upon National issues was broken this afternoon in a manner which caused a tremendous sensation among the delegates to the Democratic National Convention, which at an early hour this morning had nominated him on the first ballot as the Democratic candidate for President.

While the convention was in session listening to nominating speeches for Vice Presidential candidates William F. Sheehan, who has been the recognized personal representative of Judge Parker, received a telegram from Esopus in which he was informed by Judge Parker that he could not accept the nomination unless he was made the party standard-bearer with the full understanding on the part of the convention that he regarded the gold standard as irrevocably fixed.

When the existence of this telegram became known among the delegates it created the greatest indignation among the Southern supporters of the Judge, and there was immediately every indication of a revulsion from him, and a disposition to go so far as to take him off the ticket.

This feeling grew until it found sensational expression in a motion made by a Parker man, Senator Culberson, to refrain from nominating a Vice Presidential candidate and take a recess until 8:30 o'clock for the expressed reason that the convention did not know who its Presidential nominee would be.

And so, as the result of the feeling against Judge Parker aroused by a telegram which had not yet been read, and whose existence was only rumored, the convention took a recess from 7 until 8:30 despite the unavailing protests of Judge Parker's New York friends.

What made this sudden change all the more sensational was that it took place just as the ticket was about to become complete. Nominations for Vice President had been made, and the Chairman was in the act of calling for a vote when Culberson made his demand and threw the convention into turmoil.

It was significant of the feeling against Judge Parker that the man who made the motion was a supporter of his, and that Ollie James of Kentucky, who seconded it, was also a Parker man. There was every indication that the Southern supporters of the Judge were prepared to slump away from him, demand that he get off the ticket, and replace him by somebody else.

The thing came as a thunder clap to the galleries, who had known nothing of the state of affairs. To their eyes everything was proceeding smoothly up to the very time that Culberson climbed his chair.

As soon as the convention came to order at 5:35 o'clock nominating speeches for Vice President were begun. Everybody was in a peaceful and satisfied mood, looking forward to an early completion of the work. The tip had gone forth that ex-Senator Davis of West Virginia would be nominated for Vice President. The balconies were only about half full, and the galleries practically empty.

The nominating speeches were short, and the listless crowd listened with gentle affability and tolerance and no enthusiasm. Things had gone along in this way for about half an hour, when Sheehan received his telegram. He looked as if he had been hit between the eyes. He read it over three or four times, and then passed it to David B. Hill and August Belmont, who were seated alongside him.

A moment later there was an excited gabble in the New York delegation. Everybody was turning around and asking questions. Sheehan declared that it would have to be read to the convention, but Belmont suggested that it might not be genuine.

Sheehan rose from his seat and forced his way up the aisles, shouldering people out of his way. A crowd of excited politicians was following after him. He dashed up the platform steps and held a hurried consultation with Senator Daniel and two or three others, and then came down again. He seemed almost beside himself.

The rumor was spreading over the delegations thick and fast. It had leaked into the Tammany outfit, and they sat with satisfied grins on their faces, saying nothing. Charles F. Murphy looked as impassive as if nothing was happening.

The jam in the aisle about Sheehan was so great by this time, and the consultations between him and the other New Yorkers so excited, that the nominating speeches were seriously interfered with, and again and again Chairman Clark was obliged to suspend the proceedings while the force of the Sergeant at Arms cleared Sheehan and his friends out of the aisles. Some inkling of the thing had just come to Clark, and he looked exceedingly grim.

Frederick C. Robertson of Washington was nominating Turner for Vice President. Sheehan rushed past with a crowd of politicians at his heels, snapped "There is nothing to say" at a questioning newspaper man, and told the news to Col. Guffey. Guffey looked somewhat disgusted, and did not seem disposed to give Sheehan much help.

By this time it had been agreed that the telegram must be verified. They were all clinging to a forlorn hope that Belmont might be right and the telegram a forgery, but before verifying it, Sheehan went over to the South Carolina delegation and consulted Senator Tillman about the probable effect on the Southern delegates if the telegram should prove genuine.

Tillman's reply was discouraging, though Sheehan was probably aware beforehand of everything Tillman could tell him. The rumors were already spreading in the Southern delegations and they were beginning to look ugly.

Tillman rushed up to the platform and held a consultation with Senators Martin and Daniel of Virginia and ex-Senator Cannon of Utah. Their opinions all coincided with his. They came down together and went to their own delegations to talk with their associates.

Delegates from silver States crowded around Gov. Vardaman and in excited tones discussed the telegram.

"Parker had better get off the ticket," said a North Dakota delegate to the Mississippi Governor, "and we'll stand by you in this fight."

Senator Tillman and Gov. Vardaman announced in loud tones that South Carolina and Mississippi would withdraw their votes from Parker if he sent such a telegram.

"Do you think we are going to let him kick and cuff us about like that?"

Ollie James, Chairman of the Kentucky delegation, said that with a gold standard plank in the platform, Kentucky will give a Republican majority of 100,000.

Hill, Daniel, Tillman, Sheehan, and Poe retired to a corner in the hall for a conference. Senator Hill read the telegram to those gentlemen.

The conference was called at Senator Tillman's instance. He presented the importance of the subject to Senator Hill and said in a loud voice:

"The Democratic Party can always be relied upon to make a damn fool of itself at the critical time."

"Please wait, Senator," said Senator Hill, putting his hand on Tillman's shoulder, "we'll have a conference."

Mr. Sheehan said to some delegates who surrounded him: "Please let me alone. I am half crazy."

Mr. Sheehan then hastened off to get Judge Parker on the long-distance telephone.

In a conference between Senator Hill and Senator Daniel, the latter said:

"I say most positively that the Committee on Resolutions cannot meet again. We have finished our work." Several other members of the committee joined in echoing this sentiment.

The action of Judge Parker was taken by some to mean dictation to the Convention, and this roused the greatest anger. Gov. Vardamann of Mississippi said that the delegation of that State would not consent that any gentleman shall dictate to the Convention as to what should be its platform, and would join in an effort to reconsider the nomination if such dictation should be attempted.

All this time the galleries were in their state of calm content with the situation. They had no idea that anything out of the ordinary was going on. They could see that a good many men were rushing to and fro, and they probably wondered why Chairman Clark had to order the aisles to be cleared, but they were listening to the speeches with tolerant attention and waiting for Davis to be nominated for Vice President.

When the last State had been reached on the call for nominations Sheehan was still telephoning. Chairman Clark did not want to proceed to a vote until an answer was received, and he knew that to kill time by ordering the band to play would awaken the suspicions of the crowd. So he hit on the ingenious idea of announcing: "Any State that expressed a desire to be passed and which now changes its mind and wishes to second a nomination has the right to do so."

In response to this broad hint half a dozen State Chairmen, one after the other, arose and seconded various nominations. They killed about five minutes in this way, and then Clark was at the end of his rope. He raised his gavel and said:

"The clerk will call the roll of—"

At this juncture, just as Clark was in the act of beginning the work of nominating a Vice Presidential candidate, the clear voice of Senator Culberson sounded from the Texas delegation. He was standing on a chair and his expression was ugly.

"Mr. Chairman," said he, "for reasons that are known to all of us it seems to me that we ought not to proceed at this time to nominate a candidate for Vice President, and I therefore move that the convention—"

The galleries, totally ignorant of the situation, thought this was merely another dilatory motion, and with one voice they yelled, "No, no!"

Culberson paused, turned, looked at the galleries, compressed his lips, nodded his head and said, with deep significance and heavy emphasis on the word "delegates:"

"I think the delegates understand what I mean."

He waited after these words for another demonstration, but the significance of his manner struck the galleries with a sense that something strange was going on, and they were stricken into silence.

"And I say," he continued, turning to the Chair, "that in the present exigency which confronts the convention it ought not to proceed to the nomination of a candidate for Vice President."

"Right! Right! Correct! Correct! Correct!" roared the delegates, while the galleries looked on dazed. But Culberson's next words revealed the situation and revealed, too, the intense bitterness of the Southern delegations:

"Before the candidate for Vice President is nominated we ought to know who the candidate for President will be."

"There you get it," said Col. Guffey, approvingly.

"I therefore move that this convention take a recess until 8:30 o'clock to-night," finished Culberson.

"No, no," roared the Parker men of New York, while the Tammany men smiled.

"Does any one second that motion?" inquired Chairman Clark.

"Yes," roared Ollie James of Kentucky, leaping into the aisle with flashing eyes and pointing forefinger.

G. V. Menzies of Indiana jumped upon his chair and in a voice of rage declared that,

"All the News that's Fit to Print."

# The New York Times.

THE WEATHER.
Showers, cooler; Friday fair and warmer; fresh west winds.

VOL. LIII....NO. 17,037. NEW YORK, THURSDAY, AUGUST 11, 1904.—TWELVE PAGES. ONE CENT In Greater New York, Jersey City and Newark. | Elsewhere, TWO CENTS.

## CITY IN TWO STORMS; MAN AND BOY KILLED

### Lightning Injures Several Persons in Brooklyn.

### BOLTS HIT TWO CHURCHES

### Tents at Coney Island Blown Down and Sick Children Drenched—Almost a Record Rainfall.

Two rushing storms burst over the city yesterday, carrying death and destruction, principally across the East River in Kings and Queens. Two persons, a man and a boy, were instantly killed by lightning bolts in Brooklyn during the second storm. The records show that death came to them at exactly the same time, 5:20 o'clock, although they were six miles apart at the time.

The first storm sent people scurrying everywhere for safety in the belief that something approaching a cyclone was coming. Then came a fall of rain that made it seem as if the clouds had burst. The play of lightning was almost continuous. Several hours later came the second storm, with even more brilliant electric displays and more violent thunder crashes than the first.

The boy killed in Brooklyn was Samuel Kaplan of 312 Osborne Street, East New York. Young Kaplan had been to Jamaica Bay during the day, and was returning home with two boy companions. They took shelter during the early downpour of the second storm, and during a fresh attempt to get home reached an open field at Christopher Street and Newport Avenue, which was covered by about a foot of water.

The boy sat down to take off his shoes to wade when a bolt of lightning struck him on the right side of the head, literally scalping him. The doctors said that the bolt passed clear through the boy's body. The lad was thrown over on his face and half buried in the soft sand on which he had been sitting. When the police dug him out they found that his clothing had been torn off.

Kaplan's two boy companions were thrown down by the shock, but were not badly injured.

William Hagan, a truckman, of Grand Avenue and Dean Street, was driving his truck on Seventh Avenue near Third Street, Brooklyn, when a bolt struck him on the shoulder. He was hurled from his seat and landed in the street twenty feet away. A number of persons who witnessed the occurrence said that a ball of fire seemed to strike the man and envelop him in a blue haze. When he was picked up dead it was found that Hagan's clothing had been cut down from the right shoulder to his feet, as if with a keen razor.

At about 2:40 o'clock great banks of clouds gathered in the southwest. These seemed to be driven hither and thither for a time. Then a great mass of cloud gathered over the bay, gradually becoming thicker until it resembled a huge clay bank in the sky. A blackness, almost that of night, fell over the city, and throughout the down-town section lights glimmered in the big office buildings. Except for the temperature, it looked as though the end of a Winter day had suddenly been transplanted into August.

A flash of lightning and a crash of thunder, like the boom of a hundred guns, marked the beginning of the rainfall, which for twenty minutes was little short of a cloudburst. Between 2:50 and 3:10 o'clock there fell, according to the official records, 56-100 of an inch of rain, which comes near to being a record-breaking downpour. Many, however, who were caught in the deluge and had to wade, would be willing to swear that at least a foot of rain fell.

The downpour played all kinds of pranks with shipping. Ferryboats abandoned their schedules entirely during the hour and thirteen minutes that the first storm lasted. It was impossible in midstream to see a boat's length ahead.

The damage done by the lightning during this storm was especially severe in Brooklyn. A Gates Avenue trolley car was struck at Bushwick and Gates Avenues, and if it had not been that all of the fifteen persons in it were huddled in the two front seats to get away from the rain there would have been a story of fatalities to tell. The bolt struck the trolley pole, and burned a hole through the roof of the car. It struck the back of one of the seats in the middle of the car, and ran down the side of the seat to the steps and into the ground.

The vivid flash and the thunder crash following it caused a panic among the passengers, and one woman fainted. Two others jumped off the swiftly moving car, which was then stopped. The women were picked up, suffering only from a few bruises.

Calvary Episcopal Church, on Bushwick Avenue, opposite Ralph Street, Brooklyn, has a wrecked bell tower as a result of the storm. The lightning hit the square tower in the middle of the frame structure, and, besides wrecking the tower, scattered shingles and slates for 100 feet around. A hole was burned in the roof of the church, which might well have been destroyed but for the downpour, which effectually put out the fire.

There was a lively time in the corset factory of T. J. Menahan, half a block from the church, when the lightning struck one of the chimneys. Six hundred girls are employed in the place, and when they heard the crash and saw the lightning playing about the roof, they abandoned their machines, and fled screaming to the street. Beyond a wrecked chimney no damage was done.

Anna Bennett, seventeen years old, of 125 Sumner Avenue, and Mrs. Edna Rodgers of 22 Church Street, East New York, were so badly shocked by lightning that they had to be taken to their homes in ambulances after having been brought to consciousness. The women had sought shelter from the second storm in a doorway at Jamaica and Alabama Avenues and Fulton Street. Just opposite is Charles Umlas's hotel, on which was a tall flagpole. The lightning struck the pole, shattering it, and a large section dropped to the street. The electricity then played about the net of trolley wires at this point, and several hundred people who were near were temporarily blinded by the glare. After the terrific crash of thunder that followed it was found that several people had been thrown down, but only Miss Bennett and Mrs. Rodgers were unconscious.

When lightning struck the Roman Catholic Church of Our Lady of Lourdes, at Aberdeen Street and Broadway, Brooklyn, 200 persons praying in the church were thrown into half a panic, and but for the efforts of Father Porciele, the results might have been serious. He quieted the people, mostly women, and then all prayed for the storm to abate. The heavy flagpole surmounting the northern tower of the church was cut off at the base, as if with a saw, and was hurled into the street. The roof was afire for a time, but the rain soon put it out.

The only place in which the wind did any damage was in Coney Island, where it had a full sweep during the second storm. A veritable whirlwind came from the sea at 5:30 o'clock. Directly in its path was an encampment of tents at the foot of West Thirty-first Street. In them were forty-two sick children, mostly sufferers from tuberculosis. The camp was instituted by the Society for Improving the Condition of the Poor. The tents were blown down and the little sufferers in them were drenched by the rain. The nurses, headed by Miss Alice Thompson, kept their heads about them, however, and soon had the little ones safely in the building of the society.

In lower Manhattan and Brooklyn the afternoon rainfall was heaviest; at the same time it was comparatively light in Harlem and the Bronx. Last night when the streets were dry in the lower part of the city it was raining in the upper section of Manhattan.

### WAR COLLEGE STRIKE ENDED.

#### Bricklayers, Chiefly Negroes, Take Unionists' Places in Washington.

*Special to The New York Times.*

WASHINGTON, Aug. 10.—The strike at the War College can hardly be said to exist. The union bricklayers have given up the contest and admit they are beaten. To-day Capt. Sewell set seventeen more non-union bricklayers at work within an hour after they alighted from the Philadelphia train, and there are now forty-five first-class men on the job, all that are required to complete the work.

Most of those now engaged are colored men. They lay more brick and are less inclined to discuss labor questions and hours than their striking predecessors. No further trouble is expected.

The law prohibits any discrimination in favor of labor organizations, and with non-union men holding all the places and doing the work satisfactorily that seems to settle the whole difficulty. Should there be vacancies the Government officers will fill them with eligibles from the civil lists, no matter whether the applicants are members of the union or not.

### SULTAN MAKES PROMISES.

#### Favorable Answer to Our Demands May Be Made Soon.

CONSTANTINOPLE, Tuesday, Aug. 9.—Minister Leishman has received a message from the Porte promising a favorable communication in a day or two regarding the American representation in reference to the school question and other matters.

WASHINGTON, Aug. 10.—Senator Spooner and the President had a conference to-day over the Turkish incident. The Wisconsin Senator, as a member of the Committee on Foreign Relations, confirms the action taken to impress Turkey with the hazard that lies in the fatuous course pursued by the Sultan. There can be no question that the Senate Committee on Foreign Relations supports the attitude taken by the Administration practically with unanimous agreement on the facts in the case.

There are signs here that the signatory powers to the treaty of Paris are beginning to take active interest in the policy of the Washington Government toward Turkey.

Within the last two days, although Washington has been almost completely deserted by the diplomatic body, representatives of the German, Austrian, and French Embassies have appeared here, and all of them have communicated with the State Department or the White House. The nature of the communications has not yet been disclosed.

### JIM CROW LAW DISAPPOINTS.

#### Negroes Holding Through Tickets Ride with White Passengers.

*Special to The New York Times.*

WASHINGTON, Aug. 10.—The Jim Crow law in Maryland is not working out quite as thoroughly as its authors expected. Orders have been issued on the Baltimore and Ohio to conductors to allow colored passengers holding through tickets from Hagerstown, Frederick, and Cumberland and Philadelphia to sit in the compartments with white passengers.

Only way passengers are to be compelled to sit in the pens provided for colored people. The holder of an inter-State ticket is thus protected from the operation of the law in Maryland. Some of the colored passengers take the compartment for their race without question, but if they sit with the white passengers the conductors say nothing.

On trains between Washington and Baltimore separate compartments are provided, although the inter-State principle is conceded to obtain in this case. Local sentiment, however, is strong on the matter, and the railroad company finds it the part of discretion to carry out the law notwithstanding its defects.

#### Britain to Have Finest Battleships.

LONDON, Aug. 10.—The Admiralty has invited the Clyde shipbuilders to tender for two battleships of 16,500 tons and high speed. It is said that these vessels, in the way of armament and armored protection, will eclipse anything yet attempted. That the Admiralty is in a hurry to get the vessels started is indicated by the fact that the tenders must be sent in by Sept. 9, which is unusually short notice.



### INDEX TO DEPARTMENTS.

Commercial World.—Page 9.
Amusements.—Page 7.
Arrivals at Hotels and Out-of-Town Buyers.—Page 9.
Business Troubles.—Page 9.
Court Calendars.—Page 9.
Losses by Fire.—Page 2.
Marine Intelligence and Foreign Mails.—Page 9.
New Corporations.—Page 9.
Real Estate.—Page 10.
Society.—Page 7.
United Service.—Page 8.
Weather Report.—Page 7.
Yesterday's Fires.—Page 2.

## RUSSIANS RETIRING NORTH OF LIAO-YANG

### Kuropatkin Withdraws Main Army, Leaving Rearguard.

### BUT MAY HAVE TO FIGHT

### Report of Japanese Move Toward Mukden from the West Causes Great Anxiety in St. Petersburg.

ST. PETERSBURG, Aug. 10.—Information received by The Associated Press indicates that Gen. Kuropatkin is retreating north of Liao-Yang.

It is stated that he has withdrawn the bulk of his army safely, leaving only a strong rear guard line southeast of Liao-Yang to contest the Japanese advance.

The Japanese, it is stated, have about 300,000 men in the armies operating against Kuropatkin, rendering it too hazardous for him to risk a general engagement.

This information is obtained from an excellent source, and, it is added, that the Japanese again appear to have delayed too long, and that the chances of a decisive engagement are disappearing.

The report that the Japanese are working up westward of the main Russian army, however, occasions great uneasiness. The rumor that they are moving toward Sing-min-Tung, a short distance west of Mukden, from Niu-Chwang is generally believed.

The General Staff has no information bearing on the reported presence of a large force of Japanese at Paithuho, a place that cannot be located on available maps.

According to the statement issued by the General Staff to-night rains are again falling over a wide area in Manchuria, with the prospect of impeding operations. This is regarded as greatly assisting Kuropatkin.

LONDON, Thursday, Aug. 11.—A correspondent of The Daily Mail who visited Sing-min-Tung, which is on neutral Chinese territory, about thirty miles west of Mukden, cables the following under date Aug. 10:

"There is an enormous garrison at Mukden, reinforcements having arrived very rapidly.

"There are no Japanese north of the city. A force of some strength lies twenty-five miles to the south, and there is another Japanese army five miles east of Liao-Yang.

"I learn from a reliable source that the main Russian Army has fallen back on Chiu-Tsu." (Chiu-Tsu is probably Ing-shui-Tsu, five miles north of Liao-Yang, across the Tai-Tse River.)

LIAO-YANG, Aug. 9. (Delayed.)—The Japanese are very active at Bendziko, twenty-seven miles east of here, on the Tai-Tse River. They are bridging the river at eight points to facilitate their advance.

It is reported that the Japanese have 20,000 men and twenty guns idle at Hai-Cheng awaiting the turning movement which they are now attempting around Liao-Yang. The Hai-Cheng force will be ready to advance if the flankers succeed in pocketing the Russians.

Gen. Lubavin made a reconnaissance to the eastward in the Valley of the Tai-Tse River on the night of Aug. 6, striking the Japanese at Izyanchan. It was a dark and foggy night. Three companies of Cossacks rushed the Japanese outposts in order to develop the strength of their reserves.

It was discovered that the Japanese had 30,000 men and eight guns.

### THE LATEST RAID IN KOREA.

#### Only a Few Cossacks Near Gen-San—Easily Driven Away.

LONDON TIMES—NEW YORK TIMES Special Cablegram.


TOKIO, Aug. 10.—The operations of Cossacks near Gen-San were altogether desultory. On the evening of Aug. 8 two scouting parties, each of twenty troopers, approached within long range by different roads, but retreated promptly under fire.

Yesterday morning 200 Cossacks rode into Tok-Wen, but retired after a few shots had been fired and one man had been wounded.

### CHINESE ATTACK RUSSIANS.

#### Three Thousand Bandits Surprise Camp—Czar's Troops Lose Heavily.

LONDON, Thursday, Aug. 11.—The Tien-Tsin correspondent of The Standard says that 3,000 Chinese bandits attacked the Russian camp in the Tieh Pass on Aug. 2.

The Russians were taken unawares and lost many killed. They also lost a quantity of ammunition and supplies.

### FIND JUDGE IS BRUSQUE ONLY.

#### Federal Investigation of Charges Against Him Results in His Vindication.

WASHINGTON, Aug. 10.—Numerous charges against Judge Bayard T. Hainer of the Fourth Judicial District of Oklahoma have been under investigation for several months by the Department of Justice. The department, through Special Assistant Attorney General Charles W. Russell, to-day announced its conclusion as follows:

"After a most thorough investigation and consideration, Judge Hainer is found to be somewhat irritable and brusque and sometimes precipitate, but honest, conscientious, industrious, and competent—a fine Judge. All useful men have faults, and the Judge is found to have no more than the average."



### TURKEY BELIEVES RUSSIA.

#### Accepts Verbal Assurances Regarding Volunteer Fleet Ships.

LONDON TIMES—NEW YORK TIMES Special Cablegram.


CONSTANTINOPLE, Aug. 9.—The Porte has given its consent to the passage through the Dardanelles of the remaining ships of the Russian Volunteer Fleet. The Russian Embassy has given verbal assurances that the ships will remain under the commercial flag and will not be employed as cruisers.

Turkey, it is understood, in taking note of these assurances, made it clear that only on this condition would the passage be permitted.

In some quarters doubts are expressed as to whether Russia will respect the engagement once her ships are safely out, and it is argued that she would scarcely take the trouble of sending the Volunteer Fleet through the Dardanelles if she did not intend to use the ships for purposes of war. To reason this way, however, is to ignore the excellent effect from the point of view of the Russian Government which the passage will have on public opinion in Russia, where, doubtless, it will be regarded as a diplomatic victory over Great Britain.

Moreover, it is difficult to believe that the Russian Government will be ill-advised enough to commit a breach of faith which could hardly fail to have the most serious consequences.

### CONGRESSMAN FLED FROM RAID

#### Ollie James Jumped Out of Poolroom Window and Ran Through Field.

*Special to The New York Times.*

LOUISVILLE, Ky., Aug. 10.—Congressman Ollie James of the First Kentucky District made a flying leap for liberty when the county police raided the Turf Exchange poolroom in South Louisville to-day.

When shouts of "we are raided" went up Mr. James jumped through a high window and landed in a cornfield, leaving his broad-brimmed felt hat behind. He landed on his feet, and began to run between two rows of corn. He broke all sprinting records getting to the street car track, and when he arrived minus two buttons from his trousers and with his suspenders around his neck he learned to his disgust that the officers were only after the proprietors and employes.

Mr. James recovered his hat and returned to the city. He had come to town to attend the meeting of the Democratic State Campaign Committee, and after a bootblack had removed the clay from his shoes he took a train for Atlantic City to cool off.

### UNION WON'T PAY STRIKERS.

#### Typographers in Session Vote Not to Support Members on Strike.

ST. LOUIS, Aug. 10.—The convention of the International Typographical Union to-day resumed consideration of the report of the Committee on Laws. The committee recommended that the proposition to amend Section 124 of the General Laws be not adopted. The amendment provided that when a strike has been inaugurated under the provisions of Sections 116, 117, and 118 the Executive Committee should pay to the order of the President and Secretary of the union involved, for a period not exceeding eight weeks, an amount equal to $7 per week for each member entitled thereto.

On the first ballot, by a vote of 79 to 77, the committee report was voted down. On the second ballot, by a vote of 149 to 35, the unfavorable report of the Committee of Laws was concurred in.

By an overwhelming majority the convention decided that nothing should be done to prevent members of the International Typographical Union from fighting for the Stars and Stripes.

### ORDERS MAD DOG QUARANTINE.

#### Six Towns Up State Must Muzzle or Kill Every Canine.

BINGHAMTON, N. Y., Aug. 10.—State Commissioner of Agriculture Weiting to-day issued an order placing the City of Binghamton and the towns of Binghamton and Vestal, in Broome County, and the towns of Tioga and Owego and the village of Owego, in Tioga County, under a mad dog quarantine, and for all dogs within those towns to be muzzled at once or killed.

This is the result of the work of the mad dog from Owego, which came to this city three weeks ago, and is known to have bitten over fifty dogs and cattle in this city or between here and Owego. During the past three days four of the dogs bitten in this city have gone mad and have been killed.

### NEBRASKA FUSION ROW.

#### Democrats and Populists Name Different Sets of Electors.

LINCOLN, Neb., Aug. 10.—Both Democrats and Populists are holding conventions here to-day, and at a night session the Populists named Thomas E. Watson and Thomas H. Tibbles as Electors. The Democrats named John A. Lynch and R. O. Davis as Electors at Large.

It was admitted very early in the day that fusion along the lines suggested by the Populists, the substitution of Watson and Tibbles electors for those of Parker and Davis, and an equal division of the State offices, would never be conceded by the Democrats, who insisted on fusion alone on the State ticket, each party supporting its Presidential nominee.

W. J. Bryan aroused enthusiasm in a short address, and after making the temporary organization permanent the convention adjourned until 8 o'clock in the evening. After the early night session the convention took a recess at 10:45.

### HAD ODD COLLECTION OF SHOES.

#### Vineland Man Who Kept First Footwear of Grandchildren Is Dead.

VINELAND, N. J., Aug. 10.—Stephen T. Ellis, one of the pioneers of Vineland, who died yesterday, left a collection of shoes representing the first footwear of twenty-six grandchildren, for which he made a practice of paying $1 a shoe.

Mrs. Ellis has the photographs of most of the children encased in the uppers of the shoes, which are bedecked with the first ribbons worn by the "little darlings."

## GREAT SEA FIGHTS OFF PORT ARTHUR

### Russian Fleet Emerges and All-Day Battle Follows.

### NIGHT TORPEDO ATTACK

### Results of the Engagements Unknown—Japanese Land Guns Command the Fortress.

TOKIO, Thursday, Aug. 11.—The Russian fleet emerged from Port Arthur on Wednesday and a severe engagement with the Japanese fleet, lasting all day, followed.

The Japanese destroyers attacked the Russians at night.

The results of the engagements are unknown.

The Russian battleships Retvizan and Pobieda were seen outside Port Arthur this (Thursday) morning.

CHE-FOO, Thursday, Aug. 11, 7:30 A. M.—A Russian torpedo boat destroyer entered Che-Foo Harbor at 5:30 o'clock this morning.

She reports that six Russian battleships, four cruisers, and half of the torpedo boats escaped from Port Arthur yesterday morning.

The destroyer left Port Arthur last night. She brings five passengers, who state that the Japanese fleet is pursuing the Russians and that a battle on the open sea is expected.

Admiral Sah of the Chinese Imperial Navy arrived here last night from the Miao-Tao Islands. He says the firing of Monday night was at Port Arthur and was heavy all night long.

More firing, according to the Admiral, was heard yesterday afternoon.

ST. PETERSBURG, Aug. 10.—Nervousness over the situation at the front seems to be increasing since the occupation by the Japanese of the Wolf Hills, before Port Arthur.

It is admitted that the besiegers have an elevated position, whence emplaced guns can command the fortress.

While the officials still profess confidence that Gen. Stoessel will be able to hold out with his comparatively small garrison against the enormous number of the attackers and their evident disregard of their lives, the state of affairs creates more apprehension than the War Office and Admiralty care to acknowledge.

### LOSS TO BRITISH SHIPPING.

#### Only Two or Three Firms Still Dare to Accept Cargo for Japan.

LONDON TIMES—NEW YORK TIMES Special Cablegram.


BRUSSELS, Aug. 10.—Russia's attitude in respect to contraband of war continues to cause serious apprehension in shipping circles at Antwerp.

The virtual withdrawal of the Japan service of the Peninsular and Oriental, Holt, Thompson, and other leading English companies leaves the bulk of the carrying trade to the Far East in the hands of two or three firms of lesser importance. Even these are sorely perplexed over the choice of cargo, and large consignments of rails, wire netting, and similar goods have been refused within the last few days.

Nor is confidence strengthened by the fact that a leading English counsel has pronounced some fifty articles of daily consumption liable to confiscation should Russia's pretensions be admitted on the present basis.

It is not without significance that German shipping houses at Antwerp allow themselves more latitude in regard to their freight list, while vessels privately chartered, which have little to lose, are stepping into the breach to the detriment of the British carrying trade.

### RUSSIA POLITE, BUT FIRM.

#### Insists on Right to Sink Neutral Ships Carrying Contraband.

ST. PETERSBURG, Aug. 10.—The Russian reply to Great Britain's representations on the subject of the sinking of the Knight Commander, while couched in the friendliest terms, does not recede from the Russian position as set forth in the prize regulations in regard to the exercise of the right to destroy neutral vessels carrying contraband in cases of emergency. The reply reserves the question for discussion after the war.

At the same time Russia assures Great Britain that the extreme step of sinking neutral vessels will not be resorted to unless circumstances render it impossible to take them to a prize court.

Russia points out that the prize regulations under which Russia is acting were promulgated nine years ago, and that Great Britain did not enter a protest until after the present war began.

Great Britain's proposal that the British steamer Allanton (captured June 16 by the Vladivostok squadron) be liberated upon the deposit of security has not been accepted, Russia replying that the documents in this case are already on their way to St. Petersburg, and will have to be submitted to the Admiralty Court before further action is taken.

#### Fatal Windstorm Hits Fair Grounds.

INDIANAPOLIS, Ind., Aug. 10.—A severe windstorm struck the State Fair Grounds this afternoon while a large crowd had gathered for the harness races. Chairs were overturned in the grand stand, but no one was injured there. James Llewellyn, a teamster, was killed by the overturning of the gateman's house at the entrance to the grounds.

#### Bolt Kills Newark Man.

NEWARK, Aug. 10.—John McGreive of 8 Manor Avenue, Harrison, was instantly killed by lightning in the street near his home this afternoon.



### ROOSEVELT MONEY PLENTIFUL.

#### Only One Willing Parker Bettor at Odds of 10 to 7.

Roosevelt money was offered freely yesterday in the Street. Large sums were offered at 10 to 7. The largest bet, one of $5,000 to $3,500, was made by W. Marko, a representative of an important Stock Exchange firm, which it is reported had another $25,000 at the same odds.

None of this money was covered, and, with the exception of a single offer of $70 to $100 by J. C. McCormack on Parker, no Parker money at prevailing odds came out. No bets were reported yesterday on the Curb.

### FINDS DUBUQUE GIRL SPONSOR.

#### Mayor Selects Miss Treadway to Name Gunboat at Morris Heights.

WASHINGTON, Aug. 10.—Mayor Berg of Dubuque, Iowa, has concluded that it would be desirable for him to name a sponsor for the gunboat Dubuque, which is to be launched at Morris Heights, N. Y., on Aug. 27. A few days ago he notified the Navy Department that he was unable to find in Dubuque a young woman whom he could designate as the vessel's sponsor.

To-day he notified Secretary Morton that he had named Miss Margaret Treadway, a daughter of the President of the Dubuque Club, as sponsor for the vessel. His action in the matter terminates an incident without parallel in the annals of the Navy Department.

### FUGITIVE PAYS CREDITORS.

#### Cattle Plunger Returns from Mexico, Where He Made New Fortune.

*Special to The New York Times.*

AUSTIN, Texas, Aug. 10.—According to advices received here to-day from Parral, Mexico, Grant B. Gillett, the Kansas cattle plunger, who fled to Mexico six years ago to escape his creditors, has at last settled all the claims against him and has gone to Fostoria, Ohio, to make his future home.

It is stated that he has turned over to his creditors the Quebridillas Iguala and Grenadena Mines, all situated in the Parral district. Gillett left Mexico with a comfortable fortune after settling with his creditors. He made $37,000 gold in a mining deal a few weeks ago.

### ROB CEDARHURST HUNTSMEN.

#### Clothes, Jewelry, and Money Taken—Club Employe Arrested.

Members of the Cedarhurst Hunt Club of Far Rockaway were afield on Tuesday, and when they returned from the hunt to the clubhouse many of those who had changed their street apparel for their riding costumes there missed their clothes. In other cases jewelry and money were missing from pockets. James Parker, a hallboy, whose address is unknown and who had been hired but a short time before by Superintendent Wellington Cantor of the club, had also disappeared.

The boy, it was known, often went to the Tenderloin, and there he was caught yesterday. He was remanded by Magistrate Ommen in the Jefferson Market Court, and later the police announced that he had confessed and told where the stolen articles could be recovered.

### LA FOLLETTE SNUBS MICKEY.

#### Nebraska Executive and Staff Are Told to Wait His Pleasure.

*Special to The New York Times.*

LINCOLN, Neb., Aug. 10.—When Gov. Mickey and his official staff, forming a reception committee, called on Gov. La Follette of Wisconsin at his hotel here yesterday, they were given so cool a reception that the entire party withdrew without seeing the Wisconsin Executive at all. La Follette came to Lincoln to lecture.

The Nebraska Executive and his staff soon after Gov. La Follette's arrival called at the hotel and sent up their cards. The cards were returned with the information that when the Governor of Wisconsin got ready to receive the reception committee he would notify them.

### SOLDIERS OFF ON LONG MARCH.

#### Vermont Troopers Start for Army Manoeuvres in Virginia.

WASHINGTON, Aug. 10.—Orders were issued at the War Department to-day for the Twenty-third and Twenty-seventh Batteries of field artillery and two squadrons of the Fifteenth Cavalry, stationed at Fort Ethan Allen, Vt., to march from that post to Manassas, Va., to take part in the manoeuvres next month, a distance of about 700 miles.

It is calculated that the trip will occupy about five weeks. This probably is the longest march of United States troops in recent times, and is in the nature of an experiment.

BURLINGTON, Vt., Aug. 10.—Six troops of the Fifteenth United States Cavalry and the Twenty-third and Twenty-seventh Batteries of field artillery left Fort Ethan Allen to-day for Manassas, Va., where they will participate in the September manoeuvres of the United States Army.

The entire detachment is in command of Col. Alexander Rogers.

### THREATEN MINERS' BONDSMEN.

#### Cripple Creek Merchants Withdraw from Accused Dynamiters' Bail.

DENVER, Col., Aug. 10.—Information was received to-day at the headquarters of the Western Federation of Miners that the bondsmen for the men charged with connection with the Victor dynamiting outrage of June who have been released on bail have been notified by a committee representing the Citizens' Alliance and Mine Owners' Association that unless they withdraw from the bonds they will be deported.

All the bondsmen, except one, called at the office of the District Attorney to-day and asked to be relieved of their responsibility. The request has been granted in the cases of the men who are in Cripple Creek. Several of the accused, however, have left the district and their bonds will stand until they are again taken into custody and returned to Cripple Creek.

#### Carrie Nation Aids Drunkards' Wives.

RICHMOND, Ind., Aug. 10.—Carrie Nation, the temperance advocate, while passing through Indiana to-day, mailed a check for $1.150 to the Home for Wives of Drunkards, at Topeka, Kan., as a personal gift. Mrs. Nation still carries marks of the recent encounter with saloon keepers in Kentucky, when she was hit with a chair.

## PARKER ACCEPTS FOR SINGLE TERM

### Qualifying Declaration Electrifies Audience.

### CROWD'S INTEREST EAGER

### Rain Soaked, It Gives Candidate a Remarkable Ovation.

### ARCHDEACON BRADY'S TRIBUTE

### Nominee's Oratorical Powers Surprise Hearers—Ceremony on Home-Made Platform.

*Special to The New York Times.*

ESOPUS, N. Y., Aug. 10.—With the declaration that if elected he would not be a candidate for re-election, and that he would not accept a renomination, Mr. Parker closed his speech to-day accepting the Democratic nomination for President.

It electrified the crowd that was gathered under the trees at Rosemount. The audience had been a remarkable one for its intent, earnest, almost fervent attitude toward the speaker and the speech. Col. John I. Martin, Sergeant-at-Arms of the Democratic National Committee, said afterward: "I have attended the notification of quite a number of Presidential candidates, and I never observed on the countenances of such an audience such an expression of almost religious fervor."

When the announcement, however, came point blank, "I shall not be a candidate for nor shall I accept a renomination," the surprise was so great that the crowd seemed paralyzed. It recovered its breath in time to applaud, but everybody was agape. Then Judge Parker, raising his voice, set forth in clear, emphatic tones his reasons for his attitude.

"Several reasons," he said, "might be advanced for this position, but the controlling one with me is that I am fully persuaded that no incumbent of that office should ever be placed in a situation of possible temptation to consider what the effect of action taken by him in an administrative matter might have upon his political fortunes."

At this utterance the crowd went wild. The Notification Committee members and the spectators rose, cheering wildly, shouting "Good boy!" and waving hats, flags, umbrellas, and everything else at hand. After the crowd had broken up, this utterance continued to be the chief topic of conversation, and the interest in it became all the greater when a prominent Democrat who was present informed his friends, according to information which he declared to be absolutely reliable, that efforts had been made to get President Roosevelt to incorporate in his speech a refusal to accept a third term, and that the President had firmly refused.

#### Parker Insisted on the Renunciation.

It is a fact that some people who were aware of Judge Parker's purpose endeavored to dissuade him from making this renunciation, and that the Judge insisted upon doing it.

The general opinion was summed up as follows by Archdeacon Cyrus Townsend Brady, who, in his clerical garb, was a striking figure in the audience: "It was a great opportunity," he said, "completely lived up to. The speech was as honest, as peaceful, as honorable, and as courageous as the man himself. Its final declaration that he would not accept a renomination if elected will inevitably in some form or other become the law of the future."

The day was as unpropitious as possible. It was the first really rainy day that Rosemount had seen in many weeks. The roads were a mass of mud hours before the notification, and rubbers were at a premium. The sudden demand taxed the capacity of Ames's general store, and every wagon that wound up the hill to Rosemount was splashed with mud and the occupants wet and dirty.

There was no prospect of a let-up in the rain when the early visitors began to arrive. By noon the porch was well filled with personal friends of the Judge, who had come to see the ceremony. Ex-Senator Hill sent from Wolfert's Roost a fine lot of flowers, some of which were placed in vases in the reception room, while others formed a centre piece for the dining room table. Mr. and Mrs. Charles F. Neidlinger also brought an armful of flowers for Mrs. Parker.

Carriages were streaming continually up the hill and discharging their wet and muddy occupants on the porch. The rain was a steady pour, and people who walked over the hill were almost unrecognizable. Judge Parker declared that the plans for a notification under the trees must be abandoned, and that the ceremony would have to be held on the Sagamore, the steamboat which was bringing the committee up the river.

#### Rain Stops for Ceremony.

By the time the boat arrived, however, the rain had stopped. The skies were still black, gloomy, and forbidding, but it was decided to go ahead with the original plan and let the candidate get wet if necessary. His brother, Fred Parker, and other people in the house were busy hanging flags over the porch. Freddie, the dog, was parading proudly up and down with a flag wrapped around him. A man with a load of Parker medallions was doing a rushing business on the lawn, shouting, "Finest picture ever made of the Judge, boys."

The Sagamore hove into sight shortly after 1 o'clock and tied up at the Rosemount dock. There was a rush down the hill to meet her, and then the people on board began the heart-breaking climb up the almost perpendicular hill to the house.

"It's a sure thing that Roosevelt couldn't charge up this hill," gasped one perspiring citizen as he bent almost double in his climb. August Belmont tumbled down, Senator McCarren, who was just behind him, stopped and lifted him up by the shoulders. Belmont, who was wearing a dim

"All the News That's Fit to Print"

# The New York Times

LATE CITY EDITION

Weather: Fair, very cold today and tonight. Chance of snow tomorrow. Temp. range: today 24-14; Sunday 33-26. Full U.S. report on Page 30.

VOL. LIV....NO. 17,069. NEW YORK, SUNDAY, SEPTEMBER 18, 1904.—FORTY PAGES. PRICE FIVE CENTS.

## DEMOCRATS ARRIVING AT SARATOGA SPRINGS

### Feeling Prevails That Shepard Will Be the Nominee.

### ROD IN PICKLE FOR McCARREN

#### Foes Plan to Make Him a Caucus Bolter—Tammany for Shepard, Palmer, Gaynor, or Herrick.

*Special to The New York Times.*

SARATOGA, Sept. 17.—Democrats are piling into town on every train, and all is in readiness for the State Convention, which will be called to order on Tuesday at noon. Apparently Saratoga entirely has changed its political complexion since Thursday, for to-night nothing but Parker and Davis banners, lithographs, and signs are to be seen where earlier in the week were testimonials to the merits of Roosevelt and Fairbanks.

Since early morning decorators have been at work, and as a result the hotels show far more in the line of decoration than was to be found when the Republicans were in town. The Grand Union, where the various headquarters are to be located, presents a gala day appearance, bunting being draped around the big columns at the front of the hotel, while fully fifty big pictures of Judge Parker, four by ten feet in dimensions were hung at various points.

Even the United States Hotel, where the Republicans always have headquarters, is fairly well plastered with Parker pictures and with bunting.

Among the leaders and delegates who have arrived so far there is a feeling that Edward M. Shepard will be the candidate, although both the Grout and Stanchfield booms have arrived in town and apparently are thriving. At the same time, practically everybody declares frankly that no candidate for any office as yet has been definitely settled upon, and that an open convention is in sight.

James Shevlin of Brooklyn, who has been here for two days, said:

"So far, at least, this looks like an open convention. It would be folly for anybody to think that David B. Hill cannot go ahead and put through any programme that suits him. Most of the convincing to be done will be in conference with Senator Hill. In the preparation of the slate the backers of each candidate will have to demonstrate the strength of their man to Hill, who then will decide.

"It seems to me that an agreement can and will be reached by the various leaders in conference, so that we shall be able to go into convention with a good slate that will suit everybody."

SHEPARD WANTS NO HEADQUARTERS.

Mr. Shepard came to Saratoga this afternoon, but did not get off the train, going right through the town to his Lake George Summer home, where he said he would remain during the convention. On the train that brought him up from New York was John B. McDonald. The two spent some time together on the train, but neither had anything to say for publication.

Mr. Shepard declined to discuss politics while his train was at the station here, and he also refused to allow Herman A. Metz of Brooklyn to open Shepard headquarters here at any of the hotels. Mr. Metz came to town Thursday night and met Mr. Shepard at the station this afternoon, accompanying him to Lake George to remain over Sunday.

Mr Metz, who is the President of the old Shepard Democracy organization in Brooklyn, the Brooklyn Democratic Club, and who also is President of the newly formed Kings County Democratic Club, in which Controller Grout and Senator McCarren are prominent, is to be the active manager of the Shepard boom while the convention lasts.

Ex-Senator Michael J. Coffey of Brooklyn, the Red Hook statesman, who has successfully fought McCarren in the Ninth Brooklyn District at the last two primaries, just as he has for years successfully fought the old Willoughby Street organization there, arrived this evening and registered at the United States Hotel. He spent much time with James Shevlin. During the old days when Coffey was fighting McLaughlin and the auction-room contingent he and Shevlin were bitter enemies, but now Coffey and Shevlin are together fighting McCarren.

After Shevlin and Coffey had spent some time together this evening it became known positively that Senator McCarren would not get the fifteen anti-McCarren delegates to the convention into any caucus of the Kings County delegation. It also became known that a clever scheme had been concocted to put the forty-eight Brooklyn delegates controlled by McCarren into the position of bolting a caucus, instead of placing the fifteen Doyle-Coffey-Shevlin delegates in such a position.

At the Aug. 30 primaries McCarren carried sixteen districts with forty-eight State Convention delegates, while the anti-McCarren men carried five districts with fifteen delegates. Their districts are the Second, Seventh, Ninth, Eleventh, and Twelfth.

Now the plan is to have a caucus of the Greater New York delegates called by Tammany Hall for Monday night. Into such a caucus the fifteen anti-McCarren delegates would go, and they would stand by the caucus action.

PLAN AGAINST McCARREN.

Into any caucus of the Kings County contingent alone they would refuse to go on the ground that the caucus should be by the city delegates as a whole and not by counties or boroughs. Of course, Tammany absolutely would control any Greater New York caucus having of itself 105 delegates, while a Greater New York caucus, counting in the entire County of Westchester, would have 180 delegates.

The nine votes of Queens, the nine votes of Westchester, and the three votes of Richmond, as well as the fifteen anti-McCarren votes in Brooklyn, all would be with Charles F. Murphy and Tammany Hall, making a total of 141 votes in such a caucus. In such a gathering the forty-eight votes controlled by McCarren would be absolutely lost.

Tammanyites, of course, do not expect that the McCarren men would go into such a caucus, but they have decided upon this plan to place the burden of bolting a caucus, if any such burden is to be placed, on the shoulders of the McCarren men instead of on the shoulders of the fifteen Doyle delegates from Brooklyn. Neither Shevlin nor Coffey would actually admit the existence of this plan to-night, although neither would deny it.

"Our delegates certainly would decline to go into a caucus where McCarren would unfairly muzzle us," said Senator Coffey. "The Greater New York caucus is the cau-

Continued on Page 3, Col. 4

## JAPAN BOWS TO THE PRESS.

### Oyama Is Instructed to Treat Attaches and Correspondents Better.

TOKIO, Sept. 17—9 P. M.—Owing to the friction between the military authorities and field attaches and correspondents, Field Marshal Yamagata, Chief of the General Staff, to-day telegraphed to Field Marshal Oyama, commander in chief of the Japanese forces in the field, as follows:

"The imperial declaration of war as proclaimed to the people is universally recognized as being based on the broad principles of justice. It makes no distinction of race, religion, or national manners or customs.

"The sole object of the war is to insure the safety of this empire, guarantee the peace of the Orient, spread the blessings of civilization, and promote the general interests of all nations.

"It is therefore hoped that these principles will also find expression in the treatment of foreign officers and correspondents attached to our armies, and that, so long as the rule of military secrecy is not infringed, a frank and candid consideration be extended to them, so that the spirit of sincerity, which animates this empire, be fully demonstrated to the whole world."

## GIRL STUCK IN CAR TRACK.

### Traffic Held Up Until Policeman Got Her Shoe Heel Free from Slot.

A daintily gowned young woman stood directly in the path of a south-bound Broadway car at Thirty-fourth Street about 7:30 o'clock last evening. The rush to the theatres was on, and several more cars were held up.

"Get out of the way, Miss!" bawled the first motorman. "I ain't got no time to be bothering with youse."

But the young woman only waved her left hand and made no reply. Just then Policeman Walsh, the Beau Brummel of the Broadway squad, came up.

"What's the matter?" he queried.

"I'm stuck here; I can't move," said the young woman. "If you'll look at my feet I guess you'll see why. Oh, I never was in such a fix."

Walsh, getting down on one knee, soon saw what the trouble was. The tapering heel of her shoe had become wedged in the slot and the wearer was held fast. Walsh unlaced the shoe and the girl withdrew her foot. Then Walsh wriggled the shoe free. She slipped it on again, thanked Walsh profusely, and hurried off in the direction of Fifth Avenue.

## TOOK BAG CONTAINING $20,000.

### Man Helped Himself in Bank—Money Recovered, but Thief Escaped.

SAN FRANCISCO, Sept. 17.—Just at the close of banking hours to-day a man in the lobby of the First National Bank here, observing the cage door leading behind the counter ajar, pushed it open, walked in, and, helping himself to a bag containing $20,000 in gold coin, made a rapid exit.

He immediately slowed down his pace and walked into a side entrance of the Brooklyn Hotel, closely followed by C. K. MacIntosh, an employe of the bank, who had witnessed the theft.

Seeing he was pursued, the thief turned into the hotel office, where he was overtaken and seized by MacIntosh. When asked to turn over the money he said it was his own.

The bag was taken from him, however, and its contents were found to be undisturbed.

The daring robber, who is about thirty-five years old and was well dressed, then asked the people in the hotel office to see if he had not told the truth by accompanying him to the bank, only a few feet away. He walked to the corner undisturbed, boarded a street car which was passing, and soon was out of sight. He is now being searched for by the police.

## WOMEN'S COLLEGE CRUSADE.

### Greek Letter Societies Unite to Protect Girl Students.

CHICAGO, Sept. 17.—Professing alarm at the moral dangers said to surround young women in American colleges, nine National Greek-letter societies have started a crusade in Chicago, aimed at conditions in every co-educational college in the United States.

Resolutions have been adopted declaring for co-operation with Faculties of colleges to improve social conditions and placing upon the Grand Presidents of the societies responsibility for prosecution of the reform movement.

Mrs. E. Jean Nelson Penfield of New York, wife of Judge William Warner Penfield, as representative of the Kappa Kappa Gamma Sorority, was the moving spirit at the inter-sorority conference, which decided upon a reform movement.

The women, with the societies they represent, who decided upon the movement to improve the morals and social conditions of American colleges, are Mrs. Laura H. Norton, Chicago, Kappa Alpha Theta Sorority; Miss Elizabeth Gamble, Detroit, Pi Beta Phi Sorority; Miss Lilian W. Thompson, Chicago, Gamma Phi Beta Sorority; Mrs. T. C. Kimble, Abingdon, Ill., Alpha Pi Delta; Miss Bessie M. Krape, Freeport, Ill., Chi Omega; Miss Grace E. Telling, Chicago, Delta Gamma; Miss Amy Olgen, Chicago, Delta Delta Delta; Miss Ruth Terry, Chicago, Alpha Phi.

## PASSED SCHOONER ON FIRE.

### Steamer Chatham Saw No One on Board the Emily F. Northam.

*Special to The New York Times.*

BALTIMORE, Md., Sept. 17.—The steamer Chatham, from Savannah to-day, reports that last Thursday night, off the South Carolina coast, the three-masted schooner Emily F. Northam of Philadelphia was seen ablaze amidships.

A strong wind carried showers of sparks from the burning vessel. Her decks were awash, her masts standing, and her burgee still flying, but all her gaffs and booms were gone with the exception of the main gaff, and her yawl boat was missing.

Capt. Hudgins of the Chatham got as close as safety would permit, but could discover no signs of life aboard, and he believes the crew got away in their yawl. The schooner was lumber laden, and may have become water logged in the cyclone Thursday night, the crew setting fire to her before leaving.

## TWO HARRISONS' TOMB WRECKED BY VANDALS

### New Rochelle Boatman Makes Discovery—No Motive Suggested.

### CASKETS WERE BROKEN OPEN

#### Remains of David Harrison, Formerly Large Property Owner, and Son Found on Floor.

NEW ROCHELLE, Sept. 17.—The police of this place were notified late this afternoon that vandals had desecrated the private tomb of the Harrison family, on a small island in Echo Bay, back of Harrison Island, which was formerly the home of the Harrison family, for many years residents of Westchester County. An investigation showed that the culprits had broken open the tomb, smashed portions of the caskets, and scattered the contents about the tomb.

The desecration was discovered by Louis Pagan, who is employed by the New Rochelle Yacht Club. He was rowing along the shore, when he noticed that the door of the vault was open. Going ashore, he looked in and found everything in the tomb in confusion. He went back to New Rochelle and reported the matter to Police Sergeant Cody. Patrolman Bender was at once sent to investigate and found the remains of the two Harrison members that had been buried there scattered about the floor of the vault.

An iron pipe five feet long and three inches in diameter was near the entrance to the tomb. This had evidently been used to gain admission. Inside was found a shovel. The large stone slab used as a door was smashed into small pieces, and the two stones used to form the base on which the caskets rested was pulled out of place.

The catacomb was broken, and the brickwork was also demolished. The slab that was behind the caskets had also been pulled from its position. None of the ornaments on the caskets, however, had been disturbed.

The vault was built by David Harrison, Sr., many years ago. Mr. Harrison died in 1878 and his body was placed in the vault. His son David Harrison, Jr., died in 1882 and his body was laid beside that of his father.

The elder Harrison was at one time the largest property owner in Westchester County. He lived in a mansion on Harrison Island, where the New Rochelle Yacht Club has its home.

The police say they were in communication to-night with Frank Harrison, a Brooklyn lawyer, who is a son of the late David Harrison, Jr., but so far as known no light has been thrown on the motive for the desecration. That the culprits were not simply seeking plunder appears to be shown by the fact that they did not carry off the heavy silver handles and plates on the caskets.

## NORDICA ON AUTO DASH.

### Races from Late Liner's Pier to Dinner at Ardsley.

The American Line steamship New York got in from Southampton at 9 o'clock last evening with a heavy load of passengers, many of whom are notables. The boat was twelve hours late, and none of those aboard bemoaned that fact more than Mme. Nordica.

Just before she sailed for this side, Mme. Nordica received an invitation to sing at a private gathering at Ardsley. She cabled that she would gladly sing. She then thought that the steamship would arrive here early in the day, and she would be able to make the trip to Ardsley at her leisure.

For two days the New York battled with storms that beat up the sea into mountainous high waves, while an unfavorable gale constantly cut down the ship's days' runs. She passed in Sandy Hook shortly after 6 o'clock. Allowing for stops at Quarantine and for the time it takes to turn the ship in, Mme. Nordica figured that she would reach the pier at about 8 o'clock. She determined to reach her destination if such a thing were possible, and she sent a telegram from Quarentine to those excepting her that she would be there. She also sent a telegram to a local automobile stable to have their fastest machine at the American Line pier as soon as the vessel should dock.

The gangways had scarcely touched the pier when the prima donna, in an evening gown, with a great cloak thrown over it, rushed past the gang of longshoremen, past the customs officials, and through the crowd down into the street unaccompanied. A big, red racing machine was waiting for her. She was in it in a second, and like a shot the machine was off at wonderful speed. Cabmen, policemen, and pedestrians stood open-mouthed looking at the fast-disappearing machine as it whirled up West Street, flying across car tracks and bad spots, and making probably nearly the fastest time ever made in down-town New York.

Mme. Nordica's chauffeur escaped the vigilance of New York policemen and the constables on the road to the club. The automobile went past in a cloud of dust at such a rate that if any guardian of the highway saw it he failed to catch it.

The engagement which Mme. Nordica had was to sing at a dinner given by Charles S. Eldridge at the Ardsley Club in honor of the prima donna. She kept it all right.

Covers were laid for twelve, and after the dinner there was an entertainment at which Mme. Nordica sang to the members of the club.

## PUSHES CHAIR TO STUDY MEN.

### Beloit College Professor's Self-Imposed Task at World's Fair.

*Special to The New York Times.*

BELOIT, Wis., Sept. 17.—Last year a psychological department was established in Beloit College and Prof. Guy A. Tawney, head of the department, became so deeply interested in his experiments that this Summer he decided to sacrifice his rest and pleasure to original work. The exposition at St. Louis, with its wealth of people from all countries and all classes, was his opportunity.

Since college closed Prof. Tawney has been pushing a wheeled chair up hill and down, over the large grounds of the World's Fair. From this favorable viewpoint he has studied the actions of the crowds of people and of individuals of many types and all sorts and conditions.



## "NO PERSONAL ATTACKS ON PRESIDENT ROOSEVELT," SAYS JUDGE PARKER.

THE DEMOCRATIC CANDIDATE FORBIDS ANY REJOINDER IN KIND TO THE PERSONALITIES OF THE REPUBLICAN TEXT BOOK.

ROSEMOUNT.
ESOPUS, NEW YORK.

August 17th, 1904.

My dear Mr. Parker:-

The Times of this morning says that the party text book is about prepared, and that it will go to the printer in a few days. Therefore I hasten to beg you to see to it that there is no word in it that reflects upon the personal honor and integrity of President Roosevelt.

An Evening Post editorial indicates but little care was taken in that direction toward myself by the compiler of the Republican text book, but let there be no rejoinder in kind or otherwise.

I feel confident that you need no reminder, still my anxiety impels me to send this caution.

Very truly yours,

Alton B. Parker

Mr. George F. Parker.

## WILL MAKE MANILA A BRAND NEW CITY

### We Are to Transform and Beautify the Philippine Town.

### AND ADD A SUMMER CAPITAL

#### Latter Is to be in Mountains—Secretary Taft Sends an Architect to Prepare Plans.

*Special to The New York Times.*

CHICAGO, Sept. 17.—The National Government has plans under way for the transformation of the City of Manila into a modern capital after the manner of the scheme proposed, but not carried out, for the City of Washington, and the changes already in process of execution at Cleveland.

It also is intended to found a Summer capital—a Philippine Simla—in the mountains 100 miles north of Manila.

The Manila project has progressed so far that the task of working out the detailed plans of the undertaking has been committed within the last week by Secretary of War Taft to Daniel H. Burnham of Chicago.

The news was received in this city from Washington to-day, and was confirmed to-night by Mr. Burnham. The Chicago architect will leave next week for San Francisco, and will sail next month for Manila by way of Japan. He will be accompanied only by a professional assistant, and expects to be gone five months.

Secretary Taft has had in view not only the scheme for the reconstruction of Manila but the man who he believed would be best fitted for the undertaking. At the time the Washington commission of architects, of which Mr. Burnham was President, made its tour of Europe to gather ideas for the design of a reconstructed capital, Gov. Taft of the Philippines cabled to Secretary Root suggesting that the party be permitted to return by way of the Philippines in order to study the problem of rehabilitating Manila.

The suggestion was not acted on, but Gov. Taft kept his scheme in mind, and when he returned to become Secretary of War he seized the first opportunity to consult Mr. Burnham. The result of the conference was the appointment of the Chicago man to the staff of Government architects and engineers connected with the work of the War Department.

Mr. Burnham's plans and his report on the problems with which he finds himself confronted in the reconstruction of Manila will be submitted to the Philippine Commission and then forwarded to the War Department. The estimates of the cost of the entire project will then be made and submitted to Congress in a bill providing for the expenditure of the necessary money.

Mr. Burnham said to-night that he would not venture to discuss the extent of the reconstruction of the capital until he has made a thorough study of the city. He never has been in the Far East and his knowledge of the Philippine capital he has obtained only from books and conversations with Secretary Taft. Other Government experts already have submitted plans for the reform of the sanitation, the street car, and lighting systems of the capital, and it will be the province of Mr. Burnham to design the most effective grouping of public buildings and the laying out of parks and boulevards.

The problem before the Chicago architect is to plan a new city which will conflict as little as possible with the present arrangement. The elements of this puzzle consist of the old or "walled" city, in which are situated the cathedral and the palace, and the outer or modern city, which is divided between the Europeans, Chinese, and Filipinos.

Through the city runs the Pasig River, filled with shipping and arched with numerous bridges. Beyond is the Luneta, the fashionable driveway and park, which constitutes the only attempt at landscape architecture in the city. These elements Mr. Burnham will seek to preserve so far as possible.

The central idea of the whole plan will be found in a series of administration buildings for the department, which now are scattered all over the city in temporary and often miserable quarters. There will be a residence for the Governor, a public library, museum, public baths, and a large park to be designed.

Mr. Burnham said his greatest interest is wrapped up in the possibilities of the plans for the Summer capital. This Philippine Simla, to which the entire American administrative colony will migrate in the heated term, will be located at Beguio, in the Province of Benguet, 100 miles north of Manila.

It is a great mountain meadow, twenty miles from the sea, and 4,500 feet above its level. The climate there is cool and equable all the year, and is free from the diseases of malarial character which make life at a sea level a menace in the Summer.

"The Manila problem is one of suiting new plans as far as possible to existing conditions," said Mr. Burnham this evening. "I am, therefore, more deeply interested in the Summer capital project. There I shall be able to formulate my plans untrammeled by any but natural conditions.

"I shall make an extended study of the buildings best suited to the climate and other demands of Philippine life, and then go ahead with the creation of a brand-new city.

"This dream of a Summer capital has come down from the days of the Spanish Governors. They always were going to build a retreat in the mountains where they might administer the Government in the disease-ridden season. But it was always mañana with the Spanish rulers, and they never got around to actual work in realizing the dream."

Mr. Burnham said he could not tell just how many millions of dollars it will take to carry out the plans. He is going ahead regardless of expense, and Congress will look after that.

## LOU DILLON'S RECORD TROT.

### Champion Goes Half Mile in 58¾ Seconds.

*Special to The New York Times.*

CLEVELAND, Ohio, Sept. 17.—Three new world's records were made this afternoon during the fourteenth matinée of the Gentleman's Driving Club, at the Glenville track. All the record-breaking performances were made by horses owned by C. K. G. Billings, and were especially pleasing to him, as they celebrated his forty-third birthday. The first record to go was that for a half mile, trotting. Lou Dillon, driven by Millard Sanders, with a runner on the outside driven by "Doc" Tanner, made the half in 0:58¾, slipping a quarter of a second off the mark made by the trotting queen at Memphis last Fall, when she set the trotting record at 1:58½. At that time the first half was made in 0:59 and the last half in 0:59½. To-day, owing to the recent illness of the champion mare, Mr. Billings would not let her trot more than a half mile at top speed.

To the horsemen present this was the most impressive performance of the afternoon, but to the matinée crowd of 2,000 in the grand stand the performance of Prince Direct and Hontas Crook, Mr. Billings's crack pacing team, driven to wagon, was the most interesting. The heavy wind made it impossible to attempt a mile record, and it was announced that the team would be driven a fast half. How fast they went is best shown in the time, which was 0:29½ for the first quarter, while the half mile was finished in 1:00¼, making another world's record.

The third race that went to Mr. Billings's credit during the afternoon was when he rode Charlie Mac in an effort to beat the world's record of 2:14¾ trotting to saddle. A good track made it possible for Charlie Mac, despite the wind on the first quarter and in the stretch, to clip a second off his former mark, placing it at 2:13¾.

## CAT TURNED ON THE GAS.

### Young Man Killed—Father Found Unconscious and May Die.

NEWARK, Sept. 17.—Edward Whalen, Jr., twenty-two years old, was found dead in bed in his home, at 421 Third Street, East Newark, to-day. He had been suffocated by gas. His father, sixty years old, was found unconscious in the same room. He is in a critical condition and may die.

Two valves of a gas range in the kitchen adjoining were open. It is supposed that the cat, playing about the range, opened them.

## OUTLOOK IN ITALY IS VERY SERIOUS

### Agitation in Some Places Has Character of Rebellion.

### STRIKE IN ROME IS BEGUN

#### To Begin in Naples To-morrow—Another Fight Between Strikers and Police in Genoa.

ROME, Sept. 17.—The strike here has begun, but is not yet general.

The Socialist agitation is on the increase, especially in the northern part of Italy. In some places it is assuming the character of a rebellion.

At Naples it has been decided to strike on Monday.

In other towns troops are kept in readiness, and the police everywhere have been reinforced.

Another fight has occurred at Genoa between the strikers and police. The whole night was passed in darkness there, owing to the strike.

The Mayor and other municipal officers of Milan came to Rome to-day to present to the Government an expression of the indignation of the population of Milan as a result of what they term the slaughter of the people.

The real cause of the whole agitation is an attempt on the part of the Extreme Party to overthrow the Cabinet, as, in spite of the fact that it is a Liberal Ministry, it energetically keeps the Extremists in hand.

## AUTO GOES OVER PRECIPICE.

### New Yorker Killed and the Other Occupants Injured.

*Special to The New York Times.*

ST. LOUIS, Sept. 17.—Racing along Manchester Road, near Ballwin, St. Louis County, early this morning, a merry automobile party of four plunged over the edge of a steep declivity to the rockbed of a creek. The heavy machine crushed and almost instantly killed the chauffeur, Jack Killeen, or Kolleen, or Cullen, aged twenty-one, a telegraph operator from New York City. Miss Lulu Marquitz of St. Louis received dangerous injuries. Miss Nellie Marquitz, her sister, and Edward Parkhurst, son of a Ballwin, Mo., dentist, were less seriously injured.

With another automobile party, also of four members, the four had left the city early in the evening. Both machines, $7,000 French importations, were taken out by the chauffeurs without consulting the owners, it appears.

According to Parkhurst, the lights of the machine driven by Killeen went out on the return trip, but Killeen did not slow down. He steered his machine to destruction in dodging a farmer's wagon.

William Sauer, aged eleven, of Manchester, was watching the removal of the wrecked automobile late this afternoon, when he was run over by its hind wheel and probably fatally injured.

## A GAIN FOR JEROME.

### De Witt Boom for Controller Gives Votes to District Attorney.

*Special to The New York Times.*

BINGHAMTON, N. Y., Sept. 17.—The boom of Jerome De Witt for State Controller on the Democratic ticket was formally launched at the Democratic Assembly and County Conventions here to-day, when resolutions were passed instructing the delegates for Jerome De Witt and empowering him to choose the men who are to represent the County in Saratoga. Mr. De Witt has been in the field for several months.

He is an ex-Mayor, who was twice elected in a Republican city by overwhelming majorities, and is credited with being the strongest candidate in the Southern tier.

His candidacy makes the support of John B. Stanchfield by the Broome delegation impracticable, and they will vote for Jerome or Shepard.



## FORBADE ANY ATTACK ON PRESIDENT'S HONOR

### Parker Cautioned Compilers of the Campaign Book.

### "NO REJOINDER IN KIND"

#### Letter Made Public with Advance Sheets of Book, Which Discuss Tariff and Reciprocity at Length.

Although several pages of the Republican campaign book are given over to an attack on the character of Judge Parker, particularly in regard to his motives in sending the famous gold telegram, "no rejoinder in kind or otherwise," and no attack on the honor or integrity of President Roosevelt appear in the advance proofs of the Democratic Campaign Textbook.

In making the first installment of the advance sheets public yesterday, George F. Parker, chief of the Literary Department of the National Committee, gave out for publication this letter from Judge Parker:

Rosemount, Esopus, N. Y., Aug. 17, 1904.

My Dear Mr. Parker:

THE TIMES of this morning says that the party textbook is about prepared, and that it will go to the printer in a few days. Therefore I hasten to beg you to see to it that there is no word in it that reflects upon the personal honor and integrity of President Roosevelt.

An Evening Post editorial indicates that but little care was taken in that direction toward myself by the compiler of the Republication textbook, but let there be no rejoinder in kind or otherwise.

I feel confident that you need no reminder; still my anxiety impels me to send this caution. Very truly yours,

ALTON B. PARKER.

Mr. George F. Parker.

The book, which will be issued in a few days by the Democratic National Committee, was prepared under the direction of a committee consisting of ex-Mayor Josiah Quincy of Boston, William S. Cowherd, Chairman of the Democratic Congressional Committee, and George F. Parker.

#### The Constitution, a Preface.

By way of emphasizing the Democratic contention that the "return to the Constitution" is one of the principal issues in this campaign, the book will be prefaced with a full copy of the Constitution of the United States. The subject discussed at greatest length is the tariff. Considerable attention is also devoted to the record of the Republican Party on reciprocity.

Discussing the tariff and the trusts, the authors of the book assert that Americans are forced to pay from 5 per cent. to 200 per cent. more for the products of their own country than the same products are sold for abroad. The authority for this statement is to be found in the export trade journals of the trusts containing full lists of export prices, several copies of which have recently been obtained by the National Democratic Committee. These journals circulate only in foreign countries, and the trusts are said to use every means in their power to prevent their falling into the hands of American buyers, lest the latter may learn the truth concerning this feature of the manufacturers' business. It is asserted that the committee has employed an expert familiar with all the ins and outs of the export business who has visited the offices of exporters and received from them, in their own handwriting, many of the prices quoted in the book.

Here is an extract on the effect of the Dingley tariff law:

During the year ended June 30, 1904, the sale of American-manufactured products to foreigners amounted to $452,000,000, of which fully 85 per cent., according to estimates of well-informed exporters, was sold at cheaper prices than are charged for precisely the same goods when sold to Americans. The average price of these goods in the foreign market is 20 per cent. less than the selling price in the home market. On some goods, such as paints and varnishes, the difference between the price to foreigners and to Americans is only 5 per cent., but on agricultural implements, tools, machines, and hardware the difference in the price to the foreigner and to the American varies from 10 to 50 per cent. On wire, cartridges, playing cards, &c., the difference is more than 100 per cent., and on such articles as wire rope and borax the difference exceeds 200 per cent.

Were there nothing else to condemn the Republican policy of high tariff taxes, this one fact ought to be sufficient to cause the American people to repudiate it, for surely nothing can be more unjust than for the American Government to tax its own people to the end that American steel rails, plows, shoes, and other articles of prime necessity may be sold cheaper to the people of Japan, Europe, and foreign countries generally than they are sold at home to Americans.

It is absurd to speak of "infant industries" like the Steel Trust, which is able to compete with the so-called pauper labor of foreign countries, and which makes enough profit on its export sales, even at prices far below its domestic prices, to enable it to pay dividends upon millions of dollars of watered capital.

When the voters of America—the farmers, mechanics, clerks, and professional men—realize the extent of the difference between export and home prices they will speedily withdraw "protection" from such "infants" as the Steel and other giant trusts of this country.

#### Some Prices.

In a table giving the domestic and foreign prices of articles in daily use are to be found, for example, the following:

Table knives, per gross, foreign price, $12; domestic price, $15.

Barbed wire, per 100 pounds, foreign price, $2; domestic price, $3.

Typewriters, foreign price, $60; domestic price, $100.

Sewing machines, fine, foreign price, $20.75; domestic price, $27.50.

Sewing machines, medium, foreign price, $17.50; domestic price, $22.

Sewing machines, cheap, foreign price, $12; domestic price, $18.

Long tables obtained from export trade periodicals of the trusts and published in this country are given to show the differences in discounts from price lists for foreign and home consumers, and also the percentage of difference between export and home prices. This percentage is found to range from 10 to 72 per cent. on such articles as bells, bolts, chains, augurs, locks, saws, and so on.

The difference between the domestic and export prices of implements, tools, utensils, and other wares and goods is shown by percentages varying from 5 per cent. to 68 per cent., and the difference between the prices of a long list of miscellaneous articles by percentages varying from 10 per cent. to 50 per cent.

"While," it is stated, "the accuracy of the export prices may be challenged by Republican politicians, it is not probable that they will be questioned by the manufacturers whose names are mentioned in the list."

Under the head of "Export Values versus Home Values," it is asserted that an

"All the News That's Fit to Print."

# The New York Times

THE WEATHER.

Fair; brisk north winds.

VOL. LIV....NO. 17,111. NEW YORK, SUNDAY, NOVEMBER 6, 1904.—36 Pages and Financial Supplement. PRICE FIVE CENTS.

## PARKER BARRED THE TRUSTS FROM DEMOCRATIC FUND

### Says His Party Managers Carried Out His Explicit Instructions.

### HIS ANSWER TO ROOSEVELT

### Would Make Corporation Gifts to Parties a Crime.

### SAYS THE PRESIDENT DODGED

### Calls His Statement a Plea of Avoidance, a Confession.

### ORIGINAL CHARGE UNDEFENDED

### Judge Had Hoped Roosevelt Might Rally to His Aid to Destroy Political Election Bribery.

After a triumphal progress through the streets of Brooklyn, and in the presence of all the leading Democrats of the borough at the Kings County Democratic Club, Judge Parker last night made answer to the attack made upon him in President Roosevelt's statement of the night before.

The part of his reply that evoked the wildest cheers was his answer to the President's insinuation that corporations had contributed to the Democratic fund as well as to the Republican fund. He said that this insinuation had forced him to make a revelation that he had not intended to make. By this time the enthusiasm of the Democrats over the points he had already made had risen to such a degree that they broke out into cheering at the very announcement. The Judge impatiently stilled the cheering with his hand, and in a sharp, clear voice made his revelation.

It was that he had personally requested the National Committee to accept no contributions whatever from any trust, and that they had complied with his request.

**Uproar of Excitement.**

The Kings County Democrats simply went wild at this announcement. Hats went into the air, and, instead of cheering, they yelled like men beside themselves. In the midst of the uproar men were saying to each other, "That statement elects him President."

After that he declared that the appearance of what he called "corrupt combinations" in politics was the greatest issue presented to the people to-day, and that laws must be enacted which would pursue with drastic penalties any trust which attempted to control the Presidency by making contributions to campaign funds.
the passage of such laws. The cheering over his announcement of his purpose was second only to that which greeted his statement about his own refusal to accept campaign contributions from the trusts.

**No Abuse of Roosevelt.**

In contrast to his own attitude Judge Parker presented Mr. Roosevelt's action in appointing the Secretary of Commerce, the official investigator and custodian of trust secrets, to the post of campaign collector. He did not abuse the President, and those who expected a tart response in kind to the President's language of Friday night were destined to be disappointed; but he made it clear that the President's denial was only a denial that any "formal promise of immunity" had been given to the trusts.

The real charge, he said, the President had not met. The real charge was not that any formal promise of immunity had been given, but that the trusts were paying money to secure the election of an Administration which would have the power to prosecute them or to leave them alone.

Tremendous cheering greeted his statement of what the President ought to have done when the charge was first made. He said that the President should have co-operated with him in the effort to have an election held in which the trusts should take no financial part; the President should have cleared his skirts by refusing to allow any more contributions to be received from trusts; and he pointed out that the President's statement practically admitted that the Republicans were receiving contributions from trusts.

Judge Parker was to have been entertained at dinner, but he arrived late, and the dinner was nearly over when he got there. In the meantime the 300 police under Inspector Weigand had had the job of their lives keeping back the crowd of 5,000 or so which was held outside the lines on Smith Street and Boerum Place. The clubhouse is on Schermerhorn Street, between the other two, and at one time the crowd drove the police lines back nearly to the clubhouse before the men could be reinforced and could restore the original lines.

The Judge was cheered enthusiastically all along the line. He came in accompanied by his brother Frederick, Senator McCarren, and President Herman A. Metz of the club. The dinner was served in a room off the reception room on the third floor, where the reception was to be held.

**Cheer Parker the Man.**

At 9:03 o'clock, nearly an hour after the time set, Judge Parker came out of the dining room into the reception room The cheer he got was enthusiastic. He was taken by Mr. Metz, who was followed by the other diners, to a platform, where he faced the members of the club and such outsiders as could jam in. Mr. Metz then addressed the Judge, saying:

"Judge Parker, before introducing to you the members of the Kings County Democratic Club, and the Democrats of Brooklyn, permit me to recall to your mind the fact that Samuel J. Tilden and Grover Cleveland both closed their campaigns in Brooklyn, and to express the hope that Kings County will give you as large a majority as it gave to them; and that as Kings County goes, so will go the State of New York and the rest of the country.

"It is our sincere belief that history will repeat itself, and the members of the Kings County Democratic Club here and now pledge themselves to attend in a body your inauguration as President of the United States on March 4 next."

**The Judge Speaks.**

Then the Judge took up his manuscript and read his prepared speech. He read it emphatically, sharply, but with no trace of heat or anger. He seemed deeply in earnest, and continually tapped the air in front of him with his forefinger, as if driving his points home. He said:

**JUDGE PARKER'S REPLY TO ROOSEVELT.**

"Mr. President and Gentlemen: It gives me great pleasure to be with you to-night—the last opportunity I shall probably have to look any considerable number of Democrats in the face at one time until after election on Tuesday; and it gives me pleasure to be able to say that the outlook for us is very promising to-night. [Applause.]

"The Democracy has had a very considerable task this year, as you know, in fixing the fences over the country and getting them in good condition for work; but those of you who have kept track of the situation as it has progressed from day to day realize, I have no doubt, that the party is organized in better working condition, more harmoniously all over the country, than it has been in many years before. [Applause.]

"The purpose of my address to-night is to call attention to the fact that in his strangely belated reply to my speech of twelve days ago the President has not met the issue created since the platforms were adopted, namely: Can the trusts purchase the election? Whatever results may follow from his address, the campaign fund cannot be interfered with. It has been raised.

**The Charge Made.**

"My first utterance on the subject is to be found in an address delivered on the 24th day of October, in which I said:

"Many years have passed since my active participation in politics. In the meantime a startling change has taken place in the method of conducting campaigns, a change not for the better, but for the worse; a change that has introduced debasing and corrupt methods which threaten the integrity of our Government, leaving it perhaps a Republic in form, but not a Republic in substance, no longer a Government of the people, by the people, for the people, but a Government whose officers are practically chosen by a handful of corporate managers, who levy upon the assets of the stockholders they represent such sums of money as they deem requisite to place the conduct of the Government in such hands as they consider best for their private interests.

"I make no complaint, nor should complaint be made, of an individual who contributes toward the many legitimate expenses of a great campaign. The capitalist as an individual has as much right to contribute to such purposes and in proportion to his means as has his less wealthy fellow-citizen. Whatever he may do, based on a patriotic desire to help elect the candidates of that party which it seems to him will best serve the interests of the country, should be encouraged.

**All Used to Contribute.**

"'It is but a little while since the body of the people at large provided the legitimate expenses of a campaign. Then farmer and lawyer, doctor and mechanic, day laborer and banker, each contributed something toward the erection of banners, the circulation of literature, and the expenses of public meetings, and each contributor was a better citizen for it. It stimulated his patriotism, and the contributions were devoted to the legitimate advancement of the cause, not made for the deliberate corruption of masses of electors.

"'Gradually and effectively, but surely not permanently, has all this been changed. Some of the enterprises which have unduly thrived through favoritism, and which have been permitted by statute to indirectly levy tribute upon the people, have in the course of time become so rich and strong that they can and do contribute vast sums when it is made clear that it will advantage them, and they contribute upon the promise, direct or implied, that they shall be permitted to continue to tax the people for their own benefit. Upon such promises contributions have been not infrequently made in such large measure as to induce and procure colonization, repeating, and bribery in doubtful States.

**Growth of 'Floaters.'**

"'This has built up a class of voters known to local leaders as "floaters," a class so numerous that party canvassers allot to them in their canvass books a separate column headed with that name. This condition is recognized by party workers, local, State, and National. They are no longer shocked by it. It has become so prevalent that they are becoming hardened to it. They sometimes wonder where it is to end, but under the stress of a campaign they postpone consideration until the next election.

"'I am persuaded the time to begin the fight against those who would control the results of election contests for their private corporate interests, as distinguished from the public interest, should begin now, and whatever the result of the election may be, it should be continued until the evil is checked.

"'The excessively protected interests, which formerly poured out their treasure in order to continue existing and procure the passage of new laws permitting its further accumulation, have been joined by the combinations popularly called trusts. Their plan is to perpetuate the present Administration. Such of the combinations or trusts as do not profit by the aid of the tariff secure their profits by the exercise of monopolies. Hence their officers are opposed to the enforcement of law as against them.

**Purpose Clear as Noonday.**

"'When such forces unite to furnish the money which they are promised will control the election their purpose is as clear as noonday. It is to buy protection, to purchase four years more of profit by tariff taxation and four years more of extortion from the public by means of monopoly.

"'Political contributions by corporations and trusts mean corruption. They cannot be honest. Merely business interests are moved by merely business considerations. A corporation will subscribe to a political party only because the corporation expects that party, through its control of public officers—executive or legislative—to do something for the benefit of the corporations or to refrain from doing something to its injury. No other motive can be imagined. In the nature of things no other motive can exist. The relations established mean the expectation, if not an agreement, actual or implied, that Governmental action is to be influenced by and for corporation interests. No sophistry can give any other aspect to the transaction in the minds of reasonable men.

"'Let the defenders of the practice, if it has defenders, answer these questions:

**Why Corporations Pay.**

"'Why do corporations and trusts subscribe to political campaigns?

"'What would a trust think of a party which, after accepting from the trust a campaign contribution of $500,000, should permit the party's representatives in office to take action inimical to the trust?

"'Would the public interests be safe in the hands of a party the greater part of whose campaign funds had been contributed by corporations and trusts?

"'If the public welfare and the interests of subscribing corporation or trust should conflict, which would likely be protected?

"'The scheme of our Government opposes favoritism, but in its administration there has been much of it. Indeed it has been growing with such rapidity in recent years that these few that have enjoyed favors contributed either directly by statute or indirectly by the non-prosecution of violations of law, represent, control, and are possessed of many hundreds of millions of dollars. These interests have decided to attempt to continue the present Administration in power. Their representatives scolded about the President for some months, and thus contributed their part toward the effort which was assiduously made to satisfy the country that the trusts were opposed to the present Administration.

**Trusts and Roosevelt.**

"Whether there were real difficulties between these great powers and the Administration, difficulties which have since been settled to the satisfaction of all parties concerned, or whether there were no difficulties to be compromised and adjusted, their action being but a play to deceive the voters, the fact remains that the trusts are not now opposed to the continuance of the present Administration.

"'On the contrary, it is common knowledge that they have determined to furnish such a sum of money to the Republican National Committee as it is hoped will secure the 'floaters' in the doubtful States for the Republican ticket. Such an attempt constitutes both a menace and a challenge to every patriotic and law abiding person in this country, a challenge which ought to be accepted. The question ought to be settled now whether the floaters and illegal combinations can together control an election in this country. Such a contest means on one side vast sums of money and every man with an itching palm. It ought to array every honest, independent and patriotic citizen on the other side.

**Great Moral Issue.**

"You have learned from its reading that the purpose of that address was to warn the people against the corrupting of the electorate by tariff-bred trusts and other monopolies. It contained no criticism of the President. It simply called attention to a notorious and offensive situation—a situation which presented to my mind the greatest of the moral issues of the campaign, yes, of many campaigns.

"If he had said, on the day after the delivery of my address, after the consultation about it which he and Senator Knox had:

"'Yes, I never thought of it before, but Parker is right. Why would a trust take money out of its treasury, money belonging to its stockholders, consisting of women and children, as well as men of both parties, unless its purpose is to get something in return, something which its officers regard as more than an equivalent for the moneys taken out of the treasury?

"'Now, he is right, and I am going to stop it. Perhaps the National Committee cannot pay back the moneys contributed in this way, that they have already expended, but there shall be no more such contributions. I will join Parker in an effort to protect the ballot of the honest citizen from being overridden by merchandise ballots.'

**Roosevelt We Once Knew.**

"If he had said that, it would have sounded like the Roosevelt we once knew. And if he had followed it by acts in execution of his words it would have been of far less consequence to the people which one of us should be elected than it is now. But he did not do it. He shut his eyes to what was going on, and since that time there has been the frequent meeting of the trust magnates, and the moneys have been pouring into the treasury all the more freely and all the more plentifully because of the attitude taken by me, and which, it is true, I have enforced from day to day.

"The President does not deny these contributions now. This is what he says: 'That contributions have been made to the Republican Committee, as contributions have been made to the Democratic Committee, is not the question at issue. Mr. Parker's assertion is in effect that such contributions have been made for improper motives either in consequence of the act or in consequence of improper promises, direct or indirect, on the part of the recipients.'

"That is the only paragraph in President Roosevelt's statement which touches either directly or indirectly on the question as to whether the trusts have made contributions to the Republican campaign fund. It is almost in terms an admission that the trusts have contributed to the Republican fund.

"In coupling the Democratic campaign fund with the Republican campaign fund the President attempted to so associate the two that a denial of his assertion could not be made without implicating the Democratic Committee.

**Confession, Not Answer.**

"He is in a position to know what contributions have been made to the Republican National Committee by the trusts. If there had been no trust contributions he could easily have said so. He did not say so. He cannot say so. He has waited until the closing hour of the campaign to make easier the pretense of an answer. But it is not an answer. It is a confession with a plea in avoidance addressed to a kindly and generous people.

"If there was any doubt of the source of this great campaign fund it is no longer a matter of suspicion, for Mr. Elihu Root, the former Secretary of War, frankly admitted last night that trusts and corporations were heavy contributors. He denied only that the total amount thus acquired or utilized was as large as in previous years.

**The "Square Deal" Promise.**

"Moreover, the Republican candidate himself denies only that definite immunity from prosecution has been promised trusts for their assistance. He declares that he is merely to give them a 'square deal,' as the terms may be interpreted not by the laws of the land but by himself.

"It is plain that when the time shall come to determine what a 'square deal' between the Government of the United States and the contributing trusts really is, the beneficiary of the generosity of the latter must either recognize their service or confess himself guilty of base ingratitude.

"The President's argument and his position seem to justify trust contributions, and the inference he would have the public draw from his utterance is of course that contributions have been made by the trusts to the Democratic National Committee. At this time, therefore, I am justified in making a statement which I had not intended to make.

**Took No Trust Money.**

"I requested the Democratic National campaign managers, Mr. President, that they should not receive, directly or indirectly, from any trust, money for campaign purposes. I notified them that I proposed, if elected, to enter upon the discharge of the duties of that great office unhampered by any obligation to interests or to men.

"I said to them that I would rather be defeated than be fettered in the effort to accomplish reforms that are sorely needed. And I am advised by them that my request has been scrupulously respected.

"Instead of co-operating with me in checking this monstrous evil, which seriously threatens the liberties of our people, you called into consultation your late Attorney General, and from that consultation he came out to make an attack upon me for venturing to criticise the attempt of the trusts to control the election. He did not answer the charges or attempt to. He did attempt to divert public attention.

"I regret to say to you that it then seemed apparent to me, Mr. President, that you regarded the election of more importance than the checking of this evil.

"Later I called attention to events which have been presented and frequently discussed by leading newspapers in this city and this country following the enactment of a statute authorizing the creation of the Bureau of Labor and Commerce, a discussion which began so long ago as the first day of October.

**A Recital of Facts.**

"Now let me recite them here as I have recited them before.

"A new department of the Government was created—the Department of Commerce. To that department was intrusted inquisitorial power over the great trusts and corporations of the country. Its head, the Secretary of Commerce, was made a Cabinet officer. A half a million dollars was appropriated for its work, of which sum very little has been expended.

"The President placed at the head of this great department—empowered to probe the secrets of all the trusts and corporations engaged in inter-State commerce—his private secretary, who held that position for some months, when he resigned and was made Chairman of the National Committee.

"Now these facts are not challenged in the statement of the President, nor can they be. The statute was passed and money was appropriated to probe the trusts; Cortelyou was appointed at the head of it. He was without experience in National politics, and yet the President says in his statement, 'I chose Mr. Cortelyou as Chairman of the National Committee.'

**Rebuke at Polls Needed.**

"Now that this intended crime against the franchise has been exposed in time, now that the contributions of this money by these great monopolies looking for the continuance of old favors, or seeking new ones, stands admitted, now that these contributions have been made in such sums as to induce and permit the most lavish expenditures ever made, we, as a people, will fail in our duty if we shall not rebuke at the polls this latest and most flagrant attempt to control the election—not for legitimate business conducted for proper ends—but in order that the few may still further strengthen their hold upon our industries. We shall rue it, if, as a people, we do not make this rebuke so emphatic that the offense will never again be repeated.

**Corporations Must Not Pay.**

"But this is not enough. We should take every possible precaution to secure both Congress and the Presidency in order to assure legislation which will remove this illegal business from politics. All along the line of our official life the purpose should be avowed, and it should be pursued, with unrelenting fidelity, to procure legislation which shall make it a crime for the officers of a trust or corporation to contribute money for the control of an election of any kind, and, if it should do so, to provide for their punishment in the most effective way.

"This is not the time to consider the details of such a remedy, but one is needed which shall be so far-reaching and so drastic as to dissolve all partnerships between corrupt business interests and the Government and to make their renewal forever impossible.

"As this is a Government of laws and not of men, it does not seriously matter whether one man or another holds the great office of President of the United States, but the opportunities in that place for doing a great good are so apparent that they should be employed for the highest purposes.

**Must Destroy Bribery.**

"Great as are the problems before us in the near future—political, industrial, and social—in my judgment none is so pressing as this, the greatest of moral questions. It includes all other issues, it lies at the foundation of all other problems, and its settlement by the absolute and final exclusion of bribery or the threat of bribery or of the raising of money for this foul purpose is, to my mind, the most important question that can come before a free and moral people.

"If my countrymen shall call me to take up this work I will, God helping me, use every faculty of my mind, and will employ every power that legally and constitutionally inheres to that great office to accomplish this most beneficent result."

There was a rapturous demonstration after he had finished, and then the thousands of people who wanted to shake the Judge's hand were invited to come forward and be introduced by Mr. Metz.

The reception room is a small one, and the most of it was roped in. Around the outside of these ropes a narrow alley was left through which the people were to pass. They were not in line, and the first forward movement was a jammed rush in which everybody was powerless to move except as he was hurled forward by the others.

**Rapturous Demonstration.**

The crowd thus hurled itself up against the platform. The palms there were thrown over, shouts arose, and for a moment it looked as if a panic were in prospect. The police acted with their usual admirable efficiency, and in a minute or two had the crowd righted and able to move in something like order.

The Judge was kept handshaking there for about an hour, and then returned with his brother to the Hotel Seville. This morning, at 10 o'clock, he will return to Esopus, there to stay till after election.



## PARKER TO ROOSEVELT:

### I Forbade Trust Contributions; Why Did Not You?—A Pledge to Make Trust Contributions Criminal.

**The President's argument and his position seem to justify trust contributions, and the inference he would have the public draw from his utterance is, of course, that contributions have been made by the trusts to the Democratic National Committee. At this time, therefore, I am justified in making a statement which I had not intended to make.**

**I requested the Democratic National Campaign Managers, Mr. President, that they should not receive, directly or indirectly, from any trust, money for campaign purposes. I notified them that I proposed, if elected, to enter upon the discharge of the duties of that great office unhampered by any obligation to interests or to men.**

**I said to them that I would rather be defeated than be fettered in the effort to accomplish reforms that are sorely needed. And I am advised by them that my request has been scrupulously respected.**

**Instead of co-operating with me in checking this monstrous evil, which seriously threatens the liberties of our people, you called into consultation your late Attorney General, and from that consultation he came out to make an attack upon me for venturing to criticise the attempt of the trusts to control the election. He did not answer the charges or attempt to. He did attempt to divert public attention. I regret to say to you that it then seemed apparent to me, Mr. President, that you regarded the election of more importance than the checking of this evil.**

**We should take every possible precaution to secure both Congress and the Presidency in order to assure legislation which shall remove this illegal business from politics * * * legislation which shall make it a crime for the officers of a trust or corporation to contribute money for the control of an election of any kind. * * ***

**If my countrymen shall call me to take up this work, I will, God helping me, use every faculty of my mind, and will employ every power that legally and constitutionally inheres in that great office, to accomplish this most beneficent result.**

## MR. CORTELYOU CALLS CAMPAIGN FUND CLEAN

### In Midnight Statement Says It Was Given Voluntarily.

### NO PLEDGE OR ASSURANCE

### Chairman Claims 314 of the 476 Electoral Votes for Roosevelt—Issues Committee's Thanks.

George B. Cortelyou, Chairman of the Republican National Committee, close to midnight last night gave out the following statement:

"To all supporters of Roosevelt and Fairbanks:

"The Presidential campaign has reached its final stage, and the reports to the Republican National Committee from all parts of the country seem to be as complete as it is possible for ante-election reports to be. Upon these and upon all the information which the committee has been able to obtain, I am satisfied that the Republican candidates for President and Vice President will carry every Northern State with the possible exception of Maryland and Nevada, and will not have less than 314 of the 476 votes in the Electoral College.

"The campaign has been conducted with a much smaller fund than any Presidential campaign for the last twelve years. The fund this year, although made up of contributions from more than 4,000 persons, has been about one-half as large as the Republican fund when President McKinley was elected in 1896, and about one-half as large as the Democratic fund when President Cleveland was elected in 1892.

"Every part of this fund has come from voluntary contributions made without demand, importunity, or pressure; and without any agreements, pledge, promise, assurance, or understanding, express or implied, regarding the policy or the action of the Administration, or looking to any benefit or advantage to any contributor except the benefit which will come to all business and to all our people from the continuance of Republican policies and Republican administration.

"To the great body of public spirited citizens who from their means and by their personal efforts have aided in the arduous labors of the campaign, I return the heartfelt thanks of the National Committee of 1904.

"GEORGE B. CORTELYOU,
"Chairman."

Chairman Cortelyou declined to make any comment on the speech of Judge Parker before the Kings County Democratic Club.

## MR. ROOSEVELT SILENT.

### Declines to Discuss Judge Parker's Speech on Campaign Funds.

WASHINGTON, Nov. 5.—President Roosevelt to-night read a copy of Judge Parker's reply to his statement published this morning. It was announced by Secretary Loeb that the President had no statement to make.

Secretary Loeb was at his desk in the executive offices during the evening, and carried the speech to the President. With Mr. Loeb were Postmaster General Wynne and Assistant Secretary of State Loomis, neither of whom commented upon the speech.

## CLEVELAND TALKS OF CHAIRMAN CORTELYOU

### Regrets His Decline from Merited Office to Partisan Work.

### LOSS TO CIVIL SERVICE

### Earned His Public Positions by Merit, But Partisan Management Grieves His Old Friends.

*Special to The New York Times.*

PRINCETON, N. J., Nov. 5.—Ex-President Grover Cleveland received a representative of THE NEW YORK TIMES at his home here to-night, and when asked for his views about the letter of President Roosevelt and the previous remarks of Judge Parker in regard to Chairman Cortelyou's connection with the trusts, said that he refused to enter into any controversy which seemed to intervene between Judge Parker and President Roosevelt in relation to Mr. Cortelyou's conduct as the Chairman of the Republican National Committee.

Mr. Cleveland said, however, that there was a point in regard to Mr. Cortelyou, bearing on the civil service, which had not been called to the attention of the public by the press, and that for this reason he took the opportunity through THE NEW YORK TIMES to make the following statement, which he wrote out in his own hand:

"I see that Mr. Roosevelt in his statement published this morning in defense of himself and Mr. Cortelyou speaks of the latter as having been my Executive Clerk in the White House. He might have gone further and spoken of my high opinion of Mr. Cortelyou, amounting to personal attachment.

"From this arises my condemnation of the action of Mr. Roosevelt in putting him at the head of the Republican National Committee; and this has nothing to do with the question as to whether or not Mr. Cortelyou has or has not improperly or otherwise extorted or obtained contributions from trusts and combinations for campaign purposes. With this contention I have nothing to do. My complaint is of a different sort.

"Mr. Cortelyou before his selection as the head of a partisan National Committee, with all it implies, was pre-eminently the best illustration the country afforded of the useful and beneficent operation of civil service reform. Without influence or powerful friends he earned a humble place in the public service through civil service examination. He rose step by step through his own merits to positions of the most delicate and confidential character; and when he was put at the head of an important and new department of the Government and took a place among the members of the President's Cabinet, I believe there was not a right-thinking man in the United States who did not rejoice in his advancement as well earned, and I am sure every sincere civil service reformer was gratified by the opportunity afforded to point to so convincing a justification of the reform.

"The last place his friends or the friends of civil service reform would have thought of as one he could appropriately occupy was Chairman of the Republican National Committee, and the last thing they could have expected him to do was to resign his well-earned and befitting Cabinet position to take such a place.

"I regard it a distinct loss to the cause of civil service reform that he should have gravitated to duties and work so far and so distinctly removed from any relationship to this reform, or even to the best things in politics.

"It is in my belief most unfortunate that when Mr. Cortelyou assumes again Cabinet duties, as it seems to be conceded he will after the election, he will be given the place not in illustration of civil service reform, but in payment of the work performed, and, to say the least of it, the most suspicious partisan service.

"GROVER CLEVELAND."

## FINDS ASBURY PARK SHORTAGE.

### Town Committee Chairman Puts Lost $8,000 Up to ex-Collectors.

ASBURY PARK, N. J., Nov. 5.—Chairman Dodd of the Township Committeemen stated last night that shortages and irregularities of former Township Collectors had been discovered, and that the facts had been carefully suppressed by the Auditing Committee after a recent examination of the township books.

Justice Dodd said in estimating the alleged shortages that there would be $8,000 lost to the township. The charges will be investigated at a special meeting to be held Monday night.

"All the News That's Fit to Print"

# The New York Times

LATE CITY EDITION

Weather: Sunny, mild today; cool tonight. Chance of rain tomorrow. Temperature range: today 40-63; Tuesday 30-52. Details on page 78.

VOL. LIV....NO. 17,114. NEW YORK, WEDNESDAY, NOVEMBER 9, 1904.--SIXTEEN PAGES. ONE CENT In Greater New York, Jersey City and Newark. Elsewhere, TWO CENTS

# ROOSEVELT

## Sweeps North and West and Is Elected President.

## SAYS HE WILL NOT RUN AGAIN

### Will Have 325 Electoral Votes—Republican Gains in Congress—Folk, La Follette and Douglas Win Governorship Fights.

Theodore Roosevelt was yesterday elected President of the United States for four years more, overwhelming majorities having been given to the Republican Electoral tickets in all of the States which had been classed as doubtful. The returns received up to midnight indicate that Roosevelt will have **325** votes in the Electoral College to **151** for his opponent, Alton B. Parker. The total number of votes in the Electoral College is **476**, of which **239** are necessary to a choice. Mr. Roosevelt, therefore, will have a majority in the Electoral College of **174**. The only State about whose Electoral vote there was any doubt at a late hour was Maryland. The returns indicated that it had gone Republican by several thousand, but the Democratic State Committee had not abandoned hope.

As soon as it became certain that he had carried the country Mr. Roosevelt issued the following statement at the White House, in Washington:

**"Washington, Nov. 8, 1904.**

**"I am deeply sensible of the honor done me by the American people in thus expressing their confidence in what I have done and have tried to do. I appreciate to the full the solemn responsibility this confidence imposes upon me, and I shall do all that in my power lies not to forfeit it. On the Fourth of March next I shall have served three and one-half years, and this three and one-half years constitutes my first term. The wise custom which limits the President to two terms regards the substance and not the form. Under no circumstances will I be a candidate for or accept another nomination."**

The polls closed in New York at 5 o'clock, and the people were not kept long in suspense as to the result in New York State and the Nation. As early as 7:30 o'clock August Belmont, who was at the Democratic National headquarters receiving returns, conceded the election of President Roosevelt by "an overwhelming majority." By 8 o'clock those in charge of returns at Democratic headquarters were willing to concede that Mr. Roosevelt had carried every doubtful State in the country.

The figures which came in from New York, New Jersey, Connecticut, Indiana, and West Virginia were stunning to the Democratic managers. In none of the bulletins was there a single ray of hope for the Democrats, and as early as 8:30 o'clock a telegram was sent to Judge Parker informing him of his defeat.

Returns from New York State up to midnight indicated that Roosevelt would have a plurality of **186,000** in the State. His indicated plurality above the Bronx line was **223,000**, while Parker's indicated plurality in New York City was **37,000**. Higgins's plurality for Governor will be about **85,000**.

The Republicans of the State of New York retained their hold on the Legislature, electing on the face of the returns as this edition of THE TIMES went to press, **36** members of the Senate, to **14** Democrats, and **104** members of Assembly to **46** Democrats. This is a clean Republican gain of **7** in the Senate and **7** in the Assembly. Districts that went Republican only when McKinley ran in 1896 were this year again turned into the Republican column.

The returns for Congress show that the Republicans have elected **220** members of the House, and the Democrats **137**, thus giving the Republicans **72** majority.

In New Jersey the indicated plurality for Roosevelt is **60,000**, and the Republican candidate for Governor, Edward C. Stokes, will have about **35,000**.

Connecticut gave a plurality of **25,000** for Roosevelt. A. Heaton Robertson, the Democratic candidate for Governor, ran ahead of his ticket, but Henry Roberts, the present Lieutenant Governor, was elected by a plurality of about **20,000**.

Indiana went **50,000** for Roosevelt.

The latest returns indicated **30,000** plurality for the Republican Electoral ticket in Wisconsin. La Follette, the regular Republican candidate for Governor in Wisconsin, ran behind the Electoral ticket, but the returns indicate his election.

West Virginia, the home State of Henry Gassaway Davis, the Democratic candidate for Vice President, gave **23,000** plurality for Roosevelt and Fairbanks.

The latest returns from Colorado indicate that the State went for Roosevelt by a small plurality and that Peabody, the Republican candidate for Governor, won by a narrow margin.

Maryland was claimed by both sides at midnight, but the latest returns indicated that the State would be Republican by a small plurality.

Massachusetts furnished a surprise by electing William L. Douglas, Democrat, Governor of the State, although the plurality for Roosevelt and Fairbanks was in the neighborhood of **80,000**.

Joseph W. Folk is elected Governor of Missouri by a plurality estimated at **40,000**, but the returns indicated that Parker was running behind. He probably will carry the State by **35,000**.

While complete returns were lacking at 1:30 o'clock it seemed probable that the Democrats had elected Governors in Nebraska and possibly West Virginia. In the latter State the vote is very close, but the indications are that Cornwell, the Democratic candidate, has outrun the National ticket and will pull through.

Montana also reverses her Electoral vote on State issues and elects a Democratic Governor.

### PARKER TO ROOSEVELT.

**Sends His Congratulations at 8:30 P. M. —The President Replies.**

ESOPUS, Nov. 8.—Judge Parker to-night sent this telegram to the President:

"Rosemount,

"Esopus, N. Y., 8:30 P. M., Nov. 8.

"The President, Washington, D. C.:

"The people by their votes have emphatically approved your Administration and I congratulate you.

"ALTON B. PARKER."

WASHINGTON, Nov. 8.—President Roosevelt's reply to Judge Parker's telegram was as follows:

"Alton B. Parker, Rosemount, N. Y.:

"I thank you for your congratulations.

"THEODORE ROOSEVELT."



### THE ELECTORAL VOTE.

**ROOSEVELT.**

| State | Votes |
|---|---|
| California | 10 |
| Colorado | 5 |
| Connecticut | 7 |
| Delaware | 3 |
| Idaho | 3 |
| Illinois | 27 |
| Indiana | 15 |
| Iowa | 13 |
| Kansas | 10 |
| Maine | 6 |
| Maryland | 8 |
| Massachusetts | 16 |
| Michigan | 14 |
| Minnesota | 11 |
| Montana | 3 |
| Nebraska | 8 |
| New Hampshire | 4 |
| New Jersey | 12 |
| New York | 39 |
| North Dakota | 4 |
| Nevada | 3 |
| Ohio | 23 |
| Oregon | 4 |
| Pennsylvania | 34 |
| Rhode Island | 4 |
| South Dakota | 4 |
| Utah | 3 |
| Vermont | 4 |
| Washington | 5 |
| West Virginia | 7 |
| Wisconsin | 13 |
| Wyoming | 3 |
| Total | 325 |

**PARKER.**

| State | Votes |
|---|---|
| Alabama | 11 |
| Arkansas | 9 |
| Florida | 5 |
| Georgia | 13 |
| Kentucky | 13 |
| Louisiana | 9 |
| Mississippi | 10 |
| Missouri | 18 |
| North Carolina | 12 |
| South Carolina | 9 |
| Tennessee | 12 |
| Texas | 18 |
| Virginia | 12 |
| Total | 151 |

**Total number of votes in Electoral College, 476. Necessary to a choice, 239.**

### HIGGINS THANKS THE TIMES.

**In Message on Election Result He Recalls the Furnaceville Case.**

*Special to The New York Times.*

Olean, N. Y., Nov. 8.

*To the Editor of The New York Times:*

The magnificent majority received by President Roosevelt in his home State, in my opinion, is due to his unquestioned integrity, high character, great ability, and devotion to the welfare of the masses of the people.

In my recent campaign tour through the State the Republicans were all united and earnest for his election, and at every place we visited Democrats openly and frankly expressed their intention of supporting him.

I feel that the Republicans of the State, as well as myself, personally are indebted to THE NEW YORK TIMES for the broad integrity with which they handled the Furnaceville case.

FRANK W. HIGGINS.

# CITY VOTE

## Parker's Plurality Over 37,000.

## HERRICK BY 76,000.

### Roosevelt Carries Brooklyn by Narrow Margin—Republicans Win 19 Assembly Districts in the City.

Alton B. Parker's plurality in the City of New York will be more than **37,000** when the final count is made. With fifty-five election districts still to be heard from, he ran about **36,000** ahead of Roosevelt in the five boroughs, but the Republican candidate carried Brooklyn by about **2,000** votes.

D. Cady Herrick, Democratic candidate for Governor, carried every borough, and his plurality in the city will be about **76,000**.

Parker made a little better showing than Bryan in 1900. The Democratic plurality in the city that year was **29,181**, while Brooklyn Borough went for McKinley by **2,745**.

Manhattan and the Bronx gave Parker a plurality of more than **34,000**. In Queens he won by about **4,000** and in Richmond by nearly **600** votes.

The Republican Presidential candidate carried nineteen Assembly districts in the greater city.

In Manhattan the districts that went for Roosevelt were the Fifth, Eighth, Tenth, Sixteenth, Nineteenth, Twenty-first, Twenty-fifth, Twenty-seventh, Twenty-ninth, and Thirty-first, and probably the Twelfth and Twenty-third, where the voting was very close. In this number are three that were not carried by McKinley in 1900—the Eighth, Tenth, and Sixteenth.

The Brooklyn districts that went for Roosevelt were the First, Fourth, Fifth, Sixth, Tenth, Twelfth, Sixteenth, Seventeenth, Eighteenth, Twentieth, and Twenty-first, while the result in the Thirteenth was very close, Parker winning by less than **100** votes. The Eleventh, which was carried by McKinley [illegible] to the Democratic column.

Of the twelve State Senators chosen in New York County, nine will be Democrats. Three out of seven in Brooklyn, too, belong to the victorious party. The one Queens Senator is a Democrat.

Democratic Assemblymen were successful in twenty-six districts and Republicans in nine in New York City. In Brooklyn there are twelve Democratic and nine Republican Assemblymen. The two from Queens and the one from Richmond are Democrats.

Victor J. Dowling (Dem.) was elected Justice of the Supreme Court in New York County, and Joseph I. Green (Dem.) Judge of the City Court.

The votes for the Presidential candidates of the other parties—Thomas E. Watson, Populist; Dr. Silas E. Swallow, Prohibitionist, and Eugene V. Debs, Social Democrat—are not estimated at more than **35,000** or **40,000** altogether.

### STATE PLURALITIES.

**REPUBLICAN.**

| | |
|---|---|
| California | 40,000 |
| Colorado | 5,000 |
| Connecticut | 25,000 |
| Delaware | 2,500 |
| Idaho | 5,000 |
| Illinois | 100,000 |
| Indiana | 70,000 |
| Iowa | 150,000 |
| Kansas | 80,000 |
| Maine | 37,000 |
| Maryland | 2,000 |
| Massachusetts | 82,000 |
| Michigan | 125,000 |
| Minnesota | 100,000 |
| Montana | 2,000 |
| Nebraska | 30,000 |
| New Hampshire | 18,000 |
| New Jersey | 50,000 |
| New York | 186,000 |
| Nevada | 4,000 |
| North Dakota | 25,000 |
| Ohio | 125,000 |
| Oregon | 30,000 |
| Pennsylvania | 370,000 |
| Rhode Island | 5,000 |
| South Dakota | 15,000 |
| Utah | 8,000 |
| Vermont | 31,000 |
| Washington | 20,000 |
| West Virginia | 20,000 |
| Wisconsin | 75,000 |
| Wyoming | 7,000 |

**DEMOCRATIC.**

| | |
|---|---|
| Alabama | 25,000 |
| Arkansas | 40,000 |
| Florida | 15,000 |
| Georgia | 45,000 |
| Kentucky | 12,000 |
| Louisiana | 35,000 |
| Mississippi | 47,000 |
| Missouri | 35,000 |
| North Carolina | 22,000 |
| South Carolina | 40,000 |
| Tennessee | 15,000 |
| Texas | 250,000 |
| Virginia | 30,000 |

### NEBRASKA.

(Voted for Presidential Electors, Congressmen, Governor and State officers, and a Legislature, to elect a United States Senator. Vote in 1900: Rep., 121,835; Dem., 114,013.)

LINCOLN, Neb., Nov. 8.—Roosevelt will probably carry Nebraska by 30,000. This is the estimate of the State Central Committee. Roosevelt's election is conceded by the Fusion Committee. Berge, Fusionist for Governor, seems to be elected. The Legislature will probably be Republican. The Watson vote seems to be a trifle smaller in Nebraska than Parker's vote. Five precincts in this (Lancaster) county outside of Lincoln show a net loss to Mickey (Rep.) for Governor of 52. A loss of three votes to the precinct for the State would defeat Mickey.

Precincts in Omaha reporting thus far indicate a Republican gain on the National ticket and a corresponding loss on the State ticket.

Outside returns are similar, and with the present ratio of Republican loss on the State ticket, Berge will be elected. The Republican State Committee claims the State for Roosevelt by 30,000.

Ten out of twenty-six voting precincts in the city of Lincoln give Roosevelt a plurality of 928. The same precincts gave McKinley a plurality of 840. The city of Lincoln will give Roosevelt close to 1,900 plurality against 1,777 for McKinley. Eleven Lincoln precincts show a net loss for Mickey (Rep.) for Governor, of 161.

# HIGGINS, TOO

## Behind His Ticket, But Elected Governor by 85,000.

## UP-STATE PLURALITY 162,000

### Legislature Will Be Republican by a Majority of 80 on Joint Ballot—Depew's Successor To Be a Republican

Frank W. Higgins was swept into the Governorship yesterday by the tidal wave which gave Roosevelt a record-breaking plurality in New York State, but the "Odell tag" caused his plurality to fall to about **85,000**. His plurality north of the Bronx was probably about **162,000**, but Herrick's great vote in the city reduced this figure.

The Republicans made important gains in the Legislature. The indications are now that they have gained **7** Senators and **7** Assemblymen, thus making the Senate stand **36** Republicans to **14** Democrats, and the Assembly **104** Republicans to **46** Democrats. On joint ballot the Republicans have a majority of **80** votes. This insures the election of a Republican to succeed Chauncey M. Depew in the Senate of the United States.

### WISCONSIN REPUBLICAN.

**Roosevelt Carries the State—La Follette Wins.**

(Voted for Presidential Electors, Congressmen, Governor and State officers and a Legislature, to elect a United States Senator. Vote in 1900: Rep., 265,866; Dem., 159,285.)

*Special to The New York Times.*

MILWAUKEE, Nov. 8.—The latest returns received from the election in Wisconsin indicate that Roosevelt has carried the State by a large plurality, probably 75,000, and La Follette, (Rep.), has been elected Governor over Peck, Dem., by 25,000 plurality.

There are no figures at this time upon which to make an estimate on the next Legislature.

So far seven Republicans and one Democrat have been elected to Congress, and three districts are to be heard from.

### MINNESOTA, 100,000.

**Democratic Governor Elected by 10,000 Majority—One Congress District in Doubt.**

(Voted for Presidential Electors, Congressmen, Governor and State officers and a Legislature, to elect a United States Senator. Vote in 1900: Rep., 190,461; Dem., 112,901.)

*Special to The New York Times.*

ST. PAUL, Nov. 8.—Chairman Martin of the Minnesota State Central Committee claims a plurality for Roosevelt of 100,000. The great contest here was on Governor. The Republicans cut their nominee to such an extent that Johnson (Dem.) was elected by from 10,000 to 20,000 majority.

The Fifth Congressional District is in doubt. Figures at a late hour give the Democratic candidate a good lead, but only half the returns are completed. All other Congressmen are Republicans.

### WASHINGTON.

**Conceded to Roosevelt—State Ticket Is Still in Doubt.**

(Voted for Presidential Electors, Congressmen, Governor and State officers and a Legislature, to elect a United States Senator. Vote in 1900: Rep., 57,456; Dem., 44,833.)

*Special to The New York Times.*

TACOMA, Nov. 8.—The Democrats concede Washington on National issues, but claim the State ticket, which is still in doubt.

The candidates for Governor are Albert E. Mead (Rep.) and George Turner, (Dem.) There are also Prohibition, Socialist, and Socialist-Labor tickets.

### STATE VOTE FOR GOVERNOR.

| County. | Pluralities— Higgins, Rep. | Herrick, Dem. |
|---|---|---|
| Albany | 4,000 | ...... |
| Allegany | 3,300 | ...... |
| Broome | 2,550 | ...... |
| Cattaraugus | 3,716 | ...... |
| Cayuga | 3,789 | ...... |
| Chautauqua | 9,316 | ...... |
| Chemung | 1,108 | ...... |
| Chenango | 2,187 | ...... |
| Clinton | 1,975 | ...... |
| Columbia | 1,600 | ...... |
| Cortland | 2,100 | ...... |
| Delaware | 3,500 | ...... |
| Dutchess | 2,603 | ...... |
| Erie | 8,300 | ...... |
| Essex | 2,907 | ...... |
| Franklin | 3,319 | ...... |
| Fulton | 1,920 | ...... |
| Genesee | 2,676 | ...... |
| Greene | 584 | ...... |
| Hamilton | 100 | ...... |
| Herkimer | 1,885 | ...... |
| Jefferson | 4,929 | ...... |
| Kings | ...... | 13,096 |
| Lewis | 1,200 | ...... |
| Livingston | 2,079 | ...... |
| Madison | 3,801 | ...... |
| Monroe | 8,000 | ...... |
| Montgomery | 1,375 | ...... |
| New York | ...... | 51,497 |
| Nassau | 2,500 | ...... |
| Niagara | 2,500 | ...... |
| Oneida | 500 | ...... |
| Onondaga | 6,164 | ...... |
| Ontario | 2,002 | ...... |
| Orange | 4,500 | ...... |
| Orleans | 173 | ...... |
| Oswego | 4,150 | ...... |
| Otsego | 1,090 | ...... |
| Putnam | 730 | ...... |
| Queens | ...... | 5,097 |
| Rensselaer | 3,200 | ...... |
| Richmond | ...... | 804 |
| Rockland | ...... | 162 |
| St. Lawrence | 9,103 | ...... |
| Saratoga | 2,100 | ...... |
| Schenectady | 2,740 | ...... |
| Schoharie | ...... | 465 |
| Schuyler | 1,250 | ...... |
| Seneca | 300 | ...... |
| Steuben | 4,317 | ...... |
| Suffolk | 2,434 | ...... |
| Sullivan | 400 | ...... |
| Tioga | 1,394 | ...... |
| Tompkins | 1,346 | ...... |
| Ulster | 2,300 | ...... |
| Warren | 1,940 | ...... |
| Washington | 5,200 | ...... |
| Wayne | 3,418 | ...... |
| Westchester | 6,000 | ...... |
| Wyoming | 2,038 | ...... |
| Yates | 1,000 | ...... |
| Total | 168,478 | 96,097 |

*Estimated.

### 200,000 IN ILLINOIS.

**Gain of Three Republican Congressmen —W. P. Harrison Defeated.**

(Voted for Presidential Electors, Congressmen, Governor and State officers, and a Legislature. Vote in 1900: Rep., 597,985; Dem., 503,061.)

CHICAGO, Nov. 8.—The latest indications are that the Republican National ticket had carried Illinois by about 150,000. The Chairman of the Republican State Central Committee asserted that Roosevelt would certainly have a plurality of 200,000. The Democrats declared that the figures were greatly exaggerated, but admitted that Roosevelt would have a plurality not far from 100,000.

The returns on Congressmen are slow, but it looks as if the Republicans had gained at least three Congressmen, two of them in Chicago. William P. Harrison, the brother of Mayor Harrison of Chicago, is defeated for Congress.

Roosevelt has apparently carried Chicago by about 80,000 and Cook County by 90,000 to 100,000.

Charles S. Deneen, the Republican candidate for Governor, will have about the same plurality.

The Republicans have probably carried the First and Eighth Congressional Districts, hitherto Democratic.



## MAP SHOWING HOW THE DIFFERENT STATES VOTED.

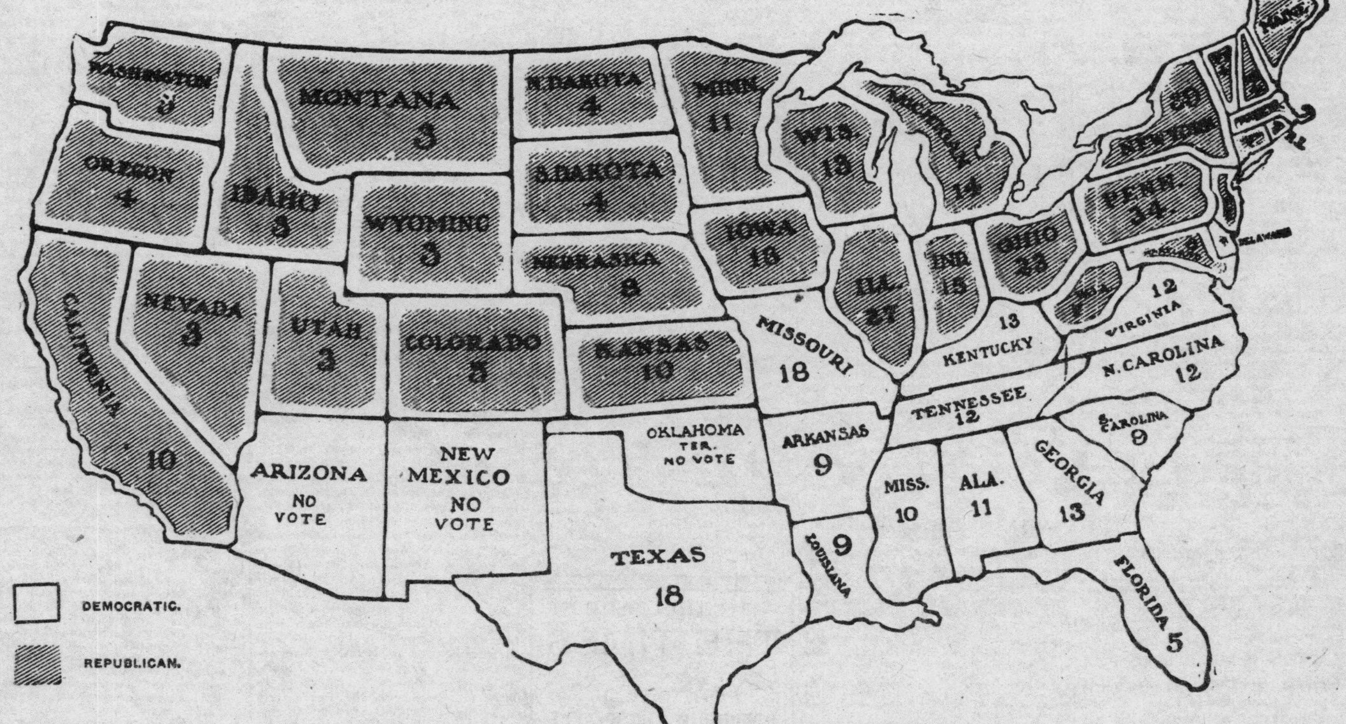

DEMOCRATIC.

REPUBLICAN.

"All the News That's Fit to Print."

# The New York Times.

THE WEATHER.
Fair, slightly warmer Thursday; Friday, fair, warmer; moderate winds, becoming south.
For full weather report see Page 22.

VOL. LIV....NO. 17,213. NEW YORK, SUNDAY, MARCH 5, 1905.—44 Pages and Financial Review. PRICE FIVE CENTS.

## RUSSIANS AFRAID ARMY IS CRUSHED

### All News Stopped—Bourse Hears of Disaster.

### ADVANCE ON RAILWAY

### Japanese Movement from Sing-min-Tung Reported.

### FEARFUL LOSS OF LIFE

### Japanese Casualties Up to Friday Said to Have Numbered 40,000 and Russians 30,000.

ST. PETERSBURG, Sunday, March 5.—With the ink of the imperial rescript announcing that the Emperor had decided to convene an assembly of elected representatives of the people scarcely dry, the overshadowing topic of conversation in St. Petersburg yesterday was the critical condition of Gen. Kuropatkin's army and the continued absence of news of the result of the day's fighting.

Gen. Kuropatkin, in a report dated Friday, announced that the Russians had been compelled to evacuate their position at Gaoto Pass.

The most startling rumors afloat yesterday had their origin on the Bourse. According to these Field Marshal Oyama had cut Gen. Kuropatkin's army in two, overwhelming the sections in detail, but the latest dispatches from the front report comparative quiet on the centre and did not indicate a movement there of importance.

The situation, however, is sufficiently grave. During the fighting at Sanlinpou on Friday the Russians were facing only a division of Japanese in the Liao Valley, and with the utmost difficulty repulsed these. Correspondents, telegraphing Friday at midnight, prophesied a renewal of the fight yesterday morning against a reinforced Japanese army.

The War Office is guarding well the secret of the outcome of the fight, and no dispatches, official or otherwise, were permitted to pass the censos yesterday. The General Staff declines to say whether Gen. Kuropatkin is standing his ground or if he is already retiring.

The battle on Friday had assumed enormous proportions. One of The Associated Press's Russian correspondents placed the Russian losses at 30,000 men and those of the Japanese at 40,000. He added that the attempt to draw a net around Gen. Kuropatkin had not yet succeeded, but that the Japanese from Sing-min-Tung were attempting by forced marches to cut the Russian line of communications.

Another report is that the Japanese flanking column at Sing-min-Tung divided, part of it moving straight east to roll up the Russian right wing, while the other was making forced marches north with the purpose of cutting the Russian line of communications with Tie Pass and closing the line of retreat. Should this operation prove successful the Russian army might be surrounded.

Gen. Kuroki, according to the latest reports received, was stalled by the Russian left, but the Russian centre yas yielding slowly before the Japanese onslaughts.

On Thursday Field Marshal Oyama shifted the weight to his left, seeking to envelope the Russian right eight miles southwest of Mukden. In the bloody hand-to-hand fighting which followed and continued for hours the losses on both sides were enormous.

Two lengthy dispatches received from Gen. Kuropatkin, respectively dated March 2 and March 3, detail the movements in various directions. The dispatch of March 2 says:

"The enemy to-day adopted vigorous offensive tactics, conducting a turning movement on our right flank before the villages of Sakhotun and Linziatun. After a strong preparatory cannonade they attacked, but were repulsed with great loss.

"The Japanese vigorously attacked the Gauto Pass position and took one of our intrenchments, from which they were dislodged by our counter-attack; but we finally abandoned this intrenchment because it was entirely destroyed.

"The Japanese to-day several times attacked our detachments on the left flank, and at about 1 P. M. carried the heights in the centre of our position. Our troops, however, counter-attacked, dislodged the enemy, and gained a footing on the crest of a neighboring hill.

"Our detachment near the village of Kudiaza, after repulsing five violent attacks and inflicting great loss, assumed the offensive."

Teh dispatch of arch 3 says:

"The offensive movement commenced in the evening of March 2 against the Japanese occupying Sanlinpou and neighboring villages was continued this morning. At the same time reinforcements arrived at Mukden.

"Early this morning the Japanese attacked our positions on the left flank in the region of Mandolesan, more than twenty Japanese battalions participating. All the atacks were repulsed with great loss to the Japanese front ranks.

"Our detachment on the left flank repulsed three attacks to-day, inflicting great loss on the enemy.

"I have thanked these valiant troops in his Majesty's name for their splendid defense.

"The losses of the Japanese attacking our left flank are so great that they are constructing defenses with the dead bodies of their fallen comrades."

An important council of war was held here on Friday, and another will be held to-day, which indicates the gravity of the situation.

In military circles it is believed that the landing of Japanese forces north of Korea and the movements of a mysterious flying column outside the extreme Russian left indicate a campaign against Vladivostok.

BERLIN, Sunday, March 5.—The Tageblatt to-day says it learns from a person in the confidence of the Russian Embassy here that the Russian authorities are convinced that Gen. Kuropatkin will soon find it necessary to evacuate Mukden and retreat to Tie Pass, where he will give decisive battle.

This, the paper's informant adds, was Gen. Kuropatkin's plan from the first, and plans have already been made for the arrival of Russian troops at Tie Pass.

The same paper yesterday printed a St. Petersburg dispatch saying:

"Gen. Kuropatkin in a telegram which arrived here at 7 o'clock last evening said 260,000 Japanese had broken through the Russian left wing, and that it was cut off from the remainder of the army.

"At 10 o'clock came another dispatch from eGn. Kuropatkin which read:

"'The Japanese are marching on Mukden. My position is extremely dangerous.'"

In Government circles here there is a conviction that Gen. Kuropatkin has been fully beaten; that part of his army has been dispersed, and that the railroad north of Mukden will probably be cut.

GEN. OKU'S HEADQUARTERS IN THE FIELD, March 3, via Fun-San.—Last night the Japanese occupied three more villages in the Russian second line of defenses, carrying the captured lines twelve miles east of Changtan. The Russians are falling back on their heavy defenses south of Mukden.

The Japanese movement is entirely successful.

The Japanese losses have not been reported, but it is probable that they will be heavy considering the importance of the movement.

The pursuit of the Russians continues.

A heavy bombardment is in progress.

MUKDEN, March 4.—1 A. M.—The Russians are holding on desperately to their positions.

On Thursday and yesterday Japanese corps gave battle on the southwest within sight of Mukden.

Russians report that a Japanese force has broken around the right and is moving north, though it is believed the Russians hold the Sing-min-Tung Road at the Liao River.

Although the fighting has now been in progress for six days, the officers here are mystified to know whether the actions at the wings are not big demonstrations to facilitate the chief Japanese object—that of breaking through the Russian centre—or, if it is Field Marshal Oyama's real intention to turn Mukden, on which side is the real movement and on which the feint.

One of Gen. Kuropatkin's staff officers said:

"Oyama's strategy is to break the centre, and then inclose the wings and compel a demoralized retreat, but till now the Japanese attacks against the centre have been only measurably successful."

Trains are leaving Mukden ceaselessly for the north with wounded men and stores.

### FIERCELY OPPOSE KUROKI.

#### Russians Making Good Resistance—Cold Hampers Japanese.

GEN. KUROKI'S HEADQUARTERS IN THE FIELD, via Fu-San, March 4.—It is believed that the Japanese attack will succeed.

The hotly contested engagement begun at midnight March 2 across the Sha River from Witosan proceeded yesterday under conditions entailing great harpships upon the attacking force and favoring those defending the intrenchments. A large Japanese contingent which crossed the plain directly west of Witosan in darkness succeeded in gaining the first line of the Russian trenches, to the great astonishment of the Russians.

The Russians afterward made a fierce resistance in the second line of trenches on the summits of the foothills, and the Japanese attacked them spiritedly.

The Russian artillery kept up a heavy fire on the Japanese guns most of to-day and also fired shrapnel at the attacking forces.

The Japanese are gathered on the slopes so close to the Russian trenches that in some places their artillery cannot give the best support. The Russians have largely abandoned their old method of volley firing.

The Japanese are obliged to wear the heaviest clothing, which, with the bitter cold and continued snow flurries, handicaps them.

### "STEADY JAPANESE GAINS."

#### Announcement in Tokio—Victory at Sing-min-Tung.

TOKIO, March 4.—It is announced today from the headquarters of the Japanese armies in Manchuria that the fighting on the right, centre, and left is resulting in steady Japanese gains.

The Japanese, it is added, have defeated the Russians at Sing-min-Tung.

An official dispatch received yesterday from Manchurian headquarters says:

"Many counter attacks in the direction of Sing-Ching have been repulsed by the Japanese.

"In the direction of Ben-tsia-pu-Tse the Japanese pressed the enemy to his main defenses, and are now engaging him.

"The Japanese have captured Sun-nu-pao-Tse and the heights north of Tang-chia-Tun, east of the Sha River Railroad, and have since been engaging the enemy's infantry.

"About a battalion of Russians attempted to penetrate Shang-wa-Fang from the direction of Fen-chia-Pao, but were repulsed.

"Paying no attention to the enemy's defenses west of the railroad, the Japanese are pressing northeast. Part of the Japanese force dislodged the enemy from Ta-min-Tun and Sing-min-Tung. The Japanese at the latter place captured quantity of provisions."

### WHERE IS THE REGIMENT?

#### Japanese Have Clothes of Men Set to Guard Gaotu Pass.

ST. PETERSBURG, March 4.—Gen. Kuropatkin, in a report to the Emperor dated yesterday, says:

"The Japanese attacking our right flank are dressed in the uniforms of our Chembarsky Regiment, which was posted at Gauto Pass," (on the Russian left flank.)



## MR. CARNEGIE ON HAND FOR CHADWICK TRIAL

### Ironmaster Arrived in Cleveland Last Evening.

### CONFERENCE ON THE CASE

#### Woman's Real Estate in Cleveland Appraised at $41,190, and Personal Property at $31,123.

*Special to The New York Times.*

CLEVELAND, March 4.—With the arrival of Andrew Carnegie in the city this evening all is now in readiness for the trial of Mrs. Cassie L. Chadwick, which will begin the Federal Court Monday morning. The trial will probably last ten days or more as a stubborn defense will be put up. Among the witnesses will be leading bankers of a dozen cities. Secretary Shaw is among the number, but will probably send a representative.

Mr. Carnegie came in at 7 o'clock this evening, his private car being attached to the train that brought the dead bodies of seven members of the engineers' battalion that was in the fatal wreck at Pittsburg last evening.

He was met at the train and will be entertained while in the city by Sylvester Everett, a financier who is an old-time friend of the ironmaster. To-night Mr. Carnegie had a conference with District Attorney Sullivan on the Chadwick case. He will probably have to stay in Cleveland until Wednesday, as it will take one or two days to secure a jury.

Nathan Loeser, trustee in bankruptcy for Cassie L. Chadwick, to-day filed in the United States District Court an inventory and appraisal of the real estate and personal property of Cassie L. Chadwick, located at the homestead, 1,824 Euclid Avenue. It covers everything from the mammoth pipe organ, which cost $8,000, and is valued in the appraisal at $2,000 down to the smallest article. The laces seized by Collector Leach are placed at $1,981. rs. Chadwick paid $5,000 for them. Two elaborate revolving urns of French cina are valued at $600. A dozen rare Coalport china plates are appraised at $300, and the silk rugs at $3,000.

Numerous paintings and pieces of china ware, for which Mrs. Chadwick is said to have paid fancy prices, are put in at much lower figures. The total valuation of personal property is $31,123. The real estate is appraised at $41,190.

The personal property will be sold the latter part of next week. The trustee will receive bids therefor in bulk, and if a satisfactory price may be obtained in that way, the court will order a sale. Otherwise the goods will be sold by auction.

### DIES ON ELEVATED TRAIN.

#### Hermann Hoffleit, Williamsburg Manufacturer, Drops in Arms of Passengers.

Herrmann Hoffleit, sixty-five years old, manufacturer of tortoise shell articles living at 210 Bradford Street, East New York, died suddenly last evening on an elevated train of the Broadway Ferry Division. He was on his way home from business at 431 Broadway, Williamsburg.

A son had started with him, but left at the loop station, as he had an appointment. The train had not reached the next station when passengers noticed that the old man was ill. Peter J. Kelleher of 49 Dresden Street, sitting next, caught Hoffleit as he was falling, and the conductor, George Gregory, came to his assistance, but Mr. Hoffleit gasped and died. The body was taken from the train at Van Sicklen Avenue.

Dr. Meister of the Bradford Street Hospital said death was due either to apoplexy or heart disease. One hundred and eight dollars and identifying papers were found in the pockets. Just as the body was being carried into his home, the son arrived. Mr. Hoffleit was born in Germany. He leaves a widow, two sons, and a daughter.

### TRY TO SINK THE CARLISLE?

#### Japanese in Sampans Said to Have Made Attempts at Manila.

that Japanese embarked in fishing sampans made four attempts to sink the

MANILA, March 4.—It is reported here British steamer Carlisle last night, but were repulsed by the customs guards on board the vessel, who fired upon the sampans.

The steamer Carlisle, now lying in Manila Harbor, was towed in there recently from San Miguel Bay, at the southern end of the Island of Luzon, where she was lying disabled.

She was under charter to the Russian Government to carry supplies from Vladivostok to Port Arthur, but lost her propeller, finally drifting to San Miguel Bay, where her Captain brought up while he went to Manila for assistance.

### JIU-JITSU KILLS ATHLETE.

#### Samuel Goodman Dies a Month After He Is Hurt in Bout.

*Special to The New York Times.*

PHILADELPHIA, March 4.—Samuel Goodman, Jr., one of the most prominent athletes in this city, died early this morning at his home in Chestnut Hill, as the result of injuries received in a friendly jiu jitsu bout more than a month ago.

With a friend, Mr. Goodman was practicing the Japanese method of self-defense in the First City Troop Armory, when he was thrown, injuring the muscles of his back and right side.

A few days afterward he was taken ill with pleuro-pneumonia. An operation was performed, but Mr. Goodman failed to recover.

### KANSAS INDORSES WARNER.

#### House Wants Missouri to Elect Him to Succeed Cockrell.

TOPEKA, Kan., March 4.—The House to-day adopted a concurrent resolution earnestly requesting the Republicans of the Missouri Legislature "to use all honorable means to elect Major William Warner United States Senator, to succeed Senator Cockrell." The resolutions say:

"We feel that he does not belong to Missouri alone, but to the Nation. His election would reflect honor upon the State of Missouri."



### PIPE, POWDER, EXPLOSION.

#### Store Destroyed, but Man Who Carried the Keg Is Alive.

OGDENSBURG, N. Y., March 4.—Thomas Hamilton's store at Brinston's Corners, on the Canadian side, was wrecked to-day by the explosion of a keg of gunpowder which Hamilton was carrying under his arm, a spark from his pipe falling into it.

He escaped with serious injuries, but the building was completely destroyed.

### PSYCHE'S BATH IMMORAL.

#### Richmond Exhibitor Sentenced to Pay Fine and Go to Jail.

*Special to The New York Times.*

RICHMOND, Va., March 4.—Police Justice Crutchfield to-day decided that Sir Frederick Leighton's picture, "Psyche's Bath," is immoral, and the proprietor of the Richmond Art Company was fined $25 and sentenced to a day in jail for exhibiting it and six other pictures in his store window in Broad Street.

An appeal was taken, and a jury will sit in judgment in the Hustings Court in what promises to be a novel trial.

### CHARCOT EXPEDITION SAFE?

#### French Explorer's Party Said to be at an Argentine Port.

BUENOS AYRES, March 4.—A telegram to The Standard says that the antarctic ship Le Francais, with the entire Charcot expedition, has arrived at Puerto Madrin, Argentina.

There is no official confirmation of the news.

PARIS, March 4.—The report from Buenos Ayres of the arrival of the Charcot antarctic expedition at Puerto Madrin, Argentina, was warmly welcomed, but the Government and the family are without confirmation of the announcement.

### HAD $5,000, DISAPPEARS.

#### Prospective Purchaser of White Plains Property Is Missing.

*Special to The New York Times.*

WHITE PLAINS, March 4.—Relatives of Charles Gamples of New York, who came to White Plains with $5,000 to buy property, are investigating his strange disappearance. Gamples came to White Plains on Feb. 22 and has not been seen since.

According to the description given to the police, the missing man is a German, about thirty-six years old, smooth shaven, and well dressed. He was about five feet seven inches tall.

### GOULDS BACK FROM MEXICO.

#### Are Now in St. Louis and Will Start for the East To-day.

*Special to The New York Times.*

ST. LOUIS, March 4.—The "Gould Special," consisting of four of the handsomest private cars in America, returned to Union Station to-day from Mexico, with Mr. and Mrs. George J. Gould, Benjamin Nicoll of New York, R. H. Russell, E. J. Jefferies, President of the Denver and Rio Grande system, and Mr. Jefferies's son, James C. Jefferies.

Mr. and Mrs. Gould and their guests will remain in St. Louis until to-morrow morning, when they will depart for the East.

Mr. Gould stated that the trip had been one of the most enjoyable ever taken by him, and had included hunting and fishing along the Gulf.

### BEEF INQUIRY GOES ON.

#### Garfield's Report Will Not Affect Grand Jury's Work.

CHICAGO, March 4.—Grand Jury investigation of the "beef trust" will go ahead regardless of the report made by Commissioner Garfield to President Roosevelt and transmitted to Congress.

When asked if it was not a peculiar condition when one department of the Government asserted the existence of a beef trust and another discredited it, Assistant District Attorney Morrison to-day said:

"It doesn't make any difference what the Department of Commerce and Labor does, we will go on and conduct our investigation as intended. Mr. Garfield's men were sent out to gather facts and figures, and not to look into the business methods of these concerns. They were not sent out to find violations of the Sherman act. The report has nothing to do with the Grand Jury investigation."

### EXPRESS KILLS A DEER.

#### The Animals Plentiful in Litchfield and Berkshire Hills.

*Special to The New York Times.*

WINSTED, Conn., March 4.—Deer are becoming so plentiful in the Litchfield and Berkshire Hills that hardly a day passes that one is not killed by a train, dogs, or some unscrupulous hunter.

A young deer, weighing 115 pounds, was struck by an express on the Berkshire Division of the New York, New Haven and Hartford Railroad at Cornwall Thursday and thrown down an embankment into a brook. The animal got up and ran, but fell dead after going a short distance.

E. R. Lorraine of Canaan, a contractor, counted thirteen in one herd this week, and driving parties are encountering the animals on the highways in the country districts.

The severe Winter and deep snow in the woods are believed to have driven the deer nearer civilization. There is a heavy penalty for killing a deer in this State.

WITH THIS ISSUE OF THE TIMES Is Given a New PORTRAIT OF PRESIDENT ROOSEVELT in four colors, in addition to the two Magazine Supplements and the new Pictorial Supplement.

## ROOSEVELT HERO OF BRILLIANT DAY

### Climax of His Career at Inauguration.

### IN HIGH SPIRITS ALL DAY

### "Great, It Touched Me to the Heart," He Says.

### CROWD JAMS THE CAPITAL

#### Greatest Parade in Washington's History the Feature of a Day of Pageants and Festivities.

*Special to The New York Times.*

WASHINGTON, March 4.—This was Theodore Roosevelt's day. The President has had other days of magnificent triumph during his strenuous and eventful life; but in his inauguration it seems as though he must have reached the climax of his remarkable career.

Ceremonies that have been superb in their solemnity and splendor, pageants that have never been equaled in Presidential inaugurations, and festivities planned with amazing prodigality have followed each other from early morning until midnight. In all of them the President has received homage that is little short of hero worship.

Throughout the day the spirit of the people has been to show their joy over the fact that they had elected Mr. Roosevelt to the great office in which fate first placed him. This they have done with a degree of acclammation such as was never before given to a candidate for the Presidency. The atmosphere has been fairly charged with this spirit of admiration and satisfaction.

#### The President De-light-ed.

The President himself has been just as much De-light-ed with the doings of the day as has the multitude. He has accepted the overwhelming evidences of approval showered upon him with the outward evidences of keen enjoyment that are characteristic of him and his exuberance has been contagious to all about him.

This inauguration attracted the greatest outside crowd to the Nation's seat of government that has ever been brought here. But with all the vastness of the crowd, there was not an accident of a serious character.

Picturesqueness and novelty were given to the inauguration ceremonies and the parade by the fact that they were participated in not only by the usual Federal and State dignitaries and troops and the foreign representatives, but by the representative and armed forces of the countries which Uncle Sam has acquired since the preceding President was inaugurated.

The weather conditions were almost perfect. "Roosevelt's luck," everybody said; but nobody envied him the luck. A warm sun tempered a breeze that was never cold enough to chill. Only once during the day—just before noon—did a shower threaten; but the cloud quickly passed.

#### Rapid Succession of Events.

With wonderful promptness the events of the day succeeded each other, so that the crowd never grew restless. Quick action was the rule all along the line. The inauguration speeches of both the President and the Vice President were brief.

The inauguration of Vice President Fairbanks in the Senate Chamber took place in the presence of a brilliant gathering of invited guests.

The scene then shifted to the east front of the Capitol, where a great crowd witnessed the inauguration of the President.

The President reviewed the inaugural procession from a stand on Pennsylvania Avenue, just in front of the White House, standing in the reviewing box from a few minutes before 3 until 6:15 o'clock. The parade included a wide range of types, all the way from a delegation of conquered Indian chiefs to half a hundred Harvard undergraduates. It was composed of about 35,000 men. The Governors of fifteen States rode by the stand at the head of their militia.

At midnight the inauguration ball in the enormous Pension Building was in full swing. President Roosevelt and the members of his family and immediate friends were there for two hours. He acted as though he longed to go down and mix with the throng and shake hands with everybody in the place. It surpassed all previous inauguration bals so far that comparisons scarcely can be made.

The President's jubilation was manifested during the parade by his unrestrained characteristic comments.

Soon after the parade began, the marching of the West Point cadets and the middies from the Naval Academy excited his admiration. "Those are the boys," he exclaimed, enthusiastically. "They're superb."

Presently the Porto Rican military contingent, marching in perfect order, came along. Turning to Senator Bacon of Georgia, the President remarked: "They look pretty well for an oppressed people, eh, Senator?" And then, aside, with a merry laugh: "I really shuddered slightly to-day as I swore to obey the Constitution!"

When the fine Filipino band, playing the President's favorite tune, "Garry Owen," passed at the head of the Filipino scouts, beautifully drilled and disciplined, the President again turned to Senator Bacon and remarked with a chuckle: "The wretched serfs disguise their feelings admirably," and he chuckled significantly.

"Two more battleships," again said the President, as the "jackies" from the war vessels in the harbor marched by. He applauded them enthusiastically, and, turning to his party, said: "Those are the men who will help to avert the danger of an international war. And, by the way, one of the new battleships is to be named South Carolina, in honor of Legare," referring to Representative Legare of Charleston, who worked for the appropriations for the navy requested by the Administration.

When the Seventh Cavalry of the army was passing the reviewing stand its band also playing "Garry Owen," President Roosevelt remarked enthusiastically, "That is a bully fighting tune, and this is Custer's old regiment, one of the finest in the service."

As the Ninth Cavalry went by, the President remarked: "These boys were with me at Saniago."

Senator Lodge during the review changed his seat to one just behind the President. Laughingly, the President turned to him and said, so that Senator Bacon might hear it: "You should have seen Bacon hide his face when the Filipinos came by. The 'slaves' were rejoicing in their shackles."

As a band heading the Delaware military contingent played "Dixie," the President said: "That is one of the best tunes in the lot." Again when one of the Pennsylvania bands played "There'll be a hot time in the old town to-night," he swung himself from side to side in time with the music and remarked, as he glanced down the long line of advancing Pennsylvanians: "Here is some of that half-million majority."

At the conclusion of the parade, as he left the reviewing stand, he said: "It was a great success. Great. And did you note that 'bunch' of cowboys. Oh, they are the boys who can ride. It all was superb. It really touched me to the heart."

It is going to be hard for the army of visitors to get out of town. Railroad time schedules have been smashed all to smithereens, and it will take a long time to straighten them out. This would not be so bad if it were not for the fact that the hotel and restaurant accommodations have been horribly overtaxed and prices for rooms and food are outrageously high.

### ROYAL RIDE TO CAPITOL.

#### Crowd Likes Military Pomp of the Procession.

*Special to The New York Times.*

WASHINGTON, March 4.—One prolonged demonstration greeted President Roosevelt to-day as he was driven under escort from the White House to the Capitol for the inaugural ceremonies, and then back to the White House again.

Both rides were impressive, the more so because of the elaborate escort which accompanied the President. At previous inaugurations only police and Secret Service men have accompanied the President on such trips, but to-day Squadron A of the New York National Guard, together with other commands, formed the escort.

Long before 10 o'clock, the hour set for the President to leave the White House, the crowds of spectators began to gather along the streets to the Capitol, while the various grand stands and windows rapidly filled. Yet the crowd that saw the President pass to the Capitol, and which greeted him enthusiastically along the line, was small compared to that which jammed the streets and the grand stands on his return to the White House in the afternoon, after he had been sworn in for the new term, and prior to his reviewing the big inaugural parade from the stand in front of the White House.

On the return Mr. Roosevelt, instead of merely raising his hat and bowing to the right and left, was compelled frequently to rise in his seat as he lifted his hat and bowed.

#### President's Hours Undisturbed.

None of the President's hours of arising and breakfasting were changed because of the day. He arose shortly before 7:30 o'clock, read the morning papers, and at 8:30 o'clock was at the breakfast table as usual, with his family. By 9 o'clock he was in the Executive offices with Secretary Loeb and Assistant Secretary Barnes, going over the papers and dispatches which had come in, most of them being telegrams of congratulation from friends in all parts of the country.

While he was being shaved Attorney General Moody, Secretary of the Navy Morton, and Jacob A. Riis chatted with him. Never before had the President appeared in better spirits, and as various telegrams were handed to him or read to him his animation increased. Shortly before 10 o'clock, bareheaded and unattended, the President crossed the roof of the west wing between the office building and the White House and entered through one of the long windows of the state dining room.

There he greeted the members of the Presidential party, including Senators Spooner, Lodge, and Bacon of the State Inaugural Committee; Representatives Dalzell, Williams, and Crumpacker of the House Committee; Brig. Gen. John M. Wilson, the Chairman of the Inaugural Committee of Citizens; Col. Bromwell, Col. McKensie, and Major McCawley; the members of the Cabinet and their wives, Secretary Loeb and Assistant Secretary Barnes, Mr. and Mrs. Douglas Robinson of New York, Miss Robinson, and others of his relatives, and the personal friends who had been invited.

#### Only Two Minutes Late.

Less than two minutes after 10 o'clock, the hour set for the ride to the Capitol, Mr. Roosevelt walked out of the north door of the Executive Mansion and saluted his aides, who were standing on the portico. The military aides stood at attention with their heads bared, while the President raised his hat and bowed gravely.

The President entered the landau which was waiting, and Senators Spooner and Lodge and Representative Dalzell of the Inaugural Committee followed, Mr. Roosevelt taking the right side of the back seat, facing forward. The four horses drawing the landau started off carefully toward the northwest gate, while all those who had cards of admission to the White House grounds started to cheer and applaud.

The others of the party took their places quickly in the other carriages, Vice President Fairbanks, Senator Bacon, and Representatives Williams and Crumpacker taking the second. In the other carriages were the aides, and the Cabinet members. Secretaries Hay, Shaw, Taft, and Attorney General Moody were in the third carriage; Secretaries Hitchcock, Morton, Wilson, and Postmaster General Wynne in the fourth, with Secretary Metcalf, Mr. Loeb, Col. Bromwell, and Commander Winslow in the last.

#### Squadron A Looks Well.

Squadron A, spick and span in their brilliant uniforms, was lined up in Pennsylvania Avenue, facing the northwest gate, ready to act as escort of honor on the trip to the Capitol just as the command had acted as escort of honor at Albany six years ago when Mr. Roosevelt was inaugurated Governor of New York.

With Squadron A were the Rough Riders and the Grand Army of the Republic uniformed command known as the "Old Guard." Both sides of the avenue were lined with people, and there were mighty cheers when the President's carriage rolled out of the gate and the bugles sounded for Squadron A to take its place.

In his accustomed place right behind the President's carriage was Sergt. McDermott of the regular ramy, the special orderly to the President. McDermott is the crack revolver shot of the army and also is one of the best horsemen in the service. At his hip hung his Colt six-shooter.

Secret Service men to the number of fourteen, together with city detectives detailed for the service, also lined themselves at either side of the carriage. The thirty Rough Riders, commanded by Col. Brodie, lined up around the carriage also protecting the President, so that it would have been practically impossible for any one to have reached his side.

#### Police at Head of Column.

The procession then moved forward, with Major Sylvester, the head of the Washington police, at the head of the column with his platoon of eighteen mounted policemen. The escort to the Presidential party had formed in Fifteenth Street and in Pennsylvania Avenue, between Fifteenth and Seventeenth Streets. As the procession moved Lieut. Gen. Chaffee, the Grand Marshal of the parade, with his staff, took place behind the police and the Artillery Corps Band.

Gen. Chaffee's staff consisted of military officials and of civilians representing the various organizations which participated in the big parade of the afternoon. Following the staff came the carriages bearing the President and his party, and then came Squadron A, headed by its own mounted band, which won frequent applause along the line of march. The Washington National Guard Band furnished music for the Grand Army of the Republic and Spanish War Veterans in the line. The Squadron A men and the detachment of Rough Riders were cheered repeatedly. Following the squadron came Gen. O. O. Howard and his staff, then the National Guard Band of the Department of the Potomac and the veterans' organizations.

#### Waves Hand to Mrs. Roosevelt.

Mr. and Mrs. Douglas Robinson, the latter a sister of the President, together with other ladies of the White House party, ran across the White House grounds after the President's carriage had departed, and went into the reviewing stand on Pennsylvania Avenue, where, in the afternoon, the President reviewed the general parade. As the President's carriage passed the stand Mr. Roosevelt bowed and raised his hat to his friends and waved his hand to Mrs. Roosevelt, Miss Roosevelt and others who stood out on the east wing of the White House and watched the procession move.

Later the Roosevelt party entered other carriages and proceeded to the Capitol to witness the inauguration ceremonies. Noisy greetings of the waiting crowd began as soon as the President's carriage was sighted at each succeeding block, and cheering was general also for Mr. Fairbanks. The sky was sunny and the air was warm, with not any more breeze than enough to half straighten out the flags of the city when the start for the Capitol was made, but before the President's carriage had reached the end of his ride the sky had become overcast, and typical March weather was threatened. By the time the return trip was started, however, regular Roosevelt weather again was on tap, and continued for the remainder of the day.

#### Presidential Horse Tumbles.

Once during the drive down Pennsylvania Avenue, when the procession halted for a moment at the corner of Fourteenth Street, the left lead horse drawing the President's carriage slipped and fell. Charles Reeder, the negro footman, leaped to the animal's side, and it regained its feet quickly.

A few minutes later, as the procession was passing through B Street, Northeast, Senator Lodge, who was in the President's carriage, called attention to a particularly persistent photographer, who had been following alongside for many blocks. President Roosevelt showed evidence of displeasure, and with repeated waving of his arm indicated his wish that the offender be removed. A Rough Rider and a policeman backed the photographer through the ropes.

When the President had entered the Capitol the mounted troops drew off to the driveways facing the inaugural stand, the Rough Riders falling in with the New York cavalrymen. The Rough Riders in fact had a rough riding time of it all the way from the White House to the Capitol. The quiet, peaceful artillery horses

"All the News That's Fit to Print."

# The New York Times.

THE WEATHER.
Snow to-day, cold wave to-night; fair, cold to-morrow; wind west.

VOL. LVII...NO. 18,267. * * * NEW YORK, WEDNESDAY, JANUARY 29, 1908—FOURTEEN PAGES. ONE CENT In Greater New York, Jersey City and Newark. { Elsewhere, TWO CENTS.

## BRYAN PLANS TO BE ROOSEVELT'S HEIR

### Tells Democratic Senators He Would Be Accepted as Such by the People.

### TO PUSH ROOSEVELT IDEAS

### Congress Minority Instructed to Show That the Republicans Are Not in Sympathy with Him.

*Special to The New York Times.*

WASHINGTON, Jan. 28.—William Jennings Bryan is convinced that he is the proper legatee of the Roosevelt Administration, the most efficient executor of the Roosevelt policies, and the one most acceptable to the voters of the country, and that, in effect, is what he told the Democratic Senators who dined with Senator Newlands in his honor last night. Mr. Bryan did not put it in that blunt fashion. He coated his pill with sugared words, but he let them know that he was the man they were after and they didn't need to seek further.

Then he proceeded to tell the Senators how the Democrats ought to work in Congress to make more certain and easy his election by bringing forward measures in accordance with the recommendations of President Roosevelt in his messages. The strategy of this is to put the Republicans in a bad hole, either by forcing them to kill Roosevelt legislation or to adopt it on Democratic initiative.

Mr. Bryan has handled his campaign on this visit to Washington with consummate skill. He has taken a leaf out of the Roosevelt book and has become master, with a big stick. He has greeted every one of the men who secretly cherished the intention of telling him that he ought to be the Warwick and not the candidate of the Democracy with very much the same sort of cheerful glare that John L. Sullivan used to employ on his antagonists in the ring. As a result that secretly cherished intention has remained secret.

Mr. Bryan carried off the Newlands dinner last night on just that plan. When the cigars were reached and the guests moved out to the smoking-room, Mr. Bryan took charge of the conversation, and thereafter the Senators listened dutifully to what he had to say.

He began by telling them he had heard of but one candidate for the Presidency who had been defeated three times; that there might have been a man defeated four times, but he was absolutely certain no man had ever been defeated on his fifth campaign. Then, apropos, perhaps, of something he felt in the atmosphere, he told the story of a cow puncher in Texas who went unbidden to a ranch dance. The floor manager took him by the arm and somewhat abruptly conducted him outside. In a short time the cow puncher tried again. Then the manager tackled him with violence and threw him out. As he picked himself up the cow puncher turned to some loungers and said:

"Those fellows can't fool me. I know what they mean. They don't want me."

After that the Senators listened with a solemn hush while Mr. Bryan lectured them on what they ought to do. He told them that the so-called "Roosevelt policies," which are, in fact, the "Bryan policies," were without doubt the most popular ones likely to come before the country in the approaching campaign. The contest would be fought out on those policies as the main issue. Then with delicacy of phraseology he confided to the Senators his belief that, as between the Democrats represented by Bryan and the Republicans represented by Taft, the country would surely select the Democrats to continue the enforcement of those policies. "There is no question where Bryan stands," the country would tell itself, for these policies were really his, and Roosevelt had but been masquerading in his clothing. As to Taft, there would be a question, and the decision would be against the President's nominee.

That assurance given Mr. Bryan turned to what his close friends have said all along was his real business here on this trip, the direction of a campaign in Congress. He called their attention to several recommendations for legislation made by the President to which the Republicans have made no response. For instance, there is an income tax. Also measures for closer Federal control of corporations in inter-State commerce; a Federal franchise, a scheme for securing the physical valuation of railroad properties, and measures to prevent overcapitalization.

All these things, he said, should be brought forward in the Senate and House by Democrats at once. By such tactics the Republicans would be forced into the open, and either be compelled to defeat the Roosevelt recommendations or accept them at the hands of the Democrats. Carried to its logical conclusion the programme would require the Denver Convention to indorse the Roosevelt policies and arraign the Republican Party for not carrying them out more fully.

The Senators sat dutifully through it all, and there was no "back talk." To-day there has been some muttering of protest, but it has all been sub rosa.

Mr. Bryan went up to the Capitol again this afternoon, and held a reception in Champ Clark's headquarters in the Ways and Means Committee room in the House. The flood of assistant Republican bills is expected to begin to appear in a short time.

An interesting contribution to the literature of the situation came to-night to the local Bryan headquarters in the shape of a poll of the House Democrats, which, it asserts, was made by four responsible Washington correspondents, "no one of whom had any sort of political bias." It shows the delegations by States, and gives Bryan 107, Johnson 16, and Gray 7, with 19 non-committal, 10 absent, and only 2 anti-Bryan. It tabulated 7 as scattering, 4 being for Culberson, and 1 each for Justice White, Judson Harmon, and Hoke Smith. The poll recently taken by The Washington Post, which this poll denounces as a "hostile newspaper," gave Bryan 98 and Johnson 31. But that poll was completed before Bryan came to town.

## DIED TO SAVE HIS SON.

### Machinist Shoved the Boy from Before a Train, but Lost His Own Life.

In an effort to save his eleven-year-old son from under the wheels of a Staten Island Rapid Transit train at the station at Great Kills yesterday, John Gladys, 37 years old, of Anandale, a machinist employed in the White Dental Works at Prince's Bay, was so badly injured that he died before he could be taken to the hospital.

Gladys and his son Harry were on their way home, but as no train was in sight they went into a waiting room close by. The boy was watching for the train, and when he saw it coming he shouted to his father to "come on" and ran toward the station. It was necessary to cross the tracks to get to the station, and the boy ran too close to the engine. The father, seeing the peril of the boy, ran after him, and just had time to shove him out of danger when he himself slipped on the snow and ice and fell directly in front of the oncoming train.

## SUBMARINES FOR PACIFIC.

### Two to be Sent from Here on Colliers to Join the Fleet.

WASHINGTON, Jan. 28.—The Navy Department is about to undertake a set of experiments to demonstrate the utility of the submarine as an adjunct in naval warfare. The longest endurance test yet made, covering a little over 100 miles, has developed the difficulty of sending these boats unaided any considerable distance from their base.

Yet in time of war the presence of a submarine might mean the successful defense of a harbor from a hostile fleet. So the naval strategists have exerted themselves to find a solution of the problem of how to give these boats the mobility desired for naval purposes.

While the Russo-Japanese war was being waged the Russian Government actually succeeded in taking submarines more than half way around the world to Vladivostok, but in that case the boats were cut into sections and reassembled upon reaching their destination. The Navy Department now desires to demonstrate the possibility of conveying these boats long distances without "knocking down" in any way.

The first step in the experiment will consist in the transportation to the Pacific of two of the smaller type of submarines, and if that is successful the effort will be made to handle the larger boats in the same way. The Shark and the Porpoise, because they are small, have been selected for the test. They are now at the New York Navy Yard, and the fact that the Equipment Bureau is soon to dispatch some colliers to the Pacific with coal for the naval vessels now on that station and for the battleship fleet has decided the naval officials to avail of this opportunity to make this test. The little boats will be picked up by one of the big floating cranes at the New York Navy Yard and deposited on the decks of two of the big colliers and thoroughly secured against the possibility of being torn away by the waves. An alternative plan contemplates the removal of some of the deck beams of the colliers, which would admit of slipping the submarines directly into the hold.

The naval constructors are studying the transportation problem thus presented, and if it is worked out successfully in this case the experiment may be extended to larger boats.

## ESCORTED EVANS'S FLEET.

### Argentine Squadron Showed Honors at Sea—Chileans at Punta Arenas.

BUENOS AYRES, Argentina, Jan. 28.—Rear Admiral Betbeder, the Minister of Marine, this afternoon received the following radiogram from Admiral Hipolita Oliva, who is in command of the Argentine squadron ordered to meet the American battleships and escort them down the coast:

At 7 o'clock on the morning of Jan. 26 we had the first radiographic communication with the battleship Connecticut, flagship of Rear Admiral Evans, which we joined at 9:30 o'clock at night. The Argentine vessels escorted the American squadron until 8:30 o'clock on Jan. 27, when flag salutes were exchanged with full ceremonial. Having effected the salute we made two runs around the squadron at a speed of fourteen knots, and then left the American vessels about 125 miles from Mar del Plata.

Rear Admiral Evans asked me to transmit his thanks to the Argentine Government for having sent the naval division to meet the American squadron, and begged me to have transmitted to the Government at Washington the radiogram sent separately.

The officers of the American torpedoboat flotilla who arrived here Sunday from Rio Janeiro were received to-day by President Alcorta and the Ministers of War, Marine, and Foreign Affairs, Gen. Fraga, Admiral Betbeder, and Señor Zeballos, respectively. President Alcorta spoke pleasantly to each one of the officers, and to Lieut. Cone, who is in command of the flotilla, he expressed his great pleasure and satisfaction in the visit to the Argentine of the American warships. To these words of welcome Lieut. Cone made a suitable reply.

PUNTA ARENAS, Chile, Jan. 28.—The Chilean cruiser Chacabuco, with the United States Minister, Mr. Hicks, and a number of Chilean officials on board, arrived here last evening. The cruiser comes to welcome the American fleet of battleships to Chilean waters.

Various entertainments have been arranged to make the time pass enjoyably while waiting the arrival of the battleships, which are expected here on Friday.

## HOLD POLICEMAN AS A THIEF.

### Patrolman Dawkins Arrested on Old Charge—Burglar Implicates Him.

On the strength of a story told by an accused thief, who alleged that the policeman had aided him in committing a burglary, Patrolman George Dawkins of the Adams Street Station, Brooklyn, was arrested yesterday by Capt. Max Steinbruck.

Dawkins was arrested last March on the accusation of John Farley of 98 Orange Street, who asserted that he had been held up and robbed on Myrtle Avenue by a stranger who was assisted by Policeman Dawkins, who was in uniform and on post. The complaint against Dawkins was dismissed because of lack of evidence.

Early Monday morning Patrolman Wendeberg of the Adams Street Station arrested two young men for robbing a hardware store at Myrtle Avenue and Duffield Street. The store was on Dawkins' post. One of the prisoners, Scott Ryan, told Capt. Steinbruck that Dawkins had "put him up" to robbing the store. Ryan further astonished the Captain by asserting that he had robbed a man outside a saloon in Myrtle Avenue last March at the suggestion of Dawkins. This, it is supposed, was the robbery complained of by John Farley.

Capt. Steinbruck laid the case before Inspector Flood, and the two discussed the matter with Assistant District Attorney Elder. It was then decided to arrest Dawkins again on the old charge.

Dawkins vigorously denied the stories told by Ryan.

## BANKER FISK'S GARAGE BURNS

### Chauffeur and Butler Hurt by Gasoline Explosion at Milton Point.

*Special to The New York Times.*

RYE, N. Y., Jan. 28.—Fire this afternoon destroyed the large garage of Pliny Fisk, the New York banker, who recently built a $1,000,000 mansion on Milton Point on the Sound. The fire was caused by an explosion while chauffeur, Martin Muller, and the butler, William Arnold, were repairing a large touring machine.

They were working on the car when suddenly a gasoline tank exploded and both men were thrown some distance. The efforts of the Rye and Milton Point Fire Departments failed to check the flames. The chauffeur was badly burned, but despite his injuries endeavored to drag the machine from the burning structure. The butler escaped serious injury by jumping through a window.

The machine and several carriages were destroyed. The loss is $10,000.

### Latest Shipping News.

Arrived—SS Prinz August Wilhelm, Kingston, Jan. 23.



## CARS LEAVE PARIS FOR NEW YORK RACE

### Three French Machines and One Italian Begin Trip Around the World.

### OVATION GREETS DRIVERS

### Throng Blocks Boulevard as Heavily Accoutred Autos Start for Havre —Spent Night at Rouen.

*Special Cable to THE NEW YORK TIMES.*

PARIS, Jan. 28.—With flags flying, amid the cheers of a dense throng that blocked all traffic on the boulevard in front of the offices of Le Matin, four of the contestants in the New York to Paris auto race left this city this morning on their way to New York to start in the historic contest. There were three French machines and one Italian, each carrying its full heavy equipment which it will take through the United States and Alaska. Each was draped with French, American, Italian, and Russian flags, and made a gallant show.

The four cars which started were:

The forty-horse-power De Dion, France; driven by G. B. St. Chaffray.

The forty-horse-power Moto-Bloc, France; driven by M. Godard.

The thirty-horse-power Brixia-Zust, Italy; driven by Antonio Scafoglio.

The twelve-horse-power Sizaire et Naudin, France; driven by M. Pons.

The four competitors were followed by a large escort of automobiles and made a circuit of the principal boulevards of the city before passing out through the Porte Maillot on the road to Rouen. Crowds gathered everywhere along the route and cheered the brave drivers heartily.

At Rouen the men were met by a delegation of automobile enthusiasts and escorted into the city, where they were entertained at a banquet and toasted by the city officials. The houses were decorated and the streets crowded as on a holiday, and there was everywhere evinced the liveliest interest in the contest. A public reception was attended by them in the evening.

A dispatch to Le Matin from Rouen announces that they will leave early to-morrow morning for Havre and will embark on La Lorraine on Saturday morning.

Of the four men in comand of the various cars, St. Chaffray is the proposer of the race and has been its organizer in Paris. Godard was a competitor in the Peking to Paris race, driving one of the De Dion cars, which finished two weeks behind the victorious Itala car. Scafoglio is an Italian journalist, while Pons was also a competitor in the Peking to Paris race, but failed to finish. He has been represented in most of the international motor races on the European Continent, and is widely known as a skillful driver. His little voiturette attracted more attention than any of the other cars.

## DULL WITH JACK LONDON.

### Old Crew Disappointed, Quits Because There's No Excitement.

Jack London, who has been making a tour of the world in his boat, the Snark, for the Woman's Home Companion, has notified that magazine that he will have to ship a new crew when he returns from his visit to San Francisco, where he now is, to Papeiti Island of Tahiti, where his boat is undergoing repairs.

According to Mr. London, Capt. Warein and Martin Johnson, his engineer, as well as a sailor and his two Japanese servants have been bitterly disappointed at their failure to meet with the adventures which they were sure must result from a trip with Jack London.

The dull routine life on shipboard has palled on the mariners, but Mr. London expects to have no difficulty in shipping a less adventure-desirous crew for the remainder of his world tour.

## PHYSICIAN DIES OF OPIUM.

### Dr. Sizer Found Unconscious in His Brooklyn Home from an Overdose.

It was learned last night that opium poisoning caused the death of Dr. Nelson Buell Sizer on Monday night at his home, 536 Greene Avenue, Brooklyn. Whether or not the poison was taken with suicidal intent is not known. Two weeks ago Dr. Sizer's brother died in the same house.

Dr. William A. Little of 923 Bedford Avenue says that he found Dr. Sizer in a comatose condition and evidently suffering from opium poisoning. Dr. Thoms, who was also called in, and Dr. Little express the highest regard for the dead physician, who was their personal friend. Dr. Thoms is a Chinese physician, who studied with Dr. Sizer in Long Island College Hospital.

## GATES SWEARS OFF TAXES.

### John W.'s $250,000 Assessment Reduced to $1,000—Texas His Home.

John W. Gates swore off his personal taxes yesterday. His name was down on the tentative non-resident books as owning personal property to the value of $250,000, and he appeared at the Tax Department yesterday and swore off all but $1,000 worth. He gave his residence as Texas, although he is credited with having a sixty-thousand-dollar apartment at the Hotel Plaza.

President Lawson Purdy of the Department of Taxes made public some figures yesterday of the number of corporations assessed in all the boroughs for the last ten years. It shows that 19,058 corporations have been assessed this year, against 18,018 last year and 8,760 in 1899. Manhattan has 16,630 assessed corporations for 1908, against 15,787 for 1907.



## OUIDA AN AMERICAN.

### Widow of Southern Officer Claims Dead Novelist as Sister-in-Law.

*Special Cable to THE NEW YORK TIMES.*

LONDON, Jan. 28.—A dispatch from Florence, Italy, says that an American woman, widow of Col. George Roy Gliddoth, who fought in the Confederate Army and died twenty years ago, told a remarkable story of the parentage of the novelist Ouida, after her funeral yesterday.

According to Mrs. Gliddoth, Louisa de la Ramée, which was the novelist's supposed real name, was none other than Col. Gliddoth's sister. This sister left her home in America at a tender age under the care of a woman who adopted her as a daughter.

Mrs. Gliddoth explained that she came from America for the purpose of aiding Ouida after writing several letters which the novelist disdained to answer. Her husband, she said, never spoke of Ouida without weeping. A photograph of him, which she showed, bore a striking resemblance, in the high forehead, penetrating glance, and other family characteristics, to Ouida.

Mrs. Gliddoth casually remarked that Ouida's father had made and lost two fortunes, disclosing the same financial weakness in the father and the daughter.

Mrs. Gliddoth's story recalls the fact that there had always been more or less mystery concerning Ouida's parentage. Some say that both her father and mother were French, and that she was born in France. Others say that her father was French, while her mother was an English lady, a native of Bury St. Edmund's, where Ouida is said to have been born in 1830. Ouida always refused to talk about her relatives, as indeed she did about any private affairs.

## PROF. GILLET IS DEAD.

### Normal College, in Which He Was Senior Professor, Left Without a Head.

Prof. Joseph A. Gillet, senior professor of the Normal College, who for more than a year has been acting head of that institution, died yesterday afternoon in the Hahnemann Hospital after an operation for appendicitis.

Prof. Gillet was 70 years old. He had been connected with the Normal College for its entire history, a span of forty years. His death, so soon after the retirement of President Hunter, leaves the college practically without a head and with the executive committee in charge of the selection of a new President uncertain as to its choice.

When President Hunter retired last May Prof. Gillet was himself contemplating laying aside active work. After much urging he decided to meet new duties as head of the college until a President was agreed upon. He remained at his post until about ten days ago, when he suffered an attack of appendicitis and was removed to Hahnemann Hospital for an operation. It was believed for a time that he would recover, but his age was too severe a handicap.

Prof. Gillet was an ante-bellum graduate of Harvard. He was a native of Massachusetts, and his body will be taken to that State for burial. He leaves a widow and two children, Louis Bliss Gillet and Mrs. James G. MacLean. Funeral arrangements will be announced later.

The Normal College is the women's college of the city's educational department, corresponding to the City College for youths. A proposal was made some time ago that the two institutions be amalgamated, and a commission was appointed by the Mayor to consider this suggestion. The commission, however, found the plan impracticable. Some of the delay in finding a new head to relieve Prof. Gillet of his onerous duties as acting President has been attributed to the appointment of this commission.

## TRIES TO CUT OFF HIS HAND.

### Port Chester Man Follows Biblical Admonition—Had Hit His Father.

*Special to The New York Times.*

PORT CHESTER, N. Y., Jan. 28.—Following the Biblical admonition, "If thy right hand offend thee, cut it off," Rainsford Ferris, a well-known resident of Port Chester, went into his cellar to-day and nearly severed his right hand at the wrist by laying it on a block and striking it with a hatchet. He is now in the hospital, and upon his recovery will be committed to the Poughkeepsie Insane Asylum.

Several years ago, Ferris had an altercation with his father and struck him with his fist. He was afterward seized with remorse, and began brooding and reading the Bible. Several times he has attempted to do bodily harm to himself, but has been restrained by his family. Physicians who have examined him say that he is suffering from insanity caused by religious mania.

## SAYS ENGINE WAS DEFECTIVE.

### Jury Holds Erie Responsible for Engineer's and Fireman's Death.

*Special to The New York Times.*

RUTHERFORD, N. J., Jan. 28.—The inquest held by Coroner Collins at Rutherford to-day on the death of John Waidler, an engineer, and his fireman, Otto Wagner, who were killed near Rutherford two weeks ago by the explosion of an Erie locomotive boiler, was attended by two expert mechanics. The Erie expert said that the fireman allowed the water to run low in the boiler, and so caused the explosion.

The Coroner's expert said the weak and defective condition of the boiler led to the explosion, and the jury returned a verdict saying that the two lives were sacrificed because of defective machinery.

## NEW WAR ON CIGARETTES.

### Another Aldermanic Ordinance to Stop Their Sale to Minors.

Another cigarette ordinance turned up at the meeting of the Aldermen yesterday. This one was introduced by Alderman Velton and was entitled "an ordinance to prevent the sale of cigarettes or tobacco to minors under the age of eighteen."

The penalty is fixed at from $10 to $25 fine, ten days' imprisonment, or both. The resolution was referred to the Committee on Laws and Legislation.



## CLYDE LINER SINKS TUG LUCKENBACH

### She Goes Down Off the Battery and One of Her Thirteen Men Is Lost.

### CAPTAIN BLAMES LINER

### Says She Did Not Follow Signals—Tugboat Goes to the Bottom in Three Minutes.

The oceangoing tugboat Edgar F. Luckenbach collided with the Clyde Line freighter Pawnee at 7:30 o'clock last night midway between the Battery and Governors Island, and in just three minutes the tugboat went to the bottom. The Pawnee got her bows jammed, but was able to continue on her trip to Philadelphia.

There were thirteen men on board the tugboat. They were all rescued from the water except Edward Nielson, a deckhand, who was reported missing. Omnah King, a Japanese oiler, was hauled out unconscious, but it was said at the Hudson Street Hospital, to which he was taken, that he had responded to treatment well and would recover in a day or two.

Some of the tug's crew said that the Pawnee had been stove in, but the police thought they were wrong.

The Luckenbach was of 227 tons, and had two masts. She was to leave the Atlantic Docks at midnight with two barges for Norfolk. She had been all day at Point Liberty, Communipaw, coaling for the trip. The Captain, Peter Nielson, and most of the crew were new to the tug.

Late in the afternoon she left her coaling point. About 6 o'clock the thirteen men ate their supper, and half of the crew stretched out in their bunks below deck to rest. With Capt. Nielson in the pilot house was Jack Farrell, the retiring mate.

The Pawnee had left Pier 29, East River, bound for Philadelphia. Just about midway between the Battery and Governors Island Capt. Nielson saw the Pawnee coming. He said that he gave the signal indicating that he was going straight on his course, and that then the Pawnee did exactly the opposite of what he had been led to expect from his understanding of her signal in reply.

The big freighter ran across the tug, cutting a huge hole about ten feet back from the bow. At the time the tug was going at slow speed, while the Pawnee was spinning along as fast as she could at that point in the channel.

The water began to pour into the tug through the hole that reached far below the water line. Capt. Nielson had given the signal to stop, following it with one to put on full speed astern.

C. F. Frye, the Chief Engineer, said afterward that he stuck to his post till the water was above his waist.

"It all happened quickly," he said. "Three minutes after the Pawnee struck us the tug was resting on the bottom, and she didn't go down so fast at that.

"Two other men and myself stuck to the Luckenbach. When I felt her going down I jumped on to the pilot house. I felt her sinking lower and jumped on to the smokestack, which was then cool as you please. The others were holding to the main mast.

"I saw the Pawnee stop. A boat was sent out to gather up the ten men in the water, but they didn't get us hanging on to the tug. We saw Tug No. 9 of the Pennsylvania Railroad coming by with two barges, and hailed her. She dropped her barges, and rescued us.

"But that was fifteen minutes later. We had been hanging on and a-shivering. The harbor lights looked like devil's eyes to us. Then came the Police Patrol boat, Sergt. Halleck commanding, and took us all off the tug and the others off the Pawnee, which went on her way. We can't find Edward Nielson, but all the rest of us are safe."

H. McNamara, the new mate, who was one of those taken on board the Pawnee, said that two or three life preservers were thrown out from the stern of the freighter, but no one got to them. He and his companions in the water swam around until boats from the Pawnee picked them up.

McNamara could not remember whether the missing Edward Nielson was swimming around in the water or whether he had stuck by the tug as she sank. He may have been one of the six or seven who were lying in their bunks smoking when the crash came, and did not get out before the water caught him.

The shivering crew got plenty of liquor on board the Pawnee and Tug No. 9. They got still more on board the Police Patrol, and then at the Harbor Squad Station, Pier A, they got more. The Patrol took them on board about 9 o'clock. At 10 o'clock they all declared they felt fine—and looked it.

## HOLDS HUSBAND FOR PERJURY

### Court Dissatisfied with Rober's Statements as to His Income in Wife's Suit.

In the separation suit of Mrs. Lilly Rober against her husband, Edward N. Rober, a real estate broker of 4,505 Third Avenue, which was heard yesterday before Justice Marean in the Supreme Court, Brooklyn, the Justice decided to hold the defendant in $1,000 bail for the Grand Jury on a charge of perjury.

Rober's bookkeeper, who had been called by Daniel F. Kiely, counsel for the plaintiff, testified that his employer had made $26,785 between 1903 and 1906 from his realty ventures alone. Rober denied this, asserting that his income never exceeded $2,500 a year. The discrepancy in the figures was so great that Justice Marean became angry.

"Either you or your bookkeeper is committing perjury, and one of you ought to be in jail," he declared.

Rober stuck to his statement, and Justice Marean decided to hold him for the Grand Jury.

The Robers have been married since Dec. 24, 1903, and have one child, Lilly, who is 2 years old. The plaintiff alleges that her husband treated her brutally and compelled her to live at his mother's home, which she said was unpleasant to her because of the character of some of the inmates. Justice Marean granted her a separation and ordered the defendant to pay her $25 a week alimony.



## LAHM LANDS IN BALLOON.

### Started from Canton, Ohio, and Alights Near Oil City, Penn.

CANTON, Ohio, Jan. 28.—A telephone message from Oil City, Penn., says the balloon Ohio with Lieut. Lahm and party landed near that city about midnight.

*Special to The New York Times.*

CANTON, Ohio, Jan. 28.—The balloon with Lieut. Lahm, U. S. A., as pilot, and two civilian passengers, merchants of Canton, ascended to-day, under the auspices of the Aero Club of Ohio.

NEW CASTLE, Penn., Jan. 28.—The balloon Ohio, in charge of Lieut. Frank P. Lahm, U. S. A., was seen at New Bedford, a small village without railroad connections, fifteen miles northwest of here, at 4:15 this afternoon. The balloon was traveling very fast in a northeasterly direction. It was estimated to be 3,000 feet in the air. Rain was falling at the time, but now it is snowing.

## DR. OSLER SENT CHLOROFORM

### Twins of Sixty Invited Him to Their Birthday Party.

*Special to The New York Times.*

ALBION, Mich., Jan. 28.—Delos Fall, senior professor in Albion College and delegate to the Constitutional Convention, and his twin brother, Dewitt Fall of Jackson, will celebrate their sixtieth birthday to-morrow, with a joint house party here.

They invited Dr. William Osler to be a guest. Dr. Osler evidently took the invitation as a joke, for he sent not only his regrets, but a bottle of chloroform to each of the brothers.

## PELL COUNTRY HOME BURNED

### Owner and Guest Escaped, but Dog That Gave the Alarm Perished.

*Special to The New York Times.*

PITTSFIELD, Mass., Jan. 28.—The country residence of John L. E. Pell of New York, at Great Barrington, was burned this morning. Mr. Pell was aroused by a pet dog, and he and his guest, Robert Clark of New York, barely escaped with their lives. The dog that gave the alarm was burned to death. The loss on the house and contents is $20,000.

Mrs. Pell, who was a daughter of the late William E. Tefft of New York, was in New York.

## PUBLIC MEN IRRELIGIOUS.

### Cardinal Gibbons Deplores Lack of Biblical Quotations in Speeches.

*Special to The New York Times.*

BOSTON, Jan. 28.—Cardinal Gibbons, who was here to-day, when asked if he believed the people of America were growing better or worse, from a religious standpoint, said:

"The people of America are showing less respect for religion than fifty or sixty years ago. For instance, the statesmen of America of those days showed in their public addresses a familiarity with and regard for the Holy Scriptures and the word of God which I am sorry does not present itself to-day.

"Webster used frequently to dovetail into his public speeches quotations from Scripture, showing his respect for the word of God. This practice is neglected by the speakers of to-day."

## NIGHT FERRIES CUT OFF.

### Subway Reduces Traffic and River Lines Retrench.

Because of the falling off of traffic on the boats caused by the opening of the new East River tunnel, the Union Ferry Company has decided to cut down the night service on the Wall Street, Fulton Street, Catharine Street, and Hamilton Ferries, beginning on Friday night.

On the Wall Street line boats will be run only from 7 o'clock A. M. to 7 o'clock P. M. There will be no service on the Fulton Ferry between 9:50 P. M. and 5 A. M. No boats will be run on the Catharine Street line between 9 P. M. and 5 A. M., and none on the Hamilton Ferry between 10:15 P. M. and 5 A. M.

## CHICAGO HAS $1,000,000 FIRE.

### Third Big Blaze in the Business District in Three Days.

CHICAGO, Jan. 28.—The third disastrous fire in the business district of the city in as many days caused a loss to-night estimated at more than $1,000,000 in the almost complete destruction of the building at 144 Wabash Avenue, occupied by Alfred Peats & Co., dealers in wall paper; the building adjoining it, occupied by John A. Colby & Sons, furniture dealers, and that in the rear, fronting on Michigan Avenue, occupied by the millinery firm of Edson, Keith & Co. Gage Brothers & Co. and Theodore Ascher & Co., millinery firms, were damaged by fire and water.

The fire started in the engine room of the Peats Building and raged for three hours. Street car lines throughout the downtown district and the elevated lines were tied up.

## FLEE FROM FIRE TO THE HILLS

### Four Burning Oil Tanks Drive Out Port Harford, Cal., Residents.

SAN LUIS OBISPO, Cal., Jan. 28.—Fire, which started late yesterday afternoon in an oil tank of the Union Oil Company at Port Harford by a stroke of lightning, burned all of last night and until late this afternoon, consuming the tank which was first set on fire and three others belonging to the Standard Oil Company. No other damage was done, although it was thought at one time that nothing could save the Marie Hotel and the Port Harford wharf.

All of the contents of the hotel and the cottages were removed to the decks of steamers or to surrounding hills and the inhabitants fled to the hills, scantily clad, in a heavy snowstorm.

Débris from one of the tanks which exploded this afternoon was blown more than a mile away. Thirty-seven thousand barrels of oil were in the tank of the Union Oil Company, which was struck by lightning, but at least half of this was pumped out. Total loss is estimated at $150,000.

### Italy Discourages Emigration.

ROME, Jan. 28.—The Government through the emigration office has issued another notice with the object of discouraging emigration to the United States. The notice states that the Italian Consul in New York has telegraphed here urging Italians to remain at home while the present industrial depression and scarcity of work in the United States continue.



## FIGHT ON GOV. HUGHES BY PARTY LEADERS

### Contest Over Delegates to the National Convention and Control of the State Committee.

### WOODRUFF FOR CHAIRMAN

### Brackett, Speaking for Hughes League, Says Parsons Was Caught with Treasonable Letters on Him.

*Special to The New York Times.*

ALBANY, Jan. 28.—All prospects of peace, as a result of the letter from Secretary of War Taft to Chairman Parsons of the New York County Republican Committee, calling off the contest for the New York delegation to the Republican National Convention, are vanishing before the developments of the last two or three days.

Everything now points to war all along the line between the friends of Gov. Hughes in the organization and the so-called "Roosevelt leaders" under the leadership of State Chairman Woodruff, Herbert Parsons, William Barnes, Jr., of Albany, and Francis Hendricks of Syracuse.

The fight will be over two propositions, the delegates at large to the Republican National Convention and the control of the Republican State Committee, which carries with it control of the Republican machine in the State.

Any attempt by the Taft forces to have Gov. Hughes's name go on the ticket for second place would be futile, according to authoritative statements made to-day. The Governor has made it plain of late that he would not consider any such plan.

The programme of the "Roosevelt leaders" is, according to a report emanating from a friend of State Chairman Woodruff, to have elected as Delegates at Large men who, while apparently for Hughes, will in reality be devoted to the interests of Secretary of War Taft and who will also fight against the proposition of sending an instructed delegation to Chicago. The Delegates at Large favored by the "Roosevelt leaders" are: Secretary of State Elihu Root, State Chairman Woodruff, William Barnes, Jr., of Albany, and Francis Hendricks of Syracuse.

#### Decided at White House.

This, according to Mr. Woodruff's friend, was virtually decided upon at the conferences held last week at the White House between President Roosevelt and several New York Congressmen.

The friends of Gov. Hughes will declare against any Hughes delegation with a Roosevelt or Taft string to it, and will demand that only men who have been whole hearted in their support of Gov. Hughes shall be sent to Chicago. They have tentatively selected the following men for these positions:

Seth Low, ex-Gov. Black, ex-Senator Brackett, and State Superintendent of Public Works Frederick C. Stevens or George W. Aldridge from Western New York.

Ex-Senator Brackett sounded the war note of the Hughes League to-day in reply to a question regarding the attitude of the League on the proposition of Chairman Parsons of the New York County Republican Committee to substitute at the special meeting of that body to-morrow evening for the resolution indorsing Gov. Hughes a resolution of his own, in place of the resolution introduced by Harry W. Mack, and sidetracked by Mr. Parsons and his friends.

"I do not understand," said Mr. Brackett, "that it is a good proposition in war to place on sentry duty, when in the presence of the enemy, one just captured with treasonable correspondence on his person. Brother Parsons seems to have been caught with such a letter on him."

"You think, then, that the friends of Gov. Hughes in the New York County Republican Committee should fight the Parsons resolution?" Mr. Brackett was asked.

"I think the friends of Gov. Hughes should fight these scuttlers everywhere," he replied. "Why, take Brother Barnes. He is shouting as loudly now as he did when he was looking for that 'honorarium.'"

#### To Control State Committee.

In regard to the fight for the control of the State Committee and the Republican organization in the State, which by the local leaders is regarded as of far more consequence than the character of the delegation, it was learned to-day that State Chairman Woodruff had been advised by his friends to become a candidate for re-election as Chairman. The committee will reorganize after the State Convention in New York on April 11.

The Woodruff machine is in the fight for its own existence. Woodruff and his friends have looked over the field and decided that the State Committee cannot be wrested from them this Spring.

If they have made no mistakes in their count, the Woodruff supporters will have twenty votes at least in the committee, and twenty is a bare majority.

#### Fight Against Parsons.

The first fight will probably occur at the special meeting of the Republican County Committee in New York to-morrow evening. Senator Saxe announced to-day that the Governor's friends would combat vigorously the attempt of County Chairman Parsons to substitute his resolution for that introduced by the Governor's friends. Senator Saxe said:

"The purposes of the Taft people under the leadership of Mr. Parsons is to substitute their resolution, with the obvious intent of demonstrating that they have not lost control of the county committee. It is an effort to demonstrate to the National Republican Party that the enemies of Gov. Hughes have captured the Hughes movement."

When asked regarding the attitude the friends of Gov. Hughes in the committee would take in case the friends of Mr. Parsons, as contemplated, sprung a resolution expressing confidence in the county Chairman, Senator Saxe said:

"I shall fight that, and take the stand that it is not necessary to give Mr. Parsons a vote of confidence every time he makes a mistake—that it is no more necessary to do so at this juncture than it was three months ago, when he made

"All the News That's Fit to Print."

# The New York Times.

THE WEATHER.
Fair; warmer to-day; fair to-morrow; fresh south winds.

VOL. LVII...NO. 18,409. * * * NEW YORK, FRIDAY, JUNE 19, 1908.—SIXTEEN PAGES ONE CENT In Greater New York, Jersey City, and Newark. { Elsewhere, TWO CENTS.

## PLATFORM THE ONE THE TIMES PRINTED

### Except Change in Injunction Plank Alterations Were Slight and Immaterial.

### SOME ADDITIONS MADE

### Wisconsin Made Effort in Convention to Force La Follette's Policies Into Platform, but Was Defeated.

*Special to The New York Times.*

CHICAGO, June 18.—Despite the official statement from the White House three days ago that the Republican platform, printed exclusively in THE NEW YORK TIMES that morning, was only a tentative draft which had been prepared for submission to the Committee on Resolutions of the convention, the convention this morning adopted that platform word for word and line for line, with only a few slight alterations in phraseology, and after all the hard fighting to change it the platform was adopted by a unanimous viva voce vote.

Thus the Administration demonstrated again the power of its control of affairs here, and showed that its "tentative suggestion" could easily be made the will of the convention.

The great fight made by the "allies" against the adoption of the "tentative suggestion" resulted in the drafting of two planks and the elimination of one clause to which some importance had been attached. The redrawn planks were that on injunctions and court procedure, which was made stronger and clearer, so that it now has a positive meaning and stands for a specific thing; and that which declared for the establishment of a National Department of Health, which was weakened to a mere commendation of the efforts to obtain greater efficiency in National public health agencies.

**Changes Were Slight.**

The clause dropped was that at the end of the paragraph on trust regulation, where in specifying the amendments of the Sherman anti-trust law desired and recommended the tentative draft included those which "at the same time will not interfere with the operation of such associations among business men, farmers, and wage earners as result in a positive benefit to the public."

The dropping of this clause abandons the proposition to enact such an amendment of the Sherman law as would discriminate in favor of labor organizations, and is a victory for the allies. It is the only one they have scored in all their desperate and bitter fighting. It defeats the Administration plan to throw a sop to organized labor.

The redrafting of the injunction plank may also be considered something of a victory for the allies in that the plank as adopted, includes a specific declaration of the intention of the party to uphold at all times the authority and integrity of all courts, State and Federal.

But the new draft of the plank which covers the issuance of writs of injunction abandons the futile straddle of the tentative plank, and comes out squarely for a definite thing, using almost exactly the language which Secretary Taft has employed in several of his speeches on labor and capital. In this respect the injunction plank as adopted is much stronger and more honest than the tentative proposition which stood nowhere and faced both ways.

**Most Notable Change.**

The most important alteration of phraseology besides those already mentioned was at the conclusion of the paragraph on railroads. The first draft read: "Favor the enactment of such legislation as will prevent, by Federal restriction, the future overissue of stocks and bonds by inter-State carriers." The plank as adopted reads: "We favor such National legislation and supervision as will prevent the future overissue of stocks and bonds by inter-State carriers."

The Committee on Resolutions swallowed cheerfully nearly all the heroics about President Roosevelt, but balked a little on the subject of the "exalted servant" and eliminated entirely the reference to his "political sovereignty," that having been more than amply demonstrated in other ways since this convention began. So now the platform, instead of saying that their "most exalted servant has come to represent not only political sovereignty alone, but the best aims," &c., says their "most exalted servant represents the best aims," &c.

The smallest alteration contained the hardest crack delivered at the Administration. It was a personal blow to President Roosevelt. This was simply the elimination of the word "model" from the reference to the Child Labor bill for the District of Columbia. In all his advocacy of that measure, and in every one of his public references to it, the President has spoken of it as a "model" for the States, and he has often expressed the desire to have the different States accept it as a model and copy it in their own legislation. But the unfeeling Committee on Resolutions, perhaps recognizing what a futile bill it is, struck out the "model" and left the States to flounder along as best they can without the benefit of that guidance.

Five new planks, one clause, and one sentence were added. The clause goes into the middle of the plank on resources and waterways, and "reaffirms the Republican policy of the free distribution of the available areas of the public domain to the landless settler." The new sentence goes into two planks on insular affairs, and declares for granting immediate citizenship to natives of Perto Rico and for the naturalization of other inhabitants of that island.

**The New Planks.**

Two of the new planks refer to foreign affairs and declare for the protection of American citizens abroad and commend the party's efforts to build up foreign commerce. One declares for the creation of a Bureau of Mines and Mining. One favors the admission of New Mexico and Arizona as States, and the fifth recommends the celebration of the centenary of Lincoln's birthday.

With these few alterations, only two of which, that about trusts and that about courts and injunctions, are material, the platform adopted unanimously this morning is almost literally that printed in THE NEW YORK TIMES before the convention had been called to order for the first time and before there was any Committee on Resolutions.

Immediately upon the opening of the session this morning Senator Hopkins, Chairman of the Resolutions Committee, presented his report, and read the platform in full. He raised a laugh right at the start by reciting how the Republican Party had "expended" the National domain, instead of "expanding" it, as the platform says. Hopkins has a good voice, but it was not strong enough to fill the great hall, and he was frequently interrupted by calls for more vigor in his tones.

When the crowd found that they could not follow what he was saying they went to talking among themselves, and for the most part the platform was read in the midst of such a tumult that only those in immediate proximity to the reader could distinguish what he was saying.

Thus they missed his remark about the "interests of the oil roads," instead of the "inter-State railroads," a remark which if it had been heard would have awakened the liveliest appreciation from a large part of the crowd.

When the Committee on Resolutions concluded its labors at an early hour this morning, the word went around that there would be no minority report. The audience was surprised, therefore, when Senator Hopkins, on the conclusion of his reading, moved the previous question upon the report "and upon the minority report to be submitted by Mr. Cooper." This was Representative Cooper of Wisconsin, one of the untamed and unterrified "La Follette radicals." Cooper presented his report at once, and it evoked a mixture of howls and "boos" from all over the hall, with wild shouts of approval from the Wisconsin delegation.

**The La Follette Demands.**

It declared for the La Follette idea of tariff revision, for physical valuation of railroads, for direct election of Senators, for publicity of campaign contributions and expenditures, and for the prohibition of injunction in labor cases. When Cooper began his speech in support of this platform a Pennsylvania delegate bobbed up with a demand to be informed how many names were signed to the minority report. Hopkins cut in to announce that he would cover that in his part of the debate, but Cooper forestalled him by shouting:

"I am the minority. I am the only man who signed the report, and I have no apology to make for it."

Cooper made a first-class La Follette argument for his platform, and was supported by two or three of the Wisconsin men in very brief talks. Then Hopkins went after the Wisconsin ideas with unsalted language. The gist of his denunciation was contained in his reference to the minority report, and the Cooper speech as the "Socialistic-Democratic utterances from Wisconsin."

The Wisconsin delegation demanded a roll call on the adoption of the minority report, and South Dakota seconded the demand. Gov. Hanly of Indiana wanted a separate vote on the campaign fund publicity plank. South Dakota demanded a separate vote on physical valuation of railroads, and Nebraska made a similar demand for the plank on the election of Senators. Sereno Payne wanted to lay the whole thing on the table. But Senator Lodge ruled that it was too late, the previous question having been ordered.

**Against Campaign Publicity.**

So the roll was called and one by one the Republican Convention went on record as solidly against campaign publicity, despite Secretary Taft's letter to Senator Burrows: against the physical valuation of railroads and the direct election of Senators, and then against the remainder of the La Follette scheme. There were loud cries from all over the hall against having to go on record in this fashion, but Lodge ruled in favor of the demand at every point and the roll was called. When Wisconsin was out of the way it took only a viva voce vote to adopt the whole platform unanimously, not even a single Wisconsin delegate shouting "No!"

**The full text of the platform will be found on Page 4.**

## MOLDING INJUNCTION PLANK.

### Senator Crane Forced Incorporation of Ideas of Choate and Butler.

*Special to The New York Times.*

CHICAGO, June 18.—Inasmuch as Senator Murray Crane of Massachusetts has been one of the most determined opponents of the insertion of an anti-injunction plank in the platform, a good deal of surprise was expressed to-day when it became known that in the full committee he had voted for the modified declaration agreed upon. His attitude was explained and much of the mystery which surrounds the contest over this plank cleared up when one or two of the chapters of the inner history of its construction became known.

The insistence of the Administration upon an anti-injunction plank is accounted for by the fact that some time ago President Roosevelt and Secretary Taft promised Mr. Gompers that the platform should declare for a limitation of the power of the courts in respect to restraining orders. To the plank, as originally drawn, Mr. Crane and the conservative members of the committee were bitterly opposed. The terms of the compromise which obtained Mr. Crane's support were dictated by himself. They were, first, that the declaration of the memorial of Nicholas Murray Butler, Joseph H. Choate, and their associates should be in spirit, if not in terms, incorporated. The phraseology of the memorial, but not its meaning, was changed and the party was pledged to uphold the authority and the integrity of the courts. That was the first point.

In the second place, Mr. Crane insisted that the declaration exempting bodies of farmers and wage-earners not organized for profit from the operation of the Anti-Trust act must go out. That point was yielded by the Administration forces. For a third consideration there was the plank for which Mr. Gompers has been laboring night and day for the practical legalization of the boycott. That, too, was left out.

Then Mr. Crane and many of his conservative associates consented to the compromise form of the anti-injunction plank, and it was approved by a large majority of the committee and adopted by the convention.



## TAFT, HEARING NEWS, TURNS TO MRS. TAFT

### "Oh, Will!" She Cries and Kisses Him, While His Daughter Squeezes His Arm.

### ROOSEVELT IS AT TENNIS

### Pauses to Praise the Nominee—Taft's Resignation as War Secretary Will Go to President To-day.

*Special to The New York Times.*

WASHINGTON, June 18.—When William Howard Taft, Secretary of War and Republican nominee for the Presidency, received the news late this afternoon of the action of the Chicago Convention, he turned first to his wife. Mrs. Taft glanced at the white slip of paper that had come from the telegraph operator's machine and promptly let it drop to the floor.

"Oh, Will!" she cried, and kissed him.

Then from the room outside the Secretary's private office came a rattle of hand clapping, followed by a lusty cheer. The door was burst open and in poured half a hundred clerks of the department, each striving to be the first to congratulate the nominee. The negro doorkeeper, who sits outside the office, fought his way forward with a big bunch of white roses.

Mr. Taft was as happy as a big boy. His face glowed with pleasure, and he used both hands in gripping those outstretched to him. Behind him were Mrs. Taft, his daughter, Miss Helen, and Charlie, his youngest son. Immediately behind them stood Brig. Gen. and Mrs. Bell, Mrs. Darlington, wife of the Inspector General, and Gen. Clarence Edwards.

"I haven't a word to say," said Secretary Taft, and his voice shook just a little with excitement. "To tell you the truth, I can't find words. They won't come. But I don't need to tell you that I'm very proud and very happy."

**Roosevelt Plays Tennis.**

Across the street, immediately behind the Executice office, the President was playing tennis with Assistant Secretary of State Bacon. Mr. Roosevelt did not seem to be giving a thought to the convention that was making history. Just as the word of Taft's victory was flashed from the convention hall he was shouting with laughter at a trick drive that fooled the active Mr. Bacon. When he did learn of it, however, he paused long enough to issue his statement praising Mr. Taft. Then he apparently became absorbed in his game.

Mrs. Taft came down early, appearing at the War Department shortly after the Secretary had arrived. She was ensconced in a big easy chair, within hearing distance of the long-distance telephone, and directly opposite the door leading to the room in which the private telegraph instrument was clicking busily.

Charlie Taft, wearing a broad grin, khaki trousers, and no coat, was everywhere. Later in the day he made himself useful by carrying the bulletins from the operator to his father's desk. Only once did young Charlie disappear. Then he returned with a rush, bearing a bag of peanuts and two big apples. By this time he had struck up a firm friendship with the telegraph operator and insisted on sharing the peanuts with him. The operator, however, was too busy to take the proffered apple, which Charlie demolished himself.

Miss Helen Taft made her appearance in the middle of the afternoon, fresh from honors won at the Baldwin School, in Bryn Mawr. She remained with her parents until the bulletin came in announcing the nomination of her father. Then she squeezed his big arm in her joy and excitement until he winced.

**Sorry for Jeering of Fairbanks.**

The humanity of the Secretary was shown in a little incident in the middle of the afternoon. He came out of his inner office just as his private secretary, Fred W. Carpenter, was reading aloud to a number of newspaper men a bulletin saying that the name of Vice President Fairbanks, who was being placed in nomination by Gov. J. Frank Hanly, was being received with jeers.

"What is that?" he asked sharply. Carpenter told him.

"I'm sorry that has happened," he said, slowly. "It's too bad. In fact, it's bad enough to have your name presented to a convention without being subjected to such treatment. Every one who has passed through it, or is going to pass through it," and he smiled, for his name had not been presented then, "has my warmest sympathy."

It had been the Secretary's intention to attend the exercises this afternoon that marked the closing of the term of the War College, but the desire to learn the action of the convention impelled him to give up the plan. At 5 o'clock Gen. Edwards, booted and spurred, strode through the crowded anteroom and informed the Secretary that the horses were waiting.

"I'm afraid I can't make it," said Mr. Taft, smiling under the approving pressure of Mrs. Taft's hand upon his arm. "I've got to stay here to satisfy my family, and, to tell you the truth, my own curiosity." This last was in a low and solemn tone, punctuated with a laugh. The trip was given up, but Secretary Root and some other officials represented the Administration at the exercises. Later Mr. Taft went to the War College for a time. Then he returned to the department.

**Big Reception at His Home.**

It was late when the Secretary and his family left the War Department and were driven home. They dined quietly, but shortly after 8 o'clock they were brought to the porch by a cheering crowd from the University Club, of which the Secretary is a member. The Army Engineers' Band was there also, and between the music and the hurrahs the quiet residence neighborhood in which is the Taft home never before has experienced such a pandemonium.

The enthusiasts refused to leave before they had shaken the Taft hand. Then there were insistent calls for a speech. The Secretary shook his head and acted very much like the little schoolgirl who is called upon for the first time to recite

**Continued on Page 3.**

### ROOSEVELT LAUDS TAFT.

White House,
Washington, June 18, 1908.

**I feel that the country is indeed to be congratulated upon the nomination of Mr. Taft. I have known him intimately for many years and I have a peculiar feeling for him, because throughout that time we have worked for the same objects with the same purposes and ideals.**

**I do not believe there could be found in all the country a man so well fitted to be President. He is not only absolutely fearless, absolutely disinterested and upright, but he has the widest acquaintance with the Nation's needs, without and within, and the broadest sympathies with all our citizens. He would be as emphatically a President of the plain people as Lincoln himself; yet not Lincoln himself would be freer from the least taint of demagogy, the least tendency to arouse or appeal to class hatred of any kind.**

**He has a peculiar and intimate knowledge of and sympathy with the needs of all our people—of the farmer, of the wage worker, of the business man, of the property owner. No matter what a man's occupation or social position, no matter what his creed, his color, or the section of the country from which he comes, if he is an honest, hard-working man who tries to do his duty toward his neighbor and toward the country, he can rest assured that he will have in Mr. Taft the most upright of representatives and the most fearless of champions.**

**Mr. Taft stands against all privilege, and he stands pre-eminently for the broad principles of American citizenship which lie at the foundation of our National well-being.**

THEODORE ROOSEVELT.

## MAY CHOOSE MEYER TO RUN CAMPAIGN

### Rivalry Between Hitchcock and Vorys Likely to Force Choice of Compromise Chairman.

### CRANE DOESN'T WANT PLACE

### Would Be Acceptable to All Factions—Committee Will Meet To-day to Organize.

*Special to The New York Times.*

CHICAGO, June 18.—There is a situation in the Taft camp that is giving lively concern to the real friends of the Secretary of War. Two factions have developed, one led by Frank Hitchcock, who was the engineer of the steam roller that flattened out the opposition to the Secretary's nomination, and the other by Arthur I. Vorys, the original manager of the Taft campaign.

The tension between these factions is such that it is doubtful if either Hitchcock or Vorys will be named as the Chairman of the National Committee. This matter will be taken up immediately by the President and Mr. Taft and decided within the next week. It is predicted that Postmaster General Meyer will be selected, and if he should fail to obtain the place it may go to some other outside man. It is certain that Vorys would not work under Hitchcock, and the latter probably would not feel like accepting a subordinate job under the man from whom he lifted the laurels.

The Treasurer of the campaign in all probability will be Charles G. Dawes of Chicago.

Outwardly, the relations between Hitchcock and Vorys are pleasant. Those who know the inside, however, say there is absolutely no sympathy between them. In the first place, Vorys is the kind of a man who believes in harmonizing. Hitchcock allied himself with factions in various doubtful States. Vorys started the campaign, and it is asserted made the nomination of the Secretary possible by the way he manoeuvred in Ohio, the Central, Western, and Far Western States, but on behalf of Hitchcock it is asserted that he cinched the nomination for Mr. Taft by his manipulation of affairs in the South.

Had Mr. Vorys continued in complete control, it is asserted, not half the contests which were decided by the National Committee would have been presented, and much of the bitterness which developed would have been avoided.

Since Mr. Vorys arrived in Chicago and established the Taft headquarters in the Auditorium Annex Mr. Hitchcock has not put his foot inside the rooms. He has had his own headquarters in another part of the hotel, and he has summoned delegates there without consultation with Mr. Vorys. It is also asserted that Mr. Hitchcock has adopted the habit of issuing statements of what he proposed to do without first getting the approval of the Ohioan, and the latter has never objected because he did not want to handicap the Secretary in the race.

Several members of the National Committee, which will be reorganized immediately after adjournment of the convention to-morrow, have informed the Secretary, it is stated, that they do not believe it would be in the interest of good politics to make Hitchcock Chairman of the Committee to manage the campaign.

Mr. Hitchcock has friends, however, upon the committee, and they want him. It is their view that he deserves reward for the splendid way in which he obtained the support of practically all the Southern States for Mr. Taft.

Senator W. Murray Crane of Massachusetts would make an ideal campaign manager, but he has indicated his unwillingness to serve as Chairman of the committee. With Mr. Crane at the head of the committee there would be no question as to the attitude of the business interests of the country.

The personal relations between Taft and Crane always have been of the most friendly character, so that if the Bay State man should be selected it is declared it would be an excellent solution of a very troublesome question.

With Crane out of the running, the general opinion here seems to be that Postmaster General Meyer will be named as Chairman. Mr. Meyer is believed in by the President. He enjoys intimate relations with Mr. Taft. He is a business man, and as such has the confidence of the business community.

There was a proposal to-night to summon Secretary Taft to Chicago to confer with the committee on the Chairmanship, but after some discussion it was abandoned.

## SAYS IT IS SHERMAN FOR SECOND PLACE

### Representative Bennet Makes the Announcement After Leaving Big Conference.

### WASHINGTON IS CONSULTED

### New York Delegation Unitedly Booms Sherman and Other States Quickly Fall Into Line.

*Special to The New York Times.*

CHICAGO, Friday, June 19.—It was announced at half-past 1 o'clock this morning by Representative Wilson S. Bennet of New York that Representative James S. Sherman of that State would be the Republican nominee for the Vice Presidency. Mr. Bennett had just come from the rooms in the Auditorium Hotel, where the Taft managers had been in consultation with leaders of the various elements in the convention. They had also been in communication with Washington for several hours.

When Mr. Bennet came out, he said: "Congressman Sherman will be nominated. You can quote me as saying so."

"Has Washington assented to Mr. Sherman's nomination?" asked THE TIMES correspondent.

"I am not authorized to speak for Washington, but I told you what you could tell your readers," was the reply.

It was learned that Congressman Parsons had made a strong fight for the New York man at the conference.

Previously the Iowa delegation had decided not to present either Dolliver or Cummins, and an effort by the Administration to find a suitable Western man had failed.

Just as soon as the Presidential nomination was settled the clans at the Republican National Convention cut loose in the struggle for second place. All the booms, big and little, that had been in retirement for the last two or three days were trotted out again for public inspection, and on the way downtown the palavering for votes for second place was resumed with energy.

By common consent the choice was admitted to lie between Senator Dolliver of Iowa and Representative Sherman of New York. The repeated assertions of friends of Vice President Fairbanks that under no circumstances would he take another nomination, were at least accepted at their face value, and the Indiana man disappeared from the canvass.

The Sherman boom came on with more enthusiasm than has been shown over any matter that has come before the convention. On every hand the question was heard, "What is the Administration going to do?" or "What does Washington say?" That was the only thing that held any of the delegates back from definite expression of preference.

The Taft managers took steps at once to get into communication with the President and Secretary, and a conference was called in rooms of Frank H. Hitchcock in the course of which there was continued consultation with Washington over the long distance telephone. Several members of the new National Committee were gathered with Mr. Hitchcock, and there was a general discussion of the situation at both ends of the wire. Word came that Secretary Taft was in consultation with the President and that when the choice of running mate should be made it would undoubtedly be either Dolliver or Sherman.

**Administration Not Decided.**

At 11:20 the consultation over the Vice Presidency was still on, with Washington not yet decided as to what should be done. Cummins had been abandoned as a possibility. Earlier in the evening the name of Attorney General Herbert Hadley of Missouri had been suggested from Washington, where the President and Secretary Taft were in conference. It was discussed here, and there was talk with some of the Missouri delegation. It was finally concluded that Hadley would not fill the bill, and so this suggestion was dropped.

The question then fell back to the choice between Dolliver and Sherman, with Sherman gaining strength. The success made by his boomers was recognized by the Administration as making it increasingly difficult to put Dolliver through. Senator Lodge came out for Sherman late in the evening. The indications were that the discussion will continue until a very late hour, but the trend was unquestionably toward Sherman.

**New Yorkers Choose Sherman.**

Meantime the New York delegation was more than busy. The first thing it did was to hold a caucus and get solidly behind the Sherman candidacy. It was decided that Sherman's name should be presented to the convention this morning by State Chairman Woodruff, and that he should have the 78 votes of the Empire State. Gen. Woodford and Seth Low both declared themselves in favor of Sherman, and the united delegation set out to round up all the strength it could collect.

The Sherman boom was helped by a tip which was industriously spread by ex-Congressman Lucius N. Littauer that he had received a telegram from Mr. Loeb, secretary to the President, to the effect that Sherman would be acceptable to the Administration as Taft's running mate.

There was a tremendous difference between the enthusiasm over the Vice Presidential fight and that which had not marked the contest for the first place. As soon as the lid was off the shouting began and it was the real kind, with genuine vim in it.

**Noisy Parades for Sherman.**

Sherman's Congressional friends came to the front with loud hurrahs. They set up huge pictures of him in the hotel lobbies and gathered in front of them, shouting and singing. The favorite song was rendered by an ever-increasing volunteer glee club, led by Representative Rodenburg of Illinois. This is it:

Hurrah for Sherman, he is a dandy,
He is a blamed fine man.
He's the whole blame candy.
He is a daisy, he drives us crazy.
Eins, swei, drei, vier,
Sherman is the winner here,
He is a blamed fine man.

Over and over they shouted this ditty.

**Continued on Page 3.**



## GOT NEWS FROM THE TIMES.

### Chicago Paper Got Platform from New York by Wire in 38 Minutes.

*Special to The New York Times.*

CHICAGO, June 18.—The much-talked-of "beat" achieved by THE NEW YORK TIMES in obtaining and printing in advance on last Tuesday morning a draft of the tentative platform from the Committee on Resolutions of the Republican National Convention furnished the telegraph companies an opportunity to show what they can do in an emergency.

To one Chicago paper, in which the tentative platform appeared the same morning on which it was printed in THE NEW YORK TIMES, the article was telegraphed from New York in just thirty-eight minutes. It ran well over 5,000 words.

It was possible for two Chicago papers to print the platform story simultaneously with THE TIMES only by reason of the difference of an hour in time between New York and Chicago. The enterprising papers in this Western city could not possibly have got the platform story, which they featured heavily in their front-page columns, except from the first edition of THE NEW YORK TIMES, which is not turned over to the various distribution agencies until about 1:30 in the morning, or 12:30 Chicago time.

One of the newspapers here, in order to get the story into the office in time, cleared all its wires the moment their New York correspondent sent them a "flash" that THE TIMES had secured a "beat" of the first magnitude in their own city. THE TIMES's "beat" came into this office over six wires, and a good deal faster than the copy could be edited and sent down to the composing rooms to be set up in type.

Immediately after the first edition of THE TIMES had left the press a New York news syndicate which had obtained a copy of the paper rushed messages all over the country offering THE TIMES's "beat" for sale to their clients. Here is a dispatch received by the representative of a Kansas City newspaper at the convention from his managing editor at 2:18 A. M., indicating how busy the wires were at that hour in the morning with THE TIMES's "beat":

"Hearst just announces will send 4,000 words of the platform taken from THE NEW YORK TIMES."

## CONGRATULATIONS TO TAFT.

### Gov. Hughes Tells Him the Welfare of the Country Is Assured.

*Special to The New York Times.*

ALBANY, June 18.—Gov. Hughes was about to leave the Executive Chamber for his home when a press dispatch giving the vote for President in the Chicago Convention arrived. He exhibited no surprise, for he had known for several days what the result would be. He expressed genuine satisfaction over the outcome, having a warm regard and great admiration for Secretary Taft.

He talked for a few minutes with the newspaper men and others present, and sitting at the big desk in his outer office he penned the following telegram which he handed to Secretary Fuller to be transmitted to Washington:

The Hon. William H. Taft, Secretary of War, Washington, D. C.:
I heartily congratulate you upon your nomination. Under your administration the welfare of the country will be assured.
CHARLES E. HUGHES.

The Governor then went direct to the Executive Mansion, where he remained all evening. His attitude toward the Vice Presidency is unchanged. His positive refusal of some days since to allow his name to be presented is unaltered.

The announcement of Taft's nomination was celebrated by the Barnes Republicans here by the booming of cannon.

## KNOX PRAISES CONVENTION.

### Pledges Great Majority in Pennsylvania for the Ticket.

PITTSBURG, June 18.—Senator Philander C. Knox received news of the Chicago Convention at the home of his former law partner, George E. Shaw, in Coraopolis, a suburb, and immediately, upon learning of Secretary Taft's nomination, sent this message to the telegraph office:

Secretary William H. Taft, Washington:
I sincerely congratulate you on the result at Chicago. Pennsylvania, as usual, will lead the list of your enthusiastic supporters.
P. C. KNOX.

Of the work of the convention, he said: "It is an excellent nomination. The party will support Mr. Taft with enthusiastic loyalty. He will be elected because the country has confidence in his ability, his integrity, and his good sense.

## WILL BE ELECTED—CANNON.

### Pledges His Services to Taft Before Roll Call Is Finished.

CHICAGO, June 18.—Speaker Cannon sent this message to Secretary Taft this afternoon:

Chicago, June 18.
Hon. William H. Taft, Washington:
You have been nominated as candidate for President by the Republican National Convention. I heartily congratulate you. You will be elected by the people in November. Illinois will cast her electoral vote for you. Whatever I can do for your success and that of the party will be done.
CANNON.

The message was sent before the convention roll call was finished.

## FAIRBANKS'S BEST WISHES.

### Hopes That Taft Will Have a Successful Administration.

INDIANAPOLIS, June 18.—Vice President Fairbanks to-night sent the following telegram:

Hon. William H. Taft, Washington:
Accept my most cordial congratulations upon your nomination, and best wishes for a successful administration.
C. W. FAIRBANKS.

Mr. Fairbanks awaited the outcome of the convention at his home here.

### Longworth's Message to Taft.

WASHINGTON, June 18.—Among the telegrams received by Secretary Taft to-night was one from Chicago reading:

"Hon. William H. Taft: The greatest triumph all way through. Best love from us both. NICK and ALICE."

## FORAKER PLEDGES SUPPORT.

### Republicans Will Quit Contending Among Themselves, Says Senator.

WASHINGTON, June 18.—"Until the convention made a nomination every Republican had a right to have his choice," said Senator Foraker to-night after hearing of the nomination of Secretary Taft for the Presidency.

"But now it is no longer a question of men, but a question of party. In this way Secretary Taft becomes my candidate for the Presidency, and while, under all the circumstances, I can probably do but little, yet I shall do all I can to help elect him. Republicans will now quit contending among themselves and turn all their guns on the common enemy."



## TAFT NAMED; FIRST BALLOT

### Throng in Galleries Vainly Makes a Great Demonstration for Roosevelt.

### 702 VOTES FOR SECRETARY

### Gov. Hughes Gets 67, All the Other Allies 207, and Roosevelt 3.

### SESSION IS DISORDERLY

### Speaker for Candidates Jeered Until Threat Is Made to Clear Galleries.

### LODGE AVERTS STAMPEDE

### Has the Roll Called in the Midst of Roosevelt Outburst—Convention Adjourns Till To-day.

### HOW THE STATES VOTED.

| | Taft. | Knox. | Hughes. | Fairbanks. | Cannon. | Foraker. | La Follette. |
|---|---|---|---|---|---|---|---|
| Alabama | 22 | | | | | | |
| Arkansas | 18 | | | | | | |
| California | 20 | | | | | | |
| Colorado | 10 | | | | | | |
| Connecticut | 14 | | | | | | |
| Delaware | 6 | | | | | | |
| Florida | 10 | | | | | | |
| Georgia | 17 | | | 1 | | 8 | |
| Idaho | 6 | | | | | | |
| Illinois | 3 | | | | 51 | | |
| Indiana | | | | 30 | | | |
| Iowa | 26 | | | | | | |
| Kansas | 20 | | | | | | |
| Kentucky | 24 | | | 2 | | | |
| Louisiana | 18 | | | | | | |
| Maine | 12 | | | | | | |
| Maryland | 16 | | | | | | |
| Massachusetts | 32 | | | | | | |
| Michigan | 27 | | | | 1 | | |
| Minnesota | 22 | | | | | | |
| Mississippi | 20 | | | | | | |
| Missouri | 36 | | | | | | |
| Montana | 6 | | | | | | |
| Nebraska | 16 | | | | | | |
| Nevada | 6 | | | | | | |
| New Hampshire | 5 | | | 3 | | | |
| New Jersey | 15 | 4 | | 2 | 3 | | |
| New York | 10 | | 65 | | 3 | | |
| North Carolina | 24 | | | | | | |
| North Dakota | 8 | | | | | | |
| Ohio | 42 | | | | | 4 | |
| Oklahoma | 14 | | | | | | |
| Oregon | 8 | | | | | | |
| *Pennsylvania | 1 | 64 | | | | | |
| Rhode Island | 8 | | | | | | |
| †South Carolina | 13 | | | 2 | | 2 | |
| South Dakota | 8 | | | | | | |
| Tennessee | 24 | | | | | | |
| Texas | 36 | | | | | | |
| Utah | 6 | | | | | | |
| Vermont | 8 | | | | | | |
| Virginia | 21 | | 2 | | | 1 | |
| Washington | 10 | | | | | | |
| West Virginia | 14 | | | | | | |
| Wisconsin | 1 | | | | | | 25 |
| Wyoming | 6 | | | | | | |
| Alaska | 2 | | | | | | |
| Arizona | 2 | | | | | | |
| District of Columbia | 1 | | | | | 1 | |
| Hawaii | 2 | | | | | | |
| New Mexico | 2 | | | | | | |
| Philippines | 2 | | | | | | |
| Porto Rico | 2 | | | | | | |
| Totals | 702 | 68 | 67 | 40 | 58 | 16 | 25 |

*Pennsylvania gave Roosevelt 3 votes.
†One South Carolina delegate absent.
Total number of delegates, 980.
Necessary to a choice, 491.

*Special to The New York Times.*

CHICAGO, June 18.—William Howard Taft of Ohio was nominated for the Presidency of the United States on the first ballot by the Republican Party assembled in convention here to-day. The roll was called in the midst of a deafening uproar and an attempt to stampede the convention for Roosevelt. The call was completed at 5:10, and at 5:16 Senator Lodge, the permanent Chairman of the convention, announced that Mr. Taft had received 702 votes. At 5:23, on the motion of Gen. Stewart L. Woodford of New York, the nomination was made unanimous. The convention then adjourned until 10 o'clock to-morrow morning.

For more than seven hours the delegates and 10,000 visitors had sweltered in the almost overpowering heat of the packed Coliseum. For many hours the task of nominating various candidates had been going on. Then at the close came the attempt at a stampede, and the ovation accorded President Roosevelt yesterday was repeated. Weary and warm though every one in the hall was, the tremendous outburst swept every one but the delegates and the Chairman from their feet, metaphorically, and had it not been for the fact that the delegates were not to be stampeded under any circumstances the result of the convention might have been different.

**Delegates Not to be Stampeded.**

As it was, there never was one minute when there was a chance of a real stampede; there never was an instant when Taft's nomination was in doubt. From first to last the machine worked to perfection, and nothing could have interfered with its action.

Except for the Roosevelt outburst, which followed close upon and was really a part of a demonstration in favor of Senator La Follette of Wisconsin, the whole proceedings of the session were marked with artificiality. The applause for Taft when his name was first mentioned was artificial to a large degree, coming only from those of the delegates who were of the Taft crowd, and from a few, a very few, people in the gallery. There was no spontaneity about it, and though it lasted fairly long, it was not to be compared to the enthusiasm manifested at the mention of the name of Roosevelt yesterday, nor to the outburst that followed later in the day.

This convention will probably be known

"All the News That's Fit to Print."

# The New York Times.

THE WEATHER.
Thunderstorms to-day; generally fair Sunday; wind southwest.

VOL. LVII...NO. 18,410. * * * NEW YORK, SATURDAY, JUNE 20, 1908.—SIXTEEN PAGES and Section Devoted to Review of Books. ONE CENT In Greater New York, Jersey City, and Newark. { Elsewhere, TWO CENTS.

## KEENE'S BALLOT WINS SUBURBAN

### Crack Four-Year-Old Establishes a Record of 2:03 for the Great Handicap.

### PUZZLED OVER INJUNCTION

### New Conditions Keep Down Attendance at Sheepshead Bay — King James Second, Fair Play Third.

SUBURBAN HANDICAP.
TWENTY-SECOND RUNNING.
Sheepshead Bay, L. I.
Distance, one mile and a quarter.

| | | Estimated. |
|---|---|---|
| 1.. | Ballot, (Notter) | 8 to 5 |
| 2.. | King James, (G. Burns) | 6 to 1 |
| 3.. | Fair Play, (E. Dugan) | 7 to 1 |
| 4.. | Master Robert, (Garner) | 4 to 1 |
| 5.. | Dandelion, (J. Lee) | 20 to 1 |
| 6.. | Bedouin, (Shreve) | 20 to 1 |
| 7.. | Frank Gill, (McDaniel) | 12 to 1 |
| 8.. | Montgomery, (Miller) | 10 to 1 |
| 9.. | Gold Lady, (Koerner) | 10 to 1 |
| 10.. | Tourenne, (Musgrave) | 20 to 1 |
| 11.. | Running Water, (McCarthy) | 20 to 1 |
| 12.. | Fillicott, (Walsh,) | 80 to 1 |

Time—2:03.
Former record for Suburban Handicap, 2:05, made by Hermis in 1904.
Former track record for distance, 2:04 3-5.
Value of stakes, $25,000.
To the winner, $20,000; to the second horse, $3,000; to the third horse, $2,000.
Owner of the winner, James R. Keene.
Trainer, James Rowe.

James R. Keene's four-year-old colt Ballot won the fastest Suburban Handicap in the history of the great event at Sheepshead Bay yesterday.

It took nothing short of the brilliant and popular victory of the great horse in 2:03, record time for the course, to give the race precedence in the popular mind over the extraordinary public patronage that the racing in itself induced, in the face of the strict suppression of all forms of betting that has been ordered under the new law, and which nearly 300 policemen were on duty to enforce. There was much speculation at the track as to the effect and significance of the injunction issued by Justice Bischoff restraining the police from interfering with the association carrying on its business.

Enthusiasm swept from the far end of the field stand through the crowded grand and club stands to the uttermost corner of the paddock, when Ballot, racing in front under the top weight for nearly a mile, passed the winning post first by two lengths from his only opponent at the end, King James, in time that was only a fifth of a second behind the American record for the mile and a quarter.

The attendance was far from the best that racing at the Sheepshead Bay course has drawn under the conditions of open betting tolerated under the law, but it was surprising alike to the holiday visitors and veterans of the turf in the generous response that the public made to the attractions of a great race alone, for there was absolutely no anticipation of open betting, and, so far as the police records for the day could show, no authenticated attempt to evade or violate the law against gambling by any among the vast crowd that filled the lawns and stands.

#### Betting Rings Were Empty.

Under the changed conditions of racing, as governed by the restrictions of the Hart-Agnew law, the betting rings were empty of all except the police, and in consequence the crowds were thoroughly in evidence through the racing.

Conservative estimates by racing officials placed the size of the attendance at from 18,000 to 20,000, divided with the greater portion of the visitors in the grand and club stands and in the private boxes. The gathering was singularly brilliant, for the fashionable world had an extraordinary representation, and the bright hats and gowns of women bloomed through the length and breadth of the stands, and made the bravest and most brilliant showing in the two tiers of the club and private boxes, which the remodeling of the main stand has provided. An uncommonly large proportion of the assembly was made up of holiday-making parties in automobiles, coaches, and carriages, and the array of automobiles parked behind the grand stand was the largest and most impressive in the history of racing at the Coney Island Jockey Club's course.

The professional horsemen were out in full force, but there was much more than a leaven of recruits to the sport of racing as a spectacle simply. A conversation which did not even arouse a laugh gave fair indication of the character of the patronage. A group of women surrounding a single man in the stand wondered where the horses were when the field was at the post for the Double Event. "Why, they've gone away," one of the women complained. The perplexed man, looking all around, exclaimed just as the horses were started with a cloud of dust streaming behind them. "No, there they are. See the smoke?"

For the men whose interest was keenest in the possibilities of betting, a ripple of excitement was caused by the report early in the afternoon that an injunction had been secured by the racing interests for the protection of the personal rights of visitors. The betting men to a unit refused to believe the reports which first reached the track, and even after confirmation of the news declined to take chances of arrest by either accepting bets or offering wagers openly. As a matter of course, the dyed-in-the-wool betting men did some betting among themselves in secret and without the exchange of money, so far as the police were able to detect it, and prices on the horses that started in the course of the day were established after a fashion, the odds laid in this manner making the basis of the reported starting prices, published in the newspapers. The amount of betting that could have gone on at the track was indicated by the fact that with more than 15,000 people in attendance the 300 policemen present made two arrests, both prisoners being implicated in a supposed single case, which was found in the field. The prisoners were unknown to the old managers of the betting ring.

#### Bets Down on Ballot.

When Ballot galloped home first in the Suburban, however, there was general and unrestrained admission among the spectators that there had been betting on that event, anyhow. The method employed was simplicity in itself, for since the repression of betting at the race

Continued on Page 4.

## ROOSEVELT'S HOLIDAY BEGINS

### Denies Hint of Fatigue—Says He's Had "Perfectly Corking Time."

WASHINGTON, June 19.—On the eve of his departure for Oyster Bay for his Summer vacation, the President was reminded that he perhaps of all men had fairly earned a rest, to which he replied:

"Do not waste any sympathy on me. I have enjoyed every minute of my stay here, and my thanks are due to the American people and not theirs to me for the opportunity I have had to serve them. I have had a perfectly corking time," he added with a characteristic Roosevelt smile and a final handshake.

All preparations have been made for the President's departure for Oyster Bay to-morrow morning. He will go on a special train, accompanied by Mrs. Roosevelt and other members of his family, and will reach Oyster Bay about 5:35 o'clock.

The President's train will consist of a private car, a Pullman, and a baggage car, and will leave the Union Station at 9:15 A. M. over the Pennsylvania Railroad. At Jersey City the party will go by boat to Long Island City. Secretary and Mrs. Loeb and officials and employes of the White House to the number of about thirty will accompany the President.

The meeting of the Cabinet at the White House to-day, the last until the President returns from his Summer vacation, was more of an occasion for a vacation farewell and for exchanging views on the work of the convention than it was for the transaction of business. Some business was disposed of, but it related mostly to minor matters which it was desired to complete before the President's departure.

## DELAGRANGE COMING HERE.

### Frenchman Signs Contract to Fly His Aeroplane at St. Louis.

Delagrange, the famous French aviator, who has been making successful long-distance aeroplane flights in different parts of Europe, will visit America this Summer. He has been secured by a coterie of enthusiastic aeronauts of St. Louis, including many members of the St. Louis Aero Club, and while it was impossible to ascertain the details of his visit yesterday, it is believed that virtually all of his flights with his famous aeroplane will be made in the West.

A. B. Lambert, a Director of the St. Louis Club, who recently qualified as a balloon pilot in the Aero Club of France, has assisted in concluding the negotiations. It was learned that a sufficient sum of money to insure the visit of Delagrange has been secured by the St. Louis syndicate, and that the contract has actually been signed.

Delagrange made his most notable achievement on May 30 in Rome, when he surpassed all of his previous records by remaining in the air for 15 minutes and 30 seconds, traveling about 9 9-10 miles. He got $8,000 for his flights in Rome, and as the gate receipts were larger the syndicate made a good profit. His flights in America will be made in some large inclosed grounds, and admission will be charged.

#### Zeppelin Again Postpones Flight.

FRIEDRICHSHAFEN, June 19.—Owing to a defect in the motor of his airship, Count Zeppelin to-day again postponed his scheduled attempt at an ascension.

## BANKER'S SON DROWNED.

### William Bourbet of New York City Lost While Swimming in a Pond.

*Special to The New York Times.*

GREENWICH, Conn., June 19.—William Bourbet, son of a New York banker, was drowned while swimming in a small pond on the Summer estate of W. T. Carrington, the New York grain broker, at 2 o'clock this afternoon.

Bourbet, who was 17 years old, was a good swimmer, and was enjoying the water with a friend, Alexander Leighton, 16 years old. The young men swam several times around the pond, and had finally reached a point about seventy-five feet above the dam, when the Bourbet boy, being somewhat exhausted, got on a floating log. While on the log something in the water bit him, and, shouting to his companion that he was going to see what bit him, he pushed the log away. Either the log struck him on the head, or he was seized with cramps, for he immediately tried to get on the log again. The log turned over with him, and Leighton, who was only a few feet away, heard him cry for help and saw him go down. He swam to the spot, but his companion had disappeared. Then he summoned help.

The pond is drained by a twelve-inch pipe, and this was opened, letting off the water. The body was discovered in eight feet of water. Bourbet was spending his vacation from the bank here with his grandfather, Carl Drinkhorn, a retired New York banker, and had come here only a few days ago. His mother also arrived for a visit just as the body was being brought ashore.

## KILLED IN MINE EXPLOSION.

### 3 Miners Dead, 2 Mortally Hurt, and 15 Entombed Near Monongahela.

MONONGAHELA, Penn., June 19.—Three miners are dead, two others perhaps fatally burned, and fifteen entombed, many of whom are supposed to be dead from an explosion at the Ellsworth No. 1 Mine of the Pittsburg Coal Company, near here to-day. Of the victims taken from the mine, John Beal is the only one identified. The others are foreigners, whose features were too scorched to be recognized.

The two burned men were hurried to the hospital here, and it was said they would probably die. Little is known as to the cause of the explosion. It occurred when all but thirty miners working on the day shift had left the workings.

Of this number fifteen were near the mouth of the slope and ran out before the force of the explosion reached them. Had the explosion occurred five minutes earlier the entire force of over 500 men would have been entrapped with probably many fatalities. Little is known here about the men still in the mines, but most of them are thought to have perished in the fumes, which are still so strong that rescuers cannot enter far into the slope.

#### Democratic Senator for Oregon.

SALEM, Oregon, June 19.—Complete but unofficial primary returns on the nomination of candidate for United States Senator give H. M. Cake, (Rep.,) 50,899, and George Chamberlain, (Dem.,) 52,421.



## BOMB EXPLODED IN PERCY NAGLE'S CLUB

### Meeting Room Wrecked, Place Set Afire, Either for Robbery or Revenge.

### NAGLE HIMSELF NOT THERE

### Clubmen Who Were in the Building and Were Unhurt Put Blaze Out —Nagle Has Many Enemies.

A bomb was exploded at 8:40 o'clock last night in the meeting room in the basement of the Kanawha Club, Percy Nagle's Democratic Club of the Thirtieth Assembly District, at 129 East 128th Street. It shook the house and other buildings adjoining, made havoc of the meeting room, and set fire to the basement stairs, which open directly into the room, the hallway partition having been removed when Percy Nagle had the building remodeled some time ago at a cost of more than $2,000.

No one was hurt in the explosion, and beyond the damage to the meeting room and stairs, the building escaped injury, although several windows in the basement were broken by the concussion. Two explanations for the attempt to blow up the building were offered by members of the club.

Thomas Lloyd, one of those in the building at the time of the explosion, called attention to the fact that last night was the night upon which dues were payable, and Secretary John Coleman had collected abot $1,000 or $1,200 in his office on the second floor. He suggested that the man who placed the bomb might have expected that every one in the building would run out when the explosion occurred, and thus give him an opportunity to get the money.

The second explanation was that the explosion was simply due to a grudge on the part of some one against Percy Nagle. Nagle has many enemies, and it was recalled that he has been assaulted by political opponents and two years ago was shot while in the street, receiving an injury which caused his retirement from active work for some time.

If Lloyd's explanation of the explosion be the correct one, the man who placed the bomb was disappointed in the result of his work. There were several dozen men in the building, most of them upon the second floor with Secretary Coleman, and instead of running out of the building, they all, including Coleman, who held on to the money, ran into the basement to the scene of the explosion.

When they reached the head of the basement stairs they were met by a cloud of smoke which poured up from below, and it was discovered that the stairs had been wrecked and that the débris was on fire. Coleman, with Michael Howell of the Fire Department's dynamite squad, Frank Schaffer, Eugene Gilligan, and Philip Gallagher, son of Mrs. James Gallagher, caretaker of the club, ran out into the street and entered the basement by the area door.

The men formed a bucket brigade extending from the kitchen in the rear of the basement into the meeting room, and by the time that firemen reached the building they had the fire out. Police Inspector Walsh was one of the hundreds of persons in the neighborhood who had heard the explosion, and he ran into the clubhouse, and when the fire was out started an investigation.

Walsh and several detectives found the broken and twisted pieces of a tin box scattered about the wrecked room, and a number of pieces of burned and singed cotton. There was also the neck of a five-ounce bottle of very heavy glass, in which the cork still remained, and also a number of pieces of tire tape. The police decided that the explosive had been contained in this bottle which had probably been wrapped around with the cotton and then put in the tin box which was bound with the tire tape.

The only clue to the identity of the man who placed the bomb was furnished by Mrs. Gallagher. She said that a few minutes before the explosion she had been in the basement and had chanced to glance out the basement window. She saw a young man leaving the basement, but said that although she did not recognize him as one of the members of the club she supposed nevertheless that he was one of the members, of whom there are about 900.

The police believe that this man placed the bomb in position, and they are searching Harlem for him. Mrs. Gallagher could give only a meagre description of the man, however, as there were no lights in the basement and it was quite dark on the sidewalk.

Percy Nagle, who is a Lieutenant in the Sixty-ninth Regiment, N. G. N. Y., is in camp with his company at Peekskill and will not return to the city until this morning. This fact caused some of the members to doubt the generally accepted explanation of the affair, as they argued that any one who would try to blow up the club would probably wait until Nagle was in it.

The explosion recalled to Harlemites who heard about it the similar attempt which was made upon Nicholas Hayes's club, the Pocassett, in 116th Street, a year ago.

## GET WESTCHESTER'S TERROR.

### Young Bostonian Confesses Sending Black Hand Death Threats.

*Special to The New York Times.*

WHITE PLAINS, June 19.—In the arrest of Walter Bernigan, 28 years old, of Boston, to-day at Armonk, Westchester County, Sheriff Charles M. Lane has captured the so-called "Black Hand" agent who has been writing death threats in letters to President Isaac W. Turner of Mount Kisco, George V. Raymond of Bedford, and other prominent residents of the northern section of Westchester County. Several of the persons threatened, fearing for their lives, had left their homes.

The letters said that unless $1,000 was sent to a certain place the homes of the receivers of the letters would be blown up by dynamite.

The prisoner's home is in Boston, but about a year ago he married Miss Hynes of Mount Kisco, a niece of Raymond, who has been a recipient of four "Black Hand" letters. When arrested Bernigan was armed with a big revolver, fully loaded. He was taken by surprise at the home of a friend, where he took refuge on Thursday night after an attempt was made to arrest him in Mount Kisco.

The prisoner was speedily disarmed, and confessed to writing the "Black Hand" letters to both President Turner and his wife's uncle, George Raymond. He also admitted that he was the man who held up the two watchmen, Weber and Russell, at the Raymond home at the point of a revolver.

Sheriff Lane of Westchester County had his suspicions directed to Bernigan, who had gone through his wife's marriage portion of $2,500 in less than a year after he married her, by the latter's talk about making the "Black Hand" business pay.

The Sheriff learned that Bernigan had given up his position in Mount Kisco and was supposed to be working in New York. In Manhattan it was found that he lived at the Olive Tree Inn, Twenty-third Street and First Avenue, under the name of John Condin. All of the Black Hand letters were mailed from Stations F and D, which are near this hotel. He must have suspected that he was being shadowed, as he did not appear at the hotel to get the decoy letters that had been sent to him.

At 10:30 o'clock last night Bernigan went to his former employer, Mr. Olem, and attempted to extort a loan from him at the point of a revolver. Olem grabbed the Black Hand agent and tried to disarm him. Bernigan escaped, but Sheriff Lane and his deputies joined in the hunt and finally captured him.

## LEGLESS BOY SAVES TWO.

### Cripple Also Minus Part of an Arm Rescues Boys from Drowning.

*Special to The New York Times.*

MORRISTOWN, N. J., June 19.—With stumps for legs and a stump for his right arm and his left arm minus several fingers, Joe Gilligan, 18 years old, this afternoon swam to the rescue of two boys in the Gravel Pit Pond and saved their lives.

Alexander Patterson and Augustus Monohan, boys of 12, were out in an old boat on the little pond near the Lackawanna Railroad tracks at Morris Plains. The pond is about ten feet deep where the boys upset the boat while playing. Patterson could not swim, and he clasped the Monohan boy around the neck. Before he was dragged under Monohan cried lustily for help.

Gilligan was sitting with other boys on the bank showing them the artificial legs his parents had bought for him. He had unstrapped them, but when he heard the cries for help he did not stop to put them on. Plunging in, he swam to the spot where the boys had come to the surface for the second time.

He grasped the two lads, pushing them apart and, swimming with one hand, pushed the Patterson lad ashore. Going back, Gilligan went for Monohan and pushed him ashore in safety.

Gilligan was run over by a trolley car in Brooklyn ten years ago. He lost one leg above the knee and the other below the knee, his right arm was taken off at the elbow, and three fingers from his left hand.

## HELD AS A FAKE LOBBYIST.

### Pittsburg Police Say Prisoner Collected $200,000.

*Special to The New York Times.*

PITTSBURG, June 19.—By far the most distinguished-looking prisoner ever in Central Police Station is D. G. Miller, arrested this afternoon by Detectives Lally and Leff. The police accuse him of having fleeced prominent people of New York, Boston, Philadelphia, St. Louis, Chicago, and Pittsburg out of $200,000.

Miller professed to be a lobbyist representing the Republican Party, and authorized to solicit funds to secure the passage through the next Congress of a two-cent fare law. He had letters alleged to be signed by Govs. Guild, Hughes and Folk; Senators Penrose, Knox, and La Follette; Congressman John Dalzell, Secretary Taft, and a score of others.

Miller came to Pittsburg from Chicago, where he made his biggest clean-up, but was forced to leave there by the approaching convention. He came to Pittsburg, and since then Chief of Police Shippey of Chicago has been trying to locate him. Among Miller's papers was a list of his victims, which contains the names of almost 5,000 persons. He had just obtained $50 from a Pittsburg business man when arrested. Miller is supposed to have a large sum of money "planted" in Chicago, but he withstood the "third degree" this afternoon without telling where it is concealed.

## GALE HITS WILD WEST SHOW.

### Tears Down Part of Buffalo Bill's Canvas at Pittsburg.

*Special to The New York Times.*

PITTSBURG, Penn., June 19.—A terrific storm broke over Pittsburg about 7:30 o'clock, just as an immense audience was assembling to witness the evening performance of Buffalo Bill's Wild West Show. A sudden gust of wind caught the canvas wall that surrounds the grounds and a section of it was blown down.

Charles S. Howell, a well-known real estate man and formerly claim agent of the Baltimore & Ohio Railroad, was caught under a falling pole and sustained a severe scalp wound. He was the only person badly hurt.

Women and children made a wild rush for the exits. Just when it appeared that many people would be crushed or trampled to death, Col. Cody appeared in the arena mounted on a horse. He circled around the ring, assuring the people that there was no danger, and begged them to remain in their seats. It was fully fifteen minutes, however, before order was restored.

A number of women fainted and had to be carried from the grounds. Little damage was done, and after the storm subsided the performance was given.

## DEER KILLS BULLDOG.

### Onlookers in Pittsburg Park See a Desperate Fight.

*Special to The New York Times.*

PITTSBURG, Penn., June 19.—A forty-pound bulldog and a large buck deer came together in Riverview Park this afternoon. The dog was killed by the buck after about ten minutes of fighting, witnessed by hundreds. The dog was owned by Mrs. Walter Dunk of Perrysville Avenue, and while she had him on a chain in the park this afternoon he broke away and attacked the buck, which was browsing quietly near by.

The buck managed to shake off the dog's hold, and the next rush of the bulldog was checked by a kick which sent the dog flying through the air. Again and again the dog came back, sometimes gaining a tooth hold, only to be shaken off by the buck. Finally the buck jumped on the prostrate dog and tore him to pieces with his sharp hoofs. Mrs. Dunk was injured trying to tear down a fence to get a club to help her dog.

#### Girl Gets $12,500 for Torn Scalp.

WHITE PLAINS, June 19.—Mary Affelt, formerly employed in the American Felt Company's Mills at Glenville, as a weaver, received a verdict to-day in the Supreme Court at White Plains for $12,500 against the company for having her hair and part of her scalp torn off by one of the looms.

#### Mrs. Ladew Wins New Haven Suit.

MINEOLA, L. I., June 19.—A jury in the Nassau County Supreme Court gave a verdict of $3,000 to-day against the New Haven Railroad in Mrs. H. B. W. Ladew's suit for injury to seven show horses while they were in a car being shipped from Simsbury, Conn., to Elsnore Farms, the Ladew country place, on Long Island.



## PROTOS TWO DAYS IN LEAD OF THOMAS

### American Car's Crew Has Thrilling Experiences on 54-Hour Run from Chita.

### ANIMALS ARE A HINDRANCE

### Machine Has Many a Wild Race with Stampeded Herds—Towed Across a River—Germans Nearing Irkutsk.

Special Cable from THE NEW YORK TIMES'S Staff Correspondent with the Racers.

VERKHNIEOUDINSK, Transbaikalia, June 19.—The Thomas car in the New York to Paris race arrived here after fifty-four hours' running from Chita, still two days behind the German Protos car. The run from Chita has been replete with thrilling experiences and full of hardship and has taxed the endurance of the men severely.

The crew got to bed at Chita at 2 o'clock on Wednesday morning, and arose at 6 ready to set out again, but after a breakfast of eggs, coffee, and black bread we were compelled to wait until noon for the arrival of our supply of gasoline. We finally got away in a drizzling rain.

We ran through a dreary mountain valley, occasionally widening into a narrow plain, making our way over grass bottomlands. The only inhabitants were migratory bands, living in tents and tending vast herds of cattle, horses, sheep, or goats. The automobile caused the greatest consternation among the animals and stampeded herd after herd.

When the herds see or hear the auto they run toward it with one accord, even from great distances. Then, when fairly close at hand, they turn, and bellowing or neighing madly in their fright, they run ahead in a wild panic, sometimes for a couple of miles before they swerve from the path the car is following. The animals in front of it have been a great hindrance to the machine, and to avoid them the car has made many a wild race for the right of way through a narrow defile with a flying herd running parallel but ahead.

#### Caravans Are Upset.

We have met long caravans of two-wheeled carts frequently. One man drives the leading cart, and the other carts follow driverless. The commotion caused by the machine among these caravans may be well imagined. While the driver clings to the horse on the leading cart, the others scatter in all directions, many upsetting and emptying the load upon the ground, while the horses drag the overturned cart until it is dashed to pieces.

When possible to get near enough to the caravans before the stampede occurs, the crew of the racing car has dismounted and, walking ahead, held the horses until the car gets by. There was one exception to the universal panic that caused more delay than all the others. This was occasioned by a colt, which, instead of rushing off, left its mother and followed the car, neighing happily. When the machine stopped it stopped, and started again when the car resumed its way. Finally, for fear that the little fellow would starve if separated from its mother, the crew got out and caught the colt after much dodging, leading it back to its mother after a long struggle.

We had a 4 o'clock lunch of bread and Bologna sausage on the first day on the moving automobile, and did not stop until 10 o'clock at night, when we reached a post house. Then, after a supper of eggs and black bread, we slept on the floor without bed clothes. We had not even overcoats or blankets to cover us, since all the baggage had been expressed ahead to reduce the weight on the car. It was still raining and intensely cold, and we were numb with chill when we set out over the very bad roads against a bleak wind in the morning.

We had not followed the post road long when it suddenly ended in a huge bog. We could see the place where the Protos had been mired and turned back, so we scattered to hunt for the Germans' tracks. After a long, tiresome search we came upon a Buriat camp and induced one of the men to show us the way around the bog.

We lunched at a post house on eggs and black tea, Shuster twice falling asleep from exhaustion while eating, but we set out again after an hour's delay, when the sun shone once more and promised a fine afternoon.

#### Crew Are Thrown Into a Ditch.

The rivers were badly swollen, and to cross one we had to be towed by eight horses led by a Buriat postillion. The water was over our hubs and in the swift current one horse lost his footing and almost drowned all by entangling the lines. We finally got across after further delays that were maddening to the impatient crew. The machine shot through a number of smaller streams, over which the bridges had been carried away.

We stopped at a Buriat camp fire for bread and tea, and then, with headlights to show the way, started over good roads at high speed. While the Thomas was dashing along we came suddenly upon a washout three feet wide. Shuster managed to swing the automobile about in time to avoid the drop and narrowly missed a deep roadside gully, but the sharp turn threw the unprepared crew out into the ditch.

We stopped again at a road house and slept without bed clothes on the floor in spite of the frost, and arose at daylight and proceeded, after a hasty breakfast, reaching Verkhnieoudinsk at 9 o'clock. We will depart at 2 to try to cut down the two days' lead which the Germans have maintained.

Verkhnieoudinsk is situated about half way between Chita and Irkoutsk, near the shores of Lake Baikal. It is 1,760 miles from Vladivostok, while Irkoutsk is 210 miles further on. With its two-day lead the German car should be nearing Irkoutsk, where the remainder of the run to Paris is believed to be possible in forty days' time, duplicating the record of the Itala car in the Peking to Paris race. No confirmation has yet been received of the reported destruction of the Italian Zust car by fire at Imianpo, 384 miles from Vladivostok.

## INTERNATIONAL STEEL TRUST.

### Additional Capital Required for Project Nearing Completion.

Special Cable to THE NEW YORK TIMES.

LONDON, June 19.—Despite denials which were professed to be given on authority, but which in several particulars tended rather to confirm the previous announcement of a great international steel combination in which the largest firms of Europe and America are included, The Iron and Steel Trades Journal maintains that the trust is now nearing completion.

Additional capital, it is said, will be required to the original amount of £150,000,000, as a large outlay will be necessary under the new British patent act, which shortly comes into force, for the construction in Great Britain of works which will give employment to many thousands of men.

## H. H. ROGERS SUIT SETTLED.

### Compromise in $50,000,000 Boston Case Over Old Oil Patent.

*Special to The New York Times.*

BOSTON, Mass., June 19.—Judgment for the defendant, by agreement, was entered to-day in the suit for $50,000,000 brought by Cadwallader M. Raymond of Somerville against Henry H. Rogers of the Standard Oil Company in the Supreme Court.

Raymond acted as the assignee of a claim which the late Benjamin F. Greenough of New York had against Mr. Rogers and his former partner, the late Charles Pratt, under a contract made in 1878, for selling them a secret process for making crude petroleum and its products non-explosive. Mr. Rogers claimed that the process was never a success and was not used.

## KEENE RACERS FOR ENGLAND.

### Turfman Ships Yearlings To-day—Horses in Training Not to Go Yet.

Several dozen yearlings from the stock farm of James R. Keene will be shipped to England to-day, according to a statement made last night by Mr. Keene to a reporter for THE TIMES. He would not say, however, that his action had been caused by the recent anti-betting law. He declined to discuss this law at all or prophesy what may be the future of racing in this State.

"I have maintained silence on that subject up to date," said Mr. Keene, "and I do not mean to break my record."

As yet, however, Mr. Keene said, he had made no arrangements to send his racing stable abroad. The yearlings that go to-morrow will be put in training on the other side and kept at work for a year, at least, before being sent to the post.

## ACCEPTS PHIPPS'S GIFT.

### Johns Hopkins University Thanks Donor of New Hospital.

*Special to The New York Times.*

BALTIMORE, June 19.—The Trustees of Johns Hopkins University, at a meeting this afternoon, accepted Henry Phipps's gift of $750,000 for the erection of a hospital building and the establishment of a Professorship of Psychiatry. A resolution adopted expresses grateful appreciation of Mr. Phipps's "enlightened generosity, recognizes in the foundation of this chair an opportunity long desired to advance in new and important directions in this country the investigation and treatment of mental diseases, and pledges co-operation of the Trustees of both university and hospital in the effort to fulfill the humane purposes of the founder."

John S. Phipps of New York, son of the donor, was here yesterday in company with the New York architect, Mr. Atterbury, who will design the building. They met the Trustees and inspected the hospital grounds.

## GETS 2,300 VOLTS AND LIVES.

### Electrician Revived by His Fellow-Workmen Pouring Water on Him.

LONG BRANCH, N. J., June 19.—Charles Cornell, an electrician of New York City, received a charge of 2,300 volts in his body this morning and lives. According to Supt. A. C. Swan of the New Jersey Consolidated Water and Light Company, who was working beside Cornell in the company's plant, Cornell touched the heavily charged wire with his finger and doubled up in a knot and was held rigid until the current was shut off.

He fell to the ground unconscious when the current was cut off and was thought to be dead. But fellow workmen dragged him outside on damp ground and poured water on him. He soon regained consciousness, and an hour later was walking about complaining of nothing but a headache.

## FOR DEMOCRATIC HOME RULE.

### "Utica Conference" Men Agree to Work for Better Representation.

ALBANY, June 19.—The Executive Committee of the Home Rule Democracy, appointed at the so-called Utica conference, met to-day, and, according to a statement given out by Chairman W. G. Rice, it was determined that its "work within party lines should be continued actively until representation for the Democracy as a whole has been regained in State Convention and State Committee."

"This movement," continues the statement in part, "is not for or against any man or set of men. It is not anti-anybody, but pro-home rule. Principles, not men, is the platform of the home rule Democracy."

#### Say Cornell Men Drink Too Much.

*Special to The New York Times.*

ITHACA, N. Y., June 19.—A petition 46 feet long has been presented to President Schurman and the Board of Trustees of Cornell University by the Ithaca Women's Christian Temperance Union asking that the Trustees stop drunkenness among students at class banquets, and that the senior banquet be held in the armory hereafter. The petitioners say that the conduct of the students "is most disgraceful," and that the alumni are as bad as the undergraduates.

#### Latest Shipping News.

Sailed—SS Italian Prince, from Santos, June 17.



## SHERMAN GOES ON TAFT TICKET

### New Yorker Named for Vice President After Administration Gives Up Contest.

### VAIN OFFER TO BEVERIDGE

### Politicians Glad That the Delegates Had a Chance to Act for Themselves.

### FINAL SESSION IS SHORT

### Small Crowd in Coliseum and Everybody Anxious to Get Away—Cannon Gets an Ovation.

*Special to The New York Times.*

CHICAGO, June 19.

**For President—William Howard Taft of Ohio.**

**For Vice President—James S. Sherman of New York.**

The fourteenth National Republican Convention, which nominated the above ticket, adjourned to-day at 11:49 A. M. after a session of about an hour and a half, during which the nomination of Mr. Sherman was rushed through without much ceremony, and the delegates, all of whom were anxious to get away, refrained from any remarkable demonstrations. The one exception was the New York delegation.

Congressman Sherman's nomination did not come as a surprise to any one at the convention. It was well understood two hours before the session was called to order by Senator Lodge, the permanent Chairman, that the New Yorker was to be named. His boom had been taken up in earnest the night before by the New York delegation. An offer of the nomination had been made by the Administration to Senator Beveridge of Indiana as late as this morning, but he refused it. With Senator Dolliver eliminated, Mr. Sherman was evidently considered the best man to fall back on in the hope that he would bring strength to the ticket in the State from which he hails.

#### Choice Left to Convention.

It is the almost universal opinion here that the Administration did a wise thing in leaving the nomination of the Vice Presidential candidate very largely to the convention. That Mr. Sherman was not the choice of Mr. Taft and the White House in the first place, is well known but of late so much has been said in the newspapers about this having been a Roosevelt bossed convention that the nomination of Mr. Sherman, and the manner in which it came about is looked upon as a good stroke. It will afford an answer in part at least to the Democrats who will charge while the convention was held in Chicago its work was done in Washington.

Mr. Sherman, of course, was acceptable to the Administration and to Mr. Taft. Otherwise he would not have been nominated. At the same time there was a real question to decide in the choosing of a man for second place, and the White House did not have any fixed choice after Mr. Dolliver left the race for good. That the matter was left to the convention was a fortunate thing for the New Yorkers, who seized the opportunity and began to boom Sherman in earnest.

It can now be said truthfully that the nomination of the Presidential candidate was the work of the Administration, that the platform was an Administration platform, put through after a fight, and that the choice of the man for second place was the work of the convention itself to the extent that the Administration did not oppose it.

#### Little Interest in Session.

The galleries of the Coliseum were more than half empty and the floor itself but partly filled when at 10:20 this morning Senator Lodge called the last session of the convention to order in the Coliseum. The gathering was noticeably different from those of the preceding days on the part of the delegates.

The always immaculate Mr. Beveridge wore his "going-away clothes," a sack suit and tan shoes. Other delegates who on previous days had attempted more or less style appeared in very light Summer things—linen suits, flannels, and checked outing clothes. To nominate a Vice President, it was evident, was not as dignified a business as nominating a President.

Rabbi Schoenfarber of Chicago said the prayer, and then Senator Lodge announced that he had omitted in the hurry and confusion of the session of yesterday to make the announcement that the convention had chosen as its candidate for President William Howard Taft. The mention of the name, of course, brought forth a shout. However, it did not last long.

#### Arrival of the Sherman Boom.

A band outside the building, which had interrupted the prayer of Rabbi Schoenfarber and been stopped, began to play again, much to Mr. Lodge's disgust. The band passed through the doors, and was held up by a messenger from Mr. Lodge and the playing stopped. The delegates, however, wanted to see what it was all about, and they shouted "Let 'em in," so Mr. Lodge acquiesced and the musicians marched in.

It was the Sherman boom arriving in the convention hall for the first time. At the head of the procession was an enormous picture of the Congressman, framed. Then came the band, playing "Marching Through Georgia," then a banner with Sherman's picture on it, and then the New York stalwarts who had worked so hard for Gov. Hughes's nomination, and were working as hard, if not a little harder, for the nomination of Mr. Sherman.

#### Other Delegates Join In.

The delegates from other States who were already in the hall joined in the demonstration for Sherman with a will, and there was a lot of cheering and applause from the floor. The gallery took no interest whatever. The band played "A Hot Time in the Old Town," and somewhere in the back of the hall a lot of young men who had boomed Sher-

"All the News That's Fit to Print."

# The New York Times.

EXTRA 5:15 A. M.

THE WEATHER—Fair to-day; fair, warmer to-morrow; wind east.

VOL. LVII...NO. 18,430. * * * * * NEW YORK, FRIDAY, JULY 10, 1908.—FOURTEEN PAGES. ONE CENT In Greater New York, Jersey City, and Newark. { Elsewhere, TWO CENTS.

## VENEZUELA RECALLS HER REPRESENTATIVE

### Senor Veloz Goiticoa, Charge in Washington, Says Good-Bye and Closes the Legation.

### ACTION DOESN'T MEAN WAR

### Thought Castro, Following American Lead, Will Not Close Consulates and Trade Will Not Be Interrupted.

*Special to The New York Times.*

WASHINGTON, July 9.—President Castro retaliated on the United States in kind to-day by withdrawing the Venezuelan representative to the United States and closing the legation of that country here. The action, following so swiftly on the report of Jacob Sleeper, Secretary of the American Legation at the Venezuelan capital, to Acting Secretary Bacon yesterday, was as unexpected as it was sudden. The belief was held generally that Castro would ignore the withdrawal of Minister Russell, thus placing this Government in the attitude of having endeavored unsuccessfully to force an issue.

Señor Veloz Goiticoa, the Venezuelan Chargé d'Affaires, has been in charge of the legation for some time in the absence of Señor Guzman, nominally the Minister. Venezuela has not maintained a regularly accredited Minister here for several months.

Señor Veloz Goiticoa made no demand for his passports, nor could he do so consistently, in view of the fact that Foreign Minister Paul had declined to issue such passports to the American Chargé when he withdrew from Caracas, on the ground that there was no necessity for passports, the country being in profound peace and his person not being threatened in any way. The señor did communicate to Mr. Bacon the fact that the files and papers of the Venezuelan Legation would be placed in the custody of Señor Jacobo Pimental, the Venezuelan Consul General in New York.

This statement is regarded as an indication that the Venezuelan Government will follow the precedent established by the United States in refraining from interfering with trade by closing the consulates, notwithstanding the breach in diplomatic relations. No arrangement has been made for the transaction of any diplomatic business which Venezuela might find it necessary to transact in the future.

Taking leave of Acting Secretary Bacon and accepting the suggestion that he communicate in writing to Secretary Root the direction of his Government in this matter, Señor Veloz paid hasty calls upon Assistant Secretaries Adee and Huntington Wilson and other officials of the State Department whom he has long and intimately known. Señor Veloz Goiticoa has come to be very highly regarded in the diplomatic circles. Indeed, it may be stated positively that his personality has gone far toward deferring the rupture which came to-day.

It is pointed out by officials who have followed closely the developments in the Venezuelan situation that there is not the slightest danger of war in the immediate future, or indeed at all. Rather will the situation resemble that following the rupture of diplomatic relations between France and Venezuela, for instance, where legations were closed on both sides and all official relations terminated while trade between the two countries continued and Frenchmen came to Venezuela and rich Venezuelans made their annual pilgrimages to Paris as if nothing had occurred.

The history of these episodes in the case of Venezuela is very much alike the feeling of resentment bred by the rupture gradually becomes less acute, and at the proper moment a friendly third party steps in and brings about restoration of amicable relations. It is even possible in our own case that the process may be more rapid than usual for two reasons.

In the first place there must be some limit to the number of powers from which Venezuela can safely separate herself, and with the termination of her relations with America to-day she has added a very potent force to the opposition, while reports from Caracas received to-day indicate that the Minister of the Netherlands is on the point of closing his legation.

In the second place, there is some ground for the belief that President Castro has been acting in a half light; that for some reason he has not been in possession of all of the facts in the case of the controversy with the United States, or, if he has, then he has been completely misled as to the motives which have impelled Secretary Root to request the Venezuelan Government to join America in having recourse to arbitration.

The State Department to-night protests, however, that it has no plans, and will make no overtures for a resumption of diplomatic amenities. The affair is regarded as an unfortunate outcome of a series of misunderstandings that has long taxed the patience of this Government.

As has been said, the Administration is not excited over President Castro's action. Complications may nevertheless follow the report of the Senate Committee on Foreign Relations, which has before it all the correspondence that has passed between this country and Venezuela.

Only a short time ago Senator Cullom, Chairman of the committee, expressed himself vigorously with regard to the manner in which President Castro should be handled. He was asked if his committee would pass on the Venezuelan matter before adjournment, and, if so, what probable line of action would be recommended.

"No, we shall have no report ready," he said. "But, in my opinion, that man Castro should be spanked soundly."

## A. T. DEMAREST POISONED.

### New York Manufacturer Is Taken Violently Ill After Eating Clams.

GREENWICH, Conn., July 9.—A. T. Demarest, a wealthy carriage manufacturer of New York City, is seriously ill at the Kent House, a Summer resort, the victim of ptomaine poisoning contracted two weeks ago while attending the graduation at Yale of his grandson, Francesco Whitenmore.

On the day following the commencement he went to a shore dinner at Savin Rock, and it was there, he believes, he was poisoned eating clams. On his return to Greenwich he was taken violently ill. For several days he was in a dangerous condition.

## DIDN'T TELL HOBSON SO.

### Emphatic Denial of "Probable War" Story Issued from Sagamore Hill.

*Special to The New York Times.*

OYSTER BAY, L. I., July 9.—In reply to the passage in Congressman Hobson's speech at Denver in which Mr. Hobson said "not so very long ago the President of the United States said in my presence, 'There exists the greatest probability of a war with Japan,'" this official statement was issued by Secretary Loeb after a long conference with Mr. Roosevelt to-night:

> In reference to the speech of Congressman Hobson, Secretary Loeb stated that the Congressman must, of course, have been misquoted. The President not only never made such a remark, but never made any remark even remotely resembling it. All that the President has ever said is that if there was a sufficient navy there would never be any possibility of this country getting into a foreign war.

Mr. Loeb said that the report that Mr. Roosevelt would take the stump in Indiana for Mr. Taft was not worth submitting to the President.

Mr. Roosevelt spent the day camping at Lloyd's Neck, Mrs. Roosevelt being his camping companion. On his return to Sagamore Hill the President's day off was upset by Mr. Loeb's visit to tell about the Hobson speech. Mr. Loeb was held at the hill for an hour past his usual time for departure. The result was the typewritten statement concerning Mr. Hobson's statement.

## ADMITS SCRIBNER CONTRACT.

### President Will Write His Hunting Trip Solely for Them, Loeb Says.

*Special to The New York Times.*

OYSTER BAY, July 9.—President Roosevelt, through Secretary Loeb, to-day confirmed the story in THE NEW YORK TIMES that he had signed a contract with the Scribners to write his hunting adventures in Africa for that firm. Mr. Loeb said that Mr. Roosevelt would write exclusively for the Scribners, giving them serial and book rights. He declined to tell the monetary consideration, but it is understood, as was told yesterday, that Mr. Roosevelt will receive a large royalty.

## JOHN G. HECKSCHER'S WILL.

### Mrs. McClellan and Mrs. Winthrop, Daughters, Get $100 Each.

Mrs. Georgiana McClellan, wife of Mayor McClellan, and Mrs. Emeline D. Winthrop, wife of Egerton L. Winthrop, benefit only to the extent of $100 each under the will of their father, John G. Heckscher, the well-known turfman and yachtsman, which was filed for probate in the Surrogate's office yesterday. The will was dated Dec. 20, 1905, and contains two codicils. It was presented by W. J. Worcester, assistant secretary of the United States Trust Company, which is named as executor and trustee. The value of the estate is given as more than $10,000 each of real and personal property.

The only public bequest is one of $5,000 to St. Rose's Free Home for Incurable Cancer at 426 Cherry Street. In his will Mr. Heckscher left his library to the New York Public Library, Astor, Lenox, and Tilden Foundations, but this was revoked in a codicil dated June 5, 1906, and instructions given that the library be sold and the proceeds be given two-thirds to his widow and a third to his brother.

To Mrs. Virginia Otis Heckscher, widow of the testator, is also left all her husband's household furniture and effects, jewelry, &c., with the exception of a few articles specifically bequeathed. She is also to receive $50,000 in cash, the income from a $100,000 trust fund, the principal of which is to revert to the residuary estate at her death, and the testator's interest in the Valley Farms Company, near Yonkers.

To Charles A. Heckscher, brother of the testator, is left a miniature of their mother, two prize shooting cups, all the testator's guns, fishing rods, reels, and other shooting, fishing, and sporting implements, seventy-five shares in the Coney Island Jockey Club, and a share in the South Side Sportsmen's Club.

Mrs. Katherine Mackay, wife of Clarence H. Mackay, is to receive a crayon portrait of the mother of the testator, Mary Travers Hecksher. To Capt. William H. Emory of the United States Navy is left $5,000 "as a token of my love and esteem," while the residue of the estate is to be divided equally between the testator's three nephews and two nieces, John C. Wilmerding, E. Coster Wilmerding, and John P. De Saules, and Matilda Van Rensselaer and Georgiana L. Heckscher. They each receive also a specific bequest of $10,000.

In his will Mr. Heckscher named his brother, Charles A. Heckscher, and his friend, Hoffman Miller, as executors and trustees, but these appointments were revoked in a codicil and the United States Trust Company substituted.

No official announcement was forthcoming yesterday as to the reason for the smallness of the bequests to Mr. Heckscher's two daughters. It was said, however, that they had been recipients of settlements at the time of their marriage, while, on the other hand, a story was in circulation which gave as the reason the disapproval of the two daughters to their father's third marriage, which took place over three years ago.

## NEW BOSTON & MAINE DEAL.

### New Haven's Control Transferred to Interests Friendly to It.

BOSTON, July 9.—The Boston & Maine Railroad, it was learned to-night, is no longer controlled by the New York, New Haven & Hartford Railroad Company. Shares of the Boston & Maine to the number of about 110,000, owned by corporations controlled by the New Haven Road, have been sold to John L. Billard of Meriden, Conn. The sale took place on June 30, and the transfers were effected on July 1. Mr. Billard is President of the Meriden Savings Bank and an extensive dealer in coal and lumber.

The decision of the New Haven Railroad to cause the corporations controlled by it to sell the Boston & Maine stock was reached at a meeting of the New Haven Directors, the purpose being to avoid the annoyances of litigation and an indisposition to combat the Commonwealth of Massachusetts.

Mr. Billard owns the Boston & Maine stock outright. He is associated with men of wealth not connected with the New Haven Company, but will himself vote the stock of the Boston & Maine. He is on friendly terms with the officers of the New Haven Railroad, and, while his purchase of the stock does not partake in any sense of a merger proposition, it is understood that his influence will be in favor of harmony in the administration of the two railroad properties.

### Latest Shipping News.

Arrived—Steamer Lusitania, from Liverpool July 4, east of Fire Island at 12:35 A. M.

## THOMAS CAR LEADS RACERS INTO EUROPE

### Has Crossed Asia and Was Reported at Obansk, West of the Urals, Yesterday.

### TWO WEEKS TO PARIS

### The Distance to French Capital About 5,000 Miles—Zust Car Has Reached Irkutsk.

POSITION OF THE NEW YORK TO PARIS RACERS.
145th Day of Race.

| Car. | Last Reported. | From New York. | To Paris. |
|---|---|---|---|
| Thomas, | Obansk, July 9 | 16,002 | 5,078 |
| Protos, | Omsk, July 4 | 15,208 | 5,872 |
| Zust | Irkutsk | 13,779 | 7,301 |

Distance from New York to Paris, 21,080 miles.
From New York to Vladivostok, 11,800 miles.

| From Vladivostok. | Miles. | From Vladivostok. | Miles. |
|---|---|---|---|
| To Harbin | 557 | To Obi | 3,017 |
| To Tsitzikar | 706 | To Kainsk | 3,204 |
| To Chita | 1,420 | To Omsk | 3,408 |
| To Verkhnieoudinsk | 1,760 | To Oufa | 4,202 |
| To Missovaia | 1,872 | To Verda | 4,982 |
| To Irkutsk | 1,979 | To Moscow | 5,268 |
| To Kansk | 2,375 | To St. Petersburg | 5,693 |
| To Tomsk | 2,960 | To Paris | 9,280 |

*Special to The New York Times.*

BUFFALO, N. Y., July 9.—A telegram received by the E. R. Thomas Motor Company from Shuster, dated from Obansk, Russia, announces the arrival of the American car in the New York to Paris race at that place, and estimates that the car will reach Paris on July 24. The telegram reads:

"Obansk, Russia, July 9.—Arrived to-day. Expect to reach Paris on July 24.—Shuster."

Special Cable to THE NEW YORK TIMES.

LONDON, July 9.—Scarfoglio, in a dispatch to The Daily Mail dated Irkutsk, Thursday, says: "The crew of the Italian Zust car in the New York to Paris race saluted this morning the little hills where Irkutsk, the Siberian capital, rises above the plain as the soldiers of Alexander the Great saluted the Indian Ocean. Yet the town has a miserable appearance. It is sunk in mud, the smoke is dense about it, and rain was falling at the time. Not the less Irkutsk seemed beautiful in our eyes, tired of the monotonous, eternal green and flowery plain, with tiny Siberian villages built of wood squatting about in it like tired cattle. Huge Mongolian caravans met us as we crossed this plain, the horses richly caparisoned and adorned with silver bands.

"The town is very large, and in spite of its appearance it seems to us a paradise, for our nerves are worn out by the constant strain of life on a racing motorcar, with its interminable delays.

"The bridges on our way had fallen to pieces, owing to deluges and inundations. We have crossed seventeen such bridges. The roads were in a hopeless condition from the overflow of the River Shilka. Once in the village of Yourba we were blocked in an old Mongolian house for two days.

"Really, ever since we left Harbin, the roads have been detestable. The way is long and the goal still far off, but human energy has its limits. We will take a short rest here.

"In a day or two we start west again, and may Siberia be kind to us."

The arrival of the Thomas car at Obansk means that it has crossed Asia successfully and is at last in European territory. The ascent of the Ural steppes has been negotiated successfully, and the roads from there on to Paris are relatively boulevards.

Obansk is off the route of the Trans-Siberian Railroad, which the car was supposed to follow, and is considerably north of the railroad. In distance it is about as far from Vladivostok as Oufa on the Trans-Siberian line. This distance is officially recorded as 4,202 miles from the Pacific terminal. It appears then that the car had traveled since July 4, when it got away from Marianovka, 763 miles, an average of about 150 miles a day.

The German Protos car was 80 miles behind on July 4, but was not expected to leave Omsk, where it then was, until Monday morning on account of the necessity of repairs.

The correspondent of THE NEW YORK TIMES with the New York to Paris racers left the Thomas car last week in order to lighten the load over the rough Siberian trail. As Obansk is off the line of the railway it is likely that he had not yet been able to rejoin the car at the time Shuster's dispatch was sent.

## MRS. LONGWORTH ANGRY.

### Listens to Convention Chairman's Attack on Her Father.

*Special to The New York Times.*

DENVER, July 9.—Mrs. Nicholas Longworth was as angry as the proverbial hornet at Permanent Chairman Clayton to-day. She had occupied a box in the convention auditorium since noon. As point after point was scored against Roosevelt in the Alabaman's speech Mrs. Longworth's nose tilted toward the sky, her jaw set in a manner that suggested her father, and her eyes snapped fire.

Congressman Longworth watched her from behind a fan, with a twinkle in his eye. When the Chairman referred ironically to "My Policies" she stamped her feet. Then Longworth's grin grew wider. His wife looked across the box, caught the twinkle in her husband's eye, flushed angrily, then both burst into a laugh, and the storm was over.

Afterward Mrs. Longworth listened to the address of Clayton without a show of temper.

### Think Thaw Will Get a Jury Trial.

WHITE PLAINS, N. Y., July 9.—It is the general belief around the Court House here that Judge Mills's decision, to be given next Monday in the Thaw case, will be that Harry K. Thaw is entitled to have the question of his sanity passed upon by a jury. It is also believed that Judge Mills will not submit the case to an ordinary Sheriff's jury, but will call a special panel of 200, from which to select the jury, and will himself preside at the trial.

## LOVE IN AN ART GALLERY.

### American Sees a Painting and Finds and Marries the Original.

Special Cable to THE NEW YORK TIMES.

LONDON, July 9.—A romantic story of Harold Abbott Titcomb, a wealthy American mining engineer, who fell in love with a picture in the Tate Gallery and married the original of it yesterday is being told here to-day. Mr. Titcomb is a direct descendant of John and Priscilla Alden, the lovers in Longfellow's "Courtship of Miles Standish."

Visiting two years ago the Tate Gallery, he fell in love with the face of the younger girl in Ralph Peacock's painting "The Sisters."

So fascinated was he with the beauty of the girl that he wrote to the artist asking for a copy of the painting. Some time later he met at the artist's house Miss Ethel Brignall, the original of the picture, and sister-in-law of the artist.

Like his ancestor, Mr. Titcomb was successful in his wooing. He spoke for himself, and married the maiden yesterday in the pretty little parish church of Beddington. The bride, in a classical gown of white embroidered with silver, and the bridegroom, dark and good looking, made a remarkably handsome couple.

The bride's train was carried by a tiny nephew, Roydon Peacock, the original of Ralph Peacock's picture, "Roydon," exhibited at this year's Academy. Mr. Peacock's present to the bridegroom was his latest painting of the bride.

## ALL RIGHT, SAYS CLANCARTY.

### Earl Will Not Name Rich New York Widow He Is to Marry.

Special Cable to THE NEW YORK TIMES.

LONDON, July 9.—The mystery shrouding the identity of the wealthy New York widow who is reported to be engaged to the Earl of Clancarty thickened to-day when numberless inquiries failed to elicit the lady's name. The first report of the engagement came here from the New York correspondent of certain London newspapers, which thereupon telegraphed the Earl of Clancarty at his Irish residence, Garbally Park, County Galway, asking if the statement was correct.

His lordship responded by a brief telegram, as follows: "All right."

This was on Wednesday. Inquiries were then set on foot in London and Dublin to ascertain the name of the lady, but all proved fruitless. Lord Clancarty himself made no answer to further telegrams addressed him on the subject.

## COREYS ENTERTAIN ROYALTY.

### Reception in Paris to Duke of Sparta, Crown Prince of Greece.

Special Cable to THE NEW YORK TIMES.

PARIS, July 9.—W. E. Corey, President of the United States Steel Corporation, and Mrs. Corey gave a reception to-night at the Hotel Ritz in honor of the Duke of Sparta. The reception was followed by dinner in the garden, which was beautifully decorated with flowers and plants.

After dinner a burlesque, "Pall Mall Revue," was acted by French players, and Mlle. Norcy sang French chansons.

Among those present were Princess Hohenlohe, Duc and Duchesse de Morny, Marquis de Turenne, Comte Talleyrand-Perigord, Comte Louis Perigord, Comtesse Hocquart de Turgot, Comte de Contades, Comtesse Divonne, Comte de Lamotte, Lady Robert Peel, Comte Robert de Lesseps, Comte de Laskeyne, Miss Bradley, Montgomery Roosevelt, Frank Munsey, and Mr. and Mrs. Douglass Story.

## SIX MONTHS FOR AN EDITOR

### Convicted of Criminal Libel for Calling Sheriff a Benedict Arnold.

*Special to The New York Times.*

PHILADELPHIA, July 9.—Much interest is being shown by lawyers and newspaper men here in the final outcome of a case of criminal libel brought against David M. Pascoe, managing editor of The Germantown Telegraph, by Sheriff Brown.

Pascoe was convicted yesterday of libeling Brown during the February political campaign by calling him a "Benedict Arnold," and sentenced to serve six months in jail and fined $200. This was the first conviction of an editor for criminal libel in Pennsylvania for many years.

Pascoe's lawyer went to Wilkesbarre to-day and got Judge Rice of the Superior Court to grant a supersedeas, on the ground that the indictment should be quashed, because Brown, as Sheriff, summoned the jury which heard the case. Judge Rice goes back to cases in Blackstone's time to prove that the Coroner should have summoned the talesmen in a case where the Sheriff personally was a party.

Pascoe, after spending twenty-four hours in jail, was released to-night on $2,500 bail.

The appeal will be heard in October.

## MRS. RING WANTS NEW TRIAL.

### Has Letters from Miss Richmond to Mr. Ring, in Slander Suit, She Says.

*Special to The New York Times.*

NYACK, N. Y., July 9.—Counsel for Mrs. Naomi Ring of Mount Vernon made a motion before Supreme Court Justice Tompkins to-day for a new trial of the suit in which Miss Grace Richmond, also of Mount Vernon, recovered a verdict for $8,000 damages for slander from Mrs. Ring in April, 1907. The suit grew out of Mrs. Ring's assertion that Miss Richmond had been seen coming out of the Mount Vernon Opera House, where P. J. Ring, the defendant's husband, had sleeping quarters.

Mrs. Ring's attorney based his argument for a new trial on the grounds of newly discovered evidence. He asserts that half a dozen love letters from Miss Richmond to Mr. Ring were found six months after the trial. In the letters, it is alleged, Miss Richmond addressed Mr. Ring as "My Love," "My Own Sweetheart," &c. They were found by a Mr. Rosenberg, a tenant in the Opera House building, in an old pocket case.

Justice Tompkins reserved decision.



## BRYAN HEARS CHEERS OVER THE 'PHONE

### Listens to the Demonstration in the Convention Hall When His Name Is Presented.

### SPENT THE DAY QUIETLY

### Reclined on the Shady Lawn and Talked with a Visiting Delegation of Nebraska Farmers.

*Special to The New York Times.*

LINCOLN, Neb., Friday, July 10.—William J. Bryan kept in touch with the convention all night by telegraph and telephone.

When the nominating speeches began Mr. Bryan went to a telephone which was connected with the convention hall and, in the midst of his family, listened to the wild demonstration which interrupted the speech of I. J. Dunn nominating him as the Democratic candidate for President. He heard the voice of Sergeant-at-Arms Martin, the music of bands, and voices raised in song.

"Clayton says the Tammany tiger will make a meal of the G. O. P. elephant next Fall," said Mr. Martin through the telephone, and his voice was mingled with the dull roar of other voices and an occasional strain of music or song, and the high-pitched comments of those near the megaphone in the auditorium.

A piping voice cried "Hurrah for Bryan!" and then the wire failed. It came up a minute later.

When the cheering was over Mr. Bryan appeared with a supply of cigars for his fellow-watchers and sank for a moment into a steamer chair, yawned heartily, and remarked that the present convention reminded him of the one at St. Louis. Then he returned to his office.

Miss Grace Bryan, who is 17 years old, was enjoying the whole proceedings immensely. Her chief pleasure was in listening at the convention telephone.

"Oh, my, they're cheering, and some one says the cheers are for Bryan. That's you, father."

In the little family party excitement kept tired eyes open. Eleven o'clock in Denver was midnight here, and the decision to cut seconding speeches to five minutes met with unqualified approval, although Mr. Bryan felt regretful that most of them pertaining to himself could not be heard, as they had been prepared by masters of oratory.

When Mr. Bryan learned of the completion of the committee's work on the platform, he said: "I am very much pleased with the platform. It is clear, specific, and strong, and I am grateful to the committee for the work that they have done in stating the issues. I am sure that the platform will greatly strengthen us in the fight upon which we are entering."

Mr. Bryan had spent a quiet day. The candidate and his secretary, Robert F. Rose, adjourned early to the shaded portion of the lawn near the kennel back of the house. Mose, the venerable bulldog; Rocker, a dachshund, two puppies, and a homeless yellow wanderer, who has adopted Fairview as a home, were blinking placidly in the grass. They looked comfortable, and Mr. Bryan learned from the lowly canines. He procured a pillow and presently with his coat off and his hands under his head, he formed a part of the recumbent picture. Messages from Denver were few, and Mr. Rose rested likewise.

The telegrapher read the private messages through the window, and Mr. Bryan, without arising, dictated the answers. Mr. Bryan did not sleep, but he talked very little to his companion. If the greatness of the impending events affected him he did not show it. His nerves are steady. It is related of him that after the adverse returns were in in 1896, and weeping and unstrung friends surrounded him, the defeated candidate alone was calm, and when McKinley's election at about 10 o'clock in the evening was absolutely confirmed he retired and slept the night through.

Judge Tait, a visitor from Oklahoma, was admitted during the afternoon.

"Brother," said the Oklahoman, "I am glad to meet you. Next to Theodore Roosevelt you are the greatest man on earth."

"It is pleasant," said Bryan, "to be next to the greatest man on earth when that man isn't a candidate."

"I have four sons in Oklahoma," said the Southerner. "They all voted for Gov. Haskell, and they will all vote for you."

"That is good," said Mr. Bryan; "that makes me almost declare in favor of large families."

Newspaper men lounged about the place all afternoon and the candidate was rarely alone, but he cautiously avoided conversation and refused in any way to discuss the destruction of the costly Taft and Sherman banner which had been cut down and burned by vandals the night before in Lincoln. He held that his first statement that he was sorry that the banner had been destroyed covered the ground thoroughly.

A half dozen farmers called to pay their respects, but they did not lure Bryan from his couch on the sod. All sat down in a row, and Mr. Bryan, leaning on his elbow, talked with them on many things besides politics.

"It's the first rest I have had in a long time," he said as he regretfully rose and entered the house.

After dinner and before the telegraph had again taken up the burden of the convention report, the candidate walked about his farm with Mrs. Bryan, his daughter Grace, and Mr. Rose.

While Mr. Bryan was listening over the telephone to the demonstration in the Denver convention hall C. O. Whedon, a lawyer neighbor of Mr. Bryan, was making a speech at a veterans' Republican rally. Mr. Whedon denounced the pictures in the windows of business houses offering "Welcome to Bryan's town." He said: "This is not Bryan's town; it was not in 1896; it was not in 1900; it is not now, and it will never be."

The Bryan Club, which had planned to have a demonstration at Fairview at night, decided in view of the lateness of the convention action to postpone it until Friday. Probably a hundred people, nearly all women, who had not heard of the delay, called early in the evening. A few automobiles, laden with Mr. Bryan's fellow-townsmen, also swept up the driveway at frequent intervals, but their visits were brief. All were greeted cordially and bidden to the formal reception later.

## BISHOP POTTER HAS RELAPSE.

### After Continued Improvement Patient Loses His Strength Slightly.

*Special to The New York Times.*

COOPERSTOWN, N. Y., July 9.—Bishop Potter's condition to-night is not quite as hopeful as yesterday. He rested very comfortably last night, and at 9 o'clock this morning Dr. Janvrin stated that his improvement had continued. To-day, however, he has suffered a slight setback, and to-night at 9 o'clock the physicians issued the following bulletin:

"Bishop Potter continued to improve slightly until to-day. During the day he has lost strength to a slight extent and the prognosis is not quite as favorable as yesterday. J. E. JANVRIN, M. D."

## LUSITANIA OFF SANDY HOOK.

### Sighted at 2 A. M. and Very Close to a New Record.

The big Cunarder Lusitania, from Liverpool, passed Nantucket at 6:45 P. M. last night, and was sighted off Sandy Hook at 2:58 this (Friday) morning. Owing to the haze observation was difficult, and the exact time of her arrival off the lightship is not known.

If she had arrived at 2 A. M., as Capt. Watts's wireless message to the company's office said she would, she would have made the 2,890 knots of the long course in 4 days 19 hours and 25 minutes, eclipsing by some 43 minutes her best previous run over the same course, which was 4 days 20 hours and 8 minutes.

Besides making a quick trip, the Lusitania has made the best day's run ever done by a steamship. On the first day out she logged 648 miles at an average speed of 25.43 knots. Her best previous day's run was 641 knots. She passed Daunt's Rock at 11:35 A. M. on Sunday. Her succeeding days' runs have been, to noon on Sunday, 21 knots; to Monday, 643 knots; Tuesday, 625 knots; Wednesday, 622 knots, and to Thursday noon 623 knots. The last twenty-four hours' run is estimated. Her estimated average speed has been about 25 knots.

The turbiner came across with a new set of propellers. The company has been experimenting with a view to obtaining the greatest amount of speed out of the vessel. Its experiments led it to substitute three-blade propellers for those of four blades, and her performance seems to have justified the change.

The Lusitania will reach her pier about 8 o'clock this morning.

## PARIS TO LONDON BY AIR.

### $5,000 to First Dirigible Machine That Carries a Passenger.

PARIS, July 9.—Henry Deutsch de la Meurthe has offered a new airship prize of $5,000.

It is to go to the first aeronaut who succeeds in conveying a passenger aboard a dirigible airship or aeroplane from Paris to London.

## TEST WIRELESS TELEPHONE.

### Messages Said to Have Been Sent from Newark to This City.

A test of a wireless telephone invented by A. Frederick Collins was made last evening between Newark and this city. Messages were received and transmitted, it is said, between the Collins laboratory, in Clinton Street, Newark, and an upper story of the Singer Building, in New York. The messages, according to a representative of the concern, were sent from the laboratory in Newark from phosphor bronze radiating aerial wires strung about ninety feet above the ground, and were received in the tower of the Singer Building, twelve miles away.

The apparatus at the receiving station in the Singer Building was extremely light and very compact. To one receptive terminal was attached an aluminum wire hanging from the top of the flagstaff and extending down to about the twenty-fifth story, while the apparatus was grounded by means of the copper sheathing of the building.

The sending equipment utilized as its initial energy a current of 500 volts derived from the Public Service Corporation's plant in Newark, and this was converted into a current of 5,000 volts by means of a specially designed high tension generator.

## WERE WOMEN BURGLARS.

### Lace Handkerchief Dropped by Thieves Who Robbed Dressmaker of $2,000.

*Special to The New York Times.*

PHILADELPHIA, July 9.—Burglars broke into the dressmaking establishment of Mrs. Agnes Howard, on South Fifteenth Street, to-day and took away more than $2,000 worth of gowns, jewelry, and silverware. Mrs. Howard left the house for her country home at Highland Park about 7 o'clock last night. Returning this morning a few minutes after 7 o'clock she opened the front door, entered the house, and found it in confusion.

Furniture and clothing were scattered around the floors from the third story to the basement. Upon investigation it was learned that the thieves, presumably two, because of the amount carried away, had climbed over the back fence, ascended a shed, and broken open a second-story window.

A small lace handkerchief left by the thieves is the only clue found, and from this has arisen the theory that the culprits were women, especially because of their excellent knowledge of the value of gowns.

## ROCKEFELLER TELLS A STORY.

### It Was Really Funny, Baptists Said, After You Figured It Out.

*Special to The New York Times.*

CLEVELAND, Ohio, July 9.—John D. Rockefeller responded to nearly ten minutes of noisy welcome at Western Reserve University campus to the Baptist Young People's Union of America in session here this week. After explaining the joy it gave him to see so many bright, happy, young faces around him, and expressing appreciation of the work of Dr. Charles Thwing, President of the university, and of the Rev. Dr. Charles A. Eaton, pastor of the Euclid Avenue Church, Mr. Rockefeller ventured on a funny story, which in time brought roars of laughter and applause from his audience.

As the older members of the convention who knew their Bible best, explained afterward, the point to it was something like this:

A country minister was explaining in humble way the parable of the Prodigal Son. He spoke of the son selling first his overcoat, then his coat, then his waistcoat, then his shirt, then his shoes, and so on through the haberdashery department. "Then," said Mr. Rockefeller impressively, "he came to himself."

Meaning, it is explained, that the prodigal realized what he was doing after all his clothes had reached the pawnshop. The story was really very funny, the Baptists said, after you figured it out, and Mr. Rockefeller told it very humorously.

### Son Born to Mrs. J. D. Rockefeller, Jr.

BAR HARBOR, Me., July 9.—A son was born to Mrs. John D. Rockefeller, Jr., late yesterday at the Rockefeller Summer home here. This is the third child, the others being a boy and a girl.

## BRYAN NAMED; FIRST BALLOT

### Denver Convention Nominates Nebraskan in the Early Morning.

### ANOTHER GREAT OUTBURST

### Noise Is Kept Going for Seventy Minutes by Huge Crowd in the Hall.

### BIG TRIBUTE TO JOHNSON

### He Is Cheered for 22 Minutes, Despite the Efforts of Chairman Clayton.

### GRAY MEN UNFORTUNATE

### Demonstration Nipped by Report of the Resolutions Committee—Platform Is Adopted Unanimously.

*Special to The New York Times.*

DENVER, Friday, 3:05 A. M., (5:05 New York Time,) July 10.—William Jennings Bryan, twice nominated and twice defeated for the Presidency, was nominated for a third time by the Democratic National Convention early this morning.

The roll call on the nomination began at 3 A. M., (5 o'clock New York time.) The roll call had not proceeded more than four minutes before it was evident that Bryan was nominated.

The convention clock had been stopped at midnight Thursday to avoid the Friday "hoodoo."

A demonstration second only to that of Wednesday was given when Bryan's name was placed before the convention. It started at 9:06 o'clock, (11:06 New York time,) and it was 10:16, or seventy minutes later, before order was restored. It was necessary to turn out most of the lights in the hall before the Bryan boomers would give up their efforts to exceed the record of the day before.

After more than two days of wrangling over the platform the Committee on Resolutions was not ready to report at 7 o'clock, the hour set for the night session. The convention waited until 8:35 o'clock, and then was told that a report would not be made till midnight. A motion was carried to hear the nominating speeches, with the understanding that the vote on the Presidency would not be taken until the platform had been adopted.

Ignatius J. Dunn of Nebraska placed Mr. Bryan in nomination. When his speech was concluded the great outburst took place.

Gov. Johnson of Minnesota was placed in nomination by Congressman Hammond at 11:05. Immediately a big demonstration began for him, Georgia joining with Minnesota. Chairman Clayton tried to stop the cheering, but despite his efforts it went on for twenty-two minutes.

Judge Gray was placed in nomination by L. Irving Handy just before midnight. As the Resolutions Committee was ready to report the Delawarean got only a minute's cheering.

Gov. Haskell began reading the platform, on which the report was unanimous, at 12:02.

The report of the committee was adopted unanimously at 12:56, and after many seconding speeches had been made the ballot was taken.

### GREAT CROWD IN THE HALL.

#### After Wait for Platform Nominating Speeches Are Heard.

*Special to The New York Times.*

DENVER, Friday, July 10.—This was the big show session at the Democratic Convention for the adoption of the platform, which it had taken the Committee on Resolutions more than forty-eight hours to prepare, and then for the nomination of Bryan, and the Auditorium was packed to the roof long before the hour set for the session. The crowd early made a rush for the galleries, filling them to overflowing.

There were few of the delegates in their places at 7 o'clock last (Thursday) night. They had lingered long at dinner, the slow dying of the twilight of the Colorado evening proving deceptive. They were rapidly arriving, however, and, like the crowd, seemed to be in splendid temper for the long session through which they must sit.

Small American flags had been placed in every chair, for when the time came for the grand whoop there must be every accessory for making it a record-breaker.

In order that the music might not fail a Chicago band relieved the cowboy musicians, most of whom never were cowboys, but who had served so loyally since the opening of the convention on Tuesday. The bandsmen of the plains, it was generally agreed, had earned their rest.

A man with a baritone voice of phenomenal power sang "Rocked in the Cradle of the Deep," and the crowd shouted for more. A quartet also sang through big megaphones and got a royal reception.

#### Sea of Red, White, and Blue.

The playing of "The Star-Spangled Banner" by the band, with a sextet of trombones carrying the air, brought the crowd to its feet, and the 12,000 small American flags beat time to the music. Everywhere was a moving sea of red, white, and blue, except in the press inclosure, where flags were not distributed to what the Bryan orators are pleased to refer as "the prostituted hirelings of a plutocratic press."

The auditorium was so crowded at 7:45 o'clock that it looked as though there would be difficulty in clearing the aisles. It was evident that there had been laxity on the doors and that thousands more had been passed in than there were seats for. There could not be less than 6,000 women in the crowd of 14,000 persons in the hall, and as they were nearly all in

"All the News That's Fit to Print."

# The New York Times.

THE WEATHER.
Fair, warmer, to-day and Sunday; east shifting to south winds.

VOL. LVII...NO. 18,431. * * * NEW YORK, SATURDAY, JULY 11, 1908.—FOURTEEN PAGES. and Section Devoted to Review of Books. ONE CENT In Greater New York, Jersey City, and Newark. { Elsewhere, TWO CENTS.

## MELLEN CONFIRMS BOSTON & MAINE SALE

### But Banker Billard Thinks There May Be Others Interested in His Purchase.

### YES, HE HOLDS ALL STOCK

**Isn't a Railroad Man, He Says, and Isn't Telling Why He Paid $14,-850,000 Cash for Shares.**

Following a meeting of the Directors of the New York, New Haven & Hartford Railroad here yesterday, President Mellen confirmed the report of the sale of the road's holdings of Boston & Maine stock to John L. Billard, a Meriden, Conn., banker, in this statement:

The New Haven Road has sold its Boston & Maine stock absolutely without any further agreement, expressed or implied. Delivery of the stock has been made, and the proceeds of the sale are now in the New Haven's treasury.

The New Haven Railroad has been of the opinion that the control of the Boston & Maine by the New Haven would have beneficial results for the Boston & Maine and New Haven Roads, their stockholders, and for the people in the territories served by these two companies. It was undoubtedly an opportunity to perform a much-needed service.

But however much the New Haven Road may have desired to bring about this new relationship between the two systems and work out these changes, it has decided to sell its Boston & Maine stock rather than combat with the Commonwealth of Massachusetts.

In addition to expressing a natural curiosity over the personality of Mr. Billard, a man never heard of here until he bought 110,000 shares of Boston & Maine stock, of a market value of some $14,-850,000, Wall Street wondered how this transaction left the Ontario & Western deal, which the New Haven also has on its hands.

It was generally assumed that Mr. Billard had been aided in his purchase by the regular New Haven banking interests, since the transaction was too big for any individual to swing.

The position of the New Haven in reference to its control of the New York, Ontario & Western was said yesterday to be that the policy adopted by the New Haven in respect to controlling an entrance to the coal fields would require it to retain control of the Ontario & Western, now that it has given up its effort to obtain formal control of the Boston & Maine. In connection with the New Haven's plan to buy a majority of Boston & Maine stock the New Haven gave an option to the New York Central to purchase the New Haven's Ontario & Western holdings. It was made clear at the time, however, that this option was contingent upon the New Haven's success in carrying through its plan for the control of the Boston & Maine.

After an hour's session the New Haven Directors adjourned to meet again on the new Fall River Line boat Commonwealth, on which they sailed for Fall River at 5:30 P. M. It was stated that the Boston & Maine sale would be formally ratified on the trip up the Sound.

*Special to The New York Times.*

BOSTON, July 10.—The announcement authoritatively made to-day that the New Haven Road had sold to John L. Billard of Meriden, Conn., its 110,000 shares of Boston & Maine stock is variously regarded here. An interview with Mr. Billard is published in which he says:

"I own the stock personally, I understand, but there are others interested. But the stock is all in my name, and I am to vote."

"Then there are others interested with you in this purchase?"

"Well, I suppose so, but it is something I cannot talk about. The facts have all been given, and if there was anything more that I could tell you about it I would be glad to do so."

"Have you ever had any experience in railroad matters before, Mr. Billard?"

"No, I have never been interested in railroad matters in any way. I have had no experience in that line whatever."

"How long have you been considering the purchase of the Boston & Maine stock held by the New Haven?"

"Oh, for some little time. I had several interviews about it before the deal was closed."

"What led you to make the purchase at this time, if you have not heretofore been interested in railroad matters?"

"That is something I cannot discuss. I said I had no experience in railroad matters. I have been for fifty years right here in Meriden, Conn., and I am President of the Meriden Savings Bank and of the Lyon & Billard Company, which deals in lumber and coal.

"All that I can say in addition to what I have already told you is that the property of the road will be cared for in good shape."

"We understand in Boston that it is your intention to work in harmony with both the Boston & Maine and the New Haven. Is that so?"

"Yes, that is true. I shall try to work in harmony with the interests of both roads and for the interests of the merchants and people of New England."

President Tuttle of the Boston & Maine said to-day:

"All I can say with regard to this transaction is that 109,948 shares of Boston & Maine controlled by the New York, New Haven & Hartford Railroad were put in for transfer on July 1. Our transfer agent, the Old Colony Trust Company, notified my by telephone that this stock had been presented for transfer and that it had been placed in the name of John L. Billard.

"I saw President Mellen a few days later, and he informed me that the stock had been sold to Mr. Billard, and that it was an actual sale.

"Mr. Billard is a man of affairs at Meriden, Conn., is President of the Meriden Savings Bank, and, so far as I know, is not generally understood to have any particular interest in the affairs of the New Haven Company.

"I do not know the price paid for the stock, but I am disposed to believe there has been an actual sale sufficient to satisfy all legal requirements.

"It is not to be presumed that Mr. Billard paid $10,000,000 or $15,000,000 of his own cash for this stock. He may have banking connections which would be glad to finance such a purchase, and if he has not, the bankers interested in the New Haven road could easily arrange the matter, but whether or not any one else has assisted in the purchase is immaterial. The stock has been bought by Mr. Billard and placed in his name. Just how he has financed it I have no knowledge, neither is it material to the fact."

Despite the fact that Mr. Billard is the nominal owner of the stock Attorney General Dana Malone says he will press the suit which the State has instituted against the New Haven Road.

The writ in the State's case is returnable the first Monday in August, and the company has thirty days in which to file an answer.

Until such an answer is forthcoming, the Attorney General and the courts will

**Continued on Page 4.**

## JAPAN SHUDDERS AT WAR.

**Mikado's Representative Says His Country Is Grateful to United States.**

*Special to The New York Times.*

WASHINGTON, July 10.—Weighing his words carefully, Kametaro Hayashida declared to-day that Japan not only shuddered at the idea of war with the United States, but could not dream of anything arising that would make it possible because of the debt Nippon owed this Government for bringing it into the Council of Nations. Mr. Hayashida is the Mikado's personal representative in the Japanese Parliament, its chief Secretary, and the author of many of the Nation's parliamentary and election reforms.

"Talk of war is not the talk of the people of Japan," he said earnestly. "Some few, unfortunately, fail to appreciate the great responsibility of the two countries. Japan has owed a debt of gratitude to America since your offer of friendship and good will when Commodore Perry visited us. All Japan is waiting to greet your great fleet. When you warships were invited to our shores the invitation was extended because we wished to show your officers and men our hospitality and demonstrate that we really do feel our indebtedness to your great Nation."

Mr. Hayashida, accompanied by a suite of expert architects and attendants, is here getting ideas for a building suitable for the Capitol of Japan. The Japanese Diet has appropriated $12,000,000 for the construction of the building. Mr. Hayashida has made a close study of many of the public structures here.

## LAKE OF OIL BURNING.

**Mexican Workman Sets Fire to Underground Workings—Explosion Follows.**

*Special to The New York Times.*

CITY OF MEXICO, Mexico, July 10.—A lake of oil covering an area of more than one square mile and of unknown depth in the State of Vera Cruz, is on fire. It has been burning for five days and has created the wildest terror among the natives of that section.

The lake is about seventy-five miles southeast of Tampico, near the San Geronimo River. It is remote from any railroad. An oil field was being developed at that place by the Pennsylvania Oil Company, which is composed of Pittsburg (Penn.) men. A careless workman accidentally set fire to one of the wells, and the flames were in some manner communicated to the underground reservoir of oil.

A terrific explosion occurred, which uplifted the earth's surface throughout the whole field. The explosion shook the earth and was plainly heard for seventy-five miles around. It was thought that an earthquake had occurred. The fire quickly spread underneath the uplift, and 1,000 feet of surface earth and rock were quickly melted down, leaving a vast open pit of burning oil.

The Pennsylvania Oil Company lost $200,000 worth of machinery. No estimate can be made of the quantity of oil which has been burned already. It will run into the millions of barrels. The entire oil field will be destroyed.

## FIVE SERENADERS WOUNDED.

**Angry Bridegroom Fires Shotgun Into a Crowd—One Fatally Hurt.**

*Special to The New York Times.*

ALLENTOWN, Penn., July 10.—Five young men were shot by an angry bridegroom, who fired with a double-barreled gun into a crowd of wedding serenadors at Danielsville early this evening. It did not become known until to-day that Amandes Miller, a widower of 49, and Miss Tessie Hardwick, who is a few years his junior, had been married secretly two weeks ago. Instead of receiving the serenaders with customary hospitality, Miller and his seventeen-year-old son William fired three shots at them.

Stewart Gable, aged 22, is in the Allentown Hospital with a mangled arm and several pellets in his heart. The surgeons say he will die. About seventy-five shot have been removed from Charles Easterday. Some unremoved shot, the doctors say, are in his body.

Both were taken to the hospital in an automobile by William Bryan, a member of the band, who also received several of the pellets.

Albert Zimmerman, Walter Minnich, and Howard Newhard are laid up in bed at their homes from wounds. Dr. Kemmerer of Danielsville is attending them and also several young women who were struck by stray shots.

In default of $2,000 bail each, Miller and his son were to-night committed to prison by Squire Eigosser to await the result of the injuries they inflicted.

## LABOR LEADERS SUED.

**Gompers, Mitchell, and Others Defendants in $50,000 Damage Action.**

*Special to The New York Times.*

DENVER, Col., July 10.—While Samuel Gompers, John Mitchell, John H. Lennon, Frank Morrison, Joseph Valentine, James Duncan, and Max Morris were holding a conference on labor matters to-day, Deputy Sheriff Thomas Lawson served them with papers calling on them to appear as defendants in a suit brought by the W. R. Thompson Marble Company.

The suit is against them as leading officers of the American Federation of Labor, the officers of the Colorado State Federation of Labor, officers of the Denver Building Trades Council, and about fifty other labor men of local or National prominence for $50,000 for alleged damages to its business by a strike and boycott. These officers will have to appear in Denver before Ellis J. Lewis on July 17 to give testimony, and the action will keep them in Denver a week longer than they had anticipated.

They are all named as joint defendants. The trial has been set for Aug. 4, and it will probably be necessary for the leaders to again return to Denver at that time also. The marble company asserts that, while paying the scale and working eight hours, the union called its men from several buildings, and alleges that Gompers, Mitchell, and the others are partly responsible.

## TWO DROWN FROM CANOE.

**New Yorker Was Trying Boat He Built, with Five-Year-Old Son.**

*Special to The New York Times.*

POUGHKEEPSIE, N. Y., July 10.—Theodore Barringer, a New York letter carrier, and his five-year-old son, Harry, were drowned this evening in Bowman's Pond at Pleasant Valley. They were in a canoe made by Barringer out of canvas and barrel staves. The frail affair overturned, throwing Barringer, his son, and another man from the canoe. The third man, whose name was not learned, was saved.

## CLEVELAND'S WILL FILED AT PRINCETON

### Ex-President Leaves Mementos to Friends and $10,000 to Each of His Children.

### THE REST GOES TO HIS WIFE

**With the Exception of $3,000 to a Niece and $2,000 Each to His Four Grand-Nephews—Wants Simple Monument.**

*Special to The New York Times.*

TRENTON, N. J., July 10.—The last will and testament of Grover Cleveland, written with his own hand two years ago, was probated to-day. Surrogate John Wesley Cornell of this county went to Princeton to meet Mrs. Cleveland so as to give her as much privacy as possible.

Bayard Stockton, Mrs. Cleveland's lawyer, met her as she left the train in Princeton. They, with Surrogate Cornell and the two witnesses to the document, were the only persons present at the Cleveland home when the document was probated. The witnesses were Prof. Andrew F. West, Dean of the Princeton Graduate School, and John H. Finley, President of the College of the City of New York.

No inventory was filed with the instrument, and the value of the estate is not mentioned. The will prescribes that the testator's body should be buried out of the proceeds of the estate, and that only a modest monument should be erected to his memory. He also expresses a wish to be buried in Princeton and not removed therefrom except to be buried beside his wife, if she cannot be buried by his body.

There are $51,000 in bequests, $10,000 to each of his four children, $3,000 to his niece, and $2,000 each to the four children of his nephew. He gives his gold watch to Richard Watson Gilder and seal ring to Frank E. Hastings. This is the text of the will:

"I, Grover Cleveland, of the Borough of Princeton, in the State of New Jersey, do make, publish, and declare this my last will and testament, hereby expressly revoking all previous wills by me made:

"First—I hereby direct that after the payment of all my debts and funeral expenses an appropriate monument, with brief inscription and only moderately expensive, be erected at my grave and paid for out of my estate. I desire to be buried wherever I may reside at the time of my death, and that my body shall always remain where it shall be at first buried subject to its removal only if it shall be absolutely necessary in order that it shall repose by the side of my wife and in accordance with her desire.

"Second—I give to my niece, Mary Hastings, daughter of my sister, Anna Hastings, the sum of $3,000, to be paid to her as soon as practicable after my death.

"Third—I give to my friend Richard Watson Gilder the watch given to me in 1893 by the said Gilder and E. C. Benedict and J. J. Sinclair, and also the chain attached to the same when last worn by me.

"Fourth—I give to each of the four daughters of my nephew, Richard Hastings, now or lately living with my sister, Anna Hastings, the sum of $2,000 each.

"Fifth—I give to Frank S. Hastings, my good friend and executor of this will, as the most personal memento I can leave to him, the seal ring I have worn for many years, which was given to me by my dear wife, and with whose hearty concurrence this gift is made.

"Sixth—I give to my two daughters, Esther and Marion, and to my two sons, Richard F. and Francis G., the sum of $10,000 each, to be paid to them, respectively, as they each shall arrive at the age of 21 years. Until these legacies are paid, or shall lapse, they shall be kept invested and the income derived therefrom shall be paid to my wife, and the aggregate of said income shall be applied by her to the support, maintenance, and education of said children in such manner and in such proportions as she shall deem best, without any liability to any of said children on account thereof. If, however, either of my said daughters shall before her legacy becomes payable cease for any reason to reside with her mother, then, and from that time, the income arising from the investment of her legacy shall be paid to said daughter. In case either of my said children shall die before his or her legacy shall be actualy paid, leaving a child or children, then said legacy shall be paid to such child or children, but otherwise the said legacy shall lapse and become a part of the residuary estate disposed by this instrument.

"Seventh—All the rest and residue of my estate and property of which I may die seized or possessed, of every kind and nature, and wheresoever the same may be situated, I give, devise, and bequeath to my dear wife, Frances F. Cleveland, and to her heirs and assigns forever, and I hereby appoint her guardian of all my children during their minority.

"Eighth—I hereby appoint my wife, Frances F. Cleveland, executrix and Frank S. Hastings executor of this my last will and testament.

"Witness my hand and seal at Princeton, New Jersey, this twenty-first day of February, one thousand nine hundred and six. GROVER CLEVELAND."

"The foregoing instrument was on the day it bears date signed by Grover Cleveland, the testator therein named, in the presence of each of us, and we both being present at the same time. And the said testator did then and there acknowledge and declare, to us and each of us, that said instrument was his last will and testament, and thereupon we did in the presence of each other and of said testator, and at his request, subscribe our names hereto as attesting witnesses.

"ANDREW F. WEST,
"Princeton, N. J.
"JOHN H. FINLEY,
"New York City, N. Y."

### Mrs. Sage's Way with a Race Track.

SAG HARBOR, L. I., July 10.—One way of settling a race-track question was evolved the other day by Mrs. Russell Sage, who bought the old forty-two-acre race track and athletic field situated about a mile from the centre of this village, and presented it to the village as a playground and athletic field for the school children. There is a fine growth of timber on one-sixth of the land, and it is understood that Mrs. Sage paid $5,000 for the tract.



## CLANCARTY WITHHOLDS NAME.

**Earl's Lawyer in America Inquiring as to Prospective Bride's Fortune.**

*Special Cable to THE NEW YORK TIMES.*

LONDON, July 10.—The Earl of Clancarty, who is now in London, today informed THE NEW YORK TIMES's correspondent, in response to his request for the name of the wealthy New York widow to whom he is reported to be engaged, that the announcement made in the newspapers was premature and that he could not give the name of the lady for publication at present.

From other sources it was learned that the legal representative of the Earl is now in America making inquiries relative to the fortune of the prospective bride, who, according to one informant, is a Canadian-born woman whose son, now 15 years of age, is preparing to enter the American Navy as a cadet at Annapolis. She is about the same age as Clancarty, 38.

The Earl was adjudged a bankrupt a year ago, and all his unentailed property, even race horses, was sold off and bailiffs took possession of his ancestral home in County Galway.

## EPISCOPAL NUNS CHANGE.

**Mother Edith of Peekskill and Two Sisters Become Catholics.**

*Special to The New York Times.*

PHILADELPHIA, July 10.—This city continues a Mecca for those affected by the pro-Roman movement in the Episcopal Church. Three Episcopal nuns are now in the Catholic convent of the Blessed Sacrament at Cornwells.

Dr. William McGarvey while an Episcopal clergyman filled the office of Chaplain General to the Sisters of the Community of St. Mary, whose mother house is St. Gabriel's School, Peekskill, N. Y. Shortly after the reception last May of Dr. McGarvey and six associates of the Companions of the Saviour into the Catholic Church Mother Katharine Drexel, superioress of the Sisters of the Blessed Sacrament, and herself a convert, called on Dr. McGarvey and tendered the hospitality of her community to such Episcopal nuns as contemplated changing their faith.

The three nuns who have accepted the invitation are Mother Edith, Mother General of the Sisters of St. Mary in the United States, and Sisters Eliza and Marina. Sister Eliza has been received into the Catholic Church by Archbishop Ryan. Mother Edith and Sister Marina are under preparatory instruction. Archbishop Ryan has promised to be present at their reception, which will take place shortly.

It is said that the purpose of Mother Edith in quitting Peekskill was unknown to her community, which was as a consequence nearly demoralized upon hearing of her whereabouts.

## METROPOLITAN TOWER BELLS.

**Four of the Largest in the World to be Placed in 46th Story.**

Four of the largest and costliest bells in the world are to be placed in the forty-sixth story of the new tower of the Metropolitan Life Insurance Company's building, in Madison Square, and from a position about 650 feet above the pavement, nearly twice as high as any in the world, their deep tones will announce each quarter of an hour.

An order for the bells was yesterday placed with the Meneely Bell Company of Troy, N. Y. The work of casting them will be begun at once, and it is expected that they will be in place in time to welcome the new year.

The largest bell, toned to B flat, will be 70 inches at the mouth and weigh 7,000 pounds; the second in E flat, will weigh 3,000 pounds; the third, in F natural, will weigh 2,000 pounds, and the fourth, in G, will weigh 1,500 pounds. They will play every fifteen minutes and strike each hour. They are to be mounted on pedestals between the marble pillars outside the forty-sixth story.

They will give what is known as the Cambridge quarters, four blows each quarter of an hour, eight blows on the half, twelve blows on the three-quarters, and sixteen blows each hour, followed by a striking of the hour.

## CASTELLANE BEGINS FIGHT.

**Court Appoints a Medical Expert to Examine Count's Youngest Son.**

PARIS, July 10.—Judge Henri Ditte, President of the Tribunal of First Instance of the Seine, to-day appointed a medical expert to make a physical examination of Jay de Castellane, youngest son of Count Boni de Castellane and his divorced wife, who is now the Princess Helie de Sagan, and decide when the condition of the boy will permit his removal from the home of his grandmother, the Marquise de Castellane.

Count Boni last week, in the absence of the boy's mother, took Jay, who was ill, from Versailles to the home of the Marquise.

It is understood that the suit of Count Boni to have the custody of his children restored to him on account of his former wife's marriage to Prince Helie de Sagan will be begun next week.

## TRAIN HOLD-UP MAN SHOT.

**Lone Operator Had Battle with Great Northern Conductor.**

SPOKANE, Wash., July 10.—Robert Roman, highwayman, attempted to hold up west-bound Passenger Train 3 on the Great Northern Railroad near Naples, Idaho, yesterday afternoon. He got nothing, but fled after exchanging several shots with Conductor Mathews and passengers of the train.

The conductor was the better marksman, and shot the robber through the lungs, breaking a rib. His wounds are probably fatal. The officers and train crew tracked him to Naples and captured him. He declares he was the only man concerned in the attempt.

## OSTEND GAMBLING TO GO.

**Raids Decide Proprietor of Famous Rooms to Remove to Scheveningen.**

OSTEND, July 10.—Hotel proprietors and store keepers here are greatly excited over a report that the proprietor of the famous gambling rooms, which bring thousands of visitors to Ostend, has decided to transfer his establishment to Scheveningen, a fashionable bathing resort in The Netherlands, because of the vigorous application of the anti-gambling law.

Recently the police have raided several of these establishments in Ostend, arrested the occupants of the rooms, and seized stakes valued at thousands of dollars.

### Latest Shipping News.

Arrived—Steamer Kaiserin Auguste Victoria, from Hamburg July 2.

## TRAIN HITS AUTO; MAN AND WIFE DIE

### Mr. and Mrs. Hutchings Killed by Long Island Express—Daughter Mortally Hurt.

### DIDN'T HEAR WARNING BELL

**Auto Ran On to the Crossing Near Centre Moriches Directly in Front of the Hampton Express.**

*Special to The New York Times.*

EASTPORT, L. I., July 10.—The grade crossing which is one and a half miles west of Centre Moriches station on the Long Island Railroad was the scene to-night of a collision between the Hampton express, crowded with fashionable members of the Hampton Summer colony, and a large Stearns limousine automobile containing its owner, W. R. Hutchings, a chandler, of 289 Sterling Place, Brooklyn; his wife, and their ten-year-old daughter Lillian. Mrs. Hutchings was killed outright. Her husband suffered such serious injuries that he died several hours after the crash. The young girl is still alive, but her injuries are considered mortal.

The Hutchings family have a Summer cottage in Union Avenue, Centre Moriches. Mr. Hutchings recently purchased a new Stearns car, and last night took his wife and daughter out in it. At the wheel was Frederick Clough, the chauffeur. The auto ran at fair speed along the South Shore Road, as it is known at this point.

Running parallel to the road are the tracks of the Long Island Railroad. They are, however, hidden from view by a tall bank which skirts the road. The grade crossing where the accident occurred is on a bend of the road. There is nothing to warn persons of the approach of a train except an electric bell, which is set ringing automatically by the approaching train itself. The noise made by a large automobile, it is said, is almost sufficient to drown the sound of it.

The automobile party was unaware of the approaching train, as Clough ran the machine on to the crossing. He said he had heard no bell. As the auto reached the tracks, the express—the fastest on the Long Island Railroad—which was running at about sixty-five miles an hour, was seen but a few yards away. It was too late to do anything. All in the car saw their danger and shrieked. The next moment the engine crashed into the rear part of the automobile, which was smashed to splinters. Mr. Hutchings was thrown 160 feet in one direction, while his wife and daughter were thrown about half that distance in the other. Clough, being on the front of the machine, missed the full force of the impact, and was thrown to the ground, escaping with a few bruises and cuts.

As quickly as possible the engineer brought his train to a stop. The passengers were all more or less frightened by the sudden checking of the speed. The train does not stop between Jamaica and Quogue, a run of seventy miles, and was making up the five minutes it was late. After stopping his train, the engineer backed it to the scene of the accident. Then the trainmen carried the injured persons to the porch of Mrs. T. S. Homan's house, which is opposite the crossing. A hurry call for doctors was sent out, and Drs. Fowler, Warner, and Rogers attended quickly. They found Mrs. Hutchings dead. Mr. Hutchings was so seriously injured that there is no hope of his recovery, and the ten-year-old daughter was hurt so badly that it is a question whether she will live. All three were borne to the family's Summer cottage.

The express only runs on Fridays, and then only in the Summer season. It carries the week-end parties from New York to the country homes along the South Shore. Its presence on the time table was unknown to Clough or any of the members of the Hutchings family.

Passengers on the train saw the car following alongside for several miles, and say that the automobile, which was being run at terrific speed, was endeavoring to beat it.

## BISHOP POTTER UNCHANGED.

**Some Concern Over His Failure to Gain Strength.**

*Special to The New York Times.*

COOPERSTOWN, N. Y., July 10.—Bishop Potter has been very comfortable to-day. After the slight set-back of yesterday the Bishop had a restful night. Dr. Henry T. Hun of Albany was called yesterday and will remain here a few days.

At 1 o'clock to-day the following bulletin was issued:

There has been no material change in Bishop Potter's condition since yesterday.
J. E. JANVRIN,
M. C. BASSETT,
HENRY T. HUN.

The physicians are very conservative in their statements regarding the Bishop's condition. The hope that the patient may get up again is freely indulged in, and yet his slowness to improve is a matter of grave concern. However, no immediate change for the worse is anticipated.

## JERSEY TOWN SET ABLAZE.

**Forest Fire Burns Many Buildings in South River, N. J.**

*Special to The New York Times.*

SOUTH RIVER, N. J., July 10.—A fire started here this afternoon which threatened for a time to wipe out the town. It was controlled at nightfall, but more than $50,000 damage had been done then, and many buildings had been destroyed. Among them were the Whitehead Building, in which was the Post Office, Citizens' Hall, Undertaker Morgan's establishment, Silk's drug store, Arthur Levy's jewelry store, George Serviss's confectionery shop, and nearly all the rest of the business section of the town.

The handsome residences of ex-Mayor Bissett and Dr. A. L. Wood were also destroyed. The fire started in Schroeder's barber shop, and an inadequate water supply allowed the flames to get beyond control. Fire apparatus was sent from New Brunswick. Three persons were slightly hurt.



## NEW CURRENCY APPEARS.

**Aldrich-Vreeland Law Bills Shown in Wall Street for First Time.**

Much interest was taken yesterday in the appearance in Wall Street of the first of the new form of National bank currency, drawn in conformity with the recently enacted Aldrich-Vreeland law, which requires that all additional National bank circulation shall be of the same form provided for the emergency currency, which the banks are free to take out under this law.

The new bills are printed in blue, and, besides bearing the announcement that the currency is secured by United States bonds "or other securities," differ in some other details from the old bank-notes.

The new bills are part of the currency issued to newly organized National banks which have just taken out their circulation.

## TAMMANYITE FOR TAFT.

**Loeb Says an ex-Senator Has Told Mr. Roosevelt He'll Vote Republican.**

*Special to The New York Times.*

OYSTER BAY, L. I., July 10.—Secretary Loeb said he had received a letter from a former Democratic State Senator and member of Tammany Hall telling him that the ex-Senator would vote for Taft and had offered to bet "Tom" Taggart $10,000 against $5,000 that Bryan would not be elected, and also $10,000 to $5,000 that Bryan would not carry New York State.

## WARRANT FOR DAN HANNA.

**Son of Late Senator Said to Have Used Whip on Automobilist.**

*Special to The New York Times.*

CLEVELAND, Ohio, July 10.—A warrant for the arrest of Dan R. Hanna, son of the late Senator, was issued by Prosecutor Dan Cull to-day. Hanna is charged with striking Claude M. Logan, salesman for the Oldsmobile Company, with a whip.

Logan disputed the right of way in a park and Hanna is said to have struck him with a driving whip.

## PARDON WAS 17 YEARS LATE.

**Letter Releasing Violator of Pension Law Went Astray.**

COLUMBUS, Ohio, July 10.—Eighteen years after George Swanston completed his one-year sentence in the penitentiary here for violating the United States pension laws, a full and complete pardon arrived at the institution to-day, signed by Benjamin Harrison, then President of the United States, and William F. Wharton, his Acting Secretary of State.

The original letter containing the pardon was received here yesterday from St. Louis. It is dated at Washington, Sept. 3, 1890, at 6 P. M. It was stamped at Columbus, Sept. 4, in the evening. It is probable that the letter has been lying in some Post Office for years.

## MISS BRICE'S DOG LOST.

**He's a Japanese and His Disappearance Agitates Newport.**

*Special to The New York Times.*

NEWPORT, R. I., July 10.—Miss Helen Brice, who returned from Europe yesterday to Newport, has been automobiling through the cottage colony most of today, assisted by her sister, Miss Kate Brice and several men, looking everywhere for her black and white Japanese dog.

Early this morning Miss Brice called for him, but there was no response. A reward has been offered, and Miss Brice continues to look for her pet. This afternoon every one was asking every one else, "Have you seen Miss Brice's dog?"

## ELOPER OF 77 FORGIVEN.

**His Mother, 95, Agrees Not to Disinherit Peck and His Bride of 22.**

*Special to The New York Times.*

NEW HAVEN, Conn., July 10.—Burr S. Peck, the 77-year-old bridegroom, returned from his elopement in New York this morning, and announced that he had left his 22-year-old bride, Mamie O'Brien, in New Rochelle with relatives.

Peck was surprised when newspaper men asked him whether his 95-year-old mother would disinherit him for marrying without her consent. She had a long talk with her wayward son, and finally agreed not to disinherit him. As there are no other near relatives chances seem remote for any annulment suit being brought.

Peck again left town, and it was said at his house to-night that he and his bride would not arrive here till next week.

## TO ACCUSE RECTOR KEMP.

**Chicago Congregation Is Preparing Charges—He Is in Sanitarium.**

*Special to The New York Times.*

CHICAGO, July 10.—The sudden departure of the Rev. Morris Kemp, rector of St. Chrysostom's Episcopal Church and formerly assistant rector of Trinity Church, New York, was explained to-day by members of the congregation who are framing charges against him, based on complaints of members of the choir, to be presented to Bishop C. P. Anderson.

The Rev. Mr. Kemp left Chicago May 22 for his home near Albany, N. Y., where he was placed in a sanitarium for treatment.

Mr. Kemp is 46 years old, and was popular with all the members of the fashionable congregation. He had acted as rector of the church for nearly a year.

## MAYOR IN MONASTERY.

**Was Saloon Owner and Politics Led Him to Shun the World.**

*Special to The New York Times.*

DUBUQUE, Iowa, July 10.—Mayor H. A. Schunk, saloon owner and politician, who disappeared recently, was to-day found in the Trappist Monastery, eighteen miles from here.

Troubles in legal and political affairs are assigned as the cause for the official's desire to shun the world. It is said that he is following out the rigid discipline of the monks, arising at 2 A. M. and attending devotions as prescribed by the order.

Simultaneously with Mr. Schunk's disappearance there was filed a suit for an injunction by ex-Alderman Joseph Needham, seeking to enjoin the Mayor from operating the liquor store run in his name while discharging the duties of Mayor. It was charged that the Mayor violated the law in that his place of business was kept open on June 2, an election day.

## BRYAN AND KERN PUT ON TICKET

### Convention Chooses Twice-Defeated Indianan as Nebraskan's Running Mate and Adjourns.

### FINAL SESSION IS QUIET

### After Turbulence Over Bryan Little Enthusiasm Is Shown for Second Place.

### WAS DECLINED BY MANY

**Cohalan Pledges All Efforts in New York, Including Force, to Elect the Candidates.**

THE DEMOCRATIC TICKET.

**For President—WILLIAM JENNINGS BRYAN of Nebraska.**

**For Vice President—JOHN WORTH KERN of Indiana.**

*Special to The New York Times.*

DENVER, Col., July 10.—With one turbulent session that lasted until the dawn was breaking and ended with the nomination of William Jennings Bryan for President, and a quiet afternoon session that resulted in the nomination of John Worth Kern of Indiana for Vice President, the Democratic National Convention ended its labors to-day. It had completed a ticket that was consistent, at any rate, for a man twice defeated for the Presidency was at the head of it, and a man twice defeated for Governor of his State was at the tail of it.

Only the reluctance of the New York leaders to present a candidate for second place on the Bryan ticket was responsible for the nomination of Mr. Kern. William J. Bryan, according to his spokesmen here, since it became certain that Judge Gray of Delaware would not consent to become his running mate, was very anxious to have the New York delegation unite on some conservative Democrat who could lend prestige to the ticket in the East.

**Place Went Begging.**

To state facts, the Vice Presidential nomination has gone begging for many days, though there was a superabundance of small fry candidates, who would have been only too happy to accept it. At the session this afternoon the one salient feature in all the speechmaking was the announcement on the part of the men who had been chosen spokesmen of the several States which were heard from that "they had intended to present" such and such a man's name, but that the candidate had begged that his name be not presented.

It was this situation that the managers of the Kern boom used to advantage. They got to work immediately after the word had come authoritatively from Tammany Leader Murphy that New York would have no candidate. The Indiana delegation appointed a committee to promote it.

Mr. Kern had exacted one condition from his friends—that his name should not go before the convention unless there was reasonable assurance that the required two-thirds vote could be rallied to his support. His boom had been little heard of since the early stage of the pre-convention activities. It had been completely eclipsed by the booms of men like Judge Gray of Delaware, Judge Gaynor of New York, and John Mitchell, the labor leader. When it became evident that men of this calibre were unwilling to go on the Bryan ticket the Kern boom took a new lease of life.

**Round-Up By Indiana Men.**

Thomas Taggart, Chairman of the Democratic National Committee, was the most persistent advocate of Mr. Kern's nomination, and it was he who engineered the appointment of the boom committee. It was composed of former Mayor John N. Holtzman of Indianapolis, Democratic State Chairman U. S. Jackson, and Congressman Lincoln Dickson. They were instructed to visit all the delegations.

With the Vice Presidential candidates at a premium, the committee found the outlook good. They worked all night and practically up to the last minute before the convention went into session this afternoon. At that time they made their report to Mr. Taggart, Roger Sullivan of Illinois, Mayor Brown of Lincoln, and Charles W. Bryan, the Presidential candidate's brother. These leaders felt satisfied that Kern could unite the delegates.

Mr. Bryan was consulted and sent a telegram to his brother in which he declared that he would be satisfied with Kern or any other candidate who looked good enough to the convention to be its nominee. It should be stated, perhaps, that en route for the convention city Mr. Kern and Chairman Jackson stopped off at Lincoln and had a talk with Mr. Bryan.

"Mr. Bryan received us very pleasantly, and said he would be quite delighted to have Mr. Kern for his running mate," said Mr. Jackson to a correspondent for THE TIMES on his arrival. "But I suppose," he added somewhat ruefully, "that he told all the other Vice Presidential aspirants the same."

When the delegates gathered at the Auditorium between 1 and 2 o'clock the word had already gone forth that Kern was to be the nominee, but as the leaders had heard the final word from Lincoln only half an hour earlier the fact was not known among the visitors, and there were hopes that there would be a fight. It was known that names of several candidates would be presented.

**Clayton Unable to Preside.**

Ollie James of Kentucky called the convention to order for the last time, Mr. Clayton of Alabama, the permanent Chairman, suffering from a sore throat. The session began at 1:50. Senator Stone of Missouri moved that the nominating speeches be limited to ten minutes and the seconding speeches to five minutes. The delegates as well as the visitors had

"All the News That's Fit to Print."

FOURTH EDITION

# The New York Times.

THE WEATHER. Fair to-day; fair, colder to-morrow; westerly gales.

4 A. M.

VOL. LVIII...NO. 18,547. **** NEW YORK, WEDNESDAY, NOVEMBER 4, 1908.—SIXTEEN PAGES. ONE CENT In Greater New York, Jersey City, and Newark | Elsewhere, TWO CENTS.

# TAFT WINS

## Falls Only 22 Short of Roosevelt's Electoral Vote.

## GETS 187,902 IN THIS STATE

### Has 314 Electoral Votes—The House Republican by Increased Majority—But Some Western States Vote for Bryan.

William H. Taft will be the twenty-seventh President of the United States, having swept the country by a vote which will give him **314** ballots in the Electoral College against Mr. Bryan's **169**, or only **22** less than Mr. Roosevelt had in 1904. His majority will be **145**. William J. Bryan yesterday suffered his third and most crushing defeat in his twelve-year run for President of the United States.

To enforce his policies President Taft will have an overwhelmingly Republican Congress, the Senate being as strongly Republican as before, and the House increasing its Republican majority from **57** to **65**.

About every so-called doubtful State went Republican, though Indiana is still in doubt. It was noticeable that the majorities in the East were greater than those in the West. In New York, for instance, Taft beat the great Roosevelt majority of 1904, getting **187,902** majority, as against Roosevelt's **175,000**.

The greatest surprise of the election was the Republican victory in New York City, where Taft's majority was **9,378**. Never before this has this city gone Republican in a Presidential election except in 1900, when it voted for McKinley as against Bryan. Chanler's plurality in the city was **56,000**.

Taft's plurality on the popular vote is estimated at **1,098,000**, as against Roosevelt's plurality of **[illegible]** over Parker.

Bryan, however, has improved on Parker's run by carrying Missouri, Nevada, and apparently his own State of Nebraska, though later returns may change the last-named State's position in the Electoral College.

In his great sweep of this State Taft carried with him Gov. Hughes, though the Governor's majority fell far below his, being only **71,189**.

Speaker Cannon will be able to make the race to succeed himself, having downed his opponent in the Danville district by about **10,500** majority in spite of Samuel Gompers's efforts.

Morris Hillquit, the Socialist candidate for Congress in the Ninth New York District, was defeated by Republican votes which were cast for his opponent Judge Goldfogle.

A noticeable feature of the election was the increase of the Republican vote in the Southern States. In Florida, for example it increased so much that early in the evening there was a report that the State had gone Republican. Everywhere in the Southern States along the Atlantic Coast there was this unusual Republican vote.

In Illinois, which Bryan's managers had claimed, there was a smashing vote against him. Cook County, where Roger Sullivan is supreme, went against him by **50,000**. The majority in the State is estimated at **170,000**.

Indiana is still in doubt, and it seems likely that Thomas R. Marshall, the Democratic candidate for Governor, has been elected, though the State may have cast its vote for Taft.

Maryland, which was claimed by the Democrats and almost conceded by the Republicans—actually conceded, in fact, by President Roosevelt—has gone Republican by a majority of about **5,000**. Kentucky is for Bryan by about **15,000**.

The biggest surprise was in Senator La Follette's State of Wisconsin, where knifing of the ticket was freely predicted even by Republican observers, and where nobody looked to see Taft do more than squeeze through. He has bettered Roosevelt's 1904 majority there, and the La Follette men have apparently played fair.

Michigan may have elected a Democratic Governor. That State is still in doubt on its Gubernatorial ticket, though it has voted for Taft.

Connecticut's majority is as usual, and Representative Lilley has been elected Governor by **15,000**.

Taft carried his own State, Ohio, by **40,000**, but Harmon (Dem.) is elected Governor.

New Jersey went Republican by over **65,000**.

The city election was full of surprises, not the least being the victory here of Taft and Chanler. In Kings County McCarren made good by carrying it for Chanler by **5,241**, though it went for Taft by **22,500**. These extraordinary results led to the report that wholesale trading had been going on in the greater city.

Texas is actually in doubt on the Governorship. Cecil Lyon's prediction, at which everybody laughed at Chicago last June, that a Republican might be elected Governor this year, may come true. Col. Simpson, an old Confederate cavalryman, is Boss Lyon's candidate.



### STATE VOTE FOR PRESIDENT.

| County. | Pluralities. Taft. Rep. | Bryan. Dem. |
|---|---|---|
| Albany | 5,500 | |
| Allegany | 4,000 | |
| Broome | 4,100 | |
| Cattaraugus | 3,187 | |
| Cayuga | 4,000 | |
| Chautauqua | 3,230 | |
| Chemung | 1,500 | |
| Chenango | 2,231 | |
| Clinton | 1,503 | |
| Columbia | 500 | |
| Cortland | 2,000 | |
| Delaware | 2,522 | |
| Dutchess | 452 | |
| Erie | 6,870 | |
| Essex | 2,940 | |
| Franklin | 3,100 | |
| Fulton | 2,000 | |
| Genesee | 2,533 | |
| Greene | 450 | |
| Hamilton | 400 | |
| Herkimer | 2,460 | |
| Jefferson | 5,072 | |
| Kings | 21,864 | |
| Lewis | 1,400 | |
| Livingston | 2,100 | |
| Madison | 3,400 | |
| Monroe | 10,353 | |
| Montgomery | 2,344 | |
| New York | | 9,835 |
| Nassau | 4,622 | |
| Niagara | 2,500 | |
| Oneida | 5,000 | |
| Onondaga | 10,370 | |
| Ontario | 2,800 | |
| Orange | 4,000 | |
| Orleans | 2,274 | |
| Oswego | 4,500 | |
| Otsego | 1,800 | |
| Putnam | 813 | |
| Queens | | 1,456 |
| Rensselaer | 4,026 | |
| Richmond | | 695 |
| Rockland | 700 | |
| St. Lawrence | 8,000 | |
| Saratoga | 1,500 | |
| Schenectady | 2,947 | |
| Schoharie | | 500 |
| Schuyler | 600 | |
| Seneca | 1,000 | |
| Steuben | 4,084 | |
| Suffolk | 4,500 | |
| Sullivan | 3,048 | |
| Tioga | 1,573 | |
| Tompkins | 1,236 | |
| Ulster | 1,650 | |
| Warren | 1,800 | |
| Washington | 4,400 | |
| Wayne | 3,582 | |
| Westchester | 9,000 | |
| Wyoming | 3,200 | |
| Yates | 1,400 | |
| Total | 200,388 | 12,486 |
| Taft's plurality | | 187,902 |

### THE ELECTORAL VOTE.

**TAFT.**

| State | Votes |
|---|---|
| California | 10 |
| Colorado | 5 |
| Connecticut | 7 |
| Delaware | 3 |
| Idaho | 3 |
| Illinois | 27 |
| Indiana | 15 |
| Iowa | 13 |
| Kansas | 10 |
| Maine | 6 |
| Maryland | 8 |
| Massachusetts | 16 |
| Michigan | 14 |
| Minnesota | 11 |
| Montana | 3 |
| New Hampshire | 4 |
| New Jersey | 12 |
| New York | 39 |
| North Dakota | 4 |
| Ohio | 23 |
| Oregon | 4 |
| Pennsylvania | 34 |
| Rhode Island | 4 |
| South Dakota | 4 |
| Utah | 3 |
| Vermont | 4 |
| Washington | 5 |
| West Virginia | 7 |
| Wisconsin | 13 |
| Wyoming | 3 |
| Total | 314 |

**BRYAN.**

| State | Votes |
|---|---|
| Alabama | 11 |
| Arkansas | 9 |
| Florida | 5 |
| Georgia | 13 |
| Kentucky | 13 |
| Louisiana | 9 |
| Missouri | 18 |
| Mississippi | 10 |
| North Carolina | 12 |
| Nevada | 3 |
| Nebraska | 8 |
| Oklahoma | 7 |
| South Carolina | 9 |
| Tennessee | 12 |
| Texas | 18 |
| Virginia | 12 |
| Total | 169 |

Total number of votes in Electoral College, 483; necessary to a choice, 242.

### PARIS HEARS NEWS.

Taft's Election Known to Throng of Americans in Cafes at 2 A. M.

PARIS, Nov. 4.—The cafés and restaurants, where the election returns from the United States were received, were thronged until early morning by Americans.

Definite news of Mr. Taft's election reached here about 2 o'clock and was made the occasion of great merrymaking, as the supporters of the Republican nominee were largely in the majority.

### LAMB CONCEDES NOTHING.

CHICAGO, Nov. 3.—At midnight John E. Lamb, Vice Chairman of the Democratic National Committee, in charge of Western headquarters, refusing to admit defeat, issued the following statement:

"I do not care to estimate the probable final result, although we do not concede anything. It looks as though we had won Montana, Nebraska, and Colorado. We have not enough from Ohio, West Virginia, or Maryland to give any indications."

# CITY VOTE

## Taft Carries New York by 9,378.

## CHANLER BY 56,000

### Hughes Loses Kings by 5,241 and Queens by 4,635—Trading at Bryan's Expense Shown in Brooklyn.

This city contributed one of the great surprises of the election, William H. Taft carrying it by a probable plurality of 9,378. The heaviest Taft vote was in Kings County, where the Republican plurality of about 22,500 was amply sufficient to overcome the Bryan plurality of 9,835 in Manhattan and the Bronx. This is with some ninety districts missing.

Chanler's vote in the city ran far below the expectations of every one, including the Republican leaders. He developed great strength in Kings County, and this, taken in connection with the heavy Taft vote there, was regarded as evidence of trading, the assumption being that Senator McCarren traded Bryan votes for Chanler votes very successfully.

In Manhattan and the Bronx, while Bryan ran behind Chanler, there was not so much evidence of trading. Chanler's plurality in the whole city will not be above 56,000, about half what was expected.

Gov. Hughes developed great strength in New York County especially, and Queens did not do as well by Chanler as the Democrats had hoped. Chanler's plurality in that borough will be apparently about 5,146.

There will be no change in the city's representation in Congress as a result of the election. Morris Hillquit, the Socialist, running in the Ninth District was again beaten by Goldfogle. Bennet and Olcott both hold their districts, though hard fights were made on them. In Brooklyn, Foelker, who as Senator, saved the anti-race track gambling bills, was elected to Congress from the Third District.

As far as the Assembly is concerned, the representation from this city will be about the same. The Republicans make a gain in the First and Fifteenth Districts of Kings, but two districts in New York County which were won last time by Republicans with Independence League indorsements have gone Democratic again. The State Senate remains practically as it was as far as this city's representation is concerned.

The Independence League ticket did not poll as heavy a vote as was expected Hisgen and Shearn ran about evenly, getting approximately 28,000 votes in the whole city.

The Tammany county ticket has seemingly been elected by a reduced plurality. The general belief is that the new registration law is responsible for the reduced Tammany pluralities.

Surrogate Beckett, whose nomination was indorsed by practically the whole of the New York Bar, was defeated by John P. Cohalan, 640 districts out of 891 in Manhattan and the Bronx, giving Cohalan a lead of something like 28,000.

Mr. Beckett early this morning, however, was still hopeful that complete returns might show his election.

"I have the greatest confidence," he said, "and if this is justified my success will be due to the strenuous support given to my cause by the whole bar."

Tammany's two City Court Judges, La Fetra and Lynch, were elected by pluralities of approximately 34,000, Wasservogel and Matthewson going down to defeat.

### STATE PLURALITIES.

**REPUBLICAN.**

| | |
|---|---|
| California | 45,000 |
| Colorado | 20,000 |
| Connecticut | 40,000 |
| Delaware | 3,500 |
| Idaho | 20,000 |
| Illinois | 175,000 |
| Indiana | 5,000 |
| Iowa | 45,000 |
| Kansas | 26,000 |
| Maine | 31,500 |
| Maryland | 5,000 |
| Massachusetts | 70,000 |
| Michigan | 100,000 |
| Minnesota | 80,000 |
| Montana | 7,000 |
| New Hampshire | 20,000 |
| New Jersey | 65,000 |
| New York | 190,000 |
| North Dakota | 10,000 |
| Ohio | 40,000 |
| Oregon | 25,000 |
| Pennsylvania | 350,000 |
| Rhode Island | 16,000 |
| South Dakota | 32,000 |
| Utah | 20,000 |
| Vermont | 28,000 |
| Washington | 40,000 |
| West Virginia | 10,000 |
| Wisconsin | 100,000 |
| Wyoming | 1,000 |
| Total | 1,629,000 |

**DEMOCRATIC.**

| | |
|---|---|
| Alabama | 45,000 |
| Arkansas | 30,000 |
| Florida | 21,000 |
| Georgia | 40,000 |
| Kentucky | 15,000 |
| Louisiana | 40,000 |
| Mississippi | 50,000 |
| Missouri | 30,000 |
| Nevada | 3,000 |
| Nebraska | 10,000 |
| North Carolina | 40,000 |
| Oklahoma | 25,000 |
| South Carolina | 40,000 |
| Tennessee | 20,000 |
| Texas | 100,000 |
| Virginia | 30,000 |
| Total | 581,000 |

Taft's Plurality over Bryan, 1,098,000.

### TIMES'S BULLETINS IN BERLIN

American Colony Cheers Taft Victory at Hotel Adlon.

Special Cable to THE NEW YORK TIMES.

BERLIN, Nov. 4.—At 4 A. M. Wednesday Berlin's American colony, headed by Ambassador Hill, is bivouacked in the lobby of the Hotel Adlon. All through the night they have been awaiting the bulletins from THE NEW YORK TIMES.

Early indications of Taft's victory were greeted vociferously, men and women breaking out into cheers, while the orchestra struck up "Yankee Doodle."

Among those who held the long vigil were American Minister to Persia Jackson, Consul General Thackara of Berlin, Consul General Gaffney of Dresden, Secretaries Hitt, Grew, and Orr of the American Embassy; Vice Consul General Cauldwell of Berlin and President Hessenberg of the American Chamber of Commerce.

# HUGHES, TOO

## Runs Behind Taft, but Wins by 71,189 Plurality.

## BIG CUT IN UP-STATE CITIES

### Rural Districts Return Large Vote for Republican Candidate, Offsetting Democratic Gains Elsewhere.

Charles Evans Hughes was re-elected Governor of New York State yesterday by a plurality of **71,189**. His plurality two years ago when he ran against William Randolph Hearst was **57,897**. In nearly all the counties of the State Gov. Hughes ran behind the Republican candidate for President, whereas in 1906 the votes cast for Hughes exceeded by from about **60,000** to **70,000** the votes cast for his running mates on the Republican State ticket.

The early returns which came from the cities up the State showed that the Governor had been cut to the extent, in some of the larger cities, of many thousand votes. The returns from the rural districts of the up-State counties, however, saved the day for the Republican candidate for Governor, bringing him down to the Bronx with a plurality of about 127,500 over Lewis Stuyvesant Chanler, his Democratic opponent. Chanler's plurality in New York City was **56,000**, reducing Gov. Hughes's net plurality to **71,189**.

In Erie and Saratoga Counties, where the Personal Liberty League was very active, the fight against Gov. Hughes was reflected in heavy losses from the Republican vote two years ago in Buffalo and Saratoga Springs. In Buffalo, where Taft received yesterday a plurality over Bryan of over **4,000** votes, Chanler piled up a plurality against Hughes of over **5,000** votes. The Saratoga Springs vote for Chanler was offset by the returns from other districts in that county, and Saratoga County remained in the Republican column with a plurality of about **1,000** for Hughes and about **1,500** for Taft. The total vote in Erie County gave Taft a plurality of **7,000** and Chanler a plurality of about **3,000**. Two years ago Hughes had a plurality of **1,282** in Erie County.

In Onondaga County Gov. Hughes proved stronger than the rest of his ticket, running several hundred votes ahead of Horace White, candidate for Lieutenant Governor on the Republican ticket.

### FORAKER EXPECTED IT, TOO.

Ohio Senator Says So—Will Not Comment Further on Result.

CINCINNATI, Nov. 3.—Senator Joseph B. Foraker, when asked for an expression on the election said:

"It is just as I expected."

He would not discuss the matter further.

### STATE VOTE FOR GOVERNOR.

| County | Pluralities. Hughes Rep. | Ch'nl'r Dem. |
|---|---|---|
| Albany | 3,900 | |
| Allegany | 3,900 | |
| Broome | 3,300 | |
| Cattaraugus | 3,150 | |
| Cayuga | 2,786 | |
| Chautauqua | 3,100 | |
| Chemung | 1,000 | |
| Chenango | 2,200 | |
| Clinton | 1,134 | |
| Columbia | 300 | |
| Cortland | 2,425 | |
| Delaware | 2,200 | |
| Dutchess | 200 | |
| Erie | | [illegible] |
| Essex | 2,980 | |
| Franklin | 2,761 | |
| Fulton | 1,900 | |
| Genesee | 2,221 | |
| Greene | 460 | |
| Hamilton | 100 | |
| Herkimer | 1,950 | |
| Jefferson | 3,765 | |
| Kings | | [illegible] |
| Lewis | 1,260 | |
| Livingston | 1,900 | |
| Madison | 2,897 | |
| Monroe | 7,599 | |
| Montgomery | 1,700 | |
| New York | | [illegible] |
| Nassau | 2,700 | |
| Niagara | 1,000 | |
| Oneida | 4,000 | |
| Onondaga | 8,167 | |
| Ontario | 2,500 | |
| Orange | 2,700 | |
| Orleans | 2,095 | |
| Oswego | 3,600 | |
| Otsego | 1,700 | |
| Putnam | | |
| Queens | | 5,146 |
| Rensselaer | 2,479 | |
| Richmond | | 1,519 |
| Rockland | | |
| St. Lawrence | 6,800 | |
| Saratoga | 141 | |
| Schenectady | 1,612 | |
| Schoharie | | 589 |
| Schuyler | 500 | |
| Seneca | 480 | |
| Steuben | 3,015 | |
| Suffolk | 3,500 | |
| Sullivan | 650 | |
| Tioga | 1,561 | |
| Tompkins | 1,175 | |
| Ulster | 1,475 | |
| Warren | 1,460 | |
| Washington | 3,200 | |
| Wayne | 3,426 | |
| Westchester | 7,000 | [illegible] |
| Wyoming | 2,400 | |
| Yates | 1,429 | |
| Total | 131,552 | 60,[illegible] |

Hughes's plurality, 71,189.

### NEBRASKA FOR BRYAN.

His Plurality 10,000—Republican Precincts Change.

NEBRASKA—Voted for Presidential electors, Congressmen, Governor, and State officers, and a Legislature. Vote in 1904: Republican, 138,558; Democrat, 51,876.

Special to The New York Times.

LINCOLN, Neb., Nov. 4, 1 A. M.—Nebraska has gone Democratic. The State may give more than 10,000 majority for Bryan if returns now on hand hold good throughout. T. S. Allen, Chairman of the Democratic State Central Committee, claims the State by 15,000 and the Republican State Committee has no statement to make. Many Republican precincts in the State have given a strong Democratic majority.

Shallenberger, (Dem.) for Governor is also elected.

OMAHA, Neb., Nov. 3.—At midnight only 264 out of the 1,800 precincts outside of Omaha and Douglas Counties had reported. In those precincts Bryan's plurality is 1,550. At this ratio Bryan's majority in the State will not reach the figures named. Shallenberger, the Democratic candidate for Governor, is losing his heavy lead over Gov. Sheldon. However, he will carry the State by about 8,000. The entire Democratic State ticket was elected.

The Omaha Bee claims that Taft has carried Nebraska by 12,000.

Omaha complete gives Bryan, 10,[illegible]; Taft, 10,609; Shallenberger, (Dem.) for Governor, 10,913; Sheldon, (Rep.,) [illegible]. The first precinct to come in gave Taft, 205; Bryan, 405, a gain of 100 for Bryan.

Indications are that Bryan has nearly overturned a normal Republican plurality of 1,600 in the City of Lincoln. Three precincts complete give Bryan 542; Taft [illegible]. Estimates on the remainder show that Taft will not carry the city by more than 200 plurality.

Bryan carried his precinct 106 to 52 for Taft.

Scattering returns from Nebraska indicate a heavy loss to Bryan in the country precincts, with a gain in Omaha and Lincoln. The State is claimed for Taft by Republican managers by between [illegible] and 10,000 majority.

The first country precinct reporting, Ravenna, Buffalo County, showed a gain for Taft of 54 over that for McKinley eight years ago, and a gain for Bryan of 15 over his own vote eight years ago.

Blue Springs, Gage County, showed a net gain of one vote for Taft.

Bryan is making slight gains over eight years ago at Grand Island, and Taft shows a loss compared with the vote for McKinley.

Forty-one precincts outside of Lincoln and Omaha give: Taft, [illegible]; Bryan, [illegible]. The same precincts in 1900 gave: McKinley, 4,778; Bryan, 4,812. Bryan probably has carried the State by from [illegible] to 14,000.

Nine precincts out of a total of twenty-one in Lincoln gave Bryan a plurality of 388 votes. The Republicans are already conceding the city and county to Bryan. Returns from thirty precincts throughout the State give Bryan a plurality of [illegible]. With this gain it is estimated that Bryan will carry the State by about [illegible]. Mr. Bryan carried his home district by [illegible] votes.

### Map Showing How the Country Voted.

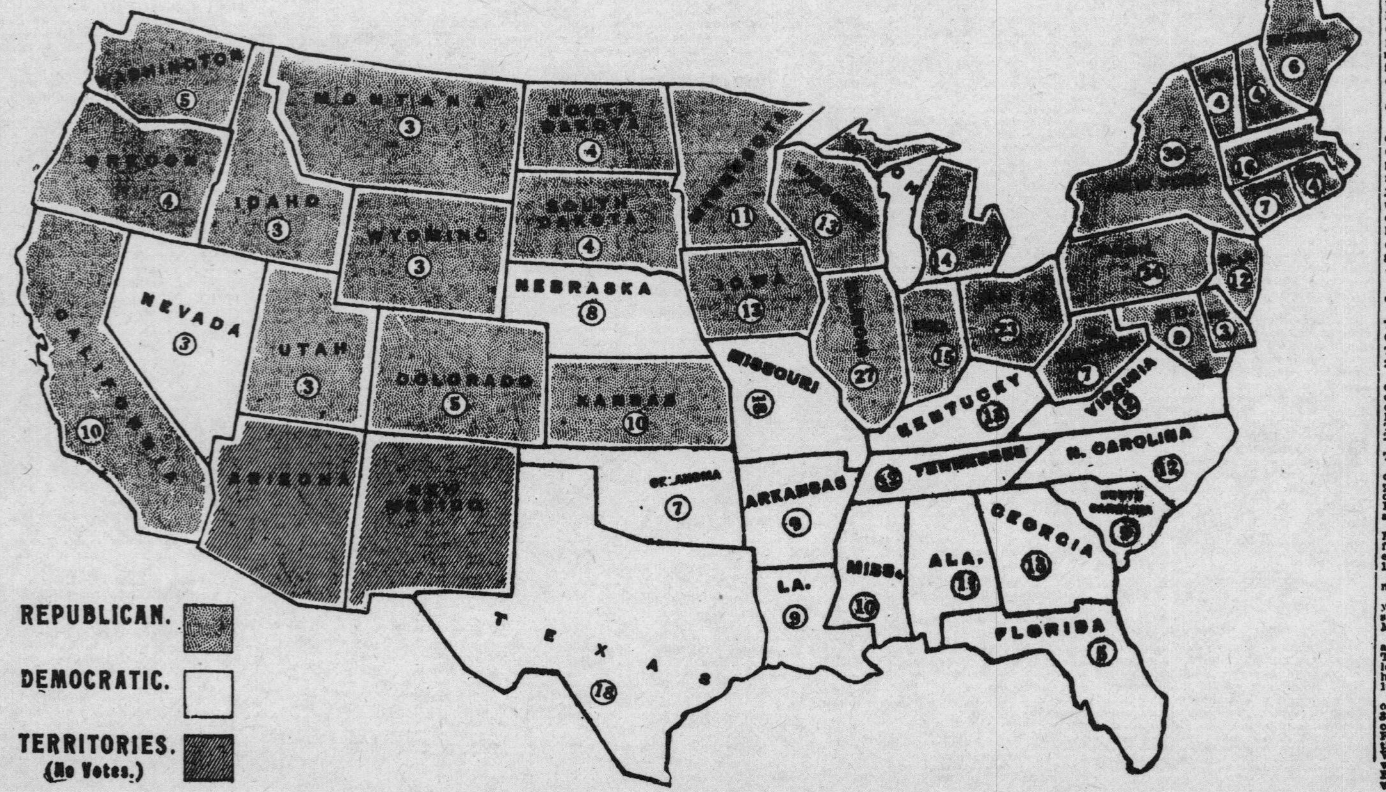

WILLIAM H. TAFT

"All the News That's Fit to Print."

# The New York Times.

THE WEATHER.
Fair to-day; fair, warmer, to-morrow; northwesterly winds.

VOL. LVIII...NO. 18,668. * * * NEW YORK, FRIDAY, MARCH 5, 1909.—EIGHTEEN PAGES. ONE CENT In Greater New York, Jersey City, and Newark { Elsewhere, TWO CENTS.

## MUTUAL GETS $815,000 ENDS M'CURDY SUITS

### Of the Sum Received, $750,000 Is Cash, Accepted to End Its Claims to Millions.

### AFFECTS ALL OFFICERS SUED

**Suits Were to Recover Alleged Unauthorized Salary and Excessive Commissions — Conspiracy Charges Behind Some.**

The Mutual Life Insurance Company has settled the suits which it brought in 1906 against its former President, Richard A. McCurdy, and others, officers and agents of the company, for the recovery of moneys alleged to have been obtained by the defendants or improperly expended by them from the funds of the Mutual Life.

Stipulations were filed in the Supreme Court in this city yesterday by counsel for the Mutual Life, agreeing to the discontinuance of about a dozen suits in which the gross amount claimed from the McCurdys and others was about $6,000,000, though the net amount was much less. The Mutual Life has received from the defendants in these suits, collectively, $815,000.

With the payment of this money and the filing of discontinuances of the suits yesterday, the litigation against the officers and agents of the Mutual Life which grew out of the insurance investigation four years ago has been brought to a close.

**Peabody Tells the Reasons.**

President Charles A. Peabody of the Mutual Life, when asked yesterday regarding the discontinuance of these suits, made this statement:

"Proposals looking to an adjustment of the litigations pending between the Mutual Life Insurance Company and certain of its former officers and others have been under negotiation for several months. They were referred by the Board of Trustees some time ago to a committee consisting of Benjamin F. Tracy, Henry W. Taft, Frederick H. Eaton, Edwin S. Marston, and H. Rieman Duval. The committee carefully examined the situation, and decided that in view of all the conditions and circumstances it would be wise to settle the controversies upon the terms proposed. This decision of the committee was approved by Joseph H. Choate, the company's special counsel in the litigation, and by James McKeen, general counsel of the company, and was duly reported to the board and approved.

"The result of the settlement is that all of the claims in dispute by and against the company have been settled and released, and the company has received the equivalent in value of the sum of $815,000."

**Whom the Mutual Sued.**

The suits instituted in 1906 by the Mutual Life included actions against Richard A. McCurdy, former President, his son, Robert H. McCurdy, son-in-law Louis A. Thebaud, and Charles H. Raymond, who with Mr. Thebaud formed the firm of Charles H. Raymond & Co., metropolitan agents for the Mutual. Actions were also begun against Robert A. Grannis and Dr. Walter R. Gillette, Vice Presidents under the old régime, and L. W. Lawrence, the stationer, who for long years supplied the company with stationery and supplies.

The members of the Committee on Expenditures were also sued, actions being brought against Robert Olyphant, James C. Holden, Charles E. Miller, and the executrix of Jacob Hobart Herrick.

The special committee of five, upon whose recommendation the settlement of these suits was decided on, submitted recently its findings in the matter to the Trustees of the Mutual Life, and its recommendations were approved. While this report has not been made public, it is understood that among the motives which prompted the recommendation that this settlement be made were the belief that judgments could be had only after long litigation, at best, and that in the case of some of the defendants, at least, there was doubt of their financial responsibility to meet judgments which might be obtained.

Furthermore, it was felt that the litigation involved would take close attention of many officers of the company for a long period. Moreover, while the gross amount claimed in these suits was about $6,000,000, this sum represented many duplications, and the net amount which under the most favorable conditions for the company could be recovered would be about $3,000,000. Again, if the contention of some of the defendants that the three-year statute of limitations applied in these cases were upheld, this sum would be still further reduced.

**Charges Behind the Suits.**

The Truesdale committee recommended several changes in the company's methods, and these have been put in effect under the direction of President Peabody and the reorganized Board of Trustees of the Mutual. The report of the committee found that the company in some respects had been managed with the seeming purpose of satisfying the ambition of the management to exert power and influence in the world of business and finance, and to make the company bigger than any other institution of its kind. Very lax methods were alleged against many of the officers of the company in the expenditure of company moneys, and improvidence and worse was charged in the making of some of the agency contracts.

In the suits filed later, conspiracy improperly to obtain money from the company without giving the company equitable value therefor was charged against some of the defendants in these actions. The committee found—and the suits brought later were based on these findings—that the committee on expenditures improperly permitted expenditures running into large sums, including about $600,000 paid over a series of years into the so-called "confidential fund." It was from this fund that political contributions amounting to more than $92,000, including contributions made to the McKinley Presidential campaign fund, were understood to have been made.

**McCurdy Sued for $3,371,341.**

The largest of the claims made in these suits against any one individual were those against ex-President McCurdy, from whom the Mutual sought to collect $3,371,341. This included claims for additional salary of $30,000 a year paid to the President from 1901 to 1905, with the knowledge, it is alleged, of only two of the Trustees of the company; sums paid on agency contracts with the metropolitan agents of the company alleged to have been excessive, and other items. These claims were, in part, duplicated in the suits against the members of C. H. Raymond & Co., who accepted commissions which President McCurdy and other officers of the company were alleged to have allowed this firm. This, in part, accounts for the duplication by which the aggregate of the claims was brought up to the large sum of $6,000,000.

**Three Years' Litigation Ended.**

Many disputed points were raised in the suits, and already nearly three years have been taken up by this litigation, although so far not one of the suits has been brought to trial on its merits. Many other legal steps which would further indefinitely postpone the actual trial of the suits could be resorted to, and meanwhile important witnesses have died. All these considerations are believed to have entered into the decision of the committee and of the officers and Trustees of the Mutual Life to settle these suits by the acceptance of about one-third of the maximum amount which the company could have hoped to obtain had it been entirely successful in every point it raised against its former officers and agents.

**Choate Approved Settlement.**

Joseph H. Choate, who has approved the settlement, was retained in 1906 as the special counsel of the Truesdale Committee, upon whose report these suits were begun. This committee was named by the Trustees of the Mutual in October, 1905, following the investigation of the life insurance companies by the Armstrong Legislative Committee, while Richard A. McCurdy was still President of the Mutual.

It was Mr. McCurdy himself who made the announcement of the appointment of this committee. It consisted of W. H. Truesdale, President of the Delaware, Lackawanna & Western; Effingham B. Morris, President of the Girard Trust Company of Philadelphia, and John W. Auchincloss. Stuyvesant Fish, then President of the Illinois Central, was added to the committee later, but he resigned in February, 1906, before the filing of the committee's final report. So, too, did Mr. Morris.

Messrs. Truesdale and Auchincloss continued their investigation, and at the end of March submitted to the Trustees of the Mutual their report on the irregularities in the management of the company which they had discovered existed under the McCurdy régime. The management of the company by that time had already been reorganized. Mr. McCurdy having resigned and Charles A. Peabody having been elected President in his place in December, 1905.

**Conspiracy Allegations.**

The contracts made with the firm of C. H. Raymond & Co. were alleged in these suits to have been due to conspiracy with the object of obtaining excessive commissions from the Mutual Life. Moreover, an important item in these claims was for the amount of money, said to be about $500,000, paid to this firm as commissions or collection charges on a large part of the premiums paid to the home office of the company. L. A. Thebaud, son-in-law of former President McCurdy, and one of the members of the firm of Charles H. Raymond & Co., was alleged in the suits filed against him to have received as profits on his partnership in this firm from 1895 to 1904, a total of $771,678 in addition to the special allowances on the part of the premiums paid at the home office of the company.

In the suit against ex-Vice President Granniss the amount sought to be recovered was $917,500. In the Gillette suit an accounting was asked. The claims against these two former officers were based on the passing of vouchers which came to them in the ordinary routine of the company's business as it was then managed, but which were alleged to have been the means of improvident or otherwise improper expenditure of the company's funds. The amount specifically claimed in the suit brought against the members of the Committee on Expenditures was $327,000.

The "confidential fund" which figured prominently in some of these suits was made up, the records showed, by quarterly payments of $25,000 over a period of six years. The officers who countersigned the vouchers for these transfers of money to this special fund were themselves unaware, it developed in the course of the insurance investigation, of some of the purposes to which the money later was put by other officers of the company.

**Mutual Gets $750,000 Cash.**

The $815,000 which the Mutual has accepted in settlement of all of these claims was paid in cash to the extent of $750,000. The balance was represented by a claim against the company for supplies delivered to it amounting to a trifle over $65,000. The company acknowledged this as a valid claim, and only held up its payment on account of counter-claims against those to whom it was due.

The settlement effected includes as one of its features the relinquishment of all claims against the company raised by some of the defendants in these suits. The commissions on renewals, to which the agents of the company against whom suits were brought might be entitled, have been commuted on terms which are regarded as advantageous to the company.

## MILLIONS TO ROAD'S WORKERS

**Pennsylvania Employes' Relief Fund Has Paid Out $25,765,403.**

*Special to The New York Times.*

PHILADELPHIA, March 4.—Reports of the Employes' Relief Fund of the Pennsylvania Railroad system, issued to-day, show that the total payments since the organization of the relief departments on Feb. 15, 1886, amount to $25,765,403.

On the lines east of Pittsburg and Erie, $112,687 was paid out in January. Of this, $42,076 went to families of members who had died, while $70,611 was paid to members who were incapacitated for work.

In January the payments of the relief fund on the lines West to members unable to work amounted to $27,711, and to families of members who died $7,750, a total of $35,461 for the month.



## OMAHA GREEK HAS MRS. HEINZE'S PEARLS

### Says He Found Them Outside the Knickerbocker Hotel, Where He Was a Sweeper.

### THOUGHT PEARLS GLASS

**He Is Arrested for Trying to Sell Them —Necklace Was Lost on Thanksgiving Night.**

*Special to The New York Times.*

OMAHA, Neb., March 4.—John Savis, a Greek railroad laborer, was to-day arrested in Omaha for having in his possession a pearl necklace, the value of which has been variously estimated from $30,000 to $100,000, and supposed to have been lost by, or stolen from, Mrs. Otto C. Heinze at the Knickerbocker Hotel, New York City, on the night of Dec. 26, 1908. The Greek to-night is in the city jail, while the necklace lies in a safe deposit vault awaiting positive identification.

Savis claims to have been formerly employed at the Knickerbocker as a sidewalk man, and says he found the necklace in the driveway, about the middle of December, nearly a month after it was lost by Mrs. Heinze. He says he showed the jewel to employes of the Knickerbocker, and continued working there until Feb. 1, when he started west. He did not know the value of the pearls, he says, and was assured in New York that they were only glass beads.

Savis walked into a jewelry store this afternoon and stepping up to the manager extended a dirty hand in which lay a pearl the size of a pigeon egg.

"What will you pay for that?" he asked. At a glance the jeweler saw that the object was a flawless pearl. On examination he also saw that the pearl had been drilled as though it had been one of a necklace.

The Greek was engaged in conversation and finally told the jeweler that he had a handful of them and would bring them to him later in the day.

In the meantime, the jeweler gave a signal to an employe who quickly informed the police. While the Greek was talking to the jeweler two detectives entered the store and, grabbing the Greek from either side, pinioned his arms.

Savis put up a good fight, and attempted to draw a pistol. He was quickly handcuffed, and a revolver taken from him. At the police station he refused to talk, and a thorough search of his person was made for the "handful" of pearls he had assured the jeweler he had.

Wrapped up in cotton batting and tied around his waist next to the skin, the pearls were found still strung on the thin gold wire chain. Savis had taken the largest one to the jeweler. There are sixty-three of the pearls, and the clasp is of gold, studded with a number of diamonds of seven-eighths carat. The pearls are perfectly matched, ranging from the size of a pea up to the centre one, which is as large as a fair-sized marble.

Savis's explanation is as follows:

"I worked at the Knickerbocker Hotel as sidewalk man. About the middle of December, one night, I found the necklace near the driveway, which in the Summer is grass. The next day I showed it to people around the hotel. They said it was glass beads.

"I worked at the Knickerbocker until the middle of February, and then I quit to come to Omaha. Some Greeks here who cannot talk English wrote me to come and act as interpreter for a railroad gang. I came here two weeks ago. I thought I would see if I couldn't sell the beads for almost anything. I took them to one watchmaker and he said they were worth about 30 cents. Then I went to Joe Mandanis, the Union Pacific interpreter, and he told me to go to another jeweler. I did and they arrested me.

"If I had known the value of the pearls and had wanted to steal them I would not have come to Omaha. I would have gone to Europe."

The police believe that Savis did not know the full value of his find, but that he considered them valuable is shown by the care he took to conceal them on his person.

---

Mrs. Otto C. Heinze of 14 East Seventy-second Street, wife of the banker and broker Otto C. Heinze, lost a necklace of sixty-three matched pearls of fine lustre on Thanksgiving night, Nov. 26 last. With her husband and several relatives she had attended a performance at the Astor Theatre and later dined at the Hotel Knickerbocker. Mr. Heinze was certain that he had seen the necklace on his wife's dress in the grill room of the hotel, and when, shortly after midnight, the loss of the necklace was discovered the matter was reported to the hotel management.

A thorough search of the waiters and maids in the hotel was made by the Pinkerton and city detectives, lasting through several days, but the necklace could not be found. A reward of $1,000 was offered for its return.

"No one by the name of Savis was employed at this hotel," said P. C. Geier, assistant manager of the Hotel Knickerbocker, last night. "He was probably a street cleaner, who found the necklace where it had fallen in the street when Mrs. Heinze stepped into a cab. After the careful search we made I felt certain that it had not been lost in the hotel."

## CLOSED SEASON FOR 'POSSUM.

**Law of Georgia Protects the New National Beast Till October.**

ATLANTA, Ga., March 4.—"Marsupial blind tiger" is the correct appellation of the concern in Georgia which deals in 'possums between the first day of March and the first day of October, and unless the violator of the law continues to supply the mad demand of the Eastern market there will be no more 'possums shipped from this State for the next seven months.

A rise in the market price of from 50 cents to $10 is recorded within less than a month, but the hopes of Georgia 'possum hunters of amassing fortunes have been ruthlessly cast to the ground by the discovery of a forgotten State law which prohibits the hunting or catching of 'possums between the dates named.



## EMBASSY FOR O. S. STRAUS.

**Roosevelt Cabinet Officer Will Be Sent to Japan by Taft.**

*Special to The New York Times.*

WASHINGTON, March 4.—President Taft has offered the Embassy to Japan to Oscar S. Straus, Secretary of Commerce and Labor in President Roosevelt's Cabinet, and Mr. Straus has accepted it. He will succeed Thomas J. O'Brien, who became Ambassador at Tokio in the Fall of 1907. Mr. O'Brien went to Tokio with Mr. Taft when he was on his way to the Philippines to open the first Philippine Assembly.

Mr. Straus has had considerable diplomatic experience, having been Minister to Turkey under President Harrison and McKinley. He has made a special study of international law and diplomacy, and is the author of several works on the subjects.

In his capacity as Secretary of Commerce and Labor Mr. Straus has had a great deal to do with the handling of the delicate subject of Japanese immigration into this country. It has fallen to him to administer the United States regulations made under authority of the immigration act of 1907 designed to diminish the immigration of Japanese laborers.

He has handled the matter with conspicuous success, and in the later dealings with Japan on the questions that have arisen out of the anti-Japanese agitation in this country, particularly on the Pacific Coast, his advice has been constantly required by Mr. Roosevelt.

## OFFERS PLACE TO NEWBERRY.

**Present Naval Secretary Could Have an Important European Embassy.**

*Special to The New York Times.*

WASHINGTON, March 4.—President Taft has offered a diplomatic mission in Europe to Secretary Newberry, who has been at the head of the Navy Department for the last three months.

It is understood Mr. Newberry could have one of the more important embassies in Europe but that he is disinclined to accept any diplomatic post.

## DEATHS AT INAUGURATION.

**One Due to Exposure—Many Ill from This Cause.**

WASHINGTON, March 4.—Much suffering was caused in the inauguration crowd here to-day by the wintry winds, the slush under foot, and freezing temperature.

Andrew Derah, 55 years old, a Pullman conductor, died at the Union Station to-night from exposure.

All of the hospitals to-night report that they have treated numerous cases of exhaustion among persons who stood for many hours in the slush and snow viewing the inaugural parade.

Another death in the crowd of visitors was that of Norman A. Stall, 45 years old, of Richmond, Va., who was stricken with apoplexy while viewing the parade.

## NO FARMERS IN KINGS COUNTY

**Only Subway Boomers with Building Lot Farms, Says Metz.**

Controller Metz has put himself on record that there are no farmers in Kings County, only "public officials and boomers of the Fourth Avenue subway who want to sell their farms for building lots."

This declaration was made by him in a letter sent yesterday to a South Bend, Ind., plow manufacturing concern from which he had received a letter asking for a list of "the farmers in Kings County with their Post Office addresses." The firm had learned from the last census that there should be about 400 farms in the county.

## WOMAN'S SUFFRAGE LOSES.

**Massachusetts Legislative Committee Rejects Bill for Equal Franchise.**

BOSTON, March 4.—A bill, designed to grant equal suffrage to women, was rejected to-day by the Legislative Committee on Constitutional Amendments.

The vote in the committee stood 8 to 4.

## SACKVILLE ACTION DROPPED.

**Charge of Tampering with Church Records Withdrawn.**

MADRID, March 4.—The Public Prosecutor to-day withdrew the charges in the criminal action recently begun against a church employe named Rolfis, in connection with the case of Ernest Henri Batiste West, claimant of the Sackville peerage and estates, against Lionel Sackville-West, to whom the estates have passed.

The Prosecutor stated that there was no evidence against the defendant, who was accused of having altered the church records of the marriage of Josephine Duran de Ortega, a Spanish dancer, to a Spaniard named Oliva.

This marriage was relied on to bar the claim of Ernest Henri Batiste West, who alleges that he is a son of the late Lord Sackville, sometime British Minister in Washington, by the dancer.

## ASKS ASIATICS BE EXCLUDED.

**California Senate Adopts Resolution Calling Upon Congress to Act.**

SACRAMENTO, Cal., March 4.—In lieu of an anti-Japanese statute, the Senate to-day expressed its views on the subject of Asiatic immigration by adopting a resolution calling upon Congress to enact an Asiatic exclusion law that would keep Japanese as well as Chinese aliens out of the country.

Senator J. B. Sanford tried to amend the resolution so that Japanese would be denied the right of naturalization, but this was voted down, the vote being 28 to 7.



## TAFT IS SWORN IN SENATE HALL

### Blizzard Compels Abandonment of Outdoor Inauguration of the President.

### SKIES CLEAR FOR PARADE

### Snow Is Swept Away and Great Procession Passes Before Taft and Sherman.

### BRILLIANT BALL AT NIGHT

### Tafts Take Possession of White House and New President Meets Yale Men.

### ROOSEVELT HURRIES HOME

### Cheered as He Leaves—He and Taft Exchange Jokes About the Blizzard.

### WIRES TO CAPITAL DOWN

**Communication Almost Cut Off All Day and Night—Trains, Including Roosevelt's, Delayed.**

*Special to The New York Times.*

By train to Philadelphia; thence by telegraph.

WASHINGTON, March 4.—William Howard Taft is President of the United States, and Theodore Roosevelt is again a private citizen.

With the weather worse than it has been at any time since the great March blizzard of twenty-one years ago, the ceremony of inaugurating Mr. Taft was carried through to-day. There was only one change of the carefully arranged programme, and that was made by resolution of Congress, which directed that the ceremony of taking the oath which made Mr. Taft President and the delivery of his inaugural address should take place in the Senate Chamber instead of upon the stand which had been erected for that purpose at the east front of the Capitol.

The change stirred to disappointed wrath thousands of men and women who had dared the howling snowstorm and gathered on the stands and about the Capitol to witness the inauguration. No man in Washington remembers another inauguration ceremony inside the Capitol. It is the breaking of a line of precedents that have been followed since a blizzard compelled Andrew Jackson to take the oath for his second term in the Senate Chamber.

**Hoped for Fair Weather.**

The official forecasters of the Weather Bureau to the very last stuck to their prediction of fair, cold weather for the day, and despite the pouring rain of yesterday afternoon and the heavy fall of wind-driven soggy snow that kept up all night optimistic Washington hoped that the prediction would come true.

Even when President Roosevelt and President-elect Taft left the White House in the midst of the whirling snow a little after 10 o'clock there were cheerful seers scattered about through the crowd who fancied they saw the sun breaking through the clouds, and prophesied a fair afternoon for the parade, the great spectacle of all inaugurations.

It was announced early that there would be no change in the parade programme because of weather, and that feature of the celebration was in fact carried out as nearly as possible according to schedule, with only a slight diminution of the number of paraders, who being volunteers had the right to fall out if they wanted to.

The going of Mr. Roosevelt was in sharp contrast to his own inauguration four years ago. Then the sun shone brightly, and, although there were traces of snow under foot, the sky was as benignant as could be. But to-day there was every justification for his remark to Mr. Taft at breakfast in the White House:

"I knew there would be a blizzard before I got out."

**Contrast of Administrations.**

There were many people in Washington to-day who applied the old weather saw about March coming in like a lamb and going out like a lion to both Mr. Roosevelt and President Taft and their administrations. Mr. Roosevelt became President first by the accident of assassination that took away his predecessor.

For the first years of his Administration of the Government his course was marked by no such strife, turmoil, and criticism as has raged during the years of the Administration to which the people elected him. He came in like the lamb, and goes out like the lion.

Mr. Taft comes in with raging weather, the political skies disturbed, and all interests, commercial and financial, as well as political, anxiously watching developments. But he comes with the confident promise of those who know him best that he will clear all skies by his course in office, and leave the country at the close of his Administration in the quiet of industrial and commercial peace.

**Difference of Methods.**

The change of Administration marks not so much a change of attitude on the great questions that have occupied public attention during the last four years as upon the methods by which the same policy will be followed.

There is no vital difference between the beliefs of Mr. Roosevelt and Mr. Taft upon such matters as the Federal control of inter-State commerce and its agencies, but there is a vital difference between the methods of Mr. Roosevelt in seeking the accomplishment of his purposes and those of Mr. Taft.

Mr. Taft is a great lawyer and Judge. He has been accustomed for years to the careful weighing of all the evidence on both sides of every question submitted to him. He makes up his mind calmly and with deliberation, and then his conclusions are fixed. He acts with the same calmness and deliberation and just the same firmness. He has surrounded himself in the Cabinet with eminent members of his own profession, whose principal experience has been in dealing with matters affecting inter-State commerce and its agencies.

Mr. Taft believes that there is need for some further legislation to complete the proper position of the Federal Government on these matters, but that none of it involves great or radical changes.

He believes that the recommendations on the subject which come from his Cabinet, composed as it will be of lawyers who have devoted years to the careful study of the problems dealt with, will secure a consideration from Congress and will have a prospect of favorable action which has not been the case with Mr. Roosevelt's recommendations, especially since the development of the breach between Mr. Roosevelt and Congress.

Mr. Taft agrees with the so-called "Roosevelt policies" thoroughly. He has believed in them for years, and first openly advocated the most far-reaching of them when he was a Judge on the Federal bench and Mr. Roosevelt was Police Commissioner in New York City. It is only natural now that he is in the White House he should seek to carry them out. But he will seek to do so with the same judicial equability that marked his service on the bench.

**Taft Reviews Parade.**

Accompanied to the Capitol by President Roosevelt and a guard of honor through a swirl of snow, that did not stop crowds from cheering, Mr. Taft returned to the White House just as the sun began to come out. Mrs. Taft accompanied the newly made President and Mrs. Sherman the new Vice President from the Capitol at the head of the imposing parade to the White House, a passageway having been cleared along Pennsylvania Avenue.

The Presidential carriage, drawn by four bay horses, which had been closed against the storm as President Roosevelt and Mr. Taft made their way to the Capitol, was thrown open as the return journey was begun, and President Taft, quickly recognized by the crowds which stood unmindful of the ankle-deep snow and slush about them, were acclaimed all along the great distances of the avenue.

For nearly three hours after that President Taft and Vice President Sherman reviewed a passing column, which was replete with martial splendor and picturesque with civic display.

President and Mrs. Taft were the centre of interest at the culminating feature of the memorable day—the inaugural ball in the Pension Building. The cavernous building had been transformed into a canopied court of ivory and white, and in it gathered a brilliant assemblage from every section of the country. While the ball was in progress indoors a display of fireworks on the Monument lot in the rear of the White House marked the end of the outdoor celebration.

Prior to his visit to the ball President Taft had entertained at tea in the White House the members of the Yale Club; had dined with Mrs. Taft at 7 o'clock, and had stopped at the Metropolitan Club to say a few words at the dinner of the class of '78, Yale.

**Roosevelt Takes His Leave.**

Following the ceremonies in the Senate President Roosevelt, again a private citizen, bade an affectionate adieu to his successor, and then hurried away through a side door to take a train for New York. As he passed out he got an ovation.

Outside the Capitol he was met by 800 members of the New York County Committee and under their escort was driven to the Union Station, a short three blocks away. He was compelled time and again to acknowledge the cheers from the throng which lined his way.

There was a wait of nearly two hours at the station, during which Mr. Roosevelt held an impromptu reception in the Presidential suite, many of his old friends among Government officials and the Diplomatic Corps saying farewell. As he made his way to the train shortly after 3 o'clock he was cheered by thousands.

To all with whom he spoke Mr. Roosevelt declared that while he had "a bully time" as President, he was glad to lay down the duties of office.

The capital was almost cut off from communication by wire to-day and to-night, because of the havoc wrought by the storm on the telegraph and telephone lines between Washington and Philadelphia.

It was possible to couple up some lines by way of the South, but correspondents were compelled to send out the bulk of their accounts of the day's proceedings by train to Philadelphia and other points where wires could be had.

## RIDE TO THE CAPITOL.

**Takes Place Under Leaden Skies, Amid Flurries of Snow.**

*Special to The New York Times.*

By train to Philadelphia; thence by telegraph.

WASHINGTON, D. C., March 4.—Under leaden skies from which swept flurries of heavy snow flakes; over pavements three inches deep in a mixture of melted snow and rain-water; yet still between lines of people three deep on both sides of Pennsylvania Avenue, President-elect William Howard Taft and President Roosevelt drove this morning from the White House to the Capitol, the former to take the oath of office as President of the United States, the latter to relinquish the position he had held for seven years.

There could have been no less auspicious day for the inauguration ceremony. Starting soon after 6 o'clock last night, a light snow, which presently developed into a near approach to a blizzard, covered sidewalks and pavements with a foot-wetting slush.

Dawn to-day revealed an overcast sky; a chill wind hurtled the snowflakes about in flurries, and when Washington and its inaugural guests awoke to find that telegraph wires were down, trains neither entering nor leaving the city, and trolley cars not running on many lines and on others only under reduced schedules, it became a question whether or not the ride from the White House to the Capitol would be accompanied by the pomp and ceremony that had been planned.

**Preparations at White House.**

At the White House, however, preparations went on as though the weather had not made itself a factor in the situation. As early as 9 o'clock and before members of Troop A of Cleveland, the crack organization of the State, which was to have the honor of escorting the Presidential party on the inaugural ride, were formed in Pennsylvania Avenue, opposite the west approach to the White House.

Major Sylvester, Chief of the Washington police, with a squad of mounted policemen, was on hand also, and several score more uniformed and ununiformed police kept the avenue in front of the White House and the driveways leading to it clear of people. In this they did not have very difficult work, as up to the very moment of the President's and President-elect's departure the people in the big stand of seats facing the White House grounds between Jackson and Madison Places did not number more than 100 or so.

Inside the White House preparations were going on also. One by one the members of the Cabinet began to arrive to accompany the President and the President-elect to the Capitol. Carriage after carriage drove up the east path, and under the big porte-cochere, and Cabinet members, Senators, and Congressmen alighted.

**Secretary Wright Arrives.**

Secretary of War Wright was the first to reach the mansion. Capt. Archibald Butt, the President's aid and the master of ceremonies, received him at the entrance and escorted him inside.

After Mr. Wright came Secretary Newberry of the Navy, followed in a few moments by Secretary of Agriculture Wilson, Secretary Garfield of the Interior, Secretary Cortelyou of the Treasury, and Secretary of State Bacon.

Vice President Fairbanks drove up accompanied by Representative Burke of the Congressional Committee of Arrangements and Chairman Stelwagen of the Inaugural Committee. Attorney General Bonaparte arrived a few minutes later, and then came Senators Knox and Lodge of the Congressional Committee.

Postmaster General Meyer was next to reach the White House and, completing the list of Cabinet officers, Secretary Straus of the Department of Commerce and Labor arrived at the Executive Mansion shortly before 10 o'clock.

**Taft Jokes Over Weather.**

Meanwhile President Roosevelt was acting as host at breakfast for the last time to President-elect Taft. The meal over, Mr. Taft stepped from the room, and in greeting a friend who was present remarked:

"I knew it would be a cold day when I was made President."

Previously Mr. Taft had remarked on the weather, when he first greeted President Roosevelt at breakfast. President Roosevelt chuckled:

"I knew there'd be a blizzard until I got out," he laughed.

The President and the President-elect were busied receiving callers until the time for the departure to the Capitol arrived.

This was at 10 o'clock, and Capt. Butt summoned the carriage to the door. An instant afterward he hurried from the White House and ordered that the carriage drive out from beneath the porte-cochere. It had been discovered that Vice President-elect Sherman had not reached the Executive Mansion yet.

It was eight minutes past the hour set for starting when Mr. Sherman, accompanied by Senator Frye, Chairman pro tem. of the Senate, reached the White House. Both hurried inside, and seven minutes later Capt. Butt again stepped through the big glass doors. Other military men followed him and took up positions beside the carriage door.

**President Roosevelt Appears.**

On the left of the big entrance stood a group of photographers and newspaper men. On the right was Gen. Bell, who had in charge the ceremonies of the day, and several policemen and attachés of the White House. An instant after Capt. Butt appeared, President Roosevelt, followed by Mr. Taft and Senators Lodge and Knox, suddenly stepped from the doorway.

The President was conventionally attired from knee to head, but over both feet and embracing his legs tightly almost to the knees he wore a big pair of golashes, sometimes called Boston gaiters. In his hand he grasped an umbrella and a copy of a weekly periodical.

As soon as he was well outside the swing of the glass doors he exclaimed loudly and heartily:

"Well, good-bye, boys, good-bye! Good luck!"

He bowed to the newspaper men, shook hands with several, and then stopped to bid adieu to several other friends, shaking hands with each.

"Good-bye! Good luck!" was all he said, but he repeated this a dozen times, smiling and nodding as he spoke. Then he popped into the carriage, seating himself on the right-hand side of the rear seat.

**Taft Gets in with Roosevelt.**

Mr. Taft, who had stood behind him smiling and nodding as the President took characteristic leave of his friends, followed him to the carriage, and the door was slammed shut.

With two members of Troop A on guard before the carriage door, the carriage moved away from the White House steps on the last trip on which Mr. Roosevelt might occupy the right hand rear seat.

The horses were skittish, and the carriage had not moved a dozen yards before the leaders and the wheel animals got into a snarl. Secret Service men and others sprang to their heads, and after a moment's delay the carriage moved off again. It passed slowly down the West Drive and out the West Gate turning east into Pennsylvania Avenue.

Troop A, the police, and Gen. Bell and his staff swung into position in front of the Presidential carriage and the procession started slowly down the avenue. There were a few shouts from the handful of people in the big shed of seats opposite the White House grounds, but there was nothing like an ovation.

**Not Like Four Years Ago.**

Compared with Mr. Roosevelt's triumphal ride four years ago the whole trip to-day was mild and unenthusiastic. Then the President rode to renew his pledge to the people as the Chief Ex-

"All the News That's Fit to Print."

# The New York Times.

THE WEATHER. Unsettled Wednesday and Thursday; cooler Wednesday; moderate variable winds. For full weather report see Page 23.

VOL. LXI...NO. 19,842. NEW YORK, WEDNESDAY, MAY 22, 1912.—TWENTY-FOUR PAGES. ONE CENT In Greater New York, Jersey City, and Newark. | Elsewhere, TWO CENTS.

## HAITIAN NEGROES AID CUBAN REBELS

### Revolt Grows Rapidly—Americans' Property Raided—Protection Demanded.

### RURALES SLAIN IN FIGHT

### Striking Santiago Longshoremen Join the Insurgents—Government Suppressing News Dispatches.

HAVANA, May 21.—While the situation arising from the racial revolutionary movement is unquestionably serious and apparently growing more dangerous, the reticence of the Government renders impossible a precise determination of its gravity.

The only thing absolutely certain is that a condition of insurgency exists among the negroes of Matanzas, Santa Clara, and Oriente Provinces, especially in the last named, and that the Government is straining every nerve to stamp out the rebellion by the use of all the military forces at its disposal, even at the cost of reducing the garrison at Havana to a few companies.

Additional troops were rushed by railroad to Oriente this afternoon, a force of 1,200 men having been dispatched to that province last night.

The new cruiser Cuba, which arrived here to-day and to which was accorded, with her consort, La Patria, a great popular demonstration of welcome, had hardly anchored before she received orders to take aboard 600 infantry and artillery and proceed to-night to Guantanamo. It is expected that La Patria will take more troops aboard to-morrow. Several carloads of ammunition were sent to Oriente to-night.

The Secretary of the Interior, Señor Bru, said this evening that the newspaper report alleging that there were 2,000 insurgents in Oriente was greatly exaggerated. The Government, he added, had positive information that the insurgents under Gens. Estenoz and Ivonét did not exceed 150.

In spite of this, reliable reports indicate that Estenoz and Ivonet have fully 600 armed and mounted followers.

The Secretary also said that the Government had not received any reports of casualties among the rural guards in engagements with the insurgents. He stated that the rural guards up to the present had held the insurgents in check, and that the arrival of heavy reinforcements now on the way would result in the speedy hunting down of all armed bands, restoring complete tranquillity throughout the island.

The American Minister, Arthur M. Beaupré, visited Secretary of State Sanguily this afternoon to demand protection for the property of the Juragua Iron Company, on which a band under Ibonet is reported to be committing depredations. The Secretary gave assurance of protection.

It is reported, but without confirmation, that Col. Armenteros, who has been operating in Santa Clara, and threatening to destroy all foreign property, has been killed in an encounter with rural guards.

Two armed parties are said to be operating to-night in the southern part of Havana Province.

A serious feature of the situation in Oriente Province, in which is the main focus of the negro insurrectionary movement, is the presence of many Haitian negroes, who recently surreptitiously entered the province and who are reported to be inflaming the Cuban negroes by citing the example of the Haitians in exterminating the whites in their country and urging the establishment of a black republic in the eastern end of Cuba. These Haitians, it is said, number several thousand.

It is rumored that several schooners from Haiti have landed cargoes of arms. Gen. Ivonet recently received $10,000 in payment for his services as a General during the revolution. It is believed that he is using this to purchase arms for the present rising.

The newspapers complain that the Government is holding up all press dispatches from the disturbed districts.

The Government continues to receive from all quarters assurances of support. Gen. Emilio Nunez, President of the Association of Veterans, and Alfredo Zayas, Vice President of the republic, as leader of the Liberal Party, have both explained that they deplore the fact that the anniversary of the birth of the nation should be marked by an attempt on the life of the republic, and urge all patriotic Cubans to rally loyally in defence of the Government.

SANTIAGO, Cuba, May 21.—Parties of armed negroes, headed by Gens. Estenoz and Ivonet, are reported to be operating in the vicinity of El Caney, El Cobre, and San Luis, and also at various points close to this city.

The band led by Ivonet passed through the Firmeza property of the Juragua Iron Company and seized a large number of horses and a quantity of explosives.

It is reported that a party of armed negroes has passed through the town of Siboney, near the coast, with a number of horses stolen from an American citizen.

The authorities consider the situation serious, but refuse to give out news.

At Sevilla and Ocana the insurgents attacked and looted stores owned by Spaniards, who have protested to the Spanish Consul at Guasimas.

An encounter is reported between insurgents and rural guards at Yerbaguinea, the guards losing two men killed and several wounded.

The strike of the longshoremen has taken on a serious aspect, as it is impossible to load steamers, and the authorities are not able to give protection. Many of the longshoremen on strike are missing to-day, and it is reported that they have joined the armed parties in the field.

WASHINGTON, May 21.—President Taft has cabled the following message of congratulation to President Gomez on the tenth anniversary yesterday of Cuban independence:

"On this anniversary, which the people of Cuba are celebrating to-day, I take pleasure in tendering to your Excellency, in the name of the people of the United States and in my own, sincere congratulations and earnest wishes for the continued peace and prosperity of the republic."



## FATHER CUTS OFF HER HAIR.

### Girl's Punishment for Going Out with a Young Man.

Miss Edna Palmer, a nineteen-year-old girl of 226 Emmet Street, Newark, told Judge Hahn in the Third Precinct Police Court of Newark yesterday how her father had cut off her hair because she had disobeyed him and had gone out with a young man her father objected to. She removed her hat and heavy veil just long enough to show that her brown hair had been cut away. She said that on several occasions her father had threatened to cut off her hair if she did not give up the young man.

On Sunday, the girl said, she kept an appointment with her friend and spent most of the day in the country. She returned early in the evening, and, upon her arrival in the house, she says, her father began to upbraid her. He again threatened to cut off her hair. She told him to do it if he dared. The father then caught hold of her, the girl said, seized a pair of shears, and cut her hair close to her head.

When questioned by Judge Hahn the father declared that he strongly objected to the young man his daughter was going with and sheared off the girl's hair to "save her soul."

"It was not that I wanted to cut off her hair," he said, "but she tormented me and held it out for me to cut."

The court asked the girl about this, but she denied it. She declared that before she went out on Sunday her father said he would cut her hair when she returned.

Judge Hahn, after he had heard the girl's complete story, told the father in no uncertain terms that he ought to be ashamed. The girl refused to enter a complaint against her father.

## CONTROL VESSEL BY MOTORS

### Man at Wheel Can Start or Stop Ship by New Invention.

*Special to The New York Times.*

SCHENECTADY, N. Y., May 21.—The two motors for the collier Jupiter, now being built at the Mare Island Navy Yard, at San Francisco, were tested at the General Electric Works to-day, in the presence of United States Navy and shipbuilding officials.

The plan to propel vessels of large size with the big electrical motors is the work of W. L. R. Emmet of this city, engineer in the lighting department of the General Electric Company. It is expected that the plan will prove highly successful and that it will in time revolutionize the method of ship propulsion, the electrical method taking the place of driving the propellers direct from the steam engines.

One feature of the equipment is the simplicity of control, it being possible for the men on the bridge to check the speed, stop or start the vessel, or back the engines from the bridge. In steam-driven vessels all this has to be done on signal from the bridge or pilot house to the engine room. With the General Electric Company apparatus the whole operation can be performed by using a simple mechanism right at the hand of the man at the wheel.

The turbine engine, generator, and motors from the works in this city will be shipped within two months.

## DIDN'T PASS, KILLS HIMSELF.

### Father Sure Son's Failure to Get Diploma Caused His Suicide.

Charles Faupel, a barber, returned from his shop to his home, 1,322 Fulton Street, Brooklyn, about 11 o'clock last night, and was met at the door by his nine-year-old daughter, Margaret, who told him that her brother, Louis, 12 years old, was moaning in his bed. The father ran to the boy, whom he found unconscious, and leaving him with the little girl, hurried to the corner, where he telephoned to Dr. Binford C. Thorne of 2 Macon Street.

The physician found the boy was poisoned and a bottle which had contained insect poison was found in his room. Dr. Thorne worked over him for nearly an hour, but the boy died.

Mr. Faupel said afterward that he was sure his boy had killed himself because he feared that he would not graduate from Public School 93 at New York Avenue and Herkimer Street. He had not been told that he was to be left back, but yesterday the names of pupils sure of their diplomas were read out in class and Louis, apparently broken-hearted, reported to his father at noon that his name was not among them.

Mrs. Faupel was visiting friends in Hoboken, N. J., and knew nothing of the death of her boy till her husband telephoned to her.

## AUTO A "DEADLY WEAPON."

### So Regarding It, a Chicago Judge Fines a Reckless Driver $1,000.

CHICAGO, May 21.—An unprecedented series of automobile accidents the past week has caused city and county officers to take drastic measures to stop reckless driving.

Judge Gemmill to-day started an active crusade against "speeders" by fining George S. Scott, who was driving an automobile that injured Anna Falkenberg, 14 years old, $1,000. The charge was assault with a deadly weapon, a new ground for the prosecution of automobile drivers.

County Prosecutor Wayman declared his intention to take personal charge of all automobile accident cases that reach his office. He favors an amendment to the State law on speeding, making it a criminal offense.

Mayor Harrison in a message to the City Council urged a revision of the city ordinances regulating the speed of machines, and followed this with a letter to Judge Olson, protesting against the release of speeders on payment of nominal fines.

## KILLED BY ROCK FROM BLAST.

### Conklin Was 1,200 Feet Away—Stone Weighed 20 Pounds.

*Special to The New York Times.*

TUXEDO PARK, N. Y., May 21.—Irving Conklin, a plumber, son of David Conklin of Johnsontown, was instantly killed last night by a rock hurled nearly 1,200 feet from a blast on the new State road.

Conklin was standing outside his home. His father hearing the blasts and seeing a large stone flying through the air, went to see where it struck and found his son dead.

Coroner Heaton of Orange County and Capt. Bush of the Tuxedo police investigated the case to-day. The rock weighed over twenty pounds, and buried itself out of sight in the soil after it struck the young man.

The State road is being constructed in this section by Sproule & Elson of Peekskill, N. Y.



## HER HORSE KILLS HER IN CENTRAL PARK

### Falls on Mrs. Knapp, Crushing Her Chest, While She Is Riding with Daughter.

### LITTLE GIRL PROSTRATED

### Policeman Finds Her Trying to Stanch Blood Flowing from Her Mother's Wounds.

Mrs. Wallace Percy Knapp, a skillful horsewoman, was killed on the West Bridle Path in Central Park at 5:30 o'clock yesterday afternoon. Her horse became unmanageable near Ninety-fourth Street, and threw Mrs. Knapp and fell upon her. The big horn of the saddle crushed her chest, breaking four ribs on the left side and three on the right side. Mrs. Knapp's 12-year-old daughter, Emma, was with her, and she screamed loudly and tried to drag her mother from beneath the fallen animal.

The daughter's cries called Policeman McLaughlin to the spot, and he succeeded in dragging the animal away. A passing automobile, owned and driven by William Wright, a member of the Automobile Club, was stopped, and Mrs. Knapp was taken in it to the Red Cross Hospital, at 100th Street and Central Park West, but she was dead when she arrived there. Her family was notified, and in a short time the hospital was thronged with her weeping relatives.

Mrs. Knapp was 35 years old and was the wife of a well-known lawyer of 2 Rector Street. Her home was at 68 East Fifty-fourth Street. She was a vigorous woman. Her favorite diversion was riding, and she indulged her love for the sport at all seasons and in all weathers. Her husband is a noted traveler, having spent much time in Europe and Africa. Mrs. Knapp traveled wth him, and so her experience in handling horses extended over a large part of the world.

She had trained her daughter to ride, and it was the pleasure of mother and daughter to spend a great deal of their spare time in the saddle. At 4:30 o'clock yesterday afternoon they decided to take a ride in the Park before dinner. It was a favorite time with them, for in the late afternoon the Bridle Paths are nearly deserted. Those who can afford this sport are mostly at home at that hour, dressing for dinner and the night's amusements.

They obtained horses at the Fifth Avenue Riding Academy, and, cutting across the Park near its southerly end, struck into the West Bridle Path and rode toward the north. Thero were few other equestrians abroad, and when they entered the path near Ninetieth Street they had the Park to themselves. Suddenly the horse that Mrs. Knapp was riding grew restless and began to prance. Mrs. Knapp sought to soothe him, but he rapidly grew worse. Then he reared, until he stood upright, and then fell over on his side, crushing Mrs. Knapp beneath him.

Norman Maul, who was on foot, heard the screams of Mrs. Knapp's daughter and hurried to the injured woman with Policeman McLaughlin. They found the daughter crying and trying to staunch the flow of blood that streamed from the nose and mouth of her mother. Policemen attached to the Arsenal, in Central Park, came up, and they caught the horse and sent it to the sheep fold. It was found that the horn of the saddle had been broken off. It was thought by Drs. Meagher and Munkittrick of the hospital staff that it had pierced the chest of Mrs. Knapp. The broken horn could not be found. The body of Mrs. Kapp was taken to her home late last night.

## LADY SUFFOLK THROWN.

### Former Miss Leiter Suffers Severe Shock—Narrowly Escapes Death.

*By Marconi Transatlantic Wireless Telegraph to The New York Times.*

LONDON, May 21.—The Countess of Suffolk (née Leiter) suffered a serious riding accident yesterday at the Suffolk seat, Charlton Park, Malmesbury. With Lord Suffolk she was taking her customary morning ride when her horse bolted.

Lady Suffolk was in peril of being thrown first into a quarry and then into a reservoir. The horse dashed at a gate across the roadway and broke it. The Countess was thrown heavily.

Lord Suffolk followed as fast as he could gallop, and, assistance being quickly summoned, Lady Suffolk was removed to the house, suffering from severe shock.

She is slightly better to-day.

Lady Suffolk was Miss Margaret (Daisy) Leiter, and is the youngest of the daughters of the late Levi Z. Leiter of Chicago and Washington. She married Lord Suffolk in 1904. Her eldest sister, Miss Mary Leiter, married Lord Curzon of Kedleston. Lady Curzon died in 1906.

## RAILROAD BARS RED GARB.

### Chicago Great Western's Rule for Employes Is a Safety Device.

*Special to The New York Times.*

CHICAGO, May 21.—"Don't wear any red clothing, because you might thereby cause the wreck of a train."

"Be courteous, because it pays in real money."

These are the latest rules promulgated for its employes by the Chicago Great Western Railroad Company. In some way the new order traveled East before it became known in the West. Then there was a procession of conductors, brakemen, engineers, firemen, and trainhands to the office of the Division Superintendent to see if the order was authentic.

Under the new regulations section hands are no longer to be permitted to wear red undershirts; brakemen must abandon their favorite vests and neckties if they are red. The idea is that if engineers are constantly seeing flashes of red, the color may become so familiar to them that a real danger signal may not be recognized.

The company has also issued a circular to its employes on the value of courtesy toward the public.

"A soft answer turneth away wrath," says the circular, "and we might add, 'A harsh answer turneth away cash.'"





## SUFFRAGE PARADER LOSES TEACHING JOB

### Dismissed from Parochial School by Parish Priest for Setting Bad Example.

### NEXT TO SOCIALISM, HE SAID

### Suffrage Leaders Espouse Her Cause and Will Find Employment for Her—An Ardent Suffragist Now.

Miss Aimée Hutchinson, who was a teacher-clerk in the parochial school connected with the Church of the Blessed Sacrament, at Seventy-first Street and Broadway, says that she lost her position because she marched in the Woman Suffrage Parade. Mrs. Harriot Stanton Blatch, speaking for the suffragists, said yesterday that Miss Hutchinson certainly should have a new position. Miss Hutchinson, who formerly was only a lukewarm suffragist, has become an ardent one. Mrs. Blatch will confer with several other leaders to-day at suffrage headquarters in regard to the girl.

Miss Hutchinson is the daughter of Mme. Torriani, a singing teacher connected with the Institute of Musical Art. She lives at 385 West End Avenue. She will be twenty-two years old on June 1. She was baptized by Father Mathew A. Taylor of the Church of the Blessed Sacrament and has always been a particular pet of his. He has never, in fact, according to Mme. Torriani, referred to her by her own name, but always calls her "Pettie."

"Several days after the parade," said Miss Hutchinson yesterday to a reporter for THE TIMES, "Father Taylor called me to his study and said: 'I am very fond of you. You know how much I like you and your work, but since you have marched in the parade of suffragists I cannot have you any longer in the school. The woman suffrage movement is the next thing to socialism, and I cannot countenance it. I have thought the whole thing over carefully, and there is nothing else to do. No matter how much I understand your own character, it is not a good example.'

"'Why didn't you tell me before, Father?' I asked, 'that you were opposed to my marching in the parade, and I would not have done so. I could still have had my convictions, but I would not have marched.'

"'I did not know that you were going to march,' he answered.

**Her Case Reported to Mrs. Blatch.**

"Well, I was out of a position, and under the circumstances it seemed only fair that the suffragists should know that I lost my position through marching in the parade. Mrs. Frederick Nathan very kindly helped me by giving me several letters, and I have been on the search for something to do ever since."

"My daughter has many talents," said Mme. Torriani. "She sings well, (her voice is a contralto,) and she plays the violin well. I do not think she will have trouble in finding something to do. She has a great many friends and no enemies. We can't help but believe that Father Taylor has made a mistake in taking the stand he has, but that cannot be helped now."

Mrs. Harriot Stanton Blatch said yesterday that the suffragists would see that Miss Hutchinson got work to do.

"She is entirely charming," said Mrs. Blatch, "and with great personality and force of character. When she came to me with a note of introduction from Mrs. Nathan I said to myself before I went into the drawing room to speak to her: 'It is just another case of a girl with a grievance. She has been discharged for some other reason than marching in the parade.' But I had not spoken two words with her before I entirely revised my opinion. She was so intelligent and so charming. She had only good words for Father Taylor. It was simply a mistaken idea of his, was all she would say.

"One result the action has had is to make her the strongest kind of a suffragist. She will devote herself heart and soul to that cause now. She is so very talented that I think she will have no difficulty whatever in getting another position, but if she does have we shall be glad to have her work with us.

**Called First Martyr of the Cause.**

"She is exactly the kind of worker that the suffrage movement needs. We wouldn't have her doing clerk's work, either. She would be the best kind of an outside worker. When I go to headquarters to-day I shall talk over the matter with some of my colaborers.

"Of course, we can really do nothing but make the matter public and permit the people to know what a young woman has suffered because she dared to assert her rights to entertain a conviction to parade with us in support of her ideas.

"Miss Hutchinson is our first martyr, and we will do our utmost to see that she loses nothing by the sacrifice she has had to make to uphold her principles. There have been others who told us that their employers threatened them with the loss of their places if they paraded, but Miss Hutchinson is the only one who really has suffered such a loss through asserting her right to think and act for what she believes to be right."

Miss Hutchinson's case was also brought to the attention of Mrs. James L. Laidlaw, who has been making an investigation. Mrs. Laidlaw is expected to come in from her country home at Port Washington, L. I., for the conference to-day.

"Persecution and tyranny will not be permitted in this country," said Mrs. Frederick Nathan. "It will awaken man to the injustice women have to bear."

It is said that there are many Roman Catholic priests who are in favor of suffrage and who are doing their utmost to bring it about. Father Taylor's position is said to be an entirely personal one. Yesterday he could not be found in his residence on West Seventy-first Street or at the parochial school. No one in authority at the archiepiscopal residence would comment on Father Taylor's action.



# ROOSEVELT TRIUMPHANT IN OHIO; CLAIMS 15 DISTRICTS OUT OF THE 21; HARMON WINS, 2 TO 1, FROM WILSON

## Victory and Defeat Explained.

### Roosevelt Manager Sees Overwhelming Triumph—Misrepresentation Did It, Says Taft Representative.

By LEWIS C. LAYLIN, Manager of the Taft Campaign in Ohio.

*By Telegraph to the Editor of The New York Times.*

COLUMBUS, Ohio, May 22.—Misrepresentation and prejudice against President Taft took early root in Ohio. The results in Illinois and Pennsylvania encouraged the opposition. But a great change and trend to Taft have occurred in the last ten days. Another week's deliberation would have meant a sweeping victory for the President. Meager returns indicate that Taft will have the State Convention and the delegates at large. Probably Roosevelt will have a majority of the district delegates. It is impossible now to make an accurate statement of the results.

LEWIS C. LAYLIN.

By WALTER F. BROWN, Chairman Republican State Central Committee.

*By Telegraph to the Editor of The New York Times.*

COLUMBUS, Ohio, May 22.—At midnight it is certain that the Roosevelt delegates have been elected in 13 districts out of 21. Complete returns will, in all probability, increase this number to 15 or 16.

The verdict of Ohio Republicans means that the Republican Party is to take up its forward movement again. under the leadership of Theodore Roosevelt.

WALTER F. BROWN.

## CRANE TO RETIRE FROM THE SENATE

### Massachusetts Senator, Following Other Old Guard Leaders, Won't Seek Re-election.

### NOT DUE TO PRIMARY DEFEAT

### Finds the Atmosphere of the Upper Chamber, Now Dominated by Progressives, Not to His Liking.

*Special to The New York Times.*

WASHINGTON, May 21.—Following the example of most of the other Old Guard leaders in the Senate, Murray Crane of Massachusetts announced to-day that he would not be a candidate for re-election. He is really the last of the Mohicans. Spooner quit in 1906, Allison, Hanna, and Platt of Connecticut are dead, and Aldrich and Hale, seeing, as Spooner did, and as Crane has now done, the handwriting on the wall, announced their retirement in 1910.

Senator Crane's retirement will be ascribed to the fear of defeat, but such an inference is unfair and untrue. He is retiring for the same reason that Aldrich and Hale did—because the atmosphere of the Senate has become distasteful to him. There is no room left for Senators of the old stripe. Men like Bristow, Borah, and La Follette have come to the front and have so jostled and bewildered the old-timers that they find no joy in serving. Of late years the Senate atmosphere has closely approximated the bustling Democratic atmosphere of the House.

This is not a theoretical view of Senator Crane's position. It is a free translation of what he has said over and over again in private conversation with personal friends the last month. He has said that there is no longer any real leadership in the Senate and that he has ceased to find pleasure there. Virtually the same thing was said by Aldrich and Hale before their retirement.

But for the fear that his action would be misconstrued Senator Crane would have made this announcement after the Massachusetts primaries, in which he was defeated for delegate to the Chicago Convention. He saw, however, that if he did so his action would be interpreted as due to pique or the fear of defeat, and he deferred it. Now he thinks the primaries are sufficiently far in the background for him to make the announcement without fear of misconstruction.

With him out of the Senate there will be nobody left who represents the old system in an adequate way. Gallinger, Penrose, and a few others will still be on guard, but none of them is a leader of the Aldrich type. Crane was the last refuge of the Old Guard. It will be a La Folletteized Senate which will run things after he quits.

Representative Weeks announced himself to-night as a candidate for Crane's place. Representative Gardner, (Senator Lodge's son-in-law;) Gov. Guild, Representative McCall, and Secretary of the Navy Meyer are spoken of as candidates, but there has always been a tradition that one of the Massachusetts Senatorships must go to the western part of the State, and all these men are from the east. Representative George P. Lawrence is the only man so far mentioned who comes from the west. Mr. Crane, in announcing his intention of retiring, issued the following statement:

"Some months ago I definitely decided not to become a candidate for re-election as United States Senator, but I intended to defer making a statement to that effect until after the Republican National Convention. There is, however, a proposition pending in the Massachusetts Legislature for the nomination of United States Senators substantially similar to the existing law relating to the nominations of candidates for the Presidency, representatives in Congress and State elective offices. If this proposed law is enacted a much earlier campaign for this office will be necessary, and I, therefore, make known my position at this time in order that those who may be interested in becoming candidates may have the fullest opportunity to have their candidacies considered.

"In making public my decision not to become a candidate again I wish to assure the people of Massachusetts of my deep appreciation of the loyal support and confidence which they have always given me."

Senator Crane is also Republican National Committeeman from Massachusetts. His term in the Senate expires March 3 next.

BOSTON, May 21.—Mayor John F. Fitzgerald announced his candidacy to-night for the nomination for United States Senator to succeed Senator Winthrop Murray Crane. Mayor Fitzgerald, in a statement, declared the withdrawal of Senator Crane to foreshadow the passage of the Senatorial Primary Preference bill now before the Massachusetts Legislature.



## BROKEN DAM WRECKS FARMS.

### Concrete Structure Near Westport Bursts After Heavy Rains.

*Special to The New York Times.*

WESTPORT, N. Y., May 21.—A large power dam seven miles west of this village, in Essex County, owned by D. F. Payne of Wadhams, gave way last night, inundating ten miles of choice farm land and causing thousands of dollars' damage to farm property, stock, sawmills, and grist mills. The heavy rains of the last two weeks, together with the fall of snow on Monday, brought heavy pressure on the mammoth concrete dam. It furnished electric power for Mineville, Elizabethtown, and Westport.

A new power house just completed by Mr. Payne was swept away, also the steel bridge and several hundred feet of the Elizabethtown Terminal Railroad embankment.

Telegraph and telephone lines are down and the roads are in bad condition.

## FIND A. B. YOUNG IN CANADA.

### New York Agent of Potomac Refining Co. Arrested at Trenton, Ont.

*Special to The New York Times.*

BALTIMORE, Md., May 21.—Alfred B. Young, stock salesman and for a time representative in New York City of the Potomac Refining Company, the officials of which were indicted by the Federal Grand Jury here on the charge of conspiring to make false representations to sell the company's stock, was arrested in Trenton, Ontario, where his relatives live, and last night was brought to Baltimore and gave bail of $5,000.

Young was at first thought to be in Europe and the Government officials made efforts to locate him there. New clues led to Canada, however, and after a conference with the law officers of the Canadian Government Post Office Inspector Carter B. Keene served Young on Saturday last with the necessary papers requiring his return to the United States.

## SAY MORSE PAID BIG FEE.

### Atlanta Hears He Gave Counsel $100,000 for Getting Him Free.

*Special to The New York Times.*

ATLANTA, May 21.—Charles W. Morse, who was reported penniless after he was sent to the penitentiary for misuse of funds in one of his banks, paid his attorneys $100,000 for obtaining his release, it is reported here. Felder, Anderson, Roundtree & Wilson of Atlanta represented Morse, and his contract, it is said, called for a fee of $100,000 if they could get him free.

Through their efforts President Taft was induced to free Morse, it being represented that the ex-banker was at the point of death. Soon after Morse was released he paid more than half of the $100,000, and the rest will soon be due. Mr. Felder, who handled the case, said:

"We certainly received sufficient compensation for obtaining Mr. Morse's release, but I do not think it would be ethical to disclose the amount."

It is stated by those in Morse's confidence that he is still wealthy. It is said that he had more than $2,000,000 when he entered prison. The $100,000 fee paid by Morse is said to be the largest ever received by an Atlanta legal firm.

## A SURE SIGN OF SUMMER.

### Not the Temperature, but the Boys in the City Hall Fountain.

Summer has arrived, and by this sign be it known. Ten youngsters eluded the vigilance of the police and went in bathing at nightfall yesterday in the fountain in City Hall Park. All day the boys selling newspapers in Park Row gazed longingly at the fountain and the policemen, always a prominent feature of the landscape. Toward evening scouts were sent out to watch the policemen. When time came for them to end their tours of duty the scouts faithfully reported their departure.

The last visible policeman had no sooner got across the park than ten little boys were lined up pulling off their clothing in feverish haste. They had made provision for the occasion, and each little boy wore a pair of trunks underneath his clothing. Hats, stockings, and other articles of clothing they handed to another boy who acted as clothes bearer and lookout.

For nearly half an hour the boys enjoyed themselves in the fountain, jumping from the edge splashing each other, and sometimes spectators.

Suddenly from somewhere out in the park came a shrill cry, and the bathers decamped, followed by the little boy with their clothes.

The policeman, who gave a not too enthusiastic pursuit, caught two of the culprits. He looked them over, smiled, and said gruffly, "Run for home before you catch cold."



### Colonel's Vote 59,054 to Taft's 41,435 with One-Fourth of Returns In.

### TAFT CARRIES CINCINNATI

### But Cleveland, Which Senator Burton Hoped to Win for Him, Goes for Roosevelt.

### TAFT MEN CLAIM HALF

### Declare Roosevelt Estimate Exaggerated, but Give Out No Figures.

### FIGHT WON, SAYS ROOSEVELT

### Gets the News at Oyster Bay and Beams with Delight at His Victory.

### FARMERS SAVED HARMON

### Gave the Governor a 7 to 1 Vote to Offset Wilson's Lead in the Cities.

*Special to The New York Times.*

COLUMBUS, Ohio, Wednesday, May 22.—Theodore Roosevelt has won a sweeping victory in the Presidential primaries in Ohio. His managers claim 30 out of the 42 district delegates chosen to-day.

Gov. Judson Harmon, according to the latest returns, will have a substantial majority over Gov. Woodrow Wilson of New Jersey on the preferential primary ballot, which will give him the control of the six delegates at large.

It is claimed by his campaign managers also that he will have a majority of the district delegates to the Democratic National Convention, and that with control of the State Democratic Convention his supporters will be able to impose the unit rule and put through a resolution indorsing him as Ohio's choice for the Presidential nomination.

While the election officials are not prepared to give in detail the pluralities rolled up in various localities by the successful candidates, there was nothing in the late returns to make the situation more hopeful to the friends of President Taft. Thick gloom pervaded the Taft headquarters here, while Lewis C. Laylin, the Taft manager, was trying to gather some grain of comfort out of what appeared to be a crushing defeat.

**Taft Leads in Cincinnati.**

Walter F. Brown, Col. Roosevelt's manager, said at 1 o'clock this morning that he was willing to concede only one of the two Congress Districts in the President's home county—Hamilton, in which is Cincinnati—to Taft. The First Congress District, according to returns received at Roosevelt headquarters at 1 o'clock this morning, had been carried for the delegates pledged to President Taft by the slim majority of 500. The Second District at that time was still in doubt, with the Roosevelt delegates gaining.

Chairman Brown claimed as certain for Col. Roosevelt fifteen out of the twenty-one districts, giving thirty out of the forty-two district delegates to the Colonel and making certain the election at the State Convention of six delegates at large pledged to Col. Roosevelt. Five districts—the Second, Third, Seventh, Thirteenth, and Sixteenth—Mr. Brown placed in the doubtful column.

The districts that Brown claims for Roosevelt are the Third, Fourth, Fifth, Sixth, Seventh, Eighth, Ninth, Eleventh, Twelfth, Thirteenth, Fourteenth, Seventeenth, Nineteenth, Twentieth, and Twenty-first.

Although Roosevelt's victory in the election of district delegates to the National Convention gives him a majority of the State's 42 delegates, it is possible that the Taft forces may control the State Convention and elect the six delegates at large. This situation arises because delegates to the State Convention were voted for to-day apart from the district delegates to the National Convention. The Roosevelt leaders hope, however, that if the Taft delegates to the State Convention are in the majority they will "see the handwriting in the wall" and shift to the Colonel.

**Returns Slow Coming In.**

Owing to the complicated ballot and the novelty of the present primary system, returns were exceedingly slow in coming in. Only a small percentage of the 5,192 voting precincts in the States had been heard from at midnight.

Complete returns from 1,325 precincts out of 5,192 in the State gave Roosevelt delegates a total of 59,054 and the Taft delegates 41,435.

Returns from 481 precincts in the Democratic returns give Harmon 7,774 and Wilson 6,875.

At midnight it was announced at the

"All the News That's Fit to Print"

# The New York Times

THE WEATHER. Showers, warmer to-day and Sunday; moderate to brisk east winds. For full weather report see Page 21.

VOL. LXI...NO. 19,866. * * * NEW YORK, SATURDAY, JUNE 15, 1912.—TWENTY-TWO PAGES. ONE CENT In Greater New York, Elsewhere, Jersey City, and Newark. TWO CENTS.

# TAFT MEN CONFIDENT OF VICTORY; SHERMAN NOT TO BE ON THE TICKET

## SHERMAN WON'T RUN AGAIN.

### Finds Vice Presidency Lacks Further Attractions for Him—Won't Go to Chicago.

*Special to The New York Time*

WASHINGTON, June 14.—It was stated here to-day on excellent authority that Vice President Sherman has decided that a renomination for the Vice Presidency has no attractions for him. This was the most significant of to-day's developments at the capital.

Mr. Sherman, who was regarded as a candidate a month or six weeks ago, and whose friends were threatening all sorts of dire calamities to President Taft's candidacy unless Mr. Sherman was slated for Vice President, has wiped his name off the slate, where it was put at his insistence, and has beaten a retreat. Four years ago Mr. Sherman was at Chicago battling for a place on the ticket with Mr. Taft. This year he will not go near the convention city. He will bury himself in the depths of the Adirondacks, far away from the zone of political brickbats and out of touch with the world. Senator Bacon has been designated to act as President pro tem. of the Senate while he is away.

This report, which was disclosed to-day for the first time, was confirmed by Senator Bradley of Kentucky, his close friend, although the Kentucky Senator did not admit that the Vice President had ever been seeking a renomination.

"Mr. Sherman informs me that he does not want a renomination. His name will not go before the convention," said Senator Bradley.

Former Speaker Cannon, who had more to do with the nomination of Mr. Sherman for Vice President four years ago than any one else, and who a few weeks ago was insisting that Mr. Sherman must be renominated, has lost interest in the subject and will not attend the convention.

There is much speculation as to the reasons for Mr. Sherman's change of mind. The most plausible theory advanced was that the Taft people, who were never anxious that Mr. Sherman should be the President's running mate, had at last carried their point, which was that the Vice Presidency should be left open for a Progressive. The President himself is objected to on the ground of being too conservative, and under the circumstances the nomination of Mr. Sherman would be regarded as a dead weight to the ticket. With Mr. Sherman out of the running, it is said, the Taft managers will make haste to bid for the Progressive vote by putting a Progressive in his place.

# COLONEL DEPARTS; TRAIN HITS ROCK

### Starts for Chicago on Lake Shore Limited, Which Narrowly Escapes Wreck.

## BOYS BLOCK THE TRACK

### Roll Heavy Boulder On to the Line Two Miles North of Tarrytown.

## AIR BRAKES SAVE TRAIN

### Ex-President Dodges Demonstration Here, but Plans for Receptions in Other Places.

Col. Roosevelt, after a long talk on the telephone with his managers in Chicago, decided at noon yesterday to start for that city on the Lake Shore Limited, which departed from the Grand Central Station at 5:30 o'clock in the afternoon. Eluding a great crowd which gathered at the station to see him off, he was taken to his private car in a freight elevator. Within an hour after the train had started, the Colonel's friends in this city were startled to hear that in rounding a curve on the New York Central line near Tarrytown, the locomotive of the limited had hit a boulder some two feet in diameter, which had been rolled to the track by mischievous boys.

The train was brought to a sudden stop when a fragment of the rock punctured an air brake pipe and while the passengers, including Col. Roosevelt, were much startled, no one was hurt. It was said later that only the setting of the air brakes saved the train from derailment. The train was sent on after considerable delay to Poughkeepsie where the damaged locomotive was taken off and another substituted.

**Eluded Crowd at Station.**

The Colonel announced his decision to go to Chicago at The Outlook office, to which he had motored from Oyster Bay. As soon as his supporters here heard the news, they arranged to make his departure noteworthy, but their plan to give him a demonstration was frustrated, as the candidate entered at a side entrance to the Grand Central Station in a taxicab and was taken to his car at once through private passages.

The Roosevelt party consisted of Col. and Mrs. Roosevelt, their son Kermit, Secretary Frank Harper and his wife, ex-Gov. Regis H. Post of Porto Rico, Theodore Douglas Robinson, a nephew of Col. Roosevelt; George D. Roosevelt, a cousin, and W. B. Howland and Travers B. Carmen. Theodore Roosevelt, Jr., met the party at the Lexington Avenue entrance to the Grand Central Station, but did not go to Chicago. The crowd waited until the train started from the station and when it was learned that the Colonel had purposely evaded the demonstration planned in his honor much surprise was expressed. Col. Roosevelt all the time the crowd was waiting for him to pass through the gates was busy writing telegrams to his campaign managers throughout the country. His first act on arriving in his car was to call for his secretary and some writing paper.

**Colonel Reading When Shock Came.**

He was engaged on his correspondence up to the time the train started and then retired to his stateroom. Two miles north of Tarrytown, as the train was sweeping around a curve at a speed of some sixty miles an hour, the locomotive crashed into the boulder.

The cow catcher of the train was crushed by the impact and a fragment of the rock tore a hole in the pipe connecting the air brakes. As a result, the brakes on all the cars of the train, including that occupied by Col. Roosevelt and his party, were suddenly locked and several of the passengers were thrown violently forward in their seats.

Col. Roosevelt's car was fourth from the engine, and he was reading when the crash came. The book was all but jerked from his hands by the shock of the sudden stop.

"I could not imagine what had happened," the Colonel said later.

That Col. Roosevelt and the other passengers were in grave danger, and that the cutting of the airbrake pipe probably prevented the derailment of the train, was the opinion of the engineer, John McAuliff, and the conductor.

"I did not see the rock as we went around the curve," said McAuliff. "I can't imagine how it got on the tracks. All I know is that the train came to an abrupt stop. The boulder must have been at least two feet in diameter, if not larger, to have smashed the cow catcher as it did."

All doubt as to how the stone got on the track was set at rest by a track walker who ran up after the train had come to a halt and said he had seen three boys roll a big boulder down the side of the cut to the rails near the Beekman Avenue bridge. Railroad detectives were sent to find the boys and arrested three youngsters, all under 10 years old. The prisoners were taken to Police Headquarters in North Tarrytown. One boy gave his name as Pollock, and the police did not take the names of his companions. They were ordered to appear before Judge Armstrong at 9 o'clock this morning.

**Train Crawls to Poughkeepsie.**

It took just thirty minutes to repair the train so that it could crawl into Poughkeepsie. There was no scheduled stop at that town, but it was decided to hold the train in the yards there. An inspector of the New York Central condemned the locomotive at Poughkeepsie. It took another twenty minutes to get a relief engine. Then the train proceeded at top speed in an attempt to make up lost time.

The collision with the boulder caused

Continued on Page 2.

## STOTESBURY IS FOR TAFT.

### Talk of Wall Street Favoring Roosevelt "All Wrong," He Says.

*By Marconi Transatlantic Wireless Telegraph to The New York Times.*

LONDON, June 14.—During a talk with THE NEW YORK TIMES correspondent to-night E. T. Stotesbury, the Philadelphia banker, said that the statements to the effect that Wall Street and other moneyed interests of America were in favor of the nomination and election of Roosevelt as President were "all wrong."

"Just as soon as I get back home," said Mr. Stotesbury, "I will use all my influence to elect President Taft if he is nominated, which I hope he will be. I am for Taft, and any statements that Wall Street and other moneyed interests are in favor of the nomination and election of Roosevelt are all wrong, so far as I gather. It is unfortunate that President Taft got drawn into a personal controversy with Roosevelt, but that does not affect the situation.

"I was elected a delegate to the convention, but had to come to Europe, so in my absence a substitute will act for me. I can only say and hope and think that Mr. Taft will get the nomination. He deserves it."

Mr. Stotesbury left Philadelphia May 14, since when he has been staying in Paris. He came here to attend the Horse Show, of which he is one of the American Directors, after which he goes on a motoring tour through England and Scotland, and thence to the Continent.

He and Mrs. Stotesbury were to-day guests of Judge and Mrs. W. H. Moore on Mr. Moore's coach during the winning ride from London to Richmond in the Richmond Horse Show Marathon coaching event.

## HOLD WOMAN FOR 5 DEATHS.

### Police Suspect Mrs. Lindorf of Poisoning All Her Family.

*Special to The New York Times.*

CHICAGO, June 14.—Mrs. Louise Lindorf, a Spiritualist, was arrested this afternoon on suspicion of having poisoned her two husbands and her three grown children. Henry Kuby, a boarder in Mrs. Lindorf's home, is also being detained by the police, who believe that he may be able to throw some light on the many deaths that have occurred in the Lindorff household within the last three years.

The arrests were made after Coroner Hoffman and Dr. H. S. Lecount had made a post mortem examination of the body of Arthur Lindorf, who died this afternoon. The death was reported to the Coroner by a physician who had attended the boy and had become suspicious that death was due to poison. The vital organs of the youth will be subjected to a chemical analysis.

Coroner Hoffman said to-night: "From what I know now, young Lindorf's death is very suspicious."

The police issued a statement that there had been a number of other deaths in the Lindorf family, which were suspicious, and on account of which they will demand an explanation. The deaths being investigated are:

Julius Granke, first husband of Mrs. Lindorf, died suddenly Aug. 12, 1905, at Milwaukee, Wis., where the family lived at that time. Carried insurance of $2,000; died supposedly as result of a sunstroke.

William Lindorf, 22 years old, died Jan. 11, 1908, supposedly of typhoid fever; insured for $1,000.

Alma Granke Lindorf, died Aug. 4, 1911, supposedly from heart disease; insured for $2,500.

Arthur Lindorf, the boy who died today, was insured for $3,500.

## EAGLE SEIZES LITTLE GIRL.

### Fiercely Attacks Father of Child, Who Finally Kills It.

*Special to The New York Times.*

BRIDGEPORT, Conn., June 14.—A huge eagle swooped down on the home of Randolph Creewald, Compo Street, Westport, on Thursday evening and seized Anna, the two-year-old daughter, in its talons, and attempted to fly away with her.

The screams of the child brought the father to the yard. The bird dropped the little one and Mr. Creewald seized her and ran into the house. As he closed the door, the eagle dashed against the panel. The eagle then flew into a nearby tree.

Mr. Creewald got his gun and fired at the bird but only stunned it. The eagle then flew toward Mr. Creewald, who fired the second barrel at ten feet, killing the eagle instantly.

The bird weighed twenty-seven pounds and was seven feet in wing measurement and over three feet from beak to tail. It it the largest eagle seen in this vicinity recently. The little girl's clothes were torn by the bird's talons, but she was not even scratched.

## CASTS FIRST VOTE AT 76.

### Commodore Swain of Japanese Navy Has Picked Out Roosevelt.

*Special to The New York Times.*

BOSTON, June 14.—Commodore Richard Swain of the Japanese naval reserve, who, despite a long service under a foreign flag, has been a good American citizen all of his 76 years, has come here to cast his first vote for President. He thinks he will vote for Roosevelt if he is nominated, but he also likes Taft.

As the Commodore, who reached Boston on the White Star liner Cymric today, stood on the pier, he showed as intense interest in voting for the first time next November as would a youth of 21.

Commodore Swain is accompanied by his wife. They will stay one year at Nantucket and then return to Japan. He is the only American in the Japanese naval service. He commands one of the ships of the Nippon Yusen Kaisha.

## DIES TALKING TO CLASS.

### Clarence F. Carroll Stricken at Warner High School Exercises.

WARNER, N. H., June 14.—While Clarence F. Carroll, formerly Superintendent of Schools at Rochester, N. Y., was delivering an address before the graduating class of the Warner High School to-day he was taken suddenly ill and died a few minutes later.

Mr. Carroll was for many years engaged in normal school work in Pennsylvania, New Jersey, and Connecticut. He was graduated from Yale in the class of 1875.



# TWELVE IN MOB SHOT, SOME WHILE RUNNING

### Guards Check with Rifles Assault on Perth Amboy Smelter—Two Dead.

## OTHERS MORTALLY WOUNDED

### Seven Inoffensive Young Men Holding Passes to Cross the "Dead Line" Fired Upon and Wounded.

*Special to The New York Times.*

PERTH AMBOY, N. J., June 14.—Two strikers are dead, two are dying in the hospital, another is there less seriously wounded, and seven young men of the city, who innocently attempted to cross the dead line, are shot in the legs—twelve in all dead or injured—as a result of the strike riots here to-day and to-night.

Following a calm which ensued after an attack upon the strikers by armed guards within the grounds of the American Smelting and Refining Company's works on State Street, in which one man was killed and two mortally wounded, the strikers were stirred to renewed activity to-night by the arrival of 300 additional Sheriff's deputies, armed with magazine rifles, from Newark and Jersey City. With these reinforcements a dead line was established 300 feet on each side of the plant, and orders were given to permit no person inside the lines. As soon as the deputies had taken their places the strikers began to assemble in large numbers until finally a mob of 2,000 had gathered on the east side of the factory.

The crowd jeered the deputies and finally some of the bolder spirits threw rocks. Finally a shower of stones began to drive the deputies back, and they resisted by opening fire on the crowd with the result that two of the rioers fell. Anthony Gerhardy was shot through the head and instantly killed, while Joseph Pedok got a bullet in the calf of the righ leg. The rioters immediately gave ground and began to run headlong to get out of rifle range. They were charged by the deputies and driven into the swamps a quarter of a mile away in the direction of the city.

As a result of the encounter many of the Deputies appeared to lose their heads and several scattering volleys were fired from time to time with the evident intention of discouraging any of the strikers who might muster up sufficient courage to attempt to return. Things remained quiet until shortly after 11 o'clock, when a group of young men, all members of respected families in the city, none of them in any way connected with the strikers, attempted to pass through the lines on the west side of the factory. They had passes and had gotten safely by the first line of Deputies and were approaching those who had taken part in the first fracas, when they were suddenly challenged.

They announced that they were not strikers and that they had passes from the Sheriff which entitled them to go through on their back from Boynton Beach to the city.

"Move along, then!" came the order from one of the Deputies, and the group accelerated their pace.

"Faster," came the second challenge, and they broke into a run.

As they did so, a volley was fired without orders, and seven of the young men fell. The wounded victims are: John Bresgaard, 20 years old, of Washington Street, shot in the right leg; Stanley Schultz, 20 years old, also wounded in the right leg; William Dockwell, 19 years old, shot through the left hip; Herbert Gillies, 20 years old, shot in the left leg and right arm; Michael Dallman, 20 years old, of State Street, wounded in both legs; Leslie Tooker, 18 years old, of Washington Street, shot in the left leg, and Andrew Nelson, 18 years of age, wounded in the right leg and left arm. All seven of the wounded youths were hurried to the City Hospital. None of them is seriously injured.

As the result of the last shooting the entire city has been thrown into a state of indignation, and prominent citizens have already announced their intention of demanding that the Governor send the militia at once. There are open declarations to-night that Sheriff Bollschweiler has been using the strike for political purposes. The Deputies are all paid by the county, and are for the most part political hangers-on who have been recruited in the neighboring townships. Sheriff Bollschweiler, it is alleged, has refused to admit that the situation has gotten beyond him.

One man was killed and two were mortally wounded about noon as the result of a clash between 2,000 strikers and the armed guards posted within the grounds of the American Smelting and Refining Company.

At 10 o'clock a group of strikers approached the main body from the direction of the city, and it was observed that these newcomers carried axes, crowbars, and sledge hammers. A sudden cheer went up among those assembled, and the new arrivals pushed and jostled their way to the front of the mob, and, as if by magic, a dozen red flags waved over the heads of the crowd.

A blue-shirted, stalwart ironworker placed himself in front of the assemblage and held up his hand for attention.

"There are scabs in the works?" he cried. "They have been brought here to take your jobs away from you. What are you going to do about it?"

"Kill them. Drag them out," shouted a score of voices in English, while from the majority of the mob cries arose in several foreign tongues from those who evidently understood the purport of the speaker's words.

The mob moved slowly forward, pushing, jostling, and cursing in a dozen tongues. Several of the guards within the works showed themselves inside the fence and called upon the crowd to fall back. No heed was paid to the warning, and the guards dropped ont of sight. Suddenly from a loophole in the fence came a puff of smoke and the report of a magazine rifle followed. No one fell, and immediately a shout of fury went up from the strikers and a hundred voices cried in chorus: "Blanks! They're using blanks! Don't mind the guards; get the scabs! Bring them out!"

Axes, crowbars, and sledgehammers were raised aloft; heavy logs were picked up from a pile of railroad ties near the ruins of the ruined trolley station, and with a yell like madmen the strikers charged for the fence pell-mell, with here and there the red banner of the Industrial Workers of the World tossing over their heads. The crack of a score of rifles halted them for a moment, and as the gray curling smoke lifted in thin spirals from loopholes in the fence the mob saw three of their number stretched on the ground almost in front of the great gate and with cries of terror they broke and ran. As soon as the rout was over and the last of the retreating strikers had passed from sight about a bend in the road the gate swung open and half a dozen unarmed guards ran to the spot where the three victims of the battle were lying, and, picking them up, hurried back inside the grounds.

A hasty examination revealed that one of the men was dead and that the other two were seriously wounded. The dead man was Stephen Burachak, a striker, who, with his wife and three small children, lived in Wayne Street in this city. The two wounded men were Jacob Powell, also married, with four children, and George Laguada, single, both of whom lived in Elizabeth Street. Powell was shot through the left lung and Laguada received a rifle bullet in the groin. Both victims were hurried to the City Hospital, where the physicians entertain slight hopes for the recovery of either.

Late this afternoon the State militia in Red Bank, consisting of the Second Troop of Cavalry, received orders to get in readiness to come here to assist the civil authorities in preserving order.

**OWEN JOHNSON PRIZE AWARDS TO-MORROW**

From the many essays on social organization of colleges that were submitted two have been selected as winners of the $150 and $100 prizes offered by the author of "Stover at Yale." Names of winners and their essays will be printed in the College Section of TO-MORROW'S SUNDAY TIMES.

# ASQUITH ATTACKED BY SUFFRAGETTES

### First Woman Assails the British Premier to Rip Off His Epaulets.

## NEXT ASSAULTS WITH FAN

### Youth Adds to Turmoil at Reception from Which the Disturbers Are Dragged by Force.

*Special Cable to THE NEW YORK TIMES.*

LONDON, June 14.—An amazing scene took place at the India office tonight when a militant suffragette attacked Premier Asquith during his official reception, held in honor of the King's birthday.

Mr. Asquith, accompanied by Mrs. Asquith and his daughter, was receiving the guests as they arrived. A well-dressed woman, about 30 years of age, when announced, instead of shaking the Premier's extended hand, said a few words and then suddenly placed both hands on Mr. Asquith's shoulder and began tugging violently at the epaulettes of the Premier's official coat.

Mr. Asquith showed considerable sang-froid and managed to shake off the woman, but she returned to the attack and tried with all her might to wrench off the epaulette from his right shoulder.

In the meantime an usher seized the woman by the waist, while Mrs. Asquith also helped to extricate her husband from his assailant's unwelcome attentions. Finally the woman was dragged away, resisting stubbornly.

All this while Mr. Asquith showed remarkable restraint and treated the woman with chivalrous forbearance, as if fearing to hurt her. He and Mrs. Asquith then continued to receive the guests.

A couple of minutes after the woman was ejected, a pale-faced youth, about 20 years old, on being introduced to the Premier, took hold of him rudely by the arms and shouted something inaudible.

Instantly Sir Henry Lunn rushed forward, took the youth by the scruff of the neck, and literally ran him out of the hall. When he reached the corridor, he consigned the youth into the care of John Ward, M. P. That giant unceremoniously flung the intruder out of the building.

Soon after the youth was thrown out another well-dressed young woman seized the Premier's arm, and in the ensuing struggle beat him on the head with her fan with considerable violence. It was necessary to use force to free Mr. Asquith from the woman's clutches.

The Premier was much perturbed over the third assault and expressed himself in very forcible terms.

Those attending the reception included Princess Henry of Battenberg, Prince Arthur of Connaught, Prince and Princess Alexander of Teck, Princess Louise of Battenberg, Prince Albert, and Princess Marie Louise of Schleswig-Holstein, Prince Alexander of Battenberg, Prince Maurice of Battenberg, Prince Louis of Battenberg, Grand Duke Michael, several Ambassadors, including Mr. Reid, and many titled persons.

## OXFORD ROUTS SUFFRAGISTS.

### "We Want Christabel," Cry Students and Speakers Flee in Cabs.

*By Marconi Transatlantic Wireless Telegraph to The New York Times.*

LONDON, June 14.—Hundreds of undergraduates mingled with the crowds that gathered at an open-air suffragette demonstration in Oxford this evening and subjected the speakers, Annie Kenney, Sylvia Pankhurst, and Rachel Barrett, to many interruptions.

The college men repeatedly shouted, "We want Christabel!" Evil-smelling gases were also liberated.

Toward the end of the meeting the "ragging" became more vigorous. In the rush for the speakers' trucks several women and children were rather badly hustled. Eventually a number of the undergraduates seized one of the trucks and dragged it toward where Miss Barrett was speaking. Another section dragged the truck on which the speakers were standing backward and forward along the thoroughfare.

The suffragist flags were broken, but amid the uproar the speakers escaped in cabs.

The uproar was not quieted until after a conflict with the police.

## STOP FOR DANGER CALLS.

### Wireless Conference Suggests Three Minutes of Silence in Every Fifteen.

LONDON, June 14.—At the session today of the International radio-telegraphic conference a resolution was adopted suggesting that wireless operators on ships at sea reserve three minutes out of each fifteen minutes they are on duty and cease sending and listen for danger calls.

# LYDDITE BOMB SENT TO IMPORTER'S WIFE

### Mrs. Henry Sidenberg's Mail at Hastings-on-Hudson Brings Infernal Machine.

## SHE OPENS IT CAREFULLY

### Yonkers Bureau of Combustibles Finds Enough of the Explosive to Blow Up a House.

Mrs. Henry Sidenberg, the wife of Henry Sidenberg, a silk importer of 305 Broadway, now at her Summer home, Pinehurst, Hastings-on-Hudson, received through the mail yesterday a package from Germany containing enough lyddite to blow a house to atoms, according to Chief Landy of the Yonkers Bureau of Combustibles.

Mrs. Sidenberg said she hadn't the least idea who sent it. Last night the police heard a report that a certain relative of Mr. Sidenberg, living in Germany, who had recently applied to him for financial aid and had been refused, had threatened to kill his wife in revenge. This was denied by Mr. Sidenberg. His city home is at 14 West Fifty-first Street.

A Yonkers police official said that he understood that Post Office Inspectors had been notified that threatening letters had been received. There was also a report that Judge Rosalsky, who is said to be related to the Sidenbergs, was visiting the family and that the bomb was intended for him. There was nothing to substantiate this.

The package was received by Mrs. Sidenberg yesterday morning. It consisted of a pasteboard box about 6 inches long, 2 inches high, and 4 inches wide. Wrapped in excelsior was a steel tube 2 inches in diameter and 6 inches long, containing what was afterward found to be lyddite. This tube was connected with a platinum wire, which protruded from its sealed end, which connected with a zinc and lead "base." The contrivance was so constructed that it would be set in action if squeezed, or if the excelsior was hastily or carelessly removed. But Mrs. Sidenberg opened the box with great caution.

Though the box was addressed in English it appeared that the writer was more used to the German letters. The box had no wrapper, and bore German postage stamps and postage marks. The name in the postage mark was indecipherable. On the top of the package was written: "Of No Value, Duty Free."

Upon opening the box Mrs. Sidenberg immediately became suspicious, and sent it by a servant to the electrical supply store of Otto E. Wagner of Hastings. A superficial examination convinced him that it was some sort of an infernal machine, so he notified the Bureau of Combustibles at Yonkers. Chief Landy called for it, and after putting it in a pail of water containing acids which tend to cause a chemical reaction and render the explosive useless, he gingerly carried the box into a vacant lot.

Attaching a string several hundred feet long, and, after yanking it around considerably to induce an explosion, he decided that it was safe to open it.

The box contained enough lyddite to blast a 2,000-ton rock, the Chief declared.

## KIMBERLEY CLUB RAIDED.

### House Deserted, but Much Gambling Paraphernalia Is Seized, Police Say.

Several men, frequenters of the Kimberley Club, occupying a four-story brownstone house at 120 West Sixty-fifth Street, who had been warned that the police were about to make a raid last night, stood across the street and laughed at detectives, in charge of Inspector Hayes, as they demolished the vestibule doors with axes.

On the third floor the raiders say they found a quantity of gambling paraphernalia, including a roulette wheel and a faro outfit. It was confiscated. No arrests were made, the house being deserted when the police made their appearance. A crowd of more than 500 people gathered.



## LONGWORTH TO FIDDLE.

### Roosevelt's Son-in-Law Will Play in a Violin Contest To-day.

*Special to The New York Times.*

CHICAGO, Ill., June 14.—Congressman Longworth, son-in-law of Col. Roosevelt, will fiddle for a prize at the Hotel Sherman to-morrow afternoon. The contest is being staged by the American Guild of Violinists to test the relative qualities of old and new violins.

Mr. Longworth is the owner of a valuable violin made by Guarnerius, and has studied under some well-known masters. When a similar contest was held in Paris last year the new violins were victorious. The audience voted that they were richer in tone than those made by the old craftsmen.

It is the intention of the guild to put the American violinist on a similar footing with the European. Violinists from the principal cities of the United States are present at the guild's convention.

The aggregate value of the violins displayed is estimated to be $250,000.

## WOULD FAVOR ROOSEVELT.

### Seven Maryland Electors for Him, Says D. M. Newbold.

BALTIMORE, June 14.—David M. Newbold, named by the Republican State Convention as one of the Presidential Electors, said to-day that seven of the eight Maryland Electors would cast their ballots in the Electoral College for Col. Roosevelt rather than President Taft, in case both were candidates for President, regardless of which was the regular nominee of the Republican Party at the Chicago Convention.

Mr. Newbold is the legal adviser of the Roosevelt forces in this State.

## CANCER FOUND IN PLANTS.

### Government Botanist Discovers Disease Like That in Human Family.

WASHINGTON, June 14.—Crown gall, a disease found in many plants, is analogous to cancer in the human family, according to Dr. Erwin Smith of the Bureau of Plant Pathology, Department of Agriculture, after a long study of the plant affection.

The similarity of manner in which crown galls spread, as compared with the insidious method in which cancer creeps along the various channels of the human body from diseased to healthy parts, is the striking part of the discovery.

It is believed here that the work of Dr. Smith will be of value in studying the cause of cancer, of which practically nothing is known.

## $250,000 TO GATES NEPHEW.

### Financier's Son Allows Henry Baker His Heritage, Disregarding Will.

*Special to The New York Times.*

AURORA, Ill., June 14.—On the eve of departing with Henry Baker, nephew and an heir of the late John W. Gates, for California, in the hope of his recovery from tuberculosis, Mr. and Mrs. Charles Gates, other heirs, agreed to give him the $250,000 left him by his uncle without any of the conditions imposed in the will. One condition was that the young man must complete his college course while unmarried.

Mr. and Mrs. Gates arrived here on Tuesday from St. Louis.

## WEST POINT HOTEL BURNS.

### Cadets and Officers Fight Fire and Help Remove Furniture.

WEST POINT, N. Y., June 14.—The old West Point Hotel, a four-story brick structure owned by the Government, was burned to-day. Most of the contents were saved. The entire military force at the academy turned out and fought the flames and helped remove the furniture.

After thirty years under one management the hotel was taken over by the new lessees two months ago and refitted throughout. The fire is thought to have originated from a defective flue.



### Vice-President to Give Way to a Progressive Running Mate.

## SCOFF AT ROOSEVELT [illegible]

### First Ballot Will Beat Him, the President's Managers Declare.

## LESS COMPROMISE TALK NOW

### Taft Sends Word He [illegible] Such a [illegible]—[illegible] Confidence in Committee.

## DELEGATES STANDING FIRM

### Long-Predicted Swing to the Colonel in the South Has Not Materialized.

## EXCHANGE BRIBERY CHARGES

### Negro Delegate Says Money Was Given to Him by Taft Men—[illegible] to Account to Vote.

*Special to The New York Times.*

CHICAGO, June 14.—The situation here is pretty much all for the nomination of Theodore Roosevelt, and [illegible] the injection of his strenuous personality into the contest to work his followers into frenzy. He will be here to-morrow afternoon.

The hard, cold figures, however, still seem to justify the predictions of the Taft managers that he will be nominated for President on the first ballot. [illegible] of New York gives him a [illegible] of [illegible] votes on the first ballot. Manager McKinley says he will have at least [illegible]. The National Committee added six votes net to the Taft forces to-day, making the net result of the contests to date 225 to 9 in President Taft's favor.

In the Roosevelt camp the figures of the Taft managers are either [illegible] or else met with disclaimers not supported with detailed lists of delegates for Roosevelt, such as the Taft managers produce. The Roosevelt men talk [illegible] about a great swing of delegates [illegible] for Taft over to Roosevelt, but those who sit down in cold blood to figure out this prophesied desertion of Taft cannot do it.

In the meantime the American [illegible] are being regaled with an exhibition of verbal mud slinging such as has never before been witnessed in a convention fight. Furious over the decisions of the National Committee favoring the Taft delegates and throwing out the Roosevelt contestants, the Roosevelt managers have become masters of denunciation, and the Taft managers are retorting in kind. Discreet men are holding their peace in the hotel corridors for fear of becoming involved in fist fights.

**Both Sides Charge Bribery.**

Bribery of delegates is being openly charged in both the Taft and the Roosevelt camps. It started with Mr. McKinley saying that the Taft forces had proof that the Roosevelt managers had been trying to bribe Southern delegates, but the proof was not produced.

To-day the Roosevelt manager, Senator Dixon, retaliated by making public a letter from Charles Banks, a negro delegate from Mississippi, returning to Manager McKinley of the Taft forces some money which he said had been paid him for his own expenses and those of other Taft delegates from his own State.

The Taft managers flout the statement of the Roosevelt men that Roosevelt will win over a great number of Southern delegates pledged to Taft by pointing out that there are only eleven who may desert Taft.

Furthermore, they boldly make the statement that if any delegates instructed for or pledged to Taft turn to Roosevelt they have assurance from thirty-five delegates from Northern Republican [illegible] instructed for or pledged to Roosevelt that they will feel free then to swing to Taft. There are said to be twenty Illinois delegates alone in this position.

There is another point that the Taft managers are making much of. In many States, notably Arizona and Arkansas, delegations were elected in which there were Roosevelt men, although the Taft men were in the majority. The Roosevelt managers sent entire contesting delegations here.

The Roosevelt contestants were thrown out by the National Committee and the divided delegations seated. Thereupon Mr. Roosevelt proceeded to brand the delegations seated, among which he had many supporters, as "thieves"; hence his supporters on those delegations say they can no longer support him and will be for Taft.

**Root Also to Arrive To-day.**

Senator Root, who is to be the Temporary Chairman and the Permanent Chairman of the convention if the Taft forces prevail, will be here to-morrow about the same time as his old friend and admirer, Roosevelt.

The Roosevelt men will try to prevent Senator Root's selection as Chairman if they dare do so, but are afraid that they

"All the News That's Fit to Print."

# The New York Times.

THE WEATHER.

Generally fair Thursday and Friday; light to moderate southwest to west winds.

For full weather report see Page 22.

VOL. LXI...NO. 19,871. * * * * NEW YORK, THURSDAY, JUNE 20, 1912.—TWENTY-FOUR PAGES. ONE CENT In Greater New York, Jersey City, and Newark. { Elsewhere, TWO CENTS.

# BOLT STARTS IN CREDENTIALS COMMITTEE AND ROOSEVELT MEN ALL WALK OUT; PLAN NOW IS FOR A THIRD PARTY

## Hot-headed Roosevelt Men Force Action Ahead of Schedule.

## IN ROW OVER CONTEST

### Quit Room Once, Ordered Back, and Then All But One Quit for Good.

## COLONEL'S PARTY PLANS

### Full Ticket in Every State Which He Believes He Can Control.

## TO SPLIT THE SOLID SOUTH

### Also Confident of Winning the West, Pennsylvania, and West Virginia.

## HADLEY FOR RUNNING MATE

### Wants the Missouri Governor Because He is a Fighting Man—May Be at Convention To-day.

CHICAGO, June 19.—After bolting once from the Credentials Committee "under the orders of Col. Roosevelt," and being called back by Roosevelt managers to the committee room, all of the Roosevelt members of the Credentials Committee except R. R. McCormick of Chicago left again at 11:45 o'clock to-night, declaring they were out for good.

The cause of the bolt was the refusal of the committee to give a full hearing on all contest cases. After the Roosevelt men had left, the committee took up the cases, but had not proceeded far when a motion to adjourn until 9 o'clock to-morrow morning was proposed and carried.

Senator Dixon, the Roosevelt campaign manager, who had been hurriedly summoned after the first bolt, left with the Roosevelt men.

"These men are tired and will go home and go to bed," he said. "I think the other fellows are wasting time to stay here to-night."

Francis H. Heney and Hugh T. Halbert of Minnesota, who had led the bolt, were the only ones who would talk at length on the situation.

"Is this a bolt?" Mr. Heney was asked.

"You can call it what you want to," he said. "These are the facts: Every Roosevelt man with the exception of McCormick has walked out because he was convinced from the rules which were proposed that there was no intention of giving a valid hearing.

"The cases that were heard before the National Committee were a farce, and this is a worse one. The line-up was perfectly plain, 32 to 19."

Mr. Halbert declared the break came because the committee limited time and excluded evidence.

"We claimed and insisted that the Credentials Committee should hear all evidence, as a court of original jurisdiction, and that the National Convention, not the Credentials Committee, should be the court of last resort."

Before adjourning the committee adopted the amended rules by a vote of 36 to 4.

Chairman Devine said the adjournment was taken because most of the contesting had left the Coliseum.

**How the Bolt Started.**

Th Roosevelt men broke out of the comtee room at 10:30 o'clock to-night, after attempting to break open the doors and bring all newspaper men into the room.

The doors of the committee room were suddenly thrown open by J. J. Sullivan of Ohio, who rushed out with the cry: "All Roosevelt men walk out."

He was followed by Hugh T. Halbert of Minnesota, Francis H. Heney of California, Georgt L. Record of New Jersey, and other Roosevelt men.

As they pushed open the swinging doors after Sullivan, they cried out to the newspaper men:

"All newspaper men come inside and see what they are trying to do to us."

Col. Shay, assistant sergeant at arms, shouted to the doorkeeper to admit no one. The Roosevelt forces shouted again for every one to come in. Mr. Thayer called for policemen, who pushed their way through, and kept the crowd from coming in.

The Roosevelt men poured from the room, declaring they were acting under orders from Col. Roosevelt.

"Everybody go to the Florentine Room at the Congress," shouted one man.

They rushed out, followed by the crowd, and in the street outside of the Coliseum they were overtaken by Secretary Hayward.

**Roosevelt's Orders, They Say.**

"Why did you act that way?" he demanded of Heney. "Why didn't you wait until some rules had been passed?"

"We are acting under the direct orders of Col. Roosevelt," retorted Heney.

"We are obeying a better General than you," shouted George Record of New Jersey. "He told us to leave that room and we did it."

Hugh T. Halbert declared the break came as the result of the refusal of the majority in the committee to open all evidence in the cases. Mr. Halbert presented resolutions asking that the temporary roll of the convention be considered as only prima facie evidence of the right of delegates to sit, and that all evidence, testimony, and the like be gone into.

He declared the committee refused to do this, and attempted to "gag" the minority by making rules that would have left the action of the National Committe as practically decisive in all the contests.

Mr. Heney later came back to the lobby and urged the Roosevelt contestants to go to the Florentine Room of the Congress, where the Roosevelt headquarters are located, and be heard by the members of the Credentials Committee representing Roosevelt.

Believing they had acted too hastily some of the Roosevelt men, including Mr. Halbert, returned to the committee room after a short conference in the street. While Mr. Record and Mr. Heney declared they were acting under Mr. Roosevelt's direct orders, others believed they should have remained until definite action was taken by the committee upon the time for argument, and the character of evidence to be considered.

R. R. McCormick of Chicago also remained in the committee room. Mr. Halbert declared they would stay until they had obtained a vote on his resolution for consideration of all evidence in the contest cases, and would then again leave.

James R. Garfield of Ohio, former Secretary of the Interior, came to the door and attempted to enter the room. It was understood he had some message from Col. Roosevelt. The police and doorkeepers thrust him back, although one of the committeemen attempted to pull him in.

With the aid of Ormsby McHarg, he was ushered into a committee waiting room through a side door. Later the full bolt was ordered.

The rules which brought on the fight were presented by James A. Hemenway of Indiana. They provided:

"That no contest cases should be considered except those appealed from the decisions of the National Committee.

"That none should be taken up where the decision of the National Committee had been unanimous.

"That cases should be consolidated where such action had been taken at the previous hearing.

"That the contestants who were not seated (usually the Roosevelt men) should open the arguments.

"That ten minutes be allowed for State cases and five for district cases for counsel on each side.

"That no evidence be considered that was not considered at the previous hearing."

The last two provisions brought on the fight, Hugh T. Halbert of Minnesota and other Roosevelt men claiming the committee should open all evidence in all cases.

After the return of the Roosevelt members an amendment was introduced making the limit of time on State cases thirty minutes for each side and for district cases fifteen minutes.

On the roll call adopting the rules R. R. McCormick of Illinois, C. St. Clair of Idaho, W. S. Lauder of North Dakota, and John M. Early of Tennessee voted "No."

The Roosevelt men who were shown by this roll call to be absent were: F. J. Heney of California, Ralph Harris, Kansas; Lex N. Mitchell, Pennsylvania; Jesse H. Libby, Maine; Edward G. Carrington, Jr., Maryland; Hugh T. Halbert, Minnesota; H. E. Sackett, Nebraska; C. H. Cowles, North Carolina; J. J. Sullivan, Ohio; Don L. Norton, Oklahoma; A. V. Swift, Oregon, and S. X. Way, South Dakota.

Jesse A. Tolerton of Missouri, who was one of those who made the first rush to the door during the first bolt, declared that he had never intended to leave the meeting, but had rushed outside to bring in the newspaper men.

"Missouri is not bolting," he said, "but will vote for Roosevelt in the convention."

R. R. McCormick, when he came out of the room, said he was "with the Roosevelt men in spirit, but perhaps not to the extent of leaving the hall."

"They were forced out of the committee," he said. "Rules were adopted that were outrageous."

After adjournment Chairman Devine declared that the committee would take up the contests to-morrow morning, and finish them as rapidly as possible, in their regular order.

**Before the Row.**

The Credentials Committee organized immediately after the adjournment of the convention, and in the first test the Taft forces elected Thomas H. Devine Chairman over the Roosevelt candidate, W. T. Lauder of North Dakota, by a vote of 30 to 18, four members being absent or not voting.

The Taft forces expected the vote on the majority of the contest cases to be 33 to 19, basing their prediction on the attitude of the respective delegations on the convention roll calls of the last two days.

Immediately after the election of Mr. Devine a recess was taken until 9:30 P. M. Soon after the night session opened the row started.

### ROOSEVELT PLANS THIRD PARTY

#### To Name Full Ticket in States He Controls and Split Solid South.

*Special to The New York Times.*

CHICAGO, June 19.—Col. Roosevelt intends to hold a bolting Republican Convention if what he calls the "rotten" delegates, who were seated by the National Committee, and who were permitted to vote in the convention to-day, are left on the permanent roll of the convention by the report of the Committee on Credentials.

As nobody doubts that these delegates will be left on the roll by the Committee on Credentials and as there is nothing in the situation to warrant the assumption that the majority of the delegates in the convention will not approve the report of its Credentials Committee, the Colonel apparently will have to bolt if he does not change his mind before the crisis comes.

This bolt will occur, if at all, after the Colonel is defeated by the throwing out of any minority report which his friends on the Credentials Committee may present. He figures that he could justify a bolt at that stage of the proceedings. If he bolted after the names of President Taft and himself had been put in nomination and voted upon, it would appear to be too much of a personal issue.

Gov. Deneen of Illinois, who for several days was "on the fence" but finally came over to Roosevelt, was told flatly of the course the Colonel intended to pursue in an interview at which several others, including William Allen White of Kansas, were present. Said Roosevelt:

**Roosevelt's Threat to Bolt.**

"The Roosevelt delegates will hold their own convention if the crooked delegates are seated, and afterwards, there will be nominations made in every State where the Roosevelt forces control for Governor, Senator and other offices."

At recent conferences Roosevelt had been asked by some of his managers if he was not afraid to head a third ticket. To this he replied that he had never shown fear in any crisis; disaster might face him, but the situation which had arisen had made the fight necessary.

In his address to the delegates last night Col. Roosevelt served notice on the convention that he would not consider himself bound for a moment by the action of the "stolen" delegates and would leave the convention with his followers if these delegates were finally seated. This address was given to the newspapers early this morning by the direct order of Roosevelt after it had been suppressed by some of his managers for several hours. The Colonel did not retract to-day from the position he had taken.

Whether the Colonel can carry out the programme he has arranged is a question which is not yet satisfactorily answered. Senator Dixon, his campaign manager, it is reported, was responsible for the suppression of the Colonel's fiery address to the delegates, and there are others among his supporters who have been trying to soften his utterances on the subject of a bolt. Serious clashes have been numerous, it is declared, but the Colonel has overruled his more conservative backers, who hesitate before taking a step which would bring on such a grave crisis in the Republican Party.

**The States He Relies On.**

The Western States, Roosevelt believes, will be with him, and he counts on Pennsylvania, West Virginia, and delegates from other States aside from the Western line-up to stand by him. California and Pennsylvania delegates, the latter under the control of Boss Flinn of Pittsburgh, were ready to leave the convention to-day, is the report from the bolt camp. To leave the convention at that time, however, was considered "bad politics" by the Roosevelt men, especially as the delegates from Maine and New York who are for the Colonel were against it.

They felt that there was still a chance to win without resorting to such revolutionary procedure. In fact, these delegates and some others as well urged that the bolt talk be dropped, at least until after the vote on the nomination. Their attitude satisfied the bolt camp that they would only grumble and cry fraud even afer that and then go home without taking a definite stand.

Col. Roosevelt has not yet given up all hope of winning out on the report of the Credentials Committee to-morrow or Friday, but this new and definite cry of bolt, coming as it does on the heels of the defeat to-day of Gov. Deneen's motion, has left a feeling that the Roosevelt followers are satisfied that the parting of the ways has come, and that it will eventually have to be a clean break, regardless of consequences, or a dismal and sorrowful retreat to Oyster Bay and seclusion. The latter course makes no appeal to Col. Roosevelt.

**Would Call Taft Men Bolters.**

With his talk of a bolt comes the assertion that it will not be a bolt at all, and that the Roosevelt supporters, having the delegates from the majority of the States that cast Republican votes in the Electoral College, are the regular Republicans. This declaration has been made by Roosevelt before, and its reaffirmation makes it evident that should he carry out this daring plan, as all things now seem to indicate, he will enter the race on that basis. Roosevelt will never admit that he is bolting. He believes the use of that word is unnecessary except as applied to his opponents.

The direct declaration that the Roosevelt forces will hold a convention of their own if defeated on the next test vote, coming as it does almost at the climax of the convention, has caused not a little excitement. As the evening passed the impression grew among the hundreds of politicians here that Roosevelt would really, after all, carry out his threat if he could hold his supporters in line. It is the last touch that was needed to bring on turmoil.

And while the excitement was at its height in the corridor of the conference rooms Col. Roosevelt remained quietly in seclusion receiving reports over the telegraph and telephone wires from the convention hall. Late in the afternoon as reports were coming in that there was a big demonstration going on for Gov. Hadley, who had appeared on the platform of the Coliseum to second the motion made by Gov. Deneen of Illinois, he talked to a few of the newspaper correspondents.

The Colonel was sitting in his main reception room, and if what was going on at the convention was discouraging him he did not show it. Every few minutes messengers ran in and out with telegrams direct from his leaders who were conducting the fight. As he read the dispatches telling of the Hadley demonstration he laughed, and then told the newspaper men what they contained.

"The cheering for Hadley has now lasted twenty minutes," he exclaimed. "That's right. There is nothing too good for him. He is splendid. He deserves it."

Another message brought the news that the Hadley demonstration had resolved itself into a Roosevelt demonstration, and the Colonel laughed heartily.

"Girls carrying Teddy bears were carried upon the platform," he read between chuckles, and then he read still another to the effect that it was a good thing it was a Roosevelt convention. He took that as an indication that otherwise Hadley might be named as the choice of the convention in the end.

**Hadley His Running Mate.**

Roosevelt wants Hadley as the candidate for Vice President on his ticket whether he bolts or not. That much he indicated clearly. He was full of praise for the Missouri Governor, who is recognised as one of the "fighting men," and Hadley, Roosevelt let it be known, could not be weaned from him by any promise.

The Colonel talked over the situation in some detail, and he seemed full of confidence that he was not losing his grip. He was as buoyant and cheerful as ever, and yet there was something in his attitude that brought with it convictoin that he feared all might not be going well. When he heard how the vote at the Coliseum on Gov. Deneen's motion was going, however, he would not admit that it discouraged him.

Roosevelt feels that if an attempt is made to name a compromise candidate the Taft forces will be unable to hold their delegates in line, and that there will be enough desertions from the Taft ranks to the Roosevelt ranks while the "switch" is in progress to assure him the nomination. His managers feel that Hadley is proof against any wiles. They do not deny that an acceptable compromise candidate might carry with him most of the Missouri delegates, but not Hadley.

The Colonel let it be known that he did not expect to attend the convention to-morrow, but he made no positive denial. Indications to-night are that he will not storm the present convention, although it is known that he at first contemplated such a move, and told his managers of the plan. But if the bolt is carried into effect it is practically certain that he will be on hand to keep his bolters in line.

**Hears Compromise Talk.**

The Colonel has received advices also that the Taft people are looking about for a compromise candidate. These reports are that Senator Penrose and Senator Murray Crane of the Taft camp have approached Gov. Hadley, Senator Cummins of Iowa, and Senator La Follette of Wisconsin.

Gov. Hadley was the first to receive an offer of the nomination as Vice President on a ticket headed by President Taft, it is declared, in an attempt to win him over from Roosevelt, but he refused and declared that such a nomination was worth nothing, as Taft, even if nominated, could not win. Just what offers were made to Cummins and La Follette the Colonel's supporters did not exactly say, but they indicated that the Taft forces would go to any length to beat Roosevelt, and did not care much about Taft so long as they furthered their own ends.

And it is not denied either that there are some among the Roosevelt supporters who would drop the Colonel if they felt that they could hold their leadership in their own States. No names were mentioned, but it was apparent that the threat to nominate full tickets in every State where the Roosevelt forces are in control, when a bolt is made, was decided upon as necessary to hold some of the Colonel's luke-warm supporters in line.

The Colonel has no intention of giving these men an opportunity to leave him in the lurch and look solely after their own interests. If they try such a course he has the threat hanging over their heads that he will do his best to see that they are defeated in their State organizations by putting up tickets to oppose them, and practically assuring the success of the Democrats.

**Colonel Sure of His Men.**

The bolt element of the Roosevelt boomers made to-day a careful analysis of the situation and it was after that that the bolt talk was openly published. Roosevelt feels, it is said, that he can count on a large majority of his delegates going with him on any proposition that he may make. And he believes also that, in the campaign to come, he will be able to win many votes away from the "bosses" of the party. He thinks there are a lot of the voters in New York State who will be with him also because they are sick of "Boss" Barnes. Sixty per cent. of the Republicans west of the Palisades is the Roosevelt estimate.

The fact that Roosevelt had been making so careful a study of the situation in preparation for a bolt was taken as proof that he was practically ready to ad-

Continued on Page 4.



# EXTRA 4 A. M.

# ROOSEVELT, BEATEN, TO BOLT TO-DAY; GIVES THE WORD IN EARLY MORNING; TAFT'S NOMINATION SEEMS ASSURED

## Many of Colonel's Delegates Will Not Follow Him from Convention.

## COMPROMISE TALK, TOO

### Hadley Looms Up, but Men Who Have Led Taft Fight Give No Sign of Change.

## TAFT STRENGTH GROWS

### Yesterday's Vote, 564 to 510, Believed to Represent the Actual Line-Up.

## WOMAN LEADS CHEERING

### Starts a Demonstration for the Colonel That Lasts Almost an Hour—Hadley Shares in It.

## ROOT QUELLS DISORDER

### Proves a Firm Chairman, but There Is a Great Deal of Confusion During the Speeches.

*Special to The New York Times.*

CHICAGO, Thursday, June 20, 2 A. M.—Col. Roosevelt in a belligerent speech before a conference of his delegates early this morning, after the Roosevelt members had quit the Credentials Committee, openly advised a bolt to-day, if the convention should not recede from its stand against his contesting delegates.

"My position is perfectly clear," he shouted. "If these fraudulently seated delegates are admitted then it is not a Republican Convention, and it is not entitled to recognition as such."

The Colonel then asked the delegates to wait in the room for an hour while he conferred with his inner circle.

"We'll wait all night for you," shouted a number of delegates.

**Advises His Delegates to Bolt.**

At 2 o'clock this morning Col. Roosevelt said in a talk to his delegates and advisers:

"So far as I am concerned, I am through. If you are voted down I hope you, the real and lawful majority of the convention, will organise as such, and you will do it if you have the courage and loyalty of your convictions.

"I am speaking to you," said Col. Roosevelt, "as a man to whom some of you have done the honor to state that you wish to nominate as President. When I went into the race I made my appeal to the people. Most of the delegates were chosen at direct primaries by the people. I made my fight squarely. I said, and some of you heard me, that if the people decided against me I would have nothing to say, but that if the people were for me and the politicians tried to cheat me out of the nomination, I would have a great deal to say.

**Cheating Him, He Says.**

"I went before the people, and I won. Now the National Committee and a portion of the convention, which is made a majority only by the aid of delegates not elected but chosen by the National Committee, are trying to cheat me out of the nomination. They can't do it. As far as I am concerned, it makes no difference. But it is not me they are cheating, it is the people, the rank and file of the Republican Party.

"I did not want to give you any advice, as I preferred to let you decide what to do, but I am going to give you my advice.

"Gov. Deneen to-day introduced a very moderate resolution in dealing with the four flagrant steals. It asked that the delegates from California, Washington, Texas and Arizona should not be permitted to vote, and that the three States stolen bodily—Washington, Arizona and Texas—should not put their representatives on the Credentials Committee. That motion was voted down by substantially the same vote that elected Root over McGovern. In each case the majority was a majority only because the votes of the fraudulently seated delegates were counted.

**Declares Root Won by Fraud.**

"Mr. Root received seventy or eighty stolen votes," continued Mr. Roosevelt. "Mr. Deneen's resolution was beaten to-day by fraudulent votes which in that resolution were named—by the votes of Texas, Arizona, Washington and the two fraudulent votes from California. If these votes had been changed the resolution would have been carried.

"To add insult to injury, the Committee on Credentials organized by choosing as Chairman Mr. Devine, the committeeman who had taken part in the very theft on which he had passed as a member of the National Committee.

"As far as I am concerned I am through. I hope that to-morrow when you go back to the convention hall you will at once introduce a resolution that not one of those fraudulently seated delegates shall vote on any question in the Credentials Committee or in the convention.

**"Don't Lie Down," He Says.**

"Don't lie down again if they beat you by fraudulent votes. There is no use in voting to cut out the fraudulent votes and then being beaten by the fraudulent votes and say you are very sorry, and go home. I hope you will then take the position that you decline longer to submit to having any delegates fraudulently seated allowed to sit as judges on their cases or vote on the report of the Credentials Committee.

"I hope you will refuse any longer to recognize a majority thus composed as having any title in law or morals to be called a Republican convention. We have by fair means elected a clear majority of the delegates, and I hope that you will not permit our opponents, having failed by fair means, to beat you by foul means and swindle the people out of the victory that they have won.

"Let's find out whether the Republican Party is still the party of the plain people, the people of the United States, or the party of the bosses, and the professional politicians acting in the interests of special privilege.

**Advises Them to Hurry.**

"If you want my advice, I would advise that you place no further trust, I would advise that you waste no further time, I would advise that you do not permit yourselves to be committed in any further way, shape, or form, by further association with these men as long as they retain control of the Republican Convention by means of a majority composed in an essential part of fraudulently seated delegates, who haven't the slightest right or title to represent the rank and file of the Republican Party and are without the slightest right or title to seats in the Republican Convention."

**Gov. Johnson Proclaims New Party.**

Gov. Johnson of California reached the Florentine room a few minutes after Mr. Roosevelt had concluded his address. Many were leaving the room when Gov. Johnson entered. A score of men seized him and rushed him to a table. Immediately the room filled up again with delegates.

"Gentlemen," Gov. Johnson began, "you have heard what we are going to do to-morrow. We are going to stop dillydallying with this robbing convention. We are going in there to fight, and we are prepared for the birth of a new Republican Party which will nominate for President Theodore Roosevelt."

"And he will be elected," shouted in chorus the delegates.

As Gov. Johnson proceeded some one in the crowd shouted the name of Hadley.

"Hadley! Hadley!" was the cry.

A mingled roar of cheers and hisses greeted this, but quiet was soon restored, and Gov. Johnson proceeded.

"This new party, which is inevitable, will be an honest party," he continued, "A party that will not countenance robbery, thievery, and dishonesty such as we have experienced here."

Some of the leaders of the progressive States declared this morning that they would not lend countenance to a bolt.

"North Dakota will remain regular and will not bolt," said Senator Gronna. "I have seen several of the Wisconsin delegates and they assure me that they, too, will remain in the regular convention."

Senator Kenyon gave the same assurance as to the ten Cummins votes in Iowa.

It was reported that Senator Clapp, the Roosevelt leader in Minnesota, had also announced that he would not bolt.

A man close to the Roosevelt leaders asserted that Col. Roosevelt could not control more than 200 votes on a bolt.

**Bolters' Meeting in an Uproar.**

After the bolt of the Roosevelt members of the Credentials Committee, Roosevelt delegates poured into the Florentine room of the Congress Hotel, where it was announced that the bolting contingent would assemble. Edward C. Carrington of Maryland, the first member of the Credentials Committee to arrive, precipitated a debate when he announced the action he and his fellow members had taken.

The delegates split into factions, some urging that the committee men should go

### ROOSEVELT CALLS FOR A BOLT.

*Special to The New York Times.*

CHICAGO, Thursday, June 20, 2:30 A. M.—"So far as I am concerned," declared Col. Roosevelt to his delegates and advisers in an address this morning, "I am through. If you are voted down I hope you, the real and lawful majority of the convention, will organize as such, and you will do it if you have the courage and loyalty of your convictions."

### Sure Now of Victory for Taft.

**By Congressman McKinley, the President's Manager.**

*Special to The New York Times.*

CHICAGO, June 19.—President Taft will be renominated by the National Republican Convention now in session.

Theodore Roosevelt has been eliminated as a candidate. Two test votes, one yesterday and another forced by his leaders to-day, have demonstrated that he cannot be nominated. The delegates have repudiated his third-term pretensions.

His managers have resorted to every known method of political strategy, but without success. They have attempted combinations with other candidates; they have adroitly presented unfair and revolutionary plans of procedure under the pretense of honesty, and they have endeavored by every means to make Taft's delegates break their pledges and instructions. In the face of these desperate efforts, the Taft column has steadily grown. Taft's majority to-day was larger than it was yesterday.

The Roosevelt followers, knowing that their candidate can never get enough votes to give him a majority of the Convention, are now seeking in hopeless and discouraged fashion for another leader. Their search will be in vain. President Taft's demonstrated majority represents delegates who have come to Chicago determined to renominate him and they will not be swerved from that purpose. They have shown their loyalty and devotion to the President upon two occasions and their solidity was not in the least affected by a deliberate attempt to stampede the Convention through a carefully planned demonstration. They gave their answer to the demonstration by casting more votes to-day than they did yesterday.

They have shown that they propose to remain with the President until his renomination is an accomplished fact and they will receive accessions to their ranks from those who have been temporarily carried away by a noisy, braggadocio campaign. The balloon-like character of the campaign has twice been punctured by decisive majority votes.

The Southern colored delegates instructed for Taft are carrying out their instructions with courage and fidelity, in spite of money and political promises. They have shown a laudable regard for loyalty to party pledges.

Roosevelt not only lost in votes to-day, but his delegates indulged in forty minutes of continuous cheering for Gov. Hadley, out of his campaign managers, showing a decided tendency to desert the Roosevelt standard.

Roosevelt's repeated threat to bolt has not materialized, and statements are made by many of his leaders that should a bolt be attempted, it will not be participated in.

The solidarity of President Taft's lines and the wavering weakness of the Roosevelt forces tell their own story of victory for the President and the bursting of the Roosevelt bubble.

WILLIAM B. McKINLEY.

"All the News That's Fit to Print."

# The New York Times.

THE WEATHER. Fair Sunday and Monday; light, variable winds. For full weather report see Page 16, Part III.

VOL. LXI...NO. 19,874. * * * NEW YORK, SUNDAY, JUNE 23, 1912.—90 PAGES, In Eight Parts, Including Picture Section and Review of Books. PRICE FIVE CENTS.

# TAFT RENOMINATED BY THE REPUBLICAN CONVENTION; ROOSEVELT NAMED AS CANDIDATE BY BOLTERS WILSON BACKS BRYAN'S STAND AT BALTIMORE

## Parker Issue Makes Sharp Line-up Between Party Factions.

### EXPECT JUDGE'S DEFEAT

**Bryanites Say Majority of the National Committee Oppose Him for Chairman.**

**DENY PARKER IS RYAN MAN**

**Bryan Said to Have Welcomed Injection of Judge to Project His Own Nomination.**

**ALL EYES ON NEBRASKAN**

**Some Leaders Fear Situation Will Develop Similar to That at Chicago.**

**FOR A LABOR TARIFF PLANK**

**Redfield Would Feature the Tariff's Human Side as Being a Burden to Modest Homes.**

*Special to The New York Times.*

BALTIMORE, June 22.—This convention is going to develop into a straight line-up between the Progressive and the conservative wings of the Democratic Party. The correspondent of THE NEW YORK TIMES who writes this, having arrived to-day from the Republican National Convention at Chicago, during the sessions of which he had the pleasure of sitting next to William Jennings Bryan, can see nothing so important as this in the situation here to-night, particularly in view of this answer sent by Gov. Wilson of New Jersey to Mr. Bryan's message asking him to stand out against Alton B. Parker as Temporary Chairman of this convention on the ground that the Temporary Chairman should be a Progressive:

"You are quite right. Before hearing of your message I clearly stated my position. The Baltimore convention is to be a convention of Progressives, of men who are Progressives in principle and by conviction. It must, if it is not to be put in a wrong light before the convention, express its convictions in its organization and in its choice of men who are to speak for it.

"You are to be a member of this convention, and are entirely within your rights in doing everything within your power to bring that result about. No one will doubt where my sympathies lie, and you will, I am sure, find my friends in the convention acting upon clear conviction and always in the interest of the people's cause. I am happy in the confidence that they need no suggestion from me."

There is to be seen a community of interest between Gov. Wilson, an avowed candidate claiming about 300 pledged votes in this convention, and Mr. Bryan, who is not an avowed candidate, but who certainly has the candidate habit, which will be watched closely.

Charles F. Murphy of New York is watching it. Roger Sullivan of Illinois is watching it. Tom Taggart is watching it, and the leaders of the Clark, Gaynor, Marshall, Harmon, and Underwood booms are watching it. You can't blame them, for while Mr. Bryan has always expressed his liking for Gov. Wilson as a candidate their union on an issue that will unquestionably be decisive is one to make the managers of Presidential aspirants sit up and take notice.

**Says Bryan Isn't in the Race.**

Everybody is, of course, asking whether Bryan is going to stay out of the race for the Presidential nomination, as he has repeatedly said he would. Dr. P. L. Hall of Nebraska, who has been a Bryan man ever since Bryan went to congress in 1890, and who usually knows just what plans the Peerless Leader has in mind, was told this afternoon that the word was being passed around here that Bryan's declaration of his opposition to Judge Parker as Temporary Chairman was very ill-timed.

"Why, how can that be?" said Dr. Hall. "This is a convention dominated by the progressive element. Bryan is progressive. Parker is not. Why, then, should Bryan be criticised for opposing Parker to be Temporary Chairman?"

"But," was suggested, "it is being said that Bryan is really promoting his own candidacy and that the purpose of bringing on this fight against Parker is to get the centre of the stage, so that he can have an issue on which to appeal to the delegates and turn them toward him from candidates who think they have them lined up for themselves. They say he has been a candidate all along."

"I have a letter here that should settle all that talk," said Dr. Hall, reaching into his coat pocket. "It is from Bryan. Came since I arrived here. It was very frank and straightforward."

But Dr. Hall did not have the letter. H said it was in his room, and that its substance was that Bryan was not a candidate for the nomination, and did not want to be nominated. Bryan said further in the letter, Dr. Hall stated, that he would not allow his name to be used, as he was sure he could do more for the Democratic Party by promoting harmony and the adoption of a real Democratic platform if he was not to run upon it.

That was important news indeed, and Dr. Hall was urged to go to his room and get the letter. Its publication, he was told, would be a real service to the Democratic Party at this time. Dr. Hall seemed to agree with this, and started for his room to give the letter out for publication. But Dr. Hall never got back with that letter, so the public for the present must be satisfied with his verbal summary of it.

The reason that Dr. Hall changed his mind about giving the letter out was that he was waylaid by some Bryan men, who pleaded that its publication would be doing Mr. Bryan a great injustice. Dr. Hall finally agreed to wait until to-morrow and let Mr. Bryan speak for himself.

Gov. Wilson certainly played a master stroke by replying to Mr. Bryan's request to stand out against Alton B. Parker as Temporary Chairman as promptly and as flatly as he did. The other candidates either could not or did not reply as definitely, and that is the reason why Gov. Wilson is being advertised throughout the land, and particularly to all the State delegations traveling in this direction, as standing shoulder to shoulder with Mr. Bryan for a Progressive ticket and a Progressive platform, while the position of the other candidates is negative.

**Parker Row Up To-morrow.**

The row over the selection of Alton B. Parker will be settled on Monday if Mr. Parker's name is not withdrawn in the meantime. There was a good deal of talk all day about Mr. Bryan having already beaten the Parker plan, but this talk was confined to the Bryan men. The face of the situation makes it appear that Judge Parker will be set aside by the National Committee. Both sides of the controversy were busy for many hours to-day lining up their forces. After this work had been completed, the statement was made that Judge Parker would lack enough votes to seat him in the temporary chair. Plenty of figures were forthcoming to prove this assertion. All of these figures are based on past performances. The men who were known to have been friends and supporters of the Nebraska leader were placed on his side of the score, and all of the others were set down on the Parker side. The result showed thirty-two National Committeemen in opposition to Parker and twenty in favor of him.

After these figures had been given out by the Bryan men there was a rumor that a meeting of the sub-committee had been celled for to-night for the purpose of selecting a less objectionable man for the Chairmanship. Charles F. Murphy was asked about Parker, and he said: "We will stick to Parker to the last."

Later came a story saying that Parker had sent word to his friends here that in view of the opposition to his selection he desired to have his name withdrawn as a candidate for the place, but this report could not be verified. If it should happen that the Bryan matter is disposed of by Parker's withdrawal either by his own action or by the action of the sub-committee the Bryan men say they will be sorry.

**Instructed Against Parker.**

The Kansas delegation held a meeting this evening and instructed National Committeeman Sapp not to vote for Parker for Temporary Chairman at the meeting of the National Committee on Monday. The delegation is instructed for Clark and backers of the other candidates hailed their action as a verification of their predictions that the Clark strength can't be delivered to the support of the New York man, as the leaders have been trying to arrange.

By injecting Parker into the situation the issue between the Bryan Progressives and the conservatives, say the Bryan men, has been made sharp and clear. Reports from the headquarters of the Nebraska man indicated that the selection of Parker tickled Bryan more than any political happening since he was last nominated for the Presidency. It is said for him that the selection of Parker was instigated by the financial interests, that Parker is the counsel for all of the interests that put Root in the Presidential chair at the Chicago Convention, and that to permit him to preside will place the Democratic Party on the same level as the Republican Party, and might lead to the defeat of the Democratic candidate. Anyway, it is certain that the Bryan men have gone into the fight to beat Parker with the highest spirits. It is a fight that has made many of them hopeful of the nomination of the candidate that will represent everything that Bryan stands for now, but not any of the things that he stood for in his three campaigns.

The Bryan men always make this clear. They want everybody to understand that the Bryan of 1912 is a made-over Bryan and that he has been through the fire and been purged of all the heresies that brought him three defeats. His friends say that as Bryan stands for progress he must himself have advanced. Whatever platform is adopted by this convention will suit Bryan, it is said, so long as it advocates progress.

While the enthusiasm for Bryan is brisk enough in many quarters, there is no little talk of his nomination. One of his closest friends said: "His nomination is possible, but not probable."

A glance at the National Committeemen who, it is said, will resist the selection of Parker as Temporary Chairman would indicate that Bryan's strength was sufficient to control the convention absolutely and all of the preliminaries. But

Continued on Page 8.



## Roosevelt Delegates Go from the Regular to Rump Convention.

### GOV. JOHNSON PRESIDES

**Scores the National Committee as Thieves and Promises Them a Lesson.**

**NEW PARTY ON RUINS OF OLD.**

**Prendergast Makes the Nominating Speech He Had Prepared for Regular Convention.**

**COMMANDMENT AS PLATFORM**

**It Is "Thou Shalt Not Steal" Applied to All the Affairs of Life.**

**WIFE AND DAUGHTERS THERE**

**News That Bolting Convention Was to be Held Drew a Great Crowd and the Police Reserves.**

*Special to The New York Times.*

CHICAGO, June 22.—Col. Roosevelt has at last openly broken off all connection with the Republican Party as represented in the National Convention.

He was nominated for President on an independent ticket to-night in the dying hours of the Republican National Convention in which he had met a defeat.

The followers of Col. Roosevelt gathered in Orchestra Hall, less than a mile from the Coliseum, and pledged their support to the former President. In accepting the nomination, Col. Roosevelt appealed to the people of all sections, regardless of party affiliations, to stand with the founders of the new party, one of whose cardinal principles, he said, was to be "Thou Shalt Not Steal."

The informal nomination of Col. Roosevelt was said to be chiefly for the purpose of effecting a temporary organization. Beginning to-morrow, when a call is to be issued for a State convention in Illinois, the work of organization will be pushed forward rapidly, State by State. At a later time, probably early in August, it is intended that a National convention shall be held.

Col. Roosevelt, in accepting the nomination to-night, said he did so on the understanding that he would willingly step aside if it should be the desire of the new party when organized to select another standard bearer.

**Prendergast Presents His Name.**

The speech nominating Col. Roosevelt was made by Controller William Prendergast of New York, who was to have presented the Colonel's name to the regular convention. Dean William Draper Lewis of the University of Pennsylvania Law School, who was to have made one of the seconding speeches, delivered to-night the address which he had prepared for the Republican Convention.

Representatives of twenty-two States composed the Notification Committee which informed Col. Roosevelt of his nomination, and in a sense stood sponsors for the movement. The committee consisted of Controller Prendergast of New York, Meyer Lissner of California, former Congressman Richmond Pearson of North Carolina, Frank Knox of Michigan, Matthew Hale of Massachusetts, A. R. Garford of Ohio, David Browning of Kentucky, Everard Bierer, Jr., of Utah, Walter Thompson of Vermont, Judge Oscar R. E. Hundley of Alabama, Judge Ben B. Lindsey of Colorado, Andrew R. Rahn of Minnesota, Judge Stevens of Iowa, Judge W. S. Lander of North Dakota, William Allen White of Kansas, John C. Greenway of Arizona, ex-Gov. John Franklin Fort of New Jersey, Col. E. C. Carrington of Maryland, Pearl Wight of Louisiana, Lorenzo Dow of Washington, Walter Clyde Jones of Illinois, and Frank Frantz of Oklahoma.

Although no public announcement was made until very late in the day of the meeting, which was expected to result in the formation of a new party, word of the plan was then flashed about the city, and before the doors were opened a crowd had collected, extending for nearly a block on Michigan Avenue. Police reserves were summoned to handle the crowd.

When the doors were thrown open the people streamed in quickly, filling all the seats except those reserved for the Roosevelt delegates to the Republican National Convention, their alternates, and the Roosevelt delegates to whom seats in the convention were refused.

Telegraph and telephone linemen were rushed to Orchestra Hall to install wires over which news of the nomination of Col. Roosevelt was to be flashed out. A huge painting of Col. Roosevelt was hung behind the stage, which was all that was done in the way of decorations.

**Roosevelt Men Gather.**

Francis J. Heney, one of the most radical of Roosevelt's supporters arrived at 9:40 and as he stepped on the platform was given a hearty cheer. There were cries of "Where is Teddy?"

As the time passed the crowd in the balcony and galleries grew impatient. It broke into applause whenever there was any excuse for a demonstration. Word received from the Coliseum that President Taft had been placed in nomination was received in silence. A moving picture concern set up a machine on the rear of the platform.

Mrs. Roosevelt, Mrs. Nicholas Longworth, and Miss Ethel Roosevelt are occupying a box.

George P. Brown and Edgar Keith of the Young Men's Roosevelt League got an enthusiastic greeting as they appeared on the stage.

At 10 o'clock the meeting had not been called to order, and the crowd began to shout:

"We want Teddy."

The California delegates arrived at 10 o'clock, headed by Gov. Johnson, and were received with a great outburst of applause. Medill McCormick and Gifford Pinchot were the next to get to the hall.

The crowd outside the hall at this time was tremendous, and the police had their hands full keeping order.

Once the crowd rushed an alley and was driven back after a hard struggle. Gov. Johnson was enthusiastic and said that Roosevelt would be the big man in the coming fight.

"He will break the solid South and be elected despite all the bosses," he declared.

**Perkins Encounters Trouble.**

When the Roosevelt family appeared Mrs. Roosevelt and Mrs. Longworth waved and smiled a welcome in recognition of the cheers. While this demonstration was going on some of the Ohio delegation arrived and received a tumultuous welcome.

Mississippi Roosevelt delegates entered the hall fresh from a meeting in their headquarters, and announced the election of S. D. Redmond of Jackson as the State's National Committeeman of the new party. Massachusetts delegates with their cry, "Massachusetts, Roosevelt 18, first, last, and all the time," next arrived.

When George W. Perkins started to mount the steps to the stage a policeman stopped him, and he had some difficulty in explaining his right to a stage seat. Mrs. Roosevelt, who witnessed the encounter, was observed to laugh heartily.

When the hall had been packed the entire audience joined in singing "America," after which the Roosevelt delegates greeted Gov. Johnson as he opened the formal part of the meeting. The Governor was preparing to speak when the Oklahoma delegation arrived. By this time the non-arrival of the Pennsylvania delegation was causing comment.

**Gov. Johnson's Speech.**

"To any man with red blood in his veins," said Gov. Johnson, "it's always a pleasure to fight a fraud, and especially to fight a fraudulent convention.

"The delegates present represent a majority of the legally elected delegates to the National Republican Convention. They propose to do right here and now just what they were elected to do."

The Governor's speech was interrupted with a wild burst of cheering.

"We came here with the mandate of the people of California. You came here with the like design to carry out, not the will of a rotten boss in Pennsylvania or a crooked one in New York, or a United States Senator in Massachusetts, but to carry out the mandate of the people to nominate Theodore Roosevelt.

"By a fraudulent vote he has been robbed of what was his. We delegates, free and untrammeled, have come here to nominate him to-night."

These words brought the great audience to its feet with a shout and for some time there was an uproar of applause.

**People Will Take Up Fight, He Says.**

"The time has gone by when in this country any self-constituted representative of the people can deny to the people that which is theirs," Gov. Johnson continued. "The time has passed when men can foist by chicane or unfair means a candidate upon the people whom the people don't want.

"So we have come here to-night to right a wrong, and just as certain as we are here to-night the people will rule. Every man who embarks in this course understands full well the responsibility which is his, recognizes the obstacles to be overcome, but we've learned out in the West that whenever there is a great wrong to be righted, the people will take up the fight and win it.

**A New Party on the Ruins of the Old**

"Beyond the mere personality of the candidate," Gov. Johnson continued, "there is much to interest every person in this movement. It has come out of the West, stalking toward benighted New York, and endeavoring even in darkest Philadelphia to make understood the principle upon which this Republic was founded. This principle was trampled under foot at the Republican National Convention. Then it was that the people of all this country rebelled.

"A National committee has endeavored to assassinate the Republican party. If it has succeeded, there are left enough patriotic, honest citizens to erect upon the ruins another party that represents progress. That is the main purpose that brings us here."

Gov. Johnson described the campaign of Col. Roosevelt against the bosses and clared that the delegates assembled proposed to "see that Mr. Roosevelt gets

(Continued on Page 7.)



## Sherman Again Chosen Running Mate of the President.

### VOTE FOR TAFT WAS 561

**107 for Roosevelt, but 344 Obeyed Him and Refused to Vote.**

**DELEGATES COME TO BLOWS**

**Convention on the Verge of Riots Several Times While the Balloting Was On.**

**ROOSEVELT SENDS DEFIANCE**

**Through Allen of Kansas the Colonel Repeats His Cry of Fraud and Theft.**

**WOMAN LEADS TAFT CHEERS**

**Widow of Gen. Logan Starts Demonstration as Harding of Ohio Ends Nominating Speech.**

*Special to The New York Times.*

CHICAGO, June 22.—Amid scenes of turbulence and disorder, which at times bordered upon a riot, the Republican National Convention wound up its labors late to-night by nominating William Howard Taft of Ohio for President and James Schoolcraft Sherman of New York for Vice President.

President Taft was renominated at 9:28 o'clock by the narrow majority of 21 votes. The total vote cast for him was 561. Vice President Sherman did much better. His vote was announced as 597.

The vote on the Presidential candidates was:

| | |
|---|---|
| Taft | 561 |
| Roosevelt | 107 |
| Cummins | 17 |
| La Follette | 41 |
| Hughes | 2 |
| Not voting | 344 |
| Absent | 6 |
| Total | 1,078 |

President Taft's and Senator La Follette's names were the only ones formally presented to the convention. The votes for the others were cast by delegates who insisted on following their instructions and two who favored Justice Hughes.

While this nomination was made Col. Roosevelt had declared himself a 'candidate for President, and announced the organization of a third party to meet in convention in August. The Grand Old Party is for the moment smashed to pieces.

Before it proceeded to its final business Col. Roosevelt informed the convention through Henry J. Allen of Kansas that his delegates would not vote on any proposition that came before it. The reason given was that robbery and fraud controlled the convention and that it was not a Republican convention any more, but an illegal and unofficial body. These unpalatable things were said to the convention in so many words. It howled and protested, but not for long, and the amazing thing about it was that such statements could be made without evoking more of a fight.

**Listen to Bitter Attack.**

There has always been a tradition that no matter how bitter your feelings may be against the man who is opposing your candidate you must preserve the fiction of its all being a friendly disagreement, your real antagonism being to the party which is to nominate the opposing candidate. To-day that fiction ws entirely disregarded. Taft was renominated in the face of a plain declaration to the convention by some of its own members that it was fraudulent and crooked, and that its ticket would be defeated at the polls.

Any other convention would have roared such a speaker off the platform in a tempest of indignation. This one kept silent during most of these assaults and merely barked sullenly at the worst of them.

By the Colonel's orders the Roosevelt men sat mute during the session and refused to vote on any proposition. His name was not presented to the convention. Both the Colonel and Allen explained that this was because, having exhausted every means of protest and finding that they were the victims of plain, ordinary burglary and highway robbery, they refused any longer to take part in or sanction by their participation the proceedings of such an assemblage.

Allen, speaking for the Colonel, and the Colonel, speaking for himself through a printed statement, read by Allen, declared that this was not a convention at all; that it was made up by the seating of men who had no right to sit in it, and that to countenance such performances by taking part in the deliberations of such a body was impossible. Therefore the Colonel ordered his followers not to vote either on the rules, the platform, the nominations, or anything else that might dome before this illegal and pirat-

## Vote That Renominated President Taft.

| State | Taft | Roosevelt | Cummins | La Follette | Hughes | Not Voting |
|---|---|---|---|---|---|---|
| 24—Alabama | 22 | .. | .. | .. | .. | 2 |
| 6—Arizona | 6 | .. | .. | .. | .. | .. |
| 18—Arkansas | 17 | .. | .. | .. | .. | 1 |
| 26—California | 2 | .. | .. | .. | .. | 24 |
| 12—Colorado | 12 | .. | .. | .. | .. | .. |
| 14—Connecticut | 14 | .. | .. | .. | .. | .. |
| 6—Delaware | 6 | .. | .. | .. | .. | .. |
| 12—Florida | 12 | .. | .. | .. | .. | .. |
| 28—Georgia | 28 | .. | .. | .. | .. | .. |
| 8—Idaho | 1 | .. | 7 | .. | .. | .. |
| 58—Illinois | 2 | 53 | .. | .. | .. | 2 |
| 30—Indiana | 20 | 3 | .. | .. | .. | 7 |
| 26—Iowa | 16 | .. | 10 | .. | .. | .. |
| 20—Kansas | 2 | .. | .. | .. | .. | 18 |
| 26—Kentucky | 24 | 2 | .. | .. | .. | .. |
| 20—Louisiana | 20 | .. | .. | .. | .. | .. |
| 12—Maine | .. | .. | .. | .. | .. | 12 |
| 16—Maryland | 1 | 9 | .. | .. | .. | 5 |
| 36—Mass. | 20 | .. | .. | .. | .. | 16 |
| 30—Michigan | 20 | 9 | .. | .. | .. | 1 |
| 24—Minnesota | .. | .. | .. | .. | .. | 24 |
| 20—Mississippi | 17 | .. | .. | .. | .. | 3 |
| 36—Missouri | 16 | .. | .. | .. | .. | 20 |
| 8—Montana | 8 | .. | .. | .. | .. | .. |
| 16—Nebraska | .. | 2 | .. | .. | .. | 14 |
| 6—Nevada | 6 | .. | .. | .. | .. | .. |
| 8—N. Hampshire. | 8 | .. | .. | .. | .. | .. |
| 28—New Jersey | .. | 2 | — | .. | .. | 26 |
| 8—New Mexico | 7 | 1 | .. | .. | .. | .. |
| 90—New York | 76 | 8 | .. | .. | .. | 6 |
| 24—N. Carolina | 1 | 1 | .. | .. | .. | 22 |
| 10—N. Dakota | .. | .. | .. | 10 | .. | .. |
| 48—Ohio | 14 | .. | .. | .. | .. | 34 |
| 20—Oklahoma | 4 | 1 | .. | .. | .. | 15 |
| 10—Oregon | .. | 8 | .. | .. | .. | 2 |
| 76—Pennsylvania | 9 | 2 | .. | .. | 2 | 62 |
| 10—Rhode Island | 10 | .. | .. | .. | .. | .. |
| 18—S. Carolina | 16 | .. | .. | .. | .. | 1 |
| 10—S. Dakota | .. | 5 | .. | 5 | .. | .. |
| 24—Tennessee | 23 | 1 | .. | .. | .. | .. |
| 40—Texas | 31 | .. | .. | .. | .. | 8 |
| 8—Utah | 8 | .. | .. | .. | .. | .. |
| 8—Vermont | 6 | .. | .. | .. | .. | 2 |
| 24—Virginia | 22 | .. | .. | .. | .. | 1 |
| 14—Washington | 14 | .. | .. | .. | .. | .. |
| 16—W. Virginia | .. | .. | .. | .. | .. | 16 |
| 26—Wisconsin | .. | .. | .. | 26 | .. | .. |
| 6—Wyoming | 6 | .. | .. | .. | .. | .. |
| 6—Alaska | 2 | .. | .. | .. | .. | .. |
| 6—Dist. of Col. | 2 | .. | .. | .. | .. | .. |
| 6—Hawaii | 6 | .. | .. | .. | .. | .. |
| 6—Philippines | 2 | .. | .. | .. | .. | .. |
| 6—Porto Rico | 2 | .. | .. | .. | .. | .. |
| Total | 561 | 107 | 17 | 41 | 2 | 344 |

Necessary to nominate, 540.
Absent, 6.

## PRESIDENT TAFT TO THE TIMES.

**A National Calamity Averted in Roosevelt's Defeat—Course Justified by the Result.**

*Special to The New York Times.*

THE WHITE HOUSE, WASHINGTON, D. C., June 22.—President Taft gave the following statement to The New York Times to-night:

"Never before in the history of the country was such a pre-convention campaign fought. Precedents of propriety were broken in a President's taking the stump, much to the pain and discomfort of many patriotic, high-minded citizens, but the emergency was great and the course thus taken was necessary to avert a National calamity, and in view of the result it was justified.

"A National convention of one of the great parties is ordinarily important only as a preliminary to a National campaign for the election of a President.

"The Chicago Convention just ended is much more than this, and is in itself the end of a pre-convention campaign presenting a crisis more threatening and issues more important than those of the election campaign which is to follow between the two great National parties.

"The question here at stake was whether the Republican Party was to change its attitude as the chief conservator in the Nation of constitutional representative government and was to weaken the constitutional guarantees of life, liberty, and property, and all other rights declared sacred in the Bill of Rights, by abandoning the principle of absolute independence of the Judiciary essential to the maintenance of those rights.

"The campaign carried on to seize the Republican Party and make it the instrument of reckless ambition and the unsettling of the fundamental principles of our Government was so sudden and unexpected that time was not given clearly to show the people and the party the dangers which confronted them.

"It was sought to break the wise and valuable tradition against giving more than two terms to any one man in the Presidency, and the dangers from its breach could not be measured.

"The importance of the great victory which has been achieved cannot be overestimated.

"All over this country patriotic people to-night are breathing more freely, that a most serious menace to our republican institutions has been averted.

"It is not necessary to-night to speak of the result in November or of the issues which will arise between the Republican and Democratic Parties in the Presidential campaign to follow.

"It will be time enough to do that after the action of the Baltimore Convention.

"It is enough now to say that, whatever may happen in November, a great victory for the Republican Party and the people of the United States has already been won.

"The party remains as a great, powerful organization for carrying out its patriotic principles, as an agency of real progress in the development of the Nation along the constitutional lines upon which it was constructed and has ever been maintained, and its future opportunity for usefulness is as great as its achievements in the past. WILLIAM H. TAFT."

## WHO WOULD BE PRESIDENT,

**If No Candidate Carried the Electoral College?—House's Duty to Elect, but on Division by States Neither Party Has a Majority—Senate Would Choose a Republican Vice President.**

The three important candidacies for the Presidency—those of President Taft, ex-President Roosevelt, and the Democratic candidate to be nominated at Baltimore this week—present the possibility that none may receive a majority of the votes in the Electoral College. In that case the next President will be chosen by the House of Representatives, the delegation from each State having one vote, a majority of all the States to elect, and no other candidates to be voted for than the three who lead in the Electoral College.

These conditions would bring about an extraordinary situation, for the State delegations in the present House of Representatives number twenty-three Democratic, twenty-two Republican, and three divided evenly. The evenly divided delegations are those of Maine, Nebraska, and Rhode Island. These three States would apparently hold the balance of power, and how they would vote is, in the circumstances, an interesting subject for speculation. If the Republican States divided between Taft and Roosevelt, the twenty-three Democratic States being less than a majority, could not elect a President. The Constitution says nothing about half votes, but if one-half of one vote from each of the three equally divided States were added to the Democratic roll the Democrats would have 24½ votes, electing their candidate by one-half of one vote.

The Vice President would be chosen by the United States Senate, and would be a Republican, the present division of the Senate being 51 Republicans and 44 Democrats.

The provision for the election of a President in this contingency is contained in the twelfth amendment to the Constitution of the United States, and is as follows:

"The person having the highest number of votes [in the Electoral College] for President shall be the President, if such number be a majority of the whole number of Electors appointed; and if no person has such majority, then from the persons having the highest numbers, not exceeding three, on the list of those voted for as President, the House of Representatives shall choose immediately, by ballot, the President. But in choosing the President, the vote shall be taken by States, the representation from each State having one vote; a quorum for this purpose shall consist of a member or members from two-thirds of the States, and a majority of all the States shall be necessary to a choice.

"And if the House of Representatives shall not choose a President, whenever the right of choice shall devolve upon them, before the fourth day of March next following, then the Vice President shall act as President, as in the case of the death or other constitutional disability of the President."

"All the News That's Fit to Print."

# The New York Times.

THE WEATHER.

Cloudy Tuesday; Wednesday, unsettled; light to moderate variable winds.

For full weather report see Page 21.

VOL. LXI...NO. 19,876. * * * * NEW YORK, TUESDAY, JUNE 25, 1912.—TWENTY-TWO PAGES. ONE CENT In Greater New York, Elsewhere, Jersey City, and Newark. TWO CENTS.

## ALFRED L. SELIGMAN DEAD IN AUTO CRASH

### Former Banker and Musician Thrown from Motor Car When Another Hits It.

### HEAD STRIKES AGAINST CURB

### Collision Occurs at Seventy-second Street and West End Avenue—R. W. Stuart in Other Car.

Alfred L. Seligman, the youngest brother of Isaac N. Seligman of J. & W. Seligman & Co., bankers, was thrown from his automobile and killed early last night in a collision with another automobile at Seventy-second Street and West End Avenue.

He left his apartments, 16 East Sixtieth Street, and started for his Summer home at Greenwich, Conn. His car was northbound in West End Avenue, and a large car, in which four men were seated, was making west along Seventy-second Street. The two machines reached the corner at the same time and were upon each other before the chauffeurs saw their danger. Mr. Seligman's chauffeur attempted to put on speed and shoot ahead of the machine that was bearing down on it. But he was a second too late, and the other car plunged into the left rear wheel of Seligman's machine. The tire and rim were smashed off the wheel and the car made a complete circle, striking the sidewalk on the northeast corner of the street.

Mr. Seligman was on the left hand side in the rear seat. The impact when the automobile hit the curb was so great that he was shot over the head of his companion and landed on his head against the sharp curb.

Morris Ranger, 2,374 Seventh Avenue, a distant relative of Mr. Seligman, was his companion on the rear seat and was also thrown out of the machine, his body falling beside that of Mr. Seligman.

**R. W. Stuart in Other Car.**

In the other car were Russell W. Stuart, manager of the Tire Core Company, 246 West Fifty-ninth Street, and three friends. It was brought to a stop at once and the occupants hurried to the aid of Mr. Seligman. He was dead, however. Mr. Ranger was not seriously hurt. The chauffeur, Harry Larkin, had managed to stick to his wheel and escape injury.

A large crowd soon collected and extra policemen were put on duty to preserve order. The body of Mr. Seligman was carried into the residence of Mrs. John S. Huyler, widow of the candy manufacturer, at 301 West Seventy-second Street, and was later removed to the West Sixty-eighth Street Police Station.

Coroner Feinberg arrived at the station later in the evening and held a preliminary hearing, at which the two chauffeurs testified under oath. Assistant District Attorney McDonald assisted the Coroner. George Nobac, who drove the machine for Stuart, said that just before the accident his eyes had been fixed on a car just ahead of him. He expected this car to turn either to the right or left, and was prepared to make a quick turn to avoid it when the car in which Mr. Seligman was riding shot ahead of him. He said his speed was about ten miles an hour. The other occupants of this car told practically the same story.

The chauffeur for Mr. Seligman estimated the speed of Stuart's car at between twenty and twenty-five miles an hour. He insisted that if the speed had been lower the machines could have gone through the collision without serious accident.

**Devoted Life to Art.**

Mr. Seligman was a widower, 46 years old. He was formerly treasurer of the Anglo-California Bank, but retired some years ago to devote all his time to art. He kept a bachelor apartment and studio at 16 East Sixtieth Street, where he spent much of his time painting and modeling in clay. He was also a musician. He was the financial backer of the Young Men's Symphony Orchestra, in which he himself played the first 'cello.

He was a great friend of Henry B. Harris, who was lost on the Titanic. A few weeks before Mr. Harris's death he donated the use of the Hudson Theatre for the orchestra's tenth anniversary. This was the occasion of a public demonstration in Mr. Seligman's honor by scores of musicians of the city, who owed their start in the profession to the opportunity which the Young Men's Symphony Orchestra gave them. Arnold Volpe, conductor of the Young Men's Symphony Orchestra, said on that occasion that Mr. Seligman's generous backing and personal interest had done great things for the development of orchestral music, not only in this city, but throughout the country.

Mr. Seligman's three brothers are George W. Seligman of the law firm of Seligman & Seligman, Isaac Newton Seligman, and Prof. E. A. R. Seligman, who holds the MacVickar chair of economics at Columbia University. Isaac N. Seligman, the eldest of the house, is in London at present. News of his brother's death was cabled to him last night.

The dead man was the youngest son of Joseph Seligman of Bavaria and Babette Steinhart Seligman. He was graduated from Columbia University in 1882, and immediately went West. Prof. Seligman said last night that Mr. Seligman was composing a symphony, and owned one of the most valuable collections of stringed musical instruments in the world. Relative to this collection, Prof. Seligman said:

"My brother kept this collection in his home in East Sixtieth Street. His generous spirit was well shown in the way he allowed the valuable instruments to be used by poor musicians. I have often seen him lend instruments, for which he had paid fabulous amounts to men who were struggling to achieve fame as musicians."

George Seligman of 23 West Ninety-fifth Street said he would take charge of his brother's body, and ordered its removal to an undertaking establishment. The funeral, he said, would probably be held from his home.

## AUTO HITS TELEPHONE POLE.

### Father and Son Thrown Out—The Former Seriously Hurt.

WESTFIELD, N. J., June 24.—Hiram I. Fink and his son, H. C. Fink, automobile dealers in this town, were out in one of their cars to-day when the front tire exploded, causing the steering wheel to swerve to one side, and before young Fink, who was driving, had a chance to recover control of the car it ran up on the sidewalk, striking a telephone pole and throwing both men out.

The older man struck the sidewalk head first and was unconscious when picked up, while his son was more fortunate, escaping serious injury, although he was out of his mind for several hours. His father was hurriedly taken to his home on Walnut Street. He is suffering from concussion of the brain, as well as other internal injuries. The car was completely wrecked.



## CLIMBS MT. McKINLEY.

### Parker's Companion Tells Mother They Reached Summit in April.

*Special to The New York Times.*

SEATTLE, June 24.—Prof. Herschel Parker of Columbia University has reached the top of Mount McKinley, America's highest peak, which has hitherto been unscaled, and is now on his way back to tell the world of his success.

This word was received to-day by letter by Mrs. George Brown of Tacoma, mother of Belmore Browne, Prof. Parker's companion. The letter, which was dated April 15, said that at the time the party were on the summit. They had but little difficulty, and would reach Cook Inlet on their way out before July 1.

Important geographical discoveries, including a new route to the peak, and two new glaciers were reported by Browne.

The letter was sent to Fairbanks by a prospector from Glacier City, a mining camp which Prof. Parker visited after leaving the mountain to obtain provisions and send out mail. All the members of the party, including the professor, were reported in the best of health.

Browne wrote that the passes used in the expedition were much easier than those discovered on previous expeditions.

Prof. Parker and Browne left Seattle in January. Twice before the party attempted to scale the peak and failed. The start was made unusually early this year and every precaution was taken to obtain success in their climb.

Prof. Parker left Brooklyn Jan. 12 to make his third attempt to reach the top of Mt. McKinley. He first attempted to scale the mountain in 1903 with Dr. Cook, whose story of having accomplished the feat alone he never credited. In 1910 he tried again, but failed.

This year he purposed to attack the northern side of the mountain, whereas before he had tried to climb the southern flank. Besides Browne, who wrote the letter, telling of the expedition's success, he had with him as another assistant Arthur Aten of Valdez, Alaska.

## LUSITANIA GOING SLOW.

### Blades of Centre Propeller the Cause of Her Reduced Speed.

*Special Cable to THE NEW YORK TIMES.*

LONDON, June 24.—The Lusitania is reported to be nearing the West Irish coast at reduced speed. Something is wrong with the blades of the centre propeller.

The liner is expected to pass Queenstown at 3 o'clock this morning.

The Lusitania's place next Sunday, when she was to sail for New York, will be taken by the California of the Anchor Line.

## BETTING ON BRYAN NOW.

### $500 Offered at 1 to 3 That He Will Be Named at Baltimore.

Bets made in the financial district on the nomination of Taft were paid yesterday and there were few of more than $100. The sporting event in the Street now is Bryan's chance of the nomination.

One man had $500 of real money to bet at 1 to 3 that Bryan would be named. He found one man willing to risk $1,000 on his conviction that the Peerless Leader would not get the prize of the Baltimore Convention and he still has $166.66 to bet against $500.

## CANADIAN TOWN FIRE-SWEPT.

### Cathedral, Town Hall, and Chateau Saguenay at Chicoutimi Burned.

QUEBEC, June 24.—Fire this afternoon destroyed many buildings, including the Chateau Saguenay, the cathedral, the town hall and the Chicoutimi Hotel at Chicoutimi, in the district of Saguenay.

Several blocks of stores and private residences were within the fire-swept area.

It was several hours before the blaze was brought within control.

## WARD BUYS DUDLEY HOUSE.

### Son-in-Law of Ambassador Reid Gets Famous London Mansion.

LONDON, June 24.—The Hon. John Hubert Ward, brother of the Earl of Dudley, has purchased Dudley House, Park Lane, one of the most noted of London mansions. It has lately been occupied by the South African millionaire J. B. Robinson.

Mrs. John Ward is the daughter of the American Ambassador, Whitelaw Reid. She married Mr. Ward in 1908.

## TICKET TAKER DIES AT POST.

### Joseph Sturges Found Dead in His Chair at Polo Grounds.

Joseph Sturges, formerly a bookmaker and for the last six years a ticket-taker at the Polo Grounds, was found dead yesterday afternoon in his chair, at the ticket office.

Sturges was fifty-two years old and resided at 59 Vermilye Avenue, the Bronx. Shortly after two o'clock yesterday he went into the enclosure where he was in the habit of collecting tickets for the ball games. At 2.40 he was found dead. The cause was heart disease.

## DECAPITATED IN LIFT SHAFT.

### Laborer Put His Head Into It, Looking for Elevator.

Thomas Daly, twenty-five years old of 3 Greenwich Street, Long Island City, a laborer employed by an electrical contracting firm which is doing repair work in Havemeyer Hall, Columbia University, thrust his head through a hole in the wall abutting on the elevator shaft on the sixth floor, yesterday morning, to see where the car was.

He forgot the counterweights of the mechanism, which were coming down at the time he put his head out, and was decapitated. His body fell to the floor, the head into the shaft.

### Latest Shipping News.

REPORTED BY WIRELESS, (Marconi.)—SS Caronia, Liverpool to New York, was 810 miles E. of Sandy Hook at 7:05 P. M.; due 25th, 7 P. M.



## COULD HAVE WON, ROOSEVELT SAYS

### Thirty Southern Delegates Offered to Switch, but He Would Not Stand for Taint.

### WANTED IT ALL BEGUN OVER

### They Weren't Willing to Unseat "Fraudulent Delegates," So—Well, Taft Got It.

### HIS STRATEGY BOARD NAMED

### Seventeen Republicans and One Democrat on It—On His Way Home to Plan General Attack.

*Special to The New York Times.*

TOLEDO, Ohio, June 24, (On the Twentieth Century Limited with Roosevelt, en route to Oyster Bay.)—The fight to form a third party is now on in earnest. To-day Theodore Roosevelt started back to Oyster Bay to map out his plans, after announcing that the mass convention to nominate him would be held not earlier than three weeks from to-day nor later than six weeks. It is probable that either Chicago or St. Louis will be selected as the place.

The names of eighteen of the men who will serve on the Organization Committee of the new party were given out to-day by Mr. Roosevelt, who said that there was no truth in the statement that it had been planned to delay the announcement until after the Democratic Convention.

The committee is to be larger than at first announced. Judge Ben Lindsey of Denver is the only Democrat on it to date. Others will be added if they can be induced to follow the Roosevelt lead later on. Here is the line-up, which gives some idea of just which leaders Roosevelt knows he can absolutely depend on:

**Organizers of the New Party.**

Gov. HIRAM W. JOHNSON, California, Chairman.

Senator MOSES E. CLAPP, Minnesota.

Senator JOSEPH M. DIXON, Montana.

Senator MILES POINDEXTER, Washington.

Gov. C. A. ALDRICH, Nebraska.

Gov. R. S. VESSEY, South Dakota.

E. A. VAN VALKENBURG, editor Philadelphia North American.

Col. W. R. NELSON, owner and publisher Kansas City Star.

Former Congressman RICHMOND PEARSON, North Carolina.

WILLIAM A. PRENDERGAST, New York.

JAMES R. GARFIELD, Ohio.

WILLIAM ALLEN WHITE, Kansas.

GIFFORD PINCHOT, California.

Judge BEN D. LINDSEY, Colorado.

MATTHEW HALE, Massachusetts.

GEORGE L. RECORD, New Jersey.

CHARLES H THOMPSON, Vermont.

Col. E. C. CARRINGTON, Maryland.

The fact that Gov. Hadley of Missouri and Senator Borah of Idaho are not on the list is taken as final proof that they have deserted the Roosevelt following. The position of Gov. Stubbs of Kansas is still left in doubt.

The third party candidate was as aggressive as ever to-day and the mention of a report that the nomination of a Progressive by the Democrats at Baltimore might end the third party talk drew a quick retort.

**Says He'll Stick to the End.**

"My position will not be influenced by any action of the Baltimore Convention," he declared. "I will not depart from what I said Saturday night. I shall accept the Progressive nomination on a Progressive platform, and I shall fight the battle through to the end."

"The retreat from Moscow" some called the departure of Roosevelt from Chicago to-day, but he seemed to think that it was more like a triumphal march. The crowds at the La Salle Street station gave him a rousing cheer as he walked along waving his hat. A moment later he appeared on the observation platform, and there were shouts of "Four years more for you, Colonel."

"I'll stick," he called back. "I'll fight them to the end, and I'll give you a square deal."

"We'll give you a square deal, too," yelled a loud-voiced man, and the crowd cheered wildly. As Mr. Roosevelt was about to enter his car again the crowd surged forward and a dozen flash lights, exploded almost simultaneously by photographers, added a bit to the excitement.

"It's terrible to be a defeated and discredited man, Colonel," one of his leaders said to him, jokingly, and Roosevelt gleefully replied: "Yes, look at them. It's awful, terrible, isn't it?"

To-day Mr. Roosevelt's followers are asserting that if he had been willing to accept the nomination at the hands of the "tainted" delegates he so bitterly attacked he could have won it.

**Says He Refused Tainted Nomination.**

On the morning of the day Taft and Sherman were nominated, Mr. Roosevelt said, a number of Southern delegates sent word to him that if he would enter the fight in the convention again they would assure him enough votes to win.

He sent back word that he would agree only if thirty of the delegates would pledge themselves in writing that they would join with the Roosevelt delegates, start all over again, elect a new Temporary Chairman, and purge the convention of the seventy-eight delegates he declares were fraudulently seated by the National Committee.

Nineteen delegates agreed to do so, Mr. Roosevelt said, but the thirty he demanded did not send their pledge. And so the plan fell through. Mr. Roosevelt

Continued on Page 5.



### The New York Times Special Train to Baltimore.

The New York Times Special Train over the Pennsylvania Railroad to Baltimore carrying the CITY EDITION of The Times, containing the latest political, general, and sporting news, is running this morning on the following schedule:

| | | |
|---|---|---|
| Leave Penn. Station, N. Y. | 3:25 | A. M. |
| Arrive Trenton | 4:35 | " |
| " West Philadelphia | 5:15 | " |
| " Wilmington | 5:50 | " |
| " Baltimore | 7:10 | " |
| " Washington (by regular Pennsylvania train leaving Baltimore at 7:38 A. M.) | 8:40 | " |

## TAFT IS STUDYING ELECTORAL MIX-UP

### Roosevelt Men Control Ten States Where Electors Already Have Been Chosen.

### ALL THESE WILL BE SOUNDED

### Those Opposed to Taft Will Be Removed and Others Named—Litigation Likely in Some States.

*Special to The New York Times.*

WASHINGTON, D. C., June 24.—One of the first things to be considered by President Taft and his advisers at the outset of the campaign is the status of the Electoral tickets named in the various States during the recent primaries.

The Republican managers are confronted by the fact that these Electors were placed upon regular Republican tickets, and unless steps are taken to place other tickets in the field they will be voted for in November under the Republican emblem.

There are ten or twelve States under the domination of Progressive Republicans where the electors already are in the field, nominated by State and district conventions under the sway of the Roosevelt people. Pennsylvania, Maryland, and West Virginia are in this list.

Flinn, the new Pennsylvania boss, picked all that State's electors in the convention that sent delegates at large to Chicago. He has threatened that every one of the Pennsylvania electors will vote for Roosevelt in the Electoral College if they are elected. The Taft leaders will ascertain from each elector what he would do, and will obtain a new set of electors if necessary.

There may be litigation in the courts on the subject. Having been nominated as regular Republicans in a regular Republican State Convention, the electors might claim regularity and fight efforts to remove them. The suggestion now is that Flinn will appropriate these electors as the electors for the new Progressive Party.

In most States it is possible for new electors to be put in the field by means of petitions filed with the State authorities, but if attempts are made to put these tickets under the regular Republican heading, the electors already nominated would be able to complicate things by going to the courts.

The policy of the Republican National Committee under the leadership of its new Chairman, who probably will be Charles D. Hilles, the President's private secretary, will be to sift the sentiments and records of every man named as an elector.

In many States Roosevelt will have to get into the running by petitions circulated among the people. In some States the number of signers is, as in New York, necessarily large. It is predicted that Roosevelt's managers will have a hard job getting 50,000 signers in that State. The cost, too, will be large.

The Roosevelt programme is to hold State Conventions of the Progressive Party and nominate their electors and State and legislative tickets where they think they have a chance to win.

## T. R. MAY WIN JERSEY ELECTORS

### Will Fight Taft for Them at the Primaries in September.

*Special to The New York Times.*

TRENTON, N. J., June 24.—Either Taft or Roosevelt may be without an electoral ticket in New Jersey next November. This peculiar condition is possible by reason of the provisions of an amendment to the Geran election law embodied in a bill introduced by Senator Leavitt of Mercer County, passed at the last session of the Legislature.

Former Gov. Fort, one of the Roosevelt leaders in the State, is quoted by a friend here as saying that the Roosevelt element would take advantage of the situation and bend every effort to name Roosevelt electors at the Fall primaries in September next with the unanimity shown in the choice of National delegates.

Formerly Jersey Republicans nominated candidates for electors in their State Conventions. The Geran law of 1910 changed this by providing for nomination by direct primaries, but before this act could become effective as respects Presidential electors the law was amended by the Leavitt bill.

As the law now stands, the Presidential preference primary relates only to preferences and to National delegates and alternates. Presidential electors are to be chosen by a unique convention, composed of the men nominated in September for the lower house and the Senate, the hold-over Senators and the Governor, who sits only in the convention of his own party.

Thus the September primaries will witness another vigorous contest between the Taft and Roosevelt forces, and candidates for the Assembly and the Senate will be required to pledge themselves to vote for Taft or Roosevelt electoral nominees, as the case may be.

The provision of the amended Geran law, which constitutes Assembly nominees members of a convention to determine who shall be the party nominees on the electoral ticket, has been closely studied by lawyers here, and they declare that a majority in this convention will have the right to name all of the electors.

## TO CAPTURE STATE MACHINE.

### Roosevelt Men in Colorado Start at Once on Their Campaign.

DENVER, Colo., June 24.—The Roosevelt Progressive Republican League of Colorado will start work at once to obtain control of the State Republican organization and send Roosevelt men to the electoral college.

An announcement was made at headquarters to-day that an address to the

Continued on Page 6.

## BRYAN, REPULSED, TO OPEN BITTER FIGHT IN DEMOCRATIC CONVENTION TO-DAY

### Will Offer Himself as Temporary Chairman to Defeat Parker.

### BEATEN IN COMMITTEE

### 31 Votes Cast for Parker, the Clark Men Lining Up with Murphy.

### ISSUE NOW PLAINLY DRAWN

### Conservatives Declare That the Nebraskan's Power Must Be Broken at the Start.

### HE MEETS THE CHALLENGE

### Says He Is Fighting Predatory Interests That Have Led the Party to Defeat.

### CONVENTION CITY SWAMPED

### Crowds Far Too Large for Baltimore's Facilities, but the Delegates Are Good-Natured.

*Special to The New York Times.*

BALTIMORE, Md., June 24.—William Jennings Bryan, backed by the Wilson and other Progressive leaders, is standing against the field to-night on the question whether the Progressives shall organize and run the Democratic National Convention, or whether it shall be opened with a reactionary keynote in an address by ex-Judge Alton B. Parker as Temporary Chairman. Judge Parker and his friends say he is not a reactionary, and that he would make a speech that would suit the Progressives, but the Bryan and Wilson leaders point to the fact that Judge Parker's campaign for the Temporary Chairmanship has the backing of the "Wall Street interests," and for that reason they are against him.

Nine out of ten of the delegates when questioned, will say that the hope of Democratic success is in following the course of the Progressive leaders, that being the only way to poll the full Democratic vote, and win over to the party the Republican votes that were alienated at Chicago. They declared that if the Bryan-Wilson Progressive programme is carried out here it will sound the death knell of the proposed Roosevelt third party movement. Of course, the fact that 90 per cent. of the delegates are talking this way does not mean that they will finally vote the same way.

The National Committee of the Democratic Party evidently did not believe that the delegates would vote thus on a roll call, for at their meeting to-night the National Committee indorsed the action of half of the members of its sub-committee by voting for Judge Parker for Temporary Chairman.

Judge Parker received thirty-one votes in the committee. Ollie James of Kentucky, who was not the Bryan candidate for the place, but merely an anti-Parker candidate, received twenty votes. Senator O'Gorman of New York, who has all along been talked of as a compromise candidate, received two votes.

**New York Dicker with Clark Men.**

This vote in the National Committee—an apparent defeat for Bryan—came at the close of a second session of that body. The first session adjourned for the announced purpose of seeing whether a compromise could be effected. Mr. Bryan and Judge Parker met, but could reach no agreement. During the recess it is said that Charles F. Murphy and the other interests who are trying to knock out Bryan at any cost won over the followers of Champ Clark in the National Committee to Judge Parker's cause by promising them that if they would stand for Judge Parker as Temporary Chairman Champ Clark should have their votes on the first ballot for nomination for President.

Such a promise would be quite in keeping with the decision reached early this morning at a conference between the leaders in the rooms of Charles F. Murphy. Attending that conference were August Belmont, DeLancey Nicoll, William F. Sheehan, Samuel Untermyer, Joseph Auerbach, Senator O'Gorman, John B. Stanchfield, Judge Morgan J. O'Brien, and many of the old-time Democratic leaders like Norman E. Mack, Thomas Taggart, Roger Sullivan, and James Guffey. The voice of that conference was that Bryan had to be eliminated from the Democratic situation, no matter what sacrifice it entailed.

If the Champ Clark votes in the National Committee were purchased by a promise of support for his boom for the Presidential nomination, it may not avail, for, while Clark has the greatest number of instructed and pledged delegates, most of them are only tied up for the first ballot, and the very men who are going to cast their first votes for Clark are of the type that cannot naturally help cheering for Bryan whenever his name is mentioned. The "Houn' Dawg" is their new fetich, but the Peerless Leader is their ancient idol.

When the Wilson leaders heard that those who were determined to defeat Bryan by making Parker Temporary Chairman were dickering with the Clark men on the basis above mentioned for their votes in the National Committee, they tried to offset it by presenting the name of a Clark man to the National Committee meeting for Temporary Chairman. The Clark National Committeemen were too foxy to nibble at that bait, though, and voted solidly for Parker.

**Bryan Issues Battle Call.**

Hence there is nothing in sight but a big fight to-morrow on the floor of the convention between Bryan and his followers and the leaders of the element which controls the National Committee and which Bryan designates "the predatory interests which have no politics."

Mr. Bryan himself said after the result in the National Committee was made known to-night:

"I had expected this. When Mr. Guffey was seated in the National Committee against the protest of the Democrats in Pennsylvania I learned what I had expected—that the majority of the committee has no conception of Democracy or is so slavishly under the control of the predatory interests as not to be free to follow their convictions. The reasons they give are like all reasons given in defense of wrong. They are insincere, and are not the reasons that in reality influence them.

"The fight will be resumed to-morrow, at which time a Progressive candidate will be presented for the convention to vote for as Temporary Chairman, and the line will be drawn so that the delegates can decide whether they will ally themselves with the Belmont-Ryan-Murphy crod that brought overwhelming defeat on the party eight years ago, and which is in close and continuous co-partnership with the crowd that nominated Mr. Taft in Chicago.

"The predatory interests have no politics, no policies. They are with the party that serves them. Having enabled a minority of the Republicans to override the will of a majority of Republicans at Chicago, they are now here to enable a minority of the Democrats to override the majority in this convention.

"There is not a great exploiting interest that is not represented in the lobbies of the hotels here. There is not a corrupting influence in American politics that is not being used, and the delegates to this convention underestimate the intelligence of the men who sent them here if they think that they can go back and deceive them into believing that the support of Mr. Parker came from any worthy motive.

"The talk of harmony is too absurd to receive consideration. I tried to secure harmony by urging several weeks ago that the committee invite Mr. Clark and Mr. Wilson, whose instructed delegates constitute maybe two-thirds of the convention, to agree on a candidate for the Temporary Chairmanship. They not only failed to do this, but refused to take the choice of either candidate. At Mr. Murphy's dictation they are trying to compel the nomination of Mr. Parker.

"I shall discuss Mr. Parker's fitness for the position to-morrow. It is enough to-night to say that if he does not know whose agent he is he lacks the intelligence necessary for a presiding officer, and if he does know he does not deserve the support of any man who has the right to call himself a Democrat.

"I expect to present the name of some Progressive for the Temporary Chairmanship and to support his claims before the convention. If I fail to find a man to lead the fight, my name will be presented as a candidate for Temporary Chairman.

"I have no way of knowing how the convention stands, but the Democrats of the Nation have done enough for me to justify me in suffering defeat if necessary in their defense. One Republican Party is enough in this country, for whatever we may call ourselves, if we cannot distinguish ourselves from them in our actions the people will not pay much attention to our words."

Senator-elect Ollie James said to-night that he had been asked by Mr. Bryan to put him in nomination to-morrow for Temporary Chairman. He said he had to decline as he was for Champ Clark first, last and all the time. This is a pretty clear indication of the Clark alliance with the anti-Bryan leaders on the question of Temporary Chairmanship.

Though besieged at Tammany headquarters with inquirers for an answer to Mr. Bryan's statement concerning the nomination of Judge Parker, Charles F. Murphy had nothing to say.

"What do you think," he was asked, "of Mr. Bryan's charge that Judge Parker represents predatory wealth?"

"He has a right to say what he chooses," replied Mr. Murphy, "and I have a right to be silent."

William R. Hearst is here, conferring first with Bryan, then with Murphy, and so down along the line. Little is known about Mr. Hearst and his plans except that he is for anything that will beat Gov. Wilson for the nomination.

Before retiring to-night Mr. Bryan said:

"I have not thought it proper to discuss with anybody what Mr. Parker said to me or what I said to him, but in answer to a rumor that is now being circulated that he read his speech to me and that I approve it, I feel justified in saying that he never read a single sentence of his speech or showed me any manuscript. He referred in a very general way to what he intends to say, but what he said only referred to two or three subjects, and no one could judge from what he said whether the speech would be acceptable or not. A very small part of the interview was spent on the question of what Mr. Parker would say. It cut no figure in either his decision or mine."

**Bryan Won't Talk on Candidacy.**

The flat declaration from Bryan that he was not going to permit the Democratic National Committee's steam roller to flatten him out came as the climax of a day during which he had been receiving the delegates by the score. The burden of his talk with all these delegates was that he believed that if this convention was not dominated by the Progressives, Roosevelt might have a chance to hold a convention for his own nomination, and might win out. He tried to dodge all questions as to his choice for the Presidential nomination, saying that the issue must first be settled as to whether "Wall Street and other corrupt influences" or the Progressives were to control the convention machinery. He replied to the direct question of whether or not he would be the standard bearer in this way:

"Eliminate me from the situation as an individual. I am here to fight for the Progressive Democracy and against the predatory interests, which will surely drag the party down to defeat again if they control. Get behind me in that fight, and if we can win on that let the delegates choose any candidate who honestly represents our cause."

How earnestly the backers of Judge Parker for Temporary Chairman are in the intent to down Mr. Bryan in the convention at its very opening was shown to-day when they engaged a suite of rooms in the Belvedere Hotel close to those of the Democratic Committee and of Mr. Bryan. De Lancey Nicoll is in charge there, and a trained band of lieutenants are out corralling leaders of delegations and bringing them in for consultation.

**Bryan's Chance to Control.**

Mr. Bryan's declaration that he will himself be a candidate for Temporary Chairman if nobody else comes forward as the candidate of the Progressives makes it pretty certain that he will be the candidate for that place. If he wins it will mean possibly another of his great 1896 "cross of gold and crown of thorns" speeches with which he will sweep the convention off its feet, so that it will follow him wildly from then to the close. If he loses the fight for Temporary Chairman he and his friends will stand right by their guns and battle at every stage of the proceedings for Progressive supremacy.

The shouters for the leading political candidates are all awaiting the result of this Temporary Chairmanship fight. The report that Champ Clark's leaders have thrown his fortunes in with the Parker leaders is given general credence. Wilson's leaders have staked their all with Mr. Bryan on the subject of the Progressive fight, and while Mr. Bryan and his friends have not declared for Wilson, it is not hard to see that the Bryan strength will go to Wilson if Bryan does not finally appear as the candidate himself.

## BRYAN'S DECLARATION OF WAR.

*Special to The New York Times.*

BALTIMORE, June 24.—William Jennings Bryan, speaking of the action of the National Committee in selecting Alton B. Parker as Temporary Chairman of the Convention, said:

"The majority of the committee has no conception of Democracy, or is so slavishly under the control of the predatory interests as not to be free to follow their convictions.

"To-morrow a Progressive candidate will be presented for the Convention to vote for as Temporary Chairman, and the line will be drawn so that the delegates can decide whether they will ally themselves with the Belmont-Ryan-Murphy crowd that brought overwhelming defeat on the party eight years ago, and which is in close and continuous copartnership with the crowd that nominated Mr. Taft in Chicago.

"The predatory interests have no politics, no policies. They are with the party that serves them. Having enabled a minority of the Republicans to override the will of a majority of Republicans at Chicago, they are now here to enable a minority of the Democrats to override the majority in this convention. * * *

"The talk of harmony is too absurd to receive consideration. * * * I shall discuss Mr. Parker's fitness for the position to-morrow. It is enough to-night to say that if he does not know whose agent he is he lacks the intelligence necessary for a presiding officer, and if he does know he does not deserve the support of any man who has the right to call himself a Democrat.

"I expect to present the name of some Progressive for the Temporary Chairmanship and to support his claims before the Convention. If I fail to find a man to lead the fight, my name will be presented as a candidate for Temporary Chairman.

"I have no way of knowing how the Convention stands, but the Democrats of the Nation have done enough for me to justify me in suffering defeat if necessary in their defense."

"All the News That's Fit to Print."

# The New York Times.

THE WEATHER.
Fair Wednesday; Thursday, unsettled; light to moderate southerly winds.
For full weather report see Page 23.

VOL. LXI...NO. 19,884. * * * * NEW YORK, WEDNESDAY, JULY 3, 1912.—TWENTY-FOUR PAGES. ONE CENT In Greater New York, Elsewhere, Jersey City, and Newark. TWO CENTS.

# WOODROW WILSON IS NOMINATED FOR PRESIDENT; GOV. MARSHALL OF INDIANA FOR VICE PRESIDENT

## Convention Deadlock Is Broken on Forty-sixth Ballot at 3:30 P. M.

### ACTION MADE UNANIMOUS

After 990 Votes Had Been Cast for the New Jersey Governor and 84 for Clark.

### ILLINOIS STARTS THE SLIDE

Then Underwood Is Withdrawn as a Candidate and Clark Delegates Are Released.

### NEW YORK GETS INTO LINE

No Protest from Bryan When Her Ninety Votes Are Cast For Wilson.

### CHEERS BY TIRED DELEGATES

Demonstration in Honor of the Nominee Hearty but Not of Long Duration.

*Special to The New York Times.*

BALTIMORE, July 2.—Woodrow Wilson was nominated for President on the forty-sixth ballot this afternoon at 3:30 o'clock. The vote was never announced, for it was made unanimous before the clerk could finish counting it up, but on the last roll call Wilson had received 990 votes to 84 for Champ Clark and 12 for Judson Harmon.

The first ballot of the convention was taken in the early hours of Saturday morning, after an all-night session, and the convention had remained deadlocked through Saturday and Monday.

The final ballot was preceded by a sort of love feast in which the spokesmen for the other candidates pledged their hearty and enthusiastic support to Wilson, despite the fact that he had not been nominated. New York went so far as to propose, through Representative Fitzgerald, that the forty-sixth ballot be dispensed with and that Wilson be nominated by acclamation.

The only reason why this was not done was that the supporters of Clark desired to place themselves on record once more—for the purpose of demonstrating their love for "Old Champ Clark," as their spokesmen all called him.

It was 12:05 when Chairman James ascended the platform and called the convention to order in the broken and husky tones which are all that remain of the voice that a week ago sounded like a forest storm.

He immediately called for the forty-third ballot. Mr. James was weary and worn, and although he kept himself under admirable control and won the respect of everybody for his patience and firmness in dealing with the hard task before him, he had none of that patience for the people who clogged the aisles and made the voices of the clerks inaudible.

#### Trouble Restoring Order.

"Please cease conversation or get out," he shouted at them, "to some place where you can talk without disturbing the convention."

Forty times during the day he had to suspend the proceedings to order the police to clear the aisles. Those wonderful Baltimore policemen only grinned sheepishly each time, and now and then one would timidly lay his hand on the shoulder of some disturber and then take it off again when he saw the disturber paid no attention to him.

This forty-sixth ballot was to be the ballot whereon Illinois was to start an expected stampede. Everybody was waiting for the vote of that State. It was, indeed, the vote of Illinois which made Wilson's nomination sure, but the other candidates managed to hold on for two more ballots, the forty-fourth and forty-fifth.

On the forty-third ballot the first change was in Arizona, where Clark lost a vote to W. J. Bryan. Connecticut followed by taking two votes from the Clark column and turning them over to Wilson, amid a "rebel yell" from the irrepressible Texans.

Idaho gave Wilson one additional vote and then Roger Sullivan arose in the Illinois delegates. Every face was turned expectantly toward him.

"Eighteen for Clark, forty for Wilson," announced Sullivan briskly. The stampede had begun. The Texans arose and cheered Illinois, facing the delegation and waving their hats at it. Many of the Wilson men cheered Sullivan individually. Under the unit rule the whole of Illinois, 58 votes, had to be counted for Wilson.

But the Clark and Underwood men hung on grimly, and it was soon evident that whatever might be the ultimate effect of Sullivan's announcement, it would not succeed in bringing about a nomination on this ballot, nor, perhaps for several more. The avalanche was starting slowly.

Iowa gave Wilson a gain of 1½, Louisiana 2, Michigan 8, North Carolina 2, and then there came a gain of real importance. Virginia cast her entire 24 votes for Wilson. Up to that time she had been casting 12 of them for Clark.

"Hurrah for Virginia," shouted a delegate from Texas, and the Old Dominion got nearly as big a welcome into the Wilson camp as had Illinois. So did West Virginia when she followed her older sister and Illinois into the Wilson ranks.

#### West Virginia Helps Wilson.

West Virginia had been particularly active and prominent on the Clark side from the beginning of the convention, so that her surrender was specially welcome. Through ex-Governor McCorkle she had done a lot of talking, and it had all been done on the Murphy side. The delegation had always been divided, but as the majority was against Wilson her votes had to be cast under the unit rule. Now they were cast the other way under the same rule, and she contributed 16 toward starting the landslide.

While this was going on Senator-elect Vardaman of Mississippi was over in the Alabama delegation urging upon Senator Bankhead that the time to withdraw Underwood had come. Mississippi wanted to join the procession, but could not do so as long as Underwood was a candidate. Bankhead and his fellow-Alabamans insisted on sticking it out a little longer.

Wisconsin gave Wilson a gain of 1, Alaska 1, and Hawaii 1. The District of Columbia, in announcing her vote, said she was casting it for "Dear Old Champ Clark." Maryland had asked to be passed when her turn came for the reason that the Wilson men in her delegation were making a dead-lift effort to bring over the others and vote Maryland solid. They failed, however, and Wilson gained only half a vote in that State.

Wilson went up to 602 on this ballot. Clark was down to 329 and Underwood to 98½. Harmon had 28, Foss 27, Kern 1, and Bryan 1.

On the forty-fourth ballot the Arizona man who had voted for Bryan went over to Wilson. Colorado gave Wilson ten out of her twelve, which was a gain of nine for him. He gained two in Indiana, one from Clark and one from Kern, and this gave him Indiana's solid vote of 30.

But it was evident that there was no chance of nomination on this ballot. No big delegations were going to swing. He kept on picking up delegates here and there, but his gains were not sufficient to promise anything definite. Wilson gained a vote in Louisiana, one and a half in Maryland, two in Pennsylvania, and four in Wisconsin. Utah's eight went over in a body.

#### Trouble Over the Proxies.

A poll of Washington developed that some of the votes were being cast by men who were not delegates, but held proxies, the delegates having gone back home to save the remnant of their bank rolls Chairman James promptly ruled that no man but a delegate or alternate could vote.

"But the State of Washington has no alternates," cried one of the proxies, "and these delegates have gone home."

"The fact that Washington has no alternates is her misfortune," replied Chairman James calmly.

"I object to the ruling of the chair," shouted one of the Washington men, "as being part of the fraud that has been practiced."

This did not ruffle Mr. James, who looked at him with patient placidity and replied: "The gentleman has the privilege of appealing from the decision of the chair."

The man was misguided enough to take this hint, and his appeal was laid on the table with a mighty shout of "aye" from the whole convention. A call for the noes brought only a feeble and lonely cry from the Washington men themselves.

The forty-fourth ballot resulted as follows: Wilson, 629; Clark, 306; Underwood, 99; Harmon, 27; Foss, 27.

While the forty-fifth ballot was proceeding there were signs of great activity in the New York delegation. All the leaders were busy conferring over the question, "Shall we do it now?" It was finally decided to wait until Alabama broke, and Murphy again cast New York's 90 votes for Clark.

The changes on this ballot were so unimportant as not to be worth chronicling. Mississippi asked to be passed, while Vardaman made another effort to get Alabama in line, but, though Senator Bankhead was now ready to withdraw Underwood, he wanted the record to stand as it was made on this ballot.

Those who were expecting the find break thought it would come from New York, not from Alabama, because of their knowledge of the close relations between Murphy, Sullivan and Taggart. Sullivan and Taggart had already thrown Illinois and Indiana to Wilson, and it seemed likely that the third of the three musketeers would come next. Murphy, however, still stood out, and it was Bankhead who was destined to put an end to the deadlock and bring about a nomination. Yet so general was the belief that Murphy was to start it that when he arose this time there was a breathless hush over the whole convention, hitherto so noisy, and every eye was fixed on him.

On this, the last real ballot, Wilson received 633, Clark 306, Underwood 97, Foss 27 and Harmon 25. It was commented on as a sinister omen for Clark that for the last two ballots he had been sticking at 306, the number which stood out to the last for Grant in the deadlocked Republican convention of 1880.

#### Underwood Quits the Race.

Chairman James now ordered the forty-sixth ballot, and the clerk was preparing to call the roll when Senator Bankhead appeared on the platform and spoke to Chairman James. The Chairman announced that the Senator wished unanimous consent to make a statement, and his manner as he pleaded for silence and attention indicated that the statement was to be one of the utmost importance. No one had any doubt what it was to be, and the convention listened in eager silence. Senator Bankhead said:

> Mr. Underwood entered this contest hoping that he might secure the nomination from this convention, but I desire to say for him that his first and greatest hope was that through this movement he might be able to eliminate and eradicate for all time every remaining vestige of factional feeling in this country.
>
> Mr. Underwood to-day would willingly, anxiously forego this nomination if he has succeeded and if the country has concluded that the Mason and Dixon line has been tramped out and this is once more a united

Continued on Page 2.

Gov. Woodrow Wilson of New Jersey

Democratic Candidate for the Presidency.

The honor is as great as can come to any man by the nomination of a party, especially in the circumstances, and I hope I appreciate it at its true value, but just at this moment I feel the tremendous responsibility it involves even more than I feel the honor.

I hope with all my heart that the party will never have reason to regret it.—*Gov. Wilson's acceptance.*

**UNPUBLISHED STORY BY DE MAUPASSANT**

Discovered among a pile of old papers, it will be published for the first time in English in NEXT SUNDAY'S TIMES.

## GOV. WILSON NOT ELATED BY VICTORY

Feels the Tremendous Responsibility Even More Than Honor of the Nomination.

### CHEERED BY BAND SERENADE

Whole Town Marches Behind It to the Strains of "Old Nassau" and Congratulates Him.

### MRS. WILSON TELLS A SECRET

Husband Gave Up Hope When Clark Polled a Majority and Formally Released His Delegates.

*Special to The New York Times.*

SEA GIRT, N. J., July 2.—Gov. Woodrow Wilson received word of his impending nomination over the telephone from Baltimore at 2:48 o'clock, went upstairs to notify Mrs. Wilson, and, on coming down again, made this statement:

"The honor is as great as can come to any man by the nomination of a party, especially in the circumstances, and I hope I appreciate it at its true value; but just as this moment I feel the tremendous responsibility it involves even more than I feel the honor. I hope with all my heart that the party will never have reason to regret it."

The word that the nomination had been made brought to an end an even week of tense feeling and suspense that wrecked nerves indiscriminately in Sea Girt, leaving to all appearances only the Governor unmoved and undisturbed.

The news was received in a spirit of solemnity. There were no cheers, no exclamations, no shouts. Even the soldiers on the rifle range near by ceased firing, and it was more than an hour later before the first demonstration commenced. The telegraph lines were clogged within ten minutes after the nomination was announced with more than a thousand personal messages to Gov. Wilson. Four extra telegraphers were sent for, and these, in addition to those already here, hoped to be able to handle the flood of work.

Mrs. Wilson's only sorrow as the break to her husband came was that Georgia, her native State, had not come to her husband's cause earlier in the battle. Gov. Wilson's final smile before he became the candidate was inspired by the switch of Virginia, the State of his birth.

"That is fine," he said, "to feel my own native State coming over for me."

#### Doesn't Know Who Sent the News.

Informal receptions during the afternoon and the reading of personal messages of congratulation occupied the Governor's time until he retired. He found an opportunity, however, to summon to Sea Girt Edward I. Edwards, State Controller, who with the Governor comprises New Jersey's State House Commission. Edwards was in conference with the Governor for thirty minutes. He emerged with eyes bulging, to declare in startled phrases that the Governor had remembered it was the scheduled day for the State House Commission to meet and that the meeting had been held in all its routine details.

"He never once mentioned the Presidency," said the puzzled State Controller.

In the Wilson home when the nomination was announced were seven persons—Gov. Wilson himself, his wife, his three daughters, Miss Hester Hasford, author of a biography of Gov. Wilson, and Miss Mary Hoyt of Baltimore, a cousin of Mrs. Wilson.

Gov. Wilson received the news over the telephone from some one whose identity he did not learn. As he came from his library into the main reception room of his home his face was lighted by a characteristic expression of suppressed solemnity and strain under perfect control. He glanced about for the members of his family. They were nowhere in sight. Under sheer strain of the final minutes they had gone, one at a time, to their rooms upstairs.

Gov. Wilson walked slowly up the stairs, and in a minute came down again with Mrs. Wilson on his arm. There was a suspicious moisture in the Governor's eyes, but Mrs. Wilson, the strain broken, was smiling at the group of reporters, who had planned to do a serpentine dance to the home, but actually came hats in hands and in sober silence. Mrs. Wilson broke the strain for all.

#### Mrs. Wilson Tells of Hope Given Up.

"Isn't it fine?" she said. "I didn't think the hard, pounding battle could win. It is a hopeful thing, a beautiful thing, to see what the people can do when they take the case in their own hands. It renews hope for the people in me. Now I'm going to quit worrying. I never had a moment's fear about the outcome if Woodrow could only get the nomination, but I did fear he'd be defeated in the convention."

Mrs. Wilson was in a confidential mood, and she confided things that the colony of reporters stationed here through all the period of stress had not guessed. She confided that her husband had abandoned

Continued on Page 4.

## Indiana Governor Is Named for Vice President at 1:56 A. M.

### TWO BALLOTS WERE TAKEN

Marshall's Lead Over Gov. Burke Then Brought His Nomination by Acclamation.

### VALEDICTORY BY BRYAN

Nebraskan, in Early Morning Speech, Hands Over the Leadership of the Party.

### NO FIGHT ON PLATFORM

Declaration of Principles Is Read and Adopted Unanimously.

### BIG CROWD AT LAST SESSION

Pennsylvania Delegates Enter Singing a Song of Loyalty to Gov. Wilson.

*Special to The New York Times.*

BALTIMORE, Md., Wednesday, July 3.—Gov. Thomas R. Marshall of Indiana was nominated for Vice President by the Democratic Convention at 1:56 o'clock this morning, and the convention adjourned. The nomination was made by acclamation after two ballots had been taken.

The first ballot was taken at 1 o'clock this morning and resulted in no choice. Gov. Marshall of Indiana received 389 votes; Gov. Burke of North Dakota, 305 2-3; Senator Chamberlain of Oregon, 157; Elmore Hurst of Illinois, 77, and Mayor Preston of Baltimore, 58. Scattering votes were cast for William F. McCombs, Congressman Sulzer, Judge Wade of Iowa, and Osborne of Wyoming.

A sensational incident of the night session occurred when W. J. Bryan was placed in nomination by a delegate from the District of Columbia. This started a demonstration for the Nebraskan. This gave Mr. Bryan an opportunity to deliver his valedictory as leader of the party. He used that exact word in describing it. He was wildly applauded. He said:

#### Bryan's Valedictory.

"Mr. Chairman and members of the convention: You have been so generous with me in the allowance of time that I had not expected to transgress upon your patience again, but the compliment that has been paid me by the gentleman from the District of Columbia justifies, I hope, a word in the form of a valedictory.

"For sixteen years I have been a fighting man. Performing what I regard as a public duty, I have not hesitated to speak out on any public question that was before the people of the Nation for settlement, and I have not hesitated to raise the hostility and the enmity of individuals where I felt it my duty to do so in behalf of my country.

"I have not ever advocated a man except with gladness, and I have never opposed a man except in sadness. If I have any enemies in this country, those who are my enemies had a monopoly of hatred. There is not one single human being for whom I feel a hatred. Nor is there one American citizen in my own party or in any other that I would oppose for anything except that I believed in not opposing him I was surrendering the interests of my country, which I hold above any person.

"I recognise that a man who fights must carry scars, and I decided long before this campaign commenced that I had been in so many battles and had alienated so many that my party ought to have the leadership of some one who had not thus offended and who thus might lead with greater hope of victory.

"And to-night I come with joy to surrender into the hands of the one chosen by this convention a standard which I have carried in three campaigns, and I challenge my enemies to declare that it has ever been lowered in the face of the enemy. The same belief that led me to prefer another for the Presidency rather than to be a candidate myself leads me to prefer another than to be a candidate myself.

"It is not because the Vice Presidency is lower in importance than the Presidency that I decline. There is no office in this nation so low that I would not take it if I could serve my country by accepting it.

"I believe that I can render more service to my country when I have not the embarrassment of a nomination and have not the suspicion of a selfish itnerest, more service than I could be as a candidate, and your candidates will not be more active in this campaign than I shall be. My services are at the command of the party, and I feel a relief now that the burden of leadership is transferred to other shoulders.

"All I ask is that, having given us a platform the most progressive that any party of any size has ever adopted in this Nation, and having given us a candidate who, I believe, will appeal not only to the Democratic vote, but to some three or four millions of Republicans who have been alienated by the policies of their party, there is but one thing left, and that is, to give us a Vice President with our President who is also progressive, so that there will be no joint debate between our candidates.

"I shall, therefore, conclude what I have to say to you, after thanking you for the very generous treatment that I have received at your hands. Let me in conclusion second the nomination, not of one man but of two men, Gov. Burke of North Dakota and Senator Chamberlain of Oregon."

#### Songs Open Night Session.

The convention was somewhat late in reassembling for its night session and it spent its time in cheering for Wilson and singing. The Pennsylvania delegation lustily sang to the air of "John Brown's Body."

Pennsyl, Pennsyl, Pennsylvania.
Pennsyl, Pennsyl, Pennsylvania.
Pennsyl, Pennsyl, Pennsylvania,
Will vote for Wilson, too.

They were presently joined by some women standing on chairs, who were loudly cheered. After about the twentieth time they had sung the stanza they improved it by the refrain: "Every State that's in the Union will vote for Wilson, too." The words were taken up all over the hall and created the greatest enthusiasm.

This and a lot like it lasted for half an hour and stopped only when Chairman James made his appearance at 9:30 o'clock. They promptly gave him three cheers.

When the roll was called for nominations for Vice President, H. H. Dean of Georgia took the platform. He caught the crowd at first by eulogizing Chairman Ollie James. But when he said "a great people demands a great man," some one yelled "Marshall of Indiana." Thereafter Mr. Dean was continually interrupted by shouts of "name him," "who is it?" "spit it out."

Nobody had the faintest idea what he was going to do, or he would have got a better hearing. He electrified the convention when he proposed the unanimous nomination of Champ Clark. It was believed that he was speaking for Clark, for the talk of nominating the Speaker for second place was rather widely spread, but ex-Gov. Dockery of Missouri immediately announced that after consultation with Mr. Clark and others this afternoon the Speaker had decided to decline the honor if it were offered to him.

"Mr. Clark," he said, "prefers his present position as Speaker or a position in the House of Representatives to any other place. But I am here to tell you that Champ Clark and his friends are as loyal to this convention and its nominee as anybody here. While I was with him this afternoon he sent a telegram of congratulation to Gov. Wilson, and I tell you that Champ Clark and Missouri are for Wilson first, last, and all the time."

#### Burke, Hurst, and Marshall.

Delaware yielded to North Dakota, and former Senator W. E. Purcell of that State went to the platform to place in nomination Gov. John Burke of North Dakota. Gov. Burke had asked the delegates of his State who wanted him to run for the Presidential nomination not to present his name, and the delegates voted for Gov. Wilson. Senator Purcell spoke of the record of Gov. Burke, and sai dhe was a simon-pure Progressive. Idaho seconded Gov. Burke's nomination, and State Senator Altscher of Illinois arose to put in nomination for the Vice Presidency Elmore Hurst of Illinois.

Senator Altscher took so long to describe the virtues of his candidate that the convention shouted: "Name him," and then so much confusion ensued that few heard the name of the nominee. Many thought he referred to William R. Hearst, and there was a big laugh. Altscher accomplished one thing, though, that pleased the weary throng. He forced the Chairman to limit the speechmaking to strictly five minutes

Major G. V. Menzies of Indiana put in nomination Gov. Thomas R. Marshall of that State. Marshall's name got a real cheer.

"Indiana makes no demand upon the convention," shouted Major Menzies. "We simply present his name; we will carry the State, no matter who is nominated. We ask you to come over to Macedonia and help us to victory."

Henry Farmer of Iowa, who looks like a boy orator, nominated Judge Martin J. Wade. His speech had to do almost entirely with a funeral, and then Judge Wade himself got up and informed the crowd that he wasn't going to second his own nomination.

"Woodrow Wilson needs by his side a man of Democratic principles," said Judge Wade, and then he mentioned Gov. Burke as the man to be nominated. Louisiana seconded the nomination of Gov. Marshall.

Alonzo L. Miles of Baltimore made a flowery speech, naming Mayor Preston of the convention city and the Baltimoreans in the audience applauded when he spoke of the war record of Maryland. In fact, Mr. Miles said more about Maryland and Baltimore than he did about Mayor Preston.

#### Baltimore and Boston Twisted.

The audience was in a gale of laughter when Mr. Miles told of the manifold virtues of Baltimore, and the speaker had to stop for five minutes. The Baltimoreans hissed the laughter, and ex-Gov. Brewer of Mississippi got up to demand a respectful hearing for Mr. Miles. But Mr. Brewer made the blunder of calling Baltimore Boston.

The audience was again convulsed, and it simply howled when the speaker in trying to compliment Mr. Brewer mispronounced the name of Mississippi. When Mr. Miles mentioned Mayor Preston's name a wave of hisses started, and almost drowned the cheers that followed. Apparently Mayor Preston is not popular with the delegates. Every time the speaker referred to Mr. Preston the hisses increased.

The delegates remembered that the Mayor was responsible for the police force of the city, and consequently of the convention hall. It is remarkable that a convention should hiss the name of the Mayor and the city where a convention is being held, but this is what happened to Mr. Peraton. Mr. Miles finally had to sit down before he had half finished.

The weary delegates then began shouting for the rollcall, but A. Mitchell Palmer, the Wilson floor leader, got a chance to say that it was time to give consideration to the report of the Resolutions Committee, which had the platform read Mr. Palmer wanted to take up the platform immediately and lay over the Vice Presidential nomination until midnight.

#### The Platform Presented.

There was such a violent protest at this that Chairman James made a special plea to the delegates in the interest of party harmony to take up the platform, and the convention agreed.

Chairman Kern of the Resolutions Committee then stepped forward to read the platform. Hundreds of persons who had come to see a Vice President nominated got up and slowly filed ont, creating so much noise that all business was suspended several minutes.

There was so much confusion in the hall that only those within a few feet of Mr. Kern could hear a word he said. There was a rumor that the sudden switch from the Vice Presidential nominations to the

Gov Thomas R. Marshall of Indiana.

Democratic Candidate for the Vice Presidency.

"All the News That's Fit to Print."

# The New York Times.

THE WEATHER.
Cloudy Thursday, followed probably by showers Friday.
For full weather report see Page 16.

VOL. LXI...NO. 19,830. * * * NEW YORK, THURSDAY, AUGUST 8, 1912.—EIGHTEEN PAGES. ONE CENT In Greater New York, Jersey City, and Newark. | Elsewhere, TWO CENTS.

## THOUSANDS HEAR WILSON ACCEPT

### Crowds Make Open-Air Ceremonies the Occasion for a Great Jersey Field Day.

### SOLEMN NOTE; FEW CHEERS

### "There's No Indispensable Man," Says Candidate, and Hearers Greet Slap at the Colonel.

### PICNICKERS ON HIS LAWNS

### Sandwich Men and Popcorn Men on Hand and Hundreds of the Handshakers Have Their Chance.

*Special to The New York Times.*

SEA GIRT, N. J., Aug. 7.—At exactly nineteen minutes after 3 o'clock a point was reached in the notification ceremonies here this afternoon, at which Gov. Woodrow Wilson, standing in a group of nine Democratic Governors, had to pronounce the fateful sentence which was to make him formally the Democratic Presidential nominee. He had already spoken the first eighty-one words of his speech of acceptance, (which is printed in full on Page 6 of THE TIMES,) and after a slight pause he launched, with quick, exclamatory effect, the direct statement: "I accept the nomination."

Gov. Dix, who was standing at Gov. Wilson's left, interrupted the speech of acceptance to launch a cheer. Mrs. C. P. Overfield, a diminutive woman member of the Notification Committee, added a woman's treble to Gov. Dix's bass, and slowly the enthusiasm spread in a ripple out over the heads of the multitude and surged back again to the speaker's stand, a mighty wave of open-air approval.

The cheering that accompanied Gov. Wilson's formal assumption of his duties as a candidate was not of a boisterous kind. Ollie James made the people roar with laughter and shout salvos of approval to his thundering periods as he told Gov. Wilson what the Democrats expected of him. But in all that Gov. Wilson had to say there was a tone of solemnity that the crowd quickly caught. At times, in consequence, it held a tense silence that was far more impressive than would have been the wildest kind of screaming and yelling.

Through the entire speech the most vociferous cheer lasted less than forty seconds. Gov. Wilson time and time again departed from the text to cut in some quiet side thrust in the humorous tone for which he is becoming famous. Once, while speaking of the tariff, he reached down to the realms of near profanity and caught up a word that censors of stage morals sometimes have objected to on the part of actors.

"The tariff," said Gov. Wilson, "is a dam; and you can spell the word," he quickly added, "either way you want to."

The crowd indicated in a series of cheerful comments that it preferred the unphonetic spelling.

Outside of the slight sally at the tariff the crowd liked best what Gov. Wilson had to say about Col. Roosevelt. Of course, he did not mention that candidate by name, but he slashed at him in a sudden verbal sally that left no doubt as to whom he had in mind.

"There is no indispensable man," was the Governor's reference to his opponent.

The crowd let itself out of leash at once, and when its hilarity had subsided Gov. Wilson added:

"The Government will not go to pieces if any one of the people who are seeking to be intrusted with its guidance should be left at home."

That set the people's cheering loose again.

**Some Extemporaneous Remarks.**

Gov. Wilson had been urged by Ollie James not to read his speech, but to memorize it, as he, the notifier, had done. But for all the warning the candidate brought his speech in manuscript form and read it from beginning to end. Sometimes the text became irksome to him and once he stopped reading altogether while he seemed to hesitate as to whether to proceed or to cut loose entirely into an extemporaneous burst.

"Oh, I wish I didn't have to read this," he said, "it would be so much more interesting if I didn't have to."

But Walter Measday, the Governor's Secretary, who was sitting close by, shook his head and Gov. Wilson finally went back to his manuscript. A little later he reached a paragraph describing the manner in which the trusts had been able to get what they wanted from the Government.

"But the next chapter will set us free again," he read from his manuscript, "there will be no tragedy in it. It will be a chapter of readjustment, not of pain and rough disturbance."

That was as far as the manuscript went and it was meant to be reassuring. But a sudden smile came over the candidate's countenance and he caught the crowd with an interpolation—"that is, there will be no pain except for a select few."

Another interpolation which pleased the crowd was put in while Gov. Wilson was outlining the part the judiciary shall play in reforming Governmental methods.

"We must absolutely overcome," he added, to the manuscript, "the shrinking modesty of our courts."

At the conclusion of his speech Gov. Wilson announced that he was going to New York early to-morrow morning. He said he expected to be engaged in New York until Friday evening, and that he had made up his mind not to go to Maine for a speaking tour. While he is in New York he will sit for his portrait in the studio of Seymour Thomas, an artist who had contributed a portrait of the Governor to the campaign fund.

Gov. Marshall of Indiana, Gov. Wilson's running mate, will make four speeches in Maine. The situation in Maine was, in

Continued on Page 2.

## REBELS CUT RAILWAY.

### Communication Between Nicaragua Coast and the Capital Severed.

*Special to The New York Times.*

WASHINGTON, Aug. 7.—The Nicaraguan news was more serious to-day. The rebels have not only cut the telegraph wires to Corinto, but have succeeded in breaking railroad communication between the capital, Managua, and the coast. No fear is felt for the safety of the United States detachment on guard at Managua, although Commander Terhune, who is at Corinto, cannot get in touch with that city.

The report of the fighting between the Diaz forces and the rebels at Rivas yesterday is confirmed, with the intelligence that the rebels were repulsed.

Conditions throughout the country continue to border on the desperate, with many persons starving, and the chances of large additions to the rebel forces increasing from day to day.

To-day the Red Cross ordered the purchase of $1,000 worth of food and medicine at Panama, to be put aboard the collier Justin when she takes on the 230 marines who are to go to the support of the bluejackets at Managua. It is believed that the chances of a general rebellion can be lessened by feeding the starving and guarding the capital and seaports, so that the troops of the Nicaraguan Government can close in on the main force of Gen. Mena.

BLUEFIELDS, Aug. 7.—The United States cruiser Tacoma arrived here today.

Conditions at Bluefields are quiet.

## MOTHER SAVES CHILDREN.

### Throws Them Out of Runaways' Path, but Is Herself Struck Down.

Mrs. Abraham Schatz was walking along East New York Avenue, Brownsville, yesterday afternoon, from the grocery to her home at No. 1,391, when down the street came a runaway team, the driver clinging helpless to the seat of a heavy truck. They were headed straight for a sidewalk crowded with playing children, and among these children Mrs. Schatz say her own little sons Harry and Julius.

There was only a moment to spare, but in that moment the mother sped across the street, seized her boys by the arms, threw them out of harm's way, and then tossed two other children to safety before she was struck by the horses and thrown beneath the truck as the runaways plunged head on into a wall. A policeman jumped from a passing trolley and stunned one of the horses with a blow of his club. Then Mrs. Schatz was lifted out of the wreck and an ambulance called for her, for William Katz of 282 Christopher Street, Brownsville, the driver of the truck, and for little Ida Lederson, one of the children of the neighborhood, who did not escape from the runaways' path.

But Mrs. Schatz insisted upon being taken to her home. There her life is despaired of, for an hour after the accident a baby was born to her. The child was dead.

Neither the driver nor the little Lederson girl was seriously hurt. The team had taken fright at Eastern Parkway and Saratoga Avenue while the truck was being unloaded and Katz was off the seat. He leaped on the truck as the horses started off at full speed, but he was unable to control them, and during the race of half a dozen blocks several collisions were narrowly escaped.

## TRAIN ROBBER NOMINATED.

### "Better Than a Public Yegg," Is Platform of Oklahoma City Candidate.

*Special to The New York Times.*

OKLAHOMA CITY, Okla., Aug. 7.—"A train robber is better than a public yegg" has been the campaign slogan of A. L. Jennings, train robber and member of the famous Dalton gang, who was nominated in to-day's primaries for County Attorney over a half dozen opponents. Jennings declared on the stump that the Dalton gang was a tame affair as compared to the present "Court House gang," who were embezzlers to the amount of $50,000.

"I have stolen more than that amount from trains in this territory," he declared, "and I have ridden away with it tied behind my saddle in a seamless sack, but I was caught at last, and now my greatest desire is to prove that I can be an honest official.

"A train robber who is trying to lead an honest life is far better than a public official who under the guise of respectability and honesty robs the people."

Jennings drew large crowds nightly to hear him narrate his bandit experiences. He was serving a ten-year sentence in the penitentiary for robbing the mails when he was pardoned by President Roosevelt.

## MAY HOLD UP HIS SALARY.

### President May Veto Bill Limiting Civil Service and Abolishing a Court.

WASHINGTON, Aug. 7.—Proposals for limited terms for civil service employes, the abolition of the Commerce Court, and the retention of its five Judges as extra Circuit Court Judges, will be submitted to President Taft as provisions of the Legislative, Executive, and Judicial Appropriation bill.

These proposals, already approved by the House, were adopted by the Senate to-day by a vote of 30 to 19 against the opposition of Senators, Cummins, Crawford, Burton, Lodge, and several others.

Some of President Taft's friends say he will veto the bill, although in doing so he will hold up his own salary, that of every member of Congress, and every United States Judge. Such action on the President's part would also further delay the annual appropriation overdue since July 1. The President opposes the abandonment of life tenure for civil service employes, and also the abolition of the Commerce Court.

The bill carries an appropriation of $34,000,000.

## TELLS OF LOST BROTHER.

### W. C. Russell Says He Intended to Share Estate with Him.

CAMBRIDGE, Mass., Aug. 7.—It was the wish of the late Daniel Russell of Melrose that his son, Daniel Blake Russell, who left home many years ago, should be found, according to the testimony of the other son, William C. Russell of Melrose, at to-day's session of the masters' hearing to determine the identity of the man from Dickinson, N. D., who asserts he is Daniel Blake Russell.

Questioned regarding the man from Fresno, Cal., whom he had taken into his home and recognized as his long lost brother, Mr. Russell said that he never had talked with him regarding the disposition of the Russell estate. He said that it always had been his intention to carry out his father's wishes and to share the estate with his brother if he found him.



## BECKER'S FRIEND IN MURDER CAR

### New Witness Says That Sullivan, After Leaving Lieutenant, Fled in It.

### TWO INSPECTORS ACCUSED

### May Be Indicted with Civilian Employe on Graft Charges—Webber a Collector, Too.

### VILE PLOT, SAYS McINTYRE

### Declares Becker Will Be Acquitted—Hunt Still On in Catskills for Missing Slayers.

District Attorney Whitman has found a reliable witness who is willing to testify that Jacob A. Reich, better known as Jack Sullivan, the friend of Lieut. Becker, the man who rode uptown with him on the morning of the Rosenthal murder, fled with the assassins in Shapiro's gray automobile. The District Attorney expects the Grand Jury to find an indictment against Sullivan for murder in the first degree on the evidence of this witness.

As for Lieut. Becker himself, Mr. Whitman is sincerely of the opinion that Becker did instigate the Rosenthal crime, and testimony corroborative of the confessions of Rose, Webber, and Vallon to that effect is in the possession of the District Attorney. At Mr. Whitman's service in the Becker case are at least ten witnesses whom the prosecution considers reputable and who are in no way involved in the murder plot.

Evidence is piling up so fast in the District Attorney's office that Mr. Whitman and Mr. Moss and Mr. Smith, the two assistants who are helping him to prepare the case, can hardly find time to handle it as it should be handled.

**Indictment of Inspectors Expected.**

Evidence corroborating the confession of Rose as to the collection of graft by the police is also accumulating rapidly, and no surprise will be occasioned in the District Attorney's office if the Grand Jury finds three indictments for this crime within the next few days. Two of the men against whom indictments are expected are Inspectors of Police, and the third is a civilian employe of the department.

"Bridgey" Webber, it is understood, collected graft for one of these Inspectors, and there is every reason to believe that he is ready now to tell the District Attorney the entire story of his relations with this Inspector, one of the best-known in the department and who is in command of one of the most important districts in the city.

The second Inspector is not in command of any district. He does, however, hold a position of great power in the department.

The civilian employe, in the direction of whom much of the damaging testimony in the hands of District Attorney Whitman points, has an office in Police Headquarters and numbers among his close personal friends some influential public officials, who are, however, not in the Police Department.

**Becker's Counsel Talk of a Plot.**

The first authoritative statement from Becker's side of the case was made yesterday by John F. McIntyre, his newly retained leading counsel. It was accepted by many as an indication of the line of defense that Becker will offer when he is placed on trial for his life at the October term of court. Mr. McIntyre stated that his client was the victim of "a diabolical plot," and he added that when Rose, Webber, and Vallon were on the stand he would be able to show this and destroy the force of their so-called confessions.

Mr. McIntyre said he was confident that Becker would be acquitted.

Mr. Whitman, when his attention was called to Mr. McIntyre's statement, said he was glad that a man of Mr. McIntyre's experience and ability had entered the case in behalf of Becker. The District Attorney concedes to Becker the benefit of every reasonable doubt, and if Becker is innocent, he declares, he above all other men wants him so adjudged.

"The evidence against Becker," said Mr. Whitman last night, "fully justified an indictment for murder in the first degree. Becker, however, is entitled to every doubt. He must be proved guilty. Until so proved the public should suspend judgment on him, and I hope they will. No man could be more anxious than I am to see Becker establish his innocence. But I believe that he is guilty."

**Important Witnesses for Grand Jury.**

The District Attorney is carefully guarding the identity of the ten or more persons who are ready to come forward at the proper time to corroborate the confessions of Rose, Webber, and Vallon. Nearly all these witnesses are strangers to the principal actors in the tragedy, and it was only by the hardest kind of work that Mr. Whitman found and persuaded them to tell what they know.

The Grand Jury will be in session today, and will devote its entire attention to hearing witnesses whose testimony is expected to establish beyond possibility of contradiction that the relations existing between Becker and Rose prior to the murder were those described in the graft collector's story to the District Attorney. Some of these witnesses are expected to tell of certain conversations bearing on the present case of murder and graft that took Rose and Becker in their presence; others to offer proof that the telephone conversations referred to by Rose in his confession did, in fact, take place, and still others to testify that the graft money Rose tells about was passed to Becker on many occasions in the presence of themselves.

Several servants, who have at different times been employed by Jack Rose, will be called before the Grand Jury, and these witnesses are expected to testify that not only did they see Rose hand the money collected as graft to Becker, but that they also heard and have remembered the conversations that passed between the graft collector and the Police Lieutenant.

**Mrs. Rose to Testify.**

Mrs. Jack Rose also is to be a witness before the Grand Jury, but she will not

Continued on Page 2.



## AUTO BUS CRASHES INTO ASTOR HOME

### Plunges Into Areaway Under Window of Mrs. Madeleine Astor's Room.

### SHE WATCHES RESCUE WORK

### House Thrown Open to Receive the Eight Victims—Police Out to Handle Big Crowd.

A Fifth Avenue bus running northward became entangled with a department store delivery car at the corner of Sixty-fifth Street about 7 o'clock last night, and, pitching across the sidewalk, plunged into the areaway of the Astor home at 840 Fifth Avenue, directly under the room of Mrs. Madeleine Force Astor. The crash of the big car as it struck the building and the cries of its occupants, more frightened than injured, brought the Astor household to the windows in alarm. The throng which during the last few days has loitered around the house formed the nucleus for a crowd which soon numbered more than a thousand and blocked traffic on the three sides of the house.

Both cars were proceeding northward when the accident happened. At the corner of Sixty-fifth Street is an excavation, where the workmen have ceased operations so as not to disturb Mrs. Astor. In passing this the Central Park bus swerved out into the middle of the roadway just as the department store car tried to pass from behind. The wheels of the latter struck the front axle of the motor bus, throwing it to the right, toward the Astor home. Mathew Mullin, the driver of the bus, was thrown to the floor unconscious, and without control the bus plunged across the sidewalk, through the heavy imported stone balustrade and iron railing, and against the building itself, where it hung in the areaway.

**Six Riders on the Bus.**

Only six persons were on the bus at the time and none inside. These, with the driver and conductor, were tossed about on the floor, but were not thrown off.

Astor servants rushed forth and helped extricate the passengers from the wreckage. Mrs. Astor, who watched the rescue work from her window, ordered that the injured be brought into the house and cared for there. Dr. Edwin B. Cragin, who for the last two days has been in constant attendance, sent down word that unless there had been serious injury he could not leave Mrs. Astor.

In the meantime the victims had been taken from the car and led to the servants' entrance on Sixty-fifth Street, where everything was done for their comfort. All refused to have an ambulance called. Mr. and Mrs. Astarita of 824 Sterling Place, Brooklyn, sent for their family doctor, but before his arrival they had a taxicab called and went away. Both were suffering from shock and slight bruises and cuts.

Miss Attig of 312 East Thirty-third Street sustained slight bruises and a sprained ankle. Jack W. Brown of 315 West Forty-second Street, an actor, formerly of the Little Theatre company, had contusions and cuts on his face and back. Both departed after being attended to in the Astor house for a few minutes. The two other passengers, an elderly couple, who refused to give their names, received some scratches.

**Auto Crash Raises Din.**

At the time when the accident happened there were hundreds of automobiles coming up Fifth Avenue from the downtown business district, and as these piled up in the crowd before the Astor house a hubbub started of cars coming to a halt, starting up again, horns blowing, and men shouting for a clear way. Fearing that the noise might disturb Mrs. Astor, Dr. Cragin telephoned to the police station and six policemen were sent from the East Sixty-seventh Street Station to keep order before the house.

Within half an hour the crowd was cleared away, and all that remained was a score or so of the curious and the big bus hanging over the areaway, with a litter of stone and broken iron lying around.

Dr. Cragin sent down word that he believed that the shock which Mrs. Astor sustained on hearing the crash and cries below her window would have no ill consequences and that his patient was doing nicely.

At the police station, where the drivers of the two cars were taken, Mullin lodged a complaint for reckless driving against Paul Pincus, chauffeur of the store car. Pincus was later arraigned before Magistrate House in the Men's Night Court and was fined $10, which he paid.

## A 1 A. M. WEDDING AT CONEY.

### Young Folk on an Outing Suddenly Decide to Get Married.

Mounted Policeman Edward Cody was on his post in Surf Avenue, Coney Island, at 1 o'clock yesterday morning, when two young men and two young women approached and, after exhibiting a marriage license, asked to be directed to an Alderman or a minister. Cody sent them in a taxicab to the home of the Rev. J. W. Kitsmeyer, pastor of the Lutheran Church of St. Paul, Coney Island, and there a few moments later Mark A. Vance, a newspaper man living at the Elks' Club, New York, and Edna F. Finn of 237 West Sixteenth Street, were married.

The bride told all about it over the telephone last evening. They had obtained the license earlier in the day in New York, with no thought of being married that evening, and with no engagement announced, but on the spur of the moment, when they had gone down to the shore for a Coney Island evening, they decided not to postpone the ceremony, and their friends, John R. Wall and Miss Maynard Roselle of Chicago, were drafted as witnesses. There is to be another ceremony to-day in St. Bernard's Catholic Church in West Fourteenth Street.

## $100,000 TO OUST LORIMER.

### Senate Committee Foots Up Expenses of Second Investigation.

WASHINGTON, Aug. 7.—When the Senate Lorimer Committee met to-day to foot up the expenses of the second investigation into the election of the former junior Illinois Senator, it found more than $100,000 had been spent.

Of that sum each of the attorneys for the committee, John H. Marble and John Healy, received in the neighborhood of $10,000.

Chairman Dillingham is preparing a resolution and a statement of the expenses for presentation to the Senate.

## FOR FREE CANAL TO OUR SHIPPING

### Senate, 44 to 11, Refuses to Strike Out Toll Exemption Clause in Bill.

### CONFINED TO COAST CRAFT

### Question Is Considered Purely Domestic, with No International Aspect.

### ARBITRATION OUTLOOK POOR

### Opposing Senators Vainly Urge That the Terms of the Hay-Pauncefote Treaty Be Respected.

*Special to The New York Times.*

WASHINGTON, Aug. 7.—By a vote of 44 to 11 the Senate at 11:30 o'clock tonight refused to strike from the Panama Canal bill the provision granting free passage through the canal to American ships. The only amendment of importance in this connection adopted by the Senate inserted the word "exclusively," so that the favors granted to American shipping may apply exclusively to the coastwise trade, in which theoretically there is no competition and therefore no discrimination against foreign bottoms.

The overwhelming nature of the vote shows that there is no chance that further debate will change the matter before the bill is finally disposed of. It also raises the far more important question as to whether this country will ever permit the treaty rights involved under the Hay-Pauncefote treaty to be arbitrated. The prevailing opinion is that so many of the Senators insist that the whole subject is purely domestic, involving no international aspects, that they will now assert that even a suggestion of arbitration is an impertinence.

Senators who have fought for the strict observance of the treaty and the equal treatment of American and foreign ships have openly stated on the floor of the Senate that if Congress voted free passage for American ships in the face of the Hay-Pauncefote treaty they would also in the face of an arbitration treaty refuse to arbitrate the question. That has been denied, and the feeling here to-night is that arbitration will never be reached.

The debate on the toll feature of the Panama Canal bill was mostly made up of set speeches by the supporters of free transit for American ships. The one exception was Senator McCumber of North Dakota, who for the third time urged the Senate strictly to observe our treaty obligations. Mr. McCumber, who had gone thoroughly into the subject, answered one of the most important points of his adversaries when he said that if another nation should pay the tolls of its ships through the canal the United States would be justified in considering that that nation had put itself outside the neutrality provisions. What steps would be taken to penalize that nation Mr. McCumber did not say. But it is suggested that an additional toll, something like countervailing duties, provided in the tariff law might be used against the shipping of such a nation. That suggestion seemed to satisfy Mr. Simmons of North Carolina, who from the Democratic side of the chamber had seriously questioned the tenability of any interpretation of the treaty that would bar American shipping from the assistance which their commercial rivals would get from their mother countries.

Speeches against the treaty were made by Mr. Works of California and Mr. Chamberlain of Oregon, with many interruptions from the floor. Their position in general was that the Hay-Pauncefote treaty committed this country to such a bad bargain that we could not be expected to abide by it. The logical conclusion of this question was seriously presented by Mr. Martine of New Jersey, when, to the amusement of the Senate, he shouted huskily:

"The Hay-Pauncefote treaty was the act of diplomatic imbecility. Treaty rights are sacred, but we come now to the still more imperative need for self-preservation. To prevent us from being starved out I want the canal to American ships to be as free as God's air."

Mr. McCumber said that he could easily understand the strong sentiment that had been developed against the treaties when he looked at a map of the United States and saw the number of the senators who came from the coast. It was natural, he said, that their views should be colored by the wishes of their constituents. He predicted that if Congress decided on favors for American shipping the question would never go to The Hague. The same construction of the treaty, he said, which would justify Senators in voting no tolls for American ships would also justify them in voting down a proposal for arbitration.

The defeat of the Burton amendment to strike out the discrimination in favor of American ships was the Senate's answer to the protest of the British Government against the legislation. It was this clause of the bill which led Great Britain to send a formal protest to the State Department.

The Senators who voted in favor of the Burton amendment were Brandegee, Burton, Crane, Fall, Gronna, Lodge, Nelson, Oliver, Penrose, Root, and Wetmore.

Because of the delicacy of the situation Senator Stone asked that the order directing a rollcall on the amendment be vacated and a rising vote taken instead. Objection to this procedure from Senator O'Gorman resulted in the rollcall being taken.

An amendment by Senator Hoke Smith requiring owners of coastwise vessels to keep the United States free from liabilities for damages resulting from their passage through the canal was defeated. So was an amendment by Senator Percy, which provided that vessels owned by Americans but built abroad should be entitled to registration for the coastwise trade.



## CARNEGIE DESIRES TAXES.

### Declares This Country Ought to Get More from Millionaires.

*Special Cable to THE NEW YORK TIMES.*

LONDON, Aug. 7.—Andrew Carnegie, in unveiling a statue of Robert Burns at Montrose, to-day said:

"In one department the motherland is ahead of the dominions and the United States. She has established the law, first proclaimed by Adam Smith, that every subject should contribute to the support of the Government in proportion to the income he enjoys under the protection of the State.

"This just taxation the millionaires of the dominions and the United States have so far escaped, but their day is coming. The hoards of millionaires should be so treated, not as a punishment, but for their good, because it is just, and justice alone insures general contentment."

## HOMER CRANDELL, 2D, KILLED

### Accidental Blow Fatal to Edwin Hawley's Little Grandnephew.

CHATHAM, N. Y., Aug. 7.—Homer Crandell, 2d, the seven-year-old son of Frederick Crandell of New York, the nephew whose marriage incurred the enmity of Edwin Hawley, but who received a large share of the railroad owner's estate, died to-day as the result of being hit accidentally on the head by a stone thrown by his ten-year-old brother Richard. Blood poisoning developed from the wound and the lad's death was very sudden.

On the day of the boy's death the funeral of his grandfather, Homer Crandell of Chatham, was held.

## TEMPLE FOR MILADY'S GARB.

### Fashion Show Folk Plan a Permanent Exhibition Building.

At preliminary meetings of the exhibitors of the fashion show to be held in the New Grand Central Palace beginning on Saturday, it has been decided to form a company to build a permanent structure similar to the Furniture Exchange, for the display of women's garments. The project was taken into consideration by reason of the fact that the manufacture of women's wear ranks as the fifth industry in magnitude in this country. The proposal of a permanent exposition building is said to have met with approval on all sides.

On the opening night of the fashion show Lillian Russell will be a visitor, and on succeeding nights other actresses will be on hand.

## PRIVATE CAR FOR HER DOGS.

### Mrs. Malcolm Whitman, San Francisco Bride, Coming Here with Pets.

*Special to The New York Times.*

OMAHA, Neb., Aug. 7.—Mrs. Malcolm Whitman, formerly Miss Jenny Crocker of San Francisco, will invade New York next week with a carload of dogs. Railroad officials in Omaha to-day were notified that Mrs. Whitman would leave California the latter part of this week with two private cars, one of which she and her maids would occupy. The other private car would be for Mrs. Whitman's dogs.

The officials were instructed to pay all attention to the comfort of the dogs. No orders were received concerning the welfare of Mrs. Whitman or the maids. Just how many dogs may be expected was not mentioned.

Mrs. Whitman was married last month. Her wedding, which cost $60,000, was the most elaborate California has ever known.

## FIGHT WESTERN UNION RELIEF

### Union Orders Telegraphers Not to Vote on Insurance Plan.

President S. J. Konenkamp of the Commercial Telegraphers' Union of America reported last evening that the New York local, at a meeting held during the day, passed a resolution instructing its members to refrain from voting on the insurance proposition of the Western Union Company.

He said that it had also been decided to instruct all the telegraphers not to vote on the plan. The benefit to the employes, he said, would be but 50 cents a month.

## HELD FOR WIFE MURDER.

### Gordon Priest, Farmer, Said to Have Confessed at Watertown.

WATERTOWN, N. Y., Aug. 7.—Gordon Priest, a yong farmer who notified the county authorities early to-day that he had found his wife robbed and murdered in their home near Evans Hills when he returned from driving the cows, was arrested to-night charged with the murder and locked up in the county jail here.

The farmer's wife, who was 32 years old, was slain in her bed. Her head was split open with the blunt end of a hatchet. Beside her body, her year old baby was found unharmed. Although Priest first asserted he was altogether innocent of the crime, and believed that his wife was the victim of a unknown robber, it is alleged by the county officers that Priest has confessed that he himself committed the crime.

A hundred dollars which Priest said had been stolen from his wife was found in the barn where, the officers say, he admitted he had hidden it.

## NO 'ROCKEFELLER' ON BRIDGE

### He Changes Tablet for Irving Memorial He Gave to Village.

*Special to The New York Times.*

TARRYTOWN, N. Y., Aug. 7.—William Rockefeller has ordered that his name be taken off the tablet to be placed on the new Washington Irving memorial bridge which he gave to the local authorities. The new bridge, which is to cost about $15,000, is rapidly nearing completion and arrangements are being made for the opening ceremonies. A local founder has been at work on the tablet and has the mold completed. It is inscribed with the year, Mr. Rockefeller's name as donor, the names of the village officers, the engineer, and contractor.

When Mr. Rockefeller learned what was on the tablet he became indignant and issued orders that his name be taken off. He was told that the work was nearly finished and the cost was $200. He said he did not care, his name must come off, and he would stand all expense. What he wants on the tablet is not yet known, but it is understood that he will have a conference with the authorities to-morrow to settle the matter.

It has been suggested that Mr. Rockefeller did not like the idea of riding over the bridge every day and being [illegible]

## ROOSEVELT NAMED SHOWS EMOTION

### "Of Course, I Accept," He Tells Progressives Who Give Him Third Term Nomination.

### JOHNSON FOR SECOND PLACE

### Dramatic Scene as Candidates Join Delegates in Singing of the Battle Hymn.

### TAKE UP ROLE OF CRUSADERS

### Colonel, Much Affected, and Happy, Plans to Open a Vigorous Campaign.

*Special to The New York Times.*

CHICAGO, Ill., Aug. 7.—Col. Theodore Roosevelt has attained the goal of his ambition. Before the first National Convention of his new party passed into history to-night it handed him on a silver platter the honor that Washington and Jefferson modestly declined and Ulysses S. Grant, though crowned with a hero's laurels, sought in vain. He was nominated as a third-term candidate for President of the United States.

Hiram W. Johnson, the militant and Progressive Governor of California, who was a Republican until the Republican Convention, six weeks ago, refused Col. Roosevelt the coveted glory of a third term, was chosen as his running mate. Both nominations were made by acclamation under a suspension of the convention rules and amid scenes which fluctuated strangely between the solemn and impressive and the merely spectacular and melodramatic.

The closing scenes of the first National Convention of the Progressive Party were unlike the scenes that have marked the closing of any National Convention within the memory of living politicians of any party. Amid an ovation that was as striking and sincere as it was impressive the two candidates were brought out on the platform to face the delegates and to deliver in their hearing, and with crowded galleries looking on, their pledges to fight manfully for the principles and policies of this new party for which it is claimed that it will usher in a new dispensation in politics and in public life. Both nominees, but the Colonel especially, seemed deeply affected as they stood face to face with the men and women who are to shape the destinies of the new party and who had selected them as their standard bearers to do "battle for the Lord."

**Tremor in Colonel's Voice.**

There was a suspicious tremor in the Colonel's voice as he acknowledged the nomination. Nor was it strange that he and his running fate should display such evidence of feeling. Wave upon wave of emotion swept over the audience as men and women joined in singing the stirring patriotic and partly religious airs which the band played. It was more like a Methodist consecration meeting than a political gathering.

It was after the Colonel's platform, embodying the vast scheme for "social and industrial justice," that he has advocated in recent public utterances, had been adopted, and after a dozen men had made nominating and seconding speeches of varying length for Gov. Johnson, that Senator Albert J. Beveridge of Indiana, Permanent Chairman of the convention, declared that Col. Roosevelt and Gov. Johnson had been duly nominated for President and Vice President, respectively.

It was nearly 7 o'clock, and the delegates and spectators had been through a long and wearing day of speeches and routine business, but there was no sign of apathy in the tremendous cheer that broke when it was proclaimed from the platform that the most important business of the convention had been completed and that the hat of the new party was in the ring.

The two nominees at that time were behind the convention scenes waiting for their cue. The two Committees of Notification, made up each of one or more members from every State delegation, had assembled on the rostrum and formed in a semi-circle very much like the chorus in an opera the moment before the hero makes his entry.

Into this semi-circle the Colonel and Gov. Johnson were conducted. Slowly they were led to the little inclosure in front of a sounding board under a brightly gleaming electric lamp. The Colonel was on the right, his running mate on the left. Between stood Chairman Beveridge.

**Mrs. Roosevelt Waves Bandanna.**

The convention stood up and cheered and cheered, but for the first few seconds the Colonel seemed oblivious of what was going on in the hall and in the galleries. He shot a rapid glance toward what in other conventions has been known as "Purple Row." In the first row of seats in that section a woman dressed in black stood up and waved a red bandanna, the favored emblem of the Bull Moosers, in the most frantic fashion. The woman was beaming, and the Colonel's lips parted in a smile as he saw the happy expression on her face. The woman was Mrs. Roosevelt, who for seven years was mistress of the White House and leading lady of the land, but who seemed to thrill with the scene before her as though it had been the Colonel's first experience at being nominated for President.

After a while the Colonel's glance shifted to the audience. Delegates stood on their feet and cheered. The hired band had gone to supper, but there was a volunteer band on the platform. It began to play, but the music was drowned in the thunder of acclaim that rolled up from the hall and down from the galleries where men and women waved flags and bandanas.

"All the News That's Fit to Print"

# The New York Times

THE WEATHER.
Fair Tuesday and Wednesday; moderate west winds.
For full weather report see Page 22.

VOL. LXII...NO. 19,988. NEW YORK, TUESDAY, OCTOBER 15, 1912.—TWENTY-FOUR PAGES. ONE CENT In Greater New York, Jersey City, and Newark. | Elsewhere, TWO CENTS.

# MANIAC IN MILWAUKEE SHOOTS COL. ROOSEVELT; HE IGNORES WOUND, SPEAKS AN HOUR, GOES TO HOSPITAL

## Bullet In Right Breast, Doctors Say Wound Is Not Serious.

## LUNG NOT PENETRATED

### Roosevelt Walks from Hospital Unassisted, and Starts for Chicago.

## MANUSCRIPT WAS A SHIELD

### Assassin's Aim Good, but Papers in the Colonel's Pockets Save Him.

## CALM ON OPERATING TABLE

### Talks Politics with Physicians While Waiting for X-Ray Machine.

## COLONEL CHECKS CROWD

### "Don't Touch Him," He Says, as Rush is Made for His Assailant—Secretary Martin Fells Maniac.

*Special to The New York Times.*

MILWAUKEE, October 14.—Col. Theodore Roosevelt was shot and wounded in the right breast in front of the Hotel Gilpatrick shortly before 8 o'clock to-night. Col. Roosevelt was about to enter his automobile to go to the Auditorium for his evening address, when a man rushed up and fired at close range.

The bullet entered the flesh under the right nipple, but its force was broken by the manuscript of the speech which Col. Roosevelt had prepared for this evening. He at first declared he had not been wounded, but on the way to the hall a hole was noticed in his overcoat and it was found that his shirt was covered with blood. Nevertheless he insisted on delivering his speech, and went on, for fifty minutes, even though his weakness became so apparent that physicians insisted that he should stop.

**Talked Politics at Hospital.**

After his speech he was taken to the Emergency Hospital to have his wound examined.

At 10:30 o'clock Col. Roosevelt was sitting on the operating table talking politics with the physicians while they were awaiting the arrival of an X-ray machine.

Col. Roosevelt left the hospital at 11:25 P. M. He was able to walk unassisted.

"I am feeling fine," he said.

**Surgeons Say Wound Is Slight.**

Col. Roosevelt left at 12:50 A. M. for Chicago. Before he left surgeons who had attended him gave out the following statement:

"Col. Roosevelt is suffering from a superficial flesh wound in the right breast. There is no evidence of injury to the lungs. The bullet is probably somewhere in the chest wall. There is only one wound and no sign of injury to the lung. The bleeding is insignificant. The wound has been sterilized externally with gauze by Dr. R. T. Fayle, the consulting surgeon of the Emergency Hospital. The bullet passed through Col. Roosevelt's army overcoat and other clothing and through a manuscript and spectacle case in his breast pocket, and its force was nearly spent before it penetrated the chest. The appearance of the wound also showed evidence of a much-spent bullet.

"Col. Roosevelt is not suffering from the shock and is in no pain. His condition is so good that surgeons did not object to his continuing his journey to Chicago in his private car. In Chicago he will be placed under surgical care.

"The X-ray photograph has been finished and the Colonel is feeling fine. He is seeing the newspaper men, and presently will go to his car to start for Chicago.

"Dr. F. L. TERRELL,
"Dr. R. G. FAYLE,
"Dr. JOSEPH COLT BLOODGOOD of Johns Hopkins.
"Dr. F. A. STRATTON."

The X-ray of Col. Roosevelt's wound shows that the bullet lodged in the abdominal wall and did not penetrate the lung.

Just as the Roosevelt special train was leaving here a sudden change in plans was made and the engineer was ordered to hold the train.

It was stated that the bullet penetrated three inches of the abdominal wall, and the wound is more serious that at first thought. This was shown by the X-ray photograph which has just been developed.

A special train was to bring from Chicago four surgeons. They are Drs. John B. Murphy, Arthur Bevan, A. R. Ochsner and L. L. McArthur.

It was finally decided at 12:45 that Col. Roosevelt should go on to Chicago, and the train started.

The positive statement that Col. Roosevelt was not injured seriously was made by Dr. Stratton, who said that there was no cause for alarm as to the Colonel's condition.

'The wound was a superficial one," said Dr. Stratton. "The bullet is imbedded in the muscular tissue. All that we did at the hospital was to put on an antiseptic dressing. You may say Col. Roosevelt is not in a dangerous condition. There is no truth in the report that the bullet penetrated the abdominal wall. If the bullet had reached his lungs it would have been evident and he would have had coughing spells."

**How the Shooting Occurred.**

The man who did the shooting said he was John Schrank of 370 East Tenth Street, New York City. Papers found on him showed he had been following Col. Roosevelt for some time, and that he was a crank on the subject of the third term.

As no secret had been made of the plans of Col. Roosevelt, a crowd was in front of the hotel to see him leave for the Auditorium. When he came out a cheer was set up and to it he responded smilingly, raising his hat and bowing. Several persons pushed to the front to see him better or to try to shake his hand, as is usual. There were cries of encouragement from all sides.

No special pains had been taken to protect the Colonel under the circumstances, and the members of his party—Philip Roosevelt, a cousin; Henry F. Cochems, the Bull Moose leader here; Albert H. Martin, one of his secretaries, and Capt. A. O. Girard of this city—were not on guard.

When the party had crossed the sidewalk to the automobile Col. Roosevelt's companions stood aside and let him step in. Mr. Martin entered immediately after him. There was another cheer and Col. Roosevelt faced the crowd and raised his hat, smiling.

A stocky man had been standing at the edge of the sidewalk only a few feet from the Colonel. When he pushed his way forward little attention was paid to him because many admirers of the Colonel have done such things.

COL. THEODORE ROOSEVELT

Col. Roosevelt, in fact, looked benevolently upon him and smiled. The man suddenly produced a pistol and fired point-blank.

**Football Player Fells Man.**

The fellow still had his pistol raised and seemed about to fire again, but here Mr. Martin saved his chief. He had seen the pistol and had leaped forward to shield the Colonel. Too late for that, he jumped just as the shot was fired and landed on the assailant.

Martin, who is six feet tall and a former football player struck squarely on the man's shouders and bore him to the ground. He threw his right arm about the man's neck with a deathlike grip and with his left arm seized the hand that held the pistol. In another second he had disarmed the fellow.

Col. Roosevelt had barely moved when the shot was fired, and stood calmly looking on, as though nothing had happened. Martin picked the man up as though he were a child and carried him the few feet which separated them from the car, almost to the side of the Colonel.

**Roosevelt Averts Lynching.**

"Here he is," said Martin, "look at him Colonel."

All this happened within a few seconds and Col. Roosevelt stood gazing rather curiously at the man who attempted his life before the stunned crowd realized what was going on. Then a howl of rage went up.

"Lynch him! Kill him!" cried a hundred men.

The crowd pressed in on the man and Mr. Martin and Capt. Girard, who had followed Mr. Martin over the side of the automobile, were caught with their prisoner in the midst of a struggling throng of maddened men. It seemed for the moment that he would be torn to pieces, and it was Col. Roosevelt himself who intervened. He raised his hand and motioned to the crowd to fall back.

"Stop, stop!" he cried. "Stand back! Don't hurt him!"

The crowd at first was not disposed to heed his words, but at length fell back and permitted Mr. Martin and Capt. Girard to carry the man into the hotel. After a short struggle he gave up and was taken without resistance out of the reach of the crowd.

"Are you hurt, Colonel?" a hundred voices called out.

"Oh, no!" he responded, with a smile. "Missed me that time; I'm not hurt a bit."

"I think we'd better be going on," he said to the other members of his party, "or we will be late."

**Colonel Learns He Is Wounded.**

No one in the party, including Col. Roosevelt himself, entertained the slightest notion that he had been shot. He felt no shock or pain at the time, and it was assumed that the bullet went wild. As soon as Col. Roosevelt had assured himself that the assassin was safe in the hands of the police he gave orders to drive on to the Auditorium.

The party had driven hardly one of the four blocks from the hotel to the Auditorium when John McGrath, another of Col. Roosevelt's secretaries, uttered a sharp exclamation and pointed to the Colonel's breast.

"Look, Colonel," he said. "There is a hole in your overcoat."

Col. Roosevelt looked down, saw the hole, then unbuttoned the big brown army coat which he was wearing and thrust his hand beneath it. When he withdrew it, his fingers were stained with blood.

He was not at all dismayed.

"It looks as though I had been hit," he said, "but I don't think it is anything serious."

Dr. Scurry Terrell of Dallas, Tex., Col. Roosevelt's physician, who had entered the automobile just before it started, insisted that the Colonel return to the hotel. He would not hear of it, however, and the car was driven on to the Auditorium.

**Speaks Despite Doctors' Protest.**

As soon as they reached the building, Col. Roosevelt was taken into a dressing room and his outer garments were removed. Dr. Terrell, with the help of Dr. John Stratton of Milwaukee and Dr. S. S. Sorenzon of Racine, Wis., who had been in the audience and came to the dressing room on a call from the platform, made a superficial examination of the wound. They agreed that it was impossible to hazard a guess as to the extent of the Colonel's injuries and that he should by all means go at once to a hospital.

"I will deliver this speech or die, one or the other," was Col. Roosevelt's reply.

Despite the protests of his physicians, he strode out of the dressing room and onto the stage.

**Audience Shocked by the News.**

A large crowd packed into the big building, cheered loudly as he entered, and without a word to indicate what had happened went to his seat. For several minutes the crowd, no man of whom suspected that the Colonel bore a bullet in his body, kept up its cheering.

Then Mr. Cochems stepped to the front of the platform and held up his hand. There was something in his manner which had its effect upon the crowd and the cheering died suddenly away.

"I have something to tell you," said Mr. Cochems, "and I hope you will receive the news with calmness."

His voice shook as he spoke and a deathlike stillness settled over the throng.

"Col. Roosevelt has been shot. He is wounded."

**Shows His Blood-stained Shirt.**

He spoke in a low tone, but such was the stillness that every one heard him. A cry of astonishment and horror went up from the crowd, which was thrown into confusion in an instant. Mr. Cochems turned and looked inquiringly at Col. Roosevelt.

"Tell us, are you hurt?"

Men and women shouted wildly. Some of them rose from their seats and rushed forward to look more closely at the Colonel.

Col. Roosevelt arose and walked to the edge of the platform to quiet the crowd. He raised his hand and instantly there was silence.

"It's true," he said. Then slowly he unbuttoned his coat and placed his hand on his breast. Those in the front of the crowd could catch a sight of the blood-stained garment. "I'm going to ask you to be very quiet," said Col. Roosevelt, "and please excuse me from making you a very long speech.

"I'll do the best I can, but you see there is a bullet in my body. But it's nothing. I'm not hurt badly," he went on.

A sigh of relief went up from the crowd, and then an outburst of tumultuous cheering. Thoroughly reassured by the Colonel's action that he was in no serious danger, the people settled back in their seats to hear his speech.

Col. Roosevelt began to speak in a firm voice, somewhat lower than its usual tone, and except that his gestures were less emphatic than usual there was nothing about the man to indicate his condition. After he had been speaking a few minutes, however, his voice sank somewhat and he seemed to stand rather unsteadily.

Dr. Terrell and Col. Cecil Lyon stepped up to him and the doctor insisted that he stop.

"I'm going to finish this speech," said the Colonel, ener-

Continued on Page 2.

## Crank's Reasons for the Shooting in Two Documents.

MILWAUKEE, Oct. 14.—A written proclamation found in the clothing of the man who shot Col. Roosevelt to-night read:

September 15, 1912, 1:30 A. M.—In a dream I saw President McKinley set up in a Monk's attire in whom I recognized Theodore Roosevelt. The President said: "This is my murderer; avenge my death."

September 12, 1912, 1:30 A. M.—While writing a poem some one tapped me on the shoulder and said: "Let not a murderer take the Presidential chair. Avenge my death."

I could plainly see Mr. McKinley's features.

Before the Almighty God, I swear this above writing is nothing but the truth.

Another note found in the man's pocket reads:

So long as Japan could rise to the greatest power of the world despite her surviving a tradition more than 2,000 years old, as General Nogi so nobly demonstrated, it is the duty of the United States of America to uphold the third term tradition. Let every third termer be regarded as a traitor to the American cause. Let it be the right and duty of every citizen to forcibly remove a third termer. Never let a third term party emblem appear on the official ballot.

I am willing to die for my country. God has called me to be his instrument, so help me God.

INNOCENT GUILTY.

Written in German at the end of this note was: "A strong tower is our God."

## Would-be Assassin Is John Schrank, Once Saloonkeeper Here.

## A MANIAC ON THIRD TERM

### Obsessed with Belief That He Was Commissioned to Remove Peril to Nation.

## HAD DREAM OF McKINLEY

### Martyred President, He Says, Told Him That Roosevelt Had Him Slain.

## STARTED ON COLONEL'S TRAIL

### Went South After Buying Revolver and Followed ex-President Closely.

## WAS BAFFLED IN CHICAGO

### Then He Went Early to Milwaukee and Planned Carefully to Make Sure of His Victim.

*Special to The New York Times.*

MILWAUKEE, Wis., Oct. 14.—For a time the man who shot ex-President Roosevelt refused to give his name, but he finally admitted that he was John Schrank of 370 East Tenth Street, New York.

In making a full confession he told of a carefully laid plot to shoot the Colonel, often frustrated, but finally successful. The man talked freely after his first refusal to give his name. He said:

"I formerly ran a saloon at 410 East Tenth Street, between Avenues D and C, New York City. I was born in Erding, Bavaria, two hours out of Munich, the capital. I am 36 years old and came to this country when 9 years old, with my parents. I have been engaged in the saloon business as proprietor and as an employe nearly all my life, until I decided that it was my duty to kill Col. Roosevelt.

"I have been personally acquainted with Roosevelt since the former President was Police Commissioner of New York in 1895. I was first attracted to him as a politician during the convention in Chicago. Then I began to think seriously of him as a menace to his country, when he cried 'Thief' at that convention. I looked upon his plan to start a third party as a danger to the country.

"My knowledge of history, gained through much reading, convinced me that Roosevelt was engaged in a dangerous undertaking. I was convinced that if he was defeated at the Fall election he would again cry 'Thief,' and that his action would plunge the country into a bloody civil war.

**Dreamed McKinley Came to Him.**

"I deemed it my duty, after much consideration of the situation, to put him out of the way. I was living at my home address at the time, but soon after I had a dream in which former President McKinley appeared to me. I was told by McKinley in this dream that it was not Czolgosz who murdered him, but Roosevelt. McKinley, in this dream, told me that his blood was on Roosevelt's hand, and that Roosevelt had killed him so that he might become President.

"I was more deeply impressed by what I read in the newspapers than others, and after having this dream was more convinced than ever that I should free the country from the menace of Roosevelt's ambition.

"On Sept. 21 I removed to the White Hotel at 156 Canal Street, near the Bowery. I did this as my first step in a plan to kill Roosevelt. I went soon afterward to a gun store on Broadway and purchased a revolver.

"I then purchased a ticket to Charleston, S. C., and went to that city by steamer. My first plan was to catch the Roosevelt party in New Orleans, but I found that to be impossible.

**Starts on Colonel's Trail.**

"I accordingly went to Charleston, and upon my arrival there had $300 left. I left a bag at the Hosley House in that city, which contained, besides the box in which the revolver I had purchased, had been packed, a deed to property on Eighty-first Street, in New York, worth $25,000, and my naturalization papers. That bag is there now.

"Not being able to carry out my plan in Charlestown I proceeded to Atlanta, Ga., thence to Chattanooga, Tenn., and from there to Evansville and Indianapolis, Ind., and to Chicago.

"In each one of these cities I tried

"All the News That's Fit to Print."

# The New York Times.

THE WEATHER.
Increasing Cloudiness to-day and probably followed by rain to-night or to-morrow.
For full weather report see Page 22.

VOL. LXII...NO. 20,010. NEW YORK, WEDNESDAY, NOVEMBER 6, 1912—TWENTY-FOUR PAGES. ONE CENT In Greater New York, Jersey City, and Newark. | Elsewhere, TWO CENTS.

# WILSON WINS

## He Gets 409 Electoral Votes; Roosevelt, 107, and Taft, 15.

## 206,000 OVER TAFT IN NEW YORK

### Illinois and Pennsylvania for Roosevelt, but Close—House Democratic By 157—May be Senate, Too—Cannon Beaten

Woodrow Wilson was elected President yesterday and Thomas R. Marshall Vice President by an Electoral majority which challenged comparison with the year in which Horace Greeley was defeated by Grant. Until now that year has always been the standard of comparison for disastrous defeats, but the downfall of the Republican Party this year runs it a close second.

The apparent results at 4 o'clock this morning gave Wilson **409** Electoral votes, Roosevelt **107**, and Taft **15**.

Wilson carried 38 States, Roosevelt 6, and Taft 4.

The Republican Party is wiped off the map. Nearly everywhere Taft ran third, with Roosevelt capturing a large majority of the old Republican vote, and in many States Taft's vote was almost negligible.

New York gave Wilson a plurality over Taft of about 206,000. Wilson's vote in the State was 698,000, Taft's 493,000, and Roosevelt's 419,000.

The Democratic plurality in the House of Representatives will not be less than **157**, and the United States Senate will probably be Democratic also.

The Democrats swept New York, electing Sulzer Governor, with Hedges running second and Straus a poor third.

Throughout the night the most interesting features were the fluctuations in Illinois and Pennsylvania, the returns from which every minute or two put first one candidate and then another in possession of the two States. This morning it is apparently certain that Roosevelt has carried them both.

New Jersey produced a majority of about **50,000** for Wilson over Roosevelt, and the Democrats have apparently gained three Congressmen. The Legislature is overwhelmingly Democratic, insuring the election of a Democrat to succeed Senator Briggs and Democratic Governor to succeed Wilson.

In Idaho, where Senator William E. Borah is running for re-election as a Republican, though a Progressive at heart, the Legislature is badly split.

There is a close race for the Senate in Oregon, with Senator Bourne, who ran independently, utterly out of it.

Maine went for Wilson by probably [illegible] with Roosevelt second. The indications are that Wilson has 47,500, Roosevelt 40,000, and Taft 27,000.

The returns from California, which Roosevelt has been expected to carry, are naturally meagre, owing to the three hours' difference in time to New York, but Wilson has carried San Francisco by 20,000 and the State seems to have gone for Wilson. The reason, of course, is that the Taft Republicans, having no opportunity to vote for candidates of their own under the California law, have voted in a body for Wilson.

Ohio has gone overwhelmingly for Wilson, electing Cox (Dem.) for Governor. President Taft's defeat in his own State was as complete as Col. Roosevelt's in his State.

Massachusetts's not only went for Wilson by a great majority, but for the first time in her history she elected a Democratic State ticket and a Democratic Legislature. This means a Democratic Senator from the Bay State in the place of Winthrop Murray Crane.

One of the features of the election was the heavy vote Roosevelt polled in the South, particularly Alabama and Georgia. At one time it seemed as if Congressman Underwood, the Democratic leader in the House, might be defeated because of the heavy vote for the Bull Moose in his district. The first three counties to be heard from in Georgia reported that Roosevelt had carried them.

Iowa has apparently gone for Roosevelt by between 4,000 and 5,000, despite Gov. Cummins's failure to take any active part in the campaign after Mr. Roosevelt's failure to take his advice about not running a State ticket.

Nebraska, which had been expected to cast an overwhelming majority for the Democrats since Mr. Bryan took an active part in the campaign, did not do so well as had been expected. Wilson has apparently carried the State, but the fight over both the Senatorship and the Governorship is close, and it is possible that Senator Brown, (Rep.,) who was looked upon as a sure loser, may win.

"Uncle Joe" Cannon went down to defeat in the Danville district, and will be missing from the Capitol for the first time since his defeat in 1890, the only other defeat he has ever met with since he began representing that district in the 70's of the last century.

Roosevelt and Taft each carried their home towns handsomely. Oyster Bay went for Roosevelt by a majority of 292, giving him 510, Wilson, 218, and Taft, 67. Gov. Wilson's birthplace, Staunton, Va., gave him 632, Taft, 287, and Roosevelt, 65.

In Vermont Taft won by 924 votes, but Roosevelt is close behind him.

New Hampshire is Democratic. Wilson carried Connecticut by nearly 7,000, and Baldwin was re-elected Governor.

Victor L. Berger, the Socialist Congressman from Milwaukee, is defeated by William H. Stafford, the Republican candidate. His majority was over **2,000**.

In New York City Wilson defeated Roosevelt by 123,000, but Roosevelt had 59,000 more than Taft.

Wilson lost 6,000 votes in Erie because of the double ballot. They have voting machines there, and that many voters pushed the knob for Sulzer, but did not push the knob for Wilson, forgetting that both knobs had to be pushed.



## The Electoral Vote

**Wilson**

| State | Votes |
|---|---|
| Alabama | 12 |
| Arizona | 3 |
| Arkansas | 9 |
| California | 13 |
| Colorado | 6 |
| Connecticut | 7 |
| Delaware | 3 |
| Florida | 6 |
| Georgia | 14 |
| Indiana | 15 |
| Kansas | 10 |
| Kentucky | 13 |
| Louisiana | 10 |
| Maine | 6 |
| Maryland | 8 |
| Massachusetts | 18 |
| Minnesota | 12 |
| Mississippi | 10 |
| Missouri | 18 |
| Montana | 4 |
| Nebraska | 8 |
| Nevada | 3 |
| New Hampshire | 4 |
| New Jersey | 14 |
| New Mexico | 3 |
| New York | 45 |
| North Carolina | 12 |
| North Dakota | 5 |
| Ohio | 24 |
| Oklahoma | 10 |
| Oregon | 5 |
| Rhode Island | 5 |
| South Carolina | 9 |
| Tennessee | 12 |
| Texas | 20 |
| Virginia | 12 |
| West Virginia | 8 |
| Wisconsin | 13 |
| Total | 409 |

**Roosevelt**

| State | Votes |
|---|---|
| Illinois | 29 |
| Iowa | 13 |
| Michigan | 15 |
| Pennsylvania | 38 |
| South Dakota | 5 |
| Washington | 7 |
| Total | 107 |

**Taft**

| State | Votes |
|---|---|
| Idaho | 4 |
| Utah | 4 |
| Vermont | 4 |
| Wyoming | 3 |
| Total | 15 |

Total number of votes in Electoral College, 531; necessary to a choice, 266.

### NEBRASKA.

NEBRASKA.—Voted for Presidential Electors, Congressmen, Governor, and State officers and a Legislature to choose a successor to United States Senator Brown, (Rep.,) and a Constitutional amendment. Vote in 1908: Democratic, 131,099; Republican, 126,997.

OMAHA, Nov. 5.—Returns from Omaha and Lincoln and scattered precincts over the State show a clear plurality for Gov. Wilson. Should the remainder of the State show the same results the New Jersey Governor will have the electoral vote by a safe plurality.

William J. Bryan to-night sent the following telegram to Gov. Wilson:

"I most heartily congratulate you and the country upon your election. Your splendid campaign has borne fruit in a great victory. I am sure your administration will prove a blessing to the Nation and a source of strength to our party."

Normal precinct, where William J. Bryan voted, gave Wilson 77; Roosevelt, 47; Taft, 26. This precinct, which is just outside Lincoln, in 1908 gave Bryan 111; Taft, 52.

# CITY VOTE

## Wilson Takes New York by 122,777 Plurality.

## SULZER BY 110,529

### All Minor Democratic Candidates In on the Party Tide—Roosevelt and Straus Second.

Woodrow Wilson carried New York City by a plurality of **122,777** over Theodore Roosevelt, and beat President Taft by **182,262** votes.

With complete returns in from all but eighteen election districts the totals of the city vote for President were: Wilson, **309,202**; Roosevelt, **186,425**, and Taft, **126,940**. Manhattan and the Bronx gave Wilson **164,211** votes, against **96,929** for Roosevelt and **61,577** for the President.

The city voted for William Sulzer for Governor by a plurality of **110,529** over Oscar S. Straus, who ran second. The vote, with 97 election districts missing, was: Sulzer, **287,980**, Straus **105,775**, Hedges **177,451**.

The county ticket, the judiciary ticket, the Congressional and Legislative tickets followed the Presidential and Gubernatorial; all the Democratic candidates, according to the early returns, being victors by substantial margins.

New York County will send a solid Democratic delegation to support President Wilson in the next Congress. In Kings County Calder is apparently the only Republican Congressman who will save his seat. Ex-Controller Herman Metz is one of the new Democratic Congressmen.

In the First Congressional, Col. Roosevelt's own district, which is partly in Queens and partly in Nassau, Lathrop Brown, Democrat, has a strong lead over W. Bourke Cockran, the Bull Moose nominee, and is likely to be elected.

In the judiciary contests the Democratic nominees for Supreme Court in Manhattan, Donnelly and Whittaker, each polled more votes than were cast for the Republican and Bull Moose candidates together.

Returns from the Senate and Assembly contests were extremely scant at midnight, but the indications are that the Democratic hold upon both houses of the Legislature has been greatly strengthened.

In fact from end to end of the city it was a clean Democratic sweep.

Apparently the Bronx voted "Yes" on the constitutional amendment to create a new county for the borough. With nineteen election districts out of 205 missing the vote on the amendment was: Ayes, **33,532**; noes, **23,607**; majority for the amendment was **9,925**.

**Wilson to the People.**

A great cause has triumphed. Every Democrat, every true progressive of whatever alliance, must now lend his full force and enthusiasm to the fulfillment of the people's hopes, the establishment of the people's rights, so that justice and progress may go hand in hand.

—*First statement of President-elect Wilson in a telegram to Chairman McCombs.*

### MICHIGAN.

MICHIGAN.—Voted for Presidential Electors, Congressmen, Governor, and State officers, and a Legislature to choose a successor to United States Senator Smith, (Rep.) Vote in 1908: Democratic, 175,771; Republican, 335,580.

DETROIT, Mich., Nov. 5.—Col. Roosevelt appears to have carried the State by 30,000. Gov. Wilson ran second and President Taft third.

The State was divided between the three Presidential candidates. The upper peninsula was apparently Taft's, but Roosevelt was strong in the lower peninsula.

In 350 out 2,048 precincts outside of Detroit the vote was: Roosevelt, 47,136; Wilson, 40,502, and Taft, 30,273.

The vote for Governor in 221 precincts was Ferris, (Dem.,) 18,085; Musselman, (Rep.,) 15,711, and Watkins, (Prog.,) 15,380.

Roosevelt's best vote was in Grand Rapids, where the early returns gave him a clear majority. In Detroit, with 8,000 ballots counted, Taft had a lead of 750. The total vote will exceed 600,000.

Woodbridge N. Ferris, Democratic candidate for Governor, is running ahead of Wilson everywhere, and the Democratic State Committee claims his election.

The vote on woman suffrage apparently is close. In Detroit it is a few votes behind. In Grand Rapids it was turned down by a two to one vote, but in other up-State towns it has a majority. The suffragists have claimed that if they made even a fair showing in Detroit the farmers would pull them through.

Congressman Doremus, Democrat, in the First (or Detroit) District, in all probability has been re-elected, being within 200 votes of Beechler, the Republican candidate, in precincts which two years ago gave Debs a plurality of 2,000.

The Legislature probably will be Republican, and will re-elect United States Senator William Alden Smith.

### NORTH DAKOTA.

NORTH DAKOTA.—Voted for Presidential Electors, Congressmen, Governor, and State officers. Vote in 1908: Democratic, 32,885; Republican, 57,680.

GRAND FORKS, N. D., Nov. 5.—With the returns at hand at 11:45 o'clock to-night the indications were that Gov. Wilson had carried North Dakota, but by what majority it was at that time impossible to estimate. Taft and Roosevelt ran close together, but far behind Wilson.

Indications were that the Republican State ticket, headed by Congressman L. B. Hanna for Governor, had won.

### SOUTH DAKOTA.

SOUTH DAKOTA.—Voted for Presidential Electors, Congressmen, Governor, and State officers, and a Legislature to elect a successor to United States Senator Gamble, (Rep.) Vote in 1908: Democratic, 40,266; Republican, 67,536.

YANKTON, S. D., Nov. 6.—With fully half the precincts missing and many counties yet to hear from, the returns from South Dakota at 1 o'clock this morning indicate that Roosevelt has carried the State by not less than 5,000.

### MINNESOTA.

MINNESOTA.—Voted for Presidential Electors, Congressmen, Governor, and State officers, and a Legislature to choose a successor to United States Senator Nelson, (Rep.) Vote in 1908: Democratic, 109,401; Republican, 195,843.

*Special to The New York Times.*

ST. PAUL, Minn., Nov. 5.—It looked at 11:30 P. M. as if Wilson had won in Minnesota. Returns from 105 precincts out of 3,963 in Minnesota gave Taft, 6,350; Wilson, 9,176; Roosevelt, 8,188.

Gov. Eberhardt, Republican, up for re-election, was leading the State ticket.

# SULZER, TOO

## Elected Governor of New York by 215,000 Over Hedges.

## STRAUS SECOND IN THE CITY

### Sulzer's Lead in Greater New York About 110,000—Hedges Beaten Only 21,000 Up the State.

William Sulzer, Democrat, was elected Governor of New York by an estimated plurality of **215,000** over Job E. Hedges, Republican.

Hedges ran a close second up the State, where he was beaten by only about **21,000**.

In Greater New York Oscar S. Straus, Progressive, ran second to Sulzer, who defeated him by **110,000**.

The total vote in the entire State was:

Sulzer, **664,488**.
Hedges, **448,918**.
Straus, **380,899**.

In the city the vote was:

Sulzer, **287,980**.
Hedges, **105,775**.
Straus, **117,451**.

Above the Bronx the vote was:

Sulzer, **358,000**.
Hedges, **337,000**.
Straus, **201,000**.

Buffalo gave Sulzer **29,326**, Hedges **16,979**, Straus **20,801**.

Rochester gave Sulzer **14,887**, Hedges **14,626**, Straus **12,092**.

Both branches of the Legislature will be Democratic by splendid majorities. Only half a dozen Progressives were elected to the law-making body. Schenectady replaced its present Socialist member in the lower house with a Democrat.

In the City of Schenectady the Socialists polled a heavy vote, their candidate, Russell, receiving **1,500** votes more than Straus, and nearly as many as Hedges. The vote was: Sulzer **4,760**, Hedges **3,944**, Straus **2,199**, Russell **3,641**.

In Auburn Sulzer beat Hedges out by **2,552** to **2,497**, Straus receiving **1,050**.

Troy gave Sulzer **8,561**, Hedges **6,061**, and Straus **2,328**.

Of the up State counties Sulzer carried Columbia, Erie, Greene, Rensselaer, Seneca, Suffolk, Sullivan, Tompkins, Ulster, Westchester.

### CALIFORNIA.

CALIFORNIA.—Voted for Presidential Electors and Congressmen and on three proposed Constitutional amendments. Vote in 1908: Democratic, 127,492; Republican, 214,398.

*Special to The New York Times.*

SAN FRANCISCO, Nov. 5.—"Wilson by 20,000," says Chairman Davis. Scattering returns from forty precincts in this city give Wilson 2,507, Roosevelt, 1,829. This means a plurality of 15,000 in the city. Roosevelt will come from the South with a lead of 25,000, but a heavy Wilson vote in the interior valleys will probably be enough to break it down.

### STATE VOTE FOR PRESIDENT.

| County. | WILSON Dem. | TAFT Rep. | ROOSEVELT Prog. |
|---|---|---|---|
| Albany | 19,300 | 15,400 | [illegible] |
| Allegany | 3,200 | 4,000 | [illegible] |
| Broome | 6,681 | 8,313 | 2,560 |
| Cattaraugus | 6,500 | 6,000 | 4,400 |
| Cayuga | 6,800 | 6,700 | [illegible] |
| Chautauqua | 4,000 | 10,000 | [illegible] |
| Chemung | 7,200 | 4,000 | [illegible] |
| Chenango | 4,100 | 4,800 | 1,700 |
| Clinton | 3,267 | 3,827 | 1,187 |
| Columbia | 5,598 | 4,820 | [illegible] |
| Cortland | 2,560 | 3,800 | [illegible] |
| Delaware | 5,746 | 5,702 | 2,444 |
| Dutchess | 9,600 | 10,000 | [illegible] |
| Erie | 40,000 | 25,000 | [illegible] |
| Essex | 1,740 | 3,020 | [illegible] |
| Franklin | 3,790 | 4,700 | [illegible] |
| Fulton | 2,550 | 3,762 | 2,167 |
| Genesee | 2,484 | 3,238 | 2,019 |
| Greene | 3,104 | 2,242 | 700 |
| Hamilton | 600 | 400 | 200 |
| Herkimer | 6,400 | 5,300 | [illegible] |
| Jefferson | 7,100 | 8,400 | [illegible] |
| Kings | 108,199 | 50,590 | [illegible] |
| Lewis | 2,500 | 2,100 | [illegible] |
| Livingston | 3,600 | 4,300 | [illegible] |
| Madison | 3,600 | 4,000 | [illegible] |
| Monroe | 18,211 | 16,902 | [illegible] |
| Montgomery | 5,200 | 6,100 | [illegible] |
| Nassau | 6,800 | 4,500 | [illegible] |
| New York | 161,220 | 60,627 | [illegible] |
| Niagara | 8,600 | 7,000 | [illegible] |
| Oneida | 14,600 | 18,100 | [illegible] |
| Onondaga | 19,000 | 18,000 | [illegible] |
| Ontario | 5,500 | 5,625 | [illegible] |
| Orange | 9,000 | 11,500 | [illegible] |
| Orleans | 3,100 | 3,800 | [illegible] |
| Oswego | 5,800 | 7,600 | [illegible] |
| Otsego | 6,600 | 6,300 | [illegible] |
| Putnam | 1,256 | 1,428 | 547 |
| Queens | 27,421 | 9,282 | 14,519 |
| Rensselaer | 14,500 | 11,500 | [illegible] |
| Richmond | 8,448 | 8,083 | 3,741 |
| Rockland | 4,233 | 2,096 | 2,319 |
| St. Lawrence | 5,900 | 9,600 | [illegible] |
| Saratoga | 6,500 | 6,000 | [illegible] |
| Schenectady | 5,572 | 5,430 | 2,718 |
| Schoharie | 3,800 | 2,200 | [illegible] |
| Schuyler | 1,700 | 1,500 | [illegible] |
| Seneca | 2,482 | 2,235 | [illegible] |
| Steuben | 8,880 | 7,594 | [illegible] |
| Suffolk | 7,000 | 5,100 | [illegible] |
| Sullivan | 4,600 | 4,300 | [illegible] |
| Tioga | 2,600 | 3,200 | [illegible] |
| Tompkins | 3,204 | 2,112 | [illegible] |
| Ulster | 9,940 | 8,075 | [illegible] |
| Warren | 3,000 | 2,800 | 2,000 |
| Washington | 3,900 | 5,400 | [illegible] |
| Wayne | 4,142 | 4,938 | [illegible] |
| Wyoming | 2,900 | 3,100 | 2,200 |
| Westchester | 22,600 | 15,730 | 11,700 |
| Yates | 1,518 | 2,028 | 795 |
| Total | 681,299 | 474,716 | 389,149 |

Plurality for Wilson, 206,533.

### STATE VOTE FOR GOVERNOR.

| County. | SULZER Dem. | HEDGES Rep. | STRAUS Prog. |
|---|---|---|---|
| Albany | 1,900 | 21,500 | [illegible] |
| Allegany | 2,175 | 2,835 | 1,918 |
| Broome | 5,741 | 7,201 | 1,889 |
| Cattaraugus | 6,500 | 6,000 | 4,400 |
| Cayuga | 4,873 | 6,249 | 2,475 |
| Chautauqua | 4,823 | 8,088 | [illegible] |
| Chemung | 7,300 | 4,130 | 3,200 |
| Chenango | 3,193 | 4,239 | 1,365 |
| Clinton | 3,276 | 3,827 | 1,187 |
| Columbia | 5,600 | 5,010 | 1,425 |
| Cortland | 2,200 | 3,150 | 2,200 |
| Delaware | 5,746 | 5,702 | 2,444 |
| Dutchess | 9,550 | 10,030 | 1,820 |
| Erie | 37,041 | 22,473 | 25,303 |
| Essex | 1,830 | 3,100 | [illegible] |
| Franklin | 2,780 | 4,025 | 1,410 |
| Fulton | 2,550 | 3,762 | 2,167 |
| Genesee | 2,484 | 3,238 | 2,019 |
| Greene | 3,623 | 2,850 | [illegible] |
| Hamilton | 600 | 400 | 200 |
| Herkimer | 8,400 | 7,172 | [illegible] |
| Jefferson | 5,412 | 3,668 | [illegible] |
| Kings | 101,720 | 48,004 | 62,851 |
| Lewis | 2,276 | 1,990 | 1,206 |
| Livingston | 3,600 | 4,300 | 2,100 |
| Madison | 3,221 | 3,231 | [illegible] |
| Monroe | 18,716 | 18,801 | [illegible] |
| Montgomery | 5,200 | 6,100 | [illegible] |
| Nassau | 6,404 | 4,172 | [illegible] |
| New York | 149,728 | 46,187 | [illegible] |
| Niagara | 8,600 | 7,000 | [illegible] |
| Oneida | 14,600 | 18,100 | [illegible] |
| Onondaga | 19,000 | 18,000 | [illegible] |
| Ontario | 5,500 | 5,000 | [illegible] |
| Orange | 10,390 | 11,400 | [illegible] |
| Orleans | 2,412 | [illegible] | [illegible] |
| Oswego | 2,627 | [illegible] | [illegible] |
| Otsego | 6,600 | 6,800 | [illegible] |
| Putnam | 1,350 | 1,400 | [illegible] |
| Queens | 22,871 | 6,937 | [illegible] |
| Rensselaer | 11,676 | 9,280 | [illegible] |
| Richmond | 7,016 | 2,599 | [illegible] |
| Rockland | 4,238 | 2,096 | [illegible] |
| St. Lawrence | 5,900 | 9,000 | [illegible] |
| Saratoga | 6,500 | 5,000 | [illegible] |
| Schenectady | 5,572 | 5,430 | 2,718 |
| Schoharie | 3,800 | 2,200 | [illegible] |
| Schuyler | 1,210 | 1,200 | [illegible] |
| Seneca | 2,490 | 2,810 | [illegible] |
| Steuben | 8,880 | 2,900 | [illegible] |
| Suffolk | 7,586 | 5,275 | [illegible] |
| Sullivan | 4,550 | 4,450 | [illegible] |
| Tioga | 1,531 | 1,761 | [illegible] |
| Tompkins | 2,300 | 2,180 | 3,100 |
| Ulster | 11,278 | 9,197 | [illegible] |
| Warren | 3,800 | 4,200 | [illegible] |
| Washington | 3,211 | 4,250 | [illegible] |
| Wayne | 4,142 | 4,939 | [illegible] |
| Wyoming | 1,616 | 2,890 | 1,647 |
| Westchester | 23,350 | 16,800 | [illegible] |
| Yates | 1,518 | 2,028 | [illegible] |
| Total | 664,468 | 448,570 | [illegible] |

Plurality for Sulzer, 215,918.

### KANSAS.

KANSAS.—Voted for Presidential Electors, Congressmen, Governor, and State officers, and a Legislature to choose a United States Senator. Preference vote for United States Senator. Vote in 1908: Democratic, 161,209; Republican, 197,216.

TOPEKA, Kan., Nov. 5.—Thirty-three scattered precincts in Kansas of 2,300 give Wilson a lead over Roosevelt of 563. On the basis of these returns Wilson will carry the State by from 35,000 to 40,000 over Roosevelt.

Indications are that Taft will have a total of 70,000 votes in the State. Judge Thompson (Dem.) has certainly defeated Gov. Stubb (Bull Moose) for Senator.

The estimated Thompson majority will be 40,000.

The Democrats claim the election of Congressmen in the Second, Fourth, Fifth, Sixth, and Seventh Districts.

Wilson's lead indicates the election of the Democratic State ticket by from 15,000 to 20,000.

Returns received indicate that woman suffrage has carried by a small majority.



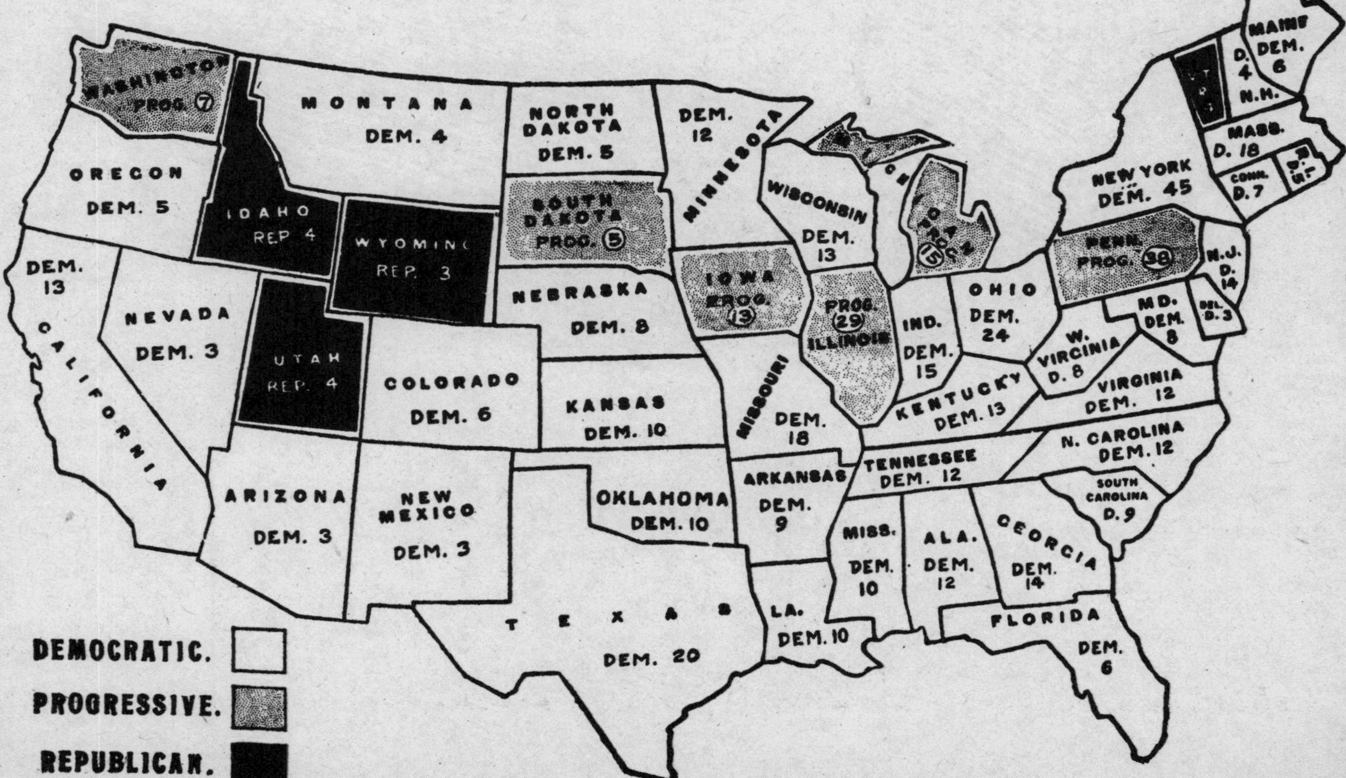

WOODROW WILSON

"All the News That's Fit to Print."

# The New York Times.

THE WEATHER.
Weather: Fair, very cold today and tonight. Chance of snow tomorrow.
Temp. range: today 24-14; Sunday 33-26. Full U.S. report on Page 30.

VOL. LXII...NO. 20,129. NEW YORK, WEDNESDAY, MARCH 5, 1913.—TWENTY-EIGHT PAGES. ONE CENT In Greater New York, Jersey City and Newark. | Elsewhere, TWO CENTS.

# WILSON SWORN IN AS PRESIDENT; PLEDGES HIMSELF TO JUSTICE; BIGGEST INAUGURAL THRONG

## DUAL SUBWAY NOW ADOPTED

### [illegible]rman McCall Accepts Willcox [illegible]—Objections Only from Maltbie and Cram.

### [illegible]ENDMENTS VOTED DOWN

### [illegible]boro and B. R. T. Contracts Passed on to the Board of Estimate for Approval.

### [illegible]LIC HEARING COMES NEXT

### [illegible] That the Signatures—Elevated Third-Tracking Certificate Held Back for the Present.

[illegible] Public Service Commission [illegible] yesterday all the contracts necessary [illegible] establishing the dual subway [illegible], with the exception of the certificate [illegible] the Interborough for third tracking [illegible] elevated lines. Chairman McCall [illegible] out for the contracts as prepared under his predecessor, William R. Willcox, with practically no alterations. [illegible] opposition came from Commissioners Maltbie and Cram, who were [illegible] down repeatedly with the aid of Commissioners Eustis and Williams. The [illegible] to transmit the contracts and certificates to the Board of Estimate was [illegible] by a vote of 3 to 2.

[illegible] agreements were immediately sent [illegible] to the City Hall and were received [illegible] the clerk of the Board of Estimate. [illegible] will be put on the calendar for consideration by the board at its regular [illegible] to-morrow. A day will then be [illegible] for a public hearing, probably at the beginning of next week, and there is no doubt that after this formality has been completed the board will give its approval.

Unless some entirely unforeseen legal obstacle is again thrown in the way, it is believed that Edward E. McCall, Chairman, and Travis H. Whitney, Secretary of the Public Service Commission, will execute the agreements with the companies before the end of next week, and that the bargain, which has been formed after five years of negotiation, by which the city will lay out a comprehensive scheme of rapid transit to meet all its future developments, will be finally completed.

**Manhattan Directors Conciliatory.**

Only the arrangements for the third tracking of the elevated lines in Manhattan and the Bronx remain as a possible cause of trouble. The certificate which was first made out to the Manhattan Railway Company, as the owner of the road, has now been transferred to the Interborough, as the lessee, and is likely, after a public hearing on March 15, to be adopted by the commission. After that its speedy passage through the Board of Estimate is assured.

The Manhattan Railway Co. held a meeting of its directors yesterday with George J. Gould, who is now in Florida, and Alfred Skitt, the vice-president, absent. No definite action was taken, but at its close Edward T. Jeffrey, who presided, said that some of the directors wished to be informed of the provisions of the Interborough's lease and had asked to have several points explained. This was done and the meeting adjourned subject to the call of the chair.

"The company" said Mr. Jeffrey, "has no desire to interfere with the development of rapid transit, but the contractual relations between the Interborough and the Manhattan companies must be determined on a fair and equitable basis. Only such a determination will stand the test of time."

The meeting of the Public Service Commission at which the contracts were adopted was entirely lacking in the spectacular features which have characterized so many of the public hearings upon them. It was held in the large hearing room of the commission on the third floor of the Tribune Building; but a number of the spectators were connected with the commission and had assembled to see an important step taken after years of deliberation. There was no demonstration.

**MALTBIE'S AMENDMENTS.**

Commissioners Maltbie and Cram had reduced their objections to writing and read them as each document came up for action, but there were no long speeches.

So soon as the proposed subway contract with the New York Municipal Railway Corporation, that is the B. R. T., was taken up Commissioner Maltbie handed this up:

I move that the proposed subway contract with the New York Municipal Railway Corporation be amended as follows:

1. That the fixed preferential allowed the company be reduced from $3,500,000 to $3,200,000 to more nearly correspond with the present earnings of the Brooklyn elevated lines.
2. That the preferential allowed to the company for new capital be limited to the interest actually paid and to amortization charges actually needed, instead of 6 per cent., which is unnecessarily high.
3. That the allowance for amortization on the cost of reconstruction of the existing railroads for initial operation be stricken out, inasmuch as the existing railroads are to remain the property of the company after the expiration of the contract.
4. That the allowance for interest on money provided prior to the commencement of construction be stricken out, and provision be made for the supply of money by the company in accordance with quarterly estimates by the commission.
5. That the provision permitting the capitalization of replacements be eliminated.
6. That the profit paid in case of recapture be limited to 5 per cent. instead of 15 per cent. in the case of initial capital and 7½ per cent. in the case of additions.
7. That clauses be inserted providing for the sale of the company's bonds to the public through competitive public bidding as in the case of municipal bonds.

**Cram's Objections.**

Commissioner Cram then entered his protest against what he termed the bargain of the city with the traction trust. His objections were thus written:

When the Public Service Commission decided against municipal operation of the mu-

Continued on Page 9.

## THE COLONEL, TOO, ON PAGE 1

### Third-Term Futurist Consults Third-Dimension Oracles on Inaugural Day.

Just at noon yesterday, when President Taft, retiring, was turning over the reins of the National Government to the incoming President, Mr. Wilson, in Washington, Col. Roosevelt took the time to view the collection of paintings of the Futurists at the Sixty-ninth Regiment Armory, Lexington Avenue and Twenty-fifth Street. It will be remembered that up to a few months ago Col. Roosevelt had expected to spend yesterday in Washington.

Other visitors suggested that perhaps something in the word "futurist" appealed to the Colonel at the fateful hour of midday, March 4. He wandered about the improvised gallery and seemed to take the greatest delight in trying to solve the hidden meanings of the cubic paintings he found there. Secretary Walt Kuhn of the Association of American Painters and Sculptors, which is giving the exhibition, spied the Colonel pondering deeply before one painting, which has been described as resembling a Bull Moose argument put into concrete form, and asked:

"Have you seen anything like this before, Mr. Roosevelt?"

"The only things I have seen that resembled some of these pictures," replied the Colonel, "were certain animals in Africa."

Col. Roosevelt, accompanied by William B. Howland of The Outlook, also visited the Lower Rents Exhibit, at Sixteenth Street and Union Square in the afternoon.

Col. Roosevelt said he was tremendously impressed with the exhibit, and believed that the question of halving the tax rate on buildings in New York City should be submitted to a referendum vote, as provided in the Salant-Schaap bill. He urged that every one in the city should visit the exhibit, and said that if they should do so there would be little doubt that a referendum on this proposal would carry.

The Colonel showed great interest in the cartoons and placards. He expressed surprise that the yearly rent for a three-room apartment, such as is one of the features, was about twice as much as the cost of a complete outfit of furnishings.

## McCOMBS FOR PARIS EMBASSY

### Said to Have Accepted Wilson's Offer—Other Likely Ambassadors.

WASHINGTON, March 4.—With the names of the new Cabinet known beyond doubt, interest turned to-night toward President Wilson's next appointments.

The Diplomatic Service will receive Mr. Wilson's first attention. The President has not yet decided upon an Ambassador to Great Britain, but for other European posts, it was stated to-night on reliable authority, Thomas Nelson Page, William F. McCombs, and Henry [illegible], and Frederic [illegible] of New York were practically certain to be chosen. Definite information is lacking as to which posts they will occupy.

Mr. McCombs will be sent to France if he desires that post, though he said today he had not made up his mind whether his proposed trip abroad on account of his health would be burdened with official duties.

Members of President Wilson's party asserted that he had definitely accepted the post at Paris. He will succeed Myron T. Herrick.

Augustus Thomas, Col. Thomas H. Birch of New Jersey, and Charles R. Crane of Chicago, it was also learned, are being considered for the foreign service.

It was said to-night that Louis D. Brandeis of Boston, who had repeatedly been mentioned as a Cabinet possibility, would be offered, and probably accept, the post of Solicitor-General. According to the story, Mr. Brandeis was to have been appointed Secretary of Commerce, but withdrew his name before the slate was finally completed.

Joseph Davies, Democratic National Committeeman from Wisconsin, it is understood, has the option of refusing the Ambassadorship to Italy, Mr. Wilson having offered him that post.

## IMPERATOR TO SAIL MAY 24.

### Kaiser May Be on Great Liner on Trial Trip to Mediterranean.

Special Cable to THE NEW YORK TIMES.

BERLIN, March 4.—The maiden voyage to New York of the Hamburg-American liner Imperator is now definitely fixed to begin on May 24.

The Kaiser has notified Herr Ballin, Chairman of the line, that he is desirous, if his arrangements permit, of taking part in the trial trip of the vessel, which may take place in the first half of May and extend to the Mediterranean.

The Imperator's sister ship will be launched at the dockyard of Blohm & Voss, at Hamburg, on April 3.

It is now understood here that the delay in the Imperator's maiden transatlantic voyage is due to the time required for the lengthening of the Hoboken dock, which work, it is expected, will be completed by the middle of May.

## RAID WIDOW AND CHILDREN.

### Police and Dwyer Find No Gambling in Yesterday's Hunt.

Acting on a report that there was gambling going on in an apartment on the sixth floor of the fashionable La Rochelle Apartments at 57 West Seventy-fifth Street, Inspector Dwyer and half a dozen detectives from the West Sixty-eighth Street Station made a raid late yesterday afternoon. They pushed aside the boy at the door and before Supt. Battle could be called made their way upstairs. The apartment they entered was occupied by a widow and her children, who became hysterical when they saw the police. No gambling apparatus was found, and the detectives withdrew.

At the station Inspector Dwyer afterward admitted that there had been no arrests, and that no gambling paraphernalia was taken. Supt. Battle said the police had made a mistake. Dwyer and his men, he said, smashed in a glass door in their excitement. He refused to give the name of the woman who occupied the apartment. She was a widow, he said, and lived there with her children.

"I suppose," he said, "that the Inspector received some report which was untrue. There isn't any gambling in this house. We know every one who is living here and wouldn't allow it."



**Inauguration Pictures.**

Two pages of photographs of yesterday's scenes in Washington will be found on Pages 6 and 7 of this issue of The Times.

**Special Half-Tone Section**

A special half-tone section, on fine paper, devoted entirely to pictures of Mr. Wilson's inauguration, will be published with The Sunday Times of next Sunday in addition to the usual Pictorial and the Fashion Sections.

To be sure of getting this pictorial history of a great National event, put in an advance order for

THE SUNDAY TIMES

## POLICEMAN SAVES DR. WEBB FROM FIRE

### Finds Old Financier Asleep in Blazing Fifth Avenue Home and Carries Him Out.

### FORCES HIS WAY INTO HOUSE

### "Was Just Concluding Cops Wasn't Worth 20 Cents the Barrel," Says Policeman.

While Traffic Policeman Emil Spies was attending to the stream of automobiles at Fifth Avenue and Fifty-third Street late yesterday afternoon he caught sight of smoke and fire issuing from the second story windows of the residence of Dr. W. Seward Webb at 680 Fifth Avenue.

The traffic policeman let the traffic tend to itself and ran north past the new St. Thomas's Church blowing his police whistle as he ran. There was no response to the door bell at Dr. Webb's home, so the policeman rapped on the plate glass of the door with his police whistle. This brought a sleepy butler to the door who, opening it very slightly, demanded to know what was wanted.

Spies merely brushed the butler aside, walked to the foot of a staircase leading upstairs and shouted "Fire!" at the top of his voice.

"Is there any one upstairs?" demanded the policeman.

"Yes," the butler answered, "but there isn't any fire except in the fireplaces, and Dr. Webb doesn't like to be disturbed. He's sleeping, Sir, by the doctor's orders."

The policeman made for the second floor landing. The first door he opened he closed again as quickly as he could for it opened into a room filled with burning walnut dressing tables and bed and a large Turkish rug.

Trying another door the policeman found a man well advanced in life sound asleep in bed. He did not stop to wake the sleeper. He went to the bed, gathered him up in his arms and made for the staircase. By this time the hallway was filling with smoke. The butler, who had come upstairs after the policeman, seized Dr. Webb's clothes and started downstairs after the policeman.

Dr. Webb, who is chiefly known as a financier who had much to do with the building of the Boston & Albany Railroad and is the owner of a magnificent country home, Shelburne Farms, at Shelburne, Vt., insisted, when halfway down the stairs, that he could walk, that he was not ill, and that he had only dropped off to sleep while resting through the afternoon as a doctor he had called at 9 o'clock in the morning had suggested.

**Plate Glass Hits Pavement.**

The traffic policeman put him down after the zone of smoke had been cleared and the butler dressed him in his street clothes. Between the policeman and the butler, each one holding an arm, Dr. Webb then walked out into the street. Plate glass was falling over the sidewalk, and women and men, participating in the 1 o'clock parade, stepped out into the roadway to avoid being hit.

A passing citizen to whom the traffic policeman had waved as he entered the house had turned in an alarm and the fire engines were already approaching. Dr. Webb was put into the automobile of a friend who drove up to the curb and was driven to the home of his son, Watson Webb, at 753 Fifth Avenue. The automobile carrying him got away from the burning residence just before the first fire engine put in its appearance, and he was thus spared the sight of seeing fire hose play over expensive paintings and hand-carved mahogany furniture, while a red glow that told of the burning up of rich tapestries flashed out of the windows.

Mrs. Webb, who was Lila Osgood Vanderbilt, a daughter of William H. Vanderbilt, had gone out for an automobile drive just before the fire was discovered, and she did not return until after the firemen had extinguished the flames, which were confined to the second floor, and had drenched most of the remaining rooms of the house.

While the fire was at its height spectators gathered at the windows of the residence of John D. Rockefeller, which adjoins the Webb residence on the west; the residence of Hamilton McK. Twombly, next to it on the north, and the residences of Samuel Untermyer, Cornelius Vanderbilt, C. H. Harkness, and William Rockefeller on the east side of Fifth Avenue, facing the Webb residence.

Mrs. Twombly was Florence A. Vanderbilt, a sister of Mrs. Webb. She was not at home when her sister's rooms were being burned out.

The cause of the fire, so far as could be learned by Battalion Chief Duffy, who responded to the fire call with three engine companies, was a large log fire left blazing in an open fireplace in Mrs. Webb's bedroom when she went out to drive. Both Mr. and Mrs. Webb, it was explained, were very fond of open fireplaces, and admired those in the residence of William H. Vanderbilt before they were married.

**Big Fireplaces Built.**

After the wedding Mr. Vanderbilt decided to build the residence at 680 Fifth Avenue as a gift for Mrs. Webb. He made large open fireplaces one of its features, and they have ever since been used in place of a furnace to heat the house.

Never before was it considered that the fireplaces were a source of any particular danger. Once one of them caught on fire in the chimney and the Fire Department had to be called to extinguish the

Continued on Page 9.

### Sun Bursting Through Clouds Brings Bright Omen to Nation's New Leader.

### CROWD THRILLED BY APPEAL

### "So Shall I Keep Thy Law," Part of the Psalm He Kissed as He Was Sworn In.

### TAFT SHARES IN THE OVATION

### Party Spirit Lost in Joint Acclamation of Winner and Loser by Democratic Hosts.

### IMPRESSIVE SENATE SCENE

### Vice President Marshall Sworn in While His Chief and Members of New Cabinet Look On.

### 40,000 IN THE GREAT PARADE

### Strains of "Old Nassau" at White House Summon Wilson to Join—Brilliant Night Spectacle.

Greeting of Wilson and Taft.

The Retiring President Welcoming His Successor in Office.

*Special to The New York Times.*

WASHINGTON, March 4.—The retiring President of the United States, ending sixteen years of Republican rule, passed the Government over to his successor, representing a new era of Democratic rule, at 1:10 o'clock this afternoon.

Then Woodrow Wilson took the oath of office at the hands of a Confederate soldier, Chief Justice White of the Supreme Court, and with President Taft was driven back to the White House for luncheon. Afterward the retired Chief Magistrate, in an automobile, driven by the same chauffeur who took him to the White House four years ago, went to the railroad station to take a train for Augusta, Ga.

President Wilson went out to the reviewing stand in front of the White House, where he saw pass before him the longest parade in the history of inaugurations. It was 40,000 strong, and whereas the usual inaugural parade ends at 4 or 5 in the afternoon, this one was marching long after dark and did not finish passing the reviewing stand until 7:15 o'clock, though it started soon after 3 o'clock.

The largest crowd ever seen at an inauguration watched the change of government from Republican to Democratic hands. It is estimated that there are more than 300,000 people in town, and that more than 100,000 of them were massed in front of the Capitol when the President delivered his short inaugural address.

Those who heard him deliver it were rapt and attentive, applauded oftener than is the case with most inaugurals, and applauded most frequently at his references to the necessity of obtaining social justice. The greatest applause came for the paragraph in which he said:

"This is not a day of triumph; it is a day of dedication. Here muster not the forces of party, but the forces of humanity. Men's hearts wait upon us; men's lives hang in the balance; men's hopes call upon us to say what we will do.

"Who shall live up to the great trust? Who dares fail to try?

"I summon all honest men, all patriotic, all forward-looking men, to my side. God helping me, I will not fail them, if they will but counsel and sustain me."

**Scene Dignified and Brilliant.**

Thomas R. Marshall of Indiana took the vacant place left by the late James S. Sherman as Vice President half an hour before Mr. Wilson succeeded Mr. Taft.

The scene both in the Senate and on the Capitol front bore its usual dignity and its usual brilliancy, the dignity being that of the solemn and impressive ceremony, so different from the oftentimes helter-skelter character of the inauguration of the President out in the open air before a peanut-chewing crowd—though on this occasion that feature was for some reason happily absent—and the brilliancy, furnished by the great array of the eminent of all nations and the beauty of the women's gowns.

Mr. Wilson's luck in weather stood by him, and though the day began under cloudy skies the sun came out before the inauguration reached its climax. It was a delightful day, warm, but not too warm, with a pleasant little breeze blowing. All things considered, nobody ever took the oath under better omens.

It was a Princeton inauguration, with the Princeton men in evidence everywhere, and no more unusual scene has ever been witnessed than when the incoming President, in conference at the White House with the outgoing President, heard his guard of a thousand students singing "Old Nassau" on the west drive and came out of the White House with bared head to join in the singing.

When Mr. Wilson went to call on President Taft, he passed from the Shoreham Hotel to the White House between a double line of college boys, some from Princeton and some from the University of Virginia, where he first studied.

**Generous Cheers for Taft.**

Mr. Taft took him down to the Capitol, and the two were applauded all the way. The applause was as much for Mr. Taft as for Mr. Wilson, and later, as Taft was going to the station in his automobile and passed through the crowd assembled to witness the inaugural parade in honor of his successor, they cheered him wildly.

It is doubtful if such generous and impartial good feeling has ever been manifested on an inauguration occasion as was shown to-day. It must be remembered that most of those who formed that crowd were Democrats, who had come to Washington to exult over their party being restored to power. The prevailing sentiment seemed to be that Mr. Taft was a "good loser," and some of the crowd shouted that phrase.

Mr. Taft and Mr. Wilson went into the Senate Chamber together, accompanied by the members of Congress, the foreign diplomats, and the Supreme Court, and watched the swearing in of Vice President Marshall. Then all in the Senate Chamber, headed by the Supreme Court, went out on the east front of the Capitol, where Chief Justice White administered the oath.

When Mr. Wilson swore to uphold and defend the Constitution, he stooped and kissed the opened Bible, held in the hands of James B. Maher, Deputy Clerk of the Supreme Court. His lips touched the page, turned to at random, and fell upon the 119th Psalm, verses 43 and 48 inclusive. The verses, beginning with the Forty-first, read:

**Psalms That He Kissed.**

Let Thy mercies come also unto me, O Lord, even Thy salvation according to Thy word.

So shall I have wherewith to answer him that reproacheth me; for I trust in Thy word.

And take not the word of truth utterly out of my mouth; for I have hoped in Thy judgments.

So shall I keep Thy law continually forever and ever.

And I will walk at liberty; for I seek Thy precepts.

I will speak of Thy testimonies also before kings, and will not be ashamed.

And I will delight myself in Thy commandments, which I have loved.

My hands also will I lift up unto Thy commandments, which I have loved; and I will meditate in Thy statutes.

This ended the ceremony, and Mr. Wilson, now become the twenty-seventh President of the United States, (if Grover Cleveland's two terms be considered as virtually one,) left with Vice President Marshall for the reviewing stand.

The parade is generally conceded the best that was ever held at an inauguration. The perfect weather was matched by the marching, and there was not a mishap. Gov. Sulzer, at the head of the New York troops, was warmly received all along the line, especially in front of the reviewing stand, and he took off his soft hat and bowed every few seconds in recognition of the applause.

After reviewing the parade, President Wilson rested for an hour and dressed for the dinner at a near-by hotel given him by the class of '79 of Princeton, of which he is a member. His family saw the fireworks from the rear of the White House.

On the streets to-night the crowds flowed back and forth in strong currents. The brilliantly lighted thoroughfares presented a carnival-like appearance, and the merriment and jubilation of the visiting throng continued until a late hour.

**Coming Cabinet in Senate Seats.**

Mr. Wilson made another of his innovations at the inaugural ceremonies by requesting that seats be reserved in the Senate Chamber for the members of his coming Cabinet. They sat there, with Vice Chancellor Garrison of New Jersey, who is to be Secretary of War, at their head, and Mr. Bryan next to him, in the most informal manner. Mr. Bryan was later taken into the little stand from which the President delivered his speech, Mr. Bryan sitting beside Mr. Taft, who defeated him four years ago. It is evident that Mr. Wilson is going to be a very unconventional President. Certainly this action of his was unprecedented.

Among those who are to be in Mr. Wilson's new Cabinet is [illegible] William B. [illegible]

## PRESIDENT WILSON'S EPIGRAMS.

The great Government we loved has too often been made use of for private and selfish purposes, and those who used it had forgotten the people.

The evil has come with the good, and much fine gold has been corroded. With riches has come inexcusable waste.

Our duty is to cleanse, to reconsider, to restore, to correct the evil without impairing the good.

We were very heedless and in a hurry to be great.

Our work is a work of restoration.

We have studied, as perhaps no other nation has, the most effective means of production, but we have not studied cost or economy.

This is no sentimental duty. The firm basis of government is justice, not pity.

These are some of the things we ought to do, and not leave the others undone, the old-fashioned, never-to-be-neglected, fundamental safeguarding of property and of individual right.

We shall restore, not destroy. We shall deal with our economic system as it is and as it may be modified, not as it might be if we had a clean sheet of paper to write upon.

We know our task to be no more task of politics, but a task which shall search us through and through.

This is not a day of triumph; it is a day of dedication.

"All the News That's Fit to Print."

# The New York Times.

THE WEATHER
Thunder Showers Sunday; Monday partly cloudy; moderate winds, mostly south.
For full weather report see Page 21.

VOL. LXV...NO. 21,809. NEW YORK, SUNDAY, MAY 28, 1916.—98 PAGES, In Seven Parts, Including Picture and Rotogravure Section and Review of Books. PRICE FIVE CENTS.

# AMERICA READY TO JOIN A PEACE LEAGUE, SAYS WILSON, AFTER EUROPE HAS ENDED THE WAR AS ITS INTERESTS DEMAND

## SUGGESTS NO PEACE TERMS

### But Insists Settlement Concerns Us as Much as Belligerents.

### SETS FORTH BIG PRINCIPLES

### United Nations Should Maintain the Integrity of All States, Great and Small.

### RULE BY FORCE SHOULD END

### America's Sole Desire, He Tells Peace League, Is to See That Justice Is Done to All.

*Special to The New York Times.*

WASHINGTON, May 27.—The United States must be reckoned with in the settlement of the great European war and the United States is willing to join a league of nations to maintain the freedom of the seas, protect small States from aggression, and stop wars begun in violation of treaties or begun without giving the world an opportunity to pass upon the causes.

That, in substance, is the program of American action, outlined tonight by President Wilson in the most important speech he has delivered since the beginning of hostilities in Europe. The occasion for this utterance was the banquet of the League to Enforce Peace which has been holding a two days' session here under the Presidency of William H. Taft, former President of the United States. Although President Wilson said at the beginning of his remarks that it would not be expected that he should discuss the program of the league, he showed, before he concluded, that he was in sympathy with the league's cardinal principle which its name suggests.

The President led up to his enunciation of policy by telling what he conceived to be the fundamental things in which the American people believed. These were:

First, that every people has a right to choose the sovereignty under which they shall live.

Second, that the small States of the world have a right to enjoy the same respect for their sovereignty and for their territorial integrity that great and powerful nations expect and insist upon.

Third, that the world has a right to be free from every disturbance of its peace that has its origin in aggression and disregard for the rights of people and nations.

"So sincerely do we believe these things," the President went on, "that I am sure that I speak the mind and wish of the people of America when I say that the United States is willing to become a partner in any feasible association of nations formed in order to realize these objects and make them secure against violation."

A minute later he made a statement that suggested that the time would be ripe for forming the proposed league of nations when the present war was ended. It was at this period of his remarks that the President made his most important utterance, saying:

"If it should ever be our privilege to suggest or initiate a movement for peace among the nations at war, I am sure that the people of the United States would wish their Government to move along these lines:

"First—Such a settlement with regard to their own immediate interests as the belligerents may agree upon. We have nothing material of any kind to ask for ourselves, and are quite aware that we are in no sense or degree parties to the present quarrel. Our interest is only in peace and its future guarantees.

"Second—A universal association of nations to maintain the inviolate security of the highway of the seas for the common and unhindered use of the nations of the world, and to prevent any war begun either contrary to treaty covenants or without warning and full submission of the causes to the opinion of the world—a virtual guarantee of territorial integrity and political independence."

Apparently the President, in making these important utterances, had in mind the invasion of Belgium and the German methods of submarine warfare, which nearly involved that nation in hostilities with the United States. Under the plan suggested the nations associated in the international league would step in to protect a small State like Belgium from the aggression of a great power which was bound by treaty pledges to respect its neutrality.

There were many at the banquet who expected the President to indicate that he was about to take the initiative in behalf of the United States toward bringing the European belligerents together to discuss peace. But the President did not go that far. At the conclusion of his address, however, he expressed confidence [illegible]

## Text of the President's Speech Discussing Peace and Our Part in a Future League to Prevent War

*Special to The New York Times.*

WASHINGTON, May 27.—Following is the text of the President's speech tonight at the banquet of the League to Enforce Peace:

When the invitation to be here tonight came to me, I was glad to accept it, not because it offered me an opportunity to discuss the program of the league, (that you will, I am sure, not expect of me,) but because the desire of the whole world now turns eagerly, more and more eagerly, toward the hope of peace, and there is just reason why we should take our part in counsel upon this great theme. It is right that I, as spokesman of our Government, should attempt to give expression to what I believe to be the thought and purpose of the people of the United States in this vital matter.

This great war that broke so suddenly upon the world two years ago, and which has swept within its flame so great a part of the civilized world, has affected us very profoundly, and we are not only at liberty, it is perhaps our duty, to speak very frankly of it and of the great interests of civilization which it affects.

With its causes and its objects we are not concerned. The obscure fountains from which its stupendous flood has burst forth we are not interested to search for or explore. But so great a flood, spread far and wide to every quarter of the globe, has of necessity engulfed many a fair province of right that lies very near to us. Our own rights as a nation, the liberties, the privileges, and the property of our people have been profoundly affected.

We are not mere disconnected lookers-on. The longer the war lasts the more deeply do we become concerned that it should be brought to an end and the world be permitted to resume its normal life and course again. And when it does come to an end, we shall be as much concerned as the nations at war to see peace assume an aspect of permanence, give promise of days from which the anxiety of uncertainty shall be lifted, bring some assurance that peace and war shall always hereafter be reckoned part of the common interest of mankind.

We are participants, whether we would or not, in the life of the world. The interests of all nations are our own also. We are partners with the rest. What affects mankind is inevitably our affair as well as the affair of the nations of Europe and of Asia.

One observation on the causes of the present war we are at liberty to make, and to make it may throw some light forward upon the future, as well as backward upon the past. It is plain that this war could have come only as it did, suddenly and out of secret counsels, without warning to the world, without discussion, without any of the deliberate movements of counsel with which it would seem natural to approach so stupendous a contest. It is probable that if it had been foreseen just what would happen, just what alliances would be formed, just what forces arrayed against one another, those who brought the great contest on would have been glad to substitute conference for force.

If we ourselves had been afforded some opportunity to apprise the belligerents of the attitude which it would be our duty to take, of the policies and practices against which we would feel bound to use all our moral and economic strength, and in certain circumstances even our physical strength also, our own contribution to the counsel, which might have averted the struggle, would have been considered worth weighing and regarding.

And the lesson, which the shock of being taken by surprise in a matter so deeply vital to all the nations of the world has made poignantly clear, is that the peace of the world must henceforth depend upon a new and more wholesome diplomacy. Only when the great nations of the world have reached some sort of agreement as to what they hold to be fundamental to their common interest, and as to some feasible method of acting in concert when any nation or group of nations seeks to disturb those fundamental things, can we feel that civilization is at last in a way of justifying its existence and claiming to be finally established. It is clear that nations must in the future be governed by the same high code of honor that we demand of individuals.

We must, indeed, in the very same breath with which we avow this conviction admit that we have ourselves upon occasion in the past been offenders against the law of diplomacy, which we thus forecast; but our conviction is not the less clear, but rather the more clear, on that account.

If this war has accomplished nothing else for the benefit of the world, it has at least disclosed a great moral necessity and set forward the thinking of the statesmen of the world by a whole age. Repeated utterances of the leading statesmen of most of the great nations now engaged in war have made it plain that their thought has come to this: That the principle of public right must henceforth take precedence over the individual interests of particular nations and that the nations of the world must in some way band themselves together to see that that right prevails as against any sort of selfish aggression; that henceforth alliance must not be set up against alliance, understanding against understanding, but that there must be a common agreement for a common object, and that at the heart of that common object must lie the inviolable rights of peoples and of mankind.

The nations of the world have become each other's neighbors. It is to their interest that they should understand each other. In order that they may understand each other it is imperative that they should agree to cooperate in a common cause and that they should so act that the guiding principle of that common cause shall be even-handed and impartial justice.

This is undoubtedly the thought of America. This is what we ourselves will say when there comes proper occasion to say it. In the dealings of nations with one another arbitrary force must be rejected and we must move forward to the thought of the modern world, the thought of which peace is the very atmosphere. That thought constitutes a chief part of the passionate conviction of America.

We believe these fundamental things:

First, that every people has a right to choose the sovereignty under which they shall live. Like other nations, we have ourselves no doubt once and again offended against that principle when for a little while controlled by selfish passion, as our franker historians have been honorable enough to admit; but it has become more and more our rule of life and action.

Second, that the small States of the world have a right to enjoy the same respect for their sovereignty and for their territorial integrity that great and powerful nations expect and insist upon.

And, third, that the world has a right to be free from every disturbance of its peace that has its origin in aggression and disregard of the rights of peoples and nations.

So sincerely do we believe in these things that I am sure that I speak the mind and wish of the people of America when I say that the United States is willing to become a partner in any feasible association of nations formed in order to realize these objects and make them secure against violation.

There is nothing that the United States wants for itself that any other nation has. We are willing, on the contrary, to limit ourselves along with them to a prescribed course of duty and respect for the rights of others, which will check any selfish passion of our own, as it will check any aggressive impulse of theirs.

If it should ever be our privilege to suggest or initiate a movement for peace among the nations now at war, I am sure that the people of the United States would wish their Government to move along these lines:

First—Such a settlement with regard to their own immediate interests as the belligerents may agree upon. We have nothing material of any kind to ask for ourselves, and are quite aware that we are in no sense or degree parties to the present quarrel. Our interest is only in peace and its future guarantees.

Second—A universal association of the nations to maintain the inviolate security of the highway of the seas for the common and unhindered use of all the nations of the world, and to prevent any war, begun either contrary to treaty covenants or without warning, and full submission of the causes to the opinion of the world—a virtual guarantee of territorial integrity and political independence.

But I did not come here, let me repeat, to discuss a program. I came only to avow a creed and give expression to the confidence I feel that the world is even now upon the eve of a great consummation, when some common force will be brought into existence which shall safeguard right as the first and most fundamental interest of all peoples and all Governments, when coercion shall be summoned not to the service of political ambition or selfish hostility, but to the service of a common order, a common justice, and a common peace.

God grant that the dawn of that day of frank dealing and of settled peace, concord, and co-operation may be near at hand!

# DR. WAITE, GUILTY, ACCEPTS VERDICT AS IF GRATEFUL

### Stands Smiling Before Jurors as One Upon Whom an Honor Is About to be Conferred.

### WHISTLES ON WAY TO CELL

### Surprised It Took More Than an Hour to Decide—Maintains Appetite and Amazing Nerve.

### MRS. HORTON SORRY FOR ALL

### Attorney Deuel Says Prisoner Had a Fair Trial—Death Sentence to be Pronounced on June 1.

Dr. Arthur Warren Waite was found guilty of murder in the first degree yesterday afternoon for killing his wealthy father-in-law, John E. Peck, at the close of the swiftest trial of a sensational murder case in New York County in years.

The jury returned its verdict at 2:46 P. M. on the sixth day of the trial after deliberation of one hour and twenty-five minutes. This period was spent in discussing the case, and the verdict was declared on the first ballot.

Waite stood up at the direction of Clerk Penny, who has been the master of ceremonies at most of the important murder trials for nearly two generations, and faced the twelve men with a deferential inclination of his head and a pleasantly expectant expression on his face, as if some honor were about to be conferred upon him. The jurymen stared back at him with faces severely set. When Clerk Penny asked for the verdict Foreman Robert Neill said in a voice little above a whisper:

"Guilty as charged."

The condemned man's self-possession did not depart for an instant. His wife, whose father and mother were killed by Waite, heard the verdict from a chair where she sat with her relatives, between the jury box and the Justice's bench, and gave a slight exclamation. Her brother, Percy Peck, sat apart from the other members of the family, a few feet to the left of the defendant, in the seat which he had occupied since the first day of the trial, and gazed at the murderer with a slight gleam of satisfaction in his eyes. It was the moment that the son of Waite's two victims had been waiting for. At the beginning of the trial Percy Peck had said to one of the Assistant District Attorneys:

"I have one favor to ask, and that is that I can have a seat through every minute of the trial near that man so that I can see the last gleam of hope gradually fade from his face."

**Waite Gives Pedigree.**

Waite's father and two brothers bowed their heads at the verdict, although it had been fully expected by them, as by all others in the courtroom.

The jury was polled at the request of Walter Rogers Deuel, attorney for the defendant, and each man confirmed the verdict.

Waite raised a hand slightly to take an oath administered by Acting Police Captain Cavanaugh, and calmly answered the questions of Clerk Penny. He said he was 29 years old, was born in Michigan, had lived at 435 Riverside Drive, was a dentist, was married, was a Protestant, that both parents were living, that he was temperate in his habits, and that he had never been convicted of an offense before. Justice Shearn ordered that he should be remanded until June 1 for sentence.

"This is a relief," Waite exclaimed to the Deputy Sheriff who left the courtroom with him. He walked with a light step past the spectators, and began to whistle and then to hum a tune when he was alone with the Deputy Sheriff on the way through the Criminal Courts Building and across the Bridge of Sighs to the Tombs.

Waite had expected that the jurors would find him guilty with briefer deliberation than took place. When the jury retired, after the charge of Justice Shearn, Clerk Penny told the Deputy Sheriff in charge to be ready to return with his prisoner on short notice.

"Yes," said Waite. "They will be out about fifteen minutes."

The prisoner, who is usually a hearty eater, was so confident of his estimate of the time it would take to convict him that he postponed his usual midday meal and took a luncheon of coffee and cake. After the verdict he went to his cell with a good appetite and ordered a substantial dinner.

**Only Becker Had Such Nerve.**

Head Keeper Julius Bremel of the Tombs, who has had charge of most of the notable criminals in this city in recent years, said that the only man convicted of murder in his recollection who had shown nerve equal to Waite's was Charles Becker.

"Harry Thaw bore no comparison to him," he said. "Neither of the four gunmen had anything like the nerve this man has. Charles Becker was about the same. Becker and Waite are the only two men I have seen in their situation who possessed perfect self-control."

Waite refused to be seen in his cell, and sent this reply to a note:

"I have nothing to say at this time. A little later I might write down my impressions."

Mrs. Waite, her brother and other members of the family left the building without making any statement, after they had remained to express their thanks to members of the District Attorney's staff. Mrs. Margaret Horton, Waite's former companion and fellow-student, who had been forced to become one of the deadliest witnesses

Continued on Page 6.

# J. J. HILL UNDER KNIFE; CONDITION IS SERIOUS

### Veteran Railway Builder Suffers from Infection—Son Leaves Here for West.

*Special to The New York Times.*

ST. PAUL, Minn., May 27.—The condition of James J. Hill, the veteran railroad builder, was pronounced tonight as serious following an operation by Dr. W. J. Mayo and Dr. C. H. Mayo of Rochester, Minn., and Dr. J. S. Gilfillan, Mr. Hill's physician.

The operation was performed at the Hill residence. In a bulletin made public following the operation it was said that he was suffering from an infection of the buttock and thigh.

"It is serious at his age," the bulletin read. "He is being carefully watched. The infection was opened and drained. He came through the operation nicely and is resting quietly."

This was the first intimation from official sources that the condition of Mr. Hill was serious. The operation followed a trip by the Drs. Mayo from Rochester to St. Paul in a special train. The train arrived at St. Paul at 3 P. M. The two famous surgeons, accompanied by assistants, were taken in automobiles to the Hill residence, where they immediately prepared for the operation. Louis W. Hill, a son; Miss Clara Hill, a daughter, and George T. Slade, a son-in-law, were waiting for the surgeons, who were familiar with his condition from a thorough examination the previous day.

Throughout the night eminent surgeons and physicians, nurses, members of the Hill family and a few close friends kept vigil at the Hill home. Archbishop John Ireland, long-time friend of the "Empire Builder," was among those who visited the sick room. A bulletin tonight, issued by Dr. Gilfillan, said:

"Mr. Hill rallied quickly and favorably from the operation. There was no alarming fever, and his temperature was very good. We are only fearful because of the patient's extreme age. The critical point in his condition will not be reached for a few days, but I anticipate favorable results."

Dr. Gilfillan, on leaving the Hill residence at 11 o'clock tonight, said:

"Mr. Hill is doing very nicely. There is no fever, and I do not expect any dangerous developments."

James N. Hill, son of James J. Hill, left last night for the West. Information as to his destination was refused at his home. Mr. Hill is a Director in the Texas Company and several other corporations.

# THREE MORE SHIPS SUNK, ONE WITHOUT WARNING

### Crew of Italian Vessel Abandoned After Ship Is Torpedoed—A British Steamer Destroyed.

LONDON, May 27.—The British steamship Danewood has been sunk. Her crew has been landed.

Lloyd's announces that the steamer Hercules, nationality unknown, has been sunk.

More than a score of steamers named Hercules are listed in the shipping registers, several of them being British and others the property of various neutrals.

PARIS, May 27.—A Havas dispatch from Port Vendres says that two French torpedo boats arrived there yesterday bringing thirty members of the crew of the Italian steamer Moravia, which was torpedoed by a German submarine on Thursday afternoon without warning. The crew was abandoned in two lifeboats. The Moravia was on her way from New York to Genoa with a cargo of flour.

The Moravia was a steamer of 2,268 tons. She sailed from New York on May 5 and was last reported passing Gibraltar on May 22.

# KAISER PUTS SOCIALIST IN IMPERIAL OFFICE

### August Mueller, Food Commissioner, First of His Party Ever So Honored.

BERLIN, May 27, (via London.)—"Finally Herr August Mueller of Hamburg."

This concluding phrase in the semi-official announcement of the names of the new "food dictatorship" is significant of the new current in Germany, for not only is Herr Mueller one of the so-called common people, without the slightest glimmer of official status, but he is also a Social Democrat—the first to grace an imperial office in Germany.

August Mueller started in life as a gardener's apprentice. He educated himself by reading to a point where he obtained a degree in a Swiss university. Later he became editor of a Hamburg Socialist newspaper. He gained prominence in his management of the co-operative organization of the Hamburg Socialists. He is a registered member of the Socialist Party and belongs to the moderate school, and is therefore repeatedly in conflict with Vorwärts and other radical organs.

In the semi-official enumeration of the colleagues of Adolph von Batocki, President of the Food Regulation Board, bearing imposing titles such as Major General, Overburgomaster, Ministerial Councillor of Commerce, the simple "Finally Herr August Mueller of Hamburg" has a twang of unconscious humor. But the new phrase promises to become a classic quotation as a tangible sign of the growing democratization of the higher German bureaucracy.

LONDON, May 27.—The commune of Griedenau, near Berlin, has decided to number all meat tickets as a measure to check rioting outside butchers' shops, according to an Amsterdam dispatch to the Exchange Telegraph Company, which quotes the Berlin Tageblatt. Holders of tickets must take their turn, according to number, and those unable to go on the specified date will get no meat for that week.



# 2,500 AMERICANS CALL ROOSEVELT TO GUIDE NATION

### With Flags, Cheers, and Songs Throng Marches Three Dusty Miles to Sagamore Hill.

### COLONEL GIVES HIS PLEDGE

### Would Demand of Every Man Who Comes Here That He Become a Citizen and American.

### 'NO ONE LOYAL TO A COWARD'

### Quotes and Commends Lowell's Line: "Peace Won't Keep House with Fear"—Off for West Today.

*Special to The New York Times.*

OYSTER BAY, L. I., May 27.—Colonel Theodore Roosevelt was called to arms today by 2,500 dusty, leg-weary pilgrims, more than 2,000 of whom came from New York and not a few from more distant points. They marched the three miles from the railroad station to Sagamore Hill to demand his leadership. They received his promise to serve his country with an outburst of enthusiasm and cries of "Our next President." The pilgrimage was made under the call of the Roosevelt Non-partisan League.

Colonel Roosevelt said it was one of the most impressive days in a lifetime. He was affected deeply, and he made no effort to conceal it. In his address, made from the porch of his home while the marchers, massed on the lawn, gave cheer after cheer, he told of his beliefs as to the country's needs.

Three special trains of eight cars each brought 2,100 of the pilgrims and Oyster Bay and nearby communities sent 400 more. There were besides at least 100 automobile parties.

Oyster Bay was ready for the demonstration. The town was gay with flags and bunting, and automobiles rushing through the streets carried pennants that whipped in the breeze and added to the prevalence of the red, white, and blue color scheme.

The first train reached Oyster Bay at 3 o'clock and freed its band of cheering men. They were greeted by the croak of automobile horns. The other trains followed at five-minute intervals and then the line of march was formed.

**No Terror in Storm Threat.**

A storm threatened but the "army" laughed at that. Some commented on the fact that the stiff breeze which carried the storm clouds "tossed the flag" at the head of the column. None thought of seeking shelter. Fortunately the storm passed off over the bay.

The Seventh Regiment Band struck up a patriotic air; the marchers, four abreast, did their best for soldierlike precision, and at the command to advance, raised the cry, "We want Teddy."

Passing through the principal streets of the village the marchers swung into East Main Street, and then to the Cove Road, which leads along the Bay to Sagamore Hill. The line stretched out a full half mile.

A banner bearer tore by the marchers at double quick, waving above his head a big American flag. "Teddy's flag and ours," shouted a man in the ranks, and that started the cheering. When they were tired of cheering the marchers broke into song.

The trip to the entrance of Sagamore Hill was made in forty-five minutes, and as the line swung up to the stiff ascent through the Roosevelt estate the band struck up "Glory, Glory, Hallelujah," one of the songs used in the convention days of 1912, when the Colonel was fighting for the nomination. A stentorian voice in the front ranks took it up and soon the entire body of marchers were singing.

We'll vote for Theodore Roosevelt
Because we know that he'll be true,
He loves our starry banner—
Our own red, white, and blue;
We know that he'll defend it
From the enemy in view,
As we go marching on.

**Start With a Rah Rah.**

There was a crowd of 500 collected on the lawns when the advance guard of the marchers appeared over the brow of the hill and put aside song for cheers. The "Mollycoddles" who had come on in advance in automobiles—that was what the marchers called them—were not lacking in enthusiasm at least. Their welcoming shouts were met by the army with this reply:

President! President!
His Boom! Bah!
Theodore Roosevelt!
Rah, rah, rah!

It was at this moment that the Colonel appeared, and he fairly burst out of the house and onto the broad back porch which overlooked the lawns where the throng was gathered. He was dressed in a khaki riding suit with riding boots. He started to say something, but never had a chance. The men and the few women who had marched three miles to tell him they wanted him for President had to let off steam first.

Hats were tossed into the air, and restraint was forgotten for the moment. There were cries of "We want Teddy," and a sea of flags tossing and fluttering in the breeze.

The Colonel stood quietly for a moment to take in the details of the scene before him. Then he waved his hand to the crowd and greeted a few of his personal friends.

"By George!" he exclaimed, "this is wonderful."

A woman standing near the Colonel

Continued on Page 7.



## American Teacher Freed by Germany Blames Student for Code Found in Trunk

BERLIN, May 27, (via London.)—Announcement was made today of the release of Miss Mary Silliman, a teacher in the American School for Girls at Constantinople, who was arrested on suspicion of espionage at Warnemunde, Germany, a month ago, while on her way to the United States. Miss Silliman has been allowed to resume her journey home and is returning to America by way of Holland.

At the time of her arrest it was alleged that the draft of a code for the transmission of messages had been discovered in her trunk when it was examined at the frontier. Miss Silliman explained that the papers probably were placed in her trunk by a revengeful pupil at the school.

The American Ambassador, James W. Gerard, has been active in her behalf.

# RIGGS BANK HEADS FOUND NOT GUILTY

### Jury Hastens to Acquit Three Washingtonians Accused in Perjury Trial.

### TREASURY CROWD CHEERS

### Employes Join Street Throngs in Tribute to Glover—Political Effect Seen.

*Special to The New York Times.*

WASHINGTON, May 27.—After being out nine minutes, part of which time was taken up in walking to the jury room and electing a foreman, the jury in the local criminal court today agreed on a verdict of acquittal in the case of Charles C. Glover, President; W. J. Flather, Vice President, and H. H. Flather, former cashier, of the Riggs National Bank, who were charged with having uttered a false affidavit in the equity proceedings growing out of the troubles between the bank and William G. McAdoo, Secretary of the Treasury, and John Skelton Williams, Controller of the Currency. Only one ballot was taken.

There was no demonstration in the court room, but a scene remarkable for Washington occurred in front of the bank. Many business men, officers of other banking institutions and depositors of the bank assembled there awaiting for news of the outcome of the trial. When it was announced that all three defendants had ben acquitted the crowd began to cheer. Right across the street from the bank is the Treasury building, and the cheers could be heard plainly in the office of Controller Williams, who was accused by the bank of a malicious intent to ruin it. A big new American flag was run up over the bank building in celebration of the acquittal, and there was more cheering.

The crowd lingered, cheering occasionally, in the hope that the acquitted men would appear. Soon President Glover arrived in a motor car. Shouting their congratulations the people in the crowd, who had increased in number, surrounded the car. Bank employes came running out and insisted on shaking the acquitted President by the hand. Every window on the north front of the Treasury Department facing the bank was crowded with officials and clerks. When President Glover appeared the Treasury contingent began waving handkerchiefs.

The crowd in front of the bank cheered at this, and the Treasury people cheered in response. It was apparent that the exoneration of the officers of the bank was popular in the building, whose heads have been at outs with the bank since the incoming of the present Administration.

Controller Williams said he had no comment to make on the outcome of the trial. President Glover said: "Of course I am greatly gratified, but as a matter of fact I never had a moment's doubt as to the outcome."

Frank J. Hogan, one of the attorneys for the defense, said: "On Oct. 1 last I said that this indictment was the result of malice. Today I say that the shafts of malice have failed to reach their targets."

The verdict of not guilty marks another stage in the controversy between officers of the bank and Secretary McAdoo and Controller Williams. An important outcome to the bank may depend on the verdict. The bank had insisted on an early trial of the perjury case, making the point that Controller Williams had indicated that he would not renew the charter of any national bank whose officers were under charges affecting their integrity. The bank's charter will expire on June 27, and the bank's officers claimed that if they were still under charges when that time arrived the Controller of the Currency would use it as an excuse to refuse to renew the charter.

An effort to expedite the trial failed, but when the case was called on May 8, the original date set, every means was taken to hurry it to a conclusion. The bank has made arrangements to take out a State bank charter to prevent the institution from closing if the Controller declines to issue a new national charter.

The Riggs Bank case has been a matter of national interest on account of the important forces involved. Bankers all over the country have followed every development and financial circles have watched it for its possible disclosure of the attitude of the Controller's office toward banking institutions. Accusations between Secretary McAdoo and Controller Williams and the bank's officers have gone back and forth, the bank claiming that the Controller was actuated by reasons of personal malice, and the Controller, backed by Mr. McAdoo, charging that the bank had been violating the national banking act.

What the effect, if any, of the acquittal will be politically and in developing sentiment in financial circles is something that cannot be foretold. The Riggs Bank is said to have received many letters from national banks, large and small, expressing sympathy and criticising the methods of the Controller. The impression prevails here that financial circles have been deeply aroused over the case, and that this feeling is reflected in the suggestion that the powers of the Controller's office should be curtailed. Politically there has been no outward reflection of the case, but some friends of the Administration have been concerned over the possible effect in a political way of the influence of bankers who share the contention of the Riggs Bank that the bank has been treated harshly.



# ASK GOV. WHITMAN TO REMOVE MITCHEL

### United Independent Democrats of Kings County Send Charges to Albany.

### MAYOR ANSWERS MGR. DUNN

### Burns Says He Found Crime Evidence in Seymour Office—Moss Criticises Wiretapping.

The removal of Mayor John Purroy Mitchel from office was asked in resolutions adopted and sent to Governor Whitman last night by the United Independent Democrats of Kings County. The resolutions said that Mayor Mitchel's usefulness to the city had "ended in disgrace."

The technical basis for the request for the Mayor's removal was that he had failed in his duty as a citizen to notify the District Attorneys of Kings and Manhattan of the knowledge he said he had that clergymen were conspiring criminally for illegal purposes. The resolution cited that in his wiretapping testimony and in public statements the Mayor repeatedly said that he had such knowledge.

The resolutions were drafted by W. F. Connell, President of the organization, the man who requested District Attorney Lewis of Kings to investigate the wiretapping which led to the indictment of Commissioner of Charities Kingsbury and William H. Hotchkiss. The resolutions were drawn at a meeting of the Executive Committee of the organization yesterday morning and adopted at a meeting at the Assembly, Fulton and Johnson Streets, last night.

**Committee Will See Governor.**

The resolutions read:

"Whereas, The Mayor of the City of New York has under oath and for several weeks in public speeches stated that he has been in possession of evidence proving that certain clergymen of the City of New York had committed crimes against the State of New York; and,

"Whereas, it is the duty of every citizen of the city, including the Mayor, having knowledge of the commission of crime to file such information with the District Attorney of the county wherein such crimes are alleged to have been committed, to the end that justice be done and the offenders punished, and,

"Whereas, the said Mayor had not filed any such information with any District Attorney within the City of New York or with any Magistrate, although publicly proclaiming his absolute knowledge of the same, and as his failure to do so has created in the public mind mistrust of his actions as a public official and led to the unanimous belief that he is using his office and powers as Mayor of the City of New York to aid and assist private interests in their attacks upon religious institutions of all denominations and that his usefulness as representative of the Government of the great City of New York has come to an end in disgrace.

"Resolved, That the United Independent Democrats of Kings County present this matter to the Governor of the State of New York and that he be requested to take the necessary procedure for the removal of John Purroy Mitchel as Mayor of the City of New York, and that a committee of five members be appointed to present these resolutions to said Governor for action thereon by him."

**News to Father Farrell.**

Frank Moss, counsel to the Thompson committee, which investigated wiretapping, and Father Farrell, whose wires were tapped, said last night they had no knowledge of any such action.

"I think the report of such a movement is a fake," said Mr. Moss. "I don't believe Governor Whitman would entertain seriously a request for the Mayor's removal. Anyhow, I don't know anything about any such action."

Father Farrell said he had not been consulted about any request for Mayor Mitchel's removal.

Mr. Connell was asked last night why the priests who had criticised the Mayor at the hearings of the Thompson committee had played no part in the action last night.

"That is because they are one of the parties concerned and their action would not be considered as unprejudiced," he said. "We have no personal interest in the matter and are acting only as citizens."

Mr. Connell said late last night that the resolutions were on their way to the Governor.

**Governor Has Left Albany.**

It had been reported for several days that Governor Whitman was considering the appointment of a commissioner under the Moreland act to investigate the subject of telephone wiretapping in New York.

News of the proposed action of the United Independent Democrats reached Albany yesterday before the action of the organization last night. But Governor hitman had left the Capitol for Medina, to be absent for four days. Certain of the Governor's advisers have told him that the wiretapping matter should not be let go without an inquiry by the Executive.

Governor Whitman has persistently refused to comment publicly on the appearance of Mayor Mitchel before the Thompson Committee, but it is known that when he was in New York a few days ago he was in communication with Senator Thompson and several clergymen involved in the controversy.

The day before Mayor Mitchel went on the stand the Governor and Senator Thompson had a long conference, it was reliably reported. Since then they have conferred over the long-distance telephone.

**Whitman Friendly to Mayor.**

Politicians believe that the Governor would be slow in taking any drastic action against Mayor Mitchel. Irrespective of their feelings toward each other personally, the Governor is politically friendly to the Mayor. He was particularly kind to the New York City bills the Mayor wished passed during the legislative session last Winter.

It was also pointed out that the New York County and Kings County Republican organizations are both friendly to Mayor Mitchel. Mayor Mitchel is very

Continued on Page 15.

"All the News That's Fit to Print."

# The New York Times.

THE WEATHER
Local showers Sunday; Monday probably showers; light to moderate variable winds.
For full weather report see Page 20.

VOL. LXV...NO. 21,323. NEW YORK, SUNDAY, JUNE 11, 1916.—102 PAGES, In Eight Parts, Including Picture and Rotogravure Section and Review of Books. PRICE FIVE CENTS.

# HUGHES ACCEPTS REPUBLICAN NOMINATION FOR PRESIDENT; DECLARES FOR UPHOLDING AMERICAN RIGHTS ON LAND AND SEA; ROOSEVELT, NAMED BY MOOSE, DECLINES; HE'S 'OUT OF POLITICS'

## COLONEL ABANDONS FIGHT

### Friends Believe He Will Quit Active Politics and Only Write.

**BULL MOOSE FATE IN DOUBT**

**Leader Is Expected to Let Matters Simmer Down and Then Meet Committeemen.**

**TAKES DEFEAT CHEERFULLY**

**Delegates Who Indorsed His Suggestion Lodge Be Nominated Shifted to Hughes.**

*Special to The New York Times.*

OYSTER BAY, N. Y., June 10.—Colonel Theodore Roosevelt will not head a third ticket in opposition to Justice Charles E. Hughes. The only debatable question is what attitude he will take in connection with the Hughes campaign. He may take the stump for Mr. Hughes. But it is more probable that he will not, and will insist that the Republican nominee make his own fight for election on the issues of Americanism, preparedness, and preservation of national honor.

As for the Colonel, he has to all intents and purposes made his last political fight. He will keep up the fight for his convictions, but hereafter it will be on an entirely different basis. He will be the writer rather than the orator.

Colonel Roosevelt has come to the decision that the best interests of the country are to be served by his refusing to head a third ticket. He feels that the worst menace to the country would be the re-election of President Wilson. He may not be satisfied entirely with the statement by Mr. Hughes, but he is thoroughly satisfied that it is better to aid, by his own elimination from the race, the election of Mr. Hughes than to promote four more years of President Wilson.

**Colonel Announces Retirement.**

The Colonel was in his library at Sagamore Hill, where many a momentous political question has been decided, when he made known his decision to decline the Progressive nomination. A score of correspondents were his guests, and not a man was there who did not want him to fight. A photographer who had edged his way into the group unnoticed in the excitement of the moment asked the Colonel for a photograph.

"Not now," he said. "No, it would not interest you. I am out of politics."

The Colonel said that he had written his message to the Progressive Convention—a tentative, and all felt, a positive, refusal—before he had read the statement by Justice Hughes accepting the Republican nomination. It was evident in his demeanor, if not in his words, that the statement had not met his expectations, but it was just as apparent that it would suffice as far as he was concerned.

There was every indication of finality in the Colonel's attitude despite the outlet from direct refusal to run on a ticket named by the Progressives, which he included in the message to the men who supported him in 1912, and were rallying again to him in the emergency of 1916.

Colonel Roosevelt left the question of a decision up to the National Committee of the Progressive Party, but that means only that the fight was over.

**Phone Conferences At Night.**

The Colonel gave no evidence of depression this evening when he received the correspondents, but it was evident that he was a bit worn by the constant demand upon him which had given him scarcely an hour for rest. All through the night he had conferred over the long distance telephone with his leaders in Chicago, never giving up the fight, although information conveyed to him early this morning showed that there was little hope of getting the support of the Republicans.

It was shortly after receiving a message to the effect that his cause in the Republican Convention was hopeless that he sent his message to the Conference Committee suggesting the name of Senator Lodge as a compromise candidate. He sent the Lodge message at 5 o'clock. It developed tonight that at 4 o'clock in the morning he had received a message from two Republican delegates on that subject.

When the Colonel told them of his intention to issue the statement in support of Lodge they said it was just what they wanted. And yet, he said tonight, both of these men had cast their ballots for Hughes when the test came in the convention.

It is believed things of this kind influenced the Colonel in his decision that to run a third ticket against Hughes simply would mean defeat for both of them, with the probability that Hughes would run second in the race. It was such instances as this, at any rate, which forced him to the decision that the most patriotic course would be to withdraw in the

Continued on Page 2.

### *Colonel Roosevelt's Conditional Refusal*

AUDITORIUM HALL, CHICAGO, June 10.—Colonel Roosevelt's message to the Progressive Convention declining the nomination was as follows:

Oyster Bay, N. Y., June 10.

To the Progressive Convention:
I am very grateful for the honor you confer upon me by nominating me as President. I cannot accept it at this time. I do not know the attitude of the candidate of the Republican Party toward the vital questions of the day. Therefore, if you desire an immediate decision, I must decline the nomination.

But if you prefer to, I suggest that my conditional refusal to run be placed in the hands of the Progressive National Committee. If Mr. Hughes's statements, when he makes them, shall satisfy the committee that it is for the interest of the country that he be elected, they can act accordingly and treat my refusal as definitely accepted.

If they are not satisfied, they can so notify the Progressive Party, and at the same time they can confer with me, and then determine on whatever action we may severally deem appropriate to meet the needs of the country.

THEODORE ROOSEVELT.

## EXPECT ROOSEVELT TO SUPPORT TICKET

**Republican Leaders Believe He Will Bury the Animosities Engendered in 1908.**

**GRATIFIED AT NOMINATION**

**Penrose and Others Confident of a Victory and Pleased That Party Is Reunited.**

*Special to The New York Times.*

CHICAGO, June 10.—Everywhere among Republican politicians appears to be a disposition to believe that Colonel Roosevelt will give his support to the Hughes-Fairbanks ticket nominated today. It is realized by the leaders that there has been some feeling on Colonel Roosevelt's part against Justice Hughes on the ground that Mr. Hughes did not show proper appreciation of the Colonel's efforts to have him renominated for Governor of New York in 1908 and to help in his fight to reorganize the State Insurance Department, but they contend that the Colonel will not let these past animosities influence him at this time.

The Colonel's message to the Progressive Convention is regarded as indicating that he will decline the Progressive nomination and find a means of coming out strongly in support of the Republican candidate. The main consideration with Colonel Roosevelt, according to the rather general view of Republicans, is the defeat of President Wilson, and they contend that it would be inconsistent for him, after all he has said in condemnation of the Wilson policies, to take measures that would give material aid to the Democratic Party.

Senator Harding of Ohio, who was both temporary and permanent Chairman of the Republican Convention, is one of those who believe that Colonel Roosevelt will not be a candidate for President on the third party ticket.

**Harding Predicts Victory.**

In speaking of the nomination of Justice Hughes, the Senator said:

"No stronger nomination could have been made. Because of his position on the bench the public had taken little notice of the vigorous Americanism and strong character of Justice Hughes. He will now put aside the judicial robes and emerge a militant and inspiring party leader. I have every confidence that there will be but two parties enlisting the attention of the American people this year, and I feel absolutely certain that November will witness the election of Hughes and Fairbanks."

Congressman W. S. Vare of Philadelphia, who favored the nomination of Colonel Roosevelt by the Republican convention, and was one of the Pennsylvania delegates who voted for the Colonel last night, is another Republican who believes that the Colonel will support Hughes and Fairbanks. Said Mr. Vare:

"The nomination of Mr. Hughes for President and Mr. Fairbanks for Vice President should prove effective in reuniting the Republican Party. I do believe that Colonel Roosevelt will give his enthusiastic support to the Republican ticket.

"Justice Hughes is a strong American. His public record is ample assurance. He will have the confidence of the Republican voters. I feel sure that Colonel Roosevelt, with his loyalty to Americanism, and his characteristic singleness of purpose, will be the ablest supporter that Hughes and Fairbanks will have.

"The spirit of progress and unity which has dominated the present convention, and the evident desire of the delegates themselves to do what is best for the Republican Party and nation make certain that there will be complete unity of purpose in the party, and that the Republicans will be restored to power in the executive and legislative branches of the Federal Government."

**People's Choice, Says Tanner.**

Frederick C. Tanner, Chairman of the New York State Republican Committee, said:

"Governor Hughes was chosen because he was the people's choice. The people will support him because they

Continued on Page 6.



## MOOSE ANGRY AND BITTER

### Convention Ends in Gloom After Long Fight for Roosevelt.

**NAME HIM AMID CHEERS**

**Three Minutes Afterward They Hear of the Republican Stampede to Hughes.**

**COLONEL'S LETTER A BOMB**

**Delegates Disperse Sadly When They Hear That He Conditionally Declines to Run.**

*Special to The New York Times.*

CHICAGO, June 10.—After having nominated Theodore Roosevelt of New York for President and John M. Parker of Louisiana for Vice President, and having listened to a communication from Colonel Roosevelt, in which was embodied a conditional refusal to lead the fight, the Progressive convention dispersed at 5 o'clock this afternoon.

It was a thoroughly resentful and indignant, if not a disheartened body of men, that filed out of the Auditorium, but, apparently, they were determined that the third party must keep to the middle of the road at all costs.

The Progressive leaders had been engaged all day in a dramatic struggle with a convention plainly out of sympathy with all plans for reconciliation with the Republicans not involving the nomination of Colonel Roosevelt on the Republican ticket as well as on the Progressive. They did not dare spring the Colonel's message on the convention until the work of the final day was done and it was ready to adjourn. Then, as it was read, it came as a stunning blow to the men who had burned all their political bridges behind them four years ago to join the Colonel in his exodus and who by this time have had more than enough of their sojourn in the wilderness.

**Silent, Cheerless Procession.**

At the closing session of the convention there had been in evidence the first flickering away of the old Bull Moose spirit which was so conspicuous in the earlier stages of the convention. The delegates and spectators who had sat through it all did not have time to realize what it all meant before the final gavel fell and the band broke into the solemn strains of "America." The Progressives are much given to fervent singing, but even the cherished strains of that old melody held no lure for them. The Colonel's message had taken all song out of them, and they started for the doors a silent and cheerless procession. Some were complaining bitterly that after all their sacrifices, the Colonel was preparing "to run out on them."

Many of the delegates went straight from the Auditorium to the nearest telegraph offices. Tonight, and for days to come, Colonel Roosevelt will be bombarded with messages, urging it upon him as a duty to run, in language probably more direct than any to which he has been accustomed, from members of his Bull Moose flock. Everybody here seems to realize that the Colonel's "conditional refusal," hinging on the attitude of Justice Hughes with regard to Americanism and preparedness, might just as well have been made absolute, especially in the light of the published statement from Justice Hughes accepting the nomination and outlining his position on the issues.

Colonel Roosevelt's message was carried to the convention by John W. McGrath, his private secretary. It was read by Raymond Robins, who presided. Amid tense silence the convention listened. It was what it had been waiting for all afternoon. When the final session began announcement was made that the Colonel should be heard from during recess, and that his communication would be read before the final adjournment.

"I am now going to read to this convention a statement from Theodore Roosevelt," said Chairman Robins. "In accordance with a lifelong practice, he refuses to act hastily in a matter of importance to all the people of this country. He wants to hear from the people first, and I imagine he has heard from them by this time."

Then Mr. Robins read the following:

To the Progressive Convention: I am very grateful for the honor you confer upon me by nominating me as President. I cannot accept it at this time. I do not know the attitude of the candidate of the Republican Party toward the vital questions of the day. Therefore, if you desire an immediate decision, I must decline the nomination. But if you prefer it, I suggest that my conditional refusal to run be placed in the hands of the Progressive National Committee.

If Mr. Hughes's statements, when he makes them, shall satisfy the committee that it is for the interest of the country that he be elected, they can act accordingly and treat my refusal as definitely accepted. If they are not satisfied they can so notify the

Continued on Page 3.

### *Republican Nominees Felicitate Each Other*

INDIANAPOLIS, June 10.—Charles W. Fairbanks this afternoon sent the following telegram to Mr. Hughes:

Indianapolis, Ind., June 10, 1916.
Hon. Charles E. Hughes,
Washington, D. C.:
I most heartily congratulate you upon your selection as the leader of the Republican Party in the present national contest.
CHARLES W. FAIRBANKS.

He received this evening the following reply:

Washington, D. C., June 10, 1916.
Your telegram deeply appreciated. I heartily congratulate you on your nomination. It is most gratifying.
CHARLES E. HUGHES.

## HITCHCOCK TRIUMPH OVER THE OLD GUARD

**Without Sleep for Two Nights, Hughes Manager Directed Defeat of "Allies."**

**WON PENNSYLVANIANS FIRST**

**How the Tide Turned as Sherman, La Follette, and Others Retired from the Contest.**

*Special to The New York Times.*

CHICAGO, Ill., June 10.—When the Republican convention met this morning the nomination of Justice Hughes was inevitable. The forces of the Old Guard had begun to disintegrate during the night. In the wee small hours of morning the leadership of the men who had formed a close corporation within the Republican ranks faded away. They could not control their following, and sadly but with resignation they reached the conclusion that organization methods would avail nothing against the desire of the majority of delegates to follow their own course, which was to get on the Hughes band wagon as quickly as possible.

Frank H. Hitchcock, who made the strategic plans that brought about the nomination of Justice Hughes, worked all night to prevent his program from being overthrown. He had slept little the night before and was fairly staggering with fatigue while he talked with men in hostile delegations whose help he needed. Last night he went without sleep again, but was at the Convention Hall bright and early this morning marshaling his forces for the supreme test of strength.

Hitchcock realized that a tactical error had been made by the Hughes supporters at Friday evening's session of the convention when they voted against the adjournment asked for by the Old Guard under the leadership of Senator Penrose of Pennsylvania. That error was due to a mistake in the delivery of a message sent by Mr. Hitchcock to the Oregon delegation, which was representing the Hughes interests on the floor, not to oppose a motion to adjourn.

**Oregon Men Misunderstood.**

The Oregon men understood that Mr. Hitchcock wanted them to vote against the motion and they sent word to other delegations friendly to Justice Hughes that the Hughes following would vote against its adoption.

The overwhelming majority cast in favor of the motion to adjourn encouraged the Old Guard contingent, which had in view the defeat of both Hughes and Roosevelt, but was all at sea as to how that result might be accomplished. As soon as possible after the convention adjourned last night some of the Old Guard leaders got together to decide on a plan of campaign, while others attended meetings of their State delegations with the object of guiding them away from the Hughes camp.

Some of these meetings lasted far into the night. The object of the Old Guard, whose combination against Hughes this week received the name of "the Allies," was to determine on a candidate to whom the strength of the anti-Hughes forces should be thrown when it became apparent that the Justice was bound to be the party's nominee unless all the contingents opposed to him were concentrated.

The allies appeared, however, to have been unduly encouraged over the showing made in the vote on Senator Penrose's motion to adjourn the convention until morning. They seemed to think that this meant the Hughes cause was weakening. On the second ballot the vote for the Justice was 328½. On the motion to adjourn the opposition, generally regarded as composed of Hughes sympathizers, showed a marked falling off from the second ballot vote for Hughes, and the Old Guard leaders seemed to get the idea that the sentiment for the jurist had begun to wane. How much mistaken they were they did not find out until this morning when they went to the convention hall prepared to administer a defeat to Justice Hughes.

**First Shift to Hughes.**

Perhaps the first break in the columns of opposition to Hughes occurred in the evening, when the two Vares of Philadelphia—William S., a Congressman, and his brother, Edwin H., a contractor—both powers in the Republican politics of the Quaker City called on Mr. Hitchcock and asked him to tell them frankly what the chances were for the nomination of Justice Hughes. The Vares had quarreled with Penrose and had cast their lot with Governor Brumbaugh. Colonel Roosevelt was the favorite of the Brumbaugh-Vare combination.

Tired as he was, Hitchcock made an eloquent argument to show that nobody but Hughes could be nominated. The

Continued on Page 4.

## HUGHES TOLD AT LUNCHEON

### Tears in His Eyes as He Greets Reporters, Then Turns to Acceptance.

**PROMPTLY RESIGNS OFFICE**

**And Abandons His Judicial Mien, Talking Smilingly to the Host of Newspapermen.**

**TELEGRAMS COME IN FLOOD**

**Nominee Is Silent on Roosevelt's Action, but His Friends Express Satisfaction.**

*Special to The New York Times.*

WASHINGTON, June 10.—Ten minutes after the first unofficial news of his nomination at Chicago had been communicated to Justice Hughes this afternoon messenger boys began to wheel up to his front door with telegrams of congratulations, camera and movie men arrived with their batteries, and the vanguard of newspaper men that had been waiting all morning on the "dog watch" was rapidly reinforced by other newspaper men, who seemed to drop out of the clouds.

Taxicabs in which they had hurried to the Hughes residence, at Sixteenth and V Streets, a mile due north of the White House, lined V Street for a block, and the entire neighborhood suddenly assumed an unwonted atmosphere of activity.

Justice Hughes received first word of his nomination at 1:35 o'clock this afternoon. He was at luncheon at the time with Mrs. Hughes and their children in the oak-paneled dining room on the second floor of the residence. Below, in the office of Lawrence H. Green, private secretary of the Justice, a group of newspaper men, who had been waiting all the morning, receiving news bulletins, which were given by them to Mr. Green for delivery to the Justice, had just received a telegraphic flash telling of the nomination of the jurist on the third ballot.

Until that moment everything had been serene and silent around the Hughes residence. Of course, the new Republican "man of the hour," being human and aware of what was taking place at the Coliseum in Chicago, was interested and undoubtedly eager, but he had not been nominated, he still wore the long black judicial robe, and there was not the slightest evidence that he cared a whit about politics.

The veil of silence remained impenetrable and passersby scarcely noticed the large, square, three-story red brick building, which was built on Colonial lines by the Justice soon after he was made a member of the Supreme Court. Then came the magic word from Chicago that meant so much to Mr. Hughes, and, perhaps, a great deal to his party, as well as the country, and ten minutes later the entire neighborhood began to buzz.

Pickaninnies who live in that part of V Street, extending a block west of the Hughes residence and lined mainly with small, but neat-looking negro residences, were attracted by the movie men and newspaper correspondents, who had assembled under the small green maples in front of the Hughes home, and they transferred their play activities from the vacant lots to that part of the sidewalk, just before the entrance to the Hughes house. In their midst was a 6-year-old kiddy in blue jumpers leading a squirrel by a string.

Across the street one of Mr. Hughes's neighbors sent a butler to the third-story windows and flung out two large American flags to the breeze in full view of the jurist's residence. Messenger boys, arriving with telegrams, were reluctant to leave after delivering their missives, and soon there was a dozen of them loitering around the movie men, who stood under a maple tree training their "guns" on the main entrance of the Justice's home and relying on their persuasive powers to induce the nominee to step outside the front portal to pose for them.

The crowd of news-gatherers and photographers assembled outside the door attracted the attention of every passerby, whether afoot or in vehicle. Upon learning the cause of the commotion many passersby forgot business or social duties and remained to augment the throng.

**Simple Drama of the Day.**

Probably no man about to be nominated to the highest office within the gift of the American people has ever been obliged to receive the preliminary news of the high honors bestowed upon him under such simple but dramatic circumstances as those under which Justice Hughes has lived in Washington the last few days.

He had but one visitor of importance yesterday, and but one caller of distinction Thursday, as he sat in the library of his home. Today there was equal respect for his reserve on the part of those who wished him well, hoped he would be nominated, and desired to say so personally, but have refrained from following the natural inclination of friends to gather about him at a time when his name was on the lips of hundreds of thousands of Americans.

Throughout the pre-convention campaign, Justice Hughes had insisted that he would not be nominated. Not until last night after the balloting began did he admit to his intimates that he might be drafted to lead his party. Even then he made no statement as to what action he would take.

Justice Hughes's last day as a member of the Supreme Court was striking in its contrasts. He spent the morning as usual in the daily routine of a member of the court. Immediately after breakfast at 8 o'clock, he went out for a stroll. The walk was shorter than usual, and merely covered the immediate vicinity of his home. Returning he went to his library and worked on decisions.

A bulletin, received by telephone by one of the group of newspaper men, assembled in the office of Mr. Green, Private Secretary of the Justice, brought the word of the nomination.

Secretary Green mounted the stairs, three at a time, to inform Mr. Hughes.

"I simply told the Justice he had been nominated and turned my back," he remarked later.

Mr. Hughes came down stairs immediately to meet the newspaper men. There were tears in his eyes as he greeted the reporters.

They then realized for the first time that Justice Hughes has a real smile. Since he came here to go on the Supreme Bench, he had conducted himself strictly according to the staid rule of the court. His manner was never effusive.

Today he seemed to throw off the judicial bearing, without losing a whit of his dignity. He beamed at the reporters, called them "you boys," and shook hands as cordially when they congratulated him as he used to shake hands when he was a plain citizen or Governor of New York.

He admitted in an aside to one of the older newspaper men that he "hadn't seen as much of the newspaper boys as he has wanted to since coming to Washington."

"I thank you for the news," said the Justice to the group, "but I have nothing to say. I have no doubt that the news is reliable, but cannot say anything until I have been officially notified by the convention. Should I hear from the convention by 3 o'clock, I will have something to say at that time."

Soon after this Chairman Harding's telegram, informing Mr. Hughes of the nomination, was received. Mr. Hughes thereupon sent his resignation by messenger to the White House. The letter read as follows:

Washington, June 10, 1916.
To the President:
I hereby resign the office of Associate Justice of the Supreme Court of the United States.
I am, sir, respectfully yours,
CHARLES E. HUGHES.

The letter reached the White House at 3:45 P. M., and was taken immediately by Secretary Tumulty to President Wilson, who dictated the following acceptance a few minutes later:

The White House.
Washington, June 10, 1916.
Dear Mr. Justice Hughes:
I am in receipt of your letter of resignation and feel constrained to yield to your desire.
I, therefore, accept your resignation as Justice of the Supreme Court of the United States to take effect at once.
Sincerely yours,
WOODROW WILSON.

Meanwhile Mr. Hughes had shut himself up in his study with his secretary

Continued on Page 4.

### *Text of Hughes's Message, Accepting the Nomination, and Attacking the Wilson Administration*

WASHINGTON, June 10.—Following is the text of the message of acceptance sent by Charles E. Hughes to the Republican National Convention at Chicago:

Washington, D. C., June 10, 1916.

Mr. Chairman and Delegates:

I have not desired the nomination. I have wished to remain on the bench. But in this critical period in our national history, I recognize that it is your right to summon and that it is my paramount duty to respond. You speak at a time of national exigency, transcending merely partisan considerations. You voice the demand for a dominant, thoroughgoing Americanism with firm protective upbuilding policies, essential to our peace and security; and to that call, in this crisis, I cannot fail to answer with the pledge of all that is in me to the service of our country. Therefore I accept the nomination.

I stand for the firm and unflinching maintenance of all the rights of American citizens on land and sea. I neither impugn motives nor underestimate difficulties. But it is most regrettably true that in our foreign relations we have suffered incalculably from the weak and vacillating course which has been taken with regard to Mexico—a course lamentably wrong with regard to both our rights and our duties. We interfered without consistency; and while seeking to dictate when we were not concerned, we utterly failed to appreciate and discharge our plain duty to our own citizens.

At the outset of the Administration the high responsibilities of our diplomatic intercourse with foreign nations were subordinated to a conception of partisan requirements, and we presented to the world a humiliating spectacle of ineptitude. Belated efforts have not availed to recover the influence and prestige so unfortunately sacrificed; and brave words have been stripped of their force by indecision.

I desire to see our diplomacy restored to its best standards and to have these advanced; to have no sacrifices of national interest to partisan expediencies; to have the first ability of the country always at its command here and abroad in diplomatic intercourse; to maintain firmly our rights under international law; insisting steadfastly upon all our rights as neutrals, and fully performing our international obligations; and by the clear correctness and justness of our position and our manifest ability and disposition to sustain them to dignify our place among the nations.

I stand for an Americanism that knows no ulterior purpose; for a patriotism that is single and complete. Whether native or naturalized, of whatever race or creed, we have but one country, and we do not for an instant tolerate any division of allegiance.

I believe in making prompt provision to assure absolutely our national security. I believe in preparedness, not only entirely adequate for our defense with respect to numbers and equipment in both army and navy, but with all thoroughness to the end that in each branch of the service there may be the utmost efficiency under the most competent administrative heads. We are devoted to the ideals of honorable peace. We wish to promote all wise and practicable measures for the just settlement of the international disputes.

In view of our abiding ideals, there is no danger of militarism in this country. We have no policy of aggression; no lust for territory, no zeal for strife. It is in this spirit that we demand adequate provision for national defense, and we condemn the inexcusable neglect that has been shown in this matter of first national importance. We must have the strength which self-respect demands, the strength of an efficient nation ready for every emergency.

Our preparation must be industrial and economic as well as military. Our severest tests will come after the war is over. We must make a fair and wise readjustment of the tariff, in accordance with sound protective principle, to insure our economic independence and to maintain American standards of living. We must conserve the just interests of labor, realizing that in democracy patriotism and national strength must be rooted in even-handed justice. In preventing, as we must, unjust discriminations and monopolistic practices, we must still be zealous to assure the foundations of honest business. Particularly should we seek the expansion of foreign trade. We must not throttle American enterprise here or abroad, but rather promote it and take pride in honorable achievements.

We must take up the serious problems of transportation, of interstate and foreign commerce, in a sensible and candid manner, and provide an enduring basis for prosperity by the intelligent use of the constitutional powers of Congress, so as adequately to protect the public on the one hand, and, on the other, to conserve the essential instrumentalities of progress.

I stand for the principles of our civil service laws. In every department of government the highest efficiency must be insisted upon. For all laws and programs are vain without efficient and impartial administration.

I cannot within the limits of this statement speak upon all the subjects that will require attention. I can only say that I fully indorse the platform you have adopted.

I deeply appreciate the responsibility you impose. I should have been glad to have that responsibility placed upon another. But I shall undertake to meet it, grateful for the confidence you express. I sincerely trust that all former differences may be forgotten and that we may have united effort in a patriotic realization of our national need and opportunity.

I have resigned my judicial office and I am ready to devote myself unreservedly to the campaign. CHARLES E. HUGHES.

## LANDSLIDE FOR HUGHES

### 949½ Votes on Day's Sole Ballot—Fairbanks His Running Mate.

**EXPECT COLONEL'S SUPPORT**

**Fuller Statement from Hughes Alone Deemed Necessary—May Mean End of Moose.**

**T. R. FORESAW THE RESULT**

**Quick Acceptance by Hughes in Line with Tacit Agreement—Conventions Adjourned.**

*Special to The New York Times.*

CHICAGO, June 10.—Charles E. Hughes and Theodore Roosevelt, both of New York, were nominated for President by the Republican and Progressive conventions at 12:49 and 12:47 o'clock today, respectively, the Roosevelt nomination beating the Hughes nomination by exactly two minutes. Charles Warren Fairbanks of Indiana was nominated for Vice President on the Republican ticket and John M. Parker of Louisiana on the Progressive. The Hughes nomination was made on the third ballot of the convention, the Roosevelt nomination by acclamation.

Colonel Roosevelt sent a tentative declination of the nomination, with the understanding that it was to stand if Hughes turned out to be sound on the issues of Americanism and preparedness, and that if Hughes turned out to be pacifistic, pussy-footed, or pro-German he would accept and make the race as the Progressive candidate.

Justice Hughes broke all records by accepting the nomination by telegraph without waiting for a formal notification by the regularly appointed committee, and declared his position not only on the issues regarded by Colonel Roosevelt as the test issues, but also on the other principal questions raised by the Republican platform. For a long time a third telegram, this one from Mr. Fairbanks declining the Vice Presidential nomination, was anticipated, because he already had sent a private one to that effect, but, instead, he accepted over the telephone. The Republicans went home stolidly and apathetically, the Progressives gloomily.

The Conference Committee scheme failed because the Republicans would name no candidate. At the last minute, after every effort to induce them to do so had proved ineffective, Colonel Roosevelt himself proposed union on Senator Henry Cabot Lodge of Massachusetts. The two Conference Committees so reported, but the Progressive Convention laid the telegram on the table and the Republicans paid no attention to it.

**Hughes Statement Criticised.**

Nevertheless, union against Wilson, though it was not handsomely accomplished, and though technically it was not accomplished at all, is regarded here as practically in effect. It is not yet complete because Justice Hughes has not yet shown how far he is in agreement with the Roosevelt position. His telegram of acceptance does declare emphatically that he stands for the protection of American rights and would have passed as a complete indorsement of the Roosevelt position if he had not specifically emphasized the Mexican question.

That emphasis raises in the Progressive mind the question why he should pick out only one phase of the Wilson foreign policy and not couple it with greater infractions of American rights from other countries, as in the case of the Lusitania. He follows closely the lines of the Republican platform, but the Progressives will want more; they will want a declaration as clear and specific as those which Colonel Roosevelt has been making.

The general tone of the Hughes telegram, however, is such as to warrant the expectation that when he speaks more in detail he will not refer solely to the Mexican question and that his expressed intention to safeguard American rights "on land or sea" will be explained so fully that no one will have any excuse for coupling it with similar utterances by, for instance, President Wilson or Secretary Lansing, and maintaining that there is no difference between the candidates. The Progressives do expect that that will come to pass, and in that case Colonel Roosevelt's tentative declination will stand.

**A Rump Ticket Probable.**

If it does stand, there will be union on Hughes so far as practical effectiveness goes. The Roosevelt men in the Republican Party will not bolt, and the Roosevelt men among the Progressives will vote for Hughes. There may even then be a bolting ticket, and very likely there will be, but it will be a rump ticket. When Henry George withdrew from the United Labor Party, (which he had built up and which he carried near to victory in 1886,) and supported Cleveland as representing the nearest available approach to the principles of that party, the irreconcilables kept the United Labor Party together.

Since they could not nominate George

"All the News That's Fit to Print."

# The New York Times.

THE WEATHER
Showers today and probably tomorrow; fresh east and southeast winds.
☞For full weather report see Page 23.

VOL. LXV...NO. 21,328. .... NEW YORK, FRIDAY, JUNE 16, 1916.—TWENTY-FOUR PAGES. ONE CENT In Greater New York, Jersey City and Newark. | Elsewhere, TWO CENTS.

# DEMOCRATS AT MIDNIGHT RENOMINATE WILSON AND MARSHALL; FIGHT OVER PLATFORM AND ADJOURN UNTIL 11 A. M. TODAY; HEAR BRYAN AND CHEER THE PRESIDENT'S WORK FOR PEACE

## PLATFORM FULL OF PROBLEMS

### Resolutions Committee, Still in Session, May Work All Night.

### STRONG ON "AMERICANISM"

### Declaration, Which Wilson Wanted as He Wrote It, Will Satisfy Him, It Is Asserted.

### DISCORD OVER SUFFRAGE

### Mexico Proves a Minor Difficulty —Tentative Draft Followed the President's Ideas.

*Special to The New York Times.*

ST. LOUIS, June 15.—The Committee on Resolutions of the Democratic National Convention was in session at 1 o'clock this morning, going over the final draft of the party platform.

Senator Stone, Chairman of the committee, announced soon after 1 o'clock that the committee had approved planks, dealing with foreign questions, the tariff, and preparedness, and that the suffrage and other planks were still under consideration. Senator Stone added that the committee would probably sit all night.

Differences over some of the planks, as reported by the sub-committee, developed and it was made evident that an effort would be made to modify or reject the declaration of the sub-committee on equal suffrage. This plank, as presented, recognized the right of women to vote and recommended to the individual States that the franchise be granted to women. Members of the committee said that this plank was stronger than the Republican suffrage plank in that it contained the recommendation, whereas the Republican plank, after recognizing the principle, merely declared without recommendation, that the granting of the suffrage to women should be left to the determination of the States.

Keenest interest was shown in the plank on Americanism, and word came from Washington that President Wilson would refuse to accept the platform unless the Americanism plank he had prepared was adopted.

Members of the Committee on Resolutions, while declining to say whether the President's plank had been changed by the sub-committee, asserted that it was so strong that it would satisfy the President and all patriotic Americans.

The plank, as reported by the sub-committee in its platform draft, presented to the Resolutions Committee when it met at 10:30 o'clock, summons all men of whatever origin or creed to unite in making clear the unity of America, but whoever, actuated by any purpose, disregards America's welfare, injures the Government, cripples industry or arouses prejudice, based on race or creed, is denounced as faithless to the trust his citizenship imposes on him.

The plank also condemns all organizations or individuals who conspire to weaken the Government or improperly influence or coerce public representatives treating or negotiating with any foreign power. While these conspiracies exist among a limited number, the plank asserts that they have been instigated to advance the interests of foreign countries to the prejudice and detriment of the United States.

At 2 o'clock the Resolutions Committee was engaged in a lively debate over the Mexican plank. This plank had been adopted tentatively before a quorum of the committee reached the conference room, but it was reconsidered after a quorum appeared. As presented by the sub-committee, the plank declared that intervention should be resorted to by the United States only as a last resort.

To this phrase Congressman Ferguson, the New Mexican member of the Resolutions Committee, objected and pleaded for its elimination. He was supported by other committeemen from border States.

Senator Martin of Virginia, who left the committee room at 2 o'clock, estimated that the committee would not finish its work before 10 o'clock, an hour prior to the meeting of the convention.

The draft of the platform as worked out by the sub-committee contained about 4,000 words and included twenty-five planks.

In general, the platform throughout followed the President's suggestions. It adopted his recommendations regarding the statement of the attitude of this country toward foreign powers, except that the sub-committee added a paragraph regarding Mexico, declaring it to be the duty of this country to hold American forces in Mexico until danger to American interests should be virtually over.

Representative John J. Fitzgerald of New York, a member of the sub-committee, made a spirited effort in behalf of the adoption of a plank calling for a liberal appropriation for the improvement of the East River to make it navigable to the Brooklyn Navy Yard for the heaviest dreadnoughts. This plank was rejected by a majority of one vote.

### President Was Insistent on His Americanism Plank

WASHINGTON, June 15. — Reports from St. Louis that some Democratic leaders favored modifying President Wilson's Americanism plank to make its denunciation of political activities by foreign-born citizens less specific brought an emphatic statement from the White House late tonight that the President would not consent to such a change under any circumstances. The President's position was made unmistakably clear to his personal advisers at the convention by telephone and telegraph.

Later the President's representatives in St. Louis telephoned him assurances that the plank would be adopted exactly as approved at the White House.

#### The Platform Preamble.

The preamble to the platform as completed by the sub-committee and submitted to the full Committee on Resolutions is as follows:

"The Democratic Party, in national convention assembled, adopts the following declaration to the end that the people of the United States may realize the achievements wrought by four years of Democratic Administration and be apprised of the policies to which the party is committed for the further conduct of national affairs.

"We indorse the Administration of Woodrow Wilson. It speaks for itself. It is the best exposition of sound Democratic policy at home and abroad.

"We challenge comparison of our record, our keeping of pledges, and our constructive legislation with those of any party of any time.

"We found our country hampered by special privilege, a vicious tariff, obsolete banking laws, and an inelastic currency. Our foreign affairs were dominated by commercial interests for their selfish ends.

"The Republican Party, despite repeated pledges, was impotent to correct abuses which it had fostered. Under our administration, under a leadership which has never faltered, these abuses have been corrected, and our people have been freed.

"Our archaic banking and currency system, prolific of panic and disaster under Republican Administrations—long the refuge of the money trust—has been supplanted by the Federal Reserve act, a true democracy of credit under Government control, already proved a financial bulwark in a world crisis, mobilizing our resources, placing abundant credit at the disposal of legitimate industry and making a currency panic impossible.

"We have created a Federal Trade Commission to accommodate vexing questions arising under the anti-trust laws so that monopoly may be strangled at its birth and legitimate industry encouraged. Fair competition in business is now assured.

"We have effected an adjustment of the tariff, adequate for revenue under peace conditions and fair to the consumer and to the producer. We have adjusted the burdens of taxation so that swollen incomes bear their equitable share. Our revenues have been sufficient in times of world stress.

"We have lifted human labor from the category of commodities and have secured to the working man the right of voluntary association for his protection and welfare. We have protected the rights of the laborer against the unwarranted issuance of writs of injunction, and have guaranteed to him the right of trial by jury in alleged contempt cases committed outside of the presence of the court.

"We have advanced the parcel post to genuine efficiency, enlarged the postal savings system, added 10,000 rural delivery routes and extensions, thus reaching two and one-half millions additional people, improved the postal service in every branch, and for the first time in our history placed the Post Office system on a self-supporting basis, with actual surplus in 1913, 1914, and 1915."

#### Busy Day for Sub-Committee.

In its all-day session the sub-committee of the Resolutions Committee faced many knotty problems. More than 1,000 suggestions for planks of all sorts were laid before it, but hundreds of these were laid aside in the preliminary stages and were not taken up at all.

Copies of the President's suggestions for the platform were given to each member. The original draft, brought to St. Louis by Secretary Baker and turned over to Chairman Stone, had many interlineations in the President's handwriting.

The most contentious questions when the sub-committee met were Americanism, Mexico, and "votes for women."

President Wilson telegraphed last night to the Committee on Resolutions, urging a strong declaration against the activity of hyphenates in American politics. It was to be virtually a challenge to the Republicans in the statement that any political party seeking to take advantage of these pro-foreign influences deserved condemnation. The plank was to state, however, that it was not to be taken as a reflection upon the greater portion of the foreign-born population of the United States.

When the sub-committee took up the President's suggestion differences developed. Some members were said to be strongly opposed to such a plank and others were insistent that the plank should go in.

The attitude shown by some delegates yesterday during the delivery of the key-

Continued on Page 3.



## BRYAN EXTOLS PRESIDENT

### Draws Volleys of Cheers from Throng by Praise of Wilson.

### BURIES ALL DIFFERENCES

### Credits Administration with More Popular Laws Than Any in Nation's History.

### MAKES APPEAL FOR PEACE

### Wants the President to Have the Honor of Bringing End to the Conflict.

*Special to The New York Times.*

COLISEUM, St. Louis, June 15.—The high moments of Democratic conventions have come mostly at night sessions, and the stage at the Coliseum was set to continue the old tradition. For the first time since the convention began the galleries were filled to the high roof. Blue-bulbed incandescent lights made the hall as bright as day, and every one was plainly keyed up to make a night of it.

Senator Reed of Missouri had brought about the postponement of the night session until 9 o'clock so that delegates could be entertained by the city of St. Louis. Presumably they had been entertained; at any rate there was an air of larking good humor on the faces of the crowd that at 9 o'clock was already waiting for events.

Applause for patriotic music came more full-throatedly than in the daytime; everything and anything was signal enough for ripples of laughing applause that meant more of coolness and comfort than of enthusiasm. Senator James's appearance on the rostrum brought one loud burst of applause. William Jennings Bryan's appearance in the press gallery brought another, and when a flashlight was set off near Mrs. Bryan by a busy photographer the merry crowd took it as a good joke.

The night session gave an opportunity for a red-fire parade, which many loyal Democrats have missed in recent years; but it wasn't a parade for any one the delegates knew; it was a parade to announce in letters of fire the candidacy of Governor Major of Missouri for the Vice Presidency. The parade was a minute and twelve seconds passing a given peanut stand outside the Coliseum. What happened to the parade when it reached the Coliseum no one inside ever knew.

#### Shouts for Bryan.

When Senator James called the convention to order at 9:18 cries of "Bryan! Bryan!" showed the heads of entertainment what the convention was looking for. Mr. James is an old-time Bryan follower, but he thundered for order. The guests of the convention, he said, must not abuse their privileges. The cheery crowd applauded this rebuke and a resolution at once was offered by Senator Thompson of Kansas to suspend the rules and hear Mr. Bryan. The motion was carried, though not without scattering "noes."

A committee headed by Senator Kern of Indiana escorted Mr. Bryan to the speaker's place, while the floor and galleries roared their approval.

Senator James introduced Mr. Bryan as "one of the leading citizens of the world and America's greatest Democrat."

Mr. Bryan set no limit to his admiration of the President nor to the party's claim for continuance in power. He said he had had differences of opinion with President Wilson, but, raising his head and his voice, while the packed Coliseum gave a mighty shout of joy and relief, he said:

"I join the people in thanking God that we have a President who does not want the nation to fight."

Manifestly there had been uneasiness lest Mr. Bryan should limit his indorsement to domestic matters, if he did not actually assail the President to justify his own resignation as Secretary of State, but he did nothing of the sort. He surprised his hearers, many of whom remembered his warlike raids on party harmony in the past by saying that all Democratic conventions were love feasts to him. But as he proceeded it was evident that he meant the description to apply truly to this convention. He was truly back with the party that had nominated him three times for the Presidency, and in his closing sentence he asked that the nomination this time be given to President Wilson.

Referring to his hope for the restoration of peace, he said:

"As a Democrat I want my party to have the honor of bringing the peace about and I want the country to give Woodrow Wilson a chance to bring it about."

It has been a long time since Mr. Bryan had his party leaders so solidly with him. Murmurs ran through the delegation that Mr. Bryan was making the greatest convention speech of his life. In a sense this was true, though not as to oratory. Mr. Bryan's friends have said that he caused Woodrow Wilson's nomination four years ago, but his enemies said that he couldn't prevent it. Tonight, however, there was no doubt that Mr. Bryan had put his personal political ambition away from him. He set at rest the one possibility of Democratic dissension here and, praising Mr. Wilson's domestic and foreign policies and his courage against the interests of those who want war, he urged a united Democracy to rally for the President's re-election.

Mr. Bryan referred to his long service for the party and the long friendships he had derived from the political wars he had waged. He praised Governor Glynn's speech of yesterday and said he had met him years ago when he threw into the Bryan campaign the vigor of a young man of promise that yesterday had been made good. He praised Senator James, and he did not fail to include in his friends, his old enemy, Senator Stone of Missouri, Chairman of the Committee on Foreign Relations, and the Committee on Resolutions here, who has been working to avoid a too warlike denunciation of hyphenated citizens in the Democratic platform.

For Mr. Bryan, in making peace with his own party, was also making a peace speech to the country on foreign affairs. The one point he stressed in his reference to the European difficulties was that President Wilson had kept the country out of war. That was his point of praise too regarding the President's handling of the Mexican situation. His view was that intervention would lead to annexation and his praise was that the President had prevented that.

Considerable attention was attracted to Mr. Bryan's failure to make any distinction between the American foreign policy during his service in the State Department. He seemed to assume that no change had come, and that the policy before and after his resignation was equally good. He applied his praise to the European as well as to the Mexican policy of the Administration.

#### Eulogizes the President.

Reviewing the struggles of the Democratic Party, Mr. Bryan said:

"After sixteen years of waiting, our party entered the White House, and fortunately we won the Senate and the House at the same time. Our party became responsible for national affairs, and now we come, after three years of labor, to make our plans for the future and to submit to the American people the claims of our party to continued confidence.

"Whatever differences of opinion may exist, or may have existed, as to particular measures or particular acts, we are here to begin the fight of 1916, a united party in every State in the Union, ready for battle.

"Today those who stand for the Democratic Party are able to go before this nation and not only give a reason for the faith that is in them, but give a defense of the Administration's claims to the confidence of the people.

"You may take all the Administrations from the beginning of our history as a Republic to the beginning of the present one, and you will not find as many laws written upon the statute books, of great importance to the people, as you will find written in the last three years by Woodrow Wilson, a Democratic President."

Briefly, Mr. Bryan then referred to the tariff revision, the Federal Reserve law, and the strengthening of the anti-trust laws.

"No President since Jackson," he continued, "has had to meet such an unholy combination of the powers of high finance, and even Jackson himself never met the situation better than Woodrow Wilson met it. We have just commenced to learn what the Federal Reserve law means for this nation. This great piece of legislation, the greatest piece of constructive statesmanship in a generation, has not only broken the hold of Wall Street upon the business of the nation, but it has broken the grip of Wall Street upon the politics of the United States. For twenty years there has not been an election but what a hundred men in Wall Street could, by coercion they had in their power, change the result of the election. And one who like myself has felt their power must be pardoned if he rejoices that we have an Administration that has broken that power and set a nation free.

"Here were three great measures, carrying out the promise of a Democratic platform, and these three great measures constitute a record of achievement which the Republican Party dare not attack. The electorate before which the Republican Party must now go is not controlled, as the convention at Chicago was, by the expert representatives of the favor-seeking corporations.

"While our President and our Congress were at work conducting this splendid pyramid of performance a war came that threw upon this Administration such burdens as no President has had to bear within the last fifty years. We inherited from a Republican Administration an insurrection in Mexico. This Administration has dealt with that situation, and the Republican Party dares not challenge a verdict before the country on the Mexican question.

"We have a few men interested in ranches and a few interested in mines who would use the blood of American soldiers to guarantee profits and their investments in a foreign land. But that is not the sentiment of the American people. The people of this country stand back of Woodrow Wilson in his determination not to interfere in the affairs of Mexico.

"Why, my friends, if President Wilson had yielded to the demand of those who have clamored for intervention in Mexico we would no sooner have crossed the line than the same men would tell him that the soldiers never must come out, for, my friends, annexation is the next step after intervention has been undertaken. And if we invaded Mexico, these same men would say, 'On to Panama!'

"But, my friends, the President not

Continued on Page 2.



## DELEGATES HASTEN ACTION

### Threat to Go Home and Not Wait for Saturday Proves Effective.

### 21-MINUTE DEMONSTRATION

### Dramatic Outburst Interrupts Chairman James's Eulogy of President Wilson.

### AVERTING WAR THE THEME

### Convention Again Enthusiastic Over Success of Administration's Diplomatic Policy.

*Special to The New York Times.*

ST. LOUIS, June 15.—The acceleration of the work of the Democratic National Convention today was the result of the delegates taking the bit between their teeth and putting their feet down on one of the time-honored stupidities of the national convention system, the custom whereby a convention must remain in session for a certain number of days, whether it has any business to transact or not, in order that the inhabitants of the convention city may have a chance to make a lot of money out of the crowds.

The original program was that Thursday was to be devoted to spellbinding speeches and that the nominations were not to be reached before Saturday morning. The delegates revolted and threatened that if the convention sat until Saturday it would sit without them, as they were going home. The leaders had to give in, the day of spellbinding was omitted, and nominating speeches were ordered for Thursday night.

A rule was brought in immediately after permanent Chairman Ollie James's speech, providing that an adjournment be had until 8 P. M., and that the order of business then be nominating speeches, with the adoption of the platform inserted whenever the Resolutions Committee was ready to report, and then the nomination of Mr. Wilson, with the nominating speeches and nomination of the Vice President to follow.

The galleries protested and yelled for the spellbinders, demanding Bryan first, but the convention paid no attention to them. The only concession it made was to amend the rule and fix the hour of reconvening at 9 o'clock, instead of 8, so as not to derange the plans for their entertainment made by the people of St. Louis. This was not done until Senator James A. Reed of Missouri had made a speech pointing out the discourtesy that would be inflicted upon their hosts if they upset these plans by the 8 o'clock rule.

The action of the convention is regarded here as the first dawning indication of a disgust with the fetish customs of national conventions and as giving a promise of better things. The most encouraging thing about it is that in any previous convention the day of useless spellbinding would have been had anyway, whether the extra day was cut out or not. There was plenty of time for it, for Senator James's speech was finished soon after 2 o'clock, and the rest of the afternoon could have been devoted to wearisome speechmaking in a hot hall. In Denver, eight years ago, when the convention proceedings were as cut-and-dried as here, that is precisely what was done. This time, however, the delegates wanted nothing but business. Even the so-called "demonstrations" were made short and divested of most of the silliest of their features.

The delegates repeated and emphasized their enthusiasm over peace by wildly cheering every one of Chairman James's references to it. There was a heartfelt and enthusiastic outburst over his declaration that the President had maintained American rights "without the shedding of a drop of blood." Mr. James repeated the effect created by ex-Governor Glynn in his speech as Temporary Chairman. Those of the leaders who were concerned over Wednesday's demonstration made no attempt to control expression of feeling by the delegates, and were concentrating their efforts on the platform, in the hope of making it strong enough to counteract and overcome any interpretation of the demonstrations as indicating a sentiment for "peace at any price."

William J. Bryan is highly satisfied and regards the events of the last two days as a great vindication for himself. Mr. Bryan delivered a speech against preparedness this afternoon at the City Club amid a tremendous burst of enthusiasm. He was cheered enthusiastically when he came into the press section this morning, and whether in the councils of the leaders or in the hall of the delegates, he is admitted to be the outstanding figure of the convention, to which he is not a delegate, and in which he has had no part.

### "I Am Very Grateful," President Wilson Says, on Receiving the News of His Renomination

*Special to The New York Times.*

WASHINGTON, Friday, June 16.—"I am very grateful to my generous friends."

This was President Wilson's only comment when told of his nomination by acclamation this morning. The President, who earlier in the evening had taken a walk in the rain with Mrs. Wilson, returned to the White House at 10:30 o'clock.

Bulletins were sent to him from the White House offices until 11:30 o'clock, when word was returned to the executive offices that the President had gone to bed. The President was not disturbed again until 12:55 o'clock this morning, when Joseph P. Tumulty, his private secretary, telephoned to him that he had been nominated by acclamation. The secretary was talking to the President when news arrived that Vice President Marshall had also been nominated by acclamation.

President Wilson slipped out the main door of the White House at 10 o'clock last night in a driving rain when nobody was about but the ushers and policemen at the front door. With him was Mrs. Wilson. Neither had an umbrella, although the rain was coming down strongly and there was a strong southeastern wind. Both wore rubber coats and rubber hats. The Secret Service men in the executive offices were promptly advised by the policeman at the front door, and took up the trail, followed by several newspaper men. Swinging around the eastern side of the White House President and Mrs. Wilson walked briskly into the Mall and the monument grounds, following the path to the Washington Monument. They went to the base of the monument, and, after tarrying several minutes, returned to the White House. Their walk lasted about half an hour.

Returning to the White House, the President and Mrs. Wilson went to the library. The White House was in direct telegraphic and telephonic communication with the St. Louis Convention hall tonight. Over the telephone line, which ran from Secretary Tumulty's offices to the platform in the convention hall, the cheering during the demonstration at midnight was easily audible.

## CONVENTION ROUSED BY JAMES'S SPEECH

### Whirlwind Demonstration of 21 Minutes Over Wilson's Success in Averting War.

*Special to The New York Times.*

ST. LOUIS, June 15.—"I can see the accusing picture of Christ on the battlefield, with the dead and dying all around him, with the scream of shrapnel and the roll of cannon, and I can hear the Master say to Woodrow Wilson, 'Blessed are the peacemakers, for they shall be called the children of God.'"

The Democratic National Convention, deaf and idle when he had referred to Wilson's achievements in upbuilding the army and navy, came to life with a wild scream today at these words of Senator Ollie James.

The Senator succeeded ex-Governor Glynn as presiding officer, and he practiced the lesson he had learned from Glynn. He took peace as his keynote, and he used it to even better advantage than Glynn, because he had been able to observe wherein Glynn made his biggest hits and had profited by it.

Ollie James is an orator of power and force. His voice is irresistible and compelling, strong enough to match well with his gigantic physique, yet melodious and full of lights and shades. His presence is eye-filling, his manner and gestures wonderfully light and supple for so big a man. He has the face of a prizefighter, the body of an oak, and the voice of a pipe organ, and he has all the tricks of the orator at the tip of his tongue.

#### Enthusiasm for W. J. B.

The first event of the morning came before the convention was called to order. It was the appearance of William J. Bryan in his place among the newspaper reporters, of whom he is one. The convention rose and cheered him—with great enthusiasm and warm personal feeling. The Commoner responded to the greeting in the old Bryan manner, so lost of late. The anxious and careworn look he had worn was all gone. Yesterday the convention took Bryan from the scrapheap and elevated him to the ridgepole. It brought back with a rush all his old self-confidence, and it was as plain as the nose on his face that he saw 1920 in his mind's eye.

"The Star-Spangled Banner" and "Dixie" were sung. Senator James, as Permanent Chairman, then took the gavel from Mr. Glynn and started in on his speech. He began with the tariff and other domestic issues, and received a cordial indorsement of his most telling points, but there was nothing beyond cordiality in it. The convention was waiting for him to get to the one subject dearest to its heart and to see whether he would voice its views as well as Glynn had done, or better. There was no question that he would voice them; the demonstration of yesterday had made it certain that he must talk peace or make a fizzle of it.

Mr. James dealt lightly with hyphenism and switched immediately to the subject of President Wilson's achievements in the cause of peace. His manner became more assured; he had been feeling his way to avoid mistake, but he had found it, and now he went on with big strides.

#### A Spontaneous Demonstration.

"There are two kinds of courage," he suddenly roared out, leaning his great body over the platform and bringing his mighty arm around in a long sweep over his head, "the courage of the man who is willing to go to the conflict himself and the courage of the man who is willing to send others there."

He got the expected result. The convention was enchanted. The cheer was spontaneous and hot from its heart.

"Some of them tell us," he said, "that the President's foreign policy has been evil and vacillating. Tonight 20,000,000 American fathers will gather around an unbroken family fireside with their wives at their sides and their children around their knees, and contrast that with the Old World, the world of broken firesides and gloom and mourning upon every hand. If that is evil and vacillating, may God prosper it and teach it to the rulers of the Old World."

The convention waited in breathless and painful silence to catch the last word of this, and with its coming there was a rush of cheers. There was no need for Sergeant at Arms John I. Martin to give his hands-up signal. He did give it, but the convention was ahead of him. The delegates did not rise to their feet, they leaped. Everything that could be waved—hats, fans, flags, articles of clothing—was tossing wildly about the bobbing heads and jumping figures of a thousand men. Nor was there any attempt to prolong this into a "demonstration" to be timed by watches and egged on by cheer leaders; it was too spontaneous, too heartfelt, too genuine. When they sat down they began to yell, "Keep it up, Ollie, keep it up," and the smile on the Senator's face showed that he intended to keep it up. There was only one note to charm them, and from that time on he sounded it without ceasing.

He did, it is true, make a short and necessary diversion to the subject of preparedness, for that is an essential part of the platform and policy of the Democratic candidate and cannot be omitted. The convention listened patiently, fully satisfied that James would make this part of the speech as brief as possible and get down immediately to the subject of which alone they wanted to hear and of which they could not hear too much. There was the usual brief handclapping for this reference, and then James dropped it.

"Four years ago they sneeringly called him a school teacher," he said, referring to President Wilson. "Today he is a world teacher. His class is made up of Kings, Kaisers, Princes, and potentates, and the schoolroom circle is the globe."

#### A Novel, Dramatic Thing.

And then came the big hit of the day, the biggest hit of the whole convention, compared with which all the bogus demonstrations here and in Chicago look pallid and puny.

"Without orphaning a single American child, without widowing a single American mother, without firing a single gun or shedding a drop of blood, he wrung from the most militant spirit that ever brooded above a battlefield the concession of American demands and American rights."

The last part of this sentence was unheard, although James bellowed it forth at the height of his great voice. Before he had uttered the word "spirit" there came a sound like the rush of a storm, and a great wave of sound broke over him. And then there was a strange thing, one not seen before. This crowd had burst out with that mighty roar the moment it caught his meaning and without waiting to hear his words; but as it shouted it wanted to hear the lost words, and spontaneously it checked itself and cleared a silence before it, and shouted, still standing and waiting to go on with its own interrupted cheer, "Repeat! Repeat!"

The thing was so novel, so unexpected, so dramatic, that Ollie James could not understand it. It was something outside his experience, outside the experience of any orator. He stood there with his mouth open, his eyes darting inquiry here and there into the crowd. His lips were motionless, but his eyes were asking what it was that they wanted him to do, what was the meaning of that sudden and breathless silence in the very midst of a cheer; for it was plainly not ended yet.

"Repeat! Repeat!" they shouted again, and James, understanding at last and realizing the great opportunity before him, stepped to the edge of the platform, raised his immense voice to its highest pitch, and sent the sentence rolling again over the heads of the men before him. This time he uttered it with great deliberation and without emphasis, relying upon the steady beat of the syllables as they slowly connected themselves to take the place of all tricks of voice or manner.

The effect was cumulative and stunning. The crowd listened in a silence so intense that it seemed as if he might have spoken in a whisper and still be heard. The delegates all stood before him with their eyes fixed on his face; the lips of many were moving as his moved, and heads were nodding as the syllables ticked off.

#### Now a Whirlwind of Sound.

The whirlwind of sound that followed the last word lasted for twenty-one minutes. The first part of it differed from the usual convention demonstration in the fact that it was not a demonstration at all: it was a shouted prayer. No attempt was made to begin it or to keep it up; it went on of itself. It was made almost entirely by the delegates, and it was made by all of them. In the galleries many persons were standing, but more were sitting. It was not the spectators who were

Continued on Page 2.

## WESCOTT NOMINATES WILSON

### New Jersey Judge Performs Same Service As He Did at Baltimore.

### MEXICAN POLICY CHEERED

### Applause Also Interrupts His References to President's Maintaining Law of Nations.

### SIGNAL FOR DEMONSTRATION

### Mention of Wilson's Name Sets Convention Cheering and Tumult Lasts 45 Minutes.

*Special to The New York Times.*

ST. LOUIS, Friday, June 16.—After a demonstration of approval of President Wilson late in the night which lasted forty-five minutes the Democratic National Convention renominated President Wilson and Vice President Marshall by acclamation. Mr. Wilson was renominated at 11:53 and Mr. Marshall at 11:55.

President Wilson was placed in nomination by Judge John W. Wescott of New Jersey.

The program called for a seconding speech from every delegation in the case of President Wilson, but after ex-Governor Harmon of Ohio and Governor Stuart of Virginia had made seconding speeches the delegates called vociferously for a vote and the nominations followed immediately.

Robert E. Burke of Illinois refused his consent to the unanimous nomination of the President amid a storm of hisses. No further attention was paid to him, and Chairman Ollie James declared the motion to nominate by acclamation carried.

Senator Kern of Indiana immediately nominated Mr. Marshall for Vice President without making a speech, and on motion the nomination was made by acclamation. The Friday hoodoo was escaped by four minutes.

At 11:59 the Notification Committees had been authorized and Chairmen Glynn and James had been appointed to the respective chairmanships of them.

#### Platform Report Delayed.

The routine motions of thanks and routine announcements of committee meetings, which are usually made at the end of a convention, were made, and then nothing remained but the platform. Chairman James's call for it brought no response, and a committee consisting of Senators Hughes, Vardaman, and Taggart was appointed to wait on the Resolutions Committee and find out what was the matter.

This was at 12:07 A. M. The convention waited impatiently for the committee to return. Many of the delegates had their hats on and were moving restlessly about the hall, while the galleries were shouting for Senator James Hamilton Lewis to make a speech.

Senators Hughes and Taggart returned at 12:20 and informed Chairman James that the Resolutions Committee had agreed on a report and was whipping it into shape, but would not be ready for two hours. There was nothing to do but while away the time with speechmaking for those two hours, and Representative Thomas J. Heflin of Alabama started it.

At 12:32 Senator Hughes informed the convention that the committee was not able to say when it would be ready with its report and a recess was taken until 11 o'clock today.

Nominating speeches were to have begun at the opening of the night session, but before getting to work William J. Bryan was invited to address the convention as an honored guest. He was greeted with great enthusiasm. The compliment conveyed in the invitation gained weight from the fact that no other man outside the convention had been either invited or permitted to address it.

It was at 10:14 P. M. that nominations for President were called for. Alabama yielded to New Jersey, and Judge Wescott, who placed Woodrow Wilson in nomination at Baltimore four years ago took the platform. Applause greeted his remarks on the policy toward Mexico. The crowd was attentive and quiet. It voiced approval of America's maintenance of international law. Some of the crowd, however, were eager for the nomination.

"Name him! Name him!" came cries from the galleries. Judge Wescott hurried his speech a little. He made such good time that he got into the peroration of his speech at 10:42 o'clock.

"The prophecy is fulfilled," said Judge Wescott; "the right has prevailed. Undisturbed by vituperation, the schoolmaster, the statesman, the financier, the emancipator, the pacificator, the moral leader of democracy has prevailed. The nation is at work, the nation is at peace. It is accomplishing the destiny of democracy."

Mr. Wescott said that four years ago the nation was not at work and men were idle. He struck a responsive chord when he referred to Mexico.

"Help Mexico!" he shouted, "or over

"All the News That's Fit to Print"

# The New York Times

LATE CITY EDITION

THE WEATHER
Showers today and probably Sunday; fresh southeast winds.
For full weather report see Page 19.

VOL. LXV...NO. 21,329. NEW YORK, SATURDAY, JUNE 17, 1916.—TWENTY PAGES. ONE CENT In Greater New York, Jersey City and Newark. Elsewhere, TWO CENTS.

# CARRANZA THREATENS OPEN WARFARE IF OUR ARMY MAKES FURTHER MOVE; CRISIS WITH MEXICO BROUGHT NEARER

## CONVENTION ENDS; PLATFORM VOTED RAPS HYPHENISM

**Plank on Americanism Sent to St. Louis by President Adopted Without Opposition.**

**NOT FIGHT OVER SUFFRAGE**

**Recommendation for Favorable State Action Wins on Roll Call, 888½ to 181½.**

**WOMEN'S DAY IN GALLERIES**

**Advocates Shrilly Cheered, Opponents Hissed—Gov. Ferguson Leads Non-Action Forces.**

*Special to The New York Times.*

ST. LOUIS, June 16.—The Democratic National Convention came to an end at 5:12 o'clock this afternoon, after the adoption of the platform, the only contest over which outside of the Committee on Resolutions related to woman suffrage and resulted in a rollcall by which the advocates of votes for women won what they considered a hollow victory.

The platform was adopted by a viva voce vote, exactly as approved by President Wilson and submitted by the Resolutions Committee, including the plank on Americanism and that favoring woman suffrage. No voice was raised against the vigorous declarations of the Americanism plank. The reading of the plank, which was drawn by President Wilson himself, was interrupted by handclapping. Its denunciation of conspirators for the advancement of foreign influence in this country was roundly applauded, as was its criticism of the disloyalty of some Americans. Excoriation of a political party that should receive such support received similar approval. Declarations for military preparedness were also uniformly applauded.

Close attention was given the plank relating to foreign policies. There was occasional scattering applause and cheers. The Latin-American policy plank got some applause, but more greeted the Mexican plank and frequently interrupted its reading, especially the reaffirmation of the Monroe Doctrine. The assertion that American troops should be kept in Mexico until danger of raids subsided was loudly applauded. The assertion that intervention is a "last recourse" received applause, but generous approval was given to the indorsement of the President's attempt to prevent intervention.

**The Hand on the Convention.**

"The hand that rocks the cradle rules the world," yelled a delegate from the Pacific Coast in reply to the speech of Governor Ferguson of Texas opposing the woman suffrage plank in the platform. Whether it ruled the world or not, that hand lay heavy on the last session of the Democratic Convention.

The galleries looking down on the convention were filled with women and bright with yellow sashes, yellow ribbons, yellow parasols. The cheering was shot through with soprano voices, and often the soprano dominated. The only subject discussed was the woman suffrage question, and on that the women in the galleries gave direction to the discussion.

A woman suffrage plank was to be adopted, and men who voted against it were hissed fiercely and without rebuke by the women in the galleries, while those who favored it were encouraged and rewarded with feminine cheers. Scattered throughout the convention were women with rollcall forms, waiting to take down the vote and register the opponents of their cause. The galleries ruled the convention and the women ruled the galleries. It was like the French Convention of the Revolution, gallery ruled, and the women with the rollcall blanks, noting down their enemies and the way they voted, suggested the knitting women of the Reign of Terror.

There was no dispute over the platform as a whole, or over any part of it, except the woman suffrage plank. The planks dealing with Americanism, with the tariff, and with other subjects received mechanical applause, but no comment or objection. But a minority report was made on the suffrage plank, and the last session of the convention was taken up with the fight over that. It was the first time that the question of votes for women had been the star feature of a session of a national convention of any party, and the change was very great from the old days when women suffragists used to besiege vainly the doors of platform committees, to be heard, if at all, merely as a reluctant courtesy.

**Big Majority for Suffrage.**

The minority report of Governor Ferguson was rejected by a vote of 888½ to 181½, and the majority report, recommending woman suffrage favorably to the States, was adopted by a viva voce vote.

Furthermore, the convention gave this overwhelming vote right on the heels of a speech by Senator Walsh of Montana, in which he swung the club of the women's vote over its head. He wasted no words on sentiment, he didn't talk about the hand that rocks the cradle, he made no appeal for equal justice to the sexes. He told the convention to adopt the suffrage plank or give up the electoral votes of the States where the woman's party has the ballot and to give up the control of the United States Senate. He told them that the women had the votes to beat the Democratic Party, to give the Presidency and the Senate to the Republicans, and that unless this plank were adopted they would do it.

It was not an idle threat. Whatever the more conservative suffragists may think or say and however they may

Continued on Page 2.

### Cabinet Congratulates Wilson; Marshall Wires: "You'll Win."

*Special to The New York Times.*

WASHINGTON, June 16.—President Wilson received the congratulations of members of the Cabinet over his renomination when he met them at the regular Friday Cabinet meeting this morning. Not until a few minutes before 11 o'clock, when the Cabinet was scheduled to meet, did the President go to the executive offices. There he found large stacks of telegrams congratulating him on his renomination, and predicting his election. Among them was one from Vice President Marshall, from Indianapolis, which the President read to members of his Cabinet. It said:

"In the fight which you are to win I am always yours to command."

President Wilson will probably go to his summer home at Shadow Lawn, in New Jersey, for the official notification of his nomination. New Jersey members of Congress have urged him to do this, and the President will probably accept. The date for his notification has, of course, not been fixed. The President will not remain at his Summer home more than a few days, but will return to Washington and stay here so long as Congress is in session.

## ELECT M'CORMICK TO RUN CAMPAIGN

**President's Choice for Chairman Grudgingly Approved by National Committee.**

**HIS SELECTION FOUGHT**

**Members Complain of Dictation and Desire for Party Harmony Alone Prevents a Rupture.**

*Special to The New York Times.*

ST. LOUIS, Saturday, June 17.—The election of a Chairman of the Democratic National Committee precipitated a fight in the organization which was livelier than any that developed during the entire convention. The quarrel was because of the deep resentment of a number of the committeemen because President Wilson personally selected a Chairman in the person of Vance McCormick of Pennsylvania. Mr. McCormick is not even a member of the National Committee.

After wrangling from 1:30 o'clock last night until after midnight, during which time many committeemen roundly scored the President for trying to run everything himself, the committeemen reached an agreement early this morning, and Mr. McCormick was elected Chairman.

The committeemen opposing the President wanted to pick their own head and were ready to unite on Homer S. Cummings of Connecticut. When they saw, however, that the President was going to take things into his own hands, they tried to "get from under," and throw the full responsibility for the campaign upon Mr. Wilson himself.

They put forward a resolution vesting in the President the power to select the full Campaign Committee to conduct his campaign as he might see fit, leaving the National Committee free from all responsibility. It was this resolution that furnished most of the debate, and it was withdrawn only after urgent appeals for harmony had been made by the cooler heads in the committee, who said they did not want the impression to get abroad that the Democrats were beginning their campaign with a free-for-all fight among themselves.

**Fight Started by Moore of Ohio.**

The resolution was presented by Judge E. H. Moore, National Committeeman from Ohio. It set forth that the committee was willing to pledge its support to the President, but wished him to assume full responsibility.

The fight got under way when Judge Moore offered his proposal. A. Mitchell Palmer of Pennsylvania made strenuous objection to it. Mr. Moore said he did not want any gag rule to obtain, and explained that the resolution had been given to him by Clark Howell of Georgia, whose proxy he held. Committeeman Barnett of Colorado moved that the resolution be tabled. John J. McGraw of West Virginia then introduced another resolution, which provided that the committee should select its own officers from within the membership.

There was some debate on this, and Mr. Moore announced that he would withdraw his own resolution and offer a substitute. The substitute read as follows:

Resolved, That the Democratic nominee for President of the United States be and he is hereby empowered to select a campaign committee of such number as he shall see fit, and a Chairman and other officers thereof, which committee and its Chairman and other officers may or may not be members of the National Committee, as such nominee shall determine; that such committee, when so selected, be in, and it is hereby empowered to have, subject to the supervision of such nominee, sole and exclusive control, conduct, and direction of the ensuing Presidential campaign; that no officer or member of the National Committee shall have or exercise any authority in the direction, control, or management of such campaign, except as such authority shall be derived from such Campaign Committee; and

Resolved, further, That we pledge to such campaign committee so selected our unqualified, earnest and enthusiastic co-operation and support in its endeavors to bring about the triumphant re-election of the Democratic candidate for President the Democratic candidates for President

When the vote on the above resolution was taken it was defeated, 46 to 2. The committee thereupon took a viva voce vote on Mr. McCormick. All present voted for him for the chairmanship.

**Fears Presidential Dynasty.**

In presenting his substitute resolution Mr. Moore said that it was meant to turn over the entire campaign to the President. He read extracts from speeches and letters of Mr. Wilson to show that the President had himself announced he would take orders from nobody. Yet, Mr. Moore continued, the President was now trying to order the National Committee how to conduct its own affairs. This power, he said, no American should have. No man, he declared, should have the power to create a Presidential dynasty.

Homer S. Cummings, the committee's own choice for Chairman, was the first to try to smooth over the trouble. He announced that he was against the Moore resolution and urged the com-

Continued on Page 2.

## ROOSEVELT WILL INDORSE HUGHES; PARTY HEADS MEET

**Colonel Said to Have Assurance Nominee in Accepting Will Bar Hyphenism.**

**PERKINS VISITS WHITMAN**

**And Governor Calls on Republican Candidate in Negotiations with Progressives.**

**COLONEL MUM ON POLITICS**

**Refuses to Give Interviews and Asserts He Will Make Announcements Only Under His Signature.**

Colonel Roosevelt will make a statement early next week indorsing Charles E. Hughes. This was positively asserted last night by a man who took an active part in negotiations intended to bring together the Republican candidate and the leader of the Progressives.

Colonel Roosevelt's expected statement is to follow the declaration of principles which Mr. Hughes will make after he is formally notified of his nomination. This was taken to mean that the statement of Mr. Hughes will contain a rebuke to German-American interference in American politics and a characterization of hyphenism sufficiently clear and vigorous to suit Mr. Roosevelt.

Governor Whitman had a long conference with Mr. Hughes yesterday. He then returned to the Hotel St. Regis where George W. Perkins called on him. After their conference Mr. Perkins went to the Hotel Langdon where he talked for some time to Colonel Roosevelt. Early last night Mr. Perkins called again on Mr. Whitman. When he left it was said that he was to make another visit to Colonel Roosevelt. Governor Whitman returned to Albany at midnight.

Mr. Perkins is regarded as the man closest to Colonel Roosevelt, and Governor Whitman is as close as any one to Mr. Hughes. It was declared last night on good authority that Mr. Whitman had learned the views of Mr. Hughes on the question of the German-American invasion of politics with more particularity than Mr. Hughes has made them known in his telegram of acceptance and statements since then, and that Colonel Roosevelt had found them strong enough, as they were transmitted by Mr. Perkins, to cause him to decide to throw his influence unreservedly in favor of the Republican candidate.

**Admits Talks Are Political.**

Mr. Perkins admitted yesterday that his talks with Colonel Roosevelt and Mr. Whitman were on politics, but he would not say anything specific. Governor Whitman refused to be quoted, although he discussed some features of the situation guardedly. After his second visit to Mr. Perkins, Governor Whitman took no pains to conceal the fact that he was in a jubilant frame of mind.

Colonel Roosevelt, who was still very much under the weather, refused to talk politics yesterday, but his friends insisted that nothing but a firm and unmistakable stand by Mr. Hughes, completely dispelling the belief of German-American propagandists that he sympathizes with their principles, would induce Colonel Roosevelt to give him active support or to take any steps to lead his Progressive followers back into the Republican ranks.

Governor Johnson, Chester Rowell, Raymond Robbins, and other Progressive leaders, who are in this city and have held discussions with Colonel Roosevelt, have refused to say anything about Colonel Roosevelt's present views or to indicate what course they are likely to pursue in the future. All that any of them would admit was that Colonel Roosevelt's stand would probably be shaped by the words of Mr. Hughes.

**Whitman Well Satisfied.**

Governor Whitman appeared last night to be well satisfied with the part that he was playing in the effort to bring the two parties together. It is said that if it is completely successful not only is his State leadership unassailable, but his prominence as a national figure is bound to be greatly increased by the credit he will receive, first as the Warwick of Mr. Hughes and secondly as the reconstructor of the Republican Party.

What part the prominence of Governor Whitman in the negotiations will have with the more radical wing of the Republican Party is at least uncertain. Many Progressives profess bitter opposition to him, and a resolution was introduced, though not adopted, at the meeting of Progressive leaders at Hotel Manhattan on Thursday night, favoring the indorsement of Judge Seabury, who may be the Democratic candidate for Governor.

While Governor Whitman and Colonel Roosevelt have not personally met, their close communication through a mutual friend, Mr. Perkins, is believed to indicate that there has been a softening of the feeling of hostility between the two men which dates back to the last campaign for the Governorship. Colonel Roosevelt charged that Governor Whitman through an intermediary had asked his support, but that the latter refused to qualify for it by making a statement denouncing William Barnes. Governor Whitman denied that the intermediary had been authorized to act for him, and Colonel Roosevelt throughout the campaign charged Mr. Whitman with untruthfulness.

After he had become Governor, Mr. Whitman recognized the Progressives liberally, appointing William H. Hotchkiss to conduct an important investigation, and later naming Oscar S. Straus as head of the Public Service Commission. The first sign that Colonel Roosevelt's opinion of the Governor was undergoing a change was his characteriza-

Continued on Page 2.

## Heavy Artillery Battles on Greek Border; Bulgars Said to be Moving Toward Rumania

PARIS, June 16.—The French War Office tonight issued the following report of operations of the army in the Balkans from June 1 to 15:

In the region of the Vardar River and of Lake Doiran both artilleries have been active during the whole fortnight. The bombardment was violent on the 4th, 8th, 10th, and 15th of June. There has been no infantry action of importance. A few patrol encounters have taken place in the mountainous region west of the Vardar. On the Struma the Bulgarians fortified themselves hastily in the region of Fort Rupel without penetrating any further into Greek territory.

Aviation—The enemy's aeroplanes have shown little activity during the last fortnight. Our machines bombarded enemy camps and organizations at Petris on June 1; at Petrio, Gievgeli, Istip, and Radovitza on the 7th; at Fort Rupel the 11th, and at Petrio and Strumitsa on the 14th.

Martial law was proclaimed in Saloniki on June 3. Its application did not cause any incidents.

ATHENS, June 16, (via London.)—It was reported in Athens today that the Bulgarians were withdrawing the majority of their forces from Saloniki to the Rumanian frontier.

PARIS, June 16.—It is reported from Saloniki, says a Havas dispatch from Athens today, that in consequence of the establishment of martial law by the Allies in that district and the taking over by them of the postal, telegraph, railway, and customs administration, the Greek military base, as well as the troops occupying the forts around Than, has been transferred to Volo, on the coast in Thessaly, about 100 miles northwest of Athens.

## RUSSIAN ARMIES ARE SWEEPING ON

**Ford River and Capture Strong Austrian Line—Entire Company Drowned.**

**14,100 MORE PRISONERS**

**6,000 Taken in Great Battle with Austrians and Germans Raging on the Stripa.**

PETROGRAD, June 16.—The capture of an additional 100 officers and 14,000 men was announced today by the War Office. The Russian successes in the offensive along the southern front are continuing, the statement declares. Its text follows:

On the front of the armies south of Poliessie the fighting continues. The enemy has suffered heavy losses in encounters with our troops. The following details of the operations in many sectors have been received:

In the course of a powerful but fruitless counterattack by the enemy in the region of Sokul, north of Rojitche, we took as prisoners twenty officers and 1,750 men.

In the region west and southwest of Lutsk during the pursuit of the enemy our cavalry fought several successful actions. Northwest of Kremenez our bold soldiers of General Sakharoff's force, after a desperate fight, dislodged the enemy from his fortified positions on the River Bluichevka between Kozin and Tarnovka by a vigorous assault. One of our young regiments, led by Colonel Tatarnoff, after a fierce fight, forded the deep river which was up to their chins. One company was engulfed and died a heroic death, but the valor of their comrades and their officers resulted in the disorderly flight of the enemy. Seventy officers and 5,000 men were taken prisoners, and two guns, a great many machine guns, 1,000 rifles, cartridges and enormous reserves of barbed wire were captured in this action.

By an equally impetuous coup, our infantry, with powerful support from the artillery, captured Rostok Wood, south of the lower Potchaieff, taking prisoners, machine guns, and bomb throwers.

By a heroic effort, the troops of General Stcherbatchoff's army yesterday overthrew the Austrians in the region of Gouvoronka and Guilovody, on the west bank of the Stripa.

Northwest of Buczacz the engagement with the Austrians and the Germans continues unceasingly. So far we have captured 6,000 prisoners, guns, and machine guns.

An enemy aeroplane has dropped bombs on Tarnopol.

Our brave Don Cossacks have taken prisoner seven officers and 600 men. The approximate total of yesterday's captures is 100 officers, 14,000 men, and a quantity of war material.

On the Dvina front and further south, in the region of Popesle, there has been an exchange of artillery and rifle fire. Our artillery made a violent attack yesterday in the region of Dvinsk. Enemy attempts to take the offensive in many sectors were everywhere repulsed by our fire.

A semi-official communication issued here today says:

"The operations near Baranovichi, to which some persons were inclined to attach importance, were nothing more serious than a reconnaissance in force undertaken to obtain information as to the enemy's strength which the simpler forms of scouting had failed to reveal. The German attacks in the Narocz and Dvina districts differed in no essentials from the local lunges which the enemy has frequently made on these sectors."

Details of the reported evacuation of Czernowitz by the Austrians are given in a dispatch from Bukowina, by way of Bucharest, received by the semi-official Petrograd News Agency. The dispatch says that before abandoning the city the Austrian authorities arrested a number of persons, who were forced to accompany the retreating troops. The railway rolling stock was sent to Ilskani and the tracks about the city were destroyed. Trainloads of wounded were dispatched to Dornavatra, seventy-seven miles southwest of Czernowitz.

BERLIN, June 16, (via London.)—The War Office today issued the following bulletin:

The Russians continued their efforts yesterday against General von Bothmer's front north of Przewloka, (on the Stripa River, north of Buczacz.) During the repulse of the enemy more than 400 men were taken prisoner by the defenders.

Special Cable to THE NEW YORK TIMES.

PETROGRAD, June 16, (Dispatch to The London Daily News.)—It is reported that the Austrian authorities have already left Czernowitz after entrusting a small committee of various nationalities with the handing over of the town to the Russians.

### CONGRATULATES THE CZAR.

**King Victor, for Italy, Expresses Admiration of Army's Success.**

PETROGRAD, June 16.—The following was issued tonight by the War Office:

The Supreme Commander, the Czar, has received the following telegram from the King of Italy:

"I am in harmony with the whole Italian people in expressing the sentiment of profound admiration for the victorious development of the powerful offensive of your Majesty's armies, and in sending to you the warmest and most friendly congratulations. Being convinced that the efforts thus happily commenced will lead to definite success, I pray you to accept the

Continued on Page 4.

## FRENCH CHECK VERDUN ASSAULTS

**Night Attempts by Germans in Great Force East of the Meuse Result in Failure.**

**BERLIN TELLS OF SUCCESS**

**Counter-Drive at French at Dead Man Hill Won Back Lost Line—Other Attacks Repulsed.**

LONDON, June 16.—In the continued heavy fighting on the Verdun front both French and Germans assert that attacks by hostile forces were repulsed.

Powerful assaults made last night on the French position southeast of Thiaumont Farm, on the east of the Meuse, broke down under the French machine gun and infantry fire, according to Paris. One assault was directed at the line from Hill 321 to the edge of Hill 320, and another at the southern edge of the Caillette Wood.

Berlin says two attacks were delivered by the French yesterday and last night on the German line along the southern slope of Dead Man Hill, west of the Meuse, but were unsuccessful. In the first attack the French temporarily gained some ground, it is stated, but a counterattack drove them back.

The Paris night report, on the contrary, reaffirms the statement of yesterday concerning the gain at Dead Man Hill, saying that trenches on a front of one kilometer (five-eighths of a mile) were captured.

The afternoon bulletin of the French War Office reads:

On the left bank of the River Meuse the Germans last night delivered several counterattacks upon the trenches on the southern slopes of Dead Man Hill, which were occupied by us yesterday. All their endeavors failed under the French fire. The total number of German prisoners taken at this point reaches 5 officers and 180 men.

On the right bank of the river the enemy, at 6 o'clock yesterday evening, directed a powerful offensive movement against our positions to the north of the Thiaumont fortifications, from Hill No. 321, as far as the sides of Hill No. 320. The successive attacks of this movement broke down under the fire of our machine guns and our infantry, and it resulted in heavy losses to our assailants.

Further to the east, following a violent bombardment with large calibre shells, the Germans undertook an attack at about 10 P. M. upon our trenches on the southern side of the Caillette Wood. Our curtain of fire, at once brought into play, prevented the enemy from coming out of his trenches.

On the remainder of the front there have been intermittent artillery exchanges.

This bulletin was issued by the French War Office this evening:

On both banks of the Meuse the activity of the artillery was intermittent during the course of the day. There was no infantry action.

It has been confirmed that the attack we made yesterday on the slope south of Le Mort Homme gave us a portion of enemy trenches on a front of about one kilometer. All the attempts made by the enemy to drive us back from there have completely failed. The number of prisoners taken exceeds 200, including six officers.

There has been no important event on the other parts of the front.

The German Army Headquarters' statement reads:

On the left bank of the Meuse the French attacked the southern slope of Dead Man Hill with strong forces. They succeeded temporarily in gaining some ground, but were driven back again by a brief counterattack. We took prisoner 8 officers and 238 men and captured several machine guns.

A repetition of the enemy attack during the late evening, and operations against German positions adjoining on both sides, were completely unsuccessful. The enemy suffered heavy, sanguinary losses.

On the right bank of the Meuse, apart from minor infantry engagements in the Thiaumont ravine, which were favorable to us, the activity was limited chiefly to violent artillery actions on both sides.

The official statement of the British War Office says:

Last night we successfully exploded mines in the neighborhood of the Souchez Quarries and Cuinchy. An enemy mine was exploded near Givenchy, but did no damage.

Today the hostile artillery was unusually active immediately north of La Bassée Canal and in the Loos salient.

Our trenches east of Zillebeke were shelled heavily for a short period this afternoon.

The remainder of the front was quiet.

### FOUND VAUX FORT A RUIN.

**Germans Captured a Few Wornout Men Among the Wreckage.**

PARIS, June 16.—The last message received from Major Reynal, commander of Fort de Vaux, before it fell into the hands of the Germans a week ago, was made public here today. The message read:

"We are reaching the limit. Officers and soldiers have all done their duty. Vive la France!"

Since the beginning of the real attack on the fort in March the Germans fired no less than 8,000 projectiles daily, and

Continued on Page 4.

### Carranza Warning to Gen. Pershing of Warfare If Our Troops in Mexico Move South, East, or West

CHIHUAHUA CITY, Mexico, June 16.—General Jacinto Trevino, commanding the Carranza Army of the North, today advised General J. J. Pershing, American expeditionary commander, that any movement of American troops from their present line to the south, east, or west would be considered a hostile act and a signal to commence warfare. General Trevino acted upon specific instructions from Carranza. He also announced today that he had received acknowledgment from General Pershing of the recent order nullifying any agreement made with General Gabriel Gavira.

Anti-American feeling here, which had died down materially, was provoked again by exaggerated reports of a recent encounter between American soldiers and natives in a saloon in Casas Grandes in which a Mexican policeman was wounded.

*Another Clash With Mexican Bandits.*

BROWNSVILLE, Texas, June 16.—United States troops came upon a band of between twenty-five and thirty Mexican bandits about ten miles east of San Benito, Texas, late tonight, and, after exchanging a few shots, the Mexicans scattered. It is reported three Mexicans were killed. So far as known, there were no American casualties.

The troops engaged came from San Benito. Two companies of the Twenty-sixth Infantry were immediately dispatched in automobiles from Harlingen, Texas, to Olmito, ten miles north of Brownsville, in an effort to cut off the bandits, who at midnight were headed for the Rio Grande.

## ARMY MONEY BILL REPORTED TO HOUSE

**Measure Intended to Carry Out Preparedness Program Calls for $157,123,099.**

**PROVIDES FOR WAR COUNCIL**

**$500,000 Set Aside for Summer Camps and $9,975,000 for National Guard Salaries.**

*Special to The New York Times.*

WASHINGTON, June 16.—The measure which will carry the actual appropriations to back up the Administration's plan for national preparedness so far as the army is concerned—the Army Appropriation bill—was reported to the House today from the Military Committee by Chairman Hay of Virginia. The bill carries $157,123,099, an increase of $55,000,000 over last year. The estimates on which the bill was based aggregated $200,000,000.

In addition to the important appropriations for the army the bill contains provision for the organization of a Council of Executive Information for the Co-ordination of Industries and Resources for the National Security and Welfare. This council is to be composed of the Secretaries of War, the Navy, Commerce, Agriculture, Labor, and the Interior.

An advisory commission of seven experts in industries, public utilities, and national resources, to be nominated by the council and appointed by the President, is made possible in the bill by a proposed appropriation of $200,000. This commission is to serve without pay. Its duty will be to recommend to the President and to department heads the location of railroads strategically with reference to the American frontier, so as to make possible the quick concentration of troops and supplies to defense points; co-ordination for military, industrial, and commercial purposes in the location of extensive highways and branches of railroads; mobilization of military and naval resources for defense purposes; increase of production of domestic articles necessary in case of interrupting commerce, and informing American producers of these needs. Although the Army Reorganization bill approved by the President on June 3 authorizes increases in the line of the regular army to 175,000 men, the Appropriation bill provides pay for only about 105,000 men, exclusive of the staff corps.

Aviation receives $1,222,000, of which $50,000 is to be devoted to experimental development of an aeroplane motor. Summer military training camps receive $500,000, and an appropriation of $9,975,000 is authorized for salaries for officers and men of the National Guard. Enlisted men in the line of active service obtain about one-sixth of the total in the bill for pay and bonuses for length of service.

Mobilization of industries in case of war is provided for by an appropriation of $200,000 for purchases of jigs, dies, and gauges to equip private plants for manufacture of standard army ordnance supplies.

Chairman Hay and the Military Affairs Committee provide in the bill for tardy recognition of the heroism of Major James Carroll, who, as a member of the Army Medical Corps, sacrificed his life in the discovery and proof of the menace of the mosquito as a carrier of yellow fever germs. Major Carroll's mother, Mrs. Harriet C. Carroll, now said to be dependent upon charity of friends, receives a pension of $600 annually in the bill.

Army officers detailed at all army posts except at West Point are prohibited from maintaining polo ponies. The bill provides for purchase of such ponies for West Point, while prohibiting their maintenance elsewhere.

### DOMINICANS TALK OF WAR.

**Movement to Drive Out American Forces Reported in Havana.**

Special Cable to THE NEW YORK TIMES.

HAVANA, June 16.—Dominicans here are collecting money to help San Domingo fight the American forces. They said Haitians had agreed to join a movement to drive the Americans from the island.

They also said Desiderio Arais, who is organizing the Dominican movement, already has sufficient ammunition stored in the mountains to fight the Americans several years.



## MEXICANS IN JUAREZ ARE CALLED TO ARMS

**Proclamation Is Posted Which Urges Citizens to Drill Against Invasion.**

**OUR TROOPS SENT TO POSTS**

**New Mexico Battery Ordered from Columbus to Strengthen the Army Force in El Paso.**

*Special to The New York Times.*

EL PASO, June 16.—All male residents of Juarez have been called to arms, the American troops hereabouts are under orders in their camps and at Fort Bliss, and tonight the feeling along the border is more tense than it has been for over a month. Street car traffic from here to Juarez was stopped tonight.

The order for all men in Juarez to report for military duty was posted in Juarez today by the military authorities. The notice, which was in Spanish and signed by Jesus Valdez, called upon citizens, both old and young, to meet in the principal plaza "to prepare for a break with the United States." The notice, as it appears on the bulletin boards and poles in the Mexican town, reads:

"We invite all the citizens and inhabitants of this town who care to receive military instruction free and voluntarily to meet in the plaza in order to practice and prepare in the event that there is a break with the United States. Please put yourself in readiness for service each afternoon at 5:30 in the Plaza Principal, opposite the headquarters of the Twenty-eighth Battalion, in order to receive the arms and ammunition necessary for closing the port if necessary."

The order for all troops to report at their camps or at the fort tonight to remain under arms was issued by General George Bell this afternoon after he learned that the notices had been posted in Juarez. The provost guards, who patrol the downtown streets, received copies of the order and notified all soldiers on liberty to report at camp or barracks at once.

It is admitted here that the situation in Juarez is causing the military and civil authorities much concern. The town is filling up with Mexican refugees from the interior, who are being given railway tickets to come to the border in search of work. These men are to be armed along with the residents of Juarez, and it is feared they will start trouble.

General Bell called up General Francisco Gonzales, commander of the Juarez garrison today, and told him that he had placed a detachment of the best sharpshooters on the border, and that they had orders to shoot to kill at the first man who fired across the line from Juarez, whether he was a civilian or soldier. The city has also armed its inspectors and health officers who work in the Mexican quarter. They have received rifles and have been ordered to return any firing from the Mexican side.

H. Marrow, an American mining man employed by the Alvarado Mining and Milling Company in the Parral district, arrived here today with the report that General Calexico Contreras, a former Villista commander, had defeated and captured a detachment of Carranza troops from the Parral garrison across the line in Durango, and had cut off the ears of thirty-five of the prisoners. There is no other confirmation of Marrow's story.

COLUMBUS, N. M., June 16.—Battery A of the New Mexico National Guard, recently mustered into the United States service, was ordered today to report for duty to General George Bell at El Paso. No explanation of the order was available here.

### CALL OUR ARMY WEAK.

**Carranza Officials Say Recent Raids Prove Inability.**

Special Cable to THE NEW YORK TIMES.

MEXICO CITY, June 16, (via Galveston.)—Regarding the border situation, Carranza officials say, the recent raids show the inability of the United States to guard its own borders. They say the United States Government will see the justice of the Mexican claims. It is asserted that Carranza is doing all possible to avoid a conflict. It is learned, unofficially, that the Carranza Government will repeat the statement made by Minister of War Obregon in his conference with General Hugh L. Scott, that no new troops will be allowed to pass the border with the permission of the de facto Government.

The Government will undoubtedly oppose any attempt to send troops into other points in Mexico.

## WARNING SENT TO PERSHING

**President and His Cabinet Discuss Most Serious Breach Since Vera Cruz.**

**NOTE TO FIRST CHIEF READY**

**Administration Has No Intention of Withdrawing Troops from Their Present Lines.**

**CROSS RIVER AT SAN IGNACIO**

**Detachment of Soldiers Defies Peril of Attack, but Fails to Find Bandits' Trail.**

### Carranza Resents Talk of Occupying Mexico

Special Cable to THE NEW YORK TIMES.

MEXICO CITY, June 15, (via Galveston.)—THE NEW YORK TIMES correspondent had a brief interview with the First Chief of the de facto Government today.

"Have you read the declarations Mr. Hughes made after his nomination by the Republican Convention?" General Carranza was asked. "What is your opinion of his declaration referring to Mexico?" He replied:

"Yes, I have read them, and to my mind there is no more occasion for Mr. Hughes discussing the occupation of Mexico than there would be for him to discuss the occupation of Germany."

In response to other questions, such as his opinion of the Democratic platform and the attitude of the United States, General Carranza promised a further statement in a few days.

*Special to The New York Times.*

WASHINGTON, June 16.—The Mexican situation tonight is forging headlong toward what promises to be the most serious crisis that President Wilson will have faced since the American occupation of Vera Cruz.

All reports reaching Washington—official as well as unofficial—indicate the possibility of a clash between the military forces of the de facto Government and American troops on Mexican soil. There is grave fear that such a clash may come before the American reply is delivered to the Carranza note, which demanded the immediate withdrawal of the American troops from Mexico.

The tension of the Mexican situation was considerably increased tonight when reports reached Washington to the effect that General Jacinto Trevino, commanding the Carranza army of the North, had today advised General J. J. Pershing, American expeditionary commander, that any movement of American troops from their present lines to the south, east, or west would be considered a hostile act and as a signal to commence warfare. The report stated that General Trevino acted upon specific instructions from Carranza.

Despite this move, however, American troops crossed the border today in pursuit of the bandits who raided the camp of the Fourteenth Cavalry at San Ignacio, Texas, yesterday morning. Near here a force of Carranzistas, under General Ricaut, is reported moving northward. It is recalled that the Carranza Government objected strenuously to the dispatch of the second punitive expedition, commanded by Colonel Sibley, in pursuit of the raiders who attacked Glenn Springs and Boquillas last month.

**Early Clash Thought Inevitable.**

In his recent note demanding the immediate withdrawal of all troops from Mexico, General Carranza bluntly told this Government that orders had been given to the de facto Government forces to resist the troops commanded by Colonel Sibley. Fortunately, that expedition went approximately 200 miles into Mexico without running into Mexican troops and a clash was avoided.

General Pershing's forces, according to the official reports received from time to time by the War Department, which were generally encamped or intrenched along a certain definite and well-marked line since the re-alignment of troops was made have gone beyond that line in numerous instances in pursuit of bandits known to be within striking distance of the expedition. Only yesterday the War Department received word that a detachment of the Thirteenth Cavalry, under Captain Turner, had proceeded as far as Tepehuanes, twenty-five miles south of Santa Clara, arriving there on Monday morning, where they captured Piedro Lujan.

This is only one of numerous instances in which, since the conference between Generals Scott and Obregon, small detachments of American soldiers have been sent outside the American lines in pursuance of the American Government's policy of having its forces attack raiders and bandits whenever they come within striking distance of the expeditionary force. General Trevino's reported warning to General Pershing that the American forces will be attacked if they move south, west or east, [illegible]

"All the News That's Fit to Print."

# The New York Times.

THE WEATHER
Fair, moderate temperature today and tomorrow; west winds.
For full weather report see Page 23.

VOL. LXVI...NO. 21,468. NEW YORK, FRIDAY, NOVEMBER 3, 1916.—TWENTY-FOUR PAGES. ONE CENT In Greater New York, Jersey City and Newark. | Elsewhere, TWO CENTS.

# CARLSTROM FLIES 652 MILES FROM CHICAGO; DOWN FOR THE NIGHT AT HAMMONDSPORT; TO ARRIVE HERE AT 9 A. M. TODAY

## WINS NEW NON-STOP RECORD

### Flies the 452 Miles to Erie in 4 Hours 17½ Minutes.

### HALTED BY SLIGHT MISHAP

### Discovers Gasoline Leaking Where Nut on Feed Pipe Had Become Loose.

### 700,000 WITNESS PROGRESS

### Reported to Everybody by Telephone at Almost Every Mile on the Way.

Victor Carlstrom, who undertook yesterday to fly the Curtiss 200-horse power military biplane, "The New York Times," from Chicago to New York between sunrise and sunset and without a stop, did not achieve all that he had planned, but he did travel 652 miles in six hours seven and one-half minutes, actual flying time, the 452 miles of this distance that lay between Chicago and Erie, Penn., being traversed without a stop in four hours, seventeen and one-half minutes, constituting a new American non-stop record.

The previous record was Carlstrom's own, made on May 21 last, when he flew from Newport News, Va., to New York, 400 miles, in four hours and one minute. Carlstrom's average per hour on that occasion was 104 miles. His average yesterday was 107 miles.

Carlstrom spent last night at Hammondsport, N. Y. He descended there at 4:24 P. M., because continuing on to New York would have involved two hours' flying in the dark, making any necessary descent on the way extremely dangerous to him and his machine. Hammondsport is a few miles north of Carlstrom's route, but one of the Curtiss factories, with its spacious aviation grounds, is there, and he will therefore have proper facilities for getting away this morning, when he will finish his journey to New York.

Hammondsport is about 315 miles from New York, a three-hour journey as Carlstrom flies. He plans to start at 6 o'clock this morning and to arrive at Governors Island at 9 o'clock or a few minutes after. He will probably reach the Hudson at Fort Lee a few minutes before 9 o'clock, and his flight down the river to Governors Island will be visible from Riverside Drive. On his arrival the mail he brings from Chicago will be distributed.

While Carlstrom did not accomplish all that was planned, it was only a loose nut, corrected later by a single turn of a wrench, that caused his descent at Erie, Penn., delaying him three hours, and it is clear that a non-stop flight between Chicago and New York in eight or nine hours is practicable, probably if the attempt were made again tomorrow it would succeed.

**Every Move Recorded.**

But if the flight itself fell short of what was desired it was attended by a demonstration of capacity to mobilize large and widely separated units of industry that was extremely impressive to those who witnessed it. From the moment that Carlstrom rose into the air at Chicago until he descended at Hammondsport, his movements were constantly observed and instantly reported. This was accomplished by the American Telephone and Telegraph Company and its associated companies. To the listener on the wire in New York it seemed that wherever Carlstrom passed over a telephone he was reported, and almost always without more than a minute's delay. Had Carlstrom been an enemy aviator in wartime there could have been no complaint of slackness or delay in gathering intelligence of his movements.

It was over the telephone that THE TIMES got its first news of Carlstrom's start. He rose into the air in Chicago at 6:09½ A. M., Western time, and at 6:10 (7:10 New York time) THE TIMES was told about it. Thereafter news came almost every minute, and not to THE TIMES alone, for it spread out over all the vast network of telephone lines for fifteen or twenty miles on either side the line of flight, heralding the flier's advance and bringing out thousands to see him—in some of the larger towns tens and scores of thousands. The telephone people estimated last night that probably 700,000 persons had witnessed Carlstrom's flight between Chicago and Hammondsport, and that had it been continued to New York the number would easily have exceeded a million.

**Bulletins of the Start.**

The first bulletin which left the aviation field at 5:45 A. M., Central time, or 6:45 New York time, said it was getting light and that Carlstrom was tuning up the aeroplane. Five minutes later came the news that he was ready to start and was loading the mail sacks. Then at 6:01 Central time it was said that Carlstrom had settled himself in the machine, half a minute later that he was ready to start, and one minute later that the motor was running.

Then come a delay of seven minutes and Carlstrom started on his record-breaking flight—at exactly 7:09½ New York time. The observers announced

Continued on Page 4.

## Carlstrom's Own Story of His Flight and of the Trifling Mishap That Delayed It

By VICTOR CARLSTROM.

Telephoned by him to THE TIMES from Hammondsport, N. Y.

I don't know what to say about my flight, except that I'm here now when I expected to be in New York. It's hard luck, and, of course, I'm disappointed. But I'll make it tomorrow.

I got away from Chicago about 6:10 o'clock, and everything was going fine until I got a little past Erie. Then I noticed that gasoline was running out beneath the machine. Something was wrong, of course, and I knew I had to stop and investigate. There wasn't any telling how much gas I had lost nor how much I had left to go on. I was right past Erie, but I turned around and went back there because I knew I would want to be near a big city and near a telephone.

I made an easy landing and jumped out to examine the machine. I found that the nut holding the pipe from the gasoline tank in connection with the carburetor had worked loose and gas was flowing out from this leak. It wasn't much of an accident to hold up a flight from Chicago to New York, but it held it up all right.

A big crowd of people began to gather round after I had landed, and I got the manager of the Bell Telephone Company to help me. He had an automobile, and I got him to drive me to the nearest telephone. I was nearly a mile, or maybe more, out of the city, and we drove to a grocery store, where I put in calls for Elmer Davis, THE NEW YORK TIMES man, and for Charles B. Kirkham, the chief engineer of the Curtiss Company. I'd left them both in Chicago. I couldn't get Mr. Davis, but I got Mr. Kirkham, and talked over the situation with him. I wanted to let him know where I was and to ask him about what he thought I'd better try to do; whether he thought I ought to keep on as far as I could or what else.

He advised me to go as far as I could, and suggested that I could make Buffalo. I was pretty sure I could make Binghamton instead, but after I had started I decided to head for here for two reasons: first, I would have a place to leave the machine, and second, I would have expert help to start the motor in the morning.

You know it's pretty hard to start an aeroplane motor like mine. That's one reason I was delayed so long in Erie. There were plenty of people around, but there weren't many who knew much about aeroplanes. First off it was hard to get the gasoline I wanted and had to have. When I finally bought fifty gallons in town I had to have it carted out in a truck and poured into my tank. The minutes flew. Time goes fast when you've got a lot to do and are all alone doing it.

Fixing the motor was a cinch. It just needed a turn of the wrench to take up on that loose nut, and then the machine was as good as ever. I can't imagine how it ever came to go wrong. It's the first time I ever had an accident of the kind. Of course I found the trouble at once, for all I had to do was to trace up the leaking gasoline to its source, and I fixed it at once, but it was some time before I was ready to start out again.

Then I had to crank that motor single handed. I got some of the crowd to hold the machine and I got a man who knew something about automobiles to throw the switch on and off as I cranked. But even at that it took me a lot of time

When I got going again I made good speed, just as I had the whole trip. No, I don't think there was anything exceptional about my time. It was about the rate the machine usually flies, though the wind helped a little. There was a southwest wind blowing, and it aided some. I flew from 4,000 to 8,000 feet up, varying the altitude as I found the better wind. It was steadier up above, not so puffy. It was pretty rough down below, and it wasn't any place to fly if you wanted to make speed.

At the rate I was going I'd have made Governors Island before 4 o'clock. It seems a shame that a little thing like a nut had to stop me, and I'm pretty disappointed, but it couldn't be helped.

My machine is all right now, and I'll finish the trip tomorrow pretty fast. In fact, there wasn't a thing the matter with the machine all day except that loose nut, and after I had that made fast the machine was as good as the day we finished the final test. It was only a question of how far I could fly before darkness made flying and landing too dangerous to attempt. Only a couple of hours more of daylight would have landed me in New York. Now I'll have to finish it another day.

I expect to leave here at about 6 o'clock in the morning, and I figure I ought to reach Governors Island about 9 o'clock, or perhaps a little before. I'll come right down a-flying.

# WALL ST. ODDS HANG AT 10 TO 7 ON HUGHES

### Waldorf Bettors Hold Wilson a Point or Two Higher, at 10 to 8 and 10 to 9.

### BROOKLYN QUOTES 10 TO 8

### Wagers Indicate Growing Faith That Hughes Will Win in New York and Wilson in Ohio.

Betting odds quoted yesterday indicated that the Wall Street opinion of the Presidential race differed from that of the uptown hotels. On the Curb the commissioners reported that about $25,000 was wagered at odds of 10 on Hughes to 7 on Wilson, while at the Waldorf Tex Rickard said he had tried vainly all day to get money down on Wilson at anything better than 10 to 8 and 10 to 9.

Rickard said the day's total of wagers was smaller than that of any other day this week, due largely to the decision of Wilson supporters to wait until the effect of the President's speeches in this city could be sized up. This view was expressed in Wall Street also. The largest wager handled by Rickard was $4,000 on Wilson against $5,000 Hughes money. He said he had placed $1,900 more at the same odds.

"The big men in Wall Street," Rickard added, "are mostly for Hughes, and they can afford to lay their money at wide odds. I don't believe the opinion down there represents the sentiment of the country. The voters who will swing the election are the farmers of the West and Southwest. My friends out there tell me that the farmer says to himself: 'Here, I'm getting more for my hogs than I ever got before, and wheat and corn are mighty high. This is no time to change things. Wilson gets my vote.' A lot of them have been Republicans before.'

Fred Schumm in Brooklyn said he had placed $3,000 on Hughes against $2,400 on Wilson and $2,000 against $1,600 with Hughes the favorite. These wagers were at 10 to 8, but the Brooklyn quotations in the afternoon, according too Schumm, swung to 10 to 7.

The odds quoted on results in New York and Ohio indicated belief that Hughes was gaining strength in New York, while Wilson's chances were improving in Ohio. Rickard said he had $25,000 Wilson money to bet even that the President would carry Ohio, and he planned to telegraph the Cleveland men who had sent money to bet on the President to offer odds today.

The New York State odds were firm both on the Curb and in Brooklyn sporting circles at 2½ on Hughes to 1 on Wilson, and Edward McQuade quoted the same figures on Whitman's chances. A bet of $3,000 against $1,000 that Hughes would carry the State was reported in Broad Street. Even money was offered that Hughes would not get a plurality of 80,000 in New York.

# HUGHES ANSWERS WILSON'S PROTEST

### Defends Discussion of Foreign Relations When People Are Assessing Stewardship.

### DEMANDS FIRMER POLICIES

### Criticises Preparedness Measures Adopted—Big Up-State Crowds—Barnes Introduces Hughes.

*Special to The New York Times.*

ALBANY, N. Y., Nov. 2.—On the final tour of his campaign in his home State today Charles E. Hughes took issue with President Wilson on the subject of Americanism. Replying to the assertion made by the President in Buffalo on Wednesday that he could not regard as a patriot any man who used "our foreign relations for political advantage," Mr. Hughes charged that the President's conduct of international relations was well described, in the words of Disraeli, as "a muddle of meddle" that invited insult, hampered the advance of American trade, and endangered the lives of American citizens on land and on sea.

"When a matter is so important as the maintenance of American rights," he said, "it is highly necessary that American opinion should be expressed, and I have no apology to make in standing before you and saying that if I am elected President I propose that the American flag shall be not only a symbol of courtesy, a symbol of justice, but it shall be the symbol of firmness and consistency in maintaining our known rights on land and on sea throughout the world."

Speaking tonight in Harmanus Bleecker Hall in Albany, where he was introduced by William Barnes, who opposed him bitterly when he was Governor of New York, Mr. Hughes added to his criticism of the President.

"I like the phrase, 'The peace of a gentleman,'" he said, quoting from one of the President's addresses, "but it is the peace of a gentleman unafraid, alert in self-respect, and getting his rights, quietly and calmly ready to maintain them. That is the peace of a gentleman."

In regard to the resignation of Secretary Garrison, Mr. Hughes said:

"We did have in the Cabinet of this Administration a first-class man as our first Secretary of War, but he could not live with the Administration and had to get out."

**The Meeting with Barnes.**

Mr. Hughes received a five-minute demonstration when he entered the hall here. His meeting with Mr. Barnes passed off without much stir, although

Continued on Page 5.



## Constantine Orders Army to Fight Venizelists Marching on Larissa

ATHENS, Nov. 2, (via London.)—King Constantine issued orders this morning to the royalist troops to prevent the advance of the revolutionist forces at all costs.

One hundred and fifty loyal troops had previously evacuated Katerina before 600 insurgents armed with machine guns, withdrawing to Larissa to join reinforcements.

The evacuation of Katerina is confirmed by the General Staff.

LONDON, Friday, Nov. 3.—According to special dispatches from Athens the Venizelist National Defense Army has seized and occupied Katerina, a few miles southwest of Saloniki, after a short fight with the Greek royalist troops. A dispatch to The Daily Mail from Athens says:

"An extraordinary situation has been created by the action of the officers of the Larissa Railway, which is controlled by the Entente Allies, in allowing royalist military officers to send reenforcements to oppose the advance of the Venizelists.

"That the Entente should permit the lending of assistance in military measures against their own allies, namely, the Venizelist troops, is considered incoherent and naturally surprises the Venizelists."

The Venizelist army now numbers 30,000.

Telegraphing from Athens, Reuter's correspondent says the Greek Government has sent reinforcements of infantry and artillery to Katerina. The correspondent adds that Admiral du Fournet, commander of the allied fleet in the Mediterranean, has sent notice to the Greek harbor authorities indicating a danger zone for vessels entering or leaving Piraeus Harbor.

Other dispatches from Athens give details of the alleged arrest at Larissa of a German officer who was proceeding in a motor car with the German Legation mail pouch, bound for the Bulgarian line.

It is said that the pouch contained important messages to the Military Attachés at Sofia and Constantinople and also detailed plans of the Suez Canal defenses.

In addition, the dispatches say it contained "compromising" letters from the Greek King and Queen to the German Emperor.

The above dispatch from Athens is the first indication that the soldiers of the Provisional Government are advancing southward on the mainland of Greece, all movements reported hitherto having been toward Saloniki. Katerina is on the northeast coast of Thesaly on the Gulf of Saloniki, and twenty-five miles from the northern terminus of the Athens-Larissa railroad at Karali-Zerven, which in turn is twenty-five miles north of the Greek military base of Larissa.

The railroad is in the hands of the French, who took it over at the time they seized the Greek fleet a few weeks ago, when it was learned that artillery and large stores of ammunition were being sent up the road from Athens to the Greek forces concentrated at Larissa.

# GERMANS GIVE UP LAST VERDUN FORT

### Withdraw from Vaux Fort Because of the Terrific French Fire, Berlin Says.

### POSITION WAS UNTENABLE

### Paris Silent on the Matter—French Gain More Ground on the Somme.

BERLIN, Nov. 2, (by Wireless to Sayville.)—Fort Vaux, on the Verdun front, has been evacuated by the Germans, says today's official report issued by Army Headquarters. The statement reads:

Army Group of the German Crown Prince: An artillery engagement on the right bank of the Meuse was repeatedly increased to great intensity.

The French up to the present have directed an especially heavy and destructive fire against Fort Vaux, which had been evacuated already in the night time by our troops, following a given order and without being disturbed by the enemy. Important parts of the fort were blasted by us before we left the position.

Fort Vaux at Verdun was evacuated on the night of Nov. 1-2 in accordance with prearranged plans, according to the German military leaders, who indicated that they considered the sacrifices involved in its retention out of proportion to its value in the present German strategic scheme.

The Associated Press representative was informed on the evening of Nov. 1 from German Headquarters of the impending evacuation and the retirement of the German lines to positions better adapted to defense, and at the same time was given an explanation of the withdrawal.

Forts Douaumont and Vaux, it was explained, formed such a material element in the defense of Verdun so long as they remained with unimpaired armament in French hands that they had to be put out of action in order to cripple the fortress, and once this was accomplished the ruins of the forts, with the armaments removed, possessed no such importance to the Germans and served chiefly as targets for the French artillery.

Now that Fort Douaumont had passed again into French possession, Fort Vaux no longer in the opinion of the German leaders justified the heavy sacrifices necessary to retain the ground about the fort, which is ill-adapted to defense against attacks from the south and west. Fort Vaux was therefore abandoned and the German lines retired to positions less exposed to the French artillery.

**Paris Silent About Fort Vaux.**

PARIS, Nov. 2.—The War Office issued the following statement today concerning operations on the Verdun front:

On the right bank of the Meuse the night was relatively calm.

**Vaux Was Captured June 6.**

The French have now recovered the only two permanent fortifications of Verdun captured by the Germans since the campaign began on Feb. 21.

Douaumont, which had been in the possession of the Germans since May 24, was recaptured on Oct. 24. It had taken the Germans from March 11, when they captured the village of Vaux, over two months to capture Fort Douaumont and had cost them over 100,000 men. The French recaptured it in two hours with small loss.

The direct German assault on Fort de Vaux began on June 1 with the capture of the Caillette Wood between the two forts. It fell on June 6, and until yesterday had been occupied by the Germans.

Fort de Douaumont is 388 meters high and Fort de Vaux, 2,500 yards to the southeast, is 349 meters. They are the highest elevations of the terrain on the Lorraine watershed of the Meuse and the Moselle.

## FRENCH ON SOMME WIN MORE GROUND

### *Advance Northeast of Morval Despite Weather—Take 736 Prisoners in Two Days.*

LONDON, Nov. 2.—In spite of the rain, accompanied by fog, and the mud, the French troops have gained considerable ground north of the Somme in the last twenty-four hours. Methodical attacks have been delivered on the short sector from Les Boeufs to Sailly-Saillisel, where the Germans hold a ridge which forms a salient in the French line.

General Fayolle's troops, according to

Continued on Page 3.

# MARINA'S GUN NO VALID EXCUSE

### Washington Holds Germany Cannot Uphold Sinking Because Ship Was Armed.

### SO VIEWS GERMAN PLEDGE

### Facts Cannot Be Learned Till Next Week—Lansing Goes Home to Vote.

*Special to The New York Times.*

WASHINGTON, Nov. 2.—Robert Lansing, Secretary of State, went today to his home in Watertown, N. Y., to remain until Election Day and cast his vote. Before leaving Washington he said there would be no action in the case of the torpedoing of the steamship Marina until his return, for the reason that the Government was not in possession of information upon which to take any action.

It is expected that by the time he returns, if not soon thereafter, sufficient evidence will be at hand to enable the President and the Secretary of State to determine the attitude of this Government toward the case of the Marina, as well as that of the British freighter Rowanmore, which was sunk almost at the same time off the southern coast of Ireland.

It was made plain today that the Government was not in possession of sufficient facts to form a conclusion as to what actually occurred, and Secretary Lansing said reports indicated that it would be impossible to obtain the facts before next week. Otherwise, he explained, he would not be leaving Washington at this time. Meanwhile, Ambassador Page at London is endeavoring to obtain the affidavits of the officers of the Marina and surviving Americans among the crew and the American Chargé at Berlin is endeavoring to get the German Government's version of the attack.

Mr. Lansing said that no further particulars regarding the Marina and Rowanmore cases had been received from Wesley Frost, Consul at Queenstown, or from the Embassy at London during the past twenty-four hours. The information received prior to today, Mr. Lansing said, was substantially the same as had been cabled to American newspapers, but he declined to disclose further details than were contained in the two original messages from Mr. Frost. It is known, however, that the official reports thus far received are rather incomplete on some important points.

**Armed Ship Question.**

There is a growing belief that the Marina case is destined to become entangled in the meshes of a technical controversy over the question as to whether Germany's pledges are broad enough to cover merchantmen carrying a defensive armament. The Marina carried a 4.7-inch gun to be used for defensive purposes. If the submarine commander's report shows that the Marina was sunk without warning, it is thought in some quarters here that he may set up the defense that his action was justified by the fact that the Marina was armed.

Should the German Government support such an explanation and set up the claim that armed merchantmen are subject to attack without warning, a most complex and difficult issue would be presented. In high official quarters today it was asserted that this Government's interpretation of the German pledges given on the demand of President Wilson in the Sussex case was that the declaration that merchantmen would not be sunk without warning or without safety to human life was broad enough to apply to merchant ships carrying defensive armament.

Nothing is to be found in the German pledge drawing any distinction between "armed" and "unarmed" merchant vessels. The language is broad enough to embrace both classes of merchant ships. Whether Germany intended this Government to understand it to be broad enough to cover both armed and unarmed merchantmen, or only intended it to apply to "unarmed" merchant vessels, has not been disclosed. Prior to the giving of this guarantee, the German Government insisted that armed merchant vessels, especially armed merchant vessels, subject to the British Admiralty instructions for firing on enemy submarines, were not entitled to exemption.

**Halted by Sussex Disaster.**

In fact, the Sussex was sunk in the very midst of a hot discussion over the right of Germany to sink armed British merchant ships on sight. It will be recalled that the diplomatic controversy over the armed ship question last March led to the debate in Congress over the McLemore and other resolutions, which had for their purpose the warning of

Continued on Page 7.

# GREAT THRONG IN GARDEN HEARS WILSON APPEAL FOR JUSTICE TO ALL MANKIND; HITS AT WALL ST. IN WALDORF SPEECH

## Wilson Hopes the Poor Have Found Him a Friend; His Account of Some of the Appeals to Him

In his address to business men at the Waldorf yesterday President Wilson made this reference to some of his experiences in campaigning in the last two or three weeks:

I have seen some things within the last two or three weeks, my fellow-citizens, that have touched me very deeply, in the great crowds that one encounters in going about in a season like this. I have seen poorly dressed women, tears streaming down their faces, holding up little children to me, as if they had discovered a friend when, God knows, all I was trying to do was to be just. I hope I am their friend; I shall always try to be. But why should they pick me out? I can think of only one thing, they have thought that men in prominent places were not giving them any consideration at all, and the minute any one of us who is supposed to have influence shows that our heart beats with theirs and that we regard them as like ourselves in all that touches their welfare, whether of the body or of the mind, they come to us with tears on their faces and outstretched arms and thank God for a friend.

# 30,000 IN PARADE CHEER PRESIDENT

### Hosts of Tammany, Led by Murphy, March Down 5th Av. to Greet Wilson.

### 50,000 SEE THEM PASS

### Silk-Hatted Democrats Carry Banners, Wave Flags, and Burn Redfire.

Thirty thousand Democrats marched in honor of President Wilson last night. In the ranks were 15,000 Tammany voters, delegations from every district in the city, as well as 6,000 Democratic youths. Sheriff Alfred E. Smith was Grand Marshal, and Thomas Smith, Secretary of Tammany Hall, acted as chief aide.

Directly behind the Grand Marshal marched the Grand Sachems of Tammany Hall, led by John R. Vorhees, 86 years old, and in the line of Sachems walked the Tammany leader himself, Charles F. Murphy. In conjunction with the Tammany delegations, 10,000 members of Wilson and Marshall clubs, and the Wilson College Men's League, led by "Big Bill" Edwards, marched along a different route to Madison Square Garden, where both parades merged.

The Democratic paraders assembled at various points along the line of march, the head of the parade extending from Columbus Circle, where the Wilson and Marshall clubs gathered, to Fifty-eighth Street and Fifth Avenue, where the Tammanyites mobilized. Fifth Avenue was thronged with spectators when, at 8 o'clock, Marshal Smith gave the command to march. Each marcher carried a small American flag and many banners were displayed bearing slogans of the party.

Some of these legends said: "Wilson is for peace and prosperity"; "Tammany is for Wilson because Wilson is for the United States of America"; "Tammany will give the biggest vote in its history to Woodrow Wilson"; "Roosevelt wants war—'I'm in complete accord with Roosevelt'—Hughes"; "'Our honor is safe with Wilson'—Ex-President Taft"; "I am a Democrat with a big D and a little d."

The Tammany parade comprised five divisions and each delegation representing the assembly districts of the greater city, was led by its district leader. The first division was composed of the Manhattan districts, which marched in their numerical order—the First Assembly District, headed by Thomas Foley, marching behind the Sachems.

**Cheering Greets the President.**

When the parade had reached Twenty-eighth Street word reached Grand Marshal Smith that President Wilson was about to leave the Waldorf-Astoria for Madison Square Garden and, after a conference with Leader Murphy, the parade was halted, while the leading band played "The Star-Spangled Banner." The sidewalks were jammed with spectators, who raised their hats and at the conclusion of the national anthem vociferously cheered the President.

As the President appeared, a prolonged cheer went up from the thousands of marchers and spectators, and a lane was opened up in the line of the parade for the Presidential party. Surrounded by a cordon of mounted police, the President's motor car moved slowly down Fifth Avenue, with the President standing in the car, with bared head. A smile of appreciation lighted up his face.

As the President passed the Grand Sachems, it was noticed that Leader Murphy was one of the first to remove his hat. Mr. Murphy received a bow of welcome from the President as the head of the parade was reached and the order to resume marching was given.

Early in the evening delegations from at a premium, and it was estimated that the different districts began to assemble from Fiftieth to Fifty-eighth Streets. It was originally planned to have a torchlight procession, but this was abandoned and flags were substituted. When the command to march was given, Fifth Avenue was thronged with people, who frequently joined in the cheering of the Tammany followers. On the steps of St. Patrick's Cathedral space was fully 50,000 spectators watched the parade.

Many of the Tammany delegations wore silk top hats and frock coats, and when the members of the Executive Committee of the Fifth Assembly District, headed by Charles Culkin, appeared wearing their formal attire the crowds applauded.

**Shouts Drown Bands' Music.**

In front of the National Democratic Club, near Forty-eighth Street, the marchers cheered a large electric sign

Continued on Page 3.

# PRESIDENT IN CROWD CLIMBS FIRE ESCAPE

### Neither He Nor Mrs. Wilson Is Able to Penetrate Jam as 40,000 Besiege Garden.

### THRONG BREAKS BOUNDS

### Women Are Crushed and Prominent Men Are Rebuffed as Police Lose Control of Throngs.

A crowd that at its height was estimated by the police at 40,000 besieged Madison Square Garden between 6 and 10 o'clock last night to get a glimpse of President Wilson or to hear his speech. Except the crowd that gathered in the neighborhood of the Garden in 1896, when William Jennings Bryan spoke there, it was the largest outpouring in the history of the big amphitheatre. After his speech at the Garden, the President motored to Cooper Union, where a crowd of 15,000 persons fairly mobbed the stand from which he attempted to address them after he had finished his speech within the hall.

The size of the crowd that began closing in about the Garden as early as 4 o'clock in the afternoon proved too great for the police arrangements, and as a result of this inadequacy scenes of the greatest disorder prevailed. The police heads blamed the trouble on the management of the Garden and of the meeting, and, while observers conceded that their charge may have been just, it seemed equally true that the police themselves were largely to blame for the situation.

One of the results of the confusion that existed from 7 until 9 o'clock was the exclusion of many prominent men from the Garden who held tickets entitling them to seats on the platform or in the boxes. Some of these men were accompanied by women, and in some cases the women were jostled with the men.

**President Climbs Fire Escape.**

People began to gather at Madison Square Garden long before 6 o'clock in the evening. An hour later every inch of the building was jammed, but still the crowd continued to fight to get inside, and soon the police were powerless. A number of women were crushed and had to be carried to safety by the police. Men, too, had their coats torn and hats smashed.

Unable to get through the mob that was still surging about the Garden entrances shortly before 9 o'clock, the President and his party, including Mrs. Wilson, had to climb up a fire escape on the Twenty-seventh Street side and get to the speaker's platform in that way.

There was no discrimination in the handling of late comers. Samuel Seabury, Democratic candidate for Governor, arrived about 8:30 o'clock and went to the entrance in Twenty-seventh Street, reserved for the President and special guests. He gained admittance, but members of his party were kept outside. Mrs. E. M. House, wife of the President's chief adviser, was announced to the cordon of police in front of the same door, but the name meant nothing to them, apparently, for she and the group of men and women with her were hustled to the north side of the street. Mrs. House later was escorted up the fire escape and allowed to enter.

A man protested when a policeman shoved him. "I am Al Smith, Sheriff of this country," he said. Sheriff Smith's announcement didn't save him and he was brushed back, though he was a marshal of the big parade.

Charles F. Murphy, Cleveland H. Dodge, Chairman Vance McCormick, William Church Osborne, George Gordon Battle, and Ralph Pulitzer were some of the other prominent men who didn't reach the inside, or who had trouble getting there.

Deputy Commissioner Dunham, Chief Inspector Schmittberger, and Inspector Morris had charge of police arrangements. They started late in the afternoon with 440 policemen. The crowd was fairly easy to handle until after 6 o'clock, when every street and avenue began to empty its hundreds in the streets rusrounding the Garden. The doors were opened between 6 and 7 o'clock. At 7:30 they were closed and only those having tickets were allowed to enter.

**Break Through Police Lines.**

Then the trouble began. The crowd at Fourth Avenue and Twenty-sixth Street broke through the police lines thrown around the building when the doors were closed and swarmed in both directions around the Garden. When the first tide reached the main entrance in Madison Avenue it swept aside the big iron gates that guard the entrance to the lobby that had been closed and carried the doorkeepers before it. Before the police inside could form a phalanx to stem the tide of invasion several hundred had reached the auditorium.

At 8:22 the Fire Department gave notice that the building was full to capacity and that no one else could be admitted. It was this ruling, made necessary by the fire regulations, that prevented late-comers holding stage and box tickets from entering.

The crowd was largest between 7 and 8 o'clock, when Inspector Schmittberger

Continued on Page 3.

# THREE BIG MEETINGS HERE

### President Says Some in Campaign Have Tried to Discredit Government.

### EFFORT TO DIVIDE CLASSES

### Tells 15,000 in Madison Square Garden the Country Stands at a Serious Turning Point.

### PREDICTS HIS RE-ELECTION

### President and Mrs. Wilson Scale Fire Escape to Get Into Garden.

To a crowd of 15,000 persons who fought for hours to get into the structure, Woodrow Wilson delivered last night at Madison Square Garden his final message of the campaign and predicted his re-election "by a demonstration of power on the part of public opinion such as has never been displayed in the world before."

Yesterday was the President's first and only public appearance in New York during the campaign, and he was greeted at the Garden with an acclaim that will mark an epoch in his career. His entrance was the signal for a demonstration of applause and cheers that lasted for thirty minutes. Seldom has the city witnessed a more fervid outburst.

It was the President's second speech of the day. In the afternoon he addressed a gathering of business men at the Waldorf-Astoria, centring his attack on what he styled the "underworld" of business and the reactionary tendencies of certain elements in Wall Street. After the Garden speech he went to Cooper Union, where, as at the Garden, he spoke mainly on human rights as affecting the man and woman who work.

Today the President returns to Shadow Lawn on the yacht Mayflower, having spent the night aboard her after his arduous day in New York.

**25,000 Outside Building.**

Political speakers at Madison Square Garden may have had longer demonstrations, but none ever was more enthusiastic. Old-timers, used to sizing up big crowds, asserted that 25,000 were massed about the building outside. Inside extra chairs had been placed on the main floor, but so many people crowded between them that a large part of the audience was standing. Even the topmost gallery was jammed and men held for support on the rafters of the roof. The hall was decorated with American flags, hundreds of them hanging from ropes stretched across the building. The speakers' stand was placed at the north side of the building, and on this sat the committee to welcome the distinguished speaker. Two bands, at either end of the hall, played popular airs.

When the President climbed to the stage ex-Governor Martin H. Glynn had just completed a perfervid oration, and it was the signal for the crowd to let loose. With the President was Mrs. Wilson, and as the two stood smiling before the roaring multitude the audience frantically waved flags, hats, and handkerchiefs. The President appeared to enjoy the scene hugely. Again and again he stretched forth his hands, vainly trying to get order, but it was always the cue for another mad outburst of cheering and whistling and waving, while the noise of the bands became totally lost. When the cheering died down the audience began to stamp until the noise sounded like thunder.

**"We Want Wilson."**

Then some one raised the cry, "We want Wilson!" It became a chant that swept the hall, and was taken up by the crowd outside. This pleased the President even more than the cheering. After the noise had kept up for just thirty minutes the band switched to "Are You from Dixie?" There was another wild outburst, and then the President began to speak.

Unfortunately for the great crowd the President was not in strong voice, and many in the far reaches of the big auditorium could not hear him at all. They cheered themselves hoarse while the demonstration was on, but having vented their enthusiasm they wanted to get outside where bands were blaring and the outside crowd was yelling. Others left the galleries to get nearer the speakers' stand, and there was considerable confusion. But those within sound of Mr. Wilson's voice cheered wildly every point he made.

It was 8:20 when ex-Judge Seabury walked to the edge of the platform and held up his hand for silence. He didn't get it for about ten minutes. There were deafening cheers for the Gubernatorial candidate, and order was obtained only after "Big Bill" Edwards seized an enormous gavel and pounded with all his might. When Mr. Seabury remarked that the audience appeared to appreciate the great debt of gratitude that they owed to the President of the United States, the crowd responded with a roar. During the cheering Charles F. Murphy was seen to take a seat near the speakers' stand. In his speech Mr. Seabury made no reference to his own candidacy, but confined his remarks to a eulogy of the President.

**Augustus Thomas Presides.**

Augustus Thomas, who presided, and whose voice could be heard in all corners of the hall, next stepped to the

"All the News That's Fit to Print"

# The New York Times

LATE CITY EDITION

Weather: Sunny and milder today; fair and mild tonight, tomorrow. Temp. range: today 58-77; Tuesday 57-74. Temp.-Hum. Index yesterday 67. Full U.S. report on Page 90.

VOL. LXVI...NO. 21,473. NEW YORK, WEDNESDAY, NOVEMBER 8, 1916.—TWENTY PAGES. ONE CENT In Greater New York, Jersey City and Newark. | Elsewhere TWO CENTS.

# ELECTION CLOSE, WILSON 264, HUGHES 251; TWO STATES IN DOUBT; HOUSE MAY BE A TIE

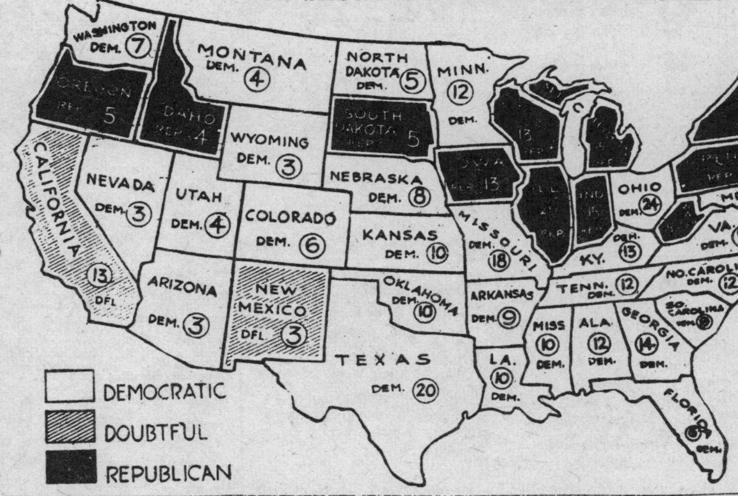

## WHITMAN BEATS SEABURY; CALDER CHOSEN SENATOR

### Governor Has a Margin of 144,000 Over His Democratic Opponent.

### WINS STRONG IN THE CITY

### Tammany Springs Surprise in the Metropolis, with Only 40,000 Majority.

### HUGHES PLURALITY 147,860

### Democrats Gain in Municipalities Up-State, but Not in the Country Districts.

### RIVALS HOLD LEGISLATURE

### Republicans Add at Least One More Congressman to the Party's Strength.

The Republicans made a clean sweep of New York yesterday. The State gave Charles E. Hughes a plurality of 147,860. Former Congressman William M. Calder was chosen United States senator, Governor Charles S. Whitman was re-elected, carrying the entire State ticket with him, and the Republicans retained control of the Legislature.

It was the same old story of New York State politics—the up-State Republican majority was too great to be overcome by the Democratic margin of the metropolis, and that Democratic majority was unusually small. Instead of the 75,000 or 100,000 margin Tammany Hall had been expected to give President Wilson in New York City, the Democratic candidate beat the Republican candidate by only 40,000 votes, while Hughes came down to the Bronx with a margin of 187,000 votes.

Tammany Hall "fell down" even harder in its support of William F. McCombs, former Democratic National Chairman, who was candidate for United States Senator, against Mr. Calder. Mr. McCombs lost New York City by a margin estimated at 10,000 or more, while Mr. Calder came down to the city with a big majority, making him the leader of the ticket, with a total vote of about 185,000.

**Democratic Gains in Cities.**

The Democrats made gains in a number of industrial cities up-State, but the country districts remained overwhelmingly Republican. The most striking Democratic gains were made in Buffalo, second largest city of the State. Slighter Democratic gains were shown also in Rochester, Syracuse, Albany, the banner Republican strongholds of the State.

Governor Whitman ran slightly behind Hughes and Calder, making a remarkably close race behind the candidate for President. Samuel Seabury, the Democratic candidate for Governor, ran far behind Wilson in New York City, polling a majority of only 22,000, against Wilson's 40,000. Governor Whitman's up-State margin was 165,000, giving him a lead over Seabury of 144,000 votes.

Frank H. Hiscock of Syracuse, the Republican candidate for Chief Judge of the Court of Appeals, defeated the Democratic candidate, Almet F. Jenks, of Brooklyn, by a substantial majority. C. W. Pound of Brooklyn defeated John T. Norton, the Democratic candidate for Associate Judge of the Court of Appeals.

Edward Schoeneck of Syracuse was re-elected Lieutenant Governor; Francis M. Hugo of Watertown, Secretary of State; Eugene M. Travis of Kings, State Controller; James M. Wells of the Bronx, State Treasurer; E. E. Woodbury of Jamestown, Attorney General; Frank M. Williams of Goshen, State Engineer and Surveyor.

**Changes in Legislature.**

The Republicans made a gain of five in the State Senate. They will have 36 out of 51 members in the 1917 Senate. In the Assembly the majority party made a gain of seven members. In the last Legislature the Republicans had 96 members; next year they will have 108. Thaddeus C. Sweet, Speaker of the Assembly, was re-elected from Oswego County, and Senator Elon R. Brown, President pro tem. of the Senate, was re-elected from the Thirty-fifth Senatorial District.

Returns were late on the vote for the propositions on the State ticket, but the indications were that the people voted against having a constitutional convention in 1918, and in favor of the issuing of $10,000,000 bonds for the purchase of additional forest lands for State reservations.

The Republicans in Albany, William Barnes's own stronghold, did not give Hughes the 12,000 majority their leaders had predicted. Hughes received in the

Continued on Page 4.

## State Pluralities

| Republican. | |
|---|---|
| Delaware | 1,000 |
| Connecticut | 6,000 |
| Illinois | 175,000 |
| Indiana | 25,000 |
| Iowa | 50,000 |
| Maine | 5,000 |
| Massachusetts | 17,000 |
| Michigan | 40,000 |
| New Hampshire | 1,000 |
| New Jersey | 35,000 |
| New York | 148,000 |
| North Dakota | 10,000 |
| Oregon | 15,000 |
| Pennsylvania | 300,000 |
| Rhode Island | 4,000 |
| South Dakota | 15,000 |
| Vermont | 28,000 |
| Wisconsin | 20,000 |
| **Democratic** | |
| Alabama | 25,000 |
| Arizona | 5,000 |
| Arkansas | 20,000 |
| Colorado | 15,000 |
| Florida | 20,000 |
| Georgia | 50,000 |
| Kansas (Est.) | 12,000 |
| Kentucky | 20,000 |
| Louisiana | 30,000 |
| Maryland | 10,000 |
| Mississippi | 30,000 |
| Missouri | 20,000 |
| Montana | 5,000 |
| Nebraska | 20,000 |
| Nevada | 5,000 |
| Ohio (Est.) | 40,000 |
| Oklahoma | 20,000 |
| North Carolina | 20,000 |
| South Carolina | 20,000 |
| Tennessee | 20,000 |
| Utah | 10,000 |
| Virginia | 15,000 |
| Washington | 20,000 |

## HUGHES WINS IN WILSON'S STATE

### Senator Martine Defeated by Frelinghuysen and Edge Is Elected Governor.

### LEGISLATURE REPUBLICAN

### Democrats Probably Retain Four of New Jersey's Twelve Seats in the House.

NEW JERSEY.—Voted for Presidential Electors, United States Senator, Congressmen, and Governor. Vote in 1912: Democratic, 178,569; Republican and Progressive, 234,721.

President Wilson has lost his own State of New Jersey to Mr. Hughes by a vote estimated, on scant returns, at about 35,000. With few exceptions all the other Democratic nominees on national, State, and local tickets of Jersey have been defeated, too.

This estimated plurality of the Republican national ticket is approximately the figure by which President Wilson carried New Jersey in 1912, but considerably less than the excess of the combined Taft and Roosevelt vote over the Wilson vote, which would indicate that all the Progressives have not gone back to the Republican Party.

Walter E. Edge, the Republican nominee for Governor, modestly claims his own election over Otto H. Wittpenn by 18,000, but available figures from the slowest State in the Union to learn what its voters have done indicate that the ex-Senator of Atlantic County has been chosen Chief Executive of the State by a much larger majority than that named by him. The worst-beaten man in the State is United States Senator James E. Martine, the "Farmer Jim" who has been a thorn in the side of Woodrow Wilson ever since the latter forced the election of Martine six years ago, thereby compelling his party to make good its bluff on the Senate primaries.

The Republican who will succeed Martine in the United States Senate is Joseph S. Frelinghuysen.

The Democrats have probably elected their candidates for Congress in the Third, Sixth, Eleventh, and Twelfth Districts.

The State Legislature, already Republican, will have a still smaller Democratic representation after inauguration of the new State Government. Returns show that President Wilson has run ahead of his ticket in nearly all of the twenty-one counties in the State, making a slightly better showing than Wittpenn and far ahead of Martine.

The vote everywhere in the State was heavy and complete returns may show the total to be a record breaker. Republicans claim that the Hughes majority in Essex County will also break all the records for that Republican stronghold.

Passaic County, which Stokes carried by about 1,000 majority at the last Gubernatorial election in 1913, claimed a Republican plurality for Hughes and Edge of about 7,000.

Monmouth County, normally Democratic, has swung the other way by something over 1,000 votes.

Other county plurality claims of the Republicans which are fully justified by the returns so far received are: Burlington, by 2,500; Cumberland, by 1,500; Mercer, by 3,500; Salem, by 1,000; Union, by 4,000; Gloucester, by 1,500.

The Republicans carried Union County by from 3,000 to 3,500. President Wilson ran 500 ahead of his ticket, Edge led Wittpenn in the county by 3,000. Congressman Kapstick, Republican, whose vote against the tabling of the

Continued on Page 2.

MAP SHOWING HOW THE STATES VOTED.

DEMOCRATIC
DOUBTFUL
REPUBLICAN

## WILSON CARRIES BUCKEYE STATE

### With More Than Half of Ohio Heard From, His Plurality Is 26,000 and Rising.

### GAINS IN RURAL SECTIONS

### Cox Leading Willis for Governor and Pomerene and Herrick Neck and Neck.

OHIO.—Voted for Presidential Electors, United States Senator, Congressmen, Governor, and other State officials. Vote in 1912: Democratic, 423,152; Republican and Progressive, 506,393.

CINCINNATI, Ohio, Wednesday, Nov. 8.—The indications early this morning were that President Wilson had carried Ohio by safe plurality.

Returns from 3,110 precincts of the 5,570 in Ohio gave Wilson 283,045, Hughes 256,282.

For Governor 2,997 precincts gave Cox, (Dem.,) 263,717; Willis, (Rep.,) 260,036.

For United States Senator 2,951 precincts gave Pomerene 254,955, Herrick, 255,023.

The returns came in slowly all night. The Democratic candidate held a slight advantage during the entire count, except for a period when the returns from Cincinnati predominated and the total for Hughes went into the lead. This was overcome by the first returns from Dayton, Columbus, and Cleveland.

Republicans were returned to the House of Representatives from five districts—the First, Seventh, Tenth, Sixteenth, and Twenty-second. The re-election of seven Democrats was assured at that hour, in the Third, Ninth, Twelfth, Thirteenth, Seventeenth, Twentieth, and Twenty-first.

In the Second District there was a close contest between S. Bowdle, Democratic member of the Sixty-third Congress, and Victor Heintz. Heintz was elected. He will succeed Alfred Allen, a Democrat.

Returns from 542 of the 556 precincts in Hamilton County give Wilson, 50,503; Hughes, 62,234; Cox, 52,901; Willis, 60,627; Pomerene, 49,865; Herrick, 62,184. The fourteen missing precincts are in that part of the county outside of the city of Cincinnati.

The German vote is said to be going almost solid for Hughes.

TOLEDO, Ohio, Nov. 7.—Forty precincts out of a total of 202 in Lucas County, which includes Toledo, give Hughes 3,045, Wilson 3,525. In fifty precincts on Governor the vote is: Willis, (R.,) 2,055; Cox, (D.,) 4,198.

## HUGHES AND HOLCOMB WIN IN CONNECTICUT

### Republicans Have Safe Lead for President, Senator, and Legislature.

CONNECTICUT.—Voted for Presidential Electors, United States Senator, Congressmen, Governor, and other State officials. Vote in 1912: Democratic, 74,561; Republican and Progressive, 102,453.

*Special to The New York Times.*

NEW HAVEN, Wednesday, Nov. 8.—With only the towns of Guilford, in New Haven County, and Windham, in Windham County, missing from Connecticut's 168 towns at 1 o'clock this morning, Hughes had a plurality of 6,726 over Wilson, the unofficial totals being: Hughes, 105,050; Wilson, 98,324.

Governor Holcomb, with an unofficial plurality of 11,091, is re-elected, with the whole Republican State ticket.

Congressman Lonergan of Hartford is the only Democrat to win a seat in Congress, and Senator McLean, triumphant over Homer S. Cummings, retains his seat in the United States Senate.

The Republicans made substantial gains in both branches of the State Legislature and will control both houses.

*Special to The New York Times.*

BRIDGEPORT, Conn., Nov. 7.—Bridgeport's munition vote went to Charles Evans Hughes. He carried the city by 1,201 votes. Twenty-three thousand ballots were cast.

## Roosevelt Will Not Advise Mr. Hughes on Appointments or Legislation

*Special to The New York Times.*

OYSTER BAY, N. Y., Nov. 7.—When informed of the lead of Hughes over President Wilson, according to the returns up to 9:45 o'clock tonight, Colonel Roosevelt issued the following statement:

In view of the latest returns I have received, it appears that Mr. Hughes is elected. I wish to express my profound gratitude, as an American proud of his country, that the American people have repudiated the man who coined the phrase about this country, that is, "Too proud to fight," and whose Administration had done so much to relax the fibre of the American conscience and to dull the sense of honorable obligations in the American people. We are all of us sincerely to be congratulated on the victory of Mr. Hughes.

Let me add, in view of certain letters and telegrams which already have begun to come in to me, that I will not make any recommendations to Mr. Hughes for appointments, nor any requests about legislation.

## Indiana and Michigan for Hughes; Wilson Is Leading in Minnesota

### Small Pluralities for Both Candidates in Several Other Western States Shown in the Scattered Returns Thus Far Available.

### CALIFORNIA.

CALIFORNIA.—Voted for Presidential Electors, United States Senator and Congressmen. Vote in 1912: Democratic, 283,436; Republican and Progressive, 287,524.

*Special to The New York Times.*

SAN FRANCISCO, Wednesday, Nov. 8.—Governor Hiram W. Johnson was elected to the Senate from California yesterday by a majority estimated by his friends to be as much as 200,000.

At midnight, on the face of available returns, the result of the Presidential vote was in doubt. With Los Angeles and San Francisco Counties virtually unreported, Republicans claimed the State for Hughes, asserting that the returns from those cities and from the rest of the counties indicated victory for their candidate. Democratic Headquarters claimed the State for Wilson by 25,000.

With returns in from 1,264 out of the 5,917 precincts, the Wilson vote is 60,734, that of Hughes 59,000. Johnson's election to the United States Senate is indicated by a big plurality.

In 1,557 precincts Hughes had 78,849 votes and Wilson 79,136.

At 3 A. M. on returns from 1,784 precincts, Hughes had 107,846, Wilson 106,445, a lead of 1,401 for Hughes.

Early in the evening Chester H. Rowell, Chairman of the Republican State Central Committee, claimed the State by 40,000 for Hughes.

"Los Angeles is going better than we figured," said his statement, "and also Alameda County. One or two interior counties are not coming up to expectations. Los Angeles should go, on present indications, at least 35,000 for Hughes, and this will be largely increased by other counties in the South. San Francisco will fall short of Democratic claims. For Governor Johnson, it is of course, a landslide.

"Returns are very incomplete," the statement adds, "but in most cases they about confirm our previous estimates. On present estimates California is absolutely safe for Hughes."

The Republican State Committee late this evening announced that Hughes had carried the State by a safe vote. The Democrats say that their information is that California will go for Wilson. They point to the fact that the women have been strong for the President, and that there has been a pronounced sentiment for him in Northern and Central California. No estimates, however, are being offered.

The polls closed at 7 o'clock. The reports are that an unprecedented vote was cast, a very large percentage of the women registered casting their ballots. It is admitted that in central California, especially in San Francisco, the women voted for Wilson three to one.

LOS ANGELES, Cal., Nov. 7.—Republican headquarters claims the election of Hiram Johnson as United States Senator by nearly 200,000. Hughes is conceded to have carried Los Angeles city and county by 25,000.

### NEW MEXICO.

NEW MEXICO.—Voted for Presidential Electors, United States Senator, Congressmen, Governor, and other State officials. Vote in 1912: Democratic, 20,437; Republican and Progressive, 26,080.

*Special to The New York Times.*

ALBUQUERQUE, N. M., Nov. 7.—Incomplete returns from twenty scattered New Mexico precincts, including the two precincts of the City of Albuquerque, give Hughes 1,389 and Wilson 1,369. Reports from various points which do not give tabulated figures show Wilson in the lead, and the chances are that Wilson has carried the State, and that Jones, Democrat, has been elected to the Senate to succeed Catron, the Republican incumbent.

The strong Democratic counties of the Pecos Valley and the strong Republican counties of Northern New Mexico have not yet reported definitely, and returns from remote precincts may alter the figures here indicated.

At 3 A. M. Hughes had a lead of 56 votes.

### MINNESOTA.

MINNESOTA.—Voted for Presidential Electors, United States Senator, Congressmen, Governor and other State officials. Vote in 1912: Democratic, 106,426; Republican and Progressive, 190,190.

ST. PAUL, Wednesday, Nov. 8.—When returns from one-tenth of the precincts in Minnesota had been tabulated early today President Wilson was leading Charles E. Hughes by nearly 5,000 votes, the count for 301 of the 3,024 precincts being: Wilson, 30,340; Hughes, 25,433.

Most of the returns were from the three largest cities of the State—Minneapolis, St. Paul, and Duluth. Republicans expressed confidence that full returns from rural districts would turn the tide to Hughes, while Democratic spokesmen maintained that the present ratio, giving Wilson a plurality of 48,342, would be maintained. Available returns showed Kellogg, (Rep.,) for Senator, leading Daniel W. Lawler, (Dem.,) of St. Paul.

The election of Governor J. J. Burnquist Republican, was indicated.

Although Republican leaders admit the vote in the three cities, St. Paul, Minneapolis, and Duluth, gives President Wilson a lead of from 8,000 to 12,000 over Charles E. Hughes, they are confident the returns from the country precincts will show a plurality of between 15,000 and 25,000 for Hughes.

### WYOMING.

WYOMING.—Voted for Presidential Electors, United States Senator, Congressmen and on amendments to State Constitution affecting school funds and construction of public roads. Vote in 1912: Democratic, 15,310; Republican and Progressive, 24,792.

CHEYENNE, Wyo., Wednesday, Nov. 8.—At a late hour this morning the result in this State was in doubt, with Wilson's lead increasing. In 128 precincts out of 588 Wilson had 5,270 and Hughes 4,483.

Indications point to the re-election of Senator Clark, who is running ahead of his ticket, and Congressman Mondell. Returns are delayed by a snowstorm.

### KANSAS.

KANSAS.—Voted for Presidential Electors, Congressmen, Governor, and other State officials. Vote in 1912: Democratic, 143,663; Republican and Progressive, 195,055.

TOPEKA, Wednesday, Nov. 8.—President Wilson had a lead of 4,119 votes at 2 o'clock this morning over Charles E. Hughes in one of the closest election races the State of Kansas has ever known.

Returns from 862 precincts out of 2,474 in Kansas give Wilson 122,503; Hughes 118,382.

Returns from 780 precincts give Capper, (Rep.,) 122,080; Lansdon, (Dem.,) 60,780 in the race for Governor.

### IDAHO.

IDAHO.—Voted for Presidential Electors, Congressmen, Governor, and other State officials and on amendments to the State Constitution. Vote in 1912: Democratic, 33,921; Republican and Progressive, 58,337.

BOISE, Idaho, Wednesday, Nov. 8.—At 2:30 o'clock this morning, with 143 out of 743 precincts counted, Wilson had

Continued on Page 3.

## ILLINOIS GIVES HUGHES 175,000

### Republicans Elect Lowden Governor and Their Entire State Ticket.

### WOMEN'S VOTE AS A FACTOR

### Divide on Party Lines in About Same Ratio That the Men Did.

ILLINOIS.—Voted for Presidential Electors, Congressmen, Governor, and other State officials. Vote in 1912: Democratic, 404,990; Republican and Progressive, 639,839.

*Special to The New York Times.*

CHICAGO, Nov. 7.—Charles Evans Hughes has carried the State of Illinois with a plurality estimated at not less than 175,000, and the entire Republican State ticket, headed by Frank O. Lowden for Governor, has been elected by about the same figure over Governor Dunne. Hughes has apparently carried the City of Chicago by 20,000, and his plurality may reach 40,000.

With Cook County going to the Republicans, the Democratic chances in the State went glimmering. The Democrats at a late hour tonight were still contending that down-State returns might somehow turn the tables. The Republicans took a quick look at the first flashes, and, as the totals kept running up all in one direction, they put out a claim that Illinois had fallen to Hughes and Lowden by 200,000 plurality.

Most of down-State returns so far in are from Republican strongholds and the figures from the strong Democratic counties may scale down the pluralities somewhat.

The women's vote ran close to the men's vote. This was the puzzling factor in the fight. It worried the politicians for months. Figures from precinct after precinct in Chicago and from county after county down-State indicate that the women's vote operated this way:

In Republican sections the women were more Republican than the men.

In Democratic territory the women were more Democratic than the men.

In Democratic wards the tendency was for Wilson to get a larger proportion of women's votes than of men's. In Republican bailiwicks Hughes generally got a larger share of the women's votes than of men's.

The rest of the Republican State ticket appears to have gone over with Lowden.

**McCormick Far in Lead.**

Medill McCormick, Republican candidate for Congressman at Large, was piling up a tremendous vote on the early returns. In scattering precincts he was polling more votes than Lowden.

The incomplete returns indicate a vast preponderance of "straight" tickets in both parties.

Fred E. Sterling, Republican State Chairman, issued this claim: "Indications are that both Hughes and Lowden will carry Illinois by over 200,000. Heavy gains are being made in many Democratic counties. For instance, La Salle County was figured on for 3,000 and it cast 5,000 for Hughes. Lowden is running about 50,000 ahead of his ticket. Hughes's majority in Cook County appears to be about 30,000."

A switch of a large part of the Socialist vote to Wilson is indicated by the early returns. It bears out reports current for weeks that the Socialists would split for Wilson on account of his "human justice" record. There is a marked falling off in the straight Socialist vote. Debs got 81,278 votes in Illinois in 1912. Incomplete returns indicate that Benson got 40,000 votes or less.

The vote was the largest in the history of Illinois. The women voted for the first time. Estimates based upon the incomplete returns are that a vote of between 1,800,000 and 1,900,000 was cast. The estimates are: Men, 1,200,000; women, 650,000.

The returns indicate that in the industrial centres down State Wilson cut down the Republican pluralities. He cut into the Progressive strongholds of 1912

Continued on Page 2.

## Electoral Vote

| Wilson | |
|---|---|
| Alabama | 12 |
| Arizona | 3 |
| Arkansas | 9 |
| Colorado | 6 |
| Florida | 6 |
| Georgia | 14 |
| Kansas | 10 |
| Kentucky | 13 |
| Louisiana | 10 |
| Maryland | 8 |
| Minnesota | 12 |
| Mississippi | 10 |
| Missouri | 18 |
| Montana | 4 |
| Nebraska | 8 |
| Nevada | 3 |
| North Carolina | 12 |
| North Dakota | 5 |
| Ohio | 24 |
| Oklahoma | 10 |
| South Carolina | 9 |
| Tennessee | 12 |
| Texas | 20 |
| Utah | 4 |
| Virginia | 12 |
| Washington | 7 |
| Wyoming | 3 |
| Total | 264 |
| **Hughes** | |
| Connecticut | 7 |
| Delaware | 3 |
| Idaho | 4 |
| Illinois | 29 |
| Indiana | 15 |
| Iowa | 13 |
| Maine | 6 |
| Massachusetts | 18 |
| Michigan | 15 |
| New Hampshire | 4 |
| New Jersey | 14 |
| New York | 45 |
| Oregon | 5 |
| Pennsylvania | 38 |
| Rhode Island | 5 |
| South Dakota | 5 |
| Vermont | 4 |
| West Virginia | 8 |
| Wisconsin | 13 |
| Total | 251 |
| **Doubtful** | |
| California | 13 |
| New Mexico | 3 |
| Total | 16 |

Total number of votes in Electoral College, 531; necessary to a choice, 266.

## CITY FOR WILSON BY ONLY 40,069

### Seabury's Plurality a Mere 21,978 in the Metropolitan Vote for Governor.

### HUGHES CARRIES QUEENS

### Calder Defeats McCombs for Senatorship—Curran Beaten for Aldermanic Presidency.

New York City gave Woodrow Wilson a scant plurality of 40,069 to offset the 186,930 plurality for Charles E. Hughes which the up-State counties sent down to the Bronx line. The city's vote for Wilson was 351,539, compared with 312,386 which it gave him for President four years ago. Hughes's city vote was 311,470, as against 126,582 for Taft and 188,896 for Roosevelt (total 315,478) in 1912.

For Governor, Samuel Seabury carried the city by a plurality of only 21,978, as against 165,000 for Whitman up-State. The total city vote, with only sixty districts missing, was, Seabury, 316,132; Whitman, 294,154.

For Senator, the indications early this morning were that Calder, Republican, had carried the Democratic City of New York against McCombs, Democrat, by about 25,000. With 367 election districts out of 2,167 Calder had then 248,896 votes against 225,874 for McCombs, showing a plurality of about 23,022 for Calder. In Mr. Calder's home borough, Brooklyn, he defeated McCombs by almost 2 to 1.

For President of the Board of Aldermen, Curran (Rep.) was beaten by Frank L. Dowling (Dem.) by about 45,000 votes.

Several odd points stood out in the voting. Wilson carried Brooklyn by about 6,800. Seabury lost the borough by 11,014. Calder, for Senator, carried it by more than 38,000. Queens, the home of the Schützenfest, normally Democratic by some 3,000 votes, gave Hughes a plurality of 2,958. Yet the Bronx, where the German-American vote was also expected to cut a large figure, went for Wilson by about 7,389.

In the city Congressional elections there is one certain Republican gain. In the Twentieth Congressional District, where B. Rosenblatt (Democrat) opposed Isaac Siegel (Republican and Progressive) one of the city Congressmen who voted against tabling the McLemore resolution, Siegel is apparently re-elected. In the Eighteenth District G. B. Francis (Republican) defeats T. G. Patten, the sitting Democratic Representative. The election of Meyer London, the lone Socialist Congressman from New York City, was, however, in doubt in the Twelfth District early this morning. The indications were that Judge Leon Sanders, his Democratic opponent, had won by a small plurality.

Eight Republican Senators are elected

Continued on Page 2.



## CALIFORNIA IN DOUBT

### Majority for Wilson Changes to 1400 Lead for Hughes.

### MAY DEPEND ON NEW MEXICO

### Hughes Leads There With No More Than 2 Score or So.

### NEW HAMPSHIRE CLOSE, TOO

### Kansas, Apparently for Wilson, Also Shows a Declining Plurality.

### NEW YORK GOES TO HUGHES

### Also Illinois, Indiana, Michigan, Iowa, and South Dakota by Large Pluralities.

### ODD RESULT IN CONGRESS

### Two Socialists, a Prohibitionist, a Progressive, and a 'Protectionist' May Hold Balance of Power.

Although Charles Evans Hughes of New York had apparently been elected President and Charles W. Fairbanks of Indiana Vice President, on returns received up to 3 A. M. today there were important shifts after that hour which leave the result undetermined, but indicating strongly the re-election of President Wilson. At this writing Mr. Wilson has 264 electoral votes and Mr. Hughes, 251, with 16 still in doubt in two States.

The still doubtful States are California, with 13 votes and New Mexico with 3.

There were landslide majorities for Hughes in the bigger States, and he may prove to have a landslide majority on the popular vote, but he will have no landslide majority in the Electoral College. The States which went for Wilson by smaller but still safe majorities have prevented that.

The East went for Hughes by overwhelming majorities, and Wilson did not carry a single State in this section, unless, as is unlikely, he has carried Delaware. The Democrats had been counting on the Middle West, but they reckoned on it in vain. The Middle West as a section went for Hughes, and most of its more important States went for him by majorities as great proportionately as those in the East.

Hughes's majority in the so-called "doubtful" States of the East were: New York, 146,800; New Jersey, 45,000; Connecticut, 10,000; West Virginia, 8,000.

In the "doubtful" States of the Middle West Hughes's majorities were: Illinois, 175,000; Indiana, 20,000; Michigan, 40,000; Wisconsin, 15,000. In this section Wilson has saved Nebraska by 10,000 and Kansas by 15,000. He seems also to have carried Ohio and Minnesota.

Pennsylvania, which went for Roosevelt four years ago, leads the Hughes majorities with 200,000.

The vote in New York State was impressive. In this Democratic city Wilson was slaughtered right and left, and he carried by the small majority of 40,000. He was expected by the Democrats to carry Buffalo, but he lost it by 3,500. The State went for Hughes by 148,000.

Hughes carried Queens by 2,900, and in Brooklyn Wilson had the surprisingly small majority of 6,000.

Whitman was re-elected Governor by 144,000, running behind Hughes through the State as a whole. He was cut heavily in some places, noticeably in Rochester, despite the fact that Rochester is the balliwick of his political friend, George W. Aldridge.

William M. Calder was elected United States Senator from this State by a majority of 187,000 over his Democratic opponent, William F. McCombs. He ran far ahead of both the other leading candidates on the Republican ticket, Hughes and Whitman.

The next President will have a difficult task on his hands so far as Congress is concerned, for his party cannot control it. The Senate is apparently Democratic by the unworkably small majority of 4, and the House is tied, 215 Democrats and 215 Republicans. Neither party can even elect a Speaker or organize the House except by dealing with the other party or with the Representatives of minor parties, who will hold the balance of power.

Of these Representatives of minor par-

"All the News That's Fit to Print."

# The New York Times.

THE WEATHER
Partly cloudy, colder; tomorrow overcast; strong west winds.
For full weather report see Page 21.

VOL. LXVI...NO. 21,475. NEW YORK, FRIDAY, NOVEMBER 10, 1916.—TWENTY-TWO PAGES. ONE CENT In Greater New York, Jersey City and Newark. | Elsewhere, TWO CENTS.

# WITH 272 ELECTORAL VOTES, WILSON WINS; GETS CALIFORNIA, NORTH DAKOTA, NEW MEXICO

## GERMANY FAVORS LEAGUE OF PEACE WITH CONDITIONS

But Bethmann Hollweg Says the Entente Allies Must Renounce Their Annexation Schemes.

DENOUNCES "BRUTE FORCE"

Abolition of "Aggressive Coalitions" Put as First Step Toward International Harmony.

ANSWERS VISCOUNT GREY

Asserts That England Plunged Europe Into War by Encouraging France and Russia.

Special Cable to THE NEW YORK TIMES.

BERLIN, Nov. 9.—Answering Viscount Grey, Chancellor von Bethmann Hollweg, in the course of his speech before the Main Committee of the Reichstag today said:

"Germany is at all times ready to join a league of nations—yes, even to place herself at the head of such a league—to keep in check the disturbers of peace."

BERLIN, Nov. 9, (by Wireless to Sayville.)—Chancellor von Bethmann Hollweg announced today before the Main Committee of the Reichstag that after the end of the war Germany would co-operate in an endeavor to find a practical means for procuring a lasting peace by means of an international league. The Chancellor also presented a new version of events in the last days before the outbreak of the war, particularly in connection with Russia's mobilization and efforts to avert hostilities.

The Chancellor, according to the Overseas News Agency, connected the two subjects in his speech, and in doing so replied to the speech made by Lord Grey, the British Foreign Secretary, to foreign newspapermen, in which he said that the origin of the present war must influence peace conditions, and that Germany would be entitled to ask for guarantees against future attacks if the present war really were forced upon Germany. Of course, Lord Grey at once added that Germany's interpretation of the origin of the war was incorrect, and that the war was not forced upon Germany, but was forced by Germany upon Europe.

**Little Faith in Arbitration Courts.**

Referring to the question of an international league for the preservation of peace, the Chancellor said:

[...]

Continued on Page 3.

## *Suffrage Amendment Defeated in Two States*

Woman suffrage amendments were evidently beaten in the two States that voted on the question last Tuesday. In South Dakota, with 200 precincts still to be heard from, the vote stood 23,934 for and 25,248 against the amendment.

West Virginia, the other State to vote on the proposition, rejected it overwhelmingly. The returns from 842 out of the 1,713 precincts in the State showed 33,887 for and 72,473 against it.

## ASQUITH EXPOUNDS ESSENTIALS OF PEACE

Must Insure Security of Weak, Liberties of Europe, and Free Future of World.

TRADE OF NEUTRALS SAFE

German Talk of Wall Against It Called Childish Fiction—Ready for Next Channel Raid.

[...]

Continued on Page 3.

## WON'T CONCEDE WILSON VICTORY WITHOUT RECOUNT

Both Sides Should Be Anxious to Remove All Doubt, Willcox Says.

FOUR STATES IN QUESTION

New Hampshire, New Mexico, North Dakota, and California Returns Scrutinized.

THE OLD GUARD CONFERS

Willcox Not Invited to Meeting of Crane, Barnes, and Others Ignored in the Campaign.

[...]

Continued on Page 2.

## *News of Wilson's Election Sent to Him by Wireless*

*Special to The New York Times.*

ASBURY PARK, N. J., Nov. 9.—To President Wilson aboard the yacht Mayflower, en route to Williamstown, Mass., this message was wirelessed shortly before midnight tonight by Secretary Tumulty:

"I am here surrounded by the loyal Democrats of old Monmouth, and beg leave to send you our greeting and congratulations. The cause you have so nobly represented has at last triumphed, and we greet you. Our hearts, our thoughts and our affections go to you."

## M'CORMICK JOYFUL AT NEWS OF VICTORY

Crowd in Democratic National Headquarters Cheers as California Goes to Wilson.

HIS OPTIMISM UNFLAGGING

Chairman All Day Had Claimed 288 Votes, and Announced: "We've Got It Sewed Up!"

Scenes of growing jubilation at Democratic National headquarters here, which were in evidence throughout the day yesterday, reached a culmination last night when word was received that THE TIMES had bulletined that California had gone for President Wilson, and that the President was re-elected. Face to face with the success which they had hoped for confidently for many anxious [...]

Continued on Page 2.

## WILSON AHEAD IN CALIFORNIA BY OVER 3,100

Republican Chairman Concedes State on Face of the Returns.

36 PRECINCTS ARE MISSING

These Cannot Change Result, Reached After Day of Great Political Tension.

FULL RECOUNT IS CERTAIN

Both Sides Carefully Watching the Canvass—Much Talk of a Split Vote.

SAN FRANCISCO, Cal., Nov. 9.—California has given her electoral vote to Woodrow Wilson.

The Republican Chairman, C. H. Rowell, admitted at 8:25 o'clock tonight that, barring some exceptional errors in the count, the President had carried the State.

Mr. Rowell conceded the State after reviewing returns showing a plurality of 2,970 for Wilson, with only forty-eight scattered precincts of the 5,870 in the State not complete. These figures were: Wilson, 465,194; Hughes, 462,224.

[...]

Continued on Page 2.

## THE ELECTORAL VOTE.

Total, 531; necessary to a choice, 266.

| State. WILSON | Vote. | State. HUGHES | Vote. |
|---|---|---|---|
| Alabama | 12 | Connecticut | 7 |
| Arizona | 3 | Delaware | 3 |
| Arkansas | 9 | Illinois | 29 |
| California (By 3,181 votes, 36 precincts missing.) | 13 | Indiana | 15 |
| Colorado | 6 | Iowa | 13 |
| Florida | 6 | Maine | 6 |
| Georgia | 14 | Massachusetts | 18 |
| Idaho | 4 | Michigan | 15 |
| Kansas | 10 | Minnesota (By 1,094 votes, 85 precincts missing.) | 12 |
| Kentucky | 13 | New Hampshire (By 131 votes, 25 precincts missing.) | 4 |
| Louisiana | 10 | New Jersey | 14 |
| Maryland | 8 | New York | 45 |
| Mississippi | 10 | Oregon | 5 |
| Missouri | 18 | Pennsylvania | 38 |
| Montana | 4 | Rhode Island | 5 |
| Nebraska | 8 | South Dakota | 5 |
| Nevada | 3 | Vermont | 4 |
| New Mexico (By 1,730 votes, 105 precincts missing.) | 3 | *West Virginia | 8 |
| North Carolina | 12 | Wisconsin | 13 |
| North Dakota (By 1,018 votes, 28 precincts missing.) | 5 | | |
| Ohio | 24 | | |
| Oklahoma | 10 | | |
| South Carolina | 9 | | |
| Tennessee | 12 | | |
| Texas | 20 | | |
| Utah | 4 | | |
| Virginia | 12 | | |
| *Washington | 7 | | |
| Wyoming | 3 | | |
| Total | 272 | Total | 259 |

*Vote for deceased Democratic Elector may give one Elector to Hughes.

*Substituted elector's name omitted from some ballots; may give one elector to Wilson.

No States are classified as doubtful in the above table. Under the close States the latest returns are given.

## *Hughes's Lead Is Up in Minnesota; Wilson Holds N. Dakota, New Mexico*

*New Hampshire, on Latest Returns, Shows a Hughes Lead of 131, With Twenty-five Districts Missing—Democrats Claim the State.*

### MINNESOTA.

[...]

### NORTH DAKOTA.

[...]

Continued on Page 4.

## CALIFORNIA DECIDES

Result Was in Doubt Till Republicans Gave It Up at 11:25 P. M.

MINNESOTA STILL CLOSE

Hughes's Lead Going Up There; Wilson Gains in Other Close States.

CONTESTS ARE PROMISED

Charges of Fraud Are Already Under Investigation in Some Districts.

ONE CITY PLAYS BIG PART

Women and Progressives of San Francisco Deciding Factor in National Result.

HOUSE CONTROL IN DOUBT

Minor Parties May Have Balance of Power—Senate Is Safely Democratic.

Woodrow Wilson and Thomas R. Marshall have been again elected President and Vice President. Soon after 11 o'clock last night all the doubtful States, except New Hampshire and Minnesota, had given Wilson such a steady lead that his election was no longer in doubt. When, at 11:25, the news came that Chester H. Rowell, the Republican State Chairman in California, had conceded the State [...]

Continued on Page 4.

"All the News That's Fit to Print."

# The New York Times.

THE WEATHER
Fair, cold, falling westerly winds today; tomorrow fair, warmer.
For full weather report see Page 21.

VOL. LXVI...NO. 21,591. NEW YORK, TUESDAY, MARCH 6, 1917.—TWENTY-TWO PAGES. ONE CENT In Greater New York. | TWO CENTS New England and Middle States. | [illegible]

# PRESIDENT INAUGURATED, CALLS FOR A UNITED NATION; 'MAY BE DRAWN ON TO A MORE ACTIVE ASSERTION OF OUR RIGHTS'; MAY YET FIND A WAY TO ARM SHIPS WITHOUT SENATE ACTION

## GREAT MASS MEETING HERE

### Cries of "Hang Them!" Greet Filibusters' Names at Carnegie Hall.

### ASK PRESIDENT TO ACT

### Beck Cheered When He Says Law Permits Wilson to Put Naval Men on Ships.

### WANTS COALITION CABINET

### Speaker Suggests Root for Secretary of State and Roosevelt for the Navy.

In a spirit of grim earnestness, 3,000 persons at a great mass meeting of Americans in Carnegie Hall last night cheered every declaration of the speakers that Germany was now at war with the United States, sprang to their feet at every demand for pledges to support the President in protecting American lives and American honor, and waved flags and shouted approval of the declaration of James M. Beck that no ancient law prevented American naval gunners on merchant ships from firing at every German submarine that tried to molest an American ship. Each mention of the Senators who talked the armed ship bill to death brought cries of "Traitor!" and "Hang them!" while boos and groans greeted reference to William Jennings Bryan. References [illegible]

Before the close of the meeting, from [illegible] turned away, resolutions were adopted with cheers, condemning the pacifists and declaring those present regarded Senator O'Gorman—mentioned specifically—and his associates with contempt, that they insisted that Germany for two years had been warring continually on the United States, and that they would not be content until the United States answered with armed force.

**Hearty Cheers for Roosevelt.**

Before it passed those resolutions and concluded the evening with singing "The Star-Spangled Banner," the huge crowd, gathered under the auspices of the American Rights League and presided over by Major George Haven Putnam, greeted with enthusiasm the mention of the name of Theodore Roosevelt as "the foremost exponent of preparedness," and had shown its approval of the wartime lessons of other countries by acclaiming a suggestion from Mr. Beck that at this time of crisis President Wilson should avail himself of the services of a coalition Cabinet, substituting former President Roosevelt for Secretary of the Navy Daniels and using the services of Elihu Root in his old place, Secretary of State.

The gathering was made up about equally of men and women, many of whom were in evening dress. The demeanor of the audience was calm at the outset, but the strong feeling underlying this calm was shown when many of those present mistook a speech by Irving T. Bush of the Bush Terminal Company as a pro-German utterance. Mr. Bush after a long plea for sympathy for President Wilson and the end of criticism of him, turned to a discussion of the war, and remarked that some "felt that Germany was a Fatherland struggling against oppression." He got no further. For more than ten minutes there were boos and hisses, cries of "Shut up!" "Throw him out!" "He's a German!" and other accusations.

**Opposed Plea for Germany.**

Time and again Major Putnam waved his arms in an endeavor to quiet the tumult, which was general throughout the house. At last Mr. Bush got a chance to finish his speech. He did so, to the accompaniment of scattering applause and a chorus of hisses whenever an opportunity offered. The speaker explained that he was not pro-German but pro-Ally, and that he merely was trying to present all sides of American feeling because there could not be unanimity of action without mutual understanding.

Except for the Bush incident and the struggles of the crowd outside with police reserves, who closed the doors on Fire Department orders when the seats were filled, there was but one feature not on the program that occasioned comment. A man in the middle of the orchestra shouted in condemnation at every mention of Germany. His loud cries aroused laughter in those about him, for each time he called out: "Shyme, shyme!"

These were the resolutions adopted at the meeting:

Resolved, That we, loyal American citizens, without distinction of party, in mass meeting assembled in the City of New York, this 5th day of March, 1917, do hereby unequivocally approve the action of the President in severing diplomatic relations with the German Government.

Resolved, That we call upon the President immediately to exercise his constitutional authority for the arming of American ships passing through the barred zone insolently established by the German de-

Continued on Page 4.



### Huge Cargoes of Food Brought Into Great Britain

Special Cable to THE NEW YORK TIMES.

LONDON, March 5.—A party of neutral journalists who made a tour of London's docks yesterday were impressed by the sight of the tremendous cargoes of food brought in by newly arrived ships, the aggregate running into hundreds of thousands of tons. Fifty ships were unloading grain and chilled beef from America, South America, and Canada, sugar from Bombay and other cargoes to augment Britain's supply.

The brisk activity impressed the newspaper correspondents as a vivid reply to Germany's boast that she was going to starve Britain out within a few weeks by her submarine campaign and bring an end to the war.

"We're getting all the ships we can handle," said a dock official. "German submarine frightfulness is not felt here."

## GERMAN ARRESTED FOR MAKING BOMBS

### Deadly Missiles and High Explosives Found in His Room in a Hoboken Hotel.

### PLOT STORIES ARE DENIED

### No Proof Found of Rumors That Prisoner Had Intended to Attack President Wilson.

Fritz Kolb, a young German, was arrested yesterday afternoon by detectives from Captain Tunney's "Bomb" Squad [illegible] in the Commercial Hotel [illegible] Street, Hoboken. In his room two well-made bombs were found complete except for the fuses and small amounts of trinitrotoluol and picric acid. Kolb came under suspicion first, according to the Hoboken police, because he boasted while drinking that he intended to cause another explosion of munitions at Black Tom. It was rumored that he was connected with many Teuton plots in this country, including a plan to send bombs to President Wilson, but nothing was brought out after his arrest to substantiate these stories.

Kolb had been watched for three weeks before he was arrested. It was known, the police say, that he had taken explosives and other materials for bombmaking to his room, and the delay in arresting him was due to the hope that, by watching him, the detectives could find out whether other persons were working with him. Chief of Police Hayes of Hoboken said yesterday that evidence had been obtained that Kolb was only one of those taking part in a widespread conspiracy to destroy munitions factories, and that several arrests might follow, including the apprehension of one of two "big men." Captain Tunney did not sustain this view. He said that the watch kept on Kolb had indicated that he was working alone, and that his arrest completed the case.

The two bombs found in Kolb's rooms were made of steel pipe, cut in seven-inch lengths, with threads worked at either end. Steel caps had been screwed on the pipe after it had been loaded with a powder thought to be picric acid, which is now in the hands of the Bureau of Combustibles in this city for analysis. Wound around the steel pipe was a copper tube perforated at intervals of every half inch. The fuse was to be inserted in this and the holes in the tube were to let in air so that the fuse would burn. The pipes and copper wire fitted perfectly into two cylindrical containers of thin lead.

All that Kolb would say after his arrest, according to Chief of Police Hayes, was that the bombs had been made by a man known to him only as "Karl." Kolb said that about five weeks ago he met this man in a saloon and allowed him to use his room. Kolb said that he did not know what his acquaintance intended to do with the bombs.

Kolb is about five feet five inches tall, and says he is 33 years old. He has brown hair, very thin in front, and a close-cropped red mustache, which is curled upward at the ends, after the fashion adopted by the Kaiser. Kolb said that he was born in Cologne, and came to this country on a German ship in 1914. He said he was not a reservist, as he was disqualified by a physical defect. He added that he had worked as a porter, waiter, cook, and bartender in this country. The police learned that for several months he had been employed as a bartender at Kemper's saloon, Fourteenth Street and Madison Avenue, Newark. Kolb was held on a charge of having explosives in his possession without a license.

EL PASO, Texas, March 5.—Fritz Kolb, arrested in Hoboken, N. J., is believed to be the man of that name who spent some time here in 1915, associated with E. F. Haagsmar, a German reserve officer, who acted as military observer with President Huerta's forces in Mexico. Kolb was known to have some connection with the German Government.



## BERLIN SEES A WILSON TRICK

### Says He Invented a 'Plot' in Order to Stampede Congress.

### LONG "SCHEMING FOR WAR"

### Failure to Incite Mexico to Attack Us Would Have Been "Criminal Negligence."

### PLOT DISGUSTS REVENTLOW

### He Blames Zimmermann for Urging Mexico to Action She Would Have Taken in Time.

By Wireless to THE NEW YORK TIMES.

BERLIN, Saturday, March 3, (via Tuckerton, March 5.)—The American situation still appears somewhat confused even to trained observers in Germany. It seems incomprehensible to them that President Wilson's coup, "splendidly stage-managed as it was," should have captured so many level-headed legislators. One of the morning papers interprets what has happened in Washington as follows:

"To remove all objections against his policy by one stroke, Wilson decided to make his revelations, which were especially calculated to impress the Western States, whose fear of Japan has thus far prevented them backing the President. He meant to open the public's eyes to 'the dark conspiracy threatening the nation.' He is evidently a [illegible] of psychological [illegible], as well as the House, immediately after his revelations complied with his wishes without the slightest suspicion that the President might have set a trap for them. Otherwise, wouldn't they have asked the question why the Government, if it was really in possession of the great secret since the day of the rupture of relations, kept silence for a whole month and only now exploded its mine?

"The natural answer to this question would have been that what is now called a dark conspiracy was really no conspiracy at all, but merely a cautious measure by the German Government to prepare defense in case of war, which, considering Wilson's menacing policy during the last two years, had to be reckoned with. Had the German Government acted differently it would have been guilty of criminal negligence."

This, indeed, is the attitude of the whole German press without any exception, and, so far as one can judge here, it is also that of the neutral European press. Much is made of the fact that Dr. Zimmermann gave Minister Eckhardt strict instructions not to approach Mexico until after America had taken the fatal step. Therefore, it is argued, Wilson's revelations must come to the Mexicans as a great surprise.

Reviewing Wilson's attitude from the beginning of the world war, the newspapers come to the conclusion that he was all the while only dreaming and scheming to inveigle his country into war with Germany—a policy which even now is gratefully recognized by the English press. Germany gave in again, but her statesmen had to prepare for the time when Wilson's demands would become intolerable. Still, they never meant their precautionary measures to become effective until after Wilson had declared war. But after that—"à la guerre comme à la guerre." No sane person would blame Germany for fortifying her position against "the eleventh enemy."

The public remains very quiet, although the newspaper articles are not always calculated to smooth things over. Today the newspapers recall the fact that in the Mexican troubles of 1914 the German cruiser Dresden saved many hundreds of Americans living in Tampico from the hands of the infuriated native populace, for which the American Admiral Mayo thanked the Dresden's commander, saying that it would give him the greatest pleasure to inform his Government of the most kindly and effective help rendered by him and his officers. It is pointed out that in an interview with an American journalist reproduced in The Army and Navy Journal Mayo mentions only the English ship Hermione as having accomplished the rescue of the Americans at Tampico, whereas the Dresden had by far the largest share. "Another proof of the American Government's blind partiality for the English" is the German comment.

**Reventlow Blames Zimmermann.**

BERLIN, Sunday, March 4, (via London, March 5.)—While some of the German papers have received the news of the German-Mexican intrigue with comparative indifference, others have vigorously denounced the policy of Foreign Secretary Zimmermann. Count von Reventlow, formerly one of the most ardent advocates of unrestricted submarine warfare and a general supporter of extreme measures, writes in the Tageszeitung:

"As a result of the publication of the

Continued on Page 4.



### American Ship Seized; Tried to Run Blockade

LONDON, March 5.—The American schooner John G. McCullough has been captured on the charge of attempting to run the blockade. She was taken to Falmouth, where her cargo is being removed for the prize court.

The steamer, not schooner, John G. McCullough left here Dec. 10 for Gothenburg. She was cleared by the United States Steamship Company, and it was said yesterday at its office here that she carried a general cargo, including a quantity of wax. The vessel was reported by cable as having put into the Azores to repair damage sustained in a storm.

Cable reports from London on Dec. 16 said that the McCullough appeared on a new list of ships blacklisted by the British Admiralty. Officials of the company said the ship put into Falmouth upon their orders for examination of her cargo, and that by doing so her name was automatically removed from the list.

## THREATEN RECALL OF SENATOR LANE

### Oregon Boils with Rage at 'Misrepresentative' Who Aided Armed-Ship Filibuster.

### STATES SUPPORT WILSON

### Ohio Deplores Filibuster—Kentucky Urges Censure—Action in Washington and Arkansas.

Special to The New York Times.

PORTLAND, Ore., March 5.—[illegible] will be invoked on United States Senator Harry Lane on June 4, if it can be found that the law applies to a Senator sent to Washington. That question is now being studied.

The whole State is bitterly aroused over the action of the junior Senator from Oregon in joining the filibuster against the Armed Ship bill, and, as in Idaho, where former Iowa citizens are planning to burn in effigy Senator Cummins, Oregonians are talking of doing the same with Lane, against whom a State-wide movement is forming.

Never has the State been so aroused over anything. Democrats joining with other parties in denunciation of the man who is described as the State's "misrepresentative." Comment received here tonight from all parts of Oregon denounced Lane, and many persons urged drastic action immediately on the man who was called by some "Oregon's traitor." One message sent to Senator Lane follows:

"As Oregonians and loyal American citizens we note with chagrin your act of participating in the Senate filibuster to defeat the Armed Neutrality bill and embarrass the President. Your action does not sit well with your constituents."

A message to President Wilson opens with the following paragraph:

"As private citizens of the State of Oregon we wish thus to apprise you of our repudiation of the act of Senator Lane in his failure to co-operate with you. Senator Lane does not represent the sentiment of his constituents."

### OHIO INDORSES PRESIDENT.

#### General Assembly Unanimously Deplores Senate Minority's Work.

Special to The New York Times.

COLUMBUS, Ohio, March 5.—Under a suspension of the rules the Ohio General Assembly today unanimously adopted these resolutions:

"Resolved, That the General Assembly of Ohio deplores the situation it has been possible to create by a pitiful minority of the United States Senate through simple lack of cloture; and, be it further

"Resolved, That in calm survey of menacing international conditions we record ourselves in sympathy with the aims and purposes of the President, and wish to lend our cheers to that great majority of the National Congress which has been standing behind him with heart and vote."

### WASHINGTON GIVES PLEDGE.

#### Legislature Promises Full Support to the Federal Government.

OLYMPIA, Wash., March 5.—Both houses of Washington's Legislature today adopted a resolution pledging men and resources to the Federal Government in the foreign crisis.

Efforts in the lower house failed to change the resolution to read "violence" instead of "murder" referring to Americans killed in the submarine warfare.

### WOULD CENSURE SENATORS.

#### Resolution in Kentucky Legislature —Members Cheer the Flag.

FRANKFORT, Ky., March 5.—The lower branch of the Kentucky Legislature, in special session here today, first passed, then reconsidered and finally referred to a committee a resolution condemning the United States Senators who blocked the enactment of the Armed Ship bill in Congress.

The resolution approved the stand of the United States Senators from Ken-

Continued on Page 2.



## 50,000 SEE INAUGURATION

### President at East Front of Capitol Again Takes the Oath of Office.

### TROOPS FEATURE OF PARADE

### Festivity Lacking and the Spirit of the Occasion Serious and Businesslike.

### MARSHALL ALSO SWORN IN

### Oath Administered in Senate Chamber in Presence of a Distinguished Company.

Special to The New York Times.

WASHINGTON, March 5.—Probably 50,000 people saw President Wilson repeat, on the east front of the Capitol today, the oath of fidelity he took yesterday in the building itself. He came out to the east front from the Senate Chamber, where he had participated in the inauguration of Thomas R. Marshall, the first Vice President to succeed himself since John C. Calhoun. He delivered his inaugural address and then went to the reviewing stand, where he reviewed a military and civic parade that lasted four hours, in which 19,000 men were in line.

This ended the official ceremonies. There was no inaugural ball. The parade was only about half as long as that of four years ago, the smallest, in fact, in many years. There was no [illegible] in authority was to minimize, not to accentuate, the spectacular and the picturesque. It was necessary that the function be gone through, but it was not necessary to emphasize it—that was the feeling which supplied the keynote. It was not a festive occasion, it was not a holiday, it was not a merrymaking, and to pretend that it was any of these things would have made the occasion grotesque; that was the governing sentiment of everybody, from the President down through all the grades of officials to the Secret Service and the police.

In other and more fortunate times inauguration day has been an innocent spree by the American people, a day of light hearts and care-free heads, a sort of political New Year's Eve, in which the old was running out and the new running in. There was the same difference between such inauguration days and this one that there is between the North Atlantic squadron on a Summer cruise, painted white and assisting at social activities, and the battleship fleet steaming out for unknown waters painted gray.

**Curt and Businesslike.**

To this stripped-for-action environment the circumstances contributed. The Senate adjourned yesterday, so that the usual pastime of watching its closing hours had to be omitted, and that has always supplied a good deal of spice to inauguration. The authorities, desirous as they were to cut the festive side of the occasion to the very bone and make it as curt and businesslike as possible, were glad of this; but the people, to whom the official frame of mind had communicated itself, helped them further and unexpectedly, for the galleries did their part too.

At all previous inaugurations this gathering in the galleries has been of a gala sort; women have vied with one another to justify the reporters in describing the scene as a "riot of color;" it has been a dress parade of gay, excited spectators, full of laughter and gossip. As if there had been an order to that effect, this whole atmosphere vanished like magic at this inauguration. The galleries were filled with soberly-dressed, quiet people, who looked down upon the Senate Chamber with earnest faces, and the usual demonstrations did not take place. The new Senators, usually greeted with outbursts from the galleries, were sworn in in silence. There were only two things that could be called demonstrations, and one was when the President came in. That was expected, but the other was unexpected, and was called forth by these words:

"I ought to be willing to live or to die, as God decrees, that it (this Government) may not perish from off the earth through treachery within or through assault from without."

The words were uttered by Vice President Marshall in his inaugural address, and they were words of the kind for which this great and grave and earnest multitude has been waiting since it came to Washington; and the silent gallery broke forth in a deep thunder of applause, that ended and then broke forth again with a depth and volume greater than at first.

**Armed Guards on Housetops.**

Coming down to the Capitol they had seen an eloquent dramatization of that part of the Vice President's phrase in which he hinted at "treachery within." On the tops of buildings in every block along the President's route and the line of march of the parade were posted armed men ready for action—policemen.

Continued on Page 3.



### Broad Principles Stated by President Wilson as "the Things We Shall Stand For" in War or Peace

*From the President's Inaugural Address.*

We stand firm in armed neutrality, since it seems that in no other way we can demonstrate what it is we insist upon and cannot forego. We may even be drawn on, by circumstances, not by our own purpose or desire, to a more active assertion of our rights as we see them and a more immediate association with the great struggle itself. * * *

We are provincials no longer. The tragical events of the thirty months of vital turmoil through which we have just passed have made us citizens of the world. There can be no turning back. Our own fortunes as a nation are involved, whether we would have it so or not.

And yet we are not the less Americans on that account. We shall be the more American if we but remain true to the principles in which we have been bred. They are not the principles of a province or of a single continent. We have known and boasted all along that they were the principles of a liberated mankind. These, therefore, are the things we shall stand for, whether in war or in peace:

That all nations are equally interested in the peace of the world and in the political stability of free peoples, and equally responsible for their maintenance:

That the essential principle of peace is the actual equality of nations in all matters of right or privilege.

That peace cannot securely or justly rest upon an armed balance of power.

That Governments derive all their just powers from the consent of the governed and that no other powers should be supported by the common thought, purpose, or power of the family of nations.

That the seas should be equally free and safe for the use of all peoples, under rules set up by common agreement and consent, and that, so far as practicable, they should be accessible to all upon equal terms.

That national armaments should be limited to the necessities of national order and domestic safety.

That the community of interest and of power upon which peace must henceforth depend imposes upon each nation the duty of seeing to it that all influences proceeding from its own citizens meant to encourage or assist revolution in other States should be sternly and effectually suppressed and prevented.

## WILSON SOUNDS A SOLEMN NOTE

### His Inaugural Address Portrays Our Perils and Duties Amid the World Strife.

### "SHOULD STAND TOGETHER"

### And Beware of Intrigue—Sets Forth America's Principles for Coming Peace.

Special to The New York Times.

WASHINGTON, March 5.—President Wilson devoted practically the whole of his short and solemn inaugural address to the foreign relations of the United States. Not once did he mention Germany by name, but the thought in every one of his measured sentences was the thought of Germany, of "the more active assertion of our rights" to which Germany might force the United States and of a "more immediate association with the great struggle itself" into which the United States might be drawn, "by circumstances, not by our own purpose or desire." But such a climax to the long-drawn-out crisis, said he, "will not alter our thought or our purpose. We desire neither conquest nor advantage."

The burden of the address seemed to be so placed that it would press upon public attention preparation for possible events of the gravest sort. Only in his opening paragraph did he mention the domestic legislation of the last four years. It was a record, he said, of singular variety and singular distinction. Then, with slow emphasis, he dismissed the subject, as this was not "the time for retrospect." "It is time rather to speak our thought concerning the present and the immediate future."

The address might be divided according to the grammatical tenses—past, present, and future. He said that since foreign currents and influence began drawing the country more and more irresistibly, "we have grown more and more aware, more and more certain that the part we wished to play was the part of those who mean to vindicate and fortify peace." There he used the past tense. His statement in the present was that, "We stand firm in armed neutrality, since it seems that in no other way can we demonstrate what it is we insist upon and cannot forego." His reference to the future was this:

"We may even be drawn on, by circumstances, not by our own purpose or desire, to a more active assertion of our rights as we see them and a more active association with the great struggle itself."

It was to this future that he particularly directed his word. He declared himself still for peace, but the easy inference from what he said was that he looked to peace now as something to come after the great European war was fought out, not as something to be achieved by proposals and parlovings. He was certain that the United States would play its rôle in making that peace, and he expressed the hope that in the "ardent heat" of the "fires that now blaze throughout the world," the United States would "be purged of faction and division, purified of the errant humors of party and of private interest, and stand forth in days to come with a new dignity of national pride and spirit."

His address, in so far as it was not a statement of the present grave situation and a warning of a possibly graver future, was a plea for unity in this "composite and cosmopolitan people."

This unity, he said, had already been in great measure brought about by the stress of outside things, things that had increased the American consciousness that America was not part of this foreign struggle, that, though America had been "deeply wronged upon the seas," she did not wish to wrong in return and was "still standing in some sort apart intent upon an interest that transcended the immediate issues of the war itself."

But the President said in unmistakable terms that America was interested in

Continued on Page 3.



## PRESIDENT RODE IN LANE OF STEEL

### Unusual Measures to Guard the Executive's Safety Recall Lincoln's Inauguration.

### DETECTIVES SURROUND HIM

### Guardsmen of Two New York Regiments Line Pennsylvania Av.—Marksmen on Roofs.

Special to The New York Times.

WASHINGTON, March 5.—Not since the first inauguration of Abraham Lincoln, fifty-six years ago, have there been such precautions as were taken today to guard the life an incoming President of the United States. Secret Service men, troops of the regular army, detectives, and policemen formed a hollow square about President Wilson as he rode to and from the Capitol Building. The roofs of buildings overlooking Pennsylvania Avenue were guarded by plain clothes men. The roof of the Capitol was similarly under surveillance.

The men of the Sixty-ninth and Twelfth Regiments, N. Y. N. G., lined Pennsylvania Avenue from the Capitol to the White House. Their guns were loaded. The State militiamen, backs to the crowds that lined the sidewalks, took their places at 10 o'clock, an hour before the President left the White House for the ride down Pennsylvania Avenue to the Senate Chamber. The guardsmen stood about twenty paces apart. They stood at attention, ready for action, while the President passed any given point.

Along the line of march and supporting the New York regiments in the task of protecting the President from bodily harm were detectives from the Central Office of this city and numerous policemen and special officers. The President literally rode to the Capitol and back again through a lane of armed men.

Members of the Sixty-ninth and Twelfth Regiments were in fighting trim. The service on the border had bronzed their faces. They were dressed in field uniforms of olive-drab—the fighting color of the army.

Surrounding the President's carriage, drawn by four horses, were thirty-two Secret Service men. Eight walked ahead of the carriage, eight behind and eight on each side. Supplementing these guards, and formed in a hollow square outside the ranks of Secret Service men, were troopers of the Second Cavalry, stationed at Fort Myer. Fifteen troopers rode abreast at the head of the carriage and as many more immediately behind. A half dozen troopers, in single file, rode nearer the curbing on each side of the President's carriage.

Near by, closely following the President, were twenty-five plain-clothes policemen from Washington and other cities. At street intersections guardsmen were stationed to face the crowd at the particular moment the President's carriage passed.

Special guards with loaded rifles and authority to act were stationed on the roofs of buildings overlooking the line of march. That extraordinary precautions as the guarding of roofs had been taken did not become generally known until the parade was actually formed. The plans of the police with respect to this were kept secret. They are understood to have been perfected by William J. Flynn, Chief of the Secret Service, and Major Raymond W. Pullman, Chief of Police of Washington.

Chief Flynn stationed himself on the platform while the President was taking the oath of office. Directly below were companies of bluejackets and marines and all about the President were detectives. Secret Service men from all parts of the country were called to Washington for the inaugural.

The zeal with which the President was guarded recalled the first inauguration of President Lincoln in 1861. The President-elect started from Spring-

Continued on Page 3.



## GREGORY ASKED FOR OPINION

### President Requests Reply in 24 Hours on Right to Arm Vessels.

### LANSING THINKS HE HAS IT

### Meanwhile Movement to Change Senate Rules to Stop Filibusters Gains Headway.

### DEMOCRATIC CAUCUS TODAY

### Hard Contest Lies Ahead, as Republicans May Oppose and La Follette Group Is Bitter.

Special to The New York Times.

WASHINGTON, March 5.—There is still a chance that President Wilson will give the order to the Secretary of the Navy to arm merchant vessel without waiting for Congress to enact a law empowering him to do so.

After he issued his statement last night, saying that old statutes prevented him from taking the responsibility of arming ships, a doubt arose in the President's mind as to the applicability of these statutes. Today he took steps to ascertain definitely whether these statutes forbade him to arm ships without special congressional sanction.

It was stated today that the President had directed Attorney General Gregory to examine the [illegible] encouraging to members of the [illegible] trade, who are anxious to have merchant ships armed without delay and the semi-blockade of American commerce ended. They believe that the President's action means that if there is any possible way legally for him to provide armament for American merchant vessels he will issue orders at once.

According to statements by officials, the doubt in President Wilson's mind as to the applicability of the statute of 1819 to the armed ship situation was raised after a talk with Secretary Lansing. It is believed that after he had issued his statement to the country the President got in touch with Secretary Lansing and found that he did not agree with the asertions made in the Senate by Senator Lodge and others that the law of nearly 100 years ago was a bar to furnishing guns to merchantmen.

The Secretary of State is said to hold that the general powers given to the President by the Constitution to provide for the common defense would enable him to order the Secretary of the Navy to furnish guns for defensive purposes to private vessels flying the American flag.

Today's inaugural ceremonies have taken up practically all the time of officials, but the President's directions to the legal officers of the Government are of such a mandatory character, it was said today, that Attorney General Gregory or his assistants will be obliged to burn the midnight oil to let the President know by tomorrow afternoon, when a Cabinet meeting may be held, whether he could take the responsibility of furnishing guns to merchant vessels without specific authority from Congress.

**Moving to Amend Senate Rules.**

The excitement of the inauguration has prevented Senators from exchanging views in regard to the ringing indictment of the Senate which the President made in his statement of last night. The Senate majority leaders, however, were so impressed by the President's language that in a brief period allowed for consultation this morning prior to the beginning of the inaugural ceremonies they decided to hold a caucus without delay to discuss the insistence of the President that the rules of the Senate should be revised so as to prevent one Senator or a small group of Senators from defeating the will of the majority of their associates, as was done in the case of the Armed Ship bill. The caucus will be held at 10:30 o'clock tomorrow morning.

The temper of the great majority of the Senate, both Democrats and Republicans, is such that no more propitious opportunity could have been afforded for undertaking to change the Senate rules so as to provide some form of cloture. Prominent Senators of both parties, who supported the President in the armed ship legislation, feel the justice of Mr. Wilson's comments on the "little group of willful men" who had made the country "helpless and contemptible" at this time of crisis.

Attempts have been made in the past to amend the Senate rules so as to provide for cloture. These were unsuccessful, as most Senators held to the tradition that the Senate was intentionally a deliberative body invested with powers which enabled it to check a too rapid House of Representatives. The fact stands out at this time, however, that a considerable number of these conservative members of the Senate now agree with President Wilson in holding that freedom of debate can be [illegible]

"All the News That's Fit to Print"

# The New York Times

THE WEATHER
Fair today; Monday, probably fair and warmer; moderate northerly winds.
For full weather report see Page 23.

VOL. LXIX...No. 22,772 •••• NEW YORK, SUNDAY, MAY 30, 1920. In Nine Parts, Including Rotogravure Picture Sections and Book Section. FIVE CENTS In Manhattan, Bronx, and Brooklyn } Elsewhere TEN CENTS

## OFFERS COMMISSION PLAN FOR ARMENIA WITH LOAN FROM US

### Hitchcock Makes New Proposal in Senate as Mandate Debate Opens.

### THREE AMERICANS ON BOARD

### Three Armenians Would Also Be Named and Another Would Be Elected by the Six.

### LODGE CORDIAL TO IDEA

### Says Republicans Are Willing to Aid Any Practicable Measure.

WASHINGTON, May 29.—President Wilson's request that Congress authorize a mandate over Armenia came under fire from both Democrats and Republicans today when the resolution to deny such authorization was brought up in the Senate.

From the Democratic side, however, came a proposal to soften the resolution by adding a provision extending American aid in the economic upbuilding of the new Near Eastern republic. The plan was taken under advisement by the Republican leaders. In order that Senators might have an opportunity to study it, an agreement was made to defer until Monday any attempt to set a date for a vote.

Under the suggested provision, which was presented by Senator Hitchcock of Nebraska, Administration leader in the treaty fight, a joint commission of Americans and Armenians would be authorized to supervise the sale here of $50,000,000 in Armenian bonds. The proceeds would go to buy railroad and agricultural materials and similar equipment and to the establishment of an Armenian banking system.

In urging his proposal, Senator Hitchcock said that he felt that the resolution as reported by the Foreign Relations Committee would have the effect of "discouraging" the Armenian people.

Senator Lodge of Massachusetts, the Republican leader, replied that proposals to aid Armenia would be received with much sympathy on his side of the chamber, but he added that there were many ways in which aid could be extended.

There was only a brief discussion of the merits of the President's request, which Senator Hitchcock said he did not intend to support. Several other Democratic Senators also indicated their disapproval, but Senator Williams, Democrat, of Mississippi, declared the United States would be unfaithful to its responsibilities if it declined to accept the mandate.

Senator Jones of New Mexico and Robinson of Arkansas, Democrats, said that the resolution involved an important question and a vote should not be taken without giving it serious consideration. The former called attention to the fact that the committee had presented no written report.

Senator Lodge replied that the matter had been considered for months, and added that only lack of time and a belief that the reasons for refusing a mandate were so plain a "child could understand them" were responsible for the absence of a formal report.

When Senator Wadsworth, Republican, of New York, expressed the opinion that the report of the Harbord Commission had thoroughly digested the facts surrounding the situation, the New Mexico Senator replied that he had not read the report.

"The committee assumes," said Senator Jones, "that a mandate carrying out the elaborate proposal outlined in the Harbord report, but the Covenant of the League of Nations says specifically that it may be limited to furnishing of administrative advice." Senator Lenroot, Republican, of Wisconsin, declared acceptance of the limited mandate suggested by Senator Jones would "leave the Armenian people in a worse state than before."

Acceptance of a mandate was opposed by Senator Smith, Democrat, of Georgia, who suggested that Congress had no constitutional authority to use public money for such a purpose and added that in any case blanket authority in the matter should not be given the President without knowing the attitude of Armenia's neighbors.

"Why, even the boundaries of Armenia have not yet been fixed," interrupted Senator Lodge.

## FURIOUS ENGAGEMENTS ON THE DNIEPER RIVER

### Bolsheviki Assault Polish Fortified Positions and the Issue Is Still Doubtful.

LONDON, May 29.—Furious fighting is in progress on the left bank of the Dneiper River, where the Bolsheviki are attempting to dislodge the Poles from their fortified positions, according to an official statement sent out by the Soviet Government at Moscow Friday.

The Poles are offering stubborn resistance, the statement says, first one side and then the other holding the first line positions.

"In the Tarashtcha region (sixty miles south of Kiev), our troops, overcoming the enemy's resistance, captured Tarashtcha with a number of villages some twenty-seven miles distant Tarashtcha," the statement adds.



## French Troops Relieve Aintab After Fighting Way Into Town

LONDON, May 29.—A French column fought its way into Aintab, Syria, and after heavy fighting succeeded in relieving the town, it was officially announced today.

The Turks suffered heavy casualties.

An unconfirmed report from Beyrut, that the Turks besieging Aintab had raised the siege and surrendered to the French, was received in cable advices last night by the Near East Relief from Major James H. Nicol, Managing Director for Syria. The siege of Aintab by the Turkish Nationalists has lasted nearly sixty days.

## WOMAN PROSECUTOR NAMED PALMER AID

### President Nominates Mrs. Adams of San Francisco for Assistant Attorney General.

### GOOD RECORD IN CALIFORNIA

### As Federal Attorney Convicted German Plotters—W. L. Frierson Made Solicitor General.

*Special to The New York Times.*

WASHINGTON, May 29.—Mrs. Annette Adams of San Francisco was nominated by President Wilson today to be an Assistant Attorney General for the United States. Mrs. Adams is now the United States Attorney for the Northern District of California. It was declared here in Washington that the office for which she was nominated today is the most important and lucrative of any office to which a woman has been appointed in the Federal service.

The President at the same time sent to the Senate the nomination of William L. Frierson of Chattanooga, Tenn., to be Solicitor General of the United States. Mr. Frierson is now an Assistant Attorney General, and Mrs. Adams was nominated to succeed him.

Mrs. Adams, it was said at the Department of Justice today, would be assigned to duties upon her qualification as an Assistant Attorney General. It was said that she will not take over Mr. Frierson's duties in connection with the prohibition law.

Mr. Frierson, as Solicitor General, will assume an office that is looked upon as one of the most important in the Government. It has been held in comparatively recent years by William H. Taft, the late Henry Hoyt of Pennsylvania, later a United States Judge and Counselor of the State Department; Frederick W. Lehmann of Missouri, the late Lloyd W. Bowers of Illinois, and John W. Davis of West Virginia, now the American Ambassador to London.

The Solicitor General presents cases for the Government to the United States Supreme Court, and is the principal assistant of the Attorney General in all matters involving major Constitutional and legal questions.

Mr. Frierson is to succeed Alexander C. King of Georgia, recently nominated for the United States Circuit bench, who in turn succeeded Ambassador Davis. He has been Assistant Attorney General since September, 1917, and as such was in charge of the enforcement of the Pure Food law, customs laws, and the Federal prohibition law. He was City Attorney of Chattanooga and was Mayor of that city from 1905 to 1907. He is 51 years old.

**California Proud of Mrs. Adams.**

*Special to The New York Times.*

SAN FRANCISCO, May 29.—From country school teacher to Assistant United States Attorney General is the record made by Annette Abbott Adams within a few brief years. She was Principal of a high school in Plumas County, Cal., when she decided to study law, entered the University of California in 1904, took her bachelor's degree, and in 1912 received her degree of Doctor of Jurisprudence.

She was appointed Assistant United States Attorney—the first woman in the United States to receive such an appointment—in 1913, as aide to John W. Preston, the United States Attorney here. Mrs. Adams's appointment did not meet with favor in Washington from the then Attorney General McReynolds. Upon his appointment to the United States Supreme Court, his successor, Attorney General Gregory, promptly confirmed Mrs. Adams's appointment.

Mrs. Adams won her laurels in the prosecution of neutrality cases during the war, especially the famous case of Franz Bopp, former German Consul General in San Francisco, and also in the Hindu conspiracy cases shortly after. It was in these trials that Mrs. Adams gained the reputation of drawing "demurrer proof" indictments.

When United States Attorney Preston was appointed to handle war work for the Government Senator Phelan recommended Mrs. Adams for the position vacated by Preston.

Her work as United States attorney for the Northern District of California drew the attention of Attorney-General A. Mitchell Palmer, whose impression of her record led him to send for her to proceed to Washington to attend a conference of District Attorneys throughout the nation.

Mr. Palmer did not notify Mrs. Adams of her promotion and the announcement from Washington came to her as a complete surprise.

During her visit in Washington in April Mrs. Adams was admitted to prac-

Continued on Page Six.



## DEBS IN PRISON GARB TAKES NOMINATION FOR PRESIDENCY

### Formally Apprised of His Selection Behind Bars of Atlanta Penitentiary.

### SAYS HE'S STILL BOLSHEVIK

### Declares Socialist Party Should Support Russian Revolution with All Its Power.

### HE KISSES THE COMMITTEE

### Woman Member Presents Bouquet to Leader, While Warden and Guards Watch Ceremony.

*Special to The New York Times.*

ATLANTA, May 29.—Clad in the prison uniform of blue denim which has superseded the traditional stripes, Eugene V. Debs, for many years the standard bearer of the Socialist Party, today received formal notification that he had again been nominated for the Presidency of the United States, and in a carefully prepared and slowly delivered address he accepted the honor paid him by his comrades.

It was a scene unique in the history of American politics—the tendering of a nomination for the Presidency of a nation to a man serving a prison term for violating the laws of that nation, a man whose prison term would outlast two terms as President if he were elected, who can make no campaign addresses, who will not be permitted even to issue campaign statements or to write political letters.

The official notification took place in the office of Warden Zerbst, at the front of the big prison, after Debs and the party of Socialists who had called upon him had gone into the May sunshine outside the main entrance and posed for innumerable photographs and many feet of movie film. It was here that Debs was kissed on the cheek by Seymour Stedman, Socialist candidate for Vice President; was kissed by and received from Dr. Madge Patton Stephens, a member of his own Socialist local at Terre Haute, a bouquet of roses, all of which was duly recorded by the movie camera.

**Debs Kisses Committee.**

Debs's blue eyes blinked in the bright sunshine, made glaring by the white marble steps and the tall walls. His bald head glistened as he bent forward to greet the comrades who shook hands with him. Composing the committee were Mr. Stedman, James Oneal, associate editor of The New York Call and a member of the National Socialist Executive Committee; Julius Gerber, Secretary of the Socialist Party in New York; Otto Branstetter, Secretary of the National Socialist Executive Committee, and Mrs. Stephens. All of the members of the committee have been friends of Debs for years, but none of them had seen him since he was sent to prison.

At 9 o'clock the party set out for the prison in automobiles. Warden Zerbst had informed them they could see Debs, and the Socialist leader was waiting in the Warden's office, in the front part of the prison, when the automobiles drove up, and the party was admitted.

Gerber was first in the line. As Debs stepped into the corridor they flung their arms about each other, Debs kissing Gerber on both cheeks. Thus he greeted each of the others, including Mrs. Stephens, who pressed the flowers upon him. They drew back to look at him and Debs beamed. The Socialist candidate is a tall, spare man, baldheaded and lank of limb and slightly stooped shouldered. He wore the regulation prison garb—blue denim trousers and coat, the "sneaker" shoes of the prison and pink flannel socks.

The proverbial prison pallor was conspicuous by its absence. In fact, every member of the visiting party was much paler than Debs. His thin, almost bony, face, creased with wrinkles, was tanned a bright brown, and even the top of his bald head, where the straggling brown hair had worn away, was pink.

Through large spectacles his blue eyes twinkled at them in a positively fatherly manner.

"Well, Gene, how goes it?" asked Oneal. "You certainly look fine."

"See!" said one of the party, pointing to a button on his coat lapel bearing Debs's picture and the announcement of his candidacy.

"Better take that off," laughed Debs. "They'll put you in the penitentiary for wearing that."

After pictures had been taken in the Warden's office the party went outside, where more pictures were taken. The kissing episode was repeated and the roses were presented again while Debs smiled, waved his hands and performed other motions at the direction of the photographers.

"That's all," said one of them. "You're a fine actor, Mr. Debs—a bully actor."

The nomination ceremony waited a few minutes for the arrival of one of Debs's fellow prisoners, Joseph Caldwell, former State Secretary of the Socialist Party in Rhode Island, who was sentenced to five years on the same charge as that on which Debs was convicted. Caldwell was warmly greeted as he was brought out by a guard and with the others took a seat in the Warden's office. Then the nomination was formally tendered.

Debs sat in a little chair at one end of a long table, hunched forward, with

Continued on Page Three.



## French Premier Pays Tribute to Our Dead; America's Grief a 'Ransom of a Better Future'



Special Cable to THE NEW YORK TIMES.

PARIS, May 29.—Premier Millerand gave through THE NEW YORK TIMES correspondent today the following message to the American people on the occasion of Memorial Day:

"The feeling of France and of the French Government toward the American people and public powers of America are today (need one say it?) what they were in the hour of common sacrifice and armed struggle to assure the triumph of liberty in the world.

"We have won the results for which we fought together. The principle of democracy is saved. The reign of democracy is assured for the future. The war has been won.

"In the presence of the tombs which hold the perishable and sacred dust of your children, fallen side by side with ours in the great world war, we can state truly that they have not died in vain. The sacrifice of these precious lives, the tears of those dear to them who remain, the grief of their country, have been the ransom of a better future.

"The way in which these heroes did their duty dictates the conduct of those Frenchmen and Americans who have survived the tempest; peace will not be truly re-established in the world till that day when the ruins which the war caused have been wiped away and its economic disasters overcome.

"We have to unite to repair for those who suffered everywhere across the world the consequences of the universal struggle. We must get back to the normal order in human relations, to a stable peace based on political and economic equilibrium.

"The Government of the French Republic salutes with emotion the American people at the moment that they weep for their dead, fallen in the great war. A. MILLERAND."

## LEASES 13 SHIPS TO NEW MAIL LINE

### Board Gives 5-Year Charter for George Washington and Other Former German Liners.

### NET $20,000,000 TO NATION

### '100% American' Concern Is Unconditional Guarantor—Service to Bremen and Danzig.

*Special to The New York Times.*

WASHINGTON, May 29.—The Shipping Board announced today that it had chartered thirteen former German passenger steamships, of a total of 90,000 tonnage, to the United States Mail Steamship Company, a new organization controlled by the France and Canada Steamship Corporation. The Shipping Board stated that the stock ownership and management of both the United States Mail Steamship Company and the France and Canada Steamship Corporation "are 100 per cent. American." Under the terms of the charter, the France and Canada Corporation is the unconditional guarantor of the United States Mail Steamship Company in the arrangement with the Shipping Board.

The George Washington, formerly of the North German Lloyd Company, carried President Wilson four times across the Atlantic in connection with the Paris Peace Conference; the Mount Vernon, one attacked and badly damaged by a German submarine; the President Grant, sister ship of the President Lincoln, which was sunk by an enemy submarine, and the America are among the vessels chartered to the United States Mail Steamship Company.

These thirteen vessels are to ply routes from New York and Boston to British, French and German ports and to Danzig. The chartering company is also to have the right to run services to Mediterranean ports. At the expiration of the five-year period of charter the chartering company is to have the first chance to purchase the vessels at prices and under terms to be then fixed by the Shipping Board.

The vessels chartered are the George Washington, Pocahontas, Mount Vernon, Callao, Susquehanna, President Grant, America, Princess Matoika, Agamemnon, Antigone, Amphion, Freedom and Madawaska.

Two more vessels, the Aeolus and the Huron, are to be chartered under the same conditions if the Shipping Board can obtain their release from present obligation.

The essential terms of the contract between the Shipping Board and the United States Mail Steamship Company are told in a statement from the Shipping Board, as follows:

"The United States Mail Steamship Company is to recondition these vessels for passenger service at its own expense. The plans for reconditioning are to be subject to the approval of the Shipping Board. The steamship company is to pay the Government a bare boat charter hire at the rate of $3.50 per net registered ton per month. 'Off hire' for overhauling and repairing is permitted, but not to exceed thirty days in any one year.

"The charter is to run for a period of five years. At the termination thereof the steamship company has the first chance to purchase the vessels at prices and terms then to be fixed by the board. In case of purchase the steamship company is to be credited on the purchase price with the amount of money spent in reconditioning vessels for service, minus depreciation, at the rate of 7½ per cent. per annum. If the steamship company does not purchase the amount so spent in reconditioning, minus depreciation, is to be returned in cash.

"Under the charter, all of the expenses of operation of these vessels, including insurance, are to be borne by the steamship company, and the return to the Government is net.

"The contract also provides that, in the event that the steamship company enters into any contract with the North German Lloyd Steamship Company or the Hamburg-American Lines for the use of the piers, warehouses, facilities, &c., of either of said companies, such agreement shall be subject to the approval of the Shipping Board.

"The steamship company also agrees to take the Aeolus and the Huron under the same conditions, provided the Shipping Board can secure their release from their present commitments to the South American service by the substitution of other suitable vessels.

"The routes for which the vessels are chartered are as follows:

"New York - Queenstown - Cherbourg-Bremen. Returning via Cherbourg-Southampton. Alternative route, New York-Dover-Boulogne-Danzig.

"Boston-Queenstown-Cherbourg-Bremen. Returning via Southampton-Cherbourg."

Under the terms of this charter, it was said, the net return to the Government for the five-year period has been estimated at $20,000,000.



## LABOR UNYIELDING ON COLISEUM WIRES

### Leader Declares Western Union Cannot Run Lines Into Chicago Convention Hall.

### WON'T CONSIDER A DEAL

### Insists Company Must Meet the Union's Terms or Stay Out of the Building.

*Special to The New York Times.*

CHICAGO, May 29.—Labor leaders here, headed by Simon O'Donnell, President of the Chicago Building Trades Council, were standing pat tonight on their declaration that not a wire of the Western Union Telegraph Company shall be put into the Coliseum, where the Republican National Convention is to be held on June 8.

O'Donnell told THE NEW YORK TIMES correspondent that there was going to be a showdown, and that he would not give an inch. He charged that the Western Union had double-crossed labor in the past, and that there could be no talk of compromise, either "the Western Union must meet the terms of labor or stay out—unless the Republican National Committee wishes to start a war with labor over the matter, which, apparently, it does not.

The row has apparently resolved itself into a fight over local labor troubles, and this may let the *Postal Telegraph* Company into the Coliseum. When the battle started the Postal Company was put into the same boat as the Western Union, and the hue and cry of past differences—the old telegraphers' strike, which has never been called off, for instance—was drawn in.

O'Donnell said tonight, however, that there might be a chance for the Postal Company; that the fight would be restricted to a local matter, and that, in his opinion, it would not spread to the Democratic National Convention at San Francisco, as some had feared.

"The Western Union will never get into the Coliseum so long as it continues to employ non-union labor and refuses to recognize the unions," said O'Donnell. "It does not look to me now that any compromise can be reached.

"When the Western Union erected the new building we played fair with them. They promised to meet our conditions, but afterward they did not, and so we have got to meet this situation. They have continued to employ non-union labor. We have not been approached by the Western Union since we made our stand, and certainly we will not make any offer. If the Western Union gets into the Coliseum it will be on our conditions."

Mr. O'Donnell was asked if the Building Trades Council controlled the men who would give service at the convention after it opened, such as the electricians.

"Yes," he said, "we will call all of our men out if the situation requires such action. We are not going to let the Western Union get away with a scab labor proposition again."

And there the matter stood tonight. If the Postal Company cannot give service, only the American Telephone and Telegraph Company will string wires into the hall to send news of the convention out to the country. The Western Union will have to open headquarters in its branch office across the alley.

At the Western Union office here it was said there had been no change in the situation; that the Western Union would not make any concession to the Building Trades Council, and that other arrangements would be made if necessary. There is some talk that a compromise may be reached, but the stand taken by O'Donnell seems to make that impossible.

The Republican National Committee has shown no disposition to enter into the fight.

## ARRESTED AS PLOTTING TO KILL GRAND VIZIER

### Two Generals Among Those Implicated and Imprisoned by Constantinople Authorities.

CONSTANTINOPLE, May 27 (Associated Press).—Kasad Riza Pasha, a General of artillery; Michad Pasha, former commander of Turkish troops along the Dardanelles, and several other persons were arrested here today, charged with plotting to kill Damad Ferid, the Grand Vizier.

The assassination was to have taken place today, according to the authorities, but Damad Ferid was warned of the plot and for the last three days has not been at the War Office.



## BONUS BILL PASSED UNDER GAG IN HOUSE BY VOTE OF 289-92

### Measure to Raise $1,600,000,000 Forced Through Under Suspension of Rules.

### DEBATE LASTS 40 MINUTES

### Opponents Fight Desperately to Prevent Adoption of Rule Preventing Amendments.

### 112 DEMOCRATS VOTE "YES"

### Forty Republicans in Negative—Mann and Clark Denounce Majority Tyranny.

*Special to The New York Times.*

WASHINGTON, May 29.—By a vote of 289 to 92 the House today passed the bill to provide bonuses for ex-service men, and in doing so broke legislative precedents by suspending the rules and passing, after forty minutes' debate, a measure which calls for an expenditure of more than $1,600,000,000. Under the gag rule plan devised to compel voting directly upon the bill it was necessary to obtain a two-thirds vote instead of a majority. This was accomplished, with 35 more than required.

Forty Republicans, including Representatives Mann, ex-Speaker Cannon, S. D. Fess, Chairman of the Congressional Campaign Committee, and Representative Kahn, Chairman of the Military Affairs Committee, deserted their colleagues, while 112 Democrats joined the majority and supported the measure after Representative Rainey of Illinois had urged them to do so.

Before the way was paved for the House to vote upon the bill without having an opportunity to offer amendments the party leaders had to resort to vigorous methods. A special rule to make "suspension days" in order in the last six days of the session, beginning today, was reported. This precipitated the real battle.

**Mann Opposed Suspension Rule.**

Representative James R. Mann, regarded as the leading parliamentarian in the House, opposed the adoption of this rule, which he denounced as an "unprecedented, outrageous and iniquitous proposition," savoring of gag rule.

Despite his protest and that of Representative Garrett of Tennessee, Speaker Gillett overruled the point of order raised by Mr. Mann, namely, that the special rule violated the House rules in that it dispensed with calendar Wednesday without a two-thirds vote, and forestalled a motion to recommit being made as provided in another House rule.

Upon an appeal by Representative Garrett from the Chair's decision that the special rule offered did not conflict with these two objections, the Speaker was sustained by a vote of 192 to 189, with two voting "present." The ruling was objected to so strongly that eleven of the twelve Massachusetts Republicans voted against sustaining the Speaker, who is the dean of the Massachusetts delegation, while the three Democrats of the State voted to uphold the ruling. Representative Green of Massachusetts supported the Chair's decision.

After the point of order had been sustained another bitter contest arose over the adoption of the rule itself. Again the leading Republicans inveighed against the procedure, but the rule was adopted by a vote of 220 to 165. In this vote 45 Republicans voted with the minority and 45 Democrats supported the position of the Republican majority. To sustain the decision of the Chair in the first test vote 34 Republicans voted against laying the appeal on the table and 13 Democrats voted to lay it on the table.

After Representative Garrett appealed from the Chair's decision Representative Mondell, the Republican floor leader, moved to lay the appeal on the table, and therefore the vote to sustain the Chair came upon the motion to table.

**Vote Against Tabling Appeal.**

Republicans voting against laying on the table were:

| | | |
|---|---|---|
| Ackerman, N.J. | Kahn, Cal. | Rowe, N. Y. |
| Burroughs, N. H. | Luce, Mass. | Sanford, N. Y. |
| | Lufkin, Mass. | Tilson, Conn. |
| Cannon, Ill. | Magee, N. Y. | Tinkham, Mass |
| Dallinger, Mass | Merritt, Conn. | Treadway, Mass. |
| Dempsey, N.Y. | Moores, Ind. | |
| Freeman, Conn. | Paige, Mass. | Walsh, Mass. |
| Fuller, Mass. | Parker, N. Y. | Ward, N. Y. |
| Glynn, Conn. | Peters, Me. | Wason, N. H. |
| Good, Iowa. | Platt, N. Y. | Winslow, Mass |
| Greene, Vt. | Ramsey, N. J. | Wood, Ind. |
| Husted, N. Y. | Rogers, Mass. | |

Democrats voting for laying the appeal on the table were:

| | | |
|---|---|---|
| Ashbrook, Ohio | Mead, N. Y. | Rubey, Mo. |
| Evans, Mon. | Mooney, Ohio. | Tague, Mass. |
| Gallivan, Mass | O'Connor, Iowa | Thomas, Ky. |
| Hamill, N. J. | Olney, Mass. | |
| Maher, N. Y. | Quin, Miss. | |

**Hilarious Scene in the House.**

The real fight was waged against the adoption of the rule. Those opposing the legislation or desirous of delay recognized that with the rules suspended and the membership forced to vote directly upon the bill, further opposition would be futile. Just as soon as the rule was adopted the House began to accept the situation. In the forty minutes allowed for debate the scene resembled that of a college campus on class day. Those who spoke were heckled. Some were cheered so loudly that Speaker Gillett could not make himself heard in calling for order. Hilarity prevailed.

Twenty minutes for debate was apportioned to each side. Member after member spoke one or two minutes, while

Continued on Page Eight.



## House Adopts Budget System And Bill Now Goes to Wilson

WASHINGTON, May 28.—Without a record vote the House adopted late today the conference report on the McCormick-Good bill providing for a Federal budget system.

The bill now goes to the President.

## ALLEN TO PRESENT WOOD AS CANDIDATE

### Kansas Governor Accepts the General's Invitation to Put Him in Nomination.

### FOR HIM FROM THE START

### Believes Republicans Will Indorse Industrial Court—Expects Democrats to Nominate McAdoo.

Governor Henry J. Allen of Kansas, who has himself been mentioned as a Presidential possibility, will place the name of Maj. Gen. Leonard Wood before the Republican National Convention for President. Governor Allen's consent to make the nominating speech was obtained yesterday at breakfast by Colonel William Cooper Procter, head of the Wood Campaign Committee, as a result of a personal telegraphic message to Governor Allen from General Wood.

Governor Allen, who said later that he had been for General Wood from the start, stated that a plank calling for the establishment of a judicial tribunal for the settlement of industrial disputes, along the lines of the Kansas State Industrial Court, the subject of his debate with Samuel Gompers, President of the American Federation of Labor, the night before, would be presented to the Republican National Convention.

The Governor said that the party which refused to meet the issue of protection of the public from the evils and dangers of industrial warfare, would go down to defeat. He said he believed the Republican Party would adopt a plank calling for the establishment of an industrial tribunal, and called attention to the fact that such a plank was contained in the platform adopted by the last New York State Republican Convention, which was written by Elihu Root. He said he expected the Democrats to nominate William G. McAdoo and make a play for the organized labor vote.

General Wood's telegram to Governor Allen stated that he and his friends realized the importance of the personality of the man to present his name and closed by asking Governor Allen to accept the invitation to make the nominating speech. Concerning his breakfast table talk with Colonel Procter, Governor Allen said:

"I received a telegram from General Wood, dated at Charlottesville, Va., last night as I was starting for my debate with Samuel Gompers, President of the American Federation of Labor. "Although I have not yet replied directly to General Wood, I got in touch this morning with Colonel William C. Procter, and assured him I would consider it a great privilege to present the General's name."

"I think the Republican National Convention will make a pledge in the platform guaranteeing protection to the public against the waste and danger of industrial warfare," said Governor Allen in reply to a question. "You will recall that the platform of the last Republican Convention in New York State, written by Elihu Root, declared for the establishment of an impartial Federal tribunal to adjudicate labor difficulties.

"If it does not do that, and tries to make a bargain with any class, its candidate will lose the great strength that comes from that great reservoir, the public. Any bargain the Republican Party has even made before has amounted to less than nothing."

Governor Allen said he expected the Democrats to nominate William G. McAdoo for President. "They might as well name Gompers," he added.

He said he expected the Republican Convention to declare for an industrial tribunal for the protection of the public in labor disputes. "That will mean, of course," he continued, "that the Democratic Party will bid for the labor vote."

The Governor said he estimated that about 20 per cent. of union labor in the country as a whole usually voted the Republican ticket. He said he did not believe that the union labor leaders could take away any appreciable part of this Republican labor vote.

He said he believed Mr. Gompers and other labor leaders would undoubtedly support the Democratic ticket, but said they were usually sympathetic with the Democratic Party. He stated that they should be sympathetic, in view of the friendliness to labor displayed by the present national Administration, and said he was surprised during his debate with Mr. Gompers that his reference to President Wilson, as a supporter of the industrial tribunal idea did not receive greater applause.

"I do not look for much opposition," said Governor Allen, when asked if he expected the Republican National Convention to adopt his proposed plank. "The temper of the people, not of resentment but of realization that we cannot go further with the present industrial conflict, is such that some party must pledge protection to the public."

Governor Allen is a member of the Committee on Policies and Platform of the Republican National Committee, which is now engaged, he said, in fighting the matter out.

Governor Allen will go to Washington today to testify before the Labor Com-

Continued on Page Eighteen.



## $1,180,043 RAISED FOR WOOD; JOHNSON HAD OVER $200,000

### Senator's California Treasurer Asserts $125,000 Was Raised in His Home State.

### PROCTER ADVANCED $721,000

### General's National Treasurer Says A. E. Monell Also Signed Note for $100,000.

### DOUBTS THEIR REPAYMENT

### Wilbur W. Marsh Brands as Absurd the Story of a $10,000,000 Fund to Elect McAdoo.

*Special to The New York Times.*

WASHINGTON, May 29.—Further revelations on the pre-convention campaign expenditures of candidates for the Presidential nominations were heard today by the Senate Investigating Committee.

A. A. Sprague of Chicago, National Treasurer of the Wood campaign, testified that $1,180,043.20 had been raised in support of the General's candidacy, of which $821,000 was advanced and is yet to be paid.

Alexander McCabe, Treasurer of the Johnson California campaign, admitted that upward of $200,000 had been subscribed, $125,000 in California alone, to further the Senator's aspirations, of which a considerable amount had been sent into other States.

Senator Hitchcock, appearing in his own behalf, said that there was no fund and no campaign to promote him as a candidate, but that the Hitchcock Club of Nebraska had spent $3,337, made up of forty-seven contributions, in the primary in that State.

Continuing efforts to discover a fund for Mr. McAdoo the committee this afternoon questioned Evan S. Harris of Albany, former Chairman of the Democratic State Committee, who denied any knowledge of any fund for campaign.

Holding its first night session the committee turned once more to the alleged fund for Mr. McAdoo. Wilbur W. Marsh, Treasurer of the Democratic National Committee, was called, and Chairman Kenyon questioned him on rumors which he said were circulated to the effect that B. M. Baruch had given pledges to the Democratic Committee to raise a $10,000,000 fund from big corporations if Mr. McAdoo were nominated.

Mr. Marsh replied that the reports were absurd.

Mr. Sprague's testimony was the first which gave any definite approximation of the Wood fund, though the committee obtained the impression from William Cooper Procter the other day that at least $1,000,000 had been raised.

**Says Col. Procter Advanced $721,000.**

Colonel Procter has borne the financial brunt of the campaign, Mr. Sprague's testimony revealed. For, in addition to the $10,000 he contributed outright and advances totaling $521,000, he indorsed two notes at Chicago banks totaling $200,000. One of these notes was also indorsed by Mr. Sprague, who said that, though there was a distinct understanding that Mr. Procter's advances and the two notes were loans and not contributions, it seemed unlikely that either he or Colonel Procter would ever be reimbursed.

"I expect to have to pay my share of the $100,000 note," said Mr. Sprague. "I feel quite sure Colonel Procter will not get back his money."

"Then there is no agreement or understanding that you and Colonel Procter will be paid back by any man or group of men?" asked Senator Reed.

"There is not and has not been."

The $1,180,000.20 fund was made up, Mr. Sprague said, of $358,768 in contributions, $200,000 in bank loans and $621,275 in other loans.

The bank loans were two notes of $100,000 each, one at the Corn Exchange Bank, Chicago, indorsed by Colonel Procter alone, the other on the Merchants' Loan and Trust, Chicago, indorsed by Colonel Procter and Mr. Sprague.

The other loans were $521,000 from Colonel Procter and $100,000 from Ambrose Monell, New York.

**Names Chief Contributors.**

He named among the chief contributors to the $358,768 John D. Rockefeller, Jr., $25,000; William Wrigley, Jr., of Chicago, $10,000; Ambrose Monell, New York, $20,000; Smathers, New York, whose first name he did not know, $20,000; H. M. Billesby, Chicago, $15,000; C. D. Shaffer, Chicago, $10,000; William C. Procter, $10,000. From William Loeb, Jr., of New York, Mr. Sprague said he received a total of $225,000, but was unable to give the names of any contributors who made up that amount.

He submitted a detailed report of expenditures covering the States into which the Wood national organization sent funds, which showed the following sums:

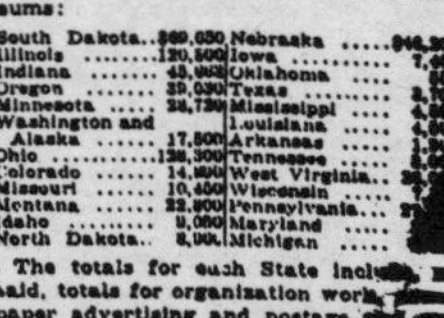

| | | | |
|---|---|---|---|
| South Dakota | $69,650 | Nebraska | [illegible] |
| Illinois | 120,500 | Iowa | [illegible] |
| Indiana | [illegible] | Oklahoma | [illegible] |
| Oregon | 39,030 | Texas | [illegible] |
| Minnesota | 24,730 | Mississippi | [illegible] |
| Washington and Alaska | 17,500 | Louisiana | [illegible] |
| Ohio | 138,300 | Arkansas | [illegible] |
| Colorado | 14,800 | Tennessee | [illegible] |
| Missouri | 10,400 | West Virginia | [illegible] |
| Montana | 22,800 | Wisconsin | [illegible] |
| Idaho | 9,080 | Pennsylvania | [illegible] |
| North Dakota | [illegible] | Maryland | [illegible] |
| | | Michigan | [illegible] |

The totals for each State include, he said, totals for organization work, newspaper advertising and postage and circularizing.

Mr. Sprague's figures showed that in Ohio, where charges of excessive expenditures in the Wood-Harding primary

Section 1

"All the News That's Fit to Print."

# The New York Times.

THE WEATHER
Generally fair today and Monday, except possible local thunder showers.
For full weather report see Page 22.

Section 1

VOL. LXIX...No. 22,786 *** NEW YORK, SUNDAY, JUNE 13, 1920. In Nine Parts. Including Rotogravure Picture Sections and Book Section. FIVE CENTS In Manhattan, Bronx, and Brooklyn | Elsewhere TEN CENTS

# HARDING NOMINATED FOR PRESIDENT ON THE TENTH BALLOT AT CHICAGO; COOLIDGE CHOSEN FOR VICE PRESIDENT

The New York Times
"All the News That's Fit to Print."
PUBLISHED EVERY DAY IN THE YEAR BY THE NEW YORK TIMES COMPANY.

NEW YORK, SUNDAY, JUNE 13, 1920.

### THE NOMINATION OF HARDING.

Upon a platform that has produced general dissatisfaction, the Chicago convention presents a candidate whose nomination will be received with astonishment and dismay by the party whose suffrages he invites. WARREN G. HARDING is a very respectable Ohio politician of the second class. He has never been a leader of men or a director of policies. For years a protégé of FORAKER, he rose to a subordinate office by favor of "Boss" Cox of Cincinnati. Beaten by JUDSON HARMON in the contest for the Governorship in 1910, he has never shown independent strength in his own State save when he was named for Senator in 1914, having a majority of a little more than 100,000 over his Democratic competitor; and outside of Ohio he has only such strength as he now derives from his place at the head of the Republican ticket. Senator HARDING's record at Washington has been faint and colorless. He was an undistinguished and indistinguishable unit in the ruck of Republican Senators who obediently followed Mr. LODGE in the twistings and turnings of that statesman's foray upon the Treaty and the Covenant.

The nomination of HARDING, for whose counterpart we must go back to FRANKLIN PIERCE if we would seek a President who measures down to his political stature, is the fine and perfect flower of the cowardice and imbecility of the Senatorial cabal that charged itself with the management of the Republican Convention, against whose control Governor BEECKMAN so vehemently protested. Rejecting LEONARD WOOD, probably the strongest candidate with the people the party could have chosen, because they knew he would never be dictated to by them, they favored Governor LOWDEN until BORAH served upon them his notice of a veto of that nomination. BORAH was commanding and truculent because he knew that he had to deal with a group of white-livered and incompetent politicians. If Republican leadership had not fallen into the hands of pigmies the chief men at Chicago would have told BORAH to bolt and be hanged, just as upon the issue of the League they would have defied JOHNSON to do his worst. But they ran like a frightened flock, surrendered everything, Mr. LODGE finally throwing off all disguises and standing out as the open foe of the Covenant of the League of Nations, even with his own reservations.

What has befallen the Republican Party of the early days, the party of sixty years ago, when it was possessed of moral purposes, or of forty and thirty years ago, when it could still profess to have them and find believers?

Where are its leaders that can be compared to MORRILL, SEWARD, HALE, PLATT of Connecticut, OLIVER P. MORTON, SUMNER, BLAINE, CONKLING and a dozen others who rose to high places in the party councils? And, if the question be not too unfeeling, where and what are its principles, if any it have? Party control, exercised by a group of Senators, is divided between LODGE on the one hand and BORAH and JOHNSON on the other. None of them, none of their accomplices in party degradation, would have come within hailing distance of the foremost rank of party chiefs in the brilliant days of Republicanism. And for principles, they have only hatred of Mr. WILSON and a ravening hunger for the offices.

Governor COOLIDGE for Vice President really shines by comparison with the head of the ticket. He at least is a man of achievement, he is known to the party and to the nation. When the police force of Boston went on strike he showed himself to be a man. He met that menace to the public safety with courage and determination, and the nation rang with praise of him. It is fortunate that not a word is to be said against the character of either candidate. They are irreproachable. But that does not compensate for the lack of achievement, for the colorlessness of the candidate for first place, or for the manner in which his nomination was brought about. It will be felt and said everywhere that the Democrats at San Francisco have received from their opponents at Chicago the gift of a splendid opportunity.



## HOW THE CONVENTION DID IT

### Delegates Had Word Early That Leaders Were for Harding.

### RECESS HASTENED CHANGE

### Two Ballots Taken After Reassembling Brought Ohio Man's Nomination.

### PENNSYLVANIA CLINCHED IT

### Big Block of New York Votes Also Helped to Decide the Struggle.

*Special to The New York Times.*

CHICAGO, June 12.—The afternoon session of the Republican National Convention on its fifth day, which reached a climax in the nomination for the Presidency of Senator Warren G. Harding of Ohio, was more like a rehearsal than a star performance in the great national political drama.

Not a single time-honored device was neglected in the effort to give the performance a touch of spontaneity, a dash of surprise and setting of overwhelming approval. But the convention had "gone dead" about 2 o'clock this morning when it was first learned that conferences of Senators and other party leaders had chosen the Harding way out of the deadlock dilemma. And all the efforts of G. O. P. pulmotor—lacking as it did any modern and novel attachments—to revive it failed.

Just as the limp, wet, worn men balloting in the pit waited until they were sure the tide really was running strong, so did the throng of spectators wait to make very sure.

**Harding Boom Starts Early.**

The suddenly revivified Harding boom started at the morning session. From that moment to the end it was a process of very slow and orderly rising enthusiasm to which gratitude at getting a hot and tedious job done contributed no mean element.

None of the stampede tricks of time-honored reliability worked this time. The crowd and the delegates in their separate ways seemed deliberately to prepare themselves for the finale.

As soon as it was recognized in high places that Senator Harding was to be the victor, the proper sort of stage management was set in motion. The galleries, in which were many of Mayor William Hale Thompson's supporters, who were Johnson men out of antagonism to Lowden and Wood, were glad enough to lend themselves to the task of furnishing an appropriate setting for the drama. But with all the stage management and all the willingness of the crowd to do what was expected to the best of its ability when the switching of big delegations made it a certainty, as the ninth ballot was being tallied, that Senator Harding was to be the nominee, and later, when the tenth ended the tiny remaining speck of suspense, the performance lacked great enthusiasm.

**Victory Outburst Soon Over.**

Perhaps two-thirds of the delegates got to their feet. Maybe a hundred climbed on chairs. A few women waved damp handkerchiefs in a valiant effort to add the orthodox feminine touch to the first national convention in which they had participated.

But there was no frenzy, no hat-smashing, no parading worthy of the name, and so little cheering that three minutes after the nomination was announced those on their feet, including virtually every one in the spectators' parts of the Coliseum, were standing listlessly.

It is a safe assertion that if Senator Lodge had elected to pound once with his cumbersome gavel, which looked to have been destined originally to be a potato masher, the hall would have been hushed in an instant.

**Announced Lowden by Mistake.**

There was just one touch of humor—though the coatless, sopping delegates didn't see it in that way. In announcing that Senator Harding had the necessary majority the Secretary inadvertently used the name of Lowden instead of that of the successful candidate. There was a howl of protest and very manifestly even the Lowden men didn't think the mistake was funny.

Senator Lodge made the formal announcement that the Ohio Senator had become the party choice in a tired voice that reflected the weariness in his pale cheeks and dark-ringed eyes. It didn't penetrate through the remnants of the din that the real, genuine Harding men were struggling desperately to accelerate into at least the semblance of a great occasion.

Senator McCormick of Illinois then strode to a point of strategic advantage under the mechanical amplifying de-

Continued on Page Four.

REPUBLICAN NOMINEE FOR PRESIDENT
SENATOR WARREN G. HARDING
OF OHIO

## WADSWORTH THREW NEW YORKERS' VOTE

### Delivered 68 to Harding on Last Ballot, Acting with Senate Leaders.

### 20 REMAINED UNBOSSED

### Organization Men Assert That They Alone Prevented Wood's Nomination.

*Special to The New York Times.*

CHICAGO, June 12.—The delegates from New York kept up a show of independence until the last hour of today's convention session, but then, when orders were given by the leaders of the organization, sixty-eight responded to the lash and voted for Harding. Their choice lay elsewhere, but they followed instructions. That was more votes than the organization leaders needed, yet they could have obtained several additional delegates had they been necessary. After Harding's nomination was assured these delegates were not asked to make the sacrifice.

Among the unbossed delegates who stood out on the final ballot were six Wood men. Robert L. Bacon of the First District, Henry L. Stimson of the Sixteenth District, George Henry Payne, alternate for George Z. Medalie of the Twenty-second District, and Lansing G. Hoskins and John Taber of the Thirty-sixth District. They voted for Wood throughout and refused to yield to the wishes of Barnes, Wadsworth and the other leaders.

In the same class was Fiorella H. LaGuardia, President of the New York Board of Aldermen. His choice was Lenroot, and he voted for him to the last.

Other delegates who were not called upon to support Harding were two who favored Butler—Miss Katherine Hammer, alternate from Butler's district, and William Brice Thompson, one of

Continued on Page Three.

## JOHNSON IS SILENT ON HARDING VICTORY

### But Intimates He May Have Something to Say Today on Combination.

### THANKS HIS SUPPORTERS

### Says There Is No Rancor and That Their Hands Are Clean—Borah Also Refuses Comment.

*Special to The New York Times.*

CHICAGO, June 12.—Senator Hiram W. Johnson, a deeply disappointed man, refused to comment tonight upon the nomination of Senator Harding, but, according to his close friends and associates, he will not bolt the Republican nominee.

Mr. Johnson was approached during the noon recess of the convention by emissaries from the Harding camp with an offer to nominate him for Vice President. He is said to have turned down this offer very testily and to have said that he was after the Presidency, not the Vice Presidency. His remarks, however, are said to have indicated that he will support Senator Harding.

The news that the Vice Presidential nomination had been offered to Mr. Johnson was in line with the report, after the adoption of the foreign relations plank, that he (Johnson) could have about anything he wanted in the convention except the nomination for President. His friends said tonight that he would make a statement concerning Senator Harding's nomination tomorrow.

When Johnson stepped before the "Battalion of Death" at his headquarters tonight to bid them good-bye he was greeted with "For He's a Jolly Good Fellow." The crowd sang lustily and with no signs of depression. When the demonstration had died down Johnson said:

"There are no tears to be shed. There is no rancor. We come out of this fight

Continued on Page Three.

## Lowden Defends Release of Delegates; Hert Says Wood Would Have Won Otherwise

CHICAGO, June 12.—Fear of a deadlock which he believed would prove detrimental to his party caused Governor Lowden to release his delegates on the convention floor at today's session, according to a statement made by him tonight. Governor Lowden said:

"After the eighth ballot, upon which I received a plurality of all votes cast, it was represented to me that the delegates were becoming restive under the delay. Fearing a protracted deadlock, which I believed would have been detrimental to the interests of the country, I decided to release all delegates and advised them to use their best judgment as to whom they should support. I have great confidence in the ability and character of the successful candidate, shall support him with all heartiness and believe the ticket will be elected. The Republican Party has not had such an opportunity for service in half a century.

"For the friendships formed during this campaign and for the loyal support of so many fine patriotic men and women I shall never cease to be grateful."

"Governor Lowden withdrew in the interest of party harmony," A. T. Hert, National Committeeman from Kentucky and one of the Lowden leaders, said tonight. Hert was a prime mover in transferring the Lowden votes to Harding and cast Kentucky's 26 for the victor.

Asked if he believed Lowden had reached the height of his strength on the eighth ballot, Hert said:

"It is my judgment that Wood would have been nominated had Lowden stayed in the fight."



## 4 NAMED FOR SECOND PLACE

### But Tired Delegates Turn To Coolidge and First Ballot Is Decisive.

### LENROOT NEXT IN FAVOR

### Votes Cast Also for Johnson, Allen, Anderson, Pritchard and Gronna.

### DELEGATES EAGER TO LEAVE

### Adjourned at 7:30 P. M., Many Leaving the Hall Before Roll Call Was Ended.

*Special to The New York Times.*

CHICAGO, June 12.—Governor Calvin Coolidge of Massachusetts was nominated for the Vice Presidency by the Republican Convention tonight by an overwhelming vote on the first ballot. The nomination was immediately made unanimous.

As soon as the Presidential nomination had been made, the call for Vice Presidential nominations was made by Chairman Lodge.

Medill McCormick went to the speakers' stand, and in a short address nominated Senator Lenroot of Wisconsin for the Vice Presidency. There were cheers and hisses, and the suggestion that Senator Lenroot be the running mate of Senator Harding didn't seem at first to captivate the audience.

Lenroot's nomination was seconded by A. T. Hert, National Committeeman for Kentucky; Senator Calder for New York and ex-Governor Herrick for Ohio.

The Chairman of the Oregon delegation placed in nomination Governor Calvin Coolidge of Massachusetts, and the Kansas delegation nominated Governor Henry J. Allen of Kansas. The convention presented a scene of disorder while various delegations were endavoring to make themselves heard to second the nomination. Massachusetts started a demonstration for its Governor. The Virginia delegation presented the name of Colonel Henry J. Anderson of Virginia for the post, in the hope that the Republicans would turn to the South for second place on the ticket.

The most enthusiastic demonstration was for Coolidge. The delegates were worn by the hard day's work behind them, and the nomination for the Vice Presidency did not seem to give much of a thrill. Those who attempted to make seconding addresses received scant attention. It was evident that what the delegates wanted most of all was to get away. In fact, many left the hall before the rollcall on the nomination was complete.

Coolidge had a runaway for the Vice Presidential nomination as soon as the balloting began. The big Eastern States, Massachusetts, New York and Pennsylvania, were lined up solidly for him, and he also got a heavy vote in the Middle West.

When Wisconsin was polled it cast two votes for Lenroot and twenty-four for Senator Gronna of North Dakota. Coolidge gained a lead so rapidly that the result was soon a foregone conclusion. When it became obvious that Coolidge would win the States down on the roll call followed the lead of the others.

The vote was:

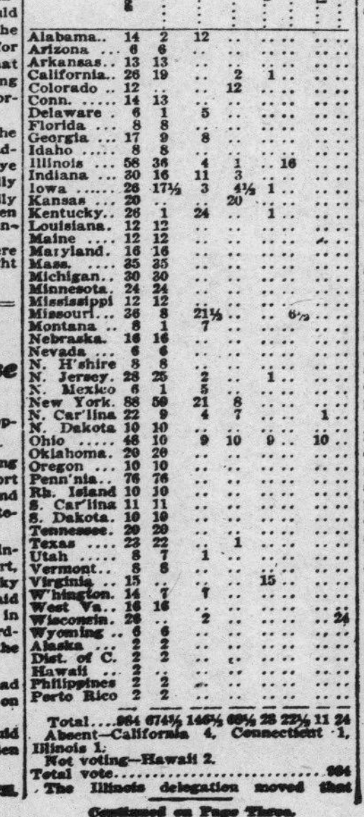

**Vote for Vice President.**

| State. | No. of Delegates | Coolidge | Lenroot | Allen | Anderson | Johnson | Pritchard | Gronna |
|---|---|---|---|---|---|---|---|---|
| Alabama | 14 | 2 | 12 | | | | | |
| Arizona | 6 | 6 | | | | | | |
| Arkansas | 13 | 13 | | | | | | |
| California | 26 | 19 | | 2 | 1 | | | |
| Colorado | 12 | | | 12 | | | | |
| Conn. | 14 | 13 | | | | | | |
| Delaware | 6 | 1 | 5 | | | | | |
| Florida | 8 | 8 | | | | | | |
| Georgia | 17 | 9 | 8 | | | | | |
| Idaho | 8 | 8 | | | | | | |
| Illinois | 58 | 36 | 4 | 1 | | 16 | | |
| Indiana | 30 | 16 | 11 | 3 | | | | |
| Iowa | 26 | 17½ | 3 | 4½ | 1 | | | |
| Kansas | 20 | | | 20 | | | | |
| Kentucky | 26 | 1 | 24 | | 1 | | | |
| Louisiana | 12 | 12 | | | | | | |
| Maine | 12 | 12 | | | | | | |
| Maryland | 16 | 16 | | | | | | |
| Mass. | 35 | 35 | | | | | | |
| Michigan | 30 | 30 | | | | | | |
| Minnesota | 24 | 24 | | | | | | |
| Mississippi | 12 | 12 | | | | | | |
| Missouri | 36 | 8 | 21½ | | | 6½ | | |
| Montana | 8 | 1 | 7 | | | | | |
| Nebraska | 16 | 16 | | | | | | |
| Nevada | 6 | 6 | | | | | | |
| N. H'shire | 8 | 8 | | | | | | |
| N. Jersey | 28 | 25 | 2 | | 1 | | | |
| N. Mexico | 6 | 1 | 5 | | | | | |
| New York | 88 | 50 | 21 | 8 | | | | |
| N. Car'lina | 22 | 9 | 4 | 7 | | | 1 | |
| N. Dakota | 10 | 10 | | | | | | |
| Ohio | 48 | 10 | 9 | 10 | 9 | | 10 | |
| Oklahoma | 20 | 20 | | | | | | |
| Oregon | 10 | 10 | | | | | | |
| Penn'nia | 76 | 76 | | | | | | |
| Rh. Island | 10 | 10 | | | | | | |
| S. Car'lina | 11 | 11 | | | | | | |
| S. Dakota | 10 | 10 | | | | | | |
| Tennessee | 20 | 20 | | | | | | |
| Texas | 23 | 22 | | 1 | | | | |
| Utah | 8 | 7 | 1 | | | | | |
| Vermont | 8 | 8 | | | | | | |
| Virginia | 15 | | | | 15 | | | |
| W'hington | 14 | 7 | 1 | | | | | |
| West Va. | 16 | 16 | | | | | | |
| Wisconsin | 26 | | 2 | | | | | 24 |
| Wyoming | 6 | 6 | | | | | | |
| Alaska | 2 | 2 | | | | | | |
| Dist. of C. | 2 | 2 | | | | | | |
| Hawaii | 2 | | | | | | | |
| Philippines | 2 | 2 | | | | | | |
| Porto Rico | 2 | 2 | | | | | | |
| Total | 984 | 674½ | 146½ | 68½ | 28 | 22½ | 11 | 24 |

Absent—California 4, Connecticut 1, Illinois 1.
Not voting—Hawaii 2.
Total vote....................984

The Illinois delegation moved that

Continued on Page Three.

FROM PHOTO ©BY GARO

REPUBLICAN NOMINEE FOR VICE PRESIDENT
GOVERNOR CALVIN COOLIDGE
OF MASSACHUSETTS

## HARDING DECLARES HE IS 'VERY HAPPY'

### Proud to Receive "This Great Honor from the Republican Party."

### COOLIDGE ACCEPTS PLACE

### Taft, Hughes, Hoover and Others Congratulate Head of Ticket.

*Special to The New York Times.*

CHICAGO, June 12.—Senator Harding, General Wood and Governor Lowden were in rooms adjoining the Coliseum during the final balloting today. They were in different parts of the Coliseum Annex. The result of each ballot was delivered to them by messengers.

It was a bulletin flash for a press association that gave Mr. Harding the thrill of his life. It read:

"Harding nominated."

When the news was given to the first editor ever nominated by the Republican Party for President he did not lose his equanimity. He said he was "very happy."

Later he said:

"I am very proud, as any American would be, to receive this great honor from the Republican Party. I am not unmindful of the obligations and responsibilities that come with it."

**Manager Predicts Harmony.**

Henry M. Daugherty, national manager for Senator Harding, issued the following statement late tonight:

"On behalf of the Republicans of Ohio, and especially on behalf of Senator Harding, his family and friends, I desire to express to Republicans of the country, men and women, our sincere gratitude for the confidence expressed in this wonderful man by nominating him as the candidate of the party for the Presidency.

"We entered this campaign with considerable reluctance because Senator Harding did not desire to make a high-powered organization campaign for the Presidency. Our plan, as is now well known, was carried out, whereby we conducted rather a modest campaign and left the selection to the Republicans of the country without too much pressure.

"We have throughout the campaign had the highest respect for opposition candidates and for their supporters. At no time have we made any attacks upon any candidate or any candidate's supporters, and Senator Harding will receive the support no doubt of every man and woman in the country who desires to vote the Republican ticket. The ticket will be elected overwhelmingly in November."

**Harding Receives Correspondents.**

With his accustomed simplicity of manner Senator Harding received the newspaper correspondents tonight on the fifth floor of the Hotel La Salle, in a hall adjoining his rooms. With him were a number of old friends, including Will H. Hays, just re-elected Chairman of the Republican National Committee, who will direct the Harding campaign.

The Senator made it plain that he realized the new responsibilities which

Continued on Page Four.

## PROPHESIED HOW HARDING WOULD WIN

### Daugherty, His Campaign Manager, Said Fifteen Tired Men Would Put Him Over.

### SENATE "JUNTA" MADE DEAL

### Attended All Conferences Behind Scenes and Blocked Move to Let Wood Bolster Forces.

*Special to The New York Times.*

CHICAGO, June 12.—"At the proper time after Republican National Convention meets some fifteen men, bleary eyed with loss of sleep and perspiring profusely with the excessive heat, will sit down in seclusion around a big table. I will be with them and will present the name of Senator Harding to them, and before we get through they will put him over."

This statement, substantially as written here, was made by Harry K. Daugherty, campaign manager for Senator Warren G. Harding, Ohio, shortly before the Presidential primaries were held in that State. Daugherty afterward entered the primaries as a candidate for delegate at large, pledged to support Senator Harding. He was beaten but the utterance which led the Republican voters in his own State to oppose him in view of unfolding events at the national party gathering here, appears to have been full of prophetic meaning.

The sweltering crowd which sat down in the Coliseum this morning gazed on the usual picture of a national convention bent on getting through with its business of nominating a candidate for the President of the United States and preparing to go back home. That picture may have appeared to many of the onlookers as one fraught with unusual interest and importance, but the history of this final day of Republican Convention was really made behind the scenes and very much after the fashion suggested in Daugherty's statement.

Two days ago Senator Harding's fight was looked upon as a forlorn hope by practically every trained political observer at the convention. In fact, up to the very moment the convention took its adjournment last night his prospects were not regarded as rosy. As recently as last night Senator Harding himself could not have entertained much hope of a successful issue, for at three minutes before midnight he filed with the Secretary of State at Columbus, Ohio, the necessary papers to qualify him as a candidate for re-election to his present position in the United States Senate.

**Conferences Held Friday Night.**

The conference at which steps were taken to break the deadlock by steering the convention toward Harding were begun soon after it finished its big day's job yesterday. During the night the conferees divided into several small groups, which kept in communication with each other by members intervisiting, in two Chicago clubs and at the Blackstone and the Congress Hotels.

While the convention was sitting today a dozen or so leaders met on the res-

Continued on Page Three.



## ARRANGED DURING RECESS

### Deal for Harding Goes Through When Lowden Frees Delegates.

### BIG GAIN ON NINTH BALLOT

### When the New York Delegates Swing to Him the Shouting Begins.

### URGED AT NIGHT COUNCILS

### But Leaders in the Race Refused to Yield at That Time—Later the Break Came.

*Special to The New York Times.*

CHICAGO, June 12.—Senator Warren G. Harding of Marion, Ohio, was nominated for President of the United States by the Republican Party represented by its delegates assembled in national convention at the Coliseum this evening. Calvin Coolidge, Governor of Massachusetts, was nominated for Vice President.

The nomination of the Presidential candidate came on the tenth ballot. In the ninth ballot the whole trend of the convention sentiment was toward Harding. When New York, with its heavy representation, went to him on the tenth, everything was over except the shouting—and the shouting began immediately.

Senator Harding's nomination was the outcome of a complex situation that did not begin to clear until last evening. After four ineffective ballots yesterday the convention had adjourned until this morning. Four additional ballots in the forenoon and early afternoon of today had developed Harding strength, but General Leonard Wood and Governor Frank O. Lowden had remained in the lead. A recess was taken for two hours, and during that short period combinations were formed that made Harding's nomination certain.

The real stampede of delegates to Harding began when Governor Lowden, abandoning his intention to address the conveintion, issued instead a formal announcement that his delegates were released from their pledges to him.

Interesting, and even thrilling, as the open proceedings in the convention were, moves behind the scenes, of which most of the convention knew nothing, had their dramatic side. The nomination of the candidate for President was arranged in conferences in hotel rooms. The prediction made in Washington weeks ago that the convention would get into a deadlock over candidates that would necessitate a combination arranged by a comparatively few of the party's dominating spirits was fulfilled to the letter.

**Johnson's Strength Disintegrated.**

Johnson's strength in the convention, never very potent, had begun to disintegrate this morning, under the influence of the understanding that Harding was the choice of the leaders represented by the Senate group. All along it had been taken for granted that when Johnson saw that he could not be nominated he would ask his supporters to go to Knox. In conferences in which he took part last night, however, he failed to intimate that he was willing to abandon his candidacy, and no efofrt was made to persuade him.

In the two-hour recess this afternoon pressure seems to have been brought upon Johnson to throw his influence to Knox or some other aspirant for the Presidential honor. It is the understanding that at this juncture Johnson indicated that he was not satisfied with Knox's views on taxation, and perhaps on other public questions. So Johnson failed to place his indorsement on the Knox boom.

Senator Borah entered the conference of the conservative group of Senators and asked them to consider Knox. He was asked if he came from Senator Johnson. Borah answered that he acted only for himself. Thereupon various objections to Mr. Knox as a Presidential candidate were raised. He was too old. It was said that he was not in good health. He had voted against woman suffrage and for prohibition. He was from a State that did not need a favorite son at the head of the Presidential ticket to keep it in the Republican Party. And the Knox boom died then and there.

**Thought Out of the Race.**

Harding gained the Presidential nomination within twenty-four hours after he was looked upon as out of the race. He had made a poor showing in convention balloting yesterday and just before midnight last night papers had been filed at Columbus entering him as a candidate for re-election to the United States Senate.

These papers had been prepared in advance and were left with friends in Columbus to whom Senator Harding gave discretion to file or not to file as they saw fit. These friends, probably ad-

"All the News That's Fit to Print."

# The New York Times.

THE WEATHER.
Fair, slightly warmer Thursday; Friday, fair, warmer; moderate winds, becoming south.
For full weather report see Page 22.

VOL. LXIX...No. 22,802 NEW YORK, TUESDAY, JUNE 29, 1920. TWO CENTS In Greater New York

# DEMOCRATS WILDLY ACCLAIM WILSON, TAMMANY ALONE SILENT; CHAIRMAN PUTS LEAGUE TO THE FORE AND DELEGATES CHEER; WITH 21 CANDIDATES, IT IS NOW THE FIELD AGAINST M'ADOO

## BOOTLEGGER' CLUE IN ELWELL CASE BARED BY CHECK

### Drawn for $12,700, Then Held Up, It Is Believed to Have Led to Death Quarrel.

### WHISKY DELIVERED, BILL UNPAID

### Several Men Said to Have Been Associated with Turfman in Illicit Traffic.

### PENDLETON IS ELIMINATED

### Inference Erroneous, Says Swann; There Is No Suspect and No Arrest Is Contemplated.

Joseph Bowne Elwell, who was murdered in his home at 244 West Seventieth Street, on Friday, June 11, was engaged in illicit whisky transactions mounting into large figures immediately before his death, according to information which was offered yesterday to District Attorney Swann.

Elwell had raised, or had been entrusted with raising, $12,700 for the purchase of whisky, during the week of the murder, according to this account, and the whisky had been actually delivered into the hands of an organization to which he belonged. A check for this amount, drawn by Elwell and said to have been deposited on the day before his death, was hastily withdrawn on the day of his death, it was stated.

The alleged "bootlegging" transactions were said to have been revealed by a German wholesale liquor dealer, who said that, because of the withdrawal of the check, he had never been paid for the whisky. The dealer was quoted as saying that the transaction had been negotiated for Elwell by a man who had at one time been in Elwell's employ. This man pointed out the danger of discovery and arrest if an examination of Elwell's account led to the uncovering of wholesale trading in violation of the Volstead Act.

**Desperate Efforts at Settlement.**

The German, as the matter was related to Judge Swann, has since made desperate but futile efforts to effect a settlement with the representative of Elwell. The whisky dealer, it was stated, only wanted $6,700, that being the actual price of the whisky, the other $6,000 being described as graft levied by Elwell, or his representative, or both of them, against the principals for whom the whisky was purchased. The whisky is now said to be on the premises of one of the various organizations with which Elwell was connected.

The theory advanced from this is that Elwell's inability to raise the money necessary to cover the check led to a quarrel between the turfman and either one of his associates or an associate of the liquor dealer; that Elwell's frantic efforts to telephone his friends early on the morning he was killed were made in an attempt to raise this money; that the assassin called upon him the morning of the murder in an effort to effect a settlement; that a heated quarrel ensued; that Elwell perhaps sought to stave off payment because of the illicit nature of the deal and that the shooting followed.

Mr. Swann appeared interested in the story and said he had not heard of it before. He refused to say whether he would investigate it. He said it did not seem to him to suggest any cause for the murder and that he would not have the present investigation set aside in order to look into the matter. The man who told the story said he had personally talked to the whisky dealer and got the account from his own lips.

**Pendleton Is Eliminated.**

William H. Pendleton, whose name has been prominently mentioned in connection with the mystery, has been eliminated. After he called on Mr. Swann yesterday with his attorney, Neilson Olcott, Mr. Swann issued this statement:

"I was amazed to read in Saturday's and Sunday's papers erroneous statements in regard to the Elwell case, and in fairness to the public, they are entitled to have these erroneous statements corrected.

"There is no 'suspect' in the Elwell murder case. This statement in the newspapers is a grave injustice to the man referred to by them, against whom we have no legal evidence to justify the publication.

"In connection with the creation of a suspect, the further statement is published that it has been intimated that an arrest is likely in the near future. There is no legal evidence that would justify an arrest in this case or even the detention of any person as a material witness at this time. Such statements may make interesting newspaper

Continued on Page Eight.



### *Lloyd George Sees No Support For Irish Independence Here*

LONDON, June 28.—With a view to forcing the Government to disclose its complete financial proposals for Ireland, the Opposition leaders in the House of Commons today moved amendments seeking postponement of the clause in the Home Rule bill repealing the 1914 act. The amendments, however, were rejected.

Premier Lloyd George, taking part in the debate, was again conciliatory toward Ireland, but insisted that nobody now would be satisfied with the 1914 act and that it was impossible to grant the demands of the Irish extremists.

He was convinced that things would improve in Ireland when the genius and common sense of her people realized that the British people would never consent to the extreme demands of the Sinn Feiners and that America would not support the demand for an independent Ireland.

## SOLDIERS RUN RIOT IN AN IRISH TOWN

### Demolish Shops in Fermoy in Revenge for Kidnapping of General Lucas.

### SINN FEIN PLAN TRANSPORT

### Anticipate Complete Stoppage of Railways—Steamer Refuses to Sail with Police.


Special Cable to THE NEW YORK TIMES.

CORK, Ireland, June 28.—A serious sequel to the kidnapping of General Lucas occurred at Fermoy last night, when damage to the extent of many thousands of pounds was done in the town by troops who, it is alleged, definitely stated they were acting in this manner as retaliation for the kidnapping of the General.

A large number of soldiers gathered in groups in Fermoy during the evening, and noisy scenes were witnessed until a late hour. At midnight the attitude of the soldiers crystallized in an attack upon various shops throughout the principal thoroughfares. Men broke out of barracks and ranged through the streets, smashing plate glass windows in every direction, and throwing the contents of shops out into the roadway.

A jeweler's shop was attacked and stripped of thousands of pounds worth of jewelry, which was thrown about the streets. Two motorcycles from a cycle shop were thrown into the river.

The disturbances continued for two hours, during which in a single street thirty-five shops were more or less destroyed, the splintering of windows being hailed with violent cheering. It is declared that shots were also fired. At 2 o'clock the men voluntarily returned to barracks, and eventually a strong picket, fully armed and supported by police, patrolled the town.

A meeting of townspeople this afternoon made an appeal to General Strickland, commander of the southern area, to prevent a repetition of the outbreak.

In September last considerable damage was inflicted upon property in Fermoy, following the shooting of Private Jones, one of a party of soldiers who were held up on their way to church parade. The present occurrence has produced a condition of terror among the inhabitants.

**No Clue to General's Prison.**


Special Cable to THE NEW YORK TIMES.

DUBLIN, June 28.—No clue is yet forthcoming as to the whereabouts of the kidnapped General, although an extremely thorough and systematic search of the district is being conducted by the military.

An anonymous letter reached the authorities in Cork stating that the cause of the arrest is that in the seizure of mails recently correspondence was discovered addressed to him in connection with Sinn Fein matters. The letter said the General will be kept in safe confinement and will be accorded the care and respect due to his rank while he is a "prisoner of war."

Colonel Dunford, who was shot when trying to escape, is reported to be making satisfactory progress.

LISMORE, Ireland, June 28 (Associated Press).—Several private houses and places of business here were sacked Sunday evening by soldiers in reprisal for the kidnapping of Brig. Gen. Lucas Saturday night.

There was some firing in the streets, but nobody was killed.

**Sinn Fein Plan Transport.**

DUBLIN, June 28 (Associated Press).—Sinn Feiners are preparing for a possible stoppage of all railway traffic and arranging to commandeer motor cars,

Continued on Page Eleven.



## OPENING SESSION SPIRITED

### Twenty-Minute Outburst for Wilson and Message of Support.

### NEW YORKERS IN FIST FIGHT

### F. D. Roosevelt and Small Group Join Procession After Battle for State Standard.

### CUMMINGS GETS OVATION

### Big Demonstration for League of Nations—A Few Shouts for Ireland.

*Special to The New York Times.*

SAN FRANCISCO, June 28.—The Democratic National Convention exploded a big sensation at its opening session today. New York delegates refused to join in a procession in honor of President Wilson until Franklin D. Roosevelt, Assistant Secretary of the Navy, and George R. Lunn of Schenectady had torn the State standard from protesting Tammany hands after a fist fight, and had carried it into the aisle with a successful football rush.

Even then only George E. Kent of Jericho and three others out of the whole delegation joined in the march around the auditorium that fast mounted into an ovation for the President. The rest of New York's contingent, including Governor Alfred E. Smith, Charles F. Murphy, W. Bourke Cockran and Miss Elisabeth Marbury, remained in their seats.

Later New York tried to atone with half-hearted demonstrations whenever the President was mentioned or allusion was made to his Administration, but the indignation of the delegations grew hourly, and the importance of the incident became more and more apparent.

**Police Rush to Disturbance.**

It was only through the majority's sudden realization of the magnitude of the spectacle they were creating that police intervention was avoided. Half a dozen policemen had rushed to the local spot of the disturbance. The whole place was ringing with excitement, fists were swinging, contesting hands were snatching at the State standard, men were pulling and hauling, when suddenly a realization came over the delegates and they subsided just as Lunn and Roosevelt and their few supporters gave a mighty tug at the standard and bore it into the aisle to the acclaim of a roaring cheer of triumph.

Though New York's unexpected contribution to the proceedings occupied no more than three minutes of the opening session, which convened at 12:20 o'clock [4:20 New York time], and though the delegates and visitors soon were settling back to listen to the keynote speech of Homer S. Cummings of Connecticut, Chairman of the National Committee and Temporary Chairman of the convention, it caused more hubbub of discussion and denunciation than any other convention incident.

According to one view, the Empire State delegates took snap judgment that the tribute might be turned into a third term stampede. Their refusal to accord acclamation to the President and the titular head of the party was much criticised.

**Blame Put on Mahoney.**

While apologists for the incident were explaining that Murphy, Smith and Cockran sat too far away from the central point of the room to stop it, it is a fact that the delegates of New York alone of the forty-eight States refused to rise in honor of the President when some 10,000 others present were on their feet.

The man who first clung to the State standard and precipitated the row was Judge Jeremiah Mahoney of the General Sessions bench. Mr. Roosevelt had looked toward Governor Smith, sitting some distance away, and indicated by motions that he wished New York to join the procession. The Governor had nodded in the affirmative, but Mahoney failed to get the signal.

By the time word was passed along to him to "let go" the fight was all over and it was too late to stop the spectacle. Both Murphy and W. W. Farley, State Chairman, declared afterward that it was all a misunderstanding, and both insisted that they had no objection to Tammany participating in a Wilson demonstration.

Tammany tonight is busily trying to make Judge Mahoney the "goat" of the whole incident, seeking to spread the impression that it was an unfortunate misunderstanding, due to him.

**Great Tribute to Wilson.**

The aloofness of the mass of New York delegates served to emphasize the conspicuous triumph of and tributes to President Wilson, into which the first session of the convention resolved itself. There were sporadic cheers for McAdoo, there was noise in behalf of Attorney General Palmer, there were banners for Governor Cox of Ohio. Yet, on the whole, candidacies came very

Continued on Page Two.



### *McAdoo Displaces Cox In Wall Street Betting*

Interest in making wagers on the chances of the various candidates for the Democratic Presidential nomination was at low ebb in Wall Street yesterday, but lack of actual bets did not prevent a shift in the odds. William G. McAdoo became the favorite for the nomination, the odds against his nomination shortening to 2 to 1. Governor Cox, who has been the favorite heretofore, dropped back to second place, 2½ to 1 being obtainable that he would not be nominated.

## GLASS CAPTURES RESOLUTIONS POST

### Wins Chairmanship from Senator Walsh—Robinson Permanent Chairman.

### RULES COMMITTEE ACTS

### Plans for Nominating Speeches, but No Balloting Before Platform Is Adopted.

*Special to The New York Times.*

SAN FRANCISCO, June 28.—Senator Glass, representing the Administration and author of a platform approved by President Wilson, was elected Chairman of the Resolutions Committee on its organization tonight. He had been strenuously opposed by the so-called Senate cabal—those Democratic Senators who fought the Wilson treaty—but Senator Walsh of Montana, who had been the opposition candidate, seconded Mr. Glass's nomination for the place and the choice was made unanimous.

Senator Robinson of Arkansas was chosen by the Committee on Permanent Organization for the permanent Chairmanship of the convention.

Other temporary officers of the convention were recommended by the convention to continue their duties as permanent officers.

**The Order of Business.**

The wets got their first real beating tonight when they tried to induce the Rules Committee to agree to have the Presidential candidate selected before the platform is considered. The drys were so overwhelmingly in control that Representative John J. Fitzgerald of Brooklyn, who led the wets fight, gracefully withdrew opposition to adopting a platform first. The dry leaders were from Tennessee, West Virginia and Kentucky, all known as liquor States.

This is the order of business for future sessions of the convention as finally adopted:

Report of the Credentials Committee.

Report of the Committee on Permanent Organization.

Report of the Rules Committee.

Nominations for the Presidency.

Report of the Committee on Resolutions (platform).

Balloting for candidates.

After some arguing and confusion as to the order of business Mr. Fitzgerald, who meantime had capitulated good-naturedly to the will of the majority, suggested that the convention adopt the rules of the Sixty-fifth Congress under which to all intents and purposes the 1916 convention operated. This was done.

The prospect as the result of the committee's decision is that the nominating speeches will begin on Wednesday, the platform will be disposed of on Thursday and the balloting will start Friday morning.

The Credentials Committee was in session late tonight to hear contests. The Georgia cases were finished and only four States voted for the Smith-Watson faction, all the rest supporting the Clark Howell delegation which is pledged to Palmer.

After 11 o'clock, when the committee began consideration of the case of Senator Reed of Missouri, there was a likelihood that the meeting would last all night.

**The Full Committees.**

Following are the two important committees as organized at the opening day's session of the Democratic Convention:

COMMITTEE ON RESOLUTIONS.

| State. | Name. | State. | Name. |
|---|---|---|---|
| Ala. | Bordon Burr. | N. M. | J. L. Lawson. |
| Ariz. | P. W. O'Sullivan. | N. Y. | W. B. Cockran. |
| Ark. | C. A. Fuller. | N. C. | J. O. Carr. |
| Cal. | E. L. Doheny. | N. D. | R. B. Murphy. |
| Col. | H. Hawkins. | Ohio | Senator Atlee Pomerene. |
| Conn. | Gus J. Ross | Okla. | Tom Lyons. |
| Del. | Senator J. O. Wolcott. | Ore. | T. E. Crawford. |
| Fla. | T. J. Appleyard. | Pa. | V. C. McCormick. |
| Ga. | W. F. Anderson. | R. I. | P. H. Quinn |
| Idaho | Senator J. F. Nugent. | S. C. | Senator E. D. Smith. |
| Ill. | A. J. Sabath. | S. D. | O. W. Iuehart. |
| Ind. | T. R. Marshall. | Tenn. | Senator McKellar. |
| Iowa | Emmit Tinley. | Texas | M. M. Crane. |
| Kan. | G. Hodges. | Utah | Senator W. H. King |
| Ky. | Senator J. C. W. Beckham. | Vt. | H. C. Churtleft. |
| La. | F. P. Stubbs. | Va. | Senator Carter Glass. |
| Me. | W. R. Pattengall | Wash. | M. A. Langhorne. |
| Md. | Governor Albert C. Ritchie. | W. Va. | W. A. McCorkle. |
| Mass. | Senator D. I. Walsh. | Wis. | J. C. Carl. |
| Mich. | E. C. Shields. | Wyo. | T. C. Dires. |
| Minn. | J. E. O'Brien. | Alaska | G. B. Grigsby. |
| Miss. | Senator Pat Harrison. | Dist. of C. | B. Colby. |
| Mo. | W. W. Graves. | Hawaii | L. L. McCandless. |
| Mon. | Senator T. J. Walsh. | Philippines | Robert E. Manley. |
| Neb. | W. J. Bryan. | Porto Rico | H. Doley. |
| Nev. | John F. Kunz. | | |
| N. H. | G. Woodbury. | | |
| N. J. | J. R. Nugent. | | |

The full Committee on Credentials as

Continued on Page Six.



## FIGHT NOW IS ON M'ADOO

### All Others United in Effort to Hold Down His Vote.

### FIRST MOVES UNDER WAY

### New York and Ohio Delegations Decide to Keep Favorite Sons in Race.

### WILL CONTEST UNIT RULE

### Marshall Talk Spreading and His Name Certain to Go Before the Convention.

*By Direct Telephone to THE TIMES at 2:15 A. M. today.*

SAN FRANCISCO, June 28, 10:15 P. M.—A poll of Democratic leaders that included four-fifths of their number, taken late tonight, indicated strongly that William G. McAdoo will be nominated before Friday.

The combination against McAdoo, however, developed strength, and indications were that it might become sufficiently powerful to beat the former Secretary of the Treasury.

Prominent leaders consider Governor Cox out of the race. Supporters of Cox, however, said late tonight that they hadn't given up hope. They continue to express confidence that their candidate will be nominated.

Others high in the councils of the party are expressing the belief that neither Cox nor McAdoo will win. They believe that a dark horse will be chosen.

Many "dark horses" are mentioned, but none appears to have the solid support that is accorded Vice President Marshall. So far as the "dark horses" are concerned, he appears to be a strong favorite.

Nevertheless, there is a strong undercurrent in favor of John W. Davis, Ambassador to England. Many delegates appear to believe that there may be a shift in Mr. Davis's favor.

For the first time there were parades for candidates tonight. The McAdoo marchers wore badges labelled "Mac'll do."

The Rules Committee decided tonight that there will be no balloting until after the platform is adopted.

**The Field Against McAdoo.**

*Special to The New York Times.*

SAN FRANCISCO, June 28.—As the Democratic National Convention is getting under way, the situation affecting candidates has narrowed down to where William Gibbs McAdoo, ex-Secretary of the Treasury and son-in-law of President Wilson, will be the target for the promoters of all other booms.

The field is a big one. It includes almost a score of candidates for the Presidential nomination, each contending for the prize along different lines. It is a battle royal, with the hand of every candidate raised against that of every other, but in the earlier stages of the convention, owing to the rapid and spectacular rise of McAdoo sentiment which has been the feature of the last forty-eight hours, the managers of other candidates are likely to be actuated by a common purpose—that of keeping the McAdoo vote down.

For that reason favorite son booms, as a rule doomed to evaporate after two or three ballots, probably will be unusually enduring in the convention which opened here at noon today.

The first aim of the anti-McAdoo forces will be to hold the groups of delegates which they control behind their respective first ballot candidates, with a view to blocking the way of McAdoo to the two-thirds majority which he must have to land the nomination, and, if possible, throw the convention into a prolonged deadlock.

The delegation from Ohio, pledged to Governor James M. Cox, prepared for such a contest at its caucus last night when it adopted a resolution binding the Buckeye delegates to vote as a unit for the nomination of Cox.

**Community of Interest.**

The action of the New York delegation in proposing Governor Alfred E. Smith as its candidate, although there is little or no chance of the convention giving more than the usual favorite son consideration to the Smith boom, and in adopting a resolution under which the delegates will be held behind the Governor until a new caucus has revised the program, is also regarded as directly in line with that purpose. Everything indicates a community of interest among

Continued on Page Six.



### *Text of Message Acclaiming President Wilson Adopted Unanimously by Democratic Convention*

SAN FRANCISCO, June 28.—The Democratic National Convention today, on motion of Governor Gardner of Missouri, directed Chairman Cummings to send to President Wilson this message, which was adopted by unanimous vote of the convention:

In recognition of the fact that the mantle of Jackson and Jefferson has fallen on your shoulders as the unquestioned leader of our party, the hosts of democracy, in national convention assembled, have directed me to send you the following resolution of appreciation and greeting:

The Democratic Party, assembled in national convention, extends to the President of the United States its admiring and respectful greetings.

For seven of the most fateful years in the history of our country Woodrow Wilson has occupied and by his character, learning and power has adorned the highest office in the gift of his countrymen.

He has initiated and secured the adoption of great progressive measures of immeasurable value and benefit to the people of the United States.

As the Commander in Chief of the Army and Navy of the United States he has led the patriotic forces of his country through the most momentous struggle in history and, without check, reserve or retardation to an honorable part in the immortal victory for liberty and democracy won by the free nations of the world.

We hail these achievements, Sir, and are proud that they have been accomplished under your Administration.

We rejoice in the recovery of your health and strength after months of suffering and affliction, which you have borne with courage and without complaint.

We deeply resent the malignant onset which you have most undeservedly been called upon to sustain from partisan foes, whose judgment is warped and whose perceptions are obscured by a party malice which constitutes a lamentable and disgraceful page in our history.

At this moment, when the delegates to this convention from every State in the Union are about to enter upon their formal proceedings, we pause to send an expression of cheer and admiration and of congratulation.

We rejoice and felicitate you upon your speedy recovery from your recent illness and congratulate America that, though temporarily broken in body, you have been able, with unclouded vision and undaunted courage, to press on for the great reforms which you have fathered for the preservation of peace throughout the world in the interest of humanity and the advancement of civilization. Long may you live to serve America and the world!

## NEW YORK VOTES FOR A 'WET' PLANK

### Also Favors Independence of Ireland and Support of Italy's Fiume Claims.

### SHARP TALK ON PROHIBITION

### Lunn Opposes Reviving Issue—Mack Favors It on Political Grounds.

*Special to The New York Times.*

SAN FRANCISCO, June 28.—The New York delegation at a meeting tonight voted to instruct W. Bourke Cockran, its member of the Committee on Resolutions, to endeavor to obtain a platform plank legalizing the manufacture and sale of light wines and beer.

The delegation also approved planks declaring for the independence of Ireland and American assistance for the settlement of the Fiume matter in accordance with the aspirations of Italy, ratification of the woman suffrage amendment by Democratic States and a labor plank satisfactory to the representatives of organized labor.

The delegates also voted in favor of a Federal workmen's compensation law and decided to oppose any plank advocating a canal from the Great Lakes to the sea by way of Canada.

The wine and beer plank was not adopted without strong opposition. Mayor George R. Lunn of Schenectady, who led the dissenters, said that such a plank would mean political suicide for the Democratic Party nationally, however much it might affect New York City.

The majority, headed by William Farley, State Chairman, who took Governor Smith's place in the chair, ran roughshod over Lunn on the ground that he was an alternate and not a delegate and denied Lunn's demand for a roll call on the resolution.

The temper of the majority was shown by the applause which greeted the introduction of the beer-wine resolution by Norman E. Mack, National Committeeman, whose argument was based almost entirely upon political expediency.

There was no record vote on this resolution, but the number opposed to it seemed to be 15 to 20. The other resolutions were adopted unanimously, except that declaring for the independence of Ireland. On that Hiram Wood of Rochester voted a loud "No."

The proposed wine and beer plank reads as follows:

"We heartily approve the abolition of the saloon and we are unalterably opposed to any attempt to revive it.

"In the personal liberty and of conserving the rights of the States, we favor legislation by Congress, allowing the manufacture and sale for home consumption of light wines and beer, re-

Continued on Page Three.



## BRYAN PUBLISHES HIS TREATY PLANK

### It Flatly Opposes Wilson, Urging Prompt Ratification with Majority Reservations.

### AMENDMENT IS CALLED FOR

### But Before This Constitutional Change President Would Name Our League Delegates.

*Special to The New York Times.*

SAN FRANCISCO, June 28.—William Jennings Bryan made public this afternoon the platform plank which he will propose on the League of Nations. It differs entirely from the Administration's suggestion and places the Commoner unequivocally in the attitude of fighting President Wilson. In brief, the Bryan plank aims to get the Peace Treaty adopted without delay and offers a way for the appointment of delegates to the League of Nations and the entrance of the United States into the organization without breaking down American traditions generally. It follows his recently announced program, namely, the ratification of the treaty with such reservations as a "majority of the Senators may agree upon, reserving for the future the making of such changes as we may deem necessary."

The Bryan plank demands an amendment of the Federal Constitution to provide for a ratification of treaties by a majority vote and favors the immediate reconvening of the Senate to ratify the Treaty of Versailles with reservations agreeable to the majority.

The plank then proposes these steps to make the League of Nations effective and safeguard American institutions:

Appointment by the President, with the consent of the Senate, of delegates to represent the United States in the league until chosen delegates are elected and qualified.

Election of the regular delegates to the league by a nation-wide vote, conducted as Congressional elections are.

Delegates to be instructed not to vote for war without specific instructions from Congress or from the people by a referendum vote.

American delegates to be instructed to insist upon disarmament.

**Text of Bryan Treaty Plank.**

This is the text of the Bryan plank:

"The Democratic Party demands an amendment to the Federal Constitution providing for ratification of treaties by a majority vote, so that it will be as easy to end a war as it is to declare war. Planting ourselves upon the most fundamental principle of popular Government, namely, the right of the people to rule—a doctrine in support of which we have recently spent over 25,000,000,000 of dollars and for which we have sacrificed 100,000 precious lives—we fa-

Continued on Page Three.



## CUMMINGS DEFENDS LEAGUE

### Treaty Presented to Convention as Great Issue of the Campaign.

### NOT A WORD ON PROHIBITION

### Although Disposition of That Problem Looms Largest to the Delegates.

### TO ADOPT PLATFORM FIRST

### Leaders Hope to See That Done Tomorrow Night—May Complete Ticket by Friday.

*Special to The New York Times.*

SAN FRANCISCO, June 28.—When Homer S. Cummings, Chairman of the Democratic National Committee, addressed the National Convention as its Temporary Chairman at the opening session today he used his eloquence to clothe the thoughts of Woodrow Wilson. His keynote speech was an amplification of the principles upon which the President desires the party to go before the country in the campaign.

Mr. Cummings spoke for President Wilson. His speech was prepared after he had obtained the President's views as to what its scope and character should be, and he came to San Francisco as the President's representative.

In this knowledge the speech has a deeper significance. It shows that to the President's mind the paramount issue of the campaign is the League of Nations.

Secondary only to his exploitation of this primary principle was the severity of Mr. Cummings's attack upon the Republican Party and particularly upon the attitude of Senator Lodge and the other Republican Senators toward the Versailles treaty. Mr. Cummings went so far as to accuse Lodge and his associates of physically wounding the President just as certainly as were Garfield and McKinley and Lincoln, for, said the Chairman, it is but a difference of degree between fanatics and partisans.

**Applause for Cummings Speech.**

Much applause was given by the delegates to Mr. Cummings's denunciation of Republican opposition to the President's attitude on the League covenant and to his explanation of the President's stand. But in the minds of the great mass of delegates the main question of policy before the convention is the prohibition issue, and to their way of thinking this dovetails into the sharp contest over the nomination of a candidate for President.

From all that has happened since the delegates began to arrive in San Francisco in numbers, it is evident that the candidacy of Governor Cox has been materially weakened by his accepted connection with the wet cause, and the indications today are that Cox is steadily losing ground to the advantage of William G. McAdoo.

No reference was made by Chairman Cummings in his keynote speech to the prohibition issue. But to the delegates generally it is a living question upon which the convention must take action. Most of them seem to think that it would be well to follow the example of the Republican Convention and ignore it—stamp it by this neglect as a settled question upon which no party declaration is necessary.

It is a toss-up whether this may properly be called a dry convention. Certainly it is not a wet convention. It is somewhat moist, particularly in those spots where the influence of politicians from the large cities is manifest. On the whole, however, it stands for a compromise between wet and dry with an apparent willingness to avoid all mention of the matter in the platform.

**Cox Hurt by Prohibition Snarl.**

The wet and dry issue has seriously affected the chances of Governor Cox as a candidate for President but it does not seem to have had any effect on the chances of McAdoo or Palmer. The Attorney General is accounted a "liberal" and obtained some wet support originally in that understanding of his position. He is said to hold that the liquor question has been settled by the adoption of the prohibition amendment and the decision of the Supreme Court in upholding the Volstead act.

McAdoo is looked upon as a dry. He is the only major aspirant for Presidential honors who has received the indorsement of the Anti-Saloon League. In the face of this William J. Bryan, champion of the bitter-end dry forces, is against him, just as Bryan is against everybody who seems to have the ghost of a show for the nomination.

McAdoo's popularity among the delegates does not seem to draw material strength from his supposedly "dry" position on liquor, but comes from other causes, one of which at the present moment is the prevailing belief that he is likely to be nominated. In a gathering made up largely of politicians the dominating desire is to be on the side of the man who will carry off the prize.

McAdoo has no visible organization. That is part of the strategy of those

"All the News That's Fit to Print"

# The New York Times

LATE CITY EDITION

Weather: Fair, very cold today and tonight. Chance of snow tomorrow. Temp. range: today 24-14; Sunday 33-26. Full U.S. report on Page 30.

VOL. LXIX...No. 22,806 NEW YORK, SATURDAY, JULY 3, 1920. TWO CENTS In Greater New York | THREE CENTS Within 200 Miles | FOUR CENTS Elsewhere

# M'ADOO LEADS; 289 VOTES ON SECOND BALLOT; CONVENTION ADJOURNS TO 9:30 A. M. TODAY; PLATFORM ADOPTED AND BRYAN DEFEATED

## PUSH BOOMS AFTER VOTING

### M'Adoo Backers Hard at Work, but Opponents Are Confident.

### DAVIS IN STRONG POSITION

### Generally Regarded as the Likely Winner if McAdoo Is Blocked.

### PLATFORM FIGHT ABSORBING

### And Managers Lay Aside Their Booming During Convention Struggle.

**Latest on Candidates.**

*By Direct Telephone to The Times at 2:15 A. M. Today.*

SAN FRANCISCO, July 2, 10:15 P. M. (2:15 A. M. Saturday, New York Time).—The principal impression here late tonight is that it is a perfectly open convention. The Administration forces demonstrated that they were in complete control and carried out their program without any serious opposition. At the same time the opposition had all the chance it wanted to make the fight to the floor of the convention.

Every issue was discussed before the convention and those who dissented from the details of the party platform as adopted by the Resolutions Committee had every opportunity to present their case. In spite of that the Administration supporters carried the plan of the committee.

The general impression is that McAdoo has a tremendous potential strength exceeding that of any other candidate. His managers are saying tonight that the balloting tomorrow will surely result in his selection as the Democratic standard-bearer.

There is the usual talk of dark horses, and many rumors are afloat of plans for switches to various candidates when the convention meets tomorrow.

Joseph M. Guffey, one of the leaders of the Palmer campaign, declared tonight that McAdoo's maximum strength would not exceed 343 votes. Mr. Guffey asserted that Palmer would forge ahead in the early balloting tomorrow, and that there was every prospect that he would be nominated before tomorrow's session adjourned.

Even the Palmer leaders, however, admitted that McAdoo would make many gains tomorrow. Mr. Guffey declared that his information was that North Carolina, whose 28 votes were cast for Senator Simmons in the preliminary balloting, would turn them to McAdoo whenever his managers want them.

*By Telegraph to The Times.*

10:20 P. M.—E. H. Moore, manager of the Cox campaign, said at 10:15 o'clock tonight that today's ballots showed that McAdoo would never get even a third of the voting strength of the convention. Moore estimated that Mr. McAdoo might get as many as 64 more votes, which would make a total of 353 if he should hold all he had on the second ballot, but he declared that this was the limit and that McAdoo could not be nominated.

Joseph M. Guffey, one of the leaders of the Palmer forces, had made a practically identical statement a little before that, giving McAdoo a maximum of 343. This similarity in predictions is one sign of the movement for a combination between the Cox and Palmer forces, negotiations for which are going on tonight.

It is believed that as yet neither of these candidates is willing to admit defeat and yield to the other, but after the developments of the early

Continued on Page Two.



### Delegates Begin to Worry About Getting Trains Home

SAN FRANCISCO, July 2.—Delegates and alternates to the convention were in a fearful mood today. There are more than two thousand of them here and many of them are thousands of miles from home. Almost every delegate was seeking information about the probability of the convention ending within the next forty-eight hours. The majority of them have made reservations on trains for tomorrow night or Sunday and have been told by railroad officials that there will be a fine mixup if reservations have to be canceled and new ones made.

## M'ADOO IN BED BEFORE VOTE BEGAN

### Balloting for President Started in San Francisco After He Had Retired for Night.

### REMAINED SILENT ALL DAY

### His Special Guard, Ed Hewman, Plants Turtle Eggs to Raise Pets for McAdoo Children.

*Special to The New York Times.*

HUNTINGTON, L. I., July 2.—William G. McAdoo went to bed early again tonight before balloting for the Presidential nomination began at the San Francisco convention. He continued to deny himself to interviewers today, both at his office and at his Huntington, L. I., home. He boarded his usual train in the morning for the city and returned by automobile at 5 o'clock.

After dinner tonight, Mr. McAdoo, the members of his family and Oscar Price, a friend, sat on the back porch overlooking Huntington Bay. Mr. McAdoo appeared calm, and the porch talk seemed to be light and cheerful.

During the last twenty-four hours the residents of Huntington have become quite warmed up to the possibility of the guest in their midst being the Democratic nominee, and possibly the next President. The interest of the villagers has not yet reached the cracker barrel stage, but there has been some talk as to what form their celebration might take if Mr. McAdoo is nominated. A constable has gone so far as to refer to him as "Mr. President."

It may be said on the best authority that if Mr. McAdoo is nominated and if the turtle eggs planted today by Ed Hewman, village watchman and special guard at the McAdoo residence, are hatched, the nominee will receive at least one young turtle. Ed Hewman, once a very able seaman, guards Mr. McAdoo's premises at night and does odd jobs, such as egg gardening, during the day. Today he planted a handful of turtle eggs on the beach, half way between the high and low water marks. Mrs. Augusta Strickland brought the eggs from Florida and presented them to Hewman, who makes no secret that if the sun continues warm and if the eggs hatch and if Mr. McAdoo is nominated the McAdoo children will have a pet turtle.

## EDWARDS LEADER STARTS HOMEWARD

### Governor's Managers Disgruntled When Nugent and Essex County Delegation Suddenly Leave.

*Special to The New York Times.*

SAN FRANCISCO, July 2.—Supporters of Governor Edward I. Edwards of New Jersey, candidate for the Democratic nomination for President on a personal liberty platform, were displeased tonight when they learned that James R. Nugent of Newark, Democratic leader of Essex County and a delegate at large, intended to leave San Francisco tonight before the nomination was made, and that the entire Essex County delegation would go with him.

Proxies for Mr. Nugent and the Essex County delegates were given to the Edwards campaign managers and were filled out in the names of the Edwards headquarters staff, who will hereafter sit in the convention. Considerable soreness was shown by Governor Edwards's managers, not because it injured the chance of his nomination—for the impossibility of that was conceded—but because they felt it looked like quitting before the battle was really on.

Mr. Nugent was not in his seat in the New Jersey delegation tonight while the vote on the Bryan dry plank was being taken, and it was said to be doubtful whether he would return. It was said for him that he had been interested principally in the platform and that he had lost interest in the convention when he found it would be impossible to put over a wet plank.

The Essex County delegates gave as the reason for their departure the impossibility of getting transportation East other than that reserved for tonight. Other delegates found no such difficulty.



## COLBY PLEASES TAMMANY

### New Yorkers Disposed to Favor Him After His Speech.

### LOOKING TO LOCAL TICKET

### Believe Secretary's Nomination Would Help Them in City and State Elections.

### GIVES UP UNIT RULE FIGHT

### Murphy Notifies "Insurgents" Delegates Will Be Permitted to Vote as Individuals.

*Special to The New York Times.*

SAN FRANCISCO, July 2.—Tammany would welcome the chance of voting for Secretary of State Bainbridge Colby, reported to be the second choice of the national Administration forces, in the event of the failure of William G. McAdoo to obtain the nomination, leaders of that organization said today.

After Mr. Colby's speech the movement in his favor gained considerable impetus in the New York delegation, and it is believed that he will be assured of the majority of New York's ninety votes if the Administration forces should swing to him as an alternative candidate for Mr. McAdoo.

The increase in the talk for Mr. Colby, as yet purely a second choice candidate, strengthened the determination of the New York State leaders to continue voting for Governor Alfred E. Smith until a break should come, and strengthened the combination against Mr. McAdoo. As explained by two Tammany leaders of the greatest prominence, Tammany would prefer Secretary Colby to Mr. McAdoo, both on personal grounds and because they believe the nomination of Mr. Colby would help their State and local tickets, while the nomination of McAdoo probably would defeat both.

With twelve judgeships at stake in New York County and with Governor Smith practically certain to be renominated, Tammany would like to enter the campaign with some chance of victory. The leaders believe this might be possible in New York State with Mr. Colby the nominee. He is considered "right" from the Tammany viewpoint on both prohibition and the Irish question, both of which are considered necessary qualifications for the head of the Democratic national ticket, if he is to do anything in New York this year, and if the State and New York City Democratic candidates are to have a chance of success.

**Drops Fight on Unit Rule.**

Charles F. Murphy and the other Tammany and up-State organization leaders reconsidered today their intention of making a fight for the unit rule before the convention. This decision was reached just before the vote on the prohibition plank submitted by William J. Bryan, and as a result neither Murphy nor any other Tammany leader will ever again cast the entire ninety votes of New York solidly in a Democratic National Convention.

Mayor Lunn of Schenectady, leader of the "insurgent" members of the delegation, was notified by National Committeeman Mack, Governor Smith and State Chairman Farley that, rather than disclose a break in the delegation by a fight on the convention floor, the organization would accept the rule, reported by the Rules Committee and accepted by the convention, as applying to New York, and would permit the delegates to vote as individuals instead of as a unit.

Mr. Farley announced New York's vote on the Bryan prohibition plank as 3 for and 87 against. Those voting for the Bryan plank were Mayor Lunn, Manton M. Wyvell of Alleghany County and Mrs. Susannah Thompson of Steuben County.

The abrogation of the unit rule will have some effect on the vote for candidates. At least fifteen of the New York delegates are now expected to vote for McAdoo after two or three complimentary ballots for Smith. Mayor Lunn estimated a greater strength for McAdoo in the delegation, and said the number voting for him probably would reach twenty-five.

The action of the McAdoo men in the New York delegation in voting as a unit with Tammany for Governor Smith on both of the first two ballots had a bit of tragedy in it. During the afternoon, while the fight over the platform was in progress, the Tammanyites had informed Mayor Lunn of Schenectady that they would not insist upon their contention that in spite of the action of the convention in breaking the unit rule procedure the delegation was still legally bound by the unit rule.

This ended the contest that had been waged in the delegation. In the platform battle its members split up according to their individual preference for or

Continued on Page Two.



### Telegram from Wilson Will Be Read Today

*Special to The New York Times.*

SAN FRANCISCO, July 2.—Homer S. Cummings, Chairman of the National Democratic Committee, said tonight that he had received from President Wilson a telegram which he would read to the convention tomorrow morning.

It was learned that the message had been sent early in the day, presumably for reading at the convention session this evening in the course of or at the close of the platform debate, but it was delayed either in transmission or in delivery to Mr. Cummings after reaching San Francisco.

At any rate, he did not receive it until tonight, after he had heard by telephone from Washington that it had been sent to him. The contents were not made public.

## ANTI-M'ADOO MEN UNABLE TO UNITE

### Murphy and Brennan Firm, but Taggart Reported Less Uncompromising.

### NEW YORK DELEGATES SPLIT

### Burleson Takes Over Active Management of Political End of McAdoo Movement.

*Special to The New York Times.*

SAN FRANCISCO, July 2.—The movement to head off the nomination of William Gibbs McAdoo for President was continued by the anti-McAdoo leaders late today while the battle over the platform was stirring the great crowd of delegates and guests at the Auditorium. George E. Brennan, leader of the Illinois Democrats, and Charles F. Murphy of Tammany Hall are standing firmly by their early decision to stop McAdoo if enough delegates can be held in line.

Thomas Taggart of Indiana, who wants to be elected United States Senator and thinks his chances are favorable if there is not a serious split that would dash hope of his getting Administration support, is reported less certain in his opposition, and possibly prepared to swing to McAdoo if it appears that the latter is the best bet where the local Indiana situation is concerned.

National Committeeman Fred Lynch, however, has lost control of the Minnesota delegates, and ten at least are outspoken for McAdoo. The Mississippi delegation is still held in line with a majority prepared to support Cox. What the Mississippi delegates will do if it is demonstrated that the Cox cause is hopeless is giving both the McAdoo and anti-McAdoo forces much cause for concern.

Postmaster General Burleson has taken over the McAdoo leadership, so far as the practical politics of the situation is concerned. Under his direction efforts are being made to obtain an agreement which would give McAdoo the bulk of the delegates pledged to Attorney General Palmer, if the early balloting shows that Palmer is out of the race. It is predicted that McAdoo may lead Palmer in the early balloting, and that the Palmer strength may not exceed 270 at the start.

Some of the Palmer supporters are prepared to grant McAdoo more than 300 votes on the early balloting, but hold that he will begin to go down hill after reaching possibly 450 votes.

**May Swing to Dark Horse.**

There is some talk that the anti-McAdoo leaders suddenly may swing their support to Ambassador John W. Davis, Chairman Cummings of the National Committee, or another dark horse, after the third or fourth ballot, if McAdoo seems to be making dangerous headway.

The leaders who are against McAdoo do not look with favor on Bainbridge Colby. While Colby represents liberalism in their minds, the fear is expressed that he would not hold the Democratic ranks together—that the party would be torn by doubt and wonder at his nomination and be delivered into the hands of a group which might destroy its integrity and cause it to disintegrate.

The tendency of both the McAdoo and anti-McAdoo forces is toward having the party's nominee represent liberalism as opposed to the conservative form taken by the Republican platform and nominee. There is agreement on one thing, if on not other, and that is that a candidate who represents the liberal movement in the country would have the best chance to win in face of the situation created by the action of the Republican Convention.

Brennan, Murphy, Lynch, Taggart and others who don't want McAdoo have felt that Governor Cox would serve this object not only where the prohibition issue was concerned, but in connection with

Continued on Page Two.



## LONG FIGHT OVER PLATFORM

### Adopted Without Change—Bryan's Plank Loses, 929 1-2 to 155 1-2.

### NO PROHIBITION PLANK

### Cockran's Beer, Wine and Cider Proposal Defeated by 726½ to 356.

### BIG BRYAN DEMONSTRATION

### Colby and Glass Defend Platform—Fight for Stronger Irish Declaration Lost.

*Special to The New York Times.*

SAN FRANCISCO, July 2.—The Democratic National Convention, at 7:15 o'clock tonight, adopted the party platform as reported by the Resolutions Committee. Every proposed change was voted down.

The convention discussed the platform for many hours. William J. Bryan's proposal of a bone dry plank, went down to defeat by a vote of 929½ to 155½.

W. Bourke Cockran, acting for Tammany and the "liberal" interests, sought to have the convention approve a plank favoring light wines, beer and cider. This was defeated by 726½ to 356.

A dry plank offered by Richmond Pearson Hobson of Alabama was defeated also, and the convention went on record as approving the decision of its Resolutions Committee in omitting all reference to the prohibition question from the platform.

Mr. Bryan lost also in his effort to have the convention modify the committee's plank concerning the League of Nations. A plank going beyond the committee's expression of sympathy with the aspirations of the Irish people met a like fate.

**Platform Adopted Unanimously.**

Once the oratorical battle of many hours was over, the convention proceeded to adopt unanimously the platform as written by the Resolutions Committee, which had labored by day and night to unite the factions into which its members were divided, notably on the League of Nations, prohibition and Irish questions.

The only planks on which there was need even for a roll call of States were Mr. Bryan's "bone dry" proposal, Mr. Cockran's "moist," one, and the Irish plank offered as a minority report by E. L. Doheny, Los Angeles oil man.

The delegates listened eagerly to the platform debate, responded readily and noisily, and voted about as they had been expected to vote. The galleries enjoyed the proceedings to the utmost, showering applause impartially upon the performances and proving so momentarily fickle that at one moment they appeared to be in a rhapsody of wet sentiment and the next moment hysterically dry.

**Bryan Shows Old-Time Fire.**

There were periods when the delegates really got warmed up over the debate, but these were rare and confined almost entirely to the prohibition issue. When Mr. Bryan, speaking in a style that oldtimers said reminded them of his oration of '96, literally hurled defiance in the teeth of the Tammany delegation, the braves rose almost in a body, while wet delegates from other States jumped to their feet and for a few moments there was a babel of taunts.

Otherwise the whole body of delegates evidently had made up its mind to leave the fighting to its chosen champions, and for its own part to settle back and take in the elocutionary display, extracting such entertainment as it could.

The demonstration for Bryan was one of the real surprises of the convention. It came at the conclusion of his terrific effort, in which he had called into play every device of oratory to win the delegates to his minority planks. In minutes it was shorter than some of the machine-made demonstrations for candidates, but in sincerity it far outdid even the ovation for President Wilson on the first day.

Mr. Bryan had been manifestly sincere in his arguments, and besides he had manifested a cleverness and gift of keen repartee in parrying the arguments of his opponents that won him admiration. No one who had sat through the convention suspected how noisy the auditorium crowd could be until the yells and shrieks and whistles and stampings for the Nebraskan burst out when he had concluded.

**Warmed to Glass and Colby.**

Though Mr. Bryan carried off the oratorical honors and proved that despite all the years that had intervened since 1896 he still had a big personal following, there were others who won

Continued on Page Three.



### First Ballot for President.

| State. | Total Delegates | McAdoo | Cox | Palmer | Cummings | Davis | Edwards | Gerard | Glass | Hitchcock | Meredith | Owen | Smith |
|---|---|---|---|---|---|---|---|---|---|---|---|---|---|
| Alabama | 24 | 9 | 3 | 6 | | 3 | | | | | | 1 | 2 |
| Arizona | 6 | 4 | 1 | | 1 | | | | | | | | |
| Arkansas | 18 | 3 | 7 | 2 | 2 | | | | | | | 4 | |
| California | 26 | 10 | 4 | 3 | 2 | 2 | 1 | 1 | 1 | | | | 1 |
| Colorado | 12 | 3 | | 8 | 1 | | | | | | | | |
| Connecticut | 14 | | | | 14 | | | | | | | | |
| Delaware | 6 | 4 | | | | | | | | | | | |
| Florida | 12 | 1 | | 8 | | | | | | | | | |
| Georgia | 28 | | | 28 | | | | | | | | | |
| Idaho | 8 | 8 | | | | | | | | | | | |
| Illinois | 58 | 9 | 9 | 35 | | | | | | | | | 5 |
| Indiana | 30 | | | | | | | | | | | | |
| Iowa | 26 | | | | | | | | | | 26 | | |
| Kansas | 20 | 20 | | | | | | | | | | | |
| Kentucky | 26 | 3 | 23 | | | | | | | | | | |
| Louisiana | 20 | 5 | 2 | 2 | | 2 | | | | | | | |
| Maine | 12 | 5 | | 5 | | | 1 | | | | | 1 | |
| Maryland | 16 | 5½ | 5½ | | | 3 | 1 | | ½ | | | | |
| Mass | 36 | 4 | 4 | 17 | | | | | | | | 2 | 7 |
| Michigan | 30 | 15 | | 13 | | | | | | | | | |
| Minnesota | 24 | 10 | 2 | 7 | | | 4 | | | | | | |
| Mississippi | 20 | | | | | | | | | | | | |
| Missouri | 36 | 15½ | 2½ | 10 | | | 5 | 1 | | | | 1 | |
| Montana | 8 | 1 | | | | | | 7 | | | | | |
| Nebraska | 16 | | | | | | | | | 16 | | | |
| Nevada | 6 | | 6 | | | | | | | | | | |
| N. Hampshire | 8 | 4 | | 1 | | | | | | | | | |
| New Jersey | 28 | | | | | | 28 | | | | | | |
| New Mexico | 6 | 2 | | 1 | 1 | | | | | | | 2 | |
| New York | 90 | | | | | | | | | | | | 90 |
| N. Carolina | 24 | | | | | | | | | | | | |
| North Dakota | 10 | 6 | 1 | 2 | | | 1 | | | | | | |
| Ohio | 48 | | 48 | | | | | | | | | | |
| Oklahoma | 20 | | | | | | | | | | | 20 | |
| Oregon | 10 | 10 | | | | | | | | | | | |
| Pennsylvania | 76 | 2 | | 73 | | | | | | | | | |
| R. Island | 10 | 2 | | 5 | | 1 | | | | | | | 2 |
| S. Carolina | 18 | 18 | | | | | | | | | | | |
| South Dakota | 10 | | | | | | | 10 | | | | | |
| Tennessee | 24 | 2 | 8 | 9 | 1 | 2 | | | | | | 1 | |
| Texas | 40 | 40 | | | | | | | | | | | |
| Utah | 8 | 8 | | | | | | | | | | | |
| Vermont | 8 | 4 | 2 | 1 | | | | | | | | | 1 |
| Virginia | 24 | | | | | | | | 24 | | | | |
| Washington | 14 | 10 | | | 1 | 1 | | 1 | | | | 1 | |
| West Virginia | 16 | | | | | 16 | | | | | | | |
| Wisconsin | 26 | 11 | 5 | 2 | 1 | 1 | | 1 | | 2 | 1 | | 1 |
| Wyoming | 6 | 6 | | | | | | | | | | | |
| Alaska | 6 | 2 | 1 | 3 | | | | | | | | | |
| Dist. of Col. | 6 | | | 6 | | | | | | | | | |
| Hawaii | 6 | 2 | | 4 | | | | | | | | | |
| Philippines | 6 | | | | | | | | | | | | |
| Porto Rico | 6 | 1 | | 2 | 1 | 1 | | | 1 | | | | |
| Canal Zone | 2 | 1 | | 1 | | | | | | | | | |
| Total | | 266 | 134 | 256 | 25 | 32 | 42 | 21 | 26½ | 18 | 27 | 33 | 109 |

Scattering—102.
Colby, Calif., 1—Total, 1.
Marshall, Del., 2; Fla., 1; Ind., 30; Mich., 1; Penn., 1—Total, 35.
Daniels, Fla., 1—Total, 1.
Clark, La., 9—Total, 9.
Underwood, Md., ½—Total, ½.
Wood, Mass., 1; N. H., 3—Total, 4.
Hearst, Mass., 1—Total, 1.
Bryan, Mich., 1—Total, 1.
Williams, Miss., 20—Total, 20.
Simmons, N. C., 24—Total, 24.
Harrison, Philippines, 6—Total, 6.
Total—1,094.
Necessary for a choice—729.

### Second Ballot

| State. | Total Delegates | McAdoo | Cox | Palmer | Cummings | Davis | Edwards | Gerard | Glass | Hitchcock | Meredith | Owen | Smith |
|---|---|---|---|---|---|---|---|---|---|---|---|---|---|
| Alabama | 24 | 10 | 3 | 6 | | 4 | | | | | | | 1 |
| Arizona | 6 | 4 | 1 | | 1 | | | | | | | | |
| Arkansas | 18 | 4 | 10 | 2 | | | | | | | | 2 | |
| California | 26 | 13 | 4 | 3 | 5 | | | | | | | | 1 |
| Colorado | 12 | 3 | | 8 | 1 | | | | | | | | |
| Connecticut | 14 | | | | 14 | | | | | | | | |
| Delaware | 6 | 4 | | | | | | | | | | | |
| Florida | 12 | 2 | | 7 | | | 1 | | | | | | |
| Georgia | 28 | | | 28 | | | | | | | | | |
| Idaho | 8 | 8 | | | | | | | | | | | |
| Illinois | 58 | 12 | 10 | 36 | | | | | | | | | |
| Indiana | 30 | | | | | | | | | | | | |
| Iowa | 26 | | | | | | | | | | 26 | | |
| Kansas | 20 | 20 | | | | | | | | | | | |
| Kentucky | 26 | 3 | 23 | | | | | | | | | | |
| Louisiana | 20 | 5 | 5 | 3 | | 1 | | | | | | | |
| Maine | 12 | 5 | | 5 | | | | 1 | | | | 1 | |
| Maryland | 16 | 5½ | 6½ | | | 2½ | 1 | | ½ | | | | |
| Mass. | 36 | 6 | 5 | 20 | | | | | | | | 2 | 3 |
| Michigan | 30 | 14 | | 13 | | | | | | | | | |
| Minnesota | 24 | 12 | | 9 | | | 2 | | | | | | |
| Mississippi | 20 | | 20 | | | | | | | | | | |
| Missouri | 36 | 17½ | 2½ | 14 | | | | | | | | 1 | |
| Montana | 8 | 2 | | 2 | 2 | | | | | | | | 2 |
| Nebraska | 16 | | | | | | | | | 16 | | | |
| Nevada | 6 | | 6 | | | | | | | | | | |
| N. Hampshire | 8 | 4 | | 2 | | | | 1 | | | | | |
| New Jersey | 28 | | | | | | 28 | | | | | | |
| New Mexico | 6 | 3 | | 1 | | | | | | | | 1 | |
| New York | 90 | | | | | | | | | | | | 90 |
| N. Carolina | 24 | | | | | | | | | | | | |
| N. Dakota | 10 | 6 | | 2 | | | 2 | | | | | | |
| Ohio | 48 | | 48 | | | | | | | | | | |
| Oklahoma | 20 | | | | | | | | | | | 20 | |
| Oregon | 10 | 10 | | | | | | | | | | | |
| Pennsylvania | 76 | 2 | | 73 | | | | | | | | | |
| Rhode Island | 10 | 2 | | 4 | | 1 | | | | | | | 3 |
| S. Carolina | 18 | 18 | | | | | | | | | | | |
| South Dakota | 10 | | | | | | | 10 | | | | | |
| Tennessee | 24 | 4 | 8 | 6 | 3 | 3 | | | | | | | |
| Texas | 40 | 40 | | | | | | | | | | | |
| Utah | 8 | 8 | | | | | | | | | | | |
| Vermont | 8 | 4 | 2 | 2 | | | | | | | | | |
| Virginia | 24 | | | | | | | | 24 | | | | |
| Washington | 14 | 10 | | | | 1 | | | | | | 2 | 1 |
| West Virginia | 16 | | | | | 16 | | | | | | | |
| Wisconsin | 26 | 16 | 5 | 2 | 1 | 2 | | | | | | | |
| Wyoming | 6 | 6 | | | | | | | | | | | |
| Alaska | 6 | 2 | | 3 | | | | | | | | | |
| Dist. of Col. | 6 | | | 6 | | | | | | | | | |
| Hawaii | 6 | 2 | | 4 | | | | | | | | | |
| Philippines | 6 | | | | | | | | | | | | |
| Porto Rico | 6 | 1 | | 2 | 1 | 1 | | | 1 | | | | |
| Canal Zone | 2 | 1 | | 1 | | | | | | | | | |
| Total | 1,093 | 289 | 159 | 264 | 27 | 31½ | 34 | 12 | 25½ | 16 | 26 | 29 | 101 |

Scattering—76
Marshall, Del., 2; Fla., 1; Ind., 30; Mich., 1; Penn., 1; Alaska, 1—Total, 36.
Daniels, Fla., 1—Total, 1.
Clark, La., 6—Total, 6.
Bryan, Mich., 1—Total, 1.
Harrison, N. H., 1; Philippines, 6—Total, 7.
Simmons, N. M., 1; N. C., 24—Total, 25.
Total, 1,094.
Necessary for choice, 729.

## NO CHOICE ON TWO BALLOTS

### McAdoo and Palmer Close Together and Cox in Third Place.

### SMITH IS RUNNING FOURTH

### Twenty-one Candidates on the First Ballot, Four with One Vote Each.

### CHANGES NOT SIGNIFICANT

### Few Shifts Between Ballots—Even Leading Three Have Not Two-thirds of Vote.

*Special to The New York Times.*

SAN FRANCISCO, July 2.—At 9:45 o'clock this evening (12:45 A. M. Saturday, New York time) the Democratic National Convention adjourned until Saturday morning after having taken two ineffectual ballots in an effort to nominate a Presidential candidate.

On both ballots William G. McAdoo of New York led the list of contenders, who numbered twenty-one at the outset.

On the second ballot McAdoo had 289 votes, a gain of 23 from the first.

A. Mitchell Palmer of Pennsylvania had 264, a gain of 8.

Governor James M. Cox of Ohio was third with 159, a gain of 25.

Thus all of the three most conspicuous candidates made gains from the first clash but maintained the same standing.

Governor Smith of New York was fourth in the list, having 109 votes on the first ballot and 101 on the second.

**End Not Yet in Sight.**

As the situation stands tonight there is no certainty as to how or when the contest will end. Judged by the manner in which the lines stood firm the convention may have a day of balloting tomorrow with a chance of a deadlock that will prolong the proceedings into next week. A Sunday session does not seem likely.

It would have taken 729 votes to make a nomination on each of the two ballots tonight. This means that none of the leading contenders is anywhere within reach of the goal. The combined votes received by McAdoo, Palmer and Cox on the second ballot lacked 17 of the necessary two-thirds.

The situation lies in the hands of the delegates who voted for the many favorite sons, including Governor Smith, whose names were before the convention.

Governor Edwards, who started off with 42 votes, 28 of which came from New Jersey, dropped to 34 on the second ballot. John W. Davis, Ambassador to Great Britain, got 32 votes on the first ballot and 21½ on the second.

On the second ballot, Vice President Marshall had 37 votes, a loss of 1; Secretary Meredith, 27, a loss of 1; Champ Clark, 6, a loss of 3; Senator Owen, 33, a loss of 9; Ambassador Gerard, 21, a loss of 12; Senator Hitchcock, 18, a loss of 16; Homer S. Cummings, 27, a gain of 2, and Senator Glass, 25½, a loss of 1.

The other votes were divided between William R. Hearst, who got 1 vote, Alfred M. Wood of Massachusetts, William J. Bryan, who got 1, Senator Williams of Mississippi, Senator Simmonds of North Carolina, Francis Burton Harrison, Governor General of the Philippines, Senator Underwood of Alabama, for whom half a vote was cast, Secretary Daniels and Secretary Colby.

**Working Hard on New Deals.**

These breaks in the favorite sons' lines are infinitesimal and mean nothing with reference to the final result. Tonight the managers of the leading candidates are busy endeavoring to make new deals that will prevent a deadlock that would carry the convention over into next week.

The expectation that existed before the balloting began that the Palmer strength would begin to disintegrate after a few ballots had been taken has not changed as a result of tonight's test. Palmer made a smaller gain than either of his two principal competitors, McAdoo and Cox.

Proportionately the gain of twenty-five by Cox is greater than McAdoo's gain of twenty-three. But there is nothing in the situation developed by the balloting to give an inkling of what the future has in store.

The McAdoo workers assert that they have assurances of enough votes to give their candidate a majority of the convention on the third or fourth ballot.

On the first ballot tonight 1,092 of the 1,094 votes in the convention were cast and on the second ballot 1,090. In each case the two-thirds majority remained the same at 729.

If McAdoo should realize the prediction of his managers by getting a majority of the full voting strength of the

"All the News That's Fit to Print."

# The New York Times.

EXTRA 6:00 A. M. THE WEATHER—Fair Today.

VOL. LXIX...No. 22,809. NEW YORK, TUESDAY, JULY 6, 1920. TWO CENTS In Greater New York | THREE CENTS Within 200 Miles | FOUR CENTS Elsewhere

# COX NOMINATED FOR PRESIDENT ON 44TH BALLOT, AFTER PALMER QUIT

## MAY BUY FRENCH TOBACCO MONOPOLY FOR $400,000,000

### American and British Interests Reported to be Negotiating with France.

### BANKS TO SHARE IN DEAL

### War Debts Are Said to Have Impelled Government to Consider the Sale.

### RYAN NAMED IN SYNDICATE

### Can Give No Information, He Says—J. B. Duke Asserts He is Not Interested.

According to reports in tobacco circles yesterday, American and British tobacco interests, together with bankers in the United States, England, France and Belgium, are negotiating with the French Government for the purchase of that Government's tobacco monopoly for $400,000,000. The report stated that France was considering the sale of her tobacco monopoly to meet war debts, including her share of the Anglo-French bonds due on Oct. 1.

The names of George J. Whelan, President of the Tobacco Products Corporation; James B. Duke of the British-American Tobacco Company and Thomas F. Ryan were mentioned in the report, which stated also that after a year or more of negotiation between the parties interested the deal seemed about on the eve of closing. The report had it that Mr. Ryan would sail this week to consummate the deal.

Mr. Ryan, at his town house, 858 Fifth Avenue, last night said that he had heard nothing definite about the matter but that he expected to see Mr. Duke and Mr. Whelan today and that he would sail on the Olympic on Thursday for a two months' stay in Paris.

Asked whether the purchase of the French tobacco monopoly would be included in his business transactions in Paris, Mr. Ryan said he did not know.

**Preferred That Nothing Be Said.**

"I have not seen Mr. Duke or Mr. Whelan," he said, "and I do not know much about this matter. I have not seen anybody about it. I can't give you any information about it."

"Would you care to make an absolute denial that there is anything in the report?" Mr. Ryan was asked.

"No," said Mr. Ryan. "So far as I am concerned I would rather you said nothing about it."

Mr. Whelan was out of town last night and could not be reached.

James B. Duke, at his home in Somerville, N. J., informed THE TIMES over the telephone last night that he knew nothing about the reported transaction.

"I heard about it from someone in my office about four or five weeks ago," he said, "but I said at that time that I was not interested in it, and I did not want to be interested in it. I know nothing about it."

Mr. Duke expressed himself in an emphatic manner regarding his desire to refrain from having anything to do with the matter, and when he was asked why he seemed so emphatic he said "I don't want to put my money into any of these countries now. They are too unsettled."

According to the report the negotiations were begun about a year ago and have proceeded busily ever since with exchanges of cable messages sometimes mounting to 10,000 words each, interspersed with visits abroad by Mr. Whelan.

**Earns $80,000,000 a Year.**

The French tobacco monopoly, it was said, earns a net profit of $80,000,000 annually. With efficient management, and with the application of American business methods of advertising and selling, and the elimination of waste, it was stated that this profit could readily be increased from 5 0to 100 per cent., amounting to from $120,000,000 to $160,000,000 a year.

France, unable to raise her share of the principal of the Anglo-French bonds due in October, has, at last, on certain conditions, the report said, consented to sell the tobacco monopoly.

If the transaction should go through, it was said that holders of stock in the tobacco concerns involved would receive the opportunity to purchase stock in the French organization to be formed and outsiders would than be permitted to buy stock.

The banks involved in the transaction are said to be in New York, Chicago, London, Paris, and Belgium. These banks, it was said, are ready to underwrite the transaction and place credit to the extent of $400,000,000 at the disposal of the French Government.

France is said to desire the retention of a certain portion of the annual profits

Continued on Page Seven.



### Miss Clay and Mrs. Stewart Get A Vote Each in Convention

SAN FRANCISCO, July 5.—The first vote to be cast for a woman for the Democratic Presidential nomination came today from the Kentucky delegation, when Chairman Stanley cast it for Miss Laura M. Clay, a prominent suffragist of the delegation.

So far as convention observers could remember it was the first vote cast for a woman in a convention of either of the two great parties.

Later one Kentucky vote was cast for Mrs. Cora Wilson Stewart, another member of the delegation.

## GERMANS JOLTED BY ALLIES AT SPA

### Come Unprepared to Furnish Disarmament Facts and Session Is Abruptly Ended.

### HELD TO THE PEACE TERMS

### Order of Program After Disarmament Is Reparations, Coal, War Guilty, Danzig Situation.

By EDWIN L. JAMES.

Copyright, 1920, by The New York Times Company.
Special Cable to THE NEW YORK TIMES.

SPA, Belgium, July 5.—The conference between the Allies and Germany opened today with a short, sharp clash, in which the Germans had decidedly the worst of it. The first meeting made it plain, once for all, that the Allies are boss of the Spa negotiations, something the Germans had not realized until it was brought to their attention.

The trouble came over the fact that the Germans thought they could postpone the disarmament discussion by not bringing with them the Minister of National Defense or the Chief of Staff. Inasmuch as France demands that settlement of the disarmament problem precede any economic discussion and that the Allies had agreed that the conference should begin by considering disarmament, the allied Supreme Council adjourned the conference, in reply to Germany's request to go ahead with economic matters, and notified the Germans to have their Defense Minister and the Chief of the Reichswehr troops here by 2 o'clock tomorrow.

There will not be any further negotiations until the disarmament question is disposed of.

This beginning does not argue well for the success of the conference. The Germans knew perfectly well that they had first to explain how they were going to disarm. Their newspapers have discussed it for weeks and it is only a few days since Foch sent three notes on the subject. In coming to Spa they knew that they had to face the question and of their omission to bring competent authorities there is only one explanation, and that is that they hoped to tackle the economic question first in order to use the disarmament agreement as the card of the conference table.

**Allies' Suspicions Aroused.**

But with the Allies disarmament is a sine qua non. The result of this attempt to dodge the issue has persuaded all the allied diplomats that the Germans must be watched very closely. Furthermore, Germans have been saying freely that they will make no reparation offer until the Allies agree to help their country, and that has put the French especially very much on the alert not to lose any move in the early part of the game.

Such a feeling does not aid the prospects of a common understanding. Furthermore, the Germans are saying freely that they will make no reparation offer until after the Allies have agreed to help their country. They give very plausible arguments, naturally, but that does not change the fact that they are running counter to the allied program.

The first meeting of the allied and German diplomats, a meeting which the hopeful construe as finally ending the war, took place at 11 o'clock at the Villa Fraineuse, atop the hill back of Spa, where Kaiser Wilhelm used to live from time to time in 1918, his year of dwindling hopes.

After a day of rain the sun was shining brightly when cars bearing the Belgian delegation drew up to the door. The British delegation was next and one noticed that Mr. Lloyd George was dressed with a pomp and style which are not generally his. Next came M. Millerand, wearing his well-known grey felt hat, and after him the Italians and Japanese.

"Promptly at the appointed hour" a big gray car pulled up at the front door, followed by two others. Out of the first machine stepped a man who might well have been a farmer dressed up for County Court Day. With a kindly, well-lined face and drooping

Continued on Page Eight.



## 14 BALLOTS AT DAY SESSION

### McAdoo Takes Lead from Cox on the 30th and Holds It During Day.

### PALMER SHOWS BIG GAIN

### Davis Reaches a Maximum of 63 Votes and Then Drops to 28.

### MANY SCATTERING VOTES

### Irvin Cobb and Ring Lardner Are Among Those Who Figure in Balloting.

### DAY SESSION

23d to 36th Ballot, Inclusive

Special to The New York Times.

SAN FRANCISCO, July 5.—After sitting for nearly seven hours and taking fourteen ballots without any candidate reaching within 300 votes of a two-thirds majority, the Democratic National Convention at 4:59 o'clock this evening (8:59 New York time) took a recess until 8:30.

It was McAdoo's day, with some encouragement for Palmer at the finish. On the twenty-ninth ballot, the seventh of the day, the shift of Indiana and Washington to McAdoo started his upward movement, and on the thirtieth, the ballot on which Woodrow Wilson passed Champ Clark at the Baltimore convention in 1912, McAdoo passed Cox.

On the thirty-second ballot McAdoo reached 421 votes. He held that figure through the thirty-third, lost half a vote on the thirty-fourth, dropped to 409 on the thirty-fifth and to 399 on the thirty-sixth ballot, the last taken at the day session.

Attorney General Palmer picked up on the later ballots of the day, rising to 222 on the thirty-fifth and 241 on the thirty-sixth, but at no time showing a prospect of reaching a figure as large as that of Cox or McAdoo. Cox fell to 376½ on the thirty-fifth ballot and received 377 on the last.

**Vote for Davis Fluctuates.**

Of the other candidates whose vote fluctuated, John W. Davis was the most prominent, receiving a miximum of sixty-three votes on the twenty-ninth ballot. On the last ballot taken in the afternoon, however, he had only twenty-eight.

It was, in fact, a day of trench warfare, dull for spectators and participants, except perhaps for a few of the leaders who put in their time in constant efforts to organize a winning combination. The speculative shift of some of the Cox votes, such as those of Indiana, to McAdoo, was for the purpose of trying out the strength of the ex-Secretary to see if he could approach the required majority.

From the opening of the session to its close there was little to see or hear but the monotonous roll call of States on ballot after ballot. Occasionally supporters of some candidate would get up a demonstration, but as a rule the outbursts were spiritless and unconvincing. The demonstration for McAdoo on the thirtieth ballot, when he passed Cox, was the best of the day, but the convention stubbornly refused to stampede.

On the thirty-fifth ballot the Palmer supporters set their somewhat theatrical program of celebration to work once more, but it did not make much of an impression. The galleries appeared to be thinking chiefly of the monotony of the session, and those on the floor were for the most part affected by the sharp antagonisms which still persisted under the surface of the convention.

**Called to Order at 10:12 o'Clock.**

As the delegates hurried to the convention hall for the opening of the convention in the morning they enjoyed the good San Francisco weather. There was a bright sun with a cold wind, and fog banks poised on the surrounding hills threatened to roll down at any moment and chill the convention.

Chairman Robinson arrived in the hall at five minutes past ten o'clock and five minutes later he was pounding on the table and ordering the delegates to their seats. There were still a good many vacancies in the ranks, and those delegates who were on hand were slow in obeying the Chairman's order. Earnest workers in behalf of many candidates were busily moving about over the floor trying to get another vote here and there to boost the showing on the critical first ballots. The galleries were filled.

Senator Robinson evidently meant business. Despite the empty seats he definitely and finally called the House to order at 10:12, the high point of punctuality for the whole convention. The Rev. Dr. Peter V. Ross offered the invocation, and varied the custom by calling for a moment of silent prayer, with repetition of the Lord's Prayer by the

Continued on Page Three.



JAMES M. COX
DEMOCRATIC NOMINEE FOR PRESIDENT.

### FORTY-FOURTH BALLOT

SAN FRANCISCO, Tuesday, July 6.—The voting by States on the forty-fourth ballot was as follows:

Alabama, 24 Votes—Davis 3, McAdoo 8, Cox 13.
Arizona, 6 Votes—Cox 3, McAdoo 3.
Arkansas, 18 Votes—Cox 18.
California, 26 Votes — McAdoo 13, Cox 13.
Colorado, 12 Votes—Cox 9, McAdoo 3.
Connecticut, 14 Votes — McAdoo 2, Cox 12.
Delaware, 6 Votes—McAdoo 3, Cox 3.
Florida, 12 Votes—Cox 12.
Georgia, 28 Votes—Cox 28.
Idaho, 8 Votes—McAdoo 8.
Illinois, 58 Votes—Davis 1, McAdoo 13, Cox 44.
Indiana, 30 Votes—Cox 30.
Iowa, 26 Votes—Cox 26.
Kansas, 20 Votes—McAdoo 20.
Kentucky, 26 Votes—Cox 26.
Louisiana, 20 Votes—Cox 20.
Maine, 12 Votes—Coc 5, McAdoo 5, absent 2.
Maryland, 16 Votes—Passed.
Massachusetts, 36 Votes—Colby 1, Cox 35.
Maryland, 16 Votes—Cox 13½, Davis 2½.
Michigan, 30 Votes—Passed.
Minnesota, 24 Votes—McAdoo 15, Cox 8, absent 1.
Mississippi, 20 Votes—Cox 20.
Missouri, 36 Votes—Cox 18, McAdoo 17, absent 1.
Montana, 8 Votes—McAdoo 2, Cox 6.
Nebraska, 16 Votes—Owen 9, Cox 5, McAdoo 2.
Nevada, 6 Votes—Cox 6.
New Hampshire, 8 Votes — Cox 2, McAdoo 6.
New Jersey, 28 Votes—Cox 28.
New Mexico, 6 Votes—McAdoo 6.
New York, 90 Votes—McAdoo 20, Cox 70.
North Carolina, 24 Votes— McAdoo 24.
North Dakota, 10 Votes—Cox 2, McAdoo 4, Owen 4.
Ohio, 48 Votes—Cox 48.
Oklahoma, 20 Votes—Owen 20.
Oregon, 10 Votes—McAdoo 10.
Pennsylvania, 76 Votes—Palmer 1, Davis 2, McAdoo 4, Cox 68, absent 1.
Rhode Island, 10 Votes—Cox 9, McAdoo 1.
South Carolina, 18 Votes—McAdoo 18.
South Dakota, 10 Votes—Owen 1, McAdoo 3, Cox 5, absent 1.
Tennessee, 24 Votes—Davis 24.
Texas, 40 Votes—McAdoo 40.
Utah, 8 Votes—Cox 1, McAdoo 7.
Vermont, 8 Votes—Cox 8.
Virginia, 24 Votes—McAdoo 2½, Davis 2½, Glass 1½, Cox 18½, absent 1.
Washington, 14 Votes—Davis 1, Cox 13.
West Virginia, 16 Votes—Davis 16.
Wisconsin, 26 Votes—McAdoo 3, Cox 23.
Wyoming, 6 Votes—McAdoo 3, Cox 3.
Alaska, 6 Votes—Cox 6.
District of Columbia, 6 Votes—Cox 6.
Hawaii, 6 Votes—Cox 6.
Philippines, 6 Votes—McAdoo 2, Cox 4.
Porto Rico, 6 Votes—McAdoo 1, Cox 5.
Canal Zone, 2 Votes—McAdoo 2.
Nomination by acclamation before ballot is completed.

## 'Leaders Cannot Win,' Says Palmer, Just Before Night Session Begins

### Various Informal Conferences Bring No Result, and Leaders Abandon a General Conference That Had Been Arranged.

By Direct Telephone to THE TIMES at 12:15 A. M. Today.

SAN FRANCISCO, July 5, 8:15 P. M. (12:15 A. M. Tuesday, New York Time).—During the dinner interval the leaders of the Cox, McAdoo, Palmer and some of the other forces tried in vain to arrive at an agreement which would break the deadlock in the balloting.

A general conference of the leaders that had been planned to meet at the St. Francis Hotel at 7:30 o'clock was abandoned when it became apparent that such a conference could accomplish nothing.

Attorney General Palmer said just before the night session of the convention opened:

"It is apparent that none of the three leading candidates can win. We have had some informal conferences, but they have not resulted in any decision as to a compromise candidate."

The McAdoo and Palmer groups made several attempts during the recess to get together, but none of them bore fruit. Each side wants the other to give way first, and the workers for both candidates insist that they will not forsake their candidate.

The Cox leaders had a long conference at the St. Francis Hotel and they decided to stick. George E. Brennan, the Illinois leader of the Ohio Governor's boom, predicted that the McAdoo boom was due to burst either early at tonight's session or tomorrow when the balloting is resumed.

Mr. Brennan declared that the McAdoo leaders could not hold their strength together any longer and that as soon as it began to fall away, the former Secretary of the Treasury would be completely deserted.

Despite the confident assertions

Continued on Page Two.





## COX TOOK LEAD AT NIGHT

### Passed McAdoo Early In Session on the 39th Ballot.

### PALMER DELEGATES FREED

### Announcement Was Made from Platform After the 38th Ballot.

### BLOCKED MOVE TO ADJOURN

### Cox Men Voted Down Proposal to Quit After the Forty-first Ballot Was Taken.

### NIGHT SESSION

Beginning With the 37th Ballot

By Direct Leased Wire to THE NEW YORK TIMES.

CONVENTION HALL, SAN FRANCISCO, Tuesday, July 6, 1:39 A. M. (5:39 New York time).—Governor James M. Cox of Ohio was nominated for President by the Democratic National Convention at 1:39 A. M. today.

The nomination came on the forty-fourth ballot. When the night session began, the thirty-seventh and thirty-eighth ballots were taken. Attorney General Palmer then released his delegates. In the succeeding ballots Cox gained steadily, until on the forty-fourth he had secured 699 votes and it was apparent that before the ballot was completed he would obtain more than 729 votes, the two-thirds majority required to nominate.

Vice Chairman Amidon of the Democratic National Committee, manager for McAdoo, interrupted the voting and moved to make the nomination unanimous which was done amid uproarious applause.

It was 1:43 o'clock A. M. (5:43 o'clock A. M. New York time) when Cox was declared the nominee.

Thereupon the convention adjourned until noon today (Tuesday), when it will complete the work by nominating a candidate for Vice President.

Cox was nominated by acclamation before the finish of the ballot. He had 699 votes at that time and McAdoo 270 when the motion was made to declare the nomination unanimous.

SAN FRANCISCO, July 5.—The Democratic convention was called to order by Chairman Robinson for its night session at 8:44 o'clock (12:44 Tuesday morning, New York time).

The thirty-seventh and thirty-eighth ballots were taken, with no material change, and then came the sensation of the night. Charles C. Carlin, manager for Attorney General Palmer, took the platform and announced that the Palmer delegates were released. The convention quickly voted a recess of twenty minutes to allow caucuses on the new situation.

It was called to order again at 10:15 P. M.

Balloting was resumed, and at the end of the fortieth ballot it was admitted by both Cox and McAdoo leaders that no break of the deadlock could be effected tonight.

They could not reach an agreement on a proposition to vote on adjournment. It was said, however, that such a bargain would be struck after the forty-first ballot, which the secretary was instructed to get under way at once.

But despite the announcement the Cox leaders declined at the close of the forty-first ballot to agree to an adjournment.

E. H. Moore, manager for the Ohio Governor, said he would not consent to stop balloting until the nomination of Cox. Representative Linebaugh of Oklahoma moved an adjournment to 10 A. M. He was greeted with howls of "No!" mingled with cries of "Yes!"

On a roll call the motion for adjournment was beaten.

The forty-second ballot was completed at 12:45 (4:45 A. M. New York time) and on this ballot Cox for the first time passed the 500 mark. The results were:

Cox 540½, McAdoo 427, Davis 49½, Owen 34, Glass 24, Palmer 8, Cummings 3, Clark 2, Colby 1.

Cox was only 7½ votes short of a majority.

On the forty-third ballot finished at 1:10 A. M. Tuesday (5:10 A. M. New York time) Cox gained still further. The result of this ballot was: Cox 567, McAdoo 412, Davis 57½, Owen 34, Palmer 7, Glass 5½, Cummings 2.

When the night session was opened the thirty-seventh and thirty-eighth ballots were put through rapidly. The result of the thirty-seventh ballot was: McAdoo 405, Palmer 202½, Cox 386, Davis 50½, Owen 33. The scattering votes weren egligible.

The ballot showed a gain of 6 for McAdoo, a loss of 38½ for Palmer and a gain of 9 for Cox.

An incipient demonstration for McAdoo following the announcement of the result of the thirty-seventh ballot was easily nipped, but not before a parade of McAdoo boosters had gone around the hall. The Chairman showed every disposition to let it linger but the punch was lacking. A few raps of the gavel brought enough order to allow the taking of the thirty-eighth ballot.

On the thirty-eighth ballot the first change came when California was called. Palmer gained three in that State, taking two from McAdoo and one from Cox. In Florida Palmer gained four, taking them from Cox. Illinois reduced McAdoo's strength in the State to 16, giving two to Davis, two to Palmer and 38 to Cox.

Massachusetts took one vote from Cox and gave it to Owen. Missouri took two from Palmer and divided them equally between Cox and McAdoo. Montana took two from Palmer and gave its entire strength to McAdoo.

New York underwent no change on this ballot. Pennsylvania gave McAdoo two of its votes. Rhode Island took one away from Palmer and two from McAdoo, giving them to Cox. South Dakota took one from Palmer and one from McAdoo. These also went to Cox.

Tennessee again gave its entire vote to Davis, while Virginia gave Palmer 3½ and McAdoo the same number, switching them from Glass.

There were no changes in the Territories and the tellers began to count up the vote. The result was as follows: McAdoo, 405½; Cox, 383½; Palmer, 211; Cummings, 4; Owen, 33; Davis, 50; Glass, 1, and Clark 3.

After the thirty-eighth ballot, at [illegible] o'clock, it became known that A. Mitchell Palmer's managers were releasing the delegates pledged to Palmer. They were going about the auditorium giving the releases, and it was prophesied that the deadlock would be broken within the next few ballots, possibly on the thirty-ninth.

Chairman Robinson introduced Charles C. Carlin of Virginia, who is Palmer's campaign manager. There was a hush as Mr. Carlin went to the platform and announced that he had been requested by Mr. Palmer to make an important announcement. Mr. Carlin said:

"I am going to make an important announcement, at the end of which I shall move a recess of twenty minutes in order that you may have an opportunity to deliberate. I am requested by the Hon. A. Mitchell Palmer to express to the delegates who have so faithfully supported him his sincere gratitude and to advise this convention that Mr. Palmer is unwilling to delay the deliberations longer.

"He feels that you should have the opportunity tonight to nominate the next President of the United States, and with that object in view I am also authorized by him unreservedly, absolutely and finally to release his delegates. Mr. Chairman, I move a recess for twenty minutes."

A shout went up as delegates and spectators realized that Palmer had finally withdrawn. When the proposal was made to take a recess of 20 minutes there were shouts of "No." If Chairman Robinson put the motion, nobody heard it. The convention simply suspended business to give the leaders a chance to consult.

Such leaders as could be reached amid the confusion were of the opinion, however, that, while there would be accessions to the Cox vote, they would not be sufficient to nominate him. The prevalent view accorded with what Mr. Palmer had said in his statement to THE NEW YORK TIMES at 8 o'clock that a dark horse would be the victor in the end.

The delegates seemed to appreciate the opportunity to stretch themselves for a few minutes. Many crowded around the Pennsylvania standard and showered congratulations upon the Palmer men for deciding to "end the agony," as one Eastern delegate expressed it.

The air was more vibrant with excitement than at any time since the balloting began. Every one knew that something was about to happen, and every one was discussing what it would be. When the end of the twenty-minute recess came the delegates began to shout "time's up."

A woman delegate, evidently grievously disappointed over Palmer's withdrawal, got into a violent quarrel with several men. One of the men talked to her rather roughly and bystanders interfered. The incident was typical. The nerves of the delegates were on edge.

During the intermission the Cox and



### Summary of the Ballots

[Ballots 1 and 2 in the table below were cast on Friday; from 3 to 22 inclusive on Saturday, and those beginning with 23 were cast yesterday. A summary of yesterday's balloting by States will be found on Pages 4 and 5.]

| Ballot. | McAdoo. | Cox. | Palmer. | Davis. | Marshall. | Cummings. | Owen. | Glass. |
|---|---|---|---|---|---|---|---|---|
| 1st | 266 | 134 | 256 | 32 | 35 | 25 | 33 | 26½ |
| 2d | 289 | 159 | 264 | 31½ | 36 | 27 | 29 | 25½ |
| 3d | 323½ | 177 | 251½ | 28½ | 26 | 26 | 25 | 27 |
| 4th | 335 | 178 | 254 | 31 | 34 | 24 | 32 | 27 |
| 5th | 357 | 181 | 244 | 29 | 29 | 21 | 34 | 27 |
| 6th | 368½ | 195 | 265 | 29 | 13 | 20 | 36 | 27 |
| 7th | 384 | 295½ | 267½ | 33 | 14 | 19 | 25 | 27 |
| 8th | 380 | 315 | 262 | 32 | 12 | 18 | 36 | 27 |
| 9th | 386 | 321½ | 257 | 34 | 7 | 18 | 37 | 25 |
| 10th | 385 | 321 | 257 | 34 | 7 | 19 | 37 | 25 |
| 11th | 380 | 332 | 255 | 33 | 7 | 19 | 35 | 25 |
| 12th | 375½ | 404 | 201 | 31 | 7 | 8 | 34 | 25 |
| 13th | 363½ | 428½ | 193½ | 29½ | 7 | 7 | 32 | 25 |
| 14th | 355½ | 443½ | 182 | 33 | 7 | 7 | 34 | 25 |
| 15th | 344½ | 468½ | 167 | 32 | .. | 19 | 31 | 25 |
| 16th | 337 | 454½ | 164½ | 52 | .. | 20 | 34 | 25 |
| 17th | 332 | 442 | 176 | 57 | .. | 19 | 36 | 26 |
| 18th | 330½ | 458 | 174½ | 42 | .. | 19 | 38 | 26 |
| 19th | 327½ | 468 | 179½ | 31 | .. | 19 | 37 | 26 |
| 20th | 340½ | 456½ | 178 | 36 | .. | 10 | 41 | 26 |
| 21st | 395½ | 426½ | 144 | 54 | .. | 7 | 36 | 26 |
| 22d | 372½ | 430 | 166½ | 52 | .. | 6 | 35 | 25 |
| 23d | 364½ | 425 | 181½ | 50½ | .. | 5 | 34 | 25 |
| 24th | 364½ | 429 | 178 | 54½ | .. | 5 | 34 | 25 |
| 25th | 364½ | 424 | 169 | 58½ | .. | 4 | 34 | 25 |
| 26th | 371 | 424½ | 167 | 55½ | .. | 3 | 33 | 25 |
| 27th | 371½ | 423½ | 166½ | 60½ | 1 | 3 | 34 | 25 |
| 28th | 368½ | 423 | 165½ | 62½ | .. | 4 | 35½ | 24 |
| 29th | 399½ | 404½ | 166 | 63 | .. | 4 | 33 | 24 |
| 30th | 403½ | 400½ | 165 | 58 | .. | 5 | 33 | 24 |
| 31st | 415½ | 391½ | 174 | 57½ | 1 | 3 | 34 | 12½ |
| 32d | 421 | 391 | 176 | 55½ | .. | 3 | 34 | 9½ |
| 33d | 421 | 380½ | 180 | 56 | .. | 3 | 34 | 13 |
| 34th | 420½ | 379½ | 184 | 54 | .. | 3 | 37 | 7½ |
| 35th | 409 | 376½ | 222 | 39 | .. | 1 | 38½ | 5 |
| 36th | 399 | 377 | 241 | 28 | .. | 3 | 36 | 4 |
| 37th | 405 | 386 | 202½ | 50½ | .. | 3 | 33 | 1 |
| 38th | 405½ | 383½ | 211 | 50 | .. | 4 | 33 | 1 |
| 39th | 440 | 468½ | 74 | 71½ | .. | 2 | 32 | .. |
| 40th | 467 | 490 | 19 | 76 | .. | 2 | 33 | .. |
| 41st | 460 | 497½ | 12 | 55½ | .. | 2 | 36 | 24 |
| 42d | 427 | 540½ | 8 | 49½ | .. | 3 | 34 | 24 |
| 43d | 412 | 567 | 7 | 57½ | .. | 2 | 34 | 5½ |

"All the News That's Fit to Print."

# The New York Times.

THE WEATHER
Thunder showers today and probably Thursday; moderate to fresh south winds.
For weather report see next to last page.

VOL. LXIX...No. 22,810 — NEW YORK, WEDNESDAY, JULY 7, 1920. — TWO CENTS In Greater New York | THREE CENTS Within 200 Miles | FOUR CENTS Elsewhere

# DEMOCRATIC TICKET IS COX AND ROOSEVELT; NEW YORKER UNOPPOSED AS RUNNING MATE; BRYAN IS SAD, BUT OTHER LEADERS REJOICE

## LLOYD GEORGE PINS GERMANY DOWN AT SPA MEETING

### In Dramatic Scene He Demands Yes or No Answer on Disarmament Question.

### HERR FEHRENBACH WEEPS

### Offers His Chances of Salvation as Pledge He Speaks for an Unrevengeful People.

### TOLD TALK IS VALUELESS

### Must Present to Conference Today a Definite Statement—Poles' Plead for Aid Is Refused.

By EDWIN L. JAMES.



Special Cable to THE NEW YORK TIMES.

SPA, July 6.—The Spa conference, with all its possibilities, hangs in the balance tonight. The Allies have served an ultimatum on Germany to present tomorrow a definite statement of how it proposes to meet the treaty disarmament terms or the conference will at once be discontinued.

The meeting today, when the Germans tried to drive the Allies backward from their firm stand on disarmament, was dramatic in the extreme. Premier Lloyd George spoke for the Allies in magnificent style. He met the German arguments and did not budge an inch. No less dramatic was the Pan-German, Fehrenbach, trying to tell the Allies that Germany had no revenge, but only good will to all men in her heart.

Human drama indeed seldom reaches the grandeur of the situation this episode presented—one statesman speaking for millions of free people who won the war and the other just as surely for the minority, the Prussianism which was defeated. Tears flowed down Fehrenbach's face as after he had offered his chances of eternal rest as a pledge that he spoke for a gentle Germany the little Welshman who led the Allies told him that vague promises by Germany were of no more value, and that her days of evasion were ended. He said Germans would now say whether or not they intended to disarm or all negotiations would be broken off.

**Marshal Foch First to Arrive.**

Yesterday when the Germans first met the Allies they tried to dodge the disarmament question, but were told they could not. The conference was adjourned until Defense Minister Gessler and General von Seecht could reach Spa. They arrived today and the conference was set for 4:30. Marshal Foch, with a smile on his face and cap on his ear, reached the Villa Fraineuse at 4 o'clock. Various delegations arrived at 4:30, and two minutes later the Germans came. Von Seecht, with a staff of half a dozen, made a handsome showing.

The conference was opened by M. Delacroix asking what was the reply to the Allies, notes on disarmament.

Herr Gessler replied, saying that Germany had done her best to carry out the treaty provisions, but had serious internal troubles. He said the Reichswehr had been reduced to 200,000 men and the navy to the treaty terms. He then sought sympathy by painting a picture of the scarcity of food. Continuing his plea, he asserted that Germany was "overheated," and "it is impossible in the present state of unrest to reduce the army to 100,000 men."

Premier Lloyd George interrupted:

"Is that a declaration that the German Government does not intend to fulfill the terms of the treaty?"

"No," was the reply, "but we ask for special consideration for conditions which have arisen since the armistice."

Lloyd George retorted:

"We don't need explanations of the past. We are concerned for the future."

He said Herr Gessler had not spoken of what Germany intended to do, but only that Germany had not fulfilled the treaty.

Here the Defense Minister sat down.

Foreign Minister Simons, remarking that Gessler had not clearly explained himself, said Germany intended eventually to reduce the army because of its expense, but she asked for time.

**Premiers Hold Private Conference.**

At this juncture Lloyd George asked for an adjournment.

While every one else took tea, the Germans and allied diplomats and Generals leaving together,, Lloyd George, Millerand and Delacroix held a private conference.

After the resumption of the session Lloyd George declared that Germany did not seem to realize the gap between the treaty terms and the execution of the treaty. The treaty, he said, left to Germany 100,000 men, 100,000 rifles and 2,000 machine guns. Germany still had 200,000 men, 20,000 machine guns and 12,-

Continued on Page Eleven.



## Gompers Glad Cox Was Named; Calls Him Clean and Fair

Special to The New York Times.

CHICAGO, July 6.—Samuel Gompers, President of the American Federation of Labor, who was in Chicago for a few hours today, expressed his pleasure at the action of the Democratic National Convention in nominating Governor Cox.

"He is a good, clean, fair man," said Mr. Gompers. "He was the logical candidate. Palmer's candidacy, though, was ridiculous. He never had a chance. Those Cox delegates would have stuck if they deadlocked the convention all Summer."

Mr. Gompers had been to San Francisco with a delegation interested in the labor plank in the Democratic platform, and which will discuss the labor planks of both parties and place its views before the public.

## GOV. COX ACCEPTS; MAY TOUR COUNTRY

### He Intimates to Convention Chairman That He Favors a Wide Campaign.

### PLEASED WITH ROOSEVELT

### The Governor Calls Him a Strong Running Mate—Visits His Mother's Grave.

DAYTON, Ohio, July 6.—In a telegram to the Democratic National Convention accepting the Presidential nomination and thanking the delegates for their support Governor James M. Cox today intimated that he is ready to make an intensive speaking campaign in every State.

Following is the text of the telegram:

"Hon. Joseph T. Robinson, Chairman, Democratic Convention, San Francisco, Cal.:

"Let me thank you for your felicitous message. I shall accept the standard from the Democracy of America, conscious not only of the honor but the great responsibility conferred.

"As Providence gives to me strength and vision, my firm resolve will be to justify the confidence which has been officially expressed.

"The shrine of government is in the communities of the land near to the homes that have given service and sacrifice. To them we will carry our cause with the assurance that the faith shall be kept and that the institutions of a free people are always sufficient to the needs of time, if they are held to the causes which we pledged.

"Please convey to the delegates of the convention my grateful acknowledgments. JAMES M. COX."

The message to the convention was timed so that it was expected to reach San Francisco shortly before the convention reconvened to nominate a Vice Presidential candidate.

It followed a message from Senator Robinson, permanent chairman of the convention, unofficially informing the Governor of his nomination and congratulating him.

Governor Cox also sent a reply to the greetings received earlier in the day from Senator Harding, the Republican Presidential nominee. His telegram to Senator Harding read:

"I accept your message as an evidence of the fraternal impulse which has always characterized the craft to which you and I belong. I heartily reciprocate the felicitous spirit which you have expressed."

Congratulations from President Wilson were received by Governor Cox this morning upon his nomination. The message from the White House, received at the Governor's office in Columbus this morning and transmitted to his home, in Dayton, read:

"Please accept my hearty congratulations and cordial best wishes.

"WOODROW WILSON."

Governor Cox sent this reply:

"I am deeply appreciative of your message of congratulations and good wishes. May I in turn felicitate you on your restoration to health?"

**Pleased With Roosevelt.**

Governor Cox tonight expressed his approval of Franklin D. Roosevelt as his running mate in the coming election.

A telegram of congratulation sent by Governor Cox to Mr. Roosevelt late this afternoon said:

"Please accept my earnest congratulation over the honor that has come to you. I am very delighted that we are associated together in the contest."

In discussing Mr. Roosevelt, Governor Cox characterized him as a very vigorous, upstanding, courageous and progressive Democrat.

"Mr. Roosevelt's speech before the National Committee in Chicago last Winter made a very strong impression," said the Governor. "He spoke in Dayton on Americanization, and his address at that time was very favorably commented

Continued on Page Three.



## FEW TO WITNESS THE CLIMAX

### Final Convention Thrills Staged Before Only 800 Spectators.

### DETAILS OF COX LANDSLIDE

### Colorado's Switch Marked the Moment When the Ohioan's Victory Became Assured.

### TEXAS HEADED COX PARADE

### McAdoo's Stanchest Supporters Carried Lone Star Standard to Strains of "Ohio! Ohio!"

Special to The New York Times.

SAN FRANCISCO, July 6.—There are in San Francisco today somewhat more than 9,000 angry people. Their rage is not at all lessened by the fact that they have nobody but themselves to be angry at, nor because they have no real reason to blame themselves; but still they are angry. They are the people who either held tickets for last night's session and didn't go, having heard what a deadly bore the long day session had been to all who participated in it or looked at it, or who went to the night session, concluded that it would be merely another chapter of the Democratic deadlock and went home before the delegates got out of the trenches and nominated James M. Cox for President of the United States.

The last half hour of that session was packed with drama, sparkling with thrills. It led up to an outburst of excited enthusiasm such as would have been impossible in the limp and exhausted Republican Convention which obeyed orders and nominated Harding in order to get out of Chicago before Sunday—an outburst which surpassed anything previously seen in this Democratic Convention, even on the day of the great debate between W. Bourke Cockran and William Jennings Bryan. The presence of 300 women delegates didn't seem to lower the temperature at all; they not only did not shut off excitement, but they helped a good deal in creating it.

**Relatively Few Saw the Climax.**

The last half hour of Monday night, or rather of Tuesday morning, was a properly exciting climax to a gathering which had already furnished a good deal of spectacular display between intervals of murderous dullness; and it was seen by perhaps 800 people outside of the delegates and alternates, the newspaper correspondents, the police, and the employes of the convention and the hall.

The excitement did not really begin till the fortieth ballot, when the Pennsylvanians, who had given Palmer their complimentary vote on the thirty-ninth, despite his withdrawal, divided according to their own preferences. The delegation had to be polled, a long and tiring interlude, but when the poll was complete it was found that McAdoo had gathered in the bulk of the residuary estate. For half an hour or so the McAdoo managers were hopeful, despite the fact that the breakup of the Palmer bloc had put Cox ahead once more.

As for the newspaper men, the supporters of the dark horses, and the few spectators who had stayed on after it had become apparent that the withdrawal of Palmer was not going to start an instantaneous landslide, they were dismayed and sore of heart. It looked as if nobody would be nominated at the night session, and everything would be left over to another day of monotonous and exhausting struggle between two deadlocked candidates.

But the forty-first ballot dulled the expectations of the McAdoo forces. Despite Pennsylvania, McAdoo had gained seven and Cox had lost seven. With the forty-second ballot Cox took a big leap forward, getting 540 votes to McAdoo's 427. This was the highest point yet reached by any candidate, and all over the hall people began to sit up and pinch themselves into wakefulness. Something might happen yet.

Here the McAdoo people threw in their reserves and tried to force an overnight adjournment. The Cox leaders stood out against it, and the house was with them. A ballot or two earlier the convention might have passed such a motion, while the galleries and the press section would have voted for it unanimously.

**Hopes of Late Stayers Revived.**

But things had changed now. Something might happen. The spectators who had stayed on for five hours hoping for some excitement, and who didn't have tickets for Tuesday's session, quivered with the hope that they were going to see something that the nine thousand deserters had missed. Delegates who when the triangular deadlock had apparently transformed itself into a dead-

Continued on Page Two.



JAMES M. COX
DEMOCRATIC NOMINEE FOR PRESIDENT.

## BRENNAN NOW RANKS AS A PARTY LEADER

### Conceded Title as Result of His Successful Fight Against McAdoo.

### PUT THROUGH COMBINATION

### Illinois Man Credited with Holding Anti-McAdoo Forces in Line to the End.

Special to The New York Times.

SAN FRANCISCO, July 6.—For fully half an hour after the Democratic National Convention had nominated James M. Cox for President and taken a recess early this morning, a rotund, middle-aged little man, with a beatific smile on his face, sat quietly in one of the seats assigned to the Illinois delegation. He was a picture of whole-hearted satisfaction.

The galleries had cleared of the few hundreds who remained into the early hours to join in the demonstration for Cox. All except a handful of the thousand or more delegates had left the hall, worn out. The last of the newspaper correspondents were deserting the press stands, and still the thick-set, smiling man remained. A few friends stepped up to shake hands and offer congratulations. His smile developed into a laugh of utter contentment.

The thick-set little man, who resembles a McManus cartoon of "Father" so faithfully that many have commented upon the fact, was George E. Brennan, leader of the Democratic forces of Illinois, which sent fifty-eight delegates to the convention. The State ranks third in importance where the size of delegations is concerned, giving ground only to New York and Pennsylvania. It had been held in line against McAdoo. In fact, it had assumed the rôle of leadership in the fight to prevent McAdoo's nomination.

Brennan was looking over the empty seats which represented all that was left of the air castles the McAdoo forces had built and which had come crashing down about their heads. He was content with the world.

**Congratulated by Leaders.**

While Brennan sat there, Charles F. Murphy, leader of Tammany, stepped up, shook hands and said "Good night." The Ohio National Committeeman, E. F. Moore, who managed the pre-convention campaign for Governor Cox, stopped to chat for a few moments and went to his hotel. Several minor leaders from New York, Illinois, Ohio and other States which had stood against McAdoo when the final test came and had thrown their support to Cox, smilingly offered their congratulations.

An attendant of the auditorium dimmed the lights. Finally Brennan arose and walked toward one of the exits, accompanied by two of his

Continued on Page Three.

## BRYAN IN DESPAIR OVER HIS DEFEAT

### "My Heart Is in the Grave with Our Cause," He Says as Convention Ends.

### UNCERTAIN OF HIS FUTURE

### He Will "Hesitate," He Asserts, but Democrats Fear He Will Join Prohibition Party.

Special to The New York Times.

SAN FRANCISCO, July 6.—William Jennings Bryan, eliminated as a factor and influence in Democratic politics, and smarting under defeat on his dry plank, coupled with the nomination of Cox, whom he characterizes as a "wet," may go into retirement from Democratic activity or get behind the not yet ended prohibition movement.

In the quiet of his own rooms at the St. Francis Hotel, overlooking a beautiful park, while the street crowds were happy and the delegates were breathing relief, the Nebraskan showed himself sad and depressed today, a broken hearted patriot. He did not hesitate to express his feeling and indicated that he knew not what his attitude would be toward the Democratic ticket or politics in general.

After discussing the action of the convention and its long drawn-out proceeding, Mr. Bryan remarked:

"My heart is in the grave with our cause. It must pause until it comes back to me."

"Do you interpret Governor Cox's nomination as a complete victory for the 'wets'?" was asked by one of the interviewers.

"It cannot be interpreted in any other way," was his reply.

"Do you not charge some anti-Administration influences with being responsible for his nomination, too?"

"Yes; but the wet forces were the moving influences and the deciding causes."

"Do you mean that you will hesitate, and pause and try to disinter your heart before you decide what you will do regarding the ticket?"

"Just that," was the reply of the peerless one.

"The convention consumed more than the usual time in reaching a decision," he continued, "and the voters now have about four months to decide. I shall use some of that time, to paraphrase a well known excuse, for hesitation.

"I regard the action of the convention in nominating Cox as a very serious mistake, in that it opened the door for the nomination of a wet candidate. I need not repeat what I have said before in regard to the evasion of other issues. I do not wish to discuss my future plans, but the public cannot overlook the importance of selecting a Senate and

Continued on Page Three.

## UNANIMOUS FOR ROOSEVELT

### Other Candidates for Vice President Withdrawn Without Vote.

### GOV. COX WAS CONSULTED

### Approved the Choice After Murphy, Brennan and Others Had Agreed.

### SMITH SWAYS CONVENTION

### New York Governor's Speech for Roosevelt Puts End to Other Booms.

Special to The New York Times.

SAN FRANCISCO, July 6.—Franklin D. Roosevelt of New York, Assistant Secretary of the Navy, was chosen by acclamation by the Democratic National Convention today as the party's candidate for Vice President. The convention, which had been in session since June 28 and had been deadlocked up to the forty-fourth ballot on the selection of a Presidential nominee, chose Mr. Roosevelt in a few minutes.

The question of selecting a Vice Presidential candidate had not consumed much of the time or thought of the leaders here, but with the Presidential nomination out of the way, it was taken up for serious discussion for the first time early this morning. First of all, the leaders got in communication with Governor Cox over the long-distance telephone at his home, in Dayton, Ohio. His advice as to a running mate was asked. He wanted to know who was in the field. When the list was given, he was also informed that Mr. Roosevelt was acceptable to the leaders, and he gave his approval.

Mr. Roosevelt was selected after the names of seven other candidates had been presented to the delegates. When it became apparent that the powers that be had made a decision there was a scramble to get on the band wagon and make the selection unanimous.

The list of other aspirants included David R. Francis of Missouri, ex-Ambassador to Russia; Maj. Gen. L. D. Tyson of Tennessee, Governor Samuel D. Stewart of Montana, ex-Governor James H. Hawley of Idaho, Joseph S. Davies of Wisconsin, T. T. Vaughan of Oregon and Edward L. Doheny of California.

**Rush to Withdraw Names.**

When these candidates or their representatives got the drift of the Roosevelt sentiment, one after the other mounted the platform and either withdrew their own names or had them withdrawn. Several other embryo candidates were not even presented to the convention. Ex-Senator James Hamilton Lewis of Illinois refused to have his name offered.

Charles F. Murphy of New York, George E. Brennan of Illinois and E. H. Moore of Ohio, leaders of the Cox forces, had united on Roosevelt before the convention was called to order. From delegation to delegation the word was passed that Roosevelt had been agreed upon, and that it was merely a waste of time to proceed with presentation of other names. But a surge of oratory was waiting to be let loose, and the convention managers, having nothing else to do for a few hours, thought it well to let the speakers have their chance.

It remained for Governor Alfred E. Smith of New York to give the quietus to all the other booms. He mounted the platform, amid the plaudits of the delegates, and in a vigorous speech seconded the nomination of Mr. Roosevelt. The scramble for the Roosevelt band wagon immediately followed and for the next fifteen minutes every candidate or his representative was busy nullifying what had been said a few minutes before.

At 3:15 o'clock it was suggested that the nomination of Mr. Roosevelt be made unanimous, and the convention by a vive voce vote ratified that proposal. The convention then wound up in a spirit of harmony.

Homer S. Cummings, Chairman of the National Committee, and Josephus Daniels, Secretary of the Navy, both of whom were McAdoo supporters to the last, made short speeches in favor of the nominees and predicted victory at the November election. The cry of "Cox and Roosevelt" went up and the weary delegates filed out of San Francisco's convention hall apparently well satisfied with what had been accomplished.

**Delegates Late in Assembling.**

The hour for the convention to reassemble had been fixed for noon, but half an hour later a mere handful of spectators were in the galleries, while groups of yawning delegates came slowly into the hall. Many of the delegates did not bother to return to the convention at all after the Presidential nomination, but left town as soon as the trains could take them.

Chairman Robinson called the convention to order at 12:45 P. M. After prayer had been offered, the preliminaries were hurried through with. The men and women members of the new National Committee were formally chosen. W. W. Farley of New York moved that the list be adopted by the convention and it was unanimously done.

Gavin McNab of California moved that the doors of the convention be thrown open to the public and any one allowed to come in, but it was not necessary, for the police had already seen to that. A resolution was adopted praising the local Police Department for the manner in which it had handled the convention crowds.

The thanks of the convention were also tendered to Temporary Chairman Cummings, Permanent Chairman Robinson and the other officers for the manner in which they had discharged their duties.

Mrs. George Bass of the women's Executive Committee received the thanks of the convention for her work among the women Democrats. The California women were thanked for their hospitality.

Mr. McNab wanted to keep the delegates longer in San Francisco, and offered a resolution that the convention take an adjournment, but a chorus of disapproval almost rent the roof. Put to a vote, the resolution was immediately lost.

**Tyson's Name Presented First.**

Nominations for Vice President were then in order. Alabama yielded to Tennessee and the flood of oratory was unloosed. Chairman Robinson limited the nominating speeches to seven minutes each.

The first candidate placed in nomination was Major Gen. Lawrence D. Tyson of Tennessee, whose name was presented by Harvey H. Hannah of Nashville. The speaker referred to President Wilson as "the greatest Democrat in the tide of time." General Tyson, he said, was a first citizen in the time of peace, but was not afraid to respond to the summons for war. For fifty years, he declared, the people of Tennessee had been perfectly happy to worship God and vote the Democratic ticket, but he thought the time had come for the South to be represented on the National ticket.

The reading of the telegram from Governor Cox accepting the Presidential nomination aroused the delegates from their lethargy. A delegate from each State seized a standard and began to march around the hall while the band played "He Rambled." After the circle of the room had been made a dozen times and the delegates had given cheers, in which the galleries took no part, the demonstration was over and quietly subsided. In their march around the hall a number of the delegates carried children on their shoulders.

The next speaker was Richard Seeley Jones of the State of Washington, who seconded by Miss Alice Reynolds of Utah and Senator Key Pittman of Nevada, did a like service for the same candidate.

Arizona yielded to Arkansas and Arkansas yielded to Montana, with the result that Senator Walsh of the last named State placed in nomination Governor Samuel D. Stewart of Montana.

Governor Stewart's nomination was seconded by Miss Alice Reynolds of Uath and Senator Key Pittman of Vevada. The independent Democrats of the West, Senator Pittman said, needed Governor Stewart on the ticket.

L. A. Hanly of California presented a native son, Edward L. Doheny, for the nomination.

**Enthusiasm for F. D. Roosevelt.**

Franklin D. Roosevelt was next placed in nomination by Timothy L. Ansberry, a former Congressman from Ohio, who sat in the convention as a delegate from the District of Columbia. The presentation of his name aroused the first genuine cheer. New York gave him a hearty send-off. The nomination was seconded by Judge K. U. M. Jackson of Kansas, and by Walter Myers of Indiana.

Senator Nugent of Idaho placed in nomination "Idaho's grand old Democrat," former Governor James H. Hawley. There were no seconding speeches for him.

Former Governor Dunne of Illinois sprang a surprise by announcing that former Senator James Hamilton Lewis had withdrawn from the race. Mr. Dunne stated that Senator Lewis had decided to withdraw because he believed that with the Presidential nomination having gone to Ohio, the candidate for Vice President should be taken from outside of the Mississippi Valley.

Governor Alfred E. Smith of New York then took the platform to second Mr. Roosevelt's nomination. The Governor, who had been honored with a half hour's demonstration when his name was presented to the convention as a Presidential candidate, also got a rousing reception when he went to the platform to make his only speech since the convention has been in session. Some one in the New York delegation proposed "three cheers for Al Smith," and the whole convention joined in giving them.

**Speech of Governor Smith.**

Governor Smith said in part:

"I very keenly appreciate the fact that we have had a long and tiresome session. Like most of the rest of you, I am keenly anxious to see other parts of the United States as much as we all appreciate the wonderful hospitality of California.

"For more than a week the eyes of the country and all the world have been on the Democratic Convention. We can fell well satisfied that so far as the platform and candidate are concerned, we have not disappointed the hopes and aspirations of humanity. We have given to the rank and file of the American people a clear and unequivocal program of Democratic doctrine and Democratic beliefs, standing forth in sharp contrast to the platform adopted by the Republicans at Chicago, in which every principle had to be a compromise to satisfy the whims of the delegates.

"When the Republican Convention was over, I met a Republican friend of mine who said to me 'Al, it makes me think of picking up a fish in cold weather. We have allowed Chicago to adopt the Lodge-Penrose theory that the Government exists for the benefit of special groups and that the Constitution and statute law stand for the protection of money and property.' As against that theory we put forward a Democratic belief that America is made up of men, women and children and that what concerns their health and welfare is a concern to Government.

"No man typifies to a greater extent the principles set forth in our platform than the candidate of this convention, Governor Cox of Ohio. New York goes back to the East with a candidate and platform that she can make a square, stand-up fight on. Democracy has the greatest chance at any time in my polit-

FRANKLIN D. ROOSEVELT
DEMOCRATIC NOMINEE FOR VICE PRESIDENT.

"All the News That's Fit to Print."

# The New York Times.

THE WEATHER
Fair and colder today; Thursday fair; strong southwest to west winds.
For full weather report see Page 15.

VOL. LXX....No. 22,929. NEW YORK, WEDNESDAY, NOVEMBER 3, 1920. TWO CENTS In Greater New York | THREE CENTS Within 200 Miles | FOUR CENTS Elsewhere

# HARDING WINS; MILLION LEAD HERE; BIG REPUBLICAN GAINS IN CONGRESS; MILLER LEADS SMITH FOR GOVERNOR

## MILLER BY 57,000

### But Democrats Refuse to Concede Governor's Defeat.

### SMITH'S SURPRISING RUN

### In Some Up-State Strongholds He Surpassed His Former Vote.

### WINS EVERY CITY BOROUGH

### Strongest in Manhattan, but Could Not Overcome Miller's Up-State Lead.

### 75,000 VICTORY, GLYNN SAYS

### Republicans Here Accuse Tammany of Holding Back City Returns.

### WADSWORTH IS ELECTED

### Plurality Betters Miller's, but Is Far Behind That on Presidential Ticket.

NEW YORK—Voted for Presidential Electors, United States Senator, Congressmen, Governor and other State officials and on an amendment to the Constitution. Vote in 1916: Democratic, 759,426; Republican, 869,115.

Polls closed at 6 P. M.

After a neck-and-neck race all evening ex-Judge Nathan L. Miller defeated Alfred E. Smith, his Democratic opponent, for the Governorship on the latest returns by about 57,000 plurality. Despite the big Harding landslide, it seemed probable for some time that Governor Smith would be able to pull through, but late returns from rural Republican districts overcame a record vote for him in New York City.

The Democratic managers refused, however, to give up hope, and early this morning still claimed the election of Mr. Smith. The Governor did not put forth any claim himself, asserting that he preferred to wait until remote up-State districts had been heard from. The Democratic leaders based their hopes for final success upon the fact that late returns showed that the Governor had increased his average majority in each election district in the city from 115 to 118 votes. They did not take into account, however, that Mr. Miller had also increased his average in up-State districts from 75 to 83.

If the present ratios are maintained, ex-Judge Miller will have an up-State lead of 379,725, while Governor Smith's plurality in New York City will be 322,494, giving the Republican candidate a plurality in the entire State of 57,231. Republican leaders claimed the election of Mr. Miller by approximately 75,000. Democratic leaders said Smith's plurality would be around 40,000.

**Smith Led at First.**

Early reports all evening showed the Tammany Governor in the lead, but when reports from rural Republican strongholds came in Mr. Miller's vote picked up considerably and shoved him well into the lead. At the same time Smith's vote in outlying districts in New York City did not keep pace with the huge vote he received in other parts of the city, and the indications were that ex-Judge Miller would be elected by a small plurality.

Some of the members of the Republican County Committee shortly before midnight made the charge that election returns were being held up in some Tammany districts until Mr. Miller's full strength had been reported. The First, Third and Fourth Assembly Districts, in lower Manhattan, where Tammany's strength is greatest, were among those mentioned at Republican county headquarters.

Deputy Attorney General Berger, accompanied by several members of the committee, set out for the polling places in the districts to learn the true state of affairs.

**Wadsworth Elected.**

United States Senator James W. Wadsworth, Jr., although running behind Senator Harding did not have any difficulty in defeating his Democratic

Continued on Page Four.



## State Pluralities.

FOR PRESIDENT.

REPUBLICAN.

| | |
|---|---|
| California | 500,000 |
| Connecticut | 100,000 |
| Colorado | 40,000 |
| Delaware | 5,000 |
| Idaho | 25,000 |
| Illinois | 800,000 |
| Indiana | 200,000 |
| Iowa | 200,000 |
| Kansas | 200,000 |
| Maine | 75,000 |
| Maryland | 20,000 |
| Massachusetts | 300,000 |
| Michigan | 400,000 |
| Minnesota | 100,000 |
| Missouri | 40,000 |
| Montana | 50,000 |
| Nebraska | 100,000 |
| New Hampshire | 30,000 |
| Nevada | 4,000 |
| New Jersey | 200,000 |
| New York | 1,000,000 |
| Ohio | 400,000 |
| Oregon | 5,000 |
| Pennsylvania | 750,000 |
| Rhode Island | 50,000 |
| South Dakota | 80,000 |
| Utah | 30,000 |
| Vermont | 40,000 |
| Washington | 150,000 |
| West Virginia | 50,000 |
| Wisconsin | 300,000 |
| Wyoming | 8,000 |

DEMOCRATIC.

| | |
|---|---|
| Alabama | 70,000 |
| Arkansas | 100,000 |
| Florida | |
| Georgia | |
| Kentucky | 20,000 |
| Louisiana | |
| Mississippi | |
| New Mexico | |
| North Carolina | 60,000 |
| Oklahoma | 7,500 |
| South Carolina | |
| Tennessee | 40,000 |
| Texas | 50,000 |
| Virginia | 75,000 |

DOUBTFUL.

| | |
|---|---|
| Arizona | |
| North Dakota | |

## CITY'S VOTE GOES TO HARDING AND SMITH

### For Republican President by 443,000 and Democratic Governor by 325,000.

### SEPARATE BALLOTS HELPED

### But Some Charges Heard That Tammany Traded Votes—Socialists Make Gains.

New York City, in yesterday's election, gave its vote overwhelmingly to Senator Warren G. Harding, Republican candidate for President; to Calvin Coolidge, Republican candidate for Vice President, and to Alfred E Smith, Democratic candidate for Governor.

Senator Harding carried every Assembly District in the Greater City with one exception—the First Assembly District, which is Governor Smith's home district. This gave Cox a plurality of about 400 votes.

In the minor contests the Republicans made some gains, although these were nothing like what might have been expected from the overwhelming sweep made by the Presidential ticket.

This result was greatly facilitated by the three ballots instituted by the Board of Elections, one for the Presidency, one for the State ticket (which also included the Congressional candidates), and one for the constitutional amendment and bonus proposal. The separation made ticket splitting easy, and the voters took full advantage of it.

Harding's victory in the city was overwhelming. At 3 A. M. today, on the returns then available, the plurality of the Republican candidate for the Presidency in the city was indicated as about 443,000.

Manhattan gave a Republican Presidential plurality of about 136,000; the Bronx, 62,000; Brooklyn, 177,000; Queens, 61,000, and Richmond, 7,000.

**Striking Support of Smith.**

But on the State ticket it was quite a different story. The same hour that found Harding victorious by 443,000 in the normally Democratic city of New York, showed Alfred E. Smith, Democrat, leading Judge Nathan Miller, his

Continued on Page Three.



## OHIO FOR HARDING; 400,000 PLURALITY IS NOW ESTIMATED

### Republicans Ahead in Nearly All the Large Cities of the State.

### BIG LEAD IN CINCINNATI

### Harding's Margin in Hamilton County Believed to be 20,000.

### VICTORY IN CLEVELAND

### Cuyahoga County About Two to One—Sweep in Toledo Also.

OHIO—Voted for Presidential Electors, United States Senator, Congressmen, Governor and other State officials. Vote in 1916: Democratic, 604,161; Republican, 516,733.

Polls closed at 5:30 P. M. (6:30 P. M. New York time).

COLUMBUS, Ohio, Nov. 2.—Returns from 2,987 precincts out of a total of 7,145 in the State give Harding 499,355, Cox 336,352.

If this ratio is maintained, the indications are that Senator Harding carried Ohio by more than 400,000 plurality.

Under instructions from State officials county election boards counted Presidential returns first. This made returns on the State ticket and the United States Senatorship unusually slow. Many scratched ballots were voted on the State ticket.

Returns from 128 precincts on the Governorship race show Davis (R), 15,690; Donahey (D), 10,833.

Returns from 66 precincts for United States Senator give Willis (R), 6,341; Julian (D), 4,794.

Senator Harding has probably carried every large city in the State from which normally the Democrats get their majorities. In some instances his pluralities have been tremendous. He is running even in Columbus, and may have carried it.

Many of the country districts are holding up to normal for Governor Cox. In some instances he is making slight gains there.

Chairman Clark claims the election of the Republican State ticket, including Harry L. Davis for Governor, by 100,000, while Chairman Durbin claims the election of A. V. Donahey (Dem.) for Governor by at least 50,000.

The vote in Cuyahoga County, including Cleveland, is running about two to one for Harding, indicating the sentiment in Northern Ohio. Four years ago Wilson carried the county two to one. Seventy-eight precincts out of 571 in the city of Cleveland gave Harding 13,840, Cox 7,937. In Cuyahoga County, outside of Cleveland, nine precincts out of 133 give Harding 2,826, Cox 830.

Hamilton County, in which Cincinnati is situated, will give 20,000 plurality for Harding.

The first twenty-two precincts to re-

Continued on Page Three.

## United States Senators Elected.

| REPUBLICANS, 20. | DEMOCRATS, 14. |
|---|---|
| S. Shortridge, Calif. | O. W. Underwood, Ala. |
| S. D. Nicholson, Col. | J. T. Heflin, Ala. |
| F. B. Brandegee, Conn. | M. A. Smith, Ariz. |
| F. R. Gooding, Idaho. | T. H. Caraway, Ark. |
| W. B. McKinley, Ill. | D. U. Fletcher, Fla. |
| J. E. Watson, Ind. | T. E. Watson, Ga. |
| A. B. Cummins, Iowa. | J. C. W. Beckham, Ky. |
| C. Curtis, Kan. | E. S. Broussard, La. |
| O. E. Weller, Md. | C. B. Henderson, Nev. |
| S. P. Spencer, Mo. | L. S. Overman, N. C. |
| G. H. Moses, N. H. | S. Ferris, Okla. |
| J. W. Wadsworth, Jr., N. Y. | G. E. Chamberlain, Ore. |
| E. F. Ladd, N. Dakota. | E. D. Smith, S. C. |
| F. B. Willis, Ohio. | C. Glass, Va. |
| B. Penrose, Pa. | |
| P. Norbeck, S. Dakota. | |
| R. Smoot, Utah. | |
| W. P. Dillingham, Vt. | |
| W. L. Jones, Wash. | |
| I. L. Lenroot, Wis. | |

## INDIANA IS SWEPT BY REPUBLICANS

### Early Returns Indicate That Harding Will Carry State by Upward of 200,000.

### WATSON LEADING TAGGART

### He Trails Ticket, but on Basis of Returns His Election Is Expected by 185,000 Plurality.

INDIANA—Voted for Presidential Electors, United States Senator, Congressmen, Governor and other State officials. Vote in 1916: Democratic, 334,063; Republican, 341,005.

Polls closed at 6 P. M. (7 P. M. New York time).

*Special to The New York Times.*

INDIANAPOLIS, Ind., Nov. 2.—Late returns coming in from the rural districts have piled up the Harding plurality in the State with every indication pointing that the Republican landslide will be the largest in the history of Indiana. It was estimated late tonight that Cox will be defeated by at least 200,000 votes. The former Republican plurality record for Indiana in a Presidential race was held by Roosevelt with 93,000.

Of 1,002 precincts out of the 3,384 in the State, Harding has received 330,767 votes and Cox, 239,621.

Warren T. McCray of Kentland, Republican Gubernatorial nominee, has been swept into office by an overwhelming plurality over Dr. Carlton B. McCulloch of Indianapolis, his Democratic opponent. Although James E. Watson ran behind the ticket in several districts in his race for re-election to the Senate against Thomas Taggart, it is estimated that he will trail Harding less than 15,000 votes. Watson ran especially strong in the rural districts, while Taggart made his best showing in the laboring centres.

On the face of incomplete returns it appears that eleven of the thirteen Congressional Districts have piled up a suf-

Continued on Page Three.

## ILLINOIS TREBLES REPUBLICAN VOTE

### Returns Indicate Harding Has More Than 800,000 Plurality in the State.

### McKINLEY CHOSEN SENATOR

### Governor, State Officers and Entire Delegation to Congress Probably Republican.

ILLINOIS—Voted for Presidential Electors, United States Senator, Congressmen, Governor and other State officials and on an amendment to the Constitution. Vote in 1916: Democratic, 950,229; Republican, 1,152,549.

Polls closed at 5 P. M. (6 P. M. New York time).

CHICAGO, Nov. 2.—Upon the basis of returns received up to a late hour tonight Harding and Coolidge have carried Illinois by a plurality of more than 800,000. At this hour Harding has an indicated plurality of 331,000 in Chicago. His plurality down State is estimated to be not less than 316,000.

Harding's plurality in Chicago is apparently larger than any ever given a candidate by the city. It exceeds the famous 147,477 which Mayor Thompson got in 1915.

In 966 of 5,730 Illinois precincts, including 475 in Chicago, Harding had 218,913 votes, against 78,906 for Cox.

McKinley, for Senator, had a plurality of 57,621 over Waller, and Small was leading Lewis nearly two to one for Governor.

The Republican sweep apparently is even stronger than in 1904, when Roosevelt carried Cook County by 126,000, the women not voting then. Four years ago Hughes carried the county by 56,000 over Wilson, but Harding's lead over Cox is more than five times greater.

By 1 o'clock it was estimated that 60 per cent. of the 884,000 registered voters had visited the polls. During the afternoon they kept swarming in, and closing time saw many still waiting in line.

Early returns indicate about 825,000 votes were cast in Chicago. The plurality

Continued on Page Three.

## CONGRESS HEAVILY REPUBLICAN, GAINS IN BOTH HOUSES

### Party Will Have a Majority of 12 in the Senate and 113 in the House.

### 54 REPUBLICAN SENATORS

### House Stands: Republicans 274, Democrats 158, Independents 2, Drys 1

### IRRECONCILABLES ELECTED

### Brandegee in Connecticut and Moses in New Hampshire Returned.

President Harding will have a Republican Congress to support his policies in the first two years at least of his Administration. Returns received up until the time this edition of THE TIMES goes to press show that the party which was triumphant at the polls yesterday will have increased majorities in both Houses, with that in the House approaching 300.

Returns in the elections for Senators and Representatives are meager from some important States, but the trend of voting in those States in the Presidential and Gubernatorial contests indicates the probable result as far as the Senate is concerned. The returns received indicate that the two houses in the next Congress will stand as follows:

Senate—Republicans, 54 Democrats, 42.

House—Republicans, 274; Democrats, 158; Independents, 2; Prohibitionist, 1.

This gives the Republicans a majority of 12 in the Senate and a majority of 113 in the House. The present Republican majority in the Senate is 2 and in the House 39.

Senator Moses of New Hampshire and Senator Brandegee of Connecticut, both Republicans of the irreconcilable treaty group in the Senate, were strongly opposed on account of their opposition to the League of Nations, but have carried their States by substantial majorities. Senator Brandegee also had the opposition of many women on account of his effort to prevent the ratification of the Nineteenth Amendment.

**Phelan Loses California.**

Samuel Shortridge, Republican, who supported Senator Hiram Johnson's irreconcilable opposition to the League of Nations, appears to have been elected to the Senate, defeating Senator James D. Phelan, Democrat, a firm friend of the Wilson Administration. Senator James E. Watson, Republican, has been re-elected from Indiana, defeating ex-Senator Thomas Taggart, Democrat. Returns from Iowa are not nearly complete, but they indicate that in spite of the opposition of organizations of farmers and laborers and a great many Re-

Continued on Page Three.

## MAP SHOWING HOW THE STATES VOTED

KEY
DEMOCRATIC
REPUBLICAN
DOUBTFUL or Insufficiently Reported.

FIGURES IN CIRCLES INDICATE NUMBER OF ELECTORAL VOTES

## Electoral Vote.

HARDING.

| State | Votes |
|---|---|
| California | 13 |
| Colorado | 6 |
| Connecticut | 7 |
| Delaware | 3 |
| Illinois | 29 |
| Indiana | 15 |
| Idaho | 4 |
| Iowa | 13 |
| Kansas | 10 |
| Maine | 6 |
| Maryland | 8 |
| Massachusetts | 18 |
| Michigan | 15 |
| Minnesota | 12 |
| Missouri | 18 |
| Montana | 4 |
| Nebraska | 8 |
| Nevada | 3 |
| New Hampshire | 4 |
| New Jersey | 14 |
| New York | 45 |
| Ohio | 24 |
| Oregon | 5 |
| Pennsylvania | 38 |
| Rhode Island | 5 |
| South Dakota | 5 |
| Utah | 4 |
| Vermont | 4 |
| Washington | 7 |
| West Virginia | 8 |
| Wisconsin | 13 |
| Wyoming | 3 |
| Total | 371 |

COX.

| State | Votes |
|---|---|
| Alabama | 12 |
| Arkansas | 9 |
| Florida | 6 |
| Georgia | 14 |
| Kentucky | 13 |
| Louisiana | 10 |
| Mississippi | 10 |
| New Mexico | 3 |
| North Carolina | 12 |
| Oklahoma | 10 |
| South Carolina | 9 |
| Tennessee | 12 |
| Texas | 20 |
| Virginia | 12 |
| Total | 152 |

Doubtful or Insufficiently Reported

| State | Votes |
|---|---|
| Arizona | 3 |
| North Dakota | 5 |
| Total | 8 |

Total number of votes in Electoral College, 531; necessary to a choice, 266.

## PRESIDENT HEARD FIRST VOTES ONLY

### He Retired at 9 o'Clock, His Physician Leaving the White House Earlier.

### NO COMMENT ON RETURNS

### Wilson at Afternoon Cabinet Meeting Expressed Confidence in Success of League.

*Special to The New York Times.*

WASHINGTON, Nov. 2.—Although messages to the White House tonight brought the news that Harding was leading in very nearly all the doubtful localities the attitude seemed to be sit tight and concede nothing until the actual result was ascertained. The experience of the Hughes débâcle four years ago appeared to hold out a lesson in the wisdom of this course for the White House circle.

No public expressions of any kind were made. The atmosphere lacked the gloom usually associated with the news of a reversal. Visitors to the White House found the Secretaries and other members of the staff in perfect good humor.

President Wilson heard bulletins until about 9 o'clock, and this being his usual bed hour, he retired, so it was said. Admiral Cary T. Grayson, his personal physician, left the White House for his home about 8:30 o'clock. This fact seemed to set aside theories that the President would be in a nervous condition if he realized that Senator Harding was far ahead in the Presidential race.

Joseph P. Tumulty, Private Secretary

Continued on Page Four.



## GIGANTIC MAJORITIES

### Pennsylvania, 750,000; Illinois, 800,000; Ohio, 400,000.

### MAY BE 6,000,000 IN ALL

### More Than 370 Electoral Votes Won by Harding and Coolidge.

### BIG GAINS IN THE WEST

### Indiana, Wisconsin, Michigan, Iowa, Kansas, Nebraska and California Won.

### NEW JERSEY BY 200,000

### Maine, with 75,000, Beats the Plurality She Gave in September.

### SOLID SOUTH UNBROKEN

### Unless Late Figures Change Tennessee—Cox May Lose All Western States.

By majorities unprecedented in American politics, Warren G. Harding was elected President and Calvin Coolidge Vice President yesterday on Senator Harding's fifty-fifth birthday. Though the addition of women to the electorate might have been expected to make the margins of successful candidates somewhat larger than in past years, it could hardly account for any such unheard of majorities as were rolled up yesterday. From coast to coast records were broken.

Harding's total pluralities in the States he carried may reach 6,500,000 and his net plurality over Cox may be 6,000,000. This surpasses by 3,500,000 the previous record, which was that of Theodore Roosevelt's victory over Alton B. Parker.

The highest State plurality ever previously recorded, Roosevelt's margin of 500,000 over Parker in Pennsylvania in 1904, was surpassed by at least four States yesterday. New York State went for Harding by nearly 1,100,000; Pennsylvania gave him a plurality of 750,000; Illinois gave him 800,000; California, which went for Wilson four years ago by a majority of 2,700, gave Harding a plurality of perhaps 500,000 over James M. Cox. Ohio, the home State of both candidates, went for Harding by 400,000.

At 4 o'clock this morning it seemed that Harding's majority on electoral votes would equal or surpass the record-breaking landslide by which Roosevelt beat Alton B. Parker.

Cox held the solid South, and Kentucky and perhaps Oklahoma among the border States; but West Virginia and Missouri had apparently gone for Harding, as they went for Roosevelt in 1904. Late reports indicate that Cox might possibly lose Tennessee.

The latest reports give Harding 371 electoral votes and Cox 152, with eight votes—those of Arizona and North Dakota—still uncertain. This, however, seems to be due to inadequate reports; the probability is that they are all for Harding.

All over the country the Harding pluralities broke records. Boston, which has been consistently Democratic in recent years, except in 1896, when McKinley carried it over Bryan, showed the effect of the drift of the Irish vote by giving Harding a plurality of more than 20,000.

New York City, however, was even more surprising. The city went for Taft in 1908 by less than 16,000; it seems to have given Harding a plurality of more than 443,000. Buffalo gave Harding a plurality of 46,247.

The effect of the Harding sweep showed everywhere. Though the Southern States stood fast, Harding had carried two wards in Atlanta and two Louisiana parishes. In the Middle West, Indiana and Kansas each gave him more than 200,000 plurality, Iowa about the same; Michigan nearly 400,000; Wisconsin nearly 300,000.

Maine, which surprised observers last September by a Republican plurality of 70,000 in the Gubernatorial election, surpassed this figure by several thousand

WARREN G. HARDING

"All the News That's Fit to Print."

# The New York Times.

THE WEATHER
Warmer, with rain or snow, today; Sunday, unsettled, rising temperature; east and southeast winds.
For full weather report see Page 27.

VOL. LXX....No. 23,051. ••• NEW YORK, SATURDAY, MARCH 5, 1921. TWO CENTS In Greater New York | THREE CENTS Within 200 Miles | FOUR CENTS Elsewhere

# HARDING INAUGURATED, DECLARES AGAINST ENTANGLEMENTS; WILSON, WEAKENED BY ILLNESS, UNABLE TO JOIN IN CEREMONY; GEN. PERSHING SLATED TO GO TO FRANCE AS AMBASSADOR

## SIMONS, ADVISED BY BERLIN, WORKS ON A NEW OFFER

### Believed in London He Will Present Terms Experts Proposed, With Additions.

### GERMANS LESS HOPEFUL

### Prepare Answer to Lloyd George's Arguments—Refuse to Acknowledge War Guilt.

### UPROAR IN THE REICHSTAG

### President Called Upon to Read All of Lloyd George's Speech After Denouncing Penalties.


Special Cable to THE NEW YORK TIMES.

LONDON, March 4.—The German Government forwarded its instructions to Dr. Simons late today and the chief German delegates spent the evening considering them. Tomorrow they will be taken in hand by the experts of the mission, and his expected statement to be presented to the conference on Monday will be completed by Sunday afternoon.

What the Germans will offer then cannot definitely be stated, but the belief in well informed quarters is that the proposals will be those which Simons, so it is said, should have originally produced, together with some additions. The presentation of these proposals would mean a victory for the experts of the mission, who, according to The Daily Chronicle's diplomatic correspondent, are strongly dissatisfied with the manner in which Simons conducted the German case.

"The tone of the German delegates underwent a good deal of change today," writes that correspondent. "There is no longer any talk of having offered the uttermost pfennig. The mission is indeed badly split. What I may call the political fraction, headed by the chief delegate, professes optimism; the experts are exceedingly pessimistic. That a tremendous blunder was made by Simons in presenting a whittled-down version of the counter-proposals he brought from Berlin is now more or less frankly admitted. Indeed, this is realized to such an extent that had there been time to bring along a substitute from Berlin, Simons would have been recalled. As it is, his position as Foreign Minister is badly shaken."

Lloyd George had a long conference today with Lord Beatty, First Sea Lord, with reference to the situation which will arise if the penalties have to be applied.

**Refuse to Admit War Guilt.**

LONDON, March 4 (Associated Press).—Dr. Simons, the Foreign Secretary, and the German experts are busy preparing a reply to some of the arguments used by Premier Lloyd George in delivering the allied ultimatum yesterday.

The Germans strongly object to the verdict of the Allies that they were entirely responsible for the war and the Premier's argument that if they taxed themselves as France and England had done they would be able to pay what is demanded of them. They maintain internal taxes, such as those on sugar, tobacco and spirits, have not been taken into account, and they are prepared to produce figures showing the Allies have underrated their impositions.

With regard to the question of responsibility for the war, the Germans maintain the European powers were equally at fault and cite a recent speech by Mr. Lloyd George in which he is quoted as saying that the world drifted into the war.

"It is hard to make a man who believes he is innocent say he is guilty," said one of the delegates today. "As for myself, I would rather commit suicide than admit Germany alone was responsible. Any Government which made such an admission would promptly be overthrown. So, if the Allies are determined to carry out their demands they must impose them upon us. They soon will find that the penalties which they outlined yesterday will not produce what they expect."

It is the general opinion of Germans in London that new propositions will be laid before the Supreme Council, but they have no hope they will satisfy the Allies. They say it is impossible to satisfy France, and they now fear Premier Lloyd George, from whom they had expected more lenient treatment, considering that he committed himself so far to the French view in his speech yesterday that it is impossible for him to recede.

Besides, the Germans hold, the firm attitude displayed in yesterday's speech has met with such approval in Great Britain that the Prime Minister must realize he followed the popular view. They believe approval was particularly noticeable respecting the decision to occupy Duisburg, Ruhrort and Düssel-

Continued on Page Nine.

### *Soviet Troops Hold Moscow To Prevent an Outbreak*

RIGA, March 4 (Associated Press).—It is reported that there is great excitement in Moscow over the events in Petrograd and that extraordinary steps have been taken to prevent revolts. The city of Moscow has been divided into four districts for defense and troops are concentrated at strategic points during the night.

STOCKHOLM, March 4 (Associated Press).—White flags are floating from the Winter palace at Petrograd and the Kremlin at Moscow, according to Helsingfors reports received here. In Moscow 30,000 troops are declared to have refused to march against the revolutionaries.

Revolutionary troops from the southern front are marching on Petrograd. Mariners at Kronstadt have sent out a wireless message exhorting all Russian troops to participate in the revolution against the Soviet.

## LEGION POST ASKS REMOVAL OF HYLAN

### Formal Request Sent to Gov. Miller as Result of "Horror on the Rhine" Meeting.

### HEARST PAPERS CONDEMNED

### Veterans of Foreign Wars Post Also Denounce Official Action as Un-American.

Formal request has been made to Governor Nathan L. Miller to remove Mayor Hylan for having allowed the "Horror on the Rhine" mass meeting in Madison Square Garden to take place. The protestants, who also condemn the Hearst newspapers for their attitude in reporting the affair, are the members of Richmond Hill Post, No. 212, of the American Legion.

On Thursday last the post adopted the following resolutions, which were attested by Frederick M. Clouter, Post Adjutant:

Whereas on Monday evening, Feb. 28, at Madison Square Garden, New York City, a pro-German mass meeting was held, conducted by enemy aliens and sympathizers styling themselves "The Horror on the Rhine" Committee, whose alleged purpose was to protest the presence of French colored troops in Germany, and whose real objective was to stir up strife between the United States and its allies, in order to obtain easier peace terms for a nation that is directly responsible for the sacrifice of 10,000,000 lives—a nation directly responsible for the wanton destruction of peaceful lands—a nation directly responsible for atrocities too inhuman to even think about—a nation that disregards treaties and international law—and a nation that defies Christian principles; and

Whereas the New York State Department of the American Legion and scores of other patriotic organizations sternly protested against the holding of said meeting to the Mayor of the City of New York; and

Whereas the Mayor ignored all protests and allowed this outrageous expression of vicious anti-American and pro-German propaganda to continue in its defiance of every instinct of red-blooded Americanism; therefore be it

Resolved, That Richmond Hill Post 212, American Legion, Department of New York, in regular meeting March 3, 1921, protests with the utmost vigor at its command such base demonstration of foul German propaganda; and be it further

Resolved, That Richmond Hill Post also condemns the Mayor of New York City for allowing this meeting to be held, and includes in this condemnation the Hearst newspapers of New York City for the attitude shown in reporting this meeting; and be it further

Resolved, That a copy of this resolution be forwarded to Governor Nathan Miller of the State of New York requesting him to remove the Mayor of New York City from office

A letter from Mr. Clouter, enclosing a copy of the resolution, said:

"The presentation of the enclosed resolution provoked many vigorous denunciations of Mayor Hylan, W. R. Hearst, and those who are pushing the sort of propaganda as was displayed at Madison Square Garden. Richmond Hill Post is the largest in Queens County, and had 395 paid-up members at the end of 1920.

"The resolution was introduced by Robert Quafle Jr. of 10,424 127th Street, Richmond Hill, Chairman of the Americanization Committee."

Resolutions adopted by Major Gen. J. Franklin Bell Post 103, Veterans of Foreign Wars of the United States, said in part:

Whereas, at the time the meeting was held thousands of our comrades were in hospitals suffering from wounds received from our country's enemies, and each day sees some of them departing from this life as a result of such wounds; therefore

Resolved, That the Major Gen. J. Franklin Bell Post 103, Veterans of Foreign Wars of the United States, go on record as being opposed to the holding of public meetings for the furtherance of the interests of any coun-

Continued on Page Eight.

## ENVOY'S POST FOR PERSHING

### General's Appointment Is Expected in Administration Circles.

### COUNT ON FRENCH ACCLAIM

### Selection Would Adjust Problem of Pershing's Vague Military Status.

### WANT A DEMOCRAT TO STAY

### Gov. W. P. G. Harding of Federal Reserve Board Counted On to Retain Place.

*Special to The New York Times.*

WASHINGTON, March 4.—It is the understanding among members of the new Republican Administration that President Harding intends to appoint General John J. Pershing as Ambassador to France. This decision will adjust what might have been a troublesome problem in connection with the military establishment, for General Pershing's status of military authority is somewhat shrouded in vagueness.

As General of the Armies of the United States General Pershing occupies a peculiar office. The Chief of the Army General Staff, a position now held by General Peyton C. March, and to which it is expected Major Gen. John C. Harbord will be appointed, is the actual head of the military service, although he ranks below General Pershing, whose commission is permanent, while that of Chief of Staff is temporary.

To assign General Pershing to specific military duty would, in a military sense, subject him to the orders of an officer junior to him in rank, and it is considered to be poor military policy to permit such a state of affairs.

**Believe French Would Hail Him.**

With General Pershing as Ambassador to France the problem would be solved, temporarily at least, and the appointment of General Pershing would have the additional advantage of tending to bring the relations of France and the United States into a more cordial atmosphere, for General Pershing is regarded as a hero by the French people and his appointment to the diplomatic mission at Paris would be extremely popular in that country.

It had been believed here that Myron T. Herrick, former Ambassador to France, would again receive an offer of the French mission. He preferred the Ambassadorship to Great Britain, but President Harding is said to have Colonel George Harvey in mind for that post.

If General Pershing should be designated for the French Mission it probably would be necessary for him to take advantage of his privilege to retire from active service. The Constitution prohibits any person from holding two offices under the Federal Government at the same time. While a retired officer of the army is still subject to call for active service, the Supreme Court has construed retired pay as in the nature of a pension and therefore not to be considered as compensation for a Federal office within the meaning of the Constitutional inhibition.

In the case of the late Nathan B. Goff, a Senator from West Virginia, the Supreme Court held that his pay as a retired Judge of the Federal Circuit bench was not a salary but a pension for past services. This decision apparently applies to General Pershing's case should he retire from active service.

As General of the Armies of the United States, General Pershing receives annual pay of $13,500, and has, in addition, allowances for quarters and other things amounting to about $8,000, so that his yearly compensation from the Government is $21,500. The salary of the Ambassador to France is $17,500, but the Congress which expired today has enacted a law providing for the building or purchase of an embassy in Paris, which the American Ambassador would have the right to occupy rent free. Under the law creating the office of General of the Armies of the United States, General Pershing is permitted to retire on full pay and allowances, so that he would lose none of his army compensation if he should accept the French mission, and at the same time would be privileged to receive the pay of an Ambassador.

**W. P. G. Harding Expected to Remain.**

The understanding also prevails in Harding Administration quarters that William P. G. Harding of Alabama has consented to remain as Governor of the Federal Reserve Board for an indefinite period.

Mr. Harding is a Democrat. He was arranging to leave the Government service to become the head of the new Foreign Trade Finance Corporation now in process of formation, but it was said tonight that he had been persuaded to defer handing in his resignation from the Federal Reserve Board so that the new Administration would have the benefit of his services at this period of business depression.

President Harding and the new Secretary of the Treasury, Andrew W. Mellon, are credited with having a profound admiration for the manner in which Governor Harding has handled financial matters recently and with being anxious to have him continue in office for as long a time as he feels that he can conveniently give his services to the Government.

### *Governor Miller Confident Harding Will Be Successful*

*Special to The New York Times.*

ALBANY, March 4.—Governor Miller thinks the Harding Administration has opportunity for great service to the country and he believes it will be equal to the opportunity.

"I think," said the Governor today, "that the new Administration holds out great promise to the people of this country. The President has surrounded himself with men who have great ability to serve as well as the disposition to serve.

"The opportunity for very great service is presented, and I have no doubt that the new Administration will be equal to the opportunity."

## HARDING IN PERSON PRESENTS CABINET

### Appears at Senate Executive Session and Reads the List of Nominees.

### ALL PROMPTLY CONFIRMED

### New President Says He Feels Sure of "Close Friendly and Personal Relations."

*Special to The New York Times.*

WASHINGTON, March 4.—President Harding personally presented to the Senate this afternoon the nominations of the men whom he had selected to head the executive departments, and in record time the Senate confirmed all of them.

The appearance of the new President before an executive session of the Senate revived a custom which Washington started and which Jefferson was the last to follow.

The President was in the Senate not more than fifteen minutes, and himself read the names of the new Cabinet officers in their constitutional order. He received a warm welcome from his former colleagues of both parties, who crowded about him as he was leaving the Chamber and wished him the best of fortune in days that are ahead of him.

"I feel no hesitancy," said President Harding as he stood beside the Vice President, "in coming to you at this time, feeling assured of the close friendly and personal relations that exist between us. Therefore, I have taken advantage of the opportunity to appear personally and communicate to you the list of the nominations for the Cabinet. It is a list that appeals to my judgment and desires, and I hope that it will make a similar appeal to the judgment and desires of the Senate."

**Read List to the Senate.**

President Harding then read to the Senate the Cabinet nominations in the following order:

*Secretary of State*—CHARLES EVANS HUGHES of New York.

*Secretary of the Treasury*—ANDREW W. MELLON of Pennsylvania.

*Secretary of War*—JOHN W. WEEKS of Massachusetts.

*Attorney General*—HARRY M. DAUGHERTY of Ohio.

*Postmaster General*—WILL H. HAYS of Indiana.

*Secretary of the Navy*—EDWIN DENBY of Michigan.

*Secretary of the Interior*—ALBERT B. FALL of New Mexico.

*Secretary of Agriculture*—HENRY C. WALLACE of Iowa.

*Secretary of Commerce*—HERBERT C. HOOVER of California.

*Secretary of Labor*—JAMES J. DAVIS of Indiana.

Immediately after he had concluded the reading of the names of the new Cabinet the President left the chamber. He departed from the Democratic side, and as he was passing out grasped the hand of Senator Underwood, the Democratic leader, and chatted with him for a moment or two. Mr. Underwood is a close personal friend of Mr. Harding and during his service in the Senate was his general pair.

**Confirmation Methods Spurred.**

When the President had passed out of the chamber the consideration of the nominations began. The committees to which the various nominations were referred had been previously polled and everything was ready to expedite confirmation in every instance, the confirmation papers having been signed by the committee members of both parties prior to the appearance of President Harding.

Mr. Hughes's name was referred to the Committee on Foreign Relations and the Chairman, Senator Lodge, immediately reported in favor of confirmation. Senator Penrose from the Committee on Finance reported the name of Mr. Mellon for the Treasury portfolio, Senator Wadsworth for the Military Affairs Committee the name of Mr. Weeks, Senator Poindexter for the Committee on Naval Affairs the name of Mr. Denby, and so on down the list. Rumors that Senator Reed of Missouri would oppose confirming Mr. Hoover proved to be unfounded and there was no opposition to any of the appointees.

When Chairman Kenyon had reported for favorable consideration the last of the new Cabinet officers, Mr. Davis for Secretary of Labor, the nominations were offered to the Senate for confirmation as a whole. Every Senator voted

Continued on Page Six.

## WILSON'S EXIT IS TRAGIC

### Limping on Cane, But Smiling, He Goes to Capitol With Harding.

### THERE HE SIGNS LAST BILLS

### But Fearing to Venture Out on East Portico, He Regretfully Leaves for His New Home.

### HE IS CORDIAL WITH HARDING

### Last Formal Statement Shows Coldness to Lodge—Gets Big Ovation at His Home.

*Special to The New York Times.*

WASHINGTON, March 4.—Dramatic and touchingly pathetic were the circumstances and incidents connected with the departure of Woodrow Wilson from the Presidency into the rôle of private American citizen. During a large part of his incumbency of the White House he had been a towering figure in the affairs of the world. He had gone abroad to fight for the incorporation into the Treaty of Versailles of the project for a League of Nations; he had been received almost as a conquering hero, and, returning, faced a fight for the object dear to his heart, and so shattered his health that there was something tragic about the broken frame of the man who limped from the White House to accompany his successor to the Capitol.

While it had been the sincere desire of Mr. Wilson to participate to the fullest extent as a witness of the swearing in of the new Administration, the closing hours of his own term of office, both in the White House and at the Capitol, had fatigued the President to a point where, at the eleventh hour, he decided to forego the inaugural ceremonies, both within the Senate Chamber and on the eastern portico of the Capitol.

The first of these was scheduled to open on the stroke of noon. Five minutes before that hour the President left the President's Room, in the Senate wing of the Capitol, was escorted to a private elevator by Senator Knox, walked with a limp and a cane slowly to a waiting automobile, and was driven around the city to his new home.

He had accompanied Mr. Harding and the rest of the official inaugural party from the White House to the Capitol, under escort of a squadron of cavalry moving at a quick trot and with flying colors between the lines of people along Pennsylvania Avenue. But when he left the Capitol at noon he was accompanied only by Mrs. Wilson, Secretary Tumulty, Admiral Grayson, secret service men and a valet. There was no cavalry escort and the automobile of the outgoing President was accompanied only by two motorcycle policemen and a party of newspaper men. The route along Pennsylvania Avenue toward the Capitol was retraced, there were flurries of applause, the party passed the White House, and before the ceremonies incidental to the inauguration of Vice President Coolidge had been completed Mr. Wilson was at his residence at 2,340 S Street, Northwest.

**Crowds Cheer Him at New Home.**

There he enjoyed a brief rest and after luncheon he figured in a series of ovations tendered by a throng of several thousand persons who assembled in front of his home when the inauguration ceremonies for his successor had concluded. Delegations representing the Democratic Central Committee of the District of Columbia and the League of Nations Association of Washington marched to the Wilson residence at 3 o'clock and for more than an hour participated in a demonstration in appreciation of his advocacy of the League of Nations. The former President appeared more than a dozen times at the front window and bowed or waved his hand in acknowledgment.

There were demands for a speech, but he waved these aside. He received a delegation of four from the two organizations who presented to him a large basket of flowers, and he told them how profoundly he was touched at these evidences of regard and esteem.

Woodrow Wilson was not by any means the tragic figure as he bowed his salutations to the throngs before his private residence that he was as he limped with the aid of a cane across the White House front portico for the last time as President earlier in the day. Whether it was because he had shaken the heavy burdens of the Presidency from his shoulders or was inspired by the cheering of the crowd, Mr. Wilson appeared to have gained in vigor. During the hour that these demonstrations lasted it was difficult for the President to remain away from the front windows of his new home.

**Grayson Had to Restrain Him.**

Men who had served in his Cabinet and Congressional members of the Democratic party were dropping in upon the ex-President in a steady string as [illegible], but from time to time he appeared at one and then another second-story window with Mrs. Wilson, who

Continued on Page Five.

### *Harding's First Order Opens White House Gates; Visitors to Be Allowed in Part of Mansion Also*

*Special to The New York Times.*

WASHINGTON, March 4.—For the first time since the United States entered the World War, April 6, 1917, the gates to the White House were opened this afternoon, scarcely two hours after President Harding arrived there from the Capitol, and the public was permitted to roam over the grounds of the executive mansion.

The President's order to open the gates, his first in the new office, came without warning. The White House luncheon with Harding relatives was over, Marion friends were leaving, and 200 members of the Hamilton Club of Chicago were filing into the executive offices under appointment to meet the new President. At 4:55 o'clock policemen at the gates were ordered to open them immediately, and crowds poured through all the entrances like water through a broken dam.

The crowds streamed across the lawns from all four sides and some pressed their faces against the White House windows. They were orderly and there was nothing resembling the scenes at the inauguration of Jackson in 1829, when supporters of Jackson broke into the White House, wrecked some of the furniture, and left muddy tracks on the carpets.

From now on the White House grounds will remain open to the public, and it was said unofficially at the executive offices tonight that the practice of admission to the lower floor of the White House by card would be resumed. The Blue, Red, Green and East Rooms will be open to any visitor who obtains a pass.

## COOLIDGE INDUCTED WITH STATELY FORM

### Full Senate Ceremonial Carried Out in the Presence of a Distinguished Crowd.

### HARDING APPLAUDS SPEECH

### Marshall Draws Laugh With Sally in Valedictory at "Legislative Cracked Ice."

*Special to The New York Times.*

WASHINGTON, March 4.—What there was of ceremonial in connection with the inauguration took place within the sympathetic environment of the Senate, a chamber of architectural dignity that lends itself to ceremonial. It was here that Calvin Coolidge was inaugurated as Vice President of the United States in the presence of a notable gathering, including President-elect Harding, whose inauguration was to follow shortly.

The new Vice President was sworn in at 12:21 o'clock. Mr. Marshall, the retiring Vice President, announced that the Senate of the Sixty-sixth Congress was adjourned sine die and handed the gavel of authority to his successor. As Mr. Coolidge took the gavel every one present rose and there was applause.

The new Vice President had been coached in his initial duties. He announced that the chaplain would offer prayer. After the prayer had been delivered Mr. Coolidge began the delivery of his inaugural address. He spoke in a deep, rather low voice, with a metallic ring, and was clearly heard throughout the chamber.

Mr. Coolidge's address was comparatively brief. He declared that the Senate was a "citadel of liberty" in the constitutional structure of the United States, and declared that its record for wisdom had never been surpassed by any legislative body.

The valedictory of Mr. Marshall preceding the speech of his successor was an expression of deep faith in the American form of government and a warning against hasty reforms. His voice rang out clearly and distinctly. Some of his sentiments were applauded, and there was both applause and laughter when he declared that those who represented the old ideals must not be "mere bellboys, subject to calls for legislative cracked ice every time the victims of a debauch of greed, gambling or improvidence feel the fever of frenzied need." Mr. Marshall received an ovation when he concluded.

[The texts of the addresses of Messrs. Coolidge and Marshall are printed elsewhere in this issue.]

Throughout these proceedings Mr. Harding sat easily in a big armchair with his knees crossed. When Vice President Coolidge finished his address Mr. Harding rose, turned out to face the rostrum and joined in the handclapping.

**Distinguished Guests Look On.**

Besides Mr. Harding, those who saw the inauguration of the Vice President included Ambassadors and Ministers of foreign countries, whose gold-braided uniforms gave a touch of color to the proceedings; the black-robed justices of the Federal Supreme Court, the members of the Senate and the House, the members of the outgoing and incoming Cabinets, officers of the army and navy, and many unofficial spectators, including Mrs. Harding, Mrs. Coolidge, and several hundred favored ones, with women in bright and hued gowns predominating, who had the good fortune to obtain cards of admission from Senators and Representatives.

The entire membership of the Wilson Cabinet was there, seated in chairs, on the floor of the chamber, but what is known as "the President's pew," always at the disposal of the President, was empty. Mr. Wilson was still President, and to him the Congressional Committee on Arrangements had left the issuing of cards for this space. Apparently the holders of these cards, if any were issued, had not availed themselves of the opportunity to witness the Senate ceremonies from this position of vantage.

Mrs. Harding sat in "the Vice President's pew," the front row on the op-

Continued on Page Three.

## SENATORS COMMEND NEW FOREIGN POLICY

### Interpret Harding's Address as Repudiation of League of Nations and Like It.

### JOHNSON GREATLY PLEASED

### Other Senators Believe President Means to Ignore Those Who Favor Reservations.

*Special to The New York Times.*

WASHINGTON, March 4.—Senators who heard President Harding's inaugural address took a lively interest in his reference to the foreign policy of the nation. There was great applause, led chiefly by the Senators on the inaugural stand, when the President, raising his voice, exclaimed:

"We do not mean to be entangled. We will accept no responsibility except as our conscience and judgment in each instance dictate."

This sentence and others in the address dealing with the foreign policy were accepted by some Senators as expressive of the desire of President Harding to refuse to accept the League of Nations. The President, in the opinion of these Senators, intends to ignore those members of his party who favored the adoption of the treaty with reservations.

Mr. Harding indicated that his move in international affairs as a means of establishing some plan to prevent wars would be to call the nations of the world into a conference to discuss the situation that grew out of the war, in the hope of arriving at a plan to establish an international court and reach an agreement as to a limitation of armament.

That some association of nations might be formed in which President Harding is willing the United States should enter, and that an international court should be formed, with the United States as a sitting member, were expressed as policies he would support.

"We are ready," said Mr. Harding, "to associate ourselves with the nations of the world, great and small, for conference, for counsel, to seek the expressed views of world opinion, to recommend a way to approximate disarmament and relieve the crushing burdens of military and naval establishments."

**Regarded as Against League.**

That sentence, some of the Senators say, defines a policy as against a league of nations and would seem to suggest that, as the result of the conference Mr. Harding is said to contemplate calling, some association of nations that will take the place of the League of Nations might be formed, with the United States taking the lead.

Accepting the world court to settle international disputes was advocated notably and conspicuously by ex-Secretary of State Root. Mr. Harding favored such a court, expressing his views in these words:

"We elect to participate in suggesting plans for mediation, conciliation and arbitration, and would gladly join in that expressed conscience and progress which seeks to clarify and write the laws of international relationship and establish a world court for the disposition of such justiciable questions as nations are agreed to submit thereto."

But in the very next sentence he seemed to take a decided stand against the League of Nations as negotiated at Versailles by President Wilson, saying:

"In expressing aspirations, in seeking practical plans, in translating humanity's concept of righteousness, justice and its hatred of war into recommended action, we are ready most heartily to unite, but every commitment must be made in the exercise of our national sovereignty."

Those who think they can interpret the President's mind on the international policy are confident, as the result of this speech and the sentiment in the country, that this Administration will evolve an association of nations

Continued on Page Four.

## HARDING FOR WORLD COURT

### Would Confer With Nations But Make No Advance Commitments.

### GIVES PLEDGE TO SOLDIERS

### Calls for a Return to Normal and for Protection of Industries.

### THOUSANDS CHEER WORDS

### Capitol Plaza Throng, a Picture of Color, Easily Hears by Aid of Amplifier.

*Special to The New York Times.*

WASHINGTON, March 4.—Under a brilliant sky and in a keen atmosphere that had more than the ordinary tang in it, Warren G. Harding took the oath of office as twenty-ninth President of the United States at 1:18 o'clock this afternoon, just eight years and eight minutes from the first time that his Democratic predecessor was sworn in.

The new Republican Executive was the sole focus of attention in the severely simple exercises that marked his induction on the east portico of the Capitol. President Wilson, who had accompanied him in an automobile from the White House, had given up his purpose to attend the ceremonies, and departed for his new home after signing a few belated bills, not even staying to see Vice President Coolidge assume his duties in the crowded Senate chamber.

Coming from that event which reached its official climax at 12:21 o'clock, when Mr. Coolidge took the oath, Mr. Harding found a good sized crowd awaiting him in the great plaza facing the little kiosk of Corinthian architecture on the Capitol steps erected to shelter the chief participants in the outdoor ceremony.

**A Colorful Picture.**

Steps and portico had been roped off for distinguished spectators, while flanking the kiosk at a little distance and at about the same level were two small stands to which admission was by ticket.

In front of the kiosk and below it sat the Marine Band, gay in scarlet coats and bright blue trousers, while the steps of the Capitol were guarded by marines, with color guards of regulars and sailors. Filling the middle ground of the scene were the spectators.

The composition and coloring of the picture were in excellent taste, and the good weather, permitting a mitigation of the drabness of Winter apparel in the crowd, furnished the last item necessary to what was pictorially one of the most satisfactory of inaugurations.

It was just before 1 o'clock that forerunners from the press gallery found their way out through the Capitol corridors and into the space allotted to them, and the crowd began to show signs of expectancy as the portico of the Capitol began to fill with distinguished guests.

In front of the stand to the left of the kiosk a group of members of the outgoing Administration gathered, Josephus Daniels and A. Mitchell Palmer conspicuous in the front row. There Andrew W. Mellon, the new Secretary of the Treasury, tall and thin, presently joined them.

Senator Lodge, smiling, stood with them for a moment or two, and then faded back into the mass of men behind them. Into the crowd on the steps came members of the diplomatic corps, shining in gold braid and white plumed hats.

**Cheers for Mrs. Harding.**

Bustling functionaries strove to clear a way down the steps to the kiosk, and army officers, diplomats and pretty girls were pressed into service and held up long white ribbons to keep back the spectators on both sides and open a path.

There was a pause, then the band struck up a lively air and Mrs. Harding, in a long fur coat, black with a broad gray collar, came down the steps escorted by a military aid and followed by other women of the new President's family. The crowd broke into a cheer as she took her stand by the front railing, on the right of the desk which was to hold the Bible used in taking the oath. In the Senate Chamber her mood had been rather serious, but now she was gay and smiling, nodding in response to the cheers of the crowd and swaying slightly in time to the music.

Some members of the new Cabinet were already in place, and now Charles E. Hughes arrived, made his way toward the front of the kiosk and then, taking off his hat, crossed to greet Mrs. Harding before finding a place in the second row. Then came Vice President Calvin Coolidge and ex-Vice President Thomas R. Marshall, who stood by the railing just left of the desk.

Another pause, and then the members of the Supreme Court, black-capped and black-gowned, descended the steps two by two, preceded by the marshal of the court, bearing the old Bible, belonging to St. John's Masonic Lodge of New York, on which George Washington had taken the oath of office as President.

When all had taken places behind the desk there was barely space enough for the last comers—President-elect Harding, escorted by Senator Knox, who

"All the News That's Fit to Print."

# The New York Times.

EXTRA 6 A. M.

THE WEATHER: Fair Today.

VOL. LXXII....No. 23,932. NEW YORK, FRIDAY, AUGUST 3, 1923. TWO CENTS In Greater New York | THREE CENTS Within 200 Miles | FOUR CENTS Elsewhere

# PRESIDENT HARDING DIES SUDDENLY; STROKE OF APOPLEXY AT 7:30 P. M.; CALVIN COOLIDGE IS PRESIDENT

## COOLIDGE TAKES THE OATH OF OFFICE

### His Father, Who Is a Notary Public, Administers It After Form Is Found By Him in His Library.

### ANNOUNCES HE WILL FOLLOW THE HARDING POLICIES

### Wants All Who Aided Harding to Remain in Office—Roused After Midnight to Be Told the News of the President's Death.

### Statement by President Coolidge

*Special to The New York Times.*

PLYMOUTH, Vt., Aug. 3.—*President Calvin Coolidge issued the following statement early this morning:*

Reports have reached me, which I fear are correct, that President Harding is gone. The world has lost a great and good man. I mourn his loss. He was my chief and my friend.

It will be my purpose to carry out the policies which he has begun for the service of the American people and for meeting their responsibilities wherever they may arise.

For this purpose I shall seek the co-operation of all those who have been associated with the President during his term of office.

Those who have given their efforts to assist him I wish to remain in office that they may assist me. I have faith that God will direct the destinies of our nation.

It is my intention to remain here until I can secure the correct form for the oath of office, which will be administered to me by my father, who is a notary public, if that will meet the necessary requirement. I expect to leave for Washington during the day.

CALVIN COOLIDGE.

**Takes the Oath of Office.**

*Special to The New York Times.*

PLYMOUTH, Vt. (Friday), Aug. 3.—Calvin Coolidge took the oath of office as President of the United States at 2:47, Eastern Standard Time, this morning (3:47 New York time). The oath was administered by his father, John C. Coolidge, who found the text in a book in his library, after having expected to wait until it was received from Washington.

The taking of the oath was a simple and solmn scene. Those who gathered in the living room of the Coolidge rome at Plymouth Notch, besides the President and his father, were Mrs. Coolidge, L. L. Lane, President of the Railway Mail Association of New England; Congressman Porter H. Dale, of Vermont; Joseph H. Fountain, editor of the Springfield Reporter, and Erwin C. Geisser, Mr. Coolidge's Assistant Secretary.

As the elder Mr. Coolidge read the oath Mrs. Coolidge looked on with wet eyes. As the end was reached, President Coolidge, raising his right hand, said in a low, clear voice:

"I do, so help me God."

A moment later the group dissolved, and President and Mrs. Coolidge retired.

*Special to The New York Times.*

PLYMOUTH, Vt., Friday, Aug. 3.—Calvin Coolidge received the news of the death of President Harding and of his own elevation to the Presidency at ten minutes before 1 o'clock this morning, Daylight Saving Time.

Mr. Coolidge received the first news of President Harding's death from telegrams signed by George C. Christian, the late President's secretary, and from THE NEW YORK TIMES, whose telegram reached him at the same moment.

These telegrams were brought to the Coolidge home at Plymouth Notch by W. A. Perkins of Bridgewater, who owns the telephone line running from Bridgewater to Plymouth. About five minutes later the newspaper men arrived in Ludlow.

The following telegram was sent to Mrs. Harding:

Plymouth, Vt., Aug. 3, 1923.

Mrs. Warren G. Harding,
San Francisco, Cal.

We offer you our deepest sympathy. May God bless you and keep you.

CALVIN COOLIDGE.
GRACE COOLIDGE.

The following telegrams announcing the death of President Harding

Continued on Page Five.

FROM PHOTO. © BY BARO

CALVIN COOLIDGE
Thirtieth President of the United States by the Death of President Harding.

WARREN GAMALIEL HARDING
Twenty-ninth President of the United States, Who Died Yesterday in San Francisco.

## Public Men Voice Tributes To Harding's Worth and Record

### Hughes Says He Was a Brave and Strong Leader—Marshall Calls Him a Great Human American—Honored as Martyr to His Duty—Sympathy Goes Out to Mrs. Harding.

*Special to The New York Times.*

WASHINGTON, Friday, Aug. 3.—Politics was forgotten in comment by public men in Washington when informed of the death of President Harding. On account of the late hour at which the news was received it was difficult to reach officials.

Secretary Hughes, who came to his office in the State Department at an early hour this morning, was shaken by the news.

"No words can express," he said, "the grief into which we are plunged by this calamity. "The nation has suffered an irreparable loss. A quiet, brave, strong leader has fallen, overborne by the burden he was carrying.

"He was not only an able and faithful public servant but one of nature's noblemen. A true hearted, generous spirit, he has left with the people he loved a rare example of gentleness in high office, and of the most conscientious and unselfish devotion to public duty."

**Marshall Found Him High Minded.**

Thomas R. Marshall, former Vice President of the United States, expressed the deepest sorrow and paid high tribute to the integrity and worth of Mr. Harding.

"The sad intelligence of the President's death has just been communicated to me," said Mr. Marshall. "These are times when all party considerations sink into insignificance. The right kind of a man thinks of the death of his President.

"This has been the death not only of my President but of a man who for many years in the Senate had been my friend of the personal and intimate kind. There is nothing that any man can say, on an occasion like this beyond bearing testimony that aside from political opinions he was a great human American who patriotically and honestly tried to serve his country.

"This is a tribute from a man who did not agree with his political principles, but it is not necessary to agree with his political principles in order to admire the integrity, patriotism and high-mindedness of a man. I think that as the years go by the people will realize that Mr. Harding tried to serve his country well."

**Loss to the World, Says New.**

Postmaster General New was at his home when the news of President Harding's death was flashed to him from San Francisco.

"I am simply overhelmed," he said. "There are times when a man can not express his grief. This is one of them. The passing of President Harding is a loss to the world, the magnitude of which can not be overestimated."

Joseph P. Tumulty said:

"The new is a dreadful shock to me, as it must be to all who knew President Harding well. While at the White House I had many delightful associations with President Harding, who then was a member of the Senate. Like all men who came in contact with the President I knew him as a kindly gentleman and a true friend."

**Says He Had People's Affection.**

Senator Walsh of Massachusetts, Chairman of the Democratic Senatorial Campaign Committee, said:

"The President's death is a terrible shock, coming as it does so soon after it was believed that he was on the way to speedy recovery. His death will be mourned in every corner of the land by every class.

"Few Presidents have had a stronger grip upon the affections of our people. His dignity, simplicity, sincerity and graciousness won the hearts of all. His personality, however, did not alone account for his popularity. He has won a place in our history among the most worthy of those who have occupied the Presidency.

"His views were statesmanlike and the honor of our nation was safe and secure in his hands. The nation has lost a noble man, and a sound and safe leader."

**Roosevelt Tells of Sacrifice.**

Colonel Theodore Roosevelt, Acting Secretary of the Navy in the absence of Secretary Denby, said:

"Words cannot express my grief at the death of my chief, President Harding. It is idle to say that his death is a calamity for the United States, for every one knows it. He gave his life to the service of our country as truly as any one in our history."

Representative Stephen G. Porter of Pennsylvania, Chairman of the House Foreign Affairs Committee, a personal admirer as well as a friend of Mr. Harding said:

"I am simply overwhelmed. I hardly know what to say. He was so gentle, so kind, his every act was in the public interest. It is a terrible shock. I really can't understand it."

Mr. Porter returned recently from Europe, where he represented this country at teh sessions of the commission of the League of Nations on the opium traffic. He was selected for the work by the President.

Senator Curtis of Kansas, Republican whip of the Senate, said:

"The entire world will be shocked at the death of President Harding. His passing at this time was very unfortunate. The extent of his loss cannot be expressed in words. The entire country

Continued on Page Four.

## President's Death Shocks Capital, Which Had Expected Recovery

### News Telephoned to Executive Clerk From San Francisco—Effort Made to Reach Coolidge in Vermont—Only Two Members of Cabinet in Washington.

*Special to The New York Times.*

WASHINGTON, Friday, Aug. 3.—News of the death of President Harding not only greatly shocked official and Washington but took the capital completely by surprise.

It was the sixth time in the history of the nation that the city had been brought face to face with the death of a President, but the shocking word was received under circumstances wholly different from those surrounding the death of any former President.

The only high officials of the Harding Administration in Washington are Secretary of State Hughes and Postmaster General New. All the other members of the Cabinet are out of the city, and two of them, Secretaries Mellon and Davis, are in Europe, while most of the others, with the exception of Secretaries Weeks and Denby, are in the Far West.

Calvin Coolidge, until last night Vice President, and who will immediately be sworn in as the next President of the United Sates, is likewise absent from Washington, but it has occurred several times in American annals that Vice Presidents have been absent from the capital on occasions of deaths of former Presidents.

When last heard from, Mr. Coolidge was at Plymouth, Vt. A message was sent direct from San Francisco notifying him of the death of Mr. Harding. From the Presidential party in San Francisco communications, the White House was advised late tonight, were sent direct to all other members of the Cabinet not now in San Francisco and to personal friends of the President.

Rudolph Forster, Executive Clerk at the White House, was communicated with direct from San Francisco shortly before midnight by long distance telephone. He talked with Mr. Smithers, the ranking member of the White House executive force in San Francisco in the absence of Mr. Christian who had gone to Los Angeles. Mr. Smithers confirmed the death of the President and informed Mr. Forster that messages were being sent to the Vice President and other Cabinet members.

Mr. Hughes is the ranking member of the Administration now in Washington, so that he will take such steps as are necessary in the present situation.

It will also be the duty of the Secretary of State to notify the members of the Diplomatic Corps, who will in turn officially cable their Governments that Mr. Harding is dead.

No plans have or can be made immediately for the swearing in of Mr. Coolidge as President. It is not necessary for him to take the oath from a member of the United States Supreme Court. Another Judge or other officer qualified to administer an oath can act in that capacity. Even a Justice of the Peace back in Vermont, where Mr. Coolidge was last known to be located, can administer the oath.

The first knowledge the White House had of the President's death came from the Rev. Dr. Freeman Anderson, assistant pastor of the Calvary Baptist Church, which President Harding attended. He telephoned to the Executive Mansion and the message was received by E. C. Goss, one of the White House police force, who was one of the few men on duty at that time of the night, as the President had been away since June 20.

In turn Patrolman Goss telephoned to Mr. Forster, who at once summoned the entire White House force. One of the first to arrive was Isaac Hoover for years chief usher at the mansion, and who has known many Presidents intimately, and Joseph Murphy, assistant chief of the Secret Service.

Pedestrians who passed the White House after the news of the President's death noticed that the iron gates on Pennsylvania Avenue were shut and locked, something which has been unknown since the advent of the Harding regime. It was explained, however, that the gates have been shut every night at 8 o'clock since the extensive repairs to the house and grounds have been going on.

Mr. Hoover, who has charge of the renovation of the White House, said at midnight that the mansion could be put in order in two days. In fact, preparations had been made to do this ever since the first news of the President's illness was received in Washington. At any time that notification was sent here that the President was to leave San Francisco the house could have been put in readiness for his reception. Workmen will begin at once this morning arranging the furniture and placing the draperies as usual.

**Dancing Stops at the Hotels.**

At the big hotels dancing was immediately stopped and a hush and gloom settled over the crowds who slowly began to leave. Extras were on the streets fairly early and residents ran out from their homes to call newsboys, and automobilists stopped their machines to buy the ink-wet sheets. Newsboys were crying extras in Executive Avenue and Pennsylvania Avenue, the two streets bounding the White House on the west and north at midnight, their cries coming clearly into the Executive Offices.

When the news was communicated to William H. Beck, private secretary to the Secretary of State, at midnight, he started by automobile for the State Department and sent word to Mr. Hughes's [illegible]

[illegible] on Page Six.

## DEATH STROKE CAME WITHOUT WARNING

### Mrs. Harding Was Reading to Her Husband When First Sign Appeared —She Ran for Doctor

### BUT NOTHING COULD BE DONE TO REVIVE PATIENT

### News of Tragic End Shocks Everybody, Coming After Day Said to Have Been the Best Since His Illness Began a Week Ago.

*Special to The New York Times.*

SAN FRANCISCO, Aug. 2.—President Harding died at 7:30 o'clock tonight [11:30 o'clock New York time] of a stroke of apoplexy.

The end came suddenly while Mrs. Harding was reading to him from the evening newspaper, and after what had been called the best day he had had since the beginning of his illness exactly one week ago.

A shudder ran through the President's frame and he collapsed.

Mrs. Harding and the two nurses in the sick room knew the end had come, and Mrs. Harding rushed out of the room and asked for Dr. Boone and the others to "come quick."

Dr. Boone and Brig. Gen. Sawyer reached the President before he passed away, but were not able to avert the inevitable.

This formal announcement following soon after told the story of the tragic end:

"The President died at 7:30 P. M. Mrs. Harding and the two nurses, Miss Ruth Powderly and Miss Sue Drusser, were in the room at the time. Mrs. Harding was reading to the President, when, utterly without warning, a slight shudder passed through his frame; he collapsed, and all recognized that the end had come. A stroke of apoplexy was the cause of his death.

"Within a few moments all of the President's official party had been summoned."

**Shocking in Its Suddenness.**

Nothing could have been a more shocking surprise. Shortly before the President's sudden collapse General Sawyer had been telling newspaper men that Mr. Harding had had the best day since he became seriously ill. He said that the President had definitely entered upon the stage of convalescence and that everything went to show that Mr. Harding was on the road to ultimate recovery.

The members of the official party had no warning that the President was in danger. They, like the newspaper men, had been assured that a fatal termination of the President's illness was a thing not likely and with good care he would be able to recover health and strength. Most of the members of the official party were at dinner when the news came. George B. Christian Jr., secretary to the President and his devoted friend, was in Los Angeles with Mrs. Christian. He had gone there at the President's solicitation to read at a gathering of the Knights Templar tonight an address which the President had prepared in the expectation that he would deliver it in person. Mr. Christian had declined to leave San Francisco until he was positively assured by the President's physicians that there was no likelihood of any set-back in the President's condition.

The newspaper men had an engagement with General Sawyer for 8 o'clock. He was to tell them of how the President was progressing toward recovery. In view of what he had said on prior occasions during the day and statements in two official bulletins, the newspaper men had every expectation that they would be able to record that Mr. Harding was one step nearer the goal of recovery.

"There will be a bulletin," said one of the White House messengers gathered in the corridor of the Presidential suite. In a few minutes copies of the bulletin on thin white paper were handed to the waiting reporters. Instead of informing them that the President's condition continued to improve, it gave them the astounding information that he was dead.

**Mrs. Harding Is Brave to the End.**

First reports that Mrs. Harding had collapsed were denied. The official version indicates that she was calm throughout her husband's last illness. She has been extremely courageous and by her manner and words helped him when he was suffering intensely and was apprehensive of a fatal termination. The official account says:

"Mrs. Harding, who from the beginning of the President's illness had expressed confidence in his recovery, did not break down. On the other hand, she continued, as from the beginning, the bravest member of the group.

"When it was realized that the President had actually passed away, she turned to those in the room, whose concern had turned to her, and said, 'I am not going to break down.'"

Mrs. Harding was seated by the bedside when at 7:10 o'clock the President suddenly collapsed. His breathing, which had been quick ever since the illness overtook him, suddenly became spasmodic. Mrs. Harding, leaving the two nurses to take whatever steps they could in the emergency, ran to the door of the Presidential suite.

"Dr. Boone!" she called, as she ran part way into the almost deserted corridor. A Secret Service operative was seated about twenty feet down the hall. She hurriedly told the Secret Service man that the President had had a sudden and severe relapse and begged the detective to try to locate Dr. Boone or any of the other physicians.

The Secret Service man took up the search for the physicians, while

CALVIN COOLIDGE

"All the News That's Fit to Print."

# The New York Times.

THE WEATHER
Mostly cloudy today; tomorrow, probably showers; east winds.
Temperature yesterday: Max., 57; Min., 41.
For weather report see next to last page.

VOL. LXXIII....No. 24,189. ***** NEW YORK, WEDNESDAY, APRIL 16, 1924. TWO CENTS Greater New York | THREE CENTS Within 200 Miles | FOUR CENTS Elsewhere

## BAN ON JAPANESE ADOPTED BY SENATE WITHOUT ROLL-CALL

**Action Would End Possibility of 'Gentlemen's Agreement' Continuing in Force.**

**HINTS OF VETO ARE HEARD**

**Lodge Sees Coolidge, Who Seems to Face Likelihood of Trade and Political Backfire.**

**MATSUI APPEALS TO PRESS**

**Foreign Minister Asserts That Action Hurts Japan and Does America No Good.**

*Special to The New York Times.*

WASHINGTON, April 15.—Total exclusion of Japanese from admission to the United States, except the professional classes which are specifically exempt, was voted by the Senate late today without a rollcall or any debate.

This was the sequence to yesterday's action when, with only two opposing, the "gentlemen's agreement" was abrogated. The language adopted today coincides with that previously written into the immigration measure by the House and precludes the possibility of exclusion being an issue between the two houses when the bill goes to the Conference Committee.

The text of the exclusion amendment as adopted is as follows:

(C) No alien ineligible to citizenship shall be admitted to the United States unless such alien

1. Is admissible as a non-immigrant under the provision of Section 3; or

2. Unless such alien is an immigrant who continually for at least two years immediately preceding the time of his application for admission to the United States has been and who seeks to enter the United States solely for the purpose of carrying on the vocation of minister of a religious denomination or professor of a college, academy, seminary or university or

3. Unless such alien is an immigrant who is a bona fide student over 18 years of age and who seeks to enter the United States solely for the purpose of studying at an accredited school, college, academy, seminary or university particularly designated by him and approved by the Secretary of Labor; or

4. Unless such alien is the wife or the unmarried child under 18 years of age of an immigrant admissible under Sub-division 2 of this paragraph and is accompanied or following to join him.

Attention is now focused on the fate of the immigration bill when it reaches President Coolidge for his signature, as it is sure to do in a short time. Senator Lodge called on the President today and informed him of the situation in the Senate. Mr. Coolidge was advised that the bill will pass in a day or two by an overwhelming vote. The President learned also the probable fate of a veto message in the face of the heavy major[illegible] expected in the Senate and the four[illegible] vote by which the measure passed [illegible] House.

**Coolidge Faces Complications.**

Several complications have arisen to trouble the President.

Secretary Hughes, it is presumed, will advise the Executive veto if he follows the tenor of his recent letter to Chairman Albert Johnson of the House Committee on Immigration and Naturalization, in which he protested against any language in the immigration bill that would violate the "gentlemen's agreement."

The possible effects of the exclusion on trade in the Orient, the likelihood of reprisals, the recent efforts of this country to develop its business opportunities across the Pacific, all will have to be weighed by the President.

Politically, the consequences of a veto may be of vital importance, especially as to the effect it would have on the votes of those States along the Pacific Coast, which have always demanded Asiatic exclusion.

President Coolidge does not intend to discuss for the present the situation that has arisen in Congress. A White House spokesman declined today to indicate whether the President would exercise the veto or not.

**Hanihara Acted Under Orders.**

Official denials were given to reports [illegible] Mr. Hanihara had acted without [illegible]ions from his Government in [illegible] his strong letter of protest to [illegible]y of State Hughes. It was [illegible]od that the principal arguments [illegible] message were transmitted from [illegible] office. It was believed that [illegible] Government would stand squarely [illegible] Mr. Hanihara. Press reports, it [illegible]d, have indicated popular ap[illegible] of his stand.

[illegible] there was a conference at the [illegible] between Senators Reed of Penn[illegible] and Shortridge of California [illegible]presentative Albert Johnson of [illegible]ton, State Chairman of the [illegible] Immigration Committee. The [illegible] in the Senate was agreed upon [illegible] decision to present the amend[illegible], which had been introduced by [illegible] Shortridge, modified to conform [illegible] House text.

[illegible]nihara will confer tomorrow [illegible]etary Hughes on the subject. [illegible] of town today.

[illegible] nearly 5 o'clock when Senator [illegible], [illegible]owing his promise yesterday [illegible] an amendment that will "defi[illegible] and effectively" exclude the [illegible], arose and had the proposal [illegible] explained briefly that it had [illegible] been made known to the Senate in yesterday's debate and that it would perfect the action taken on the "gentlemen's agreement." The question was

Continued on Page Three.



### *Fulton's Famous Ice King Succumbs to Venerable Age*

The steamboat Norwich, said to have been designed by Robert Fulton and once known as The Ice King, has been dismantled. Its historic bell has been presented by its owner, the Cornell Steamboat Company, to the Senate House at Kingston, the meeting place of the first assembly held in New York State.

For the last five years the Norwich has been idle, almost too obsolete for service. Before that, when the Erie Railroad ran into Piermont, the Norwich made many trips through the Hudson ice floes. When it quit the service it was the oldest ship on the Hudson.

## WANT PARCEL POST TO PAY SALARY RISE

**Congress Committees Agree on Increase to Postal Employes and Seek the Means.**

**NEW FEARS COMPETITION**

**Postmaster General Says Other Carriers Would Get Business—Urges Other Rate Changes.**

*Special to The New York Times.*

WASHINGTON, April 15.—A substantial increase in the rates in parcel post mail to provide means to advance salaries of postal clerks and carriers is under serious consideration by the two Post Office Committees in Congress.

Postmaster General New has notified Congress that if this additional charge on the postal service is authorized it will have to be met either by direct drafts on the Treasury or by increases in postal rates. He is opposed to the increase bills now under discussion and has recommended a salary readjustment that would add $43,000,000 to the payroll instead of $150,000,000 as provided in the Paige bill and the Edge-Kelly bill now pending.

"The Postmaster General has outlined a plan under which this $43,000,000 may be raised without enlarging the postal deficit. It provides for increases in the parcel post rates, increase in the fees for registering and insuring mails. It also provides with respect to second class matter "for increasing the rates on advertising matter in the first, second, third and fourth zones; in the first and second zones one and one-half cents per pound, in the third zone one and one-quarter cents per pound, and in the fourth zone one-fourth cent per pound."

**Pay Increase Means Rate Rise.**

To date the House committee has given little attention to increase in postal rates, other than those relating to parcel post. Department officials as well as leaders in Congress are agreed that salaries should be advanced to figures more in keeping with the increased cost of living, but they are not in accord as to the method of providing the money.

Congress leaders are disposed to get the needed funds by increasing the rates on parcel post, whereas the Postmaster General would make a general increase in rates on all mail matter except letter mail. He has warned Congress that the rates on parcel post deliveries proposed by the Paige bill, which had been given a position of priority in committee, would divert a large part of this traffic to other transportation agencies and might result in a loss instead of an increase in revenues.

At a meeting of the House Committee on Post Offices to be held at an early date further consideration will be given the salary increase bills as well as the recommendation of the Postmaster General for rate increases. Rate increases of some kind, it is indicated, will be authorized in the event that Congress provides for a general advance in salaries.

The section of the Paige bill dealing with parcel post, increases the pound rate from 5 cents to 10 cents for local deliveries. It increases the pound rate in the eight zones, which now range

Continued on Page Five.

## FRANCE AND BRITAIN APPROVE IN FULL THE DAWES REPORT

**Germany's Acceptance of It as Basis of Discussion Is on Way to Paris.**

**POINCARE EXTOLS SCHEME**

**Intimates France Will Make Concessions Necessary to Effect Reparation Settlement.**

**NATION BACKS MACDONALD**

**He Tells Commons German Debt Total Can Be Fixed When Experts' Plan Is in Operation.**

By EDWIN L. JAMES.

Copyright, 1924, by The New York Times Company.
Special Cable to THE NEW YORK TIMES.

PARIS, April 15.—Four events in Europe today taken together make it reasonably certain that the Dawes plan for reparations will have an honest trial. These events in the order of their importance are as follows:

First, a declaration by Premier Poincaré tonight in a speech which sounded the campaign keynote of the French Nationalists that France expected the Dawes plan to be put in operation and was ready to make the necessary concessions.

Second, an announcement by Prime Minister MacDonald that London had notified Paris and Washington of its willingness to accept the experts' report as an "indivisible whole."

Third, authoritative reports from Berlin that the Government is ready to accept the Dawes plan as the basis of a reparations arrangement, which is taken as an official declaration of the end of the German policy of resistance to the reparation clauses of the Treaty of Versailles.

Fourth, the renewal of the accords between the Allied Control Mission and the Ruhr [illegible] for a period of two months to give [illegible] necessary to the inauguration of the plan which bears the name of an American who fought in France.

**Champions the Dawes Plan.**

It was expected that Premier Poincaré in his speech at a dinner of the Democratic Social Republican Party at Luna Park tonight would deal almost exclusively with questions of domestic politics. Instead he devoted more than half his speech to the reparations problem. The Premier, who was expected by the experts to make haste very slowly and put forward many conditions, appeared as the valiant champion of the Dawes plan, defending it against criticism and proclaiming its virtues. It suited him from the ground up. In it he saw justification of his Ruhr policy, of his thesis that Germany could pay and of his contention that now is not the time to fix what Germany can pay two decades hence. He saw also an opportunity to carry out his policy of linking reparations to interallied debts, which is to say to lay upon Germany not only the burden of French reconstruction but the load France must pay England and America.

Drawing in vivid colors a picture of a France most glorious in peace, shedding in years of tranquility a glory over the world superior to the brilliance of her military feats, he proclaimed that the Republic sought no conquest but only its due. If France pursued a policy of firmness that policy was strictly limited by justice, he said, and added: "I have read in the German newspapers and even in some French newspapers that the reports of the experts were a condemnation of our foreign policy and especially of occupation of the Ruhr. On the contrary, those reports are the most brilliant justification of the votes of the French Parliament. They prove that in despite of all her denials Germany put herself into fraudulent bankruptcy and that she is able to pay." Turning to the details of the

Continued on Page Seven.

### *Kills His Wife, Flees, Shoots Himself; Fellows Found Dying in Auto in Woods*

*Special to The New York Times.*

SOMERVILLE, N. J., April 15.—Andrew Fellows, 23 years old, left two friends in an automobile tonight in front of the home of his mother-in-law in Fairview Avenue, cornered his wife, from whom he had been separated, in one of the upper rooms and shot and killed her. Then he ran back to the automobile with the pistol in his hand and drove off.

Captain Carter, who was in the headquarters of the State Police here, was notified of the murder a few minutes later over the telephone. He obtained a description of the car in which the slayer and his friends disappeared and sent out a general alarm to the police of the surrounding communities.

Troopers Cibulla, Daly and Haussling hurried to the house on motorcycles. They got a more detailed description of Fellows and the car and went in quest of him. They also enlisted the aid of motorists on the State road leading out of Somerville in the direction of Bound Brook. One motorist told of seeing a car answering the description turning into an unfrequented dirt road about a mile from here in the direction of Bound Brook. The troopers sped through the road, and about three hundred yards from the main highway came across the car. Fellows was alone, bending over the steering wheel with a bullet in his head. He was hurried to the Somerville Hospital, where the surgeons said that he would die.

Meantime Captain Carter had questioned the mother of the slain woman. She said that Fellows was a native of Oneida, N. Y., and that the couple were married about three years ago. They could not agree from the start and separated several times, the last time about a month ago. Mrs. Fellows then returned to her mother's home, and said that she would not try another reconciliation.

Tonight Mrs. Fellows was in her room on the top floor and her mother was seated at a window in the parlor of the house when Fellows drove up in a motor car with two other men. He gained entrance to the house before his mother-in-law could bar him and ran up the stairs to his wife's room. In a few minutes the mother-in-law heard angry words coming from the room and her daughter order Fellows to leave. There was a pause and then two shots.

Fellows came bounding down the stairs three at a time. His mother-in-law followed him to the door and saw him jump into the automobile and drive off. Then she ran to her daughter's room and found that Mrs. Fellows, shot through the head and body, had been instantly killed.

Captain Carter ordered State troopers to arrest the two men who accompanied Fellows to the house, and who are believed to have made their escape before Fellows shot himself.



### *Senate Rejects Knight As Counsel in Oil Suit*

WASHINGTON, April 15.—After weeks of delay the Senate today rejected the nomination of Samuel Knight of San Francisco to be special Government counsel in litigation looking to the recovery of Sections 16 and 36 within the confines of California Naval Reserve No. 2.

Action was in executive session, but it was reported that the vote was 39 to 26 to uphold the adverse recommendation made on the nomination by the oil committee, which disclosed the circumstances that caused Congress to direct President Coolidge to employ special counsel to prosecute suits for the recovery of the oil land.

Senator Walsh of Montana, the committee prosecutor, led the fight against Mr. Knight on the ground that he had acted as counsel for the Equitable Trust Company, in which the Rockefellers were large stockholders. Section 36 is operated by the Standard Oil Company of California.

## CHARGES FUND GIFTS FOR LIQUOR PERMITS

**C. H. Kerns Tells Daugherty Inquiry of $50,000 in Ohio and $40,000 in Kentucky.**

**MANNINGTON IS DEFIANT**

**He Refuses to Appear to Testify, Declaring the Committee Unfair and Incompetent.**

*Special to The New York Times.*

WASHINGTON, April 15.—A sensational story of alleged liquor operations in Ohio and Kentucky, with alleged contributions of $50,000 and $40,000 to Republican campaign funds in 1920 in return for promises of withdrawal permits, was told today to the special Senate committee investigating ex-Attorney General Daugherty by Cecil H. Kerns, who was sentenced to the Atlanta Penitentiary for two years for his part in wholesale violations of the liquor laws and released recently on parole. He said that withdrawal permits had been on sale in Ohio at the rate of $17 a case, or $2 more than the price which other witnesses have testified were paid in New York State.

Howard Mannington, one-time occupant of the "little green house on K Street," and the late Jess Smith were named by the witness as the men who managed affairs in Washington for the bootleg ring, and he said that Samuel Ungerleider and "Abe" Ungerleider, members of the brokerage firm of Ungerleider & Co. of Cleveland; former Representative Ralph Cole and William Halley were the most conspicuous figures in the ring in Ohio.

"Abe" Ungerleider, according to Mr. Kerns, said that he had contributed $50,000 to the Republican campaign fund in 1920 in return for liquor deals. The witness also said that two men, whom he named, had told of contributing $40,000 to the Republican State campaign fund in Kentucky to obtain similar privileges there, and had "looted" one distillery.

**Says Russell Issued Permits.**

Permits in Ohio, the witness said, were obtained from Prohibition Director Russell and the liquor flowed freely. A man named Remus, in Cincinnati, was known as "one of the bootleg kings," Mr. Kerns added, and was reputed to have made $6,000,000 and paid heavily for protection. Remus, said the witness, is now serving a sentence at the Atlanta Penitentiary, because his operations became so bold as to force prosecution. Remus, he said, went to the penitentiary because he was a fool, and he added that there were more men in the penitentiary because they were fools than because they were knaves.

Mr. Kerns said that he was notified that he must return to the penitentiary at Atlanta after it became known that he intended to appear as a witness before the Senate committee.

The names of C. Bascom Slemp, secretary to President Coolidge, and Walter F. Brown, a prominent Ohio political leader, who was named as Chairman of the joint committee on reorganization of the administrative branch of the Government by President Harding, were brought into the inquiry by Mr. Kerns during a discussion of efforts which had been made to obtain pardons.

The witness said he had heard Mr. Slemp's name mentioned at the prison in connection with a pardon for which an attorney was supposed to get a retainer of $25,000. The pardon, he said, was to be obtained because of the influence of Mr. Slemp. He admitted, however, that he had no knowledge that Mr. Slemp had received any money or participated in such a deal.

Mr. Brown was reported at the prison, Mr. Kerns said, to have been instrumental in obtaining a pardon for a negro physician of Ohio convicted for violating the narotic laws.

Howard Mannington refused today to testify or even to appear in the committee room. Mr. Mannington's name was called and his attorney, a Mr. Whiteford, appeared and said that he was prepared to make a statement.

"Well, we subpoenaed Mannington, not you," exclaimed Chairman Brookhart. "We want Mannington."

"Well, then you will have to get him under a process by which you have a right to get him, if at all, sir," retorted the attorney.

"All right; we will get him," said the Chairman.

**Tosses Statement on Table.**

Mr. Whiteford then tossed a copy of a statement and a letter from Mr. Mannington on the table, exclaiming:

"If you don't want it, you don't need to take it."

That ended the incident.

Senator Brookhart was not certain as to just what action would be taken against Mr. Mannington.

In his letter to Senator Brookhart Mr. Mannington said that when he was advised in Paris that the committee desired to examine him he returned with the purpose "of aiding in your work,

Continued on Page Eight.



## COOLIDGE'S MESSAGE OF REBUKE ASSAILED IN SENATE BY GLASS

**Virginia Democrat Says Senators Should Resent 'Amazing Imputations' of Executive.**

**MELLON ALSO ATTACKED**

**Reed of Pennsylvania Defends Coolidge—Calls Country 'Fed Up' on Investigations.**

**PRESIDENT WILL FIGHT ON**

**Callers at White House Hear Him Explain Andrew Jackson's Precedent for Stand.**

*Special to The New York Times.*

WASHINGTON, April 15.—While President Coolidge was studying today the record of Andrew Jackson in fighting what he regarded as a legislative encroachment on the powers of the executive, Senator Carter Glass of Virginia attacked the President in the Senate for his letter on the conduct of the investigations.

Senator Reed of Pennsylvania spoke in defense of the President.

Senator Glass, while upholding the integrity of Secretary Mellon of the Treasury Department, severely criticized him for his communication, as well as Mr. Coolidge for an "amazing imputation" upon the Senate.

Mr. Glass held that the President's protest against what he had construed as an effort to discredit Secretary Mellon implied some uneasiness that the prohibition unit of the Treasury Department would undergo an inquiry.

Unlike previous occasions when Mr. Coolidge and his Administration have been under fire, all of the regular Republican Senators did not sit silent and let the Democratic strictures on the President go unchallenged. Part was taken in the debate also by Senator Brookhart of the Radical Republicans.

While this was going on in the Senate, the President told Senatorial callers at the White House that he would resist any further investigations of executive departments which are proposed for political effect.

The Virginian Senator drew a distinction between what he termed "a dignified, unyielding assertion of constitutional prerogative," and Mr. Coolidge's course in leveling at the Senate "accusations which gravely impeach its honor, in justification of which indictments, he does not, as I am sure he can not, offer any proof from the record."

In responding to Senator Glass, Senator Reed insisted that President Coolidge had the support of the whole country in his protest against the trend of the investigation into Secretary Mellon's conduct of the Treasury Department.

"I have just this to say," Senator Reed asserted, "that in saying what he did the President is speaking the best thought of the country. It will not be admitted here in this chamber, our friends on the other side of the chamber will not admit it, but you will know it and you know it already from your mail and your correspondence that what the President said has the support of the whole country; that what he said met with the approval of the whole country; that the country is sick and tired of these investigations which you have been making."

Senator Reed said that certain of the investigations were proper, referring particularly to that into the Veterans' Bureau.

"The Senator from Montana did a fine piece of work in what he unearthed in the Interior Department and disclosures that he secured there in showing dishonesty on the part of Mr. Fall," Senator Reed added. "But since that was done there has not been one single thing that was useful brought out by all these investigations, and the country knows it."

**Senator Glass Criticizes Coolidge.**

On beginning his address Senator Glass acknowledged President Coolidge's right to resent Senate encroachment on the Executive's prerogatives, and paid a tribute to Mr. Mellon's ability and honesty. Then he contrasted the rights which the President possessed with the language in which the President had reproved the Senate.

"Until now, sir," Senator Glass said, "when has any Executive of the nation, in a mood of uncontrolled irritation, abruptly faced the Senate of the United States with the official charge of having instituted a Government of lawlessness?

"Until now, when has it happened, if ever before, that the President of the

Continued on Page Three.

## STATE DEMOCRATS PUT SMITH IN THE RACE FOR PRESIDENCY AND GIVE HIM OVATION; HUGHES SAYS PEOPLE WILL KEEP COOLIDGE

**GIVES REPUBLICAN KEYNOTE**

**Hughes Declares Every Guilty Person Will Be Punished.**

**CROOKS IN EVERY PARTY**

**"Let Not Partisan Pecksniffs" Assume a "Holier Than Thou" Attitude.**

**SCANDAL MONGERS SCORED**

**State Convention in Town Hall Cheers Eulogy of National Administration.**

Condemning talehearers and scandal-mongers, but at the same time stressing the declaration that the Republican Administration in Washington would neither condone wrong nor extenuate crime, Secretary of State Charles E. Hughes, as temporary Chairman of the Republican State Convention, at Town Hall last night, sounded the Administration's own keynote for the coming political campaign. He emphasized what he termed the record of Republican achievement, asserting that the President is his own platform and that "the best assurance of the future is in the character of Calvin Coolidge."

Secretary Hughes was warmly welcomed. Every mention of President Coolidge's name was applauded, and at the end of the Secretary's speech the cheering and handclapping was long sustained. Aside from the speech the convention was of so thoroughly a cut-and-dried character that the delegates laughed at the efficiency of their own machinery, and even Mr. Hughes smiled broadly. The Secretary's speech lasted for sixty-five minutes; the convention proceedings after he had concluded lasted just thirteen minutes.

**Senator Swift Permanent Chairman.**

This morning, at 10 o'clock, also in the Town Hall, the second and concluding session will begin with the report of the committee on permanent organization, which will propose State Senator Parton Swift of Buffalo for permanent Chairman of the convention. Mr. Swift will be elected and will then speak on the achievements of the Republican Party in the State, Secretary Hughes having devoted his address to the work of the National Administration. Following Mr. Swift's address, a platform will be adopted and delegates and alternates at large from this State to the National Convention at Cleveland in June will be chosen. Some minor formalities will be gone through, and then the convention will adjourn.

The Town Hall was crowded to its capacity of 1,600, and there were scores on the sidewalks who had no tickets and could not get in, and dozens on the platform who came a little late and could not get chairs. The meeting was called to order by State Chairman George K. Morris, who had been re-elected to that position in the afternoon at the meeting of the State Committee. Then a prayer was said by the Rev. De Witt C. Pelton of St. James's Episcopal Church in the Bronx, and the call for the convention was read by Secretary Lafayette B. Gleason of the State Committee. The delegates and alternates and the fortunate part of the public were still oozing into the hall.

Mr Morris announced that the State Committee recommended, for the place of Temporary Chairman of the Convention, Secretary of State Hughes, and there was an immediate burst of applause. It was then nearly 8:30 o'clock. Mr. Morris ordered the roll-call on the selection of Mr. Hughes which is required by law. Mr. Gleason was mindful, however, of the time and he told the convention with a laugh:

"Inasmuch as the radio is to start at 8:30 exactly, we'll have to have a ragged roll-call."

**Hughes Escorted to the Chair.**

The delegates had hardly finished laughing before Mr. Gleason was more than half way through his ragged roll-call. He had finished, Ogden Mills and Nicholas Murray Butler had been ap-

Continued on Page Six.

### *Back Smith's Nomination For Presidency at 1 to 4*

The launching of the Smith boom for President at the New York State Democratic Convention at Albany has brought considerable money to Wall Street to be bet on the proposition that Alfred E. Smith not only will be the nominee of his party but will be elected. J. S. Fried & Co., 20 Broad Street, announced yesterday that they had received $1,000 to be placed against $4,000 that Smith will be the Democratic Presidential nominee, and $1,000 to lay against $8,000 that he will be elected.

Odds of 5 to 1 are offered by the betting commissioners that President Coolidge will be nominated to succeed himself, and of 7 to 5 that he will be the next President. A few scattered bets have been made at 1 to 8, according to Fried & Co., that President Coolidge will not be named as the choice of the Cleveland Convention. Fried & Co. announce that they have $5,000 to place against $20,000, or on the basis of 1 to 4, that the next President will be a Democrat.

## DEMOCRATS KEEP MADISON SQ. GARDEN

**Committee Decides Against Proposed Move to a Bronx Armory With More Seats.**

**GREAT CLAMOR FOR TICKETS**

**Convention Here Brings an Overwhelming Demand—Many to Be Disap[illegible]**

Members of the Democratic National Committee definitely decided late yesterday afternoon that the National Convention of the party would be held in Madison Square Garden, as originally planned, and not in the 258th Field Artillery Armory, in the Bronx, as had been suggested by some members in order to seat more spectators.

This decision was reached after members of the committee had visited the Bronx Armory, which is [illegible] forty minutes by subway from the hotel and theatre district, and it was said the subject would not even be discussed by a subcommittee on arrangements which meets at the Waldorf on April 23.

An unprecedented demand for seats, once it had been decided to hold the convention in New York, led committee members, with George Mara, who is in charge of the preliminary preparations, and Henry Ives Cobb, an architect who has been trying to replan the Garden seating, to consider the Bronx armory seriously for a while.

There are to be about 1,000 delegates to the convention, a like number of alternates, just about as many press representatives and a few hundred additional officials and employes. And the general public has shown such deep interest that pleas for admission have mounted almost beyond belief.

**Can't Make Garden Big Enough.**

The normal seating capacity of Madison Square Garden is 13,000. It had been hoped to increase this to 18,000. It was found, however, that there was no possibility of adding 5,000 seats under plans which would pass the city's Building Department. It was pointed out, unofficially, it is understood, that the department would not approve plans which contemplated hanging a great amount of extra weight on the walls of the old structure. If plans could be devised by which the additional seating capacity could be supported from the foundation, all might be well. This has not been found possible, inasmuch as the very nature of a convention requires a great open space where the delegates are seated.

Plans have been devised whereby the seating capacity can be increased to between 14,000 and 15,000. This is greater than that of any national convention hall in recent years. The hall in San Francisco seated 11,200 persons. The Coliseum, in Chicago, where the Republicans held conventions for many years, seats 13,000 people and the hall to be used for the forthcoming Republican Convention in Cleveland will seat 13,161 people.

Even with the proposed increase in the Garden's capacity it is already evident that thousands who want to attend the sessions must be disappointed. Many members of the National Committee report that they have been literally swamped with requests from people whom they do not feel that they can ignore. One of the committeemen who has had this experience is Norman E. Mack of this State. There is, too, the fact that the New York National Convention Committee, which brought the convention to this city, committed itself for a large sum, a considerable portion of which was to be raised through the distribution of tickets to the convention on the basis of one ticket for every contribution of $100 to the fund.

**Rejected Hall Seats 30,000.**

When a subcommittee of the Committee on Arrangements met last Tuesday one of those present mentioned the Bronx armory and said he understood it would seat 30,000 people, which is approximately correct. As a consequence J. Bruce Kramer, Vice Chairman of the National Committee; Homer S. Cummings, former National Committee

Continued on Page Two.



**CONVENTION BOOMS SMITH**

**Up-State Delegates Join in Wild Demonstration for His Nomination.**

**GOVERNOR TELLS HIS STAND**

**Promises, if Nominated and Elected, No One Will Regret the Confidence Put in Him.**

**WILL STICK TO STATE WORK**

**Prohibition Question Ignored in Speeches and Declaration of Party Principles.**

### *Delegates and Alternates Chosen by State Democrats*

*Special to The New York Times.*

ALBANY, April 15.— Difficulties over the selection of delegates and alternates were smoothed over at a meeting of the newly elected Democratic State Committee, and the following were elected without opposition:

**Delegates at Large.**

Senator R. S. COPELAND of New York.
F. D. ROOSEVELT of Hyde Park.
W. H. KELLY of Syracuse.
MEYER JACOBSTEIN of Rochester.
Miss ELISABETH MARBURY of New York.
Mrs. CAROLINE O'DAY of Rye.
Mrs. ALICE C. GOOD of Brooklyn.
Mrs. K. S. PROHL of Buffalo.

**Alternates at Large.**

Lieutenant Governor G. R. LUNN of Schenectady.
EDWARD RIEGELMANN of Brooklyn.
WILLIAM F. FITZPATRICK of Buffalo.
WILLIAM F. GREEL of New York.
Miss DOROTHEA COURTEN of Richmond Hill.
Mrs. ELIZABETH COLBERT of Albany.
Miss HARRIET MAY MILLS of Syracuse.
Miss JESSIE R. NICOLL of Elmira.

*Special to The New York Times.*

ALBANY, April 15.—The Democratic Party of the State of New York, by action of its State Convention here today, formally placed Governor Alfred E. Smith in the race for the Democratic nomination for President. Governor Smith, in a speech to the convention, expressed his willingness to be a candidate.

The casting of the Governor's hat into the ring was accompanied by an unusual display of enthusiasm, which indicated that he will not be merely a Tammany candidate, but will have complete support of the party in the State. With his candidacy now in the open, an aggressive campaign will be begun to try to bring about his nomination at the National Convention, although the Governor said he had done, and would do, nothing personally to further what he admitted was his ambition.

Party leaders here, including Charles F. Murphy, leader of Tammany; Norman E. Mack of Buffalo and William E. Kelly of Syracuse, were said to be confident that Governor Smith has an excellent chance for the nomination. Many of the lesser leaders expressed belief that his nomination was inevitable. In the lobby of the Hotel Ten Eyck and the corridors of the convention hall this was the one topic of conversation. It was asserted everywhere that Governor Smith was the one candidate for President with whom the Democratic Party could hope to win.

"I want to step out of my character as Governor and have a personal word with you," Governor Smith said to the delegates after the adoption of the resolution pledging support for his candidacy for the Presidential nomination. "I heard the resolution that you passed. In fact, I read it before it came up here. It would be a difficult task for any man to stand before an audience of this kind and be able to adequately express the appreciation he would have to feel for the great compliment, the great honor and the high distinction that comes to him to be spoken of as the choice of the party in the greatest State in the Union for the highest office in all the world.

**"Done Nothing About It."**

"If I were to tell you that I haven't heard anything on this particular subject for the last year, you wouldn't believe it, because it wouldn't be true. I have heard a great deal about it, but, in the frankness that ought to exist among friends and comrades together, let me say this to you:

"I have done absolutely nothing about it, either inside or outside the State, and I do not intend to do anything about it.

"The man who would not have an ambition for that office would have a dead heart. But I stand exactly in the position today that I stood in [illegible] floor of the Constitutional Convention in 1915, when I said that a man who [illegible]

### *Wheeler Indictment Justified, Stone Finds; Senator's Arrest Now Expected in a Few Days*

*Special to The New York Times.*

WASHINGTON, April 15.—The evidence upon which a Federal Grand Jury at Great Falls, Mont., returned an indictment against Senator Burton K. Wheeler of that State has been examined by Attorney General Harlon F. Stone and in his opinion the action of the Grand Jury was justified. Senator Wheeler's arrest here is now expected in a few days. He will be taken before a United States Commissioner here and allowed to give bail for his appearance for trial.

It is learned that officials having knowledge of the evidence then at hand, and some additional evidence obtained later, express the view that it warrants the Federal Government in presenting the case to a petit jury. This, it was said, would be done in an orderly way, without in any manner interfering with the investigation into the conduct of the Department of Justice under Harry M. Daugherty, in which Senator Wheeler is now engaged.

The indictment of Senator Wheeler, it was asserted in an informed quarter today, has no relationship to his activities as the "prosecutor" of the investigation into the Department of Justice. The evidence, it was said, was obtained by the merest chance, according to the account given Government investigators who were assigned to a number of cases of alleged violation of the postal laws and investigation of one of these produced the evidence presented to the Grand Jury at Great Falls.

It was said also that the evidence was laid before the Grand Jury by the United States Attorney for the Federal Judicial District of Montana was without any suggestion from Washington.

"All the News That's Fit to Print."

# The New York Times.

THE WEATHER
Unsettled, with showers today; tomorrow unsettled and warmer.
Temperature Yesterday—Max. 59; Min. 52.
For weather report see Page 23.

VOL. LXXIII....No. 24,246. • • • • NEW YORK, THURSDAY, JUNE 12, 1924. TWO CENTS in Greater New York | THREE CENTS Within 200 Miles | FOUR CENTS Elsewhere

# BORAH AGREED UPON AS VICE PRESIDENTIAL NOMINEE IN MIDNIGHT CONFERENCE OF CONVENTION LEADERS; COOLIDGE'S PLATFORM ADOPTED, WISCONSIN'S SPURNED

## HOLD UP MAIL TRUCK ON A BUSY CORNER; GET $100,000 GEMS

### Ten Armed Men in Two Touring Cars Then Kidnap Driver and Escape.

### TRAFFIC POLICEMAN NEAR

### Robbers Subdue Other Occupant of Looted Auto by Blow With Revolver.

### WAVE PISTOLS AT CROWD

### Truck, Attacked at Abingdon Square, Is on Way to the Appraiser's Stores.

Ten armed men in two touring cars selected broad daylight and one of the busiest trucking points of the city yesterday, with a policeman seventy-five feet away, to hold up a truck conveying $100,000 worth of jewelry and diamonds from the General Post Office to the United States Appraiser's Stores for assessment of duties. The hold-up men got away with the mail pouch containing the valuables and kidnapped one of the two men on the truck. The other man put up such a stiff fight that he eluded the robbers and got to a telephone. Though many passers-by watched the robbery none interfered. Some of the witnesses, however, jotted down license plates numbers for the police.

Two suspects were questioned last evening in the Charles Street Police Station, but later were let go. In addition to the police, Department of Justice men, Post Office Inspectors and Customs Inspectors were on the case. It was the consensus of these investigators that the robbery was an "inside" case, with information furnished by somebody who knew the route usually taken and the nature of the contents of the pouch. The investigators also believed that the hold-up men, knowing they would have to get near a traffic policeman, were prepared to use their weapons against him, if necessary. Such action was not necessary, however, the policeman being in a store writing out a summons for an automobilist.

**Some of the Goods for Tiffany.**

Among the houses to which the twenty-nine packages stolen were consigned was Tiffany's. The valuables had arrived Monday on the steamship Aquitania and were on the way to the Customs authorities for appraisal. The hold-up was carried out with such clock-work precision in every detail that the police and Federal investigators were inclined to think it possible that Gerald Chapman was a member of the gang. Chapman is a fugitive from justice, having escaped a year ago from the Federal Penitentiary at Atlanta, where he was under sentence for the $2,000,000 mail truck robbery at Broadway and Leonard Street two years ago.

Yesterday's robbery, while the loss was smaller, was even more spectacular than that at Broadway and Leonard Street. The latter was in the evening, with little traffic at the scene of the hold-up. The robbery yesterday was at 10:15 o'clock in the morning, with traffic so heavy as to require the presence of a policeman.

In accordance with the daily custom of many years, a light one-ton motor truck of the Patrick H. Keahon Company, Inc., truckmen, of 108 Tenth Avenue, left the General Post Office at Thirty-third Street and Eighth Avenue with a mail pouch in which were valuables contained in a strong box. The pouch was locked. Often, the trucking company, under contract with the Government to convey jewelry from piers or from the Post Office to the Appraiser's Stores, had carried as much as $1,000,000 worth of gems. Yesterday, however, the lot was one of the lightest in many weeks.

**Policeman Off His Post.**

The strong box was being taken to the Appraiser's stores at 641 Washington Street. The invariable route was down Eighth Avenue, west on Twelfth Street, south on Washington Street. At Twelfth Street, Abingdon Square is formed by a junction of Eighth Avenue, Bank Street, Bleecker Street, Hudson Street and Twelfth Street, one of the busiest trucking areas in the city, being at that point only two blocks from the North River piers.

Driving the truck was Edward Foy, employed by the company for five years. Beside him sat Daniel Keahon, 37 years old, of Ramsay, N. J., Vice President of the corporation. Neither was armed.

A moment before the truck reached Abingdon Square, Traffic Policeman Metzler, stationed at Twelfth Street and Eighth Avenue, stepped into a store for ink with which to make out a summons for an automobilist. The store was less than seventy-five feet from the spot at which the truck was held up.

Foy had just swung west into Twelfth Street when a Cadillac touring car swerved sharply in front of him from behind. Foy jammed on the brakes and drew up against the north curb. As he came to a stop a second Cadillac touring car swung in behind him, pocketing in the truck. From the first Cadillac sprang four young men, each bearing what appeared to be a .45 calibre revolver. They climbed aboard the truck. Foy yielded readily, saying later he was thinking of his wife and two children. He obeyed the command to go into the first Cadillac. But Keahon resisted. He kept up the fight even when the six men in the second Cadillac sprang at him, one of them dazing Keahon with a blow on the head with the butt of a revolver. Finally realizing that further resistance was futile he decided to run for help.

Continued on Page Ten.



### Mr. and Mrs. Coolidge Hear The Convention Proceedings

*Special to The New York Times.*

WASHINGTON, June 11.—President and Mrs. Coolidge in the White House tonight "listened in" on the proceedings of the Republican National Convention at Cleveland, and heard the music, noise and echoes of the remarkable demonstration of more than twenty minutes' duration that was precipitated at the first mention of the President's name toward the beginning of the reading of the platform.

There were no visitors at the White House, and with the use of his eight-tube radio set, as well as over the loud speaker that had been installed in the President's study, the President and his wife were able to hear distinctly every word uttered by Charles B. Warren.

## MILLERAND QUITS; ELYSEE IS FLAGLESS

### French President's Formal Resignation Is Read in Both Houses of Parliament.

### LEFT SPLIT ON CANDIDATE

### Doumergue Refuses to Withdraw, but It Is Believed Painleve Will Be Elected Tomorrow.

By EDWIN L. JAMES.


Special Cable to THE NEW YORK TIMES.

PARIS, June 11.—Because he wanted to be a President like the President of the United States and because the majority in Parliament wanted a figure-head, President Alexandre Millerand is no longer head of the French State.

At 3 o'clock this afternoon, while the Garde Républicaine stood at attention, the tricolor on the Elysée flagmast was lowered, to signify that beneath its roof there was no longer a President of France. At the same hour his formal resignation was read before the Senate and Chamber.

The act of M. Millerand today was the logical consequence of his defeat in both Houses of Parliament yesterday, when the majority voted not to sustain any Government named by him. Tomorrow M. Millerand will move to his villa at Versailles, while the Left majority caucuses meet to nominate his successor, in preparation for the meeting of the National Assembly at Versailles at 2 o'clock Friday afternoon, the thirteenth day of the month and the thirteenth day of the existence of the thirteenth Parliament of the French Republic.

**Resignation Note Brief.**

The Senate listened in dignified silence while the Minister of Justice read the following communication from the Elysée:

> Mr. President: I have the honor to place on the table of the Senate my resignation as President of the republic.
>
> Please accept, Mr. President, the assurance of my high consideration.
>
> ALEXANDRE MILLERAND.

In the Chamber there was neither dignity nor silence. Above the cheers and yelling of the Communists and the replies of the Right, President Painlevé could not make himself heard as he read the message. As a tribute to the departing President the Nationalist side of the Chamber rose to its feet, while the Left counter-cheered this display of loyalty. The whole session lasted only twenty minutes.

After his resignation M. Millerand made public an address to the French people, in which he reviewed the war, the recovery of France since he had been in office, and said he had never done anything that was not intended for the peace and tranquillity of his country. If he had personal opinions they were the personal opinions of a Frenchman devoted to France. After the election of the 11th of May he was ready to cooperate with the majority, but they had refused and demanded his resignation. Their action was "an unjustifiable pretension violently opposed

Continued on Page Six.

## PLATFORM WINS AMID CHEERS

### 20-Minute Demonstration, for President, Then It Goes Through.

### ALL WISCONSIN PLANKS FAIL

### But La Follette Spokesman Gets a Hearing After Being Jeered as an Insurgent.

### DELEGATION SITS UNMOVED

### Neither Hisses Nor Taunts Could Win the 28 Badger Men to Rise for Coolidge.

**Full text of the Republican platform as adopted by the convention is printed on Page 4.**

By ELMER DAVIS.

*Special to The New York Times.*

CLEVELAND, June 11.—At 10:35 tonight the Republican National Convention adopted the platform prepared by the Committee on Resolutions, indorsing the policies of President Coolidge, including the World Court nd the Mellon tax plan, and adjourned until tomorrow morning, when it will reassemble to nominate the President as candidate for another term.

The platform, presented to the convention by Charles B. Warren, Ambassador to Mexico and Chairman of the Committee on Resolutions, was carried by a vote of about 13,000 to 28. None voted against it but the La Follette delegates from Wisconsin; and 12,000 spectators in the galleries and the rear of the hall joined with the delegates in the viva voce vote for the Coolidge declaration of policy.

Just before its adoption the La Follette radical platform, presented in a minority report by Representative Henry A. Cooper of Wisconsin, which may later reappear as the platform of a new third party, had been voted down, none but the Wisconsin delegation voting for it, and everybody, delegates and spectators alike, shouting their noes.

The formal trampling on the Wisconsin program was the culmination of a day devoted chiefly to the glorification of old-fashioned Republican orthodoxy, in which Coolidge men and old-line Republicans united, as against the radical program of the Northwest.

It began in the morning session with the speech of Frank W. Mondell, Permanent Chairman of the convention, which avoided the attacks on orthodox Republican leadership in Congress such as had been made in the keynote speech of Theodore E. Burton the day before, but was full of denunciation of insurgent movements such as that of the La Follette group.

**Demonstration for President.**

In tonight's session, made dull and dolorous by the reading of the orthodox platform, which occupied nearly an hour, and of the Wisconsin platform, which took up half an hour more, there were interludes of excitement when the resentment of the regulars against Wisconsin insurgency broke out.

The first display of this feeling came just after Mr. Warren had begun the reading of the regular platform, when he first mentioned the name of President Coolidge. This led to a demonstration in which the delegates rose and shouted for twenty minutes—some old-timers making it a trifle more—the spectators standing and shouting too. Everybody stood and shouted for Coolidge but the

Continued on Page Two.

### Today's Official Program.

CLEVELAND, June 12.—The official convention program for today is as follows:

Meets at 10 A. M.

Prayer by Bishop Schrembs of the Roman Catholic diocese of Cleveland.

Dr. Marion Leroy Burton, President of the University of Michigan, places President Coolidge in nomination.

Speeches seconding the nomination of President Coolidge.

Balloting on President's nomination of President Coolidge.

Speeches placing in nomination the candidate or candidates for the Vice Presidency.

Balloting on the Vice Presidential nomination.

Announcement of committees to formally notify the nominees for President and Vice President of their nominations.

Adoption of a resolution authorizing the Republican National Committee to fill any vacancies on the national ticket which may occur by death, resignation or otherwise.

Adoption of miscellaneous resolutions and motions.

Adjournment sine die.

## PLATFORM DRAFTED AFTER LONG SIEGE

### President's World Court Plank Wins in Committee, With but Two Opposing.

### FIGHT ON ANTI-KLAN PLANK

### Agricultural States Demanded More Definite Declarations—Wisconsin Movement Fails.

*Special to The New York Times.*

CLEVELAND, June 11.—President Coolidge's self-prepared plank on the World Court, reaffirming the position taken by him and by President Harding, was adopted by the Resolutions Committee of the Republican Convention tonight after the subcommittee had struggled for many weary hours in the drafting of one of the longest national party platforms presented to the voters in recent years.

The document in every respect represents the views of the Administration, as the draft formulated by Charles B. Warren, Chairman of the committee, who was selected by the President for the task, was accepted by the committee tonight, without substantial change. There was only one dissenting vote, that of Representative Henry A. Cooper of Wisconsin, spokesman on the committee for the La Follette radicals.

In the seven hours consumed by the Resolutions Committee in the consideration of the subcommittee draft, there was a long and animated discussion on the anti-Klan plank, and the planks dealing with the agricultural situation and the railroads. Chairman Warren was patient with those proposing objections to the Administration's ideas, but finally the policies dictated by the President in defining the party issues for the 1924 campaign were adhered to in the planks adopted.

The fight against the Administration World Court plank was led by Senator Harreld of Oklahoma, and Senator Watson of Indiana. Senator Harreld offered a plank which made it very clear that the United States would not enter the League of Nations and would not assume any obligations of the League, if it became a part of an International Court of Justice.

**Two Votes for Harreld's Plank.**

Senator Harreld spoke briefly on the resolution, and appeared to hold the interest of some of his colleagues. Then Chairman Warren announced that the plank which he himself had presented to the committee was written by President Coolidge and represented all that the President desired to put in the platform on this subject. This ended any effective effort to organize a revolt in the committee.

Senator Harreld's proposed plank read in part:

"We favor a World Court or tribunal, judicial rather than political, so grounded and created, as to permit our adherence thereto without impairment or sacrifice of any of the principles enunciated in the Republican platform of 1920."

The suggestion advanced by Senator Watson proposed to add an abstract of the President's message of Dec. 6, wherein he stated that the League of Nations was dead.

Senator Harreld's proposal received only two votes, those of himself and Senator Watson. Senator Watson then withdrew his suggestions.

A fight waged for a long time after decision on the World Court plank, upon the anti-Klan plank, and the demands of the farmer States members for a more definite declaration in favor of the agricultural interests. There also was an unsuccessful fight sponsored by Senator Cummins for a plank proposing compulsory arbitration of railroad labor disputes and compulsory consolidation of the carriers.

Toward the end of the conference came protests from Representative Cooper, who offered the platform, setting for the La Follette views. This was presented without argument. Chairman Warren, although the motion was not seconded, asked for a vote. The sub-platform was rejected with only one vote, that of the proposer, in support.

Mr. Cooper said that the fight would be carried to the floor, although he did not expect favorable action.

The most forceful feature of the plat-

Continued on Page Three.

## START REVOLT ON BUTLER

### Indianians Are Led By Watson, Who Now Seeks Second Place.

### RESENTFUL OF "DICTATION"

### Cabinet Group, and Especially New, Are Targets of Sharp Attack.

### OUTSIDE BACKING SOUGHT

### Movement Brings to Head a Strong Feeling Against Coolidge's Manager.

*Special to The New York Times.*

CLEVELAND, June 11.—Dissatisfaction in the Republican Convention with the alleged autocratic rule of William M. Butler, National Committeeman from Massachusetts, and President Coolidge's campaign manager, culminated tonight in open revolt against Mr. Butler's leadership.

The revolt is led by Senator James E. Watson of Indiana, who is now sending out his lieutenants of the Indiana delegation and friends in other State delegations to sound sentiment among delegates with a view to having them join in the revolt.

The emissaries of Mr. Watson were instructed by him to ask delegates whether they would vote to support Mr. Watson in his candidacy for the Vice Presidential nomination, which was announced definitely this afternoon after a meeting of the Indiana delegation.

While the fires of resentment against Mr. Butler had been smoldering ever since the Republican Convention assembled in Cleveland they did not blaze up until the meeting of the Indiana delegation today, when the situation in the convention was discussed by several speakers.

It was apparent from what was said that a considerable number of the Indiana delegates resented the apparent effort of Cabinet officers and others associated with the Coolidge Administration to determine the choice for the Vice Presidential nomination without respect to sentiment in the convention itself.

The spirited criticism heard in the meeting was directed mainly against Postmaster General New and former Governor Goodrich, both Indianans. Mr. New has taken part in the conferences of the Cabinet group in Cleveland, which had to do with determining upon the choice of the party's candidate for the second place on the ticket.

While Senator Watson was directing his forces from a room on the mezzanine floor of the Cleveland Hotel, members of the Cabinet group were conferring on the fourth floor of the same hotel with Mr. Butler.

Their call on Mr. Butler was to acquaint him with the outcome of the consideration they had given to the names of prominent Republicans who might be available Vice Presidential timber. With the Cabinet group was C. Bascom Slemp, Secretary to President Coolidge.

Senator Watson was endorsed for the Vice Presidential nomination by the Indiana convention, which he attended. This convention was alleged to have a distinct Ku Klux tinge. It was pretty well understood that there was no other serious purpose in the endorsement of Senator Watson for Vice Presidential honors than to head off any chance of a boom for that office in behalf of former Senator Albert J. Beveridge.

Since he has been in Cleveland, Mr. Watson has told leading Republicans that if they desired he would pass the word to the Indiana delegation not to present his name to the convention.

But this evening a change came in the situation when the Indiana delegation held a meeting. The principal speech was made by Joseph B. Kealing, national committeeman. Among other things he said:

"The man who does not follow out his instructions and vote for Watson is a traitor to his party."

This was intended, according to members of the delegation, as a direct thrust at Postmaster General New and ex-Governor Goodrich.

Mr. Kealing told his auditors that he had every reason to believe that the Coolidge Administration representatives here had failed to find a candidate for the Vice Presidential nomination. He said he had talked with delegates from other States and knew they were not disposed to vote "for whomever they are told to vote."

He said also that he had definite information that Secretary Hoover would not take the nomination, and with the remark that "we have no walkaway in Indiana this Fall," asserted that Senator Ralston would be on the Democratic national ticket.

The direct outcome of the meeting was that Governor Branch was chosen to make a formal statement announcing Watson's candidacy.

The leading members of the Indiana delegation have been stewing ever since they heard within twenty-four hours that Postmaster General New had told Mr. Butler, Secretary Mellon and Secretary Weeks that Watson should not be

Continued on Page Three.



### Borah Says He Will Not Accept the Nomination When Told in Washington of His Selection

WASHINGTON, Thursday, June 12, 3:30 A. M.—"I am not going to accept the nomination for Vice President," Senator Borah declared here early today after being informed that Republican leaders at Cleveland had agreed on him for the nomination.

The Idaho Senator had nothing to add to this brief statement when awakened at his residence and informed of the trend of events at Cleveland.

*Special to The New York Times.*

CLEVELAND, Thursday, June 12, 3:05 A. M. (4:05 A. M. New York time).—Attempts to reach members of the conference after the announcement had come from Washington that Senator Borah said that he would not accept, are unavailing. All had retired after making known the decision that they had reached, and refused to be disturbed afterward.

## PLEDGE MAY FORCE WISCONSIN TO BOLT

### Move for Promises of Loyalty, Now Rumored, Would Be Followed by Open Break.

### WILL DEFY MAJORITY TODAY

### La Follette Men Expect to Start a Storm—Prepare to Attend Third Party Convention.

*Special to The New York Times.*

CLEVELAND, June 11.—There is just one possibility that the Wisconsin delegates may be forced to leave their seats in the Republican National Convention and walk out before the final gavel falls. That is in the event that gossip current in the convention crowd tonight should materialize and a resolution be introduced at tomorrow's session of the convention, demanding from delegates ironclad pledges that they will abide by the action of that body, support the candidates it nominates and the platform it adopts.

Since the first batch of leaders arrived here for the convention preliminaries, there has been more or less discussion of taking such action in view of the foregone conclusion that the twenty-eight delegates from Wisconsin, who follow the leadership of Senator La Follette, would be active in a third party campaign with the Wisconsin Senator as the standard bearer. Old-line Republican leaders, under the circumstances, would much prefer to have the delegates from Wisconsin bolt and in a party sense be outlawed.

It had been expected that the convention Committee on Rules might bring in a resolution of that character, but this expectation was not fulfilled when the committee made its report to the convention today.

To be sure, there was contained in the report a clause giving the National Committee power of removal over members failing to give loyal support to the ticket, or, in other words, using their party position for the purpose of giving aid and comfort to the prospective third party enemy. But this clause was merely a strong reiteration of an old rule made to fit the present situation and did not in reality lodge in the National Committee any power which it does not now possess.

The more drastic rule for which some look tomorrow would be based on a precedent established in the convention that nominated Garfield in 1880 and for which the late Senator Roscoe Conkling of New York was the sponsor. Under this rule a loyalty pledge to candidates and platform could be enacted from all delegates remaining in the convention until final adjournment.

**Blaine Expects Loyalty Pledge.**

Governor John J. Blaine of Wisconsin, head of the La Follette delegation, is one member of the representatives from Wisconsin who fully expects action of that sort tomorrow. He would not, however, in advance of such a resolution actually coming before the convention, make any comment on what the delegates from the Badger State would do under the circumstances.

When a similar question was put to Attorney General Herman L. Ekern of Wisconsin he replied:

"Well, I do not think the Wisconsin delegates will support President Coolidge."

As at yesterday's session of the convention, the Wisconsin delegates today were the butts of jeers and hisses and the recipients of blunt and loud invitations to leave the hall. Such hostile demonstrations did not appear to disturb their equanimity. They sat stolid-

Continued on Page Three.



## FARM BLOC SUBMITS CHOICES TO BUTLER

### Asks That Vice Presidential Candidate Be Selected From Its List.

### 12 STATES VOTED ON NAMES

### Kenyon Led With 8 Votes—Curtis Got 7, and Dickinson and Gov. Hyde Each 6.

*Special to The New York Times.*

CLEVELAND, Thursday, June 12.—A committee of one delegate from each of twelve Western States, after a conference in the Kansas headquarters, at the Hotel Hollenden, called on William M. Butler, President Coolidge's campaign manager, early this morning to submit a list of candidates from which they desired the candidate for Vice President to be picked.

Each State participating fully in the conference suggested four candidates. The list of candidates submitted to Mr. Butler and the vote for each follows:

Representative L. J. Dickinson of Iowa, 6; Judge William S. Kenyon of Iowa, 8; Charles H. March of Minnesota, 2; Brig. Gen. Charles G. Dawes of Illinois, 5; Secretary Hoover, 3; Senator Lawrence C. Phipps of Colorado, 1; Senator Curtis of Kansas, 7; Governor Hyde of Missouri, 6; Major Gen. F. T. Hines of Utah, 2; Major Gen. Harbord of Kansas, 3; Senator Norbeck of South Dakota, 3, and Frank W. Mondell of Wyoming, 1.

Preference by States was expressed as follows:

Oklahoma—Curtis, Kenyon, Dickinson and Hyde.

North Dakota—Hines, March Hoover and Dawes.

Montana—Hyde, Dawes, Curtis and Kenyon.

Utah—Hines, Curtis, Kenyon and Dickinson.

Washington—Hoover, Dawes, Curtis and Hines.

Wyoming—Mondell, Kenyon, Hoover and Harbord.

Kansas—Curtis, Hyde, Dickinson and Dawes.

Michigan—Curtis, Kenyon, Harbord and Dawes.

Iowa—Dickinson, Kenyon, Hyde and Norbeck.

Missouri—Hyde, Curtis, Dickinson and Phipps.

South Dakota—Norbeck, Dickinson, Kenyon and Harbord.

Minnesota—March, Dawes, Norbeck and Kenyon.

The Nebraska delegation announced that it was pledged to General Dawes and for that reason could not submit four names but was in sympathy with the movement.

Hanford MacNider, a delegate from Iowa and former national commander of the American Legion, presided at the conference, which seemed at first likely to eliminate some of the candidates for whom there was comparatively little support and concentrate upon three or four.

Objection was made to such procedure and there was also objection to sending a committee to Mr. Butler. W. Glenn, Cowell of Michigan urged the elimination of the weaker candidates and the presentation of one candidate to the convention as the choice of an important section of the country.

"If we submit the names to any one for his O. K. we put ourselves in the position of submitting to dictation," Mr. Cowell said. "If we submit the list to

Continued on Page Five.



## EXPECT BORAH TO CONSENT

### Several Conferees Intimate He Will Accept If Nominated.

### URGED BY KENYON, CURTIS

### Latter, in Washington, Said to Have Been in Touch With Fellow Senator.

### A SURPRISE TO RADICALS

### But Knowledge That Choice Will Gratify the President Expected to Clinch Selection.

By RICHARD V. OULAHAN.

*Special to The New York Times.*

CLEVELAND, Thursday, June 12, 2 A. M. (3 A. M. New York Time).—Senator William E. Borah of Idaho was chosen at an early hour this morning to be the candidate for the nomination for Vice President of the United States. The choice was made by a conference of members of the Cabinet, Senators and Representatives and others prominent in the Republican Party affairs.

No formal announcement was made of the action of the conferees, but it was admitted informally that Senator Borah was the choice.

While there was no direct admission that the conferees had reason to believe that Senator Borah would accept the nomination, if it were conferred upon him, direct intimations that he would accept came from several members of the conference.

When one of the conferees was asked if he believed that Senator Borah would accept the Vice Presidential nomination, he said:

"If I were a newspaper man, I would say that Borah would be the nominee."

**Had Strong Backing.**

One statement made was that Judge William S. Kenyon, former Senator from Iowa, and Senator Charles Curtis of Kansas had both urged that Senator Borah be selected for President Coolidge's running mate on the Republican national ticket.

Both Judge Kenyon and Senator Curtis were on the tentative list of prospective candidates for the Vice Presidential nomination considered by the conferees. Their names were under consideration at a late hour last evening.

Senator Curtis was in Washington, and it is supposed that he has been in communication with Senator Borah. The fact that Senator Curtis has communicated with the conferees in Cleveland and that they appeared confident that Senator Borah would accept the Vice Presidential nomination indicated this.

Senator Pepper of Pennsylvania said that he had talked over the Vice Presidential situation with Senator Reed and other members of the delegation and that they would recommend that the Pennsylvania delegation favor Senator Borah. Senator Pepper added that he realized that this was one of the most important questions before the convention and that Senator Borah would be nominated and would accept.

He added, however, that neither he nor Senator Reed had any direct statement from Senator Borah, but he thought that the Pennsylvania delegation would vote for him.

**Coolidge Favored Him.**

A canvass by the conferees of the situation, effecting others who are to be proposed in the convention for the Vice Presidential nomination indicated a situation which might prevent Senator Borah's selection from being made on the first ballot. Borah's popularity in the convention is such, however, that no doubt is felt that he will be nominated ultimately.

Senator Borah was President Coolidge's first choice for the nomination. He has conferred with Senator Borah several times recently and, while the President made it known that he intended the convention should have free choice of the Vice Presidential candidate without

## Japanese Planned to Kill Our Consul, But Is Seized by Police in Yokohama

By WILFRID FLEISHER.


By Wireless to THE NEW YORK TIMES.

TOKIO, June 11.—Threats were made against the life of Graham Kemper, the American Consul at Yokohama, by Masanosuke Yamamoto, a laborer at the Yokohama dock yard, who called at the Consulate in Yokohama on Sunday afternoon to protest against the American immigration bill. He is now being held by the Yokohama police.

Yamamoto, who is 30 years of age, appeared at the Consulate, armed with a short dagger, and demanded to see the Consul. He was met by Kaneo Yoshida, an employe of the Consulate, with whom he began to remonstrate over the immigration bill. He told Yoshida that he intended to ask the Consul to intercede with the American Government regarding the bill and that in the event of the Consul's refusal he intended to kill him and then commit suicide.

Yamamoto appeared slightly unbalanced.

The Consulate employe led him by his arm to what he said was the Consul's home, but in reality he took him to a police station and handed him over.

Consul Kemper saw the intruder arguing with Yoshida, but did not see that he carried a dagger, although he noticed that Yoshida led him away.

Reports in the Japanese newspapers this evening state that Yamamoto was greatly inspired by the recent example of the unknown man who committed hara-kiri.

The American Embassy in Tokio learned from the Consulate General here that a Japanese workman had called at the American Consulate in Yokohama on Sunday afternoon and had protested against exclusion, but the embassy had received no direct report from Yokohama and had no knowledge that the intruder had threatened the life of Mr. Kemper.

Chargé d'Affaires Jefferson Caffery has asked Mr. Kemper to come to Tokio tomorrow morning and report the facts.

The Foreign Office, upon hearing the news this evening, expressed regret at the incident, but it was stated that it is impossible to prevent isolated outbursts when no intimation is given in advance. Officials said the American Embassy is now being guarded and that six policemen have been detailed to the Imperial Hotel for this purpose and to prevent any further disturbance there.

Orders would now be given, it was said, to guard both the American Consulate General in Tokio and the Consulate in Yokohama.

Public opinion here remains in an excitable frame of mind. The anti-American movement appears to have slipped beyond the grasp of those prominent leaders who hoped to keep the masses in hand by persuasion, and unless the Government takes forceful means to meet the situation it is likely that other outbursts may occur.

"All the News That's Fit to Print."

# The New York Times.

THE WEATHER
Partly cloudy and warmer today; tomorrow probably showers.
Temperature Yesterday—Max. 60; Min. 34.
For weather report see next to last page.

VOL. LXXIII....No. 24,247. NEW YORK, FRIDAY, JUNE 13, 1924. TWO CENTS in Greater New York | THREE CENTS Within 200 Miles | FOUR CENTS Elsewhere

# COOLIDGE AND DAWES NOMINATED; GENERAL IS NAMED FOR SECOND PLACE AFTER LOWDEN, CHOSEN, REFUSES IT

## EXPLOSIONS KILL 48 ON U. S. S. MISSISSIPPI; NEW BLAST FEARED

### Firing Crew Wiped Out When Back-Fire Sets Off Store of Powder in Turret.

### PASSENGER SHIP IN DANGER

### 14-Inch Gun Is Discharged in San Pedro Harbor, Shell Causing Panic on the Yale.

### THIRD GUN STILL LOADED

### After Landing Dead and Injured, Dreadnought Puts Back to Sea for Safety.

*Special to The New York Times.*

LOS ANGELES, Cal., June 12.—Three officers and forty-five enlisted men are known to have been killed, nine others probably fatally injured, and a score more hurt in various degree in an explosion in a gun turret on the U. S. S. Mississippi, off San Pedro Harbor this afternoon.

There were two separate blasts—the first was that of 1,800 pounds of powder and a charge of a fourteen-inch rifle.

The second came as the dreadnought dropped anchor near the hospital ship Relief in the harbor proper; the charge in the second great rifle in the turret exploding, the shell was hurled out to sea, missing the outgoing liner Yale by a few hundred feet and creating a panic among its passengers.

The battleships Mississippi, Tennessee, Idaho and California, comprising a division under the command of Rear Admiral William V. Pratt, left Los Angeles Harbor today for the San Clemente drill grounds for secret practice.

Part of this consisted in concentrated fire by the Mississippi, Idaho and Tennessee against a giant target to be towed by the California.

According to the reports of men on the other ships, the three dreadnoughts were lined up. In the far distance, a tiny speck showed the California.

In gun turret No. 2, situated above and slightly abaft of gun turret No. 1, forward of the ship, were the eighty-odd men comprising the gun crews for guns Nos. 4, 5 and 6.

Part of these eighty-odd were stationed at the guns themselves; the remainder of the crews were occupied in the handling rooms and in the twin tunnels leading from the ammunition stores. In command of the turret was Lieutenant Thomas Edward Zellars, a Long Beach, Cal., man. With him were Ensigns Marcus Erwin, J. J. Levasseur and James McCrea, the last two being observers from the U. S. S. New Mexico detailed to witness the target practice.

The command was given to load; the guns were elevated for the long shot.

The monster shells were brought from the ammunition stores by their mechanical carriers, lifted and shoved home in the gun barrels. Then came the great sacks of powder, 450 pounds of it in each sack, and four sacks in each charge of each gun. The three guns were loaded, and four sacks of the explosives still lay on the floor.

**Gun Breech Not Closed.**

The breeches in guns 5 and 6 swung slowly shut and tightly locked. In gun 4 the breech likewise swung toward closure, but something jammed. And in that moment when the breech hung slightly open, some one—no one knows who that some one was—gave the command to turn on the electrical current which detonated the explosive in gun 4. The charge exploded. The eighty-odd men, trapped in a steel cage designed to withstand the mightiest blow of an enemy fleet, were burned and crushed and mangled and gassed. Those within the turret proper were instantly killed.

The four sacks of powder still on the floor joined in the mighty blast—and the armor-plated roof of the turret dissolved into fragments.

In the handling rooms those closest to the door were instantly killed; those further away are in the list of the injured. The fireproof doors to the ammunition tunnels were blown from their hinges; the trap-doors leading to the handling rooms were totally destroyed.

Ensign Levasseur out of the corner of one eye had caught sight of that open gun-breech when the command to fire had been given. He unhesitatingly dove forty feet from the shell deck, where he was standing, down the shaft of the endless chain powder bucket. He was cut and bruised but is still alive. Ensign Erwin, by whom he was standing, was instantly killed.

The blast shook the ship from stem to stern. It seemed minutes, almost, before even the commanding officers knew what had happened. Then Ensign H. D. Smith of the U. S. S. New Mexico, also detailed as an observer on the Mississippi, grabbed an air hose and, with a squad of volunteers, pushed his way into the door of the wrecked turret. A blast of flame met him. A fire had started which for a while menaced the safety of the entire ship. The air from the hose fanned the flames. The rescue squad was forced to retreat. Fire hose was hastily rigged and several streams poured through every point of entrance. Shortly thereafter the rescuers were able to start their work of bringing out the bodies.

**Dreadnaught Rushes to Port.**

The Mississippi was at once put under full speed, heading for Los Angeles Harbor, and the hospital ship relief. A radio message to the latter vessel to prepare at once for fifty victims was hurriedly sent. It was this message which gave the first news of the affair to Los Angeles.

As the dreadnought cut through the waves the medical officers did their best

Continued on Page Eight.

## BURTON NAMES COOLIDGE

### Professor Breaks Traditions and Talks Out Like a Modern Salesman.

### POPULARIZES HIS VIRTUES

### And Carries Audience With Him All the Way With Homely Metaphors.

### JEERS AGAIN FOR WISCONSIN

### But Only Laughter Greets the South Dakota Vote for Hiram Johnson.

*Special to The New York Times.*

CLEVELAND, Ohio, June 12.—Calvin Coolidge was nominated for the Presidency at 1:57 o'clock this afternoon on the first ballot taken in the Republican National Convention.

He received 1,065 of the 1,109 votes. Robert Marion La Follette got 34—28 of the 29 from Wisconsin and six of the 13 from North Dakota—and Hiram Johnson got 10 of the 13 votes from South Dakota.

As usual, the galleries received every mention of La Follette's name, and the report of the votes cast for him, with jeers and hisses, but they had only laughter for the name of Hiram Johnson.

When the result of the ballot had been announced, S. X. Way of South Dakota moved that the nomination be made unanimous, and Thomas Scott of Wisconsin, who cast that State's only vote for Coolidge, seconded the motion. When Chairman Frank W. Mondell put it to a viva voce vote everybody shouted "Aye," but the recalcitrant handful of La Follette men in Wisconsin and North Dakota, and Mr. Mondell announced that "with the exception of a very few voices," Coolidge had been nominated by acclamation.

All this had been expected. There was no excitement about it and no novelty. But in at least two respects this morning's session showed a tendency to a change of long settled habits of American politics. The conventional "demonstration" for President Coolidge, following the speech in which he was nominated, was not stretched out to the fantastic and artificial length that has been common in past conventions. It stopped after thirteen minutes, although it was two minutes later before all the delegates were in their seats.

**Nominating Speech a "Sales Talk."**

And the speech which had provoked it, the speech in which Dr. Marion Leroy Burton, President of the University of Michigan, placed President Coolidge in nomination, was of a type wholly new to national conventions though not unfamiliar in the commercial-cultural life of the United States. It was a sales talk, and a good sales talk at that. From some viewpoints it might be open to criticism, but it was perfectly adapted to the object for which it was designed.

The full text of Dr. Burton's speech is printed on page 6.

Dr. Burton is not a delegate. He was picked by President Coolidge himself to deliver the official advertisement for the candidate—for that is what it was, not an address to a convention already wrapped up, sealed and delivered for Coolidge, but an advertisement to the country of the personality and virtues of the head of the Republican ticket.

When the roll of States was called for nominations for the Presidency, Alabama, head of the list, yielded to Massachusetts, President Coolidge's home State, and Governor Channing Cox of Massachusetts moved that Dr. Burton "be accorded the privilege of nominating the candidate of Massachusetts."

That was in accordance with the sacred ritual of American State religion—that the candidate must not be named until the very end of the nominating speech, when his identity is disclosed suddenly to a surprised convention. It seems to be felt that if the name is spoken during the performance of the rites the omens will be inauspicious.

But a moment later Chairman Mondell incautiously let slip the President's name, and Dr. Burton broke with tradition and told the audience right away whom he was going to nominate.

Burton—his manner today suggests that he would feel insulted by continuing the use of his academic title—Burton looks no more like a college President than he does like a politician. Tall—taller than Coolidge—almost as redheaded as Coolidge, smooth faced and brisk and snappy, he can accurately be described only by those hackneyed terms "clean-cut" and "full of pep." He looks like a real estate agent and he talked today like a real estate agent selling a building lot in a suburban home development to an unwilling but a hypnotized and unresisting purchaser.

He talked for fifty-one minutes, and so fast that he finished in that time a speech that an ordinary orator would have lingered over for an hour and a quarter.

He omitted two sections of his prepared speech, those dealing with women, a topic already much overdone in this convention, and with capital and labor. Even so, it was so very long, unusually long for a nominating speech, but he talked so fast and played with

Continued on Page Three.

REPUBLICAN NOMINEE FOR PRESIDENT.
CALVIN COOLIDGE
OF MASSACHUSETTS.

## COOLIDGE IS SILENT ON HIS NOMINATION

### President Feels He Can Express His Appreciation Best in His Acceptance Speech.

### GETS NEWS AT LUNCHEON

### Talks With Borah Before Convention Meets, and Then Listens to Its Proceedings.

*Special to The New York Times.*

WASHINGTON, June 12.—The White House was silent on the nomination of former Governor Lowden for Vice President, and equally uncommunicative after word was flashed to Washington that Mr. Lowden had announced his declination.

President Coolidge, it was stated by his spokesmen at the White House, was maintaining his attitude of "hands off" with respect to the selection of a running mate, and had not during the day communicated any preference to Mr. Butler or any other person in the convention city.

Nor would the President comment on his own nomination by the convention. Edward Clark, his personal secretary, in answer to inquiries by newspaper correspondents, stated that the President had requested him to say there would be no statement coming from the White House.

Mr. Coolidge intimated to friends several days ago that what he had to say in the way of appreciation could be most fittingly said when the Notification Committee arrives with the formal information of the action of the National Convention. On that occasion he will read a carefully prepared acceptance speech.

**At Lunch When Nominated.**

The President was at lunch at the White House when the vote of the convention was conveyed to him by Isaac Hoover, chief usher at the White House. He is reported to have nodded his acknowledgment of these tidings and resumed his meal.

President Coolidge spent practically all of the time the convention was in session "listening in" upon the convention proceedings over his radio set. Consequently he had up-to-the-minute information as to the progress of the open proceedings, and through his secretary he obtained information as to what was going on behind the scenes at Cleveland.

The President did not go to his executive office during the afternoon because of the desire of himself and Mrs. Coolidge to hear the convention speeches and votes. So far as known, there was no one with President and Mrs. Coolidge while they were listening in except Henry Long of Massachusetts, who was Mr. Coolidge's private secretary when he was Governor of Massachusetts.

Senator Borah of Idaho announced at the White House this forenoon, after a

Continued on Page Two.



## LA FOLLETTE GROUP PREDICTS DEFEAT

### Declare Blunders of Butler and Cabinet Advisers Have Beaten Coolidge.

### PRAISE LEADERS' STRATEGY

### Say Voters Are Alienated From Regulars and Prepare for Third Party Convention.

*Special to The New York Times.*

CLEVELAND, June 12.—At what one of their number referred to as "the end of a perfect day," the La Follette delegates from Wisconsin tonight are busy making hotel reservations in preparation for their attendance at what they term the "second Cleveland convention," scheduled to convene on July 4 for the purpose of nominating Senator La Follette for President of the United States on a third party ticket, which they hope, and seem to believe, will prove an insurmountable obstacle in the way of a Republican victory.

Robert M. La Follette Jr., son of the Wisconsin Senator and Chairman of the Central Republican Committee of Wisconsin, said tonight that in his opinion nothing could save the candidates nominated at the "first" Cleveland convention from defeat.

Blunders on the part of the Coolidge managers, a group of Cabinet members who have operated under the supervision of William M. Butler, Republican National Committeeman from Massachusetts, in connection with the selection of a candidate for second place on the ticket, in the opinion of the La Follette men, has shattered what slender hope there ever was of Republican success in the national election this year.

The younger La Follette has been in frequent communication with his father throughout the day. The successive moves of the La Follette delegates since they arrived at the convention, there is every reason to believe, have been in pursuance of strategy dictated by the Wisconsin Senator himself with a view to putting the convention and the party of which nominally he is an exalted member "in wrong" with the voters.

The consensus among the La Follette delegates tonight is that this purpose has been successful beyond their fondest expectations.

Tonight while the convention was in recess preparatory to a new start in the selection of a running mate for Mr. Coolidge, Mr. Butler, in his capacity of campaign manager for President Coolidge, was being "knocked" by sore and gloomy delegates, impatient to get away, in the headquarters of practically every delegation, excepting that of the La Follette group from Wisconsin.

They said they were much obliged to Mr. Butler and the members of the Cabinet who have been participating in his councils for more perfect cooperation

Continued on Page Seven.



## REVOLT PUTS DAWES OVER

### Old Timers Resent Butler's Domination of the Convention.

### HE ASKED FIRST FOR KENYON

### Regulars Named Lowden Instead and Then He Switched to Hoover.

### DISAFFECTION SPREADING

### Talk of Asking Coolidge to Select Another Man to Conduct Campaign.

By RICHARD V. OULAHAN.
*Special to The New York Times.*

CLEVELAND, June 12.—The Republican National Convention completed its work tonight and adjourned sine die after having chosen Calvin Coolidge of Massachusetts as its candidate for President and General Charles G. Dawes of Illinois as its candidate for Vice President.

Three sessions of the convention were held on the concluding day. The night session was made necessary by an extraordinary situation produced by the refusal of former Governor Frank O. Lowden of Illinois to be the party's candidate for Vice President after the convention had conferred that honor on him.

Mr. Lowden had been chosen on the second Vice Presidential ballot at the afternoon, or second session. Messages from him refusing to accept the nomination, written in advance, were produced after some of Lowden's friends had sought to prevent their being presented.

This remarkable state of affairs compelled a recess to give the party leaders an opportunity to lead the party out of the maze in which it found itself. At the night session the situation was remedied by undoing the nomination of Mr. Lowden and proceeding to ballot again for a candidate for Vice President. On the first ballot at the night session, its third ballot on a candidate for Vice President, victory went to the supporters of General Dawes.

**Convention Revolts on Butler.**

While only a gesture of protest was made against choosing President Coolidge to head the Republican national ticket in the campaign of 1924, the effort to nominate the candidate for Vice President put a fly in the Republican ointment and threatened to produce serious differences within the party management. Lack of harmony is already apparent among those who are charged with the conduct of the Presidential campaign this year.

The futile nomination of Mr. Lowden for Vice President was in part the outcome of an abortive, inept effort to draft Senator William E. Borah of Idaho for second place on the national ticket.

At an early hour this morning William M. Butler, political manager for President Coolidge, had made known that President Coolidge desired that Senator Borah should be the Vice Presidential nominee, and that Mr. Butler had assurances that Mr. Borah would accept. The Borah boom collapsed when Mr. Borah positively refused to accept the honor.

Mr. Butler countered on the disappearance of Mr. Borah from the Vice Presidential picture by offering Judge William S. Kenyon of Iowa. Leading men of the party who made wry faces when they were asked to support Judge Kenyon, whom they regarded as a near radical and not too loyal to the Republican cause, demanded a request direct from the White House that they put Judge Kenyon in second place on the National ticket. President Coolidge declined to comply with the request.

After that the leaders felt free to make their own choice of a Vice Presidential candidate. Out of their attitude in this connection came the nomination of former Governor Lowden and brought about the embarrassing situation with which the party was confronted when the convention assembled this evening for its third session.

The embarrassment was remedied, as far as straightening out the physical difficulties of the tangle was concerned, by the acceptance of Mr. Lowden's declination and the subsequent nomination of General Dawes.

But the Vice Presidential maze had another and more important phase than was apparent from surface indications. Mr. Lowden's nomination marked a revolt against the domination of Mr. Butler.

**Accuse Butler as Dictator.**

Feeling against him has been growing on the part of leading party workers, especially members of the National Committee, ever since they began gathering in Cleveland. He was charged with being dictatorial, with paying no attention to the counsel of veterans in party affairs, and generally with attempting to use his authority as President Coolidge's agent in a way detrimental

Continued on Page Two.

REPUBLICAN NOMINEE FOR VICE PRESIDENT.
CHARLES G. DAWES
OF ILLINOIS.

## BITTER FIGHT SPLITS NEW YORK GROUP

### Wadsworth and Hayward Factions Engage in War of Words at Secret Conference.

### EFFECT ON CAMPAIGN SEEN

### "Old Guard" and Progressives Line Up in Opposition Through the Whole State Organization.

*Special to The New York Times.*

CLEVELAND, June 12.—A split that may have far-reaching consequences in the New York State fight this Fall developed in the New York delegation this afternoon just before the convention opened to nominate a Vice President. Seventy-seven of the delegates held a secret conference at their headquarters in the Cleveland hotel and the so-called Old Guard element, led by Senator Wadsworth, sought to take control. Mr. Wadsworth was denounced for trying to wreck the party and the meeting ended in great bitterness.

Wadsworth, National Committeeman Charles D. Hilles and Representative Ogden L. Mills stood together against the demand of the so-called Progressive element that a Western candidate with progressive ideas be selected for Vice President. The Progressives united on Judge Kenyon of Iowa, but Wadsworth and his followers declared he would never do, because he was not conservative enough and was not even a regular organization Republican. They declared him a follower of La Follette and not in sympathy with President Coolidge. For their candidate they brought forward Theodore E. Burton, temporary Chairman of the convention.

State Senator Frederick M. Davenport of Oneida led the Kenyon faction, and several delgates made fiery speeches sustaining his choice. One speaker declared that Kenyon had been acceptable to two Republican Presidents, Harding and Coolidge, the former having made him a Federal Judge, and therefore should be acceptable to the convention. On the vote which followed, Kenyon received 23 votes and Burton 54. There were ten absentees.

**Hayward Supports Kenyon.**

Colonel William Hayward, United States District Attorney for the Southern District of New York, whose candidacy for the Republican nomination for Governor is being vigorously opposed by Senator Wadsworth, sided with Davenport and advocated the selection of Kenyon. The delegates holding Federal positions in the State lined up behind Wadsworth. The vote showed a split in the organization extending throughout the State and it is sure to have important results if it is not healed before the Fall campaign.

Samuel S. Koenig, Chairman of the New York Republican County Committee, broke away from Representative Mills and he was followed by George W. Morris, State Chairman; Senator Charles

Continued on Page Five.



## DAWES PROMPTLY ACCEPTS NOMINATION

### Issues Statement at Old Home in Marietta, Saying He Is "Very Grateful."

### COOLIDGE CONGRATULATES

### Promptly Sends Message to Running Mate—Lowden Pleased With Choice.

MARIETTA, Ohio, June 12 (Associated Press).—Brig. Gen. Charles G. Dawes, who is at the home of his sister, Mrs. A. Beach, here, said tonight:

"I accept the nomination by the Republican Party for the Vice Presidency. I deeply appreciate the honor conferred."

When the Republican Convention was taking the roll-call on the Vice Presidency, Brig. Gen. Dawes was "listening in" surrounded by two brothers with their families and friends.

When The Associated Press notified him of his nomination, General Dawes was already aware of it.

"Charley," said his brother, Henry M. Dawes, Controller of the Currency, "it's up to you again."

General Dawes came to Marietta, his native town, on Monday to attend the fortieth annual reunion of his class in Marietta College, where he was graduated in 1884.

With him tonight also was another brother, Beeman G. Dawes of Columbus.

General Dawes will leave tomorrow afternoon for Chicago.

The nomination came as a surprise to General Dawes and his relatives. He knew that he had been mentioned in connection with the office but had no idea that he would be named as President Coolidge's running mate.

He will not receive the telegrams of congratulation sent by President Coolidge, Governor Lowden and others tonight, as the telegraph office here closes early in the evening.

**Coolidge Congratulates Dawes.**

*Special to The New York Times.*

WASHINGTON, June 12.—President Coolidge sent this telegram to General Dawes late this evening:

"It will be a pleasure to be associated with you in the public service. Best wishes to you and Mrs. Dawes, in which Mrs. Coolidge joins.
"CALVIN COOLIDGE."

The President wrote this in longhand and sent it by Edward B. Clark, his personal secretary, from the main part of the White House, where he had been listening in by radio, to the telegraph room of the Executive office, to be sent immediately to General Dawes.

Herbert Hoover sent the following telegram to General Dawes:

Charles G. Dawes, Chicago, Ill.
I am more than happy at your selection and the assurance of your being again drafted to public service. The country is to be congratulated.
HERBERT HOOVER.

**Lowden Much Pleased.**

OREGON, Ill., June 12 (Associated Press).—Frank O. Lowden, former Governor of Illinois, who tonight was nomi-

Continued on Page Seven.

## DAWES WINS ON 3D BALLOT

### Gets 682½ to 234½ for Hoover on Opening of Night Session.

### CONVENTION THEN ADJOURNS

### Lowden, Chosen First With Ovation Rivalling President's, Refuses to Accept.

### KENYON AND BURTON STRONG

### They Shared Lead on Early Ballots, With Watson, Dawes and Others.

By ELMER DAVIS.
*Special to The New York Times.*

PUBLIC HALL, CLEVELAND, Ohio, June 12.—The Republican National Convention of 1924 adjourned at 10:35 tonight, Eastern Standard Time, having renominated President Calvin Coolidge and placed Brig. Gen. Charles G. Dawes of Illinois on the ticket with him as a candidate for Vice President.

The last day of the convention, the only one that had decently comfortable weather, the only one that saw the auditorium filled with spectators, was also the busiest and most entertaining of the three days of sessions.

The nomination of President Coolidge at the morning session, by 1,065 votes to 34 for Senator Robert M. La Follette and 10 for Senator Hiram Johnson, had, of course, long been foreseen; but the selection of a Vice President developed quite a struggle. Some of the struggling was done by gentlemen who wanted to be Vice President and much more of it was done by gentlemen who would not be Vice President under any circumstances and objected to being drafted.

General Dawes was nominated on the first ballot tonight, at the last of the day's three sessions, receiving 682½ votes, as against 234½ for Herbert Hoover, Secretary of Commerce, and 75 for Judge William S. Kenyon and a few scattering. But at the afternoon session former Governor Frank O. Lowden of Illinois had been nominated despite his frequently expressed refusal to be a candidate, and it took two or three more refusals before the convention took him at his word.

**Hoover Was Butler's Choice.**

General Dawes was second choice, but Mr. Hoover, whom he defeated, was not even that. Hoover was the final candidate picked by William M. Butler, President Coolidge's campaign manager, and he was defeated by Dawes, not because the delegates had anything against Hoover, but because they had a great deal against William M. Butler.

President Coolidge and Vizier Butler have ruled this convention in everything but the nomination for Vice-President, and the discontent against their domination, which has been loudly expressed in words all week, finally blossomed out into action today. The delegates couldn't beat Coolidge, nor the Coolidge platform, but they could and did beat whatever Vice-Presidential candidate was unfortunate enough to have Mr. Butler's approval. They beat one this afternoon and they beat another tonight. And neither of these was Butler's first choice, or even his fourth or fifth choice.

All the week the Administration forces have been trying to find somebody to take the Vice Presidential nomination. Borah refused, Kenyon was cold, Lowden refused; when the convention finally started balloting for a Vice President in its second session of the day Mr. Butler had been forced to recognize that though Judge Kenyon had been placed in nomination he stood small chance of being selected as the candidate of the party. In that situation Mr. Butler was forced reluctantly to give such support as he could to Representative Theodore E. Burton, Temporary Chairman of the convention, who is a Clevelander, and has, besides the support of Ohio, that of most of the leaders in the Eastern industrial States.

But the convention had a mind of its own and power to take action of its own—on the Vice Presidency.

Half a dozen other candidates had been placed in nomination at the afternoon session, among them ex-Governor Lowden. He had repeatedly refused to let himself be considered for a place on the ticket; his nomination, when first made this afternoon, brought another statement from his friends that he wouldn't take it; but he was nominated again and on the second ballot he was chosen as the Vice Presidential candidate. At the end of the roll call on the ballot he had only 413 votes, as against 286 for Burton, 555 being necessary for a choice; but there was a rush of States to change their votes before another roll call, and New York and Pennsylvania put Lowden over.

**Lowden's Refusal Causes a Snarl.**

Then it was learned that Lowden, foreseeing something of the sort, had given to friends at the convention a sealed letter, to be read in case he were nominated, absolutely refusing to be a candidate. The letter was read and William M. Butler began to cheer up. Maybe he had a chance to put over a Vice President after all. By this time it was half past seven and the conven-

Section 1

"All the News That's Fit to Print."

# The New York Times.

THE WEATHER
Showers and thunderstorms today; tomorrow probably fair.
Temperature yesterday—Max., 76; min., 60.
For weather report see Page 20.

Section 1

VOL. LXXIII....No. 24,263. • • • • NEW YORK, SUNDAY, JUNE 29, 1924. Including Rotogravure Picture Section in two parts—Magazine and Book Sections in Rotogravure. FIVE CENTS In Manhattan, Bronx and Brooklyn | Elsewhere TEN CENTS

# CONVENTION, BY ONE VOTE, DEFEATS PLANK NAMING KLAN, BRYAN, IN BITTER DEBATE, PLEADING FOR PARTY UNITY; PROPOSAL FOR LEAGUE REFERENDUM WINS, DESPITE BAKER

## HUNDREDS KILLED BY TORNADO IN OHIO; 80 IN LORAIN THEATRE

### 1,500 Injured in Lorain—100 Are Said to Have Lost Lives in Sandusky.

### FRANTIC CALLS FOR RELIEF

### Looting Breaks Out in Lorain—City Without Food—Red Cross Aid Rushed.

### TROOPS ARE CALLED OUT

### Relief and Rescue Parties Dispatched From Cleveland, Elyria and Other Points.

CLEVELAND, June 28 (Associated Press)—Three hundred are dead and at least 1,500 are injured in Lorain alone as a result of a tornado today, according to reports reaching Colonel D. H. Pond, Director of Red Cross civilian relief, here early tonight. Colonel Pond announced that he had arranged for tents for 1,000 persons to be shipped directly to Lorain from Camp Perry.

Eighty dead have been taken from the State Theatre in Lorain, the chief of police of Elyria reported at 9:30 tonight. Estimates of 300 dead and 1,500 injured are not exaggerated, the chief says.

The storm carried telegraph and telephone wires down with it, isolating Sandusky, Lorain and other points in the northern part of the State, making confirmation of reports impossible.

A motorist who drove from Loraine notified The Cleveland Plain Dealer that not only was East Lorain demolished, but the city of Lorain itself was swept away.

Reports received over crippled railroad wires from Sandusky late tonight state that between fifty and seventy-five persons were killed or drowned there today when the tornado struck that city. The Sandusky water works and several large buildings along the lake front were blown down.

Considerable damage along the shore line east of Cedar Point is reported. Some Summer homes are said to have been blown down and several persons killed.

**Martial Law Declared in Lorain.**

An automobile ferry plying between Sandusky and Marblehead broke loose from its moorings at Sandusky and struck a pier. Fifteen passengers on the ferry are reported to have been drowned.

Martial law has been declared in Lorain by Mayor George Hoffman. Police deputized American Legion members to cooperate with them and the National Guard. Looting is said to be going on freely.

Lorain is without water, light, telephones and food, and has little gas.

First reports received here from a staff correspondent of The Plain Dealer, who motored back to the first available telephone east of Lorain, were to the effect that 200 were killed in the collapse of the State Theatre at Lorain, and that forty others were dead in other parts of the city.

Reports from various other sources place the number of the dead as high as 500.

Rain continued to fall in Lorain for several hours.

Confirmation of the collapse of the theatre and washout of the Black River bridge at Lorain was brought to Cleveland by A. Downer, conductor on the Lake Shore Electric Railway, the first eyewitness of the disaster to reach this city. Many women and children were killed, motorists told him.

Practically every house on Broadway, the main street of the city east and west, was blown down, Downer reported, and automobiles were picked up and overturned on the sidewalks.

**Eyewitness Describes Scene.**

The American Shipyards at Lorain are reported to have been razed. Two boats belonging to Henry Ford were reported to have broken loose.

Reports here that small passenger steamers plying between Sandusky and Lake Erie Island resorts have been lost, but could not be confirmed late tonight.

One of the first eyewitness stories of the cyclone to reach Cleveland was brought back by L. F. Forster of Bay Village. He was in Lorain within a few minutes after the cyclone struck and he walked over several blocks of the devastated area, saw unroofed buildings, fallen trees and telephone poles, heard screams of some of the injured and afterward saw refugees fleeing the city.

"My wife and I and a party of friends were driving toward Lorain," he said. "It must have been 5:30 when the storm struck. We were about three or four miles east of the city and a heavy rain was falling.

**Saw Fires in Wrecked Town.**

"At a gasoline station we met another automobile that had stopped there. It had just come from Lorain and from the man and woman in it we learned there had been a cyclone. They said they had seen houses toppling over, roofs flying through the air, and trees and telephone poles mowed down as by a huge scythe.

"Their car was a sedan. They said the wind blew so hard that they had to sit on the floor to keep it from shattering their ear drums.

"We drove on toward Lorain until a tangle of fallen trees made further progress impossible. Then we got out and walked into the town.

"The town was a wreck. I had an uncanny feeling as I looked at houses without roofs or without walls, as I

Continued on Page Twenty-two.



## TENSE FEELING ON KU KLUX

### Strong Efforts for Harmony Were Kept Up All Day.

### ANTIS FORCED THE ISSUE

### Insisting on Repudiation by Name, They Rejected All Compromises.

### ISSUE OVERSHADOWS MEN

### It Is Admitted That Choice of Nominee Will Be Affected by Action on Religious Liberty.

By RICHARD V. OULAHAN.

When the Democratic National Convention adjourned at 1:50 o'clock this morning until 9:30 o'clock Monday morning it had reached the point of being ready to ballot on the nomination of a Presidential candidate.

Leaders of the McAdoo and anti-McAdoo forces had reached a tentative agreement that after the platform reported yesterday afternoon by the Committee on Resolutions had been adopted the convention should take one and perhaps as many as three ballots to determine the choice of a Presidential candidate.

As matters turned out, the convention became involved in a long contest over the anti-Klan plank offered by the minority of the Committee on Resolutions representing the anti-McAdoo contingents. When this plank was ultimately rejected and the platform adopted without change from the recommendations of the Resolutions Committee, it was decided that it was too late to undertake balloting, and on motion of Franklin D. Roosevelt, one of the managers for Governor Smith's candidacy, the convention adjourned.

The motion to adjourn came at the end of a session which began eleven hours before. Most of the tired delegates had sat in their seats continuously since 3 o'clock yesterday afternoon. The Committee on Resolutions was not ready to report its platform, however, until a considerable time after Madison Square Garden was crowded with delegates and spectators for the session.

All through the remaining hours of yesterday and until adjournment was taken this morning, the convention was engaged in a mighty struggle over the absorbing issue presented by the effort to have the Democratic Party go on record as condemning the Ku Klux Klan by name.

**Oratorical Battle Rages.**

Before the Klan issue was disposed of by the vote announced just before adjournment this morning there was an oratorical battle in which party chiefs of country-wide reputation participated, and an even more extensive struggle between the contending factions while the voting was in progress.

While this oratory was in progress the agreement was reached to begin balloting on the Presidential nomination as soon as the platform was out of the way. The purpose of this agreement was to try out the strength of the various candidates for the Presidential nomination with a view to giving an inkling to the managers of the chief contenders, Smith and McAdoo, as to how the sentiment of the convention was divided.

Behind this purpose was the desire to have conferences Sunday to determine upon what lines the battle for the nomination should be conducted when the convention reassembled on Monday morning after its Sunday rest.

It was the understanding that today should be a day of conferences in which the various managers of Presidential booms would have an opportunity to take account of stock and lay their plans for the final test of strength between the sundry aspirants for the honor of leading the Democratic hosts in the contest with the ticket headed by Calvin Coolidge.

**Great Crowd Waits Patiently.**

It was 5:30 o'clock when the reading of the platform presented by the Committee on Resolutions was completed. The vast audience in Madison Square Garden breathed a deep and heartfelt sigh of relief from what obviously was a strain. For three hours, delegates, alternates and the many thousand spectators in the galleries had sat patiently, held to their seats by the knowledge that the session promised sensations of momentous importance to the Democratic Party and possibly to the country, and the conclusion of the reading was accepted as a signal that the time for action was at hand.

The motion for a recess at the end of the session held yesterday morning provided that the convention should reassemble at 2:30 o'clock in the afternoon as usual. The participants in the convention and the spectators were slow in entering the Garden, but they might have been even slower without losing an opportunity of seeing all that was to be seen and listening to the discussion which the platform evoked.

To people with strained nerves the wait was trying, but everybody appeared to be in a mood to stand it without complaint. There was no move on the part of the convention officers, whose appearance on the platform was watched closely by the audience, to indicate that the proceedings were about to be begun, until just after 4 o'clock, when Senator Walsh of Montana, the

Continued on Page Seven.

### *Vote on Substituting The Baker League Plank*

| State. | Yes. | No. |
|---|---|---|
| Alabama | 11½ | 11½ |
| Arizona | 1½ | 4½ |
| Arkansas | 3 | 13 |
| California | 4 | 22 |
| Colorado | 9½ | 2½ |
| Connecticut | 5 | 9 |
| Delaware | 6 | .. |
| Florida | 5 | 7 |
| Georgia | .. | 28 |
| Idaho | 8 | .. |
| Illinois | 10 | 48 |
| Indiana | .. | 30 |
| Iowa | .. | 26 |
| Kansas | .. | 20 |
| Kentucky | 9½ | 16½ |
| Louisiana | .. | 20 |
| Maine | 11 | 1 |
| Maryland | .. | 16 |
| Massachusetts | 8 | 28 |
| Michigan | 6 | 24 |
| Minnesota | 10 | 14 |
| Mississippi | .. | 20 |
| Missouri | 2 | 34 |
| Montana | .. | 8 |
| Nebraska | .. | 16 |
| Nevada | .. | 6 |
| New Hampshire | 8 | .. |
| New Jersey | .. | 28 |
| New Mexico | .. | 6 |
| New York | 35 | 55 |
| North Carolina | 6 | 18 |
| North Dakota | 1 | 9 |
| Ohio | 48 | .. |
| Oklahoma | .. | 20 |
| Oregon | 1 | 9 |
| Pennsylvania | 52 | 22 |
| Rhode Island | .. | 10 |
| South Carolina | 18 | .. |
| South Dakota | .. | 10 |
| Tennessee | 15 | 9 |
| Texas | .. | 40 |
| Utah | 6½ | 2½ |
| Vermont | 2 | 6 |
| Virginia | 24 | .. |
| Washington | .. | 14 |
| West Virginia | 16 | .. |
| Wisconsin | 4 | 22 |
| Wyoming | 3 | 3 |
| Alaska | 1 | 5 |
| District of Columbia | .. | 6 |
| Hawaii | .. | 6 |
| Philippines | 2 | 4 |
| Porto Rico | 1 | 5 |
| Panama Canal Zone | .. | 6 |
| Totals | 353½ | 742½ |

## KLAN FIGHT STIRS THE 'DARK HORSES'

### Their Managers Striving to Line Up Possible Bolters From the Leaders.

### FIGURE ON CLOSE CONTEST

### Each Counts on Support From the Losers in the Battle Over Klanism.

With the secondary stage of the balloting for candidates, in which they are most vitally interested, definitely deferred until the Democratic National Convention resumes its labors tomorrow, groomers of the long string of "dark horses" which were entered in the race for Presidential nomination last week spent the interval between the two sessions yesterday in an endeavor to marshal their forces for the fight over the Ku Klux Klan plank.

At least two of the candidates prominently before the convention have taken their stand definitely in favor of a plank naming the Klan and condemning all that it stands for in thought and action. Governor Smith is out openly in favor of all-the-way denunciation of the hooded order. Senator Oscar W. Underwood of Alabama made his primary fight for delegates on a personal platform in which the central plank was a pronunciamento against the Ku Klux Klan.

With the forces behind Governor Smith and Senator Underwood united in the fight for such a plank, the managers of those campaigns were busily at work, before the afternoon session began, lining up delegates from other camps who, while not committed to either the Governor or the Senator from Alabama, were expected to ally themselves with the Smith and Underwood contingent in the fight for an outspoken anti-Klan plank.

There was the keenest realization in the camp of the "dark horses" that candidates might stand or fall by the outcome of the fight that was to be staged in the Garden later in the day. Should the McAdoo forces, for instance, find themselves in a position to keep out of the platform an open denunciation of the Klan, the elimination of Senator Underwood as a candidate would almost inevitably follow, while it would most seriously affect the prospects of Governor Smith, who next to McAdoo has the greatest number of delegates supporting him.

An inventory of their strength convinced the Smith and Underwood managers that the fight over the Klan plank was bound to be a close one. In addition to the two considerable groups of delegates, numbering from three to four hundred, which are firmly committed to Governor Smith and Senator Underwood, the managers of those

Continued on Page Nine.



## TEXT OF DEBATE ON LEAGUE

### Baker Refers to Majority Plank as Repudiation of Woodrow Wilson.

### CALLS IT UNCONSTITUTIONAL

### Rabbi Wise Supports Him and Terms Referendum Plan a Subterfuge.

### LUCKING OPENS ARGUMENT

### Senator Pittman, Defending Proposal, Booed and Jeered for Attack on Baker.

One of the greatest demonstrations since the convention has been under way occurred when Newton D. Baker, former Secretary of War, in an impassioned appeal, urged that the party adopt a strong and unequivocal pledge for participation of this country in the League of Nations.

Mr. Baker, who was President Wilson's close personal and political friend, summoned the party, through its platform, to take up the forward march with the soul of Woodrow Wilson, for the policies he had fought for. The convention responded to this appeal with a mighty roar and a demonstration which kept the delegates on their feet cheering for several moments.

For a little time it looked like the beginning of a foreshadowed stampede of the convention for President Wilson's Secretary of War.

Secretary Baker spoke in support of a minority plank providing for full participation of this country in the League of Nations and in opposition to a plank reported by the Resolutions Committee under the terms of which entry of this country into the League would be subject to a Federal referendum.

Alfred Lucking, counsel for Henry Ford and representative of Michigan on the Resolutions Committee, spoke for the majority plank, as also did Senator Pittman of Nevada. Mr. Baker contended that the proposed referendum was impracticable and unconstitutional and the proposal a subterfuge and Rabbi Stephen Wise, urged the adoption of the minority plank proposed by the former War Secretary.

**Full Text of the Debate.**

Following is the full text of the stenographic record of the debate:

The Chairman—The Chair recognizes the Hon. Newton D. Baker of Ohio.

Mr. Baker—Mr. Chairman and Ladies and Gentlemen of the Convention: It will be assumed that I would not venture to ask your consideration at this late day in this long conversation upon a minority report unless I felt that the gravity of the subject justified it.

I respect my associates on this committee. If in what I am about to say and in hurried speech it should seem at any time, by unfortunate accident, that I am showing less respect than I should for the gravity of their judgment or the courage and earnestness of their purpose, I ask you to excuse in me what only accident could cause.

There is no subject on this earth, apart from my relations to my God and my duty to my family, which compares even remotely with me with the League of Nations. (Great applause.)

There are men and women in this assembly whom I have met in other conventions. There are people here with whom for twenty-five years I have marched and fought for causes which we deemed great. If in that time it ever seemed to you that I deserved or might sometimes deserve your sympathy, support and help, give it to me now! I need it! (Applause.)

The man who ought to be pleading this cause is dead and lies in consecrated ground. (Applause.)

And all that is here to state his cause, weak, inadequate—all that is here is what is left of me at the end of five days, with about two hours' sleep in each night of the five.

**Would Appeal to Every Emotion.**

I do not like to appeal to your sympathy, but I want to appeal to every emotion you have in your hearts and to every thought that your intellects can generate, for we are now dealing with the gravest question, as the majority say, that can possibly be considered by man. (Applause.)

Some of this has got to be a bit technical, for again asserting my respect for this majority, I want to say that in no convention of a political character, outside of the one recently in Milwaukee, that I have ever heard in the United States has so phantastic a proposition ever been proposed with regard to American constitutional practice as is proposed by the revolutionary report of a majority of the committee on this subject. (Applause.)

Examine with me just a moment now those two reports. What does the majority report do? With praiseful and perfumed voice it praises the League of Nations as a lover would address his sweetheart. Everything that fanciful words and artistic and cunning expressions of praise can do are done to express the admiration and approval of the majority of the committee for the League of Nations. These praises, some of them chosen from the plank submitted by the Non-Partisan Association for the League of Nations, some of them out of drafts which came through me to the

Continued on Page Three.

### *Vote by States on Plank Condemning Ku Klux Klan*

The vote was on the proposed amendment of the committee minority, expressly naming the Klan. The "ayes" favored the more drastic anti-Klan plank.

| State. | Yes. | No. |
|---|---|---|
| Alabama | 24 | .. |
| Arizona | 1 | 5 |
| Arkansas | .. | 18 |
| California | 7 | 19 |
| Colorado | 6 | 6 |
| Connecticut | 13 | 1 |
| Delaware | 6 | .. |
| Florida | 1 | 11 |
| Georgia | 1 | 22 |
| Idaho | .. | 8 |
| Illinois | 45 | 13 |
| Indiana | 5 | 25 |
| Iowa | 13½ | 12½ |
| Kansas | .. | 20 |
| Kentucky | 9½ | 16½ |
| Louisiana | .. | 20 |
| Maine | 8 | 4 |
| Maryland | 16 | .. |
| Massachusetts | 35½ | ½ |
| Michigan | 12½ | 16½ |
| Minnesota | 17 | 7 |
| Mississippi | .. | 20 |
| Missouri | 10½ | [illegible] |
| Montana | 1 | 7 |
| Nebraska | 3 | 13 |
| Nevada | .. | 6 |
| New Hampshire | 2½ | 5½ |
| New Jersey | 28 | .. |
| New Mexico | 1 | 5 |
| New York | 90 | .. |
| North Carolina | 3.85 | 20.15 |
| North Dakota | 10 | .. |
| Ohio | 32 | 16 |
| Oklahoma | .. | 20 |
| Oregon | .. | 10 |
| Pennsylvania | 49½ | 26½ |
| Rhode Island | 10 | .. |
| South Carolina | .. | 18 |
| South Dakota | 6 | 4 |
| Tennessee | 3 | 21 |
| Texas | .. | 46 |
| Utah | 4 | 4 |
| Vermont | 8 | .. |
| Virginia | 2½ | 21½ |
| Washington | .. | 14 |
| West Virginia | 7 | 9 |
| Wisconsin | 25 | 1 |
| Wyoming | 2 | 4 |
| Alaska | 6 | .. |
| District of Columbia | 6 | .. |
| Hawaii | 4 | 2 |
| Philippine Islands | 2 | 3 |
| Porto Rico | 2 | 4 |
| Canal Zone | 2 | 4 |
| Total | 541 3-20 | 542 3-20 |

Amendment rejected by 1 vote.

[The totals given are those officially announced as the result, but the votes do not check, owing to the confusion over the numerous charges.]

## MAKERS OF PLATFORM IN MORNING PRAYER

### Solemn Scene After Prolonged Session of the Committee.

### KLAN DISCUSSION SHARP

### But Completed Platform Is Called Progressive, Not Radical.

The platform as presented to the Democratic Convention yesterday was conceived amid the most fervid and tense atmosphere. For three days and nights the leaders in the party discussed the big issues. By late Friday morning they had agreed upon the non-controversial planks. In the morning hours from midnight on Friday until sunrise yesterday morning these men, who had wrestled off and on with the big disturbing issues, the League of Nations and the Klan, prayed for light as the sun was shining over the housetops.

Before the prayers these committeemen had disposed of the League of Nations plank to the satisfaction of the majority and had likewise framed a plank on the Klan that was acceptable to the large majority of the committee.

But a minority of the committee voted to report a plank expressly naming the Klan. Their report was signed by William P. Pattengall of Maine and the following twelve other committee members: Frederick I. Thompson of Alabama, Senator David I. Walsh of Massachusetts, P. H. Quinn of Rhode Island, C. C. Carlin of District of Columbia, John H. McCann of Pennsylvania, Francis X. Busch of Illinois, Joseph A. Kellogg of New York, Harry Heher of New Jersey, James A. Nowell of Minnesota, James P. Leamy of Vermont, E. Brooke Lee of Maryland and John W. Troy of Alaska.

The plank on the League of Nations is interpreted by peace advocates and the ardent Wilson supporters as a straddle on the League, but it is not generally regarded as a repudiation of the League, which was one of the chief issues in the 1920 campaign. The platform makers sought to make it a secondary issue, without abandoning the pro-League policy, and aimed by the referendum proposal to take it out of the 1924 campaign, putting off consideration to a non-political election.

The railroad plank lacks the specific

Continued on Page Seven.



## TEXT OF THE KLAN DEBATE

### Arguments For and Against Censuring Order by Name.

### SENATOR OWEN FOR UNITY

### He Opposes Condemning the Klan Unheard as Inducing Religious Dissension.

### PATTENGALL ASSAILS ORDER

### Colby, David I. Walsh and Others Back Him, While W. J. Bryan Opposes.

The Democratic Convention began debate on the Klan issue last night immediately after the balloting on the League of Nations amendment offered by Mr. Baker.

The climax of a bitter debate, interrupted by applause, hisses and boos from both floor and galleries, came with the final plea of William J. Bryan against adoption of the amendment naming the Klan. He appealed for party harmony and exhorted his hearers to avoid causing dissension among Christians and perhaps a religious war.

The textual report of Mr. Bryan's address follows:

The Chairman—Mr. Cummings yields twenty-five minutes to that revered Democrat, the Hon. William J. Bryan from Florida. [Loud applause.]

A Voice—The head of the party, Mr. Bryan.

Mr. Chairman, ladies and gentlemen, members of the convention: It is now twenty-eight years since Democratic conventions became gracious enough to invite me and patient enough to listen to me, and I have not words in which to express my gratitude for the love and loyalty of millions of Democrats who have been my co-laborers for more than a quarter of a century. [Applause.]

I have spoken to you on many themes, never on themes more important than today; and since they take applause out of my time, and since I am speaking to your hearts and heads and not to your hands, keep still and let me speak to you. [Cries of "We'll do it."]

I have only a short time in which to lay before you the arguments that seem to me pertinent to this occasion, when we are about to decide not only the line of our campaign this Fall, but in which we may affect larger things than parties.

Let's understand each other. Let's eliminate the things that are not in this issue and come down to the three words that these, our good friends, as honest, as patriotic and as anxious for the welfare of the party, take out of the language and exalt above any other three words that will be used in this campaign. Note, my friends, that they take our report, every word of it, and note also that we offered to take every word of their report, but three. We said: "Strike out three words and there will be no objection." But three words were more to them than the welfare of a party in a great campaign. [Applause.]

You have listened to the applause when we have had read to you the best Democratic platform that was ever written, the noblest principles that have ever been written into a platform. We have there pleas pathetic for people in distress, but none of our principles, none of our pleas stirred the hearts of these men like the words, "Ku Klux Klan." [Long and continued hisses, boos and jeers.]

[The Chairman raps for order.]

The Chairman—The delegates of the convention will preserve order. I shall have to call Mr. Bryan when the time has expired unless you permit him to proceed.

Mr. Bryan—I call you to witness, I call you to witness that these men never took the standards of their States and marched when we appealed on grand principles. It was only when they said the Ku Klux Klan, that's the only thing—— [Hisses, boos and jeers.]

**Walsh Threatens to Clear Galleries.**

The Chairman—The officers will preserve order——

A Voice—Clear the galleries of the hoodlums.

The Chairman—Or these proceedings will cease. Please let us have order here.

Mr. Bryan—Citizens of New York, you show your appreciation of the honor we did you in holding our convention here. [A confusion of cries from the floor with the Chairman rapping for order.]

The Chairman—If the speaker is again interrupted by the galleries, they will be cleared. [Applause and some hisses.]. I shall order this in the name of the delegates of this convention, for whom I speak. I warn the delegates that this speaker is to continue, and without interruption from them.

Mr. Bryan—Let me place before you the five reasons which I submit to your judgments and your consciences. First,

Continued on Page Six.



### *Anti-Klan Plank That Won And Amendment That Was Lost*

*This is the text of the anti-Klan plank adopted:*

FREEDOM OF RELIGION, FREEDOM OF SPEECH, FREEDOM OF PRESS.

The Democratic Party reaffirms its adherence and devotion to those cardinal principles contained in the Constitution and the precepts upon which our Government is founded, that Congress shall make no laws respecting the establishment of religion or prohibiting the free exercise thereof, or abridging the freedom of speech or of the press, or the right of the people peaceably to assemble and to petition the Government for a redress of grievances; that the Church and the State shall be and remain separate, and that no religious test shall ever be required as a qualification to any office of public trust under the United States.

These principles we pledge ourselves ever to defend and maintain.

We insist at all times upon obedience to the orderly processes of the law and deplore and condemn any effort to arouse religious or racial dissension.

*This is the stronger addition to the above which the convention rejected:*

We condemn political secret societies as opposed to the exercise of free government and contrary to the spirit of the Declaration of Independence and of the Constitution of the United States.

We pledge the Democratic Party to oppose any effort on the part of the Ku Klux Klan or any organization to interfere with the religious liberty or political freedom of any citizen, or to limit the civic rights of any citizen or body of citizens because of religion, birthplace or racial origin.

## PREDICT KLAN ROW WILL INJURE PARTY

### Leaders of Masked Order See Split in South, No Matter How Platform Reads.

### OPPOSITION A SURPRISE

### Strength of Its Enemies Here Led to a Hurry Call for Klan Reinforcements.

Klan leaders were predicting yesterday that as the result of the injection of the Klan issue into the Democratic Convention the nominees of the party, no matter who they might be, would shoulder the heaviest burden ever bequeathed to the candidates of any party.

A delegate to the convention, a man who is a member of the House of Representatives and whose election was said to be the result of Klan endorsement, even went so far as to express the opinion that the party, having challenged the Klan, should be consistent and nominate an out-and-out anti-Klan candidate for President.

"We might just as well make it a clean cut issue between the Klan and the anti-Klan," said this man, "and go to the country with a candidate who stands four square on the platform, instead of pussy-footing in an effort to win votes both ways."

This man declared himself in full sympathy with Senator Underwood's public statement that the convention, if it approved the Klan, should say so, and on the other hand, if it was against the hooded organization, it should say so just as frankly. He said it would do no good to denounce the Klan without naming it, "for the damage is done and the issue is here."

In the opinion of many of the leaders in the convention, men who are not of the Klan, the handling of the Klan issue in this convention is one of the worst bungles in the history of the party. These men insist that the wise course would have been to have passed a simple resolution, if necessary, reaffirming the Jeffersonian principles of religious freedom, and then leave the Klan to go its own way, a way which they declared was becoming more and more downhill every day.

Klansmen express the opinion that the convention has handled the problem in such fashion as will in the end bring thousands of new members into the "invisible empire" in all parts of the Union. As the situation now is, the Republican Party, they say, is certain to be chief beneficiary of the Madison Square Garden row.

The defeat in committee of the plank which mentioned the Klan by name was looked on by the White-robed Knights as a victory, but they conceded that it was not a decisive one. After all the publicity of the last few days and the big anti-Klan demonstration which followed the nomination of Senator Underwood, putting in or omitting the name of the organization, they argued, is a minor consideration.

**Klan Surprised by Opposition.**

An outstanding fact of the situation disclosed in the proceedings of the last two days, is that the Klan came to New York confident that it would be able to block the anti-Klan forces just as it did at Cleveland. When it found opponents in the majority it was one of the biggest political surprises in the history of the Klan. It was something the Klonclilium did not think possible.

When the Klan leaders, who had come

Continued on Page Seven.



## GEORGIA BEATS KLAN PLANK

### Changes Vote and a Half, Some Say on Order by McAdoo Leaders.

### UNIT RULE ALSO HAS EFFECT

### Many States Challenged and Repolled, and One Fist Fight Mars Dramatic Session.

### BAKER ALSO LOSES BATTLE

### His Plea for League Wins Him an Ovation, but Delegates Reject His Plank.

By ELMER DAVIS.

An effort to incorporate in the Democratic platform a plank condemning the Ku Klux Klan by name was lost early this morning by a single vote, 541 3-20 votes having been cast for it and 542 3-20 against it.

The motion was defeated largely by virtue of the unit rule, under which only one State, Alabama, with a dissenting minority, voted for it, while a number voted against.

Even so, it could not have been beaten without the forced changes of one and a half votes in the Georgia delegation, originally cast for the motion but turned against it, according to rumor, by instructions from the McAdoo headquarters.

The resolution that was beaten was offered by fourteen of the fifty-four members of the Platform Committee as a minority report. It was advocated most vigorously by William Pattangall of Maine and Edmond H. Moore of Ohio. In its place there was adopted the Klan plank recommended by a majority of the committee, which merely advocated religious liberty and equality without mentioning the name of any order which opposes them.

**Struggle Lasts Four Hours.**

The fight over the Klan plank lasted from 8:45 o'clock at night till nearly 2 o'clock in the morning. Before it began a minority plank, calling for immediate entry into the League of Nations, offered by Newton D. Baker of Ohio and advocated by him in a passionate speech, which won him a personal triumph, was defeated by a vote of 742½ to 353½. The majority plank which was adopted, called for a popular referendum which the Government should regard as advisory.

With the majority planks thus supported in both the controversial cases, the platform as a whole was put to the convention and declared carried by a viva voce vote, although there were loud shouts against it.

At 1:55 o'clock, after nearly ten hours of continuous session, the convention adjourned until 9:30 o'clock Monday morning, when balloting on the candidates for President will begin.

The effort to get the name of the Ku Klux Klan into the platform resulted in one of the most entertaining evenings that have been seen in recent national conventions. There was, to begin with, two hours of oratory for and against the proposal, which was closed for the defense—that is for the majority of the Resolutions Committee who did not want to name the Klan—by William Jennings Bryan, who spoke with his old-time fire and enthusiasm and very nearly with his old-time success.

**Bryan Often Hissed and Booed.**

Unfortunately the galleries happened to be passionately interested in the side of the case which he was against, and he was hissed and booed again and again.

Once the chorus of hoots became so loud that Senator Thomas J. Walsh, Chairman of the convention, threatened to have them cleared if the offense were repeated. That kept the galleries fairly quiet.

Mr. Bryan was perhaps the most brilliant speaker of the evening, but the hero of the session was Andrew C. Erwin of Athens, Ga., who made a three-minute speech of extraordinary fire in favor of naming the Klan and declared that Georgians who didn't support him were unworthy of their ancestry.

This provoked a wild demonstration and the parade of twenty-three State standards around the Georgian delegation, the crowd pushing in so hard that police had to protect the Georgians.

Erwin nearly saved the anti-Klan motion again when he demanded a poll of the Georgia delegation after it had been announced by its Chairman, Hollins Randolph, as having voted three ayes and 25 noes. On Mr. Erwin's insistence, the roll of the delegation was called and it was discovered that several members were absent so that the roll showed 2½ votes aye and 17 [illegible]

**Tries Hard to Get Votes.**

But Mr. Randolph labored hard to get the votes for the motion changed and he finally worked on three of the five half-vote delegates who had voted for it and persuaded them to come around to the negative. Two or three delegates who had been absent when the first vote

"All the News That's Fit to Print."

# The New York Times.

THE WEATHER
Unsettled; local showers today; probably fair and warmer tomorrow.
Temperature yesterday—Max., 81; min., 70.
For weather report see Page 24.

VOL. LXXIII....No. 24,273. NEW YORK, WEDNESDAY, JULY 9, 1924. TWO CENTS In Greater New York | THREE CENTS Within 200 Miles | FOUR CENTS Elsewhere

# M'ADOO FREES DELEGATES FOR MEREDITH; J. W. DAVIS GETS 203½ ON THE 100TH BALLOT, THEN CONVENTION AT 4 A. M. QUITS TILL NOON

## GALLERIES BARE AT BREAK

### Hardly 500 There When Deadlock Is Broken—Delegates Down to 800.

### McADOO LETTER A PUZZLE

### Some Hearers Thought He Had Withdrawn—Others That He Only Released Forces.

### WOMEN ASKED HIM TO STICK

### And Followers Determined to Show Strength After Smith Quit as 'Leading Candidate.'

By ELMER DAVIS.

Hope deferred maketh the heart faint but realization deferred is just about as bad.

For about the tenth time a capacity crowd assembled at Madison Square Garden yesterday evening, having got the tip that this time at last a candidate was to be put over. The day session, with the usual vain balloting, had ended in a plea for harmony and a six-hour adjournment, and it had been rumored that McAdoo and Smith were going to get together and agree on a joint withdrawal.

Smith was ready but McAdoo—then—was not. And when David Ladd Rockwell, McAdoo's manager, finally announced his candidate's willingness to leave his supporters to their own devices at 2:45 o'clock this morning, there were hardly 500 people in the galleries.

Unless this reporter's estimate of a crowd is far less accurate than it has usually been, there were not more than 800 of the 1,098 delegates on the floor, though by a combination of unit rules, gentlemen's agreements and courtesy they were voting for their absent brothers.

Worn out by a night of futile balloting, the exhausted survivors of the ninety-ninth ballot suddenly sat up and stopped buzzing when Chairman Walsh announced the receipt of a letter from William G. McAdoo. Franklin D. Roosevelt, manager for Governor Smith, had announced at the beginning of the night session that Smith would withdraw if McAdoo did. McAdoo's letter might mean the break-up of the deadlock which had lasted forty ballots longer than any deadlock ever lasted before, and it would normally have been welcomed by everybody; but the final blast in Mr. McAdoo's declaration about progressive principles and the defeat of the reactionary and "wet" elements to which he professed himself opposed were greeted by hisses from the anti-McAdoo delegates.

For they were already angry at McAdoo for forcing them to spend six hours of the night and morning balloting after Smith had offered to withdraw if McAdoo would.

**Women Plead With McAdoo.**

Al Smith had proposed in a conference with McAdoo before dinner that they both withdraw, but McAdoo refused, then. When a swarm of delegates, mostly women, beset his headquarters after the conference and begged him not to withdraw he had promised to stick. Moreover, when Mr. Roosevelt announced that Governor Smith would withdraw if McAdoo would, he had incautiously called attention to the fact that Smith was at that time the leader in the balloting, having run some 40 votes beyond McAdoo.

This annoyed the McAdoo delegates, who at once decided to show the Smith people that McAdoo did have reserve strength. On the first ballot of the night session McAdoo jumped 81 votes, from 314 to 395. On the next he went over 400. The rest of the evening was spent in a demonstration that McAdoo could keep ahead of Smith and when at last the McAdoo letter was read, in the early hours of the morning, its phraseology was so ambiguous that nobody in the house knew whether it was a real withdrawal at all.

Still, there it was. McAdoo had said that his delegates could do as they liked and Smith had previously said that he would withdraw if McAdoo would. Instantly a joyful delegate from Ohio moved that the convention adjourn until 2 o'clock this afternoon. After the long and weary grind which had already taken ninety-nine ballots and used up all the nerve force and spending money in the Democratic Party, it seemed likely that with the leading candidates out of the way—if they were out of the way—which nobody seemed to be sure of—something could be done this afternoon. But the roll-call of States on the motion to adjourn showed that a big majority was in favor of going on with the hundredth ballot.

For, of course, while McAdoo had in a way released his delegates by the terms of his letter, it was not in form a withdrawal and apparently some of the McAdoo leaders wanted to show

Continued on Page Two.



## LATEST (ONE HUNDREDTH) BALLOT.

| Total Vote | STATE | McAdoo | Smith | J. W. Davis | Underwood | Meredith | Glass | Robinson | Ritchie | Walsh |
|---|---|---|---|---|---|---|---|---|---|---|
| 24 | Alabama | | | | 24 | | | | | |
| 6 | Arizona | 3 | | | 3 | | | | | |
| 18 | Arkansas | | | | | | | 18 | | |
| 26 | California | 16½ | | | | 6 | | | | 3½ |
| 12 | Colorado | ½ | 3½ | 1½ | 1 | 1 | | | | |
| 14 | Connecticut | 2 | 12 | | | | | | | |
| 6 | Delaware | | | | | | | | | |
| 12 | Florida | 9 | | 3 | | | | | | |
| 28 | Georgia | 28 | | | | | | | | |
| 8 | Idaho | | | | | | | | | |
| 58 | Illinois | | 36 | 6 | | 12 | 1 | 2 | 1 | 1 |
| 30 | Indiana | | | 14 | 4 | 11 | | | | |
| 26 | Iowa | | | | | 26 | | | | |
| 20 | Kansas | | | 20 | | | | | | |
| 26 | Kentucky | 12 | | 8½ | | | | | | 1 |
| 20 | Louisiana | | | 20 | | | | | | |
| 12 | Maine | 1 | 2 | 8 | 1 | | | | | |
| 16 | Maryland | | | | | | | | | |
| 36 | Massachus'ts | 2½ | 33½ | | | | | | | |
| 30 | Michigan | | 10 | 15 | | | | | | 5 |
| 24 | Minnesota | 6 | 15 | 1 | | | 1 | 1 | | |
| 20 | Mississippi | | | | | | | 20 | | |
| 36 | Missouri | | | 36 | | | | | | |
| 8 | Montana | 1 | | | | | | | | 7 |
| 16 | Nebraska | | 2 | | | 11 | | | | |
| 6 | Nevada | | 6 | | | | | | | |
| 8 | N. Ham'hire | | 1 | 2 | | 1½ | | | | 3½ |
| 28 | New Jersey | | 28 | | | | | | | |
| 6 | New Mexico | 6 | | | | | | | | |
| 90 | New York | 2 | 88 | | | | | | | |
| 24 | No. Carolina | | | | | | | | | |
| 10 | No. Dakota | 3 | 5 | | | 1 | | 1 | | |
| 48 | Ohio | | 15 | 23 | | 5 | 5 | | | |
| 20 | Oklahoma | | | | | | | | | |
| 10 | Oregon | 10 | | | | | | | | |
| 76 | Pennsylv'nia | 17½ | 39½ | 9 | 3½ | | 1 | | ½ | |
| 10 | Rhode Isl'nd | | 10 | | | | | | | |
| 18 | So. Carolina | 18 | | | | | | | | |
| 10 | So. Dakota | | | | | | | | | |
| 24 | Tennessee | 6 | | 8 | 2 | | 3 | 4 | | |
| 40 | Texas | 40 | | | | | | | | |
| 8 | Utah | | | 4 | | | | | | 4 |
| 8 | Vermont | | 8 | | | | | | | |
| 24 | Virginia | | | | | | 24 | | | |
| 14 | Washington | | | | | | | | | 14 |
| 16 | W. Virginia | | | 16 | | | | | | |
| 26 | Wisconsin | | 22 | | 2 | 1 | | | | 1 |
| 6 | Wyoming | | 3 | ½ | | | | | | 2½ |
| 6 | Alaska | | 6 | | | | | | | |
| 6 | Dist. of Col. | | | | | | | | | 6 |
| 6 | Hawaii | 1 | 1 | 3 | 1 | | | | | |
| 6 | Philippines | 2 | 2 | | | | | | | 2 |
| 6 | Porto Rico | | 1 | 5 | | | | | | |
| 6 | Canal Zone | 3 | 3 | | | | | | | |
| 1098 | Totals | 190 | 351½ | 203½ | 41½ | 75½ | 35 | 46 | 17½ | 52½ |

Total votes cast, 1089. Necessary to a choice, 726.

SCATTERING, 76. HOUSTON—Ida. 8, Tenn. 1. Total 9. BRYAN—Neb. 2. Total 2. SAULSBURY—Del. 6. Total 6. DANIELS—North Caro. 24. Total 24. OWEN—Okla. 20. Total 20. BAKER—Pa. 4. Total 4. GERARD—So. Dak. 10. Total 10. BERRY—Col. 1. Total 1.

## RALSTON ANNOUNCES HE WILL NOT ACCEPT

### Sends Word to Taggart That He Wants His Name Withdrawn From Race.

### HEARS CONVENTION BY RADIO

### Is Showered With Telegrams—Has Home Anxiety in Son's Illness.

INDIANAPOLIS, Ind., July 8.—Senator Samuel M. Ralston late today definitely instructed Thomas Taggart to withdraw his name from further consideration as a candidate for the Democratic nomination for President.

He had listened during the day on the radio at his farm home when the eighty-ninth ballot taken in the National Convention was announced, showing that he had received 100½ votes, his high mark.

Mr. Ralston declined to comment at that time, but later he said he was puzzled by his sudden acquisition of strength in the voting. He said he had not been in communication with Mr. Taggart, leader of the Indiana delegation; Fred Van Nuys, his law partner and a member of the delegation, or any others in New York, before the eighty-ninth ballot was taken.

The Senator continued to receive telegrams today declaring that his nomination would restore harmony in the Democratic Party. He made public one such message, received just after the eighty-ninth ballot, from B. F. Yoakum, a New York business man widely known in farming circles, as follows:

"The Democratic National Convention is becoming a joke throughout the country. Your nomination would restore its respect and confidence not only among the delegates but the country at large."

The Senator said he was not replying to messages received since he requested the withdrawal of his name from consideration by the convention on July 4.

When asked regarding the reports that he might be chosen as the candidate for the Vice Presidency, Mr. Ralston said:

"I am giving that matter no consideration whatever."

Sorrow over the death of Calvin Coolidge Jr. and anxiety over the serious illness of their own son, Emmet, 34, pervaded the Ralston home this morning, overshadowing the trend of

Continued on Page Four.



## SMITH AND M'ADOO HELD SECRET PARLEY

### Before Night Session Governor Appealed in Vain to Rival to Withdraw.

### CLOSETED FOR AN HOUR

### New Yorker Was Overheard to Accuse Californian of Trying to Wreck the Party.

Governor Alfred E. Smith and William G. McAdoo, leaders in the fight for the Democratic nomination for the Presidency, were brought together in conference yesterday afternoon by Cordell Hull, Chairman of the National Democratic Committee, and Senator Thomas P. Walsh, Permanent Chairman of the convention, in an effort to break the convention deadlock.

The meeting took place in the apartment of Hugh Wallace, former Ambassador to France, at the Ritz-Carlton.

Friends of Mr. McAdoo circulated a rumor in the convention hall during the evening that Governor Smith had pleaded with the former to get out of the race.

The Smith people promptly denied the story and said quite the opposite was true. They said the Governor not only had not pleaded with Mr. McAdoo but took an aggressive attitude toward his rival. They said that the party in the adjoining room, waiting for the meeting between the two candidates to end, heard Governor Smith's voice raised to a high pitch several times and heard the Governor tell Mr. McAdoo that his attitude was indefensible, that he was trying to wreck the party and that the Democrats would hold him responsible for what was going on. Mr. McAdoo, they said, seemed to have very little to say.

**Governor Smith Silent on Details.**

In the party that went to the Ritz-Carlton besides Governor Smith and Mr. McAdoo were Senator Walsh, Chairman Hull, Thomas L. Chadbourne and George Van Namee, former secretary to the Governor. After Mr. McAdoo and Governor Smith had shaken hands they retired to a private room and were closeted together for a full hour.

When the Smith party returned to the Manhattan Club, Governor Smith readily admitted that he had met Mr. McAdoo.

"We had known each other in the tube days," said the Governor. "And I had no trouble in recognizing him. We retired to a private room and we talked for an hour. We discussed at length

Continued on Page Three.

## Text of Mr. Roosevelt's Speech With Smith Offer to Quit

The official stenographic report of Franklin D. Roosevelt's speech, containing Governor Smith's offer to withdraw from the contest for the Presidential nomination, is as follows:

"Mr. Chairman and fellow-delegates: You have been far too good to me, much better than I deserve, [cries of "No," "No," and applause] but all the same I want to say to you that this is, I hope, the last time that I shall address a Democratic convention until 1928. [Cries of "Good," and applause.] Tonight I am here to make a very brief and very simple statement on behalf of Governor Smith. [Applause and "Hurrah for Smith."] The candidate for whom I speak now leads the poll in this convention. We have advocated his nomination as the representative of great Democratic principles, but the future of the Democratic Party rises far above the success of any candidate. ["Atta Boy" and applause.]

"After nearly one hundred ballots it is quite apparent to him and to me that the forces in this convention behind Governor Smith, the leader in the race, and those behind Mr. McAdoo, a close second, cannot be amalgamated. For the sake of the party, therefore, Governor Smith authorizes me to say that immediately upon the withdrawal by Mr. McAdoo of his name, Governor Smith will withdraw his name also from the consideration of the convention. [Loud applause.]

"And as one of the representatives of Governor Smith I would add only this: That until such withdrawal has been made by Mr. McAdoo, I can say that Governor Smith's supporters will continue to vote for Governor Smith." [Loud applause and cries of "Atta Boy."]

## CONVENTION COSTS PRODUCE A CRISIS

### Exceeded $800,000 as Local Committee Turn Over Management Saturday.

### NOW UP TO NATIONAL BODY

### Committee Had but $100,000 and at Once Began to Prune Expenses.

The New York Convention Committee has turned over the further management of the convention to the Democratic National Committee, after having expended approximately $800,000, and because its own funds are limited to about $100,000 the National Committee has begun cutting down expenses, one of the marked cuts being in the matter of ushers.

The New York committee carried practically the entire expense of the convention up to last Saturday night, or for two weeks, as the Garden was turned over to the Convention Committee and the National Committee several days before the first session was held. It was then thought the convention would last possibly ten days at the longest.

The New York committee informed the National Committee last Saturday, through George Mara, who has had charge of the arrangements, that it had fulfilled its obligations, and expenses arising after that day would have to be met by the National Committee. It was following this announcement that the force of ushers was cut.

It is not the fact that the New York Committee is in financial straits, or that it will require additional funds to meet its obligations. The expenses of the band, for one thing, are to be met by the Mayor's Committee.

As to the general situation between the National Committee and the New York Committe, Stanley J. Quinn made the following statement last night to THE NEW YORK TIMES:

"The New York Convention Committee, at the beginning of its preparations for the convention, budgeted all its ex

Continued on Page Four.

## TURMOIL IN M'ADOO CAMP

### Some of His Leaders Opposed His Abandoning Fight.

### "CHIEF" CALLS IN EACH ONE

### His Decision Is Quickly Followed by Concerted Drive on the Floor for Meredith.

### ROCKWELL HIMSELF ACTIVE

### Joins in the Proselyting for the Iowan, Who Was One of McAdoo's Stalwarts.

At 2:30 o'clock this morning, after a series of conferences with his supporters in his convention headquarters in the Madison Square Hotel, William G. McAdoo prepared a letter offering to release the delegates supporting him and intimating that he was ready to withdraw. It was said that the McAdoo forces might support Edwin T. Meredith of Iowa, formerly Secretary of Agriculture in the Wilson Cabinet, and that an effort would be made to get the convention to nominate him.

Mr. McAdoo apparently decided to abandon what appeared to be a hopeless fight for the Democratic nomination about 1 o'clock. Leader after leader of the McAdoo forces was summoned before "the chief," as he is known to his followers. The McAdoo vote had not gone up as rapidly as had been expected and the suggestion of offering a McAdoo supporter as a compromise candidate began to be discussed.

The first report was that Senator Thomas J. Walsh, Permanent Chairman of the convention, would probably be the choice of Mr. McAdoo and his leading supporters to be the candidate of the faction supporting Mr. McAdoo.

This was denied by several of those who came from the conference rooms, and it was learned about 2 o'clock that Mr. Meredith, who has been one of Mr. McAdoo's most stalwart supporters, was the most probable choice of the McAdoo forces.

Leader after leader dashed into the Madison Square Hotel, climbed the twisting flight of stairs leading to Mr. Mcdoo's headquarters in Suite 201, hurried down again, and in some instances almost ran through the halls in their hurry to get back to the convention hall.

At 2:30 Bryce Claggett, Mr. McAdoo's executive secretary, went to the speaker's platform with the expected letter from Mr. McAdoo.

Judge David Ladd Rockwell, the McAdoo campaign manager, went on the floor and held whispered conversations with various McAdoo leaders who had not been at the Madison Square Hotel conference.

It was learned definitely that some of the McAdoo delegates had been directed to vote for Mr. Meredith, presumably for the purpose of building up a vote for him so that he might be in a position to take advantage of any announcement that might be made.

Not all of the McAdoo leaders took kindly to the suggestion that Mr. McAdoo retire. Among those called in conference were Jouett Shouse of Kansas, Colonel Thomas B. Love of Texas, Clyde L. Herring and E. T. Meredith of Iowa; Thomas L. Chadbourne of New York, one of Mr. McAdoo's principal backers; William L. O'Connell of Illinois, J. Bruce Kremer of Montana, the McAdoo floor leader; Breckenridge Long of Missouri, Angus McLean of North Carolina, and William J. Bryan of Florida.

## Text of McAdoo's Letter to the Convention Freeing His Delegates from All Pledges to Him

The Madison Square Hotel, July 9, 1924.

Honorable Thomas J. Walsh, Chairman, Democratic National Convention, Madison Square Garden, New York City.

Dear Senator Walsh:

I am profoundly grateful to the splendid men and women who have with such extraordinary loyalty supported me in this unprecedented struggle for a great cause.

The convention has been in session two weeks and appears to be unable to make a nomination under the two-thirds rule. This is an unfortunate situation, imperiling party success.

I feel that if I should withdraw my name from the convention I should betray the trust confided in me by the people in many States, which have sent delegates here to support me.

And yet I am unwilling to contribute to the continuation of a hopeless deadlock. Therefore I have determined to leave my friends and supporters free to take such action as in their judgment may best serve the interests of the party.

I have made this fight for the principles and ideals of progressive Democracy and righteousness and for the defeat of the reactionary and wet elements in the party which threaten to dominate it. For these principles and ideals I shall continue to fight. I hope that this convention will never yield to reaction and privilege and that the Democratic Party will always hold aloft the torch which was carried to such noble heights by Woodrow Wilson. Cordially yours,

W. G. McADOO.

## Thrills Come Early in Morning After Session Opens Tamely

### Galleries Cheer Steadfast Stand of Smith Supporters and Boo Unyielding McAdoo States—'Dark Horses' Make Gains After Ralston Goes.

Before the gavel fell opening the twenty-first session of the Democratic Convention last night women in the California delegation staged a small demonstration for William G. McAdoo. Standing on chairs and waving bunches of varicolored sashes fastened to flag handles, they sang a McAdoo song to the tune of "John Brown's Body," repeating again and again the chorus:

Glory, glory, glory, hallelujah,
Glory, glory, glory, hallelujah;
Glory, glory, glory, hallelujah,
We're all for McAdoo.

There was the usual stir when Franklin D. Roosevelt made his appearance. He was escorted to the rostrum, where he took his seat as the crowd in the Garden hailed him with a vigorous volley of applause. Then the delegates settled down to await developments, there being a general feeling that the campaign manager of Governor Smith was about to make a momentous announcement.

It was 9:15 o'clock when the convention was called to order by Permanent Chairman Walsh. In the space set aside for the delegates there were any number of vacant seats. The boxes and galleries were well filled with as expectant an audience as has attended any session since the convention began.

**Ralston's Withdrawal Read.**

In the invocation the Rev. Wythe Leigh Kinsolving, chaplain of the Virginia Society, prayed for a spirit of sacrifice which would place men in a mood to give up personal ambition for the good of party and of country. He also prayed that religious bigotry and racial intolerance be laid aside in the deliberations which were to follow. The prayer was followed by singing by a male quartet, which won the singers as much applause as any of the candidates have received since the present period of waning enthusiasm began.

First, as the convention began its work, a resolution offered by James A. Watson of the Eleventh Massachusetts District, offering congratulations to the American Olympic team for its achievements yesterday and expressing the hope that the final victory would be theirs, was read and adopted.

Next the secretary was directed to read a telegram to Thomas Taggart, the Hoosier Democratic leader, from Senator Ralston of Indiana, who had received nearly 200 votes during the afternoon session, insisting that his name be withdrawn from further consideration by the convention. The telegram read:

Indianapolis, Ind., July 8.

Senator Thomas Taggart,
Hotel Waldorf-Astoria, New York:

Withdraw my name from further consideration by the convention. Great as the honor would be, I do not want the nomination. Everlastingly obliged to those who have voted for me. Assure the convention of my unswerving support to whoever the convention nominates.

(Signed) SAMUEL M. RALSTON.

**Roosevelt Makes Smith Offer.**

Amid great cheering and applause, Franklin D. Roosevelt was then brought forward and five minutes was allowed him in which to make an announcement.

"You have been far too good to me," Mr. Roosevelt began.

"No, no, no," came vigorous shouts from all parts of the Garden.

"I think I can assure you," Mr. Roosevelt went on when quiet had been restored, "that this will be the last time I address a Democratic National Convention—until 1928. Tonight I am here to make a brief and very simple statement on behalf of Governor Smith.

"After nearly one hundred ballots it is quite apparent to him and to me that the forces behind him, the leader in the race, and behind McAdoo, who is second, cannot be amalgamated. For the good of the party Governor Smith authorizes me to say that immediately after Mr. McAdoo withdraws Governor Smith will withdraw his name. As his representative, I think I can say further that until such withdrawal those delegates who have supported Governor Smith will continue to vote for him."

There was vigorous applause as Mr. Roosevelt ended his statement and withdrew from the rostrum. After a stern warning against intrusion by visitors upon the space set aside for the delegates, Permanent Chairman Walsh then directed the Secretary to call the roll for the ninety-fourth ballot.

**THE NINETY-FOURTH BALLOT.**

Alabama continued to vote for Senator Underwood. When Arizona was reached Fred. T. Colter, Delegate at Large, arose, threw both arms in the air and exclaimed with tremendous fervor:

"Before God, before Christ, we want McAdoo!"

"McAdoo has won!" cried another delegate from Arizona, amid cheering from some and tremendous booing and hissing in the galleries. The women in the California delegation stood up in a double row, cheering shrilly and fervently waving flags.

There were continuous outbursts of cheering and applause, mingled with boos and derisive yells from the galleries, as McAdoo won back 6 votes from Nevada and 20 from Mississippi, which earlier had gone to Senator Ralston. Nebraska's vote was again a split among a number of candidates. Ida M. Thurber of Lincoln, a delegate, challenged the vote, and Nebraska was passed.

"Oregon casts her 10 votes for the people's choice, William G. McAdoo," shrilly cried a woman delegate when that State was reached. Nebraska's controversy was over the right to vote for an alternate who had been substituted for a regular alternate by a delegate after both of the last-named had left the convention. After listening to Senator Hitchcock of Nebraska, Chairman Walsh ruled against his contention that the vote of the substitute alternate should be accepted.

Oklahoma found her way back to McAdoo after voting for Ralston on many ballots. Tennessee, whose vote was deferred until after the roll-call, also decided to stay with the Californian.

United States Senator Royal S. Copeland got seventeen votes on this ballot. McAdoo recovered eighty-one votes of those previously lost and ran ahead of Governor Smith, who gained nine votes and finished this ballot with 364½ to his credit. John W. Davis gained thirteen and three-quarters, Senator Glass twelve and Senator Robinson

Continued on Page Two.



## SMITH FORCES HOLD FIRM

### Poll 351½ on the 100th Ballot—McAdoo Drops to 190.

### CANDIDATES TO CONFER

### Action Is Urged to Seek Agreement Before Convention Meets Again Today.

### FEW TURN TO MEREDITH

### Walsh, Robinson, Gerard, Houston, Glass and Underwood Still in the Race.

**Changes in Candidates' Votes Between 1st and 100th Ballots**

This table shows how the candidates for President stood on the first ballot, taken on Monday of last week, and on the one-hundredth ballot, the latest cast, with the net change in the vote for each contender:

| Candidate. | 1st Ballot. | 100th Ballot. | Net Ch'ge. |
|---|---|---|---|
| McAdoo | 431½ | 190 | —241½ |
| Smith | 241 | 351½ | +110½ |
| Cox | 59 | 0 | — 59 |
| Harrison | 43½ | 0 | —43½ |
| Underwood | 42½ | 41½ | — 1 |
| Silzer | 38 | 0 | — 38 |
| J. W. Davis | 31 | 203½ | +172½ |
| Ralston | 30 | 0 | — 30 |
| Ferris | 30 | 0 | — 30 |
| Glass | 25 | 35 | + 10 |
| Ritchie | 22½ | 17½ | — 5 |
| Robinson | 21 | 46 | + 25 |
| J. M. Davis | 20 | 0 | — 20 |
| C. W. Bryan | 18 | 2 | — 16 |
| Brown | 17 | 0 | — 17 |
| Sweet | 12 | 0 | — 12 |
| Kendrick | 6 | 0 | — 6 |
| Thompson | 1 | 0 | — 1 |
| Walsh | 0 | 52½ | + 52½ |
| Owen | 0 | 20 | + 20 |
| Saulsbury | 7 | 6 | — 1 |
| Meredith | 0 | 75½ | + 75½ |
| Berry | 0 | 1 | + 1 |
| Gerard | 0 | 10 | + 10 |
| Houston | 0 | 9 | + 9 |
| Daniels | 0 | 24 | + 24 |
| Baker | 0 | 1 | + 1 |

The results of the 100th ballot were:

McAdoo ........................190
Smith ........................351½
J. W. Davis....................203½
Meredith ........................75½
Robinson ........................46

The convention adjourned at 3:56 A. M., after the announcement of the results of the 100th ballot, and will meet again at 12 o'clock noon today.

The delegate from Minnesota who moved the adjournment announced that there was to be an immediate conference of the candidates.

By RICHARD V. OULAHAN.

Early this morning while the Democratic National Convention was still in session a letter was read from William G. McAdoo, in which he released his supporters from any obligation to vote for him, but did not withdraw as a candidate.

Mr. McAdoo in his letter made a plea to those who had supported him to resist any effort to nominate a candidate of reactionary or wet tendencies.

Immediately after the letter was read, at 2:30 o'clock, a motion to adjourn was made, but it was shouted down, and the convention prepared to resume balloting for the choice of a nominee for President. It was then on the 100th ballot.

Early last evening, soon after the convention assembled, announcement was made in behalf of Governor Smith that he would withdraw if Mr. McAdoo would do likewise. Nothing was heard from Mr. McAdoo until his letter was read to the convention several hours later.

According to some informed McAdoo workers, Mr. McAdoo hoped that the mantle of his candidacy would fall upon the shoulders of E. T. Meredith of Iowa, who was Secretary of Agriculture under Woodrow Wilson. Others said that Mr. McAdoo had indicated orally that he would be satisfied if either Mr. Meredith or Senator Thomas J. Walsh of Montana, Permanent Chairman of the Democratic Convention, was chosen.

At the opening of the night session Franklin D. Roosevelt, Governor Smith's manager, told the convention that Governor Smith had authorized him to say "that immediately upon the withdrawal of his name (McAdoo's), Governor Smith would withdraw his name also from the consideration of the convention."

This announcement followed an interview between Governor Smith and Mr. McAdoo in the room of former Ambassador Hugh C. Wallace in the Ritz-Carlton Hotel.

After Mr. Roosevelt had made his announcement to the convention in behalf of Governor Smith, the only response of the McAdoo managers was to institute a drive for votes which brought McAdoo's waning strength up again beyond the 400 mark, displacing Governor

## Summary of Yesterday's Ballots

| Candidates | Day Session 88 | 89 | 90 | 91 | 92 | 93 | Night Session 94 | 95 | 96 | 97 | 98 | 99 | 100 |
|---|---|---|---|---|---|---|---|---|---|---|---|---|---|
| Smith | 362 | 358 | 354½ | 355½ | 355½ | 355½ | 364½ | 367½ | 359½ | 359½ | 354 | 353 | 351½ |
| McAdoo | 315½ | 318½ | 314 | 318 | 310 | 314 | 395 | 417½ | 421 | 415½ | 406½ | 353½ | 190 |
| Ralston | 98 | 99½ | 159½ | 187½ | 196¾ | 196¼ | 37 | .... | .... | .... | .... | .... | .... |
| Glass | 66½ | 66½ | 30½ | 28½ | 26½ | 27 | 37 | 34 | 39 | 39 | 36 | 38 | 35 |
| J. W. Davis | 59½ | 64½ | 65½ | 66½ | 69½ | 68 | 81¾ | 139¼ | 171½ | 183¼ | 194¾ | 210 | 203½ |
| Underwood | 39 | 41 | 42½ | 46½ | 45¼ | 44¼ | 46¼ | 44¼ | 38½ | 37¼ | 38¼ | 39½ | 41½ |
| Meredith | 26 | 26 | 26 | 26 | 26 | 26 | 26 | 26 | .... | .... | .... | 37 | 75½ |
| Robinson | 23 | 20½ | 20 | 20 | 20 | 19 | 37 | 31 | 32 | 22 | 25 | 25 | 46 |
| Daniels | 23 | 19½ | 19 | .... | .... | .... | .... | .... | .... | .... | .... | .... | 24 |
| Ritchie | 22½ | 22½ | 16½ | 16½ | 16½ | 16½ | 16½ | 20½ | 21½ | 19½ | 18½ | 17½ | 17½ |
| J. M. Davis | 20 | 20 | 22 | 4 | .... | .... | 20 | .... | .... | .... | .... | .... | .... |
| Owen | 20 | 20 | .... | .... | .... | .... | .... | .... | .... | 1 | 1 | 3 | 20 |
| Bryan | 9 | 9 | 15 | 8 | 8 | 8 | 9 | 9 | 7 | 6 | 5 | 5 | 2 |
| Saulsbury | 6 | 6 | 6 | 6 | 6 | 6 | .... | .... | .... | 6 | 6 | 6 | 6 |
| Walsh | 5 | 3½ | 5 | 4½ | 4½ | 4½ | 4 | 2 | 4 | 4 | 6 | 4 | 52½ |
| Roosevelt | 1 | 1 | .... | .... | .... | .... | 2 | 2 | 1 | .... | .... | .... | .... |
| Cummings | .... | .... | .... | 8½ | 8½ | 8½ | 1 | .... | .... | .... | .... | .... | .... |
| Houston | .... | .... | .... | .... | 2 | .... | .... | .... | .... | .... | .... | .... | 9 |
| Callahan | .... | .... | .... | .... | 1 | .... | .... | .... | .... | .... | .... | .... | .... |
| Baker | .... | .... | .... | .... | .... | 2 | .... | .... | .... | .... | .... | .... | 4 |
| Copeland | .... | .... | .... | .... | .... | .... | 17 | 2 | .... | .... | .... | .... | .... |
| Stewart | .... | .... | .... | .... | .... | .... | 1 | .... | .... | .... | .... | .... | .... |
| Marshall | .... | .... | .... | .... | .... | .... | .... | .... | .... | 2 | 3 | 2 | .... |

"All the News That's Fit to Print."

# The New York Times.

THE WEATHER
Showers today; tomorrow, fair and slightly cooler; westerly winds.
Temperature yesterday—Max. 88, min. 69.
For weather report see Page 43.

VOL. LXXIII....No. 24,274. NEW YORK, THURSDAY, JULY 10, 1924. TWO CENTS in Greater New York | THREE CENTS Within 200 Miles | FOUR CENTS Elsewhere

# DEMOCRATS NOMINATE DAVIS AND C. W. BRYAN; FORMER, ACCLAIMED, CALLS PARTY TO BATTLE; SMITH PROMISES TO WORK HARD FOR THE TICKET

## DEMOCRATS FILL THEIR TICKET

### Choose Davis and Bryan After Another Day of Balloting.

### CHOICE OF DAVIS UNANIMOUS

### Convention Adopts Taggart Motion With a Shout While a Stampede Is On.

### HE HAD MADE STEADY GAINS

### Beginning the Day With 203½ Votes, He Advanced as Meredith and Others Slumped.

By RICHARD V. OULAHAN.

Rising superior to the intra-party differences that have marked its session in New York, the Democratic National Convention yesterday, with impressive unanimity, ended its deadlock by choosing John W. Davis of West Virginia as its candidate for President.

At 2:30 o'clock this morning, in a session that was begun at 8:30 o'clock last night, while shouts of protest came from many delegates, the convention followed this action by choosing Governor Charles W. Bryan of Nebraska as its candidate for Vice President. With that done the convention at 2:35 o'clock adjourned sine die, thus ending one of the longest and momentous national party gatherings ever held in America.

Governor Bryan's selection was a great surprise. His name had not been placed formally before the convention. He was picked for second place on the ticket at a midnight conference between Mr. Davis and other party leaders during a recess, and when the convention reassembled at 1:15 o'clock this morning word was passed that he was satisfactory to the new party leader.

William Jennings Bryan was active in the effort to have his brother named for Vice President, although he had declared his hostility to Mr. Davis's candidacy and had threatened to attack him in a speech before the convention.

**One Ballot on Vice President.**

Only one ballot was taken on the choice of a Vice Presidential candidate, with more than a dozen persons, including one woman, voted for. Before the result of the ballot, which was inconclusive, was announced State delegations began to change their votes, and the swing to Bryan was on.

New York gave Bryan is ninety votes on the first roll-call. Connecticut, Kentucky, Virginia, Texas, Ohio and Oklahoma went to him as fast as the Chairman of the delegations could be recognized. Then Gavin McNab of California moved that Governor Bryan be nominated by acclamation. Booing came from the floor and galleries and the protests were so many and so loud that Mr. McNab withdrew his motion.

But in the end Governor Bryan was chosen to be the partner of Mr. Davis on the Democratic National ticket. He received 739 votes or seven more than the necessary two thirds majority. Announcement of his selection was received with cheers, jeers and hisses.

Immediately following the selection of Mr. Davis for the Presidential candidate at the first two sessions held yesterday a dramatic effort was made to give the Vice Presidential nomination to Senator Thomas J. Walsh of Montana by acclamation. Only by an appeal not to take snap judgment did Senator Walsh stay the overwhelming desire of shouting delegates to commandeer him for second place.

**Walsh Declines the Honor.**

At last night's session a letter was read in which Senator Walsh declined in advance the honor the convention sought to thrust upon him and took himself definitely out of consideration.

Edwin T. Meredith of Iowa, former Secretary of Agriculture who had been the choice of William G. McAdoo after Mr. McAdoo's retirement from the contest appeared to be most in the minds of delegates for a running mate to Mr. Davis until the formal announcement that he did not desire to be so honored was made to the convention.

Shortly before midnight Mr. Davis was escorted to the platform in Madison Square Garden and got a rousing reception. His white hair and his erect bearing gave him an attractive appearance. He spoke easily and gracefully and in a clear voice. Mr. Davis caught the fancy of his audience in a way to bring loud laughter when he said no one could claim that this convention acted in haste and without deliberation. Laying down the creed of the Democratic Party, with "honesty in Government" its first tenet, Mr. Davis brought applause from his hearers when he said "In this cause I know all Democrats will unite." He expressed confidence that he would be able to lead a united and victorious party.

The convention was also addressed by Governor Alfred E. Smith of New York.

Continued on Page Seven.

JOHN WILLIAM DAVIS
OF WEST VIRGINIA,
Democratic Candidate for President.

## DAVIS IS PUT OVER IN WILD STAMPEDE

### Weary Delegates Jump for Band Wagon and Then All Join Big Demonstration.

### IT IS WEST VIRGINIA'S DAY

### Convention Pays Tribute to the Men and the State That Gave It the New Leader.

By ELMER DAVIS.

The Democrats have finally nominated and gone home. John W. Davis was selected as the Presidential candidate yesterday afternoon, on the 103d ballot. At 2:25 o'clock this morning Governor Charles W. Bryan of Nebraska was nominated as Vice President.

The fierce tension had been relaxed by the long days of fruitless balloting. The two men in this convention who have inspired the bitterest ecstasies of love and hate had been driven out of the running after a struggle that had endured too long, so there was not the frenzied joy springing from the release of pent-up feeling such as greeted the nomination of James M. Cox in San Francisco four years ago. The delegates had fought each other to a standstill and themselves to exhaustion. They had no spirit left for the revival that should have come with the dismissal of the two leading candidates, the settlement by treaty of that endless war, and the turning toward more productive effort.

There were cheers for Davis as State after State piled up its ballot on his rising total, there was a demonstration when his nomination was finally confirmed by acclamation at the end of the 103d ballot, but it was less a demonstration for Davis, or even for the Democratic Party, than for West Virginia, the Cinderella among the States, come into her own.

**It Was West Virginia's Day.**

As West Virginia's day, it was successful. As the great climactic festival of a confident party pushing on to the hope of victory, it was not. Too many personal and sectional and sectarian hatreds have been fought out in this convention. If the spirit of this convention is a key to the spirit in which the party will fight the campaign, Mr. Davis has a hard life ahead of him. But he can always cherish the consoling thought that he gave West Virginia her great day among the States.

This convention has a gift for missing fire on its psychological moment. The withdrawal of Smith and McAdoo ought to have been a high point of emotion, a chance for reconsecration for repentance and the determination of the assembled Democrats to live a better life hereafter. But McAdoo withdrew so reluctantly and ambiguously and hedged

Continued on Page Four.



## WIFE FIRST TO TELL DAVIS HE HAD WON

### Nominee Was Having a Quiet Smoke While She Listened In on the Radio

### AT HOME OF FRANK L. POLK

### Reporters, Camera Men and Personal Callers Soon Brought an End to His Solitude.

John W. Davis sat alone, smoking, in the reception room of the home of his close friend and legal associate, Frank L. Polk, at 6 East Sixty-eighth Street, when he received the news of his nomination for the Presidency yesterday afternoon. It was called to him by Mrs. Davis, who, with Mrs. Polk, had been listening in on the radio. Running from the sitting room on the second floor to the head of the stairs Mrs. Davis cried: "You've won—you're nominated!"

Mr. Davis put down his cigar, sprang up the stairs to meet Mrs. Davis, embraced her and—just smiled.

Within a few minutes the inevitable rush of friends and supporters to congratulate Mr. Davis began. The street quickly filled with visitors' automobiles, newspaper men, movie cameras and extra policemen. And Mr. Davis's re-entry into public life was well under way.

When the newspaper men arrived Mr. Davis greeted them in the hallway of the Polk home. Mr. Polk had arrived by that time and at once took up the task of reinforcing Mr. Davis in his stand against the reportorial onslaught.

**Greets Reporters Cordially.**

Mr. Davis greeted the reporters cordially. He singled out those he knew and chatted with them personally. He apparently was willing to attempt to answer the questions which were being fired at him from all sides, but Mr. Polk warded off some which were considered irrelevant or premature and they went unanswered. One of these was the query as to how the candidate "squared" his position on the League of Nations (Mr. Davis having been an ardent supporter of President Wilson and his League proposals) with the Democratic platform's declaration on the League. Mr. Polk "ruled out" this question as "unfair at this time."

Mr. Davis told the newspaper men that his views on all public issues which might not be fully known would be set forth in his speech of acceptance and during the campaign. Later the reporters received from Mr. Polk a prepared statement from Mr. Davis. [The text of this statement is printed elsewhere.]

While the statement was being typed for the reporters, Mr. Davis "appeased" the clamor of the motion picture camera men. As he stepped from the doorway of the Polk home scores of cameras clicked and the crowd which had gathered cheered, while some acclaimed him "the next President." He wore a [illegible]

Continued on Page Nine.



### "There Can Be No Compromise With Reaction," Says Davis in First Statement After Nomination

*John W. Davis, the Democratic Presidential nominee, gave out the following statement last night:*

The history of national conventions may be searched in vain for one which has excelled this in freedom or frankness of discussion, or whose actions have been more clearly the result of the unfettered wishes of the assembled delegates. The resolution and endurance they have exhibited is but proof of their sense of the solemn responsibilities to the country under which they acted and of the supreme vitality of democracy.

I cannot but feel deeply sensible of the honor done by the convention and am even more conscious of the weighty obligations that have fallen to me by its deliberate and unanimous choice. Not least of these is the duty to put before the country, as clearly as my powers permit, the Democratic creed and the Democratic policy as the convention has declared them.

That this creed and this policy will receive the militant support of all those who call themselves by the Democratic name I do not doubt for an instant. I shall hope to rally to their aid that great body of liberal, progressive and independent thought which believes that "progress is motion, Government is action," which detests privilege in whatever form and which does not wish the American people or their Government to stand still or retreat from the midst of a changing world.

There can be no compromise with reaction. Liberal principles must and will prevail. This is the mandate of the hour and I shall obey it.

## DAVIS GETS BY WIRE CONGRATULATIONS OF SMITH AND M'ADOO

### Governor Announces That He Will Aid in Campaign if the Nominee Desires.

### McADOO IS GOING ABROAD

### With Family, He Will Spend Several Weeks in Europe—Discord Among His Workers.

Among the hundreds of persons in all walks of life who sent their congratulations to John W. Davis following his nomination for the Presidency by the Democrats yesterday were Governor Alfred E. Smith and William Gibbs McAdoo, the leading candidates through many ballots for the place.

Governor Smith sent this telegram to Mr. Davis:

Hon. John W. Davis, care Frank L. Polk, 6 East Sixty-eighth Street, New York City.

Sincere congratulations and best wishes for success and my promise of hearty support.

ALFRED E. SMITH.

The Governor said he would not make a long statement because he expected to go before the convention at the night session and "say a few things." The Governor did say, however, that in selecting Mr. Davis he thought the convention made a good choice. He said he considered Mr. Davis to be of Presidential size and that he would make a great campaign. The Governor added that he would heartily support the ticket and do anything the nominee desired him to do. He said he expected to make speeches, either in New York State or throughout the country.

Mr. McAdoo sent the following telegram of congratulation:

Hon. John W. Davis, New York City.

Please accept my congratulations on your nomination. W. G. McADOO.

This was Mr. McAdoo's only public comment on Mr. Davis's nomination.

**How McAdoo Boom Ended.**

Surrounded by a group of his supporters, part of whom were still willing to go down fighting, Mr. McAdoo sat in a room of Suite 201 of the Madison Square Hotel early yesterday morning and saw the collapse of his six-year campaign for the Democratic nomination for President.

It was 1 o'clock when Mr. McAdoo acquiesced in the demand of some of his supporters that he withdraw in the interest of party harmony after a last, desperate drive for him had failed. This decision was reached in the absence of Judge David Ladd Rockwell, Mr. McAdoo's campaign manager, who was making a fight for him on the floor.

A long discussion followed when Judge Rockwell was sent for and told of the situation. It was largely this discussion and failure of the McAdoo leaders to agree on a second choice candidate that delayed, until after 3 A. M., the sending of Mr. McAdoo's letter, releasing his delegates, to Senator Walsh, Chairman of the convention.

Although Mr. McAdoo did not withdraw in his letter, but merely announced that he released his delegates, the letter had all the effect of a withdrawal. The McAdoo forces, which had held together so long and so firmly, disintegrated rapidly. The Southern McAdoo States, always cold to the suggestion that they support either Senator Walsh of Montana or Edwin T. Meredith of Iowa, formerly Secretary of Agriculture, gradually shifted to John W. Davis. Mr. McAdoo immediately after the reading of his letter ceased to be a political factor almost before he had returned

Continued on Page Eight.

## LEADERS ACCLAIM CHOICE OF DAVIS; SEE PARTY UNITED

### "Shows Democrats Have Feet on the Ground," Says Former Governor Cox.

### DANIELS PAYS TRIBUTE

### Brennan of Illinois and Moore of Ohio See Breaches Healed—Bryan Pledges Support.

The nomination of John W. Davis as Democratic candidate for President was received yesterday with general acclaim by the party leaders and Democrats of prominence. Among those commenting were the following, who said:

William Jennings Bryan (who the other day omitted from his list of candidates meeting his approval the name of John W. Davis).—"You can say that I shall support the ticket. That is all—for the present."

James M. Cox, former Governor of Ohio.—"It is an instance of the party nominating one of the most conspicuously able men of his generation, and it is an evidence of the fact that notwithstanding the spirit of contest over controverted questions the Democratic Party, in the last analysis, had its feet on the ground. The country has always found the Democratic Party safe in an emergency.

"This is merely a matter of history repeating itself. Mr. Davis will make a profound impression on the country at the very outset of the campaign. None of the elements which make him an able man are more conspicuous than his intellectual courage and honesty."

**"Biggest and Brainiest Available."**

George E. Brennan, Democratic leader of Illinois—"We are more than pleased with the nomination of John W. Davis. We are delighted. The hard work of weeks has been rewarded. We now present to the voters as our candidate the biggest and brainiest man available for the honor. Behind him is arrayed the entire Democratic Party, united for the campaign as it was united in the tremendous enthusiasm that broke forth when Mr. Davis's nomination became assured. We look forward to an unbroken continuance of this good feeling among all Democrats, right up to the day of election. That can mean only one thing, the election of Mr. Davis."

Edmund H. Moore, Democratic leader of Ohio—"John W. Davis is the biggest man who has run for President, with the possible exception of Wilson, since 1876."

Josephus Daniels—"I think they nominated a man whom the whole country recognizes as a great man in learning, in character, and one who measures up to the highest of those who have held the position of President. He stands for independence and equality and illustrates how a man of ambition and poise can reach the heights. He has illustrated his ability for public service as legislator in West Virginia, in the House of Congress as Solicitor General and as an Ambassador. He is a great American."

Franklin D. Roosevelt—"In John W. Davis the Democratic Party has found a candidate of whom it can be proud and the voters of the country a man on whom they can unite with confidence that he will make a President worthy to rank with the other great Democrats who have held that office.

"A warm personal friend of mine, I have found him to be a man of splendid intellect, clear thinking and high, progressive ideals. Mr. Davis will have my heartiest support and I intend to

Continued on Page Ten.

CHARLES W. BRYAN
OF NEBRASKA
Democratic Candidate for Vice President

## *Davis and Smith Are Cheered In Speeches at the Night Session*

### *Presidential Candidate Appeals for Party Harmony and Gives Creed as Honesty in Government—Governor Pledges Full Support to Ticket.*

John W. Davis, the Democratic candidate for President, and Governor Alfred E. Smith addressed the Democratic National Committee last night.

Both had rousing receptions, Mr. Davis when he appealed for party harmony and said that the Democratic creed was "honesty in Government" and "public office is a public trust," and Mr. Smith when he declared that he was ready to take off his coat and vest to fight for the ticket headed by Mr. Davis.

His speech was as follows:

Mr. Chairman, ladies and gentlemen of the Convention: The most solemn announcement which can be made to any American is the information that he has been elected President of the United States. [Cries of "Good," "Pardon me, that is good"] And second only to that message in weight and dignity is the information that he has been chosen by one of the great parties of the United States to lead their forces in the national campaign. [Applause.] You will not be surprised, then, if I say to you at this moment, grateful as I am for this great honor, I think even more of the burdens and the duties you have given me to bear and to perform. But I take heart of grace, and I realize that whatever may be said of the wisdom of your selection, no one, I think, in all this land will contend that this convention has acted in haste and without deliberation. [Laughter and applause.]

And I take comfort again when I look at the banners that are erected throughout this hall, and reflect that the signs of all these States and Territories are not the emblem of a phantom army, but that they represent millions of Democrats all over this broad land ready to do as they have been for 100 years—to do battle for the cause of liberty and freedom. [Applause.] We are a national party, and in every State and Territory whose banner rests upon this floor we do battle and we win our party victory; and if we are a national party it must be, as I think, because we profess a truly national creed.

The great principles of the Democratic Party: Honesty in Government [applause]; all public office is a public trust [applause]; equal rights to all men [applause]; and special privilege to none [applause]; fair and equal taxation; an open door of opportunity to the humblest citizen in all the land [applause]; loyalty at home, courage and honor and helpfulness abroad. [Applause.]

These principles are as dear to the American of the East as the American of the West, as highly revered by the American of the North as they are by the American of the South [Applause], and in the name of this truly national creed, this truly and national party, it is ready again to do battle with all, those who challenge this creed or any part of it. [Applause.] On this platform all progressives in this country can stand; to this banner all liberals can rally, and in this cause all Democrats can—aye, more, all Democrats will unite. [Applause.]

As a more or less interested bystander I can not be ignorant of the fact that this convention has had its debates and its differences, and in the truly Democratic fashion has fought out its conflicts of opinion, and all these things, disturbing as they may have seemed at the moment, were but the thunderstorm that has cleared the clouds away and left shining on us the sun of coming victory and success. [Applause.]

It may be, and I think when I am duly advised of your mandate it will be, my duty to speak further on these and kindred themes. I shall, therefore, add no more at this moment than to express my appreciation of the great honor you have done me, and my confident belief that I shall lead in this campaign a united and militant and a victorious party. (Long and extended applause.)

**The Governor's Address.**

Governor Smith's speech was as follows:

"Mr. Chairman: Not being familiar with the rules of the convention, I am the least bit afraid that any applause may be taken out of my time [Laughter] and I will therefore very respectfully request you refrain from applause until I finish.

"I feel that it would be senseless, if not entirely useless, for me to extend any word of welcome to the delegates and their friends from the different States who are here gathered, because I think that the great City of New York has made about as complete a job as could be made of the business of extending a welcome to our friends from various sections of the country.

"If you have been annoyed in any way by the various people with whom you have come in contact, in their zeal to explain to you why in their opinion I am the greatest man in the world, overlook it. [Applause.]

"For the first time in a very great many years the Democratic Convention has been held in this city, although it is conceded that New York is the greatest city in the world, and that it is the very centre and the very heart, not only of this country, but practically of all the world. Naturally, we felt very proud. We felt particularly proud to have the convention come into this State at a time when we were able to point to a record of progress in this State under Democratic administration which cannot be equaled by any State of the Union. [Applause.]

"The State of New York has performed its full duty to the soldier. We bonded ourselves for $45,000,000 to pay the soldiers a bonus. A little more than a year ago I laid the corner stone of a memorial hospital at Kings Park, on Long Island, for the soldiers who came

Continued on Page Two.



## BRYAN PICKED BY LEADERS

### Daniels Suggests Him When Group Confers With John W. Davis.

### ALL FACTIONS AGREEABLE

### Head of Ticket Accepts Choice of Bryan's Brother as Running Mate.

### SETTLED ON FIRST BALLOT

### After 24 Candidates Are Voted On Host of States Swing Over to Bryan.

Governor Charles W. Bryan of Nebraska, brother of William J. Bryan, was nominated for Vice President on the first ballot, with a vote of 739, after a sweeping number of changes were recorded from the original votes of the States. The announcement of his nomination came at 2:30 A. M.

The convention adjourned sine die at 2:30 A. M. on motion of Senator King of Utah.

A resolution was passed in the last moments providing that the Permanent Chairman, Senator Thomas J. Walsh, be appointed Chairman of the committee to notify J. W. Davis of his nomination for President and that Senator Harrison be Chairman of the committee to notify Bryan of his selection for Vice President.

The totals on the ballot for the principal candidates were announced as follows:

|  |  |
|---|---|
| Governor C. W. Bryan | 739 |
| Major George Berry | 212½ |
| Bennett Clark | 42 |
| Mrs. Leroy Springs | 18 |
| Colonel Alvin Owsley | 18 |
| Governor George S. Silzer | 16 |
| Mayor John F. Hylan | 6 |
| Governor Jonathan M. Davis | 4 |

The nomination of Governor Bryan for second place was the direct result of a conference held by leaders with John W. Davis, the Presidential nominee, at the Manhattan Club, between 12 and 1 o'clock this morning when the convention was in recess, pending some decision on a candidate. More than a dozen men had been put in nomination, besides Mrs. Spring of South Carolina.

The meeting was held in Governor Smith's rooms. Every one deferred to the nominee's own preference, but he said that he had no choice in the matter and was there merely to hear the suggestions.

Besides Mr. Davis and Governor Smith there were present Joseph F. Guffey, Pennsylvania; George E. Brennan of Illinois, Mayor Hague of Jersey City, Josephus Daniels, Frank L. Polk, the manager of the Davis pre-convention campaign; Isidore Dockweiler of California, J. Bruce Kremer of Montana, Gavin McNab of California, ex-Governor Stuart of Montana and Thomas Taggart of Indiana.

Governor Smith was asked whom he favored and he replied that he thought the selection should be Governor Silzer of New Jersey. He said he was willing to accede to the judgment of the other leaders. Some one suggested Governor Ritchie of Maryland, and another suggestion was Newton D. Baker of Ohio. It was recalled, however, that Mr. Baker had already refused the nomination.

Senator Walsh was brought into a side conference and was pressed to take the nomination. He said that his refusal was final and he left the conference early.

Josephus Daniels then proposed Governor Bryan. This was agreeable to the McAdooites while the Smith element made no objection. It was argued that his selection would tend to bring together all the warring factions of the party and that he would be the ideal candidate to run with Mr. Davis.

The advice of Mr. Davis was asked regarding the Bryan choice and he declared that the selection in his opinion was an excellent one.

It became known at the conference that William J. Bryan had asked a delegate from Maryland to put his brother in nomination for the Vice Presidency. This delegate, however, did not desire to do anything which was not acceptable to the leaders and he declined to do so when the nominations were made by roll-call of States.

The conference had taken up the full hour of the recess and immediately broke up when Mr. Bryan's name had been agreed upon. The party left the Club and Mr. Davis returned to the home of Mr. Polk, where he spent the night.

The convention started on the roll-call of States for second position on the ticket.

Several States passed and others scattered their votes among twenty-four candidates with Governor Bryan leading with 332 votes, George L. Berry getting 270½, Mayor Hylan of New York [illegible] and Mrs. Le Roy Springs of South Carolina 42.

There ensued about a half hour of jockeying, it becoming rapidly evident that the convention would nominate on a single ballot as State after State switched its vote to Governor Bryan. New York was one of the first to change its vote, putting the entire ninety [illegible] to the credit of the Nebraska Governor. Then came a rush to [illegible] to Bryan and the [illegible] quickly.

"All the News That's Fit to Print."

# The New York Times.

EXTRA
5 A.M.
THE WEATHER—Fair today.

VOL. LXXIV....No. 24,392. NEW YORK, WEDNESDAY, NOVEMBER 5, 1924. TWO CENTS In Greater New York | THREE CENTS Within 200 Miles | FOUR CENTS Elsewhere

# COOLIDGE WINS, 357 TO DAVIS'S 136; LA FOLLETTE CARRIES WISCONSIN; SMITH BEATS ROOSEVELT BY 140,000

## CITY ELECTS SMITH

### Big Manhattan and Bronx Vote Wins for Governor.

### UP-STATE STRONGLY G. O. P.

### Roosevelt Carries Buffalo and Several Large Industrial Centres.

### BROOKLYN GOES TO SMITH

### Kings County Gives Him 152,000 Plurality, Although Coolidge Carries It by 80,000.

### LEGISLATURE REPUBLICAN

### Democrats Lose Control of Senate and Their Numbers in Assembly Are Reduced.

### SOME OFFICES IN DOUBT

### Whole Smith Ticket May Not Be Elected—Vote for the Socialist Nominee, Thomas, Is Small.

Overcoming a Republican Presidential sweep that reached nearly a million plurality, Alfred E. Smith was re-elected Governor of New York in yesterday's election, defeating his Republican opponent, Colonel Theodore Roosevelt, by an estimated plurality of 140,000.

As a vote-getter the Governor surpassed his performance of four years ago when, in the Harding landslide, he went down to defeat, although running more than a million votes ahead of his ticket.

By an enormous city vote the Governor overcame a heavy handicap, for Colonel Roosevelt captured the rock-ribbed Republican counties up-State. The Colonel, reversing the record of Nathan L. Miller, also carried Democratic city strongholds above the Bronx which Governor Smith easily carried two and four years ago.

At 1:30 o'clock this morning Colonel Roosevelt at Oyster Bay issued a statement conceding the election of Governor Smith. He said he congratulated the Governor and also expressed satisfaction over the election of President Coolidge.

While the Governor was taking the measure of his Gubernatorial opponent, President Calvin Coolidge carried the State by 920,000 plurality. His vote up-State not only reached 800,000, but he carried every borough in the City of New York with a plurality over John W. Davis, his Democratic opponent, of 130,000.

**La Follette Polls 450,000.**

Senator Robert M. La Follette, running for President on a Third Party ticket, polled 466,000 votes in the State but ran third.

While Governor Smith was elected by a safe margin there was considerable uncertainty as to the fate of the rest of the State Democratic ticket. Lieutenant Governor George R. Lunn appeared to be safe although he ran fully 100,000 votes behind the Governor in the city. The rest of the ticket was lost in the count of votes for the Governorship.

The Governor's triumph was marred somewhat by the Republican gains in the Legislature. It was admitted by the Democrats that the Republicans elected enough State Senators to take control of that body from the Democrats and had materially increased their majority in the Assembly.

George K. Morris, Republican State Chairman, made the following statement at 1:30 o'clock this morning:

"Indications are that Governor Smith has been re-elected by between 50,000 and 65,000. But we have made substantial gains in the Assembly and have regained control of the State Senate, which will now be 28 to 23 in favor of the Republicans, instead of 26 to 25 in favor of the Democrats. We gained two Senators in Erie County, one in Rensselaer County and one in New York County, with probably an additional gain of one or more in other Senatorial districts. We have undoubtedly elected the entire State ticket with the exception of Colonel Roosevelt

Continued on Page Two.

**GOVERNORS ELECTED.**

**REPUBLICAN.**

| | |
|---|---|
| Connecticut | Hiram Bingham |
| Delaware | Robert P. Robinson |
| Illinois | Len Small* |
| Idaho | Charles C. Moore* |
| Indiana | Ed Jackson |
| Iowa | John Hammill |
| Kansas | Ben S. Paulen |
| Massachusetts | Alvan T. Fuller |
| Michigan | Alex J. Groesbeck |
| Nebraska | Adam McMullen |
| New Hampshire | John G. Winant |
| Rhode Island | Aram J. Pothier |
| South Dakota | Carl Gunderson |
| Vermont | Franklin K. Billings |
| Washington | Roland H. Hartley |
| West Virginia | Howard M. Gore |
| Wisconsin | John J. Blaine* |

**DEMOCRATIC.**

| | |
|---|---|
| Florida | John W. Martin |
| Georgia | Clifford Walker* |
| New York | Alfred E. Smith* |
| North Carolina | A. W. McLean |
| South Carolina | T. G. McLeod |
| Tennessee | Austin Peay* |
| Texas | Mrs. Miriam A. Ferguson |

*Re-elected.

## COOLIDGE AND SMITH CARRY THIS CITY

### The President's Plurality About 130,000 and the Governor's About 500,000.

### LA FOLLETTE VOTE 250,000

### Coolidge Wins in Every Borough—Democrats Elect All Local Officers.

New York City gave its vote at yesterday's election to Calvin Coolidge, Republican nominee for President, and Charles G. Dawes, Republican nominee for Vice President, and at the same time rolled up a record plurality for Governor Alfred E. Smith, electing him Chief Executive of New York State for the third time.

As in the Presidential election of 1920, Governor Smith's personal popularity, apparent satisfaction with his administration and possibly some weakness of his opponent, Colonel Theodore Roosevelt, combined to give the Governor a lead never before obtained by any candidate for any office in this city.

President Coolidge obtained a total of approximately 130,000 plurality in New York City and carried every borough, according to fairly complete returns.

The indications were that he would have a plurality of about 9,000 in Manhattan, 4,300 in the Bronx, 75,000 in Brooklyn, 39,000 in Queens and 2,200 in Richmond.

**500,000 Plurality for Smith.**

Governor Smith, however, carried the city by about 500,000, the "spread between his vote and that for Davis, the Democratic Presidential candidate, being about 630,000, or nearly equal to the difference between his vote and that for Cox four years ago. Governor Smith carried every borough heavily.

The indications on incomplete returns were that he had carried Manhattan by more than 195,000, Brooklyn by approximately 150,000, the Bronx by 105,000, Queens by 42,000 and Richmond by 8,800.

Governor Smith apparently carried every Assembly district in the city but one, the Twenty-first District, in Brooklyn. La Follette showed his greatest proportionate strength in the Bronx, where he led in the Third, Fourth and Fifth Assembly Districts and was running close in the Seventh.

The vote in the Nineteenth, Manhattan, Assembly District, which includes a large part of Harlem's "black belt," showed that the negroes here remained true to the Republican Party's national candidates, but voted for Governor Smith on the Ku Klux Klan issue. With seven districts missing out of forty-four, the

Continued on Page Five.

## MRS. FERGUSON WINS 2 TO 1 IN TEXAS RACE FOR GOVERNORSHIP

### Incomplete Returns Indicate That She Will Have a Majority of 225,000 Over Republican.

### RUNS BEHIND IN CITIES

### But the Big Majorities in the Rural Districts Carry Her to Victory.

### LARGE KLAN VOTE IS CAST

### Party Lines Are Ignored as Ku Klux Vote for Republican, While Negroes Vote for Democrat.

*Special to The New York Times.*

AUSTIN, Texas, Nov. 4.—Returns from the rural districts of Texas coming in late this evening show that Mrs. Miriam A. Ferguson will probably receive a majority of about 225,000 votes over Dr. George C. Butte, Republican, for Governor.

Of a total of about 700,000 votes cast about 218,000 have been counted, giving Mrs. Ferguson a lead of 62,000 votes. According to unofficial returns, the lead which Dr. Butte started with by returns from the larger cities was quickly overcome by the rural returns.

At 10 o'clock the vote for Governor, including returns from 310 towns and cities, stood:

Mrs. Ferguson, 117,345.
Dr. Butte, 68,145.

Interest in the election was intensified by the prominence of the Ku Klux Klan issue in the campaign and it caused an outpouring of people at the polls. It is estimated that nearly 800,000 votes were cast. This is only a few thousand less than the total number polled in the run-off primary. Perfect weather prevailed all over the State, and this was a factor in favor of Mrs. Ferguson, as it meant passable roads for the farmer to travel to the precinct voting boxes.

The early returns show that Mrs. Ferguson's principal strength was in the rural districts. The count in the larger cities is progressing slowly. It shows that Dr. George C. Butte, the Republican candidate for Governor, is running well ahead of Mrs. Ferguson in Dallas, Austin, Houston, Beaumont and other of the larger cities.

Butte is also running ahead of Mrs. Ferguson in a number of the populous counties of North Texas and is making a strong showing in parts of Central Texas. The rural districts, however, are piling up in the early count an almost solid vote for Mrs. Ferguson.

According to these returns, she swept East Texas and the territory south of San Antonio and more than broke even with Butte in other rural districts. It is practically conceded by the Republican leaders that if the estimate that 800,000 votes were polled is correct Mrs. Ferguson's election by the usual big Democratic majority is assured. These leaders contend, however, that the total vote was not more than 600,000 and that this means that Butte has a chance of winning.

The Ku Klux Klan strongholds gave a surprisingly large vote for Butte. It is apparent that he received the bulk of the Klan vote. Party lines were largely lost sight of and thousands of veteran Democrats today cast their first vote for a Republican candidate for office. The election marked the greatest political revolution that ever took place in Texas. Irrespective of the indication that Butte was not elected. Practically all of the German vote, more than 30,000 in number, which is nominally Republican, went to Mrs. Ferguson because of the Klan issue. The same is true of the negro vote which went solid for the woman candidate.

TEMPLE, Texas, Nov. 4.—Mrs. Miriam A. Ferguson of Temple, who on the face of returns in today's general election

Continued on Page Five.

## United States Senators Elected

**REPUBLICANS—18.**

| | |
|---|---|
| Colorado | *L. C. Phipps |
| Colorado | †Rice W. Means |
| Delaware | T. C. du Pont |
| Idaho | *William E. Borah |
| Illinois | C. S. Deneen |
| Kansas | *Arthur Capper |
| Kentucky | F. M. Sackett |
| Massachusetts | F. H. Gillett |
| Michigan | ‡James Couzens |
| Nebraska | *G. W. Norris |
| New Hampshire | *H. W. Keyes |
| New Jersey | *W. E. Edge |
| Oklahoma | W. B. Pine |
| Oregon | *C. L. McNary |
| Rhode Island | ‡J. H. Metcalf |
| South Dakota | W. H. McMaster |
| West Virginia | Guy D. Goff |
| Wyoming | *F. E. Warren |

**DEMOCRATS—10.**

| | |
|---|---|
| Alabama | *J. T. Heflin |
| Arkansas | *J. T. Robinson |
| Georgia | *W. J. Harris |
| Louisiana | *J. E. Ransdell |
| Mississippi | *Pat Harrison |
| North Carolina | *F. M. Simmons |
| South Carolina | C. L. Blease |
| Tennessee | L. D. Tyson |
| Texas | *M. Sheppard |
| Virginia | *Carter Glass |

Result in Iowa, Minnesota, Montana and New Mexico is in doubt.

*Re-elected.
†Elected for short term to fill vacancy in present Senate.
‡Elected for both short and long terms.

## LEGISLATURE AGAIN SOLIDLY REPUBLICAN

### Party Recovers Control of the Senate, With a Probable Majority of Four.

### STRONGER IN THE ASSEMBLY

### J. A. McGinnies of Chautauqua Is Slated for Speaker—One Woman Elected.

Returns from the legislative elections throughout New York State yesterday showed that the Republicans had recaptured control of the State Senate, which during the last two years has been Democratic by the slender majority of one vote. The returns indicated also that the Republicans had increased their lead in the Assembly, which remained Republican during the two years of Governor Smith's present Administration.

Figures, which in some instances have been estimated, give the Republicans a working majority of four in the upper house of the Legislature, with the possibility that this may be increased through changes based on more complete returns.

In the normally Republican Fifteenth Senate District on the upper west side in Manhattan, Senator Nathan Straus won a signal victory, which will return him to the Senate for a third term. He defeated Assemblyman Victor R. Kaufman, whom the Republicans had nominated.

The latest figures received indicate that the Republicans, who have twenty-five members in the present Senate, will have at least twenty-nine in the body elected yesterday.

They gained one Senator in the Seventeenth District, located on the upper west side in Manhattan, where, on partial returns, the election of Courtland Nicoll, the Republican candidate, appeared assured. His Democratic opponent was the present incumbent, Senator Meyer Levy.

In the Eighth Senatorial District in Brooklyn, where early returns indicated re-election of the present incumbent, Dr. W. L. Love, more nearly complete figures pointed to his defeat by R. C. Ellis, his Republican opponent.

**Gains by Republicans.**

Other gains by the Republicans included the Thirty-first Senate District, which takes in Rensselaer County, where Senator John T. Williams, the Democratic incumbent, was defeated by John R. Williams, a Republican newcomer in the Legislature. In the Forty-ninth, which takes in part of Erie County, Robert C. Lacey, the present Democratic Senator, who enjoyed wide popularity in labor circles and has served two years in the Senate, will be replaced by L. R. Lipowicz, his Republican opponent.

Returns from the Assembly elections showed an increased Republican majority in the lower house of next year's Legislature, where the Republicans this year have a working majority of twelve. In the table a number of the districts within the city were estimated on partial returns from a small number of election districts and the result was subject to change on more complete returns.

Despite the huge pluralities run up by the Republicans for Coolidge and Dawes in New York City, the Democrats retained their hold, with few exceptions, on Senate and Assembly districts in the city which are represented by Democrats in the present Legislature.

The Republican Assembly gains were made up-State for the most part. There they won in Sullivan County, in the First District of Rensselaer, in the First and Third Albany Districts, in the Second Onondaga District and the First District in Schenectady County, all of which sent Democrats to the present Legislature in the election a year ago.

**Republican Gain in Kings.**

About the only gain made by the Republicans in this city was in the Seventeenth Assembly District in Kings, normally Republican, but for the last two or three years represented by a Demo-

Continued on Page Two.

## COOLIDGE AND EDGE WINNERS IN JERSEY

### Record Vote Gives President Plurality Which Is Estimated at 350,000.

### MRS. NORTON IS ELECTED

### First Woman in Congress From the East—Tunnel Bond Issue Adopted.

New Jersey, breaking all previous records in the size of its vote, gave large pluralities to Coolidge and Senator Edge, and increased the Republican majorities in both branches of the State Legislature. The proposed $8,000,000 bond issue for finishing the Hudson vehicular tunnels and the Camden Bridge was receiving large majorities.

The polls were closed at 7 o'clock and the size of the vote was so unprecedented that the first returns were made long after the customary time for reporting them. At 3 o'clock this morning Coolidge had a lead of 167,686 in 1,191 of the 2,559 election districts in New Jersey. On the basis of these figures his estimated plurality reached 350,000 for all the districts.

In the Senatorial contest Edge was leading Donnelly by 27,537 in 324 of the 2,559 districts. Senator Edge declared last night that the Coolidge-Dawes plurality as well as his own would reach 200,000.

The Republicans elected ten members of Congress and the Democrats only two, including Mrs. Mary T. Norton of Jersey City, who won a sweeping victory in the Twelfth District in Hudson County, a Democratic stronghold. Mrs. Norton ran against Douglas D. T. Storey, Republican, and she will be the first woman to go to Congress to represent an Eastern State.

**She Thanks the Voters.**

When her election was assured Mrs. Norton, in an interview, expressed her gratitude to Mayor Frank Hague of Jersey City for having placed her in nomination in the Twelfth District, which is a Democratic stronghold.

"I congratulate Mayor Hague," she said, "on his foresight and justice in placing New Jersey among the first States of the Union to send a woman to Congress. I thank the organization and I thank the voters. I shall do everything in my power for the people of New Jersey and for the nation."

The success of the Democratic candidate in the Twelfth District of New Jersey was a foregone conclusion. Mrs. Norton was nominated by Mayor Hague with the full approval of other Democratic leaders. Her nomination was hailed at the time as a tribute to her years of work in the interests of the party.

Mrs. Norton cast her ballot in the Twenty-first Election District, in the Eleventh Ward, Jersey City. She was accompanied by her husband when she went to the polling place in a small candy store. Her husband is Robert E. Norton, who is in the cooperage business in Jersey City.

Five election districts in Camden County gave Coolidge 705 votes, Davis 360 and La Follette 80. One election district in Morris County gave Coolidge 118, Davis 25 and La Follette 4. Twenty of the 2,559 election districts in

Continued on Page Seven.

## THIRD PARTY POLLS 4,000,000 VOTES IN WHOLE COUNTRY

### Showing in Electoral College Far Behind Strength in Popular Support.

### CARRIED ONLY WISCONSIN

### Mid-West Deserted the Senator but Industrial Districts in Cities Helped Him.

### COLLAPSE IN CALIFORNIA

### But the Senator Ran Second in That State, the Dakotas, Minnesota, Montana and Nevada.

Returns from the Eastern and Southern States, and a few States in the West, showed that the Progressive Party movement, headed by Senator Robert M. La Follette of Wisconsin, fell far short of the expectations of its leaders. Senator La Follette, apparently, has run a poor third in all States east of the Mississippi River, except his own State of Wisconsin, which he carried and Minnesota, where he is running second. He is running second in Montana, Nevada, California, Iowa and the two Dakotas. Apparently his total vote in the country is about 4,000,000.

La Follette's greatest collapse was in California, where, so far from his carrying the State, as he expected, the Republians have it by a great majority.

The following table shows the estimated La Follette vote in the various States.

| | |
|---|---|
| California | 350,000 |
| Illinois | 350,000 |
| Iowa | 275,000 |
| Indiana | 80,000 |
| Kansas | 90,000 |
| Michigan | 125,000 |
| Minnesota | 450,000 |
| New York | 410,000 |
| Montana | 50,000 |
| Nebraska | 90,000 |
| North Dakota | 100,000 |
| New Jersey | 60,000 |
| Ohio | 200,000 |
| Pennsylvania | 250,000 |
| South Dakota | 90,000 |
| Washington | 120,000 |
| Wisconsin | 375,000 |

His vote in other States varied from 1,000 or less in Arizona to about 45,000 in Maryland.

The forecasts by the Progressive Party leaders that La Follette and Wheeler would carry Illinois, Ohio and probably a few Eastern States were not made good. In both Illinois and Ohio Senator La Follette was many thousand votes behind John W. Davis, Democratic nominee, and the Wisconsin Senator received only a fraction of the total vote given to President Coolidge.

In New York State, where the backers of La Follette had predicted that the Progressive ticket would carry New York City, La Follette was a bad third. La Follette received fewer than half the votes recorded for Mr. Davis, and President Coolidge beat the Third Party candidate in New York five or six to one. Most of the La Follette strength in New York, as in other Eastern States, was concenerated in a few industrial centres.

In Massachusetts, where President Coolidge beat Mr. Davis six or seven to one, Mr. Davis beat La Follette more than two to one. Even in Boston, a city which La Follette leaders had professed confidence of carrying, Senator La Follette received but a negligible vote.

In Connecticut, another State where the Progressive Party leaders claimed great strength, early returns showed that President Coolidge was getting more than six votes for each given La Follette and that Mr. Davis was leading La Follette about two to one.

**Poor Showing in South and West.**

The Progressive Party had expected to run first or second in New Hampshire, according to the predictions made, but the returns indicated that President Coolidge would beat Senator La Follette by fifteen to one or better, and that Davis was running ahead of La Follette at the rate of eight votes to one.

Another example of the collapse of the La Follette movement was supplied

Continued on Page Five.

## Electoral Vote

**COOLIDGE.**

| State | Votes |
|---|---|
| California | 13 |
| Colorado | 6 |
| Connecticut | 7 |
| Delaware | 3 |
| Idaho | 4 |
| Illinois | 29 |
| Indiana | 15 |
| Iowa | 13 |
| Kansas | 10 |
| Kentucky | 13 |
| Maine | 6 |
| Maryland | 8 |
| Massachusetts | 18 |
| Michigan | 15 |
| Missouri | 18 |
| Nebraska | 8 |
| New Hampshire | 4 |
| New Jersey | 14 |
| New York | 45 |
| North Dakota | 5 |
| Ohio | 24 |
| Oregon | 5 |
| Pennsylvania | 38 |
| Rhode Island | 5 |
| South Dakota | 5 |
| Vermont | 4 |
| Utah | 4 |
| Washington | 7 |
| West Virginia | 8 |
| Wyoming | 3 |
| Total | 357 |

**DAVIS.**

| State | Votes |
|---|---|
| Alabama | 12 |
| Arkansas | 9 |
| Florida | 6 |
| Georgia | 14 |
| Louisiana | 10 |
| Mississippi | 10 |
| North Carolina | 12 |
| Oklahoma | 10 |
| South Carolina | 9 |
| Tennessee | 12 |
| Texas | 20 |
| Virginia | 12 |
| Total: | 136 |

**LA FOLLETTE.**

| State | Votes |
|---|---|
| Wisconsin | 13 |
| Total | 13 |

**DOUBTFUL.**

| State | Votes |
|---|---|
| Arizona | 3 |
| Minnesota | 12 |
| Montana | 4 |
| Nevada | 3 |
| New Mexico | 3 |
| Total | 25 |

Total number of votes in Electoral College, 531; necessary to a choice, 266.

Some of the States in the above list are placed as doubtful only because, due to the difference in time, the returns are inadequate.

## REPUBLICANS MAKE GAINS IN CONGRESS

### Retain Control of Senate and May Increase House Majority to 50.

### BROOKHART LIKELY TO LOSE

### Stanley of Kentucky and Walsh of Massachusetts, Democratic Senators, Apparently Beaten.

While the returns on the elections of United States Senators and members of the House of Representatives are incomplete, the indications early this morning were that the Republican Party would retain majorities in both houses of Congress for the two-year period beginning March 4, 1925, the first half of President Coolidge's new administration.

There have been Republican gains in the House sufficiently large to make it apparent that the present majority in that body, which was fifteen when the Congress adjourned in June and has been reduced to ten by resignations and deaths of Republican members, will be considerably exceeded. As for the Senate, Republican candidates have very generally held their own in States from which complete or fairly complete returns have been received.

Figures compiled from the latest returns give the following showing for the next Senate as a result of the elections yesterday:

Republicans, 52; Democrats, 38; Farmer-Labor, 1; four in doubt, with one vacancy not filled yesterday.

The majority the Republicans will have in the House is uncertain but that it will be much larger than the mere nominal majority obtained by the Republicans in the Congressional elections of two years ago is indicated by the following political alignment, based on returns up to an early hour this morning:

Republicans, 2[illegible]; Democrats, 1[illegible]; Socialists, 1, Farmer-Labor, 2; in doubt, [illegible]

## NEW YORK BY 900,000

### Coolidge's Plurality in This State Little Below Harding's

### DAVIS GETS THE SOUTH ONLY

### La Follette Apparently Only His Own State, but Large Industrial Vote

### CALIFORNIA FOR COOLIDGE

### Doubtful States of the Far West Lean to the President as Returns Increase.

### DAVIS LOSES WEST VIRGINIA

### Refused at Late Hour to Concede Defeat and Hoped for Upset From the West.

### BRYAN'S STATE TO COOLIDGE

### Plurality of 50,000 in Nebraska for the President Indicated in Latest Dispatches.

Calvin Coolidge has been elected President of the United States in a victory of impressive proportions.

At 5 o'clock this morning the returns indicated that President Coolidge had secured 357 electoral votes, Davis 136 and La Follette 13, and that 25 votes in five Western States were still in doubt. The principal overtures in the late returns were in Kentucky and Missouri. In Kentucky, in 3,431 out of 3,971 precincts, seven-eighths of the State, Coolidge had 337,838, against 331,244 for Davis. It was the opinion of the most competent observers in the State that later returns would not take the State away from the President.

In Missouri Coolidge has 251,602, against Davis's 238,896 in 1,934 out of 4,089 precincts. Correspondents in the State believed that the Republican rural precincts were sure to give the State to the President. The St. Louis Globe-Democrat estimates that Coolidge will carry the State by 50,000.

The five States remaining in doubt are Minnesota, Montana, Nevada, Arizona and New Mexico.

In Montana Coolidge has a slight lead, but the returns are too scant to justify giving the State to him at present. Arizona and New Mexico are close, with indications of going for Davis. In Nevada Coolidge has a lead of 600 votes over La Follette, who is running second, in a little less than one-half the State.

It is not probable that Davis's vote in the Electoral College will exceed 142, which it will be if he carries Arizona and New Mexico. Apparently he has no chance in Minnesota, Montana and Nevada, where he is running third, La Follette being second. On the other hand, it is possible that Coolidge may carry Minnesota, Montana and Nevada, giving him a total of 376, or, with Arizona and New Mexico added, 382 as his utmost limit.

An extreme possibility, but not a very strong one, for La Follette, is the addition of Minnesota, Montana and Nevada, to the one State that he has surely carried, Wisconsin, which would give him a total of 32.

Senator Robert M. La Follette is leading in his home State, Wisconsin, and will undoubtedly win there and get its 13 electoral votes.

Mr. Coolidge is the sixth Vice President to become President through the death of the incumbent and the second to be elected President immediately afterward. The other was Theodore Roosevelt.

**Coolidge Victory Overwhelming.**

The victory which returns President Coolidge to office and elects Brig. Gen. Charles G. Dawes of Illinois Vice President is overwhelming in the East and Middle West, and early indications are that the Republicans have registered heavily even in the Far West. Such States as North and South Dakota, which the La Follettites claimed for the Third Party, have gone to President Coolidge. So also has Oregon, which some expected to see in the Third Party column.

Nebraska also has apparently gone for Coolidge by about [illegible], according to

## La Follette Wins Koenig's Home District; Coolidge Captures Davis's and Olvany's

Senator La Follette carried the home election district of Samuel S. Koenig, Manhattan Republican leader, with a vote of 206 to 158 for Coolidge and 109 for Davis. La Follette received 175 of these votes as the Progressive candidate and 111 as the Socialist candidate. Four years ago the same district gave Cox 40 and Harding 285.

The Rev. Norman Thomas, the Socialist Gubernatorial candidate, ran a poor third in his own home district, polling only 16 votes as compared with 232 for Smith and 152 for Roosevelt.

Governor Smith's district on the lower east side was carried by Davis with a vote of 165. La Follette ran second with 116 and Coolidge third with 34. Four years ago this district gave Cox 250 and Harding 278.

Governor Smith carried his home district by a vote of 494 to 40 for Roosevelt and 2 for Thomas. Two years ago the same district gave Smith 484 and Miller 29.

President Coolidge carried the home district of Tammany Leader George W. Olvany with a vote of [illegible]. Davis had 181 [illegible]. The President also defeated John W. Davis in the [illegible] ter's district [illegible] L. J. [illegible] Davis [illegible]

Colonel Roosevelt at Oyster Bay received [illegible] Temple, a smaller [illegible] Coolidge in the [illegible] received [illegible] polled [illegible]

The home city of Lieut. Governor Lunn was carried by Colonel Roosevelt by a [illegible]

## State Pluralities Rolled Up by Coolidge.

The following table shows President Coolidge's estimated pluralities on the returns so far received from the States carried by him:

| | | | |
|---|---|---|---|
| California | *800,000 | New Jersey | 350,000 |
| Colorado | 70,000 | New York | 900,000 |
| Delaware | 15,000 | North Dakota | *120,000 |
| Illinois | 750,000 | Ohio | 500,000 |
| Indiana | 400,000 | Pennsylvania | 1,100,000 |
| Iowa | *225,000 | Rhode Island | 35,000 |
| Kansas | 250,000 | South Dakota | *45,000 |
| Maine | 80,000 | Utah | 4,000 |
| Maryland | 10,000 | Washington | 100,000 |
| Massachusetts | 250,000 | West Virginia | 35,000 |
| Michigan | 400,000 | | |
| Nebraska | 50,000 | | |

*Over La Follette.

"All the News That's Fit to Print."

# The New York Times.

THE WEATHER
Fair and colder today; tomorrow, cloudy and warmer; north winds.
Temperature yesterday—Max., 47; Min., 34.
For weather report see next to last page.

VOL. LXXIV....No. 24,512. NEW YORK, THURSDAY, MARCH 5, 1925. TWO CENTS In Greater New York | THREE CENTS Within 200 Miles | FOUR CENTS Elsewhere in the U. S.

# COOLIDGE IS INAUGURATED WITH SIMPLE CEREMONIES; URGES ECONOMY AT HOME, PEACE AND COOPERATION ABROAD; DAWES CAUSES A SENSATION BY ATTACKING SENATE RULES

## VAST BERLIN CROWD SWEPT BY EMOTION AT EBERT FUNERAL

### Men and Women Shriek and Faint Along Line of March—First Aid Given to 1,000.

### ROYAL HONOR FOR THE DEAD

### Cortege Moves Through Kaiser's Arch of Brandenburg Gate to Reichstag Building.

### CRUSH AT POTSDAM STATION

### Thousands Pass the Catafalque Before Funeral Train Bears the Body to Heidelberg.

By T. R. YBARRA.


By Wireless to THE NEW YORK TIMES.

BERLIN, March 4.—Friedrich Ebert, in youth a wandering manual laborer, in manhood a saddler and Socialist vowed to enmity against monarchs, and when death felled him, the first President of a Republic founded upon the ruins of one of the world's proudest empires, passed today in the stark majesty of death through the heart of a metropolis sacrosanct for decades to monarchy.

Past funeral pyres sending up forked flames and black smoke clouds, amid the crash of martial music and the roll of muffled drums and the thundering tread of booted soldiery, the body of Ebert the saddler moved slowly along Wilhelmstrasse, peopled with ghosts of Hohenzollerns and Bismarck, across the Pariserplatz, sacred to the victories of dead Prussian kings, and then squarely through the middle opening of the Brandenburg Gate, that superb stone emblem of Kaiserism, through which, while Imperial Germany lived, only her Kaiser could pass.

But today framed in funeral pomp, which for all its simplicity would have well befitted the proudest of kings, the body of Ebert the saddler, President of Germany, passed beneath that hallowed archway. And as the simple coffin draped with black, red and gold, the Republican colors which have ousted the black, white and red of the German Empire, emerged through that arch and stood revealed to thousands massed under a cloudless sky along the green reaches of Tiergarten parkways, the poignant strains of Chopin's Funeral March and the thud of soldiers' boots against the cobblestones were suddenly blended with another sound—hysterical shrieks from women, heartbroken wails like the keening of savage Irish tribeswomen of old, the bursting of emotion pent up beyond endurance in the breasts of Berlin workingwomen—and men too—belonging to the class to which Ebert belonged, in whom control broke and consciousness snapped when they saw him who had been one of themselves lying before their eyes in death.

**March to the Reichstag Building.**

Slowly the funeral cortège veered rightward from the Brandenburg Gate toward the Reichstag building. Squads of cavalry before and behind the coffin kept their horses pacing in funeral step. Solid squares of trench-helmeted German infantry, though a mere shadow of Germany's terrific militarism, still marched and wheeled and glared straight ahead with all the soldierliness bred by iron discipline.

And as the procession slowly progressed those hysterical shrieks still punctured the wail of the funeral marches and the thud of hoofs and boots, and stretcherbearers flitted constantly into the crowd and out again bearing disheveled women of the poorer classes, their tawdry finery in disarray, their limbs limp, their faces white—paying tribute in this helpless surrender to surging emotion to the man of the people who before their eyes was smashing the tradition of generals and kings, marshals and emperors.

Before the Reichstag Building, where stands the colossal bronze statue of Bismark, scorner of the common people and hater of socialism, the body of Friedrich Ebert, worker and Socialist, halted a few brief moments while Reichstag President Löbe, also a Socialist, spoke from the top of the great stone entrance stairway a short and feeling tribute to the dead leader—spoke it as by strange coincidence while the colossal bronze Bismark stood with his back haughtily turned to both corpse and speaker as all his life he had stood uncompromisingly contemptuous of all savoring of democracy.

Then once more the funeral cortège moved. This time it went along the tree-lined Friedensallée packed even to the uttermost treetops with onlookers, again past the Brandenburg Gate and thence along Budapesterstrasse, fringing the garden behind the palace where Bismark used to pace in deep thought framing his schemes for making the German Empire proof for all time against Socialists and Republicans, to Potsdamerplatz.

In front of the Potsdamer Railway

Continued on Page Fifteen.



## Vienna's 17-Ton Bell Is Rung, 200 Years Old, Silent for 50


Special Cable to THE NEW YORK TIMES.

VIENNA, March 4.—The big bell of famous St. Stephen's Cathedral, weighing seventeen tons, that has been silent for fifty years was rung again today.

The bell was made 200 years ago. It has not been rung for the last five decades because of the tower being thought unsafe.

The Vienna bell shares the distinction of the bells of Olmutz and Notre Dame of being the fourth largest bell in active use. It was cast in 1711 from 180 cannon taken from the Turks when the siege of Vienna was raised by the Polish army of Sobieski.

For a century it hung on the second landing of the tower. The tower soon afterward became unsafe and was removed to be rebuilt in 1860-64, when the bell was restored.

The tower with the spire is 450 feet high.

## BEEBE DREDGES SITE OF FABLED ATLANTIS

### First Yield From Bed of the Sargasso Sea Contains Glass Sponges and Volcanic Rock.

### SURFACE INSECTS CAUGHT

### High Waves Continue to Hamper Arcturus Party, Now Midway Between America and Africa.

By WILLIAM BEEBE.

By Wireless from the S. S. Arcturus, Via East Moriches, L. I.



S. S. ARCTURUS, Sargasso Sea, March 4.—We are now at the site of the fabled Atlantis on Atlantic Ridge, midway between America and Africa, with 2,300 fathoms of sea below us, and this morning our radio receiving set brought to us a lively Pittsburgh orchestra playing "Hands Across the Sea," Sousa's march.

Even with continued heavy seas we have brought our heavy dredging apparatus into play, and yesterday our first bottom dredge brought up glass sponges and volcanic rock from a sea abyss three and one-half miles down.

As this first yield from the bed of the little known Sargasso Sea emerged, and our staff of scientists viewed it with the same avaricious eagerness to analyze it as if it had been treasure trove, one of the bow winches yielded, and but for quick work by mate and crew the dredging would have ended with a bad accident.

Our trawl has brought up huge-mouthed fishes from the submarine region of darkness and also a male pipefish with a brood pouch full of eggs.

It is with vast pleasure that I report the capture of our first specimens of marine surface walking insects, safely collected, and, with the other specimens, they are now engaging the attention of our laboratory specialists in "heaven," our upper laboratory.

In the midst of these engrossing labors it has been necessary to take account of the coal bunkers of the good ship Arcturus, which, by the way, is a noble craft and endeared to us forever by her sedate carriage in the very heavy seas we are weathering.

For the high waves keep up, much to our chagrin. The Sargasso Sea, instead of being as quiet as a mill-pond, is upset by storms.

**Sargasso Sea Finds Explained.**

The glass sponges mentioned in the radio from the Arcturus have been dredged before and described, according to Dr. J. J. Galloway, Assistant Professor of Paleontology at Columbia University.

"They resemble ordinary sponges, except that they have skeletons resembling glass," he said. "Some of them are very beautiful. One type is called Venus's Flower Basket. Many of them are cup-shaped. Several specimens are on display at the American Museum of Natural History.

"As to the surface insects, I do not recall hearing of them before. There are insects which live some distance off shore but I don't remember that any lived on the ocean itself."

D. W. John, Professor of Physiography at Columbia, said last night that it was not unusual to find lava on the ocean bottom.

"It is distributed so widely that it might be found almost anywhere," he said. "It might be volcanic rock which has sunk, but volcanoes do occur at the bottom of the ocean and it might be lava which has never been above water."

In dredging the bottom in the region where the lost continent of Atlantis has been fancied to be, Dr. Beebe and his party are following in the tracks of the United States Navy, which has had the last word to say about Atlantis. The ocean bottom in the supposed locality of the mysterious sunken continent was surveyed two years ago by the United States Navy with the new sonic depth finder which measures depths by the length of time it requires for sound waves to travel to the ocean bottom and return. Dr. Harvey C. Hayes, in charge of these measurements, was deeply interested to find an area rising from the ocean bottom which suggested a sunken continent. He found an old coast line with shelving beaches of sand and gravel and other characteristics indicating that what was then the floor of the ocean might once have been at the surface.



## BIG CROWD SEES PARADE

### Crack Units of Army, Navy and Marine Reviewed by President.

### TAKES 50 MINUTES TO PASS

### They Are Followed by the Governors of 19 States With Their Military Escorts.

### MRS. ROSS GETS CHEERS

### Gifford Pinchot of Pennsylvania Alone Rides a Horse, the Others Driving in Automobiles.

*Special to The New York Times.*

WASHINGTON, March 4.—Thousands of persons lined Pennsylvania Avenue this afternoon, from the Capitol to the White House, as 5,000 picked men from the army, the navy and the marines, vanguard to the Governors of nineteen States, swung past the President in the inaugural parade. The marchers went by the glass-enclosed reviewing kiosk, where stood President Coolidge, surrounded by members of his Cabinet and gold-laced army and navy officers of high rank, in slightly less than an hour. The blaring of the bands and the spots of vivid color provided by some of the detachments kept the spectators enthused.

Thirty-two tanks, spurting smoke, rumbled past. The scarlet coated Marine Band and the United States Army Band stirred the watchers. The evenly rising and falling ranks of the blue-jacketed sailors and the tanned files of the marines all got their share of the applause. But the greatest applause of it all went to Governor Nellie E. Ross of Wyoming, bringing up the end of the Governors' automobiles. As the woman Governor passed the President's stand he smiled broadly at the shouts of "Oh, you Governor!" from the crowd, while Mrs. Coolidge clapped her hands.

Early indications were that the parade, smaller than any of recent inaugurations, would fail to attract much of a crowd. At 10 o'clock in the morning, an hour before the President was due to leave the White House and escorted by a detachment of cavalry, Secret Service operatives and Cabinet Ministers, drove down the avenue to the Capitol for the inaugural ceremonies, there were few persons indeed along the line of march. There were many streets where not more than a half dozen persons were in place awaiting the spectacle.

**Stands Slow in Filling.**

The stands also were empty. The two big official stands, extending from beyond the White House down Pennsylvania Avenue to Fifteenth Street, had an explanation for their absence of people, in that ticket holders were not admitted there until noon. But the private stands put up along the thoroughfare from Fifteenth Street to the Capitol itself were yawning for the crowds. The entire length of the parade route had been heavily policed, an officer standing every twenty feet. Thin steel cables were strung along the curb to hold the crowd back.

Not more than 5,000 were out and waiting at 11 o'clock when the President was escorted from his official home to the Capitol for the ceremonies. Here and there along the line as his automobile passed were spurts of handclapping, which he recognized by lifting his hat. By the side of her silent husband Mrs. Coolidge smiled radiantly and chatted animatedly to Senator Charles G. Curtis, Chairman of the Joint Congressional Committee on Arrangements, who was the only other occupant of the President's car.

While the inauguration was proceeding at the Capitol, however, the tardy spectators began to put in an appearance. They came fast when they started and were chiefly recruited from Washington itself. The last-minute rush of visitors from out of town failed to materialize to any extent. Good places along the route were quickly snapped up and the proprietors of the small private stands began to cheer up.

In front of the White House, where the Presidential reviewing stand had been erected, a dozen workmen were engaged until the last minute getting in readiness for the distinguished party. The chairs in the kiosk were arranged and rearranged, two huge baskets of red roses were rushed up and set in place, and finally the officials had everything in order.

**Guard Draws Up at Reviewing Stand.**

This brought the time to 1:30 o'clock. The lines of sergeants and corporals assigned from the headquarters of the Washington army area to act as guard at the reviewing stand formed, and, fixing bayonets, came to attention to await the return of President Coolidge and his party from the inaugural ceremonies and address at the Capitol, a mile and a quarter from the White House.

As soon as the inauguration was ended those waiting in line blocks away soon knew it through the swarm of persons that came hurrying down Pennsylvania

Continued on Page Five.



## Ginger, Cavalry Dog, Sees The Inauguration Through

WASHINGTON, March 4 (Associated Press).—President Coolidge had an uninvited but not unwelcome guest at his inauguration, one who, though uninvited, came early, stayed late, saw the show through to the end and had a very busy time.

He was Ginger, the dog of Troop F, Third Cavalry. Some folks might call Ginger a bulldog; perhaps he thinks he is, but he bears without shame on his escutcheon the bar sinister. First Sergeant Joe Rock says Ginger is his dog, but every other man in the troop says Ginger is the troop's dog and is ready to fight to prove it.

Ginger made the long trip from Fort Myer afoot and arrived feeling frisky. He capered right into the White House grounds, shielded by two of his friends, horses, and when President Coolidge and Vice President Dawes came out for the trip to the Capitol Ginger trotted along Pennsylvania Avenue with the procession.

## SENATORS COMMENT BITTERLY ON DAWES

### His Speech Was in Bad Taste and Will Defeat Its Object, Many Assert.

### HASTE IN CEREMONY SCORED

### Senators Had Not Time to Sign the Roll and Chamber Was Left Without a Chairman.

*Special to The New York Times.*

WASHINGTON, March 4.—Some caustic Senatorial comment was voiced this afternoon on Vice President Dawes's speech and his unprecedented method of accelerating the swearing-in of Senators to office, as well as on the fact that after the President had completed his inaugural address, Mr. Dawes did not appear in the Senate chamber, where the new Senate reassembled in order to reach an agreement for adjournment until noon tomorrow.

Democratic Senators were outspoken in their remarks about the new Vice President's assault upon the Senate rules, but it was obvious that many Senators of both parties were amazed by the Vice President's speech and the manner in which he delivered it.

Comment ranged from a declaration by Senator Robinson, the Democratic floor leader, that Mr. Dawes's performance was "ridiculous," to expressions of opinion that if there had ever been a chance of changing the rules, such hope had now been dimmed.

Some Senators were so much interested in the Dawes speech that, instead of leaving the Senate chamber to hear President Coolidge make his inaugural address, they remained in their seats and conversed in tones audible in the galleries, commenting on the fact that Mr. Dawes had spoken so remarkably before an official gathering at which not only American notables but the diplomats representing foreign nations had been guests. Mr. Dawes's manner of delivery, his gestures, waving his arms, shouting, pounding with his fists were all noted.

Among these Senators were said to be Mr. Robinson of Arkansas, the Democratic floor leader; Senator Jones of Washington, Republican; Senator McNary of Oregon, Republican; Senator Swanson of Virginia, Democrat; Senator George of Georgia, Democrat, and Senator Borah of Idaho, Republican.

**Senate Left Without a Chairman.**

Fuel was added to the flames when Mr. Dawes failed to come back to the Senate, over which he is destined to preside, after President Coolidge had completed his speech. Some parliamentarians said tonight there was no necessity for Mr. Dawes to return, and that Senator Cummins, President pro tempore of the Senate, should have arranged for some one to preside.

At any rate, Mr. Dawes did not appear, and as a result the Senators sat around, looking vaguely at each other and wondering what to do. Senator Curtis, the Republican leader, had escorted President and Mrs. Coolidge to the White House, and there seemed to be no one to suggest a move.

Finally Senator Watson of Indiana took the chair and called the Senate to order. Senator Ashurst of Arizona, Democrat, spoke immediately on the haste in which the swearing-in had been conducted, his remarks being stimulated by suggestions that some Senators had not even had time to sign the book in which signatures are always written after the swearing-in ceremony.

"This is an important matter," said Senator Ashurst. "Not only has a Senator a right to sign the roll in the presence of the Senate and of his fellow Senators, but it is his duty to do so; it is a part of the oath. We could no more dispense with his signing the roster of members in the presence of fellow Senators than we could interrupt the oath in the middle of its administration and leave the Chamber."

The Senate then adjourned until tomorrow at noon. On the way out of the chamber, Senator Caraway of Arkansas said that Mr. Dawes's failure to return, and his leaving the Senate to its own

Continued on Page Four.



## VICE PRESIDENT CAUSES STIR

### Accuses Senate of Wasting Time, and Shakes His Finger at It.

### THUMPS DESK VIGOROUSLY

### Rushes Swearing-In Ceremony and Dismisses Senators With a Wave of His Hand.

### SENATORS APPEAR ANGERED

### But the Galleries Make Merry—Dawes's Criticism Is Aimed at Unlimited Debate.

*Special to The New York Times.*

WASHINGTON, March 4.—The inauguration of Charles G. Dawes as Vice President in the Senate Chamber today preceding the inauguration of President Coolidge, was not the cut-and-dried affair that custom and precedent have sought to make it.

Precedent and custom were thrown to the winds by the new Vice President himself, when in a prepared address he accused the Senate of being recreant to its duty to the people through waste of time and its willingness to let a solitary Senator prevent the enactment of legislation. He called for a revision of rules of procedure held sacred by many of the elder statesmen of the upper house.

Not alone in that respect did the Vice President, within a few minutes after he assumed his duties as presiding officer of the Senate, make the scene one long to be remembered. His spirited personality was more in evidence through his manner than his critical utterances. He shook his forefinger at the Senate and pounded his desk to emphasize his words. He fairly shouted at those over whose deliberations he will preside.

Part of the Senatorial contingent of his audience was shocked and angered. Apparently the dominating effect on many of the others who heard and saw was amusement. A considerable proportion, mainly in the galleries, where women predominated, showed that it approved or at least did not dislike the words, if not the manner, of the Vice President's delivery.

**Curtails Swearing In Ceremony.**

Later, in the solemn proceedings—or proceedings intended to be solemn—Vice President Dawes again showed his contempt for precedent. It was his duty to administer the oath to new Senators and those who had been re-elected for the six-year term beginning today. Those who were to take the oath were called up in batches, and to each batch Vice President Dawes was obliged to repeat the words of the required pledge to support the Constitution.

It was a rather tiresome proceeding, and the Vice President showed that he found it irksome. He waved his hand toward the clerk who was calling the names of the Senator to be sworn in.

"Bring them all up together," he said, or something like it. So the remaining Senators were sworn in as a mass, instead of in several batches.

Then there was a laugh when the company was about to adjourn to the east portico of the Capitol to see President Coolidge inaugurated. The Vice President announced that the audience would retire for this purpose, and he accompanied the announcement with a wave of the hand that indicated he desired to "shoo out" the whole crowd. The galleries made merry. They enjoyed it, if the Senators did not.

After the inauguration of President Coolidge the storm broke among the Senators. Their indignation was pronounced. Some of them said very unkind things of their new presiding officer. What they intend to do about it was not determined, but it was evident this evening that some grave and reverend members of the Senate were going to bed tonight feeling that it was not the end of a perfect day.

**VICE PRESIDENT'S SPEECH.**

The speech of the Vice President was as follows:

What I say upon entering this office should relate to its administration and the conditions under which it is administered. Unlike the vast majority of deliberative and legislative bodies, the Senate does not elect its presiding officer. He is designated for his duty by the Constitution of the United States.

In the administration of this office his duty is to be concerned with methods of effective procedure, as distinguished from any legislative policy of the body over which he presides. It is not for the Vice President to be personally concerned with the interests of political parties or with the policies or projects involved in legislative action, save in that unusual contingency where, under the Constitution, it becomes necessary for him to cast the deciding vote in case of a tie.

Nor should he, in view of that unusual contingency, assume any attitude toward prospective legislation until the contingency occurs. Any other course would inevitably lessen the weight of his influence in those impartial and nonpartisan matters with which it is

Continued on Page Four.

THE PRESIDENT SMILES.



## Text of the Inaugural Address Outlining Coolidge's Policies

### The President, While Seeing Much to Be Thankful for, Urges the Need of Further Tax Cuts, Not to Save Money, but to Save People.

WASHINGTON, March 4.—The text of President Coolidge's inaugural address follows:

*My Countrymen:*

No one can contemplate current conditions without finding much that is satisfying and still more that is encouraging. Our own country is leading the world in the general readjustment to the results of the great conflict. Many of its burdens will bear heavily upon us for years, and the secondary and indirect effects we must expect to experience for some time. But we are beginning to comprehend more definitely what course should be pursued, what remedies ought to be applied, what actions should be taken for our deliverance, and are clearly manifesting a determined will faithfully and conscientiously to adopt these methods of relief.

Already we have sufficiently rearranged our domestic affairs so that confidence has returned, business has revived, and we appear to be entering an era of prosperity which is gradually reaching into every part of the nation. Realizing that we cannot live unto ourselves alone, we have contributed of our resources and our counsel to the relief of the suffering and the settlement of the disputes among the European nations. Because of what America is and what America has done, a firmer courage, a higher hope, inspires the heart of all humanity.

These results have not occurred by mere chance. They have been secured by a constant and enlightened effort marked by many sacrifices and extending over many generations. We cannot continue these brilliant successes in the future unless we continue to learn from the past. It is necessary to keep the former experiences of our country, both at home and abroad, continually before us if we are to have any science of government.

**Taking the Bearings.**

If we wish to erect new structures, we must have a definite knowledge of the old foundations. We must realize that human nature is about the most constant thing in the universe and that the essentials of human relationship do not change. We must frequently take our bearings from these fixed stars of our political firmament if we expect to hold a true course. If we examine carefully what we have done, we can determine the more accurately what we can do.

We stand at the opening of the one hundred and fiftieth year since our national consciousness first asserted itself by unmistakable action with an array of force. The old sentiment of detached and dependent Colonies disappeared in the new sentiment of a united and independent nation. Men began to discard the narrow confines of a local charter for the broader opportunities of a national Constitution. Under the eternal urge of freedom we became an independent nation.

A little less than fifty years later that freedom and independence were reasserted in the face of all the world and guarded, supported and secured by the Monroe Doctrine. The narrow fringe of States along the Atlantic seaboard advanced its frontiers across the hills and plains of an intervening continent until it passed down the golden slope to the Pacific. We made freedom a birthright. We extended our dominion over distant islands in order to safeguard our own interests and accepted the consequent obligations to bestow justice and liberty upon less favored peoples. In the defense of our own ideals and in the general cause of liberty we entered the great war. When victory had been fully secured, we withdrew to our own shores unrecompensed save in the consciousness of duty done.

Throughout all these experiences we have enlarged our freedom, we have strengthened our independence. We have been, and propose to be, more and more American. We believe that we can best serve our own country and most successfully discharge our obligations to humanity by continuing to be openly and candidly, intensely and scrupulously American. If we have any heritage, it has been that. If we have any destiny, we have found it in that direction.

But if we wish to continue to be distinctively American, we must continue to make that term comprehensive enough to embrace the legitimate desires of a civilized and enlightened people determined in all their relations to pursue a conscientious and religious life. We cannot permit ourselves to be narrowed and dwarfed by slogans and phrases. It is not the adjective but the substantive which is of real importance. It is not the name of the action, but the result of the action which is the chief concern.

**America a Balanced Force.**

It will be well not to be too much disturbed by the thought of either isolation or entanglement of pacifists and militarists. The physical configuration of the earth has separated us from all of the Old World, but the common brotherhood of man, the highest law of all our being, has united us by inseparable bonds with all humanity. Our country represents nothing but peaceful intentions toward all the earth, but it ought not to fail to maintain such a military force as comports with the dignity and security of a great people. It ought to be a balanced force, intensely modern, capable of defense by sea and land, beneath the surface and in the air. But it should be so conducted that all the world may see in it not a menace but an instrument of security and peace.

This nation believes thoroughly in an honorable peace under which the rights of its citizens are to be everywhere protected. It has never found that the necessary enjoyment of such a peace could be maintained only by a great and threatening array of arms. In common with other nations, it is now more determined than ever to promote peace through friendliness and good-will, through mutual understandings and mutual forbearance. We have never practiced the policy of competitive armaments. We have recently committed ourselves by covenants with the other great nations to a limitation of our sea power. As one result of this, our navy ranks larger, in comparison, than it ever did before.

Removing the burden of expense and jealousy which must always accrue from a keen rivalry is one of the most effective methods of diminishing that unreasonable hysteria and misunderstanding which are the most potent means of fomenting war. This policy represents a new departure in the world. It is a thought, an ideal, which has led to an entirely new line of action. It will not be easy to maintain. Some never move from their old position, some are constantly slipping back to the old ways of thought

Continued on Page Two.



## CAPITOL SCENE IMPRESSIVE

### Coolidge Takes Oath, Surrounded by National Leaders and Diplomats.

### HE IS SERENE THROUGHOUT

### Never Resorting to the Dramatic, He Gets Frequent Applause From the Crowds.

### ADDRESS TAKES 41 MINUTES

### He Stresses Need for a Purer and Better Americanism and Calls Again for World Court.

By RICHARD V. OULAHAN.

*Special to The New York Times.*

WASHINGTON, March 4.—At 12:59 o'clock this afternoon, surrounded by most of those high in the nation's affairs and in the presence of a multitude that filled the broad and deep plaza upon which the stately Capitol faces, Calvin Coolidge took the solemn oath prescribed for the President of the United States, and thus entered upon the term of four years to which he had been elected last November.

Brilliant sunshine, a breeze with a nip and a tang in it, made weather conditions all that could be desired for the comfort of participants in the inaugural ceremony and the tens of thousands who stood in the Capitol plaza or along the route of the Presidential progress from the White House to the Capitol and back again and to view the military parade which concluded the official observance of the occasion.

This quadrennial open air ceremonial at the Capitol, always impressive and dignified despite its democratic flavor, was preceded by the indoor ceremony, held within the Senate chamber, of inducting Charles G. Dawes into the office of Vice President. Ordinarily that ceremony has as much impressiveness and dignity as the Presidential inauguration, and proceeds without incident in accordance with prescribed forms. But today it was marked by diversion furnished by the dynamic manner and equally dynamic words of the new Vice President in taking up his official duties.

**Dawes Stirs the Senate.**

A few minutes after he had taken the required oath and declared the Senate convened in special session by proclamation of President Coolidge, Vice President Dawes delivered an inaugural address which caused a stir in the audience crowded into the Senate's hall. Those who had expected to hear a mere perfunctory salutatory heard something far different. It was dramatic; it was spectacular.

Vice President Dawes virtually told the Senate that it was false to the duty it owed the American people. He condemned it for waste of time. Its methods, he declared, especially the opportunity it permitted for one Senator to stop the wheels of the legislative machinery, might arouse an outraged public opinion to demand reform. He called for modification of the Senate rules, with the power they placed in the hands of a single member of the upper house to defeat a measure desired by a two-thirds majority. "Who would dare maintain," he cried—and "cried" in that sense is no exaggeration—"that in the last analysis the right of the Senate itself to act should ever be subordinated to the right of one Senator to make a speech?"

Some Senators looked aghast. Others leaned forward, amazement in their faces. Others took it humorously, and a few put their hands over their mouths as if to stifle laughter. Explosion was deferred until the inaugural ceremonies were over. Some were plainly nervous. President Coolidge, seated beneath the rostrum from which his running mate delivered his broadside of criticism, wore a face that gave no indication of what was taking place in his mind.

**Galleries Laugh and Applaud.**

But the greater part of the new Vice President's auditors on floor and in the crowded galleries enjoyed it all immensely. They laughed frequently; occasionally they applauded—a gross violation of the rules of the supposedly dignified Senate. Their laughter, however, was due more to the Vice President's vivid oratorical mannerisms than to his frank words. He waved his arms, he pounded the desk in front of him with loud, resounding thumps and he shook an admonitory finger toward the section where Senators were seated. His voice, a trifle husky, rang out. At times he shouted. Obviously he intended to be emphatic. He furnished the sensation of the day.

Otherwise it was what might be called a quiet inauguration. It was Calvin Coolidge's second inauguration. In most respects, save in the form of the pledge he gave, it differed radically from his first installation into the office of President. Near him sat his venerable father, sturdy and erect still, despite his years, who had administered the first oath in the simple and unromantic setting of a Vermont farmhouse nineteen months ago. Today the oath was administered by William Howard Taft, Chief Justice of the United States, clad in flowing judicial robes of black, who had himself stood in the same spot sixteen years ago and subscribed to the Presidential oath.

There also was the President's wife

"All the News That's Fit to Print."

# The New York Times.

THE WEATHER
Cloudy and warmer today, rain tonight; colder tomorrow.
Temperature yesterday—Max., 37; min., 24.
For weather report see Page 20.

VOL. LXXVII....No. 25,587. NEW YORK, MONDAY, FEBRUARY 13, 1928. TWO CENTS In Greater New York | THREE CENTS Within 200 Miles | FOUR CENTS Elsewhere in the U. S.

# HOOVER COMES OUT FOR THE PRESIDENCY ON A PLATFORM OF COOLIDGE POLICIES; ENTERS OHIO PRIMARY; BARS ANY BIG FUND

## CITY TO NEGOTIATE FOR ELEVATED ROAD IN FIGHT ON I. R. T.

### Seeks an Operating Alliance With Owners as Part of Plan to Seize Subways.

### STOCKHOLDERS ARE UNEASY

### Fear Contest Over Fares Will Result in Voiding Manhattan Line Lease.

### UNTERMYER LAUDS WALKER

### Asserts Mayor Is in Dead Earnest and With Proper Support by Public Will Get Relief.

Transit officials of the City Administration and the Transit Commission plan to enlist the aid of the owners of the Manhattan elevated lines in their fight to prevent the Interborough Rapid Transit Company, which operates the elevated under a lease, from collecting a seven-cent fare on both systems.

The plan to form an alliance with the elevated owners, as divulged yesterday, is part of the larger scheme, which involves seizure or recapture of the subway lines if the Interborough puts the higher fare into effect. The city, it was learned, hopes to effect an agreement with the Manhattan stockholders, whereby the elevated lines would be turned over to the city for operation with the subway system in order that the two systems might be continued as one in operation.

Information has reached the authorities that the principal owners of the Manhattan are greatly concerned over the Interborough's increased fare move, feeling that the probable effect of it would be the repudiation of the Manhattan lease, with the consequent return of the elevated lines to them for operation.

**Sees Violation of Contracts.**

Samuel Untermyer, the Transit Commission's special counsel in charge of the unification efforts and counsel for both city and the State in the forthcoming 7-cent fare litigation, declared yesterday in a guarded statement that the Interborough's contract with the city "has for years been flagrantly violated." While not admitting in so many words that the authorities planned to seize the Interborough lines under the default provisions of the contract, he agreed with city officials who favor that move that the actual putting of an increased fare into effect would be a violation of the contract which would entitle the city to take over the lines forthwith. He said he did not believe the Interborough would be foolhardy enough to put the increase into effect over the ruling of the Transit Commission.

The plans of the city and the Transit Commission, it developed yesterday, were now in definite shape. The program includes court action of a temporary nature to restrain the Interborough from raising the fare and practical steps looking to the elimination of the Interborough from the transit situation entirely.

The move to obtain an understanding with the Manhattan owners is part of the practical end of the program. In the event the city is enabled to take over the Interborough system on the ground of default the I. R. T. will be left with the elevated lines alone. At present these lines are not earning the 5 per cent. which the Interborough has to pay to the Manhattan owners under their lease of the property.

**Fear Voiding of Lease.**

It is understood that the Manhattan interests were fearful lest the Interborough's attempt to increase the rate of fare provided in the contract with the city would be construed as a breach of the contract. Should the Interborough be left with merely the elevated lines to operate, it was figured, the company would probably go into receivership and the courts would void the Manhattan lease.

The present owners of the Manhattan are not the original owners who operated the elevated lines long before the Interborough came into being with the construction of the first subway. The present owners have no facilities for operation and would be greatly embarrassed if forced to take the lines back.

The elevated system, however, is regarded by the city authorities as an important part of the rapid transit facilities of the city and cannot be abandoned without serious congestion in the subways resulting. To guard against the possibility of service on the elevated being halted, therefore, some of Mayor Walker's advisers favor an arrangement whereby the Manhattan interests would turn the elevated lines over to the city.

**To Start Negotiations Soon.**

It is understood that negotiations with this end in view are to be undertaken probably before the end of this week. The city officials, it was said last night, would urge that the elevated lines would have to be torn down within a few years anyway and that it would be to the interest of the Manhattan owners to cooperate with the city at this time, since they could then expect more favorable terms. It is planned eventually to substitute subways for the present elevated lines.

Although the Interborough's lease on the elevated lines runs for 999 years, it is inevitable, it was pointed out, that this lease would be voided

Continued on Page Eleven.

## 'Big Stick' of Kipling's Pen Is Defied by Rural Council

TICEHURST, England, Feb. 12 (AP).—Rudyard Kipling's pen looks more like a big stick than it does a sword to the Ticehurst Rural District Council.

In a dispute regarding flood damages to Kipling's Burwash property, the author recently wrote the council that, although he was "extremely adverse to litigation," he would place the matter in the hands of his solicitors unless the council soon made amends. After reading the letter to his colleagues, Chairman Spring-Rice declared:

"We can see the big stick which Kipling has waved at us, and I consider it most uncalled for."

The council then unanimously adopted a resolution denying all responsibility.

## CLUB DANCER TRIES TO DIE IN PARK LAKE

### Vainly Fights Off Young Man Who Breaks Ice to Swim to Her in the Darkness.

### CARRIED PICTURE OF LOPEZ

### Mlle. Roseray, a Night Club Performer, Refuses to Explain Her Act.

Mlle. Simone Roseray, Paris dancer starring at the Casa Lopez night club, Fiftieth Street and Broadway, was rescued against her will from drowning in the lake in the middle of Central Park early yesterday morning by Thomas Moore, 25 years old, a security company investigator, of 22 Post Avenue, who broke his way through the ice as he swam toward her.

A photograph of Vincent Lopez, orchestra leader and proprietor of the night club where she began a contract a week ago, was found among her belongings after she had been taken to the Lexington Hospital, a private institution in Lexington Avenue near Fifty-seventh Street. Detectives said words of endearment, in French, were written on the photograph.

Restored to consciousness after Dr. J. M. Blank of 15 Central Park West had worked over her for nearly three hours, the dancer would give only her name and occupation to detectives of the Arsenal Station, declining to tell why she had jumped into the lake or to reveal the names of friends or relatives, saying it would only "embarrass them."

**Knows of No Romance.**

Lopez spent yesterday at New Rochelle and his partner, Eugene Geiger, who occupies an apartment with him at 200 West Fifty-seventh Street, said late in the afternoon that he did not believe the orchestra leader knew of the affair.

"No, I don't know if there was any romance between the two," Geiger said, "but if there was, it was very secret, because there was nothing to show on the surface. Besides, I know Lopez was interested in another girl. Whether that had anything to do with the occurrence, I don't know."

Geiger said he had tried to see the dancer at the hospital to ascertain when she might be able to resume her appearances at the night club, but she had refused to see him. He added that she was suffering from shock and submersion. The hospital Superintendent declined to discuss Mlle. Roseray's condition.

The dancer's rescuer, who also was taken to the hospital suffering from chill, was discharged yesterday afternoon. Moore's family, talking over the telephone, said they had "heard something" about the rescue, but did not know the details, "as Tom hasn't come home yet."

Moore and a companion, John Reagan, of 141 West Ninety-fourth Street, were driving through Central Park toward Fifth Avenue at 4:30 A. M., when they heard screams from the direction of the lake. Without even slipping off his coat, Moore jumped from the car, ran to the edge of the lake and started out on the thin ice. He had gone only a few feet when he crashed through. Breaking the ice ahead of him with his hands, he threshed his way

Continued on Page Eight.

## LINDBERGH LEAVES HAVANA AT 2:26 A.M., FLYING TO ST. LOUIS

### Hops Off by Moonlight on 1,250-Mile Trip, Which Concludes His Tour.

### THRONG SEES HIM START

### And Cuban Band Plays a March for His Plane—Takes Sandwiches as Only Food.

### TOOK UP CUBAN PRESIDENT

### He Piloted Machado and Pan-American Conference Delegates in Nine Flights Yesterday.

By The Associated Press.

HAVANA, Monday, Feb. 13.—Colonel Charles A. Lindbergh hopped off at 2:26 o'clock this morning on his return trip to St. Louis.

Eager to see the "Lone Eagle" start on his flight of about 1,250 miles to his home port of St. Louis, spectators began arriving at Columbia Field at 1:15 o'clock.

His route is from Havana to Key West, Fla., the only hop over water. Then he will go along the Gulf of Mexico to a point directly south of St. Louis and then turn directly north.

The moon rose soon after 1 o'clock, and arrangements were being made for the flight, although the Spirit of St. Louis was still in the hangar.

Colonel Lindbergh arrived at the field at 1:50. He was accompanied by the United States Ambassador, Noble Brandon Judah.

The Spirit of St. Louis was taken out of the hangar immediately after Colonel Lindbergh's arrival.

The flier walked about the field looking for a suitable place from which to take off. He announced he would start as soon as possible.

As the Spirit of St. Louis appeared on the field, accompanied by twenty-five attendants, the Cuban band struck up a spirited march.

Soon after 2 o'clock, Lindbergh started the plane's motor.

"The motor sounds perfect," he announced.

Before starting, Colonel Lindbergh stowed several sandwiches in the plane.

He decided to taxi the plane the whole length of the field to the far end from the hangar. He would then be able to take off in the face of the wind and have the whole length of the field before him.

Lindbergh appeared rested and smiling. Mrs. Judah arrived at the field with the flier and the Ambassador.

As the flier taxied down the field an automobile preceded him to show the way over the bumpy ground.

**FLIER BUSY ON LAST DAY.**

**Takes Ninety Passengers Into Air in a Series of Flights.**

By RUSSELL OWEN.


Special Cable to THE NEW YORK TIMES.

HAVANA, Feb. 12.—Colonel Charles A. Lindbergh made another Presidential convert to aviation today when he took up President Machado of Cuba for his first airplane ride. The President was as pleased as a child, and when he came down seemed eager to go again.

While he was in the air in a big three-motor Fokker of the Pan-American Airways, which plies between Key West and Havana, he could not keep still and walked up and down the aisle talking to his wife and members of his Cabinet who were in the party and looking out of the windows.

President Machado was much delighted with the view of the National Palace from the air and the old Spanish forts, which form such a picturesque part of Cuban scenery. Once he stuck his hand out of a window in the plane and laughed like a boy when the wind slammed it back against the casing.

It was a busy day for the "flying Colonel," for he took up most

Continued on Page Three.

## Clear, Crisp Weather Draws Throngs to Seaside Resorts

Yesterday's clear, crisp weather sent city dwellers in thousands to near-by resorts. Coney Island, the Rockaways, Asbury Park and scores of other places along the seaboard were thronged. A crowd estimated at more than 100,000 at Coney Island caused the Police Department to detail about fifty additional traffic policemen for duty.

A continuous stream of automobiles passed over the Cross Bay Boulevard and Beach Channel Drive to the Rockaways throughout the day, and Asbury Park accommodated an unusually large number of visitors. Atlantic City reported the largest Lincoln Day crowd in its history.

The coldest hour of the day in this city was at 7 o'clock, when the temperature was 24 degrees. At 4 o'clock in the afternoon the mercury had risen to 37. According to the Weather Bureau forecast last night, today should be warmer, with rain probably this evening and tomorrow.

## FIND QUEEN'S TOMB AND RICH ART IN UR

### U. of P. Excavators Bare Gold Crowns and Rings, Vases and Other Sumerian Treasures.

### ARCHES OLDEST EVER FOUND

### Date to Fourth Millennium, B. C., Director Says—Attendants Lie With Queen.

Special to The New York Times.

PHILADELPHIA, Feb. 12.—From the tomb of a Sumerian Queen just discovered in Ur of the Chaldees by the joint expedition of the University of Pennsylvania and the British Museum have come contributions to archaeology and the history of architecture that may rival in importance the secrets given up by the tomb of King Tut-ankh-Amen in Egypt, a report received here from C. Leonard Woolley, director of the expedition, today indicated.

Besides the rich treasures surrounding the body of the Queen, Shub-ad, whose name appeared on a cylinder seal worn on her head with two crowns, the excavators brought to light what are declared to be the oldest arches ever discovered.

The tomb of the Queen adjoined that of a King, which was discovered recently and with which were found the bodies of his grooms, servitors, musicians and wives who had been slain to accompany the King into the next world.

Each of these tombs had a doorway, above which was a true arch of baked bricks. The chambers were vaulted with arches, of which a few rings still remained.

**Date Put at 5,000 Years Ago.**

Director Woolley said that the oldest previous arch known to archaeologists was that found over a drain at Nippur, a Babylonian city, dating back to the third millenium, B. C.

Excavation of the tombs in Ur reveals," the director said, "that corbel vaulting, the true arch and the dome all were familiar to the Sumerian builder and were carried out both in brick and stone in the fourth millenium, B. C."

Archaeologists in charge of the expedition have concluded, on the basis of the evidence they found, that the robbery of the King's tomb adjoining was done by the persons who buried the Queen, and done at the very time of her burial, probably 5,000 years ago.

Queen Shub-ad's tomb had evidently been left undisturbed by the vandals. The director described it as follows:

"The main interest here centered in the tomb itself. There were vessels of clay and copper, stone and silver, many of them broken and distorted, but others wonderfully preserved. At the other end, on a wooden bier, at the head and foot of which were crouched the bodies of attendants, lay the bones of the Queen, Shub-ad.

**Marvelous Headdress.**

"The Queen's headdress, worn originally over a great wig, was a marvelous sight as it was laboriously disengaged from stones and earth. Coil after coil of gold ribbon surrounded the hair. Above these and across the forehead ran a frontlet of lapis and carnelian beads, from which hung heavy rings of gold.

"Higher up was a wreath of large gold mulberry leaves hanging from another string of beads, and above this another wreath of leaves resembling willow leaves, with large gold flowers, whose petals were inlaid with lapis and white shell.

"Under the edge of the ribbon hung enormous gold earrings, and towering over the top of the head was a golden ornament like a Spanish comb, shaped like a hand with seven fingers, each of which ended in a gold flower.

"The Queen wore a tight-fitting necklace of lapis and gold and a cloak entirely covered with beadwork, vertical rows of beads in gold and lapis, carnelian and agate, with a border of beads set in horizontal groups of ten and fringed with dangling gold rings.

"The cloak was fastened on the right shoulder with three gold pins with lapis heads, and by the fastening were amulets—two goldfish and one of lapis—a lapis fringe of a re-

Continued on Page Four.

## SMITH TO OPPOSE AN EVASIVE PLANK ON PROHIBITION

### Friends Expect Him to Fight a Straddle if He Is to Be the Candidate.

### FOR CONSTRUCTIVE STAND

### He Would Expect the Party Declaration to Set Forth His Views, Supporters Say.

### HE NEVER URGED REPEAL

### But Has Advocated Right of States to Fix Non-Intoxicating Alcoholic Percentage.

By W. A. WARN.

Special to The New York Times.

ALBANY, Feb. 12.—No mild or evasive plank on prohibition for the Democratic national platform will have the approval of Governor Smith, in the event he should be the choice of the Houston convention for the Presidential nomination. No plank merely pledging the party to law enforcement, following the pattern of other Presidential years since the Eighteenth Amendment has been in force, will pass muster with him. That is what his friends are saying.

There has been no departure by the Governor from the policy of aloofness he has adopted for himself and consistently pursued with regard to the activities in which his friends throughout the country are engaging, to clinch what now appears to be his firm hold on the Democratic nomination.

Even though they believe now that it is nearly a foregone conclusion that he will be picked at Houston, the Governor consistently has declined to be drawn into any full discussion of national policies or the prospect of the nomination coming his way, and this in the face of much pressure brought to bear on him to toss his hat into the ring and give public expression to his views on questions that will figure prominently in the campaign this year.

**For a Constructive Platform.**

But in recent weeks, especially before the meeting of the Democratic National Committee and the Jackson Day Dinner in Washington last month, the Governor discussed with some of his friends and advisers in advance the contents of his letter, read at the dinner, which formed his first public expression upon matters having a bearing on the Presidential fight.

According to friends and advisers, the Governor strongly feels that in order to do justice to the opportunity that will come to it to win a victory this year, the party should provide a platform constructive from beginning to end; upon prohibition as well as upon all other questions of national import.

While there is no desire on the part of Governor Smith or his friends unduly to feature the prohibition question in the platform, the Governor is said to feel that if he should run it must be on a platform containing a prohibition plank that would leave no room for suspicion that he had sought to evade that issue, controversial though it be even within his own party. Consequently the Governor is credited with a determination to have the prohibition plank, in the event that he should be the standard bearer, set forth the views he has consistently expressed since prohibition in its present stage has been a topic of public discussion.

**His Record for Enforcement.**

The Governor, despite his approval of the repeal of the State Prohibition Enforcement law in 1923, has always strongly advocated rigid enforcement of the Volstead law, not only by Federal enforcement officials but by the peace officers of the State and of localities.

In connection with this it was recalled that after President Coolidge had summoned the Governors of the several Commonwealths to Washington for a discussion of ways and means for better prohibition enforcement throughout the country, Governor Smith was the only Chief Executive of a State to follow up the decisions reached at that gathering by calling together a council of public prosecutors and peace officers for the purpose of impressing upon

Continued on Page Two.

## Text of Secretary Hoover's Letter to Ohioans Announcing Candidacy for the Presidency

Special to The New York Times.

WASHINGTON, D. C., Feb. 12.—The text of Secretary Hoover's letter to his Ohio supporters is as follows:

Feb. 12, 1928.

Colonel Thad. H. Brown, Columbus Ohio.

My Dear Colonel Brown: I have received through you and others requests from very many Republicans of Ohio that I permit my name to be entered in the Presidential primaries of that State. I do so.

I shall be deeply honored by whatever support the people of Ohio may decide to give me at the Republican National Convention. I shall be glad to serve the American people through the Republican Party in any way that I can in finding constructive solution to the many problems which confront our country.

My conviction that I should not strive for the nomination and my obligations as Secretary of Commerce preclude me from making any personal campaign. I must rely wholly upon my friends in Ohio to conduct it and to conduct it in a fair manner and with steadfast regard for Republican success in the State and the nation. It is my special desire that expenditure of money shall be strictly limited and rigidly accounted for.

If the greatest trust which can be given by our people should come to me, I should consider it my duty to carry forward the principles of the Republican Party and the great objectives of President Coolidge's policies—all of which have brought to our country such a high degree of happiness, progress and security.

Yours faithfuly,

(Signed) HERBERT HOOVER.

## CRITICIZED OFFICIAL RAIDS A PUBLISHER

### But Westchester Prosecutor Denies It Is in Retaliation Against Brady Press.

### TRIP TO EUROPE ATTACKED

### Rowland Planned to Go Abroad Again for Prisoner—Won't Tell Why He Seized Books.

Books and accounts of Terence A. Brady of Yonkers, whose newspapers have been attacking District Attorney Arthur Rowland of Westchester County for planning a second trip to Europe to bring home a criminal, were seized in Mount Vernon last Thursday at the instance of District Attorney Rowland, it was learned yesterday.

Mr. Rowland said yesterday that the books and accounts had been seized because of a complaint made to his office and that the attacks on him had no bearing on the case.

"I am not at liberty to divulge the nature of the complaint at present," Mr. Rowland said. "I have no malice or enmity against Mr. Brady. The attacks on me have not annoyed me in any way and have nothing to do with the matter. It is unfortunate that the complaint came at such a time as to suggest that it was a retaliatory act on my part."

The attack by the Brady newspapers, which are The Yonkers Sunday Record, The Yonkers Star and The Mount Vernon Star, began on the announcement of Mr. Rowland that he planned to go to Europe personally to bring home a prisoner, John Wenzel of Yonkers, who is under arrest in England on a charge of stealing bonds from his wife.

The Brady newspapers criticized the District Attorney on the ground that his duties required his presence in the county; that he had no authority outside of Westchester, and that the duty of bringing home criminals from foreign parts should be performed by ordinary peace officers. Mr. Rowland went abroad a year ago on a similar mission, which, according to the Brady newspapers, involved a waste of the money of Westchester County taxpayers. In their campaign against him the Brady newspapers referred to the official as "Westchester County's seagoing District Attorney."

Terence A. Brady said he did not know the cause of the seizure of his

Continued on Page Ten.

## NAVY TUG HITS ROCK; 5 OF CREW MISSING

### The Mohave Smashes Her Hull on a Ledge Outside of Boston Harbor.

### RESCUE SHIPS SPEED TO HER

### Fourteen Men Taken Off, Six Others Reach Shore in Boat.

Special to The New York Times.

BOSTON, Mass., Feb. 12.—Five members of the crew of the navy tug Mohave are missing as the result of the craft striking on Harding's Ledge off Point Allerton late this evening while she was returning to Boston from Provincetown. Six others reached shore in a dingy and the remaining fourteen were rescued by naval vessels.

A big hole was smashed in the tug's bow by the collision in the darkness and water began to pour in. The radio operator at once sent out S O S signals and Admiral Andrews, commander of the naval district, started all available craft to the scene.

Thanks to this swift action, Patrol Boat 242 was able to reach the Mohave and take off the survivors. Because of the near-by rocks no attempt was made to salvage the Mohave, and with the waves breaking over her bow it was feared that she would probably become a total loss.

According to survivors, the Mohave struck with a tremendous crash just before 9 o'clock. She was carried high on the rocks and her hull was ripped for several feet.

Most of the crew were in their bunks when she struck, the impact hurling them on the deck. Wearing meager attire, the men rushed out and were drenched by the high waves breaking over the tug.

Two men were found to have disappeared overboard. After a few minutes the radio apparatus went dead and the commander of the tug, Boatswain Powers, sent three sailors off in a punt to carry news ashore of the disaster. Soon after they put off they shouted for help, and six more of the crew lowered a dingy and started on a vain hunt for them.

The six men in the dingy came ashore later on Nantasket Beach, but those in the punt have not been seen since. Late tonight the rescue force was still hunting for them in the near-by waters.

When the first S O S messages from the Mohave were picked up, naval officers here realized that they were confronted with an unusual accident and with the fate of the lost S-4 still fresh in their minds made all haste to render aid.

Admiral Andrews ordered the navy tug No. 71 to proceed at once to Point Allerton while the Coast Guard vessels 78, 244 and the Dix departed on the same mission.

Later the navy destroyer Maury left the Navy Yard for the scene.

Other vessels which raced to the assistance of the Mohave were the Bushnell, mother ship of the S-4, and the naval tug Sagamore, which steamed out from Provincetown.

The names of the six men who reached Nantasket on the dinghy are Charles Thompson, Clifford Alexander, Francis Sliney, Edgar Townsend, Richard Connelley and James Colbert.

Meanwhile the Coast Guard crew at Point Allerton had been notified by telephone of the wreck. They launched a surfboat and were forced to go by way of the Gut to reach the tug.

## WRITES TO OHIO BACKERS

### 'Shall Be Glad to Serve the American People,' Secretary Says.

### INSISTS ON A FAIR FIGHT

### Believes He Should Not Strive for Nomination and Will Make No Personal Campaign.

### HE'S WELCOME, SAYS WILLIS

### Senator Ready for Knockdown Battle—Hoover Soon to Enter Other State Contests.

Special to The New York Times.

WASHINGTON, Feb. 12.—Herbert Hoover, Secretary of Commerce, tossed his hat into the ring today when, in a letter to Thad Brown, leader of his Ohio supporters, in which he consented to have his name entered in the Republican Presidential primaries in that State, he announced that if nominated and elected he would carry forward the principles of the Republican Party and "the great objectives of President Coolidge's policies."

Mr. Hoover writes that his conviction that he should not strive for the nomination and his obligations as Secretary of Commerce preclude him from making any personal campaign, and he must rely wholly upon his friends in Ohio to conduct it. He says he wants the campaign conducted "in a fair manner," and emphasizes his desire that "expenditure of money shall be strictly limited and rigidly accounted for."

The decision by Mr. Hoover to get out in the open and fight was generally accepted in political circles here as the most important development in the pre-convention campaign since President Coolidge made his "I-do-not-choose" statement at Rapid City in August. It is expected that the Secretary's message to Mr. Brown will be accepted by his backers in all parts of the country as a signal to go into action in his behalf.

**"Perfectly Welcome," Says Willis.**

Senator Frank B. Willis, who will appear as a favorite-son candidate in Ohio and whose attitude in refusing to permit Hoover to appear as a second-choice candidate is held to be in part responsible for the bitter party contest which is now certain in that State, had just returned from delivering a political address in Utica, N. Y., when the Hoover message was made public.

"Oh, very well," said Mr. Willis. "He's perfectly welcome to come in. I have been known to the people of Ohio for about thirty years. I know them and they know me. He will find out at the close of the primary contest whether he has been correctly advised by those assuming to be his friends."

Despite Mr. Hoover's expressed hope that the fight in Ohio will be carried on with "steadfast regard for Republican success in the State and in the nation," there is every indication that the campaign leading up to the primary election on April 24 will be marked by such warfare as the party has not known since 1912. Senator Willis in a recent statement following Representative Burton's first suggestion that Mr. Hoover enter the Ohio contest said that it would be no kid glove affair and, in effect, that he intended to call a spade a spade.

**Complete Hoover Ticket in Ohio.**

Hoover candidates for delegates and alternates will be entered in each of the twenty-two Congressional districts of Ohio and for the seven delegates-at-large. Each district elects two delegates, thus giving a total of fifty-one, and the Hoover campaigners are going to battle for them all.

There is held in Ohio also a State-wide preference vote, which, however, is not legally binding on any of the delegates after the first ballot in the convention. While a final decision has not been made, it was indicated tonight that the Secretary, now that he was in the battle, would try to win this preference vote as well.

In 1920, when Leonard Wood contested the Ohio delegates with Warren G. Harding, the General won nine of them but was defeated by about 15,000 ballots in the preference vote. The backers of Hoover feel confident that they will win the preference vote and also get at least twenty of the district delegates and the seven delegates-at-large. To the Hoover forces thus are virtually conceded twelve delegates, including six from the three Cleveland districts, four from the two Cincinnati districts and two from Toledo.

**Burton May Head Hoover List.**

It is expected here that Representative Burton will head the list of Hoover candidates for delegates-at-large. The name of William Cooper Procter of Cincinnati, who was in command of the Leonard Wood campaign in 1920, has been suggested as another candidate for delegate-at-

## Olympic Crowd Rebels When Swiss Ski Race Utterly Exhausts Youths on 20-Mile Trail

ST. MORITZ, Switzerland, Feb. 12 (AP).—Popular feeling was aroused to a high pitch at the utter state of exhaustion of the young soldiers finishing the twenty-mile military patrol ski race today and may cause an elimination of the event from future Winter Olympic sports.

France, it is understood, is preparing to present a motion to eliminate the race at the next meeting of the International Olympic Committee.

The rules provide that contestants, carrying a rifle, rations and other field equipment, must be soldiers in active service. Many of the nations with military service requirements of a year or eighteen months had mere youths of 20 and 21 years in the event.

Gendre, a French youngster who collapsed three miles from the finish and was carried on the shoulders of his comrades the rest of the way, is reported to be delirious and to have a high fever tonight. He is a slender youth of 20. The Finns recovered quickly from the effects of the long hike and were up and around after a few hours of rest.

Norway won the event, with Finland second and Switzerland third. Two of the four members of the Finnish team collapsed after crossing the finish line and had to be carried tot a hotel, where hot grog and other stimulants were administered.

Some of the youthful soldiers dropped exhausted in the mountain passes and others staggered over the finish line to fall headlong in the snow.

Norway's winning time over the twenty-mile course, in which the difference of altitudes between the start and finish at some points was 3,000 feet, was 3 hours 50 minutes 47 seconds. The hardy men from the Northland, fresh and erect, finished, singing the national anthem of Norway at the top of their lungs, five minutes ahead of the Finns.

## Klan to Establish National Headquarters Near Large Catholic Church in Washington

Special to The New York Times.

WASHINGTON, Feb. 12.—The Ku Klux Klan is to establish a new national headquarters in this city at 1,723 Rhode Island Avenue, Northwest, which is separated by only one residence from St. Matthew's Church, one of the most imposing Roman Catholic edifices in the capital. The property is but two squares from Dupont Circle, around which are grouped many of Washington's fashionable residences, including the mansion which President Coolidge occupied during the recent renovation of the White House roof and attic.

Arrangements by the Ku Klux Klan for leasing the property were made a few days ago with Miss Laura Harlan, a real estate agent here. She said today, however, that she had no detailed information as to the plans of those with whom the lease was negotiated.

The lease, which will expire in the Fall unless renewed, she added, has not yet been returned to her. It was sent to Atlanta following the call of the persons wanting the property, who saw her sign as the real estate agent.

The residence belongs to the estate of former Representative Richard Wayne Parker of New Jersey, and has been vacant since his death. It is a substantial old house, semi-detached, and was built some fifty years ago. Its construction is of brick, there are four floors and about twelve rooms.

None of the klan's officials could be reached here for details of plans for moving the national headquarters into the building.

"All the News That's Fit to Print."

# The New York Times.

THE WEATHER
Fair today and tomorrow; fresh west and northwest winds.
Temperature yesterday—Max. 82, min. 64.
For weather report see Page 10.

Copyright, 1928, by The New York Times Company.

VOL. LXXVII....No. 25,710. NEW YORK, FRIDAY, JUNE 15, 1928. TWO CENTS In Greater New York | THREE CENTS Within 200 miles | FOUR CENTS Elsewhere in the U. S.

# HOOVER NAMED ON FIRST BALLOT BY 837; LOWDEN SECOND WITH 74; CURTIS GETS 64; FARMERS SQUELCHED ON FLOOR, 807 TO 277

## 3 ITALIA SCOUTS REPORTED FOUND BY SLED SEARCHERS

### Copenhagen Hears Dr. Malmgren and Companions Reached Northeast Land.

### NOBILE PARTY OPTIMISTIC

### Are Now Near Brock or Foyne Island and Think They Are Safe.

### ICE BALKS RESCUE PLANES

### Wilkins Thinks Nobile's Position Not Necessarily Dangerous—Pictures Castaways' Sufferings.

Special Cable to THE NEW YORK TIMES.

COPENHAGEN, Friday, June 15.—The Politiken this morning publishes a dispatch from its Kings Bay correspondent mentioning rumors there that searchers with dog sledges sent from the sealer Hobby have found the Swedish meteorologist, Dr. Malmgren, and his two companions of the Italia, who succeeded in reaching the cosat of Northeast Land.

These rumors had not been confirmed.

By The Associated Press.

KINGS BAY, Spitsbergen, Friday, June 15.—In need of equipment to enable them to withstand the rigors of the arctic until rescued, General Umberto Nobile and five other survivors of the dirigible Italia were near land today but unable to reach it.

The General's injuries and the broken leg of Natale Ceccioni prevented them from leaving the ice floe on which they have been drifting since May 25.

General Nobile was optimistic, however. In a message to the base ship Citta di Milano he said he believed his party was in a position of safety. They were near Rock Island or Foyne Island and only a short distance from the mainland. They have drifted to this position since Tuesday night.

The glare of the sun on the ice was believed to have affected their eyesight and to have softened the snow as the commander asked for snow spectacles and rubber boots. Medicine was also requested for frost bitten hands and feet.

**Polar Bears Are Friendly.**

Polar bears prowled near the Nobile party. They have not molested the castaways but firearms were requested. The guns would also offer an opportunity to replenish a dwindling larder, consisting principally of pemmican and chocolate, with bear meat.

In the hope that the three missing men, who started afoot for land from the Nobile party, might be found, dog teams were sent out from the sealing ship Hobby to patrol the route that the men were to take. The rescue parties were also to establish depots at Cape Platen, North Cape, Beverly Sound and Dove Bay.

**Fate of Seven Uncertain.**

The trio, Dr. Finn Malmgren and Captains A. Mariano and Filippo Zappi, took no skiis with them when they started for North Cape, since the ice hummocks would have prevented their use.

The fate of seven men carried off in the balloon part of the Italia continued to be uncertain. They were well supplied with food unless the balloon was caught up by the wind and carried off after the men had reached the ice and before they had time to unload their supplies.

Captain Riiser-Larsen and Lieutenant Luetzow Holm, airmen aboard the Hobby, have been prevented from making any flights to the rescue because of the extent of the pack ice.

**France Offers Plane to Amundsen.**

Special Cable to THE NEW YORK TIMES.

PARIS, June 14.—The French Government tonight announced its decision to place at the disposal of Captain Roald Amundsen the big bimotor seaplane in which Captain Guilbaud has been preparing for a transatlantic flight.

Work was immediately started by an emergency corps of mechanics to effect alterations in the transatlantic plane to adapt it to the uses of a party seeking to aid General Nobile and his companions. It was stated that the plane would be in readiness by Saturday when Guilbaud would start at once from Caudebec-sur-Seine for Bergen.

Guilbaud is one of the most experienced French Navy pilots. With Rapin he made a noteworthy flight to Africa and this year, in the plane he will fly north, he accomplished

Continued on Page Thirteen.



### Convention's Only Ballot for President Which Made Hoover the Nominee

| Total Vote | STATE | Coolidge | Hoover | Lowden | Watson | Curtis | Goff | Norris |
|---|---|---|---|---|---|---|---|---|
| 15 | Alabama | .. | 15 | .. | .. | .. | .. | .. |
| 9 | Arizona | .. | 9 | .. | .. | .. | .. | .. |
| 11 | Arkansas | .. | 11 | .. | .. | .. | .. | .. |
| 29 | California | .. | 29 | .. | .. | .. | .. | .. |
| 15 | Colorado | .. | 15 | .. | .. | .. | .. | .. |
| 17 | Connecticut | .. | 17 | .. | .. | .. | .. | .. |
| 9 | Delaware | .. | 9 | .. | .. | .. | .. | .. |
| 10 | Florida | .. | 9 | .. | .. | 1 | .. | .. |
| 16 | Georgia | .. | 15 | .. | .. | 1 | .. | .. |
| 11 | Idaho | .. | 11 | .. | .. | .. | .. | .. |
| 61 | Illinois | 13 | 24 | 16 | 4 | .. | .. | .. |
| 33 | Indiana | .. | .. | .. | 33 | .. | .. | .. |
| 29 | Iowa | .. | 7 | 22 | .. | .. | .. | .. |
| 23 | Kansas | .. | .. | .. | .. | 23 | .. | .. |
| 29 | Kentucky | .. | 29 | .. | .. | .. | .. | .. |
| 12 | Louisiana | .. | 11 | .. | .. | 1 | .. | .. |
| 15 | Maine | .. | 15 | .. | .. | .. | .. | .. |
| 19 | Maryland | .. | 19 | .. | .. | .. | .. | .. |
| 39 | Mass. | .. | 39 | .. | .. | .. | .. | .. |
| 33 | Michigan | .. | 33 | .. | .. | .. | .. | .. |
| 27 | Minnesota | .. | 11 | 15 | .. | 1 | .. | .. |
| 12 | Mississippi | .. | 12 | .. | .. | .. | .. | .. |
| 39 | Missouri | .. | 28 | 1 | 3 | 4 | .. | .. |
| 11 | Montana | .. | 10 | .. | 1 | .. | .. | .. |
| 19 | Nebraska | .. | 11 | .. | .. | .. | .. | 8 |
| 9 | Nevada | .. | 9 | .. | .. | .. | .. | .. |
| 11 | New Hamp. | .. | 11 | .. | .. | .. | .. | .. |
| 31 | New Jersey | .. | 31 | .. | .. | .. | .. | .. |
| 9 | New Mexico | .. | 7 | .. | .. | 2 | .. | .. |
| 90 | New York | .. | 90 | .. | .. | .. | .. | .. |
| 20 | North Caro. | .. | 17 | 3 | .. | .. | .. | .. |
| 13 | N. Dakota | .. | 4 | 8 | .. | .. | .. | 1 |
| 51 | Ohio | 4 | 36 | .. | .. | 10 | .. | .. |
| 20 | Oklahoma | .. | .. | .. | .. | 20 | .. | .. |
| 13 | Oregon | .. | 13 | .. | .. | .. | .. | .. |
| 79 | Penn. | .. | 79 | .. | .. | .. | .. | .. |
| 13 | Rhode Island | .. | 12 | .. | .. | 1 | .. | .. |
| 11 | S. Carolina | .. | 11 | .. | .. | .. | .. | .. |
| 13 | S. Dakota | .. | 2 | 9 | 2 | .. | .. | .. |
| 19 | Tennessee | .. | 19 | .. | .. | .. | .. | .. |
| 26 | Texas | .. | 26 | .. | .. | .. | .. | .. |
| 11 | Utah | .. | 9 | .. | 2 | .. | .. | .. |
| 11 | Vermont | .. | 11 | .. | .. | .. | .. | .. |
| 15 | Virginia | .. | 15 | .. | .. | .. | .. | .. |
| 17 | Washington | .. | 17 | .. | .. | .. | .. | .. |
| 19 | W. Virginia | .. | 1 | .. | .. | .. | 18 | .. |
| 26 | Wisconsin | .. | 9 | .. | .. | .. | .. | 15 |
| 9 | Wyoming | .. | 9 | .. | .. | .. | .. | .. |
| 2 | Alaska | .. | 2 | .. | .. | .. | .. | .. |
| 2 | Dist. of Col. | .. | 2 | .. | .. | .. | .. | .. |
| 2 | Hawaii | .. | 2 | .. | .. | .. | .. | .. |
| 2 | Philippines | .. | 2 | .. | .. | .. | .. | .. |
| 2 | Porto Rico | .. | 2 | .. | .. | .. | .. | .. |
| 1,089 | Totals | 17 | 837 | 74 | 45 | 64 | 18 | 24 |

TOTAL VOTES CAST, 1,084 NECESSARY TO A CHOICE, 543

SCATTERING VOTES—5. DAWES—Illinois, 1; Ohio, 1; Missouri, 2. Total, 4. HUGHES—Missouri, 1. NOT VOTING—Illinois, 3; Wisconsin, 2. Total, 5.

## NEW PRAYER BOOK IS AGAIN REJECTED

### House of Commons Finally Disposes of Revised Version by Vote of 266 to 220.

Wireless to THE NEW YORK TIMES.

LONDON, June 14.—The House of Commons rejected the 1928 Prayer Book measure shortly before midnight tonight by 266 votes to 220, or a majority of 46, after two days of earnest debate. Once again, as when practically the same revision of the Prayer Book was rejected last Winter, the representatives of Nonconformist England intervened when the majority of Anglican churchmen wished to alter the formula of the State Church in a direction which the Free Churches believed led toward Roman Catholicism. The majority against revision was 13 greater than the opponents of the measure obtained last December. A strong campaign to induce non-Anglicans to abstain from voting proved a failure.

**Semi-Hysteria Lacking This Time.**

The final verdict of the House of Commons against the result of twenty years of effort within the Church of England to frame a workable compromise in the ritual between High and Low churchmen was not accompanied by the semi-hysteria which marked the amazing upset of the prayer book in the first debate. Debate itself was not so impassioned. But the atmosphere within the cathedral-like Hall of the Commons and the fervent "hear, hears" which hailed speeches insisting upon "preserving the fruits of the Reformation" showed that the dominant spirit of the adverse majority was the same.

It was a striking blow for Protestantism, which, it was held, was endangered in the national church by the clerical hierarchy. The crux of the debate, as on the last occasion, was the question of reservation of the Sacrament, which Sir William Joynson-Hicks declared led straight to adoration of the real Presence.

Lord Hugh Cecil pointed vainly to the existence of the reservation for 800 years in the primitive Christian church before the appearance of adoration in its services as evidence that the practice Low churchmen

Continued on Page Eleven.

## COOLIDGE NEARING HIS SUMMER HOME

### President's Only Appearance to Crowds Gathering at Stops Is at Chicago.

Special to The New York Times.

ON BOARD PRESIDENTIAL SPECIAL TRAIN, June 14.—Under blue skies the special train carrying President Coolidge to his Summer vacation raced through Pennsylvania, Ohio, Indiana and Illinois today, and tonight was speeding across Wisconsin, the State where Mr. Coolidge will spend his holiday. Precisely one year ago to a day the President traveled the same route to Chicago on his way to the Black Hills.

So far as could be learned the President was apparently oblivious to the events at the Kansas City convention. His private car was equipped with a high-powered radio receiving set, but Mr. Coolidge did not avail himself of it, at least before Chicago was reached this afternoon.

Whether Mr. Coolidge was in touch with the political situation or not, no word came from him regarding it. Anticipations were that he would not express himself before arriving at the Pierce camp at Brule tomorrow.

Mrs. Coolidge, whose sudden indisposition forced postponement of the journey Monday evening, was said to have spent an excellent night and to be in very cheerful and optimistic spirits. While Colonel James F. Coupal, the White House physician, anticipated no untoward circumstances, he ordered his patient to conserve her strength by lying down almost throughout the day.

**Crowds Gather at Stops.**

Arising for an early breakfast, the President received some telegrams while eating this meal. But if they contained any political news, he did not reveal it, merely looking over the messages and thrusting them into one of his pockets.

Whenever the special stopped at a station for water, supplies, or to change locomotives, crowds gathered around the private car, but the President did not show himself to the eager spectators.

In the afternoon at Garrett, Ohio,

Continued on Page Sixteen.

## FEE PROPOSAL DEFEATED

### Convention Accepts the Majority Report After Stormy Debate.

### AGRARIAN BLOC INSISTENT

### Demands Seat at the Tariff Banquet Instead of 'Lazarus's Crumbs.'

### WET PLANK ALSO REJECTED

### Dr. Butler Speaks for His Plan, but Delegates Make Short Work of It.

*Full text of the platform adopted by the Republican Convention yesterday will be found on Page 8.*

Special to The New York Times.

KANSAS CITY, June 14.—Prospects of fights on the floor over the farm relief and prohibition platform planks brought out a fairly good crowd at the beginning of the morning session of the third day of the Republican National Convention.

Senator George H. Moses, the Permanent Chairman, lost no time in starting the session. At three minutes before 10 o'clock Senator Moses asked all delegates to take their seats. He repeated the request several times, with little success at first.

The weather was much warmer than during the first two days of the convention, and many of the delegates appeared in midsummer attire. Senator Moses, who wore a business suit yesterday, was today attired in blue serge coat and white flannel trousers.

With the convention called to reconvene at the comparatively early hour of 10 o'clock, the delegates were slow in arriving. Hardly one-fourth of the New York delegation were in their seats at that time.

Three minutes after 10 o'clock Senator Moses called the convention to order. Less than one-fourth of the seats in the galleries were occupied at the time.

Prayer was offered by Rabbi Herman M. Cohen of Kansas City.

Senator Moses reminded the convention that this was Flag Day.

"We claim no monopoly of this flag," he said, pointing to a flag in a standard just behind him, "but we doy say that the Republican Party made this flag the symbol of freedom."

Led by the band, the audience joined in singing the national anthem. The band followed with "The Stars and Stripes."

**Mellon Arrives Unnoticed.**

Just before the singing of the anthem Andrew W. Mellon, Secretary of the Treasury, one of the chief figures of the convention, appeared in the rear of the hall, paused a moment and then walked to his seat with the Pennsylvania delegation directly in front of the speakers' platform.

The lack of spirit in this convention was shown by the fact that he took his seat entirely unnoticed, either by the delegates or by the spectators. Four years ago at the Cleveland convention Secretary Mellon was applauded at every appearance.

The convention got to its real business when Chairman Moses announced that the next order was the report of the Committee on Resolutions. The failure of the members to agree on a farm relief plank caused abandonment of the evening session last night.

Senator Moses stated the rules which would prevail in debate on the proposed platform.

"The five-minute rule will be general in this convention except for the placing of candidates in nomination," he said. "The Chair, however, entertains motions to extend to any speaker in the debate on the platform ten minutes, but no more. The Chair recognizes the delegate from Utah, Senator Reed Smoot, Chairman of the Committee on Resolutions."

Senator Smoot began to read the majority report of the committee. His voice at first was weak and there were shouts of "Louder!" from all over the hall.

There was a steady stream of delegates and spectators arriving as Senator Smoot began to read the report, and Chairman Moses had to rap for order several times and request the delegates to keep their seats. The Chairman shifted the reading stand to bring Senator Smoot directly in front of the microphones.

There were brief ripples of applause as Senator Smoot read the earlier part of the proposed plat-

Continued on Page Four.

HERBERT CLARK HOOVER.

Copyright Harris & Ewing.

Nominated at Kansas City Last Night as the Republican Candidate for President of the United States.

## QUICK VICTORY FOR HOOVER

### His Nomination Follows a Night of Long and Fervid Oratory.

### LOWDEN WITHDRAWS NAME

### Acts at Last Minute as Protest Over Farm Declaration He Regards as Inadequate.

### BUT HE LEADS THE RIVALS

### Coolidge Gets 17 Votes, Hughes 1, Dawes 4, Watson 45 and Norris 24.

By RICHARD V. OULAHAN.

Special to The New York Times.

KANSAS CITY, June 14.—Herbert Hoover of California was nominated for President of the United States by the Republican National Convention at 11:20 o'clock tonight (1:20 o'clock Friday morning, New York Daylight Saving Time).

The nomination came to Mr. Hoover on the first ballot. He received 827 votes.

The other 200-odd represented in the convention went to the various contenders for the nomination and to some whose names had not been presented when nominating speeches were made at a session that began at 7 o'clock this evening and ended just after Mr. Hoover's victory was announced officially.

The vote in detail was as follows:

| | |
|---|---|
| Hoover | 837 |
| Lowden | 74 |
| Curtis | 64 |
| Watson | 45 |
| Norris | 24 |
| Goff | 18 |
| Coolidge | 17 |
| Dawes | 4 |
| Hughes | 1 |
| Not voting | 5 |
| Total | 1,089 |

The convention adjourned until noon tomorrow, when it will devote itself to its concluding duty of choosing a candidate for Vice President.

**Seeks Vice Presidency Solution.**

When the convention adjourned, various groups of leading Republicans went into conference in the hope of being able to adjust the conflicting and embarrassing Vice Presidential situation before the convention convened for its final session.

Late tonight the chief conference was in progress in the headquarters of Secretary Mellon in the Hotel Muehlbach. Prior to the time the conferees met the understanding prevailed that the principal contest over Vice Presidential honors had narrowed down to a choice between Senator Moses of New Hampshire and Senator Deneen of Illinois, with Deneen reluctant to have his name presented to the convention, and Moses seemingly having a shade the better of it.

A new name was brought into the situation in that of former Governor Channing Cox of Massachusetts, who was proposed on the ground that his candidacy on the Hoover ticket may save his State from going Democratic in the Presidential elections. The Pennsylvania delegation strongly urged that he be selected for second place on the national ticket.

**Convention Quiet at Climax.**

That Hoover would be chosen to lead the party in this year's Presidential campaign had been certain for days. The honor came to him at a time when the convention, tired out after two long sessions and fatigued by the cheering that marked tonight's proceedings, was not in a mood for a demonstration.

There was no outburst of enthusiasm such as might have been expected when victory perched itself at last on the Hoover banner. A cheer or two went up and then the convention was quiet while delegates from three States that had opposed Hoover's candidacy—Kansas, Oklahoma and West Virginia—moved that the nomination be made unanimous.

Senator Moses, the presiding officer, called for a viva voce expression. There was a great chorus of "aye." When he called for the nays, delegates from Wisconsin shouted a loud "no." But Moses declared that the motion to make the nomination unanimous had been carried and he read to the convention a telegram which he said had already been sent to Secretary Hoover notifying him of his nomination and congratulating him in the convention's name.

**Text of the Telegram.**

The text of the telegram as he read it to the convention was:

The Honorable Herbert Hoover,
2,300 S Street, Washington D. C.:

The Republican National Convention by a sweeping majority, which has since been made unani-

## ACTIVE HUNT STARTS FOR VICE PRESIDENT

### Ex-Gov. Cox of Massachusetts Now Suggested—Deneen and Moses Also Discussed.

Special to The New York Times.

KANSAS CITY, Friday, June 15.—Leaders from many camps were busy early this morning in an endeavor to solve the Republican Convention problem of a candidate for the Vice Presidency. Out of all this activity, results were expected in time for action when the convention is called to order this noon.

At 1 o'clock this morning (3 A. M. New York Daylight Saving Time), Secretary Mellon, representing Pennsylvania; former Senator James W. Wadsworth, representing New York; General W. B. Atterbury of Pennsylvania, and Mrs. Ruth Hannah McCormick, representing Illinois, were in conference over the Vice Presidential situation.

While the names of Senator Deneen of Illinois and Senator Moses of New Hampshire are foremost in the consideration being given to the Vice Presidential question, the name of former Governor Channing Cox of Massachusetts was entered in the list of those regarded as available for second place on the Hoover ticket.

Mr. Cox's qualifications are being strongly urged by the Pennsylvania delegation on the ground that if he were Hoover's running mate the chance of Governor Smith carrying Massachusetts as the Democratic candidate for President would be materially reduced.

**Cox Known as a Campaigner.**

Mr. Cox has the reputation of being a great campaigner, and this is a qualification ardently desired by Republican leaders for the Vice Presidential nominee, as it is felt that there should be somebody on the Republican national ticket to combat Governor Smith's remarkable stump speaking ability.

At 1:15 o'clock this morning Secretary Work and Ogden L. Mills, as spokesmen for the Hoover headquarters, entered the conference in Secretary Mellon's rooms at which the New York, Connecticut, Pennsylvania and other States were represented. Apparently the group was waiting for some word from Secretary Hoover and were prepared to agree upon a candidate for Vice President acceptable to him.

Secretary Work announced that he

Continued on Page Six.

### Hoover's Iowa Home Town Prepares to Celebrate

WEST BRANCH, Iowa, June 14 (AP).—Herbert Hoover's old home town was in a state of suspense today as its residents grouped around radio receivers waiting for word of his nomination at Kansas City. Pride was felt by all the residents in the man who left here as an orphan when 10 years old.

Tomorrow night this little Quaker village will indulge in such festivities as a parade, noisemakers and fireworks. A speaker has been engaged. He is A. F. Dawson of Davenport, a banker, former Representative in Congress and supporter of Secretary Hoover.

## CONVENTION OVATION FOR THE CANDIDATE

### Two Demonstrations Sweep the Hall as Secretary's Name Is Presented.

Special to The New York Times.

KANSAS CITY, June 14.—With the nomination of Herbert Hoover a foregone conclusion, the tense air of expectancy that usually pervades a convention on the verge of naming its candidates naturally was missing as the delegates and visitors flocked into the convention hall for the night session at which the party standard-bearer for the coming national campaign was to be selected.

The crowd was slow in assembling, too. The hour fixed for the evening session at which the real convention history was to be made was 7 o'clock. When the band in the gallery half an hour earlier began to tune up its instruments preparatory to bursting forth in music the convention hall was virtually empty.

From that time on, however, there was an unbroken flow of humanity through the aisles. A very large proportion of the crowd that flocked into the galleries and other spaces set aside for visitors were Kansas City people who had been waiting for the nominating stage of the convention to "take in" what to them is the biggest show the town has seen since 1900 when William J. Bryan received the Democratic nomination for President in this very hall.

**Prepare Hoover Demonstration.**

Long before the hall began to fill, workers for Hoover were on hand distributing American flags to the

Continued on Page Three.

## HOOVER VERY HAPPY, HAS 'NO COMMENT'

### Hears Vote Over Radio at Home in Capital—Will Meet Party Chiefs There Next Week.

Special to The New York Times.

WASHINGTON, Friday, June 15.—"I have no comment to make tonight," was the first utterance of Herbert Hoover to newspaper men at his residence immediately after the radio had flashed the news that the Secretary of Commerce had been chosen as the Republican Presidential nominee at the party convention at Kansas City

Mr. Hoover added that he might make an extended statement tomorrow, but George Akerson, his private secretary, shook his head in dissent.

Mr. Hoover looked supremely happy as he greeted members of the press, but before the brief interview was over his countenance assumed a grim and serious appearance, as if he had been suddenly sobered by the realization of a great responsibility.

After Mr. Hoover had received the congratulations of his guests, there was a brief exchange of pleasantries, and the Hoover neighbors and friends who had gathered at the house with the Secretary and his wife departed. A few minutes after midnight, Eastern Standard Time, there were no signs of life in the Hoover home.

**Party Gathered for Occasion.**

Mr. and Mrs. Hoover spent the evening in the drawing room of their S Street home in a company especially gathered for the occasion. The news coming by radio was followed with keen interest by all present. In the adjoining dining room the newspaper men followed the radio reports.

The invited guests included Mrs. William E. Borah, Associate Justice Harlan F. Stone of the Supreme Court and Mrs. Stone, John T. White of Germantown, Pa.; Edgar Rickard of New York City, William J. Donovan, Assistant Attorney General; Adolph C. Miller of the Federal Reserve Board and Mrs Miller, Ernest I. Lewis of the Interstate Commerce Commission and Mrs. Lewis, Mrs. Mark Sullivan, George Barr Baker, Herbert Hoover Jr. and his wife, Dr. and Mrs. Vernon Kellogg and George L. Akerson, Mr. Hoover's private secretary, who returned yesterday from Kansas City.

Surrounded by their guests, Secretary and Mrs. Hoover "listened in" on the proceedings of the convention and heard the nominating speeches and the din of the Hoover demon-

Continued on Page Nine.

"All the News That's Fit to Print."

# The New York Times.

THE WEATHER
Fair today; tomorrow cloudy and warmer, probably showers at night.
Temperature yesterday—Max. 73, min. 62.
For weather report see Page 25.



VOL. LXXVII....No. 25,711. NEW YORK, SATURDAY, JUNE 16, 1928. TWO CENTS In Greater New York | THREE CENTS Within 200 Miles | FOUR CENTS Elsewhere in the U. S.

# SENATOR CURTIS NAMED FOR VICE PRESIDENT ON FIRST BALLOT WITH 1,052 VOTES TO 34; HOOVER PROMISES REAL RELIEF TO FARMERS

## ANTI-WAR TREATY MAY GO TO POWERS EARLY NEXT WEEK

### Kellogg Spurs Work on It as South Africa's Reply Is Received.

### ALL ANSWERS NOW ARE IN

### Compact Will Be Submitted for Approval to the Fourteen Nations Concerned.

### KELLOGG GIVES UP HOLIDAY

### Plans to Stay in Washington Till Task Is Finished — Denmark Signs Arbitration Treaty.

*Special to The New York Times.*

WASHINGTON, June 15.—The Union of South Africa replied favorably today to the invitation of Secretary Kellogg to become a party to the proceedings looking to a multilateral treaty outlawing war.

It contained the express understanding on the part of General Hertzog, Minister of External Affairs of the South African Government, that the proposed treaty would not impair the right of legitimate self-defense or obligation under the Covenant of the League of Nations, nor be binding upon signatories as against any participant that should violate it.

This reply completes the answers from the Governments addressed by Secretary Kellogg on the subject and enables him to proceed with plans for submitting a definite draft treaty to the powers for signature. This will be done without delay, possibly early next week.

**Will First Consult Envoys.**

It is probable, however, that before dispatching the new notes, Mr. Kellogg will discuss them with the Ambassadors and Ministers of the Governments concerned who are now in Washington. Such conversations have been in progress for some time and are understood to have revealed a substantial accord. They have included the diplomatic representatives of Belgium, Poland and Czechoslovakia, so as to take into the scope of the proposed treaty all nations parties to the Locarno compacts.

By this procedure the total of Governments directly concerned in the project has been increased to fifteen, as follows: The United States, Great Britain, France, Germany, Italy, Japan, Canada, the Irish Free State, Australia, New Zealand, South Africa, India, Belgium, Poland and Czechoslovakia.

Secretary Kellogg intends to press the issue vigorously, and this was indicated in an announcement by him today that, largely on account of the outlawry of war negotiations, he would remain in the capital this Summer and not attempt to take a vacation.

Announcement of the receipt of the reply from South Africa was made contemporaneously with one that a new arbitration treaty had been signed between the United States and Denmark. It is identical in effect with the arbitration treaties recently concluded with France, Italy and Germany. The signatories were Secretary Kellogg and Constantine [illegible] the Danish Minister. The [illegible] States signed on May 18 with [illegible] a conciliation treaty modeled on the so-called Bryan compacts.

**Text of South African Reply.**

The text of the South African reply on outlawry of war read as follows:

Ray Atherton, Esq., American Chargé d'Affaires ad Interim, London.

Sir:

With reference to the note which Mr. Houghton was so good as to address to me on May 22, conveying an invitation to his Majesty's Government in the Union of South Africa to become an original party to the proposed treaty for the renunciation of war, I have the honor to inform you that the following message has been received by telegraph from General Hertzog, Minister of External Affairs of State, the Union of South Africa, for communication to you:

"Through the good offices of his Majesty's Government in the United Kingdom, the contents of the note addressed by your Excellency to his Excellency, the British Secretary of State for Foreign Affairs on the 22d of May were duly conveyed to me. On behalf of his Majesty's Government in the Union of South Africa, I beg to state that the cordial invitation of the Government of the United States extended to his Majesty's Government in the Union of South Africa to participate individually and as an orginal signatory in the treaty for the renunciation of war which the United States Government proposed to various Governments on the 13th of April last, is highly appreciated and that his Majesty's Government in the Union of South Africa will gladly take part therein as invited, together with the other Governments whose participation in the proposed treaty was invited in the first instance.

"In expressing their willingness to be a party to the proposed treaty his Majesty's Government in the Union of South Africa take it for granted:

"(a) That it is not intended to deprive any party to the proposed treaty of any of its natural right of legitimate self-defense.

"(b) That a violation by any one of the parties of any of the provi-

Continued on Page Nine.



## Port Authority Bonds Ruined By Literal-Minded Office Boy

George S. Silzer, former Governor of New Jersey, who is now President of the Interstate Trust Company and Chairman of the Port of New York Authority, related yesterday the following office boy anecdote.

Recently a broker gave his new office boy a block of Port Authority bonds and, with a view to making a record of the transaction, said: "John, take off the numbers of these bonds and deliver them to Blank & Co. and get a check."

About an hour later the boy returned with the announcement that the purchaser had refused to accept the bonds on the ground that they were mutilated. Examination showed that the conscientious messenger had taken the numbers off the bonds with a penknife. As a result, the Port Authority had to correct the young man's mistake by adopting a resolution to redeem the bonds and replace them with new ones.

## BLACKMER INDICTED; FACES EXTRADITION

### Warrant to Follow Perjury and Tax Evasion Charges of Denver Grand Jury.

### OIL MAN 'EXILE' IN FRANCE

### Juror in Stewart Acquittal Says Action Was Protest of the "Slipshod" Inquiry.

*Special to The New York Times.*

DENVER, Col., June 15.—A warrant for the arrest of Henry M. Blackmer, long sought by the Government as a key witness in the Teapot Dome and Continental Trading Company inquiries will be issued early tomorrow by the Clerk of the United States District Court here as a result of six indictments returned against him today by a Federal Grand Jury.

The indictments contain fourteen counts, charging perjury in connection with income tax returns and attempting to evade and defeat income tax payments.

Four of the indictments specifically charge the wealthy oil man with perjury in connection with his income tax return for the years 1920 and 1921, there being two indictments for each of these years.

The other two charge attempting to defeat and evade income taxes for the years 1920 to 1923 inclusive.

Federal officials said today that they believed Blackmer could not evade extradiction on the indictments charging him with perjury, although he might be able to fight it successfully on the true bills alleging attempts to evade the income tax.

Bond was set at $25,000 for each indictment, making a total of $150,000.

**Probable Warrant Procedure.**

Under the method of procedure it undoubtedly will be some time before the oil man will actually face French Magistrates to fight against being brought back here.

George Stephan, United States District Attorney, will probably order the clerk of the Federal Court to issue a warrant for Blackmer's arrest. The warrant will then be turned over to Richard Callen, Federal Marshal, to serve.

Gallen will then report back to the clerk that Blackmer cannot be found. He will return the warrant to Stephan, who will forward a certified copy of it to the Department of Justice in Washington.

The matter then will be referred to the State Department, which will take it up with the French Foreign Office. Then Blackmer will probably be placed under arrest and an extradition hearing held in France. On the outcome of this hearing will depend whether he will be returned to Denver to face trial.

Local federal authorities expressed the belief today that French law would permit Blackmer to post a bond in France after he was technically placed under arrest.

**$8,500,000 Liens Against Him.**

DENVER, June 15 (AP).—Notices of liens against Henry M. Blackmer's property were filed in New York City and Denver recently. Simultaneously, the Government made an arbitrary income tax assessment against Blackmer, which, with interest and penalty, amounts to about $8,500,000. Income tax delinquencies for the period from 1916 to 1923 were charged at that time.

Blackmer has been the enigma of the Teapot Dome case ever since the Senate Public Lands Committee began its investigation of the leasing of the Teapot Dome oil field to Harry F. Sinclair by Albert B. Fall, former Secretary of the Interior.

Soon after the investigation started Blackmer went to Europe. As the Senate committee delved into the leasing of the Dome discovery was made of the existence of the Continental Trading Company, Ltd., an oil-purchasing company incorporated in Canada. Blackmer, according to the evidence, was one of the organizers.

Eventually the Government investigators traced $736,000 in Liberty bonds, alleged to have been Blackmer's share of profits from operations of the Continental, to a New York safety deposit box. Karl C. Schuyler, Denver attorney for Black-

Continued on Page Eight



## TWO ICEBREAKERS NOW ARE NEARING ITALIA CASTAWAYS

### The Braganza Joins the Hobby and Both Are in Sight of North Cape.

### WIND AIDS THEIR PROGRESS

### But Fog Again Balks Larsen and Holm Planes After Take-Off From Hobby.

### OTHER RESCUERS ARRIVING

### Planes of Four Nations Are Speeding to Spitsbergen—Malmgren Trio Not Yet Found.

By The Associated Press.

ROME, June 15.—An official communication from the Citta di Milano, base ship at Kings Bay of the Nobile arctic expedition, reports that the Braganza has joined up with the Hobby and that the two vessels are sailing with a northeast wind, which is helping to open up the ice. They are in sight of North Cape.

The communication adds that the Norwegian airplanes piloted by Captain Riiser-Larsen and Lieutenant Holm took off from the Hobby today, but were forced to return about noon because of heavy fog.

The weather at Kings Bay was reported as of the very best brand for that region.

It was also officially announced that the Dornier-Wahl plane, which took off from Pisa Wednesday with two tons of relief supplies aboard, had arrived at Amsterdam. Major Penso is piloting this plane.

**Nobile Floe Drifting Eastward.**

Copyright, 1928, by The Associated Press.

KINGS BAY, Spitzbergen, June 15.—Instead of drifting to the westward, as at first supposed, General Umberto Nobile and his five companions of the dirigible Italia, marooned on an ice floe, are drifting to the east.

It had been supposed that, owing to the east wind prevailing at Kings Bay, the Nobile party had been blown westward, but it is learned now that a west wind prevailed in the northern region and the position of this group of castaways at midnight last night was reported as 80.38 north latitude, 27.49 east longitude, or about ten miles east of their original location.

The watchers at this place are anxiously awaiting the arrival of Major Maddelena, the Italian aviator flying the Savoia 55. He is due here tomorrow and as soon as possible after that the base ship Citta di Milano will get into communication with General Nobile. The commander of the Italia will inform the ship as to the condition of the ice in his neighborhood and whether it would be possible to rescue his men by plane.

**Equipment All Ready.**

All equipment is ready for Major Maddelena, including provisions, shoes, medicines, guns and collapsible rubber boats. Within a period of ten hours Maddelena can search over a wide area, communicating the results by wireless to the Citta di Milano.

It is understood that the powerful Russian icebreaker Maligin will not proceed to Kings Bay, but will steam directly for General Nobile's position, thus saving time.

The steamer Braganza arrived at Brandy Bay this afternoon and reported that the weather in that vicinity was fine. It is hoped, therefore, that Captain Riiser-Larsen and Lieutenant Holm will soon be able to make another scouting flight from the Hobby in search of the missing explorers, especially Dr. Malmgren and his two companions.

The dog team which the Hobby put ashore covered about nine miles today searching for the trio, but without success.

**Amundsen Will Go in French Plane.**

By The Associated Press.

OSLO, Norway, June 14.—A report from Kings Bay that the sealer Hobby had succeeded in rescuing three members of the crew of the dirigible Italia is denied here.

Captain Roald Amundsen today telegraphed the French Ministry of Marine, which placed Commander Guilbaud and a seaplane at his dis-

Continued on Page Nine.

## HOOVER SENDS MESSAGE

### He Expresses Gratitude for Nomination in a Telegram to Moses.

### SUMS UP PLATFORM AIMS

### He Sees Problems of Next Four Years as Profoundly Moral and Spiritual.

### PROMISES 'BEST IN ME'

### Will Work to Advance Welfare of the People and Uphold Coolidge Policies.

*Special to The New York Times.*

KANSAS CITY, June 15.—Herbert Hoover sent a telegram today from Washington to Senator Moses, Permanent Chairman of the Republican National Convention, in reply to the message sent to him last night by the Senator notifying him of his nomination. Following is Mr. Hoover's message, as read to the convention:

I have your telegram and I sincerely appreciate the confidence which the party has shown in me and the honor bestowed upon me. You convey too great a compliment when you say I have earned the right to the Presidential nomination. No man can establish an obligation upon any part of the American people. My country owes me nothing. It gave me, as it gives every boy and girl, a chance. It gave me schooling, independence of action, opportunity for service and honor. In no other land could a boy from a country village, without inheritance or influential friends, look forward with unbounded hope.

My whole life has taught me what America means. I am indebted to my country beyond any human power to repay. It conferred upon me the mission to administer America's response to the appeal of afflicted nations during the war. It has called me into the Cabinets of two Presidents. By these experiences I have observed the burdens and responsibilities of the greatest office in the world. That office touches the happiness of every home. It deals with the peace of nations. No man could think of it except in terms of solemn consecration.

**Must Find a Farm Solution.**

You ask me for a message.

A new era and new forces have come into our economic life and our setting among the nations of the world. These forces demand of us constant study and effort, if prosperity, peace and contentment shall be maintained.

This convention, like those which have preceded it for two generations, has affirmed the principles of our party and defined its policy upon the problems which now confront us. I stand upon that platform. At a later date I shall discuss it fully, but in the meantime I may well say that under the principles the victory of the party will assure national defense, maintain economy in the administration of government, protect workmen, farmers and business men alike from competition arising out of lower standards of living abroad, foster individual initiative, insure stability of business and employment, promote our foreign commerce and develop our national resources.

You have manifested a deep concern in the problems of agriculture. You have pledged the party to support specific and constructive relief upon a nationwide scale backed by the resources of the Federal Government.

We will and must find a sound solution that will bring security and contentment to this great section of our people.

**Problems of Next Four Years.**

But the problems of the next four years are more than economic. In a profound sense they are moral

Continued on Page Two.

## Curtis Congratulates Hoover; Welcomed as Running Mate

*Special to The New York Times.*

WASHINGTON, June 15.—One of the first messages to reach Secretary Hoover this morning was this from Senator Curtis, filed before voting on a Vice President began at Kansas City:

Kansas City, Mo.
June 15, 1928.

Hon. Herbert Hoover,
Washington.

Please accept my congratulations on your nomination. I will exert every effort for the success of yourself and the party ticket in November.

CHARLES CURTIS,
Senator from Kansas.

Later when the news came that Senator Curtis had been nominated Mr. Hoover sent the following to his running mate:

I wish you to know how greatly I welcome your nomination and your cooperation in the task we have before us. The party is to be congratulated on your selection.

## HOOVER ACCLAIMED BY CAPITAL THRONGS

### Popularity There of Nomination Is Evident—He Attends to Department Duties.

### TO DELAY LEAVING CABINET

### He Will Be in Washington Until About July 1 Clearing Up Affairs and Meeting Campaign Chiefs.

*Special to The New York Times.*

WASHINGTON, June 15.—Herbert Hoover today passed through experiences that gave him an inkling of the tumult and shouting that awaits him as he journeys toward the setting sun to his home in California, there to receive official notification of his nomination as the Republican Presidential candidate, and later as he appears before the people from time to time in the campaign that will get under way as soon as the Democrats have concluded their labors at Houston.

Mr. Hoover stepped out of the doorway of his home at 2,300 S Street a few minutes before 9 o'clock in the morning and found confronting him a battery of still and motion picture cameras. He hesitated for a moment, clenched his teeth and then stepped boldly forward and descended to the sidewalk below.

Once he had resigned himself to the inevitable Mr. Hoover proved to be a good subject for the photographers. He posed alone as directed and again surrounded by members of his family. A crowd that lined both sides of the street near the Hoover home cheered the candidate enthusiastically.

While Washington is normally phlegmatic in its dealings with dignitaries, it gave Mr. Hoover to understand that he was in the midst of friends who rejoiced in his victory. During the pre-convention fight, the capital was a hotbed of Hoover sentiment, and today the city seemed possessed of a gala spirit.

**Hailed on Ride to His Office.**

Mrs. Hoover was not the only one to accompany the Secretary of Commerce to his office this morning. Mr. and Mrs. Herbert Hoover Jr., who came from Boston to be with the head of the family during the Kansas City Convention, occupied seats in the automobile with the senior Hoovers for the trip down town.

Mr. Hoover was recognized as he sped along the streets and was acclaimed repeatedly in the two-mile drive to the Department of Commerce Building. Many persons on terms of intimacy with Mr. Hoover shouted their greetings.

The candidate apparently was surprised at the reception accorded him by the members of his office force. They stood in throngs in the lower hall of the building and another group awaited him on the floor where he makes his headquarters. Here the employes clapped and cheered. Mr. Hoover flushed with pleasure, raised his hat and bowed and beat a hasty retreat into his office.

"He really doesn't look any different than he has on the many occasions that we have seen him for more than seven years, but somehow he seems more interesting," said a pretty girl.

Owing to the rising temperature in Washington, Mr. Hoover had donned Summer attire. He wore a new straw hat, white flannel trousers and a double breasted blue serge coat, and despite the heat appeared cool and collected.

His new honors did not effect any substantial change in the customary daily routine of the Secretary, except that he reported for duty a little later than usual. As a rule he shows up at his desk at 8 A. M. This morn-

Continued on Page Three.

Associated Press Telephoto.

CHARLES CURTIS,
United States Senator From Kansas, Who Was Nominated for the Vice Presidency on the Republican Ticket. This Photograph Was Taken in Kansas City Yesterday.

## LEADERS DECIDE ON CURTIS

### Four Other Candidates Quit as the Roll-Call Is About to Start.

### BORAH DOMINATES CHOICE

### Presses Demand for a Man From the West as Group Considers Easterners.

### HOOVER WAS CONSULTED

### But Left Selection to Convention—Dawes Refused to Make Public Statement on Farmers.

By RICHARD V. OULAHAN.

*Special to The New York Times.*

KANSAS CITY, Mo., June 15.—Senator Charles Curtis of Kansas was nominated for Vice President by the Republican National Convention at 2:08 o'clock this afternoon by a vote of 1,052, to 34 cast for those of a scattering field, thus completing the party's national ticket which will be headed by Herbert Hoover of California, chosen by the convention late last night as its candidate for President.

For the first time in the history of national political parties in this country the candidates for both President and Vice President were taken from States west of the Mississippi River. In choosing Senator Curtis the party also set another precedent, for heretofore no candidate on a national ticket has had Indian blood in his veins.

Like the nomination of Mr. Hoover that of Curtis was determined by a single ballot. After casting it and then making the nomination unanimous the convention transacted some routine business and adjourned.

The scattering vote on the nominating ballot was:

Colonel Hanford MacNider of Iowa, 2.

Vice President Charles G. Dawes of Illinois, 13.

Former Attorney General Herman L. Ekern of Wisconsin, 19.

Not voting, 3.

**Curtis Thanks Convention.**

With the delegates and spectators cheering as they rose to their feet, Senator Curtis, escorted from his hotel, was brought to the platform. Rather diffident he appeared, but his face was covered with smiles. In a low, melodious voice he thanked the convention for the honor it had done him and said complimentary things about President Coolidge and Secretary Hoover. There were more cheers.

Comparatively few of those who witnessed the closing scene of the Republican convention were aware of the circumstances which brought about the adjustment of the Vice Presidential situation without prolonged balloting. Charles G. Dawes, Vice President of the United States, stationed at a telephone that connected his home at Evanston, Ill., with Kansas City, had a conspicuous part in those circumstances. It would have been Dawes in all probability to whom the Vice Presidential nomination would have gone today but for an unwillingness on his part to take a course which was regarded as essential to giving him this honor for a second time.

**Dawes Balked on Farm Relief.**

That General Dawes was willing to accept a renomination appears to be clear from all that is known of what went on last night and in the couple of hours before the convention met today at noon. The chief bit of evidence of that willingness was his assurance over the telephone that if renominated he would take the position that his pet measure, the McNary-Haugen bill, which President Coolidge vetoed and thereby killed for the time being, had been laid on the shelf for at least four years by the farm relief plank of the party platform adopted yesterday. But when General Dawes was asked to give this assurance in a public way before his name was presented to the convention for renomination he demurred. Certain Eastern leaders were dissatisfied with this reluctance, and the Dawes boom died. To have put him forth for renomination would have produced a spirited controversy. Thus the way was paved for the selection of Curtis.

When the result of the ballot which insured Curtis's selection was announced to the convention a shout went up from the delegates and spectators, a shout of relief as much as any other emotion, for the completion of the national ticket had been accomplished under conditions indicating that the party had not lost its old-time ability to harmonize its differences.

**Had Criticized Hoover.**

Without reference to Senator Curtis's Indian strain, he and some other party regulars had been off the Republican reservation since they came to Kansas City to be confronted by the growing indication that Secre-

## EUROPE APPLAUDS NAMING OF HOOVER

### London Praises His Genius for Leadership and Understanding of Foreign Affairs.

### LIKED IN BERLIN AND ROME

### World War Relief Recalled in Both Capitals—League Looks to Stronger Policy Here.

Wireless to THE NEW YORK TIMES.

LONDON, June 15.—A general note of friendly satisfaction will be voiced tomorrow in the British press over the Republican Party's nomination of Herbert Hoover for President. Except for one brief interval of unpopularity, the Republican nominee has been one of the best-known and most-admired Americans in this country ever since war times when his work of relief in Belgium first brought him into international prominence.

The brief period when Hoover fell from the good graces of British public opinion was when he was countering with all his might the effects of the British restriction on the export of rubber, known as the Stevenson Act, whereby the British rubber producers kept up the prices of American automobile tires by protecting themselves against glutting the market with surplus rubber.

**America's "Super-Organizer."**

Naturally, he was then regarded as an opponent by the British business world, and his repute as an opponent, in some sense, to Britain, leaked down dimly to the man in the street who had only a hazy notion of what all the shouting was for.

Now that Britain itself has abandoned the Stevenson restrictions and is leaving authorities on economics here casting aspersions upon the value they had, all recollection of this brief difference of view with Hoover is forgotten.

He emerges in the old light as the man who fed the hungry during the World War, the friend of the Allies in the great struggle, and since then a pre-eminent type of America's "super-organizer."

The dominant sentiment expressed in the editorials which will appear tomorrow is that Hoover will understand world problems and world conditions probably better than any President America has ever had.

**Confidence in His Election.**

The press here is already portraying him as probably the next occupant of the White House, because a Republican victory in times of prosperity has become somewhat axiomatic in British eyes. There are some faint indications in the news that comes from overseas that all is not perhaps so well with American prosperity as might be desired, but "rich" is still the ultimate adjective applied to the United States in Britain as elsewhere in Europe.

"Rich" America is expected to choose the continuation of the Re-

Continued on Page Seven.

## TOPEKA WELCOMES CURTIS BACK HOME

### Thousands Greet Him at Great Impromptu Reception at the State Capitol.

### RUSH THERE BY AUTOMOBILE

### Overjoyed Kansans Hail His Choice for Vice Presidency as Strengthening Ticket.

*Special to The New York Times.*

TOPEKA, Kan., June 15.—A great welcome home for Senator Charles Curtis, back from the Republican National Convention at Kansas City, which today nominated him for the Vice Presidency, was staged tonight on the steps of the State Capitol by thousands of his admirers and neighbors. Senator Curtis addressed the throng.

Senator Curtis traveled from Kansas City to Topeka by automobile, and so the exact hour of his arrival was uncertain. For this reason a street parade was dispensed with and the outdoor reception on the State House grounds quickly arranged. Addresses by several prominent Kansans, including Governor Ben S. Paulen, preceded the address of Senator Curtis.

Rushing here by automobiles to be present at the impromptu welcome, the people of Topeka and Kansas gave expression to their joy at the honoring of a native son of this capital city. Every band in the city was requisitioned to furnish music.

**Speakers Pay Tribute to Him.**

The speaking led off with Senator Arthur Capper, the colleague of Senator Curtis, who paid a high tribute to the Vice Presidential candidate. Governor Paulen and other prominent speakers all expressed the opinion that Senator Curtis's name will greatly strengthen the Republican national ticket, stressing the point that Senator Curtis had not been a candidate for Vice President.

The speakers declared that he yielded when the call came for service to the Republican Party. It was also declared that the vote by which he was selected as running mate for Secretary Hoover, 1,052 of 1,086 casting ballots, revealed that the nation had come to know the Kansas Senator in something of the manner in which his neighbors had always regarded him.

"In his nomination Iowa and Kansas, the home of the 'tall corn' and the State that 'grows the best wheat in the world,'" one speaker said, "have united to give the Republicans an all-Western ticket whose election would mark the beginning of a new day in national recognition for this region."

**Avoids Politics in Speech.**

In his short speech in reply Senator Curtis said he could not touch on politics before the crowd assembled to greet him without regard to

Continued on Page Five.



## Smith Orders Police Protection for Heflin At Senator's Meeting Near Albany Tomorrow

*Special to The New York Times.*

ALBANY, June 15.—Governor Smith today directed Major John A. Warner, superintendent of the State Troopers, to see to it that those who wish to hear Senator J. Thomas Heflin of Alabama, when he speaks Sunday outside the city limits, shall be enabled to do so without interference.

"I ask the people of New York to cooperate with the Governor in offering to the Senator of a sister State full opportunity to say anything he desires without interruption or discourtesy," the Governor's order read, in part. He also said:

"It is our duty to take every reasonable measure to assure to him his constitutional right of free speech. I therefore direct you to see to it that he and his meetings are fully protected."

The meeting is scheduled for 2 o'clock Sunday afternoon in a field. It is announced on a small handbill that it is to be a "patriotic rally, admission free, parking 25 cents."

The arrangements have been clothed more or less in mystery although there is a report that the affair is sponsored by the Ku Klux Klan.

Senator Heflin recently stated in Washington that he had been informed that "Governor Smith's Roman Catholic friends" would endeavor to interfere with the Senator's Albany meeting.

Section 1

"All the News That's Fit to Print."

# The New York Times.

Copyright, 1928, by The New York Times Company.

THE WEATHER
Today partly cloudy, preceded by showers; tomorrow fair.
Temperature yesterday: Max. 78, min. 70.
For weather report see Page 22, Sec. 2.

Section 1

VOL. LXXVII....No. 25,768. ••••+ NEW YORK, SUNDAY, AUGUST 12, 1928. Including Rotogravure Picture Section in two parts—Magazine and Book Sections in Rotogravure. FIVE CENTS In Manhattan, Bronx and Brooklyn | Elsewhere TEN CENTS Except in 7th and 8th Postal Zones

# HOOVER FORMALLY NOTIFIED, VOICES ISSUES; OPPOSES DRY LAW REPEAL OR NULLIFICATION; FAVORS HUNDREDS OF MILLIONS FOR FARM AID

## COOLIDGE'S VIEWS ON TREATY AND ARMY PLEASING TO PARIS

### French Had Expected American Disarmament Drive to Follow Kellogg Compact.

### EASES WAY AT GENEVA

### Only Germany and Russia Now Seen as Likely to Oppose French Stand at Parley.

### SOVIET SEEKS POWERS' AID

### Wants France and Germany to Press for Russia's Inclusion as Original Treaty Signatory.

By EDWIN L. JAMES.

Special Cable to THE NEW YORK TIMES.

PARIS, Aug. 11.—President Coolidge's declaration that the signing of the Kellogg anti-war compact would not necessarily involve a reduction of the American army and navy, makes refreshing hot weather reading for French Government officials.

France and her allies had been looking forward to a new disarmament drive directed especially against land armaments as a result of the treaty. Always too logical, the French had feared that the Americans would come forward with the argument that since everyone had agreed that there would be no more war, it was useless for France and her allies to keep large armies.

Of course, that advice may come, but now that the American President has said that the anti-war compact need not affect the American army and navy the French will be in a much better position to continue to do what they like about their armies. President Coolidge says the American army and navy are intended only for defense. That is what they all say, and how much more so since in signing the Kellogg treaty France and her allies promise never to attack any one!

So with England agreeing as a corollary to the naval agreement not to oppose the French trained reserve program, and with America indicating that she will make no disarmament drive following the signing of the Kellogg compact, the French and their partners face the prospect of having opposed to them at the coming Geneva discussions only Germany and Russia. That makes it look easy for them.

Of course something may be done in the direction of naval disarmament, but that does not greatly concern the French, since England, the chief opponent of submarines, will now make no further opposition to the French building smaller defensive undersea boats on which they wish to concentrate.

The French expect replies in the coming week to the invitations for the signing ceremony. It is believed here that Dr. Stresemann will attend if his physicians permit. There is strong sentiment in Berlin in favor of his attending. There seems no reason to believe that, with the exception of Sir Austen Chamberlain, there will be any defections from the list of Foreign Ministers originally expected to attend.

Since Lord Cushendun has been officially named Acting Foreign Secretary he will legally represent Britain as fully as would have done Sir Austen Chamberlain.

It is remarked here that Mr. Kellogg will have every prospect of spending a quiet sight-seeing week between the signing of the treaty and the sailing of the Leviathan, since the other Foreign Ministers will be leaving quickly after the ceremony for the League of Nations Council meeting in Geneva.

**SOVIET TRIES A NEW MOVE.**

**Seeks to Get Powers to Press Russian Participation in Treaty.**

Wireless to THE NEW YORK TIMES.

MOSCOW, Aug. 11.—The Soviet Government through an editorial in the official Izvestiy, today tries to press the powers to take a stand on the participation of Russia in the Kellogg compact.

The article first reviews the reactions of the international press to the interview given by Tchitcherin. Commenting on a statement by The Washington Post that the Soviet is the enemy of the United States, the article says:

"The Soviet public would be the last to hide from itself and others that the United States and Russia stand at opposite poles in contemporary development. But a quarrel between the two opposing principles of human society undoubtedly will be decided not by inter-governmental battles but by the profound processes of history developing simultaneously in every country of the world.

"If the capitalist Governments had considered it possible to decide the historic conflict by international fighting, they would long ago have renewed such attempts. But while they refrain there should follow logical deductions from the fact of the co-existence of two different social economic systems.

"There is another group of the press that, while denying opposition to participation of the Soviet, seems to fear that if discussions were begun with the Soviet, excessive frankness might compromise the whole under-

Continued on Page Twenty-three.

### Woman Jumper Clings To Balloon for Two Hours

PHILADELPHIA, Aug. 11 (AP).—For two hours Mrs. Ruby Johnson, 22-year-old parachute jumper, clung desperately through rain and mist last night to the cords of a smoke balloon that carried her eight miles before she was able to make a descent.

Just as her husband, Albert, of Toronto, and a number of persons who had followed the balloon's progress by automobile after the ascent at Roxborough, saw the big bag start to descend as the smoke gave out, Mrs. Johnson cut loose.

The balloon by that time was only 1,000 feet in the air, but the parachute opened and Mrs. Johnson landed on an estate in a suburb of Philadelphia. She was slightly dazed, but unhurt, when her husband found her. She said she had been unable to jump sooner because the ground beneath was of a character to make a landing extremely hazardous.

The ascension was made in connection with an American Legion post carnival.

## MANCHURIAN CRISIS UPSETS TOKIO PLANS

### Premier Tanaka and Cabinet Stay in Capital Over Week-end to Watch Developments.

### STATEMENT IN PREPARATION

### Nippon Is Expected to Cite Bloody Cost of Acquired Rights and Bolshevik Danger.

By The Associated Press.

TOKIO, Aug. 11.—Premier Tanaka has abandoned his usual week-end and is remaining in Tokio owing to the Manchurian crisis.

It is known that the Premier is concentrating his energies in the preparation of a statement to be issued soon. This is expected to present the historical background of the Manchurian problem and to plead Japan's claims in regard to a special position there.

Members of the Government believe that such a declaration is necessitated by developments in Manchuria and the keenness with which the world's Chancelleries are awaiting Japan's next move, some of them critically.

The Premier in a speech yesterday said that Japan would not necessarily oppose an agreement between the Chinese Nationalists and Manchuria provided Japan's rights and interests in Manchuria were not endangered. Despite this speech it was not clear today whether Tokio was willing to see a compromise between Mukden and Nanking actually effected and then wait to see the effects on Japan's interests. This question the Premier and the members of the Cabinet are considering over the week-end in connection with the expected declaration of Manchurian policies.

**May Cite Cost in Blood.**

In authoritative circles it is said that the declaration will probably recall Russian aggression in Manchuria prior to 1904, Japan's purchase by blood of a special position there in defeating Russia, Manchuria's development into a stable and prosperous region under Japan's economic aegis and Japan's purpose of maintaining that peace and prosperity.

It is believed that the declaration will further recite a list of Chinese Nationalism's recent alleged breaches of international faith, especially those aimed against Japan, such as abrogation of the Chinese-Japanese commercial treaty, and deduce these as proofs that Japan must view with alarm the extension of Nationalist control over Manchuria's foreign relations.

It is also thought that the declaration will set forth Tokio's fears for the future of the 1915 treaties on which Japan's economic empire in Manchuria is based if the Nationalists gain such control. Japan is also said to fear internal disorders in Manchuria and anti-Japanese strikes there which would cripple Japan's great railway and mining interests if the Nationalist agitators were permitted to enter.

**Tokio Fears Radicalism.**

A Government spokesman today said that Tokio was afraid that an extension of nationalism to Manchuria might bring radicalism closer to Korea and even closer to Japan proper, where suppression of communism and subversive radicalism is one of the Government's greatest worries.

The Minseito, or opposition party, has issued a manifesto interpreting the Premier's speech of yesterday as a complete change of policy, "a surrender," and an admission of failure of a "positive policy in Manchuria." This, the manifesto declared, would result in the loss of Japanese prestige in China and also in the eyes of the powers.

Neither the Minseito nor the press advocates, however, any yielding of Japan's vital interests in Manchuria, which all sections of opinion are agreed must be maintained whatever the costs.

Tokio is closely watching the Kuomintang plenary session at Nan-

Continued on Page Nineteen.



## PLANE CRASHES KILL 3 FLIERS IN JERSEY, 2 ON LONG ISLAND

### Veteran Pilot, Student Airman and a Passenger Fall Into Swamp at New Market.

### CHILDREN SEE SHIP PLUNGE

### Watch From Hepler Farm, Scene of Second Mishap in a Year—Say Craft Was Looping.

### OTHER WRECK DUE TO STUNT

### Waco Drops 2,000 Feet at Roosevelt Field—Brooklyn Pilot and His Companion Are Victims.

Special to The New York Times.

NEW BRUNSWICK, N. J., Aug. 11.—Major Lee J. Mason, veteran army pilot and war veteran and a year ago chief of the Diaz Air Service in Nicaragua, and two companions were instantly killed early this evening when their plane crashed in a cedar swamp on the farm of Samuel Hepler at New Market, near here. It was the second fatal airplane accident on the Hepler farm within a year.

Last October L. H. Thomson, pilot for the Colonial Air Transport, Inc., and three passengers crashed and were killed a short distance from the swamp in which the wreckage and bodies of Major Mason and his companions were found tonight.

Mason, Robert Powell, a student flier of Newark, and Henry H. Hack, the son of H. W. Hack of Short Hills, N. J., and New York went to Hadley Field early this evening and took the plane, a Travelair biplane, which belonged to Howell, from its hangar. They planned a short flight at the airport, it was said, and Mason was to give Howell instruction in the more intricate operations of handling a plane.

**Children See Plane Fall.**

Some children at the Hepler farm said that they saw the plane in a loop and that while it was flying upside down it fell to the ground. The Hepler farm is about 200 yards from the field.

Other witnesses told Coroner Charles Darling of Middlesex County that the plane had apparently turned to come back toward the field when it went into a spin. All three were killed instantly. The bodies were removed to a New Brunswick morgue. The plane, mechanics said, was beyond salvage.

Mason and Howell, it was said, were both employed in Newark by the Public Service Corporation. Mason had been a pilot for ten years or more. When the United States entered the World War he was employed in Detroit as an automobile mechanic. He enlisted in the aviation branch and learned to fly, but failed to see service in France. After the war he returned to the home of his parents at Yates Centre, Kan., where he worked on his father's farm for several months.

After a few months of farm work he purchased a plane and toured the country barnstorming. Early in 1927, Mason with William Brooks, another American pilot, went to Nicaragua and undertook to convert some small commercial planes into effective bombers for the air service of the Nicaraguan Government. They took part in several battles against the Liberals and their activities resulted in a protest at Washington by representatives of the Liberal Party.

**Two Killed on Long Island.**

Special to The New York Times.

ROOSEVELT FIELD, L. I., Aug. 11.—A Waco biplane, a small two passenger sport model, crashed here this afternoon and killed its pilot, Max Scherberger of 559 Decatur Street, Brooklyn, and his passenger John Bracken of 1,155 Rogers Avenue, Brooklyn.

Witnesses said that the pilot was putting the plane through a series of stunts, placing stresses upon it that were obviously more than its light structure could stand. It fell off on one wing from a height of more than 2,000 feet, apparently be-

Continued on Page Fourteen.

### Prince George Twice Halted Boarding Ship for Quebec

SOUTHAMPTON, Eng., Aug. 11 (AP).—Prince George, youngest son of King George and Queen Mary, today started for Canada to join H. M. S. Durban, aboard which he will serve as a French interpreter, but had some difficulty in getting under way.

As he was about to board the Empress of Australia, which left for Quebec, admission was flatly refused the Prince by a policeman at the barrier because he had been expected to arrive elsewhere. After an explanation the Prince was able to pass, but then encountered a stolid master-at-arms at the gangway, who declared that nobody was allowed aboard without a permit. The Prince at length went through his pockets, found his tickets and passed on.

## FOUR DEAD IN STORM IN SOUTHERN STATES

### Victims in Piedmont Section of South Carolina—Seven Hurt in Wrecking of Homes.

### FLOODS MENACE WIDE AREA

### Central Florida, Georgia and Carolinas Suffer in Disturbance Extending to Virginia.

The Associated Press.

ATLANTA, Ga., Aug. 11.—The Carolinas today felt the effects of the tropical storm as it moved slowly up the Atlantic seaboard while sections of Florida and Georgia continued to wrestle with its aftermath.

A toll of four dead, several injured, scores homeless and much property damage marked its progress late yesterday and last night through the rich Piedmont section of South and North Carolina. Tonight flood conditions caused by unprecedented rains menaced several communities, crippling communications, disrupting power service and paralyzing railroad and highway traffic.

As the disturbance passed over into Western North Carolina and Virginia during the day, the weather bureau ordered southwest storm warnings posted from Washington to Norfolk and southeast warnings from Norfolk to Delaware breakwater, saying that strong winds were in prospect.

At the same time, the centre of a new tropical storm approaching from the West Indies temporarily was "lost" by the Weather Bureau, which, however, reported that still another probably might be located south of Jamaica. Caution was advised for all vessels in the north and central portions of the western Caribbean.

**Central South Carolina Hit.**

Central and Southern South Carolina apparently were the hardest hit, high winds wrecking a number of scattered homes in that area and torrential rains drenching most of the territory. Most of the injuries occurred near Batesburg, in which vicinity seven persons were reported hurt by flying débris and in the wreckage of houses.

Jasper J. Harltye died of injuries when his home at Batesburg collapsed in the gale, an unidentified man was found dead on the highway near Cowpens and Grover Hollabough, a Southern Railway freight conductor, was killed when a high tension wire fell across his cab. The other victim was a twelve-year old negro girl who was killed when her home was demolished near Union.

Spartanburg was the greatest suf-

Continued on Page Fifteen.

## Five Hurt as Fire Truck Dashes Into Crowd; Swerves to Avoid Fatality in Nassau Contest

Special to The New York Times.

FLORAL PARK, L. I., Aug. 11.—Five persons were seriously injured and a dozen more were cut and bruised this afternoon when a motor fire truck dashed into a crowd lining the course at a tournament in which the fire departments of many Nassau County towns and villages were competing.

The five badly hurt were taken to Nassau County Hospital at Mineola. They are:

STEPHEN GOZLEY, 54 years old, 38 Vanderbilt Avenue, Floral Park; broken leg and broken arm.

JOHN STRISKO, 25 years old, 16 Emerson Avenue, Baldwin, L. I.; broken leg.

RICHARD SWANSON, 6 years old, 251 Jericho Turnpike, Floral Park; lacerations of the head.

LOUIS ULENDORF, 27 years old, of 15 Charles Street, Roosevelt, L. I.; broken leg.

ANTHONY ZEIBERT, 20 years old, 48 North Road, Great Neck, L. I.; broken jaw and broken right arm.

The Roosevelt Fire Department's hook and ladder truck, manned by the "Brush Rabbits," as the volunteers are known, and driven by Jack Bier of Roosevelt, was at the head of a runway preparing to speed several hundred yards, stop, raise a ladder and send a man to the top. David Herk, a Floral Park motorcycle policeman, rode down the runway to clear the spectators from the course. The crowd gave way and the truck started. Then Bier, with his machine gathering speed every second, saw that Herk had turned his motorcycle and was riding back directly in the path of the fire wagon.

He threw on his brakes and swerved his truck to the right to avoid killing the policeman and the heavy truck dashed into the throng. Men, women and children were bowled over before Bier could stop.

## SMITH LISTENS IN ON HOOVER SPEECH, RESERVING OPINION

### Rival's Remarks Will Affect Own Address but Little, It Is Indicated.

### MAY TAKE UP FEW POINTS

### But Governor Intends Democratic Statement to Be Independently Constructive.

### HE WILL FINISH IT SOON

### Back in Albany From Chicago Trip, He Plans Conferences the Coming Week With Party Heads.

From a Staff Correspondent of The New York Times.

ALBANY, Aug. 11.—Governor Smith, back from Chicago, listened in over the radio tonight to the speech of acceptance of the Republican nomination delivered by his political opponent, Herbert Hoover, on the other side of the continent at Stanford University, Palo Alto, Cal.

Sitting in his easy chair beside his radio set in the reception room of the Executive Mansion, the Governor was an interested auditor. Almost as attentive were his wife and Mr. and Mrs. Arthur Smith, his son and daughter-in-law, who sat with him about the loud speaker. What observations the Governor made on the notification proceedings to newspaper men who had been invited to join the family for the evening were "off the record," but there was no sign that he considered the Hoover address a serious blow to Democratic hopes.

"I have nothing to say about it; not a word," was the Governor's pre-arranged comment on the speech, to which he later adhered.

**Dines Early to Hear Speech.**

The Governor had an early dinner to be ready for the beginning of the proceedings, and was in good humor as he took his place. The scene much resembled the occasion when he listened in on the Democratic National Convention, although Mrs. Smith, who had gone to Houston, was not then in the family circle, and his eldest daughter, Mrs. John A. Warner, then always beside him, was in Maine today with Major Warner, her husband.

Although the Governor did not speak of it, it is understood that Mr. Hoover's speech may influence the handling of some phases of his own address, to be delivered here a week from Wednesday, accepting the Democratic Presidential nomination. He may stress some points and change others, although he wants his document to be independently constructive. Three or four days remain in which Governor Smith will complete his speech, for he is anxious to have it out for distribution to the press a week ahead of time.

In announcing he was going to play golf this afternoon with his son, Arthur, the Governor disclosed that he had written most of his acceptance speech at his home at night.

"A man can play a little golf and still face three days of hard work," he said. "The great bulk of the message has been written in the night time. I can play some golf in the daytime and still work nights."

**Back in Albany at 7 A. M.**

Having been forced to rise at 6:30 o'clock this morning to get off at 7 from the train which brought him back from Chicago and the funeral services of George E. Brennan, Governor Smith retired to bed again in the Executive Mansion for a part of the morning, and reported later that the interruption caused by traveling from the station to his home had hardly disturbed his sleep.

He has now before him not only the completion of his acceptance speech, but a series of conferences next week with political leaders. He expects the coming days, therefore, to be the busiest for some time.

The Governor would make no comment on the approval by the Public Service Commission of the Consolidated Gas-Brooklyn Edison merger.

He also was silent on the matter of his proposed debate with Dr. John Roach Straton. If the Baptist clergyman is content to have the debate in Calvary Church, where he delivered the sermon attacking the Governor's record, the candidate is said to be prepared to go ahead with arrangements. According to his friends, he considers as frivolous the suggestion that a second debate be held in St. Patrick's Cathedral or that the Cathedral or its parishioners be drawn into the matter at all.

Copyright by John Doctoroff.

HERBERT HOOVER.

Crayon Drawing by John Doctoroff, Chosen by the Candidate as the Official Campaign Picture.

**Extracts From What He Says on Prohibition:**

I do not favor the repeal of the Eighteenth Amendment. I stand for the efficient enforcement of the laws enacted thereunder. Crime and disobedience of law cannot be permitted to break down the Constitution and laws of the United States.

Modification of the enforcement laws which would permit that which the Constitution forbids is nullification. This the American people will not countenance * * * There are those who do not believe in the purposes of the several provisions of the Constitution. No one denies their right to seek to amend it. * * * But the Republican Party does deny the right of any one to seek to destroy the purposes of the Constitution by indirection.

## CAPITAL COMMENT ON HOOVER DIVIDED

### Pittman Lauds Tolerance Plea in 'Able Message' but Says Liquor Stand Lacks Courage.

### SEES NO NEW FARM HOPE

### Smoot Calls Address Master's Work and Mrs. Hert Says It Should Go to Hearts of All.

Special to The New York Times.

WASHINGTON, Aug. 11.—Herbert Hoover, in his speech today accepting the Republican nomination for the Presidency, displayed a "lack of courage" in his treatment of the liquor issue, offered no new hope of relief to agriculture, and as a whole clung to the party declarations contained in the Kansas City platform, according to Senator Key Pittman of Nevada, Chairman of the Resolutions Committee at the Democratic convention in Houston.

He described the speech as "an able message" that testified to the political acumen rather than to the courage of the candidate.

Senator Pittman will head the committee named to notify Governor Smith of his nomination.

On the other hand, the Hoover speech was indorsed in strong terms by Senator Reed Smoot of Utah, Chairman of the Senate Finance Committee and Chairman of the Resolutions Committee at the Republican convention in Kansas City.

Mrs. Alvin T. Hert, Vice Chairman of the Republican National Committee, also extolled the candidate as embodying aspirations of the people, and especially of American women.

**Admits Evils, Pittman Notes.**

"It is an able message," said Senator Pittman. "It is the best defense of eight years of Republican administration that could be made. It is a testimonial to the sagacity and political acumen rather than the courage of the candidate.

"There are no surprises to the public. He hangs to the platform as closely as if he had drawn it. His speech is but an echo of previous Republican acceptance speeches, with one exception—he breaks the custom of candidates by boldly admitting the evils that exist, which is a testimo-

Continued on Page Eight.

## HOW THE PRESS SEES HOOVER ACCEPTANCE

### Republican Papers Laudatory, but Democrats Call the Nominee Evasive.

### MID-WESTERN VIEWS CLASH

### Some Hail Speech as Friendly to Farmers—Others View It as Non-Constructive.

Extracts from editorials of leading newspapers in various sections of the country commenting on Mr. Hoover's speech accepting the Republican nomination for the Presidency are as follows:

**NEW YORK CITY.**

**Says Speech Strengthens Nominee.**

From The Herald-Tribune.

The faith and character of Herbert Hoover are written large for all men to see in his first speech as a candidate for the Presidency. What might have been, for a different type of candidate, a perfunctory reiteration of partisanship becomes a declaration of vital convictions. He speaks in general accord with the sound Republicanism of the Kansas City platform, but the phrases are vitalized by a stirring personal faith, keen definition and the will to execute.

Whether Mr. Hoover is setting forth the constructive labors which will confront the next Administration, or defining poverty and the hopes of its abolition, or analyzing the problems of the farmer, or tracing the relation of Republican tariffs and Republican restriction of immigration to current prosperity, he impresses by the careful accuracy of his phraseology and the clarity of his approach. Whatever aid modern engineering skill, American organizing ability, American business acumen can lend to the solution of America's current governmental problems, Mr. Hoover is pre-eminently equipped to bring to the White House.

There is scant comfort for the soft-minded, the idealist-in-a-hurry or the excited reformer in Mr. Hoover's speech. He reiterates his attitude toward prohibition as "an experiment noble in motive," and we commend a more careful study of his phraseology to the hasty Mr. du Pont, who misquoted this particular phrase. The best hope, in fact the only hope,

Continued on Page Six.

## 70,000 FLOCK TO STADIUM

### Nominee Addresses the Nation Through Radio in Ceremony at Stanford.

### SEES PROHIBITION ABUSES

### Fact Finding Inquiry to Correct Them Proposed—Republican Tariff Is Lauded.

### INTOLERANCE IS DENOUNCED

### League Cooperation Favored—Tribute to Coolidge as a Great President.

From a Staff Correspondent of The New York Times.

PALO ALTO, Cal., Aug. 11.—Before 70,000 who faced him in the great stadium of Stanford University and in the hearing of millions in all parts of the nation to whom his words were carried by radio, Herbert Hoover this afternoon formally accepted the nomination of the Republican Party as its candidate for President of the United States.

The speech, representing the careful thought of weeks, is the battle cry of the Republican Party, the real platform on which Mr. Hoover goes to the electorate. It was an extended discussion of the issues, such as farm relief, prohibition, the tariff, foreign affairs, immigration and honesty in public life.

The exercises in the stadium began nearly two hours before Mr. Hoover was scheduled to appear. Four brass bands, including the student bands of Stanford and the municipal bands of San Francisco, had a part in the preliminary program. The Stanford cheer leaders were early in position to direct the cheering in honor of their illustrious alumnus.

**Candidate Enters the Stadium.**

Senator Moses, who, because of his position as Permanent Chairman of the Kansas City convention, notified Mr. Hoover of his nomination, came into the stadium immediately after the candidate. Governor C. C. Young of California, in a speech less than five minutes long, introduced Senator Moses. In the stadium were the members of the Notification Committee, one from each State, the District of Columbia and the insular possessions.

Senator Moses, in notifying Mr. Hoover, declared at one point in his address:

"We know that you will not seek to transcend or to distort or to nullify any portion of your party's platform or any portion of the Constitution of the United States from which our platform springs. Knowing your exceptional sense of organization; knowing the intrinsic merit of your character, and knowing the fine executive powers which you possess, we have turned to you to lead us in these immediate years when the greatest need for our country is the application of sound economic principles—in which you possess an unquestioned mastery."

**Nominee's Stand on Prohibition.**

Prohibition was one of the outstanding features of Mr. Hoover's speech. He declared that he was against the repeal of the Eighteenth Amendment, and he stood for the rigid enforcement of the law. The amendment, he declared, must not be nullified by indirection. There is just one way, he said, by which the country can rid itself of prohibition, and that is by changing the Constitution.

The candidate repeated his recent statement on prohibition:

"Our country has deliberately undertaken a great social and economic experiment, noble in motive and far-reaching in purpose. It must be worked out constructively."

He added:

"Modification of the enforcement laws which would permit that which the Constitution forbids is nullification. This the American people will not countenance. Change in the Constitution can and must be brought about only by the straightforward methods provided in the Constitution itself."

The nominee said "common sense" compels the realization that "grave abuses" have occurred under prohibition—"abuses which must be remedied."

"An organized searching investigation of fact and causes can alone determine the wise method of correcting them," he added. "Crime and disobedience to law cannot be permitted to break down the Constitution and laws of the United States."

There was no question that in the opinion of the throng prohibition was the real point of cleavage in the campaign of 1928. There was approval of what Mr. Hoover said about the tariff, of his promise to account for every penny expended in the campaign, his denunciation of dishonesty in high official places, his stand on immigration, but it was his position on prohibition that brought him what came nearer to

Continued on Page Two.

"All the News That's Fit to Print."

# The New York Times.

Copyright, 1928, by The New York Times Company.

THE WEATHER
Cloudy, possibly showers, today; tomorrow, fair and warmer.
Temperature yesterday: Max. [illegible], Min. [illegible].
For weather report see Page 42.

VOL. LXXVII....No. 25,779. NEW YORK, THURSDAY, AUGUST 23, 1928. TWO CENTS in Greater New York | THREE CENTS Within 200 Miles | FOUR CENTS Elsewhere in the U. S.

# SMITH FOR STATE CONTROL OF LIQUOR TRAFFIC, CHANGES IN 18TH AMENDMENT AND VOLSTEAD LAW; RAIN CUTS CROWD AT ACCEPTANCE CEREMONY

## TUNNEY BESIEGED BY BRITISH CROWDS; GETS NO PRIVACY

### Throngs Pursue Him From Early Landing at Plymouth to Royal Suite in London.

### ENGLISH FIND HIM "UNIQUE"

### Praise His Looks, Voice and Demeanor—He Expresses Wish to See G. B. Shaw.

### HE IS SILENT ON MARRIAGE

### But Is Adamant on Retirement, Saying He Will No Longer Be a "Goldfish in a Bowl."

Wireless to THE NEW YORK TIMES.

LONDON, Aug. 22.—Gene Tunney, the retired champion, who arrived in England today on the Mauretania, is spending the night in the gorgeous royal suite of the Savoy Hotel in London and will go to Dublin tomorrow morning to visit the country where his parents were born. Tunney allowed Plymouth ship reporters to interview him on landing, vouchsafed a few words to London interviewers at Paddington station and posed good-naturedly for photographers on the roof of the Savoy. He has now denied himself to newspaper men.

"I want to sink as far into obscurity as possible," he declared. "The next time I come I hope I shall not even have the restrained attentions of your English press men."

No one observing how he shrank from the attentions of the crowd that awaited him at Paddington could doubt Tunney's sincerity. He gave every indication of wishing not only to avoid publicity but to forget the rôle in which he has earned it.

**Marvels at Guards Officer.**

Tunney had no reason to cavil at the warmth of his reception. As soon as he left the train at Paddington carrying a bag of very new golf clubs he was swallowed up in a hysterical crowd of hero worshipers, shouting "Good old Gene!" and brandishing autograph books.

The boxer darted into a taxicab and escaped with a huge sigh of relief. As the cab whirled past Buckingham Palace he caught sight of a Guards officer in scarlet uniform.

"Say, what's he doing, dolled up like that?" asked Gene with amazement. "Say, what's that boy, tell me, some one."

He also marveled at exponents of Hyde Park oratory, two or three of whom were in full swing. Then the taxicab swung into the Strand.

"Shaw used to live there," said some one as it passed the Adelphi.

"What? In there? Say, how could he write in that place?" asked Tunney.

"Extremely shy, handsome, with fine eyes, quietly dressed in a light brown suit and looking as unlike a prizefighter as it would be possible to picture," was how English newspaper men saw him. In fact, it was rather an "out-size" in American tourists than the world's boxing champion who landed from the Mauretania this morning not far from the spot whence the Mayflower set sail. Tunney knew all about the Mayflower.

**Recalls Drake as He Lands.**

"By Jove," he said, "aren't some of those cliffs the ones that Drake played bowls on before he went out to lick the Spaniards, and wasn't it from somewhere around here that the Pilgrims sailed?" he asked. He got the decision on both counts.

Some one in Tunney's party had confused Plymouth with Portsmouth and thought that it was only a two hours' journey from London. Tunney accordingly started for the metropolis by automobile, but as rain and mist, characteristic of the English Summer, made it difficult to see the scenery he gave up at Exeter and took a train the rest of the way. Arriving at his hotel he again showed a lack of acquaintance with English geography.

"Will you ring up Surrey and ask for Thornton Wilder?" he requested. It was explained to him that ringing up Surrey was the English equivalent of calling up Ohio.

England's preliminary verdict on Tunney is highly favorable. It finds him less of a "highbrow" than America thinks him, shyer than any world's champion can ever have been before, and as boyishly eager to soak up Old World impressions as a piece of blotting paper.

"His quiet voice is almost musical, his smile is contagious and his bearing is modest and unassuming," said one interviewer.

"It would probably be true to say that he was the most popular passenger aboard the Mauretania," wrote another. "His shy manner and soft voice, combined with his thoughtfulness for others, won him universal affection."

**Refuses to Discuss Wedding.**

Tunney will cross to Dublin tomorrow to officiate at the close of the Tailteann games. Then he will go west to try to find where his forefathers lived.

"It is sentiment with me, for I am half Irish and very sentimental," he explained today.

Then he will come back to England for a fortnight, and he expects to spend a good deal of that time with his friend Thornton Wilder.

Tunney firmly refused to discuss his coming marriage and the only

Continued on Page Seventeen.

### *Famous Peter Pan Statue Is Desecrated in London*

Wireless to THE NEW YORK TIMES.

LONDON, Aug. 22.—The statue of Peter Pan—the dainty windblown figure of a barefoot child engaged in blowing a reed flute—which for years has been the most loved statue in Kensington Gardens, was covered with tar and feathers before dawn today by unidentified vandals.

All day it was shrouded with a heavy tarpaulin tent under which workmen of the Department of Parks are cleaning it. At the department's office it was stated this afternoon that the statue was not damaged.

Scotland Yard is seeking the guilty vandals.

The sculpture of the late Sir George Frampton is so noted a sight of London that mothers from the suburbs and from distant cities on visits to the capital bring their children to see it. There were several groups of these personally conducted small sightseers disappointed during the day's enforced repairs.

## MAYOR GILLIS FACES 330 DAYS IN PRISON

### Newburyport's Vivid Executive Also Fined $1,140 for Illegal Gasoline Station.

### JUDGE CALLS HIM 'OUTLAW'

### Emerging After Appeal, 'Bossy' Says He'll Run for Governor to Get Revenge.

*Special to The New York Times.*

NEWBURYPORT, Mass., Aug. 22.—Mayor Andrew J. (Bossy) Gillis was sentenced today in Newburyport District Court to 330 days in the House of Correction and ordered to pay fines totaling $1,140.

The sentence and fines were imposed after Mayor Gillis, termed an "outlaw" by Judge Nathaniel N. Jones, had been found guilty in eleven counts on charges of illegally storing gasoline, illegally selling gasoline and violating city ordinances by removing sidewalks and changing street levels.

The Mayor's predicament was brought about through his insisting on opening and operating a gasoline filling station in a restricted residential section of the city.

**Judge Severe in Remarks.**

At the end of the hearing, while Mayor Gillis listened intently, Judge Jones, after commenting on the fact that Mr. Gillis two years ago in Superior Court had promised to remove the gasoline tanks from the same site, said:

"This man is an outlaw. Such a man as this can be described only by that term. He has broken his word to the Courts. He seems to forget he is a Mayor. He seems to forget that he no longer is a private character, but a public figure whose acts and omissions are placed in more prominence before the public eye because of his station.

"Such a man, committing such acts as have been described here, deserves little consideration."

"I appeal," the Mayor said simply, after the denunciation. He was released on his own recognizance for trial next month in Superior Court at Salem.

Mr. Gillis two years ago attempted to operate the disputed gasoline station on the same site. At that time he was the "town bum," in his own expression. The City Fathers promptly haled him into court and forced him to give up the station. He swore he would reopen the station if he had to become a city official to do it. The issue followed exactly that sequence, with the intervention of the law again.

**"Gillis Day in Court."**

The tumult and the shouting in anticipation of "Gillis day in court" were dimmed a bit when the hearing opened, with the frown of Judge Jones sending down a gray veil over the proceedings.

The long list of counts was read. Mayor Gillis listened intently.

Seven prosecution witnesses were sworn. They included wealthy Newburyport residents, abutters of the Mayor's gasoline station and also persons who had purchased gasoline from the disputed station.

City Solicitor Kelliher acted as counsel for Mayor Gillis and said that defense admitted the truth of all charges in the complaint, except the alleged illegalities. Ernest Foss of Newburyport appeared as counsel complainant. The testimony had to do with the sales from the Gillis station, the taking away of a curbstone for a drive into the station, the matter of city and state permits and the storage of gasoline.

The Judge announced his findings on the law, with his opinion on Newburyport's Mayor, and pronounced sentence.

"What a sleigh ride!" exclaimed the chunky, red-headed Mr. Gillis when he had taken appeal and had emerged into the open air.

"You can tell the world I'm going to run for Governor, and when I'm elected I'll fire Judge Jones.

"That gas station of mine will run on like a brook. They can't scare Bossy Gillis."



## WILLEBRANDT AIDE PUSHES DRY INQUIRY IN SPITE OF TUTTLE

### Night Club Drive Goes On and Woman Chief Has 'No Comment on What Subordinate Says.'

### HE IS OUT OF CITY FOR A DAY

### Silent at Lake George Home on the Washington Assertion He Knew of 125 Subpoenas.

### POLICE OFFICERS HEARD

### Inspector Bolan, One of 37 Called, Reports to Morrison—Staff Here Also Conducts Hearing.

Indications were yesterday that Mrs. Mabel Walker Willebrandt, Assistant Federal Attorney General in charge of dry law prosecutions throughout the country, was not inclined to abide by the announcement of United States Attorney Charles H. Tuttle that a halt would be called on the manner of examining witnesses in the Federal Grand Jury's investigation of the twenty-six night clubs raided by prohibition agents sent here from Washington. Through her special assistant, Norman Morrison, Mrs. Willebrandt was in full control here yesterday and the Grand Jury proceedings went right ahead.

Mr. Tuttle interrupted his vacation last Monday and returned to his office in the Federal Building when he learned that subpoenas had been issued for 125 patrons of night clubs and others to appear before the Grand Jury. Thirty-seven of those who had been named in the subpoenaes were police officials or former police officials.

Although the subpoenas had been issued in his name, Mr. Tuttle on his arrival declared that he knew nothing of them and was not aware of the plan of Mrs. Willebrandt and others high in the Attorney General's office in Washington to hale the club patrons before the Grand Jury to obtain information of alleged dry law violations in the clubs.

**Says Tuttle Knew of Subpoenas.**

This statement of Mr. Tuttle was contradicted Tuesday night by Mrs. Willebrandt, however, in a statement over the telephone from Washington. Mrs. Willebrandt declared that "Mr. Tuttle personally knew of the calling of the additional witnesses and set the date when the Grand Jury was to come back for the purpose of hearing their testimony, and all the subpoenaes were issued from his office and he appointed his assistant who has been working on the case."

Mrs. Willebrandt followed this with the announcement that she "did not intend to enter into any public comment about what any subordinate officer of the Department of Justice may or may not say to the press with respect either to the method of the investigation or the policies that are or are not to be followed."

The latter part of Mrs. Willebrandt's statement was taken to refer to the announcement of Mr. Tuttle last Monday, when, on learning that four patrons of night clubs already had been questioned in the Grand Jury inquiry, he declared that "it wasn't right to subject all these New Yorkers to pitiless publicity which wasn't necessary," and that the inquiry would be continued, but "along other lines."

**Police Officials Are Called.**

Mr. Tuttle was not at the Federal Building yesterday when Mr. Morrison began the interrogation of the additional witnesses before the Grand Jury by calling two police officials, a detective and several others to testify. The prosecutor the night before had left for his country home at Lake George, to preside yesterday at a meeting of the Lake George Association, of which he is President. The police officials were Deputy Chief Inspector James S. Bolan, Commander of the uniformed and plain clothes force in the midtown district, and Lieutenant John Bulkley of the Mercer Street Station, and

Continued on Page Ten.

### *Hoover 'Band Wagon' Gives Talks, Tunes and Pictures*

A Hoover-Curtis "band wagon," a motor bus equipped with amplifying apparatus, four loud-speakers and motion picture projector apparatus, arrived in the city yesterday and was placed at the disposition of the Republican Speakers' Bureau, which has headquarters at the Waldorf.

The bus is painted red, white and blue. Its apparatus enables it to receive and amplify music or a speech received from a radio station, to amplify the voice of a speaker and to project motion pictures at night. Eighteen of these buses will be used by the Republicans in this campaign and two already are in use. The bus which arrived here yesterday is on its way to Rocky Point, R. I., to amplify the first speech of Senator Charles Curtis, nominee for Vice President, there today.

## WORK TO KEEP ALOOF IN FIGHT ON MACHOLD

### Will Not Intervene in Choice of State Chairman, Washington Aide Asserts.

### HOOVER ACTION UNLIKELY

### Nominee's Original Backers Here Suggest Compromise Candidates for Post.

*Special to The New York Times.*

WASHINGTON, Aug. 22.—Dr. Hubert Work, Chairman of the Republican National Committee, will not intervene in the selection of a chairman of the New York State Republican Committee to fill the vacancy created by the death of George K. Morris, according to a statement made in behalf of Dr. Work today by one of his aides at Washington headquarters.

Hoover leaders here appear to be satisfied that the State Committee will elect E. Edmund Machold to the chairmanship at the meeting in New York on Friday. They do not believe that either Mr. Hoover or Dr. Work could be persuaded to take a hand in the contest that has been started by Hoover men in New York.

**Work Shuns Local Fight.**

Chairman Work, it was explained, has adopted the policy of keeping hands off in factional differences that develop in state party organizations, and will not depart from this rule in the controversy that has been aroused over the apparent determination of the Hilles group to elevate Mr. Machold to the chairmanship. Dr. Work, it was said, made no comment on the New York situation today, and it could not be learned whether a direct appeal had been made to him by Hoover men that the choosing of a chairman in New York be delayed until an opportunity had been given to consult Mr. Hoover on the subject.

Certain Republicans here take the view that as William M. Hill, Chairman of the New York State Hoover Campaign Committee, and Ogden L. Mills, Under-Secretary of the Treasury, both of whom were active Hoover men prior to the Kansas City convention, have acquiesced in the proposal to make Mr. Machold the new State Chairman this should prompt other New York Hoover men to fall into line with what is obviously the wish of a majority of the State Com-

Continued on Page Twenty-one.

## HOOVER ENCOURAGED AT ALL-DAY PARLEY WITH FARM LEADERS

### Nominee Visits Cedar Rapids and Gets Favorable Reports From the Corn Belt.

### RESTATES HIS OWN POLICY

### But His Remarks Made at Closed Conference Are Not Publicly Revealed.

### RECEIVES HEARTY GREETING

### Listens to Governor Smith's Speech of Acceptance, but Withholds Comment.

From a Staff Correspondent of The New York Times.

CEDAR RAPIDS, Iowa, Aug. 22.—Herbert Hoover spent today in Cedar Rapids and for practically the entire time he was in conference with farm leaders of the Corn Belt States, who reported on the political situation in Iowa, the Dakotas, Nebraska, Missouri, Indiana, Minnesota, Wisconsin, Tennessee and Illinois. This evening he listened over the radio to Governor Smith's speech. He made no comment on it.

Some of those who saw Mr. Hoover today told him that everything was rose-tinted so far as the Republican ticket is concerned. Others reported that a real fight is ahead in some of the States west of the Mississippi, notably in Montana, the Dakotas, Wisconsin and Minnesota.

In the main, however, the reports were optimistic. Opinion seemed to be that while there is dissension in the agricultural West at this time, it is not so serious that it cannot be eliminated by missionary work between now and election day in November.

Mr. Hoover knows that a fight has to be made in some of these Middle and Northwestern States. It is not denied in high quarters that large areas in the farming West must receive serious consideration if Republican victory is to be assured. A member of the United States Senate, who is in Cedar Rapids today, said that if the election were held tomorrow North Dakota and Montana would go for Mr. Smith, that Wisconsin, South Dakota and Nebraska would be in doubt.

Another United States Senator was quoted as saying that in Indiana a majority of the farmers are for Governor Smith. He said, however, that there is enough time left to win the State provided those in command of the Republicans get busy.

**Thousands Greet the Nominee.**

Mr. Hoover arrived in Cedar Rapids from West Branch at 11 o'clock this morning. As he entered the city he was cheered by thousands who lined the sidewalks. To these people he was not Herbert Hoover of California but Herbert Hoover the native Iowan. Nowhere has the welcome been more enthusiastic or more sincere than here in Cedar Rapids and it so happens Cedar Rapids is one of the few cities in Iowa where the normal Democratic vote is worth counting.

At noon Mr. Hoover had a conference with the editors of about seventy farm newspapers, who reported on every State in the corn belt as well as Pennsylvania, Tennessee, Nebraska, Oklahoma and other States outside the corn growing areas.

The meeting was executive. None of the newspaper men accompanying Mr. Hoover was admitted. So far as is known no stenographic report of proceedings was made.

Mr. Hoover stated his position on the farm problem. He was asked no questions. And it was stipulated that he was not to be quoted for publication. The talk, however, is that in explaining his stand he emphasized the necessity of bringing about a coordination of the agricultural and other industries in the solving of the problem which he has declared to be the most important that awaits the attention of the next Administration.

The nominee was with the farm newspaper men about one hour. It was said that the papers represent an agricultural reading public of not less than 8,000,000 persons. It was also said that among the editors present were some who are inclined to support Governor Smith.

Those who were present included Senators Watson and Robinson of Indiana, Capper of Kansas, Brookhart of Iowa, Pine of Oklahoma and Nye of North Dakota; Representatives Wood of Indiana, Johnson of South Dakota, Faust of Missouri and the entire House delegation from Iowa. Some of them say the election is already won. Others are not so optimistic.

On one phase of the situation, however, all appear to be in agreement and that is the McNary-Haugen bill has passed into history. That that proposition for the relief of the farmers is as dead as a door nail, is the admission of most of those who

Continued on Page Twelve.

Times Wide World Photo.

**GOVERNOR ALFRED E. SMITH.**

**Democratic Candidate for President Delivering His Acceptance Speech in the Assembly Chamber at Albany.**

### *Extracts From What He Says on Prohibition:*

I shall to the very limit execute the pledge of our platform "to make an honorable endeavor to enforce the Eighteenth Amendment and all other provisions of the Federal Constitution and all laws enacted pursuant thereto. * * * The corruption in enforcement activities * * * I will ruthlessly stamp out. * * * Today disregard of the prohibition law is insidiously sapping respect for all law. I raise therefore what I profoundly believe to be a great moral issue involving the righteousness of our national conduct and the protection of our children's morals. * * * Some immediate relief would come from an amendment to the Volstead law giving a scientific definition of the alcoholic content of an intoxicating beverage. * * * I personally believe in an amendment in the Eighteenth Amendment which would give to each individual State itself only after approval by a referendum popular vote of its people, the right wholly within its borders to import, manufacture or cause to be manufactured and sell alcoholic beverages, the sale to be made only by the State itself and not for consumption in any public place. * * * Our Canadian neighbors have gone far in this manner to solve this problem. * * * I will never advocate nor approve any law which directly or indirectly permits the return of the saloon.

*Full text, Page 2, Cols. 7 and 8, Page 3, Cols. 1 and 2.*

## WASHINGTON VIEWS DIVIDED ON SPEECH

### Smoot Says Smith Sets Up a Straw Man in Attack on Reaction.

### PRAISE BY SENATOR GEORGE

### Declares Enforcement Pledge Carries Conviction—New Criticizes Farm Proposals.

*Special to The New York Times.*

WASHINGTON, Aug. 22.—Comment in Washington today on Governor Smith's speech was divided to a great degree, according to political party affiliations.

Senator Smoot denounced as an "untruth" what he termed the Governor's description of the Republican Party as a party of reaction. The Senator saw in the address a promise of another Underwood tariff law, to which he contrasted the Democratic nominee's declaration against any sudden revision of the economic system. The Underwood law, he said, would "have ruined" the country.

On the other hand, Senator Fletcher declared the address demonstrates that Governor Smith measures up to the standards of a great statesman and predicted a wave of popular approval for his doctrine of equalized opportunity.

Senator George, dry, who was among the contenders for the Democratic nomination at Houston, said it was "the speech of an honest man with an honest mind and a human heart." The Governor's assurance that he will ruthlessly stamp out corruption in prohibition enforcement agencies "carries conviction," the Georgian declared.

Former Senator Hansbrough, Chairman of the Smith Independent League, declared the speech showed that the farmer at last "is in a position to take a step toward relief by voting for a man whose record for constructive achievement is beyond reproach"; but Postmaster General New criticized the handling of the agrarian subject. The Governor's stand on prohibition, he added, promises "the administration of the temperance laws by Tammany."

SENATOR REED SMOOT, Republican, of Utah. He lays great stress

Continued on Page Five.

## HEAVY RAIN FORCES INDOOR EXERCISES

### Only 2,000 Able to Get Into Capitol—Throng Stands on Lawn in Downpour.

### LATER REWARDED BY SMITH

### In a Panama Hat and a Raincoat the Governor Introduces Robinson and Raskob.

*Special to The New York Times.*

ALBANY, Aug. 22.—Although rain prevented the outdoor ceremony which had been planned for the formal notification of Governor Smith of his nomination as candidate for the Presidency of the Democratic Party, the nominee nevertheless did addres in the open later the patient thousands who listened under umbrellas to the words, carried to them by amplifiers, he spoke in the Assembly chamber.

By the time the indoor ceremony had reached the stage where the Governor had mounted the rostrum and begun the delivery of his speech of acceptance, the outdoor crowd had been swelled by the arrival of new thousands who had come out to listen where they could not look and for whom the inclement weather appeared to hold no terrors.

Under raised umbrellas they stood in the drenched park, men and women, for more than an hour while the Governor's address came to them. Governor Smith, when he learned this, told Chairman Raskob of the national committee, who acted as master of ceremonies, to announce through the microphone so word would reach the outdoor thousands that at the end of the proceedings he would make a brief appearance on the speaker's platform erected in the park at the foot of the majestic flight of steps that form the eastern approach to the capitol building.

This announcement was greeted with applause by the audience in the Assembly chamber and with a mighty roar of gratitude from the drenched multitude without.

By the time the Governor appeared outdoors, the open air audience had grown enormously. It was estimated

Continued on Page Four.



## STILL BARS THE SALOON

### Smith's New Plan Would Ban Sale of Liquor in Public Places.

### PLEDGES AID TO FARMERS

### Governor Would Ask First Congress Session for Relief Devised by Experts.

### PROMISES TARIFF REFORM

### But Would Not Disturb Business —Not a 'Jingo,' but Hostile to Isolation Policy.

By W. A. WARN.

*Special to The New York Times.*

ALBANY, Aug. 22.—Giving voice to the conviction that victory would surmount the Democratic banner in November because his party was "right" and its triumph would mean progress for the nation, Governor Smith this evening was formally notified of and formally accepted his nomination for the Presidency of the United States.

The ceremony was held in the Assembly Chamber instead of outdoors in Capitol Park as had been the original intention, for a dismal rain began in the morning and continued throughout the day and early evening hours.

Hence a slim 2,000, all the chamber would hold, heard the Governor deliver his speech of acceptance in which, with characteristic frankness and clarity of expression, he defined his personal views on the important issues of the campaign and his personal reaction to pledges contained in the national platform of his party.

**Thousands Listen Under Umbrellas.**

Included in the audience were prominent Democrats from different parts of the country, many members of the National Committee and practically all the members of the notification committee, headed by Senator Key Pittman of Nevada.

Had the heavens smiled on what undoubtedly was the greatest hour in the eventful life of Alfred E. Smith, he would have spoken before a throng which advance estimates put at 100,000, and arrangements had been made to care for that number in the outdoor ceremony program.

As it was when the indoor ceremonies began, a crowd estimated to number 10,000 stood under raised umbrellas on the spot selected for the outdoor notification. The address was carried to them through amplifiers of which big clusters were hung to the trees at different points.

In addition to the indoor and outdoor audiences, there were invisible millions who heard the Governor's speech as it came to them over the most extensive radio hook-up on record. This embraced 104 transmitting stations, a network spanning the continent from coast to coast and reaching out to every section of the country.

**New Dry Law Stand a Surprise.**

The Governor's words were fraught with one big surprise. In the main he hewed closely to the platform of his party on the chief issues of the political battle, but on prohibition, amid great applause, he took an even more advanced stand than he has in any of his earlier public utterances.

He came out squarely and bluntly in favor of an amendment to the Eighteenth Amendment under which individual States, subject only to a popular referendum, would be empowered to manufacture and traffic in alcoholic beverages for home consumption solely along lines akin to the so-called Quebec system now in force in most of the Provinces of Canada.

This was taken by the listening Democratic leaders clearly to indicate that the Governor would make prohibition the leading issue in his campaign and would stake his all on wet support in the big Eastern States, trusting to Southern States to perform true to tradition and return the usual Democratic majorities, despite the aversion of Democrats there to any liberalization of the dry laws.

**Inspired by Great Democrats.**

Governor Smith at the very beginning of his speech proclaimed himself a believer in "the idealism of Jefferson, Cleveland and Woodrow Wilson." The names of these great leaders of Democratic thought and legislation at different periods of the nation's history recurred in his address again and again.

The dominant note in the early part of his speech gave assurance of a new sort of leaderships in the Democratic Party and at Washington should the speaker be elected President.

He invoked the name of Woodrow Wilson at the opening of his speech when he voiced his formal acceptance of the "summons to a wider field." He quoted Grover Cleveland's his-

Continued on Page Two.

## *Russia Bars British Warship Seeking Dead; Would Agree to One From 'Friendly Nation'*

MOSCOW, Aug. 22 (AP).—The Soviet News Agency, Tass, says that in response to a British request through the Norwegian Mission at Moscow that she be allowed to send a warship to transfer the bodies of the crew of the recently raised submarine L-55 from Leningrad to England, the Soviet Government has replied that it cannot consent to a British warship entering Soviet territorial waters.

The Soviet Government, however, would not object to a warship of a friendly nation, such as Norway, or a British merchantman coming.

Regarding reports of alleged delay by the Soviet Government in replying to the British request, the agency said that this was only received in Moscow on Aug. 20.

The L-55 was sunk in 1919 while assisting the "White" Russians against the Bolshevist Government, but recently was raised by the Soviet authorities who found a number of skeletons and decomposed bodies of British seamen.

By declining to give permission for a British warship to visit Russian waters the Moscow Government is merely following international usage where diplomatic relations have been ruptured. Great Britain severed diplomatic and commercial relations with Soviet Russia on May 24, 1927.

The authentic first news to reach the British Admiralty in regard to the loss of the L-55 came through the press on Aug. 17, although the submarine had been missing since June, 1919. On the 12th of that month the relatives and next of kin of the personnel were officially informed that during operations in the Baltic Sea the vessel had probably been lost with all on board.

This was a fact then known absolutely to the Soviet Government, which a month ago made preparations to raise the craft in order to see whether the cause of her sinking had been gun fire from the Russian destroyers, Azard and Gavril, or collision with a mine. Investigation proved the former cause.

"All the News That's Fit to Print."

# The New York Times.

Copyright, 1928, by The New York Times Company.

THE WEATHER
Cloudy today, followed by showers, colder at night; tomorrow fair.
Temperature yesterday—Max., 63; min., 54.
U. S. Weather Forecast—For details see Page 50.

VOL. LXXVIII....No. 25,840. **** + NEW YORK, TUESDAY, OCTOBER 23, 1928. TWO CENTS In Greater New York | THREE CENTS Within 200 Miles | FOUR CENTS Elsewhere in the U. S.

# THRONG OF 22,000 IN THE GARDEN HEARS HOOVER ASSAIL SMITH'S POLICIES AS 'STATE SOCIALISM'; OPPOSES PUTTING GOVERNMENT INTO BUSINESS

## FRANCE AND BRITAIN PUBLISH NAVY NOTES; NEW BID TO US HINTED

### Paris Forecasts Invitation to America to Have Gibson Confer With Chamberlain and Briand.

### AT GENEVA IN DECEMBER

### Official Documents Emphasize Effort to Meet Our Views on Naval Limitation.

### PROOF OF LAND-NAVY DEAL

### Britain Dropped Opposition to French Conscription—Paris Says This Still Holds.

Special Cable to THE NEW YORK TIMES.

PARIS, Oct. 22.—A French "blue book" and a British "white paper" were published today in Paris and London, respectively, giving the correspondence exchanged between the two capitals, instructions sent to their respective envoys in Washington and other correspondence on the Franco-British naval limitation understanding.

Following the publication, inquiry was made this evening in competent quarters as to what the next step might be, in view of the fact that both diplomatic books close with the American refusal to accept the compromise elaborated by London and Paris.

The reply was given that Sir Austen Chamberlain and M. Briand would be at Geneva in December for the meeting of the League of Nations Council, and that they would welcome the presence there of an American representative to consider whether a basis could not be laid for a revision of the naval proposal into a form which might be acceptable to Washington.

It was even mentioned that Hugh Gibson, American Minister to Brussels, would not be far away. Mr. Gibson headed the American delegation at the abortive naval conference in Geneva last year.

Incidentally, an opinion was expressed in authoritative quarters that the Franco-British agreement on military disarmament subsisted, regardless of what might happen to their naval understanding.

The French and British books are virtually identical, with the exception of the instructions to the Washington Ambassadors of France and Britain, each book giving, naturally, the instructions issued by the respective Governments, although fundamentally there is small divergence.

**Sought Formula Suitable to Us.**

The French blue book contains thirty-five exhibits and fills sixty-three printed pages.

The purpose of both books is to prove to world opinion that the understanding between London and Paris on naval limitation represents no selfish bargain to serve national ends, but a sincere effort to iron out the differences separating the English and the French views in order to promote the prospects of a naval agreement at Geneva.

The documents are filled with references to the American position, and declarations that it was desired to find a formula which America would accept. Emphasis is laid by the French n a statement that the Ambassador of Washington in Paris had accepted the proposal "on the condition that a general accord be reached on these bases by all the great naval powers, and notably the United States."

The first twelve documents of the French blue book review the naval discussions prior to the meeting of the Geneva conference of June, 1927, and bring into the limelight the opposing views of the French and British, the latter asking for a division of fighting ships into eleven categories, while the French wished one tonnage allotment for each nation, out of which each nation could build the ships it liked.

Document 13 contains excerpts from the address by Mr. Gibson at the close of the naval conference on Aug. 4, 1927, in which he advised the various Governments to consider, through diplomatic channels, a settlement of the differences which separated them.

Document 14 is the letter of instruction sent by M. Briand to Paul Claudel, the French Ambassador at Washington, on Dec. 31, 1927, calling attention to the compromise suggested some months before by France at the Geneva meeting of the Preparatory Disarmament Commission whereby warships would be divided into four classes, with a certain elasticity in the partition of cruisers and submarines, and asking him to try to obtain the American reaction to this plan and urging that the League must make progress in its disarmament work.

**Gibson's Speeches Quoted.**

M. Briand expressed the opinion that within the frame of these French propositions the tripartite conference at Geneva indicated there might be ground for an agreement.

Document 18 reports Mr. Gibson's speech of March 23, this year, at the Geneva preparatory meeting, in which the American Minister again advocated diplomatic efforts to settle differences among the naval nations on the limitation of cruisers.

The same day, as shown by Documents 16, 17, 19, 20, 21 and 22, the French and British delegates announced they had already begun negotiations to settle their differences. This referred largely to what is set

Continued on Page Twenty-two.

## Mussolini Gives His Royalties On Writings Here to Charity

ROME, Oct. 22 (AP).—Premier Mussolini has donated 100,000 lire (about $5,230), which he announced represented his royalties from his writings for American papers and magazines, to charitable works of the Fascist Party.

The money will be used to aid the vacation colonies for children at the seashore or in the mountains next Summer.

Augusto Turati, Secretary of the Fascisti, announced that the gift would be used for an important project connected with those charities.

## SEELY GETS YEAR AND FINE OF $500

### Sewer Engineer, Convicted With Connolly, Freed in $5,000 Bail Pending Appeal.

### PLEA FOR MERCY DENIED

### Court Says He Is Sorry for Defendant, but Cannot Show Discrimination.

Supreme Court Justice Arthur S. Tompkins sentenced Frederick Seely, former design engineer in the Queens Sewer Bureau, to one year in the New York Penitentiary and $500 fine yesterday in the Supreme Court in Long Island City. This was the same sentence that Justice Tompkins imposed upon former Borough President Maurice E. Connolly of Queens last week.

Like Connolly, Seely obtained a certificate of reasonable doubt from Supreme Court Justice Edward Riegelmann and thereby got his freedom on $5,000 bail pending appeal.

Seely asked for mercy when arraigned for sentence before Justice Tompkins.

"I want the Court to take into consideration," he said, "the fact that I spent half my life in the service of the city and the construction of public works. By reason of my conviction, my reputation is gone and my life is ruined. I will be unable in the future to earn a livelihood."

**"Cannot Show Discrimination."**

"I am very sorry for you, Mr. Seely," said Justice Tompkins, shaking his head, "but I cannot show any discrimination between you and Mr. Connolly."

Justice Tompkins then imposed the sentence while Seely stood with bowed head. The engineer's lips trembled and he shook his head in the negative when reporters asked him if he had anything to say while deputy sheriffs led him away.

Seely was taken back to the Queens County Jail, where he had been held without bail after his conviction last Wednesday. Two hours later he was freed from jail on Justice Riegelmann's writ of reasonable doubt. As in the case of Connolly, Emory R. Buckner, the special prosecutor in charge of the case, did not oppose the granting of the writ.

Mr. Buckner declined to comment on reports that Seely might turn State's evidence against Connolly and others before the Extraordinary Grand Jury which indicted Connolly and Seely and which will resume its work, Justice Tompkins announced yesterd..y, on Monday, Nov. 5.

Seely left jail in the automobile of Fred R. Curran, who was secretary to the late John M. Phillips, sewer pipe manufacturer, with whom Connolly and Seely were convicted of conspiracy to defraud the city in sewer contracts.

"I feel the sentence is too severe and I propose to appeal it to the highest court in order to vindicate my innocence," said Seely. "I am going to get down to business and try to get a job and earn my living in the meanwhile."

Dana Wallace, chief counsel for Seely, said:

"Seely isn't going to do any squealing, for there is nothing to squeal about."

**Motion for Re-Trial Denied.**

Wallace applied to Justice Tompkins for a new trial for Seely, but the motion, together with other motions in the engineer's behalf, was denied.

Connolly did not appear at his office in Long Island City yesterday. He was released from Welfare Island on $5,000 bail pending appeal last Saturday.

"He isn't worried," said his brother, Alderman John Connolly. "I saw him yesterday and he was cheerful and quite confident of victory in the end."

Henry H. Klein, attorney for the Queens taxpayers, who first brought the sewer scandal to public attention last Winter, said yesterday that he intended to press his demand that the city bring a civil action against Connolly, the Phillips estate and the Queens sewer contractors to recover the money of which the city was defrauded in the sewer contracts. He also said he intended to file a complaint with the Grievance Committee of the Queens Bar Association to disbar Connolly from the practice of law.



## 649 DISTRICTS SPLIT BY ELECTIONS BOARD; $35,000 FUND ASKED

### New Decision to Care for Huge City Registration Calls for Employing 400 Clerks.

### TWO RULINGS BY OTTINGER

### Backs Paper Ballots in Oneida County and Decides Those in Line at Closing May Vote.

### HARVEY AGAIN TO SEEK WRIT

### Petition for Mandamus to Compel Use of Machines in Queens Comes Up Tomorrow.

The Board of Elections changed its mind again yesterday and authorized the creation of 649 new election districts in the greater city to handle the unprecedented increase in the number of registered voters. Earlier in the day 650 new districts were authorized but it was found possible to reduce that number by one. Last Friday the board adopted a resolution authorizing 2,000 new districts, but cut the number to 705 the following day. Yesterday it was found that splitting up all districts containing more than 800 registered voters made it possible to get along with only 649.

Making public a list of the existing election districts to be divided under its latest ruling, the board sent to the Board of Estmate a request for $35,000 appropriation to pay for the services of the 400 clerks who will be needed to establish the new districts. These clerks will work not more than fifteen days at a daily wage of $7.50 for a twelve-hour day.

Of the 649 new districts 121 will be in Manhattan, 303 in Brooklyn, 89 in the Bronx, 132 in Queens and 4 in Richmond. The division will be made along geographical lines and the work of putting it into effect will start at once.

**Harvey in New Move.**

John Holley Clark Jr., counsel for Alderman George U. Harvey, Republican candidate for President of Queens, prepared yesterday a new petition for a Supreme Court writ of mandamus to compel the use of voting machines in Queens, which together with the Bronx and Richmond has been left by the Board of Elections to the use of paper ballots. The petition will be served on Assistant Corporation Counsel Hilly today and argued before Justice Ingraham tomorrow morning. Mr. Clark was unable yesterday to obtain the consent of Mr. Hilly to a rehearing on a similar petition which was denied by Justice Ingraham last Friday.

The motion for mandamus will be opposed by Mr. Hilly who is confident that it will be denied. Members of the Board of Elections, informed of a ruling yesterday by Attorney General Albert Ottinger, who held that the Oneida County board had the authority to restrict districts to paper ballots, although lacking power to order the use of both paper ballots and machines in the same district, declared that it sustained their action in this city.

In his petition Mr. Harvey asks that the Board of Elections be directed to arrange the districts to permit the use of voting machines in all of them; or to place a machine in each of the existing 619 districts in Queens; or to arrange that voting in all districts with more than 600 voters be by machine and in other districts, if necessary, by paper ballot. Mr. Clark said yesterday that he would carry the case to the highest State court if relief was denied tomorrow.

By its action the Board of Elections increased the number of election districts from 2,845 to 3,494, a gain of 22 per cent. The resolution provided for two voting machines in all districts in Manhattan and Brooklyn listing more than 650 and fewer than 800 voters, and two ballot boxes

Continued on Page Twelve.

## HE IS CONFIDENT OF VICTORY

### Tells Party Leaders the Only Danger to Success Is Overconfidence.

### BUSIEST DAY OF CAMPAIGN

### Assured That the State Is His by Chieftains at Breakfast—Greets Many Delegations.

### SPEAKS FOR STATE TICKET

### At Luncheon He Praises Aides for Patriotic Services—Spends Whole Day at Hotel.

Herbert Hoover confidently predicted his election yesterday. He said he had not the slightest doubt, if the present activity was continued, as to what the electorate of the nation would do on Nov. 6.

This optimistic forecast was made in the course of one of the busiest days of the campaign for him, in which he received the assurances of New York State and city leaders that he would capture the electoral vote of the Empire State in his battle against New York's own native son, Governor Alfred E. Smith.

Mr. Hoover first voiced his confidence in his campaign in a conference with newspapermen following his talks with the leaders of his campaign here. He reiterated it at a luncheon at which he was guest of honor and both times he said that only overconfidence could prevent the outcome which he expected.

**Grateful for Aides' Efforts.**

Mr. Hoover added to his luncheon address an expression of gratitude for the activity for him here by party workers and he lauded the labors of party organizations as contributing genuine patriotic services which were not to be considered as solely partisan. He urged the election of Alanson B. Houghton, ambassador to the Court of St. James's and Republican candidate for United States Senator, who was on the dais. He also called for the election of Albert Ottinger, Republican candidate for Governor.

Vice President Dawes, State Chairman H. Edmund Machold, Senator George H. Moses of the national campaign forces, and Louis Marshall, New York attorney, also spoke at the luncheon.

Mr. Marshall brought into his address the religious question, which he asserted had been aroused not by any party organization, but by the "idiosyncracies" of Southern Democrats. He also praised Mr. Hoover's immigration stand against the national origins test for a quota basis.

**Whole Day of Conferences.**

Mr. Hoover's day of activity began early and went on until late in the afternoon, when he retired to dine in privacy and obtain some rest before the main address at Madison Square Garden. All day long he received delegations of supporters and conferred with campaign backers.

The entire day was spent within the confines of the Waldorf, where he has established headquarters for his stay in the city. A steady stream of visitors passed into his private rooms on the third floor to assure him of the success of his candidacy, and when not occupied with these visitors he ventured forth to other parts of the hotel to greet various delegations.

The first event of the day brought the roseate reports of victory in New York. They came from the leaders

Continued on Page Four.

Times Wide World Photo.

HERBERT HOOVER AT MADISON SQUARE GARDEN.

The Republican Candidate Photographed Last Night as He Acknowledged the Cheers of the Throng That Jammed the Garden to Hear His Address.

## SMITH ARRANGES WHIRLWIND FINISH

### Will Open in Boston, Swing to Baltimore and Philadelphia and Wind Up Here.

### PROHIBITION MAIN TOPIC

### Nominee Also Will Discuss Labor, Foreign Affairs and Bureau Reorganization.

From a Staff Correspondent of The New York Times.

ALBANY, Oct. 22.—A spectacular drive that will give him opportunity to make the sort of whirlwind finish which he has had in mind from the beginning will conclude Governor Smith's campaign for the Presidency.

It will start in Boston Wednesday with a parade and a speech to be delivered to an audience of 30,000 in three halls linked by loud speakers. It will sweep down the Atlantic seaboard with an accompaniment of processions and expected demonstrations to Philadelphia and Baltimore and return through Newark to a final culmination in New York City.

It will bring forth other campaign notes not yet sounded, but its dominant refrain will be prohibition. The Governor has not given particular emphasis heretofore to his plea for modification of the Volstead act and the Eighteenth Amendment. He made one speech on the subject in Milwaukee. He touched upon it again at Nashville, Tenn., and at Chicago. In Omaha, Neb., he replied to a newspaper question by declaring that he did not consider it the foremost issue. Farm relief, if anything, was the topic to which he referred most frequently.

With the battleground shifted to the urban and industrial East a different emphasis will be required, although the Governor's announced opinion that no one individual issue overshadows the others will not be changed.

**Leaders Urge Prohibition Issue.**

The leaders and local candidates whose districts Governor Smith will enter, his party Chairman, John J. Raskob, and his own ideas of the campaign strategy demand that he hammer upon the prohibition question. There is no doubt here that he will do so. In some seventeen formal and informal speeches in the West and South he has urged his views on the matter only three times. In the six remaining addresses now on the schedule he is expected to stress them on every occasion.

Senator David I. Walsh of Massachusetts, who called upon the Governor today, and Thomas J. Spellacy, National Committeeman from Connecticut, who was a visitor yesterday, urged him to bring prohibition to the fore. Governor Albert C. Ritchie of Maryland and the Senators of his State have already given similar advice for his address in their State, and the sentiment of leaders in other States in the section is well known.

"What if you do repeat yourself? Dispense with the radio if you are afraid of taxing the patience of the national audience and give our people what they are waiting for—straight talks on prohibition," one of the Democratic leaders told the Presidential candidate.

When Governor Smith started his second campaign tour Mr. Raskob is understood to have expressed fear that the wet and dry issue was being submerged. His influence, too, is supposed to have been mustered to the side of the Eastern party chieftains. The population in their territory has been unanimously repre-

Continued on Page Sixteen.

## Mrs. Woodrow Wilson Home; Expects Gov. Smith to Win

Mrs. Woodrow Wilson returned yesterday from Europe on the Leviathan and said she was enthusiastic about Governor Smith and felt confident that he would be elected.

Mrs. Wilson added that she would not do any campaigning for the Democratic candidate and would not vote for him because she had no vote since she lived in the District of Columbia, but that if she had one to give it would certainly be cast for Governor Smith.

Mrs. Wilson was accompanied by Mrs. Bernard Baruch and her daughter, Miss Belle Baruch. The party was met at the pier by Mr. Baruch.

## DRAFT HOUGHTON TO AID HOOVER IN WEST

### The Senatorial Candidate's Own Drive to Halt for Talks in St. Louis and Milwaukee.

### GERMAN SUPPORT IS SOUGHT

### Change in Plans Is Made at the Personal Request of the Presidential Nominee.

Alanson B. Houghton, Republican candidate for United States Senator, is going to the Middle West to try to keep the so-called German vote in line for Herbert Hoover.

The Ambassador to the Court of St. James's at the personal request of the Republican Presidential candidate, will cut his own campaign here to two speeches in the final week of the election drive so that he can talk for the national ticket in St. Louis and Milwaukee.

Mr. Houghton, according to an announcement yesterday by H. Edmund Machold, Republican State Chairman, will speak in St. Louis on Friday night and in Milwaukee on Saturday night. He will return to New York Monday. On his return Mr. Houghton will speak once in New York City and once in some up-State city, not yet decided on. It was said he would ignore prohibition as an issue. He is expected to follow the program set forth in his speech of acceptance in which he stressed the tariff issue.

His supporters were reluctant to have him go out of the State with only two weeks left to election day, but the Ambassador put himself at the disposal of the Presidential candidate and announced himself ready to do whatever was desired.

As the first Ambassador to Germany after the World War his work attracted the favorable attention of the German-Americans in this country. This year Governor Smith, because of his stand on prohibition and other issues, had admittedly made big inroads in Republican territory in St. Louis and Wisconsin, where there is a big German-American voting population.

St. Louis is normally Republican while rural Missouri is Democratic, but this year the Governor is expected to get a big part of his support in the city, with Mr. Hoover running stronger than usual for a Republican in the rural districts. Wisconsin is being claimed by the Democrats and even the Republicans admit their chances are doubtful there due to the support of the Democratic nominee by many backers of the forces headed by Senator La Follette and Senator Blaine. Senator Blaine has declared for Governor Smith.



## OTTINGER PROMISES WATER-POWER PLAN

### Declares at Oswego He Will Call Experts to Speed Development in State.

### DEFENDS PROPOSED LEASE

### Under Its Provisions People Could Have Reclaimed Property, He Asserts.

Special to The New York Times.

OSWEGO, Oct. 22.—Attorney General Ottinger, Republican Gubernatorial candidate, charged his Democratic opponents here tonight with deliberate political misrepresentation of his position on State water power development.

"I propose when Governor, immediately after my election," he said, "to call together a non-partisan group of experts. I shall ask this committee to study this question of power development, to weigh the merits of the leasing plan, the merits of the so-called Water Power Authority plan and the merits of any other plan which may be suggested, and to report at the earliest possible date its conclusions and recommendations as to how the present tremendous waste of water power can be avoided and the people derive the benefits to which they are entitled from its development.

"The character, integrity and ability of those who I believe will accept the call to serve the State and its people in a matter of such vital importance should secure a plan that could be put into operation without further opposition. I will accept any plan that such a committee pronounces the best plan to secure what I propose—the immediate development of our water resources.

**Promises to Thwart Delay.**

"I am ready to make every sacrifice of opinion on detail to see to it that this 'white coal' is carried to every home and industry at the earliest possible moment, and so far as it is in my power I will thwart every carefully hidden effort to accomplish further delay."

Mr. Ottinger spoke before an audience which filled Robinson Auditorium here after having discussed prosperity, the tariff and national issues at meetings in Ogdensburg and Watertown during the day.

"There has been so much misunderstanding and misconstruction of views on the subject of water power," the Republican candidate said tonight, "that I am going to ask your indulgence while I state the actual facts. I am not exaggerating when I say that there has been a deliberate attempt to smear this issue with political paint so as to confuse the average man and woman. We have had words about water power for the last quarter of a century, but no power.

"The people today are justly tired of a do-nothing political expediency while our great water energy in this State continues to run unharnessed to the sea.

"It is possible to increase by nearly 3,960,000 horse power the energy produced in this State from water.

"While we have been talking instead of acting, manufacturing enterprises have been moving into the South, where low-priced power is offered. We must not only hold within our borders such concerns, but we must do the thing to attract new industry. If New York State is

Continued on Page Eighteen.



## SPECIFIES THREE ISSUES

### Attacks Farm Aid, Power and Dry Plans of His Opponent.

### STRIKES AT PATERNALISM

### Candidate Declares It Would Cripple Energies of People and Destroy Initiative.

### CHEERED FOR MANY MINUTES

### Throng Hails Mrs. Hoover Also—Dawes Calls Prosperity the Sole Campaign Issue.

Speaking to an immediate audience of about 22,000, and to a vastly greater number of radio listeners, Herbert Hoover, Republican nominee for President, declared last evening at Madison Square Garden that the policies advocated by Governor Smith, his Democratic opponent, for the solution of the prohibition, farm relief and electrical power problems, constituted State socialism. Such policies, he said, are an abandonment of the traditional American policy of private initiative in business under which the United States has become the most prosperous nation in the world.

It was Mr. Hoover's first speech in New York City since his nomination. His address was an appeal for the continued support of the business element in New York City and elsewhere, which has been an important factor in Republican success in past Presidential campaigns. Declaring himself opposed to the Government engaging in business, Mr. Hoover asserted that evils that might result from great private business units could be corrected by regulation, but indicated a belief that there should not be too much of that.

**Prosperity the Issue, Says Dawes.**

Vice President Charles G. Dawes, seconded Mr. Hoover's appeal to the business element by declaring that the issue of the campaign was the maintenance of prosperity. Mr. Dawes, who had been a receptive candidate for the nomination for President, asserted that a Republican national administration meant prosperity, and declared that a revision of the tariff by its enemies, the Democrats, instead of by its friends, the Republicans, would unsettle business confidence and destroy prosperity. Mr. Dawes declared that prohibition was not an issue and that, with both major parties pledged in their platforms to attempt to bring about farm relief, this could not become a major issue.

Mr. Hoover's speech at Madison Square Garden marked the climax of a busy day, passed almost entirely under the roof of the Waldorf. During the morning and afternoon Mr. Hoover conferred with the leading party chieftains and obtained from them assurances he would carry New York State. He received delegations of those who had aided him in relief work abroad and in the food administration here, foreign-born voters, theatrical folk, disabled veterans and members of the Hoover Service League. He was entertained at luncheon by Charles D. Hilles, National Committeeman; State Chairman H. Edmund Machold and Samuel S. Koenig, Chairman of the New York County Committee, and told the men and women County Chairmen and Vice Chairmen of the State that he had no doubt of his election.

**Cheered for Many Minutes.**

Mr. Hoover received an enthusiastic welcome in the home city of his opponent. There were two demonstrations for him at the meeting, the first of nine minutes' duration on his appearance on the platform and the second, which lasted twelve and a half minutes, when he rose to speak.

The first ovation was the more spontaneous. A roar went up when he appeared on the platform, accompanied by James R. Sheffield, former Ambassador to Mexico and Chairman of the meeting; his son, Allan Hoover, and George Akerson, his assistant. The cheers drowned out the sound of the bands, and the waving of thousands of American flags sent a ripple of color around the huge hall which, with its arena seats and balconies, resembles a stadium. Mr. Hoover, who had come from the Waldorf by automobile, smiled and waved his hand.

The number present was estimated by the Garden management as 22,000, and of these probably about two-fifths were women, a large fraction for a political meeting. It was noticeable during the cheering that the women seemed to be even more enthusiastic than the men.

There was another outburst of cheering for Mrs. Hoover, when Mr. Sheffield in his opening remarks

Continued on Page Three.

## Dry Agent Shot in Back in Chicago Court; Spectators Searched, but No Pistol Is Found

Special to The New York Times.

CHICAGO, Oct. 22.—Thomas Ryan, fifty-five-year-old veteran of the prohibition force, was shot in the back and seriously wounded this afternoon as he was standing in the court room of United States Commissioner Edwin H. Walker, waiting to testify in a liquor case.

Panic broke out among the forty persons in the court room as Ryan, tottering, shouted, "I'm shot!" and collapsed in the arms of Edward A. Fisher, Assistant United States District Attorney, who was sitting directly in front of the dry agent.

A systematic search of every one in the room was made without finding a weapon that had been discharged or any one toward whom suspicion might be directed.

The theory that the shot might have been fired by a man standing on the stone ledge outside the room was discarded by Patrick Roche, special intelligence agent of the Internal Revenue Bureau, because all of the windows had been closed, with the exception of one, which was opened six inches from the top. The course of the bullet was upward and could have come from there.

After three hours of investigation, Mr. Roche expressed the theory that the would-be murderer had been sitting behind Ryan, where he could command a clear view of each witness, and was waiting to kill Policeman Michael Shannon, who was to have been the next witness in a liquor case. The killer evidently had his pistol in his side pocket, and in getting it out to shoot Shannon, accidentally discharged it, according to Mr. Roche.

This theory was rejected by United States District Attorney Johnson.

"It was a cold-blooded attempt at murder," Mr. Johnson said.

Shannon was the policeman who shot and killed Silvio Colombo on Oct. 11 in a raid on a garage on East 115th Street, the battle following discovery of a still. Shannon was wounded in the forehead. Nick Beomsterboer was captured and it was during his trial that Ryan was shot.

"All the News That's Fit to Print."

# The New York Times.

LATE EDITION 5:30 A.M. WEATHER—Fair today; cloudy tomorrow.



VOL. LXXVIII....No. 25,855. NEW YORK, WEDNESDAY, NOVEMBER 7, 1928. TWO CENTS In Greater New York | THREE CENTS Within 200 Miles | FOUR CENTS Elsewhere in the U. S.

# HOOVER WINS 407 TO 69; DOUBTFUL 55; SMITH LOSES STATE; SOUTH BROKEN; ROOSEVELT IS ELECTED GOVERNOR

## HOOVER CARRIES ILLINOIS, SWEEPING IN THE STATE TICKET

### Smith Wins in Chicago, but His Republican Rival Gets Big Down-State Vote.

### IOWA STRONG FOR HOOVER

### Nebraska Puts Republican in Lead and His Victory Seems Certain.

### MICHIGAN ALSO REPUBLICAN

### Hoover Sweeps Ohio by a Big Majority—Entire State Ticket Elected.

*Special to The New York Times.*

CHICAGO, Nov. 6.—Illinois went Republican today. Herbert Hoover and the State ticket, headed by Louis L. Emmerson, candidate for Governor, and Otis F. Glenn, nominee for United States Senator, won by such large figures in down-State territory that close battles over some of the places in Cook County were eliminated.

Although he apparently lost Chicago to Governor Smith, incomplete returns indicated that Hoover had carried Cook County, which was counted upon by the Democrats as certain for their entire ticket.

The figures received as this is written forecast a Smith victory in Chicago by about 40,000 and informal reports from the suburbs of the county promised a Republican lead of 75,000.

The vote of 3,208 precincts out of 6,942, including 1,816 from Cook County, gave Hoover 741,167; Smith 604,811. The Republican nominee for President apparently won the State by about 400,000.

Emmerson and his fellow contestants for State executive office apparently fell considerably behind Hoover both in Cook County and down-State, but all apparently were safe on the face of the incomplete figures.

**Close Race for Senatorship.**

The closest race of all was that for United States Senator which the first reports indicated might be a neck and neck race because of the way that Anton J. Cermak, the "wet" Democrat ran ahead of Governor Smith in Chicago. The first big batch of city precincts to be heard from promised him a Chicago lead of from 250,000 to 275,000.

It was thought that Glenn might not be able to overcome this in the down-State territory because the figures on the Governorship which had been received more fully did not indicate that Emmerson would carry down-State by quite that big a margin. But when the outside counties began to report the returns forecast a margin for Glenn outside Chicago in excess of 350,000.

Cermak was the only Democrat who leaped ahead of his national ticket in Chicago. Floyd E. Thompson, Democratic gubernatorial entry, was allowed by his party to trail Governor Smith and also Thomas J. Courtney, nominee for Attorney General against Oscar E. Carlstrom, the Republican who now holds that office.

The returns on these offices were far ahead of those for the rest of the offices on the State ticket, but Hoover's lead and the leads of Glenn, Emmerson and Carlstrom were taken as proof that all the Republican entries had carried the State.

On incomplete returns Judge William J. Lindsay, Democrat, was leading Judge John A. Swanson, Republican, for State's Attorney, the centre of the battle over Cook County offices.

In the battle over lucrative berths on the Board of Review, Thomas D. Nash, Democrat, is leading Edward R. Litsinger, Republican.

**Much Splitting of Votes.**

Scattering precinct figures from all the wards, indicate a day of prodigious vote splitting.

The Crowe-Thompsonites whetted their axes for the Dineen Republican candidates, and vice versa. Indications are that if Judge Lindsay maintains his early lead, the entire Democratic ticket may win. Figures on other candidates are slow in arriving but they indicate that the Crowe-Thompson machine was caught in another avalanche, similar to the one that struck it in the popular uprising at the April primaries.

In the fight for drainage trusteeships, where the Crowe-Thompson

Continued on Page Four.

## U.S. Senators Elected

**REPUBLICAN—18**

California.......*H. W. Johnson
Connecticut.......‡F. C. Walcott
Delaware..John G. Townsend Jr.
Idaho.......§John Thomas
Illinois.......§Otis F. Glenn
Indiana.......*A. R. Robinson
Maine.......¶Frederick Hale
Maryland...‡P. L. Goldsborough
Michigan....†A. H. Vanderberg
Nebraska.....*Robert B. Howell
New Jersey...‡Hamilton F. Kean
North Dakota..*Lynn J. Frazier
Ohio.......*Simeon D. Fess
Ohio.......§T. E. Burton
Pennsylvania....*David A. Reed
Rhode Island......‡Felix Hebert
Vermont.......*Frank L. Greene
Wisconsin..*R. M. La Follette Jr.

**DEMOCRATS—9**

Arizona.....*Henry F. Ashurst
Florida.......*Park Trammell
Massachusetts..*David I. Walsh
Mississippi.....*H. D. Stephens
New York.......*R. S. Copeland
Tennessee...*Kenneth McKellar
Texas.......‡Tom Connally
Utah.......*William H. King
Virginia.........*C. A. Swanson

**FARMER-LABORITE—1**

Minnesota...*Henrik Shipstead

**IN DOUBT—7**

Missouri — New Mexico
Montana — Washington
Nevada — West Virginia
Wyoming

*Re-elected for full term ending March 3, 1935.
†Elected for both long and short terms.
‡Elected for full term ending March 3, 1935.
¶Re-elected Sept. 10, 1928, for full term ending March 3, 1935.
§Elected for short term ending March 3, 1933.

## BAY STATE IS CLOSE, WITH SMITH AHEAD

### Walsh, Democrat, Re-elected to Senate and Cole Is in Front for Governor.

### SMITH WINS RHODE ISLAND

### But State Ticket Goes Republican—Other New England States for Hoover.

*Special to The New York Times.*

BOSTON, Mass., Nov. 7.—At 4:30 o'clock this morning, after one of the liveliest election nights ever known in Massachusetts, and when it appeared that the Democrats had swept the State, there was a possibility that Herbert Hoover, though trailing Governor Smith, might receive the eighteen electoral votes of this State.

At the same time there was a probability that the fianl returns would show Frank G. Allen winner of the Gubernatorial contest over his Democratic opponent, General Charles H. Cole, despite the latter's lead.

Senator David D. Walsh, Democrat, running 10,000 votes ahead of Governor Smith, was clearly re-elected over Benjamin Loring Young, Republican.

**Smith Carries Textile Cities.**

From early in the evening, when Hoover had built up a substantial lead, the returns from Boston and some textile centres pulled him down and pushed Smith out in front.

Then followed a see-sawing back and forth, with Smith slowly forging ahead in the early morning hours, largely as a result of 10,000-vote margins which were given to him in Fall River and Lowell, 4,000 in New Bedford, 5,000 in Salem, 7,000 in Holyoke, and lesser votes in other cities.

For President, 952 precincts out of the 1,605 in the State gave Hoover 405,125, Smith 426,509.

For Governor, 848 precincts, including 300 of the 339 in Boston, gave Allen (R.) 346,495, Cole (D.) 351,091.

For Senator, 848 precincts gave Young (R.) 312,886, Walsh (D.) 321,002.

Unofficial Boston figures for 310 precincts out of 339 gave Hoover

Continued on Page Two.

## NEW JERSEY GIVES REPUBLICAN SLATE A HEAVY MAJORITY

### Incomplete Figures for State Show Hoover Leads Smith by 116,944.

### LARSON AHEAD OF DILL

### Victory for Republican by 166,340 Is Indicated in Gubernatorial Race.

### KEAN BEATING EDWARDS

### Strong Republican Showing Is a Damaging Blow to Prestige of Hague as Leader.

Herbert Hoover's indicated plurality in New Jersey was 309,420 early this morning when the tabulation of returns from 1,102 of the 2,920 districts gave Hoover 303,792 and Smith 186,848. In the metropolitan district of New Jersey the Republican and Democratic candidates ran a close race.

In Essex County, which includes Newark, tabulation of the vote in 150 of the 481 districts showed that it stood, Hoover, 39,122; Smith, 31,810.

Hamilton F. Kean was leading Senator Edward I. Edwards, Democrat, by 91,021 in 1,102 districts and his indicated plurality was 239,440.

**Larson in the Lead.**

In the Gubernatorial contest the returns from 1,102 districts gave Larson 269,391 and Dill 205,692, giving Larson, Republican, a lead of 63,699 and an indicated plurality of 166,340.

In 75 of 506 districts in Hudson County, the stronghold of Mayor Frank Hague, the vote was: Hoover 9,106, Smith, 18,302, Kean 10,204, Edwards 18,896, Larson 10,302, Dill 18,107.

Increasing Republican pluralities reported from the counties of Southern New Jersey were not offset by expected Democratic gains in the metropolitan area.

Republican candidates for Congress were leading their opponents in all counties except Hudson, and Republican candidates for the Assembly were reported generally in the lead in all but counties which are now represented in the Assembly by Democrats.

While the Republicans of Camden County were celebrating the success of their State and national tickets there, State Senator Joseph H. Forsyth was reported to be dying from influenza at his home at Haddonfield. He was stricken several days ago. He was elected in 1926 for three years.

Reports from Trenton were to the effect that a plurality of from 150,000 to 200,000 for Hoover was indicated by the early returns. According to The Associated Press fifty-six districts out of 2,920 in strongly Republican territory gave Hoover a lead of 5,456 over Smith. The vote was Hoover 9,078 and Smith 3,622.

The first 12,000 ballots tabulated in Jersey City gave Smith 7,761 votes, Hoover 4,024, Edwards 7,405, Kean 4,037, Dill 7,276, Larson 4,320.

Forty-five districts reported in the United States Senatorial and Gubernatorial races. These gave Kean, Republican, 7,080; Senator Edwards, Democrat, 3,217. The Governorship figures were William L. Dill, Democrat, 3,580; Morgan F. Larson, Republican, 6,989.

The indicated heavy pluralities of the Republican candidates for United States Senator and Governor were a damaging blow to the prestige of Mayor Hague, Vice Chairman of the Democratic National Committee, whose Democratic stronghold in Hudson has been sufficiently powerful in three Gubernatorial elections to stem the Republican tide in other sections of New Jersey and send Democratic candidates to the Governor's Mansion and to the Senate.

**Fight in Hudson County.**

The fight of Mayor Frank Hague of Jersey City, Democratic leader in Hudson County, was responsible for the action of election officials in striking the names of apporximately 29,000 voters from the enrollment lists. It was reported that several thousand voters had been disfranchised in Hudson County because of inability of the Commissioner of Registration to deal with the situation resulting from the County Board of Election's ruling at the eleventh hour. Election officials re-

Continued on Page Eighteen.

## Gov. Smith's Message to Mr. Hoover

Governor Smith sent the following telegram just after midnight to his successful rival:

*Hon. Herbert Hoover,*
*Palo Alto, Cal.:*

I congratulate you heartily on your victory, and extend to you my sincere good wishes for your health and happiness and for the success of your Administration.

ALFRED E. SMITH.

## Electoral Vote

**HOOVER.**

| State | Votes | State | Votes |
|---|---|---|---|
| Arizona | 3 | Nevada | 3 |
| California | 13 | New Hampshire | 4 |
| Colorado | 6 | New Jersey | 14 |
| Connecticut | 7 | New Mexico | 3 |
| Delaware | 3 | New York | 45 |
| Florida | 6 | Ohio | 24 |
| Idaho | 4 | Oklahoma | 10 |
| Illinois | 29 | Oregon | 5 |
| Indiana | 15 | Pennsylvania | 38 |
| Iowa | 13 | South Dakota | 5 |
| Kansas | 10 | Tennessee | 12 |
| Kentucky | 13 | Utah | 4 |
| Maine | 6 | Vermont | 4 |
| Maryland | 8 | Virginia | 12 |
| Michigan | 15 | Washington | 7 |
| Minnesota | 12 | West Virginia | 8 |
| Missouri | 18 | Wisconsin | 13 |
| Montana | 4 | Wyoming | 3 |
| Nebraska | 8 | | |
| | | Total | 407 |

**SMITH.**

| State | Votes | State | Votes |
|---|---|---|---|
| Alabama | 12 | Mississippi | 10 |
| Arkansas | 9 | Rhode Island | 5 |
| Georgia | 14 | South Carolina | 9 |
| Louisiana | 10 | Total | 69 |

**DOUBTFUL.**

| State | Votes | State | Votes |
|---|---|---|---|
| Massachusetts | 18 | Texas | 20 |
| North Carolina | 12 | Total | 55 |
| North Dakota | 5 | | |

**Total number of votes in Electoral College, 531; necessary to a choice, 266.**

## HOOVER BREAKS THE SOLID SOUTH

### He Carries Virginia and Probably Florida and North Carolina—Leads in Texas Also.

*Special to The New York Times.*

RICHMOND, Va., Nov. 6.—Herbert Hoover has carried the Old Dominion and broken the Solid South.

State Democratic headquarters authorized the statement before midnight:

"he unofficial returns indicate that Virginia has gone for Hoover."

At a late hour he had obtained a 21,000 lead over Governor Smith, with two-thirds of the State polled. His plurality had been steadily mounting from the start.

The totals in 1,429 precincts out of 1,665 were: Hoover, 145,641; Smith, 124,520.

Fifteen of forty precincts in Richmond gave Hoover 2,253 and Smith 2,391.

Danville has gone for Hoover. It is a Ku Klux Klan stronghold, but Democrats were as thoroughly organized there as anywhere in the State.

Hoover, as expected, polled heavy votes in the first and second districts while Smith showed great strength in the fourth.

Only in the ninth district did the returns look normal. There were fewer Democratic defections than in other parts of the State, and Hoover and Smith were running neck and neck.

**Hoover Leads in Texas.**

DALLAS, Texas, Nov. 6 (AP).—The possibility that a Republican Presidential candidate might carry Texas for the first time in history loomed late tonight as Herbert Hoover, for the third time during the tabulation of the vote, went into the lead.

The 11 o'clock tabulation of the Texas Election Bureau showed the Republican ahead by 2,355 votes, with more than half of the ballots counted. It was the largest lead either candidate had gained in the nip and tuck race. Hoover's total, as computed by the bureau, was 208,415, Smith's 205,860. Later a count of 214 counties out of 253, four

Continued on Page Two.

## CITY GIVES SMITH 430,000 MAJORITY

### Incomplete Count Also Indicates Like Lead for Roosevelt for Governor.

Governor Smith carried New York City by about 430,000 plurality over Mr. Hoover, or about 88,000 less than the plurality he received over Theodore Roosevelt in 1924, which was the largest plurality the city gave him in any of his Gubernatorial campaigns.

With only 28 out of the 3,493 election districts of the city missing, Smith had 1,106,524 against 680,074 for Hoover, a plurality of 426,450. Norman Thomas, Socialist candidate, received less than 50,000 in the city.

Franklin D. Roosevelt, Democratic candidate for Governor, ran behind Smith in the city. With 90 districts missing, Roosevelt had 1,087,418 against 699,441 for his Republican opponent, Attorney General Albert Ottinger, a plurality of 387,977.

Herbert H. Lehman, Democratic candidate for Lieutenant Governor, and United States Senator Royal S. Copeland, Democratic candidate for re-election to the Senate, ran ahead of their ticket in the city.

**Lehman Has Big Lead.**

With 193 districts missing, Lehman received 1,106,086 votes, against 614,241 for Mr. Lockwood, his Republican opponent, a plurality of 491,847.

With 668 districts missing, Copeland had 958,401 to 498,699 for Alanson B. Houghton, former Ambassador to Germany and Great Britain, the Republican candidate, a plurality of 459,702 for Copeland.

Albert Conway, Democratic candidate for Attorney General, and Maurice S. Tremaine, Democratic candidate for re-election as State Controller, also ran ahead of Smith in the city. With 382 districts missing, Conway had 1,020,620 votes against 564,486 for Hamilton Ward, Republican, a plurality of 456,134. With 286 districts missing, Tremaine had 1,056,027, against 568,380 for

Continued on Page Seven.

## ROOSEVELT IS VICTOR BY SLIM PLURALITY; COPELAND ALSO WINS

### Democratic Nominee Captures Governorship by Margin Indicated to Be 40,000.

### SENATOR IN BY 56,000

### Re-elected Over Houghton After Running Up Lead of 523,000 in the City.

### LEAVES SMITH FAR BEHIND

### Polls 90,000 More Votes Than the Governor—Lehman, Conway and Tremaine Leading.

Franklin D. Roosevelt, Democrat, defeated Attorney General Albert Ottinger, Republican, for the Governorship of New York State, on the basis of returns from 7,718 election districts out of the 8,267 in the State. A plurality of about 40,000 for Mr. Roosevelt was indicated on these figures, and it is possible that this plurality might be cut somewhat by the returns from the missing districts but not enough to give Mr. Ottinger the State.

Senator Royal S. Copeland, candidate for re-election on the Democratic ticket, apparently had won from former Ambassador Alanson B. Houghton by an indicated plurality of about 56,000. Senator Copeland ran surprisingly well in New York City, where his plurality seems likely to reach 523,000, or about 90,000 more than the plurality received by Governor Smith, heretofore regarded as the strongest candidate in the city, personally.

The victories for Mr. Roosevelt and Senator Copeland went some distance toward assuaging the local Democrats for Governor Smith's defeat. Governor Smith's indicated plurality in New York City was about 430,000, and his defeat in the State by about 125,000 was indicated.

**Roosevelt Lead 68,568.**

Mr. Roosevelt had an actual lead of 68,568, with 549 out of the 8,267 election districts in the State missing, the vote being Roosevelt 2,073,372 and Ottinger 1,954,754.

Outside New York City 4,298 election districts out of 4,774 gave Roosevelt 929,953 and Ottinger 1,257,002, an actual plurality of 327,049 and an indicated up-State plurality for Ottinger of 367,598.

In New York City 3,400 out of 3,393 election districts gave Roosevelt 1,093,369 and Ottinger 697,752, an actual plurality of 395,617 and an indicated plurality of 405,188.

Mr. Roosevelt ran ahead of Governor Smith in virtually every county up-State, while Mr. Ottinger cut into the Democratic vote somewhat in New York City, but not as much as expected.

Senator Copeland's run in New York City was surprising. In 3,144 out of the 3,493 election districts in the city he received 1,033,048 and Houghton 561,539, an actual plurality of 471,509 and an indicated plurality of 523,950.

To offset this tremendous plurality, seemingly the largest ever received in the city by any candidate, Mr. Houghton in 3,645 out of 4,774 Up-state election districts received 1,069,464 to 713,173 for Senator Copeland. This is an actual plurality of 356,291 and an indicated plurality of 467,852 for Mr. Houghton Upstate.

The delay in the returns from about a thousand up-State districts led Mr. Roosevelt to charge early this morning that there were indications which led him to suspect fraud up-State. He announced that Edward S. Dore, Chairman of the Law Committee of the Democratic State Committee, would leave for up-State this morning with a hundred lawyers ready to resist or prevent any fraud which might be attempted.

"Owing to the extreme delay with which about 1,000 districts up-State are sending in election returns, the Democratic State Committee has become convinced that fraud is being committed in an attempt to elect Ottinger as Governor of the State of New York," Mr. Roosevelt said.

"Accordingly, Mr. Dore, John Godfrey Saxe and Maurice Bloch, minority leader of the Assembly, are leaving New York City on the Empire State Express this (Wednesday) morning for up-State cities, together with a staff of 100 lawyers to uncover such frauds as have been com-

Continued on Page Two.

## HOOVER CARRIES NEW YORK BY 125,000

### Republican Nominee Captures New Jersey, Takes Wisconsin; Breaks Solid South, Winning Virginia, Florida

### GAINING IN NORTH CAROLINA AND BAY STATE

### Most of Farm Belt in Republican Column in Record-Breaking Vote—Kentucky, Missouri and Tennessee Lost to Democrats.

Voting in unprecedented numbers, a myriad of American citizens yesterday chose Herbert Hoover of California for President of the United States and Charles Curtis of Kansas for Vice President.

How pronounced is the victory of these candidates of the Republican Party over their Democratic competitors, Governor Alfred E. Smith of New York, nominee for President, and Joseph T. Robinson of Arkansas, the Vice Presidential nominee, cannot be determined until the stupendous task of counting 40,000,000 or more votes is completed, but a Republican landslide took place at the polls, and it will be reflected in a heavy Hoover-Curtis majority of the 531 ballots in the Electoral College.

**400 Electoral Votes for Hoover**

Mr. Hoover is assured of more than 400 electoral votes. It is probable that his majority will increase as further returns are received. He has broken the traditionally Democratic Solid South. He has carried Virginia and returns from Florida indicate that he has won in that State. His tally in the Electoral College may go as high as 444 votes if North Carolina, North Dakota and Texas, which are very close, are added to his strength, or even to the stupendous total of 462, if the count now proceeding in Massachusetts turns in his favor.

Such an outcome would give Mr. Hoover a majority of 397 electoral votes over Governor Smith. It is already apparent that no Presidential candidate of any major party has been beaten as badly as Governor Smith, with the exception of William H. Taft, who got only 8 votes in the Electoral College in his contest for re-election against Woodrow Wilson and Theodore Roosevelt.

According to the latest returns received from Massachusetts, North Carolina, North Dakota and Texas, these States are still in the doubtful column either by reason of inadequate returns or on account of the closeness of contests as the count proceeds, and while Governor Smith may be shown to have carried some of them, his tally of electoral votes may not exceed seventy.

**New York Spells Smith's Doom.**

Governor Smith's hope of victory began to fade within a few hours after the polls closed in New York State when it was indicated that he had carried New York City, his great stronghold, by less than 450,000, which was much short of the estimate of his managers. As returns began to roll in from up-State it became apparent that the Hoover plurality in that strong Republican area would materially overcome the showing for Governor Smith in New York City, with the prospect that the Republican nominee would carry the State by a lead in the neighborhood of 125,000.

With New York's forty-five electoral votes placed in the Hoover column it became merely a matter of waiting until the full returns determined what the Republican candidates' majority will be in the Electoral College. The tremendous onsweep of the Hoover following was emphasized when State after State in which the Democrats had placed hope of victory went over into the Republican camp.

New Jersey was carried by the Republican national ticket by a heavy majority. Maryland followed suit. Late returns show that Hoover also took Missouri. Of other border States, he captured Kentucky and Oklahoma. Minnesota, which the Smith management was also hopeful of carrying on account of the defection among Republican voters because of Mr. Hoover's attitude on the McNary-Haugen bill, gave him a heavy plurality.

**Smith States Only in South.**

As for Governor Smith, there is no assurance that he has carried any State outside of the South. With the results in Florida and Texas still in doubt he seems to be certain of having carried only Alabama, Georgia, Louisiana, Mississippi and South Carolina. In the early morning hours late returns had Hoover forging ahead even in North Carolina. Tennessee was conceded to the Republican candidate.

His victories in Alabama and North Carolina are a set back for Senator J. Thomas Heflin and Senator Furnifold M. Simmons, who deserted their party allegiances to oppose him, Simmons on the ground of Governor Smith's anti-prohibition policy and Senator Heflin for the openly stated reason that Governor Smith was a Catholic.

In the early morning hours returns from Wisconsin indicated that the portion of the State outside of Milwaukee had voted so heavily for Hoover that Smith's lead in the metropolis made famous by beer had been overcome and that the State's thirteen electoral votes would be added to the steadily mounting Hoover column.

It was after 4 o'clock this morning before virtually complete returns from Rhode Island showed that Smith had carried Rhode Island, the only State outside the Solid South that can with certainty be placed to his credit. He seems to have carried it by a small majority, probably not exceeding 2,000.

Maine, New Hampshire, Vermont and Connecticut joined the Republican procession. At an early hour this morning the prospect was that where the eighteen electoral votes of Massachusetts would go could not be made certain until late today.

**Republican Congress Assured.**

The victory for the Republican national ticket is accompanied by the assurance that, as President, Mr. Hoover will have the support of a Congress controlled by those of his own party. While returns are incomplete, the indications are that the Republican majority in the House of Representatives

HERBERT C. HOOVER

"All the News That's Fit to Print."

# The New York Times.

THE WEATHER
Rain today, colder at night; fair Wednesday.
Temperature yesterday—Max., 50; min., 34.
U. S. Weather Forecast—For details see Page 52.

VOL. LXXVIII....No. 25,973. NEW YORK, TUESDAY, MARCH 5, 1929. TWO CENTS in Greater New York | THREE CENTS Within 200 Miles | FOUR CENTS Elsewhere Except 7th and 8th Postal Zones



# HOOVER INAUGURATED BEFORE THRONG OF 50,000 IN RAIN; PLEDGES EFFORT TO ENFORCE LAWS, AID WORLD PEACE; PARTING WITH COOLIDGE IS CLIMAX OF DAY'S CEREMONY

## MEXICAN REBELS WIN VITAL BORDER CITIES; NOW CLAIM 9 STATES

### Portes Gil, Preparing to Quell Revolt, Ch[illegible] Leaders Aim at Military Dictatorship.

### CALLES WILL HEAD AN ARMY

### Will Fight Sonora Insurgents—Rebels Name Escobar Chief and End Religious Laws.

### BID FOR CATHOLIC AID SEEN

### 5,000 Rebels Reported Marching on Guadalajara—Hoover Tackles Issue Today—Securities Fall Here.

**Four-Hour Battle Is Reported, With 5,000 Federals Engaged**

By The Associated Press.

EL PASO, Texas, March 4.—Five thousand Federal troops under the command of General Francisco Urbalege engaged a large body of revolutionists in a pitched battle that lasted four hours this afternoon, according to reports received here tonight.

An unconfirmed report stated that one Mexican Federal soldier and two rebels had been killed in a skirmish at Cannea, Sonora.

MEXICO CITY, March 4 (11 P. M.) (AP).—The government announced tonight that no armed clash had occurred with forces of the rebel armies during the last twenty-four hours.

Special Cable to THE NEW YORK TIMES.

MEXICO CITY, March 4.—President Emilio Portes Gil acknowledged in a statement today that three of the nine States claimed by rebel leaders in revolt had joined the revolutionary movement. The rising in Sonora and Vera Cruz already had been admitted and today's statement added Coahuila, with the announcement that General J. Gonzalo Escobar, commander of the Federal troops in that State, had gone over to the rebels.

Former President Plutarco Elias Calles, who was appointed Secretary of War yesterday, will leave the capital Wednesday to take command of the Federal forces in Sonora. Meanwhile troops are being mobilized to fight the rebels.

The statement issued by President Portes Gil reads as follows:

"I consider the rebel movement headed by Generals Jesus M. Aguirre of the State of Vera Cruz; Francisco R. Manzo of Sonora and J. Gonzalo Escobar in Laguna is the most unjustified of all those which have occurred within the republic in recent times.

These unfaithful leaders, not satisfied with the rank which they enjoy and abusing the confidence placed in them, taking advantage of the resources which the nation placed in their hands for the purpose of safeguarding national institutions, and taking advantage of futile excuses, declared themselves in open rebellion, assuredly with the purpose of establishing a military dictatorship within the Republic.

"No program, no noble ideas have these military leaders presented in the declarations which they issued in starting their movements. In their attitude there is seen nothing more than the idea of personal gain.

"Fortunately, the major portion of the army loyally responded to the call to sustain our institutions. The entire nation, by means of various organizations, has disapproved energetically of the shameful uprising for which under no circumstances can the Mexican nation be held responsible.

"The nation will defend its institutions.

"EMILIO PORTES GIL."

**Troops Are Mobilized.**

The only evidence here that there is any revolt in the republic is the unwonted movement of columns of troops throughout the day. No secret is being made of this movement, the men marching through the main thoroughfares that lead toward the railway stations. All troops are in campaign kit and well equipped.

The entire city is calm. The average man in the street tonight was just awaiting what news Presidential headquarters might give out before forming opinions as to what might

Continued on Page Eleven.



**Mexican Leader in Revolt Specifies Its Objectives**

*In response to a cable inquiry asking him for a statement as to the present situation in Vera Cruz and as to the aims of the revolutionists, General Jesus M. Aguirre, in command of the troops which have seized the Mexican seaport, sent this reply:*

By Cable to the Editor of THE NEW YORK TIMES. [Translation].

VERA CRUZ, Mexico, March 4.—The movement which began the day before yesterday against the Federal Government has the support of the troops of this district, of the navy of the Gulf, under the command of Commodore Hiram Hernandez, and of numerous groups of Agrarians and of the people in general.

No arrests have been made and the authorities of the State, as well as the local authorities, continue in their posts.

The movement is supported by forces in the States of Sonora, Sinaloa, Chihuahua, Durango, Coahuila, as well as by large contingents from the States of Jalisco, Michoacan, Colima and Guanajuato. Minor movements have also sprung up all over the republic.

The movement has for its purpose the overthrow of the Federal Government because of its endeavor to impose [upon the country] the unpopular candidate Ortiz Rubio. We want effective suffrage and a popular and earnest government that will respect all of the liberties of the people.

(Signed) JESUS M. AGUIRRE,
General of Division.

## DEBT EXPERTS AGREE TO YOUNG PROPOSAL

### They Will Seek Plan to Set Up New International Body to Replace Reparation Board.

### TO HANDLE REICH PAYMENTS

### Project Would Make Indemnity Business Matter—Paris Subcommittees to Collaborate.

Special Cable to THE NEW YORK TIMES.

PARIS, March 4.—Adoption of a proposal by the chairman, Owen D. Young, that the Experts' Conference direct its efforts toward the creation of a central organism in the form of an international corporate body which would take the place of the Reparation Commission and the Dawes Plan organization was the principal act of the plenary session today, which lasted less than an hour.

The reports from the three subcommittees were heard and approved and it was decided that each committee would continue its labors in the light of Mr. Young's proposal, and that their work be correlated in a general recommendation to be submitted to another plenary session on Wednesday.

**Respite For Germans.**

Until then there will be only informal meetings and the hour when the Germans must face the question of the amounts and the number of the annuities they must pay was thus once more postponed.

Approval of Mr. Young's motion signified, however, that the experts had progressed sufficiently to obtain agreement on a general method by which they purpose to deal with the reparations problem. Summarized by a member of the committee, this method is "to treat reparations as an international commercial question in an international way."

The functions of the new body which would supersede the Dawes organizations and as far as possible remove the question from the atmosphere of the World War would be fourfold: First, receiving and disbursing all Germany's reparation annuities; second, handling all deliveries in kind; third, arranging all details with regard to the proposed commercialization and mobilization of German payments; fourth, executing all functions relating to protection in case of any delays in conditional annuities.

The probability is that the international organism would be governed by a board of directors representing all the countries interested, whose chairman would be selected as the most capable international banker or expert available regardless of nationality. He might be an American though from an authoritative source

Continued on Page Twenty-four.

## ADDRESS BACKS DRY LAW

### President Declares the Violators' Activities Must Be Stopped.

### PLANS FOR COURT REFORM

### Commission Will Be Named to Devise Ways to Strengthen Criminal Procedure.

### STRESSES PARTY PROMISES

### Executive Says Tariff Should Be Altered to Aid Farmers, Labor and Business.

By JAMES A. HAGERTY.

*Special to The New York Times.*

WASHINGTON, March 4.—A pledge for a more vigorous enforcement of the Eighteenth Amendment and a promise that his administration would do all in its power to advance the cause of world peace were among the outstanding features of President Hoover's address.

The President made formal announcement of his intention to appoint a national commission to investigate the Federal System of criminal justice, including the method of prohibition enforcement and the causes of abuses under it, with the purpose of making recommendations for the reorganization of the Federal laws and court procedure.

Mr. Hoover omitted from his address his suggestion for the transfer of a large part of the prohibition enforcement activities from the Treasury Department to the Department of Justice, as an essential step for a more effective enforcement organization. This suggestion was contained in the advance copy of his speech given to the press.

Some confusion resulted from this omission, but it was stated by members of the President's staff that the paragraph referring to the proposed transfer was omitted inadvertently. The President, it was said, stood by every statement in the text of the speech given to the press.

The paragraph omitted reads as follows:

"In the meantime, it is essential that a large part of the enforcement activities be transferred from the Treasury Department to the Department of Justice as a beginning of more effective organization."

Mr. Hoover expressed belief that the increase of crime and the decrease of confidence in rigid and speedy justice were due only in part to the additional burdens imposed upon the Federal judicial system by prohibition. He declared that steps toward reform, reorganization and strengthening of the system, both civil and criminal, should not be delayed.

**Appeals for Cooperation.**

The President attributed the abuses which he admitted had grown up under prohibition, as due in part to the failure of some of the States to accept their share of responsibility for concurrent enforcement by passing State prohibition enforcement acts and to the failure of many State and local officials to accept the obligations of their oath of office to enforce the law.

Saying that criminals would have no opportunity to deal in illegal liquor if large numbers of otherwise law-abiding citizens did not purchase it from them, President Hoover declared that the success of the government in enforcing law depended upon the support of the citizens, and he appealed to them to aid in stamping out outlawry and crime by refusing to participate in illegal transactions.

The whole system of self-government would crumble if officials chose what laws they would support, said Mr. Hoover. He asserted that the worst evil of disregard for some law was that it destroyed respect for all law. He added that, if citizens did not like a law, it still was their duty to discourage its violation, but that they still had a right to work openly for its repeal.

Mr. Hoover indicated that so far as it lay in the power of the Federal Government there would be short shrift during his administration for the bootlegger and dealer in forbidden beverages.

"To those of criminal mind there can be no appeal but vigorous enforcement of the law," he said. "Fortunately they are but a small percentage of our people. Their activities must be stopped."

In his discussion of world peace Mr. Hoover praised the Kellogg-Briand treaty for the renunciation of war and declared that as an in-

Continued on Page Six.



**Roosevelt Sends Greeting Of New York to Hoover**

*Special to The New York Times.*

ALBANY, March 4.—Both the Executive and legislative chambers observed the Presidential inauguration at Washington today. In a telegram to President Hoover, Governor Roosevelt said:

"Please let me extend to you the felicitations and good wishes of the people of the State of New York on your inauguration. Mrs. Roosevelt and I also send you and Mrs. Hoover our personal congratulations and good wishes."

In the Senate chamber all through the day a radio receiver on the rostrum detailed the proceedings in Washington, while legislators and clerks grouped around to listen at intervals.

## HOOVER WON'T OFFER NAME OF MELLON

### In Submitting Cabinet Today He Will Also Withhold Davis as Unnecessary to Confirm.

### NO OPPOSITION EXPECTED

### New Senate Abruptly Opened and Adjourned by Curtis, Using Fist as Gavel.

By LEWIS WOOD.

*Special to The New York Times.*

WASHINGTON, March 4.—Although President Hoover had intended to send the nominations of his new Cabinet members to the Senate for confirmation immediately after the close of the inaugural ceremonies today, he postponed that program until tomorrow because a large number of the members of the Senate wished to participate in various events this afternoon.

As a result, the names of all the Cabinet members, except those of Andrew W. Mellon as Secretary of the Treasury, and James J. Davis as Secretary of Labor, will be forwarded to the Senaate when it meets at noon tomorrow.

It was learned on excellent authority tonight that the names of Mr. Mellon and Mr. Davis will not be sent to the Senate, as this is considered unnecessary under law. They will continue into the Hoover Cabinet without the asking of Senate action.

The decision not to place Mr. Mellon's name before the Senate will avoid what would have been a stern fight against him by Republican insurgents and Democrats. According to Republican and Democratic Senate leaders, it will also greatly shorten the executive session necessary for confirmation of the Hoover Cabinet.

**Open Session Sought on Cabinet.**

Virtually no opposition is expected by the leaders even though it had been previously reported that objection would be brought against James W. Good as Secretary of War and Walter F. Brown as Postmaster General. It is hoped that the confirmations will be approved within a few days.

There is a possibility, however, that Republican insurgents and some Democrats may endeavor to force an open discussion of the nominations. Sentiment in favor of open executive sessions gained considerable new strength in the Senate sessions ending today, even such conservatives as Senator Jones, the Republican whip, introducing a resolution to discard the rule of secrecy.

But despite the fact that insurgents and Democrats may use part of the executive session this week in a demand for open doors, it is not believed they will win. Conservatives fear that debating nominations in open session would afford such a chance to seek to make political capital, that confirmation might be delayed for weeks.

President Hoover now hopes to have his first meeting with his Cabinet on Friday. The new President will hold a conference with members of the press at noon tomorrow and the executive offices at the White House will be organized.

George K. Ackerson and Lawrence Richey, two of his secretaries, will be sworn in and take charge at once. Many members of the present staff, including Rudolph Forster, the executive clerk, will remain in the new régime.

The Senate, which had expected to receive the Cabinet nominations, was in session only a few minutes. Vice President Curtis took charge of the body in a manner suggesting the swift methods of his spectacular pred-

Continued on Page Four.



## CROWD HOLDS ITS GROUND

### Masses in Downpour at Capitol to Watch the Inauguration.

### SPELLBOUND AT SPECTACLE

### Approves New President's Policies and Gives Farewell Plaudit to Coolidge.

### HOOVER KISSES THE BIBLE

### Book Open at Page Which Refers to Happiness of Those Observing the Law.

By BRUCE RAE.

*Special to The New York Times.*

WASHINGTON, March 4.—More than 50,000 persons, at least a quarter of them women, stood fast today beneath the pelting blows of a drenching downpour as Herbert Hoover, in sombre settings on the East portico of the Capitol assumed the Presidency and delivered his inaugural address.

Fear that the rainfall, which began just before the incoming President appeared on the platform, might ruin the picture proved unfounded. Rather it added to the solemnity as the oath of office was administered and it seemed to increase the seriousness with which the new President's message was received.

Remarkable was the picture of the broad, strong figure of the President-elect, rain-spattered, as he stood bareheaded before Chief Justice Taft. There was not a sound from the vast concourse, not a sound anywhere except on the platform, as the former President sonorously recited the words of the Presidential oath.

On the platform the newly chosen leader of the nation, his face graven with consciousness of the high moment, and the learned Chief Justice, graven and deliberate.

Out on the plaza, where the erratic wind was whipping the rain gusts about, a great assemblage, motionless in the grip of tension, heedless of the downpour.

**Spell Holds Crowd in Silence.**

This spell held the crowd throughout the delivery of the inaugural address. There were not any great outbursts of enthusiasm until the newly inducted President was about to read his address. Before he could actually turn to the reading-stand, Calvin Coolidge, a second before retired to private citizenship, moved to his side.

He extended his hand to his successor. President Hoover gripped it. Both smiled and exchanged a word or two, unheard even by those nearest them on the platform. The simple gesture did not seem to have been made as a salute from a retiring President to an incoming one, but as man to man.

The action caught the fancy of the crowd instantly. Applause started near the white, elevated platform and spread rapidly through the crowd. It became a roar of handclapping interspersed with shouts that caused the President to pause before beginning his address.

**Throngs Gather at Capitol.**

The crowd began to gather at the east front of the Capitol hours before the ceremony there was scheduled to take place. More than 8,000 pine benches had been set in place, extending in great rows out from the platform to the asphalt pathways through the plaza. Chairs had been placed on the platform itself and on the approaches leading to it from the Capitol steps.

The chairs were for the use of the members of the Senate, the House, the Diplomatic Corps and the Commanders of the Army, the Navy and the Marine Corps and their staffs. Seats also were in place on the platform for the Governors of the States and their staffs.

Trudging down Pennsylvania Avenue to the Capitol or seeking the slightly less congested streets paralleling the parade thoroughfare, the crowd surged in force. Thousands came by automobile from their hotels or homes in the city and the streets soon became so congested that reinforcements were called to handle the traffic snarls.

Mobilizing rapidly, the multitude soon began to blot out the grass plots and asphalt of the plaza. The seating accommodations were quickly filled by the fortunate ones who had managed to obtain tickets. Within an hour of the time set for the administration of the oath, which was 12:45 P. M., all seats had been taken save about 500 directly

Continued on Page Two.

Times Wide World Photo.

STARTING FOR THE INAUGURATION.
President Coolidge and President-elect Hoover Leaving the White House for the Capitol.

## COOLIDGE GIVES UP CARES OF OFFICE

### Returns With Relief to Private Life Amid the Acclaim of Great Throngs.

### SAYS FAREWELL OVER RADIO

### Then He and Mrs. Coolidge Start Trip to Old Home in Northampton.

By CHARLES R. MICHAEL.

*Special to The New York Times.*

WASHINGTON, March 4.—Calvin Coolidge, the thirtieth President of the United States, became a private citizen today. His departure from the scene which he has dominated for five years and a half was taken amidst a tumultuous demonstration as, with Mrs Coolidge, he drove away from the Capitol. Having witnessed the inaugural ceremonies, he departed a few minutes after Mr. Hoover, seeking to fall at once into the rôle of a private citizen and leave the honors to the new President.

In the drive with Mr. Hoover down Pennsylvania Avenue shortly after 11 o'clock, and everywhere he appeared, the crowds greeted the retiring President heartily, and again when he left the inaugural stand. The demonstration for him reached a climax at the station, where fully 5,000 people, crowded into the train shed and overflowing into the concourse, waved and cheered.

**Endeavors to Efface Himself.**

President Coolidge sought to efface himself from the nation's tribute to Herbert Hoover as much as possible. He participated in the exercises only where tradition dictated. He followed the precedent of President Roosevelt, and instead of returning to the White House with the new President, formally bade his successor goodbye at the Capitol.

Mr. Coolidge established another precedent when he requested his Cabinet to accompany the new President, and not escort him and Mrs. Coolidge to the station. The Cabinet members said their farewells in the President's room in the Capitol. Their wives had extended their good wishes to Mrs. Coolidge in the White House this morning.

"You are still Cabinet members," Mr. Coolidge informed his official family when they expressed a wish to accompany him to the station. "It is your duty to get behind President Hoover and be with him. I wish to get accustomed to being a private citizen and I might as well start this afternoon."

As Mr. and Mrs. Coolidge stood on the rear platform of their special car there arose from thousands of throats the cry of "Good-bye, good luck." Then a mighty roar shook the train shed as the distinguished travelers sped away to take up their

Continued on Page Three.



## HOOVER ENJOYS DAY; BUSY FROM THE DAWN

### He Is Up and Has Breakfast Before Others of Family in S Street House.

### ATTENDS TO EARLY MAIL

### While Appreciating Inauguration Exercises, He Is Ready to Get at Tasks of Presidency.

By L. C. SPEERS.

*Special to The New York Times.*

WASHINGTON, March 4.—Herbert Hoover's day, the first half of which embraced his final hours as a private citizen, was as simple and devoid of display as have been most previous days in the life of the new President.

The dawn found him awake. By 7 o'clock he was dressed and at the desk in the library of his S Street home. Seeing him, no one not cognizant of the facts of the situation would have imagined that in a few hours he was to be Chief Executive of the United States. He read the papers, attended to some private correspondence and chatted with members of his family and his personal staff.

Before 8 o'clock Mr. Hoover breakfasted. He was alone. Not even Mrs. Hoover was at the table. He was back in the library when Mrs. Hoover and W. H. Henry, her venerable uncle from South Dakota, appeared in the dining room. With them were Herbert Hoover Jr. and his wife and Mrs. May Hoover Leavitt, sister of the President.

There was an air of suppressed excitement in the big mansion. It affected, it seemed, everybody except Mr. Hoover. He was as calm and unperturbed as ever. So far as actions and words are concerned, the day to him was just another work day.

As fast as his secretaries sorted the early morning mail, Mr. Hoover glanced over the more important items in it. Letters calling for personal attention he laid aside. Others he turned back to the secretaries.

**His Grandchildren Pay Visit.**

The two little grandchildren, Herbert 3d and Peggy, children of Herbert Jr., came into the room. For a while Mr. Hoover played with them before sending them on their way.

Ten o'clock came and it was time for Mr. Hoover to get ready for his induction into office. That meant donning clothes of the kind he does not like, morning coat and trousers and a silk hat. It is a hundred-to-one bet that tomorrow morning he will appear in the usual double-breasted suit, blue or gray in color, and the pearl gray fedora that is his

Continued on Page Two.



## A NEW HOOVER IS HEARD

### President's Voice Rings With Confidence as He States Policies.

### RAIN SPATTERS HIS FACE

### Tense Audience Cheers as He Begins Inaugural Address After Taking Oath.

### CURTIS ASSUMES OFFICE

### Uniforms of Army, Navy and Diplomats Heighten Colorful Scene in Senate.

By RICHARD V. OULAHAN.

*Special to The New York Times.*

WASHINGTON, March 4.—Before a great throng, soaked by a cold, penetrating rain, as it stood in the open air at the Capitol this afternoon to witness his inauguration as President of the United States for a term of four years, Herbert Hoover asked God's help "in this service to my country to which you have called me."

The solemn ceremony of administering the constitutional oath of office, performed by the black-robed Chief Justice of the United States Supreme Court, William Howard Taft, at 1:10 o'clock, was broken by a cheer that marked the passing of Calvin Coolidge to private life and the incoming of a new administration.

Shortly before that impressive scene was enacted Charles Curtis of Kansas had been installed as Vice President, with the required oath administered to him by that man of colorful personality, Charles G. Dawes, whom he succeeded in office.

**Scene in the Senate Chamber.**

The setting for the Vice Presidential installation was the sheltered Senate chamber, into whose limited space were crowded somber-gowned justices of the nation's highest judicial tribunal, ambassadors and ministers of foreign countries, most of them in ceremonial uniforms brilliant with gold and silver, the members of the retiring Cabinet and those who will compose the new, Senators, Representatives, Governors of States and the highest ranking officers of the military and naval services.

From the galleries hundreds of spectators, mostly women in their best gowns, including the wives of the outgoing President and his successor, looked down on this striking spectacle of the workings of the American democracy.

Tonight Mr. Hoover is in the White House as President, his family with him, while Mr. Coolidge, accompanied by his wife, is traveling on a train to his home town, Northampton, Mass., to take up again the life of a private citizen.

It was all very simple, in spite of the ceremonial attaching to it, this transfer of governmental direction from one man to another, but it was a simplicity impressive in its orderly, peaceful details.

**Central Figures Ride Together.**

Escorted by troops of cavalry, Mr. Coolidge, as President, and Mr. Hoover, as President-elect, had gone together from the White House to the Capitol, followed by Vice President Dawes and Vice President-elect Curtis. When the proceedings at the Capitol had been completed, the former President said good-bye to his successor and went to the Union Station to take his train for Northampton.

As it was drawing out of Washington the new President was receiving the acclamations of a multitude while he reviewed the most elaborate military and civic parade that Washington had seen on a Presidential inauguration day since a devastating blizzard wrecked the outdoor ceremonies prepared for the induction of William Howard Taft as President just twenty years ago. And the rain kept coming down.

The first drops of the sprinkle that later became a downpour were pattering on the massive white dome of the Capitol as the protagonists of the Senate ceremonies passed in dignified procession from the great central rotunda into the open air. The Presidential oath-taking function took place on a far-reaching wooden platform erected over the long flight of stone steps leading to the Capitol's east entrance, where nearly all other Presidents have been inducted into office. Its chief feature was a covered pavilion without sides and here Mr. Hoover stood as he delivered his inaugural address after affirming the oath.

Near him sat Mr. and Mrs. Coolidge and Mrs. Hoover, Herbert Hoo-

"All the News That's Fit to Print."

# The New York Times.

LATE CITY EDITION
POSTSCRIPT
WEATHER—Showers and thunderstorms today and tomorrow.
Temperatures Yesterday—Max., 80; Min., 60.



VOL. LXXXI....No. 27,172. **** + NEW YORK, THURSDAY, JUNE 16, 1932. TWO CENTS In New York City | THREE CENTS Within 200 Miles | FOUR CENTS Elsewhere Except 7th and 8th Postal Zones

# CONVENTION ADOPTS HOOVER DRY-WET PLANK; REPEALISTS WAGE A FUTILE BATTLE ON FLOOR; UPROAR AMONG DELEGATES AND IN GALLERIES

## PLEA TO US ON DEBTS PUSHED IN LAUSANNE ON CONFERENCE EVE

### Leaders Discuss a Resolution Asking Cancellation as 600 Gather for Opening Today.

### MacDONALD TO PRESIDE

### Determined to Achieve Results—Another German Moratorium Is Believed to Be Likely.

### REICH'S ATTITUDE DECISIVE

### Papen and Neurath Indicate Stand Will Be That She Cannot Pay, Not That She Will Not.

By The Associated Press.

LAUSANNE, Switzerland, June 15.—A request that the United States cancel all war debts was being discussed tonight as the 600 delegates of thirteen nations assembled here for tomorrow's opening session of the conference on debts and reparations at which a way to world economic recovery will be sought.

The request to the United States—in the event that it is decided on—will be presented to the conference in the form of a resolution. Whether such drastic action would be advisable was debated tonight at many private gatherings of the delegates.

Meanwhile Prime Minister Ramsay MacDonald of Great Britain, who is slated to serve as president of the conference, prepared the speech with which he will open the proceedings.

**Determined on a Decision.**

British spokesmen were authority for the statement that Mr. MacDonald was determined to lead the way to some definite accomplishment before the conference adjourned.

There had been some objection to the selection of the British Prime Minister as presiding officer, but Foreign Minister Dino Grandi of Italy apparently disposed of it in conversations with the leaders of the delegations from the important countries.

On July 15 German reparations of more than $300,000,000 fall due. The Berlin Government has announced that it cannot pay them. Tonight a new moratorium of one to five years seemed the most likely method of dealing with this problem.

The first session will open in an atmosphere of uneasiness caused largely by the recent government upset in Germany, an event that was particularly displeasing to France.

The German delegation is headed by the new Chancellor, Franz von Papen, whose Cabinet is predominantly composed of titled Junkers who were powers in the old imperial régime. Incidentally, Lieut. Col. von Papen has brought with him sixty assistants, one of the largest staffs at the meeting.

**Leaders Prepare Program.**

Mr. MacDonald was host this afternoon at his hotel to Premier Edouard Herriot of France, Signor Grandi and Foreign Minister Paul Hymans of Belgium, all veterans of numerous international conferences. At this conference the program of the meeting was prepared.

The United States is not represented, but the Washington Government's "off-stage" part is of extreme importance, for the deliberations will be carried on in an atmosphere made uncertain, by the possible attitude of the United States toward proposals affecting war debts.

After the problem of German reparations has been taken care of, the conference will consider Hungarian and Bulgarian payments. Then the floor will be free for general discussion of the monetary and economic troubles that have been afflicting the world.

Those hoping for the success of the conference laid stress on the importance of the understanding reached by Mr. MacDonald and M. Herriot in Paris over the week-end. Mr. MacDonald said he and his colleague had arrived at the basis of a common viewpoint that they were thinking along the same lines.

The Germans enter the meeting with the backing of the Young Plan advisory committee for their contention that they are unable to pay. The committee found six months ago that the Reich for the time being was at the bottom of its purse.

Remembering the assassination of Vaslav Vorowski, Russian delegate to the Lausanne conference of 1924, the Swiss police have taken extraordinary precautions to protect the delegates to this meeting.

Two hundred newspaper men are here to inform the world of what takes place.

**German Attitude Crucial.**

Wireless to The New York Times.

LAUSANNE, June 15.—It is on the attitude of Germany that the fate

Continued on Page Five.

## Robinson Laughs at 'Optimist' Who Sees Congress Near End

By The Associated Press.

WASHINGTON, June 15.—Senator Robinson of Arkansas, Democratic leader in the Senate, today called attention to the statement of Senator McNary of Oregon, assistant Republican leader, that he hoped the Senate would be able to adjourn by the end of this week, characterizing Mr. McNary as "an amazing optimist."

"I still cling to the dim hope," said Mr. McNary, "that we may conclude our work by Saturday."

"Then," replied Mr. Robinson, "I must characterize my good friend, the Senator from Oregon, as an amazing optimist."

Meanwhile Acting Speaker Rainey told newspaper men that "we will be lucky if we are able to adjourn by Saturday week."

## STORM OFFICE TO GET JOBS ON CITY SUBWAY

### 5,000 Await Opening of Board's Quarters to Seek Work on Eighth Avenue Line.

### FIND MOST POSTS FILLED

### 20,000 Applications on File for 1,500 Positions—Service Likely to Start Before Fall.

Nearly all of the 1,500 men required for municipal operation of the Eighth Avenue subway have been chosen by the Board of Transportation, it was disclosed yesterday. Not only that, but for the past two weeks motormen, switchmen, signal men and other classes of specialized employes have been under training in the 207th Street yards and on the twelve-mile stretch of new subway.

Formal appointment of the new employes, who were tentatively chosen from a list of more than 20,000 applicants on file in the Board of Transportation offices for many months, will be announced as soon as the Board of Estimate has formally adopted the resolution on municipal operation which was approved last Tuesday in committee of the whole and municipal and State Civil Service Commissioners have approved the personnel set-up with its 108 different classifications.

Opening of the Eighth Avenue line before next Fall is now believed probable. It will be preceded by a week or two of non-revenue operation on the same headways and with the same operating personnel as required for revenue operation.

**Storm Offices for Jobs.**

Announcement of the approval of municipal operation by the committee of the whole brought to the offices of the Board of Transportation at 250 Hudson Street a throng of about 5,000 job-seekers who milled about the entrance of the building for more than an hour before the board's offices were opened. Soon after the opening hour it was found necessary to send for a detail of ten patrolmen to maintain order and keep the applicants in line. They received blanks to fill out and leave with clerks assigned to handle applications.

The great majority of the applicants were lacking in practical railroad experience, although a few were younger employes of the Interborough and B. M. T. Placards on the corridor walls informed the job-seekers that it was useless to apply unless they had actual railroad experience. In a few days the board will make public a set of regulations covering the qualifications for jobs.

The process of selecting trained employes has been going on quietly for several weeks. The list of 20,000 applicants, compiled over a period of months, includes men trained in every branch of rapid transit operations, including motormen, switchmen, guards, signal and tower men, car inspectors, maintainers and all the other special branches listed in the 108 classifications created by the Board of Transportation. More than enough material is now on hand, it was indicated, than would be required to man the completed independent city system.

**Recruits from Old Lines.**

The training of motormen has been under the direction of Arthur M. Green, the board's motor instructor, while tower and signal men have been trained by its division engineers. Most of the motormen, switchmen and signal crew have been recruited from the Interborough, B. M. T. and the Union Switch & Signal Company, which installed the signal system on the new line.

The men tentatively chosen will pass examinations by the special boards set up by the Board of Transportation and will be placed on the Municipal Civil Service Commission's list after passing its examinations for physical and moral fitness.

Some 200 positions as station agents, platform men and porters will be filled, it was indicated, by

Continued on Page Three.

## BONUS BILL PASSES IN HOUSE, 209-176; SENATE TO RUSH VOTE

### Veterans Cheer in Gallery as Plan for $2,400,000,000 in New Currency Is Approved.

### REPUBLICANS ARE ASSAILED

### Backers of Measure Say They "Sold Out to Administration" as 126 Vote Against It.

### SENATE DEFEAT EXPECTED

### Leaders Will Try to Get Action Today—Evacuation of "Army" Is Predicted After Test.

From a Staff Correspondent.
Special to The New York Times.

WASHINGTON, June 15.—The House today passed the Patman bill for the issuance of $2,400,000,000 additional currency to pay off the remaining half of the soldiers' bonus certificates, and sent the measure immediately to the Senate. The vote was 209 to 176.

Senator Thomas of Oklahoma, one of the Senate's most ardent advocates of immediate payment of the bonus certificates, which will not become due until 1945, sent word to Representative Patman and others in the House that he would seek to have the bill brought up in the Senate tomorrow so that it could be voted upon during the day.

Whether the "fiat," or "printing press money," as it was characterized in the House today, will be approved by the Senate is problematical. Proponents of the measure in the House, disappointed at their showing, were plainly disturbed tonight, and they admitted that they held no hopes of passing the bill over President Hoover's veto.

The President has let it be known that he will not approve the bill. He is reliably reported to have the pledges of fifty-six Senators to support his veto, in the event the Senate approves the bill and sends it to the White House for his action. The House proponents, in view of this situation, are basing their sole hope on the theory that the President "will not dare" veto the measure.

In the words of one of the strongest supporters of the Patman bill, the Republicans in the House "sold out to the administration after they had individually promised ex-service men in their respective districts to support the bonus bill."

Only fifty-six Republicans and one Farm-Labor member voted with the 152 Democrats who supported the Patman bill, while fifty Democrats sided with 126 Republicans in opposing it.

**Veterans in Gallery Keep Count.**

Several hundred men of the bonus army sat in the House gallery this afternoon and watched tensely as the vote was being taken. Some tried to keep count on their fingers, and in the front row a Negro veteran marked each vote down with a pencil. He smiled broadly and communicated the news to his comrades when it was evident the bill had passed.

When the vote giving the veterans their first victory in this session of Congress was complete, they forgot the warning against demonstrations and started applause, in which many women in the galleries joined. Their breach of the rules was unrebuked, however, and they rushed out of the chamber to spread the tidings among their comrades.

The news of the vote was taken

Continued on Page Two.

## MILLS RULED IN DRAFTING

### 37 Planks in Platform Please President in Every Respect.

### MONETARY PARLEY IS URGED

### Demand of Silver States Met—Gold Standard Sustained and Inflation Is Assailed.

### UTILITY REGULATION ASKED

### Sets Up Challenge to Roosevelt—Tariffs in Act Upheld, Others Promised.

By CHARLES R. MICHAEL.
Special to The New York Times.

CHICAGO, June 15.—Under administration control, with Secretary Mills dominating the situation, the resolutions committee after long hours of argument agreed today on the prohibition plank and the party's declaration on other matters of vital interest for the twentieth Republican National Convention.

At 6:40 P. M. the platform was made public and it was submitted to the convention in night session.

Written by Cabinet members and others friendly to the administration, the platform from beginning to end is thoroughly acceptable to President Hoover, who was informed by telephone of every action of the resolutions committee in its twenty-five hours' deliberation on its most important feature.

Throughout the long sessions of the committee Secretaries Mills and Hyde presented the views of the administration, and these, without any verbal changes in the rough draft presented to the full committee, were accepted.

The platform represents President Hoover's ideas on government and the questions to be decided in the Presidential campaign. Old-time Republican leaders, including William M. Butler, chairman of the Republican National Committee in 1924, while disagreeing on many points, accepted the platform on the ground that President Hoover must make his fight for re-election on his record and the promises he is willing to make to bring about economic recovery and stabilization of industrial conditions.

**Platform Embraces 37 Planks.**

He and others who are regarded as men of political wisdom mildly disagreed during consideration of the platform, but surrendered to the administration's demands.

Mr. Butler and other men who have defined former policies of the Republican party were opposed rather pronouncedly to the prohibition declaration, arguing that it was not explicit, that it required almost a legal explanation as to its purposes and would place the party in a position of explanation rather than on the offensive.

The platform contains about 8,500 words and consists of thirty-seven planks. Besides prohibition, the

Continued on Page Thirteen.

## Means Is Sentenced to 15 Years in Prison; Judge Denounces Lindbergh Baby Fraud

By The Associated Press.

WASHINGTON, June 15.—Gaston B. Means, former Department of Justice agent, stood again today in the shadow of prison walls.

Sentences of ten years' imprisonment for larceny of $100,000 paid him by Mrs. Evalyn Walsh McLean to ransom the kidnapped Lindbergh baby and an added five years for larceny of $4,000 "expense money," were pronounced against the ex-convict by Justice James M. Proctor.

Means stood with arms akimbo and a grin on his dimpled face as the justice censured him strongly for his "clever and adroit plan."

"The Lindbergh case," Justice Proctor said before pronouncing judgment, "brought out all the best in the hearts of men, but also gave the opportunity to some to display the weakness and wickedness of human nature.

"The verdict of the jury in this case reveals that the defendant capitalized not only on the sweetest and tenderest emotions of the human heart, but also the basest."

T. Morris Wampler, one of Means's counsel, immediately noted an appeal to the District of Columbia Court of Appeals. It will be heard during the October term.

Means, grinning broadly, was led away to the District of Columbia jail, where he will remain unless application for bail is accepted. A decision will be made tomorrow.

This is the third time in Means's sensational career, which has been a jumble of suits, trials, adventure and misadventure, that he has been sentenced to prison.

He once drew a two-year sentence and a $10,000 fine for conspiracy to violate the Volstead act and for swindling men who paid to get whisky out of bonded warehouses.

Later, he received the same penalty when convicted of conspiring to obstruct justice in a case involving the Glass Casket Company of Altoona, Pa.

His connection with Mrs. McLean, estranged wife of the former publisher of The Washington Post, was revealed last May 5 when he was arrested for taking the money on a representation that he knew the whereabouts of the kidnapped son of Colonel and Mrs. Charles A. Lindbergh.

## The Prohibition Plank Which Was Adopted

Special to The New York Times.

*CHICAGO, June 15.—The prohibition plank of the platform agreed upon late this afternoon by the Resolutions Committee and adopted tonight by the convention reads as follows:*

### THE EIGHTEENTH AMENDMENT.

The Republican party has always stood and stands today for obedience to and enforcement of the law as the very foundation of orderly government and civilization. There can be no national security otherwise. The duty of the President of the United States and the officers of the law is clear. The law must be enforced as they find it enacted by the people. To these courses of action we pledge our nominees.

The Republican party is and always has been the party of the Constitution. Nullification by non-observance by individuals or State action threatens the stability of government.

While the Constitution makers sought a high degree of permanence, they foresaw the need of changes and provided for them. Article V limits the proposals of amendments to two methods: (1) Two-thirds of both houses of Congress may propose amendments or (2) on application of the Legislatures of two-thirds of the States a national convention shall be called by Congress to propose amendments. Thereafter ratification must be had in one of two ways: (1) By the Legislatures of three-fourths of the several States or (2) by conventions held in three-fourths of the several States. Congress is given power to determine the mode of ratification.

Referendums without constitutional sanction cannot furnish a decisive answer. Those who propose them innocently are deluded by false hopes; those who propose them knowingly are deceiving the people.

A nation-wide controversy over the Eighteenth Amendment now distracts attention from the constructive solution of many pressing national problems. The principle of national prohibition as embodied in the amendment was supported and opposed by members of both great political parties. It was submitted to the States by members of Congress of different political faith and ratified by State Legislatures of different political majorities. It was not then and is not now a partisan political question.

Members of the Republican party hold different opinions with respect to it and no public official or member of the party should be pledged or forced to choose between his party affiliations and his honest convictions upon this question.

We do not favor a submission limited to the issue of retention or repeal, for the American nation never in its history has gone backward, and in this case the progress which has been thus far made must be preserved, while the evils must be eliminated.

We therefore believe that the people should have an opportunity to pass upon a proposed amendment the provision of which, while retaining in the Federal Government power to preserve the gains already made in dealing with the evils inherent in the liquor traffic, shall allow States to deal with the problem as their citizens may determine, but subject always to the power of the Federal Government to protect those States where prohibition may exist and safeguard our citizens everywhere from the return of the saloon and attendant abuses.

Such an amendment should be promptly submitted to the States by Congress, to be acted upon by State conventions called for that sole purpose in accordance with the provisions of Article V of the Constitution and adequately safeguarded so as to be truly representative.

*The remainder of the platform submitted to the convention is printed an page 15.*

## DAWES'S 'NO' CRUSHES ANTI-CURTIS DRIVE

### Plans for Nominating General Were Being Perfected When His Statement Arrived.

### ILLINOIS STILL HOLDS OUT

### But Texans, Who Led Boom, Say No One Is in Sight to Fight For.

By L. C. SPEERS.
Special to The New York Times.

CHICAGO, June 15.—The backbone of the anti-Curtis movement, which had assumed such menacing proportions that the renomination of the Vice President was seriously in doubt, appears to have been broken as a result of Charles G. Dawes's definite refusal to make the race. Final plans for the nomination of General Dawes were being perfected when word came from Washington that he "could not" accept if nominated.

The Dawes bandwagon was running full speed and, according to National Committeeman Creager of Texas, who engineered the boom, twenty-four States were ready to vote for him with six others in doubt, and veering to the side of the former Vice President. Illinois endorsed Dawes at the very time the "could not" message was being released in Washington.

**Had "Definite" Information.**

According to the Texans, they had good reason to believe that General Dawes would accept if nominated, and it was this "definite" information, said Captain J. W. Lucey of Dallas, who started the boom, which caused Texas to lead off in the movement to prevent the renomination of Mr. Curtis. The Texans still oppose the Vice President, but with General Dawes apparently out of the picture they do not know where to turn. There is no one in sight, at this time, they say, who can "bat for Dawes."

Iowa tonight endorsed Hanford McNider, American Minister to Canada, and appointed a committee to solicit support from other delegations. The boom is not making the headway, however, which made the Dawes movement so serious a menace to the plans of Vice President Curtis for a renomination.

Other suggestions for the nomination include Secretary of the Treasury Mills, Secretary of War Hurley, Representative Snell of New York, the permanent chairman of the convention; Walter E. Edge of New Jersey, Ambassador to France, and Secretary of Agriculture Hyde. All of these men are administration support-

Continued on Page Twelve.

## The Convention's Second Day; Resubmission Plank Accepted

Special to The New York Times.

CHICAGO, June 15.—The chief developments of the second day of the Republican National Convention were:

1. The acceptance of the platform, chief interest being in the prohibition plank.

2. The convention, following the administration dictum, reversed the national committee and threw out the Tolbert delegation from South Carolina.

3. The anti-Curtis renomination move was threatened with collapse when General Dawes announced that he would not accept if nominated for Vice President.

## THE VOTE ON REPEAL

Special to The New York Times.

*CHICAGO, Thursday, June 16.—Following is the official vote on the motion to amend the majority report of the resolutions committee by adopting the Bingham report urging repeal, fractional votes being approximated:*

| State. | Delegates. | Yes. | No. |
|---|---|---|---|
| Alabama | 19 | .. | 19 |
| Arizona | 9 | 9 | .. |
| Arkansas | 15 | .. | 15 |
| California | 47 | 6 | 41 |
| Colorado | 15 | 1 | 14 |
| Connecticut | 19 | 19 | .. |
| Delaware | 9 | .. | 9 |
| Florida | 16 | .. | 16 |
| Georgia | 16 | 2 | 14 |
| Idaho | 11 | .. | 11 |
| Illinois | 61 | 45 | 15½ |
| Indiana | 31 | 23 | 3 |
| Iowa | 25 | 3 | 22 |
| Kansas | 21 | 4 | 17 |
| Kentucky | 25 | 14 | 10 |
| Louisiana | 12 | .. | 12 |
| Maine | 13 | 5 | 8 |
| Maryland | 19 | .. | 19 |
| Massachusetts | 34 | 16 | 17 |
| Michigan | 41 | 25½ | 15½ |
| Minnesota | 25 | .. | 25 |
| Mississippi | 11 | 11 | .. |
| Missouri | 33 | 8¼ | 23¾ |
| Montana | 11 | .. | 11 |
| Nebraska | 17 | 1 | 16 |
| Nevada | 9 | 8 | 1 |
| New Hampshire | 11 | .. | 11 |
| New Jersey | 35 | 35 | .. |
| New Mexico | 9 | 2 | 7 |
| New York | 97 | 76 | 21 |
| North Carolina | 28 | 3 | 25 |
| North Dakota | 11 | .. | 11 |
| Ohio | 55 | 12 2-9 | 42 7-9 |
| Oklahoma | 25 | .. | 25 |
| Oregon | 13 | 3 | 10 |
| *Pennsylvania | 75 | 51 | 23 |
| Rhode Island | 8 | 8 | .. |
| South Carolina | 10 | .. | 10 |
| South Dakota | 11 | 3 | 8 |
| Tennessee | 24 | 1 | 23 |
| Texas | 49 | .. | 49 |
| Utah | 11 | 10 | 1 |
| Vermont | 9 | 9 | .. |
| Virginia | 25 | .. | 25 |
| Washington | 19 | 11 | 8 |
| West Virginia | 19 | 4 | 15 |
| Wisconsin | 27 | 22 | 5 |
| Wyoming | 9 | 9 | .. |
| Alaska | 2 | .. | 2 |
| District of Col. | 2 | .. | 2 |
| Hawaii | 2 | 2 | .. |
| Philippines | 2 | 1 | 1 |
| Puerto Rico | 2 | .. | 2 |
| Total | 1,154 | 472 | 681 |

*One delegate absent.

## GALLERIES AT NIGHT JEER AND CHEER

### 15,000 Join in Booing Leaders Advocating Administration's Prohibition Proposal.

### SILENCED BY FINAL VOTE

### Partisan Crowd, Which Snell Once Threatened to Expel, Sticks to Guns to the Last.

By JAMES A. HAGERTY.
Special to The New York Times.

CHICAGO, Thursday, June 16.—Throughout the night battle over the prohibition plank a crowd of 15,000 men and women packing the galleries, jeered and booed the party leaders advocating adoption of the administration's proposal and wildly cheered the repealists pleading for the minority plank.

Their disapproval centred upon James R. Garfield, chairman of the resolutions committee, who presented the majority report and their acclaim upon Senator Hiram Bingham of Connecticut, who offered the minority plank. At one time Chairman Snell threatened to clear the galleries, but the spectators stuck to their places till the conflict ended in the early morning and only the defeat of the extremists silenced them.

**Gallery Vociferously Partisan.**

The partisanship of the galleries was evident before the opening of the session, the men and women in them, presumably largely Republicans, cheered the playing of "East Side, West Side" by the organ, thereby paying a tribute to former Governor Alfred E. Smith, Democratic nominee for President in 1928 and candidate for the nomination again this year. They jeered virtually every administration speaker, including Ogden L. Mills Secretary of the Treasury, whose forceful speech gained him the hearing that the milder manner of Mr. Garfield failed to obtain.

Of the advocates of repeal, Dr. Nicholas Murray Butler of New York got the most enthusiastic reception. He was applauded at the end of nearly every sentence. Senator Bingham and the other repeal speakers also came in for repeated applause.

But if the repeal advocates had the galleries, the administration leaders had the votes, as the roll-call demonstrated. The spectators cheered at every announcement of a vote for Bingham repeal plank by a State delegation, and the announcement of the result was received with comparative silence by the galleries and with cheers by the delegates on the floor.

At the outset of the night session

Continued on Page Sixteen.

## REPEAL REJECTED, 681-472

### Hoover Leaders Keep Grip on Delegates in a Stiff Battle.

### EXTREME DRYS ALSO LOSE

### Measure Calls for Conventions on New Amendment for State and Federal Control.

### FULL PLATFORM ADOPTED

### Final Refusal of Dawes to Run Spikes the Guns of the Anti-Curtis Forces.

*The text of Chairman Snell's speech is printed on Page 16.*

By ARTHUR KROCK.
Special to The New York Times.

CHICAGO, Thursday, June 16.—Under the pressure of the administration, a reluctant Republican National Convention shortly before 1:30 o'clock this morning voted down the minority's effort to have flat repeal of prohibition submitted to the American people.

The vote on the plank offered for the minority of the resolutions committee by Senator Hiram Bingham of Connecticut was 681 against, 472 for, with one absentee. Only Mississippi broke away from the powerful control of the administration.

After the minority report had been defeated the entire platform was adopted by a viva voce vote and the convention adjourned until 11 A. M. today.

Though the most serious economic problems press for solution, and the platform was full of discussions of these and plans for the reconstruction of the nation, the convention debated only the subject of prohibition.

**The Question, as Presented.**

The question was whether, as Senator Bingham put it, the party would offer a clean-cut chance for a yes and no vote on the Eighteenth Amendment or whether, as Secretary Mills defined it, a new amendment should be recommended, which would give the Federal Government, should the adoption of the new amendment make prohibition a matter for State instead of national solution, the power to keep dry those States which wished to remain that way and to prevent the open saloon from being established in States which choose to be wet.

The debate began in an atmosphere of heat and emotion, much stimulated by galleries devoted to the idea of flat repeal. Chairman James R. Garfield of the resolutions committee was hissed and booed, and so were other speakers for the compromise plank. But as the night wore on, the galleries wearied, and the epochal decision was taken in a quiet stadium.

Before it ended a personal appeal to the convention to stand by the majority report in the name of President Hoover was made by John McNab, a California delegate, who put Mr. Hoover in nomination at Kansas City in 1928. This is the first time that there has been public admission that the President has been directing the decisions of the convention.

**President in Full Control.**

Though what was tonight publicly confessed had been well known unofficially for weeks, New York, Pennsylvania, New Jersey, Illinois, Indiana and Michigan, all Republican stalwarts, cast more votes for the Bingham motion than for the proposal sanctioned by Mr. Hoover. It was evident that the sentiment of the convention was overwhelmingly for repeal But the word had been passed down the line from the White House and, as is the unvarying rule of American politics, a President on renomination eve controlled the declarations of his party.

If it is the wish of the President, tomorrow the Vice President will be renominated along with him, although the sentiment in the convention against Charles Curtis is as strong as it was against the "new amendment" plan. Whatever the result in that matter, the fiction that this convention was to be permitted to work its untrammeled will is gone into limbo.

Not since the Republican regulars in 1912 nominated William H. Taft

Continued on Page Twelve.

"All the News That's Fit to Print."

# The New York Times.

LATE CITY EDITION
POSTSCRIPT
WEATHER—Possibly showers today; tomorrow fair and warmer.
Temperatures Yesterday—Max., 85; Min., 64.



VOL. LXXXI....No. 27,173. ****+ NEW YORK, FRIDAY, JUNE 17, 1932. TWO CENTS In New York City | THREE CENTS Within 200 Miles | FOUR CENTS Elsewhere Except 7th and 8th Postal Zones

# HOOVER, CURTIS RENAMED ON FIRST BALLOTS; DRY-WET PLANK IS DEFENDED BY STIMSON

## LAUSANNE TO OFFER REPARATIONS TRUCE TILL FINAL SOLUTION

**Britain and France Agree on Plan to Be Put to Reich at Closed Session Today.**

**IDEA IS TO SATISFY PAPEN**

**Proposal Can Be Interpreted Fairly in Germany as Virtual End to War Debts.**

**M'DONALD ASKS BOLDNESS**

**In Opening Speech He Holds Out Hope That We May Cooperate in Solving Economic Problems.**

By FREDERICK T. BIRCHALL.
Wireless to THE NEW YORK TIMES.

LAUSANNE, June 16.—To a private plenary meeting of the Lausanne conference tomorrow will be presented a memorandum, to which Great Britain and France have already agreed, extending the suspension of all reparations payments, including the French unconditional annuities under the Young Plan, until a final settlement can be worked out.

The idea behind this move is that it will give Chancellor von Papen of Germany something to take home that can be fairly interpreted as a practical ending of reparation payments and therefore something to talk about in the German elections. A second advantage of the step is that it removes from the Lausanne conference the curse of having to work in a hurry before payments by Germany should begin again on July 2.

Third, it is believed it will satisfy French opinion as preparing the way for a larger consideration of the entire economic problem, for which Prime Minister MacDonald appealed in his opening speech today.

**Not Moratorium Extension.**

It is to be noted that this proposal is not for an "extension of the moratorium," which would bring in the matter of United States debts. It is rather for a continuation of the European status quo and therefore in full accord with the purpose of this conference. Germany, however, would not be obligated to pay indemnities to the Bank for International Settlements on the next instalments, due July 2, of non-postponable reparations she owes France, which under the present arrangement are returned to Germany in the form of railway bonds redeemable in ten years. Thereby will be removed the metaphorical sword overhanging Chancellor von Papen's head. Yet, at the same time, the end of reparations is not formally acknowledged, which satisfies Premier Herriot of France.

Should the proposal prove acceptable tomorrow it will be in fact a success for the method of temporizing as against the clean-cut method of cancellation which Germany came here to demand. On that point Lieut. Col. von Papen is still to be heard from, but the friendliness toward him manifested by frequent visits from M. Herriot and Mr. MacDonald may not be without reward.

Pending the complete economic discussion and final settlement that Mr. MacDonald envisages, the work of exploration and liquidation, if the proposal carries, will be continued by technicians and experts. Thus the conference will in truth have fulfilled some of the expectations based on it as a preparatory movement toward a real world adjustment.

**MacDonald Sounds Keynote.**

By P. J. PHILIP.
Wireless to THE NEW YORK TIMES.

LAUSANNE, June 16. — Elected unanimously as president of the Lausanne conference, Prime Minister Ramsay MacDonald in a speech that strongly set forth the principles that must be established began the work of trying to get Europe to put its financial house in order.

He mentioned the United States twice, both times to emphasize her unity with the rest of the world. But there was no mention, and from the British delegation there will be no mention, of Europe's debts to the United States. That is another problem to be settled at some other time

Continued on Page Four.



## *12-Year Sentence on American In Assault Protested to Spain*

Special to THE NEW YORK TIMES.

WASHINGTON, June 16.—United States Consular officers at Malaga and Seville, Spain, have intervened with the military authorities in behalf of John C. Wiley of Inglewood, Cal., who has been sentenced by a military tribunal to twelve years' imprisonment, with recommendation for commutation, on charges of assaulting a carabinero in Malaga on March 10.

The carabinero is said to have suffered a broken nose and to have been incapacitated for duty for nineteen days.

The State Department said today that the case would come up for review soon and the American officials had been promised that it would be submitted to the Premier. The consuls contend that the sentence was out of all proportion to the offense and have urged commutation or deportation.

## CHILE OVERTHROWS REGIME AS TOO RED

**Army Storms Palace and Captures General Grove as His Guards Quit Him.**

**DAVILA'S FRIENDS IN POWER**

**Mobs Fight in Streets as Planes Circle Overhead, Dropping Flares.**

Special Cable to THE NEW YORK TIMES.

SANTIAGO, Chile, Friday, June 17.—Colonel Marmaduque Grove was overthrown early today as provisional head of the Chilean Government, according to a manifesto by army leaders who launched a counter-revolt against him last night.

Troops opposed to communism surrounded the government palace and demanded Colonel Grove's surrender by midnight. An earlier manifesto signed by General Agustin Moreno on behalf of all garrisons of the army said if he did not yield by that time, planes and troops would bombard the palace if necessary to obtain control of the government.

Colonel Grove replied that he would die rather than surrender. Shortly after midnight troops began attacking the palace and soon afterward it was announced by the counter-revolutionists that their drive had been successful.

At an early hour the army leaders had not yet named the new junta to take over the government, but it was assumed that Carlos G. Dávila, who, because of his moderate views, was driven out of the junta dominated by Colonel Grove, would be a member.

**Coup a Blow at Communism.**

Both manifestos declared the counter-revolt was intended to prevent the establishment of communistic practices and to carry forward the socialistic principles enunciated by the junta which seized power from former President Juan Esteban Montero on June 4.

Early last evening rebellious troops began marching on the palace and surrounded it, facing a loyal guard of carabineers. Soon after the midnight attack began, it was observed that the members of the Presidential guard were quietly abandoning their arms and slipping out of the courtyard and palace. When the surrender of the men was practically complete General Moreno announced the success of the counter-revolt.

Earlier there had been considerable disorder in the city, with mobs parading and shouting for and against Colonel Grove.

The rising was made necessary, according to the counter-revolutionists, by the failure of Colonel Grove to keep promises made before the revolution of June 4 and by his encouragement of Communism. The new régime, it was declared, has the support of the entire army, will put down Communism with a firm hand and will maintain order throughout the country.

**Colonel Grove Captured.**

SANTIAGO, Chile, Friday, June 17 (AP).—Colonel Marmaduque Grove, leading member of the new Socialist junta that deposed President Montero twelve days ago, was captured early today in a counter-revolutionary overthrow of his régime.

When the troops first approached the palace several officers got past the guards and demanded the surrender of General Grove, who re-

Continued on Page Three.

## BONUS BILL REPORTED ADVERSELY, 14 TO 2; CAMP MORALE SAGS

**Break-Up Starts After Senate Delays Action Till Today and Defeat Appears Likely.**

**CRUCIAL PERIOD AT HAND**

**Officials Believe Jobless Men Will Roam Nation in Bands, Hungry and Penniless.**

**TEMPER OF MEN ON EDGE**

**Former Leader Flares at the Police, Saying Veterans Are Going to Quit "Soft-Pedaling."**

From a Staff Correspondent.
Special to THE NEW YORK TIMES.

WASHINGTON, June 16.—The Senate vote on the Patman bill for the payment of $2,400,000,000 to World War veterans, which was passed by the House yesterday and was scheduled for action by the upper body today, was deferred until tomorrow after the Finance Committee had reported it adversely following a swift consideration this morning.

Late this afternoon Senator Smoot, chairman of the Finance Committee, gave formal notice that the bonus bill would be taken up as soon as the Senate met tomorrow morning. Opponents of the measure say that it will be defeated in the Senate, and even should it unexpectedly succeed, its veto by President Hoover is assured. Its friends admit that it could not possibly be passed over his veto.

Just before the Senate recessed tonight Senator Watson obtained unanimous consent to have the bonus made unfinished business. He remarked that he hoped for a final vote tomorrow, and said that if this did not materialize there would be ample time for discussion anyway.

With today's developments the morale of the bonus expeditionary force, which has remained high in the face of amazing difficulties, began almost visibly to sag. The unexpected delay, the adverse report of the committee and the growing expectation of defeat began to weigh heavily on the thousands of destitute ex-service men encamped here, and the movement of the veterans homeward, only a trickle thus far, was notably increased.

Officials believed that the beginning of the long-expected break-up of the camp was at hand, and would begin in earnest after the Senate vote.

**Officials Plan Evacuation.**

Hence they began planning for what they concede is the most dangerous period of the bonus army's existence—the period in which the men will start roving about the country as isolated bands of unemployed, without funds, without food and without the discipline to which they submitted voluntarily when they thought there was a chance of achieving their objective.

The bill was opposed in the Finance Committee by fourteen of the sixteen members present. Those voting for the adverse report were Senators Watson, Reed, Shortridge, Couzens, Keyes, Thomas of Idaho, Metcalf and Smoot, all Republicans, and King, George, Walsh of Massachusetts, Connally, Gore and Harrison, Democrats. Those voting favorably were Senators La Follette and Jones of Washington, both Republicans.

Senator La Follette later explained on the floor that he felt that a measure so important should not have had an adverse report, but should have been reported without recommendation.

A motion by Senator Connally to pay the present value of the adjusted compensation certificates, giving the veterans the option of cashing and surrendering them now or of holding them until 1945, was defeated by vote of 11 to 4.

Senator Connally then proposed an amendment to change the interest rate on loans on the certificates from 4 per cent to 3, but this also was voted down. A similar fate met a proposal of Senator Thomas of Oklahoma, principal proponent of the bonus payment in the Senate, that the certificates be cashed when the holders presented proof of absolute want.

When the bill was reported to the

Continued on Page Two.

## DENIES IT IS A 'STRADDLE'

**Secretary, Over Radio, Says Liquor Plan Is 'Definite and Logical.'**

**'FAITH' WITH PEOPLE KEPT**

**'Real Gains' Under Dry Law Must Be 'Disentangled From Evils Incurred,' He Holds.**

**THE ADMINISTRATION REPLY**

**Mr. Stimson's Address Is First Move to Justify the Party's Stand to Country.**

Special to THE NEW YORK TIMES.

CHICAGO, June 16.—Defending the prohibition plank in the Republican platform, Secretary of State Stimson declared over the radio tonight that instead of being a "straddle," the proposed method of dealing with the prohibition problem was "consistent, definite, logical and well-founded in law and fact."

Secretary Stimson was speaking over a nation-wide radio hook-up of the National Broadcasting Company and his was the first move on the part of the administration to justify the party's stand before the country.

Asserting that the Eighteenth Amendment represented in its adoption the hopes of millions of American wives and mothers, he added:

"To ruthlessly destroy such a faith by indiscriminately condemning an effort like the Eighteenth Amendment, instead of taking the trouble to disentangle the real gains that have been accomplished from the evils which have been incurred, would be an act of social folly and national wrong."

**MR. STIMSON'S ADDRESS.**

Secretary Stimson's address was as follows:

"My friends of the radio audience:

"At their meeting last night the members of the Republican National Convention took a momentous step in the direction of American constitutional history. By a vote of 1,153 they have unanimously recommended to submit to the voters of this country a proposal to change the Eighteenth Amendment.

"They divided by a vote of 681 to 472 as to the form of the proposed change which should be submitted. But they were unanimous in recommending the submission of a proposal to change. Should the Democratic party in its approaching convention take similar action, the constitutional steps toward this momentous change will be well under way.

"There has been so much misunderstanding on the subject that it is well to analyze carefully the nature of what has been done. In the first place, both parties, in the convention last evening, advocated a new amendment to the Constitution. Even those who seek solely the repeal of the Eighteenth Amendment require a new amendment to accomplish such a repeal.

"The two proposals which were before the Republican National Convention last evening differed only as to the form which the new amendment should take.

**Basis of the Majority Plank.**

"In the second place, both propositions were clear and explicit, and the difference between them was fundamental and easily understood. The newspaper criticism that the majority plank was a straddle is quite unfounded. It is perfectly consistent, perfectly definite and perfectly logical. It is well founded in law and fact.

"Let us see what this fundamental difference between the two proposals was, and the reason for that difference. One proposal was an impatient demand to abrogate the entire work of the past thirteen years under the prohibition amendment, and to confess it to be an entire failure; to do away with all direct power on the part of the Federal Government in regard to the liquor traffic, and to leave the situation in respect to liquor as it was before 1919.

"This proposal was tantamount to asserting that everything which we have done during those years was useless or evil, that we should confess it to be a great and complete failure and go back and start over again.

"Right here it is well to remind you of what is frequently forgotten, namely, that the Eighteenth Amendment did not come out of thin air

Continued on Page Seventeen.

AGAIN THE REPUBLICAN STANDARD BEARERS

Harris & Ewing Photo.
HERBERT HOOVER.

Harris & Ewing Photo.
CHARLES CURTIS.

## HOOVER LAYS PLANS FOR COMING FIGHT

**His First Move Is Selection of Everett Sanders to Be Head of Committee.**

**SPEAKING TOURS UNLIKELY**

**Friends of Executive Expect Him to Direct Much of Fight From His Camp on the Rapidan.**

Special to THE NEW YORK TIMES.

WASHINGTON, June 16.—Gratified by the outcome of the Republican convention, President Hoover began preparations this afternoon for the campaign for his re-election.

His first move, after sending a message of appreciation for his nomination to Chairman Snell of the convention, was to let the national committee know that he preferred the election of Everett Sanders of Indiana as chairman of the committee.

Mr. Sanders is a former Representative, was secretary to President Coolidge and is experienced in national politics and national campaigns. Since 1929 he has been practicing law here and in Chicago.

The new chairman and the executive committee of the national committee are expected to come here shortly and map out campaign plans with the President. No definite word escaped from the White House on the question today, but it was predicted by Mr. Hoover's close political advisers that he would conduct the campaign from here and make relatively few speeches. It was pointed out that this would be in accordance with past custom when Presidents standing for re-election have attended to the duties of their high office and not engaged in far-flung campaign trips or many speeches.

**Trip to California Suggested.**

There is some talk among friends of the President of his going to California by warship through the Panama Canal to keep an engagement tentatively set for him to open the Olympic Games at Los Angeles late in July. This would permit a campaign trip back across the country.

Close friends of the President, however, declared that practically all chance of his going to California for notification ceremonies at his Palo Alto home had disappeared, due to the pressure of public business and the efforts he is making to combat the economic depression.

The ceremonies notifying him of the nomination and his acceptance speech, it was predicted, would be held either here or at his Rapidan camp in about six weeks. The chances were said to favor Washington and there were suggestions by his advisers that his acceptance speech might be delivered from the south portico of the White House. President Coolidge, it was recalled, delivered his acceptance speech here in 1924 at a night meeting in Memorial Continental Hall.

In any event the Rapidan camp will be the scene of important campaign activities, since the President intends to spend week-ends there during the Summer as often as pos-

Continued on Page Fourteen.

## Ballot for President

Special to THE NEW YORK TIMES.

*CHICAGO, June 16.—The vote of the Republican National Convention by which President Hoover was renominated here today was as follows:*

| State. | Delegates. | France. | Coolidge. | Dawes. | Blaine. | Wadsworth. | Hoover. |
|---|---|---|---|---|---|---|---|
| Alabama | 19 | .. | .. | .. | .. | .. | 19 |
| Arizona | 9 | .. | .. | .. | .. | .. | 9 |
| Arkansas | 15 | .. | .. | .. | .. | .. | 15 |
| California | 47 | .. | .. | .. | .. | .. | 47 |
| Colorado | 15 | .. | .. | .. | .. | .. | 15 |
| Connecticut | 19 | .. | .. | .. | .. | .. | 19 |
| Delaware | 9 | .. | .. | .. | .. | .. | 9 |
| Florida | 16 | .. | .. | .. | .. | .. | 16 |
| Georgia | 16 | .. | .. | .. | .. | .. | 16 |
| Idaho | 11 | .. | .. | .. | .. | .. | 11 |
| *Illinois | 61 | .. | 3½ | .. | .. | .. | 54½ |
| Indiana | 31 | .. | .. | .. | .. | .. | 31 |
| Iowa | 25 | .. | .. | .. | .. | .. | 25 |
| Kansas | 21 | .. | .. | .. | .. | .. | 21 |
| Kentucky | 25 | .. | .. | .. | .. | .. | 25 |
| Louisiana | 12 | .. | .. | .. | .. | .. | 13 |
| Maine | 13 | .. | .. | .. | .. | .. | 13 |
| Maryland | 19 | .. | .. | .. | .. | .. | 19 |
| Massachusetts | 34 | .. | .. | .. | .. | .. | 34 |
| Michigan | 41 | .. | .. | .. | .. | .. | 41 |
| Minnesota | 25 | .. | .. | .. | .. | .. | 25 |
| Mississippi | 11 | .. | .. | .. | .. | .. | 11 |
| Missouri | 23 | .. | .. | .. | .. | .. | 33 |
| Montana | 11 | .. | .. | .. | .. | .. | 11 |
| Nebraska | 17 | .. | .. | .. | .. | .. | 17 |
| Nevada | 9 | .. | .. | .. | .. | .. | 9 |
| N. Hampshire | 11 | .. | .. | .. | .. | .. | 11 |
| New Jersey | 35 | .. | .. | .. | .. | .. | 35 |
| New Mexico | 9 | .. | .. | 1 | .. | .. | 8 |
| New York | 97 | .. | .. | .. | .. | .. | 97 |
| No. Carolina | 28 | .. | .. | .. | .. | .. | 28 |
| No. Dakota | 11 | .. | .. | .. | 2 | .. | 9 |
| Ohio | 55 | .. | .. | .. | .. | .. | 55 |
| Oklahoma | 25 | .. | .. | .. | .. | .. | 25 |
| †Oregon | 13 | 3 | .. | .. | .. | .. | 9 |
| Pennsylvania | 75 | 1 | .. | .. | .. | 1 | 73 |
| Rhode Island | 8 | .. | .. | .. | .. | .. | 8 |
| So. Carolina | 10 | .. | .. | .. | .. | .. | 10 |
| So. Dakota | 11 | .. | .. | .. | .. | .. | 11 |
| Tennessee | 24 | .. | .. | .. | .. | .. | 24 |
| Texas | 49 | .. | .. | .. | .. | .. | 49 |
| Utah | 11 | .. | .. | .. | .. | .. | 11 |
| Vermont | 9 | .. | .. | .. | .. | .. | 9 |
| Virginia | 25 | .. | .. | .. | .. | .. | 25 |
| Washington | 19 | .. | .. | .. | .. | .. | 19 |
| W. Virginia | 19 | .. | .. | .. | .. | .. | 19 |
| Wisconsin | 27 | .. | 1 | .. | 11 | .. | 15 |
| Wyoming | 9 | .. | .. | .. | .. | .. | 9 |
| Alaska | 2 | .. | .. | .. | .. | .. | 2 |
| Dist. of Col. | 2 | .. | .. | .. | .. | .. | 2 |
| Hawaii | 2 | .. | .. | .. | .. | .. | 2 |
| Philippines | 2 | .. | .. | .. | .. | .. | 2 |
| Puerto Rico | 2 | .. | .. | .. | .. | .. | 2 |
| Total | 1,154 | 4 | 4½ | 1 | 13 | 1 | 1,126½ |

*Three not voting.
†One absent.

## REPUBLICAN PRESS SPLIT ON 'WET' PLANK

**Many Papers Hold That It Is a 'Meaningless Evasion'—Others See Notable Step.**

Editorial comment of Republican and independent newspapers over the nation differs on the merits of the prohibition plank in the Republican platform, telegraphed excerpts of editorials to THE NEW YORK TIMES indicated last night, with the wet papers bitter at what they called a "straddle."

In New York, The Sun declared that out of the "mountain of minds at Chicago comes a ridiculous mouse." The evident purpose of its authors "was to be obscure, and they have succeeded."

The Post, also Republican, headed its editorial "A moral failure at Chicago," and The World-Telegram, wet and independent, agreed with numerous other newspapers in calling the plank a "meaningless evasion."

The Herald Tribune, wet and Republican, declared that "in some paradise for politicians may yet be devised a compromise more inclusive and vague than the wet-moist-dry plank. * * * To date it has no rival." It added that the "great compromisers of Chicago can retire for a long rest, assured of the hearty disapproval of every one with an honest conviction on the subject."

The Chicago Tribune, Republican,

Continued on Page Fifteen.

## CURTIS VICTORY WON AGAINST FIELD OF 12

**Snell, Harbord, Alvin Fuller, Replogle and MacNider Were Put in Nomination.**

**PENNSYLVANIA TURNS TIDE**

**Suddenly Gives 75 to Kansan—Foes Unable to Muster Behind One Candidate.**

By L. C. SPEERS.
Special to THE NEW YORK TIMES.

CHICAGO, June 16.—Charles Curtis of Kansas won renomination as the Republican Vice Presidential candidate, but it was not an easy victory, and save for the fact that Pennsylvania swung its seventy-five votes to him after the roll-call of the States was concluded, he would have been 19¼ ballots short of the majority necessary for nomination.

The anti-Curtis elements in the convention fought to the last, but were unable to concentrate on any one candidate. With General Charles G. Dawes standing as their candidate, there was apparently every justification for their boast they had Mr. Curtis stopped, but with the Illinoisan out of the picture the backbone of the opposition was broken.

Six nominations were made for Vice President, and thirteen names, all told, were on the tally sheet when the roll-call was completed. One of them was that of Senator Couzens of Michigan, who received two of the eleven "Progressive" votes in the Wisconsin delegation. The fact that Mr. Couzens was born in Canada, and therefore ineligible, did not deter the La Follettites from allotting him a share of their honorary vote.

Three ex-soldiers constituted the main opposition to the renomination of Mr. Curtis—Hanford MacNider of Iowa, former National Commander of the American Legion; Major Gen. James G. Harbord of New York, chief of staff of the A. E. F., and General Edward Martin, chairman of the Republican State Committee of Pennsylvania.

**Six Placed in Nomination.**

Mrs. Edward Everett Gann, sister of the Vice President, was on the firing line to the end. She was tired and smiling when Pennsylvania withdrew the name of General Martin and cast its seventy-five votes for her brother, which assured his renomination on the first ballot.

The six nominations placed before the convention were those of Mr. Curtis, former Governor Alvin E. Fuller of Massachusetts, Mr. MacNider, J. Leonard Replogle of Florida, Representative Bertrand Snell of New York, the permanent chairman of the convention, and General Harbord.

Those who in addition to these were named in the voting that followed were Mr. Dawes, Judge William S. Kenyon of the United States Circuit Court of Appeals, Senator Couzens, Secretary Hurley of Oklahoma, David Ingalls, Republican

Continued on Page Thirteen.

## CHEER HOOVER 27 MINUTES

**Delegates Give 1,126 1-2 Votes on First Ballot, 634 1-4 to Curtis.**

**NEW YORK FOR HARBORD**

**France Ejected From Rostrum —Coolidge's Name Fails to Stir Convention.**

**HOOVER VICTORY COMPLETE**

**Administration Had 200 Votes in Reserve—Convention Ends After Nominations.**

By ARTHUR KROCK.
Special to THE NEW YORK TIMES.

CHICAGO, June 16.—Under the disclosed domination of the President, the Republican national convention at its closing session today renominated Herbert Hoover and gave a grudging but safe majority to Charles Curtis of Kansas, renominated as the party candidate for Vice President.

Mr. Hoover received 1,126½ votes on the first ballot, his nomination immediately thereafter being made unanimous. Mr. Curtis, the beneficiary of a last-minute switch of Pennsylvania's 75 votes from its Republican State Chairman, General Edward Martin, to the Vice President, had a first ballot majority of 55¾, with a total of 634¼. His nomination also was made unanimous. Until Pennsylvania responded to the Administration goad, Mr. Curtis lacked 19¼ votes of the sum required for his renomination.

It has been twenty years since the obvious will of a Republican National Committee has been so completely and publicly subordinated to a President's program. In 1912, as today, both President and Vice President were renominated, the only time in its history that the Republican party has repeated its ticket.

But then Theodore Roosevelt bolted the convention and formed the Bull Moose party, badly defeating the regular Republicans under William H. Taft in the election and assuring the victory of the Democratic ticket headed by Woodrow Wilson.

**No Prospect of a Bolt.**

So far as the political elements of the Republican party are concerned, there were no prospects of a bolt as the result of the defeat of the repeal plank last night and the renomination of Mr. Curtis today. The only menacing element was the insurgency of the New York delegation. Today its members cast ninety-five of their ninety-seven votes for General J. G. Harbord for Vice President, ignoring the plain warning which lay in the fact that the two New Yorkers who voted for Mr. Curtis were the Secretary of State, Henry L. Stimson, and the Secretary of the Treasury, Ogden L. Mills.

Last night the New Yorkers cast seventy-six of their votes for the Bingham repeal plank. The administration, which made that struggle the test of its control, had only twenty-one. Had not Charles D. Hilles, the national committeeman, declined to aid the State chairman, W. Kingsland Macy, in his effort to supplant Representative Ruth B. Pratt as national committee woman, this steadfast friend of the President would have been defeated.

The church drys, and those who are dry before they are Republican or Democratic, will not be heard from until they meet in national conclave in August, after they have examined the prohibition plank which the Democrats will adopt in Chicago the week after next.

It may be that then, as they did against James W. Wadsworth Jr. and Charles H. Tuttle, they will put independent New York State and national tickets in the field. Should this happen, the effect of that action, joined to the demonstrated dissatisfaction with Mr. Hoover's program of New York's regular Republicans, may be as disastrous to the national Republican candidates as was Colonel Roosevelt's third-party movement twenty years ago.

For days before this convention opened, and for the first day of the session, administration leaders maintained the strategic fiction that the delegates were to "work their will" on all points. In every respect save

Continued on Page Thirteen.

Section 1

"All the News That's Fit to Print."

# The New York Times.

LATE CITY EDITION
WEATHER—Cloudy, preceded by showers today; tomorrow showers.
Temperatures Yesterday—Max., 78; Min., 60.

Section 1

Copyright, 1932, by The New York Times Company.

VOL. LXXXI....No. 27,182. **** NEW YORK, SUNDAY, JUNE 26, 1932. Including Rotogravure Picture Section in one part—Magazine and Book Sections in Rotogravure. TEN CENTS

# LEWIS QUITS RACE, FREES DELEGATES; ROOSEVELT GETS 28 OF ILLINOIS VOTES; PLANK FOR SUBMISSION OF REPEAL READY

## 1,000,000 TO MARCH IN EUCHARISTIC FETE AS CLIMAX TODAY

### Four Huge Processions to File Through Dublin After Solemn Pontifical High Mass in Park.

### PAPAL BROADCAST PLANNED

### Archbishop Curley Is Selected to Celebrate Mass—His Mother, 92, Is Dying.

### PILGRIMS POUR INTO CITY

### Religious Exaltation at Its Peak—100,000 White-Clad Children Attend Special Service.

Special Cable to THE NEW YORK TIMES.

DUBLIN, June 25.—The religious exaltation of the Irish Catholics mounted hourly tonight as the climax of the Eucharistic Congress, with a solemn pontifical high mass and procession for almost 1,000,000 worshipers, drew near.

After a week of spiritual fervor such as they have never known, Ireland's devout Catholics are keyed to a high pitch of emotion awaiting the moment when, if possible, the Pope will broadcast to them tomorrow from the Vatican.

Those who have come from abroad for this Eucharistic Congress have seen great sights before and know something of the world they live in, but thousands of the Irish here are simple peasants from remote villages or farmhouses, and for them tomorrow will be the greatest day of their lives.

One could feel the fervor of the whole city rising today as thousands of pilgrims poured in to participate in the great closing ceremony of the congress.

**Special Trains on Way.**

The first of a fleet of special trains arrived in Dublin from Northern Ireland tonight, disgorging thousands into a city already packed to the bursting point, and between now and noon tomorrow 130 special trains will roll into Dublin's stations carrying approximately 150,000 persons from all parts of Ireland.

An armada of cross-Channel boats is en route from England crowded with Catholics from Glasgow, Liverpool and Birmingham, and there were so many thousands that a Cunarder had to be chartered to provide for the overflow crowd.

With almost 1,000,000 persons marching in the procession tomorrow, the congress authorities are taking every precaution against accidents. Ten thousand uniformed soldiers and policemen will be on duty while four endless processions converge on O'Connell Bridge in the heart of the city.

First-aid stations have been built at intervals between Phoenix Park and the bridge, two miles away, and all vehicular traffic into Dublin will be prohibited until the procession is over.

**100,000 Children in Service.**

Today an army of 100,000 children took possession of the open-air cathedral in Phoenix Park, where tomorrow's culminating ceremony will be held. They were like the sands of the sea—there was no counting them—as they streamed across the park to take their places before the great white altar.

It was an army in white, the girls in long silk dresses with white veils over their heads and the boys' costumes including white trousers and white shoes. Many of them had come from pitifully poor homes in Dublin's slums and more than a few families had gone hungry to dress them properly for the occasion.

Irish mischief was in their eyes when they started, but soon it changed to wide-eyed wonder when they saw the altar with scarlet-robed Cardinals sitting alongside the Papal Legate's throne.

The clear voices of the children floated in "Ave Maria" through the park and out over Dublin, being carried far and wide by loud-speakers. Their chubby hands were cupped in prayer and their faces solemn with the mysteries of the faith.

**Archbishop Curley Chosen.**

DUBLIN, June 25 (AP).—A signal honor was conferred upon American Catholicism today when Archbishop Michael J. Curley of Baltimore was selected to celebrate the solemn pontifical high mass that will conclude the Eucharistic Congress tomorrow.

"I can only say that this is a very moving recognition of the premier See of America," the Archbishop said when he had been informed of his selection. He characterized the congress as the greatest demonstration of faith he had ever seen.

It was disclosed today that Arch-

Continued on Page Seven.



## 500,000 Are Slain and Missing In Chinese Communist Drives

By The Associated Press.

SHANGHAI, June 25.—Reports published by the Chinese Government today declared that the Communist and bandit scourge sweeping Kiangsi Province had resulted in 500,000 persons slain and missing.

This huge total has been piled up during the last three months, the reports said.

The Chinese Communists have recently won startling victories, on one occasion causing the loss of two entire Nanking divisions.

It was reported a few days ago that Marshal Chiang Kai-shek himself was preparing to start a drive against them up the Yangtse Valley.

## KING HAD EXPECTED REVOLUTION IN SIAM

### People's Party Insists He Had Consented to the Move for Constitutional Monarchy.

### ECONOMIC CAUSES SEEN

### Drop in Rice Sales a Factor, Says the Legation in Paris—Prince Guarded Here.

By The Associated Press.

BANGKOK, Siam, Sunday, June 26.—King Prajadhipok cordially accepted today the end of his absolute power and the establishment of a constitutional monarchy by leaders of the People's party.

In a telegram from Huahin, on his way back to the capital, he said he was in entire agreement with the requirements of the new form of government set up by an almost bloodless revolt of the army and navy on Friday.

The King, who was on a holiday with his consort when his absolute monarchy was overturned, said he had recognised the desirability of a governmental change for some time.

He was willing, he added, to act as head of the new administration, although the period during which he would do so might not be very long because of the state of his health.

Leaders of the People's party objected to the use of the word revolution in connection with their movement against the government.

They asserted that they were establishing a government "by and for the people with the King's consent."

**All Treaties Are to Be Kept.**

The capital was peaceful after the military coup, the royal Princes having spent a nervous but safe night in chairs and on cots in the throne hall, where leaders of the People's party established headquarters of the Provisional Government.

Legations were informed by the Foreign Office that all treaties would be kept and that the lives and property of all foreign residents were safe.

The Prince of Nagor Svarga, who was a member of the Supreme Council, and other members of the royal family were seized before dawn Friday and taken from their beds to the throne hall, where they were heavily guarded.

The coup d'état was led by the chief of the Army and Navy General Staff.

A manifesto issued to the people accused King Prajadhipok of favoring his own family at the country's expense.

Prince Kambaeng Beura, Minister of Commerce and Communications, was reported to have escaped in the roundup of the nobles, and his whereabouts was unknown.

Newspapers, including the American-edited Daily Mail, were not closed, but were urged to print details of the movement.

Following the brief activity on Friday that established a constitutional monarchy, a warship was sent to Huahin to bring the King and Queen back to the capital.

**Economic Cause Is Seen.**

PARIS, June 25 (AP).—The Siamese Legation here said today that the inability of the peasants to sell rice and rubber was the chief cause of the economic problems which led to the Siamese upset.

A sliding-scale salary reduction for government employes, put into effect six months ago, was a contributing cause, legation officials said.

A grave export situation was caused, they said, by a drastic reduction of Chinese and Japanese imports of Siamese rice.

The legation officials said they believed the situation at Bangkok was "grave enough" since they had received no official word from the capital since the overturn took place.

**Our Recognition Continues.**

Special to THE NEW YORK TIMES.

WASHINGTON, June 25.—Prince Subba Svasti, brother of the Queen of Siam, who is traveling incognito in this country as Major Svasti, arrived here tonight from New York

Continued on Page Five.

## HERRIOT AND CABINET OPPOSE HOOVER PLAN; INSIST ON SECURITY

### Premier in Statement Admits He Tried to Forestall Proposal at Geneva Conference.

### REPARATIONS ACCORD SEEN

### French Believe Germans Will Agree to Compromise and Offer Compensation.

### SMALL POWERS AID HOOVER

### Delegates to Disarmament Parley Plan to Force Action on Project for Reductions.

Wireless to THE NEW YORK TIMES.

PARIS, June 25.—Premier Herriot returned here this morning from Lausanne for a second week-end trip to Paris and as swiftly as last Saturday got a unanimous Cabinet agreement to his and Joseph Paul-Boncour's negotiations. However, his support this time is not for a constructive accomplishment such as a five-power declaration but for virtually destroying the hope of making President Hoover's arms plan a genuine basis for discussion.

In a carefully prepared statement he read to newspaper men after the Cabinet council, M. Herriot admitted he had tried to forestall the Hoover message when he first heard of it, stated his opposition to much of it and reiterated the French desire for security by means of international force.

Moreover, Le Temps tonight, in what is accepted as an inspired editorial, gives an analysis intended to show the impossibility for France to accept the American suggestions. Until today, Paris, even in the best informed circles, had retained some doubt as to whether France would accept the plan as a basis of negotiations but no hopes remain tonight.

**"Satisfied" With Reparations Talks.**

Being in the midst of the conversations with the Germans on reparations, M. Herriot was unable to discuss the matter publicly except to say that he was "very satisfied" with the way things were going. Despite the fact that Camille Chautemps, Minister of the Interior, admitted afterward that "nothing has yet been accomplished," from unofficial but well-informed sources it was learned that the French really expected the Germans to abandon their unwillingness to compromise and make satisfactory compensation.

The French are just as tired of those "definite and final" reparations agreements as the Germans are and M. Herriot's original demand for the continuance of the Young Plan is understood to be merely a bargaining point. When it comes to a showdown the French will not oppose the abandonment of reparations as such as soon as the Germans make a fair offer, which they are expected to do next week.

M. Herriot, discussing the Hoover Plan in his declaration, said that when he was warned it was coming he felt concerned and expressed that concern to the American delegates, but nevertheless the message came out. Although he agreed with certain passages, such as those relating to fortifications and the interdependence of land, air and naval forces, obviously inserted out of regard for the French, he said he could not help feeling that certain articles must have been "garbled in transmission, for example, that part of the document where the German forces are evaluated at 100,000 men."

He said he also felt that the American program failed to take into account possible coalitions of two countries against a third.

"Therefore," he continued, "we French always have demanded and still demand international organization and control."

There was no hint from either M. Herriot or his associates that they would consider disarmament as connected with war debts. The Premier, however, did say that no European settlement was possible without universal settlement, by which he means that unless the United States cancels the war debts, reparations cannot be settled.

The editorial in Le Temps, after accusing President Hoover of issuing a campaign document which had merely complicated matters at Geneva and even had risked wrecking the progress made to date, launches into a careful and detailed analysis of what the plan would mean for France. It says, for instance, that it would impose naval parity with Italy, which "is absolutely unacceptable to a world and colonial power such as France," it would mean a 36.6 per cent reduction for France, 8.7 per cent for Italy and 25 per cent for Britain, Japan and the United States. Whereas the French Navy would possess

Continued on Page Two.



### Major Sports Results.

**Golf**—Gene Sarazen added the national open championship to the British open title which he won recently by scoring 70 and 66 for the last two rounds at Fresh Meadow, giving him a 72-hole total of 286. His score equaled the record for this event. Phil Perkins and Bobby Cruickshank tied for second at 289.

**Tennis**—Frank Shields and Sidney B. Wood Jr. reached the quarter-finals of the British singles championship. Wilmer Allison lost to Frederick Perry of England.

**Baseball** — Gehrig's nineteenth home run helped the Yankees turn back the Athletics, 7—4. The Giants lost to the Phillies, 9—8, and Brooklyn bowed to the Braves, 6—5. Harvard beat Yale, 6—0, winning the series.

**Racing**—Blenheim captured the Brookdale Handicap at Aqueduct.

*(Complete Details in Sports Section)*

## HOOVER 'WRONG,' SAY RELIEF BILL BACKERS

### Wagner Denies Threat to Budget and Asserts Public Works Would Employ 2,500,000.

### CONFEREES ARE AT ODDS

### They Adjourn After a Brief Session—Norbeck Doubts "President Can Tell Us What to Do."

Special to THE NEW YORK TIMES.

WASHINGTON, June 25.—Aroused by the President's criticism of his unemployment relief bill because of the $500,000,000 appropriated in it for public works, Senator Wagner today delivered a final plea for the measure as it was taken up by a conference of members of the House and Senate.

"Today the informed and expert opinion of the nation and the great body of its citizens approve and commend this legislation," Senator Wagner said. "And Mr. Hoover is again defying the light and the truth, obstinately resisting the persuasion of fact and logic and contributing to the despair which is all too prevalent."

The conferees considering the bill, headed by Senator Norbeck and Representative McDuffie, adjourned after a brief meeting during which they voted to have the Congressional legislative counsel prepare a brief explaining the wide differences between the Wagner bill and the Garner bill passed by the House, the two measures which they must reconcile or leave Federal unemployment relief in a hopeless deadlock.

The Wagner bill provides $300,000,000 for immediate loans to States for emergency relief work, $500,000,000 for public works to be financed by bond issues and $1,500,000,000 to be loaned by the Reconstruction Finance Corporation to States and municipalities for self-liquidating construction projects.

The Garner bill provides $1,190,000,000 for public works financed by bond issues, $1,000,000,000 for Reconstruction Finance Corporation loans for self-liquidating projects and $100,000,000 to be administered as an emergency fund by the President.

**Conferees See Difficult Task.**

Senator Norbeck, speaking for the conferees after this morning's meeting, said that the administration effort to have private industries included among the recipients of Reconstruction Finance Corporation loans was considered favorably by the House conferees but was opposed by the Senate conferees.

No secret was made by the conferees that they doubt they can frame a measure acceptable to Congress, both houses of which demand

Continued on Page Twenty-One.

## ROUGH DRAFT COMPLETED

### It Proposes Conventions by States, Protection of Dry Areas.

### SALOON BAN IS DEMANDED

### Tumult of Wets Booing Cannon Marks Conclusion of Public Hearings on Question.

### BISHOP WARNS OF A BOLT

### He Is Jeered for Five Minutes After Declaring Repeal Will Lose South as in 1928.

By CHARLES R. MICHAEL.

Special to THE NEW YORK TIMES.

CHICAGO, June 25.—The subcommittee of the unofficial Democratic platform committee this afternoon began consideration of a tentative prohibition plank of unprecedented brevity, which will be reported to the committee on resolutions when that body has been appointed by the national convention on Monday. The subcommittee took up the proposal after listening for three hours to wets and drys at a hearing which was featured by many and heated verbal exchanges.

This is the text of the plank, which provides for submission of an amendment to the Federal Constitution repealing the Eighteenth Amendment, but not pledging the party to support of repeal:

> We favor submission to State conventions of an amendment repealing the Eighteenth Amendment submitted to the people in such manner as to assure a choice between the present system and return to the States of the power and responsibilities to prohibit liquors by such means as will promote temperance, prevent the return of the saloon, and protect the dry States in their enforcement of laws and permit the taxing of liquor by Federal or State Governments.

It was explained after the hearing that the subcommittee of the unofficial platform committee before which the hearing was held had not agreed to the plank, but may report it with its own plank and others to the resolutions committee for consideration.

Senator Hull was of the opinion that the rough draft represented ideas that will be finally embodied in the prohibition plank. Both he and A. Mitchell Palmer indicated that the plank would be modified greatly in language but would stand for the principle of submission to allow the people to determine whether they desired to repeal or retain the Eighteenth Amendment, without committing members of Congress to support the amendment.

**Market Regulation Proposed.**

Mr. Palmer, Attorney General in the Wilson Administration, who is drafting a platform for the Democratic National Convention, said tonight that a strong plank providing for Federal regulation of stock ex-

Continued on Page Twenty-five.

### *How Democratic Leaders View Roosevelt Move To Do Away With Two-Thirds Nomination Rule*

Special to THE NEW YORK TIMES.

*CHICAGO, June 25.—Following are among the sentiments expressed by party leaders over the plan of the Roosevelt management to provide for the nominations this year by a simple majority:*

JAMES A. FARLEY—The thing must be done, should have been done before and will be done now.

CARTER GLASS—I cannot support any candidate who takes the short cut to the nomination that way.

NEWTON D. BAKER—Sensitive men would find it difficult to defend a candidate who started out with a moral flaw in his title.

JAMES M. COX—It threatens that the councils of the party may be dominated by those who think only of the nomination in June, defying the possibilities of November.

JOHN W. DAVIS—They're hanging a millstone around his (Roosevelt's) neck.

JOHN SHARP WILLIAMS—The two-thirds rule has been for a century the South's defense. It would be idiotic on her part to surrender it.

## ROOSEVELT DECIDES ON FIGHT TO FINISH

### Farley, After Phone Talk, Commits Him to Stand or Fall on Two-thirds Rule Issue.

### TEXAS SPURNS A CHANGE

### Garner Attends Caucus of State Delegates, Which Also Votes to Support Shouse.

By JAMES A. HAGERTY.

Special to THE NEW YORK TIMES.

CHICAGO, June 25.—The forces of Governor Franklin D. Roosevelt, leading candidate for the Democratic nomination for President, seemed to hold firm all along the line today.

Despite reports to the contrary, they persisted in their determination to elect Senator Thomas J. Walsh permanent chairman of the convention and to force the fight for the abandonment of the two-thirds rule to an issue in the convention.

James A. Farley, the campaign manager, announced that the Roosevelt leaders had no intention of receding from their position in refusing to accept any of the several proposed compromises.

Mr. Farley issued his statement after a talk over the telephone with Governor Roosevelt and conferences with leading supporters. In this statement he definitely committed not only the Roosevelt managers here but also the Governor himself to the fight for the elimination of the two-thirds rule, which now has become the vital issue of the convention.

**Acts After Compromise Fails.**

The announcement that Governor Roosevelt had decided to stand or fall on the result of the fight to change the two-thirds rule was made to newspaper reporters in the early afternoon following attempts by some of the more pacific of the Roosevelt leaders to get an agreement on a compromise.

Under this compromise, sponsored by Senator Harrison of Mississippi, the convention rules would be changed so that the majority rule on nominations would not be invoked until ten ballots had been cast without a choice under the two-thirds rule.

Most of the leaders in the Roosevelt camp opposed this compromise because they felt that any recession on their part would result in getting no rule change at all and destroy or impair the chance of Roosevelt's nomination.

**Farley Explains Stand.**

Mr. Farley's statement was as follows:

"It is a grossly inaccurate statement to say that the friends of Governor Roosevelt have decided to 'abrogate' the two-thirds rule. There is no two-thirds rule at the present binding the convention which will meet next Monday. Nor will that convention be bound by any rule whatever except such rules as the delegates deliberately vote for after the convention is organized.

"The two-thirds rule can only be imposed upon the convention by a deliberate and affirmative action of the convention itself. Our contention is that this affirmative action should not be taken—that the two-thirds rule has been outgrown and has been productive of disruption even to the extent of undoubtedly ruining all chance of Democratic success in 1924.

"That we should again deliberately

Continued on Page Twenty-three.

## LINES SHIFT ON RULE, WITH SOUTH DIVIDED

### Opposition Arises in States Which Roosevelt Claimed as a Unit for Abrogation.

### MISSISSIPPI DEALS BLOW

### Williams Calls Change "Idiotic"—Gardiner and Daniels at Odds in North Carolina.

By L. C. SPEERS

Special to THE NEW YORK TIMES.

CHICAGO, June 25.—Reaction to the Roosevelt proposal to abrogate the Democratic two-thirds rule continues to indicate opposition to the change in quarters where the Roosevelt managers had been counting on solid support.

This is especially true in many Southern delegations which the Roosevelt management has been claiming as practically a unit for abolition of the rule to clear the way for the nomination of Governor Roosevelt by a majority vote.

The hardest blows to the Roosevelt move came from Mississippi and Ohio. Ex-Senator John Sharp Williams of Mississippi, from the shades of his Cedar Grove plantation, nineteen miles from Yazoo City, telegraphed ex-Senator James A. Reed of Missouri that it would be "idiotic" for the South to turn against the rule.

From Cleveland, Newton D. Baker, the most talked of "dark horse" in the convention, sent word of his opposition to a change, while simultaneously came the announcement that the Ohio delegation would vote solidly to retain the rule, so far as this convention was concerned.

The first Southern State to indicate its opposition to the abrogation movement was North Carolina, whose twenty-six votes had been listed as solid for a change.

The North Carolinians, of whom Governor Max Gardiner is the chairman, will caucus Monday morning, and the indications are that the vote to sustain the rule will be, to use the words of one of its most influential delegates, "overwhelmingly" against the Roosevelt proposal.

**Daniels and Gardiner Differ.**

At the caucus of the "friends" of Governor Roosevelt Thursday night, ex-Secretary of the Navy Daniels agreed to the abrogation program. Other delegates subsequently arriving remarked that Mr. Daniels spoke only for himself and Mr. Daniels, when asked if this was true, answered that it was. Governor Gardiner is opposed to abrogation now and there will be no surprise if the delegation votes three "ayes" and twenty-three "noes."

Mississippi now appears clearly out of the abrogating column by a substantial majority of its twenty delegates. Representative John E. Rankin of Tupelo, leader of the abrogation element in the delegation, was busy today trying to rally his Mississippians against the rule, when the telegram came from Mr. Williams.

Mr. Rankin had just issued a statement in which he claimed all the Southern States as favoring abolition of the rule, when Mr. Reed received the message from Mr. Williams, which read as follows:

"Two-thirds rule has been for a century the South's defense and it would be idiotic on her part to surrender it."

This declaration from the Sage

Continued on Page Twenty-two.

## LEWIS CAUSES SENSATION

### Withdrawal of Senator Is First Break in Ranks of 'Favorite Sons.'

### CONCILIATION TALK STARTS

### Some of Governor's Supporters Think New Gains Insure His Nomination.

### BAKER ENTERS RULES FRAY

### Joins Opponents of Change as Both Sides Gain and Lose Adherents on Question.

By ARTHUR KROCK.

Special to THE NEW YORK TIMES.

CHICAGO, June 25.—The first wide breach in the "favorite-son" entrenchments appeared swiftly and dramatically today when a telegram to an Illinois editor from Senator James Hamilton Lewis, withdrawing as a Presidential candidate, was issued from Roosevelt headquarters.

The breach was not made by any foray on the part of the Governor's managers. They were, they said, as much surprised as any one else. Senator Lewis simply wired Vincent Y. Dahlman of Springfield that he is out of the race and left the fifty-eight Illinois delegates pledged to him to choose their own course.

Since from twenty to thirty of the delegates are favorable to Governor Roosevelt, the advantage to him on all controversial questions before the convention is obvious. So far as the nomination is concerned, Senator Lewis's withdrawal adds a new element of Roosevelt strength for the first ballot.

In the opinion of many this new element of strength clinches the nomination by repairing any damage caused by the sudden decision of the Roosevelt leaders Thursday midnight to apply the simple majority rule to the nomination of this convention. The managers of New York's Governor were confirmed in their belief that the race was over.

An immediate consequence of this spreading opinion was a move to find some means to alleviate the feelings wounded by the decision of the Roosevelt group to support Senator Thomas F. Walsh of Montana against Jouett Shouse of Kansas for permanent chairman and to pass the new majority rule.

Conciliation filled the air of Chicago tonight. By several influential leaders the hope was expressed that "some way" would be found to abandon the new rule plan, to reach an accommodation in the Shouse-Walsh fight and to nominate the Governor of New York by two-thirds on the first ballot without any taint on his title or burning wounds in the breasts of his opponents. How this was to be achieved no one tonight seemed to know. But a spirit of compromise permeated the more cautious section of the Roosevelt group.

Another contingent of leaders met the talk of compromise with the word that it was too late; that to let go at any point was to risk the loss of everything.

While this division of council was appearing, supporters and foes of the new convention rule swooped down upon the freed delegates from Illinois.

**Roosevelt the Chief Gainer.**

Until news of Mr. Lewis's decision came from Roosevelt sources the day had been devoted to systematic roost-robbing by both factions. The captives of both sides were in twos and threes until the release of the Illinois delegates offered an opportunity for wholesale operations. By the expressions on the faces in the various candidates' rooms, it was easy to see that the Roosevelt managers were the only ones made happy by Senator Lewis's action.

James A. Farley, Governor Roosevelt's chief-of-staff, reverted to his prediction of a first-ballot nomination, but this time he did not say whether it would be a new-rule or an old-rule majority.

The "stop-Roosevelt" leaders, already handicapped by inability and unwillingness to make a fast alliance, went separately to Mayor Anton J. Cermak of Chicago, boss of the urban areas up-State, to find out how badly they were hurt and to help a concentration against the released Roosevelt energy down-State.

Mr. Cermak offered no great comfort. He said that he thought Mr.

Continued on Page Twenty-two.

## *Father Duffy, Ill Nine Days, Growing Weaker; Little Hope for Chaplain of "Fighting 69th"*

The Rev. Francis P. Duffy, World War chaplain of the 165th (the Fighting Sixty-ninth) Infantry, was in a coma early this morning at St. Vincent's Hospital, where he was taken nine days ago suffering from colitis. Little hope was held out that he would survive the night.

At his bedside were his brother and sister, three priests from his parish and Colonel Alexander E. Anderson of the 165th. When Colonel Anderson left soon after 1 o'clock this morning he said Father Duffy had not roused from the coma since 5 o'clock yesterday afternoon.

Father Duffy rallied after a severe relapse several days ago, but his condition became very unfavorable yesterday, according to his attending physician, Dr. George R. Stewart.

In addition to the intestinal ailment, which was a consequence of the hardships he endured in his campaigning, Father Duffy is suffering from an acute infection of the liver and gradual loss of strength, Dr. Stewart said.

Father Duffy, who is pastor of Holy Cross Church, Forty-second Street West of Eighth Avenue was seriously ill last Spring with influenza but has since been recuperating.

Once described by Cardinal Hayes as "the ideal army chaplain and the ideal parish priest," Father Duffy won fame and decorations from the United States and France for his devotion to his men under fire during the World War. Few clergymen have been held in more affectionate regard by persons of many faiths. Father Duffy was 61 years old on May 2.

Father Duffy is the holder of the Distinguished Service Cross and the Croix de Guerre for his heroism when his regiment crossed the Ourcq under heavy fire during the battle that lasted from July 28 to July 31, 1918. He was also promoted from First Lieutenant to Major at that time.

His citation for the Distinguished Service Cross said:

"Despite constant and severe bombardment with shells and aerial bombs, he continued to circulate in and about two aid stations and hospitals, creating an atmosphere of cheerfulness and confidence by his courageous and inspiring example."

"All the News That's Fit to Print."

# The New York Times.

LATE CITY EDITION
WEATHER—Fair today and tomorrow, temperature unchanged.
Temperatures Yesterday—Max., 88; Min., 65.



VOL. LXXXI....No. 27,186. + * * * * NEW YORK, THURSDAY, JUNE 30, 1932. TWO CENTS In New York City | THREE CENTS Within 200 Miles | FOUR CENTS Elsewhere Except 7th and 8th Postal Zones

# DEMOCRATS PLEDGE PARTY TO REPEAL OF THE DRY LAW AND QUICK MODIFICATION TO LEGALIZE BEER, 934¾-213¾; PLANK AGAINST WAR DEBT CANCELLATION IS SUBMITTED

## BRITAIN TO DELIVER SWIFT TARIFF BLOW IF IRISH DO NOT PAY

### Parliament Will Rush Taxes if £1,500,000 Annuities Are Not Met by Midnight.

### TREASURY TO PAY DIVIDENDS

### Funds Will Be Given to the Bank of England to Protect the Holders of Irish Stock.

### OTHER SUMS ALSO SOON DUE

### Levies Will Be Devised, Effective Before July 14, to Raise Total of £5,000,000 a Year.

Special Cable to THE NEW YORK TIMES.

LONDON, June 29.—As reprisal for the refusal of the Free State to pay the half-yearly land annuities amounting to £1,500,000 (the pound was quoted at $3.60 yesterday) which are now due, Britain proposes to impose a sweeping tax on Free State goods entering Britain. Unless the money is in the hands of the British National Debt Commissioners by midnight tomorrow, machinery will be put in motion for rushing a tax bill through all stages of Parliament next week to become law before the Summer recess on July 14.

The Irish land stock is guaranteed by the British Treasury and the holders will receive their dividends as usual on Friday. The Treasury will provide the money to enable the Bank of England to make the payments, but the Cabinet is determined that the burden shall not be borne by the British taxpayer.

To this end it has now been arranged that taxes shall be imposed even on Irish live stock and dairy produce, notwithstanding a provision in the import duties act that all goods imported from the dominions shall enter Britain free of duty until Nov. 15.

The British Cabinet is agreed that President de Valera's attitude has left it no choice but to insist on the recovery of sums due to Britain by an alternative method.

**Britain's Last Note Ignored.**

Thus far no reply has been received from the Free State to the last note of Britain, which made it clear that the United Kingdom could not agree to arbitration by a tribunal the personnel of which was not confined to citizens of the British Commonwealth of Nations. Mr. de Valera suggested in his last note that other financial matters should be referred to arbitration, and Britain assumes that other moneys due will not be handed over. The moneys payable amount altogether to about £5,000,000 in a full year, including the land annuities of £3,000,000, the Royal Irish Constabulary pensions of £1,000,000, local loan annuities of £600,000, compensation for damage to property in the Free State in 1919 and 1921 of £250,000 and small amounts for pensions and allowances to judges and civil servants.

As the value of imports from the Free State during the present financial year are estimated at about £30,000,000, it is realized that it will not be an easy matter to levy duties amounting to £5,000,000, and one of the principal tasks of the government framing any new proposals will be to see that the duties do not cease to be revenue duties and become protective duties.

**Payment Stoppage Campaign Pledge**

In the campaign leading to his recent election as President of the Irish Free State Council, Eamon de Valera announced his intention of withholding the £3,000,000 of annual land payments due to the British Treasury under the treaty of 1920. These annuities, payable for some fifty years or more, are collected from Irish Free State farmers in repayment of the amount borrowed on their behalf to buy out their landlords.

The British Treasury acts as an intermediary between the tenants and those from whom the money was borrowed. Mr. de Valera contends that this is neither morally nor legally correct and that Britain must prove her right to these monies before a court acceptable to both parties.

Great Britain threatened several months ago that if Mr. de Valera should ever succeed in abolishing the oath of allegiance to the King—another of the Free State Council President's objectives—and repudiating the payment of the land annuities that it would resort to tariff weapons instead of troops and guns.

**Economic Strangulation Possible.**

Under these conditions, the Free State would be regarded simply as a seceder from the empire and be cut off automatically from the tariff privileges she now enjoys with the other British dominions. The British market absorbs 90 per cent of the Free State's products. Britain

Continued on Page Three.

## 274 Speakeasies to Be Locked; June Figures Set a Record

As a result of United States Attorney Medalie's new policy of bringing padlock suits against all places raided by prohibition agents, Raymond J. Mulligan, United States Marshal, will snap locks on 274 speakeasies which were named defendants and tried in June. The number is a record for the Southern District of New York. Federal Judge Alfred C. Coxe signed 200 decrees yesterday. Decrees against seventy-four resorts had been signed before.

Of the 200 places, 137 were ordered closed for six months and the rest for a year each. Thirty-two defendants were directed by the court to file bonds of from $500 to $1,000 each to guarantee observance of the law, and thirty-six complaints were dropped for technical reasons.

## POLICE HAVE A CLUE, CURTIS TRIAL SHOWS

### Federal Investigator Says Definite Group Is Suspected in Lindbergh Case.

### SWEARS HOAX BALKED HUNT

### Norfolk Man Said He Signed Confession "to Get Some Sleep," Another Testifies.

From a Staff Correspondent.
Special to THE NEW YORK TIMES.

FLEMINGTON, N. J., June 29.—The New Jersey State police, who for nearly four months have been vainly trying to find the kidnappers of the Lindbergh baby, have a definite group of men under suspicion. This much and no more about the hunt was revealed here today, the third of the trial of John H. Curtis, Norfolk boat builder, on a charge of willfully misleading the police in their efforts to arrest the kidnappers and murderers of Charles A. Lindbergh Jr.

The revelation came while Lloyd Fisher, the young Flemington lawyer who is heading the defense, was cross-examining Frank J. Wilson of Baltimore, investigator for the Department of Internal Revenue, who has been associated for many weeks with the hunt. Wilson, a bland and obviously experienced court witness, is one of the government's expert investigators who spent two years accumulating under-cover evidence on which the government finally sent Al Capone to jail.

**Insists Hoax Aided Kidnappers.**

Wilson had testified for more than an hour and had told of meeting Curtis for the first time on the night of May 12 at the Lindbergh home after the body of the child had been discovered. Mr. Fisher was seeking to break down the assertion of the witness that Curtis had caused attention to be taken from important clues and diverted to checking up his tales of Gloucester fishing boats, kidnappers with hide-outs in Cape May, with the witness sticking stoutly to his opinion.

Finally Wilson admitted that in one case he questioned some one at the instigation of Curtis, and that but for Curtis he would have let this unnamed person alone for the time being.

Wilson, under questioning, declared further that on May 13 he was convinced that Curtis did not have actual knowledge of the kidnappers. The defense lawyer picked him up quickly and reached for a copy of Colonel Lindbergh's testimony yesterday morning.

"Then you disagreed with Colonel Lindbergh's testimony?" he asked sharply as he prepared to read it. Harry Stout, associate prosecutor, interrupted and Judge Robbins ruled that the Lindbergh testimony should not be read.

The cross-examination continued as follows:

Q.—What other things did you do or not do as a result of Curtis's information? A.—It is possible that interviewing a certain man at a certain time interfered with the apprehension of the kidnappers.

**Refuses to Detail Suspicion.**

Q.—Who was the man you normally would not have interviewed that you did interview because of Curtis? A.—I can't answer that question.

Here Mr. Stout interceded again and over Mr. Fischer's protest obtained permission from the court to ask the witness why he could not tell the story of this mysterious man.

"We have a right to know who that man is," protested the defense counsel.

Mr. Stout continued:

Q.—Mr. Wilson, is the person in question suspected of being implicated in the crime? A.—No, not he, but he is in touch with others who we strongly suspect.

Q.—If you disclose this man's name, would it affect the people with whom he is in touch? A.—I think it would.

Q.—The exposure of the person to whom you refer might prevent the

Continued on Page Two.

## Vote by the States on the Prohibition Plank; Majority for Outright Repeal Overwhelming

Special to THE NEW YORK TIMES.

*CHICAGO, Thursday, June 30.—Following is the vote in detail as taken by the Democratic convention early this morning on the question of substituting the minority for the majority (wet) report on the prohibition plank in the platform, the "no" votes standing for outright repeal and legalized beer, the "yes" votes for resubmission:*

| State or Territory. | Votes. | Yes. | No. | State or Territory. | Votes. | Yes. | No. |
|---|---|---|---|---|---|---|---|
| Alabama | 24 | 21 | 3 | North Dakota | 10 | .. | 10 |
| Arizona | 6 | .. | 6 | ‡Ohio | 52 | 2 | 49 |
| Arkansas | 18 | 13 | 5 | Oklahoma | 22 | 22 | .. |
| California | 44 | 11 | 33 | Oregon | 10 | 3 | 7 |
| Colorado | 12 | 1 | 11 | Pennsylvania | 76 | .. | 76 |
| Connecticut | 16 | ¼ | 15¾ | Rhode Island | 10 | .. | 10 |
| Delaware | 6 | 4 | 2 | South Carolina | 18 | .. | 18 |
| Florida | 14 | 1 | 13 | South Dakota | 10 | 6 | 4 |
| Georgia | 28 | 28 | .. | Tennessee | 24 | 6 | 18 |
| Idaho | 8 | .. | 8 | Texas | 46 | .. | 46 |
| Illinois | 58 | .. | 58 | Utah | 8 | .. | 8 |
| Indiana | 30 | .. | 30 | Vermont | 8 | .. | 8 |
| Iowa | 26 | .. | 26 | Virginia | 24 | 13 | 11 |
| Kansas | 20 | 12 | 8 | Washington | 16 | 1½ | 14½ |
| Kentucky | 26 | .. | 26 | *West Virginia | 16 | 8½ | 7 |
| Louisiana | 20 | 3 | 17 | Wisconsin | 26 | .. | 26 |
| Maine | 12 | 2 | 10 | Wyoming | 6 | .. | 6 |
| Maryland | 16 | .. | 16 | Alaska | 6 | .. | 6 |
| Massachusetts | 36 | .. | 36 | Dist. of Columbia | 6 | .. | 6 |
| Michigan | 38 | .. | 38 | Hawaii | 6 | .. | 6 |
| xMinnesota | 24 | 4 | 18 | Philippines | 6 | .. | 6 |
| Mississippi | 20 | 20 | .. | Porto Rico | 6 | .. | 6 |
| Missouri | 36 | 7½ | 28½ | Canal Zone | 6 | .. | 6 |
| Montana | 8 | .. | 8 | Virgin Islands | 2 | .. | 2 |
| ††Nebraska | 16 | 5 | 9 | Totals | 1,154 | 213¾ | 934¾ |
| Nevada | 6 | .. | 6 | | | | |
| New Hampshire | 8 | .. | 8 | | | | |
| New Jersey | 32 | .. | 32 | | | | |
| New Mexico | 6 | 1 | 5 | | | | |
| New York | 94 | .. | 94 | | | | |
| North Carolina | 26 | 18 | 8 | | | | |

†One refused to vote.
‡One absent.
*One-half absent.
xTwo absent.

## RIVAL MANOEUVRES KEEP LEADERS BUSY

### Reports of Gains and Losses in Various Delegations Bring Rumors of Trading.

### BOTH SIDES TELL OF BREAKS

### Roosevelt Managers Concentrate on Winning 6 States and Opposition Centres on 5.

By L. C. SPEERS.
Special to THE NEW YORK TIMES.

CHICAGO, June 29.—With political eyes turning to all points of the compass, with rumblings heard in at least four of the Roosevelt delegations and with echoes audible in four or five others in the same column, the strategy of the Roosevelt managers is centred tonight in a last-minute drive to win the nomination for Governor Roosevelt on the first two ballots.

The friends of Governor Roosevelt are bringing their heavy artillery into action in an effort to break the opposition strength in the New York, Illinois, Texas, California, Missouri and Oklahoma delegations. Of these, Missouri is considered the best bet from the Roosevelt standpoint. Under the instructions the unit rule binding the forty-six votes of Texas can be broken only with the consent of Speaker Garner.

Senator Jim Reed is still in control of a majority of the Missourians, while California is linked to Texas with instructions almost as binding as those voted by the Texans in their State convention. Oklahoma must stand by Governor Murray as long as he cares to hold them.

**Tammany Support in Demand.**

The Tammany element in the New York delegation and the Illinois delegation are therefore the "mystery" of the situation. They are under fire from both sides of the controversy, the anti-Roosevelt forces seeking to hold them in line for any candidate just so long as it isn't Roosevelt, while the Roosevelt organization is hammering away day and night to bring them into the Roosevelt camp, believing that success in that direction probably would start a band-wagon movement and bring about the nomination of Governor Roosevelt.

The Roosevelt opposition is concentrating on the Indiana, Mississippi, Iowa, Minnesota and Alabama delegations, in all of which there is a strong anti-Roosevelt movement under way. The situation in these five States is tonight the most serious menace facing the Roosevelt management.

The votes involved total 124, every one of them figuring in the original forecasts made by Chairman Farley

Continued on Page Sixteen.

## ROOSEVELT RANKS FIRM, FARLEY SAYS

### Defections Denied as Manager Predicts 690 on First Ballot and Possibly Two-thirds.

### LIQUOR FIGHT DISCOUNTED

### Chairman Holds It Will Not Affect Candidate—Declares No Pact Made on Second Place.

By JAMES A. HAGERTY.
Special to THE NEW YORK TIMES.

CHICAGO, June 29.—Reports of defections in the Roosevelt ranks were denied today by James A. Farley, campaign manager for the Governor. Mr. Farley declared that the contrary was the case and that Mr. Roosevelt would pick up votes when the test comes on the first ballot.

"Governor Roosevelt will have between 690 and 700 votes on the first ballot," Mr. Farley said, sticking to his original prediction. "We hope there will be a sufficient number of shifts to give him two-thirds and bring about his nomination on the first ballot."

Mr. Farley's optimistic statement followed a day of pulling and hauling by the campaign managers of the various candidates.

Taking the vote of 626 for Senator Walsh in the permanent chairmanship fight as the low point of Roosevelt strength so far revealed, the supporters of the Governor asserted that they would have at least fifty or sixty more votes for Governor Roosevelt on the first ballot.

The Roosevelt men admitted that on the first ballot they would lose the 6½ votes which Senator Walsh received from Connecticut and the 19½ from Missouri, a total of 26.

They claimed as prospective gains on the first ballot 4½ cast for Jouett Shouse in Alabama, 1 in Delaware, 10 in Iowa, 6½ in Kansas, 7 in Maine, 1 in Nebraska, 3 in New Mexico and 4 in North Carolina, a total of 37.

The Roosevelt managers also expect 22 or 25 votes from Indiana and to gain 5 or 6 in New York.

Mr. Farley declined in his interview to give any details of his first-ballot expectations.

"How is New York going to vote?" he was asked.

"I don't know about New York," he replied, "but I hope for the best."

"How about reports that Governor Roosevelt is losing votes in Mississippi, Iowa, West Virginia, Minnesota and Alabama?" he was asked.

"There is no danger there," he said.

"Do you think the coming fight over the prohibition plank will affect Roosevelt adversely?" was the next question.

"I see no reason why it should,"

Continued on Page Eighteen.

## RESULT CHEERED WILDLY

### Crowd Roars Approval of the Wet Plank After 4-Hour Debate.

### LONG OVATION FOR SMITH

### Gets 10-Minute Demonstration on Making First Appearance on Convention Platform.

### RITCHIE JOINS IN APPEAL

### David I. Walsh Also Takes Part —Hull Booed When He Champions the Prohibition Cause.

By W. A. WARN.
Special to THE NEW YORK TIMES.

CHICAGO, Thursday, June 30.—A tumultuous night session of almost five hours in which the repeal champions of the Democratic party debated with the advocates of moderation, while packed galleries cheered or jeered or laughed and delegates broke into two impromptu parades, led up to the convention's rejection of the minority report on its prohibition plank early today.

The decision was greeted with a thunder of applause by the throng which had listened to former Governor Alfred E. Smith of New York, Senator David I. Walsh of Massachusetts and Governor Albert C. Ritchie of Maryland demanding the end of prohibition by outright repeal and to Senator Cordell Hull of Tennessee pleading for submission of the Eighteenth Amendment without making acceptance of repeal a test of party loyalty.

**Roar of Welcome for Smith.**

When Mr. Smith's turn came and he appeared on the rostrum the convention rose to acclaim him with a roar of welcome.

The delegates, alternates and visitors, as he made his way to the front of the platform, let loose a tumult of cheering and for nearly ten minutes he was compelled to wait for it to subside before he could begin to speak.

The former Governor of New York, a pioneer in the movement for the repeal, stood smiling, but it was very evident that as wave after wave of cheers swept through the stadium a lump was rising in his throat.

It was not long before the giant organ started out to fill the stadium with the east side melodies that signalize public appearances of Mr. Smith. The organist took the audience on a prolonged tour of "The Sidewalks of New York." After a while delegations pledged to Smith took the cue and began marching behind their standards.

**New York Aloof in Parade.**

The New York banner remained anchored to its moorings where the delegation sat. The standards of Connecticut, Massachusetts, Rhode Island and New Jersey had been bobbing up and down for a while and then they began to move through the aisles in the most spontaneous of all the demonstrations that have marked the convention.

Ohio was followed by Pennsylvania's standard as the demonstration was drawing to a close.

The Smith demonstration followed the reading of the minority plank by Senator Hull, who proceeded to defend its refraining from pledging the party to repeal on the ground that politics should be eliminated from the elections for conventions in the several States set up to act on the question of repeal following submission from Congress.

The convention did not seem to take kindly to the discourse, and even when he mentioned the name of Woodrow Wilson, whom he quoted in support of his own contention, it failed to stir the delegates.

Mr. Smith in his address declared that the failure of the Republican National Convention to write into its platform a clear-cut, forthright declaration on prohibition had provoked country-wide distrust. He was applauded vigorously and cheered when at the close of his short address he called upon the convention to adopt the majority plank presented by the resolutions committee.

"I ask that for the sake of the party, for the sake of the country and for the sake of the taxpayers," he said.

Maury Hughes of Texas, scheduled to speak for the minority report,

Continued on Page Fourteen.

## Texts of the Democratic Plank on Prohibition And the Minority Report Which Was Defeated

Special to THE NEW YORK TIMES.

*CHICAGO, June 30.—The text of the majority prohibition plank, adopted by the Democratic convention early this morning, and that of the rejected minority plank are as follows:*

### The Majority Plank

We favor the repeal of the Eighteenth Amendment.

To effect such repeal, we demand that the Congress immediately propose a constitutional amendment to truly representative conventions in the States called to act solely on that proposal.

We urge the enactment of such measures by the several States as will actually promote temperance, effectively prevent the return of the saloon and bring the liquor traffic into the open under complete supervision and control by the States.

We demand that the Federal Government effectively exercise its power to enable the States to protect themselves against importation of intoxicating liquors in violation of their laws.

Pending repeal, we favor immediate modification of the Volstead act to legalize the manufacture and sale of beer and other beverages of such alcoholic content as is permissible under the Constitution and to provide therefrom a proper and needed revenue.

### The Minority Plank

We advocate that the Congress immediately propose to truly representative conventions in the States, called to meet solely on the proposal, a repeal of the Eighteenth Amendment.

In the event of repeal, we urge that the Democratic party cooperate in the enactment of such measures in the several States as will actually promote temperance, effectively prevent the return of the saloon and bring the liquor traffic under complete supervision and control by the States and that the Federal Government effectively exercise its power to protect States against importation of intoxicating liquors in violation of their laws.

*The text of the majority prohibition plank which was adopted by the Republican National Convention and that of the minority report for repeal, which was rejected by a vote of 681 to 422, will be found on page 17.*

## ROOSEVELT IS READY FOR CHICAGO FLIGHT

### Plane Waiting at Albany Would Also Carry Mrs. Roosevelt and Their Sons.

### TRIP WOULD TAKE 7 HOURS

### Governor's Friends Say Presence at Convention Would End Physical Incapacity Rumor.

From a Staff Correspondent.
Special to THE NEW YORK TIMES.

ALBANY, June 29.—With an airplane poised for a flight to Chicago if he is nominated, Governor Roosevelt gathered the members of his family about him in the Executive Mansion tonight to listen to the session of the Democratic National Convention over the radio.

The Governor maintained his usual silence about flying to the convention to address the delegates if chosen as their standard bearer, and, if anything, was more uncommunicative than on other convention developments of the past few days. If he does make the air trip, his wife and sons will probably accompany him.

It has been known for some days that the Governor would probably hurry to the convention if selected in the hope of reaching Chicago before the final adjournment. A trimortored passenger plane has been sent to the Albany airport from Cleveland by the American Airways, Inc., and is ready to depart on short notice.

The Governor turned aside all questions concerning the flying trip, but did not deny that he would choose that spectacular method of going to the convention city.

"I may go in a submarine," he bantered.

He was in excellent spirits and continued to exchange badinage with the correspondents about the Chicago trip while steadfastly refusing to commit himself.

**Trip Would Take Seven Hours.**

The plane, according to an announcement of the Airways Company, was brought to Albany after Guernsey Cross, secretary to the Governor, had intimated that the Executive might want to use it.

In the face of the Governor's silence concerning the plane, Walter Pollock, manager of the Airways station here, declined to permit the taking of photographs in the hangar, on orders from Mr. Cross.

If the Governor should use the plane, it is estimated that the trip would take about seven hours. If a nomination were made tomorrow night he could leave early Friday morning and arrive in Chicago just

Continued on Page Eighteen.

## PLATFORM DEMANDS TARIFF FOR REVENUE

### Lays Depression to Disastrous Policies Pursued "Since the World War."

### FOR ECONOMIC PARLEY

### Party's Declaration of Policies Set Forth With Record-Breaking Brevity.

By CHARLES R. MICHAEL.
Special to THE NEW YORK TIMES.

CHICAGO, June 29.—The extreme wets crushed the moderate submissionist group and the chief spokesmen for Governor Roosevelt in the Democratic convention's resolutions committee late today, and by a vote of 35 to 17 forced the insertion of a wringing wet and modification plank into the platform, which was submitted to the convention tonight.

This step, representing chiefly a victory for the opponents of Governor Roosevelt, was taken under the leadership of Senator David I. Walsh of Massachusetts, a Smith adherent, who, however, received support from Senator Wheeler of Montana, one of the Roosevelt leaders. Senators Glass and Hull, William G. McAdoo and A. Mitchell Palmer fought the ultra-wets, who commanded nearly two-thirds of the membership of the resolutions committee.

The platform, of about 1,400 words, is concise in its definition of party principles and is regarded as the shortest one ever produced by the Democratic party.

The platform does not mention the names of President Hoover or of the Republican party. It has a preamble charging present economic conditions to "the disastrous policies pursued by our government since the World War," and urges a complete change in government as a cure.

**Points of the Platform.**

With the introductory words "we advocate," the platform favors a 25 per cent cut in the costs of government; a balanced budget; non-confiscatory taxation; a sound currency; an international silver conference; a tariff for revenue with a tariff commission "free from executive interferences"; an international economic conference; the form of unemployment relief passed by the Senate; State unemployment and old-age insurance; broad farm relief; a frugal armed service, but one qualified for national defense; strict enforcement of the Sherman law; divorce of the government from private business connection; greater regulation of utility and holding companies and stock exchanges; detailed advertising of flotation costs in stock offerings; quicker liquidation of deposits in closed banks; separation of affiliates from commer-

Continued on Page Sixteen.

## BIG MAJORITY FOR REPEAL

### Only Seven States Vote in Favor of the Mild Wet Plank.

### THREE CANDIDATES DEBATE

### All the Contenders Release Their Delegates to Vote Their Own Opinions.

### ARENA IN WILD ACCLAIM

### Southern and Western States Which Helped Adopt Prohibition Reverse Former Stand.

*Text of Democratic platform as submitted to convention, Page 15.*

By ARTHUR KROCK.
Special to THE NEW YORK TIMES.

CHICAGO, Thursday, June 30.—Early this morning the Democratic party went as wet as the seven seas at the fourth session of its national convention in the Stadium. By an overwhelming majority the delegates sustained the majority plank in the platform which puts the party on record as favoring outright repeal of the Eighteenth Amendment and immediate modification of the Volstead act to permit the manufacture and sale of beer.

The vote was 934¾ against substitution of the minority report and 213¾ for.

The minority proposal was that the party merely pledge prompt submission of repeal to State conventions and guarantee Federal protection to those which desire to remain dry.

Although Senator Cordell Hull of Tennessee pleaded with the convention not to make prohibition a party question, and W. A. Fitts of Alabama said that the committee action would make doubtful the vote of five States in the election, the majority proposal carried overwhelmingly.

Only from Alabama, Arkansas, Georgia, Kansas, Mississippi, North Carolina and Oklahoma did the minority plank command the support of a majority.

Kentucky was the first State to vote for the dripping wet plank, followed by Louisiana, South Carolina and Texas.

The once dry South and West deserted the amendment which they put in the Constitution in 1919 after fifty years of agitation. California, Florida, Indiana (which had the driest of bone-dry enforcement acts), Iowa, Kentucky, Louisiana, Maine (the first dry State), Michigan, Minnesota, Missouri, Montana, Nebraska, Nevada, North Dakota, Ohio, Oregon, South Carolina, Tennessee, Texas, Utah, Washington—all these gave majorities of their total strength to the party advocacy of repeal.

**Debate Thrills Hearers.**

The convention action was preceded by a thrilling debate in which three Presidential candidates made their first appearances on the platform, Alfred E. Smith, Governor Ritchie and Governor Murray. The first two were for the majority plank. Mr. Murray was on the other side.

Not since the convention began has there been such a demonstration as was given to Mr. Smith. Galleries and delegates joined in the storm of applause which greeted the candidate of 1928 and roared out approval of a statement by a delegate from Texas who followed him with the statement that it was not prohibition but religious prejudice which lost Texas for Mr. Smith in 1928.

Every seat in the galleries and on the floor was filled and during the four-hour debate few left the hall. The galleries were almost always turbulent, their wet sentiments leading them to give the minority plank orators indifferent attention.

Other dissents to the platform planks on the veterans' bonus, farm relief, guarantee of bank deposits and home rule for Hawaii were noted in other minority reports made by Governor Murray, W. G. McAdoo and others. These will be voted on tomorrow when the platform as a whole is considered.

But tonight's vote demonstrated that the platform as written by the full committee will be overwhelmingly

Continued on Page Fifteen.

"All the News That's Fit to Print."

# The New York Times.

LATE CITY EDITION
WEATHER—Clearing and cooler today; tomorrow fair.
Temperatures Yesterday—Max., 86; Min., 70.



VOL. LXXXI....No. 27,188. ++**** NEW YORK, SATURDAY, JULY 2, 1932. TWO CENTS In New York City | THREE CENTS Within 200 Miles | FOUR CENTS Elsewhere Except 7th and 8th Postal Zones

# ROOSEVELT NOMINATED ON FOURTH BALLOT; GARNER EXPECTED TO BE HIS RUNNING MATE; GOVERNOR WILL FLY TO CONVENTION TODAY

## CONFEREES REACH RELIEF COMPROMISE UPON $2,100,000,000

### Use Parts of Both Wagner and Garner Bills in Report to Reach Congress Tuesday.

### BOND ISSUES ARE BARRED

### $1,500,000,000 Provided for R. F. C. Loans—$300,000,000 Available for Public Works.

### GRANTS TO STATES SPLIT

### $200,000,000 Allowed, According to Population—$100,000,000 on a Basis of Need.

*Text of Secretary Mills's review of government finances, page 2.*

Special to THE NEW YORK TIMES.

WASHINGTON, July 1.—Agreement on relief legislation, the most important subject before Congress, was reached by the conferees tonight just after the Senate and House recessed until Tuesday, when they will take up the conference report.

Compromising between the Wagner and Garner bills, each involving about $2,300,000,000, the conferees drew up a program of $2,100,000,000 divided as follows:

$1,500,000,000 for loans by the Reconstruction Finance Corporation to public and private enterprises, but only to the latter where money is unavailable elsewhere.

$300,000,000 for construction of public works, this money not to be financed by bond issues, but by the Treasury.

$200,000,000 for direct loans to the States on a basis of population.

$100,000,000 for direct loans to the States on a basis of need.

**Points of Difference in Bills.**

For a week the conferees have been struggling to adjust the administration's viewpoint, as well as differences between the Wagner and Garner bills, as follows:

Wagner Bill—$1,500,000,000 for loans by the Reconstruction Finance Corporation to self-liquidating enterprises of a public character; $500,000,000 for public works, financed by bond issues; $300,000,000 for loans to the States on a population basis.

Garner Bill—$1,000,000,000 for loans by the Reconstruction Finance Corporation to public and private enterprises; $1,190,000,000 for public works financed by bond issues; $100,000,000 for a Presidential emergency fund.

The administration vigorously opposed bond issues, demanded that private business as well as self-liquidating public enterprises be allowed to obtain loans from the Reconstruction Finance Corporation and desired that the loans to States be granted on a need instead of a population basis.

**Character and Purposes of Loans.**

Announcing the agreement by the conferees, Senator Norbeck explained that the parts of the Garner bill regarding Reconstruction Finance Corporation loans had been accepted with certain restrictions and suitable safeguards.

He said the loans to private enterprises could be made only when it was impossible to obtain money from other sources, and that the loans could be granted for only four purposes—"agriculture, industry, commerce and employment."

Loans to municipalities would be permitted, he stated, only for future needs and not to settle debts already contracted. He said that this meant that no loans would be granted for long-due payment of school teachers, as in Chicago, but might be allowed to continue employment of the teachers and other city employes.

The loans could also be made for public works and to the small as well as the large merchant, the Senator stated, but in all cases they would have to be adequately secured.

Continued on Page Two.



## The Fourth and Decisive Ballot

Special to THE NEW YORK TIMES.

*CHICAGO, July 1.—The detailed vote on the fourth ballot of the Democratic National Convention nominating Franklin D. Roosevelt for President follows:*

| Total Vote | STATE | Roosevelt | Smith | Garner | Ritchie | Baker | Reed | Traylor | White | Byrd |
|---|---|---|---|---|---|---|---|---|---|---|
| 24 | Alabama | 24 | .. | .. | .. | .. | .. | .. | .. | .. |
| 6 | Arizona | 6 | .. | .. | .. | .. | .. | .. | .. | .. |
| 18 | Arkansas | 18 | .. | .. | .. | .. | .. | .. | .. | .. |
| 44 | California | 44 | .. | .. | .. | .. | .. | .. | .. | .. |
| 12 | Colorado | 12 | .. | .. | .. | .. | .. | .. | .. | .. |
| 16 | Connecticut | .. | 16 | .. | .. | .. | .. | .. | .. | .. |
| 6 | Delaware | 6 | .. | .. | .. | .. | .. | .. | .. | .. |
| 14 | Florida | 14 | .. | .. | .. | .. | .. | .. | .. | .. |
| 28 | Georgia | 28 | .. | .. | .. | .. | .. | .. | .. | .. |
| 8 | Idaho | 8 | .. | .. | .. | .. | .. | .. | .. | .. |
| 58 | Illinois | 58 | .. | .. | .. | .. | .. | .. | .. | .. |
| 30 | Indiana | 30 | .. | .. | .. | .. | .. | .. | .. | .. |
| 26 | Iowa | 26 | .. | .. | .. | .. | .. | .. | .. | .. |
| 20 | Kansas | 20 | .. | .. | .. | .. | .. | .. | .. | .. |
| 26 | Kentucky | 26 | .. | .. | .. | .. | .. | .. | .. | .. |
| 20 | Louisiana | 20 | .. | .. | .. | .. | .. | .. | .. | .. |
| 12 | Maine | 12 | .. | .. | .. | .. | .. | .. | .. | .. |
| 16 | Maryland | 16 | .. | .. | .. | .. | .. | .. | .. | .. |
| 36 | Mas'chusetts | .. | 36 | .. | .. | .. | .. | .. | .. | .. |
| 38 | Michigan | 38 | .. | .. | .. | .. | .. | .. | .. | .. |
| 24 | Minnesota | 24 | .. | .. | .. | .. | .. | .. | .. | .. |
| 20 | Mississippi | 20 | .. | .. | .. | .. | .. | .. | .. | .. |
| 36 | Missouri | 36 | .. | .. | .. | .. | .. | .. | .. | .. |
| 8 | Montana | 8 | .. | .. | .. | .. | .. | .. | .. | .. |
| 16 | Nebraska | 16 | .. | .. | .. | .. | .. | .. | .. | .. |
| 6 | Nevada | 6 | .. | .. | .. | .. | .. | .. | .. | .. |
| 8 | N. Ham'hire | 8 | .. | .. | .. | .. | .. | .. | .. | .. |
| 32 | New Jersey | .. | 32 | .. | .. | .. | .. | .. | .. | .. |
| 6 | New Mexico | 6 | .. | .. | .. | .. | .. | .. | .. | .. |
| 94 | New York | 31 | 63 | .. | .. | .. | .. | .. | .. | .. |
| 26 | No. Carolina | 26 | .. | .. | .. | .. | .. | .. | .. | .. |
| 10 | No. Dakota | 10 | .. | .. | .. | .. | .. | .. | .. | .. |
| *52 | Ohio | 29 | 17 | .. | 2 | .. | .. | .. | 3 | .. |
| 22 | Oklahoma | 22 | .. | .. | .. | .. | .. | .. | .. | .. |
| 10 | Oregon | 10 | .. | .. | .. | .. | .. | .. | .. | .. |
| 76 | Pennsylv'a.* | 49 | 14½ | .. | 1½ | 5½ | .. | .. | .. | .. |
| 10 | Rhode Isl. | .. | 10 | .. | .. | .. | .. | .. | .. | .. |
| 18 | So. Carolina | 18 | .. | .. | .. | .. | .. | .. | .. | .. |
| 10 | So. Dakota | 10 | .. | .. | .. | .. | .. | .. | .. | .. |
| 24 | Tennessee | 24 | .. | .. | .. | .. | .. | .. | .. | .. |
| 46 | Texas | 46 | .. | .. | .. | .. | .. | .. | .. | .. |
| 8 | Utah | 8 | .. | .. | .. | .. | .. | .. | .. | .. |
| 8 | Vermont | 8 | .. | .. | .. | .. | .. | .. | .. | .. |
| 24 | Virginia | 24 | .. | .. | .. | .. | .. | .. | .. | .. |
| 16 | Washington | 16 | .. | .. | .. | .. | .. | .. | .. | .. |
| 16 | West Va. | 16 | .. | .. | .. | .. | .. | .. | .. | .. |
| 26 | Wisconsin | 24 | 2 | .. | .. | .. | .. | .. | .. | .. |
| 6 | Wyoming | 6 | .. | .. | .. | .. | .. | .. | .. | .. |
| 6 | Alaska | 6 | .. | .. | .. | .. | .. | .. | .. | .. |
| 6 | Dist. of Col. | 6 | .. | .. | .. | .. | .. | .. | .. | .. |
| 6 | Hawaii | 6 | .. | .. | .. | .. | .. | .. | .. | .. |
| 6 | Philippines | 6 | .. | .. | .. | .. | .. | .. | .. | .. |
| 6 | Puerto Rico | 6 | .. | .. | .. | .. | .. | .. | .. | .. |
| 6 | Canal Zone | 6 | .. | .. | .. | .. | .. | .. | .. | .. |
| 2 | Virgin Islds. | 2 | .. | .. | .. | .. | .. | .. | .. | .. |
| 1,154. | Totals | 945 | 190½ | .. | 3½ | 5½ | .. | .. | 3 | .. |

*Five 1½ votes not cast.
Ohio cast one vote for Cox.

## MADDEN MUST GO TO PRISON AGAIN

### High Court Holds He and Three Others Still Under Parole, Upsetting Levy Ruling.

The police are looking for Owen Madden, former convict, and three of his associates, former Sing Sing inmates.

The search began yesterday when the Appellate Division of the Supreme Court unanimously reversed the decision of Supreme Court Justice Aaron J. Levy, who sustained a writ of habeas corpus last April freeing the four ex-convicts from the custody of the State Parole Board. Madden and his companions, Jeremiah J. Sullivan, Terence Reilly, alias Thomas Robinson, and Gustave Guillaume, alias Little Frenchy, are wanted for violation of parole.

Justice Levy, in sustaining the writ releasing Madden, had ruled that Madden was arrested on flimsy and highly technical grounds and that Madden had been discharged from parole in 1929. He also held that Madden's arrest "was an attempt to convict under color of law for wrongs which cannot be brought home to him by competent evidence." He ruled that the other three had also been discharged from parole.

**Dispute Levy's Findings.**

The five justices of the Appellate Division, Presiding Justice Finch and Justices Martin, Townley, McAvoy and Merrill, in their review of the proceedings before Justice Levy, commented: "No evidence, either documentary or otherwise, of the

Continued on Page Three.

## BINGHAM OFFERS SENATE BEER TEST

### Puts 4 Per Cent Beverage Plan Into Rider for Home Loan Bank Bill—Wets Count on 49 Votes.

Special to THE NEW YORK TIMES.

WASHINGTON, July 1.—A test in the Senate on modification of the Volstead act seemed likely when Senator Bingham today offered a proposal to legalize beer of 3.2 per cent alcoholic content by weight, or 4 per cent by volume, as an amendment to the Home Loan Bank bill.

He announced that he would not press for a vote on his amendment until the Democratic Senators returned from Chicago, where their party convention has gone on record for immediate liberalization of the Volstead act. The Senate recessed tonight until Tuesday, when the Home Loan Bank bill will come up again.

Through his rider to the bill, the Connecticut Republican hopes to force a House vote also on the proposals.

Prohibition leaders in that body recently made a point of order against another vote on modification as an independent proposal, but wets now consider that attaching the Bingham plan to the Home Loan Bank bill will overcome parliamentary objection.

**Conflicting Views of Prospects.**

Wet leaders in the Senate drew up tentative polls on their prospects if a vote can be had on the Bingham scheme. Their computations, manifestly speculative, indicated a hope

Continued on Page Nine.

## HE IS 'READY FOR ACTION'

### Plane Starts With Him at 8 A. M. for Chicago to Open Campaign.

### WIFE AND BOYS GOING, TOO

### On Way Governor Will Work on Speech Accepting His Party's Nomination.

### EXPECTS TO MEET SMITH

### Addressing 1,000 Neighbors on Lawn, He Predicts Harmony and Certain Victory.

By JAMES A. KIERAN.
Special to THE NEW YORK TIMES.

ALBANY, N. Y., Saturday, July 2.—Wreathed in smiles, Governor Roosevelt sat in his armchair in the Executive Mansion early this morning, jubilant at his nomination and all ready with plans for an intensive campaign to win his way to the White House.

With his wife, his sons and close friends around him, he had heard a short time before the balloting that chose him as the candidate of the Democratic party for the Presidency as it came from the radio in the corner of the room.

Then, as he received newspaper correspondents, he heard coming back over the radio from Chicago the message he had sent telling of his prospective appearance before the convention today, together with the announcement that a meeting of the national committee had been requested for tonight at the Congress Hotel to launch the campaign.

"We are ready for action," the Governor said.

**Joyous Night in Mansion.**

All through the evening the Executive Mansion, where four years ago Alfred E. Smith received the news of his nomination at Houston, had an atmosphere of suppressed elation. It had been intimated that Texas and California might come to the Roosevelt banner, but nothing was certain.

Just before the radio broadcast started the definite news was circulated and as members of the Governor's family and his aides hurried about the mansion they clearly showed their joy.

Throughout the broadcast the Governor sat in the workroom on the south side with his small party which included Supreme Court Justice Samuel I. Rosenman and Mrs. Rosenman, Miss Marguerite Lehand and Miss Grace Tully, his private secretaries; Detective "Gus" Gennerich, his New York City bodyguard, and several others.

When the doors were finally opened and the Governor officially became the candidate of his party, he was quick to extend the olive branch to Alfred E. Smith.

"Do you expect to see Governor Smith soon?" he was asked.

"I certainly hope so," said the Executive, smiling.

**Family to Fly With Him.**

"I haven't any particular statement," said the Governor. "I sent it to Chicago and there it is coming back now. The speech tomorrow will be the official notification so that we can save the expense of bringing people here from all over the country later.

"I am going to leave at 8 o'clock in the morning by airplane and expect to reach Chicago by about 2:30 our time. I am going to do some final work on the speech on the trip out.

"Mrs. Roosevelt will go along, and my two boys, Elliott and John. That's four. Then Miss Lehand, Miss Tully, Sergeant Earl Miller and Gus Gennerich and"——

Here he paused and turned toward Justice Rosenman, who has been his constant companion for a week.

"And Sam, will he go?" interjected Mrs. Rosenman. The justice had previously indicated that he did not intend to make the trip.

"Sure he'll go," said the Governor. The justice laughed.

"We expect to have a good trip," said the Governor. Then he went on to banter with some of the correspondents whom he has known for some time, posing for a photograph

Continued on Page Four.

## The Democratic Nominee

© New York Times Studio Photo.

FRANKLIN DELANO ROOSEVELT.

## GARNER WITHDRAWS, AIDING ROOSEVELT

### 'Politics Is Funny,' the Speaker Philosophizes as He Reveals His Decision.

### PLACE ON TICKET IS SEEN

### Capital Democrats Look Upon Texan as Logical Nominee for Vice Presidency.

Special to THE NEW YORK TIMES.

WASHINGTON, July 1.—Speaker Garner, until this evening a stubborn candidate for the Democratic nomination for the Presidency, telephoned orders to Representative Rayburn and William G. McAdoo, his campaign managers, tonight to release the California and Texas delegations pledged to his support.

He ordered them to be released in favor of Governor Roosevelt, heightening, in the opinion of the capital, the chances of Mr. Roosevelt for winning the nomination.

The Speaker's action is viewed here as making himself Governor Roosevelt's logical running mate.

His announcement of withdrawal from the Presidential race was made to THE NEW YORK TIMES shortly before 9 o'clock tonight.

Long past his customary bedtime, Mr. Garner was on the roof garden of the hotel where he makes his home. He was alone and apparently unrecognized by others seeking relief from the heat.

"You've gone to Roosevelt?" a reporter asked him.

"That's right, son," the Speaker replied. "And that is all I am going to say to you."

His cigar glowed against the night. To a comment from the reporter, he replied:

"I'm a little older than you are, son. And politics is funny."

"You may become the first man in

Continued on Page Six.

*Democratic Nominee's Name Is Pronounced "Rose-velt"*

By The Associated Press.

ALBANY, N. Y., July 1.—The Democratic Presidential nominee pronounces his name "Rose-velt" in two syllables and with a long "o," instead of the way it looks as if it should be pronounced.

The name Roosevelt came over with the old Dutch patroons, and in the Dutch language double o is pronounced as a single long "o."

## SMITH HEARS NEWS IN GRIM SILENCE

### Refuses Comment on Rival's Victory—Friends Say He May Not Support Ticket.

By The Associated Press.

CHICAGO, July 1.—Alfred E. Smith, sitting in his hotel headquarters facing a radio and a poster urging "Smith for President," heard, without formal comment, tonight the nomination of Governor Roosevelt.

"Do you intend to support the nominee?" he was asked.

"I have no comment to make," Mr. Smith replied, chewing vigorously at a cigar. Then he turned back to the radio and resumed his grim silence.

Mr. Smith's associates and political backers said they did not believe he would support the Democratic ticket in November.

An expression of bitter sadness came to the face of the "Happy Warrior of 1928" as soon as William G. McAdoo began to announce the switch of California's votes. There was a change in that expression only once during the rest of the evening, when Connecticut's votes for Smith launched an outburst of cheering. He smiled slightly for the moment.

The outcome of the convention was not a complete surprise to the former New York Governor, for the report of the switch had filtered

Continued on Page Five.

## 15,000 IN STADIUM FOR CLIMAX SCENE

### Galleries Unaware as Ballot Began That Garner Action Made Outcome Certain.

### WALKER SILENT ON RESULT

### He Lets Curry Acknowledge for Tammany Its Defeat in Overwhelming Vote.

From a Staff Correspondent.
Special to THE NEW YORK TIMES.

CHICAGO, July 1.—Fifteen thousand persons who crowded the Stadium for the Democratic convention session tonight expecting drama were not disappointed in the spectacle they saw when Franklin D. Roosevelt was nominated, amid the cheers of delegates, and groans and boos from those in the galleries.

It was more than ordinary drama when William G. McAdoo, whose nomination Alfred E. Smith blocked at the Madison Square Garden convention in New York City, went to the platform to announce that California and Texas would give ninety votes for Roosevelt, making the latter's nomination certain and preventing Mr. Smith from continuing any longer at this convention the blocking rôle he filled in 1924.

With the local sentiment, as revealed by the gallery demonstrations, bitterly opposed to Mr. Roosevelt, the roll-call was attended with great disorder caused by interruptions from the galleries.

As State after State recorded their support for Roosevelt, the men and women in the galleries roared their disapproval and resentment and cheered wildly at the announcement of the votes which stayed with Mr. Smith.

While the Smith States stuck by their candidate, the support of favorite sons disintegrated.

As Missouri broke from former

Continued on Page Six.

## ROOSEVELT VOTE IS 945

### Smith His Nearest Rival, With 190 1-2 as Four States Stick to End.

### McADOO, BREAKS DEADLOCK

### Casts California's 44 Amid Wild Demonstration After Garner Releases Texans.

### RITCHIE MEN FALL IN LINE

### Tammany Holds Aloof—Cermak Forced to Appeal to the Booing Galleries.

By ARTHUR KROCK.
Special to THE NEW YORK TIMES.

CHICAGO, July 1.—California and Texas, which came to Chicago pledged to Speaker John N. Garner, broke the deadlock on the Presidential nomination in the Democratic National Convention on the fourth ballot tonight by casting their ninety votes for Governor Franklin D. Roosevelt of New York.

This started a bandwagon rush, in which only New York—the nominee's home State—Massachusetts, Rhode Island, New Jersey and Connecticut declined to join, and Mr. Roosevelt was selected by a vote of 945, the convention's two-thirds requirement being 769 1-3. His nearest rival, Alfred E. Smith, received 190½ votes, the four States named sticking to him to the last.

**Roosevelt to Fly to Chicago.**

Governor Roosevelt, as soon as he heard of his success, sent a message which the permanent chairman, Senator Thomas J. Walsh of Montana read to the convention. The Governor announced that he will be here tomorrow, coming by airplane from Albany, to address the convention and to receive his formal notification, thus avoiding the expense of a more formal and distant ceremony.

The national committee will also be reorganized under the eye of the nominee tomorrow with his convention manager, James A. Farley of New York, as chairman. A great occasion, led by Senator Walsh, with bands and speeches, is to be made of the notification ceremonies.

Senator Walsh, the permanent chairman, sent the following telegram to Governor Roosevelt:

"The convention extends its greetings and assurance of fealty to our nominee and welcomes the news that he will be here with us tomorrow."

William G. McAdoo, former Secretary of the Treasury, was the voice of Mr. Roosevelt's destiny. When the name of California was called by the reading clerk he took the platform to explain the change of the vote in the Western States. The news of the impending action had spread throughout the delegates.

But the galleries had not heard about it, and, when they sensed what was happening, the boos and yells with which they expressed their anger over the defeat of Alfred E. Smith required the efforts of Mayor Anthony J. Cermak of Chicago, whose presence was demanded by Permanent Chairman Thomas J. Walsh, to restore a measure of quiet.

**McAdoo Speaks for West.**

Mr. McAdoo said that California had not come to Chicago to deadlock the convention, that Democracy had suffered enough, as in 1924 when he himself had almost polled a majority, by such methods. He said that the opinion of the West, in which Speaker Garner joined, was that Democrats should fight Republicans and not one another.

He did not say what has been known here for several days, that William Randolph Hearst, who has great influence in the California delegation and who "discovered" the qualification of Mr. Garner as a candidate, pressed the shift to Mr. Roosevelt because he feared that a deadlock might produce Newton D. Baker or another candidate with whose international policies he is not in agreement. Mr. Hearst also is a believer in majority rule and the Texas-California contingent was responding to his ideas on that subject.

Throughout a feverish day in

Continued on Page Four.

Sections 1 AND 4

"All the News That's Fit to Print"

# The New York Times.

LATE CITY EDITION
WEATHER—Fair, moderate temperature; Monday fair and warmer.
Temperatures Yesterday—Max., 75; Min., 66.

Sections 1 AND 4

Copyright, 1932, by The New York Times Company.

VOL. LXXXI....No. 27,189. **** NEW YORK, SUNDAY, JULY 3, 1932. Including Rotogravure Picture Section in one part—Magazine and Book Sections in Rotogravure TEN CENTS

# ROOSEVELT PUTS ECONOMIC RECOVERY FIRST IN HIS ACCEPTANCE SPEECH AT CONVENTION; GARNER FOR VICE PRESIDENT BY ACCLAMATION

## CURTIS IS CONVICTED; JURY FINDS HE KNEW ACTUAL KIDNAPPERS

### Lindbergh "Negotiator" Faces a 3-Year Term for Story He "Confessed" Was Hoax.

### LENIENCY IS RECOMMENDED

### Judge Had Ordered Acquittal Unless Accused Was Held to Have Dealt With Gang.

### PROMPT APPEAL IS PLANNED

### Verdict Reached in Four Hours With Six Ballots Taken—Majority for Conviction From First.

From a Staff Correspondent.
Special to The New York Times.

FLEMINGTON, N. J., July 2.—John Hughes Curtis, the Norfolk boat builder and self-styled "intermediary" for the return of the Lindbergh baby, was found guilty here today of deliberately giving false information for the purpose of preventing the arrest of the kidnappers.

The tall, rugged Norfolk manufacturer, who for many years had been a man of high repute in his own community, now stands convicted, under the indictment and the charge, as Judge Robbins gave it to the jury, not only of lying but of having actually known who the kidnappers were. Curtis had "confessed" that his entire story was a hoax.

Sentence was deferred until July 11. The maximum penalty is three years in prison and a fine of $1,000.

The jury was out four hours and five minutes. As is the Hunterdon County custom, the court house bell was tolled when it was ready to return.

From store and hotel porch spectators came on the run. Curtis, who had been in the jail, entered the court room head erect, facing the eyes of the curious who have been watching him throughout the five days of the trial. Until today he has been smiling, confident and affable. When he entered the room this afternoon the smile was gone, his normally ruddy face was white and the blue eyes stared straight ahead.

He took his seat behind his counsel table. The jury filed in, and Judge Adam O. Robbins, dressed in a linen suit and without his robe, ascended the bench.

**Woman Announces Verdict.**

"Have you reached a verdict?" asked C. Leon Fells, clerk of the court.

"We have," the five women and seven men answered in chorus.

"What is your verdict?" demanded Mr. Fells.

Miss Leila Alpaugh, forewoman, then read from a slip of paper:

"We, the jurors in the State of New Jersey, in the County of Hunterdon, find the defendant guilty with recommendation of mercy by the court."

Instantly the defendant's brothers, Sandusky and George, jumped to his side and put their arms about him. He held himself erect, staring straight ahead.

Lloyd Fisher for the defense asked that the jury be polled and each of the twelve pronounced the word "guilty."

There was a moment of silence and Mr. Fisher bent over Curtis, with his brothers. Suddenly the defendant jumped to his feet, hurled his great bulk through the little group of brothers and friends and ran to the door leading to the jail.

Photographers snapped him as he went out and bailiffs hurried after him. In the home of Warden George Anderson, which is in the jail building, his 11-year-old daughter, Constance, who has been at his side all through the trial, was awaiting him. The little girl remained with him until evening.

The twenty-four-hour guard which has watched Curtis since his arrest on March 18 resumed its duties tonight to avoid any risk of suicide.

**Immediate Appeal Planned.**

The convicted man's counsel went to work preparing their appeal to be presented Tuesday. Lloyd Fisher, who has led the defense forces, declared that he would carry the case to the highest court of the State, the Court of Errors and Appeals, if he could not get a reversal in the State Supreme Court.

Colonel Charles A. Lindbergh, who has sat through all the sessions of the trial itself at the State counsel's table, did not appear today, nor did Colonel Schwarzkopf. Colonel Lindbergh learned of the verdict by telephone at his home. He had no comment to make. Staying with him through the trial has been Edwin Bruce, the Elmira business man who accompanied Colonel Lindbergh and Curtis on many of their boat trips. He will stay at the Hopewell home over the week-end. Colonel Lindbergh, it is understood, feels that Mr. Bruce has been most self-

Continued on Page Six.

## Major Sports Results.

**Track**—William Carr of Penn broke the accepted world's record for the 440-yard run in defeating Ben Eastman of Stanford in the Intercollegiate A. A. A. A. meet at Berkeley, Cal.

**Tennis**—Ellsworth Vines Jr., American tennis champion, overwhelmed H. W. (Bunny) Austin of England, 6—4, 6—2, 6—0, to win the Wimbledon tennis championship.

**Rowing**—The Penn A. C. four and Bachelors Barge Club double won national rowing championships and will represent the United States in the Olympics. The Leander Rowing Club captured the Grand Challenge Cup in the Royal Henley Regatta.

**Racing**—Faireno defeated Gusto in the Dwyer stakes at Aqueduct. Top Flight annexed the Arlington Oaks at Chicago, while Stepenfetchit won the Latonia Derby.

*Complete details in Sports Section.*

## PRIEST DEFIES CITY ON QUITTING RECTORY

### Mgr. Cashin of St. Andrew's Will Stay "Until Marshal Puts Us on Street."

### HOLDS PLEDGE NOT KEPT

### Property of Historic Church in Federal Deal—Land for New Buildings Not Provided.

Faced with a city order to vacate the rectory of St. Andrew's Roman Catholic Church, at Duane Street and City Hall Place, by Aug. 1, Mgr. William E. Cashin, pastor of the church, declared yesterday that he and his staff would remain until the "marshal puts us on the street," because the city had failed to carry out its share of an agreement to exchange other land for the rectory site.

The small red brick church in the old part of New York has been known for years as the home of the printers' mass. Mass has been celebrated there at 2:30 every Sunday morning since the time when most of the daily newspapers had their plants along Park Row.

The first church there was built about 1796 and was used by Methodists. After the Methodists abandoned it with the drift of population uptown, the church building was used as a wine warehouse for a time. In 1840 it became a Catholic club and was used as a rallying place for Catholics in the city. Two years later it became a Catholic church and is now the ninth oldest Catholic church in the city.

The church's difficulties with the city arise from the city's sale of a new site for a court house to the Federal Government. The courthouse site lies to the north and east of the church property, forming a triangular plot just south of the State Courts Building. In assembling the site the city agreed to give the church additional land on the south of the church building in exchange for an equal acreage in the bed of City Hall Place owned by the church.

**Says City Failed to Keep Bargain.**

"The city promptly took over the land in the bed of City Hall Place and opened a street there," Mgr. Cashin said yesterday. "The city, however, has failed to give us the land promised in exchange in the rear of our church. Under those conditions we have not been able to go ahead with plans for a new church and rectory which were drawn three years ago, because we do not know exactly what the site for these buildings will be. If we vacate the parish house on the first of August we will have no rectory. I think we are entitled to stay, and we will stay until the city marshal puts us on the street."

Cardinal Hayes was born at 17 City Hall Place and was baptized in St. Andrew's, where he later served as an altar boy. The site of his birthplace has been cleared, but the church was anxious to obtain it for sentimental reasons. Under its agreement with the city, the church agreed to cede its rectory, at 20 City Hall Place. The city agreed to give the church title to 15, 17 and 19 City Hall Place, in the rear of the church building. The city further agreed to give additional land on the south side of the church in return for the rights to land in the bed of City Hall Place, but this part of the bargain has not been fulfilled.

Plans for the new church and rectory involve an expenditure of about $500,000. It will require about a year to complete the new buildings. The same type of structure as now exists will be built, to preserve the character of the old church. In addition to the attendance at the printers' mass, now in its thirty-second year, the church has an average daily congregation of 600 worshipers, while it is overcrowded on Easter, Christmas and other holy days.

The church was remodeled about 1860 after the widening of Duane

Continued on Page Two.

## REICH BALKS AT PLAN FOR FINAL PAYMENT THROUGH BOND ISSUE

### Berlin Is Expected to Announce at Lausanne Today Its Refusal to Meet Creditors' Terms.

### SOME REMAIN OPTIMISTIC

### British Delegation Still Believes Settlement Will Be Reached at Powers' Parley.

### DEBTS NOT NOW INVOLVED

### Other Nations Owing Reparations Meet at Lausanne to Follow Course Set for Germany.

By P. J. PHILIP.
Wireless to The New York Times.

LAUSANNE, July 2.—Final agreement was reached today among Germany's governmental creditors on the terms of a reparations settlement. The plan will be officially communicated to the German delegation tomorrow.

The capital amount to be paid by Germany has been fixed, as anticipated at 4,000,000,000 marks [$952,000,000]. Germany will, according to the plan, hand over bonds to that amount which will be put on the market when conditions are favorable but not before three years. The interest rate will be 5 per cent on the marketed bonds.

**No Mention of War Debts.**

In the scheme no mention is made of the creditor powers' indebtedness to the United States. Prime Minister MacDonald from the first insisted and today obtained Premier Herriot's consent that this should be so and that this settlement should be exclusively a European concern and not have the appearance of being conditional on United States action on debts. At the same time Germany's creditors will retain this juridical right, that they can defer ratification for at least three years, that is to say, until after they and others have reached a new settlement with the United States.

Furthermore, the French are satisfied with having obtained from the British Government a promise that there will be no separate settlement with the United States without consultation and agreement with the other debtors. This formula provides for a united front.

The whole future, however, still remains dependent on Germany's attitude toward the capital payment plan. Under the pressure and persuasion of Prime Minister MacDonald the Reich delegation here seems perfectly willing to consent in the belief that this proposed bond issue will never be made but will join the bonds handed over many years ago to the Reparation Commission.

**Many Expect Rejection Today.**

Berlin still is unconvinced, and tonight it is anticipated by many that tomorrow Chancellor von Papen, in the name of his government, will reject this carefully prepared proposal. During the day telephonic communication with Berlin has been almost continuous and the capital's resistance to the proposal has not lessened.

Louis Germain-Martin, French Finance Minister, summarized the situation this morning when he said everything was going well in Lausanne and that it was a pity that all the people in Berlin had not been able to come to Lausanne.

The German opposition is partly political and partly based on the argument that it will be impossible for Germany at the end of three or even five years to add to her present burdens the service on this debt. The interests of private creditors and holders of Dawes and Young Plan bonds are being urged as a reason why the plan should not be accepted.

Continued on Page Four.

## *Women Speakers to Front In Democratic Campaign*

By The Associated Press.

CHICAGO, July 2.—This campaign is going to be a big opportunity and bring a lot of hard work for women. Among those likely to be prominent as campaign speakers for the Democratic nominee are:

Miss Frances Perkins, Industrial Commissioner of New York State, a close friend of Governor Roosevelt.

Mrs. Caspar Whitney and Mrs. H. Goddard Leach of New York, both former presidents of the State's League of Women Voters.

Mrs. John C. Greenway of Arizona, a family friend to whom was given her State's complimentary vote for the Vice Presidency.

Mrs. R. F. Lindsay of Texas, president of her State's Federation of Women's Clubs.

Mrs. Harrison Parkman of Kansas, a magazine editor, who asserted today "this is a non-political fight for the good of the country."

Mary W. Dewson, leader of the Roosevelt women's headquarters.

## DEMOCRATS NAME FARLEY CHAIRMAN

### Roosevelt Manager Assumes Charge at Once to Launch Pre-Election Campaign.

### CHEERS GREET ROOSEVELT

### Governor Praises Raskob and Shouse for Building Up the Party Nationally.

From a Staff Correspondent.
Special to The New York Times.

CHICAGO, July 2. — Governor Roosevelt and his supporters lost no time in taking control of the new Democratic National Committee, which met tonight in the Gold Room of the Congress Hotel and elected as chairman James A. Farley, who successfully conducted Governor Roosevelt's campaign for the nomination. He succeeds John J. Raskob, selected by Alfred E. Smith, the Presidential nominee in 1928.

By the election of Mr. Farley, the Roosevelt supporters wrested control of the national party organization from the friends of Governor Smith. The call for the meeting immediately after the adjournment of the convention was issued at the suggestion of Governor Roosevelt, who expressed himself as desiring immediate organization of the committee and an early start of the campaign.

Mr. Farley was placed in nomination by John H. McCooey, the new committeeman from New York, and seconded by Mrs. Bernice S. Pyke of Ohio.

Mr. Raskob appointed Mr. McCooey, Governor White of Ohio and Arthur F. Mullen of Nebraska to escort Mr. Farley to the chair. Mr. Farley was appauded as he stepped onto the platform.

**Cheers Greet Roosevelt.**

The committee re-elected Robert Jackson, another Roosevelt supporter, as secretary. A moment later Governor Roosevelt entered the room, to be received with cheers.

"Ladies and gentlemen, and fellow-Democrats," Governor Roosevelt said when the cheering died down, "this is the second time I have been

Continued on Page Ten.

## *Reynolds, a Wet, Wins in North Carolina Over Morrison, a Dry, in Senatorship Race*

Special to The New York Times.

RALEIGH, N. C., July 2.—Robert Rice Reynolds, a militant wet, won an overwhelming victory in today's Democratic primary, when he was nominated over Senator Cameron Morrison upholder of the dry cause by a majority far in excess of the 50,000 plurality Mr. Reynolds received in the first primary on June 4.

John C. B. Ehringhaus, administration candidate for Governor, ran behind Mr. Reynolds, but was leading Lieut. Gov. Richard T. Fountain, who based his campaign largely upon an attack upon the administration of Governor Max Gardner and "machine" rule. Mr. Ehringhaus had a plurality of 47,000 in the first primary.

In the Senatorship contest returns from 1,292 of the 1,829 precincts in the State gave: Reynolds, 167,710; Morrison, 115,868.

For the governorship nomination the same precincts gave: Ehringhaus 129,317, Fountain 124,736.

Reynolds and Fountain had a common cause in that both attacked the "machine."

Captain A. L. Fletcher, high man for Commissioner of Labor in the first primary, had an easy victory over Clarence E. Mitchell today.

The Reynolds campaign was undoubtedly helped by the wet position taken by the Democratic National Convention, political observers say, since Senator Morrison had expressed disapproval of the party's repeal plank.

From the earliest precincts to be reported the overwhelming nature of Mr. Reynolds's victory was apparent. He swept county after county regardless of whether Ehringhaus or Fountain was the victor in the Gubernatorial contest.

## CONVENTION HAILS GARNER

### Delegations Rush to Line Up Behind Candidate of Roosevelt Leaders.

### McDUFFIE OFFERS HIS NAME

### Alabamian, an Intimate Friend, Calls Speaker "the Man America Needs."

### LONE CONTESTANT YIELDS

### General Tinley, Nominated by Iowa, Moves Convention Make Action Unanimous.

By L. C. SPEERS.
Special to The New York Times.

CHICAGO, July 2.—John Nance Garner of Texas, Speaker of the House of Representatives, of which he has been a member nearly thirty years, was nominated at 3:40 P. M. today as the Democratic candidate for Vice President of the United States.

The convention, tired but still noisy, for once during the week was in complete agreement. Only one other nomination was made—that of General Matthew A. Tinley of Iowa. When the roll-call of the States was concluded General Tinley moved the nomination be made unanimous.

There was no excitement attending the placing in nomination, the seconding and the final action of the convention to make the man from Uvalde, Texas, the running mate of Governor Roosevelt, who was speeding by airplane to Chicago to accept the nomination for the Presidency.

It was 2 o'clock when Senator Walsh, the chairman, called the convention to order. The hall, already comfortably crowded, was gradually assuming a "standing room only" status. The big pipe organ pealed forth "The Eyes of Texas," and the final business of the convention was under way.

**Close Friend Names Garner.**

Alabama yielded to Texas, and Texas in return called on a son of Alabama, Representative John W. McDuffie of Monroeville, an intimate friend of Mr. Garner and Democratic whip of the House, to place the name of "the gentleman from the cactus country" before the convention.

It was a task Mr. McDuffie relished, for Mr. Garner in his eyes is the biggest man in public life. Mr. McDuffie, who was the leader in the fight for his own and the Garner relief plans, went at his task with a will. Others may have doubts, but he is certain a landslide is coming and that it will sweep Roosevelt and Garner into office next November.

"A few days ago," he said, "the Republicans everywhere were predicting dissension in the ranks of the Democratic party. On that prediction they based their hopes of victory. Then we named Franklin D. Roosevelt for President and in doing so chilled the heart of every Republican in the United States."

This hit a responsive chord on the floor. Texas whooped back in true cowboy style, and the others just yelled. Everywhere in the land, declared Mr. McDuffie, Democrats are happy because the people are swarming into the Democratic camp as the place where real progressive leadership awaits them.

"In any crisis," said the Alabamian, "the American people, when they are thinking, call on the Democratic party for leadership."

Naming Mr. Garner for the second place on the ticket, he lauded the Speaker as a man of "sturdy and rugged character," as the "outstanding leader in Congress," and as a "real, red-blooded he-man." "Just the kind," he exclaimed, "America needs for Vice President at this time."

**Predicts "Greatest Victory."**

"Roosevelt and Garner," concluded Mr. McDuffie, "will lead the Democratic party to the greatest victory it has ever achieved."

The Texans jumped up, waved the Lone Star flag and gave a few war whoops. California waved its own flag with its big grizzly bear, and the other delegations indicated their approval in ways less demonstrative. The demonstration was quickly over with, and then came the long roll call and its short seconding speeches and announcements.

Tammany caused a burst of real

Continued on Page Eight.

The Vice Presidential Nominee

© Harris & Ewing Photo.

JOHN NANCE GARNER.

## SMITH-HEARST FEUD AIDED ROOSEVELT

### Break to the Governor Is Looked Upon as Furnishing Revenge for the Publisher.

### GARNER SHIFT TURNED TIDE

### Ten-Year Conflict Goes Back to Smith's Ban on Hearst's Ambitions in This State.

By JAMES A. HAGERTY.
Special to The New York Times.

CHICAGO, July 2.—Last night's sensational break in the balloting for President by the delegates to the Democratic National Convention, by which Texas and California furnished ninety votes and started the stampede which resulted in the nomination of Roosevelt, furnished revenge on Alfred E. Smith for William Randolph Hearst as well as for William G. McAdoo.

Mr. Smith's feud with Mr. AcAdoo, which resulted from the defeat of the latter in the 1924 convention, was recalled immediately by most of the delegates when Mr. McAdoo took the platform to announce that California and Texas had decided to vote for Roosevelt. The part of Mr. Hearst, or his friends, in the arrangement by which Roosevelt obtained the nomination for President and Speaker John N. Garner the nomination for Vice President became known today.

The Smith-Hearst feud, although not active recently, has existed for more than ten years. It reached its highest point in the New York State convention of 1922, when Mr. Smith, a candidate for the Democratic nomination for Governor, resisted all attempts to get him to accept Mr. Hearst as a running mate as a candidate for United States Senator. Mr. Smith, it was said at the time, even disregarded the advice of the late Charles F. Murphy, leader of Tammany, who believed that the nomination of Hearst was advisable to prevent a break in the party that might bring about Mr. Smith's defeat.

Four years earlier, in 1918, when Mr. Smith was first nominated and elected to the Governorship of New York State, he clashed with Mr. Hearst at the New York State convention. Mr. Hearst also was a candidate for the nomination, and a large force of his supporters went to Saratoga Springs in an unsuccessful attempt to bring about his nomination. This clash resulted in bitterness, but later in the campaign Mr. Hearst in his newspapers supported Mr. Smith against Governor Charles S. Whitman, who had been renominated for a third term by the Republicans.

Mr. Hearst always asserted and the assertion was not denied—that

Continued on Page Ten.

## ROOSEVELT URGES EARLY CAMPAIGN

### He Declares in Interview That Object of Plane Trip Was to Spur Vote Drive.

### DISAPPOINTED OVER SMITH

### He Had Hoped to See His Rival Soon—Plans to Take Train Home From Chicago Tonight.

From a Staff Correspondent.
Special to The New York Times.

CHICAGO, July 2.—An early and vigorous Democratic campaign throughout the country was urged by Governor Roosevelt tonight as he established himself in the Presidential suite at the Congress Hotel for a brief stay in the convention city.

Holding his first "levee," for a large group of correspondents, Mr. Roosevelt set forth a supplementary reason for making an airplane trip to the convention.

"The whole idea of flying here," he said, "was to bring forward the idea of getting the campaign started. You know that August is usually the month to get stirring. But I believe that some votes can be made in July.

"I do not know just what my own plans will be for the next few months. I am starting back for Albany tomorrow night if the present schedule holds. But, of course, these plans are tentative."

The Governor was asked if he planned to speak in every State during the campaign. He smiled and replied:

"No, I hardly think so. You know, those coast-to-coast trips are all right for a young man such as I was when I was a candidate for Vice President and I was only 38, but it is a bit different now."

The Governor seemed in fine spirits, although the rush of convention congratulations was a bit overwhelming.

On one score the Governor indicated some disappointment. When asked if he expected to see Alfred E. Smith, his chief convention rival, he replied:

"I am afraid not for a few days."

Before Mr. Roosevelt left Albany he had expressed a desire to see Mr. Smith as soon as possible, but the ex-Governor had already left Chicago when the Roosevelt plane arrived.

Governor Roosevelt's comment on the nomination of Speaker Garner for the Vice Presidency was:

"I am very happy at the selection of Jack Garner. There are two reasons for that. One is his possession of splendid ability. The other is that we are very old friends, for I have known him ever since my own Washington days."

The Governor said he had no definite schedule for tomorrow and that he planned to take a train for home about 10 o'clock in the evening.

## FAMILY FLIES TO CHICAGO

### Thundering Cheers Greet the Governor at Airport and in Stadium.

### '100%' FOR THE PLATFORM

### "Eighteenth Amendment Is Doomed From This Day," He Declares in Speech.

### PLEDGES SELF TO 'NEW DEAL'

### He Calls for Enlightened International Outlook and Shorter Work Day and Week.

*The text of Gov. Roosevelt's acceptance speech is on page 8.*

By ARTHUR KROCK.
Special to The New York Times.

CHICAGO, July 2.—Before it adjourned tonight, after unanimously nominating Speaker John N. Garner of Texas for Vice President, the Democratic National Convention saw and heard its Presidential choice of yesterday, Governor Franklin D. Roosevelt of New York.

Mr. Roosevelt confessed that in coming here he was breaking a tradition.

"Let it be from now on," he said, "the task of our party to break foolish traditions. We will break foolish traditions and leave it to the Republican leadership * * * to break promises."

**Pledges Aid to "Forgotten Man."**

His speech was aggressive. He pledged his aid, "not only to the forgotten man, but to the forgotten woman, to help them realize their hope for a return to the old standards of living and thought in the United States." He would, he said, "Restore America to its own people."

Mr. Roosevelt began with a tribute to Woodrow Wilson. He then described the economic situation from his own viewpoint, saying that swollen surpluses went into the building of "unnecessary plants and Wall Street call money." The government should be "made solvent" again, said Mr. Roosevelt.

The galleries warmed to him when he firmly endorsed the platform plank advocating repeal of the Eighteenth Amendment and modification of the Volstead act, and the Southern delegations noted his pledge to protect the dry States in their wish to keep out intoxicating liquors and to prevent the return of the saloon.

**Work and Security the Need.**

He suggested as one means of decreasing unemployment, putting men at work on reforesting waste areas. As to agriculture, he would aid that by production planning, by the adoption of a tariff equalizing world prices and by lowering interest rates of farm loans. He expressed it as his firm conviction that the popular welfare depends on the granting of what the great mass of the people want and need.

Their demand is for work and reasonable security, he declared, and he pledged his efforts to effect them.

In concluding, he told his hearers that he intended to make a number of short visits during the campaign to various parts of the country.

Jefferson, the father of the Democratic party, rode to his inaugural on horseback, but the nominee of 1932 flew to the scene of his triumph by airplane from Albany and covered the ninefold greater distance in less time. The convention rose enthusiastically to the voyager of the skies, and accepted his method of travel and the fact that he endured its rigors so well as a proof of his venturesome spirit and fine physical equipment for the office of President of the United States.

**Animosities Are Forgotten.**

Governor Roosevelt, when he had reached the platform, faced a hall almost as crowded and as emotional as at any time during the convention period. Except in small groups among the galleries and the delegates the disappointment and animosity of the preceding days were buried, and it was evident that the thousands of people believed they were in the presence, not only of the nominee of the Democratic party, but of the next President of the United States.

Before Mr. Roosevelt appeared, and his appearance was delayed by

Continued on Page Nine.

"All the News That's Fit to Print."

# The New York Times.

**5 A.M. EDITION**
WEATHER—Rain today; tomorrow fair and colder.
Temperatures Yesterday—Max., 56; Min., 50.



VOL. LXXXII....No. 27,318. Entered as Second-Class Matter, Postoffice, New York, N. Y. NEW YORK, WEDNESDAY, NOVEMBER 9, 1932. * * * * * TWO CENTS In New York City | THREE CENTS Within 200 Miles | FOUR CENTS Elsewhere Except in 7th and 8th Postal Zones

# ROOSEVELT WINNER IN LANDSLIDE! DEMOCRATS CONTROL WET CONGRESS; LEHMAN GOVERNOR, O'BRIEN MAYOR

## BIG VOTE FOR M'KEE

### O'Brien Is 245,464 Behind Ticket as Protests Rise

### BUT FINAL LEAD IS 616,736

### Pounds Concedes Defeat Early, Saying 'Day of Miracles Is Past.'

### McKEE TOTAL IS 137,538

### Thousands of "Write-In" Votes Are Wasted as Backers Fail to Record Choice Properly.

### HILLQUIT POLLS 248,425

### Gets Greatest Vote in History of City for a Socialist—Runs Far Ahead of Party.

Surrogate John P. O'Brien, Tammany's candidate, was elected Mayor of New York yesterday, but overshadowing his victory, which was a foregone conclusion, was the tremendous "write-in" vote cast for Acting Mayor Joseph V. McKee.

Final returns from the city showed Judge O'Brien to have received a plurality of 616,736 over his nearest opponent, Lewis H. Pounds, Republican. Judge O'Brien's vote was 1,055,768, Mr. Pounds polled 439,032, and Morris Hillquit, Socialist, polled the highest vote ever given a candidate of his party in the city by receiving 248,425 votes.

**Vote Listed by Boroughs.**

By boroughs, the totals were as follows:

| | O'Brien. | Pounds. | Hillquit. |
|---|---|---|---|
| Manhattan | 309,256 | 113,278 | 39,398 |
| Bronx | 181,349 | 48,284 | 67,949 |
| Brooklyn | 358,605 | 155,478 | 112,740 |
| Queens | 176,237 | 105,481 | 25,821 |
| Richmond | 30,321 | 16,511 | 2,517 |
| City total | 1,055,768 | 439,032 | 248,425 |

The vote for Mr. McKee, put early this morning at 137,538, actually was far more than that, if ballots in which the voters had abbreviated his name, or used initials, or spelled it wrongly, were counted.

The vote was unprecedented, particularly as the use of voting machines made it much more difficult for a name to be writen in than on the old paper ballots.

Judge O'Brien had a clear majority of 215,000 votes over the combined vote of Pounds, Hillquit and McKee, but the McKee ballots cast aside as void would have reduced this, it was pointed out last night.

The vote for Mr. McKee by boroughs was as follows:

Manhattan, 26,336, with ten election districts missing.
Bronx, 24,453, complete.
Brooklyn, 43,328, complete.
Queens, 36,303, complete.
Richmond, 6,790, complete.
City total, 137,538.

The vote for Mr. McKee, made without any campaign on his part, and in the face of his own disavowal of the movement, kept him in the political picture as a candidate to be reckoned with for the full four-year term, to be voted on in 1933.

The term for which Judge O'Brien was elected starts on Jan. 1, 1933, and ends on Jan. 1, 1934.

The vote for Mr. O'Brien indicated he ran 381,263 votes behind Governor Roosevelt in the city, in actual votes cast, though his plurality was only 245,464 smaller than that given to the Presidential candidate.

Mr. Pounds conceded Mr. O'Brien's victory as early as 9:30 in the evening, and he sent the latter a telegram of congratulation.

He said later he could have been elected only by a miracle, and that the days of miracles were past. Mr. McKee, receiving election returns at the Park Lane, also sent a short

Continued on Page Seven.



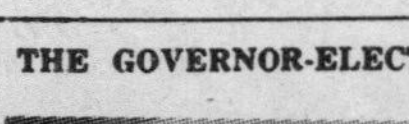
THE GOVERNOR-ELECT.

© New York Times Studio.
Colonel Herbert H. Lehman.

## JUDGES IN 'DEAL' WIN; PROTEST VOTE HEAVY

### Steuer and Hofstadter Elected With Lydon and Leary to Supreme Court Bench.

### 290,000 FOR INDEPENDENTS

### Bar Leaders Elated by Big Count for Deutsch and Alger—Call It 'Warning to Bosses.'

City Court Justice Aron Steuer and State Senator Samuel H. Hofstadter were elected yesterday over their independent opponents, Bernard S. Deutsch and George W. Alger, by a vote of about 2 to 1.

The protest vote against the so-called deal by which Senator Hofstadter and Justice Steuer received bipatrisan nominations for two of four vacancies on the Supreme Court bench in the first judicial district exceeded all expectations, but it was not enough to upset the combined strength of the Republican and Democratic organizations.

Justice Richard P. Lydon, who was nominated by both major parties for re-election, and Municipal Court Justice Timothy A. Leary, who had the Democratic nomination for the fourth vacancy on the bench, were elected with comfortable margins. Municipal Court Justice George L. Genung, who had the Republican nomination, trailed far behind the independent candidates.

Since Justice Lydon's re-election was virtually uncontested, his totals were not computed in the early returns. Of the other, Justice Steuer and Judge Leary were running slightly ahead of Senator Hofstadter, whose lead was large enough, however, to preclude the possibility of his being overtaken by Mr. Deutsch, his nearest rival.

**The Complete Returns.**

The complete returns for the entire first judicial district, comprising the boroughs of Manhattan and the Bronx, follow:

| | |
|---|---|
| Steuer | 565,405 |
| Leary | 547,112 |
| Hofstadter | 544,032 |
| Deutsch | 293,125 |
| Alger | 287,167 |
| Genung | 205,222 |

The totals recorded for the judiciary candidates in Manhattan follow:

| | |
|---|---|
| Steuer | 367,295 |
| Hofstadter | 357,430 |
| Leary | 331,442 |
| Deutsch | 147,886 |
| Alger | 145,346 |
| Genung | 138,304 |

Final returns from the Bronx, where the independent candidates ran strongest, showed the following totals:

| | |
|---|---|
| Leary | 215,670 |
| Steuer | 198,110 |
| Hofstadter | 186,602 |
| Deutsch | 145,239 |
| Alger | 141,821 |
| Genung | 66,918 |

The independent candidates did not

Continued on Page Twelve.

## STATE VICTORY SOLID

### Lehman Gets Record Party Plurality of 887,000.

### WAGNER CLOSE TO HIM

### National Ticket Has Margin of 615,000—Full Slate Is Elected.

### RELIEF BONDS ARE VOTED

### Republicans Have Narrow Edge Up-State—Hill Admits 'Protest' Defeated Them.

By JAMES A. HAGERTY.

Lieut. Gov. Herbert H. Lehman, Democratic nominee for Governor, defeated Colonel William J. Donovan, Republican, yesterday, in the Democratic whirlwind that swept New York State, by a plurality of about 887,000, a record for a Democratic candidate in this State.

Governor Franklin D. Roosevelt and Speaker John N. Garner, the Democratic candidates for President and Vice President, carried the State by a plurality of about 615,000, as against Governor Roosevelt's heretofore record Democratic plurality of 725,000, which he received as candidate for re-election to the Governorship two years ago.

With Governor Roosevelt and Colonel Lehman were swept into office the other Democratic candidates on the State-wide ticket, United States Senator Robert F. Wagner, candidate for re-election; M. William Bray, for Lieutenant Governor; State Controller Morris S. Tremaine, Attorney General John J. Bennett Jr. and the two candidates for Representatives-at-Large, Elmer E. Studley and John Fitzgibbons.

Colonel Lehman led Governor Roosevelt by 88,279 in actual votes cast in New York City and also led the Governor in many cities and counties up-State. His indicated plurality exceeded that of Governor Roosevelt by more than 250,000, but exceeded the indicated plurality for Senator Wagner by only about 35,000.

Returns on the proposition and proposed constitutional amendment were slow in coming in, but a large majority for the proposal to issue $30,000,000 in bonds for unemployment relief was indicated, and scattering returns indicated that the constitutional amendment to throw open the forest reserve to the development of recreational facilities had been beaten.

The vote for President and State-wide candidates follows:

FOR PRESIDENT.

New York City, complete—Roosevelt, Democrat, 1,437,231; Hoover, Republican, 575,031; Thomas, Socialist, 120,486; actual plurality for Roosevelt, 862,200.

Up-State, 431 election districts missing—Roosevelt, 1,022,121; Hoover, 1,254,032; actual plurality for Hoover, 231,911; indicated plurality for Hoover, 247,107; indicated plurality for Roosevelt in the entire State, 615,093.

FOR GOVERNOR.

New York City, complete—Lehman, Democrat, 1,525,510; Donovan, Republican, 542,492; plurality for Lehman, 983,018.

Up-State, 561 election districts missing—Lehman, 1,056,088; Donovan, 1,141,735; actual plurality for Donovan, 85,647; indicated plurality for Donovan, 95,817.

Indicated plurality for Lehman in the entire State, 887,201.

FOR UNITED STATES SENATOR.

New York City, complete—Wagner, Dem., 1,438,343; Medalie, Rep., 517,733; plurality for Wagner, 920,610.

Up-State, 1,301 districts missing—Wagner, 915,699; Medalie, 964,418;

Continued on Page Sixteen.



## The President's Message To the President-Elect

From a Staff Correspondent.

*PALO ALTO, Cal., Nov. 8.—President Hoover conceded his defeat for re-election at 9:17 o'clock tonight, Pacific Time, and dispatched this telegram of congratulations to Governor Roosevelt:*

Palo Alto, Cal.,
Nov. 8, 1932.

The Hon. Franklin D. Roosevelt,
Biltmore Hotel,
New York, N. Y.

I congratulate you on the opportunity that has come to you to be of service to the country and I wish for you a most successful administration. In the common purpose of all of us I shall dedicate myself to every possible helpful effort.

HERBERT HOOVER.

*Governor Roosevelt had not received President Hoover's message when he left for his home shortly before 2 o'clock this morning. Pending its receipt he said he preferred not to make reply or comment on the message.*

## DEMOCRATS CONTROL STATE SENATE, 26-25

### Republican Margin in Assembly of 6 Votes Is Reduced to 2—Lose by 4 Up-State.

### ALSO TWO SENATE SEATS

### Moffatt Is Re-elected, While Hastings and Dr. Love Are Defeated in City Race.

The slender working majority of two votes by which the Republicans control the present State Senate was swept away in yesterday's Democratic landslide. The next Senate will be made up of 25 Republicans and 26 Democrats, giving the Democrats a majority of one. The present Senate has 27 Republican and 25 Democratic members. Twenty-six votes are required to pass a bill in that branch of the Legislature.

In the Assembly, where 76 votes are required to control legislation, the Republican majority of six is cut down to two in the 1933 Legislature. The Republicans won 77 seats and the Democrats 73 at yesterday's elections for the Assembly.

The Democrats won four Assembly districts north of the Bronx away from the Republicans; one district in Monroe County, one district in Oneida and two in Sullivan and Schoharie counties. The Republicans, however, reduced the up-State Democratic gains by recapturing from them Schuyler county in the southern tier, where last year they succeeded in electing their candidate for the Lower House.

**Post Is Defeated.**

The Republicans also managed to strengthen their New York City representation by electing Herbert Brownell Jr. in the Tenth (Manhattan) District. This was the district where Langdon W. Post, Democratic incumbent was turned down by Tammany for supporting legislation to broaden the powers and continue the Hofstadter Committee and ran as an independent, polling 5,053 votes. Mr. Brownell defeated his Tammany opponent by a scant plurality of 307 votes. He received 8,907 votes, Sylva La Chappelle, the Democrat, 8,600.

The Democrats gained two Senate districts up-State, the Thirty-first, made up of Rensselaer County, and the Thirty-sixth, made up of Oneida. In the Thirty-fourth, composed of St. Lawrence and Franklin Counties, Warren T. Thayer, the present Republican incumbent, managed to win again after a hard fight.

The New York City Republicans will have three representatives in the Legislature, Senator-elect George Blumberg, who won by a plurality of approximately 500 over Senator John A. Hastings, Democratic incumbent in the Seventh Senatorial

Continued on Page Five.



## OVERTURN IN SENATE

### Bingham, Watson, Moses and Smoot Are Defeated.

### DEMOCRATIC MAJORITY 12

### Party Adds to Control in House—May Rule Both Branches This Winter.

### LA GUARDIA LOSES SEAT

### Mrs. Pratt Defeated, Wadsworth Wins—Texas Sends Garner Back to the House.

The Democratic wave of victory yesterday gave that party complete control of Congress and in its onrush carried down to defeat the four Republican leaders of the Senate.

Senator Smoot of Utah, Republican dean of the Senate and chairman of the powerful Finance Committee; Senator Watson of Indiana, floor leader; Senator Moses, president pro tempore and Senator Jones of Washington, chairman of the Appropriations Committee, all were relegated to the ranks of "lame ducks." No such upset has occurred in recent history.

While returns early this morning showed the new Senate will be Democratic by a majority of twelve and the House overwhelmingly Democratic, there was a possibility that in the session of the old Congress convening on Dec. 5, the Democrats will achieve a slender control of the whole body.

**Changes in Coming Session.**

They now have a majority of one in the House, in the old Congress that still is to hold a "lame-duck" session; in the Senate the numbers were evened with the defeat of Senator Barbour of New Jersey for the short term beginning next month, and there was, early this morning, an even chance that Colorado would elect Walter Walker, a Democrat, also for the short term. In that event the Senate in December would be: Democrats 49, Republicans 46, Farmer-Labor 1.

On the basis of incomplete returns, the new Senate stood at Democrats 54, Republicans 34, Farmer-Labor 1, and seven States still in doubt.

The next Congress not only will be Democratic; it will be wet.

New York Republicans fared especially ill in the election, which saw Representative La Guardia, fiery "liberal" Republican who led a bloc that controlled the House temporarily in the last session, defeated by J. J. Lanzetta, Democrat. Representative Ruth Pratt also failed of re-election.

**Moses Loses in Close Race.**

Of the most prominent Republicans who were unseated, Senator Watson went down first, conceding his defeat by Frederick Van Nuys, Democrat.

Senator Moses ran nip and tuck with Fred H. Brown, Democrat, until after midnight in the poll of ballots, when returns from Manchester, N. H., spelled his certain defeat.

Senator Smoot was defeated by Professor E. D. Thomas and Mr. Jones by Homer T. Bone. Both of the victors were Democrats. Senator Jones, who is better known as the author of the "five-and-ten" law than for his important committee chairmanship, was defeated coincident with adoption of a State referendum in Washington repealing that State's prohibition law.

An important Republican defeat in the House was that of Representative Haugen of Iowa, co-author of the McNary-Haugen bill, who went down before F. Bierman, Democrat.

**McAdoo Wins Seat.**

William Gibbs McAdoo, former Democratic Secretary of the Treasury, who was credited with switching the Democratic National Convention to Franklin D. Roosevelt through

Continued on Page Six.

THE PRESIDENT-ELECT.

© New York Times Studio.
Franklin D. Roosevelt.

## The Electoral Vote

ROOSEVELT 448.

| | | | |
|---|---|---|---|
| Alabama | 11 | Nebraska | 7 |
| Arizona | 3 | Nevada | 3 |
| Arkansas | 9 | New Jersey | 16 |
| California | 22 | New Mexico | 3 |
| Colorado | 6 | New York | 47 |
| Florida | 7 | North Carolina | 13 |
| Georgia | 12 | North Dakota | 4 |
| Idaho | 4 | Ohio | 26 |
| Illinois | 29 | Oklahoma | 11 |
| Indiana | 14 | Rhode Island | 4 |
| Iowa | 11 | South Carolina | 8 |
| Kansas | 9 | South Dakota | 4 |
| Kentucky | 11 | Tennessee | 11 |
| Louisiana | 10 | Texas | 23 |
| Maryland | 8 | Utah | 4 |
| Massachusetts | 17 | Virginia | 11 |
| Minnesota | 11 | Washington | 8 |
| Mississippi | 9 | West Virginia | 8 |
| Missouri | 15 | Wisconsin | 12 |
| Montana | 4 | Wyoming | 3 |
| **HOOVER 59.** | | | |
| Connecticut | 8 | New Hampshire | 4 |
| Delaware | 3 | Pennsylvania | 36 |
| Maine | 5 | Vermont | 3 |
| **DOUBTFUL 24.** | | | |
| Michigan | 19 | Oregon | 5 |

Votes in Electoral College, 531; needed to elect, 266.

## *Wets in Control in Both Houses, But Short of Two-Thirds in Senate*

### *Modification of Volstead Act Appears Certain, and House Has Easy Majority for Repeal, but Upper Chamber Support Is Uncertain on Basis of Returns.*

Complete control of the next Congress by forces opposed to Federal prohibition was one of the results which came with the political upheaval that took place with yesterday's election.

With full returns from the major portion of the country and definite trends established in the remainder, it appeared certain that those demanding a change in the dry laws would hold between fifty and fifty-five seats in the Senate and 300 or more in the House of Representatives.

Up until an early hour this morning, only nineteen outspoken drys had been returned definitely to the House, while twenty-four Senators, most of whom did not come up for re-election this year, remained among the prohibitionists. Around 100 House seats still were in doubt, and several Senators and re-elected Representatives were yet undecided how to align themselves on the question.

The aggregation chosen yesterday represented a veritable checker-board of views on prohibition reform, but the extent of the majorities indicated a good chance for immediate modification of the Volstead act to allow light wines and beer. The gains in both Houses were chiefly among Democrats, whose party has been pledged to that course.

Modification in the next Congress appeared much more probable on the basis of yesterday's election than outright repeal of the Eighteenth Amendment. Sixty-four Senate seats and 290 in the House will be required for the latter, whereas only a bare majority of 49 in the Senate and 218 in the House would be needed to change the national prohibition (Volstead) law.

The House was sure of the necessary two-thirds for repeal, as early this morning the anti-prohibitionists had already captured 292 seats; the

Continued on Page Eight.

## SWEEP IS NATIONAL

### Democrats Carry 40 States, Electoral Votes 448.

### SIX STATES FOR HOOVER

### He Loses New York, New Jersey, Bay State, Indiana and Ohio.

### DEMOCRATS WIN SENATE

### Necessary Majority for Repeal of the Volstead Act in Prospect.

### RECORD NATIONAL VOTE

### Hoover Felicitates Rival and Promises 'Every Helpful Effort for Common Purpose.'

**Roosevelt Statement.**

President-elect Roosevelt gave the following statement to THE NEW YORK TIMES early this morning:

"While I am grateful with all my heart for this expression of the confidence of my fellow-Americans, I realize keenly the responsibility I shall assume and I mean to serve with my utmost capacity the interest of the nation.

"The people could not have arrived at this result if they had not been informed properly of my views by an independent press, and I value particularly the high service of THE NEW YORK TIMES in its reporting of my speeches and in its enlightened comment."

By ARTHUR KROCK.

A political cataclysm, unprecedented in the nation's history and produced by three years of depression, thrust President Herbert Hoover and the Republican power from control of the government yesterday, elected Governor Franklin Delano Roosevelt President of the United States, provided the Democrats with a large majority in Congress and gave them administration of the affairs of many States of the Union.

Fifteen minutes after midnight, Eastern Standard Time, The Associated Press flashed from Palo Alto this line: "Hoover concedes defeat."

It was then fifteen minutes after nine in California, and the President had been in his residence on the Leland Stanford campus only a few hours, arriving with expressed confidence of victory.

A few minutes after the flash from Palo Alto the text of Mr. Hoover's message of congratulation to his successful opponent was received by THE NEW YORK TIMES, though it was delayed in direct transmission to the President-elect. After offering his felicitations to Governor Roosevelt on his "opportunity to be of service to the country," and extending wishes for success, the President "dedicated" himself to "every possible helpful effort * * * in the common purpose of us all."

This language strengthened the belief of those who expect that the relations between the victor and the vanquished, in view of the exigent condition of the country, will be more than perfunctory, and that they may soon confer in an effort to arrive at a mutual program of stabilization during the period between new

FRANKLIN D. ROOSEVELT

"All the News That's Fit to Print."

# The New York Times.

LATE CITY EDITION
POSTSCRIPT
WEATHER—Fair today; tomorrow cloudy, warmer, probably rain.
Temperature Yesterday—Max., 42; Min., 27.



VOL. LXXXII....No. 27,417. Entered as Second-Class Matter. Postoffice, New York, N. Y. NEW YORK, THURSDAY, FEBRUARY 16, 1933. TWO CENTS In New York City | THREE CENTS Within 200 Miles | FOUR CENTS Elsewhere Except in 7th and 8th Postal Zones

# ASSASSIN FIRES INTO ROOSEVELT PARTY AT MIAMI; PRESIDENT-ELECT UNINJURED; MAYOR CERMAK AND 4 OTHERS WOUNDED

## REPEAL VOTE TODAY SET IN THE SENATE; FILIBUSTER BROKEN

### Wets Win in Test Ballots as Blaine Plan Is Stripped of Protective Clauses.

### ROBINSON LEADS FIGHT

### Borah Backs Him on Removing the Anti-Saloon Section, Voted Out 33-32.

### STATE LIQUOR PLAN OUT

### Commission Proposes to Bar the Saloon—Limit on Places to Sell Beer.

*Report of the State Liquor Control Commission is on Page 15.*

Special to THE NEW YORK TIMES.

WASHINGTON, Feb. 15.—The Senate today stripped the Blaine prohibition resolution to practically "naked" repeal and agreed to vote on the measure at 3 P. M. tomorrow.

Senator Robinson, the Democratic leader, who led the fight to simplify the resolution, predicted that the Senate would furnish the necessary two-thirds majority for adoption on the morrow.

He expressed confidence, too, that the resolution as amended tonight would be acceptable to Speaker Garner and other House leaders, who announced at the outset that the House would be allowed to vote only on the Democratic repeal plan as advocated in the last campaign.

Every prediction was that the vote tomorrow would be extremely close. Senator McNary, assistant Republican leader, described the resolution as "teetering," with the possibility of going one way or the other. He would make no forecast.

Wet leaders, scanning the votes of today, were very hopeful as to the outcome tomorrow. They had succeeded in breaking the filibuster started by the drys to prevent a vote.

Coincidental with the agreement to vote tomorrow, the Senate, by a vote of 33 to 32, struck the so-called anti-saloon provisions from the Blaine resolution, and, on a ballot of 45 to 15, decreed that ratification should be by conventions in the several States instead of Legislatures.

**Passage in House Predicted.**

A deciding vote on the amendment, proposed by Senator Robinson, to strike out the anti-saloon section, was cast by Senator Borah, long a dry stalwart. He held it was impossible for the government properly to exercise any supervision over saloons once the Eighteenth Amendment was repealed.

As the resolution stood tonight, its proposal was only one degree removed from outright repeal. It carried a clause directing Federal protection of dry States which the Garner repeal resolution, submitted at the outset of the session, did not contain but which Senate leaders said tonight was not sufficiently controversial to bring a deadlock between the two branches.

The resolution as it emerged was believed to have a better chance of passage in the House than the proposal submitted by Speaker Garner the first day of Congress. The Speaker's resolution failed by only six votes of obtaining the necessary two-thirds majority, and it was pointed out tonight that the six votes from Senator Robinson's own State, which were cast in the negative at that time, were sufficient to change the tide should repeal be proposed anew to the House.

It was recalled, too, that Senator Robinson was opposed to the Garner resolution, whereas his espousal at this time of the Democratic platform plan was responsible for much of the weight given the revival of the repeal movement.

The dry filibuster against the Blaine resolution broke up in the Senate today when wets announced

Continued on Page Fourteen.



## *Illinois Senate Passes Bills For Repeal of Prohibition Laws*

By The Associated Press.

SPRINGFIELD, Ill., Feb. 15.—The State Senate today passed two prohibition repeal measures and sent them to the House for further action.

The vote on the repeal measures, which had been delayed because of Governor Henry Horner's insistence that regulatory acts should be provided first, was preceded by promises in the debate that they would not be signed until the regulatory bills also had been adopted.

The two bills would remove from the statute books State prohibition and the search and seizure acts.

A measure designed to authorize banking holidays was introduced in the House. Under its terms, the Governor would be empowered to declare a holiday for the State and Mayors authorized to do so for municipalities.

## BOY GANG CHIEF, 15, ADMITS KILLING 'FOE'

### Says He Stabbed Queens Lad, 12, for "Lying" About Him and Vowed to "Get" Him.

### VICTIM MISSING 2 WEEKS

### Found Bound in Closet of a Vacant House to Which Killer Had Lured Him by Ruse.

Bound, gagged and stabbed through the heart, the body of 12-year-old William Bender, who disappeared Jan. 31, was found yesterday in a closet in one of a row of partly-built dwellings, less than two blocks from his home at 6 Bergen Landing Road, Richmond Hill Circle, Queens. He had been dead for at least two weeks.

Nine hours after the body was found, Harry Murch, 15-year-old leader of a juvenile gang, confessed he had murdered the Bender boy. Murch and his chum, John Miller, 10, who was with him when the crime was committed, were picked up by the police yesterday afternoon. For more than five hours, despite persistent questioning by officials of the Police Department and the District Attorney's office, they calmly denied all knowledge of the crime. Then finally they broke down.

"I did it," Murch is said to have declared. "Bender lied about me. He told the whole neighborhood that I had hit Mrs. Peterson on the head with a monkey wrench. I said I'd get him and I did."

He is to be arraigned today in children's court, Jamaica, on a charge of homicide.

**Tells of Meeting Victim.**

Murch said that on the afternoon of Jan. 31 he and Miller had met Bender outside the latter's home.

"I told him," Murch said, "that I was going to stick up a peanut peddler and that if he'd come over to the houses in Maurelania Avenue with me I'd show him how I was going to do it. He came along all right. But he seemed a bit suspicious.

"So I tied up Miller first. Then I untied Miller and tied up Bender. As soon as I had him where I wanted him I took out my knife and stabbed him in the heart."

Miller corroborated Murch's story. Afterward, the boys said, they fled from the house and agreed to say nothing to any one. The knife which Murch used for the crime, they said, was taken from the kitchen of his home.

The clue that broke the case was a small piece of gingham cloth that had been used to gag the dead boy. The fact that Murch had threatened to "get Bender" was well known in the neighborhood and soon after the body was discovered detectives went to the home of Murch's parents, Mr. and Mrs. Charles Murch, in Philbert Avenue, just a short distance from the home of the Bender boy.

In the Murch garage the detectives found other pieces of gingham of exactly the same quality and pattern as that which had been used for the gag. Young Murch and Miller were immediately taken into custody.

The body of the missing boy was

Continued on Page Ten.

## TAX RATE OF $2.40 SEEN AS VALUATIONS DROP $1,195,006,742

### Sexton Estimates a 19-Point Reduction to the Lowest Basic Levy Since 1920.

### REALTY BURDEN EASED

### Assessment Totals Cut in All Boroughs—Personalty Less, Franchise Values Rise.

### ALDERMEN VOTE BUDGET

### Adopt $518,427,972 Document Without Change—Mayor Denies Plea on Sergeants-at-Arms.

Final adoption of the revised 1933 budget at a total of 18 per cent below that of the 1932 budget and announcement of a cut of $1,195,006,742 in assessed valuations of city real estate, personal property and franchises provided yesterday a substantial basis for belief that the basic tax rate this year will be appreciably lower than the 1932 rate of $2.59 per $100 of assessed valuation.

For the first time in the city's history the total of assessed valuations is lower than in a preceding year. Valuations placed upon franchises for tax purposes were increased in every borough this year. Valuations on real estate showed decreases in every borough, while in the Bronx alone the valuations on personal estate showed a rise. The total valuations for all boroughs in 1932 was $19,977,077,315. For 1933 the final valuations aggregate $18,782,070,573.

The Board of Aldermen adopted a final budget of $518,427,972.16, the same total recently approved by the Board of Estimate. This figure shows a decrease of $112,933,325.81 from the total budget for 1932, which was $631,366,297.97. The budget now goes to Mayor O'Brien for his signature. It must be filed with Controller Berry by Feb. 25.

**Nineteen-Point Tax Drop Seen.**

James J. Sexton, president of the Department of Taxes and Assessments, said that he was certain the basic tax rate would show a decided drop. He expressed the belief that the rate would not exceed $2.40, a drop of nineteen points.

Deputy Controller Frank J. Prial, in the absence of the Controller, said that no accurate estimate of the rate could be made before the amount of the city's general fund for reduction of taxation is known. The general fund, the budget and the final total of assessed valuation, are the three factors used in computing the basic rate. Borough tax rates are added to the basic rate to pay for local improvements.

Mr. Prial said that the amount of the general fund would depend

Continued on Page Nine.

SERIOUSLY WOUNDED.

Times Wide World Photo.
Mayor Anton J. Cermak of Chicago

## WOMAN DIVERTED AIM OF ASSASSIN

### 100-Pound Wife of Miami Doctor Tells How She Forced Up Man's Arm.

### HELD ON DURING SHOOTING

### Gun Had Been Pointed "Right at Mr. Roosevelt" 15 Feet Away, She Relates.

By Telephone to THE NEW YORK TIMES.

MIAMI, Fla., Feb. 15.—Mrs. Lillian Cross, 48 years old, and weighing only 100 pounds, probably saved the life of the President-elect tonight when she forced the would-be assassin's shooting arm upward and caused the bullets to go high.

"He was aiming right at the President," said Mrs. Cross. "I saw him. That's why I caught his arm and forced the gun up. I said to myself, all in a flash, 'Oh! He's going to kill the President!'"

Mrs. Cross said that she was not frightened when she saw the weapon. Her only thought was for Mr. Roosevelt.

"I didn't begin to get nervous at all until it was all over," she related after she reached her home at 1,089 Northwest Second Street.

"I drove to the park tonight with my husband, Dr. W. F. Cross (he's a physician and surgeon here) and with my friend, Mrs. Willis McCrary of Atlanta, Ga. My husband got a seat somewhere in the back of the crowd, but Mrs. McCrary and I found seats right up front, by the guard rail they'd put up.

"President Roosevelt was only about fifteen feet away from us. He finished his speech and got down from the back of the automobile—an open car it was—and had settled in the back seat. I stood up on the bench on which I'd been sitting

Continued on Page Three.

## *Cermak in Critical Condition at Hospital; "Glad It Was I, Not You," He Tells Roosevelt*

Special to THE NEW YORK TIMES.

MIAMI, Thursday, Feb. 16.—Mayor Cermak was shot in the right side, just below the ribs, and was in a critical condition at Jackson Memorial Hospital. An X-ray showed the bullet lodged in the back of the abdomen.

An emergency operation was considered at 12:30 A. M. and plans were made to undertake it at once. A short time later physicians put off the operation.

When President-elect Roosevelt called to see Mayor Cermak at the hospital the Mayor turned his head and smiled faintly, saying:

"I'm glad it was I, instead of you. I wish you would be very careful. The country needs you badly. You should not take any more such chances as you took tonight."

The President-elect replied:

"The country needs a man like you, too. I can only express my deepest regrets. I have decided not to leave tonight and will return to see you in the morning."

James B. Bowler, Chicago City Councilman, who told of the conversation, said Mr. Roosevelt was expected to call again at the hospital about 8 A. M.

Mr. Bowler was with Mayor Cermak in the emergency room and took from the front of the Mayor's shirt a .32 calibre bullet, which was believed to be a spent shot that had hit one of the other victims.

A bulletin on Mayor Cermak's condition, issued at 2 A. M., said:

"Pulse, 88; temperature, 98.6; respiration, 24. His condition is regarded as dangerous, but not immediately critical. The bullet evidently traversed the diaphragm and margin of the liver and lodged in the body of the eleventh dorsal vertebra. Surgical intervention is deemed unwise unless his condition becomes worse."

The bulletin was signed by Dr. John W. Snyder, Dr. Thomas H. Hutson and Dr. T. S. Nichol. Dr. Snyder is in charge, and at the hospital this morning he said:

"Mrs. Gill and Mayor Cermak have more than a fifty-fifty chance to recover."

## WASHINGTON IS STUNNED

### Hoover Wires Roosevelt; Rejoicing That He Was Not Wounded.

### ASKS NEWS OF CERMAK

### Senators Express Gratitude President-Elect Escaped Madman's Shots.

### RISK TO PRESIDENT SEEN

### Determination Is Voiced That Life of His Successor Be Safeguarded by All Means.

Special to THE NEW YORK TIMES.

WASHINGTON, Feb. 15.—The nation's capital was deeply shocked tonight on hearing of the attempt on the life of President-elect Roosevelt.

From President Hoover to the lowliest citizen the reaction was instant that the country cast every safeguard around the President-elect.

President Hoover himself struck the keynote when he said:

"I am deeply shocked at the news. It is a dastardly act."

**Hoover's Message to Roosevelt.**

At the same time the President sent a telegram to Mr. Roosevelt which read:

"Together with every citizen I rejoice that you have not been injured. I shall be grateful to you for news of Mayor Cermak's condition."

Official and unofficial Washington was stunned at the first reports of what appeared to be an attempt on the life of the man who within less than three weeks will become Chief Executive. Newspaper extras were on the street almost immediately, and citizens sat close to their radios, receiving the latest news flashes. General relief was expressed that Mr. Roosevelt escaped injury.

**Comment of Leaders.**

Speaker Garner said:

"I am gratified beyond words that the President-elect is uninjured and that he will assume the administration of the Government of the United States, which is desired by the American people as expressed in the overwhelming result of the November elections."

Secretary Mills said:

"I am thankful that our next President escaped injury and that the act of a misguided or crazy individual will not deprive the American people of their chosen leader."

"Of course, I am overjoyed that the President-elect escaped," said Senator Byrnes, one of Mr. Roosevelt's closest advisers, "but I deplore profoundly that such a thing could happen. It's awful!"

Senator Robinson of Arkansas, Senate minority leader, said:

"Assuming that the shots were fired at Mr. Roosevelt, it should be understood that this is the United States, not Russia. No fanatic, crank or revolutionist, or any number of them will be permitted to prevent the orderly transfer of power in the government of the United States."

**Thinks Assailant Deranged.**

"How dreadful, and how fortunate he did not hit!" said Senator Lewis of Illinois. "I do not know what to say except that it was a dastardly act. I do hope it was not attempted out of ill will. It must have been the result of a deranged mind; certainly no one in his right mind would attempt such a thing. If, as appears possible, the shots were actually fired at Mayor Cermak, it undoubtedly was some member of the old lawless element in Chicago with a fancied grievance against the Mayor."

Chief Moran of the Secret Service, ill at his home here, received a report late this evening from Joseph E. Murphy, Assistant Chief, from the hospital in Miami where Mayor Cermak had been taken.

Commenting on the shooting, Senator Shipstead said:

"This unfortunate incident shows the risk the President and the President-elect of the United States are subject to. There are always cranks in the country. Every citizen

Continued on Page Three.

ESCAPES ASSASSIN'S BULLETS.

New York Times Studio Photo.
President-Elect Franklin D. Roosevelt.

## GUNMAN LAYS ACT TO BODY 'TORMENT'

### Joe Zingara, Hackensack Bricklayer, Says Pain Made Him 'Hate All Presidents.'

### DESCRIBED AS ANARCHIST

### Man Who Fired at Roosevelt Says He Once Tried in Italy to Kill King Victor Emmanuel.

By Telephone to THE NEW YORK TIMES.

MIAMI, Feb. 15.—Surrounded by detectives and high police officials, the man who shot at President-elect Roosevelt tonight gave his name as Joe Zingara of New York and related, in spasms of words during questioning at Police Headquarters, how "constant torment from a stomach operation" had impelled him to attempt the life of the President-elect.

Zingara, a short, stocky man of about 35, a brick mason who came to Miami two months ago from Hackensack, N. J., betrayed by his manner even in the rational portions of his statement the warped mentality which resulted in his deed tonight.

In an almost boastful tone, he declared that he had attempted the life of King Victor Emmanuel of Italy ten years ago. That failed, he said, for the same reason as his attempt tonight—"there was too big a crowd."

He admitted he had no personal grievance against Mr. Roosevelt. Saying "No, I had none," he swept away questions of that nature.

Nor could the police discover that he had any personal grievance against the King of Italy. But he hated "rich and powerful persons," he said with a hiss, and they were figures, he indicated, for his wrath.

**"I Don't Like Presidents."**

"I like Roosevelt personally, but I don't like Presidents," he replied when asked if he didn't like the President-elect. He intended to kill him, he said, "and I would be glad if I had killed the President-elect."

He did not like Presidents because "rich men send their children to schools."

He said this was because "when I was a young man, rich men's sons went to school while I worked in a brick factory in Italy and burned myself."

Zingara indicated a scar on his stomach which he said was the result of the burn.

He was seized with the idea of trying to kill the President-elect only two days ago, he declared.

"About two days ago I bought a paper for 5 cents and saw that the President-elect was coming to Miami," he related.

"So yesterday I went to a place

Continued on Page Two.

## MRS. ROOSEVELT TAKES NEWS CALMLY

### She Telephones Immediately to Husband and Is Relieved to Find Him Unhurt.

### KEEPS SPEAKING PROGRAM

### Assured That "He Is Not Even Excited," She Takes Train Later for Ithaca.

Mrs. Franklin D. Roosevelt returned to her home at 49 East Sixty-fifth Street about 10:30 o'clock last night and found the household upset. The Negro butler's face betrayed his agitation as he admitted her.

"What's it all about?" she demanded.

Stammering, the butler told her that her husband, the President-elect, had been fired upon in Miami. He had only the meager information gleaned from newspapers, which called the house when the first brief reports were received.

Mrs. Roosevelt was met at her home by her daughter, Mrs. Anna Roosevelt Dall, and received the news calmly and without apparent emotion.

"Those things are to be expected," she remarked.

With a calm and steady voice she placed a long distance telephone call which reached the President-elect at the bedside of Mayor Cermak. There followed a few minutes of conversation and then Mrs. Roosevelt turned to the group in the room and said:

"He's all right. He's not the least bit excited."

**Leaves for Ithaca.**

A few minutes later Mrs. Roosevelt, accompanied only by her maid, was on a railroad train bound for Ithaca, N. Y., to fill a speaking engagement on the program of Cornell University's Home and Farm Week. The train left at 11:35.

Mrs. Roosevelt was speaking at the Warner Club at 321 West Forty-fourth Street when the first of the dramatic incident in Miami was received in New York newspaper offices. She left there without knowledge of what had happened.

In his telephone conversation with Mrs. Roosevelt, members of the household said, the President-elect informed her that it was his belief that the would-be assassin's bullets were aimed at Mayor Cermak, and not at him.

They quoted him as saying that five persons were in the hospital as a result of the shooting, and that he wasn't even scratched. Instead of starting back for New York last night, as he had planned, however,

Continued on Page Two.

## ASSASSIN SHOOTS 5 TIMES

### Police and Bystanders Leap for Him and Take Him Prisoner.

### ACCOMPLICE TAKEN LATER

### Cermak and New York Officer Rushed to Hospital—Now in Serious Condition.

### ROOSEVELT DELAYS TRIP

### Had Been Warmly Welcomed and Intended to Start for North at Once.

By JAMES A. HAGERTY.
Special to THE NEW YORK TIMES.

MIAMI, Feb. 15.—An unsuccessful attempt was made to assassinate President-elect Franklin D. Roosevelt just after he ended a speech in Bay Front Park here at 9:35 o'clock tonight, two hours after his return from an eleven-day fishing cruise on Vincent Astor's yacht Nourmahal.

Although the gunman missed the target at which he was aiming, he probably fatally wounded Mayor Anton Cermak of Chicago and four other persons were hit by five shots from his pistol before a woman destroyed his aim on the last shot by seizing his wrist and a Miami policeman felled him to the ground with a blow of his night stick.

**List of the Wounded.**

The wounded are:

Mayor Anton Cermak of Chicago, shot through the chest; condition critical.

Miss Margaret Kruis of the Henry Clay Hotel, Miami Beach, a visitor from Newark, N. J., shot through the hand.

Mrs. Joe H. Gill, wife of the president of the Florida Power and Light Company, shot in the abdomen; condition critical.

William Sinnott, a New York policeman, living at 612 West 178th Street, shot in the head; condition critical.

Russell Caldwell, 22, of Miami, shot in the head.

**Roosevelt Was Target.**

The would-be assassin, who was arrested immediately and lodged in the city prison on the nineteenth floor of Miami's skyscraper City Hall, is Giuseppe Zingara of Hackensack, N. J.

Although early reports were that he intended to kill Mayor Cermak rather than the President-elect, due to his remark, "Well, I got Cermak," it appeared later that Mr. Roosevelt was his target.

"I'd kill every President," he was reported by the police to have said after his arrest.

"I'd kill them all; I'd kill all the officers," he also is reported to have said, indicating that he may be an Anarchist.

Evidence that the attempted assassination of Roosevelt was premeditated was obtained by the police late tonight and Andrea Valenti, who lived with Zingara, was arrested on suspicion of being an accomplice.

A search of Zingara's clothing disclosed several newspaper clippings, mostly from local newspapers announcing Mr. Roosevelt's intended visit to this city.

**Clipping on McKinley.**

One clipping, however, contained an account of the assassination of President McKinley by the anarchist Czolgosz. This strengthened the police belief that Zingara might belong to some anarchist group, although no direct evidence has been obtained showing such a connection.

Detectives, deputy sheriffs and policemen were working on several clues, obtained by the questioning of Zingara and Valenti.

Zingara is charged with assault with intent to kill, pending the preferring of the more serious

Section 1 "All the News That's Fit to Print."

# The New York Times.

LATE CITY EDITION
WEATHER—Fair today and tomorrow; temperature unchanged.
Temperature Yesterday—Max., 42; Min., 34

Section 1

Copyright, 1933, by The New York Times Company.

VOL. LXXXII....No. 27,434. Entered as Second-Class Matter, Postoffice, New York, N. Y. NEW YORK, SUNDAY, MARCH 5, 1933. Including Rotogravure Picture, Magazine and Book Sections. TEN CENTS | TWELVE CENTS Beyond 200 Miles. Except in 7th and 8th Postal Zones.

# ROOSEVELT INAUGURATED, ACTS TO END THE NATIONAL BANKING CRISIS QUICKLY; WILL ASK WAR-TIME POWERS IF NEEDED

## PLAN TO USE SCRIP HERE

### Bankers Ready to Issue Clearing House Paper at End of Holiday.

### WILL MEET WOODIN TODAY

### Eastern Financiers to Join Parley at Capital on Plans to Permit Reopenings.

### STOCK EXCHANGES CLOSED

### Drain on the Gold Reserve Is Halted—Cash Being Set Aside to Meet Payrolls.

**The Banking Situation.**

The New York Clearing House Association prepared to print and issue certificates to be used by the public as substitute money.

In every State of the nation, including the District of Columbia, banking was wholly or partly suspended.

In London, Paris and other European capitals, dollar transactions were suspended.

Bankers from New York and other financial centres will confer with Secretary of the Treasury Woodin on remedial plans for presentation by the President to this afternoon's legislative conference.

**Scrip Being Rushed.**

Clearing house certificates will be used instead of currency in New York when the banks reopen on Tuesday after the two-day holiday proclaimed by Governor Herbert H. Lehman, according to present plans of the New York Clearing House Association, it was learned last night.

This was confirmed by Mortimer N. Buckner, president of the New York Clearing House Association and chairman of the board of the New York Trust Company, following a meeting of the clearing house committee at the clearing house, 77 Cedar Street.

Bankers from New York and other centres have been called to Washington to confer with William H. Woodin, Secretary of the Treasury, at 10 o'clock this morning on plans for meeting the emergency. George W. Davison, chairman of the Central Hanover Bank and Trust Company and head of the Clearing House Committee, left for Washington yesterday afternoon; and George L. Harrison, governor of the Federal Reserve Bank of New York was scheduled to go last night. Charles S. McCain, chairman of the board of the Chase National Bank, was in Washington yesterday and it was thought likely that he would remain for the conference.

In the event that the discussions of the bankers with Mr. Woodin develop a plan which can be put into effect through Congressional action, the proposals will be laid before President Roosevelt this afternoon and presented by him to a conference of legislators. It is expected that the results of the conference may have a bearing upon how quickly the new Congress is called into session.

In addition to the New York bankers, representatives from the banking communities of Philadelphia, Chicago, Baltimore and Richmond are expected to attend the conference

**Act to Meet Payrolls.**

It was indicated last night that arrangements would be made whereby payrolls due yesterday or tomorrow would be met by the withdrawal from the banks of sufficient amounts of currency to pay all or part in cash. Concerns accustomed to paying by check would be permitted to withdraw cash, it was predicted, or the banks would make special provision for cashing pay checks. Governor Lehman is expected to give his approval to a payroll plan being worked out by the banks and business houses.

The banking holiday ordered by Governor Lehman in a proclamation issued at his apartment, 820 Park Avenue, at 4:20 o'clock yesterday morning, was effective yesterday, and will expire at the

Continued on Page Twenty-five.

### *Checks Still Accepted Here For Federal Income Taxes*

Collectors of Internal Revenue in New York City were still accepting checks yesterday in payment of Federal income taxes, and it was said that checks would continue to be accepted during the bank holiday.

No consideration was yet being given to possible postponement of payments, due on March 15. This could only be granted by the Secretary of the Treasury or Commissioner of Internal Revenue in Washington, although the law allows individual applications for extension of time.

Walter E. Corwin, Collector in Brooklyn, said clearing-house certificates would not be accepted, if issued as a medium of exchange. The law permits payment in cash, checks, Treasury notes or Liberty bonds.

## VICTORY FOR HITLER IS EXPECTED TODAY

### Repression of Opponents Held to Make Election Triumph for Regime Inevitable.

### FIRES BLAZE ON BORDERS

### Nazis Light Them as Sign of "Reawakening"—Imperial Flag to Be Restored.

By FREDERICK T. BIRCHALL.

Special Cable to THE NEW YORK TIMES.

BERLIN, March 4.—In a countrywide blaze of bonfires and torchlight parades the allied National Socialist and Nationalist parties tonight closed the electoral campaign, which tomorrow is expected to entrench them securely in power not only throughout Germany as a result of the Reichstag elections but throughout Prussia, where the electorate will vote simultaneously for a separate State ticket.

Tonight, on every eminence along Germany's borders, not excluding the Polish Corridor, a bonfire flamed to signalize the Nazi ideal of an awakening nation. In Köenigeberg, East Prussia, Chancellor Adolf Hitler himself made his closing appeal to aroused patriotic fervor.

In every city and every town of considerable size uniformed Nazis marched to some centre, where amid the blare of brass bands playing partiotic songs, in which the whole assemblage joined, Nazi orators proclaimed the dawning of a new day.

In Berlin alone there were twenty-four parades to an equal number of meeting places, where through loud-speakers the voice of Herr Hitler was heard and acclaimed.

**No Counter-Demonstrations.**

There were no counter-demonstrations from the opposition. They were "verboten," for this is a one-way election. Nor, late tonight, despite the dire predictions sent to the outside world, had any serious disturbance been reported. All that is over, for what is the use of inviting inevitable and overwhelming reprisals when all the authority and all the weapons are monopolized by the other side?

In Thuringia, the only State in which a few Socialist newspapers remain unsuspended, they were all compelled by the Nazi State government today to reprint Chancellor Hitler's recent speech against "Marxism" on the front page.

The utmost left for those opposed to an all-Nazi régime is to vote against it silently and secretly tomorrow—if they dare—and to hope for the best.

So confident today are the government leaders of a verdict in their favor that even before the polls are open they are already announcing the first act of the new Reichstag. It will be to retire the Republican flag of black, red and gold under which Germany has fought her way out of the difficulties in which the World War left her and to replace it with the black-white-red banner of the former imperialism.

"We shall be happy to get rid of that emblem of 'Marxism,'" declared Captain Hermann Wilhelm Goering, Minister Without Portfolio and the spokesman of militant na-

Continued on Page Twenty.

## READY TO CALL CONGRESS

### President Probably Will Summon Extra Session for Wednesday.

### WORKS ON LEGISLATION

### Cabinet Ordered to Meet With Him Today to Draft Banking Reform Measures.

### AID LIKELY IN A WEEK

### Steps Considered Include Deposit Guarantee, Use of Scrip and Tax on Hoarded Gold.

Special to THE NEW YORK TIMES.

WASHINGTON, March 4.—President Roosevelt plunged immediately into the banking situation tonight by summoning members of his Cabinet and leaders of Congress to meet tomorrow afternoon to decide upon a program to deal with it.

As soon as the program is agreed upon. Congress will be called into special session, probably on Wednesday, and it is the expectation of administration advisers that legislation will be enacted within another week.

The White House issued the following statement at 7:20 P. M.:

"Respecting the date for the extra session of Congress, no decision has been reached tonight, but probably will be by tomorrow night.

"The Secretary of the Treasury will begin tomorrow a series of discussions called at the request of President Roosevelt, looking to prompt action in the banking situation. He is calling a number of individuals and Reserve Bank officials to Washington. Some have already been invited and more will be called tonight."

Bankers from New York, Philadelphia, Chicago, Baltimore and Richmond were invited to the conference with Secretary Woodin at 10 o'clock tomorrow morning.

After they have discussed the banking situation, whatever plan may be adopted will be transmitted to President Roosevelt for presentation to the legislative conference in the afternoon.

**Four Proposals Advanced.**

While President Roosevelt was reviewing the parade from the stand in front of the White House this afternoon, members of his Cabinet and two former Secretaries of the Treasury, David F. Houston and William G. McAdoo, were engaged in discussion of a program which will be laid before the conference tomorrow.

The main points advanced but not finally decided upon at this informal conference, in which Secretary Woodin participated for a few minutes, were:

1. The organization of a corporation to which banks must subscribe to guarantee bank deposits.

2. The issue of scrip, as was resorted to in the banking emergency in 1907, to be put out by the banks to the amount of frozen deposits.

3. A tax on hoarded gold, as high as 15 per cent.

4. Other measures to protect our gold holdings.

Secretary of State Hull said, however, that a tax on hoarded gold did not seem practicable, and probably would not be resorted to in the hope of raising any considerable amount of money, but merely as a move to force hoarders to put gold into circulation and restore confidence in the banks.

These suggestions with others will come before the conference tomorrow and the new administration leaders were confident tonight that a program could be agreed upon for submission to and prompt action by Congress by the middle of next week.

**Problem Is to Allay Fear.**

"The main thing right now," said Secretary Hull, "is to allay the unreasonable and unreasoning fear in the public mind. That in itself would be a long step in the direction toward restoration of confidence. Nothing right now is more unjustifiable than attempts to hoard money."

Former Secretary of the Treasury

Continued on Page Twenty-four.

THE NEW PRESIDENT TAKING THE OATH OF OFFICE.

Associated Press Photo.

Franklin D. Roosevelt, With Hand Raised, Being Sworn by Chief Justice Charles Evans Hughes on the Rostrum in Front of the Capitol at 1:08 P. M. Yesterday. At the Right Are His Son, James Roosevelt, and Former President Hoover.

## HOOVER, AS CITIZEN, HERE ON WAY HOME

### Spends Evening in Seclusion in Hotel After Seeing His Successor Take Office.

### SEEMS GLAD TO GET AWAY

### Bids Genial Farewell to Old Friends in Capital After Morning of Heavy Cares.

By RUSSELL OWEN.

Herbert Hoover entered private life yesterday after a day of foreboding, in which his successor addressed the nation as though it were entering upon a war. With downcast eyes and a diffident manner, Mr. Hoover went to the Capitol to see Mr. Roosevelt inaugurated as President, and left hurriedly, as if glad to throw from his shoulders the mantle of responsibility for the affairs of a country desperately distressed.

Immediately after the ceremony he left the Capitol and drove to the railroad station to take a train for New York, where he arrived at 5:50 o'clock last night. He went to the Waldorf-Astoria and spent the evening in seclusion, avoiding visitors.

Until half an hour before he stepped into the automobile that was to bear him and President Roosevelt to the inaugural ceremonies in Washington, he was busy with affairs of state. As no other man who has stepped from the office of Chief Executive, he was beset with complex problems until the end of his term. The last bills he signed were those to aid the country through the present crisis. He signed them grimly, with a grave face, realizing to the full the difficulties which he was bequeathing.

**Raises Hat Only Once.**

The drive from the White House to the Capitol was through lines of people who watched with serious, rather than enthusiastic faces. A sense of depression had ettled over the capital so that it could be felt. The two men, side by side, were looked upon as symbols of a government trying to cope with dangers which were as subtle as they were treacherous. The few cheers were for Roosevelt rather than Hoover. He realized that, and only raised his hat once during the trip, although the new President smiled and doffed his hat frequently in response to the faint cheers from the stands and sidewalk.

But once in the railroad station to take the train to New York after the inauguration, Mr. Hoover came into his own again. There were people who firmly believed in him,

Continued on Page Four.



## *Text of the Inaugural Address; President for Vigorous Action*

### *"This Is Pre-eminently the Time to Speak the Truth," He Says, in Demand That "the Temple of Our Civilization Be Restored to the Ancient Truths."*

Special to THE NEW YORK TIMES.

*WASHINGTON, March 4.—President Roosevelt's inaugural address, delivered immediately after he took the oath, was as follows:*

President Hoover, Mr. Chief Justice, my friends:

This is a day of national consecration, and I am certain that my fellow-Americans expect that on my induction into the Presidency I will address them with a candor and a decision which the present situation of our nation impels.

This is pre-eminently the time to speak the truth, the whole truth, frankly and boldly. Nor need we shrink from honestly facing conditions in our country today. This great nation will endure as it has endured, will revive and will prosper.

So first of all let me assert my firm belief that the only thing we have to fear is fear itself—nameless, unreasoning, unjustified terror which paralyzes needed efforts to convert retreat into advance.

In every dark hour of our national life a leadership of frankness and vigor has met with that understanding and support of the people themselves which is essential to victory. I am convinced that you will again give that support to leadership in these critical days.

In such a spirit on my part and on yours we face our common difficulties. They concern, thank God, only material things. Values have shrunken to fantastic levels; taxes have risen; our ability to pay has fallen; government of all kinds is faced by serious curtailment of income; the means of exchange are frozen in the currents of trade; the withered leaves of industrial enterprise lie on every side; farmers find no markets for their produce; the savings of many years in thousands of families are gone.

More important, a host of unemployed citizens face the grim problem of existence, and an equally great number toil with little return. Only a foolish optimist can deny the dark realities of the moment.

Yet our distress comes from no failure of substance. We are stricken by no plague of locusts. Compared with the perils which our forefathers conquered because they believed and were not afraid, we have still much to be thankful for. Nature still offers her bounty and human efforts have multiplied it. Plenty is at our doorstep, but a generous use of it languishes in the very sight of the supply.

**Charges "Money Changers" Lack Vision.**

Primarily, this is because the rulers of the exchange of mankind's goods have failed through their own stubbornness and their own incompetence, have admitted their failure and abdicated. Practices of the unscrupulous money changers stand indicted in the court of public opinion, rejected by the hearts and minds of men.

True, they have tried, but their efforts have been cast in the pattern of an outworn tradition. Faced by failure of credit, they have proposed only the lending of more money.

Stripped of the lure of profit by which to induce our people to follow their false leadership, they have resorted to exhortations, pleading tearfully for restored confidence. They know only the rules of a generation of self-seekers.

They have no vision, and when there is no vision the people perish.

The money changers have fled from their high seats in the temple of our civilization. We may now restore that temple to the ancient truths.

The measure of the restoration lies in the extent to which we apply social values more noble than mere monetary profit.

Happiness lies not in the mere possession of money; it lies in the joy of achievement, in the thrill of creative effort.

The joy and moral stimulation of work no longer must be forgotten in the mad chase of evanescent profits. These dark days will be worth all they cost us if they teach us that our true

Continued on Page Three.

## 500,000 IN STREETS CHEER ROOSEVELT

### Their Spirits Are Lifted by His Smile of Confidence as They Watch Parade.

### MANY ON ROOFS, IN TREES

### Throng Waiting for Ceremony Is Solemnly Silent Until New President Appears.

Special to THE NEW YORK TIMES.

WASHINGTON, March 4.—The quadrennial pageant which traditionally accompanies the inauguration of a new President was enacted here today with all the pomp and panoply of more prosperous years and with all solemnity.

Before the august Capitol, in an inadequate and windswept forty acres, 100,000 of his countrymen saw Franklin D. Roosevelt swear on the ancient Bible of his Dutch fathers to cherish and defend the Constitution of his country.

Five hundred thousand others saw his reassuringly confident smile as he rode from Capitol to White House at the head of a parade of 18,000 marching men and women, among whom were such of his formidable rivals for the nomination as Alfred E. Smith and Governor Albert C. Ritchie of Maryland.

Mr. Roosevelt became the thirty-second President of the United States on a day that was cloudy and chill, with an occasional ray of sunlight piercing the clouds below which rode majestically the navy airship Akron and ninety-six military airplanes from Bolling and Langley Fields.

Flags flew at half-taff on the Senate and House Office Buildings in memory of Senator Walsh, who was to have been Attorney General in the new Cabinet.

Over the vast throngs there hung a cloud of worry, because of the economic and business outlook. The new President's recurrent smile of confidence, his uplifted chin and the challenge of his voice did much to help the national sense of humor to assert itself.

**Reviews Parade for Three Hours.**

Again, standing throughout the afternoon while legions of men of all degrees and colors marched past his glass-enclosed reviewing stand in the Court of Honor, the new President, advocate of a new deal, set an example of resolute fortitude and cheerfulness as he doffed his hat in deference to the colors and in greeting to old friends and supporters.

He stood between Admiral William V. Pratt, Chief of Naval Operations, and General Douglas Mac-

Continued on Page Two.

## 100,000 AT INAUGURATION

### President, Grim, Terse, Pledges 'Adequate but Sound Currency.'

### SCORES 'MONEY-CHANGERS'

### In Fighting Speech He Demands Supervision of Credits and Investments.

### STICKS TO CONSTITUTION

### Calls on People and Congress to Follow Him as Leader in War on Depression.

By ARTHUR KROCK.

Special to THE NEW YORK TIMES.

WASHINGTON, March 4.—With solemn mien, Franklin D. Roosevelt of New York took the oath of office and became the thirty-second President of the United States on the main steps of the Capitol at eight minutes after 1 o'clock this afternoon.

A deep consciousness of the task before him was patent in his unusual demeanor as, his face stern, his voice grave, he repeated after Chief Justice Hughes the historic words of the oath. This realization animated also the inaugural address which Mr. Roosevelt then delivered in the presence of at least a hundred thousand persons who gathered in the Capitol grounds.

The sense of the administration's burden was apparent, too, in the manner and speech of Vice President Garner, who, an hour before the President took the oath, laid down his gavel as Speaker of the House of Representatives and was inducted into his new office in the Senate chamber, where he will henceforth preside.

**Keeps Pledge of Action.**

"Action" was the promise of Mr. Roosevelt's speech, and action was immediately forthcoming. The first moment after the ceremonies were over, the President swore in his Cabinet, summoned the party leaders to a Sunday conference to work out the plan for banking relief and arranged to call an extra session of the Seventy-third Congress, probably on Wednesday, to legislate the plan into law.

"This nation asks for action, and action now," he said on the steps of the Capitol. Within a few hours, he acted.

The President had consistently maintained his attitude that he would not accept responsibility without power in the period between his election and his inauguration. Powerful and subtle suasions could not move him. But when authority came he moved at once as he had said he would.

**Atmosphere Is Grim.**

Though the city was gay with flags and lively with the music of bands and cheers for the marchers in the inaugural parade which followed the oath taking, the atmosphere which surrounded the change of government in the United States was comparable to that which might be found in a beleaguered capital in war time.

The President in his address told the people that they were at war with the forces of depression and offered them leadership and action in the new campaign to be raged against these forces.

In words that burned and scourged he denounced the financial leaders of the nation, declared that these "money changers" should be driven from the temple and that they should not be allowed to return to their high places. No more, he declared, should those entrusted with other people's money be permitted to misuse it.

The inaugural address was a Jacksonian speech, a fighting speech, implicit with criticism of the lack of leadership and the philosophy of government which the President imputed to his predecessor, who sat there, listening. He would lead, he said, as the people expect, within the confines of the Constitution, and he will demand that Congress follow this leadership.

But if his present powers prove insufficient to win the war to which he pledged his full mind and

Continued on Page Three.

"All the News That's Fit to Print."

# The New York Times.

LATE CITY EDITION
Snow and colder today. Tomorrow fair and continued cold.
Temperatures Yesterday—Max., 29; min., 18.



VOL. LXXXV....No. 28,492. Entered as Second-Class Matter, Postoffice, New York, N. Y. NEW YORK, MONDAY, JANUARY 27, 1936. PP TWO CENTS In New York City. | THREE CENTS Within 200 Miles | FOUR CENTS Elsewhere Except in 7th and 8th Postal Zones.

# ITALIANS PUSH ON IN SOUTH; FOES RETREAT 268 MILES; FIGHT CONTINUES IN NORTH

## ETHIOPIA ORDERS A STAND

### Desta Demtu Is Told to Fight Advance From Mountain Passes.

### AIR TOLL AT 500 IN SIDAMO

### Italian Bombers Are Killing Civilians in Raids, Addis Ababa Reports.

### CHANGE IN ROME AIM SEEN

### Drive in South Is Believed to Be Related to Offer in the Hoare-Laval Plan.

By The Associated Press.

LONDON, Jan. 26.—Benito Mussolini's mechanized armies pushed through Southern and Southwestern Ethiopia at an unprecedented pace today. Reports received here from Rome said Italy's southern "hell on wheels" column rumbled onward past Noghelli, aiming seemingly at Allata, major city of Sidamo Province, hundreds of miles from the starting point of the column, at Dolo.

Heavy hostilities apparently continued, too, on the Northern Ethiopian front, with conflicting Italian and Ethiopian claims of victory still unreconciled.

**Sixteen Miles Beyond Noghelli.**

The Southern armies of General Rodolfo Graziani were reported to have marched about sixteen miles beyond Noghelli to the villages of Ducan and Bidatta, capturing many prisoners.

[Allata, the reported Italian objective, is 350 miles northwest of Dolo and on the fringes of Lake Abaya. Noghelli is approximately 250 miles from Dolo.]

Another Italian column, headed by General Agostini, was proceeding northwest along the Kenya border, said reports reaching Rome.

In Geneva some officials believed Mussolini was determined to set a furious pace in Ethiopia before the weather forced a cessation of hostilities. They thought the dictator was seeking a military position that might force a favorable peace agreement.

**Ethiopia Admits Southern Loss.**

By The Associated Press.

ADDIS ABABA, Jan. 26.—Official Ethiopian sources disclosed today the retreating Southern armies of Ras Desta Demtu had fallen back to Wadara, 268 miles northwest of Dolo.

Military strategists, however, expressed doubt that the Italians would be able to defend their communication lines from Dolo as far as Wadara, and declared the invaders were in grave danger of being trapped and massacred either there or at Noghelli.

Ras Desta Demtu, Emperor Haile Selassie's son-in-law, was ordered by the Emperor to make a stand in the mountain passes behind Wadara, which is the northern terminus of a motor road. At the same time the Ethiopians will resort to night attacks on the Italian communication lines.

The official news from the South came in the midst of "victory" celebrations for alleged northern successes. A Saturday announcement said "two important Italian fronts" had been taken following a three-day northern battle described as the biggest of the war. The announcement said Makale, key point of the northern Italian advance, was surrounded and cut off, and it contended thousands of the invaders had fallen and that tanks, cannon and machine guns had been captured.

**Reports 2 Columns Wiped Out.**

Two Fascist columns attempting to rescue besieged troops of the Makale garrison were wiped out, the government said.

[Italy rejoiced over the same battle, the Fascist high command saying the Italians had crushed an Ethiopian plan to attack west of Makale; that the Ethiopians were "beaten everywhere" and that their casualties were 5,000, compared with 743 dead and wounded for Italy.]

A fortnight's anxiety over the whereabouts of a Swedish Red Cross unit ended with the receipt of a telegram here announcing the unit's safe arrival at Igra Alem, newly built capital of Sidamo Province. To reach Igra Alem the Swedes

Continued on Page Ten.

## Munitions Blast Kills 40 In Aleppo, Beirut Hears

By The Associated Press.

BEIRUT, Syria, Jan. 26.—Reports reaching here today said forty persons had been killed in Aleppo when an ammunition storehouse blew up. Details were lacking.

The reported blast follows Nationalist rioting in Aleppo yesterday in which two persons were killed and 250 jailed. Syrian students decided to strike tomorrow in sympathy with the Nationalists.

Aleppo, important industrial city and market in North Syria, has an estimated population of about 177,000 persons.

The modern citadel, standing on a hill 200 feet high and surrounded by a moat, and the Zakaria Mosque, containing the tomb of Zacharias, father of John the Baptist, are among the most important buildings.

# FUNERAL OF GEORGE MAY AID DIPLOMACY

### Statesmen Expected to Use Chance for Talks Aimed at Winning Political Gains.

### REICH MAY GET ADVANTAGE

### Neurath, Its Envoy to Rites, Is Well Liked in Britain—Starhemberg Seeks Help.

By FREDERICK T. BIRCHALL.

Wireless to THE NEW YORK TIMES.

LONDON, Jan. 26.—Kings, Princes, Premiers or foreign Ministers from every country in Europe are arriving here daily for the royal funeral. In the aggregate they constitute a political gathering that even Geneva cannot duplicate.

Not only crowned heads, but also generals, admirals and diplomats of highest rank are in this galaxy. All come ostensibly to pay respects to the revered memory of King George and undoubtedly all the proprieties will be observed. Nevertheless, there will be many luncheons, dinners and other private and semi-private gatherings at which they will all meet socially, and amid these opportunities a certain amount of diplomatic business will be done. From time immemorial such gatherings, whether for weddings or funerals, have been used for such purposes.

A classic example was the funeral of Queen Victoria in 1901. Britain, then waging the Boer War, was universally condemned by the rest of Europe and was more isolated and better hated than at any other time within a century. The German Kaiser hated Britain, and he even telegraphed to President Paul Kruger of the Transvaal, expressing sympathy for the Boers. Britain was furious about it.

But in the atmosphere of grief over the Queen there came a

Continued on Page Nine.

# VENIZELOS VICTOR IN GREEK ELECTION; HIS RETURN LIKELY

### Liberals Whose Leader Is in Exile Pile Up Lead Over His Foe, Kondylis.

### TSALDARIS ALSO SET BACK

### Many Republicans Lose in the Poll—Communists Likely to Get 14 Seats.

By GEORGE WELLER.

Wireless to THE NEW YORK TIMES.

ATHENS, Jan. 26.—On a platform of toleration of King George II, the Venizelists defeated Field Marshal George Kondylis today in a perfectly orderly and honestly conducted election, thereby making probable an early return of Eleutherios Venizelos to Greece.

Marshal Kondylis, however, aided by John Theotokis, by an amazing spurt outran Panayoti Tsaldaris and made himself the strongest leader of the anti-Venizelists. He will command in Parliament a fighting minority, which will support his existing control of army officers.

Mr. Tsaldaris paid the penalty for vacillating over the question of restoration and the Venizelist question by heavy losses throughout the country. Many Republican leaders were annihilated. General John Metaxas lost heavily to Marshal Kondylis, and the Communists lost strength to Mr. Venizelos. The Venizelists obtained 80 per cent of the vote in Macedonia and even more in Crete.

**British Alliance Involved.**

Marshal Kondylis's unexpected strength may presage parliamentary opposition to King George's military alliance with Great Britain, for Marshal Kondylis hitherto has done his utmost in Italy's interests on every occasion. Mr. Venizelos's private agreement with King George for mutual toleration was made with the object of keeping Greece within the British camp, and Mr. Venizelos, therefore, may be publicly invited by King George to return home as early as possible as an offset to Marshal Kondylis.

The returns in Athens are nearly complete and may be taken as roughly corresponding to those which the national vote will show. They are as follows:

Venizelists, 37,000; Kondylists, 21,000; Tsaldarists, 15,000; Communists, 7,000; Republican Front (of minor republican leaders) 3,000; Metaxas party, 2,500, and Canellopoulous party, 2,500.

Premier Constantine Demerdjis prophesied tonight that the Venizelists would obtain about 125 seats out of the total of 300. The Kondylists were expected to get sixty seats and the Tsaldarists forty-five.

[An Associated Press dispatch said returns last night indicated the Liberals would get 135 seats; the parties of Mr. Tsaldaris and Marshal Kondylis, 125; the Communists, 14; the Republicans, 8; the party of General Metaxas, 9, and the Independents, 9. Thus no single party appeared able to form a government alone.]

Mr. Venizelos' photograph on the Liberal ballots drew a blast from Marshal Kondylis, who said:

"My opposition is not against the Liberals as a party but against Venizelos personally, who must never be allowed to return to the

Continued on Page Twelve.

# 'Phantom' Thief Eludes 200 Police All Day in Woolworth Building

### Skyscraper in State of Siege After Burglar Loots Five Offices and Shoots Watchman—Squads With Machine Guns and Powerful Lights Search Every Cranny in Vain.

The heavy boots of policemen and detectives echoed in the marble corridors of the Woolworth Building all yesterday afternoon and last night in futile search for a burglar who had looted five offices and wounded a building watchman.

More than 200 stalwarts of the Police Department with their squad and division leaders, armed with rifles, machine guns, small arms and powerful searchlights, covered every inch of the forty acres of floor-space from basement to tower without a sign of the wraith-like cracksman.

Wanderers in the deserted canyons of lower Broadway were astonished by the bristling display of fourteen police radio cars—some called from points as distant as Fort Hamilton in Brooklyn—detective squad cars and four emergency units that surrounded the skyscraper.

Wild rumors spread through the lower city as the search progressed. They began with reports that a daring gang had looted the mails in the City Hall branch of the post-office, just opposite the Woolworth Building. Then they switched to a story that the offices of Special Prosecutor Thomas E. Dewey on the fourteenth floor of the skyscraper had been ransacked.

Late in the afternoon it was whispered at the offices of the Brothers Osborn, handwriting experts for the State in the Hauptmann trial, in Room 4002, had been broken into in a search for new Hauptmann evidence. None of these rumors had any basis in fact.

About 9 A. M. yesterday, Ray Kelly, starter in the building, discovered that thirty pass keys for offices in various parts of the building had been stolen from the superintendent's suite in Room 2908. He immediately telephoned to Edward Stacey and Howard Downs, assistant superintendents.

About an hour later watchmen discovered that five offices on the thirty-fifth floor had been ransacked. The doors apparently had been opened with either passkeys or master keys and several desks had been jimmied. The places

Continued on Page Five.

# U. S. JEWRY BACKS REICH EXODUS PLAN

### St. Louis Assembly Endorses Proposal to Finance the Emigration of Youths.

### NAZIS EVOLVE NEW IDEA

### Exporters to 'Borrow' Wealth of Emigrants and Repay 65% Over 13 Years.

From a Staff Correspondent.

ST. LOUIS, Jan. 26.—Leaders representing the organized philanthropic effort of American Jewry voted unanimous endorsement today of the proposal outlined last night by Sir Herbert Samuel and Felix M. Warburg to finance the emigration of the younger generation of Jews from Germany, together with as many of the older generation as might be able to exist elsewhere.

Assembled at the Chase Hotel here as the National Council of Jewish Federation and Welfare Funds, representing sixty-seven local communal agencies in more than fifty cities, 500 leaders voted that they not only would continue to carry their obligations to the needy in this country but also could and would contribute as much in addition as might be necessary for the German effort, in advance of learning what sum might be required.

Leaders admitted they had been moved by Mr. Warburg's impassioned plea to leave less to their own children but to leave them their heart interest in some co-religionist of the same age for whom they had provided fair play.

Great importance was attached to Sir Herbert's declaration that the decision that the younger generation must leave Germany had been made by their own parents there, by those who were so rooted in Germany that they must remain but who recognized that their children must leave in order to live.

**Project Held Possible.**

The endorsement was led by William J. Shroder of Cincinnati, re-elected today as president of the council. Speaking before the German appeal last night, he had cautioned his audience that there were American as well as German needs, and other needs in Europe not so dramatic as those in Germany but as urgent.

Today, however, he said that it was the whole-hearted belief of the leaders present that while the American needs must be met as usual in support not only of Jewish but of nonsectarian communal services without diversion of any funds, the German effort could also be supported.

"It means more giving," said Mr. Shroder. "Those familiar with the local situations are agreed that, with some sacrifice, the extra giving can be secured. It means increasing the willingness to give rather than the ability to give. I don't think we have come to the limit even of income giving. As a personal opinion I think we could double the present amounts of giving out of income without going into capital. But if we have to go into capital before the German problem is solved, we must face that also."

The leaders present had waited before pronouncing on the project to receive the public assurance of Sir Herbert that the "rescue" of the German Jews did not entail

Continued on Page Eleven.

# BONUS ENACTMENT SCHEDULED TODAY

### Senate Defeat of Veto Appears Certain and Treasury Prepares to Print Bonds.

### FARM PROBLEM UP NEXT

### AAA Substitute to Go to Both Houses This Week—Nye Will Ask More Inquiry Funds.

Special to THE NEW YORK TIMES.

WASHINGTON, Jan. 26.—The Soldier Bonus Bill tonight was only a few hours away from the statute books, according to all indications, and before the Senate stops work for the day tomorrow the measure is expected to be sent to the State Department, there to be filed away in the archives.

Not even the most outspoken critic of the $2,491,000,000 "baby-bond" measure would predict its defeat tomorrow when the Senate votes on the question of overriding the President's veto. But instead of a vote of 74 to 16, by which the bill passed the Senate on last Monday, it was estimated tonight that "about twenty" Senators would vote to sustain the President. That number would be far short of the ballots necessary to sustain the veto, so even the White House was said to have abandoned hope.

From authoritative sources tonight it was learned that Treasury officials have started machinery for the printing of the more than 45,000,000 individual $50 baby bonds that will be required to redeem the outstanding adjusted service certificates. The bonds will not be printed, however, for some weeks.

**A Busy Week Ahead.**

With the Bonus Bill out of the way for all time, Congress faces one of the busiest weeks since it convened less than one month ago. The most important bill to follow the bonus will be proposed "stop-gap" legislation to take the place of the invalidated AAA act, and this probably will be followed by the permanent Neutrality Bill.

Another controversial matter that will come up during the week is the request of the Munitions Investigating Committee for additional funds to complete its investigation. Since Senator Nye and Senator Clark put into the record of the committee charges that President Wilson and Secretary Lansing had "falsified" about secret European treaties prior to our entrance into the World War, considerable criticism has developed. Both Senator Glass and Senator Byrnes publicly stated they did not favor additional appropriations to continue the so-called muckraking.

**Nye Will Ask for Funds.**

Senators Nye and Clark will go tomorrow before the Auditing and Control Committee, of which Senator Byrnes is chairman, to ask for about $7,500 which they deem necessary to complete the investigation.

Although many of its supporters have expressed the belief it will eventually be held unconstitutional, Senate and House Agriculture Committees plan to report favorably the AAA relief amendments before the middle of the week. Secretary Wallace and Chester C. Davis, AAA administrator, will appear before the Senate committee tomorrow, after which committee approval is expected.

The House last week authorized

Continued on Page Four.

# 1,500 on Snow Train All Night Getting Home; Stranded Skiers Riot at Bear Mountain

About 1,500 Winter sports enthusiasts spent more than twelve hours last night and early this morning trying to get back to New York after a freight train wreck between Haverstraw and West Haverstraw, N. Y., had marooned them up-State, leaving 350 of them on the unsheltered platform of the Bear Mountain station for almost four hours.

The group stranded at Bear Mountain, braving a temperature of 8 degrees above zero while icy blasts from the frozen Hudson River, a stone's throw away, whipped snow flurries about them, staged a near riot. Howling and shrieking, they tore up planks from the platform and twenty-foot beams from the park docks near by, heaping up the fuel into a giant bonfire.

In a short time flames leaped thirty feet high near the tracks, and over the crackling of the beams could be heard the war whoops of the snowbound mob. The light of the fire illuminated an area reaching up to the Bear Mountain Inn, a half mile up the mountain. Fearing the flames would start a forest fire, Sergeant John Drew and a police squad checked them and had coffee brought from the inn to the half-frozen ski jumpers and their followers.

A thirty-five-coach relief train was made up at West Haverstraw from the 5:30 P. M. snow train from Phoenicia and other sections. With some 1,000 ski enthusiasts aboard, sleeping as best they could in the crowded day coaches, the train reached Bear Mountain at 12:26 A. M. and pulled out at 1:11 A. M. One locomotive pushed it at a crawling pace. Ten minutes later a coupling knuckle broke, causing another hour's delay.

At first the New York Central Railroad planned to bring the Winter sports enthusiasts back by way of Beacon on the east shore. Finding it would take about three hours to get the group across from Newburgh by the one-way ferry running through a narrow lane in the ice-covered river, the road decided to try to bring the train down the west shore to Weehawken.

A relief train was held at Beacon with accommodations for 1,500. This could reach New York at the earliest at 7:30 P. M. It was hoped the Weehawken route would be opened so that the marooned skiers could be returned at an earlier hour.

# INDUSTRIAL OUTPUT AT FIVE-YEAR PEAK IN DECEMBER RISE

### Durable Goods Upturn Sent Reserve Board's Adjusted Index Up to 103.

### GAINED 5 POINTS IN MONTH

### Employment Rise Continued in Steel, Automobiles, Rail Cars and in Shoe Plants.

Special to THE NEW YORK TIMES.

WASHINGTON, Jan. 26.—With increases in the output of durable manufactures largely responsible, industrial production as indicated by the Federal Reserve Board's adjusted index advanced in December to the highest point since the Spring of 1930.

Among the durable goods, iron and steel and automobiles played the most important part in the upturn.

The index stood at 103, as compared with 98 in November.

Factory employment held its own between mid-November and mid-December, the board reported, whereas a small decline usually appears. In some important lines, however, there were increases.

The report, touching on general business and financial conditions, and based on statistics for December and the first three weeks of January, read as follows:

"Industrial production and employment showed a further increase in December, when allowance is made for the usual seasonal changes, and distribution of commodities was in increased volume.

**Production and Employment.**

"The board's seasonally adjusted index of industrial production, which takes account of the considerable decline that usually occurs in December, advanced from 98 per cent of the 1923-25 average in November to 103 per cent in December, the highest level reached by this index since the Spring of 1930. As in other months during the last half of 1935, the rise in the index was due in part to increases in output of durable manufactures, particularly iron and steel and automobiles.

"During the first half of January production of steel and automobiles increased somewhat, following declines in the holiday period. Output at mines also was larger in December than in November. Activity at cotton and silk textile mills declined less than is usual in December, while at woolen mills there was a more than seasonal decrease in operation. Output at shoe factories increased.

"Factory employment showed little change between the middle of November and the middle of December, when a slight decline is customary. The number employed continued to increase at steel mills, automobile factories, foundries and machine shops and at railroad car-building plants. There also was an increase in employment at shoe factories. Seasonal declines were reported by many other important industries. Factory payrolls were larger in the middle of December than a month earlier.

"The value of construction contracts awarded increased sharply in December, according to figures of the F. W. Dodge Corporation, although a decline is usual in that month. There was a furthe. substantial growth in the volume of awards for publicly financed proj-

Continued on Page Four.

# Bandsmen 'Too Cold' to Play at Park Lake; Moses Aide Ousts Them From WPA Jobs

Forty members of the Park Department Band, a WPA unit, appeared at the Fifty-ninth Street Lake in Central Park yesterday afternoon and complained about the cold. Playing their instruments in such a low temperature, they said, would place them in great danger of being frostbitten, and so they would be unable to fill their assignment to provide music for the department's annual Winter Carnival.

W. Earle Andrews, general superintendent of the Department of Parks, who was present to watch the carnival, glanced at a thermometer and the melting surface of the ice and suggested that the musicians carry on their program. They told Mr. Andrews that they had warned WPA and Park Department officials in advance that a low temperature would prevent their playing because they feared "frostbite and its consequent injuries."

Mr. Andrews pointed out that it had been planned to house them in the boathouse, where it would be warm enough for them to play without even catching a cold. The musicians persisted in their refusal to play. Mr. Andrews thereupon dismissed the band on the spot and informed the musicians that they would not be reinstated in their jobs.

Music was provided for the ice skating events of the carnival by playing phonograph records over the public address system.

On Friday the musicians' union sent a request to officials asking that the musical program for the carnival be eliminated because of the forecast of cold weather. Jacob Rosenberg, secretary of Local 802, said that the musicians should be treated just as though they were privately employed. The Park Department made plans to keep the men warm, however, and ordered them to appear.

It was said yesterday that Mr. Andrews had the authority for his action and that the dismissal would be effective because the Park Department would refuse to approve the musicians' time sheets.

The carnival, which was conducted under the direction of James V. Mulholland, supervisor of recreation, included the all-city finals in ice-skating races for the borough champions of various ages.



# SMITH EXPECTED TO LEAD OPEN FIGHT ON ROOSEVELT; WOULD GO TO CONVENTION

## Farley 'Didn't Hear' Smith, Nor Has He 'Read' Speech

Special to THE NEW YORK TIMES.

CORAL GABLES, Fla., Jan. 26.—Postmaster General Farley, chairman of the National Democratic Committee, tonight declined to comment on the speech of Alfred E. Smith at the Liberty League dinner last night in Washington.

"I didn't hear it, I haven't read it, and have no statement to make," Mr. Farley said smilingly this evening as he rested with his two daughters at the Miami Biltmore Hotel. He indicated that he would make no direct reply later to the attack of Mr. Smith on the New Deal and the Roosevelt administration.

Mr. Farley, who had just returned from a water-sports show, said that he was enjoying a complete rest from his duties, allowing nothing more serious than an effort to lower his golf score to occupy his vacation time.

# CAPITAL IS DIVIDED ON SMITH THREAT

### Some Leaders Minimize His Aim to Rebel, Others Scoff at Effect.

### 'WALL STREET' IS HEARD

### Richberg Says Socialism 'Cry' Is 'Patented by Interests'—Robinson to Go on Radio.

By TURNER CATLEDGE.

Special to THE NEW YORK TIMES.

WASHINGTON, Jan. 26.—The open threat of former Governor Alfred E. Smith to bolt the leadership of President Roosevelt in the coming campaign, made last night at the first annual dinner of the American Liberty League, resounded with baffling effect today throughout the quarters of those who feel they must carry the New Deal torch in that contest.

Such Democratic leaders as expressed themselves pretended to disbelieve that Mr. Smith intended to sound a call for party revolt when he said that he and those who felt like him would probably "take a walk" if the coming convention in Philadelphia endorsed the measures of President Roosevelt.

Mr. Smith's utterance took them completely by surprise. They had expected him to inveigh against the New Deal and to go even further than he did and criticize the President personally. They had not expected, however, that he would suggest a course of action designed deliberately to defeat the administration next November.

But to those who gave full credit to the plain language of that part of his address—and this was most convincing as the words were reread—the "Happy Warrior" appeared a much greater menace to the administration's political secur-

Continued on Page Two.

## WIDE EFFECT IS PREDICTED

### Republicans See Their Chances in the Fall Much Enhanced.

### TAMMANY MAY BE SPLIT

### Farley War on Dooling Might Involve Fate of This and Other States' Electors.

### SMITH GETS MANY CALLS

### But He Is Silent on Reaction to Speech in the Capital—Press Mostly Favorable.

By JAMES A. HAGERTY.

Former Governor Alfred E. Smith's Liberty League speech in Washington Saturday night was interpreted here yesterday as meaning that he is ready to lead a bolt from the Democratic National Convention at Philadelphia in June if, as seems inevitable, President Roosevelt is renominated and his administration is approved in the party platform.

Mr. Smith, it was learned from friends, expects to be a delegate to the convention, presumably as a Congressional District delegate from Manhattan, and his threat to "take a walk" was regarded as meaning a walk out of the convention.

His speech with its attack on the New Deal policies of President Roosevelt is expected to have important consequences in the coming Presidential campaign, which, in the opinion of Republican leaders at least, will increase greatly the chance of the election of a Republican President.

Mr. Smith's announcement of his opposition to the re-election of President Roosevelt—and his speech was interpreted here as meaning that it would be an active opposition—was declared by Republicans and anti-New Deal Democrats to mark the beginning of a definite movement to start a revolt among Democrats to oust the present administration.

His speech has intensified interest in the meeting to be held Wednesday at Macon, Ga., at which Governor Talmadge, another Democratic foe of the New Deal, will seek to unify the anti-Roosevelt forces in the South.

**The Effect on Tammany.**

Mr. Smith's scathing denunciation of the President's policies as smacking of Moscow may lead locally to a decision of the Roosevelt group, headed by Postmaster General Farley, to go ahead with a movement to try to displace James J. Dooling as leader of Tammany.

Disruption of the local Democratic organization by a fight on the New Deal issue, opponents of the President declared, might conceivably cause Mr. Roosevelt to lose the forty-seven electoral votes of New York, and the break might spread to cause him to lose other important States.

Democratic supporters of President Roosevelt took the view that Mr. Smith's speech would not have so great an adverse effect on the President's political fortunes as expected by its sponsors.

They admitted that it would give some impetus to the drift of conservative Democrats from the President, but asserted that the rank and file of the party throughout the country would remain loyal.

Local friends of the President asserted that the influence of Mr. Smith, even in New York City, was not so great as it had been, and that the election returns would bear out this assertion.

**Socialistic Portion Stressed.**

The important part of Mr. Smith's speech, as seen by political leaders here, was that portion in which he declared that it was all right with him for the New Dealers to disguise themselves as Karl Marx or Lenin, but that he would not stand for them marching under the banner of Jefferson, Jackson or Cleveland.

"Now what is worrying us is this," Mr. Smith said. "Where does that leave us millions of Democrats? My mind is fixed upon the convention in June in Philadelphia. The committee on resolutions is about to report. The preamble to the platform is:

"'We, the representatives of the

Continued on Page Three.

"All the News That's Fit to Print."

# The New York Times.

LATE CITY EDITION

Generally fair and slightly cooler today. Tomorrow fair and warmer.

Temperature Yesterday—Max., 77; Min., 62

Copyright, 1936, by The New York Times Company.

VOL. LXXXV.....No. 28,629. Entered as Second-Class Matter, Postoffice, New York, N. Y. NEW YORK, FRIDAY, JUNE 12, 1936. PP TWO CENTS In New York City. | THREE CENTS Within 200 Miles. | FOUR CENTS Elsewhere Except in 7th and 8th Postal Zones.

# REPUBLICANS NAME LANDON UNANIMOUSLY; HE ACCEPTS PLATFORM, ADDING OWN IDEAS

## SOVIET TO SET UP NEW PARLIAMENT WITH TWO HOUSES

### One Chamber to Be Composed of Deputies Elected by Secret Vote of the People.

### 'SENATE' WILL BE PICKED

### It Will Contain Delegates of the Republics—Freedom of Speech Due for All.

### PRESS ALSO IS AFFECTED

### Liberty of Worship and Equal Rights for Women Among Features of Charter.

By WALTER DURANTY

Wireless to THE NEW YORK TIMES.

MOSCOW, June 11.—The proposed new Soviet Constitution, which will be published tomorrow, is strikingly different from the earlier Constitution, which became law July 6, 1923.

The first difference is that in the initial section there is no reference as before to the severance of the world into the camps of socialism and capitalism—no mention of imperialist hostility or of a union of international workers or that "the bourgeoisie of the world have been unable to organize the collaboration of peoples."

**Allows Private Farming**

Instead, the new first section stresses the success of socialism in the Union of Soviet Socialist Republics, declares the means of production, commerce, finance, the railroads, &c., now belong to the State and outlines the position of collective farms, with the note that their property belongs to them "eternally," but the Constitution allows private farming and private sale of produce on the condition that it be direct and not involve any profit from or exploitation of a third party.

That, in short, is the basic principle of the Soviet State today as expressed by the new Constitution—that no individual or group can profit by the labor of others and that everything that matters is the property of the community, worked for the community's benefit.

The first section concludes with these significant sentences: "The economic life of the U. S. S. R. is directed by the State's economic plan toward increasing the general wealth.

"In the U. S. S. R. there is established the principle of socialism. 'From each according to his capacity, to each according to his work.'"

Here you get the basic principle of Stalinism, or Soviet socialism, at its present stage as compared with the ultimate goal of Marxian communism, the motto of which is, "From each according to his capacity, to each according to his needs." In other words, the Socialist principle of greater rewards for greater service still prevails over the ultimate ideal of Communist equality.

The second change is that instead of seven federated republics in the U. S. S. R. there will henceforth be eleven, the Caucasian Federation being split into three—Georgia, Azerbaijan and Armenia—and Kirghizia and Kazakstan are added. This is only a formal difference for administrative purposes, and the federated republics, as before, retain the right to secede from the union at will.

**New Parliament Provided**

The third change, however, is more important, affecting the whole electoral system. Instead of provincial Soviets being elected by lists on open ballot and then their choosing delegates to the All-Union Soviet Congress, there are now to be secret ballots for individual Deputies on the basis of one Deputy to each 300,000 members of the population.

These Deputies will be elected to what will be equivalent to the House of Representatives in the United States. And instead of these Deputies sitting jointly with the Congress of Nationalities, there will henceforth be two houses with equal powers of action and initiative, in which the House of Nationalities will be chosen by provincial councils in the ratio of ten Deputies from each federated republic, five from each autonomous

Continued on Page Five

## Hoover Calls Platform 'Fighting, Progressive'

Former President Herbert Hoover last night called the Republican platform and Governor Landon's specific statements upon it, as read at the Cleveland convention, "fighting and progressive."

Through his secretary Mr. Hoover made public this statement:

"The platform admirably covers the principles and methods I have so repeatedly advocated. The platform is the fighting, definite and progressive statement the country needs.

"When put into force by the American people, these principles will regenerate the country. Governor Landon's statement amply covers any other points that may be in question."

## BORAH IS 'STUNNED' BY LANDON'S PLEA

### Nominee Should Have Acted 'Sooner,' He Says When Told of Gold, Wage Demands.

### SILENT AS TO HIS SUPPORT

### Senator Leaves for Washington After Winning Victory on His Platform Goals.

By The Associated Press.

CLEVELAND, June 11.—The Plain-Dealer says Senator Borah appeared "stunned" when informed at Akron tonight that Governor Landon had declared for a gold-backed currency and a constitutional amendment, if necessary, to permit State regulation of wages and hours.

Informed of the nominee's telegram to the Republican convention, Mr. Borah said:

"Well, that's his business. Why didn't he send it sooner?"

The Plain-Dealer says Mr. Borah ran his hands over his face four or five times. Asked if he had any more comment, he said:

"I shall wait until morning and see what they do."

Mr. Borah was on a train en route to Washington, having left Cleveland just a few minutes before the delegates adopted the platform. He had fought to have any mention of the gold standard eliminated from the platform.

**Platform Pleases Him**

Special to THE NEW YORK TIMES.

CLEVELAND, June 11.—Senator Borah expressed himself this afternoon as well pleased with the platform sent to the national convention by the committee on resolutions.

But the question whether he would support the man whom the convention was to select as party standard bearer remained unanswered when the Idaho Republican left for Washington.

After the final draft of the platform had been completed and become available for examination, it was reported that Senator Borah had examined it and was satisfield with the language of the planks in

Continued on Page Fourteen

## 'VICTORY' LANDON PLEDGE

### He Promises to Wage One of Party's Most Forceful Campaigns.

### THANKS HIS TOWNSMEN

### With Wife at His Side on the Front Porch He Hails Their Loyalty.

### TOPEKA HAILS THE CHOICE

### Citizens Decorate City and Parade to Governor's Home When Nomination Is Flashed.

By WARREN MOSCOW

Special to THE NEW YORK TIMES.

TOPEKA, Kan., June 11.—With thousands of his neighbors and other citizens of Topeka gathered around the yellow brick Executive Mansion at Eighth and Buchanan Streets, Governor Alfred M. Landon delivered to them tonight a simple message of his appreciation of their loyalty and affection as they gathered to celebrate his nomination as the Republican candidate for President.

Earlier, in a statement issued to the press, he had pledged himself to lead a harmonious party to victory next November.

It was exactly 11:14 o'clock, Central standard time, when the Governor and Mrs. Landon stepped out to meet a deafening roar of applause from the crowd.

The air rang with cheers, torches and flares blazed and band after band blared "Oh, Susanna" as the Governor and Mrs. Landon left the study in which they had spent most of the evening to appear on the front porch.

**Thanks His Townsmen**

The Landons' neighbors and all Topeka had been preparing to celebrate his actual nomination and had been awaiting only a radio flash from the convention hall in Cleveland apprising them of the fact. The city was decorated with flags and bunting, and paraders formed in line, with all the city's bands and bugle and fife and drum corps ready to blow their heartiest. Finally word of the nomination came and the paraders marched to the Executive Mansion.

Governor Landon, when he stepped forward into the glare of the floodlights arranged around the house, was at ease, though toward the end of his talk he was plainly affected. He wore a gray business suit, with a white shirt and attached soft collar.

Mrs. Samuel E. Cobb, Mrs. Landon's mother, and Joe Cross, a cousin of Mrs. Landon, were with the Governor and his wife. They took seats on the porch swing, while the Governor and Mrs. Landon faced the cheers of the more than 15,000 paraders.

Governor Landon in his greeting said:

Mrs. Landon and I are deeply touched by this expression of your good will and good wishes. We are proud, too, that so many of our friends from surrounding towns

Continued on Page Thirteen

## Roll-Call of the States On Landon's Nomination

Special to THE NEW YORK TIMES.

*CLEVELAND, June 11.—Following is the vote by States for Governor Landon when roll was called on the nomination for President:*

| State or Territory. | No. of Deleg. | State or Territory | No. of Deleg. |
|---|---|---|---|
| Alabama | 13 | New Jersey | 32 |
| Arizona | 9 | New Mexico | 6 |
| Arkansas | 11 | New York | 90 |
| California | 44 | North Carolina | 23 |
| Colorado | 12 | North Dakota | 8 |
| Connecticut | 19 | Ohio | 52 |
| Delaware | 9 | Oklahoma | 21 |
| Florida | 12 | Oregon | 10 |
| Georgia | 14 | Pennsylvania | 75 |
| Idaho | 8 | Rhode Island | 8 |
| Illinois | 57 | South Carolina | 10 |
| Indiana | 28 | South Dakota | 8 |
| Iowa | 22 | Tennessee | 17 |
| Kansas | 18 | Texas | 25 |
| Kentucky | 22 | Utah | 8 |
| Louisiana | 12 | Vermont | 9 |
| Maine | 13 | Virginia | 17 |
| Maryland | 16 | Washington | 16 |
| Massachusetts | 33 | West Virginia | 15 |
| Michigan | 38 | Wisconsin | 6 |
| Minnesota | 22 | Wyoming | 6 |
| Mississippi | 11 | Alaska | 3 |
| Missouri | 30 | Dist. of Columbia | 3 |
| Montana | 8 | Hawaii | 3 |
| Nebraska | 14 | Philippine Islands | 3 |
| Nevada | 6 | Puerto Rico | 2 |
| New Hampshire | 11 | Total | 984 |

West Virginia gave one vote for Borah. Wisconsin gave 18 votes to Borah.

## VANDENBERG LOOMS AS RUNNING MATE

### Senator Agrees to Reconsider Refusal and Landon Men Believe He Will Aeccept.

### STEIWER SECOND CHOICE

### Kansans May Pick Him if Other Plan Fails—Borah Backs Gannett—Knox Boomed.

By CHARLES R. MICHAEL

Special to THE NEW YORK TIMES.

CLEVELAND, June 11.—The Landon forces have not yet abandoned the hope of persuading Senator Vandenberg to accept the nomination for Vice President, despite reiteration of his announcement of last week that his decision to remain in the Senate was "final."

Although he continued his refusal earlier in the day, the Michigan Senator agreed this evening to confer again with the Landon forces after adjournment tonight. At this time he was expected to determine whether he would bow to the request of Governor Landon.

Confidence was expressed at the Kansan's headquarters that Mr. Vandenberg would be nominated tomorrow.

There is a strong movement in favor of Colonel Knox. His selection, however, is opposed by Colonel Robert R. McCormick, publisher of The Chicago Tribune.

Frank E. Gannett of Rochester, N. Y., a Borah supporter, came into the situation as a compromise candidate. Members of the New York delegation were told that Senator Borah desired his nomination and "would vigorously support

Continued on Page Twelve

## THE PLATFORM IS VOTED

### Containing 14 Planks, It Is Declared Largely a Liberal Victory.

### WORLD COURT IS BARRED

### States' Rights Are Stressed—Social Security Would Be on Pay-as-You-Go Basis.

### BANS 'SCARCITY' POLICY

### Farm Statement Sets Broad Aims on Crops and Credit Help—Trading Act Repeal Urged.

By FELIX BELAIR Jr.

Special to THE NEW YORK TIMES.

CLEVELAND, June 11.—After laboring for three days and nights to draft a declaration of political principles that would come near to satisfying the expected Presidential candidate and placate potential party bolters, the resolutions committee of the Republican National Convention brought forth tonight a platform on which it hopes the party can carry the national elections in November.

It was a composite of compromises in which the demands of Governor Landon, the assured nominee, were subordinated in several important instances to those of the more conservative Eastern delegations on matters of social and economic progress.

Throughout its preamble and fourteen planks the document condemned abuses it connected with the present administration.

While it urged continuance of several reforms inaugurated by the Roosevelt administration, such as regulation of security markets for the protection of investors, social security and unemployment relief—with the latter two administered by the States—these were far outnumbered by the departures from present national policy that it proposed.

**Main Points of Platform**

The outstanding declarations of the platform were:

1. Constitutional and local self-government must be preserved as well as the authority of the Supreme Court as final protector of citizens' rights, and maintenance of our system of free enterprise, private competition and equality of opportunity.
2. Absorption of the unemployment by private industry and agriculture holds the only answer to that problem, and to that end restriction of production should be abolished, and all policies that raise production costs and cost of living discontinued. Legitimate business should be encouraged and the government withdrawn from competition with industry.
3. Responsibility for relief of the needy must be returned to the States, which should receive Federal grants in proportion as the States contribute. This should be combined with a system of public works, such projects to be undertaken only on their merits.
4. The States should enact Old-Age Pension Laws for persons over 65 and the government make contributions to support such systems according as States contribute, but all such programs should be financed on a pay-as-you-go policy, by widely distributed taxation.
5. Labor's right to organize and bargain collectively through representatives of its own choosing without interference must be protected. State laws and interstate compacts should be undertaken to abolish sweatshops and child labor.
6. Scarcity economics should be abolished in agriculture; a national land use program should be pursued for the protection and restoration of land resources; experimental aid to farmers should be developed for production of new crops and promotions of new industrial uses of non-food crops; farmers protected from foreign importations. Farm credits at rates comparable with those in industry should be fostered together with decentralized nonpartisan control of the farm credit administration. A form of subsidy should be instituted to take care of exportable surpluses with benefits based on the domes-

Continued on Page Fourteen

© New York Times Studio Photo.

NOMINATED FOR PRESIDENT
Alfred Mossman Landon

## The Text of the Platform

Special to THE NEW YORK TIMES.

*CLEVELAND, June 11.—Following is the text of the party platform as adopted by the Republican National Convention tonight:*

America is in peril. The welfare of American men and women and the future of our youth are at stake. We dedicate ourselves to the preservation of their political liberty, their individual opportunity and their character as free citizens, which today for the first time are threatened by government itself.

For three long years the New Deal administration has dishonored American traditions and flagrantly betrayed the pledges upon which the Democratic party sought and received public support.

The powers of Congress have been usurped by the President.

The integrity and authority of the Supreme Court have been flaunted.

The rights and liberties of American citizens have been violated.

Regulated monopoly has displaced free enterprise.

The New Deal administration constantly seeks to usurp the rights reserved to the State and to the people.

It has insisted on passage of laws contrary to the Constitution.

It has intimidated witnesses and interfered with the right of petition.

It has dishonored our country by repudiating its most sacred obligations.

It has been guilty of frightful waste and extravagance, using public funds for partisan political purposes.

It has promoted investigations to harass and intimidate American citizens, at the same time denying investigations into its own improper expenditures.

It has created a vast multitude of new offices, filled them with its favorites, set up a centralized bureaucracy and sent out swarms of inspectors to harass our people.

It has bred fear and hesitation in commerce and industry, thus discouraging new enterprises, preventing employment and prolonging the depression.

It secretly has made tariff agreements with our foreign competitors, flooding our markets with foreign commodities.

It has coerced and intimidated voters by withholding relief to those opposing its tyrannical policies.

It has destroyed the morale of many of our people and made them dependent upon government.

Appeals to passion and class prejudice have replaced reason and tolerance.

To a free people, these actions are insufferable. This campaign cannot be waged on the traditional differences between the Republican and Democratic parties.

The responsibility of this election transcends all previous political divisions. We invite all Americans, irrespective of party, to join us in defense of American institutions.

### CONSTITUTIONAL GOVERNMENT AND FREE ENTERPRISE

We pledge ourselves:

1. To maintain the American system of constitutional and local self-government, and to resist all attempts to impair the authority of the Supreme Court of the United States, the final protector of rights of our citizens against the arbitrary encroachments of the legislative and executive branches of government. There can be no individual liberty without an independent judiciary.
2. To preserve the American system of free enterprise, pri-

Continued on Page Fourteen

## LANDON SENDS TELEGRAM

### To Back Constitutional Amendment if States' Wage Laws Fail.

### FOR GOLD AT PROPER TIME

### In His Message to Convention He Specifies Exceptions in Accepting the Platform.

### BORAH WINS HIS PLANKS

### Vandenberg Is Expected to Be Vice Presidential Choice at Final Session Today.

By ARTHUR KROCK

Special to THE NEW YORK TIMES.

CLEVELAND, Ohio, June 11.—An unbossed Republican National Convention, yet working like a machine, at 11:41 o'clock tonight unanimously nominated Alfred M. Landon of Kansas for President, adopted unanimously a platform embracing certain social welfare ideas of the New Deal (which otherwise is excoriated) and seated party control in a group of young Kansas politicians and editors who entered the national political field less than two years ago.

At a final session tomorrow Arthur H. Vandenberg of Michigan is expected to accept the Vice Presidential nomination.

Eighteen Borah delegates from Wisconsin and the Senator's campaign manager (Delegate Carl G. Bachmann of West Virginia) voted for Mr. Borah on the first ballot, which prevented a nomination by acclamation under the rules. But Wisconsin then moved to make the nomination unanimous, and it was done.

**Hamilton Reads Message**

Two dramatic events colored the night session. Before John D. M. Hamilton, the chief of staff of the nominee, presented his name to the convention, he read at Mr. Landon's request a telegram from the Governor "interpreting" three planks of the platform and stating reservations. These planks, relating to currency, civil service and State control of wages and hours, had been revised by the resolutions committee from the text submitted by the Governor as a part of the week-long effort to placate Senator Borah and win his support in the campaign.

Governor Landon "interpreted" a "sound currency" to mean a currency eventually convertible into gold, insisted that the civil service should extend as far as the government's under-secretariat and pledged himself to support a constitutional amendment to permit the States to regulate wages and hours if the statutory method were not effective. He said "in good conscience" he must make these intentions known in advance.

The other element of drama was when all the other Presidential candidates but Senator Borah, who had already left for Washington, took the platform and seconded the nomination of Mr. Landon. Mr. Borah is only fairly well-pleased with the platform, and he expects to survey Mr. Landon's speeches and the personnel of his campaign cabinet for a couple of months before deciding whether to support the candidacy. Herbert Hoover, the other eminent Republican whose opposition was feared by the Landon group, phoned here today that he was satisfied with the platform.

Senator Vandenberg was among those seconding the nomination. Colonel Knox, L. J. Dickinson, Robert A. Taft and Harry Nice, the other aspirants, followed.

**Harmony the Landon Goal**

Harmony among all Republicans and the support of anti-New Deal Democrats have all along been stated as the twin goals of the Landon managers, and, except for Mr. Borah, the harmony seems to have been effected.

The end of the session, amid a series of ecstatic demonstrations for Mr. Landon and Mr. Vandenberg, came after a day of anxious concern to the Kansas syndicate which, at midnight last night believed that all its worries were over. Mr. Landon's differences with the resolutions subcommittee, and with Mr. Borah, and the latter's objections to revision of planks he had been asked to submit, caused the snarl.

But by 7 o'clock tonight, except

Continued on Page Twelve

## Gov. Landon's Statement on Platform

Special to THE NEW YORK TIMES.

*CLEVELAND, June 11.—Governor Landon, while approving most sections of the platform, sent the following message which was read to the convention before he was placed in nomination by John M. Hamilton:*

To the delegates of the Republican National Convention:

My name is to be presented for your consideration as a candidate for the nomination for President of the United States. The platform recommended by your committee on resolutions and adopted by the convention has been communicated to me.

I note that according to the terms of the platform, the nomination tendered by this convention carries with it, as a matter of private honor and public good faith, an undertaking by each candidate to be true to the principles and program herein set forth.

If nominated, I unqualifiedly accept the word and spirit of that undertaking.

However, with that candor which you and the country are entitled to expect of me, I feel compelled before you proceed with the consideration of my name to submit my interpretation of certain planks in the platform so that you may be advised as to my views. I could not in conscience do otherwise.

Under the title of Labor the platform commits the Republican party as follows:

"Support the adoption of State laws and interstate compacts to abolish sweatshops and child labor, and to protect women and children with respect to maximum hours, minimum wages, and working conditions. We believe that this can be done within the Constitution as it now stands."

I hope the opinion of the convention is correct that the aims which you have in mind may be attained within the Constitution as it now stands. But, if that opinion should prove to be erroneous, I want you to know that, if nominated and elected, I shall favor a constitutional amendment permitting States to adopt such legislation as may be necessary adequately to protect women and children in the matter of maximum hours, minimum wages and working conditions. This obligation we cannot escape.

The convention advocates "a sound currency to be preserved at all hazards." I agree that "the first requisite to a sound and stable currency is a balanced budget."

The second requisite, as I view it, is a currency expressed in terms of gold and convertible into gold. I recognize, however, that the second requisite must not be made until and unless it can be done without penalizing our democratic economy and without injury to our producers of agricultural products and other raw materials.

The convention pledges the party to the merit system and to its restoration, improvement and extension.

In carrying out this pledge I believe that there should be included within the merit system every position in the administrative service below the rank of assistant secretaries of major departments and agencies, and that this inclusion should cover the entire Postoffice Department.

ALF M. LANDON.

"All the News That's Fit to Print."

# The New York Times.

LATE CITY EDITION
Partly cloudy, possibly showers today, temperature unchanged. Tomorrow generally fair.
Temperatures Yesterday—Max., 77; Min., 61

Copyright, 1936, by The New York Times Company.

VOL. LXXXV....No. 28,630. Entered as Second-Class Matter. Postoffice, New York, N. Y. NEW YORK, SATURDAY, JUNE 13, 1936. PP TWO CENTS In New York City. | THREE CENTS Within 200 Miles. | FOUR CENTS Elsewhere Except in 7th and 8th Postal Zones.

# KNOX NOMINATED FOR VICE PRESIDENT, HAMILTON CHAIRMAN, CONVENTION ENDS; LANDON PREPARES VIGOROUS CAMPAIGN

## ROOSEVELT ASSAILS MONOPOLY AS FOE OF REAL FREEDOM

### 'Yeomanry' of Trade and Farm Must Be Saved From It, He Says in Dallas Speech.

### WARNS OF LABOR'S PERIL

### If It Is to Be a Commodity, We Shall Become a Nation of Boarding Houses, He Says.

### DEMANDS FEDERAL CURBS

### States Cannot Right Abuses, He Holds—Thousands at the Exposition Greet Him.

*Text of the President's speech at Dallas appears on Page 2.*

By CHARLES W. HURD

Special to THE NEW YORK TIMES.

DALLAS, June 12.—President Roosevelt struck out forcefully in a speech here today against monopolistic tendencies in business which he said must be eliminated to save from extinction "the yeomanry of business and industry and agriculture."

"Today we have restored democracy in government," he told a crowd of 50,000 persons who were crowded into the stadium and a nation-wide radio audience. "We are in the process of restoring democracy in opportunity."

In connection with this statement, Mr. Roosevelt said that "the net result of economic and financial control in the hands of the few has meant the ownership of labor as a commodity.

"If labor is to be a commodity in the United States," he went on, "in the final analysis it means that we shall become a nation of boarding houses instead of a nation of homes.

"If our people ever submit to that, they will have said good-bye to their historic freedom. Men do not fight for boarding houses. They will fight for their homes."

The President's speech was based, as befitted the scene of its delivery, on State laws regulating utilities, which made Texas a pioneer in this field.

**Constitutional Questions to Fore**

However, it went far beyond a mere recitation of achievement by Texas and hinted strongly at the renewal of efforts by the administration to find a method of re-enacting in permanent form social and economic reforms attempted heretofore by means of Federal legislation, but overturned by Supreme Court decisions.

This speech followed two days after one at Little Rock in which Mr. Roosevelt began a new campaign for a liberalizing interpretation of the Constitution to permit the Federal Government to assume jurisdiction in protecting public welfare whenever it appeared any problem was too great to be handled individually by the States.

To some observers, therefore, it appeared without benefit of further elucidation by the President that Mr. Roosevelt was beginning on this tour a definite political campaign to test popular sentiment at the elections in November on the constitutional question.

The audience which heard Mr. Roosevelt directly listened with evident interest and punctuated his remarks with frequent applause.

**Links Yeomanry and Democracy.**

The President opened his speech with a description of the new trend toward travel by the people of the country and expressed the hope that as many as possible might visit this exposition, the principal one commemorating Texas's liberation from Mexico.

He soon began his basic topic by recalling that Texas, "in a period of monopoly, combinations, overcapitalization, high rates and discrimination against the small shipper," had pioneered in the field of regulating utilities. He then went on to describe how this State set up anti-trust laws in "the old Texas spirit of freedom for the individual."

"In our national life," Mr. Roosevelt went on, "public and private, the very nature of free government demands that there must be a line of defense held by the yeomanry of business and industry and agriculture, not the generalissimos, but the small men, the average men in business and industry and agriculture, those men who have an ownership in their business and a responsibility which gives them stability.

"Any elemental policy, economic or political, which tends to eliminate these dependable defenders of democratic institutions, and to concentrate control in the hands of a few small, powerful groups, is directly opposed to the stability of

Continued on Page Two

## *British, Convinced Duce Is Serious, Look for a Way to End Sanctions*

### *Neville Chamberlain's Trial Balloon Indicates Public Is Weary of Futile Measures—Program of League Reform May Be the Sugar Coating for the Pill of Recantation.*

By AUGUR

Wireless to THE NEW YORK TIMES.

LONDON, June 12.—Sir Eric Drummond, the British Ambassador in Rome, has addressed an insistent warning to London that Premier Benito Mussolini's decision to leave the League of Nations unless economic sanctions are removed must be taken seriously.

Moreover, there is good reason to suspect that the Duce in this case, simultaneously with Italy's official resignation from Geneva, will mobilize several million men so as to be prepared for any emergency.

The Duce means business. In fact, he cannot help himself, because public opinion in Italy, wound up to a high pitch by successes in Africa, will not tolerate the continuance of punitive treatment.

However, the chance of Italy's deserting Geneva on this pretext is slender, because there is a strong current in London definitely set toward the removal of sanctions which have failed to prevent war, were unable to stop it and yet are utterly incapable of restoring the independence of Ethiopia. Chancellor of the Exchequer Neville Chamberlain's speech signifies that the Cabinet decision will be in favor of liquidation of the whole enterprise.

Through reports of its diplomatic representatives in European capitals, the British Government is informed that members of the League of Nations consider sanctions dead, but wait upon Great Britain to take the lead in their abolition, as she took the initiative in their being imposed.

President Eduard Benes has let it be known that Czechoslovakia remains a stanch backer of collective action, yet considers it is high time to bring Italy back to the fold by ending sanctions. Czechoslovakia refuses, however, to take the initiative, as she regards this as the duty of Britain and France.

Russia's attitude is even more definite. Foreign Commissar Maxim Litvinoff says the peril confronting Europe comes only from militarism in Germany. As Italy is willing to join a common front

Continued on Page Four

## GEOGHAN IS NAMED IN CORBETT STORY OF DRUKMAN PLOT

### Detective Believed That 'Willie,' Whom Byk Mentioned, Was Prosecutor, Not Kleinman.

### TOLD TO 'PULL OFF' CASE

### Witness Also Says Geoghan Saw an Intoxicated Aide Question Prisoners.

The name of District Attorney William F. X. Geoghan of Brooklyn was brought into the Drukman conspiracy trial by his own accused assistant yesterday in an attempt to establish the identity of the "white-hot Willie" said to have been mentioned by Leo P. Byk in an attempt to "fix" the murder case.

William W. Kleinman, the accused Assistant District Attorney and one of the five defendants on trial in Brooklyn, drew from Detective Charles S. Corbett an admission that, in the detective's opinion, the "Willie" in question was not "Willie" Kleinman, but his chief, "Willie" Geoghan.

To the evident surprise of the prosecution, but apparently to its complete satisfaction, Kleinman delved even deeper into matters which the State deliberately skirted. He obtained from the witness accusations that Mr. Geoghan stood by unprotestingly as another assistant drunkenly questioned prisoners in the Stagg Street police station on the night of the Samuel Drukman murder.

**More Damaging Accusations**

He got from the detective an accusation that Chief Assistant District Attorney Frederick L. Kopff had given the order to "pull off" from the Drukman investigation; that Assistant District Attorney Harry Sullivan had not exerted himself in presenting the Drukman case to the first grand jury, which afterward exonerated the murderers; that Assistant District Attorney Hyman Barshay, who also worked on the Drukman inquiry, was, in his opinion, "a rat."

This line of cross-examination was explained by Kleinman later as an attempt to show that Corbett, whose sanity is challenged by the defense, was hypercritical in his opinions of the persons with whom he worked on police matters.

Special Prosecutor Hiram C. Todd, who regards Corbett as one of the State's chief witnesses, indicated his opinion of the impression Corbett has made on the jury by declining to curtail the cross-examination even after Justice Erskine C. Rogers had shown a disposition to intervene.

The reference to Mr. Geoghan in connection with Byk involves an alleged relationship which figures not only in the conspiracy trial but also in the formal charges made by the Drukman grand jurors against the District Attorney in demanding his removal from office by Governor Lehman. The Governor is withholding action on that request until the completion of the conspiracy trial.

Byk is an alleged trafficker in slot machines, who has a criminal record. The special grand jury charged that Byk was an intimate friend of Mr. Geoghan and had free access to his office. He is named in the

Continued on Page Two

New York Times Studio Photo.

THE VICE PRESIDENTIAL NOMINEE

Colonel Frank Knox

## LANDON CALLS IN HIS AIDES

### Strategy, With Invasion of Enemy Country, to Be Mapped Monday.

### CONGRATULATIONS POUR IN

### Hoover, Dawes, Merriam, Mills and a Number of Democrats Pledge Their Support.

### KNOX WELCOMED AS ALLY

### They Will Renew Fight of 1912 for 'Larger Americanism,' the Governor Wires Him.

By WARREN MOSCOW

Special to THE NEW YORK TIMES.

TOPEKA, June 12.—Eager for "an immediate move on the enemy," Governor Landon laid plans today in his first busy hours as the Republican Presidential nominee for a meeting of his general staff on Monday to study campaign strategy.

Physically refreshed though he had had barely six hours' sleep, the Governor sent a message of confidence to the Republican convention in Cleveland; congratulated Colonel Frank Knox, the Vice Presidential nominee; arranged to meet Colonel Knox, John D. M. Hamilton, the new national Republican chairman, and other party chiefs here on Monday; received interviewers and read numerous congratulatory messages which poured into his office all day.

The messages included assurances of support from virtually every Republican national leader except Senator Borah and also from a number of Democrats, including former Governor William H. Murray of Oklahoma.

Former President Hoover, Charles G. Dawes, former Vice President; Representative Snell, Theodore Roosevelt and Governor Merriam of California were among the Republicans who telegraphed, Ogden L. Mills, former Secretary of the Treasury, telephoned congratulations.

**Messages to the Nominee**

Among the messages were the following:

Herbert Hoover—I send you my heartiest congratulations. You have a great task for the American people. I pray you will have divine help.

Charles G. Dawes—Your immediate demonstration of the qualities of high leadership was exactly that which was needed to make most effective the American party's fight to preserve American principles. As an old Mariettian and friend of your friends there, I send congratulations.

Colonel Frank Knox—The unanimous action of the Republican National Convention in choosing you as the standard bearer of our party has my thoroughgoing approval and I extend to you my heartiest congratulations. The tribute was a great one indeed to you personally and I am happy to be among those who will go forward under your leadership in November.

Frank F. Merriam—Congratulations and best wishes for your success in November. The people will ratify the work of the convention. Be assured of my hearty support.

Theodore Roosevelt—Congratulations on nomination and especially on superb telegram. You are a leader for whom I can fight wholeheartedly.

William H. Murray—Sincere congratulations. Now for liberty, law and Landon opposed to Russian Red revolution.

Representative Frank Crowther—Congratulations. Every Republican in New York State will support you. My Congressional district will give you 25,000 majority.

There were a number of messages also from Kansas Democrats, such as the following, signed by M. Trueheart of Sterling.

"Congratulations. I have been a lifelong Democrat, but I am for you."

Among the personal messages was this from Mrs. John D. M. Hamilton, mother of the new Republican National Chairman:

"I am proud my son had the honor of presenting the next President of the United States to the people."

Mr. Landon indicated that at the conference Monday there would be

Continued on Page Eight

## VOTE ON KNOX UNANIMOUS

### Vandenberg Rejects Bid of Landon Forces and Edge and Nice Quit.

### IT'S A BULL MOOSE TICKET

### Both Nominees Bolted in 1912, and Both Are From Midwest, Riding Into Party Control.

### HARMONY AIM TO THE FORE

### Attempt to Draft the Michigan Senator Dropped When Pennsylvania Swings Away.

By ARTHUR KROCK

Special to THE NEW YORK TIMES.

CLEVELAND, June 12.—Colonel Frank Knox of Chicago appealed to the delegates to the Republican National Convention as the strongest possible nominee for Vice President, after Senator Arthur H. Vandenberg of Michigan formally notified them today that he would not accept the second place on the ticket headed by Governor Alfred M. Landon of Kansas. Therefore, in the same free-will spirit which has characterized this remarkable gathering, the delegates unanimously nominated Colonel Knox and adjourned soon after 1 o'clock this afternoon.

The sentiment for Colonel Knox over ex-Senator Edge of New Jersey, Governor Nice of Maryland and others was made so plain by the seconding speeches for the Illinois publisher that the others, following last night's example, withdrew on the platform, and this time even Wisconsin went along on the first ballot.

When it was over the Republicans had chosen as candidates for President and Vice President of the United States two former Bull Moosers, who bolted the party in 1912; two veterans of the World War; two men from the Mississippi River basin, where party control is now lodged.

That control was sealed, in an organization sense, this afternoon by the unanimous election of John D. M. Hamilton, Governor Landon's pre-convention campaign manager, as chairman of the Republican National Committee to succeed Henry P. Fletcher of Pennsylvania.

**West in Saddle, Rides Lightly**

Although the West is in the saddle, it is riding lightly, as the process of the Vice Presidential nomination today once more revealed. Governor Landon and his young group of Kansas University classmates, Kansas politicians and Kaw Valley editors very much wanted Senator Vandenberg for second place. They carefully devised a plan to draft him today, feeling sure that he would be obliged to accept.

But Mr. Vandenberg would only consider a draft by acclamation, and did not desire even that. By the time this viewpoint was finally made known to the Landon leaders, Pennsylvania had grown tired of waiting for them to get in touch with the Senator and at 9:30 o'clock this morning pledged itself to Colonel Knox with whom Mr. Vandenberg is understood to have conferred early this morning.

Acclamation being then impossible, the Senator drafted a letter to the convention, once more taking himself out of consideration. The Kansans still insist they could have obtained acclamation if they had been able to reach the Senator by telephone last night. Yet this correspondent had a phone conversation with him as late as 1:30, an hour when the Landonites say they were informed his telephone was shut off.

Pursuing his week-long practice of attempting no dictation, Mr. Hamilton let nature take its course and Colonel Knox got every vote. With Mr. Vandenberg out of the way his only strong opposition came from his fellow-publisher, Colonel Robert R. McCormick of Chicago. The other Chicago newspaper factor in the convention—William Randolph Hearst—several months ago had publicly listed Colonel Knox among persons acceptable to him for national honors.

In addition to his personal unwillingness to run for Vice President, Mr. Vandenberg had another and very practical reason. Maine votes on its State ticket in Sep-

Continued on Page Seven

## PARIS HOTELS OPEN; VAST STRIKE WANES

### Government Plans to End Tips Because Workers Have Won Minimum Wage Scale.

### BLUM WARNS AGITATORS

### 40-Hour-Week Bill Is Passed by Chamber—Premier Asks Senate to Act Tuesday.

Wireless to THE NEW YORK TIMES.

PARIS, June 12.—Paris returned to its normal appearance and life today with the reopening of cafés, restaurants and hotels where strikes had occurred.

At the same time in the Chamber of Deputies Premier Léon Blum gave the country assurance that his government would assure order in the streets and that it would deal with fomenters of trouble who were seeking to take advantage of the strike situation. In a session which disregarded the lunch hour he pushed through the Chamber his Forty-Hour Week Bill with the whole weight of his majority behind him and, for the moment at least, set aside definitely proposals to devalue the franc.

Tips may be abolished in France as a result of the accord reached today between the employers and workers in Paris restaurants, hotels and cafés. Max Dormoy, Under-Secretary of the Premier's office, said the employes had been assured a minimum wage, so the government would submit to the Chamber a bill for the abolition of tipping in hotels and restaurants and another bill establishing government control over employment contracts.

**New Scale for Workers**

According to an agreement between the employers and the unions, the workers will receive a daily wage of 30, 35 or 40 francs. In addition, they will get two meals a day or an allowance of 6 francs per meal. For hotel employes a minimum wage of 700 francs monthly was fixed, with increases of 7 per cent to 15 per cent for all employes receiving less than 5,000 francs yearly.

"None is master of the future," Mr. Blum said today, but he and his Finance Minister, Vincent Auriol, are convinced that an appeal to the country, coupled perhaps by some threats, will be sufficient to release enough of the 45,000,000,000 francs which the French people have hidden away to set industry going again and that out of the renewed business activity the State and the employers of labor will get a sufficient share to meet all the burdens that are being placed on them.

Mr. Blum this evening made his first appearance as Premier before the Senate, where it has been predicted he will eventually meet his severest opposition. He spoke only briefly, asking the Senators to meet Tuesday to pass the five reform bills he has put through the Chamber.

He reassured the Senate concerning the strike situation and declared the government was fully resolved to maintain public order.

"It is not a government of anarchy, it is a government of order and will act firmly with any suspicious elements seeking to insinuate themselves among the strikers," he said.

Regarding his bill revising the deflation decrees in favor of State employes and veterans and fixing

Continued on Page Four

## 15 INJURED AS LIFT PLUNGES 8 FLOORS

### Elevator in 42d St. Building Shattered After Rebounding on Springs at Bottom.

### VICTIMS THROWN IN HEAP

### Nine Women Students in Car —Operator Says Emergency Brake Failed to Work.

A passenger elevator in the Wurlitzer Building, 120 West Forty-second Street, crashed eight stories to the basement last night, shattering itself on the springed base and causing injuries to the fifteen passengers, of whom nine were women. Four victims were taken to hospitals.

Ambulances and police emergency crews were rushed to the scene at 8:30 P. M. In the meantime building employes and others aided in extricating those trapped in the car. Two of the persons were taken to the Ruptured and Crippled Hospital and two to Polyclinic Hospital.

All the passengers were students of the Delehanty Institute for Civil Service taking a course in the secretarial work. The school is on the fourteenth floor.

**Unable to Check Speed**

All had boarded the car at the fourteenth floor after their classes were dismissed. The car, operated by Michael Flannagan of 369 West Forty-eighth Street, started its downward trip normally, but when it reached the twelfth floor it picked up abnormal speed. Flannagan tried to check the speed with the control lever, but this proved ineffective.

As the car reached the eighth floor, he applied the emergency

Continued on Page Three

## *Jesse Jones Saved From Fiery Air Death, Then Helps Rescue Daring Texas Pilots*

By The Associated Press.

DALLAS, June 12.—Jesse Jones, chairman of the Reconstruction Finance Corporation, and three other passengers here were saved from death today by two daring pilots who raced a flaming monoplane to earth while fire raged in their compartment.

Ed Hefley of Houston, the pilot, was seriously burned about the face and arms. Co-Pilot Eugene Schacher, also of Houston, was less seriously injured. Mr. Jones helped pull them to safety.

The RFC head gave them full credit for saving his life and the lives of his fellow passengers, former Governor and Mrs. W. P. Hobby and Joe Toomey, Mr. Jones's secretary, all of Houston. All these escaped injury excepting Mr. Hobby, who was cut slightly over the right eye.

The blazing monoplane, with the pilot and co-pilot grimly facing the flames in their compartment, dived at a rate estimated by Hefley at 275 miles an hour. It landed in a field near Ferris, twenty miles south of Dallas, skidding to a smoking halt after the landing gear had been torn off.

Mr. Jones and his fellow passengers tore open the door of the pilots' blazing compartment and dragged Hefley and Schacher to safety. A few moments later the plane was destroyed by the blaze.

Schacher said he and Hefley smelled a gasoline leak while flying, cut off the motor and began a gradual descent. A moment later, he said, there was a backfire and a flash of flame.

As fire began to eat at the single-motored ship, Hefley put it into a dive.

"Pilot Hefley told me to go back and tell the passengers what had happened," Schacher said. "I told them to fasten their safety belts, that the plane was on fire and that we would land in a hurry. They did not show any alarm, but quietly did as I told them."

Mr. Jones said Schacher then rejoined Hefley in the pilot's compartment, tightly closing the door to the passenger cabin.

"If they had not stuck to their posts," he asserted, "we all would have been killed.

"With the plane ablaze, the pilot made a quick forced landing, a beautiful piece of work. The plane hit hard and we scrambled out, pulling the pilots from the flaming compartment."

Mr. Jones said he did not have time to be frightened.

"We came down so fast that we didn't have time to think," he said.

Mr. Jones was en route home after speaking at the dedication of the statue of Robert E. Lee here in connection with the centennial celebration.

## BORAH UNDECIDED AS NORRIS BOLTS

### Ex-Candidate Withholds Commital on Landon—Colleague Out Again for Roosevelt.

### FRAZIER LEANS TO KANSAN

### But Idahoan, While Denying 'Soreness,' Lashes Out on Gold and Makes 'No Promises.'

Special to THE NEW YORK TIMES.

WASHINGTON, June 12.—Three members of the Republican party's liberal wing today expressed variant reactions to the nomination of Governor Landon for the Presidency.

Senator Norris, standing by his 1932 choice, declared himself for the re-election of President Roosevelt; Senator Frazier, who supported Mr. Roosevelt in 1932, said that he might back Mr. Landon, and Senator Borah refused to say whether he would support Governor Landon in the campaign.

Senator Norris asserted that the Republican party was again reactionary, with the Old Guard in the saddle, and that in his opinion the welfare of the nation demanded continuance of the New Deal.

Returning here from Cleveland in a grim mood, Senator Borah severely criticized Mr. Landon's statement on the gold standard, declared that he had made no promises to stump for the head of the ticket, but said that he had "no objection" to Colonel Knox as Vice Presidential choice.

He said that he left the convention with no bitterness over the failure of his own candidacy for the Presidential nomination.

**Borah Unyielding on Gold**

In a statement to the press Senator Borah said he would not discuss the campaign until he returned to Idaho and continued:

"I have not had time to study the platform as a whole, but with reference to the planks to which I gave most consideration, I am quite in harmony, particularly the foreign policy and monopoly and the omission of any pledge to return to the gold standard.

"I do not care to comment upon Governor Landon's message to the convention. I am not clear as to what it means. If it means he is

Continued on Page Nine

## KNOX LAUDS LANDON FOR 'HIGH COURAGE'

### Declares His Telegram on Platform Put Campaign on Plane of Sincerity.

### NOMINATION A SURPRISE

### On Way Home, He Learns by Radio in Indiana Hotel Room of Convention Action.

Special to THE NEW YORK TIMES.

CHICAGO, June 12. — Colonel Frank Knox, who had left the Republican Convention in Cleveland feeling his "participation all over," only to learn on the way home that he had become the party's Vice Presidential nominee by a unanimous vote, returned to his office tonight declaring that he was "honored" to have been chosen.

Surrounded by scores of reporters who crowded the publisher's office of his newspaper, The Chicago Daily News, he gave his first interview since being named by the party.

He made public a telegram to Governor Landon in which he accepted an invitation to go to Topeka Monday to confer on plans for the campaign.

"Both political and economic conditions call for a display of the same great qualities which endeared us both to Theodore Roosevelt," Colonel Knox's message said. "I know that you have them and I gladly place myself under your orders and will undertake to discharge every assignment you give me with all the vigor and ability I possess. We go forward to victory."

The publisher learned of his nomination soon after the action had been taken, but far from the convention scene; he was sitting near a radio in the dining room of a hotel in Michigan City, Ind., where he and his party, including Mrs. Knox and his secretary, John O'Keefe, had stopped for an hour or so on the way back to Chicago.

Although besieged by reporters, photographers, newsreel and radio operators, he declined to make a statement until he had reached Chicago.

When he arrived here he found a small army of press representatives awaiting him at his apart-

Continued on Page Seven

"All the News That's Fit to Print."

# The New York Times.

LATE CITY EDITION
Partly cloudy and warmer today. Tomorrow cloudy and cooler, probably showers.
Temperatures Yesterday—Max., 71; Min., 57

Copyright, 1936, by The New York Times Company.

VOL. LXXXV.....No. 28,643. Entered as Second-Class Matter, Postoffice, New York, N. Y. NEW YORK, FRIDAY, JUNE 26, 1936. PP TWO CENTS In New York City. | THREE CENTS Within 200 Miles. | FOUR CENTS Elsewhere Except in 7th and 8th Postal Zones.

# DEMOCRATS ADOPT PLATFORM CONTINUING NEW DEAL; FAVOR CONSTITUTIONAL AMENDMENTS, IF NECESSARY; CONVENTION ABROGATES CENTURY-OLD TWO-THIRDS RULE

## RUSSIA TO SPEED NEW CONSTITUTION AND PARLIAMENT

### Unanimous Approval Is Held Likely at the Congress of Soviets in November.

### ITS TEXT IS NOW PRINTED

### Charter Presented to People by Soviet Leaders Appears in This Issue of The Times.

### DRAWS ARDENT DISCUSSION

### Tens of Millions of 'Non-Party Bolsheviki' Now Back the Socialist Government.

*Text of the proposed Soviet Constitution appears on Page 10.*

By WALTER DURANTY
Special Cable to THE NEW YORK TIMES.

MOSCOW, June 25.—The new Soviet Constitution will be voted by the All-Union Congress of Soviets about the middle of November, but already it is the subject of ardent discussion throughout the Soviet Union.

The procedure to be followed in voting the Constitution will be somewhat different from that which voted the existing Constitution. In 1922 the tenth Soviet Congress of the Russian Socialist Federated Soviet Republic voted at the beginning of December for a union of the federations of Russia, White Russia, the Caucasus and the Ukraine, and on Dec. 30 the representatives of those four countries at the first Union Congress agreed unanimously that the new union should be formed.

**Dates Formally From 1923**

On July 6, 1923, the new Constitution was approved by the Central Executive Committee of the Union, which had been elected by the aforesaid first congress, but it was not until January, 1925, that the Union Constitution was formally voted by the second Union Congress of Soviets.

Next November the new Constitution with appropriate amendments will be submitted to the Soviet Congress elected according to the present rules, which give cities and towns a five times greater proportion of representation than the villages. This congress consists of two bodies—the elected Council of Soviets and the elected Council of Nationalities—which sit jointly in the Kremlin.

The basic lines of the project as published probably will remain unchanged, but there will be a number of minor amendments. For instance, there is an ambiguous phrase in one article stating that Soviet citizens vote at the age of 18. As the article runs, it would seem to imply that only 18-year-olds have the right to vote, which obviously is absurd. So here the correction will be introduced, "from 18 upward."

A more serious amendment may be required for Article 49, which states that the new presiding council shall be empowered to declare war, if the Congress is not sitting, "in the event of an armed attack on the U.S.S.R." This, however, fails to take into consideration treaty obligations already assumed by the Soviet Union in the pacts of mutual assistance with France and Czechoslovakia or such obligations of a similar character as might result from collective action by the League of Nations against an aggressor.

**Unanimous Vote Seen**

There probably will be some days of discussion of the amendments, and the delegates in both houses will have a right to propose others. Then the Constitution will be voted by a show of hands requiring a two-thirds majority of the joint assembly for its adoption. In point of fact, the vote will almost certainly be unanimous.

The probable composition of the congress will be about 70 per cent Communist party members and 30 per cent "sympathizers," or "non-party Bolsheviki," which is a phrase introduced by Joseph Stalin in a speech to collective farm workers in May of last year.

As far back as 1903 Lenin split the Bolsheviki from the Mensheviki on the ground that the former must be "active" always—that is to say, prepared to live or die only for the Communist party and to obey its orders with unflinching discipline.

Nowadays the battle for socialism in the U.S.S.R. is definitely won, and behind the vanguard of the Communist party there are tens of millions of Soviet citizens who fully sympathize with the Socialist system and can rightly be designated as "non-party Bolsheviki."

After voting the Constitution, the congress will set a date for the election of a new Parliament—which probably will be held late in January or early in February of next year.

## British Spinsters Seek Pensions of Government

By The Canadian Press.

LONDON, June 25.—Five thousand spinsters from every part of the country will journey to London Saturday for a demonstration in Hyde Park demanding pensions.

Specifically, they seek pensions for spinsters at the age of 55 under the national insurance scheme.

Spinsters' associations were started last year by Florence White, well-known Bradford business woman. Their membership now totals 35,000.

## ESTES PARK CHEERS LANDON'S ARRIVAL

### 1,000 Mounted Coloradoans Encircle Governor's Auto in Tumultuous Welcome.

### SNOWY PEAKS RIM SCENE

### Kansan Shuns Politics in 'Big Rush to Go Fishing'—Warm Reception in Denver.

By WARREN MOSCOW
Special to THE NEW YORK TIMES.

ESTES PARK, Col., June 25.—A vacation trip which turned into a miniature campaign tour ended this afternoon with Governor Landon, Republican Presidential nominee, and his family resting comfortably at the McGraw ranch, six miles from here, in the heart of Colorado's Rockies.

Snow-tipped mountain peaks, ranged in rows like sentinels, marked the route of the Governor and his family, as they neared the end of the seventy-five-mile drive from Denver, over rough mountain roads, to their vacation place, 7,600 feet high.

Earlier on that trip, from the time the Governor and his party left Topeka last night, thousands of Kansans, Coloradoans and even some from Arizona turned out to give him hearty greetings.

It was "Hyah, Alf," from Topeka onward, with hundreds turning out at the hamlets en route, and nearly all succeeding in shaking the Governor's hand. "Glad to see you, it was good of you to come down to the station," would be a typical reply on Mr. Landon's part.

Although the train drawing the Governor's private car reached Denver at the early hour of 7:30 this morning, Rocky Mountain time, there were many on the sidewalks in front of the Union station who had been there for at least an hour before that. Republican National Committeeman Lawrence C. Phipps and State Chairman Charles R. Enos headed a small party which boarded the train at Watkins, thirty miles from Denver.

**Welcomed by Governor**

At Denver, Governor Ed C. Johnson and Mayor Benjamin F. Stapleton, both Democrats, were at the train to welcome the Republican nominee to the State. With Governor Landon were Mrs. Landon, Peggy Anne, Nancy Jo and Jackie, the three children; Mrs. Samuel E. Cobb, Mrs. Landon's mother, and Mrs. Lucy McCue, governess.

Both Mr. and Mrs. Landon were presented with bouquets of flowers at the station. Mr. Landon was wearing a plain blue suit, straw hat, white shirt, and the same blue tie with white spots that he wore the night he was nominated.

In Denver he exchanged greetings, in speeches that were broadcast with those of members of the welcoming committee. Mr. Enos introduced him as "our next President," and the crowd of about 3,000 cheered.

At Denver, the first thing on the program was a press interview, and the first question, from a local newspaper man, was, "Where do you stand on the silver question?"

**Defers Stand on Silver**

"That's shooting them right from the hip," the Governor replied, laughing.

"That, and other similar questions, must be discussed in the regular way, in the formal addresses that I will make, starting with the acceptance speech on July 23. After that they will be the proper subjects for questions and for interpretation."

The subject switched to fishing. The Governor again stated that while he might use worms in Kansas, and get away with it, he might lose Colorado if he used anything but dry flies out here.

The final question, shot at him by a woman reporter, was:

"Are you going to put any women in your Cabinet?"

"Mrs. Landon," the Governor said without hesitation.

The Governor, in his radio address, broadcast from the station entrance, expressed the pleasure that he and Mrs. Landon felt in being in "cool Colorado," and added that the intermingling of the citizenry of the two States gave them more in common than a mere 200 miles of boundary line.

After this came a drive through

Continued on Page Five

## Delegate Got $4 for Cow, Is Charged $4 for Steak

Special to THE NEW YORK TIMES.

PHILADELPHIA, June 25.—While Philadelphia hotel and restaurant prices have not invoked the escalator clause every day as did those of Cleveland, they are still pretty high for the taste of many delegates from the rural districts.

One Democrat from Tennessee ordered a steak at a Broad Street hotel today and when his bill came he discovered that he had to pay $4. Whereupon he leaped to his feet with a wild shriek: "Why, last week I sold a whole cow for $4."

## 50 HURT IN CRASH OF PARADE STAND

### 200 Are Hurled Into Surging Crowd Watching Mummers' March in Philadelphia.

### RIOT CALLS BRING POLICE

### Mishap Comes Near Climax of Revel When Texas Girl Is Crowned 'Convention Queen.'

By LAWRENCE E. DAVIES
Special to THE NEW YORK TIMES.

PHILADELPHIA, June 25.—A 100-foot section of grand stand on the parkway collapsed tonight, injuring fifty persons, while one of the largest and most boisterous crowds in Philadelphia's history struggled to see a combined Mummers' revel, military parade and mardi gras given for Democratic National Convention visitors.

The accident, in which more than 200 spectators were thrown to the ground amid splintered boards, occurred when candidates for election as "Queen of the Convention" were starting down the Parkway on palm-decorated floats before the arrival of the paraders.

An hour and a half later, after riot calls had sent hundreds of policemen into action to control the shouting throngs, Miss Marion Fore, candidate from Texas, was chosen by a group of women judges as the convention queen.

Upon the head of the 20-year-old graduate of the University of Texas Mayor S. Davis Wilson put a crown of silver glittering with red and blue gems. For a long time she sat upon an oaken throne under the Washington statue, presiding over a fairyland of Mummers and tens of thousands of cheering spectators.

Mayor Wilson also presented a loving cup to the convention queen, who is the daughter of Sam Fore Jr. of Floresville, Texas, a publisher of several newspapers.

The Mayor gave smaller cups to Miss Mary Jane McCloskey of Pennsylvania, daughter of Matthew H. McCloskey, co-leader of the Philadelphia Democratic organization, and Miss Corinne Neely of West Virginia, daughter of Senator M. M. Neely.

Police officials said that they had never been confronted with so large and unruly a crowd over a mile and a half of central city streets. They estimated that upward of 200,000

Continued on Page Fourteen

## SOUTH BOWS TO CHANGE

### Appeased by Promise to Reapportion as Two-thirds Rule Ends.

### FIGHT ON FLOOR AVOIDED

### Committee Instructs Party Heads to Work Out New Representation Basis.

### ON DEMOCRATIC VOTE CAST

### Southerners Will Be Relatively Stronger Than Delegates of Less 'Regular' States.

By CHARLES R. MICHAEL
Special to THE NEW YORK TIMES.

PHILADELPHIA, June 25.—The century-old two-thirds rule, born in a tragic day of American history, when Jackson was President, died today in the progressive Roosevelt era. The convention tonight adopted the report of the rules committee, which recommended its abrogation and the substitution of the majority rule for the nomination of President and Vice President.

After long consideration of this troublesome issue, the rules committee, supported by administration influences, not only succeeded in overpowering the Southern opposition to a change in the rules, but avoided a fight on the floor by unanimously adopting a resolution sponsored by Senator Tydings of Maryland, which instructed the Democratic National Committee to work out a new basis of representation in the national conventions based upon the Democratic vote cast in the respective States.

The national committee was instructed to improve the system for selection of delegates and report to the 1940 convention. The present basis of apportioning delegates will be maintained until after the next convention.

Opponents of abrogation, led by Representative Eugene E. Cox of Georgia and Beeman Strong of Texas, announced themselves entirely satisfied with this action, which they said would maintain the prestige of the Solid South and ensure the building up of the party in other sections of the country. Sectionalism is removed by the abolition of the two-thirds rule and the proposed plan of representation in the convention based upon Democratic strength in each State.

**Text of Resolution**

The resolution which effected a peaceful solution and satisfied those opposing repeal reads:

"Be it resolved that the Democratic National Committee is hereby instructed to formulate and recommend to the next national convention a plan for improving the system by which delegates and alternates to Democratic National Conventions are apportioned, and be it further resolved that in formulating this plan the national committee shall take into account the Democratic strength within each State, the District of Columbia,

Continued on Page Fourteen

## Voting 'Aid' Offered to 115,073 Job Holders By Democratic Committee in Washington

Special to THE NEW YORK TIMES.

WASHINGTON, June 25.—The Democratic National Committee has opened a campaign to encourage 115,073 government officeholders in the District of Columbia to vote in their own States, since no elections are held in the District and its residents have no vote unless they establish voting status in their home States.

According to a spokesman of the Democratic absentee voters' committee, the national organization has sent letters to government employes who received Democratic endorsements for their jobs, informing them of registration dates in their States before the Presidential election.

A typical letter, signed by W. Forbes Morgan of the Democratic National Committee, contains this statement:

"The following information relating to elections in your State this year will no doubt be of interest to you."

The Civil Service Commission stated today there is no objection to this procedure since the letters do not infringe civil service laws by urging votes for any party or candidate. Absentee voters are informed that registration blanks, applications for absentee ballots and notarial service are available to Democrats.

Republican leaders here today said that this step was an innovation and condemned it heartily. E. F. Colloday, Republican National Committeeman from the District of Columbia, declared:

"It is a palpable attempt to influence these officeholders to register as Democrats in support of the New Deal. It is an application of undue influence."

Republicans have opened an absentee voters' office under the auspices of the Republican committee of the District of Columbia, but they are said to have confined their activities to advising applicants how to go about voting and to supplying notarial service.

Attempts have been made by the District of Columbia Commissioners to have planks advocating suffrage for the District inserted in the Republican and Democratic platforms this year.

## Text of the Democratic Platform

Special to THE NEW YORK TIMES.

*THE MUNICIPAL AUDITORIUM, PHILADELPHIA, June 25.—Following is the text of the platform as adopted by the Democratic National Convention:*

We hold this truth to be self-evident—that the test of a representative government is its ability to promote the safety and happiness of the people.

We hold this truth to be self-evident—that twelve years of Republican leadership left our nation sorely stricken in body, mind and spirit; and that three years of Democratic leadership have put it back on the road to restored health and prosperity.

We hold this truth to be self-evident—that twelve years of Republican surrender to the dictatorship of a privileged few have been supplanted by a Democratic leadership which has returned the people themselves to the places of authority, and has revived in them new faith and restored the hope which they had almost lost.

We hold this truth to be self-evident—that this three-year recovery in all the basic values of life and the re-establishment of the American way of living has been brought about by humanizing the policies of the Federal Government as they affect the personal, financial, industrial and agricultural well-being of the American people.

**PROTECTION OF FAMILY, HOME**

We hold this truth to be self-evident—that government in a modern civilization has certain inescapable obligations to its citizens, among which are:

(1) Protection of the family and the home.

(2) Establishment of a democracy of opportunity for all the people.

(3) Aid to those overtaken by disaster.

These obligations, neglected through twelve years of the old leadership, have once more been recognized by American government. Under the new leadership they will never be neglected.

For the protection of the family and home:

(1) We have begun and shall continue the successful drive to rid our land of kidnappers and bandits. We shall continue to use the powers of government to end the activities of the malefactors of great wealth who defraud and exploit the people.

**SAVINGS AND INVESTMENTS**

(2) We have safeguarded the thrift of our citizens by restraining those who would gamble with other people's savings, by requiring truth in the sale of securities; by putting the brakes upon the use of credit for speculation; by outlawing the manipulation of prices in stock and commodity markets; by curbing the overweening power and unholy practices of utility holding companies; by insuring fifty million bank accounts.

**OLD AGE AND SOCIAL SECURITY**

(3) We have built foundations for the security of those who are faced with the hazards of unemployment and old age; for the orphaned, the crippled and the blind. On the foundation of the Social Security Act we are determined to erect a structure of economic security for all our people, making sure that this benefit shall keep step with the ever-increasing capacity of Amer-

Continued on Page Thirteen

## PLEDGES THE PARTY TO CONTINUE RELIEF

### Platform Also Promises Labor Efforts for Shorter Hours and 'Prevailing Wages.'

### WALLACE VIEWS ADOPTED

### He Obtains Commitment for Further Steps Toward Farm Production Control.

By FELIX BELAIR Jr.
Special to THE NEW YORK TIMES.

PHILADELPHIA, June 25.—The 1936 platform of the Democratic party, pledging a continuance of the social and economic objectives of the New Deal and asking a return to power on those grounds, was completed here late today and adopted unanimously by the convention late in the evening.

Committee agreement on the document was reached after night and day sessions in which proposed changes in the draft, completed by a subcommittee headed by Senator Wagner of New York, were intermittently referred by telephone to President Roosevelt at Washington for his approval.

Somewhat longer and more specific than any of the tentative drafts, the completed platform was in many respects a compromise between a detailed campaign document and one reciting only the record of the administration without promise of further specific economic or social reforms in the future.

**Outstanding Planks**

Outstanding planks included a definite pledge to seek an amendment to the Constitution whereby the Federal Government, acting with the States, might enjoy ample power "adequately to regulate commerce, protect public health and safety and safeguard economic security."

Specifically mentioned in this connection were administration efforts to date to legislate to relieve drought, dust storms and floods, prescribe minimum wages, maximum hours, child labor and working conditions in industry, and curb monopolistic and unfair business practices.

Such things as these could never adequately be handled by the forty-eight States acting independently of one another, the platform stated, and added that "we have sought and will continue to seek to meet these problems through legislation within the Constitution."

**To Maintain Constitution**

It was emphasized, however, that even should an effort be launched to amend the basic law, this would be "to maintain the letter and spirit of the Constitution."

It was clear from the text that the resolutions committee had been at considerable pains not to men-

Continued on Page Thirteen

## Five Women to Second Roosevelt's Nomination

Special to THE NEW YORK TIMES.

PHILADELPHIA, June 25.—Seconders of the nomination of President Roosevelt will include at least five women.

They are Mrs. Frank E. Johnesse of Boise, Idaho, the only woman chairman of a State delegation; Mrs. Lucretia del Valle Grady of California, Mrs. Emma Guffey Miller of Pennsylvania, Mrs. Mary T. Norton of New Jersey and Mrs. Nanny Wood Honeyman of Oregon, who was the victor in a strongly contested primary and is a nominee for Congress.

## O'CONNOR ASSAILED FOR BACKING 2/3 RULE

### New Yorkers Charge He Violated Caucus Wish by Vote Against Abrogation.

By JAMES P. McCAFFREY
Special to THE NEW YORK TIMES.

PHILADELPHIA, June 25.—The action of Representative John J. O'Connor, as New York member on the rules committee, in voting against the abolition of the two-thirds rule in Democratic conventions surprised the New York delegation today. Only Tuesday afternoon the delegates had unanimously voted at a caucus to favor majority rule for the nomination of Presidential and Vice Presidential candidates.

While Mr. O'Connor belittled his action in going against the wishes of the caucus, delegates not only from New York City but from upState showed indignation at his vote.

For the most part the delegates were guarded in their comment, but a few of Mr. O'Connor's friends from Manhattan heard that the Representative was seeking favor among delegates from the Southern States, who were against abrogation of the rule.

They suggested that Mr. O'Connor had the ambition to become Speaker of the House at the next session. At present he is chairman of the House Rules Committee. It is expected, however, that he will have opposition, either in his party primary or from the Rev. Charles E. Coughlin's supporters, for re-election in his district.

**O'Connor Minimizes Action**

Mr. O'Connor freely discussed his vote, but would not explain his action in reversing the sentiment of his colleagues. Soon after the rules committee had drawn up its report, Mr. O'Connor visited Chairman Farley at Democratic national headquarters.

"What was the reason for your voting against abolition of the two-thirds rule?" Mr. O'Connor was asked.

"Why, it's only much ado about nothing," he replied.

"Is there anything to the sugges-

Continued on Page Fourteen

## 'AL SMITH' BANNERS INCITE WILD FRACAS

### Fists Fly in the Crowded Balcony as Police Eject Party of Demonstrators.

### CALLED REPUBLICAN PLOT

### Leader Blames Philadelphia 'Machine'—Delegates Shout for 'Lynching.'

By F. RAYMOND DANIELL
Special to THE NEW YORK TIMES.

THE MUNICIPAL AUDITORIUM, PHILADELPHIA, June 25.—The sudden appearance of Al Smith banners in a corner of the upper balcony here tonight caused a free-for-all fight which was quelled by police.

David L. Lawrence, chairman of the Pennsylvania Democratic State Committee, brought the delegates to their feet later by making a charge that the whole thing was plotted by Republicans and that such "skullduggery" must stop.

Senator Clark, chairman of the Rules Committee, before reading his committee's report, declared that the country could judge for itself where the party's sympathies lay by comparing the "funny demonstration in the balcony for Mr. Smith with the fine enthusiasm displayed by the followers of the New Deal."

The hero of the little incident was Joe Marinelli, Deputy Attorney General of Pennsylvania, who, alone and unaided at first, stormed the citadel of the disturbers, seized their banners and trampled them beneath his feet. A left hook to the jaw sent him tumbling over three rows of seats, but he came up fighting.

State highway patrolmen and city police rounded up the disturbing element, comprising, officials said, about fifty young men from the Republican Second Ward, and rushed them out of the hall after escorting them through a threatening crowd in the basement.

**Admitted as "Loyal Democrats"**

Police Captain Charles Kane said the whole group entered the hall at 8:35 equipped with noise makers but without tickets. They were admitted, he said, upon their protestations that they were "loyal Democrats." While police said the leader was identified as a Republican ward politician, Assistant Attorney General Margiotti began an investigation to determine whether the plot originated in "higher circles."

The balcony delegation broke out its banners just as the convention delegations were marching around on the floor below waving banners and wearing paper caps. In the midst of this official celebration, the three Smith banners were unfurled.

"Al Smith—We Want Al Smith,"

Continued on Page Twelve

## A ROOSEVELT DOCUMENT

### Platform Draft Is Flown to the Capital for His Final Alterations.

### HAS HIS LITERARY STYLE

### Reference to Silver Purchase Act Is Ruled Out in Party's Currency Declaration.

### AGAINST ALL WAR PROFITS

### True Neutrality and Continuance of the Good Neighbor Policy Are Pledged.

By ARTHUR KROCK
Special to THE NEW YORK TIMES.

PHILADELPHIA, June 25.—A platform emphatically endorsing and continuing the New Deal to the point of amending the Constitution to make room for it if the Supreme Court persists in the narrow constructions of recent times was submitted to the Democratic National Convention tonight by a unanimous committee on resolutions and unanimously adopted. The convention also rescinded the two-thirds majority rule, a century old this year.

Franklin Delano Roosevelt, the candidate who will stand upon the platform in the campaign, had approved it completely before it was offered to the convention. There are two commanding reasons why he accepted it without reservation:

One—With Senator Wagner, chairman of the committee, he directed the preparation of the preliminary draft.

Two—As edited and slightly revised to meet all influential opinions, it was sent to him, by plane, by him remanded, and then adopted by the committee.

**Science Aids in Coordination**

The devices of modern science and invention—the airplane and the long-distance telephone—were summoned to the task of coordinating the wishes of the President and the suggestions of the resolutions committee. When the original draft of the platform was completed this morning by a subcommittee it was sent to the White House by air and, with certain revisions, returned to Philadelphia by the same means. In the interval, committee members discussed points at issue with the President over the telephone. It is general in treatment, and divided into subjects, not planks.

The declaration on the Constitution says that the Republicans propose to meet national problems by State means. But, the Democrats continue, forty-eight Legislatures, State houses and State courts cannot adequately handle problems arising from droughts, dust storms, wages and hours, monopolistic practices, &c. Both Federal and State treatment are demanded.

The Democratic party will continue to seek remedies within the Constitution. But if legislation cannot provide these within the present Constitution, it will seek such clarifying amendments as will enable Congress and the Legislatures—each in its proper jurisdiction—to enact laws which will adequately regulate commerce, protect public health and safety and safeguard economic security.

No mention is made in the platform of the pledges of 1932, the Silver Purchase Act and execution, the World Court, the League of Nations, the NRA, the AAA, the "holding company death sentence" that tied up Congress for half a year, or of several other matters which the Republicans will seek to translate into issues. The President personally ruled against any of the specifications.

**President's Style Reflected**

The platform definitely reflects the literary style and political attacks of the President. These features of it especially are his: The preamble, paraphrasing parts of the Declaration of Independence ("We hold these truths to be self-evident"), which the Republicans at Cleveland also paraphrased; the reiteration of the statement about the farmer, the business man, youth, labor and other groups, after recounting measures taken to put them on the path to recovery: "We will keep him (or them) on that road," and the avoidance of specific planks to permit a general re-

Continued on Page Twelve

"All the News That's Fit to Print."

# The New York Times.

LATE CITY EDITION
Cloudy, possibly showers today, somewhat cooler. Tomorrow cloudy, possibly showers and cooler.
Temperatures Yesterday—Max., 86; Min., 63



VOL. LXXXV....No. 28,644. Entered as Second-Class Matter, Postoffice, New York, N. Y. NEW YORK, SATURDAY, JUNE 27, 1936. PP TWO CENTS In New York City. | THREE CENTS Within 200 Miles. | FOUR CENTS Elsewhere Except in 7th and 8th Postal Zones.

# *ROOSEVELT NOMINATED BY ACCLAMATION; DEMONSTRATIONS FOR HIM AND LEHMAN*

## RAIL PENSION LAW VOIDED BY COURT; WRIT HALTS TAXES

District of Columbia Court Rules 1935 Act and Its Tax Legislation Unconstitutional.

CITES FINDING ON 1934 LAW

Bailey Holds Supreme Court Decision on This Also Invalidates Substitute Measures.

CARRIERS WIN INJUNCTIONS

Federal Board Plans a Quick Appeal as 1,000,000 Workers Face Loss of the Benefits.

*Text of Justice Bailey's decision on rail pensions is on Page 28.*

By LOUIS STARK
Special to THE NEW YORK TIMES.

WASHINGTON, June 26.—On grounds similar in part to those expounded by the United States Supreme Court majority on May 6, 1935, in invalidating the 1934 Railroad Retirement Act, Justice Jennings Bailey in the District of Columbia Supreme Court today declared unconstitutional the 1935 Railroad Pension Law and its companion tax measure, providing the levying and collection of taxes to finance railway men's pensions.

The Tax Act and the Pension Act itself were "inseparable," the two dovetailing "into one another so as to create a complete system," the court declared in the ruling.

The decision was the second blow delivered to the pension aspirations of a million railway workers in the last fourteen months, the Supreme Court having previously held the first Pension Law invalid as a violation of the due process clause of the Constitution.

The first decision was announced while the Social Security Act was pending, and gave rise to the question whether the taxation feature of the Social Security Act would stand up when attacked in the Supreme Court. Today's decision revived the doubts as to the constitutionality of the Social Security Act.

In today's decision, Justice Bailey stated that on Aug. 29, 1935, Congress had approved two acts, one creating a pension system for railway employes and the other levying an excise tax of 3½ per cent of the payrolls, to be paid by the carriers, and a similar tax to be deducted from the employes earning up to $300 a month.

**Laws Held Interdependent**

"The provisions of the two acts in question are so interrelated and interdependent that each is a necessary part of one entire scheme," the opinion stated. "This is not only apparent from the terms of the acts themselves but is shown by their legislative history. It was clearly the intention of Congress that the pension system created by the Retirement Act should be supported by the taxes levied upon the carriers and their employes."

Holding that the Taxing Act was unconstitutional, Justice Bailey said that it sought to collect revenue, not to provide for the expenses of government, "but solely for a purpose which the United States Supreme Court has held not to be within the domain of the Fedetral Government."

Whether the twenty-one standard railway unions would attempt to open direct negotiations with the Class I roads, wnich won a victory by the decision today, in an effort for an agreement on a voluntary pension arrangement, could not be ascertained in advance of early conferences among the unions.

**Counsel Will Meet Judge**

It was assumed that the decision would be appealed to the Supreme Court, but in the absence of Attorney General Cummings no statement was forthcoming from the Department of Justice.

Counsel for the Railroad Retirement Board and the Federal law officers will meet in Justice Bailey's chambers on Tuesday to draw up the formal court order.

The decision enjoined the Railroad Retirement Board from compelling the railroads to "assemble, compile or furnish any of the information and records required, or which may be required to be furnished under said Retirement Act."

It also enjoins Commissioner of Internal Revenue Guy T. Helvering

Continued on Page Twenty-eight

## *Warships of Five Nations To Meet in Chilean Fete*

Special Cable to THE NEW YORK TIMES.

SANTIAGO, Chile, June 26.—Warships of five Latin American nations—Argentina, Brazil, Peru, Ecuador and Chile—will meet in Valparaiso Bay early in September, it was announced today.

They will be present to participate in celebrations marking the 400th anniversary of the founding of the city of Valparaiso.

The meeting is considered an excellent occasion to reawaken cordiality among Latin Americans.

A great display of Chile's air forces is contemplated.

## DRUKMAN JURORS DEBATE FOR HOURS

Get Case Accusing Five of Plot in Brooklyn Murder at 2 P. M. and Sit Into the Morning.

POLICE GUARD JURY ROOM

Judge Holds Charges 'of Great Importance' and Menace to the Jury System.

The Brooklyn blue ribbon jury which listened for four weeks to testimony in the Drukman conspiracy trial had not yet agreed, at 3:30 A. M. today, on verdicts for the five defendants charged with plotting to obstruct justice in the Samuel Drukman murder case.

Shortly before midnight the police cleared hundreds of persons out of the building and an army of scrubwomen took possession of the marble floors and corridors. The ousted crowds milled about in the street where ordinarily the sidewalks are deserted at that hour of the night. Scores of persons coming from the theatres drew up in taxicabs to get news.

At that time there had been no word from the jury room since the jurors returned from dinner. No persons were allowed above the ground floor of the building, except the uniformed court officers guarding the vicinity of the jury room. Justice Rogers had given no indication whether he would lock up the jury for the night.

**Get Case at 2 P. M.**

The jury had been deliberating, with time out for dinner, since 2 P. M. yesterday. Supreme Court Justice Erskine C. Rogers, presiding at the extraordinary term of the court, charged the jury for an hour and forty-five minutes in the morning. Then the jurors went out to lunch, and at 2 o'clock began their deliberations.

Shortly before 5 o'clock they sent two communications to the judge, one asking for testimony dealing with certain tapped-wire conversations and for the testimony of witnesses whose stories, partly contradicting each other, dealt with the State's charge that the defendant, William W. Kleinman, had been seen in an automo-

Continued on Page Four

## LEHMAN FOR SOCIAL ISSUE

He Denounces 'Callous' Republican Fight on Security Plan.

'GHASTLY' PHILOSOPHY HIT

President's Program Is Held 'Most Humane Measure of Our Lifetime.'

'MIRACLE' UPTURN HAILED

Governor Also Predicts Fresh Business Expansion—He Will Confer With Roosevelt.

*Text of Governor Lehman's seconding speech is on Page 7.*

By W. A. WARN
Special to THE NEW YORK TIMES.

THE MUNICIPAL AUDITORIUM, PHILADELPHIA, June 26.—In one of the most impressive addresses of his public career, Governor Lehman of New York appeared before the Democratic National Convention tonight amid a great ovation to second the nomination of President Roosevelt on behalf of the President's and his own home State. He painted a picture of the reaction which would follow in the event of a Republican election victory this Autumn.

Governor Lehman said that in New York the Republicans in the Legislature had bitterly fought progressive measures, especially the social welfare legislation that had been recommended by himself and his immediate predecessor in the Governorship, now the President.

At no time did Governor Lehman mention former Governor Smith, with whom he has been on terms of warm friendship since he entered public life.

**"Callous" Policies Scored**

In his arraignment of Republican leaders in New York Governor Lehman described their policies as "cruel," "callous" and "reactionary," and declared that the social philosophy which inspired their action was undoubtedly the guiding star of Republican leaders in the nation.

Mr. Lehman declared that President Roosevelt had supplied leadership which was needed as never before when he took office and had lifted the country out of an abyss of despair and panic as by "a miracle." The Governor predicted that upon the foundation laid by the President there would be witnessed an expanding improvement in business during the present year.

"For the real progress that has been made, for the great economic reconstruction of this country, for the hope and confidence that again lie in the breasts of millions of our people—one man above all others deserves our gratitude—Franklin D. Roosevelt," Governor Lehman said.

Governor Lehman met a charge

Continued on Page Seven

## *President Thanks Lehman, Hails Tribute to Him*

Special to THE NEW YORK TIMES.

MUNICIPAL AUDITORIUM, PHILADELPHIA, June 26.—President Roosevelt tonight sent the following telegram to Governor Lehman:

"I thank you, my old friend, from the bottom of my heart for all you said tonight.

"That wonderful tribute to you came from the hearts of every State, and you rightly deserved it. My love to you both.

"FRANKLIN D. ROOSEVELT."

The both includes Mrs. Lehman.

## ROOSEVELT HINTS OF FARLEY DECISION

His Deferring of Reply Till End of Convention Is Construed as Forecasting Cabinet Change.

CLOSER TO PHILADELPHIA

President Keeps Telephone Busy—Acceptance Speech Will Dwell on Platform.

By CHARLES W. HURD
Special to THE NEW YORK TIMES.

WASHINGTON, June 26.—President Roosevelt hinted today of early settlement of the question as to how long Postmaster General Farley would remain in the dual position of Cabinet member and chairman of the Democratic National Committee.

In response to a question at a White House press conference whether he was prepared to discuss Mr. Farley's expected resignation, President Roosevelt replied that he could not say anything until after the convention. His remark was construed as at least partial confirmation of reports that Mr. Farley would resign from the Cabinet in the near future.

Mr. Farley has remained in the Cabinet for more than two years since the President issued a dictum that party officials could not also hold government office, a rule which he enforced with severity except in the case of the party chairman.

**Keen Over Convention**

The press conference, the President's last before he will go to Philadelphia tomorrow night to accept renomination, came in the midst of a day divided about equally between routine work on bills left by Congress and political work, including the polishing of his speech of acceptance.

The President was cheerful over the smooth running of the Philadelphia convention, but marks of fatigue on his face reflected the late and irregular hours he has kept during the week.

For the first time he admitted an active interest in the convention, saying that he had used the telephone at 1:30 this morning. Denying reports that memoranda on the final draft of the platform had been sent to him by airplane for approval, he laughingly asked newspaper correspondents if they did not agree that the telephone was a simpler means of communication.

His early morning call to Philadelphia was made to congratulate Senator Wagner, chairman of the resolutions committee, on his delivery of the platform before the convention. The radio brought it to the White House.

Mr. Roosevelt said that he also tried to reach Marvin H. McIntyre, one of his secretaries sent to Philadelphia as an observer, but was unable to do so at that hour.

**Rough Draft Still "Too Rough"**

As for the platform, much of which obviously was substantially written in advance of the convention with the close cooperation of, if not by, Mr. Roosevelt, he said that he had only read part of the final text.

What the President wishes to say publicly about the platform will constitute the main portion of his speech tomorrow night.

This speech, a comparatively brief document of about 2,000 words, was almost completed, having been dictated last night by the President, but he said that he probably would make several changes in it because the rough draft, in second reading this morning, appeared to be literally "too rough" in spots

In further conversation the President said that he intended to stay within the borders of the United States until after election and that there would be no cruises to Hawaii

Continued on Page Nine

## DRAMA IN NIGHT SESSION

One Big Moment Is Held Back When Lehman Speech Is Delayed.

HE GETS TWO OVATIONS

Acclaim in Drafting Movement Rivals That for President as Name Is Ratified.

DOOLING LEADS PARADE

'It Was Swell,' Says Governor, but Gives No Intimation of What Answer Will Be.

By TURNER CATLEDGE
Special to THE NEW YORK TIMES.

THE MUNICIPAL AUDITORIUM, PHILADELPHIA, Saturday, June 27.—With two prolonged demonstrations for Governor Herbert H. Lehman and another for President Roosevelt, the Democratic National Convention, at its session which ended nearly an hour after midnight this morning, attempted by a frank show of its enthusiasm to tie together the personalities of these two leaders for the campaign.

When the convention adjourned at 12:55 this morning until 10 A. M. today, it was in the midst of an ovation to President Roosevelt. It was the second given him during the day's two sessions, the other, lasting an hour and four minutes, being when he was placed in nomination in the afternoon.

The first outburst for Governor Lehman rivaled anything seen at this convention. It came when Chairman Robinson announced at about 10 P. M. that the New York Governor would take the rostrum to second the nomination of President Roosevelt.

**Culmination of "Draft" Move**

It was the culmination of the "draft Lehman" movement which started even before the convention began and which last night saw every State, Territory and district represented here join in a concerted movement to add what they all considered a "dynamo of strength" to the Democratic ticket next Fall.

The demonstration was started by the New York delegation, led by James J. Dooling, leader of Tammany; Frank V. Kelly, Brooklyn leader; Senator Robert F. Wagner, and Borough President James J. Lyons of the Bronx. Just behind came George Gordon Battle. The New Yorkers were smiling and shouting as they were joined by delegates from other States.

The instant Governor Lehman's name was mentioned by Senator Robinson, permanent chairman of the convention, the delegates, alternates and spectators literally exploded with enthusiasm. They had been waiting impatiently for nearly an hour while representatives of other States paid their respects to the candidacy of Mr. Roosevelt.

The demonstration bade fair to go on and on, but Senator Robinson pleaded for quiet so that Governor Lehman could begin his speech. When he began the aisles were jammed with marching delegates and alternates, each delegation headed by a banner advocating the drafting of the Governor for renomination.

**Lehman Stops the Outburst**

As Mr. Lehman raised his voice, however, the demonstration quickly subsided. The demonstration lasted eleven minutes and might have gone on for an hour had it not been halted.

The New York delegation started a new demonstration for Governor Lehman after he had completed his speech. The Buffalo women's drum and bugle corps started playing again and the "Lehman Must Run" banners began moving in all sections of the hall.

Chairman Robinson rapped for order and tried to stop it. He wanted to proceed with the seconding speeches and was ready to present Mrs. Emma Guffey Miller to speak for Pennsylvania, but the New Yorkers kept parading, Alabama joined in, then followed Pennsylvania, Minnesota, Texas, Kansas—headed by a banner making light of Governor Landon's claims of balancing his budget—a delegate bearing the standard of the National Colored Democratic Association, North Dakota, Michigan, the Virgin Islands and others.

Other delegations waved their standards.

The second Lehman demonstration continued for ten minutes be-

Continued on Page Nine

© Photo by New York Times Studio.

RENOMINATED FOR PRESIDENT
Franklin Delano Roosevelt,
from a photograph for which he posed at the White House last Saturday

## ENTHUSIASM RUNS HIGH

Eight Hours of Oratory Precede Acclamation in Early Morning.

CHEER PRESIDENT AN HOUR

Delegates in Ecstatic Climax When Name Is Presented to Convention by Mack.

LEHMAN TOPS SECONDERS

Received So Enthusiastically as to Leave No Doubt of Desire That He Run Again.

*Text of former Justice Mack's nominating speech is on Page 6.*

By ARTHUR KROCK
Special to THE NEW YORK TIMES.

THE MUNICIPAL AUDITORIUM, PHILADELPHIA, Saturday, June 27.—After more than eight hours of eulogistic oratory and demonstrations, which kept the Democratic National Convention in session from 1 P. M. yesterday until 12:55 o'clock this morning, Franklin Delano Roosevelt was nominated for re-election by acclamation. Vice President Garner will be similarly honored this afternoon.

Fifty-seven speeches were made by the orators in the seconding talkathon, representing every State, territory, possession and the District of Columbia. They included twelve Governors, eight Senators, one Senator-elect, eight women, a Cabinet officer and the Governor General of the Philippine Islands. Senator McAdoo, when called to the chair, also spoke in favor of the nomination but his was not strictly a seconding speech.

On motion of Governor Berry of South Dakota the rules were suspended and the roll-call was dispensed with, the nomination coming at 12:42 A. M.

**Final, Noisy Celebration**

Senator Robinson's announcement from the platform that the President had been chosen by acclamation—thus "beating Cleveland"—loosed another and the final demonstration of the all-day, all-night session. It was just like the rest and was still in progress when the chairman heard, put and declared passed a motion to recess until 10 o'clock this morning—an action unknown to nearly all the shouting, parading, horn-tooting demonstrators.

Rarely has the flow of harmonious oratory been equaled in a national political gathering as a few conservatives joined a long parade of New Dealers in extolling the President. Going a step beyond the Repubican convention at Cleveland two weeks ago, the Philadelphia delegates cast not a single vote against Mr. Roosevelt. A score of votes from Wisconsin and West Virginia kept Governor Alf M. Landon from enjoying the same distinction.

Much more exciting than the actual nomination was a series of tumultuous uprisings to honor Governor Herbert H. Lehman of New York, who made the chief seconding speech at 10 o'clock last night. The effort was in part prearranged to convince Mr. Lehman that he must stand for re-election. At the same time a great deal of it was spontaneous and sincere. When Mr. Lehman was finally permitted to leave the platform he received a telegram of thanks from the President at Washington. Though beset with importunities, he declined to admit any change in his intention to retire.

**Stresses President's Record**

The Governor stressed the President's bent and record in behalf of social welfare, and, by his scathing attack upon the Republican leadership at Albany, intimated what the chief campaign issue in that State will be if the Democrats can make it so.

When the President's name was formally proposed by John E. Mack of Poughkeepsie, who rendered the same service in 1932, a demonstration of more than an hour's duration interrupted the proceedings. Whatever the feelings of many Democrats who will go along this year for a number of reasons, and some of whom excused themselves from prominent participation in the oratory of the day, there is no doubt that the tumult expressed the feeling of the overwhelming majority of the delegates.

Although a fair percentage of the

Continued on Page Eight

## *3 Guilty of Fraud, Fourth's Fate in Doubt In Failure of $81,000,000 Title Company*

J. Crawford Stevens, president, and Reginald P. Ray, vice president, of the defunct Westchester Title and Trust Company, were found guilty at 12:20 A. M. today on all counts of a twenty-count mail fraud indictment by a Federal court jury which had deliberated for more than eight hours.

Philip H. Kuss, also a vice president, was found guilty on twelve of the twenty counts, and the jury failed to reach an agreement on the guilt or innocence of Frederick P. Condit, chairman of the executive committee, who is also a vice president and trustee of the Title Guarantee and Trust Company.

Judge Robert P. Patterson ordered the jury locked up for the night. It will continue its deliberation this morning on Condit.

Stevens and Ray face prison terms up to ninety-seven years and fines totaling $29,000 each, while Kuss is subject to imprisonment for up to fifty-seven years and fines totaling $22,000.

Shortly before midnight Judge Patterson called the jury into the court room and asked whether they had been able to approach a verdict. Fletcher Swain, foreman, said that agreement had been reached regarding three of the defendants but that the jury was deadlocked as to the fourth. Judge Patterson then said that he would accept a partial verdict and the jury retired, to return about twenty minutes later.

Former Mayor John J. Fogarty, of Yonkers, representing Stevens and Kuss, and Monroe Cahn, attorney for Ray, objected strenuously to the court's procedure in accepting an incomplete verdict.

The Westchester Title and Trust Company failed in August, 1933, with $81,000,000 of its securities in the hands of the public. The trial has been in progress for more than seven weeks.

Of the twenty counts in the indictments, nineteen concerned the mailing of sales-promotion literature containing statements which the government charges were misleading. The twentieth charged conspiracy. Some of the challenged statements were that mortgage certificates issued by the company were absolutely safe, depression proof and secured by Westchester County homes or improved property.

Judge Patterson pointed out that Mr. Condit was not a salaried officer of the company and was not active in its affairs. The jury's duty, he explained, was to determine only whether he participated in arranging for year-end loans in 193[illegible] and 1932 and whether, if he did so, he knew this was done to produce financial statements which might mislead the public.

## OUTBURSTS ALARM PROF. CEREBELLUM

Psychiatrist Diagnoses Campaignomania Which Affects Delegates at Times.

By F. RAYMOND DANIELL
Special to THE NEW YORK TIMES.

THE MUNICIPAL AUDITORIUM, PHILADELPHIA, June 26.—Campaignomania, an occupational disease common to politicians at recurrent intervals, notably in Presidential years, broke out on the floor of the Democratic convention today and spread rapidly until a large proportion of the visitors in the balconies was infected.

Isolated cases of the malady have been noted among the delegates since they began assembling here early this week, but the outbreak did not reach epidemic proportions until this afternoon, when the magic name of Franklin Delano Roosevelt fell from the lips of John E. Mack into the cluster of microphones before him.

The symptoms were recognized and the diagnosis provided by Professor Cerebrus Cerebellum, a noted psychiatrist from Brownsville, Brown County, Ind., close friend of those other Brown countians, Godfrey Gloom and Abe Martin, who once remarked that a "lot of people believe in Providence who never heard of Rhode Island."

As the professor explained it, campaignomania is a disease characterized by more or less violent manifestations of short duration. There is no immunization against it, he said, and the more dignified statesmen are especially susceptible to its ravages at convention time.

**Case History Is Revealing**

In the interest of science, the professor suggested that a detailed and objective study of the apparent aberrations of reflexes of the patients be made and published for the benefit of students of psychiatry and politics. Therefore the following:

At 1:28 P. M. when Mr. Mack mentioned the name of Mr. Roosevelt, the delegates and guests were slumped in their seats, listening politely and to all outward appearances behaving like perfectly normal average citizens.

A second later the entire scene had changed from a relatively dignified assemblage of patriots to one resembling what might take place in the psychopathic ward of a great

Continued on Page Eight

## GARNER ON SCENE, MET WITH ACCLAIM

Vice President Passes Through Cheering Crowds From Station to His Hotel.

By CHARLES R. MICHAEL
Special to THE NEW YORK TIMES.

PHILADELPHIA, June 26.—Jovial Jack Garner, Vice President, arrived here at 7 o'clock tonight to participate with President Roosevelt in the notification ceremonies tomorrow night. Escorted by 175 mounted policemen from the Thirtieth Street station, he was cheered by the crowds, whose attention was attracted by shrieking sirens as he and the reception committee proceeded to his hotel. He acknowledged the acclaim from the sidewalks by standing up in his car.

At the hotel the Texas delegates, massed in the street under their Lone Star banner, gave him a rousing welcome.

Mr. Garner was met at the station by a committee composed of Attorney General Cummings, Postmaster General Farley, Senators Robinson and Connally and Governor and Mrs. Earle. As he left his car he turned to the captain commanding the police escort and said:

"I have never seen a better lot of officers than you have here. You remind me of the Texas Rangers and your presence makes it homelike."

**Is Guest at Reception**

The Vice President attended a reception given in his honor by the Texas delegation and later participated briefly in the dinner of the Young Democrats. He did not make a speech and tarried only long enough to greet them. He told them as he left that the future of the country and the Democratic party depended upon their efforts.

Mr. Garner spent the evening in his hotel chatting with old friends. Many came to visit him. He will not make any public appearance until tomorrow night, when he is scheduled to accept renomination for the Vice Presidency before President Roosevelt makes his acceptance speech.

Since becoming Vice President, Mr. Garner has refrained from discussing public questions. He remained true to that policy tonight and declined to comment upon the platform.

He, however, did discuss the political outlook with Chairman Farley and other Democratic chieftains

Continued on Page Nine

"All the News That's Fit to Print."

# The New York Times.

LATE CITY EDITION
Partly cloudy, with moderate temperatures today. Tomorrow fair, with little change in temperature.
Temperatures yesterday—Max., 76; min., 70.

Section 1



VOL. LXXXV....No. 28,645. | Entered as Second-Class Matter, Postoffice, New York, N. Y. | NEW YORK, SUNDAY, JUNE 28, 1936. | Including Rotogravure Picture, Magazine and Book Review. | PP | TEN CENTS | TWELVE CENTS Beyond 200 Miles Except in 7th and 8th Postal Zones.

# ROOSEVELT TO WAR ON 'ECONOMIC ROYALISTS'; HAILED BY THRONGS IN ACCEPTANCE CEREMONY; GARNER NAMED AS WEARY CONVENTION CLOSES

## NEW 'FIXING' BARED BY DRUKMAN JURY AS 3 ARE CONVICTED

### Court Orders an Inquiry After Juror Finds Note in Pocket —He Voted All Guilty.

### SPLIT ON GEOGHAN AIDE

### Two Hold Out for Acquittal of W. W. Kleinman and Dardis, City Detective.

### SENTENCES TO BE TUESDAY

### Maximum Term Is Year in Jail and $500 Fine—Todd Weighs Trying Two Again.

An attempt to "reach" the blue-ribbon jury that heard jury-tampering evidence in the Drukman conspiracy case for the last four weeks was disclosed yesterday afternoon when the jurors, unable to agree on verdicts in the cases of Assistant District Attorney William W. Kleinman and Detective Giuseppe F. L. Dardis, were discharged after more than twenty-seven hours' deliberation.

The jury stood ten to two for conviction of both defendants.

Earlier in the day the jury had convicted the three other defendants. They were Henry G. Singer, former Assistant United States Attorney in Brooklyn; James J. Kleinman, father of the Assistant District Attorney, and Jacob Silverman, a bakery products dealer who was said to have been friendly with notorious Brooklyn characters.

All were charged with conspiracy to obstruct justice, a misdemeanor, punishable by a maximum penalty of $500 in fines and one year in the penitentiary.

They will be sentenced by Supreme Court Justice Erskine C. Rogers in Brooklyn on Tuesday. At the same time Special Prosecutor Hiram C. Todd will announce whether the State intends to re-try the younger Kleinman and Dardis.

**Todd Praised by Mayor**

Mayor La Guardia was watching the Police and Fire Departments baseball game in the Yankee Stadium yesterday when he was informed of the outcome of the Drukman case. He said:

"Hiram Todd has certainly rendered a great public service. Now that it is over I believe that the people of the City of New York and of Brooklyn, particularly, will be well able to size up the situation in Brooklyn.

"Knowing of the conditions prevailing there that were disclosed in the Drukman case and the convictions of today, the people of New York ought to go out and build a monument for great public service to Asa B. Gardner."

The reference was to a former District Attorney of New York County who was removed from office thirty years ago.

No sooner had the court reluctantly discharged the weary jurors than Mr. Todd called newspaper men into his temporary office to hear him read a formal statement indicating that an attempt had been made last Thursday to influence a juror. The juror had reported the matter immediately and had, it was shown, voted for a conviction of all the defendants.

**Court Orders Inquiry**

Justice Rogers directed the prosecutor to begin immediately an inquiry to determine how a note, the contents of which were not disclosed, found its way into the pockets of the juror's suit, which had been sent out to be cleaned. The jurors had been locked up from the opening day of the trial, under constant guard. They were picked from a special panel after three days of exhaustive questioning by attorneys.

The juror to whom the note was sent was said to be Charles Sayles Jr., an insurance broker, who lives at the Towers Hotel, which also was the place where the jury was locked up each night during the trial. His name was not mentioned in Mr. Todd's statement, but other jurors said that he was the man. A telephone call to his room reached a man who said he was Mr. Sayles. He said he "would not discuss that matter," and referred all questions "to the judge."

Mr. Todd's statement, which he would not elaborate, said:

"Yesterday morning, before Judge Rogers charged the jury, he convened counsel for both sides in his chambers and stated that there had been called to his attention an attempt to improperly influence one of the members of the trial jury.

"In substance, Judge Rogers stated that on Thursday morning one of the jurors found an anonymous note in his coat pocket, which note stated an opinion as to the guilt or innocence of the defendants on trial.

"The juror who so found the note

Continued on Page Twenty-one

## Major Sports Results

**Track**—Bill Bonthron sprang a surprise by beating Gene Venzke by a foot in the 1,500-meter run at the semi-final Olympic trials at Cambridge. Both qualified for the final tryouts.

**Yachting**—Robert P. Baruch's new sloop Kirawan won the Bermuda race, which started Monday from Newport. She was one of thirteen finishers reported.

**Racing**—Alfred Gwynne Vanderbilt's Discovery took the Brooklyn Handicap at Aqueduct, beating his stable-mate, Good Gamble, by four lengths. The entry was favored at 2—7.

**Golf**—Alfred Padgham, home-bred pro, captured the British open with a total of 287. Gene Sarazen led the American contingent with 291.

**Tennis**—Bryan M. (Bitsy) Grant of Atlanta routed Vivian McGrath of Australia, 6—3, 6—4, 6—0, to reach the quarter-finals at Wimbledon.

**Baseball**—The Giants triumphed over the Cubs, 11—2. The Yanks downed the Browns, 10—6. Rain prevented the Dodger-Cardinal game.

*(Full details in Section 5.)*

## REICH BACKS MOVE BY NAZIS IN DANZIG

### Foreign Office Newspaper Is Emphatic in Asserting League Control Is Useless.

### ISSUE STUDIED IN GENEVA

### Some Fear Dictatorship Will Be Established—Poles Await Next Step in Free City.

By The Associated Press.

BERLIN, June 27.—The Foreign Office, through its mouthpiece, the Deutsche Diplomatische Korrespondenz, openly backed the Danzig Nazis' independence move tonight.

"A State with many centuries of old traditions and culture such as Danzig does not need a governor or governess," it said in commenting on the Nazi declaration in the Free City of Danzig that League of Nations supervision was "superfluous."

"For this reason," it added, "the expectation must be voiced that the League of Nations henceforth will refrain from inappropriate methods which in the end could only lead to the question of whether the League really sees its task as a furtherance of peace or perhaps the creation of dissension."

**Danzig Sees Reich Moves**

DANZIG, June 27 (AP).—Germany plans further steps soon to return this free area to the Reich, foreign observers predicted tonight following a Nazi independence declaration.

The declaration by Albert Forster, Nazi leader, that the League of Nations and its High Commissioner had become "superfluous" in Danzig affairs caused a sensation when published today. It was published throughout Germany at the same time.

Opposition members regarded the declaration as a trial balloon on the part of Chancellor Adolf Hitler.

Foreign observers said High Commissioner Sean Lester had a mere shadow of political power. This opinion was shared by Opposition leaders.

The Opposition members now pin their hopes on the Polish Government rather than on the League commissioner, it was said. Because of the tenseness of the situation, however, no responsible person, not even Commissioner Lester, would allow himself to be quoted tonight.

[League supervision over Danzig became effective in 1920 and constituted a compromise between Poland's demands for a sea outlet for shipping and the Versailles peace treaty negotiators' fears of placing an essentially German population under another nation's sovereignty.]

Opposition leaders freely admitted that without Polish protection their existence would be precarious. They contended the High Commissioner's intervention was futile during recent riots and brawls. The Opposition leaders said the Polish Government was able to force the Senate to introduce measures guaranteeing peace and security for all inhabitants.

Diplomatic quarters believe the position of Mr. Lester and the League of Nations generally has become precarious. They contend that Great Britain, whose support the Danzig Opposition counted on, is losing interest in Danzig.

Polish circles said their attitude was one of watchful waiting.

**Geneva Debates Problem**

GENEVA, June 27 (AP).—Nazi Germany and Nazi problems in Danzig stirred the anxiety of League of Nations powers today.

Germany's rearmament, informed

Continued on Page Eight

## 4 REPORTED KILLED AS PLANE CRASHES IN LAKE CHAMPLAIN

### 'Good-Will' Craft Plunges Into 300 Feet of Water With 3 Men and a Girl.

### 2 OTHERS FORCED DOWN

### Flight to Canada Is Cancelled, After 29 Craft Set Out Here, Because of Weather.

An airplane crash in which four persons were believed killed, and the forced landing of two other planes, marred the fifth annual flying yesterday of the Roosevelt Field-Montreal good-will flight.

Twenty-nine planes left Roosevelt Field, L. I., between 9 A. M. and 11 A. M. in the air tour, and moved north into extremely bad flying weather, upon which a complete report was not received before the flight started.

Fifteen of the planes were officially grounded at Albany, one was forced down at Westport, N. Y., and one at Pittsfield, Mass., and five found refuge at Burlington, Vt.

The disaster taking four lives occurred several miles from Burlington, when the plane fell into Lake Champlain, more than a mile from the New York shore, at a point where the depth is estimated at more than 300 feet.

Only remnants of the plane, including a part of the wing, from which the identity of the ship was established, had been found last night. State troopers and lake lifeguards were attempting to recover the bodies.

Everett Moniz, a pilot of Richmond Hill, Queens, one of the participants in the informal mass flight to Montreal, who stopped at Albany but later flew on to the scene, made the identification of the plane.

**Reported Victims of Crash**

On the basis of his identification, officials at Roosevelt Field reported the victims of the crash as follows:

FRANK ZAGLIMENE, pilot, 30 years old, of 1,851 Eastern Parkway, Brooklyn.
ERIC ERICKSON, 59-11 Queens Boulevard, Woodside, L. I.
STEPHEN (Steve Kay) ZOZAKIEWICZ, 29-09 Twenty-third Avenue, Astoria, L. I.
KATHERINE ZARLING, 24, of 113 East 32-201 Street, Hollis, Queens.

A plane piloted by Henry Schiebel, who had three passengers, A. G. Dezzary, Mrs. Mary Baudossi and her daughter, Irene Baudossi, was forced down at Pittsfield, Mass. Injuries were reported here not to be serious.

Blinding rain forced down at Westport, N. Y., a plane piloted by Richard Blythe of New York, who had as his passenger Philip Dorrler, also of New York.

Blythe, piloting one of the planes which pushed beyond Albany in the face of threatening weather, was on his course when forced down. The undercarriage of the plane was sheared off when the plane landed. Neither the pilot nor his passenger was seriously injured.

**Boys Tell of Plane's Fall**

The fall of the plane into Lake Champlain was seen by Reginald and Edmond Johnson of Pittsburgh, two boys vacationing on a farm near Charlotte, Vt. The ship came out of the mists shortly after noon and was losing altitude rapidly, they reported. Just before it would

Continued on Page Twenty-nine

## *Roosevelt and Landon To Be Targets for Drys*

By The Associated Press.

CHICAGO, June 27.—D. Leigh Colvin, the Prohibition party's candidate for President, declared today that he would attack Governor Landon as well as President Roosevelt in his Fall campaign.

Mr. Colvin asserted that Kansas, which he called "the premier dry State," had become wet during the Landon administration.

"There's a startling amount of liquor there," he asserted in an interview. "More than at any time since 1880."

That was the year Kansas voted constitutional prohibition.

"I just spent two days in Topeka," Mr. Colvin continued. "There are 244 beer saloons there in a city of 64,000.

"Why, some sections are as bad as the Bowery—six saloons to a block."

He said it was "Governor Landon's associates" who blocked passage in 1935 of a bill forbidding anything stronger than 1½ per cent beer in Kansas.

The Prohibition party's complaint against President Roosevelt, Mr. Colvin explained, is that he sponsored repeal.

## SALVOS OF CHEERS GREET PRESIDENT

### Serried Banks of Humanity on Field Hang on the Words of His Acceptance Speech.

### APPLAUD MANDATE CALL

### Garner Ceremony Speeded to Bring Roosevelt Before Party as Standard-Bearer Again.

By TURNER CATLEDGE
Special to THE NEW YORK TIMES.

FRANKLIN FIELD, PHILADELPHIA, June 27.—Probably the most impressive setting for a notification ceremony in the history of the United States was that witnessed here tonight when President Roosevelt and Vice President Garner were notified by the officials and delegates of the recently adjourned Democratic National Convention that they had been called to carry the party's standard again in the campaign of 1936.

More than 100,000 persons (some put it at 110,000), the largest crowd ever gathered in Franklin Field, exploded into one great cheer when at 9:37 there came the announcement over the loudspeaker system that "your President has arrived." They refrained from the convention practice of marching only because Philadelphia safety officials had requested that they keep their seats.

The light in the demonstration meter to the left of the speakers' stand had reached 100 before the

Continued on Page Twenty-five.

## LEHMAN GETS NEW PLEA

### State Delegates Cite 'Duty' in a Request That He Run Again.

### FIGHT FOR ISSUES ASKED

### 'We Have Not Failed You; Do Not Fail Us,' Unanimous Statement Pleads.

### GOVERNOR STILL SILENT

### Sits as Chairman of Session but Refuses Comment on Move to Draft Him.

By JAMES P. McCAFFREY
Special to THE NEW YORK TIMES.

PHILADELPHIA, June 27.—The New York delegation, assembling for the last time at today's session, went on record unanimously in demanding that Governor Lehman consent to head the State ticket again this Fall.

Asserting that the issue of the coming convention would be centered on President Roosevelt and those aligned with him in "the battle for popular rights," the statement declared that there was no one in the country except the President himself who personified those principles more than Governor Lehman.

The statement said further that Mr. Lehman had "valid reasons" to retire, but it urged him "to disregard his personal inclination and hear the call of duty."

"Governor Lehman, we have not failed you," said the statement; "do not, we ask, fail us."

Nevertheless, Mr. Lehman, who sat through most of today's session as the chairman of the State delegation, declined again to be quoted on the "draft Lehman movement."

**Link State-National Campaigns**

The statement was presented by Herbert Bayard Swope, delegate from the First New York district, and was seconded by Representative Caroline O'Day, delegate-at-large. A large number of the delegates voiced their enthusiasm for the plea.

The statement follows:

"The delegation from New York to the Democratic National Convention, recognizing that the struggle for victory is one and the same in the nation and the State, unanimously adopts the following statement as bespeaking the sentiments of the Democracy of the State and of the country:

"The issue in the coming election is squarely centered upon Franklin D. Roosevelt and those aligned with him in the battle for popular rights.

"There is no individual in all America, next to the President, who better personifies those principles than Herbert Lehman. The four years of his two terms as Governor have been rich in accomplishment. His true sense of social responsibility has risen above party lines.

**Say People Believe in Him**

"The people of New York believe in Herbert Lehman, and they insist upon his remaining in office. With him as their guide, they are safe. Prudent in plan, bold in execution, he has contributed a bright new chapter to the splendid record made by the Democratic Governors since the war.

"Governor Lehman's reelection will be proof of the sound working of our democratic processes.

"The Democratic party of New York enters the campaign serene in the conviction that no political organization has ever had greater right, based on performance, to ask from the voters of the nation and the State a mandate of continuance. The record spells the victory.

"But to make certain that there shall be no misadventure, it is necessary to have our forces, united by a common purpose, led by the same captains. We have just chosen unanimously the national leader; we must be no less fortunate within our State.

**Point to Uncompleted Work**

"Admitting that valid reasons may animate Herbert Lehman in his desire to return to private life, we, his fellow-New Yorkers, proud of his courage and secure in his capacity, entreat him to disregard

Continued on Page Twenty-seven

Buckingham Studios Photo.

RENOMINATED FOR VICE PRESIDENT
John Nance Garner,
from his most recent—and his favorite—photograph

## Text of Roosevelt Address

Special to THE NEW YORK TIMES.

*PHILADELPHIA, June 27.—The text of President Roosevelt's speech of acceptance was as follows:*

Senator Robinson, members of the Democratic convention, my friends:

We meet at a time of great moment to the future of the nation. It is an occasion to be dedicated to the simple and sincere expression of an attitude toward problems, the determination of which will profoundly affect America.

I come not only as the leader of a party—not only as a candidate for high office, but as one upon whom many critical hours have imposed and still impose a grave responsibility.

For the sympathy, help and confidence with which Americans have sustained me in my task I am grateful. For their loyalty I salute the members of our great party, in and out of official life in every part of the Union. I salute those of other parties, especially those in the Congress who on so many occasions put partisanship aside. I thank the Governors of the several States, their Legislatures, their State and local officials who participated unselfishly and regardless of party in our efforts to achieve recovery and destroy abuses. Above all, I thank the millions of Americans who have borne disaster bravely and have dared to smile through the storm.

**Declares Nation Has Conquered Fear**

America will not forget these recent years—will not forget that the rescue was not a mere party task—it was the concern of all of us. In our strength we rose together, rallied our energies together, applied the old rules of common sense, and together survived.

In those days we feared fear. That was why we fought fear. And today, my friends, we have won against the most dangerous of our foes—we have conquered fear.

But I cannot, with candor, tell you that all is well with the world. Clouds of suspicion, tides of ill-will and intolerance gather darkly in many places. In our own land we enjoy, indeed, a fullness of life greater than that of most nations. But the rush of modern civilization itself has raised for us new difficulties, new problems which must be solved if we are to preserve to the United States the political and economic freedom for which Washington and Jefferson planned and fought.

Philadelphia is a good city in which to write American history. This is fitting ground on which to reaffirm the faith of our fathers; to pledge ourselves to restore to the people a wider freedom—to give to 1936 as the founders gave to 1776—an American way of life.

**'Economic Royalists' Carve New Dynasties**

The very word freedom, in itself and of necessity, suggests freedom from some restraining power. In 1776, we sought freedom from the tyranny of a political autocracy—from the eighteenth century royalists who held special privileges from the crown. It was to perpetuate their privilege that they governed without the consent of the governed; that they denied the right of free assembly and free speech; that they restricted the worship of God; that they put the average man's property and the average man's life in pawn to the mercenaries of dynastic power—that they regimented the people.

And so it was to win freedom from the tyranny of political autocracy that the American Revolution was fought. That victory gave the business of governing into the hands of the average man, who won the right with his neighbors to make and order his own

Continued on Page Twenty-five.

## CAMPAIGN ISSUE DEFINED

### The President Avoids All Personalities in His Philadelphia Speech.

### FIGHT FOR FREEDOM SEEN

### Battle Today Is Like That of 1776, He Says, With New Set of 'Royalists' in Power.

### GARNER RENEWS PLEDGE

### Renominated by Acclamation, Vice President Vows His Fealty to New Deal.

By ARTHUR KROCK
Special to THE NEW YORK TIMES.

FRANKLIN FIELD, PHILADELPHIA, June 27.—Under a cloud-veiled moon, in skies suddenly cleared of rain, to a mass of more than 100,000 people gathered in the stadium of the University of Pennsylvania, and by radio to unnumbered millions all over the nation and world, Franklin Delano Roosevelt tonight accepted the renomination of the Democratic party for President of the United States and, avoiding personalities of any description, defined the issue of this campaign as it appears to him.

The President said that, as the fathers of the Republic had achieved political freedom from the eighteenth-century royalists, so it was the function of those who stand with him in this campaign to establish the economic freedom they also sought to establish, and which was lost in the industrial and corporate growth of the nineteenth and twentieth centuries.

Vice President John N. Garner of Texas, in this same place, renewed his pledge of allegiance to the President, made four years ago, and added a vow of fealty to the New Deal. The President was notified of his renomination by Senator Robinson of Arkansas, permanent chairman of the Democratic National Convention that closed today. Senator Harrison of Mississippi acted as proxy for Senator Barkley of Kentucky, temporary chairman, whose function it was to notify the Vice President, but who sailed for Europe on official business today.

**Crowd Roars Its Enthusiasm**

The arrival of the President in the stadium was greeted by a real demonstration, as distinguished from the artificial efforts of conventions. One hundred thousand people rose and roared unmistakable acclaim as Mr. Roosevelt entered the platform on the arm of his eldest son and clasped the hand of Vice President Garner while "The Star-Spangled Banner" was sung.

Thunderous cheer after cheer rolled out as the President finished, and, led by his mother, members of his family gathered about him. He mopped his brow, drank copiously of ice water and then stood waving his clasped hands above his head, while the tumult continued and the band played. Before Mr. Roosevelt left the stand on the arm of his son, James—as he entered—he waited for "Auld Lang Syne," and cheered its last echoes with the crowd. It was a personal triumph of the kind given to few men.

If the high tenor of his speech can be taken as an indication of what sort of campaign the President will conduct, Postmaster General Farley's prediction of the "dirtiest" contest of recent times will not be realized, so far as the chief protagonists of the parties are concerned, for Governor Alf M. Landon has implied the same tactics.

**For Those Who Weary of Struggle**

The only conceivable reference to Alfred E. Smith and other Democrats who have attacked him that the President made was when he said that some had grown weary of the struggle and relinquished their hope of democracy "for the illusion of a living." The crowd roared approval.

Informed by Senator Robinson that the administration "has vindicated the faith of plain people in the processes of democracy," and confounded those who demanded a dictatorship in 1933, the President took up this major theme, which is also sounded in the Philadelphia platform.

The following is a summary of the President's speech, which was more of a rededication of the New

Continued on Page Twenty-five

## *Last Jeffersonian Expires With Convention; Godfrey Gloom a Victim of Modern Devices*

By ELMER DAVIS
Special to THE NEW YORK TIMES.

PHILADELPHIA, June 27.—Godfrey G. Gloom, the aged Jeffersonian from Amity, Ind., died this evening as a result of injuries sustained when he was crossing a street in West Philadelphia on his way to Franklin Field.

Mr. Gloom had leaped, with an agility hardly to be expected in one of his years, out of the way of a car carrying a radio commentator, only to be knocked headlong by a motor cycle bearing the plates of a newspaper photographer. Stunned by the impact, Mr. Gloom was carried by passers-by to the sidewalk, where, before the arrival of the ambulance, he recovered consciousness and lifted himself on one elbow.

"My time has come," said the veteran, articulating with some difficulty. "But when, on visits to my granddaughter in New York I used to be taken to the opera, I observed that the tenor, even though mortally wounded, was always able to lift himself on one elbow and deliver his self of some farewell remarks.

"And while in my younger days I sang bass in the church choir, I purpose as my final gesture to show that I am as good a man as any German or Italian tenor."

"It is entirely fitting," Mr. Gloom pursued, "that I should meet my end through the agency of those gadgets of modern progress, the radio and newspaper photography. It is these more than anything else that have ruined what was the most cherished pastime of my declining years, attendance at national conventions.

"Whatever happens, whether on the rostrum or at some statesman's press conference, the newspaper photographers are always down there in front, shoving other people out of the way, snapping their flashlights in everybody's eyes, throwing their used flash bulbs under your feet, and in general so comporting themselves that you figure that they might as well tell the delegates, reporters and spectators to stay at home and let the photographers hold a national convention all by themselves, where they could have a good time taking one another's pictures.

"As for the radio, its demoralizing effect on convention oratory is well known. If it had taken the roaring out of oratory it could well be commended, but it has merely taken out the spontaneity and left all the roars in, with the sole qualification that the roarer has to take the proper stance so that he can roar into the microphone.

"Nowadays, if you attend a con-

Continued on Page Twenty-eight

"All the News That's Fit to Print."

# The New York Times.

LATE CITY EDITION
Partly cloudy, possibly scattered showers today. Tomorrow showers and cooler.
Temperatures Yesterday—Max., 84; Min., 72

Section 1

Copyright, 1936, by The New York Times Company.

VOL. LXXXV....No. 28,694. Entered as Second-Class Matter, Postoffice, New York, N. Y. NEW YORK, SUNDAY, AUGUST 16, 1936. Including Rotogravure Picture, Magazine and Book Review. P TEN CENTS | TWELVE CENTS Beyond 200 Miles Except in 7th and 8th Postal Zones.

# 733 EXECUTED IN MADRID, 7,000 OTHERS IN CITY SEIZED; REBELS NEAR PORT OF IRUN

## LEMKE ENDORSED BY COUGHLINITES; VOTE IS 8,152 TO 1

### Lone Dissenter Stirs Rumpus, and Police Protect Him as He Explains Stand.

### HE HINTS AT HEARST LINK

### Priest Scoffs at This and Tells of Fight on Liberty League and du Ponts.

### HE IS ELECTED PRESIDENT

### Constitution and Platform Are Adopted at Cleveland—Smith and Dr. Townsend Speak.

*Text of Coughlin convention's platform is printed on Page 27.*

By F. RAYMOND DANIELL
Special to THE NEW YORK TIMES.

CLEVELAND, Aug. 15.—The National Union for Social Justice in convention assembled voted 8,152 to 1 today to get behind the third party candidacies of William Lemke and Thomas C. O'Brien, but on the advice of the Rev. Charles E. Coughlin, their omnipotent leader, the delegates turned their backs unanimously on proposals that they endorse the Union party or its platform.

Even the almost insignificant division of opinion reflected in the vote for endorsement of Mr. Lemke and Mr. O'Brien, Presidential and Vice Presidential candidates respectively of the Union party, provoked a minor rumpus in this amazingly unanimous gathering of the followers of a potent radio voice.

John O'Donnell an alternate from Pittsburgh who turned out to be the lone "No" man of this convention and a figure almost unique in this Presidential year of one-man conventions, was seized by the local constabulary and hauled upon the platform to explain himself to Father Coughlin, who waived the right of cross-examination and threw the culprit to the delegates.

**Dissenter Scores Hearst**

Blinking a little from the glare of flashlights, Mr. O'Donnell took a stance before the microphones and allowed that he yielded to no man in his admiration for Father Coughlin and his loyalty to the radio priest's sixteen points of social justice. What burned him up, he told the booing delegates, was to see them become victims of "mob psychology," and "humbly and ignorantly serve the purposes of the Liberty League and William Randolph Hearst."

Charles J. Madden, who hails from the same Pennsylvania Congressional district as Mr. O'Donnell, popped onto the platform when the latter's three minutes expired, to render public apology for having among his delegation "one of Jim Farley's stooges," and to proclaim that Pennsylvania's Thirty-third district was "100 per cent behind the National Union and Father Coughlin," whom he called a worthy successor to Washington, Lincoln and Jefferson.

All this discussion called, of course, for a few words from Father Coughlin, who was seemingly more pleased than irked by the turn events had taken. He delivered a renunciation of Mr. Hearst and the Liberty League into the microphones to the intense pleasure of the delegates out front, who were being prepared for the rhetorical talents of Dr. Francis E. Townsend and the Rev. Gerald L. K. Smith of Louisiana, the latter the peer of the priest of Royal Oak, Mich., in arousing an audience.

**Smith Fears Communist Plot**

The Rev. Mr. Smith, who lays claim to the following of Share-the Wealthers that Huey Long enlisted, arrived here this afternoon complaining about a Communist plot to kill him. If he had his way, he said, he would outlaw the Communists, suppress their publications and forbid them to hold meetings in the United States. He declared the way they plotted and carried on under the protection of the Constitution was terrible.

Hobnobbing with the Rev. Mr. Smith and his patron, Dr. Townsend of $200-a-month pension fame, was Eugene Daniell of Boston, the young man who once showed his disapproval of the President and the nation's financial policies by sending a pop bomb through the mails and putting a stench bomb in the ventilating system of the New York Stock Exchange.

The Bostonian did not commit himself, but his presence here led to the conclusion that he had decided to throw himself also behind the Lemke candidacy.

It was nearly 7 P. M. before Dr. Townsend, who is here in connection with a lawsuit over the finances of his troubled organization,

Continued on Page Twenty-seven

## Great Crowds Acclaim Roosevelt On Inspection Tour in Pennsylvania

### Police Batter Way Through Throngs Lining 30-Mile Drive in Flood Area—Reception Milder in Binghamton Region, Where He Allocates $2,568,000 for Dam Work.

By CHARLES W. HURD
Special to THE NEW YORK TIMES.

WILKES-BARRE, Pa., Aug. 15.—President Roosevelt's three-day trip through Pennsylvania, Ohio and New York on a "non-political" tour of regions which were stricken with serious floods last March ended in Northeastern Pennsylvania this afternoon with one of the most impressive popular demonstrations that has marked his administration.

Solid ranks of persons cheered him through Scranton and Wilkes-Barre and the succession of towns between which run together in a continuous line, broke through police lines to get a closer view of him and repeatedly choked wide thoroughfares in congested areas of these cities, where motorcycle police had to use bodily force to open lanes through which the official procession of automobiles could pass.

Some members of the President's party estimated the number of persons who cheered the President as exceeding 500,000, while more conservative persons cut this figure in half. But the crowds, close-packed in cities and unusually large in the towns, lined a route of thirty miles over which the President drove.

It was impossible to determine how much political support was indicated in the demonstration, or how much of it represented only mass curiosity, but persons of all ages and types literally fought good-naturedly to get as close to the President as possible, in a manner which those who travel habitually with Presidents have seldom seen before. They not only applauded but shouted and whistled and greeted Mr. Roosevelt by name in a manner that left even the optimistic Democratic leaders of Pennsylvania astounded.

The demonstration completely dwarfed the announced purpose of the President's visit here, to "see with his own eyes" the flood problem that faces this city and the Susquehanna Valley.

It supplied the greatest possible contrast with a visit this morning to Binghamton, N. Y., at the head of the Susquehanna watershed and

Continued on Page Twenty-six

## PEEK IN FARM PLEA 'INDICTS' NEW DEAL

### Agriculture Has Lost Ground to Industry Under Its Policies, He Asserts.

### ASKS CURB ON IMPORTS

### Roosevelt's Ex-Adviser in Radio Talk for Grange Demands Shift in Tariff Aims.

*The text of Mr. Peek's address is printed on Page 29.*

Special to THE NEW YORK TIMES.

CHICAGO, Aug. 15.—The New Deal farm program was indicted on four counts today by George N. Peek, who charged that under the administration's operations "agriculture has definitely lost ground in its fight for equality with industry."

Mr. Peek, who was formerly foreign trade adviser to President Roosevelt, spoke over a radio hookup sponsored by the National Grange. He asserted that Secretary Wallace had refused to speak on the same program, saying that he was talking on a nonpartisan basis while the Secretary preferred to treat the farm problem on a partisan basis.

Agriculture, under the New Deal, he asserted, "has definitely lost ground in its fight for equality with industry."

His first "count" against the New Dealers is that they gave no adequate consideration to the fact that "the laws of nature transcend the laws of men."

By controlling the farmer's individual initiative they thought they could control his production, he said.

**Soil Act Held Political Move**

The program of "regimented production," Mr. Peek said, was checked only for a short time by the Supreme Court's AAA decision and the subsequent repeal of the "clearly unconstitutional" potato, tobacco and cotton acts.

"The so-called Soil Conservation Bill was hastily patched up and railroaded through Congress," he went on. "The great principle of soil conservation was thus prostituted to serve the political ends of an administration determined to evade the decision of the Supreme Court.

"Even the drought of 1934 and the black rust in the Spring wheat belt in 1935 taught New Dealers nothing. If they learn anything in 1936 it will not be from the drought but from the farm vote at the polls."

The second "count" in Mr. Peek's indictment is that the administration's "prates" about the loss of foreign markets on one hand, ignoring the fact that other nations have found ways to trade among themselves, while on the other hand "responsible administration officials have refused to trade and have prevented important sales of farm products to foreign nations."

**Foreign Credit Policy Assailed**

Mr. Peek's third and fourth "counts" were based on imports and exports of farm products and the foreign credits involved. He asserted that the New Dealers had attempted to deceive the farmer by "misleading" language on export increases, while ignoring the extent and effect of competitive farm imports.

Asserting that the administration

Continued on Page Twenty-nine

## LANDON WIDENS SPEAKING PLANS

### He Will Make 15 Rear-Platform Talks on Return Trip From the East.

### SPECIAL TRAIN ASSEMBLED

### Important Conferences With Party Leaders Along the Way Will Mark His Journey.

By JAMES A. HAGERTY
Special to THE NEW YORK TIMES.

ESTES PARK, Col., Aug. 15.—Governor Landon will make eleven rear platform appearances in Illinois and four in Missouri on his return from Buffalo on Aug. 27, it became known today when the itinerary for his trip was made public.

All of the stops will be for three minutes each, except the one in Springfield, Ill., which will be for forty minutes, long enough for him to make a half hour speech or visit the tomb of Abraham Lincoln, if the Governor should decide to do so.

The Presidential candidate's party is scheduled to return to Topeka at 11:45 P. M., Aug. 27. Governor Landon will leave Buffalo an hour after completing his speech there on the night of Aug. 26. No stops will be made between Buffalo and Chicago, except for railroad operating purposes.

Governor Landon's first stop in Illinois will be at Joliet at 9 A. M. Other Illinois cities at which he will make appearances are Dwight, Pontiac, Bloomington, Lincoln, Springfield, Virden, Carlinville, Alton, Granite City and East St. Louis. The Missouri stops will be at Washington, Jefferson City, Sedalia and Warrensburg.

Cars for the special train on which the candidate and his party will travel were being assembled today at Denver. It will be an eight-car train—a private car for Governor Landon with sleeping quarters for twelve persons, two compartment cars, two sleeping cars, a lounge car, a dining car and a baggage car.

The private car has been equipped with loud-speakers and special lights for the news reel photographers.

Besides his three main speeches at his birthplace at West Middlesex, Pa., Chautauqua and Buffalo and his rear platform appearances, Governor Landon will hold an important series of conferences on his Eastern trip.

When the train leaves Denver Thursday, it will have on board Charles Enos, Republican State Chairman, and fifty leading Colorado Republicans, who will call on Governor Landon when he boards the train at La Salle and continue with him to Julesburg, near the State line.

At North Platte, Hugh A. Bullen, national committeeman for Nebraska; former Representative Robert Simmons, candidate for Senator, and other party leaders will meet the train and continue with the Governor to Omaha, where the latter will pass the night. A delegation of Iowa Republicans will board the train at Council Bluffs the following day and an Illinois delegation will meet the Governor at Clinton, Iowa, and continue on the train to Chicago.

John D. M. Hamilton, national chairman, is expected to join the party at Omaha and participate in

Continued on Page Twenty-eight

## MAYOR ORDERS CUT IN SHERIFFS' COSTS; DENOUNCES 'SPOILS'

### Instructs Budget Director to Slash Officials' Requests—Scores Pleas for Rises.

### WOULD ABOLISH THE JOBS

### Acting on Blanshard Report Charging Political Waste, He Urges Consolidation.

Declaring that the expenditures of the Sheriffs' offices in the five counties were almost entirely waste, Mayor La Guardia asked Budget Director Leo J. McDermott yesterday to wield the pruning knife on their 1937 budget requests.

The Mayor based his recommendations on a report made to him yesterday by Paul Blanshard, Commissioner of Accounts, covering a nineteen-month survey of the offices. Mr. Blanshard found the Sheriffs' offices were grossly overmanned; that they were a haven for political plum-pickers, and that their operation constituted a heavy expense on the city.

The report, Mr. Blanshard said, was factual only, adding that it was the task of the Municipal Assembly to reorganize county government in line with the recent constitutional amendment.

In a foreword to the Blanshard report, the Mayor said the five county governments had outlived their usefulness and had become an annoying burden to the taxpayers. Reform of county government was one of his major objectives, he declared.

**Hopes for Consolidation**

With a constitutional amendment in effect permitting abolition of all county offices except those of judges, District Attorneys and County Clerks, the Mayor said he hoped the political leaders of all groups would get together on a constructive program of consolidation.

The Municipal Assembly has already named for this work a committee consisting of representatives of both the Board of Estimate and the Board of Aldermen. Since holding its organization meeting, the Mayor was informed, the committee has made no progress with its task.

Peter J. McGuinness, Sheriff of Kings County, bore the brunt of the Mayor's wrath, though the Mayor is known to like him personally. Sheriff Daniel E. Finn of New York County was joined with Mr. McGuinness in the report as an outstanding example of official waste and extravagance.

**Mayor Assails Requests**

In his letter to the Budget Director, Mayor La Guardia said:

"You have recently received from several Sheriffs requests for substantial increases in their budgets for the year 1937. In considering these requests it is only right that you should have all official information available concerning the practices prevailing in the Sheriffs' offices.

"You will note that this study shows that the Sheriffs' offices of the five counties are 'grossly overmanned and expensively operated.' The Commissioner of Accounts and his special counsel have reached the conclusion after a careful analysis of the operations of these offices that a large part of the $800,000 spent upon them is waste.

"In the light of these findings, the applications for increased salaries for the various political ap-

Continued on Page Fifteen

## EX-SOVIET LEADERS ARE LIKELY TO DIE FOR 'TERROR PLOT'

### Zinovieff and Kameneff Are Expected to Be First 'Old Bolsheviki' Executed.

### TROTSKY SCORES CHARGE

### Offers to Testify at Inquiry to Prove Innocence—Wants a Board to Go to Russia.

By HAROLD DENNY
Special Cable to THE NEW YORK TIMES.

MOSCOW, Aug. 15.—The death penalty for Gregory Zinovieff, Leon Kameneff and the fourteen others named in the charges of a Trotskyist plot to kill Joseph Stalin and other Soviet leaders was demanded today in violently worded resolutions adopted by factory meetings, workers' clubs and Soviet organizations in general.

These, together with an editorial declaration by Pravda that no mercy must be shown to "enemies who try to rob the people of their leaders," make it a virtual certainty that this fate is in store for the once honored members of the Soviet oligarchy. Russians are convinced the accused will be found guilty of the sensational charges made public last night.

**Only One Penalty Seen**

In the opinion of Russians an offense involving the life of Stalin can have but one penalty. "The law knows only one measure for crimes committed by the Trotsky-Zinovieff gang," said Pravda significantly.

Thus in all probability there will be the unprecedented spectacle of the Communist State taking the lives of men who were once high among its rulers—Zinovieff, head of the Communist International's world revolutionary activity through the stormiest years, and Kameneff, who helped to steer the Soviet ship of State before Stalin forged to the top and took command.

Until now the Soviet government has never executed old "Bolsheviki," although it has demoted, disgraced, exiled and even imprisoned many of them.

The trial beginning Wednesday, which is expected to be dramatic, will fall into two parts. First, it will be a virtual retrial of Zinovieff and Kameneff and associates, who were convicted as the creators of a counter-revolutionary center following the assassination of Sergei Kiroff, Leningrad Communist leader, in December, 1934.

They were charged with planting counter-revolutionary ideas that inspired a plot to assassinate Soviet leaders and with thus being morally responsible, although they were not charged with having consciously instigated the plot. Zinovieff and Kameneff made abject confessions of these charges.

Now, however, they are charged with the vastly more serious offense of having at Leon Trotsky's behest plotted the assassination of Kiroff and of Stalin and other leaders. So far as is known there is no accusation that Zinovieff and Kameneff hatched a new plot while in prison. The new defendants, including five said to have been sent into Russia from abroad, are accused of a new plot, however.

Although there is no additional official information there is a widespread rumor that Nov. 6 had been set as the day for assassination of

Continued on Page Ten

## Major Sports Yesterday

**OLYMPIC GAMES**

Both the men's and women's team swimming championships were captured by the United States as the aquatic program came to an end. Under the unofficial scoring system, the American men amassed 83 points to 77 for the second-place Japanese, who won the title at the last Olympics, and the American women finished with 55 points to 52½ for the Netherlands squad, which was the runner-up. Marshall Wayne of Miami triumphed in the platform event to give the United States a sweep in the four diving contests.

**TRACK AND FIELD**

Four world marks were smashed as the United States Olympians routed the British Empire's stars, 11 to 3, before 90,000 at White City Stadium in London. A feature was the four-mile relay performance of Charles Hornbostel, Gene Venzke, Archie San Romani and Glenn Cunningham, who scored in the record time of 17:17.2.

**BASEBALL**

By defeating the Phillies, 4—1, while the Cardinals lost to the Pirates, 7—1, the Giants advanced to within a game and a half of the league-leading St. Louis team. The New Yorkers also cut to one game the advantage of the second-place Cubs, who were beaten by the Reds, 5—4. The Dodgers turned back the Bees, 6—2, and the Yankees overwhelmed the Athletics, 16—2.

**RACING**

William Woodward's Granville bolstered his claim to the 3-year-old championship, winning the $19,700 Travers Stakes by a head through the mud at Saratoga.

**GOLF**

Miss Jean Bauer of Providence took the women's New York State title, beating Miss Betsy MacLeod of Buffalo in the final, 4 and 3. Willie Turnesa of Fairview downed Charles H. Mayo Jr. of Lido, 2 and 1, to win the Green Meadow invitation tourney.

*(Complete Details of These and Other Sports Events in Section 5.)*

## LOYALISTS LOSE IN NORTH

### Insurgent Column Is on Outskirts of Irun After an Earlier Setback.

### STORM HIDES ATTACKERS

### Residents Flee as Men and Women Leftists Retreat to Barricades in City.

### AIR RAID KILLS ONE GIRL

### Santander Is Said to Have 1,200 Prisoners on Ships Loaded With Dynamite.

By The Associated Press.

HENDAYE, France, Aug. 15.—Advancing Spanish Rebels tonight occupied Endarlaza, the gateway to the northern Spanish city of Irun, after a day's fighting. They stopped, however, before the town of Behoria on the outskirts of Irun.

Government forces, battling desperately in the northern mountains, sent an armored train to cut off the stream of refugees going toward France. Hundreds crossed the international bridge into this French border city as the Insurgents pushed toward Irun.

The Rebel campaign to smash government resistance around Irun culminated in a drive by 1,500 Rebels. At least fifty were killed and 100 were reported wounded on both sides.

Some of a group of forty-two refugees who reached here aboard the Italian freighter Giorgio Ohlsen said many casualties were suffered in the Loyalist-held city of Gijon which Rebels bombarded. They related reports that Leftists at Gijon had shot great numbers of suspected Rightists in prison.

**Loyalists Gain at First**

The tide of battle swung in favor of the government forces for a while this morning when the insurgents were driven back while their airplanes dropped bombs inside Irun.

The second Rebel attack was launched during the evening under cover of a heavy thunderstorm. The Leftists were routed from the gorge at Endarlaza Pass.

The Loyalists fled from the positions gained earlier with Rebel infantry pursuing them down the highway along the Bidassoa River. Government leaders attempted a counter-attack on the outskirts of Behobia but they were driven back.

While men and women members of the Popular Front militia waited at street barricades constructed weeks ago other inhabitants gathered their possessions and fled.

Some fugitives hurried westward toward San Sebastian, where the Leftists were fighting off a Rebel attack on Renteria. Others sought safety by crossing the international bridge into France. Frontier police, aided by Mobile Guards who had been posted on the border in anticipation of such a rout, permitted only a few hundred to cross.

The French police said the fleeing Spaniards would have temporary refuge in France provided they remained south of Bordeaux.

**Fight on Six-Mile Front**

By The Associated Press.

BIRATOU, Franco-Spanish Frontier, Aug. 15.—Loyalists were successful early today in holding back Rebels who fought for five hours on a six-mile front to capture Irun.

The government forts in the northern sector, Guadalupe, San Marcos and San Marcia, drove back the Rebels with heavy artillery fire.

Loyalist infantry followed the fleeing Fascists, opened machine gun fire and took up strong positions in the hills. During the advance Fascists were within two and one-half miles of Irun.

Under cover of a barrage laid down by their artillery, 3,000 Rebels, mostly volunteers, massed on a road leading into Irun only to meet with a withering fire from government forts. They were beaten back, suffering heavy losses.

The old government fort and munitions dump at Piña de Aya, southeast of the shell-torn town of Oyarzun, was blown up by the

Continued on Page Two



## Most Envoys to Madrid Decide to Remain There

By The Associated Press.

MADRID, Aug. 15.—The diplomatic corps conferred here today and most of the envoys decided to continue operations of embassies and legations.

The United States, British and French embassies indicated they had no immediate intentions to depart but it was said the German embassy might be closed.

The German diplomats were busy evacuating their nationals and indicated that when this was done they would depart, leaving about eighty Germans in Madrid.

The Italian Ambassador has permission to close the embassy when he considers it necessary but has reached no decision.

## BRITONS WARNED ON SPANISH TRADE

### Foreign Office Frowns Upon Dealings With Either Side in the Civil War.

### NEUTRALITY DEADLOCKED

### French Unable to Get Germany and Italy to Cooperate on Non-Intervention Plan.

By CHARLES A. SELDEN
Wireless to THE NEW YORK TIMES.

LONDON, Aug. 15.—The example set by President Roosevelt in cautioning American citizens that their dealings with belligerents in the Ethiopian war would be at their own risk was followed today by the British Government with reference to citizens of this country and the Spanish civil war.

In an official communiqué of the Foreign Office concerning the proposed non-intervention agreement and the export of munitions, there is the following warning:

"British subjects who assist either side in Spain by land, sea or air not only are running grave risks for themselves, but are rendering it more difficult to arrive at proposed agreements. They must not expect to receive any assistance or support whatever in the difficulties which they may meet with during an such enterprises which run counter to the object which His Majesty's Government is seeking to obtain."

The above warning was issued after Foreign Secretary Anthony Eden, who is still in the country, had given his approval by telephone.

It was also announced at the Foreign Office today that at a conference in Paris this afternoon between Foreign Secretary Yvon Delbos and the British Ambassador, Sir George Clerk, the two governments had reached a complete accord on details of the non-intervention agreement which the two governments have accepted in principle. But it was said that they have not yet given any definite promise of adherence.

At the moment the Foreign Office was issuing an appeal to Britain not to assist either side in the Spanish civil war three more airplanes left Croydon for Spain.

They were bound for Barcelona. They carried sufficient fuel to reach there non-stop so as to avoid landing in France.

**Text of the Communiqué**

The text of the the Foreign Office communiqué follows:

His Majesty's Government have for their part declared their willingness when a general agreement is reached to prohibit the export of arms to either side, and that they will also take every measure open to them to prevent the supply of civil aircraft.

It is hoped that an agreement of other governments to this effect will be obtained in the very near future.

In the meantime, no licenses have been issued since the commencement of the present troubles in Spain for the export to that country of arms or munitions under the arms export prohibition orders of 1931; and it should be realized that maintenance of a strict, impartial attitude of non-intervention is essential if any happy events in Spain are to be prevented from having serious repercussions elsewhere.

British subjects who assist either side in Spain by land, sea or air are not only running grave risks for themselves but are rendering it more difficult to arrive at a proposed agreement, whatever

Continued on Page Two

## RED MILITIA IS ACCUSED

### Rightists Taken in Night to Park to Be Killed by the Leftists.

### MANY NOTABLES MISSING

### Bodies of Slain Are Dumped From Trucks Into Big Pits Without Identification.

### ALL CLERGY ARE IN HIDING

### Hundreds of Priests Believed to Have Been Shot Since Church Fires July 19.

Wireless to THE NEW YORK TIMES.

MADRID, Aug. 12 (Delayed; Uncensored).—Leftist militiamen executed 733 priests, Rightists, Royalists and avowed Fascists in the first three weeks of the civil war, according to information obtained by the writer from doctors, from wives of Monarchists and Right Wing Republicans and other fairly reliable sources.

These men were removed from their homes by militiamen in the middle of the night and taken to their deaths in the Casa de Campo, a vast park on the outskirts of Madrid, although Premier José Giral, a mild-mannered little apothecary and close friend and President Manuel Azaña's close friend, said there had been no wholesale slaughter of Conservatives in Madrid as there had been in Barcelona.

**Curb on Militia Stressed**

"It is possible," said Premier Giral, "that there have been some excesses, for it must be remembered we are living in exceptional circumstances. But militiamen are forbidden to arrest private citizens unless they are accompanied by a policeman, and this rule is being enforced.

"People are arrested usually on suspicion of activities against the State. If nothing can be proved against them they are released. If any charges are brought against them they appear before the normal emergency courts, which function whenever constitutional guarantees are suspended."

It has been officially admitted that 7,000 persons were arrested in Madrid in the three weeks ended Aug. 9.

Emiliano Iglesias, former Ambassador to Mexico and right-hand man of former Premier Alejandro Lerroux, whose Radical party is Spain's oldest republican party, was arrested with his wife by proletarian militiamen in the Palace Hotel. Their names, which are the only journals published in the capital.

**Couple Reported Slain**

It is rumored that Mr. Iglesias and his wife were executed by Red vigilantes in the Casa de Campo instead of being taken to prison. All the Rightist prisoners are held incomunicado so it is impossible to confirm or deny this rumor.

Among those who disappeared, whose families and friends mourn them as dead, was José María Carretero, a well-known Royalist writer and former King Alfonso's close friend, who under the pen name of El Caballero Audaz wrote a book "Was Alfonso XIII a Good King?" and a long series of articles discussing the republic's failure from the Monarchist viewpoint.

Others missing are Marquis de la Torrencilla, Francisco Alvial, a son of Marquis de la Frontera, and Domingo Ortega, a celebrated matador with Rightist sympathies.

It is difficult to give an approximate number of those slain in the Casa de Campo. A Red Cross doctor said the bodies picked up in what used to be Madrid's private royal park were piled into trucks at night to be used for hauling coal and sand and dumped into big pits in the municipal cemetery. No effort at identification was made before these mass burials.

The trucks are the type used in construction work with mechanism for raising the forward end and tilting the contents. Thus the bodies rolled out like sand and gravel into the common graves, without coffins.

**2,000 Killed in Barracks**

On July 19 and 20, when the militiamen stormed the Montana and Carabanchel barracks in Madrid, at least 2,000 were killed, according to reliable Red Cross workers. After a

Continued on Page Three

"All the News That's Fit to Print."

# The New York Times.

LATE CITY EDITION
Partly cloudy and warmer today.
Tomorrow cloudy with little change in temperature.
Temperatures Yesterday—Max., [illegible]; Min., [illegible]



VOL. LXXXVI.....No. 28,768. | Entered as Second-Class Matter, Postoffice, New York, N. Y. | NEW YORK, THURSDAY, OCTOBER 29, 1936. | PP | TWO CENTS in New York City. | THREE CENTS Within 200 Miles. | FOUR CENTS Elsewhere Except in 7th and 8th Postal Zones.

# CITY THRONGS CHEER ROOSEVELT AND LANDON AS THEY OPEN FINAL BATTLE FOR THE EAST; REPUBLICAN CANDIDATE GREETED BY SMITH

## NEUTRALS ABSOLVE ROME AND LISBON OF ARMING REBELS

### Russia Dissents From Decision of London Committee but Continues as Member.

### FACES ITALIAN CHARGES

### Rome's Envoy Lists Twenty Alleged Violations of 'Hands-Off' Pact by Soviet.

### MADRID DRAWS IN TROOPS

### Main Army Recalled for Stand in Capital, Rebel Fliers Find—Rightist Air Bases Raided.

By FREDERICK T. BIRCHALL
Special Cable to THE NEW YORK TIMES.

LONDON, Oct. 28.—For almost six hours the International Committee for the Application of the Non-intervention Agreement on Spain wrangled again today and with scant results. Russia alone dissenting, the committee exonerated Portugal and Italy of the charges against them, holding the charges "unproved."

The committee was silent about the charges against Russia, but it presented to the Soviet Union new charges made by Italy, with a request for "observations" on them.

With this mild distribution of whitewash the committee exhausted itself, and as if in despair of accomplishing anything real it will not attempt further action for the present. However, despite all threats of retirement, no power has left the committee.

**Will Meet Next Week**

It will meet again a week hence, and its subcommittee will meet next Friday. Before then Madrid will probably have fallen and the position will be clearer. Meantime the committee will do nothing.

In today's meeting Ivan M. Maisky, Soviet Ambassador to London, submitted a reply to the request for elucidation of Russia's declaration that she would not be bound by the non-intervention agreement to any further extent than other governments. The reply was almost as ambiguous as the previous document.

It was, in effect, that the violation of obligations by even a single participant in the agreement relieved the other participants of their obligations. Mr. Maisky's reply said the Soviet Government was convinced that after the agreement had come into effect the governments sympathizing with the Spanish Rebels had continued abundantly to supply them with war materials. The proceedings of the committee had convinced the Soviet Government, the reply continued, that there were now no guarantees against further supply of these war materials.

"In these circumstances," Mr. Maisky stated, "the Soviet Government is of the opinion that until such guarantees are created and effective control over the strict fulfilment of obligations is established, those governments who consider supplying the legitimate Spanish Government as conforming with international law, order and justice are morally entitled not to consider themselves more bound by the agreement than those governments who supply the Rebels in contravention of the agreement."

Mr. Maisky then proceeded to renew and argue his previous proposal for control of Portuguese frontier ports and, in addition, Spanish ports and borders, including "points along the frontier not occupied by the Rebels, provided the consent of the Spanish Government is obtained."

**Italy Accuses Russia**

The Soviet representative wanted discussion of this proposal to begin immediately, but he did not get his wish. Dino Grandi, Italian Ambassador to London, presented a note making twenty new allegations that Russia had supplied arms to the Madrid Government. Fifteen of the allegations purported to give details of the loading of war material destined for Spain at Black Sea ports.

Portugal contended Great Britain had broken the rules of procedure by submitting Madrid's complaints to the committee before satisfying itself that these were based on satisfactory evidence. The Earl of Plymouth, chairman of the committee, defended himself on this charge and declared it unfounded.

The Portuguese representative submitted two notes, the first dealing with this charge, the second indignantly denying the Russian allegations and including counter-

Continued on Page Three



## Bad Scenario Helps Send Soviet Film Men to Jail

By The Associated Press.

MOSCOW, Oct. 28.—Three executives who "went Hollywood" in Russia were sentenced to labor camps today. The men, former executives of the Eastern Film Trust, were convicted of frittering away State money for the production of movies.

The manager was sentenced to serve four years, the director to two years and a bookkeeper to one. They were charged with purchasing a bad scenario, countenancing excessive production expense and with wasting money searching for talent.

During their trial it was testified that out of forty employes of the movie company two were Trotskyists, six thieves, one a murderer and two embezzlers.

## GOERING DEFIANT OF 'FOREIGN FIST'

### Plan to Make Third Reich Self-Sufficient Forced on Her by Powers, He Tells Rally.

### HOLDS COLONIES 'STOLEN'

### Economic Leader Utters Dire Threats Against All Those Impeding His Program.

By OTTO D. TOLISCHUS
Wireless to THE NEW YORK TIMES.

BERLIN, Oct. 28.—What was described as the opening gun in the execution of Chancellor Adolf Hitler's second Four-Year Plan was fired by Col. Gen. Hermann Goering tonight in an impassioned speech in the Sportpalast. He appealed to the entire German people to work together in the common cause even at the price of temporary sacrifices and uttered dire threats against all daring to interfere with the new aim.

The first Four-Year Plan, General Goering said, achieved Germany's armament freedom, created a new German army and restored Germany to the rank of a big power, besides abolishing unemployment and saving agriculture from ruin. The second Four-Year Plan, he said, must achieve Germany's economic independence and his special task, he explained, was to coordinate all the forces in a common cause.

General Goering paid, significantly enough, equal tribute to both Dr. Hjalmar Schacht, head of the Reichsbank, and Dr. Schacht's opponent, Wilhelm Keppler, Hitler's economic adviser, for what has been achieved so far. But he emphasized that much greater things must still be achieved, and though he admitted that he was no economic expert he emphasized that he had the will and a "passionate heart to carry the new plan through even better than contemplated."

**To Break "Foreign Fist"**

There was rousing applause when he exclaimed:

"We must prevent that fist from abroad from grabbing at our throat. We will break this fist during the next four years finger by finger. We know that others begrudge us our place in the sun. But we shall not capitulate."

The new plan, he insisted, was forced on Germany and Germany would gladly renounce it if a crazy world would permit her to do so. But the outside world, he said, had no reason to reproach Germany for wanting to have her share of this world's riches and should be thankful that through the Four-Year Plan Germany was trying to equalize, in a peaceful way, what has been kept from her.

"Our colonies have been stolen from us," he exclaimed amid thunderous applause, "Our gold has been stolen from us. Germany was bled white by reparations. Then came the Chosen People and plundered Germany through the inflation. It is bitter mockery to say 'Why don't you buy your raw materials?' Give us back our gold and we shall.

**Attacks Foreign Journalists**

"Britain has one-third of the world as her colonies. We have nothing. If we had only a fraction of these colonies we would not need to talk about raw materials or food shortages."

He turned against those foreign journalists who write about a food shortage in Germany and told them they had better write about Russia, Spain and the rest of the world where "unrest, democracy, communism, anarchy, destruction, robbery and murder prevail." Thereupon he admitted that an occasional "tension" in the supply of foodstuffs did exist because human wisdom had failed so far to make hens lay eggs or cows give milk in equal quantities the year around.

He assured the German nation that at the moment the German cupboard perhaps was somewhat empty but that even in a half-year there would be much more than today. Nobody would ever starve in

Continued on Page Six

## SEA STRIKE HELD UP ON PACIFIC COAST; THREAT MADE HERE

### As Midnight Deadline Passed, Negotiations to Avert a Walkout Continued.

### NEW YORK GROUP'S STAND

### Seamen's Defense Committee Empowered to Call for Sympathetic Action.

By The Associated Press.

SAN FRANCISCO, Thursday, Oct. 29.—The midnight deadline for calling a coastwide maritime strike passed without announcement from the joint union negotiating committee. It apparently was awaiting outcome of conferences between coast freight operators and seagoing unions.

Shortly before last midnight the Sailors Union of the Pacific announced tentative accord on a new agreement for one year with the coastwise shippers which would raise wages $10 to $80 per month and provide a slight raise in overtime pay rates.

A little later, it was unofficially announced that a similar accord had been reached with the firemen. The coastwise operators continued conferences with cooks and stewards.

The Shipowners' Association of the Pacific, operators of the so-called Coast steam schooner trade, a separate organization from the deep sea lines, anounced last night that further negotiations with unions would be "useless."

**Employers Tell Stand**

The employers sent letters to the various unions detailing what they said took place in "final" peace meetings during the day. They rejected not only the conditions proposed by the unions but also refused to consider the workers' "solid front" demands which prevented any union from accepting peace terms until the others had been satisfied.

Meanwhile, paralysis began spreading along the waterfronts. Police in San Francisco, Los Angeles and other coast cities prepared for extra duty in the event of trouble.

With the midnight deadline only a few hours away, seven ships were reported tied up by "crew action." Ship movements decreased sharply. Mail was transferred to foreign vessels.

Rear Admiral H. G. Hamlet of the Federal Maritime Commission and Edward F. McGrady, assistant Secretary of Labor, stood by awaiting developments. Their weeks of effort to avert a tie-up appeared to have gone for nothing.

**Hope for Intervention**

Mr. McGrady said he attempted to communicate by telephone with one of President Roosevelt's secretaries at the White House but was unable to make connections. Previously some union circles had expressed the belief that only Presidential intervention could avert a walkout, which would involve 37,000 men and tie up West Coast shipping.

The shipowners' letter to Harry Lundberg of the Sailors Union said the following ships were tied up:

The Mapele at San Pedro, "the crew of which has deserted."

The Maui in San Francisco,

Continued on Page Eight

## Mormons Soon to Open Storehouses for Needy

By The Associated Press.

SALT LAKE CITY, Oct. 28.—Bounteous storehouses, filled in a program to take all unemployed members "off relief," will be opened to the needy Nov. 1 by the Latter Day Saints Church.

The "budget system" will govern distribution of food, clothing and medical supplies to about 15,000 persons reported eligible for aid.

A dozen strategically situated storehouses were crammed with preserved food and home-made clothing throughout the Summer. The church created work projects and ward-farms, those employed receiving certificates redeemable in goods.

A similar program is planned for next year.

## KELLY COMES OUT AGAINST CHARTER

### Brooklyn Democratic Leader Opposed to Proportional Voting and Revision.

### REFORM BACKED AT RALLY

### The Mayor, Ingersoll and Seabury at Mass Meeting Attack Machine Fight on Change.

Frank V. Kelly, Brooklyn Democratic leader, formally announced yesterday his opposition to the proposed city charter and proportional representation, which will be voted on Tuesday.

In an interview at Brooklyn Democratic headquarters yesterday morning, the county chieftain said the new charter "destroys borough autonomy" and proportional representation "thwarts the people's will." Mr. Kelly, however, urged the voters to support the referendum for the three-platoon system in the New York Fire Department.

Support for the charter and proportional representation, on the other hand, was urged later yesterday by Borough President Raymond V. Ingersoll of Brooklyn at a mass meeting held by the Citizens Union at Cooper Union. Mr. Ingersoll said "the proposed charter gives due weight to the spirit of local autonomy, and is a careful and painstaking piece of modernization work which, in my opinion, will be a step forward for our city."

**Seabury Speaks for Charter**

On the same platform as the Brooklyn Borough President, in support of the charter and proportional representation, Samuel Seabury denounced "the regency of Tammany Hall for the opposition which it announced on Tuesday," and Mayor La Guardia said "there are no reasons for the opposition except selfish reasons—the charter is bad for politicians."

The Tammany regency was called

Continued on Page Eleven

## British Freighter Adrift in Atlantic Gale; Little Hope of Immediate Assistance Seen

The 5,000-ton British freighter Afghanistan was tossing helplessly in a gale last night half way across the North Atlantic and far above the regular ship routes. There was little hope that immediate aid could be sent to the vessel.

A brief wireless message picked up here by Mackay Radio from the ship shortly after 5 P. M. yesterday reported that her rudder had been swept away by high seas and that her exact position could not be determined. An approximate position given placed the ship near the center of a northerly Great Circle course, which curves on an arc below Greenland between the northern tip of Newfoundland and Glasgow, Scotland.

The vessel, which is owned by the Hindustan Steam Shipping Company, Ltd., of London, has been plying between Montreal and British ports. The number of persons on board was not revealed in the message.

The course that the vessel was following is about 500 miles above the paths of transatlantic liners.

The Gdynia-America liner Batory, en route to New York from Copenhagen over a northerly course, was believed to be closest to the drifting vessel.

LONDON, Oct. 28 (AP).—The tail of one of the worst storms in years lashed itself out in the North Sea, Northern Ireland and Scotland today, leaving a wake of death and destruction. Strong northwesterly winds still were blowing in many sections, and communication with storm-torn areas remained cut.

Fourteen sailors were believed drowned when the 1,951-ton Latvian steamer Helena Faulbaums foundered fifteen minutes after she had gone on the rocks off the island of Mull, west of Scotland. The four survivors were brought in safely from the island. Five bodies were recovered.

The Swedish steamer Bona, with a crew of twelve, was reported in distress off Karlskrona, in the Baltic Sea. Hope for the safety of the lightship Elbe and her crew of fifteen was abandoned at Cuxhaven, Germany, after tugs had failed to reach the spot where the craft capsized and foundered.

DUBLIN, Oct. 28 (AP).—Sixteen passengers, four of them children, landed at Dublin tonight from the American Shipper, showing no effects of the buffeting the United States Line's ship received as she drifted helplessly in heavy seas off the Irish coast Sunday night. The vessel proceeded to Liverpool in tow for repairs.



## LANDON ROUTE THRONGED

### 200,000 in the Streets Between the Station and Hotel.

### RALLY AT GARDEN TONIGHT

### State Candidates Will Join Leader on Platform—Overflow Session Outside.

### 3,000 HEAR HIM IN NEWARK

### Candidate Assails Bids for 'Class' Votes as Violation of the American Creed.

*Text of Governor Landon's speech in Newark is on Page 19.*

By JAMES A. HAGERTY

New York City Republicans and anti-New Deal Democrats gave their standard bearer, Governor Alf M. Landon, a rousing reception when he arrived here yesterday for the Republican rally tonight at Madison Square Garden.

The Republican Presidential candidate had previously spoken to an enthusiastic audience of between 3,000 and 4,000 at the Mosque Theatre in Newark.

He quoted the late Samuel Gompers, for years president of the American Federation of Labor, to sustain his contention that it was against the interest of organized labor to ally itself with any political party and assailed those who sought to deliver the labor, farm or any "class" vote as betrayers of the "creed of America," which he said holds that there are no classes in this country.

**Thousands Throng Station**

Nearly 10,000 persons were on hand at Pennsylvania Station when the Governor's train arrived at 4:28 P. M., while a crowd estimated by the police at more than 200,000 lined the streets and cheered from office building windows as the candidate drove from the station to the Murray Hill Hotel, Park Avenue and Forty-first Street.

With the exception of his arrival at the station, where some boos mingled with the cheers, Governor Landon received a cordial welcome to the city. Along the route on Thirty-fourth Street to Fifth Avenue, up that thoroughfare to Forty-second Street and across Forty-second Street to Park Avenue, his supporters greeted him with ticker tape, horns and shouts.

As the Landon special train pulled into the Pennsylvania Station, a welcoming committee headed by William F. Bleakley, Republican candidate for Governor; Melvin C. Eaton, Republican State chairman, and Kenneth F. Simpson, New York County leader, greeted the Governor on the platform.

When he ascended to the main section of the station from Track 12, the waiting crowd, which had been gathered for more than an hour, burst into a roar of greeting. The Governor, in excellent spirits, smiled and waved his hat at them.

Proceeded by a phalanx of newspaper photographers and reporters, the Governor and his party were conducted through the station toward the Seventh Avenue entrance. As the group reached the Seventh Avenue arcade, just before leaving the building, a loud wave of boos swept through the crowd waiting there.

The Governor's expression changed only slightly and he merely waved his hat at the hostile crowd, which by that time had been drowned out by cheers from the Republicans who had followed their candidate through the station.

**Police Lines Are Broken**

As Governor Landon stepped into the open touring car outside the station the large crowd, overflowing through the police lines, almost overwhelmed the Governor in attempting to shake his hand. Finally after some delay the procession, led by ten mounted policemen and a band, started for the hotel.

Riding in the motorcade, which included forty autos, were a group of Republicans who had formed the welcoming committee. They included W. Kingsland Macy, former Republican State Chairman; Mrs. Ruth Pratt, Republican National Committeewoman; Special Sessions Judge Nathan D. Perlman, Republican candidate for Attorney General; John R. Crews, Republican

Continued on Page Nineteen

## Smith May Introduce Landon; Two Meet for First Time Here

### *Leaders Debate Plan to Have Ex-Governor Present the Nominee—'Going to Stick Together for a Long Time,' Kansan Says After Genial Chat in Hotel Suite.*

The possibility that former Governor Alfred E. Smith, Democratic nominee for President in 1928, may introduce Governor Alf M. Landon at the rally in Madison Square Garden tonight was indicated last night when it was learned that the selection of Mr. Smith was under consideration.

Opposition to giving this rôle to Mr. Smith developed among Republican leaders here. John D. M. Hamilton, Republican National Chairman, will arrive this morning and the matter will be referred to him.

Governor Landon was reported to be keeping out of anything that might cause a dispute, but some of his closest advisers are understood to favor the selection of Mr. Smith if he would consent to make the presentation.

It is their theory that the spectacle of a former Democratic Presidential candidate introducing the present Republican Presidential nominee would have a favorable effect throughout the country upon those Democrats who disapprove of the New Deal but have not determined definitely that they will vote for Governor Landon.

Mr. Smith called on Governor Landon just before 7:30 last night and talked with him for half an hour in the nominee's suite at the Murray Hill Hotel. It was the first time they had met.

The two later went into a side room to pose for newspaper photographers, who snapped them with Governor Landon's hand on Mr. Smith's shoulder and with the two shaking hands. After the "stills" had been taken they went to an adjoining room to face the newsreel cameras.

"I am delighted to be in the great City of New York," Governor Landon said, extending his hand. "And I am delighted to meet you, sir."

"Well, Governor," Mr. Smith replied with a wide grin, "I am sure that the splendid reception you received must have convinced you that you are very welcome in New York, and I want to tell you that you have more friends among the

Continued on Page Eighteen

## BLEAKLEY PLEDGES AID ON MORTGAGES

### Will Continue Moratorium, He Tells Queens Rally, and Work for Reapportionment.

### AGAIN ATTACKS GOVERNOR

### Accuses Him of Misquotation—Charges 'Certain Influences' Got Crime Bill Veto.

In a speech devoted to questions of particular interest to the voters of Queens County, William F. Bleakley, Republican candidate for Governor, pledged his support last night to legislative reapportionment and to a continuance of the mortgage moratorium.

The address was made at a Republican rally at Public School 93, Forest Avenue and Madison Street, Ridgewood. It was the most important address in a full day which began with a speech in the Union League Club, in which the candidate renewed his attack on Governor Lehman for conducting a "campaign of misquotation."

He charged the Governor with inconsistency and insincerity in supporting the crime bills. As proof of this he cited the legislative bills that gave Westchester and Nassau County courts jurisdiction in gambling cases. He declared that the bill for Westchester and that for Nassau were identical, but that the Governor, after signing the one for Westchester, had vetoed that for the island county.

"Of course," he said, "it becomes plain that certain influences in Nassau County were brought to bear."

During the afternoon Mr. Bleakley met Governor Landon at the Pennsylvania Station. Both will appear on the platform at the big Madison Square Garden rally tonight. Mr. Bleakley rode with his party's Presidential candidate at the head of the procession that escorted them across town to the Murray Hill Hotel, where Mr. Landon is stopping.

**Pledges Voice to Queens**

Concerning reapportionment, Mr. Bleakley said:

"As I view it, there should be no question that Queens, because of its growth, resources, potentialities and the vision and character of its people, is entitled to her full share of representation in the Legislature, something which has been withheld from her for years.

"And it is my similar view that Queens is entitled to a prominent place and a definite and separate political voice in the councils of the State.

"I will work honestly and sincerely for reapportionment, if I am elected, and, as to Queens having a stronger voice in political councils, whether I am elected or not, I will exert every effort within my own party to see to it that the voice of Queens is heard in greater volume in Republican councils and that more recognition and attention be

Continued on Page Fourteen

## LEHMAN URGES CITY RESTORE PAY CUTS

### Governor, Carrying Campaign to Queens, Demands Former Level for Salaries.

### FIGHTS FOR REDISTRICTING

### He Wins Applause by Praising Saving of Borough Homes With Federal Funds.

Invading Queens last night in his campaign for re-election, Governor Lehman demanded that the New York City government provide full salary restorations for school teachers and city employes at "the earliest possible time." He went on to pledge himself to continue his fight for reapportionment of Congressional and legislative districts.

The Governor addressed a large crowd at the Jamaica High School, which applauded as he declared he would recommend continuation of the mortgage moratorium and deficiency judgment laws for another year. He hailed the Home Owners Loan Corporation for saving thousands of homes to the owners and declared this constituted a reply to Republican charges of extravagance leveled against the Roosevelt administration.

Governor Lehman spoke in Queens after traveling all day with President Roosevelt in various parts of the city and sharing with the President the many cheers along the route. He dined with James C. Sheridan, Queens Democratic leader, at the Pomonok Country Club at Parsons Boulevard before going to the Jamaica rally. William F. Brunner, candidate for Aldermanic President, was another guest.

**Issue Put Up to City**

The Governor's demand that the city take action to restore the salaries of school teachers and city employes, which were cut as economy moves, puts the issue squarely up to the city government. The State government, he said, had made full restoration of cuts in 1935. He defended his veto of a bill which would have made it mandatory for the city to restore the cuts imposed on school teachers and city employes and declared that the city itself had full power to take such action.

"And it is my earnest hope," he said, "and a sincere hope, that the officials of the City of New York, who now possess all the power they need, will decide to restore salaries at the very earliest possible time."

The Governor's pledge to keep on fighting for reapportionment, a subject dear to the heart of Queens, also won applause. He asserted that if "political" opposition continued to block redistricting he would urge again an amendment to the State Constitution to devise "some more certain method" for achieving reapportionment.

The Democratic Gubernatorial candidate assailed the Republican controlled Assembly at the past legis-

Continued on Page Fifteen

## 300,000 SEE PRESIDENT

### Crowds Line His 30-Mile Route Through Three Boroughs.

### HE BRINGS PEACE MESSAGE

### Predicts Better Civilization for World at Statue of Liberty Celebration.

### PLEDGES FIGHT ON SLUMS

### Acclaimed on East Side and in Brooklyn—Waves to Landon Procession at End of Day.

*Texts of President Roosevelt's speeches appear on Pages 20, 21.*

By RUSSELL B. PORTER

A tremendous outpouring of men, women and children welcomed President Roosevelt to New York City yesterday as he began the last week of his campaign for re-election.

Crowds estimated at no fewer than 300,000 persons, perhaps as many as 500,000, surrounded him at places where he stopped for brief addresses, and lined the streets of Manhattan, Brooklyn, Staten Island and near-by Bayonne, N. J., as he passed in his automobile procession with a smiling, confident air.

Nowhere was there any incident to mar the warmth of the city's ovation except for one brief interlude of booing as he passed down lower Broadway. Even there the volume of cheers and applause was so great as to make the demonstration against him seem insignificant.

Time after time he received New York's typical greeting in artificial showers of paper, ticker tape and confetti, falling like garlands over his head from high office buildings and tossed upon his car from the throngs in the streets. During the morning, afternoon and evening that he spent in the city and its environs, he traveled more than thirty miles without passing a block whose sidewalks were not jammed with enthusiastic crowds.

**Pledges Housing Program**

Speaking in the densely populated lower East Side, at a celebration of the fiftieth anniversary of the dedication of the Statue of Liberty, the President deviated from the "non-political" nature of his day's program by promising that, if re-elected, he would begin a housing program for the masses who live in overcrowded city districts. Immigrants and children and grandchildren of immigrants constituted a large part of the thickly packed gathering that cheered him in this statement, made in the playground at Roosevelt Park. It was his first visit to this part of New York since his election in 1932.

In the same address the President attacked speculators who "gamble with and lose the savings of the clients of their banks." He commended the immigrants to America for their contributions to American civilization and culture.

President Roosevelt also spoke at the main Statue of Liberty celebration on Bedloes Island, and at the laying of the cornerstone of a new gymnasium at Brooklyn College.

He went to his home at 49 East Sixty-fifth Street for dinner. At 10:53 P. M., at Pennsylvania Station, he boarded his campaign train, which had dropped him at Bayonne yesterday morning. The train left at 2:30 A. M to take the President on a speaking tour of Pennsylvania, Delaware and New Jersey. He will return here for an address at the Brooklyn Academy of Music tomorrow night and his final major campaign speech at Madison Square Garden on Saturday night.

**Children Crowd Streets**

For an hour before the Presidential special was due to arrive in Bayonne, the streets of that city were crowded with people, including thousands of school children, who had a holiday for the occasion. He arrived at 9:30 o'clock and was greeted by Mayor Lucius Donohoe, who introduced him to the crowd at the West Eighth Street railroad station. Aerial bombs were exploded as part of the demonstration.

The President told his welcomers that he had tried to "achieve for the people of this country a greater security and a greater prosperity

Continued on Page Twenty

"All the News That's Fit to Print."

# The New York Times.

FINAL EXTRA

Rain and much colder today. Tomorrow fair, with little change in temperature.

Temperatures Yesterday—Max., 73; Min., 65

Copyright, 1936, by The New York Times Company.

VOL. LXXXVI....No. 28,774. Entered as Second-Class Matter, Postoffice, New York, N. Y. NEW YORK, WEDNESDAY, NOVEMBER 4, 1936. TWO CENTS In New York City. | THREE CENTS Within 200 Miles. | FOUR CENTS Elsewhere Except in 7th and 8th Postal Zones.

# ROOSEVELT SWEEPS THE NATION; HIS ELECTORAL VOTE EXCEEDS 500; LEHMAN WINS; CHARTER ADOPTED

## FEW HOUSE SHIFTS

### Democrats May Add to Vast Majorities in Both Chambers

### THREE SENATORS TRAIL

### Barbour, Hastings and Metcalf Appear to Have Lost Seats.

### 90 HOUSE RACES IN DOUBT

### Democrats Elect 254, While Republicans Obtain 84, and Progressives 6.

By TURNER CATLEDGE

Republican hopes of making heavy inroads upon the huge Democratic majorities in Congress were apparently smothered under the pro-Roosevelt landslide in yesterday's election.

As the size of the New Deal avalanche continued to grow into the early morning hours the Democrats gave promise of actually increasing their lop-sided majority in the Senate and were offsetting Republican gains of new House seats by capturing places now held by anti-New Dealers. If the trend of the count persists in the tardy tabulations today the Democrats may hold their own or actually add to their majorities in both branches of Congress.

In the wreckage left by the Democratic sweep also appeared the Senatorial careers of three outstanding Republican Senators—Barbour of New Jersey, Hastings of Delaware and Metcalf of Rhode Island. As the count from their respective States stood early today, these three incumbents appeared defeated.

Moreover, the Democrats threatened to pick up still another Republican Senate seat, that formerly occupied by the late Senator Couzens, and they were pressing hard upon Senator Lester J. Dickinson of Iowa, whose opposition to the administration's farm relief program won for him the enmity of many farmers in his State.

**Lodge Leading Curley**

The only present Democratic Senate seat which appeared definitely lost to the Democrats was that held by Senator Marcus Coolidge of Massachusetts. Henry Cabot Lodge 2d, Republican, was well ahead of Governor James M. Curley for this post, despite the State's substantial majority for the remainder of the Democratic national and State ticket.

Still another Democratic berth was threatened. Senator W. J. Bulow, Democrat, was trailing Chandler Gurney, Republican, by a slight margin in South Dakota.

The veteran Senator Norris, who left the Republican fold to stand for re-election as an Independent in Nebraska, was increasing his lead over former Representative Robert G. Simmons, Republican, and Terry Carpenter, "regular" Democrat.

Representative Ernest Lundeen, Farmer-Labor candidate, was piling up a commanding lead over former Governor Theodore Christianson, Republican, in Minnesota.

Senator Borah, Republican dean of the Senate, was doing the same to his opponent, Governor C. Ben Ross, Democrat.

As the Senate count stood early today, the Democrats appeared to have elected twenty of the thirty-six Senators who were up for election this year and the Republicans six, while ten were still in doubt. On this showing the Democrats would have a membership of at least sixty-seven Democrats in the new Congress, the Republicans seventeen, Farmer-Laborites one, and Progressives one. The Democrats stood a good chance to pick up still others out of the ten in

Continued on Page Three



### Landon Congratulates President, Who Replies

Special to THE NEW YORK TIMES.

TOPEKA, Wednesday, Nov. 4.—Governor Landon conceded his defeat in a message of congratulation to President Roosevelt at 1:30 o'clock this morning, Eastern standard time.

His message read as follows:

"The nation has spoken. Every American will accept the verdict and work for the common cause of the good of our country. That is the spirit of democracy. You have my sincere congratulations.

"ALF M. LANDON."

Governor Landon decided to send the message after he had retired for the night at the Exective Mansion, with the word that no statement would be issued during the night.

Special to THE NEW YORK TIMES.

HYDE PARK, N. Y., Wednesday, Nov. 4.—Half an hour after receiving Governor Landon's message President Roosevelt sent the following reply:

"I am grateful to you for your generous telegram and I am confident that all of us Americans will now pull together for the common good. I send you every good wish."

## UNION PARTY VOTE FAR BELOW BOASTS

### Coughlin Group Appears to Have Exercised Little Influence on the Electorate.

### SUPPORT OF LEMKE WEAK

### Even in Ohio and South Dakota His Showing in the Early Returns Is Poor.

By F. RAYMOND DANIELL

Representative William Lemke, the Presidential candidate of the so-called "lunatic fringe," made scarcely a dent in the great totals the nation piled up for President Roosevelt and Alfred M. Landon in yesterday's voting.

Showing his greatest strength in Illinois, Pennsylvania and Massachusetts, the North Dakota Representative, who had the backing of the Rev. Charles E. Coughlin, Dr. Francis E. Townsend and the Rev. Gerald L. K. Smith, still remained a negligible factor in the outcome of the election.

Despite confident predictions by the Union party's backers last August that Mr. Lemke would take enough votes from Mr. Roosevelt to deprive him of a majority in the Electoral College, thus throwing the election into the House of Representatives, nowhere did he poll a substantial enough vote to hurt either major party candidate.

In his home State of North Dakota the co-author of the Frazier-Lemke bill was trailing far behind the President and his Republican opponent. The first seventy-eight precincts reporting gave Mr. Lemke only 1,280 to Mr. Roosevelt's 11,644 and Mr. Landon's 5,333.

Here in New York, Father Coughlin's candidate for the House of Representatives in the Sixteenth Assembly District was snowed under. He was former State Senator John A. Hastings, an intimate friend of former Mayor James J. Walker. His opponent was Representative John J. O'Connor, who incurred Father Coughlin's wrath by threatening to kick the priest of Royal Oak from the Capitol to the White House. Mr. O'Connor seemed an easy winner in the Sixteenth.

Two reasons were advanced to explain the failure of Mr. Lemke to make a better showing. The first was that Father Coughlin, the Rev. Mr. Smith and Dr. Townsend all were inflationists when it came to estimating the size of their following, which each placed in the neighborhood of 6,000,000 voters. The second was that the men and women who cheered so loudly at the Cleveland conventions of the National Union for Social Justice and Old Age Revolving Pensions Ltd., became Republicans and Democrats again after returning home.

The early vote for Representative William Lemke, even in States where Father Coughlin's National Union for Social Justice boasts a

Continued on Page Five

## BIG CHARTER VOTE

### 8-Hour System for Firemen Also Wins Easily

### VOTING CHANGE APPROVED

### Brunner Is Victor Over Morris by Large Plurality.

### ROOSEVELT SWEEP HERE

### President's Vote and Margin, Which Reached 1,356,458, Set Highest City Record.

By RUSSELL B. PORTER

President Roosevelt piled up the largest vote and plurality ever accorded to a candidate for any office in the history of New York City at yesterday's election.

With all the city's 3,799 election districts in, the President had the extraordinary plurality of 1,356,458, which was considerably larger even that his campaign managers had estimated.

This was about 50 per cent larger than his 1932 plurality and about three times former Governor Alfred E. Smith's city plurality when he ran against Herbert Hoover for the Presidency in 1928.

The total Presidential vote was 2,747,240, or over 500,000 more than the total vote cast in the 1932 Presidential election and the 1933 Mayoralty election, the previous records.

Governor Lehman ran behind the President, but had a plurality of 921,938 with no election districts missing. He ran about 2 to 1 ahead of William F. Bleakley, his Republican opponent, while President Roosevelt's ratio was 3 to 1 over Governor Landon. Governor Lehman's plurality was not as large as in 1932, when it was 989,844, but was larger than two years ago, when it was 803,956.

**Brunner an Easy Winner**

In the day's only election for city office, William F. Brunner, Democrat, had a final plurality of 891,880 over Newbold Morris, Republican, in the contest for president of the Board of Aldermen, with no election districts missing.

The voters approved all three local questions on which referenda were taken. They accepted the new city charter by 927,396 to 583,044, an affirmative majority of 344,354, with 689 election districts missing.

With 78 election districts missing, they voted 898,389 for and 551,914

Continued on Page Four

### Smith Plans Comment On the Election Today

Alfred E. Smith, former Democratic candidate for President who espoused the cause of Alfred M. Landon in this campaign said last night that he probably would issue a statement today setting forth his views on President Roosevelt's sweeping victory.

Earlier in the evening he had called THE NEW YORK TIMES to ask how the election was going. He was informed that President Roosevelt was leading in all but a handful of States. He made no comment but when he was asked if he were going to a party of Jeffersonian Democrats in the apartment of Raoul Desvernine, Liberty League lawyer, to which he had been invited, he replied:

"No, I'm going to bed."

P. S.—The former Governor did not retire at once. He called up an hour later to get the latest returns.

## DEMOCRATS RETAIN STATE SENATE LEAD

### They Are Assured of 30 Seats of the 51, One More Than Their Previous Number.

### FAIL TO WIN ASSEMBLY

### Republicans Are Beaten for Five Places, but Still Hold a Bare Working Majority.

By W. A. WARN

The Democrats will control the State Senate by a subsantial majority and the Republicans will have a bare working majority in the Assembly, according to complete returns from the legislative elections.

The latest returns give the Democrats thirty seats out of fifty-one in the Senate, a net gain of one over their present quota. The Republicans suffered a loss of five seats in the Assembly, but still retain seventy-six seats, which gives them the constitutional majority necessary to pass bills and prevail on important parliamentary motions.

The result in not a few of the districts, however, on the face of the latest returns was so close that in some instances a demand may be made by the losers for recount proceedings.

This city will lose its only Republican Senator through the defeat of Senator Joseph C. Baldwin 3d in the Seventeenth Senatorial District, situated in Manhattan. Leon A. Fischel, Democrat, carried the district by a plurality somewhat below 5,000.

The Democratic solidarity of Albany County in its legislative representatives surprisingly was broken. A Republican candidate for Assembly, John McBain, nominated in

Continued on Page Five

### Roosevelt, Speaking to Victory Procession At Hyde Park, Predicted Record Sweep

By CHARLES W. HURD

Special to THE NEW YORK TIMES.

HYDE PARK, Nov. 3.—With wire returns indicating a landslide for President Roosevelt far in excess of the majority necessary to re-elect him, President Roosevelt said tonight that he thought the "sweep" might carry every section of the United States.

Speaking to several hundred loyal followers who staged a victory procession through rain from Hyde Park to Mr. Roosevelt's home, Hyde Park House, at 10:30 P. M., he said:

"The returns are not all in yet, so I can't say anything official or final, but it looks as though we are going to have one of the largest sweeps ever heard of in the United States."

"As a matter of fact, from the returns now, it looks as though this sweep has carried every single section of the country," he exclaimed.

The President, laughing and happy, spoke while standing on the open porch of his house, looking out over a crowd whose faces were illuminated by red-fire torches and the calcium flares used for light for motion pictures.

He waved aside sound microphones, saying: "This is just a home party."

The crowd cheered the President, Mrs. Roosevelt, and his mother, Mrs. Sara Delano Roosevelt.

The assemblage cheered loudly when Mr. Roosevelt said one of his happiest moments came with the word that he had carried the village of Hyde Park, although he lost the township.

The crowd remained for half an hour, with some enthusiastic persons shouting "How about 1940?"

Mr. Roosevelt leaned on the arm of his son, Franklin Jr. Beside him were his wife and mother. Grouped behind him was a small party including his daughter, Mrs. Anna Boettiger, and Mr. Boettiger, Mrs. James Roosevelt, his daughter-in-law, and other relatives.

Others in the party included Secretary and Mrs. Morgenthau, Judge and Mrs. Sam Rosenman, Frederick A. Delano and members of the White House staff and newspaper correspondents.

## LEHMAN VOTE CUT

### Bleakley Gets a Surprising Total in the City

### SWEEP HELPS GOVERNOR

### Roosevelt Strong in Industrial Cities—Gets Big Up-State Poll.

### OTHER DEMOCRATS SAFE

### Bray, Tremaine, Bennett and Others of State Ticket Regarded Certain of Victory.

By JAMES A. HAGERTY

Governor Herbert H. Lehman was re-elected Governor of New York yesterday for a third term. The indicated plurality for the Governor over former Supreme Court Justice William F. Bleakley, his Republican opponent, was about 600,000.

Governor Lehman, who was urged to become a candidate for re-election to help President Roosevelt, ran far behind the President in New York City. With all the election districts reported, his plurality in New York City was 921,938 as compared with the city plurality of 1,356,458, or more than the million and a quarter predicted by Postmaster General Farley, for President Roosevelt. President Roosevelt's plurality in the State was indicated at about 1,150,000.

The tremendous vote for President Roosevelt in New York City and the failure of Governor Landon to carry up-State by much more than 200,000 indicated that the defection of former Governor Alfred E. Smith and other Jeffersonian Democrats had little effect on the Presidential vote, although there apparently were influences within the Democratic party working against Governor Lehman in New York City.

With New York City complete and 480 election districts missing out of 5,151 up-State, the vote for President was:

| | Roosevelt. | Landon. |
|---|---|---|
| Up-State | 1,197,201 | 1,370,516 |
| New York City | 2,016,204 | 659,746 |
| Totals | 3,213,405 | 2,030,262 |

Actual plurality for Roosevelt, 1,183,143.

With New York City complete and 892 election districts missing up-State, the vote for Governor was:

| | Lehman. | Bleakley. |
|---|---|---|
| Up-State | 1,060,564 | 1,338,892 |
| New York City | 1,795,124 | 873,186 |
| Totals | 2,855,688 | 2,212,078 |

Actual plurality for Lehman, 643,610.

The tremendous vote for President Roosevelt swept to victory the other State-wide Democratic candidates for re-election, Lieut. Gov. M. William Bray, Controller Morris S. Tremaine, Attorney General John J. Bennett Jr., and Mrs. Caroline O'Day and Matthew J. Merritt, Representatives at Large.

Incomplete returns also indicated the election of Harlan W. Rippey, Democratic candidate for Associate Judge of the Court of Appeals over Supreme Court Justice James P. Hill, Republican candidate.

**City Margin Is Unprecedented**

President Roosevelt carried New York City by the unprecedented plurality of 1,356,458, the total vote being 2,016,204 for the President and 659,746 for Governor Landon. This was more than 50,000 in excess of the results forecast in the surveys made by the five Democratic county leaders, which they believed should be scaled down 10 per cent to give the probable results.

Governor Lehman's New York City plurality increased with the late returns, and he did not run as far behind the President as the early returns had indicated he would do.

With all election districts reported, the vote for Governor in New

Continued on Page Five

©New York Times Studio Photo.

FRANKLIN D. ROOSEVELT

## DEMOCRATS SWEEP ALL PENNSYLVANIA

### President Wins by More Than 550,000 in First National Party Victory in 70 Years.

### PHILADELPHIA IS CARRIED

### Whole State Government and the Legislature Go to Democratic Control.

Special to THE NEW YORK TIMES.

PHILADELPHIA, Wednesday, Nov. 4.—Pennsylvania, the Keystone State of Republicanism, was swept yesterday by the Democrats for the first time in a Presidential election since the Civil War era.

With unprecedented Democratic pluralities in Philadelphia and Allegheny Counties, with greatly diminished Republican pluralities in the commuting counties about Philadelphia, and with even the rural districts only half heartedly Republican, President Roosevelt carried the State by a margin which exceeded 550,000 votes.

Returns from 6,733 of the State's 8,010 divisions gave:

Roosevelt, 2,010,343.

Landon, 1,469,679.

Lemke, 44,253.

Complete returns from the 1,291 divisions in this city gave:

Roosevelt 521,941.

Landon, 322,229.

This city plurality of 199,712 exceeds that for Herbert Hoover in 1932 for the whole State by 40,000.

The Democratic victory, the size of which amazed even the leaders of that party, not only gave to President Roosevelt this State's thirty-six electoral votes, but put the State government wholly in the hands of the Democrats.

**Democrats Get Legislature**

George H. Earle in 1934 seized the Governorship for the Democrats for the first time in forty-four years. Since assuming office he has been at odds constantly with a Republican-controlled State Senate, which has succeeded in balking many of his plans for putting a "little New Deal" in effect in Pennsylvania.

As a result of yesterday's election

Continued on Page Three

## JERSEY'S 16 VOTES SAFE FOR NEW DEAL

### Upsets in Republican Areas Add to Huge Pluralities in Democratic Counties.

### SMATHERS SEEMS WINNER

### Senate Aspirant Runs Behind Roosevelt but Has Lead Over Barbour, Incumbent.

New Jersey's sixteen electoral votes seemed at 5 o'clock this morning in possession of President Roosevelt. Reports from 1,719 of the State's 3,551 election districts gave him 493,071 votes to 295,794 for Governor Landon.

Hudson County, the great Democratic stronghold run by the State leader, Mayor Frank Hague of Jersey City, was responsible for this tremendous lead in what had been a doubtful State until the count began. It seemed quite likely that, although Mr. Landon made gains in other areas, he never could overcome the Hudson County handicap, particularly since several normally powerful Republican communities deserted Landon for Roosevelt.

Keeping pace with President Roosevelt in the Democratic territories, but dropping behind him in many Republican sections which the President dominated, State Senator William H. Smathers, Democrat, had in 1,656 districts a total of 404,546 for United States Senator.

His Republican opponent, W. Warren Barbour, the incumbent, was gathering many hundreds here and there, outside Hudson County, having a total in the same districts of 297,000. Though this seemed a difficult lead to overcome, Mr. Barbour was quite confident that the great number of unreported districts would offset the Smathers advantage and pull him through for another stay in Washington.

Even Mayor Hague's prediction of 125,000 plurality in Hudson County for Roosevelt was so far surpassed as to give him a happy surprise. In 545 districts out of 684 in that county, the President received 294,-

Continued on Page Eleven

## POLL SETS RECORD

### Roosevelt Electoral Vote of 519 Seen as a Minimum

### NO SWING TO THE BOLTERS

### 'Jeffersonian Democrats' Fail to Cause Rift as Expected.

### NEIGHBORS HAIL PRESIDENT

### Landon Concedes Defeat and Sends His Congratulations to Victorious Rival.

By ARTHUR KROCK

Accepting the President as the issue, nearly eight million more voters than ever before had gone to the polls in the United States—about 45,000,000 persons—yesterday gave to Franklin Delano Roosevelt the most overwhelming testimonial of approval ever received by a national candidate in the history of the nation.

Except for the small corner of New England occupied by Maine, Vermont and New Hampshire—which was oscillating between Republican and Democratic in the early morning hours of Wednesday—the President was the choice of a vast preponderance of the voters in all parts of the country, and with him were re-elected as Vice President John N. Garner of Texas and an almost untouched Democratic majority in the House of Representatives. The Democratic national ticket will have a minimum of 519 electoral votes and a possible popular majority of ten millions.

The Republican candidates for President and Vice President, Governor Alfred M. Landon of Kansas and Colonel Frank Knox of Illinois, are the worst-beaten aspirants for these offices in the political annals of the United States, with the exception of William H. Taft in 1912, when Colonel Theodore Roosevelt led a formidable revolt in the Republican party and Mr. Taft carried only Vermont and Utah. Yesterday Utah was also in the President's campaign bag. He had carried forty-five States as contrasted with the forty-two he won from Herbert Hoover in 1932. And to assure his reputation as the greatest vote-getter in the annals of the United States he—a Democrat—had overwhelmingly swept Pennsylvania, unfailingly Republican for generations in national elections.

The following table contains a list of the States carried by the President, with a total of 519 electoral votes, to which the four of New Hampshire may yet be added:

| State | Votes | State | Votes |
|---|---|---|---|
| Alabama | 11 | Nebraska | 7 |
| Arizona | 3 | Nevada | 3 |
| Arkansas | 9 | New Jersey | 16 |
| California | 22 | New Mexico | 3 |
| Colorado | 6 | New York | 47 |
| Connecticut | 8 | North Carolina | 13 |
| Delaware | 3 | North Dakota | 4 |
| Florida | 7 | Ohio | 26 |
| Georgia | 12 | Oklahoma | 11 |
| Idaho | 4 | Oregon | 5 |
| Illinois | 29 | Pennsylvania | 36 |
| Indiana | 14 | Rhode Island | 4 |
| Iowa | 11 | South Carolina | 8 |
| Kansas | 9 | South Dakota | 4 |
| Kentucky | 11 | Tennessee | 11 |
| Louisiana | 10 | Texas | 23 |
| Maryland | 8 | Utah | 4 |
| Massachusetts | 17 | Virginia | 11 |
| Michigan | 19 | Washington | 8 |
| Minnesota | 11 | West Virginia | 8 |
| Mississippi | 9 | Wisconsin | 12 |
| Missouri | 15 | Wyoming | 3 |
| Montana | 4 | | |

**Landon Sends Congratulations**

After hours of hopeful waiting on rural districts in the Northeast States, Mr. Landon and the Republican national chairman, John D. M. Hamilton, announced their intentions of letting the night pass before agreeing to the fact of the stupendous party defeat. But about 1 A. M. in Topeka, Mr. Landon sent the customary message of congratulation to the President at Hyde Park, and at 1:45 A. M., at headquarters in Chicago, Mr. Hamilton followed suit. All the important newspapers supporting the Republican ticket (about 90 per cent of the metropolitan and country

Continued on Page Three

"All the News That's Fit to Print."

# The New York Times.

LATE CITY EDITION
Rain and warmer today. Tomorrow rain and colder.
Temperatures Yesterday—Max., 35; Min., 30



VOL. LXXXVI....No. 28,852. Entered as Second-Class Matter, Postoffice, New York, N. Y. NEW YORK, THURSDAY, JANUARY 21, 1937. P TWO CENTS In New York City. | THREE CENTS Within 200 Miles. | FOUR CENTS Elsewhere Except in 7th and 8th Postal Zones.

# ROOSEVELT PLEDGES WARFARE AGAINST POVERTY, BROADER AID FOR 'THOSE WHO HAVE TOO LITTLE'; THRONGS SEE INAUGURATION IN PELTING RAIN

## NEW AUTO PARLEY IN CAPITAL FAILS; MURPHY GLOOMY

### Sloan, Knudsen and Aides Meet All Afternoon With Governor and Miss Perkins

### CONFEREES ARE ANXIOUS

### But Secretary Is Hopeful—Further Talks in the East May Be Arranged

### ENTIRE BUICK PLANT SHUT

### Closedown Makes Total of Flint Idle 38,000 and Accentuates Relief Problem

**Day's Strike Developments**

WASHINGTON—A parley in which Secretary Perkins, Governor Murphy and General Motors officials participated failed to find a solution of difficulties.

FLINT—The Buick plant shut down completely last night, adding 10,000 to the ranks of the idle, which previously numbered 28,000. Danger that the relief problem will soon become acute is seen.

DETROIT—As a matter of strategy, affiliates of the C.I.O. moved to settle the local Bohn Aluminum plant strike and the glass strike in Pittsburgh.

PITTSBURGH—Union and Pittsburgh Plate Glass officials reached an agreement on wages in five company plants which will send 7,000 back to work at once. The workers will get 8 cents an hour more.

**Capital Negotiations Futile**

Special to THE NEW YORK TIMES.

WASHINGTON, Jan. 20.—Governor Murphy of Michigan, at the end of another long conference here today on the General Motors strike situation indicated that it seemed difficult, if not impossible, to break the deadlock through State action.

Possibility of Presidential intervention within a week loomed as the eventual action to end the strike.

This was the conclusion forced on observers, after Governor Murphy had participated in an all-afternoon conference with Secretary Perkins, Alfred P. Sloan, president of General Motors; William S. Knudsen, executive vice president; Donaldson Brown, chairman of the corporation's finance committee, and John Thomas Smith, general counsel.

There was a possibility that Mr. Murphy might go to New York to continue his efforts to arrange resumption of the truce which he had brought about last Friday at Lansing where, for the first time, he had General Motors officers and the union officials in one room at the same time.

Following today's meeting neither the Governor nor any participant concealed his anxiety over the fact that the situation was reaching a critical stage.

For the present it appeared that President Roosevelt would not be called upon to mediate the strike issues, for Secretary Perkins was determined to avoid this if possible. However another week, it was said, will probably tell another story.

**Negotiations Kept Secret**

The utmost secrecy surrounded the afternoon deliberations. All sorts of reports were current, including one that the parley would be resumed tomorrow and that John L. Lewis, chairman of the Committee for Industrial Organization, might then be called into a conference with Mr. Sloan.

Governor Murphy said that he would exhaust all efforts "in the East" to arrange for resumption of joint negotiations, but did not explain what he meant. He was holding further talks tonight.

Mr. Lewis has repeatedly charged that a "united front" of financial groups interested in the steel, automobile, rubber and glass and coal industries is intent on ending what they consider the "menace" of the C. I. O., which has for its objective the organization of these mass production industries.

Mr. Murphy would not say whether he would confer tomorrow with officers of the United Automobile Workers of America, who left Detroit tonight for Washington, nor would he indicate whether he would again see Mr. Lewis.

Secretary Perkins declined to discuss the situation with reporters, but a statement was issued in her behalf to the effect that she and the Governor were still striving to reopen negotiations on a "fair and honorable" basis.

**Statement by Miss Perkins**

Her statement was as follows:

"We discussed all aspects of the problem and particularly the break-

Continued on Page Four

## Berlin-Tokyo Body Named To Carry Out Agreement

By The Associated Press.

BERLIN, Jan. 20.—A mixed German-Japanese commission has been named to carry out provisions of the anti-Comintern agreement of last November, it was learned from a semi-official source tonight.

Names of the members have not been disclosed.

The agreement binds the two nations "to execute in close cooperation with each other" such measures as are deemed necessary to counteract "the disruptive activities of the Communist International."

## EX-CONVICT SLAYS SHACKLED TROOPER

### Prisoner Attacks Michigan Officer in Patrol Car and Handcuffs Him to a Mail Box

### CAUGHT IN 3-STATE HUNT

### Gunman Cornered on Highway in a Commandeered Car—Confesses to Murder

By The Associated Press.

MONROE, Mich., Jan. 20.—State Trooper Richards G. Hammond was killed early today after he had been overpowered by a prisoner in a patrol car and had been shackled to a rural mail box with his own handcuffs. The prisoner, a paroled convict, shot the trooper through the head.

Tonight, after the most intensive man-hunt in Michigan's history had spread to the States of Ohio and Indiana, the fugitive felon, Alcide (Frenchy) Benoit, 24 years old, was captured by State Police and, according to Sheriff Joseph J. Bairley of Monroe County, later confessed that he had slain the policeman.

Sheriff Bairley said that Benoit admitted after questioning that he slugged Hammond following his arrest at midnight last night at almost the exact spot where he was captured tonight, and that he had dragged the dazed trooper from his automobile, handcuffed him to the mail box post and then shot him.

Prosecutor Francis C. Ready and State Police Captain Lawrence A. Lyon declared that Benoit admitted in an oral statement that he fired the fatal shot, but insisted that it was fired during a fight he had with the trooper, and not while the officer was in a dazed condition.

**Escaped With Posse Near By**

After handcuffing Trooper Hammond to the mailbox post, the officials quoted Benoit as saying, and firing the fatal shot, he fled, hiding in a field while a posse flashed lights within a few feet of him. After the posse had gone, he said, he spent the remainder of the night and all of today in a barn near Monroe.

He admitted, the officials said, that he had committed robberies in Detroit, Flint, Grand Rapids, Lansing and Pontiac, Mich.; Toledo, Cleveland and Chicago.

The capture of Benoit came after Captain Lyon had expressed fear early in the evening that Benoit had eluded the net set for him.

At 7 P. M., a man later identified as Benoit, knocked on the door of a farmhouse near Fetterman, occupied by Paul Balog, 56; his wife and two children. The man asked Balog and his son, Steve, 16, to help him dig his car out of the mud. Balog said later that the man threatened to shoot them if they did not help.

They went to the barnyard, Balog said, where the man declared he was the man who had shot the trooper, and with two guns—one his own and other taken from Trooper Hammond—forced the Balogs to start their pick-up truck and drive him toward Monroe.

At the edge of the city they were met by State police, but Benoit, who was driving, swerved his car, narrowly missing a trooper who sought to question him, and eluded capture.

Balog said that they drove around in the vicinity of Monroe for an hour, dodging police cars by driving in private lanes and leaving lights off, but finally again approached the intersection of Michigan State Route No. 50 and Telegraph Road, where Benoit and John Smith, 29, alias Delberto, also a former convict, had been arrested by Troopers Hammond and Sam Sineni last night as suspects in the kidnapping of Fred Williams, a Detroit used-car salesman.

**Surrenders to Four Troopers**

As Benoit dodged into a driveway tonight, a State police car followed and fired one rifle shot into the back of the truck, Balog told newspaper men. The bullet penetrated the end gate and the seat on which the three sat, but failed to strike any of them.

Balog said that Benoit resisted when four troopers sought to handcuff him, but that when he saw the

Continued on Page Two

## OPEN DOOR URGED IN WORLD COLONIES BY TOKYO MINISTER

### Arita Says This Is Way to End Much Unrest Among Lands Lacking Raw Materials

### DEFENDS PACT WITH REICH

### Attributes World's Troubles to Communism—Sees Gain in Relations With U. S.

By HUGH BYAS

Wireless to THE NEW YORK TIMES.

TOKYO, Thursday, Jan. 21.—An appeal that the world adopt an "open door" policy of free trade in all colonies to give poor nations access to essential raw materials was made at the opening of the Diet (Parliament) today by Foreign Minister Hachiro Arita.

Mr. Arita declared that if the colony-owning nations would agree to pursue this policy, it would go far toward eliminating world unrest and dissatisfaction.

He defended the Japanese "anti-Communist" pact with Germany by describing how he felt communism was menacing the world, but added that the accord had no ulterior implications and was not a threat to any country. He went further, in fact, and urged that other lands join in it.

Both Mr. Arita and Premier Koki Hirota, who opened the Diet session, laid great emphasis on Japan's efforts to promote friendship with the United States and Britain.

**Defense Needs Stressed**

Mr. Hirota also emphasized the necessity for rapidly expanding Japan's armaments.

"Of all the questions before the House, promotion of defense is the most important," he said. "We require this in order to insure the safety of the country, to carry out its policies and to maintain our position as the stabilizing power of East Asia. No weakness in defense can be permitted at this time.

"The reason is apparent when we survey the international situation. The army is compelled to expand its defenses without delay in order to attain security."

His references to the navy were expressed in milder terms. The navy, also, he said, is obliged to adjust its defenses to meet the new non-treaty situation, but it goes without saying that Japan will not be the first to start a naval race.

"Our naval program will continue to be governed by the principle of non-menace and non-aggression," he declared.

Mr. Hirota also defended the German pact, asserting that the Comintern's activities had been increasing in recent years.

Japan, he said, will continue to seek a settlement of outstanding problems with the Soviet.

**Treaty Plan Suggested**

Special to THE NEW YORK TIMES.

WASHINGTON, Jan. 20.—Foreign Minister Arita suggested to the Tokyo Diet that the problem of colonial trade be settled universally in the spirit of the Congo Basin treaty, according to the text of his address as given out here by the Japanese Embassy.

It was assumed that Mr. Arita referred to the rules and regulations established in 1884 in the Congo Basin for States that had obtained grants of territory there under the supervision of the International Association of the Congo.

By declaration of the association, foreign citizens who established themselves in the Congo received

Continued on Page Ten

## ADDRESS IS PRAISED

### Many Republicans Join Democrats in Hailing Tone of the Speech

### CALLED A 'FINE SERMON'

### Senator McNary's Remark Gets No Disagreement Even From the Partisan Critics

### NO DETAILS OF PROGRAM

### Those Who Expected Outline of the Next Four Years Alone Voice Disappointment

By TURNER CATLEDGE

Special to THE NEW YORK TIMES.

WASHINGTON, Jan. 20.—The elevated tone of President Roosevelt's inaugural address, especially his redeclaration of the principle that government should be the instrument of our "united purpose to solve for the individual the ever-rising problems of a complex civilization," was the memory which thousands of visitors took home with them tonight.

Democrats, of whom there were hundreds of thousands in Washington, hailed the address, in the words of Senator Harrison, as the "Roosevelt gospel of real democracy," and Republicans could do nothing but agree that it was "a fine sermon," as Senator McNary of Oregon, Republican leader of the Senate, commented.

Those who had looked for a detailed outline of the President's purposes for the next four years, especially for an elaboration of his program for the new Congress, were in part disappointed. Those who had expected that he would expand upon his view of international relations, particularly his plans for keeping the United States out of war, were also short of specifications. But within the 2,000 words of his address could be read the credo of his whole political philosophy, which, as he asserted, was ratified by the American people in the most recent expression of the popular will.

**Many in Crowd Fail to Hear**

The address brought no wild burst of applause from the rain-drenched audience. In fact, it was hardly heard by many of the thousands who gathered in the Capitol plaza. Those who were more interested in what he had to say than in the spectacle stayed by their radios to hear the words which the falling sleet and rain prevented the crowd from hearing.

There was a rush for copies of the address tonight, however, and newspapers carrying it in full were much in demand. It was a speech which provoked reference to no particular part. It was interesting from the standpoint of the whole, for it was the overtone that was significant: "Forward! Forward! Forward!"

Contrary to expectations, even to

Continued on Page Fifteen

## Rail Brotherhoods to Ask 20% Wage Jump; $116,500,000 Annual Rise in Joint Demand

Special to THE NEW YORK TIMES.

CHICAGO, Jan. 20.—Leaders of the five big railroad brotherhoods voted here tonight to demand a 20 per cent pay increase for about 300,000 members of the unions.

The vote came after nine days of negotiations among the brotherhood chiefs in conference here. The brotherhoods embrace all employes in the train service classifications.

Based on the October, 1936, payroll statistics issued by the Interstate Commerce Commission, the 20 per cent rise would require an increase of $116,500,000 in the annual payrolls of the country's railroads.

Formal notice of the demand for increased pay will be served on the country's carriers as soon as the necessary steps can be taken, David B. Robertson of Cleveland, president of the Brotherhood of Locomotive Firemen and Enginemen, asserted.

The brotherhood leaders did not act on a six-hour day, thirty-hour week proposal, presented at the start of their meeting.

Besides the firemen's brotherhood, the unions involved in the joint demand are the Brotherhood of Railway Trainmen, Brotherhood of Locomotive Engineers, Order of Railway Conductors and the Switchmen's Union of North America.

Mr. Robertson's group has 65,000 members. The largest brotherhood is that of the railroad trainmen, headed by A. F. Whitney of Cleveland, which has 145,000 members. The conductors have 20,000 members; engineers, 65,000, and the switchmen, 7,000.

James A. Phillips of Cedar Rapids, Iowa, is president of the conductors; Alvaney Johnson of Cleveland is president of the engineers, and Thomas C. Cashen of Buffalo is chief of the switchmen. The latter union is the only one of the five affiliated with the American Federation of Labor.

Under the Railway Labor Act the railroads of the country within thirty days after the filing of notice of demands by the unions must set a time and place for meeting with brotherhood leaders for the opening of wage negotiations. If no agreement can be reached the whole matter is then referred to Railway Labor Board for adjudication.

Times Wide World Photo.

**FRANKLIN D. ROOSEVELT BEGINS HIS SECOND TERM**

Chief Justice Charles Evans Hughes administering the oath of office to the President

## CROWD UNDAUNTED BY STREET FLOODS

### Mud, Rain and Sleet Forgotten as Thousands Cheer the President's 'Challenge'

### STAY THROUGH PARADE

### Army and Naval Units March Over an Hour in Storm—Governors Ride in Autos

By F. RAYMOND DANIELL

Special to THE NEW YORK TIMES.

WASHINGTON, Jan. 20.—Ankle deep in mud, huddled under umbrellas, with rain that was half sleet pelting them in the face, thousands stood shivering in a raw wind today while Franklin D. Roosevelt swore for the second time, upon the Bible of his ancestors, to "preserve, protect and defend" the Constitution of the United States.

These and other thousands scrambled over pavements running with water like trout streams to places along Pennsylvania Avenue to see the procession of military strength, actual and potential, which the President, scorning the protection of bullet-proof glass, reviewed as he stood for more than an hour and a half on the portico of a replica of Andrew Jackson's Hermitage after his inauguration.

When the President in his inaugural address, delivered immediately after he took the oath, promised to carry on the reforms as well as the reconstruction that he had begun in the name of the New Deal, he made this "challenge:"

"The test of our progress is not whether we add more to the abundance of those who have much; it is whether we provide enough for those who have too little."

At these words, the crowd forgot its umbrellas, forgot its wet feet, forgot its discomfort and cheered and applauded. These were the sort of words that the New Dealers, engaged in a devotional demonstration of patriotism, with their acres of umbrellas swinging like black mushrooms in a mucky field, had come to hear.

**Taking of the Oath Is Dramatic**

The unexpected, the unscheduled, the more dramatic incident took place before the President began his inaugural address. It was indefinable, intangible and yet it impinged upon the consciousness of almost every one there as Lincoln's eloquence at Gettysburg must have impressed those fortunates who heard it. It came as he repeated after Chief Justice Charles Evans Hughes the traditional oath of office taken by the thirty-one Presidents who have preceded him.

John N. Garner, who was sworn in by Senator Joseph T. Robinson, majority leader of the Senate, responded with the simple words, "I do," after the senior Senator from Arkansas had administered the oath. Not so the President when he took the oath from Chief Justice Hughes, who has been lined up with the anti-New Deal majority of the Supreme Court on most admin-

Continued on Page Fifteen



## The Inaugural Address

By The Associated Press.

*WASHINGTON, Jan. 20.—The text of President Roosevelt's inaugural address, delivered immediately after he took the oath, was as follows:*

My Fellow-Countrymen:

When four years ago we met to inaugurate a President, the Republic, single-minded in anxiety, stood in spirit here. We dedicated ourselves to the fulfillment of a vision—to speed the time when there would be for all the people that security and peace essential to the pursuit of happiness. We of the Republic pledged ourselves to drive from the temple of our ancient faith those who had profaned it; to end by action, tireless and unafraid, the stagnation and despair of that day.

We did those first things first.

Our covenant with ourselves did not stop there. Instinctively we recognized a deeper need—the need to find through government the instrument of our united purpose to solve for the individual the ever-rising problems of a complex civilization.

Repeated attempts at their solution without the aid of government had left us baffled and bewildered. For, without that aid, we had been unable to create those moral controls over the services of science which are necessary to make science a useful servant instead of a ruthless master of mankind. To do this we knew that we must find practical controls over blind economic forces and blindly selfish men.

We of the Republic sensed the truth that democratic government has innate capacity to protect its people against disasters once considered inevitable—to solve problems once considered unsolvable. We would not admit that we could not find a way to master economic epidemics just as, after centuries of fatalistic suffering, we had found a way to master epidemics of disease. We refused to leave the problems of our common welfare to be solved by the winds of chance and the hurricanes of disaster.

In this we Americans were discovering no wholly new truth; we were writing a new chapter in our book of self-government.

**Forefathers Found Way Out of Chaos**

This year marks the one hundred and fiftieth anniversary of the constitutional convention which made us a nation. At that convention our forefathers found the way out of the chaos which followed the Revolutionary War; they created a strong government with powers of united action sufficient then and now to solve problems utterly beyond individual or local solution. A century and a half ago they established the Federal Government in order to promote the general welfare and secure the blessings of liberty to the American people.

Today we invoke those same powers of government to achieve the same objectives.

Four years of new experience have not belied our historic instinct. They hold out the clear hope that government within communities, government within the separate Sates, and government of the United States can do the things the times require, without yielding its democracy. Our tasks in the last four years did not force democracy to take a holiday.

Nearly all of us recognize that as intricacies of human relationships increase, so power to govern them also must increase—power to stop evil; power to do good. The essential democracy of our nation and the safety of our people depend not upon the absence of power but upon lodging it with those whom the people can change or continue at stated intervals through an honest and free system of elections. The Constitution of 1787 did not make our democracy impotent.

In fact, in these last four years, we have made the exercise of all power more democratic; for we have begun to bring private autocratic powers into their proper subordination to the public's government. The legend that they were invincible—above and beyond the processes of a democracy—has been shattered. They have been challenged and beaten.

Our progress out of the depression is obvious.

**Seeks More Enduring Social Structure**

But that is not all that you and I mean by the new order of things. Our pledge was not merely to do a patchwork job with second-hand materials. By using the new materials of social justice we have undertaken to erect on the old foundations a more enduring structure for the better use of future generations.

In that purpose we have been helped by achievements of mind and spirit. Old truths have been relearned, untruths have been unlearned. We have always known that heedless self-interest was bad morals; we know now that it is bad economics. Out of the collapse of a prosperity whose builders boasted their practicality has come the conviction that in the long run economic morality pays.

We are beginning to wipe out the line that divides the practical from the ideal, and in so doing we are fashioning an instrument of unimagined power for the establishment of a morally better world.

This new understanding undermines the old admiration of

Continued on Page Fourteen

## PRESIDENT SPEAKS

### Calls for Leadership of the People Along Road They Have Chosen

### SCORNS 'BLINDLY SELFISH'

### But He Repeats His Reliance on 'General Welfare' Clause of the Constitution

### HEAD BARED TO DOWNPOUR

### 'If Crowd Can Take It, I Can,' He Says—Mrs. Roosevelt Joins Him in Open Car

By ARTHUR KROCK

Special to THE NEW YORK TIMES.

WASHINGTON, Jan. 20.—On the main portico of the Capitol, his head bared to a chill, driving rain, Franklin Delano Roosevelt soon after noon today took for the second time the oath as President of the United States; and to a streaming crowd in front of, beside and behind him reconsecrated the government to leadership of "the American people forward along the road over which they have chosen to advance."

Under the terms of the Norris Amendment to the Constitution, adopted Feb. 6, 1933, this was the first inaugural to be solemnized on a date other than March 4. But the elements made it one to be remembered for another reason by visiting the capital city with a frigid downpour which was responsible for many empty places, a bedraggled parade and a rush of auditors from the space in front of the Capitol as soon as the President completed his address.

His reconsecration was in general terms, omitting specifications of program which members of his Cabinet had expected. The President briefly reviewed the dispersal of "stagnation and despair" after he took office in 1933 and pledged government to "solve for the individual the ever-rising problems of a complex civilization." He spoke scornfully of "blind economic forces" and castigated "blindly selfish men"; and once more he admonished any who may doubt it (courts, people or Congress) that the powers implied in the Constitution of 1787 were "sufficient then and now to solve problems utterly beyond individual or local action."

**As to the Law and Welfare**

The President, stressing once more the preamble of the national charter, emphasized that by it government is ungrudgingly entrusted with the "general welfare," and indicated that he expects from all concerned a liberal construction of laws which have general welfare for their purpose.

Of his own four-year record, this was his epitome:

"By using the new materials of social justice we have undertaken to erect on the old foundation a more enduring structure for the better use of future generations."

Again, as on March 4, 1933, the President won a shower of golden opinions by his inaugural address. Among his divergent groups of political supporters none saw in its general terms any policy in conflict with their own. Praise came from all types of political partisans in the capital (Republicans referred to the speech as a "sermon" and Democrats as a "gospel"); and there was a bull market in Wall Street.

**"A Change in Moral Climate"**

The President selected as the greatest alteration in the nation since he first took office "a change in moral climate" and expressed confidence that there were enough men and women of "good-will" in the country to make permanent that change. He did not find that the "happy valley" had been reached in his four years, pointing to the "indecent" living conditions of millions, with education, recreation and advancement denied them, a third of the nation ill-housed, ill-clad and ill-nourished, their poverty a brake on prosperity's wheel. Because of that prevailing condition, he said, the government will "carry on" until the happy valley is reached, paying no heed to the counsels of comfort, opportunism or timidity.

Despite the cold, pitiless beat of the rain, the President's speech was continuously interrupted with applause. And though the crowd

Continued on Page Fourteen

"All the News That's Fit to Print."

# The New York Times.

LATE CITY EDITION
Fair today, little change in temperature. Showers late tomorrow, not much change in temperature.
Temperatures Yesterday—Max., 78; Min., 54

Copyright, 1940, by The New York Times Company.

VOL. LXXXIX. No. 30,106. Entered as Second-Class Matter, Postoffice, New York, N. Y. NEW YORK, FRIDAY, JUNE 28, 1940. THREE CENTS NEW YORK CITY and Vicinity | FOUR CENTS Elsewhere Except in 7th and 8th Postal Zones.

# REPUBLICANS NOMINATE WENDELL WILLKIE FOR THE PRESIDENCY ON THE 6TH BALLOT; RUMANIA GIVES UP BESSARABIA TO RUSSIA

## BUKOVINA SLICED

### Part of Province, Ports on Black Sea and the Danube Also Ceded

## HUNGARY IS WATCHED

### Carol Prepares to Resist Blow From That Nation—Will Meet Russians

By The Associated Press.

BUCHAREST, Rumania, Friday, June 28—Rumania bowed last night to a Soviet demand for great areas of her territory and moved nearly 2,000,000 men into Transylvania to meet an expected Hungarian attempt to get that province.

Despite earlier reports that Red troops already were on the march, it was disclosed late last night that Russia had agreed to hold back from the actual occupation of the ceded areas—Bessarabia and Northern Bukovina—until the last details of the cessions had been worked out. Diplomats labored at that task. It is expected to be completed today. Soviet troops then would cross the frontier.

[An authoritative diplomatic source in London said early today that Rumania had yielded to Russia on the cession of Bessarabia and Northern Bukovina and that King Carol had asked a conference with the Russians to bid for Russian aid in case of attacks by Hungary and Bulgaria, which also claim Rumanian territory, according to a dispatch to THE NEW YORK TIMES.]

The capital was quiet. The officially censored press still was not permitted to publish a word of the Red ultimatum or of King Carol's acceptance.

**The Road From Munich**

Whether she fights Hungary or not, whether Bulgaria presses her own territorial claim for Southern Dobruja or lets it lie, Rumania, World War heir to Balkan supremacy, was well on the road to dismemberment. It is a road that winds from Munich, through Czecho-Slovakia and Poland to Finland and back again to France.

Apparently Germany and Italy gave their consent to Russia's latest coup. Axis Ministers were in long and earnest consultation with King Carol in his hours of deliberation and decision.

Rumania, rich in oil and grain, but poor in strategic location and useful alliances, decided she must give in to Russia—that no calling into force of her months of military preparations could alter the final result. Hence she yielded just short of a 10 o'clock deadline last night for her peaceful assent and agreed to discuss details later.

She had invoked a virtually general mobilization while the Grand Council considered Russia's demands. The council first accepted them in principle, pleaded unavailingly for time to dicker and finally capitulated.

The decision disposed only of Russia's claims. Now will come Hungary, with the reported backing of Adolf Hitler, to ask for Transylvania. Bulgaria, a friend of Russia, may seek the return of Southern Dobruja.

All told, Rumania stands to lose nearly half of her 113,884 square miles and return to Balkan obscurity—a satellite wavering between the gravitational pulls of the Axis powers in the west and the Red empire in the east.

**The Reported Demands**

Amid reports that Red Army planes were darkening the horizon and that Red troops, tanks and artillery were massing at her frontier, Rumania's Grand Council, under the presidency of the 46-year-old King, gave reluctant consent to demands that authoritative sources outlined as follows:

Return of Bessarabia, 17,146 square miles of fertile country, inhabited by more than 3,000,000 persons.

Cession of the northern part of Bukovina Province, but how much of Bukovina's 4,030 square miles and 911,000 inhabitants Russia wanted was not known.

Control of Rumania's big Black Sea port, Constanta, as a Red naval base.

Supervision of Galati and Braila, two Rumanian ports controlling

Continued on Page Twelve

## The International Situation

**Developments in Europe**

Soviet Russia apparently made a bloodless attainment of her claims against Rumania yesterday. A Rumanian communiqué indicated that a Soviet ultimatum demanding two large slices of territory and concessions for Red naval forces in Black Sea ports had been accepted.

Bessarabia, once a province of Imperial Russia, and Bukovina, of the old kingdom of Austria-Hungary, were reported ceded outright, with Constanta becoming a Soviet naval base and other concessions granted in the Danubian delta ports of Galati and Braila. [All the foregoing, Page 1, Column 1.]

London heard that King Carol, after yielding to the ultimatum, sought Soviet aid against expected demands by Hungary and Bulgaria for return of their lost territories of Transylvania and Dobruja, respectively. [Page 14, Column 2.]

A well-informed Nazi source in Berlin indicated the Soviet move was within the scope of a tri-partite agreement with Germany and Italy for division of the Balkans. [Page 1, Column 3.]

In Rome, however, the Soviet grab caused undisguised surprise. Observers saw it as a contravention of the reported Axis plan to maintain the neutrality of the Balkans. It was feared that if the Russian war machine once started rolling it would not stop until the Red flag waved over the Dardanelles. [Page 13, Column 1.]

There was no official statement from Turkey, but a Turkish naval squadron moved through the Bosporus into the Black Sea, war planes patrolled the air lanes over the Dardanelles and anti-aircraft batteries went on the alert. [Page 1, Column 2.]

While London heard further reports of German troop transport concentrations in French, Belgian and Netherland ports, another British Cabinet leader—Minister of Supply Herbert Morrison—told the world by radio that Britain would hold the fort despite all odds until "the rest of the civilized world" could mobilize against the dictators. Earlier he had told the House of Commons that British war production and imports, although not satisfactory as yet, were approaching that state. [Page 1, Column 4.]

Meanwhile, Britain continued her air raids on harbors, oil refineries and airdromes in Germany and German-occupied territory. Daylight raids on refineries at Misburg and Bremen were reported especially damaging. Damage in the German raids on the East Coast Thursday night was said to have been relatively unimportant. German planes raided Britain again early today. [Page 16, Column 6.]

**Repercussions Elsewhere**

A proclamation controlling the movement of any foreign or American ships in domestic waters or the Panama Canal area was signed by President Roosevelt. It was believed five French ships in American ports would be affected. The President also signed the $1,768,913,000 Army-Navy Appropriation Bill. [Page 1, Column 5.]

Washington received reports from Europe that peace feelers had been put out for a settlement between Britain and Germany. These persisted despite British denials. Some indication of Germany's attitude might be revealed in an expected speech by Chancellor Hitler today, the capital believed. [Page 1, Column 4.]

A "last warning" to United States citizens in Britain to go home was issued by Ambassador Kennedy in London. He said the sailing of the liner Washington from Galway July 4 might be the last by an American ship "until after the war." [Page 16, Column 4.]

## TURKISH WARSHIPS GO INTO BLACK SEA

### Ankara Prepares to Defend Straits in Face of Soviet Demands on Rumania

By The Associated Press.

ANKARA, Turkey, June 27—A Turkish naval squadron steamed through the Bosporus today to the Black Sea, ready to defend the Straits against attack. [Turkey only Wednesday announced her non-participation in the European war.]

This historic guardian of the Dardanelles felt deep concern over Russia's ultimatum to Rumania demanding not only large land concessions but also naval bases on the Black Sea and Danube.

Turkish planes circled over the Straits and anti-aircraft guns were in position. Turkey's main fear was of a general move in this direction, with the Straits as the ultimate goal.

**Assurance on Syria Doubted**

Wireless to THE NEW YORK TIMES.

ANKARA, Turkey, June 26 (delayed)—It was reported tonight without confirmation that Germany had assured Turkey that Italy would not be allowed to take Syria, which this country regards as its back door.

Diplomats here, however, are inclined to discredit this report. It is held significant that it should circulate just as Turkey had decided formally to announce her invocation of the escape clause in her pact with Great Britain and France.

Apart from this it is considered interesting that Syria and Lebanon are not mentioned in the Italian-French armistice terms. There is speculation as to whether this is because of German influence on Italy or because Italy does not wish to make demands on territory where a large army is established when she already has a full job with Britain in the Mediterranean.

The future of Syria is of vital interest to Turkey. As yet there is

Continued on Page Fourteen

## NAZIS INSIST SOVIET ACTS UNDER ACCORD

### Zones of Interest Reported to Have Been Determined by Axis and Moscow

By The United Press.

BERLIN, Friday, June 28—A tri-power agreement between Germany, Italy and Russia dividing zones of interest in Southeastern Europe opened the way for the Soviets' ultimatum against Rumania, it was stated in well-informed Nazi quarters early today.

Joseph Stalin's demands, under an ultimatum expiring at 10 o'clock last night, that Rumania surrender Bessarabia and the northern part of Bukovina Province were said to have been a direct result of this general understanding.

Germany and Italy, according to Nazi informants, agreed to recognize Russia's territorial claims as a means of making good the "injustices" of the settlements following the World War.

Chancellor Hitler and Premier Mussolini, both of whom have vital interests in Rumania and the Balkans and look to Southeastern Europe for supplies to keep their war machines going, were said to have attached conditions to the "go ahead" signal to Mr. Stalin.

The satisfaction of Russia's territorial claims must be brought about in such a manner, they were reported to have stated, as to prevent any general outbreak of war or economic disturbance in the Balkans.

Even an economic disturbance there would severely hamper Germany and Italy, it was pointed out, at a time when they are massing all their strength in preparation for a promised "knockout blow" against Britain.

This understanding with Russia regarding Southeastern Europe was understood to have been reached at a somewhat later date and in considerably "looser" form than Germany's agreement with Russia

Continued on Page Thirteen

## BRITISH DIGGING IN

### Speed Efforts to Make Islands a Fortress—Rise in Output Noted

## NAZIS MASS A FLEET

### 'Hundreds' of Craft Are Assembling in Invasion Move, London Hears

By ROBERT P. POST

Special Cable to THE NEW YORK TIMES.

LONDON, June 27—The British pushed forward today with their preparations for turning these islands into a fortress to withstand the siege and the attacks that most people here are convinced are coming.

The conception of Britain as an outpost of civilization was perhaps best summed up today by Herbert Morrison, the Minister of Supply, who followed up a fighting speech in the House of Commons with a broadcast to the United States in which he said that Britain was a strong point "which will hold on and hold out in the very jaws of the enemy while the rest of the civilized world mobilizes its resources for victory."

Earlier Mr. Morrison had given percentage figures to show how British production had been raised since the Churchill government took office. The increase in production of cruiser and infantry tanks between April and June was 115 per cent, Mr. Morrison said, and the increase in Bren gun carriers was 64 per cent. These were only indications of enormous increases that included artillery and small arms, the Minister told Parliament.

**Labor Volunteers Discussed**

Other indications of the speed with which Britain is moving to make this land a fortress—always with the provision that it will be a fortress from which sorties can and will be made—were also provided today. Ernest Bevin, the Minister of Labor, told the Commons he was consulting the War Office on the possibility of calling volunteer labor for construction of defenses to supplement the full-time work now being done. At the same time Mr. Bevin said that while the number of persons now being trained for skilled factory labor in government training centers was at 10,700, a new record, "we need thousands more."

Mr. Bevin appealed to any skilled fitters, machine operators and instrument makers who were not now employed and were capable of instructing others to come forward at once. The Minister said he had no women in training, but was getting ready to establish a system whereby each factory would take some.

Another facet of the plan for making Britain, uninvaded for centuries, a fortress also was discussed today. This was the question of getting women and children out. Geoffrey H. Shakespeare, Under-Secretary for Dominions, head of the scheme, told the Commons that

Continued on Page Fifteen

## U. S. ACTS ON SHIPS

### President to Exercise His Emergency Power Over Foreign Craft

## CANAL IS INCLUDED

### Bill Signed to Increase Army and Start on 68 New Warships

Special to THE NEW YORK TIMES.

WASHINGTON, June 27—President Roosevelt today declared by proclamation the existence of a national emergency to the extent necessary to control the movement of all American and foreign shipping in United States continental waters and around the Panama Canal, and "to take full possession and control of such vessels" and remove their officers and crews.

The invocation of this war-time authority was described in a White House statement as supplementary to the proclamation last September of a "limited emergency," under which Mr. Roosevelt directed immediate expansion of the Army, Navy and Marine Corps and the Coast Guard. The President acted today under Section 1 of Title II of the Espionage Act of June 15, 1917.

Presumably subject to the proclamation were at least five French ships.

The text of the proclamation was not immediately available. Neither were the specific regulations, which the White House said were to be issued by the Treasury Department. As a result, it could not be ascertained positively that the President had proclaimed a state of national emergency beyond the language he used in the limited emergency proclamation following the outbreak of war in Europe last September.

**New Defense Bill Signed**

Throughout the day, plans to safeguard the security and economic welfare of the Western Hemisphere dominated White House activity. The President signed the $1,768,913,908 supplemental defense appropriation of funds to increase the Army's enlisted strength to 375,000 men, to buy 3,000 more planes and to authorize the Navy to begin the construction of sixty-eight new warships.

Before issuing the emergency proclamation, the President conferred with the Advisory Defense Commission and received a report on progress toward rapid expansion of the armed forces and for raising the output of fighting planes to a mass production basis.

With his special Cabinet committee, composed of the Secretaries of State, Treasury, Agriculture and Commerce, Mr. Roosevelt also reviewed plans for a Pan-American economic union to guard this hemisphere against totalitarian economic aggression. The plan is reported unofficially to be meeting with a cool reception from South American countries, but there was no confirmation from the White House conferees.

The text of the section of the Espionage Act under which the

Continued on Page Seven

## Washington Hears of Peace Talk, But British Deny Nazi Overtures

By BERTRAM D. HULEN

Special to THE NEW YORK TIMES.

WASHINGTON, June 27—Diplomatic circles were convinced today on the basis of confidential advices that soundings were being made in Europe for a negotiated peace between Britain and Germany, but they were far from certain that the effort would get anywhere.

The possibilities are such, however, that the attention of the diplomats was directed with more than usual interest to the speech that Chancellor Hitler is reported preparing to make tomorrow, and their immediate attention was diverted from the Russian move against Rumania.

The conviction that feelers had been put out for possible peace negotiations between the two major belligerents persisted in the face of denials from British Government spokesmen that such a move was in the wind and assertions in London that the reports were nothing more than German propaganda.

The reports have been circulated in Berlin. They also have appeared with some definiteness in Italian official quarters.

But diplomats here pointed out that, granting all this, it did not follow that the soundings would get anywhere. The possibilities, it is assumed, will be known better in a few days. It is taken for granted that if nothing comes of them the German attack on Britain will not be long delayed.

The State Department said it had no information other than dispatches that mentioned the current reports in European capitals. These reports, the department said, could not be confirmed officially. Department officials were disposed to accept at face value British declara-

Continued on Page Fifteen

THE REPUBLICAN NOMINEE
Wendell Lewis Willkie
Times Studio, 1940

## Summary of the Ballots

*Following are the total votes received by candidates in the balloting at the Republican convention last night:*

| Candidate. | First Ballot. | Second Ballot. | Third Ballot. | Fourth Ballot. | Fifth Ballot. | *Sixth Ballot. |
|---|---|---|---|---|---|---|
| Dewey | 360 | 338 | 315 | 250 | 57 | 8 |
| Taft | 129 | 203 | 212 | 254 | 377 | 312 |
| Willkie | 105 | 171 | 259 | 306 | 429 | 659 |
| Vandenberg | 76 | 73 | 72 | 61 | 42 | 0 |
| James | 74 | 66 | 59 | 56 | 59 | 1 |
| Martin | 44 | 26 | 0 | 0 | 0 | 1 |
| MacNider | 34 | 34 | 28 | 26 | 4 | 2 |
| Gannett | 33 | 30 | 11 | 4 | 1 | 1 |
| Bridges | 28 | 9 | 1 | 1 | 0 | 0 |
| Capper | 18 | 18 | 0 | 0 | 0 | 0 |
| Hoover | 17 | 21 | 32 | 31 | 20 | 9 |
| McNary | 13 | 10 | 10 | 8 | 9 | 0 |
| Bushfield | 9 | 0 | 0 | 0 | 0 | 0 |
| La Guardia | 0 | 1 | 0 | 0 | 0 | 0 |

*Unofficial.

## WILLKIE CREDITED FOR OWN VICTORY

### Convincing Delegates of His Meeting Challenge of Day Said to Have Defeated Foes

By ARTHUR KROCK

Special to THE NEW YORK TIMES.

MUNICIPAL AUDITORIUM, Philadelphia, Friday, June 28—The nomination of Wendell L. Willkie was a political revolution, but peaceful by contrast with others which have shaken the rest of the world. In normal times it could not possibly have happened.

The professional politicians, unaware that changed times and the impact of thunderous events have cracked the system which they long have practiced, sought to prevent the miracle by the usual methods.

These included an appeal to partisanship, because Mr. Willkie has so recently become a Republican; an attempt to match the personality of Thomas E. Dewey against him; an effort to overcome the tide with Senator Robert A. Taft, bred in the tradition and the son of a Republican President and Chief Justice, and finally one of those old-fashioned combinations which often have been successfully employed to "stop" a political intruder.

None of it worked because, as they compared the candidates put

Continued on Page Six



## DEWEY WEAKENED BY PARTY RIFT HERE

### His Vote in State Delegation, Smaller Than Expected, Drops to Four on the Fifth Ballot

By WARREN MOSCOW

Special to THE NEW YORK TIMES.

MUNICIPAL AUDITORIUM, PHILADELPHIA, June 27—Thomas E. Dewey's Presidential boom, always weak in his home State, was formally buried tonight, at exactly 11:30 P. M., when the New York delegation swung 75 of its 92 votes to Wendell Willkie on the fifth ballot. This move came after Mr. Dewey had released his delegates, at their request, relayed to him by J. Russel Sprague, the Dewey campaign manager. The prosecutor got only four votes on this roll-call.

Dewey had started off with 61 votes, fewer than expected, while Frank E. Gannett got 17; Willkie, 6; Herbert Hoover, 4; Senator Vandenberg, 1, and Joseph W. Martin Jr., 1.

Then, on the second ballot, secret as was the first, Dewey dropped to 58; Gennett got 16; Willkie, 13; Hoover, 3; Vandenberg, 1, and Mayor La Guardia, 1.

The third ballot, the first public ballot, found Dewey getting only 54 votes, and on the fourth, with Gannett releasing his votes, 6 more pledged to Dewey dropped off, and Westchester, Long Island and Brooklyn began to put the pressure

Continued on Page Four

## RIVALS WORN DOWN

### Willkie Garners Votes as His Opponents Free Their Delegates

## MANY STATES SWITCH

### Convention Adjourns in the Early Morning, Hailing Victor

By TURNER CATLEDGE

Special to THE NEW YORK TIMES.

MUNICIPAL AUDITORIUM, Philadelphia, Friday, June 28—Wendell Lewis Willkie of New York, Indiana-born president of the Commonwealth & Southern Corporation, former Democrat who has been a foe of the New Deal, was nominated early this morning for President of the United States by the Republican party.

His nomination came on the sixth ballot of the party's twenty-second annual convention, marking one of the greatest upsets in the history of the convention system in America. A newcomer to the party, opposed by its veteran leaders, and lacking the usual organization to build up a candidate's strength, Mr. Willkie came into the picture here on the crest of a popular wave which not only did not diminish but finally asserted itself on the convention delegates themselves.

Starting out in tonight's balloting in third place, Mr. Willkie went forward in a series of thrusts until he went over on the sixth. He first eliminated Thomas E. Dewey, who came to the convention with the largest number of delegates, then Senator Taft, who was supported by many of the regular leaders. He outran a challenge which Senator Taft's smooth-operating machine was finally able to start.

**Rush to Willkie Is Begun**

After the middle of the sixth ballot the convention turned into a rush for the Willkie standard. Governor Bricker of Ohio, who had led Mr. Taft's largest single block of delegates on the floor, sought at that time to make the convention's vote unanimous, but Joseph W. Martin Jr., the permanent chairman, ordered the roll-call to proceed to the end. Finally, however, the ballot was made unanimous at 998, two of the 1,000 delegates being absent from the hall.

Managers of other candidates at once offered their congratulations and those of their principals. All sought to close ranks in the spirit of the enthusiasm which swept the hall and the galleries when it became apparent that Mr. Willkie had been nominated.

The main business now left to the convention is the selection of a candidate for Vice President. Mr. Willkie will be requested tomorrow to indicate his desires as to a running mate. That the second-place candidate will come from the West is practically certain, and suggestions already were being made as to the availability of Senator Charles L. McNary, Minority leader of the Senate, while some of the defeated Presidential candidates also were discussed.

**Rivals to Support Willkie**

After the nomination had been made unanimous, J. Russell Sprague, manager of Mr. Dewey's campaign, said the young prosecutor had asked him to express his thanks to his supporters and his assurance that he would give Mr. Willkie his whole-hearted support in the coming campaign.

David S. Ingalls, Senator Taft's campaign manager, said it had been a great fight and that Senator Taft and those who supported him would be behind Mr. Willkie, whom he acclaimed as the next President.

Governor James of Pennsylvania and Senator John Thomas of Idaho joined in making the nomination unanimous.

Former President Hoover sent his congratulations directly to the winner stressing that Mr. Willkie was the choice of a free convention and undoubtedly would move on to victory.

Mr. Willkie considered for a while going before the convention tonight and accepting the nomination, but canceled the plan because of extreme fatigue. He had been constantly on the move, with hardly three full hours of sleep a night

Continued on Page Five

"All the News That's Fit to Print."

# The New York Times.

LATE CITY EDITION
Mostly cloudy today, cooler tonight. Tomorrow fair, little change in temperature.
Temperatures Yesterday—Max., 75; Min., 69

Copyright, 1940, by The New York Times Company.

VOL. LXXXIX..No. 30,107. Entered as Second-Class Matter, Postoffice, New York, N. Y. NEW YORK, SATURDAY, JUNE 29, 1940. THREE CENTS New York City and Vicinity | FOUR CENTS Elsewhere Except in 7th and 8th Postal Zones.

# REPUBLICANS NAME M'NARY FOR VICE PRESIDENT; WILLKIE AIMS AT UNITY, DEFENSE AND RECOVERY; RUSSIANS INVADE RUMANIA, HUNGARY THREATENS

## REDS ARE FIRED ON

### Many Killed as Russians Battle Rumanians for Hours in Cernauti

### OLD BORDER PASSED

### Soviet Units in Moldavia —Carol Calls on Hitler, Mobilizes Fully

By The Associated Press.

BUCHAREST, Rumania, Saturday, June 29—Embattled Rumanian citizens fought Red Army troops for hours today in the border town of Cernauti as the Russian Army of Occupation swept into ceded parts of Rumania and moved beyond those areas into old Rumania. Scores of civilians were killed and wounded.

The fighting at Cernauti started between Communists and anti-Communists hours before the troops arrived in midafternoon and hurled tanks at barricades thrown up in the streets.

After being driven from the streets the anti-Communists took to housetops and sniped at the vanguard of the Russian Army marching in to take over territory the Bucharest government handed over in response to Moscow demands.

From before dawn until Russian infantry marched in at 2 P. M. the snipers blazed away. They finally were killed or dispersed.

Many Russians were killed at an undisclosed point on the Bessarabian frontier when Rumanian forces opened up on the Red forces which continued on past the limits of ceded Bessarabia and Bukovina into old Rumania.

**Full Mobilization Ordered**

King Carol ordered complete mobilization—"to the last man"—effective at midnight, and all taxis and private vehicles here disappeared from the streets during the early morning hours.

Cafes and restaurants closed as waiters hastily doffed their aprons and hurried to concentration points to join the 2,000,000 men already under arms in this war-threatened Balkan kingdom.

It was learned that the German Legation warned the Rumanian Government to increase internal police measures against possible "revolutionary activity by Communists and Jews."

A complicated situation fell on the Rumanian General Staff with the revelation that many of Rumania's troops on the Hungarian frontier—another trouble spot—are from ceded Bessarabia.

According to the Russian demands to which King Carol capitulated, they must return to their Bessarabian homes as new Russian citizens.

Besides losing some of its best fighters, the General Staff must find replacements quickly on the Hungarian frontier, which threatens to develop trouble over Budapest's demands for Transylvania, territory lost to Rumania after the World War.

After taking over Cernauti, a city of 110,000 population, the Russians swept into Dorohio, a town in the Province of Moldavia.

As soon as this news seeped out the Rumanian Government filed an urgent appeal with the German Minister that Berlin put hard pressure on Moscow to halt the Red advance and force the Russians to retire to the line named in their original, and accepted, demand.

Already, Red troops have occupied surrendered sections of Rumania in a political conquest that may yet bring conflict between Germany and Russia.

**Nazi Military Mission Arrives**

A German military mission, arriving here last night was understood to have come to see to it that the Soviet kept to the original territorial demands.

Red soldiers were reported without official confirmation to be moving on Botoshani, which, like Dorohoi, is in the northernmost district of old Rumania.

The Russian move brought unrest to the entire European southeast and to Asia Minor.

Dr. Wilhelm Fabricius, the German Minister to Rumania, went to Vienna yesterday in a special airplane, apparently to get new instructions from Chancellor Hitler, to whom Carol had appealed for help.

While Bulgaria and Hungary—

Continued on Page Eight

## The International Situation

### Developments in Europe

Sharp fighting broke out between Rumanian citizens and soldiers and Red Army troops as the Soviet war machine rolled through the ceded territories of Rumania and beyond.

King Carol ordered mobilization "to the last man." The Rumanian Government appealed to the German Minister for Nazi pressure on Moscow to hold the Soviet to the terms of the cession agreement. [All the foregoing Page 1, Column 1.]

On word of the Red advance Hungary sent her troops marching toward the Rumanian border, with the possibility that they might not stop at the frontier. Previously it had been indicated that Hungary viewed the Soviet move into the Balkans with equanimity and would await an Axis triumph in the war with Britain for settlement of her claims for Transylvania. [Page 1, Column 4.]

Turkey said nothing, but added to her fleet concentration in the Black Sea and increased her mobilized land troops to an estimated 500,000. [Page 1, Column 3.]

Reports of peace moves continued. Berlin's answer was that the cannons were still speaking and no other voice would be listened to. An Associated Press dispatch from London quoted a neutral diplomatic source as saying the German invasion of the British Isles would await disposition of peace possibilities. [Page 9, Column 1.]

Former Prime Minister Neville Chamberlain denied in an interview in London that he was leading any peace move, that he was at odds with Prime Minister Churchill or that there was any disunity among the British. [Page 9, Column 6.]

The British recognized the de Gaulle French National Committee in London as the "leader of all free Frenchmen" and an ally against the Axis. It was problematical, however, how much of the French Empire General de Gaulle could rally. General Mittelhauser of France was reported to have ordered cessation of hostilities of his command in Syria, and Bordeaux reported a declaration of support by general Nogues, commander in North Africa. [Page 1, Column 2.]

Bracing herself for invasion, Britain declared a new defensive area stretching 230 miles north along the east coast of England and Scotland from the previous zone, which ended at The Wash, near Nottingham. The area will be taken over by the military and all civilians may be evacuated. [Page 7, Column 5.]

Unremitting air warfare between Germany and Britain continued. As the British completed evacuation of the Channel Islands Nazi raids caused twenty-nine deaths. New waves of German bombers also flew over Britain this morning, dropping their deadly cargoes. The British, in turn, said their raids against shipping bases and oil refineries on the Continent continued day and night. [Page 7, Column 1.]

### Repercussions Elsewhere

Torpedoing of the "S. S. Edgehill" off Ireland was reported by a Gibraltar radio station. The one-time United States freighter Edgehill, now the Oremar, is at Baltimore dock, and there was no clue to the vessel's identity. The station said its source was the American Export liner Excalibur, which left Naples, Italy, yesterday with refugees. [Page 1, Column 4.]

Additional billions for defense may be asked of Congress soon, President Roosevelt indicated, to finance a long-term buying plan for Army supplies. He set no figure, but War Department sources recently have said the Army will need equipment costing $3,000,000,000 above that already authorized. [Page 1, Column 5.]

The Japanese Government was said to be dissatisfied with the economic concessions already offered in the Netherlands Indies and to have demanded freedom of entry for Japanese nationals and Japanese economic enterprises. A Foreign Office statement said the Japanese must have airtight assurances of an increased flow of necessary supplies from the Indies. [Page 34, Column 1.]

## HUNGARIANS MARCH

### Will Go Into Rumania if Red Army Pushes On, Spokesmen Warn

### CLAIM AXIS SUPPORT

### Bulgaria Holding Off on Dobruja—Nazi-Soviet Rift Deemed Nearer

By The Associated Press.

BUDAPEST, Hungary, June 28—Hungary sent her troops marching to the Rumanian frontier tonight and official quarters said they would continue across the border with the full support of Germany and Italy if the Russian Army of Occupation in Rumania kept moving toward the Carpathian Mountains.

Officials here asserted that the continuing Russian advance into old Rumania after the occupation of ceded Bessarabia and Northern Bukovina would change entirely Hungary's attitude heretofore of watchful waiting. They said Germany, although desirous of keeping Hungary out of war, would certainly give Hungary the go-ahead signal "with full Axis support" if the Russians failed to apply the brakes.

The entire question of peace or war in Southeastern Europe appeared to hang on how far Russia would go into Rumania. An open break between Moscow and Berlin over the Rumanian issue seemed a growing possibility.

**Soviet Ultimatum Denied**

Hungarian officials denied a Rumanian press assertion that Russia had sent Hungary an ultimatum demanding Carpatho-Ukraine [Ruthenia]. They said it was "typical Rumanian gangsterism" and asserted they had received no communication from Moscow.

[The inspired Rumanian press, The Associated Press reported, carried under a Budapest dateline a dispatch that said: "Diplomatic circles here in Budapest say the Moscow government has sent a note to the Hungarian Government demanding a protectorate over the Ukrainian elements of Ruthenia." Diplomatic quarters in Bucharest said they expected a similar move by Germany, the United Press reported.]

The Hungarian troops were ordered to advance tonight, the official news agency said, because of the complicated situation in Rumania. It was explained that this meant that troops had been sent up to the line a short distance from the Rumanian frontier.

Hungary appeared ready to go into Transylvania, a Rumanian agricultural area formerly Hungary's, at a moment's notice if the Soviet advance continued. A communiqué of the news agency said:

"The Hungarian Government, owing to the unclear situation in Rumania, has decided to make its preparations more severe all along the Rumanian border and to order the frontier chasseur [light cavalry or infantry] troops to advance."

The inspired press expressed concern over the welfare of the 1,500,-

Continued on Page Eight

THE REPUBLICAN CANDIDATES

Wendell Lewis Willkie
*For President*

Charles Linza McNary
*For Vice President*

Times Studio, 1940

## SENATOR DRAFTED

### New Party Rulers Pick Veteran Farm Leader to Balance Ticket

### OVATION TO WILLKIE

### Convention Din Greets Nominee—He Asks Battle for Liberty

By TURNER CATLEDGE
Special to THE NEW YORK TIMES.

PHILADELPHIA, June 28—The Republican National Convention drafted today Senator Charles L. McNary of Oregon as the party's candidate for the Vice Presidency on the ticket with Wendell L. Willkie and thus set the stage for a vigorous campaign.

The convention ended at 5 P. M. in a final burst of political zeal, with Mr. Willkie standing before the cheering delegates and spectators, summoning them to battle for the preservation of liberty in the last great free democracy on earth.

Shaking his tousled hair and thrusting out his fists to emphasize his challenges, Mr. Willkie gave the assembled Republicans the assurance they were seeking that here was a man who would fight. If the reaction of the throng could have been reduced to a single sentence of the street it probably would have been:

"Oh boy! He's got the stuff!"

Mr. Willkie thanked the delegates. He complimented Representative Joseph W. Martin Jr. of Massachusetts for his fair and impartial performance as permanent chairman of the convention. He stood beside Mrs. Willkie, a neatly dressed, attractive little woman dressed in a combination of blue and white, for the photographers, sound and television camera men. As he started to leave the platform he turned to the crowd for one last word.

"Going Away to Sleep"

"Now, I'm going away to sleep for a week," he said.

A more formal notification ceremony and acceptance are expected to take place later at his birthplace in Elwood, Ind. He will leave the convention city tomorrow aboard the yacht of Roy W. Howard, newspaper publisher.

Other candidates who fell by the wayside in last night's balloting already were leaving. Their headquarters at the various hotels were deserted except for a few loyal workers in each who were packing up the remaining effects.

Mr. McNary's nomination was unanimous. It was made so after the Missouri delegation and Congressmen scattered throughout numerous State contingents had given a complimentary vote to Representative Dewey Short of the "Show Me State." When, at the end of the first roll-call, the vote stood McNary 890, Short 108, the latter moved to make the decision unanimous and there followed a roar of "ayes."

Mr. McNary was an agreed choice of the many forces who converged at the last minute behind Mr. Willkie. The Senate leader was said to have declined the honor at the first suggestion, but later said that if the convention wanted him he would accept. His nomination was in reality a draft.

**McNary's Farm Role Stressed**

The Senator was placed in nomination by W. S. Moscrip, Minnesota farm leader. His work in behalf of agriculture was cited throughout a number of seconding speeches. He is remembered among Republicans as co-author of the celebrated McNary-Haugen farm bill, forerunner of recent farm aid programs.

In moving to make Mr. McNary the solid choice of the convention, Mr. Short predicted that the tie-up of Willkie and McNary, the one speaking for business in government and the other for assistance to agriculture, the Republicans would certainly win in November.

Senator Arthur H. Vandenberg, whose Michigan delegates really started the bandwagon move to Mr. Willkie last night after the Senator had released them, received a tremendous ovation when he took the rostrum to second the nomination of his Senate colleague.

Backers of Mr. Short had no idea of putting him over. They merely wanted to give a compliment to,

Continued on Page Three

## BILLIONS MORE AIM OF ARMS PROGRAM

### President to Ask Congress Soon to Make Purchases Possible on Even Larger Scale

Special to THE NEW YORK TIMES.

WASHINGTON, June 28—President Roosevelt indicated today that he would ask Congress soon to appropriate more billions for national defense in order to reduce the cost to the government of planes, tanks and other mechanized equipment and provide manufacturers with a backlog of orders on which to plan production.

The President told a press conference that the question was being studied, but that he was unable to give the exact amount of the appropriation to be asked. War Department sources have indicated, however, the need for equipment costing $5,000,000,000 over and above that already authorized. Other authorities said any further defense appropriations would go to the Army.

As defense plans continued to dominate White House conferences, Secretary Morgenthau acted under the President's proclamation of yesterday to forbid any ships to leave an American port on a foreign cruise without express permission of the Treasury Department. To enforce regulations carrying out the order the Secretary set up a new office of merchant ship movements under the direction of Assistant Secretary Herbert E. Gaston.

Besides forbidding unauthorized departures the rules establish close supervision over the handling and

Continued on Page Sixteen

## Willkie Approves Platform, Opposes Big Campaign Gifts

By JAMES A. HAGERTY
Special to THE NEW YORK TIMES.

PHILADELPHIA, June 28—In an interview with nearly 300 newspaper correspondents, editors and magazine writers at the Hotel Warwick, Wendell L. Willkie, Republican nominee for President, announced today that he would resign on Monday as president of the Commonwealth and Southern Corporation in preparation for an extensive and intensive campaign.

Saying that he did not wish at this time to go into detail on questions of policy, Mr. Willkie stated that he already had accepted the nomination, but that he expected to make an acceptance speech at a formal notification, which probably would be at Elwood, Ind., his birthplace.

Asked what he regarded as the outstanding issues of the campaign, he replied:

"National unity, the speedy building of an adequate national defense and rehabilitation of our economic system."

Sitting on the end of a table in the grand ballroom of the hotel, Mr. Willkie smilingly faced a battery of five motion picture cameras with their blinding lights and the flashlights of thirty newspaper photographers with composure.

He talked easily and informally, parrying some of the questions about policies with a pleasant smile. The general impression made by the Republican presidential nominee was that of a pleasant and able personality who was ready to make a hard fight for election, once he started out on the stump.

**Confers With Party Leaders**

It was nearly 1 o'clock, two hours after the interview had been scheduled, when Mr. Willkie entered the ballroom. He had been delayed by conferences with party leaders, presumably by discussion over the selection of the nominee for Vice President and the chairman of the new national committee.

Preceding Mr. Willkie's arrival, his young son, Philip, wearing a brown plaid sports coat, brown gabardine trousers and a brown shirt and necktie, posed for the photographers. Addressing the reporters, he said:

"I just want to say that I am very happy and to thank you for the fine press reports my father has received."

After saying that he would resign as president of the Commonwealth and Southern Corporation at once, Mr. Willkie remarked that he expected to go to the convention later in the day.

"I am just going to say 'Hello,'" he added. "I want to go out to the convention to see the delegates, not to make a speech."

"Will you accept the nomination?" he was asked.

"I have accepted already, so far as that is concerned," he replied.

Mr. Willkie was asked whether, in the event of his election, he would confer with President Roosevelt if the foreign situation should

Continued on Page Three

## ROOSEVELT WILLING TO TALK TO WILLKIE

### Would Be 'Very Glad' to See Him if He Cares to Discuss Our International Relations

Special to THE NEW YORK TIMES.

WASHINGTON, June 28—President Roosevelt said today that he would be very glad to see Wendell L. Willkie if the Republican Presidential nominee felt inclined to come to the White House to talk over international relations.

The reference to Mr. Willkie was made by Mr. Roosevelt at his press conference when he was asked if he planned to invite the Republican candidate to Washington to talk about a "common front" on foreign affairs. The President said he had not thought of it and then made his statement that he would be very glad to see Mr. Willkie.

Mr. Roosevelt's own reaction to the nomination of Mr. Willkie could only be guessed by those attending his press conference and the Cabinet meeting.

To the newspaper men Mr. Roosevelt suggested Mr. Willkie's electric utility connections only indirectly. He began his conference with an apology for being late—something he has rarely done in the past. He said the reason was that some one had turned off the power on the elevator to the second floor of the Executive Mansion. With a laugh he said he hoped the incident had no connection with what happened in Philadelphia last night.

**Farley and Ickes Comment**

Postmaster General Farley, on leaving the White House, asked to be excused from further comment, and laughingly called attention to the following statement which he issued earlier in the day:

"The nomination greatly clarifies the issue before the nation—which is a good thing. The question is, of course, what set of forces, economic and social, are to control our government—the historic American processes, or some new and somewhat foreign methods of concentrated control.

"Most of the rank and file Republicans will understand this as well as most of the rank and file Democrats."

Secretary Ickes said:

"Franklin D. Roosevelt will be re-

Continued on Page Three

## TRUCE IS ACCEPTED BY FRENCH IN SYRIA

### Leader of 500,000 Troops to Abide by Petain's Decision—North Africa Backs Him

Wireless to THE NEW YORK TIMES.

BEIRUT, Syria, June 28—General Eugene Mittelhauser, French Commander in Chief in the Middle East, announced today the cessation of hostilities in Syria. He declared the French flag would continue to fly over Syria.

His announcement was made over the Beirut radio yesterday, but was released for publication only today. The announcer said General Mittelhauser, in agreement with the French High Commissioner, Gabriel Puaux, had decided that the armistice conditions signed by France did not change the situation of the mandated territories and therefore Syria and Lebanon should cease hostilities against Germany and Italy.

It is understood the French administration of the two mandated territories will continue as before, the French forces remaining in the country. Relations with Palestine will not be materially affected, it is stated, and Palestine's trade with Syria is expected to continue normally.

**Tunisia and Algeria Report**

BORDEAUX, France, June 26 (Delayed) (UP)—General Auguste Nogues, French commander in North Africa and Governor General of Tunisia, issued the following declaration of loyalty to the government of Premier Henri Philippe Petain to the Moroccan press, it was said here today:

"North Africa is a part of French territory. It intends to remain French and its big army has remained loyal.

"We must work for France's re-

Continued on Page Nine

## TURKEY SPEEDS UP WAR PREPARATIONS

### 500,000 Men Under Arms as Fleet Sails Into Black Sea to Warn Bulgaria

By The Associated Press.

ISTANBUL, Turkey, June 28—Turkey mobilized more men tonight, raising to more than 500,000 the number of troops under arms, and poured both surface warships and submarines into the Black Sea. Significantly the Turkish fleet, followed by a submarine flotilla, was headed north, probably to cruise past the coast of Bulgaria, a former segment of the Ottoman Empire.

There were intensive troop movements throughout the country, mainly in the direction of the Bulgarian frontier. Aside from this manifest warning to Bulgaria and what might stand behind her, the Turks were taking every precaution to defend their heritage, the Dardanelles, from attack from the east. Turkey was vitally concerned by Soviet Russia's thrust into Rumania.

**Plan to Double Fighting Force**

In addition to the new mobilization, the Turkish Government was understood to have completed a plan to double the fighting force of half a million within twenty-four hours if need be.

Before the Turkish fleet entered the Black Sea it was fully fueled and supplied in the Bosporus. It was headed by the 23,100-ton battle cruiser Yavuz, a product of Imperial Germany, Turkey's flagship. Turkish mine sweepers plied the waters outside the Straits and mine layers planted explosives along the Turkish Black Sea coast.

The action was regarded here as serving notice to all, and to Bulgaria in particular, that Turkey was

Continued on Page Seven

## Ship Bearing Name of U. S. Steamer Is Reported Torpedoed Off Ireland

A radio message from Station GYW, Gibraltar, relaying a message purported to have been received from the American Export liner Excalibur, was picked up by the Mackay Radio and the RCA-Radiomarine stations here early today reporting that the steamer Edgehill and Empire Toucan had been torpedoed in the Atlantic Ocean southwest of the Irish coast.

The one-time United States freighter Edgehill, now known as the Oremar and still under the United States flag, is tied up at the dock at the Lower Yard of the Bethlehem Shipbuilding Corporation in Baltimore, undergoing engine repairs. Officials of the Calmar Steamship Company, 25 Broadway, owners of the vessel, said the freighter had not made a European voyage since they acquired her in January, 1939, and they knew of no other freighter named Edgehill.

Maritime records listed no other vessel named Edgehill and, since there was no further identification in the message, there was no indication that the vessel reported torpedoed was a United States ship.

Station GYW frequently relays marine information, it was said at the radio stations here. The Gibraltar station said the message had originated from the Excalibur, which left Naples, Italy, yesterday with some 300 American refugees bound home, after having sailed from Genoa, Italy, on Wednesday.

The Empire Toucan is believed to be a British freighter that left a southern part recently for an undisclosed destination. Whether she was near the position given in the unconfirmed message could not be learned in shipping circles, but the departure of a ship of the same

Continued on Page Six

"All the News That's Fit to Print."

# The New York Times.

LATE CITY EDITION
Fair with moderate temperatures today. Tomorrow fair, somewhat warmer.
Temperatures Yesterday—Max.,83; Min.,68



VOL. LXXXIX...No. 30,125. Entered as Second-Class Matter, Postoffice, New York, N. Y. NEW YORK, WEDNESDAY, JULY 17, 1940. THREE CENTS NEW YORK CITY and Vicinity | FOUR CENTS Elsewhere Except in 7th and 8th Postal Zones.

# ROOSEVELT LEAVES THIRD TERM TO PARTY; RELEASES DELEGATES FOR A FREE CHOICE; MOVE TO DRAFT HIM IS SET FOR TONIGHT

## U. S. RESISTS CLOSING OF THE BURMA ROAD, HULL MAKES CLEAR

### Secretary, After Talking to Stimson, Asserts American Interest in Trade Lanes

### BRITISH ARE SURPRISED

### Think Declaration, Warning That We Will Not Retreat, Comes Rather Late

By BERTRAM D. HULEN
Special to THE NEW YORK TIMES.

WASHINGTON, July 16—Secretary of State Cordell Hull took direct issue with Great Britain and Japan today over the proposed closing of the Burma route for supplies to China, serving notice through a statement issued by the State Department of opposition to the closing of the road.

Whether this means that steps may be taken to support this opposition or only that the United States is merely giving notice that she does not acquiesce in the stopping of essential traffic over the road will become known only as events unfold.

The possibility also exists that the effect of the declaration may be to support and therefore to stiffen Britain's position regarding Japan.

The position was similar to the one taken by Mr. Hull several weeks ago, when Japan demanded the closing of the Indo-China railway to military supplies and he reminded Japan that the United States had a vital interest in the trade arteries over which world commerce moves.

The statement today again emphasized this point, namely, that the American Government "has a legitimate interest in the keeping open of arteries of commerce in every part of the world."

**TEXT OF STATEMENT**

The text of the State Department's statement follows:

The Secretary of State, in reply to inquiries by press correspondents for comment in regard to reports that, at the instance of the Japanese Government, the British Government would prohibit temporarily the movement of certain commodities through Burma into China over what is known as the Burma route, said that this government has a legitimate interest in the keeping open of arteries of commerce in every part of the world and considers that action such as this, if taken, and such as was taken recently in relation to the Indo-China railway, would constitute unwarranted interpositions of obstacles to world trade.

The statement embodied Mr. Hull's well known views, that there is no way to carry on world commerce if trade arteries are to be closed at the instance of any country. It is a position of which Great Britain is well aware, although it was not disclosed whether Britain had been informed in advance of the American attitude.

It was on this basic position that Mr. Hull rested his case, rather than on the Open Door policy, the Nine-power treaty, or other international engagements. The bare fact is that closing the Burma route will shut off American products from China, and so the interests of the United States are affected.

Figures are not available as to the extent of this traffic, but trucks, gasoline and other supplies move over the route, which is the principal artery into China and the region being defended by General Chiang Kai-shek.

**Divergence in Policy**

The declaration, however, took on far broader significance than this, for it appeared to place the United States at odds with both Britain and Japan. From this standpoint it was regarded as possibly as significant as the historic break on Far Eastern policy between Britain and the United States in January, 1932, when London refused to go along with Secretary of State Henry L. Stimson on his vigorous Manchurian diplomacy.

It may or may not have been significant that Secretary Stimson, now occupying the War portfolio, conferred with Secretary Hull this morning, before the statement was issued. However, Mr. Hull said it was just a call in a general sense,

Continued on Page Twelve

## The International Situation

Secretary of State Hull issued a statement yesterday in which he said that the closing of the Burma road, chief supply route of the Chinese Government, was an unwarranted obstacle to world trade. Under pressure from Japan, Britain recently agreed to close that road. Thus Mr. Hull's statement put him in opposition to both London and Tokyo. [Page 1, Column 1.]

The Japanese Army forced the resignation of the Cabinet of Premier Yonai, apparently because the Cabinet's policy against the United States and Britain was considered insufficiently strong. Indications were that Prince Konoye would establish a one-party government on the German-Italian model. Such a government would be expected to seek control over French Indo-China, the Netherlands Indies and other Far Eastern possessions of non-Asiatic nations. [Page 1, Column 2.]

Reports received by President Roosevelt showed that the Advisory Defense Commission had cleared Army and Navy contracts totaling $1,661,891,494 since July 6. [Page 1, Column 4.]

His friends in Rome expect Chancellor Hitler to convoke a meeting of the Reichstag late this week or early next, at which he will offer Britain one last chance to submit. Count Ciano, the Italian Foreign Minister, will visit Berlin before that meeting. In Rome it was reported that among the terms of peace would be the yielding up of the colonies lost by Germany after the last war and a British commitment to stay aloof from the affairs of Europe, which would in effect be split between Germany and Italy. [Page 1, Column 3.]

A newspaper in Grenoble, France, published reports that Germany had 600,000 troops massed for an attempt to invade Britain and that action might start Friday night if the weather were right. The same paper said the original take-off had been set for the night of July 9-10 but had been postponed because of dissension in the German High Command. Observers held that this publication of supposed plans might be German propaganda pressure on Britain to submit. [Page 15, Column 2.]

An announcement in the British House of Commons that evacuation of children to the United States and Canada must be halted brought criticism that the sons and daughters of the wealthy were being removed to safety but that the children of the poor must face war. Lack of naval escorts was the reason given for stopping the evacuation. [Page 19, Column 1.]

Bad weather prevented any major series of daylight German raids on Britain, but the British said they had shot down three of the comparatively few bombers that did come over. Monday night the British and Germans exchanged raids on airdromes, ports and industrial objectives. [Page 14, Column 2.]

London reported that in the week ended July 7 a total of 114,137 tons of British, Allied and neutral merchant shipping had been destroyed. Berlin asserted that the British convoy system had been proved a failure. [Page 15, Column 1.]

Italy claimed to have eliminated the important Dolo salient on the Kenya-Ethiopia frontier, shortening her line by almost 200 miles. Britain denied that the salient had been cut off. [Page 16, Column 3.]

On the ground that Chile was tolerating an anti-Nationalist campaign, Spain — which is friendly to Germany—severed diplomatic relations with Chile. The Chilean Government has been combating a pro-Nazi movement, said by the authorities to have been aimed at the overthrow of the government. [Page 11, Column 1.]

## JAPANESE CABINET FORCED TO RESIGN

### Army Men Withdraw Support From Yonai, Ending Regime —Konoye Likely Choice

By HUGH BYAS
Wireless to THE NEW YORK TIMES.

TOKYO, Wednesday, July 17—The Japanese Cabinet of Premier Mitsumasa Yonai resigned last night after General Shunroku Hata, the War Minister, by resigning yesterday afternoon, forced its hand. It is expected that Prince Fumimaro Konoye, a former Premier, who will return to Tokyo at midnight, will be the next Prime Minister.

An official announcement did not disclose the nature of the differences that caused General Hata to resign. The newspaper Asahi states that the reason was "his conviction that a renovation of the internal structure had become necessary in order to cope with the world situation."

Differences regarding Prince Konoye's still nebulous plans for a new political structure cannot account for the fall of the Cabinet. The Japanese Army is more likely to have been responsible and its motives must be sought in urgent questions of policy connected with its plans for a settlement in China.

Recently the Sunday edition of Nichi Nichi, one of the leading newspapers, demanded the conclusion of an alliance with Germany and Italy. Such views go further than any probable Japanese Government seems prepared to go, but they are supported by a strong faction, and until the situation clears there must be grave anxiety regarding the future policy of Japan.

**Consultations With Leaders**

Yesterday's events followed a series of consultations that General Hata had been holding with army leaders. These are presumed to have been connected with Prince Konoye's project.

Yesterday morning General Hata visited Premier Yonai. Both expressed views friendly to the Konoye project. Later, General Hata held consultations, first with his principal subordinates in the War Office and then with his fellow tri-

Continued on Page Twelve

## WARNING TO BRITAIN BY HITLER EXPECTED

### Ciano Reported Planning to Go to Reichstag Session, Where Ultimatum May Be Issued

By HERBERT L. MATTHEWS
By Telephone to THE NEW YORK TIMES.

ROME, July 16—Count Ciano, the Italian Foreign Minister, is leaving for Berlin very soon, according to reliable information, and this is a sure sign that the offensive against Great Britain cannot be far off. There were even strong reports in Rome this evening that the Foreign Minister had already left, but this is denied in authoritative circles.

Count Ciano is understood to be going to Berlin to be present at the Reichstag meeting in which Chancellor Hitler is expected to sound the trumpet for the forthcoming battle, and, at the same time, to offer the British their last chance to submit peacefully.

Since German circles think that the Reichstag will meet the end of this week or the beginning of next, one may suppose that the great attack is due within a week or ten days.

There has been much discussion in the last twenty-four hours of Virginio Gayda's statement that the British will have to choose between submission or war. In some quarters this is taken as a warning to the British that Chancellor Hitler is going to give them an ultimatum before he attacks and, thanks to Signor Gayda's "letting the cat out of the bag," the British have some extra days to think it over.

**"New Economic Order" Discussed**

The customary "Italian political circles" this morning denied that Signor Gayda's statement was to be taken at its face value, or that it forecasts what is going to happen at the Reichstag meeting. He was just writing in general terms, it was stated.

Signor Gayda today devotes a long and important article to a discussion of the "new economic order in Europe" after the war is over.

"The basis," he writes, "will be the creation of vast European

Continued on Page Fifteen

## CLEARS CONTRACTS OF $1,661,891,494 TO SPEED DEFENSE

### Advisory Commission's Production Figures Since June 6 Revealed by President

### GASOLINE TO BE STORED

### Knudsen and Stettinius Report Decreasing Tool Bottleneck, Synthetic Rubber Gain

*Text of report to the President on defense program, Page 10.*

Special to THE NEW YORK TIMES.

WASHINGTON, July 16—A picture of how the National Advisory Defense Commission had cleared since July 6 contracts totaling $1,661,891,494 for the Army and Navy and of the progress made by the commission in developing its preparedness program was drawn by President Roosevelt today at his press conference.

He read reports from each of the commission's seven departments, giving the first details of what has been done toward mobilizing men, materials and machines in the $10,000,000,000 rearmament program.

The reports had been presented to him at an earlier meeting with the commission and several members of the Defense Council of the Cabinet.

**Mr. Knudsen's Report**

In reporting the total amount of contracts cleared, William S. Knudsen, chief of the commission's production division, said that $1,390,575,404 was for the Navy and $271,316,089 for the Army. The contracts were for airplanes, tanks, battleships, ammunition, anti-tank guns, anti-aircraft searchlights, machine guns, various fire-control precision instruments, tractors, trucks, blankets, overcoating, serge cloth, worsted shirting, service shoes, ship propulsion machinery, storage batteries for submarines, airport and air station construction, barracks and many other items.

"Evidence has developed indicating progress toward solution, for the time being at least, of the bottlenecks in the machine tool industry," Mr. Knudsen reported. "The embargo authority has contributed substantially to the retention in this country of vital machine tool units which otherwise would have been exported."

Plans had been worked out under which a definite percentage of machine-tool manufacturing facilities would be reserved for defense needs and would be discussed further at a meeting tomorrow of the Machine Tool Defense Committee with the production division and the coordinator of defense purchases.

"Awarding of contracts for the Army for tank construction has begun through a commitment with

Continued on Page Ten

## PLATFORM IS READY

### Full Agreement on the Foreign Policy Plank Is Reached

### FIRM AGAINST WAR

### Wheeler Group Satisfied, but Proviso for Private Aid to Allies Is Seen

By TURNER CATLEDGE
Special to THE NEW YORK TIMES.

CHICAGO, July 16 — Complete agreement on all important provisions of the Democratic platform, particularly the declaration on foreign policy, was reported tonight by the resolution committee's subcommittee of seventeen which had spent all day and most of the evening drafting the document.

All factions were reticent to discuss what the platform contained, but Senators Wheeler of Montana and McCarran of Nevada claimed a victory for the strict non-interventionists on what the party would be asked to say about international relations and defense.

**Minority Report Is Obviated**

"It's a good platform and there'll be no minority plank," Senator Wheeler said.

"It's emphatic and satisfactory to me," Senator McCarran said of the foreign affairs declaration.

Mr. McCarran said that the proposal of himself and several others for a plank pledging the party against the principle of a third term for President would probably be dropped in view of Mr. Roosevelt's views, as presented to the convention tonight by Senator Barkley. He took the position that the President himself had declared in favor of his (McCarran's) position and there was no need to press the proposal further. No effort toward its adoption was made by the group in the subcommittee tonight.

Senator Walsh, another non-interventionist, said of the foreign-policy plan:

"It's excellent and will meet the objections of those people most scrupulous in their desire to keep this country out of war."

**Military Help Is Proscribed**

It was reported from good sources at midnight that the foreign policy statement pledges the party to oppose sending any part of the Army, Navy or air force to fight in foreign lands.

Also included, according to this authority, is a defense of the Monroe Doctrine, a statement of sympathy for the Allies, or countries fighting aggression, and a pledge to encourage such aid as may be extended within the laws of this country and without impairment of American defenses.

Administration forces deferred to the strict non-interventionists in the drafting of the plank and only once made a serious effort to write in a clause over their protest.

This clause, it was said, would

Continued on Page Three

## *Willkie Serves Notice on the Democrats He Will Combat 'Mud Slinging' Campaign*

By JAMES C. HAGERTY
Special to THE NEW YORK TIMES.

COLORADO SPRINGS, July 16—Wendell L. Willkie replied here today to last night's keynote speech by Speaker Bankhead at the Democratic national convention, and countered the keynoter's charges that the Republican party had permitted conditions to exist which led to the market crash in the late Twenties, by saying:

"I am very proud that I had absolutely nothing to do with that phase of American economic life."

Declaring that he had devoted "a substantial part" of his time in the last seven and a half years "to protecting the investments of the people against the assault of their own government," Mr. Willkie referred to speculation in stocks of utility companies, vending machine companies and "gambling in foreign exchange, such as German marks," a charge which Republicans have frequently raised against President Roosevelt during the Nineteen Twenties before he became President.

In addition, the statement, it is believed, was made to serve notice on the Democratic party that the nominee would not stand for any attempt to link him in the public mind with the stock manipulations of the Twenties, or any whispering or direct campaign to characterize him as "a second Insull."

It is known that Mr. Willkie resents these tactics, views them as "mud-slinging" and will campaign vigorously against any attempt to accuse him, as the candidate of the Republican party, of "robber-baron methods."

"I found myself in complete accord with Speaker Bankhead in his condemnation of the speculative orgies of the Nineteen Twenties," Mr. Willkie said when asked for comment on the keynote address. "I agreed with him in his strictures about the unloading of the public during the same period of common stocks beyond their true value.

"I have always thought that such speculation was to be condemned whether it was in the securities of

Continued on Page Eight

## Third-Term Statement

Special to THE NEW YORK TIMES.

*CHICAGO, July 16—At the close of his formal speech as permanent chairman tonight Senator Barkley said:*

And now, my friends, I have an additional statement to make on behalf of the President of the United States.

I and other close friends of the President have long known that he had no wish to be a candidate again. We knew, too, that in no way whatsoever has he exerted any influence in the selection of delegates or upon the opinions of the delegates to this convention.

Tonight, at the specific request and authorization of the President, I am making this simple fact clear to this convention.

The President has never had and has not today any desire or purpose to continue in the office of the President, to be a candidate for that office, or to be nominated by the convention for that office.

He wishes in all earnestness and sincerity to make it clear that all the delegates to this convention are free to vote for any candidate.

That is the message which I bring to you tonight from the President of the United States by authority of his word.

## WOMEN WIN VOICE IN POLICY MAKING

### Get Equal Membership With Men on the Democratic Platform Committee

By KATHLEEN McLAUGHLIN
Special to THE NEW YORK TIMES.

CHICAGO, July 16—Equal membership with men on the resolutions committee was accorded Democratic women tonight as the first business of the night session of the party's convention. The "ayes" were declared by Speaker Bankhead, temporary chairman, to have won over a loud chorus of "noes" from the masculine protesters against the move among the delegates.

Incorporated as part of the machinery of permanent organization of the convention, the proposal was offered by Mrs. Thomas J. Buckley of Massachusetts, and seconded by Representative Mary T. Norton of New Jersey. Its passage, Mrs. Norton asserted, was a matter of simple justice to the women who had worked as hard as the men campaigners for the twenty years since they had the vote, and who deserved a voice in the development of the policies which they promoted.

**Women United Behind Plank**

As firmly welded in their demands for "fifty-fifty" representation with men on the important policy-shaping committee as they had been divided in their demands for a plank calling for an equal rights amendment to the Constitution, the Democratic women had expected the equal-representation proposal to be presented at the first session today, but the matter encountered a parliamentary snarl and was deferred until the night session.

The plank was acknowledged to have the blessing of President Roosevelt and the tacit approval of Chairman Farley. Nevertheless, a prediction of opposition made by Senator Pepper of Florida had kept the women anxious until the vote was cast. Senator Pepper expressed the opinion that the committee, comprising one representative from each State, already was unwieldy in size and that doubling its membership would only complicate matters farther.

**Full Membership Provided**

When presented this morning to a breakfast gathering of the women's division of the Democratic party by Representative Norton, the resolution received the unanimous endorsement of the 1,800 women present. It provided that "there should be elected from each State two members of the committee on platform or resolutions; that in every State district and territory having women delegates, or women alternates, one of those two members shall be a man and one a woman."

Even Mrs. Emma Guffey Miller of Pennsylvania, whose lambasting of the opponents of the suggested equal rights plank has been a highlight of the proceedings to date, was in accord with the proposal and said that she would support it with her vote.

The resolution was drawn up as part of the procedure of setting up a permanent organization for the convention. It represents a natural development of the fight made so successfully four years ago at Philadelphia, where women delegates won the right to act as alternates to men members of the resolutions

Continued on Page Six

## CLAMOR FOR DRAFT SWEEPS THE FLOOR

### Answer to Roosevelt, Byrnes Says, but Anti-Third Term Sentiment Persists

By The Associated Press.

CHICAGO, July 16 — Although President Roosevelt dramatically informed the Democratic National Convention tonight that he had no "desire or purpose" to be renominated, his declaration decreased not one whit the determination of party leaders to draft him for a third-term campaign.

Senator Byrnes of South Carolina, floor leader of the "Draft Roosevelt" forces, quickly sounded the viewpoint of the third term contingent by telling reporters that the demonstration on the floor and the cries of "We want Roosevelt" had answered the President.

"I know that the President's statement represents his sincere views," Senator Byrnes said. "However, it is for the delegates to say who shall be the nominee and in this emergency the President cannot refuse to serve the American people."

**"Not Definite" to Worth Clark**

But from Senator D. Worth Clark of Idaho, a supporter of Senator Wheeler's Presidential aspirations, came a different reaction.

"The statement is not definite," Senator Clark said. "It leaves the convention, the delegates and the candidates in the same uncertain condition they were before. As far as I am concerned, unless Senator Wheeler decides otherwise, his name will be placed in nomination before the convention by me."

James A. Farley, chairman of the national committee and a candidate, said:

"I have no comment to make. The statement speaks for itself."

Another opponent of third terms, Senator Millard E. Tydings of Maryland, said:

"I admire the President for the statesmanlike stand he has taken." He added:

"I think he is sincere in not desiring to continue. There is no doubt that he would have gotten the full support of two-thirds of the delegates had he been a candidate."

Representative Elmer J. Ryan, a Minnesota delegate, issued a statement saying that the convention was "being run by a group of White House manipulators."

**Assails "Small Clique"**

"The Corcoran-Cohen-Hopkins group has induced a tired President to accede to a third-term draft," he declared. "By White House influence, this small clique has so far been able to kill off the candidacies of other capable Democrats."

E. B. Germany, campaign manager for Vice President Garner, told reporters:

"The situation hasn't been changed. We have felt this was the President's sentiment all the time.

"The whole Garner campaign has been predicated upon the assumption that Roosevelt would not be a candidate. The Garner campaign has never been an anti-Roosevelt movement."

Mr. Germany added that he was unable to guess how the President's declaration would affect the chances of Mr. Garner's nomination.

The "draft Roosevelt" interpreta-

Continued on Page Four

## CHOICE LEFT OPEN

### Barkley Tells Delegates President Has 'No Desire' to Run

### ACCEPTANCE IS SEEN

### Demonstration Quickly Starts—Senator Hits New Deal Critics

*Address of Senator Barkley as permanent chairman, Page 4.*

By JAMES A. HAGERTY
Special to THE NEW YORK TIMES.

STADIUM, CHICAGO, July 16—President Roosevelt broke the silence of months tonight on his attitude toward renomination for a third term and through Senator Alben W. Barkley, Permanent Chairman of the Democratic National Convention, informed the delegates that he had no wish to run again, and released all delegates pledged to or instructed for him to vote for any candidates they might be pleased to support.

This announcement, which was made by the Senator at the end of his formal address as Permanent Chairman, was taken as the basis on which to accord the President a virtually unanimous nomination later, and an implicit promise on his part that he would accept renomination if drafted by a united convention.

The demonstration which followed announcement of Mr. Roosevelt's attitude was seen as proof that sponsors of the draft movement, including Senator James F. Byrnes of South Carolina, the floor leader, and Harry L. Hopkins, Secretary of Commerce and liaison officer with the White House, were ready to complete tomorrow their plan to draft the President.

The intention of the Roosevelt supporters to proceed with their plan to renominate President Roosevelt was shown by Senator Byrnes's announcement in moving for adjournment until noon tomorrow.

"I move that the convention adjourn until 12 o'clock tomorrow," Senator Byrnes said, "and that the convention then take up the adoption of the platform at the afternoon session, so that we can proceed at the evening session with the nomination of a candidate for President and finish the job which we came here to do by renominating Franklin D. Roosevelt."

**Message Phoned to Barkley**

The President's message to the convention was transmitted to Senator Barkley in the afternoon by telephone from the White House. The Kentucky Senator spoke slowly and impressively in delivering it to the delegates.

Leaders of the draft Roosevelt movement, including Senator Byrnes and Secretary Hopkins, earlier in the evening contemplated a coup by which an attempt would be made to renominate the President by acclamation after delivery of his message by Senator Barkley, and it was part of this plan to have a tremendous Roosevelt demonstration.

Abandonment of this plan seemingly was due to the opposition of Postmaster General Farley and other party leaders. Mr. Farley, when asked what he thought of such a plan, replied:

"If that should be done, there would be no necessity of having an election."

Asked to comment on the President's message, Mr. Farley said:

"It speaks for itself."

**Says He Has Not Campaigned**

Senator Barkley said that he and other close friends of Mr. Roosevelt had known for some time that he had no wish to be a candidate again. The Kentucky Senator added that the President had in no way exerted influence on the election of delegates or upon the opinion of delegates, and that at the specific request and authorization of the President he was making this fact clear to the convention.

Many of the delegates seemed for a moment to be partly stunned by Senator Barkley's announcement. After a moment they rallied and a demonstration for the President started with a parade of standards

Continued on Page Five

"All the News That's Fit to Print."

# The New York Times.

LATE CITY EDITION
Mostly cloudy with scattered showers and not much change in temperature today and tomorrow.
Temperatures Yesterday—Max.,74; Min.,66

Copyright, 1940, by The New York Times Company.

VOL. LXXXIX..No. 30,126. Entered as Second-Class Matter, Postoffice, New York, N. Y. NEW YORK, THURSDAY, JULY 18, 1940. THREE CENTS NEW YORK CITY and Vicinity | FOUR CENTS Elsewhere Except in 7th and 8th Postal Zones

# ROOSEVELT RENOMINATED ON FIRST BALLOT; STRICT ANTI-WAR PLATFORM IS ADOPTED; NO ARMY ABROAD UNLESS U. S. IS ATTACKED

## BURMA ROAD PACT AROUSES COMMONS; PEACE DEMAND MET

### Japan Reported Ready to Deal With China, but Britons Call 'New Munich' Shameful

### QUESTION ON U. S. EVADED

### Konoye Forms a Centralized Regime in Tokyo—South Seas Drive Expected

By The United Press.

LONDON, July 17—Japan promised to attempt to reach a general peace settlement with China before Oct. 18 as part of the agreement reached today with Great Britain to close for three months the Burma supply route to China, it was learned authoritatively tonight.

British quarters reaffirmed their readiness to offer their good offices to end the long Chinese-Japanese war, provided their services were desired by the governments in Tokyo and Chungking.

Announcement in Parliament of the Anglo-Japanese agreement, forced by Japan, caused an uproar and the deal was called "shameful." It was consummated despite the declaration of Cordell Hull, American Secretary of State, that it would be considered by the United States an unwarranted obstacle to world trade.

**U. S. Policy "Ambiguous"**

Although the United States' continued shipments of strategic raw materials to Japan frequently has been regarded in London as making Washington's Far Eastern policy "ambiguous," it is generally believed that today's agreement probably will provoke severe criticism in the United States.

Coupled with the continuance in office of Chamberlain "appeasers," today's partial acceptance of Japan's demands is expected also to increase home dissatisfaction with the policies of the Churchill government, although the position of Prime Minister Winston Churchill himself still appears to be impregnable.

Geoffrey Mander, Liberal, who attacked the agreement, demanded sarcastically whether it was likely to be more successful than previous attempts at appeasement such as Munich. The Speaker ruled him out of order, but amid shouts of "order, order," Mr. Mander asked whether the British Government, in view of Mr. Hull's statement, was going to refuse transit to United States goods consigned to China, most of which has been going by the Burma Road.

**Questions Are Evaded**

"I think it rather irresponsible to make statements of that sort," replied Richard Austen Butler, Foreign Under-Secretary, whose announcement had set off the uproar.

Wilfred Roberts, who sided with Mr. Mander, asked Mr. Butler pointblank whether the United States had expressed approval or disapproval of the agreement in advance of the accord.

Mr. Butler replied evasively: "We must leave interpretation of the American statement to Americans." Mr. Roberts said he was not satisfied and would raise the question later.

Chinese circles here bitterly compared Britain's action to the position that would arise if the United States prevented war material from reaching Britain and then offered to promote Anglo-German peace talks.

British commentators said this comparison was irrelevant because the United States was not engaged in a life-and-death struggle in the West.

**Halifax Speaks in Lords**

In the House of Lords, Foreign Secretary Viscount Halifax made a statement similar to that of Mr. Butler in the Commons.

Viscount Cecil of Chelwood, friend of China, cautioned the government against closing the Burma Road or putting pressure on China to make peace.

Responsible quarters here said, regarding one point of the agreement, the Japanese consular officials would not have the right to inspect and prohibit traffic through Burma but that British authorities

Continued on Page Fifteen



## 3 British Ports Wrecked By Nazis, Say Dutch Crew

By The Associated Press.

BOSTON, July 17—Members of the crew of the Netherland freighter Zypenberg, arriving to load scrap metal for United Kingdom ports, asserted today that Plymouth, England, and Pembroke and Cardiff, Wales, had been devastated by almost continuous raids by Nazi bombing planes and that many ships had been sunk in British harbors. [London issued a denial.]

The Zypenberg was among vessels taken over by the British Ministry of Shipping after the German invasion of the Netherlands. Officers and crew said they had had a 50 per cent wage reduction and had been forced to operate unarmed in dangerous waters.

They said that while their vessel was anchored in one British port, a Nazi bomber sank a British ship anchored close astern. Wharves in the three British ports they mentioned had been demolished, they added.

## GIBRALTAR DEMAND VOICED BY FRANCO

### Chief of State Gives Notice Spain Expects a Part in Post-War Settlement

By T. J. HAMILTON
Wireless to The New York Times.

MADRID, July 17—General Francisco Franco told army, navy and air force officers today that "there remains for us as a duty and a national mission control of Gibraltar, expansion in Africa and continuance in the policy of unity."

Speaking at a ceremony at which he conferred Spain's highest military award, the Grand Laureate Cross of San Fernando, General Franco added that these aspirations were embodied in the will of Queen Isabella and after centuries "are still binding upon us."

The radio and press today were busy presenting Spain's claims on Morocco, the newspapers insisting that it was time that Spanish and French Morocco, each with its own Caliph, were united.

Rumors of peace negotiations here continue.

British sympathizers here got some encouragement out of the fact that the new Ambassador, Sir Samuel Hoare, was the guest of honor tonight at a dinner given by Colonel Juan Beigbeder, the Foreign Minister, even though this is a courtesy usually extended to newly arrived diplomats.

Otherwise, however, the increasing popularity of the Germans is illustrated by the reappearance of swastika flags, which had once virtually disappeared, at a majority of shops and cafes and many private homes. An interesting example

Continued on Page Ten

## ARMY OF 2,000,000 A MINIMUM NEED, MARSHALL INSISTS

### 45 Infantry Divisions and 10 Armored Divisions Are the Objective, General Says

### STIMSON HAILS BURKE BILL

### Ludicrous for Any One to Oppose Compulsory Service Plan, He Tells Civilian Aides

By FRANK L. KLUCKHOHN
Special to The New York Times.

WASHINGTON, July 17—A trained and fully equipped army of 2,000,000 men is the minimum necessary for adequate defense of this hemisphere, even with Navy and Air Force cooperation, General George C. Marshall, Chief of Staff, declared today in disclosing that the War Department had as its objective the formation of forty-five streamlined infantry divisions and ten armored divisions.

Both General Marshall and Secretary Stimson again urged the passage of compulsory selective service legislation in addressing a meeting today at the War Department of Civilian Aides to the Secretary of War from nine corps areas and forty-four States.

Secretary Stimson declared this legislation "the very foundation stone of preparedness," and added: "Congress has appropriated billions of dollars for material to save the country, but we have not yet taken the step necessary to get the men to run the matériel."

General Marshall, in a subsequent press conference, said that Army plans were based as much on trained man power as matériel. The nine Regular Army infantry divisions and the four National Guard divisions, which it is planned to call to service as soon as Congress will authorize the step, would be fully equipped by Jan. 1, the general said, stressing that this was merely a first step toward preparedness.

**"Poker With Every One Looking"**

The Army could not adequately defend this hemisphere even with the 1,200,000 in the proposed Protective Mobilization Force, under all conditions, he said frankly in deploring that "we're playing poker with every one looking at our hand."

Reiterating that the entire National Guard should be called to service at least thirty days before the compulsory training becomes effective, around Sept. 1 if possible, General Marshall held that "the greatest mistake we can make is to flood the carburetor on the first jump" in explaining that, if

Continued on Page Eight

## The Only Ballot

| Votes. STATES. | Farley. | Garner. | Roosevelt. | Tydings. |
|---|---|---|---|---|
| 22—Alabama | 1 | .. | 20 | 1 |
| 6—Arizona | .. | .. | 6 | .. |
| 18—Arkansas | .. | .. | 18 | .. |
| 44—California | .. | 1 | 43 | .. |
| 12—Colorado | .. | .. | 12 | .. |
| 16—Connecticut | .. | .. | 16 | .. |
| 6—Delaware | .. | .. | 6 | .. |
| 14—Florida | .. | 1½ | 12½ | .. |
| 24—Georgia | .. | .. | 24 | .. |
| 8—Idaho | .. | .. | 8 | .. |
| 58—Illinois | .. | .. | 58 | .. |
| 28—Indiana | .. | .. | 28 | .. |
| 22—Iowa | .. | .. | 22 | .. |
| 18—Kansas | .. | .. | 18 | .. |
| 22—Kentucky | .. | .. | 22 | .. |
| 20—Louisiana | .. | .. | 20 | .. |
| 10—Maine | .. | .. | 10 | .. |
| 16—Maryland | .. | .. | 7½ | 8½ |
| 34—Massachusetts | 12½ | .. | 21½ | .. |
| 38—Michigan | .. | .. | 38 | .. |
| 22—Minnesota | .. | .. | 22 | .. |
| 18—Mississippi | .. | .. | 18 | .. |
| 30—Missouri | 2 | 1½ | 26½ | .. |
| 8—Montana | .. | .. | 8 | .. |
| 14—Nebraska | 1 | .. | 13 | .. |
| 6—Nevada | 4 | .. | 2 | .. |
| 8—N. Hampshire | .. | .. | 8 | .. |
| 32—New Jersey | .. | .. | 32 | .. |
| 6—New Mexico | .. | .. | 6 | .. |
| 94—New York | 25 | .. | 64½ | .. |
| 26—North Carolina | .. | .. | 26 | .. |
| 8—North Dakota | .. | .. | 8 | .. |
| 52—Ohio | .. | .. | 52 | .. |
| 22—Oklahoma | .. | .. | 22 | .. |
| 10—Oregon | .. | .. | 10 | .. |
| 72—Pennsylvania | .. | .. | 72 | .. |
| 8—Rhode Island | .. | .. | 8 | .. |
| 16—South Carolina | .. | .. | 16 | .. |
| 8—South Dakota | 5 | .. | 3 | .. |
| 22—Tennessee | .. | .. | 22 | .. |
| 46—Texas | .. | 46 | .. | .. |
| 8—Utah | .. | .. | 8 | .. |
| 6—Vermont | .. | .. | 6 | .. |
| 22—Virginia | 8 | 8 | 5 | .. |
| 16—Washington | .. | .. | 15 | .. |
| 16—West Virginia | 4 | .. | 12 | .. |
| 24—Wisconsin | .. | 3 | 21 | .. |
| 6—Wyoming | .. | .. | 6 | .. |
| 6—Alaska | 6 | .. | .. | .. |
| 6—D. of Columbia | .. | .. | 6 | .. |
| 6—Hawaii | .. | .. | 6 | .. |
| 6—Puerto Rico | 3 | .. | 3 | .. |
| 6—Canal Zone | 6 | .. | .. | .. |
| 6—Philippine Isl. | .. | .. | 6 | .. |
| 2—Virgin Islands | .. | .. | 2 | .. |
| Total | 72 | 61 | 946 | 9½ |

The totals of the ballot prior to announcement of the official result were: Roosevelt, 946 13/30; Farley, 72 27/30; Garner, 61; Tydings, 9½; Hull, 5 2-3. Absent 3½; not voting 1.

## CONFUSION RISES OVER SECOND PLACE

### Some Hold Roosevelt Means to Select a Running Mate When the Time Comes

By HENRY N. DORRIS
Special to The New York Times.

CHICAGO, July 17—Far from having cleared up the confused race for Vice President, the message of President Roosevelt to the convention was thought tonight to have further complicated the situation.

There was a feeling among the delegates, despite the tenor of the Presidential message, that there would be a definite White House selection of a running mate after the convention had disposed of the first place.

Nevertheless, the score or more of candidates for running mate doubled their efforts on the theory that, after all, the delegates might be allowed to choose their favorite.

One of the developments of the day was a movement among the Texas delegation to obtain Vice President Garner's consent to support Representative Rayburn of Texas, the House majority leader, who continued his activity among other delegations today.

The Texans were said to feel that Mr. Rayburn is acceptable to the President. They say that Mr. Garner is entirely out of the picture, so far as Mr. Roosevelt's acceptance is concerned.

**Activity for Bankhead**

There was renewed vigor among the Alabama delegation, which is instructed for Speaker Bankhead for Vice President. Since so many candidates are pressing their cases and the time is short, several delegations were reported today to have looked with favor upon Mr. Bankhead's candidacy, on the ground that he is at once a loyal supporter of the President and the symbol of traditional Democratic conservatism.

Governor Stark of Missouri, who is described by his adherents as "the perfect candidate" because of

Continued on Page Five

## 'STAY OUT' PLANK

### Goes Slightly Beyond the Recent Pledge of the President

### FOR MONROE POLICY

### All Material Aid Pledged for Peoples Attacked by Aggressors

*Text of the platform as adopted will be found on Page 4.*

By JAMES A. HAGERTY
Special to The New York Times.

CHICAGO, July 17—After a long delay due to differences of opinion among members of the committee on resolutions on the foreign relations plank, Senator Wagner of New York, chairman of the committee, presented the final draft of the platform to the Democratic convention tonight. It was adopted by a voice vote.

Controversy in the committee centered on the phrasing of the foreign relations plank, which as finally submitted was strictly noninterventionist, calling for non-participation in foreign wars and expanding the recent pledge of President Roosevelt not to send troops to fight in Europe by a definite declaration against sending the military, naval or air forces to fight in foreign lands outside of America, except in case of attack.

This strong isolation declaration was modified only by a pledge to support the Monroe Doctrine and a pledge to send "to peace-loving and liberty loving people wantonly attacked by ruthless aggressors" all material aid "consistent with law and not inconsistent with the interests of our own national self-defense."

**Agreement Is Reached**

Unanimous agreement by members of the resolutions committee on the final draft was reached while Senator Claude H. Pepper of Florida, who led the fight for a strong declaration for aid to Great Britain was absent. Senator Burton K. Wheeler of Montana, a leader of the anti-war group, entered the meeting room just after the agreement was reached. He pronounced the foreign relations plank satisfactory as the meeting broke up.

Secretary Hopkins said tonight: "There is nothing on the foreign policy plank which changes by one jot or tittle the foreign policies of the President and the Secretary of State. I refer not only to the present policies, but future policies. I cannot believe that any one can mislead the American people on this point. The foreign policy of the President has the overwhelming approval of the American people."

After Senator Wagner finished reading the platform and moved for its adoption, Elmer J. Ryan of Minnesota offered an amendment to insert the declaration of the 1896 convention declaring against a third term as a violation of American tradition. The reading of the amendment was greeted with groans and jeers. There was a faint shout of ayes when Chairman Barkley asked for a vote on the amendment and then a thundering chorus of noes. The platform was then adopted with a loud shout of ayes.

**Says Party Aided Democracy**

The committee's report, as presented by Senator Wagner, declared that the Democratic party had labored successfully:

"1. To strengthen democracy by defensive preparedness against aggression, whether by open attack or secret infiltration;

"2. To strengthen democracy by increasing our economic efficiency and

"3. To strengthen democracy by improving the welfare of the people."

The platform endorses the leadership and statesmanship of President Roosevelt during the past seven years and declares that he has for years warned the people of the nation that our peace and security were threatened. The platform proposes to provide America "with an invincible air force, a Navy strong enough to protect all our seacoasts

Continued on Page Six

AGAIN THE DEMOCRATIC NOMINEE
Franklin Delano Roosevelt
Times Studio

## PLATFORM MARKED BY DOUBT ON FUTURE

### Anti-War Plank and Sympathy Expressed for Victims of Attacks Reflect Uncertainties

By ANNE O'HARE McCORMICK
Special to The New York Times.

CHICAGO, July 17—As finally patched up out of bitterly divergent opinions and adopted by the convention tonight, the foreign policy declaration in the Democratic platform turns out to be a plank that makes up in breadth what it lacks in thickness. It is obviously hewn to cover many points of view and to bear almost any interpretation the candidate wishes to place on it.

The isolationist Senators on the committee and their outside supporters were not able to write their own ticket, as they expected to do a week ago today. But they received satisfaction in being permitted to dictate a strong anti-war pledge and to go much farther than the President in his recent declaration to Congress that American soldiers would never be sent to fight in "European wars" by asserting that "we will not send our Army, naval or air forces to fight in foreign lands outside of the Americas, except in case of attack."

The last phrase is typical of the leeway left to the interpreters of the platform. Its meaning depends altogether on the construction placed on "attack" and may easily be extended to mean any assault on American interests, wherever it takes place.

**Roosevelt Backers Placated**

On the other hand, the committee members who held out for a statement of policy more in line with the stand of the Administration which this convention seeks to keep in power were placated by the expression of sympathy and support given to the nations fighting against aggression.

Great Britain was not mentioned by name, though Senator Pepper and several members of the committee fought hard for a pledge of "aid to Britain," but the Democrats affirm that "the world's greatest democracy cannot afford heartlessly or in a spirit of appeasement—a significant and holy argued point—"to ignore the peace-loving and liberty-loving peoples

Continued on Page Six

## NATION WILL HEAR PRESIDENT TONIGHT

### Roosevelt Expected to Address Convention on Radio After Notification

Special to The New York Times.

WASHINGTON, Thursday, July 18—President Roosevelt is expected to address the Democratic National Convention and the nation in a radio address tonight, following his official notification of his nomination for a third term.

The President listened for several hours to the radio broadcast of the convention proceedings into the early hours of the morning and sent out word that he would have nothing to say until formally notified of his nomination.

White House aides said that they could not confirm officially the President's reported intention to address the convention by radio, but added that he expected the notification before noon tomorrow. All indications were that he would acknowledge it before the day was out.

The President had only two callers during the day. Secretary Stephen T. Early said he "purposely kept his engagements down to the minimum in order to listen in on the radio to what happened at Chicago and to be available in case any of his key men should want to reach him over the special telephone set-up in the White House."

To all such callers over the private telephone from Chicago, Mr. Early said the President was "open and available."

Any idea among the few Democrats and Republicans left in Washington that Mr. Roosevelt would refuse renomination for a third term faded with his message to the convention Tuesday through Senator Barkley. The certainty that the President would accept a renomination was shared by the White House staff although Mr. Early answered a question by saying he was "not thinking about it just now."

Mr. Early did say, however, that he would be available to the newspaper men should the President be placed in nomination tonight. All other attempts to draw him out on the President's plan ran into a blank wall. He volunteered the information that Mr. Roosevelt

Continued on Page Six

## BY 'ACCLAMATION'

### Farley, Who Remained in Race, Makes the Vote Unanimous

### RIVALS' POLL IS 150

### Third-Term Tradition Is Upset—Garner, Tydings Stay to End

By TURNER CATLEDGE
Special to The New York Times.

CHICAGO, Thursday, July 18—President Roosevelt was renominated early this morning for a third term for President of the United States by the Democratic National Convention.

The President's renomination, which climaxed a "draft" movement carried out in contravention of one of the oldest and best established traditions in American politics, came theoretically by "acclamation," but the move to nominate unanimously or by acclamation came in a dramatic surrender by Postmaster General James A. Farley and others who had stood with him against a third-term nomination.

Mr. Farley, Vice President Garner and Senator Millard E. Tydings of Maryland all had been placed in nomination in pursuance of the third-term protest. Before the move to nominate by acclamation was made by Mr. Farley more than 150 of the convention delegates had cast votes against Mr. Roosevelt, distributing them among the three named above and Secretary Cordell Hull. Governor Cooper of Tennessee explained to the convention that Mr. Hull was not and had never been a candidate.

**How the Ballot Stood**

The total vote before it was made unanimous was Roosevelt 946 13/30, Farley 72 27/30, Garner 61, Tydings 9½ and Hull 5 2/3.

There was but little demonstration when the convention made its momentous decision. The first thing that happened was a song led by Phil Regan, "When Irish Eyes Are Smiling," the convention's song to Mr. Farley.

Mr. Roosevelt's nomination was clinched when New York voted, giving 64½ votes for him, 25 for Farley, 1 for Secretary Hull, with 3½ missing. New York's sixty-four votes put the President over the 548 votes needed for renomination. There was no notice given by the delegates of this momentous hour. It was shortly before 1 A. M.

Senator Barkley, Permanent Chairman of the Convention, appointed a committee composed of Senators Byrnes of South Carolina, Charles F. Sawyer of Ohio and Mayor Edward F. Kelly of Chicago to notify the President of his renomination.

The convention adjourned shortly before 2 A. M. until 2 o'clock in the afternoon, when it will meet to name a candidate for Vice President.

**Acceptance Held Certain**

The President is counted as certain to accept the nomination, despite a statement made to the convention in his behalf that he did not desire to run again. His acceptance is expected to come in a radio message to the convention before it adjourns.

He also will be expected now to indicate his choice for Vice President from among a growing list of potential candidates. He may also take occasion in replying to the Convention "draft" to express his ideas on a platform adopted by the party and which, it is understood, did not satisfy him completely by the language of its statement against intervention by the United States in foreign wars.

The Roosevelt "draft" had been indicated from a time long before the delegates assembled in Chicago, and it moved relentlessly to its successful conclusion under the management of inner circle New Dealers, assisted by Senator James F. Byrnes of South Carolina as floor leader.

Just before the roll-call of States started for the nomination, the convention howled down a proposal of Representative Elmer J. Ryan of

Continued on Page Five



## The International Situation

The Anglo-Japanese agreement, by which the Burma road to China has been closed and Japan, it is reported, has promised to seek peace with China, was attacked in the British House of Commons yesterday as a "shameful deal." [Page 1, Column 1.]

Prince Konoye, head of the one-party-government movement in Japan, named his Foreign, Navy and War Ministers. They will join him in a strong centralized government. No immediate alliance with Germany and Italy is expected from his government, but attempts at expansion southward are likely. [Page 14, Column 2.]

Sir Archibald Sinclair, British Air Minister, took advantage of a let-up in the German raids on Britain to warn his countrymen by radio that they must expect much greater bombardments from the sky than any yet experienced. He admitted Germany had air superiority. For the first time in weeks the Royal Air Force did not visit Germany Tuesday night. [Page 12, Column 2.]

The Wehrmacht, organ of the German High Command, published an article saying that vessels ready at French ports could cross the Channel to Britain in from forty minutes to four hours, that airplanes could effectively support such attacks, and that ten French points of departure, all equipped with proper defenses and with good rail connections, had been completely prepared. [Page 12, Column 3.]

Sir Stafford Cripps, Britain's new Ambassador to Moscow, recently had an interview with Joseph Stalin, it was revealed. Among matters discussed, it was understood, were some of interest to the United States. London reported that the Russian dictator had said Russia was determined to stay neutral, and that he saw no reason to fear German domination of Europe. [Page 13, Column 2.]

General Franco, chief of the Spanish Government, warned Britain in a speech that Spain expected to get Gibraltar back. This was the first official endorsement of the Gibraltar campaign carried on by students and Falangists. [Page 1, Column 2.]

An army of 2,000,000 men is the minimum for defense of this hemisphere, General Marshall, chief of staff, told a meeting at Washington of civilian aides to the Secretary of War. The War Department wants forty-five streamlined infantry divisions and ten armored divisions. [Page 1, Column 3.]

"All the News That's Fit to Print."

# The New York Times.

LATE CITY EDITION

Fair with little change in temperature today and tomorrow.

Temperatures Yesterday—Max., 83; Min., 67



VOL. LXXXIX..No. 30,127. Entered as Second-Class Matter, Postoffice, New York, N. Y. NEW YORK, FRIDAY, JULY 19, 1940. THREE CENTS NEW YORK CITY and Vicinity | FOUR CENTS Elsewhere Except in 7th and 8th Postal Zones.

# ROOSEVELT, ACCEPTING, FEELS HE MUST SERVE WITH OTHERS IN CRISIS; FOR MILITARY DRAFT; WINS FIGHT FOR WALLACE AS HIS RUNNING MATE

## NAZI BOMBS SMASH SCOTTISH TENEMENT, HIT NEAR TROLLEY

### Gardens Around Girls' School in Wales Torn Up—Several Civilians Are Killed

### ALDERSHOT RAID REPORTED

### Berlin Claims Damage to Big British Military Base, Arms Factories and Ships

By JAMES MacDONALD

Special Cable to THE NEW YORK TIMES.

LONDON, July 18—In sporadic German bombings that extended today from Southeast Scotland to Wales, the chief results reported here were destruction of a Scottish tenement, a narrow escape for passengers in a street car, heavy bombing of gardens around a girls' school and death or injury to several civilians in isolated fields and villages.

Whether the raiders did any damage to shipping, factories or military bases was not stated in the official communiqué.

[The German High Command declared its planes carried out destructive attacks against the Aldershot military center, the harbor at Portland and various arms and other factories and set fire to four merchant ships near Scapa Flow, according to The United Press.]

Eighteen persons were in the street car in Scotland when a bomb burst near by, shattering the car windows but injuring no one inside. The blast tore up a one-ton chunk of track and hurled it 100 yards away. A youth standing at some distance was knocked off his feet and slightly hurt.

**Several Buried in Debris**

Several occupants of the tenement building were buried in the debris but later rescued by firemen and taken to hospitals.

A man working in a field in Southeast England was killed and three persons, including a 97-year-old woman, injured when a lone raider dropped two bombs this afternoon.

During the raids on Wales, screaming bombs burst in the gardens of houses and around a girls' private school, injuring four children but failing to do any other serious damage.

The Ministry of Home Security said one German plane machine-gunned a cottage in Northeastern England, but did not say whether any one was hit.

Officially it was announced that one German bomber was shot down off the south coast and one British fighter failed to return from his attempt to drive off the raiders. Unofficial reports said two German planes were destroyed.

[Early this morning The United Press reported that four raiders were destroyed.]

**British Retaliate**

The Royal Air Force made some raids on barge concentrations and air bases in the Netherlands and Belgium last night and early this morning, but bad weather curtailed their bombing operations, according to the Air Ministry. The weather was so thick some British raiders could not locate their objectives and returned to their bases with full bomb loads.

However, the British say they succeeded in bombing an oil plant at Gelsenkirchen in the Ruhr and an oil depot at Ghent, starting fires in both places. Also they reported attacking air bases at Merville and Hertogenbosch in South Holland.

The Air Ministry said one coastal command plane was lost while on reconnaissance duty over the Channel yesterday. While searching for it some British fliers encountered a German bomber and shot it down, it was added.

**Ships Fight Off Planes**

LONDON, July 18 (AP)—British ships off the northeast coast of Scotland tonight fought off an attack by German war planes amid shelling and bomb explosions so intense that houses ashore rocked with the vibration.

The sky was lit by the flashes of anti-aircraft shells exploding like fireworks, accompanied by the thunder of bombs.

Five persons were injured and many houses were damaged in one

Continued on Page Eleven

## *Nazis Take French Island Commanding Channel Gate*

By The Associated Press.

BERLIN, July 18—Germany, broadening her front line for the threatened invasion of Britain, announced today she had landed forces on the French island of Ouessant in the Atlantic off the jutting coast of Brittany and 120 miles south of Land's End.

The island commands the southern entrance to the English Channel and is the westernmost territory of France proper. To the north, Land's End is on the extreme tip of England's Channel coastline.

## CHURCHILL DEFENDS BURMA ROAD PACT

### Says Accord With Japan Wins 'Time and Relief of Tension' in British Fight to Survive

*Text of Prime Minister Churchill's statement, Page 10, Col. 2.*

By ROBERT P. POST

Wireless to THE NEW YORK TIMES.

LONDON, July 18—Prime Minister Winston Churchill put his seal on the British negotiations with Japan by announcing in the House of Commons today that an agreement had been reached whereby the Burma road would be closed for three months to the transit of arms, ammunition, gasoline, trucks and railroad supplies for China.

The same agreement applies to Hong Kong, although Mr. Churchill said no arms, ammunition or any other goods that the Japanese Government had mentioned were now being exported to the Chinese Government from that Crown Colony.

Mr. Churchill and Viscount Halifax, the Foreign Secretary, who made a similar statement in the House of Lords, were subjected to some crticism. The Prime Minister defended the government's move on the ground that it provided two necessary things—"time and relief of tension."

**Notes Struggle to Survive**

Britain is "engaged in a life-or-death struggle," Mr. Churchill said. He declared that it was obvious that two factors were to be considered. One was the increasing tension between the British and the Japanese because of Japanese demands about the Burma Road; the other was that permanent closure of the route would be a default from British obligations as a power friendly to China.

"What we have therefore made is a temporary arrangement," Mr. Churchill said, "in the hope that the time so gained may lead to a solution just and equitable to both parties of the dispute and freely accepted by them both."

The Prime Minister added that Britain wished to see both Japan and China happy under a peace settlement. Britain will be quite willing after the conclusion of a Sino-Japanese peace, he said, to negotiate the abolition of extraterritorial rights, the return of concessions and the revision of all treaties applicable to China.

**Wants Prosperous Japan**

"We wish to see Japan attain that state of prosperity which will ensure to her population the welfare and economic security which every Japanese naturally desires," he added. "Toward the attainment of the aims of both these countries we are prepared to offer our collaboration as our contribution. But it must be clear that if they are to be attained it must be by a process of peace and conciliation, not by war or the threat of war."

Mr. Churchill did not bother to conceal from the world that Britain was playing for time in the Far East. In fact, when asked by former War Secretary Leslie Hore-Belisha whether the concession to Japan would in fact obtain the good-will of that country, Mr. Churchill replied:

"I can give no such assurance. I don't know at all, and I think that all that happens to us in the Far East is probably likely to be very much influenced by what happens over here."

Mr. Churchill added in reply to questions that the decision on the Burma Road had not been reached without taking into consideration the attitudes of the United States and Russia.

Lord Halifax was badgered in the House of Lords after he had made his statement, but he refused to go

Continued on Page Ten

## REALISM AT PARLEY IS PLEDGED BY HULL, ON WAY TO HAVANA

### Secretary Says Republics Take a Practical View of Their Security Problems

### ARGENTINA SEEN AS SNAG

### Some Believe Her Reluctance to Follow U. S. Lead May Bring a Definite Split

Special to THE NEW YORK TIMES.

WASHINGTON, July 18—Promising "realistic" treatment of "immediate problems of economic and political security" facing the Western Hemisphere as a result of Nazi victories in Europe, Secretary of State Cordell Hull and his staff entrained this afternoon for the trip to Havana, where a Pan-American conference of Foreign Ministers, or their representatives, of the twenty-one republics will convene Sunday.

Among numerous matters dealing with the military, economic and spiritual defense of the New World against Nazi penetration and ideology that it is planned to discuss are the treatment of New World islands belonging to European nations dominated by Germany, methods of keeping the Nazis from forcing a barter system upon this hemisphere and means of dealing with fifth columns.

**"Friendliness Toward All"**

Secretary Hull stressed that the meeting would be conducted "in a spirit of complete friendliness toward all nations demonstrating their will to conduct international relations upon a basis of peace and friendship." His statement read as follows:

"The twenty-one American republics, pursuant to procedures agreed to at the Buenos Aires, Lima and Panama conferences, are once again about to meet in conference through their Foreign Ministers or their representatives.

"A major purpose of the Havana meeting is full and free consultation among the American republics with respect to the conditions, problems, difficulties and dangers confronting each of them. The complete exchange of information enables each government thoroughly to understand the problems, needs and viewpoints of the others. The ground will thus be prepared for the adoption of basic and concrete measures, having common support, for the common benefit of each and all of the republics.

"The agenda of the forthcoming meeting calls for the consideration of certain immediate problems of economic and political security. The American republics approach their task in a spirit of complete friendliness toward all nations demonstrating their will to conduct in-

Continued on Page Seven

## SHARP FLOOR FIGHT

### Wallace Won Majority Against Eight Rivals for the Post

### BANKHEAD'S VOTE BIG

### Lively Revolt Was Waged Against Candidate the President Sought

*The ballot for the nomination for Vice President, Page 3.*

Special to THE NEW YORK TIMES.

CHICAGO, Friday, July 19—Acting under orders from President Roosevelt, the Democratic National Convention after a stormy session early this morning nominated Henry A. Wallace, Secretary of Agriculture for Vice President.

The nomination went to Secretary Wallace on the only ballot. The unofficial count showed 627 7-10 for Mr. Wallace; 327 4-15 for Speaker Bankhead. Other unofficial figures were: Jesse Jones, 59 1-10; Senator Adams of Colorado, 11½; Senator Brown of Michigan, 1; Senator Lucas of Illinois, 1; James A. Farley, 8; Senator Barkley, 2, and Louis Johnson, 1.

Mr. Wallace's nomination will show in the record as having been made unanimously, but there were sizable quantities of "no" votes when Senator Barkley, permanent convention chairman, put the motion of Senator Bankhead of Alabama to suspend the rules and make the choice complete.

**Barkley Rules on the Vote**

Senator Barkley ruled that two-thirds of the convention had voted in the affirmative on the motion, and therefore it was carried as provided in the rules.

Mr. Wallace was in the Convention Hall and there was a rush of friends and well-wishers to his side. He had sat practically unnoticed throughout. He refused to make a statement.

Mr. Wallace's nomination came at the end of an uproarous session which threatened at times to get out of control of the New Deal high command. Hundreds of the delegates, supported by thousands of spectators in the galleries, were openly resentful of the Administration attempt to dictate the choice for Vice President. The dissenting delegates sought to rally around Speaker Bankhead, but the Administration's pressure was too great.

**Delegates in a Testy Mood**

It seemed for a time that the opposition movement might center around Paul V. McNutt, Federal Security Administrator, instead of Speaker Bankhead, whose supporters were in a determined mood, but Mr. McNutt personally went before the delegates to urge them to fol-

Continued on Page Three

## The International Situation

Defending British closure of the Burma road for a three-month period, Prime Minister Churchill told the House of Commons the purpose was twofold: (1) to relieve tension with Japan while Britain was fighting a life-or-death struggle at home; (2) provide an interval during which China and Japan might arrive at a settlement. He said Britain was willing to consider abolition of extraterritoriality in China, rendition of British concessions and revision of treaties once peace was established. [Page 1, Column 2.]

Operating despite bad weather, German fliers continued aerial harassment of the embattled Britons. Some of the bombs fell in crowded cities; one near a street car load of Scots; another on a Scottish tenement. The British communiqué listed no military objectives hit. The German High Command, however, said an armament factory at Greenock, a factory at Eastbourne, an airfield at Tunbridge and the great British military center at Aldershot had been effectively attacked. The British claimed success in raids on Channel ports, an oil plant and an oil supply depot. [Page 1, Column 1.]

There was no hint from Berlin as to when the drive on Britain would start, but Propaganda Minister Goebbels told parading German soldiers there that "you have just one more battle to win—then bells of peace will ring." [Page 7, Column 2.]

Secretary Hull, departing with his staff for the Pan American conference at Havana, promised "realistic" treatment of the economic and political problems of the Western Hemisphere. Among these problems he listed disposition of New World islands belonging to conquered countries, means of combating totalitarian trade barter systems and "fifth columns." [Page 1, Column 3.]

Indications that the United States was seeking a legal basis for withholding from the Pétain Government the $2,000,000,000 in French credits here was given by Secretary Morgenthau. He said the decision as to their release would be made by the President and Secretary Hull. It was believed the credits would find their way to Germany if the United States released them. [Page 8, Column 2.]

## THE DEMOCRATIC CANDIDATES

Franklin Delano Roosevelt
*for President*
Associated Press

Henry Agard Wallace
*for Vice President*
Associated Press

## NO CAMPAIGNING, FIRST LADY STATES

### In Address to Convention, She Says at Chicago That Duty Keeps President at Post

By KATHLEEN McLAUGHLIN

Special to THE NEW YORK TIMES.

CHICAGO, July 18—Eight years after her husband shattered the tradition of the non-appearance of Presidential candidates before the conventions which nominated them, Mrs. Franklin D. Roosevelt, in the same hall and on the same platform, established another tonight, the first wife of a President or nominee ever to address a major political party conclave.

Her talk was brief, her word was not the last word by many thousands in the convention record. But the message she brought and the tribute she got, of sustained silence for an impressively delivered appeal for a united country, loomed as another peak in a turbulent evening.

She was introduced at 10:30 o'clock while the State delegations were at fever heat over contests for the Vice Presidential nomination and before the President had addressed the assembly, because she was due to return East in a specially chartered plane tonight.

She arrived just before sunset, in a plane which left New York at 2:45 o'clock, with her son, Franklin D. Roosevelt Jr., as her only companion on the flight. She was, in effect, the deputy of the President to the convention in this city where he was nominated for the Presidency in 1932.

She brought the news to the delegates that the President, who sent word earlier that he "had no wish to be a candidate," did not plan a campaign, due to the heavy burden involved in the conduct of the nation's affairs during the world crisis.

In her address she disclosed this important fact after a special tribute to Postmaster General James A. Farley, who met her plane at the Municipal Airport.

**Gravity Marks Interview**

An unusual gravity was reflected in Mrs. Roosevelt's demeanor both during a mass interview to which she submitted immediately after her arrival in Chicago and as she stood on the platform facing the packed throng in the Stadium waiting for Chairman Barkley to complete his introduction of her.

When she stepped off the plane at the American Air Lines hangar she told a press corps that she could not say whether she would speak at the evening session, "because I have just arrived and I have not been told what the schedule is."

She received reporters in an upstairs office of the air lines company, isolated from the union pas-

Continued on Page Five

## *Garner Wins a $10 Bet For Guessing Roosevelt*

By The Associated Press.

CHICAGO, July 18—Vice President Garner bet on March 30, 1940, that President Roosevelt would be nominated for a third term.

At that time Mr. Garner was a candidate. Everett Watkins, Washington correspondent of The Indianapolis Star, exhibited today a card on one side of which had been written.

"I bet $10 to $1 that Mr. Garner can't name the nominee for President. Everett Watkins."

On the back, with Mr. Garner's signature, was: "F. D. Roosevelt."

He placed it in an envelope. He gave it to Mr. Watkins just before the latter left for Chicago and with instructions that the envelope was not to be opened until after nomination.

Today Mr. Watkins mailed Mr. Garner a check for $10.

## BURKE BOLTS PARTY OVER THIRD TERM

### Senator Calls It Threat to Freedom—Holt Asks Senate Rebuke to Roosevelt

Special to THE NEW YORK TIMES.

WASHINGTON, July 18—Condemning President Roosevelt's third term nomination as "fraught with peril to our free institutions," Senator Edward R. Burke of Nebraska bolted the Democratic party today and pledged his support to Wendell L. Willkie, the Republican nominee.

Almost simultaneously Senator Rush Holt, Democrat, of West Virginia, announced he would seek a record vote on his anti-third term resolution which has been pending in the Senate for months but allowed to lie dormant by its author at the urgent request of his Democratic colleagues. Senator Holt refused to say whether he would bolt his party and become an active worker against the President's reelection.

Representative Coffee, Democrat, of Nebraska, anounced that he would not support Mr. Roosevelt for a third term, although he refused to say whether he would support Mr. Willkie in the campaign.

Senator Norris, Independent, of Nebraska, contended that the argument of Senator Burke, his junior colleague "falls flat in the face of modern world and domestic conditions."

Senator Burke, in a telegram to Mr. Willkie, criticized the party leadership for the third-term nomination and predicted that "a host of citisens nurtured in the Democratic faith" would support his

Continued on Page Six

## PRESIDENT SPEAKS AS IF IN PRESENCE

### Talks Amid Small Group Over Radio to Nation—Message Hinged on Running Mate

Special to THE NEW YORK TIMES.

WASHINGTON, Friday, July 19—President Roosevelt sat in the big oval room of the executive offices in the presence of his immediate secretarial staff early this morning when he spoke over the radio to the Democratic National Convention in Chicago, with the country listening in over nation-wide networks.

His message accepting nomination for re-election was delivered as quietly and intimately as if his hearers were in his presence. The personal note was sensed by the group who were there with him.

This was especially recognized when he said that the "call of party alone would not prevail upon me" and that, while "self-appointed commentators and interpreters" would "seek to misinterpret or question motives," he was "thinking only of the national good and the international scene" and would have to bow to "the invisible thing called 'conscience'" and accept his nomination.

**Night Hours of Waiting**

There had been a question during the evening hours whether the address of acceptance would ever be delivered. Insistent upon the choice of a running mate satisfactory to him, the President had withheld the message pending the convention's action on the Vice Presidency.

When the President had been informed late in the day that party leaders in Chicago were unable to agree on the selection of Secretary Wallace, he sent word through his secretary, Stephen T. Early, that his address might be postponed or canceled.

"The President is determined not to address the convention unless and until its work has been completed," Mr. Early said at the time, although he did not mention Mr. Wallace.

Mr. Early went so far as to say that nomination of the running mate agreeable to the President might mean the difference between his acceptance or rejection of the third-term nomination. White House sources stressed that the selection of a Vice Presidential candidate would be of the convention's choosing rather than that of Mr. Roosevelt.

**No Callers at the White House**

It was plain last night, however, that President Roosevelt had not changed his mind about Mr. Wallace as the one man acceptable to him on the third-term ticket.

I[illegible] the day and evening the "b[illegible] end of the White House" too[illegible] on the appearance of

Continued on Page Four

## PRESIDENT ON RADIO

### 'Draft' Must Be Made by People, He Asserts as Convention Ends

### ASSAILS CONQUEST

### Won't Have Time, He Says, for 'Purely Political Debate' This Year

*The text of Roosevelt acceptance speech, page 2.*

By TURNER CATLEDGE

Special to THE NEW YORK TIMES.

CHICAGO, Friday, July 19—President Roosevelt accepted early today the third-term nomination tendered him early yesterday by the Democratic National Convention.

He did it by a dramatic radio address from the White House, after the convention had followed his direct orders in nominating Secretary Henry A. Wallace as his Vice Presidential running mate in the campaign.

Mr. Roosevelt thus became the first President in the history of the United States to gain or accept a third-term nomination for the high office. Only two nights ago he had sent a statement to the convention disclaiming his desire to run.

He told the convention in his address that "no call of party alone" would change a decision he had previously made not to run. But he added that the need to serve was a different matter.

He put his decision, therefore, squarely on the basis of the national defense, to which he has been giving of late practically all his effort. He could not call other people to serve, he said, and decline to serve himself if he were summoned by the people.

Because of the millions of citizens involved in the conduct of defense, "most right thinking people," the President said, are agreed that some form of selection for military service by draft is as necessary as it was in 1917.

**Contest Delays Address**

The length of the Vice Presidential nominating contest delayed Mr. Roosevelt's message for several hours, but soon after midnight, at a signal from Senator Barkley, permanent chairman of the Convention, the familiar voice came in clear and strong. A spotlight was thrown on a huge picture of the President at one end of the hall. Delegates and spectators fell into dead silence.

Mr. Roosevelt's voice came into the Convention Hall at the end of one of the most uproarious sessions of a Democratic assemblage in recent years. It was occasioned by a resistance of many delegates to the bald attempt of the Administration to put over a candidate for Vice-President whom many of them did not prefer. The convention adjourned sine die at 1:05 A. M.

"My conscience will not let me turn my back on a call to serve," the President said.

But he added:

"Only the people themselves can 'draft' a President."

He expressed gratitude for the selection of Mr. Wallace. He said that Mr. Wallace's "practical idealism" would be of great service to him and the people.

He took occasion, too, to send "most affectionate greetings" to "my old friend, Jim Farley." He felt sure, he said, that Mr. Farley would continue to give all the aid he possibly could to the Democracy.

**To Stay Close to Washington**

He predicted that the type of campaign soon to come would be quite different from such contests in the past. He intimated that he would keep close to his desk in Washington, where he could get in touch with any part of this country or with Europe or Asia, if necessary.

He would not have the time, he said, to engage in "purely political debate," although he would never be loath to call attention to misinterpretation and "mis-statements" of facts that might me made by political candidates.

The delegates and spectators stood and sat in absolute silence as the President spoke. His voice came over the system of loud

Continued on Page Three

"All the News That's Fit to Print."

# The New York Times.

LATE CITY EDITION
Fair and continued cool today. Tomorrow increasing cloudiness and continued cool.
Temperatures Yesterday—Max., 56; Min., 47

Copyright, 1940, by The New York Times Company.

VOL. XC....No. 30,226. Entered as Second-Class Matter, Postoffice, New York, N. Y. NEW YORK, SATURDAY, OCTOBER 26, 1940. THREE CENTS NEW YORK CITY and Vicinity | FOUR CENTS Elsewhere Except in 7th and 8th Postal Zones.

# LEWIS DECLARES FOR WILLKIE; SAYS ROOSEVELT MEANS WAR AND DICTATORSHIP IN NATION

## STAKES C. I. O. RULE

### Tells Wide Audience on Radio He Will Quit Office if President Wins

### SPEAKS IN 'CITIZEN' ROLE

### Roosevelt's Objective Is 'War,' He Charges, Declaring New Deal Has Not Kept Faith

*The text of Mr. Lewis's address will be found on Page 12.*

By LOUIS STARK
Special to THE NEW YORK TIMES.

WASHINGTON, Oct. 25—John L. Lewis threw his support tonight to Wendell L. Willkie, Republican candidate for President, in an address in which he attacked President Roosevelt as seeking a dictatorship by asking for re-election to a third term.

Speaking over some 322 radio stations on three broadcasting chains, the president of the Congress of Industrial Organizations and of the United Mine Workers of America charged President Roosevelt with leading the nation toward war. He asserted that the New Deal had not kept faith with the people, that it had failed to solve the problem of unemployment, and that even when the defense program reached the maximum of employment some 5,000,000 persons would still be idle.

Mr. Lewis gave his followers and supporters in the C. I. O. a mandate to go out and defeat Mr. Roosevelt, gambling his future leadership of the C. I. O. on his stand for Mr. Willkie by saying that if the President were re-elected he (Mr. Lewis) would "accept the result as being the equivalent of a vote of no confidence and will retire as president of the C. I. O. at its convention in November."

**Makes Vote a Direct Issue**

"Sustain me now or repudiate me," he urged his followers in a personal appeal, making the issue, in effect, "a vote for Roosevelt is a vote against Lewis."

"I will not chide you and will even hope that you will not regret your action," he said in his speech.

Thus Mr. Lewis presented his followers with a dilemma, since many of them have already indicated their support of Mr. Roosevelt. At the last convention of the miners' union, speaker after speaker made it clear that he held both Mr. Roosevelt and Mr. Lewis in esteem.

In the most bitter assaults on President Roosevelt which he had ever uttered, Mr. Lewis denounced the Administration for alleged failure to plan for the day when the nearly 100,000,000 soldiers and citizens serving European armies would be demobilized and, he said, would then begin to dump their commercial products into South American markets in competition with those of the United States.

Mr. Lewis partly cleared up the uncertainty which had preceded his address by announcing that he was speaking not as president of the C. I. O. or of the United Mine Workers, but "only in the rôle of a citizen and an American."

**Speaks "To All My Countrymen"**

"I do not speak for labor, but on the contrary I speak to labor and to all my countrymen," he declared.

Mr. Lewis kept secret until the last minute the name of the sponsor for his speech. Just before he went on the air it was announced that the sponsor was the National Committee of Democrats for Willkie.

Concerning the contents of his address Mr. Lewis had kept even his closest intimates in the dark. He let it be known that he had no assistance in writing the speech, not even from persons who are said to advise him on important matters. Mrs. Lewis and his daughter, Kathryn, are believed by many labor leaders to have been the only ones to have known in advance what he intended to say.

The address went out on what was said to have been the most costly radio network ever organized for a labor speaker. Mr. Lewis spoke over the N. B. C., C. B. S. and Mutual Broadcasting systems, at a cost of about $45,000. It was estimated that the speech may have reached 25,000,000 to 30,000,000 listeners.

"If President Roosevelt is re-established in office in the forthcoming election he will answer to no man, including the Congress, for his executive acts, that may create a dictatorship in the land," he declared.

"This election may be historically comparable to the controlled elec-

Continued on Page Twelve

## President Speaks in Boston Oct. 30; Says He Would Serve Full 4 Years

### Trip to Contested Area Will Fill Baltimore Gap in Schedule—Roosevelt Spikes Rumor He Might Resign

By CHARLES HURD
Special to THE NEW YORK TIMES.

WASHINGTON, Oct. 25—President Roosevelt intends to make a major political address in Boston on the night of Oct. 30, the White House announced tonight. This will fill a gap in his speaking schedule which was created by cancellation of plans to speak that night in Baltimore.

"The President probably will visit Massachusetts and deliver a major political address in Boston on the night of Oct. 30," the White House announcement said. "Detailed arrangements have not been worked out."

The trip is expected to include other stops in Massachusetts, perhaps at defense establishments.

The announcement of the President's intention to carry his campaign into a territory in which the Republicans have claimed gains for Wendell Willkie followed an earlier declaration that "of course" Mr. Roosevelt planned to serve out his full four-year-term if he was re-elected.

Rumors have been widely circulated that the President might resign at the end of what he considered the current emergency and turn over the office to the Vice President.

Mr. Roosevelt took cognizance of the rumors for the first time when he responded to a question asked at his press conference by Edward E. Wilcox, a member of the Washington Bureau of The Philadelphia Bulletin.

The question was as follows:

"In your Philadelphia address you said, 'We are determined during the next four years to make our objective of a job for every young man and woman in the United States a living fact.' Does this mean, Mr. President, that if reelected, God willing, you will serve out a full four-year term?"

The President smiled, and replied that, of course, he planned to serve for another full term, if given the opportunity. He thanked the reporter for saying "God willing," and then authorized the reporters present to use quotation marks with the words "of course."

The rumor, circulated before the national convention, gained in force after Mr. Roosevelt's renomination. Many persons in Washington, discussing it as a potentiality, pointed to the President's preference for

Continued on Page Eight

## AUTO PLANTS POOL DEFENSE EFFORTS

### Capacity Pledged at a Meeting in Detroit to Speed Share of Work on 12,000 Planes

Special to THE NEW YORK TIMES.

DETROIT, Oct. 25—Leaders of the automobile industry today pledged a pooling of their efforts in pushing the production of 12,000 airplanes for the national defense. This was the result of a meeting between the company heads and William S. Knudsen, production director for the National Defense Advisory Commission, in the offices of the Automobile Manufacturers Association. The closed session lasted for nearly five hours.

Afterward Mr. Knudsen said the aircraft industry soon will be subletting contracts to automobile companies in the amount of about $500,000,000.

The orders, Mr. Knudsen said, will start flowing by next Spring, and will be mostly for parts and tooling for bomber production. The amount does not include contracts already awarded for airplane engines.

Whether this added burden on automobile production capacity will eliminate 1942 motor car models remains to be seen.

**"Wait and See," Says Knudsen**

Mr. Knudsen said he saw no reason why the project should interfere with the normal production activities of the industry.

"Let us wait until the contracts are allotted next Spring," he said. "Maybe the industry can superimpose the normal production on top of the defense load, but we will have to wait and see."

There are about 400 separate parts used in bomber construction, Mr. Knudsen pointed out. The automobile manufacturers will be asked to fabricate fuselage, tail and wing assemblies.

Two types of bombers were under discussion. One is a smaller, two-motor type, weighing 24,000 pounds, the other a larger ship weighing about 40,000 pounds.

Mr. Knudsen told the officials that difficulty with the construction of the smaller ships was not expected, but that trouble had developed in the plans for the larger type, believed similar to that now

Continued on Page Seven

## Last Days of the Fair

Today and tomorrow are the last days of the World's Fair.

The final festivities tomorrow night will open at 7 P. M. when a new and powerful light will be used to illuminate the Trylon and Perisphere, symbols of the World of Tomorrow. From that hour on until the last light flickers out in the Amusement area, it will be every man to his own pleasure. Good luck, last Fair goer.

## WILLKIE PROMISES EXPANDED INDUSTRY

### This Will Employ Idle, Swell Farm Sales Where New Deal Failed, He Declares

*The texts of Mr. Willkie's addresses appear on Page 10.*

By JAMES A. HAGERTY
Special to THE NEW YORK TIMES.

WILKES-BARRE, Pa., Oct. 25—Declaring that the Roosevelt Administration had failed to bring about recovery because it had not understood the true relationship between various elements of our economy, particularly between industry and agriculture, Wendell L. Willkie said tonight in an address in the Wilkes-Barre Armory that the American people had a management in government which for nearly eight years had had a fair trial and had been unable to solve the farm problem, revive industry or provide jobs and now says that it cannot be done.

"Under such circumstances what have you to lose in making a change?" the Republican Presidential candidate said. Isn't it about time to get new management into your government? Isn't it about time to get management that believes in the future of the country and believes that the job can be done?

"I ask you to put me to work. I know that this job can be done."

Mr. Willkie asserted that solution of the problem of industry did not lie entirely in industry and that the solution of the problem of the farmer did not lie entirely in the farms. The solution of the industrial and unemployment problems, he said, lies largely in the expansion of the purchasing powers of the farmers and the solution of the farm problem lies very largely in the farmer's market, the industrial workers who buy the food raised on the farms.

**New Deal Is Arraigned**

Mr. Willkie said that the United States for seven and a half years had had an Administration that tried to divide the nation into classes, and had sought to solve the problem of the farmer by paying him needed benefits without affording him a market and to solve the problems of the workers by passing social legislation and providing relief. He said that the purpose of these efforts were good but were not enough.

"They do not solve the basic problems," Mr. Willkie continued. "They do not bring about a unified recovery of improvement of industrial activity and of farm prosperity. The farmer is entitled to a fair income that will make him independent of benefit payments. The worker is entitled to a job at fair wages so that he can be inde-

Continued on Page Ten

## WALLACE CHARGES NAZIS ARE ORDERED TO ASSIST WILLKIE

### Told to Use Money and Effort, He Says, as Roosevelt Defeat Is Necessary to Hitler

### HE ALSO LINKS APPEASERS

### Republican Held Patriotic but Confused in Mind on World Cross Currents

Special to THE NEW YORK TIMES.

PHILADELPHIA, Oct. 25—Charging that Nazi agents had been ordered to spend money and effort to accomplish the defeat of President Roosevelt next month, Henry A. Wallace asserted at a campaign rally tonight that a Republican victory was a necessity for the plans of Adolf Hitler and his fellow-dictators.

"We cannot shut our eyes," he said, "to the fact that a part of their plan is to remove from their path the greatest power for the protection of our peace, the Administration and leadership of Franklin D. Roosevelt."

The Democratic nominee for Vice President described Wendell Willkie as a "well meaning" campaigner who had "shown that his mind is in a state of confusion"; in other words, he said, a Presidential candidate who "often tries to make up for lack of knowledge by shouting and waving his arms."

"This fact explains, I believe, why the Nazi agents in this country have been ordered to work for his election," Mr. Wallace went on. "The friends of the totalitarian powers have decided that the ignorance and lack of leadership of the Republican candidate qualify him as their candidate."

In his attack upon Mr. Willkie and in terming him the candidate of the dictators and the appeasers, Mr. Wallace emphasized that he was not questioning the patriotism of the nominee or the rank and file of the Republican party. Nevertheless, he contended, Nazi leaders had found in Mr. Willkie and his party qualities which appeared to them as "the element of weakness that they need for their designs."

**La Guardia Speaks to Labor**

The former Secretary of Agriculture, with Mayor La Guardia of New York, addressed a crowd which packed the Third Regiment Armory. The meeting was arranged by the Amalgamated Clothing Workers of America and the Independent Voters for Roosevelt and Wallace. About 6,000 persons were jammed into the hall, and there was an overflow crowd of 3,000.

Mayor La Guardia directed his remarks to labor, charging that Mr. Willkie had been "picked" as the Republican candidate for President because of "his anti-labor record and his utility background." He asserted that in no previous Presidential campaign had there been "such a bold front, such premeditated plans and such determined efforts to fight labor."

In presenting his case of Mr. Willkie as the candidate of Hitler and the appeasers Mr. Wallace described the propaganda methods of the dictators and quoted from the Nazi press "expressing Hitler's feelings about President Roosevelt."

"It is now necessary," Mr. Wallace said, "that we understand why he has decided to apply pressure in this country for a Republican victory in this election. The answer is to be found in the short-sightedness and blind obstruction among the Republican leaders, as well as in the weaknesses shown by their chief candidate.

"The contrast between the Demo-

Continued on Page Eight

## Japanese Bid High to Russia For Amity, Seeing War With Us

By HUGH BYAS
Wireless to THE NEW YORK TIMES.

TOKYO, Oct. 25—Japan is getting ready to make substantial offers to Russia in return for an agreement removing the fear of Russian pressure in the Far East.

The government's precise intentions are effectively concealed, but when Lieut. Gen. Yoshitsugo Tatekawa, the Japanese Ambassador to Moscow, negotiates he will be fortified by the knowledge that Japanese informed opinion, especially in Nationalist ranks, favors discussion of concessions that formerly would have been incredible.

Japanese opinion has made a complete about face since the German-Italian-Japanese pact was signed, and Russia, formerly regarded as a pariah, is now being courted with brilliant offers. It is even suggested that Russia needs Afghanistan and India to make Soviet economy truly self-sufficient.

The expert on Russian affairs of the newspaper Asahi, a former Moscow correspondent, suggests that the Portsmouth treaty between Russia and Japan be abrogated. That treaty constitutes the legal basis for Japan's immensely valuable Siberian fisheries and the mere suggestion of a concession in that direction shows the length to which the advocates of a Japanese-Russian entente are willing to go.

Nothing short of a major turn in the policy toward Russia can save Japan in "the eventual struggle with the United States" in the view of Masao Maruyama, the Asahi expert. That struggle, he believes, is inherent in Japan's pact with the Axis powers.

"That Japan will find herself confronted across the Pacific by a resentful and powerful United States is inevitable," he said. "Without a determined stand on our part cooperation with Germany is impossible."

Even if Japan incidentally pro-

Continued on Page Six

# U. S. ASKS FRANCE TO STATE HER AIMS; HOPES SHE WON'T JOIN WAR ON BRITAIN; R. A. F. POUNDS BERLIN; LONDON HARD HIT

## NAZI CITIES RAIDED

### Vital Targets in Berlin and Other Centers Are Reported Bombed

### 35 OBJECTIVES ATTACKED

### Systematic Pattern Seen to Demolish Reich's Military and Industrial Bases

By RAYMOND DANIELL
Special Cable to THE NEW YORK TIMES.

LONDON, Oct. 25—Berlin was bombed again last night by aircraft of the Royal Air Force. There, as in other parts of the Reich and German-occupied territory, objectives already bombed again were sought out and attacked. [A total of thirty-five targets in Western Europe were raided, according to The United Press.]

Today's communiqué telling of last night's assaults indicated more plainly than ever that the British air force instead of resorting to senseless retaliation against German civilians for what is happening here are concentrating on a systematic pattern of attack designed completely to demolish objectives considered worth destroying.

In Berlin, the Putlitzstrasse and Lehrter railroad yards, damaged in earlier raids, were bombed again. So were Hamburg, Wilhelmshaven and other cities whose names recur often in the communiqués. The very familiarity of the objectives is taken to mean that the British air force is not content to leave a job half done, but once it is undertaken returns night after night to make sure that railroad yards, oil refineries and ports damaged in earlier raids are not allowed to complete repairs and go on about their business.

[British bombing planes again last night attacked German naval bases and oil targets in Northern and Central Germany, airdromes in Nazi occupied territory and Nazi gun emplacements on the Channel coast, the Air Ministry said this morning, according to a United Press dispatch.]

**Attack Lasts Three Hours**

The attack on Berlin itself lasted for more than three hours. Rail centers in the German capital and other objectives in the center of the city were heavily attacked, it was announced. Weather conditions were not favorable for high altitude bombing, as thick clouds covered the city from 4,000 feet above the ground to more than 12,000 feet. Nevertheless, the Air Ministry said, British bombers despite anti-aircraft fire managed to come down low enough to spot their objectives.

While the raid still was progressing gaps in the cloud layer made it possible for raiding planes to climb beyond accurate fire from ground batteries and still see what they were bombing.

The first raiders released salvos of incendiary and explosive bombs on the Putlitzstrasse and Lehrter yards. The second wave sighted the fires and continued the attack. Other raiders started a huge fire in the center of the Berlin target area, which served as a beacon for late arrivals.

The British did not use all their raiders over Berlin, where, accord-

Continued on Page Two

## The International Situation

United States concern over the prospect that France, under German pressure, may commit herself to military action against Britain has been expressed to Ambassador Henry-Haye for transmission to Vichy. Pending exact information on the subject of the conversation Thursday between Adolf Hitler and Marshal Pétain, it was said that Under-Secretary of State Welles told the Ambassador Thursday night of this government's anxiety over the situation. Mr. Welles was reported to have made a formal request for a full report through official channels on what was planned and France's attitude toward the rumored German demands for political, economic and military collaboration. [Page 1, Column 8.]

There still was no official information in Vichy as the French Chief of State returned to France's provisional capital and called a meeting of his Cabinet for today. Meanwhile Vice Premier Laval, who had held preliminary conversations with the Germans before Marshal Pétain talked to Herr Hitler, met Italian Foreign Minister Ciano to discuss Italian-French relations. Unofficial quarters in Vichy believed Germany was attempting to form a Pan-European bloc preparatory to a peace offer to Britain. It was the belief in Vichy that the Axis was hurrying to perfect such a bloc and offer a "compromise" peace before the United States Presidential election Nov. 5. [Page 1, Column 7.]

Neutral Switzerland heard that Marshal Pétain had refused a categoric demand from Herr Hitler for French military aid against Britain. In holding out against the Germans it was believed he might have the backing of General Franco, whose continued failure to put Spain openly with the Axis has caused speculation. The French and Spanish leaders are old personal friends. A possible compromise solution of the French-German question, some circles in Berne believed, might be French agreement to political and economic collaboration in the suggested Pan-European bloc, which Berne also heard the Axis was anxious to present to the United States as an accomplished fact on or before election day. [Page 4, Column 1.]

With the diplomatic offensive apparently in full swing, the Germans yesterday renewed their aerial siege of Britain, which had been lagging for several days. Mass raids by fast fighter-bomber planes were resumed during the daylight hours not only on London but elsewhere over the United Kingdom, and darkness brought no surcease from the bombs and the gunfire. A string of bombs landing in a London street in midafternoon hit directly on one street car and damaged four others and a passing bus. A number were injured, but only two persons were killed. The British said at least twelve of the raiders had been shot down. [Page 1, Column 6.]

The Germans said Italian planes were aiding in the aerial siege of Britain for the first time. This was confirmed by Rome, which said that an Italian air base had been established on the French coast. Their first action came on Thursday night. Planes especially designed for raids on England were being used, the Fascist press reported. [Page 2, Column 1.]

The Royal Air Force gave Berlin its twenty-third taste of aerial warfare Thursday night, the British Air Ministry reported, dropping bombs on two big railway yards and setting a great fire in the center of the city. News trickling out of the German capital said the German populace was not showing the same spirit as the people of London in facing sudden death from the sky. The Nazis said that damage was slight, but that there had been a number of casualties in Berlin and in the raids elsewhere. Thirty-four other targets, including four German naval bases, were reported attacked by the British bombing squadrons. [Page 1, Column 5.]

On the African front it appeared the Italian Army, which has been consolidating its advance base in Egypt at Sidi Barrani for several weeks, was getting ready to move again. The official Rome communiqué reported patrol clashes east of the city and increased air activity. The Fascist press said Marshal Graziani's forces already were established forty miles east of Sidi Barrani, only thirty-five miles from the well-fortified British base at Matruh. [Page 2, Column 6.]

On the eve of the opening in Moscow of negotiations for a Japanese-Russian non-aggression pact, authoritative Japanese commentators indicated Tokyo was ready to reverse its former policy toward the Soviet and make concessions undreamed of a few months ago in order to secure Russian compliance with the Japanese drive for control of East Asia. [Page 1, Column 4.]

## NAZIS AGAIN STRIKE HEAVILY AT LONDON

### Severe Day and Night Raids End the Respite—Liverpool, Scotland and Midlands Hit

By ROBERT P. POST
Special Cable to THE NEW YORK TIMES.

LONDON, Saturday, Oct. 26—German raiders swarmed over London and other sections of Britain with increased fury last night and early today after two heavy daylight attacks in which the Nazis used almost 400 planes.

The British had no confirmation of German reports that Italians had been taking part in the raids. They were willing to believe the reports, but they had not shot down any Italians.

As the night assault on London developed into the heaviest of the week, many parts of Scotland were attacked by low-flying planes. Besides wrecking homes and killing many persons outright, bombs brought down telephone lines and damaged electricity cables.

It was reported from Eastern Scotland that a train had been machine-gunned. A guard saw a German raider flying almost level with the train. One bullet hit a dispatch case and broke a mirror. Another bullet struck the shoulder strap of a woman in a service uniform. The train did not stop.

A lone Nazi raider also machine-gunned a town on the east coast of Scotland and bombed one building and partly demolished a row of cottages. Nobody was in the building or in the cottages. A British plane chased the raider away.

A Midlands town that has under-

Continued on Page Three

## LAVAL SEES CIANO ON 'EUROPEAN BLOC'

### Meeting Held Part of Plan to Make British Sue for Peace —Petain Returns to Vichy

By The United Press.

VICHY, France, Oct. 25—The French Vice Premier, Pierre Laval, conferred today with the Italian Foreign Minister, Count Ciano, on Chancellor Hitler's reported efforts to create a "Pan-European bloc" and force Britain to make peace.

M. Laval conferred with Count Ciano, presumably in or around Paris, as Marshal Henri Philippe Pétain returned to Vichy from the conference which he and M. Laval had yesterday with Herr Hitler in occupied France.

Meanwhile the Pétain Government was reported to have accepted Herr Hitler's terms for a permanent peace treaty.

Herr Hitler's terms were not disclosed, but it was understood that he demanded that France divide control of her strategic African possessions with Germany, Italy and Spain.

It was understood that M. Laval was trying to negotiate with Italy the same sort of "reconciliation and collaboration."

In exchange for her territorial and strategic surrenders, it was understood, France would obtain from Germany and Italy a permanent peace agreement "without punitive measures" such as Marshal Pétain pleaded for in his recent radio manifesto to the French people.

VICHY, France, Oct. 25 (AP)—Marshal Henri Philippe Pétain

Continued on Page Five

## VICHY DATA SOUGHT

### Events in France, Spain, Balkans and Far East Studied by President

### U. S. RESERVES ATTITUDE

### Roosevelt Said to Have Banned Warning to French—Sees No Threat to Us of War

By BERTRAM D. HULEN
Special to THE NEW YORK TIMES.

WASHINGTON, Oct. 25 — The United States has expressed its anxiety to France over the prospect that she may become involved in war against Britain and has requested that the Vichy government forward as promptly as possible a report on the latest developments and diplomatic conferences.

This was learned today in diplomatic circles which made clear that the United States Government was reserving its attitude pending the receipt of exact information concerning the trend of the rapidly moving events in Europe.

Reports that the State Department had warned France that she could expect no more aid from the United States if she went to war against Britain were discounted by officials, who said that such a warning had been recommended to the White House but not adopted for the reason that about the only way the United States could make a warning effective would be to enter the war.

France is not receiving food from this country. There was also a suggestion that President Roosevelt make an appeal to Marshal Henri Philippe Pétain, but this, too, was said to have been laid aside.

**President Watching Events**

President Roosevelt is watching closely events in France, Spain, the Balkans and the Far East, but it is reported authoritatively that he does not consider that these situations carry any threat of American involvement in the war.

In response to a question at his press conference this morning he indicated that the United States will consider the Vichy government friendly, despite the conferences of Marshal Pétain and Vice Premier Pierre Laval with Chancellor Hitler and his aides.

The President said that the United States still maintains diplomatic relations with Vichy. When a reporter interjected that "we still have diplomatic relations with Germany also," Mr. Roosevelt laughed.

Until some definite information has been received from France President Roosevelt, who conferred at some length yesterday with Secretary of State Cordell Hull, is giving particular attention to four phases of the international situation. They are:

1. Spain, where the German Chancellor and German diplomats are working hard to develop more aggressive support for the Axis.
2. The ultimate disposition of the French fleet and the role its disposition will play in the future developments of the European war. This situation might affect developments in the Caribbean, where the American republics would prevent any change in the status of French possessions.
3. Greece and the Balkans, where an explosive situation is developing as Germany extends her pressure eastward.
4. The Far East, where American nationals have been advised to come home, where Japan is eyeing rich oil and other resources of the Netherlands Indies, and where reports are current regarding the possibility of a Japanese-Russian non-aggression pact.

While Mr. Roosevelt does not consider that these four situations carry any threat of American involvement in war, he is seeking to prepare machinery to offset the shock in this country from any developments in any one of the four trouble zones.

**Plans Laid to Freeze Credits**

The arrangements include machinery to freeze credits and cash balances in this country held in the name of the involved countries in case of Axis domination, preparations to get American nationals out of trouble zones, and the drafting of proclamations to set up necessary American safeguards in event of eventualities.

The anxiety of the United States over the prospects of French entry into the war against Britain and the desire for information were transmitted through Gaston Henry-Haye, the French Ambassador, who

Continued on Page Four

"All the News That's Fit to Print."

# The New York Times.

LATE CITY EDITION
Cloudy, much colder today. Tomorrow partly cloudy and rather cold
Temperatures Yesterday—Max., 68; Min., 52

Copyright, 1940, by The New York Times Company.

VOL. XC..No. 30,237. Entered as Second-Class Matter, Postoffice, New York, N. Y. NEW YORK, WEDNESDAY, NOVEMBER 6, 1940. THREE CENTS NEW YORK CITY and Vicinity | FOUR CENTS Elsewhere Except in 7th and 8th Postal Zones.

# ROOSEVELT ELECTED PRESIDENT; CERTAIN OF 429 ELECTORAL VOTES; DEMOCRATS KEEP HOUSE CONTROL

## RETAIN HOUSE GRIP

### Democrats, Holding 225 Seats, Gain at Least Ten From Rivals

### 65 ARE NOW IN DOUBT

### Latest Figures Indicate Republican Gain of 1 to 3 Senators

By TURNER CATLEDGE

Unless further complete returns today show more Republican winners in yesterday's election, the Democrats not only will have met successfully the challenge of their opponents to control the house but may actually repair some of the damage to their huge majority in cthe 1938 Congressional election.

The Republicans, on the other hand, may have added from one to three to their roster in the Senate, but this remains to be determined by complete reports.

Returns received up to 4 o'clock this morning indicated that the President's party had dropped only four seats to the opposition, while they had picked up at least ten now held by Republicans. This made the count 225 Democrats, 143 Republicans, one Independent Democrat and one American Labor ,with sixty-five seats still in doubt.

The present House is composed of 259 Democrats, 167 Republicans, one Farmer-Laborite, two Progressives and one American Labor member, with five vacancies due to deaths and resignations.

The status of the Senatorial tabulation at that hour, with thirty-six States in contest—thirty-three for full and three for unexpired terms—showed Democrats, 18; Republicans, 7, and 11 still in doubt. This made sure that the new Senate would have at least 62 Democrats, 22 Republicans, 1 Independent, leaving the 11 in doubt. The present ratio of the Senate is 69 Democrats, 24 Republicans, 1 Progressive, 1 Independent and 1 Farmer-Laborite (Senator Shipstead of Minnesota, who ran this year as a Republican).

The Senate's lone Progressive, Senator Robert M. La Follette, trailed Fred H. Clausen, his Republican opponent, in the earlier returns from Wisconsin, but along in the morning hours he forged ahead and word from the Badger State indicated that he might pull through in the toughest fight of his career.

The four seats dropped by Democrats to Republicans were in the Eighth Oklahoma, Sixteenth New York, Fourth California and the Sixth Misouri districts. More than offsetting these were the ten picked up by the Democrats, including the First, Second and Fourth Connecticut districts and the Congressman at Large of that State; the First and Second Rhode Island districts, the Fift and Twenty-second Pennsylvania districts and the Forty-first New York and the Sixteenth Ohio districts. The Democrats made a clean sweep of the delegations in Connecticut and Rhode Island, annexing six seats held in these two States. Perhaps the greatest upsets in the House were the defeats of Representative Phil Ferguson, Democrat, of Oklahoma by Ross Rizley, Republican, and of the Democratic Representative James Fay of the Sixteenth New York by William E. Pheiffer, Republican.

**Incumbent Democrats Sticking**

Incumbent Democrats were holding tenaciously to leads in most of the other contests in which they were involved and New Deal nominees were threatening sitting Republican Congressman in a number of districts, particularly in States where the Roosevelt victory was assuming landslide proportions in the popular vote.

The Republicans had entertained no hope from the start of capturing the leadership of the Senate, but they claimed chances of picking up from five to ten new seats to add to the twenty-four they now have.

Continued on Page Two



## THE VOTE FOR PRESIDENT

| State. | Districts Total. | Districts Reported. | Roosevelt, Democrat. | Willkie, Republican. | Thomas, Socialist. | Electoral Vote Roosevelt. | Electoral Vote Willkie. |
|---|---|---|---|---|---|---|---|
| Alabama | 2,300 | 1,107 | 140,984 | 21,224 | ........ | 11 | .. |
| Arizona | 430 | 270 | 40,287 | 21,603 | ........ | 3 | .. |
| Arkansas | 2,169 | 642 | 37,258 | 8,586 | ........ | 9 | .. |
| California | 13,692 | 9,594 | 1,043,200 | 743,522 | ........ | 22 | .. |
| Colorado | 1,610 | 387 | 43,150 | 54,301 | ........ | .. | .. |
| Connecticut | 169 | 166 | 412,648 | 358,159 | ........ | 8 | .. |
| Delaware | 249 | 200 | 50,890 | 40,312 | ........ | 3 | .. |
| Florida | 1,451 | 895 | 246,183 | 82,531 | ........ | 7 | — |
| Georgia | 1,720 | 895 | 196,657 | 29,046 | ........ | 12 | .. |
| Idaho | 792 | 300 | 36,113 | 30,155 | ........ | .. | .. |
| Illinois | 8,378 | 6,017 | 1,514,763 | 1,375,092 | ........ | 29 | — |
| Indiana | 3,898 | 2,185 | 576,754 | 576,872 | ........ | .. | .. |
| Iowa | 2,453 | 1,505 | 356,657 | 376,859 | ........ | — | .. |
| Kansas | 2,734 | 1,377 | 147,821 | 216,802 | ........ | .. | 9 |
| Kentucky | 4,341 | 2,240 | 297,223 | 193,622 | ........ | 11 | .. |
| Louisiana | 1,712 | 481 | 137,518 | 22,987 | ........ | 10 | .. |
| Maine | 629 | 623 | 154,732 | 163,782 | ........ | .. | 5 |
| Maryland | 1,331 | 1,194 | 351,234 | 241,447 | ........ | 8 | .. |
| Massachusetts | 1,810 | 1,151 | 636,856 | 575,950 | ........ | 17 | .. |
| Michigan | 3,630 | 1,349 | 287,245 | 387,758 | ........ | .. | 19 |
| Minnesota | 3,696 | 910 | 258,715 | 216,433 | ........ | 11 | .. |
| Mississippi | 1,668 | 635 | 87,190 | 4,179 | ........ | 9 | .. |
| Missouri | 4,479 | 2,914 | 526,667 | 480,110 | ........ | .. | .. |
| Montana | 1,195 | 262 | 43,057 | 26,829 | ........ | 4 | .. |
| Nebraska | 2,043 | 1,227 | 124,825 | 169,083 | ........ | .. | 7 |
| Nevada | 260 | 177 | 15,545 | 11,213 | ........ | 3 | .. |
| New Hampshire. | 294 | 287 | 115,932 | 103,671 | ........ | 4 | .. |
| New Jersey | 3,630 | 2,038 | 529,922 | 564,294* | ........ | .. | 16 |
| New Mexico | 914 | 413 | 60,999 | 39,300 | ........ | 3 | .. |
| New York | 9,319 | 9,297 | 3,231,032 | 3,021,536 | ........ | 47 | .. |
| North Carolina | 1,926 | -,686 | 560,558 | 175,507 | ........ | 13 | .. |
| North Dakota | 2,262 | 631 | 73,669 | 73,330 | ........ | .. | .. |
| Ohio | 8,675 | 7,722 | 1,485,514 | 1,385,759 | ........ | 26 | .. |
| Oklahoma | 3,613 | 2,805 | 355,766 | 249,117 | ........ | 11 | .. |
| Oregon | 1,693 | 923 | 89,971 | 89,639 | ........ | .. | .. |
| Pennsylvania | 8,113 | 7,132 | 1,912,401 | 1,670,032 | ........ | 36 | .. |
| Rhode Island | 259 | 259 | 181,881 | 138,432 | ........ | 4 | .. |
| South Carolina | 1,277 | 953 | 81,867 | 4,144 | ........ | 8 | .. |
| South Dakota | 1,936 | 1,034 | 61,211 | 83,369 | ........ | .. | 4 |
| Tennessee | 2,300 | 1,891 | 257,724 | 119,836 | ........ | 11 | .. |
| Texas | 254 | 244 | 504,433 | 118,198 | ........ | 23 | .. |
| Utah | 831 | 345 | 63,298 | 39,941 | ........ | 4 | .. |
| Vermont | 246 | 246 | 64,244 | 78,355 | ........ | .. | 3 |
| Virginia | 1,714 | 1,622 | 223,388 | 103,030 | ........ | 11 | .. |
| Washington | 3,018 | 1,063 | 154,500 | 102,082 | ........ | 8 | .. |
| West Virginia | 2,300 | 1,016 | 217,064 | 155,580 | ........ | 8 | — |
| Wisconsin | 3,038 | 1,782 | 408,666 | 377,717 | ........ | 12 | .. |
| Wyoming | 696 | 490 | 32,889 | 31,765 | ........ | .. | .. |
| | | | | | | 429 | 51 |

*Hudson County returns incomplete.

## ROOSEVELT WINNER IN MASSACHUSETTS

### Indicated Margin Is Below That of 1936—Saltonstall Ahead in a Close Race

Special to THE NEW YORK TIMES.

BOSTON, Nov. 5—President Roosevelt carried Massachusetts over Wendell Willkie in today's election. Indications tonight were that his margin would be smaller than the 174,000 by which he captured the State's 17 electoral votes four years ago.

The Democratic surge was great enough to re-elect Senator Walsh over Henry Parkman Jr. by a substantial margin and to endanger Governor Leverett Saltonstall's re-election in his contest with Attorney General Paul A. Dever.

Lieut. Gov. Cahill, State Secretary Cook, State Treasurer Hurley and State Auditor Cook apparently were re-elected, while Robert T. Bushnell seemed to have won his contest for Attorney General on the basis of returns which had been counted late tonight.

President Roosevelt was Strongest in the industrial cities outside Boston. He carried Lynn by almost 6,000 votes and New Bedford by a ratio of nearly 2 to 1. It was estimated that Roosevelt's margin in Boston would approach 100,000. He carried Somerville by 4,100 votes.

Governor Saltonstall fared much

Continued on Page Four

## The War

Leading developments yesterday in the war, accounts of which appear on Page 25—the first page of the second section, —were as follows:

1. A German pocket battleship appeared in mid-Atlantic and shelled a British convoy.

2. Prime Minister Churchill emphasized before the Commons the growing U-boat threat and said bases in Ireland were needed by Britain.

3. In the Greek-Italian hostilities Rome reported an advance in the Yanina sector, the Greeks were said to be closing in on Koritza and a Yugoslav town was bombed by Italian-type planes.

The summary headed "International Situation" also appears on Page 25.

## NEW JERSEY VOTE GOES TO PRESIDENT

### Willkie Margin Cut in Normal Republican Areas—Edison and Barbour Win

By RUSSELL B. PORTER

On the basis of incomplete returns at 4 o'clock this morning, President Roosevelt appeared to have carried New Jersey with its sixteen electoral votes by a safe plurality—over Wendell Willkie—drastically reduced from 364,000 margin in 1936. and closer to his 31,000 edge in 1932.

The same returns indicated the election of Charles Edison, former Secretary of the Navy and son of the late Thomas A. Edison, the inventor, over his Republican opponent, State Senator Robert C. Hendrickson. Mr. Edison appeared to have polled more votes than the President.

United States Senator W. Warren Barbour, Republican candidate for re-election, ran far ahead of his ticket, and decisively defeated James H. R. Cromwell, former Minister to Canada and husband of Doris Duke, the tobacco heiress.

Eight hours after the polls closed at 8 P. M. there was still uncertainty over State-wide totals. Only one-half of the State's 3.631 election districts had reported their results by that time, and only a few comparatively of these were from the strong Democratic counties—Hudson, where Mayor Frank Hague of Jersey City, vice chairman of the Democratic National Committee, piled up a big Roosevelt vote, and Camden and Middlesex, where big industries with strong Roosevelt labor strength are located.

**Big Vote Adds to Delay**

The delay in recording the vote from these counties was caused partly by the record-breaking vote, brought out by perfect weather and unprecedentedly heavy registration, partly by the fact that voting machines are not used in these counties, and partly by the traditional withholding of the Hudson County vote until after the Republican counties have reported.

Surrogate John H. Gavin of Hudson County, spokesman for Mayor Hague, estimated early this morning, with the vote still incomplete, that Hudson would give the President and Mr. Edison a plurality of 110,000, including 60,000 in Jersey City. Mr. Cromwell was running far behind.

Four years ago Mr. Roosevelt re-

Continued on Page Twelve

## CITY MARGIN WIDE

### Lead Totals 727,254—Queens, Richmond Won by Willkie

### P. R. SYSTEM UPHELD

### Abolition Move Defeated by About 206,550—Simpson Is Elected

By LEO EGAN

Franklin D. Roosevelt piled up a plurality of 727,254 in New York City yesterday as voters in record-breaking numbers went to the polls under clear skies to record their choice for President. This was far short of the 1,375,396 plurality given to him in 1936, when he was a candidate for a second term.

The President carried the three most populous counties in the city but lost Queens and Richmond. Queens gave Wendell Willkie a plurality of 36,875.

Senator James M. Mead, seeking re-election on the Democratic ticket, ran slightly ahead of the President. He carried the city by 845,063, carrying all five counties.

The President's pluralities of 350,-610 in Kings, 219,066 in the Bronx and 195,017 in Manhattan were much less than his supporters had counted on except in Manhattan, but they were enough to please them. The Manhattan plurality was larger than expected.

**Results in Other Contests**

Other features of yesterday's voting in the city were the defeat by an indicated plurality of 206,550 of the proposal to repeal the proportional representation method of selecting members of the City Council, the apparent defeat of Representative James H. Fay in the Sixteenth District, the election of Kenneth F. Simpson, New York County Republican leader, for the Congressional seat now held by Representative Bruce Barton; the election of John Cashmore and Samuel S. Leibowitz, the Democratic candidates for Borough President and County Judge, respectively, in Brooklyn, and the re-election of Representative Vito Marcantonio, outstanding Congressional foe of conscription and the Roosevelt defense program, in the Twentieth Congressional District on Manhattan's upper East Side.

The President carried all but two Assembly districts in Manhattan, losing the Fifteenth and Tenth, and all but three in King's losing the Ninth, Tenth and Twentieth. He swept all eight districts in the Bronx and lost three out of six in Queens.

In all but one borough the friends of proportional representation were able to beat down the proposal to repeal it. If the proposal had been carried the voters would have elected Councilmen next year on the basis of State Senate districts with

Continued on Page Four

WINNERS OF PRESIDENCY AND VICE PRESIDENCY
Franklin Dèlano Roosevelt — Henry Agard Wallace

## DEMOCRATS CARRY STATE BY 230,000

### Mead, O'Day, Merritt and Desmond Join President in New York Victory Column

By JAMES A. HAGERTY

For the third time President Franklin D. Roosevelt carried his home State of New York with its forty-seven electoral votes in yesterday's election, this time by a plurality of about 230,000, over Wendell L. Willkie, his Republican opponent.

The vote in New York City with 40 election districts missing out of 4,051 gave Willkie 1,241,501 and Roosevelt 1,937,017, an actual plurality for Roosevelt of 695,516 and an indicated plurality of 700,823.

Outside New York City in 5,004 out of 5,268 election districts, the vote was Willkie 1.685,043, Roosevelt 1,219,817, an actual plurality of 465,276 for Willkie and an indicated plurality of 489,924. This gave the President an actual plurality of 230,240 on these returnst and an indicated plurality of 215,000, which may be slightly higher because of the small number of votes in the unreported districts.

Bruce Barton, Republican candi-

Continued on Page Ten

## *Bonfires of All Buttons Urged to Heal Bitterness*

Public bonfires of all the Democratic and Republican campaign literature and buttons was suggested yesterday by William Allen White, national chairman of the Committee to Defend America by Aiding the Allies, as a means of "healing partisan bitterness and for launching a nation-wide campaign to safeguard American democracy."

Mr. White, in a statement issued last night, urged "unity mass meetings" as soon as possible after election, in a message to the representatives of the group's 717 local chapters in the forty-eight States.

The meetings should be held, he said, "not in the spirit of exaltation on the part of the victorious party but with the idea that we destroy the symbols of partisan bitterness and unite now on a national program of safeguarding American democracy."

## PRESIDENT TAKES KEYSTONE STATE

### Republican Chairman Concedes Pennsylvania—Guffey Ahead in Senate Race

Special to THE NEW YORK TIMES.

PHILADELPHIA, Wednesday, Nov. 6—Aided by impressive strength in the industrial areas, President Roosevelt apparently duplicated his feat of 1936 and won the thirty-six electoral votes of traditionally Republican Pennsylvania in yesterday's election.

The trend in the senatorial contest between Senator Joseph F. Guffey, Democrat, and Jay Cooke, chairman of the Philadelphia Republican Committee, was in the direction of the re-election of Mr. Guffey, who campaigned on his record of "100 per cent Roosevelt support."

The Democrats, it seemed likely, would gain an undetermined number of seats in the State's Congressional delegation, which had been Republican by nineteen to fifteen, and they appeared to have an even chance of wresting control of the State House of Representatives from the Republicans, who took it over with the election of Governor James two years ago. The Republicans were hopeful of salvaging their majority in the State Senate.

James F. Torrance, Republican State Chairman, conceded Pennsyl-

Continued on Page Four

## *Willkie Retires Refusing to Give Up; He Declines Any Statement Before Today*

Grimly clinging to his avowed determination not to give up the fight, Wendell L. Willkie said at 1:30 this morning that he intended to go to bed in his suite at the Hotel Commodore, and that he would have no statement to make concerning the election until some time after he wakes up this morning.

This information, relayed from his fourteenth-floor suite to the waiting crowd of reporters in the press headquarters downstairs, was the only word that came from Mr. Willkie after he had briefly appeared before a crowd of cheering campaign workers at 12:20 A. M., to say that he was neither afraid nor disheartened, and repudiate indignantly suggestions that he should concede his defeat.

When he appeared at that time before about 1,500 faithful supporters in the Grand Ball Room of the Commodore Hotel, Mr. Willkie pleaded with them not to quit and expressed his confidence that the fight they had jointly waged would eventually be won.

His appearance before his campaign workers came after hours of seclusion in his private suite, where he repeatedly characterized the election as "a horse race" and predicted that the result would not be known definitely until some time today. Mr. Willkie appeared before the crowd of campaign workers at 12:19 A. M.

Holding up both hands to ask for silence while they gave him an ear-splitting ovation, Mr. Willkie said:

"Fellow workers: I first want to say to you that I never felt better in my life. I congratulate you in being a part of the greatest crusade of this century. And that the principles for which we have fought will prevail is as sure as that the truth will always prevail.

"And I hope that none of you are either afraid or disheartened because I am not in the slightest.

"I just wanted to come down and thank you so much for being my fellow fighters in this struggle—to

Continued on Page Five

## ROOSEVELT LOOKS TO 'DIFFICULT DAYS'

### But Tells Celebrators That He Will Carry On for the Country 'Just the Same'

By CHARLES HURD

Special to THE NEW YORK TIMES.

HYDE PARK, Wednesday, Nov. 6—Standing on the portico of his mother's home here, Franklin D. Roosevelt early today acknowledged his re-election with a promise to continue to be "the same Franklin Roosevelt you have known."

He made this statement to several hundred residents of Hyde Park and vicinity who formed a torchlight procession that carried out a tradition marking Democratic political victories with rallies at the old house, a parade formed by Democrats as soon as returns indicated the victory.

"We are facing difficult days in this country," Mr. Roosevelt told the throng, "but I think you will find me in the future just the same Franklin Roosevelt you have known a great many years."

The President beamed on the crowd as he leaned on the arm of his third son, Franklin Jr., in the bright light of flares set in place by motion-picture camera men.

He smiled and waved while hundreds of persons trooped through the grounds from cars parked first in the driveways and afterward on the Albany Post Road, some of them a quarter of a mile away.

**President Faces His Neighbors**

Behind the President were grouped about forty guests who had been entertained by Mrs. Roosevelt at supper at her cottage at Val-Kill. But the President faced a crowd in which there were no prominent politicians, no industrial leaders.

These were exclusively his neighbors, who bear to him the same relationship as the villagers bore to his father when he was a minor Democratic leader and a friend of President Cleveland.

President Roosevelt walked on to the front porch of Hyde Park house just before midnight, when he finally broke a vigil over tables on which he marked election returns behind locked doors in the dining room of his home.

The first glare of red flares was seen far off down the driveway. Ten minutes later, exactly at midnight, a town band marched into the car park in front of the house.

The President, with Franklin Jr., stood at the right side of the porch.

Continued on Page Two

## BIG ELECTORAL VOTE

### Large Pivotal States Swing to Democrats in East and West

### POPULAR VOTE CUT

### First Time in History That Third Term Is Granted President

By ARTHUR KROCK

Over an apparently huge popular minority, which under the electoral college system was not able to register its proportion of the total vote in terms of electors, President Roosevelt was chosen yesterday for a third term, the first American in history to break the tradition which began with the Republic. He carried to victory with him Henry A. Wallace to be Vice President, and continued control of the House of Representatives by the Democrats was also indicated in the returns.

But in many of the larger States so many precincts were still missing early this morning, and the contest in these States was so close, that Wendell L. Willkie, the Republican opponent, whose name Mr. Roosevelt never mentioned throughout the campaign, refused to concede defeat. He said it was a "horse race," and that the result would not be known until today. He went to bed in that frame of mind.

As the returns mounted there seemed little, however, to sustain Mr. Willkie's hope. New York, Massachusetts, Connecticut, Rhode Island, Pennsylvania, Ohio and Illinois, of the greater States, all appeared to have been carried safely by the President. The Solid South had resisted all appeals to revolt against Mr. Roosevelt's quest for a third term. The Pacific and Mountain States were following the national trend.

**States for Mr. Roosevelt**

States sure or probable for the President are:

Alabama, Arizona, Arkansas, California, Connecticut, Delaware, Florida, Georgia, Illinois, Kentucky, Louisiana, Maryland, Massachusetts, Missouri, Minnesota, Mississippi, Montana, Nevada, New Hampshire, New Jersey, New Mexico, New York, North Carolina, Ohio, Oklahoma. Pennsylvania, Rhode Island, South Carolina, Tennessee, Texas, Utah, Virginia, West Virginia and Wisconsin—electoral votes, 429.

States sure or probable for Mr. Willkie:

Kansas, Maine, Michigan, Nebraska, North Dakota, South Dakota, Vermont—electoral votes 51.

States doubtful or insufficiently reported:

Colorado, Idaho, Indiana, Iowa, Oregon, Washington and Wyoming—electoral votes, 51.

**The Electoral Vote**

Listing as doubtful nine States, including several like California, Ohio and Indiana, which seem certain to join the Democratic column, there were at 3 A. M. only 51 electoral votes in possible dispute. The President had an apparently certain total of 429, while with more or less security in Mr. Willkie's column were only 51 votes.

No shift or series of shifts could affect the electoral result and the indications were that the President's total would reach from 420 to 470.

Either figure would be much less than the nearly clean sweeps he had in 1932, when he carried forty-two States, and in 1936, when only Maine and Vermont went Republican. And unless the Far West and the Mountain States shall be shown to have given incredible majorities and late returns from the Eastern States pile up the President's votes higher than indications seem to make possible, Mr. Roosevelt's popular majority will be far less than he had against Herbert Hoover and Alf M. Landon.

It appeared early this morning that a maximum of 5,000,000 and a minimum of 2,000,000 would represent the final difference between the popular votes cast for the two major Presidential candidates. The Associated Press tabulation at 1:50 A. M. was 14,879,930 for Mr. Roose-

Continued on Page Two

"All the News That's Fit to Print."

# The New York Times.

LATE CITY EDITION
Fair with slowly rising temperature today. Tomorrow increasing cloudiness and warmer.
Temperatures Yesterday—Max., 29; Min. 17



VOL. XC..No. 30,313. Entered as Second-Class Matter, Postoffice, New York, N. Y. NEW YORK, TUESDAY, JANUARY 21, 1941. THREE CENTS NEW YORK CITY and Vicinity | FOUR CENTS Elsewhere Except in 7th and 8th Postal Zones.

# ROOSEVELT INAUGURATED FOR THE THIRD TIME; WINANT TO BE NAMED AMBASSADOR TO LONDON; BRITISH INVADE ERITREA; DICTATORS SET COURSE

## FASCISTI IN FLIGHT

### Desert Fighters Driving Italians Toward Vital Red Sea Port

### R. A. F. BOMBS BASES

### Clashes on Kenya Front Widen New Threat to African Colonies

Wireless to THE NEW YORK TIMES.

CAIRO, Egypt, Jan. 20—Italian troops continued an orderly retreat from Kassala into Eritrea today, closely followed by British mobile forces, which continually harassed the Fascist rear guard. Fortifications around Sabderat and Tesenei were occupied yesterday without opposition, thus again making the results of many months' labor useless to the Italians.

The advancing British forces now are more than thirty miles inside Eritrea, headed east through foothills along the southern section of a road that makes a flat loop south from Sabderat, which is ten miles inside the border, to the Tesenei area, about twenty miles inside. The road then turns east and then north again directly south of Agordat, where it meets the railway from the Red Sea port of Massawa.

The railway extends west from Agordat to within sixty miles of Kassala, but the road in that region is not comparable with the southern route.

**Supply Problem Difficult**

The British units are now somewhat reinforced, but all the action thus far has been a mere series of patrol forays. The Italians apparently are withdrawing according to plan in good order. It is possible that they will retreat to Agordat to eliminate the extremely difficult problem of supplying a rather large force over rough and rutty roads under frequent bombing and subject to daily attacks of British patrols, which had continually threatened to isolate Kassala.

From Agordat the Italians will have the advantage of easy supplies unless the R. A. F. destroys the railway. The British, on the other hand, would be forced to supply their forces over the road previously used by the Italians, should they decide to penetrate that far.

This action on the part of the Italians is strangely similar to that of the British last Summer when they withdrew to the railhead at Matruh, forcing the Italians to lengthen their lines of communication. However, it is likely that the British also learned a lesson from the subsequent events and that they are unlikely to take such chances as those that made the Italians a prey to flanking movements.

**R. A. F. Hampers Retreat**

Early yesterday morning R. A. F. bombers attacked gun positions southeast of Tesenei and further hampered the Italian retreat by bombing and machine-gunning truck concentrations in the same area. Massawa, Assab and Hargeisa also were bombed. The attackers braved an intensive anti-aircraft fire at Massawa, setting many fires at this port, where supplies going inland to Agordat must be landed.

Blinding sand storms again swept Northern Libya yesterday, considerably hampering air activity, but R. A. F. patrols were carried out in the Tobruk area.

On the Kenya front British motorized units continued their offensive patrol activities, which are steadily reducing the Italian gains made last Summer.

**Clashes on Kenya Border**

NAIROBI, Kenya, Jan. 20 (UP)—South African forces, part of the southern jaw of a British pincer campaign against the Italians in East Africa, reported today the capture of prisoners in clashes on the Kenya-Italian Somaliland and Kenya-Ethiopian borders.

Prisoners were taken in the El Yibo area, near Lake Rudolf along the border between Kenya and Western Ethiopia, said a communiqué, and eleven dead, including two European officers, were left behind by the dispersed Fascist unit.

In a patrol clash on the El Wak road, near the Kenya-Italian So-

Continued on Page Ten



## The International Situation

TUESDAY, JAN. 21, 1941

President Roosevelt took office for his tradition-breaking third term in a historic inaugural ceremony on the Capitol steps yesterday. In an address broadcast throughout the world he considered the status, the strength and the future of free democracies in the present menaced world. As to this nation, he said: "We do not retreat. We are not content to stand still. As Americans, we go forward, in the service of our country, by the will of God." The speech and the occasion were marked by a solemnity that seemed to reflect the grave international events. [Page 1, Column 8.]

The inaugural parade foreshadowed the new military role that this country is preparing to play in defense of the democracies. Instead of the panoply of floats, and the colorful uniforms of club and fraternal organizations it was primarily a military spectacle, which some 500,000 persons viewed from every available vantage point. [Page 1, Column 6.]

As if further to emphasize the international wartime aspect of the occasion, the members of the diplomatic corps attending included representatives of nations that are fighting each other, as well as those of nations that have been occupied or overrun. [Page 4, Column 6.]

The next United States Ambassador to London to succeed Joseph P. Kennedy, who is retiring, will be John Gilbert Winant, former Governor of New Hampshire and former Director of the International Labor Office at Geneva, it was learned in London. It is understood he will be accompanied by a business man having the rank of Minister who will serve as liaison officer to handle United States supplies to Britain. [Page 1, Column 4.]

Reichsfuehrer Hitler and Premier Mussolini have held their meeting, but just when, or where, or what was discussed has not been disclosed. The official German news agency said merely that the leaders had met in the presence of their Foreign Ministers and "had a comprehensive exchange of views relative to the situation." [Page 1, Column 2.] The Italian communiqué was identically worded. It was thought in Rome that the obvious matters discussed were Axis policy regarding the Balkans, the Mediterranean, Britain and developments in the United States and France. [Page 11, Column 3.]

Colonel William J. Donovan arrived in Sofia, Bulgaria, to be received by King Boris. Although he has no official rank, it was believed in diplomatic circles in Sofia that his mission was to provide information concerning the help the United States was prepared to give Britain, and that King Boris's decision regarding any future German pressure might be guided by what the Colonel had to say. [Page 10, Column 2.]

The "dissipation of all misunderstanding" between Marshal Pétain and Pierre Laval was explained in Vichy as a move initiated by the Marshal to curb a violent press campaign in Paris against the Vichy government and to unify French opinion. The step will not alter French policy and France will not turn over her immobilized fleet to Germany for use against Britain, an official spokesman said. [Page 1, Column 3.]

Italian forces retreating from the Kassala area withdrew into Eritrea, Italian East Africa, followed by pursuing British mobile units, according to Cairo. The British already were more than thirty miles inside Eritrea. [Page 1, Column 1.]

Italian air formations dropped tons of explosives on the Athens district and on Crete, but without doing much damage, according to Athens reports. The Greeks reported having sunk an Italian submarine. [Page 11, Column 1.]

Bad flying weather over the Strait of Dover prevented German bombers from getting through to England last night. There were a few scattered daylight attacks, which caused only slight damage. [Page 9, Column 1.]

*Communiqués of the belligerents are on Page 10*

## AXIS CHIEFS DRAFT NEXT MOVE IN WAR

### Quick New Action Is Expected After Hitler-Mussolini Talk —U. S. Believed a Topic

By C. BROOKS PETERS

Wireless to THE NEW YORK TIMES.

BERLIN, Jan. 20—The veil of secrecy that shrouded the movements of Reichsfuehrer Hitler and Premier Mussolini for forty-eight hours was lifted slightly this afternoon when the official German news agency released a communiqué declaring that a meeting between the two leaders and their Foreign Ministers had taken place.

The communiqué did not reveal when or where the conversations had been held nor what decisions had been reached. It said merely:

"On the occasion of a meeting in the presence of the Foreign Ministers of the Axis, the Fuehrer and the Duce had a comprehensive exchange of views relative to the situation. This exchange took place in the spirit of the hearty friendship between the two government heads and of the intimate comradeship in arms between the German and Italian peoples. It resulted in complete agreement of mutual opinions on all questions."

The issuance of this communiqué was somewhat surprising, for two hours earlier—shortly after 1 o'clock—three score foreign correspondents had been informed in a press conference that reports of a meeting between Herr Hitler and Signor Mussolini could be categorically denied.

Later the semi-official commentary Dienst aus Deutschland declared that the meeting had taken place over the week-end, but it did not say where. Since the previous meeting between the two men was held in Florence, Italy, when Herr Hitler learned of the Italian ultimatum to Greece, and since the German communiqué today was released before the Italian announce-

Continued on Page Twelve

## VICHY INSISTS REICH WILL NOT GET NAVY

### Petain Held Still Master—Talk With Laval Termed Merely a Move for Unity

By The United Press.

VICHY, France, Jan. 20—France refuses to turn over her immobilized fleet to Germany for use against Great Britain and insists upon full observance of the French-German armistice, despite the reconciliation of Marshal Henri Philippe Pétain and Pierre Laval, an official spokesman said today.

The "dissipation of all misunderstandings" between Marshal Pétain and the man he ousted as Vice Premier on Dec. 13 was undertaken by the 84-year-old marshal in a move to curb a violent campaign in the Paris press against the Vichy government, it was stated.

"France lives in the same regime as before and France's policy consists of respecting to the letter every line of the armistice convention," said a spokesman.

"It must be perfectly understood that our fleet will not be used against our former allies, just as it must be understood that we will continue to assure and safeguard our empire overseas.

"Marshal Pétain remains the chief of all France—free France, occupied France and overseas France," the spokesman continued.

"He remains the man who represents integral authority. Tomorrow, the same as today and yesterday, his Ministers, whoever they may be, will be responsible only to him. To use his own words, it is he whom history must judge."

The official French radio today broadcast the following explanation of the meeting of Marshal Pétain and M. Laval:

"It was for imperious reasons of domestic policy that Marshal Pétain decided to deprive himself on Dec. 13 of the aid of M. Laval, as

Continued on Page Twelve

## ENVOY IS SELECTED

### Former Head of World Labor Office Picked to Succeed Kennedy

### BUSINESS MAN TO AID

### Will Be Named Minister for Liaison in Supply of U. S. War Goods

By DAVID ANDERSON

Special Cable to THE NEW YORK TIMES.

LONDON, Jan. 20—John G. Winant will be the next United States Ambassador to the Court of St. James, it was learned today. He is expected to be accompanied by a business man who will have the rank of Minister and liaison duties in connection with the United States' production of war materials, which is becoming more essential to Great Britain daily.

The former Governor of New Hampshire has been mentioned often by the British press as a possible successor to Ambassador Joseph P. Kennedy since the latter faded from the scene. His appointment will cause little surprise and will be received with pleasure by his many friends here.

Mr. Winant entered the European picture in 1935 when he became assistant director of the International Labor Office at Geneva, moving up to the directorship two years ago. His record as an administrator, coupled with his personality, stamped on the minds of influential Britishers a most favorable impression.

The Foreign Office here would not discuss the Ambassadorship until the appointment had passed through. It would not even confirm that its assent had been asked to Mr. Winant's appointment.

With Viscount Halifax, Foreign Secretary until he was named Ambassador to the United States, expected in Washington soon, it was a question of absorbing interest here who would be his opposite number in London. Since Lord Halifax has been selected to carry on the mission of his predecessor, the Marquess of Lothian, in explaining to Americans what their stake is in Britain's battle, it is safe to assume that the selection of Mr. Winant means that he will carry on President Roosevelt's policy whereby arms and machines will be hastened to this country.

**A Liberal Republican**

John Gilbert Winant is a liberal Republican whose humanitarian principles have far transcended party or class lines. As a prominent member of the Republican party, he has been a stanch supporter of President Roosevelt's New Deal program, and as a wealthy New England aristocrat he has devoted his mature years to an intensive study of labor and social welfare problems.

Tall, deliberate and earnest, "an aristocratic version of Abraham Lincoln," he has often been mentioned as a possible Presidential candidate on a liberal Republican platform. He was mentioned as a

Continued on Page Nine

AGAIN THE NATION'S CHIEF EXECUTIVE
Franklin Delano Roosevelt taking the oath from Chief Justice Charles Evans Hughes
Times Wide World

## Hull to Refuse to Disclose Envoys' Data to Congress

### He Will Reject Demands for Access to Reports by Bullitt and Kennedy on European Affairs

By The Associated Press.

WASHINGTON, Jan. 20—The State Department will reject legislative demands that the department make public the diplomatic reports of Joseph P. Kennedy and William C. Bullitt, according to rumors on Capitol Hill. Mr. Kennedy, who will retire soon as Ambassador to Great Britain, and Mr. Bullitt, former Ambassador to France, were said by Senator Wheeler of Montana to have disagreed sharply on the course the United States should pursue in the European war.

One legislator told reporters that the State Department would decline to release the reports, even to Congressional committees, on the ground that they were confidential documents of the Executive branch of the government.

This informant said that Administration officials believed publication of the documents would shed little light on the lend-lease legislation and might create an unnecessary side issue in the fight over the program.

Mr. Kennedy is scheduled to testify before the House Foreign Affairs Committee tomorrow.

Representative Fish, ranking minority member of the committee, said today that opposition witnesses "definitely will answer the absurd charges made by Government officials that we are in danger of immediate invasion and that this bill has something to do with a crisis in England in sixty or ninety days."

Fish declared it was "absurd" to talk of aiding Britain in a period of sixty to ninety days because, he added, none of the equipment leased or loaned to the British would reach them during that period.

There were reports on the Senate side today that opposition members were seeking to draft a substitute for the lend-lease legislation which would provide an outright cash gift to Britain of $1,000,000,000 to $2,000,000,000.

Indications that this "gift" strategy would be employed in the determined fight for defeat of the lease-lend legislation served to give notice that inauguration day signified

Continued on Page Eight

## DEFENSE PROGRAM IS PARADE KEYNOTE

### Mechanized Units, Coast Guard and Soldiers, Sailors and Marines Salute President

Special to THE NEW YORK TIMES.

WASHINGTON, Jan. 20—The inaugural parade which marched "the historic mile" down Pennsylvania Avenue today and past the White House to salute President Roosevelt for the third time provided a dramatic foretaste of things to come in the military program of the United States.

Soldiers on foot and on wheel, airplanes in mass formations and sailors and marines marching with fixed bayonets, these component parts of the parade virtually swamped the few civilian units, which themselves were barely sufficient to represent the civilian activities of the Federal Government.

This was an inaugural parade without floats, without civilian drum and bugle corps, without drum majors or "drum majorettes," without club and fraternal bands and without the delegations of silk-hatted marchers whom States have sent to the Capitol ever since Thomas Jefferson was first inaugurated here in 1801.

Even the tempo was different, for the mechanized mass of the parade, the gigantic wheel and tractor implements of mechanized warfare roared past the reviewing stand at forty miles an hour.

There were only two bits of color in the whole parade. The first was furnished by the Marine Band, which wore the traditional scarlet coats with blue trousers and yellow chevrons and stripes. The other was provided by a National Youth Administration unit, dressed in Russian-type blouses colored bright red or bright blue, accompanied by a band wearing flowing capes.

Otherwise the military and naval display was characterized by khaki or blue or gray uniforms, by riflemen marching with fixed bayonets and soldiers equipped for field service, including steel helmets.

About thirty Governors had a prominent place in the parade, each having three small sedans for his official party. The rest of the parade was confined to the preparedness program which formed the

Continued on Page Seven

## 'New World Order' Only a Matter of Time, Says Matsuoka, Urging U. S. to 'Allay' Crisis

By The Associated Press.

TOKYO, Tuesday, Jan. 21—Foreign Minister Yosuke Matsuoka told the Japanese Diet today that Japan, Germany and Italy certainly would accomplish their goal of a new world order "if only given time" and expressed hope that the United States "will bend her utmost efforts to allay the impending crisis of civilization."

Should both the United States and Japan become involved in a new world war because of the triple military alliance, he said "no one could guarantee that it could not develop into a war spelling the downfall of modern civilization."

United States trade embargoes against Japan, he said, left his country no alternative save to build up a self-sufficient trade sphere in "Greater East Asia" and he declared that the United States "has evinced no adequate understanding" that such a sphere "is truly a matter of vital concern to Japan."

"British dominions and colonies in various ways interfering with Japan's shipping," he said.

He represented the military alliance with Germany and Italy as a device designed to "prevent further extension of present disturbances," and declared that Germany and Italy shared his country's desire to remove mutual Japanese-Russian misunderstandings.

"Some of these pending issues [with Russia] are now well on the way to settlement," he said.

"Establishment of a new world order, the goal of the powerful triple pact, if only given time, will surely be accomplished," he continued.

"There is no room for doubt that it will be crowned with brilliant success. If the Japanese people are fully and firmly prepared for this task, the future of our empire will indeed be great and glorious."

"The United States," the Foreign Minister said in his lengthy foreign

Continued on Page Fourteen

## PRESIDENT FINDS IT EXHILARATING DAY

### Attends the Many Ceremonies in High Spirits, His Mien Turning Grim at Times

By FRANK L. KLUCKHOHN

Special to THE NEW YORK TIMES.

WASHINGTON, Jan. 20 — One word describes the way the first American President to win a third term felt on the first day of his third Administration—exhilaration.

It was with obvious zest and joy that President Roosevelt went through a long day of ceremonies which began with a church service at 10:30 A. M., came to a climax with the precedent-shattering taking of his third oath of the office at 12:11 P. M. and, after a colorful parade, an air demonstration by 235 planes and various receptions, ended with a family dinner at the White House at 8 P. M.

The President clearly was in high spirits as he drove down Pennsylvania Avenue to the Capitol in an open car. He chatted animatedly with Speaker Rayburn, who sat next to him, and waved his tall silk hat with his right hand to the crowds, smiling and nodding to those thousands upon thousands lining the streets whose eyes were focused upon him.

He was in just as happy a mood when he drove back to the White House with Mrs. Roosevelt beside him amidst the same acclaim.

**Face Shows Solemnity, Too**

There were grim moments and solemn moments during the day, and these were reflected in Mr. Roosevelt's face, such as when he prayed in church, delivered his philosophical inaugural address, and alertly watched mechanized equipment, including light tanks and scout cars, future officers in the form of West Point and Annapolis cadets, fighting contingents and uniformed NYA and CCC boys parade by him after luncheon.

By and large, however, the President appeared to enjoy keenly the glittering display and pageantry of the day, the color of foreign and American uniforms of many hues and the good-fellowship involved in lunching with 1,300 dignitaries and other guests, receiving Governors and members of the Electoral College and meeting 2,000 more guests at a 5 o'clock tea. His enjoyment was manifested by his frequent smile, his eagerness and his constant conversation.

The services at St. John's Episcopal Church this morning were brief, but to some extent they set the tone of the day. There were three hymns, "O God, Our Help in Ages Past," "America," and "Faith of Our Fathers." The Rev. Frank R. Wilson of the Roosevelts' home church, St. James of Hyde Park, read a general confessional; the Rev. Howard S. Wilkinson of St. Thomas's Church of Washington read the Twentieth Psalm and the Rev. C. Leslie Glenn of St. John's read from II Kings 6:8-17.

As the President's mother, Captain James Roosevelt of the Marines, Crown Prince Olaf and Crown Princess Martha of Norway and the other members of the President's personal party, as well as the Cabinet members and dignitaries in the congregation knelt, the clergyman, standing before the

Continued on Page Six

## NO RETREAT HERE

### Democracy Won't Die and Nation Proves It, President Asserts

### INACTION A DANGER

### Sacrifices Justified, He Adds, if Spirit of the Land Is Saved

*Text of the President's speech will be found on Page 2.*

By TURNER CATLEDGE

Special to THE NEW YORK TIMES.

WASHINGTON, Jan. 20—On the exact spot on the Capitol steps where, with few exceptions, Presidents have taken the oath since the time of James Monroe, Franklin Delano Roosevelt was inaugurated again today as President of the United States. While one tradition was thus observed, another was shattered, for Mr. Roosevelt was the first person in American history to win or accept more than two terms in the White House.

The Constitutional oath was intoned by Chief Justice Hughes, and with his hand on an opened page of an old family bible, Mr. Roosevelt turned to an immense crowd shivering in the bright cold sunshine, and to them and millions listening in on the radio throughout the world he voiced the challenge:

"We do not retreat. We are not content to stand still. As Americans, we go forward, in the service of our country, by the will of God."

After uttering these words, interpreted here as summing up the aspirations represented in the domestic and foreign policies of his Administration, Mr. Roosevelt, as Commander in Chief of the Army and Navy, reviewed a military parade intended to impress upon the visiting multitudes the results of their own efforts toward national defense.

**Against Disruption From Without**

The President made it clear that he considered it an historic occasion.

In his clear, modulated voice, the President likened the trials now before the country to those of the times of Washington and Lincoln. In Washington's day the task of the people was to create and weld together a nation. In Lincoln's, it was to preserve the nation from disruption from within.

"In this day," he said, "the task of the people is to save that nation and its institutions from disruption from without."

Although conceived and delivered under the stress of the international crisis, the address did not chart by specification the future course of the Administration. Rather, it was a philosophic dissertation on the status and strength of free institutions in this troubled world—a prelude to a declaration that "our strong purpose is to protect and perpetuate the integrity of democracy."

The inauguration ceremony in itself was over in less than half an hour. Mr. Roosevelt took the oath at 12:11 P. M., and sixteen and one-half minutes later he had completed his address, one of the shortest on record.

**Wallace Takes the Oath**

Five minutes before the President faced Chief Justice Hughes, Henry Agard Wallace took the oath as Vice President, receiving it at the hands of his predecessor, John Nance Garner. Incidentally, one of Mr. Roosevelt's first acts in his new Administration was to turn and embrace his former team-mate whom he once referred to as "Old Man Commonsense," and to bid him God's speed on his journey back to Texas and retirement.

After the ceremony at the Capitol the President rode to the White House with Mrs. Roosevelt down lanes of cheering thousands along Constitution and Pennsylvania Avenue. After an inaugural luncheon at the White House, attended by more than 1,000 guests, the President reviewed the troops as they passed through a Court of Freedom in front of the Executive Mansion.

Nearest the President at this function were Vice President Wallace, Mrs. Roosevelt and the Presi-

Continued on Page Three

"All the News That's Fit to Print"

# The New York Times.

LATE CITY EDITION
POSTSCRIPT
Warm and humid today.
Temperatures Yesterday—Max.,87; Min.,70
Sunrise, 5:27 A. M.; Sunset, 8:32 P. M.



VOL. XCIII..No. 31,568. Entered as Second-Class Matter. Postoffice, New York, N. Y. NEW YORK, THURSDAY, JUNE 29, 1944. THREE CENTS IN NEW YORK CITY

# DEWEY AND BRICKER NAMED ON 1ST BALLOT; BRITISH TANKS FORGING RING AROUND CAEN; RUSSIANS TAKE MOGILEV, DRIVE FOR MINSK

## ORNE RIVER NEARED

### British Win a Great Tank Battle and Put Foe in Turmoil

### VITAL EXITS ARE CUT

### Maupertus Falls to U. S. Forces—Enemy Clings to Cap de la Hague

**5 A. M. Communique**

By The Associated Press.

SUPREME HEADQUARTERS, Allied Expeditionary Force, Thursday, June 29—Strong new Allied forces have thrust across the Odon River southwest of Caen, the bridgehead in that sector has been widened, and British and German tank forces have clashed strongly south of the river, Supreme Headquarters announced today.

Armored clashes also were announced north and northwest of Caen by communiqué No. 47.

All organized Nazi resistance apparently has ended on the Cherbourg Peninsula, although isolated enemy pockets were reported still holding out on Cap de la Hague.

The communiqué added that "bad weather again restricted air activity." Allied planes flew on armed reconnaissance southeast of Caen and attacked enemy road transport.

By DREW MIDDLETON

By Cable to The New York Times.

SUPREME HEADQUARTERS, Allied Expeditionary Force, Thursday, June 29—An iron ring of tanks and men is closing around Caen to the north, west and south of that ancient city, which today forms the hinge of the German battle line in Normandy.

Tanks and Tommies of the British Second Army have swept across Odon River and smashed forward nearly three and a half miles to Maltot, less than 4,000 yards from the Orne River and four and three-quarters miles southwest of Caen. The scythe-like offensive toward the southeast around Caen has now progressed ten miles from its starting line back of Tilly-sur-Seulles and is lopping off German arteries of communication with Caen one by one.

While the Germans are fighting desperately but unsuccessfully to stem this movement across their supply lines, fierce fighting suddenly flared up directly north of the city in the area between Epron and Herouville, which lie two and a half miles to the north and northeast, respectively, of Caen.

**U. S. Drive Reported by Foe**

[The German-controlled Paris radio said early Thursday that the American Second Corps had launched an attack in the direction of St. Lo and that violent fighting was in progress, according to an Associated Press dispatch from London.]

Twenty-five German tanks were destroyed by British anti-tank guns and tanks yesterday, boosting the total for the offensive to more than sixty, more than a battalion, or half the strength of an armored regiment.

A staff officer at the front last night described the action as a "very big battle and a highly successful one," and he declared that the seven-mile advance of British tanks over difficult country in the face of "an extremely tough position" was "a tremendous achievement."

These are bold words for a staff officer in the midst of a battle that is not yet won. As yet no enemy movement out of Caen has been reported, despite the cutting of the two roads to Villers-Bocage and Aunay-sur-Odon and the threat to three more east of the Orne, which should be under the fire of British

Continued on Page 3

## U. S. Invasion Force Has 28,849 Captives

By The Associated Press.

CHERBOURG, June 28—Germans captured by American forces in France from D-day, June 6, to last night totaled 28,849, it was reported officially today, and others still are being brought in.

The biggest day's haul was June 26, when 9,381 enemy troops were captured. Yesterday's figure was 8,592.

## ADVANCE ON SAIPAN IS OUTFLANKING FOE

### Forrestal Says Next Blows by Navy Will Be at Philippines, Japan and Indies

By GEORGE F. HORNE

By Telephone to The New York Times.

PEARL HARBOR, June 28—The most substantial gains yet made in the Battle of Saipan were reported today by Admiral Chester W. Nimitz, Commander in Chief of the Pacific Fleet and Pacific Ocean areas.

[Secretary of the Navy James V. Forrestal announced Wednesday that after the complete occupation of Saipan the next targets would be Japan, the Philippines and Netherlands Indies in offensives by surface ships and planes.]

On the eastern shore of Saipan the marines and Army troops have pushed two miles northward above Kagman Point, threatening the enemy's left flank. We have pushed past the villages of Donnay and Hashigoru and on the western coast have pushed farther into the town of Garapan.

Two hundred enemy troops were killed two days ago in a small sector of the island at the extreme southeastern point where they made a lunging counter-attack and broke through our lines above Nafutan Point.

**Foe in Desperate Attacks**

They tried to drive on northward to escape the contracting of the band of steel holding them on the point but our secondary lines blunted the thrust and they were slashed and forced back again. Yesterday they launched four desperate attacks, but they are still contained in the point's extreme tip and it appears that they are doomed.

The enemy is making repeated attempts to reach and damage our sea forces covering the assault. They have launched two futile air attacks while we continue to bomb hard near-by Tinian Island every day and hammer away at airfields and installations on Rota and Guam.

Our carrier aircraft attacked Guam and Rota on Monday, striking fuel reservoirs and coastal defense guns on Guam and destroying three small craft in Port Apra. Another cargo vessel, previously damaged in the harbor, has now sunk.

At Rota the airstrip was strafed and buildings set afire. Neither

Continued on Page 8

## RED ARMY STABS ON

### 50 Miles From Gateway to Warsaw in Wide Pincer Thrusts

### NEAR POLISH BORDER

### Nazi Division Wiped Out, Two Generals Seized as Mogilev Falls

By The United Press.

LONDON, Thursday, June 29—Onrushing Soviet troops overwhelmed and captured Mogilev yesterday and launched a frontal assault on Minsk, gateway to Warsaw and Berlin, while other Russian forces, advancing twenty-three miles, rolled to within fifty miles of the White Russian capital and rapidly closed a great pincers on the city.

While Gen. Ivan D. Chernyakhovsky's Third White Russian Army drove to Kostritsa, eight miles northeast of Borisov and fifty miles northeast of Minsk, Gen. Konstantin K. Rokossovsky's First White Russian Army captured Osipovichi, sixty miles southeast of Minsk, in an outflanking movement that carried the irresistible westward drive twenty-six miles northwest of encircled Bobruisk.

At the same time Soviet troops took Lepel, twenty-two miles from the Polish border, launched a new drive toward Baranovichi and Brest-Litovsk and, on the Finnish battle fronts, smashed to within eighteen miles of Petrozavodsk, capital of the Karelian Soviet Republic.

**Fall of Bobruisk Expected**

More than 1,150 other towns and settlements fell yesterday under the Russian avalanche in White Russia, which crumbled all Nazi strongholds before Minsk with the exception of Bobruisk, outflanked and encircled and expected to fall within a matter of hours.

The complete German Twelfth Infantry Division at Mogilev—possibly 15,000 men—was wiped out, its commanders were captured and more than 1,600 other Germans were killed or captured on the sixth day of the Red Army's White Russian offensive, which has cost Adolf Hitler up to 94,500 men killed or captured.

Five German infantry divisions were encircled at Bobruisk and Soviet forces, fighting in the suburbs, were systematically wiping them out. Within the closing prongs of the Minsk pincers a new pincer movement was initiated to trap and cut off the remnants of German troops thrown back along a seventy-five mile front north and south of Mogilev.

It was the Second White Russian Army of Col. Gen. Matvei Zakharoff that captured Mogilev, a town of 100,000 persons, the towns of Shklov and Bykhov, eighteen miles north and twenty-three miles south, and nine other rail stations north and south, clearing the most

Continued on Page 6

## THE CANDIDATES OF THE REPUBLICAN PARTY

Thomas E. Dewey
*For President*
The New York Times Studio, 1939

John W. Bricker
*For Vice President*
The New York Times Studio, 1939

## BOND SALES TOTAL 59% OF U. S. QUOTA

### Soar to $9,374,000,000 — City and State Pass the Billion-Dollar Mark

New York City and New York State have both passed the billion-dollar milestone in the Fifth War Loan, it was announced yesterday by Nevil Ford, State chairman of the War Finance Committee. He disclosed that the city's all-investors' total at the close of business on Tuesday was $1,046,552,432, and that of the State was $1,241,300,000.

These totals represent 25.1 per cent of the city's quota of $4,167,-

Continued on Page 24

## *Throng at Airport Cheers Dewey Arrival in Chicago*

By JAMES A. HAGERTY

Special to The New York Times.

CHICAGO, June 28—A crowd of a thousand persons raised a mighty cheer as Governor Dewey arrived at the Municipal Airport at 7:30 (Central time) tonight at the end of his now historic flight from Albany to face the Republican National Convention and accept its nomination for President.

The sun was setting when the plane of the United Air Lines, approaching from the east, circled over the field and slowed down after making a perfect three-point landing directed by Capt. Lee C. Brown, the pilot, who was a flier in the first World War.

As the craft came to a stop the name on its prow became visible. A laugh went up spontaneously as the crowd read "State of Ohio"

Continued on Page 10

## War News Summarized

THURSDAY, JUNE 29, 1944

The British offensive against Caen ground out important gains in Normandy and the enemy stronghold was being gripped from north, west and south. Allied tanks and infantry pushed forward as much as three and one-half miles yesterday for a total advance of ten miles from the starting point at Tilly-sur-Seulles. The enemy was driven from Rauray, southeast of Fontenay, and the Odon River was crossed on a two-mile front. Twenty-five German tanks were knocked out during the day. The Cherbourg peninsula was being cleared of enemy pockets and the badly damaged Maupertus airfield was in American hands. [1:1; map, P. 2.]

Military authorities in Washington said the American Fourth, Ninth and Seventy-ninth Divisions, after a brief rest, would be available for action elsewhere in France. [3:1.]

The French underground assassinated Philippe Henriot, Vichy Minister of Propaganda, in his Paris apartment, Berlin reported. [1:2-3.] General de Gaulle was expected to take to Washington for this country's approval a draft agreement with Britain on questions not involving recognition of the French Committee. [5:5.]

Allied planes from Britain and Italy rained destruction on many vital targets. The Fifteenth Air Force struck oil refineries and rail centers near Bucharest, Rumania. The Eighth Air Force hit airfields in the Laon area of France and rail yards at Saarbruecken in Germany. With the RAF it blasted flying-bomb emplacements along the Channel and enemy communications centering on Paris. [4:1.]

The German defeat in Russia grew as the Red armies captured Lepel, forced the Dnieper on a seventy-five-mile front and drove the enemy out of Mogilev. More than 1,150 communities were liberated during the day. Soviet forces were within fifty miles of Minsk and twenty-two of the old Polish border. Gains were also scored on the Finnish front. [1:3; map P. 6.]

Washington sources expected the United States to break diplomatic relations with Finland following her "perfect understanding" with Germany. [6:3.]

Fifth Army troops were within thirty miles of Leghorn in Italy, and the Eighth Army on the Adriatic side of the peninsula was within twenty-five miles of Ancona. [5:1.]

Americans on Saipan in the Marianas pushed ahead nearly two miles to threaten the Japanese left flank. Land-based planes from Aslito airfield were supporting the troops. Japanese positions from Paramushiru through Guam and Rota to Truk and the Marshalls were pounded by American planes on Sunday and Monday. [1:2; map, P. 8.] Allied gains were reported from all Burma fronts [7:3] and in China the Japanese were fighting close to surrounded Hengyang. [9:1.]

Secretary of the Navy Forrestal declared that after Saipan the United States would strike at Japan, the Philippines and the Netherlands Indies. [8:1.]

## CONVENTION GIVES DEWEY AN OVATION

### State Standards and Posters of Candidate, Bands and Organ and Delegates Lend Color

By MEYER BERGER

Special to The New York Times.

CHICAGO, June 28—Twenty-five thousand Republicans met Gov. Thomas E. Dewey of New York, their Presidential nominee, in the stadium tonight.

They cheered him a full five minutes, with State standards and Dewey posters waving, with bands blaring and Stadium organ thundering. Mrs. Dewey stood beside him smiling.

In their first glimpse of the man they have chosen as standard bearer the crowd saw a trim figure, tonsorially and sartorially perfect, a man who showed his teeth when he smiled.

He seemed self-assured, master of the studied gesture. Throughout the cheering he turned slowly un-

Continued on Page 11

## BRICKER NOMINATED FOR SECOND PLACE

### Selection Follows Withdrawal From Presidency Race and His Seconding of Dewey

By CHARLES E. EGAN

Special to The New York Times.

CHICAGO, June 28—Gov. John W. Bricker of Ohio won the Republican nomination for Vice President today on a first ballot which was unanimous.

Governor Bricker's nomination followed swiftly after he had removed himself from the contest with Governor Dewey for first place and walked to the microphones to second the Dewey nomination.

Although cries of "No" came from Ohio's delegates, Governor Bricker told his supporters that it was evident that sentiment for Mr. Dewey for the Presidential nomination was "overwhelming." He urged his backers to vote for the New Yorker.

The Ohioan's withdrawal and his appeal for support for Mr. Dewey surprised most of the delegates, but party leaders had been aware of a change since 2 o'clock this morning. At that time word circulated that Governor Bricker for the first time had conceded that he could not defeat Mr. Dewey and had expressed a willingness to accept the Vice Presidential nomination.

The withdrawal of Gov. Earl Warren, head of the California delegation, left the second-place

Continued on Page 13

## DEWEY AT STADIUM

### Says Plank on Foreign Policy Represents Big Area of Agreement

### ASKS AID OF YOUTH

### Military Phase of War Will Not Be Part of Campaign, He Vows

*Dewey's acceptance speech Page 10; Bricker's, Page 13.*

By TURNER CATLEDGE

Special to The New York Times.

CHICAGO, June 28—Thomas E. Dewey, Michigan-born, racket-breaking Governor of New York, was overwhelmingly chosen by the Republican convention today as its Presidential candidate to meet the fourth term bid of President Franklin D. Roosevelt, who is expected to be nominated by the Democrats in this same hall three weeks from today.

The New York Governor, who until today had maintained publicly that he was not a candidate, flew from Albany with Mrs. Dewey to accept the nomination and to meet the Vice Presidential nominee, Gov. John W. Bricker of Ohio, who was named unanimously a few hours earlier.

In the final night session, which was the most crowded and most enthusiastic of the whole convention, Mr. Dewey pledged his utmost efforts to lead the party back to power in Washington and to new conquests in the States and Congress in the November election.

Answering the challenge of former President Hoover, who last night called for a new generation to take over the helm of the Republican party, Mr. Dewey exhorted his followers to a finish fight to drive out "the 'tired and quarrelsome' Administration which has ruled in Washington for eleven years.

**Says War Command Will Stand**

Taking a leaf out of the book of President Roosevelt, who flew to Chicago twelve years ago to accept his first nomination, Mr. Dewey responded with the same fighting type of speech.

He brought his audience up in cheers time after time as he delivered thrusts at the New Deal, but especially where he declared that "the military conduct of the war is outside this campaign."

"It is and must remain completely out of politics," he said. General Marshall and Admiral King are doing a superb job. Let me make it crystal clear that a change in Administration next January cannot and will not involve any change in the military conduct of the war."

The change in Administration, he confidently predicted, would bring "an end to one-man government in Washington."

After Jan. 20, inauguration Day, he said, the Government would have a Cabinet of the "ablest men and women to be found in America" who would receive full delegation of the powers of their office.

He made an appeal time after time to youth—youth to win the war, youth to keep the peace.

No organization of peace can last if it is slipped through by "stealth or trickery," he said. Making and keeping the peace was "not a task for men who specialize in dividing our people."

"It is no task to be entrusted to stubborn men, grown old and tired and quarrelsome in office," he said. "We learned that in 1919."

America's duty to win the peace was parallel with its duty to win the war, he said. Recently there had been a growing area of agreement among the American people on foreign policy. Only a few, "a very few," maintained that America could remain aloof any longer, he said, and only a few believed it

Continued on Page 12

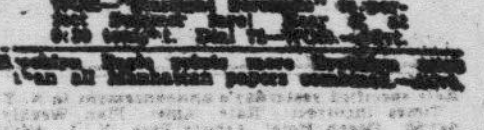

## *Patriots Execute Vichy Minister; Henriot Slain in His Room in Paris*

By E. C. DANIEL

By Wireless to The New York Times.

LONDON, June 28—Philippe Henriot, eloquent and implacable foe of the French resistance movement, was executed before the eyes of his wife in their Paris bedchamber shortly after dawn this morning. Nine bullets from the revolvers of guerrillas disguised as militiamen or policemen ended the life of the Vichy Minister of Propaganda.

That is Berlin's version of his death. It is accepted with satisfaction by the command of the French Forces of the Interior in London. The French also admit the German charge that the assassination was inspired from London, although disavowing any advance knowledge of this specific act. Within an hour after the assassination had been announced by DNB, Brig. Gen. Joseph-Pierre Koenig, commander of the French underground army, sat down smiling to a gay luncheon in London, served with German white wine.

The execution of Henriot, who twice a day for months past has been attempting by radio to talk French patriots out of their intransigeance toward the Germans, was another demonstration of the thoroughness and precision of the French underground's operations. Henriot arrived in Paris yesterday with Pierre Laval. He went to bed last night in the Vichy Ministry of Information in Paris.

Shortly before 6 A. M., DNB

Continued on Page 5

## *Willkie Congratulates Dewey, But Is Silent on Campaign Help*

Wendell L. Willkie, with the help of the press associations, got a message to Governor Dewey yesterday that said, "Hearty congratulations on your nomination. You have one of the great opportunities of history." Observers immediately noted that it omitted any promise of support in the Presidential campaign.

The 1940 Republican nominee had attempted to transmit the message by telegraph, but was blocked by wartime restrictions on congratulatory messages.

Informed at Albany of the message just before he boarded a plane for Chicago, Governor Dewey sent the following reply by telegram:

"Many thanks for your gracious wire and for your good wishes. I appreciate them ever so much."

Mr. Willkie's telegram was written after Mr. Dewey's name had been put before the convention, but before he was nominated. Copies were given to the press services at the time the message was turned over to a Western Union messenger. James C. Hagerty, the Governor's executive assistant, called Mr. Dewey's attention to the message after hearing a radio broadcast which carried a press association report on the "dispatch" of the telegram.

Failure to include in the message a mention of help during the campaign was taken to indicate that Mr. Willkie wants further information about Mr. Dewey's

Continued on Page 14

"All the News That's Fit to Print"

# The New York Times.

LATE CITY EDITION
POSTSCRIPT
Continued warm and humid today.
Temperatures Yesterday—Max., 89; Min., 71
Sunrise, 5:34 A. M.; Sunset, 8:28 P. M.



VOL. XCIII..No. 31,581. Entered as Second-Class Matter, Postoffice, New York, N. Y. NEW YORK, WEDNESDAY, JULY 12, 1944. THREE CENTS IN NEW YORK CITY

# ROOSEVELT AGREES TO RUN FOR A FOURTH TERM, HE IS SILENT ON WALLACE FOR VICE PRESIDENCY; AMERICANS DRIVE ON ST. LO, FOE LASHES AT CAEN

## ALLIED LINE ERUPTS

### Germans Expend Men and Arms in Futile Blows at British

### RECAPTURE MALTOT

### U. S. Troops Smash on Junction—Advance Down West Coast

**5 A. M. Communique**

By The Associated Press.

SUPREME HEADQUARTERS, Allied Expeditionary Force, Wednesday, July 12 — The Germans made heavy counter-attacks all along the Normandy front yesterday but they were held and the Allies made some gains, communiqué No. 73 said today.

The Americans encountered heavy opposition in the vicinity of St. Lô but captured Pont-Hébert, the communiqué said.

Lieut. Gen. Omar N. Bradley's forces advanced further down the road from La Haye du Puits toward Lessay and enlarged the bulge past Sainteny.

On the east of the line, where the British were stopping enemy thrusts, the "strongest German counter-blow was in the area of Colombelles-Ste. Honorine," the communiqué stated.

By E. C. DANIEL

By Cable to The New York Times.

SUPREME HEADQUARTERS, Allied Expeditionary Force, Wednesday, July 12—Tenacious German forces, extravagantly expending men and matériel have struck back with a series of vicious counter-attacks against the British efforts to break out across the Orne River into the open battleground south of Caen.

But, despite the German counteraction, the British Second Army has obtained a lodgment of indeterminate length along the west bank of the Orne between Louvigny and Maltot, southwest of Caen, in the tumultuous triangle between the Odon and Orne Rivers. Winning the admiration of Gen. Sir Bernard L. Montgomery himself, the Germans shrewdly employed hard-punching combat teams of infantry bolstered by groups of as many as thirty tanks to win back Maltot on Monday night and to reoccupy Louvigny yesterday morning, fighting with demoniac fury for every foot of ground in the bridgehead.

Three times yesterday, reports from the front said, the Germans stormed up Hill 112, northeast of Esquay, which gives the masses of the Allies' artillery observation over the seething battle area. Each time the British swept the Germans off again, but last night, a front dispatch said, three German tanks were still milling about the summit.

Against less fanatical resistance,

Continued on Page 3

## CANADIAN TROOPS MOVE THROUGH RUBBLE OF CAEN

Searching for isolated pockets of resistance and snipers

The New York Times (Canadian Army via U. S. Signal Corps Radiotelephoto)

## CAPITAL WAS SURE

### Few in Congress Voice Surprise Over News From White House

### WAVER ON 4TH TERM

### Some Democrats Marked as Opponents Now See a Wartime Need

Special to The New York Times.

WASHINGTON, July 11—Members of Congress remaining in Washington received generally without surprise today President Roosevelt's announcement that he would accept a renomination. Only one, a Republican, professed to having "played a hunch that he would not run."

Democrats, for the most part, expressed great satisfaction and confidence in the November outcome. Opposition to a fourth term was voiced where it had been voiced before, but in some instances this objection gave way in the case of Mr. Roosevelt. In some Democratic quarters where relationships with the White House are strained, inquiry brought the "no comment" response.

Republicans accepted the challenge of the Roosevelt candidacy. "Let the chips and candidates fall where they may," said Senator Guy Cordon of Oregon.

At the State Department, Secretary Hull was asked to comment at his news conference, soon after the President made his announcement. He said he had no comment, but added that he had just heard that the President had made a statement which spoke exceedingly well for itself.

**Democrats See Call of War**

At the Capitol, Democrats, receiving the news in the course of hearings, in their offices and while at the Senate Office Buildings Cafeteria, accepted the President's decision as the carrying out of a mission essential to the winning of the war and unbroken international relationships.

"The Commander in Chief, like any good soldier," said Senator Claude Pepper of Florida, "is going to stay at his post of duty. The nation expected this of the President and it will approve his decision."

Senator Charles O. Andrews of

Continued on Page 12

## The President's Letter

By The Associated Press.

*WASHINGTON, July 11—The text of President Roosevelt's letter to Chairman Hannegan, saying he will accept a nomination by the Democratic National Convention is as follows:*

Dear Mr. Hannegan:

You have written me that in accordance with the records a majority of the delegates have been directed to vote for my renomination for the office of President, and I feel that I owe to you, in candor, a simple statement of my position.

If the convention should carry this out, and nominate me for the Presidency, I shall accept. If the people elect me, I will serve.

Every one of our sons serving in this war has officers from whom he takes his orders. Such officers have superior officers. The President is the Commander in Chief and he, too, has his superior officer—the people of the United States.

I would accept and serve, but I would not run, in the usual partisan, political sense. But if the people command me to continue in this office and in this war I have as little right to withdraw as the soldier has to leave his post in the line.

At the same time, I think I have a right to say to you and to the delegates to the coming convention something which is personal—purely personal.

For myself, I do not want to run. By next spring, I shall have been President and Commander in Chief of the armed forces for twelve years—three times elected by the people of this country under the American constitutional system.

From the personal point of view, I believe that our economic system is on a sounder, more human basis than it was at the time of my first inauguration.

It is perhaps unnecessary to say that I have thought only of the good of the American people. My principal objective, as you know, has been the protection of the rights and privileges and fortunes of what has been so well called the average of American citizens.

After many years of public service, therefore, my personal thoughts have turned to the day when I could return to civil life. All that is within me cries out to go back to my home on the Hudson River, to avoid public responsibilities, and to avoid also the

Continued on Page 12

## PRESIDENT'S STAND

### Says He Is No More Free to Withdraw in War Than Is a Soldier

### DELEGATES PLEDGED

### Announcement Is Reply to Hannegan Report on Clear Majority

By CHARLES HURD

Special to The New York Times.

WASHINGTON, July 11—President Roosevelt will accept a nomination for a fourth term from the Democratic National Convention. He will serve if elected.

He announced that he would run again for the office he has held longer than any other man by disclosing at his press conference today his reply to a letter from Robert E. Hannegan, chairman of the Democratic National Committee, officially notifying him that "more than a clear majority" of the delegates to the party convention will go to Chicago next week bound to support his candidacy.

"If the convention should carry this out," the President wrote, "and nominate me for the Presidency, I shall accept. If the people elect me, I will serve."

**No Mention Made of Wallace**

The President's announcement solved a political riddle which has been the subject of much speculation and prognostication, but it emphasized the growing question as to whom he will support for second place on the Democratic ticket.

Vice President Henry A. Wallace returned yesterday from a trip to Russia and China and talked for two hours with the President in a visit that was publicly recorded. He had luncheon with the President today, but under such private circumstances that the White House offices declined to confirm his visit.

The complete omission of Mr. Wallace's name from the correspondence between the President and Mr. Hannegan indicated to political observers that Mr. Wallace's future position at least is open to question. It was recalled that four years ago Mr. Roosevelt withheld notice of his intention to accept nomination for a third term until literally the last minute—and then he set up the condition that Mr. Wallace, who was somewhat less than universally popular with Democratic political leaders—should be his running mate.

**President to Run 'Reluctantly'**

Mr. Roosevelt wrote that he would run "reluctantly, but as a good soldier," obedient to "the Commander in Chief of us all—the sovereign people of the United States." He dwelt at length on the duties of soldiers serving in the war and taking orders from their superior officers.

"I would accept and serve," he wrote, "but I would not run, in the usual partisan, political sense. But if the people command me to continue in this office and in this war, I have as little right to withdraw as the soldier has to leave his post in the line."

His whole personal desire, he said, was to retire to private life, "to go back to my home on the Hudson River, to avoid public responsibilities and to avoid also the publicity which in our democracy follows every step of the nation's Chief Executive."

"Such would be my choice," he emphasized. "But we of this generation chance to live in a day and hour when our nation has been attacked, and when its future existence and the future existence of our chosen method of government are at stake.

"To win this war whole-heartedly, unequivocally and as quickly as we can is our task of the first importance. To win this war in such a way that there be no further

Continued on Page 12

## ROOSEVELT GIVES ALGIERS A TOP ROLE

### President Recognizes It as De Facto Authority Subject to Eisenhower's Needs

Special to The New York Times.

WASHINGTON, July 11 — The United States has granted to the French Committee of National Liberation the status of a working "de facto authority" in French civil affairs in liberated areas but has left full authority to handle occupation matters to Gen. Dwight D. Eisenhower, President Roosevelt announced today.

The substance of the President's informal, oral announcement, made at a White House press conference, consisted of a promise to consider the Committee as the dominant political authority in France until an election could be held. However, he left the door open to consideration of the claims of other French groups in liberated areas by saying that, in cases of conflicting recommendations, General Eisenhower would act on the final basis of maintaining peace.

All in all, it appeared to observers, in the light of the President's complete remarks, that the situation as between the United States and Gen. Charles de Gaulle was relatively unchanged by the general's visit to Washington except that there now existed a new spirit of cordiality, resulting from the talks between Mr. Roosevelt and General de Gaulle.

The President voluntarily made his statement, without awaiting questions on the subject, when he

Continued on Page 6

## Russians Grind On 18 Miles In New Push to East Prussia

By The United Press.

LONDON, Wednesday, July 12—Soviet tanks and infantry, cutting through stiffening enemy resistance, smashed forward eighteen miles yesterday in a new drive toward East Prussia, while northeast of embattled Vilna other Red Army forces broadened their wedge between the German strongholds of Dvinsk and Kaunas.

Russian troops battled in Vilna's streets for the fourth day, wiping out separated enemy groups in the center of the city.

Far to the south other Soviet army units advanced nineteen miles toward Volkovysk, where the Germans are expected to make their main stand before Bialystok. The Russians also were within eight miles of Pinsk.

More than 390 towns and settlements were freed by four Soviet armies on the main Eastern Front.

In Finland the Red Army captured the vital rail station of Suojaervi, clearing the seventy-mile length of a railroad from Petro-

Continued on Page 9

## HIGH NAZI WARNS GERMANY OF PERIL

### Dittmar Sees Fight Now for Own Soil—Miscalculations Charged to Staff in Russia

By DANIEL T. BRIGHAM

By Telephone to The New York Times.

BERNE, Switzerland, July 11—Implicitly condemning Adolf Hitler's "intuitive" generalship, in a broadcast to the Reich home front tonight, Lieut. Gen. Kurt Dittmar, Dr. Joseph Goebbels' "bad news breaker," told the German people that the Wehrmacht High Command's underestimation of the Russian potential and subsequent miscalculation of Germany's strategic reserves had created a situation in which the Reich today was fighting on the defensive on three main fronts, "on every one of which the enemy enjoys considerable superiority in manpower and material."

He spoke of the need now "to protect German soil."

[While emphasizing the Eastern Front, General Dittmar warned that the Western Front still represented the "focal point" of current military devel-

Continued on Page 9

## President Seen as Agreeable To Change in Running Mate

By ARTHUR KROCK

Special to The New York Times.

WASHINGTON, July 11—Four years ago, when the President was informed on the telephone by his floor managers at the Chicago convention that the leaders were about to nominate him for a third term but were resisting his selection of Henry A. Wallace as running-mate, Mr. Roosevelt sent word that his acceptance would be conditional on the choice of Mr. Wallace.

Today, through the medium of a letter to National Chairman Robert E. Hannegan, the President announced without reservation that he will accept a nomination for a fourth term.

Since he knows that the convention's resistance to renominating Mr. Wallace for Vice President will be even greater than it was to the original selection, the lack of conditions in his letter amounts to notice from the President to the convention that he will accept a running mate other than the Vice President this year. It is understood he has a list of acceptable substitutes for consideration by the delegates and their leaders at Chicago, and, while the convention may go outside this list, it is reasonably certain that no one will be chosen for second place who is objectionable to Mr. Roosevelt.

**Names Reported to Be on List**

The list is said to include James F. Byrnes, former Supreme Court Justice and now "deputy President"; William O. Douglas, a member of the Supreme Court; John G. Winant, Ambassador to Great Britain, and Senator Scott Lucas of Illinois—in the order of their preference. Additional names have been on the list since the day the President was persuaded by Mr. Hannegan, Mayor Edward Kelly

Continued on Page 12

## WPB WILL START NELSON'S PROGRAM

### Byrnes Orders End of Dispute and the First Step Will Be Taken on Saturday

By WALTER H. WAGGONER

Special to The New York Times.

WASHINGTON, July 11—At the insistence of James F. Byrnes, Director of War Mobilization, a compromise was reached today which is likely to end the dispute between Donald M. Nelson, chairman of the War Production Board, and the Armed Services over the matter of reconverting industry to civilian production.

Guided virtually from the bedside of Mr. Nelson, who is confined to his apartment following an attack of pneumonia, members of the WPB representing all phases of war production agreed to postpone to varying times from today the effective dates of four specific orders in a reconversion program outlined by Mr. Nelson on June 19.

It was these orders, scheduled to have become effective July 1, which provoked protests from

Continued on Page 27

## War News Summarized

WEDNESDAY, JULY 12, 1944

German commanders threw men and matériel with reckless prodigality against Allied lines in France yesterday but failed to stem the relentless progress of the Anglo-American drives. Near Caen, British and Canadians had established a hold on the west bank of the Orne between Louvigny and Maltot, although the enemy recaptured both those villages. United States troops extended their positions on both sides of the Carentan road to Périers and drew ever closer to St. Lô. [1:1; map P. 2.]

Artillery and bombers saturated Hill 192 overlooking St. Lô in advance of an infantry and tank assault that drove the dazed Germans from their strongly fortified positions. [1:2-3.] A powerful enemy tank force ordered to take Isigny, far back of the lines, was shattered by Allied fighter-bombers near Pont-Hébert. Twenty-one German tanks were destroyed and six damaged out of a total of thirty-five. [4:1.]

More than 1,100 escorted Fortresses and Liberators flew through bad weather to attack Munich by instrument. Twenty bombers and two fighters failed to return but some landed in Switzerland. Italian-based aircraft struck the naval docks at Toulon and on Monday night the RAF stabbed at Berlin. In the first month of the invasion 1,284 Allied planes were lost on 158,000 sorties; 1,067 German planes were destroyed. [5:1.]

that General de Gaulle's French Committee would be recognized as the de facto political authority in liberated areas until a free election could be held in France. General Eisenhower would determine what were military and what were freed areas. [1:2.]

Soviet armies widened their Polish front yesterday and gained as much as eighteen miles along a bulge aimed at Grodno, Bialystok and Brest-Litovsk. [1:3-4; map P. 9.] In Italy, French troops were within twenty miles of Florence and were reported to have captured Poggibonsi. [8:2-3.]

The Nazi military expert, General Dittmar, admitted in a broadcast that the German situation was serious because of mistakes of military leadership and said the defense of the Reich demanded "a radical straightening of the whole front." [1:3.]

Guam was shelled again by American warships and bombers struck at the Kuriles and Truk. [10:2.] A full-scale Chinese assault on Tengyueh, Lungling, Mangshih and Sungshan, the last major barriers blocking the road into Burma, was reported ready. [10:3.] In Hunan Province Yungfeng was recaptured. [10:5.]

President Roosevelt said he would run for a fourth time despite his desire to retire from public office. "If the people command me to continue in this office and in this war," he declared, "I have as little right to withdraw as the soldier has to

## U. S. Submarine Lost With a Crew of 60

Special to The New York Times.

WASHINGTON, July 11—The United States submarine S-28, an 800-ton veteran, authorized during World War I and launched in 1922, was accidentally lost recently while engaged in training exercises in the Pacific, the Navy Department announced today.

All hands—about sixty in all—were lost, including the commanding officer, Lieut. Comdr. Jack Gordon Campbell, 28 years old, of Chicago, Ill.

"The depth of water makes it impossible to salvage the submarine and hope has been abandoned for the recovery of the missing personnel," the Navy said. "An investigation is now in progress to determine the available facts in the case."



## U. S. Planes and Guns Hammer Foe Into Grogginess on Hill Near St. Lo

By HAROLD DENNY

By Wireless to The New York Times.

WITH AMERICAN FORCES, in Normandy, July 11—Fighting hard over most of a forty-eight-mile front today, American troops captured a height overlooking the important transportation center of St. Lô.

The victory was accomplished by the most impressive and spectacular attack since Cherbourg—an attack in which our artillery and dive-bombers hammered the Germans until they were groggy and then our tanks went in with the infantry and beat down the remaining resistance. In the past week there had been only slow advances on the American front, with little but La Haye du Puits to show as concrete results. Today, however, the American C

power into the drive and wrested important ground from the hard-fighting enemy, who had evidently been ordered to oppose every foot of our advance.

The spearhead of the Americans' heaviest attack today was directed against a height known only by its designation on contour maps as Hill 192. It had been a thorn in the side of our troops ever since they had arrived in front of it ten days after D-day. It is not very high, but it is just enough higher than any other near-by ground so that the Germans there, as an American officer in today's attack put it, "have been looking down our throats."

For about one hour our troops

Continued on Page

## Taft Doubts Congress Will Approve World Financial Stabilization Plan

Special to The New York Times.

WASHINGTON, July 11—Senator Taft of Ohio predicted today that no agreement for an international monetary fund drafted on the terms of the original joint statement of experts, sent out by Secretary Morgenthau to the representatives of the other United Nations at the Bretton Woods conference, would be approved by either Senate or House.

The Senator said in a statement that although he believed Congress would adopt a pact providing for continuous consultations with other countries and would authorize the Secretary to use the stabilization fund as he has in the past to stabilize foreign exchange, it would not endorse any plan based on the terms of the original state-

In his statement, Senator Taft said:

"I have been asked by many correspondents and press representatives what the terms of the agreements now being negotiated at Bretton Woods are to be, and whether they have been or will be approved by Congress. I can't answer the first of these questions because of the secrecy which surrounds the Bretton Woods conference, but I can say that in my opinion no agreement for an international monetary fund on the terms of the original joint statement of experts will be approved

Continued on Page 32



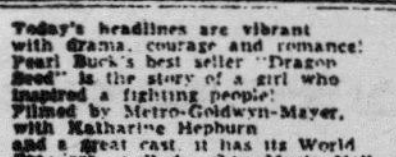

"All the News That's Fit to Print"

# The New York Times.

LATE CITY EDITION
Sunny with moderate winds today.
Temperatures Yesterday—Max., 80; Min., 65
Sunrise, 5:40 A. M.; Sunset, 8:24 P. M.



VOL. XCIII..No. 31,587. Entered as Second-Class Matter. Postoffice, New York, N. Y. NEW YORK, TUESDAY, JULY 18, 1944. THREE CENTS IN NEW YORK CITY

# U. S. TROOPS HACK WAY INTO ST. LO; BRITISH DEEPEN PUSH BELOW CAEN; RUSSIANS FLANKING BREST-LITOVSK

## WALLACE LEFT TO DELEGATES BY ROOSEVELT

### HIS LETTER PUBLIC

**Praises Vice President but Says Convention Must Decide**

**OTHER CANDIDATES ACTIVE**

**Contest Becomes More Spirited With Byrnes, Barkley, Truman in Lead**

By TURNER CATLEDGE
Special to THE NEW YORK TIMES.

CHICAGO, July 17—The choice of a Democratic candidate for Vice President was thrown wide open for the party's forthcoming national convention tonight when a letter was received here from President Roosevelt saying, in effect, that he would not dictate the renomination of Vice President Henry A. Wallace.

The President's communication, written at Hyde Park July 14 and addressed to Senator Samuel D. Jackson of Indiana, who is slated to be permanent chairman of the convention, which opens Wednesday, endorsed Mr. Wallace warmly as "my personal friend."

He said he had been associated with Mr. Wallace during his Vice-Presidential tenure of the last four years, for eight years previously when he was Secretary of Agriculture, and "well before that." He liked Mr. Wallace, and Mr. Wallace was his "personal friend," said the President, adding:

"For these reasons I personally would vote for his renomination if I were a delegate to the convention."

The President went on to say that he did not "wish to appear to be in any way dictating to the convention." The convention, he said, must decide the Vice-Presidential choice "and it should—and I am sure it will—give great consideration to the pros and cons of its choice."

The letter, dated three days ago, did not reach Mr. Jackson until late today, and he made it public at an 8 P. M. press conference.

**THE PRESIDENT'S LETTER**

The President's letter was as follows:

THE WHITE HOUSE
Washington
Hyde Park, N. Y., July 14, 1944.

My dear Senator Jackson:

In the light of the probability that you will be chosen as permanent chairman of the convention, and because I know that many rumors accompany all conventions, I am wholly willing to give you my own personal thought in regard to the selection of a candidate for Vice President. I do this at this time because I expect to be away from Washington for the next few days

The easiest way of putting it is this: I have been associated with Henry Wallace during his past four years as Vice President, for eight years earlier while he was Secretary of Agriculture, and well before that. I like him and I respect him and he is my personal friend. For these reasons I personally would vote for his renomination if I were a delegate to the convention.

At the same time I do not wish to appear in any way as dictating to the convention. Obviously the convention must do the deciding. And it should—and I am sure it will—give great consideration to the pros and cons of its choice.

Very sincerely yours,
FRANKLIN D. ROOSEVELT.

Honorable Samuel D. Jackson,
Stevens Hotel,
Chicago, Ill.

**"Green Light" Is Seen**

All afternoon speculation grew as to the content of the letter especially as the hours wore on and it did not arrive, as predicted yesterday by Robert E. Hannegan, national chairman. One word got around that the President had withdrawn the message to make it stronger in Mr. Wallace's behalf, and other speculation had it that he had decided to have nothing to say at all.

Senator Jackson said he could not explain the delay. It was

Continued on Page 9



## *Heavy Death Toll Reported in Blast*

By The Associated Press.

MARTINEZ, Calif., July 17—Scores of persons were reported killed tonight and hundreds injured in a terrific explosion in a naval ammunition dump at nearby Port Chicago. The blast was felt more than fifty miles away.

First reports from the scene estimated the dead as high as 650. Hospitals were jammed with the injured, many of them naval personnel from the big base thirty-five miles from San Francisco.

The blast, from an unknown cause, partially disrupted communication lines and virtually leveled the small town of Port Chicago. Plate glass windows were blown out in Martinez and other neighboring communities.

An under sheriff said he understood two navy ships loading ammunition at Port Chicago had blown up.

## WALLACE THROUGH, OPPONENTS ASSERT

**But Vice President's Friends Do Not Agree Letter Ends Chances**

By WARREN MOSCOW
Special to THE NEW YORK TIMES.

CHICAGO, July 17—While the reaction of many delegates and observers tonight to the Roosevelt letter on Vice President Henry A. Wallace was that it had "finished" Mr. Wallace so far as the renomination for the Vice-Presidency was concerned, Mr. Wallace's supporters took an entirely different point of view.

Public expressions on the letter were polite, while privately the lobby of the Stevens Hotel buzzed with comment that the President had administered the coup de grace to the man whose nomination he dictated in 1940 and whom he publicly rebuked for an intra-Administration controversy with Jesse Jones only a year and a half ago. With this point of view the Wallace backers definitely did not agree.

Wallace headquarters at the Hotel Sherman had, officially, no comment to make on the President's letter. However, the attitude of the Wallace supporters, as expressed by a spokesman, was that they were "very happy" over the letter.

They argued that had the President gone any stronger in his letter than expressing his "personal preference" he would have been accused of attempting to dictate to the convention, and when he carefully refrained from dictating he was bound to be interpreted, by those opposed to Mr. Wallace, as being only lukewarm to the renomination of the Vice President.

The President, and the people through polls, have spoken and expressed their preference for Mr. Wallace, the latter's supporters argued in the face of a general opinion that the President's letter had not helped his 1940 running-mate. If, in the face of this endorsement, the convention rejects Mr. Wallace, it will be flying in the face of public opinion, as well as the President's "personal

Continued on Page 11

## CONFERENCE ADDS 3 DAYS TO TALKS; SNARLED ON BANK

**Russia and Some Torn by War Lead Protest on Fund Quotas as Subscription Basis**

**OTHER AMERICAS DIVIDED**

**Hotel Protests Extension but Yields and Wires Hundreds of Patrons to Delay Arrival**

By RUSSELL PORTER
Special to THE NEW YORK TIMES.

BRETTON WOODS, N. H., July 17—The closing date of the United Nations Monetary and Financial Conference, originally scheduled for Wednesday, was postponed today until Saturday because discussions of the proposed $10,000,000,000 International Bank for Reconstruction and Development have been stalled by demands of various countries for lower capital subscriptions.

At a caucus last night attended by representatives of about fifteen countries, including the United States, Great Britain, Canada, some of the western European nations and some Latin-American countries, the United States presented its view that every country joining the bank should be required to make the same subscription as its quota in the $8,800,000,000 International Monetary Fund, which was agreed upon Saturday night.

The American plan also provided that any nation wishing to do so might increase its subscription. It is understood that the United States and perhaps some other countries would be willing to increase their subscriptions enough to bring the total to $10,000,000,000 if other countries met their quotas.

**Russians in Opposition**

It is also understood that all fifteen countries at the caucus agreed to the American plan. When it was presented to the Russians, however, they rejected it. So did some of the Latin-American nations. The opposing countries asked for time in which to communicate with their home Governments for further instructions. Meantime, they pressed their case for lower subscriptions.

The Russians, it is understood, did not give any reasons. It is known, however, that they are disappointed over the two-to-one defeat by the conference of their proposal that the devastated countries should be allowed to reduce their gold payments to the fund by a quarter to a half, depending on the amount of damage a country has suffered.

The Russians are said unofficially to take the position that they should be allowed to make a smaller subscription to the bank for the same reasons they wanted a larger quota and a smaller gold payment in the fund. They argue that they need their gold and other resources to pay for the reconstruction of their cities, factories and homes ruined by the Nazis. The larger their quota in the fund, the more American dollars and other foreign exchange they can acquire to finance post-war buying of machinery and other goods abroad. The less they subscribe to the bank the more they will be able to buy in the foreign market without borrowing. Some of the other invaded and occupied countries are understood to have supported the Russian position.

The Latin-American countries, which formed a solid group which won the right to two permanent members of the twelve-man executive committee which will manage the fund, split over the question of

Continued on Page 26

## *Zoo Bear Tears Arm Off Girl; Baited by Pranksters at 2 A. M.*

The prank of a skylarking young foursome who invaded the Central Park Zoo at 2 A. M. yesterday and clambered over a 3-foot protective railing to bait a polar bear ended disastrously when the aroused animal turned on one of the girls and tore her arm off at the elbow.

The girl, who was the only one injured, is Miss Catherine Searles, 24 years old, of 1155 Park Avenue, the daughter of Henry Malcolm Searles, a Rahway, N. J., manufacturer. She was taken to Roosevelt Hospital, where, after an emergency operation to remove the rest of the arm, her condition was described as "satisfactory."

Police reconstructing what had happened said that Miss Searles had entered the park at the Sixty-fourth Street and Fifth Avenue entrance shortly before 2 A. M. yesterday. She was in the company of Miss Gertrude Brady of 610 Park Avenue, daughter of Henry Brady, New York City auctioneer; Corp. Edward Cheney of Manchester, Conn., on furlough from Camp Shelby, Miss., and William Chick of Boston.

Earlier they had attended a party at a residence at 152 East Eighty-fourth Street, and from there had gone on to the Stork Club. Leaving the night club, the group walked to the zoo grounds, where they found all the animal houses shut. They passed the line of cages adjacent to the lion house and then went on to the outdoor bear cages at the north end of the grounds.

The bears were asleep, and in order to awaken them, the police

Continued on Page 21

## REACH CURZON LINE

**Red Army Advances 25 Miles North of Central Poland Bastion**

**LATVIAN BORDER CROSSED**

**Petrucenki, 2 Miles Beyond Frontier, Captured—Niemen Bridgehead Reinforced**

By The United Press.

LONDON, Tuesday, July 18—Red Army forces, in a sensational twenty-five-mile advance down the Minsk-Warsaw highway, pushed to within fifteen miles north of the Polish fortress city of Brest-Litovsk yesterday, while a northern Soviet spearhead smashed two miles into Latvia.

After having thrust a wedge between the twin German bastions of Bialystok and Brest-Litovsk guarding Warsaw, the gateway to the Polish plains, Marshal Konstantin K. Rokossovsky's First White Russian Army captured the town of Vydomlya, fifteen miles north of Brest-Litovsk, where the Russo-German peace was signed during the last war.

The twenty-five-mile advance to Vydomlya put the Russians 113 miles east of Warsaw—less than half the distance covered in the twenty-five-day old Soviet offensive—and fifteen miles from the Bug River border of German-occupied Poland.

**Latvian Junction Is Goal**

At the northern end of the 550-mile front rambling from the Pripet Marshes to Latvia, Gen. Andrei I. Yeremenko's Second Baltic Army made the first Soviet crossing of the Latvian border, capturing the town of Petrucenki, two miles across the frontier and twenty-five miles east of the big Latvian rail junction of Rezekne. Russian troops now are fighting in all three of the Baltic states—Estonia, Latvia and Lithuania.

The Second Baltic Army and Gen. Ivan C. Bagramian's First Baltic Army captured more than ninety towns, including the important localities of Sebezh, forty-two miles, and Osveya, forty-five miles southeast of Rezekne, as they drove on the rail junction from three directions.

The Moscow midnight bulletin announced that the Russians had put to flight units of two German infantry divisions and seized more

Continued on Page 5

**AMERICAN REINFORCEMENTS ON WAY TO FRANCE**

Soldiers on deck of an Allied ship crossing the English Channel on their way to Normandy to fight the Nazis. This photo was made on Thursday.

The New York Times (U. S. Signal Corps)

## BOMBERS RIP RAILS ALL ACROSS FRANCE

**U. S. Planes Tear Nazi Traffic Net in Arc From Belgium to Lower Rhone Valley**

By E. C. DANIEL
By Wireless to THE NEW YORK TIMES.

SUPREME HEADQUARTERS, Allied Expeditionary Force, Tuesday, July 18—Detour signs on railways, roads and bridges leading from the German supply pools to the Normandy battle front began to appear almost on the very borders of France yesterday after American heavy bombers from Britain and Italy and the Royal Air Force's big planes made one of the strongest series of attacks yet undertaken against enemy communications in France.

More than 750 Flying Fortresses and Liberators of the Britain-based

Continued on Page 4

## War News Summarized

TUESDAY, JULY 18, 1944

American troops in France battled their way into St. Lô, then withdrew to the outskirts under murderous German counter-attacks and artillery fire, and later began to drift back into the city upon whose possession rests the fate of the whole enemy line at the base of the Cherbourg Peninsula. The British engaged in a furious day-long tank battle in the Caen area, and hard-won advances were reported from the entire front. Allied bombers and fighters battered German supply dumps and front positions. [1:8; map P. 2.]

The battle for St. Lô is the hardest fought engagement since the Allied armies of liberation landed in France. The timely arrival of planes to bomb and strafe the enemy halted the most ambitious German counter-attack in its tracks. [3:3-4.]

Isolation of France and paralysis of all rail lines used by the Germans were brought a step nearer yesterday when Allied planes swung down from Britain and up from Italy to blast key junctions, bridges and similar targets. [1:5.]

The German radio rejected General Eisenhower's classification of the French resistance movement as part of the Allied military machine. Berlin declared all Frenchmen were bound by the terms of the armistice and resisters would be treated as terrorists. [3:1.]

Soviet forces, in a day of extensive gains, drove two miles into Latvia and were, elsewhere along the border, leaving few German invaders on Russian soil. The Red Army was thirty-four miles from Bialystok at one point and at another, after gaining twenty-five miles, was within fifteen miles of Brest-Litovsk. [1:4; map P. 5.] Some 57,000 Germans marched through Moscow yesterday. They were prisoners of war on their way to the east. [1:6-7.]

British units of the Eighth Army in a surprise dash crossed the Arno River beyond Arezzo on the way to Florence. On Italy's west coast American troops were less than two miles from Leghorn. [1:7.]

Reinforced Japanese in China were striking in many sectors, and although the defenders reported successes at some places the situation was considered serious. [6:5.] The Japanese were being pushed back on all active fronts in Burma. [6:2.]

Premier Curtin told the Australian Parliament that Britain would send powerful forces into the Pacific this year but that the main effort would be delayed until after defeat of Germany. [7:1.] The "present grave war situation" caused Premier Tojo to replace Admiral Shimada as Navy Minister with Admiral Naokuni Nomura. [7:5.]

Britain, Russia, China and the United States will open exploratory discussions on an international security organization in Washington next month. Because Russia is not at war with Japan she will not sit at the sessions attended by China. Other United Nations will be called into the discussions later. [1:6-7.]

## *Talks on Peace Council Set; Russia Not to Sit With China*

By BERTRAM D. HULEN
Special to THE NEW YORK TIMES.

WASHINGTON, July 17—Long under consideration among the four big powers, exploratory conversations on an international organization for maintaining peace have been agreed upon and will be held here, beginning probably early next month, Secretary of State Cordell Hull announced tonight.

The discussions will be in two parallel sets, as at Teheran and Cairo, so Russia and China will not meet around the conference table, since the Soviet Union is not at war with Japan.

"The four Governments signatory to the declaration of Moscow," Secretary Hull said, "are agreed that informal conversations and exchanges of views on the general subject of an international security organization will soon begin in Washington, probably early in August.

"It has been decided, following discussions with the other Governments, that the first phase of the conversations will be between representatives of the United Kingdom, the United States and the Soviet Union and that conversations on the same subject between representatives of the United States, the United Kingdom and China will be carried on either at the same time or shortly thereafter.

"These conversations will be followed by discussions with the other United Nations."

It had been hoped that Russia would consent to sit with the delegates of China, inasmuch as the discussions will concern post-war security. Separate conferences of Marshal Joseph Stalin and Generalissimo Chiang Kai-shek with President Roosevelt and Prime Minister Churchill were arranged

Continued on Page 5

## 8TH ARMY SURGES ACROSS ARNO RIVER

**British Trap Germans Waiting to Raze Span—Americans 2 Miles From Leghorn**

By HERBERT L. MATTHEWS
By Wireless to THE NEW YORK TIMES.

ROME, July 17—The Arno River was crossed yesterday in a surprise dash by British Eighth Army units that had taken Arezzo.

They came on so fast and hard that the Germans had no time to blow up one bridge and the British established their first bridgehead across the historic river just south of Castiglion Fibocchi. This is mountainous terrain, leading finally to the strong point of Pontassieve, which covers Florence on the east, so one must not jump to the hasty conclusion that the fall of Florence is necessarily near.

However, progress has been made at many points. Everywhere except around Poggibonsi, where the French have been fighting off counter-attacks and are barely hanging on to the town, the Germans are being pushed back to-

Continued on Page 3

## *57,000 Nazis Parade in Moscow As Prisoners From White Russia*

By W. H. LAWRENCE
By Wireless to THE NEW YORK TIMES.

MOSCOW, July 17—A part of the German Army—57,000 "strong"—marched through the streets of Moscow today, but not in the role of conquerors, as Chancellor Hitler mistakenly dreamed three years ago.

The Germans were prisoners of war, headed east from the White Russian front, where they had been trapped and captured by swiftly advancing Soviet forces.

It was the first time that Moscow's residents had seen such a spectacle. They turned out in thousands to line the route of march. For the most part they watched silently as the weary, unshaven prisoners plodded by in groups ranging from 1,000 to 3,000, guarded by mounted police.

Diplomats of many countries, including United States Ambassador W. Averell Harriman, were in the crowd that watched the prisoners march from the railway stations. This correspondent also observed a Japanese diplomat as he watched the soldiers of his ally.

There were few demonstrations from the crowd, which had been advised this morning by Pravda that there should not be any. But at one place, witnesses said, a woman cried out to passing Germans: "Give me back my daughter, give me back my daughter."

Others in the crowd, who comforted her, said that she explained

Continued on Page 5



## ALLIES INCH AHEAD

**House-to-House Battle Rages in Pivotal Base of Foe's Norman Line**

**BRITISH PUSH INTO EVRECY**

**Nazis Lose 31 Tanks in Vain Counter-Attacks—Planes Bombard German Supplies**

By DREW MIDDLETON
By Cable to THE NEW YORK TIMES.

SUPREME HEADQUARTERS, Allied Expeditionary Force, Tuesday, July 18—Infantrymen of the United States First Army hacked a path through stubborn German defenses east of St. Lô yesterday and by last night they had established positions in the outskirts of the shattered town while combat patrols were smashing their way from house to house toward the heart of the town on which Field Marshal Gen. Erwin Rommel's line in western Normandy is anchored.

While the Americans tightened their arc about St. Lô and pushed closer to Périers in what was generally described as one of the fiercest battles of the campaign, in which sixteen German tanks were destroyed by American anti-tank guns and bazookas, the British Second Army drove steadily forward on a six-mile front southwest of Caen, pushing into the eastern outskirts of Evrecy.

**British Front Confused**

From Vendes, on the right flank to Evrecy on the left, British and German tanks, infantry and artillery mixed up in a confused and furious battle that rolled over fields and through battered villages from dawn to dusk. British tanks hammered a path through enemy armor into Noyers in the center of the battle sector on the Caen-Villers-Bocage road, engaging German tanks and infantry along dusty roads from which great plumes of smoke and dust rose to the hot, blue sky overhead. Fifteen German tanks were destroyed by British armor in the tank battles in this sector.

The British took Haut des Forges, Bas des Forges and Vendes, but their control of the later was uncertain, since the enemy counter-attacked violently later with elements of five armored divisions.

The Germans' ability to maintain a static defense position across the base of the Cherbourg Peninsula depends on their retention of St. Lô, hinge for their present line through Périers to Lessay, which, despite the presence of American patrols in the outskirts of the town, has not been captured yet. St. Lô would also be a hinge of a switch line running westward to Coutances.

**German Stand Expected**

Observers in London believe that the Germans probably will make a maximum effort first to hold St. Lô and then, if that becomes impossible, to deny its use by the First Army very much as they have denied Lieut. Gen. Miles C. Dempsey the use of Caen.

Forward supply dumps of German Seventh and Fifth Armies opposing the British Second and American First Armies underwent a sustained aerial attack yesterday. Fighter-bombers sought out and bombed stores of gasoline, oil and ammunition and vehicle parks behind the German front. Simultaneously, German infantry and artillery positions were harried, bombed and machine-gunned by fighter-bombers.

There is a great test of strength going on between the American and German armies at St. Lô, easternmost point on the fifty-five miles of the active American front in Normandy. Here the Germans have thrown in artillery, tanks and infantry without stint. Here American doughboys are proving themselves superior to the finest German troops.

In this positional warfare the tactics of the last years of World War I are coming to the fore. Lieut. Gen. Omar N. Bradley's infantry advanced east of St. Lô at dawn yesterday morning without the artillery preparation that usually heralds an attack. Driving

Continued on Page 3

"All the News That's Fit to Print"

# The New York Times.

LATE CITY EDITION
Partly cloudy with moderate winds today.
Temperatures Yesterday—Max.,80; Min.,66
Sunrise, 5:42 A. M.; Sunset, 8:22 P. M.



VOL. XCIII..No. 31,590. Entered as Second-Class Matter, Postoffice, New York, N. Y. NEW YORK, FRIDAY, JULY 21, 1944. THREE CENTS IN NEW YORK CITY

# ROOSEVELT NOMINATED FOR FOURTH TERM; HITLER ESCAPES BOMB, PURGES GENERALS; CAEN DRIVE GAINS; RUSSIA OPENS NEW PUSH

## FUEHRER 'BRUISED'

### Bomb Wounds 13 Staff Officers, One Fatally—Assassin Is Dead

### 'USURPERS' BLAMED

### Hitler Names New Chief of Staff—Himmler to Rule Home Front

*Texts of Hitler, Doenitz and Goering speeches, Page 3.*

By JOSEPH SHAPLEN

Adolf Hitler had a narrow escape from death by assassination at his secret headquarters, the Berlin radio reported yesterday, and a few hours later in a radio broadcast to the German people he blamed an "officers' clique" for the attempt to kill him. His address disclosed a movement in the armed forces to overthrow him and his regime. He announced that a purge of the conspirators was under way.

Thirteen members of his military staff were injured, one fatally and two seriously, by a bomb set off at an undisclosed place while many of his highest advisers were assembled around him. The man who played the role of assassin, Hitler said, was Colonel Count von Stauffenberg, one of his collaborators, who stood only six feet away from him as he hurled the bomb. Von Stauffenberg is dead, Hitler announced.

Waiting to see Hitler before the assassination attempt was Benito Mussolini. Reich Marshal Hermann Goering, who rushed to Hitler's side, was in the immediate vicinity. Hitler escaped with singes and bruises.

**Army Clique Blamed**

While Dr. Joseph Goebbels and Nazi radio propagandists at first tried to put the blame for the attempt to kill the Fuehrer upon the Allies, Hitler himself exploded the bombshell by announcing that the culprits were a group of German Army officers. He thus confirmed reports of a serious rift between the Nazi High Command and German military elements.

In his broadcast, recorded by the Federal Communications Commission, Hitler told the German people: "If I address you today I am doing so for two reasons: first, so that you shall hear my voice and know that I personally am unhurt and well, and, second, so that you shall hear the details about a crime that has no equal in German history.

"An extremely small clique of ambitious, unscrupulous and at the same time foolish, criminally stupid officers hatched a plot to re-

Continued on Page 3

## Nazi Party Clashes With Army Reported

BERNE, Switzerland, July 20 (UP)—Skirmishes took place in various parts of Germany today between Nazi party members, led by SS [Elite Guard] Troopers, and groups of the regular army, according to unconfirmed reports reaching here tonight.

Conferences of the Nazi party organization were held in all principal cities of the Reich this evening, and members were asked to reaffirm their loyalty to the party and to Adolf Hitler, according to reliable information.

Zurich reported that responsible quarters there had information that a subversive movement was under way in various parts of the Reich.

By Wireless to The New York Times.

BERNE, Friday, July 21—There were unconfirmed reports at the Swiss-German frontier shortly after 1 o'clock this morning that some shooting had occurred on the other side of the line, but whether or not it indicated mutiny could not yet be ascertained.



## Nazi-Army Rift Is Revealed In Gravest Reich War Crisis

### 'Usurpers' Who Hatched Plot Not Named—Accused of Being Officer Group Wanting to Repeat the 1918 'Stab in the Back'

By RAYMOND DANIELL
By Cable to The New York Times.

LONDON, July 20—Broadcasting so that the German people could hear his voice and know that he was unhurt after the attempt to assassinate him, Chancellor Adolf Hitler confirmed tonight all rumors and suspicions of disaffection and unrest in the Reich.

Heinrich Himmler, the Fuehrer said, has been made commander in chief of the home army to "create order once and for all." Hitler also ordered that no "military authority, no leader of any unit, no private in the field" was to obey any orders emanating from "usurpers" who were seeking peace.

He left the identity of those usurpers something of a mystery, for he referred to them as "a small group that emerged in Germany, just as in Italy, in the belief that they could repeat the 1918 stab in the back." Later he said they had "no bond with or nothing in common with the Wehrmacht, and, above all, none with the German people."

It is clear that a real crisis has arisen in the Reich and it remains to be seen whether the Nazis have chosen the wisest way to deal with it. A purge is as likely to widen the schism as not, and the German people, with their traditional respect for their officer class, may feel that if the Nazis choose war, and the old officers favor peace, the time may have come to question the infallibility of the Fuehrer.

The announcement left open to speculation the question of not only who was behind the assassination attempt but, even more interesting, the question of who in Germany was in position to make the attempt.

That Germany is going through

Continued on Page 5

## Admiral and General Told To Form New Tokyo Regime

Gen. Kuniaki Koiso, a member of the same Kwantung Army group to which former Premier Gen. Hideki Tojo belongs, arrived in Tokyo from Korea yesterday to participate with Admiral Mitsumasa Yonai in the formation of a new "critical decisive wartime" Cabinet by "command" of Emperor Hirohito, it was disclosed in Japanese broadcasts and press dispatches reported to the Office of War Information by the Federal Communications Commission.

General Koiso, Governor General of Korea, and Admiral Yonai, a former Premier and member of the Supreme War Council, were summoned as "senior leaders of the army and navy," the Japanese Domei agency said. Each is 64 years old.

Meanwhile, the Domei agency, in a wireless dispatch to the controlled East Asia press, warned its bureaus to be "on the alert" for new developments, presumably regarding an announcement of the new Cabinet's membership.

"Competent political observers expect that the new Cabinet will be formed swiftly," Domei said. Another Japanese account predicted that the new Government would be formed by "Friday morning at the latest."

**Co-Premiership Doubted**

Koiso and Yonai were designated to form a new Government after Emperor Hirohito had called in Marquis Koichi Kido, Lord Keeper of the Privy Seal, to sound out Japan's "elder statesmen" for candidates to serve as the nucleus for what Domei termed a "more powerful Cabinet."

In a continuation of the "elder statesman" system of choosing Cabinet leaders, Kido then called a caucus of former Premiers. After this meeting, the following an-

Continued on Page 3

## ALLIES STORM ARNO ON A 25-MILE FRONT

### Americans, in Hot Pursuit of Bewildered Germans, Plunge to Town 12 Miles From Pisa

By The Associated Press.

ROME, July 20—American troops battered their way across the Arno River Valley on a 25-mile front between Pisa and Florence today as German forces, bewildered by the sudden breakthrough, retreated across the Arno into the mountain defenses of their Gothic Line.

Lieut. Gen. Mark W. Clark's doughboys held complete control of hill masses overlooking the Arno from the south, and American artillery raked the entire valley in search of German rear-guard units protecting the withdrawal of the main body of enemy forces to the north of the stream.

German resistance was confined almost entirely to these small groups armed with automatic weapons—tactics similar to those that delayed the entry of General Clark's troops into Rome an entire day. One American column was firmly established on the south bank of the Arno at Pontedera, twelve miles inland from Pisa.

An Allied spokesman said Ger-

Continued on Page 5

## Allies Report Belgian Uprising Comparable to French Sabotage

By Wireless to The New York Times.

SUPREME HEADQUARTERS, Allied Expeditionary Force, July 20—Belgium's extensive and complicated network of rail and road communications was reported in a special Allied communiqué today to have been "largely disrupted" as the result of the "highly satisfactory" operations of the Belgian underground. The communiqué was the first from Supreme Headquarters to mention the Belgian resistance movement that has been declared by Belgian authorities to be a formal military organization the same as the French Forces of the Interior.

Reporting that Belgian operations "throughout the entire country" had "contributed substantially to the delaying movement of enemy reinforcements to the battle area," the communiqué also said that French forces had detained a Panzer division moving toward Normandy for thirty hours and had wrecked twenty-six strategic bridges between June 24 and July 6.

Eighty Germans were killed and 300 wounded in the attack on the Panzer division, said the communiqué, which also confirmed an earlier French report that patriots had destroyed a train carrying flying bombs in eastern France.

From July 4 to 15, the communiqué said, the French forces continued operations "in face of violent German attacks," defeating or eluding the Germans in every case.

In addition, the French slowed traffic on the "whole railway sys-

Continued on Page 4



## BRITISH PUSH SOUTH

### Take Troarn Rail Depot While Second Column Captures Bourguebus

### ENEMY SLOWS DRIVE

### Strong Anti-Tank Belt Checks Smash Toward Plains Before Paris

By DREW MIDDLETON
By Wireless to The New York Times.

SUPREME HEADQUARTERS, Allied Expeditionary Force, Friday, July 21—Tanks and infantry of the British Second Army, battling stubborn German rearguards at Troarn and St. André-sur-Orne, yesterday, widened the eleven-mile front south and east of Caen that Lieut. Gen. Miles C. Dempsey's troops have punched out in three days of audacious and arduous fighting.

Strong German anti-tank positions northwest of Vimont slowed down the advance to the southeast toward Vimont, momentarily at least. However, British artillery and infantry were assaulting these positions last night as the second stage of the great trial of strength with the Seventh German Army opened.

**British Positions Solid**

Bourguebus, five and a quarter miles southeast of Caen, was the most important of a dozen towns and villages taken by the British in the twenty-four hours ended at midnight last night. It is almost in the center of an arc extending from the Orne west of St. André to the railroad station at Caen, which marks the area in which the Second Army is solidly established.

Farther to the south, southeast and east, in front of the main positions, British tanks were operating against the German lines, seek-

Continued on Page 4

## LWOW IS MENACED

### Red Army Near Polish City—New Wedge Is Driven From Kovel

### GRIP ON BUG WIDENS

### Foe's Supply Lines Cut—Dvinsk Rail Link Slashed on West

By W. H. LAWRENCE
By Wireless to The New York Times.

MOSCOW, Friday, July 21—Revealing another terrific Red Army offensive, Marshal Joseph Stalin announced last night that forces led by Marshal Konstantin K. Rokossovsky, after three days' fighting in the Kovel sector, had driven a wedge thirty-one miles deep on a 123-mile front, pushing the Germans back to the western Bug River.

He disclosed, also, that Marshal Ivan S. Koneff's First Ukrainian Army had captured Rawa Ruska, an important rail junction, severing the most direct supply and retreat route for the Germans' outflanked Lwow garrison.

These new triumphs over the battered, reeling German Army at the southern end of the eastern front were celebrated in Moscow at 10 and 11 P. M. by two salutes of twenty salvos each from 224 guns—demonstrations that brought hundreds of thousands of Muscovites into the streets.

The first salute was directed to Marshal Rokossovsky in tribute to the drive of his forces from Kovel through the strongly fortified German defense line, which culminated in reaching the western Bug at Opalin and in the capture of more than 400 inhabited points. Opalin, on the eastern side of the Bug, is less than fifteen miles from Chelm on the road to Lublin.

Other forces under Marshal Kon-

Continued on Page 6

## War News Summarized

FRIDAY, JULY 21, 1944

An almost successful attempt on Hitler's life and Emperor Hirohito's command to two jingo war lords to form a new Japanese Cabinet pushed actual battlefield developments into the background yesterday.

Hitler was conferring at his secret headquarters with the staff of the German High Command, Berlin said, when Col. Count von Stauffenberg, one of his collaborators, threw a bomb at the Fuehrer. Although the assassin was only six feet away Hitler escaped with bruises and burns. One of the thirteen staff officers was killed and two others were seriously injured.

Shortly after the explosion Hitler informed the German people of what had happened, blaming an "officers' clique" that wished to bring about a revolt. He immediately placed Gestapo Chief Himmler in absolute command within the Reich, said the "criminal elements" would be ruthlessly exterminated and indicated grave concern by warning all soldiers and civilians not to obey orders unless they had come from him. He also named Col. Gen. Guderian Chief of Staff, replacing Field Marshal Gen. Keitel. [All the foregoing 1:1.]

In Japan, Admiral Mitsumasa Yonai, Premier during the tense days of early 1940, and his then Overseas Minister and later Governor General of Korea, Gen. Kuniaki Koiso, were commissioned to form a "critical decisive wartime" Cabinet. Both men are militarists and expansionists of the Tojo type. [1:2-3.]

Allied statesmen saw in both developments evidence of crisis in the enemy camps. London observers believed that Hitler's order for a new purge indicated clearly that unrest within Germany was general [1:2-3], while former Ambassador Grew and Secretary of State Hull in Washington expressed the prevalent opinion that Tokyo had at last admitted the gravity of the military situation. They warned, however, against expecting a Japanese collapse. [3:6.]

On the actual war fronts Allied gains were reported everywhere. The British Second Army in France was widening its eleven-mile bulge south and east of Caen and trying to force Field Marshal Rommel into a decisive tank battle. Americans advanced in the St. Lô area and crossed the River Ay to a depth of 300 yards in the Lessay sector. [1:4, map P. 2.] The resistance movement that has proved so effective in France has spread into Belgium. [1:2-3.]

Although torrential rains slowed Allied progress in Italy the Fifth Army reached the Arno River along a twenty-five-mile front above Leghorn and was close to Pisa. [1:3.]

Overhead some 2,000 planes from Britain and nearly 1,000 from Italy teamed in a coordinated attack on aircraft plants, ball-bearing factories, airfields and other targets in southeast Germany. It was one of the war's most concentrated blows. [5:1.]

The Russians scored the most impressive gains in a new offensive in the Kovel area. The Red Army reached the western Bug River on a wide front after driving as deep as thirty-one miles on a 123-mile line in three days. Another advance brought Soviet troops to within five miles of Lwow and a flanking thrust cut the main German supply and escape railroad. [1:5; map P. 6.]

Action in the Pacific was on a lesser scale. American planes blasted Guam with 721 tons of bombs in two days. [7:5.] Chinese troops were attacking the Japanese from within Hengyang and from outside the Hunan city [7:1] while along the Burma front other Chinese routed an enemy relief force trying to reach Pingka. [6:6.]

AGAIN NAMED FOR PRESIDENCY

Franklin Delano Roosevelt
Associated Press, 1944

## Roosevelt's Acceptance

*Following is the text of President Roosevelt's acceptance speech from a Pacific Coast naval base, as recorded and transcribed by* The New York Times:

Mr. Chairman, ladies and gentlemen of the convention, my friends:

I have already indicated to you why I accept the nomination that you have offered me, in spite of my desire to retire to the quiet of private life.

You in this convention are aware of what I have sought to gain for the nation, and you have asked me to continue.

It seems wholly likely that within the next four years our armed forces, and those of our Allies, will have gained a complete victory over Germany and Japan, sooner or later, and that the world once more will be at peace, under a system, we hope, that will prevent a new world war. In any event, whenever that time comes new hands will then have full opportunity to realize the ideals which we seek.

In the last three elections the people of the United States have transcended party affiliation. Not only Democrats but also forward-looking Republicans and millions of

Continued on Page 8

## PRESIDENT FAVORS TRUMAN, DOUGLAS

### Would Take Either as Running Mate, Letter to Hannegan Says—Battle Gets Hotter

By JAMES A. HAGERTY
Special to The New York Times.

CHICAGO, July 20—In an attempt to bolster the waning strength of Senator Harry S. Truman of Missouri for the nomination for Vice President, Robert E. Hannegan, Democratic national chairman, made public tonight the letter written to him by President Roosevelt, saying that either Senator Truman or William O. Douglas, justice of the United States Supreme Court, would be satisfactory to him as a running mate and would add strength to the ticket.

Mr. Hannegan said he had not made the letter public earlier because he considered it necessary to obtain the consent of the sender before releasing a personal letter for publication. He said he had talked today with President Roosevelt by telephone and had received such consent.

The letter, which was written on White House stationery and dated July 19, 1944, was as follows:

"Dear Bob:

"You have written me about Harry Truman and Bill Douglas. I should, of course, be very glad to run with either of them and believe that either one of them would bring real strength to the ticket.

"Always sincerely,
"FRANKLIN D. ROOSEVELT."

The letter was addressed to

Continued on Page 10

## ARMS USE TO KEEP PEACE IS PLEDGED

### Platform Backs World Role on Sovereignty Basis—Opposes Racial Vote Ban

*Text of the Democratic platform is on Page 12.*

By CHARLES E. EGAN
Special to The New York Times.

CHICAGO, July 20—A platform calling for the participation of this country with the United Nations in a world organization, empowered to use armed force when necessary to preserve international peace, was adopted by the Democratic convention tonight.

It committed the party to support a program to have the United States join in "the establishment of an international organization based on the principle of the sovereign equality of all peace-loving states, open to membership by all such states, large and small, for the prevention of aggression and the maintenance of international peace and security."

Embodied also in the platform was a plank stating that racial and religious minorities "have the right to live, develop and vote equally with all citizens and share the rights that are guaranteed by our Constitution."

The platform, of 1,500 words, carried expressions in favor of the opening of Palestine to unrestricted Jewish immigration and

Continued on Page 12



## VOTE IS 1,086 TO 90

### Byrd Gets 89, Farley One—President on Radio Accepts

### STANDS ON RECORD

### Says 'Experience,' Not 'Immaturity,' Will Win War, Peace and Jobs

*Wallace and Barkley texts, Page 10; Jackson's, Page 11.*

By TURNER CATLEDGE
Special to The New York Times.

CHICAGO, July 20—Franklin Delano Roosevelt of New York was nominated today for a fourth term as President of the United States by a noisy, irritable Democratic convention, meeting in the same hall where he was chosen for his first term in 1932 and for a third in 1940.

A few hours later, speaking to the convention directly by radio from his train at a Pacific Coast naval base, he accepted the nomination and opened his re-election bid on the note of "experience" versus "immaturity."

Mr. Roosevelt asserted that he considered the convention's action as a call upon him to serve. He said it was up to the American people in the November election to decide whether plans already made and men already serving to achieve victory and make America and the world a better place in which to live were to be continued or supplanted by an administration with no program but to oppose.

**His Three-Point Program**

He presented a three-point program—to win the war, to secure the peace with force if necessary, and to build an economy with full employment and a high standard of living—as a promise of himself and the party which had called him again to lead.

In this election, he said, the people would not consider "glowing words or platform pledges," but would decide on the record made in the war and in "domestic achievements."

The President said he was too busy, and the emergency too serious, to permit him to engage in an active campaign for re-election.

But he added that he should "feel free" to report to the American people from time to time on the progress of their efforts and to "correct misstatements of fact" which might be made by the Republican opposition.

He disclosed that he was on the West Coast now in pursuance of his "constitutional duties" in connection with the war.

**Roar of Cheering for Speech**

The President's words came strong and magic-like through the loud speaker system—just as it did in his acceptance speech at his third-term nomination in this hall four years ago.

At the end the crowd in the arena and galleries broke into uproarious cheering. People were still shouting in a deafening roar when the motion was made. They attempted to shout down the motion.

The motion was carried, however, and the convention recessed at 10:55 o'clock until 11:30 tomorrow morning when it will reassemble to settle the Vice Presidential nomination.

The renomination of the President went through swiftly.

Mr. Roosevelt received 1,086 votes on the first roll call. Senator Harry F. Byrd, who was not a candidate, received 89, and James A. Farley, former chairman of the Democratic National Committee, who would not let his name go before the convention, received one from his home State of New York.

A telegram notifying the President of his nomination was dispatched to him immediately by Senator Samuel D. Jackson, Per-

Continued on Page 9

"All the News That's Fit to Print"

# The New York Times.

LATE CITY EDITION
Clear with light to moderate winds today.
Temperatures Yesterday—Max., 76; Min., 66
Sunrise, 5:43 A. M.; Sunset, 8:21 P. M.

Copyright, 1944, by The New York Times Company.

VOL. XCIII..No. 31,591. Entered as Second-Class Matter, Postoffice, New York, N. Y. NEW YORK, SATURDAY, JULY 22, 1944. THREE CENTS IN NEW YORK CITY

# NAZIS BLOCK PLOT TO SEIZE GOVERNMENT; AMERICANS LAND ON GUAM, PUSH INLAND; TRUMAN NOMINATED FOR VICE PRESIDENCY

## 2D BALLOT DECIDES

### Wallace, Leading 429½ to 319½ on First, Is Crushed 1,100 to 66

### BREAK BY MARYLAND

### Real Fight Ends With Big Shift by Illinois—Ready, Says Senator

By TURNER CATLEDGE
Special to THE NEW YORK TIMES.

CHICAGO, July 21—Senator Harry S. Truman of Missouri was nominated tonight as the Democratic candidate for Vice President in the fifth and final session of the twenty-eighth national convention of the party.

He appeared immediately before the cheering delegates massed in the arena of the great hall to accept his "responsibility" as a running mate in President Roosevelt's bid for a fourth term in the White House.

Directly following the nomination, support of the ticket was pledged by Vice President Henry A. Wallace, James A. Farley, former National Chairman, and Sidney Hillman, head of the CIO Political Action Committee, which had supported Mr. Wallace.

Mr. Truman's victory, which was also an overwhelming defeat for the renomination hopes of Vice President Wallace, came on the second ballot. The official announcement of the tally clerks gave the Missouri Senator 1,100 votes to 66 for Mr. Wallace and 4 for Associate Justice William O. Douglas.

[A tabulation of this ballot by The Associated Press from official records of the convention gave: Truman 1,031, Wallace 105. Other votes in the compilation were: Governor Cooper of Tennessee, 26; Senator Barkley of Kentucky, 6; Justice Douglas, 4 and Paul V. McNutt, 1.]

**Truman Speaks to Throng**

Mr. Truman, who rose from comparative political obscurity in Kansas City to win the second highest honor of his party, was sitting on the platform eating a sandwich when the result was announced.

Pulled up to the microphone by Senator Samuel D. Jackson of Indiana, permanent chairman of the convention, Senator Truman responded to the demands from the crowd for a word.

"You don't know how very much I appreciate the very great honor which has come to the State of Missouri," he said in a halting, shy manner. "It is also a great responsibility which I am perfectly willing to assume.

"Nine years and five months ago I came to the Senate. I expect to continue the efforts I have made there to help shorten the war and to win the peace under the great leader, Franklin D. Roosevelt.

"I don't know what else I can say, except that I accept this great honor with all humility. I thank you."

It was the shortest speech of the day and was appreciatively applauded by a crowd that literally had become surfeited with oratory. A moment later the convention passed into history on a motion by Governor Herbert O'Conor of Maryland to adjourn sine die.

"This convention has completed the business for which it was assembled, to nominate the next President and Vice President of the United States," he said.

**Swing Led by Maryland**

Senator Truman, President Roosevelt's second choice for place, ran through to win the nomination after having trailed Vice President Wallace on the first ballot by 110 votes.

On the opening roll-call Mr. Wallace received 429½ ballots and Mr. Truman 319½, with the remainder scattered among fourteen other candidates who had been named in nominating speeches or

Continued on Page 5



ROOSEVELT'S RUNNING MATE

Harry S. Truman — Blackstone, 1944

## Monetary Parley Agrees On Terms of World Bank

By RUSSELL PORTER
Special to THE NEW YORK TIMES.

BRETTON WOODS, N. H., July 21—The United Nations Monetary and Financial Conference reached an agreement today on a plan for an $8,800,000,000 International Bank of Reconstruction and Development to guarantee post-war international investments. The total capital of the world bank is the same as the aggregate of the international monetary fund to stabilize currencies which was accepted last week. Thus two vital parts of the post-war program to try to insure world peace and prosperity have been accepted, with some reservations, by all the forty-four United and Associated Nations participating in the conference, subject to the approval of the Congress of the United States and the executive and legislative branches of other Governments.

In order to reach an agreement, the United States delegation had to abandon its position that the subscriptions to the bank, which represent each country's risks in guaranteeing international loans, should be the same as the quotas in the fund, which represent a country's rights to acquire foreign exchange with which to buy goods in the world market.

However, it is the opinion of the United States delegation, after receiving the advice of its four members of Congress, two Republicans and two Democrats, and its one banker member, Edward E. Brown, president of the First National Bank of Chicago, that the fund and bank agreements have been

Continued on Page 28

## BIG CITY BOSSES WON OVER HILLMAN

### Two Presidential Letters Had Important Influence on Convention Strategy

By JAMES A. HAGERTY
Special to THE NEW YORK TIMES.

CHICAGO, July 21—Somewhat belatedly, leaders of the Democratic organizations in a score and a half of States, headed by big city bosses, Edward J. Flynn and Frank V. Kelly of New York, Mayor Edward J. Kelly of Chicago, Mayor Frank Hague of Jersey City and Robert E. Hannegan, national chairman, of St. Louis, brought about the nomination of Senator Harry S. Truman of Missouri for Vice President by the Democratic National Convention.

By the nomination the Democratic politicians won a victory over Sidney Hillman, chairman of the Congress of Industrial Organizations Political Action Committee, who stuck to Vice President Henry A. Wallace to the last and whose influence had been suffi-

Continued on Page 10

## Farley Pledges Roosevelt Backing, Accepting Decision or Convention

Special to THE NEW YORK TIMES.

CHICAGO, July 21—James A. Farley, former Democratic national chairman and former Postmaster General, announced tonight that he would support President Roosevelt for re-election despite his opposition to a fourth term.

"I have been opposed on principle to a third or fourth Presidential term," Mr. Farley said in a statement, which he released just after the nomination of Senator Truman for Vice President. "For that reason, I voted for the nomination of Senator Harry F. Byrd of Virginia for President.

"Having participated in the proceedings of the convention, I accept its decision and will support the party nominees."

Mr. Farley declined to amplify his statement. He resigned recently as chairman of the New York State Democratic Committee and is not expected to take an active part in the campaign.

Mr. Farley, who was of great help to Mr. Roosevelt in the latter's first nomination for President and in his first and second campaigns for election, broke with the Chief Executive during the latter part of Mr. Roosevelt's second term.

Secretary of the New York State Democratic Committee in 1928, when Mr. Roosevelt was first elected Governor of New York, Mr. Farley was promoted to State chairman and managed Mr. Roosevelt's campaign for re-election as Governor in 1930. Mr. Roosevelt's plurality of 730,000 at that elec-

Continued on Page 9

## RUSSIANS RACE ON

### Bug River Is Crossed Again on Wide Front Due East of Lublin

### LWOW BATTLE BEGUN

### Brest-Litovsk Railway to Chelm Cut—Ostrov Is Captured in North

By W. H. LAWRENCE
By Cable to THE NEW YORK TIMES.

MOSCOW, Saturday, July 22—The Soviet battle for the liberation of Poland began in earnest yesterday as the Red Army smashed across the Bug River from Lyuboml on a thirty-seven-mile front and advanced up to nine miles beyond the west bank. In that operation the railroad between Chelm and Brest-Litovsk was severed.

Other Red Army forces moved closer to Lwow and to Brest-Litovsk, and the Soviet High Command announced that Soviet troops had captured 570 inhabited points on both the northernmost and the southernmost sections of the front.

At the northern end of the front, troops of the Third Baltic Front executed an outflanking maneuver and captured the important enemy stronghold and communications hub of Ostrov—a victory that Moscow celebrated with a salute of twelve salvos from 124 guns.

Although the capture of Ostrov won the salute, from a military and strategic point of view the biggest news was the crossing of the Bug west of Lyuboml by Marshal Konstantin K. Rokossovsky's First White Russian Army and the nine-mile advance beyond it, which sent his troops streaming toward Lublin and Warsaw.

In the sector southwest of Brody, where four or five German divisions are encircled, Marshal Ivan S. Koneff's First Ukrainian Army continued the process of extermination, capturing 2,000 more prisoners and 100 artillery pieces. The

Continued on Page 5

## BEACHHEADS SET UP

### Americans Invade Guam After Mighty U.S. Blow From Sea and Air

### OPPOSITION IS LIGHT

### Resistance Increases as Japanese Are Pushed Toward Inland Hills

By GEORGE F. HORNE
By Telephone to THE NEW YORK TIMES.

PEARL HARBOR, July 21—United States assault troops and sea forces began yesterday the long awaited invasion of the big island of Guam and have established good beachheads against light opposition, although resistance increased in some sectors as the Americans drove inland.

[Front dispatches reported that the landings were made on either side of Port Apra, The Associated Press said. From the shore areas, where Japanese defenses had been blown to pieces, the invaders drove swiftly toward a range of hills in the interior.]

They stormed ashore after enemy defenses received their seventeenth straight day of heavy attack from the air. All this week, up to the time of the landings, surface units of the Fifth Fleet had battered the island with tons of steel. They continued yesterday, covering the marines and Army assault troops making the invasion. A terrific rain of 627 tons of bombs and 147 rockets was unloosed by our planes in the day preceding the landings.

Admiral Chester W. Nimitz, Commander in Chief of the Pacific Fleet and Pacific Ocean areas, announced the landings at 1:30 o'clock this morning.

**Japanese Are Weakened**

With Saipan securely in our hands, the tremendous Pacific forces have turned, as was expected, to carry retribution to the Japanese where their strongly armed and confident forces poured ashore

Continued on Page 7

## War News Summarized

SATURDAY, JULY 22, 1944

The few facts seeping through the tight German censorship yesterday indicated that the anti-Hitler revolt was still alive and that a purge of anti-Nazi leaders was still under way. German army officers who attempted to take Hitler's life simultaneously tried to take over the government offices in Berlin, the German radio said. The same source declared the revolt had been mercilessly suppressed and that Propaganda Minister Goebbels had frustrated the attempt to seize the Government offices. A Stockholm report said two German divisions had revolted Wednesday in East Prussia, while another dispatch from Switzerland relayed unconfirmed reports of a revolt among German naval units at Kiel and Stettin. [1:8.]

Secretary of State Hull attributed the unrest in Germany and the attack on Hitler to a spreading realization in the Reich of impending defeat. He cautioned, however, against overoptimism on an early end of the war in Europe. [3:2-3.]

Red Army forces blasted a thirty-seven-mile-wide hole in Hitler's much-publicized "East Wall" defenses along the Bug River and are threatening to crumble the whole German defense structure guarding Warsaw, now only eighty-two miles away. Other Russian troops seized Ostrov, the last Nazi fortress before the Latvian border on the direct route to Riga. The Red Army was increasing its threat to the imperiled strongholds of Lwow, Brest-Litovsk, Kaunas and Dvinsk by the hour, as beaten German armies fell back everywhere along an almost continuous 800-mile front from Finland to the Carpathian foothills. [1:4; map P. 5.]

Allied troops in Normandy slugged through rain and mud to cement positions below Caen to a depth of five miles. Canadians seized St. André-sur-Orne and St. Martin-de-Fontenay near Caen as the enemy gave ground slowly. American forces increased their pressure on Périers after winning a foothold on the road from St. Lô to Périers. [1:6-7; map P. 3.]

The two-way aerial offensive from Britain and Italy continued for the fourth consecutive day as nearly 3,000 American bombers and fighters pounded a dozen German targets. [4:1.] Ground troops in Italy pierced strong German Arno River defenses, forcing the water barrier into the mountain fringes of the "Gothic Line" in at least one place. [1:7.]

Striking at Japan's inner defense zone, American assault troops landed on Guam Island, first American territory seized by the Japanese, early Thursday and have established good beachheads. Admiral Nimitz reported that additional troops were landing against light initial Japanese resistance, and that casualties were moderate. A terrific naval and aerial bombardment of the strategic island, 1,565 miles southeast of Tokyo, softened up the enemy defense before our landings. As our troops moved inland the Japanese put up stiffened resistance in some sectors. [1:5; map P. 7.]

In China fierce fighting raged around Hengyang for the twenty-sixth day as relief forces attacking Japanese troops who have besieged that major junction on the Canton-Hankow railroad drove deeper into the enemy lines. [6:1.]

## Drive South of Caen Stalls As Rain Floods Battle Area

### British Forced to Withdraw Armored Units—Canadians Beat Off Fierce German Counter-Attacks in Mud and Mists

By DREW MIDDLETON
By Cable to THE NEW YORK TIMES.

SUPREME HEADQUARTERS, Allied Expeditionary Force, Saturday, July 22—British and Canadian infantrymen, their uniforms muddy and sodden after thirty-six hours of heavy rains, were fighting a grim, bloody battle for Verriers and St. Martin-de-Fontenay on the British Second Army sector south of Caen last night, but the remainder of the Allied front in Normandy was quiet save for the measured pounding of cannon and mortars.

The offensive launched by the Second Army Tuesday morning with such high hopes had stalled, frustrated as much by the thick doughlike mud that covered the roads and fields as by the lethal fire of German anti-tank positions around Vimont. These positions now must be rooted out by infantry and artillery, under adverse conditions for the attackers, while British armored divisions follow the example of German Panzer units and retire from the battlefield until the stage has been set for a great armored battle for the road to Paris.

The gains registered yesterday were all on the western flank of the Second Army's salient along the east bank of the Orne River. Canadians were fighting German infantrymen for Etavaux and St. André-sur-Orne in conditions reminiscent of World War I.

At St. Martin-de Fontenay, half a mile south of St. André-sur-Orne, the Canadians took the village and then stood off a heavy German counter-attack supported by tanks. When the counter-attack was over the Canadians went forward to find German dead lying thick on the muddy ground. The enemy casualties were "satisfactory," a report from the front said.

There was mud and mist everywhere and little knots of men were fighting silently with bayonets in a dank, dripping world where gun flashes were the only light.

The weather, which has favored the enemy since D-day, has imposed a stalemate on the operations in this sector, although farther west British infantrymen

Continued on Page 3

## British Label Hitler Attack Rivals' Bid for False Peace

By Cable to THE NEW YORK TIMES.

LONDON, July 21—Although the news from Germany is taken as an indication of a grave crisis within the Reich, there is no disposition here to regard it as a ground for hoping for an early termination of hostilities. As The Times of London will say tomorrow, when the enemy "wavers," that is the time for throwing in reserves, not for relaxing.

It is strongly felt here that Adolf Hitler's rivals, far from being converts to the Allied cause, are merely another brand of champions of militarism who merely believe themselves better able to rescue the Reich from disaster than the present Nazi leaders.

Their game, it was said, is to supplant Hitler so as to try to make peace on terms that would preserve the Wehrmacht for another war under more favorable conditions. Therefore, it is recognized by the people as well as officials that even had the officers' coup succeeded, peace would still be a long way off.

**Generals Reach Conclusion**

"Unconditional surrender" is still an Allied condition of an armistice, and there is little conviction here that even the generals who would like to rid their country of Hitler would accept that without continuing the struggle in the hope of getting better terms later.

However, this evidence of a rift in the façade of German unity is recognized as important evidence that at least some German military leaders have reached the conclusion that the Nazi direction of the war has brought Germany to a

Continued on Page 3

## U. S. PATROLS STAB ACROSS ARNO RIVER

### Pierce Mountain Fringes of Gothic Line While British Thrust Nearer Florence

By The United Press.

ROME, July 21—American Fifth Army combat patrols pierced strong German Arno River defenses today, forcing the river into the mountain fringes of the Gothic Line in at least one point, while artillery blasted German installations north of the river from captured high points on the south bank.

The Americans took advantage of improved weather to roll up scattered German resistance groups south of the river, while on the coast German guns of all calibers hammered the battered port of Leghorn from advantageous positions on Mount Pisano, northeast of Pisa.

This height, on which the Germans have installed many field guns, anti-aircraft batteries, machine guns and pillboxes, affords

Continued on Page 5

## Invaders Find Defenses of Guam Blown to Shreds by Our Attacks

By JOHN R. HENRY
Of International News Service
For the Combined Allied Press

ABOARD A FLAGSHIP AT GUAM, July 21 (Guam Time)—A liberation force of Third Amphibious Corps marines and Army troops thundered ashore at Guam today with the destructive blast of a Pacific typhoon.

The Leathernecks spearheaded two separate beachhead assaults, storming across coral-studded shorelines in the wake of a 17-day sea and air bombardment that reached a stupefying crescendo as landing craft churned into remnants of the Japanese coast defenses.

Casualties were described as "light" for United States forces. The Japanese dead were uncounted.

At nightfall Maj. Gen. Roy Geiger's Third Amphibious Corps troops dug in on perimeters between Adlup and Asan, a point north of Orote Peninsula, and from the shattered town of Agat to Bangi Point, south of the rocky finger of land.

The northern beachhead, where the terrain was most rugged, stretched in an arc several thousand yards. The southern force shoved inland and established its own substantial beachhead. General Geiger is a marine aviator and veteran South Pacific commander.

So effective had been the preparatory barrages that troops flowed ashore with negligible initial resistance and in record time.

Despite sprinkling enemy fire

Continued on Page 7

## HITLER HUNTS FOES

### Thousands of Officers Reported Arrested in Purge of Army

### MUTINY IS RUMORED

### Sailors at Kiel, Stettin and Troops in East Said to Revolt

By RAYMOND DANIELL
By Cable to THE NEW YORK TIMES.

LONDON, Saturday, July 22—Although reports from Berlin insist that the plot of army officers to overthrow the Nazi regime and seize power themselves has been suppressed and its instigators liquidated, the isolation of the Reich from the rest of the world continues and it is apparent that counter-measures are being pressed.

[A Swiss report to The United Press said it was understood that German naval units had revolted at Kiel and Stettin. Stockholm dispatches said 5,500 German officers had been arrested throughout Germany and that there had been disorders in eastern Germany and East Prussia.]

Everything suggests that the plot that had its climax in the attempt to assassinate Adolf Hitler was deep and well laid, with far-reaching ramifications. On evidence supplied by the highest Nazi authorities it is known that the plotters, who included Col. Gen. Ludwig Beck, who was dismissed as Chief of Staff by Hitler in November, 1938, attempted to kill Hitler and bring off a coup d'état.

The scheme apparently succeeded to the point where the conspirators were able to issue orders in conflict with the plans of Hitler and other Nazi leaders.

**Leaders Revealed Troubles**

The extent of the disaffection seemingly caused such consternation in the Nazi camp that Hitler, Reichmarshal Hermann Goering and Grand Admiral Karl Doenitz felt impelled in the small hours yesterday morning to try to set things straight by urgent appeals, even though their action involved disclosure to a hostile world that a rift had developed between some high army officers and the Nazi party on the best way to save Germany from destruction.

There is no evidence to show that the challenge to Hitler's leadership and domination of the Nazi party has spread to the civilian population but Transocean, German news agency, revealed that certain "precautionary measures" had been taken in the center of Berlin.

Alfred Rosenberg, Nazi party "philosopher," writing in a special edition of the Voelkischer Beobachter yesterday morning, called the attempt on Hitler's life the opening of hostilities on a "fifth front."

Some additional light on what happened in the Reich in those crucial hours preceding Hitler's broadcast was provided last night from Berlin. According to the official story, provided for soldiers in the field, a clique that was connected with "an enemy power" had obtained control of "certain means of communications" through a subordinate officer.

**Major Informed Goebbels**

Through these channels, it was said, orders were sent to Major Remer, commandant of a battalion of the Berlin guard, telling him Hitler was dead, that disorders had been reported in the Reich and that the Wehrmacht had taken over the government. Major Remer was directed to occupy with his force the administrative headquarters at Berlin, which he did.

But then, according to this account, Major Remer immediately communicated with Propaganda Minister Joseph Goebbels, head of the Berlin municipal administration, who convinced him that he had been obeying faked orders. The fact that "traitors" had laid hands on certain communications systems brought about yesterday

Continued on Page 3

"All the News That's Fit to Print"

# The New York Times.

LATE CITY EDITION
POSTSCRIPT
Considerable cloudiness and milder today; moderate winds.
Temperatures Yesterday—Max., 51; Min., 37
Sunrise, 7:15 A. M.; Sunset, 5:43 P. M.

Copyright, 1938, by The New York Times Company.

VOL. XCIV. No. 31,700. Entered as Second-Class Matter, Postoffice, New York, N. Y. NEW YORK, WEDNESDAY, NOVEMBER 8, 1944. THREE CENTS IN NEW YORK CITY

# ROOSEVELT WINS FOURTH TERM; RECORD POPULAR VOTE IS CLOSE; DEMOCRATS GAIN IN THE HOUSE

## 2-DAY LUZON BLOWS SMASH 440 PLANES, 30 JAPANESE SHIPS

### Halsey's Fliers Destroy 249 Aircraft, Sink Four Vessels in Sunday Sweep

### MANILA FIELDS RAVAGED

### Ports and Installations Hit Hard—Enemy Lines to Leyte Defenders Are Strained

By GEORGE HORNE

By Telephone to THE NEW YORK TIMES.

PEARL HARBOR, Nov. 7—Admiral William F. Halsey's Third Fleet carriers spread death and damage over southern Luzon Island in the Philippines for the second successive day on Sunday, sinking another five ships and destroying 249 additional enemy aircraft.

It was a major air strike, apparently an all-out effort to annihilate the Japanese air forces supporting enemy counter-attacks on Leyte, where American military leaders have reported the campaign nearing its final stages.

Over the two days, according to Admiral Chester W. Nimitz's communiqué today, the enemy has lost 440 aircraft, 327 of which were caught and destroyed on the ground and 113 shot down in the air. The principal plane concentrations were found on seven fields in the Manila network. They were Nichols, Clark, Nielson, Lipa, Tarlac, Bambam and Mabalacat.

[The two-day toll of enemy ships sunk or damaged was about thirty.]

**Unable to Rise in Strength**

As the widespread attacks continue, the enemy air opposition is becoming steadily weaker, as is evidenced by the fact that on the second day all but a few of the lost enemy aircraft were caught on the ground, unable to get into the air.

Terrific damage is being inflicted on port facilities and ground installations in and around Manila harbor. In addition to ships sunk and planes destroyed, many air and surface craft were listed as damaged. Reports on the action were still of a preliminary nature and there was no count of our own losses.

Admiral Nimitz said three oil storage areas were left blazing at the northern section of Clark Field and at the northeast of the field a tremendous explosion was observed, followed by fire. North of Malvar a railroad engine and five tank cars were blown up.

**Five Ships Sunk at Manila**

In the harbor of Manila the fighters, torpedo planes and dive-bombers sank three cargo ships and an oil tanker, probably sank a destroyer and damaged two destroyers, two destroyer escorts, a trawler and several cargo ships. Fourteen cargo ships were damaged during the two-day attack, in which wave after wave of American planes swept in from the sea to wipe out available enemy strength that might be used to bolster the hard-pressed Japanese forces on Leyte.

Meanwhile the steady attacks on the Bonins and Kuriles are continuing. On Sunday a Liberator of the Eleventh Army Air Force, flying hundreds of miles from our Aleutian bases, hit three small transports off Onnekotan Island in the Kuriles and other Liberators flying with it concentrated on land targets of the island base.

Seven enemy fighters fought the big bombers in a running battle, and guns from three Liberators brought down one and probably destroyed another. Two Liberators were damaged.

Otomari and Tori Island, also in the Kuriles, were attacked. Seventh Air Force Liberators

Continued on Page 19, Column 3



## War News Summarized

WEDNESDAY, NOVEMBER 8, 1944

**Japanese Lose 440 Planes**

Japanese air power in the Philippines received a staggering blow on Saturday and Sunday when Third Fleet carrier planes destroyed 440 enemy aircraft in the Manila and southern Luzon areas. Nearly thirty ships, including a number of warcraft, were also destroyed or damaged. Our fliers reaped their greatest harvest at seven airfields where they wiped out 327 planes on the ground. Port and ground installations suffered terrific damage. Reports were still incomplete and our own losses were not known. [1:1.]

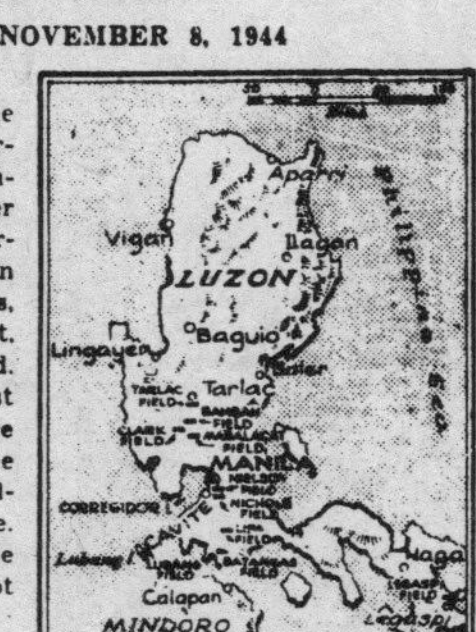


Luzon fields pounded from air

**Battle Joined on Leyte**

American troops on Leyte were battling elements of four Japanese divisions in the hills north of Ormoc and repulsed three heavy attacks, inflicting great loss on the enemy. The area of Valencia, north of Ormoc, was under American artillery fire. [19:2, with map.]

**Tokyo Sees B-29's**

The jittery Japanese reported more Superfortresses on reconnaissance flights over Tokyo and surrounding territory. They also said that the Bonins and Volcanos had been bombed. [19:2.] In China the enemy scored by driving to within twenty miles of Liuchow, but in Burma the British captured Kennedy Peak and threatened Fort White and Paletwa. [21:1.]

**Grim Fight Below Aachen**

The United States First Army fought its way back into the streets of Vossenack in some of the bitterest fighting of the war. Three German counter-attacks from Schmidt were repulsed. The Sixth Army Group made important advances in the Vosges Mountains and in the Netherlands Allied troops were mopping up the liberated areas. [19:8, with map.]

**Soviet Drive Forecast**

Behind the lull on Russia's fighting fronts the Red Army was reported to be preparing for a great new offensive. [19:4.] The Athens radio announced that the Greek Government had ordered dissolution of the guerrilla bands Edes and Elas. [19:5.]

**Robot Blows at U. S. 'Possible'**

A joint Army-Navy statement said that it was "entirely possible" for flying bombs to reach the United States from Europe, but gave no indication such an attack was expected. [19:6-7.]

## FISH IS DEFEATED; CLARE LUCE WINS

### Congress Veteran Concedes Bennet's Victory—Close Finish in Connecticut

Special to THE NEW YORK TIMES.

NEWBURGH, N. Y., Wednesday, Nov. 8—Representative Hamilton Fish, for twelve terms a Republican member of the House and a leading isolationist and critic of President Roosevelt's foreign policy, conceded his defeat by Augustus W. Bennet just before 1 o'clock this morning.

"From reports I have received to date, it looks like I have lost the district by a 5,000 vote majority," he said.

"It looks as if the Republicans have lost the House, and if that is so, as much as I regret it, I have no great desire to continue to serve as a minority member, which I have for the last fourteen years in an uphill fight."

Mr. Bennet, in a victory statement, paid tribute to those who had supported him from all parties, "including the much-abused Political Action Committee." He hailed his election as the result of the citizens' determination "to eliminate Ham Fish from Congress."

**Factors in the Result**

Heavy Republican defections to Mr. Bennet in Orange County and strong support for Mr. Fish's opponent in the parts of the district in Rockland, Sullivan and Delaware counties sent the Republican nominee down to defeat in the bitterest Congressional election in this part of the State in years.

Complete returns from Orange County gave Fish 35,126 votes to 27,371 for Bennet, a majority for Fish of 7,755. This indicated that Mr. Bennet's majority for the whole Twenty-ninth Congressional District would be about 5,600.

Complete returns from Rockland County gave Bennet 19,706 votes to 12,323 for Fish, a majority of 7,383.

In Sullivan County, with twenty-four election districts missing, including those where Mr. Bennet was expected to run strongest, the vote was Fish 3,877, Bennet 3,776,

Continued on Page 2, Column 7

## ROOSEVELT VICTORY CLAIMED IN JERSEY

### Hague Spokesmen Also Say Wene Will Win—Constitution Revision Is Rejected

Despite greatly reduced pluralities in Hudson County, Democratic stronghold of New Jersey, lieutenants of Mayor Frank Hague of Jersey City, Democratic boss of the State, predicted shortly before 4 A. M. today that the State's sixteen electoral votes would be delivered to President Roosevelt, largely by virtue of an estimated plurality of 75,000 votes in Hudson. In 1940 Mr. Roosevelt carried the county by a plurality of 100,877.

Mayor Hague's spokesman also predicted victory for the party nominee for the United States Senate, Representative Elmer H. Wene, although by a close vote, and rejection of the proposed revised State Constitution by a substantial margin.

Mr. Hague himself left headquarters in Jersey City early today without making any statement.

The Jersey City predictions were made despite the fact that eight of the twelve wards in the city had not reported returns up to that hour, but the estimates on the fate of charter revision appeared to be borne out by Statewide returns. At 4 A. M., with 1,311 of the State's 3,657 election districts missing, the vote for rejection was 480,503 to 381,686 for approval.

At the same hour Mr. Dewey was leading Roosevelt by a vote of 481,677 to 456,275, with 1,819 districts missing, and H. Alexander Smith, Mr. Wene's Republican opponent, was leading the Democratic nominee by a vote of 562,251 to 503,763, on the basis of returns from 2,226 districts.

**Five Hudson Communities Bolt**

The apparent failure of the Hague machine earlier to deliver the expected large Democratic plurality in the county had caused some political observers to place the State in the doubtful class.

Continued on Page 9, Column 4



## GET 11 TO 20 SEATS

### Victories Blast Hopes of Rivals to Control the House

### SENATE UNCHANGED

### Democrats Have 180 in House, Republicans 155, 98 in Doubt

By TURNER CATLEDGE

Democratic gains of from eleven to twenty seats in the House and a possible new place or two in the already one-sided Senate, appeared on returns received up to 5 A. M. today to have followed in the wake of yesterday's fourth-term landslide for President Roosevelt.

Republican hopes of controlling the House appeared to have been blasted beyond any possibility of realization and what in the earlier count seemed to portend a G. O. P. gain in the Senate began to fade with the later returns.

These same reports showed the defeat of Representative Hamilton Fish, Republican, of New York, one of the most controversial figures in the lower house; the possible defeat of Senator John A. Danaher, Republican, of Connecticut; a victory for Mrs. Clare Luce, Republican, in a close race in the Fourth Connecticut Congressional District; a trend in the early count against Senator Gerald P. Nye, Republican "isolationist" of North Dakota, and a neck-and-neck contest in which Senator James J. Davis, Republican, of Pennsylvania, was trailing his Democratic opponent, Representative Francis J. Myers, by a slight margin.

**Leading Senators Re-elected**

These returns also revealed the re-election of Senator Alben W. Barkley, Democratic Majority Leader, in Kentucky; of Senator Scott Lucas, Democrat, in Illinois; of Senator Robert A. Taft, Republican, in Ohio; of Senator Millard Tydings, Democrat, in Maryland, and numerous other sitting Senators, both Democratic and Republican.

With 98 House seats still in doubt, the Democrats had clinched 180 seats in the House of Representatives of the Seventy-ninth Congress; the Republicans were certain of at least 155; the American Labor party of 1 and the Progressives of 1.

Seventeen Senate places were still awaiting the decision of the final count, but the Democrats were certain of 49, or an actual majority. The Republicans appeared certain of thirty-one and the Progressives of one.

With the latest returns received the Democrats had garnered a net

Continued on Page 2, Column 5

ELECTED TO PRESIDENCY AND VICE PRESIDENCY

Franklin D. Roosevelt — C. Perskie
Harry S. Truman — Chase Statler

## ROOSEVELT STRONG IN WAR VOTE TALLY

### Partial Count of Ballots of Armed Forces Increases President's Majority

By CHARLES GRUTZNER Jr.

The majority given to President Roosevelt by civilian voters who went to the polls throughout the nation yesterday was increased by the count of war ballots marked, some of them as long as two months ago, by members of the armed forces in camps here and in far-flung theatres of operations.

The decisiveness of the President's victory over Governor Dewey removed the possibility that the outcome of the election might hinge on the soldier vote in some of the eleven States that delayed counting their war ballots, but partial returns from States that counted their war ballots yesterday made it clear that the support of the men and women in the armed forces would be a strong factor in building up the final majority of their Commander in Chief.

A breakdown of the vote into civilian and war ballots was slow in coming in from nearly all of the thirty-seven States that counted their soldier vote yesterday, because election officials were concerned chiefly with transmitting

Continued on Page 4, Column 2

## New York for Roosevelt; Wagner Re-elected Senator

By JAMES A. HAGERTY

For the sixth consecutive time, four times as a candidate for President and twice as a candidate for Governor, President Roosevelt carried his home State of New York in yesterday's election and won its forty-seven electoral votes. With 3,609 of the 3,700 election districts in New York City and with 4,978 of the 5,421 election districts outside New York City reporting, President Roosevelt had an actual lead over Governor Dewey, his Republican opponent, of 300,831 and a plurality of about 283,000 for the President in the State was indicated.

Returns from 3,609 election districts out of 3,700 in New York City gave Dewey 1,240,216, Roosevelt 1,966,539. This is an actual plurality of 726,273 and an indicated plurality of 743,700 for Roosevelt.

Returns from 4,978 election districts out of 5,421 outside New York City gave Dewey 1,585,771, Roosevelt 1,160,329. This is an actual plurality of 425,442 and an indicated plurality of 460,785 for Dewey.

Re-elected in the sweep for the President was United States Senator Robert F. Wagner, who defeated Secretary of State Thomas J. Curran by a plurality probably greater than that for Mr. Roosevelt. Also elected was Associate Judge of the Court of Appeals Marvin R. Dye, who defeated John Van Voorhis, Republican. The President, Senator Harry S. Truman, candidate for Vice President, Senator Wagner and Mr. Dye, all Democrats, also were nominees of the American Labor and Liberal parties.

Returns from 3,566 election districts out of 3,700 in New York City gave Curran 1,183,020, Wagner 1,957,026. This is an actual plurality of 774,006, and an indicated plurality of 802,900 for Wagner.

Returns from 4,797 of 5,421 election districts outside of New York City gave Curran 1,468,965, Wagner 1,086,736. This is an actual plurality of 382,249, and an indicated plurality of 433,680 for Curran.

Both Houses of the State Legislature remain Republican. Among the greatest upsets in the State was the defeat of former Mayor Rolland B. Marvin of Syracuse, Republican candidate for State Senator in the Forty-third Senatorial District, by Richard P. Byrne, Democratic and American Labor party nominee. On incomplete returns, Senator John J. Dunnigan, Democratic leader of the

Continued on Page 6, Column 4

## DEWEY STATEMENT ADMITS HIS DEFEAT

### Candidate Concedes Loss of Election at 3:12 A. M. and Congratulates Victor

Gov. Thomas E. Dewey, Republican candidate for President, conceded defeat at 3:12 o'clock this morning.

His statement was made at Republican National Headquarters in the Hotel Roosevelt, where both he and Herbert Brownell Jr., chairman of the National Committee, earlier had refused comment on the growing indication of a lopsided electrical college vote for his Democratic opponent, President Franklin D. Roosevelt.

Mr. Dewey said:

It is clear that Mr. Roosevelt has been re-elected for a fourth term, and every good American will whole-heartedly accept the will of the people.

I extend to President Roosevelt my hearty congratulations and my earnest hope that his next term will see speedy victory in the war, the establishment of lasting peace and the restoration of tranquillity among our peoples.

I am deeply grateful for the confidence expressed by so many million Americans for their labors in the campaign.

The Republican party emerges from the election revitalized and a great force for the good of the country and for the preservation of free government in America.

I am confident that all Americans will join me in a devout hope that in the years ahead Divine Providence will guide and protect the President of the United States.

President Roosevelt, from his Hyde Park home, acknowledged, at 3:28 o'clock this morning Gov-

Continued on Page 3, Column 2



## Roosevelt Leads as Davis Trails, In Mounting Pennsylvania Count

Special to THE NEW YORK TIMES.

PHILADELPHIA, Wednesday, Nov. 8—On the basis of partial returns from all but three of the sixty-seven counties in Pennsylvania, it appeared early that President Roosevelt for the third successive time had captured the State's electoral votes.

Swept on the Roosevelt wave, it appeared, was Representative Francis J. Myers in his race to unseat James J. Davis, 71-year-old Republican Senator who was elected first in 1932 and re-elected six years ago.

Whether the Roosevelt impetus would be sufficient to sweep into office the Democratic candidates for the five State offices remained in doubt. Reports in these instances, lagging far behind the count on the two top contests, were inconclusive.

With 6,013 of 8,202 precincts reporting, President Roosevelt was leading Governor Dewey, 1,282,392, to 1,238,986. Among the returns were all the 1,338 precincts in this city where the President gained a lead of 117,000.

The returns showed that once again the soft coal miners in western Pennsylvania and the anthracite miners in the East repudiated John L. Lewis, president of the United Mine Workers of America, by turning in thumping pluralities for Mr. Roosevelt.

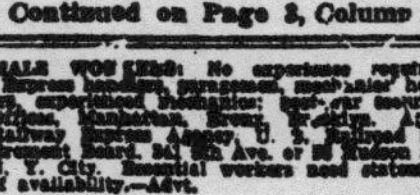

On the other hand, with less than half the precincts reporting and Governor Dewey reducing the President's lead, Republican leaders were hoping that late returns and a fair share of the soldier vote, to be counted on Nov. 22, would mean victory for the party in the State.

Although the President seemed

Continued on Page 8, Column 4

## DEWEY CONCEDES

### His Action Comes as Roosevelt Leads in 33 States

### BIG ELECTORAL VOTE

### Late Returns in Seesaw Battles May Push Total Beyond 400

By ARTHUR KROCK

Franklin Delano Roosevelt, who broke more than a century-old tradition in 1940 when he was elected to a third term as President, made another political record yesterday when he was chosen for a fourth term by a heavy electoral but much narrower popular majority over Thomas E. Dewey, Governor of New York.

At 3:15 A. M. Governor Dewey conceded Mr. Roosevelt's re-election, sending his best wishes by radio, to which the President quickly responded with an appreciative telegram.

Early this morning Mr. Roosevelt was leading in mounting returns in thirty-three States with a total of 391 electoral votes and in half a dozen more a trend was developing that could increase this figure to more than 400. Governor Dewey was ahead in fifteen States with 140 electoral votes, but some were see-sawing away from him and back again. Typical of these was Wisconsin, where he overtook the President's lead about 2 A. M.; Nevada, where Mr. Roosevelt passed him at about the same time, and Missouri.

In the contests for seats in Congress, the Democrats had shown gains of 11 to 20 in the House of Representatives, assuring that party's continued control of this branch. In the Senate the net of losses and gains appeared to be an addition of one Republican to the Senate, which would give that party twenty-eight members—far short of the forty-nine necessary to a majority. A surprise was the indicated defeat of the veteran Pennsylvania Republican, Senator James J. Davis.

**Mrs. Luce's Opponent Concedes**

The Congressional races were featured by a mass Democratic attempt, in which the President and Vice President Henry A. Wallace personally participated, to unseat Representative Clare Boothe Luce of Connecticut. But shortly after 3 A. M., following a night in which the lead had swung back and forth, her election was conceded by her opponent, Miss Margaret Connors. Some hours before, to his neighbors at Hyde Park, the President had expressed rejoicing over Mrs. Luce's "defeat." Her success is the vitriol in the Democratic honey.

Despite the great general victories by the Democrats, the popular vote will evidently show a huge minority protest against a fourth term for the President. Tabulations by the press associations indicated that the disparity between the ballots cast for the two candidates will be so small that a change of several hundred thousand votes in the key States, distributed in a certain way, would have reversed the electoral majority. At 4:40 A. M. The Associated Press reported 16,387,999 for Mr. Roosevelt and 14,235,051 for Mr. Dewey from more than one-third of the country's election districts. This ratio, if carried through, would leave only about 3,000,000 votes between the candidates.

One of the most interesting struggles for the Presidency was that in Wisconsin, where Mr. Dewey took an early lead, lost it and regained it again. Wisconsin is the State where the late Wendell L. Willkie made his stand for renomination, posing the issue of

Continued on Page 2, Column 3

"All the News That's Fit to Print"

NEWS INDEX, PAGE 41, THIS SECTION

The New York Times

Copyright, 1945, by The New York Times Company.

LATE CITY EDITION
Fair with gentle to moderate winds today.
Temperatures Yesterday—Max., 34; Min., 29
Sunrise, 8:16 A. M.; Sunset, 6:00 P. M.

Section 1

VOL. XCIV..No. 31,774. Entered as Second-Class Matter, Postoffice, New York, N. Y. NEW YORK, SUNDAY, JANUARY 21, 1945. Including Magazine and Book Sections. TEN CENTS New York City and Suburban Area (15c Elsewhere)

# ROOSEVELT SWORN IN FOR FOURTH TERM; EXTENDS GOOD NEIGHBOR POLICY TO WORLD; RUSSIANS GAIN 25 MILES; FRENCH OPEN DRIVE

## TILSIT IS CAPTURED

### A Second Soviet Army Enters East Prussia in South, Foe Says

### SILESIAN ENTRY SEEN

### 6-Mile Dent Made, Nazis Assert—Chief Strides Taken on Berlin Road

By The Associated Press.

LONDON, Sunday, Jan. 21—The Red Army, killing or capturing 90,000 Germans in a week of its lightning offensive across Poland, yesterday forced the Warta River in a twenty-five mile advance, and the German radio said early today that other Soviet spearheads to the southwest had crossed the embattled Silesian frontier 200 miles from Berlin.

Simultaneously, other Soviet forces invading German East Prussia to a depth of forty-six miles in a seventeen-mile advance toppled the great stronghold of Tilsit and reached to within forty-five miles of Koenigsberg, while another army coming up from the south reached the lower East Prussian frontier on a wide front.

Berlin said the Russians had crossed into southern East Prussia on a thirty-seven mile front in a great pincers movement that carried to within sixty-five miles of the Baltic behind Koenigsberg and which seemed aimed at lopping off that entire German province.

**Silesia Reported Invaded**

In eastern Slovakia the strongholds of Kosice, Presov and Bardejov fell, and the Russians also seized Nowy Sacz in southern Poland southeast of Cracow.

Berlin indicated that the crossing into Silesia, the "Ruhr of the East," was made by the Russians in the area of Namslau, six miles inside Silesia, twenty-seven miles east of Breslau, the provincial capital, and 200 miles southeast of Berlin.

The situation at the Silesian frontier is "critical," Berlin said, with schoolboys, business men, clerks and others of the Volkssturm, or Home Army, being thrown into the struggle to save Breslau—once considered a "safe city" by those who had fled there from much-bombed Berlin.

Even miners from the Silesian coal fields have been sent into the front line, Berlin said. "They marched all night in grim weather from their pits to take up positions in front of the Russians at dawn," the Berlin radio report said.

**Industrial Cities Being Flanked**

Moscow did not mention a crossing into Silesia, but said that Marshal Ivan S. Koneff's First Ukrainian Army had reached the frontier or was within five miles of it on a winding sixty-five-mile front from captured Mieleszyn, forty-five miles east of Breslau, down to occupied Lubliniec, strategic road junction thirty-two miles east of the German industrial city of Oppeln.

Koneff's troops steadily were outflanking the rich southeastern corner of Silesia, and in fifteen-mile advances had rolled to within nine miles northeast of Dabrowa, Polish Silesian coal center, by the capture of Lazy. The seizure of Lazy also put this Russian spearhead within twenty miles of the German frontier where are clustered the German industrial cities of Beuthen, Hindenburg and Gleiwitz.

A German commentator, Col. Ernst von Hammer, in explaining the steady Russian strides westward, said Russian artillery fire was "murderous."

The Soviet communiqué said that between Jan. 12, when the big winter offensive got under way, and Jan. 19, the three Soviet armies in Poland alone had killed 65,000 Germans and captured

Continued on Page 13, Column 1



## British Submarines Sink 84 Craft in East

By The Associated Press.

LONDON, Jan. 20—The Admiralty announced tonight that British submarines in Japanese-controlled waters had sunk eighty-four supply ships.

Many of the ships were small, the communiqué said. Many were carrying fuel and other supplies to Burma and enemy-held islands.

The submarines also bombarded shore installations in several instances.

The latest bag brought the total kills by British submarines in Japan's theatre to more than 200 craft in the last six months. This figure does not include ships hit by gunfire, driven ashore or otherwise damaged. Five more ships were damaged in the latest series of operations, the Admiralty said.

## SIXTH ARMY SPLITS JAPANESE ON LUZON

### Overruns 37-Mile Stretch of Vital North-South Highway, Smashes Enemy in North

By LINDESAY PARROTT

By Wireless to The New York Times.

ALLIED HEADQUARTERS, on Leyte, Sunday, Jan. 21—Striking eastward from their Luzon wedge Gen. Douglas MacArthur's Sixth Army troops have occupied a continuous thirty-seven-mile stretch of the strategic north-south highway from Panaqui in the south to Sison in an action that, today's communiqué said, practically cut the enemy forces in two.

Firm possession of the highway virtually isolates Japanese forces in the western mountains, the Baguio district and in northern Luzon, severing their only feasible road communication with enemy troops to the southward of our salient.

While the eastern road leading from Manila to the northern coast of Luzon at Aparri along the wide Cagayan Valley still remains open, the only route through which the Japanese in the western hills can reach that thoroughfare is over narrow mountain trails. Nor can such Japanese troops as are grouped around the capital come to the assistance of their northern forces without facing the same difficult if not impossible task.

**A Principal Objective Attained**

Thus, according to the communiqué, one of the principal objectives for which the Lingayen landings were made—the severance of the two large bodies of the enemy in Luzon—now has been accomplished.

Northward of the long stretch of highway now in our hands enemy resistance has crumbled after a series of vicious but uncoordinated counter-attacks into which the Japanese flung tanks and artillery. These attacks, launched on Thursday and during

Continued on Page 3, Column 2

## RHINE PUSH BEGUN

### French Strike as Enemy Forces 7th Army Back 5 Miles in Alsace

### BRITISH GAIN 3 MILES

### U. S. 1st and 3d Armies Further Compress the Belgian Salient

By The Associated Press.

SUPREME HEADQUARTERS, Allied Expeditionary Force, Paris, Jan. 20—The French First Army struck a surprise blow for Alsace's liberation today with a new offensive on a twenty-five-mile front that rolled up three-mile gains seventy miles south of where American comrades-in-arms battled to save the imperiled capital of Strasbourg.

The French jumped into the mounting battle, with the fate of Alsace and Strasbourg in the balance, after tank-led German troops drove United States Seventh Army lines back five miles and threatened to undermine American positions in the northeast corner of France.

**French Surprise Germans**

The assault, rolling out under the cover of a blinding snowstorm from the Vosges eastward to the Rhine in the Mulhouse area, achieved complete surprise and still was pressing forward tonight against that tough German core known as the Colmar pocket from which the enemy was menacing Strasbourg from the south.

At the opposite end of the 300-mile western front, the British Second Army ran into enemy tanks for the first time, but plowed on three miles into western Germany and the Netherlands appendix, seizing at least six more towns.

The British cut off a German area five miles by three miles with a pincers movement of two armored columns northeast of Sittard. One British unit attacked eastward from Echt and the other pushed north from Hoengen until the junction was made. More than 400 prisoners were taken by the British.

The American First Army was methodically tightening the screws on St. Vith, the Belgian highway and rail center four miles from the Reich border through which the Germans must retire.

**Third Nears Vianden**

The American Third Army was driving in from the west against stout resistance, and to the east was battling over northern Luxembourg's snow-clad hills within three miles of Vianden, on the Reich border where Hitler's legions swept across in the Ardennes offensive.

A dispatch from the front said there were signs that the Germans were withdrawing into the Sieg-

Continued on Page 17, Column 1

FRANKLIN D. ROOSEVELT TAKING PRESIDENTIAL OATH FOR FOURTH TIME

Repeating the constitutional pledge after Chief Justice Harlan F. Stone (obscured by flag at left) on the south portico of the White House. Secretary of Senate Edwin Halsey is on extreme left and Col. James Roosevelt, the President's son, on right.

Associated Press Wirephoto

## ALLIES SIGN TRUCE WITH HUNGARIANS

### Voroshiloff Acts for All in Pact With Provisional Body—U. S., Britain Represented

By The United Press.

LONDON, Jan. 20—Representatives of the Provisional National Government of Hungary, formed less than a month ago in Debrecen, signed an armistice agreement with the United States, the Soviet Union and Great Britain in Moscow today, the Moscow radio said.

The three major powers acted in the name of all the United Nations at war with Hungary, Moscow said. The Czechoslovak and Yugoslav Ambassadors witnessed the signing. The text of the armistice will be published separately, the broadcast added. It gave no hint of the terms.

W. Averell Harriman, United States Ambassador to Moscow, was chief American representative at the negotiations, which began Thursday. His assistants included Maj. Gen. John R. Deane. John Balfour, British Chargé d'Affaires,

Continued on Page 14, Column 1

## Shivering Thousands Stamp In the Snow at Inauguration

By BERTRAM D. HULEN

Special to The New York Times.

WASHINGTON, Jan. 20—An overcast sky parted and a patch of blue appeared overhead just as President Roosevelt took his position at the speaker's stand on the south portico of the White House at noon today for his fourth inauguration as the Chief Magistrate of the country.

An overnight storm had left a light fall of snow, which glistened on the ground and on the leaves of the near-by magnolia trees. The thermometer stood at one degree above freezing but, unlike all others, the President stood without an overcoat.

Bareheaded and attired in a dark business suit, Mr. Roosevelt looked down upon the guests who stood below him on the grounds of the White House and beyond to Constitution Avenue, where several thousand of the public had gathered to witness the ceremony from afar.

Farther on and slightly to the left, the President looked to the Washington Monument, and directly before him in the far distance to the Jefferson Memorial, glistening in the reflected light of the snow.

By his side stood Col. James

Continued on Page 27, Column 7

## PERKINS TO REMAIN LABOR SECRETARY

### Cabinet Changes Limited to Commerce Post, Reported Assigned to Wallace

By JOSEPH A. LOFTUS

Special to The New York Times.

WASHINGTON, Jan. 20—Miss Frances Perkins will remain as Secretary of Labor, it was learned today, and speculation on fourth-term Cabinet changes was confined to the post of Secretary of Commerce.

Official Washington was confident that Henry Wallace, who retired as Vice President, would continue in a high post, and his close associates say that he will be Secretary of Commerce.

Friends of Jesse H. Jones, who is Secretary of Commerce as well as directing head of the Reconstruction Finance Corporation and its several subsidiary financial agencies, insists that he has had no word that he is to be relieved of any of his duties.

It is reported that Mr. Jones would retain his directorship of the RFC and related agencies, which have been the basis of his authority.

Those who discount the information that Mr. Wallace will be named Secretary of Commerce ground their position on the known conflict of views between Secretary Jones and the former Vice

Continued on Page 26, Column 4

## TRUMAN HASTENS TO CALL MOTHER

### 'Now You Behave Yourself' She Cautions, After He Hitch-hikes to Capitol

By C. P. TRUSSELL

Special to The New York Times.

WASHINGTON, Jan. 20—Vice President Harry S. Truman slipped away from the post-inaugural White House luncheon forty minutes ahead of time today, hitch-hiked a ride to Capitol Hill and telephoned his mother, Mrs. Martha Truman, who is 91 years old, at Grandview, Mo. She told him she had "heard it all over the radio," referring to the induction ceremony, and admonished him:

"Now you behave yourself!"

After a brief conversation Mr. Truman went to work clearing up the mail he had received as a Senator. Atop one of two heaps of correspondence was a telegram from five farmer neighbors in Jackson County, Mo. Addressed to "Harry S. Truman, Vice President, United States," it read:

"Dear Harry: When you came home from World War I to the home farm you sold your mules and saddle horse. We all knew you were going somewhere. Congratulations."

It was signed by Charles D. Davis, John Slaughter, Ray W. Moore, R. D. Barrey and John H. Perkins.

**Missourians on Hand**

Missouri felt close to Harry Truman today, and many of its citizens were on hand to see him take the second highest office in the land. A group moved to his office and had steaming coffee and sandwiches in an adjoining room while the new Vice President signed mail and joined in conversation now and then when snatches of it reached his ears.

One friend, Ted Mark of Kansas

Continued on Page 27, Column 5

## STONE GIVES OATH

### President Then Pledges Victory for Allies and 'a Durable Peace'

### RULES ISOLATION OUT

### Solemn Ceremony Lasts 15 Minutes—Truman Is Sworn by Wallace

*The text of the inaugural address is on Page 26.*

By JOHN H. CRIDER

Special to The New York Times.

WASHINGTON, Jan. 20—Franklin Delano Roosevelt, nearing his sixty-third birthday, stood today on the south portico of the White House bareheaded and without an outside coat, despite raw, wintry weather, to become the nation's first fourth-term President.

It was the simplest inauguration on record, and the crowd, which stretched out over the snow-covered south grounds of the White House and into the Ellipse beyond, was the smallest ever to witness such a ceremony.

In the shortest inauguration address he has ever given, Mr. Roosevelt drew a distinction between the perfection for which we would strive in the peace to come and the something less than perfection we would achieve in the immediate future.

He took a philosophical view of history, noting its ups and downs, but quoted his old Groton schoolmaster, the late Dr. Endicott Peabody, that despite its valleys and peaks "the trend of civilization itself is forever upward."

President Roosevelt took the oath of office from Chief Justice Harlan F. Stone about two minutes after Harry S. Truman of Missouri had been sworn in as Vice President by his predecessor, Henry A. Wallace.

The sun of high noon barely broke through an overcast sky to shed a half light on the historic scene of the thirty-ninth inauguration in the country's history.

**Sums Up the Lessons**

The President, in his address, summed up the lessons learned by the country in recent arduous years as follows:

"We must live as men, not as ostriches, nor as dogs in the manger."

After thus burying "isolationism," so far as his Administration was concerned, he held forth the prospect of "a human community," declaring:

"We have learned to be citizens of the world."

And then, as if to extend the "Good Neighbor" policy around the world, he added:

"We have learned the simple truth, as Emerson said, that 'the only way to have a friend is to be one.'"

The President stressed, more heavily than any other passage in his address, that it was "at a fearful cost" that we had learned the lessons of recent years. Many standing there before him on the thin blanket of snow were thinking of the gigantic battles in snow and ice raging on European battlefields at that very moment.

**Calls for a "Better Life"**

Another phrase given special emphasis in the unusually slow-spoken and carefully enunciated address were the words "for all our fellow-men," where Mr. Roosevelt expressed hope for a "better life" for everyone, in the final passage of his address. His words were carried by loudspeakers to the most distant of his immediate audience and to radio listeners throughout the country and the world.

Although Mr. Roosevelt's demeanor during the ceremony was as solemn as the moment in his-

Continued on Page 26, Column 2



## War News Summarized

SUNDAY, JANUARY 21, 1945

The Red Army, in another day of great triumphs, swept twenty-five miles along the highway from Warsaw to reach 100 miles west of the fallen Polish capital, seized the important East Prussian industrial city and stronghold of Tilsit and, according to German reports, advanced to within 200 miles of Berlin in its South Poland drive.

Berlin reported that Russian troops had penetrated southern East Prussia, reaching within seventy-five miles of Danzig in their apparent drive to pinch off the Junkers province. The enemy also acknowledged that the Russians were fighting in the Namslau area six miles inside German Silesia, after having gained the border in western Poland on a wide front. Farther south, still other Russian armies seized four more strongholds, including Nowy Sacz, as they pursued the enemy across southern Poland and eastern Slovakia. [All the foregoing, 1:1; map, P. 13.]

As the German threat to Strasbourg, capital of Alsace, increased, the French First Army launched an offensive seventy miles south of the battle lines along which the American Seventh Army was striving to guard the city. The French advanced three miles on a twenty-five-mile front in their drive intended to erase the Colmar pocket, from which the enemy menaced Strasbourg from the south. North of Strasbourg, German troops forced back our troops five miles.

The British Second Army, meanwhile, advanced another three miles into western Germany on the other end of the western front. The American First Army maintained its pressure on St. Vith and the American Third Army advanced over northern Luxembourg's snow-swept hills to within three miles of Vianden on the German border. [All the foregoing 1:3; maps, P. 17.]

In the Philippines, our troops isolated Japanese forces in the western mountains of northern Luzon from those in the Manila area when they cut the only feasible enemy line of communication by occupying a continuous thirty-seven-mile stretch of a strategic north-south highway. [1:2; map, P. 3.]

Aerial photographs showed that during the Superfortress raid on the Osaka-Kobe industrial area of Japan on Friday at least 315 direct bomb hits were scored in a 4,000-foot radius of the big Kawasaki aircraft plant, all but completely destroying the engine factory. [5:1.]

The new Ledo-Burma Road was opened as a supply route to China following the capture of Wanting. [1:6-7.]

An armistice was signed in Moscow between the representatives of the Provisional National Government of Hungary and the Soviet Union, the United States and Great Britain. The terms are expected to be made public today. [1:4.]

President Roosevelt, inaugurated as the nation's first fourth-term Chief Executive, told the world that "we shall work for a just and durable peace as today we work and fight for total victory in war. We can and we will achieve such a peace." [1:8.]

## 6,300 Canadian Soldiers AWOL Of 15,600 Called to Go Overseas

By P. J. PHILIP

By Wireless to The New York Times.

OTTAWA, Jan. 20—Out of 15,600 draftees designated for overseas service and sent on embarkation leave, 6,300 have not yet reported back for duty, National Defense Headquarters revealed today.

Their action has not affected the steady dispatch of reinforcements overseas, defense officials said. In the official account of the situation Defense Headquarters said that already more than 8,300 draftees, recruited for home defense, had been debarked in Britain under the new order in addition to the normal quota of volunteer reinforcements.

The arrival of these troops, the official statement said, has brought the normal reinforcement program fully up to the strength planned for overseas to date, while the special program arranged for the use of national defense draftees overseas also is progressing according to schedule.

In so far as the actual dispatch of reinforcements was concerned, the Defense Department said that the promise made in Parliament last month had been kept and that the front-line needs would be fully maintained.

The other side of the picture, however, is admittedly discouraging. Of the 15,600 draftees who received embarkation leave during the Christmas and New Year holi-

Continued on Page 22, Column 3



## New Road From India to China Is Opened by Trucks and Jeeps

By The United Press.

CHUNGKING, China, Sunday, Jan. 21—Central Chinese News Agency dispatches reported today the opening of the new Myitkyina-Tengyueh supply route between India and China and the recapture of Wanting, last Japanese stronghold on the old Burma Road.

A news agency dispatch from Lungling said that Chinese forces on the Sino-Burma border had recaptured the Burma Road town of Wanting. The defeated Wanting garrison is retreating in the direction of Lashio, to the south, with the Chinese in hot pursuit, the dispatch said.

The capture of Wanting, taken and lost again by the Chinese several weeks ago, eliminated the last pocket of Japanese resistance along the old land route to India through North Burma, closed since the Japanese invasion of Burma in 1942.

A Chinese news agency dispatch from Mangshih in Yunnan said the first convoy to China had passed over the newly constructed highway between Myitkyina in Burma and Tengyueh in China and was due at Paoshan today. Composed of nearly 100 American trucks and jeeps, the convoy traversed Burma along the Ledo Road route built by American engineers and assembled at Myitkyina last week, waiting for the new link with Tengyueh to be completed.

The Myitkyina-Tengyueh road was designed as an alternate route to the regular Ledo-Burma Road

Continued on Page 7, Column 3

"All the News That's Fit to Print"

# The New York Times.

Copyright, 1945, by The New York Times Company.

LATE CITY EDITION
Clearing and warm today.
Fair, continued warm tomorrow.
Temperatures Yesterday—Max., 74; Min., 54
Sunrise today, 6:21 A. M.; Sunset, 7:33 P. M.

VOL. XCIV...No. 31,856. Entered as Second-Class Matter, Postoffice, New York, N. Y. NEW YORK, FRIDAY, APRIL 13, 1945. THREE CENTS IN NEW YORK CITY

# PRESIDENT ROOSEVELT IS DEAD; TRUMAN TO CONTINUE POLICIES; 9TH CROSSES ELBE, NEARS BERLIN

## U. S. AND RED ARMIES DRIVE TO MEET

### Americans Across the Elbe in Strength Race Toward Russians Who Have Opened Offensive From Oder

### WEIMAR TAKEN, RUHR POCKET SLASHED

### Third Army Reported 19 Miles From Czechoslovak Border—British Drive Deeper in the North, Seizing Celle—Canadians Freeing Holland

By DREW MIDDLETON
By Wireless to THE NEW YORK TIMES.

PARIS, April 12—Thousands of tanks and a half million doughboys of the United States First, Third and Ninth Armies are racing through the heart of the Reich on a front of 150 miles, threatening Berlin, Leipzig and the last citadels of the Nazi power.

The Second Armored Division of the Ninth Army has crossed the Elbe River in force and is striking eastward toward Berlin, whose outskirts lie less than sixty miles to the east, according to reports from the front. [A report quoted by The United Press placed the Americans less than fifty miles from the capital.] Beyond Berlin the First White Russian Army has crossed the Oder on a wide front and a junction between the western and eastern Allies is not far off.

[The Moscow radio reported that heavy battles were raging west of the Oder before Berlin, indicating that Marshal Gregory K. Zhukoff had launched his drive toward the Reich's capital. The Soviet communiqué announced further progress by the Red Army forces in and around Vienna.]

Paris is wild with excitement tonight. A special edition of the newspaper France-Soir carries a report by the radio station "Voice of America" that places American forces fifteen and five-eighths miles from Berlin after an airborne landing that had linked up with Lieut. Gen. William H. Simpson's forces advancing eastward from the Elbe. This would put American forces only seventy-five miles from the Red Army vanguard.

**No Confirmation at Headquarters**

There was no confirmation of this report at Allied Supreme Headquarters, which by its own admission was thirty-six hours behind developments on some sectors of the front.

Resistance was continuing only on the northern and southern flanks. The center had burst wide open. Weimar fell to Lieut. Gen. George S. Patton's infantry, and reports from the front said Erfurt also had been cleared. Schweinfurt and Heilbronn, two German bastions on the south, had fallen to United States Seventh Army forces, who were driving on Bamberg, while farther north Third Army forces were about thirty-five miles from the Czechoslovak frontier in the area east of Coburg.

[The German radio reported American Third Army forces at Lichtenberg, nineteen miles from the Czechoslovak border, The United Press said.]

The offensives to liberate the Netherlands and reduce the Ruhr

Continued on Page 12, Column 2

## OUR OKINAWA GUNS DOWN 118 PLANES

### Japanese Fliers Start 'Suicide' Attacks on Fleet, Sink a Destroyer, Hit Other Ships

By W. H. LAWRENCE
By Wireless to THE NEW YORK TIMES.

GUAM, Friday, April 13—Japanese attempting to halt the American march to Tokyo, have started "desperate, suicidal" aerial attacks upon our ships and men in the Okinawa area, losing 118 planes on Thursday alone, Fleet Admiral Chester W. Nimitz announced today.

The Japanese succeeded in sinking a destroyer and damaging several other surface units, the communiqué said. All of the damaged vessels remained in action.

It was the first time that the Navy had revealed the suicidal nature of the Japanese air missions against our ships and men. The Japanese radio has been saying that this type of assault was being carried on by a "special attack corps" known in Japanese as "kamakazi," which, translated literally, means "divine wind."

**Attack at Low Levels**

The Japanese fliers launched their attacks upon our ships and men at a high speed and from low levels, diving directly into a ship or troop concentration to explode their bombs as they crashed.

There was no official estimate of the total number of enemy aircraft engaged in the Okinawa area attack other than the report of the 118 enemy planes destroyed.

Admiral Nimitz reported that the attacks began early on April 12 (Eastern Longitude time) with seven enemy planes shot down during the morning in the vicinity of the Hagushi beaches.

The tempo of the attack was stepped up in the afternoon as the Japanese bore in on our ships in wave after wave. Admiral Nimitz said that ships' guns, carrier aircraft and shore-based anti-aircraft shot down 111 of the attackers.

The revelation of the suicidal Japanese air attacks was the highlight of Admiral Nimitz' regular morning communiqué, which also disclosed the identity of two Marine and two Army divisions that have gone into action on Okinawa. These included the Twenty-seventh Army Division, formed from New York National Guard units, which are seeing action for the first time since the Saipan campaign and previously had engaged in the Gilbert Islands assault. It is com-

Continued on Page 13, Column 3

## *Army Leaders See Reich End at Hand*

By The Associated Press.

WASHINGTON, April 12—High Army officials told Senators today that the end of organized fighting in Germany probably would come within a few days.

Describing the pell-mell dash of American Armies across Germany, General Staff officers expressed the opinion to members of the Senate Military Committee that a collapse of German arms was imminent.

Those who attended said the army chiefs declared that they were so sure of the results that orders had been drawn for a drastic reduction in shipments of durable equipment to Europe.

Franklin Delano Roosevelt
1882-1945

## SECURITY PARLEY WON'T BE DELAYED

### State Department Urges That World Be Shown We Plan No Changes in Policy

By JAMES B. RESTON
Special to THE NEW YORK TIMES.

WASHINGTON, April 12—The United Nations Security Conference will open in San Francisco on April 25, despite the death of President Roosevelt, Secretary of State Edward R. Stettinius Jr. announced tonight.

Mr. Stettinius said that he had been authorized by President Harry Truman to make this announcement after a meeting of the Cabinet at the White House.

Most of the overseas delegations to the San Francisco conference have either arrived in this country or are now on their way, but while this was said to have been a factor in the decision to proceed with the conference, State Department officials urged that every attempt be made to give immediate evidence to the world that President Roosevelt's foreign policy would be sustained by the new Administration.

President Roosevelt had planned to address the San Francisco conference. His interest in an international organization of nations to maintain peace and security had gone back to his service in the Wilson Administration, when he sat in the gallery of the Senate and listened to the debate that resulted in the rejection of the League of Nations Covenant. He had expressed to friends his desire to participate in the San Francisco conference and to see the United States enter the new league during his term in office.

The sudden elevation of Presi-

Continued on Page 2, Column 1

## War News Summarized

FRIDAY, APRIL 13, 1945

President Roosevelt died yesterday afternoon, suddenly and unexpectedly. He was stricken with a massive cerebral hemorrhage at Warm Springs, Ga., on the eve of his greatest military and diplomatic successes—the impending fall of Berlin and the opening of the San Francisco Conference to set up a World Security Organization that would make the world free from martial and economic strife [1:7-8.]

Mr. Roosevelt had been sitting in front of the fireplace of his Little White House, having gone to Warm Springs on March 30 for a three-week rest. About 2:15 Eastern war time he said, "I have a terrific headache," lost consciousness in a few moments and died at 4:35. He was 63 years old. [1:6.]

The tragic word spread quickly around the world. Expressions of sorrow poured in from all sections. [4:5.] American soldiers and sailors refused to believe the reports until there was no longer doubt that their Commander in Chief had gone. [4:2-3.]

Harry S. Truman was sworn in as President at 7:09 o'clock last night, and a few minutes later Mrs. Roosevelt left for Warm Springs. [1:7.] The new President immediately called a Cabinet meeting and declared that Mr. Roosevelt's policies would be continued, that the war would be carried on until Germany and Japan surrendered unconditionally and that the San Francisco Conference would open April 25 as scheduled. [1:3.]

Some 500,000 American soldiers of the Third and Ninth Armies, and thousands of tanks, sped along a 150-mile front toward Berlin and Leipzig. The Ninth, surging across the Elbe, according to delayed reports was less than fifty miles from the German capital and 115 from the Russians along the Oder. The Third Army captured Weimar, home of the late German Republic, and was twenty-three miles below Leipzig, with the First closing a pincers from the north. [1:1-2; map P. 2.]

The Moscow radio reported that the Red Army was waging fierce battles east of Berlin, indicating resumption of the drive on that city. Elsewhere Russian troops scored wide gains and cut the last escape railroad from Vienna. [13:1.]

Open cities were ruled out and every German was ordered by Himmler to fight to the death, although Goebbels said "the war cannot last much longer." [12:6-7.]

The Ninth Air Force destroyed at least 117 more German planes yesterday. [11:8.]

In Italy the Eighth Army advanced along a thirty-mile front toward Bologna and the Po Valley; the Fifth Army also made good gains and was eleven miles from La Spezia. [13:8, with map.]

Japanese planes resumed their suicide attacks on American ships off Okinawa, sinking a destroyer and damaging several other vessels. One hundred and eighteen enemy planes were shot down. [1:2.] The Americal Division invaded Bohol, last of the enemy-held central Philippines. [18:6.] The B-29 attack on Koriyama, 110 miles north of Tokyo, set a new Superfortress distance record. [18:2.]

Secretary of State Stettinius and Secretary of War Stimson, denouncing Germany's "steadily increasing" mistreatment of American prisoners, said those responsible would be brought to justice. [13:6-7.]

Clashes between Right and Left wing elements in Iran were reported from Moscow. [13:2.]

## LAST WORDS: 'I HAVE TERRIFIC HEADACHE'

### Roosevelt Was Posing for Artist When Hemorrhage Struck —He Died in Bedroom

By The Associated Press.

WARM SPRINGS, Ga., April 12—President Franklin D. Roosevelt's last words were:

"I have a terrific headache."

He spoke them to Comdr. Howard G. Bruenn, naval physician.

Mr. Roosevelt was sitting in front of a fireplace in the Little White House here atop Pine Mountain when what was described as a massive cerebral hemorrhage struck him.

The President's Negro valet, Arthur Prettyman, and a Filipino messboy carried him to his bedroom. He was unconscious at the end. It came without pain.

Dr. Bruenn said that he saw the President this morning and he was in excellent spirits at 9:30 A. M.

"At 1 o'clock," Dr. Bruenn added, "he was sitting in a chair while sketches were being made of him by an artist. He suddenly complained of a very severe occipital headache (back of the head).

"Within a very few minutes he lost consciousness. He was seen by me at 1:30 P. M., fifteen minutes after the episode had started.

"He did not regain consciousness, and he died at 3:35 P. M. (Georgia time)."

The artist sketching Mr. Roosevelt was N. Robbins of 520 West 139th Street, New York.

Only others present in the cottage were Comdr. George Fox, White House pharmacist and long an attendant on the President; William D. Hassett, Presidential secretary; Miss Grace Tully, con-

Continued on Page 4, Column 2

## END COMES SUDDENLY AT WARM SPRINGS

### Even His Family Unaware of Condition as Cerebral Stroke Brings Death to Nation's Leader at 63

### ALL CABINET MEMBERS TO KEEP POSTS

### Funeral to Be at White House Tomorrow, With Burial at Hyde Park Home—Impact of News Tremendous

By ARTHUR KROCK
Special to THE NEW YORK TIMES.

WASHINGTON, April 12—Franklin Delano Roosevelt, War President of the United States and the only Chief Executive in history who was chosen for more than two terms, died suddenly and unexpectedly at 4:35 P. M. today at Warm Springs, Ga., and the White House announced his death at 5:48 o'clock. He was 63.

The President, stricken by a cerebral hemorrhage, passed from unconsciousness to death on the eighty-third day of his fourth term and in an hour of high triumph. The armies and fleets under his direction as Commander in Chief were at the gates of Berlin and the shores of Japan's home islands as Mr. Roosevelt died, and the cause he represented and led was nearing the conclusive phase of success.

Less than two hours after the official announcement, Harry S. Truman of Missouri, the Vice President, took the oath as the thirty-second President. The oath was administered by the Chief Justice of the United States, Harlan F. Stone, in a one-minute ceremony at the White House. Mr. Truman immediately let it be known that Mr. Roosevelt's Cabinet is remaining in office at his request, and that he had authorized Secretary of State Edward R. Stettinius Jr. to proceed with plans for the United Nations Conference on international organization at San Francisco, scheduled to begin April 25. A report was circulated that he leans somewhat to the idea of a coalition Cabinet, but this is unsubstantiated.

**Funeral Tomorrow Afternoon**

It was disclosed by the White House that funeral services for Mr. Roosevelt would take place at 4 P. M. (E. W. T.) Saturday in the East Room of the Executive Mansion. The Rev. Angus Dun, Episcopal Bishop of Washington; the Rev. Howard S. Wilkinson of St. Thomas's Church in Washington and the Rev. John G. McGee of St. John's in Washington will conduct the services.

The body will be interred at Hyde Park, N. Y., Sunday, with the Rev. George W. Anthony of St. James Church officiating. The time has not yet been fixed.

Jonathan Daniels, White House secretary, said Mr. Roosevelt's body would not lie in state. He added that, in view of the limited size of the East Room, which holds only about 200 persons, the list of those attending the funeral services would be limited to high Government officials, representatives of the membership of both

Continued on Page 3, Column 2

## TRUMAN IS SWORN IN THE WHITE HOUSE

### Members of Cabinet on Hand as Chief Justice Stone Administers the Oath

By C. P. TRUSSELL
Special to THE NEW YORK TIMES.

WASHINGTON, April 12—Vice President Harry S. Truman of Missouri, standing erect, with his sharp features taut and looking straight ahead through his large, round glasses, became the thirty-second President of the United States in a ceremony lasting not more than a minute in the Cabinet Room of the White House at 7:09 o'clock tonight.

The oath was administered by Chief Justice Harlan F. Stone two hours and thirty-four minutes after the sudden death of President Roosevelt at Warm Springs. Mr. Truman had picked up a Bible from the end of the big Cabinet conference table, held it with his left hand and placed his right hand upon the upper cover. After repeating the oath, he bowed his head, lifted the Bible to his lips and kissed it.

Even before he had taken the oath Mr. Truman had asked President Roosevelt's Cabinet to continue in service. He also authorized Edward R. Stettinius Jr., Secretary of State, to announce that the United Nations Conference for International Organization would go on as scheduled.

To the newsmen at the White House he sent this word, through Stephen Early, press secretary:

"For the time being I prefer not to hold a press conference. It will be my effort to carry on as I believe the President would have done, and to that end I have asked the Cabinet to stay on with me."

Soon after he became President, Mr. Truman left the White House for the five-room Connecticut Avenue apartment where he has resided with Mrs. Truman and their 20-year-old daughter, Mary Margaret, for four years. He said he was "going home, to bed."

It was shortly after he had finished presiding over the Senate debate on the United States-Mexican Water Treaty late this afternoon that Mr. Truman received word from the White House of President Roosevelt's death. This was at about 5:15 P. M., a half hour before the news was made public. Reaching for his hat, he dashed out of the office, calling back to his staff that he was going to the White House.

Arriving at the White House, the

Continued on Page 3, Column 6

## *Byrnes May Take Post With Truman*

Special to THE NEW YORK TIMES.

WASHINGTON, April 12—James F. Byrnes, recently resigned as Director of War Mobilization and Reconversion, known to be one of President Truman's warmest friends in official Washington, is expected to be called to the White House for consultation, and possibly to take an important post in the Cabinet, in the immediate future.

President Truman's admiration of former Justice Byrnes is well known here. He undoubtedly would have been Mr. Truman's choice as a successor to Cordell Hull as Secretary of State.

HARRY S. TRUMAN

"All the News That's Fit to Print"

# The New York Times

LATE CITY EDITION

Mostly sunny today. Tomorrow rain, or snow changing to rain.

Temperature Range Today-Max.,47; Min.,28
Temperatures Yesterday—Max.,45; Min.,34
Full U. S. Weather Bureau Report, Page 47

VOL. XCVII..No. 32,917. Entered as Second-Class Matter. Postoffice, New York, N. Y. NEW YORK, TUESDAY, MARCH 9, 1948. Times Square, New York 18, N. Y. Telephone LAckawanna 4-1000 THREE CENTS IN NEW YORK CITY

# TRUMAN AND M'ARTHUR WILL ACCEPT NOMINATIONS FOR THE PRESIDENCY, THEY SAY, IF CHOSEN BY CONVENTIONS

## RUSSIA REPORTED URGING PARTITION IN PALESTINE NOW

### First Meeting of Powers Said to Have Heard Vigorous Appeal by Gromyko

### U. S. AIMS AT SETTLEMENT

### Both Countries Expected to Hold Individual Parleys With Jews and Arabs

By THOMAS J. HAMILTON

Special to The New York Times.

LAKE SUCCESS, N. Y., March 8—The Soviet Union is pressing for a prompt decision on steps to carry out the partition of Palestine while the United States still hopes that a settlement satisfactory to both Jews and Arabs can be worked out, it was learned tonight after the first meeting of the great powers on the question.

The meeting, attended by representatives of the United States, the Soviet Union, China and France, was held this morning in the Park Avenue office of Andrei A. Gromyko, Soviet Deputy Foreign Minister.

According to some accounts, both Mr. Gromyko and Warren R. Austin, United States representative, made it plain that they had planned to hold individual conferences with both Arabs and Jews in an attempt to find a solution.

It was understood, however, that Mr. Gromyko, regardless of such action, had laid great stress on the language of the resolution adopted Friday by the United Nations Security Council, which asked the five great powers to consult "with a view of implementing" the partition resolution adopted last November by the General Assembly.

**To Support Positive Measures**

The Security Council resolution specifies that these consultations should take place merely for the purpose of making recommendations to the council on what instructions it should give the Palestine Commission. However, it was understood that Mr. Gromyko, who has not thus far disclosed the Soviet position, indicated that he would support positive measures.

The United States position, as laid down by Mr. Austin in his statement to the council on Feb. 24, is that the council does not have the power to send an international force to implement partition, but does have the right to take the necessary steps to maintain peace and security in Palestine.

Mr. Austin had proposed that the council ask the great powers to consult with Jewish and Arab representatives as well as with Great Britain, the mandatory power, concerning the implementation of the assembly resolution. However, this part of the United States resolution failed of passage last Friday because of the abstentions of the Soviet Union and the Ukraine.

United States sources, however, said that the council had not forbidden the great powers to hold such conferences, and it was understood that Mr. Austin had planned to go ahead. The Arab Higher Committee, spokesman for Palestinian Arabs, boycotted the United Nations Special Committee for Palestine, which recommended parti-

Continued on Page 3, Column 2

## Red Star Planes Fire At Chennault Craft

By The Associated Press.

SHANGHAI, Tuesday, March 9—Two P-39 fighter planes with Soviet markings attacked a Chennault commercial transport plane late yesterday while it was over the Gulf of Po en route from Mukden to Tsingtao, North China, the airline reported today.

Whiting Willauer of the airline staff said the fighter planes made five passes at the transport, firing each time. He said the transport pilot stated they must have had no intention of hitting his craft, otherwise they couldn't have missed.

Mr. Willauer said the transport's pilot, L. B. Buol of Stockton, Calif., a former Marine flier, took pictures of the attacking planes. They were marked with red stars, Mr. Willauer said.

Mr. Willauer's report did not say whether the pilots of the fighter planes were Russian or Chinese. The Chinese Government has charged Russia with providing arms for the Chinese Communist forces.



## MAYOR GREETS VISITOR FROM IRELAND

Mr. O'Dwyer with Eamon de Valera at Gracie Mansion
The New York Times

## De Valera Is City's Guest; Official Welcome Today

By MARSHALL E. NEWTON

Eamon de Valera, American-born former Premier of Ireland, returned yesterday for a visit to his native land—his first in eighteen years. He arrived at La Guardia Field at 4:58 A. M. on an American Overseas Airlines plane from Shannon Airport, accompanied by Frank Aiken, former Irish Minister for Finance, and Liam MacGowan of the Dublin Irish Press, a publication supporting the Fiana Fail party, of which Mr. de Valera is leader.

Despite the early hour a large crowd gathered to meet the tall, scholarly-appearing Irish leader, who recently surrendered the reins of government to James Costello. Grover A. Whalen, chairman of the Mayor's Reception Committee, was there to bid him welcome. Garth Healy, Irish Consul General in New York, representatives of Irish-American societies and old friends of his early days in New York also were at the airport.

The former Prime Minister spent a busy day in conferences a lunch with Mayor O'Dwyer, a press interview and talks with local Irish leaders. So busy, in fact, that he remarked he had had no time to form any impression of New York.

Today he will be the guest of the city at an official reception at City Hall at 11 A. M. after a parade up lower Broadway from Bowling Green. This will be followed by an official luncheon at the Waldorf-Astoria Hotel. Tonight he will be the guest of Cardinal Spellman at a private dinner at the Cardinal's residence, Fiftieth Street and Madison Avenue. Tomorrow he will pay a courtesy call on President Truman at the White House in Washington.

Asked if any official matters would be discussed with President Truman, Mr. de Valera said: "I am in the hands of the President. He will determine what we discuss."

For more than an hour in the afternoon Mr. de Valera discussed world affairs, in response to questions from reporters, barring only one subject—domestic Irish politics. As he seated himself before

Continued on Page 2, Column 2

## SOVIET ACCUSES U. S. OF AIM TO WAR ON IT

### Note on London Talks Charges Plot to Split Europe, Rearm Ruhr, End Big 4 Council

By The Associated Press.

MOSCOW, March 8—Russia charged tonight that the United States was leading a Western power plot to split Europe and build up military might in Germany "with the purpose of aggression against the Union of Soviet Socialist Republics."

A Soviet note to the United States, Britain and France charged that in the attempt to carry out the plot the major Western powers were trying deliberately to liquidate the Big Four Council of Foreign Ministers.

The note rejected a British reply to an original protest that the three-power conference in London on Germany's future violated the Potsdam agreement. Russian authorities said that the note was delivered Saturday to the Governments of the Western powers. It was made public today at a news conference.

It accused the Western Allies of "paralyzing" the Allied Control Council in Germany. It added that the British and Americans had merged their zones in western Germany so they would not have to demilitarize the region "nor liquidate their military enterprises in Germany."

The Russians said that the United States had decided to:

(1) "Split Europe into two camps."

(2) "Include schismatic western Germany in the Western bloc" with the purpose of "building up

Continued on Page 8, Column 2

## Commodity Markets in New Slump; Weather and U. S. Buying Factors

Prices broke yesterday on the nation's commodity markets in the sharpest decline since the slump of a month ago. The new break came suddenly after a week in which prices had made their biggest advances in three months.

The slide was along a wide front, including grain, hogs and cotton on the commodity markets. By afternoon a sympathetic decline had set in on the New York Stock Exchange, where combined averages were off 0.37 point. All sections of the stock list were down except aircrafts, which showed some gains.

Business observers attributed the price breaks to the weather, uncertainty over Government purchases and heavier shipments from farm to market.

Wheat, corn and soy bean futures dropped the limit permitted for a day's trading on the Chicago Board of Trade, but wheat recovered slightly.

At the close of yesterday's trading in Chicago May wheat sold at $2.36½ a bushel, off 7½ cents from the previous close. May futures in corn sold at $2.16⅛, off 7⅞ cents; in oats at $1.10½, off 4¼ cents, and in soy beans at $3.48, off 8 cents. The low prices reached by May futures in the break that culminated on Feb. 14 were: Wheat, $2.32; corn, $1.96¾; oats, 96⅜ cents, and soy beans, $3.25.

Hog prices in the Midwest stockyards were 25 cents to $1.50 lower a 100 pounds, top hogs selling at Chicago for $23.50 a hundredweight.

Cotton quotations on the New York market were off $4.30 to $6.75 a bale, the largest drop in recent trading. Cotton for March delivery was down to $3.03 cents a pound and for May to a range of 33.08 to 33.14 cents.

The Associated Press index of thirty-five wholesale commodity prices had its sharpest break since Feb. 10. It dropped 2.11 points to

Continued on Page 19, Column 1



## RELIGIOUS TEACHING IN SCHOOLS BARRED BY SUPREME COURT

### 8-1 Decision in Champaign, Ill., Case Holds Such Use of Public Buildings Unconstitutional

### CHURCH AND STATE APART

### Atheist's Successful Protest May Bring Fight Here on the Released-Time Program

By JAY WALZ

Special to The New York Times.

WASHINGTON, March 8—The Supreme Court declared today that religious instruction in public school buildings was unconstitutional.

An 8-to-1 decision upheld the complaint of a mother in Champaign, Ill., an avowed atheist, who said that her son had been "embarrassed" by being the only child in his room not attending religious classes under a local plan.

The majority rejected the Champaign program because it involved use of public school buildings for classes taught once a week on school time. Justice Hugo L. Black stated for the court that the use of tax-supported property for dissemination of religious doctrines violated the Constitutional concept of separation of church and state.

Justice Stanley F. Reed, in dissent, said the decision threw into doubt all forms of religious instruction connected in any way with school systems.

**Pupils Released Early Here**

Such classes are now attended by thousands of pupils under programs set up in scores of communities throughout the country, including New York City, where children may be excused during specified school hours for religious classes held elsewhere.

Justice Robert H. Jackson, while joining the majority, said he believed it went too far and argued that the decision would open the gates to a flood of litigation by groups that did not like local practices.

Under the Champaign plan, set up in 1940, the school board cooperated with the local Council on Religious Education by offering the needed facilities. The Council provided outside teachers representing the Protestant, Roman Catholic and Jewish faiths. Pupils, with the consent of their parents,

Continued on Page 26, Column 2

## WOULD MEET 'DUTY'

### General Says He Would Be 'Recreant' to Balk Call of the People

### DOES NOT 'COVET' OFFICE

### 'Go Ahead' Signal for Boom Is Linked to Rise in Nation of Anti-Communist Views

By The Associated Press.

TOKYO, Tuesday, March 9—Gen. Douglas MacArthur said today he would accept the Presidency "if called by the American people," but would not actively seek it.

A special statement commenting upon Wisconsin Republican nominating petitions filed in his behalf was issued by the supreme commander for the Allied powers here. Its text was as follows:

"I have been informed that petitions have been filed in Madison signed by many of my fellow citizens of Wisconsin presenting my name to the electorate for consideration at the primary on April 6. I am deeply grateful for this spontaneous display of friendly confidence. No man could fail to be profoundly stirred by such a public movement in this hour of momentous import, national and international, temporal and spiritual.

"While it seems unnecessary for me to repeat that I do not actively seek or covet any office and have no plans for leaving my post in Japan, I can say, and with due humility, that I would be recreant to all my concept of good citizenship were I to shrink because of the hazards and responsibilities involved from accepting any public duty to which I might be called by the American people."

In addition to the Wisconsin move in behalf of General MacArthur, Hearst newspapers have begun a "MacArthur for America" boom, seeking his nomination as Republican candidate for President.

Until his public statement today,

Continued on Page 14, Column 3

## World News Summarized

TUESDAY, MARCH 9, 1948

President Truman and General MacArthur announced yesterday that they would accept nomination for the Presidency. Mr. Truman told party leaders he would run, if named, and declared he would not alter his stand on civil rights, which has antagonized the South, or on Palestine, which has alienated other supporters. [1:8.] General MacArthur, commenting in Tokyo on petitions filed in his behalf in Wisconsin, said he would "not actively seek or covet any office," but would accept if "called by the American people." [1:5.]

Both issues complicating the President's chances were in the news. Republicans teamed with Southern Democrats in the House to overwhelm a proposal to restore anti-discrimination provisions to an appropriation bill. [18:3.] While Russia was said to have pressed for prompt decision on implementing partition of Palestine, the United States, at a big powers' talk, urged an opportunity to bring Jews and Arabs together. [1:1.] United Nations legal experts held that the Security Council had the right to take enforcement action if the Arabs resisted partition. [3:5.]

The Senate, in its first decisive test, defeated, 53 to 19, a restrictive amendment to the European Recovery Program. Secretary Marshall pleaded for final Congressional action by April 1 with Speaker Martin, who could only promise a vote probably before April 10. [1:6-7.] A survey of 430 community leaders showed overwhelming endorsement of the Marshall Plan in principle, although some doubts about details. [13:1.]

A purely economic aid program for China would fail and must be backed by adequate military help, several witnesses told a House committee. [12:6.]

After conferring privately with the four top defense officials, a Senate committee voted unanimously to hold public hearings on universal military training and push to a vote at this session. [1:7.]

Former Premier de Valera, welcomed on his arrival in this city from Ireland, took a dim view of the future of the United Nations and was fearful of a new war. [1:2-3.]

Russia accused the United States of seeking a divided Europe, a militarized Germany and aggression against the Soviet Union. In a new note protesting against the London conference on Germany's future Moscow said the major Western powers sought to end the Foreign Ministers Council. [1:2.]

Finland has agreed to talks on a pact with Russia and will suggest that they be held in Moscow. [4:4-5.]

An American soldier was shot and seriously wounded by a Russian guard in Vienna. [6:1.] In Indo-China two women employed by the State Department were murdered. [12:4.]

Religious instruction in American public schools involves use of tax-supported property and is unconstitutional, the Supreme Court ruled, 8 to 1. [1:4.]

In Albany, the Board of Regents denounced the State University bill supported by Governor Dewey, holding the proposed dual authority would set education back. [19:2-3.]

Political differences made it appear that Mayor O'Dwyer's financial bills, including a higher transit fare, would be killed by the Legislature. [1:6-7.] A committee recommended a one-year extension of the state's stand-by rent-control law and this city's curbs on rentals, but opposed controls on garage rentals. [17:1.] Governor Dewey signed the $20,000,000 emergency pay-increase bill. [17:2-3.]

*This is Meatless Tuesday*

## LINE UP FOR THE PRESIDENTIAL RACE

Gen. Douglas MacArthur
Associated Press

President Truman
The New York Times (Washington Bureau)

## Senate by 53 to 19 Rejects A Move to Change Aid Plan

By FELIX BELAIR Jr.

Special to The New York Times

WASHINGTON, March 8—The Senate voted by 53 to 19 today to reject the first attempt to amend the European Recovery Program legislation in a manner not welcome to Senator Arthur H. Vandenberg and the Senate Foreign Relations Committee. The first test of revisionist strength came a few hours after Secretary of State George C. Marshall made a personal appeal to Speaker of the House Joseph W. Martin Jr. for all possible speed on the legislation in view of accelerated Communist activity in western Europe.

Accompanied by Under-Secretary Robert A. Lovett and Ambassador Lewis W. Douglas, Secretary Marshall went to the Capitol to stress the greater importance of the Administration's April 1 deadline on the program in the light of recent developments in Czechoslovakia and Finland and the coming important elections in Italy.

Aside from the Speaker's expression of confidence that final action on the legislation would come before April 10, the State Department group received no assurances. However, Representative Martin arranged for a meeting of House and Senate leaders tomorrow to synchronize disposition of the measure in the two branches of Congress.

It was understood, meanwhile, that an effort would be made in the House to seek action on the plan before taking up aid to China, Greece, Turkey and other areas. The Foreign Affairs Committee of the House has already voted to report a foreign aid bill in omnibus fashion and a reversal of that decision would first be in order.

Such a move would not come until after tomorrow's conference between House and Senate leaders in which Chairman Charles A. Eaton of the Foreign Affairs group was invited to participate with Speaker

Continued on Page 13, Column 4

## HEARINGS ON UMT TO BEGIN IN SENATE

### Armed Services Group Votes Action After Defense Chiefs Call Step 'Mandatory'

By C. P. TRUSSELL

Special to The New York Times.

WASHINGTON, March 8—Public hearings on measures designed to build up the nation's defense—with universal military training as the base—were ordered today by the unanimous vote of the Senate Armed Services Committee.

The decision was made after the committee had conferred in private with the country's four ranking defense officials on situations and needs in light of recent world developments. The committee was told, it was said later, that UMT had become "not only necessary but mandatory."

After the vote was taken, James Forrestal, Secretary of Defense, said.

"Events are making progress for us." He declined to elaborate.

With Mr. Forrestal at the closed session were Kenneth C. Royall, Secretary of the Army; John L. Sullivan, Secretary of the Navy, and W. Stuart Symington, Secretary of the Air Force.

The arguments presented by the defense chiefs left the committee, or the ten of thirteen members present, determined to open the case of the UMT to Congressional trial. The purpose behind the

Continued on Page 11, Column 2

## O'Dwyer 8c-Fare Bill Due to Die; Republicans Pass Onus to Mayor

By LEO EGAN

Special to The New York Times.

ALBANY, March 8—Mayor William O'Dwyer's transit bill, intended to pave the way for increasing New York City subway fares to 8 cents, appeared headed for the legislative scrap heap tonight as Republican and Democratic legislative leaders exchanged recriminations and charges of bad faith.

But the Republican legislative majority was put in a position at the same time to enact a fare bill of its own before the end of the week, if it so chose, through introduction of a new transit bill by the Assembly Rules Committee.

In place of the elaborate provisions of the O'Dwyer bill, the Republican substitute provides for repeal of the Muzzicato law, which permits the City Council to order a referendum on any fare rise. In addition, the new bill gives the Board of Transportation, with the approval of the Mayor, power to fix and adjust the rate of fare from time to time.

If enacted as a substitute for the O'Dwyer bill, the Rules Committee measure would make the Mayor the only elected official who would be required officially to approve a fare increase. Under the O'Dwyer bill no elected official would be required to give such approval.

The bill also provides that any change in fares could become effective only at the start of the city's fiscal year, July 1.

Mayor O'Dwyer, in a statement telephoned to Irwin Steingut, Democratic leader of the Assembly, and read on the floor tonight, said he was "unalterably opposed" to the Rules Committee's substitute for his transit bill. If enacted into law, he said, he would not use it.

The O'Dwyer transit bill started on its way to the legislative grave-

Continued on Page 16, Column 2



## PRESIDENT READY

### He Will Not Back Down on Palestine, Civil Rights Stands

### M'GRATH TELLS DECISION

### Says After Talk With Truman That Democratic Leaders Requested the Move

By ANTHONY LEVIERO

Special to The New York Times.

WASHINGTON, March 8—President Truman declared this afternoon that he was willing to be a candidate for President if the Democratic party nominated him.

Making his first formal bid for a full, four-year term in the White House, the Chief Executive affirmed that he would not back down on his civil rights policy, the most troublesome issue facing his administration and his party.

Mr. Truman also asserted that he would handle the Palestine problem without regard to politics but mindful of the security of the United States and of the world. He reiterated that decisions of the United Nations would be supported by the American Government.

The surprise announcement that Mr. Truman, heir of Franklin D. Roosevelt's unexpired term, was ready to run on his record came in undramatic circumstances.

**McGrath Tells of Decision**

Senator J. Howard McGrath of Rhode Island, chairman of the Democratic National Committee, announced the candidacy and Mr. Truman's views in the lobby of the White House executive office. Before he did so, however, he talked with Mr. Truman for ninety minutes.

"The first thing that I have to tell you," Senator McGrath told reporters, "is that in response to numerous requests from Democratic leaders throughout the country, I asked the President if I might state what his intentions are with respect to the coming Democratic National Convention.

"The President has authorized me to say that if nominated by the Democratic National Convention, he will accept and run."

Mr. McGrath came to the White House at 3:30 P. M. with a package of political woes that accumulated during Mr. Truman's recent fifteen-day Caribbean tour and vacation. With him were Gael Sullivan, executive director of the Democratic committee, and John M. Redding, publicity director. The latter remained in the lobby. At 5 P. M. Messrs. McGrath and Sullivan came out of the President's office, looking serious.

**Civil Rights Plan Stands**

The revolt of the Southern Democrats, with its rising threat of secession from the party, became acute during the President's absence from the capital. During that time, the storm also arose over the restatement of American policy on Palestine by Warren R. Austin, chief American delegate to the United Nations.

Without prompting, Senator McGrath plunged into the civil rights question.

"I talked to the President with respect to his civil rights message," Mr. McGrath said. "The President's position remains unchanged since he delivered that message.

"I might state that it is my view, which I expressed to the President, that the substance of his message is as old as the Constitution of the United States itself and as new as the 1944 Democratic national platform."

Of the ten points of the civil rights program, which the President sent to Congress on Feb. 2, seven points directly bear on the Negro issue in the South. The Administration has sent to Congress a civil rights bill, but it is being held in abeyance by Democratic Congressional leaders.

Had they discussed Palestine, Senator McGrath was asked

"I asked the President to explain the present status of the Palestine situation, which he did

Continued on Page 15, Column 4

"All the News That's Fit to Print"

# The New York Times

LATE CITY EDITION
Warmer with scattered showers today. Showers tomorrow.
Temperature Range Today—Max., 73; Min., 55
Temperatures Yesterday—Max., 66; Min., 42
Full U. S. Weather Bureau Report, Page 42

VOL. XCVII..No. 32,979. Entered as Second-Class Matter, Postoffice, New York, N. Y. NEW YORK, MONDAY, MAY 10, 1948. Times Square, New York 18, N. Y. Telephone LAckawanna 4-1000 THREE CENTS IN NEW YORK CITY

## RAIL CONFEREES DEADLOCK IN LONG WHITE HOUSE TALKS; TRUMAN SILENT ON SEIZURE

### PARLEYS RECESSED

Go Past Midnight, With New Discussions to Start at 8:30 A. M.

CLIFFORD IS CONSULTANT

Legal Adviser With President as Steelman Reports on Status of Negotiations

By JAY WALZ
Special to THE NEW YORK TIMES.

WASHINGTON, Monday, May 10—It became evident early this morning that efforts to avert the nationwide railroad strike were still unavailing. The walkout is scheduled for tomorrow at 6 A. M., standard time.

A series of separate conferences with each side, conducted at the White House by Dr. John R. Steelman, assistant to President Truman, began at 10 A. M. yesterday morning and continued past midnight, but apparently had made no progress.

However, hope was not abandoned. Dr. Steelman, ending a conference with union representatives at about 12:10 A. M., asked them to return for further talks at 8:30 A. M.

After the union leaders had left he again saw the representatives of the railroads. This meeting broke up at 12:53 A. M., with Dr. Steelman asking the group to come back at 9 A. M.

**Reports "Nothing but Talking"**

As Alvanley Johnston, one of the union conferees, left the White House he said:

"We have just been talking, talking, nothing but talking."

Whether the Government planned seizure of the roads to prevent a strike or in the event of a strike were matters left for speculation.

Observers felt generally, however, that the White House would act neither to postpone the strike deadline or to seize the roads unless it appeared at the last minute that peace efforts were futile.

Dr. Steelman had nothing official to say about the series of meetings.

The night meetings began at 9 o'clock, when the management leaders were called to the White House, with the union chiefs "on call" at a hotel.

Charles G. Ross, White House press secretary, in announcing that the management officials were being called back for a night session, stated that Dr. Steelman had spent the previous hour reporting to President Truman.

**Truman Stays Close at Hand**

The President took no direct part in the negotiations during the day, leaving them to Dr. Steelman. Except for a brief walk around the White House grounds in the morning, however, he remained in the residential quarters of the mansion all day, receiving occasional reports on the talks from Mr. Ross or other White House aides.

The conferees in their several arrivals and departures during the afternoon and evening made brief and for the most part noncommittal remarks in response to questions by reporters. Early in the afternoon the union chiefs issued a statement accusing the railroads of "inflamatory remarks" and threatening, if talks broke down, to "place the full facts before the public."

The fact that both sides met separately with Dr. Steelman led to speculation that his immediate problem was to establish some basis of agreement on which the opposing leaders could meet together.

Involved in the dispute are a 15½ cents-an-hour pay rise recommended by a Government fact-finding board and a number of operating rules, many of which also involve money payments. The railroad managements are willing to pay the recommended hourly increase but are adamant against any rules changes except those suggested by the Government board.

The unions are satisfied neither with the amount of hourly pay increase nor with the proposals for changing the rules.

Mr. Ross said that Clark Clif-

Continued on Page 3, Column 6

### N. Y. Central Sets Embargo On Perishables for Tonight

*Police Prepare for Truck, Bus and Auto Congestion if Strike Comes Tomorrow—Greenwich Plans Commuter Line*

By ALEXANDER FEINBERG

The New York Central Railroad announced yesterday an embargo on livestock, poultry and perishable freight to go into effect at one minute before midnight tonight, standard time. It was forced to this action, the company said, "to prevent the needless waste of food which would not reach its destination" if the scheduled nation-wide strike is carried through.

No word was forthcoming from the Pennsylvania Railroad, which apparently has decided to withhold a similar declaration until the last minute before the strike deadline set for 6 A. M. (standard time) tomorrow.

The two other major freight carriers here, the Erie and the Baltimore & Ohio, along with most other roads in the nation and the Railway Express Agency, had previously put an embargo on perishables that cannot reach their destination by today.

In its statement the New York Central said: "Appreciating fully the public welfare problems involved, the New York Central has for several days delayed the placing of any embargoes. Unfortunately, however, in order to prevent the needless waste of food which would not reach its destination in event of a strike it is impossible to delay further. The New York Central System therefore is forced today to impose an embargo effective at 11:59 P. M. standard time, Monday, May 10, against further carload shipments of livestock, live poultry and perishable freight."

It was the placing of these embargoes on perishables—most of them went into effect either Friday or Saturday midnight—that led Mayor O'Dwyer to warn President Truman on Friday that their continuation would send prices

Continued on Page 3, Column 1

## SOUTH KOREA VOTES AS COMMUNISTS TRY TO SABOTAGE POLL

Foes of U.N.-Directed Election Spread Violence—2 Killed Attacking Seoul Booth

BROADCAST HITS AT HODGE

6,000,000 Expected to Ballot in Spite of Intimidation, Murder, Kidnapping

By RICHARD J. H. JOHNSTON
Special to THE NEW YORK TIMES.

SEOUL, Korea, Monday, May 10—More than 6,000,000 voters are expected to go to the polls today in the first general election in the 4,000-year history of Korea.

[A heavy vote was being cast, amid considerable violence in several centers, said an Associated Press dispatch. In Seoul two Communists, suspected saboteurs, were slain after, police said, they had fired on a polling booth.]

Under the observation of the United Nations Temporary Commission on Korea the elections will reveal whether the South Koreans, at least, can successfully take this first step toward self-government. In addition, the elections will offer a supreme test of the strength and influence of Korea's small but fanatically aggressive Communist party.

Guided and instructed by the Soviet North Korean occupation authorities, and with the full weight of North Korea's Communist-controlled puppet government behind them, the South Korean Communists have announced that they will wreck the elections and plunge the American occupation zone into a blood bath if necessary.

**Attacks Aimed at U. S.**

Despite the efforts of the combined South Korean security forces to maintain order, the Communists have continued their campaign of murder, torture and intimidation up through the eve of the elections.

The Communist intention is either to prevent the elections, which prospect has completely faded, or to stir up such a degree of disorder and police counteraction as to discredit the election results and nullify the United Nations' efforts.

The North Korea Soviet-controlled radio Saturday night broadcast an open letter to Lieut. Gen. John R. Hodge, United States commander in Korea, signed by political party and Soviet organization representatives in North Korea demanding:

"Give up your attempt to carry out a separate election. You had better get out of Korea with your clothes packed."

The letter complained that General Hodge had unduly criticized the Communists.

"The people of the world," it said, "know that the patriotic fighters who have struggled against the Japanese oppressors and Hitler's political power of Germany during World War II are the Communists of Korea. The Americans should recognize it.

"We know that you have suffered much from the strikes or so-called riots and you have fallen into nerve-racking situations with which we sympathize. Why do you make such a valuable effort at the expense of your nervous system?"

**95 Per Cent Registered**

Despite ceaseless attacks on potential voters, candidates, election officials and police the Communists had failed to prevent 95 per cent of South Korea's eligible voters from registering.

Nearly 400 Koreans have died in Communist-led guerrilla warfare since Jan. 1. Thousands have been injured. Scores of homes have been burned. Election officials and candidates have disappeared. Railroads and communications lines have been damaged or destroyed.

Nevertheless, more than 8,000,000 of South Korea's 19,500,000 population have signified their desire to participate in the election, but not all of them are expected to vote.

They will choose 200 members of a Constituent Assembly upon which a national Government for Korea will be based.

This election will be confined to the American zone. The Soviet Union has refused to allow the commission to enter North Korea where the Soviet Union has set up a Communist-controlled puppet government.

The United Nations Interim Committee last February advised the commission, in the face of the

Continued on Page 3, Column 2

## Haganah Attacks to Clear Jerusalem-Tel Aviv Road

*Commandos Meet Fierce Arab Resistance—Cunningham Sends Proposals of Truce Terms for Capital to Both Sides*

By DANA ADAMS SCHMIDT
Special to THE NEW YORK TIMES.

JERUSALEM, May 9—Commandos and sappers of the Palmach, striking force of the Haganah, went into action early today to clear the 200-yard-long, three-foot-high Arab road block at Bab el Wad that has obstructed the road from Tel Aviv to Jewish Jerusalem for nineteen days.

Jews who circled through the Judean hills to attack the Arab position above a narrow gorge fifteen miles west of Jerusalem met fierce resistance. They lost five dead and eleven injured, according to first reports. Arab reinforcements converged toward the vital road block and the Haganah brought up armored cars and mortars from Jerusalem. Three aircraft, presumed to have been Jewish, circled over the area during the day.

[The Zionist forces also attacked the Arab village of Beit Mahsir, which is the chief base for the Arabs blocking the highway, The Associated Press reported.]

This was the Jews' bid to open the Tel Aviv-Jerusalem road—the central factor in current truce discussions. Control of the road is one of the few trumps remaining in Arab hands. The fight now developing may prove to be a decisive phase in the battle for Jerusalem and one of the most decisive in the entire Palestine conflict.

The cease-fire within the municipal boundaries of Jerusalem remained intact today. Lieut. Gen. Sir Alan G. Cunningham, the High Commissioner, announced that he had sent draft proposals for truce terms in the city to the Jews and Arabs at 7 P. M. He also endorsed the proposal put forward by Jacques de Reynier, chief representative here of the International Red Cross, for placing Jerusalem under the Red Cross flag.

If the Red Cross receives formal requests from non-political, non-military Arab and Jewish groups, which it has asked for, General Cunningham said that the Government would support the proposal until the British leave, in

Continued on Page 16, Column 6

## British Act in U. N. to Guard Economic Rights in Palestine

By THOMAS J. HAMILTON
Special to THE NEW YORK TIMES.

LAKE SUCCESS, N. Y., May 9—The British Government has informed the United Nations Palestine Commission that it wants assurances regarding the protection of British economic interests in Palestine, including the oil pipeline from Iraq to Haifa, after the termination of the British mandate next Saturday.

The text of the British communication on this subject was kept secret at the request of the British delegation. However, usually reliable sources said it had implied that the funds of the Palestine Currency Board, together with other assets of the British Administration in Palestine that are now held in London, would not be released until the British Government was satisfied that British and other foreign economic interests in Palestine were protected.

The funds of the Currency Board are invested mostly in British Government securities, and it is understood that the total assets of the Palestine Administration held in London approximate £50,000,000 ($200,000,000). The British letter to the Palestine Commission listed British economic interests in the following order of priority:

(1) The Iraq pipeline, owned by the Iraq Petroleum Company, owned jointly by British, Dutch, American and French oil companies, with the British the largest stock-owners; the installations at Haifa for handling the oil, which are owned by a subsidiary of the Iraq Petroleum Company; a franchise held by a British company for oil prospecting in southern Palestine.

(2) Civil aviation rights for the use of airports in Palestine by British interests.

(3) A plant for the extraction of potash from the waters of the Dead Sea. The plant is Jewish owned but is in the part of Palestine assigned under the partition plan to the proposed Arab state. Great Britain's interest in it derives from the fact that the

Continued on Page 15, Column 1

## JET FIGHTERS SCORE IN MAJOR SEA TEST

Squadron Operates Smoothly Off 600-Foot Carrier Deck in a Turbulent Sea

By JOHN STUART
Special to THE NEW YORK TIMES.

ABOARD U.S.S. SAIPAN, off Block Island, May 6 (Delayed for Navy release)—In a rough open sea naval aviation today answered affirmatively most of the questions that have been raised as to the operability of jet aircraft from carriers.

Sixteen Phantoms of Fighter Squadron 17A—air group and ship's company unite in proudly calling it "Seventeen Able"—did everything that could be asked of carrier fighters and did it all perfectly for the first time in such numbers.

Through the day the sixteen aircraft accomplished almost threescore landings and take-offs from the Saipan's deck, little more than 600 feet long and 100 feet wide.

The sea was such that the ship rolled up to 11 degrees as she pitched into a wind of 23 to 28 knots. Yet never a jet plane even approached the barriers. Most of them hooked into the first or second of the nine wires of the arresting gear. They were catapulted off and flew off at intervals that would have done credit to an old and practiced squadron using conventional aircraft.

Handling of the aircraft on the flight deck was equally good. The

Continued on Page 8, Column 4

## Socialists Name Norman Thomas A Sixth Time for the Presidency

By WILLIAM G. WEART
Special to THE NEW YORK TIMES.

READING, Pa., May 9—Nominated without opposition, Norman Thomas, veteran political campaigner, today became the Socialist party's Presidential candidate for a sixth consecutive time.

The 200 delegates, representing forty states at the party's national convention, selected Tucker P. Smith, 49, head of the Economics Department at Olivet College, Mich., as the 63-year-old New Yorker's running mate. In a secret ballot, Mr. Smith won the Vice-Presidential place over Mrs. Mary Donovan Hapgood of Indianapolis, on whose recommendation the nomination was made unanimous.

In his speech of acceptance, Mr. Thomas denounced what he termed the bipartisan failure of Republicans and Democrats to deal with the cycle "through boom toward bust," and condemned the Progressive party for its alliance with Communists.

"The best thing our confused Democratic President has done, his support of recommendations of his Civil Rights Committee, is precisely the thing that damns him worst in his own party—a fact which exposes the terrible inadequacy of that party as the servant of the people," Mr. Thomas asserted.

Referring to the record of the Republican party in the Eightieth Congress, he further maintained that it had created "the conditions which breed the industrial tempest and widespread strikes with which our nation is threatened."

In the third party movement, Mr. Thomas declared, Henry Wallace cannot succeed in his alliance with Communists when Jan Masaryk so tragically failed. On some issues, he added, the Socialists may agree with Mr. Wallace, "but we are obliged to reject any

Continued on Page 2, Column 5

## CHURCHILL ASSERTS MASSES' HOPE LIES IN UNIFIED EUROPE

Says People Must End Hatreds and Become 'Proud to Say I Am a European'

BANS ON SLAVERY ASKED

Throng in Amsterdam Urged to Fight Against Tyranny 'Whatever Liveries It Wears'

By DAVID ANDERSON
Special to THE NEW YORK TIMES.

AMSTERDAM, the Netherlands, May 9—A message of hope was addressed today by Winston Churchill to the "broad proletarian masses" when he repeated his call for a united Europe.

The cause of the European union was transferred from The Hague to this city, where a crowd of 10,000 packed old, sun-lit Dam Square to listen to speeches by the leaders of the movement and catch a glimpse of Mr. Churchill, who is revered by the people of the Netherlands.

"I invoke the interest of the broad proletarian masses," he said, speaking in English. "We see before our eyes scores of millions of humble homes in Europe and in lands outside which have been afflicted by war.

"Are they never to have a chance to thrive and flourish? Is the honest, faithful breadwinner never to reap the fruits of his labor? May he never bring up his children in health and joy and with the hopes of better days? Can he never be free of the fear of foreign invasion, the crash of bomb and shell, the tramp of hostile patrol or what is even worse, the knock upon his door by the political police?"

The remedy for better days lies in the first place in conquering ourselves, Mr. Churchill asserted. Old feuds must die and territorial ambitions be set aside, he added.

He said he looked forward to seeing a council of Europe comprising as many states as possible on the Continent of Europe. Members of all European countries should be proud to say "I am a European," and wherever they went to feel that "here I am at home," he declared.

His audience was greatly amused

Continued on Page 11, Column 3

## NEW TRAFFIC BODY ENLISTING BUSINESS PROPOSED FOR CITY

Service of Leaders of Trade for 'Most-Pressing Problem' Sought by Commerce Chief

'SUBSTANTIAL' COST SEEN

Maguire Decries 'Makeshift' Aid and Calls for Action—Mayor to Discuss Plan

Describing traffic congestion as the city's most pressing problem, Edward C. Maguire, Commerce Commissioner, recommended to Mayor O'Dwyer yesterday that the city enlist its business leaders in a new Traffic Commission specifically charged with solving the problem.

Mr. Maguire said sufficient information had been gathered through numerous surveys and that the time for action had arrived. He added that up to now no full-scale effort had been made to untie the traffic knot.

Since community support was required for success, the commissioner said, leaders in finance, real estate, the trades and professions and other callings should be enlisted at the outset. His report urged both short-term and long-range programs to relieve congestion.

Members of the Board of Estimate and business leaders will hear the Mayor discuss the proposals at a luncheon today at 12:30 P. M. in the Commodore Hotel.

"Unless we act promptly," Mr. Maguire reported, "irremediable damage to business and industry will result, adversely affecting the general welfare and prosperity of our citizens, the business man, the employe, the property owner and the rent-payer alike. Unless some comprehensive and definite course is charted, forcefully implemented and translated into performance, any relief obtained must necessarily be makeshift and transitory."

For the new Traffic Commission Mr. Maguire recommended two divisions, one dealing with traffic control and the other with planning and performance.

Police Commissioner Arthur W.

Continued on Page 5, Column 2

## World News Summarized

MONDAY, MAY 10, 1948

Despite a series of White House conferences that ended early today, there was no indication that the Government had made any progress toward averting the nation-wide rail strike, set for 6 A. M. tomorrow. Operators and unions, reportedly as far apart as ever, were scheduled to resume talks this morning. [1:8.]

Merchants here declared that a railroad strike would affect only a small part of this city's supplies of fresh produce. Seventy per cent of New York's fruits and vegetables, 85 per cent of its poultry, 90 per cent of its fish and 50 per cent of its meat are brought in by truck or boat. [1:7.] The New York Central Railroad announced an embargo on perishables and city officials discussed new traffic-control measures. [1:6-7.]

Commerce Commissioner Maguire, calling general traffic congestion the city's major problem, urged Mayor O'Dwyer to name business leaders to a new traffic commission. [1:5.]

The Amalgamated Clothing Workers, CIO, and the New York Clothing Manufacturers Exchange will open a $1,000,000 union health center in Manhattan. [1:6-7.]

A Federal program of compulsory health insurance, advocated by President Truman, was called "unwise" in a report drafted by the Brookings Institution for a Senate subcommittee. [1:6-7.]

Millions in South Korea began voting today for a Constituent Assembly in an election supervised by the United Nations. There was increased violence on the part of Communists. [1:1.]

Zionists attacked strong Arab positions west of Jerusalem in an effort to reopen the road from Tel Aviv. [1:2-3; map P. 16.] Britain, reported to be holding Palestine funds as security, asked the United Nations Palestine Commission for assurance that British and other foreign property would be safe after the mandate expired next Saturday. [1:2-3.] At Lake Success, delegates worked in an atmosphere of mounting gloom to set up "caretaker governments" in Palestine. [13:1.]

The six-power conference in London is nearing an end with no agreement in sight on Germany's economic and political future. Foreign Minister Bidault insisted that France would never abandon her claims for security against Germany. [8:2.] In Vienna, American and Austrian experts agreed that Washington, in making Marshall Plan allotments, had seriously over-estimated Austria's capacity to trade with countries in the Soviet sphere. [7:2.]

Winston Churchill said the hope of the "broad proletarian masses" lay in a Europe united for peace and security. [1:4.]

In this country the Socialists for the sixth consecutive time nominated Norman Thomas for President. [1:2-3.]

The Navy and the Army have conducted successful maneuvers. Jet planes easily operated from a carrier [1:2] and transport planes landed 2,300 troops with full equipment. [31:5.]

**Winston Churchill's War Memoirs**

See Page 23 for today's installment in which Mr. Churchill tells how the British Fleet planned to combat the menace of Germany's pocket battleships.

## $1,000,000 Health Center For Clothing Workers Here

By A. H. RASKIN
Special to THE NEW YORK TIMES.

ATLANTIC CITY, N. J., May 9—Plans for establishment of a $1,000,000 union health center in Manhattan were announced here today by the Amalgamated Clothing Workers, CIO, and the New York Clothing Manufacturers Exchange. The announcement was made on the eve of the opening tomorrow of the union's sixteenth biennial convention.

The health center, which is expected to begin operations within three months, will provide free medical service to 60,000 men's clothing workers in the metropolitan area. The annual operating budget of $500,000, as well as the funds necessary to set up the clinic, will be contributed by the employers.

The New York project will be the forerunner of similar centers to be established by the union and the industry in Chicago and Philadelphia. All three centers will supplement the surgical, maternity and hospital benefits Amalgamated members receive under their industry-wide health insurance program.

Development of the medical plans shared interest in the minds of the 1,500 convention delegates with speculation about the union's probable course in the Presidential election this fall. It was taken for granted that the convention would repudiate the third party movement headed by Henry A. Wallace, but it was not expected that it would give its endorsement to any prospective major party candidate.

Union leaders predicted that the Amalgamated, a bellwether of the middle-of-the-road forces in the Congress of Industrial Organiza-

Continued on Page 4, Column 2

## FRUIT, VEGETABLES TO COME BY TRUCK

Near-By Farms Can Supply Most of City's Needs—Air Transport Suggested

Truck transport from near-by farms will meet most of the fresh fruit and vegetable requirements of the metropolitan area in the event of a railroad strike, trade spokesmen said yesterday.

Edward A. Hausman, executive secretary of the Allboro Retail Fruit Association, who said that 70 per cent of the city's supply of fresh produce customarily came by truck, declared that the major farm products that might run short here if railroads became idle would be lettuce, tomatoes, citrus fruits, asparagus and onions.

Mr. Hausman sent a telegram last night to Mayor O'Dwyer suggesting that he call a meeting of produce wholesalers and retailers to discuss a joint venture for bringing in by plane such fruits and vegetables as are now dependent upon rail shipment.

Despite assurances by the city Department of Markets that New

Continued on Page 4, Column 6

## Doctors Too Few to Run System Of National Care, Says Brookings

Special to THE NEW YORK TIMES.

WASHINGTON, May 9—The United States does not have enough physicians to meet all demands likely to be made under a Federal program of compulsory health insurance, a study made by the Brookings Institution said today.

Moreover, it said there were not enough dentists to meet present yearly demands and there was a great shortage of nurses. Further complication of the situation was seen in the building of numerous hospitals, as additional requirements imposed upon the present active medical personnel could only lead to deterioration of quality of medical care, according to the report.

The Brookings study, made for a subcommittee of the Senate Committee on Labor and Public Welfare, concluded that it would "seem unwise" to adopt a compulsory health insurance system.

The report, a blow at President Truman and other proponents of such a program, was released less than a week after the close of the National Health Assembly, called at the request of the President "to find some way to meet the health situation in this country."

The report, prepared by George W. Bachman and Lewis Meriam, of the institution's staff, declared that the movement for a compulsory program had not only ignored the fact of good and improving conditions, as revealed by mortality rates, but had misused statistics to show evidence of need for medical care.

Dr. Bachman has served on the faculties of leading medical colleges and for eleven years headed the Institute of Tropical Medicine at Puerto Rico. During the war he headed the mission of the American Bureau of Medical Aid to China. Dr. Meriam is author of numerous studies on Government administration and of a recent

Continued on Page 31, Column 7

"All the News That's Fit to Print"

# The New York Times.

LATE CITY EDITION
Cloudy, warm with evening showers today. Fair, cooler tomorrow.
Temperature Range Today—Max.,[illegible]; Min.,[illegible]
Temperatures Yesterday—Max.,[illegible]; Min.,[illegible]
Full U. S. Weather Bureau Report, Page 47

Copyright, 1948, by The New York Times Company.

VOL. XCVII..No. 33,025. | Entered as Second-Class Matter, Postoffice, New York, N. Y. | NEW YORK, FRIDAY, JUNE 25, 1948. | Times Square, New York 18, N. Y. Telephone LAckawanna 4-1000 | THREE CENTS NEW YORK CITY

# DEWEY UNANIMOUS REPUBLICAN CHOICE FOR PRESIDENT ON THE THIRD BALLOT; RUNNING MATE WILL BE NAMED TODAY

## CLAY DECLARES U.S. WON'T QUIT BERLIN SHORT OF WARFARE

### But Military Sources Imply West May Go if Germans Suffer Under Soviet Curb

### TENSION IN CITY MOUNTS

### British Stop Ruhr Shipments to Russians as Latter Cut Electricity and Milk Supply

By JACK RAYMOND
Special to THE NEW YORK TIMES

HEIDELBERG, Germany, June 24—In a serious appraisal of the Berlin situation and the attendant policy in Germany, Gen. Lucius D. Clay, United States Military Governor, concluded today that the Russians were exerting their "final pressure to drive us out of Berlin."

He added, however, that the Western Allies would consider nothing short of war as a reason for withdrawal, and that the Russian tactics would not delay the program to create a German government in the Western zones.

There was an impression here, however, as General Clay met with United States military commanders and Military Government officials in a regularly scheduled meeting, that the Western Allies would consider leaving the former German capital if the suffering of the populace became too great.

**Supply By Air Impossible**

Should the Russians maintain transport restriction, the city, which requires 2,500 tons of supplies daily, could not be fed by air. In that case a Western Allies' decision to leave could be explained as a diplomatic sacrifice in the interests of Germans.

[The Soviet Military Administration increased its pressure against the Western sectors Thursday, Berlin dispatches reported. It cut off electricity from the United States sector, announced that further power cuts would be made and stopped the delivery of fresh milk from the Soviet zone into the United States area.

[The British, in return, halted the shipment of the monthly allotment of coal and steel from the Ruhr to the Soviet zone over railway lines other than the Soviet-blocked Helmstedt-Berlin route. Infantry and armored cars moved through the United States and British sectors, causing considerable alarm among Western Berliners.]

In an interview at newly established European Command headquarters General Clay declared: "They can't drive us out by any action short of war as far as we are concerned."

**Says Germans Are Sufferers**

The real sufferers in the former capital, he emphasized, are the Germans. The Russian acts against the Western Allies hurt not only the Germans in the Western sectors but those of the Soviet sector as well, he added. "It would be hard for the Russians to maintain the squeeze without hurting their sector unless they built an iron gate through the city," he said.

"The Germans of Berlin apparently are prepared to take considerable suffering," the general declared.

General Clay declared that the families of United States personnel would be ordered out of the city "only if war were around the corner."

Another impression gained here is that the United States Military Government feels the Berlin situation has long since passed into the governmental level. There appears to be no way to retaliate against the Russians in Germany without making a possibly regrettable error.

Yet, it is felt that the Republican convention appears to have engrossed Washington. In contrast with the April crisis, military sources said, Washington authorities who then seemed "over-

Continued on Page 18, Column 4

## *Draft Bill Signed by Truman; Youths Register in Six Weeks*

### *President Acts Without Comment—Rush Into Guard Units for Exemption Is Halted —Big Defense Funds Also Approved*

By ANTHONY LEVIERO
Special to THE NEW YORK TIMES.

WASHINGTON, June 24—The draft act requiring military service of men from 19 through 25 years of age became law at 5:40 P. M. today when President Truman signed the measure without comment.

Registration of youths was expected to begin within six weeks, but under the law no one could be drafted until ninety days from today.

In the first year 200,000 to 225,000 men would be called. A provision of the law also permitted 161,000 youths of 18 to volunteer for one year in any of the regular services.

The signing of the bill cut off an unparalleled recruiting stimulus which had more than filled the post-war strength of the National Guard and swelled the ranks of other reserve components. Under the terms of the measure, youths who joined the civilian components were exempt from the draft.

President Truman signed the measure, cornerstone of the Administration rearmament program, within twenty-four hours after it had reached him, squelching reports that he would delay as long as possible in order to fill the ranks of the reserve units.

Members of the National Guard and other part-time units need drill only once a week and go to camp for only about two weeks in a year for three years, whereas drafted men must serve full time for twenty-one months.

The draft bill was the second major measure of the 263 passed in the closing days of the Congressional session to reach the President's desk. Earlier in the day he signed a bill appropriating $3,749,059,250 for the Navy and Marine Corps in fiscal 1949.

The Navy funds included construction of a mammoth carrier of

Continued on Page 7, Column 2

## *Louis Fight Off to Tonight When Rain Drenches City*

By JAMES P. DAWSON

A near-cloudburst which deluged the Yankee Stadium commencing at 7:40 o'clock last night forced a second postponement of the scheduled fifteen-round heavyweight championship bout between Joe Louis, the titleholder, and Jersey Joe Walcott, Camden, N. J., challenger. The bout was postponed until tonight.

In the meantime, Louis has returned to his training quarters at Pompton Lakes, N. J. Walcott will spend the time at the Capitol Hotel, where he has been staying since weighing in at Madison Square Garden on Wednesday, the original date of the battle.

If there's more rain today—and the forecast is for late-afternoon or evening thunder showers—the contest will be postponed to tomorrow night. Monday night also may be available if inclement weather continues.

Neither champion nor challenger plans any extra training work of a strenuous nature. Louis' manager, Marshall Miles, said the titleholder would engage in a brief road workout this morning. Walcott's trainer, Dan Florio, satisfied that the challenger will be unaffected by the double postponement, said Walcott would probably confine his exercise to a walk in Central Park this morning.

Louis and Walcott were at the Stadium prepared to don ring togs when the postponement announcement was made at 8:15. It had been held off until the last minute while officials of the Twentieth

Continued on Page 29, Column 1

## BEN-GURION UPHELD BY ISRAELI COUNCIL

### 2 Rejoin Cabinet on Amnesty Pledge — Unified Army Is Mapped, 400 'Rebels' Held

By GENE CURRIVAN
Special to THE NEW YORK TIMES.

TEL AVIV, Israel, June 24—The Provisional Government of Israel passed its first important political crisis tonight when it received a vote of confidence from the State Council. The possibility that dissident groups might overthrow the Government as an aftermath of Tuesday's rebellion was thus averted.

[Heavy explosions were heard Thursday night and early Friday south of Tel Aviv, The Associated Press said. Reports circulated in Tel Aviv that the Israeli Army was attacking Irgun Zvai Leumi strongholds in the vicinity of Abu Kebir.]

The vote was 24 against 7, with 5 abstaining.

At the same time the two Cab-

Continued on Page 12, Column 3

## *Soviet Bloc Urges 4-Power Accord On German Rule, Occupation End*

Special to THE NEW YORK TIMES.

LONDON, June 24—In a five-point program for the unification of Germany issued tonight through the Moscow radio, the eight Eastern European Foreign Ministers proposed the formulation of a German peace treaty providing for the withdrawal of occupation troops within one year of signature.

The points that the Moscow radio said the conference had agreed upon in the Warsaw parley presided over by Soviet Foreign Minister Molotov were:

(1) That Great Britain, the United States, France and the Soviet Union implement agreements for the completion of Germany's demilitarization.

(2) That the Ruhr's heavy industry be placed under four-power control for a definite period.

(3) That a provisional government for all Germany be established, consisting of representatives of the democratic parties and organizations of Germany, with the objective of creating guarantees against a repetition of German aggression.

(4) That a peace treaty be concluded in accordance with the Potsdam decisions and that occupation forces be withdrawn.

(5) That arrangements be made for Germany to fulfill her reparations obligations to the countries that suffered from German aggression.

The Warsaw conference was called to consider the six-power Western proposals for the setting up of a provisional government in Western Germany and internationalization of the Ruhr.

The broadcast, which was received here by the Soviet monitor, said that the proposals had been adopted today at the conference of the Foreign Ministers of the Soviet Union, Albania, Bulgaria, Czechoslovakia, Yugoslavia, Poland, Rumania and Hungary.

It said the Ministers considered "the solution of the following

Continued on Page 16, Column 1

## COAL OWNERS YIELD ON PAY AND RELIEF TO PREVENT STRIKE

### $1-a-Day More in Wages With Relief Fund of 100 Million a Year Won in Lewis Victory

### AGREEMENT BEING DRAWN

### 'Onerous' Clauses Retained by Union—Steel Company Plants Go Along 'Reluctantly'

By LOUIS STARK
Special to THE NEW YORK TIMES.

WASHINGTON, June 24—John L. Lewis and the United Mine Workers of America today won a smashing victory in forcing bituminous coal operators to agree on a wage increase of $1 a day for 400,000 mine workers and a doubling of their payments into the welfare fund.

The union's price for averting a nation-wide coal strike when the present agreements expire on June 30 came high. The concession on the welfare fund alone means that the operators will pay 20 cents a ton into the fund instead of 10 cents. This will increase the fund from $50,000,000 to $100,000,000 annually.

President Truman's Board of Inquiry, which was to have turned in its report to the White House tonight, deferred action for another day after being advised that operators and miners had reported "progress toward a complete agreement."

In the hope of completing their agreement tonight operators and miners resumed conferences after dinner.

However, at 10 P. M., operators who left the conference room for a few minutes declared that they were "disgusted" with Mr. Lewis' methods at this evening's session.

They asserted that despite their major concessions, the union chief-

Continued on Page 6, Column 4

## DEWEY GIVES CALL

### Accepting Nomination, He Bids People Seek Unity in New Faith

### UNFETTERED, HE SAYS

### Praises All Opponents and Avoids Partisan Attack on Truman

*Text of Governor Dewey's address to convention, Page 2.*

Special to THE NEW YORK TIMES.

PHILADELPHIA, June 24—Gov. Thomas E. Dewey accepted the nomination tonight and immediately appealed to the party and the country for unity on the basis of a new spiritual faith.

The unity America sought, the nominee told a cheering audience, was more than material. Spiritually, he said, the people had yet to find the means to put together the world's broken pieces.

Mr. Dewey, who was accompanied to the platform by his wife and a big group of supporters, told the delegates that he had accepted the nomination and that he came to the convention hall and the nomination "unfettered by a single obligation or promise to any living person, free to join with you in selecting to serve our nation the finest men and women in the nation."

Mr. Dewey was generous in victory to his opponents for the nomination. He praised them all—and called them out by name. When he came to that of Harold E. Stassen, the galleries burst into one of the loudest tributes of the night, and loud, though somewhat less responsive shouts, greeted the names of Senators Robert A. Taft and Arthur H. Vandenberg.

The Governor avoided any partisan attack on the Truman Ad-

Continued on Page 4, Column 5

## World News Summarized

FRIDAY, JUNE 25, 1948

Gov. Thomas E. Dewey of New York was unanimously nominated as the Republican candidate for President on the third ballot of the party's national convention in Philadelphia last night. [1:8.] The "stop Dewey" coalition fell apart even before the roll could be called, leading contenders publicly releasing their delegates. [2:6.]

On the first ballot Mr. Dewey took a commanding lead, with 434 votes to 224 for Senator Taft, 157 for Harold E. Stassen and others far behind. On the second ballot the Dewey vote reached 515, thirty-three less than the required majority. [2:2.] Mr. Dewey would have been nominated on that ballot if the opposing group had not forced a recess and Senator Baldwin had not delayed switching Connecticut's vote for him to Dewey. [1:7.]

Governor Dewey went immediately to the convention hall to accept the nomination. He told the delegates he had made not a single pledge to anyone to obtain the nomination. In a move to erase battle scars, he paid tribute to his six rivals by name. [1:5.]

The convention will select a candidate for Vice President today. House Majority Leader Halleck, who had been looked upon as the almost certain nominee, was said to be strongly challenged by advocates of Mr. Stassen and Senator Knowland of California. [1:6-7.]

In Washington, President Truman signed the Selective Service Act. Although the draft will not become effective for ninety days, registration of men from 19 through 25 is expected to start within six weeks. The President also signed a $3,749,059,250 Navy and Marine Corps appropriation bill. [1:2-3.]

Soft-coal operators and miners agreed on a new contract, lessening the danger of a strike next month. The pact, a sweeping victory for John L. Lewis, provides a $1-a-day pay increase and doubles industry payments into the welfare fund. [1:4.]

A Federal statutory court here reserved decision in the first action directly challenging the constitutionality of the non-Communist affidavit section of the Taft-Hartley Act. [6:1.]

The City Planning Commission made public plans for an integrated Manhattan civic center, with parks, tunnels, public buildings and the elimination of slums in the Brooklyn Bridge-Manhattan Bridge area. [1:6.7.]

The Russians "can't drive us out" of Berlin "by any action short of war," General Clay declared. It was indicated that the Western powers might consider leaving the city if Russian action imposed too great suffering on the Germans. [1:1.] American and British forces patrolled the streets of their sectors and the British placed an economic sanction on the entire Soviet zone of occupation in Germany. [19:1.] A French Foreign Office spokesman said the real issue was not that of currency but of Russia's desire to rule all of Berlin. [17:2.]

A German peace treaty calling for the withdrawal of occupation troops within a year after the signing of the pact and agreement on a provisional government of all Germany, with the Ruhr under four-power control, was demanded by the Foreign Ministers of Russia and her seven satellites at their Warsaw conference. [1:2-2.]

The Provisional Government of Israel, threatened by dissident forces, won a 24-to-7 vote of confidence in the State Council. There were seven abstentions. Plans were laid for a single Israeli army. [1:2.] Britain was reported urging the Arabs to prolong the truce. [12:1.]

NOMINATED FOR PRESIDENT

Thomas E. Dewey The New York Times (by Tames)

## *Stassen-for-Vice-President Urged, Challenging Halleck*

By C. P. TRUSSELL
Special to THE NEW YORK TIMES.

PHILADELPHIA, Friday, June 25—Harold E. Stassen was represented by a spokesman early today as being willing to submit to "a real draft" by the Republican National Convention for nomination for Vice President. This spokesman added, however, that Mr. Stassen did not expect such a draft as he believed Gov. Thomas E. Dewey had another nominee in mind.

Mr. Dewey consulted by telephone with Senator Robert A. Taft and Mr. Stassen before calling a conference on the Vice Presidential nomination in his room at the Bellevue-Stratford early today.

In the course of this communication, it was reported authoritatively that Senator Taft had said that if Senator John W. Bricker of Ohio should be nominated he, Mr. Taft, would fight for his election. Mr. Bricker was Governor Dewey's running mate on the Presidential ticket of 1944.

The commanding lead of Charles A. Halleck of Indiana, majority leader of the House, had been challenged at high party levels. There remained signs that Mr. Halleck might still win, however, unless he faced Mr. Stassen. Mr. Bricker also might make the vote nip and tuck.

Opposition to the Indiana Representative, largely because of his record on foreign policy, spurred a Stassen-for-Vice-President drive. Early today there gathered in the Dewey suite a widely representa-

Continued on Page 4, Column 2

## CONNECTICUT LOST CHANCE TO BE KEY

### Would Have Gone to Dewey on Second Test, Taking Others, Except for Baldwin Word

By FELIX BELAIR Jr.
Special to THE NEW YORK TIMES.

PHILADELPHIA, June 24—Connecticut's delegation to the Republican National Convention almost, but not quite, achieved the role here today that the key California and Texas delegations held in the nomination of Franklin D. Roosevelt by the Democrats in 1932.

Connecticut would have switched to Governor Dewey before the result of the second ballot was announced but for one thing—a promise made by Senator Raymond E. Baldwin. But it still was clear that Harold E. Mitchell, Connecticut's national committeeman and boss, had taken the decisive step and the recess between the second

Continued on Page 3, Column 6

## *Downtown Manhattan Face-Lifting Proposed by City Planning Board*

A blueprint for changing the face of the entire downtown Manhattan area surrounding the Civic Center was made public yesterday by the City Planning Commission.

The long-range plan calls for an integrated Manhattan Civic Center combined with sweeping street, building and park improvements designed to rehabilitate an area that has endured without plan or alteration for almost a century, except for the comparatively new public and private buildings in Foley Square. The area encompasses the approaches to Brooklyn Bridge and City Hall Park on the south and extends north between Broadway and the East River to Canal and Pike Streets.

Salient features of the plan include tunnel approaches and improvements to Brooklyn Bridge; the marking out of proposed sites for a Municipal Courts Building, an office building to house the city's engineering and building staffs, a new Police Headquarters, and other public buildings; the widening of Park Row and other streets and the closing of some; construction of a bus terminal and public parking garage, and the transformation of Foley Square into a single large park area as the heart of the integrated Civic Center.

It envisages also the demolition of the old Tweed Court House and consequent improvement of City Hall Park, the rehabilitation of squalid slum areas for residential purposes, the reconstruction of the projecting decks of the Brooklyn Bridge and the razing of its honeycomb of warehouses at arch openings and in streets under the bridge.

The plan, prepared by the Commission in collaboration with the office of Manhattan Borough President Hugo E. Rogers and other city agencies, will be the subject of discussion at a "preview luncheon" today at the Downtown Ath-

Continued on Page 25, Column 3

## OPPOSITION FALLS

### Taft and Stassen Join in Urging Selection of New Yorker

### GOP PRECEDENT SET

### Dewey Is First Defeated Candidate to Be Chosen Again

By WILLIAM S. WHITE
Special to THE NEW YORK TIMES.

PHILADELPHIA, June 24—Thomas E. Dewey was nominated tonight by the Republicans for the Presidency of the United States.

His selection, on the third ballot of the twenty-fourth Republican National Convention, was unanimous after his forces had smashed an opposing coalition.

When two ballots had shown that the Governor of New York was not to be stopped, his erstwhile antagonists renounced their rivalries with him and pledged all their power to his success in November.

Mr. Dewey came at once to the convention hall and, before the hot and shouting delegates, accepted his nomination in a placating spirit toward his former opponents.

"In all humility," he said, "I pray God that I may deserve this opportunity to serve our country."

**"Lasting Peace" Put First**

Above all its efforts, he declared, the Republican party and the country must seek for the world "a just and lasting peace."

The convention will select tomorrow a Vice Presidential nominee in what is described in the most authoritative quarters as a "wide open field."

Mr. Dewey said pointedly that he was "unfettered by a single obligation or promise to any living person." It was understood that the Dewey group wanted to consider overnight the available men for second place on the ticket.

Governor Dewey is the only Republican in the party's history to be nominated for President after having been once defeated. He lost in 1944 to Franklin D. Roosevelt.

On the first ballot today the Governor got 434 votes to 224 for Senator Robert A. Taft of Ohio, his strongest opponent.

On the second ballot, he climbed to 515 votes, as compared with 274 for Mr. Taft.

The results of the three ballots for the major leaders were as follows:

First—Dewey, 434; Taft, 224; Harld E. Stassen, 157; Senator Arthur H. Vandenberg of Michigan, 62.

Second—Dewey, 515; Taft, 274; Stassen, 149; Vandenberg, 62.

Third—Dewey, all 1,094 votes.

When the second roll-call ended associates of Senator Taft, Mr.

Continued on Page 3, Column 2

## *Hottest Day of Year Cooled by Showers*

New York got its warmest weather of the year yesterday as the temperature rose to 89 degrees at 6 P. M., five notches above the previous high mark of 84 on May 12.

The heat and high humidity combined to give the city a sweltering atmosphere, but some relief came in the early evening with heavy showers. The mercury dropped from 89 at 6 P. M. to 69 degrees at 9 P. M. The humidity, 48 at 8 P. M., rose to 96 at 9 P. M. The humidity had reached the saturation point, 100, in the late morning.

The downpour caused short-circuits in signals on the Independent Subway Division at Thirty-sixth Street and Northern Boulevard in Queens, halting Jamaica and Brooklyn Crosstown trains for ten minutes after 8:39.

Steaming weather also is in prospect for today.

"All the News That's Fit to Print"

# The New York Times.

LATE CITY EDITION
Sunny and cooler today. Mild followed by showers tomorrow.
Temperature Range Today—Max.,80; Min.,70
Temperatures Yesterday—Max.,87; Min.,69
Full U. S. Weather Bureau Report, Page 31



VOL. XCVII..No. 33,026. Entered as Second-Class Matter, Postoffice, New York, N. Y. NEW YORK, SATURDAY, JUNE 26, 1948. Times Square, New York 18, N. Y. Telephone Lackawanna 4-1000 THREE CENTS IN NEW YORK CITY

# WARREN WINS 2D PLACE ON TICKET; PLEDGES A 'CRUSADE' WITH DEWEY; SLATED TO RECAST U. S. BUREAUS

## BERLIN SIEGE ON AS SOVIET BLOCKS FOOD

### CITY SUPPLY SHORT

British Report Stocks In West Lower Than Previous Estimates

RUSSIANS HALT BARGES

Clay Declares Three-Zone Regime Is Near—London Cabinet Discusses Issue

By DREW MIDDLETON
Special to THE NEW YORK TIMES.

BERLIN, June 25—About 2,250,000 Germans in the Western sectors of Berlin came face to face with the grim specter of starvation today as the siege of those sectors began in earnest.

The Soviet Military Administration banned all food shipments from the Soviet-controlled areas into Berlin as part of its calculated policy of starving the people of the Western sectors into the acceptance of the Communist demand for the withdrawal of the Western powers.

[In Frankfort on the Main, Gen. Lucius D. Clay, United States Military Governor, said the establishment of a Western tripartite military administration to supervise the establishment of a Western German Government was imminent. In London the British Cabinet considered moves to offset the Soviet curbs on supplies to Western Berlin.]

Although they see dark days ahead, the Berliners remained calm. Those in the Western sectors changed their marks for the new Deutsche mark of the Western powers with a minimum of disturbance.

Straightaway a brisk black Bourse developed in which one Deutsche mark was sold for up to thirty of the new Russian-sponsored marks, which the Germans call "tapetengeld," or wall paper money.

**Clay and Robertson Meet**

Although Generals Clay and Sir Brian Robertson, British Military Governor, conferred this afternoon, no announcement of policy toward the Russian siege was made after their conference.

The desperate situation in which the strategy of starvation is being exerted ruthlessly by the Russians for political ends, has been lifted out of the hands of the Military Governors to Washington, London and Paris.

According to official figures sent to London yesterday the present food situation in the Western sectors is more serious than has been admitted.

These figures were based on the food supplies available for all of Berlin June 15. Since then there has been very little addition to the existing stocks because of the increasing severity of the Soviet blockade and, of course, constant consumption.

It is estimated that the following food stocks are on hand today for all Berlin, including the Soviet sector: Seventeen days' supply of bread grains and flour, thirty-two days' supply of cereals, forty-eight days' supply of fats, twenty-five days' supply of meat and fish, forty-two days' supply of potatoes and twenty-six days' supply of skimmed and dried milk.

**Foodstuff Stores Scattered**

These foodstuffs are scattered throughout the city in warehouses. Most of those containing bread grains and flour stocks are in the Soviet sector and henceforth the stocks will not be available to the Western sectors.

The commandants of the three Western sectors have replied to the Soviet ban by forbidding the shipment of any food from their sectors into the Russian sector. Since the people of the Soviet sector can be supplied by the entire Soviet zone, the order, although impressive in tone, means little.

A more telling blow at the economy of the Soviet zone was leveled by the bipartite Economic Commission of the United States and British zones in Frankfort on the Main, which suspended "indefinitely" the shipment of all classes of goods from coal to fountain pens into the Soviet zone. This embargo was added to that

Continued on Page 6, Column 2

## Two U. S. Educators Detained by Soviet

By The Associated Press.

BERLIN, June 25—Dr. Lester K. Ade, former State Superintendent of Education in Pennsylvania, was arrested by the Russians today and held five hours before being released.

He said his companion, Dr. Lucile Allard, Coordinator of Elementary Education in Garden City, L. I., also had been detained.

Dr. Ade said the Russians had asked them "dozens and dozens" of questions, including one about Henry A. Wallace's chances for election.

Five other Americans, including members of a constabulary patrol, also were detained, United States officials reported.

## PRESIDENT SCORES DP BILL, BUT SIGNS

Calls It Anti-Semitic Mockery and Says He Approves Only for Sake of Those Aided

*Text of President Truman's statement is on Page 7.*

By ANTHONY LEVIERO
Special to THE NEW YORK TIMES.

WASHINGTON, June 25—The displaced persons bill to admit 205,000 refugees into this country became law this afternoon, but in signing it President Truman denounced the measure as a mockery.

In a long statement filled with scathing denunciations of the compromise measure, passed in the hectic closing hours of the session, the Chief Executive declared he would have vetoed the bill if Congress had not adjourned.

Mr. Truman said the bill was anti-Semitic and he also asserted that it would exclude some Catholics who had fled into the American zone of Germany as anti-Communist refugees.

In explanation of why he had signed the bill so reluctantly, Mr. Truman said he did not wish to penalize its beneficiaries and that he did so with the hope that Congress would rectify its "injustices" as soon as possible.

Whether the bill was "worse than no bill at all" was a hairline question which Mr. Truman said he had decided in favor of the 200,000 persons who would be admitted in the next two years, along with 3,000 orphans and 2,000 recent refugees from the Communist coup in Czechoslovakia.

Against these three points of merit, the only ones he conceded in the bill, Mr. Truman listed "numerous" defects which he said had resulted from a compromise that combined "the worst features of both the Senate and House bills."

"If the Congress were still in session," Mr. Truman said, "I would return this bill without my approval and urge that a fairer,

Continued on Page 7, Column 3

## JOE LOUIS RALLIES TO STOP WALCOTT IN ELEVENTH ROUND

Trailing on Points, Champion Turns Tide With a Right to Jaw and Keeps Crown

42,667 AT THE STADIUM

Jeer Early in Bout Because of Lack of Action—Bomber Says He Is Retiring

By JAMES P. DAWSON

Because he has the punch that has made him one of the greatest heavyweights ever to hold the title, Joe Louis, the ring's Brown Bomber, still is the world champion.

He knocked out Jersey Joe Walcott of Camden, the challenger for the title, in the eleventh round of an ordinary championship battle last night in the Yankee Stadium, and plucked glorious, spectacular victory from threatened defeat.

Trailing the 34-year-old challenger through ten rounds of fighting which more than once drew jeers from the crowd of 42,667, Louis turned the tide of battle with one punch. It was a right to the jaw which shook Walcott to his toes. It was delivered as the shifty challenger was boxing in the confusing style that had baffled Louis last December and was baffling him again before a great crowd which paid $841,739 for the spectacle.

The blow provided the opening which Louis had sought from the start. The champion lost no time pressing his advantage. A savage, furious flurry of short-arm lefts and rights drilled against the head of Walcott as the challenger backed to the ropes and sought to throw up a defense of crossed arms.

**One Right—and It's All Over**

Louis' punches drilled home to the head, however, and they jarred. A right to the jaw shot through a brief opening, and the fight was over.

Walcott pitched forward on his face, rolled over on his back, lay with arms outstretched as the count was tolled over him by Referee Frank Fullam. He struggled to his knees at "seven," but was bewildered, befuddled. He knelt there apparently listening to the count, but probably hearing it not at all.

At "ten" he was struggling to get erect. But he was beyond the effort. He didn't know where he was, though he made as if he would resume fighting.

Referee Fullam clasped the beaten Walcott in his arms and guided him to his corner, knocked out after the eleventh round had gone 2 minutes 56 seconds.

**Doctor Leaps Into Ring**

Dr. Vincent A. Nardiello jumped through the ropes to examine the beaten veteran. His examination apparently showed Walcott had suffered no ill effects from the brief ordeal which brought about his downfall just when it appeared he was on the road to the heavyweight championship of the world.

Walcott was able to step to ring-center and clasp the hand of his conqueror and pose with Louis in wordless acknowledgment of the master's superiority. He was able, too, to talk into a radio microphone, and it was Walcott who led the procession from the ring when the excitement had subsided.

After the battle Walcott was critical of Referee Fullam. The

Continued on Page 11, Column 1

## $250,000 Is Hunted In Wreck of Plane

By The United Press.

MT. CARMEL, Pa., June 25—Authorities were searching today for an air-express package containing a reported $250,000 in small-denomination currency believed jettisoned before the crash of the United Airlines DC-6 near here June 17 in which forty-three persons were killed.

An Army helicopter being used in the search made a forced landing in an open field four miles north of here this morning. The occupants were not injured.

Discovery of a parcel of spun glass intact some distance from the crash scene gave strength to the theory that part of the cargo was dropped from the four-engined mainliner to reduce its weight.

A postal authority said the parcel weighed 240 pounds and contained bills in one, five and ten dollar denominations.

## LEWIS AND OWNERS SIGN NEW CONTRACT

UMW Victory Preserves the Union-Shop Clause, Causing Bolt by 'Captive' Companies

By LOUIS STARK
Special to THE NEW YORK TIMES.

WASHINGTON, June 25—John L. Lewis and the Commercial Coal Operators today signed a one-year agreement on the last effective working day of the 1947 contract. While the contract technically expires on June 30, the ten-day vacation period at midnight tonight ushered in a cessation of coal digging until July 5.

When the terms of the contract were made public shortly after 2 P. M. today, it was apparent that the magnitude of the United Mine Workers' victory was even greater than had appeared yesterday when the chief terms leaked out.

Despite a last-minute bolt by the spokesman for the "captive" mine operators, Mr. Lewis won the general operators to a renewal of

Continued on Page 5, Column 6

## DEWEY GIVES PLANS

A Major Goal Will Be to Help China Fight Communists, He Says

SCORES 'NIGGARDLY' AID

He Says 'Conference' Plan, Used to Pick Warren, Would Be Employed With Congress

By LEO EGAN
Special to THE NEW YORK TIMES.

PHILADELPHIA, June 25—In his first press interview since his nomination, Gov. Thomas E. Dewey said today that one of the cardinal principles of his administration, if elected, would be to help China combat Communist influences within its borders.

Mr. Dewey declared his complete approval of the platform adopted at the Republican National Convention, which ended today, and he described the procedure by which Gov. Earl Warren of California had been chosen as the candidate for Vice President.

Discussing China, Mr. Dewey renewed an accusation he made last year that the Truman Administration had been niggardly in financial aid for China. To preserve a free China against the Communists, the United States, he said, should provide "military advisers, the kind of material the Chinese need and far greater financial assistance."

He added that his general attitude toward China today was the same as it was last December, when he made a public appeal for Marshall Plan assistance to help it achieve stability and peace.

**Opposes Personal Diplomacy**

One reporter asked the Presidential candidate if he could handle Stalin. His answer was that he thought Russo-American relations would improve if handled through regular diplomatic channels.

"I am opposed to personal diplomacy, which always fails," he added. This did not mean, he has

Continued on Page 3, Column 6

THE REPUBLICAN TICKET FOR '48

Gov. Earl Warren and Gov. Thomas E. Dewey
The New York Times (by Tames)

## Truman Reported Confident His Chances Are Improved

By JOHN D. MORRIS

WASHINGTON, June 25—President Truman believes the Republicans' nomination of Gov. Thomas E. Dewey improved Democratic chances of retaining the Presidency in the November elections, White House callers reported today. He was represented as being "definitely encouraged about the whole political situation."

His feeling, the visitors indicated, stemmed partly from the opinion that Mr. Dewey was very much of a conservative and consequently would provide an excellent target for one of the President's favorite gibes at the Republicans—that they represented special interests while the Democrats were more solicitous of the common man.

Another consideration in Mr. Truman's appraisal of the nomination was said to be the convention's failure to choose Senator Arthur H. Vandenberg of Michigan. Many Democratic strategists feel he would have been the most dangerous opponent because of his leadership in the bipartisan foreign policy.

Reports of President Truman's reaction to Mr. Dewey's nomination came principally from Senator James E. Murray of Montana and Representative Laurie C. Battle of Alabama, Democrats, after White House visits. The Senator said Mr. Truman felt that the 1948 Republican platform was "nothing but the reiteration of promises they have failed to keep in the past."

Word that the President was "definitely encouraged" was given to reporters by Representative Battle. He also hinted at the possibility of healing the split between the President and Southern Democrats over Mr. Truman's espousal

Continued on Page 2, Column 5

## WARREN EXPLAINS HIS CHANGE OF MIND

Says Dewey's Request, Status in Cabinet Swayed Him to Seek the Nomination

*Governor Warren's speech of acceptance appears on Page 3.*

By CLAYTON KNOWLES
Special to THE NEW YORK TIMES.

PHILADELPHIA, June 25—Gov. Earl Warren of California declared today that Gov. Thomas E. Dewey's proposal to have the Vice President act as an assistant President with Cabinet status was a major factor in his decision to accept second place on the Republican ticket.

The Californian had stated emphatically as late as a few days before the convention started that he would not run for the Vice Presidency and his sudden change of plan baffled many, even within the convention itself.

Public bewilderment on the point was the greater because Mr. Warren had turned down the Vice Presidential nomination in 1944 when he would have had the same running mate.

Peppered with questions on this

Continued on Page 3, Column 2

## UNANIMOUS CHOICE

Californian Nominated by Acclamation After Dewey Selects Him

GETS CONVENTION OVATION

A Role in Cabinet and 'Full Partnership' in Work of Administration Pledged

By WILLIAM S. WHITE
Special to THE NEW YORK TIMES.

PHILADELPHIA, June 25—Gov. Earl Warren of California was nominated by acclamation today as the Republican candidate for Vice President of the United States.

He will stand with Gov. Thomas E. Dewey of New York, the Presidential nominee, in the November election.

Mr. Warren was chosen without contest and without a roll-call after the name of Harold E. Stassen of Minnesota had been provisionally offered by Arizona and then withdrawn.

The Republican party thus closed its twenty-fourth national convention here with a ticket of two Governors—the one from the Atlantic and the other from the Pacific—neither of whom has had any connection with the controversial record of the Eightieth Congress.

Mr. Warren's nomination by the weary convention required precisely thirty-two minutes. He appeared soon afterward in the hall, where the Far Western delegations led all the others in giving him a lusty, neighborly sort of greeting. He delivered a short, impromptu speech.

"I accept the nomination," he told the delegates with a smile, "before you change your mind."

**Pledges 'A Great Crusade'**

Gravely then he pledged himself "in all humility" to give to Mr. Dewey "the very best that I have and every bit of loyalty that is in my make-up."

The campaign in the fall, he declared, would be "a great crusade for the return of our Government to Republican principles."

Governor Warren was the first choice of Governor Dewey for the Vice-Presidential designation, and his nomination pleased the internationalist wing of the party, whose leaders had been strongly opposed to Representative Charles A. Halleck of Indiana.

The acceptance of the nomination by Governor Warren was made, it was learned, with reservations. Reports of an early morning talk between the Californian and Mr. Dewey varied, but on one point there was agreement. Governor Warren was represented as saying he would take the nomination, if, in the event of his election, he would not be "only a gavel-pounder in the Senate."

Governor Dewey took cognizance of this later as he discussed the Vice-Presidency with reporters.

"There is a story," he said, "that I intend to make an historical change in the position of Vice President and transform it into a working job.

**Senate Duties Would Be Eased**

"I should most earnestly hope that it would be possible, and I believe it will be entirely feasible, to take advantage of Governor Warren's superb talents in the colossal job of reorganizing the national Government and bringing some order out of the chaos.

"I should hope that he could be relieved substantially of his duties of presiding over the Senate in which the members could help and that Governor Warren would be able to give a large amount of time to administrative work of the Government and accept a full partnership in this tremendous task in these difficult times."

Mr. Dewey added that he "definitely" would want the Vice President to participate in Cabinet deliberations.

Mr. Halleck, the Republican floor leader of the House of Representatives, had come forward prominently because he had led the Indiana delegation into the Dewey camp after Governor Dewey was yet to win his own great victory

Continued on Page 2, Column 7

## Egyptians Strafe U. N. Aircraft, Block Israeli Convoy to Colonies

By GENE CURRIVAN
Special to THE NEW YORK TIMES.

TEL AVIV, Israel, June 25—The Egyptians violated the truce on two counts today by strafing a United Nations plane and refusing by force to permit an Israeli convoy to pass through their positions to colonies in the Negeb as agreed under the truce terms. The plane incident was said to have occurred in the vicinity of Negba.

As a result of these alleged infractions the United Nations has withdrawn all its representatives from Egyptian-controlled territory in Palestine and has informed the Egyptian Government that the truce was violated.

[In Cairo the Egyptian Prime Minister said the pilot of the Egyptian plane had opened fire on the United Nations craft because "he suspected that it was an enemy plane," The Associated Press reported.

[Count Folke Bernadotte, the United Nations mediator, reported to Lake Success that he had "protested vigorously" to the Egyptian Government and demanded an explanation.]

Meanwhile, according to Alexis Ladas, United Nations spokesman, the convoy was free to do as it pleased. United Nations control has been withdrawn and if the Israeli authorities decide that it should fight its way through, there are no legal ties to bind them. He pointed out that there was no general truce break, however.

The Israeli Government announced tonight that it had received the following communication from Col. Paul Bonde of the United Nations:

"The Egyptians have prevented a convoy. By decision of mediator they have therefore broken truce. Israeli forces are free to act against Egyptian forces."

The communiqué added:

"The Provisional Government desires it to be known that the defense army of Israel will exercise

Continued on Page 5, Column 2

## World News Summarized

SATURDAY, JUNE 26, 1948

Governor Earl Warren of California will be the Republican candidate for Vice President. He was nominated by acclamation to be Governor Dewey's running mate at the closing session of the Republican National Convention yesterday. Mr. Warren pledged a campaign that would be "a great crusade for the return of our Government to Republican principles." [1:8.] An offer by Governor Dewey to have the Vice President as an assistant President with Cabinet status was cited as a major factor in persuading Mr. Warren to accept the nomination. [1:7.]

Mr. Dewey voiced approval of the Republican party platform and declared that, if elected, he would give more ample support to China to combat communism within its borders. [1:5.]

President Truman was pictured by White House callers as "definitely encouraged about the whole political situation" and convinced that Governor Dewey's nomination had increased Democratic chances of retaining control of the White House. [1:6.]

The Chief Executive reluctantly signed the compromise bill to admit 205,000 refugees into this country. He criticized the measure as anti-Semitic and anti-Catholic. [1:2.]

A new one-year agreement signed by John L. Lewis and soft-coal operators gave the miners a $1-a-day wage increase and an additional 10 cents a ton, or about $50,000,000 annually, for their welfare fund. [1:4.]

The 2,250,000 inhabitants of the Berlin zones occupied by the Western powers remained calm despite the prospect of a sharp curtailment of their food supplies as Soviet authorities halted all food shipments into the areas. [1:1.] General Clay announced the imminent organization of a tripartite military government group to serve as a control agency over the projected Western German Government. [6:6.]

The proposals for the unification of Germany advanced at the Warsaw conference of eight Eastern European Foreign Ministers provided no basis for renewed talks by the major powers, in the opinion of diplomatic representatives of the Western powers in the Polish capital. These diplomats believed Moscow would form an East Germany Government after these proposals had been rejected by the Western powers. Washington received the Warsaw program with reserve. [7:1.]

The return of Italian Communist leaders from the Warsaw meeting to Rome coincided with a new outbreak of strikes in northern Italy. [6:8.]

The United Nations withdrew its representatives from Egyptian-controlled territory in Palestine after two violations of the truce agreement. The Egyptians strafed a United Nations plane and used force to bar the passage of an Israeli food convoy through their positions in the Negeb. A United Nations spokesman indicated that the convoy was free to fight its way through if it so chose. [1:2-3.]

Count Bernadotte, United Nations Mediator, reported the two Egyptian infractions to the Security Council. [5:1.]

The Security Council ignored Soviet protests as it refused to reopen debate on Generalissimo Franco's regime in Spain. [4:6-7.]

A new sharp slump in the value of Chinese currency has followed reverses suffered by the Nanking Government in its civil war with the Communists. [7:5.]

Joe Louis retained his world heavyweight championship when he knocked out Joe Walcott in the eleventh round. [1:3.]

## Vote-Buying for Valente Charged; Hogan Plans Inquiry in Tammany

By JAMES P. McCAFFREY

District Attorney Frank S. Hogan announced yesterday afternoon that he would investigate reports that three Tammany district leaders had received $1,000 each to vote for Judge Francis L. Valente of General Sessions as the Democratic designee for Surrogate of New York County.

The Criminal Court jurist was designated at a meeting of Tammany Hall's executive committee last Wednesday. He defeated Vincent R. Impellitteri, president of the City Council, who was the choice of Mayor O'Dwyer and Frank J. Sampson, Tammany leader. Judge Valente was a last-minute substitution for his uncle, Justice Louis A. Valente of the Supreme Court, who had drawn the opposition of the Association of the Bar of the City of New York.

Mr. Hogan interrupted a trip to Lake George, N. Y., to make his announcement. The District Attorney was on his way to the annual convention of the New York State District Attorneys convention when he was informed of the reports. He returned to his Manhattan office immediately.

"I have read the account of the alleged bribes and it should be unsparingly investigated up to the hilt," Mr. Hogan said. "I will call anybody and everybody who may have any information with respect to the alleged bribes."

The New York County prosecutor said that the inquiry would be started Monday morning. At that time, he added, a new grand jury would be sworn in.

Judge Valente said last night:

"This is Mr. Hogan's job. If he thinks there is anything to investigate, he should bring out all the facts."

Meanwhile, the American Labor party, through its New York County secretary, Councilman Eugene P. Connolly, announced that its organization had designated Nathan Dambroff as its candidate

Continued on Page 32, Column 2

"All the News That's Fit to Print"

# The New York Times.

LATE CITY EDITION

Partly cloudy and mild today. Increasing cloudiness tomorrow.

Temperature Range Today—Max.,82 ; Min.,67
Temperature Yesterday—Max.,81 ; Min.,60
Full U. S. Weather Bureau Report, Page 41



VOL. XCVII..No. 33,045. Entered as Second-Class Matter. Postoffice, New York, N. Y. NEW YORK, THURSDAY, JULY 15, 1948. Times Square, New York 18, N. Y. Telephone Lackawanna 4-1000 THREE CENTS IN NEW YORK CITY

# TRUMAN, BARKLEY NAMED BY DEMOCRATS; SOUTH LOSES ON CIVIL RIGHTS, 35 WALK OUT; PRESIDENT WILL RECALL CONGRESS JULY 26

## MOSCOW REJECTS PARLEY ON BERLIN TO BREAK IMPASSE

### Reply to Protests on Blockade Asserts Any Talks Must Embrace All of Germany

### BLAMES WEST FOR SPLIT

### Soviet Says Currency Reform and Proposed New State Made Its Action Necessary

*Text of Soviet reply to protest on Berlin is on page 16.*

By HERBERT L. MATTHEWS
Special to The New York Times.

LONDON, July 14—The Soviet Union rejected the Western powers' demand for the lifting of the blockade of Berlin in notes to Washington, London and Paris delivered today by Soviet Ambassadors in those capitals.

The text of the reply to the United States, as broadcast by the Moscow radio and translated here by the Soviet monitor, said the Soviet Union would conduct four-power negotiations on the "general question of quadripartite control in relation to Germany" but not only on Berlin as the Western powers had proposed. The Moscow broadcast said the replies to Great Britain and France were similar. The note to the United States repeated the Russian contention that "Berlin is in the center of the Soviet zone and is part of that zone."

**Deny Pressure Is Intended**

In reply to one crucial passage in the Western Allies' notes it had this to say:

"As regards the declaration of the Government of the United States [similar passages appeared in the British and French notes] that it will not be induced by threats of pressure or other actions to abandon its right to participate in the occupation of Berlin, the Soviet Government does not intend to enter into a discussion of this declaration for it has no need of a policy of pressure since by violation of the agreed decisions on the administration of Berlin the above mentioned Governments are themselves rendering null and void their right to participation in the occupation of Berlin."

There were a few good features in the note from the Western Allies' viewpoint, such as a reference to the blockade moves as "temporary measures" and the fact that they had been necessitated by the Western currency reform. There also was an offer to feed all of Berlin with Soviet supplies.

However the Soviet reply was basically a refusal to meet any of the Western Allies' demands and therefore it brought the United States, Britain and France face to face with further serious decisions.

[Washington sources said the Soviet reply left the Berlin situation unchanged and indicated that new Western power talks would be held.]

Discussions between these three powers began almost immediately today and will continue on a more intense basis tomorrow because many hours were lost today in translations, comparisons and preliminary soundings.

The British Foreign Office unaccountably gave out during the afternoon that there were "no major sensations" in the Soviet note and that was the official attitude up to the time the Foreign Office closed late tonight. However, the text of the note was the clearest possible demonstration that the Russians had replied with a firm categorical "no."

This was the vital passage replying to the Western Allies' demand that the blockade of Berlin be lifted preliminary to the holding of four-power talks on Berlin—not Germany as a whole—recognized as the crucial issue:

"While not objecting to negotiations, the Soviet Government, however, deems it necessary to declare that it cannot link the start of these

Continued on Page 16, Column 3

## Stalin Is 'Outraged' By Togliatti Attack

By The United Press.

LONDON, July 14—The Moscow radio declared tonight that Premier Stalin and the Soviet Communist party were "outraged" by the attempt to slay Palmiro Togliatti in Italy.

The broadcast said the following telegram was signed by Premier Stalin and sent by Russian Communists to the Italian Communist party:

"The Central Committee of the Communist party of the Soviet Union is outraged by the villainous attempt of an outcast of humanity on the life of the teacher of the working class and all the laboring people of Italy, our well-loved Comrade Togliatti.

"The Central Committee of the Communist party of the Soviet Union is grieved that Comrade Togliatti's friends were not able to protect him from the foul underhand attack."

## SOVIET BACKS U. S. ON PALESTINE EDICT

### Four Other Countries Support U. N. Threat of Sanctions to Halt War in Holy Land

By THOMAS J. HAMILTON
Special to The New York Times.

LAKE SUCCESS, N. Y., July 14—The Soviet Union and four other countries gave their support today to a United States proposal that the United Nations Security Council invoke Chapter VII of the Charter and order both sides to stop the fighting in Palestine. These announcements apparently guaranteed the passage of this part of the resolution introduced by the United States yesterday, but left in doubt the fate of the sections to which the Soviet Union objected.

It was expected that Andrei A. Gromyko, Soviet representative, or Dmitri Z. Manuilsky, Ukrainian Foreign Minister, who is this month's chairman of the Council, would demand tomorrow that it vote paragraph by paragraph on the United States resolution. Apart from these two countries, the United States can count on six votes—one short of the needed majority—for most of its resolution.

[An offensive by Israeli forces in Galilee resulted in the capture of three towns in the vicinity of Nazareth. At the same time Israeli units pressed their attack from the coastal plain in an effort to dislodge the Arabs from Latrun, key point on the Tel Aviv-Jerusalem supply road. On the Jerusalem front, the Arabs opened an attack on Israeli-held Mount Zion.]

The United States resolution would determine that the situation in Palestine constitutes a "threat to the peace" and would bind the

Continued on Page 15, Column 1

## RIOTS SWEEP ITALY AFTER AN ASSASSIN WOUNDS TOGLIATTI

### Six Dead, Scores Hurt as Reds Battle Police, Who Are Said to Be in Control

### GENERAL STRIKE IS BEGUN

### Communist Chief Improves After 3 Bullets Are Removed—Assailant Captured

By ARNALDO CORTESI
Special to The New York Times.

ROME, Thursday, July 15—Palmiro Togliatti, Italy's Communist chief, was shot three times yesterday morning outside the Chamber of Deputies by a university student who fired four revolver bullets at him at point-blank range. One bullet entered his left lung. The other wounds were not serious.

At 10 o'clock last night a bulletin issued at Polyclinic Hospital, where he was fighting for his life, said Signor Togliatti's condition was slightly improved. He was said to have a good chance of recovery from his wounds, but fear was expressed that his heart, which has been weak for some years, might not hold out.

The assassin was arrested running from the scene.

Nearly all Italian cities were swept by rioting as soon as the news of the shooting was broadcast. [Six policemen and demonstrators were killed and scores wounded, according to news agencies.]

**General Strike Called**

The Communists started a powerful campaign to force the resignation of the Government. The General Confederation of Labor, which they control, called a general strike on a national scale. It began at midnight and was to continue for an indefinite time. The strike order applies to every form of activity except a very few of the most essential public services. It applies even to the railroads and the postal and telegraph services, which have hitherto always been excluded.

In Milan generally and especially in the "red citadel" of Sesto San Giovanni, a suburb of Milan, the workers last night had begun to occupy factories and were preparing to stand a siege in them.

This is without question the most serious challenge that Communists have yet hurled at the Government. They evidently reckon that they can tie up the whole country and keep it tied up till the Government has no option but to resign.

The Government, however, has met the challenge squarely. It addressed a proclamation to the

Continued on Page 18, Column 6

## IN A FIGHTING MOOD

### 'Will Win the Election and Make the Republicans Like It'

### SCORNFUL OF RIVALS

### Housing, Education and Civil Rights Issues for Special Session

*Text of President Truman's acceptance speech, Page 4.*

By JAMES RESTON
Special to The New York Times.

PHILADELPHIA, Thursday, July 15—President Truman accepted the Democratic Presidential nomination in a fighting mood this morning, predicted victory in November and announced that he would call Congress back into session on July 26 to deal with housing, education, civil rights and other controversial measures.

The President was in turn scornful and bitter about the Republicans. They had made a lot of proud statements in their campaign platform, he said, and now he would give them a chance to prove that they meant what they said.

The Congress would have every chance later this month to deal with most of the questions that needed to be settled. These questions could be debated in a hurry, in fifteen days, he said, if the Republicans really meant what they were saying. But the real test the people would make, he emphasized, would be action not words.

The immediate reaction at Convention Hall was that the President's summons to Congress would create even more bitterness than now exists between the Republican-controlled branch and the Democratic executive. In midsummer, the inhabitants of the steaming capital are never precisely in a deliberative mood, and with an election campaign going on simultaneously the temperature is not likely to be reduced.

Housing and high prices, Mr.

Continued on Page 3, Column 5

THE DEMOCRATIC NATIONAL TICKET

Harry S. Truman
*President*

Alben W. Barkley
*Vice President*

The New York Times

## VICTORY SWEEPING

### President Wins, 947½ to 263, Over Russell on the First Ballot

### BARKLEY ACCLAIMED

### Nominees Go Before Convention to Make Acceptance Talks

*Text of the Donnelly speech nominating Truman, Page 5.*

By W. H. LAWRENCE
Special to The New York Times.

PHILADELPHIA, Thursday, July 15—President Harry S. Truman won nomination for a full term in the Democratic National Convention early today and promptly made the Republican record in Congress the 1948 key issue by calling a special session of Congress to meet July 26 to challenge the GOP to keep its platform pledges.

The President, selected by well over two-thirds of the Democratic delegates, although the Solid South dissented and thirty-five delegates from Mississippi and Alabama walked out, was in a fighting mood as he went before the convention with his running mate, Senator Alben W. Barkley, who was chosen by acclamation.

Confidently predicting his and Senator Barkley's election because "the country cannot afford another Republican Congress," the President said that the special session would be asked to act on legislation of various types.

**Cites Republican Platform**

He would call on it, he declared, to act to halt rising prices, meet the housing crisis, provide aid to education, enact a national health program, approve civil rights legislation, raise minimum wages, increase social security benefits, finance expanded public power projects and revise the present "anti-Semitic, anti-Catholic" displaced persons law.

The Republicans said they were for all these things in their 1948 platform, the President stated, and, if they really meant it, all could be enacted into law in a fifteen-day session.

President Truman set the convention on fire with his acceptance speech, which came at the end of a long, tiring, tumultuous session in which the north-south party split was deepened appreciably, although only a handful of southern delegates bolted.

The Southerners who remained were almost as angry as those in the "walk" about the convention's strong civil rights pledge and its overwhelming refusal to include a state's rights plank in the platform.

Senator Barkley promised to follow the President's leadership, agreed to carry out the platform and pledged himself to carry the story of Democratic accomplishments to every precinct to insure victory in November.

The acceptance speeches completed, the convention adjourned at 2:30 A. M.

**Truman Margin of Victory**

President Truman's margin over his chief rival, Senator Richard B. Russell of Georgia, was 947½ to 263, while Paul V. McNutt received half a vote in the final tabulation.

Senator Russell got almost the solid Southern vote remaining in the convention after the bolt by delegates from Alabama and Mississippi.

As soon as Mr. Truman was nominated, at 12:42 A. M., the convention moved ahead to the nomination of his Vice-Presidential running mate.

There was an attempt to present Senator Russell again for the Vice Presidency, but he stopped it and

Continued on Page 3, Column 1

## TRUMAN IS SHUNNED IN VOTES OF SOUTH

### Eleven States Give Him 13 of Their 278—Mississippi and Half of Alabama Bolt

By WILLIAM S. WHITE
Special to The New York Times.

PHILADELPHIA, Thursday, July 15—The eleven states of the old Confederate South gave today to the nomination of President Truman only thirteen of their 278 votes in the Democratic national convention.

The entire Mississippi delegation of twenty-two and thirteen of the Alabama delegation bolted the con-

Continued on Page 9, Column 1

## South Beaten on Race Issue As Rights Plank Is Widened

By C. P. TRUSSELL
Special to The New York Times.

PHILADELPHIA, July 14—The Democratic National Convention, by a roaring voice vote, committed its party today to what was called a straightaway Roosevelt-Truman platform for 1948. In scenes of emotional demonstration, with Southern Democrats pleading rather than demanding as Northern liberals were firmly in the saddle, the document was changed at only one point. That was where a majority of the convention, in effect, accused its platform committee of hedging on the civil rights program which had precipitated the South into bitter revolt against President Truman.

[*Text of the platform as adopted by the convention is on page 8.*]

By a roll call of 651½ to 582½, the convention demanded that four objectives of that program be spelled out: abolition of poll taxes in Federal elections, a national law against lynching, creation of a permanent fair employment practices system and non-segregation of the races in the armed services.

In another cracking-down action, the convention refused bluntly and decisively, in the face of Southern argument that the upholding or throwing down of the Constitution itself was at stake, to put a states'

Continued on Page 8, Column 7

## BARKLEY IS CHOSEN AFTER BRIEF FLURRY

### Only Rival, Senator Russell, Quits the Race—Truman Hails Kentuckian

*Text of Senator Barkley's acceptance speech, Page 7.*

By FELIX BELAIR Jr.
Special to The New York Times.

PHILADELPHIA, Thursday, July 15—Senator Alben W. Barkley of Kentucky was nominated by acclamation early today as the Democratic Vice Presidential candidate, leading even President Truman as the overwhelming choice of the delegates to the party's thirtieth national convention.

A few minutes later the man whose choice was dictated by an

Continued on Page 7, Column 2

## World News Summarized

THURSDAY, JULY 15, 1948

President Truman was nominated by the Democratic National Convention this morning as the party's Presidential candidate against Governor Dewey and Henry A. Wallace. He received 947½ votes against 263 for Senator Richard B. Russell of Georgia, named by the Southern states' rights bloc as a gesture of defiance to Mr. Truman, and ½ vote for Paul V. McNutt. Senator Barkley was nominated for Vice President by acclamation after Senator Russell, again named by the Southerners, had withdrawn as the only opposing candidate. [1:8.]

In an acceptance speech that ripped into the Republicans the President told the convention he would call Congress back into session on July 26 to act on housing, high prices and other vital measures to show "if there is any reality" behind Republican platform pledges. [1:4.]

The Southern revolt reached its climax at the night session, when the entire Mississippi delegation of twenty-two and half of Alabama's twenty-six delegates walked out of the convention hall at the start of the roll-call for Presidential nominations. Then the name of Senator Russell was presented after Governor Laney of Arkansas, around whom the opposition first rallied, had withdrawn. [1:5.]

During the afternoon a series of Southern attempts to soften the civil rights plank of the platform and to incorporate a State's rights plank went down to overwhelming defeat. The Southerners' crowning disappointment came unexpectedly when Northern liberals, rejecting Administration pleas to do nothing to upset party unity, put over by a vote of 651½ to 582½ a strengthened civil rights plank that lauded President Truman's program and called for its enactment. The platform was then adopted by voice vote. [1:6-7.]

In this city Governor Dewey criticized the Democratic plank on foreign relations as containing "extremely partisan and provocative assertions." [8:1.]

Russia rejected the protest of the Western powers on the Berlin blockade. She told Washington, London and Paris in notes that they had lost all legal status in Berlin by having broken the Yalta and Potsdam pacts for four-power rule in Germany. The Soviet Union again urged four-power talks on all of Germany, but refused to accept settlement of the Berlin dispute as a precondition. [1:1.] A record number of 500 United States and British planes flew 2,500 tons of food and supplies into Berlin. [1:2-3.]

Palmiro Togliatti, Communist leader in Italy, was shot and seriously wounded by a student. The Communists blamed the Government and demanded its resignation. Strikes, attended by fatal riots, broke out all over the country. [1:3; map P. 18.]

The United States proposal to order both sides in Palestine to cease fighting won the support of Russia and four other countries in the United Nations Security Council. [1:2.] Israeli forces captured several towns near Nazareth. [14:3.]

## West Replies to Russians' Rebuff With Another Air Tonnage Record

By DREW MIDDLETON
Special to The New York Times.

BERLIN, Thursday, July 15—The Western Powers met the Soviet refusal to raise the siege of Berlin with a record number of air supply flights carrying a record tonnage and solid determination, generally expressed, this morning, to keep the Western flags flying in the city.

News of the Soviet reply to the United States, British and French notes of protest circulated slowly through the Western sectors of the city, already darkened by electricity restrictions and facing perhaps more stringent rationing in the future.

Everywhere reaction to the wording of the Soviet note was the same: resolution in the face of the Soviet blockade of the city and hope that the Russian answer would lead to an expansion of the air lifeline into the city.

"Perhaps the tone of the Russian note will impress on the people of the United States just what we are up against here," said one senior member of Gen. Lucius D. Clay's staff. "I hope we can look forward to an early increase in the airlift as a result."

Another United States official declared he hoped that the Russian emphasis on such things as currency reform would not blind Americans to "the far larger issues at stake" in the Berlin crisis.

The tone of the Soviet note was not a surprise to United States and British military government officials who forecast the temper of the Russian reply on the basis of an editorial in the Taegliche Rundschau, Soviet Army newspaper, Wednesday morning.

The editorial called the Western proposal to negotiate a solution of the Berlin crisis "ridiculous" and demanded that any conference between the East and the West embrace the entire German question

Continued on Page 17, Column 6

## Truman, in a Gay Mood, Receives Acclaim of Big Convention Crowd

Special to The New York Times.

PHILADELPHIA, Thursday, July 15—Democratic delegates and galleries filled with guests paid dignified tribute at 1:30 A. M. to President Truman and Senator Alben W. Barkley as they came to Convention Hall platform to accept their nominations.

The President, dressed in white, moved to the rostrum to "Hail to the Chief," and Mrs. Truman and his daughter, Margaret, walked with him, all smiling. The entire audience of some thirteen to fifteen thousand delegates and visitors stood to cheer them. Confetti and streamers flew.

Then the band played "The Missouri Waltz" for the President and "My Old Kentucky Home" for the grizzled Kentucky Senator, as the two shook hands. Chairman Sam Rayburn had asked for "a short demonstration" but his attempts to choke off the band's version of "My Old Kentucky Home" went unheard. The President shook with laughter.

Mrs. C. E. Miller of Philadelphia gave the President a floral replica of the Liberty Bell, and with the statement that through him the nation expected "peace in out time, and peace for all time," released forty-eight white doves from a basket on the platform. The birds zoomed toward the brilliantly-lighted dome, some ninety feet from the floor.

They were bewildered and frightened, at first. They flew against the rafters, against the bunting and swooped and dived at the President on the platform. Most were caught within a few minutes but others flew on silent wings, circling in the harsh light, all through the acceptance speeches of Senator Barkley and the President.

The great throng in the hall listened attentively to the speeches.

The President had a friendly reception from the moment he entered the hall until he left it, at 2:20 A. M., with the cheers and "Hail to the Chief" resounding behind him.

"All the News That's Fit to Print"

# The New York Times.

LATE CITY EDITION
Rain ending tonight. Partly cloudy and mild tomorrow.
Temperature Range Today—Max., 64; Min., 58
Temperatures Yesterday—Max., 61; Min., 46
Full U. S. Weather Bureau Report, Page 46

Copyright, 1948, by The New York Times Company.

VOL. XCVIII..No. 33,157. Entered as Second-Class Matter, Postoffice, New York, N. Y. NEW YORK, THURSDAY, NOVEMBER 4, 1948. Times Square, New York 18, N. Y. Telephone Lackawanna 4-1000 THREE CENTS NEW YORK CITY

# TRUMAN WINS WITH 304 ELECTORAL VOTES; DEMOCRATS CONTROL SENATE AND HOUSE; EUROPE SEES FOREIGN POLICY CONTINUING

## NATIONS ARE UNITED IN ASSEMBLY VOTE FOR PEACE PACTS

### Marshall and Vishinsky Back Mexican Resolution in U. N. to Bring About Treaties

### ATOMIC DEBATE FOLLOWS

### Austin Expresses Hope Russia Will Accept the Majority View to Effect Control

By A. M. ROSENTHAL
Special to THE NEW YORK TIMES.

PARIS, Nov. 3—The United Nations General Assembly unanimously asked the Big Five today to start a new era of cooperation and a few hours later heard the United States invite Russia to "high level" atomic control negotiations.

Without debate the plenary session of the Assembly gave quick approval to the Mexican resolution calling on the major powers to try again to settle their quarrels and come to agreement on the terms of peace treaties with Germany and Japan.

Mexico's resolution was introduced to leaven the atmosphere of tension and animosity caused by the thrashing out of all major Soviet-West disputes in the full Assembly and in committee rooms. From the beginning it had the support of every member of the Big Five and all small and middle sized powers.

**Marshall, Vishinsky Vote Yes**

When Dr. Herbert Evatt of Australia, Assembly President, asked for a vote the delegates saw something they had not seen at a plenary session of this Assembly on any important issue. Secretary of State Marshall and Andrei Y. Vishinsky of Russia both raised their hands to vote yes.

But that about ended agreement for the day. The next major item on the agenda was the atomic control controversy, and the Assembly settled down to hear a rehashing of the arguments from the majority and the minority.

The two main documents are before the committee—the Canadian resolution adopted by the Political and Security Committee, and the rejected Soviet motion.

Canada's proposal approves the majority control plan, continues the life of the Atomic Energy Commission and suggests that the sponsors of the United Nations' atomic control idea—Canada and the Big Five—get together to try to break the deadlock.

On the other hand, the Russian resolution would ignore the majority control reports, but would instruct the Atomic Commission to continue. The Russian motion also contains a controversial proposal for simultaneous signing of conventions outlawing the atomic bomb and establishing atomic control.

**Austin Accents Talks**

The first and only speaker today was Warren R. Austin of the United States. He gave full support to the Canadian resolution, but put the accent on the paragraph dealing with private Big Five Canada talks.

"It is the desire of the United States that these consultations should be at a high level and principally concerned with the cause of the Soviet Union's finding itself at present unwilling or unable to take a cooperative part with other nations in the necessary measures for the maintenance of peace," he said.

Mr. Austin made it clear that he did not expect differences to disappear at the first consultation. But the United States, he said, believes the time is ripe for "quiet and mature discussion in an atmosphere of intelligent deliberation."

"We believe that the terrible problem of atomic energy would provide the framework which would keep constantly before the consulting powers the urgent necessity for agreements on measures which would resolve the present difficulties and which would lift from the hearts of nations the overshadowing fear of atomic warfare," said the United States delegate.

The tenor of the former Vermont Senator's speech was probably the most moderate of any made on the high-powered atomic dispute. He told the delegates that the United States felt that some day Russia would come to believe that it was in her interests to accept foolproof atomic control.

Mr. Austin acknowledged that the United States had gone into the session "just about" convinced that a continuation of the Atomic Commission would be futile. But many other delegates announced

Continued on Page 35, Column 7

## 10 U. S. Fliers Crash In B-29 in Britain

Special to THE NEW YORK TIMES.

LONDON, Nov. 3—A United States B-29 Superfortress, on a routine flight between Scampton airfield in Lincolnshire and the Burtonwood air depot in Lancashire, crashed today with its crew of three officers and seven enlisted men.

Seven bodies had been recovered by nightfall. It was presumed that all aboard had been killed. The crash occurred in one of the loneliest regions of the British Midlands — atop Kinder Scout, a 2,000-foot mountain near Glossop in Derbyshire.

United States Air Force headquarters said tonight that no identification of crew members could be made until the next of kin had been notified. The plane, however, was revealed to be part of the 301st Bomb Group in the United Kingdom.

## JAPAN HELD GUILTY OF AGGRESSIVE WAR

### Court Cites Attack on China and Designs on Allies in Prelude to Tojo Verdict

By The Associated Press.

TOKYO, Thursday, Nov. 4—The International Military Tribunal held today that Japan was guilty of waging wars of aggression against China and planning similar hostilities against the United States, Britain, Russia and other allied powers.

The ruling came in the first day's reading of the voluminous judgment in the war crimes trial of former Premier Hideki Tojo and twenty-four co-defendants. It covered the period from 1928 to 1938.

The eleven-nation court narrowed the issues down to the simplest terms:

Was Japan guilty of waging aggressive war in violation of international treaties?

Were the twenty-five defendants responsible for making and carrying out those policies?

Were the defendants responsible for crimes against humanity and violations of the laws of war?

Thus far in its reading, the tribunal has declared that "militarists and their supporters" seized control of Japan's Government. This in effect means that any who joined in the seventeen Cabinets since 1928 adopted the militarists' policy as their own.

The court ruled that the Manchurian conquest of 1931 and the full-scale war against China, which opened July 7, 1937, were instigated by militarists and deliberately provoked on the part of Japan.

Earlier, the tribunal cleared the twenty-five defendants of thirty-eight of the fifty-five counts in their war crimes indictment.

It held that in the early 1930's the Japanese Government began preparations for war not only against China but against Russia, Britain, the United States and other Western powers.

The court has not reached the individual verdicts against the prisoners, however.

The tribunal blamed the Japanese Army for fomenting the Sept. 18, 1931, Mukden incident which gave Japan the excuse to seize Manchuria. And the war with China in 1937, it said, was a direct result of the foreign policy adopted

Continued on Page 32, Column 3

## WEST IS HOPEFUL

### Sees Marshall Plan Aid and Truman Doctrine Being Carried Out

### END OF SNARLS FORECAST

### Observers on Continent Say Berlin and Other Issues Will Be Discussed Soon

By C. L. SULZBERGER
Special to THE NEW YORK TIMES.

MADRID, Nov. 3—As an immediate result of President Truman's astonishing electoral victory, many major foreign political developments that had been halted until after the voting in the United States almost certainly will be activated now more swiftly than had been expected.

Not only has Mr. Truman's reelection established his position in a fashion relatively more impressive to foreign eyes than it was in the past, but the shift in the Congressional picture is bound to convince other nations of the solidity of the United States administration and the permanence of the programs and attitudes adopted by the White House during the last two years.

[Astonishment and relief were expressed in London. Paris sources saw the continuance of the Truman Doctrine and the Marshall Plan. At the United Nations session John Foster Dulles said he believed President Truman would continue the "bipartisan foreign policies that have proved their worth." Dr. Herbert V. Evatt of Australia said the world owed Mr. Truman a tribute for his battles for mankind.]

It is obvious from the views foreign sources expressed before the vote that both the extreme Left and the extreme Right in Europe are disappointed. Likewise the center and non-Communist Left—the so-called "Third Force"—is bound to be delighted because it has derived considerable support from United States diplomacy.

It was generally considered that Moscow would have preferred a Republican victory. One Communist tactic used whenever possible was to attempt to disrupt the center forces and group the anti-Communist opposition as much as possible into coalitions that Kremlin propaganda could label the Right Wing.

One may assume that such would have been the Communist strategy in attacking a Dewey Administration as Rightist, even though it represented a scant change.

The Soviet Union obviously also must have been severely disappointed at the wretched showing of Henry A. Wallace.

Mr. Truman's moral position with "Third Force" elements must certainly now be high, because there was considerable interest abroad in his attitude on civil rights, even though this question

Continued on Page 24, Column 4

## SWEEP IN CONGRESS

### Democrats Obtain 54-42 Margin in Senate by Winning 9 GOP Seats

### CERTAIN OF 258 IN HOUSE

### Republicans Have 167, With 9 Still in Doubt—Shifts in Chairmanships Slated

By WILLIAM S. WHITE

The Democrats swept all of Congress yesterday, recapturing the supposedly impregnable Republican House by a landslide and seizing firm control of the Senate in one of the great political revolutions of American history.

As the story of Tuesday's elections yet unfolded in the late counts from the voting places, the first Republican Congress since 1932 looked out upon a scene of catastrophe as it prepared to relinquish its brief two-year tenure of leadership.

Broken were the great bastions of Republican Congressional strength; vanished was the almost universal presumption that no matter what happened to the Senate, the House would stay in Republican hands.

The labor vote, implacably angry over the Taft-Hartley Act and resentful over Republican tax reductions, had moved with strength and determination against the Republican incumbents.

**Farm Vote Disappoints GOP**

The farm vote had bitterly disappointed the Republicans. Where it did not turn upon them outright, the Democrats made deep inroads in the grain belts.

President Truman's long campaign against the Eightieth Republican Congress, which he had called either "the worst" or "the second worst" of all time, apparently had a strong appeal at the ballot boxes.

Thus, last night, with all the votes not yet counted, the Democrats had taken in overflowing measure their revenge for their own Congressional rout of 1946.

The clear prospect was that in the Eighty-first Congress of next January the House would be overwhelmingly Democratic with as

Continued on Page 6, Column 3

A VICTORY SMILE AND SALUTE GIVEN BY THE PRESIDENT

Mr. Truman acknowledging plaudits of a crowd outside his hotel in Kansas City. He had just received Governor Dewey's message of congratulations.

Associated Press Wirephoto

## DEWEY 'SURPRISED'; WILL NOT TRY AGAIN

### Congratulates Truman, Asks Support for Him to Aid National Unity, Peace

By RUSSELL PORTER

After conceding defeat and sending congratulations to President Truman yesterday, Governor Dewey announced he did not intend to seek a third Presidential nomination. He said he had "no plans" about a third term as Governor and denied a reported intention of resigning. His term has two years to run.

In his telegram and in a press conference the Governor urged public support of the President for the sake of national unity and world peace. At the press conference he emphasized "most earnest-

Continued on Page 3, Column 1

## Truman Humble in Pledging Service to American People

By ANTHONY LEVIERO
Special to THE NEW YORK TIMES.

INDEPENDENCE, Mo., Nov. 3—President Truman accepted this day of supreme triumph in a spirit of humility and with a simple pledge to serve the American people for prosperity and peace. The fire-breathing campaigner, who "passed a miracle" unsurpassed in American political history, today was more like the man who appeared so overawed when he assumed the succession to the late Franklin D. Roosevelt.

Correspondents who have been recording his words in many weeks of hard campaigning gave him an opportunity to have an "I-told-you-so" fling at Thomas E. Dewey and the poll-takers. He had said that today they would be the red-dest-faced people in the United States. Mr. Truman did not take the opportunity.

To the American people he rededicated himself to four years of the Presidency with these words:

"I feel very deeply the responsibility which has fallen to my lot as the result of the election. I shall continue to serve the American people to the best of my ability. All my efforts will be devoted to the cause of peace in the world and the prosperity and happiness of our people here at home."

In fewer words, but as feelingly expressed, was his message to Mr. Dewey, who until yesterday was the almost universally acknowledged winner.

"I thank you sincerely for your congratulations and good wishes. Your fine sportsmanship is deeply appreciated. We jointly owe

Continued on Page 7, Column 3

## CHIEF RACE DELAYS REFERENDA COUNT

### But Some States Decide Such Issues as War Bonus, Old-Age Aid, Labor Controls

By The Associated Press.

WASHINGTON, Nov. 3—In the general election voters of several states were called upon to decide upon bonuses for veterans of World War II, increased old age pensions, labor issues and various tax and bond proposals.

The closeness of the Presidential race was delaying today reports on most of the results

Twelve states posed veterans' benefit questions to their electorates. Reports from six show that Indiana, South Dakota and Louisiana approved bonuses; Nebraska and Wisconsin did not. The Indiana action is not binding on the 1949 Legislature. North Dakota defeated a proposal for a levy for a veterans' rehabilitation fund.

Eight states, in addition to Kansas, had the perennial wet vs. dry issue on the ballot in one form

Continued on Page 15, Column 4

## OHIO POLL DECIDES

### It Clinches for President in Race Called Miracle of Electioneering

### NO RECORD BALLOT IS SEEN

### Dedicating Himself to Peace, Prosperity, Truman Says He Wants to Deserve Honor

By ARTHUR KROCK

The State of Ohio, "mother of Republican Presidents," furnished the electoral bloc early yesterday forenoon which assured to President Harry S. Truman a four-year term in his own right as Chief Executive of the United States. Until this late accounting of votes cast in Tuesday's general election put Ohio firmly in Mr. Truman's column, after it had fluctuated throughout the night, he was certain of but 254 electoral votes, which were twelve less than the 266 required.

The historic role played by Ohio was only one of the dramatic and extraordinary phases of the election of 1948. The President, opposed by the extreme right and left wings of the Democratic party, won a minimum of 304 electoral votes as against 189 acquired by his Republican opponent, Gov. Thomas E. Dewey of New York; carried a Democratic majority in Congress along with him after the Republicans had held this for two years; and gained victory through a multi-sectional combination of states that did not include New York, New Jersey, Pennsylvania and four of the Southern states in normal Democratic territory.

**Miracle of Electioneering Seen**

In the political history of the United States this achievement by Mr. Truman will be set down as a miracle of electioneering for which there are few if any parallels. His victory made him the undisputed national leader of the Democratic party, which, though bitterly divided for the past few years, has acknowledged none since the death of Franklin D. Roosevelt, whom Mr. Truman succeeded from the office of Vice President.

When it was assured that he would have Ohio's electors and hence the majority he needed, and Governor Dewey had wired his congratulations and publicly conceded defeat, the President dedicated his official future to world peace and domestic prosperity and said to his brother, J. Vivian Truman, simply: "I just want to deserve the honor."

**No Record Vote Indicated**

In the result, unexpected by nearly everyone who qualified as a judge of elections except the President himself, there were these other attendant circumstances:

1. The popular vote, expected to reach 51,000,000 or 52,000,000 and thus break the record poll of about 49,548,000 in the Presidential contest of 1940, will probably be far short of the 1940 total.

2. It is possible that Mr. Truman's plurality over Mr. Dewey will not exceed 2,000,000 and may be less than that, which is smaller than the electoral division of 304 to 189 would ordinarily indicate. But this can be partly attributed to the fact that two splinter Democratic tickets were in the field—the States' Rights Democrats headed by Gov. J. Strom Thurmond of South Carolina, and the Progressives headed by Henry A. Wallace, which will poll almost 2,000,000 votes more than probably would have gone in large measure to the national Democratic ticket in normal circumstances.

3. To the vote cast for Mr. Wallace can be traced definitely the failure of the President to carry only one state, New York, with forty-seven electors.

4. California, after see-sawing all Tuesday night and yesterday morning as in 1916, and as Ohio did this year, ended in the Truman column as it did in Woodrow Wilson's contest with Charles E. Hughes thirty-two years ago. But then California made the drama of victory for Wilson: this year Ohio

Continued on Page 2, Column 4



## World News Summarized

THURSDAY, NOVEMBER 4, 1948

President Truman's victory in Tuesday's election was assured yesterday when Ohio's final figures gave him that state. He was then certain of at least 304 electoral votes, with 189 for Governor Dewey and 38 for Governor Thurmond on the States' Rights ticket. [1:8.]

The President accepted his victory with humility. Thanking Governor Dewey for his congratulations, Mr. Truman said they both were indebted to the American people, who had shown the world once again "the vitality of our free institutions." [1:6-7.] Mr. Dewey, conceding defeat, urged national unity behind the President "to keep our nation strong and free and establish peace in the world." [1:5.]

Henry A. Wallace did not congratulate the President, but called on him to fulfill his campaign promises. [20:1.]

The Democrats' sweep of Congress in all sections gives them control of the House, with a majority that may reach 100 [1:4], and of the Senate, where the majority reached twelve. [2:2.]

Few immediate changes were seen in the Cabinet. Secretary Marshall wishes to retire to his farm and Secretary Forrestal may resign upon unifying the armed forces. [15:3.]

Labor support and general dissatisfaction with high prices were held responsible for cutting Governor Dewey's plurality in New York to 42,777. [18:3.] The Democrats gained nineteen seats in the Assembly and ten in the Senate. [12:4.]

In the eyes of foreign diplomats, the Truman victory assured a steadier and more vigorous American foreign policy than was possible with a Democratic President and a Republican Congress. [1:3.] A form of lend-lease arms assistance for Western Europe, it was said in Washington, will be started even before the new Congress takes office. [33:2-3.]

Britain saw the Marshall Plan undisturbed as a result of Mr. Truman's election [22:2] and the British people admired his fight. [22:4.] The French felt that their Third Force had been strengthened. [23:2-3.] Germans were encouraged [20:3], as were the Italians. [19:4.] South America felt there would be no important change in the diplomatic corps. [23:4.] The Chinese, however, were disappointed, having looked for more liberal help from Governor Dewey. [1:2-3.] Arab states saw Israel strengthened. [23:6.]

John Foster Dulles and Warren R. Austin, both Republicans, declared in Paris that the bipartisan policy would not be disturbed. [21:3.]

The United Nations General Assembly unanimously approved a Mexican resolution urging the big powers to settle their differences and to speed peace treaties. [1:1.]

The uncoordinated state of internal security controls is a grave threat to the nation's security, Secretary Forrestal told the President and the National Security Council. [33:1.]

The International Military Tribunal for the Far East, reconvening to pass judgment on Tojo, found Japan guilty of waging aggressive war. [1:2.]

## Truman Vote Disappoints Nanking; Hope of Full Aid From Dewey Gone

By HENRY R. LIEBERMAN
Special to THE NEW YORK TIMES.

NANKING, Thursday, Nov. 4—Manifestly hoping for a Republican victory in the United States elections, high Chinese officials were unable to conceal their disappointment today as the balloting returns, broadcast by American shortwave radio, showed President Truman's re-election.

The surprising vote figures were being carefully tallied in the Government Information Office yesterday afternoon, while Generalissimo Chiang Kai-shek conferred with Premier Wong Wen-hao and tried to persuade the latter not to resign in the midst of the present military, economic and psychological crisis in China.

Other Nanking officials telephoned American correspondents for the last word on the returns that the correspondents themselves were getting by shortwave radio.

Dr. Wong has submitted his resignation three times, but it has not been accepted by the Generalissimo. Before he conferred with Generalissimo Chiang, the harassed Premier asserted his determination to resign at a full meeting of the Cabinet yesterday morning. He was authorized by the Cabinet, as a matter of formal constitutional procedure, to report its resignation to the Generalissimo orally. However, each member was reportedly left free to carry on at his own discretion.

Encouraged by the Republican party platform and Gov. Thomas E. Dewey's campaign statements asserting Democratic neglect of China, the Government had been anticipating fuller American aid under a new administration after it took office in January. But with the time factor made critical by a series of morale-shattering, civil war defeats the Government seemed to be counting even more on the immediate magic

Continued on Page 23, Column 5

## Kansas Votes Prohibition Repeal After 68 Years of Dry Experience

By The Associated Press.

TOPEKA, Kan., Nov. 3—Kansas voted repeal of its sixty-eight-year-old constitutional prohibition amendment. Wet forces piled up an apparent 46,000-vote majority in yesterday's voting.

Repeal of the amendment, however, was just the beginning of the fight for legalized liquor in Kansas. The issue now goes to the Legislature where some seats were upset as a result of the repeal vote. Many observers said the vote, which trailed the balloting for national and state offices in this Republican stronghold, was merely a division of wets and drys.

Kansas still has a "bone dry" law on the books which bans transportation and possession of liquor. The Constitution prohibited only manufacture and sale. Repeal means that the Legislature can decide what needs to be done but offers no solution for eliminating the "bone dry" law.

Prohibition leaders, apparently expecting repeal, were working on state legislators before the election. The city voting put repeal across but western dry counties control the State House.

The vote on repeal pulled with it another state matter of major interest to the legislators. They now will get a pay increase.

The end of prohibition as a political issue was predicted yesterday by leaders of the liquor industry when the repeal victory in Kansas was made known. Defeat of prohibition measures in California, Washington and Colorado acted to strengthen this belief.

Vice Admiral F. E. M. Whiting, president of the Licensed Beverage Industries, an association representing all major liquor producers, made this comment:

"Kansas can now be added to the list of seventeen countries and provinces which have tried prohibi-

Continued on Page 13, Column 2

"All the News That's Fit to Print"

# The New York Times.

LATE CITY EDITION
Mostly sunny and cool today; cloudy tonight and tomorrow.
Temperature Range Today—Max.,34; Min.,15
Temperatures Yesterday—Max.,42; Min.,31
Full U. S. Weather Bureau Report, Page 43

Copyright, 1949, by The New York Times Company.

VOL. XCVIII..No. 33,235. Entered as Second-Class Matter, Postoffice, New York, N. Y. NEW YORK, FRIDAY, JANUARY 21, 1949. Times Square, New York 18, N. Y. Telephone Lackawanna 4-1000 THREE CENTS IN NEW YORK CITY

# TRUMAN, 32D PRESIDENT, IS INAUGURATED; CALLS ON U. S. TO LEAD DEMOCRATIC WORLD; DENOUNCES COMMUNISM, PLEDGES U. N. AID

## COMMUNISTS WIN RIGHT TO WITNESSES AGAINST U. S. JURY

### Will Call First Today in Effort to Prove Illegality of Body That Indicted Them Here

### MIGHT SUMMON 12 JUDGES

### Medina Permits Defense Step While Studying Motion to Strike Out Challenge

By RUSSELL PORTER

The right to call witnesses against the grand jury that indicted them was won yesterday by the eleven Communist leaders. Defense lawyers announced they would present their first witnesses this morning. They have contended the jury was illegal and its indictment void, because it was selected by methods that excluded certain minority groups.

Defense counsel said also they might put Judge John C. Knox, senior jurist of this Federal district; Judge Harold R. Medina, who is trying this case, and the ten other judges in this district, on the witness stand.

Jurors and jury officials also may be subpoenaed. A defense agent applied for 100 subpoenas from the clerk of the court and received fifty, all that were on hand.

The defendants were indicted by a special grand jury on charges of organizing the Communist party to teach and advocate overthrow and destruction of the Government by force and violence.

**Jury Indicted Hiss Also**

The same jury later indicted Alger Hiss, former State Department official, on charges of perjury to conceal evidence of espionage in the transmission of official secrets to Russian Communist agents.

Presumably, if the Communists succeed in voiding their indictment on the ground that the grand jury was improperly constituted, this would set a precedent for voiding the Hiss indictment.

Judge Medina opened the door to the grand jury challenge when he decided to "take proofs" while reserving decision on a prosecution motion to strike out this challenge.

"My disposition has been to grant the prosecution's motion," he said, "but this will give me time to study it further."

George W. Crockett Jr. of Detroit then stood up at defense counsel table. He is attorney for Carl Winter, Michigan State chairman, and Jacob Stachel, "educational" director of the Communist party.

Mr. Crockett announced he might have to call all the Federal judges of this district to the witness stand to testify regarding discrimination against Negroes and other minorities in selecting juries. Mr. Crockett himself is a Negro.

**Says He Might Call Medina**

Looking over his glasses at Judge Medina, Mr. Crockett said grimly:

"I might have to call your honor."

Judge Medina leaned back in his big red leather chair behind the bench and smiled amiably.

"That's been done before," he said.

The judge then asked United States Attorney John F. X. McGohey and the five chief defense lawyers to submit memoranda as to the competence of a judge as a witness in a proceeding before himself.

Mr. McGohey suggested the need to find out whether the judge would be disqualified by law from continuing to sit in a case after appearing as a witness.

"It would be an extraordinary thing," the judge added, "if a maneuver of that kind could disqualify the judge. I doubt that could be the law, because if it were, and if counsel were repeatedly seeking delay for various

Continued on Page 9, Column 1



## North Ireland Votes On Eire Tie Feb. 10

By The United Press.

BELFAST, Northern Ireland, Jan. 20—A general election that is expected to determine whether Northern Ireland will remain part of the United Kingdom will be held Feb. 10, it was announced today.

It will be the first general election since Eire's declaration of independence from the British Commonwealth.

Observers here agree that the chief election issue would be Britain's plan for the establishment of federal Ireland. Under this plan, Northern Ireland and Eire would have their own parliaments but would send representatives to an All-Ireland Assembly at Dublin that would control vital matters such as defense and taxation. Both of these matters now are controlled by Britain in Northern Ireland.

## CHIANG HELD READY TO LEAVE NANKING

### Farewell Statement Reported Being Drafted in Move to Ease Parley With Reds

By HENRY R. LIEBERMAN
Special to THE NEW YORK TIMES.

NANKING, Jan. 20—Generalissimo Chiang Kai-shek's speech-writer, Tao Hsi-sheng, was again reported at work tonight on a farewell statement for the Generalissimo in the midst of a dynamic political situation that has reached a new stage for ups and downs, even in China.

According to the Generalissimo's plans, as they were said to have existed just before midnight, he is now preparing to depart for Formosa over a route that may include stop-overs of undisclosed duration at Fenghwa, his old home in Chekiang Province, and Foochow on the coast of Fukien.

Several times before this the Generalissimo is known to have told his intimates that he was planning to leave Nanking, only to alter the plan soon thereafter. Now that Premier Sun Fo's Cabinet has formally decided to propose a cease-fire order to the Communists, however, his leaving Nanking seems to have become a more pressing matter for the peacemakers, anxious to make their sincerity plain to the Communists.

Even if the Generalissimo leaves Nanking, his departure for South China, where the Government is shifting its capital, is still regarded as leaving open the possibility of the anti-Communist bloc operating under his leadership from a series of new bases in Fukien, Kwangtung and Formosa.

It is considered almost inevitable that if the Generalissimo leaves, the step will be accompanied by some face-saving formula.

With the capital no longer

Continued on Page 12, Column 3

## ASIAN LANDS URGE FREE INDIES IN '49; NEHRU INVITES BLOC

### New Delhi Delegates Agree to Bid U. N. Order Dutch Back to Pre-'Police Action' Lines

### COLONIAL RULE ASSAILED

### Indian Premier Issues Call for Permanent Gathering to Guard Area Interests

By The United Press.

NEW DELHI, India, Jan. 20—Delegates from nineteen Asian countries decided at a secret meeting tonight to ask the United Nations Security Council to order the complete independence of Indonesia by the end of this year.

They decided also to recommend to the Council that the Dutch be ordered to withdraw immediately to the lines they occupied before the Dutch "police action" last Dec. 18 and that this withdrawal be completed by March 18.

The Asian delegates met here at the request of the Indian Prime Minister, Pandit Jawaharlal Nehru, to protest the Dutch military action in Indonesia and to study the possibilities of aiding the Indonesian Republic.

At the opening plenary session this morning, Prime Minister Nehru proposed the creation of a permanent organization of Asian states to guard the interests of the Far East.

He said that the immediate aim of the conference would be to find a solution to the Indonesian problem. But he added that the delegates also should consider the creation of a "permanent arrangement for effective mutual consultation and concerted effort in the pursuit of common aims."

His statement was a clear call for a regional organization of Asian states within the framework of the United Nations. It will be discussed Saturday by the full conference.

During the secret meeting today at Hyderabad House, the Asian delegates decided also to ask the Security Council to insure the re-establishment of a recognized Indonesian interim government by March 18, the deadline for troop withdrawals.

Tomorrow the delegates will discuss the question of applying sanctions against the Netherlands, and it appeared today that such sanctions would be approved by most of the nations represented.

Prime Minister Nehru, who was elected chairman, sounded what may be the only controversial note in this conference with his proposal for a permanent Asian organization.

His plea was supported by Brig. Gen. Carlos P. Romulo of the Philippine Republic. General Romulo

Continued on Page 12, Column 5

## PRAISE IN CONGRESS

### Members Hail Truman's Bold Stand, but Are Wary on New Aid

### DETAILS ARE ASKED

### Non-Partisan Questions Raised on Extent of Loan Guarantees

By C. P. TRUSSELL
Special to THE NEW YORK TIMES.

WASHINGTON, Jan. 20—The principles and objectives enunciated by President Truman in his inaugural address today drew warm comment from members of Congress. But no guarantees were given that he would escape controversy over his "bold new program" for making American scientific advances and industrial progress available for the improvement and growth of underdeveloped areas of the world.

While the partisanship that stems usually from first reaction was almost absent, questions were raised at key points, and fuller explanation was demanded as to the proposed scope and application of the program, its possible cost and the means of financing it.

There was widespread call from members of both parties that there be a "spelling out" of details, especially that phase of the program that was interpreted by many as proposing a guaranteeing of investments in foreign countries.

**Praise of U. N. Acclaimed**

Mr. Truman's declaration of continuance of unfaltering support to the United Nations and its related agencies appeared to have won universal approval within both major parties. So did his pledge of continuing programs for world economic recovery, with reservations as to the new plan.

A strengthening of freedom-loving nations against the dangers of aggression seemed to have such widespread approval that predictions were made in some quarters that the proposed North Atlantic Collective Defense Pact would get through Congress "without trouble."

It was stated, in varied phrasing through many voices, that the President's analysis of democracy as compared with communism, and the force with which he had made the comparison, had done great

Continued on Page 5, Column 2

HARRY S. TRUMAN TAKING THE OATH AS PRESIDENT

The Chief Executive being sworn by Chief Justice Fred M. Vinson. In the center, holding Bibles, is Charles E. Cropley, clerk of the United States Supreme Court, and at the right of Mr. Truman is Vice President Alben W. Barkley.

The New York Times (by Ernest Sisto)

## SPEECH SEEN AS AID TO WESTERN WORLD

### Capital Observers Hold It Step to Expand Economic and Military Defenses Abroad

By JAMES RESTON
Special to THE NEW YORK TIMES.

WASHINGTON, Jan. 20—President Truman's inaugural address was generally interpreted in the capital as one of the most ambitious pronouncements on foreign affairs ever made by an American President.

Mr. Truman said so much about what the United States was prepared to do about opposing communism, building a collective security system and restoring the economic strength of Western Europe, however, that some of his principal advisers on foreign affairs felt that he did not put enough emphasis on the reciprocal

Continued on Page 7, Column 1

## More Than a Million Roar In Approval of Inauguration

By WILLIAM S. WHITE
Special to THE NEW YORK TIMES.

WASHINGTON, Jan. 20—The roar of a great crowd—over a million persons were here as the unofficial delegates of the people of this country—rose and fell today in broken, happy cadence for Harry S. Truman's inauguration as President of the United States.

There was elation and aggressive triumph in the voices of these men and women, the triumph of the many whose man somehow had won against all the probabilities.

In their struggling, staring mass they overran the aloof green and marble reaches of Washington; they swarmed over cold official lawns hardly used year in and year out; they struggled, sometimes angrily, for places before the great, stern façades of the Supreme Court, the Capitol, the Library of Congress, the Treasury.

For many blocks they filled the lateral streets running into Pennsylvania Avenue, the traditional way here for pageants, and a great many thousands of them never really saw the parade for which they had come so far.

Their voices, making a hoarse medley of all the accents of the United States of America, beat strongly against the endless, brass thumping of the endless bands.

The streets were filled and running with their noises, and the

Continued on Page 4, Column 6

## BARKLEY SWORN IN AS VICE PRESIDENT

### 'Happy to Be Backing Up the President,' He Says—Day Marks Turn in Career

By CLAYTON KNOWLES
Special to THE NEW YORK TIMES.

WASHINGTON, Jan. 20—With thirty-six years of continuous service in Congress behind him, Alben W. Barkley embarked upon a new career of service to the nation today as he took the oath of office as the thirty-fifth Vice President of the United States.

Erect and seemingly sturdy as an oak, the 71-year-old Kentuckian was sworn into his new office at 12:23 P. M. by Associate Justice Stanley F. Reed, a few minutes before Harry S. Truman took the

Continued on Page 3, Column 5

## PEACE A MAJOR AIM

### Truman Says America Will Not Waver From Fight on Aggressor

### TO STRENGTHEN FREE

### Proposes Sharing U. S. Scientific Gains With Undeveloped Areas

*The text of the President's Inaugural Address, Page 4.*

By ANTHONY LEVIERO
Special to THE NEW YORK TIMES.

WASHINGTON, Jan. 20—Harry S. Truman denounced communism as a false doctrine and outlined a four-point program for American world leadership, and peace, as he assumed the Presidency in his own right in the most impressive inaugural of American history.

Thus with a positive statement of American aspirations, the thirty-second President of the United States concluded the traditional ceremony on Capitol Hill which reached a tremendous global audience on the radio waves.

He took the oath of office before a throng of more than 100,000 of his fellow countrymen at 12:29 P. M., a few minutes after Senator Alben W. Barkley of Kentucky took a similar oath and became the Vice President.

Unlike many of his predecessors, whose inaugural addresses were in the nature of philosophical discourses, the plain-spoken Missourian delivered a major policy statement. It was replete, like virtually all his speeches, with concrete statements and proposals.

**Calls for Just Settlement**

Mr. Truman drew a sharp, straight line between democracy and communism, without the slightest trace of the softening toward Russia which some observers had been suspecting recently.

The Chief Executive asserted that democracy was a vitalizing force, sustaining the initiative which was in our hands, and that we would not be moved from our faith by the Soviet political philosophy.

President Truman explained he was not making his strongly contrasting definitions of democracy and totalitarianism merely to be argumentative. He saw communism as a threat to world recovery and lasting peace, he said, and he was offering what he proclaimed to be a constructive program for all nations.

He did not leave Russia and her satellites out of his hopes. Although he mentioned none of them by name, as he neared the end of his address he expressed a belief that the countries under Communistic regimes would "abandon their delusions and join with the free nations of the world in a just settlement of international differences."

**Would Share Progress**

The heart of his aims Mr. Truman set forth in one, two, three, four fashion. First he reiterated unwavering support of the United Nations and here he made a friendly gesture to such nations that are aborning, as Israel, Korea and Indonesia. He said they would strengthen the United Nations as they themselves became strong with the nourishment of democratic principles.

As his second point, Mr. Truman reiterated this country's determination to work for world recovery by giving full measure to the European Recovery Program and promoting trade for all the world's markets.

On the North Atlantic Security Plan, which is now crystallizing, Mr. Truman focused his third point. He said, "We will strengthen freedom-loving nations against the dangers of aggression," but only within the recognized framework of the United Nations Charter and

Continued on Page 2, Column 4

## Jerusalem's Fate Held Main Issue In Settlement of Palestine Question

By ANNE O'HARE McCORMICK
Special to THE NEW YORK TIMES.

JERUSALEM, Jan. 20—The best place to study both sides of the Palestine conflict is in Jerusalem. Here are two distinct cities, as far apart in aspect, time, outlook and way of life as they are near in space.

Across a narrow No Man's Land, cluttered with the debris of a passionate war—for to both sides this is an intensely desired and holy place—the New City looks upon walls of the Old and the Old City looks back on the open streets and modern buildings of the New. They are in constant sight of one another, separated only by a small guard and a few strands of barbed wire 100 feet apart, but no citizen of one town ever sets foot in the other.

Not a Jew remains in the Old City and only a few hundred Arabs, strictly confined in a small section, are left in the New City. Each community is under military rule and each lives a separate, restricted life in a world of its own so different from the other that it is hard to remember that they ever mingled.

What will happen to Jerusalem is the central question in the Palestine settlement. Control of the Negeb, desert area to the south, now an international issue, is the foremost material objective of Israel. Her determination to own this empty area and to people it with 2,000,000 settlers shows how the ideas of the new state regarding both territory and population have expanded as a result of military conquests.

A leading Zionist statesman remarked the other day with the accent of regret that Israel's problems would be simpler if she were the smaller state envisioned in the United Nations partition plan. "But too much has occurred since to make it possible for any Govern-

Continued on Page 11, Column 4

## World News Summarized

FRIDAY, JANUARY 21, 1949

Harry S. Truman, the thirty-second President of the United States, was inaugurated yesterday. He delivered a major address on foreign policy, assailing communism in a sort of parallel-column contrast of what he called communist vices with democratic virtues. He outlined a four-point program of American world leadership for peace: unfaltering devotion to the United Nations and its economic agencies, determination to carry on international recovery programs, creation of a North Atlantic security group within the United Nations framework to strengthen the democracies, and sharing of American scientific and technological progress with the rest of the world. [1:8.]

Observers called the speech the most ambitious pronouncement on foreign policy ever made by a President. They endorsed the principles but questioned some of the details. [1:5.] Congressional reaction was somewhat the same. Objection to what was felt to be a guarantee of American investments abroad was voiced. [1:4.]

President Truman started his day at an early breakfast with World War I comrades of Battery D [1:6-7] and went to the Capitol, where he and Vice President Barkley were sworn in. [1:7.] He reviewed the inaugural parade, which took nearly three hours to pass the stand [5:1], and then attended a reception at the National Gallery of Art. [6:3.] It was estimated that 1,000,000 persons had witnessed the ceremonies. [1:6-7.]

Some changes in the Taft-Hartley Law were advocated by the Chamber of Commerce of the United States. [35:6.] The United Automobile Workers will demand pensions of at least $100 a month. [16:4.] A strike caused New Jersey to cut off the supply of gas to industries in the Camden area. [16:2.]

Lawyers for the American Communist leaders on trial won the right to call witnesses against the grand jury that brought the indictments. [1:1.]

Generalissimo Chiang Kai-shek was reported ready to quit Nanking to smooth the way for peace talks with the Communists. [1:2.]

The New Delhi conference of Asiatic countries decided to ask the United Nations to order full independence for Indonesia. [1:3]

Disagreement on "important points" delayed an Israeli-Egyptian armistice. [11:2-3, with map.]

Big Four talks on an Austrian treaty will be resumed in London Feb. 7. [10:5.]

The new Greek Cabinet was sworn in. [14:2.]

*Index to other news appears on Page 22.*

## Captain Harry, Not Mr. President, Starts Day of Days With Battery D

By CHARLES HURD
Special to THE NEW YORK TIMES.

WASHINGTON, Jan. 20—From noon until late tonight President Truman's life blended into the panoply and formality of an inaugural history-making in its size, but this morning—and the morning began before sunrise—the time was his own and the man was Harry S. Truman or plain "Captain Harry."

The dividing line in the day occurred at 12:29 P. M. At that minute Mr. Truman took the oath as President of the United States and stepped into the pattern of his day of triumph. Behind him, however, even at noon, lay almost half a dozen active hours arranged as he had planned them.

He had, in those hours, spanned activities ranging from jocular chiding at a breakfast of his old companions in Battery D to attending divine services in St. John's Episcopal Church, together with doing a little work. Only two other personal intervals were left in his crowded day: one, a lunch in the office of his old friend, Leslie L. Biffle, Secretary of the Senate, and the other a private dinner late this evening with his family at Blair House.

Otherwise, Mr. Truman's time divided itself into four official parts that taxed many younger persons in his entourage, but in which he participated despite the fact that he had less than five hours' sleep last night.

On this official schedule, he first took his oath of office and delivered an inaugural address at the Capitol in ceremonies starting at noon. At 2 P. M. he belatedly led his own inaugural parade to the White House, to stay there for more than three hours watching it march past. Long after the scheduled hour of 5 P. M. he hastened to the National Gallery of Art to

Continued on Page 3, Column 2

"All the News That's Fit to Print"

# The New York Times.

LATE CITY EDITION
Mostly fair, mild in afternoon today. Partly cloudy tomorrow.
Temperature Range Today—Max., 51; Min., 37
Temperatures Yesterday—Max., 52; Min., 36
U. S. Weather Bureau Report, Page 4, Sect. 5

Section 1

NEWS SUMMARY AND INDEX, PAGE 95

Copyright, 1952, by The New York Times Company.

VOL. CI No. 34,399. Entered as Second-Class Matter, Post Office, New York, N. Y. NEW YORK, SUNDAY, MARCH 30, 1952. Including Magazine and Book Review. FIFTEEN CENTS New York City | 50 Mile Zone | Elsewhere Twenty-five Cents

# TRUMAN ANNOUNCES HE WILL NOT RUN AGAIN; SAYS HE SERVED LONG, FEELS 'NO DUTY' TO STAY; NEWS STUNS DEMOCRATIC LEADERS AT DINNER

## CATHOLIC SCHOOLS RAISE ENROLLMENT TO 4,000,000 PEAK

### $250,000,000 Expansion Plan Is Under Way for Adding of 1,000,000 by 1960

### PERSONNEL IS INADEQUATE

### Survey Discloses High Cost for Lay Teachers to Fill Gap —Curriculums Improving

By BENJAMIN FINE

Growing at a rapid rate, the Roman Catholic schools and colleges in the United States have a record enrollment of 4,000,000 students, representing an increase of more than 35 per cent in the last ten years.

For the first time, the Catholic elementary schools have exceeded 3,000,000, while the secondary schools are above 600,000. The Catholic-supported institutions of higher learning have combined enrollments of 350,000. The increase is expected to continue, estimates by school officials placing the 1960 Catholic school and college enrollment at 5,000,000.

To meet the tremendous demands placed upon it, the Catholic school plant is in the midst of an expansion program that will cost $250,000,000. Under construction are facilities valued at $130,000,000, while $110,000,000 in construction is projected for next year. Only the shortage of steel or other critical supplies will slow this all-out expansion.

These findings are based on a nation-wide study of Catholic education by THE NEW YORK TIMES. Data were obtained from more than 75 per cent of the Catholic dioceses in the United States—ninety-four out of 126. Information also was supplied by representatives of the National Catholic Welfare Conference in Washington.

**Teacher Shortage Acute**

The teacher shortage in the Catholic schools is just as acute as it is in the public institutions. Many superintendents report they are unable to obtain the necessary teachers, either lay or religious. They say that because of this shortage the Catholic schools can not expand as rapidly as they might.

Many Catholic officials report that they are turning more and more to lay teachers to fill the gap, though too often these teachers are not available because of the public schools' competition for their services. This year the Catholic schools employ a total of 199,118 teachers, of whom 97,068 are religious. Ten years ago the total number of teachers was 88,444.

In the United States today there are 11,519 Catholic schools, divided as follows: 8,845 elementary, 2,296 secondary and 378 unspecified.

The growth in Catholic school enrollment has been rapid on both the elementary and secondary levels. Each of the 126 dioceses conducts one or more schools. New York State leads with 900 elementary schools. Within the state the Archdiocese of New York (Bronx, Manhattan, Staten Island and Westchester County), with 284 elementary and ninety-nine secondary schools, and the Diocese of Brooklyn, with 227 elementary and fifty-two secondary schools, account for a majority of the Catholic-supported schools.

**Facilities Dictate Rise**

THE TIMES' survey indicates that about 60 per cent of Catholic children of school age (elementary and secondary) are attending parochial schools. The remaining 40 per cent attend public schools. In the 1951-52 school year the Catholic elementary schools have enrolled 3,035,033 children, the Catholic high schools 611,123. Approximately 350,000 students are attending Catholic-supported colleges, universities, teacher-training institutions and other postsecondary schools. In the 1950-51 school year 2,879,623 attended Catholic elementary schools and

Continued on Page 75, Column 1

## Britain and Egypt Progress Toward Suez Compromise

### London Said to Concede Troop Withdrawal and End of Sudan Condominium—Cairo Is Cautious on 'Exploratory' Talks

By ALBION ROSS
Special to THE NEW YORK TIMES.

CAIRO, March 29 — British-Egyptian talks, concerning unilateral concessions by London or mutual concessions that would start off favorably the new negotiations for settlement of the long-drawn-out and bitter British-Egyptian conflict, were moving fast today.

Sir Ralph Stevenson, the British Ambassador, saw the Egyptian Foreign Minister, Abdul Khalek Hassouna Pasha twice, once in the morning and once in the afternoon.

The general understanding was that Britain had agreed to declare her willingness to evacuate the British garrison from the Suez Canal Zone base but that the finding of a formula for settling Egypt's demands regarding the Sudan was proving difficult.

It was not known what, if anything, the Egyptians were prepared to concede in response to the British. What Britain and the West want, obviously, is a declaration that Egypt is prepared to enter some type of Middle East defense partnership with the West.

So far as the Sudan is concerned, it seemed that the British were prepared to recognize the end of the British-Egyptian condominium, which Egypt unilaterally abrogated last October at the same time that she abrogated the British-Egyptian alliance providing for the presence of a British garrison in the Suez Canal zone.

Britain would accept the proposition of a Sudan, sovereign and independent of the British crown, but whether she would be prepared formally to recognize the Egyptian claim of King Farouk as King of Sudan was not yet clear though it was believed that Britain would be willing to announce acceptance of King Farouk's sov-

Continued on Page 26, Column 5

## Foe Says U. S. Would Intern Pro-Red U. N. Korea Captives

By LINDESAY PARROTT
Special to THE NEW YORK TIMES.

TOKYO, Sunday, March 30—The Peiping radio accused the White House today of "utter callousness and ill will" toward American prisoners captured by the Communists in the Korean war. The broadcast, monitored here, asserted that "the American warmongers do not want all their prisoners who are now in care of this side to be repatriated."

The Chinese radio made the statement in a long account of supposedly secret negotiations at Panmunjom on an exchange of prisoners in an armistice. The broadcast reasserted charges that United Nations spokesmen had violated the agreement for secrecy, then itself went on to describe a "new proposal" it said had been advanced by Allied representatives in the conference tent.

No confirmation has been given here that such a proposal was made. A communiqué at Allied advance headquarters last night said only that the executive discussions had lasted three hours yesterday.

At Panmunjom today, staff officers sat through another unprofitable session, still debating the Communists' demand for inclusion of the Soviet Union as one of the "neutral" nations to police an armistice. The United Nations representative, Col. Don O. Darrow, told the Communists their persistence was simply delaying the armistice.

The Communist version of the United Nations stand broadcast by Peiping went back to Jan. 21, when, it was asserted, Rear Admiral Ruthven E. Libby, Allied delegate, told the Chinese and North Korean representatives that "only

Continued on Page 2, Column 3

## 'MET' MAY REVIVE REMODELING PLAN

### Deferred Proposal to Revamp Theatre, Erected in 1883, Is Receiving Attention

A long-dormant proposal to remodel the Metropolitan Opera House at a cost of $2,000,000 to $3,000,000 received renewed attention from officials and friends of the institution yesterday in the wake of news that the Columbus Circle site projected for a new home would not be available.

The deferred proposal, blueprinted some years ago, calls for extensive renovations inside and outside the theatre, which was built in 1883. The blueprints might have to be brought up to date it was acknowledged yesterday, but any renovation of the old theatre would have these basic aims:

¶Modernization of production facilities. This would include better quarters backstage, enlargement of the pit and perhaps a more maneuverable stage.

¶Rearrangement of the aisles and the seating plan on the orchestra floor. It has been suggested that space for 300 or 400 more

Continued on Page 75, Column 5

## Yugoslavs Stage Orderly Protest Against 3-Power Talks on Trieste

By M. S. HANDLER
Special to THE NEW YORK TIMES.

BELGRADE, Yugoslavia, March 29—Thousands of university and high school students paraded tonight through the streets of Belgrade in an orderly and disciplined manner in protest against the Western move to solve the question of Zone A of the Free Territory of Trieste without the consent or participation of Yugoslavia.

The columns of students appeared after nightfall and converged on the center of the city, carrying their national flags and big placards, the principal slogan of which read "No solution of the Trieste question without Yugoslavia." Many of the placards read "Down with the Italian Fascist warmongers," "Down with the Cominform-Fascist imperialists," "Togliatti-De Gasperi, the forerunners of fascism" (a reference to Premier Alcide De Gasperi and Palmiro Togliatti, leader of the Italian Communists), "We keep what is ours and don't want anything that belongs to anyone else."

The students chanted and sang as they marched. Some of their chants were "Trieste is ours," "No solution without Yugoslavia" and "Down with the Italian Fascists." But the more significant point was the resurrection of wartime Partisan songs and chants, such as "Tito and the army," "Long live the Yugoslav Army."

Deputy Minister of Foreign Affairs Leo Mattes told a joint session of the National Assembly tonight that the Yugoslav Government would refuse to recognize or be bound by any decision that might be reached at the forthcoming British-American-Italian conference in London on the administration of Zone A, now occu-

Continued on Page 25, Column 1

## FRENCH KEEP RIGHT TO VOTE IN TUNISIA UNDER NEW PLANS

### Schuman Outlines a Program to Transfer Internal Power to Area Within 5 Years

### DEMONSTRATION IN TUNIS

### New Premier Confers With Bey —Resident General Is Named Foreign Head in Cabinet

By ROBERT C. DOTY
Special to THE NEW YORK TIMES.

PARIS, March 29—France's new program of internal reforms for Tunisia envisages the transfer of most aspects of internal sovereignty to the North African protectorate within five years but clings to the old stumbling block of previous negotiations — voting rights for the French minority there.

The program outlined to the National Assembly's Foreign Affairs Committee today by Foreign Minister Robert Schuman is predicated on the election of municipal councils in Tunisia by popular suffrage—that is, with the protectorate's 150,000 French residents joining the 3,500,000 Tunisians at the polls. Resistance to this sharing of Tunisian sovereignty with non-Tunisians was a cardinal principle of the nationalist regime that was violently uprooted Wednesday by the French.

On the other hand, the mingling of Frenchmen and Tunisians in common institutions is an essential part of the long-term French aim.

[A late Paris dispatch of The Associated Press said telephone communication had been cut with Tunis, possibly marking a clamping on of censorship as new violence was reported.]

The parts of M. Schuman's declaration to the Assembly committee that were made public made no mention of ultimate French Union membership for Tunisia, but this goal was defined by another authoritative official source.

In Tunis meanwhile the new pro-French Premier, Salah-Eddine Ben Mohammed Baccouche, had his first interviews with Sidi Mohammed el Amin Pasha, the Bey of Tunis and the country's nominal ruler, and with the Resi-

Continued on Page 27, Column 1

## RACE IS WIDE OPEN

### Truman Decision Leaves Time for Intensive Party Contest

### STEVENSON TO FORE

### Barkley Also Mentioned in Addition to Those Already in Field

By ARTHUR KROCK
Special to THE NEW YORK TIMES.

WASHINGTON, March 29—President Truman's announcement at the Jefferson-Jackson Day dinner here tonight that he would not accept renomination threw wide open the contest for the Democratic party choice for the first time since 1932.

Though President Roosevelt in 1940 withheld announcement of his willingness to run again until just before the convention acted, and in 1944 kept the party leaders guessing until a few weeks before the hour of decision, the general belief never failed that he would accept renomination. Consequently nothing like an open contest occurred in either year.

Mr. Truman's withdrawal, however, occurs nearly four months before the Democratic national convention is to meet in Chicago, and this will afford ample time for those Democrats already in the field and others who will enter to make a positive and intensive campaign for the nomination.

Among the added starters the names most prominently mentioned tonight were those of Gov. Adlai E. Stevenson of Illinois and Vice President Alben W. Barkley.

Up to now Senators Kefauver of Tennessee, Russell of Georgia and Kerr of Oklahoma were running under the handicap of the President's silence. The fact that he could at any time cancel all their efforts by announcing that he was again a candidate, and the further fact that no one could be sure that he would not do so, had the effect of making their campaigns seem like shadow-boxing.

But now that the field is open, the more so because the President as yet has offered no public advice as to a successor, the Democratic battle has begun in earnest.

Continued on Page 66, Column 3

## Kimball Says Navy Plans to Equip All Carriers for Atomic Warfare

### Fleet to Be Able to Carry Bombs Wherever Needed, He Tells Congress—New U. S. Arms Surpass Russia's, Collins Asserts

By JOHN D. MORRIS
Special to THE NEW YORK TIMES.

WASHINGTON, March 29—Dan A. Kimball, Secretary of the Navy, has informed Congress of the Navy's intention "to develop the capability of delivering atomic bombs from all airplane carriers."

The Navy's plans for creating what would amount to a fleet of atomic carriers were sketched by the secretary to the Joint Congressional Committee on Atomic Energy in testimony made public today.

At the same time, the House Appropriations Committee published testimony by Gen. J. Lawton Collins, Army Chief of Staff, that the Army had increased its fire power by 50 per cent over World War II, and was making "superior weapons to those of the Soviets."

"The existing arsenal would be 'tremendously effective' against any mass Russian attack in Europe, he said. The power of European defense forces will be greatly enhanced in the future, he added, by "atomic artillery and guided missiles with and without atomic warheads."

The Appropriations Committee also was told that Army draft calls would rise to about 50,000 a month after July as compared with 15,000 scheduled for May. Lieut. Gen. A. C. McAuliffe, Assistant Chief of Staff for Personnel, estimated that this would be necessary because 600,000 to 700,000 inductees, reservists and guardsmen, or almost half of the Army, would have to be released during the fiscal year beginning July 1.

Mr. Kimball, testifying behind closed doors Sept. 27, told the Joint Atomic Committee that the atomic bomb "is the most efficient weapon in our general arsenal and will have a multitude of uses in the execution of the Navy's mission."

"The role of the Air Force," he said, "is to handle the strategic [air] war, but we can and I am sure will be asked to take collateral missions and we are getting our carriers ready to deliver bombs wherever they want them delivered. And tactically I think that the field has not been scratched."

The transcript of Mr. Kimball's testimony was edited for security reasons to such an extent that there were only brief and sometimes cryptic references to plans for converting the country's entire carrier force to atomic warfare. There was no indication of how long it would take.

But one implication was that the recently developed small atomic bomb could be carried by planes capable of landing and taking off from the smallest carriers. Also of possible significance was the ap-

Continued on Page 22, Column 1

'I SHALL NOT BE A CANDIDATE'

President Truman at the moment he announced his decision at Jefferson-Jackson Day dinner.

## Political Circles Surprised; Some Hope 'No' Isn't Final

President Truman's announcement that he would not be a candidate for re-election was received with surprise in most political circles, and some Democrats expressed a hope that the decision was not final. Questioning of political leaders by THE NEW YORK TIMES, The Associated Press and The United Press last night, after the President had disclosed his decision, brought the following comment:

Gov. Adlai Stevenson of Illinois, who has been reported unofficially as the man Mr. Truman favors to succeed himself, told a reporter the decision "was all a surprise to me."

"I am still a candidate for the Governor of Illinois and nothing else," Mr. Stevenson said.

Asked if he would accept the Democratic nomination, he replied:

"I'll cross that bridge when I come to it."

Senator Richard B. Russell, Democrat of Georgia, an announced candidate for the Presidential nomination, said he had been convinced for a long time that the President would not run for re-election, and had been saying so at his own news conferences.

"I hope that it means a free convention," Mr. Russell commented.

In Hastings, Neb., Senator Estes Kefauver of Tennessee, an announced candidate for the Democratic Presidential nomination, said:

"President Truman has served the nation well during many years as Senator, Vice President and President. I think history will record as outstanding his great efforts to achieve world peace.

"I am sure the Democratic party will continue with its constructive platform both in the field of for-

Continued on Page 68, Column 3

## BARKLEY ASSAILS M'ARTHUR CHARGE

### Says General Perverts Truth —Denies Policy Will Lead to War or Socialism

Special to THE NEW YORK TIMES.

WASHINGTON, March 29—Vice President Alben W. Barkley tonight charged General of the Army Douglas MacArthur with grossly perverting the truth.

In a speech at the $100-a-plate Jefferson-Jackson Day dinner here the Vice President struck back sharply at the ousted Far Eastern Commander who recently indicated that he would accept a draft to become the Republican Presidential nominee.

The Vice President's speech was in response to General MacArthur's address to the Mississippi Legislature at Jackson last Saturday, in which he asserted that "wastrel" domestic policies of the Administration were leading the nation "toward a Communist state" and that its foreign policy was "preparing us for a war in Europe."

Mr. Barkley declared that "any assertion, or claim, or pretense that either our domestic program or our foreign policy is intended or calculated to foment war in

Continued on Page 65, Column 6

## Crisis in Taft Race Seen Tuesday As Wisconsin and Nebraska Vote

By RICHARD J. H. JOHNSTON
Special to THE NEW YORK TIMES.

MILWAUKEE, March 29—The battle for Wisconsin's thirty Republican and twenty-eight Democratic convention delegates will go into its final round here tomorrow morning.

On Tuesday, from 6 A. M. to 8 P. M. in country areas and from 6 A. M. to 8 P. M. in the cities, an estimated 1,000,000 voters of this industrial, dairy and agricultural state, their ears still ringing with the echoes of campaign oratory, loud-speaker exhortations and political argument, will go to the polls and mark their Presidential preference primary ballots.

Five slates of delegates-at-large, listing ten names each, and ten of Congressional District delegates listing two names each will confront the voters.

At the top of the Republican

Continued on Page 48, Column 6

By WILLIAM M. BLAIR
Special to THE NEW YORK TIMES.

OMAHA, Neb., March 29—The big question in Nebraska today is whether the "grass roots" appeal of General of the Army Dwight D. Eisenhower, as manifested in Minnesota's write-in "miracle," can match and overcome the well-organized drive for write-in votes for Senator Robert A. Taft of Ohio in the state's Presidential preference primary on Tuesday.

Big money is being poured into the Nebraska campaigns. Every medium of mass communication is being employed. No holds are barred and the fight may go down to one of the bitterest finishes in this state's history.

The Eisenhower-Taft battle overshadows the important Demo-

Continued on Page 48, Column 4

## HE BARS ANY DRAFT

### President Also Maps the Party's Strategy, Says It Can Win Again

### ASSAILS G.O.P. DRIVE

### Lashes 'Dinosaurs' and 'Loud Talkers' Among the Republicans

*Text of the President's speech is printed on Page 64.*

By W. H. LAWRENCE
Special to THE NEW YORK TIMES.

WASHINGTON, March 29—President Truman dramatically announced tonight that he would not be a candidate for re-election and would not accept the nomination if he were drafted by the Democratic convention.

He made the announcement in almost dead-pan fashion toward the end of his speech before the 5,300 Democrats attending the party's traditional $100-a-plate Jefferson-Jackson Day dinner in the National Guard Armory here.

Following is the text of the statement interpolated into his prepared speech:

"I shall not be a candidate for re-election. I have served my country long and I think efficiently and honestly. I shall not accept a renomination. I do not feel that it is my duty to spend another four years in the White House."

The audience was taken completely by surprise by the announcement since there had been no indication anywhere in the earlier part of his speech nor in the advance word given to highest officials on his staff that he intended at this point to bow out of the 1952 political campaign.

"Oh no, oh no," shouted a few people on the floor.

**Statement Total Surprise**

But there was less demonstration than might have been expected because the huge crowd was taken totally by surprise.

Many of those in the audience appeared not to have heard or understood the import of Mr. Truman's statement. Others simply were stunned.

As soon as he had made his matter-of-fact disclaimer of any intentions to run again, Mr. Truman hurried on to finish the rest of the speech. The crowd applauded, not more vigorously than might have been expected, and the President hurriedly left the hall.

One man sitting near him said that the President's announcement, in long hand, rested on the speaker's rostrum alongside the typescript of his prepared speech.

The President inserted his statement just after he had declared that the record his administration had made would be the one on which the Democratic nominee would have to run "whoever the Democratic nominee * * * may be this year."

As the President left the armory he was stopped by reporters who asked, "Is this decision subject to any change at all?"

**Any Change Ruled Out**

"None whatsoever," Mr. Truman replied.

Mrs. Truman, who was with him, was asked whether she agreed with the decision.

"Of course," she said, "anything he says goes."

After the Trumans had returned to the White House Joseph Short, White House secretary, said that Mr. Truman had reached the decision to make his announcement tonight about a week ago while on vacation in Key West. Mr. Short underlined that the Key West decision was the timing of the announcement and not the basic decision itself. He would not say when Mr. Truman decided not to run again.

At his press conference Mr. Short was asked if he had any idea of Mr. Truman's plans for the time after he leaves the White House.

"I would suggest you ask him at

Continued on Page 65, Column 3

"All the News That's Fit to Print"

# The New York Times.

LATE CITY EDITION
Fair and warm today and tomorrow.
Temperature Range Today—Max., 85; Min., 64
Temperatures Yesterday—Max., 85; Min., 65
Full U. S. Weather Bureau Report, Page 29



VOL. CI..No. 34,503. Entered as Second-Class Matter, Post Office, New York, N. Y. NEW YORK, SATURDAY, JULY 12, 1952. Times Square, New York 36 N. Y. Telephone LAckawanna 4-1000 FIVE CENTS

# EISENHOWER NOMINATED ON THE FIRST BALLOT; SENATOR NIXON CHOSEN AS HIS RUNNING MATE; GENERAL PLEDGES 'TOTAL VICTORY' CRUSADE

## LONG U. N. AIR RAID POUNDS PYONGYANG AND REDS' BUILD-UP

### Three-Wave Daylight Attack Is Followed by Smashing B-29 Blows at Night

### NORTH'S CAPITAL AFLAME

### Allied Land, Navy and Marine Fighter-Bombers Strike as Korea Truce Talks Drag On

By LINDESAY PARROTT
Special to THE NEW YORK TIMES.

TOKYO, Saturday, July 12—Allied aircraft of many nations smashed yesterday at the North Korean capital at Pyongyang and the Communists' military build-up in western Korea in one of the largest and most devastating raids of the war.

Attacking in waves from 10 A. M. until late in the afternoon, the planes flew 1,200 sorties from ground bases and from the decks of United States and British carriers at sea

Almost 600 tons of bombs fell on the daylight targets at Pyongyang and at Hwangju and Sariwon, on the rail line south of Pyongyang, where for months the Communist armies had stockpiled supplies of arms and munitions and placed military headquarters, communications centers and repair shops.

Meanwhile, the truce talks at Panmunjom continued, the secret sessions on the vexed prisoner question producing no indicated progress. A brief sitting was held this forenoon and another meeting was set for tomorrow.

**Mass Night Strike**

Last night, in what headquarters of the Far East Air Forces here called the "largest night air-strike of the Korean conflict," B-29 Superforts from Japanese and Okinawan bases returned to the Communist capital in a new blow. The medium bombers also fanned out over North Korea, hitting supply concentrations at Hamhung, on the east coast; Kyomipo, near Pyongyang, and Sinmak, to the north.

Fifty-four of the B-29's unloaded 540 tons of high explosives over Pyongyang, still blazing from the attack of th fighter-bombers during daylight. Industrial plants, vehicle parks and repair shops were reported hit, with "excellent" results.

Sixty-five bombers participated in the attacks throughout North Korea, with major concentration over selected targets at Pyongyang. The clouds that moved in over the Pyongyang area during the afternoon had cleared at night and the bombardiers saw their projectiles fall in direct hits.

[Later, Far East Air Forces said one F-84 Thunderjet was lost in the day and night attacks. The Associated Press reported All the Superforts returned safely to base. The F-84 was shot down by Communist ground fire. The report did not cover Navy or Marine or other Allied planes.]

**Reds' Radio Makes Claim**

The Reds' Pyongyang radio, on the air a few hours after the daylight strikes, claimed ten Allied aircraft shot down.

No official estimate of the damage done in the day and night attacks had been made pending the study of aerial photographs taken from reconnaissance planes that followed close on the tails of the bombers.

Returning pilots spoke of huge secondary explosions that followed hits by bombs and rockets and big islands of fire raging last evening where hundreds of gallons of napalm—jellied gasoline—fell.

Pyongyang, the biggest railroad junction in North Korea, around which the enemy had built airfields, anti-aircraft positions and supply dumps and where some of the few remaining industrial targets north of the Thirty-eighth Parallel remained, was a mass of flames, observers said.

Pilots flying in the second wave of attack said smoke was rising thousands of feet from the Red

Continued on Page 2, Column 3

## O'Dwyer Considers Staying in Mexico

By SYDNEY GRUSON
Special to THE NEW YORK TIMES.

MEXICO CITY, July 11—Ambassador William O'Dwyer is seriously considering taking up permanent residence in Mexico when his job comes to an end.

All the Ambassador will say for public quotation at this time is that he has "made no definite plans" for the future. But he has recently told persons inquiring about his plans that settling down in Mexico is high among the possibilities.

The former New York Mayor celebrated his sixty-second birthday last Monday and in discussing the future, he has expressed concern for the financial security of his wife, the former Sloan Simpson, in the event of his death.

On his retirement from the mayoralty of New York to become Ambassador to Mexico, Mr.

Continued on Page 11, Column 5

## STEEL LEADERS SEE UNION, THEN CONFER

### Murray Awaits New Industry Offer in Pittsburgh—Talks Expected to Go On Today

By A. H. RASKIN
Special to THE NEW YORK TIMES.

PITTSBURGH, July 11—Negotiations to end the crippling national steel strike waited on a new industry offer today.

After a ninety-minute meeting this morning with Philip Murray, president of the United Steelworkers of America, C. I. O., a committee representing the major steel and iron ore producers went to the headquarters of the United States Steel Corporation where they spent the afternoon in private conference with other steel company officials.

No report came from the closely guarded industry session, but there was hope that the committee would emerge with a new peace proposal to put before the union tomorrow.

Mr. Murray announced at 8:30 P. M. that no further joint meetings would be held today but that it was "reasonable" to expect there would be an industry-union meeting tomorrow.

"We did meet with the industry today, and that's that," the union leader said.

Leaders on both sides refrained

Continued on Page 23, Column 6

## $445,560,000 SOUGHT FOR NEW SUBWAYS BY TRANSIT BOARD

### Second Avenue Network and 2 Brooklyn Extensions Put Before Estimate Body

### BENEFITS DESPITE DEFICIT

### Traffic Relief Seen—Costs of Operation 17 to 20% Above Revenue Conceded

By PAUL CROWELL

The Board of Transportation authorized yesterday, subject to approval of the Board of Estimate, eight subway construction projects in Manhattan, Brooklyn, Queens and the Bronx with a total estimated cost of $445,650,000.

The projects listed were six routes of the Second Avenue trunk line, with connections with existing subway lines, and the proposed extensions of the Utica Avenue and Nostrand Avenue I. R. T. subway lines in Brooklyn. The cost of the Second Avenue project was estimated at $363,500,000, including $41,000,000 for equipment. The two Brooklyn extensions were estimated to cost $82,150,000, including $13,990,000 for equipment.

The proposals would include also a subway link-up in the form of a new line from Fifty-third Street and Avenue of the Americas to East Seventy-sixth Street and Second Avenue and thence running under the East River to Woodside Avenue and Thirty-eighth Avenue in Queens.

**Not in Use Before 1957-58**

In a report to the Board of Estimate the transit agency expressed the belief that ground for the eight projects could not be broken before next fall. It was indicated that the operation of the Second Avenue trunk line and its connections could not begin before 1958 and that of the two Brooklyn extensions before 1957.

The transit agency's report admitted that audition of the Second Avenue line and the two Brooklyn extensions to the existing rapid transit system would create an enlarged subway network unable to earn operating expenses under a 10-cent fare.

"The most desirable benefits to be derived from the proposed routes," the report said, "are those which will be realized by the mil-

Continued on Page 29, Column 8

## Freed American Tells of Drugging With 'Truth Medicine' in China

By HENRY R. LIEBERMAN
Special to THE NEW YORK TIMES.

HONG KONG, July 11—Robert T. Bryan, China-born American lawyer who was held incomunicado for sixteen and a half months as a political prisoner in a Shanghai jail, said today that his Communist captors had drugged him with two injections of "truth medicine" to extract an acceptable "confession" and a separate statement denouncing the United States State Department.

Mr. Bryan, who served as municipal advocate for the Shanghai International Settlement from 1928 to 1941, was arrested Feb. 11, 1951.

He was subsequently accused of espionage and also charged with responsibility for extradition proceedings in which Communist political operatives had been turned over to the Nationalist Government during the days of extraterritoriality.

"They blindfolded me, put me on a table and stuck something in my spine," he said in describing the first drug injection. "After about ten or twenty minutes when they sat me down, I felt I was sitting in mid-air.

"I wrote something, but I do not remember what happened. It took my volition away. I awoke the next morning with a terrific hangover."

This was the first report by a released political prisoner that he had been drugged by the Chinese Communists to elicit a "confession." It raised immediate speculation about the "confessions" of Lieut. John Quinn and Lieut. Kenneth L. Enoch, the captured American fliers who were represented by the Peiping Government as having admitted the dropping of "germ bombs" in Korea.

In addition to the American military prisoners captured by the Chinese Reds in Korea, thirty-seven American civilians are officially listed here as being imprisoned in China. Thirteen more are reported to be under house arrest.

Mr. Bryan, who has resided in China about forty-five of his fifty-nine years, and who was also interned during World War II, said he underwent his first drug injection last April, after two of his "confession" drafts had been pronounced unacceptable. He said the second was administered last month, when he again failed to satisfy his interrogators after having received the option of "establishing merit" either by denouncing his friends or criticizing the State Department.

"I wrote something about the Foreign Service Act of 1946, but they did not like that, so I was blindfolded and doped again," he recalled. "Later, when they showed me my signature, I told them I would repudiate anything obtained by drugs. They said no, this could

Continued on Page 2, Column 3

THE 1952 STANDARD-BEARERS OF THE REPUBLICAN PARTY

Gen. Dwight D. Eisenhower, for President

Associated Press Wirephotos

Senator Richard M. Nixon, for Vice President

## TAFT GIVES WINNER HIS PLEDGE OF AID

### Pair Exchange Compliments in Cordial Chat but Supporters of Ohioan Are Bitter

By LEO EGAN
Special to THE NEW YORK TIMES.

CHICAGO, July 11—General of the Army Dwight D. Eisenhower and Senator Robert A. Taft today had their first face-to-face meeting since the Republican convention opened and exchanged mutual professions of esteem and respect in an obvious effort to allay factional bitterness within the Republican party.

Senator Taft, his brother, Charles P. Taft, Republican candidate for Governor of Ohio, and David S. Ingalls, who managed the Senator's pre-convention campaign, all pledged themselves during the day to use their full influence to persuade the Senator's friends to give full support to the convention winner.

Usually it is the loser who calls upon the winner, but General Eisenhower reversed the custom to make a personal call on Senator Taft soon after the nomination and to bespeak the Ohioan's help in the campaign ahead.

Senator Taft, with three of his four sons standing beside him, received the general in his headquarters' suite at the Conrad Hilton Hotel and offered his congratulations. Later the two fought their way, with the help of a detail of Chicago police, into the entrance hall of the Taft headquarters where television and newsreel cameras had been set up and newspaper reporters and photographers were waiting.

**General Praises Taft**

As soon as he could make himself heard, Senator Taft stepped before the microphones and said:

"I want to congratulate General Eisenhower. I shall do everything possible in the campaign to secure his election and to help in his Administration."

General Eisenhower, flashing the grin he has made famous, then turned to the crowd, jammed shoulder-to-shoulder in the hall, and said:

"I came over to pay a call of friendship on a very great American. His willingness to cooperate is absolutely necessary to the success of the Republican party in the campaign and in the Administration to follow."

General Eisenhower's statement brought a chorus of cheers from Taft followers, who slightly outnumbered the reporters and television crews in the hall. Earlier, when the general first arrived, he had been greeted by a mixture of cheers and boos, followed by a "We want Taft" chant.

Obviously disturbed by the boo-

Continued on Page 6, Column 1

## Nominee Asks Unity at Home And Just, Sure Peace Abroad

By JAMES RESTON
Special to THE NEW YORK TIMES.

CONVENTION BUILDING in Chicago, July 11—General of the Army Dwight D. Eisenhower accepted the Republican Presidential nomination tonight and summoned his party to a "great crusade" for "total victory" over the Democrats in November.

*[Text of Eisenhower speech of acceptance is on Page 4.]*

Likening his new assignment to the historic "crusade" he led against Nazi Germany, the 61-year-old retired five-star general pledged himself to "a program of progressive politics" designed to produce unity at home and peace abroad.

To the obvious delight of a convention audience, many of whose members have feared that he would not conduct a fighting campaign against the Administration, General Eisenhower defined his first aim:

"To sweep from office an Administration which has fastened on every man of us the wastefulness, the arrogance and corruption in high places; the heavy burdens and anxieties which are the bitter fruit of a party too long in power."

Remembering at the same time the acrimonious arguments and sharp divisions that preceded his nomination on the first ballot this morning, General Eisenhower appealed for an end of squabbling at home and torment abroad in these terms:

"It is our aim to give to our country a program of progressive policies drawn from our finest Republican traditions; to unite us

Continued on Page 5, Column 1

## VICTORS' STRATEGY OUTPACED RIVALS'

### Action on Doubtful Delegate Issue and on TV Ban Took Lead From Taft's Men

By JAMES A. HAGERTY
Special to THE NEW YORK TIMES.

CHICAGO, July 11—General of the Army Dwight D. Eisenhower won the Republican nomination for President because the members of his board of strategy completely outmaneuvered the supposedly adroit group of politicians who managed the campaign of Senator Robert A. Taft of Ohio.

The initial break that started the chain of events that led to the nomination of General Eisenhower came even before the convention opened last Monday when the Taft-dominated Republican National Committee and its pro-Taft chairman, Guy George Gabrielson, refused to permit television, radio and motion picture coverage of the committee's hearing on delegate contests. The committee had even barred newspaper photographers from the hearings before previous Republican conventions.

**Eisenhower Took Control**

The result was that every television and radio chain in the country filled the air with protests against what they called an "Iron Curtain" on the committee's proceedings, demanded free access to the hearings and stressed that it was supporters of Senator Taft who had imposed the ban over the objection of supporters of General Eisenhower. This television and radio barrage proved very damaging to Senator Taft's candidacy.

With supporters of Senator Taft in control of the National Committee and its Committee of Arrangements for the convention, the Eisenhower campaign managers not only overcame this handicap but in test votes involving contests in Georgia, Louisiana and Texas, took control of the convention and went on to nominate General Eisenhower.

Heading the Eisenhower group and entitled to major credit for directing the Eisenhower campaign was Senator Henry Cabot Lodge Jr., campaign manager. Others who contributed largely to the convention victory were Herbert Brownell Jr. of New

Continued on Page 3, Column 4

## NIXON, ACCEPTING, URGES G.O.P. SWEEP

### Senator Was Selected Without Opposition—His Record and Youth Strong Factors

*Text of acceptance speech by Senator Nixon, Page 4.*

By WILLIAM S. WHITE
Special to THE NEW YORK TIMES.

CONVENTION BUILDING in Chicago, July 11—Senator Richard Milhous Nixon of California was nominated without opposition today as the Republican candidate for Vice President of the United States.

The whole proceeding required less than half an hour.

Senator Nixon, who is 39 years old, was the choice of all the leaders who supported his senior on the 1952 Republican ticket, General of the Army Dwight D. Eisenhower, and was, of course, acceptable to the general.

Accepting the nomination in a short speech to the Republican National Convention tonight, Senator Nixon put in a strong appeal for the election of a Republican Congress.

Control by the G. O. P. was vital, he said, and especially to put in places of power such men as Senator Robert A. Taft of Ohio, General Eisenhower's defeated antagonist for the Presidential designation.

It was only with a Republican Congress, Mr. Nixon declared, that the Republicans could consolidate

Continued on Page 6, Column 2

## Democrats Respond to Eisenhower By Urging Liberal as His Opponent

Democratic party leaders in various parts of the country reacted yesterday to the Presidential nomination of General of the Army Dwight D. Eisenhower on the Republican ticket by emphasizing the need for a liberal nominee to oppose the general.

Although many prominent Democrats, including Averell Harriman, Senator Estes Kefauver of Tennessee and Senator Richard B. Russell of Georgia, were outspoken in their views, President Truman, who stayed close to his television set in Washington watching the Republican proceedings in Chicago, maintained silence.

Mr. Truman had only one scheduled engagement yesterday forenoon, setting aside most of his time for studying the Republican situation.

Senator Robert S. Kerr of Oklahoma, a candidate for the Democratic Presidential nomination, had this to say about the nomination of General Eisenhower:

"General Eisenhower will find as did [Wendell] Willkie and [Thomas E.] Dewey before him that no matter how hard he tries to escape it the Republican party's record will be a handicap greater than he can overcome. After Nov. 4 he will be a sadder but wiser general."

At Springfield, Ill., Gov. Adlai E. Stevenson said he had no comment on the nomination of General Eisenhower. He reiterated his assertion that he was not a candidate for the Democratic nomination.

The labor plank in the Republican platform adopted in Chicago yesterday came under attack from the International Association of Machinists, an independent union. A. J. Hayes, the president, sent telegrams, before General Eisenhower was nominated, to the four leading Republican candidates denouncing the plank as "unfriendly to labor" and adding:

"The Republican party has long had the reputation of being the

Continued on Page 10, Column 2

## REVISED VOTE 845

### Minnesota Leads Switch to Eisenhower and Others Join Rush

### BUT SOME HOLD OUT

### First Call of the States Gave General 595 to 500 for Taft

*First ballot with revised vote is printed on Page 6.*

By W. H. LAWRENCE
Special to THE NEW YORK TIMES.

CONVENTION BUILDING in Chicago, July 11—General of the Army Dwight D. Eisenhower won a hard-fought first-ballot nomination today as the Republican candidate for President and Senator Richard M. Nixon of California was chosen by acclamation as his running mate for the Vice Presidency.

The former Supreme Allied Commander in Europe went before the 1,206 Republican delegates tonight to accept the nomination and pledge that he would lead "a great crusade" for "total victory" against a Democratic Administration he described as wasteful, arrogant and corrupt and too long in power. He said he would keep "nothing in reserve" in his drive to put a Republican in the White House for the first time since March 4, 1933.

The Republican convention adjourned finally at 8:21 P. M., Central daylight time (9:21, New York time) after it had heard Senator Nixon accept the Vice-Presidential nomination. He pledged a "fighting campaign" to insure election not only of a Republican President, but also a House and Senate controlled by his party.

**Bitterly Divided Convention**

General Eisenhower won in a bitterly divided Republican convention. In the last week the general had taken leadership in the contest from Senator Robert A. Taft of Ohio, the chief party spokesman in Congress, who was making his third unsuccessful bid for nomination to the office once held by his father, William Howard Taft.

Victory came for General Eisenhower on the first ballot. The official results were 845 for General Eisenhower, 280 for Senator Taft, 77 for Gov. Earl Warren of California, and 4 for General of the Army Douglas MacArthur.

But that figure did not represent truly the voting sentiments of these delegates as they faced the crucial and final showdown between General Eisenhower and Senator Taft.

When the first roll-call of the states was completed, General Eisenhower had 595 votes—nine short of the required majority of 604—and Senator Taft had 500. The balance of power rested with favorite-son candidates, such as Governor Warren, who had 81 votes, and Harold E. Stassen, former Minnesota Governor, with 20. General MacArthur had received only 10 votes.

**Others Then Changed**

And while Governor Warren's California delegation held firm for him in the hope of a deadlock, Mr. Stassen's Minnesota delegates, no longer bound because he had received less than 10 per cent of the vote, broke away and cast nineteen votes for General Eisenhower before a first ballot result could be announced.

The nineteen, added to the General's previous total, gave him 614, or ten more than a majority. Then other states began to change their votes in order to be recorded on the side of the winner.

Thus, while General Eisenhower's nomination later was made unanimous on the motion of principal backers of Senator Taft and Governor Warren, who pledged the support for their principals to the nominee, it was made clear that General Eisenhower was the choice of a divided convention, and that one of his first tasks would be to restore party unity and heal the deep wounds inflicted during the

Continued on Page 7, Column 1

"All the News That's Fit to Print"

# The New York Times.

LATE CITY EDITION
Fair and continued pleasant today and tomorrow.
Temperature Range Today-Max., 84; Min., 66
Temperatures Yesterday—Max., 82; Min., 66
Full U. S. Weather Bureau Report, Page 2



VOL. CI..No. 34,517. Entered as Second-Class Matter, Post Office, New York, N. Y. NEW YORK, SATURDAY, JULY 26, 1952. Times Square, New York 36, N. Y. Telephone LAckawanna 4-1000 FIVE CENTS

# STEVENSON IS NOMINATED ON THE THIRD BALLOT; PLEDGES FIGHT 'WITH ALL MY HEART AND SOUL'; TRUMAN PROMISES TO 'TAKE OFF COAT' AND HELP

## MOSSADEGH HINTS AT NEW ENDEAVOR TO SOLVE OIL ISSUE

### Iranian Premier Tells Nation That 'Solution of Problem' Has Now Become 'Easier'

### EARLY REFORMS PLEDGED

### Government Leader Confers With Communists—Feeling Against U. S. Mounts

Special to THE NEW YORK TIMES.

TEHERAN, Iran, July 25 — Premier Mohammed Mossadegh told the nation in a radio broadcast tonight that the tangled oil problem had taken a turn for the better and that therefore he was resolved to initiate and carry out reform measures and to take fundamental speedy steps he believed the country direly needed now.

[The Associated Press reported that the Premier made his statement in these words: "In view of the fact that a solution to the oil problem now is easier, I intend to institute reforms which the country needs. These reforms can take place only in a calm atmosphere. So long as there is disorder, there is no opportunity for any kind of improvements."]

Dr. Mossadegh summoned George Middleton, British Chargé d'Affaires, to his office. They conferred for more than two hours. The purpose of the visit has not been disclosed but Mr. Middleton said that a guess that it concerned oil would not be far wrong.

Dr. Mossadegh's internal authority is now unchallenged and the decision of the International Court of Justice that the Anglo-Iranian oil complaint was outside its jurisdiction improved considerably his international situation in approaching the oil issue. Speculation naturally is to the effect that, starting from this position, he may seek again some type of solution of the oil problem.

**Mossadegh Sees Communists**

Dr. Mossadegh received the leaders of the Tudeh Communist organization, which now calls itself the Association to Combat Imperialism. The subject obviously was the relation between the Government and the National Front on one hand and Communist leaders on the other after their cooperation in last Monday's violent events, which drove Ahmad Ghavam from power.

In his radio address to the nation the Premier said:

"My dear compatriots, you will admit that no social reforms can be carried out without the existence of security forces. The maintenance of peace and security is the first condition of positive acts of the Government.

"The offenses and encroachments of some members of the security forces may have induced you to look askance on the entire security forces, but with the formation of a national government there is no reason why this suspicion should continue to exist,

Continued on Page 3, Column 5

## U. S. Olympian Sets Steeplechase Mark

By ALLISON DANZIG

Special to THE NEW YORK TIMES.

HELSINKI, Finland, July 25—Horace Ashenfelter won today the fastest 3,000-meter steeplechase race ever run for the United States' twelfth gold medal in track and field and its first Olympic victory ever in this event.

In the remarkable time of 8 minutes 45.4 seconds, 18.4 seconds under the Olympic record that has stood in the books since 1936, the 29-year-old Penn State graduate from Glen Ridge, N. J., ran away from the world's best to win by thirty yards as the first eight to finish excelled the old mark.

Vladimir Kazantsev of Russia, the favorite, who shadowed the special agent of the Federal Bureau of Investigation virtually all the way until he stumbled in

Continued on Page 16, Column 1

## Snag on Iron Ore Pay Blocks Order to Reopen Steel Mills

### 600,000 Union Men Await Pact for Miners —Fairless and Murray Plan to Visit Plants to Promote Labor Harmony

By A. H. RASKIN

Special to THE NEW YORK TIMES.

WASHINGTON, July 25—The longest and most costly steel strike in the country's history was officially called off today, but an unexpected snag over wage rates for 23,000 iron ore miners blocked the sending of union back-to-work orders to 600,000 striking steel workers.

The last-minute difficulty, which both sides hoped would blow over in a few hours, cast a shadow over settlement arrangements that had indicated the steel dispute might provide a foundation for a new era of cooperative labor-management relations in the industry that represents the backbone of the American economy.

With only one dissenting vote, the 175-man Wage Policy Committee of the United Steelworkers of America, C. I. O., voted this afternoon to accept the settlement terms agreed upon at the White House yesterday by Philip Murray, president of the union, and Benjamin F. Fairless, president and chairman of the United States Steel Corporation.

The agreement, which was personally announced by President Truman, provided a wage increase of 16 cents an hour, retroactive to last March 1; paid holidays, higher shift differentials and other "fringe" benefits that would cost 5.4 cent an hour more, and a modified union shop.

The agreement specified that iron-ore miners were to get all the same benefits, plus additional wage increases intended to bring their pay scales up to the steel level.

It was this provision that caused the difficulty today.

Under the agreement part of the difference in wage rates was to be made up at once and the rest at the end of the first year of the

Continued on Page 30, Column 5

## U. N. Truce Team Walks Out Of Korea Talks for a Week

By LINDESAY PARROTT

Special to THE NEW YORK TIMES.

TOKYO, Saturday, July 26—The United Nations delegates walked out of the new plenary sessions at Panmunjom today and told the Communists they would return in a week for further discussion of an armistice in the Korean war.

The senior Allied delegate, Maj. Gen. William K. Harrison Jr., led the United Nations representatives out of the conference tent after the enemy delegation had devoted much of the first of a new series of meetings to a violent repetition of charges against the United Nations Command. The two sides agreed, however, that during the week's adjournment staff officers would meet to see what could be done to draft new tentative armistice terms as a basis for further discussion.

Pooled dispatches from Korea said General Harrison was shaking with anger as he left the roadside tent, where the Chinese and North Koreans, after the breakdown of the last three weeks' se-

Continued on Page 2, Column 3

## 6 AIDES OF FAROUK RESIGN AFTER COUP

### 5 High-Ranking Police Officials Jailed as Maher Cabinet Acts Speedily in Egypt

By The Associated Press.

CAIRO, July 25—Gen. Mohammed Naguib Bey's Army-backed governmental house-cleaning reached to King Farouk's own palace today. Six of the monarch's top aides resigned.

At the same time Egypt's new strong man moved anew to crush opposition to the military coup by which he had installed the anti-corruption Government of Premier Aly Maher Pasha.

Maher Pasha's new Cabinet took over today, pledged to try to end the crisis that has swept this Middle East country for six months. The Cabinet hopes to end the corruption that, according to Maher Pasha, had brought the crisis about and to settle Egypt's dispute with Britain over the Suez Canal and the Sudan.

**Police Officials Arrested**

General Naguib Bey flew to Alexandria for a conference with Maher Pasha, leaving behind him a series of arrests. Among those held were five high-ranking political and police officials who were accused of conspiring against the public safety, an army communiqué said. Twelve generals of the Egyptian Army also were in custody.

The officials held included Maj. Gen. Mousif Mahmoud Pasha, Under Secretary of the Interior Ministry; the commandant of the Cairo police, the director of a special section of the Interior Ministry and two high officers of the political section of the police.

The communiqué said: "Although we have detained these few people * * * a much larger number of army men have been arrested."

Maj. Gen. Sirry Amer Bey, commander of Egypt's frontier corps, was arrested at Salum, on the Egyptian-Libyan border, and returned to Cairo.

General Naguib Bey received an ovation when he called on the new Premier. While they conferred for an hour, a crowd outside cheered and called the general "Protector of Egypt."

After the conference he told newsmen that his first aim was to assure the people of Alexandria,

Continued on Page 3, Column 3

## PRESIDENT IN FORM

### Talks in 'Whistle Stop' Manner, Predicting Ticket's Victory

### HITS AT EISENHOWER

### Says 'People Will Not Choose Man Without Faith in People'

*Text of the President's speech at the Convention, Page 4*

Special to THE NEW YORK TIMES.

CONVENTION BUILDING in Chicago, Saturday, July 26—President Truman told a cheering Democratic National Convention early this morning that it had nominated a winner in Gov. Adlai E. Stevenson of Illinois.

The President promised that he would "take off my coat and go out to help him win."

In a direct attack on Gen. Dwight D. Eisenhower, the Republican Presidential nominee, Mr. Truman declared that the "people won't choose a leader who does not have faith in the people." He said he did not think the country would be turned over to men "who are more concerned with cutting the budget than with the security of the United States."

This was a reference to General Eisenhower's pre-nomination pledge to reduce the Federal budget by $40,000,000,000 under certain conditions.

**How to Win Elections**

Mr. Truman started to speak at 1:42 A. M., after a four minute ovation. He reminded the delegates that four years ago at about the same hour in the morning he had predicted victory for the ticket headed by himself and Senator Alben W. Barkley of Kentucky for Vice President.

"But you didn't believe me," said the President with a grin.

"I'm telling you now that Adlai Stevenson will win in 1952."

The President said that the real reason Democrats won elections "is perfectly simple—it is because they give the American people the kind of Government they want."

"The Republicans," he declared, "are going to throw millions of dollars into an attempt to confuse

Continued on Page 8, Column 8

## GOVERNOR ACCEPTS

### Humility Marks Speech by Nominee Before Cheering Delegates

### HE HAILS PLATFORM

### Illinoisan in Tribute to Losing Candidates—Bids for Unity

*Text of the acceptance speech by Mr. Stevenson, Page 5.*

By JAMES RESTON

Special to THE NEW YORK TIMES.

CONVENTION BUILDING in Chicago, Saturday, July 26—Gov. Adlai E. Stevenson of Illinois, in a speech marked both by humility in the face of the high honor and by a vigorous determination in the face of its challenge, early today accepted the Democratic nomination for President.

"I will fight to win that office with all my heart and soul," he told the cheering delegates. "With your help, I have no doubt that we will win."

Earlier, the "no" man from the Lincoln country, had for the first time said "yes."

"I did not seek it. I did not want it," he said a moment after he had been nominated by the Democratic National Convention.

"But to shirk it would be to repay honor with dishonor," he added.

The call, he continued, "asked of me nothing except that I give such talents as I have to the services of my country. That I will do."

"I feel no exaltation or sense of triumph whatever, nothing but humility. I shall go on my knees and I shall ask my God to give me strength and courage and to nourish my spirit for this great undertaking in this great hour of history."

At the outset, he said, he had never been "more conscious of the appalling responsibility of office."

He went immediately to the convention hall from the home on Chicago's "Gold Coast" where he made his short statement.

The 52-year-old Governor developed this same solemn theme after he had been driven at breakneck speed through the late night traf-

Continued on Page 5, Column 5

## CONVENTION-BOUND PRESIDENT VOTES BY PROXY

Associated Press Wirephotos

At the precise moment Mr. Truman was waving farewell at the Washington Airport before starting for Chicago in his plane . . . . . . Thomas J. Gavin was casting his vote as the President's alternate on the convention floor in support of Adlai E. Stevenson.

THE DEMOCRATIC STANDARD-BEARER

Associated Press Wirephoto

ADLAI E. STEVENSON

## 300-VOTE SWITCH DECIDES CONTEST

### Harriman's Withdrawal Swings Big State Blocs on Third Ballot to the Governor

*Harriman statement, Kefauver and Russell talks, Page 4*

By FELIX BELAIR Jr.

Special to THE NEW YORK TIMES.

CONVENTION BUILDING in Chicago, Saturday, July 26—A sudden switch of more than 300 votes gave Gov. Adlai E. Stevenson of Illinois a third-ballot victory and the Democratic Presidential nomination here early today after Averell Harriman had announced his withdrawal from the contest and New York, Pennsylvania, Massachusetts, Michigan and Arkansas had swung in behind the choice of President Truman.

The race came out just as predicted by the managers of Governor Stevenson's floor campaign. Paul E. Fitzpatrick, the New York State party chairman, took the speaker's platform after a dinner recess to announce Mr. Harriman's withdrawal. Massachusetts' favorite son, Gov. Paul A. Dever, followed with the announcement to the convention that he, too, was withdrawing in favor of Governor Stevenson.

Mr. Fitzpatrick's statement in behalf of Mr. Harriman was followed much later in the session by speeches by Senator Estes Kefauver of Tennessee and Senator Richard B. Russell of Georgia, both conceding the nomination to the Illinoisan.

With the Harriman and Dever switches there were more than 100 votes right there to be added to Governor Stevenson's second ballot total of 423½. When Michigan switched its 40 votes from Senator Estes Kefauver it remained only for Pennsylvania to bring along the stragglers by giving the Governor all its 70 votes, a net gain of 30.

Texas held out with its big 52-vote bloc, as did other delegations favoring Senator Russell but the die was already cast.

Senator Kefauver came up the center aisle of the auditorium on the arm of Senator Paul H. Douglas of Illinois in an attempt to gain the platform to announce his plan to nominate Senator Douglas, who was not in nomination but who would then have withdrawn and urged all Kefauver delegates to vote for Governor Stevenson. But Speaker Sam Rayburn, the convention's permanent chairman, ruled that the balloting must proceed.

Governor Stevenson was within a few votes of the required 615½ majority when the roll-call of the states ended and Speaker Rayburn gave to Tennessee the first oppor-

Continued on Page 5, Column 1

## LEADERS IN HUDDLE ON VICE PRESIDENCY

### Balloting Is Postponed Until Noon Today as Kefauver Foes Present Objections

Special to THE NEW YORK TIMES.

CONVENTION BUILDING in Chicago, Saturday, July 26—Democratic party leaders went into a huddle early today immediately following the Presidential nomination of Gov. Adlai E. Stevenson for talks on the Vice Presidency.

The National Convention put off its choice until a noon session. The original program had called for selection of Governor Stevenson's running mate after his acceptance speech.

It was understood that the delay stemmed principally from some objections to Senator Estes Kefauver of Tennessee, who forged to the top of the "guess" list after he dramatically yielded in the Presidential race.

A late starter among the possibilities was Representative John W. McCormack of Massachusetts. Others mentioned were Vice President Alben W. Barkley, Senator John J. Sparkman of Alabama, Secretary of the Interior Oscar L. Chapman and Senator Richard B. Russell of Georgia.

Among those in the huddle at the near-by Stockyards Inn were Averell Harriman, who last night withdrew from the Presidential race, and Jake Arvey of Chicago, Governor Stevenson's principal backer in Illinois.

Regarding the possibility of taking the post, Senator Kefauver said:

"I haven't been offered the place and I really don't believe I would want to accept it. I haven't talked

Continued on Page 8, Column 7

## Two Coalitions Won Stevenson's Victory

By JAMES A. HAGERTY

Special to THE NEW YORK TIMES.

CHICAGO, Saturday, July 26—The strategy used by supporters of Gov. Adlai E. Stevenson to get him the Democratic nomination for President, like the horns of a dilemma, had two prongs.

First, by a coalition with supporters of Senators Richard B. Russell of Georgia and Robert S. Kerr of Oklahoma they brought about the seating of the Virginia, Louisiana and South Carolina delegations, members of which had declined to take the loyalty pledge imposed by the Credentials Committee as a condition of participation in the convention.

Having formed this temporary alliance with the conservative Southern delegates and lessened

Continued on Page 6, Column 8

## RIVALS DROP OU[T]

### Withdrawal of Harrima[n] Starts States' Rush to the Governor

### ILLINOISAN TRAILE[D]

### But Picked Up Strengt[h] From Larger States—Got C. I. O. Backing

*The three ballots of Convention are printed on Page 6.*

By WILLIAM S. WHITE

Special to THE NEW YORK TIMES.

CONVENTION BUILDING i[n] Chicago, Saturday, July 26—Go[v.] Adlai E. Stevenson of Illinois w[as] nominated early today on the thi[rd] ballot for President of the Unite[d] States by the thirty-first Demo[cratic] National Convention.

President Truman came here t[o] salute him and to stand with hi[m] before the delegates.

Mr. Truman, cheerful and smi[l]ing, declared to the Convention:

"I'm telling you now Adlai Stev[enson] is going to win in 1952 * * * I am going to take my coat off an[d] do everything I can to help hi[m] win."

Governor Stevenson told th[e] delegates that he could never hav[e] sought such an honor, and adding "I have asked the mercif[ul] Father of us all to let this cu[p] pass from me. But from suc[h] dread responsibility one does no[t] shrink in fear, in self-interest, o[r] in false humility."

"So," he went on, quoting fro[m] the Bible, "'if this cup may no[t] pass away from Me, except I drin[k] it, Thy will be done'."

**Huge Demonstration**

Mr. Truman walked, as an enormous demonstration beat the walls of this hall, the length of the platform to greet Mr. Stevenson and take him to face the crowd.

The convention adjourned at 2:35 A. M. (3:35 A. M., New York time), to meet again at 11 A. M.

Governor Stevenson's nomination—the first genuine draft since the Republicans demanded and got James A. Garfield in 1880—came after the withdrawal of Averell Harriman of New York had turned the great bulk of that delegation to the Stevenson standard.

Then Senator Estes Kefauver of Tennessee put over the Stevenson selection. Tennessee cast its 28 votes for the Governor, who was then a handful short of the required 615½ needed for a majority in a total of 1,230.

**'Did Best We Could'**

Senator Richard B. Russell of Georgia, after Mr. Stevenson's nomination, pledged to join in efforts for a party victory in November.

Senator Kefauver told the convention that it had been "quite apparent" that someone here had to yield. His intention, he said, had been to nominate Senator Paul H. Douglas of Illinois and Senator Douglas had intended in turn to give his favor to Governor Stevenson.

But this had been made impracticable by the Stevenson rush, Mr. Kefauver said, in effect, so he was simply retiring. It had been a good fight, he observed, "and we did the best we could."

Senator Kefauver, it appeared, was heading instead for the Vice Presidential nomination. The selection for Vice President is scheduled to be made today.

Mr. Stevenson to the end had not been a candidate.

Four aggressive aspirants—Mr. Harriman, Senator Kefauver, Senator Russell and Senator Robert S. Kerr of Oklahoma—had struggled with the Stevenson draft movement until it became apparent that there was to be no stopping it. Senator Kerr had retired early—before dinner-time last night—when his own Oklahoma delegation had left him, obviously with his consent, though he did not make it formal until nearly midnight.

Mr. Harriman's announcement of retirement from the race came after Mr. Truman, a Stevenson backer, had arrived here. The

Continued on Page 5, Column 1

"All the News That's Fit to Print"

NEWS SUMMARY AND INDEX, PAGE 59

# The New York Times.

LATE CITY EDITION
Mostly fair and warm today. Fair, continued warm tomorrow.
Temperature Range Today—Max., 90; Min., 70
Temperatures Yesterday—Max., 86; Min., 69
Full U. S. Weather Bureau Report, Sect. 3, P. 9

Section 1

VOL. CI No. 34,518.

Entered as Second-Class Matter, Post Office, New York, N. Y.



NEW YORK, SUNDAY, JULY 27, 1952.

Including Magazine and Book Review.

RAG PAPER EDITION
ONE DOLLAR TWENTY-FIVE CENTS

# FAROUK OUT; QUITS EGYPT AFTER COUP

## ARMY EXILES KING

### He Sails With Queen and Infant Son, Who Is Named Fuad II

### ITALY THEIR DESTINATION

### Iran Premier Reported Ready to Negotiate With British on Nationalized Oil Concern

By The Associated Press.

CAIRO, July 26—King Farouk I abdicated the ancient Egyptian throne today at the climax of a tank-supported Army clean-up campaign and sailed away in the Mediterranean aboard his Royal yacht, the Mahroussa. The Army said his family went with him for exile in Italy.

The Cabinet proclaimed Farouk's son, seven-month-old Crown Prince Ahmed Fuad, to be King Fuad II of Egypt and the Sudan.

[As Premier Mohammed Mossadegh of Iran presented his new Cabinet roster to the Shah, a National Front newspaper disclosed that the Premier had invited negotiations with Britain with a view to resolving the deadlock over the nationalized Anglo-Iranian Oil Company.]

Gen. Mohammed Naguib Bey, Egypt's new strong man and leader of the virtually bloodless Army coup, had surrounded the Royal palaces with armed forces. Soldiers arrested several officers of the Royal Guard in a showdown at Ras el Tin Palace in Alexandria, Egypt's summer capital.

In addition to 18-year-old Queen Narriman and the baby, Farouk's three daughters by former Queen Farida—Princesses Ferial, Fadia, and Fawzia—accompanied him into exile.

[The French Press Agency said it had learned authoritatively that Farouk intended eventually to go to the United States. He will sail first to Europe, it said, and will proceed to the United States when necessary formalities are completed.]

**Naguib Salutes Monarch**

General Naguib Bey, self-proclaimed Commander in Chief of the Army, shook hands with the ousted monarch and saluted him while the band played the Royal anthem. Farouk, wearing the uniform of an Egyptian admiral, waved good-by with his cap as a twenty-one-gun salute was fired.

The abdication of King Farouk, wealthy former playboy, marked the end of a reign of sixteen troubled years highlighted by World War II, during which his country occupied a vitally strategic position, and by a post-war dispute with a former mighty ally, Britain.

First reports quoted Queen Narriman as having said that she had wanted to accompany her husband but was prevented from doing so because she "must take care of the baby Crown Prince and help bring him up."

Late tonight Premier Aly Ma-

Continued on Page 3, Column 6

ABDICATES

Associated Press

King Farouk

## STAFF TALKS GO ON AMID TRUCE RECESS

### But U. N. Officers Are Doubtful That Review Asked by Foe Will Make Progress

By LINDESAY PARROTT
Special to The New York Times.

TOKYO, Sunday, July 27—Full-scale negotiations at Panmunjon for an armistice in the Korean war were in abeyance for a week today after an angry squabble yesterday when United Nations delegates walked from the conference tent, forcing a new adjournment.

Staff officers of both sides were to hold this morning the second of a new series of sessions called by the Communists to review the tentative truce agreement being used as a basis for discussion by the plenary delegations. United Nations spokesmen said they expected little progress toward settlement of the critical issue of prisoner exchange, which has blocked an armistice since December.

[The staff officers met for an hour and a half Sunday and agreed to meet again Monday forenoon, news agencies said.]

A senior United Nations staff officer, Col. Duncan S. Somerville, told correspondents after the thirty-nine-minute session yesterday that the Communists had given no indication that they placed particular emphasis on those paragraphs of the document dealing with the exchange of captives, but apparently wanted a review of the entire sixty-four-clause agreement, painfully hammered out at previous staff meetings and translated into official texts in three languages.

**Somerville Is Pessimistic**

Frankly pessimistic, Colonel Somerville told the enemy representative, Col. Chang Chun San, "Our main differences are issues that cannot be settled by editorial mumbo jumbo."

If differences are found to exist between the texts, he continued, they could be adjusted by translators without formal meetings at Panmunjom. However, the Communists apparently meant to keep the staff sessions open, possibly to communicate with the Allies if the main Chinese-North Korean delegation sought a new plenary meeting before Aug. 3.

The senior United Nations representative, Maj. Gen. William K. Harrison Jr., told his opposite number, North Korean Lieut. Gen. Nam Il, when he walked out of the tent yesterday, "If you have anything to say, you can say it through our staff officers." But General Harrison indicated that only a "very important" development would bring the Allied negotiators back before the week was out.

Yesterday's walkout was the fourth by the United Nations since the discussion of prisoner exchange began, and a week's enforced adjournment was the longest pause thus caused in the truce talks. As on previous occasions, General Harrison led the delegation from the tent after the Communists, back in an open session after

Continued on Page 2, Column 4

## Major Sports News

**OLYMPIC GAMES**

Bob Mathias broke his own world record with 7,887 points as the United States swept the first three places in the decathlon yesterday. It was the Tulare (Calif.) star's second victory in that event. Milton Campbell of Plainfield, N. J., was second and Floyd Simmons of Los Angeles third. Joseph Barthel of Luxembourg defeated Bob McMillen of the United States in a close finish in the 1,500-meter final. Both were timed in 3:45.2, a new record.

**BASEBALL**

The Giants defeated the Reds, 7—2, and moved within four and a half games of first place as the Dodgers lost again to the Cards, 5—3. The Tigers beat the Yankees, 10—6, on Steve Souchock's homer in the eleventh.

**HORSE RACING**

To Market, 2-1 choice, easily won the $152,350 Arlington Handicap. Golden Gloves led the favored Hitex home in the Saranac at Jamaica.

*(Details in Section 5).*



## 600,000 STEEL MEN ORDERED TO MILLS; ORE ISSUE SETTLED

### Murray's Bid to Union Follows Pay Increase Agreement for 23,000 Miners

### WAGE BOARD IS RESTRICTED

### Truman Puts It More Directly Under Economics Chief in Line With Congress' Plan

By A. H. RASKIN
Special to The New York Times.

WASHINGTON, July 26—The final obstacle to ending the steel strike was removed late this afternoon and union back-to-work telegrams started 600,000 strikers streaming into the steel mills after an absence of fifty-five days.

An all-day conference between industry and union leaders resulted in an agreement at 4:55 P. M. on a pay increase for 23,000 iron ore miners. This was the only issue that had stood in the way of terminating the walkout that had made 1,500,000 workers idle in steel and industries dependent on steel.

All other problems had been taken care of in a White House agreement signed on Thursday by Philip Murray, president of the United Steelworkers of America, C. I. O., and the "big six" steel companies. The agreement was ratified yesterday by the union's Wage Policy Committee.

The pact provided for a wage increase of 16 cents an hour, retroactive to March 1; paid holidays, higher shift differentials and other benefits that will cost 5.4 cents an hour more, and a modified union shop.

Pre-strike wages in the steel industry averaged $1.88 an hour.

**Miners Get Other Gains**

A companion agreement, also signed at the White House in President Truman's presence, specified that iron ore miners were to get all the same gains, plus additional wage increases intended to bring their pay scales up to the steel level.

The complication that delayed a full settlement for twenty-four hours was the timetable to be followed in equalizing the steel and the iron ore wages. Under the agreement part of the difference in pay rates was to be made up at once and the rest next July 1. The exact amount to be given each year was not set forth but was left for subsequent negotiation.

The average pay in ore mines is now 20 to 25 cents an hour below the steel average, but 8½ cents of this is offset by an agreement the employers made a year and one-half ago to put that amount into a fund to be used in equalizing iron ore wages.

Today's conference between union officials and heads of the major iron ore companies resulted in a decision to grant additional

Continued on Page 15, Column 1

# SPARKMAN CHOSEN BY DEMOCRATS AS RUNNING MATE FOR STEVENSON; SENATOR HAILS PARTY SOLIDARITY

## TEAM TAKES SHAPE

### Illinoisan Acts for Unity by Not Pressing Any Choice for Ticket

### STARTS IN MIDDLE OF ROAD

### Governor Takes Alabaman as Compromise and Introduces Him as a Real 'Prize'

By JAMES RESTON
Special to The New York Times.

CHICAGO, July 26—Gov. Adlai E. Stevenson took a position in the middle of the road today and started his journey in quest of the Presidency.

In agreeing to Senator John J. Sparkman of Alabama as the Vice Presidential nominee, the Democratic party's Presidential candidate approved the man who was least likely to upset either the North or South.

There was some feeling in the convention that Senator Estes Kefauver of Tennessee would have added more strength to the ticket or that a younger and more aggressive man would have countered the Republican Vice Presidential nominee, the 39-year-old Senator Richard M. Nixon of California, but Mr. Stevenson avoided an extreme position either way.

He did not oppose the Kefauver suggestion. He did not come out strongly for anybody. He saw that sentiment was moving toward Senator Sparkman, who is 52, as a compromise acceptable to the Old Guard in the South and the Young Turks of the North, so he pursued a policy of judicious leaving-alone.

**Drives With Harriman to Hall**

Likewise, he avoided any hasty action on the question of selecting a national chairman to see him through the campaign. He merely asked Frank E. McKinney of Indianapolis, the present chairman, to stay on for a while until he could study the situation, and Mr. McKinney agreed.

The Governor has had less physical strain on him in this convention than most other persons connected with it, but he was up until the middle of the night and then slept late this morning.

Averell Harriman of New York, who started the landslide for Mr. Stevenson last night by withdrawing from the race and urging his delegates to vote for the Illinoisan, had breakfast with the Governor late in the morning.

Both then drove behind a police

Continued on Page 21, Column 1

AT THE HEAD OF 1952 DEMOCRATIC NATIONAL TICKET

Associated Press Wirephoto

Gov. Adlai E. Stevenson, left, the nominee for President, holding up the hand of Senator John J. Sparkman, the candidate for Vice President, as the convention cheered.

## TICKET ACCLAIMED

### Nominees Pledge Strong Campaign—No Ballot Taken on 2d Place

### TWO WOMEN ARE NAMED

### India Edwards and Judge Sara Hughes Get Complimentary Mention, Then Withdraw

*Text of Sparkman's acceptance speech is on Page 19.*

By WILLIAM S. WHITE
Special to The New York Times.

CONVENTION BUILDING in Chicago, July 26 — The thirty-first Democratic National Convention nominated Senator John J Sparkman of Alabama today for Vice President on the ticket headed by Gov. Adlai E. Stevenson of Illinois, and wound up its long, weary meeting in general party harmony.

The Senator accepted the nomination with a pledge to "take the message of democracy to the people of this country."

"I believe, I earnestly believe," he said, "that we will go out of this convention with greater solidarity, greater unity in all sections of the country and in all segments of our party than we have been able to achieve in a long, long time."

Mr. Sparkman whose designation had been approved in advance by Governor Stevenson, was chosen on the motion of James A. Farley of New York that no ballot be taken. The designation of the Alabaman was described by the presiding officer, Representative Sam Rayburn of Texas, as one of acclamation on a voice vote.

At no point had there been any serious rival, though Mrs. India Edwards, vice chairman of the Democratic National Committee, and Judge Sarah Hughes of Dallas, Tex., had been put in nomination in a complimentary way.

**Pledge Hard Campaign**

Governor Stevenson came to the convention platform to stand with Senator Sparkman, their hands interlocked and raised high. They promised a hard campaign this autumn against the Republican nominees, Gen. Dwight D. Eisenhower and Senator Richard M. Nixon of California.

The convention was adjourned at 2:20 P. M., Central daylight time (3:20 New York time), on a note of North-South amity to which the selection of Senator Sparkman had contributed.

Some of the Northerners held misgivings, however, in spite of Mr. Sparkman's generally liberal political record, over what he would do in the campaign about the convention civil rights plank, which called for Federal legislation to help end racial discrimination.

Senator Herbert H. Lehman of New York called on Mr. Sparkman to embrace that plank wholeheartedly, saying that if he did not there was "no question" that the Democratic ticket would be imperiled in New York.

Mr. Sparkman, Senator Lehman said, is in every respect except possibly this one "a real fighting liberal."

**Several Walk Out**

Representative Adam Clayton Powell Jr. of New York and several other Negro delegates walked out of the hall in dissatisfaction before the nomination was achieved.

The delegates on the whole accepted the designation in good part.

Mr. Sparkman, in his speech, reminded the delegates that he had been a member of the Resolutions Committee that drafted the platform. He said there had been some difficult problems involved, but "we sat and reasoned with one another until we came out with a platform on which we can all stand."

Mr Sparkman had been agreed upon before 4 o'clock this morning in consultations among President Truman, Governor Stevenson, Frank E. McKinney, Chairman of the Democratic National Commit-

Continued on Page 18, Column 1



## M'KINNEY TO HOLD POST TEMPORARILY

### National Committee Chairman Agrees to Stay on When Nominee Requests It

By WILLIAM M. BLAIR
Special to The New York Times.

CHICAGO, July 26—Frank E. McKinney of Indianapolis was retained as chairman of the reorganized Democratic National Committee today on a temporary basis at the request of Gov. Adlai E. Stevenson of Illinois, the party's Presidential nominee.

Governor Stevenson made a personal appearance before the committee to ask that Mr. McKinney stay on in his post because he had no organization of his own and was "utterly dependent on the National Committee."

Jacob M. Arvey, Illinois National Committeeman, who made the formal motion to retain Mr. McKinney and other officers temporarily, said later that Governor Stevenson "wouldn't talk about anything until last night."

"He hasn't made a choice because he hasn't considered it," Mr. Arvey added. "He has only met Mr. McKinney twice but considers him a fine and able man, but he just wouldn't say a word about anything."

Mr. McKinney told the committee prior to the Governor's appearance that he had "every intention to ask to be relieved." But when the Governor called him he agreed to stay on "in deference to Governor Stevenson, and until he, Senator John Sparkman and the executive committee have a chance to choose a new chairman."

There were reports that Mr. McKinney would carry on permanently after the Illinois Governor had surveyed the situation and decided on the kind of organization he wanted.

**Sparkman Praises Chairman**

Senator Sparkman, chosen by the party today as its candidate for Vice President, also appeared before the committee, which has a number of new members. He commended Mr. McKinney and also alluded to the convention fight over the seating of delegations from Virginia, South Carolina and Louisiana, which had refused to take a "loyalty pledge" to the party.

"The party has worked out of a very difficult situation from a national viewpoint," said the Alabaman.

The committee, he added, has labored hard to "the end that all wounds of the party could be healed." He earnestly hoped that "we all carry away from here the belief that what we have striven so hard to accomplish has been accomplished."

Among the changes on the committee was the seating of former Gov. Fielding L. Wright of Mississippi, who was the Vice Presiden-

Continued on Page 23, Column 1

## Eisenhower Attacks Record And Platform of Democrats

By RUSSELL PORTER
Special to The New York Times.

DENVER, July 26—Commenting on the Democratic ticket nominated at Chicago, Gen. Dwight D. Eisenhower today struck the keynote of the Republican Presidential campaign. It combined a promise of lasting peace and expanding progress for the United States with an implied attack on the record of the Democratic Administration.

The general's statement follows:

"The Democrat party has named its candidates and offers them to the country on a one-plank platform: defense of the entire Administration record.

"I am confident that the American people will support the program that Senator Nixon [Richard M. Nixon of California, Republican Vice Presidential nominee] and I will outline during the campaign to retain and expand American progress and, in organizing for a lasting peace, make our country a healthier, stronger, happier and better America than anything we have yet known."

The general telephoned his statement from his fishing camp in the Colorado Rockies to James C. Hagerty, his press secretary, at summer campaign headquarters at the Brown Palace Hotel here.

In a message to the Republican state convention here General Eisenhower also promised to make an "all-out" campaign for a "smashing" victory.

"In this crusade," he said, "I urge you to encourage the support of the young men and women of America, as well as the thousands of other citizens who are eager to rally to the Republican cause."

He said his election would mean

Continued on Page 25, Column 1

## SPARKMAN WARNED ON RIGHTS PLANK

### Lehman Says Full Backing Is Vital or the Ticket Will Be Weakened in New York

By LEO EGAN
Special to The New York Times.

CONVENTION BUILDING in Chicago, July 26—Senator Herbert H. Lehman of New York today urged Senator John J. Sparkman of Alabama, following his nomination for Vice President, to embrace without reservation the civil rights plank written into the Democratic platform earlier in the week.

"If he doesn't," Senator Lehman said, "there is no question but that it will weaken the ticket in New York."

Senator Sparkman's nomination for Vice President appeared to nullify the underlying strategy of New York's ninety-four-vote delegation yesterday in throwing the bulk of its support to Gov. Adlai E. Stevenson of Illinois for the Presidential nomination on the third ballot.

Although the change was made without any prior agreement with

Continued on Page 20, Column 1

## Eva Peron Dies in Argentina; A Power as President's Wife

### Buenos Aires Sets National Mourning—End Comes After Long Illness

Special to The New York Times.

BUENOS AIRES, July 26—Señora Doña Maria Eva Duarte de Perón, wife of President Juan D. Perón, who had made herself one of the most powerful women in the history of Argentina and of the New World, died tonight at 8:25 o'clock. She had long been ill.

According to the Argentine Who's Who, she was 30 years old. [Biographical material not currently published in Argentina gave Señora Perón's age as 33, her date of birth May 17, 1919.]

The people of Argentina, who had been celebrating masses for the recovery of the First Lady, who was called "the spiritual chief of the nation," were well prepared for the event. During the course of the day the Sub-Secretariat of Information had issued three bulletins in rapid succession that clearly indicated the end was near.

President Peron, who was at her bedside when she died, had been staying nearly all week close to his wife in the Presidential Residence. Members of the Cabinet were there today.

At 9:42 P. M., all radio stations interrupted their programs to report:

"The Sub-Secretariat of Information fulfills the very sad duty of announcing that at 8:25 o'clock, Señora Eva Perón, the spiritual chief of the nation, passed away."

The announcement was followed by religious music.

Señora Perón was operated upon last November for cancer. Her last public appearance was on June 4, when, looking extremely pale and worn, she attended the ceremony at which General Perón was inaugurated to succeed himself as President—largely through her help.

As news of the death was received throughout the country, each Province decided to send here special delegations, presided over

Continued on Page 56, Column 4

Associated Press, 1952

Senora Peron

## Bank Robber Slays F. B. I. Agent In Gun Battle in W. 69th St. Hotel

By RICHARD H. PARKE

A Federal Bureau of Investigation agent was wounded fatally in the lobby of the Congress Hotel, 19 West Sixty-ninth Street, at 1:15 P. M. yesterday in a pistol battle that resulted in the capture of a Kansas bank robber sought as one of the nation's ten most-wanted criminals.

Joseph J. Brock, 44 years old, of 33-15 Eightieth Street, Jackson Heights, Queens, was shot by the robber, Gerhard A. Puff, 37, as the agent crouched behind a frosted-glass door waiting for his quarry to emerge from an elevator.

Puff, who slipped down a rear stairway and fired point-blank at the F. B. I. man, was himself brought down by a bullet in the left leg in an exchange of shots as he ran through the lobby past four other agents. He fell in the street outside.

Mr. Brock, who was married and the father of three children, was dead when an ambulance reached Roosevelt Hospital. Edward Scheidt, agent in charge of the bureau's New York office, said it was the first time in his memory that an agent on duty had met violent death in this area.

Puff, a bespectacled, mild-mannered man with a fondness for highly polished shoes, also was taken to Roosevelt Hospital, but later was transferred to the prison ward at Bellevue. He suffered a fractured leg. His condition was said to be good.

Last night, at the Federal Court House in Foley Square, James B. Kilsheimer 3d, an Assistant United States Attorney, filed a complaint signed by Arthur Duffy, an F. B. I. agent, before Federal Judge John F. X. McGohey charging Puff with murder in the first degree. The attorney's request that the prisoner be held without bail was granted.

Two young women seized in the Congress, an apartment hotel, told the F. B. I. last night that a man who had registered at the hotel on Sunday with Puff, and who later checked out, was George Arthur

Continued on Page 10, Column 3

"All the News That's Fit to Print"

# The New York Times.

LATE CITY EDITION
Mostly fair and continued cool today, tonight and tomorrow.
Temperature Range Today—Max., 68; Min., 54
Temperatures Yesterday—Max., 67; Min., 54
Full U. S. Weather Bureau Report, Page 47



VOL. CII..No. 34,577. Entered as Second-Class Matter, Post Office, New York, N. Y. NEW YORK, WEDNESDAY, SEPTEMBER 24, 1952. Times Square, New York 36, N. Y. Telephone LAckawanna 4-1000 FIVE CENTS

# NIXON LEAVES FATE TO G.O.P. CHIEFS; EISENHOWER CALLS HIM TO A TALK; STEVENSON MAPS INFLATION CURBS

## MARCIANO ANNEXES TITLE IN 13TH BY KO OVER JOE WALCOTT

### Brockton Heavyweight Ends Reign of 38-Year-Old Rival With Right to Jaw

### 40,379 FANS WATCH BOUT

### Hundreds Besiege Philadelphia Stadium in Wild Rush to Acclaim New Champion

By JAMES P. DAWSON
Special to The New York Times.

PHILADELPHIA, Sept. 23 — Rocky Marciano, undefeated Brockton, Mass., fighter, knocked out Jersey Joe Walcott, 38-year-old ring warrior from Camden, N. J., tonight to become the world heavyweight champion.

With a devastating right to the jaw, Marciano ended the reign of the old champion after forty-three seconds of the thirteenth round. Until that moment it was a bruising battle that thrilled 40,379 fans from all over America in Philadelphia's Municipal Stadium. The receipts were $504,645.

Under the impact of that one terrific blow Walcott sank against the ropes, then slid head first to the canvas, while Referee Charley Daggert counted him out of the title he had won after much desperate effort slightly more than a year ago.

The knockout was the cue for a tremendous demonstration. Fans swarmed into the ring as the unbeaten Bay State boxer with the paralyzing punch stood in his corner, winner of the ring's richest prize after a battle that he could have lost as early as the first round. He was the first white heavyweight to hold the title since Jim Braddock was stopped by Joe Louis in Chicago in 1937. Here was the new champion and nothing could halt the crowd in its eagerness to acclaim him.

**Many Trampled in Rush**

From all sections of the vast arena, where Gene Tunney had lifted the title from Jack Dempsey just twenty-six long years ago, fans rushed on the ring to greet the conqueror.

Many were trampled in the rush, which started in the lower-priced seats in the permanent stands and, under increasing momentum, moved across and through the seats at the ringside.

For a time a wall of police about the working press rows checked the rush. Police climbed into the ring. A straggler broke through the cordon back of the press rows. Then another. Then it was a steady stream of humanity climbing and clambering over the backs of the writers.

Then the crush became too much for the police. They gave up and let the demonstration run its course. Several telegraph instruments and typewriters at the ringside were kicked under the ring. A movie camera was broken.

Most of the demonstrators were young fellows with the reckless abandon that only youth can boast. They risked broken and bruised limbs to get into the ring.

When Walcott had been counted out his stricken handlers leaped through the ropes to the side of their fallen idol and carried him to his corner. It was several minutes before he could be revived sufficiently to leave the ring, with the assistance of Trainer Dan Florio and his brother Nick, and his manager Felix Bocchicchio.

Marciano, on the other hand,

Continued on Page 41, Column 1

## Dodgers Take Flag By Defeating Phils

The Brooklyn Dodgers clinched the National League pennant last night with a 5-4 victory over the Philadelphia Phillies in the twilight opener of a double-header at Ebbets Field. The Dodgers lost the second game, 1—0, in twelve innings.

A two-run double by Duke Snider during a three-run fifth inning enabled Brooklyn to take the opener. The Brooks now lead the second-place Giants by six games. The Giants have only six to play and the Dodgers four. New York's double-header yesterday with Boston was rained out.

Gran Hamner accounted for the Phillies' runs with a third-inning home run against Johnny Rutherford, the winning pitcher, with the bases filled.

Details on Page 42.

## U. N. IN NEW DRIVE ON BATTERED HILL

### Reply to 'Harassing' Jabs Hits Enemy in West—Red Probes Repulsed on Wide Front

By LINDESAY PARROTT
Special to The New York Times.

TOKYO, Wednesday, Sept. 24—United Nations troops struck back today at the Communists on the western front in Korea after the enemy, probing all along the 100-mile Allied line yesterday from Panmunjom in the west to the "Punchbowl" in the eastern Korean mountains, sought but failed to find weak spots.

Allied infantry jumped off this morning in an attack on "Kelly Hill," battered hillock in the west, which hard-fighting Chinese had captured last Thursday. Front reports said the combat still was in progress at 7:30 A. M.

For the second time United Nations infantry fought its way to the top, but resistance continued and the issue was in doubt. The Allies reached the summit Saturday, but were turned back later by an enemy counter-attack. Today's assault was the third effort to retake the hill, which is seven miles southwest of bitterly contested "Old Baldy," near Panmunjom, captured from the Chinese Sunday by a battalion from the United States Second Infantry Division.

**Attacks at 20 Points**

The enemy's series of local attacks yesterday were made in strength of no more than two platoons, but Eighth Army Headquarters said the jabs were delivered in twenty places along the outpost line. All were driven back.

A military spokesman said the Communist tactics probably were intended as "harassing actions" following the heavy local fighting of the last two weeks.

The enemy's apparent determination during the last fortnight to increase the scale of the ground fighting in a series of drives for outpost positions has cost the Chinese and North Koreans a considerable number of casualties, intelligence estimates said. Eighth Army Headquarters said 3,332 enemy were killed or wounded during the week of September 15-21, and 3,743 in the previous week. The total of more than 7,000 casualties is approximately the usual strength of an enemy division.

**South Koreans Retake Hill**

The heaviest toll in the last few days was taken during the seesaw fighting for a hill north of the "Punchbowl," a strategic cup-shaped valley that controls the best lines of communication in the rugged eastern Korean watershed. Communist casualties there in fifteen hours of fighting Tuesday were estimated at 117 killed and 322 wounded.

The troops that stormed the hill in a tank-led attack after the heights had been seized by the enemy during darkness were identified as members of the Republic of Korea Eighth Division, one of the outfits of the retrained and re-equipped South Korean Army now holding much of the front. The R. O. K.'s recaptured the hill after Allied planes had made eighty-seven strikes against North Koreans dug in there.

Four new probes were made by the enemy yesterday on a four-mile front in the eastern sector, Eighth Army Headquarters said. In each case the Communists withdrew after engagements lasting up to a half-hour and the R. O. K.'s continued to hold the contested hill.

On the central front the enemy felt out Allied advance positions northwest of Yonchon, and in the west the Chinese Communists made five light attacks against scarred "Bunker Hill," won and lost several times in recent fighting. Contact was maintained during the night and up to 6 A. M.

Continued on Page 2, Column 6

## WEST REJECTS BID FOR BIG 4 SESSION ON GERMAN TREATY

### Reply to Moscow Insists That First Such Conference Deal Only With Free Elections

### OCTOBER TALK SUGGESTED

### Identical Notes Say Russians 'Shifted' Stand Since They First Urged Peace Moves

By WALTER H. WAGGONER
Special to The New York Times

WASHINGTON, Sept. 23—The United States, Britain and France rejected today a proposal by the Soviet Union for a Big Four conference on a German peace treaty and insisted again that such a meeting be limited to making plans for free, all-German elections. The meeting "could take place in October," the Western powers said.

In identical notes delivered by their envoys in Moscow to the Soviet Ministry of Foreign Affairs, the Western Big Three restated their conviction and determination that first things come first — that machinery must be set up for carrying out free elections throughout divided Germany, that the elections must be held, and that a unified German government must be created before a German peace treaty could be discussed.

Today's note was the Western reply to the Soviet communication of Aug. 23, in which a three-point agenda for possible Big Four talks was proposed, with the "preparation of a peace treaty with Germany" at the top of the list.

**Eighth Item in Exchanges**

The reply constituted the eighth item of correspondence between the three Western capitals and the Soviet Union, with four notes issuing from each side, since Moscow first formally suggested Big Four talks on Germany last March 10.

From the beginning, the Soviet Union has proposed talks on a broader basis than the Western powers, especially the United States, have been willing to accept. Countering, Washington, London and Paris have proposed an agenda, restricted to the question of free elections, that has not been acceptable to the Kremlin.

Western diplomats have shown no enthusiasm for getting into a propaganda battle with the Soviet Government on the question of Germany, which, they feel, would be a certainty if the Russians had all of Germany's difficulties, problems and grievances to work over in a forum as important as a Big Four conference.

Today's Western note, hinting at the prospects for Soviet propaganda blasts at a meeting on Germany, called attention to the "wholly unfounded attacks" on the Atlantic pact, the European Defense Community Treaty and the Bonn peace contract with the Western Allies in the Soviet communication of Aug. 23.

Describing all those develop-

Continued on Page 9, Column 1

## PRAISE BY GENERAL

### He Commends Senator for 'Magnificent' Talk on His Finances

### STUMPS OHIO WITH TAFT

### Then Discards Cleveland Text to Laud Running Mate as a Courageous Person

*Text of the Eisenhower speech in Cleveland is on Page 24.*

By JAMES RESTON
Special to The New York Times.

CLEVELAND, Sept. 23—Gen. Dwight D. Eisenhower listened to Senator Richard M. Nixon's explanation of his defense fund tonight and immediately indicated that he would retain the Senator as his Vice Presidential running mate.

In an extraordinary evening that started with a defense of Senator Nixon's honesty and developed into a Hollywood-type story of the Senator's life, General Eisenhower told a roaring crowd of 15,000 in the Cleveland Public Auditorium that his personal admiration and affection for the Californian were "undiminished."

The Republican Presidential nominee, who watched the Nixon telecast while the audience in the Public Auditorium listened to it over a loudspeaker, withheld final judgment on the case, but he praised Senator Nixon's courage and left no doubt that, unless some wholly new element were introduced into the controversy, Senator Nixon would receive his endorsement. He also called the Senator to a personal meeting with him.

**'Affection' Is Undiminished**

General Eisenhower wired Mr. Nixon tonight as follows:

"Your presentation was magnificent. While technically no decision rests with me, yet you and I know that the realities of the situation will require a personal pronouncement, which so far as the public is concerned, will be considered decisive.

"In view of your comprehensive presentation, my personal decision is going to be based on a personal conclusion. To complete the formulation of that personal decision, I feel the need of talking to you and would be most appreciative if you could fly to see me at once. Tomorrow night I shall be at Wheeling, W. Va.

"I cannot close this telegram without saying that whatever personal admiration and affection

Continued on Page 25, Column 1

EXPLAINS SPECIAL EXPENSE FUND: Senator Richard M. Nixon, Republican Vice Presidential nominee, as seen on television screens here. The New York Times

## 'I'M NOT A QUITTER'

### Senator Says He'll Let Republican National Committee Decide

### HE REVIEWS HIS FINANCES

### Accepts Bid to Meet General—Cites Legal Opinions on Use of $18,235 Fund

*Text of Nixon speech, Page 22; financial record, Page 23.*

By GLADWIN HILL
Special to The New York Times.

LOS ANGELES, Sept. 23—Senator Richard M. Nixon, in a nation-wide television and radio broadcast tonight, defended his $18,235 "supplementary expenditures" fund as legally and morally beyond reproach.

He laid before the Republican National Committee and the American people the question of whether he should remain on the Republican party's November election ticket as the candidate for Vice President.

Rising, near the end of his talk, from the desk at which he had sat, Senator Nixon urged his auditors to "wire and write" the Republican National Committee whether they thought his explanation of the circumstances surrounding the fund was adequate.

"I know that you wonder whether or not I am going to stay on the Republican ticket or resign," he said. "I don't believe that I ought to quit, because I'm not a quitter * * *.

**Decision 'Not Mine'**

"But the decision, my friends, is not mine. I would do nothing that would harm the possibilities of Dwight Eisenhower to become President of the United States; and for that reason I am submitting to the Republican National Committee tonight, through this television broadcast, the decision which it is theirs to make. * * *.

"Wire and write the Republican National Committee whether you think I should stay or whether I should get off; and whatever their decision is, I will abide by it."

Later he accepted an invitation from General Eisenhower for a conference.

In a half-hour talk that was partly personal, including a frank exposition of his finances, and partly an appeal for support of the Republican ticket such as he has been making in his current whistle-stop tour, the Senator declared of the Southern California supporters' fund disclosed last week:

"I say that it was morally wrong if any of that $18,000 went to Senator Nixon for my personal use.

"I say that it was morally wrong if it was secretly given and secretly handled.

"And I say that it was morally wrong if any of the contributors got special favors for the contributions that they made."

But he declared that, on all three points, the factual answer was negative.

**Speaks With Assurance**

The candidate, clad in a gray suit and a dark tie, delivered his address in a Hollywood radio-television studio—from which the public was excluded—with composure and assurance. His wife, Patricia, was seated close to him, and he made frequent references to her in detailing his career.

His talk also was peppered with barbed references to the Democratic opposition.

Referring to an Illinois political fund with which Gov. Adlai E. Stevenson, Democratic Presidential nominee, has been linked, Senator Nixon, while stipulating that he did not "condemn" this, suggested that both Mr. Stevenson and his running mate, Senator John J. Sparkman of Alabama, should "come before the American people" and report on their incomes.

"If they don't," he said, "it will be an admission that they have something to hide."

In support of his position, he cited two independent reports he had prepared, one on his finances and one on the legal aspects of the "supplementary expenditures" fund, for the information of Gov. Sherman Adams of New Hampshire, campaign executive of Gen-

Continued on Page 23, Column 1

## OUSTER A MISTAKE, CAUDLE TESTIFIES

### He Says He Was Told Truman Called It 'a Great Injustice'—White House Denies This

By LUTHER A. HUSTON
Special to The New York Times.

WASHINGTON, Sept. 23—President Truman was quoted in testimony before a House of Representatives Judiciary subcommittee today as saying that he had done Theron Lamar Caudle "a great injustice" when he dismissed him as Assistant Attorney General in charge of the Tax Division of the department.

Mr. Caudle gave the testimony near the end of an emotional recital of his version of his dismissal. The President's statement, he said, had been made to Representative Frank W. Boykin, Democrat of Alabama, during a private interview at the White House last March. Mr. Boykin disclosed the conversation to Mr. Caudle and members of his family, the witness related.

When Mr. Boykin asked Mr. Truman what he was going to do to rectify the "injustice" the President answered, "What can I do?" Mr. Caudle testified.

Representative Boykin also said, according to Mr. Caudle, that Mr. Truman had told him that if Donald S. Dawson, one of the President's aides, had arrived at Key West two hours earlier "I never would have done it."

**Dismissal Ordered From Florida**

The President ordered Mr. Caudle's dismissal from Key West, Fla., where he was on vacation on Nov. 16 last. Mr. Dawson arrived soon after the action was taken.

The White House said that there was no truth in the statement that the President had told Representative Boykin he had done Mr. Caudle a great injustice.

At Mr. Boykin's office here it was said that he was in Alaska on a business trip and could not be reached immediately for comment.

Mr. Caudle was dismissed while a Congressional inquiry was under way into tax scandals in the Bureau of Internal Revenue and the Justice Department's handling of cases referred to it by the bureau. The only statement made at the time was that the President had acted because of "outside activities" incompatible with Mr. Caudle's responsibilities as a Government official.

Representative Frank L. Chelf, Democrat of Kentucky and chairman of the subcommittee, asked Mr. Caudle if he had ever heard "the basis upon which the President acted."

"No, sir," replied Mr. Caudle. "I never have found out."

Mr. Caudle said that Representative Boykin told him that during the White House interview "the

Continued on Page 12, Column 3

## Stevenson Willing to Impose Tighter Controls if Needed

By W. H. LAWRENCE
Special to The New York Times.

BALTIMORE, Sept. 23—Gov. Adlai E. Stevenson of Illinois told a cheering capacity audience of 9,000 Maryland Democrats tonight that he would not hesitate to impose tighter wage and price controls if necessary to halt inflation.

The Democratic nominee's speech was heard also by a nation-wide radio and television audience. It was made just after Senator Richard M. Nixon of California, the Republican Vice Presidential nominee, had concluded his report about his personal finances.

[The text of the Stevenson speech is printed on Page 26.]

But the Governor did not refer in any way to Senator Nixon's speech, of which he saw about two minutes on television before he left his hotel room, nor to the question of whether the Californian should be dropped from the Republican ticket.

As he was leaving the platform Mr. Stevenson was informed by a reporter of the gist of the address by Senator Nixon, in defense of his $18,235 expense fund. Asked to comment, he said:

"I'll have nothing to say on that tonight."

[The American Federation of Labor convention in New York adopted a resolution on Tuesday giving unanimous support to Governor Stevenson. Similar action had been taken previously by the executive committee of the Congress of Industrial Organizations.]

The Baltimore speech, delivered in the Fifth Regiment Armory, was Governor Stevenson's set speech on the inflationary problem, for the solution of which he

Continued on Page 27, Column 5

## U. S. WIDENS STUDY INTO NIXON'S FUND

### Aide First Affirms Then Denies That Truman Asked Inquiry—Senator Tied to Tax Case

By ANTHONY LEVIERO
Special to The New York Times.

WASHINGTON, Sept. 23 — The White House at first confirmed and later denied today that President Truman had directed James P. McGranery, Attorney General, to study the possibility of criminal prosecution of Senator Richard M. Nixon, Republican Vice Presidential candidate, and the seventy-six Californians who contributed $18,235 to his expense fund.

Before the White House had withdrawn its statement, however, a Justice Department spokesman confirmed that the study was being made. Moreover, the spokesman said that the study was wider in scope than at first indicated—wider in that he indicated an intent to assure the involvement of Senator Nixon if it was concluded that his seventy-six sponsors were liable to prosecution.

Meanwhile, The St. Louis Post-Dispatch reported that Dana C.

Continued on Page 17, Column 1

## Teachers Union Witnesses Assail Senate Red Inquiry

By CHARLES GRUTZNER

Two officers of the Teachers Union testified under oath yesterday that they were not and never had been members of the Communist party, but they joined eight other witnesses who refused to tell a Senate Internal Security subcommittee whether they were Communists in denouncing the current investigation into communism in the schools as an attack upon the concept of the open mind in education.

Several of the witnesses in the Federal Court House on Foley Square charged that the "inquisition" of teachers had been inspired in church circles that were trying to "intrude" upon public education.

Charles J. Hendley, former president of the union, named George A. Timone, prominent Roman Catholic layman and chairman of the Board of Education's law committee, as a foe of the union because it "has defended the American principle of separation of church and state and has strenuously opposed clerical interference with public education."

Mr. Hendley, one of the eight who refused to say whether they were or ever had been Communists, denied that the Teachers Union was or ever had been controlled by Communists, as he said charged by Mr. Timone and Dr. Bella V. Dodd, former Communist functionary and former legislative representative of the union, in testimony two weeks ago.

Public hearings will continue today at 9 A. M. before Senator Homer Ferguson, Republican of Michigan, sitting as a one-man subcommittee, and Robert Morris, counsel to the subcommittee. After an hour of open testimony the committee will go into closed session to examine teachers in all four of the municipal colleges and several other local institutions, including Columbia, New York and Long Island Universities.

Additional officers of the Teachers Union will be questioned at the open hearings before and after the closed session. It is expected that members of the college and university faculties will be put on the stand at an open hearing tomorrow.

James Nack, the union treasurer, and Mrs. Mildred K. Garvin, vice president in charge of elementary schools, swore they never had been Communists. Mr. Nack is a mathematics teacher, and director of the school honor society at Stuyvesant High School. Mrs. Garvin is a grade teacher at Public School 192, Manhattan.

Mr. Nack and Mrs. Garvin became the first, among twenty teachers or union officials questioned so far, to answer what have come to be known as the "$64

Continued on Page 4, Column 3

## Frauds in U. S. Grain Are Put at 10 Million

By JOHN D. MORRIS
Special to The New York Times.

WASHINGTON, Sept. 23 — The Senate Agriculture Committee blamed lax administration and poor enforcement policies today for the Federal grain storage scandals brought to light in public hearings earlier this year.

In a forty-one-page report of findings and recommendations, the committee estimated that 131 private warehouse men had embezzled about $10,000,000 of Government-owned grain over the last five years. Slightly more than $2,000,000 of the losses have been recovered, and some additional recoveries are possible.

The "conversions," as such embezzlement is called in the grain trade, were of crops stored for the Agriculture Department's Commodity Credit Corporation under the Federal farm price support program.

However, the report said, "no

Continued on Page 19, Column 1

## Truman Buys Painting for Wife, Trying His Art On First for Size

By PAUL P. KENNEDY
Special to The New York Times.

WASHINGTON, Sept. 23—President Truman took a brief recess from the affairs of state and the political turmoil this afternoon for a bit of a esthetic shopping.

After a surprise visit to a Georgetown antique shop, the President came away with a Dutch castle scene, painter unidentified, which he will present to Mrs. Truman to be hung in their Independence, Mo., home.

In the course of seventeen minutes, Mr. Truman inspected about 150 paintings in a collection bought a year ago by Charles Kohen for his shop.

Quiet Georgetown was startled at 4 P. M. when a squad of Secret Service men set up a guard around Mr. Kohen's small shop. By the time the President's limousine rolled up thirty minutes later, followed by a Secret Service car, a handful of the curious had gathered in front of the shop.

Immediately on entrance, Mr. Truman was taken to the shop's second floor by Mr. Kohen. After one look at the large room, the walls of which were lined and the floors stacked with pictures, the President, according to Mr. Kohen, exclaimed:

"You've got too damn many pictures here."

The President, Mr. Kohen said, had no clear idea about the subject matter, the school or the painter, but he knew the exact size he wanted.

"I know exactly the place I want to hang it," the President explained.

He was finally torn between the Dutch painting and a landscape by Joseph Turner. The choice went to the Dutch picture, but the President was at first insistent on knowing the painter.

"Don't ask me that, Mr. Presi-

Continued on Page 13, Column 1

"All the News That's Fit to Print"

# The New York Times.

LATE CITY EDITION

Mostly fair today and tomorrow, little change in temperature
Temperature Range Today-Max., 70; Min., 56
Temperatures Yesterday—Max., 70; Min., 50
Full U. S. Weather Bureau Report, Page 63



VOL. CII..No. 34,578. Entered as Second-Class Matter, Post Office, New York, N. Y. NEW YORK, THURSDAY, SEPTEMBER 25, 1952. Times Square, New York 36, N. Y. Telephone Lackawanna 4-1000 FIVE CENTS

# EISENHOWER CALLS NIXON VINDICATED; COMMITTEE VOTES TO RETAIN NOMINEE; STEVENSON BARS DATA ON ILLINOIS FUND

## 800 NEW POLICEMEN WILL BE APPOINTED BY CITY WEDNESDAY

### Funds for 200 Civilian Clerks to Be Asked to Release Men for Foot Patrol Duty

### $5,500,000 NEW OUTLAY

### Mayor's Move to Increase Force Prompted by Demands to Halt Crimes of Violence

By PAUL CROWELL

Mayor Impellitteri announced yesterday that 800 new policemen would be appointed next Wednesday. He announced also that the Board of Estimate would be asked at its meeting on Oct. 9 to provide funds for 200 civilian clerks to be assigned to the Police Department to make available for patrol duty an equal number of policemen now doing clerical work.

The Mayor's moves to place an additional 1,000 policemen on the streets to safeguard the city's residents from crimes of violence were made known after he had conferred at City Hall with Police Commissioner George P. Monaghan and Budget Director Abraham D. Beame.

"We have re-examined the pressing need for new patrolmen and have concluded that money must be provided even though appropriations for less essential services may have to suffer," the Mayor declared.

"These moves will give us an additional 1,000 policemen out on the streets, where they are needed. Police Commissioner Monaghan is in complete accord with me on the desirability of putting more men out on foot patrol."

**Monaghan 'Personally Delighted'**

Mr. Monaghan, when informed of the Mayor's announcement, said that he was "personally delighted" at the Mayor's decision to make more policemen available for patrol duty.

The 800 men to be appointed next Wednesday will be in addition to the 525 new policemen to be appointed between that date and July 1, 1953, in order to place the manpower of the Police Department on a forty-four-hour-week basis until Jan. 1 and on a forty-two-hour week between Jan. 1 and next July 1.

The appointment of the 800 new policemen will represent an acceleration of the program announced by the Mayor several weeks ago, when he said that 400 new men would be named Oct. 1 and 400 more every three months thereafter until a total of 1,600 has been appointed by next July 1. It was indicated at City Hall that there was a possibility that the total might be as high as 2,000.

**Demands for Drastic Action**

The moves announced by the Mayor plus the addition of 525 policemen to the force to allow for the shorter work-week program will cost the city about $5,500,000 more than is now provided in the Police Department's budget for 1952-53. The additional funds will be made available by the issuance of budget notes to be redeemed in the expense budget for 1953-54, by transfers of funds from other agency appropriations or by a combination of both methods.

The Mayor's moves to increase the police manpower available for foot-patrol duty were prompted by strong and insistent demands that drastic action be taken to prevent

Continued on Page 15, Column 4

## 28 in Police Case Identified By Gross, but Only 3 as Payees

### Weary Gambler Names Bou, Regan and Scro in Pay-Offs—Repeats the Charge He Began Payments to O'Brien in 1943

By EMANUEL PERLMUTTER

Harry Gross, sallow-faced and hollow-eyed, walked through a courtroom in the Criminal Courts Building yesterday and picked out twenty-eight suspended plainclothes men whom he said he knew. Of the remaining three defendants in the departmental graft trial, two were absent and the third was excluded from identification because his lawyer was not present.

This perfect score by the former bookmaker seemed to cast a pall over the defendants and their lawyers. It didn't appear to brighten the countenance of the witness either. He walked sullenly and wearily back to the witness stand to begin the first day of his testimony against the policemen who allegedly had been on his payroll.

In the day's proceedings Gross specifically named three of the defendants who, he said, were involved in his graft payments. He also gave details of gambling bribes he allegedly made to former Police Commissioner William P. O'Brien in 1944 when the latter was a deputy chief inspector in charge of the Thirteenth Division, Brooklyn.

The three defendants named by Gross in pay-offs were Capt. John Bou and Patrolmen Edward Scro and Danied A. Regan. He mentioned five other defendants in testimony about his operations between 1942 and 1944, but did not say he made payments to them.

The former gambler, who has already served one year of a twelve-year sentence for bookmaking, said Captain Bou was the first of the defendants to whom he paid graft. He said he paid $100 a month to the captain in 1942 when the defendant was attached to the Police Commissioner's Squad.

Under questioning by Victor J. Herwitz, assistant corporation counsel, Gross testified that the payments to Bou were made for

Continued on Page 15, Column 1

## Senate's Communist Inquiry Reaches Into Local Colleges

By CHARLES GRUTZNER

The Federal investigation into communism in the nation's schools reached yesterday into colleges in this area as faculty members of Columbia and Rutgers Universities and Hunter, Brooklyn and Queens Colleges testified at an open hearing of the Senate Internal Security Subcommittee in the Federal Court House on Foley Square.

Of ten witnesses heard yesterday, all but one refused to answer fully the twin questions whether they were or had ever been members of the Communist party. Lucille Spence, secretary of the Teachers Union and a biology teacher at Franklin K. Lane High School, Brooklyn, swore that she neither was nor had ever been a Communist.

All the witnesses denied, as had teachers from elementary and high schools at previous hearings, that they ever had seen any evidence of attempts by teachers in their schools to inculcate students with Communist ideology.

**Evidence on Proposed Texts**

The subcommittee put into its record, however, evidence that the Teachers Union suggested classroom use of material published by organizations which, according to Benjamin Mandel, research director for the Senate unit, had been listed by one or more Government agencies as subversive.

Mr. Mandel noted for the record that the union publication, The New York Teacher News, carried a regular column entitled "New Materials for Classroom Use," which frequently listed or reviewed publications of allegedly subversive groups. He said the paper also urged union members to attend meetings of such organizations.

Among the organizations listed by Mr. Mandel were the Committee for a Democratic Far Eastern Policy, the National Council of Soviet-American Friendship, the American Committee for Protection of the Foreign-Born, and the Council for African Affairs.

Three among the witnesses who refused to answer one or both of the "$64 questions" face automatic dismissal by the Board of Higher Education from their posts in municipal colleges under Section 903 of the City Charter, which provides that any city employe who refuses to testify before an authorized body on grounds of possible self-incrimination forfeits his job.

**Teachers Are Named**

They are Vera Shlakman, economics instructor at Queens College and union vice president in charge of colleges; Bernard Reiss, Professor of Psychology at Hunter, and Harry Slochower, associate professor in the Brooklyn College German Department, who has been teaching comparative and world literature.

Professor Slochower told Senator Homer Ferguson, Republican of Michigan, sitting as a one-man subcommittee, that he was not a Communist. He balked, however, at the companion question: "Have you ever been a member of the Communist party?"

A fourth employe of the Board of Higher Education, Frederic Ewen, assistant professor of English at Brooklyn College, forestalled dismissal by filing his retirement papers on Tuesday, as he was entitled to do, having put in thirty years of service. Professor Ewen announced his retirement from the witness chair. Neither

Continued on Page 11, Column 1

## RED FORCE RETAKES WEST KOREAN HILL

### Puerto Ricans Win Crest, but Shelling Beats Them Back —Clark Confers at Front

By LINDESAY PARROTT
Special to THE NEW YORK TIMES.

TOKYO, Thursday, Sept. 25—Hard-fighting Chinese Red infantry threw United Nations forces back yesterday from "Kelly Hill" on the Western Korean front. But Allied troops scored in an eastern sector, smashing two enemy attacks on ridges south of Kosong near the Japan Sea.

Puerto Rican troops of the Sixty-fifth Regiment of the United States Third Infantry Division fought their way in the morning to the top of "Kelly Hill," in the Panmunjom sector, which was seized last week by the Chinese Communists. For a few hours, the Puerto Ricans held the crest, after savage hand-to-hand combat when two assault columns converged on an enemy's trenches and bunkers.

But heavy mortar and artillery fire pounded the hill from the enemy lines, and at noon the Puerto Ricans pulled back, leaving the slopes to the Communists. It was the third try that United Nations troops have made to recapture the much-battered hillock and the second time they have reached the crest, only to withdraw under the enemy guns.

The fighting flared up on the recently quiet East coast front when North Koreans, supported by 2,500 rounds of fire, attacked two hills south of Kosong.

One Red battalion struck shortly

Continued on Page 2, Column 2

## Iran Answers British-U. S. Oil Bid; Sets Time Limit on London's Reply

By ALBION ROSS
Special to THE NEW YORK TIMES.

TEHERAN, Iran, Sept. 24—The Iranian reply to the Churchill-Truman proposals for a settlement of the British-Iranian oil dispute was presented tonight to George Middleton, British Chargé d'Affaires, and Loy W. Henderson, United States Ambassador, by Premier Mohammed Mossadegh. The text will be published here tomorrow.

The note, which contains Dr. Mossadegh's counter-proposals, described as the final Iranian offer, was to have been handed over before noon today, but it was delayed by last-minute discussion of a covering letter to Prime Minister Churchill and President Truman.

[In Washington the Iranian Ambassador informed President Truman that his country was confronted by "very dangerous" economic conditions. The envoy appealed to the United States to prevail upon Britain to drop the blockade that prevents Iran from exporting oil.]

All reports indicate that the Iranian reply does not contain an ultimatum but sets a time limit for a British answer.

It contains a demand for an advance payment by the Anglo-Iranian Oil Company of £49,000,000 ($137,200,000) that is carried on the books of the company under an agreement of 1949 that Iran did not ratify. The demand is understood to have been put in such a form that the sum could be considered as an advance payment for oil deliveries that Iran is prepared to make if the International Court of Justice should find that the sum is not due Iran.

The way has also been left free for the Court to reject the adop-

Continued on Page 5, Column 2



## 'CLIQUE' IS BLAMED IN CAUDLE OUSTER; HE QUOTES M'GRATH

### Former Official Says Superior Told Him White House Group Was 'After' Both of Them

### HINTS AT A NEW SCANDAL

### He Declares Ex-Justice Head Talked of Story That Would 'Blow White House High'

By LUTHER A. HUSTON
Special to THE NEW YORK TIMES.

WASHINGTON, Sept. 24—Theron Lamar Caudle testified today at a House of Representatives Judiciary subcommittee hearing that J. Howard McGrath, former Attorney General, had told him that a "clique in the White House" was "after him" and that the same "clique" was after Mr. McGrath.

Mr. Caudle also testified that Mr. McGrath had told him he had a story he could tell that would "blow the White House so high it would become another satellite and the force of gravity would never bring it back to earth."

The witness said Mr. McGrath did not tell him the story and he had no idea what it was. The White House said it would have no comment on Mr. Caudle's testimony.

Mr. Caudle was dismissed by President Truman last November from his post as assistant attorney general in charge of the tax division of the Department of Justice. Mr. McGrath's resignation was requested by the President in April.

**Witness Names Three Men**

The witness said Mr. McGrath did not name the members of the "clique." Asked if he knew who they were, he said he "had an idea." He then named Charles S. Murphy, David H. Stowe and the late Joseph Short.

Mr. Murphy is special counsel to the President, Mr. Stowe is an administrative assistant to the President and Mr. Short was White House press secretary until his death last week.

Mr. Caudle completed his testimony before the subcommittee, headed by Representative Frank L. Chelf, Democrat of Kentucky, that is investigating the Department of Justice.

Mr. Chelf and Representative Kenneth B. Keating of New York, the ranking Republican member of the group, issued a joint statement in which they said of Mr. Caudle that "we feel that he is an honest man who was indiscreet in his associations and a pliant conformer to the peculiar moral climate of Washington."

The conversation about the "clique in the White House" and the story that would blow the White House so high, took place, according to Mr. Caudle, in Mr. McGrath's home after Mr. Caudle was dismissed, but while Mr. McGrath was still Attorney General. Mr. Caudle had gone there, he

Continued on Page 24, Column 2

## GIFT PLAN BACKED

### Governor Says Program Lessened Sacrifice of Low-Paid Key Aides

### RECIPIENTS' NAMES SECRET

### Nominee Undecided on Listing the Identities of Donors, He Tells Baltimore Backers

*Text of the Stevenson speech in Baltimore, Page 23.*

By W. H. LAWRENCE
Special to THE NEW YORK TIMES.

SPRINGFIELD, Ill., Sept. 24—Gov. Adlai E. Stevenson of Illinois declared today that he had no intention of making public any details of the fund from which he gave secret extra compensation to some appointive Illinois state officials.

The Democratic Presidential nominee asserted he did not believe any useful purpose would be served by publicizing the names of the officials helped or the amounts they received. He also said that he did not know whether he would make public a list of the contributors who made possible these gifts "around Christmas time to a small number of key employes who were making sacrifices to stay in the state government."

The Illinois Governor gave this message to an audience of more than 500 leaders in the Volunteers for Stevenson movement at a $3-a-plate breakfast in the Sheraton Belvedere Hotel in Baltimore. He then flew back to his headquarters here for a thirty-four-hour respite before he hits the campaign trail again Friday morning. His next tour takes him to Evansville, Ind., and Indianapolis on Friday, and Paducah, Ky., and Louisville on Saturday. A big picnic will be held in midday Saturday at the farm home of Vice President Alben W. Barkley near Paducah.

**Defends the Fund**

Governor Stevenson, who has been extremely frank in discussing many of the issues of this campaign, has been reticent about telling the details of the Illinois fund, an issue raised against him by his opponents after disclosures had been made that Senator Richard M. Nixon of California, the Republican Vice Presidential nominee, had received more than $18,000 from a group of wealthy Californians to help meet heavy Senatorial and political expenses.

Governor Stevenson said that

Continued on Page 22, Column 1

Associated Press Wirephoto

THEY "STAND TOGETHER": Gen. Dwight D. Eisenhower and his running mate, Senator Richard M. Nixon, left, respond to cheers of crowd that greeted them after they met last night in Senator Nixon's plane at airport in Wheeling, W. Va.

## CANDIDATES MEET

### Airport Greeting Warm—General Calls Senator a 'Man of Honor'

### TICKET HARMONY ASSURED

### Californian Now 'Stands Higher Than Ever,' Eisenhower Says of His Explanation

*Texts of Eisenhower and Nixon speeches in Wheeling, Page 21.*

By JAMES RESTON
Special to THE NEW YORK TIMES.

WHEELING, W. Va., Sept. 24—Gen. Dwight D. Eisenhower said tonight that his Vice Presidential running mate, Senator Richard M. Nixon of California, had been "completely vindicated" of charges in connection with a privately raised expense fund.

Speaking before a cheering and enthusiastic crowd here, the Republican Presidential nominee announced that the 107 members of the Republican National Committee who could be reached had all voted for retaining Mr. Nixon on the ticket. There are 138 members on the full committee.

General Eisenhower declared he believed Senator Nixon "had been subjected to an unfair and vicious attack."

"He is not only completely vindicated as a man of honor but, as far as I am concerned, he stands higher than ever before," said the general.

Thus it was plain that, although there had been no official statement sealing the California Senator's place on the ticket, the general's statement taken with the report on the national committee, made it certain that Mr. Nixon would remain the Republican party's Vice Presidential nominee.

**'A Man of Honor'**

General Eisenhower's remarks were:

"Ladies and gentlemen, my colleague in this political campaign has been subject to a very unfair and vicious attack. So far as I am concerned, he has not only vindicated himself, but I feel that he has acted as a man of courage and honor and so far as I am concerned, stands higher than ever before.

"I am going to ask Senator Nixon to speak a few words to you this evening, but before he comes to this podium, let me read to you two messages. The first one is a tribute. This is a telegram to me:

"'Dear General: I am trusting that the absolute truth may come out concerning this attack on Richard and when it does I am sure you will be guided right in your decision to place implicit faith in his integrity and honesty. Best wishes from one who has known Richard longer than anyone else. His mother.'

"Now, as I waited on him at the plane this evening, I received a telegram from the Republican Na-

Continued on Page 20, Column 1

## MESSAGES POUR IN BACKING NOMINEE

### Wires at Rate of 4,000 an Hour Overwhelmingly in Favor of Retaining Californian

By CLAYTON KNOWLES
Special to THE NEW YORK TIMES.

WASHINGTON, Sept 24—A flood of telegrams, pouring in on the Republican National Committee at the rate of 4,000 an hour, appeared tonight to have assured Senator Richard M. Nixon's retention on the Republican national ticket even before he met with Gen. Dwight D. Eisenhower in West Virginia.

With more than 75,000 messages tallied by 5 P. M., sentiment was running overwhelmingly in favor of the Californian's remaining as his party's Vice Presidential candidate.

Samplings both by the committee and by individual reporters who had free access to the great piles of telegrams showed that by a margin of about 200 to 1 voters wiring headquarters felt that Mr. Nixon's Los Angeles speech last night had put him in the clear on the controversial $18,235 "supplementary expenditures" fund put at his disposal by a group of California supporters.

Republican leaders were elated by the reaction to the Nixon speech.

**White House Is Silent**

There was no comment at the Democratic National Committee or at the White House. Senator Clinton P. Anderson, Democrat of New Mexico, interviewed as he left the White House after a visit with the President, said that, as a Democrat, he felt any advantage arising from the incident would "be our way."

The impact of the Nixon talk also was apparent in editorial comment in the capital.

The Washington Post, supporting General Eisenhower, which last Saturday called upon the Senator to withdraw from the ticket, will say in an editorial to be printed in tomorrow morning's editions that Mr. Nixon's public report has "confirmed our belief that he has done nothing 'involving moral turpitude'—to quote the phrase he used in urging the resignations of William Boyle and Guy Gabrielson." The editorial continued:

"But we remain of the conviction that he has committed an error of judgment, however unwittingly * * *. Many people will continue to view the Nixon episode as evidence that the Eisenhower crusade is overtolerant of missteps within its own membership.

"For that reason, Senator Nixon has added a burden to the Eisen-

Continued on Page 24, Column 7

## G. O. P. HEADS RALLY TO NIXON'S SUPPORT

### Summerfield Asserts Attack Has 'Backfired'—Senator's Position Held Stronger

Before the announcement by Gen. Dwight D. Eisenhower last night that the Republican National Committee had voted 107 to 0 to retain Senator Robert M. Nixon on the ticket, a survey by THE NEW YORK TIMES showed the committee overwhelmingly in favor of the Senator.

The backers of the Republican Vice Presidential nominee included Arthur E. Summerfield, chairman of the committee.

On Tuesday night, at the end of Senator Nixon's half-hour broadcast explanation of the $18,235 expense fund donated to him by California supporters, he declared he was submitting the question whether he should stay in the race to the committee and would abide by its decision.

He made it clear that his own inclination was to remain, that his conduct was fully justified.

Mr. Summerfield declared in Cleveland that attacks on Senator Nixon because of the fund had "backfired." He predicted that Senator Nixon's speech would prove "the turning point of the campaign."

His views were echoed throughout the country by Republican officials as they attempted to dig

Continued on Page 27, Column 2

## French Submarine Vanishes In Mediterranean; 48 Aboard

### La Sibylle Fails to Surface After Dive Off Toulon—U. S. Sends Aid Team

By The United Press.

TOULON, France, Sept. 24—The French submarine La Sibylle vanished off this naval base today and ships and planes were sweeping the Mediterranean Sea near here tonight for traces of the missing craft and her forty-eight-man crew.

The alarm was sounded when La Sibylle failed to surface on schedule after anti-submarine maneuvers at 10 A. M. Late tonight no sign of the submarine had been found and the French Navy expressed "serious anxiety" about her fate.

A veritable air-sea task force was ordered from Toulon to search the sea between the craggy isle of Porquerolles, about thirty miles offshore just east of Toulon, and the Riviera resort coast.

[One ship later saw a buoy belonging to the submarine bobbing about in the water fifty miles south of Porquerolles, according to Reuters.]

Another French submarine, the 2326, was lost in approximately the same area late in 1946 with twenty-one men aboard. No trace ever was found of her or her crew.

The 2218, the only other submarine France has lost since World War II, also vanished without a trace in 1948, carrying thirty-five men to their death.

A French naval spokesman in Paris warmly welcomed a British offer to lend France a special underwater television camera developed during last year's search for the British submarine Affray. The camera found the hulk of the Affray on the bottom of the English Channel, but too late to save its seventy-five-man crew.

It was not clear how soon the TV equipment could be made available to the French search fleet in the Mediterranean.

The passing hours increased concern about La Sibylle's fate, and made it seem more and more certain that the missing submarine

Continued on Page 9, Column 4

The New York Times Sept. 25, 1952

Scene of search (cross).

## Dewey, Blaming Truman for Korea, Says Eisenhower Is Hope of Peace

Charging that the United States is in a Korean war because the Democratic National Administration invited the war by two acts of "supreme folly," Governor Dewey declared last night that the election of Gen. Dwight D. Eisenhower, Republican nominee for President, was essential to the survival of this country.

It was the Governor's first speech of the campaign and was carried by television and radio from the New York studios of the National Broadcasting Company.

Recalling that he had warned about Korea in 1947, Mr. Dewey said "the supreme folly was nevertheless committed of pulling our troops out of Korea because they [the Administration] let our Army run down, and then of announcing from the public platform that it was outside of our defense perimeter."

The Governor added that the National Administration might just as well have sent a telegram to Stalin inviting him to conquer Korea, because we had thereby created "a vacuum of power."

Mr. Dewey said that we had had 117,000 American casualties to pay for Mr. Truman's "blunder." He asserted that we could not afford to continue to pay that kind of a price for "survival by a continuation of the fumbling that brought us unprepared into World War II and bungled us into the Korean war."

In a caustic attack on the foreign policy of the Truman Administration, the Governor declared:

"The only solution I know for the survival of this country is that we've got to get rid of the traitors and the incompetents and the crooks in Washington, and get into the Government of this country the skill, the know-how and the vision to win the peace."

In discussing how we could pre-

Continued on Page 19, Column 1

*Text of the Dewey address is on Page 13.*

"All the News That's Fit to Print"

# The New York Times.

LATE CITY EDITION
Fair, windy and cooler today.
Fair and cool tomorrow.
Temperature Range Today—Max., 60; Min., 45
Temperatures Yesterday—Max., 60; Min., 47
Full U. S. Weather Bureau Report, Page 32



VOL. CII..No. 34,608. Entered as Second-Class Matter, Post Office, New York, N. Y. NEW YORK, SATURDAY, OCTOBER 25, 1952. Times Square, New York 36, N. Y. Telephone Lackawanna 4-1000 FIVE CENTS

# EISENHOWER WOULD 'GO TO KOREA'; STEVENSON ASSAILS 'SLICK' PLANS; ACHESON BARS PEACE OF DISHONOR

## SUBWAYS STALLED BY SIGNAL FAILURE AT HEIGHT OF RUSH

### Blast and Fire Halt I.R.T. and B.M.T. Trains, Then Force Them to Crawl for Hour

### THOUSANDS ARE DELAYED

### All of Brooklyn and Most of Manhattan Hit—Bingham Blames Old Equipment

By RALPH KATZ

A small explosion and fire in a manhole outside a powerhouse serving the B. M. T. and I. R. T. subway lines caused one of the city's worst delays in transportation last night at the height of the rush hour.

The fire affected the signal system on the I. R. T. throughout Brooklyn and most of Manhattan and on the B. M. T. from Times Square to the lower end of Manhattan. It caused a half-hour shutdown of service on the I. R. T. and a fifteen-minute shutdown on the B. M. T., after which there were slowdowns on most lines for nearly an hour.

When the trains resumed running they crawled through the tubes, halting intermittently between stations to make sure that all precautions were being observed.

Many thousands of homeward-bound riders and others converging into the Times Square area were caught in the tie-up and slowdown. More than 320 trains on both facilities were involved. The Times Square station became so crowded that the entrances were closed for an hour.

**60,000 Stalled on I. R. T.**

While the number of stalled trains was about equal on each line, an indication of the number of persons affected was contained in a report from the I. R. T. that between 100 and 125 of its trains held an estimated 60,000 persons.

Many left the trains and walked along subway catwalks to stations, where they sought alternate routes to their destinations.

The explosion and fire occurred at 6:03 P.M. in a manhole on Fifty-ninth Street between Eleventh and Twelfth Avenues. The fire itself was small and was easily put out, but its shorting of near-by circuits could not be handled by the circuit-breakers along the signal wires, which are designed to prevent burn-outs.

The result was a failure on the alternating current lines that feed thirteen sub-stations for the control of signal lights. The interruption of signal service advanced swiftly from breaker to breaker until it became necessary to shut down temporarily the running power in the affected areas.

**Service Slow and Erratic**

At the Times Square station, the tie-up was recorded as from 6:05 to 6:50 P. M. After that, the trains ran slowly and erratically. The shuttle service to Grand Central operated without interruption, but slowly because of the signal failure.

The seven entrances to the station were closed as soon as the halt developed as a move to prevent unusual crowding. Some of the station lights went out and others burned dimly. It was impossible to ascertain how many riders were in the station at the time, but at one entrance alone 480 accepted receipts for their fares.

A detail of police was sent to the subway station from the West Thirtieth Street police station to handle the crowds at the en-

Continued on Page 34, Column 2

## Hurricane Injures 70 As It Pounds at Cuba

By The Associated Press.

MIAMI, Fla., Oct. 24—A hurricane packing 165-mile-per-hour winds slashed a broad path across Cuba today on a course that would take it near South Florida's Gold Coast.

The storm thundered inland over Cuba, with its center near Cienfuegos on the south coast, beating a sixty-mile-wide swath through rich sugar cane and ranch land. Gales lashed outward seventy-five miles from the center of the storm, described as one of the most violent to strike land in recent years.

Seventy persons were reported injured when their homes were blown down. These casualty figures covered only two areas in the path of the storm.

Heavy damage to roads, crops and fruit trees was reported in the Cayman Islands, 125 miles below Cuba. The commissioner

Continued on Page 33, Column 4

## HARLEM TENEMENT CITED ON 91 COUNTS

### First Week of Firetrap Survey Lays 84 Violations to Same Owner in 4 Other Buildings

By CHARLES G. BENNETT

The end of the first week of the city's firetrap survey in Harlem brought a crackdown yesterday by Frederick S. Weaver, Deputy Commissioner of Housing, on the Klahr Realty Corporation, owner of a five-story tenement building at 1 West 118th Street.

Notices that ninety-one violations of the multiple dwelling law had been found at the building, the first one searched by housing inspectors, were sent yesterday by Mr. Weaver to the Klahr Corporation at 1466 Fifth Avenue.

The owner was also notified of eighty-four violations found in four buildings it operates at 1462-66-68 Fifth Avenue, around the corner from the 118th Street address.

In all, the inspectors reported they had found 617 violations in the seventy-two apartment buildings in the block bounded by West 118th Street, West 119th Street, Lenox and Fifth Avenues. A team of eleven inspectors worked under the supervision of Patrick F. Kelly, chief of the Housing and Buildings Department's rodent control section.

**Cases Going Directly to Court**

Denouncing the Klahr corporation for its large number of violations, nine of them labeled "extremely hazardous," Commissioner Weaver said he would eliminate the usual departmental hearings and take the owner directly into the Magistrates' Courts.

"Because of the serious nature of many of these violations the owner corporation is not entitled to any consideration from this department," Mr. Weaver declared, adding that the notices served yesterday would be followed by court summonses within five days.

The Klahr Corporation and other Manhattan landlords subsequently brought into court in the continuing firetrap survey are scheduled to go before a special part of Municipal Term presided over by Chief Magistrate John M. Murtagh.

Mr. Murtagh, who has pledged the magistrates' cooperation with the housing campaign, accompanied the housing inspectors last Monday when they opened their drive. Aghast at the living conditions he saw in the crowded apartments in the 1 West 118th Street building, the Chief Magistrate ex-

Continued on Page 15, Column 5

## COAL OWNERS ASK PUTNAM TO REVIEW W. S. B. WAGE CURB

### Economic Stabilizer Gets Plea for Approval of the 40c Cut From Rise of $1.90 a Day

### END OF STRIKE KEY AIM

### Moses Says Operators Want to Reopen Pits—Anthracite Negotiations Recessed

By JOSEPH A. LOFTUS
Special to The New York Times.

WASHINGTON, Oct. 24—Northern soft coal operators asked the Government tonight to reconsider the Wage Stabilization Board's refusal to approve 40 cents of the wage increase of $1.90 a day they contracted to pay the miners. About 350,000 members of the United Mine Workers have been on strike since Monday in protest against the board's decision.

Harry M. Moses, president of the Bituminous Coal Operators Association, representing mainly northern tonnage, filed a petition with Roger L. Putnam, Economic Stabilization Administrator. Whether he also filed a petition with the Wage Stabilization Board could not be learned.

Mr. Moses would not indicate whether his appeal had any basis other than the willingnes of the operators to honor the contract he made and their desire to restore production.

The Wage Board majority of public and industry members held in their decision that an increase of more than $1.50 would give to the miners a larger increase than had been received by workers in any other major industry and might set a pattern for increases that would break anti-inflation controls.

**Putnam Studying Petition**

Mr. Putnam's office acknowledged this evening that the petition had arrived "a few minutes ago." A spokesman said that Mr. Putnam was "going to study it very carefully and in the meantime he is not going to say anything about it."

John L. Lewis, president of the United Mine Workers, had stated that the miners would go back to work when the operators paid them the full $1.90 increase. He had been reported willing to join the request for reconsideration of the W. S. B. cut in the wage increase, but whether he did could not be learned tonight.

[However, in New York a spokesman for Mr. Lewis said last night that the mine chief had joined Mr. Moses in the appeal to Mr. Putnam. He added that Mr. Lewis would not release information concerning the appeal until it was made public through other sources.]

Mr. Lewis did not join in the original petition to the board for approval of the wage increase.

He left late this afternoon for Morgantown, W. Va., where he will make a speech tomorrow night in behalf of the Democratic nominee for President, Gov. Adlai E. Stevenson.

**Cole Working on Dispute**

David L. Cole, director of the Federal Mediation and Conciliation Service, has been working on the dispute for the last two days. He conferred with Mr. Moses and Mr. Lewis again today, but declined to answer questions about the nature of their talks.

He refused to give any support to assumptions that private talks with Mr. Putnam and higher officials in the Administration preceded the filing of the Moses petition.

The Administration obviously is trying to end the coal strike before the election, but whether it is willing to do it with a straight-out reversal of the Wage Stabilization Board has not been indicated.

Mr. Lewis and Mr. Moses are eager to get the mines back into production, but both are reported averse to substituting "fringe" improvements—such as higher vacation pay or welfare fund payments—for the 40-cent cut ordered in the wage agreement.

The United Mine Workers and the anthracite operators continued their negotiations for a new contract. Talks were recessed late today until tomorrow.

**Effects of Reversal Surmised**

WASHINGTON, Oct. 24 (AP)—Any reversal of the Wage Stabilization Board decision on the coal wage would be bound to anger board members and might well lead to mass resignations, at least of the industry members, according to views expressed here tonight.

A reversal of the board, it was suggested, would furnish Republican party campaigners with pow-

Continued on Page 12, Column 5

## Support of the U. N. Urged by Nominees

Gen. Dwight D. Eisenhower and Gov. Adlai E. Stevenson declared their support of the United Nations last night and called upon the people of the nation to back the world organization.

*[Texts of messages by two candidates appear on Page 2.]*

Commending the United Nations for its prompt action in Korea, General Eisenhower asked the American people "to reaffirm their devotion to the peaceful hopes of free men everywhere" and the United States "as a proud member of the United Nations pledge again our strength, our fortune and our sacred honor to the end that no free nation shall ever again be destroyed upon this earth."

In backing United Nation action in Korea, General Eisenhower supported the action taken

Continued on Page 2, Column 5

## LONG FIGHT SURGES OVER KOREAN HILLS

### U. S. and South Korean Forces Win and Lose Peaks as the Reds Pour In More Men

By LINDESAY PARROTT
Special to The New York Times.

TOKYO, Saturday, Oct. 25—United States and South Korean troops were locked today in a swaying battle with the Chinese Communists for "Triangle Hill" and "Sniper Ridge," outpost bastions of the enemy's main defenses on the central Korean front. The results were still in doubt at noon after thirty hours of continuous combat.

During the morning, weary infantrymen of the Republic of Korea's Second Division fought their way back to the crest of "Pinpoint Hill," dominating feature of "Sniper Ridge," north of Kumhwa. But the Chinese Reds were pouring a fresh regiment into the fight for the position, which had already cost the foe most of a division (12,000 men) in casualties.

Latest reports said the South Koreans held about half of "Pinpoint," the Reds the other half.

The South Koreans had gone forward through one of the heaviest barrages the Communists have fired in the current hill fighting. During the night, before the Chinese Reds' infantry drove the South Koreans off the summit, enemy guns had laid 17,000 rounds of mortar and artillery shells on the ridge.

Intermittent rain hampered close-

Continued on Page 3, Column 3

## U. S. EXPLAINS VIEW

### Secretary Tells U. N. Unit Washington Is Ready and Eager to End War

### ASKS APPROVAL OF EFFORT

### Again Rules Out Any Forcible Repatriation and Cites 17 Pacts Signed by Soviet

*Excerpts from U. N. address by Mr. Acheson are on Page 4.*

By A. M. ROSENTHAL
Special to The New York Times.

UNITED NATIONS, N. Y., Oct. 24—Secretary of State Dean Acheson told United Nations delegates today that the United States was ready and eager to end the Korean war but that peace could not be "purchased at the price of honor."

For almost three hours Mr. Acheson held the floor of the Political and Security Committee of the General Assembly, taking the sixty delegates on a carefully impassionate, calmly spoken and meticulously detailed review of the Korean war, all that led up to it and the long drawn-out attempts to end it. Several times in his speech he carefully underlined the charge that it was the Soviet Union that had trained and equipped the army of North Korea, sent it into a war of aggression and still was maintaining it in the field.

Mr. Acheson formally asked the General Assembly to give its approval to the United Nations conduct of the war through the United States, acting in its capacity as the Unified Command. Together with twenty other countries, the United States put before the committee a resolution calling on the enemy to accept the one principle that apparently has been holding up the signing of a truce, the principle that no prisoner of war should be sent back home against his will.

**Soviet Signatures Cited**

The Secretary of State, in a deliberately dry voice, read out seventeen treaties signed by the Soviet Union after World War I in which the principle of no forcible repatriation had been explicitly agreed to by the Soviet Government.

"Pretty good doctrine," Mr. Acheson said caustically.

Time and again Mr. Acheson, who spoke without a prepared text but relied on sheaves of notes, stressed the point that the United States had done everything honorable to reach a Korean peace. He revealed that not only had open

Continued on Page 4, Column 6

The New York Times (by Meyer Liebowitz)

ACHESON SPEAKS: The Secretary of State at United Nations Political and Security Committee of the General Assembly.

## GENERAL IN PLEDGE

### 'First Task' Would Be 'Early and Honorable' End of the War

### HE GIVES FOUR PROMISES

### Bars Appeasement—Declares 'Record of Failure' Led to Far East Fighting

*Text of the Eisenhower speech in Detroit is on Page 8.*

By ELIE ABEL
Special to The New York Times.

DETROIT, Oct. 24—Gen. Dwight D. Eisenhower gave the nation his pledge tonight that if elected President he would go to Korea to seek an early and honorable end of the war there.

He promised to "forego the diversions of politics" and to concentrate on the task of closing the war—a conflict that was never inevitable or inescapable, he said, but one that resulted from the Truman Administration's repeated failures to heed the warnings of Republicans. The General's statement was cheered by an overflow crowd of 5,000 in the Masonic Auditorium here.

To pledge an end of the Korean fighting by any "imminent exact date" would be dishonest, the Republican candidate for President asserted, but it would be equally dishonest to tell the United States that it could only "wait—and wait—and wait" for peace.

The quest of an honorable end of the war requires a personal trip to Korea by the new President, General Eisenhower said, and added:

"Only in that way could I learn how best to serve the American people in the cause of peace.

"I shall go to Korea."

**To 'Re-Examine Every Course'**

He also outlined these four pledges to the American people:

1. That the first task of his Administration would be to "review and re-examine every course of action open to us with one goal in view: To bring the Korean war to an early and honorable end."
2. That he would go to Korea to see for himself how best to achieve this goal.
3. That the United Nations should step up the training and arming of the South Korean forces so that they might eventually defend their own frontiers. At the same time, the free nations should shape a program of psychological warfare capable of cracking "the Communist front" in the Far East.
4. That his Administration would always reject appeasement and vacillation, because appeasement was not the road to peace, but "surrender on the installment plan," he said, quoting the late Senator Arthur H. Vandenberg of Michigan.

Coming near the end of a half-hour radio and television address on the last night of his whistle-

Continued on Page 8, Column 2

## Stevenson Fears a 'Munich' In Rival's Asian Troop Plan

By W. H. LAWRENCE
Special to The New York Times.

ABOARD STEVENSON TRAIN, in New York, Oct. 24—Gov. Adlai E. Stevenson of Illinois told upstate New York audiences today that Gen. Dwight D. Eisenhower's "proposal of a quick and a slick way out of Korea" would risk a "Munich in the Far East, with the probability of a third World War not far behind."

The Democratic Presidential nominee worked hard, at fourteen stops, for New York's vitally important forty-five electoral votes. His day began with a trainside audience of almost 1,000 at Niagara Falls, at 7:15 A. M., and wound up with a formal speech, locally televised and broadcast, at the Rensselaer Polytechnic Institute at Troy, at 9:30 P. M.

*[Text of Stevenson talk in Rochester appears on Page 10.]*

This was United Nations Day and Governor Stevenson hammered at the Republican Presidential candidate's proposal, first made in isolationist-minded Illinois, that South Korean troops should be trained and equipped to take over the Korean front lines by themselves so that American and other United Nations troops could be pulled back into reserve. In a speech at Champaign, Ill., early in October, General Eisenhower had said that if there must be a war in the Far East "let it be Asians against Asians."

"The war in Korea, my friends, is not Mr. Truman's war," Governor Stevenson told an enthusiastic audience at Rochester. "It is mankind's war. * * * The issues in this conflict are too grave and too great for partisan politics. And the proposal of a quick and a slick way out of Korea is false.

**'Would Mean Surrender'**

"My opponent has told us that we could leave the South Koreans to do the fighting alone against the Communists," Mr. Stevenson continued. "He has said that Asians should be left to fight Asians. If we were to follow the General's policy, we would risk a Munich in the Far East, with the probability of a third World War not far behind.

"Great as would be the increasing role bravely taken by the armies of the Republic of Korea, it is clear that the withdrawal of all American forces would mean ultimate surrender of South Korea to the larger, stronger forces of the Communists, and South Korea itself would become a base for further aggression and Communist pressure against Japan, Formosa and the Philippines. And, it would also release Communist forces for still greater adventures on the mainland of Asia."

Governor Stevenson asserted that Gen. James A. Van Fleet, Eighth Army commander in Korea, had declared that the South Korean army would not be strong enough to man the entire battle line by itself. Governor Stevenson went on to say that this "mistake" by General Eisenhower "could not be charged to ignorance." He said

Continued on Page 16, Column 6

## U. N. EDITORIAL AIDE ADMITS RED LINKS

### Confirms Chambers' Charges —Senator Criticizes Lie on Suspects' Paid Leaves

By RICHARD H. PARKE

A Democratic Senator acting as chairman of a Senate subcommittee strongly criticized Trygve Lie, United Nations Secretary General, yesterday for giving leaves of absence with pay to ten American United Nations employes suspected of Communist affiliations.

Senator James O. Eastland of Mississippi, who said Mr. Lie's action was "beyond my comprehension," asserted at the same time that his internal security subcommittee of the Senate Judiciary Committee had uncovered among American employes of the United Nations the "greatest concentration" of Communists in its hearings to date.

He made his statement as the committee wound up a session at the Federal Courthouse on Foley Square during which it wrung an admission from David Zablodowsky, a United Nations editorial official, that he had been a member of a Communist underground, al-

Continued on Page 5, Column 1

## Judge Hand Says U. S. Democracy Is Menaced by Suspicion and Fear

By MURRAY ILLSON
Special to The New York Times.

ALBANY, Oct. 24—Unfounded denunciations are spreading fears and suspicions that may lead to the destruction of the country's political institutions, Learned Hand, retired chief judge of the Second Federal Circuit Court of Appeals, asserted here tonight.

Making the principal address before a state-wide gathering of 600 education officials attending the eighty-sixth convocation of the Board of Regents of the University of the State of New York, Judge Hand said that the United States was threatened by internal as well as external perils and was facing "a test which it may fail to pass."

"Risk for risk, for myself I had rather take my chance that some traitors will escape detection than spread abroad a spirit of general suspicion and distrust, which accepts rumor and gossip in place of [illegible] and unintimidated inquiry," the judge said, adding.

"I believe that that community is already in the process of dissolution where each man begins to eye his neighbor as a possible enemy, where nonconformity with the accepted creed, political as well as religious, is a mark of disaffection; where denunciation, without specification or backing, takes the place of evidence; where orthodoxy chokes freedom of dissent; where faith in the eventual supremacy of reason has become so timid that we dare not enter our convictions in the open lists to win or lose."

Judge Hand, who retired last year after forty-two years on the Federal bench, said that the fears he had cited were "a solvent which can eat out the cement that binds the stones together" and that they might in the end "subject us to a despotism as evil as any that we dread."

These fears, he added, "can be

Continued on Page 5, Column 3

## Morse Resigns From G.O.P.; May Hold Key Vote in Senate

### Oregonian Says He Acts for Good of Country— Will Be Independent

By LAWRENCE E. DAVIES
Special to The New York Times.

PORTLAND, Ore., Oct. 24—Senator Wayne Morse of Oregon announced tonight that he was resigning from the Republican party because the tenets of Abraham Lincoln no longer held in a party "dominated by reactionaries running a captive general for the Presidency of the United States." Henceforth, he said, he would be an independent.

His announcement, made on a recording played at a meeting and dance of Volunteers for Stevenson, followed by less than a week the Senator's word that he was supporting Gov. Adlai E. Stevenson of Illinois, the Democratic nominee, for President.

This was despite the fact, he said in his speech, that he was the first member of the Senate publicly to declare himself for Gen. Dwight D. Eisenhower as a potential Republican nominee.

Near the close of a seventeen-minute recording Senator Morse, who has been a controversial figure among Oregon Republicans almost since his election to his first term

Continued on Page 9, Column 2

### Should Chamber Be Evenly Divided After Nov. 4, He Could Swing Control

By C. P. TRUSSELL
Special to The New York Times.

WASHINGTON, Oct. 24—Senator Wayne Morse of Oregon, who has bolted the Republican party as well as its Presidential nominee, Gen. Dwight D. Eisenhower, stepped tonight into a position where he might be able to dictate whether the United States Senate should be Republican or Democratic in the next Congress.

If the electoral battles in the various states where Senate seats are at stake this year should result in a Senate of forty-eight to forty-eight counting Mr. Morse as a Republican, under which party he was elected, the Oregon Senator could weight the scales by throwing his vote either way. The present division is forty-nine Democrats and forty-seven Republicans, counting Mr. Morse in the Republican total.

If he voted with the Democrats, they would control the Senate. If he elected to vote with his former colleagues, the Republicans, the resulting tie would have to be decided by the vote of the Vice President, and that Vice President

Continued on Page 9, Column 3

## Retail Price Index Declines 0.2% After Steady Climb Since February

Special to The New York Times.

WASHINGTON, Oct. 24—The Government's retail price index dropped 0.2 per cent between mid-August and mid-September, the first decline since last February. The index had been rising steadily since then. A drop of 1 per cent in food prices was responsible for the decline. Prices for all other major groups went up.

The drop was about 0.5 per cent in the old index, which the Bureau of Labor Statistics still compiles as a convenience for unions and managements whose cost-of-living escalator contracts are geared to it.

The modernized index as of Sept. 15 was 190.8, as against 191.1 on Aug. 15. The drop of three-tenths of a percentage point amounted to about two-tenths of a per cent. This index carries a different weight for food than the old index and includes some new items, such as television sets and frozen foods.

The index rise since the Korean fighting began in June, 1950, has been 12.1 per cent. It is up 2.3 per cent above a year ago. The index base (100) is the price average from 1935 to 1939.

The old index on Sept. 15 stood at 191.4, as against 192.3 in mid-August.

The movement of the retail price index affects most wage rates, sooner or later. Where escalator clauses are in operation, the effect is automatic, though most adjustments are made on a quarterly basis, rather than monthly. In the quarter ended Sept. 15, the rise in the old index was three-tenths of a percentage point, or about 0.2 per cent.

The price drop of 1 per cent put the food index at 233.2 per cent of the 1935-39 average. This is 2.6 per cent higher than a year ago and 14.8 per cent above June, 1950. Chiefly responsible for the food

Continued on Page 14, Column 7

"All the News That's Fit to Print"

# The New York Times.

ELECTION EXTRA

Fair, warmer today. Some cloudiness and turning cooler tomorrow.
Temperature Range Today—Max., 62; Min., 38
Temperature Yesterday—Max., 52; Min., 30
Full U. S. Weather Bureau Report, Page 55

Copyright, 1952, by The New York Times Company.

VOL. CII No. 34,619. Entered as Second-Class Matter. Post Office, New York, N. Y. NEW YORK, WEDNESDAY, NOVEMBER 5, 1952. Times Square, New York 36, N. Y. Telephone Lackawanna 4-1000 FIVE CENTS

# EISENHOWER WINS IN A LANDSLIDE; TAKES NEW YORK; IVES ELECTED; REPUBLICANS GAIN IN CONGRESS

## G.O.P. HOUSE LIKELY

### But the Senate Margin Hangs in the Balance of Two Close Races

### LODGE TRAILING RIVAL

### President Eisenhower May Lack a Working Majority in Congress

By JAMES RESTON

It appeared at 4:30 this morning that control of the United States Senate could be determined by the outcome of the Senatorial races in Michigan and Massachusetts.

At that time the Republicans appeared to have picked up five new seats and lost three others, thus enabling them to wipe out the two-seat advantage held by the Democrats at the end of the Eighty-second Congress.

To assure the power to organize the Senate and place their Republicans at the head of its important committees, however, Senator Henry Cabot Lodge Jr., Republican of Massachusetts, would have to overcome an advantage of more than 75,000 held by Representative John F. Kennedy, his opponent.

And Representative Charles E. Potter, Republican of Michigan had to retain the 47,000 lead he held over the Democratic incumbent, Senator Blair Moody of Michigan.

**Morse May Be Vital**

So close was the Senate race that there was a possibility that control of the upper chamber could be determined by the decision of Senator Wayne Morse of Oregon, who was elected as a Republican, but who broke with his party during the campaign, and announced that hereafter he was an "independent."

Though it appeared that the Republicans had won control of the House, one thing was certain: that President Dwight D. Eisenhower would not have a comfortable working majority in either house and would require all his gifts of persuasion to win consent for his policies on Capitol Hill.

Several factors in the Senate race were noteworthy:

¶Of the ten so-called isolationist or extremist Republicans who went before the voters yesterday, seven seemed fairly sure of victory. These were Senators Joseph R. McCarthy of Wisconsin; John W. Bricker of Ohio; William E. Jenner of Indiana; Edward Martin of Pennsylvania; Arthur V. Watkins of Utah, George W. Malone of Nevada and Hugh Butler of Nebraska.

Three other Republicans in this same category, however, were in serious trouble if they had not actually been defeated. They were:

Continued on Page 15, Column 1

## Electoral Vote by States

| | Eisenhower | Stev'son | | Eisenhower | Stev'son |
|---|---|---|---|---|---|
| Ala. | — | 11 | Neb. | 6 | — |
| Ariz. | 4 | — | Nev. | 3 | — |
| Ark. | — | 8 | N. H. | 4 | — |
| Calif. | 32 | — | N. J. | 16 | — |
| Colo. | 6 | — | N. M. | 4 | — |
| Conn. | 8 | — | N. Y. | 45 | — |
| Del. | 3 | — | N. C. | — | 14 |
| Fla. | 10 | — | N. D. | 4 | — |
| Ga. | — | 12 | Ohio | 25 | — |
| Idaho | 4 | — | Okla. | 8 | — |
| Ill. | 27 | — | Ore. | 6 | — |
| Ind. | 13 | — | Pa. | 32 | — |
| Iowa | 10 | — | R. Isl. | 4 | — |
| Kan. | 8 | — | S. C. | — | 8 |
| *Ky. | — | 10 | S. D. | 4 | — |
| *La. | — | 10 | *Tenn. | 11 | — |
| Me. | 5 | — | Texas | 24 | — |
| Md. | 9 | — | Utah | 4 | — |
| Mass. | 16 | — | Vt. | 3 | — |
| Mich. | 20 | — | Va. | 12 | — |
| Minn. | 11 | — | Wash. | 9 | — |
| Miss. | — | 8 | W. Va. | — | 8 |
| Mo. | 13 | — | Wisc. | 12 | — |
| Mont. | 4 | — | Wyo. | 3 | — |
| | | | Total | 442 | 89 |

*Trend.

## EISENHOWER TAKES JERSEY BY 300,000

### Senator Smith Is Re-elected—Bond Issues Supported in Record Balloting

By RUSSELL PORTER

With more than three-quarters of New Jersey's vote counted early this morning, Gen. Dwight D. Eisenhower appeared headed toward a plurality of close to 300,000 in the state over Gov. Adlai E. Stevenson. This far exceeded Governor Dewey's 1948 plurality of 85,669 over President Truman.

United States Senator H. Alexander Smith, Republican candidate for re-election, won a sweeping victory over his Democratic opponent, Archibald S. Alexander, though Mr. Smith ran behind the head of his ticket. His indicated plurality was about 200,000.

The returns were:

PRESIDENT

3,461 precincts out of 3,840:

| | |
|---|---|
| Eisenhower | 1,203,120 |
| Stevenson | 921,375 |

UNITED STATES SENATOR

3,399 precincts out of 3,840:

| | |
|---|---|
| Smith | 1,089,883 |
| Alexander | 903,533 |

The Republicans appeared to have retained their majority of nine to five in New Jersey's delegation in the House of Representatives.

Both bond issues on the ballot

Continued on Page 23, Column 2

## STATE LEAD 850,000

### General's Upstate Edge Tops Million—He Loses City by Only 362,674

### PROTEST VOTE SEEN

### Albany County, Other Areas in Democratic Column Switch

**State Presidential Vote**

CITY SUMMARY

| | Eisenhower (Rep.) | Stevenson (Dem.-Lib.) |
|---|---|---|
| Manhattan | 300,234 | 447,877 |
| Bronx | 241,545 | 393,052 |
| Brooklyn | 447,148 | 656,278 |
| Queens | 449,505 | 331,633 |
| Richmond | 55,981 | 28,247 |
| Total | 1,494,413 | 1,857,087 |
| Upstate | 2,413,299 | 1,147,510 |
| Grand total | 3,907,712 | 3,104,597 |

4,394 election districts out of 4,394 in the city reporting and 5,222 out of 5,954 upstate.

By JAMES A. HAGERTY

Gen. Dwight D. Eisenhower, Republican nominee for President, carried New York State with its forty-five electoral votes with a plurality of landslide proportions that will reach nearly 850,000.

With 33 election districts missing, all outside this city, General Eisenhower led Gov. Adlai E. Stevenson, his Democratic opponent, by an actual plurality of 846,020 and an indicated plurality of 840,034.

To carry his adopted state by this astounding plurality, General Eisenhower held Governor Stevenson down to an actual plurality of 362,674 in this city, far less than the supporters of the Democratic candidate expected.

With the 33 election districts missing, General Eisenhower carried the state outside the city by an actual plurality of 1,265,789 and, assuming that his vote held up in the missing districts, by an indicated plurality of about 1,270,000.

Governor Stevenson carried Manhattan by 147,633, the Bronx by 151,597 and Brooklyn by 209,130, all far below Democratic expectations. General Eisenhower carried Queens by 117,872 and Richmond by 27,834, well above

Continued on Page 24, Column 3

## New President and Vice President

DWIGHT D. EISENHOWER

RICHARD M. NIXON

The New York Times

## RACE IS CONCEDED

### Virginia and Florida Go to the General as Do Illinois and Ohio

### SWEEP IS NATION-WIDE

### Victor Calls for Unity and Thanks Governor for Pledging Support

By ARTHUR KROCK

Gen. Dwight D. Eisenhower was elected President of the United States yesterday in an electoral vote landslide and with an emphatic popular majority that probably will give his party a small margin of control in the House of Representatives but may leave the Senate as it is—forty-nine Democrats, forty-seven Republicans and one independent.

Senator Richard M. Nixon of California was elected Vice President.

The Democratic Presidential candidate, Gov. Adlai E. Stevenson of Illinois, shortly after midnight conceded his defeat by a record turnout of American voters.

At 4 A. M. today the Republican candidate had carried states with a total of 431 electors, or 165 more than the 266 required for the selection of a President. The Democratic candidate seemed sure of 69, with 31 doubtful in Kentucky, Louisiana and Tennessee.

General Eisenhower's landslide victory, both in electoral and popular votes, was nation-wide in its pattern, extending from New England—where Massachusetts and Rhode Island broke their Democratic voting habits of many years—down the Eastern seaboard to Maryland, Virginia and Florida and westward to almost every state between the coasts, including California.

**General Wins Illinois**

The Republican candidate took Illinois, Governor Stevenson's home state. In South Carolina, though he lost its electors on a technicality, he won a majority of the voters. And, completing the first successful Republican invasion of the States of the former Confederacy, the General carried Texas and broke the one-party system in the South.

The personal popularity that enabled him to defeat Senator Robert A. Taft of Ohio in the Republican primaries in Texas, and present him with the issue on which he defeated the Senator for the Republican nomination, crushed the regular Democratic organization of Texas that was led by Speaker Sam Rayburn of the House of Representatives and had the blessing of former Vice President John N. Garner.

The tide that bore General Eisenhower to the White House, though it did not give him a comfortable working majority in either the national House or the Senate (the Democrats may still nominally control the machinery of that branch), probably increased the number of Republican governors beyond the present twenty-five.

"My fellow citizens have made their choice and I gladly accept it," said Governor Stevenson at 1:46 A. M., Eastern standard time, and he asked all citizens to unite behind the President-elect. The defeated candidate said he had sent a telegram of congratulation to General Eisenhower.

At 2:05 A. M., from the Grand Ballroom of the Commodore Hotel, General Eisenhower said he recognized the weight of his new responsibilities and that he would not give "short weight" in their execution. He also urged "unity" and announced he had sent a telegram of thanks to the Democratic candidate for his promise of support.

The issues of the unusually vigorous campaign that was waged

Continued on Page 14, Column 3

## IVES IS RE-ELECTED BY RECORD MARGIN

### Defeats Cashmore by Biggest Plurality of Any Republican—Harding Mark Topped

**Vote for Senator**

CITY SUMMARY

| | Ives (Rep.) | Cashmore (Dem.) | Counts (Lib.) |
|---|---|---|---|
| Manh'n | 303,040 | 322,157 | 88,797 |
| Bronx | 233,548 | 277,506 | 101,014 |
| B'klyn | 398,498 | 522,751 | 147,370 |
| Queens | 429,225 | 265,812 | 62,558 |
| Rich'd | 51,939 | 28,742 | 2,044 |
| Total | 1,416,250 | 1,416,968 | 401,783 |
| Up-state | 2,399,770 | 1,099,842 | 52,259 |
| Gr Totl | 3,816,020 | 2,516,810 | 454,042 |

4,394 election districts out of 4,394 in the city reporting and 5,854 out of 5,954 up-state.

By LEO EGAN

Senator Irving M. Ives won re-election in a three-cornered race yesterday by the largest plurality ever obtained by a Republican candidate in New York State, topping President Warren G. Harding's record-setting margin of 1,089,929 in 1920 by more than 200,000 votes.

The former majority leader of the State Assembly and co-sponsor of New York's law against racial discrimination in employment thus became the first Republican Senator to win re-election in New York since the late James W. Wadsworth performed that feat in the Harding landslide of 1920.

Not only did Senator Ives carry the normally Republican upstate area by a plurality that may reach 1,297,972, but he came within 718 votes of capturing normally Democratic New York City as well.

The complete Senate vote in the city gave Senator Ives 1,416,250 to 1,416,968 for Borough President John Cashmore of Brooklyn, the Democratic candidate. Thus Mr. Cashmore's plurality within the city was held to 718 votes.

With 5,854 of the 5,954 districts outside the city totaled, Senator Ives had an actual plurality of 1,299,928. On this basis, his final up-state margin should reach 1,300,000.

Dr. George S. Counts, the Liberal party candidate, polled 454,042 votes in the same districts tabulated for Senator Ives and Mr. Cashmore. On this basis his final vote could reach 460,000. Corliss Lamont, the American Labor can-

Continued on Page 21, Column 2

NEW YORK TIMES news bulletins are broadcast over WQXR every hour.

## Eisenhower Cracks South, Heads for Victory in Texas

By WILLIAM S. WHITE

Gen. Dwight D. Eisenhower, the Republican Presidential candidate, has smashed the traditionally Democratic Solid South in his national victory over Gov. Adlai E. Stevenson. He has carried outright Florida and Virginia, with their twenty-two electoral votes. This morning unofficial observers gave him the greatest Southern prize of all—Texas and its twenty-four electoral votes, the sixth biggest bloc in the United States.

Confirmation of this indicated loss would involve a Democratic disaster.

Apart from all this and from receiving the greatest popular ballot ever given a Republican in the South, General Eisenhower was first narrowly leading and then narrowly trailing this morning in Tennessee, which has eleven electoral votes. In Tennessee, the position was so close that the result probably will not be known until late this afternoon.

In Louisiana and South Carolina Governor Stevenson had slight leads after trailing often in the early returns.

Only the hardest of the hard core of the Old South has remained wholly faithful to the old Democratic tradition.

Mississippi, Arkansas, North

Continued on Page 22, Column 3

## CONNECTICUT G. O. P. SEATS 2 IN SENATE

### Benton and Ribicoff Concede to Purtell and Bush While Eisenhower Sweeps State

Special to THE NEW YORK TIMES.

HARTFORD, Conn., Wednesday, Nov. 5—Gen. Dwight D. Eisenhower swept to an amazing landslide victory in Connecticut yesterday, winning by a margin of nearly 130,000 votes over Gov. Adlai E. Stevenson in final returns from the 169 cities and towns in the state.

The victory astounded Republicans as well as Democrats. Prior to the election, Republican leaders had made cautious claims of victory by about 25,000 or 30,000 votes, while Democrats privately thought they had a chance to win the state.

The tremendous Eisenhower sweep carried two Republican United States Senators into office with him. Senator William A. Purtell of West Hartford defeated William Benton, Democrat, for the full six-year term by a margin of 90,286, and Prescott S. Bush, Greenwich banker, defeated Representative Abraham A. Ribicoff of Hartford, Democrat, by 30,373 votes. Mr. Ribicoff made a spectacular uphill run but was edged out by Mr. Bush's lead in the small towns that are traditionally Republican.

Final returns were:

PRESIDENT

169 precincts out of 169:

| | |
|---|---|
| Eisenhower | 610,989 |
| Stevenson | 481,482 |

UNITED STATES SENATOR

(For six-year Term)

169 precincts out of 169:

| | |
|---|---|
| Purtell (R.) | 575,445 |
| Benton (D.) | 485,159 |

(For Four-year Term)

| | |
|---|---|
| Bush (R.) | 559,586 |
| Ribicoff (D) | 529,213 |

The Eisenhower sweep enabled the Republicans to win five of the six seats from Connecticut in the House of Representatives, a gain

Continued on Page 22, Column 3

## GENERAL APPEALS FOR UNITED PEOPLE

### He Vows Not to Give 'Short Weight' as President—Thanks Rival for Pledge

By WILLIAM R. CONKLIN

A jubilant Gen. Dwight D. Eisenhower accepted his election as President early this morning with a pledge to the American people that he would not give "short weight" in the execution of his new responsibilities in Washington.

With his wife by his side, the Republican President-elect told 2,000 campaign supporters in the grand ballroom of the Commodore Hotel at 2:05 A. M. that it would take the support of a united people to carry his Administration to success in its efforts to build a "better future for America."

His remarks were carried by radio and television to all parts of the country.

He read a message he had sent a few minutes before to his defeated rival, Gov. Adlai E. Stevenson of Illinois, thanking him for his promise of assistance. General Eisenhower expressed hope that Americans of both parties would speedily forget campaign bitter-

Continued on Page 20, Column 2

## Hill Battle Spurts in Korea; Allies Press 'Triangle' Fight

By LINDESAY PARROTT

Special to THE NEW YORK TIMES.

TOKYO, Wednesday, Nov. 5—The hard-fighting South Korean infantry, driving for the third time in three days up the slopes of the central Korean ridges, drove a penetration today into the Communist lines on the western flank of "Triangle Hill," a strategic position north of Kumhwa.

Early this afternoon, the Republic of Korea (R. O. K.) troops had captured one of the twin peaks that project from "Triangle"—named "Jane Russell Hill." The sharp, indecisive combat continued.

The attack on the twin peaks was tied in with a new drive against the central pyramid of "Triangle Hill." The South Koreans again thrust within yards of the crest.

The Chinese Reds struck again just to the east in a new attempt to capture the summit of "Sniper Ridge," flanking "Triangle" on the United Nations' right.

The crest of "Triangle" had been lost to the Chinese Communists after the United Nations limited objective offensive took it last month. The South Koreans pushed up southern slopes today to within fifty yards of the Reds' lines.

Some reports said the fighting again today was as furious as during the attacks Sunday and Monday, when the South Koreans desperately struggled to regain the positions.

Allied warplanes were out against the enemy guns. About fifty sorties had been flown by Fifth Air Force fighter-bombers before noon against Red artillery on high Papasan Mountain, the Communists' strongpoint just to the north of the central front.

At every opportunity, Allied guns pounded the Reds on the crest of "Triangle."

The Reds' guns dropped 5,000 rounds on the United Nations positions near "Heartbreak Ridge" and the "Punchbowl" in the mountainous eastern watershed, where the heaviest fighting of yesterday occurred. A North Korean battalion hit Allied defense positions on "Heartbreak" on the heels of the barrage, but the enemy failed to make a penetration.

On "Triangle Hill" and the twin peaks to the west of it, contact was light yesterday. At least temporarily, the South Koreans broke off attempts to storm two positions they had lost to the Chinese Reds' counter-attacks, after the United Nations limited objec-

Continued on Page 2, Column 3

## M'Carthy Is Winner, But Is Last on Ticket

By RICHARD J. H. JOHNSTON

Special to THE NEW YORK TIMES.

MILWAUKEE, Wednesday, Nov. 5—Wisconsin went to the Republicans today for the third time in a national election since 1920.

The predicted Republican sweep of the state and capture of its twelve electoral votes became a certainty a few minutes after midnight.

Gen. Dwight D. Eisenhower, the Republican Presidential nominee ran second on the G. O. P. ticket with Gov. Walter J. Kohler Jr. leading the slate in his bid for re-election.

As the returns neared the final count, Gen. Dwight D. Eisenhower's vote indicated he would emerge as leader of the G. O. P. slate in Wisconsin. With 2,036 of the state's 3,224 vtoing precincts reported, his vote was 554,369 to Gov. Adlai E. Stevenson's 356,218.

Gov. Walter J. Kohler, seeking

Continued on Page 22, Column 6

## Stevenson Concedes the Victory As Weeping Backers Cry 'No, No'

By WILLIAM M. BLAIR

Special to THE NEW YORK TIMES.

SPRINGFIELD, Ill., Wednesday, Nov. 5—Gov. Adlai E. Stevenson conceded defeat early today to his Republican opponent. Gen. Dwight D. Eisenhower, and pledged the support "he will need to carry out the great tasks that lie before him."

The Governor came from the Executive Mansion to the Democratic Headquarters in the Leland Hotel to make his announcement before a jammed ballroom of supporters, many of whom broke into tears and cried, "No, no."

Governor Stevenson said:

"General Eisenhower has been a great leader in war. He has been a vigorous and valiant opponent in the campaign. These qualities will now be dedicated to leading us all through the next four years.

"It is traditionally American to fight hard before an election.

"It is equally traditional to close ranks as soon as the people have spoken. From the depths of my heart I thank all of my party, and all of those independents and Republicans who supported Senator Sparkman and me."

The Governor said he had dispatched to General Eisenhower in New York a telegram which he read. It said:

"The people have made their choice and I congratulate you. That you may be the servant and guardian of peace and make the dale of trouble a door of hope is my earnest prayer. Best Wishes.

Adlai E. Stevenson."

Governor Stevenson did have a grin, however, for the crowd and displayed his ever-present humor to reporters. Asked how about 1956, the next presidential election year, he echoed in a loud voice and with mock surprise "56! Examine that man's head."

As for his immediate plans, he

Continued on Page 16, Column 2

"All the News That's Fit to Print"

# The New York Times.

LATE CITY EDITION
Occasional rain today, rain ending tonight. Fair, mild tomorrow.
Temperature Range Today—Max., 42; Min., 37
Temperatures Yesterday—Max., 47; Min., 37
Full U. S. Weather Bureau Report, Page 55



VOL. CII..No. 34,696. Entered as Second-Class Matter, Post Office, New York, N. Y. NEW YORK, WEDNESDAY, JANUARY 21, 1953. Entered as Second-Class Matter, Post Office, New York, N. Y. FIVE CENTS

# EISENHOWER SWORN, PLEDGES QUEST FOR PEACE; BACKS U. N., URGES WESTERN EUROPE TO UNITE; 750,000 SEE PARADE; MORSE BALKS CABINET VOTE

## QUILL GETS READY TO END BUS STRIKE ON MAYOR'S TERMS

### Gives Out Haywood Telegram Backing Arbitration and Has C. I. O. Council Approve It

### BUT HE STILL CAN DITCH IT

### Service Seen by Monday if All Goes Well—Two Companies Accept Impellitteri Plan

By A. H. RASKIN

Michael J. Quill, president of the Transport Workers Union, C. I. O., set machinery in motion yesterday for ending the twenty-day-old bus strike under Mayor Impellitteri's arbitration plan.

With the union, the bus companies and city officials jockeying over details of the plan, there was still a chance last night that the entire peace effort might collapse, but some observers expected that buses would be back in operation by Monday on routes that normally carry 3,500,000 daily riders.

Without surrendering his freedom to scuttle the Impellitteri formula if the details were not worked out to his satisfaction, Mr. Quill took two steps during the day that made it plain he was conditioning the 8,000 strikers to acceptance of the proposal in a secret-ballot vote later this week.

He made public a telegram from Allan S. Haywood, executive vice president of the Congress of Industrial Organizations, urging the union to go along with the Mayor's suggestion that the union and the struck companies pick their own three-man arbitration panel to decide the dispute over union demands for a forty-hour week with no loss in pre-strike takehome pay.

**Haywood Comes to Quill's Aid**

Mr. Haywood is always on tap when Mr. Quill needs someone to help him out of an embarrassing situation, and there was no doubt in the mind of anyone connected with the situation that the Haywood telegram was sent at Mr. Quill's instigation to combat rank-and-file resistance to arbitration of any kind.

The second development that indicated how Mr. Quill's mind was running was the decision of a delegation from the New York C. I. O. Council to recommend that the bus strikers accept the Impellitteri plan. Mr. Quill is president of the council, and the council's recommendation was in the nature of a man talking to himself.

The council committee, headed by Morris Iushewitz, secretary-treasurer, met with Mayor Impellitteri at noon to express its support of the Quill union's fight for a forty-hour week. The Mayor told the group he agreed that the bus workers were entitled to a forty-hour week, but that he opposed any settlement that would upset the 10-cent fare.

The unionists replied that they were equally concerned with keep-

Continued on Page 24, Column 7

## 12 Injured in Jersey As Bus Falls 25 Feet

Special to The New York Times.

WEEHAWKEN, N. J., Jan. 20—One person was critically injured and eleven others cut and bruised this afternoon when the bus in which they were riding plunged twenty-five feet from Pershing Road into the New York Central West Shore Division freight yard at the waterfront here.

The bus, a Public Service system vehicle owned by the Interstate Transportation Company, was en route from the Hudson Place Terminal in Hoboken to the New York Central's West Forty-second Street ferry terminal when the accident happened at 2:20 P. M.

Descending the Palisades on the steep, cliffside road, the bus went into a skid on the wet cobblestone paving when the driver, Herman Ohm, 53 years old, of 321 Seventy-ninth Street, North Bergen, applied the brakes to go into an elbow bend that the road takes

Continued on Page 26, Column 5

## Line 'Impregnable,' Korean Foe Boasts

By LINDESAY PARROTT

Special to The New York Times.

TOKYO, Wednesday, Jan. 21—The Government-controlled Peiping radio boasted today that the Communists had built a fortified line across the Korean peninsula through which United Nations troops would be unable to break.

In a broadcast this morning, possibly timed to coincide with the inauguration of President Eisenhower, who promised to work for an early and honorable end of the Korean war, Peiping called its defenses "impregnable"—never before seen in the history of war. During a year of almost static fighting along the 155-mile front, the broadcast said, the "People's forces have built 'a great wall' across Korea."

Thousands of men, working day and night, have created an intricate system of tunnels,

Continued on Page 3, Column 5

## CITY URGED TO FIGHT TO HOLD PORT RANK

### Cavanagh Tells Crime Inquiry of Trade Shifts and Offers Plans for Expansion

By CHARLES GRUTZNER

This port is "just about keeping its head above water" in competition for the post-war increase in the nation's shipping, Edward F. Cavanagh Jr., City Commissioner of Marine and Aviation, told the State Crime Commission yesterday.

He expressed the belief that this port could gain a larger share of trade through legitimate political activity in Washington and by improving its physical facilities here. He is to make further recommendations at today's public hearing, starting at 10 A. M. in the County Court House on Foley Square.

Mr. Cavanagh supported in general the findings of Dennis J. Walsh Jr., consulting engineer, who testified that a survey of seven principal Atlantic and Gulf ports showed that New York had 53 per cent of today's "competitive" business, the same percentage as before World War II, and that New Orleans had increased its share from 13 to 17½ per cent, Baltimore had increased its percentage from 10 to 13, while other cities, Boston in particular, had suffered percentage losses.

**Proskauer More Pessimistic**

Mr. Walsh is a partner in the engineering concern of Sanderson & Porter, which made a $20,000 study for the State Crime Commission of shipping in the ports of New York, Philadelphia, Baltimore, Norfolk, Boston, New Orleans and Mobile. Joseph M. Proskauer, chairman of the Crime Commission, expressed disagreement several times with Mr. Walsh's interpretations of trade figures. Mr. Proskauer took a darker view of this port's competitive position than that indicated by Mr. Walsh's testimony.

After Mr. Proskauer had stressed one phase of the survey, which showed that New York had suffered relatively in coastwise shipping, although gaining in foreign trade, Mr. Walsh said the popular notion of rating a port's competitive status on a basis of gross tonnage was inaccurate. He said most coastwise shipping—petroleum, coal and some other bulk cargoes—was routed in accordance with rail differential rates and other factors that made such things as the port facilities and pier handling costs unimportant. Because of this, he said, the volume of such cargo has nothing to do with the competitive position of the individual ports.

Neither Mr. Walsh nor Commissioner Cavanagh made any mention of racketeering, labor trouble, pier violence or any of the other waterfront evils that the Crime Commission has been exposing since early last month.

Testimony of three other witnesses, however, touched directly on the more sensational aspects of the waterfront investigation.

A 69-year-old pier watchman for the Isthmian Steamship Line tes-

Continued on Page 33, Column 4

## POSTS GO UNFILLED

### Senate Approval of Eight Nominees Delayed by Morse's Objection

### VOTE EXPECTED TODAY

### Wilson Hearings Put Off Until Friday—Brownell May Offer a Solution

By C. P. TRUSSELL

Special to The New York Times.

WASHINGTON, Jan. 20—Plans for President Eisenhower to carry eight of his nine Cabinet appointees into office with him today were blocked in the Senate within an hour after the inauguration ceremonies by Senator Wayne Morse of Oregon.

A few hours later it was announced that Senate hearings on the confirmation of the ninth appointee, Charles E. Wilson, the Secretary of Defense-designate, originally scheduled for tomorrow, had been put off until Friday.

Mr. Morse, who bolted the Republican party during the Eisenhower campaign and declared himself an independent, contended that he and perhaps others in the Senate had not had sufficient time to study the records that had prompted unanimous advance approval of appointments by Senate committees.

His single objection to immediate confirmation had the effect of delaying the votes for at least a day.

A mass Cabinet swearing-in ceremony, planned for late afternoon in the historic East Room of the White House, was called off, pending a settlement of the dilemma.

**1933 Precedent Cited**

Tonight the nine Government departments were without top officers. The Truman Cabinet left office at noon. The departments automatically went under the temporary management of officials of sub-Cabinet rank, most of them Democrats.

It had not been this way on March 4, 1933, when the late President Roosevelt took his first oath as President. His whole Cabinet was confirmed by the Senate and was sworn in that day. The Republicans, twenty years later, had cited this precedent and had tried to follow it.

The new President had given fast cooperation to carry out the Republican plan. He went directly from the inaugural stand into the Capitol and formalized the eight Cabinet nominations with his signature.

The Senate, too, planned fast work and went from the ceremonies to its chamber for action. As it re-

Continued on Page 19, Column 7

The New York Times Facsimile Transmission

"* * * I WILL FAITHFULLY EXECUTE THE OFFICE": Gen. Dwight D. Eisenhower, the thirty-fourth President of the United States, taking the oath of office, administered by Chief Justice Fred M. Vinson, on a platform in front of the Capitol. At the left are former Presidents Harry S. Truman and Herbert Hoover. At right is the new Vice President, Richard M. Nixon.

## TRUMAN, TOO, GETS HIS BLAZE OF GLORY

### 'Old Has-Beens' Party Gives Roaring Ovation and 5,000 at Station Sing Farewell

By ANTHONY LEVIERO

Special to The New York Times.

WASHINGTON, Jan. 20—Harry S. Truman headed tonight for Independence, Mo., a carefree man, leaving behind the New Deal-Fair Deal era and in a sense walking into the pages of history.

Yet he was walking off only a pace, for he expected to play a vigorous role as the Democratic party's elder statesman in the stirring times that were certain to follow the historic change of power today.

Mr. Truman has said that in about six months he would be ready for his new part.

Today, however, was somewhat symbolic of his Presidential career—he had risen to great popularity and had sunk, at times, to a low point in popular favor.

The day was symbolic of this because Mr. Truman made a backstage departure after the climactic moment on Capitol Hill.

But when he reached the home of Dean Acheson, his controversial Secretary of State, in old Georgetown, he received a tumultuous ovation that was as heart-warming as any he received during his

Continued on Page 16, Column 2

## 'Internationalist' Inaugural Acclaimed in Both Parties

By WILLIAM S. WHITE

Special to The New York Times.

WASHINGTON, Jan. 20—Congress responded with general warmth and in many cases with profound bipartisan approval today to President Eisenhower's Inaugural Address. There was an all but visible gathering behind him of great blocs of members of both houses. Democrat and Republican alike, in his strong, somber pledge to carry this nation forward in full unity with the free world.

His speech, though lacking specifications, was interpreted by many as one of the most internationalist ever delivered to the country—not excluding the addresses of Franklin D. Roosevelt and Harry S. Truman.

President Eisenhower thus was heard with what almost amounted to joy by all those in both parties who for years had fought for foreign aid and foreign association and foreign alliance.

Some of the Democrats privately and jubilantly twitted some in the isolationist or near-isolationist wing of the Republican party to show where in world affairs General Eisenhower differed in any great principle from Mr. Truman and Mr. Roosevelt.

The Senate Democratic Leader, Senator Lyndon B. Johnson of Texas, carried this theme into a public statement. Senator Johnson first had commented only that the Inaugural Address was "a dignified statement of the dreams and aspirations that motivate millions of people."

But, on encountering a large group of reporters in the Senate dining room, he added:

"It was a statement, and a very good statement, of Democratic programs of the last twenty years."

Senator Robert A. Taft of Ohio, the Republican Senate leader, declared formally:

"It was a great and inspiring beginning, a great and inspiring speech."

**Trouble Seen Later**

A conservative pro-Eisenhower Senate Democrat of great influence made this observation "as his summary of the attitude of the Taft group of Republicans, who always have differed with General Eisenhower to some extent on foreign policy:

"In the tone of this speech there is much that could cause trouble with the Taft people, if later President Eisenhower spells out, for example, what seems in some passages to be implied. Take the reciprocal trade program as an example. The General seems to be for it.

"But what is said in generalities, as in this Inaugural Speech, may differ much from what may come later on. I should say that no one thus far would be inclined to challenge General Eisenhower on anything in it. Trouble is likely to come later."

Many noted, too, that President

Continued on Page 19, Column 3

## BRITISH SEEK HINTS OF NEW U. S. POLICY

### Search for Inaugural 'Clues' on Tariff Cut—Tributes Flow From World Capitals

Special to The New York Times.

LONDON, Jan. 20—Two phrases in President Eisenhower's inaugural address aroused special interest in Government circles here today. One was his hint that the new Administration might make trade a little easier, and the other was that the United States might expect a little more British cooperation toward European unity.

There was nothing very specific in the speech on either point, but there is enough sensitivity here to read meanings between the lines.

To many persons in the British Government, the most interesting passages in the General's speech were those in which he promised to help the proved friends of freedom to "achieve their own security and well-being."

Was this a pledge to lead a crusade for a lowering of tariff barriers against British goods?—that was the question that raised itself in the minds of British exporters,

Continued on Page 17, Column 3

## LONG, GAY PARADE CHEERS PRESIDENT

### He Takes Salute of All States as 750,000 Watch Frolic and Review of Might

By HAROLD B. HINTON

Special to The New York Times.

WASHINGTON, Jan. 20—The nation's capital and its hundreds of thousands of visitors gave President Eisenhower a gay and colorful welcome today, with sunny skies bringing mild temperatures, jovial good humor and a carnival spirit to the city.

From shortly before two o'clock until long after darkness had fallen, it seemed that everybody in town was watching the parade. The police estimated that the spectacle drew 750,000 persons, probably more than any other procession in its kind in Washington's history. However some oldtimers thought otherwise and suggested that television was responsible.

**Lasts Longer Than Planned**

Although the parade lasted two and a half hours longer than planned, President Eisenhower and Vice President Richard M. Nixon held to their posts on the reviewing stand until the last two elephants wound up the procession at 6:58 P. M.

The new President saw samples of his country's military might, ranging from the eighty-five-ton cannon for atomic artillery shells to California sheriff's posse riding palomino horses; from the Governor's Foot Guards of Connecticut and the Georgia Hussars of Savannah, in their Revolutionary uniforms, to the present-day

Continued on Page 21, Column 4

## PRESIDENT'S PLAN

### He Lists 9-Point Guide for Barring War but Bans Appeasement

### ENDORSES AID ABROAD

### Asserts Nation Is Ready to Join Move Seeking 'Drastic' Arms Cuts

*Text of the inaugural address appears on Page 19.*

By W. H. LAWRENCE

Special to The New York Times.

WASHINGTON, Jan. 20—Dwight David Eisenhower was inaugurated today as the thirty-fourth President of the United States and he pledged that his Administration would "neither compromise, nor tire, nor ever cease" in its quest for an honorable world-wide peace.

While he expressed in his Inaugural Address abhorrence of war as "a chosen way" to end the threat of international communism and laid down a nine-point program to guide the nation's efforts for world peace, the new President also flatly banned appeasement of aggressor forces. He declared that "in the final choice a soldier's pack is not so heavy a burden as a prisoner's chains."

The former five-star General of the Army, who led Allied troops to victory in Europe in World War II, took the oath of office at 12:32 P. M. in solemn, moving ceremonies before the United States Capitol building. The term of office of Harry S. Truman, the retiring President, had expired constitutionally at noon, and the nation, for thirty-two minutes, technically was without a President.

**Cabinet Confirmations Delayed**

Richard Milhous Nixon, former California Senator, had been inaugurated as Vice President a few minutes earlier, succeeding Alben W. Barkley.

But these were the only two members of the new Administration team to take office today. A request of the new President that the Senate confirm at once eight members of his Cabinet, headed by John Foster Dulles as Secretary of State, was blocked by the single objection of Senator Wayne Morse, Oregon independent, who resigned from the Republican party last fall to give his support to Adlai E. Stevenson of Illinois, the Democratic Presidential nominee.

The controversial proposed appointment of Charles E. Wilson to be Secretary of Defense was not submitted to the Senate with the nominations of other Cabinet officers.

The biggest inaugural crowd in history, estimated by the police at 750,000, was on hand to celebrate the return of a Republican President to the White House for the first time since March 4, 1933. But President Eisenhower's sober appraisal of the world situation and of the steps this nation and the free world must take to meet the challenge of the forces of slavery gave his listeners few opportunities to applaud.

**'Fixed Principles' for Peace**

His comparatively short, 2,400-word Inaugural was devoted almost exclusively to foreign policy, with only passing reference to domestic concerns. He enunciated these "fixed principles" to direct the moves for world peace:

¶While the nation abhors war "as a chosen way to balk the purposes of those who threaten us, we hold it to be the first task of statesmanship to develop the strength that will deter the forces of aggression and promote the conditions of peace." The United States is willing to engage "in joint effort to remove the causes of mutual fear and distrust among nations, and so to make possible drastic reduction of armament" if methods can be provided "by which every participating nation will

Continued on Page 18, Column 4

## Croydon Hotel Hold-Up Frustrated By Policeman; 6 of 7 Thieves Seized

The alertness of a patrolman, combined with the wiles of a fast-thinking night watchman, frustrated a seven-man hold-up gang early yesterday at the Croydon Hotel, 12 East Eighty-sixth Street, off Madison Avenue, and resulted in the capture of six of the men.

One of the thugs later told the police that they were after what they believed was a large sum of money in safety deposit boxes in the hotel's safe. He said they were not out to hold up guests, none of whom were involved in the affray, during which a dozen shots were fired.

Flying bullets failed to find any marks and the only known injury was to one of the thugs who, trying to escape, leaped from a second-story window and broke an ankle. Another man fell to the sidewalk in front of the hotel as three shots were fired at him, but he got up and escaped into Central Park.

According to Deputy Inspector Francis J. M. Robb, in charge of the Sixth Detective Division, the affair began at 5 A. M. and ended about fifteen minutes later with the capture of the last three of the gang on the hotel's top floor. Detectives reconstructed the scene this way:

Patrolman Thomas Shore, 35 years old, of the East Sixty-seventh Street Precinct, who lives at 35-64 Eighty-fourth Street, Jackson Heights, Queens, and has been on the force six and a half years, was returning to the lobby from a washroom when he heard a man say: "Put your hands behind your back."

Stepping behind a pillar, he saw two men standing in front of the clerk's desk. Then he noticed five other men, apparently guests at first view, walk in the front door with three suitcases. As they joined the two men at the desk, however, the policeman stepped from behind the pillar with his pistol drawn.

One or more of the thugs immediately fired four shots at him and he emptied his own pistol at the group. As he backed out the front door to reload, one of the men darted out and fled west toward the park. Patrolman Shore fired three shots after him.

When he re-entered the hotel the six other men had disappeared and he put in a call for aid. A similar call was made from the

Continued on Page 13, Column 1

## Nixon, Though a Quaker, 'Swears' To Do His Duty as Vice President

By CLAYTON KNOWLES

Special to The New York Times.

WASHINGTON, Jan. 20—Richard Milhous Nixon took a big forward stride in a meteoric political career today as he took the oath of office as the thirty-sixth Vice President of the United States.

Just 40 years old, Mr. Nixon, second youngest Vice President in history, has been in politics just six years. Elected to the House of Representatives in 1946 in his first political venture, he served there four years before moving up to the Senate.

A native of California, he is the first American from the Far West to assume the Vice Presidency. No one west of Texas had held the job before.

Mr. Nixon took the oath of office at 12:23 P. M. It was administered by Senator William F. Knowland of California, with whom he had served as a member of Congress. Mr. Nixon, his right hand raised and his left hand resting on two old family Bibles, slowly and firmly repeated after Mr. Knowland the traditional oath of office.

This oath, which is twice as long as that which was administered to President Eisenhower, began: "I [Richard M. Nixon] do solemnly swear that I will support and defend the Constitution * * *."

It was noted that Mr. Nixon, though a Quaker, swore, rather than affirmed, as is Quaker custom, that he would faithfully perform his duties and defend the country and its institutions. He did not kiss the Bibles as Herbert Hoover, another Quaker, did on assuming the Presidency twenty-four years ago or as Alben W. Barkley did in taking the oath of office as Vice President in 1949.

The Nixon Bibles were open during the ceremony to that passage from the Sermon on the

Continued on Page 22, Column 4

DWIGHT D. EISENHOWER

"All the News That's Fit to Print"

# The New York Times.

LATE CITY EDITION
Condensation of U. S. Weather Bureau forecast: Mostly fair and somewhat milder today. Partly cloudy tomorrow.
Temp. range today: 42-25; yesterday: 35-23
Full U. S. Weather Bureau Report, Page 66



VOL. CV..No. 35,831. Entered as Second-Class Matter, Post Office, New York, N. Y. NEW YORK, THURSDAY, MARCH 1, 1956. Times Square, New York 36, N. Y. Telephone Lackawanna 4-1000 FIVE CENTS

# EISENHOWER SAYS HE WILL SEEK A 2D TERM; CONFIDENT OF HEALTH; BARS 'BARNSTORMING'; PRAISES NIXON BUT DOES NOT ENDORSE HIM

## U.S. JUDGE ORDERS ALABAMA CO-ED TO BE REINSTATED

### Bids School Admit Miss Lucy by Monday—Bars Contempt Action Against Trustees

### CITES THEIR 'GOOD FAITH'

### He Finds That Reaction Was Underestimated—Negro Says She Will Return

By WAYNE PHILLIPS
Special to The New York Times.

BIRMINGHAM, Ala., Feb. 29—The University of Alabama was ordered today to reinstate Autherine J. Lucy, its first Negro student, by Monday morning.

Miss Lucy, 26 years old, of Birmingham, was enrolled at the university Feb. 1 after a three-year court fight. She was suspended five days later after a series of campus disorders protesting her presence.

Federal Judge Hobart H. Grooms also vacated a contempt motion, sought by Miss Lucy, against the board of trustees and officials of the university. He said the trustees had acted in good faith in suspending Miss Lucy. If they had not done so, he ruled, "she might have suffered great bodily harm."

Miss Lucy sat tense and nervous today in the Federal District Court here as a succession of witnesses recounted the events leading to her suspension. Some said that if she returned to the campus she might be killed.

**Feared for Life, She Says**

She said on the witness stand that while she was a virtual prisoner in a classroom building held in a state of siege by a howling mob outside, she feared that she might be killed. She said she had prayed.

With deliberation and occasional flashes of dry wit she answered the questions of the university's attorney, Andrew J. Thomas. Beside her, when she sat at the counsel table, was a well-worn copy of the Bible.

After she heard the decision of Judge Grooms readmitting her, she said again that she would return to the campus.

"That girl sure has guts," her attorney, Thurgood Marshall, chief counsel for the National

Continued on Page 28, Column 1

## TEAMSTERS UNION FACES SUSPENSION

### Meany Weighs Tie to I. L. A. —Internal Strife Rises

By A. H. RASKIN

The International Brotherhood of Teamsters, most powerful unit in the merged labor movement, is facing possible suspension over its alliance with the exiled International Longshoremen's Association.

The possibility of punitive action by the parent federation arose yesterday amid fresh outcroppings of internal strife within the 1,300,000-member truck union. The uprisings were designed to prevent domination of the union by James R. Hoffa, international vice president and chairman of the Central States Conference of Teamsters.

The Detroit unionist announced Monday that the teamsters would deposit $400,000 to the credit of the I. L. A. to enable it to pay its debts and to participate in a joint organizing drive. The pier union was expelled from the American Federation of Labor in 1953 on charges of gang domination.

In Washington, George Meany, president of the united labor movement, announced that he had begun an investigation into the teamster-longshore pact. He pledged that he would take

Continued on Page 28, Column 3

## Testimony Clashes At Gas Gift Inquiry

By RUSSELL BAKER
Special to The New York Times.

WASHINGTON, Feb. 29—Senate investigators were told today that John M. Neff had offered a $2,500 campaign contribution in Iowa for the chance to talk with Senator Bourke B. Hickenlooper about the natural gas bill.

However, Mr. Neff, an attorney for the Superior Oil Company of California, denied the story under oath. The conflicting testimony will be sent to the Department of Justice for possible perjury action.

The witness who testified that the offer had been made was Robert K. Goodwin, a Des Moines manufacturer and banker and Republican Committeeman for Iowa.

The two men, smiling wanly, confronted each other under the great glass chandeliers in the Senate caucus room, then

Continued on Page 13, Column 3

## G.O.P. TAX CUT BILL VOTED AT ALBANY

### Legislature Acts in Face of Veto Threat—Committees Propose Budget Slash

By LEO EGAN
Special to The New York Times.

ALBANY, Feb. 29—Republican majorities rammed their $50,000,000 income tax cut bill through both Senate and Assembly this afternoon. They did this despite warnings the bill would be vetoed by Governor Harriman, a Democrat.

In the Senate the vote was 35 to 23. In the Assembly it was 84 to 58. All the Democrats voted against the measure in both houses.

The Senate deliberately voted down the Governor's plan today. The vote was 36 to 22, one Democrat, Joseph Zaretski of Manhattan, voting with the Republicans in opposition. He explained he was opposed to any tax cut this year.

While the bill was under discussion, the Republican controlled Senate Finance and Assembly Ways and Means Committees proposed reductions totaling $23,528,072 in Governor Harriman's record high $1,494,700,000 state-spending program for next year.

**Democrat Hits Action**

Among the suggested cuts were the elimination of a $9,900,000 appropriation to give New York City a share in motor vehicle license fees and the elimination of a $2,400,000 item for state subsidies for child daycare centers, most of which would have gone to New York City.

Passage of the Republican income tax cut bill today represented an abrupt termination of negotiations between the Governor and legislative leaders for a compromise on this subject.

Assemblyman Eugene F. Bannigan, the Democratic minority leader, charged on the floor that Republicans were courting a veto of the tax-cut bill to justify a refusal to increase gasoline and Diesel fuel taxes. Such increases have been recommended by the Temporary Highway Finance Commission to support a $500,000,000 highway bond issue and an expanded highway construction program.

Lacking the two-thirds majorities needed in each House to repass a bill over the Governor's veto, the Republicans are expected to abandon their efforts for an income tax cut after today.

Mr. Harriman announced that he was still willing to resume compromise tax-reduction negotiations. But his offer is unlikely to be accepted.

The Republican bill as passed today would give all taxpayers a credit of 20 per cent on the first $100 of taxes due on April 15 and a 10 per cent credit on the next $400, with a limit of $60 to any one taxpayer. Governor Harriman had proposed a sub-

Continued on Page 25, Column 4

## DULLES SUGGESTS SOVIET MAY FAVOR CUT IN ARMS COST

### Tells Senate Unit, However, U. S. Will Not Be Misled Into Weakening Defenses

By ELIE ABEL
Special to The New York Times.

WASHINGTON, Feb. 29—Secretary of State Dulles suggested today that the Soviet Union might welcome some reduction in the present burden of armaments.

Testifying before a special Senate Foreign Relations subcommittee on disarmament, Mr. Dulles qualified this statement with assurances that the Administration would not jeopardize the nation's security by accepting at face value Soviet promises to disarm.

"We do not minimize the difficulties of dealing in these matters with a potential enemy who is untrustworthy and who in manifold ways has demonstrated that he is a past master of the art of evasion and secretiveness," the Secretary of State said.

"However, there is some reason to believe that the Soviet Union itself would welcome relief from the present burden of armament," he added.

**Russians Called Dissatisfied**

Mr. Dulles said this assessment was based on the "logic" of the present situation within the Soviet Union. He depicted the Russian people as being "in a state of very considerable dissatisfaction" with their low standard of living.

It would be logical for the Soviet leaders to agree to spend less on armaments so they could apply an increased share of their production to raising the living standards of their own people, Mr. Dulles said. In addition, the Soviet Union would thus have more to spend on its new program of economic aid to underdeveloped countries in South Asia and the Middle East, he added.

The Secretary of State, who leaves for Pakistan Friday afternoon to attend the council meeting of the Southeast Asian Collective Defense Treaty in Karachi March 6 to 8, appeared before a subcommittee headed by Senator Hubert H. Humphrey, Democrat of Minnesota, which is surveying the whole disarmament problem.

Senator Leverett Saltonstall, Republican of Massachusetts, asked Mr. Dulles whether "face-to-face" meetings with the Soviet leaders offered the best hope of achieving a disarmament accord.

"I don't know any other way," Mr. Dulles replied. "I don't get

Continued on Page 6, Column 3

## Gronchi in Congress Discounts Arms Tie

By DANA ADAMS SCHMIDT
Special to The New York Times.

WASHINGTON, Feb. 29—President Giovanni Gronchi of Italy urged Congress today to lead the Western world away from military alliances and toward economic cooperation to counter Communist expansionism.

"The reorganization of the Western world is the central problem of the day," he declared in an address before a joint session of the Senate and the House of Representatives.

As an early step he proposed that the North Atlantic Treaty Organization be "brought into line" with today's realities, in which "military imbalance has been reduced," but in which, none the less, "the world is no more secure than it was one or two years ago."

The North Atlantic alliance,

Continued on Page 5, Column 3

## PARIS ARMY CHIEF QUITS ON ALGERIA

### Guillaume Out After Policy Dispute—Special Powers Asked by Government

By ROBERT C. DOTY
Special to The New York Times.

PARIS, Feb. 29—The French Government reorganized its high military command today and asked for special powers to deal with the Algerian revolt.

Gen. Augustin Guillaume was replaced as Chief of the General Staff following disagreement with his civilian chiefs over military policy in North Africa. He was succeeded by Gen. Paul Ely, a member of the high council of the armed forces.

Late today, Premier Guy Mollet submitted to Parliament a request for extensive powers in the fields of administration, economic and social affairs, and security for Robert Lacoste, Minister Residing in Algeria.

Details were not revealed, but the special powers were reported to include authority to reinstate the "state of urgency" in Algeria or even, if events should warrant it, full martial law.

Debate on this measure, probably early next week, was expected to present the left-of-center Republican Front Cabinet with its first serious political test. Some observers doubted that the National Assembly would grant the Government's request.

Neither here nor in Algeria has M. Mollet's appeal to the rebels to lay down their arms and accept the arbitration of new elections aroused any enthusiasm.

Conservatives, including most

Continued on Page 3, Column 2

## 9,000 Jam Court as Scofflaws Rush to Beat Amnesty Deadline

By JACK ROTH

The last day of the amnesty period for scofflaws found 9,000 persons in the Criminal Courts Building at 100 Centre Street yesterday. The worst jam in Manhattan Traffic Court history ensued.

About 6,000 persons waited in long lines in the lobby to pay their fines at the court clerk's windows. Three thousand of these were scofflaws. At one point the lines backed up a stairway leading to the second floor.

In addition, another 3,000 repentant drivers crowded about the Traffic Summons Control Bureau on the third floor. Tables were supplied in the corridors for the scofflaws to fill out forms.

Chief Magistrate John M. Murtagh called the amnesty a "great success" and estimated that of the 20,000 persons categorized as scofflaws all but about 6,000 had appeared.

He predicted that when all the scofflaw tickets of the amnesty period had been processed, the accounting would show that the city had collected nearly $750,000 in fines on long-ignored traffic summonses.

"Because of the last-minute influx of scofflaws," Mr. Murtagh said, "there will be a delay of perhaps a week before we can turn over the warrants to the police for the arrest of the remainder. We must make certain that none of the warrants apply to people who appeared at the last minute.

"But early next month the police will swing into action. Our goal is 100 per cent compliance with every summons issued since 1950."

He reiterated an earlier statement that this amnesty for scofflaws would be the last such grace period, because "motorists must be taught to answer summonses on time." There were two previous amnesties.

Concerning the last-minute rush, which was marked by confusion and grumbling, Mr. Murtagh admitted such great numbers had not been anticipated.

The confusion was caused by the fact that five patrolmen, suddenly called to keep the lines

Continued on Page 35, Column 3

## 2D SPOT IN DOUBT

### Foes of Vice President Now May Push Drive to Block Him

By W. H. LAWRENCE
Special to The New York Times.

WASHINGTON, Feb. 29—President Eisenhower passed up today two opportunities to give an automatic immediate endorsement to renomination of Vice President Richard M. Nixon.

General Eisenhower said he properly could not speak out on the choice of a running mate until after the Republican National Convention itself had picked its Presidential nominee.

He mixed repetition of previous high praise for Mr. Nixon with what sounded at least like indirect criticism of the Vice President for his recent effort to continue a Republican party label on Chief Justice Earl Warren. The President said he personally would never admit that any Supreme Court justice continued to have a political designation while on the high court.

President Eisenhower's failure to call at once for Vice President Nixon's renomination undoubtedly will put new steam behind an effort already under way by some influential Republicans to select another running mate. These anti-Nixon men argue that the 1956 campaign involving a President who has suffered a heart attack will place new emphasis with voters on the Vice Presidential nominee.

**Silent on Running Mate**

In his radio-television address to the nation, the President made no mention at all of Mr. Nixon or any other possible running mate.

The omission by the President may not be meaningful, however. General Eisenhower is assured of renomination by acclamation, and the convention unquestionably will nominate any man he favors for Vice President. So he could speak up for Mr. Nixon even at the last minute and insure his renomination.

The Nixon question was raised in two ways immediately after the President had disclosed he would be available for renomination and re-election if the Republican party and a majority of the people wanted him.

He was asked directly whether he would again want Mr. Nixon as his running mate.

"As a matter of fact," President Eisenhower responded, "I wouldn't mention the Vice Presidency, in spite of my tremendous admiration for Mr. Nixon, for this reason: I believe it is traditional that the Vice President is not nominated until after * * * Presidential candidate is nominated; so I think that we will have to wait and see whom the Republican convention nominates, and then it will be proper to give an expression on that point."

**Respect 'Unbounded'**

Asked whether, if nominated, he would have a personal preference for Mr. Nixon's renomination, the President responded:

"I will say nothing more about it. I have said that my admiration and my respect for Vice President Nixon is unbounded. He has been for me a loyal and dedicated associate, and a successful one.

"I am very fond of him, but I am going to say no more about it."

The indirect criticism came when President Eisenhower was asked his own reaction to the Vice President's characterization of Mr. Warren as a Republican Chief Justice.

The President said he would not comment, and never had, on a comment by someone else. He added:

"But I will say this: Once a man has passed into the Supreme Court he is an American citizen and nothing else in my book until he comes out of that court, and I believe that it would be—I would never admit that he was—longer had a political designation."

There has been sharp political controversy over the Vice President's recent contention in a New York speech that the Su-

Continued on Page 16, Column 5

Associated Press Wirephoto

EXPLAINS DECISION: President and Mrs. Eisenhower at the White House last night, before his TV-radio speech.

## Butler Questions Fitness; Republicans Hail Decision

By JOHN D. MORRIS
Special to The New York Times.

WASHINGTON, Feb. 29—The physical fitness of President Eisenhower to serve another term was challenged sharply today within minutes of his announcement that he was willing to run. "The American people will never elect a President who, at 65, has had a serious heart attack and who is unable to be a full-time Chief Executive," Paul M. Butler, the Democratic National Chairman, declared.

While Mr. Butler raised the issue of health, other leaders of

*The texts of Butler and Hall statements are on Page 17.*

both parties publicly hailed the President's decision.

The prevailing Democratic line was one of gratification that General Eisenhower considered his recovery sufficient to permit him to stand the rigors and pressures of four more years in the White House. But warnings of a hard campaign "on the issues," requiring vigorous activity by both candidates and ending in a Democratic victory, also came from leading party spokesmen.

Republicans responded to the announcement with enthusiasm that promised the President's renomination without a dissent by the national convention at San Francisco next August.

Predictions that the delegates would choose him by acclamation came from Vice President Richard M. Nixon and Senator Wi-

Continued on Page 17, Column 1

## Two Senators Ask Inquiry on Benson

By WILLIAM M. BLAIR
Special to The New York Times.

WASHINGTON, Feb. 29—Two Senate Democrats suggested today that the special lobby investigating committee explore what they charged were efforts by the Secretary of Agriculture to influence Southern Senators to vote against rigid farm-price supports.

Senator Hubert H. Humphrey of Minnesota said that Ezra Taft Benson, the Secretary, appeared to have violated a law prohibiting lobbying with Federal appropriations. The situation is "close enough to make it appear necessary for our new committee on lobbying to look into it most carefully," he declared.

Senator Allen J. Ellender of Louisiana accused Mr. Benson of "trying to buy votes of

Continued on Page 12, Column 3

## STEVENSON CALLS DECISION PROPER

### Bids President 'Set Terms of Debate' on His Health —Sees 'Vigorous' Drive

By CLAYTON KNOWLES

Adlai E. Stevenson called upon President Eisenhower yesterday to "set the terms of the debate" on the issue of his health, now that he has declared his availability for a second term.

Most active of the Democratic candidates for the Presidency, the former Illinois Governor stressed that it was General Eisenhower who had "drawn the distinction between the private matter of his personal health and the public question of how the office of President shall be conducted."

In Washington, it was felt that President Eisenhower's decision would help Mr. Stevenson's chances for the Democratic nomination.

Mr. Stevenson said it was fitting that President Eisenhower, before whom he went to defeat in 1952, should be the candidate and thus defend the policies and record of his Administration.

This view, given in a brief statement, was echoed by other Democrats across the country and by leading Republicans, too, if with a noticeable change in inflection. And Mr. Stevenson noted also that the President must look forward to carrying the "burden of what will be a very vigorous campaign."

This was a point that other Democratic candidates, announced and unannounced, stressed as well.

In Albany, Governor Harriman asserted that the President "can no longer shift responsibility to associates and subordinates." Mr. Harriman asserted that the President must now answer for "surrender to the domination of one group in our country—the big interests"—and for policies abroad that have "undermined our prestige and shaken the confidence in us of the people of the free world."

And at Milwaukee, Senator Estes Kefauver, like Mr. Steven-

Continued on Page 19, Column 3

## CAN 'LAST 5 YEARS'

### President Finds 'Not Slightest Doubt' of Fitness for Duty

*Conference transcript, Page 14; text of speech, Page 15.*

By JAMES RESTON
Special to The New York Times.

WASHINGTON, Feb. 29—He said "yes."

Dwight David Eisenhower, the thirty-third President of the United States, agreed this morning to a second-term nomination. He explained why in a television-radio report to the nation tonight.

Speaking slowly and in a slightly hoarse voice, General Eisenhower said tonight: "After the most careful and devoutly prayerful consideration * * I have decided that if the Republican party chooses to renominate me, I shall accept."

The 65-year-old President frankly told his party tonight, however, that because of his heart attack last Sept. 24, he must restrict his activities in the conduct of his office and in the Presidential campaign.

"The President had raised personally the problems created by his heart attack at a crowded news conference this morning at which he said: "I assure you of this: My answer would not be in the affirmative unless I thought I could last out the five years."

**Can Perform His Duties**

And he told the nation tonight:

"As of this moment, there is not the slightest doubt that I can perform as well as I ever have all the important duties of the Presidency. This I say because I am actually doing so and have been doing so for many weeks."

Speaking of the Presidential campaign, General Eisenhower warned that "neither for renomination nor re-election would I engage in extensive traveling and in whistle-stop speaking—normally referred to as 'barnstorming.'" He added:

"I had long ago made up my mind, before I ever dreamed of a personal heart attack, that I could never, as President of all the people, conduct the kind of political campaign where I was personally a candidate. The first duty of a President is to discharge to the limit of his ability the responsibilities of his office."

General Eisenhower did not mention the Vice-Presidency in his radio address. He was cautious about committing himself

Continued on Page 15, Column 6

## MARKET SURGES, THEN FALLS BACK

### News Sets Off Buying Wave, but Stocks End Lower

By BURTON CRANE

Wall Street had its day of anti-climax yesterday. The President's announcement that he would seek re-election brought a boiling market of 3,900,000 shares, a ticker tape that ran nineteen minutes behind the floor for a time, an uprush of prices for a single hour—and a net loss on the day.

More stocks fell than rose. Seven of the ten most heavily traded issues closed lower. The New York Times combined average of fifty stocks fell 2.62 points to 322.88, a drop of more than 4/5 of 1 per cent.

Expectations that the President would announce his decision jammed the two galleries of the New York Stock Exchange well before its opening at 10 A. M. The east gallery was largely reserved for reporters, photographers and newsreel and television cameramen. The general public thronged the west gallery.

At the opening, the market was active and strongly higher, starting with gains of 1 and 2 points on good-sized blocks. United States Steel, for example, was up ⅞ on 10,000 shares. Volume continued heavy and

Continued on Page 47, Column 8

"All the News That's Fit to Print"

# The New York Times.

LATE CITY EDITION

Condensation of U. S. Weather Bureau forecast: Cloudy, milder today, showers later. Tomorrow cloudy, occasional rain.
Temp. range today: 60-44; yesterday: 47-37.
Full U. S. Weather Bureau Report, Page 56.



VOL. CV..No. 35,888. Entered as Second-Class Matter, Post Office, New York, N. Y. NEW YORK, FRIDAY, APRIL 27, 1956. Times Square, New York 36, N. Y. Telephone Lackawanna 4-1000 FIVE CENTS

## RUSSIANS PROMISE RESTRAINT IN SALE OF MIDEAST ARMS

### Statement With Britain Also Pledges Support of U. N. Peace Bid in the Area

### WIDE CONTACTS SOUGHT

### Two Nations Favor Increase in Non-Strategic Trade and in Cultural Relations

*Texts of statements issued in London are on Page 3.*

By DREW MIDDLETON
Special to The New York Times.

LONDON, April 26—The Soviet Union has agreed to exercise restraint in the sale or arms to Egypt and other countries. It has also promised to support United Nations efforts to arrange a final settlement between Israel and the Arab states.

These steps toward an easier situation in the Middle East are regarded by the British as the most important results of talks here with the Soviet leaders. A statement on the British-Soviet discussions was signed tonight by Prime Minister Eden and Premier Nikolai A. Bulganin.

According to the statement, the two countries agreed that:

¶They will do their "utmost" to end the armaments race in all parts of the world.

¶They will try to prevent an increase of tension along the frontier between Israel and the Arab states.

¶They will do everything possible to achieve a peaceful solution of the dispute between the Arab states and Israel under the sponsorship of the United Nations.

¶They will attempt to reach an immediate agreement for substantial reduction "under appropriate international control" of armed forces and armaments.

¶They will study means of increasing trade in non-strategic goods between the two nations.

¶They will create more favorable economic conditions for further exchange of cultural missions and information.

**Optimism Is Restrained**

Restrained optimism pervades Government comment on the results of the talks. If Nikita S. Khrushchev, Soviet Communist leader, and Premier Bulganin mean what they say, then East and West are edging toward agreement, in the view of one qualified source.

But the British do not believe that the discussions, although they provided considerable insight into Soviet attitudes, revealed changes of policy significant enough to warrant another East-West conference.

The British Government, for instance, regards the reunification of Germany in peace and freedom as the most important step toward European security. But no understanding on the means of uniting Germany was attained, or even approached, during the talks.

It is probable that at their press conference tomorrow morning the Soviet leaders will announce an invitation to Prime Minister Eden to visit the Soviet Union. This visit may take place next year. It is regarded by the British as offering another opportunity to Sir Anthony to

Continued on Page 3, Column 6

## Administration Alters Tone Of Its Foreign Policy Line

### A New Note Is Sounded on Neutralism, Pacts, NATO, Atomic Energy and Disarming—No Change in Actions

By JAMES RESTON
Special to The New York Times.

WASHINGTON, April 26—The Eisenhower Administration is consciously changing the tone and emphasis of its pronouncements on foreign policy.

It has made no major change in its foreign policy actions, and it has yet to win the consent of Congress for any major changes, but it is clearly singing a different tune about the neutral nations, military pacts, the North Atlantic Treaty, atomic energy and disarmament.

President Eisenhower struck the new note in his extemporaneous remarks before the American Society of Newspaper Editors here last Saturday.

"The world changes," he said, "and in these days it changes rapidly. A policy that was good six months ago is not necessarily now of any validity. It is necessary that we find better, more effective ways of keeping ourselves in tune with the world's needs."

In keeping with this principle, the Administration is now placing new emphasis on these themes:

¶Neutrals: Instead of questioning the wisdom of neutrality, President Eisenhower and Secretary of State Dulles are now emphasizing the right of neutrality and promising aid to nations even if they do not align themselves with the Western allies.

¶Military alliances: Instead of emphasizing the military aspects of defense, the Administration is now stressing, as President Eisenhower did the last week-end, the need for "economic and social progress" in the under-developed nations. This theme is also being applied to the economic and political development of the North Atlantic Treaty Organization, and to the peaceful applications of atomic

Continued on Page 4, Column 3

## Sailors in Moscow Assert U. S. Tried to Detain Them

By The United Press.

MOSCOW, April 26—Five Soviet sailors, considered in the United States to have been the victims of a "political kidnapping," said today that American officials had tried "all means" to force them to stay in New York against their will.

They read a prepared statement to nearly 100 newsmen. It said that they had returned to Russia willingly after they were warned in the United States that "all kinds of horrors and even death" awaited them at home.

*Texts of Russian statements on five sailors, Page 12.*

Most of today's "press conference" was consumed by the reading of the long statement. The Russians, appearing fit and natty in their American suits, then consented to a short question-and-answer period.

The five seamen were among nine who sought political asylum in the United States last fall after their tanker, the Tuapse, was seized by Chinese Nationalists in Taiwan [Formosa]. They returned to Russia early this month. As a result, the United States ousted yesterday two members of the Soviet delegation to the United Nations. The State Department charged unwarranted "intervention" by the Russian delegation.

[At United Nations headquarters in New York the Soviet delegation denied that its chief, Arkady A. Sobolev or any of his staff had forced the Russian sailors to return to their homeland.]

Although there was evidence at their living quarters in the New York area that at least four of the five seamen had left for Russia on short notice, they said today that the entire plan had been preconceived.

They said the crew members

Continued on Page 12, Column 6

## NATION RELAXES EXPORTS TO REDS

### 700 Non-Strategic Items Are Freed From Requirement for Special Licensing

*List of the export items freed from controls, Page 10.*

By CHARLES E. EGAN
Special to The New York Times.

WASHINGTON, April 26—The Government smoothed the way today for a greater volume of exports to the Soviet Union and to her European satellites. It marked the first major easing of trade restrictions since the beginning of the "cold war."

In a new general license export order, Sinclair Weeks, Secretary of Commerce, made public a list of more than 700 non-strategic items that exporters now might ship to the Soviet and other Communist countries in Europe without obtaining an export license for each shipment. Hereafter, exporters sending listed items to Soviet bloc destinations will be able to handle the transactions as they would similar shipments to friendly countries in Europe.

Secretary Weeks emphasized that all the goods included on the new roster were of the type

Continued on Page 10, Column 4

## CAIRO SAYS ARABS ACCEPT U. N. IDEAS TO END TENSIONS

### Israeli Hitch at Withdrawal of Troops From Border Held Last Obstacle

By OSGOOD CARUTHERS
Special to The New York Times.

CAIRO, April 26 — Official sources said today that Egypt had accepted all of the principles and most of the specific items of Dag Hammarskjold's plan for ending the Arab-Israeli border tensions. The sources added that all the other Arab states had followed Egypt in similar acceptance.

According to the informants, the latest draft of the so-called Hammarskjold plan was received today and the Egyptians considered that the mission of the United Nations Secretary General was approaching a successful conclusion.

The only issue that threatened to throw the mission into a deadlock was the question of the withdrawal of Egyptian and Israeli forces from the demarcation line.

Premier Gamal Abdel Nasser of Egypt has proposed that the troops of both sides withdraw 500 yards from the line. The Israelis are said so far to have rejected this proposal on the ground that it would leave many of their frontier settlements unprotected against infiltration and attack.

The Hammarskjold plan was said to have mentioned only generally the troop withdrawal proposal. According to the Cairo sources the Egyptians have insisted that the Secretary General specify the exact distance of the withdrawal and try to obtain Israeli compliance.

**Withdrawn Certain Distance**

The informants said Egypt already had withdrawn her forces a certain distance from the demarcation line in the Gaza Strip where clashes and reprisals had threatened to explode into an all-out war just as Mr. Hammarskjold was beginning his peace mission to the Middle East.

Those forces had been pulled back, the informants said, as soon as Egypt and Israel agreed to Mr. Hammarskjold's first proposal for a cease-fire and a pledge that neither side would commit a hostile act in the area.

The Egyptians said today that not a single shot had been fired by either side along the Israeli-Egyptian frontier during the last seventy-two hours. They charged, however, that Israeli planes continued to fly at great altitudes over Egyptian-held territory and that these flights had been reported to the United Nations Truce Supervision Organization.

Premier Nasser and his aides were studying the Hammarskjold plan tonight and it was announced that they planned to report their views on it to the Secretary General before he arrives here Saturday for a second round of talks.

Mr. Hammarskjold went to Beirut, Lebanon, today following

Continued on Page 5, Column 4

## DEMOCRATS DROP PLAN TO PROVIDE DIRECT FARM AID

### Bow to Mounting Opposition —Compromise Bill to Be Offered in House Today

By WILLIAM M. BLAIR
Special to The New York Times.

WASHINGTON, April 26—Faced with mounting opposition, House Democrats backtracked today on their plans to push a revised farm bill with direct subsidies to farmers.

Instead they planned to offer tomorrow a compromise bill that would include the Administration soil bank plan and other features not specifically opposed by the Administration.

The Democratic shift came as Senate Republicans and a few Democratic supporters prepared to start the soil bank through the Senate unless the House acts soon on a separate soil bank bill. It was understood that the effort to get the soil bank before the Senate would be made next week if the House insisted on taking up the new Democratic bill.

The Administration's soil bank bill is sponsored in the Senate by thirty-nine Republicans and four Democrats.

Representative Harold D. Cooley, Democratic chairman of the House Agriculture Committee, said he would introduce tomorrow the revised farm bill that Democrats had hoped would be the vehicle for regaining 90 per cent of parity supports on corn, wheat, cotton, rice and peanuts.

**Fight Will Continue**

The fight for direct subsidies or payments to farmers for the difference between existing price support levels and 90 per cent of parity will not be dropped completely, however. Representative W. R. Poague, Democrat of Texas and author of the idea, will present tomorrow a bill including the feature.

The Democratic decision to set aside the direct subsidies came after Republican leaders lashed the Democratic tactics and Representative Clifford R. Hope of Kansas, top Republican of the House Agriculture Committee, refused to go along with the Democratic plan.

Mr. Hope said he believed, however, that the bill Mr. Cooley would introduce was "a fair compromise." He predicted early action on the measure.

Mr. Cooley said he did not "want to get into another party fight at this stage of the session and face another [Presidential] veto." He added that if Mr. Poague's direct payment plan was inserted in his bill he would support it.

Representative Charles A. Halleck, Republican of Indiana and principal figure in the Administration's farm fights in the House, said the revised farm bill was almost "certain to be vetoed" if it was "loaded up again."

He and Representative Leslie C. Arends of Illinois, House Republican whip, called the direct

Continued on Page 15, Column 2

# NIXON DECIDES HE WILL RUN; EISENHOWER IS 'DELIGHTED'; RENOMINATION SEEMS SURE

Associated Press Wirephoto

WILL RUN: Vice President Richard M. Nixon says he will accept renomination. Presidential Press Secretary James C. Hagerty, rear, said President Eisenhower was "delighted."

## DELAY EXPLAINED

### Vice President Says He Took Time to Weigh 'All the Factors'

By W. H. LAWRENCE
Special to The New York Times.

WASHINGTON, April 26—Vice President Richard M. Nixon formally notified President Eisenhower today that he would accept renomination.

The President made known at once that he was "delighted."

The two announcements were made from the White House at 3:45 P. M. without advance fanfare or notice. They virtually assured Mr. Nixon's renomination by acclamation on the first ballot at the Republican National Convention opening in San Francisco Aug. 20.

Mr. Nixon slipped into a side door of the White House unobserved just after 3 o'clock for a half-hour talk with the President. The news was made public immediately afterward at a news conference summoned, on thirty seconds' notice, in the office of James C. Hagerty, White House press secretary.

"I informed the President that in the event the President and the delegates to the convention reach the decision that it is in the best interest of the Republican party and his Administration for me to continue in my present office that I would be honored to accept that nomination again as I was and as I did in 1952," Mr. Nixon said in a statement filmed for later television broadcasts.

**Nixon Explains Delay**

Mr. Hagerty immediately added:

"The President has asked me to tell you gentlemen that he was delighted to hear of the Vice President's decision."

Only yesterday General Eisenhower had said at his news conference that he still had no "final and definitive" report from his 43-year-old Vice President whether he wished renomination.

The President announced on Feb. 29, after weeks of indecision following his heart attack of Sept. 24, that he would seek a second term. After that announcement he said he had told Mr. Nixon to "chart his own course."

Mr. Nixon was asked at the news conference why he had taken so long to do so.

"As you gentlemen are aware, I believe that the most important decision from the standpoint of the country that has been made is, of course, the one the President made when he indicated he would run again," the Vice President replied.

"I felt that it was most important for me to make a decision which in my judgment and in the judgment of my associates was in the best interests of the success of the President in his campaign for re-election and for the continued success of the President's Administration. Consequently, I had to weigh all the

Continued on Page 19, Column 2

## $15,000,000 Fraud On Uranium Stock Charged to Broker

A Jersey City stock broker was indicted yesterday by a Brooklyn Federal grand jury on charges of defrauding thousands of clients in a $15,000,000 uranium stock swindle.

The defendant is Walter F. Tellier, the head of Tellier & Co., a brokerage firm with offices at 1 Exchange Place, Jersey City. Previously, Tellier had pleaded not guilty in the Federal Court, Brooklyn, to a charge that he had participated in a $900,000 fraud through the sale of Alaska Telephone Company debenture bonds.

United States Attorney Leonard P. Moore said Tellier was the principal salesman for 20,000,000 shares in the Consolidated Uranium Mines, Inc. The prosecutor said there were approximately 50,000 stockholders in the United States and that most of them lived along the Atlantic Coast.

In the indictment, Tellier was accused of seven mail fraud violations and seven additional violations of the Securities Act of 1933. The indictment said the violations took place between February, 1951, and last April 15.

Assistant United States Attorney Paul Windels Jr. supervised a four-month inquiry into Tellier's operations. He was assisted by two Securities and Exchange Commission attorneys, John T. Callahan and Edward Jaegermann. They said this was

Continued on Page 19, Column 5

## NEWS PUBLISHERS SETTLE TRUST SUIT

### Consent Decree Ends Case Over Ad Policies — Judge Calls Action 'Salutary'

*Texts of the consent decree and statements, Page 17.*

By RUSSELL PORTER

The Federal Government's civil antitrust suit against the American Newspaper Publishers Association was settled yesterday by agreement.

The association consented in Federal Court to refrain from certain practices alleged to violate the Sherman Antitrust Act, and the Government dropped the suit. The court called the agreement "very salutary."

The A. N. P. A. was among six trade associations in the newspaper, magazine and advertising fields named as defendants in the action, filed last May. The Government charged them with conspiracy to violate the antitrust law by setting up a "recognition" system of accrediting agencies to place national advertising in publications and by fixing the agencies' commissions at 15 per cent.

The "recognition" system as attacked by the Government appears to have been ended by yesterday's action and by a consent decree recently accepted by another defendant, the American Association of Advertising Agencies.

**Suit Pends Against 3 Groups**

The Publishers Association of New York City, also a defendant, whose members belong to the A. N. P. A., recently agreed to abide by any settlement in the A. N. P. A. case.

The three associations against which the suit is still pending are the Associated Business Publications and the Periodical Publishers Association, both of New York, and the Agricultural Publishers Association of Chicago.

The settlement came during yesterday's final session of the A. N. P. A.'s seventieth annual convention at the Waldorf-Astoria Hotel.

Last night, at a meeting of the association's Bureau of Advertising at the Waldorf, Crawford H. Greenewalt, president of E. I. du Pont de Nemours & Co., made a plea in behalf of "the uncommon man." He said that the uncommon man was being threatened by a growing emphasis on group action and conformity. Such an emphasis on conformity, he declared, can stifle the creative individual by "submerging him into the common denominator."

At the earlier session of the

Continued on Page 16, Column 2

## Senate Inquiry Hears Imprisoned Spy Reveal Russian Espionage Tactics

Associated Press Wirephoto

Harry Gold, third from left, testifying yesterday in capital. At extreme left is David Greenglass, confessed atom spy. Beside each is a deputy U. S. Marshal. Senator Herman Welker, at microphones, is sitting as one-man subcommittee.

By The Associated Press.

WASHINGTON, April 26 —Harry Gold, convicted spy, told a story today of eleven years of espionage and the betrayal of vital chemical, photographic and atomic bomb secrets to the Russians. He was brought from prison to appear before the Senate Internal Security subcommittee, which is investigating Soviet activities in the United States. Gold told of "recognition signals," such as a tennis ball, tickets to a prize fight, matching pieces of a boxtop, and furtive meetings on deserted streets, in a zoo or at a cemetery to slip valuable papers to Soviet agents. He conceded that his activity had caused "tremendous damage" to the United States and had helped the Soviet Union get secrets of the atomic bomb, a photographic method of cutting through camouflage and formulas for varied solvents and a local anesthetic. Now, he

Continued on Page 13, Column 5

## Adenauer Says U. S. Expects Bonn Draft

By M. S. HANDLER
Special to The New York Times.

STUTTGART, Germany, April 26—Chancellor Konrad Adenauer said tonight that the United States Government expected West Germany to adopt a law for eighteen-month military conscription.

The manner in which Dr. Adenauer conveyed the United States Government's views on the highly controversial issue of conscription seemed to convey the impression that Washington was making the West Germans responsible for the success or failure of the Atlantic pact as a military alliance.

The Chancellor was reported to have put the matter to a caucus of leaders of his Christian Democratic Union substantially in the following terms:

¶If West Germany should fail to meet its military commitments, the North Atlantic

Continued on Page 4, Column 3

## Hiss Disputes Soviet On Red 20th Century

By HARRISON E. SALISBURY
Special to The New York Times.

PRINCETON, N. J., April 26—Alger Hiss said tonight that he was confident of the falseness of a Soviet prediction that the twentieth century was the century of communism

The former State Department official, who served a term for perjury, addressed an audience of 200 Princeton University students in his first speech since he was released from prison in November, 1954.

The authorities had taken extensive security precautions against violence or untoward demonstrations. They had concentrated upward of fifty university guards and an equal number of municipal policemen and plainclothes men on the campus.

Mr. Hiss' address was delivered in a calm, classroom-

Continued on Page 14, Column 3

## Nixon Plans to See Next H-Bomb Tests

Special to The New York Times.

WASHINGTON, April 26—Vice President Richard M. Nixon is expected to witness the hydrogen bomb tests in the Pacific next month. After that he may visit South Asia and the Middle East.

Officially, the plans for the Vice President to make the trip to the Pacific are still tentative. But it is understood that he expects to be there.

Plans for him to continue on around the world are understood to depend on the political and military situation in the Middle East. If the cease-fire between the Arabs and Israelis holds, some officials believe that a visit by Mr. Nixon as President Eisenhower's representative might do a lot of good.

During previous tours of the Far East and Central America the Vice President won a reputation for exerting persuasive charm.

On his way to the Middle

Continued on Page 19, Column 1

"All the News That's Fit to Print"

# The New York Times.

LATE CITY EDITION

Condensation of U. S. Weather Bureau forecast: Mostly cloudy with showers today. Fair and pleasant tomorrow. Temperature range today: 78—65. Temperature range yesterday: 78.6—59.2. Full U. S. Weather Bureau Report, Page 56.



VOL. CV..No. 35,984. Entered as Second-Class Matter, Post Office, New York, N. Y. NEW YORK, WEDNESDAY, AUGUST 1, 1956. Times Square, New York 36, N. Y. Telephone Lackawanna 4-1000 FIVE CENTS

# KEFAUVER WITHDRAWS FROM RACE, THROWING SUPPORT TO STEVENSON; HARRIMAN PROMISES FIGHT TO END

## DULLES DEPARTS FOR SUEZ TALKS; U.S. BLOCKS FUNDS

### Secretary Flies to London Suddenly After President Asks Him to Attend

### CANAL'S ASSETS FROZEN

### Treasury Acts on Company's and Egypt's Holdings Here to Protect Investors

By EDWIN L. DALE Jr.

Special to The New York Times.

WASHINGTON, July 31—Secretary of State Dulles left suddenly today for the London talks on the Suez crisis. He flew off after a ninety-minute session with the President and will be in London in the morning.

A few hours after Mr. Dulles' departure, the Treasury froze "temporarily" all the assets in the United States of the Egyptian Government and the Suez Canal Company. The order does not affect bank accounts or other assets of private persons and companies.

Mr. Dulles' trip to London was announced by the White House in these terms:

"In view of the importance of the matter being discussed in London between Foreign Ministers [Selwyn] Lloyd and [Christian] Pineau, the President has asked Secretary Dulles personally to take part in the concluding period of their talks, in which the United States also is represented by the Deputy Under Secretary of State [Robert Murphy]."

Mr. Dulles said essentially the same thing at National Airport before he took off, and refused to elaborate. Asked if his trip was "urgent" on the basis of Mr. Murphy's reports, he replied: "You will have to draw your own conclusions."

**Is Silent on Proposals**

He also refused to comment on whether he was taking with him any United States proposals for settling the crisis. Mr. Dulles said he expected to be back "in a day or two."

It was learned over the weekend that concerned officials had been alerted for a probable trip to London by Secretary Dulles at just this time. However, Mr. Dulles apparently changed his mind subsequently, and then today changed it back again.

He said at the airport that he had had "no plans up to 11 this morning." The White House statement made plain that the President had requested the trip.

It was learned that the trip was not occasioned by anything that happened yesterday at the Cairo meeting between President Gamal Abdel Nasser of Egypt and the United States Ambassador, Henry A. Byroade. That session was said not to have produced anything new of importance.

Officials here were still not at all sure what would come out of the London talks. Though obviously a plan for international supervision of the canal — if Egypt would go along—has been in the forefront of the discussions, officials said it was still premature to conclude that this would be the solution agreed upon.

One good reason for Mr. Dulles' trip may well have been simply a demonstration of American backing for the British and

Continued on Page 3, Column 2

## Khrushchev Appeals For Calm Over Suez

By JACK RAYMOND

Special to The New York Times.

MOSCOW, July 31—Nikita S. Khrushchev appealed to the Western powers today to be moderate in their reaction to Egypt's nationalization of the Suez Canal.

While endorsing the Egyptian action, Mr. Khrushchev, the Soviet Communist party chief, stressed Moscow's interest in keeping the canal free to international shipping.

He assailed the idea of military action, which, he said, had been raised by "unreasonable voices," and expressed confidence in the "common sense, experience and political sobriety of the statesmen of Britain and France."

Mr. Khrushchev commented on the Suez situation at a rally of young workers here. There

Continued on Page 2, Column 5

## Eisenhower's Four Years

### Analysis of Administration as Advocate Of Foreign Assistance and Freer Trade

*This is the eleventh in a series of articles analyzing the record of the Eisenhower Administration at the start of the Presidential election campaign.*

By DANA ADAMS SCHMIDT

Special to The New York Times.

WASHINGTON, July 31—The Eisenhower Administration has charted a course toward a liberal foreign economic policy. Here and there, under domestic political pressure, it has deviated from this course.

But Europeans who feared that a Republican Administration would mean a turn toward protection in foreign trade and the beginning of the end in foreign aid were dead wrong.

On the contrary, the two outstanding facts about this Administration's record were these:

1. It established itself as a successful advocate of freer trade.
2. It recognized foreign aid as an integral part of long-term United States foreign policy, and perhaps its most effective tool.

Thus, to the surprise of many at home and abroad, there was no break between the Truman and the Eisenhower Administrations but a continuity of ideas between them.

Fundamentally a Government of business men, the Eisenhower Administration has given these ideas a special private-enterprise accent. And it has developed them further, in response to the rapid changes in the economic world in the past four years.

In midsummer of 1952 the post-war reconstruction of Europe—what has been called the Marshall Plan phase—was just about over. The emphasis in United States foreign aid had begun to shift to Asia. The Korean war was dragging to an end. Stalin was still in the saddle, but his days were numbered.

In midsummer of 1956 the Eisenhower Administration is well on its way into a new economic era. Europe, its productivity restored, is booming. The

Continued on Page 10, Column 3

## LONDON STRESSES CRISIS ON CANAL

### British and French Compare Suez Issue to Korean War—To Press Dulles on Unity

By BENJAMIN WELLES

Special to The New York Times.

LONDON, July 31—Ranking British and French statesmen believe that the dispute over Egypt's nationalization of the Suez Canal Company has brought on the most serious international crisis since the Korean war.

The statesmen of the two nations expressed intense satisfaction today over the news that United States Secretary of State Dulles was arriving tomorrow for talks on the current Suez crisis.

For four days Selwyn Lloyd, British Foreign Secretary, and Christian Pineau, French Foreign Minister, have been pressing Robert Murphy, United States Deputy Under Secretary of State, without success to bring the United States into line with its major European allies.

The European statesmen want the United States to agree in principle with them that the Suez Canal must remain a truly "international" waterway with freedom of passage to all ships at all times effectively guaranteed by an international agency on the spot.

However, Mr. Murphy has not had powers to pledge the United States to accept this principle. He has had to refer the allied views to Washington and the process has been time-consuming and frustrating to the British and French whose interests are more immediately involved and who want to confront President Gamal Abdel Nasser with an imposing international line-up before President Nasser's coup is allowed to harden.

**Admiralty Alerts Fleet**

The Admiralty announced today that "certain naval moves have been ordered" to meet the possibility of serious trouble in the Eastern Mediterranean. Warships in Britain's three chief home posts, Portsmouth, Devonport and Chatham, have received orders to prepare for an immediate state of readiness.

Mr. Dulles will be asked tomorrow to place the United States on record as agreeing with Britain and France that the Suez Canal must be under international jurisdiction. If this can be agreed to, informants here say, Britain and France will then call a conference here of the International Chamber of Shipping, which consists of about sixteen major maritime users of the canal.

They include, besides the United States, Britain and France, such other nations as Australia, Belgium, Canada, Denmark, Finland, Greece, India, Italy, the Netherlands, New Zealand, Norway, Spain and Sweden.

With the Big Three as bellwethers and with the support of these other maritime nations whose future use of the Suez Canal appears to be jeopardized by "unfettered" Egyptian control of the vital waterway, the British-French plan will be to demand of President Nasser that he accept some form of inter-

Continued on Page 3, Column 2

## 6 More Red Leaders Are Convicted Here Under the Smith Act

By DAVID ANDERSON

All six second-string Communist leaders on trial in Federal Court here on conspiracy charges under the Smith Act were convicted yesterday by a jury of four women and eight men.

It was the swiftest disposition of any case involving important Communists. The actual trial, apart from jury selection, was completed in three months, and the jury arrived at its verdict in about ten hours of deliberation.

One hundred and eight Communists now have been convicted in seventeen Smith Act prosecutions across the country. Yesterday's was the third in New York, where there have been no jury acquittals. A Seattle jury acquitted a Communist in 1953. Other juries in New Haven and Cleveland voted one and four acquittals, respectively, earlier this year.

The indictments in these trials

Continued on Page 52, Column 3

## BURMESE TROOPS FACE RED CHINESE TO HALT INVASION

### Clashes With Peiping Forces Reported—Negotiations for Withdrawal Under Way

By The Associated Press.

RANGOON, Burma, July 31—Military sources said tonight Chinese Communist troops had occupied about 1,000 square miles of Burma's northern territory after clashes with Burmese forces. Some casualties were reported.

Burma's Government said it was "seriously concerned" about the border area developments. A Foreign Office statement, confirming reports that Red Chinese troops had established outposts in northeast Burma, said the Government had brought the matter to the attention of the Chinese Communist Government in Peiping.

"Negotiations are now in progress with a view to the withdrawal of these Chinese troops to the Chinese side of the border," the Foreign Office said.

Premier Ba Swe has been conferring with the inner circle of his Cabinet and with Burmese military chiefs. The executive committee of the Premier's party, the Anti-Fascist People's Freedom League, was informed of a "threat to Burma's security."

**Troops 200 Yards Apart**

Military informants said troops of the two armies now faced each other across a strip of land no wider than 200 yards at many points in the mountainous area known as the northern Wa State, about 100 miles east of Lashio.

Accurate reports on the strength of the Chinese force were not available, but it was estimated here at not fewer than 500 troops. The military sources said the Chinese Communists had occupied a triangular area with a fifty-four-mile base after penetrating as far as sixty miles beyond the frontiers of the Kachin and Wa States. Additional small forces of Red troops are reported in the Kachin States to the north of the Wa area.

Foreign Minister Sao Hkon Hkio met with top War Office officials, and the Foreign Office said it was keeping in close touch with the border developments.

One frontier report quoted Red

Continued on Page 4, Column 3

## McKeon Describes Fatal March

Associated Press Wirephoto

S/Sgt. Matthew C. McKeon, photographed on the witness stand yesterday during a recess at his court-martial.

By WAYNE PHILLIPS

Special to The New York Times.

PARRIS ISLAND, S. C., July 31—With tears in his eyes, S/Sgt. Matthew C. McKeon told today of the disciplinary march into Ribbon Creek that cost the lives of six Marine recruits. The sergeant testified on the eleventh day of his general court-martial on charges of drinking on duty, oppression of troops and involuntary manslaughter. Standing beside a large relief map of the area, and facing the seven commissioned officers who will decide his fate, the sergeant traced with a wooden pointer the route of the night march of April 8. He told of hearing shouts of "help" and the thrashing in the water of a half-dozen men who had drifted thirty feet into the stream. As he swam out to them, he said, one of the men grabbed him about the neck. They went under the water twice as they struggled, the sergeant testified. "I tell you,

*Excerpts from testimony by McKeon are on Page 14.*

Continued on Page 15, Column 1

## ILLINOISAN HAPPY

### Expresses 'Gratitude' for Backing—Denies Making Any Deal

By RICHARD J. H. JOHNSTON

Special to The New York Times.

CHICAGO, July 31—Beaming confidence and affability, Adlai E. Stevenson expressed "gratitude" late today to Senator Estes Kefauver for throwing his support to him.

The withdrawal of Senator Kefauver from the Democratic Presidential nomination race, Mr. Stevenson said, "was not a complete surprise."

The announcement, however, caught the former Illinois Governor's campaign headquarters here completely unaware of the development.

Shortly before 4 P. M., the headquarters learned of Senator Kefauver's decision.

Hurried telephone calls were made to the Stevenson farm home at Libertyville, Ill., thirty-five miles from the city.

It was announced one-half hour later that Mr. Stevenson was driving alone into the city.

His arrival, however, was delayed for more than an hour. It was explained later that he had been trying unsuccessfully during that time to reach Senator Kefauver in Washington to express his thanks.

Meanwhile, his campaign headquarters was hastily reorganized for a press conference.

**Reads Statement**

Mr. Stevenson strode into the room grinning broadly. He posed for photographers and then read a formal statement.

"I have been trying to reach Senator Kefauver by phone," he declared.

"I want to express to him my gratitude for his gracious and spontaneous expression of his support. He has often expressed his approval of the Presidential primaries and he has been as good as his word," Mr. Stevenson said.

"I respect Senator Kefauver as a thoughtful, liberal Democrat. We share a grave anxiety about drift at home and deterioration abroad under a faltering leadership and a divided party.

"Senator Kefauver has expressed the hope—which I share—that we Democrats, united by a common purpose, can soon close ranks and get on with this fateful campaign," he added.

Nearly forty paid and volunteer campaign office workers broke into loud applause.

Among the first questions directed at the 1952 Democratic Presidential nominee, concerned whether he had made any "understanding, arrangement or deal" with the Tennessean prior to the Kefauver announcement.

Mr. Stevenson's broad smile quickly vanished.

"No, sir," he said, sharply, "I did not."

He went on to say that Senator Kefauver's decision was "not a complete surprise" to him.

**Kefauver Aide Shocked**

Asked when he had last talked with the Tennessee Senator he responded that they had chatted at the dinner given in Washington last July 19 in honor of Senator Walter F. George of Georgia in connection with Senator George's announcement of his retirement from public office.

Steve Healey, publicity director for the Kefauver campaign headquarters here, expressed "shock" at the Senator's decision.

"It was a shock. A. Bradley Eban, his convention manager, phoned me the news before the Washington announcement. Eban emphasized there were no deals made."

Mr. Healey said that Kefauver convention headquarters, which was to go into operation in the Conrad Hilton Hotel here tomorrow, would open on schedule.

"It will continue to be maintained through the convention," Mr. Healey said.

Mr. Stevenson was asked if he could identify "any further obstacle" to his nomination by his party's convention here Aug. 13. He said, "Yes, one obstacle, Governor Harriman of New York."

Mr. Stevenson sidestepped a

Continued on Page 12, Column 5

Associated Press Wirephoto

OUT OF THE RUNNING: Senator Estes Kefauver of Tennessee announces in Washington his withdrawal as candidate for Democratic Presidential nomination. He urged support for Adlai E. Stevenson at National Convention.

## Stassen Says Nixon Would Cost Ticket 'Millions of Votes'

By JOSEPH A. LOFTUS

Special to The New York Times.

WASHINGTON, July 31—Harold E. Stassen asserted today that Vice President Richard M. Nixon would cost President Eisenhower "millions of votes" if they ran together this year.

Mr. Stassen did not say how much of a liability he thought the President could carry and still win, but he did say, in answer to a question, that "I have never considered any election, not even the 1948 one, a cinch until the ballots are counted. You have to evaluate my effort in those terms."

He spoke at a National Press Club luncheon. The President's special assistant on disarmament problems will start a voluntary four-week payless leave on Thursday to promote his campaign for Gov. Christian A. Herter of Massachusetts for the Vice Presidential nomination.

Mr. Stassen, who said he had irritated some party leaders because they wanted a "cut and dried" convention, got an answer today from Leonard W. Hall, Republican national chairman.

"I have said repeatedly," Mr. Hall asserted in a statement, "that the 1,323 delegates and the 1,323 alternates to the Republican National Convention will decide the nomination for President and Vice President. Both the President and the Vice President have publicly stated they want an open convention."

Mr. Hall visited the White House twice today. On his second trip he spent fifteen minutes with the President and also talked with staff aides. The of-

Continued on Page 11, Column 3

## Meyner Denounces Rebuff to Bigelow

By GEORGE CABLE WRIGHT

Special to The New York Times.

TRENTON, July 31 — The Republican-controlled State Senate was the target today of widespread criticism led by Gov. Robert B. Meyner for its refusal to confirm the appointment of former Superior Court Judge John O. Bigelow as a member of the board of governors of Rutgers University.

Confirmation of Judge Bigelow was denied last night solely because as a lawyer he represented a Newark teacher who invoked the Fifth Amendment while testifying before the House Committee on Un-American Activities.

The action by the Senate resulted today in the calling of an emergency meeting of the Essex County Bar Association to "consider this serious problem." The meeting, called by

Continued on Page 8, Column 5

## GOVERNOR IN RACE TO 'LAST BALLOT'

### Claims Half Kefauver Votes, Indicates View Stevenson Would Be Losing Nominee

Governor Harriman claimed last night more than half of the 200 convention votes released yesterday by Senator Estes Kefauver and declared that he would remain in the race for the Democratic nomination for President "until the last ballot is counted."

His assistant secretary, James L. Sundquist, had received from Senator Kefauver, he said, an estimate that "at least half" of the Kefauver delegates would swing to the Harriman camp.

"From indications I have now received I believe it will be more," the Governor asserted.

Governor Harriman's statement, dictated to his headquarters in the Beverly Hotel after a meeting with his advisers, was at variance with Senator Kefauver's publicly expressed opinion that "the great majority" of his delegates would follow his advice and vote for Adlai E. Stevenson.

Earlier last night, in a statement at La Guardia Airport on his return from a delegate hunt in New England, Governor Harriman gave indirectly his personal endorsement of a view that Mr. Stevenson could not win the election if nominated.

**Cites His Principles**

"This campaign is drawn on principles and I will keep fighting until the last ballot is counted," Governor Harriman told reporters. "I stand for the only principles which will win in this campaign." He said that he represented "the principles of Franklin D. Roosevelt and Harry S. Truman," obviously meaning that he stood for more "progressive" policies than were embodied in the "moderation" that has been ascribed to Mr. Stevenson.

The Governor's airport statement ran counter to some of the advice he had received after Senator Kefauver's announcement that he had withdrawn as a candidate for President and had urged his supporters to back Mr. Stevenson.

This counsel was to remain silent on the new development until there had been some indication whether Senator Kefauver's delegates would actually line up for Mr. Stevenson.

Governor Harriman had received the news of Senator Kefauver's withdrawal in Boston. Immediately thereafter he retired to his hotel room and made a number of long-distance telephone calls. Presumably, he thought over, while flying from Boston, what he would say on

Continued on Page 18, Column 1

## HARMONY IS GOAL

### Senator Expects Most of His Delegates Will Swing in Line

*Text of Kefauver's statement is printed on Page 12.*

By CHARLES E. EGAN

Special to The New York Times.

WASHINGTON, July 31—Senator Estes Kefauver of Tennessee withdrew today as a candidate for the Democratic Presidential nomination. He threw his support to Adlai E. Stevenson.

At a hastily called news conference Mr. Kefauver said he had acted for party harmony. He gave the opinion that his move would insure the nomination of Mr. Stevenson on the first, or at latest the second, ballot at the national convention in Chicago next month.

Some of his delegates may decline to follow his advice to back Mr. Stevenson, Senator Kefauver said, "but the great majority, I am sure, will go along with my advice." He said he thought that those who did not back Mr. Stevenson would support Governor Harriman of New York.

Mr. Kefauver explained that he was not a candidate for any nomination. The convention nominates only for President and Vice President.

"Would you refuse second place on the ticket?" he was asked.

"We'll cross that bridge when we come to it, if we do, at Chicago," the Senator replied.

**'No Deals' With Stevenson**

He said he did not decide to withdraw until 2 P. M. today after many "lonely hours" of consideration. He added that he had not discussed the move with Mr. Stevenson, and had made "no deals and no agreements" with his opponent.

The news conference was held at 4 P. M. Senator Kefauver apologized for the lack of advance notice but added: "I considered it necessary to get the word out just as rapidly as possible."

"It's better to have the statement made now than have the matter wait until the convention meets in Chicago," he said.

He read his prepared statement softly and then answered questions with calm and no noticeable emotion.

It was otherwise with his two principal aides who flanked him, F. Joseph (Jiggs) Donohue, campaign chairman, and J. Howard McGrath, chairman of the Kefauver executive committee. Mr. McGrath had tears in his eyes, and Mr. Donohue stared glumly at the floor as the Senator spoke.

Mr. Kefauver showed none of the bitterness with which he had attacked Mr. Stevenson in their primary fights, notably in Florida and California. He praised Mr. Stevenson as a "much more formidable campaigner today than he was four years ago." He said his erstwhile opponent had been putting more person-

Continued on Page 12, Column 1

## Union Starts Strike At Aluminum Plants

By CLAYTON KNOWLES

A strike that could knock out more than 65 per cent of the nation's aluminum production took firm hold as negotiations collapsed at 1:30 A. M. today.

At that hour the chairman of the union committee bargaining with the Aluminum Company of America stalked out of the negotiations meeting room saying:

"The strike is on!"

At 3 A. M. the United Steelworkers of America had struck or seemed about to shut down twelve Alcoa plants employing more than 17,000 persons and nine mills of the Reynolds Metals Company employing an additional 10,000.

The Aluminum Workers International Union, negotiating at Pittsburgh with Alcoa on behalf of 13,000 workers in another nine plans, withheld

Continued on Page 24, Column 3

"All the News That's Fit to Print"

# The New York Times.

LATE CITY EDITION
Condensation of U. S. Weather Bureau forecast:
Showers this morning; fair this afternoon, tonight and tomorrow.
Temperature range today: 86—72
Temperature range yesterday: 80.1—70
Full U. S. Weather Bureau Report, Page 52

VOL. CV..No. 35,997. Entered as Second-Class Matter, Post Office, New York, N. Y. NEW YORK, TUESDAY, AUGUST 14, 1956. Times Square, New York 36, N. Y. Telephone LAckawanna 4-1000 FIVE CENTS



# DEMOCRATIC KEYNOTE TALK ASSAILS NIXON AS 'HATCHET MAN' OF G. O. P.; LAYS 'INDIFFERENCE' TO PRESIDENT

## LABORITES BREAK WITH EDEN ON USE OF FORCE IN EGYPT

### Deny Backing Militant Policy —Ask Recall of Commons After 22-Nation Parley

### URGE U. N. ROLE IN CRISIS

### Britain Withdraws Some Troops From Germany—Bonn Told of Action

By KENNETT LOVE
Special to The New York Times.

LONDON, Aug. 13—Britain's united political front against Egypt broke today. The Labor party moved into full opposition to the Government's militant policy in the crisis over Cairo's nationalization of the Suez Canal operating company.

Laborite leaders demanded the recall of Parliament immediately after the end of the twenty-two nation Suez Canal conference opening here Thursday. They denied the widespread impression that they had supported the Conservative Government in its preparations to internationalize the canal, by force if necessary.

Originally twenty-four nations had been invited to attend the conference but both Egypt and Greece refused.

Shortly before the Laborite leaders published their statement, the Government announced the withdrawal of units of its North Atlantic Treaty Organization forces in West Germany as part of its military build-up in the Middle East. Reinforcements continued to move to the Mediterranean by air and sea on a round-the-clock schedule.

**Gaitskell Presides at Talk**

Hugh Gaitskell, leader of the Laborite Opposition, presided at a [illegible] meeting of party officials in Parliament who decided to dissociate the party from the Government.

In their statement, the Opposition leaders demanded assurance that the Government's military measures were "purely precautionary, solely intended for defense against possible aggression and not preparations for armed intervention outside and inconsistent with our obligations under the Charter of the United Nations."

The statement urged that the conclusions of the Suez Canal conference be submitted to a special meeting of the United Nations General Assembly. It asserted that any plan for international control of the canal should be associated with the United Nations.

The statement gave particular endorsement to reservations against the Government's forceful policy that Mr. Gaitskell made in the Suez debate in the House of Commons Aug. 2, just before Parliament began its twelve-week recess.

**Sees No Need for Force**

Mr. Gaitskell had said the actions of Lieut. Col. Gamal Abdel Nasser, President of Egypt, so far did not justify using armed force.

He likened Colonel Nasser to Hitler and Mussolini and urged the British Government to assert its prestige in the Middle East. The latter part of the statement was interpreted at that time as an enthusiastic endorsement of the Government's militant attitude in the Suez crisis.

James Griffiths, deputy leader of the Labor party, and Alfred Robens, its foreign affairs spokesman, reported to the Laborites' meeting today on their conference Friday with Prime Minister Eden on the Suez situation. Mr. Gaitskell reported on his correspondence with Sir Anthony.

An authoritative informant said the Laborite leaders had agreed the Prime Minister was bluffing in making military preparations and that his bluff had been called. This source said the Labor party's decision to steer clear of the Government had been motivated by its opinion that Sir Anthony had prepared his own political ruin.

The Opposition leaders feel that the Prime Minister will be forced to back down on the use of force, this source said. This will alienate the Conservative "Suez rebels" who number about forty members of Parliament, and wreck Sir Anthony's political prestige, according to the informant.

If the Government persists in

Continued on Page 8, Column 6

## U. S. in Full Suez Accord With Britain and France

### Dulles Is Said to Have Ordered Denial That Washington Altered Stand—Some Policy Points Unanswered

By DANA ADAMS SCHMIDT
Special to The New York Times.

WASHINGTON, Aug. 13—The State Department emphasized today its "complete agreement" with the British and the French on means of solving the Suez dispute.

Secretary of State Dulles, heading a delegation of twenty-three, will leave for the London Suez Canal conference by plane at 2:30 P. M. tomorrow in time for talks with British and French officials Wednesday. The conference, which will open Thursday, will consider Egypt's nationalization of the Suez Canal operating company.

The point on which the United States agrees fully with Britain and France, the State Department said, is "that there should be international means to insure the practical and efficient functioning of the canal as a free, open and secure international waterway in accordance with the Convention of 1888." The nine-nation pact stipulated that the canal must be open to the merchant vessels and warships of all nations in times of war and peace.

The United States denied reports that it had in any way altered its views on this subject since Mr. Dulles met Selwyn Lloyd, British Foreign Secretary, and Christian Pineau, French Foreign Minister, in London two weeks ago, or that any differences on this subject had arisen with Britain and France.

Mr. Dulles was reported to have ordered this statement to be issued. He was disturbed by a report that the United States would not back the British and French demand for an international agency to run the Suez Canal, but would be satisfied

Continued on Page 3, Column 4

## L. I. Crews Delay Trains In Dispute Over Schedules

Thousands of Long Island Rail Road riders were delayed during the morning and evening rush hours yesterday by a "timetable slowdown" by members of the trainmen's union.

Last night the Long Island, the world's busiest commuter line, with 170,000 daily passengers, said all trains were back on schedule. The union said there would be no resumption of the slowdown today.

To safeguard against future slowdowns, the Long Island went into Federal Court late yesterday afternoon and obtained a temporary injunction barring such activity.

Federal Judge Matthew T. Abruzzo set tomorrow at 10:30 A. M. for a hearing on the company's request for a permanent injunction. The railroad also asked for unspecified damages for lost revenues and added expenses resulting from the slowdown.

During the morning commuter rush, twenty-five trains on four divisions were late an average of twelve minutes—one as much as forty minutes. Twenty-six were on time. The trains of five other divisions were not affected.

During the evening rush period, sixty-five trains were late an average of ten minutes each. The longest delay was thirty-two minutes. Thirty thousand commuters were affected by the morning stoppage, and an equal number or more in the evening.

Last September members of the same union—the Brotherhood of Railroad Trainmen—conducted a similar protest against making schedule changes. That slowdown affected 90,000 passengers, 190 trains and caused delays up to an hour and fifty-seven minutes.

The reason for the job action was the same this year as last. On Aug. 1 the Long Island issued eighty-six pages of schedule changes to be pasted in the trip books carried by employes. Forty-one were to be pasted up by yesterday, the remaining forty-five by next Saturday. The pasting of schedules is standard Long Island procedure

Continued on Page 20, Column 1

## Wilson Establishes Panel to Halt Leaks Of Military Papers

By The United Press.

WASHINGTON, Aug. 13—The Secretary of Defense said today that secret military documents had been falling into the hands of "unauthorized persons for several months. He set up a special committe to stop the leaks.

Charles E. Wilson named Charles A. Coolidge of Boston, a former Assistant Secretary of Defense, to head his special committee of retired senior officers and defense officials. He directed them to tell him how best to check the leaks and "assure greater protection of classified [secret] material."

In a letter to Mr. Coolidge, Secretary Wilson said he was "seriously concerned over the unauthorized disclosure of classified military information." Declaring "this must stop," he asked Mr. Coolidge to prepare an interim report swiftly to "eliminate this threat to national security."

Mr. Wilson did not give details of the "unauthorized disclosures." But he apparently referred to publication of documents in May and June showing interservice disputes over missiles, aircraft carriers and

Continued on Page 7, Column 2

## TEEN GANGS AGREE TO 3-WEEK TRUCE

### Will Plan Community Center —Grievance Procedure Set

By CLAYTON KNOWLES

Warring East Side gangs agreed shortly before midnight last night to a three-week truce. These points were agreed upon:

¶There will be no "rumbling" (gang fighting) through Sept. 4.

¶No group larger than three persons from either side will walk through the "turf" (neighborhood) of the other side.

¶The Enchanters and the Sportsmen, allied on one side, will have one representative each on a grievance committee, and the Dragons, their neighborhood rivals, will have the third member. Differences that cannot be resolved will be referred to local clergy.

¶As evidence of good faith on both sides, a joint bus ride will be held in about two weeks. A committee representing the three gangs will make the arrangements.

¶The rival groups will work together for the establishment of a community center. Present community centers in the area have neither the space nor the money to take care of the 49,000 youngsters in the area.

The agreement was reached in a mediation session with Peter M. Brown, a former assistant

Continued on Page 26, Column 3

## CZECHS OPEN WAY FOR 160,000 TO GO TO WEST GERMANY

### Red Cross Aide Announces Accord on Repatriation of Ethnic Germans

Special to The New York Times.

BONN, Germany, Aug. 13—Up to 160,000 Czechoslovak citizens of German descent have been granted freedom to emigrate to West Germany, the West German Red Cross announced today.

Dr. Heinrich Weitz, president of the organization, said he had negotiated an agreement with the Czechoslovak Red Cross for the voluntary emigration of "ethnic Germans." Most of them live in the Sudeten area of northern Czechoslovakia. Dr. Weitz could not estimate how many of the 160,000 would take advantage of the opportunity to leave for Germany.

The agreement, which has yet to be reduced to writing, was regarded in diplomatic quarters here as further evidence of Czechoslovakia's desire to "normalize" relations with West Germany. There is some controversy within the Bonn Government as to whether West Germany should respond favorably to an apparent interest in Czechoslovakia in opening diplomatic relations.

Dr. Weitz said German inmates of Czechoslovak prisons, and former prisoners as well, were included in the migration agreement. In return, about fifty Czechoslovak children now living in West Germany will be sent home if their parents so request and about thirty Czechoslovak citizens serving sentences in West German jails will be sent across the border.

**Accord Reached in Prague**

Dr. Weitz said he had negotiated the oral agreement during a visit to Prague, Czechoslovakia. It is similar to a migration-repatriation agreement recently concluded between West Germany and Poland. The German Red Cross hopes to conclude similar arrangements with Hungary and Rumania.

Several hundred thousand ethnic Germans, descendants of ancient German colonizers who have retained a sense of nationality, live in scattered communities throughout East Europe. Millions were forcibly expelled to Germany at the end of World War II.

The largest of these German "islands" before the war was the Sudetenland community of more than 1,000,000 German-speaking persons. Hitler's insistence on "reclaiming" them for the German nation brought about the partition of Czechoslovakia in a prelude to World War II. Almost all Sudeten Germans were cast out of Czechoslovakia after the surrender of Germany in 1945.

In its recent attempts to improve relations with the West German Government, the Czechoslovak Government has permitted Germans residing on both sides to cross the border for family reunions virtually without limit.

**Returning Poles Get Land**

BUECHEN, Germany, Aug. 13 (UP)—The Polish Government is turning over to exiles returning from Canada and Australia land and houses left by German emigrants from Polish-administered territories, repatriates arriving here today said.

Associated Press Wirephoto

KEYNOTER, Gov. Frank G. Clement of Tennessee, and Mrs. Franklin D. Roosevelt acknowledging cheers of the Democratic delegates last night after he introduced her to convention.

[Photograph not detected as an image, printed above its caption]

The New York Times

STICKING TO THE RULES: The regulations of the Long Island Rail Road require trainmen and conductors to paste schedule changes into books before starting on runs. This resulted in delays up to forty minutes. Here at Jamaica station, Trainmen G. A. Fagan, left, Walter Holewinski, center, and G. P. Vanderbilt paste the new timetables.

## KNOWLAND SAYS IT'S NIXON AGAIN

### Forecast Follows Talk With Eisenhower—Hall's Mail Backs Vice President

By JOSEPH A. LOFTUS
Special to The New York Times.

WASHINGTON, Aug. 13—Senator William F. Knowland said on the White House doorstep today that the Republican party would renominate Vice President Richard M. Nixon.

The prediction by the Senate Republican leader followed a conference with President Eisenhower and a breakfast chat with Wilton B. Persons, chief of White House liaison with Congress.

The California Senator said that he and the President had discussed politics, foreign affairs and legislation at their thirty-minute conference. But he refused to say specifically that they had discussed the Vice President. Mr. Knowland said he was "not in a position to go into detail."

He said the California delegation to the Republican National Convention would be "overwhelmingly" for an Eisenhower-Nixon ticket. Such a ticket will be re-elected in November by a "substantial majority," he predicted.

President Eisenhower has said that Mr. Nixon was acceptable to him as a running mate again this year but he has not specifically ruled out others.

In the meantime, Harold E. Stassen reported progress in his campaign for the nomination of

Continued on Page 17, Column 6

## Reuther Is Backing Stevenson in Split Of Labor's Leaders

By C. P. TRUSSELL
Special to The New York Times.

CHICAGO, Aug. 13—Labor split today over a choice between Adlai E. Stevenson and Governor Harriman of New York for the Democratic Presidential nomination. Its usual united front was gone, at least for the present.

Walter P. Reuther, president of the United Automobile Workers of America, came out tonight for Mr. Stovenson. David J. McDonald, head of the United Steelworkers of America, spoke for Governor Harriman yesterday.

The U. A. W. has about 1,500,000 members. Mr. Reuther also is vice president of the combined American Federation of Labor and Congress of Industrial Organizations, whose membership totals 15,000,000.

Mr. McDonald's organization has 1,250,000 members. He is also a vice president of the A. F. L.-C. I. O.

The split was expected to widen, according to other leaders. However, both sides were "playing it carefully."

Neither of the principal lead-

Continued on Page 13, Column 6

## PRODUCTION RATE SETS U. S. RECORD

### Yearly Figure Is Estimated at $408,000,000,000

Special to The New York Times.

WASHINGTON, Aug. 13—The United States' gross national product reached a record annual rate of $408,000,000,000 in the second quarter of 1956.

The second quarter rate was $5,000,000,000 above that of the first quarter—the previous high—and $21,000,000,000 above the comparable quarter of 1955. The gross national product is the sum of goods and services produced.

The Commerce Department, in reporting the record today, estimated that one-half of the rise from the first three months to the second was caused by increasing prices. The other half, it estimated, indicated a real increase in the volume of production.

The output increase was achieved despite a substantial decline in automobile production and a lesser reduction in residential construction. Compared with the first half of 1955, gross national product this year was 6 per cent higher current dollars and 4 per cent in real value.

The Commerce Department's revised figures for gross national product for the first three months of 1956 put the rate at

Continued on Page 21, Column 6

## DEMOCRATS HEAL 'LOYALTY' BREACH

### Adopt New 'Good Faith' Rule — Seat Mississippi and South Carolina Regulars

By ANTHONY LEWIS
Special to The New York Times.

CHICAGO, Aug. 13—The "loyalty oath" issue, which tore the 1952 Democratic convention apart, was buried today in a show of party unity.

The two men who led the North-South fight on the floor in 1952, Senator Hubert H. Humphrey of Minnesota and former Gov. John S. Battle of Virginia, jointly appealed to the convention Rules Committee to adopt a new and non-controversial "good faith" rule. The committee did so unanimously.

In another important sign of harmony, the Credentials Committee voted 52 to 2 to seat the regular delegations from Mississippi and South Carolina. These had been the only two seating contests in this convention.

There can be no floor fight on the Mississippi and South Carolina decisions because the rules permit a minority report only if the challengers win at least 10 per cent of the Credentials Committee.

**Floor Battle Unlikely**

It now is certain that there will be no floor battle between North and South over any party loyalty oath or credentials. And in the important remaining area of uncertainty—the civil rights plank—the trend also seems to be toward harmony.

The defeat of the seating challenges today upset last-minute efforts to bar Senator James O. Eastland of Mississippi from the convention.

Oregon's National Committeeman, Monroe Sweetland, said this afternoon that keeping Senator Eastland out would add 1,000,000 votes to the Democratic ticket this fall. There is widespread fear in the Northern wing of the party that Senator Eastland's outspoken views on Negro rights, and his strategic position as chairman of the Senate Judiciary Committee, could cost many Negro votes this year.

In the 1952 floor battle, maverick Northern forces succeeded in forcing through a loyalty oath that bound all delegates to work to get the Democratic ticket on their state's ballot. This was a reaction to the Dixiecrat maneuver in 1948 of keeping the regular party ticket off the ballot in several Southern states.

As it turned out, the loyalty oath was not enforced. Its chief effect was to annoy Southern delegates. After 1952 a North-South committee succeeded in settling the issue.

The compromise discards loy-

Continued on Page 13, Column 2

## CLEMENT CAUSTIC

### Mrs. Roosevelt Urges Unity—Stevenson Is Still Leading

*Text of the keynote address is printed on Page 14.*

By W. H. LAWRENCE
Special to The New York Times.

CHICAGO, Aug. 13—Gov. Frank G. Clement of Tennessee set the Democratic National Convention on fire tonight with a slashing keynote address aimed at President Eisenhower and Vice President Richard M. Nixon.

The 36-year-old Tennessee Governor, who is seeking his party's Vice-Presidential nomination, stepped in where many Democrats feared to tread by striking directly at General Eisenhower. He termed him unfit by his training or his record to serve a second term as President.

Governor Clement sought to blame President Eisenhower for the violence of political attacks made on Democrats by Vice President Nixon. The Republicans, he said, waged a "double-faced campaign" with "the vice-hatchet man slinging slander and spreading half-truths while the Top Man peers down the green fairways of indifference."

The barb at the President and his golfing brought one of the biggest bursts of applause given Governor Clement. The Tennessean was interrupted forty-four times by applause during his address.

**Wild Demonstrations**

Governor Clement not only set off a wild demonstration for himself but he also started one for former President Harry S. Truman. He pledged, in Mr. Truman's behalf, that the former President would support with all his strength any candidate the convention might nominate for the Presidency.

The delegates stood cheering and looking in Mr. Truman's direction as the keynoter touched, though indirectly, on the fierce, unresolved rivalry for first place on the party ticket.

Mr. Truman has staked his personal prestige on an effort to win the Presidential nomination for Governor Harriman of New York. This effort involves stopping the acknowledged front-runner, Adlai E. Stevenson of Illinois.

Later tonight, Mrs. Franklin D. Roosevelt, herself a Stevenson supporter, struck rather directly at Mr. Truman's effort to sway the Convention's judgment on the nominee.

She told the delegates the party must have "young leadership" and that while the advice of older people was useful, the choice of a nominee was "an individual responsibility" for each delegate.

She pleaded with the Democrats to remain united, to solve their problem over civil rights with "imagination and under-

Continued on Page 12, Column 2

## Shifts to Harriman Reported Dwindling

By LEO EGAN
Special to The New York Times.

CHICAGO, Aug. 13—A drift of uncommitted delegates to Governor Harriman that started with former President Harry S. Truman's endorsement of him on Saturday appeared to have slowed today.

At the end of the day, Milton Weilenmann, Western regional manager of the Governor's campaign for the Democratic nomination for President, was contending only that Mr. Harriman would have "over 400" first-ballot votes. This is substantially the same number that was claimed the day before

What apparently was happening was that Mr. Harriman was picking up new recruits by ones and twos instead of large blocs. Even these new gains were offset by minor defections.

Mr. Harriman himself put in a busy day visiting various state delegations and receiving

Continued on Page 13, Column 4

"All the News That's Fit to Print"

# The New York Times.

LATE CITY EDITION

Condensation of U. S. Weather Bureau forecast: Warm, humid, chance of afternoon or evening showers today and tomorrow. Temperature range today: 85—72 Temperature range yesterday: 87.1—72.5 Full U. S. Weather Bureau Report, Page 45.



VOL. CV..No. 36,000. Entered as Second-Class Matter, Post Office, New York, N. Y. NEW YORK, FRIDAY, AUGUST 17, 1956. Times Square, New York 36, N. Y. Telephone LAckawanna 4-1000 FIVE CENTS

# STEVENSON NOMINATED ON THE FIRST BALLOT; OVERWHELMS HARRIMAN BY 905½ VOTES TO 210; PUTS RUNNING MATE UP TO THE CONVENTION

## DULLES PROPOSES A BOARD FOR SUEZ WITH LINK TO U. N.

### Agency Would Include Egypt —Shepilov Conciliatory As Meeting Opens

*Texts of Dulles and Shepilov statements on Page 3.*

By HAROLD CALLENDER
Special to The New York Times.

LONDON, Aug. 16—Secretary of State Dulles presented to the Suez Canal conference today what was, in effect, a United States-British-French plan for the future of the waterway.

His proposal, made on the first day of the conference of twenty-two nations, was that the operation of the canal should be entrusted to an international board established by treaty and "associated" with the United Nations. Egypt would be represented on the board.

From the Soviet Union, represented by its Foreign Minister, Dmitri T. Shepilov, came a long comment, not on the three-power plan but on the conference. Mr. Shepilov's speech reiterated the criticisms and reservations lengthily expressed in the Soviet note of Aug. 9 questioning the composition and competence of the conference. But it ended in an ostensible offer to cooperate to make the conference a "first step" in a negotiation on the Suez problem.

**Nasser Aide Is Firm**

But negotiation seemed to be rejected by an apparent spokesman for President Gamal Abdel Nasser of Egypt, who arrived here tonight by plane from Cairo. He was Wing Comdr. Ali Sabry, political adviser to the President.

To reporters who met him at London Airport he said President Nasser would not acknowledge any independent authority over the canal, which must be under Egypt's sole control. He said: "There will be no compromise that interferes with the independence and sovereignty of Egypt."

It was assumed here that Wing Commander Sabry would speak for President Nasser in the informal talks that will take place outside the conference, which decided today to meet only in the afternoons.

In a short speech welcoming the conference to London, Prime Minister Eden said the occasion

Continued on Page 3, Column 5

## POLAND TO WIDEN PRIVATE BUSINESS

### To Encourage Limited Group of Service Industries

By SYDNEY GRUSON
Special to The New York Times.

WARSAW, Aug. 16—The Polish Communist party has started to encourage limited private enterprise. Thus it is reversing one of the basic tenets of its economic philosophy.

The Government has decreed a number of inducements to rebuild small service industries where a minimum of materials is required and the main value is in the labor. Included under the decree are bakers, tailors, cobblers, plumbers, blacksmiths, mechanics and producers in the traditional cottage industries such as embroidery and woodworking.

It is not likely that this will lead to an immediate increase in retail shopkeeping because manufactured goods still will have to be bought by shopkeepers from Government stores at retail prices.

All other East European Communist countries have a small number of private shops. These are the remains of the campaign against private enterprise. But no other satellite has permitted the opening of new shops or small industries as Poland is now going to.

The Polish moves to encourage

Continued on Page 5, Column 3

## *AP Correspondent Freed by Hungary*

By JOHN MacCORMAC
Special to The New York Times.

VIENNA, Aug. 16—Dr. Endre Marton, Hungarian correspondent of The Associated Press imprisoned since February, 1955, on charges of spying, was released from prison today. Word of his release came from Budapest.

His wife, Ilona Nylas Marton, who was arrested on similar charges four months later, was set free last April when accusations against her were said to have been found baseless. She had worked as United Press correspondent in Budapest.

The arrest of the Martons came shortly after the return of Matyas Rakosi to complete power in Hungary as Com-

Continued on Page 4, Column 4

## WIDE ARAB STRIKE PROTESTS PARLEY

### Egypt Virtually at Standstill but Canal Is Unaffected— Violence in Libyan City

By OSGOOD CARUTHERS
Special to The New York Times.

CAIRO, Aug. 16—Cairo, the greatest metropolis in Africa and the Middle East, was virtually a dead city today.

A Government-sponsored twenty-four hour strike throughout Egypt brought the nation almost to a standstill. The strike was in protest against the opening today of the London conference on the status of the Suez Canal.

Reports from the rest of the Arab world said similar protest demonstrations in various forms had been staged in support of Egypt's opposition to the conference.

Among the few operations unaffected by the Egyptian strike was the passage of the daily convoys of ships through Suez Canal. The state authority that has taken over control of the canal since President Abdel Gamal Nasser nationalized the Suez Canal Company ordered that work go on there as usual.

Public utilities also were kept in operation.

**Cairo Airport Is Closed**

The international airport at Cairo was closed. All airlines using it had canceled their flights for the day.

Shops in Cairo, Port Said, Ismailia, Suez and Alexandria were shuttered. The streets of these usually teeming cities were virtually deserted.

No incidents were reported throughout the country. The Government had issued orders against either rallies or street demonstrations. Security measures imposed by Colonel Nasser's police force were totally effective.

Streets approaching foreign embassies were heavily guarded by policemen on foot, on horseback and in radio cruise cars.

Ordinary Government offices were closed. However, top officials stayed at their posts and continued intensive diplomatic and political activities in connection with the Suez Canal crisis. They studied reports from London on the progress of the Suez conference.

The Soviet Union's Cairo Embassy was reported to have kept open direct telephone and telegraph lines to London throughout the day. Western embassies worked at full pace, although some of their Egyptian employes stayed away for the day.

**Tear Gas Used in Tripoli**

CAIRO, Aug. 16 (Reuters)—Among the incidents reported today in the Moslem world was the arrest of several Libyan demonstrators in Tripoli.

Policemen there broke up a pro-Egyptian demonstration with tear gas. Also in Tripoli, a small boy threw a stone through a window of a United States cultural affairs center.

In Casablanca, Morocco, crowds thronged the streets shouting anti-British and anti-French slogans and "Vive Nas-

Continued on Page 2, Column 4

## TRUCE IN CYPRUS URGED ON BRITISH BY UNDERGROUND

### Leaflet by Pro-Greek Force Proposes Negotiations— London Awaits Word

By The United Press.

NICOSIA, Cyprus, Aug. 16—The Greek Cypriote underground organization, blamed for much of the terrorism that has swept this Mediterranean island in the last year and a half, offered Britain a military truce today.

The appeal for the truce by the National Organization of Cypriote Fighters, known as E. O. K. A., was made in leaflets distributed on the streets of Nicosia.

The leaflets said that E. O. K. A. was asking for a cease-fire to test the British Government's good faith. If the truce call was ignored, "operations will be resumed on a fiercer and more intensive scale."

Observers said the proposed truce might indicate the first sign of a take-over of underground activities by Anargyros Karadimas, who has been reported as successor of the long-hunted Col. George Grivas.

**The Underground Leadership**

The truce leaflets were signed by "Dighenis," the traditional name for a Cypriote nationalist, ethnic Greek outlaw leader. Since E. O. K. A. began its anti-British terrorism April 1, 1955, Dighenis is believed to have been Colonel Grivas, a 58-year-old former Greek Army officer.

The truce offer came shortly after Field Marshal Sir John Harding, the British Governor of Cyprus, outlined his terms in an interview with the English-language Times of Cyprus:

"Let the murderers make the first move if there is to be a stopping of violence and its consequences on this island," Governor Harding said.

The "consequences" to which he referred were a British crack-down on terrorism with added military and police force, as well as the recent hanging of at least five convicted extremists.

Governor Harding said the pro-Greek terrorists had committed more than forty murders before the first hanging took place. In July, he said, the illegal underground group committed seventeen murders.

"If we have to look for responsibility for the deaths of these men [the executed extremists], we must look back to the people who started the terrorist movement and persuaded them to take up murder," the Governor added.

The E. O. K. A. leaflets said that, awaiting a reply by the British, the underground had halted its operations. "But," the leaflets added, "E. O. K. A. is

Continued on Page 4, Column 5

## *Russians Exporting New Bible to U. S.*

By HARRISON E. SALISBURY

Godless Russia is now exporting Bibles to God-fearing America.

In the newest twist of Communist policy the Soviet state book monopoly is shipping Bibles, in the Russian language, to the United States. They are now on sale in New York at $10 a copy.

The Russian Bibles are published in excellent type on good quality paper by the Moscow Patriarchy of the Russian Orthodox Church. They are distributed abroad, however, by Mezhdunarodnaya Kniga, the Soviet state book monopoly.

An initial shipment of fifty copies of the new Bible was received by the Four Continent Book Corporation, 821 Broadway. It was said to be selling well.

The American shipment is part of a first printing of 25,000 Bibles. A second printing, numbering 75,000, is expected soon. In view of the

Continued on Page 11, Column 1

## GEROSA REBUFFED IN ECONOMY PLEA

### City Units Ask $408,335,704 More in New Capital Than His Report Had Advised

By PAUL CROWELL

City departments and agencies have asked the City Planning Commission to allocate in its 1957 capital budget $589,035,704 of new funds chargeable against the municipal debt limit. The over-all total of capital budget requests is $1,064,452,161.

The $589,035,704 in requests for new funds is $408,335,704 more than Controller Lawrence E. Gerosa believes the city can borrow for public works projects without having to impose new nuisance taxes to help balance its expense budget for 1957-58.

On Wednesday Mr. Gerosa warned the Board of Estimate and other city agencies that borrowing for public works projects must be curtailed if new nuisance taxes were to be avoided. He estimated that it would be unsafe for the city to borrow more than $180,300,000 within the debt limit for such projects in 1957.

In Chicago, where he is attending the Democratic national convention, Mayor Wagner said he was confident that the city would be able to produce a balanced budget for 1957-58 without recourse to any new nuisance taxes.

The Mayor took issue with

Continued on Page 12, Column 1

## *4 Israelis on Bus Killed, 7 Hurt In an Ambush in Southern Negev*

### *Attackers Said to Have Come From Jordan—Land Mine Blast Injures Five*

Special to The New York Times.

ELATH, Israel, Aug. 16—Gunmen who were believed to have infiltrated from Jordan killed four Israelis today in an ambush of a bus and its military escort in the Negev. Seven others were wounded in the attack on the road to this frontier town on the shore of the Red Sea.

Elsewhere in the bleak Negev today five civilians were hurt when the truck in which they were riding north of Sde Boker was blown up by a land mine.

A Government spokesman said the Foreign Ministry had apprised Maj. Gen. E. L. M. Burns of Canada, chief of the United Nations truce team in Palestine, "of the particular gravity of the situation."

Today's dead were three soldiers who had traveled in a jeep as a vanguard, and one bus pas-

Continued on Page 4, Column 4

The New York Times Aug. 17, 1956

A bus fell into an ambush in the Negev (1) as a truck was blown up by a land mine to north of Sde Boker (2).

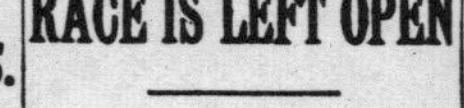

## RACE IS LEFT OPEN

### Humphrey, Kefauver Leading in Contest for Vice President

*Text of Stevenson talk after nomination is on Page 7.*

By JAMES RESTON
Special to The New York Times

CHICAGO, Aug. 16—Adlai E. Stevenson, the Democratic party's Presidential nominee, made a dramatic personal appeal to the convention tonight to make a free and solemn choice of his Vice-Presidential running-mate.

In a move designed to point up the controversy in the Republican party over the nomination in San Francisco next week of a running-mate for President Eisenhower, Mr. Stevenson told the convention that he would not try to hand-pick the Democratic Vice-Presidential nominee.

President Eisenhower has been challenged by Harold E. Stassen, his special assistant on disarmament, to give the Republican convention a similar free choice. The President has indicated that he would be "perfectly satisfied" with Vice President Richard M. Nixon on the Republican ticket this year, but has also said he wants an open convention.

"The choice will be yours," Mr. Stevenson told the delegates shortly after 11 o'clock. "The profit will be the nation's."

**Great Care Urged**

Mr. Stevenson emphasized that seven of the thirty-four Presidents in the history of the United States had reached the White House as a result of the death of the President.

This, he said, placed an especially heavy obligation on the convention to choose the Vice-Presidential nominee tomorrow with great care.

There was a prolonged back-stage dispute this afternoon and night over whether Mr. Stevenson would make his acceptance speech tonight immediately after he was nominated for the second time by acclamation.

Mr. Stevenson wanted to accept tonight rather than tomorrow, when he was scheduled to come before the convention and share the platform with former President Harry S. Truman, who waged an open campaign to defeat him here this week.

The chairman of the convention, Speaker Sam Rayburn, and the chairman of the Democratic National Committee, Paul M. Butler, insisted, however, that the original program be followed even if it was distasteful to the nominee.

Mr. Stevenson then asked and was granted permission to make his appeal on the Vice Presidential question.

**No Mention of Truman**

Unlike most of the speakers before the convention, Mr. Stevenson did not address Mr. Truman as he opened his remarks before the jammed convention hall.

Mr. Truman sat in a box on his right, but Mr. Stevenson merely addressed the chairman, Mr. Rayburn, and the delegates.

"The responsibility of the Presidency has grown so great," he said, "that the nation's attention has become focused as never before on the office of the Vice Presidency. The choice for that office has become almost as important as the choice for the Presidency."

Mr. Stevenson then added that "each political party" had the "solemn obligation" to offer the country a person fully equipped first to assist in the discharge of the duties of the most exacting job in the world, and second, "to himself assume, if need be, this highest responsibility."

"I have decided," Mr. Stevenson said, "that the selection of the Vice-Presidential nominee should be made through the free processes of this convention so that the Democratic party's candidate for this office may join me before the nation not as one man's selection but as one chosen by our great party even as I have been chosen."

He said there were several

Continued on Page 8, Column 1

Associated Press Wirephoto

THE WINNER: Adlai E. Stevenson as he appeared last night at the convention hall, after he had been nominated.

## *Stevenson Pledges to Fight 'All the Way' in Campaign*

By WILLIAM M. BLAIR
Special to The New York Times.

CHICAGO, Aug. 16—Adlai E. Stevenson, the Democratic nomination in his pocket, lost no time tonight in starting the long hard race against President Eisenhower. "This is the end of a long journey," he told his cheering campaign workers, "but it is also the beginning of a long journey. And I'm, going to fight all of the way."

The Democratic candidate addressed his supporters at the Conrad Hilton Hotel less than an hour after he told the Democratic National Convention that it would have a free choice of the Vice-Presidential candidate.

This action, together with his other activities throughout the day, was a clear indication that he had been thinking ahead and planning his campaign against the Republican President who is considered certain of renomination at San Francisco next week.

In a number of statements earlier in the day, Mr. Stevenson had shown solicitude for the big-city voters, with their concern over civil rights, and the traditionally Democratic states of the South.

First of all, he had said that he would have preferred a "specific endorsement" of the Supreme Court's decision against school segregation in the platform.

But he had balanced this with friendly words for the South. He called the Democratic party the "only North-South party." And

Continued on Page 7, Column 3

## *High Police Press Delinquency Drive*

By CLAYTON KNOWLES

An unusual meeting at Police Headquarters, called to intensify the city's war against juvenile delinquency, last night produced demands for funds fo. 5,000 more patrolmen.

The department's entire approach to the juvenile problem was reviewed in the light of a 41.3 per cent rise in crimes by youths for the first six months of the year over the comparable period of 1955.

Commissioner Stephen P. Kennedy, conceding that the police "cannot do this job alone," appealed to leaders of the Youth Councils to step up their efforts as the new school year started. The councils are citizen groups that work with the police at the precinct level. All precinct captains and the youth officers who work with them were present.

Notably absent were represen-

Continued on Page 44, Column 1

## HARRIMAN PLANS '58 ALBANY RACE

### Governor Also Pledges Aid to Stevenson in Drive to 'Put Him Over'

By LEO EGAN
Special to The New York Times.

CHICAGO, Aug. 16—Governor Harriman of New York pledged his help to Adlai E. Stevenson tonight less than half an hour after the former Illinois Governor had defeated him for the Democratic nomination for President.

Earlier, in a television appearance on the Columbia Broadcasting System, Mr. Harriman made it unmistakably clear that he intended to seek in 1958 a second term as Governor.

In the broadcast Mr. Harriman said he expected to remain as Governor of New York "for many, many years" if he failed to win the Presidential nomination. He remarked that "you know there's another election in 1958." That is the year in which the next state election of a Governor takes place.

The Governor said he intended to call on Mr. Stevenson following his television concession of defeat to congratulate the winner in person. "We are old friends, you know," he observed.

The Governor said he would campaign from one end of the state to the other because he regarded Democratic victories in the national election and in Congressional and legislative races as important.

The Governor kept score on the balloting in an air-conditioned room off the main convention hall. With him as the roll was called and his fate sealed were George Backer, a personal associate; Charles Van Devander, his press secretary; Walter Mordaunt, an assistant press secretary; Theodor Tannenwald, a friend; Daniel E. Gutman, his counsel, and Mrs. India Edwards, chairman of the women's division of his campaign committee.

Mrs. Harriman and the Governor's two daughters, Mrs. Stanley Mortimer and Mrs. Shirley

Continued on Page 7, Column 7

## VICTOR IS CHEERED

### Wins by Acclamation Upon Motion of the Harriman Camp

*Texts of Kennedy and Gary speeches are on Page 8.*

By W. H. LAWRENCE
Special to The New York Times.

CHICAGO, Aug. 16—Adlai E. Stevenson won renomination for President on the first ballot at the Democratic National Convention tonight.

The roll-call gave Mr. Stevenson 905½ votes, with only 686½ required for victory. Governor Harriman of New York ran a poor second with only 210 votes despite all the help that former President Harry S. Truman could give him.

Gov. Raymond Gary of Oklahoma, who had placed Governor Harriman in nomination, moved to give Mr. Stevenson the unanimous support of the convention.

Speaker Sam Rayburn, the Permanent Chairman, put the question as one of choosing the nominee by acclamation. There was an ear-splitting roar of "ayes."

"There are no 'noes,'" announced Speaker Rayburn without asking whether there was any opposition.

Mr. Stevenson announced at once that he wanted the convention to have a free-and-open choice of his Vice-Presidential running mate without his indicating in advance any preference. That vote will be taken tomorrow afternoon.

**Cheered by Delegates**

The Presidential nominee received a tremendous ovation when he appeared before the convention to express his thanks and to make his suggestion that the delegates themselves choose the Vice-Presidential nominee.

He did not say so, but it was obvious that the purpose of his move was to contrast the Democratic method choosing a Vice-Presidential nominee with that of the Republican party. The top G. O. P. leadership has joined in slating renomination of Vice President Richard M. Nixon as President Eisenhower's running mate.

Upon receiving news of the nomination, Mr. Stevenson said: "I feel relieved and happy." Later he told the delegates:

"My heart is full and I am deeply grateful but I did not come here to speak of the action you have just taken. That I shall

Continued on Page 6, Column 3

## DE SAPIO SUFFERS LOSS OF PRESTIGE

### But Wagner Gains Stature as Backer of Stevenson

Special to The New York Times.

CHICAGO, Aug. 16—Adlai E. Stevenson's nomination for President raised tonight the possibility of major power shifts in the Democratic party in New York State.

Carmine G. De Sapio's prestige as a state and national political leader has suffered a setback because of Governor Harriman's failure to make a better showing, in the opinion of many New York delegates.

As the leader of Tammany Hall, national committeemen for New York and unofficial manager of Mr. Harriman's campaign, Mr. De Sapio came to the convention as a prospective king-maker. He will leave as a local politician.

Mayor Wagner, on the other hand, will leave with more prestige and, possibly, political power than when he entered it. From the start, Mr. Wagner was outspoken in his preference for Mr. Stevenson over Governor Harriman. His one concession to party "unity" was an agreement to waive this preference for one ballot to give Mr. Harriman a courtesy vote.

Should Mr. Stevenson be elected, it is the view of most

Continued on Page 9, Column 1

"All the News That's Fit to Print"

# The New York Times.

LATE CITY EDITION
Condensation of U. S. Weather Bureau forecast: Hot and humid today and tonight. Hot tomorrow, thunderstorms later.
Temperature range today: 90—76.
Temperature range yesterday: 83.7—71.8.
Full U. S. Weather Bureau Report, Page 35.



VOL. CV..No. 36,001. Entered as Second-Class Matter, Post Office, New York, N. Y. NEW YORK, SATURDAY, AUGUST 18, 1956. Times Square, New York 36, N. Y. Telephone LAckawanna 4-1000 FIVE CENTS

# KEFAUVER NOMINATED FOR VICE PRESIDENT; BEATS KENNEDY, 755½-589, ON SECOND BALLOT; STEVENSON VOWS DRIVE FOR A 'NEW AMERICA'

## SHEPILOV REJECTS WEST'S SUEZ PLAN; ASKS WIDER TALK

### But Russian Stresses World Interest in Canal While Backing Egypt's Claims

*Excerpts from Shepilov and Pineau speeches, Page 3.*

By HAROLD CALLENDER
Special to The New York Times.

LONDON, Aug. 17—The Soviet Union rejected today the British - French - United States plan for international operation of the Suez Canal.

At the same time Moscow called for another and wider conference on the canal. It emphasized the international interest in the waterway as well as Egypt's rights. And it asserted that the Soviet Union, like the West, was concerned to assure free navigation through the canal. Egypt nationalized the Suez Canal Company July 26.

The Soviet view—expressed in an hour-long speech delivered to the Suez Canal conference here by Dmitri T. Shepilov, Soviet Foreign Minister—was that Egypt should assume obligations to guarantee free transit, to maintain and improve the canal and to fix tolls only after international consultation.

**Russian to See Dulles Today**

After this speech, whose negative aspects were conspicuous, it was learned that Mr. Shepilov had made an appointment to visit Secretary of State Dulles at the United States Embassy tomorrow morning. Mr. Shepilov made a similar visit Wednesday.

The United States view was that Mr. Shepilov's speech today was a moderate restatement of the Soviet Union's declaration of Aug. 9 in which it agreed to come to the present conference. Nothing very new was seen in what Mr. Shepilov said except the proposal for a committee to prepare a second conference.

French officials, however, suggested that the speech might "open a door" and that it merited close study. They stressed what they called Soviet recognition that the Suez situation could not remain in its present state and that some new kind of guarantee of freedom for shipping through the canal was necessary.

Others also saw more in Mr. Shepilov's speech than in the earlier Soviet declaration. While insisting upon respect for Egypt's rights, Mr. Shepilov spoke of international cooperation, in forms acceptable to Egypt, for the application of the convention on free navigation. His words, while not crystal clear in the English text, appeared to suggest some international supervision of Egypt's administration of the canal.

Mr. Shepilov proposed that the present conference formulate general principles for a settlement to be negotiated at a later

Continued on Page 3, Column 3

## 9 Egyptians Killed In Gaza Zone Fights

By JOSEPH O. HAFF
Special to The New York Times.

JERUSALEM, Aug. 17—Nine Egyptian soldiers were killed in two incidents near the Israeli border in the Gaza Strip last night, the United Nations Truce Supervision Organization said here tonight.

Maj. Gen. E. L. M. Burns of Canada, the United Nations Chief of Staff here, was examining all the data. He will send a report to Secretary General Dag Hammarskjold.

Following a day-long investigation into the incidents, the United Nations Truce Supervision Headquarters reported that an exchange of fire between Egyptian and Israeli patrols in the Egyptian-controlled territory south of the city of Gaza at 6:30 P. M. had resulted in the death of three Egyptian soldiers. United Na-

Continued on Page 29, Column 2

## F. B. I. Solves Riesel Case; Reports Acid-Hurler Slain

### Hoodlum Scarred in Attack Was Killed Here July 28—2 Ex-Convicts Held—Attempt to Silence Writer Charged

By STANLEY LEVEY

The Federal Bureau of Investigation untangled yesterday the mystery of the acid attack that cost the sight of Victor Riesel, labor columnist.

Two men, ex-convicts who were linked to labor rackets in the garment industry, were arrested and held in $100,000 bail each. They were accused of trying to prevent Mr. Riesel from testifying before a Federal grand jury investigating industrial rackets here.

The hired acid thrower, according to the F. B. I., was a 22-year-old petty hoodlum named Abraham Telvi of 2506 Avenue X, Brooklyn. He was murdered July 28 on the lower East Side, where he grew up. His killing may have been part of a triple gangland slaying with broad ramifications, it was indicated.

By an ironic twist, Telvi's acid attack on Mr. Riesel, which took place in the early morning hours of April 5, may have marked him for death. Some of the sulphuric acid that he dashed into the columnist's eyes splashed his own face, leaving him with scars.

Acting United States Attorney Thomas B. Gilchrist Jr. said yesterday that the underworld felt the facial burns made Telvi "too hot" and that his assassination was ordered. In fact, he added, there was an earlier attempt to take Telvi for "a ride." This failed when the thug became suspicious.

The two ex-convicts were

Continued on Page 30, Column 2

## INDONESIA URGES WARNING TO WEST

### Sukarno Proposes All Newly Free Lands Join in Saying: 'Hands Off Egypt!'

BY ROBERT ALDEN
Special to The New York Times.

JAKARTA, Indonesia, Aug. 17—President Sukarno called today upon the newly independent nations, especially those in Asia and Africa, to unite in warning: "Hands off Egypt!"

"If I were to decide, I would immediately convoke a second Asian-African conference to discuss this call," the Indonesian President declared in a major speech marking the eleventh anniversary of his country's independence. The first Asian-African conference was held in Bandung, Indonesia, in 1955.

The President said Indonesia placed complete confidence in Egypt's guarantee that the Suez Canal would always be open to international traffic. Indonesia's attendance at the London conference on the status of the Canal is in "defense of Egypt's sovereign rights and in defense of peace," he added.

The Indonesian President said that his country's stand was plain, that Egypt was acting within her inalienable rights as a sovereign state in nationaliz-

Continued on Page 2, Column 5

## Bonn's High Court Outlaws Red Party And Front Groups

By M. S. HANDLER
Special to The New York Times.

BONN, Germany, Aug. 17—The Federal Constitutional Court outlawed the West German Communist party and its numerous front organizations today.

Alerted early in the morning in anticipation of the court's decision, the state police occupied the party's headquarters in Duesseldorf. The party's central newspaper, Freies Volk, published in Duesseldorf, also was closed but only after the staff had succeeded in getting out the day's issue.

The state police in other parts of the country moved in and occupied local party headquarters and publishing offices. However, according to reports reaching Bonn, the police managed to seize only propaganda material.

Party records, membership lists and confidential documents had long since been moved to undisclosed destinations, presumably in East Germany. Several truckloads of material were intercepted at Helmstedt on the border of East Germany, but the contents have not yet been examined.

The court's decision was given in answer to a charge filed by the Bonn Government in November, 1951, that the Communist party was committed to the overthrow of the constitutional

Continued on Page 4, Column 3

## PLATFORM HAILED

### Acceptance Talk Also Welcomes Truman Aid in Campaign

*The text of Stevenson's speech appears on Page 8.*

By WILLIAM M. BLAIR
Special to The New York Times.

CHICAGO, Aug. 17—Adlai E. Stevenson called tonight for a rebirth of leadership to "give us a glimpse of the nobility and vision without which peoples and nations perish."

In a fighting speech he accepted renomination as the Democratic candidate for President with a pledge to work with all the resources at his command to carry out the Democratic platform. He called the platform "a signpost" toward a "new America."

Mr. Stevenson said:

"I mean a new America where poverty is abolished and our abundance is used to enrich the lives of every family.

"I mean a new America where freedom is made real for all without regard to race or belief or economic condition.

"I mean a New America which everlastingly attacks the ancient idea that men can solve their differences by killing each other."

Mr. Stevenson, pledging to work for these objectives, declared:

"These are the terms on which I accept your nomination."

**Scores 'Personality Cult'**

He blasted the Republicans with a charge that the Administration had not told the truth to the country.

"I say that what this country needs is not propaganda and a personality cult," he said. "What this country needs is leadership and truth, and that's what we mean to give it."

He saluted former President Harry S. Truman, who fought to block his nomination.

"I am glad to have you on my side again, sir!" he said.

He called Mr. Truman the "distinguished American who has been more than equal to the hard test of disagreement and has now reaffirmed our common cause so graciously."

He also told the cheering delegates to the national convention that their free choice of Senator Estes Kefauver of Tennessee as his running mate had "renewed and reaffirmed our faith in free Democratic processes."

The office of Vice President, he said, has been "dignified by the manner of your selection as well as by the distinction of your choice."

Before speaking Mr. Steven-

Continued on Page 7, Column 1

Associated Press Wirephoto

THE DELEGATES' CHOICE: Adlai E. Stevenson and Senator Estes Kefauver on the rostrum last night at the convention in Chicago. At the right is former President Truman.

## FINISH DRAMATIC

### Bay Stater Nearly In When Stampede to Rival Is Set Off

By W. H. LAWRENCE
Special to The New York Times.

CHICAGO, Aug. 17—Senator Estes Kefauver seized the Democratic Vice-Presidential nomination by an eyelash today.

The Tennessean edged out Senator John F. Kennedy of Massachusetts on the second ballot in an open floor fight to become the running mate of Adlai E. Stevenson of Illinois. Mr. Stevenson was renominated for the Presidency last night.

The Democrats picked two men who fought each other bitterly in the primaries to oppose the Republican slate in November. President Eisenhower and Vice President Richard M. Nixon are expected to be renominated at San Francisco next week.

The Stevenson-Kefauver team shared the spotlight at the final session tonight of the Democratic National Convention with former President Harry S. Truman, who had opposed the selection of both.

Tonight they came to accept their nominations. Mr. Truman came to bid for party unity and to take back some of the harsh things he had said against Mr. Stevenson this week. Besides saying that Mr. Stevenson was "top defeatist to win," Mr. Truman in his private conversations has mispronounced the Tennessean's name as if it were spelled "Cowfever." Tonight he pronounced it correctly.

**States Switch Votes**

After Mr. Stevenson's speech and the singing of "The Lord's Prayer" the thirty-second convention ended at 10:52 P. M., Central daylight time [11:52 P. M. Eastern daylight time].

The final ballot was as dramatic as any Democratic convention has witnessed.

Senator Kefauver's nomination was made by acclamation upon the motion of Senator Kennedy. When the second roll-call was completed, but before the result had been announced, Senator Kennedy had 648 votes, 38½ votes short of the required majority. He was far ahead of the Tennessee Senator.

Then the states began to wave their standards to switch their votes. The lead seesawed. At that point, Senator Albert Gore of Tennessee, who was running third, withdrew in favor of his colleague and released the delegates pledged to him.

That started a stampede to the 53-year-old Mr. Kefauver. The Senator went over the top on the basis of new votes that Missouri had cast for Senator Hubert H. Humphrey of Minnesota.

The final official tabulation as reported by The Associated Press gave Senator Kefauver 755½ votes and Senator Kennedy 589. This Convention had 1,372 delegates, with 686½ votes comprising a majority.

Earlier figures on the final

Continued on Page 6, Column 1

## KEFAUVER SCORES NIXON FOR 'SMEAR'

### Tells Convention That He'll Never 'Demean' Office of Vice President

*Text of the Kefauver speech is printed on Page 8.*

By ANTHONY LEWIS
Special to The New York Times.

CHICAGO, Aug. 17—Senator Estes Kefauver accepted the Democratic nomination for Vice President tonight with a jab at his prospective Republican opponent, Vice President Richard M. Nixon.

"The chief function of the Vice President should not be that of a political sharpshooter for his party," Senator Kefauver told the Democratic National Convention. "It should not be that of providing the smear under the protection of the President's smile ***.

"As your Vice-Presidential candidate, I promise you that I will never demean that high office to traduce fellow-Americans. I will never use it to sow division and distrust."

This was a reference to Democratic charges that throughout his political career, and notably in the election of 1954, Mr. Nixon used half-truths and insinuations to smear the Democrats as pro-Communist.

Senator Kefauver began his speech by saying he was proud to have been selected as the Vice-Presidential candidate by the new device of an open convention.

"It will be very interesting to

Continued on Page 7, Column 5

## Truman Terms Stevenson 'A Fighter' Who Can Win

By ANTHONY LEVIERO
Special to The New York Times.

CHICAGO, Aug. 17—Harry S. Truman declared tonight that Adlai E. Stevenson was "a real fighter." The former President came out battling for the Democratic party. He told the convention delegates that the Democratic standard-bearer had given him "a pretty good licking, and he's going to give Eisenhower a better one."

Mr. Truman reversed his bitter attitude toward Mr. Stevenson in making the opening speech at

*Text of the Truman address will be found on Page 8.*

the night session of the convention. Only two days ago he had branded the Democratic Presidential candidate as a political weakling who would deliver his party into a conservative-reactionary caretakership for the next four years.

Last night in nominating Mr. Stevenson the convention delivered a trouncing to Mr. Truman, who had headed a faltering cause in behalf of Governor Harriman. Today the convention rebuffed Mr. Truman again in nominating Senator Estes Kefauver as the Vice-Presidential candidate. The former President has a pronounced antipathy for the Tennessean.

But in returning to party regularity the former President called on every Democrat to throw "the Republicans out of office." He attacked the Eisenhower Administration on seven major issues.

**Calls Kefauver 'Able'**

Mr. Truman's speech was written before the nomination of Mr. Kefauver. After the convention had acted he applied this political benediction to Mr. Stevenson's running mate:

"The convention has given Governor Stevenson an able and efficient running mate in Estes Kefauver. He will add great strength to the ticket."

Speaker Sam Rayburn, the convention chairman, introduced the former President and said "we should not remember the shots he made from the hip—and he made many of them."

Mr. Rayburn added that Mr. Truman had made some of the most far-reaching decisions in history.

The vast audience was more than willing to forget the shots from the hip. They gave the old party warhorse a roaring ovation that echoed to the rafters until Mr. Truman himself gaveled for silence so that the program could be kept on schedule.

In no time at all he had the audience completely with him, cheering and laughing.

Mr. Truman ad libbed to make even more gracious his formal admission that he had taken a

Continued on Page 9, Column 2

## NEW YORK IS COOL TO TENNESSEAN

### Leaders Wanted Catholic on Ticket to Help Carry State in November

By LEO EGAN
Special to The New York Times.

CHICAGO, Aug. 17—A deep conviction that Adlai E. Stevenson will need help to carry New York was behind the battle waged by New York leaders today to obtain the Vice-Presidential nomination for either Mayor Wagner or Senator John F. Kennedy of Massachusetts.

Representative Charles A. Buckley said that Mr. Stevenson could not carry New York without help. He made the statement in urging the delegation to switch from Mayor Wagner to Senator Kennedy between the first and second ballots.

Mr. Buckley is the Democratic leader of the Bronx, which usually casts the highest percentage of Democratic votes of any county in the state.

"Anyone who would vote for Kefauver would vote for Stevenson," he told Carmine G. De Sapio, chairman of the New

Continued on Page 9, Column 4

## L. I. Boy Calls Nasser 'Nice Man' After Visiting Him

Associated Press Radiophoto

President Gamal Abdel Nasser, left, with Dennis Briody and his father, Charles Briody

By The United Press.

CAIRO, Aug. 17—Dennis Briody, 13 years old, of Massapequa, L. I., met Lieut. Col. Gamal Abdel Nasser, President of Egypt, today and thought he was "a real nice man." The boy came to Egypt as Colonel Nasser's personal guest Aug. 8. Today the President received the young visitor and his father, Charles, in the Presidential office. Dennis wrote Colonel Nasser that "some people in the United States have misconceptions about Egypt." Dennis told Colonel Nasser he had enjoyed his visit to points of interest. While he awaited the Nasser interview, Dennis went sight-seeing.

## Soviet Will Reverse Two Arctic Rivers

By HARRISON E. SALISBURY

Georgi M. Malenkov, former Soviet Premier, recently outlined to a visiting American publisher a plan for increasing the power output of the Volga River by reversing the flow of two Arctic rivers.

The previously undisclosed Soviet plan was discussed by Mr. Malenkov in an interview with Shelton Fisher, publisher of Power magazine, a McGraw-Hill publication. Mr. Fisher recently returned from the Soviet Union.

Mr. Malenkov, now Minister of Electric Power Stations, disclosed that the great Volga project was already on the engineering drafting boards. It is designed to stabilize the year-around waterflow in the Volga. Mr. Malenkov estimated that power production would be increased by 11,000,000,000 kilo-

Continued on Page 2, Column 4

## Republicans Hail 'Good News,' Chide Foes on 'Picking a Loser'

By LAWRENCE E. DAVIES
Special to The New York Times.

SAN FRANCISCO, Aug. 17—Republican spokesmen exuded optimism today over prospects not only of retaining the Presidency but also of obtaining control of the Senate. They did this on the basis of what they called "the good news" from Chicago.

Almost on the eve of the opening Monday of their own national convention here in the Cow Palace, party leaders chided the Democrats for "picking a loser"—Adlai E. Stevenson—to run against President Eisenhower.

Then, with Senator Andrew F. Schoeppel of Kansas, chairman of the Senate Republican Campaign Committee, in the lead, they analyzed prospective Senate battles and predicted a net gain of "four or five seats."

Senator Schoeppel was reminded that this claim was much more optimistic than a picture drawn twenty-four hours earlier by Senator William F. Knowland of California, the minority leader. Mr. Knowland had told a Western Republican conference that with work the Republicans could capture the House, but that the Senate was "going to be more difficult."

"I am more optimistic," Senator Schoeppel declared, "after seeing what the Democrats have done at Chicago. They have nominated a loser. We beat him once and we'll beat him again. He can't win. Former President Truman said that and so did John L. Lewis [president of the United Mine Workers of America]. On top of that the Democratic platform set forth the most glib

Continued on Page 10, Column 4

"All the News That's Fit to Print"

# The New York Times.

LATE CITY EDITION
Condensation of U. S. Weather Bureau forecast: Mostly fair today; showers possible tonight. Clearing tomorrow.
Temperature range today: 72—62.
Temperature range yesterday: 69.3—61.6.
Full U. S. Weather Bureau Report, Page 52.

© 1956, by The New York Times Company.

VOL. CV..No. 36,006. Entered as Second-Class Matter, Post Office, New York, N. Y. NEW YORK, THURSDAY, AUGUST 23, 1956. Times Square, New York 36, N. Y. Telephone Lackawanna 4-1000 FIVE CENTS

# EISENHOWER AND NIXON ARE RENOMINATED; G. O. P. CONVENTION IS UNANIMOUS ON BOTH; STASSEN GIVES UP, SECONDS VICE PRESIDENT

## SOVIET AND INDIA BAR BID TO EGYPT TO DISCUSS SUEZ

### Block Proposal for Talk on Canal's Regime—Action Prolongs London Parley

*The text of Selwyn Lloyd's address is on Page 2.*

By HAROLD CALLENDER
Special to The New York Times.

LONDON, Aug. 22—The Soviet Union and India joined today to block a proposal to ask Egypt to negotiate with other nations for an international regime for the Suez Canal.

They thus prolonged the Suez Canal conference of twenty-two nations, which was to have finished today. It will meet again tomorrow to try to decide how negotiations with Egypt are to begin. Egypt, which refused to attend the conference, nationalized, on July 26, the company operating the canal.

The nations supporting the United States proposal for such negotiations now number eighteen. France and Spain withdrew today the reservations they had made yesterday.

[Some diplomats in London from the smaller European countries are predicting a Western defeat in the Suez crisis. As a result, they have begun talking of a whole new European approach to the nations of the East. One diplomat said a "new way of living" would have to be worked out "without special Western spheres of influence."]

**Held Essential to Solution**

Informally declaring Britain's adherence to the United States proposal, as amended yesterday to win the backing of Eastern nations, Selwyn Lloyd, British Foreign Secretary, seemed to insist that an international operating agency for the canal was beyond negotiation. He said such an agency was "an essential part of any settlement."

British officials contended today that the United States proposal, even in its amended form, still expressed sufficiently clearly the determination of the Western powers to refuse any compromise on the principle of international operation of the canal.

The French back the same principle. They were not too pleased when the term "international board" was dropped from the United States text in favor of "a Suez Canal board" representing Egypt and other states.

Nor were they content with the terms of the New Zealand proposal put to the conference today. This suggested that negotiations be offered to Egypt "on the basis of" the United States proposal, or "statement," as it is called in the terminology of this conference. The French had urged in private talks that

Continued on Page 3, Column 5

## Cairo Issues Threat Of Canal Priorities

By OSGOOD CARUTHERS
Special to The New York Times.

CAIRO, Aug. 22—Egypt threatened today to give priority in the Suez Canal to ships other than those of Britain and France if British and French canal pilots quit their jobs.

The threat was made by Nabih Yunis, Under Secretary of the Ministry of Finance and a member of the twelve-man managing board of the Egyptian Government's new Suez Canal Authority.

[In London, the chief spokesman of the Foreign Office said the Egyptian threat "appears to be a clear case of discrimination." Selwyn Lord, Foreign Secretary, disputed Soviet contentions that the canal was being run smoothly.]

Mr. Yunis charged bitterly that "some British and French pilots resort to the trick of

Continued on Page 3, Column 1

## CYPRUS BAND GETS 3 WEEKS TO YIELD

### Terrorists Given a Deadline by British to Surrender Under Amnesty Offer

By BENJAMIN WELLES
Special to The New York Times.

LONDON, Aug. 22—The British Government has offered the Cypriote terrorists three weeks in which to surrender with their arms.

Those who take advantage of the offer, which is effective at midnight tonight, can choose either to go freely to Greece, if Greece will have them, or to remain in Cyprus under detention. Any among those who stay who are implicated in crimes of violence against persons will be tried, the Government announced.

The British offer, made today by the British Governor, Field Marshal Sir John Harding, in Nicosia, was announced by the Colonial Office. It was described officially as a move to test the value of the pamphlets recently distributed in the island crown colony by the National Organization of Cypriote Fighters, oth-

Continued on Page 9, Column 2

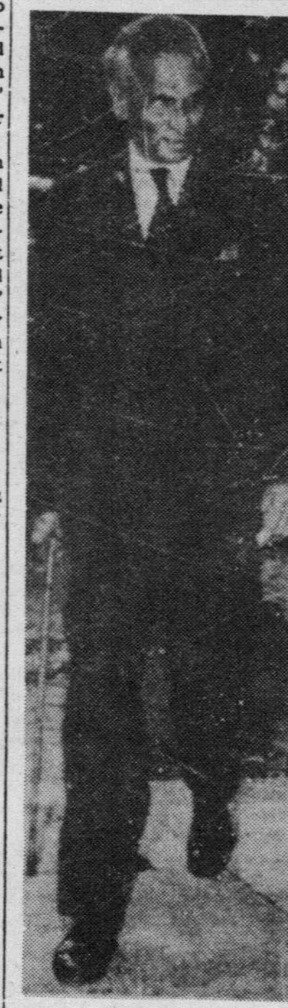

Associated Press Radiophoto

**PROLONGS SUEZ TALKS:** V. K. Krishna Menon of India. He is shown leaving Foreign Office yesterday after session with Selwyn Lloyd, British Foreign Secretary.

## U.S. NAVAL PLANE MISSING IN ATTACK OFF CHINA'S COAST

### 16 Men Aboard Patrol Craft—Fighter Cover Is Sent With the Search Party

Special to The New York Times.

WASHINGTON, Aug. 22—A Navy patrol plane is missing after having been attacked by aircraft off the coast of Communist China.

In reporting the incident tonight the Navy said an air and surface search with an "air cover" of fighting planes was under way. A brief statement by the Navy said:

"The Navy reported that one of its planes is missing and unaccounted for after having been under attack by aircraft. The identity of the attacking air craft has not yet been determined.

"The commander of the United States Seventh Fleet, Vice Admiral Stuart Ingersoll, has initiated an air and surface search for the plane or survivors and has provided air cover for the planes and ships taking part in the search.

"The plane's reported position at the time of the attack was approximately 160 miles north of Formosa [Taiwan] and about thirty-two miles off the China coast over international waters.

"The plane, a P4M Martin Mercator, is powered by two jet and two reciprocating engines. It is designed for long over-water patrols and photographic reconnaissance. It normally carries a crew of nine. The missing plane was on a routine patrol flight at the time of attack."

**Attacked at Night**

Later the Navy reported that the attack took place at 12:25 A. M. Thursday, Taiwan time (12:25 P. M. Wednesday, Eastern standard time).

[A spokesman at headquarters of the Far East Air Forces in Tokyo said Thursday the missing plane was carrying sixteen men, The Associated Press reported. Chinese Nationalist authorities on Taiwan said no plane of theirs had been involved in the attack, Reuters reported.]

Admiral Arleigh A. Burke, Chief of Naval Operations, has notified all Government authorities of the incident. It was assumed that word had been sent to President Eisenhower and Charles E. Wilson, Secretary of Defense, who are at the Republican National Convention in San Francisco, and Secretary of State Dulles, who is taking part in the London conference on the Suez Canal.

Although there had been many instances in which United States planes were shot down or attacked by planes belonging to Soviet satellite nations over the last few years, this type of incident had appeared to be occurring less frequently.

The last Navy plane to suffer

Continued on Page 5, Column 3

**NIXON FLIES TO HIS FATHER:** Vice President Richard M. Nixon and Mrs. Nixon leave San Francisco for bedside of Mr. Nixon's father, critically ill at La Habra, Calif.

Associated Press Wirephotos

**THE PRESIDENT MEETS STASSEN:** President Eisenhower confers with Harold E. Stassen, who said he was ending campaign to replace Vice President Nixon on the ticket.

## NIXON AT BEDSIDE OF AILING FATHER

### Flies to His Home on Word of Critical Illness—Return to Convention Uncertain

By The Associated Press.

WHITTIER, Calif., Aug. 22—Vice President Richard M. Nixon flew here from the Republican National Convention today to take up a vigil at the bedside of his father, who is critically ill.

Little hope was held for the recovery of 77-year-old Francis A. Nixon. He was stricken with bleeding of the major artery leading to the abdomen in his home at La Habra, near here, at 4 A. M. today. He was intermittently unconscious during the day.

The Vice President whose home is in Whittier, canceled all engagements and sped to his father. He was accompanied by his wife and brother, F. Donald Nixon of Whittier, and sister-in-law, Mrs. Clara Jane Nixon.

On learning of the convention results, Mr. Nixon said:

"We've just heard the proceedings and were very gratified by the results in the renomination of President Eisenhower and appreciative too for the support of the delegates for the nomination of Vice President.

"I'll work harder than in previous campaigns to see that leadership is available to the United States and the world for four more years."

After being with his father several hours, Mr. Nixon said his return to San Francisco depended on his father's condition

Continued on Page 15, Column 5

## Stassen Reverses Position After Visiting Eisenhower

By WILLIAM S. WHITE
Special to The New York Times.

SAN FRANCISCO, Aug. 22—Harold E. Stassen capped an unconditional surrender in his campaign to "stop" Richard M. Nixon tonight by seconding the Vice President's renomination at the Republican National Convention. Earlier, after a short talk with President Eisenhower, Mr. Stassen had phlegmatically reversed himself. He had promised to support and work for the re-election of Mr. Nixon as well as of President Eisenhower. He also had announced his intention of staying in his job as disarmament adviser to the President—and had firmly closed the door on the recent past.

At all events, Mr. Stassen came to the convention hall tonight to salute the man he had attacked as recently as yesterday as harmful to the Republican ticket this fall—Vice President Nixon.

He thus came full circle—not only now accepting Mr. Nixon but also praising him. His brief act of rebellion had represented the only breech in the picture of total unity that the Republicans had presented here.

[In La Habra, Calif., Mr. Nixon said he was "deeply appreciative" of Mr. Stassen's changed position. He said this would help the party "present a united front" for the election campaign.]

Mr. Stassen was well received—there were no boos—as a prodigal who had come home. He called Mr. Nixon "able" and "experienced," and appealed to independents, dissident Democrats and minority voters over the country to support the Vice President in the fall.

He asked to be allowed "respectfully to plead" with the party leadership not to forget these groups in their campaign plans.

He said that his own act of retreat did not foreclose others from voting for some person other than Mr. Nixon, if they chose, but he added that Mr. Nixon would "give very ounce of his intelligence and devoted efforts" toward the re-election of President Eisenhower.

He pledged his own "wholehearted and all-out efforts" for the Eisenhower-Nixon ticket, saying that when "points of decision" arose in the party he would always be "a team player."

He asserted that a continuation of the Eisenhower-Nixon leadership, with the cooperation of members of Congress of both parties, offered "the best prospect" for reaching a sound system of world disarmament in hydrogen and other weapons.

He spoke eleven minutes to a convention that seemed basically friendly but unstartled. What he would do here tonight had for hours been known.

He had an eleven-minute conference, from 10:53 A. M. to 11:04 A. M., with President

Continued on Page 15, Column 7

## DEWEY SAYS G.O.P. WILL GUARD PEACE

### Cites President's Record—Calls His Re-election Best for Nation's Prosperity

*The text of speech by Dewey will be found on Page 16.*

By LEO EGAN
Special to The New York Times.

SAN FRANCISCO, Aug. 22—Thomas E. Dewey told the Republican National Convention tonight that America's best hope of continued peace and prosperity depended on President Eisenhower's re-election.

In a speech that frequently brought outbursts of applause and cheers from the delegates, Mr. Dewey assailed Democrats for inconsistencies, past misdeeds and ineptness.

It was the kind of speech the delegates seemed to have been waiting for since the convention opened. They took full advantage of it to voice their confidence in winning this year's election.

As proof that the nation could not depend on Adlai E. Stevenson, the candidate for President named by the Democrats last week, Mr. Dewey cited opinions expressed by two outstanding Democrats at Chicago.

Averell Harriman, who succeeded him as Governor of New York, asserted, Mr. Dewey recalled, that he was the only Democrat able to deal with Communists. Harry S. Truman, who defeated Mr. Dewey for President in 1948, was quoted as having warned Democrats that the nation would face a trial-and-error period in foreign relations if Mr. Stevenson were elected.

The former Governor asserted that the nation was indebted to Mr. Truman for this "involuntary lapse into objectivity."

Mr. Dewey's gibes at the former Democratic President evoked both laughter and applause. So did later references to Mr. Truman's "squirrel head" remark to describe some military men during his recent European trip and his allusions to some letters Mr. Truman had written as President.

The speech, even more than

Continued on Page 17, Column 4

## TWO ACCEPT TODAY

### Eisenhower Says That No Rival to Nixon Came Forward

*Transcript of the Eisenhower news conference, Page 15.*

By W. H. LAWRENCE
Special to The New York Times.

SAN FRANCISCO, Aug. 22—Roaring Republicans unanimously renominated President Eisenhower and Vice President Richard M. Nixon tonight.

A "dump Nixon" movement collapsed completely with the unconditional surrender of its leader, Harold E. Stassen. Mr. Stassen had tried in vain to get Gov. Christian A. Herter of Massachusetts to oppose Mr. Nixon.

General Eisenhower summoned a special, nationally televised press conference to announce that Mr. Stassen's campaign had ended and that all barriers to Mr. Nixon's renomination had been removed. Mr. Stassen later seconded Mr. Nixon's nomination.

Mr. Nixon's victory was made unanimous and complete when a Nebraska delegate, Terry Carpenter, capitulated. On the first roll-call Mr. Carpenter had passed because the convention chairman, Representative Joseph W. Martin Jr. of Massachusetts, had ignored his joking attempt to place in nomination the name of "Joe Smith." Just before the vote was announced, Mr. Carpenter gave in, and the Nixon total climbed to 1,323 votes.

**Convention Is Jubilant**

It was a moment of triumph and tragedy for the Vice President. He was at the bedside of his critically ill father, Francis A. Nixon, at La Habra, near Los Angeles, when the convention made him its choice for a second term. The elder Nixon is 77.

The nominating processes gave the confident delegates something to cheer and demonstrate about as they sent the victorious team of 1952 back into battle against a Democratic slate again headed by Adlai E. Stevenson of Illinois. Mr. Stevenson's new running mate, picked in an open floor fight at Chicago last week, is Senator Estes Kefauver.

Both the President and Vice President are scheduled to make their acceptance speeches at the final session of this convention tomorrow afternoon. But there was doubt tonight Mr. Nixon could leave his father's bedside. And there was talk of a special television broadcast by him from Los Angeles to the delegates in this hall.

The convention recessed tonight at 9:05 P. M. (12:05 A. M. Eastern daylight time), until 4 P. M. tomorrow when it will hear the acceptance speech of President Eisenhower at least. An organizational meeting of the new national committee was called for 11:30 A. M. tomorrow by Perry W. Howard, Mississippi

Continued on Page 12, Column 1

## HALLECK, HERTER NOMINATE TICKET

### President Is Hailed as Man 'Equal to the Times'—Nixon Called Dedicated

*Texts of Halleck, Herter and Stassen speeches, Page 14.*

By ALLEN DRURY
Special to The New York Times.

SAN FRANCISCO, Aug. 22—Representative Charles A. Halleck of Indiana placed President Eisenhower's name in nomination today for a second term.

He told a cheering Republican National Convention that General Eisenhower was "the most universally respected, the most profoundly dedicated man of our times."

Later, Gov. Christian A. Herter of Massachusetts nominated Vice President Richard M. Nixon for a second term. He called him "a great Vice President" who had made his office "more significant, more influential, more useful than ever before in our history."

Mr. Halleck told the enthusiastic delegates that now, as in Abraham Lincoln's time, "a Divine Providence has again given us a man equal to the times."

Referring to Democratic charges that General Eisenhower had been "a part-time President," Mr. Halleck shouted:

"Are peace and military might—balanced budget and stable dollar—Federal payroll and tax cuts—farming at peace instead of war—huge highway program—expanded housing, Social

Continued on Page 13, Column 3

## 3d Ave. to Be Zoned For a Model Street

By CHARLES G. BENNETT

General rezoning of Third Avenue from East Fifteenth to East Ninety-sixth Street was approved yesterday by the City Planning Commission.

Essentially, the thoroughfare is to be more restricted than at present. The rezoning proposal now goes to the Board of Estimate, where prompt approval is expected.

It is proposed to make certain that stores and other commercial establishments moving to Third Avenue will conform to plans for making it one of the city's model thoroughfares.

The new zoning will introduce a "retail" classification to Third Avenue, a designation that has been written into the zoning law since the statute was adopted in 1916.

Retail designations permit residential and commercial uses while providing tighter restric-

Continued on Page 53, Column 2

## Drive to Draft Wagner Gaining Among Delegates of State C.I.O.

By STANLEY LEVEY
Special to The New York Times.

ALBANY, Aug. 22—A labor drive to draft Mayor Wagner of New York as the Democratic candidate for United States Senator was developing here today.

Leaders of the State Congress of Industrial Organizations, which will open its sixteenth annual convention tomorrow, reported strong sentiment for the Mayor among the group's 1,000,-600 members throughout the state.

Mr. Wagner, who took himself out of contention for the nomination earlier this week, will speak tomorrow afternoon. His appearance is expected to inspire a demonstration among the delegates urging him to change his mind.

Sharing the platform with him will be Senator Herbert H. Lehman. Senator Lehman announced yesterday that he would not seek re-election. At the same time he said he would support Mr. Wagner with "satisfaction pleasure and full confidence" if the Mayor were the choice of the Democratic State Convention next month.

The feeling among union delegates gathering here was that Mr. Wagner was a "natural" for the nomination. They cited his labor record as Mayor and that of his father, the late Senator Robert F. Wagner, author of the Wagner Labor Relations Act.

The State C. I. O. has indicated that its political activity in the coming campaign will be vigorous. Louis Hollander, president of the organization, said committees would be formed throughout the state to work with groups representing

Continued on Page 18, Column 6

## Character by Name of Joe Smith Nearly Opens Up the No. 2 Race

Special to The New York Times.

SAN FRANCISCO, Aug. 22—A "Democrat" bored by the unanimity of the proceedings, infiltrated the Republican National Convention tonight and nominated "Joe Smith" for Vice President.

The one lonely "no-man" in the whole convention was Terry Carpenter, a bona fide delegate from Nebraska, who served as a Democrat in Congress from 1933 to 1935.

His first effort was to put Secretary of Interior Fred A. Seaton of Nebraska in nomination as Vice President, but Joseph W. Martin Jr. of Massachusetts, convention chairman, refused on the ground that this was against Mr. Seaton's wishes.

But that did not stop Mr. Carpenter, a large, bespectacled white-haired man, who insisted on substituting the name of "Joe Smith."

"Joe who?" inquired Mr. Martin. "Joe Smith," firmly replied Mrs. George P. Abel of Lincoln, chairman of the Nebraska delegation.

Reporters and television operators immediately converged on the lone dissenter, from all over the Cow Palace, as Gov. Christian A. Herter of Massachusetts was starting to nominate Richard M. Nixon.

The commotion was too much for Chairman Martin.

Banging his gavel and leaning over the rostrum he said:

"Take your Joe Smith and get out of here."

The reporters, together with Mr. Carpenter, were pushed from the hall by the sergeants-at-arms. Once outside, Mr. Carpenter was pinned against a wall. In that uncomfortable position

Continued on Page 17, Column 3

"All the News That's Fit to Print"

# The New York Times.

LATE CITY EDITION
Condensation of U. S. Weather Bureau forecast: Some cloudiness today; cloudy tonight. Clearing, cooler tomorrow.
Temperature range today: 66—50.
Temperature range yesterday: 65.4—52.2.
Full U. S. Weather Bureau Report, Page 69.



VOL. CVI . No. 36,082. Entered as Second-Class Matter, Post Office, New York, N. Y. NEW YORK, WEDNESDAY, NOVEMBER 7, 1956. Times Square, New York 36, N. Y. Telephone LAckawanna 4-1000 FIVE CENTS

# *EISENHOWER BY A LANDSLIDE; BATTLE FOR CONGRESS CLOSE; JAVITS VICTOR OVER WAGNER*

## *Suez Warfare Stopped Under British-French Cease-Fire*

## MAYOR CONCEDES

### Javits, Swept In With the Eisenhower Tide, Wins Stiff Contest

**Vote for Senator**
CITY SUMMARY

| | Javits (Rep.) | Wagner (Dem.-Lib.) |
|---|---|---|
| Manhattan ... | 270,146 | 393,462 |
| Bronx ....... | 218,895 | 374,810 |
| Brooklyn .... | 398,088 | 605,002 |
| Queens ...... | 400,832 | 372,505 |
| Richmond ... | 49,694 | 32,881 |
| Total ...... | 1,337,655 | 1,778,660 |
| Upstate | 2,362,618 | 1,478,238 |
| Grand total | 3,700,273 | 3,256,898 |

All E. D.'s of 4,607 in city and 6,522 of 6,525 upstate.

By DOUGLAS DALES

Attorney General Jacob K. Javits was swept to victory yesterday in the Eisenhower Republican landslide in his race against Mayor Wagner for the United States Senate.

Mayor Wagner conceded defeat in a statement at 1:22 A. M. after the trend to Javits' victory became unmistakable.

Mr. Wagner carried three boroughs in the city—Manhattan, Brooklyn and the Bronx—but lost in Queens and Richmond.

The city-wide complete totals gave Mr. Javits 1,337,655 votes to 1,778,660 for Mayor Wagner. The Mayor's total included 233,560 on the Liberal party line. The Liberal line attracted 404,769 votes in the city four years ago, when the party ran its own candidate for the Senate, George S. Counts.

The victor's margin was expected to reach 444,000 with the final results. With all city districts and 6,522 of 6,525 districts upstate reported, Mr. Javits had an edge of 443,375.

Mayor Wagner carried two of the fifty-seven upstate counties, Erie and Albany. Eisenhower carried both.

Everywhere outside the city, Mr. Javits ran substantially behind the President's vote. On the other hand, Mayor Wagner ran well ahead of Adlai E. Stevenson, the Democratic candidate for President.

In view of the size of the

Continued on Page 26, Column 2

## PRESIDENT SCORES NEW HIGH IN STATE

### Plurality Tops 1,500,000 as He Cuts Rival's City Edge

**State Presidential Vote**
CITY SUMMARY

| | Eisenhower (Rep.) | Stevenson (Dem.-Lib.) |
|---|---|---|
| Manhattan .. | 299,929 | 378,018 |
| Bronx ...... | 256,909 | 343,656 |
| Brooklyn ... | 459,703 | 558,187 |
| Queens ..... | 471,144 | 313,311 |
| Richmond .. | 64,236 | 196,653 |
| Total .... | 1,551,921 | 1,614,825 |
| Upstate .... | 2,766,183 | 1,127,403 |
| Grand total | 4,318,104 | 2,742,228 |

All E. D.'s of 4,607 in city and 6,522 of 6,525 upstate.

By LEO EGAN

President Eisenhower swept New York yesterday by a plurality that dwarfed all previous records.

With sixty-one of the state's 11,132 election districts still to report this morning, General Eisenhower's margin exceeded 1,500,000.

The previous record for a Presidential plurality in New York was established in 1920, when the late Warren G. Harding, Republican, defeated James M. Cox, Democrat, by 1,139,927.

All the missing districts are in Republican territory upstate.

Continued on Page 23, Column 1

## *An International Summary: The Mideast and Hungary*

*Following are summaries of the leading developments in the Middle East and Europe. The full foreign news report begins on the first page of the second part.*

**Cease-Fire Is On**

Britain and France put a cease-fire into effect and halted their advance in Egypt. Prime Minister Eden told Commons that conditions had been established for an international police force under the United Nations to promote settlement of Middle Eastern issues.

**Invaders Hold Canal**

The invasion forces claimed control of the Suez Canal Zone. They took Port Said and drove south before the cease-fire became effective.

**Egyptians Halt Fight**

The Egyptians decided to hold their fire at the deadline in the hope that the United Nations resolution of Nov. 2, providing for withdrawal of all forces behind armistice lines, would be carried out.

**Soviet May Send 'Volunteers'**

Indications in Moscow were that Soviet "volunteers" who began applying for service with Egyptian forces might go to the Middle East despite the cease-fire. Moscow broadcast a Cairo appeal for aid.

**Troop Withdrawal Asked**

Asian and Arab states drafted a United Nations resolution calling on Britain, France and Israel to withdraw their troops from Egypt immediately. A special session of the General Assembly called for last night was postponed until this morning.

**Hungarian Battle Persists**

Stubborn Hungarian revolutionary forces are continuing to fight the Soviet army in Budapest, according to diplomatic reports received in Vienna. Women and children were said to be fighting alongside the men in a house-to-house struggle. The General Assembly scheduled a special session this afternoon to consider Soviet intervention in Hungary.

## EISENHOWER SETS RECORD IN JERSEY

### Margin of 700,000 Carries All 21 Counties—G. O. P. Wins 2 Hudson Seats

By GEORGE CABLE WRIGHT

President Eisenhower yesterday scored the greatest victory in New Jersey political history.

With most of the state's ballots tallied early this morning, his margin over Adlai E. Stevenson had soared above 700,000, almost double that of 1952. He became the first candidate in modern times to carry all twenty-one counties.

The returns were:

PRESIDENT
4,017 districts out of 4,155.

| | |
|---|---|
| Eisenhower ........... | 1,522,971 |
| Stevenson ........... | 821,067 |

The most startling aspect of his victory was the complete turnabout of Hudson County, for half a century a Democratic stronghold.

This county gave the President a majority of 76,554. In 1952 Mr. Stevenson had carried Hudson by 7,886 votes.

In fact, Republicans swept every county contest. When residents of Hudson awake this morning it is certain that many will find it hard to believe that for the next two years they will be represented in Congress by not one, but two, Republicans. There was no precedent there for that.

A third Democratic incumbent, Representative Harrison A. Williams Jr., went down to defeat in Union County.

Thus, the Democratic representation of six in the House was cut in half. All eight Republican incumbents were re-elected.

President Eisenhower became the first Presidential candidate to carry the solidly Democratic bailiwick of Jersey City since Warren G. Harding did it in 1920. Long the citadel of the late Frank Hague and now of John Kenny, it gave General Eisenhower a majority of 31,527 over Mr. Stevenson. In 1952 the Democratic candidate had carried the city by 8,251.

But the trouncing of the former Illinois Governor was by no means restricted to Hudson. Camden and Mercer Counties, which also went to Mr. Stevenson in 1952, likewise turned their backs to him this year.

Continued on Page 28, Column 5

## BUSH RE-ELECTED IN CONNECTICUT

### Plurality for Eisenhower of 303,036 Biggest in State in a Presidential Race

By RICHARD H. PARKE
Special to The New York Times.

HARTFORD, Nov 6—President Eisenhower scored an easy victory in Connecticut today. He carried to victory with him Senator Prescott S. Bush, the Republican incumbent.

The President's plurality of 303,036 votes over Adlai E. Stevenson, Democratic candidate, was the greatest margin the State ever has given a Presidential contender. The previous high figure was 136,138 votes, achieved by Prseident Coolidge in 1924.

The President, whose 1952 plurality of 129,363 was considered of landslide proportions, defeated Mr. Stevenson today by 708,995 votes to 405,959, according to complete but unofficial returns.

The Republican sweep was general throughout the state. It carried in Senator Bush by a plurality of 129,544 votes. He defeated his Democratic opponent, Representative Thomas J. Dodd, by 607,330 to 477,876.

The Republicans also retained

Continued on Page 28, Column 5

## SENATE IN DOUBT

### Democrats Lag in East on War Issue but Gain in the West

By WILLIAM S. WHITE

The Democrats and Republicans fought along a swaying electoral battle line early today for control of the oncoming Eighty-fifth Congress.

Not all the power of President Eisenhower's landslide victory had been enough to put his Republican Congressional colleagues in front.

The Senate race, in which the Republicans were attempting to overturn a present 49-to-47 Democratic margin of control, was an affair of hairbreadth drama.

Small net Republican gains for the House of Representatives were indicated. But whether these would continue or would be enough remained wholly in doubt.

The Republicans needed a net gain of 15 House seats, and the capture of 2 additional and now vacant seats that had been Republican.

The pattern of the Congressional contest was this: The East, more sensitive than other sections to the last-minute issue involved in the Middle Eastern and Central European war crises, on the whole was hitting the Democrats hard. The appeal of "don't change horses in midstream" was strong in this area. In the interior, however, Democratic organizational strength, farm discontent and other factors were turning up great Democratic strength.

**Cooper Wins in Kentucky**

The position on the Senate in some critical states was this:

KENTUCKY—A gain of one Republican seat in former Senator John Sherman Cooper's defeat of his Democratic challenger, Lawrence Wetherby, for the seat made vacant by the death of Senator Alben W. Barkley. The possibility of another gain for the Republicans in the fact that the assistant Democratic leader of the Senate, Earle C. Clements, was running behind Thruston B. Morton, a former assistant Secretary of State in the Eisenhower Administration.

NEW YORK—A Republican gain in the victory of Jacob K. Javits over Mayor Wagner for the seat being vacated by Senator Herbert H. Lehman, Democrat-Liberal.

OHIO—A Democratic gain in the defeat by Gov. Frank J. Lausche of Senator George H. Bender.

ILLINOIS—Senator Everett M. Dirksen, Republican, ran ahead of his Democratic opponent, Richard Stengel.

PENNSYLVANIA—Joseph S.

Continued on Page 3, Column 1

## *Coudert Wins in Close Contest; Vote in Queens 7th Rechecked*

By CLAYTON KNOWLES

The Republicans emerged from a hard-fought Congressional campaign early today with a possible net gain of one in the state delegation to the House of Representatives.

At 4:20 A. M. a final decision rested on the outcome of the race in the Seventh district of Queens. Here Representative James J. Delaney, Democratic incumbent, claimed victory at 4:15 A. M. by forty votes, but a final tally was unavailable.

An hour and a half earlier, Delaney supporters were conceding the election of Joseph Stockinger, a Republican, but the contest was so close that all 217 districts were being rechecked.

The announced vote for 202 districts was 72,186 for Mr. Stockinger to 72,112 for Mr. Delaney, who ran with Liberal party backing.

The prospect that the Republicans would pick up a House seat in the state, giving them twenty-seven of a total of forty-three, arose when Representative Frederic R. Coudert Jr. staged an eleventh-hour triumph in the Manhattan Seventeenth District.

He prevailed once more over Anthony B. Akers, Democrat-Liberal who had come within 314 votes of defeating him in 1954. This time Mr. Coudert won, 68,862 votes to 66,207.

If Mr. Delaney should go to defeat, the Republicans will have seven of the twenty-two House seats filled in the city.

President Eisenhower's land-

Continued on Page 29, Column 6

PRESIDENT EISENHOWER

VICE PRESIDENT NIXON

## G. O. P. MAKES BID TO CAPTURE HOUSE

### Picks Up 9 Seats in East, but Drive Eases in West —Midwest to Decide

By JOHN D. MORRIS

Republicans got off to a fast start in their bid to recapture control of the House of Representatives, but appeared to lose steam early today as returns trickled in from the West.

As of 3 A. M., results from yesterday's Congressional races indicated a decided Republican trend, with some major upsets for the Democrats. However, with control of nearly two-thirds of the 435 seats still in doubt, victory for either party was far from certain.

The undecided contests were almost entirely in the Midwest, where the issue of declining farm income was a factor favoring the Democrats, and in the Far West.

**G. O. P. Gains in East**

Such returns as were available from those areas indicated possible Democratic gains in Iowa, California and South Dakota.

Eastward, where the only decisive tallies were available, Republicans had picked up nine seats held by Democrats in the Eighty-fourth Congress while holding their own in all other contests where returns were conclusive. One, in New York City, was subpect to a recount. Democrats had failed to capture any Republican seat except one that they took in the Maine election on Sept. 10.

Republican incumbents were easy victors in a number of contests that had promised to be close.

The most outstanding upsets were in New Jersey, where the Hudson county Democratic stronghold of the late Mayor Frank Hague of Jersey City unseated its two Democratic Representatives, T. James Tumulty and Alfred D. Sieminski, in the Thirteenth and Fourteenth Congressional Districts.

Mr. Sieminski lost to Norman H. Roth, Republican. Mr. Tumulty, a 300-pound legislator, was defeated by Vincent J. Dellay, Republican.

A third Democratic incumbent in New Jersey, Harrison A. Williams, lost to Florence P. Dwyer, Republican.

Republicans also picked up one D[illegible]cratic seat in Connecticut, one in Deleware, one in Pennsylvania, one in Indiana and

Continued on Page 3, Column 3

## *Stevenson Concedes Defeat and Wishes President Success*

*Stevenson and Kefauver talks appear on Page 13.*

By HARRISON E. SALISBURY
Special to The New York Times.

CHICAGO, Wednesday, Nov. 7—Adlai E. Stevenson conceded the election of President Eisenhower in a statement made public at 12:25 A. M. Central standard time today (1:25 Eastern standard time).

In a telegram to President Eisenhower, the Democratic candidate expressed his understanding of "grave difficulties" that the Administration faced and wished all success to General Eisenhower in the years ahead.

Mr. Stevenson coupled his telegram of congratulations to the President with an appeal to his followers to carry forward in the crusade for what he called a "New America."

He called on America's leaders to recognize that the nation "wants to face up squarely to the facts of today's world."

"We don't want to draw back from them," Mr. Stevenson said. "We can't. We are ready for the test that we know history has set for us."

Mr. Stevenson in his statement took note of the troubled conditions of the world.

"Beyond the seas, in much of the world, in Russia, in China, in Hungary, in all the trembling satellites, partisan controversy is forbidden and dissent suppressed," Mr. Stevenson said.

Mr. Stevenson also took note

Continued on Page 13, Column 5

## Electoral Vote by States

| | Eisenhower | Stevenson | | Eisenhower | Stevenson |
|---|---|---|---|---|---|
| Ala. | — | 11 | Nev. | 3 | — |
| Ariz. | 4 | — | N. H. | 4 | — |
| Ark. | — | 8 | N. J. | 16 | — |
| Calif. | 32 | — | N. M. | 4 | — |
| Colo. | 6 | — | N. Y. | 45 | — |
| Conn. | 8 | — | N. C. | — | 14 |
| Del. | 3 | — | N. D. | 4 | — |
| Fla. | 10 | — | Ohio | 25 | — |
| Ga. | — | 12 | Okla. | 8 | — |
| Idaho | 4 | — | Ore. | 6 | — |
| Ill. | 27 | — | Pa. | 32 | — |
| Ind. | 13 | — | R. Isl. | 4 | — |
| Iowa | 10 | — | S. C. | — | 8 |
| Kan. | 8 | — | S. D. | 4 | — |
| Ky. | 10 | — | Tenn. | 11 | — |
| La. | 10 | — | Texas | 24 | — |
| Me. | 5 | — | Utah | 4 | — |
| Md. | 9 | — | Vt. | 3 | — |
| Mass. | 16 | — | Va. | 12 | — |
| Mich. | 20 | — | Wash. | 9 | — |
| Minn. | 11 | — | W. Va. | 8 | — |
| Miss. | — | 8 | Wisc. | 12 | — |
| Mo. | — | 13 | Wyo. | 3 | — |
| Mont. | 4 | — | | | |
| Neb. | 6 | — | Total | 457 | 74 |

## EISENHOWER VOWS TO TOIL FOR PEACE

### Hails Landslide Re-election as Proof Nation Wants 'Modern Republicanism'

*Texts of the Eisenhower and Nixon talks on Page 12.*

By RUSSELL BAKER
Special to The New York Times.

WASHINGTON, Wednesday, Nov. 7—President Eisenhower hailed his landslide re-election victory today as proof that his "modern Republicanism has now proved itself and America has approved of modern Republicanism."

He pledged in a victory statement early this morning to work with "whatever talents the good God has given me for 168,000,000 Americans here at home and for peace in the world."

Addressing a jubilant crowd of party workers at Republican election headquarters here and the nation, over television, the President declared that so long as the G.O.P. pursued the "ideals, the hopes and aspirations" of the people, it would continue to flourish.

"If it is anything less," he said, "it is only a conspiracy to seize power. And the Republican party is not that."

**'Looks to the Future'**

Thus, in his moment of triumph, General Eisenhower claimed a sweeping triumph for what his Administration's philosophers had styled the "new Republicanism" and what he himself termed this morning "modern Republicanism."

"Modern Republicanism," he said, "looks to the future and this means it will gain constantly new recruits." So long as it continued to remain "modern," he added, it would "continue to increase in power and influence for decades to come."

So long as it clings to its "modern" ideals, the President declared, it would "point the way to peace among nations and prosperity, advancing standards here at home in which everyone will share."

The President delivered his victory statement at 1:45 A. M., about fifteen minutes after this restive crowd gathered in the mammoth ballroom of the Sheraton-Park Hotel had heard Adlai E. Stevenson concede defeat in Chicago.

General Eisenhower had been waiting upstairs in a third-floor suite for three and a half hours,

Continued on Page 13, Column 1

## 41 STATES TO G.O.P.

### President Sweeps All the North and West, Scores in South

By JAMES RESTON

Dwight David Eisenhower won yesterday the most spectacular Presidential election victory since Franklin D. Roosevelt submerged Alfred M. Landon in 1936.

The smiling 66-year-old hero of the Normandy invasion, who was in a Denver hospital recuperating from a heart attack just a year ago today, thus became the first Republican in this century to win two successive Presidential elections. William McKinley did it in 1896 and 1900.

Adlai E. Stevenson of Illinois, who lost to Mr. Eisenhower four years ago, thirty-nine states to nine, conceded defeat at 1:25 this morning.

At 4:45 A. M. President Eisenhower had won forty-one states to seven for Mr. Stevenson. His electoral lead at that time was 457 to 74 for Stevenson, and his popular vote was 25,071,331 to 18,337,434—up 2 per cent over 1952. Two hundred and sixty-six electoral votes are needed for election.

**Victory in All Areas**

This was a national victory in every conceivable way. It started in Connecticut. It swept every state in New England. It took New York by a plurality of more than 1,500,000. It carried all the Middle Atlantic states, all the Midwest, all the Rocky Mountain states and everything beyond the Rockies.

More than that, the Republican tide swept along the border states and to the South, carried all the states won by the G.O.P. there in 1952—Virginia, Texas, Tennessee and Florida—and even took Louisiana for the first time since the Hayes-Tilden election of 1876.

For the President and his 43-year old Vice Presidential running mate, Richard M. Nixon of California, who carried much of the Republican campaign, it was a more impressive victory than for the Republican party.

So close were many races for

Continued on Page 2, Column 3

## CLARK LEADS DUFF IN PENNSYLVANIA

### Democrat's Edge Dropping —President Takes State

By WILLIAM G. WEART
Special to The New York Times.

PHILADELPHIA, Wednesday, Nov. 7—Joseph S. Clark Jr., former Mayor of Philadelphia, was running ahead of Senator James H. Duff early today.

But his margin was ebbing as returns from rural areas and small towns began to offset the lead he piled up in large cities.

President Eisenhower won the state's thirty-two electoral votes by a plurality that was steadily mounting.

Mr. Clark expressed disappointment at the defeat of his party's standard-bearer. He attributed General Eisenhower's victory to his "personal popularity." Mr. Clark's campaign manager, Mayor Richardson Dilworth of Philadelphia, said the President's re-election was due to the "emotion caused by the war situation."

In the event the final tally in the Senatorial race is close, an estimated 50,000 absentee votes cast by servicemen and hospitalized veterans may decide the outcome. Under the law, absentee ballots are mailed to county

Continued on Page 18, Column 6

"All the News That's Fit to Print"

# The New York Times.

LATE CITY EDITION
Condensation of U.S. Weather Bureau forecast:
Partly cloudy today and tomorrow with rising temperatures.
Temperature range today: 56—43
Temperature range yesterday: 43.8—36.6
Full U. S. Weather Bureau Report, Page 57

© 1957, by The New York Times Company.

VOL. CVI...No. 36,158. Entered as Second-Class Matter, Post Office, New York, N. Y. NEW YORK, TUESDAY, JANUARY 22, 1957. Times Square, New York 36, N. Y. Telephone Lackawanna 4-1000 FIVE CENTS

# EISENHOWER, IN SECOND INAUGURAL, CALLS UPON COUNTRY TO SACRIFICE FOR A GLOBAL 'PEACE WITH JUSTICE'

Associated Press Wirephoto

HAT'S OFF TO SPECTATORS: President Eisenhower acknowledging cheers of crowd as car moves along Constitution Avenue in Washington during the inaugural parade.

## HE BARS ISOLATION

### Stresses Duty to World as Thousands Watch Oath Ceremonies

*Text of the Inaugural address is printed on Page 17.*

By W. H. LAWRENCE

Special to The New York Times.

WASHINGTON, Jan. 21 — President Eisenhower summoned his countrymen today to pay the high, full price of building a just peace based on moral law.

This was the message of his short, thirteen-and-one-half-minute Inaugural address, as the Republicans celebrated their party's greatest Presidential electoral victory.

The President repeated at a public ceremonial before the Capitol the oath of office he had taken privately yesterday when his first term ended. Then he proclaimed a kind of global "Eisenhower doctrine."

He warned that "rarely has this earth known such peril as today." The President stated as his fixed purpose the "building of a peace with justice in a world where moral law prevails."

He termed "international communism and the power that it controls" the great "divisive force" in the world.

**Pledges Continued Aid**

General Eisenhower asserted the nation's deep involvement and responsibility in events that might lead to controversy or conflict in every part of the world "whether they touch upon the affairs of a vast region, the fate of an island in the Pacific or the use of a canal in the Middle East."

He pledged continuing United States aid to those who would be free of foreign domination or free "from grinding poverty."

The nation watched and listened by television and radio as the President and Vice President Richard M. Nixon formally undertook obligations to preserve, protect and defend the Constitution. It then looked in on the big inaugural parade.

Police officers estimated the crowd at the Capitol at 20,000, about half the size of the crowd four years ago at the President's first inauguration. Police Chief Robert V. Murray estimated the crowd along the parade route at 750,000, the same estimate he gave in 1953.

**President Appears Fit**

Standing in his open car, the President bowed, waved, and tipped his black Homburg to the cheers of the tens of thousands who lined the historic two-mile route between the Capitol and the White House. He looked remarkably fit for a man who had passed the age of 66 and in the last sixteen months had suffered a severe heart attack and an emergency abdominal operation for ileitis.

The mood of his inaugural speech contrasted sharply with the celebrations of his Republican admirers, who attended four full-dress inaugural balls tonight.

The President stated in somber tones the continuing threat

Continued on Page 16, Column 3

# SUSPECT IS HELD AS 'MAD BOMBER'; HE ADMITS ROLE

### Files of Edison Co. Lead to Ex-Employe in Waterbury —Extradition Is Planned

### NO EVIDENCE IN HOME

### Worker Quoted as Saying He Was 'Gassed' at Plant, Contracted Tuberculosis

The police here announced early today that a 54-year-old man had admitted that he is the so-called Mad Bomber. The police said the man had confessed at Waterbury, Conn., where he is being questioned. They added that "all things indicate he is the man."

"It looks good but it has to be checked out," a high police official said. It was believed the suspect would be extradited to New York.

At 3 A. M. Capt. Ernest Paul of the Waterbury Police Department said: "There's no question that he's the Mad Bomber."

At 3:30 A. M. today the suspect was still being questioned.

The suspect was identified as George Metesky of 17 Fourth Street, Waterbury. He was described as a husky well-built man who resides with his two sisters.

The police said he was a former employe of the Consolidated Edison Company.

**30 Bombs in 16 Years**

The bomber has planted more than thirty of his home-made devices in public places over the last sixteen years. With the finding of a bomb in the New York Public Library on Christmas Eve an epidemic of false bomb alarms started here.

The police had theorized the bomber harbored a grudge against the Edison company. In thirteen letters, notes or postcards written to the police or other persons, the bomber was quoted as saying he had never been compensated for a crippling injury sustained while working for Con Edison years ago.

A number of high police officials left here for Waterbury early today. They included Chief of Detectives James B. Leggett, Deputy Chief Inspector Edward Byrnes, in charge of Manhattan West detectives; Deputy Commissioner Aloysius Melia, in charge of legal matters; Acting Captain Thomas Curley, in command of the detail assigned to the bomber investigation; members of the Bomb Squad and the Police Laboratory.

The police said the suspect was arrested in his home shortly before midnight by four New York detectives. It was said no

Continued on Page 58, Column 5

# 4 Nations in Baghdad Pact Support U.S. Mideast Plan

### Moslem Leaders Regard Eisenhower Policy as Peace Effort

*Text of the communiqué will be found on Page 3.*

Special to The New York Times.

ANKARA, Turkey, Jan. 21—The four Moslem nations allied in the Baghdad Pact announced today their support of President Eisenhower's program for the Middle East.

In a communiqué issued after their meeting here, Turkey, Pakistan, Iran and Iraq described the Eisenhower proposal as "best designed to maintain peace" in the Middle East and to "advance the economic well-being of the people."

The plan "is not designed to create spheres of influence nor to enslave the peoples of the Middle East," the communiqué added.

Several seemingly ambiguous

Continued on Page 3, Column 2

### Autonomy of Jordan Is in Peril, Observers in Amman Fear

By SAM POPE BREWER

Special to The New York Times.

BEIRUT, Lebanon, Jan. 21—Jordan is in the midst of a crisis that threatens her existence as a nation.

The best-qualified observers in Amman, the Jordanian capital, say it is doubtful Jordan will last out the year as an independent state.

She has just accepted a guarantee from three Arab states to replace the annual subsidy she always has had from Britain. That is looked upon as throwing her definitely into the Egyptian camp, orienting her policy on Moscow.

Jordan is not an economically viable unit. The British are expected to stop their subsidy at the end of March. At roughly $23,000,000, it is more than half

Continued on Page 3, Column 5

# GOMULKA VICTORY AT POLLS TO BRING A PARTY SHAKE-UP

### Polish Leader Plans to Use People's Mandate to Oust Foes From Organization

By SYDNEY GRUSON

Special to The New York Times.

WARSAW, Jan. 21—A thorough housecleaning of the Polish Communist party will follow the tremendous election endorsement won by Wladyslaw Gomulka, the party's First Secretary.

M. Gomulka was reliably reported today to have finally convinced himself that a showdown struggle for control of the United Workers (Communist) party is necessary. The party machinery has remained in the hands of a pro-Soviet faction named for the suburban village of Natolin, where its leaders used to caucus.

Yesterday's election armed M. Gomulka mightily for a party fight. Although official results will not be known until tomorrow or Wednesday, it seems certain that a national turnout of more than 90 per cent of those entitled to vote was achieved without the use of direct pressure or police methods.

**Politburo Wins Seats**

The entire nine-man Politburo chosen against Soviet opposition during the political crisis last October won election to the new Sejm (Parliament). So apparently did all the preferred candidates on the single common National Front list presented to the voters.

Meeting with some of his supporters to discuss the election victory, M. Gomulka told them, "Now we are going to work on the party." One of the first consequences of his determination was a decision to postpone until 1958 the party congress originally scheduled for this March.

M. Gomulka had tried to achieve party unity by forgiving and forgetting the Natolinists' opposition to his restoration as First Secretary last October and to the program of a more liberal, moderate Communist system represented by his leadership.

**Campaign Tactics Noted**

The campaign within the election campaign waged by his opposition was the decisive factor in changing M. Gomulka's mind.

The opposition smeared M. Gomulka's closest supporters with every kind of innuendo about their personal lives and their political pasts. It used the most blatant anti-Semitic slogans to try to discredit people close to M. Gomulka and to defeat Roman Zambrowski, the only Jew in the Politburo.

As M. Gomulka's supporters see it, the Natolinists had long ago given up trying to overthrow M. Gomulka as First Secretary. But they had hoped to isolate him by defeating some of his most prominent supporters in the election for a new Parliament. They believed this would have forced M. Gomulka to make room for Natolin representatives in the Politburo again.

M. Gomulka apparently began to realize this danger only after a Natolin man who had been

Continued on Page 10, Column 5

# Doria Settlement Reported; Pool for Claims Considered

By RUSSELL PORTER

The Swedish American and Italian Lines were reported yesterday to be near an out-of-court settlement of claims against each other because of the collision of the Stockholm and the Andrea Doria. If the settlement goes through as reported, its principal terms would be:

¶The abandonment by the Italian Line of its $30,000,000 claim for the sinking of the Doria, and by the Swedish Line of its $1,000,000 claim for the crushed bow of the Stockholm.

¶The end of each line's attempt to prove the other's "privity" or corporate share in negligence as a cause of the accident and thus to remove its limitation of liability.

¶The establishment by both lines of a limited-liability pool of $4,400,000 to $6,200,000 to meet death, injury, cargo and baggage claims on behalf of passengers and shippers.

**Claimants Number 2,000**

About 2,000 claimants have filed more than $116,000,000 in damage suits against both lines. About $85,000,000 represents claims in behalf of shippers and passengers. Under the reported agreement these claims would have to be scaled down to between $4,400,000 and $6,200,000.

Some lawyers say many of the claims overlap and the total can be cut to about $5,000,000 by further negotiations if a final settlement is reached between the two lines. They say many such claims are customarily filed for sums far in excess of provable loss, as a "margin of safety" principle.

Under international practice in admiralty law shipping lines enjoy limitation of liability for a collision to the value of ships after an accident unless "privity" is proved. In the case of the Stockholm its value after the accident was $4,000,000. Thus under the reported settlement the

Continued on Page 58, Column 2

# ISRAEL TO SUBMIT GAZA AIMS TODAY

### Hammarskjold Will Receive Proposal for Rule of Strip Under U. N. Supervision

By THOMAS J. HAMILTON

Special to The New York Times.

UNITED NATIONS, N. Y., Jan. 21—Israel's plan for administering the Gaza Strip under United Nations supervision will be submitted to Secretary General Dag Hammarskjold tomorrow.

The plan calls for the withdrawal of Israeli forces, with all civil and social services placed under the direction of the United Nations. Who would administer these services was not specified in reports available here. A dispatch from Jerusalem published today said that Israel was willing to provide and pay for all the services.

Under the plan, the Israeli police would remain, but presumably the United Nations Emergency Force would be stationed in the strip pending a definitive settlement.

Several delegates, however, expressed doubt that the Secretary General would do anything more than report the Israeli offer to the General Assembly.

**Lodge Asked Deployment**

In fact, it is uncertain whether, without Assembly authorization, he would go so far as to deploy the United Nations force in the manner suggested last week by the United States.

Henry Cabot Lodge Jr. of the United States has requested that the force be deployed along the Egyptian-Israeli armistice demarcation line and in the Gulf of Aqaba area to prevent a recurrence of "hostile activities."

Mr. Lodge's request was understood by some Western European delegates to mean that the United Nations force should be stationed in both areas in such a way as to prevent the return of Egyptian forces.

Israel maintains that if Egypt regains control, the Gulf of Aqaba area will be used to blockade the Israeli port of Elath and Egyptian raids on Israel will be organized in the Gaza Strip.

**Egypt's Stand Given**

However, Egypt, with the support of the Asian-African and Soviet blocs, insists that Israel withdraw unconditionally under the Assembly's Nov. 2 cease-fire resolution. Israel's withdrawal from the rest of the Sinai Peninsula is to be completed tomorrow.

The essence of the situation is that no resolution instructing Mr. Hammarskjold to station the force in the Gaza Strip and the Gulf of Aqaba area seems likely to get the necessary two-thirds vote in the Assembly.

On the other hand, the Asian-African and Soviet blocs would probably find it impossible to produce a majority for a resolution instructing the Secretary

Continued on Page 5, Column 3

# TEAMSTERS CLASH DISTURBS MEANY

### Union Chief to Discuss Battle With Senators at Parley

By A. H. RASKIN

Special to The New York Times.

MIAMI BEACH, Jan. 21—George Meany said today he was "very much concerned" over the battle between the International Brotherhood of Teamsters and the Senate Permanent Subcommittee on Investigations.

The president of the American Federation of Labor and Congress of Industrial Organizations announced that he would make the dispute the "first order of business" at the midwinter meeting of the federation's executive council here next Monday.

At hearings in Washington last week leaders of the 1,400,000-member truck union challenged the authority of the subcommittee, headed by Senator John L. McClellan, Democrat of Arkansas. The teamsters balked at answering questions about union racketeering or the use of union funds to pay the personal bills of union officials.

Mr. Meany declined to give his own views in advance of next week's meeting. However, close associates said he believed strongly that any union leader who refused to account for his handling of union money should get out.

In pre-session discussions with other A. F. L.-C. I. O. execu-

Continued on Page 30, Column 3

# Stark Will Resist Any Attempt To Ease Him Out of City Hall Job

### Expects to Run Again for Council Head as a Step Toward Mayor's Office

By RICHARD AMPER

Abe Stark, President of the City Council, made it clear yesterday that he would resist any attempt to ease him out of City Hall and the Mayoralty picture.

The 61-year-old Brooklyn clothier declared in an interview that "under no circumstances," now or in the future, would he seek or accept the Borough Presidency of Brooklyn.

He thus put at rest assorted speculation that high Democratic party leaders had offered to back him for the Brooklyn post to remove him from the line of succession to the office of Mayor.

His automatic elevation to fill a vacancy in the Mayoralty has been used as an argument against Mayor Wagner's running for the United States Senate. The argument was used by some who contended Mr. Stark lacked qualification and stature for the job.

Mr. Stark said that no political leader had suggested, tacitly or otherwise, that he run for Borough President nor had any

The New York Times

Abe Stark

politician offered to support him for the job. Nor has he been offered any state office, he said. He added that he would not accept any.

If Mayor Wagner decides to seek re-election—and Mr. Stark said he expected the Mayor to —he will run again for Council President. He said he

Continued on Page 24, Column 7

# HARRIMAN SPURS ROAD CONTRACTS

### Asks for Special Fund to Let Construction Begin Before Federal Aid Is Available

By LEO EGAN

Special to The New York Times.

ALBANY, Jan. 21—Governor Harriman has asked Republican legislative leaders for a $194,537,384 emergency appropriation to speed construction of Federal-aid highways in New York.

In conferences with Republican chairmen of legislative fiscal committees, Paul H. Appleby, State Budget Director, has explained that an early appropriation would permit work on these highways to get under way by the summer.

Without the appropriation it would be impossible for the state to let the highway contracts until Federal funds became available. This would mean that work on some contracts could not start until next year.

The entire amount of the appropriation would be refunded to the state by the Federal Government.

**Tax Collections Rise**

Mr. Harriman's plan for speeding construction became known today as revenue reports showed that state tax collections were running even further ahead of estimates than Mr. Harriman anticipated two weeks ago when he submitted his annual message to the Legislature.

Instead of a $30,000,000 surplus of revenues over expenditures for the fiscal year that ends March 31, the surplus may reach as much as $35,000,000. On this basis, the state would wind up the fiscal year with $93,000,000 more than Mr. Harriman estimated at the close of the last legislative session. At that time he calculated that it would be necessary to draw on accumulated reserves to the extent of $58,000,000 to balance this year's budget.

In December tax collections amounted to $129,433,899, an increase of $41,200,000 over the corresponding month of 1955. About $34,000,000 of the increase was attributed to advancement of the time for paying an installment of the corporate franchise tax.

For the first nine months of the present fiscal year collections were $1,044,184,490, an increase of $91,134,629 over the

Continued on Page 22, Column 4

# Nixon Expects Wider Role In Government and Party

By WILLIAM S. WHITE

Special to The New York Times.

WASHINGTON, Jan. 21—Richard M. Nixon was sworn today for his second term as perhaps the most powerful Vice President in the country's history. Two hours before taking the oath at the Capitol he made it plain that with the President's assent he proposed to broaden in the next four years the already significant responsibilities he had increasingly exercised in the four years now gone.

The general tone of the Vice President's comments led some politicians at the Capitol to believe that he was staking out a claim to be President Eisenhower's logical successor.

All this was in the background as Mr. Nixon stood with uplifted hand to respond to the oath of his office as it was gravely and impassively read to him by his potential chief rival, Senator William F. Knowland of California.

"Congratulations, Mr. Vice President," said Senator Knowland stolidly when the brief ceremony had ended.

Mr. Knowland, the Republican Senate leader, is retiring from the Senate at the end of his term in 1958 with what are widely supposed to be plans to challenge his fellow Californian, Mr. Nixon, for future party leadership.

Senator Knowland's course, it

Continued on Page 16, Column 4

# ALIEN PLAN DROPS NATIONALITY BASIS

### 28 Democrats, Led by Celler, Ask Quota Rise to 250,000 in 5 'Class' Groupings

By The Associated Press.

WASHINGTON, Jan. 21—Twenty-eight House Democrats proposed today a major revision of the immigration and nationality laws. The proposal would eliminate the quota system based on nationality of immigrants and substitute a "class" basis without regard to national origin.

It would also establish a fixed annual quota of 250,000. The present system sets a maximum annual authorization of 154,657 quota immigrants.

Representative Emanuel Celler, Democrat of Brooklyn, chairman of the Judiciary Committee, is chief sponsor of the legislation. He said he would introduce it next week.

He and Herbert H. Lehman, the Democrat who was then Senator from New York, sponsored similar legislation last year.

**Would Ban 'Discrimination'**

In a statement today Mr. Celler said:

"Under my proposal there will be no discrimination based on national origin or race, and there will be no classification of United States citizens into two categories, native born and naturalized."

The proposal would set up five classes of immigrants, family unification, occupational, refugee, national interest and resettlement.

Within each class no more than 15 per cent of the annual allocation could be issued to inhabitants of any country. The President would submit to Congress each year the proposed allocation for each of the five classes and Congress then would have sixty days in which to approve or disapprove it.

In disagreements the allocations effective in the preceding

Continued on Page 11, Column 5

# State Votes Inquiry Of City Transit Unit

By DOUGLAS DALES

Special to The New York Times.

ALBANY, Jan. 21 — The State Senate unanimously adopted a resolution tonight authorizing an investigation of the New York City Transit Authority.

During the debate the Democrats announced they would offer a resolution tomorrow calling for an investigation of the Long Island Rail Road.

The Transit Authority resolution was bitterly assailed by the Democratic minority as a politically inspired effort to embarrass the Democratic Administration in New York during an election year.

An affirmative vote was called for by Senator Joseph Zaretzki of Manhattan, the new minority leader, as a

Continued on Page 21, Column 1

# Harriman Appoints Shapiro City Judge

By WARREN WEAVER Jr.

Special to The New York Times.

ALBANY, Jan. 21—Governor Harriman sent to the Senate for confirmation tonight the nominations of three New York City residents for vacant judgeships. Two of the seats are on the Supreme Court and the third on the City Court of New York.

Mr. Harriman named Justice Frederick Backer of the Domestic Relations Court and Judge Louis J. Capozzoli of General Sessions to the Supreme Court. The posts pay $30,000 a year.

His nominee for the City Court vacancy was J. Irwin Shapiro, the present State Commissioner of Investigation and a former Domestic Relations Court justice. City Court justices receive $22,000 a year.

Justice Backer succeeds Jus-

Continued on Page 21, Column 4

"All the News That's Fit to Print"

# The New York Times.

LATE CITY EDITION

U. S. Weather Bureau Report (Page 91) forecasts: Occasional rain today; rain ending tonight. Partly cloudy tomorrow. Temp. range: 47—40; yesterday: 45—29.9.

NEWS SUMMARY AND INDEX, PAGE 91

SECTION ONE

VOL. CIX....No. 37,234.



NEW YORK, SUNDAY, JANUARY 3, 1960.

35c outside New York City, its suburban area and Long Island. Higher in air delivery cities.

TWENTY-FIVE CENTS

## MAYOR PLEDGES FULL-SCALE STUDY OF TRANSIT CRISES

### One Aim Is to Eliminate Strike Threats—Public Is 'Sick of Them,' He Says

### 15-CENT FARE PROMISED

### Wagner Points to Burden on Budget—Notes Authority Is Creature of the State

*Text of Wagner's statement is printed on Page 63.*

By STANLEY LEVEY

Mayor Wagner announced yesterday that he had ordered the City Administrator's office to prepare "a comprehensive plan for dealing with the city's transportation problem."

The Mayor said the plan, designed to eliminate New York's biennial transit labor crises, would be "the most thoroughgoing study yet made of transportation" here.

To begin with, Mr. Wagner said, there will be a report on what the study should cover and what is needed to do the job.

Then, he declared, "I will set in motion the necessary machinery for working out our solutions, utilizing in this effort the best thinking in the community, state, region and nation."

**Atmosphere of Crisis**

The Mayor acted just two days after settlement of labor disputes between the Transport Workers Union and the Transit Authority and seven private bus companies.

The agreements were reached at City Hall as a 5 A. M. New Year's Day strike deadline approached, and with the usual atmosphere of crisis and pressure.

Both settlements were possible only as a result of financial assistance from the city. Mayor Wagner made $6,500,000 a year available to the authority to pay for the cost of its police force for two years. And he has promised to compensate the private lines for transporting school children at cut-rate fares.

**'Terrible Ordeal' Cited**

The authority-union contract calls for wage increases of 18 to 25 cents over two years plus welfare benefits that bring the total hourly cost to about 40 cents, or $35,000,000. The private lines package grants total benefits worth nearly 36 cents an hour, for a total cost of about $4,000,000.

In announcing his plan for a transportation study, the Mayor said he and the people of the city were "sick and tired of this periodic anxiety, uncertainty, pressure and near-panic."

"It simply doesn't make sense," he declared, "for the people of the city to go through this terrible ordeal every year or every second year.

"It prevents orderly development of a good transportation

Continued on Page 63, Column 5

## President and Aides Work on Messages to Congress

Associated Press Wirephoto

The President with Maurice H. Stans, director of Bureau of the Budget, at Augusta, Ga.

By FELIX BELAIR Jr.
Special to The New York Times.

AUGUSTA, Ga., Jan. 2—A blanket of fog over the Augusta National Golf Club kept President Eisenhower indoors again today for a busy round of official duties. Just after 8 A. M., the President conferred with White House aides from Washington on his State of the Union Message and his annual Budget Message. He will deliver the first message to Congress in person next Thursday. The budget document will be submitted on Jan. 18. Before taking up these major messages, the President worked for half an hour on routine reports and official correspondence, ac-

Continued on Page 40, Column 1

## EISENHOWER WARY ON PLAN TO WIDEN CIVIL RIGHTS LAW

### Unlikely to Press Congress for U. S. Vote Registrars to Protect Negroes

By ANTHONY LEWIS
Special to The New York Times.

WASHINGTON, Jan. 2—The Administration will not press for early Congressional action on a proposal to appoint Federal registrars in Southern areas where Negroes are denied the right to vote.

That was the key recommendation in the Civil Rights Commission report last Sept. 8. It has been made a rallying cry by civil rights organizations, and it is already looming as a major political issue in the new session of Congress.

Congress reconvenes next Wednesday. The President will deliver his State of the Union Message Thursday and submit his budget Jan. 18.

**Early Action Seen**

No program has been fixed for either house, but the Senate is expected to hold an early debate on Federal aid for school construction. Other big issues of the session are likely to include farm policy, Government bond interest rates and improved Social Security benefits.

The civil rights issue will be waiting in the wings. By all indications it will not wait long.

The Senate majority leader, Lyndon B. Johnson of Texas, has promised to call civil rights legislation up for debate in mid-February. In the House, backers are working, with good hopes of success, to dislodge a bill from the Rules Committee.

The Administration has not fixed its position on civil rights. But official thinking indicates strongly that it will stand pretty much on the relatively modest proposals made by President Eisenhower last year.

**Bill Whittled Down**

A truncated version of the 1959 package was approved by the House Judiciary Committee last summer and is now in the Rules Committee. The House bill would:

¶Permit inspection of state voting records by the Justice Department and require preservation of the records for two years.

¶Make it a Federal crime to interfere with court school desegregation orders by violence or threats.

¶Make it a Federal crime to cross state lines in flight from prosecution for bombing or burning any building.

¶Authorize Federal schooling for children or military personnel in communities where schools have been closed to avoid integration.

In addition to these provisions, President Eisenhower had called for technical assistance to communities ending school segregation and for creation of a permanent commission against job discrimination by Government contractors. The Judiciary

Continued on Page 54, Column 1

## Another Democrat Enters Contest

Associated Press Wirephoto

Senator John F. Kennedy at his news conference yesterday

## KENNEDY IN RACE; BARS SECOND SPOT IN ANY SITUATION

### Formal Announcement Cites Confidence He Will Win Election as President

### CHALLENGES SYMINGTON

### Insists All Aspirants Should Be Willing to Test Their Strength in Primaries

*Text of Kennedy statement will be found on Page 44.*

By RUSSELL BAKER
Special to The New York Times.

WASHINGTON, Jan. 2—Senator John F. Kennedy made it official today.

He told a news conference that he was a candidate for the Democratic Presidential nomination and was convinced that he could win both the nomination and the election.

At the same time Democratic leaders who believe that his following can be consolidated behind the Democratic ticket if Mr. Kennedy is given the Vice-Presidential nomination were given a sober warning.

If he is rejected for top place on the ticket, the Senator said, he will refuse to accept the Vice-Presidential nomination "under any condition."

**'Not Subject to Change'**

This decision, he added, "will not be subject to change under any condition."

The 42-year-old Massachusetts Democrat, first serious Roman Catholic contender for the Presidency since Alfred E. Smith ran in 1928, delivered his long-expected announcement to a crowded news conference in the Senate Caucus Room.

Of the many Democratic contenders, Senator Hubert H. Humphrey of Minnesota is the only other who has announced his candidacy for the Presidential nomination.

Regarding religion, Mr. Kennedy said:

"I would think that there is really only one issue involved in the whole question of a candidate's religion—that is, does a candidate believe in the Constitution, does he believe in the First Amendment, does he believe in the separation of church and state. When the candidate gives his views on that question, and I think I have given my views fully, I think the subject is exhausted."

**Audience Applauds**

An audience of about 300 supporters and friends applauded various answers to the reporters, giving the session the flavor of a political rally. Mrs. Kennedy also attended the conference.

Mr. Kennedy has been openly campaigning for the Democratic nomination for months. Thus today's ceremonial announcement came as no surprise.

At present the Senator is the acknowledged front-runner in

Continued on Page 44, Column 1

## BORDER BUILD-UP RUSHED IN INDIA

### Army Reinforced and Roads Built Near Tibet—Peiping Stand Is Unchanged

By PAUL GRIMES
Special to The New York Times.

NEW DELHI, India, Jan. 2—A massive campaign is under way to strengthen northeastern India against any further Chinese Communist aggression.

Army troops and paramilitary police units are being reinforced. Supply lines are being strengthened and are handling as much modern arms and equipment as India's limited resources will allow.

Top priority has been given to the construction and improvement of roads and communications. New roads are pushing into mountainous jungles that until last summer were considered nearly impenetrable.

Meanwhile, Communist China's latest note on its border claims against India has emphasized how far apart the two countries are in the dispute.

**Note Termed Friendly**

Indian sources here conceded privately that the Chinese Foreign Ministry's note of Dec. 26 appeared friendlier than early Peiping messages. Yet they noted that Peiping's claims to more than 40,000 square miles of Indian territory appeared as firm as ever.

India's defensive determination was strikingly evident to this reporter in a two-week tour of the Northeast. The tour included Himalayan highlands less than thirty-five miles from the Tibetan frontier. It included the Indian protectorate of Sikkim, sandwiched between Tibet and Nepal, and the hill city of Shillong, the command post and brain center for the remote North East Frontier Agency.

Prime Minister Jawaharlal Nehru has warned that any aggression against Sikkim would be considered an attack on India. He has rejected Peiping's claims to more than 32,000

Continued on Page 2, Column 3

## *Bonn Charges Plot To Smear Republic With Anti-Semitism*

By ARTHUR J. OLSEN
Special to The New York Times.

BONN, Germany, Jan. 2—The West German Government charged tonight that a wave of anti-Semitic incidents during the holiday season was a result of a deliberate effort to defame the republic.

A written statement made no attempt to identify the source of the alleged anti-German campaign.

It said that the police authorities were making every effort to track down the "wire-pullers" responsible for more than a dozen incidents of swastika painting and other acts of hooliganism with anti-Semitic or neo-Nazi overtones.

Several more incidents were reported today in widely separated parts of the country.

**Statement by Government**

The Government statement said:

"The Federal Government and the whole German people have followed with greatest indignation reports about the desecration of Jewish places of worship and the smearing of public and private buildings with emblems and slogans of National Socialism.

"There are signs that these actions in various parts of the country are part of a concerted plan to defame the Federal Republic in the eyes of the world public. The German police authorities are conducting extensive inquiries to identify the wire-pullers behind the acts.

"The police authorities will do everything they can to bring the guilty people to justice and prevent the repetition of incidents of this kind."

Government officials believe that some of the incidents, unheard of since the end of World War II in Germany, may be examples of "juvenile stupidities," presumably inspired by the wide publicity given to the desecration of a Cologne synagogue on Christmas Day.

Three members of the Rightist radical German Reichs party have been charged in connection with the Cologne incident.

Continued on Page 4, Column 4

## BENSON DRAFTING 40C CUT IN WHEAT

### Price Supports Geared to Open Market Planned to Reduce Surplus

By WILLIAM M. BLAIR
Special to The New York Times.

WASHINGTON, Jan. 2—The Administration is planning to ask for sharply lower price supports on wheat and an expansion of aid to low-income farmers.

Secretary of Agriculture Ezra Taft Benson has tentatively decided to seek a drop in price supports on wheat to about $1.37 a bushel under a new formula geared to open market prices. This would be 40 cents below the $1.77-a-bushel support announced for the 1960 wheat crop under the parity formula in effect for two decades.

President Eisenhower and Mr. Benson have asked Congress to abandon the parity concept as the basis for price supports. But they have not yet outlined proposals for a support level on wheat. They also want all acreage and marketing controls removed from wheat.

However, it is understood that Mr. Benson has in mind a level of 75 per cent of the average market price of the three years immediately preceding a crop year. This plan would become effective with the 1961 crop if approved by Congress.

Based on the average of the last three years of about $1.85 a bushel, this level would be about $1.37 a bushel.

If Mr. Benson compromised at

Continued on Page 58, Column 4

## *Party's Debate on Kennedy Takes Note of Catholic Vote*

By JAMES RESTON
Special to The New York Times.

WASHINGTON, Jan. 2—Senator John F. Kennedy was in the center of a controversy within the Democratic party tonight as a result of his flat and "final" statement that he would not accept the Vice-Presidential nomination "under any condition."

This was interpreted by leaders of his party as both a temporary tactical move, and as a threat, and it raised once more the question of his powerful political support among Roman Catholics.

Those who saw the Senator's public rejection of the Vice-Presidential nomination today as merely a tactic regarded it as a perfectly justifiable move to protect his campaign for the Presidential nomination.

Those, however, who really did take his statement as a "final" rejection of the Vice-Presidential nomination regarded it as something far more ominous: as a warning to the Democratic leaders not to think they can reject his bid for the Presidency on religious grounds and still retain the backing of his supporters by giving him the Vice-Presidential nomination.

**Facts Widely Known**

The facts of this controversy among Democratic leaders are widely known. Though they are seldom discussed in public they are as follows:

In the Democratic Presidential race of 1956, when Senator Kennedy sought and almost got the Vice-Presidential nomination, Theodore Sorensen, who was and still is the Senator's assistant, made a detailed study of voting records to demonstrate that a Catholic Vice-Presidential candidate would be an advantage to the Democratic ticket.

Early in that 1956 race, the Senator's father, former Ambassador Joseph P. Kennedy, opposed his son's campaign for the Vice-Presidency on the ground that President Eisenhower was probably going to win and that, if Senator Ken-

Continued on Page 44, Column 2

## DEMOCRATS PRESS CUT IN STATE TAX

### Little Chance Seen for Plan, but It Is Expected to Give Party Campaign Issue

By DOUGLAS DALES

The Democratic minority in the Legislature will make a reduction in the state income tax a main goal in its 1960 legislative program.

Tax relief will be sought chiefly through a restoration of exemptions that existed prior to changes enacted last year. The Legislature will convene Wednesday.

Little chance is seen that the Democratic proposals will succeed, but they will provide campaign ammunition next November, when a new Legislature will be elected.

The principal obstacles to an increase in the allowances for personal exemptions are the loss of revenue that would result and the efforts of the Rockefeller administration to achieve conformity between state and Federal tax practices.

The Democratic drive for a tax cut was announced in a statement yesterday by Michael H. Prendergast, state chairman, and Senator Joseph Zaretzki and Assemblyman Anthony J. Travia, the minority leaders.

They proposed that the personal exemption allowance be restored to $2,500 for a married couple and $1,000 for a single person. They also urged that the "head of family" category, with a $2,500 exemption, be restored.

With the establishment of the

Continued on Page 64, Column 4

## MAN FOUND SLAIN, SECOND WOUNDED

### Police Hunt 3 in Shootings at 13th St. and Ave. A

One man was killed and another wounded in a fusillade of bullets fired early today on the lower East Side.

The police believe they were shot by three men, who fled.

The dead man was found lying on the curb at the northeast corner of Thirteenth Street and Avenue A. He had three bullet wounds in the back of the head and another in his chest.

The dead man's last name was tentatively listed by the police as Parisi. A car registered in the name of Mario Parisi of 1651 East Seventh Street, Brooklyn, was found near the scene.

The second man staggered eight blocks to the Fifth Street police station to report the shooting. He had two bullet wounds, one in the left arm and the other in the left hand.

The wounded man was Carl Radosti, 35, of 170 Fenimore Street, Brooklyn.

Authorities began investigating a report that three young men were seen hurrying into the hallway of 214 Avenue A.

Continued on Page 51, Column 1

## *Soviet Is Believed Ahead of U. S. In Explosions for Peaceful Use*

By GLADWIN HILL
Special to The New York Times

LOS ANGELES, Jan. 2—Some of the nation's foremost atomic researchers are ruefully convinced that the Russians have quietly forged far into the lead in another important field of science.

This is the application of tremendous explosions to peaceful engineering purposes, such as mining and the development of waterways.

In this field, over the last four years, the Russians apparently have accomplished some things the United States is still talking about doing.

The advance is not just technical. In some spectacular experiments, the Russians evidently have added greatly to the scanty amount of scientific knowledge about specialized explosive phenomena.

Intelligence reports and sketchy Soviet publications about this work, for instance, have become of prime interest and concern among scientists working for the Atomic Energy Commission at the University of California Radiation Laboratory at Livermore.

This laboratory, where the hydrogen bomb development was centered, is the headquarters of the A. E. C.'s Plowshare Project for peaceful applications of nuclear explosions.

A recent and hitherto undisclosed laboratory assessment of the Soviet work concludes that

Continued on Page 28, Column 4

## *School Integration Has Passed Its Crisis, Negro Leader Says*

### *All-Out Resistance Yielding to Legal Skirmishing, Marshall Declares*

By WAYNE PHILLIPS

The period of crisis and massive resistance to school integration has passed, according to the Negro attorney who won the Supreme Court decision outlawing racial segregation in public schools.

In its place, says Thurgood Marshall, has come a period of token integration, legal maneuver and what he calls "a lot of fast play around second base."

The 51-year-old attorney gave his view of what lies ahead in the school-integration controversy on the eve of his departure for his first trip to Africa.

He flew to Liberia last Friday to attend the inauguration of President William V. S. Tubman of Liberia. He will travel for two months before returning to the seventeenth-floor office in the Coliseum Tower from which he supervises the nationwide legal struggle of the Negro for equality.

Mr. Marshall, a graduate of the Howard University Law School, has been an attorney for the National Association for the Advancement of Colored People since 1934. Since 1950 he has been director-counsel of that organization's legal defense and educational fund.

The fund provides legal assistance to Negroes who are

Continued on Page 52, Column 1

The New York Times

Thurgood Marshall

## *Doctors Find Christmas Strains Make Season Unhappy for Many*

By JOHN A. OSMUNDSEN

Relief from the pressure of having to be happy during the holidays is beginning to brighten the lives of many persons who react violently against Christmas, according to a current medical journal.

Hives, overeating, crying jags, dishonesty, sexual deviation and just plain orneriness are said to be some of the "Christmas reactions" that those people develop around Thanksgiving and carry on until after the first of the year.

Underlying those difficulties are the rituals or "rules" of Christmas, four Utah physicians and psychiatric social workers wrote in the December issue of American Practitioner and Digest of Treatment.

Those rules, they said, require that everyone celebrate, renew family ties, exchange gifts, put up holiday decorations, have a special Christmas dinner, and—above all—be happy.

The trouble is, the physicians observed, that all those rules cannot be observed by everyone, often compounding existing psychological difficulties.

In another way, such seasonal symptoms stem from the dual nature of Christmastime, according to the report.

To some, they wrote, Christmas is a time to relax and indulge oneself, to become a child again for a while.

To others, the holiday is only a reminder that life is tough enough the rest of the year.

Either way, the season is

Continued on Page 35, Column 1

## Today's Sections

| | |
|---|---|
| Section 1 (2 sections) | News |
| Section 2 | Drama, Screen, Music, TV, Radio, Gardens, Resorts |
| Section 3 | Financial and Business |
| Section 4 | Review of the Week |
| Section 5 | Sports |
| Section 6 | Magazine |
| Section 7 | Book Review |
| Section 8 | *Real Estate |
| Section 9 | *Employment Advertising |
| Section 10 | Advertising |

*Included in all copies in the New York metropolitan area and adjacent territory.

## Index to Subjects

| | Section. | Page. |
|---|---|---|
| Art | 1 | 67 |
| | 2 | 18-19 |
| Boats | 5 | 8 |
| Book Review | 7 | .. |
| Bridge | 2 | 10 |
| Camera | 2 | 17 |
| Dance | 2 | 12 |
| Decorative Arts | 6 | 34-35 |
| Drama | 2 | 1-5 |
| Editorials | 4 | 8 |
| Education | 4 | 9 |
| Fashions | 6 | 36-37 |
| Financial and Business | 3 | .. |
| Food | 6 | 30 |
| Gardens | 2 | 36-38 |
| Home Improvement | 2 | 36 |
| Letters to Editor | 4 | 8 |
| Music | 2 | 8-10 |
| News Summary & Index | 1 | 91 |
| Obituaries | 1 | 88-90 |
| Puzzles | 6 | 46 |
| Real Estate | 8 | .. |
| Records | 2 | 11 |
| Resorts | 2 | 20-35 |
| Review of Week | 4 | .. |
| Science | 4 | 9 |
| Screen | 2 | 6-8 |
| Ships & Aviation | 5 | 10-11 |
| Society | 1 | 78-86 |
| Sports | 5 | .. |
| Stamps, Coins | 2 | 11 |
| Television-Radio | 2 | 12-16 |
| Weather | 1 | 91 |

"All the News That's Fit to Print"

# The New York Times.

LATE CITY EDITION
U. S. Weather Bureau Report (Page 82) forecasts: Mostly fair and cool today; partly cloudy tonight. Mild tomorrow. Temp. range: 48—35; yesterday: 55.6—40.8

VOL. CIX. No. 37,328. NEW YORK, WEDNESDAY, APRIL 6, 1960. FIVE CENTS

10 cents beyond 50-mile zone from New York City except on Long Island. Higher in air delivery cities.

## KENNEDY BEATS HUMPHREY IN HEAVY WISCONSIN VOTE; NIXON DISPLAYS STRENGTH

## WEST TURNS DOWN KHRUSHCHEV PLAN FOR DISARMAMENT

### Rejects Premier's Proposals as Basis for Compromise at Geneva Conference

### MOCH OUTLINES STAND

### Move Is Seen as Attempt to End Stalling by Russians for Propaganda Gains

By A. M. ROSENTHAL
Special to The New York Times.

GENEVA, April 5—The West rejected today Premier Khrushchev's proposals for complete disarmament as the basis for any disarmament compromise.

More than three weeks of Western argument and pleas were summed up at the ten-nation disarmament conference in that major decision to make things clear to Moscow.

It was a decision based on the growing conviction of Western delegations that the Soviet Union was blocking a decision to move on to specific disarmament steps in an attempt to get the maximum propaganda out of the negotiations.

The West has just about given up hope that the Soviet Union will make any real move toward considering Western proposals for step-by-step disarmament before the summit meeting scheduled to open in Paris May 16.

**Negotiation Is Expected**

The rejection of the Soviet plan for complete disarmament in four years was meant as notice to the Russians that there was not much time before the summit to negotiate on specific disarmament steps.

Western delegations still believe that sooner or later the Soviet Union will drop its all-or-nothing stand and pick something for negotiation, probably a reduction of conventional armed forces. But the West also believes that unless the Russians move in the direction of specific negotiations before the summit, there will not be enough time in Paris to accomplish much.

All this was part of the thinking behind the decision to talk more plainly than ever to the Russians. There is no talk here of "breaking up" the conference. What has happened is that the conference has moved swiftly to the point where the delegates of East and West have each said "no" to the other's first-round position and the future is now out of their hands.

**Point-by-Point Rejection**

The job of speaking plainly to the Communists was handed by the West to Jules Moch of France. He had had a good deal of experience along that line as Minister of the Interior in France and as French delegate to earlier disarmament conferences.

Point by point M. Moch gave the Western rejection of the fundamentals of the Soviet plan—the timetable, the disbanding of all national forces before the creation of an international policing arm, the political commitment to the program of complete disarmament before agreement on inspection.

When he had finished ticking off the rejections, M. Moch leaned across the green baize table and told the Russians that the West was ready to hear Soviet suggestions based on the Western proposal for gradual disarmament.

But as far as Mr. Khru-

Continued on Page 12, Column 4

Associated Press Radiophoto

DISTINGUISHED VISITOR: President de Gaulle riding beside Queen Elizabeth yesterday from Victoria Station to Buckingham Palace at start of President's state visit.

## Criticism of Racial Curbs Increasing in South Africa

By LEONARD INGALLS
Special to The New York Times.

JOHANNESBURG, South Africa, April 5—Sentiment appeared to be growing among South Africans today for a softening of their country's harsh racial policies. Violence brought on by these policies continued.

Two business leaders and an important member of the Opposition United party warned of the consequences of the present state of emergency caused by racial unrest.

They called on the Government to consult African leaders and to give South Africa policies that would win her respect rather than condemnation throughout the world.

Fourteen ministers of the Anglican Church in Capetown appealed today to the Government of Prime Minister Hendrik F. Verwoerd to bring to an end the "methods of violence against individuals now openly adopted by the police." They urged restraint and regard for human dignity.

**Justice Minister Replies**

In a reply to the clergymen and others making similar protests, François C. Erasmus, Minister of Justice, said that the police were dealing with "intimidators" who try to keep Africans from their jobs.

In Capetown today the Senate approved a bill empowering the Government to outlaw the African National Congress and the Pan-Africanist Congress, the major groups representing African political aspirations. The bill had already been passed by the House of Assembly, and it now becomes law.

The death of an African tonight at the African settlement of Lamontville near Durban brought to two the number killed in violence today in South Africa. Five Africans and a white policeman were hurt when the police opened fire to break up a mob threatening African workers returning from their jobs in Durban.

**New Clash in Capetown**

Meanwhile, an outbreak of violence in the Capetown area, where the Government appears to be in control of the situation only through the use of force, led to at least one death today and injuries to five Africans. Thirty persons, some in serious condition, were still being treated for injuries suffered in yesterday's crackdown by the police on Africans in the Capetown area.

Throughout South Africa authorities reported that the African labor force, upon which the country's economy is based, was back at work. In Capetown 90 per cent of the African workers were at their jobs.

The concern of the business community over the tense situation and its economic effect was stressed by Peter Mosenthal, a

Continued on Page 4, Column 5

## BONN AVERTS RIFT IN EUROPE'S TRADE

### Agrees to Restudy Speeding of Common Market, Thus Barring Action July 1

By ARTHUR J. OLSEN
Special to The New York Times.

BONN, Germany, April 5—A threatened economic split of Western Europe July 1 was postponed today by the action of the West German Government.

The Federal Cabinet renewed its commitment to the creation of a Common Market of six Continental nations. But it tacitly agreed to give the European Economic Community and non-member nations more time to head off the division of Western Europe into rival trading blocs.

The Cabinet appointed a committee of four Ministers to study a proposal to speed the formation of the Common Market. This step, proposed for July 1, would erect a tariff wall between the "Inner Six"—West Germany, France, Italy, the Netherlands, Belgium and Luxembourg—and the rest of the world.

The "Outer Seven" nations of the European Free Trade Association—Britain, Sweden, Norway, Denmark, Austria, Switzerland and Portugal—would be particularly affected.

The decision to restudy the speed-up plan meant that the July 1 goal could not be met, regardless of West Germany's ultimate policy position.

Economic experts had already agreed that the date was unrealistic, in any event, for technical reasons. The proposal, put forth by Prof. Walter Hallstein, president of the European Economic Community, involves elaborate duty computations and

Continued on Page 8, Column 1

## DE GAULLE GETS LONDON WELCOME

### 100,000 at Palace Acclaim War Leader on His Return —Queen Stresses Unity

By DREW MIDDLETON
Special to The New York Times.

LONDON, April 5—Twenty years ago Charles de Gaulle fled to London, a little-known general of a discredited army and a beaten country. He returned today as President of France to be welcomed by Queen Elizabeth II and cheered by her subjects.

President de Gaulle stood with the Queen on the floodlit balcony of Buckingham Palace tonight to accept the cheers of a crowd estimated at nearly 100,000.

At a glittering state banquet in the palace, the Queen, toasting "General de Gaulle, our friend," emphasized that the English Channel must not form a psychological barrier to "real understanding between Britain and France, between Britain and the other countries of Western Europe."

**Economic Conflict Feared**

Prime Minister Macmillan, in the course of a sixty-five-minute talk with President de Gaulle earlier in the evening, was reported to have emphasized the danger to Western unity that might arise from trade rivalry between the six-nation European Common Market and the seven-member European Free Trade Area.

It is not European unity that Britain fears, Mr. Macmillan is understood to have told his guest, but integration of one part of Europe that inevitably would pit that part against the rest in economic and political conflict.

The two statesmen also discussed problems of aligning Western policies for the summit meeting with the Soviet Union next month, officials said. General de Gaulle gave Mr. Macmillan an account of his discussions with Premier Khrushchev during the Soviet leader's just-concluded visit to Paris.

But there was no indication thus far that President de Gaulle had been impressed by the first

Continued on Page 13, Column 1

## MAYOR DEMANDS STATE GRANT CITY MORE HOME RULE

### In Annual Report, He Also Hails Fiscal Position and Pledges Slum Fight

*Text of the Wagner message is printed on Page 36.*

By CHARLES G. BENNETT

New York City is entitled to and intends to get a far greater degree of home rule than it has, Mayor Wagner told the City Council yesterday.

The Mayor demanded that the state commission investigating New York City affairs give the matter highest priority.

"Our right to be free from the necessity of running to Albany for permission to proceed with a great variety of local matters, our right to govern ourselves with at least the powers of a small chartered city in California—this remains a major goal of my administration," the Mayor declared.

**Aid Pact a 'Giant Step'**

Mr. Wagner conceded that the March 26 agreement between the city and the state for $41,000,000 in additional state aid in the fiscal year beginning on July 1 was "a giant step forward." But the agreement, he asserted, did not touch home rule.

The Mayor gave his views in his annual message to the Council on the state of the city.

The 6,000-word message was delivered personally. It accompanied the submission to the Council of Mr. Wagner's 127-page illustrated and printed annual report for 1959 entitled "Better Government: The Measure of Achievement."

Both the report and the message found the city's economic health excellent, pledged a continued drive for the abolition of slums and improvement of housing, promised to root out any dishonesty in city inspectional services, outlined the accomplishments of many municipal agencies and set a variety of city administration goals for the coming year.

**Applauded By Officials**

An audience consisting principally of City Councilmen and about twenty department heads applauded the Mayor when he arrived and again when he finished his forty-eight-minute talk.

In emphasizing the city's desire for greater freedom in local affairs the Mayor said: "We are an old city on this continent. We have long experience in the art, science and responsibility of government. We can govern ourselves, and we should have the authority to do so.

"The means for achieving this result ought to be a matter of highest priority with the New York State Commission on Governmental Operations, now examining into city affairs."

The acting chairman of the state commission is Frank C. Moore, former Lieutenant Governor and State Controller.

In January Mayor Wagner endorsed recommendations of the Temporary State Commission on Revision and Simplification of the Constitution that home-rule powers of local governments be expanded.

At present localities can use

Continued on Page 37, Column 4

## President Called 'Happy' Over Civil Rights Measure

### Dirksen Reports View and Says G. O. P. Will Take Credit for the Bill—Final Approval in Senate Approaching

By RUSSELL BAKER
Special to The New York Times.

WASHINGTON, April 5—Republican Congressional leaders said today that President Eisenhower was "happy" with the civil rights bill awaiting passage in the Senate.

Everett McKinley Dirksen of Illinois, the Senate's Republican leader, said that in the 1960 political campaign the party would "point with pride" to the voting-rights measure as "an Administration bill."

Although claiming it as an Administration victory, Mr. Dirksen allotted some of the credit to Lyndon B. Johnson of Texas, the Senate Democratic leader. "The majority leader has certainly been cooperative," he said. "That I can say to the whole wide world."

Mr. Dirksen's comments were made at a news conference after this morning's White House meeting between Republican Congressmen and the President.

The bill, honed down to a voting-rights measure and two new general criminal statutes on bombing and obstruction of court orders, is ready for passage after a final tide of Southern oratory subsides.

Today was largely given over to voting down minor Southern amendments and giving the Southerners a last chance to

Continued on Page 27, Column 8

## White House Parley Fixes Principles for Aged Care

By JOHN D. MORRIS
Special to The New York Times.

WASHINGTON, April 5—President Eisenhower and Republican Congressional leaders moved a step toward agreement today on a subsidized program of voluntary health insurance for the aged.

They set up broad guidelines for such a program at a White House meeting in which Vice President Nixon and Arthur S. Flemming, Secretary of Health, Education and Welfare, participated.

While there were no decisions or details, the discussion encouraged predictions that the Administration would submit recommendations to Congress before the session adjourned.

Secretary Flemming may give more information on the prospect, particularly about the timing of any Administration proposals, in testimony tomorrow before a Senate subcommittee studying problems of the aged.

However, Administration sources reported that he was not ready to present a plan to Congress.

**Softening of Resistance**

The main significance of today's White House conference appeared to be a softening of resistance among Republican leaders to the principle of federally aided health insurance.

At a similar conference last week Mr. Flemming failed to win endorsement of a proposal for Federal and state subsidies to help persons over 65 years of age to pay health insurance premiums. President Eisenhower then marked the plan for further study.

There was evidence that a shift in sentiment was at least partly attributable to the presence today of Mr. Nixon, who

Continued on Page 35, Column 4

## PROSECUTORS HIT BAN ON WIRETAPS

### U. S. Rulings Seen Leading to Enforcement Collapse —Many Cases Put Off

By EMANUEL PERLMUTTER

Six New York State District Attorneys warned here yesterday that recent judicial decisions restricting the use of wiretapping by prosecutors posed an immediate and serious threat to law enforcement in the state.

These fears were expressed at an all-day public hearing on wiretapping by the State Investigation Commission at its office, 270 Broadway.

District Attorney Frank S. Hogan said he had been forced to hold up the prosecution of ten indictments and six major investigations in New York County because of the judicial rulings.

District Attorney Edward S. Silver of Brooklyn said he might have to dismiss 200 defendants and halt some prosecutions and investigations because the use of wiretaps was involved in the cases.

Mr. Silver, who is president of the National District Attorneys Association, asserted that

Continued on Page 44, Column 4

## CITY POLL IS KEY

### Bostonian Gains 20 Convention Ballots and His Rival 10

By AUSTIN C. WEHRWEIN
Special to The New York Times.

MILWAUKEE, April 6—Senator John F. Kennedy of Massachusetts defeated Senator Hubert H. Humphrey of Minnesota in yesterday's Wisconsin Democratic Presidential primary.

Early today the 42-year-old Bostonian held a comfortable and growing lead over his Minnesota rival.

Vice President Nixon ran unopposed in the Republican column. He did not campaign in the state.

Returns from 3,039 of 3,451 precincts give:

Kennedy (D.) .......... 389,41[illegible]
Humphrey (D.) .......... 318,8[illegible]
Nixon (R.) .......... 305,27[illegible]

Mr. Nixon had been written off as a factor before the election. His showing was regarded by some observers as better than expected.

**Cross-Over Assayed**

But at the same time his total was clearly cut by Republicans who crossed over into the Democratic column, either to vote for their co-religionist, Senator Kennedy, a Roman Catholic, or for other reasons.

For example in the Third Congressional District in the southeast that always votes Republican, Mr. Nixon ran third. This is a rural district, 28 per cent Catholic, and Republican farmers crossed over to vote for both Democrats.

The Eighth District is also Republican and is 47 per cent Catholic. There the cross-over was clearly in favor of Senator Kennedy alone.

The six Congressional districts won by Mr. Kennedy and his majority of the popular vote gave the Massachusetts Senator a total of 20 of the state's convention votes. Senator Humphrey's four Congressional districts were worth 10 convention votes.

**Vote Near a Record**

The heavy voting was certain to erase the record primary vote cast in 1952.

Each of the candidates had four Congressional districts apparently won before the Milwaukee County returns were counted. But in the two Milwaukee area Congressional districts, the Fourth and Fifth, Senator Kennedy piled up a 2-to-1 lead over his rival.

Senator Humphrey took an early lead as returns from the rural districts along the Minnesota border rolled in at the outset. It was in these rural areas where the Minnesota Senator wooed farmers as their "consistent friend" that he won three districts, the Third, Ninth and Tenth.

The Minnesota Senator also led in the Second that includes the state university and the state capital in Madison where liberalism is strong.

Robert Kennedy, the Senator's brother and campaign manager, discounted the effect of the Catholic vote. He said it "was a factor," but argued that his brother ran well in Pro-

Continued on Page 34, Column 2

## Religion Big Factor In Kennedy Victory

By DONALD JANSON
Special to The New York Times.

MILWAUKEE, April 5—Religion played a major role in Senator John F. Kennedy's victory in the Wisconsin Presidential primary, returns indicated tonight.

Voters in areas with a high concentration of Roman Catholics, which regularly vote Democratic, gave the Massachusetts contender a top-heavy margin there.

More significant, he scored decisive victories in some Catholic localities that usually vote Republican.

This means that Catholic Re-

Continued on Page 34, Column 1



## Plotters Still Threaten Trujillo; Leaders Plan Early Showdown

*Following is the last of three articles on the Dominican Republic by a correspondent who recently visited there.*

By EDWARD C. BURKS

The signs in the Dominican Republic point to further attempts to overthrow Generalissimo Rafael Leonidas Trujillo Molina. If the dictator is forced out, many long-suppressed forces will scramble for power.

No one has been groomed by General Trujillo as his successor in the event of his peaceful departure from the scene. If he is forced out, the military, the embattled professional class, returning exiles, peasants and workers will all be competing for power. An invasion from Premier Fidel Castro's Cuba is also a possibility.

On the other hand, if the general rides out the present crisis, it appears that he can do so only by putting down a new nation-wide plot or uprising.

A diplomat with considerable Dominican experience sums up the present situation as "very nasty."

He foresees an early showdown between General Trujillo and the harassed professional class, which is waiting to regather its strength after the smashing of its January plot.

At a meeting with this correspondent in an abandoned building, ranking members of the underground spoke of their

Continued on Page 2, Column 3

## Tiros I May Prove Unintentional Spy

By JOHN W. FINNEY
Special to The New York Times.

WASHINGTON, April 5—The Tiros I satellite is working so well that the space agency is worried that it may unintentionally have placed a blurry-eyed spy in the sky.

Officials of the National Aeronautics and Space Administration, after repeated earlier denials, conceded today that there was a possibility that Tiros I, aside from taking pictures of the earth's cloud cover, might also be obtaining rudimentary photographs of objects on the earth's surface.

It still has not been established that Tiros I is taking detailed pictures of the earth's surface, and some prominent

Continued on Page 18, Column 3

NEWS INDEX


| | Page | | Page |
|---|---|---|---|
| Art | 47 | Music | 46-49 |
| Books | 38-39 | Obituaries | 41 |
| Bridge | 38 | Real Estate | 67-68 |
| Business | 56-58 | Screen | 46-49 |
| Buyers | 57 | Ships and Air | 82 |
| Crossword | 39 | Society | 45 |
| Editorial | 40 | Sports | 52-56 |
| Events Today | 45 | TV and Radio | 83 |
| Fashions | 50-51 | Theatres | 46-49 |
| Financial | 57-67 | U. N. Proceedings | 2 |
| Food | 50-51 | Wash. Proceedings | 35 |
| Man in the News | 31 | Weather | 82 |

News Summary and Index, Page 43


The New York Times

EMPHASIZES HOME RULE: Mayor Wagner addressing City Council yesterday at City Hall

"All the News That's Fit to Print"

# The New York Times.

LATE CITY EDITION
U. S. Weather Bureau Report (Page 66) forecasts: Cloudy and mild today; fair tonight. Cloudy, chance of showers tomorrow.
Temp. range: 72—55; yesterday: 73.0—53.5.

VOL. CIX..No. 37,378.  NEW YORK, THURSDAY, MAY 26, 1960. 10 cents beyond 50-mile zone from New York City except on Long Island. Higher in air delivery cities. FIVE CENTS

## ROCKEFELLER AVAILABLE FOR PRESIDENTIAL DRAFT, BUT WON'T ENCOURAGE IT

### SEES STATE CHIEFS

### Avoids Backing Nixon —Delegates Going to Chicago Unpledged

By WARREN WEAVER Jr.
Special to The New York Times.

ALBANY, May 25—Governor Rockefeller said today that he would accept a draft for the Republican nomination for President.

"Drafts come very seldom in this country, but if a draft should come, I would be greatly honored and I would accept," the Governor declared.

However, he said he did not expect such a draft and would not encourage one.

It was the first time that Mr. Rockefeller had publicly emerged from behind his oft-repeated statement that he was not a candidate for the nomination.

In effect, he altered his position to that of an inactive candidate, something all his aides and most political observers had known him to be all along.

He also indicated that he might attend the Republican National Convention in Chicago.

**Call for National Debate**

When Governor Rockefeller proposed last Monday a national debate, devoid of partisanship, on the failure of the summit conference, observers regarded this as an indication that he had not ruled himself out of the race.

In recognition of Mr. Rockefeller's willingness to make his political position a little clearer and stronger, the executive committee of the Republican State Committee voted unanimously to send New York's ninety-six delegates to the national convention uncommitted. The convention starts July 25.

The action came after the executive committee had spent nearly two hours discussing the issue. Some party leaders felt that the Governor should either declare himself a candidate, thus binding them, or remove himself from the race, leaving them free to endorse Vice President Nixon.

The decisions reached at the executive committee meeting were not popular with some of the county chairmen who learned of them later. Many local leaders had hoped that Mr. Rockefeller would withdraw al-

Continued on Page 20, Column 6

United Press International Telephoto
REPUBLICAN LEADERS MEET IN ALBANY: Governor Rockefeller, left, and L. Judson Morhouse, the state chairman of the party, arriving for yesterday's sessions.

## State Says Track Builders Got Dual Fees for One Job

By EMANUEL PERLMUTTER

Contractors at two raceways cheated the state by billing for construction equipment listed as in use at both tracks at the same time, the State Investigation Commission charged yesterday. The asserted profiteering took place in 1957 and 1958 at Yonkers and Monticello Raceways, about seventy miles apart. It involved cranes, large shovels, bulldozers and caterpillar graders owned by Edward J. Petrillo, Inc., of Yonkers.

The work consisted of the construction of the new $7,000,000 Monticello track and a $20,000,000 rebuilding job at Yonkers Raceway. Under a law repealed last year, the state is still committed to pay for the work done at Yonkers. As a new track, Monticello did not qualify for the state aid.

**$155,000 Fraud Charged**

Besides the duplicate use of equipment, the state was defrauded of about $155,000 on steel work listed as costing $300,000 for the new $18,000,000 Yonkers clubhouse, the commission said.

These overcharges by contractors and subcontractors were cited by the commission in the second day of its public hearings into alleged profiteering on the state-financed work at Yonkers.

Yonkers Raceway, in a statement read yesterday at the hearing by Louis Haimoff, its lawyer, said it would not seek payment from the state for excessive fees charged by contractors.

"Prompt action will be taken to recover any such excess payments in appropriate legal proceedings at the earliest possible moment," Mr. Haimoff said. "We undertake that the state will not ultimately lose one cent

Continued on Page 20, Column 3

## MAYOR NOT BOUND TO BACK DE SAPIO

### Says Choice of Democratic Committeeman Should Await Convention

By LEO EGAN

Mayor Wagner declared yesterday that he was not committed to Carmine G. De Sapio's re-election as Democratic national committeeman for New York.

He also said that he was not interested in becoming national committeeman himself and that he had not yet heard of any candidate to replace Mr. De Sapio, the leader of Tammany Hall.

On May 8 the Mayor declined to say whether he would support Mr. De Sapio for re-election, but he did say he preferred Mr. De Sapio as a political leader to someone who would try to interfere with the running of City Hall.

**No City Hall Role**

Mr. Wagner said then that Mr. De Sapio "doesn't play any part" in his administration, "has never requested any legislation" and "has never attempted to interfere in my appointments."

Mr. Wagner's comments yesterday were made to reporters at a reception at Gracie Mansion for Senator Stuart Symington, Democrat of Missouri, a candidate for the Presidential nomination. Senator John F. Kennedy of Massachusetts, the leading contender for the nomination, also spent most of yesterday in New York and talked to Liberal party leaders.

The Mayor said he did not think any decision on national committeemen should be made until the delegates who will cast New York State's 114 votes at the Democratic National Convention were all selected officially.

Eighty-six district delegates will be formally elected in the June 7 primary. The new Demo-

Continued on Page 20, Column 4

## HOUSE UNIT BARS 4 BILLION TAX CUT

### Keeps Corporate and Sales Rates and Phone Levy

By JOHN D. MORRIS
Special to The New York Times.

WASHINGTON, May 25—The House Ways and Means Committee voted today to stand fast against scheduled reductions in corporation and excise taxes for another year.

Its action, if it becomes law, would forestall Federal revenue losses of more than $4,000,000,000 a year, of which $2,700,000,000 would occur in the fiscal year beginning July 1. President Eisenhower was counting on this income in projecting a surplus of $4,200,000,000 for the coming year.

The committee took the action in approving a bill to carry out Administration recommendations for continuation of the taxes at present rates. It also authorized a $293,000,000,000 ceiling on the national debt in the fiscal year that starts July 1. The present temporary ceiling is $295,000,000,000.

The committee rejected a proposal to allow the 10 per cent levy on local telephone service to expire June 30, as provided by present law. It also refused to halve the telephone tax. All decisions were by one-sided voice votes.

The bill will go to the House floor, possibly next week, under procedure prohibiting any amendments opposed by the Ways and Means Committee. Consequently, the House is ex-

Continued on Page 67, Column 1

**Adlai E. Stevenson on the National Purpose**

The second article in the debate on America's national purpose is written by the man who was the Democratic candidate for President in 1952 and 1956. It will be found

TODAY ON PAGE 30

## House Opens Debate On School Fund Bill

By TOM WICKER
Special to The New York Times.

WASHINGTON, May 25—The House of Representatives opened debate today on a $975,000,000 school construction bill, with the Administration apparently dangling a compromise before supporters of the bill.

There was no word from President Eisenhower, but Arthur S. Flemming, Secretary of Health, Education and Welfare, hinted at a veto of the measure in its original form. He suggested amendments to "improve" it.

Some of the bill's leading supporters were saying privately that they would not fight too hard against amendments favored by Mr. Flemming. Their view was that the amendments would not decisively alter the bill's purpose, but might make it acceptable to the President.

In the only vote, on procedure, ground rules for debating

Continued on Page 67, Column 4

## FOOD COSTS PUSH CONSUMER INDEX TO ANOTHER HIGH

### Prices Increase by 0.4% to 126.2—A Sharp Drop Taken by Used Cars

By RICHARD E. MOONEY
Special to The New York Times.

WASHINGTON, May 25—Rising food prices lifted the Consumer Price Index to another record in April—four-tenths of 1 per cent higher than March and almost 2 per cent higher than a year ago.

The Labor Department's Bureau of Labor Statistics reported today that the index for April was 126.2, using the 1947-1949 average as a comparison basis of 100.

The index measures changes in the prices of a selected assortment of items and services for which city wage-earners typically spend their income.

If all prices moved together, the April increase would mean that it cost $10.04 to buy in April what $10 bought in March.

**Index Fairly Steady**

Like all changes in the overall index, April's resulted from a mixture of increases and decreases, of which the most important was a 1.5 per cent increase in food prices. Food counts for almost one-third of the index.

Arnold Chase, chief of the bureau's Price Division, said he wanted to emphasize that "this does not mark the beginning of a strong upward trend" in the index, which had been fairly steady for the previous six months.

The food price increases stemmed from special factors that are not likely to be repeated, he said. He cited bad weather and the start of a new downward cycle in pork and egg production, plus the fact that food prices generally rise somewhat at this time of year. Egg prices, which often decline in April, were up almost 13 per cent.

**Gradual Rise Forecast**

Mr. Chase said it was not likely that the increases in food prices would be offset by drops later on. He thought the overall index might be steady in May, then rise gradually through the summer.

The only significant price reduction in April was for used cars. A drop of 2.1 per cent in April and 4.8 per cent in March added up to the sharpest two-month decline since the index started measuring used-car prices seven years ago. The bureau laid it to competition from compact models.

New-car prices were unusually steady in April, the report said, because sales have picked up strongly. Prices of most other consumer goods and services increased a little, with the exception of transportation fares, home repair and maintenance costs, and electricity

Continued on Page 22, Column 2

## 96 Million Co-op Will Be Built Above Railroad Yards in Bronx

### Butchers Union Gets Air Rights for Middle-Income Project Over Mott Haven Tracks

By THOMAS W. ENNIS

A $96,000,000 middle-income cooperative apartment development for 5,206 families will be built over the New York Central's Mott Haven yards in the Bronx. Work is expected to start this year.

The railroad yards are forty feet below street level. The apartment buildings—eventually there will be twenty-two, each twenty stories high—will be erected on a concrete platform spanning the tracks and flush with the street. The concrete base will be supported by columns sunk deep between the tracks below.

The cooperative, sponsored on a nonprofit basis by the Amalgamated Meat Cutters and Butcher Workmen of North America, will be known as Concourse Village. The site is one block east of the Grand Concourse and extends from East 150th Street to East 161st Street, between Sheridan and Morris Avenues.

Monthly carrying charges of $27.88 a room are planned, after a down payment of $700 a room. The down payment is the tenant-owners' contribution to the construction costs.

Amalgamated has leased the

The New York Times May 26, 1960
Project's site is in black

air rights over the forty-acre area from the New York Central System, which uses the Mott Haven yards for the maintenance and storage of its railroad cars.

Under the lease, which is for sixty years, with an option for a forty-year renewal, the railroad will receive $750,000 a year in rent when the development is completed.

Plans for the cooperative were announced yesterday by James W. Gaynor, state Housing Commissioner.

The state, under its middle-income housing program, will provide a fifty-year, low-in-

Continued on Page 24, Column 5

## EISENHOWER SAYS U.S. MUST DEAL WITH SOVIET ON BASIS OF REASON; OFFERS AIR AID IN U.N. PATROL PLAN

### ANSWERS CRITICS

### President Reports to Nation, Shows Photo Taken 13 Miles Up

*Text of the President's address is printed on Page 6.*

By DANA ADAMS SCHMIDT
Special to The New York Times.

WASHINGTON, May 25—President Eisenhower said tonight that in spite of the collapse of the summit conference "we must continue businesslike dealing with the Soviet leaders."

Undeterred by "bad deportment," the United States must make clear that "the path of reason and common sense is still open if the Soviets will but use it," he declared.

Addressing the nation by radio and television, the President said that the United States would "preserve and build on" such progress as has been made in nuclear-test and disarmament negotiations.

"We will not back away," he asserted.

Tomorrow at breakfast President Eisenhower will follow up his speech with a further report to ten leading Senators and thirteen Representatives.

**Reply on Two Fronts**

The speech, delivered five days after the President's return from the summit conference, was primarily a carefully worded reply to critics at home and abroad.

Renewing his five-year-old offer of an "open skies" agreement with the Soviet Union, the President offered to donate United States reconnaissance aircraft for any such plan set up by the United Nations.

After making this offer, he illustrated what a United Nations aircraft could do by showing a picture taken from a plane thirteen miles above a naval station north of San Diego. He pointed out that it clearly showed two intersecting runways including diagonal six-inch white lines marking off plane parking spaces. The White House later said that the lines were four inches wide.

The showing of the photograph vividly illustrated the advance in photographic techniques and materials since World War II.

It also clearly called atten-

Continued on Page 6, Column 3

Associated Press Wirephoto
PHOTO SHOWN BY EISENHOWER: This picture of a California air station, taken at altitude of 13 miles, was shown by President on TV. Noting that lines on parking lot, upper right, are four inches wide, he stressed effectiveness of aerial surveillance.

## 2 LANDS BID SOVIET AVOID VOTE IN U. N.

### Ecuador and Ceylon Urge Gromyko to Forgo Council Balloting on U-2 Charge

By THOMAS J. HAMILTON
Special to The New York Times.

UNITED NATIONS, N. Y., May 25—Ecuador and Ceylon appealed to the Soviet Union today not to press to a vote its resolution condemning flights of United States aircraft over Soviet territory.

Their requests were presented after three days of debate in the Security Council had demonstrated that the Soviet resolution would be overwhelmingly rejected.

Of the eleven members of the Council, only the Soviet Union and Poland will vote for the resolution, and there will be at least seven opposing votes. Ceylon and Tunisia are now expected to abstain, but some sources saw a possibility that Tunisia might also vote against the Soviet proposal.

Andrei A. Gromyko, Soviet Foreign Minister, did not reply to the appeals from Sir Claude Corea of Ceylon, who is president of the Security Council for May, and José A. Correa of Ecuador.

On the insistence of Henry

Continued on Page 8, Column 4

## Tiros Films Soviet Clouds Without a Moscow Protest

By JOHN W. FINNEY
Special to The New York Times.

WASHINGTON, May 25—Since the U-2 spy plane incident, the National Aeronautics and Space Administration has been taking detailed cloud pictures over the Soviet Union without Soviet objections and without the advance approval of the State Department.

The pictures have been taken for the last two weeks by the high resolution camera in the Tiros I meteorological satellite launched on April 1. The pictures are now being processed by the space agency with the expectation that they will be made public in the near future.

Past performances of the camera make it unlikely that the pictures will show any recognizable ground objects in the Soviet Union. The significance of the pictures, however, is that they will provide something of a precedent for a nation's right to use satellites for peaceful, scientific purposes and indirectly for military warning and reconnaissance purposes.

**Midas Working Well**

Meanwhile, the first of the early-warning satellites—the experimental Midas II launched yesterday from Cape Canaveral, Fla.—was reported by the Air Force today to be working perfectly.

The Air Force announced that the capability of the satellite's infrared sensors to detect ballistic missiles as they are launched would be tested early next week.

As the satellite passes overhead, large magnesium flares, visible for fifty miles, will be lighted on the ground to determine the sensitivity of the infrared sensors. Plans call for igniting one flare at Edwards

Continued on Page 8, Column 3

## Battered Chile Hit By 3 New Tremors

By The Associated Press

SANTIAGO, Chile, May 25—Three heavy quakes and fresh tidal waves spread panic in southern Chile today.

[At Honolulu, a tidal wave alert touched off a mid-day scramble to high ground throughout the Hawaiian Islands, United Press International reported. The alert was called off after minor fluctuations in the sea level.]

A new, quake-born volcano joined six older craters in spewing smoke and ash over stricken southern Chile.

The countryside's terrain was shifted by the violence of the quakes that began Saturday.

With nearly 2,000 persons dead or missing, authorities expected the recorded toll to rise considerably when reports arrive from areas still isolated by a breakdown in communications.

Perhaps 2,000,000 Chileans

Continued on Page 3, Column 4

## PEIPING'S VICTORY ON IDEOLOGY SEEN

### Sharp Rift With Moscow on Attitude Toward the West Is Tied to Summit Failure

By HARRISON E. SALISBURY

A violent ideological dispute between the Soviet Union and Communist China was raging on the eve of the summit meeting and may now have been resolved in favor of Peiping.

That conclusion has been reached by some specialists in Soviet affairs after examining texts of an unusual exchange of ideological arguments between Moscow and Peiping. The exchange occurred on the ninetieth anniversary of Lenin's birth, April 22—nine days before the U-2 incident.

The text of the Chinese arguments has been published in the April 26 issue of the English-language Peking Review, which has reached New York. The Soviet presentation was contained in an address at the Lenin stadium in Moscow by Otto V. Kuusinen, member of the Communist party's Presidium. His speech was published by Pravda, Soviet party newspaper.

**Views Radically Opposed**

It seems probable that the controversy and the radically opposed views of the Soviet and Chinese Communist parties played a major role in the evolution of Premier Khrushchev's policy on the eve of the Paris meeting.

The documents make clear that as late as April 22 the Soviet and Chinese positions were far apart. The Chinese were insisting that little or nothing might be expected from negotiation with the "imperialist West." They said that President Eisenhower had continued to conduct a warlike, aggressive policy despite the Camp David discussions with Premier Khrushchev last September.

The public Soviet position hewed strictly to Premier Khrushchev's position that discus-

Continued on Page 7, Column 1

NEWS INDEX


| | Page | | Page |
|---|---|---|---|
| Art | 67 | Music | 36-38 |
| Books | 30-31 | Obituaries | 33 |
| Bridge | 30 | Real Estate | 54 |
| Business | 44-45, 53 | Screen | 36-38 |
| Buyers | 44 | Ships and Air | 66 |
| Crossword | 31 | Society | 29 |
| Editorial | 32 | Sports | 39-44 |
| Events Today | 38 | TV and Radio | 67 |
| Fashions | 29 | Theatres | 36-38 |
| Financial | 44-54 | U. N. Proceedings | 5 |
| Food | 28-29 | Wash. Proceedings | 21 |
| Man in the News | 18 | Weather | 66 |

News Summary and Index, Page 35


## TURKISH DEPUTIES BATTLE IN HOUSE

### 15 Hurt as Rival Party Groups Hurl Furniture

Special to The New York Times.

ANKARA, Turkey, May 25—Fighting broke out in the Grand National Assembly today. Fifteen members were wounded by flying desk tops and broken chairs before the fighting between Deputies of Premier Adnan Menderes' Democratic party and of the Opposition People's Republican party was halted.

The affray started when Kasim Gulek, a former secretary general of the People's Republican party, insisted on talking after the Speaker had ruled him out of order. Under debate was a motion of the Republicans demanding that a bill amending the election law be put before Parliament without delay.

Mr. Gulek said the Opposition had persistently been denied the right of speech and, therefore, he would proceed to speak in defiance of the Speaker's ruling.

He was at once attacked by Democratic Deputies and his fellow Republicans rushed to his rescue.

As the fight developed, most of the Republican members gathered along the wall to the right of the rostrum and the Democrats withdrew along the left wall. The two sides hurled pieces of furniture, inkpots and briefcases for about fifteen minutes.

The Speaker finally stopped the battle by ordering a recess.

Continued on Page 2, Column 3

"All the News That's Fit to Print"

# The New York Times.

LATE CITY EDITION
U. S. Weather Bureau Report (Page 66) forecasts: Variable cloudiness today; fair and cool tonight. Fair tomorrow.
Temp. range: 76—60; yesterday: 75.8—61.5.
Temp.-Hum. Index: 71; yesterday: 70.

VOL. CIX..No. 37,419. NEW YORK, WEDNESDAY, JULY 6, 1960. FIVE CENTS
10 cents beyond 50-mile zone from New York City except on Long Island. Higher in air delivery cities.



## U.S. FILES PROTEST ON CUBAN SEIZURE OF OIL REFINERIES

### Strong Note Asks Return of Two Plants—Calls Action Illegal and Unethical

### SUGAR IMPORTS HALTED

### President's Move on Quota Is Awaited—Advisers on Americas to Meet

*Text of United States note is printed on Page 2.*

By WILLIAM J. JORDEN
Special to The New York Times.

WASHINGTON, July 5—The United States filed a vigorous protest today with Cuba against her seizure of two United States-owned oil refineries.

The action was one of several during the day reflecting the rising tension in relations between the two nations.

The Agriculture Department ordered a halt in any new imports of sugar from Cuba pending action by the President on a special bill that authorizes him to cut Cuba's quota in the United States market.

The State Department announced that the National Advisory Committee on Inter-American Affairs would meet tomorrow and Thursday. Informed sources said relations with Cuba would head the agenda.

**Action Called Arbitrary**

A note delivered to the Ministry of Foreign Relations in Havana described the seizure of the refineries as illegal, arbitrary and unethical. It asked the Government of Premier Fidel Castro to return the action.

There was little hope in Washington that Cuban officials would reverse their action. The expectation was for more rather than less trouble, with further seizures of property owned by foreigners.

The diplomatic protest resulted from the seizure last week of refineries owned by Texaco, Inc., and Esso (Cuba), Inc., a subsidiary of the Standard Oil Company (New Jersey). Cuban authorities said they were taking control of the refineries because of the companies' refusal to process crude oil bought by Cuba from the Soviet Union.

A refinery owned by the Royal Dutch-Shell Group was also taken over. Britain has

Continued on Page 2, Column 3

## Ex-Cuban Premier Quits Regime and Asks Asylum

### Miro Cardona, Ambassador-Designate to U. S., Cites 'Ideological' Conflict—Castro Gets Expropriation Law

By TAD SZULC
Special to The New York Times.

HAVANA, Wednesday, July 6—Dr. José Miro Cardona, Cuba's Ambassador-designate to the United States, broke with the Government of Fidel Castro yesterday. He requested asylum in the Argentine Embassy.

Dr. Miro Cardona, 58 years old, served as the first Premier of the Castro regime.

Three other Cuban ambassadors were discharged yesterday.

Both a Foreign Ministry purge of "unreliable" diplomats and the ambassadors' desire to leave the Government service appeared to be behind the dismissals.

Early today the Cuban Government established the machinery for nationalizing United States property here through "forced expropriation" in retaliation for the expected cut in the sugar quota.

The United States Congress has authorized the President to slash Cuba's annual exports into the United States. The United States has placed an embargo on imports of Cuban sugar pending action by the President.

Dr. Miro Cardona's defection considered the most significant of many defections from the top diplomatic ranks of the Castro Government, was accompanied by a letter of resignation to President Osvaldo Dorticós Torrado. Dr. Miro Cardona, a well-known lawyer, declared in the letter that he was convinced "the ideological divergencies between the policies of the Government and my conscience are already insoluble."

Dr. Miro Cardona, who played a key role in the revolution against Gen. Fulgencio Batista, former dictator, served as Premier of Cuba from Jan. 7 to Feb. 12, 1959, when Dr.

Continued on Page 3, Column 4

## Indian 5-Year Plan Needs 4.6 Billion in Foreign Aid

Special to The New York Times.

NEW DELHI, India, July 5—India will require $4,600,000,000 in foreign exchange to finance projects proposed in her third five-year-plan, which is to begin next April.

The third plan calls for a total investment of the equivalent of $23,625,000,000.

The foreign-exchange needs for development of the nation's economic programs were outlined in a report published today by the Government.

The report noted that foreign exchange constituted one of the key factors to the success of the plan because more than 50 per cent of the total investment in the public (state-owned) sector would be devoted to the expansion of heavy and basic industries and transport and communications. Foreign exchange will be needed to buy foreign supplies and equipment for expanding these industries.

**Disadvantages to Cause Strain**

The third plan, it was noted, would start with several disadvantages that would impose a heavy strain on the national economy.

The first disadvantage is that India's foreign - exchange reserves have dwindled to a level leaving no scope for further withdrawals. This means that the entire foreign-exchange requirements of the third plan will have to be met by foreign aid.

The second disadvantage is that the cost of machinery and equipment in overseas markets has risen sharply.

The third disadvantage is that India would also have to arrange for private-sector require-

Continued on Page 9, Column 3

## BONN CALLED LAX ON AID PROGRAMS

### U. S. Treasury Aide Asserts the West Germans Are Not Pulling Their Weight

By SYDNEY GRUSON
Special to The New York Times.

BONN, Germany, July 5—The United States told West Germany today that it was not pulling its weight in providing aid to the developing countries of Asia, Africa and South America.

The criticism of West Germany's past and projected aid programs was made by T. Graydon Upton, Assistant Secretary of the Treasury, at the opening session of a meeting of the nine-nation Development Assistance Group.

The organization was established this year on United States initiative to work out methods and compare information of foreign-aid programs. The delegates of Britain, Canada and France echoed Mr. Upton's criticism, according to a diplomat present at the opening session.

The Germans had been expecting the criticism and, privately acknowledged that it was justified. Dr. Hans Reinhardt of the Ministry of the Economy made a formal defense of West Germany's programs and plans, but then directed the meeting's attention to Dr. Ludwig Erhard's speech in the recent parliamentary debate on foreign aid.

Dr. Erhard, the Minister of the Economy, told Parliament that West Germany "must increase its help" to developing

Continued on Page 8, Column 3

## Khrushchev Looks To Reds' Triumph

By M. S. HANDLER
Special to The New York Times.

VILLACH, Austria, June 5—"Life is short," Premier Khrushchev said today, "and I want to see the Red Flag fly over the whole world in my lifetime."

The remark was made in a confident but bantering tone to a group of correspondents who surrounded the Soviet leader after he had viewed the Kaprun hydroelectric power dam, one of the proudest achievements of Austrian engineering in the post-war period.

Mr. Khrushchev was in excellent humor after last night's party in the Residenz, former seat of the Archbishops of Salzburg.

The sharp cold air had refreshed Mr. Khrushchev as he examined the Kaprun project,

Continued on Page 15, Column 1

## U. S. SAID TO DROP PLAN FOR SESSION OF U. N. ARMS BODY

### Reported Abandoning Its Bid for Meeting This Month to Publicize Soviet Walkout

By THOMAS J. HAMILTON
Special to The New York Times.

UNITED NATIONS, N. Y., July 5—Reliable sources said today that the United States had decided not to press for a meeting this month of the United Nations Disarmament Commission.

The United States and Canada had taken the lead in urging that the commission be called into session by July 15 to publicize the actions of the Soviet bloc, which broke up the ten-nation disarmament group in Geneva.

Two other Western members of the group, Britain and Italy, had agreed to go along with the United States in proposing the meeting.

**France Issued Warning**

However, France took the position from the beginning that the Western powers would forfeit the propaganda advantage given to them by the Soviet bloc's behavior unless they had a clear-cut program to submit to the Disarmament Commission.

[At the Geneva conference on banning nuclear tests, the Soviet Union accepted a British compromise proposal for assuring East-West parity in the top jobs of the projected international control commission. The United States was said to be giving the plan favorable consideration.]

The United States plan to seek a meeting of the Disarmament Commission aroused no enthusiasm and met with a serious setback last week from Secretary General Dag Hammarskjold of the United Nations. He said the commission should be in no "rush" to meet and should allow the dust to settle.

**Allies Delay Decision**

As a result of this reception, the representatives in Washington of the five Western powers have delayed taking a decision pending Premier Khrushchev's response to Western suggestions that the Geneva negotiations be resumed.

Reliable sources said they saw no possibility that Mr. Khrushchev would agree. They predicted that the five Western governments would simply take no action at this time regarding a meeting of the Disarmament Commission, thus allowing the matter to be decided by default.

One Western delegate said that if Canada continued to insist upon a meeting there was a faint chance that the other Western powers might agree to join in. However, the leading United Nations delegates are going ahead with their vacation plans on the basis that there will be no meeting of the Dis-

Continued on Page 6, Column 4

## JACK CASE GOES TO JURORS TODAY; UNGAR ASSAILED

### Defense Declares Realty Man 'Enmeshed' Borough Chief —Scotti Asks Conviction

By RUSSELL PORTER

The case against Borough President Hulan E. Jack of Manhattan is expected to go to the jury today.

Both the prosecution and the defense summed up their cases yesterday, depicting the Borough President in conflicting lights. The prosecution saw him as a sophisticated politician who had "degraded" his high office "with his eyes open." The defense pictured him as a "babe in the woods" misled by a "conniving" friend.

Judge Joseph A. Sarafite is scheduled to deliver his charge to the jury at 10 A. M. today in the Court of General Sessions. He will then submit the case to the jury for its deliberations and verdict.

**Renovation at Issue**

Mr. Jack has stood trial on charges of letting Sidney J. Ungar, a lawyer and real estate promoter doing business with the city, pay $4,400 for remodeling his apartment. The Borough President is also charged with conspiring to obstruct justice by concealing the source of the money.

If convicted, he would be subject to one year's imprisonment and $500 fine on each of four counts in the indictment, and would automatically lose his $25,000-a-year city job. He has suspended himself from office pending completion of the case.

Alfred J. Scotti, chief assistant district attorney, in a two-and - three - quarter - hour summary, which at times was highly impassioned, urged a verdict of guilty. He argued that the evidence showed overwhelmingly that the Borough President had "degraded" his high office by "shameful" conduct and "callous disregard of his legal and moral obligations."

**Pleads With Jury**

The prosecutor also pleaded with the jury not to let Mr. Jack off for "any strange reason that has no place in this trial."

Carson DeWitt Baker, defense counsel, in a two-hour discussion of his case, asked acquittal on the ground that the Borough President had been a "babe in the woods" who had been "ensnared" in Ungar schemes, but had refused to be corrupted. He emphasized testimony by Mayor Wagner and all other members of the Board of Estimate that Mr. Jack had never tried to influence their votes for Ungar projects.

Mr. Baker also put stress on the many character witnesses, including ministers, priests and rabbis, who had testified to the defendant's high reputation for integrity.

Mr. Scotti ridiculed the de-

Continued on Page 34, Column 1

Associated Press Wirephoto

HAT IN RING: Senator Lyndon B. Johnson of Texas formally announces his candidacy for the Democratic Presidential nomination at news conference held in Washington.

## Democratic Hopefuls Face Early Test on Voting Rule

By W. H. LAWRENCE
Special to The New York Times.

LOS ANGELES, July 5—Democrats formally opened pre-convention preparations today with the prospect of an early clear-cut test of strength between Senator John F. Kennedy and his combined opposition on a rules-change issue.

The test vote Monday night may give an indication in advance of the scheduled Wednesday night balloting on a Presidential nominee whether the Massachusetts Senator has the clear convention majority that his supporters claim and his opponents dispute.

The opposition goal, announced by backers of Senators Lyndon B. Johnson of Texas and Stuart Symington of Missouri, is a new rule that would prevent delegations from changing their vote after the initial roll-call of states and before the vote totals are announced.

**Seek to Stop Stampede**

Their aim is to prevent the early withdrawal of favorite-son candidates and a possible stampede of vote switches to Senator Kennedy at the end of the first roll-calls on which he will concededly hold the lead.

"We'll fight it if they try it," Robert F. Kennedy, a key strategist in his brother's drive for the Presidency, said.

Meanwhile, the party's Platform Committee began today a four-day series of hearings. The first session was marked by sharp debate on a proposal that the Democrats oppose use of the Social Security system for a new medical care plan for the aged. However, Paul M. Butler, Democratic National Chairman, said he expected the convention to agree on a platform without a floor fight.

Mr. Butler said at a news conference that the outlook for party unity was good. Other officials said any efforts to challenge the credentials of Southern delegates would be limited to individuals. The credentials Committee will meet on Friday to deal with any challenges that arise.

**Similar Test in 1952**

The rules-test issue recalled that eight years ago a similar test disclosed the weakness of the late Senator Robert A. Taft of Ohio in a Republican convention that later gave the nomination to President Eisenhower.

Then the question was a "fair-play" amendment, providing that delegates whose credentials were challenged could not vote until the issue of their seating had been decided finally by the convention.

Present Democratic rules permit unlimited vote switches after a roll-call, but the permanent chairman, who will be Gov. LeRoy Collins of Florida in this convention, has the sole discretion in deciding which delega-

Continued on Page 20, Column 2

## MANISCALCO CASE BRINGS NEW TRIAL

### City Buildings Aide Accused Over Garage Permit—His Clerk Is Suspended

By JOHN SIBLEY

A Buildings Department employe was suspended yesterday on charges of falsifying records for a contractor who sought special favors from Borough President Albert V. Maniscalco of Staten Island.

At the same time the employe's supervisor was accused of ordering the illegal alterations and was notified that he must face departmental trial and possible dismissal.

In a simultaneous development, Buildings Commissioner Peter J. Reidy sent to District Attorney Frank S. Hogan contradictory sworn statements by the contractor who built a garage at Mr. Maniscalco's home, reportedly in the hope of getting preferential treatment.

These developments stemmed from an investigation early this year by the State Commission on Governmental Operations of the City of New York. The commission said it had found evidence that Marvin Klein, a builder, had been favored by Mr. Maniscalco in dealings involving purchase of city real estate, zoning and in sewer connections to his projects.

The suspended employe is Clarence Martino of 44 Waterside Parkway, Great Kills, S. I., a $5,750-a-year clerk in the Staten Island office of the Department of Buildings. During a

Continued on Page 34, Column 5

## Goldfine and Aide Begin Jail Terms

By The Associated Press.

BOSTON, July 5—Bernard Goldfine went to Federal prison today for contempt of court in a tax case.

The wealthy textile manufacturer, who once boasted of friends in high political office, was handcuffed to a convicted bank embezzler as he was led away to serve ninety days in the Federal penitentiary at Danbury, Conn.

His secretary and business associate, Mildred Paperman, was taken to a county jail in Cambridge to serve ten days on a similar contempt charge.

Federal Judge Charles E. Wyzanski Jr. sent them off to jail after denying petitions by counsel and a personal appeal by Goldfine for ten days or two weeks more of freedom.

Goldfine, who is 69 years old, accepted the sentence calmly,

Continued on Page 21, Column 2

## JOHNSON ENTERS RACE OFFICIALLY; SEES 500 VOTES

### Texan Says Kennedy Will Receive Fewer Than 600 on the First Ballot

### HEALTH ISSUE IS BARRED

### Majority Leader Criticizes New Englander Obliquely —Cheered by Backers

*Transcript of Johnson news conference is on Page 18.*

By JOHN D. MORRIS
Special to The New York Times.

WASHINGTON, July 5—Senator Lyndon B. Johnson announced today that he was a candidate for the Democratic Presidential nomination.

Senator Johnson said he expected to go to the convention with more than 500 first-ballot votes against fewer than 600 for Senator John F. Kennedy of Massachusetts. The nomination requires 761.

The 51-year-old Texan, majority leader of the Senate, had been campaigning for weeks. So his announcement was no surprise to anyone.

But he carried off the ritual of making a formal declaration before television cameras, now standard procedure for Presidential aspirants, in the approved manner.

**Backers Cheer Him**

Looking self-assured and dignified, he stood before a cluster of microphones and read a fifteen-minute prepared statement, then answered reporters' questions for fifteen minutes.

The performance was punctuated by cheers and applause from several hundred Johnson partisans who packed the spacious, coldly modern auditorium of the New Senate Office Building. House Speaker Sam Rayburn, the Senator's Texas colleague and campaign adviser, was among them.

The ceremony produced one surprise. In the question - and - answer period, when Senator Johnson passed up an opportunity to rule himself out as a possible nominee for Vice President.

"I have been prepared throughout my adult life to serve my country in any capacity where my country thought my services were essential," he declared.

"However," he went on, "I am

Continued on Page 18, Column 7

## JURY TO EXAMINE TV QUIZ PERJURY

### Hogan to Offer Data Today From 1958 Rigging Inquiry

By PETER FLINT

A special grand jury will begin an inquiry here today to determine whether criminal charges should be lodged against witnesses for false testimony in the investigation of television quiz shows.

The grand jury was impaneled yesterday at the request of District Attorney Frank S. Hogan after an eight-month investigation by his office.

"A great many" of the more than 100 persons questioned during the investigation "are believed to have testified falsely" before a previous panel, Mr. Hogan said.

It was his investigation—begun in September, 1958—into the rigging of television quiz shows here that led to an inquiry by the House of Representatives that exposed widespread scandals in the industry.

Mr. Hogan announced that he would present evidence to the grand jury so it might determine whether the crimes of perjury, subornation of perjury, obstruction of justice or conspiracy had been committed.

A spokesman said that presentation of the evidence would take about three days, so that the appearance of witnesses, expected to include the major money winners on the rigged shows, would probably be delayed until next week.

The taking of testimony is expected to last at least a month. A spokesman for Mr. Hogan's office acknowledged "a possibility" that the life of the grand jury, the fourth impan-

Continued on Page 26, Column 5

## Thai Rulers Honored in Parade

The New York Times

King Phumiphol Aduldet of Thailand acknowledges cheers along route of the motorcade up Broadway to City Hall.

### King and Queen Win Applause of Crowd Along Broadway

By GREG MacGREGOR

The unassuming dignity of a young King and the captivating smile of his radiant Queen won a multitude of admirers here yesterday.

With little more than curiosity, a crowd of lunchgoers estimated at 750,000 by the police, lined the streets of lower Broadway to become a spontaneous rooting section for the royal couple—King Phumiphol Aduldet and Queen Sirikit of Thailand.

The traditional ticker-tape-and-confetti parade became a short fiesta, and New Yorkers went back to work a little happier after the occasion.

The twenty-minute parade ended at 12:25 P. M. at City Hall, where the King and Queen signed the guest book and were received by Mayor and Mrs. Wagner.

"I have seen receptions in the movies, and I am very excited to receive one," the King said.

The 27 - year - old Queen, dressed in Siamese fashion for the first time here—an ankle-length skirt of pink silk and a pink silk jacket with buttons of

Continued on Page 13, Column 1

## 3D SOVIET ROCKET SHOT INTO PACIFIC

### 8,078-Mile Flight Reported —U.S. Planes See Impact

By The Associated Press.

MOSCOW, July 5—The Soviet Union fired a rocket into the mid-Pacific today and an official announcement said it had hit close to its target 8,078 miles from the launching pad.

[United States Navy planes observed the impact in the Pacific, United Press International reported.]

Tass, the Soviet press agency, said further test shots would follow before the end of July in carrying out a program to perfect powerful multi-stage rockets capable of reaching Mars or Venus and putting a man into space.

The Soviet announced Jan. 21 that in its first test, a powerful new multi-stage rocket had come within 1.24 of a mile of a target in an area about 1,000 miles southwest of Hawaii. That rocket was said to have traveled 7,760 miles.

A second rocket, on Feb. 1, ending the first series of tests, landed in the same target area, Moscow said.

The Soviet has not disclosed the launching sites for any of the tests.

Speculation abroad was that the January shot was from a base in the area of the Caspian Sea, nearly a third of the way around the earth. The range announced for the rocket today indicated it was launched from a base still farther away.

The United States on May 20 fired a Super Atlas rocket from Cape Canaveral, Fla., past the southern tip of Africa to near the Prince Edward Islands in

Continued on Page 4, Column 3

NEWS INDEX



| | Page | | Page |
|---|---|---|---|
| Art | 29 | Music | 26-29 |
| Books | 31 | Obituaries | 31 |
| Bridge | 30 | Real Estate | 54 |
| Business | 41-42, 53 | Screen | 26-29 |
| Buyers | 53 | Ships and Air | 66 |
| Crossword | 31 | Society | 30 |
| Editorial | 32 | Sports | 36-40 |
| Events Today | 33 | TV and Radio | 67 |
| Fashions | 15 | Theatres | 26-29 |
| Financial | 41-52 | U. N. Proceedings | 6 |
| Food | 33 | Weather | 66 |
| Man in the News | 3 | | |

News Summary and Index, Page 35

"All the News That's Fit to Print"

# The New York Times.

LATE CITY EDITION
U. S. Weather Bureau Report (Page 54) forecasts: Cloudy, chance of showers today. Fair, cooler, less humid tomorrow.
Temp. range: 84—72; yesterday: 83.2—70. Temp.-Hum. Index: high 70's; yesterday: 78.

VOL. CIX—No. 37,427. © 1960, by The New York Times Company. Times Square, New York 36, N. Y. NEW YORK, THURSDAY, JULY 14, 1960. 10 cents beyond 50-mile zone from New York City except on Long Island. Higher in air delivery cities. FIVE CENTS

# KENNEDY NOMINATED ON THE FIRST BALLOT; OVERWHELMS JOHNSON BY 806 VOTES TO 409

# Security Council Authorizes U. N. Force to Aid Congo

## PEACE UNIT VOTED

### U. S. and Soviet Clash in Debate—Belgians Asked to Pull Out

*Congolese texts, resolution, debate excerpts, Page 4.*

By THOMAS J. HAMILTON
Special to The New York Times.

UNITED NATIONS, N. Y., Thursday, July 14 — The Security Council authorized Secretary General Dag Hammarskjold today to organize and send a United Nations force to the Congo.

The vote was eight in favor and none against, with Britain, France and Nationalist China abstaining.

The vote was taken at 3:03 A. M., nearly six and a half hours after the Security Council, at the request of Mr. Hammarskjold, began its urgent night session. The decision was delayed by bitter exchanges between the United States and Soviet representatives, Henry Cabot Lodge and Arkady A. Sobolev. The Council adjourned at 3:21 A. M.

**Outcome Was Uncertain**

The outcome remained uncertain until the last. It was known that Britain, France and Nationalist China would abstain. They objected to a provision in the resolution, which was introduced by Tunisia, calling for the withdrawal of Belgian troops from the Congo.

The withdrawal recommendation was included on the demand of the Soviet Union and the African states. However, word was passed during the long meeting that the Soviet Union and Poland had not received instructions on the Tunisian proposal, and would therefore abstain if the United States insisted upon a vote at this meeting.

This belief was strengthened after Walter Loridan, the Belgian representative, announced that Belgian troops would be withdrawn from the Congo when the United Nations force is able to provide "effective" maintenance of order.

Mr. Sobolev termed this statement unsatisfactory. He introduced amendments condemning Belgian "armed aggression" in the Congo, stating that the Belgian forces must be withdrawn "immediately," and limiting participation in the United Nations force to the other African states.

The first two amendments were rejected 7 to 2, with only the Soviet Union and Poland

Continued on Page 4, Column 3

## Belgian Commandos Rout Congo Troops at Airport

### Bunche Meets With Both Sides to Try to Halt Clashes—Congolese Open Fire on Convoy of Refugees

By HENRY TANNER
Special to The New York Times.

LEOPOLDVILLE, the Congo, July 13—Belgian commandos occupied Leopoldville's airport today and then clashed with Congolese troops. At least six Congolese and two Belgians were killed.

Belgian forces occupied the airport at midmorning. They went into action after Congolese soldiers had moved into the airport and had threatened to interfere with the evacuation of Belgian civilians by Sabena, the Belgian airline.

[Leopoldville was reported by press associations to be under the control of Belgian troops, but there was uncertainty over the extent of control. Congolese troops opened fire Wednesday night on a convoy of 300 Belgians heading for the airport. Reuters said the Congo Government had declared that a "state of war" existed with Belgium. The Congo has asked Ghana to send troops.

[In Brussels, the Belgian Government said it would keep troops at key points in the Congo.]

Dr. Ralph J. Bunche, United Nations Under Secretary, met with Congolese authorities and Ambassador Jean van den Bosch of Belgium this afternoon in an effort to halt the clashes.

Dr. Bunche was reported to have been called in by the Congolese to mediate a cease-fire between them and the Belgians. He left the United States Embassy, where he has an office, in the early afternoon with the blue United Nations flag flying

Continued on Page 3, Column 2

## MOSCOW BIDS U. N. CONVENE AT ONCE ON RB-47 INCIDENT

### Says Flights by U. S. Planes With Reconnaissance Aim Are Threat to Peace

By OSGOOD CARUTHERS
Special to The New York Times.

MOSCOW, July 13—The Soviet Union called today for an urgent meeting of the United Nations Security Council to discuss its charges of United States "aggressive actions."

The Soviet complaint derived from the shooting down of a United States RB-47 reconnaissance plane off the Soviet coast in the Barents Sea on July 1.

[In a statement from the summer White House at Newport, R. I., the United States backed a full investigation by the United Nations of the "wanton shooting down" of the plane.]

Moscow called for the United Nations meeting in a cablegram sent by Foreign Minister Andrei A. Gromyko today to the president of the Security Council, José A. Correa of Ecuador.

**Hammarskjold Gets Copy**

The message, a copy of which was sent to Secretary General Dag Hammarskjold, charged that the United States flights constituted "a serious threat to the preservation of peace."

The United States has denied that the RB-47 plane had violated Soviet territorial waters as alleged by the Kremlin.

The Soviet request came on the heels of a statement yesterday by Premier Khrushchev that his Government might take the matter of the plane before the Security Council.

He said he did not expect that the Security Council, which he described as an "instrument" of the United States, would take any action satisfactory to the Soviet Union. However, he said he thought it was necessary to raise the question there anyway if only to "discredit the dishonest judges once more."

Mr. Gromyko's cablegram, which he said would be followed by an explanatory letter, noted that the Security Council had discussed the previous plane incident, in which a U-2 reconnaissance jet was shot down deep inside Soviet territory on May 1.

The message asked the Security Council to "take such measures as appear necessary to put an end to these dangers

Continued on Page 6, Column 5

Associated Press Wirephoto

AFTER THE VICTORY: Senator John F. Kennedy of Massachusetts heads for rostrum at Los Angeles Memorial Sports Arena to address the Democratic National Convention.

## LONG DRIVE WINS

### Wyoming's Vote Puts Bostonian Over Top Before Acclamation

*Kennedy's talk on Page 14; nominating speeches, 16.*

By W. H. LAWRENCE
Special to The New York Times.

LOS ANGELES, Thursday, July 14—Senator John F. Kennedy smashed his way to a first-ballot Presidential nomination at the Democratic National Convention last night and won the right to oppose Vice President Nixon in November.

The 43-year-old Massachusetts Senator overwhelmed his opposition, piling up 806 votes to 409 ballots for his nearest rival, Senator Lyndon B. Johnson of Texas, the Senate majority leader. Senator Kennedy's victory came just before 11 o'clock last night [2 A. M. Thursday, New York time].

Then the convention made it unanimous on motion of Gov. James T. Blair Jr. of Missouri, who had placed Senator Stuart Symington of Missouri in nomination.

**'We Shall Win'**

Senator Kennedy, appearing before the shouting convention early today, pledged he would carry the fight to the country in the fall "and we shall win."

He thanked his defeated rivals for their generosity and appealed to all of their backers to keep the party strong and united in a tremendously important election. He spoke directly of Senators Johnson and Symington and the favorite sons, but made no reference to Adlai E. Stevenson.

The third session of the national convention adjourned after his speech. The next session will convene at 5 P. M. today.

Little Wyoming, well down the roll-call, provided the decisive fifteen votes that gave victory to Senator Kennedy. Two favorite-son states, Minnesota and New Jersey, waited in vain to give the on-rushing Kennedy bandwagon the final shove.

When Wyoming came in with its vote, the Kennedy total had mounted to 765 votes, or more than the 761 votes required for nomination.

It was a tremendous victory for Senator Kennedy. Mr. Johnson, the Senate majority leader, had fought desperately to reverse a Kennedy tide that had been running for months. But Senator Johnson quickly telephoned his congratulations to

Continued on Page 14, Column 1

## KISHI IS STABBED AT HOME IN TOKYO

### Japan's Premier Is Reported Not Badly Hurt — Ikeda Chosen His Successor

By RICHARD J. H. JOHNSTON
Special to The New York Times.

TOKYO, Thursday, July 14—Premier Nobusuke Kishi was attacked by an assassin and stabbed in the thigh within an hour after his apparent successor had been elected by his party.

The Premier was attacked at a reception in his official residence. The attacker was identified by the authorities as Taizo Aramaki, a Rightist, about 45 years old.

Mr. Kishi was removed to a nearby hospital, where it was announced that his condition was not serious.

His assailant was arrested.

The police established the time of the attack as 2:30 P. M. This would be within forty minutes of Mr. Kishi's departure from Hibiya Hall in Downtown Tokyo, where the Liberal-Democratic party convention had been held.

The reception at the Premier's home was arranged to honor Hayato Ikeda, who, less than an hour before had been elected in the convention of the governing party as its new president, replacing Mr. Kishi who had resigned in the convention a short time before.

Mr. Ikeda, now Trade Minister, backs the Kishi policies.

The attack on the 63-year-old Premier was an ironic twist in the turbulent politics of recent months in Japan.

On June 23 he had announced

Continued on Page 11, Column 2

## Peru Urges O.A.S. Debate Red Threat; U. S. Favors Parley

Special to The New York Times.

WASHINGTON, July 13 — Peru has suggested that the foreign ministers of the American nations meet soon to consider the Soviet threat to inter-American unity and democracy in the Western Hemisphere.

Informed sources said the Peruvian initiative was welcomed by the United States and that Washington would support the proposal. It is believed that the Peruvian suggestion will be considered at a meeting this week of the Council of the Organization of American States.

The Peruvian suggestion was circulated today among representatives of the twenty-one members of the O.A.S. It was also the subject of urgent consultation at embassies and in the State Department.

Peru's proposal was couched in careful diplomatic language, but its meaning was clear. The message stressed the necessity for the continued solidarity of the countries of this hemisphere. It called for the defense of the regional system in inter-American affairs and of democratic principles.

There was no specific refer-

Continued on Page 12, Column 5

## JOHNSON PLEDGES HELP TO KENNEDY

### He Assures Candidate of His Full Support and Issues a Call for Party Unity

By JOHN D. MORRIS
Special to The New York Times.

LOS ANGELES, July 13—Senator Lyndon B. Johnson accepted tonight "with all my heart" Senator John F. Kennedy's nomination for President.

The Texan, who had watched the convention proceedings by television in his suite at the Biltmore Hotel, issued a four-paragraph statement just as the first ballot ended. It had been prepared as Montana and some other Mountain States failed to provide expected shifts to the Johnson banner.

The statement follows:

"The delegates have made their decision and I accept it with all my heart.

"Senator Kennedy has my sincere congratulations, and my solemn assurance that in the coming months of this campaign, no one will be more dedicated than I—no one will work harder than I to make doubly sure of what all Democrats here and throughout the country know must come about for the good of the nation and the free world—that John F. Kennedy will be elected the next President of the United States.

"We have a winner—he has proved it here.

"Now, let our party unite behind our candidate—let us sweep the country this November, so that in January Demo-

Continued on Page 15, Column 6

## Symington Heavy Favorite For Second Place on Ticket

By LEO EGAN
Special to The New York Times.

LOS ANGELES, July 13—Senator Stuart Symington became a heavy favorite for the Vice-Presidential nomination tonight following Senator John F. Kennedy's first-ballot nomination for President. The Missouri delegation was the first to swing into line behind Senator Kennedy after the New Englander had clinched the nomination for first place.

At the Kennedy headquarters in the Biltmore Hotel it was announced that the Presidential nominee would meet with those under consideration for Vice President and with party leaders from all sections of the country before going to bed.

Before the convention opened, he had promised the New York delegation, which was an important factor in his victory, that he would consult with its leaders before making a choice on second place.

Senator Symington parried questions about the Vice-Presidential nomination with the comment that the matter was entirely up to Senator Kennedy.

**Good Word for Jackson**

Although the Missouri Senator was regarded as the front runner for the Vice-Presidential nomination, two others were receiving serious consideration.

They were Gov. Orville L. Freeman of Minnesota, who had placed the New Englander in nomination, and Senator Henry M. Jackson of Washington State.

At a meeting of the Washington delegation today, Robert F. Kennedy, the Senator's brother and floor manager, said that Senator Jackson was his (Robert's) personal choice for the place but that political considerations might force his brother to turn elsewhere.

Governor Freeman had also been informed that those around Senator Kennedy had a high regard for him and that he would be acceptable as a Vice-Presidential candidate.

Up to the hour of Senator Kennedy's nomination, Senator Symington and Representative Charles A. Brown of Missouri, his campaign manager, were declaring that Senator Symington was not a candidate. But few delegates expected him to

Continued on Page 15, Column 6

## STEVENSON GIVEN A WILD RECEPTION

### His Nomination Touches Off Roaring Demonstration—It Lasts 25 Mintues

By WILLIAM M. BLAIR
Special to The New York Times.

LOS ANGELES, July 13—A wild, emotional demonstration for Adlai E. Stevenson shook the Democratic National Convention tonight.

As the name of the man who led the Democrats in 1952 and 1956 was placed before the convention, the galleries erupted in a screaming roar that dwarfed all that went before.

A rip-roaring nominating speech by Senator Eugene J. McCarthy, an "egghead" from Minnesota, set off the nearest thing to hysteria that this convention has seen.

Although the demonstrators obviously were full of enthusiasm, it was also obvious that the demonstration was at least partly contrived.

It took the convention chairman, Gov. LeRoy Collins of Florida, twenty-five minutes to slow down the stamping, shouting show to get seconding speeches.

**Supporters Storm Floor**

Stevenson supporters from outside the convention stormed the floor, some apparently gaining entrance by ruses, to call for the man who said he did not come West to seek the nomination.

Chanting, placard-waving demonstrators jammed the aisles while the galleries suddenly came alive with thousands of placards and hundreds of demonstrators going round and round in a deafening din.

The bobbing, weaving demonstrators on the floor, many of them young persons, caused many delegates to cover their ears. And many covered their heads with their hands as the Stevenson rooters bounced a giant, white papier-mâché ball through the air. The ball represented a snowball intended to dramatize the "Draft Stevenson" effort.

For the most part, the delegates appeared unmoved by the

Continued on Page 15, Column 2

## HOGAN WILL PRESS A NEW JACK TRIAL

### Fall Date to Be Asked Today in Borough Chief's Case

By PETER FLINT

A date for a new trial for Borough President Hulan E. Jack of Manhattan on charges of conflict of interest and conspiracy will be requested by District Attorney Frank S. Hogan today in the Court of General Sessions.

Since the court is now in summer recess, with only three of the nine judges sitting, the prosecutor is expected to ask for a date in the fall.

Mr. Jack's first trial ended last Thursday night when the jury failed to agree on a verdict after two days of deliberation and was discharged.

Mr. Jack's lawyer, Carson DeWitt Baker, said he would request an immediate trial. But he expressed the view that Mr. Hogan would "have his way as usual," and that the new trial probably would begin in October.

Mr. Baker also expressed "firm conviction" that the Borough President would continue his self-suspension from office until the case was resolved. Mr.

Continued on Page 25, Column 5

## Union Forcing Plant To Return to City

By A. H. RASKIN

An arbitrator has ordered a New York clothing manufacturer to reopen his closed factory here and to pay the Amalgamated Clothing Workers union more than $200,000 in damages for having moved his work to Mississippi.

The employer, who lost a court fight to block arbitration, made it clear yesterday that he would resist the unusual award through new litigation.

The union is confident that recent decisions of the United States Supreme Court strengthening the power of arbitrators and limiting the right of judges to upset their awards will bar a successful challenge.

Jacob S. Potofsky, president of the Amalgamated, hailed the award as proof that "runaway

Continued on Page 55, Column 4

## 2 Planes Down Off Philippines; 86 of 88 Aboard Saved From Sea

### Two Lost as U. S. Airliner Ditches—Island DC-3 Also Crashes, 30 on It Safe

By United Press International.

MANILA, Thursday, July 14—An American airplane and a Philippine passenger plane went down at sea in separate accidents today with a total of eighty-eight persons aboard. But eighty-six were reported safe after swift, dramatic rescue from shark-dangerous waters.

At least thirty-four Americans were aboard one of the planes, a Northwest Orient Airlines DC7-C on the last leg of a New York-to-Manila flight with fifty-one passengers and a crew of seven.

United States air force amphibious planes from Clark Field reported the rescue of fifty-six persons from the Northwest plane. One person was reported killed and one missing.

In the southern Philippines, 500 miles from Manila between the islands of Negros and Mindanao, a Philippines Airlines plane on an inter-island flight ditched in shallow water near land and all thirty passengers and crew members were picked up.

Passengers on the Northwest

The New York Times July 14, 1960

Sites of crash of U. S. plane (1) and Philippines plane (2)

airliner included Dr. Rodrigo L. Sarmiento, Filipino surgeon banished from the United States for the confessed killing of a Brooklyn nurse, Margaret Kabak. Dr. Sarmiento was among the survivors.

The Northwest plane, which had come from New York via Seattle, Anchorage, Tokyo and Okinawa, crash-landed near the little island of Jimalog, of the Potillo group about 150 miles northeast of Manila, after a propeller "ran away" and fell off and a wing caught fire.

Capt. David Rall, 53 years old of Seattle, deliberately put the plane down at sea after radioing at 4:20 A. M. [4:20 P. M.

Continued on Page 12, Column 4

## Plan to End Strike On L.I.R.R. Offered

Governor Rockefeller's fact-finding board proposed an arbitration plan last night to bring an immediate end to the Long Island Rail Road strike.

The plan was rejected almost at once by the union's negotiating committee. It charged that most arbitrators had been "so brainwashed by the propaganda of the Association of American Railroads and the National Association of Manufacturers" that labor could not trust them.

The rejection will be reviewed by the 1,350 strikers at a meeting this morning, but union leaders said they would "bet a million dollars that the men will turn the idea down unanimously."

The company said the union's reaction made further study of the plan seem academic. It

Continued on Page 20, Column 2

## F.H.A. INVESTMENT OPENED TO PUBLIC

### Individuals Invited to Deal in U. S.-Insured Mortgages

By RICHARD E. MOONEY
Special to The New York Times.

WASHINGTON, July 13—The Government invited individuals today to invest in mortgages insured against loss by the Federal Housing Administration.

It was, in effect, an offer of a long-term investment that would earn a little more than 5 per cent and would be paid off by the Government if the mortgage went into default. The yields of representative stocks and bonds currently are lower than 5 per cent.

Investment in an F. H. A.-insured mortgage would not be riskless. The investor would have to hold his investment until the mortgage was paid off, by the homebuyer or F. H. A., if he were to realize the full return. If he sold out before that, he might sell at a loss.

Besides being an attractive offer, and a break with policy of twenty-five years' standing, today's action was the Government's third stimulant to sagging activity in home building in as many months.

In April, the F. H. A. reduced

Continued on Page 55, Column 4

NEWS INDEX



| | Page | | Page |
|---|---|---|---|
| Books | 25 | Obituaries | 27 |
| Bridge | 24 | Real Estate | 43 |
| Business | 34, 43 | Screen | 22, 23 |
| Crossword | 25 | Ships and Air | 54 |
| Editorial | 26 | Society | 24 |
| Fashions | 21 | Sports | 30-33 |
| Financial | 35-42 | TV and Radio | 55 |
| Food | 21 | Theatres | 22, 23 |
| Letters | 26 | U. N. Proceedings | 3 |
| Man in the News | 12 | Weather | 54 |
| Music | 22, 23 | | |



News Summary and Index, Page 29

"All the News That's Fit to Print"

# The New York Times.

LATE CITY EDITION

U. S. Weather Bureau Report (Page 48) (includes map)
Fair and pleasant today, tonight and tomorrow.
Temp. range: 78-64; yesterday: 72-60.
Temp.-Hum. Index: low 70's; yesterday: 71.

VOL. CIX..No. 37,428. NEW YORK, FRIDAY, JULY 15, 1960. FIVE CENTS

10 cents beyond 50-mile zone from New York City except on Long Island. Higher in air delivery cities.

# JOHNSON IS NOMINATED FOR VICE PRESIDENT; KENNEDY PICKS HIM TO PLACATE THE SOUTH

## U.S. Reaffirms Monroe Doctrine in Reply to Khrushchev

### 'KEEP OUT' POSTED

#### Note to Moscow Says 'Bolshevik Doctrine' Is Aim of Soviet

*Text of the State Department statement on Page 2.*

By DANA ADAMS SCHMIDT
Special to The New York Times.

WASHINGTON, July 14—The United States placed around the Western Hemisphere today a "keep out" sign meant for Premier Khrushchev.

Answering the Soviet Premier's comment on Tuesday that the Monroe Doctrine was dead, and his threat to use rockets to protect Cuba against United States armed intervention, the State Department reaffirmed the 137-year-old doctrine and denounced Mr. Khrushchev's "naked menace to world peace."

In a statement approved by President Eisenhower, the State Department counter-attacked with the charge that Mr. Khrushchev sought "to establish a Bolshevik doctrine providing for the use of Soviet military power in support of Communist movements anywhere in the world."

**Soviet Comment Cited**

The Soviet Premier said Tuesday at a news conference that he considered the Monroe Doctrine to have "outlived its time" and to have "died, so to say, a natural death." He said the United States was now using the doctrine "to rule all the Latin-American countries and meddle in their domestic affairs."

Mr. Khrushchev also assailed the treaty giving the United States a naval base at Guantanamo Bay in Cuba as a "sheer iniquity" for not having a time limit. He pledged Soviet support to Cuba against any United States military action that might follow moves to oust the United States from the base.

The State Department charged today that the Soviet leader had "abrogated to himself the power to determine what international agreements should or should not be binding—even though the Soviet Union is not a party thereto."

**Intervention Is Charged**

The United States statement added:

"While disregard for treaties to which it is a party may be viewed by the U. S. S. R. as a convenient approach to international relations, such an effort can only be regarded by law-abiding states as another example of Soviet intervention in the affairs of other countries."

With regard to the Monroe Doctrine, the State Department affirmed that its principles "are as valid today as they were in 1823 when the doctrine was proclaimed."

They are valid, the statement said, because they have been built into "the inter-American security system through the Organization of the American States."

Meanwhile moves began among the American states to

Continued on Page 2, Column 2

### U.N. Force Due in Congo; Disorders Continue There

#### Bunche Expects Troops by Tomorrow—U. S. Missionaries Abused

By HENRY TANNER
Special to The New York Times.

LEOPOLDVILLE, the Congo, July 14—Dr. Ralph J. Bunche announced this afternoon that United Nations troops were expected to reach Leopoldville by Saturday.

The United Nations Under Secretary said the first United Nations forces to arrive would be drawn from the African states of Ghana, Guinea, the Mali Federation, Morocco and Tunisia. By early next week at least four battalions will be here, he added.

[A European slapped Premier Patrice Lumumba at the Leopoldville airport, The Associated Press reported.]

Maj. Gen. Carl Carlsson von Horn of Sweden, now head of the United Nations truce supervision organization in Jerusalem, will head the operation

Continued on Page 3, Column 5

#### U.S. and Soviet Asked to Supply Vehicles and Food for New Unit

By THOMAS J. HAMILTON
Special to The New York Times.

UNITED NATIONS, N. Y., July 14—Secretary General Dag Hammarskjold asked the Soviet Union and the United States today to help provide the food and transportation for the United Nations force in the Congo.

Similar requests were addressed by the Secretary General to Britain, Italy and India a short time after the Security Council had authorized him to establish the force.

Under Mr. Hammarskjold's program, as outlined to the Security Council at the emergency session, the great powers will be barred from supplying contingents for the force, which is to number about 2,400 officers and men.

The Secretary General is thus adhering to the same course he followed in establishing the

Continued on Page 3, Column 2

### U. S. WILL INFORM BRITAIN OF PLANS FOR AIR MISSIONS

#### Assurance on 'Provocative' Flights Is Prompted by Criticism in London

By JACK RAYMOND
Special to The New York Times.

WASHINGTON, July 14—The United States has agreed to a formal arrangement to give Britain advance notice of Air Force flights from British bases that could be interpreted in Moscow as provocative.

Prime Minister Macmillan requested such an assurance in an exchange of messages with President Eisenhower.

The British leader acted after the running political debate in Parliament on United States bases had been intensified by the fact that an RB-47 reconnaissance bomber downed by the Soviet Union in the Barents Sea July 1 was based in Britain.

[The summer White House accused the Soviet Union of "just lying" in its charge that the RB-47 had violated Soviet air space and territorial waters. The United Nations Security Council was expected to take up the Russian complaint late next week.]

**U. N. Debate Demanded**

Moscow has demanded that the United Nations Security Council take up its charges that American reconnaissance flights are endangering peace. President Eisenhower has expressed the United States' readiness to go before the world organization with counter-charges of Soviet lawlessness.

According to authorities here, the proposed United States-British agreement on flight plans will not require an amendment to the existing bases agreements. These agreements, concluded in 1951, provide for the stationing of United States strategic bombers and other military forces in Britain.

The new document, it was said, probably will take the form of a memorandum of understanding. It is expected to be similar in its legal formulas to the agreements that were developed with the establishment of intermediate-range ballistic missile bases in Britain.

The Macmillan request grew from domestic political considerations, it is understood here. Under present arrangements, it was noted, the British are well informed of United States flying operations. There is continuous liaison between Royal Air Force and United States Air Force authorities at the

Continued on Page 2, Column 5

Associated Press Wirephoto

HIS CHOICE: Senator John F. Kennedy of Massachusetts, left, poses with Senator Lyndon B. Johnson after naming Texan as his selection for Vice-Presidential nomination.

### CHOICE A SURPRISE

#### Senator Is Selected By Acclamation—Calls for Unity

*Johnson and Lawrence texts will be found on Page 10.*

By W. H. LAWRENCE
Special to The New York Times.

LOS ANGELES, July 14—Senator Lyndon B. Johnson of Texas was nominated for Vice President tonight by the Democratic National Convention as Senator John F. Kennedy's running mate.

Senator Johnson's was the only name placed in nomination. At 9:10 P. M. [12:10 A. M. Friday New York time] the convention suspended its rules and nominated him by acclamation. On a voice vote the roar of ayes far exceeded in volume the negative votes.

The Kennedy-Johnson ticket was ready to do battle with the Republican ticket, which will be headed by Vice President Nixon and will be chosen at the Republican National Convention opening July 25 in Chicago.

**Kennedy's Choice**

Senator Johnson was nominated on the recommendation of the Massachusetts Senator. Senator Kennedy overrode protests by labor and Northern liberals in the surprise move in naming the Senate majority leader for Vice President. The Texan's acceptance of second place was equally surprising.

Senator Kennedy, a Roman Catholic, moved boldly to win party unity and new strength below the Mason-Dixon Line by choosing the Texan, a Protestant, for his running mate.

The Presidential nominee is 43 years old, and his running mate is 51.

Until yesterday, they were bitter rivals for the Presidency. Senator Kennedy smashed to a first-ballot victory, polling 806 votes to 409 for Senator Johnson.

**Convention Ends Today**

Tomorrow, the two will accept their nominations formally at an open-air rally in the Coliseum, which seats more than 100,000 persons. That event formally ends the convention.

The Johnson choice was far from universally popular, but it satisfied the overwhelming majority of the delegates. As practical politicians, most leaders believed that Senator Johnson would add more strength to the Democratic ticket in the South than he would hurt it in the North. The choice was particularly offensive to leaders of Americans for Democratic Action. Negro leaders were divided, some favoring and some opposing Senator Johnson.

Gov. David L. Lawrence of Pennsylvania nominated Senator Johnson.

He hailed the Senator as the "strongest Democratic leader in the history of the United States Senate," and as one who had been

Continued on Page 8, Column 1

### China Reds in Cuba Today To Negotiate a Sugar Deal

By TAD SZULC
Special to The New York Times.

HAVANA, July 14—A fourteen-man Communist Chinese trade mission headed by Lu Hau-chang, Deputy Minister of Foreign Commerce, will arrive in Havana tomorrow.

It is expected to negotiate an agreement with Cuba involving the purchase of a substantial amount of sugar, possibly 500,000 tons.

The establishment of formal trade relations between Peiping and the regime of Premier Fidel Castro has long been awaited. There are reports that such a step would be followed by the establishment of diplomatic relations. Cuba now maintains relations with Nationalist China. No nation in the Western Hemisphere has recognized the Peiping regime.

In preparing to negotiate a trade pact with Peiping, the Castro regime was taking another step in tightening its bonds with the Communist powers.

**Trade Accords Signed**

It has already signed trade and credit agreements with the Soviet Union, Poland, Czechoslovakia and East Germany. It has received a promise from the Soviet Union to buy the sugar the United States cut from the Cuban quota this year. It has received Premier Khrushchev's promise of military aid if Cuba is attacked.

The expected arrival of the Chinese delegation was announced late today by Foreign Minister Raul Roa. There had been no previous hint.

Communist China has bought nearly 130,000 tons of sugar in Cuba this year, but the transactions were worked out through commercial intermediaries in London. Payment was by letters of credit for British currency.

**World Group to Meet**

The expectation in trade quarters here was that the Chinese mission would conclude a formal agreement similar to those signed with the Soviet Union and East European nations for the exchange of sugar and other commodities for machinery and manufactured goods.

In its earlier sugar purchases here, China paid 2.91 and 2.93 cents a pound. This was below the world market prices as was the case with Soviet purchases. Cuba has now set 3.25 cents a pound as the minimum export price.

To overcome the problems surrounding the expected sales to China and the Soviet Union, Commerce Minister Raul Cepero Bonilla was scheduled to fly to London tomorrow to attend a meeting of the international sugar council.

Since Cuba has already sold

Continued on Page 2, Column 3

### AIRLINE TALK OFF, U.S. TELLS SOVIET

#### Washington Defers Parley to Demonstrate Vexation Over Moscow Policy

By WILLIAM J. JORDEN
Special to The New York Times.

WASHINGTON, July 14—Angered by recent Soviet statements and actions, the United States postponed today talks with the Soviet Union on a civil airline agreement.

A message informing the Soviet authorities of the decision was delivered in Moscow today. The talks were to have begun Monday.

[In Moscow, the Soviet Union protested that its vessels were being "buzzed" by military planes of the United States and its allies.]

In canceling the negotiations on a Moscow-New York air arrangement, the United States made clear that it considered that relations between the two countries had deteriorated. It said the prevailing atmosphere would have an adverse effect on the negotiations and it would be better to wait for a more suitable time.

Officials here do not hide

Continued on Page 2, Column 5

### KENNEDY ASSURES NEW YORK CHIEFS

#### Agrees to Use Regular Party Machinery and Not Create Separate Organization

By LEO EGAN
Special to The New York Times.

LOS ANGELES, July 14—Three New York Democratic leaders reached tentative agreement today with Senator John F. Kennedy on two important phases of the fall Presidential campaign in their state.

Under the agreement the Senator will neither sponsor nor authorize the creation of any organization to run his campaign separate from the Democratic State Committee.

In addition, if a mutually satisfactory date can be found, he will address this year's annual upstate Democratic fund-raising dinner in September. He will also make a large number of personal appearances in the state.

Both understandings were reached at a conference with the Democratic candidate for President this morning. It was attended by Mayor Wagner, Carmine G. De Sapio, New York national committeeman, and Michael H. Prendergast, New York state chairman. It took

Continued on Page 10, Column 1

### Some Northerners Irked By Designation of Johnson

By JOSEPH A. LOFTUS
Special to The New York Times.

LOS ANGELES, July 14—Senator John F. Kennedy's choice of Senator Lyndon B. Johnson as a campaign partner today was a swift, bold stroke to bind the wounds of the Democratic party. The new national leader from Massachusetts sought a bridge to the South. He believes that he found it by way of Texas, for the Texan was the South's candidate for President.

Senator Johnson's selection was a blow to Senator Stuart Symington of Missouri and his backers, who had had reason to believe the Missourian held top place on the "probable" list. Senator Symington, however, appeared to accept the decision as one of the realities of political life.

Senator Kennedy had faced the possibility of Southern sullenness, if not rebellion, because the convention until today had represented almost total defeat for the Southern conservative wing of the party.

**Compounded Defeat**

The defeat of Senator Johnson for first place had compounded the gash inflicted on the Southerners by a civil rights plank that was written by Northern liberals with scarcely a gesture of compromise.

Some Northerners felt affronted by the choice of Senator Johnson, although few were saying so for the record. In the end, it is not expected to change their determination to carry the fight to the Republicans in the fall.

At least two of Senator Kennedy's morning visitors had argued against Senator Johnson as a running mate. They were Gov. G. Mennen Williams of Michigan and Walter P. Reuther, president of the United Automobile Workers.

Informed sources said the two had come away feeling that they had made their case successfully.

Governor Williams later called the selection of Senator Johnson a "mistake" and a "disappointment."

Joseph L. Rauh Jr. of Washington, a founder of Americans for Democratic Action, used the term "double cross."

Not all of labor was opposed

Continued on Page 8, Column 6

### STEVENSON READY TO AID CAMPAIGN

#### He Calls on the Nominee—Cabinet Office for Him Appears in Doubt

By WILLIAM M. BLAIR
Special to The New York Times.

LOS ANGELES, July 14—Adlai E. Stevenson summed up his political situation in these words today:

"We started with nothing and we ended with nothing."

Crushed in the balloting, he called on Senator John F. Kennedy of Massachusetts, the Democratic Presidential nominee, and later said he would "support and campaign actively" for him.

It was apparent at the convention that Mr. Stevenson, who led the party in 1952 and 1956, had lost his power though retaining great affection.

By his own actions he had all but cut himself off from Senator Kennedy. It was by what he had not done as much as what he had done. This accounted perhaps for Senator Kennedy's omitting his name last night in extending the olive branch to all who had opposed

Continued on Page 11, Column 3

### F.C.C. Voids TV Channel Grants To Miami and Boston Concerns

By TOM WICKER
Special to The New York Times.

WASHINGTON, July 14—The Federal Communications Commission severely penalized today Boston and Miami television license holders accused of improper associations with former members of the commission.

The commission deprived Public Service Television, Inc., of its right to broadcast on Channel 10 from Miami and disqualified two other applicants for the channel. The channel was awarded to Public Service, a subsidiary of National Airlines, on Feb. 7, 1957.

The commission set aside its grant of Boston's Channel 5 to WHDH-TV, a station owned by The Boston Herald-Traveler newspapers. But WHDH may continue to broadcast while hearings are held on a new license and may apply for authority to broadcast on the channel.

Three other applicants for the Boston license, granted to WHDH on April 24, 1957, may also apply again.

In the Miami case, only L. B. Wilson, Inc., of the original four applicants escaped censure. Wilson was given authority to construct a station and broadcast on Channel 10 for four months after construction.

The two F. C. C. decisions were made in the first television cases remanded to the agency by the courts on grounds of ex parte, or off-the-record, approaches and improper influence. Thus, they apparently laid down a rule of toughness for similar cases.

The Miami decision in particular followed exactly recommendations made last Nov. 8 by the Justice Department. Attorney General William P. Rogers said then that he favored a clear rule that approaches to a regulatory agency, outside its regular proceedings, would automatically result in loss of the case for the offending applicant.

In both cases, however, the commission overruled the findings of Horace Stern, a former Pennsylvania judge assigned by

Continued on Page 49, Column 2

### 200 Perish in Guatemalan Fire That Traps 600 Asylum Inmates

Special to The New York Times.

GUATEMALA, July 14—More than 200 persons were believed to have perished in a fire that swept the Guatemala city hospital for the insane early today.

By this afternoon 126 bodies had been removed from the ruins of the building. Dr. Mariano Lopez, the Health Minister, said he expected that eighty additional dead would be found in the smoldering debris.

About 600 of the 1,500 men, women and children inmates were trapped by the fire. Policemen, firemen and volunteer workers, led by President Miguel Ydigoras Fuentes, brought out groups of patients, who sometimes fought their rescuers.

All the children in the asylum were believed to have been saved.

The hospital, under the national Government's jurisdiction, is in an old building in downtown Guatemala. It was opened in 1890.

The fire started shortly after last midnight in a women's section. It was feared that most of the patients in that section were dead.

Some officials thought the fire started in a sewing room where a candle, left before a religious image, ignited combustible material. Others said the cause of the fire might have been a short circuit in the electric wiring.

Scores of patients were burned

Continued on Page 2, Column 2

### $282,000 Cash Seized in House Raided as Jersey Policy Bank

By JOHN W. SLOCUM

NORTH ARLINGTON, N. J., July 14—Authorities seized $282,000 in cash tonight in a raid on a numbers bank described as the largest ever uncovered in New Jersey.

Two persons and a number of lottery slips were also seized in the raid, which was conducted by state, county and local authorities.

Arrested were Mrs. Susan Kaiser, 63 years old, and her son Harry, 45. They were accused of maintaining in their home a place where people could engage in lottery games and of running a numbers game.

Mrs. Kaiser was held in $10,000 bail and her son was held in $100,000 bail. Kaiser's wife Edna was named a material witness and released in her own recognizance, according to Assistant County Prosecutor Frank J. Cuccio.

The house that was raided is a brick and frame Cape Cod model with three bedrooms and a finished cellar. It is at 53 Forest Street.

Deputy Attorney General John J. Bergin said the cash was mostly in small bills from $1 to $50.

The money was found in all parts of the house. Adding machines, lottery books, records and other betting apparatus also were seized.

Mr. Bergin said the operation

Continued on Page 7, Column 5

### NEWS INDEX


| | Page | | Page |
|---|---|---|---|
| Books | 21 | Music | 15 |
| Bridge | 20 | Obituaries | 23 |
| Business | 30, 38 | Real Estate | 38 |
| Buyers | 38 | Screen | 12-15 |
| Crossword | 21 | Ships and Air | 48 |
| Editorial | 22 | Society | 20-21 |
| Fashions | 17 | Sports | 26-30 |
| Financial | 30-38 | TV and Radio | 49 |
| Food | 17 | Theatres | 15 |
| Letters | 22 | U. N. Proceedings | 2 |
| Man in the News | 8 | Weather | 48 |


News Summary and Index, Page 25

"All the News That's Fit to Print"

# The New York Times.

LATE CITY EDITION
U. S. Weather Bureau Report (Page 54) forecasts: Mostly fair and warm today, tonight and tomorrow.
Temp. range: 84—65; yesterday: 72.9—68.9.
Temp.-Hum. Index: 76; yesterday: 71.

VOL. CIX..No. 37,441.  NEW YORK, THURSDAY, JULY 28, 1960. 10 cents beyond 50-mile zone from New York City except on Long Island. Higher in air delivery cities. FIVE CENTS

# NIXON IS GIVEN NOMINATION BY ACCLAMATION AFTER GOLDWATER GETS 10 LOUISIANA VOTES; CANDIDATE PICKS LODGE FOR SECOND PLACE

## SANITATION UNION QUITS IN PROTEST; GARBAGE PILES UP

### 5,000 March on City Hall as Wage Talks Break Off —Walkout May Go On

By LAYHMOND ROBINSON

Thousands of tons of refuse were left lying on city streets yesterday when angry sanitation workers suddenly stopped work to protest a breakdown in wage negotiations with the city.

The Sanitation Department reported that at least 4,000 of the 5,000 garbage collectors, street cleaners and incinerator employes on the day shift had failed to report for duty at 7 A. M. They may not report today, either.

Instead, the shouting, chanting city employes, augmented by 1,000 fellow workers who were on vacation or had days off, marched to City Hall.

They besieged the building for several hours, created a traffic jam and gave a 100-man police detail some anxious moments in holding the surging crowd behind barricades. However, there was no violence, though the police took the precaution of locking the doors of City Hall.

**Meeting Collapses**

Later in the day, a collapse of a hastily arranged meeting between union and city negotiators brought predictions that the walkout, which the union has denied is a strike, might last for some time.

Last night, as a result of the walkout, Traffic Commissioner T. T. Wiley announced that alternate-side parking rules would be lifted here today. Motorists may ignore signs that normally prohibit parking on Thursdays between 8 A. M. and 11 A. M. and 11 A. M. and 2 P. M. The department has not decided yet what it will do about parking regulations tomorrow.

**City Demands Return**

At the meeting between union and city negotiators, the spokesmen for the city, acting under instruction from the Board of Estimate, demanded that the men return to work before negotiations were resumed. Union negotiators rejected the demand and vowed to stay out until the city came up with a better offer on wages and fringe benefits.

The state's Condon-Wadlin Law prohibits strikes by Civil Service employes but Mayor Wagner would not say yesterday whether he viewed the stoppage as a strike, nor would he say whether the law would be invoked for the first time here.

Union members did not report for the night shift. The Sanitation Department said only a handful had showed up for night duty, which begins at 4 P. M. Usually about 700 men work the night shift in the summer.

The Sanitation Commissioner warned the men involved that they would be docked a day's pay for each day they refused

Continued on Page 11, Column 4

## Stock Margin Rate Is Cut To 70% by Reserve Board

### Officials Deny Reduction From 90% Is Aimed at Shoring Up the Market— Economic Significance Minimized

By TOM WICKER
Special to The New York Times.

WASHINGTON, July 27—The margin requirement for purchases of stocks was reduced from 90 to 70 per cent today by the Federal Reserve Board.

The reduction is effective tomorrow. It reflects the belief of the board of governors of the Federal Reserve that stock market credit is relatively stable at this time.

The margin requirement governs the minimum cash payment a stock buyer must make. As an example, today's action will reduce from $900 to $700 the amount of cash that must be put up for each $1,000 of stock.

The reduction also applies to short sales, in which a trader borrows stock and sells it in the hope of buying it back later at a lower price and thus making a profit.

The margin requirement is a device by which the Federal Reserve attempts to prevent excessive use of credit in the stock market. A spokesman said today the board of governors "just thinks 70 per cent will do it" under today's conditions.

The price of common stocks has declined recently. But the spokesman denied that today's action was an attempt to shore up prices or to stimulate credit and speculative activity.

He conceded, however, that since a trader could pick up more stock with the same amount of money, beginning tomorrow, the reduction might have an initial effect on the volume of transactions.

Despite the fact that the latest change before today's in margin requirements—an advance from 70 to 90 per cent on Oct. 16, 1958—came when the

Continued on Page 37, Column 1

## CHIEFS CONSULTED

### Bricker Is Expected to Place U.N. Aide in Nomination

By LEO EGAN
Special to The New York Times.

CHICAGO, Thursday, July 28—Henry Cabot Lodge, delegate to the United Nations, was picked today by Vice President Richard M. Nixon to be his running mate.

Mr. Nixon revealed his preference a few hours after he himself had been nominated for President by the Republican convention.

Mr. Nixon came out of his room and made this announcement:

"I have reached a decision that I shall recommend to the convention Henry Cabot Lodge."

He said he would call Mr. Lodge at his New York home and ask if he would accept. He said he expected the decision to be affirmative.

Mr. Nixon made the announcement at 2:20 A. M. Central daylight time (3:20 A. M. New York time).

His decision all but assured Mr. Lodge's nomination for Vice President when the convention votes tonight on that post.

Mr. Nixon made the selection in consultation with leading Republicans in a meeting that began at his hotel about a half hour after the adjournment of last night's session of the convention.

**Choice Not Unanimous**

New York was represented at the meeting by L. Judson Morhouse, its Republican State Chairman.

The choice of Mr. Lodge was far from unanimous. However, Mr. Nixon insisted upon the Presidential nominee's right to choose his running mate.

Earlier yesterday, Mr. Nixon had listed the 58-year old former Massachusetts Senator as one of the four front runners for the vice-presidential nomination.

The three others were: Senator Thruston B. Morton of Kentucky, the 52-year-old Republican National Chairman.

Representative Walter H. Judd of Minnesota, now 61 years old, who delivered the keynote address to the convention on Monday.

Robert B. Anderson, the 50-year-old Secretary of the Treasury, a former Texas Democrat who became an Eisenhower Republican in 1952.

To offset Midwest opposition to Mr. Lodge, an arrangement was reported to have been made to have former Senator John W. Bricker of Ohio place his name in nomination. And Representative Gerald Ford of Michigan, a

Continued on Page 12, Column 5

Associated Press Wirephoto

AFTER THE DELEGATES VOTED: Vice President and Mrs. Nixon at their hotel in Chicago last night with their daughters, Patricia, left, 14 years old, and Julie, 12.

## UNITY IS STRESSED

### Goldwater Withdraws and Asks Backing for the Nominee

*Hatfield's speech, Page 12; Goldwater text, Page 14.*

By W. H. LAWRENCE
Special to The New York Times.

CHICAGO, Thursday, July 28—Vice President Richard M. Nixon swept to a first-ballot Republican Presidential nomination last night and the right to face Democratic Senator John F. Kennedy in the November election.

Early today, Mr. Nixon chose Henry Cabot Lodge, chief United States delegate to the United Nations, as his Vice-Presidential running mate.

Mr. Nixon received 1,321 votes on the polling of state delegations. Senator Barry Goldwater of Arizona received ten votes, cast by members of the twenty-six-vote Louisiana delegation even after the Arizonan had asked withdrawal of his name from consideration.

At the end of the roll-call, Louisiana moved to make Mr. Nixon's choice unanimous, but balked at changing its ten votes from the Goldwater to the Nixon column without a poll. When the roll-call vote was announced as 1,321 to 10, the Arizona delegation then moved to make the nomination unanimous, and this was done by acclamation.

**Goldwater Asks Unity**

The convention decision pits the 47-year-old Vice President against the 43-year-old Senator from Massachusetts. Mr. Nixon is the first Vice President in the history of the modern two-party system to win a Presidential nomination in his own right.

Senator Goldwater made the dramatic appearance of the night, calling upon all conservatives to back Mr. Nixon in November and avoid any party split or stay-at-home nonvoting attitude that would help Democrats "dedicated to the destruction of this country."

Withdrawing his own name from consideration for the Presidency, the Arizona Senator, an avowed conservative, said he had been campaigning for Mr. Nixon's nomination for the last six years and would fight for his election in November.

**Lecture to Conservatives**

"Let us put our shoulders to the wheel of Dick Nixon and push him over across the line," Senator Goldwater said.

He lectured conservatives sternly, telling them they must "grow up" and get to work "if we want to take this party back some day—and I think we can."

He said the Democratic party no longer was the party of Jefferson, Jackson and Wilson but now was ruled by "Bowles, Galbraith and Reuther." His references were to Representative Chester Bowles of Connecticut; Kenneth Galbraith, Harvard economist, and Walter P. Reu-

Continued on Page 12, Column 1

## FRENCH 'SLIGHTS' ANGER ADENAUER

### He Will Leave for Week-End Paris Talks Only Because His Hand Was Forced

By SYDNEY GRUSON
Special to The New York Times.

BONN, Germany, July 27—Chancellor Adenauer will fly to Paris for talks with President de Gaulle Friday, but in a furious mood and only because the French forced his hand.

Both Paris and Bonn announced the meeting this afternoon and said the main subject of the talks would be the political integration of Western Europe.

But the background to this laconic announcement was far more dramatic. The Chancellor had been infuriated by a number of what he considers slights to West Germany by France and had determined not to go through with the meeting this week-end.

The French, aware of his mood, let it be known last night to West German reporters in Paris and to some French newspapers that the meeting was on.

Apparently rather than permit a crack for all the world to see in the painfully restored French-German friendship, the keystone of his European policy,

Continued on Page 2, Column 5

## British Earl Named Foreign Secretary In Cabinet Shuffle

By DREW MIDDLETON
Special to The New York Times.

LONDON, July 27 — Prime Minister Macmillan chose the Earl of Home as Britain's new Foreign Secretary today in a major reconstruction of the Conservative Government.

Selwyn Lloyd leaves the Foreign Office to become Chancellor of the Exchequer. A successful tenure there would improve Mr. Lloyd's prospects as the future Prime Minister.

Lord Home (whose name is pronounced Hume) is the first peer to be Foreign Secretary since Lord Halifax held the office twenty years ago. The official announcement of his appointment this evening brought to a climax the mounting criticism of the last five days.

Mr. Macmillan will be forced to defend his choice against the Labor party's censure in a House of Commons debate tomorrow night.

The objections to the appointment of Lord Home were based on two points. First, the critics said, the Foreign Secretary should be a member of the House of Commons and answerable in the House to any questions on foreign policy. Second, the objectors maintained, there was nothing in Lord Home's career to justify the appointment.

The first newspaper comment

Continued on Page 2, Column 2

## NIXON BOLSTERS ROCKEFELLER TIE

### New York Delegation Greets Him Warmly — Governor to Campaign Anywhere

By WARREN WEAVER Jr.
Special to The New York Times.

CHICAGO, July 27—At political sword points only a week ago, Governor Rockefeller and Vice President Nixon joined today in a powerful demonstration of concord.

Mr. Nixon made a special morning trip two miles up Michigan Avenue to visit his new-found supporters in the New York delegation. The delegation endorsed him unanimously, if belatedly, yesterday.

The Governor went to the Sheraton Towers lobby to greet Mr. Nixon, like classmates at a reunion. Beaming, he escorted him to the closed caucus. They posed for pictures with arms around each other.

Mr. Rockefeller said the Vice President's visit had given the New Yorkers "a final inspiration and emotional lift."

"We're with you all the way," he promised.

Mr. Nixon was hardly less enthusiastic about the Governor. He pleaded with the New York

Continued on Page 14, Column 3

## 13 Dead in Chicago Crash Of 'Copter on Airport Run

By The Associated Press.

CHICAGO, July 27—A helicopter carrying passengers between airports suddenly lost power and plunged in a mass of flames into a suburban cemetery tonight. All thirteen persons aboard were killed. Wreckage was scattered over a wide area.

A swath of clipped tree tops almost 600 feet long indicated that the pilot had tried to gain altitude.

Witnesses said the craft, an S-58, carrying eleven passengers and a crew of two, stopped in air, zigzagged a moment and then plummeted, shooting flames.

The helicopter, owned by Chicago Helicopter Airways, Inc., was on an eleven-minute trip from Midway Airport on the Southwest side to O'Hare International Airport on the Northwest side.

**Falls Near River**

It plunged into the Forest Home Cemetery north of Roosevelt Road near the Des Plaines River. The crash site is between suburban Maywood and Forest Park.

An officer of the helicopter company landed near the crash scene and said that the pilot of the downed craft was Capt. Robert Meyer, 37 years old. The names of the other victims were not immediately available.

However, a company spokesman said "no one of national importance was known to be aboard." He apparently referred to the fact the Republican National Convention is meeting in Chicago.

The helicopter, which has a capacity of fourteen, including

Continued on Page 55, Column 2

## ROBERT KENNEDY EASES SPLIT HERE

### Candidate's Brother Wins Prendergast's Approval of Independent Group

By CLAYTON KNOWLES

Robert F. Kennedy came to New York yesterday and brought Michael H. Prendergast around to an agreement that an independent citizens' committee could work effectively in the state for the election of Senator John F. Kennedy as President.

Mr. Prendergast, the Democratic state chairman, reversed his earlier opposition to such an auxiliary campaign unit during a two-and-a-half hour luncheon meeting with Mr. Kennedy, who is the manager of his brother's campaign for the Presidency.

Carmine G. De Sapio, Democratic national committeeman, who sat in on the session at the Hampshire House, was asked if he, too, was satisfied.

"One hundred per cent!" he said with emphasis.

The conference was one of five important meetings that Mr. Kennedy held during a busy day with representatives of virtually every shade of thinking within the Democratic party.

The session with Mr. Prendergast was of particular importance because Mr. Prendergast had understood originally in talks with Senator Kennedy that the campaign would be run strictly through the Democratic state organization.

Later, when the Senator agreed to establishing a Citizens for Kennedy committee here, Mr. Prendergast viewed the enterprise as competitive with the regular organization's work. He also viewed the individuals

Continued on Page 16, Column 1

## Iran Cuts Cairo Tie In Dispute on Israel

By Reuters.

TEHERAN, Iran, July 27—Iran severed diplomatic relations with the United Arab Republic today and gave Cairo's Ambassador here twenty-four hours to get out of the country.

The severance was announced by Foreign Minister Abbas Aram after he had served the expulsion order on the Ambassador, Mahmoud Hammad.

Mr. Aram said the decision to oust Mr. Hammad was made after President Gamal Abdel Nasser attacked Shah Mohammed Riza Pahlevi of Iran yesterday in a speech at Alexandria. President Nasser assailed the Shah for his statement Saturday that Iran had recognized Israel.

The Iranian Foreign Minister described President Nasser as

Continued on Page 5, Column 1

The New York Times

PROTEST AT CITY HALL: Employes of the Department of Sanitation rally against the breakdown of wage talks

## Key Issues in Congo Awaiting U.N. Chief

By HENRY TANNER
Special to The New York Times.

LEOPOLDVILLE, the Congo, July 27 — Secretary General Dag Hammarskjold is likely to be successful in paving the way for the peaceful entry of United Nations forces into Katanga Province, diplomatic observers here predict.

Mr. Hammarskjold is scheduled to arrive here tomorrow from Brussels. Katanga, which has declared its independence of the Congo, is expected to be the dominant issue in his consultations here. He will spend four or five days talking with Congolese, Belgian and United Nations officials.

Katanga is now controlled by Belgian forces that went there at the request of the provincial Premier, Moise Tshombe. Mr.

Continued on Page 3, Column 5

## NEWS INDEX



| | Page | | Page |
|---|---|---|---|
| Books | 25 | Music | 19-20 |
| Bridge | 24 | Obituaries | 27 |
| Business | 34-35, 43 | Real Estate | 43 |
| Buyers | 43 | Screen | 19-20 |
| Crossword | 25 | Ships and Air | 54 |
| Editorial | 26 | Society | 21 |
| Fashions | 30-31 | Sports | 21-25 |
| Financial | 32-43 | TV and Radio | 53 |
| Food | 30-31 | Theatres | 19-20 |
| Letters | 26 | U. N. Proceedings | 3 |
| Man in the News | 12 | Weather | 54 |

News Summary and Index, Page 29


## Eisenhower Is Firm For Middle of Road

By DONALD JANSON
Special to The New York Times.

CHICAGO, July 27 — President Eisenhower emphasized today the superiority of a middle political course over right or left extremes.

He denounced the Socialist philosophy of a "fairly friendly European country" he said he had been reading about in the last few weeks.

"The experiment of almost complete paternalism" there, he said, has resulted in a sharp rise in the suicide rate, "more than twice our drunkenness," and a "lack of moderation discernible on all sides."

It was believed that he had alluded to Sweden. Her suicide rate is 19.9 for every 100,000 persons, compared with ten in

Continued on Page 14, Column 4

"All the News That's Fit to Print"

# The New York Times.

LATE CITY EDITION
U. S. Weather Bureau Report (Page 48) forecasts:
Fair, warm, humid today and tonight. Warm, chance of showers tomorrow.
Temp. range: 84--68; yesterday: 85.2—66.
Temp.-Hum. Index: near 76; yesterday: 79

VOL. CIX..No. 37,442.  NEW YORK, FRIDAY, JULY 29, 1960. 10 cents beyond 50-mile zone from New York City except on Long Island. Higher in air delivery cities. FIVE CENTS

# LODGE IS NOMINATED FOR VICE-PRESIDENCY; NIXON ASKS THAT FIGHT AGAINST COMMUNISM BE WAGED ON SOCIAL AND ECONOMIC FRONTS

## GARBAGE TIE-UP EASED BY UNION; TEST DUE TODAY

### Members Boo Order to End 2-Day Protest, but Many on Night Shifts Report

By LAYHMOND ROBINSON

Over the angry protests of many sanitation workers, union leaders announced the end yesterday of a two-day walkout of city garbage collectors and street cleaners.

The Sanitation Department reported last night that the men began returning to work on the shifts that started at 4 and 5 P. M. A spokesman said 263 of the 415 men scheduled to work on those shifts had reported.

At 1:15 A. M. today the department said the entire midnight-to-8 A. M. shift of about 200 men had reported for duty.

However, the real test of the back-to-work order will come with the day shift, beginning at 7 o'clock this morning. At that time 5,000 men normally report to work.

The men who reported last night and this morning were put to work removing some of the 16,000 tons of litter that accumulated during the walkout.

**No Hazard Seen**

Despite the pile-up health and sanitation officials said the accumulation did not constitute a health hazard. Sanitation officials pointed out that the two-day delay was not serious because pick-ups were made normally on alternate days.

The suspension of the walkout prompted Traffic Commissioner T. T. Wiley to announce that the alternate-side parking rules would again be enforced in Manhattan and the Bronx today. He had suspended the rules in the two boroughs because there were no street cleaners at work.

The decision to call off the walkout was highly unpopular with many of the workers who attended a mass meeting called by the union, the Uniformed Sanitation Men's Association.

Four thousand members of

Continued on Page 6, Column 5

## Capital Airlines Merger With United Is Agreed On

### C. A. B. Faces Policy Decision in Ruling on Acquisition of the Debt-Ridden Capital in an Intricate Deal

By JOHN W. FINNEY
Special to The New York Times.

WASHINGTON, July 28—United Air Lines and Capital Airlines announced plans today to merge.

Agreement on the merger plans, designed to rescue Capital from serious financial difficulties, was announced jointly at a news conference by W. A. Patterson, president of United, and T. D. Neelands Jr., chairman of Capital.

Before the merger plan can go into effect, it will have to be approved by the Civil Aeronautics Board, as well as the stockholders of the two companies, which are two of the nation's oldest and largest airlines.

The plan actually represents an acquisition of the money-losing Capital Airlines by United. In exchange for $46,-500,000 worth of preferred and common stock United would acquire Capital's fleet of airplanes, its property and facilities and, most important, its air routes, as well as an estimated $25,000,000 tax-loss carry forward.

Under the merger plan common shareholders of Capital would receive, for each seven shares of their stock, one share of United common stock plus a warrant entitling them for five years to purchase an additional one and one-half shares of United common stock at $40 a share. Holders of Capital's $12,000,000 of 4¼ per cent debentures, due in 1976, now convertible into thirty-three and a third shares of Capital, would be offered twenty shares of

Continued on Page 50, Column 1

## U. N. CHIEF HAILED BY CONGO CROWD IN LEOPOLDVILLE

### Belgians Announce Plans to Complete Withdrawal if All Goes Well

By HENRY TANNER
Special to The New York Times.

LEOPOLDVILLE, the Congo, July 28—Secretary General Dag Hammarskjold of the United Nations arrived in the Congo this morning.

He received an ovation from a crowd of about 2,000 Congolese, who lost no time telling him what they expected him to do.

Spectators waved signs that read in poorly spelled French: "Quick Liberation for the Congo," "Total Retreat of Belgians" and "Down with Tshombe."

Moise Tshombe, Premier of Katanga Province, has declared the secession of the province from the Congo.

The Belgian Ambassador, Jean van den Bosch, was loudly booed when his car, flying the Belgian flag, joined Mr. Hammarskjold's motorcade.

The welcoming scene took place on the bank of the Congo River, a few blocks from Leopoldville's business district. Mr. Hammarskjold arrived by motor launch from Brazzaville, capital of the French Community's Congo Republic across the river.

**Flight Made in Dutch Plane**

The Secretary General flew to Brazzaville in a K.L.M. Royal Dutch Airlines DC-7C.

He was met at Brazzaville by Justin Bomboko, the Congo's Foreign Minister; Dr. Ralph J. Bunche, United Nations Under Secretary, and Maj. Gen. Carl Carlsson von Horn, United Nations commander here. They then crossed the swiftly flowing river, with its floating green and blue islands of water hyacinth.

A few hours after Mr. Hammarskjold's arrival sources at the Belgian Embassy said that if all went well Belgian troops would be withdrawn from Congo territory by next week-end, except for Katanga and two bases at the mouth of the Congo River.

The sources said the timing of the withdrawal was entirely dependent on the speed with which United Nations forces were sent to the Congo interior. The Belgians will pull out of each area as soon as United Nations forces are able to protect the civilian population there, they added.

Belgian officials gave the following summary of the state of the Belgian withdrawal:

¶Equator Province—The Belgians occupy four areas. They

Continued on Page 3, Column 5

Associated Press Wirephoto

NOMINEES ACCLAIMED AT THE CONVENTION: Vice President Nixon and Henry Cabot Lodge, who make up the Republican national ticket, acknowledging the cheers of the crowd last night at the closing session in the International Amphitheatre, Chicago.

## CONVENTION ENDS

### Nixon Plans Strategy to Extend Freedom Without a War

*Nixon and Rockefeller talks will be found on Page 9.*

By W. H. LAWRENCE
Special to The New York Times.

CHICAGO, July 28—Republicans completed a Nixon-Lodge ticket tonight. Then they launched a hard-hitting campaign emphasizing international issues.

The 1,331 delegates to the twenty-seventh National Convention unanimously nominated Henry Cabot Lodge for Vice President. Mr. Lodge, delegate to the United Nations, had been hand-picked for the spot by Vice President Nixon, the Presidential nominee.

The final gavel adjourning the convention fell at 10:42 P. M. Central daylight time (11:42 P. M. New York time).

In his wildly cheered acceptance speech, Vice President Nixon said the free world must counter the Communist slogan of "victory for communism." It should do so, he said, by working toward a victory, not over other nations or peoples, but of freedom over tyranny, better health over disease and plenty over poverty.

**'Strategy for Freedom'**

Mr. Nixon pledged that his administration would take the initiative from the Communists and develop its own "worldwide strategy, an offensive for peace and freedom" designed to win the battle for freedom without war.

The major Communist threat, he said, is to be found in the non-military areas. Here, he said, aggression comes clothed as an economic and social champion. This forces the need for a new strategy for the Nineteen Sixties, he continued.

To this end he proposed reorganization of all Government agencies having responsibility for non-military aspects of the "cold war."

Mr. Nixon said he would bring under the direct supervision of the President all agencies dealing with loans and grants, technical assistance, information and exchange of persons. These diffused groups should be welded into a single powerful economic striking force, he contended.

Heading into battle with the Democratic combine of Senator John F. Kennedy for President and Senator Lyndon B. Johnson for Vice President, Mr. Nixon brought cheers when he asserted that the Republicans had given him a running mate "who shares my views on world issues and who will work with me and not against me in

Continued on Page 8, Column 1

## CITY ACCEPTS GIFT FOR CAFE IN PARK

### Unanimous Vote in Estimate Board Backs $862,500 Hartford Pavilion

By PAUL CROWELL

The Board of Estimate yesterday accepted Huntington Hartford's gift of an $862,500 cafe and pavilion to be constructed in Central Park at Fifty-ninth Street and Fifth Avenue.

The vote to accept the gift was unanimous, as was a vote by the board to approve an architect's fee of $112,500 as part of the over-all cost of the project.

Controller Lawrence E. Gerosa has already deposited in a special account a check for $862,500 received from the Huntington Hartford Family Fund, Inc., of which Mr. Hartford is president. The city will use its own funds to pay for planning and building the cafe and will be reimbursed from the special account.

Park Commissioner Newbold Morris said he hoped to have the cafe and pavilion in operation early next spring.

The vote to accept the gift followed a ten-minute executive session of the Board of Estimate at the close of a lively three-hour public hearing. Accepting the gift from the A. & P. heir was opposed by twenty-

Continued on Page 6, Column 1

## Loss to City Seen In Selling Old Buses Other Lines Re-Use

By CHARLES G. BENNETT

The Board of Estimate heard yesterday that buses sold by the Transit Authority as junk were bought, reconditioned and put back into service by private bus lines.

Mayor Wagner directed Joseph E. O'Grady, a member of the Transit Authority, to submit to the board "immediately" a report on the authority's procedures in selling its used rolling stock.

During an hour-long hearing, Bernard Shatzkin, counsel for three Queens private bus lines, said that about a year ago the Transit Authority had sold 190 of its old buses to a junk dealer who disposed of them to private bus lines for $350 each.

Mr. Shatzkin said one of his clients, the Triboro Coach Corporation, bought six of the buses and reconditioned them at a cost of about $6,000 each.

By contrast, the lawyer declared, the Triboro recently sold for $10,000 each several buses that it had bought in 1950 for $18,000 each.

He said he believed that each of the 190 buses the Transit Authority sold to the junk dealer had been resold for about $350. The junk dealer reportedly, paid the authority about $200 for each bus.

Mr. O'Grady did not deny Mr. Shatzkin's basic facts. Several Estimate Board members seemed incredulous. City Coun-

Continued on Page 7, Column 3

## KENNEDY ACCEPTS NIXON TV DEBATE

### Vice President Is Agreeable but Bars Reading Notes —8 Hours Proposed

A series of television debates this fall between the Republican and Democratic candidates for President became a likelihood last evening.

In Hyannis Port, Mass., Senator John F. Kennedy accepted an invitation by the National Broadcasting Company to appear on eight one-hour evening programs with his opponent.

In Chicago, Herbert G. Klein, Vice President Nixon's press secretary, said Mr. Nixon was "willing to debate a rival candidate, including Senator Kennedy, if this is the desire of the networks and the public."

However, Mr. Klein said, the Vice President wants to examine the format of such debates, "as Senator Kennedy is doing."

"To have a really effective debate," he added, "it should be one in which the candidates speak without notes or text. It should be a debate, as opposed to two people reading notes. It should be a free contest—an opportunity for each to examine the other's mind."

**Sent By Sarnoff**

The N. B. C. invitation was tendered in telegrams by Robert W. Sarnoff, chairman. It proposed that the two candidates meet in face-to-face debate for four hour-long programs. These would be followed by four panel discussions during which they would face questioning by newsmen.

"I wholeheartedly accept your invitation to meet on television with Vice President Nixon during the coming campaign," Senator Kennedy said in a telegram to Mr. Sarnoff. "I believe you are performing a notable public service in giving the American people a chance to see the candidates of the two major parties discuss the issues face to face."

Later last evening, the Columbia Broadcasting System and the American Broadcasting Company also offered prime evening time to the top candidates.

Dr. Frank Stanton, president of C. B. S., extended the invitation to the Vice-Presidential nominees as well. He suggested a series of eight broadcasts, with the Presidential candidates sharing the opening and closing ones, and "intervening programs devoted to discussions between opposing Presidential and Vice-Presidential candidates and press interviews."

Leonard H. Goldenson, presi-

Continued on Page 13, Column 1

## Lodge Calls U. S. Election Vital in East-West Conflict

By AUSTIN C. WEHRWEIN
Special to The New York Times.

CHICAGO, July 28—Henry Cabot Lodge said tonight that the 1960 election took on "compelling, overwhelming" urgency because of the "life and death struggle" now under way between communism and democracy.

In a speech accepting the Republican nomination for Vice President, the United States representative at the United Na-

*Lodge and Judd addresses appear on Page 10.*

tions said another Republican Administration would strengthen the nation's military power to guarantee "that no nation will ever dare attack us."

Mr. Lodge praised Vice President Nixon, the party's nominee for President, as the best man in the country "to represent us in the turmoil of world politics."

**'Remarkable Human Being'**

"He is a remarkable human being," Mr. Lodge asserted. He described the Vice President as "uniquely experienced in government, with particular emphasis on foreign affairs," and hailed him as "tough-minded" and "immensely intelligent."

Mr. Lodge told the delegates to the Republican National Convention that in the last eight years the Eisenhower Administration had put the nation's house in order, strengthened the country and brought world peace closer by promoting the

Continued on Page 8, Column 5

## NIXON PICKS BOARD TO RUN CAMPAIGN

### Heads Group as His Own Manager—3 Ex-Chiefs of Party on Panel

By WILLIAM M. BLAIR
Special to The New York Times.

CHICAGO, July 28—Vice President Nixon will run his campaign with the aid of an unusual board of strategy.

Abandoning the traditional organization headed by a campaign manager, Mr. Nixon will have a campaign-committee system, with the members interchangeable according to needs.

Some of the staff already have been assigned. Others will be announced next week. For the most part, the members are party leaders who have been working with the Vice President for months in both pre-convention and campaign planning.

**Delays Departure**

Tonight the Vice President delayed his departure from his suite in the downtown Sheraton-Blackstone Hotel until after Henry Cabot Lodge, Ambassador to the United Nations, had been chosen as the Republican Vice-Presidential nominee. He watched the Vice-Presidential nomination on television, and then went directly to the International Amphitheatre to accept his party's Presidential nomination.

In effect, Mr. Nixon will be his own campaign manager and head the committee. However, because he will be on the campaign trail in what he said today will be a "precedent-shattering campaign," the committee will function as a focal point for campaign plans.

The group now includes:

Robert H. Finch, 34-year-old administrative assistant to Mr. Nixon; Attorney General Wil-

Continued on Page 10, Column 1

## Reform Democrats Get Campaign Role

By CLAYTON KNOWLES

Robert F. Kennedy told New York political leaders yesterday how the Kennedy-Johnson campaign would be run in New York State.

His brother, Senator John F. Kennedy, the Democratic Presidential nominee, still has to approve the details, but a hard-won understanding among local leaders seemed to have been achieved on essentials.

The key decision was that the reform Democrats, who have mounted a major challenge to the regular Democratic organization in New York County, would work in the campaign through an independent Citizens for Kennedy Committee.

Mr. Kennedy said the reform group would "play a major role in the citizens' committee with other groups and organizations who will have representation within the citizens' organization."

"Details remain to be worked out," he declared, "but we think

Continued on Page 13, Column 1

## Nixon Will Consult New York Leaders

By LEO EGAN
Special to The New York Times.

CHICAGO, July 28—Vice President Nixon told the New York delegation today that he would consult Governor Rockefeller and State Chairman L. Judson Morhouse on all matters affecting New York if he is elected President.

His announcement emphasized the lack of factional differences within the Republican party in New York, such as are troubling the Democrats. Presumably Mr. Nixon's New York campaign will be directed by the Republican state organization with the help of an independent Citizens for Nixon Committee, as was done in 1952 and 1956.

The pledge heartened many delegates who have felt that President Eisenhower has too often gone outside the party organization to fill important offices at his disposal.

Mr. Nixon made his pledge

Continued on Page 10, Column 5

## IRAN BOYCOTTED BY ARAB LEAGUE

### Curbs Extended in Dispute Over Link With Israel

Special to The New York Times.

CAIRO, July 28—The Arab League extended its economic boycott of Israel to Iran today because the Iranian monarch had reaffirmed de facto recognition of Israel.

A spokesman for the Arab League Secretariat said the Arab countries would blacklist Iranian companies and ships. League sources said confidently that other Arab countries would follow Cairo's lead in severing diplomatic relations with Iran.

Meanwhile, Djamachid Gharib, Iranian Ambassador to the United Arab Republic, was closing the embassy here to leave Cairo with his staff this weekend.

President Gamal Abdel Nasser in an angry speech announced in Alexandria Tuesday that he was closing Cairo's embassy in Teheran. He accused the Shah, Mohammed Riza Pahlevi, of having bowed to the will of "imperialists" to receive a "few more dollars of American aid." Two hours later Mr. Gharib was summoned to the Foreign Office in Cairo and told that he and his staff must leave.

It appeared today that the breaking of relations between the two Moslem countries was complete.

It was announced here today that Mahmoud Moharram Hammud, U. A. R. Ambassador in Teheran, would be ready to leave the Iranian capital with all members of his staff and families within two days.

United Press International Radiophoto

U. N. CHIEF IN LEOPOLDVILLE: Dag Hammarskjold, in dark suit, after his arrival in the Congo capital. Behind and to left of him is Maj. Gen. Carl Carlsson von Horn, commander of U. N. force. Lined up for the occasion are Ghanaians aiding U. N.

NEWS INDEX



| | Page | | Page |
|---|---|---|---|
| Books | 23 | Music | 14-16 |
| Bridge | 22 | Obituaries | 25 |
| Business | 30-31 | Real Estate | 38 |
| Buyers | 30 | Screen | 14-16 |
| Crossword | 23 | Ships and Air | 48 |
| Editorial | 24 | Society | 29 |
| Fashions | 28-29 | Sports | 17-22 |
| Financial | 30-38 | TV and Radio | 49 |
| Food | 28 | Theatres | 14-16 |
| Letters | 24 | U. N. Proceedings | 3 |
| Man in the News | 8 | Weather | 48 |

News Summary and Index, Page 27

"All the News That's Fit to Print"

# The New York Times.

LATE CITY EDITION
U. S. Weather Bureau Report (Page 45) Forecasts: Mostly fair today and tonight. Partly cloudy and milder tomorrow. Temp. range: 66—50; yesterday: 65—49.4.

VOL. CX..No. 37,513.

NEW YORK, SATURDAY, OCTOBER 8, 1960.

10 cents beyond 50-mile zone from New York City except on Long Island. Higher in air delivery cities.

FIVE CENTS

# KHRUSHCHEV SAYS SUMMIT AFTER U. S. VOTE IS PRICE FOR STATUS QUO IN BERLIN

## PREMIER DISPUTED

### An Aide of Macmillan Denies Assurance of Big 4 Talk

*Excerpts from Khrushchev's speech are on Page 2.*

By THOMAS J. HAMILTON
Special to The New York Times.

UNITED NATIONS, N. Y., Oct. 7—Premier Khrushchev threatened today to sign a peace treaty with East Germany unless he was assured that the Western Big Three agreed to meet with him shortly after the United States Presidential election or voiced wish to do so.

Assurance that such a meeting would be arranged was given to him by Prime Minister Macmillan of Britain, the Soviet Premier said. This was interpreted as meaning a Big Four summit meeting would be held soon after the election. A British spokesman denied this.

Mr. Khrushchev emphasized that if arrangements for a summit meeting held good he would keep his promise not to take unilateral action regarding Germany or West Berlin. He added, however, that if there was no agreement on the date and no desire for one, the Soviet Union and other countries would sign a separate treaty with East Germany.

**Berlin's Status Threatened**

"That will mean the end of the occupation regime in West Berlin also," he declared.

However, this renewal of Soviet threats regarding West Berlin was overshadowed by the question whether Mr. Khrushchev was correct in his statement that Mr. Macmillan had "assured" him that a summit meeting would be held.

John Russell, a spokesman for Mr. Macmillan, said tonight that "no such positive assurance" had been given to Mr. Khrushchev by Mr. Macmillan. Mr. Russell conceded, however, that, as he had previously stated, "the possibility of another summit conference some time in 1961 was indeed implicit" in the talks between Mr. Macmillan and Mr. Khrushchev.

There was no word on whether the British Government had asked President de Gaulle whether he would agree to a summit meeting early next year. It was assumed that Mr. Macmillan, in view of protocol requirements, would not have asked the opinions of the two major candidates for the Presidency, Vice President Nixon and Senator John F. Kennedy.

Messrs. Nixon and Kennedy, in their television debate this evening both said they would not participate in a summit meeting unless the Soviet Union met prior conditions.

Mr. Khrushchev made his statement at a luncheon given for him by the United Nations Correspondents Association.

Mr. Macmillan, who returned to London early this week, told Mr. Khrushchev during their talks here that he hoped a sum-

Continued on Page 2, Column 4

# French Ask A-Bomb Veto On Use by West Anywhere

### *De Gaulle Details His Views on Defense —Again Insists on 'National' Force in Contrast to NATO Integration*

By ROBERT C. DOTY
Special to The New York Times.

PARIS, Oct. 7—President de Gaulle stated publicly today for the first time that France intended to seek veto rights over the use anywhere of nuclear weapons by the West.

This position, which has long been the subject of semi-secret and inconclusive exchanges by Paris, Washington and London, was detailed by the French President in a speech at Grenoble.

"So far as her defense is concerned, France believes that defense has a national character," he said. "With respect to nuclear armament, she intends to have her own instrument."

"France intends that if, by misfortune, atomic bombs were to be dropped in the world," he went on, "none should be dropped by the free world's side unless she should have accepted it, and that, from her soil, no atomic bomb should be launched unless she herself should have decided it."

In these few remarks President de Gaulle stated the core of his position on the North Atlantic Treaty Organization that has embroiled him with West Germany, his principal Continental ally, with the United States and Britain, and with a considerable part of French political opinion.

In the pursuit of his goal of a "national" defense, President

Continued on Page 3, Column 7

# HERTER CONSULTS WARSAW LEADER

### Secretary and Gomulka Are Said to Have Discussed Possible U.S. Aid Rise

By JACK RAYMOND
Special to The New York Times.

UNITED NATIONS, Oct. 7—Secretary of State Christian A. Herter and Wladyslaw Gomulka, the First Secretary of the Communist party of Poland, conferred for half an hour today.

It was understood that they had discussed possible increases in United States economic aid to Poland. The United States has provided $650,000,000 in economic assistance to Poland in the last four years, including $426,300,000 worth of surplus agricultural products for which payment was accepted in Polish currency.

Last year, almost directly as a consequence of United States dissatisfaction with Polish support of Soviet policies, the United States agreed to provide only half of a $100,000,000 request for non-agricultural economic assistance.

M. Gomulka is the only Communist chief of the Soviet bloc with whom the United States has had a high-level contact since the United Nations General

Continued on Page 2, Column 8

# 2 IN CREW VANISH AFTER RAIL CRASH

### Wreck of Central Freights Delays Thousands Here —Conductor Killed

By IRA HENRY FREEMAN

The Hudson Division of the New York Central was blocked for nine hours yesterday after a moving freight train rammed a halted one in the Bronx.

Immediately after the crash, the engineer and fireman of the oncoming train disappeared, and the railroad was still trying to locate them last night with the aid of the police. A railroad official said the engineer had run through a stop signal.

The wreck occurred about dawn on the bank of the Harlem River, a quarter of a mile below the Marble Hill Station. The moving freight, an outbound one, plowed into the rear of the one stopped on the tracks. The conductor of the stalled train was killed and a brakeman was injured.

Cars blocking the tracks forced inbound trains on the division to stop at Marble Hill, and more than 11,000 commuters from the lower Hudson River valley were delayed in reaching the city during the morning rush hours.

The stalled commuters had to

Continued on Page 48, Column 3

# TV JURY CHARGES 20 WITH PERJURY IN QUIZ INQUIRY

### Group Questioned Included Van Doren, Mrs. Nearing and Bloomgarden

By JACK ROTH

A New York County grand jury has returned second-degree perjury charges against twenty to twenty-five contestants on two television quiz shows.

The District Attorney's office said yesterday that since none of the accused had been arrested yet, it would be illegal to make their names public.

Among those who are known to have been questioned by the special television grand jury that returned the charges were Charles Van Doren, the former Columbia University instructor; Vivienne Nearing, who defeated Mr. Van Doren on the show "Twenty-one," Hank Bloomgarden and Elfrida Von Nardroff.

All those against whom the grand jury acted, it was learned yesterday, had appeared on either "Twenty-One" or "Tic Tac Dough" and all were money winners.

**Questioned on Coaching**

It was reported that the defendants were accused of lying before a grand jury when they testified under oath that they had never received assistance from anyone connected with the programs prior to their appearances.

The special panel that has been hearing evidence, the fourth July, 1960 hold-over grand jury, handed up a number of documents to General Sessions Judge Charles Marks, who had empaneled the jurors.

He directed the panel to continue its deliberations into other television matters and subsequently, it was learned, he signed an order directing that the District Attorney's office follow the mandate of the grand jury and file informations against the defendants.

All were accused, in one-count informations, of perjury in the second degree. This is a misdemeanor, punishable on conviction by a year in jail and a $500 fine.

**Jury 'Sanctity' at Stake**

First-degree perjury is defined as perjury committed in connection with a material fact and is punishable by five years in prison. Second-degree perjury is described as perjury that does not fall into the category of first-degree perjury.

A number of judges expressed the belief that one "strong reason" the grand jury had acted in the matter was because "it was felt that the sanctity of the grand jury system must be upheld."

The life of the television panel is supposed to expire on Oct. 28, but one report said that the life of the panel would be extended.

Assistant District Attorney Joseph Stone has been conduct-

Continued on Page 46, Column 3

# NIXON AND KENNEDY CLASH ON TV OVER ISSUE OF QUEMOY'S DEFENSE; U-2 'REGRETS' AND RIGHTS ARGUED

The New York Times (by John Orris)

REPUBLICAN: Vice President Nixon as he appeared last night on TV screen.

DEMOCRAT: Senator John F. Kennedy taking part in telecast from Washington.

## EXCHANGES SHARP

### Senator Is Accused of 'Woolly Thinking'—He, Too, Is Tough

*Nixon-Kennedy transcript is on Pages 10 and 11*

By RUSSELL BAKER
Special to The New York Times.

WASHINGTON, Oct. 7—Vice President Nixon and Senator John F. Kennedy raised the campaign temperature tonight, clashing sharply on foreign policy and civil rights in the second of their nation-wide television debates.

The question of who won will have to await the surveys of voters, but the equally nagging question for Republicans—of how Mr. Nixon would "project" after his unhappy appearance in the first debate—was answered immediately. The Vice President did not have the thin, emaciated appearance that worried Republicans across the nation during the first debate.

One of the high points of tonight's debate was a direct conflict between the Presidential candidates over policy for dealing with the islands of Quemoy and Matsu off the Chinese mainland.

**Criticizes Vagueness**

Mr. Kennedy took the position that the islands were militarily worthless and, lying virtually in a harbor on the Communist mainland, were indefensible.

Moreover, he said, Administration vagueness about whether the islands would be defended in case of Communist attack created a dangerous uncertainty for the Chinese about this country's intentions. While Taiwan (Formosa) should certainly be defended, he indicated, he favored a pull-back from Quemoy and Matsu by the Chinese Nationalists.

Mr. Nixon denounced this as "the same kind of woolly thinking that led to disaster in Korea." He insisted that the islands should be held. "These two islands are in the area of freedom," he said. To give them up, he argued, would only encourage the Communists to press their drive on Taiwan.

The question was not of "two tiny pieces of real estate," he said, but a matter of principle.

**Johnson Is Nixon Target**

In a long running exchange over civil rights, Mr. Nixon denounced the Democratic Vice-Presidential candidate, Senator Lyndon B. Johnson of Texas, as a man who had voted against most of the civil rights proposals in the Democratic platform and "who opposes them at the present time."

Although Mr. Johnson contends that, as Democratic Senate leader, he is responsible for the only two civil rights bills to be enacted since the Reconstruction period after the Civil War, Mr. Kennedy did not expand on this issue.

Instead, Mr. Kennedy charged

Continued on Page 12, Column 1

# SCHENECTADY ASKS AID IN G. E. STRIKE

### Emergency Is Proclaimed —Company Calls on Court to Bar Mass Picketing

Special to The New York Times.

SCHENECTADY, N. Y., Oct. 7—City officials here declared a state of emergency today after thousands of striking workers sealed off the General Electric Company main plant.

Mayor Malcolm Ellis and City Manager Arthur Blessing said the 152-man police force could not deal with a situation where "serious violence might occur at any time." Eleven persons were arrested, but no one was injured, in picket-line rushes.

Late this afternoon General Electric moved for a court order prohibiting mass picketing. The union will be required on Monday to show cause why such an injunction, limiting picketing, should not be issued.

**Production Halted**

The company also filed with the National Labor Relations Board a complaint charging that the union had engaged in unfair labor practices. A similar charge was filed today in connection with picket-line outbreaks at a G. E. plant in Syracuse.

For the second day plant production was at a standstill. Only a dozen persons were able to smash their way through dense picket lines manned by members of Local 301 of the International Union of Electrical Workers.

The emergency declaration came on the sixth day of the union's nation-wide strike against fifty-five General Electric plants. The company is attempting to keep its installations open despite the walkout, but union pickets have pre-

Continued on Page 13, Column 4

# Kennedy Protests Lighting And Cold and Wins on Both

By W. H. LAWRENCE
Special to The New York Times.

WASHINGTON, Oct. 7—Short-lived disagreements over blinding lights and a frigid studio developed tonight just before Vice President Nixon and Senator John F. Kennedy made their second joint nation-wide television appearance.

Democrats were the complainants in both instances, contending that steps taken to improve Mr. Nixon's television appearance were unfair to Senator Kennedy.

The studio had been chilled to 64 degrees to relieve Mr. Nixon's heavy perspiration problem that contributed to his generally unsatisfactory physical appearance on television last week.

Senator Kennedy tested the flood lighting from both his own lectern and Mr. Nixon's before the show began. He complained that four bright lights shone directly into his eyes from his own position but only one bright light hit him directly when he stood in Mr. Nixon's spot.

**Adjustments Made**

After the complaints, network officials adjusted the lighting to Senator Kennedy's satisfaction, and an engineer turned up the thermostat to a 70-degree temperature in the studio.

At the end of an hour-long show, the consensus among studio observers was that Mr. Nixon's make-up artist and lighting experts had done a better job for him than last time and that the physical image projected by the cameras was a vast improvement over the debate from Chicago on Sept. 26.

The Vice President wore what was described as "a mild amount of make-up."

Senator Kennedy, as before, declined all make-up assistance and appeared before the nation without applying powder.

While partisans for both sides

Continued on Page 12, Column 3

# JOBLESS LIKELY TO SHOW DECLINE

### September Figure Expected to Disclose Drop Was Greater Than Usual

By RICHARD E. MOONEY
Special to The New York Times.

WASHINGTON, Oct. 7—The official monthly estimate of unemployment is expected to show that the number of jobless declined more than usual in September.

The Labor Department will not release the estimates until Monday morning. But a source who has been right before suggested that Monday's report would show 3,400,000 unemployed in September, against 3,800,000 in August.

There is a political facet to the report on unemployment, of course, in the election campaign and the effect, real or imagined, that a good or bad report might have.

The political factor crops up every second year, as the general elections approach. Neither Vice President Nixon nor Senator John F. Kennedy mentioned the report due Monday in their television debate tonight.

**Pre-vote Report Due**

If past form is followed, there will be one more report on the job situation before the vote. The report is regularly issued on about the tenth day of each month, except in election years, when Democratic and Republican Administrations alike have found that they were able to complete the statistical work a little earlier in November.

Unemployment almost always declines in July, August, September and October, even in recession years. It has dropped in eleven of the thirteen post-war Septembers, mostly by 150,000 to 250,000. If the drop this time were greater than this, the seasonally adjusted percentage rate of unemployment would also be reduced. Assuming a 400,000 drop in unemployment this time, it is estimated that the rate would drop to 5.4 per cent, from 5.9 per cent in August. There

Continued on Page 13, Column 7

## Bronx Wreck Blocks Central, Delays Commuters

Freight cars criss-cross tracks below Marble Hill Station (at right of bridge in rear)

The New York Times (by Arthur Brower)

At the station, service is terminated and commuters are transferred to the IRT subway

# Adenauer Clashing With Erhard Again

By SYDNEY GRUSON
Special to The New York Times.

BONN, Germany, Oct. 7—Chancellor Adenauer and Dr. Ludwig Erhard, the Vice Chancellor and Minister of the Economy, are engaged in another blazing political dispute.

It is a many-sided clash involving specific economic issues and also the Chancellor's well-known antipathy to the Minister as his successor.

The specific issues are the trade sanctions against Communist East Germany ordered by Dr. Adenauer last week and the effort by the Chancellor and representatives of big industry to bypass Dr. Erhard in deciding upon measures to meet the dangers of inflation here.

When the latest Communist squeeze on Berlin began, Dr. Adenauer was on holiday and Dr. Erhard headed the Govern-

Continued on Page 8, Column 2

# British Believe Ghana Intends To Nationalize Foreign Assets

Special to The New York Times.

LONDON, Oct. 7—A report that the Government of Ghana planned to nationalize all foreign business enterprises caused considerable anxiety here today.

A dispatch from The News Chronicle's correspondent in Accra said that the nationalization would begin May 1 and be completed in three years. It said that representatives of the concerns, including seventy owned by British interests, had been told this by a Ghana official at a private meeting.

The Commonwealth Relations Office said it had received no communication from the Ghana Government, but was asking Sir Arthur Snelling, the British High Commissioner in Accra, about it.

A spokesman for the United Africa Company said, after the regular weekly meeting of the concern's board of directors, that the company was aware that proposals were being discussed in Ghana for the establishment of a national cooperative organization that would take over all imports and distributive trades.

"According to the company's information, these proposals have been drawn up in certain Government circles, but have not yet been before the Cabinet," the spokesman said.

"It appears that the proposals affect equally all private enterprise, Ghanaian and expatriate, large and small."

The United Africa Company, a subsidiary of Unilever, is an importing business that deals in a wide range of goods. Until last year, it purchased about 16 per cent of Ghana's total annual cocoa crop. Cadbury's,

Continued on Page 4, Column 5

## NEWS INDEX


| | Page | | Page |
|---|---|---|---|
| Art | 46 | Man in the News | 6 |
| Books | 21 | Music | 15 |
| Bridge | 20 | Obituaries | 23 |
| Business | 26-27 | Real Estate | 35 |
| Churches | 26 | Screen | 15 |
| Crossword | 21 | Ships and Air | 45 |
| Editorial | 22 | Society | 14 |
| Events Today | 26 | Sports | 17-21 |
| Fashions | 16 | TV and Radio | 46-47 |
| Financial | 26-34 | Theatres | 15 |
| Food | 16 | U. N. Proceedings | 3 |
| Letters | 22 | Weather | 45 |

News Summary and Index, Page 25


# Labor Sues to Halt Erie Line's Merger

By The Associated Press.

WASHINGTON, Oct. 7—Railway labor sought today to block the merger of the Erie and Lackawanna Railroads until the Interstate Commerce Commission guaranteed the jobs of union members.

A petition filed in the United States District Court in Detroit contended that the I. C. C. violated the Interstate Commerce Act when it approved on Sept. 13 the merger of the lines into the nation's twelfth largest railroad.

The unions asked the court to issue an order preventing the merger from going into effect as scheduled Oct. 17 until the question of labor protective conditions could be worked out.

Judge Thomas P. Thornton set a hearing on the request for next Wednesday and asked that

Continued on Page 23, Column 2

"All the News That's Fit to Print"

# The New York Times.

LATE CITY EDITION
U. S. Weather Bureau Report (Page 93) forecasts: Cloudy, periods of rain today. Partly cloudy, colder tomorrow. Temp. range: 55—41; yesterday: 53.8—40.4.

VOL. CX..No. 37,546.  NEW YORK, THURSDAY, NOVEMBER 10, 1960. 10 cents beyond 50-mile zone from New York City except on Long Island. Higher in air delivery cities. FIVE CENTS

# KENNEDY'S VICTORY WON BY CLOSE MARGIN; HE PROMISES FIGHT FOR WORLD FREEDOM; EISENHOWER OFFERS 'ORDERLY TRANSITION'

## DEMOCRATS HERE SPLIT IN VICTORY; LEHMAN ASSAILED

### De Sapio Accepts Challenge for Party Control—Mayor Claims Leadership

*Text of De Sapio statement appears on Page 43.*

By LEO EGAN

Less than twenty-four hours after the polls closed, the political coalition that gave Senator John F. Kennedy New York's forty-five electoral votes began coming apart at the seams.

Its disintegration was signaled by Carmine G. De Sapio in a statement assailing former Gov. Herbert H. Lehman, key figure in the Democratic reform group, and Alex Rose, Liberal party master of strategy.

The statement accepted Mr. Lehman's election night challenge to a finish fight for control of the party organization in the city and state.

At the same time it appeared to rule out any chance of a Democratic-Liberal party coalition for next year's Mayoral election in New York City and for the Governorship election in the state in 1962 if Mr. De Sapio remains in control of the party machinery.

**Kennedy's Delicate Problem**

Mr. De Sapio, leader of Tammany and Democratic National Committeeman for New York, consulted Michael H. Prendergast, the Democratic State Chairman, and a number of party leaders in the city and upstate before issuing his statement.

The collapse of the coalition so soon after it achieved its goal gave President-elect Kennedy a delicate political problem before he takes office. At some stage soon he will have to decide whom in New York to consult about appointments for the new Administration.

Thus, in so far as New York is concerned, the election appeared to raise as many questions as it settled. Control of the Democratic party machinery is one of them. Among the others are: What is Mayor Wagner's political future? And what is Governor Rockefeller's?

When told of Mr. De Sapio's statement last night, Mayor Wagner commented that he in-

Continued on Page 43, Column 1

## *Registration Set-Up Called Faulty Here*

By DOUGLAS DALES

Political leaders voiced dissatisfaction yesterday over the way permanent personal registration functioned here Tuesday in its first test in a Presidential election.

Charges were made that thousands of persons had been disfranchised because they were unable to convince election inspectors that they had registered and were eligible to vote.

How many voters may have been so affected was concededly a guess. But a check of the Supreme Courts in the five boroughs indicated that more than 1,300 persons had gone before the justices for orders directing the inspectors to permit them to vote.

"There was a minimum of 10,000 denied the right to vote," Abraham Gellinoff,

Continued on Page 43, Column 5

## ASSEMBLY DELAYS U.N. CONGO DEBATE

### Postpones It Indefinitely, 48-30, as Soviet Backs Step—U. S. Move Fails

By KATHLEEN TELTSCH
Special to The New York Times.

UNITED NATIONS, N. Y., Nov. 9—The General Assembly voted tonight to postpone the debate on the Congo indefinitely.

The 48-to-30 vote, with eighteen abstentions, was on a surprise move made by Ghana with the help of Guinea and Nigeria and the enthusiastic support of the Soviet bloc.

The United States tried to avoid the adjournment vote by asking for a suspension of the session until delegates could ponder the unexpected request.

Western sources said privately that Ghana's initiative appeared to have been prompted in part by the presence here of President Joseph Kasavubu of the Congo and the likelihood that the Assembly's Credentials Committee would agree to his request for the seating of a Congolese delegation of his supporters.

**A Two-Hour Wrangle**

Ghana, Guinea, India and five other states have joined in sponsoring a resolution that aims instead at having the Assembly seat a delegation designated by the deposed Congolese Premier, Patrice Lumumba.

The Assembly acted after a two-hour wrangle marked by two table-thumping demonstrations by the Soviet bloc and also by Ghana, both in protest against the efforts of Foreign Minister Pierre Wigny of Belgium to defend his country's position on the Congo issue.

The adjournment request was made by Alex Quaison-Sackey, Ghana's chief delegate. He appealed to the Assembly to hold off any further debate pending the efforts of a fifteen-member Asian-African commission to reconcile the clashing political factions in the Congo and restore some governmental stability.

He said that the commission probably would leave for the Congo in a week and that further acrimonious debate in the Assembly would only hamper the conciliation effort.

However, the adjournment as voted did not stipulate how long the debate should be suspended. United States sources said tonight that they understood this to mean that discussion could

Continued on Page 3, Column 1

## ATOM BILL BEATEN IN FRENCH SENATE

### Debre to Push Compromise on Nuclear Force Plan

By W. GRANGER BLAIR
Special to The New York Times.

PARIS, Thursday, Nov. 10—The Senate early today rejected President de Gaulle's project for an independent French nuclear striking force.

By a vote of 186 to 83, with seventeen abstentions, this conservative Upper House approved a procedural motion to table the national nuclear deterrent bill that had been passed to it by the National Assembly Oct. 27.

Although the Senate's action was a stinging blow to President de Gaulle and a sharp indication of mounting parliamentary opposition, it did not mean that the Government's measure would not eventually become law.

It was announced after the vote that Premier Michel Debré would call for the creation of a mixed committee of Senators and Deputies to work out a compromise measure. Should this conference committee fail to find a compromise, the Government would resubmit its measure to the Assembly for a second reading, and virtually certain approval. The measure would then become law with or without Senate's approval.

The Senate motion to table

Continued on Page 8, Column 1

## NEWS INDEX



| | Page | | Page |
|---|---|---|---|
| Books | 44-45 | Music | 59-62 |
| Bridge | 44 | Obituaries | 47 |
| Business | 72-73 | Real Estate | 83 |
| Buyers | 72 | Screen | 59-62 |
| Crossword | 45 | Ships and Air | 93 |
| Editorial | 46 | Society | 54 |
| Fashions | 56 | Sports | 65-71 |
| Financial | 73-82 | TV and Radio | 95 |
| Food | 56 | Theatres | 59-62 |
| Letters | 46 | U. N. Proceedings | 3 |
| Man in the News | 73 | Weather | 93 |



News Summary and Index, Page 49

## WINNER'S PLEDGE

### Family Is With Him as He Vows to Press Nation's Cause

*Text of Kennedy's statement is printed on Page 36.*

By HOMER BIGART
Special to The New York Times.

HYANNIS, Mass., Nov. 9—Senator John F. Kennedy accepted in solemn mood today his election as President.

He pledged all his energy to advancing "the long-range interests of the United States and the cause of freedom around the world."

He made this pledge inside the flag-decked Hyannis Armory at 1:45 P. M., an hour after Vice President Nixon, his Republican opponent, had conceded defeat.

His wife, Jacqueline, stood at his side as the 43-year-old President-elect faced 300 newsmen and massed batteries of TV cameras and gave his victory statement to the nation.

Behind him were arrayed the Kennedy family: his father, former Ambassador Joseph P. Kennedy; his mother, three sisters and three brothers.

**No Sign of Jubilation**

The Kennedys showed no evidence of jubilation. All wore expressions of solemnity. Mr. Kennedy's margin of victory was too slender to stir much elation. Some of his aides acknowledged disappointment over the startlingly narrow gap in the popular vote.

Mr. Kennedy, after responding to applause with a diffident bow and a smile, first read the telegram from Mr. Nixon conceding defeat and extending congratulations. The Senator had stayed up until 3:50 A. M. awaiting this concession and had gone to bed disappointed when the Vice President withheld it.

**Replies to Nixon**

Mr. Nixon wired the President-elect that all the nation would give him "united support" in the next four years.

Mr. Kennedy replied to Mr. Nixon:

"I know that the nation can continue to count on your unswerving loyalty in whatever effort you undertake, and that you and I can maintain our long-standing cordial relations in the years ahead."

Mr. Kennedy then read a congratulatory message from President Eisenhower.

In his message the President informed Mr. Kennedy that he would shortly receive suggestions from the President as to the change-over of responsibilities for national leadership.

To this Senator Kennedy had replied:

"I am grateful for your wire and good wishes. I look forward to working with you in the near future. The whole country is hopeful that your long ex-

Continued on Page 36, Column 7

United Press International Telephoto

THE MESSAGES WERE CONGRATULATORY: Senator John F. Kennedy displaying telegrams at Hyannis, Mass. With him are Mrs. Kennedy, his parents and Robert F. Kennedy, left, and R. Sargent Shriver, a brother-in-law.

## KHRUSHCHEV NOTE SALUTES KENNEDY

### Message of Congratulations Asks for Negotiations on Tensions in World

*Text of Khrushchev message will be found on Page 42.*

By The Associated Press.

MOSCOW, Nov. 9—Soviet Premier Khrushchev congratulated Senator John F. Kennedy today for his Presidential victory.

He expressed hope that Soviet-United States relations would "again follow the line along which they were developing in Franklin Roosevelt's time."

He urged negotiations aimed at easing the international situation.

[In Bonn, Chancellor Konrad Adenauer said he planned to go to Washington early next year for conferences with Mr. Kennedy.]

Mr. Khrushchev's statements in a congratulatory message to Mr. Kennedy coincided with Moscow's insistence that the policies of President Eisenhower had suffered a rebuff in the election.

The Soviet press contended that the election proved "the American people have blackballed the policy of the 'cold war' and the arms race, that they want changes and expect Washington to pursue a reasonable course in international affairs, a course dictated by life and the balance of forces now prevailing in the world." Mr.

Continued on Page 42, Column 4

## Electoral Vote by States

| | Rep. | Dem. | | Rep. | Dem. | | Rep. | Dem. |
|---|---|---|---|---|---|---|---|---|
| Alabama | .. | 5* | Louisiana | .. | 10 | Ohio | 25 | .. |
| Alaska | .. | .. | Maine | 5 | .. | Oklahoma | 8 | .. |
| Arizona | 4 | .. | Maryland | .. | 9 | Oregon | 6 | .. |
| Arkansas | .. | 8 | Mass. | .. | 16 | Penna. | .. | 32 |
| California | .. | .. | Michigan | .. | 20 | Rhode Island | .. | 4 |
| Colorado | 6 | .. | Minnesota | .. | 11 | So. Carolina | .. | 8 |
| Conn. | .. | 8 | Mississippi | ** | ** | So. Dakota | 4 | .. |
| Delaware | .. | 3 | Missouri | .. | 13 | Tennessee | 11 | .. |
| Florida | 10 | .. | Montana | 4 | .. | Texas | .. | 24 |
| Georgia | .. | 12 | Nebraska | 6 | .. | Utah | 4 | .. |
| Hawaii | .. | .. | Nevada | .. | 3 | Vermont | 3 | .. |
| Idaho | 4 | .. | New Hamp. | 4 | .. | Virginia | 12 | .. |
| Illinois | .. | 27 | New Jersey | .. | 16 | Washington | 9 | .. |
| Indiana | 13 | .. | New Mexico | .. | 4 | W. Virginia | .. | 8 |
| Iowa | 10 | .. | New York | .. | 45 | Wisconsin | 12 | .. |
| Kansas | 8 | .. | No. Carolina | .. | 14 | Wyoming | 3 | .. |
| Kentucky | 10 | .. | North Dakota | 4 | .. | Total | 185 | 300 |

*Five electors are pledged to Kennedy and six unpledged.
**Eight electors not pledged to vote for party candidates.

## LIBERALS SUFFER SETBACK IN HOUSE

### G. O. P. Picks Up 22 Seats to Aid Conservative Bloc

By JOHN D. MORRIS

The House of Representatives will have a more conservative tinge in the Eighty-seventh Congress.

Inroads into the present House Democratic majority of 283 to 154 scored by the Republicans in Tuesday's elections promised to strengthen their conservative coalition with Southern Democrats.

The liberal legislative program to be submitted early next year by the new Democratic President, John F. Kennedy, may consequently face handicaps in the new Congress, which convenes Jan. 3.

In the Senate, Republicans cut the Democratic margin by two seats, to 64 to 36. That chamber remains predominantly liberal in membership, although conservatives dominate key committee posts.

**Gubernatorial Shifts**

The Democrats achieved a net gain of one governorship and now control thirty-four of the fifty state houses. In twenty-seven gubernatorial contests the Democrats won fifteen and the Republicans twelve, with an exchange of party control in thirteen.

In the House races, nearly complete unofficial returns showed that the Democrats had elected 257 House candidates and the Republicans 175, with five contests still in doubt.

The Republicans captured twenty-nine seats held by Democrats and lost seven of their own, for a net gain of at least twenty-two. For a bare numerical majority of 219 they would have had to achieve a net gain of sixty-five.

Among the eleven states of the Old Confederacy the Republicans maintained their hold on seven seats of the Eighty-

Continued on Page 38, Column 4

## NIXON WIRE GIVES HIS 'BEST WISHES'

### Sends Kennedy a Message —500 in Capital Hail Him

By BILL BECKER
Special to The New York Times.

LOS ANGELES, Nov. 9—Vice President Nixon conceded today the Presidential election of his Democratic opponent, Senator John F. Kennedy.

About twelve hours after the polls had closed, the Vice President sent the following telegram to Senator Kennedy at Hyannis Port, Mass.:

"I want to repeat through this wire the congratulations and best wishes I extended to you on television last night. I know that you will have the united support of all Americans as you lead the nation in the cause of peace and freedom in the next four years."

**Read by Aide**

The telegram was read to newsmen by Mr. Nixon's press secretary, Herbert G. Klein, at 9:45 A. M., Pacific standard time (12:45 P. M., Eastern standard time).

The Vice President did not make a personal appearance. Mr. Klein said Mr. Nixon was resting with Mrs. Nixon and their two daughters in their suite at the Ambassador Hotel.

It was obvious that the Vice President had considered his remarks late on election night a virtual concession.

[A crowd of several hundred greeted Mr. Nixon as he arrived Wednesday night at Andrews Air Base, near Washington, after a flight of four and a half hours from Los Angeles.]

Mr. Nixon remained in seclusion most of the morning although Mr. Klein said he was up about 6 A. M. after little more than three hours of sleep. The secretary said Mr. Nixon

Continued on Page 42, Column 5



## PRESIDENT SENDS WIRE TO KENNEDY

### He Felicitates Senator and Orders Agency Chiefs to Cooperate With Him

By FELIX BELAIR Jr.
Special to The New York Times.

AUGUSTA, Ga., Nov. 9—President Eisenhower congratulated President-elect John F. Kennedy today on his election and then invited him to designate representatives to participate in all Federal policy discussions to assure an "orderly transition" to the new Administration.

The text of the President's telegram was withheld here at the request of Mr. Kennedy. But President Eisenhower is understood to have told the President-elect that he had instructed all heads of Federal departments and agencies to "cooperate fully" with Mr. Kennedy's representatives.

President Eisenhower arrived here for his customary fall holiday in midafternoon after a two-hour flight from Washington.

The President's message of congratulation to Mr. Kennedy was sent from the White House just before he took off for his favorite vacation retreat here at Augusta National Golf Club.

He also sent messages to the defeated Republican candidate, Vice President Nixon, and his running mate, Henry Cabot Lodge, as well as Vice President-elect Lyndon B. Johnson.

In his telegram to Mr. Nixon

Continued on Page 42, Column 7

## RESULTS DELAYED

### Popular Vote Almost Even—300-185 Is Electoral Tally

By JAMES RESTON

Senator John F. Kennedy of Massachusetts finally won the 1960 Presidential election from Vice President Nixon by the astonishing margin of less than two votes per voting precinct.

Senator Kennedy's electoral vote total stood yesterday at 300, just thirty-one more than the 269 needed for election. The Vice President's total was 185. Fifty-two additional electoral votes, including California's thirty-two, were still in doubt last night.

But the popular vote was a different story. The two candidates ran virtually even. Senator Kennedy's lead last night was little more than 300,000 in a total tabulated vote of about 66,000,000 cast in 165,826 precincts.

That was a plurality for the Senator of less than one-half of 1 per cent of the total vote—the smallest percentage difference between the popular vote of two Presidential candidates since 1880, when James A. Garfield outran Gen. Winfield Scott Hancock by 7,000 votes in a total of almost 9,000,000.

**End Divided Government**

Nevertheless, yesterday's voting radically altered the political balance of power in America in favor of the Democrats and put them in a commanding position in the Federal and state capitals unknown since the heyday of Franklin D. Roosevelt.

They regained control of the White House for the first time since 1952 and thus ended divided government in Washington. They retained control of the Senate and the House of Representatives, although with slightly reduced margins. And they increased their hold on the state governorships by one, bringing the Democratic margin to 34—16.

The President-elect is the first Roman Catholic ever to win the nation's highest office. The only other member of his church nominated for President was Alfred E. Smith, who was defeated by Herbert Hoover in 1928.

**Faces Difficult Questions**

Despite his personal triumph, President-elect Kennedy is confronted by a number of hard questions:

¶In the face of such a narrow victory how can he get through the Congress the liberal program he proposed during the campaign?

¶Can so close an election produce any impetus for loosening the conservative coalition of Republicans and Southern Democrats which has blocked most liberal legislation in the House?

¶Will the new President be able successfully to claim a mandate for legislation such as the $1.25 minimum wage, Fed-

Continued on Page 35, Column 1

## *10 Irish Soldiers Slain in Congo When U.N. Patrol Is Ambushed*

By PAUL HOFMANN
Special to The New York Times.

LEOPOLDVILLE, the Congo, Nov. 9—A patrol of eleven Irish soldiers of the United Nations force in the Congo was ambushed in the northern part of Katanga Province yesterday. The bodies of four men were sighted.

[The United Nations Command said that ten soldiers had been slain in the ambush, Reuters reported. The Irish Army announced in Dublin that one private had survived the attack. Reports received by the United Nations in New York said the surviving soldier was "badly wounded," according to United Press International.]

The patrol belonged to the Irish Thirty-third Battalion, which has headquarters in the industrial city of Albertville. The battalion, with a strength of about 550 men, is responsible for maintaining order in a vast area of North Katanga. The region has been the scene of intertribal warfare and clashes between Baluba tribesmen and the gendarmerie controlled by Moise Tshombe, President of Katanga.

United Nations officials here were unable to say who had attacked the Irish patrol. The ambush occurred south of Niemba, a village between Albertville and Kabalo. The zone is described as "Baluba country," but it is not known whether Baluba tribesmen were responsible for the assault.

Announcing the loss, a United Nations spokesman said it brought the toll of dead in the international force in the Congo to about thirty since the world organization's troops arrived

Continued on Page 2, Column 3

## *Vatican Calls Kennedy Election Proof of American Democracy*

By ARNALDO CORTESI
Special to The New York Times.

ROME, Nov. 9—The election of Senator John F. Kennedy, a Roman Catholic, to the Presidency was received with keen satisfaction in the Vatican today.

During the campaign the Vatican remained neutral. Its newspaper, L'Osservatore Romano, abstained from all comment lest it be accused of siding with one candidate against the other.

Today the editor of the newspaper, former Italian Deputy Raimondo Manzini, said:

"Kennedy's victory strengthens the appreciation for the high democratic principles of freedom that guide American public life and assure access to the highest office to every citizen regardless of social class, race, or religion.

"The effective support given by large numbers of Protestant citizens to a Catholic considered suitable for the Presidency has been significant in this respect. Catholics are, of course, satisfied at the solemn confirmation of the principle that the office of President is open to a son of the Catholic Church, which enjoys such large prestige in the United States. Catholics have, however, always admired Nixon's irreproachable attitude of deferential respect for the Catholic hierarchy."

Senator Kennedy's victory was announced under large headlines by the whole morning press in Italy today. In most newspapers it took precedence over the results of the provincial and municipal elections that were held in Italy over the week-end.

Government circles received the news without astonishment

Continued on Page 38, Column 7

JOHN F. KENNEDY

"All the News That's Fit to Print"

# The New York Times.

LATE CITY EDITION
U. S. Weather Bureau report (Page 44) forecasts
Chance of snow flurries, cold today and tonight. Fair and cold tomorrow.
Temp. range: 21—6; yesterday: 17—10

VOL. CX..No. 37,618. © 1961 by The New York Times Company. Times Square, New York 36, N. Y. NEW YORK, SATURDAY, JANUARY 21, 1961. 10 cents beyond 50-mile zone from New York City except on Long Island. Higher in air delivery cities. FIVE CENTS

# KENNEDY SWORN IN, ASKS 'GLOBAL ALLIANCE' AGAINST TYRANNY, WANT, DISEASE AND WAR; REPUBLICANS AND DIPLOMATS HAIL ADDRESS

# 24-Hour Snowstorm Ties Up City Area; Schools Closed

## COLD TO CONTINUE

### Northeast Is Crippled by Heavy Drifts—Deaths Total 47

By RUSSELL PORTER

Cold and windy weather plagued the city yesterday in the wake of a twenty-four-hour snowstorm that almost paralyzed the East.

The bitter wind here hampered the removal of the ten-inch snow, intensified suffering and delayed the restoration of normal travel.

Continued cold was predicted for the week-end, with the possibility of snow flurries today. Clear skies were expected tomorrow.

The temperature dropped to 9 degrees here at 2 A. M. today and went lower in the suburbs. A high in the twenties was expected this afternoon. The wind, which was twenty miles an hour yesterday afternoon was expected to drop to ten to fifteen miles an hour today.

Schools and colleges were closed in the city and other parts of the stormbound East. Many factories and business offices were shut down or forced to work with short staffs.

**Travel Disrupted**

Highways were blocked, auto traffic was slowed, cars were marooned in snow banks, rail and bus traffic was suspended or slowed, air travel was all but halted, mail service was interrupted and funerals were canceled.

The Associated Press counted at least forty-seven deaths attributed to the storm, including twenty in Pennsylvania, six in New York, two in New Jersey and five in Connecticut. Most of the deaths were caused by storm-induced traffic accidents and overexertion from shoveling snow.

Two Navy men and a civilian were in a truck that went off a pier into Jamaica Bay at Floyd Bennett Field in Brooklyn early yesterday. One body was found last night.

**Drifts Up to 10 Feet**

Although the Weather Bureau measured ten inches of snow near its Rockefeller Center office, it said the fall varied from six to twelve inches throughout the city. Windblown drifts were as high as ten feet in the city and suburbs.

The Weather Bureau labeled the storm a near blizzard here because the wind did not maintain the steady thirty-to-forty-mile-an-hour velocity of a blizzard. Some gusts reached fifty miles an hour, however, and the temperature dropped as low as 12 degrees early yesterday.

The storm was the city's second major one of the winter. In the first, on Dec. 11 and 12, a total of seventeen inches fell.

The new snowfall, although lighter, was considered worse in places because of the heavy drifting.

The new snowstorm began

Continued on Page 14, Column 1

Associated Press Wirephoto

NEW PRESIDENT TAKES THE OATH: John Fitzgerald Kennedy taking the oath of office yesterday. Administering it is Chief Justice Earl Warren, and holding the Bible is James R. Browning, Clerk of the Supreme Court. In the foreground, from the left, are Mrs. Kennedy; Mrs. Warren; outgoing President Eisenhower; Mrs. R. Sargent Shriver, a sister of President Kennedy; Dean Rusk and, at right, Lyndon Baines Johnson, who was sworn in as Vice President. Partly hidden behind Mrs. Shriver is Adlai E. Stevenson.

## NATION EXHORTED

### Inaugural Says U. S. Will 'Pay Any Price' to Keep Freedom

*Text of Inaugural Address will be found on Page 8.*

By W. H. LAWRENCE

Special to The New York Times

WASHINGTON, Jan. 20—John Fitzgerald Kennedy assumed the Presidency today with a call for "a grand and global alliance" to combat tyranny, poverty, disease and war.

In his Inaugural Address, he served notice on the world that the United States was ready to "pay any price, bear any burden, meet any hardship, support any friend, oppose any foe to assure the survival and the success of liberty."

But the nation is also ready, he said, to resume negotiations with the Soviet Union to ease and, if possible, remove world tensions.

"Let us begin anew," Mr. Kennedy declared. "Let us never negotiate out of fear. But let us never fear to negotiate."

**Asks Aid of Countrymen**

He called on his fellow-citizens to join his Administration's endeavor:

"Ask not what your country can do for you—ask what you can do for your country."

At 12:51 P. M., he was sworn in by Chief Justice Earl Warren as the nation's thirty-fifth President, the first Roman Catholic to hold the office.

Ten minutes earlier, Lyndon Baines Johnson of Texas took the oath as Vice President. It was administered by Sam Rayburn, Speaker of the House of Representatives.

At 43 years of age, the youngest man ever elected to the Presidency, Mr. Kennedy took over the power vested for eight years in Dwight D. Eisenhower, who, at 70, was the oldest White House occupant.

President Kennedy alluded to this change of generation in his inaugural.

**'Torch Has Passed'**

He said:

"Let the word go forth from this time and place, to friend and foe alike, that the torch has been passed to a new generation of Americans—born in this century, tempered by war, disciplined by a hard and bitter peace, proud of our ancient heritage—and unwilling to witness or permit the slow undoing of those human rights to which this nation has always been committed today at home and around the world."

A blanket of 7.7 inches of newly fallen snow, bitter winds and a sub-freezing temperature of 22 degrees held down the crowds that watched the ceremonies in front of the newly

Continued on Page 8, Column 1

## SNOW KEEPS MANY FROM JOBS IN CITY

### Airport Drifts Stop Flights—Highway Traffic Light, With Some Roads Shut

By McCANDLISH PHILLIPS

Tens of thousands of people in the metropolitan area solved their transportation problems yesterday by evading them. They stayed at home.

For the most part, the brave, the bold and the resourceful were able to get to work. But they were often delayed and in many cases had to use alternate routes.

Others, who had stayed at hotels in the city overnight, had little trouble reaching their offices.

Long-distance travelers faced greater difficulties.

Snow clogged runways at the three major airports, bringing air traffic almost to a halt. Instead of the normal 1,600 arriving and departing flights there were twelve—six at New York International Airport and six at Newark.

This situation began to be reversed by late afternoon, and La Guardia and the two other airports reported virtually normal operations. Some flights were being canceled, however,

Continued on Page 15, Column 1

## Unions Reject Plea to Halt Rail Picketing for 10 Days

By A. H. RASKIN

Leaders of the crippling harbor strike rejected early today a plea by Governor Rockefeller for a ten-day halt in their picket blockade of railroad terminals and freight yards.

The Governor had made his appeal on the basis that snow-clogged highways had aggravated the peril to the city's lifeline created by the pickets' cut-off of rail commutation and food and freight movements.

The three striking unions asserted that compliance with the Governor's request would strip them of their only effective weapon without requiring any "comparable sacrifice" by the railroads.

They said the withdrawal of pickets by the 664 ferry and tug crewmen would "completely tip the scale in favor of the employers and obviously encourage an even more unyielding position on their part."

The marine strikers were so irked by the Governor's move that they urged the New York City Central Labor Council to call a meeting of all unions here to censure him. The rail tug unions asserted that he had intervened on the side of management in a manner that endangered the security and the bargaining status of all labor.

The rejection of the armistice plan came a few minutes after new settlement negotiations sponsored by the Governor had ended in failure. The peace talks will be resumed at 10:15 A. M. today, but there was no indication last night that they were making any progress.

The outlook was for a rapid intensification of the strikers'

Continued on Page 15, Column 5

## CASTRO SUGGESTS AMITY WITH U. S.

### Premier, in Citing Kennedy's Inaugural, Says Cuba Is Ready to 'Begin Anew'

By R. HART PHILLIPS

Special to The New York Times.

HAVANA, Jan. 20—Premier Fidel Castro said tonight that the Cuban Government would "begin anew" in its relations with the United States.

The Premier stressed, however, that Cuba would hold the United States responsible for improving relations between the countries.

The Castro Government began here a demobilizing of the militia forces called up against an alleged threat of a United States "invasion."

Dr. Castro noted that President Kennedy had urged in his Inaugural Address that the United States' adversaries "begin anew the quest for peace."

"For our part," Premier Castro declared, "we are going to begin anew."

"However, we will ask nothing from Washington, nor did we expect any favors or economic assistance from Washington," he asserted. "We have no resentment of the past, but we will wait for the action of the Kennedy Administration. We

Continued on Page 4, Column 4

## Inaugural Widely Praised By Both Sides of Congress

By JOHN D. MORRIS

Special to The New York Times.

WASHINGTON, Jan. 20—President Kennedy was widely acclaimed in Congress today for an Inaugural that stirred Republicans as well as Democrats. Diplomats and other public figures also joined in the praise.

The outgoing President, Dwight D. Eisenhower, said his successor's address was "fine, very fine."

Among the other Republican comment was that of Everett McKinley Dirksen, the Senate minority leader, who described the speech as "inspiring" and "a very compact message of hope."

Charles A. Halleck, the House Republican leader, said:

"I was much impressed."

**Monroney Calls It Best**

Any prize for the most glowing reaction would probably have gone to Senator A. S. Mike Monroney of Oklahoma, who led forces seeking the nomination of Adlai E. Stevenson, one of the country's most eloquent orators, at the Democratic National Convention last July.

Senator Monroney called the speech "the best Inaugural Address I have heard in my lifetime." He said he had heard twelve in all, starting with Woodrow Wilson's second in 1917.

He and a number of others,

Continued on Page 8, Column 6

## EISENHOWER FINDS NEW LIFE 'GREAT'

### Drives to Gettysburg Farm as Private Citizen After a Luncheon in His Honor

By FELIX BELAIR Jr.

Special to The New York Times.

GETTYSBURG, Pa., Jan. 20—Dwight D. Eisenhower left the official Washington scene today and became an elder statesman.

At the same time the curtain fell on his fifty years of public service as soldier and President and a new life as a private citizen began.

Mr. Eisenhower appeared lighthearted and no little relieved to be rid of the burdens of office, and he expressed his mood several times during the afternoon.

"Great, fine," he said when asked how he liked the idea of retiring from public life.

After President Kennedy's Inaugural, Mr. Eisenhower went to the 1925 F Street Club in Washington for a farewell luncheon given in his honor by Lewis L. Strauss, former chairman of the Atomic Energy Commission.

It had been a bitterly cold morning for everybody and the cocktails and champagne flowed freely inside. The host was having trouble getting his guests away from the bar until Mr. Eisenhower put down his glass

Continued on Page 12, Column 1

## SOVIET SHAKE-UP SEEKS FOOD RISE

### Khrushchev Orders Changes in Supply and Distribution

By OSGOOD CARUTHERS

Special to The New York Times.

MOSCOW, Jan. 20—Premier Khrushchev has ordered a sweeping reorganization of supply and distribution in Soviet agriculture.

He has ordered the setting up of new agencies as middlemen between industry and the farms to insure a better supply of equipment to agriculture and a better return distribution of food to the people.

The Premier's proposals were adopted two days ago by the ruling Central Committee of the Communist party after having been outlined in a lengthy speech three days ago in the Kremlin at a plenary session of the committee.

The proposals were aimed at ending the lag in the growth of agriculture and at working out ways of better satisfying the demands of the populace for meat, milk, butter and eggs as well as the usual fare of bread and potatoes.

The most drastic divergence from the traditional Soviet sys-

Continued on Page 3, Column 2

## KHRUSHCHEV SEES HOPE FOR ACCORD

### Message to Kennedy Urges Drive to Ease Tensions

By Reuters.

LONDON, Jan. 20—Premier Khrushchev and President Leonid Brezhnev of the Soviet Union cabled President Kennedy an Inauguration Day message today extending the hope for a "radical improvement" in Soviet-American relations.

They hoped, the Soviet news agency Tass reported, that joint efforts of the United States and the Soviet Union would improve relations and therefore "make healthier the entire international climate."

[British Government officials, politicians and the press joined Friday in hailing President Kennedy's Inaugural Address. They admired its content and acclaimed its "style and flair" as symbolizing a new, dashing and dynamic approach to the world's problems.]

The cable from the Russian leaders said:

"Dear Mr. President, we congratulate you upon your inauguration. We avail ourselves of the opportunity to express the

Continued on Page 10, Column 8

## Inquiry Mystified by Jet Wreck That Killed 4 on Take-Off Here

By RICHARD WITKIN

Investigators failed yesterday to turn up any solid clue as to why an Aeronaves de Mexico jet airliner crashed on take-off from a snow-whipped runway here Thursday evening.

They found only that the DC-8 had not been overloaded, that the snowstorm had not dropped the ceiling or visibility below the legal minimum for take-offs, and that the pilot evidently had tried to stop the plane by reversing thrust on all four engines.

Most observers thought it amazing that 102 of the 106 persons on board managed to escape before the plane went up in flames. The four who died were all members of the Mexican crew: two pilots, an engineer and a woman purser.

The jet, taking off to the northeast on the 10,000-foot Runway 7 at International Airport, ripped out a 100-foot-wide section of a steel fence at the end of the strip. It then tore through a wire mesh cyclone fence in the field beyond, struck a car as it crossed Rockaway Boulevard, and came to rest in a marshy area about 900 feet from the runway.

Many of the 102 survivors were interviewed by Civil Aeronautics Board officials during the day.

George Van Epps, C. A. B. chief in the Northeast region,

Continued on Page 16, Column 5

## Capital Paraders Don Overcoats To Pass in White House Review

By RUSSELL BAKER

Special to The New York Times.

WASHINGTON, Jan. 20—President Kennedy had warned that it wouldn't be easy on "the New Frontier" and, for 32,000 marchers in today's inauguration parade, it wasn't.

A Siberian wind knifing down Pennsylvania Avenue in the wake of last night's snowfall turned majorettes' legs blue, froze baton twirlers' fingers and drove beauty queens to flannels and overcoats.

"This," said Cathy Magda, Miss Florida from Fort Lauderdale, "is the coldest parade I can ever remember."

Under her gown, she confided, she was wearing flannel pajamas.

Fear of chilblains visibly reduced attendance along the mile-and-a-half route from the Capitol to the White House but the big and ebullient Clan Kennedy obviously had the time of its life.

The President's younger brother Robert, the new Attorney General, rode down the avenue seated high on the back of his open car, hair tossing in the wind, waving and laughing in exuberant spirits.

The President's sister Eunice brought her movie camera to the reviewing stand in front of the White House and had her brother pose in the foreground as she panned across the

Continued on Page 9, Column 4

## 5 Dances Conclude Capital Festivities

By DAVID HALBERSTAM

Special to The New York Times.

WASHINGTON, Jan. 20—Some of them brought formals and tuxedos thousands of miles, then stayed in their hotels. Some of the women shivered in their fashionable and frail gowns while some of their men wore long johns under their white-tie formals at the Inaugural Ball here tonight.

The ball was the last official event of a crowded two-and-a-half-day schedule of social politicking, or political-socializing, and the exhausting pace began to show tonight.

It was cold again, and windy, and there were traffic problems. If there was any redeeming part about tonight's weather as far

Continued on Page 11, Column 8

NEWS INDEX


| | Page | | Page |
|---|---|---|---|
| Art | 45 | Music | 17-18 |
| Books | 19 | Obituaries | 21 |
| Bridge | 18 | Real Estate | 36 |
| Business | 27-28 | Screen | 17-18 |
| Churches | 24 | Ships and Air | 44 |
| Crossword | 19 | Society | 19 |
| Editorial | 20 | Sports | 25-27 |
| Events Today | 19 | TV and Radio | 45 |
| Fashions | 22 | Theatres | 17-18 |
| Financial | 27-35, 44 | U. N. Proceedings | 4 |
| Food | 22 | Wash. Proceedings | 13 |
| Man in the News | 5 | Weather | 44 |

News Summary and Index, Page 23

"All the News That's Fit to Print"

# The New York Times.

LATE CITY EDITION

U. S. Weather Bureau Report (Page 58) forecasts: Cloudy, windy, chance of showers today and tonight. Cold tomorrow.

Temp. Range: 62—54; yesterday: 64—51.

VOL. CXIII...No. 38,654.  NEW YORK, SATURDAY, NOVEMBER 23, 1963. TEN CENTS

# KENNEDY IS KILLED BY SNIPER AS HE RIDES IN CAR IN DALLAS; JOHNSON SWORN IN ON PLANE

## TEXAN ASKS UNITY

### Congressional Chiefs of Both Parties Promise Aid

By FELIX BELAIR Jr.
Special to The New York Times

WASHINGTON, Nov. 22—Lyndon B. Johnson returned to a stunned capital shortly after 6 P.M. today to assume the duties of the Presidency.

The new President asked for and received from Congressional leaders of both parties their "united support in the face of the tragedy which has befallen our country." He said it was "more essential that ever before that this country be united."

Partisan differences disappeared in the chorus of assurances with which the Congressional leaders responded.

Mr. Johnson was described by those who talked with him as "stunned and shaken" by the assassination of President Kennedy.

**Discusses U.S. Security**

But he moved quickly from problems of national security and foreign policy to funeral arrangements for Mr. Kennedy.

Across the street from the West Wing of the White House, the President conferred with officials in his old Vice-Presidential offices in the Executive Office Building.

Senator George A. Smathers, Democrat of Florida, a personal friend of the dead President, was one of those who described Mr. Johnson as shaken.

"Everyone is," he added. "But the President is the more so because he was right there when the tragedy occurred."

While flying to Washington aboard the Presidential plane, Mr. Johnson arranged for a meeting with Cabinet members to ask that they remain at their posts. He made the same request of staff members in the executive office.

**Meets With Harriman**

"Calm and contained" was the way Senator J. W. Fulbright described the President's manner during a discussion of foreign-policy matters with Under Secretary of State W. Averell Harriman. The Arkansas Senator said the President had been working on "what looked like a statement"—presumably an assurance of continuity of the nation's foreign policy.

The new President's first conference was aboard the helicopter that flew him the 15 miles from Andrews Air Force Base

Continued on Page 11, Column 3

Henry Grossman

*"This is a sad time for all people. We have suffered a loss that cannot be weighed. For me it is a deep personal tragedy. I know the world shares the sorrow that Mrs. Kennedy and her family bear. I will do my best. That is all I can do. I ask for your help—and God's."—President Lyndon Baines Johnson.*

## PRESIDENT'S BODY WILL LIE IN STATE

### Funeral Mass to Be Monday in Capital After Homage Is Paid by Public

By JACK RAYMOND
Special to The New York Times

WASHINGTON, Nov. 22—The body of John F. Kennedy will lie in state in the rotunda of the Capitol Sunday and then will be borne to St. Matthew's Roman Catholic Cathedral for a pontifical requiem mass at noon Monday.

The President's body was returned to Washington today in the same Air Force jet that carried him to Texas. The airliner, with Mrs. Kennedy, the new President, Lyndon B. Johnson, and Mrs. Johnson aboard, arrived at Andrews Air Force Base at 5:58 P.M.

It was announced later that Mr. Kennedy's body would lie in the White House tomorrow from 10 A.M. to 6 P.M., during which time Government and diplomatic officials will pay their respects.

The coffin will be taken from the White House to the Capitol rotunda Sunday morning, where

Continued on Page 9, Column 3

## PARTIES' OUTLOOK FOR '64 CONFUSED

### Republican Prospects Rise—Johnson Faces Possible Fight Against Liberals

By WARREN WEAVER Jr.
Special to The New York Times

WASHINGTON, Nov. 22—President Kennedy's assassination threw the American political scene into turmoil today.

It removed at a single blow the man who would have been renominated for a second term in the White House by acclamation nine months from now.

It elevated into the Presidency and the leadership of the Democratic party an older, more conservative man still emerging from his Southern heritage.

It increased immeasurably for the leaders of the Republican party prospects of electing a President next November.

The shock of the President's death stilled the official voices of politics in the capital. But so profound was the potential effect on the government and leadership that private consideration could not be silenced.

Before, there had been facts and strong probabilities on the

Continued on Page 6, Column 3

## LEFTIST ACCUSED

### Figure in a Pro-Castro Group Is Charged—Policeman Slain

By GLADWIN HILL
Special to The New York Times

DALLAS, Tex., Nov. 22—The Dallas police and Federal officers issued a charge of murder late tonight in the assassination of President Kennedy.

The accused is Lee Harvey Oswald, a 24-year-old former marine, who went to live in the Soviet Union in 1959 and returned to Texas last year.

Capt. Will Fritz, head of the Dallas police homicide bureau, identified Oswald as an adherent of the left-wing Fair Play for Cuba Committee.

Oswald was arrested about two hours after the shooting, in a movie theater three miles away, shortly after he allegedly shot and killed a policeman on a street nearby.

He was arraigned tonight on a charge of murdering the police officer. The charge related to the Kennedy killing was made later.

**Appears in Line-Up**

After the arraignment, the suspect, a slight, dark-haired man, was taken downstairs to appear in a line-up, presumably before witnesses of the Kennedy assassination.

While being escorted, handcuffed, through a police building corridor, he shouted: "I haven't shot anybody."

Captain Fritz said Oswald was employed—the exact job was unknown—at the Texas School Book Depository, a warehouse from which the assassin's bullets came. The captain said some witnesses had placed Oswald in the building at the time of the assassination.

The sequence of events leading to his arrest was as follows:

As a citywide manhunt began during the hour following the assassination, an unidentified man notified police headquarters, over a police-car radio, that the car's officer had been

Continued on Page 4, Column 1

**NEWS INDEX**


| | Page | | Page |
|---|---|---|---|
| Art | 24-25 | Obituaries | 29 |
| Books | 27 | Screen | 22-23 |
| Bridge | 26 | Ships and Air | 58 |
| Business | 36, 44 | Society | 32 |
| Churches | 21 | Sports | 33-35 |
| Crossword | 27 | Theaters | 22-23 |
| Editorial | 28 | TV and Radio | 59 |
| Financial | 36-44 | U. N. Proceedings | 30 |
| Food | 20 | Wash. Proceedings | 30 |
| Music | 22-23 | Weather | 58 |

News Summary and Index, Page 31


Henry Grossman

John Fitzgerald Kennedy
1917-1963

## Why America Weeps

### *Kennedy Victim of Violent Streak He Sought to Curb in the Nation*

By JAMES RESTON
Special to The New York Times

WASHINGTON, Nov. 22—America wept tonight, not alone for its dead young President, but for itself. The grief was general, for somehow the worst in the nation had prevailed over the best. The indictment extended beyond the assassin, for something in the nation itself, some strain of madness and violence, had destroyed the highest symbol of law and order.

Speaker John McCormack, now 71 and, by the peculiarities of our politics, next in line of succession after the Vice President, expressed this sense of national dismay and self-criticism:

"My God! My God! What are we coming to?"

The irony of the President's death is that his short Administration was devoted almost entirely to various attempts to curb this very streak of violence in the American character.

When the historians get around to assessing his three years in office, it is very likely that they will be impressed with just this: his efforts to restrain those who wanted to be more violent in the cold war overseas and those who wanted to be

Continued on Page 7, Column 6

## The City Goes Dark

By ROBERT C. DOTY

The center of New York, the restless night city, wore darkness and went in near silence after the murder of President Kennedy last night.

In and around Times Square, the normal, frenetic Friday night pulse slowed as near to a halt as it ever comes. Most legitimate and movie theaters, night clubs and dance halls closed their doors and darkened their marquees.

As dusk came, automatic devices turned on the huge, gaudy display signs that normally blot out the night. Then, one by one, the lights blinked out, turning the great carnival strip into what was almost a mourning band.

There were exceptions, of course. Restaurants, by decision of their trade associations, remained lighted and open as a

Continued on Page 5, Column 2

## *Gov. Connally Shot; Mrs. Kennedy Safe*

### *President Is Struck Down by a Rifle Shot From Building on Motorcade Route—Johnson, Riding Behind, Is Unhurt*

By TOM WICKER
Special to The New York Times

DALLAS, Nov. 22—President John Fitzgerald Kennedy was shot and killed by an assassin today.

He died of a wound in the brain caused by a rifle bullet that was fired at him as he was riding through downtown Dallas in a motorcade.

Vice President Lyndon Baines Johnson, who was riding in the third car behind Mr. Kennedy's, was sworn in as the 36th President of the United States 99 minutes after Mr. Kennedy's death.

Mr. Johnson is 55 years old; Mr. Kennedy was 46.

Shortly after the assassination, Lee H. Oswald, described as a one-time defector to the Soviet Union, active in the Fair Play for Cuba Committee, was arrested by the Dallas police. Tonight he was accused of the killing.

**Suspect Captured After Scuffle**

Oswald, 24 years old, was also accused of slaying a policeman who had approached him in the street. Oswald was subdued after a scuffle with a second policeman in a nearby theater.

The shooting took place at 12:30 P.M., Central standard time (1:30 P.M., New York time). Mr. Kennedy was pronounced dead at 1 P.M. and Mr. Johnson was sworn in at 2:39 P.M.

Mr. Johnson, who was uninjured in the shooting, took his oath in the Presidential jet plane as it stood on the runway at Love Field. The body of the President was aboard. Immediately after the oath-taking, the plane took off for Washington.

Standing beside the new President as Mr. Johnson took the oath of office was Mrs. John F. Kennedy. Her stocking was saturated with her husband's blood.

Gov. John B. Connally Jr. of Texas, who was riding in the same car with Mr. Kennedy, was severely wounded in the chest, ribs and arm. His condition was serious, but not critical.

The killer fired the rifle from a building just off the motorcade route. Mr. Kennedy,

Continued on Page 2,

Capt. Cecil Stoughton via United Press International

THE NEW PRESIDENT: Lyndon B. Johnson takes oath before Judge Sarah T. Hughes in plane at Dallas. Mrs. Kennedy and Representative Jack Brooks are at right. To left are Mrs. Johnson and Representative Albert Thomas.

Associated Press

WHEN THE BULLETS STRUCK: Mrs. Kennedy moving to the aid of the President after he was hit by a sniper yesterday in Dallas. A guard mounts rear bumper. Gov. John B. Connally Jr. of Texas, also in the car, was wounded.

LYNDON B. JOHNSON

"All the News That's Fit to Print"

# The New York Times.

LATE CITY EDITION

U. S. Weather Bureau Report (Page 78) forecasts: Mostly sunny today; fair tonight. Partly cloudy tomorrow. Temp. Range: 50—30; yesterday: 53—34.

VOL. CXIII..No. 38,763. © 1964 by The New York Times Company. Times Square, New York, N. Y. 10036 NEW YORK, WEDNESDAY, MARCH 11, 1964. TEN CENTS

# LODGE VICTOR IN NEW HAMPSHIRE AS GOLDWATER AND ROCKEFELLER ARE SWAMPED BY WRITE-IN VOTES

## TURKISH CYPRIOTE URGES U.N. TO ACT AS CLASHES WIDEN

### Kutchuk Says People Face 'Complete Annihilation' if Peace Force Is Delayed

### APPEAL TO ANKARA SEEN

### Greek Fighters Kill 2 and Defeat Force at Mallia—Paphos Truce Uneasy

By The Associated Press

NICOSIA, Cyprus, March 10 — The Turkish Cypriote who is Vice President of Cyprus urged the United Nations today to take swift action to save the island's Turkish minority "from complete annihilation."

The appeal of Dr. Fazil Kutchuk came as the Government announced that its forces had overwhelmed Turkish Cypriotes in a day-long battle in the village of Mallia, in southwest Cyprus.

Two Turkish Cypriotes were reported killed and five, including a young girl, were wounded in the Mallia fighting.

Other clashes erupted across Cyprus as a result of the three-day battle in the west coast town of Ktima, a suburb of Paphos, 20 miles from Mallia.

There was sporadic shooting in Ktima, where Greek and Turkish Cypriote officials met to strengthen the shaky ceasefire that ended the fighting yesterday.

**Message Sent to Thant**

Dr. Kutchuk sent messages to U Thant, Secretary General of the United Nations, and to the foreign ministers of Britain, Greece and Turkey, the three powers that guaranteed the independence of Cyprus under a treaty signed in 1960.

A Government spokesman said Dr. Kutchuk's annihilation charge was ridiculous.

President Makarios said in a message to Mr. Thant that "every effort is being made to exercise maximum restraint to avoid any act that might worsen the situation in Cyprus."

Archbishop Makarios, a Greek Cypriote, added: "It is regrettable, however, that Turkish extremists are deliberately creating incidents by armed action, endangering public safety and causing friction."

His message was in reply to one from Mr. Thant appealing for an end to bloodshed on the island.

Dr. Kutchuk's message said: "If an effective United Nations force cannot be dispatched forthwith, we beseech and call upon the guarantor powers to fulfill their treaty obligations and rescue the Turks from the threat of genocide."

That appeared to be an appeal to Turkey to come to the rescue.

Continued on Page 3, Column 1

## QUEEN ELIZABETH BEARS THIRD SON

### Both Reported Well—Child Is Fourth in Family

By JAMES FERON
Special to The New York Times

LONDON, March 10—Queen Elizabeth II gave birth tonight to her third son and her fourth child at Buckingham Palace.

A bulletin signed by five physicians said the Queen was "safely delivered of a son at 8:20 this evening" and that both were well. The weight of the infant was not given.

The baby, whose name will probably not be known for several weeks, is the second child born to a reigning British sovereign since 1857. The first was Prince Andrew, the baby's 4-year-old brother.

The baby is third in line to the throne, coming after Prince Charles, who is 15 years old, and Prince Andrew, but before the Queen's 13-year-old daughter, Princess Anne. The Queen is 37 and has reigned since 1952.

News of the birth was given quickly on radio and television. Within minutes cars were slowly circling the statue of Queen Victoria in front of the palace and a small crowd collected on the sidewalk.

People huddled in the cold, peering at the palace, which was dark except for tiny slits

Continued on Page 7, Column 1



## Soviet Bloc Talk on China Forecast as Rift Deepens

### Khrushchev Reported Losing Patience Over Peking Attacks and Planning April Conference in Budapest

By DREW MIDDLETON
Special to The New York Times

PARIS, March 10 — A meeting of Premier Khrushchev and other Communist leaders to discuss worsening relations between the Soviet and Chinese Communist parties was forecast tonight by East European sources.

The meeting will be held in Budapest, capital of Hungary next month, the sources said. Premier Khrushchev is expected to arrive there about March 30 for anniversary celebrations of the liberation of Hungary from the Nazi armies in 1945.

These celebrations are to take place April 4 and the Communist conference is expected to begin soon after.

According to both East European and Western sources Mr. Khrushchev has been consulting Communist leaders throughout the Soviet bloc and Western Europe for the last two weeks.

The Soviet Communist party he is believed to have told the other leaders, cannot continue to maintain the present tenuous relations with the Chinese Communist party unless Peking shows some willingness to cooperate.

In the consultation, Mr. Khrushchev has suggested a meeting of Communist party first secretaries. These would be from all the Communist parties that follow Moscow's ideological line, a group that includes all European Communist parties except those of Albania and Yugoslavia.

One East European source asserted that Mr. Khrushchev's patience with the Chinese was

Continued on Page 12, Column 1

## U.S. Reconnaissance Jet Downed in East Germany

By ARTHUR J. OLSEN
Special to The New York Times

BONN, March 10—A United States reconnaissance bomber strayed across the East German frontier today, the Air Force announced. The plane was brought down, and the announcement said it was uncertain whether the three airmen aboard were safe.

[A Defense Department spokesman in Washington said the three crew members had bailed out, according to The Associated Press. It said the United States protested to the Soviet Union against the "precipitous action by the Soviet military forces in shooting down" the plane and expressed regret that it had strayed into Communist East Germany.]

**Second Incident in 6 Weeks**

The Air Force's statement was issued at Wiesbaden, headquarters of its command in Europe.

The flight of the twin-engine Douglas RB-66 into East German airspace was the second such incident in six weeks.

A T-39 jet trainer, also described as having been on a routine training mission, blundered across the East German frontier Jan. 28 and was shot down by Soviet fighters. The three airmen aboard were killed. The Air Force said then that the T-39 apparently had become lost.

An Air Force official said that the possibility "was not excluded" that both planes had fallen victim to false electronic signals sent by Soviet trans-

Continued on Page 10, Column 2

## CAMBODIANS PLAN TO BUY RED ARMS

### Mission Off to Moscow and Peking—U.S. Embassy in Pnompenh Stoned

By SEYMOUR TOPPING
Special to The New York Times

SAIGON, South Vietnam, March 10 — A Cambodian military delegation left today for Peking and Moscow. The delegation, led by Lieut. Gen. Lon Nol, the army commander in chief, has been authorized to purchase arms.

Diplomatic sources said the mission had been contemplated for some time but the timing of its departure was meant to underline the dissatisfaction of Prince Norodom Sihanouk, Cambodia's chief of state, with the non-Communist world.

[Cambodian demonstrators stoned the United States Embassy in Pnompenh Wednesday, tore down its flag and set fire to the British Embassy before being dispersed by the police, United Press International reported from the Cambodian capital.]

Prince Sihanouk accused the United States last night of duplicity in its efforts to arrange a settlement of Cambodia's border differences with South Vietnam and Thailand. The Cambodian leader rejected the United States' terms for a four-power conference that would guarantee the neutrality and territorial integrity of his country.

In a broadcast made in the presence of the ruling council the Prince accused the United States, South Vietnam, Thailand and also Laos of a plot to partition his nation.

He said he would negotiate

Continued on Page 5, Column 3

## 7 More Tax Aides Accused of Bribery

Seven more employes of the Internal Revenue Service were arrested on bribery charges yesterday in a continuing investigation of corruption in the city's Federal tax bureaus.

The arrests brought to 32 the number of persons taken into custody since the investigation came to light a month ago.

William H. Sperling, Assistant United States Attorney, said that so far the inquiry showed the Government had been defrauded of $3 million in tax refunds and unpaid taxes.

Four of those arrested yesterday were auditors in the Brooklyn tax bureau at 210 Livingston Street. The three others, two of them tax examiners, were employed in the Manhattan office, 120 Church Street.

The bribes allegedly accepted by the auditors, Mr. Sperling

Continued on Page 79, Column 1

## SCHOOLS UPHELD ON ZONE CHANGES FOR INTEGRATION

### But Appellate Court Rules Pupils Have Right to Go to Classes Nearest Homes

The Appellate Division of the State Supreme Court ruled unanimously yesterday that the Board of Education had the right to rezone schools to promote racial integration.

However, the decision upheld the right of pupils to attend schools nearest their homes.

The 18-page decision handed down in Brooklyn was hailed as a victory by different factions in the school integration controversy: the Board of Education, which is seeking better school integration; civil rights groups, which favor more drastic action, and parent and taxpayer groups opposed to the transportation of children to schools outside their neighborhoods.

The only one publicly to indicate disappointment was the lawyer for a group of white parents in Brooklyn who brought the original action challenging the board's authority to assign their children to a new junior high school outside their neighborhood.

**Appeal to Be Sought**

The parents, who live in East Flatbush, contended that their children were being assigned to Junior High School 275 in Brownsville solely on the basis of race to achieve a better ethnic balance among the pupils. Brownsville is largely Negro and Puerto Rican.

Frank H. Gordon, the lawyer for the parents, said the Court of Appeals in Albany would be asked to review the Appellate Division's decision.

"We believe that the law of the State of New York, the State and Federal Constitutions, the morals and equities are all in our favor," he said.

Although the Appellate Division's ruling dealt with a specific case and somewhat unusual features, the opinion considered basic issues that have been at the heart of other integration suits in New York.

**Lower Court Reversed**

In upholding the school board, the court reversed a decision by Supreme Court Justice Edward G. Baker, who ruled last September that the proposed rezoning in Brooklyn was illegal because it violated Section 3201 of the State Education Law. This section holds that "no person shall be refused admission into or be excluded from any public school in the state of New York on account of race, creed, color or national origin."

In the Brooklyn case, the parents had contended that their children were being excluded because of race from Junior High School 285 in East

Continued on Page 28, Column 1

## PRESIDENT SILENT

### Does Not Intend to Ask Envoy to Resign Post or Curb His Actions

By TOM WICKER
Special to The New York Times

WASHINGTON, March 10—President Johnson does not regard Henry Cabot Lodge's victory in the New Hampshire Presidential primary as having compromised Mr. Lodge's position as Ambassador to South Vietnam.

Mr. Johnson, an interested watcher at the television set tonight, had no comment to make on Mr. Lodge's big write-in vote or on the sizable Democratic write-in total for Attorney General Robert F. Kennedy.

Informed sources said, however, that the President did not intend to seek Mr. Lodge's resignation, or to check his political freedom, as a result of today's primary.

A sort of gentlemen's agreement exists between the two, it was suggested. It would place the burden upon Mr. Lodge to let Mr. Johnson know when he thought he could no longer serve the Administration because of the political situation in the United States.

**Has President's Confidence**

There had been speculation that if Mr. Lodge won in New Hampshire, and if he allowed his name to remain on the ballot in the Oregon primary, he would be so nearly an active candidate against Mr. Johnson that the President would have to take action.

Mr. Lodge has engaged in no active campaigning, however, and has refused to announce his candidacy or publicly encourage his supporters.

In addition, informed sources say Mr. Johnson believes Mr. Lodge has done a good job in Saigon, still has a contribution to make there, and that his departure now might be a hard blow to South Vietnamese morale.

The sources would not concede it, but it is generally believed here that Mr. Johnson is content to have a prominent Republican associated with his conduct of the guerrilla war in Vietnam.

Nothing could be learned tonight of Mr. Johnson's personal reaction to the Lodge victory or to the vote for Robert Kennedy.

Persons close to him, however, were well satisfied with the fact that Mr. Johnson re-

Continued on Page 18, Column 2

Associated Press Wirephoto

PRIMARY DAMPENER: Snow falls as voters leave the Town Hall in Canterbury, N. H., after voting in Republican Presidential primary. Heavy snow continued all day.

## NIXON IS FOURTH

### Democratic Write-ins Link Johnson and Robert Kennedy

By JOHN H. FENTON
Special to The New York Times

CONCORD, N. H., Wednesday, March 11—Ambassador Henry Cabot Lodge won a smashing victory last night in the nation's first Presidential primary of the 1964 campaign.

In cities and hamlets alike throughout New Hampshire, voters slogged through sleet and snow yesterday to write in the name of the Ambassador to South Vietnam as their preference for the Republican nomination for President.

Mr. Lodge, an undeclared candidate in the primary, who is in Saigon, led almost from the start as the returns were counted. He slowly pulled away from the two principal declared candidates in the contest, Governor Rockefeller of New York and Senator Barry Goldwater of Arizona.

**Write-ins for Nixon**

Former Vice President Richard M. Nixon, also an undeclared candidate and the beneficiary of a write-in campaign, was running fourth.

The three other declared candidates in the Republican race were Senator Margaret Chase Smith of Maine, Harold E. Stassen of Philadelphia, a former Governor of Minnesota, and Norman LePage of Nashua, N.H., an accountant. All three were far out of contention.

At 1 A.M. the National Broadcasting Company gave these vote totals on the basis of 85 per cent of the vote: Lodge, 28,526; Goldwater, 18,989; Rockefeller, 17,192; Nixon, 14,226.

[In Washington, Senator Goldwater said he had "goofed up somewhere" during the campaign. Governor Rockefeller said in New York that the primary was "a victory for a favorite son."]

**Winning All Delegates**

Slowly counted returns also indicated that Mr. Lodge was winning all 14 of the delegates who will cast votes at the Republican National Convention July 13 in San Francisco.

In the Democratic primary, President Johnson and Attorney General Robert F. Kennedy were having their names bracketed together by the voters as write-in choices for the Presidential and Vice-Presidential nominations. There were no names printed on the Democratic ballots.

At 11:37 P.M. the American Broadcasting Company gave these vote totals: Johnson, 27,492; Kennedy, 15,167.

Shortly after 11 P.M., George Cabot Lodge, the elder son of the Ambassador, read a prepared statement from his father in Saigon, asserting that "the voters of New Hampshire have paid me the highest of compliments." He said he would "consider their action and all its meanings."

The younger Mr. Lodge said the statement had been given

Continued on Page 18, Column 1

## Auto Insurers Cut Rates 10 to 15% in 4 Boroughs

By JOSEPH C. INGRAHAM

The first major over-all cuts in automobile liability insurance rates for most of the metropolitan area since 1942 will go into effect today. The cuts range from 10 to 15 per cent in the city and from 4 to 8 per cent in the suburbs. However, there are three exceptions.

On Staten Island the rate goes up 11 per cent; in northern Westchester, up 2 per cent, and in Rockland County, up 7 per cent.

Offsetting the sharp decreases here are big increases in major cities upstate, a reversal of the rate pattern that has prevailed for more than 20 years.

The net result is a statewide reduction of 2 per cent.

The new rates apply to policyholders insured by the 225 companies affiliated with the National Bureau of Casualty Underwriters and the Mutual Insurance Rating Bureau.

The companies estimate the cuts will mean a reduction in premiums of $7 million a year.

**S. I. Claims Are Up**

Bureau members write 75 per cent of liability coverage in the state. The so-called independents, like the Allstate Insurance Company, set individual schedules, generally lower than the bureau rates. A check yesterday indicated that they, too, probably would cut their rates to meet the competition.

William Leslie Jr., general manager of the national bureau, said "a reduction in the number of questionable claims rather than a decline in accidents" was responsible for the marked drop in rates in the city area.

Mr. Leslie also stressed that "underwriters do not make rates; drivers do."

He explained that the cost of settling claims was the determining factor. In support of the rate rise on Staten Island, he noted that in 1960 it cost under-

Continued on Page 49, Column 5

## GOVERNOR YIELDS ON AID TO SCHOOLS

### Agrees to $23 Million Rise for Next Year—Decision Is Victory for Carlino

By LAYHMOND ROBINSON
Special to The New York Times

ALBANY, March 10—Governor Rockefeller and top legislative leaders broke their deadlock today over increasing state aid to public schools.

The Governor agreed to go along with a proposal calling for a $23 million increase in state assistance in the coming school year.

Under the plan, each district would get a 3 per cent increase for operating costs. This would mean $5 million to $6 million for New York City, $3 million for Nassau County and $1.5 million for Suffolk County.

Because the state budget year, which begins April 1, does not coincide with the fiscal years of the school districts, only about half of the $23 million will have to be included in the Governor's 1964-65 budget.

**Legislation Held Up**

The agreement represented a victory for Assembly Speaker Joseph F. Carlino and other suburban legislators who have spearheaded the drive for a rise in state assistance above the $61 million in mandated increases already provided in the Governor's budget.

The failure of the Governor, Mr. Carlino and Senate Majority Leader Walter J. Mahoney to reach agreement on the school-aid issue has held up action on the Rockefeller budget and a wide range of other major legislation.

The impasse had also jeopardized Mr. Rockefeller's Presidential campaign schedule. He could have been delayed on his trip to California had the deadlock persisted.

With the issue settled, he left Albany to spend the night in New York City. He is scheduled to fly to California tomorrow in pursuit of that state's convention delegates. He is not

Continued on Page 49, Column 2

## NEWS INDEX


| | Page | | Page |
|---|---|---|---|
| Books | 36-37 | Music | 32-35 |
| Bridge | 36 | Obituaries | 39 |
| Business | 50-51 | Real Estate | 62-63 |
| Buyers | 51 | Screen | 32-35 |
| Crossword | 37 | Ships and Air | 78 |
| Editorial | 38 | Society | 42 |
| Events Today | 37 | Sports | 43-49 |
| Fashions | 28-30 | Theaters | 32-35 |
| Financial | 49-61 | TV and Radio | 79 |
| Food | 28-30 | U. N. Proceedings | 6 |
| Letters | 38 | Wash. Proceedings | 13 |
| Man in the News | 2 | Weather | 78 |

News Summary and Index, Page 41


## Rights Foes Raise Constitutional Issue

By E. W. KENWORTHY
Special to The New York Times

WASHINGTON, March 10—Southern Senators began today to make their constitutional case against the civil rights bill.

In a long speech laced with legal citations and devoid of oratorical flourishes, Senator John Stennis of Mississippi argued that the section banning discrimination in public accommodations was unconstitutional because it could not rest on either the 14th Amendment or the Commerce Clause.

Under the generalship of Senator Richard B. Russell of Georgia, Mr. Stennis is one of the captains of the three platoons into which Mr. Russell has divided his "band of eighteen."

The other captains are Sena-

Continued on Page 21, Column 1



## 'Draft Kennedy' Unit Files in Wisconsin

By JOSEPH A. LOFTUS
Special to The New York Times

WASHINGTON, March 10—A committee to draft Robert F. Kennedy for Vice President filed incorporation papers in Wisconsin today.

The group is acting without the authority or permission of the Attorney General. In fact, in the light of certain recent events, Mr. Kennedy is wondering whether his friends are not causing him more trouble than his enemies.

For example, the recent departure of a Democratic National Committee employe was traced today to President Johnson's belief at one point that the employe had engineered the New Hampshire write-in for Mr. Ken-

Continued on Page 19, Column 3



## 3,000 in Rights Protest March on Albany in Snow

United Press International Telephoto

Demonstrators, after leaving buses, march past State Education Building toward Capitol

By FRED POWLEDGE
Special to The New York Times

ALBANY, March 10—More than 3,000 supporters of civil rights and social reform marched on the state capitol today in snow, freezing rain and slush. They presented their demands to Governor Rockefeller and legislative leaders, who offered their sympathy but no specific help. Leaders of the six labor and civil rights organizations that sponsored the one-day demonstration were not surprised by the Governor's reaction. A. Philip Randolph, the Negro labor leader who is heading an effort to establish a $1.50 minimum hourly wage in the state, told the demon-

Continued on Page 25, Column 5

"All the News That's Fit to Print"

# The New York Times.

LATE CITY EDITION
Fair, moderate temperatures today. Partly cloudy tomorrow.
Temperature Range Today-Max., 63; Min., 45
Temperatures Yesterday—Max., 59; Min., 47
Full U. S. Weather Bureau Report, Page 47

VOL. CXIII..No. 38,847. NEW YORK, WEDNESDAY, JUNE 3, 1964. TEN CENTS


# GOLDWATER CLINGS TO THIN LEAD IN BITTER CALIFORNIA PRIMARY; BUCKLEY AND DE SAPIO DEFEATED

## U.S. AND CAMBODIA AGREE TO SUPPORT U.N. BORDER STUDY

### Council to Get a Resolution Today on Friction With South Vietnam Regime

### AFRICANS PROPOSE PLAN

### 3-Nation Committee Would Visit Area of Dispute and Report Within 45 Days

By THOMAS J. HAMILTON
Special to The New York Times

UNITED NATIONS, N. Y., June 2—The United States and Cambodia agreed today to a proposal under which the Security Council would establish a committee of three to investigate friction along the Cambodian-South Vietnamese border. The panel would submit recommendations to prevent a recurrence.

The proposal, drafted by Morocco and the Ivory Coast, will be submitted to the Council by Ahmed Taibi Benhima, the Moroccan representative, when the Council resumes debate on the question tomorrow.

Today's meeting was canceled because Huot Sambath, Foreign Minister of Cambodia, had not yet received his instructions.

Reliable sources said the committee would be composed of representatives of three elected members of the Council.

**Group Will Visit Site**

The committee will be instructed to go to Saigon and Pnompenh, the capitals of South Vietnam and Cambodia, and also to the site of the recent frontier incidents that produced Cambodia's complaint to the Council. The Cambodians accused the United States and South Vietnam of aggressive actions.

The committee would be instructed to report its findings and recommendations to the Council within 45 days. Barring a Soviet veto, the resolution is believed to be certain of adoption.

Morocco, Brazil and possibly the Ivory Coast, it is understood, are expected to be on the committee. Norway also has been considered, but it is believed that if she is named the Soviet Union will demand inclusion of Czechoslovakia.

Although Mr. Sambath told the Council last Thursday that Cambodia would agree to a United Nations commission to help demarcate the Cambodian-South Vietnamese border, this is not included in the proposal. Reliable sources said that the Foreign Minister had withdrawn his consent for such a commission.

**Reparations Request**

According to reliable sources, the resolution will deplore the incidents cited by Cambodia and will request "those responsible" to pay reparations. It is understood, however, that it will not name either the United States or South Vietnam.

The resolution will also appeal to "all states"—including Communist China, North Vietnam and South Vietnam, which are not members of the United Nations—to help bring about a peaceful settlement and also to respect Cambodia's neutrality and independence.

The latter request would be addressed "particularly" to the states that participated in the Geneva conference of 1954. Cambodia, with French support, started the Council debate by

Continued on Page 2, Column 6

## Shastri Backs Soviet View on Laos

United Press International Radiophoto
Prime Minister-elect Lal Bahadur Shastri after the voting

By THOMAS F. BRADY
Special to The New York Times

NEW DELHI, June 2—The Prime Minister-elect of India, Lal Bahadur Shastri, declared tonight that proposals received here earlier in the day from Moscow on the problem of Laos "seem generally reasonable." He added that unless the 14 powers that met in Geneva in 1962 to guarantee Laotian neutrality "meet again it will be impossible to solve the Laos problem satisfactorily." On foreign policy in general he said: "We cannot afford to associate ourselves with any power bloc." He declared Prime Minister Nehru's policy of nonalignment "was beneficial and will

Continued on Page 11, Column 1

## President Reasserts Aim To Defend Southeast Asia

By HEDRICK SMITH
Special to The New York Times

WASHINGTON, June 2—President Johnson, in his first news conference in nearly a month, reasserted United States commitments to defend Southeast Asia today but softened the tone of recent warnings of a possible expansion of the war in Vietnam.

In response to reporters' questions, the President said he knew of no plans for the United States to carry the anti-Communist struggle in South Vietnam to the north. [Question 12, Page 25.]

The future of Southeast Asia "as a whole" is at stake in Laos and Vietnam, he said, adding that the United States intended to stand by its "solemn commitments to help defend this area against Communist encroachments." [Opening statement.]

The White House announced that Under Secretary of State George W. Ball would leave Thursday for Europe, where he will confer with President de Gaulle and with members of the British Government.

The stated purpose of the trip is to attend a United Nations trade and aid conference in Geneva, but qualified sources said Mr. Ball would be conferring with the French and British on Western moves in Southeast Asia.

So far Paris has been work-

Continued on Page 3, Column 1

## NEW CONGO FORCE IS FLOWN TO KIVU

### Bukavu, Capital of Province, Left Defenseless by Rebel Rout of its Garrison

By J. ANTHONY LUKAS
Special to The New York Times

BUKAVU, the Congo, June 2 — Fresh troops flew into rebellious Kivu Province today following a rout of Congolese forces here by Communist-directed rebels. Elements of the 13th Infantry Battalion were rushed from their base at Kamina toward this provincial capital, which has been virtually defenseless since Sunday.

Preparing for the worst, the United Nations and the United States Consulate here continued to evacuate women and children from the area.

Authorities here fear that Bukavu may be attacked at any time by the rebels, who advanced to within 25 miles of the city over the weekend.

The Congolese troops who had been holding positions south of Bukavu have fallen back in utter confusion. Many soldiers are believed to have gone over to the rebels. The troops left here have no will to fight.

Observers fear that if the rebels do attack they will be joined by most of the remaining

Continued on Page 6, Column 3

## WAGNER BOLSTERS POLICE ON SUBWAY TO DETER ATTACKS

### 700 Patrolmen to Be Added During Night Shift When Violence Is at Peak

By HOMER BIGART

Mayor Wagner, in response to angry demands for greater security against crime and racial violence, took steps yesterday to build up police strength on streets and in subways.

He ordered overtime duty for city police and Transit Authority police. This will make available an extra 700 foot patrolmen from 6 P.M. to 2 A.M., the period in which most crimes are committed.

"I am determined to see that we are going to have law and order in this city of ours," Mayor Wagner declared after an emergency conference with Police Commissioner Michael J. Murphy and Joseph E. O'Grady, chairman of the Transit Authority.

**Cost of $5 Million a Year**

The overtime police pay will cost the city $5 million a year, according to Budget Director William F. Shea.

In other moves to deter teen-age hooliganism of the kind that terrorized subway riders last weekend, the Mayor:

¶Ordered all 20,000 patrolmen to wear their uniforms to and from work.

¶Told the Transit Authority to cut through red tape and put 141 rookie patrolmen and five new sergeants on duty in the first week in July, instead of next October.

¶Ordered a speedup on the installation of an experimental two-way radio communications system for subway trains.

Mayor Wagner admitted concern over the antiwhite rampages of teen-age Negro gangs in the subways, but he added: "There are other gangs in the city besides Negro and Puerto Rican. There are white gangs."

**White Understanding Asked**

Civil rights leaders, fearful of a lasting setback as a result of the weekend disorders, asked whites to understand the frustration of Negroes.

The Rev. Dr. Martin Luther King Jr. said such incidents of "antisocial behavior" would continue "as long as you have the problems of urban dislocation growing out of poverty."

In a telephone interview from Los Angeles, where he was on a speaking tour, Dr. King said that the subway violence was caused by "individuals who are victims of chronic poverty and economic insecurity."

But Marshall England, chairman of the New York chapter of the Congress of Racial Equality, condemned the newspapers for "headlining" Negro youth delinquency.

He said the papers were guilty of discrimination because they had ignored a recent incident in which "150 white gangsters" left two young Negroes "lying in danger of death at a Far Rockaway Hospital."

The Queens assistant district attorney, Stanley J. Pryor, said

Continued on Page 26, Column 3

## WAGNER MEN WIN

### But Brooklyn Victory of Steingut Forces Tempers Success

By EARL MAZO

Reform Democrats and Rockefeller Republicans won impressive victories in city and state primaries yesterday.

The defeat of Representative Charles A. Buckley and several of his key associates in the Democratic organization in the Bronx seems certain to have a significant impact on national politics, as well as on the state and local scene.

The voter turnout in districts where there were contests was extraordinarily heavy for a primary. In the key New York City races, Democratic nomination is tantamount to election.

Jonathan B. Bingham, a newcomer to elective politics, triumphed over Mr. Buckley despite the fact that he had been supported by only one top-ranking Democratic leader, Mayor Wagner.

Mayor Wagner's power and influence in the party—and his claim on the vice presidential nomination—were advanced by the triumphs of Mr. Bingham and other candidates he had endorsed.

The Reform group suffered some important setbacks. In the most notable defeat, William F. Haddad, a founder of the movement, failed to unseat Representative Leonard Farbstein in Manhattan's 19th Congressional District.

Mr. Buckley's unsuccessful bid for his 16th nomination for Congress was backed by some the nation's most important Democrats.

**Johnson Sent Letter**

President Johnson sent a letter and then a follow-up special message of support, and Attorney General Robert F. Kennedy made a campaign appearance with Mr. Buckley to emphasize the Kennedy family's endorsement.

Mr. Buckley had urged the Attorney General's nomination for Senator to oppose Senator Kenneth B. Keating, the Republican incumbent, in the November election.

While the Buckley organization's primary losses weaken the Representative's effectiveness, the old-line political boss kept a majority on the 3,800-member county committee, which the Reform organization did not challenge. He thus is still titular head of the party in the Bronx.

In the Republican primaries, Rockefeller organization candidates for seats as delegates to the Republican National Convention won contests against supporters of Senator Barry

Continued on Page 31, Column 1

## Bingham Victor in Bronx By a 4,000-Vote Margin

### Congressman's String of Nominations Is Ended by Reform Challenger—Scheuer Wins Over Healey

By DAVID HALBERSTAM

Jonathan B. Bingham upset Charles A. Buckley yesterday for the Democratic nomination for Representative in the Bronx's 23d Congressional District.

Mr. Bingham, who had been taunted by Representative Buckley because of his patrician background, won an uphill battle in a primary that was marked by invective, innuendo and occasional discussion of the issues.

The Reform challenger ended a Buckley string of 15 consecutive Democratic nominations to Congress, where Mr. Buckley is chairman of the powerful House Public Works Committee.

With all 284 election districts reporting, Mr. Bingham had 26,473 votes to Mr. Buckley's 22,488.

Mr. Bingham's victory exceeded his own estimates. He had predicted a margin of 2,600 votes. He had carefully calculated the district and felt that a total vote of 42,000 or 43,000 was needed for his victory.

The election was a particularly bitter one for Mr. Buckley. His future as a power in New York politics was further undermined by the defeat of one of his top lieutenants, Representative James C. Healey, by another Reform Democrat, James H. Scheuer, in the 21st Congressional District.

Mr. Buckley did not concede defeat last night. The 73-year-old Congressman, who has never

Continued on Page 31, Column 4

## Koch Keeps Leadership Of 'Village' by 164 Votes

By MARTIN ARNOLD

Carmine G. De Sapio, former Tammany Hall leader and symbol of big city bossism, lost by 164 votes yesterday in his bid to return to political power. He was defeated for the second time by Edward I. Koch, a Reform Democrat backed by Mayor Wagner, for the district leadership of Greenwich Village, the First Assembly District South.

The vote was 5,904 to 5,740.

Mr. Koch, a 39-year-old, tall, lean, balding lawyer, defeated Mr. De Sapio last September by 41 votes. But the Court of Appeals upheld Mr. De Sapio's claim of irregularities and ordered the rematch election for yesterday.

Less than an hour after the polls closed Mr. De Sapio appeared before his supporters in the Tamawa Club and conceded defeat.

"Oh, no," he said when asked if he was retiring from politics. "I'll have to sleep on this."

His supporters cried "oh" and "oh my God" when the 55-year-old chief admitted defeat. Mr. De Sapio replied: "The Mets lose a lot of ball games and they still have a lot of fans."

Speaking in a gentle voice, Mr. De Sapio urged his followers to accept the outcome, saying: "As far as I know there were no irregularities. I haven't had a chance to study it."

In the Koch headquarters

Continued on Page 31, Column 5

## SALINGER WINNER IN BID FOR SENATE

### Victory Is a Blow to Brown—G.O.P. Picks Murphy for Race in November

By GLADWIN HILL
Special to The New York Times

LOS ANGELES, June 2—Pierre Salinger, former White House press secretary, emerged tonight as the winner of California's Democratic Senatorial nomination.

He swept to victory over his principal opponent, State Controller Alan Cranston, with the appeal to voters to "Let the man who spoke for Presidents speak for you."

This appeal evidently transcended the charge of "carpetbagging" leveled by Cranston forces after the chubby Presidential aide quit his Washington job in March to plunge into the California contest at the last minute.

**Murphy G.O.P. Choice**

He will be pitted in the November election against California Republicans' choice today in a three-man race: George Murphy, former movie actor who is now a Hollywood executive.

They will contest for the seat now held by Democratic Senator Clair Engle, who withdrew from the contest a month ago because of illness.

With about half of the total

Continued on Page 30, Column 5

## ROCKEFELLER GAINS

### Governor Cuts Down Gap in Late Tally —Urban Vote Key

By LAWRENCE E. DAVIES
Special to The New York Times

LOS ANGELES, Wednesday, June 3—Senator Barry Goldwater clung to a narrow and dwindling lead over Governor Rockefeller this morning in the bitter California Presidential primary.

The Arizonan had been considered the underdog in this, the last significant primary before the opening of the Republican National Convention on July 13. At stake were this state's 86 convention votes.

The Columbia Broadcasting System, after tabulating 83 per cent of the expected 2 million Republican votes, gave Senator Goldwater 864,963 votes and Governor Rockefeller 798,751—a lead of 66,212.

The National Broadcasting Company, after counting 82 per cent of the expected vote, reported 874,557 for Senator Goldwater and 842,184 for Mr. Rockefeller.

**Lead for Governor**

However, the American Broadcasting System announced at 11:35 P.M. (2:35 A.M. Wednesday, New York time) that Governor Rockefeller had 638,291 votes and Senator Goldwater 629,054.

C.B.S., using computer projections of early returns, said at 7:22 P.M. (10:22 P.M. New York time), that Mr. Goldwater would win. This was only 22 minutes after most of the polling places had closed.

A.B.C. gave victory to Mr. Goldwater at 8:12 P.M. N.B.C. said its computers indicated such a close vote that it would not name the winner last night.

Late last night neither The Associated Press nor United Press International had designated a winner. The A.P., with a tabulation from 22,841 of the state's 32,861 precincts, said Mr. Goldwater had 532,463 votes and Mr. Rockefeller 550,079.

U.P.I., with returns counted from 21,538 precincts, said the tally was 459,480 for Mr. Goldwater and 476,217 for Mr. Rockefeller.

**Goldwater Strength Noted**

Influential Republicans believe that Senator Goldwater entered the primary with about 540 convention delegates committed for first-ballot support.

Adding California's 86 delegates would mean he had fewer than 30 to pick up before he could record 655—the total needed to win the party's nomination for President.

Party professionals indicated that Mr. Goldwater would collect more delegate votes from conservative Middle West states before the convention if he won California.

Senator Goldwater himself, receiving the election returns at the Ambassador Hotel early last night, predicted "a greater and greater stop-Goldwater movement."

"It's not a victory for Barry Goldwater, It's a victory for the

Continued on Page 30, Column 1

## The Savannah, First Atom-Powered Merchant Ship, Gets Noisy Welcome

The New York Times (by Arthur Brower)
The nuclear-powered merchant ship Savannah receives the usual New York Harbor greeting as she heads for her pier

By EDWARD A. MORROW

The world's first atomic-powered merchant ship, the Savannah, received a noisy welcome yesterday morning as she made her first entry into New York. Scores of tugs and other small craft accompanied the white-hulled, 22,000-ton vessel up the Narrows as fireboats threw water into the air, helicopters buzzed overhead and conventional ocean liners saluted with their foghorns. Tugs nudged the vessel into Pier 84 at West 44th Street at 1:45 P.M., stern first, to keep her nuclear reactor as far from shore as possible. Mayor Wagner, in dockside ceremonies, proclaimed June 2 to 8 as Nuclear Ship Savannah Week. President Johnson, in a telegram read at the welcoming ceremony, said that the ship, which is scheduled to sail next Monday on the first of a series of goodwill trips to Europe, would demonstrate to the people of the world the intention of this nation to use atomic energy for peaceful purposes and for the benefit of mankind. The Savannah, a joint project of the Maritime Administration and the Atomic Energy Commis-

Continued on Page 34, Column 4

## U. S. Reprimands Arab Envoys For Criticism of Eshkol's Visit

Special to The New York Times

WASHINGTON, June 2—The United States reprimanded 13 Arab Ambassadors today for a statement criticizing the visit of Premier Levi Eshkol of Israel.

Mr. Eshkol completed two days of discussions with President Johnson with the announcement that the United States and Israel had agreed to undertake joint studies on the problems of desalting sea water.

American and Israeli officials said the Johnson-Eshkol discussions had gone extremely well. The cordiality, however, was overshadowed by the Administration's efforts to keep the Arab-Israeli feud from developing further here.

The State Department made elaborate arrangements to permit Acting Secretary of State George W. Ball to carry on his scheduled discussions with Premier Eshkol at noon and also to meet with the representatives of 13 Arab countries—without having the two parties meet.

Mr. Ball, an Under Secretary serving as Acting Secretary in the absence of Secretary Dean Rusk, summoned the Arab diplomats to rebuke them for a statement issued by Arab press

Continued on Page 13, Column 1

## Johnson Reports a 'New Vitality' In Nation's Economic Expansion

Special to The New York Times

WASHINGTON, June 2 — President Johnson said today that the nation's record-long economic expansion was showing "new vitality" and would "roll on through 1964 and we believe well into 1965."

*Transcript of news conference will be found on Page 25.*

The President told his news conference that it was "much too soon" to assess the full effects of the tax cut enacted in February, but he said the economic indicators to date strongly implied "the fresh confidence, the expanded purchasing power and the new incentives created by the Revenue Act of 1964." [Opening Statement, Page 25.]

As has become a habit with him, the President reeled off a string of the most recent economic indicators, nearly all

Continued on Page 25, Column 7

NEWS INDEX



| | Page | | Page |
|---|---|---|---|
| Art | 45 | Obituaries | 43 |
| Books | 40-41 | Real Estate | 67-68 |
| Bridge | 40 | Screen | 36-39 |
| Business | 56-58 | Ships and Air | 85 |
| Buyers | 57 | Society | 35 |
| Crossword | 41 | Sports | 48-54 |
| Editorial | 42 | Theaters | 36-39 |
| Fashions | 45 | TV and Radio | 86-87 |
| Financial | 55, 59-[illegible] | U. N. Proceedings | 6 |
| Food | [illegible] | Wash. Proceedings | 2 |
| Man in the News | 3[illegible] | Weather | 85 |
| Music | 34-3[illegible] | World's Fair | 37 |

News Summary and Index, Page 45

"All the News That's Fit to Print"

# The New York Times.

LATE CITY EDITION

U. S. Weather Bureau Report (Page 52) forecast: Partly cloudy, warm today. Cloudy, with showers tonight and tomorrow.
Temp. Range: 86—64; yesterday: 83—61.
Temp.-Hum. Index: 70's; yesterday: 72.

VOL. CXIII....No. 38,857.  NEW YORK, SATURDAY, JUNE 13, 1964. TEN CENTS

# SCRANTON ENTERS G.O.P. CONTEST UNDER A 'PROGRESSIVE' BANNER; SCORNS THE VIEWS OF GOLDWATER

HAT IN RING: Gov. William W. Scranton of Pennsylvania announces his candidacy for the Republican Presidential nomination in Baltimore. With him on platform is his wife.

Associated Press Wirephoto

## WARNS ON RIVAL

### Implies Senator Could 'Doom' Others on Party's Tickets

*Transcript of Scranton's talk will be found on Page 8.*

By JOHN D. MORRIS
Special to The New York Times

BALTIMORE, June 12—Gov. William W. Scranton entered the contest for the Republican Presidential nomination today under a banner of "progressive Republicanism."

The 46-year-old Pennsylvanian announced his candidacy in a speech laced with barbed allusions to the conservative views of Senator Barry Goldwater of Arizona, the leading contender for the nomination.

His forum was the Maryland State Republican Convention at the Lord Baltimore Hotel. Last night, shortly after deciding to become a candidate, he accepted a previously proffered invitation to address the convention.

His announcement drew cheers and chants from the several hundred delegates present. There were also some jeers and shouts of "Goldwater! Goldwater!"

**Talk Sharply Worded**

Without mentioning Mr. Goldwater by name, Mr. Scranton left no doubt that the Senator's brand of Republicanism was his target in many sharply worded passages.

"I've come here to offer our party a real choice," he declared. "I reject the echo we have thus far been handed—the echo of fear and of reaction, the echo from the never-never land that puts our nation on the road backward to a lesser place in the world of free men.

"I come here to announce that I am a candidate for the Presidency of the United States."

At another point, he called on his party to unite "behind our traditional principles and not behind some weird parody on our real beliefs."

In an obvious allusion to the campaign style of Senator Goldwater, he also denounced "the easy answer, or the fast draw or the quick solution."

**Warns of Peril to Ticket**

In a special appeal to rank-and-file Republican politicians, Governor Scranton reminded the delegates that the party's Presidential candidate could help others on the ticket or "doom them to undeserved defeat."

"Therefore," he said, "any political party which seriously undertakes to lead the Government of this nation — not only in Washington but also in the state capitols, and in the courthouses and in the city halls — such a great party will not lightly throw away the top places on its ticket."

Mr. Scranton conceded that the hour was late for progressives to challenge Senator Goldwater for the nomination. He accepted a share of the responsibility for the delay.

But he strongly disputed the view that the Goldwater forces already had all but assured the Senator's nomination.

Some persons are "so afraid

Continued on Page 8, Column 1

# GERMAN REDS SIGN FRIENDSHIP PACT WITH THE RUSSIANS

### 20-Year Treaty Proclaims 'Inviolability' of Borders Established After War

## POTSDAM TERMS CITED

### Agreement States 4-Power Accords, Affecting Berlin, Continue to Be Binding

*Text of Soviet-East German treaty is on Page 2.*

By HENRY TANNER
Special to The New York Times

MOSCOW, June 12—The Soviet Union signed a 20-year treaty of friendship and cooperation with East Germany today.

Premier Khrushchev and Walter Ulbricht, Communist party leader and chief of state of East Germany, signed the document after a three-hour rally in the Kremlin.

A member of the East German delegation said that the main importance of the treaty lay in the fact that East Germany would have the same status in relations with Moscow as all the other members of the Communist bloc.

East Germany had been the only member without a friendship treaty with the Soviet Union.

**Earlier Accords Affirmed**

The treaty stated explicitly that it did not affect the rights and obligations assumed by either of the two Governments under previous international agreements, including the Potsdam agreement of 1945.

The Potsdam agreement stipulated the conditions of four-power control of Germany, including Western access to Berlin.

The treaty said that the two sides regarded West Berlin as an "independent political entity."

East German sources hastened to explain that this had been the position of the two Governments all along. The clause does not supersede Mr. Ulbricht's earlier proposals for a demilitarized free city, they added.

Western diplomats here felt that the terms of the treaty were not so dire as some quarters had feared when it became known that the Soviet Union had given notice to the United States, Britain and France that the treaty would be signed.

**Bolstering of Regime Sought**

The consensus was that the Kremlin's purpose in its warm hospitality to Mr. Ulbricht during his state visit and the signing of the treaty was to bolster the prestige of the East German regime, both at home and abroad.

At the same time, it was felt, the Soviet leadership sought to avoid anything that would antagonize the Western allies, create new cold war tensions or render the division of Germany irremediable.

The long speeches by Mr. Khrushchev and Mr. Ulbricht at the rally were replete with pledges of peaceful intentions and with references to the necessity of upholding Mr. Khrushchev's policy of peaceful coexistence.

Both speakers used the occasion to accuse the Chinese Communist leaders of endangering world peace.

"Nuclear war is stupid, stupid,

Continued on Page 2, Column 5

# Soviet, in Shift, Supports Increase in U.N. Councils

### Backs Adding of 4 Seats to Security Body to Benefit Asians and Africans—Also Favors Larger Social Council

By THOMAS J. HAMILTON
Special to The New York Times

UNITED NATIONS, N. Y., June 12—The Soviet Union has reversed itself and agreed to the expansion of the Security Council and the Economic and Social Council to provide more seats for African and Asian members.

Reliable sources said today that the Soviet delegation had sent a note to Latin-American delegates, who also favor the expansion, stating that it would agree to broadening of the Security Council from 11 members to 15 and the Economic and Social Council from 18 to 27.

The note stated that Communist China favored the expansion and implied that the Soviet Union would ratify the proposed expansion amendments to the Charter, which were adopted by the General Assembly last December.

The fact that Communist China is not a member of the United Nations was used by the Soviet Union during the Assembly debate to justify its opposition to the expansion.

Despite the overwhelming Assembly vote in favor of expansion—97 to 11 for broadening the Security Council, 96 to 11 for expanding the Economic and Social Council—the f[illegible]re of the permanent members to support the proposed Charter amendments seemed to eliminate any possibility that they would go into effect.

No amendment to the Char-

Continued on Page 4, Column 4

# Berlin Rights Reaffirmed By President and Erhard

By MAX FRANKEL
Special to The New York Times

WASHINGTON, June 12—President Johnson and Chancellor Ludwig Erhard of West Germany reasserted today the rights of the Western powers in Germany and Berlin and their interest in working toward the peaceful reunification of Germany.

The two leaders found no ground for apprehension in the new treaty of mutual assistance between the Soviet Union and East Germany. They also found no new opportunity for reopening East-West negotiations on the various issues in Central Europe.

*Text of the joint communiqué appears on Page 3.*

The heads of government and their aides, during a day-long round of meetings, reviewed a number of ideas being pressed by Bonn to emphasize the fact that reunification has not been forgotten, as Chancellor Erhard put it.

**Allied Fleet Is Urged**

The United States, in turn, persuaded the West Germans to agree, at least in a communiqué, that various accords with Moscow, including measures of arms control, promote rather than delay the goal of reunification.

The communiqué, issued this evening before a formal White House outdoor dinner for the German guests, also stressed the importance of the North Atlantic Treaty Organization and called for the establishment of an allied nuclear navy "by the end of the year."

West German support for the United States in the "serious situation" in Southeast Asia was emphasized in the communiqué. It promised greater West German political and economic contributions to the fight against North Vietnamese "aggression."

Communist China, which is

Continued on Page 3, Column 1

# LAOS NEUTRALISTS LOSE A VITAL POST

### Hill Re-taken by Pathet Lao—Hanoi Units Reported Shown in U.S. Photos

By United Press International

VIENTIANE, Laos, June 12 — Communist-led troops drove neutralist defenders from a vital defense post west of the Plaine des Jarres today, and Premier Souvanna Phouma announced that United States jet reconnaissance planes would resume operations.

The neutralist Premier said the flights had shown "important" troop movements by Pathet Lao and North Vietnamese troops. He also said United States Navy planes had photographic proof for the first time of Communist North Vietnamese troops in Laos.

There have been earlier unofficial reports of such photographic evidence.

A right-wing general, Amkha Soukhavong, reported that the Communist-led troops had driven neutralists from Phou Kout, a hill position commanding the important east-west Highway 7. He said the attackers were only 11 miles from the neutralist strongpoint of Muong Soui.

It was the second time in a week that Pathet Lao troops had captured Phou Kout. They overran the village last Friday

Continued on Page 5, Column 3

# RIGHTS BACKERS BAR REFERENDUM ASKED BY RUSSELL

### 67-22 Rejection of Plan by Senate Typifies Day of Defeat for the South

By E. W. KENWORTHY
Special to The New York Times

WASHINGTON, June 12 — The Senate rejected overwhelmingly today a proposal by Richard B. Russell of Georgia for a national referendum on the civil rights bill.

The amendment submitted by the leader of the Southern opposition provided that the 11 titles of the bill would not take effect until approved "by the qualified voters of the several states."

The amendment was defeated, 67 to 22. Only three Republicans voted for it—Bourke B. Hickenlooper of Iowa, Karl E. Mundt of South Dakota and John J. Williams of Delaware.

Only two non-Southern Democrats voted for it—Robert C. Byrd of West Virginia and Frank J. Lausche of Ohio.

**Goldwater Misses Vote**

Senator Barry Goldwater of Arizona, the front-running candidate for the Republican Presidential nomination, did not appear for the roll-call.

Earlier, however, the Arizonan voted for three Southern amendments that would have impaired the bill or greatly complicated its administration.

The first of these, proposed by Strom Thurmond of South Carolina, would have made any violation of the ban on discrimination in public accommodations a crime punishable by a fine up to $1,000 or imprisonment up to six months, or both

**Civil Suit Required**

As the bill now stands, there are no criminal penalties, and the aggrieved person is required to institute a civil action for injunctive relief.

The purpose of the Thurmond amendment in making violations a criminal offense was to make certain that the defendant would get a jury trial. Southern juries have displayed a reluctance to convict fellow Southerners in civil rights cases.

The amendment went down by a vote of 66 to 23.

The second Southern amendment approved by Senator Goldwater was proposed by John G. Tower, Republican of Texas, one of his stanchest supporters. It would have eliminated the power of the President's Committee on Equal Employment Opportunity to deal with discrimination by employers with Government contracts.

**Union Shop Plan Loses**

At present this committee can cancel a contract if the employer continues to discriminate. Under the Tower amendment, the Equal Employment Opportunity Commission, which is created by the bill, would deal with discrimination in plants with Government contracts. Cases that come before this commission must go through an extended period of persuasion before reaching a court.

The amendment was defeated 59 to 29.

The third amendment approved by Mr. Goldwater, also sponsored by Mr. Tower, would have voided union-shop contracts, permitting compulsory unionism, if the union was guilty of discrimnation. It was rejected 62 to 27.

However, Mr. Goldwater

Continued on Page 21, Column 5

# SEGREGATION SEEN IN SCHOOL PAIRING

### Program Might Cause White Families to Leave City, Queens Court Is Told

By LEONARD BUDER

The lawyer for a group of white parents who are trying to block the pairing of two Queens elementary schools charged yesterday that the Board of Education's integration plan would actually lead to more school segregation.

Bernard Kessler, the lawyer, said that the forced transfer of children to schools outside their own neighborhoods to promote integration would result in a flight of middle-class families from the city.

Mr. Kessler appeared at a hearing in State Supreme Court in Queens on a suit brought by Remo J. Addabbo, the father of a kindergarten pupil, and 10 other parents who are seeking to have the scheduled pairing declared unconstitutional.

**Scheduled in September**

The lawyer and the parents are members of the Jackson Heights Parents and Taxpayers Association, a group favoring the preservation of neighborhood schools.

Justice Charles Margett reserved decision after hearing arguments by Mr. Kessler and Assistant Corporation Counsel Sydney Nadel, who represented the Board of Education.

The hearing was the first on a suit challenging the constitutionality of the school pairings, which are to go into effect in September. Five largely white elementary schools are to be paired with five predominantly Negro schools under the integration plan approved by the board last week.

Under the plan, Public School 149 in Jackson Heights, which is 87 per cent white, would be paired with nearby P.S. 92—in Corona, which is virtually all Negro. All first and second graders would attend P.S. 92 and all third through sixth

Continued on Page 24, Column 3

# Widening of G.O.P. Race Is Hailed by Party Leaders

Former President Eisenhower, Governor Rockefeller and other leading Republicans welcomed yesterday the entry of Gov. William W. Scranton into the race for the party's Presidential nomination. They said it was a healthy move that would mean an open convention.

Even before Governor Scranton made his announcement in Baltimore, many Republican leaders had voiced their approval with varying degrees of enthusiasm.

Supporters of Senator Barry Goldwater stiffened their backs and said it was too late; two leading supporters of Ambassador Henry Cabot Lodge said they were shifting their support to the Pennsylvania Governor; Governor Rockefeller, Gov. George Romney of Michigan and former Vice President Richard M. Nixon said they were pleased, but withheld their support.

In Gettysburg, Pa., General Eisenhower issued a statement calling the Scranton candidacy "good for the health and vigor of the party."

"It is in this conviction," the statement went on, "that I welcome the entry of Governor Scranton, whom I have long admired, into the contest for the Presidential nomination."

**Backed by Lodge Aide**

The national chairman of the campaign committee for Ambassador Lodge, Maxwell M. Rabb, said: "Lodge would have given leadership of the highest standards, but so will Scranton. We are proud to support Scranton and we know he will be victorious in July and then again in November."

Another leading Lodge supporter, Robert Mullen, who is national coordinator for the Committee to Draft Lodge, said he would urge leaders of his organization in 45 states to support Governor Scranton.

While he has not talked to the Ambassdor, Mr. Rabb said, he is sure he would agree with the organization's actions.

The man who has been an active candidate for the longest time, Governor Rockefeller, said that he was glad to see Mr. Scranton in the battle, "in the cause of moderate Republicanism."

The Governor, who has the support of more than 100 delegates to the convention, then said that he intended to remain a candidate. Mr. Rockefeller has been openly critical of other party moderates who had either failed to enter the Presidential race or back him.

Governor Romney of Michigan said that while Governor Scranton's public record and public positions indicated he would favor a platform "in

Continued on Page 8, Column 4

# SCRANTON WORDS STING GOLDWATER

### Senator Says His Foes Are 'Desperate' to Beat Him—Sees a Nixon Maneuver

By CHARLES MOHR
Special to The New York Times

WASHINGTON, June 12 — Senator Barry Goldwater was rocked today by the sharp attack from Gov. William W. Scranton of Pennsylvania, who had been his best friend among major Republican party leaders.

"The Republican establishment is desperate to defeat me," said Mr. Goldwater. "They can't stand having someone they can't control."

Mr. Goldwater and his advisers are uncertain as to how seriously Mr. Scranton's entry into the Republican Presidential race endangers the front-running Arizona conservative.

**644 Believed in Hand**

They think, it was learned, that they will enter the Republican National Convention at San Francisco on July 13 with about 644 delegates of the 655 needed to nominate.

Thus, in their view, the nomination may be won or lost in the feverish last-minute attempts to woo delegates in the convention city.

Almost everything about Mr. Scranton's hurried entry into the race surprised them. They had expected former Vice President Richard M. Nixon to be the challenger.

Nor had they expected that Mr. Scranton would attack Mr. Goldwater's brand of conservatism in such stunning terms. Mr. Scranton, in a speech to

Continued on Page 10, Column 3

United Press International Radiophoto

AT SOVIET-EAST GERMAN RALLY: Premier Khrushchev and Walter Ulbricht, the East German Communist leader, at the friendship gathering yesterday in Moscow.

# South African Court Sentences 8 to Life

By ROBERT CONLEY
Special to The New York Times

PRETORIA, South Africa, June 12 — Eight persons were sentenced to life imprisonment today on the ground that they had plotted a "violent revolution" against South Africa's racial policies.

Nelson R. Mandela, Walter M. E. Sisulu and the other defendants convicted under the antisabotage laws stood drawn and pensive before the Supreme Court here as sentence was pronounced. It ended one of South Africa's longest political trials.

Mandela, the so-called "Black Pimpernel" of the South African freedom movement, and the

Continued on Page 6, Column 1



# Turkish Premier Said to Accept Bid to Visit U.S. for Cyprus Talk

Dispatch of The Times, London

ANKARA, Turkey, June 12—Premier Ismet Inonu has accepted President Johnson's invitation to visit Washington, it was reliably reported here tonight.

The United States Ambassador, Raymond Hare, will be informed tomorrow of the Premier's acceptance. The date of the visit will be fixed later.

An official spokesman described as "completely false" reports that George W. Ball, United States Under Secretary of State, had proposed during his recent visit to Ankara and Athens an exchange of populations and territory between Turkey and Greece as a means of settling the Cyprus problem.

"There is constant speculation of this kind following these visits," the spokesman said. "We do not take it seriously."

Dr. Dirk U. Stikker, who is retiring as secretary general of the North Atlantic Treaty Organization and who is trying to relieve tension between Turkey and Greece, conferred for two hours today with Mr. Inonu. The talks were officially described as "very frank and friendly" and as "very useful for both sides." Dr. Stikker will leave Ankara tomorrow.

Special to The New York Times

WASHINGTON, June 12 — If Premier Inonu accepts the

Continued on Page 4, Column 6



NEWS INDEX



| | Page | | Page |
|---|---|---|---|
| Art | 20 | Music | 14-15 |
| Books | 21 | Obituaries | 23 |
| Bridge | 20 | Screen | 14-15 |
| Business | 27, 36 | Ships and Air | 52 |
| Chess | 20 | Society | 11 |
| Churches | 26 | Sports | 16-20 |
| Crossword | 21 | Theaters | 14-15 |
| Editorial | 22 | TV and Radio | 53 |
| Fashions | 12 | U. N. Proceedings | 2 |
| Financial | 27-36 | Wash. Proceedings | 8 |
| Food | 12 | Weather | 52 |
| Man in the News | 8 | World's Fair | 13 |

News Summary and Index, Page 25

# Draft Vatican Decree Suggests Family Planning May Be Needed

By PAUL L. MONTGOMERY
Special to The New York Times

WASHINGTON, June 12 — The principle that family limitation may be a necessity in the modern world is included in the draft of a declaration, completed this week, for the Vatican's Ecumenical Council.

The declaration, which is still subject to revision, is expected to come before the Roman Catholic bishops for approval when the third session of the council convenes in September.

An outline of the declaraton was given today by the Rev. Dr. Bernard Haring, a leading moral theologian and secretary of the commission that prepared the draft. Father Haring arrived from Rome yesterday to preside at a conference at Catholic University. While recognizing the principle of responsible parenthood and the limitation of family size that that implies, Father Haring said, the declaration is silent on the means toward this end. It would thus represent no relaxation of the church's ban on contraceptive devices.

If approved, it could serve to extend discussion on birth control, however, and provide new ground for theological work on the issue.

Many theologians believe that the responsible parenthood principle, which the council declaration would make explicit, is already implicit in the teaching of the Roman Catholic

Continued on Page 26, Column 6

"All the News That's Fit to Print"

# The New York Times.

LATE CITY EDITION
U. S. Weather Bureau Report (Page 78) forecasts: Mostly sunny, windy and cooler today; Fair and cool tonight and tomorrow.
Temp. Range: 75—62; yesterday: 82—66.
Temp.-Hum. Index: 60's; yesterday: 72.

VOL. CXIII..No. 38,860.

NEW YORK, TUESDAY, JUNE 16, 1964. TEN CENTS

# SUPREME COURT HOLDS STATES MUST APPORTION LEGISLATURES ON BASIS OF EQUAL POPULATION

## ROCKEFELLER GIVES UP RACE; AIDS SCRANTON

### VOWS FULL HELP

### Terms Pennsylvanian 'in the Mainstream' of Political Thought

*Text of Governor's statement is printed on Page 25.*

By JOSEPH LELYVELD

Governor Rockefeller, the first candidate to enter the Republican Presidential race, withdrew yesterday in favor of Gov. William W. Scranton of Pennsylvania.

In a brief statement released at his New York office, Mr. Rockefeller urged moderates in the party to unite behind Governor Scranton as "a candidate in the mainstream of American political thought and action."

This was the closest the statement came to mentioning Senator Barry Goldwater of Arizona, the leading candidate for the nomination. After he lost the California primary on June 2, Mr. Rockefeller remarked that if Senator Goldwater was in the mainstream "we've got a meandering stream."

**85 to 88 New York Votes**

The Governor's campaign aides estimated that he would be able to deliver 85 to 88 votes from the 92-member New York delegation to Governor Scranton at the Republican Convention in San Francisco next month. These delegates are not legally bound to the Governor, but since they are from his home state he is confident of his political control.

In addition, Governor Rockefeller will attempt to give Governor Scranton the 18 delegates he won in Oregon in his only victory in a contested primary. These delegates will be legally free after he releases them and for that reason the Governor's statement stopped short of a release.

There are 20 to 25 more delegates pledged to Governor Rockefeller. It is considered likely that they will follow his lead into the Scranton camp.

**Meeting With Aides Set**

The Governor scheduled a meeting for today with his representatives from across the country and a news conference for this afternoon.

Mr. Rockefeller was at his Pocantico Hills estate when the curtain fell on a campaign that began officially last Nov. 7 and unofficially as soon as the votes were counted in the 1960 election.

For more than two years, it was widely assumed that he would be the party's nominee in 1964. All this changed overnight when he remarried on May 4, 1963, after his divorce earlier. From then on, his campaign was under a cloud.

In his statement yesterday, he stressed that he had become an active candidate in November "to fight for the basic principles of progress and moderation on which the Republican party was founded and has prospered."

Now, he said, if that fight is to be won, it will be won under the Scranton banner.

"Accordingly," the statement

Continued on Page 25, Column 1

## Lodge Denies Plan To Quit as Envoy

By PETER GROSE
Special to The New York Times

SAIGON, South Vietnam, June 15—Henry Cabot Lodge firmly denied today a Washington report that he had resigned as United States Ambassador to South Vietnam for health reasons. The report, he said, is "totally false."

Mr. Lodge underwent a thorough medical checkup only a few days ago, sources said, and was reported to be in good health. At 61, he continues to go for energetic swims nearly every day during his lunch hour.

The question plaguing Ambassador Lodge today is whether he should resign for other reasons—political reasons. It is a question that remains unanswered.

As a liberal Republican and a possible though undeclared contender for the Republican

Continued on Page 24, Column 3

## SCRANTON BEGINS DRIVE IN MIDWEST

### Governor Is Critical of Both 'Dime-Store Feudalism' and Foreign Policy

By JOSEPH A. LOFTUS
Special to The New York Times

DES MOINES, Iowa, June 15—Gov. William W. Scranton of Pennsylvania opened a fighting campaign for convention delegates in the Midwest tonight, swinging to the right at Senator Barry Goldwater of Arizona and to the left at President Johnson.

With one hand he struck at "dime-store feudalism" and "extreme reactionaries." With the other he aimed blows at an Administration that he said had "put together a short-order foreign policy, serving up each day's hash from the leavings of yesterday's mistakes."

The Governor received two rousing receptions, although Goldwater enthusiasts infiltrated both and interrupted speeches with yells for the Senator.

**Response Is Warm**

A two-floor auditorium that seats more than 4,000 was nearly filled. The crowd responded to the Governor's speech with deafening approval time after time. Goldwater fans chose the quiet moments of the speech to yell, "We want Barry."

The Goldwater claque hooted the Governor's remarks that "this is not the hour for us to join those extreme reactionaries who are anything but conservative."

More than 500 persons, with a band, met the Governor at the airport.

A late starter in the race for the Republican Presidential nomination, delighted rather than dismayed by his underdog role, the Governor set out to tap in the next four weeks every state with uncommitted

Continued on Page 25, Column 5

## PEKING WARNS U.S. RISKS RETALIATION WITH LAOS FLIGHTS

### Says Southeast Asia Peace 'Is Hanging by Thread'—Renews Parley Call

By SEYMOUR TOPPING
Special to The New York Times

HONG KONG, June 15—Communist China asserted today that United States air operations in Laos were inviting retaliatory action.

Warning that "peace in Indochina and Southeast Asia is hanging by a thread," Peking pressed its demand for the prompt reconvening of the 1962 Geneva conference on Laos.

Jenmin Jih Pao, official organ of the Chinese Communist party, said in a lengthy editorial that the United States bore responsibility for the bombing Thursday of Peking's mission at the headquarters of the Communist-led Pathet Lao at Khang Khay, in north-central Laos. One Chinese was reported to have been killed and five staff members to have been injured.

**Provocation Charged**

Rejecting denials by the United States Embassy at Vientiane, Laos, that United States planes were involved in the attack Thursday, the editorial charged that the bombing had been planned by the Johnson Administration as a premeditated and deliberate provocation against Communist China.

According to information received here, the raid was carried out by T-28 trainer aircraft converted to fighter-bombers that were supplied to the right-wing Laotian Air Force by the United States. Strikes by the Laotian Air Force and reconnaissance flights by United States Navy planes began last month after Pathet Lao troops had attacked neutralist forces on the Plaine des Jarres.

Reliable sources in Washington reported last weekend that United States Air Force jets bombed Communist gun positions in Laos last Tuesday after two Navy planes had been downed. But there were no reports that United States planes were involved in the raid Thursday.

**Pressure Held Aim**

Western analysts here said the editorial had apparently been intended to exert pressure for acceptance of Peking's demand for reconvening the Geneva conference without delay. This demand was put forward in notes sent to Britain and the Soviet Union, co-chairmen of the Geneva conference, which guaranteed Laotian independence and neutrality.

The notes strongly protested the Khang Khay bombing.

However, analysts also noted that the editorial had hinted more strongly than any previous statement that Chinese Communist forces might become directly involved in the Laotian conflict.

"Having reconnoitered inten-

Continued on Page 3, Column 1

## Rights Groups, in Switch, Back Schools' Racial Plan

### 7 Organizations Drop Opposition After Gross Changes Setup on Transfers—Taxpayer Group Continues Fight

By LEONARD BUDER

Representatives of seven civil rights and community organizations switched their positions yesterday and said they would urge their members to support the Board of Education's integration plan.

The representatives acted after Dr. Calvin E. Gross, the Superintendent of Schools, agreed, as they put it, to eliminate "a number of objectionable features" in the plan, which is scheduled to go into effect in September. Dr. Gross described the changes as "refinements."

A key change will allow Negro children who were scheduled to attend sixth-grade classes in specified junior high schools next fall to transfer to specified integrated or white elementary schools. The groups had previously charged that the Negro pupils were merely being transferred from segregated elementary schools to segregated junior high schools.

Yesterday's development, which came as a surprise, ended for the time being the long controversy between civil rights groups and the school system.

All of the groups had previously denounced the board's integration plan because, they said, it did not substantially correct racial imbalance in the schools. Several had indicated that they might sponsor new demonstrations in the fall, including possibly a prolonged boycott by Negro pupils.

The organizations that an-

Continued on Page 18, Column 5

## GOMULKA ASSAILS CHINESE LEADERS

### Polish Chief Says They Are 'Dangerous'—Proposes World Red Conference

By DAVID BINDER
Special to The New York Times

WARSAW, June 15—Wladyslaw Gomulka condemned the Chinese Communist leadership today in sharp terms.

The First Secretary of the Polish United Workers (Communist) party, who was addressing the opening session of the party's fourth congress, called the Peking leaders "shortsighted and dangerous."

In a speech lasting six and a half hours he said that the Chinese, in their pursuit of "great-power ambitions," had indulged in policies "that have nothing to do with Marxism-Leninism or proletarian internationalism."

Mr. Gomulka then urged preparation of a world conference "of all parties to participate" in seeking to re-establish Communist unity. The split is over methods of achieving world Communism, with Peking advocating revolutionary tactics and Moscow favoring the co-existence approach. The Polish

Continued on Page 5, Column 1

## GREECE'S PREMIER TO VISIT JOHNSON

### Coming to U.S. for Cyprus Talks June 24-25, After President Sees Turk

By TAD SZULC
Special to The New York Times

WASHINGTON, June 15—President Johnson announced tonight that Premier George Papandreou of Greece would confer with him here on the Cyprus crisis immediately after a similar meeting with Premier Ismet Inonu of Turkey.

Mr. Inonu will meet with President Johnson next Monday. According to tonight's announcement, Mr. Papandreou will be in Washington June 24 and 25.

The Presidential invitations to the two Premiers were issued last week. This coincided with hastily arranged visits to the Greek and Turkish capitals by Under Secretary of State George W. Ball.

The Ball mission reflected the mounting concern here over the situation on the Mediterranean island, where fighting has raged between the majority Greek Cypriotes and the Turkish Cypriotes. Clashes broke out in December after the Government

Continued on Page 7, Column 2

## PRIVILEGE RULING

### Justices Widen Scope of Fifth Amendment in State Actions

Special to The New York Times

WASHINGTON, June 15—In two landmark criminal-law decisions, the Supreme Court extended today the protections of the Fifth Amendment's privilege against compelled self-incrimination.

Overruling a 56-year-old precedent, the Court held that the privilege applied in state as well as Federal proceedings. The vote was 5 to 4, but two of the Justices dissented on the facts of this case and did not necessarily disagree with the constitutional ruling.

The Court also held, again overturning a prior decision, that if a state granted a man immunity and then forced him to testify, the testimony could not be used in a Federal prosecution. This result was reached unanimously, but on diverse grounds.

The first case involved William Malloy of Windsor, Conn., who was convicted on a betting charge in Hartford in 1959. He drew a 90-day jail sentence and a $500 fine.

**Queried About Arrest**

In 1961 he was called to testify before an inquiry into gambling and other illegality in Hartford County. He was asked questions about his arrest in 1959 and about whether he knew a John Bergoti, apparently a suspect of some kind.

Mr. Malloy refused to answer, invoking the Fifth Amendment. He did not explain how answers to those questions might incriminate him. He persisted in silence even after he was told that the statute of limitations had run out on any gambling activities as early as 1959.

At the time, Mr. Malloy's invocation of the Fifth Amendment was in error. The Supreme Court had held for more than a century that the protections of the first 10 amendments to the Federal Constitution applied only to the Federal Government, not the states.

**Bill of Rights Applied**

In this century the Court has gradually applied some of the Bill of Rights protections to the states. It has found these protections encompassed in the 14th Amendment, which prohibits the states from denying any person the "due process" of law.

But in 1908 the Court specifically held that the Fifth Amendment privilege against being forced to testify against oneself was not applicable in state proceedings. It reiterated that view in a 5-to-4 decision in 1947.

Connecticut, however, like all other states, has its own protections against compulsory self-incrimination. The Connecticut Supreme Court of Errors therefore, went ahead and considered whether Mr. Malloy had come within the privilege.

The Connecticut court found

Continued on Page 32, Column 1

The New York Times

PRESENTS DECISION: Chief Justice Earl Warren, who announced Supreme Court ruling on apportionment of state legislatures.

## DEMOCRATIC GAIN IN STATE IS SEEN

### Court Ruling Is Expected to Liberalize Legislature by Shift of Influence

By DOUGLAS DALES
Special to The New York Times

ALBANY, June 15—The decision of the United States Supreme Court declaring New York's legislative apportionment formula unconstitutional is expected to have two major long-range effects upon the Legislature.

First, it will require a major political realignment of the Republican and Democratic forces. While not assuring the Democrats of majorities in the Legislature, historically dominated by Republicans, a formula based on population will put control by the Democrats within their grasp.

Second, by increasing the relative influence of the cities and suburban areas in the Legislature at the expense of upstate rural counties, the decision is almost certain to change the character of the Legislature, giving it a more liberal point of view.

**Two Questions Open**

The decision in Washington left unanswered the question when the change in districting formulas must be put into effect. And it also left open for interpretation the meaning of reapportionment based "substantially" on population.

In mandating the case back to the three-member statutory court that originally dismissed the suit, the Supreme Court gave the lower court authority to decide when the changes must go into effect.

Should the lower court order the changes effective for the 1964 elections, it could create a vast assortment of technical problems in view of the relatively short time remaining until the general election Nov. 3.

Candidates for the 150 Assembly seats and the 58 Senate seats were nominated by the political parties in the primary election June 2.

In view of the time that would be required for the statutory court to make its findings, the time required for a special session of the Legislature and the weeks required for the circulation of nominating petitions by candidates, the view here was that the implementation of today's decision probably would be put off until the 1966 legislative election.

Among those subscribing to this expectation was Assembly Speaker Joseph F. Carlino, who

Continued on Page 31, Column 1

## HISTORIC DECISION

### Both Houses Affected—Ruling Upsets 6 States' Districts

*Excerpts from decision are on Pages 28 to 31.*

By ANTHONY LEWIS
Special to The New York Times

WASHINGTON, June 15—The Supreme Court held today that the districts in both houses of state legislatures must be "substantially equal" in population.

It was a decision of historic importance. Not since the school segregation cases 10 years ago had the Court interpreted the Constitution to require so fundamental a change in this country's institutions.

A 6-to-3 majority laid down the broad rule that both houses of state legislatures "must be apportioned on a population basis."

Only a handful of states meet that standard now. While the opinions gave no specific guide, it would not be surprising if 40 of the 50 states found their districts upset.

**Suburbs Also Gain**

The big gainers from redistricting will be the cities and especially now the fast-growing suburbs. Rural areas have long had many more seats in most state legislatures than their population would indicate.

The Court said there was no valid analogy between state legislatures and the Federal Congress, in which the Senate is based not on population but on two members for each state. Today's decision does not affect the United States Senate.

The specific provision in the Constitution for the Senate, the Court said, resulted from a compromise among the sovereign states that formed the Union. But counties and other subdivisions of states have never been sovereign, and states are subject to the Constitution's overriding requirement of equality.

**Opinion by Warren**

Chief Justice Earl Warren wrote for the majority. He was joined by Justices Hugo L. Black, William O. Douglas, William J. Brennan Jr., Byron R. White and Arthur J. Goldberg.

Justice John Marshall Harlan delivered an impassioned dissent. Extemporizing from the bench, he spoke of the "solemnity of this occasion" and warned against the Court's damaging itself by sweeping a decision.

Justices Tom C. Clark and Potter Stewart did not accept the majority's reasoning. But they did agree, on narrower grounds, that some of the state legislative apportionments before the Court were unconstitutional.

The Court passed on six cases from Alabama, New York, Colorado, Maryland, Virginia and Delaware. It found the existing districts in all six legislatures unconstitutional.

Suits are pending in almost 40 states. Cases are awaiting

Continued on Page 28, Column 2

## Goldwater Joins in Futile Effort To Kill Key Part of Rights Bill

By E. W. KENWORTHY
Special to The New York Times

WASHINGTON, June 15—Senator Barry Goldwater and four of his stanchest supporters joined with the Southern bloc in the Senate today in a futile attempt to kill the public accommodations section of the civil rights bill.

The vote by which the Senate repulsed the effort to strike out what Negroes regard as the vital core of the measure was 63 to 23.

Seventeen Southerners, five Republicans and one Northern Democrat voted for the amendment. The other Republicans were Norris Cotton of New Hampshire, who was Mr. Goldwater's campaign manager in that state's Presidential primary last March; Wallace F. Bennett of Utah, Edwin L. Mechem of New Mexico and Milward L. Simpson of Wyoming.

The Northern Democrat voting for the amendment was its sponsor, Robert C. Byrd of West Virginia.

The public accommodations section, called Title II, bans discrimination or segregation in hotels, motels, restaurants, theaters and sports arenas.

Mr. Goldwater's vote for the motion to eliminate the title was expected. He has always taken the position that he deplores discrimination in public accommodations but opposes any attempt to outlaw it as

Continued on Page 17, Column 1



## After 134 Years, Soldiers of France Leave Algiers

United Press International Radiophoto

Trucks, carrying detachment of French troops sailing for home, roll onto Algiers pier

By PETER BRAESTRUP
Special to The New York Times

ALGIERS, June 15—For the first time since 1830, the French Tricolor did not fly over the port of Algiers today. The last French troops here—2,000 of them—quietly boarded transports and headed home across the Mediterranean. Few Algerians seemed to notice. Two years after independence, the French military presence, which dominated this city's life during the bitter 1954-62 war for independence, had ceased to matter. Apparently fearful of incidents, Paris decreed that the waterfront embarkation ceremonies on the Quai Gabès be brief and closed to the press and the public. Shortly after 8 P.M., a 300-man rear guard in combat dress marched across the quai behind a band. It consisted of troops of the First Spahi

Continued on Page 5, Column 4

## Moseley Gets Chair; Verdict Is Cheered

By DAVID ANDERSON

Applause broke out in State Supreme Court yesterday after a jury had voted to send Winston Moseley to the electric chair for the murder of Catherine Genovese in Kew Gardens.

The sudden hand-clapping and a few cheers, all from women, in the Queens County Criminal Courthouse caused Justice J. Irwin Shapiro to pound his desk angrily for order.

After the courtroom had quieted, however, Justice Shapiro told the jurors:

"I don't believe in capital punishment, but I must say I feel this may be improper when I see this monster. I wouldn't hesitate to pull the switch on him myself," Moseley himself

Continued on Page 53, Column 2



NEWS INDEX



| | Page | | Page |
|---|---|---|---|
| Books | 36-37 | Obituaries | 39 |
| Bridge | 36 | Real Estate | 63-64 |
| Business | 54, 62-63 | Screen | 46-48 |
| Buyers | 53 | Ships and Air | 77-78 |
| Chess | 36 | Society | 34 |
| Crossword | 37 | Sports | 49-52 |
| Editorial | 38 | Supreme Court | 31, 32 |
| Fashions | 42-43 | Theaters | 46-48 |
| Financial | 55-62 | TV and Radio | 79 |
| Food | 42 | U. N. Proceedings | 8 |
| Letters | 38 | Wash. Proceedings | 32 |
| Man in the News | 31 | Weather | 78 |
| Music | 46-48 | World's Fair | 26 |

News Summary and Index, Page 41




## Jersey Labor Split By Power Struggle

By DAMON STETSON
Special to The New York Times

NEWARK, June 15—New Jersey's merged labor organization fell apart today, broken by a power struggle between the former leaders of the Congress of Industrial Organizations and the American Federation of Labor.

The former C.I.O. unions, which formed their own Industrial Union Council last winter, said they would hold a separate convention in Atlantic City on June 26-28. If that convention, they said, they will decide whether to go it alone in the future.

The bitter division at the opening of the state A.F.L.-C.I.O. convention here today made it clear that there would

Continued on Page 50, Column 1

"All the News That's Fit to Print"

# The New York Times.

LATE CITY EDITION

U. S. Weather Bureau Report (Page 62) forecasts: Sunny, hot and humid today; fair, hot and humid tonight and tomorrow.

Temp. Range: 94—70; yesterday: 89—67. Temp.-Hum. Index: about 80; yesterday: 77.

VOL. CXIII..No. 38,890.  NEW YORK, THURSDAY, JULY 16, 1964. TEN CENTS

# GOLDWATER IS NOMINATED ON FIRST BALLOT; HE CALLS JOHNSON 'BIGGEST FAKER IN U.S.'; SELECTS REP. MILLER AS HIS RUNNING MATE

## MIKOYAN IS NAMED SOVIET PRESIDENT; BREZHNEV SHIFTED

### Former Chief to Serve Full Time as Khrushchev Aide —His Position Enhanced

By HENRY TANNER
Special to The New York Times

MOSCOW, July 15—Anastas I. Mikoyan became President of the Soviet Union today.

Leonid I. Brezhnev, who had held the post since 1960, stepped aside to devote himself full-time to his duties as Premier Khrushchev's deputy in the Secretariat of the Communist party, the center of power in the Soviet Union.

Western analysts drew the following conclusions from the change:

¶Mr. Brezhnev's chances of becoming Mr. Khrushchev's eventual successor have been substantially enhanced.

¶Mr. Khrushchev's own power has been increased, since his two closest associates now occupy the key posts of titular head of state and deputy party leader.

¶The Presidency — technically the post is the chairmanship of the Presidium of the Supreme Soviet (Parliament)—is likely to gain in importance. Mr. Mikoyan, while assuming the representative functions of his new post, is expected to continue many of his activities in the field of foreign relations.

**Step in Long-Range Plan**

Some analysts saw today's move as the first step in a long-range program to assure an orderly transition from Mr. Khrushchev to Mr. Brezhnev.

The analysts thought that the change raised a possibility that Mr. Khrushchev, when he felt the time had come, might decide to turn over the party leadership to Mr. Brezhnev and take over the Presidency from Mr. Mikoyan.

Mr. Mikoyan's rise to the Presidency came at a short and surprisingly matter-of-fact meeting of the Supreme Soviet.

Mr. Khrushchev rose and in the name of the Central Committee of the Communist party nominated Mr. Mikoyan.

He praised Mr. Mikoyan as a "true Leninist" and a "fighter for peace" and declared that the Central Committee felt he de-

Continued on Page 3, Column 1

## CONGO TO BOYCOTT AFRICAN MEETING

### Tshombe Also Says Regime Has Released Gizenga

By J. ANTHONY LUKAS
Special to The New York Times

LEOPOLDVILLE, the Congo, July 15 — Premier Moise Tshombe announced tonight that the Congo would boycott the conference of African leaders opening Friday in Cairo.

Mr. Tshombe also said that his Government had released Antoine Gizenga, the leftist leader who was held on an island in the mouth of the Congo River for the last two and a half years.

The announcements were made in a seven-paragraph declaration after a day of frantic meetings in Mr. Tshombe's home.

The decision to boycott the Cairo conference followed declarations by several African leaders that they would not sit at the conference table with Mr. Tshombe.

Among those who made statements sharply critical of Mr. Tshombe were President Ahmed Ben Bella of Algeria and President Kwame Nkrumah of Ghana.

Mr. Tshombe, who was named last week as the Congo's fourth Premier, is considered by many African leaders to be a pawn

Continued on Page 4, Column 3

Associated Press Cablephoto

SOVIET HIERARCHY: Premier Khrushchev with Leonid I. Brezhnev, center, and Anastas I. Mikoyan before Supreme Soviet. Mr. Mikoyan succeeded to the Presidency.

## SOVIET SAYS CHINA FEARS RED PARLEY

### Peking Told in Sharp Letter That It Would Get Rebuff at Conference of Parties

Special to The New York Times

MOSCOW, July 15 — The Soviet Union made public today a letter to Communist China harsher in tone than any other published Soviet document about their ideological dispute.

The long letter, sent to Peking June 15, charged that the Chinese leaders opposed a Soviet call for a world conference of Communist parties because they were "afraid" of facing the other parties at a meeting.

"You have never seriously thought of a conference . . . because you could not count on the support for your ideological and political platform on the part of a world Communist forum," the letter said.

**Tone of Letter Caustic**

The letter, though pale compared with some of the accusations made by Soviet and Chinese newspapers, was more caustic than any previous message sent to the Chinese and made public so far. It gave an insight into the tone the Russians and Chinese have been using in the private exchanges in their ideological dispute.

The Russians asserted that only two parties in the world —the Chinese and Albanian—were against a world conference.

The "overwhelming majority" of the other parties, the letter continued, are actively supporting the idea and a number of parties are for it in principle but have "reservations" about the timing.

The Soviet plan for a conference will be discussed again next week when Premier Khru-

Continued on Page 7, Column 1

## 2 More Policemen Ousted in Inquiry

By EDITH EVANS ASBURY

A police lieutenant and a patrolman were dismissed yesterday for refusing to cooperate in the investigation into alleged collusion between policemen and gamblers.

Both men had served in plainclothes in strategic posts.

Police Commissioner Michael J. Murphy, who announced the dismissals, said earlier in the day that changes had been made in his department and "there will be others" as a result of the investigation. Three grand juries in Manhattan and one in Brooklyn are questioning policemen and gamblers.

Yesterday's dismissals brought

Continued on Page 14, Column 3



## Britain Now Backs Independence Talk For South Rhodesia

By LAWRENCE FELLOWS
Special to The New York Times

LONDON, July 15 — Britain agreed tonight to call a conference of Southern Rhodesians, black and white, to discuss terms on which the self-governing colony would achieve independence.

Up until now Britain has resisted proposing such a conference, fearing that the Rhodesian Government, if pressed too hard, might unilaterally declare the colony independent.

Sir Alec Douglas-Home, the British Prime Minister, also undertook to approach Ian D. Smith, the Southern Rhodesian Prime Minister, to try to persuade him to release African nationalists now detained.

Sir Alex was supported in this by a unanimous declaration of the Prime Ministers of the British Commonwealth that none of them would recognize a declaration of independence by the Southern Rhodesian regime.

The Commonwealth Prime Ministers' conference here was supposed to have ended at noon today. The agreement on a Rhodesian conference was reached nine hours later. It helped to relieve the tension that resulted when a young white man assaulted Jomo Kenyatta, Prime

Continued on Page 5, Column 1

## STATEN ISLAND HIT BY A FERRY STRIKE

### City Employes Defy Court Order — 35,000 Daily Commuters Affected

Ferry workers walked off the job early today, tying up service between Manhattan and Staten Island that is used by more than 35,000 persons a day.

The strike, in addition to halting ferries on the Whitehall Street-St. George, S.I., run, also affects ferry service to North Brother Island, Riker's Island, City Island and Hart Island.

The walkout started at 12:20 A.M. when employes of the ferryboat Verrazano refused to open the entrance gates to the ferry at the Battery. About 150 ferry employes cheered when the gates stayed closed.

Leo Brown, Commissioner of the Department of Marine and Aviation, immediately had copies of a temporary strike injunction given to the employes of the Verrazano. The employes still refused to open the gates.

The injunction was issued Monday by Supreme Court Justice George Tilzer several hours after members of Local 333 of the United Marine Division of the National Maritime

Continued on Page 62, Column 6

## SCORNFUL ATTACK

### Senator Charges That President Changed Civil Rights Stand

By CHARLES MOHR
Special to The New York Times

SAN FRANCISCO, July 15—Senator Barry Goldwater accused President Johnson today of being "the biggest faker in the United States" and the "phoniest individual who ever came around."

The Arizona Republican made his extemporaneous remarks on his way to a service elevator in a back hall of the Mark Hopkins Hotel after addressing a "captive nations" rally.

A reporter asked him if the Republican National Convention's refusal to strengthen its civil rights plank would not give the Democrats a good issue in November.

The Senator's head snapped around. With an edge of scorn in his voice, he said:

"After Lyndon Johnson—the biggest faker in the United States? He opposed civil rights until this year. Let them make an issue of it. I'll recite the thousands of words he has spoken down the years against abolishing the poll tax and F.E.P.C. [Fair Employment Practices Commission]. He's the phoniest individual who ever came around."

**Plans 'Vigorous Campaign'**

Later in the day, after his nomination, Senator Goldwater told a news conference that he intended to wage a "vigorous campaign" but assumed that it would not be a campaign of personal attack.

He added that he expected President Johnson also to wage a vigorous campaign.

The Senator said he hoped the campaign would give the American people "time to think, and I hope that I'm the better salesman."

Senator Goldwater said that the differences within the Republican party were "rather minor" and that, "with some exceptions, we could almost overlook them."

"I can't find words to express the feeling that is in my heart," Mr. Goldwater said. "No greater honor can come to any Republican."

Mr. Goldwater said that he knew Mr. Johnson's campaign would be conducted like his own, on the issues and not on personalities.

Mr. Goldwater said he would attempt to withdraw as a candidate to succeed himself in the Senate. But he said that a "dis-

Continued on Page 17, Column 1

Associated Press Wirephoto

AFTER NOMINATION: Senator and Mrs. Barry Goldwater embrace during news conference in San Francisco.

## G.O.P. Chairman Picked For No. 2 Spot on Ticket

Special to The New York Times

SAN FRANCISCO, July 15—Senator Barry Goldwater today selected Representative William E. Miller of upstate New York as his Vice-Presidential running mate. Mr. Goldwater was reported to have asked Mr. Miller to run with him in a phone call about noon, many hours before the Arizonan was formally chosen as the Republican standard-bearer.

Reliable sources made known Mr. Goldwater's choice. Asked after his nomination whether he had phoned Mr. Miller to offer him the No. 2 position on the Republican ticket, the Senator said "No." But he added that he was "favorably inclined" toward the New Yorker.

"I didn't think it would be fair to ask him, if that was my intention, until he was through with his official duties at the convention," Mr. Goldwater said.

Mr. Miller is the Republican national chairman.

Mr. Miller, interviewed later, said he would be "delighted" to run with the Senator.

Before he made his choice, Mr. Goldwater also had been

Continued on Page 18, Column 3

## EISENHOWER CHIDES SENATOR'S FORCES

### Says Rejection of Changes in the Platform Violated Democratic Method

By FELIX BELAIR Jr.
Special to The New York Times

SAN FRANCISCO, July 15—Former President Dwight D. Eisenhower condemned today the tactics of Goldwater delegates to the Republican National Convention in rejecting efforts to strengthen a platform declaration on civil rights and to add one on "extremism."

His comment concerned two proposals by Gov. George Romney of Michigan. These, as well as others, were overwhelmingly defeated by the convention in a dramatic demonstration of the support that a majority of the delegates were giving Senator Barry Goldwater.

In a television appearance as a political consultant for the American Broadcasting Company, General Eisenhower said that he was "unhappy" about the defeat of the proposals, but even more about the way in which this was accomplished.

His earlier disappointment apparently forgotten, General

Continued on Page 18, Column 5

## U.S. Judge Orders Sheppard's Release

Special to The New York Times

DAYTON, Ohio, July 15—Dr. Samuel H. Sheppard, convicted of slaying his wife in 1954, today was ordered released from prison.

Federal District Judge Carl A. Weinman ruled that Sheppard had been denied his constitutional rights in his trial 10 years ago in Cleveland. He declared Sheppard's custody void and ordered his release in $10,000 bond.

The judge said Sheppard's trial had been "a mockery of justice." Sheppard is expected to be released from Ohio Penitentiary in Columbus tomorrow.

If Cuyahoga County (Cleve-

Continued on Page 32, Column 1



## VOTE IS 883 TO 214

### Scranton Plea to Make It Unanimous Is Then Approved

By TOM WICKER
Special to The New York Times

SAN FRANCISCO, July 15—Barry Morris Goldwater, the champion of a new American conservatism, was nominated for President tonight by the 28th Republican National Convention.

The Arizona Senator, the 20th man in the line of Republican nominees that began with John C. Frémont and Abraham Lincoln, needed only one ballot to win the nomination and crush the moderate forces that had controlled his party for a quarter-century.

The only serious challenger was Gov. William W. Scranton of Pennsylvania.

At the conclusion of the ballot he appeared on the platform to move for the unanimous nomination of Senator Goldwater. The convention then adopted by acclamation a resolution making it so.

The count of the first ballot stood as follows for the two leading contenders:

Goldwater ................883
Scranton ...................214

**Will Accept Today**

Senator Goldwater did not appear at the convention, which adjourned at 11:11 P.M. Pacific daylight time (2:11 A.M., Thursday, New York time). He will accept the nomination tomorrow, after his choice for Vice President, Representative William E. Miller of New York, is duly nominated.

There was never any contest from the moment Senator Everett McKinley Dirksen concluded his nominating speech for Senator Goldwater and set off a wild demonstration that thundered through the Cow Palace for 29 minutes.

Governor Scranton, who entered the race only a few weeks ago, nevertheless refused to withdraw before the ballot was taken. He was on the Cow Palace grounds with his wife, waiting in a trailer for the results.

As soon as the ballot was completed, however, Governor Scranton came striding briskly down the long wooden ramp to the platform, his wife just behind him, with his campaign

Continued on Page 16, Column 1

## COURT OPENS WAY ON REDISTRICTING

### U.S. Judges Give State Until July 27 to Offer Plan

By THOMAS P. RONAN

A three-judge Federal Court cleared the way yesterday for reapportionment of the New York Legislature in time for the November election, but it did not specifically order the change.

After formally declaring the present system of apportionment unconstitutional, the court recessed until July 27 "to await action, if any, by the duly constituted authorities of the State of New York in the light of this declaration."

On that date it will hear "representations" by the parties involved in the suit on how its judgment of unconstitutionality can be implemented. The representations will include suggested reapportionment plans,

Continued on Page 20, Column 3

NEWS INDEX


| | Page | | Page |
|---|---|---|---|
| Art | 28 | Man in the News | 17 |
| Books | 28-29 | Music | 22-25 |
| Bridge | 28 | Obituaries | 31 |
| Business | 41-43 | Real Estate | 50 |
| Buyers | 41 | Screen | 22-25 |
| Chess | 28 | Ships and Air | 62 |
| Crossword | 29 | Society | 21 |
| Editorial | 30 | Sports | 36-40 |
| Fashions | 34-35 | Theaters | 22-25 |
| Financial | 41-50 | TV and Radio | 63 |
| Food | 34 | Weather | 62 |
| Letters | 30 | World's Fair | 35 |

News Summary and Index, Page 33




## Prime Minister of Kenya Is Attacked by a British Fascist in London

Associated Press Cablephoto

Prime Minister Jomo Kenyatta, left, of Kenya, braces against attack by member of British National Socialist Movement, in London. Mr. Kenyatta announced that he was unhurt.

United Press International Radiophoto

Mr. Kenyatta leaving conference later in the day.

"All the News That's Fit to Print"

# The New York Times.

LATE CITY EDITION

U. S. Weather Bureau Report (Page 54) forecasts: Mostly sunny, warm and humid today; fair tonight. Fair, hot tomorrow.

Temp. Range: 90—72; yesterday: 85—70. Temp.-Hum. Index: about 80; yesterday: 76.

VOL. CXIII..No. 38,891. NEW YORK, FRIDAY, JULY 17, 1964. TEN CENTS



# GOLDWATER PROMISES PROGRAM TO MAKE COMMUNISM 'GIVE WAY'; MILLER IS NAMED RUNNING MATE

## PATHET LAO DRIVE ON VITAL BASTION REPORTED OPENED

### Regime Says Muong Soui, Neutralist Stronghold, Is Target of Pro-Reds

### ROAD NETWORK PERILED

### Defense Ministry Asserts North Vietnamese Troops Are Supporting Attack

Special to The New York Times

VIENTIANE, Laos, July 16—The National Defense Ministry announced tonight that pro-Communist Pathet Lao forces had launched an offensive against Muong Soui, the principal stronghold of the neutralist faction in Laos, in the north-central region.

A communiqué said Pathet Lao troops, supported by North Vietnamese forces, had crossed the Nam Ngum, the river below the town, and were driving westward on Muong Soui. Four battalions with three batteries of artillery were said to be involved in the attack.

Muong Soui guards the approaches to a road network leading south to Vientiane and north to Luang Prabang, the royal capital.

It was not possible to obtain confirmation immediately of the assertion that North Vietnamese troops were supporting the Pathet Lao.

**Westerners Are Convinced**

However, Western military observers are convinced that North Vietnamese cadres have operated with Pathet Lao forces, and that on occasions entire units have been committed by North Vietnam.

Gen. Kong Le, the neutralist military commander, has made Muong Soui his main base since his troops were swept westward off the Plaine des Jarres by a Pathet Lao offensive in May. The position is reported to be held by 2,500 neutralist troops, supported by a number of light tanks of Soviet origin. About 1,000 friendly Meo tribesmen guerrillas are screening the neutralist flanks.

The Defense Ministry communiqué said Laotian T-28 fighter-bombers were attacking the Pathet Lao forces.

Western military sources were unable to confirm any details of the communiqué.

**Rightist Build-Up Reported**

Earlier, a build-up of rightwing forces for a possible offensive had been reported west of Muong Soui. This could be aimed at destroying an isolated pocket of Pathet Lao troops holding positions at Vang Vieng, on the road between Vientiane, the administrative capital, and Luang Prabang, about 70 miles to the north.

If a major Pathet Lao attack is in progress, its initial objective would be to overrun Muong Soui and then press westward to join this isolated force astride a key communications route.

Earlier, Prince Souvanna Phouma, the neutralist Premier, said in an interview he no longer had any hope of arranging peace talks with the Pathet Lao.

For several weeks the Premier has exchanged messages with Prince Souphanouvong, the Pathet Lao leader, on the pos-

Continued on Page 5, Column 4

## Ferry Strike Ends After Day's Tie-Up On Staten Is. Route

A one-day wildcat strike by workers on the city-owned ferry between Staten Island and Manhattan ended early today and runs were resumed.

After a stormy 2½-hour union meeting that ended at 12:35 A.M., members of Local 333 of the United Marine Division of the National Maritime Union agreed to go back to work immediately.

Union officials would not indicate what had prompted the decision of the members. A spokesman for Mayor Wagner said that the union and the city had reached a contract settlement, but would give no details.

Earlier yesterday, Supreme Court Justice Arthur Markewich had granted the city's motion for a further temporary injunction. A restraining order had been issued on Monday but had been defied by the strikers.

The walkout, which began early yesterday, halted two

Continued on Page 28, Column 1

## NEGRO BOY KILLED; 300 HARASS POLICE

### Teen-Agers Hurl Cans and Bottles After Shooting by Off-Duty Officer

By THEODORE JONES

An off-duty police lieutenant shot and killed a 15-year-old Negro boy in Yorkville yesterday when the youngster allegedly threatened him with a knife. After the shooting about 300 teen-agers, mostly Negroes, pelted policemen with bottles and cans.

Before order had been restored by 75 steel-helmeted police reinforcements, a Negro patrolman attempting to disperse the screaming youths was hit on the head by a can of soda. He was taken to Lenox Hill Hospital, where his condition was later reported as good.

The shooting occurred at 9:20 A.M. outside a six-story white brick apartment house at 215 East 76th Street, opposite the Senator Robert F. Wagner Junior High School, where summer school classes were in progress.

The dead boy was James Powell, a student at the school, who lived at 1686 Randall Avenue, the Bronx. The police said the youth had been shot twice, in the right hand and in the abdomen, by Lieut. Thomas Gilligan of Brooklyn's 14th Division.

The trouble began when Patrick Lynch, superintendent of the building at 215 East 76th Street, sprayed water on three youths while he was washing down the sidewalk, according to Deputy Chief Inspector Joseph

Continued on Page 31, Column 1

## 2 BUILDING AIDES DISMISSED BY CITY AS EXTORTIONISTS

### Third Inspector Suspended —Birns Reports on 107 Trials Over 6 Years

By CHARLES G. BENNETT

Two of the city's building inspectors have been dismissed and one suspended on charges of extortion in the last four weeks. A fourth inspector was dismissed for misconduct early last month.

Building Commissioner Harold Birns disclosed the actions yesterday in a report to Mayor Wagner on steps taken to combat graft in his department over the last six years.

Since October, 1958, he said, there have been 107 disciplinary trials. Of those tried, 21 were dismissed, 9 resigned while on trial and 31 were suspended or fined.

A majority of the dismissals and resignations involved bribery or extortion. Each disciplinary case, he said, was announced publicly as soon as possible after its final disposition.

**Accused by Landlord**

Mr. Birns told the Mayor that the most recently suspended inspector had been arrested after a Bronx landlord had complained that the inspector had attempted to extort $50.

The two dismissed inspectors were accused by Abraham Kazan, the builder, of demanding more than $2,000 for expediting the issuance of occupancy certificates for the Penn Station South housing project.

The inspector dismissed for misconduct, Mr. Birns said, was found guilty of failing to perform his duties properly in connection with the construction of houses in Canarsie, Brooklyn.

Mr. Birns appealed to persons knowing of any misconduct by Buildings Department employes to "come forward" and tell what they know.

**Promises Prompt Action**

"Those who come forward," Mr. Birns declared, "may be assured of personal consideration and the knowledge that their information will be the subject of prompt, effective action."

Commenting on the report, Mayor Wagner said: "The public has a right to know that everything that can be done is being done to prevent dishonesty in money-sensitive branches of the city government, such as the Department of Buildings, and to punish dishonesty when it is apprehended."

The Mayor said he did not know who should be blamed more, "the inspector who takes the bribe or the man who offers it."

"In any event," Mr. Wagner declared, "there can be no rest or surcease in our efforts and vigilance in this department and in every other one which has analogous responsibilities

Continued on Page 56, Column 3

## CHAIRMAN CHOSEN

### Dean Burch, an Aide of Senator, to Take Over Miller's Post

By CHARLES MOHR

Special to The New York Times

SAN FRANCISCO, July 16—Senator Barry Goldwater took command of the Republican party today and placed its administration in the hands of his 36-year-old protégé, Dean Burch.

Mr. Goldwater told a meeting of Republican state chairmen this morning that Mr. Burch, a lawyer from Tucson, Ariz., who is the Senator's deputy campaign manager, was his choice to become the new Republican National Chairman.

The Republican National Committee will meet tomorrow with Mr. Goldwater to make the selection formal.

**Early Talks Planned**

In the meantime, some members will try to find out what they can about Mr. Burch, who is relatively unknown in national politics.

Mr. Burch said today that a meeting would be held "as quickly as possible to organize the campaign and to make the national committee the instrument of the campaign and the party."

He said that he would hold the discussions with Senator Goldwater and Representative William E. Miller of upstate New York, the Vice-Presidential nominee, who has been national chairman.

He said of the campaign that "we plan to operate through the national committee" and that that body would be "the center of operations."

**Long-Planned Move**

He confirmed a long-discussed plan for the key members of the present campaign staff to move into quarters at the national committee offices in Washington.

This will be something of a departure from the usual. In recent campaigns, special campaign organizations responsible directly to the candidate were superimposed upon the national committee, which was largely bypassed.

Mr. Goldwater, who spent an hour with Mr. Miller, let it be known that his campaign manager, Denison Kitchel, 56, of Phoenix, Ariz., would continue in that capacity. But Mr. Kitchel and the Presidential campaign staff will become a part of the national committee.

The Senator's press secretary,

Continued on Page 11, Column 1

United Press International Telephoto

THE REPUBLICAN TEAM: Senator Barry Goldwater, the Presidential nominee, and Representative William E. Miller of New York, his running mate, after acceptance speeches.

## CONVENTION ENDS

### Extremism in Defense of Liberty 'No Vice,' Arizonan Asserts

*Text of Goldwater speech is printed on Page 10.*

By TOM WICKER

Special to The New York Times

SAN FRANCISCO, July 16—Senator Barry Goldwater of Arizona accepted the Republican Presidential nomination tonight with a call to his party "to free our people and light the way for liberty throughout the world."

Communism, he said, must be made to "give way to the forces of freedom."

"The sanctity of private property," he said, "is the only durable foundation for constitutional government in a free society."

"Extremism in the defense of liberty," Senator Goldwater declared, "is no vice . . . moderation in the pursuit of justice is no virtue."

**Thunderous Ovation**

The Senator, nominated on the first ballot at last night's session of the 28th Republican National Convention, received a thunderous ovation when he appeared in the Cow Palace tonight for the closing session.

As he spoke, dedicating his campaign to what he called "the ultimate and undeniable greatness of the whole man," he was constantly interrupted by the enthusiasm of the delegates, who had never given serious thought to choosing anyone else.

Earlier tonight, the delegates nominated Senator Goldwater's choice for the Vice-Presidential nomination, Representative William E. Miller of New York, without a dissenting vote. Three delegates from Tennessee abstained, however, because they thought the convention should have made the selection.

The nomination of 50-year-old Mr. Miller was almost routine business, as the great hall waited in suspense for the appearance of its hero.

**Speaks in Quiet Tone**

Senator Goldwater, mild-mannered, bespectacled, speaking usually in a quiet voice, and with almost no gestures, did not disappoint his hearers—the conservatives who at this convention wrested the Republican party from its quarter-century of control by moderate forces.

He laid down a strong line of active resistance to Communism abroad, and what he pictured as state planning at home.

Senator Goldwater offered no quarter to the moderate Republican forces that fought him throughout his campaign for the nomination and who succumbed reluctantly to the power of his delegates here. Some moderate delegates were reported to be angered at the militant tone of the speech and the absence of an olive branch to them.

Mr. Goldwater made no direct mention of the civil rights

Continued on Page 10, Column 1

## COHN ACQUITTED IN SECOND TRIAL

### Gottesman Also Cleared of Perjury as Jury Rejects Bribery Accusation

By WILL LISSNER

Roy M. Cohn and Murray E. Gottesman were acquitted yesterday of charges that they had attempted to obstruct a Federal investigation of a $5 million stock swindle.

The retrial of Mr. Cohn in Federal District Court on charges of perjury and obstruction of justice, and of Mr. Gottesman on charges of perjury, ended at 11:38 A.M. At that moment the foreman of the jury, Claude C. Applegate, a retired advertising salesman, reported: "Not guilty on all counts."

Two dozen relatives and friends of Mr. Cohn and Mr. Gottesman—including seven of Mr. Cohn's nine law partners—began to cheer.

**Marshals Seek Quiet**

Judge Dudley B. Bonsal gave a reproving look while Federal marshals sought to hush the spectators.

Mr. Cohn put his arms in a bear hug around Thomas A. Bolan, an associate defense counsel who is one of his partners, and said: "Great! Great!"

Mr. Gottesman wept. "It's the end of a nightmare," he said later.

Mr. Cohn had a victory party at the Stork Club last night at which about 300 friends hailed the jurors' decision.

The jury, 11 men and one

Continued on Page 24, Column 6

## Johnson Notes Advances In 3 Economic Indicators

By EILEEN SHANAHAN

Special to The New York Times

WASHINGTON, July 16—President Johnson announced today that the national economy had made "notable advances" in the last three months. He predicted that the gains for the rest of the year would be "even greater."

Government reports made public today showed that the gross national product, the number of employed industrial workers and personal income had all advanced strongly in recent months.

The gross national product, the dollar figure that measures the entire output of the economy, rose by nearly $10 billion to an annual rate of $618.5 billion in the March-June quarter.

The number of workers on nonagricultural payrolls increased in June by 600,000 to a record total of 59.1 million. The rise was about 100,000 larger than is normally expected in the month.

**Gain a Near Record**

Total income received by individuals increased in the March-June quarter by $11.4 billion to a total of $491.3 billion.

The gain for the quarter was a near record, President Johnson said, and the rise of $32.3 billion from the second quarter of last year was a record.

The increase in the gross national product in the second quarter, coupled with the $9 billion rise recorded in the first quarter, puts the economy almost exactly where the Administration said it would be when it made its annual economic forecast in January.

That forecast put the gross

Continued on Page 8, Column 5

## LINDSAY PONDERS BOLT FROM TICKET

### G.O.P. Liberal Says He Will Search His Conscience—Keating in Quandary

By ANTHONY LEWIS

Special to The New York Times

SAN FRANCISCO, July 16—Representative John V. Lindsay of Manhattan said today that he would have to search his conscience before deciding whether to vote for Senator Barry Goldwater, his party's nominee for President.

Mr. Lindsay, one of the most liberal Republican members of the House, is now finishing his third term. He has built up increasingly large margins in the 17th Congressional District.

This year the leader of the Conservative party of New York, Kieran O'Doherty, is running against him. He is out here as an aide to Mr. Goldwater, and Mr. Lindsay said with some feeling that he understood that the Senator would back Mr. O'Doherty.

**Delegates Leave Early**

Senator Kenneth B. Keating and a large group of the other New York delegates walked out of the convention hall tonight after Senator Goldwater finished his acceptance speech. They left as he was applauded loudly for saying that "extremism in the defense of liberty is no vice." The delegates said, however, that they were leaving only to "avoid the crush."

Senator Jacob K. Javits and Representative Lindsay were among those who stayed. The Senator commented that he had "heard nothing new" in the acceptance speech.

"It was pretty much a fundamental generalization of the

Continued on Page 12, Column 6

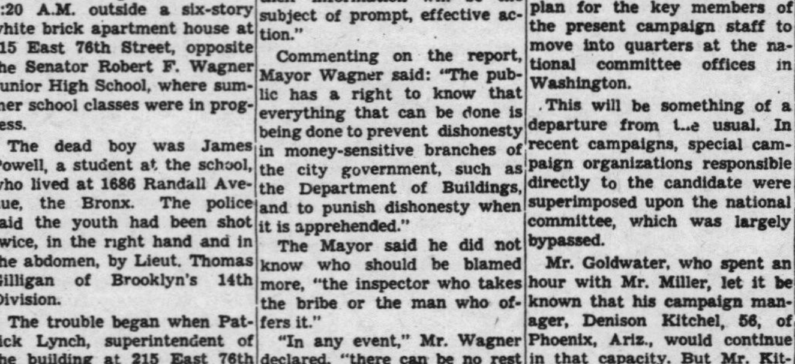

## Thant Calls for Curb On Cyprus Build-Up

By SAM POPE BREWER

Special to The New York Times

UNITED NATIONS, N. Y., July 16—A new appeal for restraint in the crisis on Cyprus was made today by the Secretary General, U Thant.

Mr. Thant stressed the danger of the arms race that has been developing in that island republic. He appealed to the governments of Cyprus, Greece and Turkey and to the Turkish Cypriote community to "do all within their power to halt this perilous trend and to reverse it before it leads to a major clash in Cyprus, with all the dangers that such a clash entails."

Mr. Thant sent cablegrams that were essentially identical

Continued on Page 2, Column 5

The New York Times

ORDER RESTORED: Policemen stand guard as summer students leave Senator Robert F. Wagner Junior High School, 215 East 76th Street. Students rioted earlier after police lieutenant shot and killed Negro youth, who reportedly attacked him with a knife.

## British Postal Strike Halts Mail; Millions of Letters Clog Offices

By CLYDE H. FARNSWORTH

Special to The New York Times

LONDON, July 16 — The mails stopped in Britain today as 120,000 deliverers and sorters staged their first national strike in 70 years to back demands for higher pay.

Wildcat strikes had slowed mail deliveries to a trickle, and the one-day official strike produced additional mountains of unsorted mail.

Angry postmen are planning to follow up the walkout with a two-week ban on overtime and a strict adherence to work rules, which will produce additional postal chaos.

In the London area alone, 21 million letters were piled up in sorting centers, twice the figure of yesterday. Additional millions of letters lay uncollected in mail boxes.

Post office officials appealed to the public not to mail letters and to report overflowing mail boxes. The London area normally handles 20 million letters daily.

Many banks and business offices were running private messenger services to handle essential missives. Telephone switchboards were unusually busy.

There were reports that, if the pay dispute went on, there would be "guerrilla strikes" at key post offices or brief strikes among the telephone staff that would disrupt that service.

Telegrams from abroad were being delivered as much as three hours late tonight and the backlog was not being dealt with quickly.

Mail from the United States

Continued on Page 3, Column 2

## U.S. and Soviet Link Desalting Programs

By JOHN W. FINNEY

Special to The New York Times

WASHINGTON, July 16 — The United States and the Soviet Union reached an informal agreement today on limited scientific cooperation in developing methods for desalting sea water, including possible use of atomic energy.

As a first step in the cooperative program, the two sides will exchange inspection visits by technical experts.

A Soviet team will visit laboratories and experimental desalinization plants in the United States in the coming week, and an American team will make a similar inspection trip to the Soviet Union later this year.

The agreement was reached during three days of discussions

Continued on Page 6, Column 6

NEWS INDEX


| | Page | | Page |
|---|---|---|---|
| Books | 25 | Music | 14-17 |
| Bridge | 24 | Obituaries | 27 |
| Business | 33, 40 | Real Estate | 41 |
| Buyers | 40 | Screen | 14-17 |
| Crossword | 25 | Ships and Air | 54 |
| Editorial | 26 | Society | 32 |
| Fashions | 30 | Sports | 18-21, 24 |
| Financial | 33-41 | Theaters | 14-17 |
| Food | 30 | TV and Radio | 55 |
| Letters | 26 | Weather | 54 |
| Man in the News | 11 | World's Fair | 31 |

News Summary and Index, Page 29




NEW NUMBER FOR ORDERING WANT ADS in The New York Times. OXford 5-3311. Fast, direct-line service to want ad takers.—Advt.

"All the News That's Fit to Print"

# The New York Times.

LATE CITY EDITION
U.S. Weather Bureau Report (Page 66) forecasts: Mostly sunny today; fair tonight. Fair and warmer tomorrow.
Temp. Range: 81–62; yesterday: 89–70.
Temp.-Hum. Index: low 70's; yesterday: 78.

VOL. CXIII . No. 38,932.  NEW YORK, THURSDAY, AUGUST 27, 1964. TEN CENTS

# DEMOCRATIC TICKET: JOHNSON AND HUMPHREY; BOTH NOMINATED BY ROARING ACCLAMATION; PRESIDENT AT SCENE, BREAKING A TRADITION

## RULERS IN SAIGON UNABLE TO AGREE ON A NEW REGIME

### Khanh and Colleagues Split—U.S. Being Consulted on Shift—Riots in Danang

By PETER GROSE
Special to The New York Times

SAIGON, South Vietnam, Aug. 26 — South Vietnam's political crisis deepened today with the failure of its military rulers to agree on a new head of state and a new form of government.

"The situation is very serious," said Major General Nguyen Khanh after emerging from protracted talks with members of the Military Revolutionary Council — talks that were supposed to formulate a new framework to supplant General Khanh's seven-month-old regime.

General Khanh was Premier until he became President Aug. 16 on the basis of a new Constitution. He and leaders of the armed forces agreed yesterday to step aside under the pressure of Buddhist and student protests against the dictatorial aspects of the Government.

**Council to Meet Again**

Today's meetings made it clear that the generals and colonels could not agree on how much power they were preparing to relinquish or to whom they would relinquish it. The council has controlled the country since the ouster and assassination of President Ngo Dinh Diem last November.

Another meeting of the council is scheduled tomorrow.

[In Washington, authoritative sources said that the crucial steps taken by the Khanh Government to deal with the political situation were made known in advance to the United States.]

Meanwhile, religious strife continued in the central Vietnamese city of Danang, where Buddhist-Roman Catholic violence has resulted in 70 casualties, including at least a dozen deaths, in the last three days.

**Taylor to Fly to U. S.**

Grim and weary after a virtually sleepless night and day of bargaining, General Khanh said, "We military men have to consider things thoroughly before offering a solution to the people."

The President's intention of achieving re-election with new support from Buddhist groups and the political parties had clearly been blocked by the leaders of the armed forces.

The crisis, which flared into violence Sunday, showed how fragile is the political structure on which the United States has based its efforts to defeat the Communist Vietcong.

An American spokesman said Ambassador Maxwell D. Taylor was adhering to plans to return to the United States by air for

Continued on Page 3, Column 5

## Goldwater Favors Some Peking Talks

By CHARLES MOHR
Special to The New York Times

AVALON, Calif., Aug. 26—Senator Barry Goldwater said today that he had long believed "talks with Red China might be profitable" to end the war in South Vietnam.

If he were elected President, he indicated, he would be willing to permit negotiations with Peking.

He also expressed a qualified belief that the Johnson Administration was working for a negotiated settlement of the war in South Vietnam.

A little later, however, Mr. Goldwater appeared to modify his remarks to indicate that he had in mind some form of ultimatum rather than negotiations in the usual sense.

Mr. Goldwater interrupted a five-day Pacific cruise to hold

Continued on Page 2, Column 3



## Pontiff Says Some Tenets Of Peace Are 'Crumbling'

### He Is Reported to Have South Vietnam, Cyprus and the Congo in Mind in Talk Deploring the Divisions Among Men

Special to The New York Times

CASTEL GANDOLFO, Italy, Aug. 26—Pope Paul VI, in a vibrant appeal for peace, said today that some of the basic principles of peace were crumbling.

The Pontiff said there were new symptoms of the reappearance of divisions among peoples, races and cultures. "This spirit of division is guided by nationalistic pride, by prestige politics, the armaments race, social and economic antagonisms," he said.

He called on all "men of goodwill" to "listen to our humble voice" and place above "every other interest" the values of human dignity and fraternal accord.

The Pontiff's appeal was made to pilgrims attending a general audience at his summer residence. It was motivated, he said, not only by the anniversary at this time of year of the start of both world wars, but also by the "acute disagreements" that he said existed between various countries today.

The Pope did not specify any areas or countries, but L'Osservatore Romano, the Vatican newspaper, remarked in commenting on the speech that "to name islands or peninsulas or near and far hinterlands in which there is fighting" was superfluous.

Vatican sources commented that there was no doubt the Pope had Cyprus, the Congo and South Vietnam in mind.

The speech amounted to another step in a peace effort that the Pope started Aug. 10 with his encyclical "Ecclesiam Suam" ("His Church"). In that encyclical he said he was willing to intervene in disputes between nations to help find solu-

Continued on Page 12, Column 3

## PRISONERS FREED BY EAST GERMANY

### Accord With Bonn Reported for Thousands Detained on Political Charges

Special to The New York Times

BERLIN, Aug. 26—Communist East Germany has quietly begun to release a large number of political prisoners, the majority of them West Germans and West Berliners, official sources said here today.

They declined to confirm or deny that the release was an outcome of secret talks between East and West German justice officials. Observers said there was evidence that West German authorities had been informed and consulted.

On Monday, West German authorities freed Günther Hofe, an East Berlin publisher. He had been held in pretrial detention for almost 11 months on charges of having acted as a Soviet and East German agent. Bonn refused to explain the release.

Informed sources said several thousand persons were involved in the East German release.

The West German news

Continued on Page 10, Column 1

## Saks Fire Forces 5,500 Into Streets, Shuts Store a Day

By THEODORE JONES

High-fashion models and beauty salon patrons with their hair in curlers were among 5,500 persons forced into the streets from Saks Fifth Avenue by a smoky fire yesterday morning.

The fire, which broke out in a subbasement shortly after 11 A.M., sent clouds of dense smoke up through elevator shafts and air-conditioning ducts, and forced the store to close for the rest of the day.

Two firemen were injured in fighting the blaze, which was brought under control an hour after it had started. An employe of the store inhaled smoke and was given oxygen at the scene.

Allen Johnson, vice president and general manager of the store, said that damage to merchandise had been slight and that the fire had been confined to the basement. He also said he could not estimate the revenue lost through the closing of the store.

Adam Gimbel, president of the store, said that Saks would open on schedule at 9:30 A.M. even "if we have to work all

Continued on Page 37, Column 5

Associated Press
BUSINESS AS USUAL—MORE OR LESS: Saks Fifth Avenue hairdresser continuing work on patron's coiffure after smoky fire in the store's basement forced evacuation of the building. Women who had been in the beauty salon wear robes provided by store.

## SENATOR PRAISED

### 'Best Man in America for the Job,' Johnson Tells Convention

By EARL MAZO
Special to The New York Times

ATLANTIC CITY, Thursday, Aug. 27—Senator Hubert H. Humphrey was nominated for Vice President by acclamation at the Democratic National Convention early today.

Mr. Humphrey's name was placed in nomination by Senator Eugene J. McCarthy, his colleague from Minnesota, after President Johnson had appeared before the convention to name Mr. Humphrey as his choice and describe him as "the best man in America for the job."

In the seats of honor at Convention Hall for the long series of speeches supporting the nomination of Mr. Humphrey were the President and the Johnson and Humphrey families.

After the voice vote by which Mr. Humphrey was unanimously nominated, the Vice-Presidential candidate joined the President in the box of honor.

Because of the late hour—about 12:30 A.M.—and the fact that most of the audience and many of the delegates had left Convention Hall, Mr. Humphrey's acceptance speech was postponed until the final convention session tonight.

**Triple Announcement**

The process by which President Johnson let out the secret of his choice for Vice President was highly unusual.

All told, he announced it three times last night.

He did so at 8:30 at Andrews Air Force Base, near Washington, before leaving for Atlantic City. He presented Mr. Humphrey to newspapermen as "the next Vice President."

On his arrival here an hour later, Mr. Johnson told newsmen at Bader Airport that Mr. Humphrey was his man. At that impromptu news conference he delivered what amounted to a preliminary nominating address, speaking at length of his high regard for Mr. Humphrey.

The Minnesotan, standing beside the President, smiled broadly and declared he was honored and proud.

The third announcement came before the convention itself.

Mr. Humphrey had gotten a glimpse, yesterday morning, of what lay ahead later in the day. And in midafternoon he had been summoned from Atlantic City to Washington by the White House.

When he returned last night at 9:30, he came to Convention

Continued on Page 21, Column 3

Associated Press Wirephoto
NOMINEE PRESENTS RUNNING MATE: President Johnson as he introduced Senator Hubert H. Humphrey to the Democratic convention. Mrs. Humphrey is at the left.

## The Choice of Humphrey, Step by Step

Special to The New York Times

*This special report on how President Johnson picked his Vice-Presidential running mate was prepared by Tom Wicker, James Reston, Anthony Lewis, Earl Mazo and E. W. Kenworthy of The New York Times staff.*

WASHINGTON, Aug. 26—President Johnson's long delay in picking Senator Hubert H. Humphrey for the Vice-Presidency was carefully planned and for a specific purpose.

He had no doubts about Senator Humphrey's qualifications, but he wanted to get the widest possible support for Mr. Humphrey within the Democratic party, and he got it before making his decision at 3 o'clock this afternoon.

Also, the President wanted to make sure at the end that he and Senator Humphrey agreed on their concept of the Vice-Presidency. When Mr. Humphrey flew in here this afternoon, they had a long talk and agreed on the following things:

¶The Vice-Presidency, if the Democrats win in November, should have important executive responsibilities.

¶The Vice President should supervise the Johnson Administration's policies on space, disarmament, the antipoverty program, health, education and welfare and other fields within Mr. Humphrey's special competence.

¶The Vice President should take on a great deal of responsibility in the field of foreign affairs. He should represent the President abroad on special missions and assume many of the ceremonial duties that President Johnson has had to carry alone in the last nine months. For this purpose, the President intends to ask the Congress to provide an official residence for the Vice President in Washington.

"I think in all my life," the President said tonight before going to the Convention Hall, "that I have never taken any decision more seriously than picking Humphrey. I have had one thing in mind above all others, that is that when fellows like you come to write the history of this period they will say that we paid attention to the main thing.

"I picked Humphrey because, in my judgment, and after checking with leaders all over the country, I was convinced that he would be the best man to be President if anything happened to me."

Having reached a decision on the principle of picking a possible President, Mr. John-

Continued on Page 22, Column 1

## NEW LAW ENDING ATOMIC MONOPOLY

### Johnson Signs Bill to Allow Private Ownership of Fuel

By JOHN W. FINNEY
Special to The New York Times

WASHINGTON, Aug. 26 — President Johnson signed legislation today that ends an 18-year government monopoly of atomic fuels. Under the law, by June 30, 1973, the nuclear power business will be on its own within the framework of the free-enterprise system.

The amendment is the most far-reaching change in atomic legislation since the postwar McMahon Act was supplanted in 1954.

The 1954 law took the first step toward ending the government monopoly, created in a postwar concern over the awesome and little understood new force that had been unleashed, by permitting private possession of nuclear fuels and private ownership and operation of atomic power plants.

Reflecting a holdover of the postwar caution, however, the 1954 law still required Government ownership of the fissionable materials, such as enriched uranium, used as fuels in atomic reactors.

The government-owned and government-produced materials were leased, or in some cases given, to the private owners of atomic power plants.

Under the new amendment, unexpectedly approved by the Joint Congressional Committee on Atomic Energy this month after two years of deliberation, the commission after 1970 will be required to sell the nuclear fuels.

After mid-1973 all nuclear

Continued on Page 19, Column 3



## Keating Declares Some Democrats Are Offering Help

By WARREN WEAVER Jr.
Special to The New York Times

ONEONTA, N.Y., Aug. 26—Senator Kenneth B. Keating said today that he had received promises of personal and political support from a number of New York Democrats in the 24 hours since Robert F. Kennedy announced his Senate candidacy.

The list of those who telephoned or sent personal messages, Mr. Keating reported, includes "some Democratic officeholders and at least two party officials," as well as others prominent in Democratic circles in New York City and upstate.

The Senator declined to identify any of the Democratic supporters, but he said their comments "certainly showed a resentment against this invasion from outside the state."

His reference was to the fact that Attorney General Kennedy is moving into New York State for the purpose of seeking the Democratic nomination for the Senate and running against Mr. Keating. For a number of years Mr. Kennedy has lived in Virginia and voted in Massachusetts.

Mr. Keating made his claims of Democratic support in an informal press conference in the office of The Oneonta Star. He said later that some of his Democratic friends had sug-

Continued on Page 25, Column 4

### NEWS INDEX


| | Page | | Page |
|---|---|---|---|
| Books | 31 | Music | 26-28 |
| Bridge | 30 | Obituaries | 33 |
| Business | 44-45, 54 | Real Estate | 54 |
| Buyers | 44 | Screen | 26-28 |
| Crossword | 31 | Ships and Air | 65-66 |
| Editorial | 32 | Society | 38 |
| Fashions | 36-37 | Sports | 39-43 |
| Financial | 45-54 | Theaters | 26-28 |
| Food | 36-37 | TV and Radio | 67 |
| Letters | 32 | Weather | 66 |
| Man in the News | 21 | World's Fair | 28 |

News Summary and Index, Page 39


## ALABAMIANS QUIT OVER PARTY OATH

### Mississippi Delegates Begin Leaving Atlantic City

By CLAUDE SITTON
Special to The New York Times

ATLANTIC CITY, Aug. 26—The Alabama delegation to the Democratic National Convention followed the Mississippi delegation today in withdrawing rather than signing pledges of loyalty to President Johnson for the coming election.

They left behind only token groups of loyalists—nine from Alabama and three from Mississippi—to take part in the President's nomination by acclamation.

Eugene Connor, Alabama's national committeeman, was turned away by sergeants-at-arms when he sought to take his seat. Mr. Connor, former Birmingham police commissioner, predicted that the action would hurt President Johnson politically in the South.

The refusals by the two delegations to participate in the proceedings came after the convention's adoption yesterday of a recommendation by the Credentials Committee that the Mississippians take the loyalty pledge. The convention had earlier approved a similar requirement for the Alabamians.

Many of the Mississippians, who had made known their intention last night to quit the convention, left Atlantic City earlier today.

Mayor Jess Lanier of Bessemer, chairman of the unpledged group in the Alabama delegation, and its other leaders said tonight before the convention opened that they would suffer no further "insults" and that they were returning to Alabama.

Seymore Trammell, Ala-

Continued on Page 24, Column 3

## JOYOUS WELCOME

### Hall Erupts in Sound as Suspense Over Ticket Is Ended

*Texts of Johnson speech and airport conference, Page 20.*

By TOM WICKER
Special to The New York Times

ATLANTIC CITY, Thursday, Aug. 27—Lyndon Baines Johnson of Texas, the man who took over the Presidency last Nov. 22 in the shattering hour of John F. Kennedy's assassination, was nominated for a term of his own last night by the 34th Democratic National Convention.

Then Mr. Johnson did what he loves to do. He smashed precedent by going before a turbulent and happy gathering of more than 5,000 delegates and alternates to name Senator Hubert H. Humphrey of Minnesota as his choice for the Vice-Presidential nomination.

The happy Democrats, and thousands of spectators jammed into Convention Hall, cheered wildly for both Mr. Johnson and Mr. Humphrey.

**Speech Put Off**

Late in the program, after Senator Humphrey had been nominated by acclamation, it was announced that he would put off his acceptance speech until tonight. The convention then adjourned, at 12:37 A.M.

After lingering for an hour and chatting with the Texas delegation, the President finally left for Washington.

The President's nomination was also by acclamation. The motion to suspend the rules and dispense with the call of the states was offered by Mrs. Lloyd Danzig of Florida. It came after the remnants of the Alabama delegation yielded to Texas, so that Gov. John B. Connally Jr. could place the Johnson name in nomination.

It also was Governor Connally who nominated Mr. Johnson in his first abortive bid for the Presidency, at the Chicago convention in 1956.

Gov. Edmund G. Brown of California shared the nominating process, and was followed by seven seconding speakers.

**Roared Into Effect**

The delegates whooped the nomination into effect with a roar. Speaker of the House John W. McCormack of Massachusetts, the permanent chairman, confirmed it with a bang of his huge gavel.

The nomination set off an enthusiastic demonstration. All over the hall banners waved, balloons soared toward the lofty curved ceiling, bands played in an ear-splitting cacophony, the great organ bellowed and men struggled through the jammed aisles, screaming at the top of their lungs.

When it was quieted with much gaveling, Mr. Johnson came to the platform and set

Continued on Page 20, Column 1

## Hurricane's Gusts Sweep Into Miami

By The Associated Press

MIAMI, Thursday, Aug. 27—A hurricane struck Miami early today with winds of 75 miles an hour.

After toying with the city for hours, the hurricane, named Cleo, sent gusts across Miami's Key Biscayne that reached hurricane intensity.

Sustained gales—winds 25 to 75 miles an hour—battered the rest of the city as the storm's center churned just 25 miles to the southeast.

Forecasters warned that the storm center might go ashore north of the city and subject the coast from Fort Lauderdale to West Palm Beach to winds of 60 to 80 miles an hour.

The island of Bimini, about 35 miles offshore, also was struck

Continued on Page 17, Column 3

"All the News That's Fit to Print"

# The New York Times.

LATE CITY EDITION

U. S. Weather Bureau Report (Page 77) forecasts: Sunny, hazy and warm today; clear tonight. Fair and warm tomorrow. Temp. Range: 81—57; yesterday: 78—52.

VOL. CXIV..No. 38,993.  NEW YORK, TUESDAY, OCTOBER 27, 1964. TEN CENTS

# BRITAIN IMPOSES 15% IMPORT TAX TO BACK POUND

## U.S. SYMPATHETIC

### But Exporters Here Fear Measure Will Cut Sales Sharply

By CLYDE H. FARNSWORTH
Special to The New York Times

LONDON, Oct. 26—The new Labor Government announced today the introduction of a temporary 15 per cent surcharge on imports and tax incentives for exports as part of a broad program to protect the pound and strengthen the British economy.

The Government said the nation this year faced the biggest balance-of-payments deficit in its history—between £700 million and £800 million ($1.96 billion and $2.24 billion).

The deficit, amounting to nearly as much as the £900 million ($2.52 billion) of British gold and convertible currency reserves, has arisen mainly because this key trading nation has been unable to sell as much as she buys overseas.

**Trade Gap Swells**

Last month, the trade gap, at £133 million ($372.4 million), was the widest this year.

The huge deficit represents a potential drain on reserves, which, if unchecked, could lead to devaluation of the pound.

[In the United States, the Government and the export trade accepted the necessity of the British program, but made it clear that sales in Britain would be reduced substantially. European Governments and businessmen were generally dissatisfied with the export levy.]

In what was billed as a "fireside" chat to the nation, Prime Minister Harold Wilson emphasized tonight the temporary nature of the new measures and said that what was basically needed was a change in the nation's approach to economic matters.

Speaking for 10 minutes over Britain's two television networks, he called the situation "extremely serious" but said it "can and will be handled."

Mr. Wilson said that, although Britain made sacrifices in two World Wars, "the world does not owe us a living."

**Hard-Sell Urged**

A more aggressive approach to winning export orders was needed in the board room, the Prime Minister said, adding in words reminiscent of those of President Kennedy:

"We have got to think less of what we can get out of the economy and a great deal more of what we can get into it. We ought to think more about earning money and less about making it."

George Brown, Minister for Economic Affairs, and James Callaghan, Chancellor of the Exchequer, stressed at a news conference that Britain was not becoming protectionist.

They said the measures would not affect Britain's determination to seek broad worldwide tariff cuts under the Kennedy round of negotiations or the elimination of tariffs in the European Free Trade Association.

A Conservative party spokesman indicated later in the day

Continued on Page 61, Column 1

George Brown, Minister for Economic Affairs, at the news conference in London.

Associated Press Cablephotos
James Callaghan, Chancellor of the Exchequer, at the conference yesterday.

# RUSK AND BRITON REVIEW ALLIANCE

### Gordon Walker Presses Bid to Alter 1962 Missile Pact —Meets Johnson Today

By TAD SZULC
Special to The New York Times

WASHINGTON, Oct. 26—Foreign Secretary Patrick Gordon Walker of Britain and Secretary of State Dean Rusk examined today the problems of the Atlantic alliance, ranging from nuclear defense to the policies of the new Moscow leadership.

In four sessions extending from a morning conference at the State Department to a formal dinner, Mr. Gordon Walker and Mr. Rusk prepared for the Briton's conference at noon tomorrow with President Johnson.

Mr. Gordon Walker's two-day visit here is designed to lay the groundwork for a meeting between the new British Prime Minister, Harold Wilson, and Mr. Johnson.

Mr. Wilson plans to come to Washington early in December to open negotiations with the United States on reorganizing

Continued on Page 14, Column 1

# SOVIET CHIEFS SET COMMUNIST UNITY AS URGENT TASK

### Editorial in Izvestia Calls Equality and Sovereignty the Bases for Action

By HENRY TANNER
Special to The New York Times

MOSCOW, Oct. 26—The new Soviet administration promised today to work for unity among Communist nations and Communist parties on the bases of equality and sovereignty.

The pledge was in the form of an editorial in the Government newspaper Izvestia. The headline said, "A Commonwealth of Equals." The editorial, unlike most Soviet writings on this subject in recent months, did not mention the Chinese Communists. Nor did it contain any reference to ideological dissension or "splitters" and "threats" to Communist unity.

Western observers saw the editorial as part of an effort by the new Soviet leaders to indicate to the world that basic Soviet policy will continue while the Khrushchev style and tactics are changed.

The editorial was also seen as evidence that the new leaders have set these principal goals of great urgency: to consolidate the bloc of Communist countries, to halt the disintegration of the international Communist movement and to get off the collision course with Communist China.

**'Boisterous' Style Decried**

It is the contention of the new leaders that the "boisterous" personal style of Nikita S. Khrushchev nearly led to catastrophe in these goals even though the Kremlin's basic policy was sound.

Charges against the former Premier that have been printed in the last 10 days have outlined this view.

The opinion is expected to be the main theme of further explanations this week. Informed sources expect Pravda, the Communist party newspaper, to publish a new set of charges against Mr. Khrushchev in a few days, probably mentioning the former Premier by name for the first time.

The most significant point in the new editorial, observers felt, was the absence of any polemics against the Chinese.

**New Freedom Seen**

The new Soviet leaders apparently believe that they have a freedom of action in the Chinese-Soviet conflict that Mr. Khrushchev did not because his personal prestige was directly committed.

Western diplomats here take it for granted that consultations between Moscow and Peking will take place sooner or later.

The emphasis in the editorial on the "equality" of all Communist parties in the international movement did not go beyond similar statements made by Mr. Khrushchev.

It was seen as an effort by the new leaders to reassure foreign Communists that there would be no change on this point as a result of Mr. Khrushchev's departure.

In the last few months, foreign Communists have oc-

Continued on Page 2, Column 3

## Prelates Bid Rome Clarify Its Message

By ROBERT C. DOTY
Special to The New York Times

ROME, Oct. 26—Bishops of the Roman Catholic Church said today that the church "must live in the midst of men" and deliver its spiritual message in terms they understand.

This was a recurring theme as the prelates of the church continued debate in the Ecumenical Council on a draft on "The Church in the Modern World."

Speakers asked for a more positive church attack on the problems of poverty, for abandonment of elaborate clerical dress and language and for avoidance of juridical, legalistic approaches to sin and science that risk making the church a "laughing stock" for nonbelievers.

The central theme in the wide range of subjects covered

Continued on Page 12, Column 3

# 9 U.S. MARINES DIE IN WAR EXERCISE

### 13 Hurt as Copters Collide in Landing Maneuvers on the Coast of Spain

By JACK RAYMOND
Special to The New York Times

HUELVA, Spain, Oct. 26—Nine American marines were killed and 13 were injured this morning when two helicopters collided over the drop zone a few hours after the start of a joint United States-Spanish amphibious assault training maneuver.

The two helicopters, Sikorsky H-34's, were consumed by the flames caused by the collision, a Navy spokesman said. Officials could not recall a bigger death toll in any similar training exercise.

The names of the victims were withheld pending official notification of their families.

The accident marred what was otherwise an impressive start in a war game with an armada of American warships ranged on an eight-mile front off Spain's southern coast, not far from where Columbus sailed for America in 1492.

**Operation Called Success**

Helicopters and fighter planes filled the air over the beaches. United States and Spanish marine units waded spiritedly ashore with rifles aloft. Heavy equipment, including tanks, bulldozers and cranes, were rolled out of specially designed landing craft. A long jetty-like pier was built in a few hours.

United States and Spanish officials termed the first day's operations a technical success. With 80 ships and nearly 60,000 men in the two-nation task force, the exercise, known as Steel Pike 1, is said to be the largest amphibious maneuver since the Korean War.

Representative L. Mendel Rivers, chairman-designate of the House Armed Services Committee, especially stressed Spain's role. He said it was indicative of "the complete confidence with which Spain is

Continued on Page 6, Column 3

# BUDGET ESTIMATE CUT $700 MILLION; RECEIPTS ALSO OFF

### Current Year's Spending Is Now Put at $97.2 Billion—Pentagon Trims Credited

Special to The New York Times

WASHINGTON, Oct. 26—The Government issued revised budget estimates today for the current fiscal year, showing expenditures at $97.2 billion, down $700 million from the estimate in the January budget.

Receipts were put at $91.5 billion. This was down $1.5 billion from January, mainly because the tax cut was passed later than the original budget had assumed. This delay will result in increased refunds next spring.

The deficit is now estimated at $5.7 billion instead of the $4.9 billion estimated in January. This is a reduction from the $8.3 billion deficit in the fiscal year 1964 that ended last June.

Although there were sizable reductions from the January spending estimates in eight Government departments, by far the biggest was in defense spending. This is now estimated at $48.6 billion compared with $50 billion in January.

The biggest increase from January was in agriculture spending, which is up nearly $1 billion.

**Campaign Statement**

In another development today the White House released another in its series of brief statements on the major economic issues in the campaign. Today's was entitled "Responsible and Effective Fiscal Policy" and essentially restated policies already announced by the Administration.

The statement reiterated the policy that the Government should aim for a balanced budget only when the economy was operating at its "full potential." At times when men and machines are idle, it said, "we must take steps to stimulate production and create jobs, to restore the health of the economy—even though these measures may temporarily add to the deficit."

The statement also said that "fiscal policy must be constantly alert to the danger that a steady growth in revenues relative to expenditures could choke off our economic expansion, as it did in the late nineteen-fifties."

**Congress Credited**

To avert such a "fiscal drag," resulting from the rapid growth of receipts, the statement said there were several possibilities. They included "further tax reductions, increases for top-priority Federal programs and an increased flow of funds to state and local authorities."

"The size of these adjustments and the choice among them at any given time," the statement concluded, "must and will depend on the changing needs of our people, the state of our economy, and the demands of national security—not on some rigid mechanical formula fixed for years in advance."

This was an apparent refer-

Continued on Page 19, Column 4

# GOLDWATER EXHORTS 18,000 IN GARDEN 'VICTORY' RALLY; HITS JOHNSON 'DADDYISM'

The New York Times (by Larry Morris)
OVATION: Crowd in Madison Square Garden hails Barry Goldwater, in the foreground

## 5,000 ON STREETS

### Candidate Is Cheered for 28 Minutes—Scores Busing

*Text of Goldwater speech will be found on Page 30.*

By PETER KIHSS

Senator Barry Goldwater received a deafening 28-minute ovation at Madison Square Garden last night and then went on to predict he would win the Presidency next week in "the major political upset of the century."

More than 18,000 persons jammed the arena, and 5,000 others who were unable to get in listened as loudspeakers brought the program out to 49th Street west of Eighth Avenue.

The Republican Presidential nominee was interrupted with applause and cheers at almost every phrase of a speech that took him 35 minutes. Some of his points appeared to be directed at his New York City audience as he made his only appearance here in the campaign.

**For Neighborhood Schools**

He set the crowd to roaring when he declared: "If you ever hear me quoted as promising to make you free by forcibly busing your children from your chosen neighborhood school to some other one just to meet an arbitrary racial quota—look again because somebody is kidding you!

"I believe in our system of neighborhood schools, and I want to see them preserved and improved. I don't want to see them destroyed or be sacrificed by a futile exercise in sociology which will accomplish nothing—but lose much."

He added, "My friends, these are not matters of civil rights—they are matters of common

Continued on Page 30, Column 1

## Johnson, in South, Decries 'Radical' Goldwater Ideas

By CHARLES MOHR
Special to The New York Times

COLUMBIA, S. C., Oct. 26—President Johnson, making a determined attempt to reverse Republican trends in the South, said today that Senator Barry Goldwater of Arizona had advanced "the most radical proposals that have ever been made to the American people."

"Under the wild charges and the impulsive statements of the opposition," Mr. Johnson said, "is hidden a deadly intention that would initiate policies which I think would radically change the American way of life."

The President also told a crowd at Jacksonville, Fla., that he could recall Presidential campaigns from those of Woodrow Wilson to those of John F. Kennedy and Richard M. Nixon.

"But none of these men tried to split our country wide open, none of these men preached hate," he said.

**Travels With Southerners**

Mr. Johnson, who spent last night in Orlando, Fla., campaigned today at Jacksonville, Macon, Ga., Augusta, Ga., and Columbia. In Florida and Georgia, he traveled under the sheltering canopy of major Southern Democratic politicians, who have rallied to the national ticket as they have not done since the days of the New Deal.

Georgia's Governor, Carl E. Sanders, said in introducing the President on the steps of the Macon City Hall that "for 100 years our hearts and our votes have belonged to the Democratic party."

The President drew large crowds along streets and highways wherever he went. They were liberally sprinkled with pro-Goldwater posters, but the political climate was warm.

**Seemed to Wince**

Mr. Johnson has shaken so many hands in recent days that he seemed to wince with pain occasionally today as overenthusiastic voters grabbed and clutched his bandaged fingers.

Mr. Johnson recalled to audiences that he was the only President born and reared in the South since Woodrow Wilson, and said:

"I know the burdens the South has borne. I know the ordeals that have tried the South through all these years."

At Augusta he spoke also of his personal vision of the Presidency, saying:

"I regard it as an office of

Continued on Page 20, Column 3

# 'UNFAIR' ASSERTION LAID TO KENNEDY

### Fair Campaign Group Says He Apparently Distorted Record of Keating

By R. W. APPLE Jr.

The Fair Campaign Practices Committee said yesterday that Robert F. Kennedy appeared to have distorted the record of Senator Kenneth B. Keating on the nuclear test-ban issue.

In a confidential letter to the former Attorney General, the committee asserted that his criticism of the Senator's position "is not only false and distorted, but also appears to be either a deliberate and cynical misrepresentation or the result of incredible carelessness, touched with luck."

Mr. Kennedy charged last week that his Republican opponent had "ridiculed" the treaty and had supported it only after its ratification by the Senate was certain.

Senator Keating replied with a denunciation of "preposterous distortions" and "outright lies" and asked the independent, nonpartisan committee to conduct an investigation.

The committee's letter, signed by Bruce L. Felknor, its executive director, listed a long series of statements by Mr. Keating in support of the treaty, including one made on May 27, 1963. The treaty was approved on

Continued on Page 26, Column 1

## Virginia Vote Lists By Race Ruled Out

By ANTHONY LEWIS
Special to The New York Times

WASHINGTON, Oct. 26—The Supreme Court struck down today Virginia laws requiring state officials to keep separate voting, property and tax records for whites and Negroes.

But the Court upheld another Virginia statute against a challenge by Negro complainants. This one requires that all divorce decrees show the race of the husband and the wife.

A three-judge Federal District Court in Alexandria, Va., had reached those conclusions about the state laws last April. Its decision was affirmed by the Supreme Court today summarily, without argument.

The Court divided 8 to 1 on

Continued on Page 18, Column 1

## London Urges Paris To Review Superjet

By SYDNEY GRUSON
Special to The New York Times

LONDON Oct. 26—Britain's new Labor Government has told France that it wants to "re-examine urgently" their joint project for the building of the world's first supersonic passenger plane, the Concorde.

This was announced today in a Government White Paper on measures to redress the deficit in Britain's balance of payments—the measure of what Britain spends and earns abroad.

The announcement confirmed reports that a number of so-called "prestige projects," including the Concorde, were un-

Continued on Page 15, Column 1

United Press International Telephoto
AMPHIBIOUS LANDING: United States Marines, in cooperation with Spanish troops, conduct maneuvers near Huelva, in southern Spain. Lying offshore is a fleet of ships supporting the troops participating in the joint exercise.

## NEWS INDEX


| | Page | | Page |
|---|---|---|---|
| Art | 41 | Music | 42-45 |
| Books | 36-37 | Obituaries | 39 |
| Bridge | 36 | Real Estate | 64 |
| Business | 52, 62-63 | Screen | 42-45 |
| Buyers | 52 | Ships and Air | 77 |
| Crossword | 37 | Society | 46 |
| Editorial | 38 | Sports | 47-50 |
| Events Today | 44 | Supreme Court | 18, 52 |
| Fashions | 32-33 | Theaters | 42-45 |
| Financial | 51-61 | TV and Radio | 78-79 |
| Food | 32-33 | U. N. Proceedings | 3 |
| Man in the News | 14 | Weather | 77 |

News Summary and Index, Page 41




## Yugoslavia May Get Fulbright Scholars

By FELIX BELAIR Jr.
Special to The New York Times

WASHINGTON, Oct. 26—The United States expects to sign soon after Election Day a treaty with Yugoslavia for the exchange of Fulbright scholars and professors between the two countries. It would be the first such agreement with a Communist country.

President Johnson has called for "building bridges" between the United States and Eastern Europe, but Congress during the last session seemed more intent on blocking existing arrangements with Communist countries than on building new links. It voted a flat ban on Food

Continued on Page 18, Column 1

"All the News That's Fit to Print"

# The New York Times.

LATE CITY EDITION
U. S. Weather Bureau Report (Page 78) forecasts:
Sunny today; clear tonight.
Fair and milder tomorrow.
Temp. Range: 63—48; yesterday: 60—48.

VOL. CXIV.... No. 39,001. NEW YORK, WEDNESDAY, NOVEMBER 4, 1964. TEN CENTS


# JOHNSON SWAMPS GOLDWATER AND KENNEDY BEATS KEATING; DEMOCRATS WIN LEGISLATURE

## KENNEDY EDGE 6-5

### Keating's Defeat Is Termed a 'Tragedy' by Rockefeller

**New York Vote**

PRESIDENT
Johnson, Dem. . . . . . 4,509,514
Goldwater, Rep. . . . . . 2,089,113
11,330 of 12,439 E.D.'s rptg.

SENATOR
Kennedy, Dem. . . . . . 3,479,976
Keating, Rep. . . . . . 2,857,023
11,318 of 12,439 E.D.'s rptg.

By R. W. APPLE Jr.

Robert F. Kennedy was elected to the United States Senate from New York yesterday in his first bid for elective office, overwhelming Republican Senator Kenneth B. Keating.

With more than 80 per cent of the vote counted, Mr. Kennedy held a 6-to-5 lead. Because most of the untallied vote was in heavily Democratic New York City, it appeared that the former Attorney General's plurality might reach 650,000.

Mr. Keating conceded defeat at 11:39 P.M. with the announcement at the Roosevelt Hotel that he had sent a congratulatory telegram to Mr. Kennedy.

Governor Rockefeller, standing beside the white-haired Rochester legislator, said Mr. Keating's defeat was "a tragedy for the state and nation."

**Runs Behind Johnson**

"Senator Keating, one of the great Senators in the history of New York, has been rolled under by a national landslide," the Governor added. "He waged a magnificent campaign."

Mr. Kennedy ran well behind President Johnson, who seemed to be headed for a record margin of 2.5 million votes or more in the state. The President won all of the state's 62 counties.

It thus appeared that about a million New York voters had split their ticket to cast votes for Mr. Johnson and Mr. Keating — but even this wasn't enough to make the Senate contest close.

A major surprise was the showing of the Liberal party, which had expected to deliver

Continued on Page 27, Column 4

## The Election at a Glance

**President**

| | Number of States* | Electoral Votes |
|---|---|---|
| Johnson | 45 | 486 |
| Goldwater | 6 | 52 |

*Includes Dist. of Columbia

**President—New York**

| | |
|---|---|
| Johnson | 4,509,514 |
| Goldwater | 2,089,113 |

Incomplete

**Senator—New York**

| | |
|---|---|
| Kennedy | 3,479,976 |
| Keating | 2,857,023 |

Incomplete

**The Senate**

| Newly Elected Senators | | Make-up of New Senate | |
|---|---|---|---|
| Democrats | 25 | Democrats | 65 |
| Republicans | 5 | Republicans | 30 |
| In doubt | 5 | In doubt | 5 |

**The House**

| | |
|---|---|
| Democrats elected | 261 |
| Republicans elected | 127 |
| In doubt | 47 |

## UPSET AT ALBANY

### Carlino and Mahoney Defeated—Special Session Expected

By LAYHMOND ROBINSON

A surge of Democratic votes swept the Republicans from control of the State Legislature yesterday for the first time in more than a quarter of a century.

The massive victory gave the Democrats a probable working majority of a dozen seats in the Assembly and a half dozen in the Senate.

Not since 1935, in the sweep of Franklin D. Roosevelt's New Deal, had the Democrats had control of both the houses. Not since 1938 had they held control of the Senate.

Toppled from their powerful posts in stunning upsets were Assembly Speaker Joseph F. Carlino of Long Beach, L. I., and Senate Majority Leader Walter J. Mahoney of Buffalo.

**Beaten by Outsiders**

Both suffered defeat at the hands of virtually unknown Democrats.

Mr. Carlino, the top Republican figure in the lower house for six years and an Assemblyman representing Nassau's Second Assembly District for 20 years, was beaten by Jerome R. McDougal Jr., a car salesman making his first race for public office.

Senator Mahoney, often called the most powerful man in the Legislature, was unseated by John H. Doerr of Buffalo in Erie County's 55th Senate District.

Another high-ranking Republican who lost was Senator MacNeil Mitchell of Manhattan, the most influential New York City member of the two houses.

In some districts in the suburbs and in upstate counties, Democrats captured Assembly and Senate seats for the first time in this century.

**Districting Fight Due**

At the last session, the G.O.P. had a 10-vote edge over the Democrats in the Assembly, holding 85 seats to 65 for the Democrats. In the Senate they had a 33-25 edge.

Although the Democrats ended this G.O.P. domination, the battle for control could be resumed again in December.

The Governor is expected to call a special session of the Legislature then to adopt a new plan for reapportioning seats in the two houses.

This reapportionment session will be controlled by the present members, with the Republicans in control.

Members elected yesterday do not take their seats until the

Continued on Page 33, Column 3

LYNDON BAINES JOHNSON

The New York Times

HUBERT HORATIO HUMPHREY

## TURNOUT IS HEAVY

### President Expected to Get 60% of Vote, With 44 States

By TOM WICKER

Lyndon Baines Johnson of Texas compiled one of the greatest landslide victories in American history yesterday to win a four-year term of his own as the 36th President of the United States.

Senator Hubert H. Humphrey of Minnesota, Mr. Johnson's running mate on the Democratic ticket, was carried into office as Vice President.

Mr. Johnson's triumph, giving him the "loud and clear" national mandate he had said he wanted, brought 44 states and the district of Columbia, with 486 electoral votes, into the Democratic column.

Senator Barry Goldwater, the Republican candidate, who sought to offer the people "a choice, not an echo" with a strongly conservative campaign, won only five states in the Deep South and gained a narrow victory in his home state of Arizona. Carrying it gave him a total of 52 electoral votes.

**Senator Plans Statement**

A heavy voter turnout favored the more numerous Democrats.

In Austin, Tex., Mr. Johnson appeared in the Municipal Auditorium to say that his victory was "a tribute to men and women of all parties."

"It is a mandate for unity, for a Government that serves no special interest," he said.

The election meant, he said, that "our nation should forget our petty differences and stand united before all the world."

Mr. Goldwater did not concede. A spokesman announced that the Senator would make no statement until 10 A.M. today in Phoenix.

**Johnson Carries Texas**

But the totals were not the only marks of the massive Democratic victory. Traditionally Republican states were bowled over like tenpins—Vermont, Indiana, Kansas, Nebraska, Wyoming, among others.

In New York, both houses of the Legislature were headed for Democratic control for the first time in years. Heralded Republicans like Charles H. Percy, the gubernatorial candidate in Illinois, went down to defeat.

Former Attorney General Robert F. Kennedy, riding Mr. Johnson's long coattails, overwhelmed Senator Kenneth B. Keating in New York.

But ticket splitting was widespread. And in the South, Georgia went Republican; never

Continued on Page 22, Column 1

## JOHNSON CRUSHES RIVAL IN JERSEY

### Lead Near 900,000, Topping Eisenhower's Record—Williams Re-elected

**New Jersey Vote**

PRESIDENT
Johnson, Dem. . . . . . 1,645,844
Goldwater, Rep. . . . . 853,708
4,001 of 4,603 E.D.'s rptg.

SENATOR
Williams, Dem. . . . . 1,474,523
Shanley, Rep. . . . . . 891,425
4,001 of 4,603 E.D.'s rptg.

By GEORGE CABLE WRIGHT

President Johnson won New Jersey's 17 electoral votes yesterday in the biggest political victory ever scored in the state.

With 91 per cent of the vote tallied, the President held a record lead of nearly 900,000 votes over his Republican opponent, Senator Barry Goldwater.

Until yesterday, the record plurality for a Presidential candidate in New Jersey was the 756,605-vote margin rolled up by President Eisenhower, a Republican, in 1956.

In sweeping at least 19, and possibly all of the state's 21 counties, Mr. Johnson carried to victory with him incumbent Democratic Senator Harrison A. Williams Jr. Democrats also captured a majority of the state's 15 seats in the House of Representatives for the first time since 1912.

In the present Congress, Republicans hold eight of the seats. On the basis of incomplete returns from yesterday's balloting, Democrats won at least 10 seats.

The Democratic candidate James J. Howard also held a narrow lead over his Republican opponent, Marcus Daly, in an

Continued on Page 32, Column 4

## Connecticut Votes 2-1 for President; All Democrats Win

**Connecticut Vote**

PRESIDENT
(Complete)
Johnson, D. . . . . . . . 825,416
Goldwater, R. . . . . . . 392,556

SENATOR
Dodd, D. . . . . . . . . . 779,252
Lodge, R. . . . . . . . . . 425,376

By RICHARD H. PARKE

President Johnson led a sweeping Democratic victory in Connecticut yesterday.

His better than 2-to-1 margin over Senator Barry Goldwater eclipsed the previous record plurality in a Presidential race in the state. Mr. Johnson's plurality was 432,860. The earlier record had been set by President Dwight D. Eisenhower in 1956 when he defeated Adlai E. Stevenson by 306,758 votes.

Senator Thomas J. Dodd, the Democratic incumbent, also triumphed easily over his Republican opponent, former Gov. John Davis Lodge. But the 57-year-old Senator ran about 75,000 votes behind the President.

One result of President Johnson's landslide was the defeat of the state's only Republican Congressman, Representative Abner W. Sibal of the Fourth (Fairfield County) District. Mr. Sibal lost the normally Republican district to former Representative Donald J. Irwin, a

Continued on Page 32, Column 1

## SOUTH REVERSES VOTING PATTERNS

### Goldwater Makes Inroads, but More Electoral Votes Go to the President

By JOHN HERBERS
Special to The New York Times

ATLANTA, Nov. 3—President Johnson carried a majority of Southern states tonight by turning the normal voting patterns inside out.

The rural Deep South, solidly Democratic in the past, voted for Senator Barry Goldwater of Arizona on the Republican ticket. The states on the border of the region, which had gone Republican in recent Presidential elections, returned to the Democrats.

But so strong was the Goldwater tide in the Deep South that seven Republican Congressional candidates rode to victory on the Senator's coattails from districts that had been Democratic since Reconstruction.

The Republicans made their biggest gains in Alabama, where five candidates for Congress defeated Democratic opponents.

President Johnson carried Virginia, North Carolina, Florida, Tennessee, Arkansas and Texas with a total of 81 electorial votes. Senator Goldwater carried Louisiana, Mississippi, Alabama, Georgia and South Carolina with a total of 47 electorial votes.

South Carolina and Mississippi had not voted for Repub-

Continued on Page 24, Column 2

## Democrats Are Assured Of Majorities in Congress

### House Gain for Democrats

By JOHN D. MORRIS

Democrats strengthened their control of the House of Representatives in yesterday's elections, scoring substantial gains in all regions except the South.

With returns from Congressional races still incomplete early this morning, the trend indicated a Democratic pickup of at least 20 seats and possibly 30 or more.

The Republicans nevertheless scored spectacular breakthroughs in the South, winning five of Alabama's eight seats, one of Mississippi's five and at least one of Georgia's 10.

Those gains were more than offset, however, by the loss of both of their Texas seats and by heavy Democratic gains in other parts of the country.

The House division in the expiring 88th Congress is 257 Democrats and 178 Republicans. This credits five vacancies to the parties last holding the seats. Three were occupied by Democrats and two by Republicans.

With 218 needed for a major-

Continued on Page 21, Column 1

### 3 G.O.P. Senators Lose

By E. W. KENWORTHY

The Democrats appeared virtually certain today of maintaining a nearly 2-to-1 majority in the United States Senate.

At 3 A.M. the Democrats had won 25 of the 35 contests in yesterday's elections. These, added to their 40 holdovers, assured them of 65 seats when the Eighty-ninth Congress convenes in January.

The Republicans, at the same hour, had won only five seats—in Vermont, Nebraska, Delaware, Arizona and Hawaii—all of which were won by incumbent Senators. These, added to 25 holdovers, assured the Republicans of at least 30 seats.

The party line-up when Congress adjourned last month was 66 Democrats and 34 Republicans.

By 3 A.M. the Democrats had captured three seats from the Republicans.

In New York, Robert F. Kennedy, former Attorney General, a brother of President Kennedy,

Continued on Page 20, Column 1

## STATE DEMOCRATS GAIN SIX IN HOUSE

### Lindsay and Other Liberal Republicans Keep Seats

By WARREN WEAVER Jr.

Democrats swept through the New York Congressional delegation in yesterday's election, unseating six Republican Representatives and threatening the House seat of a seventh.

In the wake of the Johnson victory, the Democrats increased their strength in the delegation from 20 to 26 while the number of Republicans dropped from 21 to 14, with one district in doubt.

Although they failed to dislodge any of the three New York City Republican Congressmen, Democratic candidates scored victories elsewhere across the state. They took two seats in Nassau County, one in Westchester, one in the Hudson Valley and two in Western New York.

Among the chief Republican survivors was Representative John V. Lindsay of Manhattan, who won by a 65,000-vote margin in his East Side district.

Other Republicans to retain their seats were Representative Seymour Halpern of Queens, who like Mr. Lindsay had opposed Senator Barry Goldwater, and, Representative Ogden R.

Continued on Page 24, Column 3



## G.O.P. Grip Broken In Suburban Voting

By JOHN SIBLEY

Traditional Republican bastions in the suburbs crumbled before the Johnson onslaught yesterday, and the President carried with him many local Democratic candidates in nearby New York and New Jersey communities.

Widespread ticket-splitting showed, however, that Republican suburbanites were not forsaking their party so much as they were renouncing its Presidential nominee, Senator Barry Goldwater.

Westchester County, for the first time since 1912, gave a plurality to a Democratic Presidential candidate. Rockland County went Democratic for the first time since Franklin D. Roosevelt carried the county in 1936 and for only the fourth time in 100 years.

Long Island's suburbs, too, went to the President. Mr. Johnson became the first Democratic Presidential candidate in modern

Continued on Page 33, Column 3

## ROMNEY IS VICTOR; PERCY'S BID FAILS

### Democrats Likely to Achieve Gain in Governorships

By JOSEPH A. LOFTUS

Democrats gave a good account of themselves in 25 contests for Governor yesterday, but it was a Republican who produced the spectacular.

Gov. George Romney, running aloof from Senator Barry Goldwater, set off a Michigan ticket-splitting spree to win re-election and thereby planted himself firmly in the thin front line of 1968 Presidential possibilities.

While Senator Goldwater gathered barely a third of Michigan's votes, the Governor defeated Neil Staebler with more than 55 per cent of the tally.

Strong Goldwater supporters "cut" Governor Romney, but the latter improved on his own 1962 vote totals in the labor-Democratic areas of Detroit and Flint-Saginaw.

The Republicans failed to capture a major prize, the Illinois governorship. The defeated nominee, Charles H. Percy, had figured in Presidential talk for the future.

Gov. Otto J. Kerner won a second term in Illinois despite the failure of Mayor Richard Daley's organization to deliver Chicago majorities as big as those Mr. Kerner won there four years ago.

Nationally the Democrats seemed likely to score a net

Continued on Page 24, Column 4

## Summary of International News: Wilson Acts to Nationalize Steel

*Following is a summary of foreign news. A full report begins on the first page of the second part.*

**Labor Offers Program**

Britain's new Labor Government offered a program of controversial legislation to Parliament. Headed by a demand for renationalization of the steel industry, the proposals indicate one of the bitterest sessions in parliamentary history.

**French Explain Aim**

Foreign Minister Maurice Couve de Murville told the French Parliament that the United States and Europe should develop separate, but not necessarily hostile, policies. In Washington, officials predicted that a major crisis for Atlantic unity would arise at a NATO meeting in December.

**Bolivian Troops Revolt**

A military revolt broke out in Bolivia and appeared to be spreading across the country. A truce designed to open the way for efforts "to resolve the present crisis" facing the Government of President Victor Paz Estenssoro was announced. In neighboring Chile, Eduardo Frei Montalva was inaugurated as the country's 28th President. In Cuba workers will vote Dec. 2 for worker councils.

**Soviet Voices Concern**

The Soviet Union expressed concern to the United States over the situation along the Cambodian-South Vietnamese border. In Pnompenh, Prince Norodom Sihanouk said his nation was ready to retaliate against any further border incursions by South Vietnamese forces. In Saigon, United States officials raised the casualty toll in Sunday's bombardment of the Bienhoa air base to 76 Americans, of whom four were dead.



## WHITE BACKLASH DOESN'T DEVELOP

### Vote in Suburbs in North Is Strong for President

By ANTHONY LEWIS

Rich and poor, Protestant and Roman Catholic and Jew, farmer and city-dweller and suburbanite all showed marked shifts toward President Johnson in yesterday's extraordinary election.

Only in the Deep South did Senator Barry Goldwater score any significant gains for the Republican ticket over four years ago. Riding the crest of the racial issue there, he swung Mississippi, Alabama, Georgia, South Carolina and Louisiana to his party.

The white backlash, on which Mr. Goldwater had counted so strongly, failed to materialize in most parts of the North. Only among voters of Polish and other East European origins were there signs of this resentment toward Negroes, and even this phenomenon was scattered

Continued on Page 26, Column 1

**NEWS INDEX**


| | Page | | Page |
|---|---|---|---|
| Books | 36-37 | Music | 44-47 |
| Bridge | 36 | Obituaries | 39 |
| Business | 58, 62 | Real Estate | 63 |
| Buyers | 80 | Screen | 44-47 |
| Crossword | 37 | Ships and Air | 78 |
| Editorial | 38 | Society | 50-51 |
| Events Today | 51 | Sports | 53-58 |
| Fashions | 49 | Theaters | 44-47 |
| Financial | 59-61 | TV and Radio | 79 |
| Food | 49 | U. N. Proceedings | 43 |
| Man in the News | 42 | Weather | 78 |


News Summary and Index, Page 41

## PRESIDENT SEES A UNITY MANDATE

### In Victory Talk, He Pays Tribute to Predecessor

*The text of Johnson's talk will be found on Page 22.*

By CHARLES MOHR
Special to The New York Times

AUSTIN, Tex., Wednesday, Nov. 4—President Johnson said early this morning that his election was a "mandate for unity" and for a "government that provides equal opportunity for all and special privilege for none."

Mr. Johnson, obviously deeply moved by his landslide victory, told a crowd at the Municipal Auditorium here that it was a tribute to "the program begun by our beloved President John F. Kennedy."

Of the returns, Mr. Johnson said, "I doubt there have ever been so many people seeing so many things alike" on an Election Day.

Earlier, Mr. Johnson had said of Senator Barry Goldwater's refusal to concede that it was "purely a matter for the individual involved—whatever reasons he may have, I don't know."

He also said that the election was going "about as we expected."

Mr. Johnson appeared on the Municipal Auditorium stage with his wife and two daughters to a long ovation.

He said that "no words are

Continued on Page 22, Column 6

## Salinger Is Losing; Johnson Wins State

By LAWRENCE E. DAVIES
Special to The New York Times

SAN FRANCISCO, Wednesday, Nov. 4—President Johnson captured California's 40 electoral votes in his triumph over Senator Barry Goldwater in yesterday's election.

On the basis of the incomplete count of ballots, however, the President's former press secretary, Senator Pierre Salinger, apparently lost his Senatorial battle to George Murphy, the Republican nominee.

Mr. Salinger late last night refused to concede defeat but said he "would be less than candid if I didn't say the vote doesn't look good." Some of his campaign strategists agreed that the results "looked bad" but declared they would await developments for a few hours before having anything definite to say.

Mr. Salinger, who has been

Continued on Page 34, Column 4

"All the News That's Fit to Print"

# The New York Times.

LATE CITY EDITION
U. S. Weather Bureau Report (Page 66) forecasts: Sunny and cold today; clear and cold tonight. Fair tomorrow. Temp. range: 37—24; yesterday: 38—22.

VOL. CXIV..No. 39,079. NEW YORK, THURSDAY, JANUARY 21, 1965. TEN CENTS



# JOHNSON, TAKING OATH, PLEDGES EFFORTS TO BRING AN END TO TYRANNY AND MISERY; BOTH PARTIES' LEADERS ACCLAIM ADDRESS

THE PRESIDENT: Chief Justice Earl Warren administering oath of office to President Johnson at the Capitol yesterday. Mrs. Johnson held the Bible during the ceremony. Vice President Hubert H. Humphrey is at rear.

Associated Press Wirephotos

THE VICE PRESIDENT: Hubert H. Humphrey being sworn in by Speaker of the House John W. McCormack. Fred Gates, center, an old friend of Mr. Humphrey, holds the Bible.

## NATION EXHORTED

### Thousands Hear Plea for U.S. Dedication to Justice for All

*Text of President's address will be found on Page 16.*

By TOM WICKER
Special to The New York Times

WASHINGTON, Jan. 20 — Lyndon Baines Johnson of Texas began his first full term as President today with a pledge that the nation aspired "to nothing that belongs to others" but sought only "man's dominion over tyranny and misery."

Mr. Johnson spoke for 22 minutes after being sworn in by Chief Justice Earl Warren at 12:03 P.M. A crowd of thousands, seated and standing in the east plaza of the Capitol grounds in near-freezing temperatures, saw the ceremony and heard the Inaugural Address.

Before the President took his oath, Hubert Horatio Humphrey, the former Senator from Minnesota, was sworn in by Speaker of the House John W. McCormack as Vice President. Up to that moment, Mr. McCormack had been first in the line of succession to the Presidency.

Mrs. Johnson, a colorful figure in a brilliant red outfit, held the family Bible on which her husband's left hand rested as he repeated the words that reaffirmed him as the 36th President of the United States.

Mr. Johnson had asked his wife to hold the Bible.

**Johnsons Watch Parade**

After the Inauguration ceremony, which was completed virtually on schedule just after 12:30 P.M., Mr. and Mrs. Johnson watched the Inaugural parade for about two and a half hours.

They were in a heated reviewing stand in front of the White House, and behind bulletproof glass. Stringent protective measures were invoked all day as the President appeared before large crowds.

Mr. Johnson obviously enjoyed himself as he waved to the marchers, greeted friends visiting his reviewing stand, and at one point put his beagle, Him, in the President's chair for the television cameras.

It was 5:13 P.M. and nearly dark before the President and his wife left the stand and went into the White House.

The President did not leave the crowd without a parting word. As the parade dispersed, he took the microphone in his reviewing stand and told those immediately around it:

"Thank you so much. You are very lovely people and we will try very hard to be worthy of your trust and confidence."

Mr. Johnson frequently refers to himself in the first person plural.

Mr. Johnson gave his Inau-

Continued on Page 16, Column 1

## Moses Criticizes Banker; Defends Finances of Fair

By ROBERT ALDEN

Robert Moses, president of the World's Fair Corporation, denounced yesterday as "false" charges of financial secrecy at the fair. The charges had been made by George S. Moore, chairman and president of the First National City Bank and a former fi-

*Text of Moses' statement is printed on Page 25.*

nancial adviser to the fair. Mr. Moses also made some allegations of his own.

In one instance, Mr. Moses said that the First National City Bank had "attempted to persuade the fair to make a $750,000 loan" to a pavilion—the Better Living Center—that was already $6 million in debt to the bank.

Mr. Moses said that the fair's finance committee, with Mr. Moore absent, had advised against making the loan, which was not granted.

**Documents Used**

Mr. Moses made his reply, which included several revelations on the management of the fair, as a result of the resignation on Monday of Mr. Moore, chairman of the fair's finance committee, and four other banker advisers.

In his statement, supported by 20 documents, Mr. Moses said: "Sabotaging the fair is no service to the community. We need boosters, not knockers."

The other bankers who resigned on Monday were David Rockefeller, president of the Chase Manhattan Bank; William S. Renchard, president of the Chemical Bank New York Trust Company; Dale E. Sharp, vice chairman of the board of the Morgan Guaranty Company,

Continued on Page 25, Column 4

## PARIS AND BONN SPUR UNITY MOVES

### But Little Headway Is Made by de Gaulle and Erhard on Nuclear Problem

By DREW MIDDLETON
Special to The New York Times

PARIS, Jan. 20—France and West Germany agreed today on new initiatives toward reunification of Germany and political unity in the European Common Market.

But, after six hours of discussions, President de Gaulle and Chancellor Ludwig Erhard had made little headway on the key issue of German aspirations on nuclear defenses.

The Germans still seek a role in Western nuclear strategy through the mixed-manned nuclear fleet proposed by the United States, the broader Atlantic nuclear force proposed by Britain, or a combination of the two.

The results of the two-day conference between the French and German leaders were made known by Karl Günther von Hase, German Secretary of State for Information, and Claude Lebel, official spokesman of the French Foreign Ministry, at a news conference.

The de Gaulle-Erhard talks were held at the President's chateau at Rambouillet outside Paris.

**Diplomats Assess Results**

Allied diplomats assessing results of the talks thought that, on the basis of present information, Dr. Erhard had gained more from the conference than General de Gaulle.

It was decided that discussions of plans for political unity in the Common Market trade bloc would be held at the foreign ministers' level, as Germany had proposed.

Even more advantageous for the Germans in this election year is the agreement to talk about German unity with the British and United States Governments. Reunification, one German source noted, remains a highly emotional issue in the Federal Republic.

General de Gaulle believes that reunification is incompatible with German moves for a role in nuclear defense. But Bonn's position remains little changed, according to Mr. von Hase.

The German spokesman said

Continued on Page 3, Column 5

## 3 STRIKE LEADERS GIVEN JAIL TERMS

### Welfare Unions Fined and 19 Defendants Convicted in Condon-Wadlin Case

By EMANUEL PERLMUTTER

Supreme Court Justice Irving H. Saypol found 19 leaders of the Welfare Department strike guilty of criminal contempt yesterday for flouting his order that they end the walkout. He sentenced three of them to 30 days in jail and fined them $250 each.

Justice Saypol also fined each of their two unions $250. But he withheld action until next Monday on a request by Assistant Corporation Counsel William M. Murphy that the other defendants also be fined $250 each.

The three sentenced to the New York County jail were not imprisoned yesterday. Justice Saypol stayed execution so that the city could go into court at 10 A.M. today with formal commitment orders.

Those fined and ordered to prison were Joseph Tepedino, president, and Ishmael Lahab, first vice president, of the Social Service Employes Union, and Alan R. Viani, president of Local 371 of the American Federation of State, County and Municipal Employes. All were paroled in the custody of their lawyers.

Yesterday's action came as a result of legal efforts by the city to get the welfare investigators and other workers to end their 17-day-old strike in violation of the state's Condon-Wadlin Act, which prohibits strikes by public employes. The

Continued on Page 26, Column 5

## 2 Alabama Officials Clash Over Arrests In Negro Vote Drive

By JOHN HERBERS
Special to The New York Times

SELMA, Ala., Jan. 20—A rift in the white community over Sheriff James G. Clark's militant actions in dealing with Negroes attempting to register as voters broke into the open today while the sheriff was arresting 150 applicants on a charge of unlawful assembly.

Sheriff Clark and Selma's Director of Public Safety, Wilson Baker, stood 10 feet apart in front of the Dallas County Courthouse and glared at each other. They communicated through representatives.

The city administration and a number of business leaders had been trying to adopt a more moderate course in dealing with the Rev. Dr. Martin Luther King Jr.'s direct-action campaign against voter discrimination. Sheriff Clark has angrily turned down this suggestion.

The hefty sheriff, surrounded by deputies and a special

Continued on Page 22, Column 3

## GALAMISON SEIZED IN SCHOOL BOYCOTT

### Minister Is Charged With Urging Defiance of Law

By MARTIN TOLCHIN

The Rev. Milton A. Galamison was arrested yesterday on a charge of exhorting children to defy the state's compulsory education law as he led the boycott of Public School 617, Brooklyn, into its second day.

The clergyman, who led two citywide school boycotts last winter with impunity, was paroled in the custody of his lawyers by Family Court Judge Justine Wise Polier. She set trial for Feb. 3.

That is Mr. Galamison's target date for extending the boycott to all 15 of the so-called "600" schools for violent, disruptive children. He charges that an inferior education is provided in these schools.

In the courtroom, the clergyman's counsel was served with a temporary injunction granted on Tuesday by State Supreme Court Justice M. Henry Martuscello.

The injunction was defied early yesterday morning by six adult pickets from the Citywide Committee for Integrated Schools, who intercepted children on their way to the antiquated, red brick schoolhouse. One picket shepherded some of the children

Continued on Page 22, Column 4

## HUMPHREY SWORN AS VICE PRESIDENT

### Family Watches as He Takes Over Post Vacant Since Kennedy Assassination

By E. W. KENWORTHY
Special to The New York Times

WASHINGTON, Jan. 20 — A few minutes before noon today, Hubert Horatio Humphrey —his right hand upraised and his left hand on an old Bible belonging to his wife's family—intoned after Speaker John W. McCormack, "So help me God," and the nation had a Vice President for the first time since Nov. 22, 1963.

The 38th Vice President turned and shook hands with President Johnson. Then he took two steps and kissed the girl he fell in love with back in Huron, S. D., when he worked in his father's drugstore there.

As Mr. Humphrey left the Mayflower Hotel this morning —where he and his wife occupied the suite used in 1933 by Franklin Delano Roosevelt before his inauguration — he told reporters that his working philosophy was "that you only live once and you ought to live each day as happily, fully and meaningfully as you can."

It was a happy, full and meaningful day for Hubert and Muriel Buck Humphrey.

Always the despair of his staff for his indifference to schedules, Mr. Humphrey said this morning that as Vice President he would make a major effort "to be on time."

He was on time all day — at the National City Christian

Continued on Page 18, Column 1

## Congress Praises Speech As a Call to High Purpose

By JOHN D. MORRIS
Special to The New York Times

WASHINGTON, Jan. 20—Members of Congress acclaimed President Johnson's first Inaugural Address today as a fitting statement of the country's abiding principles, aspirations and goals. Republicans and Democrats agreed that the President had sketched, in appropriately broad and nonpartisan terms, the lofty objectives behind which all patriotic Americans should unite.

In their public comments, many used the words "magnificent" and "inspirational" to describe the speech.

Some privately expressed appraisals, however, suggested that the President's style of delivery was considerably less inspirational than the substance of what he said.

**Possible Explanation**

Such remarks were volunteered by several legislators as a possible explanation why the President was not applauded more often or more enthusiastically.

It was doubtful, in any case, whether the address would affect the treatment of the President's legislative program. His State of the Union Message Jan. 4 and subsequent special messages to Congress were more to the point in that regard, members observed.

Since reaction to those messages has been largely favorable, prospects for substantial legislative achievements by the Administration were already good.

If the Inaugural improved those prospects, Congressional comments indicated that it did so by encouraging a spirit of

Continued on Page 17, Column 6

## SECURITY FORCES ARE LARGEST EVER

### Safety Is Insured by F.B.I., Secret Service and 5,000 Policemen and Troops

By FELIX BELAIR Jr.
Special to The New York Times

WASHINGTON, Jan. 20—The heaviest concentration of security forces ever assembled in the nation's capital was mobilized today to insure the safety of the President and Vice President and to control the record Inaugural crowds.

Plans worked out months ago by the Secret Service called into duty the staffs of other Treasury enforcement agencies as well as the Federal Bureau of Investigation and 5,000 metropolitan and armed forces police, National Guardsmen and regular troops.

While taking the oath of office, President Johnson and Vice President Humphrey were protected on three sides by a bulletproof glass screen. Atop the Inaugural platform and concealed from the thousands that thronged the Capitol plaza, special agents surveyed the scene with automatic weapons ready.

**A Helicopter Hovers**

A Secret Service helicopter hovered overhead, and at the base of the Capitol dome other agents with rifles, Army television scanners and walkie-talkie transmitters kept watch for any sudden or untoward movement throughout the President's Inaugural Address. Plainclothes policemen walked an unaccustomed beat on the roofs of the Senate and House wings of the Capitol building.

Most of the protective system was set in motion weeks ago, however, and remained unseen during the ceremonies today. Long before the President entered his newly armored limousine with its bulletproof glass top and rear viewing win-

Continued on Page 17, Column 8

## Young Reported Ready to Quit As State Republican Chairman

Special to The New York Times

ALBANY, Jan. 20—Fred A. Young has decided to resign as Republican state chairman.

Reliable sources reported tonight that Mr. Young's resignation would be announced within the next few days. It was not known whether a successor had been chosen.

All indications were that Mr. Young was leaving of his own volition and that his departure had no connection with the defeat his party suffered in November.

The chairman was on his way to Chicago tonight for the meeting of the Republican National Committee that begins there on Friday.

Mr. Young, who is 60 years old, is a hearty man who revels in the intrigues of politics. Before assuming the chairmanship two years ago, he served as an Assemblyman, a State Senator and Presiding Judge of the New York Court of Claims.

According to well-posted informants, Mr. Young is to undertake a study of the state's land-acquisition policies that could lead to a complete revision of the condemnation statutes.

In 1963, before Mr. Young's appointment to the $30,000-a-year party position, an attempt was made to persuade Carl Spad of Westchester County, Governor Rockefeller's appointments secretary, to become state chairman. Mr. Spad refused, but politicians here thought it possible he would be asked again.

Another possibility is William L. Pfeiffer, of Old Westbury, L. I., a former state chairman who recently joined Mr. Rocke-

Continued on Page 21, Column 3

## Paradox and Reason

### President Blends Religion and Politics In a Strong Appeal for Faith and Unity

By JAMES RESTON
Special to The New York Times

News Analysis

WASHINGTON, Jan. 20 — President Johnson's Inauguration was a dramatization of the American Dream. It was all there, "bigger and better" than ever before: The poor boy, the country boy at the pinnacle of the world; the lovely wife holding the Bible for the oath; the eternal American combination of religion and politics; and above all, the optimism of America transmitted by a man-made satellite in the sky to a distracted and pessimistic world.

The ceremony was one long paradox: A sermon and a circus; a prayer and a parade; the Bible and the ballyhoo. Change is our problem, said the 36th President of the United States; reason and faith our shield; unity our only hope—this thrown out with painfully slow evangelical overtones to an unreasoning, skeptical and disunited world.

The echoes of past Presidential inaugurals were unmistakable today. "The problems are new," said Teddy Roosevelt in his Inaugural Address, "the tasks before us differ from the tasks set before our fathers who founded and preserved this republic."

"Ours is a time of change," said President Johnson, "rapid, and fantastic change, baring the secrets of nature, multiplying

Continued on Page 17, Column 6

## President Dances With Many at Ball

Special to The New York Times

WASHINGTON, Jan. 20 — Thousands of Democrats ended hours of official celebration tonight by observing the ballroom style of Lyndon B. Johnson, one of the rare Presidents to dance at his own Inaugural ball.

The huge ball, held at five places because of the demand for tickets at $25 each, drew about 28,000 persons to the National Guard Armory and the Sheraton-Park, Mayflower, Shoreham and Statler-Hilton Hotels. Previously only at John F. Kennedy's Inaugural ball were there so many locations.

The President and his party left the White House at 9:18 P.M. to attend the inaugural balls. He was in black tie.

The Johnsons' first stop was at the Mayflower, where the dance floor in front of the Pres-

Continued on Page 18, Column 3

NEWS INDEX



| | Page | | Page |
|---|---|---|---|
| Art | 28 | Man in the News | 13 |
| Books | 28-29 | Music | 21-23 |
| Bridge | 28 | Obituaries | 31 |
| Business | 40-41, 49 | Real Estate | 50 |
| Buyers | 40 | Screen | 21-23 |
| Chess | 28 | Ships and Air | 61 |
| Crossword | 29 | Society | 36 |
| Editorial | 30 | Sports | 34-39 |
| Events Today | 36 | Theaters | 21-23 |
| Fashions | 24 | TV and Radio | 63 |
| Financial | 41-50 | U. N. Proceedings | 8 |
| Food | 24-25 | Weather | 61 |

News Summary and Index, Page 33

"All the News That's Fit to Print"

# The New York Times

LATE CITY EDITION

Weather: Partial clearing today; fair, cool tonight and tomorrow. Temp. range: today 62-53; Sunday 68-48. Full U.S. report on Page 90.

VOL. CXVII..No. 40,245 — NEW YORK, MONDAY, APRIL 1, 1968 — 10 CENTS



# JOHNSON SAYS HE WON'T RUN; HALTS NORTH VIETNAM RAIDS; BIDS HANOI JOIN PEACE MOVES

## ROCKEFELLER URGES ALBANY LEADERS TO SPEED BUDGET

### Ready to Work With Them to Provide Funds as Fiscal Year Opens Today

By PETER KIHSS

Governor Rockefeller urged Republican and Democratic legislative leaders yesterday to agree quickly on a new budget as the state moved into the 1968-69 fiscal year today without a budget.

The Republican-controlled Senate has passed one version of the budget, but the Democratic-controlled Assembly is pondering a counter-version. The Governor said in a statement he was "ready to work with the leadership in both houses" for "a budget that meets the needs of the people of our state and provides the revenues necessary to finance it."

After the Legislature does act, the Governor will presumably seek a supplemental appropriation to restore some of the spending cuts that both parties' legislative fiscal committees make in his proposed school, urban, crime and construction programs. This is a traditional technique.

**Assembly May Act Today**

Fiscal aides to Assembly Speaker Anthony J. Travia analyzed the Senate proposals through the night. Mr. Travia himself said he was considering two interim moves. One would have the Assembly approve the budget appropriations and cuts already agreed on; the other would seek a temporary authorization for state spending at the rate for the last quarter of the fiscal year just ended.

Joseph Zaretzki, Senate Democratic minority leader, charged here yesterday that the budget bills rammed through the Senate early Saturday by the Republican leader, Earl Brydges, and his party followers aimed only "to get by next November's election."

Senator Zaretzki asserted that two of its key elements—

Continued on Page 38, Column 3

## Liberals Designate Javits; Nickerson Race Confused

**Baron May Enter Race**

By CLAYTON KNOWLES

The Liberal party State Committee designated Senator Jacob K. Javits for re-election late yesterday, but under conditions that confronted him with the prospect of waging a primary fight to gain the extra line on the voting machines.

A bloc of unionists in the party, contending that an endorsement of Mr. Javits would aid Richard M. Nixon in his Presidential bid, put up Murray Baron, a long-time Liberal leader. Although Mr. Baron lost, he rolled up enough votes to qualify to run in the June 18 primary.

The Liberals acted several hours before President Johnson's withdrawal. Mr. Baron came under heavy attack in the prevote debate as "more

Continued on Page 50, Column 1

**Johnson Causes Upset**

The contest for the Democratic Senate nomination in New York was thrown into confusion last night by President Johnson's announcement that he would not seek the party's nomination for re-election.

Eugene H. Nickerson, the organization's candidate for the nomination and a supporter of Senator Robert F. Kennedy, said of the Johnson announcement: "I was very surprised. It just comes as such a complete surprise to me that I think we have to sleep on it."

Representative Joseph Y. Resnick of Ellenville, a Senate candidate who supports President Johnson, sent a telegram to the President urging the President to reconsider his decision.

"Mr. President," the Resnick

Continued on Page 50, Column 5

## 3 Beachfront Hotels Destroyed by Fire In Rockaway Park

By LAWRENCE VAN GELDER

Flames spurred by howling ocean winds raged through the Rockaway Park section of Queens yesterday, destroying three beachfront hotels, damaging small stores and bungalows, charring police and fire equipment and forcing the evacuation of hundreds of residents.

As the number of alarms climbed swiftly to eight, more than 400 firemen and 60 pieces of equipment were pitted against the intense blaze, which sent up a column of gray smoke visible for more than a dozen miles in the afternoon sky.

Despite the fury of the fire and the menacing wind-whipped embers that flew through the neighborhood around Beach 116th Street and Ocean Promenade, no serious injuries were reported from the blaze, which was attributed by officials to three small children. Four firemen, however, were reported

Continued on Page 36, Column 4

## HOUSE PLAN SPURS INVESTING ABROAD

### Committee Asks Creation of Quasi-Public Corporation to Attract Private Capital

By FELIX BELAIR Jr.
By The Associated Press

WASHINGTON, March 31—The House Foreign Affairs Committee urged in a report today that the Federal Government consider creating a quasi-public corporation to promote private American investments in underdeveloped countries.

The report, originated by Representative Leonard Farbstein, Democrat of Manhattan, won the unanimous approval of the committee.

The gist of the report was that the investment guarantee program of the Agency for International Development was no longer able to attract sufficient private capital to spur economic growth in the poor countries of Latin America,

Continued on Page 8, Column 1

## TAX RISE PUSHED

### Increase in War Costs Cited—No Specific Cuts Suggested

By EILEEN SHANAHAN
Special to The New York Times

WASHINGTON, March 31—President Johnson called on Congress tonight to "move from debate to action, from talking to voting" on a tax increase.

He pledged himself to accept any appropriate reductions in Federal spending that Congress voted, but he proposed nothing specific in the way of economy moves.

He announced, in fact, that there would be an increase in Government outlays because of the war. These, he said, would amount to $2.5-billion in the current fiscal year, which ends June 30, and $2.6-billion in the next fiscal year.

What effect the President's decision not to run for re-election might have on the long fight over the tax increase and Government spending was not immediately clear. A lame duck President is usually considered to have greatly diminished power to influence Congress, but the President's removal of himself from the campaign could also remove some of the partisanship from the tax and spending issue.

**Deficit to Increase**

The increases the President announced in defense spending would raise the deficit for the current year to $22.3-billion and for next year to $20.5-billion, if the 10 per cent tax surcharge is not enacted, and assuming that there are no other changes in spending from the official January estimates.

If the tax increase is enacted, with April 1 the effective date for individuals and Jan. 1 for corporations, as the President has asked, this year's deficit would be $20.4-billion and next year's, $10.6-billion.

"Enactment of a tax increase now, together with expenditure control, is necessary to protect our security, continue our prosperity and meet the needs of our people," Mr. Johnson said.

He said he believed there

Continued on Page 30, Column 3

## DMZ IS EXEMPTED

### Johnson Sets No Time Limit on Halting of Air and Sea Blows

By MAX FRANKEL
Special to The New York Times

WASHINGTON, March 31—President Johnson announced tonight that he had ordered a halt in the air and naval bombardment of most of North Vietnam and invited the Hanoi Government to join him in a "series of mutual moves toward peace."

The President said:

"Tonight, in the hope that this action will lead to early talks, I am taking the first step to de-escalate the conflict. We are reducing—substantially reducing—the present level of hostilities. And we are doing so unilaterally and at once."

The President said that attacks would continue only in the area just north of the demilitarized zone, which separates North Vietnam from South Vietnam, and where, he said, the "continuing enemy build-up directly threatens allied forward positions and where movements of troops and supplies are clearly related to that threat."

**Hanoi's Stand Recalled**

The President set no time limit for his restraint order. Until now, North Vietnam has demanded an "unconditional"—apparently meaning permanent—halt in the bombing of all its territory and all other acts of war against it.

North Vietnam's restraint and other unspecified events, the President indicated, can make possible an early end of "even this limited bombing."

The areas to be spared, he said, include almost 90 per cent of North Vietnam's population and "most of its territory."

The White House refused to give a more specific geographical delineation.

[In Saigon, the United States command said that the order went into effect at 9 P.M. Sunday, New York time, when President Johnson began his address, The Associated Press reported. Page 15.]

At the same time, Mr. Johnson used a televised address to the nation to urge the Soviet Union and Britain to do everything possible to move from his "unilateral act of de-escalation" toward a genuine peace.

He designated Ambassador at Large W. Averell Harriman and the American Ambassador to Moscow, Llewellyn Thomp-

Continued on Page 28, Column 1

Associated Press

ADDRESSES THE NATION: President Johnson last night

## SURPRISE DECISION

### President Steps Aside in Unity Bid—Says 'House' Is Divided

*Text of Johnson's address will be found on Page 26.*

By TOM WICKER
Special to The New York Times

WASHINGTON, March 31—Lyndon Baines Johnson announced tonight: "I shall not seek and I will not accept the nomination of my party as your President."

Later, at a White House news conference, he said his decision was "completely irrevocable."

The President told his nationwide television audience:

"What we have won when all our people were united must not be lost in partisanship. I have concluded that I should not permit the Presidency to become involved in partisan decisions."

Mr. Johnson, acknowledging that there was "division in the American house," withdrew in the name of national unity, which he said was "the ultimate strength of our country."

"With American sons in the field far away," he said, "with the American future under challenge right here at home, with our hopes and the world's hopes for peace in the balance every day, I do not believe that I should devote an hour or a day of my time to any personal partisan causes or to any duties other than the awesome duties of this office, the Presidency of your country."

**Humphrey Race Possible**

Mr. Johnson left Senator Robert F. Kennedy of New York and Senator Eugene J. McCarthy of Minnesota as the only two declared candidates for the Democratic Presidential nomination.

Vice President Humphrey, however, will be widely expected to seek the nomination now that his friend and political benefactor, Mr. Johnson, is out of the field. Mr. Humphrey indicated that he would have a statement on his plans tomorrow.

The President informed Mr. Humphrey of his decision during a conference at the latter's apartment in southwest Washington today before the Vice President flew to Mexico City. There, he will represent the United States at the signing of a treaty for a Latin-American nuclear-free zone.

**Surprise to Aides**

If Mr. Humphrey should become a candidate, he would find most of the primaries foreclosed to him. Only those in the District of Columbia, New Jersey and South Dakota remain open.

Therefore, he would have to rely on collecting delegates in states without primaries and on White House support if he were to head off Mr. Kennedy and Mr. McCarthy.

Former Vice President Richard M. Nixon is the only announced major candidate for the Republican nomination, although Governor Rockefeller has said that he would accept the nomination if drafted.

Mr. Johnson's announcement tonight came as a stunning surprise even to close associates. His main political strategists, James H. Rowe of Washington, White House Special Assistant Marvin W. Watson, and Postmaster General Lawrence F. O'Brien, spent much of today conferring on campaign plans.

They were informed of what was coming just before Mr.

Continued on Page 27, Column 1

## Political Chiefs Stunned; Kennedy Sets News Parley

By SYLVAN FOX

Political leaders across the country reacted with shock, surprise and—in some cases—admiration to President Johnson's announcement last night that he would not seek re-election in November. Some political leaders immediately focused attention on Vice President Humphrey as a possible contender for the Democratic Presidential nomination.

Others suggested that Mr. Johnson's withdrawal could alter the position of Governor Rockefeller, who pulled out of contention for the Republican Presidential nomination on March 21.

Neither Mr. Humphrey nor Mr. Rockefeller was commenting immediately on his political plans in the light of Mr. Johnson's withdrawal.

Senator Robert F. Kennedy, like many others, was left almost speechless by the President's announcement.

"I don't know quite what to say," Senator Kennedy commented when he got the word of the President's decision. The Senator, a leading contender for the Democratic Presidential nomination, scheduled a news conference for 10 A.M. today.

Continued on Page 27, Column 4

## WISCONSIN WEIGHS IMPACT ON VOTING

### Primary Excitement Turns to Surprise—McCarthy and Nixon Wind Up Campaign

By DONALD JANSON
Special to The New York Times

MILWAUKEE, March 31—Excitement over a spirited contest between Senator Eugene J. McCarthy and President Johnson in the Wisconsin Democratic Presidential primary turned to surprise tonight with the President's announcement that he was not a candidate for re-election.

Thousands of Wisconsin voters, who had expected to choose between the two on Tuesday, saw and heard the President on television take himself out of the contest.

The announcement ended speculation that the Wisconsin primary, the first in the nation to have the President's name on the ballot, would produce a record vote.

It left only Senator McCarthy as an active candidate on the Democratic ballot and only former Vice President Richard M. Nixon as a major candidate on the Republican side. It eliminated the urgency that thousands of Republicans had felt to cross over to the Democratic contest to vote against the

Continued on Page 48, Column 1

The New York Times (by William E. Sauro)

AT ROCKAWAY PARK BLAZE: More than 400 firemen were called out to fight eight-alarm fire that raged on Beach 116th Street in the Rockaway Park section of Queens. Jamaica Bay is in rear. Four firemen were slightly hurt.

## Top Saigon Officials Confused By Refusal of Johnson to Run

By GENE ROBERTS
Special to The New York Times

SAIGON, South Vietnam, Monday, April 1—President Johnson's refusal to seek re-election plunged the top level of the South Vietnamese Government into confusion today and touched off a meeting of key American officials.

It was apparent, according to Americans who were at the presidential palace at the time, that President Johnson's announcement caught the South Vietnamese by surprise.

"Top advisers and officeholders began rushing toward the Vice President's office in obvious states of agitation," said one American who was waiting for a conference with Vice President Nguyen Cao Ky. "A few minutes later, Ky's military aide appeared and said all appointments had been canceled."

There was similar excitement at the United States Embassy. A receptionist said that no high officials were available for comment and explained that they were all in a top-level meeting.

There was also a rash of meetings at the headquarters of the military command here.

While many military officers and virtually all South Vietnamese officials are op-

Continued on Page 28, Column 5

NEWS INDEX



| | Page | | Page |
|---|---|---|---|
| Books | 43 | Man in the News | 2 |
| Bridge | 42 | Music | 56-59 |
| Business | 67-73 | Obituaries | 45 |
| Buyers | 67 | Real Estate | 73 |
| Chess | 42 | Screen | 56-59 |
| Congress Vote | 32 | Ships and Air | 89 |
| Crossword | 43 | Society | 60 |
| Editorials | 44 | Sports | 61-67 |
| Fashions | 54 | Theaters | 56-59 |
| Financial | 67-73 | TV and Radio | 90-91 |
| Food | 54 | U. N. Proceedings | 3 |
| Letters | 44 | Weather | 90 |



News Summary and Index, Page 47

"All the News That's Fit to Print"

# The New York Times

LATE CITY EDITION

Weather: Mostly sunny, mild today; fair tonight. Cool tomorrow. Temp. range: today 60-46; Sat. 65-50. Full U.S. report on Page 91.

SECTION ONE

VOL. CXVII....No. 40,272 — NEW YORK, SUNDAY, APRIL 28, 1968 — 40c beyond 50-mile zone from New York City, except Long Island. 75c beyond 200-mile radius. Higher in air delivery cities. — 50 CENTS



## COLUMBIA BOARD SCORES 'MINORITY' CRIPPLING CAMPUS

### Trustees Bar Amnesty for Students Who Took Over 5 University Buildings

### KIRK STRONGLY BACKED

### President Calls All Faculties to Meeting Today to Help Settle the Disruption

*Text of Columbia trustees' statement is on Page 74.*

By MURRAY SCHUMACH

Columbia University's board of trustees denounced yesterday the "small minority" of students who have seized five buildings on the campus and said there would be no amnesty for "those who have engaged in this illegal conduct."

In a strong statement supporting the university's administration, the chairman of the board, William E. Petersen, authorized the university president, Dr. Grayson Kirk, "to take all further steps which he may deem necessary or advisable to enable the university to resume its normal activities."

The trustees said that demonstrators had introduced a "false issue" in presenting the construction of a gymnasium at Morningside Park as "a racial issue or discrimination."

**Accept Gym Suspension**

However, the trustees said they would abide by the administration's decision, made at the request of Mayor Lindsay on Thursday, to halt work on the gymnasium "temporarily" pending "further discussion by the trustees."

The controversial building would be erected on 2.1 acres of the 30-acre park. It would contain two gymnasiums. There was considerable community resentment because one would be for Columbia College undergraduates and the other for residents of the Morningside Heights and West Harlem communities.

The board's statement in midafternoon was preceded by a terse announcement by Dr. Kirk that a special meeting of all faculties of Columbia University has been called for 10 A.M. today at the Law Building to help settle the disruption

Continued on Page 74, Column 1

## 87,000 March in War Protests Here

The New York Times (by Robert Walker)

The crowd assembled yesterday for antiwar rally in the Sheep Meadow in Central Park. At rear is Central Park West.

## 143 Demonstrators Are Seized, Most in Washington Sq. Clash

By MICHAEL STERN

An estimated total of 87,000 people, marching under banners denouncing racism and the war in Vietnam, paraded down both sides of Central Park yesterday to a rally in the Sheep Meadow.

In a day marked by scattered scuffles and violence as the police tried to contain unauthorized parades, 143 persons were arrested. Most of these were at Washington Square Park, where 400 members of leftist and youth groups gathered at 11 A.M. to stage a rival peace rally and march.

Thirty-five youths were arrested when they emerged from Central Park after the Sheep Meadow rally on their way to march to Columbia University in support of the student strike there.

Among those arrested at Washington Square was Aryeh Neier, executive director of the New York Civil Liberties Union. He was charged with harassment, on the complaint of a United Press International photographer who said Mr. Neier had twice bumped him.

Mr. Neir later issued a statement in which he denounced the police action in Greenwich Village as an attempt to break up what he called a "legal demonstration."

While thousands of policemen were deployed trying to contain these troubles, still others lined Fifth Avenue where 2,700 members of veterans' and patriotic groups marched in the annual Loyalty Day Parade.

The city had been braced for traffic tieups and a sharp falloff of business in midtown stores, restaurants and theaters as the result of concurrent parades and demonstrations, but conditions appeared to be no more chaotic than on a normally busy Saturday.

The estimate of the number of marchers in the antiwar parades was made by New York Times reporters, who stood at the 72d Street entrances on both sides of the park, and ticked off the ranks of paraders on mechanical counters. The totals were 42,000 for the Central Park West parade and 45,000 for the Fifth Avenue parade.

However, many of those who trooped down the avenues did

Continued on Page 72, Column 1

## U.S. AND HANOI FAIL IN NEW LAOS TALK TO AGREE ON SITE

### Second Meeting in a Week Inconclusive—Foe in South Attacks Two Bases

By BENJAMIN WELLES
Special to The New York Times

WASHINGTON, April 27—The State Department said that United States and North Vietnamese representatives met again today in Laos but failed to break the deadlock over a site for preliminary talks on the war in Vietnam.

State Department sources said conversations in Vientiane between Ambassador William H. Sullivan and Nguyen Chan, North Vietnamese chargé d'affaires, had produced no agreement yet. It was their second meeting this week.

[While efforts continued to arrange a site, enemy forces in South Vietnam launched mortar and artillery attacks against two United States military bases in Quangtri Province, which adjoins North Vietnam. Page 4.]

**Hanoi Aide Complains**

In the diplomatic contact in Vientiane, the North Vietnamese denounced the United States mission for allegedly having violated a pledge of secrecy in regard to the periodic contacts. According to State Department sources, Mr. Chan said:

"Vientiane is the only place we are having private exchanges and we mutually agreed to keep them secret. The Americans are the ones who gave out the news."

Carl Bartch, State Department spokesmen, said there would be no comment for the moment on Mr. Chan's charge. However, he noted newsmen had known of the discussions for some time and were in fact often seen waiting outside the meeting place in Vientiane in the hope of obtaining information.

Hanoi is understood to be pressing still for at least preliminary talks in Warsaw or Pnompenh, with a possible continuation later in Paris. The United States has publicly opposed a meeting in Pnompenh or Warsaw and has countered with 15 alternative capitals, which in turn have not been accepted by the North Vietnamese in public statements.

**Dispute Unresolved**

Diplomatic sources confirmed that an official message had now been received from Hanoi, but they made it clear that it still failed to settle the dispute satisfactorily from the United States' point of view.

According to reliable sources, President Johnson was on the verge of accepting Warsaw as a point of initial contact on April 4. But when the President was handed a news-agency message indicating that Tass, the Soviet press agency, had disclosed the choice of Warsaw as the meeting place, he was said to have become exceedingly angry.

Since then White House and State Department aides have been listing a variety of reasons why Warsaw would be impossible as a site.

They have noted that Poland has shipped war matériel to North Vietnam; that the six al-

Continued on Page 2, Column 6

## HUMPHREY JOINS PRESIDENCY RACE; CALLS FOR UNITY

Associated Press

Vice President Humphrey announcing his candidacy

### Pledges Campaign of 'Maturity, Restraint and Responsibility'

By WARREN WEAVER Jr.
Special to The New York Times

WASHINGTON, April 27—Hubert Horatio Humphrey, who rose from South Dakota pharmacist to the Vice-Presidency of the United States, announced today his candidacy for the Democratic nomination for President.

The 56-year-old Minnesotan opened his bid for the White House with an appeal for renewed patriotism, a stanch declaration of optimism, a pledge of maturity and a call for unity in his party and the nation.

*Text of Humphrey's speech will be found on Page 66.*

The Vice President's well-advertised announcement came in a nationally televised speech to 1,700 friends and supporters jammed into the Regency Ballroom of the Shoreham Hotel, overlooking rain-dampened Rock Creek Park. Hundreds more watched him on television in adjoining rooms.

Known for his enthusiasm, Mr. Humphrey had never seemed quite so exuberant as he was on the threshold of his greatest challenge.

"Here we are, the way politics ought to be in America," he told the cheering audience, "the politics of happiness, the politics of purpose and the politics of joy. And that's the way it's going to be, too, all the way from here on out."

(In an interview, Mr. Humphrey recounted the difficulties in arriving at his decision. Page 66.)

The Vice President's declaration put him officially into competition with Senators Robert F. Kennedy of New York and Eugene J. McCarthy of Minnesota for the nomination left open by President Johnson's decision not to seek re-election.

Mr. Humphrey will not compete with his two adversaries in the primaries; the deadline for entering those races has passed. Backed by an organization whose leaders all turned out for the celebration today, he will campaign for delegates in the nonprimary states, working toward a first-ballot victory at the National Convention in Chicago in August.

He avoided any specific commitment on issues in his half-hour speech, which was carried to 11 Western European nations by satellite. He promised

Continued on Page 66, Column 5

## NEW SCHOOL PLAN BACKED BY MAYOR

### Supports Regents' Measure Calling for More Drastic Reform Than His Own

By LEONARD BUDER

Mayor Lindsay has dropped his original school decentralization plan and given his support to a bill that the State Board of Regents proposes to submit to the Legislature this week providing for a total reorganization of the city system.

The measure will call for the removal of the Board of Education and the creation of locally governed community school districts that would have virtually full control over the schools in their areas.

Mr. Lindsay's own bill, sent to the Legislature in January, has been bogged down in committee and is considered to have no chance of passage.

Governor Rockefeller has given assurances that he will strongly support the Regents' bill.

However, bitter opposition is certain to come from the Board of Education, the United Federation of Teachers and the Council of Supervisory Associations, which have been strong critics of the Mayor's less drastic proposal.

The Regents' bill, according to the latest draft prepared by the State Education Department in consultation with the Mayor, will contain these major provisions:

¶Replacement of the present nine-member Board of Education by a five-man body with changed powers and duties, effective July 1. The new board

Continued on Page 77, Column 1

## 6,600 IN PARADES FOR LOYALTY DAY

### Turnout for Two Marches Backing War Is Smallest in 20 Years of Event

By SETH S. KING

The annual Loyalty Day parade, consisting of 2,669 marchers, passed up Fifth Avenue yesterday morning through scattered crowds that stood quietly along the flag-draped avenue. It was the smallest Loyalty Day parade since the first one 20 years ago.

In Brooklyn, 4,000 marchers stepped along Fourth Avenue, between 66th and 86th Streets, in a second parade marking the day originally set aside to answer leftist May Day gatherings.

For the last two years the Loyalty Day parades, organized by the Veterans of Foreign Wars, have been billed as demonstrations of support for American servicemen in Vietnam and as answers to rallies calling for an end to the war.

The Fifth Avenue parade began at 11:03 A.M. as the Most Rev. Terence J. Cooke, Archbishop of the Roman Catholic Archdiocese of New York, and Frank Gigante, grand marshal of the parade and commander of the New York County Council of the Veterans of Foreign Wars, led the marchers northward from 37th to 52d Street.

The streets were dry after an early morning rain and a pale spring sun warmed the marchers, many of them members of parochial school bands and youngsters from drum and bugle corps and drill groups

Continued on Page 72, Column 5

## PHOEBUS, ORIOLES, HURLS NO-HIT GAME

### Turns Back Red Sox, 6-0—Yanks Bow, 7-0, to Tigers

Tom Phoebus, 26-year-old right-hander, who struggled through seven years in the minor leagues before joining the Baltimore Orioles last season, pitched the first no-hit no-run game of the baseball season yesterday by defeating the Boston Red Sox, 6-0. Phoebus struck out nine batters, walked three and allowed only one base runner after the first inning.

Denny McLain turned in his second complete game and his second victory as the American League-leading Detroit Tigers beat the New York Yankees, 7-0. McLain allowed five hits. Jim Merritt of the Minnesota Twins gained his third victory by defeating the Chicago White Sox, 4-1. It was Chicago's 11th defeat in 12 games.

**TRACK**

Villanova became the first team in the 74-year history of the Penn Relays to win five of the eight championship relays. Three of the victories established meet records.

**THOROUGHBRED RACING**

Cain Hoy Stable's Captain's Gig scored an eight-length victory in the Stepping Stone Purse at Churchill Downs, Ky., a prep for next Saturday's $125,000 added Kentucky Derby. Bold Hour won the 25th running of the $85,000 Grey Lag Handicap at Aqueduct.

*Details in Section 5.*

## Clocks Set Ahead For Daylight Time

Daylight saving time began today at 2 A.M. in most states, with clocks and watches set ahead one hour. Thus, today is the shortest day of the year, with only 23 hours.

Only Hawaii and Arizona exempted themselves by state law from making the time change called for in the Uniform Time Act adopted by Congress in 1966.

The act provides that all states not exempting themselves by legislative action must observe daylight time from 2 A.M. on the last Sunday in April until 2 A.M. on the last Sunday in October—this year Oct. 27—when the lost hour of sleep will be regained.

## Spiraling Medical Costs Reflect Deficiencies in U.S. Health Care

1957-'59=100

Hospital Daily Service Charges

All Medical

Physicians' Fees

Prescriptions and Drugs

200 · 180 · 160 · 140 · 120 · 100 · 80

1962 · 1963 · 1964 · 1965 · 1966 · 1967

Source: Department of Health, Education and Welfare

Medical care cost trends are indicated in percentage, with the 1957-59 cost in each category being 100%.

By HAROLD M. SCHMECK Jr.
Special to The New York Times

WASHINGTON, April 27—A patient in Massachusetts found to his dismay that his hospital clinic had raised its fee for visits from $6.50 three years ago to $12.

In Washington, a workman who had been badly burned in an accident was sent home recently after 85 days in the hospital. The bill was just over $30,000, but the patient did not seem to mind.

A schoolteacher in West Virginia went to a hospital emergency room with a pain in the right side of his chest. He emerged later with no clear diagnosis and a bill for $62.

In rural Mississippi a mother and 11 young children have grits for breakfast, pecans for lunch, rice, beans and greens for supper. One of the children has periodic blackout spells, but, until recently, had never seen a doctor in her life.

While each of these cases illustrates the rapidly rising cost of health in America, each gives a different aspect of this

Continued on Page 79, Column 3



## British Navy Frigate Rushes To Help Bermuda Quell Riots

By Reuters

HAMILTON, Bermuda, April 27—The British frigate Leopard raced toward this riot-torn tourist island today to back up the beleaguered police force.

The vessel, with 15 officers and 230 men aboard, was sent from Norfolk, Va., at the request of the Bermuda Government.

The 20-mile-square colony was under a state of emergency after two nights of rioting and arson by bands of Negro youths.

Five whites were attacked, including John Patton, deputy chairman of the majority United Bermuda party. He was hospitalized yesterday with a broken arm and face cuts after he had pleaded with the youths to "cease this senseless attempt to destroy Hamilton."

John Commodore, an American tourist, was released from a hospital yesterday. He was attacked on Thursday.

The rioting was brought under control at 3 A.M. today after the police had made 31 arrests and imposed a curfew at 2 A.M. The curfew was imposed again today until 6 A.M. tomorrow.

The Bermuda Regiment, a force of 300, and reserve policemen were ordered to report for duty.

Last night, arsonists destrayed a warehouse, one of Hamilton's most exclusive

Continued on Page 28, Column 1

## U.N. URGES ISRAEL TO CANCEL PARADE

### But Unanimous Council Vote Brings Pledge of Defiance

By SAM POPE BREWER
Special to The New York Times

UNITED NATIONS, N. Y., April 27—The Security Council voted unanimously tonight to ask Israel to cancel a projected military parade through Arab sections of Jerusalem next Thursday.

Yosef Tekoah of Israel told the Council in an emotional comment after the vote that Israel would hold the parade, celebrating the 20th anniversary of modern Israel, as planned and that "behind the parade will march 20 centuries."

Secretary General Thant had told Israel and the Council that he considered that such a demonstration would undermine current efforts toward peace talks in the Middle East.

Israel was bitterly criticized in all-day meetings of the Council for her reluctance to cooperate. Of the 15 countries in the Council, only the United States and Brazil did not speak against the parade.

It was felt that the parade would be a demonstration of

Continued on Page 8, Column 1

## Today's Sections


| | |
|---|---|
| Section 1 | (3 Parts) News |
| Section 2 | Drama, Movie, Gardens, Stamps, TV, Radio |
| Section 3 | Financial and Business |
| Section 4 | Review of the Week |
| Section 5 | Sports |
| Section 6 | Magazine |
| Section 7 | Book Review |
| Section 8 | *Real Estate |
| Section 9 | *Employment Advertising |
| Section 10 | Resorts and Travel |
| Section 11 | *Advertising |
| Section 12 | **Advertising |
| Section 13 | Advertising |
| Section 14 | ***Advertising |
| Section 15 | Boating |

*Included in all copies in the New York metropolitan area and adjacent territory.
**Included in all copies in the New York metropolitan area and suburbs plus Philadelphia.
***Included in all copies in Brooklyn, Queens and Long Island.


## Index to Subjects


| | Section | Page |
|---|---|---|
| Architecture | 2 | 34 |
| Art | 2 | 32-35 |
| Boating | 5 | 15 |
| Bridge | 2 | 6 |
| Camera | 2 | 24 |
| Coins | 2 | 37 |
| Chess | 2 | 40 |
| Dance | 2 | 23 |
| Drama | 2 | 2-10 |
| Editorial | 4 | 18 |
| Education | 4 | 15 |
| Fashions | 6 | 86 |
| Food | 6 | 92 |
| Garden | 2 | 38-46 |
| Home Fashions | 6 | 94 |
| Letters to the Editor | 4 | 19 |
| Movies | 2 | 11-16 |
| Music | 2 | 11-19 |
| News Summary & Index | 1 | 91 |
| Obituaries | 1 | 82-83 |
| Puzzles | 6 | 120 |
| Radio-TV | 2 | 25-28 |
| Records | 2 | 29-31 |
| Science | 4 | 13 |
| Ships and Aviation | 1 | 80 |
| Society | 1 | 84-104 |
| Stamps | 2 | 36-37 |
| Weather | 1 | 91 |

"All the News That's Fit to Print"

# The New York Times

LATE CITY EDITION

Weather: Windy, rain likely today. Clearing, cool, tomorrow. Temp. range: today 57-52; Tues. 56-50. Full U.S. report on Page 77.

VOL. CXVII. No. 40,303

NEW YORK, WEDNESDAY, MAY 29, 1968

10 CENTS

# M'CARTHY BEATS KENNEDY IN OREGON PRIMARY UPSET; NIXON IS A STRONG WINNER

## DRIVE TO COMPEL DE GAULLE TO QUIT PRESSED BY FOES

### Opposition Assails Regime and a Minister Resigns—Cohn-Bendit Reappears

### MITTERRAND MAKES BID

### Declares His Candidacy for President—Text Is Issued for June Referendum

*Text of referendum question is printed on Page 10.*

By HENRY TANNER

Special to The New York Times

PARIS, May 28—The Gaullist Government came under sharp pressures today from the forces that are seeking the immediate resignation of President de Gaulle and Premier Georges Pompidou.

Daniel Cohn-Bendit, the extremist student leader, showed up at the Sorbonne in defiance of a Government ban on his re-entry from Germany. The student, known as Danny the Red, had dyed his red hair black and traveled to Paris through a student underground to appear in the university's main amphitheater.

François Mitterrand, President de Gaulle's old election foe, called for the formation of a provisional government immediately after the "departure of the general on June 16 if not before." June 16 is the date of the referendum upon which President de Gaulle has staked his office. Mr. Mitterrand said he was a candidate for President.

**Accepts Under Pressure**

Education Minister Alain Peyrefitte turned in his resignation and Premier Pompidou accepted it under pressure.

Georges Séguy, secretary general of the Communist-led General Federation of Labor, in a complete reversal of his earlier position, declared that the strikes, now 11 days old, would not end until the Government made a "fundamental change" in economic and social policy. He said he did not think the Government could do so.

The federation called on workers to take to the streets in all parts of the country tomorrow to support their de-

Continued on Page 10, Column 1

## FIGHTING FLARES ON SAIGON'S EDGE

### Major Offensive Doubted—Attack on Dalat Repelled

By GENE ROBERTS

Special to The New York Times

SAIGON, South Vietnam, May 28—Enemy and allied troops fought house to house today on the outskirts of Saigon and the resort city of Dalat.

By nightfall, the allies had repelled the assault on Dalat, 140 miles northeast of Saigon, but were still trying to root out entrenched enemy units on the northeastern and southwestern fringes of the capital.

High-ranking officers said here that neither of the enemy attacks involved enough troops to pose a serious threat to the cities. They speculated that the enemy made both moves for psychological reasons and in an effort to create more refugee problems for the South Vietnamese Government.

**Psychological Drive Seen**

"He wants to show everyone he's still around," a United States general said. "He probably sees some psychological value in this."

Officers in the field tended to agree.

"He doesn't have enough troops here, or on the way here, to be carrying out any real military objective," said Maj. Arley Harper, an American adviser to South Vietnamese Rangers who were fighting on the southwestern edge of the city. "He just filters in, digs himself some holes and tries to stay. I think he's trying to

Continued on Page 12, Column 7

Associated Press

DESCRIBES SEARCH: Capt. James Hildreth, operations officer at Atlantic Fleet Headquarters, Norfolk, indicates on the map the point where the oil slick was found. This is about 650 miles west of the Azores, along the submarine's projected course.

## France Forced to Spend Dollars to Defend Franc

By CLYDE H. FARNSWORTH

Special to The New York Times

BRUSSELS, May 28—The Bank of France has started to lose some of the $6-billion worth of gold and dollars that have piled up in its coffers as official reserves for the settlement of international debts.

The Bank for International Settlements in Basel, Switzerland, acting under instructions from Paris, has begun to buy French francs that have been offered in the currency markets recently because of the economic paralysis gripping France.

Only a few months ago, the franc was in great demand, and President de Gaulle, backed by a hoard of French gold, was attempting to undermine the standing of the dollar as a currency nations hold in their reserves along with gold.

**Dollar Backed by Gold**

The United States is the only country prepared to give gold for its currency. For every $35 presented to it by foreign governments, the American Treasury will give an ounce of gold. General de Gaulle wanted a higher price for gold and wanted its exclusive use in reserves. He maintained that the United States got privileges from the reserve status of the dollar.

The weakness of the franc and the loss of French reserves could signal the end of the de Gaulle offensive against the dollar.

The Bank for International Settlements, established to facilitate intergovernmental finan-

Continued on Page 11, Column 3

## PRESIDENT PRODS HANOI ON PARLEY

### Asks End to 'Fantasy' and Work to Bring Peace—Hears Vance Report

*Transcript of news conference appears on Page 12.*

By MAX FRANKEL

Special to The New York Times

WASHINGTON, May 28—President Johnson said today that it was time for the Paris negotiations on Vietnam "to move from fantasy and propaganda to the realistic and constructive work of bringing peace."

After hearing a first-hand report on the talks from Cyrus R. Vance, the President pledged to keep searching patiently for agreement. But with Hanoi sending men and supplies into South Vietnam "at an unprecedented rate," he said, the United States will not allow itself to "be pressured" into halting the bombing of North Vietnam.

In Paris, an American spokesman indicated that recent enemy offensives and infiltration made it harder for the United States to assume, as President Johnson offered to do last fall, that North Vietnam would not take advantage of a complete halt in the bombing. [Page 12.]

Mr. Vance, who is the second-ranking man on the American negotiating team led by W. Averell Harriman, briefed the President and his senior advisers for two hours. He also reported to Prime Minis-

Continued on Page 12, Column 1

## Johnson Requests Freer World Trade

By EDWIN L. DALE Jr.

Special to The New York Times

WASHINGTON, May 28—President Johnson disclosed today that he had decided not to ask Congress, at least for the present, for special measures, such as an import surcharge, to help the nation's trade balance.

The disclosure came as the President sent a message to Congress reaffirming his Administration's support for freer world trade and asking approval of these proposals:

¶Repeal of the 47-year-old "American selling price" system of customs valuation for benzenoid chemicals, which affords special protection to domestic producers.

¶Liberalization of the test that workers and businesses must meet to receive "adjust-

Continued on Page 2, Column 6

## VAST SEARCH FAILS TO FIND SUBMARINE

### Planes and Ships Traverse 2,100-Mile Route in Vain —Johnson 'Distressed'

By WILLIAM BEECHER

Special to The New York Times

WASHINGTON, May 28—A vast air-sea search for the missing nuclear-powered attack submarine Scorpion passed the 24-hour mark today with increasing signs of doubts that her 99-man crew would be found in time.

"With the passage of time, we're more apprehensive," said Capt. John F. Davis, director of the Navy's Pentagon task group that is monitoring all search efforts.

President Johnson, asked at his news conference about the search, said there was "nothing that is encouraging to report" and that "we are all quite distressed." [Question 6, Page 12.]

By late today at least 37 ships and 16 long-range patrol planes were covering a 2,100-mile course from the Azores to Norfolk, Va. The Scorpion had planned to traverse this area on her way home from three months of exercises with the Sixth Fleet in the Mediterranean.

At midday the only possible sign of a ship in trouble, the Navy said, was the report of an oil slick about 650 miles west of the Azores along the Scorpion's projected course. A nu-

Continued on Page 16, Column 1

## Business Suits Now Proper at Ascot

Special to The New York Times

LONDON, May 28—Royal Ascot, the race meeting at which horses run second to fashion, may have a more plebeian appearance this year. Men will no longer be obliged to wear morning dress in the Royal Enclosure.

A note from the office of the Duke of Norfolk, who as Earl Marshal of England arranges a number of royal events, was mailed with Ascot tickets last night. It said that morning dress, uniforms or business suits could be worn in the Royal Enclosure at the races, which are scheduled for June 18 to June 21.

An Ascot official warned against excessive liberties, however, saying: "By a lounge suit we mean a complete suit, not just trousers and casual jacket. Gentlemen, of course, should have hats."

The easing of the rules on Royal Enclosure regalia, made internationally famous by the movie version of "My Fair Lady," was believed to reflect the wish of Queen Elizabeth II. She will be at the races.

For generations men in the Royal Enclosure have appeared in this costume: a top hat, either black or pearl gray; a stiff white collar and a four-in-hand gray tie, or an ascot worn with a wing collar; a pearl gray or oxford gray waistcoat; an oxford gray cutaway coat with a

Continued on Page 8, Column 3

Pictorial Parade

Queen Elizabeth accompanied by the Duke of Norfolk at the Royal Ascot meeting two years ago. The Earl Marshal of England wears traditional attire, optional this year.

## ROCKEFELLER LAGS

### Reagan Runs Second but Trails Badly—Winner Jubilant

By LAWRENCE E. DAVIES

Special to The New York Times

PORTLAND, Ore., May 28—Richard M. Nixon rode to a more commanding victory in the Oregon Republican Presidential primary today than his campaign managers or rivals had projected for him.

The former Vice President soundly defeated his only opponent on the ballot, Gov. Ronald Reagan of California, who did not personally campaign. Governor Rockefeller of New York, who was not on the ballot, ran third with write-in votes.

With 1,518 of 2,599 precincts reporting, the vote was:

| | | |
|---|---|---|
| Nixon | 85,303 | 71% |
| Reagan | 26,147 | 22% |
| Rockefeller | 8,041 | 7% |

Robert W. Packwood overwhelmed John S. Boyd for the Republican nomination for the United States Senate. Mr. Packwood was receiving more than 85 per cent of the vote.

The News Election Service, which collected the Oregon returns as representative of press associations and television networks, cautioned that early tabulations would not accurately reflect the size of the Rockefeller write-in vote.

In some of the counties it is the custom not to count write-in ballots until the day after the election.

The same word of caution applied to the write-in votes received by Vice President Humphrey in the Democratic primary.

Mr. Nixon, when he was commanding 74 per cent of the votes, declared, "The chances of my now being derailed are pretty well eliminated."

"I expect some phone calls tonight," he continued, "some from Republicans who believe 'Now is the time to get on the train before it leaves the station.'"

"This big win," he said, "will help in making some of the fence-sitters move over."

A jubilant Mr. Nixon, addressing a cheering crowd of

Continued on Page 18, Column 2

Associated Press

VICTORY IS HIS: Senator Eugene J. McCarthy smiling as campaign workers applaud him in Portland after victory in the Oregon primary over Senator Robert F. Kennedy.

## $5-Billion Plan on Housing Voted by Senate, 67 to 4

By JOHN W. FINNEY

Special to The New York Times

WASHINGTON, May 28—The Senate approved today a comprehensive $5-billion bill designed to provide 1.2 million new or rehabilitated housing units for lower-income families over the next three years.

The bill introduces several major innovations in the Federal housing programs, most of them intended to combat the problem of urban decay by extending Federal assistance to lower-income families seeking housing.

The legislation would inaugurate a new program of Federal subsidies on mortgage interest to encourage home ownership by lower-income families. Through liberal tax depreciation, it also seeks to enlist the support of private industry in building low and moderate income housing.

**Victory for Administration**

And it opens the door for slum families to obtain home mortgages guaranteed by the Federal Housing Administration.

Adopted by the Senate by a vote of 67 to 4 after three days of debate, the bill represents a major legislative victory for the Administration. To a degree, the bill also meets one of the demands of the Poor People's Campaign, which has been urging Federal programs to encourage the building of millions of housing units for the poor.

Only Senators Spessard L. Holland, Democrat of Florida; Richard B. Russell, Democrat of Georgia; John C. Stennis, Democrat of Mississippi, and Strom Thurmond, Republican of South Carolina, voted against the bill.

Basically, the bill follows the lines of the ambitious housing program submitted earlier this year by President Johnson. In effect, the Senate bill, which

Continued on Page 14, Column 1

## Consumer Prices Up 0.3 Per Cent in April

By The Associated Press

WASHINGTON, May 28—Living costs continued climbing in April at an annual rate of 4 per cent, the fastest in 17 years, the Labor Department announced today.

It gave as the chief reasons strong market demand and rising wages.

Some 45 million workers lost 13 cents a week in purchasing power, the department said, because prices outpaced record high pay averaging $2.79 an hour and $104.63 a week.

The department said the Consumer Price Index rose to 119.9, up three-tenths of 1 per cent for the month and 4 per cent above the figure of one year ago.

The 119.9 figure, based on 1957-59 prices, means that it cost $11.99 in April for every

Continued on Page 15, Column 3

## S. E. C. ASKS CUTS IN BROKERS' FEES

### New York Stock Exchange Gets Proposal to Benefit Investors in Big Trades

By EILEEN SHANAHAN

Special to The New York Times

WASHINGTON, May 28—The Securities and Exchange Commission formally asked the New York Stock Exchange today to reduce the commissions its member firms charge on large stock transactions.

The request for changes in the exchange's commission rate structure constituted only the first step—and an interim one—in what will be a comprehensive review not only of the exchange's schedule of commission charges but also of its practices regarding eligibility for membership and the ways in which its members do business with each other and with nonmembers.

The S.E.C. asked that the lower commission charges on large transactions go into effect on Sept. 15, or earlier, if possible.

**Purpose of Request**

At the same time, it announced that it would begin hearings on July 1 on fees, membership and all other matters relating to the commissions charged on all national securities exchanges, including the American Stock Exchange and seven regional exchanges.

The immediate purpose of today's request for a reduction in the Big Board's schedule of minimum commission rates was to give to mutual fund shareholders some or all of the benefits that the funds and brokerage firms now get from informal arrangements undercutting the prescribed minimum commission.

Principal among these arrangements are what are known as "give-ups," a system whereby the brokerage firm executing a large mutual fund order splits its commission with another brokerage firm, usually one that is selling the

Continued on Page 46, Column 5

## TURNOUT IS HEAVY

### New Yorker's Chance in California Periled by Primary Loss

By WARREN WEAVER Jr.

Special to The New York Times

PORTLAND, Ore., May 28—Senator Eugene J. McCarthy won a stunning upset victory over Senator Robert F. Kennedy in the Oregon Democratic primary tonight.

Senator Kennedy's defeat, his first in three primaries, abruptly slowed the New Yorker's drive for the Presidential nomination and threatened to endanger his chances in the California primary, which will be held a week from today.

Senator Kennedy said tonight: "It would appear that McCarthy has won the primary."

He offered his congratulations to Senator McCarthy.

Results from 1,348 of the state's 2,599 precincts were as follows:

Results from 1,520 of the state's 2,599 precincts are as follows:

**PRESIDENTIAL RACE**

| | | |
|---|---|---|
| McCarthy | 62,179 | 43% |
| Kennedy | 54,295 | 37% |
| Johnson | 18,555 | 13% |
| Humphrey | 9,722 | 7% |

Senator Wayne Morse held a slender lead over former Representative Robert S. Duncan in the primary contest for the Democratic nomination for Mr. Morse's seat. A third contestant, Phil McAlmond, trailed, but his vote was far larger than the Morse plurality.

Results from 1,301 of the state's 2,599 precincts were as follows:

Results from 1,493 of the state's 2,599 precincts are as follows:

**SENATE RACE**

| | | |
|---|---|---|
| Morse | 69,283 | 48% |
| Duncan | 66,009 | 46% |
| McAlmond | 7,937 | 6% |

Senator McCarthy told a cheering crowd of followers at his campaign headquarters here that he believed he could now go into the California primary on even terms with Senator Kennedy.

"I think we've demonstrated who has the real staying power, the real strength, the real commitment," the Minnesota Senator declared.

Senator Kennedy said tonight that Senator McCarthy had won a significant victory in the Oregon primary but that he would continue his campaign for the Presidency.

"I congratulate Senator McCarthy for what appears to be a significant victory," Senator Kennedy said when he stepped from his plane on which he returned from a day of campaigning in California.

"I would say it is not helpful," the Senator commented,

Continued on Page 18, Column 5

## Slate For Humphrey Is Elected in Florida

By MARTIN WALDRON

Special to The New York Times

TALLAHASSEE, Fla., May 28—A favorite son delegation favoring Vice President Humphrey for President today won 55 of Florida's 63 delegate votes to the Democratic National Convention in a primary election.

In a tight contest for the Democratic nomination for the Senate in Florida, former Gov. LeRoy Collins apparently won nomination over State Attorney General Earl Faircloth.

In unofficial returns from 2,640 out of 2,649 precincts the vote:

| | |
|---|---|
| Collins | 400,000 |
| Faircloth | 390,000 |

Unofficial returns showed that a slate of Democratic party leaders led by Senator George A. Smathers easily defeated two other delegate slates in state-

Continued on Page 18, Column 2

NEWS INDEX


| | Page | | Page |
|---|---|---|---|
| Books | 37 | Obituaries | 36, 39 |
| Bridge | 36 | Real Estate | 61 |
| Business | 46, 58-59 | Screen | 29-31 |
| Buyers | 61 | Ships and Air | 77 |
| Crossword | 37 | Society | 42 |
| Editorials | 38 | Sports | 29-36 |
| Fashions | 43 | Theaters | 29-31 |
| Financial | 45-57 | TV and Radio | 78-79 |
| Food | 43 | U. N. Proceedings | 9 |
| Man in the News | 10 | Wash. Proceedings | 15 |
| Music | 20-28 | Weather | 77 |

News Summary and Index, Page 41

"All the News That's Fit to Print"

# The New York Times

LATE CITY EDITION

Weather: Sunny, warm today; fair, continued warm tonight, tomorrow. Temp. range: today 83-58; Tues. 76-57. Temp.-Hum. Index 75; Tues. 70. Full U.S. report on Page 93.

VOL. CXVII. No. 40,310 — NEW YORK, WEDNESDAY, JUNE 5, 1968 — 10 CENTS



# KENNEDY SHOT AND GRAVELY WOUNDED AFTER WINNING CALIFORNIA PRIMARY; SUSPECT SEIZED IN LOS ANGELES HOTEL

## PRESIDENT INVITES SOVIET TO JOIN U.S. IN PEACE EFFORTS

### Defends Policy in Address at Glassboro Commencement, Year After Kosygin Talks

*Text of the Johnson speech appears on Page 14.*

By MAX FRANKEL

Special to The New York Times

GLASSBORO, N. J., June 4—President Johnson returned to his favorite diplomatic setting today and, in the "spirit of Glassboro" that is still evident here, invited the Soviet Union again to join in a global peacemaking effort.

Openly sentimental about his meeting here a year ago with the Soviet Premier, Aleksei N. Kosygin, Mr. Johnson delivered one of his now-frequent valedictory messages at the commencement exercises of Glassboro State College.

Standing just a few hundred yards from the house, Hollybush, in which for more than 10 hours he and the Soviet leader debated policy and dreamed for their grandchildren, the President today offered a new message of optimism about the cooperative spirit that he believed would gradually fall over mankind.

He offered more collaboration to the Soviet Union and counseled Americans against isolationism. He defended his position on Vietnam and reiterated proposals for peace in the Middle East and Soviet-American arms control.

And he admonished the political candidates who wish to succeed him to help find "answers" instead of "slogans" in foreign affairs, to help "tip the balance" from hostility to reconciliation and from stalemate to progress.

In this way, Mr. Johnson said, Americans and Russians

Continued on Page 14, Column 3

## FRENCH GET FUND TO GUARD FRANC

### Borrow $745-Million From I.M.F.—Strikes Persist

By JOHN L. HESS

Special to The New York Times

PARIS, June 4—France drew $745-million from the International Monetary Fund today to protect the value of the franc, which has been under strong pressure abroad.

The Finance Ministry accompanied an announcement of the step with the news that French reserves of gold and foreign currency dropped by $307-million during the strike-torn month of May, to $5.7-billion.

Most of the loss came last week, when France bought francs on the world market to keep the price from falling below its official rate of 4.94 to the dollar (20.26 cents). The Federal Reserve Bank of New York and the Bank for International Settlements in Switzerland acted as agents for the French in buying francs.

Across France today there were only scattered breaks in the nation's 17-day-old strike despite appeals and warnings issued by President de Gaulle, Premier Georges Pompidou and other leaders. [Page 3.]

The strike ended in the nationalized gas and electricity company, the Bank of France and several private banks, and among civilians in naval yards

Continued on Page 2, Column 4



## Marcus Testifies G.O.P. Official Urged Him to Accept a Kickback on Contract

By BARNARD L. COLLIER

James L. Marcus took the witness stand yesterday and testified that Joseph E. Ruggiero, the Republican county law chairman, and Vincent Albano, the New York County Republican chairman, both had tried to induce him to award an $840,000 city contract to companies they favored.

The former Water Commissioner and once close adviser to Mayor Lindsay said in Federal court that on Nov. 17 or 18, 1966, he told his business partner and lawyer, Herbert Itkin, that "Mr. Ruggiero had offered 10 per cent of the total contract and that 5 per cent would go to Mr. Ruggiero and 5 per cent to Mr. Itkin and myself, and I felt that we ought to award the contract to Oakhill."

Testimony showed that the reference to "Oakhill" meant the Oakhill Contracting Company, Inc., of Queens, a concern that wanted the contract to clean and refurbish the Jerome Park Reservoir in the Bronx.

Marcus testified also that Mr. Albano had asked him to give the contract to a different company, S. T. Grand, Inc., because its owner, Henry Fried, "is a big contributor to the Republican party."

The testimony was given before a 12-man jury hearing evidence in United States District Court in a bribery conspiracy trial. Marcus has pleaded guilty in the case to taking a bribe for awarding the contract.

Marcus said that Mr. Itkin, who is not on trial now but was named as one of seven co-defendants in the Federal indictment handed up last December, was opposed to making any deal with Mr. Ruggiero on the contract.

He quoted Mr. Itkin as saying:

"You've got to be crazy. We owe so much to Danny and

Continued on Page 59, Column 1

## COAST TALLY SLOW

### New Yorker Captures Lead Over McCarthy in Late Tabulation

By LAWRENCE E. DAVIES

Special to The New York Times

LOS ANGELES, Wednesday, June 5—Senator Robert F. Kennedy defeated Senator Eugene J. McCarthy yesterday in California's Democratic Presidential primary.

After trailing in the vote count for several hours after the polls closed, Mr. Kennedy overcame his rival in the tabulation early this morning.

His victory assured him of at least 172 California delegate votes at the party's national convention in Chicago.

At a victory celebration in the Ambassador Hotel, shortly before he was shot, Mr. Kennedy called for an "end to violence" in the nation.

The two Senators' slates of delegate candidates ran far ahead of an uncommitted slate headed by California's Attorney General, Thomas C. Lynch.

The Lynch slate was formed to support President Johnson before he announced he would not run again. Most of its members now favor Vice President Humphrey.

Returns from 7,277 of 21,301 precincts gave:

| | | |
|---|---|---|
| Kennedy | 413,660 | 45 % |
| McCarthy | 387,854 | 42 % |
| Unpledged | 114,351 | 12 % |

**Humphrey Challenged**

Senator Kennedy challenged Mr. Humphrey to debate him in the nonprimary states. He also said he would make a new effort to persuade Mr. McCarthy to join him in an attempt to stop Mr. Humphrey from winning the nomination.

In the Republican Senatorial primary, Senator Thomas H. Kuchel was running ahead of Dr. Max Rafferty, but the outcome appeared in doubt.

The polls closed at 8 P.M. (11 P.M. Eastern daylight time). It was hours before Los Angeles, using automated devices for the first time, began gathering any substantial figures from its computers.

These indicated that Senator Kennedy was on the way to a vote total in this most populous county that would insure him a statewide triumph.

The Los Angeles delays were caused not by voters' unfamiliarity with computer punch

Continued on Page 32, Column 4

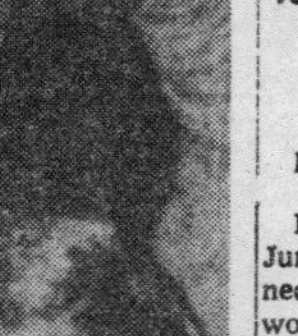

United Press International

WOUNDED BY A GUNMAN: Senator Robert F. Kennedy lying on floor of anteroom in the Ambassador Hotel in Los Angeles minutes after he was shot early this morning.

## CONDITION 'STABLE'

### Aide Reports Senator Is 'Breathing Well'—Last Rites Given

By WARREN WEAVER Jr.

Special to The New York Times

LOS ANGELES, Wednesday, June 5—Senator Robert F. Kennedy was shot and critically wounded by an unidentified gunman this morning just after he made his victory speech in the California primary election.

Moments after the shots were fired, the New York Senator lay on the cement floor of a kitchen corridor outside the ballroom of the Ambassador Hotel while crowds of screaming and wailing supporters crowded around him.

On his arrival at Good Samaritan Hospital a spokesman described Senator Kennedy's condition as "stable." He was described as breathing but not apparently conscious.

Frank Mankiewicz, Senator Kennedy's press aide, was quoted as saying, at 4:15 A.M.: "He is breathing well and has good heart. I would not expect he is conscious."

**Shot Twice in Head**

Mr. Mankiewicz said the Senator had been shot twice in the head—once in the forehead and once near the right ear. He was transferred to Good Samaritan Hospital after a brief stop at General Receiving Hospital.

The Rev. Thomas Peacha said he had administered the last rites of the Roman Catholic Church in the hospital's emergency room. This is normal procedure when a Catholic has been possibly seriously injured.

The suspected assailant, a short, dark-haired youth wearing blue denims, was immediately seized by a group of Kennedy supporters, including the huge Negro professional football player Roosevelt Grier. They pinned the assailant's arms to a stainless steel counter, the gun still in his hand.

**Wife by his Side**

Senator Kennedy lay on the floor, blood running from his back. His right eye was open but the other was partly closed as his wife, Ethel, kneeled at his side. His shirt was pulled open, and a rosary could be seen on his chest.

Richard Tuck, a Kennedy aide who was at his side at the time of the shooting, said the Senator's condition was "very bad." Within minutes he was rushed to a hospital.

Some witnesses reported that he had been shot in the back of the head or neck. Others indicated that at least one bullet had entered his torso.

A physician who gave Senator Kennedy emergency treatment before he was removed

Continued on Page 32, Column 1

## Israel and Jordan Clash; Artillery and Planes Used

By TERENCE SMITH

Special to The New York Times

JERUSALEM, June 4—Israeli and Jordanian forces fought a day-long battle across the Jordan River with artillery and aircraft today, on the eve of the first anniversary of the six-day war. Israel reported that her jet fighters had pounded artillery positions on the east bank of the river and had struck at long-range gun emplacements near Irbid, an Arab town about 12 miles east of the cease-fire line.

It was the first time planes had been called into action in nearly four months.

Three Israeli farmers were reported killed, and six civilians and one paramilitary border policeman were reported wounded during the fighting, which flared intermittently during the morning and expanded into a major exchange in the afternoon.

[The Amman radio said that Jordan had shot down four Israeli fighter planes and destroyed three Israeli artillery positions and four tanks. Forty-five Israelis were said to have been killed or wounded. Thirty-five Jordanians were reported dead—all civilians but two — and 62 were reported wounded.]

According to the Israeli military spokesmen, the Jordanians poured artillery shells into eight settlements along the west bank of the river south of the Sea of Galilee. When the

Continued on Page 16, Column 2

## 5 Killed in Saigon By New Shelling; Tie to Talks Seen

By BERNARD WEINRAUB

Special to The New York Times

SAIGON, South Vietnam, Wednesday, June 5—The Vietcong fired mortars into the southern edge of Saigon last night as entrenched Vietcong units fought South Vietnamese marine and airborne reinforcements in scattered parts of this uneasy capital.

Hours after the Vietcong had fired 40 rockets into the city, sporadic rifle fire rang out north of Saigon while fighting continued in the night in the northeast and western fringes.

Late at night the Vietcong fired 18 mortar shells into the city, which is under curfew. The shells, landing near Cholon, the Chinese quarter, killed five Vietnamese civilians and wounded 21.

One mortar shell landed on the President Hotel, less than a half mile from the Presidential Palace in the center of the city.

Meanwhile, the United States mission confirmed that a "mal-

Continued on Page 13, Column 1

## 300 AT COLUMBIA LEAVE CEREMONY

### Walk Out Quietly in Protest as Commencement Is Held at St. John Cathedral

*Excerpts from Hofstadter address are on Page 34*

By SYLVAN FOX

About 300 students in light blue academic robes and mortarboards walked out of the Columbia University commencement exercises at the Cathedral Church of St. John the Divine yesterday to bring to a climax the campus protest that began on April 23.

Two persons—a student and a junior faculty member—were arrested on charges of disorderly conduct during the walkout, which was joined by about 15 members of the teaching staff.

The demonstration was otherwise quiet and did not cause any interruption in the graduation ceremonies in progress in the huge cathedral. About 1,600 degree candidates remained in their seats.

In the commencement address, Prof. Richard Hofstadter, a Pulitzer-prize winning historian, assailed the tactics of the student protest that has crippled the university for six weeks, at times through the seizure of campus buildings. "The technique of the force-

Continued on Page 34, Column 1

## Kennedy Claims Victory, And Then Shots Ring Out

By JOHN G. MORRIS

Special to The New York Times

LOS ANGELES, Wednesday, June 5—Senator Robert F. Kennedy had just completed a statement claiming victory in the California primary. Amid cheers and flashing V-for-Victory signs from the several hundred persons gathered in the Embassy Room of the Hotel Ambassador, the Senator started to work his way off the podium and through the crowd clustered around.

He had just moved into an anteroom room cluttered with soggy coffee cups, half-eaten sandwiches and cigar butts when the shots rang out.

Those in the back of the Embassy Room could not hear the shots. But those further forward in the room were sent into hysterical screaming by what had happened.

**Screams of Hysteria**

"Oh God," one bystander cried, "It can't happen to this family again."

For five minutes, the throng in the Embassy Room was thrown into a state of panic. The cries of admiration changed to hysterical screams as the shots—muffled by the crowd noise — penetrated the consciousness of the bystanders.

There were calls for doctors. "Let me out of here," someone called. "Please clear the floor."

Jenny Rapelle of North Hollywood was standing near Senator Kennedy when the shooting broke out. She was spattered with blood.

Senator Kennedy's wife, Ethel, wearing a green silk dress, had stood at Senator Kennedy's right during his victory statement.

## HUGHES FORCES VICTOR IN JERSEY

### McCarthy Insurgents Win 20 of 80 Delegate Seats In Light Balloting

By RONALD SULLIVAN

An uncommitted slate of New Jersey delegates to the Democratic national convention led by Gov. Richard J. Hughes took a commanding lead last night over an insurgent slate pledged to Senator Eugene J. McCarthy in the state's Democratic primary.

Democratic leaders at the party's headquarters in Trenton said that the slate headed by the Governor had apparently won approximately 60 of the 80 delegates, which is just about what Mr. Hughes predicted last week.

Organizational leaders were ready to concede that all of their five-man delegate slates in the two Bergen Congressional districts had lost to the McCarthy forces. However, Democratic officials stopped counting the vote there at 1 o'clock this morning. They said a final result would not be ready until later today.

William Browne, the executive director of the Democratic state committee, said the Hughes slates appeared to have lost to Senator McCarthy in the Fifth district, which embraces Morris and Somerset Counties, and in the 12th district, which includes western portions of Union and Essex Counties.

He also said that Senator McCarthy seemed to be winning two delegates in the Fourth district, which includes Mer-

Continued on Page 35, Column 1

## Research Unit Cuts Link to Universities

By DAVID R. JONES

Special to The New York Times

WASHINGTON, June 4—The Institute for Defense Analyses changed its structure today in an effort to deflect student protests against its links with 12 major universities.

The trustees of the nonprofit, Government-sponsored research institute announced that membership in the organization, which previously consisted of the universities, would henceforth be composed only of individuals from academic and public life.

University officials who had represented their schools will remain in the institute as individuals, and a number of other leading Americans will be taken into membership.

The move was made because a number of the 12 universities

Continued on Page 33, Column 2

NEWS INDEX



| | Page | | Page |
|---|---|---|---|
| Art | 38 | Music | 35-39 |
| Books | 44 | Obituaries | 47 |
| Bridge | 44 | Real Estate | 74-75 |
| Business | 60, 72-73 | Screen | 35-39 |
| Buyers | 24 | Ships and Air | 93 |
| Crossword | 44 | Society | 42-43 |
| Editorials | 46 | Sports | 51-54 |
| Fashions | 40 | Theaters | 35-39 |
| Financial | 61-71 | TV and Radio | 94-95 |
| Food | 40 | U. N. Proceedings | 16 |
| Letters | 46 | Wash. Proceedings | 23 |
| Man in the News | 30 | Weather | 93 |

News Summary and Index, Page 49



## Kennedy Triumphs In Dakota Primary

By DONALD JANSON

Special to The New York Times

PIERRE, S. D., June 4—Senator Robert F. Kennedy scored a decisive victory today over Vice President Humphrey and Senator Eugene J. McCarthy in South Dakota's Presidential primary.

With 1,382 of 1,581 precincts reporting, the results were as follows:

| | | |
|---|---|---|
| Kennedy | 26,952 | 49% |
| Johnson* | 17,103 | 31% |
| McCarthy | 11,008 | 20% |

(* Regarded as pledged to Humphrey).

Mr. Kennedy ran strongly with every segment of South Dakota's Democratic voters—urban dwellers, farmers, ranchers, miners, Indians and residents of college towns. He took a solid early lead in the counting tonight and never re-

Continued on Page 32, Column 5

The New York Times (by Edward Hausner)

WALKOUT: Columbia graduating students, center, leaving commencement at Cathedral Church of St. John the Divine

"All the News That's Fit to Print"

# The New York Times

LATE CITY EDITION

Weather: Sunny, warm today; fair, continued warm tonight, tomorrow. Temp. range: today 88-62; Wed. 83-59. Temp.-Hum. Index 75; Wed. 74. Full U.S. report on Page 94.

VOL. CXVII..No. 40,311 — NEW YORK, THURSDAY, JUNE 6, 1968 — 10 CENTS



# KENNEDY IS DEAD, VICTIM OF ASSASSIN; SUSPECT, ARAB IMMIGRANT, ARRAIGNED; JOHNSON APPOINTS PANEL ON VIOLENCE

## MARCUS TESTIFIES DE SAPIO HAD ROLE IN A CON ED DEAL

### Says Itkin Sought Delay of Permit to Aid Own Scheme With Ex-Tammany Head

By BARNARD L. COLLIER

Former Water Commissioner James L. Marcus testified yesterday that he had been asked to delay approval of a permit to Consolidated Edison while the former Tammany Hall leader, Carmine G. De Sapio, was trying to make a deal with the utility company.

Marcus testified that the request came last September from his business partner, Herbert Itkin, who was in turn trying to negotiate a deal with Mr. De Sapio.

The testimony was elicited from Marcus under cross-examination on the third day of a Federal bribery conspiracy trial that has been marked by the mention in Marcus's testimony of several prominent members of both the Republican and Democratic parties.

Marcus was asked if there was a time when he, as Commissioner of Water Supply, Gas and Electricity, had "done business" with Con Edison. His answer was yes.

**Says Itkin Asked Delay**

"Itkin came to me," he said, "and said that Con Ed wanted a permit to increase the voltage on one of their power lines for 20 miles." He added that his approval as Commissioner was needed.

"Itkin said I should hold up for a while because he was negotiating with Carmine De Sapio, who was negotiating with Con Ed."

Marcus said that Mr. Itkin asked him to delay the approval for "a few weeks."

At that point in the trial, which came at about 4:40 P.M., Herman Zoloto, a lawyer representing Henry Fried, a contractor, and Mr. Fried's company, S. T. Grand, Inc., shouted:

"You're way ahead of your story, Mr. Marcus!"

Judge Edward Weinfeld broke in and scolded Mr. Zoloto for "a highly improper re-

Continued on Page 41, Column 1

## TRANSIT PACKAGE SUBMITTED TO CITY

### M.T.A. Seeks Approval of 8 New Subway Routes

By EMANUEL PERLMUTTER

A $1.27-billion package of subway and commuter railroad additions and improvements was submitted to the Board of Estimate and Mayor Lindsay yesterday.

The program was presented by the Metropolitan Transportation Authority and the New York City Transit Authority with a request for speedy city agreement on the new routes and engineering designs.

The over-all plan, which would take 10 years to complete, consists of eight new subway routes, including a Second Avenue subway, and Long Island Rail Road connections to the East Side of Manhattan and to Kennedy International Airport.

City approval of the routes and designs is a first step before application can be made for $60-million set aside by the Legislature for the engineering design of the mass transportation program presented by the Metropolitan Transportation

Continued on Page 55, Column 1



## France Will Meet Tariff Deadline; Strikes Dwindling

By HENRY TANNER

Special to The New York Times

PARIS, June 5 — Maurice Couve de Murville told France's partners in the Common Market today that despite the nationwide strike now coming to a close, the Government would honor the July 1 deadline for the abolition of remaining tariffs in the European trade bloc.

Today workers in the nationalized railroad company, the Paris transit system, the post and telegraph offices and other public administrations voted to go back to work. Trains are expected to start running tomorrow on several major national lines and the Paris subways.

By the end of the week, it is expected, the nationwide strike, now in its 18th day, will be all but ended.

Mr. Couve de Murville, who is the new Minister of Economy and Finance, also reassured his countrymen

Continued on Page 15, Column 1

## JERUSALEM POLICE CLASH WITH ARABS

### Israelis Halt Procession on Anniversary of War—U.N. Council Meets on Fighting

Special to The New York Times

JERUSALEM, June 5—A silent Arab procession commemorating the first anniversary of the Arab-Israeli war erupted into a violent clash today when Isareli policemen intercepted the marchers at the edge of the walled Old City of Jerusalem.

The clash was the most violent aspect of a widespread protest in which Arabs shuttered shops and other busisnesses here and elsewhere on the west bank of the Jordan and in the occupied Gaza Strip. It came after a day-long battle yesterday across the Jordan between the Israelis and Jordanians, in which aircraft and artillery were used.

[The United Nations Security Council met Wednesday at the urgent request of Israel and Jordan to consider recurrent hostilities along their cease-fire line. It postponed debate, probably until Thursday. Page 3.]

In the west-bank towns of Nablus, Jenin and Tulkarm, all centers of Arab nationalism, the general strike was 100 per cent effective. All stores, cafes and offices were closed, public transportation ceased and the streets were virtually devoid of traffic and pedestrians.

Schools throughout the west bank and Gaza Strip had no

Continued on Page 2, Column 4

## Italy's Cabinet Quits As Parliament Opens

By ROBERT C. DOTY

Special to The New York Times

ROME, June 5—Premier Aldo Moro and his center-left coalition Government, which has ruled Italy for four and a half years, resigned tonight with the convening of the new parliament, the fifth since World War II.

President Giuseppe Saragat asked Mr. Moro and his ministers to remain in office as a caretaker government while the search for a new government, which may be arduous, goes on.

Resignation of the government with the convening of a new parliament is automatic. But any hope that the Moro

Continued on Page 14, Column 3

## 6 IN RACE GUARDED

### Secret Service Given Campaign Security Task by President

*Text of the Johnson speech is printed on Page 23.*

By MAX FRANKEL

Special to The New York Times

WASHINGTON, June 5—For the second time in five years, Lyndon B. Johnson undertook today, amid national shock and outrage, to offer protection, prayer, comfort and assistance to his political rivals in the Kennedy family and then to try to heal the country's political and psychological wounds.

The President's first reaction to the shooting of Senator Robert F. Kennedy this morning was that "there are no words equal to the horror of this tragedy."

But tonight, in an emotional and at times even angry statement on television, he pleaded with all Americans to end the violence in their midst once and for all, to tolerate neither hatred nor the preaching of violence and to resolve to live under the law.

**A Guard for Candidates**

Mr. Johnson said he was appointing a commission of distinguished citizens to investigate both the circumstances and the causes of physical violence of all kinds in the United States, in the hope that the nation can learn "how we can stop it".

Earlier he had moved swiftly to provide protective Secret Service details to the six announced Presidential candidates of major parties, other than Vice President Humphrey, who already has such protection because of his office.

Meanwhile, in the House of Representatives, a vote of 317 to 60 cleared the way for the House to accept the Senate version of an anticrime bill, including controls over the interstate sale of hand guns. The vote rejected a move to send the legislation to a Senate-House conference.

**Members of Commission**

To the commission Mr. Johnson named Milton Eisenhower, former president of Johns Hopkins University; Archbishop Terence J. Cooke of New York; Albert Jenner, Chicago lawyer who worked for the commission that investigated the assassination of President Kennedy; former Ambassador Patricia Harris; Eric Hoffer, the longshoreman-turned-philosopher; Senators Philip Hart, Democrat of Michigan, and Roman L. Hruska, Republican of Nebraska; Representative Hale Boggs, Democrat of Louisiana, majority whip in the House; Representative William M. McCulloch, Republican of Ohio, and Federal Judge Leon Higginbotham of Philadelphia.

The President described himself as shocked, dismayed and deeply disturbed, as he knew all Americans were, by the shooting, which he described as the "latest spectacular example" of lawlessness and violence.

"So let us, for God's sake, re-

Continued on Page 23, Column 1

**NEWS INDEX**



| | Page | | Page |
|---|---|---|---|
| Books | 43, 45 | Music | 52-55 |
| Bridge | 44 | Obituaries | 47-48 |
| Business | 67, 78, 80 | Real Estate | 80 |
| Buyers | 78 | Screen | 52-55 |
| Chess | 44 | Ships and Air | 94 |
| Crossword | 45 | Society | 42-43 |
| Editorials | 46 | Sports | 59-64 |
| Fashions | 50 | Theaters | 52-55 |
| Financial | 67-80 | TV & Radio | 95 |
| Food | 50 | U. N. Proceedings | 3 |
| Letters | 46 | Wash. Proceedings | 56 |
| Man in the News | 21 | Weather | 94 |

News Summary and Index, Page 49



AFTER THE SHOOTING: Senator Kennedy's wife, Ethel, bends over him as a man checks pulse to determine condition

## HANOI INSISTS U.S. HALT ITS BOMBING

### Aides Call Talks Response to Johnson—Suspicion Voiced of a Plot Against Kennedy

By HEDRICK SMITH

Special to The New York Times

PARIS, June 5—North Vietnamese negotiators contended today that Hanoi had responded to President Johnson's restriction of American air attacks on the north by entering official talks here. They asserted that the next move, a total halt in bombing, was up to the United States.

The North Vietnamese argument, put forward in the seventh negotiating session between the two sides since May 13, produced one of the sharpest exchanges since the Vietnam talks began here.

The North Vietnamese made no direct comment on the shooting of Senator Robert F. Kennedy, but circles close to the delegation voiced suspicions in private, asking if the attack was not part of a conspiracy by the Johnson Administration. [Page 33.]

Near the end of today's session at the former Majestic Hotel, Hanoi's chief representative, Xuan Thuy, leaned across the negotiating table and asked the American delegates bluntly:

"When will the United States unconditionally cease the bombing and all other acts of war against the Democratic Republic of Vietnam so that other questions can be discussed?"

In response, W. Averell Har-

Continued on Page 8, Column 4

## Big Board Weighs 4 Special Closings

By VARTANIG G. VARTAN

A securities industry panel recommended yesterday that the New York Stock Exchange, the American Stock Exchange and the over-the-counter market close down for four days over the next month to cope with the deluge of paperwork in brokerage offices.

The panel proposed closing the securities markets for three Wednesdays—June 12, 19 and 26—as well as Friday, July 5.

The board of governors of the New York Stock Exchange will meet this afternoon to consider the proposal. Wall Street sources said that in view of the critical situation the governors are expected to accept the pro-

Continued on Page 73, Column 1

The New York Times (by George Tames)

ROBERT F. KENNEDY

## A Pall Over Politics

### Murder Raises Grave Questions for Presidency Races Now and in Future

By TOM WICKER

Special to The New York Times

News Analysis

WASHINGTON, Thursday, June 6—The murder of Robert F. Kennedy shattered the 1968 Presidential campaign and lowered a pall of uncertainty over American politics now and in the years to come. For the immediate future, it may well have assured the nominations by the Democrats and Republicans of the present front-running candidates — Vice President Humphrey and Richard Nixon. It raised grave questions, however, about the personal dangers of political campaigning in the United States. It added a tragic new dimension to the near-martyrdom of the Kennedy family, which has now lost two sons to assassins' bullets.

It removed forever one of the most promising young political leaders in recent American history, one with particular appeal for the poor, the downtrodden and the alienated inhabitants of the Negro slums. That appeal had been proved in all of Robert Kennedy's primary victories this year.

These elements of society also revered the Senator's brother, President Kennedy, who was assassinated on Nov. 22, 1963. How they would react to Robert Kennedy's murder—both in the immediate future and for the long political pull—was a crucial question.

The murder added sorrowful emphasis to one of Robert Kennedy's major political themes—the necessity for orderly and just redress of grievances, in place of violent action.

Ultimately, Mr. Kennedy's death—the first assassination of an American Presidential candidate—might lead to changes in campaigning practices, even to the fundamental manner in which the nation chooses its President.

The most immediate effect, however, was that for the third—and most harrowing—time a shock wave of unexpected events had completely altered the shape of the 1968 campaign.

The first came on March 12 when Senator Eugene J. McCarthy of Minnesota won 42 per cent of the Democratic vote in the New Hampshire primary, and Mr. Kennedy immediately thereafter became an active candidate.

The second transformation

Continued on Page 25, Column 6

## NOTES ON KENNEDY IN SUSPECT'S HOME

### Cite 'Necessity' to Murder Senator Before June 5, Anniversary of War

By PETER KIHSS

A notebook found in the Pasadena home of Sirhan Bishara Sirhan had "a direct reference to the necessity to assassinate Senator Kennedy before June 5, 1968," Mayor Samuel W. Yorty of Los Angeles said last night.

The date was the first anniversary of the six-day war, in which Israeli forces smashed those of the United Arab Republic, Syria and Jordan.

Sirhan, a 24-year-old Christian Arab, who has described himself as a Jerusalem-born Jordanian, is being held in the shooting of the New York Senator.

Justice Department records indicated that Sirhan came to the United States with his family in January of 1957 as immigrants, less than three months after the Suez war in 1956. Sirhan was 12 at the time.

The family quickly broke up in discord, the father staying in New York to work as a plumber and then going back to their former Palestine home, the mother taking five children to California, where a sixth child immigrated later.

Sirhan was described yesterday by Police Chief Thomas Reddin of Los Angeles as "very cool, very calm, very stable and quite lucid."

He was quoted as having said,

Continued on Page 21, Column 6

## Father of Suspect 'Sickened' by News

By TERENCE SMITH

Special to The New York Times

ET TAIYIBA, Israeli-Occupied Jordan, Thursday, June 6—Bishara Sirhan's hands trembled as he talked about his son Sirhan Bishara Sirhan, the accused assailant of Senator Robert F. Kennedy.

Mr. Sirhan dwelled on the tragedy of the shooting. He became angry as he talked, and finally said: "This news made me sick when I heard it. If my son has done this dirty thing, then let them hang him."

Mr. Sirhan's memories of his five sons are those of 10 years ago, when he last saw them and their mother. After years of fierce family quarrels, Bishara

Continued on Page 21, Column 4

## SURGERY IN VAIN

### President Calls Death Tragedy, Proclaims a Day of Mourning

*Texts of the medical reports appear on Page 22.*

By GLADWIN HILL

Special to The New York Times

LOS ANGELES, Thursday, June 6—Senator Robert F. Kennedy, the brother of a murdered President, died at 1:44 A.M. today of an assassin's shots.

The New York Senator was wounded more than 20 hours earlier, moments after he had made his victory statement in the California primary.

At his side when he died today in Good Samaritan Hospital were his wife, Ethel; his sisters, Mrs. Stephen Smith and Mrs. Patricia Lawford; his brother-in-law, Stephen Smith; and his sister-in-law, Mrs. John F. Kennedy, whose husband was assassinated 4½ years ago in Dallas.

In Washington, President Johnson issued a statement calling the death a tragedy. He proclaimed next Sunday a national day of mourning.

**The Final Report**

Hopes had risen slightly when more than eight hours went by without a new medical bulletin on the stricken Senator, but the grimness of the final announcement was signaled when Frank Mankiewicz, Mr. Kennedy's press secretary, walked slowly down the street in front of the hospital toward the littered gymnasium that served as press headquarters.

Mr. Mankiewicz bit his lip. His shoulders slumped.

He stepped to a lectern in front of a green-tinted chalkboard and bowed his head for a moment while the television lights snapped on.

Then, at one minute before 2 A.M., he told of the death of Mr. Kennedy.

Following is the text of the statement from Mr. Mankiewicz:

"I have a short announcement to read which I will read at this time. Senator Robert Francis Kennedy died at 1:44 A.M. today, June 6, 1968. With

Continued on Page 20, Column 1

## KUCHEL UNSEATED AS RAFFERTY WINS

### Conservative Beats Senator in California's Primary

By LAWRENCE E. DAVIES

Special to The New York Times

LOS ANGELES, June 5—Dr. Max Rafferty, State Superintendent of Public Instruction, defeated Senator Thomas H. Kuchel in the Republican Senatorial primary in California yesterday, cutting short Mr. Kuchel's 15-year career in the Senate.

Returns from 20,714 of 21,301 precincts gave:

| | | |
|---|---|---|
| Rafferty | 1,056,038 | 50% |
| Kuchel | 985,097 | 47% |

As the vote count continued today, it became apparent that the conservative Republicanism of Southern California had carried Dr. Rafferty to victory over the heretofore unbeatable Republican whip in the Senate.

Mr. Kuchel, an outspoken liberal-moderate who had made political extremists such as John Birch Society members his targets in recent years, was beaten by the voters in Los Angeles, San Diego and Orange Counties, after having led Dr. Rafferty last night and early today.

Dr. Rafferty, who has become

Continued on Page 28, Column 3

"All the News That's Fit to Print"

# The New York Times

LATE CITY EDITION

Weather: Partly sunny, chance of showers today. Sunny tomorrow. Temp. range: today 92-72; Tuesday 80-67. Temp.-Hum. Index yesterday 75. Complete U.S. report Page 66.

VOL. CXVII..No. 40,373  NEW YORK, WEDNESDAY, AUGUST 7, 1968 10 CENTS

## WORLD BANK'S AID TO BE INCREASED TO OFFSET U.S. CUT

### Less-Developed Countries to Receive More Funds, McNamara Announces

### BONDS SOLD IN GERMANY

### Tentative Plan Understood to Be Double This Year's Total Lending Program

By EDWIN L. DALE Jr.
Special to The New York Times

WASHINGTON, Aug. 6—The World Bank is about to begin a major expansion of lending to the less-developed countries to help offset a downtrend in the aid programs of the United States and some other industrial countries.

This was disclosed today in an announcement by Robert S. McNamara, president of the bank, known formally as the International Bank for Reconstruction and Development.

The announcement came in connection with a major borrowing by the World Bank in West Germany. The bank raises funds not from Governments or taxpayers, but by selling bonds in the world's capital markets. Any major increase in lending depends upon the bank's ability to sell more bonds.

**McNamara Explains Move**

Mr. McNamara said today:

"At a time when the flow of capital aid is lessening, and the dangerous gap between the rich countries and the poor is growing, it is essential that the World Bank expand its lending activities to prevent the development effort grinding to a halt.

"Such an expansion of lending demands a significant expansion in borrowing. The World Bank has been examining its capacity to raise in the markets the sums which are needed. I feel confident that the bank can very substantially increase its program of borrowing, and thereby expand the flow of investment funds to the developing countries."

It is understood that the tentative plan is for the bank to double its borrowings in the fiscal year that began July 1, implying an approximately equal increase in its lending.

In the last fiscal year, the bank's loans totaled $847-million. A doubling of that total would just about offset the cuts by Congress in President

Continued on Page 62, Column 4

## RUSH-HOUR TRAINS REDUCED BY L.I.R.R.

### Cancellations of 24 Runs Laid to 'Slowdown'

Harassed riders of the Long Island Rail Road who had to cope with the cancellation of nine commuter trains during the evening rush hour yesterday will have to deal with the cancellation of 15 commuter trains this morning.

The railroad said a "slowdown" of railway carmen who inspect and repair equipment at the Dunton Car Shop in the Jamaica-Richmond Hill section of Queens caused the cancellations. Consequently, the railroad said, nearly 300 of its 1,200 cars were not available for use, pending completion of inspections and necessary repairs.

More than 12,000 persons normally ride the morning trains that were canceled. They were the following:

Westbound between Babylon and Brooklyn, the 5:25, 6:03, 7:20; Freeport to New York, 8:09; Long Beach to Brooklyn,

Continued on Page 40, Column 1

NEWS INDEX


| | Page | | Page |
|---|---|---|---|
| Art | 38 | Movies | 33-39 |
| Books | 41 | Music | 33-39 |
| Bridge | 40 | Obituaries | 43 |
| Business | 56-57, 66 | Real Estate | 68 |
| Buyers | 56 | Ships and Air | 86 |
| Crossword | 41 | Society | 48 |
| Editorials | 42 | Sports | 49-52 |
| Fashions | 46 | Theaters | 33-39 |
| Financial | 56-65 | TV and Radio | 87 |
| Letters | 42 | U. N. Proceedings | 18 |
| Man in the News | 29 | Weather | 86 |

News Summary and Index, Page 45


## Panel to Pass on Candidates for Judge

### Party Leaders in Bronx and Manhattan Agree to Fitness Review

By THOMAS P. RONAN

Democratic, Republican and Liberal party leaders in Manhattan and the Bronx have agreed to nominate only those candidates for 17 Supreme Court judgeships who have been approved by a newly formed citizens' screening committee.

In announcing this yesterday, Presiding Justice Bernard Botein of the Appellate Division for the First Department said the agreement "could be the most significant breakthrough in the century-old and hitherto frustrating campaign for improved judicial selection in New York."

"I hope it might be a forerunner of a permanent sensible, statutory formula for the selection of all judges in New York," said the justice, whose department includes the two counties.

He told a news conference at the Association of the Bar of the City of New York, 42 West 44th Street, that with the consent of the leaders of the political parties he had appointed a broad-based 19-member citizens' committee to screen potential nominees for 17 Supreme Court posts in the two counties.

The New York Times
Justice Bernard Botein

### Citizens' Unit Will Check Nominees for 17 Posts on Supreme Court

The actual nominations will be made by delegates to the parties' judicial conferences next month. Normally the delegates are responsive to the wishes of their county leaders.

"This is the first time in this state that the responsible leaders of the major parties have consented to be bound by the decisions of a citizens' committee, selected under nonpolitical auspices, and representing a true cross section of the community," Justice Botein said.

He praised Francis T. P. Plimpton, president of the bar association, and his associates for their "patience, skill and dynamics" in arranging meetings with the political leaders and getting their agreement.

Justice Botein also said that the political leaders "who among themselves probably

Continued on Page 25, Column 2

## Israeli Forces, in Pursuit, Cross Into Jordan Again

By TERENCE SMITH
Special to The New York Times

JERUSALEM, Aug. 6—Israeli forces crossed the cease-fire line with Jordan today, for the second time in three days, in "hot pursuit" of what was described as an escaping band of Arab saboteurs. This time ground troops—helicopter-borne soldiers — pushed the band "a few kilometers" into Jordanian territory, according to an Israeli Army spokesman.

Of the band of nine saboteurs, five were reported killed and two wounded and captured. Two were said to have escaped. There were no Israeli casualties, the spokesman said.

**Air Raid on Sunday**

On Sunday Israeli planes crossed the Jordan River in a reprisal raid against what was called an Arab terrorist base camp 13 miles northwest of Amman, near the town of Salt. The air raid was the first action on the eastern side of the Jordan River in two months.

Until today, Israeli ground troops had not entered Jordanian territory since April 8, when an alleged commando base south of the Dead Sea was attacked.

Today's encounter took place a few miles east of Ein Yahav, an Israeli settlement near the Jordanian border

Continued on Page 17, Column 3

The New York Times Aug. 7, 1968
Cross shows site of clash

## ANGLICANS OPPOSE POPE'S BIRTH VIEW

### Bishops Reaffirm '58 Stand That Size of a Family Is Matter of Conscience

By EDWARD B. FISKE
Special to The New York Times

LONDON, Aug. 6 — Anglican bishops attending the Lambeth Conference went on record today as opposing the declaration by Pope Paul VI that mechanical or chemical birth control was contrary to divine law.

In a 500-word statement adopted after two days of debate, the leaders of the 47-million-member Anglican Communion expressed appreciation of the Roman Catholic Pontiff's "deep concern for the institution of marriage and the integrity of married life."

"Nevertheless," the statement continued, "the conference finds itself unable to agree with the Pope's conclusion that all methods of conception control other than abstinence from sexual intercourse or its confinement to the periods of infecundity are contrary to the 'order established by God.'"

The Lambeth Conference, which meets every 10 years, brings together the bishops of the Anglican Communion. It is being attended by 463 bishops, including more than 100 from the Episcopal Church in the United States.

In 1930, the Lambeth Con-

Continued on Page 10, Column 1

## STORM KING PLAN BY CON ED GAINS IN F.P.C. REPORT

### Examiner Supports Building of Power Plant on Hudson —No Peril to Fish Found

By EILEEN SHANAHAN
Special to The New York Times

WASHINGTON, Aug. 6— A Federal Power Commission hearing examiner recommended today that Consolidated Edison be permitted to build its controversial power plant at Storm King Mountain.

He said that there was no "evidentiary support" for the claims of opponents of the project "that these installations would scar and change scenic values associated with the mountain."

The examiner, Ewing G. Simpson, also found that there were no suitable alternatives to the Storm King Mountain project that would create an equally reliable power supply for New York City.

He held, in addition, that there was no proof that the installation would be a significant hazard to fish life.

**A Mixed Reaction**

Predictably, the recommendation was praised by Con Edison and criticized by the Scenic Hudson Preservation Conference, the organization whose successful court suit forced the rehearing by the F.P.C.

The utility's chairman, Charles F. Luce, said "all of us at Con Edison are most gratified at the examiner's decision and we will continue our efforts to obtain an F.P.C. license to build the Cornwall project as rapidly as possible."

The Preservation Conference, on the other hand, said: "We are disappointed by the Federal Power Commission examiner's recommendation, but this has to be acted upon by the full commission and we would expect it to take a broader view of the responsibilities imposed on it by the Court of Appeals in our case. If that fails, we shall appeal again to the courts."

Mr. Simpson's opinion, which is subject to approval or modification by the five-man Power Commission, was only the latest action in a controversy that is now more than five years old.

The commission initially approved construction of the project in 1965 after lengthy proceedings in which the company agreed to alter many of the original features of the in-

Continued on Page 20, Column 6

## GERMAN REDS END ATTACK ON PRAGUE

### Accords at Bratislava Bring Shift in Party's Stance —Ulbricht Is Silent

By DAVID BINDER
Special to The New York Times

BERLIN, Aug. 6—The compromise on Czechoslovakia reached Saturday by the leaders of six European Communist countries has forced the East German regime to shift its public stance.

As late as Friday, when Walter Ulbricht, the East German party leader, was on his way to the session in Bratislava, the Slovak capital, he was publicizing a condemnation of "antisocialist counterrevolutionary forces in Czechoslovakia" expressed in a joint communiqué with the American Communist party.

On the same day the party organ, Neues Deutschland, continued to stress the Warsaw letter of July 15, in which the Soviet Union, East Germany, Poland, Hungary and Bulgaria criticized Prague's reform movement in a letter that was conveniently forgotten 24 hours later at the Bratislava summit.

**Reports Are Ignored**

Since the meeting, East German organs and radio and television stations have refrained from ideological attacks on Czechoslovakia.

Ignoring reports that Mr. Ulbricht was booed and told to "go home" by crowds of Slovaks and some East Germans in Bratislava, Neues Deutschland said that he had taken a pleasant Sunday tour of the city, during which "passers-by waved and called out friendly greetings again and again."

Today Neues Deutschland printed some of the remarks

Continued on Page 5, Column 1

## EISENHOWER HAS 6TH HEART ATTACK

### Medical Outlook 'Guarded' After Major New Seizure

By FELIX BELAIR Jr.
Special to The New York Times

WASHINGTON, Aug. 6—Former President Dwight D. Eisenhower suffered another major heart attack early today, and attending physicians said the medical outlook was "guarded" or uncertain.

The general's third seizure since April 29 came at 6:15 A.M. when he complained of chest pains about 10 hours after addressing the Republican National Convention at Miami Beach from his suite at Walter Reed Army Medical Center here.

The attack was diagnosed later in the day as another myocardial infarction—a damaging of the myocardium or heart muscle resulting from a total or partial blocking of one of the branches of the coronary arteries that carry oxygenated blood to the heart.

It was the sixth attack of this kind suffered by the 77-year-old General of the Army. He suffered his first seizure at Denver on Sept. 24, 1955, during his first term.

He was stricken again on Nov. 9 and 11, 1965, at Augusta, Ga. The three subsequent attacks at Desert City, Calif., and later at Walter Reed Medical Center were less severe than the earlier episodes.

His doctors did not minimize

Continued on Page 32, Column 5

## Top Cubans Linked to Guevara Band

By HENRY RAYMONT

Thirteen guerrillas slain in Bolivia along with Ernesto Che Guevara are described in a new book as high-ranking Cuban Army officers, among them four members of the Central Committee of the Cuban Communist party.

The evidence is presented in a book brought out yesterday by a New York publisher, Stein & Day. The book, "The Complete Bolivian Diaries of Che Guevara and Other Captured Documents," is said to contain all the diaries of Mr. Guevara and three of his lieutenants.

Sol Stein, president of the publishing house, said at a news conference that he had received exclusive literary rights for the publication of the documents from the Bolivian Army high command. The Bolivian Army claims ownership of the original documents on the ground that they were captured through activities of war.

Mr. Stein said that a Cuban version of Mr. Guevara's diary, published here last month by Ramparts magazine and Bantam Books, had suppressed the identity of the Cuban guerrillas who accompanied Mr. Guevara in Bolivia, listing only their aliases.

"The presence in Bolivia of members of the Cuban party's Central Committee and other officers who were veterans of the Cuban revolution, in addition to Che Guevara, is one of the most remarkable facts to have come to light with the publication of the complete documents," he asserted.

**Plans Reported Concealed**

The Stein & Day book was edited by Daniel James, the author of five books on Latin America and a former editor of The New Leader, a liberal periodical. In a long introduction, Mr. James says that Mr. Guevara's plans in Bolivia were concealed from the leadership of the Bolivian Communist party until after the revolutionary and his Cuban companions had established their bases.

Even in the days before Mr. Guevara arrived in La Paz in October, 1966, disguised as a baldish Uruguayan businessman, Premier Castro was misleading Bolivian Communists into believing that the guerrilla war was to be launched in a neighboring country, Mr. James contended.

Last month, Premier Castro accused Mario Monje, head of the Bolivian Communist party, of having sabotaged the insurrectional attempt by "intercepting well - trained Communist militants in La Paz who were going to join the guerrillas."

Mr. Monje and most of the Bolivian Communist party leaders follow the Moscow line, which questions the political desirability of fomenting guerrilla operations in Latin America.

Mr. James also writes that the documents showed that Premier Castro abandoned Mr. Guevara in the last days

Continued on Page 13, Column 1

# ROCKEFELLER AND REAGAN STRUGGLE TO DENY NIXON VICTORY ON FIRST BALLOT

The New York Times (by Edward Hausner)

PLAN STRATEGY: Governor Rockefeller with Gov. Raymond P. Shafer of Pennsylvania, who will nominate the New York Governor at the Republican Convention session tonight.

United Press International

LOOKING FOR SUPPORT: Gov. Ronald Reagan talking to the delegation from Ohio at the Doral Hotel yesterday.

## TWO GAIN SUPPORT

### Platform Is Approved by the Convention— Nomination Today

By TOM WICKER
Special to The New York Times

MIAMI BEACH, Wednesday, Aug. 7—The Rockefeller-Reagan pincer movement inched ahead yesterday against Richard M. Nixon's confident drive for a first-ballot Presidential nomination at the Republican National Convention.

Pressure was building in the Southern delegations, meanwhile, to force Mr. Nixon to a conservative Vice-Presidential running mate—with Gov. Ronald Reagan of California most often cited.

Last night's session of the convention itself was devoted primarily to routine business and consideration of the 1968 platform, which was approved by the delegates just before the session adjourned at 12:25 A.M. today.

The delegates will return to Convention Hall at 5 P.M. for the crucial session of the quadrennial meeting—selection of a Presidential nominee.

**A Rousing Speech**

Although the business last night was routine, Senator Everett McKinley Dirksen of Illinois did rouse up the delegates with a stump speech in the grand style and a peroration that included a quotation from the Pledge of Allegiance to the Flag, in which the audience joined.

But yesterday and last night at Convention Hall, attention still centered on whether Mr. Nixon could be held below the magic figure of 667 on the first ballot.

Working from the left, Governor Rockefeller of New York gained the support of Gov. Daniel J. Evans of Washington, the 42-year-old keynote speaker, plus about 16 delegates in Mr. Evans's state, in Iowa and in Minnesota.

On the right, Governor Reagan continued to peck away at Mr. Nixon's strength among

Continued on Page 28, Column 1

## Nixon Says He Has Eased Views on Communist Bloc

By ROBERT B. SEMPLE Jr.
Special to The New York Times

MIAMI BEACH, Aug. 6 — Richard M. Nixon said today that some of his basic foreign policy views had changed over the last eight years and that he no longer regarded the Communist world as an unyielding, monolithic force.

The former Vice President,

*Excerpts from Nixon news conference on Page 28.*

who built his political career on opposition to Communism at home and abroad, told an early morning news conference that he had revised some of his earlier attitudes, largely because the Communist world had itself shifted in a new direction.

In 1960, Mr. Nixon said, "the Communist world was a monolithic world." "Today it is a split world, schizophrenic, with very great diversity," particularly, he said, in Eastern Europe.

Accordingly, he suggested, the "era of confrontation" with the Communist world has ended, ushering in a new "era of negotiations with the Soviet Union."

"Whoever is President, whether it is President Johnson or whether it is Humphrey or whether it is Nixon, whoever is President in the next four years and these eight years must proceed on the assumption that negotiations with the leaders of the Soviet world, negotiations eventually with the leaders of the next superpower, Communist China, must

Continued on Page 28, Column 7

## Gov. Evans Backs Rockefeller; A Gain by Reagan Is Reported

### New Yorker Buoyed

By R. W. APPLE Jr.
Special to The New York Times

MIAMI BEACH, Aug. 6—With only about 36 hours left until the first roll-call, Governor Rockefeller's campaign for the Republican Presidential nomination emerged from the doldrums today.

Gov. Daniel J. Evans of Washington, the tall, dark-haired keynoter at last night's opening convention session, endorsed Mr. Rockefeller at a news conference this morning. His action will probably bring Mr. Rockefeller's first-ballot total of Washington votes to six, a gain of four.

After a visit from Mr. Rockefeller, a Nixon backer and four uncommitted delegates in Minnesota announced for him. There were also signs of small Rockefeller gains in Missouri, where he had been thought very weak, and in other states.

In addition, seven United States Representatives, includ-

Continued on Page 29, Column 1

### Californian at Caucuses

By GLADWIN HILL
Special to The New York Times

MIAMI BEACH, Aug. 6—Gov. Ronald Reagan reportedly gathered some strength today as he industriously plied the delegate-caucus circuit in his new role of active candidate.

His camp made no specific claims of a gain in his delegate backing, which has been estimated at around 200 votes, less than one-third the number needed for the Republican Presidential nomination.

But from several Southern states came reports of polarizing sentiment in his favor. And his receptions ranged from warm to enthusiastic at all his stops.

Four more states — Maryland, Delaware, Tennessee and Missouri — were hastily added this afternoon to eight others whose contingents he addressed in a fast-paced, daylong round of appearances.

Asked if he really wanted

Continued on Page 29, Column 6

## Senator Long Loses In Missouri Primary

Special to The New York Times

ST. LOUIS, Wednesday, Aug. 7—Lieut. Gov. Thomas F. Eagleton upset Senator Edward V. Long yesterday in Missouri's Democratic primary election.

Mr. Eagleton, 39 years old, claimed victory at a midnight celebration at his campaign headquarters. He was leading Senator Long by almost 20,000 votes and had a 45,000-vote lead over the third candidate, W. True Davis, a millionaire industrialist.

With 3,762 of 4,358 precincts counted, Mr. Eagleton had 188,437 votes, Mr. Long had 170,782 and Mr. Davis 143,111.

Mr. Eagleton in November

Continued on Page 31, Column 1

"All the News That's Fit to Print"

# The New York Times

LATE CITY EDITION

Weather: Fair, seasonable today, tonight. Partly cloudy tomorrow. Temp. range: today 84-72; Wed. 94-74. Temp.-Hum. Index yesterday 82. Complete U.S. report Page 66.

VOL. CXVII. No. 40,374 — NEW YORK, THURSDAY, AUGUST 8, 1968 — 10 CENTS



# NIXON IS NOMINATED ON THE FIRST BALLOT; SUPPORT FOR LINDSAY IN 2D PLACE GROWING

## U.S. STEEL ENDS 7-DAY PRICE WAR; RISES CUT IN HALF

### Rest of Industry Accedes, Rolling Back to 2.5%—Johnson Is Pleased

By ROBERT A. WRIGHT

The steel price battle between the Government and industry ended yesterday with a compromise.

Steel prices will rise, but only by about half as much as most of the industry had planned. The Administration said it was gratified.

The détente in the seven-day war came when the United States Steel Corporation, the industry's largest producer, announced price increases on a broad range of products averaging about 2.5 per cent. That compared with increases announced by other producers last week ranging from 4.5 to 4.9 per cent.

Other producers quickly fell in line with U.S. Steel, rolling back their earlier increases.

First to rescind the higher prices was the Bethlehem Steel Corporation, the second-largest producer. Bethlehem had touched off the current round of general price increases last week following an industry labor agreement that was estimated to raise labor costs more than 6 per cent.

**Inflation Threat Reduced**

There was no evidence that U.S. Steel had negotiated the compromise increase with the Government.

Arthur M. Okun, chairman of the President's Council of Economic Advisers, told a news conference in Washington, "It is gratifying that the U.S. Steel action significantly reduces the threat of a large and general inflation in steel prices." Later, when other companies announced rollbacks, Mr. Okun said the developments were welcome and added, "Compared to the threat posed last week, the American consumer has been saved a half-billion dollars in inflation."

At the Texas White House, President Johnson termed the

Continued on Page 44, Column 3

## COUNSEL FOR JUDGE ON TRIAL IS SEIZED

### Accused of Bribe Effort—2d Defense Aide Held

By FRANCIS X. CLINES

Special to The New York Times

RIVERHEAD, L. I., Aug. 7—A defense lawyer and a private detective involved in the bribery trial here of Supreme Court Justice James A. Roe Jr. were arrested tonight on charges of having tried to bribe a prospective witness.

The two men were identified by Suffolk District Attorney George J. Aspland as Edward B. Ryder 3d, the lawyer, and William J. Lindsay, the private detective. Mr. Lindsay is a former investigator for the District Attorney's office.

Mr. Lindsay has been working as a private investigator for the Roe defense.

According to Mr. Aspland, a police detective, feigning cooperation, accepted a $40 bribe from Mr. Lindsay at about 2 P.M. today in the County Courthouse while the Roe trial was under way.

Mr. Aspland charged that the bribe had been offered on the instructions of Mr. Ryder, but no details were offered.

The bribe allegedly was paid to Detective Richard Downing, a member of the District Attorney's staff who was a principal investigator in the Roe trial.

Justice Roe is accused of having tried to bribe two Shelter

Continued on Page 19, Column 1

## U.S. Informs Hanoi It Will Soon Free 14 Captured Sailors

By HEDRICK SMITH

Special to The New York Times

PARIS, Aug. 7—The United States informed the North Vietnamese negotiators today that it planned to release 14 captured North Vietnamese seamen soon and hoped that this would lead to expanded prisoner exchanges.

The announcement, which follows the release of three captured American pilots by Hanoi, was made during the 16th negotiating session between American and North Vietnamese delegates.

Ambassador at Large W. Averell Harriman, the chief United States delegate, gave a list of the names of the seamen to Col. Ha Van Lau, who headed the North Vietnamese delegation, and appealed for a list of American airmen held by North Vietnam.

Mr. Harriman said after the three-hour negotiating session that he had told the

Continued on Page 3, Column 6

## DERAILMENT ADDS TO L.I.R.R. DELAYS

### Thousands Angrily Wait in Station as Trains Are Cut—Outlook Today Gloomy

By DAMON STETSON

Thousands of commuters on the Long Island Rail Road were delayed last night because of a derailment of a train at the east portal of the tunnel under the East River.

The railroad reported that no one was hurt on the train, which had only an operating crew aboard. An announcement over the loudspeaker system at Pennsylvania Station shortly after 5 P.M. asked waiting passengers to find other means of transportation, if possible, and warned of indefinite delays for all trains.

**More Delays Due**

The announcement threw the crowds of hot and sweaty commuters into confusion as hundreds surged forward to seek further information or ran to telephones. The station had become chaotic even before the derailment as a result of an earlier announcement by the railroad that 19 trains had been canceled because of an alleged slowdown by carmen who repair and inspect cars.

Harried Long Island commuters face more travel complications today as a result of what the railroad insists is a work slowdown that has limited the availability of passenger cars.

By midnight the derailed coaches had been removed, but "extended delays" were reported through the night as track crews worked to replace damaged sections of track. The

Continued on Page 20, Column 3

## CZECHS SEEKING WAYS TO LOOSEN SOVIET TRADE TIE

### Aides Are Scouting in West for Cash Loans to Make Industry Competitive

By PAUL HOFMANN

Special to The New York Times

PRAGUE, Aug. 7—Czechoslovakia is seeking $400-million to $500-million in hard-currency loans in Western Europe to buy equipment that would make her lagging industry competitive in world markets.

The search for financing in Western Europe is being carried out while high Czechoslovak officials shuttle between here and Moscow to renegotiate vital imports of oil, iron ore and other raw materials from the Soviet Union.

Both courses of action are being taken for the same purpose: to extricate this nation of traditionally adaptable and skilled workers from the smothering economic embrace of the Soviet Union.

**'It Must Be Done'**

"It must be done cautiously, but it must be done," a member of the Prague Chamber of Commerce said. "We just cannot afford to end our economic cooperation with the other Socialist countries abruptly, but neither can we afford to go on as we have until now."

In the view of Czechoslovak and foreign observers here, this prudent attempt at disengagement from the Soviet economic sphere may well represent the second round in the Czechoslovak regime's fight for liberalization.

The first round, according to this view, ended with the six-nation Communist meeting in Bratislava last Saturday, when Moscow apparently abandoned its attempts to intimidate Prague by military pressure.

**Sanction Possibility Cited**

By a gradual economic disengagement, the Government of Alexander Dubcek, First Secretary of the Czechoslovak Communist party, would be in a position to reduce the chances of Moscow's applying more, though subtler, pressure through economic sanctions.

At first glance, Czechoslovakia appears extremely vulnerable to Soviet sanctions. The Czechoslovaks rely on the Soviet Union for much of their gasoline and wheat, while textile mills place a good deal of cloth on the Soviet market.

But this country, Czechoslovaks point out, is also an important supplier of uranium for Soviet nuclear projects. It also sends technicians to developing countries and provides other important services, nominally for the international Communist movement but actually for Moscow. Furthermore, the Soviet economy depends to some extent on heavy machinery built in Czechoslovakia.

Continued on Page 8, Column 2

The New York Times (by William E. Sauro)

SUPPORT FOR NIXON: Demonstrators on the convention floor after Richard M. Nixon was nominated at the 29th Republican National Convention in Miami Beach. Gov. Spiro T. Agnew of Maryland made the nominating speech.

## ORIGINAL VOTE 692

### But Convention Then Makes It Unanimous on Plea by Reagan

*Excerpts from the nominating speeches are on Page 24.*

By TOM WICKER

Special to The New York Times

MIAMI BEACH, Thursday, Aug. 8—Richard Milhous Nixon, the "old pro" of American politics, was nominated for President today on the first ballot at the Republican National Convention.

Mr. Nixon, only the eighth man to be renominated by the Republicans after having lost one Presidential election, triumphed over a determined "stop Nixon" drive waged from the left by Governor Rockefeller of New York and from the right by Governor Ronald Reagan of California.

Just as the Nixon forces had steadfastly contended during a week of maneuvering at this 29th Republican National Convention, the 55-year-old former Vice President, who was also the party's nominee in 1960, proved to have the 667 votes needed for nomination "buttoned up."

The first-ballot count, before the convention made the nomination unanimous, was as follows:

| | |
|---|---|
| Nixon | 692 |
| Rockefeller | 277 |
| Reagan | 182 |
| Others | 182 |

**2 Big States Lost**

Mr. Nixon's nomination came at the end of an almost interminable evening of oratory and demonstrations, in which 12 candidates were nominated and seconded; two withdrew before the balloting began at 1:17 A.M.

As the roll-call of the states proceeded, Mr. Nixon's lead mounted steadily—even though the two largest states went elsewhere. California cast 86 votes for Governor Reagan and New York gave 88 of its 92 to Governor Rockefeller.

Wisconsin, whose 30 delegates were won by Mr. Nixon in the state primary last April, put the former Vice President over the top, giving him three votes more than the 667 he had needed.

At the completion of the roll-call, Mr. Nixon had 692 votes and the switching began with Minnesota; it had cast only 9 of its 26 votes for Mr. Nixon, but it switched all to him. One by one, the rest of the states began to fall in line.

A cheer went up when Ohio finally cast 58 votes for Mr. Nixon. Gov. James A. Rhodes had held out as a favorite son, having 55 Ohio votes on the official roll-call.

Within minutes of the clinching votes, Governor Reagan appeared on the platform.

**Reagan Barred at First**

Mr. Ford, citing the convention rules, would not immediately let Mr. Reagan come to the rostrum, however.

While Mr. Reagan was waiting, the one-time front runner and a favorite son here, Gov. George Romney of Michigan, also switched his state's 48 votes to Mr. Nixon.

Meanwhile, New York representatives were trying to get recognition, apparently under instructions to move that the nomination be made unanimous. The delegation chairman Charles Schoeneck, finally shouted into the public address system that New York so moved.

Mr. Ford, however, continued to recognize the delegations one by one, rather than entertaining a motion for unanimity.

Ultimately, he entertained a motion from Virginia to suspend the rules. It was shouted through and Mr. Reagan was allowed to come to the plat-

Continued on Page 22, Column 1

## HUMPHREY GIVEN CHICAGO PHONES

### Extra Lines Are Installed Despite Strike—Aides of McCarthy Complain

By DONALD JANSON

Special to The New York Times

CHICAGO, Aug. 7 — Representatives of Vice President Humphrey have had extra telephones installed at his Chicago offices despite a strike by electrical workers.

Spokesmen for Senator Eugene J. McCarthy, the Vice President's rival for the Democratic Presidential nomination, complained that lack of telephones was jeopardizing their operation. But they said they had not sought and would not seek to circumvent the striking International Brotherhood of Electrical Workers in acquiring extra phones.

A Humphrey spokesman at first denied that extra telephones had been installed, then conceded that Illinois Bell Telephone Company management personnel had put six in one office.

A company spokesman said other phones had been installed for Mr. Humphrey in the Sheraton-Blackstone Hotel "before the strike." These were removed last week, he said, after Mr. Humphrey decided to shift his headquarters to the Conrad Hilton Hotel.

**Calls Allocations Fair**

A spokesman in the office of Stephen A. Mitchell, former Democratic National Chairman, who is convention arrangements chairman for Senator McCarthy, said the Vice President's shift to the Hilton had resulted in a wholesale slash in the McCarthy request for 300 rooms at the Hilton.

Eden Lipson, assistant to Mr. Mitchell here, said the McCarthy request had been made in March and the McCarthy staff had assumed the request was being met.

She said the Vice President apparently had asked the Democratic National Committee to move his operations to the Hilton about two weeks ago, following rumors that additional phone service would be easier to get there.

Yesterday John Criswell, ex-

Continued on Page 26, Column 5

## Lindsay Hints Inability to Refuse Nixon

### New Yorker 'Troubled' by Prospect of Linking Name to Nominee's

Special to The New York Times

MIAMI BEACH, Thursday, Aug. 8—Despite vocal Southern opposition, strong sentiment was reported last night to be building up in the Nixon organization to choose Mayor Lindsay as the Republican Vice-Presidential candidate.

Richard M. Nixon's strategists were understood to be working on a plan that could put the New York City Mayor on the ticket without violating the Presidential nominee's pledge to keep the party united.

From Lindsay headquarters came word that the Mayor had told a few friends he might not be able to reject an offer of the Vice-Presidential nomination if Mr. Nixon went to him with a strong appeal.

At the same time, however, Mr. Lindsay, a liberal, has said privately that he was "troubled" by the thought of linking his name with the more conservative Mr. Nixon's and by the traditional inactivity of Vice Presidents.

From both camps, there was agreement that no offer of the Vice-Presidential nomination had been yet made and none had been accepted.

Should efforts to put together a Nixon-Lindsay ticket collapse, Senator Mark O. Hatfield of Oregon was regarded as the most likely running mate for the former Vice President, slightly more acceptable to the Southern critics of Mr. Lindsay because he is less identified with the urban North.

The prospects of Senator Charles H. Percy as a Nixon running mate seemed still further on the decline. Influential Republicans reported that the Illinois Senator, in the running a few days ago, was no longer on the priority list of possibilities.

In an effort to make a Lindsay selection as acceptable as possible throughout the party, Nixon strategists were experimenting with the idea of a chief of staff or campaign manager for the Vice-Presidential effort who would be welcomed by the more conservative elements in the party.

There was awareness among Nixon advisers that Mr. Lind-

Continued on Page 25, Column 3

## A Remarkable Comeback for Nixon

By JAMES RESTON

Special to The New York Times

News Analysis

MIAMI BEACH, Thursday, Aug. 8—Richard Milhous Nixon has made his way back to the top of his party. It is the greatest comeback since Lazarus, and even in this mean and vicious business there is scarcely a Nixon doubter who does not recognize it as a remarkable personal achievement. The politics of America have a way of spinning personal stories no rational novelist would dare offer to a skeptical generation. The careers of Lyndon Johnson, the Kennedys, Dwight Eisenhower and Harry Truman, who made it to the White House, and of Barry Goldwater, Adlai Stevenson and Nelson Rockefeller and the other also-rans are scarcely conceivable in American modern fiction—and Richard Nixon now joins this unbelievable company.

Rejected by the voters of his native state of California, retired by personal choice in an angry farewell from politics in 1962, rejected again by the leaders of the Republican party in his adopted state of New York, he has nevertheless won another chance for the Presidency, which he lost by only 113,000 votes in 1960.

So far Mr. Nixon's is a party victory, gained by industry and loyalty that made him more acceptable to the divergent factions of the Republican party than any other candidate, and this, of course, is now his problem and his challenge. For the record that enabled him to win a majority of the Republican delegates here, against the most progressive element in his party, is precisely the record that now stands between him and a majority of the nation as a whole.

The core of his opposition in this convention came from New York, California and Pennsylvania, which are the most formidable symbols of an increasingly urban nation. His strength, though widespread, was primarily in the South, where he will meet powerful Democratic opposition in the general election, and in the Middle West, which is likely to produce the Democratic Presidential nominee, Hubert Humphrey of Minnesota.

Political, like military, leaders have a way of preparing

Continued on Page 23, Column 7

## That Time When Minutes Last Hours

By RUSSELL BAKER

Special to The New York Times

MIAMI BEACH, Thursday, Aug. 8—The atmosphere was crackling with tedium when the Republican party assembled in the Miami Beach Convention Hall last night to pick itself a President.

It had been building relentlessly all week, the boredom, and at 5 P.M., when Chairman Gerald Ford called the faithful to order, it had reached an intensity that was scarcely bearable.

It was not so much due to the pervasive assumption, which prevailed at the cocktail hour, that Richard Milhous Nixon had actually been nominated several weeks ago and that this evening's rites were merely a charade. Not at all. As "Casablanca" and Humphrey Bogart have demonstrated, there is nothing an American enjoys more than a good show with a familiar ending.

The American nominating process, however, is a vestigial leftover from the baroque era of 19th century politics. It is capable of producing melodrama when the outcome is uncertain, but when uncertainty is minimal it becomes a vehicle for brutal and agonizing punishment of human spirit and flesh.

Hour upon hour of thundering cliché, of enervating restatement of the obvious, of prancing up and down the hall in exhaustively planned "demonstrations"—the whole soggy business relieved only by an occasional burst of asininity—this is the way it has been done for a century or more and, unless politicians change more in the next hundred years than they have in the last, the way it will doubtless be done for a century to come.

Typically, last evening's performance began with a bout of inspirational song by the "Up With People" chorus, a group of very attractive but nonetheless very square young people whose musical message is a hymn to the good old American values. They are the politician's answer to soul music. Lee Bowman, the actor, certified them orthodox with the cry, "And not a hippie among them!"

The resounding cheer sug-

Continued on Page 24, Column 5

## $25-Million Mt. Vernon Renewal Will Replace Slums With Plaza

By MERRILL FOLSOM

Special to The New York Times

MOUNT VERNON, Aug. 7—A $25-million urban redevelopment program in the decayed core of this troubled community was put in motion today, with ground to be broken Sept. 1 for stores and 732 apartments on 19 acres.

"It is the shot in the arm that Mount Vernon so badly needs," said Samuel J. Lefrak of New York, president of the Lefrak Organization, developers for the project. "It will bring new people, new industry and new prosperity to the city."

Mayor August P. Petrillo said this was "one of Mount Vernon's most memorable days." He and Mr. Lefrak were among the speakers at a meeting in the Forum Hotel at which final agreement on the project was announced to 100 civic leaders.

For nine years urban redevelopment in this tightly packed community of 4.5 square miles has been snarled in bitter political and racial controversy. Three projects have been planned but none started. Industry and many white residents have fled. The population dropped from 76,010 to 72,918 between 1960 and 1965 and is still declining.

The new project, called Mount Vernon Plaza by Mr. Lefrak and the Midtown Renewal Program by the city, will

Continued on Page 15, Column 2

NEWS INDEX



| | Page | | Page |
|---|---|---|---|
| Art | 30 | Man in the News | 22 |
| Books | 30-31 | Movies | 27-29 |
| Bridge | 30 | Music | 27-29 |
| Business | 47, 50, 53 | Obituaries | 33 |
| Buyers | 53 | Real Estate | 53 |
| Chess | 30 | Ships and Air | 66 |
| Crossword | 31 | Society | 36 |
| Editorials | 32 | Sports | 38-44 |
| Fashions | 37 | Theaters | 27-29 |
| Financial | 44-53 | TV and Radio | 67 |
| Food | 37 | U. N. Proceedings | 5 |
| Letters | 32 | Weather | 66 |

News Summary and Index, Page 35

"All the News That's Fit to Print"

# The New York Times

LATE CITY EDITION

Weather: Mostly sunny, hot today; fair and warm tonight, tomorrow. Temp. range: today 89-72; Thurs. 91-73. Temp.-Hum. Index yesterday 80. Complete U.S. report Page 69.

VOL. CXVII..No. 40,375  NEW YORK, FRIDAY, AUGUST 9, 1968 — 10 CENTS

# NIXON SELECTS AGNEW AS HIS RUNNING MATE AND WINS APPROVAL AFTER FIGHT ON FLOOR; PLEDGES END OF WAR, TOUGHNESS ON CRIME

## BIG BOARD URGES COMMISSION CUT ON LARGE TRADES

### Exchange Concedes Federal Pressure Prompted Move for Its First Reduction

By EILEEN SHANAHAN

The New York Stock Exchange, conceding that it was acting under "Government prodding," proposed yesterday the first reduction in brokerage commissions in its 176-year history.

The reduction in commissions would apply only to stock transactions involving 1,000 or more shares, on which current commissions are considered excessive by both the Exchange and the Securities and Exchange Commission. Thus, many ordinary investors, who never buy or sell as many as 1,000 shares at once, would reap no direct benefit.

Among those, however, who would profit directly would be almost all persons with money invested in mutual funds or in private or corporate pension funds that invest in common stocks.

**Fund Shareholder Would Gain**

The reduction in brokerage commissions paid by mutual-fund managers on large stock transactions would put an additional $15 to $20 each year into the pocket of a typical mutual-fund shareholder with $5,000 invested in a fund with average securities trading.

Brokerage commissions are considered part of the fund's cost of doing business, and are part of the management fee, which is, in effect, subtracted from the value of the investor's holdings. If the commission comes down, there would be less to be subtracted, so the value of the investor's holdings would go up accordingly.

Traders of substantial blocks of stock would benefit not only from reduced charges on their trades on the New York Stock Exchange, but also on almost all of their other stock transactions. New York Stock Exchange brokerage commissions set the pattern for the rest of the industry.

**Governors Approve Reduction**

For the brokerage community as a whole, the reduction in commissions would amount to an estimated $150-million a year, or about 7 per cent of total stock-exchange commissions based on the volume of trading on the New York Stock Exchange last year. Assuming continuation of this year's pace of trading, the reduction would be even greater for 1968.

The commission-cutting proposal was announced at a news conference by Robert W.

Continued on Page 56, Column 3

## President Discloses An Ailment of Colon

By NEIL SHEEHAN
Special to The New York Times

AUSTIN, Tex., Aug. 8—President Johnson has had since 1960 a common intestinal condition known as diverticulosis, White House officials said today.

The officials disclosed the presence of diverticula — pouches cropping out from the President's large intestine, or colon—while giving a report on the results of the President's annual physical examination at the Brooke Army Medical Center in San Antonio.

The President's condition is not considered an illness, officials explained, because none of the diverticula have ever become inflamed from trapped intestinal matter, a disorder known as diverticulitis. Nor have they caused Mr. Johnson any discomfort, it was said.

Continued on Page 8, Column 1

## U.S. Finds Wolfson And 3 Aides Guilty Of S.E.C. Violations

By H. J. MAIDENBERG

Louis E. Wolfson, who dazzled the world of high finance with his activities in the early nineteen-fifties, and three co-defendants were found guilty of violating the Securities and Exchange Commission Act by a Federal jury here yesterday.

The 55-year-old former scrap metal merchant and present chairman of the Merritt-Chapman & Scott Corporation was found guilty of perjury, subornation of perjury, obstruction of justice, concealing documents and filing false statements with the S.E.C. The company, a shipbuilding, construction, chemicals and money-lending concern, is now in liquidation.

He faces a maximum prison sentence of 14 years and a fine of $32,000. Fraud and stock manipulation charges against the multimillionaire financier were dropped by Federal Judge Edmund L. Palmieri early in the eight-

Continued on Page 56, Column 1

## JULY PLAN TO OUST DUBCEK REPORTED

### Sources in East Berlin Say Soviet and East Germany Considered an Invasion

By DAVID BINDER
Special to The New York Times

BERLIN, Aug. 8 — Highly placed sources in East Berlin disclosed today that the Soviet Union and East Germany seriously considered invading Czechoslovakia in mid-July.

One informant said, "I was really worried not so much by what was happening in Prague as what was happening here."

He went on to speak of a partial mobilization of the 650,000-man reserves of East Germany's People's Army, which has not yet been publicized; of the recall of hundreds of East German tourists, and of the virtual closing of the border with Czechoslovakia.

[In Warsaw, informed sources said that Soviet troops were still arriving in Poland despite the accords on Czechoslovakia. Page 4.]

An East Berlin source said

Continued on Page 5, Column 1

## 'NEW LEADERSHIP'

### 'Long Dark Night' Over, Nominee Says, Pledging Action

*Texts of Nixon and Agnew speeches, Page 20.*

Special to The New York Times

MIAMI BEACH, Aug. 8 — Richard M. Nixon called tonight for "new leadership" to restore the nation's prestige abroad and heal its wounds at home.

"The long dark night for America is about to end," the Republican Presidential nominee declared in his acceptance speech.

"The time has come for us to leave the valley of despair and climb the mountain so that we may see the glory of the dawn of a new day for America, a new dawn for peace and freedom to the world."

Mr. Nixon told the partisan audience of thousands and a nationwide television audience of millions that he would make the end of the war in Vietnam his first order of business.

Without offering specific solutions, Mr. Nixon suggested that only a new Administration "not tied to the mistakes and policies of the past" could bring a successful conclusion to the hostilities.

**'Era of Negotiation'**

Offering the hand of friendship to the nation's cold-war adversaries, he said that "after an era of confrontation, the time has come for an era of negotiation" with the leaders of Communist China and the Soviet Union.

On domestic issues, Mr. Nixon offered to solve the nation's internal difficulties by combining a firm approach to law and order with new remedies for the problems of poverty that would depend less on Government "billions" and more on activities of an enlarged private sector.

The speech was punctuated frequently by applause. The response was greatest after his appeals for law and order and his frequent references to what he portrayed as a decline in national prestige over the last eight years.

Early in his speech Mr. Nixon said that he had talked with Mrs. Dwight D. Eisenhower earlier in the day and that she had said that the best thing for the ailing former President

Continued on Page 21, Column 5

United Press International

G.O.P. CANDIDATES: Richard M. Nixon and Gov. Spiro T. Agnew of Maryland respond to cheers at Convention Hall

## 3 NEGROES KILLED IN NEW MIAMI RIOT

### Policemen Battle Snipers—Troops Hold 100 Blocks Amid Looting and Fires

Special to The New York Times

MIAMI, Friday, Aug. 9 — Two Negroes were killed yesterday and one early this morning as Miami policemen and Negroes exchanged gunfire in the northwest section of the city.

The police said that two of the victims were killed in a gun battle at an apartment house on 62d Street yesterday.

The third man was identified by the police as a sniper who was killed early today on a roof at 301 Northwest 22d Street, in the city's Central District, a Negro area.

In Liberty City, also a predominantly Negro section, where the original violence broke out two days ago, the police reported that conditions had become quiet. Today's violence erupted in adjoining Central District.

Police Lieut. Jay Golden said that the violence in the Central District was producing "firefights like in Vietnam."

Armed National Guard troops

Continued on Page 16, Column 1

## Humphrey and McCarthy Welcome G.O.P.'s Ticket

### Vice President Elated

By ROY REED
Special to The New York Times

WAVERLY, Minn., Aug. 8—Vice President Humphrey said today that the country would have a "clear choice" in this year's Presidential election if he was chosen by the Democrats to oppose Richard M. Nixon.

He also gave his first hint of a possible line of attack on the Republican ticket chosen this week in Miami Beach. Speaking of Mr. Nixon's selection of Gov. Spiro T. Agnew of Maryland as a running mate, he said:

"I have a feeling the choice represented a rather significant compromise. Mr. Nixon had a great deal of support from the South. Maryland is a border state, and I imagine the choice of Mr. Agnew was related to some of the problems in the Republican party."

**Meets With Newsmen**

The Vice President was barely able to conceal his pleasure at the prospect of running against Mr. Nixon and Mr. Agnew.

"We now have a Republican ticket we can go to the mat with," he said.

He refused to discuss his own possible running mate.

Mr. Humphrey met newsmen on the lawn of his lakeside home here a few minutes after the announcement that Mr. Nixon had picked Mr. Agnew.

The Vice President, dressed in a sports coat and turtle neck shirt and chatting informally, acknowledged that the Agnew

Continued on Page 22, Column 3

### Senator Is Confident

By E. W. KENWORTHY
Special to The New York Times

WASHINGTON, Aug. 8 — Senator Eugene J. McCarthy had praise today for the selection of Richard M. Nixon as the Republican nominee for President.

"I think the choice of Nixon is a proper choice," he said at a brief news conference. "He is truly a Republican candidate."

Earlier, when two reporters called on Mr. McCarthy in his dark-walled Senate office, they found him in a relaxed mood after a day of strenuous Ohio campaigning yesterday in Columbus and Cleveland.

**Books on His Desk**

On his desk were copies of "Poems" by George Seferis, the Greek poet; Robert Lowell's "Near the Ocean," T. S. Eliot's "The Wasteland," and Robert Bly's "The Light Around the Body."

The Senator arrived home last night in time to watch on television some of the nominating speeches and demonstrations in Miami Beach, and he said he was giving some thought to an innovation when his turn came in Chicago.

"What," he asked, "would you think of something along the line of a Greek chorus for the nominating speech?"

"You mean," one of his visitors asked, "strophe and antistrophe—with the strophe saying 'a man who' and the antistrophe saying . . .?"

"That's right," Mr. McCarthy

Continued on Page 22, Column 5

## LINDSAY RESISTS PLEA BY LIBERALS

### Rejects a Move to Nominate Him and Accepts Invitation to Speak for Agnew

By RICHARD REEVES
Special to The New York Times

MIAMI BEACH, Aug. 8—Mayor Lindsay resisted today the pleas of a group of Northern liberals who urged him for nine hours to become a candidate for the Republican Vice-Presidential nomination against Gov. Spiro T. Agnew.

The liberals, who included Gov. John Chafee of Rhode Island and several Congressmen, began telephoning the Mayor within minutes after Richard M. Nixon announced that he had selected the Maryland Governor as his running mate.

The pleas continued as Mr. Lindsay prepared to step onto the convention platform to second the nomination of Mr. Agnew and began again as soon as the Mayor left the podium.

Mr. Chafee, who later switched his insurgent support to Gov. George Romney of Michigan, said that at no time did Mr. Lindsay waver in his determination to support Mr. Nixon's choice.

Mr. Lindsay's action in supporting the established party leadership contrasted sharply with his decision in 1964 not to support the party's Presidential candidate, Barry Goldwater.

Thus, the young Mayor stepped deeper into the main-

Continued on Page 21, Column 8

## Jersey Bans New River Pollution

### Court Tells 9 Towns in Morris to Stop Construction

By RONALD SULLIVAN
Special to The New York Times

TRENTON, Aug. 8 — Nine Morris County communities, several of which have rapidly developing residential and industrial complexes, were ordered today in State Superior Court to suspend any further building until they stopped polluting the Rockaway River.

The order was praised by Richard J. Sullivan, the director of the State Division of Clean Air and Water. He said it was the first time in memory that a group of New Jersey communities had been ordered to halt major construction in the interest of keeping the state's rivers clean.

"If you're looking for a trend in water pollution control," he said today, "this is the kind of thing that's going on now."

The order, which had been sought by Mr. Sullivan, was issued this morning by Superior Court Judge James Rosen in the Hudson County Courthouse in Jersey City.

It applies to Boonton Township and Borough, Denville, Randolph, Dover, Rockaway Borough and Township, Wharton and Victory Gardens, which lie in the Rockaway Valley watershed.

Sewers in the nine municipalities lead to the Jersey City waste treatment plant, which the city built in the early

Continued on Page 56, Column 3

The New York Times Aug. 9, 1968

Court ordered all building halted in shaded communities

## Svetlana Alliluyeva Burned Her Soviet Passport

### Will Seek U.S. Citizenship, She Writes to a Friend

By HENRY RAYMONT

Svetlana Alliluyeva has written a friend that she burned her Soviet passport last summer so that no one could ever think that she might return to Moscow. She also indicated that she intended to seek United States citizenship.

In an intense, personal and sometimes caustically witty letter, Miss Alliluyeva, Stalin's daughter, vowed she would never return to the Soviet Union, "a land of uninterrupted pain and trauma" for which, she said, she felt none of the nostalgia that Russians living abroad often develop.

*Svetlana Alliluyeva's letter is printed on Page 14.*

Writing with affection about friendships she has formed with American families in Princeton, N. J., where she has lived for almost a year, she said, "My life is now really free, full of interest and significance for me."

The 1,500-word letter, dated May 11, was sent to an unidentified elderly Russian woman living in Paris with a request that it be published as a reply to an article in the French newspaper L'Aurore.

The article, written by André Vigo, depicted Miss Alliluyeva, who is in her early 40's, as lonely, longing to return to her two children in Moscow, unable to adapt to American life and heavily guarded by the police. The article was based on a visit to Princeton, the author said.

"I should be resigned by now to being lied about," Miss Alliluyeva wrote, "but somehow I cannot get reconciled to the idea that from now on and forever there will be no escape for me from lies. As a result I continue to react strongly to articles of this kind."

Her letter was first published in Russian in a small exile journal in Paris called La Pensée Russe, and more recently in La Croix, a French Roman Catholic daily. It also appeared in Russian in the July 14 issue of Novoye Russkoye Slovo, a Russian-language daily in New York.

Reached at her home in Princeton, Miss Alliluyeva made available an approved English translation of the letter. The translation was by Paul Chavchavadze, a descendant of Georgian princes who emigrated to the United States and has written several books about Czarist Russia.

In the letter, Miss Alliluyeva acknowledged that she missed her children—Iosif, 21, born during her first marriage, to

Continued on Page 14, Column 1

## REBELS PUT DOWN

### Fail in Effort to Have Convention Choose Romney Instead

By TOM WICKER
Special to The New York Times

MIAMI BEACH, Aug. 8—Richard M. Nixon accepted tonight the nomination of a Republican party that was surprised and to a large extent unhappy over his choice of Gov. Spiro T. Agnew of Maryland as his running mate.

Mr. Agnew was approved by the delegates on a roll-call vote in which Gov. George Romney of Michigan received 186 votes and 26 other delegates withheld their votes from the Marylander. Mr. Agnew got 1,128 votes.

Mr. Nixon, addressing a packed and cheering convention hall, pledged that his "first priority foreign policy objective" would be "to bring an honorable end to the war in Vietnam."

**His Domestic Policy**

Turning to domestic policy, Mr. Nixon promised a tough approach to crime and lawlessness, criticized the courts for going too far "to weaken the peace forces against the criminal forces" and pledged to maintain law and order.

Mr. Nixon's oration ended in a tremendous ovation and an enormous outpouring of orange balloons from the ceiling of the convention hall. Before and after his speech, he took Mrs. Nixon and his daughters, Patricia and Julie, to the podium.

Taking note of the battle over Mr. Agnew's nomination, Mr. Nixon said it had been a healthy thing for the party and that even after spirited contests for President and Vice President Republicans "stand united before the nation tonight."

**Hoped for Unity**

Mr. Nixon's aides said he had selected Mr. Agnew as his running mate in the belief that the Maryland Governor would help unite the party. The result was the opposite.

All day long, after the choice was announced, the delegates seethed and grumbled, particularly those in the moderate wing of the party and from the big urban states, who believed a Southern-oriented ticket could not win this fall.

When the convention was called to order at 7:30 P.M., a major revolt against Mr. Nixon's choice might have been set off had not Mayor Lindsay of New York seconded Mr. Agnew's nomination and firmly refused to have anything to do with the dissidents.

**Preference for Lindsay**

Mr. Lindsay was the alternative they preferred, and the latent support for him in the convention could be measured by the long and enthusiastic ovation he received when he went to the podium for his seconding speech. It dwarfed the tiny demonstration staged for Mr. Agnew when he was nominated by Representative Rogers C. B. Morton of Maryland.

Mr. Romney was nominated by the Nevada state chairman, George Abbott, and allowed his name to remain before the convention. He apparently made no effort either to head off or to assist the movement in his behalf.

His 186 votes included majorities of the delegations from Delaware, Michigan, Minnesota

Continued on Page 18, Column 1

NEWS INDEX


| | Page | | Page |
|---|---|---|---|
| Art | 33 | Movies | 26-31 |
| Books | 32-33 | Music | 26-31 |
| Bridge | 32 | Obituaries | 35 |
| Business | 46-47 | Real Estate | 56 |
| Buyers | 46 | Ships and Air | 69 |
| Crossword | 33 | Society | 25 |
| Editorials | 34 | Sports | 38-42 |
| Fashions | 24 | Theaters | 26-31 |
| Financial | 46-56 | TV and Radio | 71 |
| Food | 24 | U. N. Proceedings | 2 |
| Man in the News | 18 | Weather | 69 |

News Summary and Index, Page 37

"All the News That's Fit to Print"

# The New York Times

LATE CITY EDITION

Weather: Showers likely today; clearing tonight. Fair tomorrow. Temp. range: today 85-73; Friday 91-76. Temp.-Hum. Index 83; Friday 83. Complete U.S. report on Page 52.

VOL. CXVII. No. 40,376

NEW YORK, SATURDAY, AUGUST 10, 1968

10 CENTS



## ULBRICHT OFFERS TALKS WITH BONN; EASES CONDITIONS

### East German Chief Says He Is Prepared to Negotiate a Nonaggression Pact

### SILENT ON RECOGNITION

### Exchange of Special Envoys Proposed—West German Reaction Is Guarded

By DAVID BINDER

Special to The New York Times

BERLIN, Aug. 9—In a dramatic shift in policy, Walter Ulbricht, the East German Communist party leader, made a conciliatory bid today for improved relations with West Germany.

Addressing the Volkskammer, or Parliament, Mr. Ulbricht declared that the German Democratic Republic was prepared to negotiate with the Federal Republic a pact renouncing the use of force between them.

He also offered to name a special state secretary to begin talks with a similar Bonn appointee. Both offers represent positive responses to proposals by the West German coalition Government, headed by Chancellor Kurt Georg Kiesinger.

[In Bonn, a Government spokesman said that if Mr. Ulbricht's proposals contained new suggestions West Germany would "not react negatively."]

**Tone of Speech Is Sober**

The conciliatory aspect of Mr. Ulbricht's extraordinary speech appeared not only in the relatively sober tone of his address but also in the fact that he had backed away from his previous insistence on Bonn's full-scale recognition of his regime as a precondition to any talks.

Mr. Ulbricht's declaration followed by a week the meeting of six European Communist leaders at Bratislava, Czechoslovakia, and was obviously influenced a great deal by the compromise achieved there.

Political observers here called the declaration a "virtual about-face" compared with the strident animosity with which Mr. Ulbricht was treating Bonn's proposals a week ago.

The East German Government abruptly cut off all of its own attempts at conciliation with West Germany when Mr. Kiesinger's coalition took power in December, 1966. Thus, the proposals represent a new example of the extraordinary agility the 75-year-old Mr. Ulbricht has demonstrated so often in his long career as a Communist leader.

He carefully coupled his offer, however, with demands that Bonn drop its 19-year-old claim to be the sole legitimate government of Germany. He also insisted that Bonn give up the so-called Hall-

Continued on Page 2, Column 2

AT PRAGUE AIRPORT: Alexander Dubcek, left, First Secretary of Czechoslovakia's Communist party, greeting President Tito of Yugoslavia. At rear, partly obscured by Mr. Dubcek, is Ludvik Svoboda, President of Czechoslovakia.

Associated Press

## Tito and Czech Leaders Confer as Prague Exults

By HENRY KAMM

Special to The New York Times

PRAGUE, Aug. 9—President Tito of Yugoslavia, the leader of the first Communist country to break with the Soviet Union, received a publicly jubilant but officially reticent welcome today when he arrived on a visit to Czechoslovakia.

The jubilation came from the people of Prague, who see in President Tito the personification of Communist independence. But the leaders of Czechoslovakia and Marshal Tito know they must tread softly to avoid offending Moscow.

President Tito arrived in a black limousine at Hradcany Castle, high above Prague, flanked by Alexander Dubcek, First Secretary of the Czechoslovak Communist party, and President Ludvik Svoboda.

Hradcany Square was packed with people clamoring for the marshal and Mr. Dubcek. The tumult went on for nearly an hour, but none of the leaders made an appearance. Finally, word was passed that there would be a speech from the inner courtyard dividing the castle from St. Vitus Cathedral.

Thousands swept through the narrow passageways to the magnificent courtyard, where

Continued on Page 2, Column 1

## BIAFRANS REJECT NIGERIANS' OFFER

### Insisting Upon Sovereignty, They Turn Down Peace Plan at Conference

By ALFRED FRIENDLY Jr.

Special to The New York Times

ADDIS ABABA, Ethiopia, Aug. 9 — The Biafran delegates to the peace talks being held here rejected the Nigerian federal Government's nine-point peace plan today.

They insisted, as they have always done, that no solution that did not give them full sovereignty could bring lasting peace to the 56 million inhabitants of what was once widely regarded as Africa's most promising nation.

Both sides agreed to meet again Monday, but observers saw little hope that future sessions would produce the reconciliation that has not emerged during three sessions this week and eight days of talks at the end of May in Kampala, Uganda.

Where Nigeria insists that the former Eastern Region give up the independence it proclaimed May 30, 1967, Biafra replies that only autonomy can save it from a repetition of the massacres that forced its people to opt for their own nation.

"The hatred and bitterness underlying these events are so

Continued on Page 3, Column 6

## RHODESIAN JUDGE UPHOLDS REGIME

### Rules the Government Has Legal Status in Spite of British Panel's Opinion

By Reuters

SALISBURY, Rhodesia, Aug. 9—A High Court judge ruled today that the Government of Prime Minister Ian D. Smith had achieved legal status. The ruling appeared to strengthen Rhodesia's campaign for international recognition of its break from Britain in 1965.

Justice Harold E. Davies ruled that the court was not bound by a judgment last month by the Judicial Committee of the Privy Council in London that the Smith Government and its post-independence laws were illegal. The committee is the highest British legal body for members of the Commonwealth.

"It is my view that the present Government has achieved internal de jure status and that the court sits by virtue of its authority derived from recognition by the Government in terms of the 1965 Constitution," he said.

**Death Sentences Given**

Justice Davies gave his judgment when convicting 32 black Africans on charges of possessing arms. He later sentenced them to death, but said that he would draw the attention of the Government to features in the case justifying mercy.

In March Rhodesia hanged three black Africans who had been convicted of murder, thereby defying a commutation of their sentence by Queen Elizabeth, whom it still acknowledges as chief of state.

Justice Davies said that the ruling today was his personal view and that because of the "utmost importance and considerable complexity of the matter," he would accede to a defense request to refer it to the Appellate Division of the court.

**Hearing Is Due**

The Appellate Division, which ruled recently that the Government had achieved de facto but not de jure status, will consider the matter next week.

If the court upholds Justice Davies's decision, the Government will have won a major victory in its struggle for recognition of its independence.

Justice Davies ruled on an objection by defense counsel that laws made by the Smith Government were illegal. He found this submission "void and without substance."

The submission followed a Privy Council order for the im-

Continued on Page 3, Column 5

## Convention Biased Against McCarthy, Key Aide Charges

By DONALD JANSON

Special to The New York Times

CHICAGO, Aug. 9—A backer of Senator Eugene J. McCarthy for President charged today that Democratic National Committee officials arranging the party convention were "biased" in favor of Vice President Humphrey and were working to "foreclose any hope for an open convention."

Stephen A. Mitchell, former Democratic National Chairman, who is chairman of convention arrangements for Mr. McCarthy, said the Senator's allocation of space at the headquarters hotel and telephones at the convention hall were not only inadequate but also greatly inferior to allocations for Mr. Humphrey, the front-runner for the Presidential nomination.

Mr. Mitchell directed most of his fire, in a news conference in the Palmer House, at John M. Bailey, Democratic National Chairman, and John B. Criswell, party treasurer and executive director of the convention.

He said a Criswell letter Tuesday had slashed a McCarthy request for 300 rooms

Continued on Page 14, Column 4

## MOSCOW STRESSES PARTY SUPREMACY

### Warns Against Any Move Toward Liberalization

By RAYMOND H. ANDERSON

Special to The New York Times

MOSCOW, Aug. 9—The Soviet Communist party warned its members today that if any of them had any ideas about liberalization in the party along the lines of the recent Czechoslovak reforms, they had best forget about them.

Pravda, the party organ, printed a long article defending the principle of "democratic centralism" and declaring that an abandonment of this system of unquestioning obedience to decisions from the top would lead to a collapse of Communist party rule.

The paper recalled with distaste the turbulent nineteen-twenties, when left-wing and right-wing factions in the party leadership vied for power.

The left-wing faction, headed by Trotsky and others, was crushed at the 15th party congress in 1927, when Stalin, reacting to a storm of shouts that an opposition be permitted, declared, "Enough, comrades, an end must be put to this game."

Two years later, the right-wing faction, led by Bukharin, was suppressed and Stalin was in full control.

Democratic centralism, evolved before the 1917 revolution when the party was an illegal group conspiring to overthrow Czarist rule, was incorporated into the party's statutes at its sixth congress, in 1917.

Described as the guiding

Continued on Page 2, Column 2

## N.Y.U. WILL RETAIN HATCHETT IN POST

### Decision Made at Urging of Goldberg and Mrs. Motley

By LEONARD BUDER

New York University announced last night that it would keep John F. Hatchett as director of its new Martin Luther King Jr. Afro-American Student Center even though he wrote an article that has been condemned by Jewish and other groups as being anti-Semitic.

James M. Hester, the university's president, said the decision to retain Mr. Hatchett in his post was based on a plan suggested by Arthur Goldberg, former Supreme Court Justice and delegate to the United Nations, and Federal District Judge Constance Baker Motley.

Mr. Goldberg and Judge Motley, who is a university trustee, intervened in the controversy over the appointment of Mr. Hatchett at the request of Dr. Hester. In a letter to Dr. Hester made public by the university, Mr. Goldberg said:

"As a result of my frank and candid talk with Mr. Hatchett, I believe he now understands the injustice and dangers inherent in the kind of criticism he voices in the article. Mr. Hatchett strongly denies that he is anti-Semitic although the expressions in the article can be so regarded."

Mr. Hatchett said the university's decision to retain him was "a sign of the developing maturity in the university community to accommodate itself to the legitimate demands of

Continued on Page 15, Column 2

## Senator McGovern Ready To Run Against Humphrey

### He Will Open Drive Today as Peace Candidate With Some Kennedy Support

By PETER GROSE

Special to The New York Times

WASHINGTON, Aug. 9—Senator George S. McGovern of South Dakota, a dove on the Vietnam war, plans to announce tomorrow his candidacy for the Democratic Presidential nomination.

Senator George S. McGovern

According to aides on his Senate staff, the 46-year-old former history professor will declare at a nationally televised news conference at 11 A.M. that he is turning his favorite-son status into that of a serious national candidate.

He hopes to draw support from the former backers of Senator Robert F. Kennedy, who at the time of his death June 6 had more than 300 committed delegates to the national convention.

Within the last week, it is understood, Senator Edward M. Kennedy talked with Senator McGovern and offered him his fullest possible personal cooperation.

He is expected to base his campaign on a Vietnam peace proposal that will reportedly call for the following:

¶A halt in the bombing of North Vietnam.

¶A pledge against escalation of the United States war effort.

¶New South Vietnamese elections, open to all citizens, including the so far disfranchised followers of the National Liberation Front.

¶A demand that the Saigon Government open negotiations with the front and Vietcong military leaders.

These are said to be the main lines of a proposed plank for the Democratic party platform that Senator McGovern expects to present to the 110-member platform committee at a Washington meeting on Aug. 20. The

Continued on Page 18, Column 3

## JOHNSON TO BRIEF NIXON AND AGNEW ON TALKS IN PARIS

### Republican Nominees to Fly to Ranch Today—Will See Rusk, Vance and Helms

### TRIP TO SOVIET IS OFF

### Presidential Candidate Will Visit Party Chiefs in States That Opposed His Bid

By WARREN WEAVER Jr.

Special to The New York Times

MIAMI BEACH, Aug. 9—Richard M. Nixon will fly to Texas with his Republican running mate tomorrow for a Presidential briefing on progress in the Paris talks on Vietnam.

The Republican nominee for President was invited by President Johnson to take Gov. Spiro T. Agnew with him to the L.B.J. Ranch for a meeting with Secretary of State Dean Rusk; Cyrus R. Vance, one of the negotiators in Paris, and Richard C. Helms, Director of Central Intelligence.

[Vice President Humphrey had a meeting with the President Friday that was said to have been devoted largely to "all developments" in foreign affairs. The White House denied that the meetings with Mr. Humphrey and the Republican nominees had resulted from some important new development regarding Vietnam. Page 13.]

**Phone Call From President**

Mr. Nixon told a news conference this morning that Mr. Johnson initiated the invitation when he telephoned his good wishes after the former Vice President's victory at the Republican National Convention yesterday morning.

"Dick, you have my congratulations and my sympathy," was what Mr. Johnson said, according to the Republican nominee.

"He said he appreciated my statement about Vietnam and the language in the platform," Mr. Nixon continued. "I made it clear we are not going to undercut the negotiations; that will be the policy of the party and the policy of the candidates between now and the election."

**Trip to Soviet Canceled**

At the same time, Mr. Nixon announced that he had been forced to cancel his tentative plans to visit the Soviet Union for talks with Russian leaders around the time of the Democratic National Convention, which opens Aug. 26 in Chicago.

He said that he could not undertake this trip without also stopping off for consultations in London, Paris, Rome and Bonn and that his schedule would not accommodate this much time. The Russian trip

Continued on Page 12, Column 1

## Agnew Upset by Criticism; Nixon Defends His Choice

### Governor Cites Record

By DOUGLAS E. KNEELAND

Special to The New York Times

MIAMI BEACH, Aug. 9—Gov. Spiro T. Agnew, the Republican candidate for Vice President, said today he was deeply disturbed that "it's being made to appear that I'm a little to the right of King Lear."

Obviously weary but relaxed in his red-carpeted 12th-floor suite at the Eden Roc Hotel, the 49-year-old Maryland Governor smiled when he was asked if Lear was a rightist and said dryly:

"Well, he reserved to himself the right to behead people and by my definition that's a right-ist position."

Then the smile disappeared and he quietly but emphatically began a lengthy defense of his own stand on civil rights—a stand that was widely challenged by liberals of his party yesterday after Richard M. Nixon selected him as a running mate.

He said that he was not bothered by what he described as "a very weak and abortive effort" at the Republican convention last night to nominate Gov. George Romney of Michigan for the Vice Presidency.

But he declared that he was troubled by newspaper, radio and television emphasis that he was a candidate whose civil

Continued on Page 12, Column 6

### Nominee Hails Ticket

By ROBERT B. SEMPLE Jr.

Special to The New York Times

MIAMI BEACH, Aug. 9—In his first public defense of his controversial running mate, Richard M. Nixon described Spiro T. Agnew today as "one of the most underrated political men in America."

Citing the Maryland Governor's "poise under pressure," the Republican nominee declared:

"When it comes to carrying the attack and resisting the attack, he's got it.

"You can look him in the eye and you know he's got it. This guy has got it. People say he's not known. That's nonsense in this day and age. He's known now, and as the campaign goes on he'll become better known."

Mr. Nixon's views on his running mate were expressed during a 45-minute impromptu news conference at a seaside resort in Key Biscayne, south of Miami.

The Nixon forces had arranged a cocktail party for his staff and members of the press. The staff had passed the word to newsmen "not to bring your pencils," but when the nominee entered he was immediately surrounded and subjected to a barrage of questions about his running mate. Mr. Nixon's

Continued on Page 12, Column 5

## Mobile Police Unit Is Formed To Contend With Crowds Here

By JOSEPH NOVITSKI

Police Commissioner Howard R. Leary announced yesterday the creation of a mobile police unit specifically trained to control the crowds that gather in street demonstrations, at political rallies and after major sporting events.

The announcement of the formation of the group, the special events squad, came while most of the 220 volunteers for the force were undergoing the final session of a two-month training and trial period.

Small details of the squad's men, experienced veterans of the department's Safety-Emergency Division, were on the job yesterday at the United Nations Plaza, where a vigil urging assistance for starving Biafrans was in its second day.

The veteran patrolmen, 70 in all, will form the backbone of the new unit, while 130 recent graduates of the Police Academy have volunteered for the squad. Twenty sergeants complete the unit.

The crowds that will be the squad's primary assignment were previously policed by men drawn from all of the city's precincts and divisions. These men, Commissioner Leary said, will now be able to remain in the areas they know well.

A Police Department spokesman explained that the new unit would be a daytime complement to another specialized, mobile police unit, the Tactical Patrol Force. The primary assignment of the Tactical Patrol Force is in high crime areas from 6 P.M. to 2 A.M.

"We don't have the T.P.F. in the daytime," Jacques Nevard, Deputy Commissioner for Press Relations, said. He added that the special events squad, like the tactical force, is a step toward the creation of what he called a modern police force, with mobile, specialized units.

Mr. Nevard said members of the new unit could be used to quell street disorders, but he

Continued on Page 54, Column 6

## North Vietnamese Dampen Speculation on 'Signal'

### Officials in Paris Draw Back From Hint That Lull in War Has Political Significance

By HEDRICK SMITH

Special to The New York Times

PARIS, Aug. 9—North Vietnamese officials sought today to dampen speculation that they had been trying obliquely to signal the United States to interpret the seven-week-old lull on the Vietnam battlefield as a political gesture.

The officials pointedly drew back from earlier private comments to an American reporter in which they had hinted that the lull had political significance and had suggested, in effect, that if President Johnson wanted to end the war he should take advantage of the situation.

The comments, reported by Murrey Marder of The Washington Post, had attracted intense diplomatic interest here and in Washington, though most American officials considered the North Vietnamese comments too ambiguous and too indirect a signal to satisfy President Johnson's terms for a cessation of the bombing of North Vietnam.

Today authoritative North Vietnamese sources were even more cautious in discussing their Government's position. In a long, informal discussion, one North Vietnamese official complained that the press had commented too much about The Washington Post's report, though he did not disavow its contents. He said that he regarded this incident as a thing of the past.

The effect of his remarks was to undercut some of the press and diplomatic speculation that the talks between American and North Vietnamese delegations were moving into a more serious and delicate place. They also dimmed hopes among American officials that Hanoi might be edging toward a diplomatic shift.

The source agreed to discuss Hanoi's position informally on the understanding that he would not be identified by name or quoted directly. The impression in some diplomatic circles was that he was taking a harder line now either because of instructions from Hanoi or because he had been embarrassed by an exaggerated press reaction.

The dominant American view, expressed by President Johnson, is that the battlefield lull is merely the prelude to a major enemy assault, mentioned yesterday in a Vietcong broadcast to the guerrillas.

Nonetheless, it is understood that some American officials have not entirely ruled out the possibility that the combat lull is an act of restraint that the North Vietnamese have refused to identify as such because of their standing objection on principle to the American demand for restraint and reciprocity.

The duration of the lull, which the United States says dates from June 29, has impressed American officials. The longer it lasts, they note, the more opportunity there is for diplomats to seek some satisfactory secret word from Hanoi that this is a deliberate political gesture.

But so far no such word has

Continued on Page 4, Column 3

### NEWS INDEX



| | Page | | Page |
|---|---|---|---|
| Antiques | 18, 24 | Man in the News | 14 |
| Art | 25, 28 | Movies | 15-17 |
| Books | 25 | Music | 15-17 |
| Bridge | 24 | Obituaries | 27 |
| Business | 32-33 | Ships and Air | 52-53 |
| Churches | 30 | Society | 19 |
| Crossword | 25 | Sports | 20-23 |
| Editorials | 26 | Theaters | 15-17 |
| Fashions | 18 | TV and Radio | 53 |
| Financial | 31-41 | U. N. Proceedings | 3 |
| Food | 18 | Weather | 52 |

News Summary and Index, Page 29

"All the News That's Fit to Print"

# The New York Times

LATE CITY EDITION

Weather: Sunny, mild today; fair and milder tonight and tomorrow. Temp. range: today 77-56; Wed. 75-57. Temp.-Hum. Index yesterday 69. Complete U.S. report on Page 70.

VOL. CXVII..No. 40,395 · NEW YORK, THURSDAY, AUGUST 29, 1968 · 10 CENTS



# HUMPHREY NOMINATED ON THE FIRST BALLOT AFTER HIS PLANK ON VIETNAM IS APPROVED; POLICE BATTLE DEMONSTRATORS IN STREETS

## SOVIET TO LEAVE 2 BLOC DIVISIONS ON CZECHS' SOIL

### Svoboda Tells the Cabinet Other Forces Will Depart in 'Several Months'

By TAD SZULC

Special to The New York Times

PRAGUE, Aug. 28—President Ludvik Svoboda told his Cabinet today that the withdrawal of the Soviet-led occupation troops from Czechoslovakia would take "several months and stages" and that at least two divisions would remain permanently stationed on the West German border.

Authoritative sources that provided the account of the Cabinet meeting at Hradcany Castle quoted the President as having informed the ministers that no exact date had been set to begin the withdrawal of the forces of the Soviet Union and the four other Warsaw Pact countries that invaded Czechoslovakia a week ago.

The National Assembly adopted an eight-point resolution asking that a firm date be set forthwith for removal of the occupying forces and declaring that the Czechoslovak Army of 200,000 men was capable of guarding its own frontiers.

**Prague Back at Work**

Meanwhile, Prague was back at work, but a curfew was maintained and Soviet armored scout cars and motorized infantry trucks with machine guns mounted on their cabs continued to cruise through the city's crowded streets.

In a speech to the nation tonight, Premier Oldrich Cernik announced that today's Cabinet session had drafted a proposal to the Soviet Union, Poland, Hungary, Bulgaria and East Germany to begin "soon" the actual negotiations for the departure of their armies.

He said that within two weeks economic talks with the Soviet Union were to begin "during which compensation for damages" caused by the invasion would be discussed among other topics.

Czechoslovakia has long been

Continued on Page 3, Column 1

Associated Press

John Gordon Mein

## U. S. ENVOY SLAIN IN GUATEMALA

### Terrorists Shoot Mein After Ambushing Car—Johnson and Rusk Ask Inquiry

By Reuters

GUATEMALA, Aug. 28—The United States Ambassador, John Gordon Mein, was slain here this afternoon by unidentified youths who had ambushed his limousine.

The 54-year-old career Foreign Service officer tried to put up a fight, but fell under a hail of pistol and machine-gun fire, dying instantly. At least nine bullets struck his body.

As the Ambassador was driving along Avenida Reforma to the embassy, several youths leaped out of two small Japanese-made cars and opened the limousine's rear door to force him out. He resisted and they opened fire.

[In Washington, President Johnson and Secretary of State Dean Rusk expressed shock and grief and called on Guatemala to investigate the assassination.]

**Campaign of Terror**

Mr. Mein is believed to be the first United States Ambassador assassinated at his post.

The kidnapping of prominent people has been an element of the terror campaign that has been waged by extremist political elements in this uneasy Central American country, which has a population of more than 4.6 million.

The shooting occurred three blocks from the Biltmore Hotel, where Mr. Mein had attended a luncheon given by the Foreign Minister, Emilio Arenales Catalán. The scene was about 10 blocks from the embassy.

The Ambassador's chauffeur,

Continued on Page 16, Column 3

## HUNDRED INJURED

### 178 Are Arrested as Guardsmen Join in Using Tear Gas

By J. ANTHONY LUKAS

Special to The New York Times

CHICAGO, Thursday, Aug. 29—The police and National Guardsmen battled young protesters in downtown Chicago last night as the week-long demonstrations against the Democratic National Convention reached a violent and tumultuous climax.

About 100 persons, including 25 policemen, were injured and at least 178 were arrested as the security forces chased down the demonstrators. The protesting young people had broken out of Grant Park on the shore of Lake Michigan in an attempt to reach the International Amphitheatre where the Democrats were meeting, four miles away.

The police and Guardsmen used clubs, rifle butts, tear gas and Chemical Mace on virtually anything moving along Michigan Avenue and the narrow streets of the Loop area.

**Uneasy Calm**

Shortly after midnight, an uneasy calm ruled the city. However, 1,000 National Guardsmen were moved back in front of the Conrad Hilton Hotel to guard it against more than 5,000 demonstrators who had drifted back into Grant Park.

The crowd in front of the hotel was growing, booing vociferously every time new votes for Vice President Humphrey were broadcast from the convention hall.

The events in the streets stirred anger among some delegates at the convention. In a nominating speech Senator Abraham A. Ribicoff of Connecticut told the delegates that if Senator George S. McGovern were President, "we would not have these Gestapo tactics in the streets of Chicago."

When Mayor Richard J. Daley of Chicago and other Illinois delegates rose shouting angrily, Mr. Ribicoff said, "How hard it is to accept the truth."

**Crushed Against Windows**

Even elderly bystanders were caught in the police onslaught. At one point, the police turned on several dozen persons standing quietly behind police barriers in front of the Conrad Hilton Hotel watching the demonstrators across the street.

For no reason that could be immediately determined, the blue-helmeted policemen charged the barriers, crushing the spectators against the windows of the Haymarket Inn, a restaurant in the hotel. Finally the window gave way, sending screaming middle-aged women and children backward through the broken shards of glass.

The police then ran into the restaurant and beat some of the

Continued on Page 23, Column 1

The New York Times (by Neal Boenzi)

AT CONVENTION: Cheering in the amphitheatre after Vice President Humphrey's name was placed in nomination

United Press International

IN STREETS: Police attempting to clear demonstrators on Michigan Avenue outside Conrad Hilton Hotel last night

## VICTOR GETS 1,761

### Vote Taken Amid Boos For Chicago Police Tactics in Street

*Excerpts from the nominating speeches are on Page 22.*

By TOM WICKER

Special to The New York Times

CHICAGO, Thursday Aug. 29—While a pitched battle between the police and thousands of young antiwar demonstrators raged in the streets of Chicago, the Democratic National Convention nominated Hubert H. Humphrey for President last night, on a platform reflecting his and President Johnson's views on the war in Vietnam.

Mr. Humphrey, after a day of bandwagon shifts to his candidacy, and a night of turmoil in the convention hall, won nomination on the first ballot over challenges by Senator Eugene J. McCarthy of Minnesota and George S. McGovern of South Dakota.

The count at the end of the first ballot was:

| | |
|---|---|
| Humphrey | 1,761¾ |
| McCarthy | 601 |
| McGovern | 146½ |
| Phillips | 67½ |
| Others | 32¾ |

**Violence Draws Attention**

There was never a moment's suspense in the balloting, and throughout a turbulent evening, the delegates and spectators paid less attention to the proceedings than to television and radio reports of widespread violence in the streets of Chicago, and to stringent security measures within the International Amphitheatre.

Repeated denunciations of Mayor Richard J. Daley from convention speakers and repeated efforts to get an adjournment or recess were ignored by convention officials and Mr. Daley.

He sat through it all, usually grinning and always guarded by plainclothes security men, until just before the roll call. Then he left the hall. A few miles away, the young demonstrators were being clubbed, kicked and gassed by the Chicago police, who turned back a march on the convention hall.

**Watched From Hotels**

Most of the violence took place across Michigan Avenue from the convention headquarters hotel, the Conrad Hilton, in full view of delegates' wives and other watching from its windows.

From the convention rostrum, Senator Abraham A. Ribicoff of Connecticut, denounced "Gestapo tactics in the streets of Chicago."

Julian Bond, the Negro insurgent leader from Georgia, in announcing his delegation's

Continued on Page 20, Column 1

## FIGHTING INTENSE IN SAIGON REGION

### G.I.'s Battle Through Night With Foe on Infiltration Routes Near Capital

Special to The New York Times

SAIGON, South Vietnam, Thursday, Aug. 29—Sharp fighting flared around Saigon last night and this morning as United States infantrymen battled a sizable enemy force on flatland infiltration routes northwest of the capital.

The United States command said this morning that fighting had continued through the night with a company-size enemy unit 32 miles northwest of Saigon and 4 miles north of Trangbang.

So far, a total of 86 enemy soldiers have been killed in the fighting, American spokesmen said. Reports from the scene were sketchy, but United States spokesmen termed American casualties light.

**101st Division Involved**

According to the spokesman, the fighting began Tuesday after soldiers of the 101st Air Cavalry Division set up a cordon around an area and began moving in.

Fighting tapered in the evening, but by noon yesterday units of the division, trudging through muddy fields, came under sharp fire. Fighting continued into the morning.

Farther north, near another key infiltration route into Saigon, soldiers of the United States 25th Infantry Division fought two enemy companies seven miles southeast of Tayninh. During the four-hour bat-

Continued on Page 10, Column 1

## Defeat for Doves Reflects Deep Division in the Party

By JOHN W. FINNEY

Special to The New York Times

CHICAGO, Aug. 28—A deeply divided Democratic National Convention, after a climactic floor clash between the Administration's supporters and its critics, adopted today a White House-dictated plank supporting President Johnson's policy in Vietnam. The whole platform was then approved.

By a vote of 1,567¾ to 1,041¼, the convention re-

*Excerpts from the debate on platform, Page 22.*

jected a plank advanced by Democratic doves calling for an unconditional halt in the bombing of North Vietnam. Instead, it adopted a plank that called for a bombing halt but only on conditional terms.

The vote reflected the deep, emotional division within the party over the Vietnam issue. The division manifested itself in nearly three hours of increasingly acrimonious debate, conducted against a backdrop of sporadic chants of "Stop the war!" from the galleries and the New York and California delegations.

It was a division that Vice President Humphrey, in his bid for the Presidential nomination, had hoped to avoid. But he could not avoid it when Mr. Johnson intervened behind the scenes to toughen the language of the plank so that it would correspond to Administration policy.

In the wake of the policy confrontation, the major question was whether Mr. Hum-

Continued on Page 25, Column 1

## HUMPHREY AIDES LIST 4 FOR TICKET

### Say Muskie, Harris, Alioto and Shriver Are Leading for the No. 2 Spot

By STEVEN V. ROBERTS

Special to The New York Times

CHICAGO, Aug. 28—Aides of Vice President Humphrey advanced four names today as leading candidates for the Vice-Presidential nomination: Senators Edmund S. Muskie of Maine and Fred R. Harris of Oklahoma, Mayor Joseph L. Alioto of San Francisco and Sargent Shriver, the Ambassador to France.

The list contained no surprises. All four men have figured in recent speculation.

However, Mr. Humphrey met in his hotel suite today with key political figures, including Mayor Richard J. Daley of Chicago, and aides said the Vice-Presidency was one topic of discussion. It was generally believed that the final decision would not be made until tomorrow.

It was considered a remote possibility that Mr. Humphrey would try to heal the deep breach in the party over the Vietnam war by choosing a prominent war critic. Senators Eugene J. McCarthy of Minnesota, George S. McGovern of South Dakota and Edward M.

Continued on Page 22, Column 2

## PRAGUE'S LEADERS WARNED BY SOVIET

### It Says It Will Be Vigilant—Hints Doubt on Outcome

By RAYMOND H. ANDERSON

Special to The New York Times

MOSCOW, Aug. 28—The Soviet Union warned today that the reform leaders of Czechoslovakia, although allowed to return to Prague and to retain their positions after the negotiations here, were on a short leash and under the vigilant eyes of the Kremlin.

Soviet commentators asserted that a counterrevolutionary threat continued to exist in Czechoslovakia, and they indicated that Moscow had doubts that the Prague leadership could or would cope with the dangers adequately.

[In Bonn, the West German Government called for a complete restoration of Czechoslovakia's sovereignty and a pullback of all Soviet invasion forces. Page 6.]

Pravda, the Communist party organ, expressed indignation that underground radio stations in Czechoslovakia had broadcast criticism of the agreement worked out in Moscow between the Soviet leadership and a Czechoslovak delegation headed by President Ludvik Svoboda.

Yuri Zhukov, the political

Continued on Page 4, Column 3

## Dubcek Was Put in Handcuffs: An Account of Confrontation

*The following chronological account of the confrontation of Soviet and Czechoslovak leaders after the invasion of Czechoslovakia was written by Vincent Buist of Reuters.*

PRAGUE, Aug. 28—Alexander Dubcek, the Czechoslovak Communist leader, was hustled out of his party headquarters last Wednesday, handcuffed and flown to a secret destination in Slovakia in a Soviet military aircraft.

All the way he sat on the plane's metal deck.

This was disclosed in an account of Mr. Dubcek's arrest and of the Moscow negotiations given to me today by an official of the Czechoslovak Communist party's Central Committee.

The official said Mr. Dubcek was in his private room speaking on the telephone when the Central Committee building was surrounded by Soviet paratroopers with light tracked vehicles last Wednesday morning.

The party leader was trying to find out details of the extent of the invasion as a Soviet security officer and two soldiers armed with light machine guns burst into the room.

They tore the telephone out of Mr. Dubcek's hands and ripped the wire out of the wall, the official said.

The party leader was taken away and locked in a room in

Continued on Page 2, Column 5

## The Party and the Police

By JAMES RESTON

Special to The New York Times

CHICAGO, Aug. 28—The Democratic party was deeply hurt politically here tonight by the vicious clashes between demonstrators and the police in the streets of Chicago. Though the party itself had no direct responsibility for the incidents, it held its convention here knowing of the dangers of violence and counted on Mayor Daley and his police to handle the situation without embarrassment to the party. This gamble failed, despite all the barbed wire barricades, the police, secret agents and National Guardsmen. It was not only that Mayor Daley was condemned from the rostrum and

News Analysis

stood in the aisles mocking Senator Abraham Ribicoff, who had condemned the police action, but tens of millions watched the incidents on television to the obvious detriment of the Democratic party.

By the end of the night, Daley had become a symbol in the convention of the opposition within the party to the turbulent conditions of American life. So strong was the feeling against Mayor Daley and his police that even the name of Illinois was loudly booed when the roll of the states was called for nominations for the Presidency.

Thus the convention pre-

Continued on Page 20, Column 3



## Gruening Defeated In Alaska Primary

By LAWRENCE E. DAVIES

Special to The New York Times

ANCHORAGE, Alaska, Aug. 28—A dramatic, unexpected victory by a dark, good-looking, 38-year-old challenger has terminated the long political career of Senator Ernest Gruening, an 81-year-old warhorse known to his admirers as "Mr. Alaska."

Mike Gravel, a real estate developer from Anchorage and former Speaker of the state's House of Representatives, won the Democratic nomination for the Senate over Mr. Gruening in yesterday's primary election in Alaska.

Unofficial returns to Secretary of State Keith Miller in

Continued on Page 26, Column 5

NEWS INDEX



| | Page | | Page |
|---|---|---|---|
| Art | 32 | Man in the News | 20 |
| Books | 33 | Movies | 44-46 |
| Bridge | 33 | Music | 44-46 |
| Business | 57, 58 | Obituaries | 35 |
| Chess | 33 | Real Estate | 58 |
| Crossword | 33 | Ships and Air | 70 |
| Editorials | 34 | Society | 40 |
| Fashions | 42 | Sports | 47-51 |
| Financial | 51-56 | Theaters | 44-46 |
| Food | 42 | TV and Radio | 71 |
| | | Weather | 70 |

News Summary and Index, Page 37

"All the News That's Fit to Print"

# The New York Times

LATE CITY EDITION

Weather: Sunny today; clear, cool tonight. Sunny, mild tomorrow. Temp. range: today 78-58; Thursday 71-61. Temp.-Hum. Index yesterday 70. Complete U.S. report on page 66.

VOL. CXVII..No. 40,396 — NEW YORK, FRIDAY, AUGUST 30, 1968 — 10 CENTS



# HUMPHREY BARS RIGIDITY IN VIETNAM POLICY AND FLOUTING OF LAW; MUSKIE ON HIS TICKET

## CZECHS TO RENEW CURBS ON PRESS AND NONRED CLUBS

### Smrkovsky Discloses Plan for Restraint on Reform Under Moscow Pact

*Excerpts from speech giving terms of accord, Page 2.*

By TAD SZULC
Special to The New York Times

PRAGUE, Aug. 29—Plans to restore press censorship and disband non-Communist political groups were announced here today as the first steps to restrain Czechoslovakia's democratic reform in the wake of last week's invasion by the Soviet Union and four of its Warsaw Pact allies.

The measures were disclosed in a radio address to the nation by Josef Smrkovsky, President of the National Assembly. Mr. Smrkovsky was one of the Czechoslovak leaders seized by Soviet forces Aug. 21 and taken to Moscow, where they then negotiated under duress a compromise accord looking to ultimate departure of the occupation troops.

The assembly leader was vague about the scope of censorship. He said:

"We shall have to take special measures in the field of radio, television and the press to prevent writings against the foreign policy requirements and the interests of the Republic."

Mr. Smrkovsky indicated that the National Assembly, whose members have expressed disapproval of the Moscow accord, would be asked to draft legislation for the new restrictions.

**Self-Censorship Seen**

Today's Prague newspapers, the first to appear since the Soviet-Czechoslovak agreement was made public Tuesday, seemed to practice self-censorship pending restoration of official curbs. They confined themselves to publication of speeches made by Czechoslovak leaders in the last few days and other official material.

Literarni Listy, liberal weekly of the writers' union, announced in a one-page issue that it would discontinue publication if censorship was reimposed. Freedom of the press was introduced into this Communist country last January at the start of the movement toward democratization.

The radio stations, still in the hands of the resistance movement, continued to operate from their clandestine studios. But, like television, they were expected to return to the air soon as official Government institutions.

The first sign of renewed Government control came with word that Jiri Pelikan, director of national television, and Zdenek Hejzlar, head of the

Continued on Page 2, Column 2

## Moscow Says Foes Peril Czech Accord

By HENRY KAMM
Special to The New York Times

MOSCOW, Aug. 29—The Soviet Union charged today that "counterrevolutionary forces" in Czechoslovakia were trying to frustrate the carrying out of the obligations Czechoslovakia undertook in her negotiations with the Soviet Union.

These negotiations, which concluded here Tuesday, provided for restraints on the democratization program.

In a situation report published by Tass, the official press agency, Moscow accused unidentified counterrevolutionaries of attacking the leaders of the Czechoslovak party and Government in an attempt to seize power.

During the Moscow negotiations, the Soviet Union accused the so-called counterrevolutionaries of supporting Czechoslovakia's leaders. Now that Alexander Dubcek, First

Continued on Page 3, Column 1

## ECONOMIC LOSSES OF CZECHS HEAVY

### Prague Experts Say 2 Years Are Needed to Recover—Trade Dislocation Cited

Special to The New York Times

PRAGUE, Aug. 29 — Leading economists here believe it will take Czechoslovakia at least two years to recover from the economic consequences of the Soviet invasion.

This assessment came in a two-page report by the Economics Institute of the Czechoslovak Academy of Sciences.

The chief concern is not so much the physical damage and production losses suffered over the last week. Rather, it is the effect on external economic relations. The report said the invasion would have "catastrophic consequences on the complicated machinery of the Czech economy."

**Sought Western Investment**

Before the Soviet-bloc armies invaded on Aug. 20, Czechoslovakia had been making a major effort to increase her earnings of hard currency so that she could buy the Western equipment needed to modernize her industrial plant.

Czechoslovakia had to try to sell more goods in the West and attract Western capital investments. Progress was slow. There were few goods manufactured here of interest in the West. Investors were reluctant to invest their money here.

Nevertheless, before the Soviet Union and its allies struck, hundreds of Western businessmen were in Prague studying ways of developing markets, as

Continued on Page 2, Column 6

## THOUSANDS MARCH

### Scores Are Arrested, Some Delegates—Tear Gas Is Used

By J. ANTHONY LUKAS
Special to The New York Times

CHICAGO, Friday, Aug. 30—More than 150 people, including nine convention delegates, were arrested last night after National Guardsmen halted 3,000 persons marching toward the International Amphitheatre.

The guardsmen then fired tear gas to disperse the rest of the crowd. Later they fired more tear gas into ranks of demonstrators in front of the Conrad Hilton Hotel.

The first canisters of gas arched into crowds on Michigan Avenue at exactly 10:30 P.M., just as Vice President Humphrey was mounting the podium in the Amphitheatre to make his acceptance speech.

The arrests occurred at 18th Street and Michigan Avenue after the mass march, led by Dick Gregory, the comedian and black militant, was halted by guardsmen in armored personnel carriers and jeeps with barbed-wire barriers mounted on their hoods.

**Ordered to Turn**

The guardsmen told the demonstrators that they would have to turn west on 18th Street. Mr. Gregory insisted that all members of the huge throng were invited to his home on East 55th Street, south of the Amphitheatre.

"We have a right to go to my house," Mr. Gregory said.

But Brig. Gen. John R. Phipps, field commander of the National Guard contingent here, refused to let them proceed. High-ranking city officials said that the march was being blocked on the advice of the Secret Service.

The marchers decided to insist on their rights. One by one they walked through the barriers where they were seized by National Guardsmen and escorted to huge police vans.

**Other Delegates**

The first marcher through was Mr. Gregory himself, dressed in tan coveralls and a rain hat. Then came Tommy Fraser, a crippled delegate from Oklahoma riding in a wheel chair.

Then came other delegates, including Murray Kempton, the New York Post columnist, who is a delegate from Manhattan; Peter Weiss and the Rev. Richard Neuhaus of the Bronx, and Richard Samuel of Westfield, N. J.

Earlier, an enforcement officer had told the delegates that if they kept their delegates' cards on they would be escorted to the Amphitheatre, about four miles away.

The delegates caucused on the sidewalk and decided to seek arrest instead. They took off their credentials. "We have

Continued on Page 14, Column 1

Associated Press

THE DEMOCRATIC CANDIDATES: Vice President Humphrey and his wife with Senator Edmund S. Muskie and Mrs. Muskie as they acknowledged the applause at the convention, before the Vice President made his acceptance speech.

## M'CARTHY PLEDGES DRIVE WILL GO ON

### Tells Peace Demonstrators He'll Campaign for Doves but Not for Humphrey

*Excerpts from McCarthy talk appear on Page 16.*

Special to The New York Times

CHICAGO, Aug. 29 — In a farewell address to his youthful troops today, Senator Eugene J. McCarthy urged them not to despair at his defeat, the rejection of the dovish Vietnam plank by the Democratic National Convention, or "what may be accomplished in the future."

"We have not lost the fight on the [Vietnam] issue," he declared.

On the contrary, he said, "we have had a great victory to this point, one which should reassure us about the system itself."

Later, in a speech before several thousand of the young demonstrators involved in last night's clash with the police, the Senator promised to carry on his campaign against the war by helping other doves win election in the fall and by withholding his endorsement from either national ticket.

Thus did Senator McCarthy seek to keep his young supporters where he had brought them nine months ago when he announced his Presidential candidacy — within the traditional political process—and try to head off any further violence tonight.

**Talks to Demonstrators**

An hour after his farewell meeting with his supporters at the Conrad Hilton, Senator McCarthy walked out of the hotel, passed the blue line of the Chicago police, crossed Michigan Avenue, went through the olive line of National Guardsmen, and spoke to the throng of young dissidents.

The Secret Service had sought to persuade the Senator not to go into the midst of the various peace groups — some of them simply antiwar, others radical and even pro-Vietcong.

The Secret Service agents were evidently concerned that the Senator might get hurt, or that he might set off a demonstration that would bring police clubs into action again, and that Mr. McCarthy would be blamed for the violence.

The Senator was introduced by Dick Gregory, the Negro comedian, who said, "I've been trying to get this Secret Service protection for two months."

Continued on Page 16, Column 1



## Daley Defends His Police; Humphrey Scores Clashes

### Criticism Angers Mayor

By R. W. APPLE Jr.
Special to The New York Times

CHICAGO, Aug. 29 — Infuriated by attacks upon himself, his city and his police force, Mayor Richard J. Daley defended today the manner in which antiwar, anti-Humphrey demonstrations were suppressed in downtown Chicago last night.

Mr. Daley described the demonstrators as "terrorists" and said they had come here determined to "assault, harass and taunt the police into reacting before television cameras."

The Mayor flushed deeply as he denounced the reports of newspapers, radio and television last night. He asserted that "the whole purpose of the city and the law enforcement agencies" had been "distorted and twisted."

"In the heat of emotion and riot," Mr. Daley said, "some policemen may have overreacted, but to judge the entire police force by the alleged action of a few would be just as unfair as to judge our entire younger generation by the actions of the mob."

In an interview tonight on

Continued on Page 15, Column 1

### Nominee Faults Both Sides

By ROY REED
Special to The New York Times

CHICAGO, Aug. 29 — Vice President Humphrey had sharp words today for the Chicago police and the demonstrators they battled in the streets while he was being nominated for President last night.

He said he had talked to the Justice Department and been assured that the Federal Bureau of Investigation was looking into the incident.

He defended Mayor Richard J. Daley, who has been charged with permitting the police to beat demonstrators and newsmen. Mr. Daley delivered 112 of Illinois's 118 delegate votes to Mr. Humphrey at the Democratic National Convention.

The Vice President said he and Mrs. Humphrey had been threatened with assassination "half a dozen times."

"What is the Mayor of this city supposed to do about that?" he asked during an interview on the National Broadcasting Company's "Today" television show. "Everyone of us were threatened and had to be under heavy guard. Now that doesn't make you feel very happy."

"Now you don't have to be

Continued on Page 15, Column 5

## MUSKIE BIDS PARTY RESPOND TO YOUTH

### Vice-Presidential Candidate Strikes Conciliatory Tone in Acceptance Speech

*Text of the Muskie address will be found on Page 17.*

By JOHN W. FINNEY
Special to The New York Times

CHICAGO, Aug. 29—Senator Edmund S. Muskie of Maine, accepting the Democratic nomination as Vice President, called on the Democratic party tonight to respond to the protests of youth by attempting to build a society in which there would be equal respect for all as well as respect for law and order.

Speaking before a convention that had been in a state of turmoil over the clashes between youthful demonstrators and the Chicago police, the Maine Senator attempted to strike a conciliatory tone to draw the protesting youth back into the Democratic party.

The time has come, he said, to acknowledge that concealed behind the "illusion of prosperity for all, are shortcomings in our society that conceal hunger, poverty and despair."

**The Spirit of the Young**

"Freedom does not work unless we work at it," he said, "and that I believe to be part of the reason for the spirit and determination of so many of the young people, and the disadvantaged among them, to make a place for themselves in the building of our country."

Their efforts and protests, he continued, "should be viewed as the most creative expression of the human spirit."

It is "disquieting," he said, that at times this youthful unrest is expressed in unrestrained, irrational and sometimes explosive ways. Their protest, he said, may also be the result at times of "exploitation by militants whose motives are suspect."

But, he said, "We must have the patience to make the distinction between these two groups and to deal with each of them differently. We must learn to work with these people to insure their continued participation in the democratic process."

Senator Muskie's brief ac-

Continued on Page 12, Column 6

## RIOTING ASSAILED

### 2 Nominees Speak at Tumultuous Final Session of Parley

*Text of Humphrey's speech is printed on Page 17.*

By TOM WICKER
Special to The New York Times

CHICAGO, Aug. 29—Hubert H. Humphrey accepted the Democratic Presidential nomination tonight with a promise that on the issue of Vietnam "the policies of tomorrow need not be limited by the policies of yesterday."

In an emotional speech interrupted 75 times for applause, with some boos heard on three occasions, Mr. Humphrey pledged to unify his divided party and nation and call them to a "new sense of purpose as a free people."

Taking note of the street violence that has marred this convention week in Chicago, Mr. Humphrey insisted that "rioting, burning, sniping, mugging, traffic in narcotics and disregard for the law are the advance guard of anarchy" and had to be stopped.

But, he said, in a reply to the Republican nomination acceptance speech of Richard M. Nixon, "the answer does not lie in attacks on our courts or on our laws or our Attorney General."

**Voices Sadness at Violence**

"The answer lies in reasoned, effective action by state, local and Federal authority," he said. "We do not want a police state, but we do need a state of law and order," he added.

Mr. Humphrey and his handpicked Vice-Presidential running mate, Senator Edmund S. Muskie of Maine, appeared before a tumultuous final session of a Democratic National Convention that was bitterly divided on the issue of Vietnam and shocked by the violent street battle that raged here last night between antiwar demonstrators and the police.

Mr. Humphrey expressed "deep sadness" at this violence but said it had taught the lesson that "violence breeds counter-violence and it cannot be condoned whatever the sources."

**An Ovation for Johnson**

The nation should resolve tonight, he said, "that never, never again shall we see what we have seen."

When Mr. Humphrey mentioned President Johnson's name as the President who had "accomplished more of the unfinished business of America than any of his modern predecessors," some scattered booing was heard.

But a tremendous ovation for Mr. Johnson followed when Mr. Humphrey said:

"Tonight, to you, Mr. President, I say thank you, thank you, Mr. President."

Mr. Muskie was approved at

Continued on Page 12, Column 1

## Mrs. Shapiro Says Galamison Is Sabotaging Board's Sessions

By LEONARD BUDER

The president of the Board of Education yesterday accused the Rev. Milton A. Galamison, a newly appointed member, of "encouraging and condoning" disruptions of board meetings by "self-appointed community groups."

Mrs. Rose Shapiro, the president, said that Mr. Galamison had engaged in "a consistent campaign of sabotage and vilification of the board" during the current controversy over school decentralization.

Mr. Galamison, a long-time critic of the board before he was named a member last month by Mayor Lindsay, replied that the disruptions were "an indication of an absolute lack of public confidence in the Board of Education." He denied any role in the disruptions.

He declared that both Mrs. Shapiro and Dr. Aaron Brown, the vice president, should resign because "they are not in touch with reality." He added that if they did not resign, he would renew efforts to get the board to elect new officers.

Mrs. Shapiro, a member of the board since 1963, made her charges while commenting on Wednesday's tumultuous 12-hour public hearing on the board's proposed school decentralization plan.

The session ended at 9:25 P.M., with 65 speakers waiting to be heard, when the board members present could not control angry persons in the audience and restore order. A half hour earlier, Superintendent of Schools Bernard E. Donovan stormed out of the hearing at the Fashion Institute of Technology, after being jeered, taunted and insulted.

During the long session, advocates of total community control of local schools, who were in the majority, booed and interrupted speakers with different views.

Mrs. Shapiro said in an interview that the board would not hold another public hearing on decentralization. She said that the members would meet on Sept. 3 to try to work out a plan to take effect next month.

Mrs. Shapiro also indicated that the scheduled Sept. 4 public meeting, at which the board was to formally adopt its plan, might have to be put off a day or two.

She deplored the disorders that marked the hearing Wednesday and one Monday on Federally financed school programs and the Aug. 21 board meeting. All three were

Continued on Page 5, Column 1

## Zeckendorf Files Bankruptcy Plea

By TERRY ROBARDS

William Zeckendorf Sr., the real estate executive whose buildings helped shape the New York skyline, filed a petition yesterday for an arrangement with creditors under Chapter XI of the Federal Bankruptcy Act.

The petition, filed here in United States District Court, lists personal assets of $1,883,620.73 and liabilities of $79,076,100.53. It came three years after the keystone of his real estate empire, Webb & Knapp, Inc., was committed to reorganization under the Bankruptcy Act.

The 61-year-old businessman, who cut a wide swath through the financial and real estate worlds as Webb & Knapp's flamboyant chairman,

Continued on Page 54, Column 1

## Week's U.S. War Dead of 308 Highest of Summer

### Wounded Are Put at 1,134 and 4,755 of the Enemy Are Listed as Killed

By BERNARD WEINRAUB
Special to The New York Times

SAIGON, South Vietnam, Friday, Aug. 30—The United States command said yesterday that 308 Americans were killed in action last week and 1,134 wounded, the highest level of the summer.

The number of deaths was almost double the total for each of the three previous weeks and was the highest since 324 American servicemen were killed in the week that ended June 15.

The command said that the number of enemy dead for the week that ended Aug. 24 was 4,755, almost double that of the previous week.

The figures brought to 27,101 the total number of American servicemen killed in action in Vietnam. The total of wounded rose to 169,296.

The command also disclosed a slight decrease of 3,500 men in the total number of American forces in Vietnam. A spokesman said there were now 539,500 servicemen in Vietnam. A week earlier, the number was 543,000.

[In Washington, a Defense Department spokesman said Thursday that the decrease in manpower was not politically significant. He said the decrease represented a fluctuation in rotation schedules and that the long-term trend remained one of increasing United States troop strength to the authorized total of 550,000 men.]

The casualty figures reflected the fierce fighting last week in the Mekong Delta region and the northern provinces, which continued yesterday. Especially sharp clashes were reported north of Saigon, in the Central Highlands and near the old imperial capital of Hue.

Soldiers of the United States 101st Air Cavalry Division, moving along canals and swamps, fought for the third consecutive day 32 miles northwest of Saigon, in an area used by the enemy for infiltration of new troops.

The fighting, against a sizable enemy force, was supported by helicopter gunships, tactical fighters and artillery. The enemy soldiers were reported to be dug into bunkers and rice paddies about four miles north of the city of Trangbang.

Contact apparently broke off late yesterday as the enemy evaded American forces and withdrew. Military spokesmen said that 16 Americans had been killed and 25 wounded. The fighting began Tuesday

Continued on Page 7, Column 1

NEWS INDEX


| | Page | | Page |
|---|---|---|---|
| Books | 31 | Movies | 22-29 |
| Bridge | 30 | Music | 22-29 |
| Business | 54-55 | Obituaries | 33 |
| Buyers | 55 | Real Estate | 55 |
| Crossword | 31 | Ships and Air | 66 |
| Editorials | 32 | Society | 37 |
| Fashions | 36 | Sports | 38-42 |
| Financial | 45-53, 55 | Theaters | 22-29 |
| Food | 36 | TV and Radio | 67 |
| Letters | 32 | U. N. Proceedings | 2 |
| Man in the News | 12 | Weather | 66 |

News Summary and Index, Page 35

"All the News That's Fit to Print"

# The New York Times

LATE CITY EDITION

Weather: Partly sunny, windy and cool today. Fair, cool tomorrow. Temp. range: today 67-58; Thurs. 84-68. Full U.S. report on Page 93.

VOL. CXVIII . No. 40,431 — NEW YORK, FRIDAY, OCTOBER 4, 1968 — 10 CENTS



## GROMYKO, AT U.N., ASKS ARMS TALKS AS STEP TO PEACE

**Seeks 'Serious Exchange of Views' With U.S. on Curbs for Strategic Weapons**

**SPEECH IS CONCILIATORY**

**But He Terms Occupation of Czechoslovakia Vital to the 'Socialist Commonwealth'**

*Excerpts from Gromyko's talk will be found on Page 14.*

By DREW MIDDLETON
Special to The New York Times

UNITED NATIONS, N. Y., Oct. 3—The Soviet Foreign Minister, Andrei A. Gromyko, in a speech today, offered the General Assembly the prospect of progress toward peace through disarmament and arms control.

The Soviet Union, Mr. Gromyko declared, continues to be a "convinced advocate of finding possibilities of cooperation or even of joint action with the government of bourgeois countries for the common purpose of preventing a new world war."

To many delegates, Mr. Gromyko seemed to be telling the United States that a fresh start toward a détente could be made through steps toward disarmament. The Soviet Union, he declared, is ready to start "a serious exchange of views" with the United States on the mutual limitation and reduction of strategic nuclear weapons, including antimissile missiles.

**Adamant on Czechs**

The Foreign Minister, however, did not retreat from the Soviet contention that the occupation of Czechoslovakia was necessary to maintain "the socialist commonwealth." He warned that his country would "neither tolerate nor allow" any future attempts to weaken the Communist community in Eastern Europe.

United States officials on reflection said that Mr. Gromyko's speech had answered the five questions on Czechoslovakia posed yesterday by Secretary of State Dean Rusk. These included one asking for the withdrawal of Soviet and other Communist troops.

The "doctrinal" answers, these sources said, upset them because they reflected the ideological position expressed in a Pravda article on Sept. 29, which had been the target for Mr. Rusk's criticism. The answers, the officials said, should "alarm lots of people, like the Rumanians." The Rumanian Government, which has often pursued policies independent of Moscow, has shown great anxiety over the events in Czechoslovakia.

Mr. Gromyko, the Americans

Continued on Page 14, Column 1

Associated Press

IN EXILE: Fernando Belaúnde Terry, the ousted President of Peru, waving to newsmen as he arrived at Ezeiza Airport in Buenos Aires. He was replaced by a military junta.

## ARMY COUP OUSTS PERUVIAN REGIME

**President Belaunde Exiled to Argentina—Students Battle Troops in Lima**

By The Associated Press

LIMA, Peru, Oct. 3—Military leaders overthrew the Government of President Fernando Belaunde Terry before dawn today in a coup-d'état that encountered stiffening resistance as the day wore on. Students fought troops and policemen in the streets.

Whisked off by plane to Buenos Aires after the coup, Mr. Belaúnde, who is 55 years old, declared on arrival that he had been ousted in "a barracks coup," not by the armed forces of the constitutional Government.

Gen. Juan Velasco, Army Chief of Staff and President of the Joint Chiefs, was made head of the new military Government.

He issued a communiqué signed by himself and the navy and air force chiefs, indicating that the three services were involved.

The military leaders placed under house arrest all 11 members of a Cabinet that the President had sworn in only 14 hours before the coup. The Cabinet, seventh of Mr. Belaúnde's five-year regime, had been picked to deal with a

Continued on Page 2, Column 4

## DEATHS PUT AT 49 IN MEXICAN CLASH

**500 Wounded After Troops Fire on Students at Rally—1,500 Taken Prisoner**

By PAUL L. MONTGOMERY
Special to The New York Times

MEXICO CITY, Oct. 3—Student leaders struggled to regroup their forces today after a night of bloodshed that left dozens dead, hundreds wounded and 1,500 in jail.

A thousand federal soldiers fired rifles and machine guns at what had been a peaceful student rally in the plaza of a housing project last night. When the shooting ended an hour later, the plaza and an adjacent Aztec ruin were strewn with bodies.

The official toll of the battle, which has already become known as La Noche Triste—The Night of Sorrow—was 28 dead and 200 wounded. But it was virtually certain that at least 49 persons had been killed and 500 wounded.

**Olympics Planning Continues**

Despite the violence, Mexico plunged ahead with preparations for the Olympic Games, scheduled to start Oct. 12. Avery Brundage, chairman of the International Olympics Committee, said that there was no connection between the "student manifestations" and the Olympics. [Page 60.]

Reports of the street fighting between troops and students have apparently cut the number of visitors expected at the Olympics. Hotels and travel agents reported cancellations.

The Minister of Defense said

Continued on Page 3, Column 1

## EX-FISCAL OFFICER IS SEIZED ON COAST IN CITY FUND THEFT

**Dismissed Director of Human Resources Agency Accused of Embezzling $22,912**

By PETER KIHSS

The former director of fiscal affairs for the city's Human Resources Administration was arrested yesterday in California on a warrant charging she had embezzled $22,912.69 in funds of the agency, Arnold G. Fraiman, the city's Commissioner of Investigation, announced here.

The former official, Mrs. Helynn R. Lewis, was arrested at the Olympian Hotel in Los Angeles and held overnight in the women's jail in that city. She had been dismissed from her $19,000-a-year job Sept. 19 by Mitchell I. Ginsberg, head of the superagency, for refusing to answer questions by Commissioner Fraiman.

Mrs. Lewis originally entered city service as an administrative officer in the Head Start program for preschool children in December, 1966. When she was promoted to her last post last April 25, Mr. Ginsberg called her "an exceptionally competent manager" who had "made a valuable contribution to the city's antipoverty program."

**Youth Corps Not Involved**

Commissioner Fraiman, along with other local and Federal officials, has been investigating misappropriation of Neighborhood Youth Corps funds, including payrolls handled by Mrs. Lewis's staff. But he said yesterday that the funds involved in the embezzlement charge had nothing to do with the Youth Corps.

The Human Resources Administration said Mrs. Lewis, in her position as director of fiscal affairs, had been bonded for up to $5-million. In addition, the agency said, all of the persons responsible for Neighborhood Youth Corps finances in the summer had been bonded last July 18 in a package total for up to $3-million.

**U. S. May Make Claim**

Commissioner Ginsberg had estimated Wednesday that "the amount of misappropriated funds will be under $1-million" in the $16.8-million 1968 summer program of the corps. He also then said he expected the city and Federal governments would "recover all the money that may have been used" in that program.

Yesterday, however, it appeared the city may face substantial claims from the United States Department of Labor for misused funds in the corps' 1967 summer program for which there may not be bond protection. The city has estimated the 1967 losses at $250,000, but one source yesterday said further study may raise this to $450,000, largely caused by raising or duplicating of checks by low-level employes without bonding.

Representative Hugh L. Carey, a Brooklyn Democrat who has

Continued on Page 26, Column 4

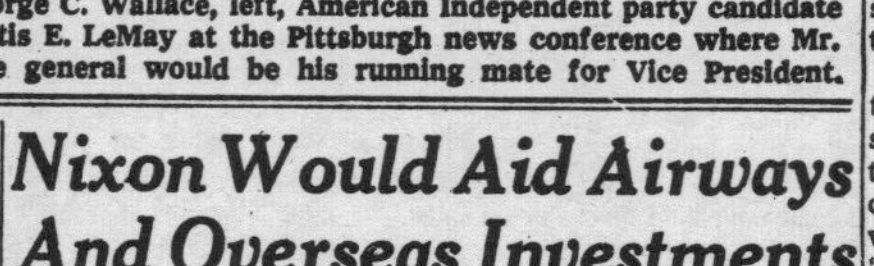

Associated Press

THE WALLACE TICKET: George C. Wallace, left, American Independent party candidate for President, with Gen. Curtis E. LeMay at the Pittsburgh news conference where Mr. Wallace announced that the general would be his running mate for Vice President.

## NEW SCHOOL PLAN STIRS PEACE HOPE

**Galamison Idea Would Link Ocean Hill to Harvard and Other Universities**

By LEONARD BUDER

A plan for ending the Ocean Hill-Brownsville school dispute that would involve giving the Brooklyn district the same powers exercised by independent school districts throughout the state was offered last night by the Rev. Milton A. Galamison, a member of the city's Board of Education.

The proposal was intended to lift the threat of a new citywide teachers' strike. Under it, the district would be linked to Harvard University and to institutions in New York City in a revised experiment to test total community control of local schools.

But Albert Shanker, the president of the United Federation of Teachers, immediately asserted that the plan was "extremely dangerous."

**Says Changes Are Needed**

Emerging from a meeting with Mr. Galamison, other city school officials and representatives of the Ocean Hill-Brownsville district, the union leader declared:

'The plan is unacceptable unless it is significantly modified."

Then he returned to the meeting at the Commodore Hotel, which had started at 6 P.M. At 1:25 this morning Mr. Shanker and Mr. Galamison came out of the session. They appeared in good spirits.

Mr. Shanker said that there had been "no resolution" but that further talks would be held later today.

Earlier, Mr. Galamison, in re-

Continued on Page 33, Column 2

## *Nixon Would Aid Airways And Overseas Investments*

By EILEEN SHANAHAN
Special to The New York Times

WASHINGTON, Oct. 3—Richard M. Nixon has pledged "swift action" to end congestion in the nation's airways and to repeal "at the earliest possible time" present Government restrictions on overseas investments by American corporations.

The promise to increase the number of air traffic controllers, airports and runways to end "years of neglect" of aviation was made in a letter dated Sept. 24, which was sent to individuals involved in both commercial and private aviation.

The text of the aviation policy letter was made public today by the Republican National Committee, following the disclosure two days ago that it existed and that another, privately circulated letter dealing with the securities industry existed as well.

**Campaigns in South**

The National Committee, at the same time, made public the text of a Nixon statement on foreign investment, which officials at the candidate's headquarters said was being circulated "approximately simultaneously" to heads of large corporations and banks and others directly interested in overseas investment.

Mr. Nixon himself, on his first sortie into the Deep South, declared in Atlanta that George C. Wallace was irresponsible and "should not be President." The attack marked a change of strategy for Mr. Nixon, who has previously been ignoring the third-party candidate in his public speeches.

Meanwhile, two Democratic Senators attacked Mr. Nixon both for the manner in which he had distributed his policy paper on the securities industry

Continued on Page 51, Column 1

## HOUSE DROPS CURB ON DESEGREGATION

**Rejects Earlier Bid to Block U.S. Efforts to End Dual School Systems in South**

By MARJORIE HUNTER
Special to The New York Times

WASHINGTON, Oct. 3—The House voted today to drop anti-integration provisions that it had written into a major appropriations bill just a few months ago.

The action was a major victory for civil rights forces and the Johnson Administration.

As approved last June by a wide margin, the provisions would have sharply limited school desegregation efforts in the South.

Federal officials would have been stripped of their one effective weapon—the withholding of Federal funds—in forcing an end to dual school systems throughout much of the South.

In backing down from its earlier stand, the House headed off a bruising fight with the Senate, where a strong move

Continued on Page 29, Column 2

## GEN. LEMAY JOINS WALLACE'S TICKET AS RUNNING MATE

**Says He Would Use Nuclear Bomb, but Rules It Out as Unnecessary in Vietnam**

**EX-GOVERNOR IS UPSET**

**Declares Former Air Force Chief 'Prefers Not to Use Any Sort of Weapon'**

*Excerpts from LeMay-Wallace news conference, Page 50.*

By WALTER RUGABER
Special to The New York Times

PITTSBURGH, Oct. 3—Gen. Curtis E. LeMay, the former Air Force Chief of Staff, became George C. Wallace's Vice-Presidential running mate today and promptly dropped some political bombs in the third-party campaign.

"If I found it necessary [in the Vietnam war]," the general said, "I would use anything that we could dream up, including nuclear weapons, if it was necessary." But he added, "I don't think it's necessary in this case or this war to use it."

Mr. Wallace, who has taken great pains to assure audiences in his Presidential bid that he would use only conventional weapons in Vietnam, appeared markedly perturbed by all the general's talk of nuclear bombs.

As his campaign plane left Pittsburgh for stops in Indianapolis and Toledo, the former Alabama Governor insisted to reporters aboard that the general also flatly ruled out a nuclear war in Vietnam.

**An Angry Response**

The general was presented by Mr. Wallace at a nationally televised news conference in the Pittsburgh Hilton Hotel.

When Jack Nelson, southern correspondent of The Los Angeles Times, asked Mr. Wallace whether he agreed with the general's position, the Alabamian, obviously nettled, snapped back:

"What you're doing, Mr. Nelson, is typical of The Los Angeles Times. You're trying to say that if the time ever came that it was necessary to use any sort of weapon in the vital interests of our national security, you wouldn't use them.

"All General LeMay has said—and I know you fellows better than he does because I've had to deal with you—he said that if the security of the country depended on the use of any weapon in the future he would use it. But he said he prefers not to use any sort of weapon. He prefers to negotiate."

Mr. Nelson again asked whether Mr. Wallace agreed

Continued on Page 50, Column 6

## *Tigers Set Back Cardinals, 8-1, Drawing Even in World Series*

By JOSEPH DURSO
Special to The New York Times

ST. LOUIS, Oct. 3—Mickey Lolich tied the World Series with flair today by pitching and batting the Detroit Tigers to an 8-1 victory over the St. Louis Cardinals.

He stopped the Cardinals on six hits, hit the first home run of his six-year major league career, forced in another run by walking with the bases loaded and hit a single.

He received plenty of help from his teammates, who had been victimized in the opening game yesterday by Bob Gibson and his record performance of 17 strike-outs.

With Gibson watching harmlessly today from the top step of the dugout, the Tigers attacked four Cardinal pitchers with 13 hits that included three home runs—one by Willie Horton in the second inning, one by Lolich in the third and one by Norm Cash in the sixth.

The series now moves to Detroit for the next three games. It will be resumed Saturday with Ray Washburn pitching for St. Louis against Earl Wilson.

Lolich, who revived Detroit's chances with a stunningly rounded effort, often takes a back seat to Denny McLain as a flamboyant personality. He won 17 games this season while McLain was winning 31. He

Continued on Page 58, Column 5

## *Turbulent Market Highest in 2 Years*

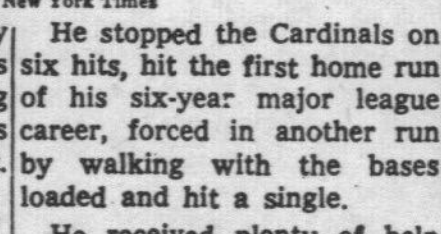

Stock market prices rose briskly yesterday to reach their highest level in two years. Volume on the New York Stock Exchange boomed to 21.11 million shares, the second busiest session on record.

On Wall Street, analysts attributed part of the strong performance to increasing talk of a "Nixon market," reflecting confidence that a Republican Administration and a conservative Congress would be good for corporate profits.

Meanwhile, the basic impetus for advancing stock prices continues to come from prospects of further inflation, an increase in the money supply and the surprising rise in the economy.

*Details on Page 69.*

Associated Press

TAKING PRISONERS: Soldier using his rifle butt to prod students captured during clash in Mexico City Wednesday

## *Humphrey Visits West Virginia, Hoping to Reverse 1960 Defeat*

By R. W. APPLE Jr.
Special to The New York Times

WOLF PEN, W. Va., Oct. 3—Eight years ago, Hubert H. Humphrey stood in a hotel room in Charleston to renounce, for the moment, his hopes for the Presidency. Today he returned to West Virginia, a candidate for the White House once more.

In 1960, the Vice President suffered the worst defeat of his long political career in this outpost of Appalachia, losing to John F. Kennedy in the state's Presidential primary. So today was full of reminders of the past as well as hopes for the future.

Jimmy Wolford, the stocky, crew-cut minstrel, brought out his battered guitar and sang again his plaintive tune about "Hubert Humphrey, your man and mine."

Marvin Crouch came along, too—a little man with a weatherbeaten face and a devotion to Mr. Humphrey so fierce that he used to get into fist fights with supporters of John F. Kennedy.

James H. Rowe Jr., the lean, rawboned old political professional from Montana, rode in the press bus, looking out at the long motorcade snaking through the hills and hollows and remembering how Mr. Humphrey campaigned here eight years ago, in a wheezing old bus adorned with a banner that proclaimed him "The Man With Heart from the Heartland of America."

And John M. Bailey of Connecticut, who was with Mr. Kennedy in 1960, sat a couple of seats farther back, with his glasses up on his forehead as always, absorbing a constant needling from Mr. Rowe.

"There's another post office back there," Mr. Rowe would call out. "You people took care of this state. Must have more new post offices than California or New York."

It was a melancholy day,

Continued on Page 52, Column 1

NEWS INDEX


| | Page | | Page |
|---|---|---|---|
| Books | 44-45 | Music | 33-43 |
| Bridge | 44 | Obituaries | 47, 57 |
| Business | 68-69, 79 | Real Estate | 80 |
| Buyers | 68 | Ships and Air | 93 |
| Crossword | 45 | Society | 56 |
| Editorials | 46 | Sports | 58-62 |
| Fashions | 54 | Theaters | 33-43 |
| Financial | 67-79 | TV and Radio | 95 |
| Food | 54 | U. N. Proceedings | 15 |
| Man in the News | 50 | Wash. Proceedings | 16 |
| Movies | 33-43 | Weather | 93 |


News Summary and Index, Page 49

"All the News That's Fit to Print"

# The New York Times

LATE CITY EDITION

Weather: Rain today and tonight. Cloudy, showers likely tomorrow. Temp. range: today 52-48; Wed. 54-45. Full U.S. report on Page 93.

VOL. CXVIII . . No. 40,465  NEW YORK, THURSDAY, NOVEMBER 7, 1968 10 CENTS

# NIXON WINS BY A THIN MARGIN, PLEADS FOR REUNITED NATION

The New York Times (by Neal Boenzi)

SHE KNEW IT ALL ALONG: President-elect Richard M. Nixon holding crewelwork, a facsimile of Presidential seal embroidered by his daughter Julie, who stands beside her fiancé, David Eisenhower. Mrs. Nixon and daughter Patricia completed the family group at the Waldorf-Astoria yesterday.

## NIXON'S ELECTION EXPECTED TO SLOW PARIS NEGOTIATION

### Allied. Diplomats Suggest All Sides May Adopt a Wait-and-See Stance

By HEDRICK SMITH

Special to The New York Times

PARIS, Nov. 6 — Allied diplomats suggested tonight that Richard M. Nixon's election victory would add, at least temporarily, to the delays and complications of getting meaningful Vietnam peace negotiations under way.

The American, the North Vietnamese and the National Liberation Front delegations here had no comment on the election results.

But allied diplomats close to the talks suggested that the Republican victory would probably bring eventual changes in the American negotiating team, encourage delays by the South Vietnamese Government, and induce a wait-and-see attitude by all sides until Mr. Nixon's own approach to the talks became clearer.

The uncertainty about the future relationship between the outgoing Johnson Administration and Mr. Nixon is considered the primary complicating factor.

**Eyes on Saigon**

"Everybody has to see how Nixon and Johnson are going to handle this period," said one Western diplomat.

The Saigon Government is reported to feel that the Johnson Administration pressed it too rapidly toward expanded talks embracing the Vietcong. It now is expected to use the change-over period in the United States to play for time.

South Vietnamese officials here made no secret that they consider Mr. Nixon more sympathetic than Mr. Johnson to their position.

They have recently dropped hints that they expect no active negotiating on issues of substance until early next year.

Western diplomats now speculate that President Nguyen Van Thieu may delay sending a delegation to the talks here until he has learned Mr. Nixon's views.

But a more common opinion is that Saigon will send a delegation soon and then try to stall until the Republicans take office in January.

The Republican victory,

Continued on Page 13, Column 1

## POLICE SEIZE 125 ON C.C.N.Y. CAMPUS

### AWOL Soldier Taken From Student Center 'Sanctuary'

About 250 members of the Tactical Patrol Force moved onto the City College campus early today at the request of the administration and arrested more than 100 students and the AWOL soldier they had been guarding in a student center.

Under the direction of Police Commissioner Howard R. Leary, Chief Inspector Sanford Garelik and a number of other high police officials, the arrests were carried out without violence following a warning from the administration to vacate the building.

In all, about 125 persons were arrested, including supporters of the peace movement and Pvt. William Brakefield, who had been in the Finley Student Center, at 133d Street and Convent Avenue, since last

Continued on Page 4, Column 4



## Soviet Bids U.S. Confer; Calls for 'Normalization'

By HENRY KAMM

Special to The New York Times

MOSCOW, Nov. 6—The Soviet Union greeted the election of a new President of the United States today with a call for the "normalization" of relations between Moscow and Washington for the sake of world peace.

The demand was put forward in a speech on behalf of the ruling Politburo of the Communist party by First Deputy Premier Kirill T. Mazurov as election returns in the United States showed that Richard M. Nixon had won the Presidency. The occasion was the traditional speech in the Kremlin on the eve of the anniversary of the Bolshevik Revolution.

To underline the importance Moscow attaches to relations with the United States, Mr. Mazurov raised the issue twice. Noting Soviet proposals for mutual limitations on nuclear weapons and delivery systems, the official said:

"It is relevant to recall in this connection that we have expressed readiness to conduct negotiations with the United States on the entire range of these problems. But their positive solution does not depend on the Soviet Union alone."

**Review of Soviet Actions**

After a review of Soviet actions on the international scene, Mr. Mazurov returned to Soviet-American relations. He said:

"We have always attached great importance to the normalization of relations between the Soviet Union and the United States, which would be important not only to both of our countries but also to world peace."

A public offer to enter into negotiations with the United States for an accommodation on vital issues was regarded as a Soviet reaction to the

Continued on Page 14, Column 1

## POSITION ON SINAI DEFINED BY ISRAEL

### Note to Jarring Links Issue of Boundaries to Security Needs and Tiran Rights

By DREW MIDDLETON

Special to The New York Times

UNITED NATIONS, N. Y., Nov. 6—Israel has told the United Arab Republic that her attitude toward the boundary problem will be governed by her security needs and the maintenance of full protection of Israeli navigation in the Strait of Tiran.

This is the first time that Israel has defined with any precision her interest in the Sinai Peninsula.

Western diplomats inferred that if Israel's security requirements were fulfilled, including protection of shipping in the Strait of Tiran, the Government would not reject an arrangement that returned a demilitarized Sinai to Egypt. The peninsula has been occupied by Israel since the Israeli-Arab war of June, 1967.

This information was in a memorandum that Foreign Minister Abba Eban gave yesterday to Dr. Gunnar V. Jarring, the United Nations intermediary. Mr. Eban went over the text of the memorandum with Dr. Jarring at meetings yesterday afternoon and last night.

Ambassador Jarring was asked to transmit the memorandum to Mahmoud Riad, the Egyptian Foreign Minister. The clarification of Israel's approach to the boundary problem apparently was intended to rebut Mr.

Continued on Page 2, Column 3

NEWS INDEX


| | Page | | Page |
|---|---|---|---|
| Books | 44-45 | Movies | 51-54 |
| Bridge | 44 | Music | 51-54 |
| Business | 65, 76-77 | Obituaries | 47, 50 |
| Buyers | 77 | Real Estate | 79 |
| Chess | 44 | Ships and Air | 93 |
| Crossword | 45 | Society | 55 |
| Editorials | 46 | Sports | 58-63 |
| Fashions | 56 | Theaters | 51-54 |
| Financial | 63-78 | TV and Radio | 95 |
| Food | 56 | U. N. Proceedings | 3 |
| Man in the News | 21 | Weather | 93 |

News Summary and Index, Page 49


## REPUBLICANS GAIN SAFE ALBANY EDGE

### Lead in Assembly Put at 77-73 and in Senate at 33-24 Unofficially

By JAMES F. CLARITY

Republican officials said yesterday that they expected to have clear majorities in both houses of the 1969 Legislature.

The Republicans, on the basis of unofficial but reliable vote-counts in the elections for the 150 Assembly and 57 Senate seats, will probably control the Assembly by 77 to 73, and the Senate by 33 to 24.

The official counts of several close Assembly races were not expected to affect lower house control, which the Republicans appeared almost certain to have wrested from the Democrats in Tuesday's election.

**Official Count Delayed**

The official count of the close races was expected to be completed early next week. The G.O.P. Senate majority was assured, regardless of the final count in a few close races.

But the Republicans' control of the Assembly, which they had lost in 1964, did not appear to give G.O.P. leaders assurance that their programs and legislation or those proposed by Governor Rockefeller would necessarily sail through the Legislature because of the majorities in both houses.

Among the Republicans who captured Democratic seats in the Assembly were several conservatives who, by combining with conservative Democrats, could obstruct, if not defeat, legislation they considered liberally oriented, or objectionable for other reasons.

Three of the newly elected Republican Assembly members

Continued on Page 40, Column 5

## The Election at a Glance

### President

Needed for Election—270 Electoral Votes

| | Number of States* | Electoral Votes |
|---|---|---|
| Humphrey | 14 | 191 |
| Nixon | 30 | 287 |
| Wallace | 5 | 45 |
| In Doubt: Alaska, Missouri. | 2 | 15 |

*Includes District of Columbia.

### The Senate

| Newly Elected Senators | | Make-up of New Senate | |
|---|---|---|---|
| Democrats | 18 | Democrats | 58 |
| Republicans | 15 | Republicans | 41 |
| In Doubt | 1 | In Doubt | 1 |

### The House

| | |
|---|---|
| Democrats Elected | 243 |
| Republicans Elected | 192 |

## Senate's Liberal Coalition Survives Gains by G.O.P.

By DAVID E. ROSENBAUM

Republicans made a net gain of at least four Senate seats in Tuesday's election, but the balance between liberals and conservatives did not appear to have changed substantially from the present Senate.

One Senate race remained in doubt last night. In Oregon, Wayne Morse, a Democrat, who served four terms, was running a close race with State Representative Robert W. Packwood, a Republican. Observers said it might be days before the outcome was certain.

Depending on the Oregon race, the Democrats will hold 58 or 59 seats in the new Senate to 41 or 42 for the Republicans. In the present Senate there are 63 Democrats and 37 Republicans.

Four conservative Republicans and one conservative Democrat were elected to seats that had been held by liberals or moderates. On the other hand, there was a shift in favor of liberals in at least two states.

Thus it appeared that a majority could still be formed from liberal Northern Democrats and moderate Republicans to pass legislation on such issues as civil rights and aid to education.

The Republicans' net gain of only four seats in the House of Representatives dashed the party's hopes of capturing control of that body.

In the Senate the Republicans picked up seats that had been held by Democrats in Arizona, Florida, Maryland, Ohio, Oklahoma and Pennsylvania. Democrats took Republican-held seats in California and Iowa.

Among the new conservatives was Barry Goldwater, the Republican Presidential nominee in 1964. He defeated Roy L. Elson for the Arizona

Continued on Page 29, Column 2

**Election Tables**

Tables reporting the vote in national, state and local contests in Tuesday's election are now scheduled for publication in The New York Times tomorrow.

The Times had expected to print them today, but breakdowns in the News Election Service's national and regional computers made a total recheck of the election results necessary. This recheck is expected to be concluded today.

## A Loser Concedes and Tries to Smile

By R. W. APPLE Jr.

Special to The New York Times

MINNEAPOLIS, Nov. 6—It was probably Hubert Horatio Humphrey's last hurrah in Presidential politics.

He had tried once before, in 1960, and had been crushed by the superb organization of John F. Kennedy in the West Virginia primary. Now he had lost again, this time to the man whom John Kennedy had defeated, in an agonizingly close finish.

*Transcript of the Humphrey statement is on Page 22.*

The Vice President—a hearty, sentimental man, given to laughter and to tears—tried to smile as he stood on the stage in the Leamington Hotel's ballroom this morning and listened to his faithful followers shout, "We Want Humphrey!" But what he brought forth was more a grimace than a grin. "Thank you very much," he said in a quavering voice. "It's nice to know."

Mr. Humphrey went through

Continued on Page 22, Column 1

Associated Press

Vice President Humphrey with his wife after conceding

## GOAL IS HARMONY

### President-Elect Vows His Administration Will Be 'Open'

By ROBERT B. SEMPLE Jr.

President-elect Richard M. Nixon turned yesterday from the business of winning elections to the business of assembling an Administration.

Weary but thankful, he appeared before an elated band of supporters gathered in the ballroom of the Waldorf-Astoria at 11:35 A.M. He expressed his gratitude for their efforts and his admiration for the "gallant and courageous fight" of his opponent.

*Transcript of Nixon's remarks will be found on Page 21.*

He also extended the hand of friendship to the disappointed partisans of Mr. Humphrey's cause—particularly the young.

Near the end of his eight-minute talk, Mr. Nixon took note of the division in the nation and pledged, in these words, to bend every effort to restore racial peace and social harmony:

"I saw many signs in this campaign. Some of them were not friendly and some were very friendly. But the one that touched me the most was one that I saw in Deshler, Ohio, at the end of a long day of whistle-stopping, a little town, I suppose five times the population was there in the dusk, almost impossible to see — but a teen-ager held up a sign, 'Bring Us Together.'

"And that will be the great objective of this Administration at the outset, to bring the American people together. This will be an open Administration, open to new ideas, open to men and women of both parties, open to the critics as well as those who support us.

"We want to bridge the generation gap. We want to bridge the gap between the races. We want to bring America together. And I am confident that this task is one that we can undertake and one in which we will be successful."

Several hours later the campaign entourage began to disassemble, its members heading home for a brief but long-overdue rest. The candidate himself flew southward for a three-day vacation in Key Biscayne, a peninsula just south of Miami where he rested occasionally during the campaign.

Although he has been urged

Continued on Page 21, Column 1

## ELECTOR VOTE 287

### Lead in Popular Tally May Be Smaller Than Kennedy's in '60

By MAX FRANKEL

Richard Milhous Nixon emerged the victor yesterday in one of the closest and most tumultuous Presidential campaigns in history and set himself the task of reuniting the nation.

Elected over Hubert H. Humphrey by the barest of margins—only four one-hundredths of a percentage point in the popular vote—and confronted by a Congress in control of the Democrats, the President-elect said it "will be the great objective of this Administration at the outset to bring the American people together."

He pledged, as the 37th President, to form "an open Administration, open to new ideas, open to men and women of both parties, open to critics as well as those who support us" so as to bridge the gap between the generations and the races.

**Details Left for Later**

But after an exhausting and tense night of awaiting the verdict at the Waldorf-Astoria Hotel here, Mr. Nixon and his closest aides were not yet prepared to suggest how they intended to organize themselves and to approach these objectives. The Republican victor expressed admiration for his opponent's challenge and reiterated his desire to help President Johnson achieve peace in Vietnam between now and Inauguration Day on Jan. 20.

The verdict of an electorate that appeared to number 73 million could not be discerned until mid-morning because Mr. Nixon and Mr. Humphrey finished in a virtual tie in the popular vote, just as Mr. Nixon and John F. Kennedy did in 1960.

With 94 per cent of the nation's election precincts reporting, Mr. Nixon's total stood last evening at 29,726,409 votes to Mr. Humphrey's 29,677,152. The margin of 49,257 was even smaller than Mr. Kennedy's margin of 112,803.

**Meaning Hard to Find**

When translated into the determining electoral votes of the states, these returns proved even more difficult to read, and the result in two states—Alaska and Missouri—was still not final last night. But the unofficial returns from elsewhere gave Mr. Nixon a minimum of 287 electoral votes, 17 more than the 270 required for election. Mr. Humphrey won 191.

Because of the tightness of the race, the third-party challenger, George C. Wallace, came close to realizing his minimum objective of denying victory to the major-party candidates and then somehow forcing a bargain for his sup-

Continued on Page 20, Column 1

## Johnson Vows Aid In Power Transfer

By NEIL SHEEHAN

Special to The New York Times

SAN ANTONIO, Tex., Nov. 6—In a telegram of congratulations this morning, President Johnson informed President-elect Richard M. Nixon that he would do "everything in my power to make your burdens lighter on that day when you assume the responsibilities of the President."

Even as Mr. Johnson's telegram was being transmitted to Mr. Nixon from the President's ranch 65 miles north of here, the machinery had been set in motion for an orderly transition from the old Administration to the new.

Lawson Knott, the administrator of the General Services

Continued on Page 20, Column 3

RICHARD M. NIXON

"All the News That's Fit to Print"

# The New York Times

LATE CITY EDITION

Weather: Occasional rain today, tonight. Cloudy, cold tomorrow. Temp. range: today 42-32; Monday 41-33. Full U.S. report on Page 94.

VOL. CXVIII...No. 40,540

NEW YORK, TUESDAY, JANUARY 21, 1969

10 CENTS

# NIXON, SWORN, DEDICATES OFFICE TO PEACE; OFFERS A ROLE TO YOUNG AND DISAFFECTED AND A CHANCE TO 'BLACK AS WELL AS WHITE'

## SOVIET TELLS U.S. THAT IT IS READY FOR MISSILE TALKS

### Terms Curb on Arms Race 'Realizable' but Not Easy —9-Point Plan Pressed

*Excerpts from the Moscow statement, Page 2.*

By THEODORE SHABAD
Special to The New York Times

MOSCOW, Jan. 20—The Soviet Government affirmed today, the day of Richard M. Nixon's inauguration, that it was ready to "start a serious exchange of views" on the control of nuclear missiles.

The Russians emphasized that they were "not more interested than the United States" in beginning the talks, which were agreed to last July but were delayed by tensions resulting from the Soviet-led military invasion of Czechoslovakia Aug. 20-21.

Soviet views on the projected missile talks and on nuclear disarmament in general were reiterated at a news conference held at the Foreign Ministry by Leonid M. Zamyatin, press chief, and Kirill V. Novikov, head of the ministry's International Organizations Department.

**Difficulties Acknowledged**

In a statement, Mr. Zamyatin reviewed a nine-point disarmament plan proposed last summer by Premier Aleksei N. Kosygin and pressed by the Soviet delegation during the session of the United Nations General Assembly last fall.

"The problem of limiting the nuclear arms race," the statement said, "is, in the opinion of the Soviet Government, a practically realizable, though not an easy, undertaking."

In answer to questions, Mr. Zamyatin denied that the news conference had been timed deliberately for Mr. Nixon's inauguration as President.

Mr. Novikov added:

"The disarmament issue has been a timely one for any government of any country, including both the old and the new Administrations in the United States. But if the Nixon Ad-

Continued on Page 2, Column 4

## Czech Sets Himself Afire In 2d Such Protest Action

By ALVIN SHUSTER
Special to The New York Times

PRAGUE, Jan. 20—A second young man set himself afire today, apparently in another protest for Czechoslovak freedom.

President Ludvik Svoboda announced the second incident in a television appearance tonight in which he urged young people to "stop these terrible acts."

The immolation occurred in Pilsen, about 50 miles southwest of Prague. The victim was identified as Josef Hlaraty, a 25-year-old brewery worker. [The Czechoslovak news agency, C.T.K., reported that Mr. Hlaraty had suffered second-degree burns and that it appeared likely that he would live, The Associated Press reported.]

Grim-faced and somber, Mr. Svoboda had just referred to the immolation on Thursday of 21-year-old student, Jan Palach, to whom tribute was paid in Prague today by tens of thousands of people.

[In Budapest, a 17-year-old student, carrying two small Hungarian flags, set himself afire. No motive for his action was made public.]

In referring to Mr. Palach, who died yesterday, as a person of "pure character and pure intentions," the President urged the country's youth not to show "their political attitudes in this way.

"I have just received a shocking report," he added, "that in Pilsen in a similar manner another young man made an attempt on his life. On behalf of your parents, of all the people in the country, and myself, and in the name of humanity, I

Continued on Page 3, Column 1

## Pueblo Skipper Says Navy Rejected 'Destruct System'

By BERNARD WEINRAUB
Special to The New York Times

CORONADO, Calif., Jan. 20—Comdr. Lloyd M. Bucher, the skipper of the Pueblo, said today that the Navy had turned down his request for a "destruct system" for the secret electronic and coding gear on the intelligence ship.

"I made the request at least two, perhaps three times," Commander Bucher said quietly at the opening of the Naval Court of Inquiry into the seizure of the ship last January by North Korea. "I'm quite sure," he said, that one letter was to the Chief of Naval Operations.

Standing stiffly beside a diagram of the Pueblo, the 41-year-old commander told the court of five admirals that his numerous requests to install such electronic equipment as a more extensive phone hookup, damage control gear and alarms had been rejected because of "money and time."

"There were never improvements that we were permitted because of money and time," said Commander Bucher, the first witness. "We did not get the improvements I requested."

Commander Bucher's failure or inability to destroy secret equipment on his ship is expected to be a key issue at the Court of Inquiry in an amphitheater on the Naval Amphibious Base here.

The fact that the North Koreans boarding the ship were not repulsed is also expected to be a key issue.

Commander Bucher testified that he had requested three gun mounts on the Pueblo. Two days before the ship left the Yokosuka Naval Base in Japan for the mission off North Korea, the Navy in-

Continued on Page 4, Column 4

## ARMS THIEVES KILL 3 GERMAN GUARDS

### 2 Other Soldiers Wounded In Raid on Ammunition Depot in the Saar

By DAVID BINDER
Special to The New York Times

BONN, Jan. 20—A German army munitions depot near Lebach in the Saarland was raided early today by a gang that shot five sentries, killing three and severely wounding two.

The federal Attorney General, Ludwig Martin, said that the gang had stolen about 1,400 rounds of small-arms ammunition and taken three carbines and two pistols from the sentries. The Lebach depot contained no other weapons and is not classified as secret. Its supplies of howitzer, mortar and small-arms ammunition are used by the 261st Parachute Battalion, garrisoned in Lebach.

At a news conference in Bonn, Government spokesmen said they had no clues to the identity or number of the raiders. It is believed that they were armed with machine pistols and knives.

The raid, described by a Defense Ministry spokesman as unparalleled in the history of

Continued on Page 3, Column 4

## TEACHER BEATEN, CLOTHING IGNITED

### Three Negro Youths Attack White Instructor at Lane

By PETER KIHSS

Three Negro youths beat a teacher and set his clothing afire yesterday in the racially tense Franklin K. Lane High School.

Frank Siracusa, the teacher, said he had dashed down the stairs to find who had tossed a stone through his classroom window, only to find himself suddenly squirted with fluid from a water pistol that was ignited by a cigarette lighter.

He escaped burns by stripping off his flaming coat and jacket, even while the shell frames of his eyeglasses melted in his pocket.

But he suffered abdominal injuries from being punched and kicked. He was taken from the school on the Brooklyn-Queens border to La Guardia Hospital in Queens, where he was kept for observation. The 30-year-old chemistry teacher was reported in good condition last night.

It was the 14th attack on a

Continued on Page 36, Column 1



## Johnson Rebuffs Udall on Plan To Set Aside Vast Park Acreage

By WILLIAM M. BLAIR
Special to The New York Times

WASHINGTON, Jan. 20—President Johnson added 384,500 acres to the national parkland system today in a rebuff to Secretary of the Interior Stewart L. Udall, who had sought to preserve 7.5 million acres.

The decision, Mr. Johnson's last official act, bowed to the demands of the Democratic chairman of the House Interior Committee, Representative Wayne N. Aspinall of Colorado.

The President's action was the culmination of more than a month of heated negotiations during which Secretary Udall was understood to have told Mr. Johnson, "You have my resignation right now."

This episode was believed to have occurred last Saturday evening after the Department of the Interior had prepared news releases announcing that the President had signed proclamations setting aside the 7.5 million acres. The White House denied he had signed, saying he still was considering the proclamations.

"I am deeply disappointed the President did not go all the way with me," Secretary Udall said with emotion today as word reached him in his office of the White House decision.

Mr. Udall, however, declined to discuss the bitter ending of eight years as Interior Secretary, during which the park-

Continued on Page 30, Column 1

The New York Times (by Edward Hausner)

THE 37TH PRESIDENT: Richard M. Nixon, his wife at his side, repeating the oath of office read by Chief Justice Earl Warren. Behind them are President Johnson and, partly hidden at right, Mr. Nixon's Vice President, Spiro T. Agnew.

## CABINET APPROVED EXCEPT FOR HICKEL

### Senate Swiftly Confirms 11 —Puts Off a Decision on Alaskan Until Today

Special to The New York Times

WASHINGTON, Jan. 20—The Senate swiftly confirmed 11 members of President Nixon's Cabinet today, but put off until tomorrow a decision on the 12th, Gov. Walter J. Hickel of Alaska, named as Secretary of the Interior.

The Alaskan, under attack as industry-oriented in his views on conservation of natural resources, won approval of the Senate Interior Committee earlier today on a 14-to-3 vote. The 11 other Cabinet members chosen by Mr. Nixon won declared or tacit approval of committees last week.

The Senate also put off for a day the nomination of Charles W. Yost to be United States representative to the United Nations. He was included in the list sent to the Senate today by Mr. Nixon shortly after he had been sworn in as President.

Senator J. W. Fulbright, Democrat of Arkansas, chairman of the Senate Foreign Relations Committee, said he knew of no objection to Mr. Yost. But he told the Senate that the committee would meet tomorrow to hear Mr. Yost.

Mr. Yost, a career diplomat, was No. 2 man in the United States mission to the United Nations under both Arthur J. Goldberg and the late Adlai E. Stevenson.

The name of David R. Packard to be Deputy Secretary of Defense was not submitted

Continued on Page 30, Column 6

## From Partisan to President of All

By JAMES RESTON
Special to The New York Times

News Analysis

WASHINGTON, Jan. 20—President Nixon has started his Administration with a simple statement of priorities: peace abroad and reconciliation at home. His inauguration speech followed the traditional appeals to unity, and invoked the normal themes of patriotism, religion and the common morality of the nation, but there was more to this than the emotion and rhetoric of a great occasion.

Mr. Nixon and his principal advisers have been talking a great deal in these last few weeks, not about their policies—it is too early for that—but about how to approach their problems, and particularly about how to keep things from getting even worse than they are now.

Out of these hurried preliminary talks with one another in New York recently, two things have emerged. The division and disruption of the nation and a really serious and uncontrollable military confrontation between the United States and the Soviet Union in the Middle East are the major problems before the new Administration, and these questions must have first priority.

It would be misleading to say that Mr. Nixon and his associates have had time to make definitive judgments about these things, but at least they have identified the disasters to be avoided and they seem to have decided on how they think they might avoid them.

Their tentative conclusions, which may help explain Mr. Nixon's speech today, are first, that Vietnam, if it continues as in the past, will increasingly divide the nation and therefore should be ended in compromise as soon as possible.

Even more important, as one understands their thinking, the Arab-Israeli controversy really might get out of hand and confront both the United States and the Soviet Union with a major war

Continued on Page 22, Column 3

The New York Times

TAKING THE OATH OF OFFICE: Spiro T. Agnew being sworn in as Vice President by Senator Everett McKinley Dirksen, chairman of the Joint Inaugural Committee and Republican Senate leader. At center is J. Mark Trice, secretary for the Senate minority.

## HAILED BY PARADE

### Cheered by 250,000 on Route—Agnew Also Takes Oath

A slip-out section on the inauguration, Pages 21-28; text of address, Page 21.

By ROBERT B. SEMPLE Jr.
Special to The New York Times

WASHINGTON, Jan. 20 — In sober pageantry, Richard M. Nixon became the 37th President of the United States today and vowed to "consecrate" himself to the cause of world peace.

Near the end of his 17-minute Inaugural Address, delivered under leaden skies to a crowd massed on the East Plaza of the Capitol grounds, the new President raised his eyes from his text and said:

"I have taken an oath today in the presence of God and my countrymen, to uphold and to defend the Constitution of the United States. To that oath, I now add this sacred commitment: I shall consecrate my office, my energies and all the wisdom I can summon to the cause of peace."

**Poets and Presidents Quoted**

Reaching widely for inspiration — he quoted from poets, past Presidents, the civil rights anthem "We Shall Overcome" and from his first campaign speech 12 months ago — Mr. Nixon promised to open his Administration to youth, to the disaffected and the alienated, to make America's promise "real for black as well as white."

He spoke hardily at all about law and order and civil disobedience, a major issue in his campaign for the Presidency.

Mr. Nixon was sworn in at 12:15 P.M. by Chief Justice Earl Warren, who was administering the oath to a new President for the fourth time. Moments earlier, Spiro T. Agnew, former Governor of Maryland and the son of a Greek immigrant, was sworn in as Vice President by the Senate Republican leader, Everett McKinley Dirksen.

**A Variety of Emotions**

The inaugural platform from which Mr. Nixon spoke supported many different emotions. Mrs. Nixon, a colorful figure in a brilliant pink outfit, held the two family Bibles on which her husband's left hand rested as he took the oath. The outgoing President, Lyndon Baines Johnson, watched intently and listened carefully during both the oath and the Inaugural Address. Mrs. Johnson smiled often, as if happy to be going home, Mrs. Humphrey less often, and Vice President Humphrey seemed subdued throughout.

After the inauguration ceremonies, President Nixon reentered the Capitol, where his first official act of office was to sign the nominations of his Cabinet. He lunched with his Cabinet and with Republican Congressional leaders and then—shortly after 2 P.M.—joined his wife in a black limousine to lead the traditional inaugural parade down Pennsylvania Avenue from the Capitol to the White House.

Throughout the day the skies were heavily overcast. But the rain held off until dusk, well after the parade was over.

Continued on Page 22, Column 1

NEWS INDEX


| | Page | | Page |
|---|---|---|---|
| Art | 43 | Movies | 39-43 |
| Books | 45 | Music | 39-43 |
| Bridge | 44 | Obituaries | 47 |
| Business | 60, 71-73 | Real Estate | 73-74 |
| Buyers | 73 | Society | 50 |
| Crossword | 45 | Sports | 53-58 |
| Editorials | 46 | Supreme Court | 16, 58 |
| Fashions | 51 | Theaters | 39-43 |
| Financial | 58-70 | Transportation | 94 |
| Food | 51 | TV and Radio | 95 |
| Letters | 46 | U. N. Proceedings | 2 |
| Man in the News | 24 | Weather | 94 |

News Summary and Index, Page 49

"All the News That's Fit to Print"

# The New York Times

LATE CITY EDITION

Weather: Partly sunny today; clear tonight. Cloudy, milder tomorrow. Temp. range: today 28-45; Tuesday 33-37. Full U.S. report on Page 94.

VOL. CXXI . No. 41,689 | NEW YORK, WEDNESDAY, MARCH 15, 1972 | 15 CENTS



# WALLACE GETS 42%, HUMPHREY 2D, JACKSON 3D, MUSKIE 4TH IN FLORIDA; LINDSAY EDGES M'GOVERN FOR 5TH

United Press International

AT I.T.T. HEARING: Former Attorney General John N. Mitchell, right, having a final word with Robert C. Mardian of the Justice Department before testifying in Washington yesterday as the Senate Judiciary Committee opened third week of hearings on case.

## HUSSEIN REPORTED PROPOSING STATE FOR PALESTINIANS

### Jordanian Said to Suggest an Autonomous West Bank Linked With East Bank

Special to The New York Times

BEIRUT, Lebanon, March 14—King Hussein has reportedly proposed to the Big Four powers a plan for rejoining the Israeli-held west bank with the east bank of Jordan in a federal system to be called the United Arab Kingdom instead of the Hashemite Kingdom of Jordan.

Informed Arab diplomatic sources said that an outline of the plan was submitted by the Jordanian King to the Ambassadors of the United States, Britain, France and the Soviet Union yesterday. The Arab governments have also been informed, the sources said.

[On the west bank, Palestinian leaders were thrown into confusion by reports of the Hussein plan. The Israeli Foreign Ministry denied that any agreement had been reached between Israel and Jordan. In Washington, King Hussein's plan was viewed as an effort to shore up his position in the Arab world. Pages 6 and 7.]

**'Serious Repercussions'**

Baghdad radio, monitored here, broke into a newscast this afternoon to broadcast news of the reported proposals by King Hussein. The Iraqi radio asserted that the plan "will have the most serious repercussions on the Arabs as a whole and on the Palestine question in particular."

The proposed plan, the state-controlled radio said, "envisions a political settlement between Jordan and the Zionist state."

It would not be possible to carry out such a plan without Israel's agreement to give up the west bank area of the Jordan River.

**Israeli Agreement Needed**

Arab diplomatic sources say that King Hussein insists that the proposed new state should have the same boundaries as those of Jordan before the 1967 Middle Eastern war. This would mean that Israel should give up all the territory she seized from Jordan, including the Old City of Jerusalem.

Diplomats consider Israel unlikely to agree. On the other hand, there have been persistent reports recently of contacts between Jordan and Israel for a settlement.

There is some speculation that King Hussein may have proposed the plan at this time to forestall the municipal elections that the Israeli authorities have ordered for next month on the west bank area.

King Hussein and other Arab

Continued on Page 4, Column 3

## NIXON MARGIN BIG

### Governor Captures 75 of 81 Delegates in Dramatic Victory

By MARTIN WALDRON

Special to The New York Times

MIAMI, March 14 — Gov. George C. Wallace of Alabama scored a dramatic victory in the Florida Presidential primary today, capturing 75 of the state's 81 delegates to the Democratic National Convention.

Riding the issue of school busing and promising to tax the rich and crack down on crime, Mr. Wallace finished far ahead of 10 other Democrats who had spent $3-million in an effort to defeat him.

Senator Hubert H. Humphrey of Minnesota, who ran here to revive his national political fortunes, finished second. Mr. Humphrey led the field in the 11th Congressional District, including parts of Miami and Miami Beach, and won six convention delegates.

Senator Henry M. Jackson of Washington ran third, firmly ahead of Senator Edmund S. Muskie of Maine, who had entered the Florida contest with strong support from party officials.

**A Major Setback**

Mr. Muskie's poor showing was a major setback, even more damaging than last week's showing in New Hampshire for the man deemed the "front runner" for more than a year. There are still 21 primaries remaining.

In the Republican primary, also held today, President Nixon easily won Florida's 40 delegates to the Republican National Convention. The President did not campaign in the state.

With 99 per cent of the state's 2,841 precincts reporting, the tally was:

| DEMOCRATS | | |
|---|---|---|
| Wallace | 514,722 | (42%) |
| Humphrey | 231,015 | (18%) |
| Jackson | 167,539 | (13%) |
| Muskie | 109,461 | (9%) |
| Lindsay | 81,075 | (7%) |
| McGovern | 74,832 | (6%) |
| Mrs. Chisholm | 44,770 | (4%) |
| McCarthy | 5,842 | (0%) |
| Mills | 4,618 | (0%) |
| Hartke | 3,536 | (0%) |
| Yorty | 2,576 | (0%) |
| **REPUBLICANS** | | |
| Nixon | 357,143 | (87%) |
| Ashbrook | 35,977 | (9%) |
| McCloskey | 16,982 | (4%) |

Governor Wallace, who spent election day sunning himself atop an Orlando hotel, smoking cigars and reading old copies of the National Geographic magazine, said he was surprised at the margin of his victory.

He said none of the other candidates "can take any comfort from being second or third."

However, Senator Humphrey's

Continued on Page 32, Column 1

Senator Hubert H. Humphrey talking to reporters.

The New York Times/Mike Lien and Dick Scoda

Gov. George C. Wallace of Alabama with wife, Cornelia, and grandson, Jimbo, watching lead build up yesterday.

## BUDGET APPROVED, BUT 2 SNAGS LOOM

### Mayor Threatens a Veto on Spending Curbs—M.T.A. Opposition Possible

By MAURICE CARROLL

A revised capital budget for New York City was adopted early today, but two possible problems were built into it—a threatened mayoral veto over restrictions on some spending and a possible confrontation between the city and the Metropolitan Transportation Authority.

After a day of private trading and public posturing at City Hall, the Board of Estimate and the City Council approved changes totaling 10 per cent of Mayor Lindsay's $1.8-billion construction budget.

A deal had been worked out late Monday by the Mayor's budget team and a coalition put together by Controller Abraham D. Beame.

Their plan was adopted by a 34-to-1 vote in the Council.

The board voted unanimously in favor of the plan, with the exception of five items, against which the Mayor's votes were cast. The most important of these were "lump sum" appropriations and a cut of $8-million in the manpower training program, originally set to get $41-million.

The only opponent in the Council was Frank J. Biondolillo, Staten Island Republican.

"This is a better, more realistic budget than the Mayor's," said Mario Merola, the Council's finance chairman.

Continued on Page 40, Column 2

## Mitchell Denies Discussing 3 Cases With I.T.T. Chief

By FRED P. GRAHAM

Special to The New York Times

WASHINGTON, March 14—Former Attorney General John N. Mitchell disclosed today that he discussed the Government's antitrust policies privately with Harold S. Geneen, the president of the International Telephone and Telegraph Corporation, for some 35 minutes during a 1970 meeting, but he said he refused to talk about the Government's three cases against the company.

In testimony before the Senate Judiciary Committee, which included searching cross-examination by some Democratic Senators, Mr. Mitchell insisted that he had not personally been involved in any way in the handling or settlement of the three suits.

He also swore that he had taken no part in negotiations that led to the selection of San Diego as the site of the 1972 Republican Convention.

He denied categorically that he had discussed the I.T.T. case at a Kentucky Derby party last year with Mrs. Dita D. Beard, the company's Washington lobbyist. When she persisted in raising the subject, Mr. Mitchell said, he told her to "in effect, shove off."

Mr. Mitchell's testimony came as the committee opened its third week of hearings growing out of allegations that I.T.T. had pledged $400,000 to the Republican convention and that simultaneously it had influenced the Justice Department to settle the three suits on a basis favorable to the company.

Having disqualified himself from I.T.T. cases because his former law firm once represented one of the company's subsidiaries, Mr. Mitchell said he had made Mr. Geneen promise not to discuss I.T.T.'s cases. The 35-minute session, held on

Continued on Page 34, Column 4

## Volpe Wants Road Funds Tapped for Mass Transit

By DAVID E. ROSENBAUM

Special to The New York Times

WASHINGTON, March 14—Transportation Secretary John A. Volpe asked Congress today to allow part of the Federal money that is earmarked for highways to be used for public transportation in the nation's cities.

Urban specialists and other supporters of increased Federal aid for mass transit saw Mr. Volpe's announcement as a major breakthrough.

But there appeared to be substantial opposition to the program in Congress, especially among some members holding key committee positions. Before the program could be enacted, it would probably have to go through six Congressional committees.

Mr. Volpe said that his plan had the complete support of President Nixon, and that the Administration's budget officials had assured him that the money he envisioned would be spent.

Under Mr. Volpe's proposal, $1.5-billion more would be made available to urban areas for public transportation in the fiscal year beginning July 1, 1973. The amount would rise to $1.85-billion in the next fiscal year and to $2.25-billion after

Continued on Page 94, Column 6

## NIXON WILL MEET TRUDEAU IN APRIL

### President Will Go to Canada on the 13th for 2 Days—Trade Major Problem

By BERNARD GWERTZMAN

Special to The New York Times

WASHINGTON, March 14—President Nixon will go to Canada on April 13 for two days of talks with Prime Minister Pierre Elliott Trudeau, the White House said today.

The announcement, made simultaneously in Ottawa, came at a time of deep strains in Canadian-American relations, caused largely by unresolved trade disagreements and Canadian concern that Washington may impose sanctions against Canadian goods.

Plans for a Canadian visit were made last year before the world monetary crisis that led on Aug. 15 to Mr. Nixon's imposition of the 10 per cent surcharge on imported goods—a move that caused considerable stir among Canadians, who send 60 per cent of their exports to

Continued on Page 13, Column 1

## Democratic Race Widens; Muskie Concedes Setback

By R. W. APPLE Jr.

Special to The New York Times

MIAMI, March 14—After a year of campaigning, during which most politicians and every poll agreed that Senator Edmund S. Muskie of Maine led the Democratic Presidential race, a new contest appeared to have started tonight.

Some of Senator Muskie's senior advisers agreed with what seemed to be the consensus—that Mr. Muskie ceased to be the front-runner when Gov. George C. Wallace of Alabama captured the bulk of Florida's 81 convention delegates. Mr. Wallace now has 75 committed convention votes, more than any other candidate.

As the returns for the Florida primary cascaded in, few people were able to name a Democratic favorite.

With an assist from the Alabama Governor's potent showing, the other national Democrats accomplished in Florida what they had been hoping for months to do: vanquish Muskie. The man from Maine finished a weak fourth after having won unimpressively in the New Hampshire primary only a week ago.

Mr. Muskie will try to recoup

Continued on Page 32, Column 3

## BUSING BAN WINS BY LARGE MARGIN

### Florida Governor's Efforts Rejected in Straw Ballot —Dual System Opposed

By DOUGLAS ROBINSON

Special to The New York Times

MIAMI, March 14 — Florida voters in a straw ballot overwhelmingly voiced today their opposition to court-ordered compulsory busing of school children to achieve racial integration.

The vote, which has no legal effect, was a rejection of efforts by Gov. Reubin Askew to halt the antibusing movement in the state and was interpreted by the Governor himself as a possible blow to his political standing.

"When a politician takes an unpopular position and the polls prove how unpopular the issue was, there's bound to be some effects," Governor Askew said tonight. "However, it will not keep me from speaking out on the issues."

The voters also came out solidly in support of a second

Continued on Page 32, Column 6

## Hughes Sees Somoza And Envoy of U.S.; Departs Nicaragua

By WALLACE TURNER

Special to The New York Times

SAN FRANCISCO, March 14—Howard R. Hughes, lean, healthy and wearing a Van Dyke beard, left Managua, Nicaragua, early today after a social visit with the President of Nicaragua and the United States Ambassador aboard his private jet.

The meeting lasted from 10:45 P.M. until "almost midnight," said Ambassador Turner B. Shelton, who arranged the meeting with President Luis Anastasio Somoza Debayle so that Mr. Hughes could express his gratitude for help in arranging a place for him when he left the Bahamas in February.

"He looks extremely well," Mr. Shelton said of Mr. Hughes. "He is slender. His health seems to be good. He was wearing a short beard that covers his face and builds into a Van Dyke on his chin. His hair is cut short. It's sort of gray and black—salt and pepper."

This was the first reliable

Continued on Page 41, Column 4



## Physician Indicted In Insurance Case

By LACEY FOSBURGH

Dr. Geoffrey Richstone, a Park Avenue internist and cardiologist, was indicted by a Manhattan grand jury yesterday on charges of conspiracy and attempted grand larceny in the death of Gail Richards, his employe and girlfriend.

She died several weeks after a $100,000 life insurance policy was taken out naming him as her beneficiary.

Edwin Weinberg, a certified public accountant and the 33-year-old doctor's insurance agent, was indicted with him.

In announcing the eight-count indictment, District Attorney Frank S. Hogan said the homicide bureau was continuing its investigation into the death of Miss Richards, who was 30 years old.

Milton Helpern, the city's

Continued on Page 36, Column 5

## Pay Board Staff Backs Coast Dock Raise Above Limit

Associated Press

George H. Boldt, left, Pay Board chairman, studies contract settlement, as Harry Bridges, right, president of longshoremen's union, and Edmund Flynn, chief negotiator for shippers in West Coast dock strike, follow testimony.

By PHILIP SHABECOFF

Special to The New York Times

WASHINGTON, March 14—The Pay Board formally took up today the potentially explosive West Coast longshore contract and heard its own staff report that there might be justification for approving a wage increase in excess of its guidelines.

Both parties to the contract—the International Longshoremen's and Warehousemen's Union and the Pacific Maritime Association—urged the board to approve the full settlement, which calls for a 25.9 per cent increase in wages and fringe benefits in the first of two years.

The staff, while refraining from any specific recommendation, suggested that the West Coast situation might meet a "test of uniqueness" permitting a special exception to the board's pay standards because of unusually high productivity gains.

The possibilities open to the board range up to the full settlement from a minimum of 8.9 per cent that the staff said was permissible under the guidelines.

Both labor and management cited big gains in productivity as justification for the size of the settlement. They pointed out that output per worker rose nearly 150 per cent over the decade.

Harry Bridges, president of the union, summed up his case by saying, "The workers I represent produce one hell of a lot for the wages they get."

The board, made up of repre-

Continued on Page 28, Column 3



## McGraw-Hill Editor Demoted Over 'Gift or Loan' by Authors

By HENRY RAYMONT

McGraw-Hill, Inc., the center of two recent book-publishing storms, removed Robert S. Stewart yesterday as editor in chief of the company's trade book division, charging he had received $1,700 as a "gift or loan" from two of his authors.

The sum—which amounted to 10 per cent of an advance on royalties and has been at least partly repaid by Mr. Stewart—was reportedly given to the editorial executive by Alfred Kantor, author of "The Book of Alfred Kantor," and his collaborator, John Wykert, a science writer.

Mr. Stewart, who was appointed to the top editorial position last June, could not be reached yesterday for comment on the charges.

Asserting that "any financial transaction between author and editor is absolutely contrary to company policy," Harold W. McGraw Jr., president of McGraw-Hill's book division, said:

"This was a very serious error in judgment on the editor's part. Mr. Stewart has been relieved, effective immediately, as editor in charge of our trade book division in the McGraw-

Continued on Page 41, Column 1



NEWS INDEX

| | Page | | Page |
|---|---|---|---|
| Art | 54 | Movies | 52-56 |
| Books | 45 | Music | 52-56 |
| Bridge | 44 | Obituaries | 50 |
| Business | 65, 76 | Op-Ed | 47 |
| Crossword | 45 | Sports | 57-60 |
| Editorials | 46 | Theaters | 52-56 |
| Family Style | 42 | Transportation | 94 |
| Financial | 65-77 | TV and Radio | 95 |
| Going Out Guide | 54 | U. N. Proceedings | 13 |
| Letters | 46 | Washington Record | 38 |
| Man in the News | 44 | Weather | 94 |

News Summary and Index, Page 49

"All the News That's Fit to Print"

# The New York Times

LATE CITY EDITION

Weather: Sunny, cool today; clear and cold tonight. Fair tomorrow. Temp. range: today 30-44; Tuesday 39-42. Full U.S. report on Page 90.

VOL. CXXI . No. 41,710



NEW YORK, WEDNESDAY, APRIL 5, 1972

15 CENTS

# FOE DRIVING ON QUANGTRI AND FOR HUE

## SITES IN NORTH HIT

### Saigon's Forces Fall Back, Abandoning Another Base

By CRAIG R. WHITNEY

Special to The New York Times

SAIGON, South Vietnam, Wednesday, April 5 — South Vietnamese troops abandoned one of their remaining defense points on the north bank of the Cua Viet last night and North Vietnamese tanks were reported moving south toward the embattled city of Quangtri, capital of South Vietnam's northernmost province.

As of this morning, no ground attacks were made by the North Vietnamese troops who swept down from the demilitarized zone over the last six days, but intense artillery shelling was reported at Quangtri.

The next major city to the south, the old imperial capital of Hue, was also said to be coming under heavy pressure as the North Vietnamese troops stepped up attacks on Government positions in the hills to the west. Officers in Hue said they expected an attack on the city soon.

The United States command announced today that American warplanes had made nine retaliatory strikes at missile-guidance radar sites and artillery positions in the northern half of the demilitarized zone, which straddles the border between North and South Vietnam, and above the zone inside North Vietnam yesterday and Monday.

All the strikes were northwest of Quangtri city, the command said, and two surface-to-air missile sites were reported destroyed and an antiaircraft position was blown up in the two-day period.

The command has now announced 120 such protective reaction "strikes in North Vietnam so far this year, almost as many as in all of last year.

**Clouds Are Lifting**

American warplanes flew 145 strikes against North Vietnamese positions in a 10-mile strip below the southern edge of the demilitarized zone yesterday, as clouds over the area lifted somewhat. The United States command said the aircraft came under intense ground fire from antiaircraft artillery sites and surface-to-air missiles.

At the same time, five United States Navy destroyers fired at North Vietnamese troop positions and at Route 1 in the same area, which was controlled by Government forces until the North Vietnamese struck there over the weekend.

But the weather, according to American commanders here, had not improved enough over North Vietnam to allow fighter-bombers to begin striking at troop positions and artillery emplacements there. The United States command is known to have planned major strikes from air bases in Thailand and

Continued on Page 16, Column 4

## Hanoi Says Threat Won't Deter Forces

Special to The New York Times

HONG KONG, Wednesday, April 5—Hanoi has declared that threats to bomb North Vietnam could not blunt the Communist forces' "determination to fight and to win" the war in Vietnam.

A statement issued by a spokesman of North Vietnam's Foreign Ministry and broadcast by the Hanoi radio said the United States had "threatened North Vietnam with heavier bombing raids" and stated that the Vietnamese people would "duly punish the U.S. imperialists" for any encroachment on the North's sovereignty and security and would "smash any of their military adventures."

Continued on Page 16, Column 1

## NIXON DISPATCHING ADDITIONAL B-52'S

### 10 to 20 Craft Are Ordered to Reinforce Air Armada to Counter Enemy Offensive

By TERENCE SMITH

Special to The New York Times

WASHINGTON, April 4—The United States tonight ordered the deployment of 10 to 20 more B-52 bombers to Indochina to strengthen the American ability to respond to the new North Vietnamese offensive.

The new planes will bolster the existing fleet of strategic fortresses by up to 25 per cent. Eighty more of the giant bombers already are stationed at airfields in Thailand and Guam.

The Pentagon spokesman, Jerry W. Friedheim, declined comment on the B-52 deployment, except to observe that President Nixon had expressed his readiness "to take whatever steps are necessary to protect the remaining United States forces in South Vietnam."

**Soviet Weapons Cited**

Meanwhile, the State Department asserted that what it said was North Vietnam's extensive use of Soviet supplied tanks and heavy artillery in its five-day offensive had added "a new factor to the battlefield situation in South Vietnam."

The department spokesman, Robert J. McCloskey, said that Soviet equipment had permitted the North Vietnamese to wage "conventional warfare rather than their traditional guerrilla-style attacks."

Mr. McCloskey's stress on Soviet equipment appeared to be an effort to provide additional public justification in case of a decision to renew the bombing of North Vietnam.

He specifically said the United States was still holding open all its retaliatory options,

Continued on Page 16, Column 7

# BANGLADESH GETS U.S. RECOGNITION, PROMISE OF HELP

### Rogers Announces the Turn in Policy—Nixon Sends a Note to Sheik Mujib

By BENJAMIN WELLES

Special to The New York Times

WASHINGTON, April 4 — The United States extended formal diplomatic recognition today to Bangladesh, the nation of 70 million Bengalis that declared independence from Pakistan in December. Some 60 other countries had already recognized the new nation.

Washington's decision marks a sharp turn in the hostile relationship that began when the United States supported Pakistan in her war to keep control of her eastern wing. American diplomacy opposed not only the Bengalis' secession but also India's military efforts on their behalf.

Secretary of State William P. Rogers, in announcing United States recognition today in a statement distributed to the press, said that "we look forward to good relations with this new country."

**Message for Leader**

"I want to reaffirm our intention to develop friendly bilateral relations and be helpful as Bangladesh faces its immense task of relief and reconstruction," Mr. Rogers said.

The Secretary of State said that Herbert D. Spivack, the principal American diplomatic officer in Dacca, the capital of Bangladesh, had been here for consultations and was returning with a message from President Nixon to Bangladesh's Prime Minister, Sheik Mujibur Rahman, officially informing him of United States recognition.

As the American decision was announced, there was a hint of another possible move to heal the wounds left by the Indian-Pakistani war. That came in New Delhi, where Prime Minister Indira Gandhi said that India was "in direct touch" with Pakistan. [Page 5.]

The State Department spokesman, Robert J. McCloskey, asked to explain the long delay in granting Bangladesh recognition—a delay that has led to criticism of the United States by Sheik Mujib and Mrs. Gandhi—replied: "There is no magic in the timing. Governments set

Continued on Page 4, Column 4

## '72 Vegas Recalled

The General Motors Corporation recalled yesterday 130,000 of its 1972 model Vega automobiles to correct a defect in the fuel and exhaust system that it said created the danger of fires. [Details on Page 90.]

# M'GOVERN WINNER IN WISCONSIN, WALLACE, HUMPHREY VIE FOR 2D; LINDSAY, TRAILING, GIVES UP RACE

## MAYOR RUNS SIXTH

### Says Returns Indicate He Cannot Continue as a Candidate

By FRANK LYNN

Special to The New York Times

MILWAUKEE, April 4 — After suffering his second decisive primary defeat, Mayor Lindsay withdrew tonight from the race for the Democratic Presidential nomination.

"The returns are clear and they mean that I cannot honestly continue as a candidate, and therefore I am withdrawing," the Mayor told about 250 supporters, almost all of them teen-agers, at the Sheraton Schroeder Hotel ballroom here.

The Mayor said he would continue his fight to end the war in Vietnam, save the cities and provide justice for all, but he added: "It cannot be as a candidate for the Presidency in 1972."

The Mayor did not endorse any other candidate. His aides predicted that he would not endorse anyone for some time, particularly while the field is wide open.

The decision to withdraw was reached at a half-hour conference of the Mayor and about a half-dozen of his top aides in his 12th-floor suite at the hotel.

**Calm in Defeat**

The Mayor, sources said, was calm but convinced that he should drop out as soon as it was clear that he would finish sixth. In Florida on March 14, the Mayor was fifth.

Some of his aides, playing the roles of devil's advocates, according to an informant, suggested that he withdraw only from the Massachusetts primary on April 25 and marshal his forces for the later primaries in Oregon and California, while others proposed that he delay a final decision on his campaign for a few days.

But Mr. Lindsay argued that his withdrawal was inevitable and that there was no sense in delaying it.

The Mayor was accompanied by his wife, Mary, and Mayor Charles Evers of Fayette, Miss., as he strode briskly through the crowd gathered for a Lindsay "Victory Party" at the ballroom.

Mr. Lindsay was unemotional and he even smiled weakly as he spoke.

He congratulated Senator Mc-

Continued on Page 32, Column 1

Associated Press — United Press International

Mayor Lindsay and Senator and Mrs. George McGovern saluting supporters last night

## VICTOR DISCERNS VOTE OF PROTEST

### McGovern, After 14-Month Effort, Is Now Established as Serious Contender

By R. W. APPLE Jr.

Special to The New York Times

MILWAUKEE, April 4—After a lonely, 14-month campaign, during which few professionals took his candidacy seriously, Senator George McGovern of South Dakota established himself in Wisconsin tonight as a serious contender for the Democratic Presidential nomination.

"We can stand at least one night of prosperity," Mr. McGovern said at a victory celebration. He said that he was hesitant to overinterpret the results but called his showing here "a vote of protest and hope."

Both Mr. McGovern and Gov. George C. Wallace of Alabama ran more strongly than they or most politicians initially expected. Both appeared to have benefited from a sense of alienation and unrest in the Wisconsin electorate, as well as from a big Republican cross-over vote.

The Alabama Governor, who demonstrated for the first time in 1972 that he could attract the votes of Northerners even where school busing was not an overt issue, claimed "a great

Continued on Page 32, Column 7

## Cross-Over a Key Factor

Senator George McGovern and Gov. George C. Wallace of Alabama appeared to have benefited strongly from a heavy Republican cross-over vote in the Wisconsin Democratic primary, according to preliminary findings of a cross-section survey of voters by The New York Times and Daniel Yankelovich, Inc.

It showed that Republicans cast at least a quarter and perhaps a third of the Democratic ballots. Senator McGovern's total included possibly a third in Republican votes. As many as half of Governor Wallace's votes appeared to come from Republicans.

Mr. McGovern, who had frequently been described as a one-issue, antiwar candidate, gave clear evidence that he has successfully broadened his base of appeal, the survey showed. Many of his supporters strongly endorsed Mr. Wallace's position on economic issues. Wallace voters also praised the Governor's stands on taxes and inflation.

By contrast, few supporters of Senator Hubert H. Humphrey said they voted for him because of his stand on issues. They emphasized, instead, reasons of background and personality, especially his long Government experience.

The Times/Yankelovich survey was one of a series being conducted in primary campaigns. The Wisconsin survey involved 378 persons who voted the Democratic ballot and who were interviewed as they left the polls. They came from 36 precincts in nine randomly selected counties.

## MUSKIE IS FOURTH

### Jackson Places Fifth—Nixon Captures 97% of Vote for G.O.P.

By DOUGLAS E. KNEELAND

Special to The New York Times

MILWAUKEE, April 4—Senator George McGovern of South Dakota won the Wisconsin Democratic Presidential primary today.

Hours after the polls closed, Mayor Lindsay, running far behind, abandoned his quest for the nomination.

Senator McGovern, riding on the strength of a closely knit campaign organization that had been working determinedly but quietly in Wisconsin for almost a year, ran well ahead of Senator Hubert H. Humphrey of neighboring Minnesota and Gov. George C. Wallace, who were battling for second place. At a late hour, the Governor edged ahead.

Senator Edmund S. Muskie of Maine, the early front-runner in the Democratic sweepstakes, suffered another blow to his Presidential aspirations by finishing a disappointing fourth as he did in Florida.

Trailing badly in fifth and sixth places, respectively, were Senator Henry M. Jackson of Washington and Mayor Lindsay.

President Nixon, who did not campaign here, swept the Republican primary with 97 per cent of the vote, easily capturing the state's 28 delegates to the national convention in San Diego.

On the ballot with Mr. Nixon were Representative Paul N. McCloskey Jr. of California, who has dropped out of the race, and Representative John M. Ashbrook of Ohio, a conservative who made no appearances in Wisconsin.

With 86% of 3,290 precincts reporting, the Democratic tally was:

| | | |
|---|---|---|
| McGovern | 288,751 | (30%) |
| Wallace | 211,335 | (22%) |
| Humphrey | 202,871 | (21%) |
| Muskie | 99,739 | (10%) |
| Jackson | 76,501 | ( 8%) |
| Lindsay | 66,202 | ( 7%) |

**McGovern Pleased**

As it became apparent that he would win, Senator McGovern termed the support he was receiving "a vote of protest and hope."

He predicted that the victory here would give his drive for the nomination the momentum that it needed to win the Massachusetts' primary April 25 and to do well in the one in Pennsylvania on the same day.

Senator McGovern won a clear victory in the popular vote, but it appeared that he might have to share the state's 67 delegates to the Democratic convention in Miami Beach in July.

As the statewide winner, Mr. McGovern received the 11 at-large delegates. The rest are apportioned among the nine Congressional districts.

The South Dakotan seemed

Continued on Page 32, Column 1

## Archdiocese of New York Puts Worth at 643-Million

By EDWARD B. FISKE

The Roman Catholic Archdiocese of New York has issued a financial report—the first of its kind by a Catholic diocese—setting its net worth at $643-million.

The report was compiled in the last few weeks with the assistance of a leading accounting company. It will be made available to the 1.8 million New York Catholics in the 10-county archdiocese later this week through the archdiocesan newspaper, The Catholic News.

Officials said that the report represented an effort to gain a more precise picture of archdiocesan assets and expenses during a time of financial difficulty. It was also seen as a response to growing pressure, both inside the Catholic Church and outside, to conduct ecclesiastical financial affairs in a more public manner.

The financial report, which is accompanied by a 45-page explanatory statement, says that nearly nine-tenths of archdiocesan net assets, or $563-million, consist of land, buildings and equipment, much of it "single purpose" properties suitable only for religious purposes.

The remaining net assets are $51-million in cash and other liquid assets and an endowment fund with a net book value of $29-million. The $29-million includes a securities portfolio with a market value of $13-million.

The accounting concern that drew up the report said the carrying value of such holdings as land and buildings was approximate because a variety of methods, including original cost as well as city assessments, had been used to estimate

Continued on Page 34, Column 1

## Adam Clayton Powell, 63, Dies in Miami

Special to The New York Times

MIAMI, April 4—Adam Clayton Powell, a Baptist minister who became a prominent spokesman and symbol for blacks during 11 successive terms he served in the House of Representatives, died in Jackson Memorial Hospital here tonight from complications that followed prostate surgery. He was 63 years old.

The New York Times/Robert Walker

Adam Clayton Powell Jr.

**A Man of Many Roles**

By THOMAS A. JOHNSON

The Rev. Adam Clayton Powell Jr. played many roles during a lengthy and controversial public career and he seemed to play each with his own special exuberance.

No matter what the dispute—and there were many—Mr. Powell could be expected, in public, to flash a big toothy smile, puff dramatically on a big cigar and come up with a quip and an insight that had escaped almost everyone else.

Then, with an enthusiasm as dependable as spring following winter, he would go about presenting the Powell side, which was invariably a spicy blend of his own great intelligence, some truths and, often, items the opposition would call untruths.

The larger ingredients in a Powellian explanation were always irascibility, irreverence and an uncompromising disdain for what he regarded as the hypocrisy of men who did in secret what he never tried to hide.

A further and more direct insight into the character of the flamboyant Mr. Powell came in his own summation of his Congressional career when he stated: "As a member of Congress, I have done nothing

Continued on Page 30, Column 1

## Moscow Refuses Swede a Visa To Give Award to Solzhenitsyn

Special to The New York Times

STOCKHOLM, April 4—The Soviet Embassy said today that it had refused to issue a visa to the secretary of the Swedish Academy to travel to Moscow to present the Nobel Prize for Literature to Aleksandr I. Solzhenitsyn.

The secretary, Dr. Karl Ragnar Gierow, was scheduled to go to Moscow Sunday to present the Nobel gold medallion and diploma originally awarded to the Russian novelist in 1970. The private ceremony was to take place in a Moscow apartment.

Originally, Mr. Solzhenitsyn planned to come to Stockholm to take part in the formal ceremony. However, on Nov. 27, 1970, seven weeks after the award announcement, he said he would not attend the ceremony because he feared that if he left his country, Soviet officials declined to comment on the return.

Today Soviet Embassy officials declined comment on the visa refusal, except to say that "the matter can be discussed again." Dr. Gierow said he did not know why the visa had been withheld and declined further comment.

Friends of Dr. Gierow said he had applied for the visa last week, apparently taking for granted that it would be issued. Normally Swedes have no difficulties getting visas to the So-

Continued on Page 7, Column 1

## U.S. Panel Urges a Drive to Control V.D.

By RICHARD D. LYONS

Special to The New York Times

WASHINGTON, April 4—Federal health officials recommended today a massive drive against venereal disease combining increased testing, stricter reporting, better education and more money.

Major facets of the campaign would include a voluntary venereal disease education program for schoolchildren starting in the seventh grade and enforcement of existing mandatory tests for syphilis and gonorrhea that would result in the testing of 40 million Americans in the fiscal year 1973, which begins July 1.

Officials of and advisers to the Department of Health, Education and Welfare estimated that there would be a record 2.5 million new cases of gonorrhea this year and 100,000 new cases of infectious syphilis, the highest number since the widespread use of antibiotic drugs started to bring the disease under control 20 years ago.

In the fiscal year 1971 there were 23,336 reported cases of syphilis and 624,371 cases of gonorrhea.

The officials reiterated warnings that venereal disease was epidemic in the United States and that gonorrhea, in particular, was "out of control."

Dr. Bruce Webster, chairman of the National Commission on Venereal Disease, made public the group's report which had 40 recommendations aimed at controlling the increasing spread of venereal disease.

To underscore the seriousness of the drive against venereal disease, the officials said that even if the campaigns were fully implemented they expected the number of cases to continue to rise in 1973.

The report of the national

Continued on Page 28, Column 4

NEWS INDEX


| | Page | | Page |
|---|---|---|---|
| Books | 43 | Music | 36-41 |
| Bridge | 42 | Obituaries | 48 |
| Business | 61, 73 | Op-Ed | 45 |
| Crossword | 43 | Society | 52 |
| Editorials | 44 | Sports | 53-57 |
| Family/Style | 50 | Theaters | 36-41 |
| Financial | 61-74 | Transportation | 90 |
| Going Out Guide | 36 | TV and Radio | 91 |
| Letters | 44 | U. N. Proceedings | 8 |
| Man in the News | 22 | Washington Record | 26 |
| Movies | 36-41 | Weather | 90 |

News Summary and Index, Page 47

"All the News That's Fit to Print"

# The New York Times

LATE CITY EDITION

Weather: Cloudy, mild with chance of showers today, tonight, tomorrow. Temp. range: today 59-73; Monday 57-74. Full U.S. report on Page 86.

VOL. CXXI . No. 41,751 · © 1972 The New York Times Company · NEW YORK, TUESDAY, MAY 16, 1972 · 15 CENTS

# WALLACE IS SHOT; CONDITION SERIOUS; A SUSPECT SEIZED AT MARYLAND RALLY

Associated Press

AFTER SPEECH: Gov. George C. Wallace takes off jacket and goes to shake hands. At front is Secret Service agent.

C.B.S. News via United Press International

DURING SHOOTING: Man at right with light hair and sun glasses holds gun as person in crowd tries to shake his arm

C.B.S. News via Associated Press

KNEELING OVER HUSBAND: Mrs. Cornelia Wallace bending over the Governor after he was shot at close range

## 3 MORE WOUNDED

### Legs of Governor Are Paralyzed but Hope Is Voiced by Doctor

By R. W. APPLE Jr.

Special to The New York Times

LAUREL, Md., Tuesday, May 16—Gov. George C. Wallace of Alabama, seemingly on the verge of his greatest electoral triumphs, was shot and gravely wounded yesterday afternoon as he campaigned for President at a shopping center in this suburb of Washington.

Late last night, after the 52-year-old Governor emerged from almost five hours of emergency surgery at the Holy Cross Hospital in nearby Silver Spring, Md., one of his surgeons said that he expected Mr. Wallace "to make a full recovery."

The surgeon, Dr. Joseph Schanno, said that Mr. Wallace had suffered at least four wounds and the doctors had removed one bullet. He said that another bullet was lodged near the spine and that the Governor's legs were paralyzed as a result.

**Will Continue Campaign**

The Governor's wife, Cornelia, said she was "very happy that he's alive and has a sound heart and a sound brain." Billy Joe Camp, his press secretary, reported this morning, after Mrs. Wallace had talked with the Governor, that he would continue his Presidential campaign and "will be at the Democratic convention as a strong, viable candidate."

The state and local police arrested a suspect, who was identified by the Justice Department as Arthur Herman Bremer, a 21-year-old white man from Milwaukee. The department said that the Secret Service had taken custody of a .38-caliber, snub-nosed, five-shot revolver allegedly used by Mr. Bremer in the shooting. Later, Federal and state charges were filed against him.

**Held in $200,000 Bond**

Mr. Bremer was taken before United States Magistrate Clarence Goetz in Baltimore last night and was ordered held under $200,000 bond.

Three persons who were with Governor Wallace as he plunged into the crowd at the Laurel Shopping Center were also hit by the four or five bullets fired by the attacker.

The shooting occurred after the Governor, having finished a speech here, shed his coat and stepped from behind the protection of his bullet-proof speaking stand.

A young man wearing sungasses and a red, white and blue shirt bedecked with Wallace buttons thrust his right hand between two other people

Continued on Page 34, Column 1

## Saigon's Forces Reoccupy Bastogne Base Near Hue

By MALCOLM W. BROWNE

Special to The New York Times

SAIGON, South Vietnam, Tuesday, May 16 — South Vietnamese troops, led by a platoon of 30 soldiers flown in by helicopters, reoccupied Fire Base Bastogne yesterday on the southwesterly approaches to Hue.

The five helicopters carrying the soldiers reportedly encountered no enemy fire as they landed at the base, which the South Vietnamese abandoned April 28 under heavy attack. The base had fallen after the North Vietnamese who had besieged it for more than three weeks sent commandos storming in to penetrate the barbed-wire defenses.

But after routing the defenders at the end of April, the North Vietnamese did not move their long-range 130-mm. artillery into Bastogne to shell Hue, the former imperial capital of Vietnam on the coast 15 miles away.

[The United States command announced the arrival of the carrier Saratoga off the Vietnamese coast Monday, bringing to six the number of attack carriers there. United Press International reported. The United States Seventh Fleet was now said to have 60 ships in the area.]

[In Washington, Secretary of State William P. Rogers angrily defended the mining of North Vietnam's harbors and said that if the Johnson Administration had taken the step earlier, the war might have ended long ago. Page 14.]

Allied officers in the Hue area said that if the re-entry into Fire Base Bastogne appeared to have been easy, this was only because it had capped more than a week of slow, hard fighting and several more days of heavy air and artillery bombardment.

South Vietnamese spokes-

Continued on Page 14, Column 3

## PRESSURE GROUPS ANGER ROCKEFELLER

### He Asserts Judges Blocked Court Reform and Lawyers Stymied 'No-Fault' Bill

By JAMES F. CLARITY

Special to The New York Times

ALBANY, May 15—Governor Rockefeller charged today that "inordinate pressures" placed on legislators by judges and lawyers had blocked two of his "vital programs"—court reform and no-fault insurance—in the 1972 Legislature.

Mr. Rockefeller, commenting on the action of the Legislature three days after it had adjourned for the year, said the

*The no-fault insurance bill was defeated through the lobbying efforts of one small group of men—the New York State Trial Lawyers Association. Article on Page 31.*

judges had stymied most of his court-reform program. The lawyers, Mr. Rockefeller said, had blocked the no-fault automobile accident insurance bill he had supported.

The Governor pledged to continue to fight for passage of the two programs next year. He said undue pressure had also been exerted on the legislators to repeal the state's liberalized abortion law. The Governor vetoed the repeal measure Saturday.

"My pledge is to make an all-out fight for no-fault automobile insurance and court reform in 1973," Mr. Rockefeller said at a news conference in the Red Room of the Capitol. "Some headlines have interpreted the failure of the Legislature to enact these two vital programs as a setback for me. The truth is that they marked a setback for the people of New York State.

"At no time," the Governor

Continued on Page 30, Column 3

## Court Exempts the Amish From Going to High School

By FRED P. GRAHAM

Special to The New York Times

WASHINGTON, May 15—The Supreme Court ruled 7 to 0 today that the Amish religious sect is exempt from state compulsory education laws that require children to attend school beyond the eighth grade.

The Amish—the rural "plain people" who cling to a horse-and-buggy way of life—believe that education beyond the eighth grade teaches worldly values at odds with the simple life required by their creed.

With this in mind, the Court held that state laws requiring children to attend school until they are 16 years of age violate the constitutional rights of the Amish to free exercise of religion.

The decision specifically applied to Wisconsin, but it was written in terms broad enough to apply to all states that require attendance in public or private schools beyond the eighth grade. Mississippi and South Carolina are the only states that do not have compulsory school attendance laws.

The opinion, written by Chief Justice Warren E. Burger, was the first by the Court holding a religious group immune from compulsory attendance requirements.

The Court stressed the 300-year resistance of the Amish to modern influences and served notice that faddish new sects or communes that reject formal education would probably not be granted similar exemptions.

"It cannot be overemphasized," Justice Burger wrote, "that we are not dealing with a way of life and mode of education by a group claiming to have recently discovered some 'progressive' or more en-

Continued on Page 28, Column 1

## Hogan Drops Jay Kriegel Case; Reports He Can't Prove Perjury

By DAVID BURNHAM

The question of whether one of Mayor Lindsay's closest aides, Jay L. Kriegel, committed perjury during his testimony before the Knapp Commission will not be presented to a grand jury, District Attorney Frank S. Hogan announced yesterday.

Mr. Hogan said his office was dropping the case because "the people would not be able to establish beyond a reasonable doubt that there was a willful, irreconcilable inconsistency" between Mr. Kriegel's testimony before the Knapp Commission on June 17, 1971, and Dec. 20, 1971.

The commission was created by Mayor Lindsay—on the recommendation of a special committee that included Mr. Hogan—to investigate allegations of widespread police corruption and of failure by officials in the Lindsay administration to follow up on information about cases of corruption brought to their attention.

Mr. Hogan, in a two-and-a-half-page statement, said another reason for not proceeding with the case was that "there is substantial doubt concerning the authority of the Knapp commission to administer the oath" at the December hearings.

Whitman Knapp, the chairman of the commission, said in

Continued on Page 28, Column 3

NEWS INDEX



| | Page | | Page |
|---|---|---|---|
| Art | 48 | Movies | 48-51 |
| Books | 41 | Music | 48-51 |
| Bridge | 40 | Obituaries | 46 |
| Business | 57, 69 | Op-Ed | 43 |
| Chess | 40 | Sports | 52-55 |
| Crossword | 41 | Theaters | 48-51 |
| Editorials | 42 | Transportation | 86 |
| Family/Style | 38 | TV and Radio | 87 |
| Financial | 57-71 | U. N. Proceedings | 4 |
| Going Out Guide | 48 | Washington Record | 10 |
| Letters | 42 | Weather | 86 |

News Summary and Index, Page 45


## GUNMAN'S ATTACK CLOUDS CAMPAIGN

### Uncertainty Created Both by Wallace's Status and Impact of Shooting

By MAX FRANKEL

Special to The New York Times

WASHINGTON, May 15—The bullets that felled George C. Wallace on the eve of his greatest achievements in national politics will also upset both the conduct and the calculations of the 1972 Presidential campaign.

If he could recover in time to resume some form of campaigning, and his press secretary says he will, the Alabama Governor may find an even more aroused constituency rallying to his cause. And some degree of sympathy vote may further swell his expected victories tomorrow in the Democratic primaries of Michigan and Maryland.

The Governor had 210 delegate votes of the 1,509 needed for nomination when he was struck down.

If he is forced out of the campaign, there is no one now in sight to pick up the banner of populism, tinged with an overtone of segregation, that brought the Governor 9.9 million votes, or 13.5 per cent of the total cast for President, in 1968 and seemed to promise him an equally strong following this year.

No one has ever quite

Continued on Page 34, Column 7

## Shooting Suspect Shouted: 'Hey, George! Over Here!'

By WARREN WEAVER Jr.

Special to The New York Times

LAUREL, Md., May 15 — George C. Wallace was shot while standing at the new crossroads of middle America today, between the drive-in bank and variety store of a suburban shopping center.

The suspected assailant, a young white man, called the Alabama Governor over to him after Mr. Wallace had stepped from behind his bullet-proof speaking stand and came down to shake hands with the crowd of about 1,000.

"Hey, George! Hey, George! Come over here! Come over here!" the man shouted insistently, according to several witnesses. The man had been standing against the ropes that cleared a space for security guards and reporters between the crowd and the small parking lot speaking stand.

Mr. Wallace heard the shouts and veered to his left, working his way down the line of admirers. He came first to Mrs. Brigitte Howkins of Hyattsville, a plump matron, who reached over a man, took Mr. Wallace's hand and said: "Good luck, Governor Wallace."

"He smiled at me," Mrs. Howkins recalled later, "dropped my hand and reached out for another when the man who had been standing on my right lifted his right arm and suddenly there were shots."

Mr. Wallace fell to the asphalt parking surface and lay on his back in the brilliant sunshine. Witnesses said he was bleeding from the chest and appeared also to have been struck in the right arm.

Val Hymes, a columnist for several Maryland newspapers, saw the Governor sprawled on the pavement, a large red splotch spreading across his shirt front. "I thought at first he was dead," she said.

Mrs. Wallace ran to his side,

Continued on Page 34, Column 4

## Kennedy Guarded By Secret Service

By BEN A. FRANKLIN

Special to The New York Times

WASHINGTON, May 15—Shortly after Gov. George C. Wallace of Alabama was shot today, President Nixon ordered Secret Service protection for Senator Edward M. Kennedy of Massachusetts, Representative Shirley Chisholm of Brooklyn and Representative Wilbur D. Mills of Arkansas.

Senator Kennedy, who has declared repeatedly that he is not a candidate for President, accepted the offer, and an unspecified number of agents were guarding his home tonight in nearby McLean, Va. Agents joined Mrs. Chisholm in Detroit, where she was stay-

Continued on Page 35, Column 1

## MILWAUKEE MAN HELD AS SUSPECT

### Seized on Weapons Charge Last October in Wisconsin —Many Paradoxes Seen

By JAMES T. WOOTEN

Special to The New York Times

WASHINGTON, May 15—The young white man arrested as a suspect today in the shooting of Gov. George C. Wallace is a 21-year-old resident of Milwaukee who pasted Wallace bumper stickers on his car and his apartment door and was exuberantly cheering the Democratic Presidential candidate only moments before the shots rang out.

Those apparent contradictions are but a small part of the paradoxical picture now being sketched of Arthur Herman Bremer, the man accused by Federal authorities today of having tried to kill the Alabama Governor at a shopping center in Laurel, Md.

It was reported that he was arrested on a charge of carrying a concealed weapon last Oct. 18 and was subsequently convicted of disorderly conduct.

A Justice Department spokesman said that the .38-caliber snub-nosed revolver allegedly used at Laurel had been purchased in Milwaukee Jan. 13 and fired five times today.

From descriptions supplied

Continued on Page 34, Column 3

"All the News That's Fit to Print"

# The New York Times

LATE CITY EDITION

Weather: Sunny, hot today; cloudy, chance of rain tonight, tomorrow. Temp. range: today 72-90; Tuesday 70-89. Temp.-Hum. Index yesterday 80. Full U.S. report on Page 82.

VOL. CXXI . . No. 41,808 | NEW YORK, WEDNESDAY, JULY 12, 1972 | 15 CENTS



# HUMPHREY AND MUSKIE YIELD TO M'GOVERN; HE MOVES TO EASE PARTY DISAGREEMENTS; WALLACE'S PLATFORM PROPOSALS REJECTED

Associated Press

Gov. George C. Wallace addressing the convention

## Wallace Tells Convention He Wants to Help Party

By JAMES T. WOOTEN

Special to The New York Times

MIAMI BEACH, July 11—Gov. George C. Wallace made a wheelchair appearance before the Democratic National Convention here tonight amid growing signs that he has abandoned the possibility of an independent candidacy and is seriously considering at least a tacit endorsement of the party's Presidential nominee.

"I am here because I want to help the Democratic party," Mr. Wallace told a courteous but restrained throng of delegates and spectators. "I want to help it become what it used to be—the party of the average working man."

In a voice noticeably stronger than in any of his previous public appearances since he was gravely wounded and partly paralyzed in May, the 52-year-old segregationist gave the crowd and a national television audience a rerun of the speech that helped win five primary elections.

Two Secret Service agents and an Alabama state trooper lifted the Governor, in his gleaming, chrome wheelchair, to the convention platform, where he was greeted with a handshake by its chairman, Lawrence F. O'Brien.

Although a number of del-

Continued on Page 19, Column 2

## DEBATE RUNS LONG

### Overwhelming Votes Affirm the Liberal Tenor of Parley

By JOHN HERBERS

Special to The New York Times

MIAMI BEACH, Wednesday, July 12—The Democratic National Convention rejected by an overwhelming majority early today a move by supporters of Gov. George C. Wallace to rewrite the party's platform along conservative, antibusing, pro-military lines.

By a thundering chorus of noes, the convention rejected eight minority planks as the convention plunged into a protracted platform debate, with the proceedings carefully scheduled for late at night, when many Americans are usually asleep.

The proposals, supported by Governor Wallace in a dramatic appearance before the convention late last night, called for a strong stand against busing to desegregate the schools, a constitutional amendment permitting prayer in the public schools, support for the constitutional right to bear arms, a strong military posture and refusal to withdraw from Vietnam without the simultaneous release of American prisoners of war.

**Voice Vote Taken**

The Wallace forces did not demand roll-call votes on their proposals and the votes were taken by voice.

Defeat of the Wallace proposals had been expected, but the overwhelming vote against them affirmed the liberal tenor of the convention, which then proceeded to consideration of minority reports from the left. Several of these had far more support than the Wallace proposals.

A minority plank on tax re-

Continued on Page 20, Column 7

United Press International

Senator and Mrs. Humphrey as he dropped from race

Senator McGovern after his rivals had left the field

The New York Times/Ann Phillips

## Humphrey Defends Race; Muskie Urges Party Unity

### Minnesotan to Campaign

By CHRISTOPHER LYDON

Special to The New York Times

MIAMI BEACH, July 11—Emotional in a final staff meeting and stoical in a public withdrawal of his candidacy, Senator Hubert H. Humphrey of Minnesota wanted more than anything today to erase two unhappy impressions of his third and probably final Presidential race.

To more than 100 under-30 advance men, researchers, baggage handlers and all-purpose aides of the last six months, he recalled apologetically and in a puzzled tone that they had won so little public attention while he was being labeled by some as the conservative candidate of "old hacks" in the Democratic party.

"Go out there into the press room and let them see you," he told the young workers, who cried when he said he was quitting.

At a news conference moments later Mr. Humphrey cocked his chin at the television cameras and sought to dismiss any idea that his five weeks of tactical maneuver since losing the California primary was somewhat unsporting.

"This has been a good fight," he said. "We've waged a good battle. We've done it within the rules of the game."

Reading from a text and declining to accept questions, Mr.

Continued on Page 21, Column 2

### Rival Ends 3d Drive

Special to The New York Times

MIAMI BEACH, July 11—Senator Edmund S. Muskie ended his campaign for the Presidency today for the third and last time, quietly abandoning not only his candidacy but also any possible role he might have chosen either as king maker or king stopper.

Pledging his support to Senator George McGovern, the sober-faced Maine Senator said in his public statement that his candidacy "would benefit neither my supporters nor the Democratic party."

His brief statement, delivered at a news conference with his wife at his side at the Americana Hotel, combined abdication with a plea for party unity.

Senator Muskie's once luminous prospects had long since dimmed. Nevertheless, he came to Miami Beach with a bloc of delegates that might have made him a powerful arbiter either in selecting the party's nominee or rejecting him.

He sought neither role, threading his way between them with such deliberation that many here ridiculed his seeming indecisiveness. While waiting for his final withdrawal statement today, one spectator won laughs by predicting that Mr. Muskie would announce only that he was undertaking "an exhaustive re-

Continued on Page 21, Column 6

United Press International

Senator Muskie addressing backers after withdrawing

## McGovern Said to Narrow Choice for Running Mate

By DOUGLAS E. KNEELAND

Special to The New York Times

MIAMI BEACH, July 11—Senator George McGovern, the Democratic Presidential nomination within his grasp, was reported by his associates today to have narrowed his choices for a running mate to three or four persons. But there was no agreement among his advisers on which three or four.

Senator Edward M. Kennedy of Massachusetts was widely acknowledged by Mr. McGovern's top advisers to be still at the head of the list, but none expressed much hope that he would accept.

"He's always been in the forefront," said Gary Hart, the national campaign director. He said that Senator McGovern still planned to consult with Senator Kennedy, as he has said he would, before making a decision on a Vice-Presidential nominee.

**Rules Out Pressure**

However, he added that he did not think earlier indications that Mr. Kennedy was not interested in a place on the ticket had changed.

"The Senator respects his judgment" he went on. "Unless he wants to run, Senator McGovern will not put any pressure on him."

Another McGovern aide said that Mr. McGovern planned to talk to Mr. Kennedy after the vote on the nomination tomorrow night.

There was some support, opposed by former associates of the Kennedys, for throwing the Vice-Presidential nomination open to the convention for a decision, with the expectation that the Massachusetts Senator would be chosen. Indications were that Mr. McGovern would oppose putting this sort of pressure on Mr. Kennedy.

In the weeks before the convention, the names dropped by Mr. McGovern and his associates as possibilities for the second spot grew to a total of more than 20, obviously at least partly a result of the normal maneuvering for delegate support.

By today, however, the South Dakotan, who has said he would prefer to suggest a running mate to the convention rather than leave the choice completely to the delegates, was getting into the final stages of the selection process.

His leading strategists, all of whom disclaimed absolute

Continued on Page 18, Column 5

## ALABAMIAN WOOED

### McGovern Supports Jackson's View on Defense Issue

By MAX FRANKEL

Special to The New York Times

MIAMI BEACH, Wednesday, July 12—Senators Hubert H. Humphrey and Edmund S. Muskie surrendered the Democratic Presidential nomination yesterday to their colleague, George McGovern, and with different degrees of enthusiasm summoned him to reunite the party.

Their action still left Gov. George C. Wallace of Alabama, Senator Henry M. Jackson of Washington and Representative Shirley Chisholm of Brooklyn as formal contenders, but the contest in the Democratic National Convention turned last night to the party's election-year program of promises and principles and to the plainly difficult task of holding the support of its traditional power blocs.

*Texts of statements issued at Miami Beach, Page 21.*

Mr. Humphrey, choked up at the end of a 12-year quest for the Presidency, released his delegates to vote as they wished but promised to battle on as a loyal Democrat for equal opportunity and social justice.

**Muskie Is Hopeful**

Mr. Muskie, the other half of the Democratic ticket in 1968, yielded with a more optimistic reading of a McGovern candidacy as one that could make the party "a lasting home" to the optimism and energy of the young. He voiced hope for the long-term health of the party.

Mr. McGovern, although momentarily elated by his rapid rise from relative obscurity, immediately showed himself sensitive to problems he will face in trying to unseat President Nixon.

His followers, now dominant in the convention, heeded the Senator's appeal to give a most polite hearing to Governor Wallace when the Alabamian appeared briefly before them to press his amendments to the platform and to give them "the benefit" of his exposure to the average American.

New Yorkers remained seated to deny him respect, and his delegates from Texas, Michigan, Florida and Alabama cheered. But most of the hall merely stood in curiosity and then heard the Governor's appeals for tax reform, against school busing and other issues.

**Changes Shouted Down**

The delegates then moved on to shout down all of Mr. Wallace's proposed changes and appeared ready to give Mr. McGovern the tone and language he wanted in the platform in almost every respect.

Senator McGovern also passed the word that he would welcome acceptance of Mr. Jackson's platform amendment calling for a stronger defense posture in Europe and the Mediterranean, particularly for the sake of Israel.

Moreover, in a brief statement accepting the support of the families of prisoners of war, Mr. McGovern slightly shaded his pledge of an Indochina withdrawal within 90 days of inauguration by saying he would keep some forces in nearby Thailand and the surrounding seas to make sure the prisoners

Continued on Page 20, Column 3

## Apollo 15 Crew Is Reprimanded

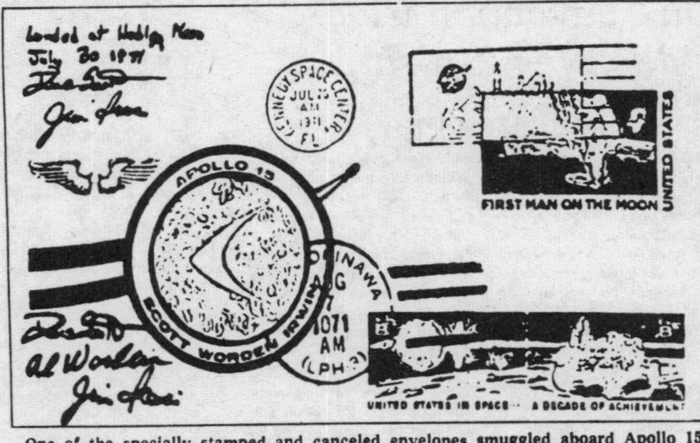


One of the specially stamped and canceled envelopes smuggled aboard Apollo 15

By HAROLD M. SCHMECK Jr.

Special to The New York Times

WASHINGTON, July 11—The Apollo 15 astronauts were reprimanded today by the space agency for smuggling 400 specially stamped and canceled envelopes to the moon and back last July. Later 100 of these were sold by a German stamp dealer for a sum reported to be more than $150,000.

The astronauts gave the envelopes to an acquaintance through whom they were sold by the dealer.

The acquaintance was to have repaid the astronauts, Col. David R. Scott, Lieut. Col. Alfred M. Worden and Col. James B. Irwin, all of the Air Force, by setting up a trust fund for their children. This part of the arrangement was never fulfilled.

A spokesman for the National Aeronautics and Space Administration said the astronauts had had second thoughts about the stamp deal after the first news of the envelopes' existence on the stamp collectors' market had been circulated in stamp magazines.

The astronauts then decided on their own, the spokesman

Continued on Page 24, Column 2

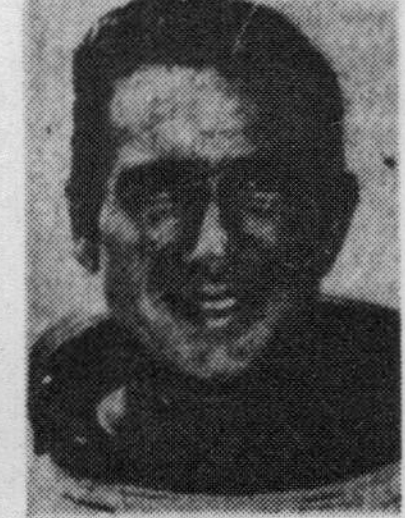

NASA

From left, Col. David R. Scott, Col. James B. Irwin and Lieut. Col. Alfred M. Worden

## Edge Is Given to Spassky In Adjourned First Game

By HAROLD C. SCHONBERG

Special to The New York Times

REYKJAVIK, Iceland, July 11—The first game of the Bobby Fischer-Boris Spassky match for the world chess championship was adjourned tonight after 40 moves.

Although the consensus of experts gave the Soviet champion the edge, it was felt that his American challenger still had good chances for a draw. The game is to resume at 5 P.M. tomorrow—1 P.M. New York time.

The game started quietly enough. Spassky opened, as many had expected, with P-Q4, and Fischer adopted a Nimzo-Indian Defense. This is a standard defense, and for a while it seemed as though both players were heading toward a routine draw.

Then, on the 29th move, the game exploded. Spassky offered a pawn that, in the opinion of the experts, could not be taken. It was what is known as a "poisoned pawn," for if Fischer took it his bishop would probably be trapped.

Fischer took it and gasps of surprise swept through the auditorium.

Had Spassky miscalculated? Or had Fischer misjudged, giving up the bishop for two pawns and a tenuous position?

It will not be known until Fischer talks whether he miscalculated or decided to take Spassky's dare, the devil take the consequences.

Even if Fischer does lose the first game, he has achieved the respect of every player here by rising to Spassky's dare and throwing away a sure draw for a speculative attack.

At adjournment, the 29-year-old American grandmaster was desperately trying to turn to advantage his pawns on the king's side. The grandmasters

Continued on Page 26, Column 1

BLACK
FISCHER

SPASSKY
WHITE

Position at adjournment, after 40 . . . P-R5.

## 39 TENNIS COURTS TO GET 'BUBBLES'

### City's Program Will Allow for Play All Winter

By RALPH BLUMENTHAL

In a major boon for the city's growing number of tennis lovers—of whom he is one—Mayor Lindsay announced yesterday a $3-million program of resurfacing, winterizing or lighting for nearly a third of the city's 515 intensively used municipal tennis courts.

The improvements, to be financed largely by private concessionaires, were described by a Park Department spokesman as probably the largest such program since the courts were built, most of them decades ago.

Coming amid what can only be seen as a runaway tennis craze here, as elsewhere around the country, the improvements stand to alter a way of life for an entire subspecies of New Yorker that now spends uncounted hours waiting to claim space at overcrowded facilities while dozens of courts lie idle, awaiting a drying sun or groundkeepers.

Under the new program, most of which is supposed to be completed before the end of

Continued on Page 66, Column 1

NEWS INDEX


| | Page | | Page |
|---|---|---|---|
| Books | 38-39 | Movies | 26-30 |
| Bridge | 38 | Music | 26-30 |
| Business | 51-66 | Obituaries | 44 |
| Crossword | 39 | Op-Ed | 41 |
| ditorials | 40 | Sports | 31-35 |
| Family/Style | 48 | Theaters | 26-30 |
| Financial | 51-66 | Transportation | 82 |
| Going Out Guide | 28 | TV and Radio | 83 |
| Letters | 40 | U. N. Proceedings | 2 |
| Man in the News | 19 | Weather | 82 |

News Summary and Index, Page 43

"All the News That's Fit to Print"

# The New York Times

LATE CITY EDITION

Weather: Periods of rain likely today, tonight. Clearing tomorrow. Temp. range: today 72-82; Wed. 74-90. Temp.-Hum. Index yesterday 81. Full U.S. report on Page 70.

VOL. CXXI . No. 41,809 | © 1972 The New York Times Company | NEW YORK, THURSDAY, JULY 13, 1972 | 15 CENTS

# M'GOVERN NOMINATED ON THE FIRST BALLOT, AND WILL RUN ON PLATFORM HE HAD SOUGHT

## Kennedy Informs Nominee He Won't Be Running Mate

By DOUGLAS E. KNEELAND

Special to The New York Times

MIAMI BEACH, Thursday, July 13—Senator Edward M. Kennedy turned down an offer this morning to run for Vice President on the ticket headed by Senator George McGovern. Mr. McGovern said through a spokesman here that he had made the offer in a telephone conversation with Mr. Kennedy after receiving the Presidential nomination at the Democratic National Convention.

Later, Mr. Kennedy said in Hyannis, Mass., that he was "honored and humbled" by the offer but had to decline for "overriding personal considerations." In particular, he cited "personal family responsibilities" to his own family and those of his late brothers, John and Robert.

### Won't Be Chairman

Mr. Kennedy added that he would consider taking a prominent role in the campaign but ruled out the possibility that he would be its national chairman. He said he would talk to Mr. McGovern again today on the matter of other possible running mates for Senator McGovern.

In his statement here, the nominee expressed regret over Mr. Kennedy's refusal but said he "fully understood the Senator's position."

"The Kennedy family has already made great sacrifices to the nation," he added.

Senators Edmund S. Muskie of Maine and Hubert H. Humphrey of Minnesota also promised in congratulatory phone conversations to suggest potential nominees. They were not asked to run.

### Askew Declines to Run

Last evening Gov. Reubin Askew of Florida, who for months was at or near the top of any roster of possible running mates put forth by Mr. McGovern himself, also insisted that he would not take the job.

The two refusals left the question of a running mate up in the air, but Mr. McGovern must decide by this afternoon, his deadline for submitting a nomination.

Governor Askew was one of at least two possible Democratic Vice-Presidential choices who were approached in recent days by political operatives for Senator McGovern and told, in effect, "to stay loose" because they were still in the running.

Despite urgings from the intermediaries that he refrain from any reiteration of his earlier public statements that he was not interested in the Vice-Presidential race, Mr.

Continued on Page 22, Column 6

## ULSTER PARADERS DISPLAY POWER

### 100,000 Protestants March on a Day of Violence—5 Persons Killed

By BERNARD WEINRAUB

Special to The New York Times

BELFAST, Northern Ireland, July 12 — Pounding drums and gripping swords and flags, nearly 100,000 men marched throughout Northern Ireland today in a vivid display of Protestant power. The day was marked by violence.

The parades — the annual July 12 Orange marches — began after three youths were shot dead, two in Belfast and one in the town of Portadown, 25 miles southwest of here, in separate incidents early in the morning. Late tonight two men were killed in a pub in Portadown.

Explosions shook downtown Londonderry and a soldier was critically wounded by snipers in the Andersonstown section of the capital.

Belfast and the rest of the embattled province remain frightened. An extraordinary mood of tension and sullen defiance has been created by the abrupt end of the cease-fire by the Irish Republican Army's militant Provisional wing, the disclosure that William Whitelaw, Northern Ireland's administrator, had been negotiating with the I.R.A. and the rapid rise of the paramilitary Protestant Ulster Defense Association.

### 'For God and Ulster'

"We're not looking to the past in this parade but to the future," said Robert Craig, a 45-year-old engineer, who was huddled under an umbrella near City Hall with his wife and 11-year-old daughter, who wore a pin on her coat reading "For God and Ulster."

"We're demonstrating our determination to keep the Protestant way of life," he said. "It's under threat as never before. We all know it."

Nearby on Royal Avenue, Billy Oliver, a 32-year-old salesman from the Shankill Road, lifted his 7-year-old son to watch a row of men in bowler

Continued on Page 14, Column 3

Associated Press

Illinois delegation members cheering after their first-ballot votes for Senator McGovern were cast at the Democratic convention in Miami Beach. The delegation, in casting 119 votes for the Senator, put him over the 1,509 votes required for the nomination.

## Two 727 Jets Hijacked; $1.1-Million Is Demanded

By RICHARD WITKIN

A National Airlines 727 jet bound from Philadelphia to New York was diverted back to Philadelphia International Airport last night by two hijackers demanding three parachutes and $600,000, including $20,000 in Mexican pesos.

Two hours later, an American Airlines 727 en route from Oklahoma City to Dallas was hijacked by a man demanding $550,000 and parachutes and, for some reason, insisting that he switch to another plane.

Carrying 51 passengers and a crew of seven, the American plane landed at Oklahoma City at 11:47 P.M. New York time after circling over Fort Worth for more than an hour in stormy weather.

An hour and 15 minutes later, the hijacker ordered it into the air to circle while the ranson was being assembled. The plane was reported still circling at 2:30 A.M.

The fact that the planes involved in both incidents were Boeing 727's was obviously no matter of chance. The three-jet craft has been a favorite of hijackers because of the rear-facing stairway that drops down beneath the belly and makes parachuting comparatively easy and safe.

The National plane, carrying 113 passengers and six crew members, was taken over as it approached Kennedy International Airport about 7:30 P.M.

Philadelphia's airport, where it landed 90 minutes later, was closed to all other traffic.

Armed law-enforcement men were deployed in large numbers as officials set about trying to

Continued on Page 71, Column 1

## Fischer Walks Out, Comes Back, Loses

By HAROLD C. SCHONBERG

Special to The New York Times

REYKJAVIK, Iceland, July 12 — Bobby Fischer lost the first game of his world championship chess match with Boris Spassky tonight after staging a 35-minute walkout.

Later, Fischer was reported to have said that he might not play tomorrow's scheduled second game.

The first game, adjourned after 40 moves, resumed at 5 P.M. An hour and five minutes later, in a hopeless position at the 56th move, the American challenger stood up and offered his hand. Spassky, the champion, took it, and the game became history.

One Fischer admirer said sor-

Continued on Page 31, Column 4

## PROTESTERS FIND CANDIDATE FIRM

### McGovern Says He Won't Shift Positions on Any Fundamental Stands

By JAMES M. NAUGHTON

Special to The New York Times

MIAMI BEACH, July 12—Senator George McGovern appeared before a group of angry young demonstrators in his Presidential campaign headquarters here tonight to assure them that he was "not shifting my positions on any of the fundamental stands that I've taken in this campaign."

His pledge—to a collection of some 300 radical students, poor blacks and war foes who had virtually tied up the Doral Hotel—was made from the steps of a lobby that glistened with crystal chandeliers and marble walls.

### 'A More Open Country'

It was the most bizarre and dramatic demonstration yet of the difference between this Democratic National Convention and the one that preceded it four years ago in Chicago.

"We are a more open country than we were four years ago at another convention," Mr. McGovern said after 20 minutes of dealing with the demonstrators' questions, not always to their satisfaction. "Four years from now," he added, "we will be a more decent country."

The confrontation, on the night capping Mr. McGovern's 18-month grass-roots campaign for the Presidential nomination, grew out of concern that the Senator was softening his position on the Vietnam war.

But Mr. McGovern reasserted as "a flat pledge" his commitment to have every American combatant and prisoner out of

Continued on Page 22, Column 7

## McGovern Forces Shape Planks to Suit Candidate

By JOHN HERBERS

Special to The New York Times

MIAMI BEACH, July 12—In an 11-hour session that ended at sunrise today, the Democratic National Convention rejected strong efforts to write into the party platform a series of New Left stands on such issues as abortion, homosexual rights, tax reform and guaranteed income. The forces of Senator George McGovern were firmly in control.

The convention, operating at full strength despite the hour, turned back by a wide margin an appeal by Gov. George C. Wallace of Alabama for planks against busing and Government spending and for a stronger military, a citizen's right to bear arms and prayer in public schools.

In the end, Senator McGovern got almost exactly the kind of platform he wanted to run on against President Nixon in November—a 24,000-word document with a liberal, Populist tone and direction, but one so worded that he could shape his own stand on the major issues of the day.

The McGovern forces did not so much fear tying the Senator's hands with a New Left platform drawn for his constituency in the primaries as they did providing targets for the Republicans to use against him in their appeal to the center of the electorate.

Only two of 20 minority reports to the document drafted by the Platform Committee in Washington last month were approved by the convention—one to extend more land rights to Indians and one to offer stronger military support for Israel.

The McGovern leaders in ef-

Continued on Page 22, Column 2

## On Convention Floor: The New Spirit of '72

By ROBERT B. SEMPLE Jr.

Special to The New York Times

MIAMI BEACH, July 12 — At 7:40 tonight, a Wallace supporter in a gaudy outfit parades around the convention hall clanging people over the head with a giant bell. Two elderly delegates wearing Jackson boaters fox-trot in the aisle.

They are regarded—even the bell-swinger—with polite curiosity. This has been, and remains, a serious convention, its disciplined cadres a full generation removed in spirit and tempo from conventions past. It is also, tonight, a bit dull, its conclusions foregone, its delegates drained by the parliamentary struggles of preceding days.

It even begins slowly, and for an hour the podium is mercifully bereft of dignitaries, leaving the field to a couple of minor folk heroes. One is Jimmy (The Greek) Snyder, the Las Vegas bookmaker, who circulates knowingly among the press.

"Three hundred and sixty electoral votes for Nixon and still climbing," says Jimmy, who seems disinclined at the moment to put a great deal of money on Senator George McGovern.

The other is Col. Harland Sanders, the white-haired symbol of a company that dispenses fried chicken, and did so tonight in remarkable quantities. "If combined into one superchicken," the Kentucky colonel informs anyone who will listen, "it would be two stories high and weigh over 7,000 pounds."

How does one maneuver a superchicken into the Democratic National Convention? First, one cuts it up and puts

Continued on Page 23, Column 1

## Nixon to Ask $1.8-Billion to Aid Flood Victims in Six-State Area

By EILEEN SHANAHAN

Special to The New York Times

SAN CLEMENTE, Calif., July 12—Homeowners and businessmen in a six-state area damaged last month by Tropical Storm Agnes would receive up to $5,000 each in an outright grant from the Federal Government to make repairs to their property and replace damaged belongings, under legislation proposed today by President Nixon.

The proposed legislation, which Mr. Nixon is expected formally to send to Congress next Monday, would constitute the most generous financial aid to disaster victims ever offered by the Federal Government. The over-all money request will total $1.8-billion.

In announcing his relief proposal, Mr. Nixon said that more than 128,000 homes and businesses had been damaged or destroyed by the storm, which swept through parts of the Southeast and East in late June, causing widespread flooding.

The six states whose residents would be eligible for the new loans are Florida, Maryland, New York, Pennsylvania, Virginia and West Virginia.

For those who suffered dam-

Continued on Page 16, Column 3

## A STUNNING SWEEP

### Senator Seeks Unity—Wallace Rules Out Third-Party Race

By MAX FRANKEL

Special to The New York Times

MIAMI BEACH, Thursday, July 13—George Stanley McGovern was proclaimed the Democrats' candidate for President here early this morning to complete a stunning sweep of the party's processes and national convention.

Without suspense, but with many raw wounds of battle, the convention registered on a single ballot the victory that was sealed in a tense credentials battle 48 hours earlier.

Inexorably, to triumphant cheers, the Senator from South Dakota, who had defied the polls, the odds and the established techniques and the established power centers of his party, cashed in his three years of dazzling organization effort.

One week before his 50th birthday, and barely three months after he first vaulted to prominence in the grass-roots primaries, Mr. McGovern claimed the prize of a reformed, restructured but also partly resentful convention. He also won the platform he had sought and gave to the party's many skeptics and holdouts a promise of conciliation and unity by November for the expected race against President Nixon.

At the moment of victory, he

*A Man in the News article on Senator McGovern appears on Page 24. A review of his record on public issues is on Page 25.*

learned that Senator Edward M. Kennedy of Massachusetts was firm in his refusal to run for Vice President and that Gov. George C. Wallace of Alabama had firmly decided to stay out of the Presidential race this year.

The formal tally at the end of the first ballot gave Mr. McGovern 1,715.35 votes, comfortably beyond the 1,509 needed for nomination. The hall exploded with joy when the decisive ballots were cast by the bitterly disputed Illinois delegation.

### TV Set Proves Balky

Mr. McGovern was fiddling with a balky television set in his hotel suite and barely got back to his chair before the moment of climax. His staff burst out with applause but he merely smiled, remarked that it was a long-awaited moment and retreated to take a telephone call from his stoutest rival, Senator Hubert H. Humphrey of Minnesota.

Mr. McGovern also received a congratulatory call from Senator Kennedy at Hyannisport, Mass., during which he formally asked the bearer of a famous name to join him as his running mate. The nominee later announced that Mr. Kennedy declined for "very personal reasons."

Expressing regret, Mr. Mc-

Continued on Page 23, Column 2

## C.B.S. Goes Afield For President, 37

By ALBIN KREBS

The Columbia Broadcasting System Inc. yesterday announced the election of Arthur R. Taylor as president and a member of the company's board of directors. The 37-year-old Mr. Taylor is executive vice president and chief financial officer of the International Paper Company.

It was the second time in less than a year that C. B. S. had gone outside its own corporate structure and outside the broadcasting industry to choose a president.

Mr. Taylor will succeed Charles T. Ireland Jr., who died June 8, only eight months after he gave up his job as senior

Continued on Page 45, Column 5

## Many Here Hold Doctorates of Unaccredited College

By LINDA CHARLTON

A number of people in the fields of education and mental health in the New York City area — some in responsible academic positions, many others treating emotional problems or teaching others how to — are equipped with doctorates from an unaccredited Bible college in Canada.

The "degrees" and the various uses to which they are being put do not seem to involve matters of legality. But particularly because persons with such doctorates are deeply involved in mental therapy and counseling, Dr. Morton Schillinger, incoming executive director of the prestigious New York State Psychological Association, said yesterday that he considered them "a serious professional and ethical problem" and a "significant hazard to the consumer."

The school, Philathea College, was set up in 1946 in London, Ont., by Benjamin C. Eckardt, a clergyman in the Church of Christ who also has the title of Bishop of Ontario in the Free Protestant Episcopal Church.

It was chartered as a religious training school that could grant only such diplomas as "Licentiate of Theology." When Philathea applied last April to the appropriate provincial agency to have its charter amended to include degree-granting powers, the request was rejected.

In fact, said H. H. Walker, Deputy Minister of the Ontario Department of Colleges and Universities: "If Philathea were to apply today for incorporation, we would not approve of their use of the word college."

In its latest catalogue, however—it is the 1969-71 catalogue, with a 1971-73 supplement and a new date pasted to its cover—Philathea offers three kinds of bachelor's degrees as well as the degree of doctor of philosophy. These degrees have been offered for some years at the college, which has a small three-part campus in London.

A survey by The New York Times reveals that the holders of Philathea doctorates—either "honorary" or "earned" — include the founder of a Long Island school for gifted children; faculty members at Fordham University and the City University of New York and the former director of a city - fi-

Continued on Page 39, Column 1

The New York Times/Frank Lodge

A Philathea College building in London, Ontario

On the college seal is the Latin motto, "God made all things."





NEWS INDEX

| | Page | | Page |
|---|---|---|---|
| Books | 33 | Movies | 27-29 |
| Bridge | 32 | Music | 27-29 |
| Business | 45-58 | Obituaries | 38 |
| Crossword | 33 | On-Ed | 35 |
| Editorials | 34 | Sports | 40-45 |
| Family/Style | 30 | Theaters | 27-29 |
| Financial | 45-58 | Transportation | 70 |
| Going Out Guide | 28 | TV and Radio | 71 |
| Man in the News | 24 | Weather | 70 |

News Summary and Index, Page 37

"All the News That's Fit to Print"

# The New York Times

LATE CITY EDITION

Weather: Partly sunny, warm today; fair, warm tonight. Hot tomorrow. Temp. range: today 70-88; Thursday 71-76. Temp.-Hum. Index yesterday 74. Full U.S. report on Page 62.

VOL. CXXI . No. 41,810 | © 1972 The New York Times Company | NEW YORK, FRIDAY, JULY 14, 1972 | 15 CENTS

# M'GOVERN NAMES EAGLETON RUNNING MATE; ASSERTS NIXON IS THE 'FUNDAMENTAL ISSUE'

## Hanoi, as Talks Resume, Appears to Hint at Shift

By FLORA LEWIS

Special to The New York Times

PARIS, July 13—The North Vietnamese delegation seemed to offer a subtle change today in its negotiating position at the Paris peace talks, which resumed after a 10-week hiatus.

The two sides exchanged restatements of familiar positions at the formal talks. Later, in impromptu remarks during the closed session, the head of the North Vietnamese delegation, Xuan Thuy, repeated Hanoi's demand that the United States abandon its support of President Nguyen Van Thieu of South Vietnam, but indicated that subsequent political arrangements could be made directly among Vietnamese without involving the United States.

Mr. Thuy, whose remarks were reported to the press by the North Vietnamese spokesman, Nguyen Thanh Le, made a distinction between "two aspects of the political question."

It is "the responsibility of the United States," Mr. Thuy said, to end its support for the Thieu Government and to end its "intervention in the internal affairs of Vietnam." But the second aspect, he said, was the question of "power in Saigon—a question for the Vietnamese people to negotiate excluding all outside influences."

[In Washington, a State Department official said that Mr. Thuy's reference to "two aspects of the political question" had caused curiosity in the American delegation, but added that it was unclear whether Mr. Thuy meant to convey a new position or another way of describing an old one. Page 5.]

In the statement—which was new more in approach than in substance—Hanoi seemed to be saying that if the United States would abandon Mr. Thieu, it need not go on to haggle over who should be in the "three-segment" coalition the Communists propose to replace him with, nor even accept responsibility for "imposing" a new government in Saigon.

Previously, the United States has suggested that all political problems be discussed among Vietnamese, but Hanoi has insisted on a full political as well

Continued on Page 4, Column 4

## 2 JET HIJACKERS GIVE UP IN TEXAS; 3 HOSTAGES FREED

### F.B.I. Recovers $500,000 Ransom 22 Hours After Plane Was Diverted

By ANTHONY RIPLEY

Special to The New York Times

HOUSTON, July 13—Two hijackers, one an Ethiopian citizen, surrendered today to a Federal Bureau of Investigation agent at a small airport south of Houston about 22 hours after they had commandeered a National Airlines jet while it was going from Philadelphia to New York.

F.B.I. officials reported that the ransom obtained by the hijackers—$500,000 in American money and 20,000 Mexican pesos, which is the equivalent of $1,600—had been recovered.

The rear ramp of the Boeing 727, a plane that is a favorite target for parachuting hijackers, suddenly dropped down at about 4 P.M., Central daylight time (5 P.M. New York time), and three stewardesses being held as hostages descended. They were followed by the two hijackers, who held their hands over their heads.

**2 Weapons Confiscated**

Agents confiscated a shotgun and a .22-caliber pistol.

The two men were identified by the F.B.I. as Michael Stanley Green, 33 years old, of Washington and Lulseged Tesfa, 22, an Ethiopian. They were handcuffed and driven to Houston for arraignment on air-piracy charges before United States Magistrate H. Lingo Platter.

The hijackers were held in $1-million bail each, and were taken to the Harris County Rehabilitation Center for transfer to Philadelphia, where they will face the charges.

Meanwhile, a second hijacking that began yesterday ended when a 49-year-old debt-ridden Oklahoman named Melvin Martin Fisher handed an empty revolver to a stewardess seven hours after he had commandeered an American Airlines 727 going from Oklahoma City to Dallas.

**Calmly Surrenders**

Only the cockpit crew and the stewardess were still on board when the hijacker, who had obtained $200,000 in extortion money, calmly gave up early today. Charged with air piracy, he waived preliminary hearing before United States Magistrate Charles R. Jones in Oklahoma City, and was ordered

Continued on Page 62, Column 1

Associated Press

Senator George McGovern and Senator Thomas F. Eagleton acknowledging the cheers of the delegates

## IMPASSIONED PLEA

### Dakotan Urges Party to Lead the Nation in Healing Itself

By MAX FRANKEL

Special to The New York Times

MIAMI BEACH, Friday, July 14—Senator George McGovern pushed through the nomination of Thomas Francis Eagleton, a freshman Senator from Missouri, as his running mate early today and then appeared with him before a singing and screeching throng of delegates to deliver an impassioned plea for the Democratic party's help in leading the nation in a vast enterprise of self-healing.

After three hours of desultory roll-calls, this most unusual of conventions rolled to a climax with bursts of song and vows of unity — and ovations for the delegates of Alabama. And the hall shook with enthusiasm when Mr. McGovern brought a prediction that he would restore unity among the fragmented Democrats and bring victory over President Nixon.

*The text of McGovern speech is printed on Page 11.*

"He is the unwitting unifier and the fundamental issue of this national campaign," he said in his acceptance address.

**"Come Home, America"**

Mr. McGovern's partisan and at times evangelical thrusts were obviously designed to tap the fervent emotion in this closing session of a most unusual nominating session. But he lost the chance to deliver it in prime evening television time because the new party rules were used to force one long ballot on a proposal to delay further party reform and to nominate a long string of favorites for the Vice-Presidency.

The speech proclaimed a rhetorical refrain for his campaign: "Come Home, America"—home from errant paths, among which he listed deception in high places, war in remote places, wasteful military spending, pandering to special privilege, waste of unemployment, prejudice of race and the loneliness of the old and the poor.

**Appeals for Faith**

He made few departures from his prepared text when he delivered the speech, starting shortly before 3 A.M.

Mr. McGovern, in his speech accepting the nomination from the more than 3,000 delegates, promised alert and sufficient military defenses, but also a "turn away from excessive preoccupation overseas to rebuilding our own nation."

"And this is the time," he said. "It is the time for this land to become again a witness to the world for what is noble and just in human affairs. It is the time to live more with faith and less with fear — with an abiding confidence that can sweep away the strongest barriers between us and teach us

Continued on Page 11, Column 1

## A Record Rainfall Snarls Road and Rail Traffic Here

By ROBERT D. McFADDEN

Eclipsing a 75-year-old record for the date, a three-inch rainfall drenched the metropolitan area yesterday, snarling road, rail and subway traffic, flooding basements in outlying sections and adding to the troubles of farmers and others hit hard by the tropical storm Agnes last month.

The rain, which reached a driving torrent at mid-morning and tapered off to an occasional drizzle in the afternoon, brought several major New Jersey rivers to flood stage and caused heavy flooding of basements and streets in low-lying areas of Queens, Staten Island and Rockland and Westchester Counties.

By late afternoon, the National Weather Service reported, 3.06 inches of rain had fallen here, breaking the record of 2.29 inches for a July 13 set in 1897 and bringing this month's total rainfall to 3.61, just a shade under the average for the whole of July.

The rain gave umbrella salesmen another field day, but kept shoppers off the streets, delayed tens of thousands of commuters, caused numerous traffic accidents and left some homeowners awash.

While there were no reports of widespread damage, the heavy summer storm produced some dismaying scenes across the metropolitan area.

A tow truck in Bronxville, in Westchester County, was seen fishing for a car completely immersed in a depression on the Bronx River Parkway.

Raw sewage backed up into

Continued on Page 35, Column 2

## Fischer Stays Out, Forfeits 2d Game; Appeal Is Expected

By HAROLD C. SCHONBERG

Special to The New York Times

REYKJAVIK, Iceland, July 13—Bobby Fischer remained in his hotel room today, refusing to show up for his scheduled game with Boris Spassky. He was declared the loser by forfeit and the score of this strange world championship chess match became 2 to 0 in favor of the Soviet titleholder.

Fischer's lawyer was expected here tomorrow to press for a reversal of the forfeit. He said before leaving New York that if chess officials refused to wipe the forfeit off the books he would sue to force them to do so.

Spassky appeared on the stage of Exhibition Hall promptly at 5 P.M. Lothar Schmid, the referee, started Fischer's clock. According to Rule 5 of this match, a player who has not appeared on time has an hour to arrive after his clock has started. When the hour is up, his game is declared forfeit.

Spassky sat before the chessboard for about five minutes, looking uncomfortable, and then left the stage. The audience of

Continued on Page 29, Column 4

## Exchange Selects Needham of S.E.C. As Chief Executive

By TERRY ROBARDS

James J. Needham, a member of the Securities and Exchange Commission, was named yesterday to be the first full-time, salaried chairman and chief executive officer of the New York Stock Exchange.

Mr. Needham, a 45-year-old former New York accountant, was selected at the first meeting of a new board of directors that was structured to give a greater voice to the public in the exchange's affairs.

He was a surprise choice for the job, which is expected to be the most prominent in the securities industry. It was estimated some time ago that the new chairman would be paid upward of $200,000 a year.

The exchange had concentrated its search for a new leader principally in Wall Street in an effort to find an individual with great expertise in the securities business. However, Mr. Needham is known to be highly regarded in the financial community.

Since his appointment to the S.E.C. by President Nixon in 1969, he has had a sympathetic ear for Wall Street's problems. He has made himself available to financial leaders to discuss the issues and questions facing the industry and has frequently made speeches to business-men's groups.

Although Mr. Needham succeeds Ralph DeNunzio in the

Continued on Page 37, Column 5

## CAMPAIGN TO USE PRIMARY TACTICS

### Big Drive for Youth, Reform Rhetoric and Grass-Roots Organizing Will Continue

By JAMES M. NAUGHTON

Special to The New York Times

MIAMI BEACH, July 13—Senator George McGovern will try to win the White House in November with the same techniques he patented in the Democratic primaries: a huge registration drive among youths, reform rhetoric and national grass-roots organizing.

With or without the active assistance of regular Democratic organizations, the Senator from South Dakota is preparing to wage a fall campaign as though the nation were one big primary state.

There are many critics in the party who doubt his campaign will overcome President Nixon. But Mr. McGovern and his strategists are beginning the campaign with expressions of the same confidence they said they felt when, according to the polls, the Senator could never be nominated.

Frank Mankiewicz, the national coordinator for the McGovern campaign, says he is convinced that "the voters are lying in the woods waiting for Richard Nixon to go by."

And Gary Hart professes to know the date when they will

Continued on Page 10, Column 5

## Marathon Session Sifted Long Roster of Candidates

By DOUGLAS E. KNEELAND

Special to The New York Times

MIAMI BEACH, July 13—Senator George McGovern and his senior staff went through a marathon session of politics and pondering, apparently laced with some hard-nosed disputes, before finally settling late this afternoon on Senator Thomas F. Eagleton of Missouri as his running mate on the Democratic ticket.

After Senator Edward M. Kennedy of Massachusetts flatly turned down the Vice-Presidential spot "for very real personal reasons" shortly after midnight, the real decision-making began in the upper reaches of the Doral Hotel, the South Dakotan's headquarters.

While Senator Kennedy had made it plain in recent weeks that he did not want to run, some leading McGovern advisers nourished until that post-midnight telephone conversation between the newly nominated Presidential candidate and Mr. Kennedy hopes that he might still be persuaded to join the ticket.

**From 24 Down to 7**

Once that verdict was in, they turned their attention to a long list of alternatives.

Although some political debts obviously were paid and some egos intentionally polished in the late flurry of phone calls to party leaders and leaks of potential candidates, much of the day's frenetic activity seems to have been a very real part of the selection process.

One of the Democratic Presidential nominee's closest advisers said that a score of senior staff members meeting throughout the day, working with Senator McGovern, pared an original list of 24 names to seven as a workable number.

But even the list of seven changed several times during the day as Mr. McGovern con-

Continued on Page 10, Column 2

## KENNEDY EXHORTS PARTY TO VICTORY

### Electrifies Convention With Praise for McGovern and Appeal for Unity

By R. W. APPLE Jr.

Special to The New York Times

MIAMI BEACH, Friday, July 14 — Senator Edward M. Kennedy of Massachusetts, the man who shunned his party's Presidential nomination this year, electrified the Democratic National Convention this morning with praise for Senator George McGovern and an exhortation to victory in November.

He brought the whistling, clapping, shouting, foot-stomping crowd to its feet time after time as he compared Senator McGovern, the Democratic Presidential nominee, to all the great men of the party's past—Jefferson and Jackson, Wilson and Franklin D. Roosevelt, Hubert H. Humphrey and Lyndon B. Johnson and his own brother, John F. Kennedy.

Mr. Kennedy quoted Woodrow Wilson's maxim to the effect that a great purpose makes a great party and said this convention and this candidate had met it.

And, indirectly, he urged party unity by admonishing the new elements who have dominated the Miami Beach meeting not to treat with disdain

Continued on Page 12, Column 5

## 'Credentials Mad' Society Called Spur to Unaccredited Colleges

By LINDA CHARLTON

For a variety of reasons, ranging from a "credentials mad" society to a new recognition of untraditional approaches, unaccredited colleges are "springing up all over the place," according to an official of the organization concerned with the accreditation of colleges and universities in this country said yesterday.

"It seems to me that in the last four or five years there's been a noticeable upsurge in this kind of development," said Norman Burns, the executive director of the Federation of Regional Accrediting Commissions of Higher Education.

Although the most effective remedy is believed to be stronger legislation by individual states, another possible remedy arises in the recent action of the Federal Trade Commission in issuing a "cease and desist" order to one such college in Ohio, according to Jerry Miller, associate director of the National Commission on Accrediting. The commission is an advisory group.

An extreme example of both academic misrepresentation and remedial action came to light yesterday in Federal Court in Brooklyn. Two Orthodox Jewish rabbis pleaded guilty to using the mails to defraud would-be students in a mythical "Marlowe University." The students paid $400 to $500 for degrees they never received.

A New York Times investiga-

Continued on Page 36, Column 7

Associated Press

United Press International

Hijackers in the custody of the Federal Bureau of Investigation in Houston after leaving the jet they had commandeered, and surrendering. Michael Stanley Green is at left and Lulseged Tesfa, wearing a light shirt, is in photo at right.

## A Fumble at the Hour of Triumph

By JAMES RESTON

Special to The New York Times

News Analysis

MIAMI BEACH, Friday, July 14—The only thing that seems to bother George McGovern and his blue-jean machine is success. They were rattling along fine until the South Dakota Senator was nominated, and then they fumbled their hour of triumph. Their first big bobble of the convention started when they made a sharp turn at high speed from the new politics to the old politics in the selection of the Vice Presidential nominee.

Mr. McGovern raced to the nomination by scalding the old pros, and their smoky room shenanigans, and then, in the exuberance of victory, he presided over a closed-door choice of Senator Thomas F. Eagleton as Vice President and sent out the word at the last minute, not only to Mr. Eagleton, but to the convention.

The result was a lovers' quarrel—as usual a protracted affair ending in reconciliation—but it took so long that even the night watchmen on the Pacific Coast were going to bed before Mr. McGovern could make the most important speech of his career.

It was an understandable mistake by tired and distracted men, but it was a serious and avoidable mistake and nobody is more critical of it than Mr. McGovern's principal aides.

By the time that Frank Mankiewicz came down and announced that Senator Eagleton was Mr. McGovern's choice for Vice President—15 minutes before the deadline for filing nominations for the Vice Presidency—there was scarcely time for the state chairmen, let alone the delegates, to get the word before making their way to the convention hall.

This threw the whole evening's proceedings off schedule. The "free delegates" and the "open convention" suddenly changed, and a lot of people in the hall began to proclaim that they were not free but trapped, and that the "openness

Continued on Page 12, Column 5

NEWS INDEX



| | Page | | Page |
|---|---|---|---|
| Art | 16 | Movies | 15-20 |
| Books | 28-29 | Music | 15-20 |
| Bridge | 28 | Obituaries | 34 |
| Business | 36-46 | Op-Ed | 31 |
| Crossword | 29 | Society | 28 |
| Editorials | 30 | Sports | 21-25, 28 |
| Family/Style | 14 | Theaters | 15-20 |
| Financial | 36-46 | Transportation | 62 |
| Going Out Guide | 16 | TV and Radio | 63 |
| Man in the News | 10 | Weather | 62 |

News Summary and Index, Page 33

"All the News That's Fit to Print"

# The New York Times

LATE CITY EDITION

Weather: Partly sunny, warm today, mild tonight. Sunny, warm tomorrow. Temp. range: today 67-85; Tuesday 76-91. Temp.-Hum. Index yesterday 79. Full U.S. report on Page 7.

VOL. CXXI ... No. 41,822  NEW YORK, WEDNESDAY, JULY 26, 1972 15 CENTS

## HOUSE COMMITTEE BACKS AMENDMENT SEEKING WAR'S END

### Foreign Affairs Panel Votes, 18 to 17, for a Measure Asking Pullout by Oct. 1

### BLOW TO WHITE HOUSE

### Group Once Strongly Upheld Vietnam Policy — Truce Conditions Softened

By JOHN W. FINNEY

Special to The New York Times

WASHINGTON, July 25—The House Foreign Affairs Committee, once an ardent backer of the Vietnam war, voted today for legislation that would order a termination of American involvement in the war, subject only to a limited cease-fire with North Vietnam and release of American prisoners.

By a vote of 18 to 17, the committee attached the end-the-war amendment to a $2.126-billion foreign military aid authorization bill. A corresponding bill in the Senate was voted down yesterday after a similar but stronger troop withdrawal amendment was added to it.

In the Senate today, a movement was under way to revive the antiwar amendment by attaching it to other legislation, a movement likely to gain impetus now that the House seems to be moving in the same direction.

**Setback for Administration**

The House committee's adoption today of the amendment sponsored by Representative Lee H. Hamilton, Democrat of Indiana, represents the first time that the group has approved an antiwar measure. In the past the Administration has relied upon the committee to block or modify end-the-war amendments approved by the Senate, an attitude that continued to prevail in the White House right up to the House committee's action today.

Just a few hours before the House committee's vote, the Presidential press secretary, Ronald L. Ziegler, said the White House was hopeful that the House of Representatives would approve a foreign aid authorization bill acceptable to the Administration, thus giving the Senate "a chance to reconsider" its action yesterday in defeating the aid legislation after an amendment calling for a troop withdrawal in four months had been added.

**Bill Going to House Floor**

Unexpectedly, the Administration now finds its Vietnam policy under legislative attack in both houses of Congress. The Administration's best hope of thwarting the attack lies in the House, which has in the past supported its Vietnam policy against Senate amendments, but it was no longer regarded as certain that the White House could block or modify the amendment approved by the Foreign Affairs Committee when the foreign aid bill reaches the House floor, probably next week.

As reflected in the House committee's action today and

Continued on Page 5, Column 1

## Dean at Columbia Is Shot; Suspended Student Sought

### College Official, at Work in Hamilton Hall Office, Struck by 3 Bullets

By ERIC PACE

Associated Press

**Dean Henry S. Coleman at Columbia in 1968 during student disorders.**

Dean Henry S. Coleman of Columbia College was shot three times and seriously wounded yesterday afternoon, and police officials said they were seeking a suspended undergraduate for questioning.

Mr. Coleman, the dean of students and one of the most popular figures on the Columbia campus, was shot in the chest, jaw and wrist while working in his office at Hamilton Hall. He was reported in good condition and "doing fine" last night after undergoing chest surgery at St. Luke's Hospital.

The undergraduate being sought was identified as Eldridge McKinney, a 20-year-old Chicagoan. The Police Department's chief spokesman, Deputy Commissioner Richard M. Kellerman, declined to say specifically whether Mr. McKinney was a suspect, but he observed that "Eldridge McKinney is currently being sought for questioning in this case—there is nothing further I can say at this time."

A Columbia University spokesman, Martin Gleason, said the assailant's identity was unknown, but he reported late yesterday that Mr. McKinney "had an appointment and saw Dean Coleman early today" about his suspension.

It was at about 2 P.M. that the shooting occurred. Mr. Gleason said the assailant had

Continued on Page 41, Column 2

## S. E. C. PROPOSES RULES TO CONTROL NEW-STOCK SALES

### Fuller Data and Additional Duties for Brokers and Underwriters Included

By EILEEN SHANAHAN

Special to The New York Times

WASHINGTON, July 25—Extensive new regulations, aimed at preventing the development, in the future, of wildly gyrating "hot-issues" markets in new stocks, were proposed today by the Securities and Exchange Commission.

The proposed new requirements go far beyond simple expansion of disclosure of the company's condition and prospects by the issuer of the stock, although such increased disclosure is a main facet of the commission's recommendations.

In addition, however, the S.E.C. would impose upon underwriters new responsibilities to make sure that the issuer was telling the truth about his company and that enough stock was sold to genuine public investors to create a true market for the stock.

**Face New Responsibility**

As for brokers, they would be subject to a new responsibility for determining whether the purchase of a newly issued stock was a "suitable" investment for a given customer.

Broad as the proposals are, they constituted only the first of several steps that the commission intends to take to protect the public from undue risk when it buys new stock issues.

The S.E.C. announced that further regulatory proposals would be forthcoming, dealing with the problems of the actual initial distribution of the stock and of the "after-market," that is, the trading after the initial distribution. Manipulation and the creation of artificial shortages of "hot issues" have occurred in the after-market in the past.

Further hearings will be held on these subjects, and the actual proposed regulations will probably not be issued until after the turn of the year, the commission indicated.

The S.E.C. would not, itself, under the proposals it made today, do the actual regulating of underwriters' or brokers' ac-

Continued on Page 57, Column 1

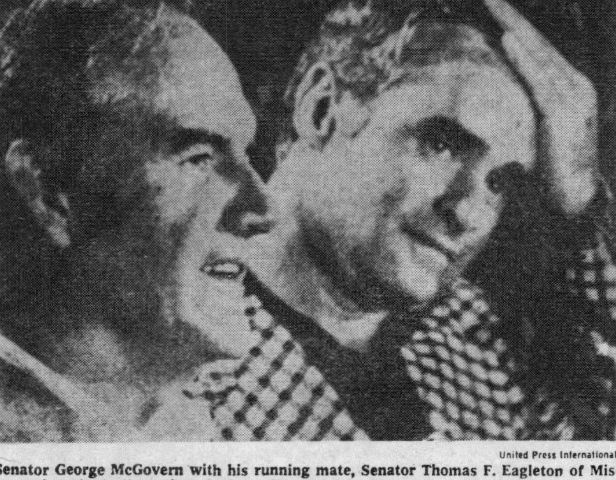

United Press International

**Senator George McGovern with his running mate, Senator Thomas F. Eagleton of Missouri, during a discussion of Mr. Eagleton's health history yesterday at Custer, S. D.**

## EAGLETON TELLS OF SHOCK THERAPY ON TWO OCCASIONS

### Says He Was in Hospital 3 Times From 1960 to 1966 for 'Nervous Exhaustion'

### SUFFERED 'DEPRESSION'

### McGovern Says He Would Have Made Same Choice if He Had Known

By CHRISTOPHER LYDON

Special to The New York Times

CUSTER, S. D., July 25—Senator Thomas F. Eagleton, the Democratic Vice-Presidential nominee, said here today that he was hospitalized three times between 1960 and 1966 for "nervous exhaustion and fatigue" and that he had undergone psychiatric treatment, including electric shock therapy, for "depression" on two of the three occasions.

The 42-year-old Missourian volunteered a review of his medical history before a surprised news conference this

*News conference excerpts appear on Page 20.*

morning at the vacation retreat of his running mate, Senator George McGovern of South Dakota.

**Checkup Last Week**

On the basis of a complete checkup in Washington last week, Senator Eagleton said laughingly that he suffered now from nothing worse than "two pounds overweight and half a hemorrhoid."

In Washington, political associates and opponents of Mr. Eagleton accepted without question his statement. Members of Congress and Missouri politicians said that his history of treatment was well known in his home state and among some associates on Capitol Hill.

Senator McGovern, acknowledging that he had not been aware of his running mate's earlier difficulties when he chose him at Miami Beach 11 days ago, said he would have picked him anyway. "There is no one sounder in body, mind and spirit than Tom Eagleton," he said.

Later, in response to questions about whether he had made "an irrevocable decision" to keep Mr. Eagleton on the ticket, Mr. McGovern replied, "Absolutely." He made the statement in an interview with Harry Reasoner to be broadcast on the American Broadcasting Company's Evening News show tomorrow night.

**No Withdrawal**

At one point Senator Eagleton offered to withdraw from the ticket. However, according to Richard Dougherty, Mr. McGovern's press spokesman, the Presidential nominee "declined even to discuss it."

Yet Mr. Eagleton himself was manifestly nervous—his hands and his face seeming to quiver slightly—as he spoke of his health record.

"As a young man, I drove myself too hard," he said.

He did not rule out a discussion of his health as an is-

Continued on Page 20, Column 3

## Nixon Accord With Soviet Embitters NATO Officials

By FLORA LEWIS

Special to The New York Times

BRUSSELS, July 20—Members of the North Atlantic Council, guiding body of the Atlantic alliance, are baffled and bitter at what they consider President Nixon's end run in signing a declaration of principles with the Soviet leader Leonid I. Brezhnev in Moscow last May.

One chief allied delegate called it "a deception." Another said the Moscow declaration was "a typical example" of current American disregard for the North Atlantic Treaty Organization and for the procedures that have become a customary and expected part of the alliance as an Atlantic institution.

The Soviet-American agreement has already produced harmful effects in their own relations with Moscow, according to officials of more than one member Government. They expect it will also serve to weaken the Western position when negotiations begin this November for an East-West European security conference.

Among countries known to be distressed are almost all the members of the Common Market, as well as other important allies. Some leading delegates have confided to American of-

Continued on Page 13, Column 1

## 10 MILLION FREED FROM WAGE CURBS

### Exemptions Are Extended by Dropping Controls on Pay Below $2.75 an Hour

By EDWARD COWAN

Special to The New York Times

WASHINGTON, July 25—The Nixon Administration announced today that it was exempting 10 million more workers from Government wage controls.

The new exemption was established by increasing to $2.75 an hour the wage level below which workers are not subject to the Pay Board's jurisdiction. The Cost of Living Council, which oversees the program of economic controls, originally set the cutoff point at $1.90 an hour.

Taking into account earlier exemptions, the council said, 56 per cent of the nation's 58 million nongovernment, nonfarm employes will be eligible for pay increases in excess of the Pay Board's guideline of 5.5 per cent. An undetermined number of farm and government employes will also be exempt.

A Federal District Court here ruled 10 days ago that $1.90 was less than Congress intended. Donald Rumsfeld, the council's director, said that, even without that ruling, the $1.90 figure would have been raised,

Continued on Page 15, Column 1

## Chess Play Adjourned

After 40 moves, Bobby Fischer and Boris Spassky adjourned the seventh game of their world championship chess match in Reykjavik, Iceland. Play is to resume today. Details on Page 16.

## U.S. JURY INDICTS AIDE OF MACKELL

### Assistant District Attorney Accused of Taking Bribe to Quash Gun Case

By ARNOLD H. LUBASCH

Norman D. Archer, an assistant district attorney of Queens, was indicted by a Federal grand jury here yesterday on charges of accepting a bribe to quash a criminal case.

Mr. Archer, who was in charge of obtaining thousands of Queens County indictments as chief of the indictment bureau in District Attorney Thomas J. Mackell's office, was charged in the indictment with sharing a $15,000 bribe to dismiss a gun-carrying case against a defendant who proved to be an undercover agent.

The indictment against the 51-year-old Mr. Archer also charged Frank R. Klein, 71, a Queens lawyer, and Leon Wasserberger, 56, a Manhattan bail bondsman's aide, with arranging the alleged bribe last spring.

This was the second indictment to result so far from an extensive corruption investigation headed by United States Attorney Whitney North Seymour Jr., who complained last month that The New York Times and The Daily News had hurt the investigation by disclosing that it was underway.

Mr. Seymour said at a news conference announcing the latest indictment that "a substan-

Continued on Page 38, Column 3

## Most Power Back in City; Voltage Cut in Some Areas

By FRANK J. PRIAL

Electricity was restored yesterday to most of the 500,000 people in areas blacked out Monday, but some Consolidated Edison customers in Brooklyn, Queens and Manhattan remained without power or with reduced power more than 32 hours after the failures first struck the city.

There were these other developments in the city's continuing power crises:

¶Charles F. Luce, Con Edison's chairman and chief executive, said the company, concerned about power shortages, had been "surprised" and "embarrassed" when the trouble came from cable failures.

¶State and city officials, as they did in previous power crises, demanded new investigations of Consolidated Edison.

¶A financial report showed net income for the utility rose sharply in the first half of 1972, but earnings for the full year are expected to fall "somewhat below" the $2.35 a share earned in 1971.

"There's no problem any place on the system except for some very scattered problems in southern Brooklyn and southern Queens," James Pastorius, a Con Edison spokesman, said early this morning. "The remaining pockets lacking service were mostly individual customers, he said.

Hundreds of repairmen working around the clock restored service in most of the affected areas of Queens by 2:45 A.M. yesterday and in most of the affected areas of Brooklyn by 5:45 A.M., Con Edison said. The company also reported that a voltage reduction that had hit Manhattan's Upper West Side had been corrected by noon yesterday.

However, there was still not sufficient power late yesterday afternoon to operate appliances and refrigerators in stores

Continued on Page 19, Column 2

## School Board Will Create Office of Safety Director

By IVER PETERSON

The Board of Education will create a new position of safety director for the city's public schools and appoint Eldridge Waith, a former commander of patrolmen in Harlem, to fill it.

The move, which was confirmed last night by board officials, is apparently designed to counter the school system's growing problems with violence, as well as to offset the United Federation of Teachers' contract demands for tougher policies on school crime.

The creation of the new post and Mr. Waith's appointment will be officially announced tomorrow. Mr. Waith broke the news yesterday in Charlotte Amalie, on St. Thomas, where he has served for the past 18 months as Commissioner of Public Safety for the United States Virgin Islands.

Dr. Harvey B. Scribner, Chancellor of the school system, would not comment publicly on the report.

Mr. Waith said he would leave his Virgin Islands job on Aug. 28. In New York, he will have under his command about 200 school guards who have been trained by the Police Department. This number is scheduled to be increased, a spokesman for the Board of Education said last night.

Mr. Waith's appointment comes at a time when the central board and the teachers union are sharply divided over the problem of handling crime in the schools, such as the sale of drugs, assaults on teachers, vandalism and shakedowns of students for pocket money.

The board has maintained that the teachers themselves are best suited to maintain con-

Continued on Page 34, Column 4

## Syphilis Victims in U.S. Study Went Untreated for 40 Years

By JEAN HELLER

The Associated Press

WASHINGTON, July 25—For 40 years the United States Public Health Service has conducted a study in which human beings with syphilis, who were induced to serve as guinea pigs, have gone without medical treatment for the disease and a few have died of its late effects, even though an effective therapy was eventually discovered.

The study was conducted to determine from autopsies what the disease does to the human body.

Officials of the health service who initiated the experiment have long since retired. Current officials, who say they have serious doubts about the morality of the study, also say that it is too late to treat the syphilis in any surviving participants.

Doctors in the service say they are now rendering whatever other medical services they can give to the survivors while the study of the disease's effects continues.

Dr. Merlin K. DuVal, Assistant Secretary of Health, Education and Welfare for Health and Scientific Affairs, expressed shock on learning of the study. He said that he was making an immediate investigation.

The experiment, called the Tuskegee Study, began in 1932 with about 600 black men,

Continued on Page 8, Column 1



## Britain Faces Paralysis in Labor Dispute

Associated Press

**Members of Britain's Trades Union Congress marching through fish market area on way to London prison where five dockers have been jailed for contempt.**

By ALVIN SHUSTER

Special to The New York Times

LONDON, July 25 — Britain approached industrial paralysis tonight as more workers left their jobs and thousands threatened to follow in support of five imprisoned dock workers. But there was a glimmer of hope.

With unrest spreading across the country, Britain's Official Solicitor, a normally obscure court official, decided to seek the dock workers' release, which could end the crisis. The decision by Norman Turner, the Solicitor, came after unofficial strikes shut all major ports, stopped publication of national and local newspapers and disrupted many industries.

More workers, including miners, truck drivers and airport workers, walked out today. And London's bus drivers and conductors voted to stop work at midnight for 24 hours, foreshadowing agony for commuters here tomorrow.

Even greater disruption is threatened on the railroads by the locomotive engineers, who will vote later this week on whether to take similar action.

The leaders of the Amalgamated Union of Engineering Workers, which has 1.5 million members, ordered a protest strike on Monday. And the general council of the Trades Union Congress, representing nine million workers, will meet

Continued on Page 12, Column 3

## Sheriff Frees Green Berets' 'P.O.W.s'

By JAMES T. WOOTEN

Special to The New York Times

ALABASTER, Ala., July 25—The Mayor of this little town and its chief of police were driving around one day last week tacking up posters for the Mayor's re-election campaign.

"All of a sudden, I looked up, and there were a lot of soldiers with guns, and they were waving them around and pointing them at us, and we just got captured," Mayor Willie Mathis said here today.

The Mayor and chief, C. E. Carter, were kidnapped last Tuesday by members of a National Guard Special Forces unit (Green Berets) that was apparently attempting to inject some hostile-village realism into summer maneuvers.

They were later rescued by a slow-talking sheriff who thwarted a second kidnapping attempt on a local judge, forced a prisoner exchange and finally frustrated the elaborate Guard plan.

"What we did was to outsmart the Vietcong," C. P. Walker, the sheriff of Shelby County, said today after the bizarre incident was disclosed in a Birmingham newspaper.

Although the National Guard was embarrassed by the incident and refused to comment on it, the Alabaster city officials offered a detailed narrative to visitors.

According to their account, Mayor Willie Mathis, 68 years old, who has been in municipal government for two decades, and Mr. Carter, the 47-year-old police chief, were driving around the town last Tuesday putting up posters for the Mayor's re-election campaign.

Neither of the men noticed a small camper-truck trailing them until its five occupants, in Army uniforms, suddenly surrounded them and with their M-16 carbines and pistols motioned them toward their vehicle.

"They kept saying, 'Keep quiet! Get Moving!' and waving those guns around, and I've got to admit that I was frightened," the Mayor said today. "I couldn't imagine what

Continued on Page 6, Column 1

NEWS INDEX



| | Page | | Page |
|---|---|---|---|
| Art | 22 | Movies | 21-26 |
| Books | 35 | Music | 21-26 |
| Bridge | 34 | Obituaries | 40 |
| Business | 45-57 | Op-Ed | 37 |
| Chess | 16 | Sports | 27-30, 34 |
| Crossword | 35 | Theaters | 21-26 |
| Editorials | 36 | Transportation | 73 |
| Family/Style | 42 | TV and Radio | 74-75 |
| Financial | 45-57 | Washington Record | 74 |
| Going Out Guide | 22 | Weather | 73 |

News Summary and Index, Page 39

"All the News That's Fit to Print"

# The New York Times

LATE CITY EDITION

Weather: Partly sunny, warm today; fair, warm tonight. Sunny tomorrow. Temp. range: today 64-84; Monday 66-71. Temp.-Hum. Index yesterday 70. Full U.S. report on Page 69.

VOL. CXXI . . No. 41,828

NEW YORK, TUESDAY, AUGUST 1, 1972

15 CENTS

# EAGLETON QUITS AT REQUEST OF M'GOVERN; SAYS HE DOES NOT WANT TO 'DIVIDE' PARTY

## 6 KILLED BY BOMBS AFTER TROOP PUSH ON I.R.A. IN ULSTER

### Blasts in Village Wound 30 as Soldiers Move Through Urban Catholic Areas

By BERNARD WEINRAUB

Special to The New York Times

BELFAST, Northern Ireland, July 31 — Six persons were killed in terrorist bomb blasts today following a predawn operation by British troops that smashed the barricades of Roman Catholic areas in Belfast and Londonderry.

As thousands of soldiers, backed by armored convoys and bulldozers, moved through silent Catholic neighborhoods this morning, three bombs exploded without warning in automobiles in the center of the tiny village of Claudy, 10 miles southeast of Londonderry. The six victims included a 9-year-old girl. Among the 30 wounded, five are in critical condition.

**Most Barricades Gone**

By tonight, almost all the barricades in Londonderry and Belfast had been swept aside. Weary British soldiers, gripping automatic weapons, were deployed beside schools, apartment houses and empty pubs in Catholic areas.

"The position now is that anyone can go anywhere at any time," Maj. Gen. Robert Ford, the commander of land forces here, said this evening.

Belfast and Londonderry are under virtual siege. Flak-jacketed soldiers — some of them with faces blackened with charcoal—patrolled such Irish Republican Army strongholds as Andersonstown, Falls Road and the Ardoyne in Belfast as well as the Bogside in Londonderry. Troop carriers, tanks and armored cars, equipped with twin Browning machine guns, rumbled down the center of Belfast.

**'Army Now in Control'**

"The army are now in occupation and control throughout Northern Ireland," William Whitelaw, the British administrator for Ulster, said this morning after the assault into so-called "no-go" areas established by the Catholics. It was the biggest military operation ever mounted in Northern Ireland.

For nearly three years, areas of Londonderry and Belfast, Northern Ireland's two principal cities, have been effectively barricaded to the army and the police, creating a haven for the I.R.A. Mr. Whitelaw had hesitated in the past to dismantle the barricades and deploy troops into these areas, fearing bitter gun-

Continued on Page 3, Column 4

## Ellsberg's Lawyers Ask Rehnquist Ban

By FRED P. GRAHAM

Special to The New York Times

LOS ANGELES, July 31—The tangled court proceedings in the Pentagon papers case were further complicated today when the defense sought to disqualify Justice William H. Rehnquist from taking part in the Supreme Court's consideration of the case.

The request that Justice Rehnquist excuse himself came in response to a Justice Department application, filed with the Supreme Court this morning, that asked the full Court to overturn Justice William O. Douglas's stay of the Pentagon papers trial.

Justice Rehnquist was asked, in a telegram to the Court, to excuse himself from any action on the stay because of his alleged connection with aspects of the Pentagon papers contro-

Continued on Page 16, Column 4



## Lend-Lease Debts Blocking A Soviet-U.S. Trade Pact

By HEDRICK SMITH

Special to The New York Times

MOSCOW, July 31—Persisting differences over Soviet repayment of a World War II lend-lease debt have prevented Secretary of Commerce Peter G. Peterson and top-level Soviet officials from achieving an over-all Soviet-American trade agreement in 10 days of talks here, diplomatic sources reported tonight.

Mr. Peterson, who had a three-hour meeting with the Communist party general secretary, Leonid I. Brezhnev, in the Crimea yesterday and a four-hour negotiating session here today with the Soviet Union's Foreign Trade Minister, Nikolai S. Patolichev, leaves for Poland tomorrow en route home.

Diplomatic sources said the joint Soviet-American Economic Commission would issue a communiqué on its work tomorrow, probably announcing plans for another meeting in Washington to make a final effort at achieving the elusive trade agreement before the November election.

The commission was established during President Nixon's May summit meeting with Soviet leaders when, despite efforts, they failed to reach a trade agreement.

Diplomatic sources said tonight that the two sides were still deadlocked over terms of Soviet repayment of the lend-lease debt. The Soviets are demanding a 2 per cent interest rate on the outstanding debt, and the Americans are asking for 6 per cent.

"We began at zero and came back to zero," was the way one negotiator described the 10 days of talks. But other officials, both Soviet and American, insisted that progress had been made, that the results had been about as expected, and that the warm atmosphere of the May summit meeting persisted.

Neutral diplomats have suggested that the White House is hesitant to make trade concessions to Moscow until it sees

Continued on Page 52, Column 3

## European Families Feel The Bite of Rising Costs

By CLYDE H. FARNSWORTH

Special to The New York Times

PARIS, July 31—Inflation, which seems to be the inevitable accompaniment of life in a modern industrial society, is changing the habits and attitudes of Europeans.

Strikes in Britain, France, Italy and elsewhere are one sign of the frustrations the working man feels in trying to keep up with the ever-mounting cost of living.

In Britain, the industrial strife is on a scale not seen since the nineteen-twenties. And Italy is already feeling the tremors heralding the quakes that will come this fall when the latest wage contracts expire.

The more prosperous European middle classes, while less afflicted, have not been spared. They are squeezed right and left, but their problem is not so much earning enough to live as keeping what they've got. The 16th century French writer Montaigne put it succinctly. "I find it more trouble to watch over money than to get it."

No issue—whether soccer or Bobby Fischer's chess antics, the topless fad at St. Tropez or new ministers in Paris, Bonn and Rome—can quite compete with the inexorable march of prices as a topic of conversation in the pubs and municipal flats of England, around the wooden kitchen tables of France, in the winehouses of Germany and Austria, in the tulip-decked living rooms of the Netherlands or in the crammed Fiat of a Neapolitan family rolling on the ramp of the ferry to the island of Ischia.

What exactly is happening to prices? How are they affecting the daily lives of Europeans? What are the Europeans doing about them? What are the attitudes of governments and the financial authorities?

Here is what the raw statistics show for latest annual inflation rates in some nations: the Netherlands, 8 per cent; Switzerland, 6.3 per cent; Britain, 6.2 per cent; France, 5.4 per cent; West Germany, 5.1 per cent; Japan, 4.5 per cent, and the United States, 3.2 per cent.

But the statistics don't tell anything like the full story. Things like this are left out:

¶Bus fares have doubled in

Continued on Page 2, Column 1

## HATCH ACT UPSET; U.S. COURT FINDS CURBS TOO VAGUE

### Civil Service Unit Enjoined From Enforcing Bars on Political Activity

By ROBERT M. SMITH

Special to The New York Times

WASHINGTON, July 31 — A three-judge panel of the United States District Court here ruled today that the Hatch Act's prohibitions on political activity by Federal civil service employes are so vague and broad that they are unconstitutional.

By a vote of 2 to 1, the panel enjoined the Civil Service Commission from enforcing the 33-year-old act. The court stayed its injunction, however, until the Supreme Court can decide the issue.

It was not clear whether the Civil Service Commission would continue to enforce the act. A spokesman for the commission said its lawyers were still analyzing the decision. Similarly, a Justice Department spokesman said that Government lawyers had not decided whether to appeal the case to the Supreme Court.

**Letter Carriers Sue**

The suit against the Civil Service Commission was brought by the National Association of Letter Carriers, six local Democratic and Republican committees and six Federal employes as a class action on behalf of all Federal and state employes covered by the Hatch Act.

The court held that the political committees had not shown that they adequately represented state employes and therefore limited its ruling to Federal employes.

In his opinion for the court, District Judge Gerhard A. Gesell took note of a 1947 decision by the Supreme Court, United Public Workers v. Mitchell, which upheld the act, but it contended that the present case was different.

Judge Gesell said that this case "focuses not on the merits of the objective of the Hatch Act but on the manner in which Congress defined the conduct it purported to prohibit." He held the Congressional definition "ambiguous and unsatisfactory."

He pointed out that the Congressional definition "incorporates by reference over 3,000

Continued on Page 25, Column 4

United Press International

Senator George McGovern announcing the withdrawal of Senator Thomas F. Eagleton

## OTTAWA REJECTS LEGAL MARIJUANA

### But Asks End to Jail Terms for Possession and to Criminal Citations

By JAY WALZ

Special to The New York Times

OTTAWA, July 31 — The Canadian Government today rejected recent recommendations that it legalize the simple possession of marijuana and hashish. However, under a new policy to be proposed to Parliament, first offenders would be treated far more leniently than in the past.

"The Government has no intention to legalize possession of cannabis in any form," Health Minister John C. Munro declared in a statement, "nor does it intend to legalize the cultivation of cannabis for personal use."

At the same time, Mr. Munro continued, the Government recognizes the need to amend laws to reduce their "impact" on users not involved in the trafficking or cultivation of the illegal drugs. To make this possible, the Government will seek to transfer all controls relating to cannabis, the group of drugs that includes marijuana and hashish, from the Narcotic

Continued on Page 6, Column 1

## Eagleton Tells McGovern It Was 'the Only Decision'

By DOUGLAS E. KNEELAND

Special to The New York Times

WASHINGTON, July 31—A little after 8:30 tonight, Senator Thomas F. Eagleton left the Marble Room just off the Senate floor for the long walk down the underground corridor to his office building.

At his side was Senator George McGovern, the Democratic candidate for the Presidency. When they went into the Marble Room, Senator Eagleton was McGovern's running mate. When they left, Senator Eagleton knew it was all over.

The 42-year-old Missourian was gaunt, red-eyed and visibly nervous. But as they walked down the corridor, he had his arm draped over Mr. McGovern's shoulder.

Over and over he said to the man who had just convinced him to resign from the ticket that it was "the correct decision, the only decision—it will prove to be the right one in the long run."

**Hands Held High**

As they reached a fork in the tunnel, they parted ways with hands held high in waves as Mr. Eagleton went to his office in one building and Mr. McGovern moved toward his in another.

A little more than an hour later, the two men thrust their way, with the aid of Secret Service agents, through the crush of newsmen and campaign aides jamming Room 318—the Caucus Room in the Old Senate Office Building.

The chamber was electric with excitement, expectant yet somehow sad about the announcement that most of those

Continued on Page 24, Column 4

## 5 THUGS AT PLAZA GET $45,000 GEMS

### 21 Employes Held Captive as Gunmen Break Open 5 Safe-Deposit Boxes

By ERIC PACE

Five dapper robbers smashed open five safe-deposit boxes at the Plaza Hotel early yesterday, the police said, and escaped with more than $45,000 worth of jewelry belonging to jewelers who had come here for a convention.

Waving pistols, the robbers herded 21 hotel employes and bystanders into a 10-by-11-foot office. Then, crouching under a crystal chandelier, they broke open the boxes, scooped up an emerald tiara and other pieces of jewelry and drove off.

"If somebody pulls a gun on you, you don't argue with him," said Jack Craver, the hotel manager, who went to the hotel at Fifth Avenue and Central Park South soon after the hour-long rain ended at 5 A.M.

He said that the two hotel security men on duty had been patrolling upstairs during the holdup and that the other employes had not sounded alarms.

No one was hurt, and no ar-

Continued on Page 70, Column 1

## SUCCESSOR SOUGHT

### O'Brien and Muskie in Running—Dakotan to Address Nation

By JAMES M. NAUGHTON

Special to The New York Times

WASHINGTON, July 31 — Senator Thomas F. Eagleton, yielding to a request from Senator George McGovern, withdrew tonight from his campaign for the Vice-Presidency. He said that he did not wish to "divide the Democratic party" by continuing as its nominee.

Eighteen days after choosing Mr. Eagleton as his running mate, Senator McGovern, the Democratic Presidential nominee, announced that they had agreed that the "best course" would be for Mr. Eagleton to step aside and thereby terminate a national debate over his health.

*Statements and excerpts are printed on Page 25.*

Thus Mr. Eagleton became the first Vice-Presidential nominee ever to withdraw from candidacy, other than by death.

Democratic leaders across the country, after learning of Mr. Eagleton's withdrawal, said that while the action was sad personally, it would strengthen the party's chances in the November election.

**May Pick O'Brien**

Senator McGovern said that he did not have a new nominee in mind, but there were reports that he would recommend to the Democratic National Committee that it select its former chairman, Lawrence F. O'Brien, to take Mr. Eagleton's place.

Among other names mentioned was that of Senator Edmund S. Muskie of Maine, whose associates said that he would be available if Mr. McGovern were to ask him to become the new Vice-Presidential nominee.

Mr. McGovern said at a news conference at which he and Mr. Eagleton announced the decision that "health was not a factor" in making it. But he added that Senator Eagleton's disclosure, six days ago, that he had been hospitalized in 1960, 1964 and 1966 for treatment of nervous exhaustion and fatigue had "dominated the political dialogue of the country" and threatened to obscure the real issue of the campaign.

**Committee to Choose**

Mr. Eagleton said he would write a letter in the morning officially informing Mrs. Jean Westwood, the chairman of the national committee, of his decision. Mrs. Westwood will then convene a meeting of the committee, which has the responsibility of choosing a new candidate.

Mr. McGovern announced that he would go on nationwide television at 9 P.M. tomorrow "to discuss the events of the campaign to date." But he said he did not expect to announce a Vice-Presidential nominee tomorrow.

It was clear that Senator Eagleton had yielded to Senator McGovern in agreeing to withdraw at a two-hour private meeting in the Marble Room off the United States Senate chamber earlier tonight.

"I would have preferred to remain on the ticket," Mr. Eagleton said at a news conference an hour later in the high-ceiling Caucus Room of the Old Senate Office Building.

He said that he had "marshaled my arguments in lawyer-like fashion" in seeking to

Continued on Page 24, Column 3

## 3 Hijack Jet, Collect $1-Million and Fly to Algeria

By RICHARD WITKIN

Three hijackers commandeered a Delta Air Lines jet yesterday, collected a major portion of the $1-million they had demanded and forced the crew to head for Algeria.

Accompanied by three women and two or three children, the hijackers released the 86 other passengers at Miami after the extortion money, stuffed in a blue suitcase, had been hauled into the cockpit by rope.

A Delta spokesman said that he could not say precisely how much money had been turned over but that it was believed to be the largest amount ever paid in a hijacking in this country. The previous high was slightly over $500,000.

**Refueled in Boston**

Having obtained the money, the hijackers, who are black, ordered the DC-8 flown to Boston to refuel and to pick up a navigator for the over-water flight. At 8:50 P.M. the plane headed out over the ocean on a nonstop flight for Algiers, which has become a haven for some black militants.

The plane was expected to reach Algiers at 3:23 A.M., Eastern daylight time.

In another hijacking to Algeria in early June, the $500,000 in extortion money collected by the two hijackers was later re-

Continued on Page 69, Column 5

Associated Press

An F.B.I. agent lugging a suitcase containing ransom money demanded by hijackers to the Delta Air Lines DC-8 at Miami Airport. As directed by the hijackers, presumably to show that he was unarmed, the agent wore only a swimsuit.

## Paul-Henri Spaak Is Dead at 73; An Architect of European Unity

By ROBERT D. McFADDEN

Paul-Henri Spaak, the Belgian statesman who was one of the chief architects of European unification and Western solidarity in the postwar era, died of kidney failure yesterday in Brussels. He was 73 years old.

The New York Times

Paul-Henri Spaak

Mr. Spaak, who came to be known as "Mr. Europe" for his international vision and towering efforts to integrate the continent, became ill while on vacation in the Azores on Saturday. He was flown home in a United States Air Force plane, entered Brugmann Hospital on Sunday and died shortly after midnight.

Although Mr. Spaak retired from political life in 1966, he had remained active, traveling, writing and speaking frequently about the institutions and peoples he loved, and was generally believed to have been in good health in recent years, apart from regular attacks of gout.

After the announcement of his death yesterday, flags were ordered flown at half-staff throughout Belgium and in many parts of Europe, and there were scores of tributes for the man with a global vision from leaders around the

Continued on Page 38, Column 2

NEWS INDEX


| | Page | | Page |
|---|---|---|---|
| Art | 28 | Movies | 28-31 |
| Books | 33 | Music | 28-31 |
| Bridge | 32 | Obituaries | 38-39 |
| Business | 45-56 | Op-Ed | 35 |
| Chess | 32 | Society | 27 |
| Crossword | 33 | Sports | 40-43 |
| Editorials | 34 | Theaters | 28-31 |
| Family/Style | 26 | Transportation | 69 |
| Financial | 45-56 | TV and Radio | 70-71 |
| Going Out Guide | 28 | U. N. Proceedings | 3 |
| Letters | 34 | Washington Record | 23 |
| Man in the News | 3 | Weather | 69 |

News Summary and Index, Page 37

"All the News That's Fit to Print"

# The New York Times

LATE CITY EDITION

Weather: Sunny and mild today; fair tonight. Partly cloudy tomorrow. Temp. range: today 60-80; Saturday 59-80. Full U.S. report on Page 75N.

News of special interest to readers in New Jersey will be found on pages 59 to 74.

VOL. CXXI .. No. 41,833 © 1972 The New York Times Company NEW YORK, SUNDAY, AUGUST 6, 1972 75c beyond 50-mile zone from New York City, except Long Island. Higher in air delivery cities. NJ 50 CENTS

# SHRIVER IS CHOSEN BY M'GOVERN TO FILL SECOND SPOT ON TICKET AFTER MUSKIE DECLINES OFFER

## Justices Decline to Upset Stay of the Ellsberg Trial

### High Court, in a Poll by Burger, Rejects Government Plea for Special Session on Delay in Pentagon Papers Case

By FRED P. GRAHAM

Special to The New York Times

LOS ANGELES, Aug. 5—Chief Justice Warren E. Burger announced today that the Supreme Court had declined to upset Justice William O. Douglas's stay of the trial of the Pentagon papers case.

In a one-paragraph order issued in Washington, the Chief Justice noted that the Justice Department had asked the Court, which is now in its summer recess, to convene a special session to consider overturning the stay.

He then announced that "after consultation with all members of the Court except Justice Douglas, who granted the stay, the motion to call a special term of the Court is denied."

With the exception of the Chief Justice and Justice Byron R. White, the other members of the Court are scattered about the country and were apparently polled by telephone. There was no indication how many, if any, had favored convening a session in Washington to consider overturning the stay.

Thus the trial of Daniel Ellsberg and Anthony J. Russo Jr. for allegedly disclosing the top secret study of the Vietnam war will apparently not begin until at least October, and possibly not for many months beyond.

The stalled Pentagon papers case has already become a legal curiosity, as it is the first trial ever to be blocked by a Supreme Court Justice after the jury was sworn in.

Justice Douglas stayed it 48 hours before the lawyers' opening arguments were to have been delivered last Monday so the defense could appeal a wiretap controversy.

The Justice Department had conceded that it had picked

Continued on Page 18, Column 3

## Czech Hostility Lingers 4 Years After Invasion

By JAMES FERON

Special to The New York Times

PRAGUE, Aug. 1—An atmosphere of hostility and protest lingers in Prague these days, four years after Soviet tanks arrived here to end the experiment in Communist reform. It is considered far short of a threat to the authorities, but they worry anyway and move quickly, sometimes sharply, to control any indication of dissent.

The result is something of a stalemate, with those who oppose the Government too feeble to express anything but token resistance and the Government seemingly indecisive about enacting reforms that are still needed.

"People are not working hard," a journalist said, "not because it's some kind of nationwide protest but because they are dispirited and feel that it won't get them anywhere. There's no incentive, no reward, so they do the minimum."

**Accent on Normalization**

Dr. Gustav Husak, the Communist party leader who replaced Alexander Dubcek after the Warsaw Pact invasion in August, 1968, has announced several times since last summer that "normalization" of the country is complete.

But it is apparently not complete enough to permit introduction of a comprehensive program, perhaps because Dr. Husak and his colleagues have been able to agree only on how to correct the past and not on how to chart the future.

The trials of dissidents who have persisted in expressing opposition to the Husak Government are intended to mark the end of the Dubcek chapter, but they have also exposed new pockets of opposition that may only delay the healing process. Evidently some Czechoslovaks

Continued on Page 2, Column 3

### Today's Sections


| Section | |
|---|---|
| Section 1 (2 Parts) | News |
| Section 2 | Drama, Movies, TV, Radio |
| Section 3 | Financial and Business |
| Section 4 | The Week in Review |
| Section 5 | Sports |
| Section 6 | Magazine |
| Section 7 | Book Review |
| Section 8 | *Real Estate |
| Section 9 | *Employment Advertising |
| Section 10 | Resort & Travel |
| Section 11 | *Advertising |

*Included in all copies distributed in New York City and its suburban areas.


### Index to Subjects


| | Section | Page |
|---|---|---|
| Art | 2 | 17-18 |
| Boating | 5 | 10-13 |
| Bridge | 6 | 50 |
| Coins | 2 | 23-24 |
| Dance | 2 | 18 |
| Editorials | 4 | 12 |
| Education | 4 | 9 |
| Fashions | 6 | 46 |
| Food | 6 | 45 |
| Gardens | 2 | 24-26 |
| Home Fashion | 6 | 48 |
| Home Improvement | 2 | 26 |
| Letters to the Editor | 4 | 12 |
| Music | 2 | 11-12 |
| News Summary & Index | 1 | 75 |
| Obituaries | 1 | 51 |
| Op-Ed | 4 | 13 |
| Photography | 2 | 24 |
| Puzzles | 6 | 52 |
| Records | 2 | 19-22 |
| Science | 4 | 6 |
| Society | 1 | 52-58 |
| Stamps | 2 | 23 |
| Transportation | 5 | 16 |
| Weather | 1 | 75 |


## THIEU ANNOUNCES HARSH NEW RULES FOR NEWSPAPERS

### His Decree, Seen as Bid to Stifle Opposition, May Close Many Dailies

By SYDNEY H. SCHANBERG

Special to The New York Times

SAIGON, South Vietnam, Aug. 5—President Nguyen Van Thieu today issued a stringent decree, aimed at controlling the press, that seems certain to close down many and perhaps most of the daily newspapers in South Vietnam. The move was viewed by South Vietnamese newsmen and diplomatic observers as an attempt to eliminate all opposition comment and criticism.

The decree requires every daily paper to deposit in the Government treasury within 30 days the amount of 20 million piasters, or about $47,000. This money, according to the decree, will be a guarantee to cover possible future fines and court charges arising from the Government's already strict press code on "national security" matters.

Many dailies here are shoestring operations, and they are expected to go out of business simply because they cannot raise that amount of money.

**Shutdown for 2d Offense**

The decree states further that when the daily issue of a newspaper is confiscated by the Government for the second time for carrying "articles detrimental to the national security and public order," the Interior Ministry can shut down the paper pending a decision in the courts.

The impact of that second-offense clause could be even more severe than the financial requirement in the decree. Hardly a day passes in Saigon without a few dailies' having their editions confiscated on grounds of their having violated the security provisions of the press code. Last week, the Government took 44 such alleged violations to court and won verdicts of guilty in 39.

There are 46 daily newspapers in South Vietnam. All but one, which is based in Can-tho, are published in Saigon. Of the 46, 29 are Vietnamese-language papers, 14 are printed in Chinese, two in English and one in French.

**Most Have Criticized Saigon**

Only four or five of these can be described as out-and-out opposition newspapers that rarely find anything favorable to say about the Thieu Government. But most of the rest are also critical from time to time, and they, too, have felt the Government's wrath.

Rumors were circulating among Vietnamese newsmen in Saigon today that President Thieu wants to reduce the number of newspapers to five, all supporting him.

Examples of the kinds of articles considered offensive

Continued on Page 4, Column 1

## U.S. PLANS DETAILS FOR P.O.W. RETURN

### Hawaii Meeting This Week Will Coordinate Program for Eventual Repatriation

By BERNARD GWERTZMAN

Special to The New York Times

WASHINGTON, Aug. 5—Although neither an end of the Vietnam war nor a release of prisoners seems imminent, the Administration has quietly drawn up a detailed program, code-named Operation Egress Recap, for the eventual return and rehabilitation of the more than 500 Americans believed held captive in Southeast Asia.

"The purpose of Operation Egress Recap is to insure that everything conceivable is anticipated ahead of time, so that when our men are released, they are treated with dignity, respect, understanding, love and kindness, all the way up and down the line," a State Department official said.

A Defense Department official said, "We want to try to return the men to their families in conditions as close as pos-

Continued on Page 3, Column 1

United Press International

Sargent Shriver signing autograph at Barnstable (Mass.) airport before flying to Washington last night.

Associated Press

Senator and Mrs. Edmund S. Muskie at their summer home in Kennebunk Beach, Me., yesterday.

## DECISION HAILED

### Successor to Eagleton Called Favorite of Nominee's Staff

By CHRISTOPHER LYDON

Special to The New York Times

WASHINGTON, Aug. 5—Senator George McGovern chose Sargent Shriver as his Vice-Presidential running mate today after Senator Edmund S. Muskie had rejected his invitation to join the Democratic ticket.

Mr. Shriver, the first director of the Peace Corps under his brother-in-law, President Kennedy, and of the antipoverty program under President Johnson, will be put in nomination before an expanded 303-mem-

*Text of McGovern statement appears on Page 28.*

ber Democratic National Committee here Tuesday night.

He will succeed Senator Thomas F. Eagleton, who resigned from the race last Monday after disclosing that he had been hospitalized three times in the nineteen-sixties for nervous exhaustion and depression.

Mr. Muskie, the Democratic Vice-Presidential nominee in 1968 and the early front runner for the Presidential nomination this year, cited family considerations in becoming the sixth man to reject Mr. McGovern's offer.

**Other Rejections**

Earlier this week, Mr. McGovern had been turned down by Senators Edward M. Kennedy of Massachusetts, Hubert H. Humphrey of Minnesota and Abraham A. Ribicoff of Connecticut. In addition, Senator Gaylord Nelson of Wisconsin and Gov. Reubin Askew were thought to have been given chances to express interest but declined.

Mr. McGovern made his announcement for television cameras, sitting before a wooden desk in front of a false marble fireplace in a small room in the Capitol.

Mr. Shriver, who had sailed this morning off Hyannis Port, Mass., was playing tennis at the Kennedy family compound there when he received Mr. McGovern's firm offer.

Before leaving for Washington from the Barnstable, Mass., airport Mr. Shriver said he was "very happy and very proud" to have been chosen.

**Staff Favorite**

Mr. Shriver had been the choice of several factions within the McGovern organization at the Democratic National Convention three weeks ago, and was the staff's favorite after Mr. Eagleton's candidacy collapsed.

He has political roots in Chicago, where he once managed the Merchandise Mart, one of the world's largest office buildings, for the late Joseph P. Kennedy, and in Maryland, where he considered running for Governor in 1970. But he has never been a candidate before, a point that

Continued on Page 28, Column 1

## 4 Sent Into Kitchen And Are Shot Dead In Chicago Suburb

By United Press International

BARRINGTON HILLS, Ill., Aug. 5 — One or two gunmen herded a retired businessman, his wife and two other members of his family into the kitchen of their suburban Chicago home last night and murdered them, the police reported. The $100,000 home was ransacked.

Those slain were Paul M. Corbett, 67 years old, a former president of Johnson & Higgins, one of the nation's largest insurance brokerage firms; his wife, Marian Boand Corbett; her daughter by a previous marriage, Barbara Boand, 22, and her sister, Mrs. Dorothy Derry, 60.

The mass slaying was discovered when Anthony Boand, Mrs. Corbett's son, went to the home to return a borrowed car and found his relatives lying in blood in the kitchen and pantry. The front door was open and a television set was on.

Police Chief Ralph Hummel of Barrington Hills said that the kitchen area of the gray brick home "looked like a slaughterhouse."

"It's the worst incident I've ever experienced," he said.

Late today, the police indicated that they thought robbery might have been a motive, although a "considerable amount" of valuable jewelry was not touched. The police theorized that the house had been searched for "documents or money."

Mr. Corbett and his wife

Continued on Page 25, Column 4

## JOINT FORCE RAIDS COAST DRUG CULT

### 57 Seized in a Group Linked to Leary—Large Illicit Narcotics Deals Alleged

By DANA ADAMS SCHMIDT

Special to The New York Times

WASHINGTON, Aug. 5 — Fifty-seven persons connected with Timothy Leary's sex and drug sect, the Brotherhood of Eternal Love, were arrested or indicted and large quantities of LSD, hashish, hashish oil, cocaine, mescaline and marijuana were seized in dawn raids in California, Oregon and Hawaii today, the Bureau of Narcotics and Dangerous Drugs announced.

Seven of those arrested by a task force combining the Federal, state and local authorities were picked up at Leary's ranch at Idyllwild in Orange County near the San Bernardino State Forest. Three were seized on the island of Maui in Hawaii and three at Grants Pass in Oregon, the bureau said.

The other arrests were made at scattered locations in San Diego, Mariposa and Orange counties in California.

Two hashish oil laboratories and $16,000 in cash were seized at unspecified locations in California.

Officials of the bureau said the haul at Leary's ranch included three hashish pipes, apparently locally made, boxed for shipment.

The raids began at 2 A.M. to-

Continued on Page 19, Column 1

## Muskie Puts Family First In His Decision Not to Run

By BILL KOVACH

Special to The New York Times

KENNEBUNK BEACH, Me., Aug. 5—Senator Edmund S. Muskie, bowing to "family duties and the interests of my growing children," rejected today Senator George McGovern's offer to be the Democratic Vice-Presidential nominee.

The decision was made after discussions with his wife, Jane, and four of his five children that lasted beyond last midnight.

"I telephoned Senator McGovern this morning to tell him that, with considerable regret, it was not possible for me to accept his offer to run on his ticket with him," Senator Muskie said at a news conference on the front lawn of his summer home.

**Cites Strain on Wife**

Surrounded by his family, Senator Muskie then explained his decision by saying:

"It was a family decision and not a political decision. We have been involved almost four years in Presidential politics. It had involved a neglect, to an extent no one finds satisfactory, to family duties and the interests of my growing children."

Citing the "heavy emotional drain, especially for Mrs. Muskie as well as the children," the Maine Senator said that he felt regret about his decision because "the challenge of Presidential politics is still very real."

Since the Presidential nominee's offer to Senator Muskie

Continued on Page 29, Column 1

## M'GOVERN ASSAILS NIXON ON JOBLESS

### Says Policy Made 5 Million Idle While Family Grocery Bill Rose $450 a Year

By United Press International

WASHINGTON, Aug. 5—Senator George McGovern charged today that President Nixon's economic policies had thrown nearly five million people out of work and added $450 a year to the grocery bill of the average family.

In what was billed as a campaign white paper, the Democratic Presidential nominee said:

"The Nixon record is one of giveaways to the big corporations and take-aways from the average taxpayer.

"By the end of Nixon's term, the average family of four will have lost about $3,000 in potential income, thanks to the stagnant Nixon economy. Nixon has thrown almost five million Americans out of work and increased the tax burden on the average taxpaying family.

"Nixonomics has raised food prices by 4 per cent a year and has added a total of well over $450 to the average family's grocery bill."

Senator McGovern, who is expected to make the economy one of his major campaign issues, declared the President's policies had turned out to be "a calamity for every man and woman in America except those with special entree to the White House."

He sharply questioned Ad-

Continued on Page 30, Column 4

## Jetport Plan for Grand Teton National Park Is Opposed

By ROBERT LINDSEY

Special to The New York Times

JACKSON HOLE, Wyo., Aug. 1—Against a backdrop of soaring mountain peaks, meandering rivers and exquisite wilderness lakes, the people of this historic valley are engaged in a bitter battle over community values — and the future of Grand Teton National Park.

Seeking to give the region's tourism-based economy a push, local business and political leaders want to expand an airport in the nearby park—it is the country's only commercial airport located within a national park — so it can accommodate jet airliners. Congress appropriated $2.1-million for the project last December after several years of lobbying by local interests.

But environmentalists and many townspeople are fighting the plan fiercely, contending that the presence of jet planes in the park — especially the noise of jets echoing across this placid valley toward the Grant Teton mountains — would destroy much of the wilderness serenity that visitors seek.

The local dispute is growing

Continued on Page 46, Column 3

The New York Times/Robert Lindsey

At the Jackson Hole airport in the Grand Teton National Park, Wyo., a turboprop is serviced. Local business and political leaders want facilities expanded to accommodate jets; environmentalists oppose the move.

## Man Arrested in Newark Called 'Prime Suspect' in Killings Here

By MURRAY SCHUMACH

A 22-year-old man arrested in Newark was described by the police yesterday as "a prime suspect" in the killing of two policemen on the Lower East Side last Jan. 27 and in the shooting of two other policemen in Harlem.

Acting Police Commissioner William H. T. Smith called the arrest "a major development" in the long hunt for the killers of Patrolmen Gregory Foster and Rocco Laurie on Avenue B and East 11th Street.

Jubilant about the breakthrough, top police officials gathered at Police Headquarters to give out the news in the absence of Police Commissioner Patrick V. Murphy. Mr. Murphy, who was personally involved in the investigation, is on vacation.

The arrest was made possible by the help of a cab driver in Newark who rode around the city with the police in the early morning and pointed out the man they sought.

Acting Commissioner Smith said there was no doubt that a man arrested in Newark Thursday after the shooting of a policeman was Robert Fitzgerald Vickers, one of nine persons in the group calling itself the Black Liberation Army. Commissioner Murphy, short-

Continued on Page 23, Column 1

"All the News That's Fit to Print"

# The New York Times

LATE CITY EDITION

Weather: Partly sunny today; partly cloudy and warm tonight, tomorrow. Temp range: today 87-68; Tuesday 86-65. Temp.-Hum. Index yesterday 82. Full U.S. report on Page 82.

VOL. CXXI . . No. 41,850 © 1972 The New York Times Company NEW YORK, WEDNESDAY, AUGUST 23, 1972 15 CENTS

# NIXON IS RENOMINATED BY 1,347-TO-1 VOTE; LIBERALS LOSE FIGHT OVER RULES FOR 1976

## 2 Hold 8 Hostages in a Bank in Brooklyn

The New York Times/Larry Morris

One of the gunmen talking with police outside the bank in front of a crowd

By FRANK J. PRIAL

Two gunmen, apparently seeking the release of a hospital mental patient, held eight hostages for more than eight hours yesterday at a bank in Brooklyn.

The gunmen's plans called for taking some or all of their hostages to Kennedy International Airport, where they hoped to commandeer a plane for a flight to freedom.

Their hostages were the bank manager and seven women, all of them said to be employes of the bank, a branch of the Chase Manhattan Bank at Avenue P and East Third Street, in the Flatbush section of Brooklyn. A security guard was held captive but released after three hours.

One of the gunmen, reached by telephone inside the bank, said to newsmen: "I'm gay. When I get Ernest back, then I'll release one of the hostages."

The gunman identified himself as John Wojtowicz. He said he was demanding the release of Ernest Aaron, a psychiatric patient at Kings County Hospital in Brooklyn whom he described as his "wife."

Soon thereafter, a young man wearing a hospital coat and identified as Mr. Aaron was brought to the scene by police. He talked briefly to Mr. Wojtowicz at the door of the bank and, later, on the

Continued on Page 45, Column 3

## PRICES RISE 0.4%; INCREASE BIGGEST IN LAST 5 MONTHS

### Consumer Index for July Is Pushed Up by Food Costs —Earnings Also Gain

By EDWIN L. DALE Jr.

Special to The New York Times

WASHINGTON Aug. 22—The Consumer Price Index, pushed upward as expected mainly by higher food prices, rose four-tenths of 1 per cent in July following four months of more moderate increases, the Labor Department reported today.

The increase in food prices had been signaled by earlier increases at the wholesale level. The rise in the consumer index of four-tenth overall, the largest since a similar upward spurt of food prices pushed the index up in February, was the same both before and after adjustment for normal seasonal changes in some prices.

The increase in the New York City metropolitan area was the same as in the nation as a whole.

The price of meat showed the biggest increase in the overall food price index. The price category covering meats, poultry and fish jumped 2.8 per cent in July and was 10.1 per cent above the like month a year ago.

**Price of Cattle Down**

A ray of hope, however, was found by Edgar R. Fiedler, Assistant Secretary of the Treasury for economic affairs, who was today's official interpreter of the index. He said that prices paid for cattle on the hoof dropped 13 per cent from their peak in mid-July and that this drop should begin showing up soon at the retail level.

In addition, it was also announced that after allowing for higher prices and changes in income and Social Security taxes, the "real" spendable earnings of the average worker in July were 4.3 per cent above those of a year earlier, the largest increase for any July since records began to be kept on a monthly basis in 1964.

This came about mainly because average weekly earnings were up 6.7 per cent to $136.47, while consumer prices were up only 3 per cent.

In a related development, the Labor Department reported a sharp drop, compared with a year ago, in the size of wage gains won by workers in the construction industry in the

Continued on Page 16, Column 3

United Press International

People cheering for President Nixon on his arrival at Miami International Airport

## A JUBILANT PARLEY

### President Appeals for Support of Youths at Key Biscayne Rally

By MAX FRANKEL

Special to The New York Times

MIAMI BEACH, Aug. 22 — The Republican party formally and jubilantly proclaimed Richard Milhous Nixon here tonight as its candidate for another term as President.

In an atmosphere of celebration, even coronation, marred only by the harassment of delegates by antiwar demonstrators outside the hall, the party's 30th national convention designated Mr. Nixon as the party's leader for the third time in 12 years. It acted with only a murmer of opposition and with hardly a doubt that he would be re-elected by a huge majority in November.

The final tally was 1,347 votes for Mr. Nixon and one, as required by New Mexico's primary law, for Representative Paul N. McCloskey Jr. of California. The projected picture tally called him "others."

**Debate Over 1976**

The nomination came after an afternoon session that brought the only open debate and the only contested roll-call of the week's events — over party rules for the 1976 convention. But the dissenters were heard and decisively voted down, leaving the delegates with nothing more to do than cheer.

Mr. Nixon, who flew to Miami this afternoon from Washington, watched the ritual of nomination at his nearby seaside home in Key Biscayne and then made his first appearance as candidate at a youth rally at Miami's Marine Stadium. He thus devoted all his public statements today to special appeals for the still elusive support of young people.

Introduced there by Sammy Davis Jr., Mr. Nixon said he did not think the youth vote "was in anybody's pocket."

**Nixon Welcomes Davis**

The convention watched him on television monitors as the President called attention to the celebrities working for his election, particularly Mr. Davis, whom he welcomed also as a Democrat, a friend of the Kennedy family and a symbol of equal opportunity for black Americans, another constituency leaning toward the Democrats.

"I believe in the American dream," the President asserted. If re-elected, he added, he would be working for young people to make them look back on their first votes for him as among their best.

Governor Rockefeller of New York, who had twice failed to wrest control of the party from Mr. Nixon, rendered the ultimate tribute of placing the President's name in nomination and describing the duty as an honor.

"We need this man of ac-

Continued on Page 26, Column 2

## McGovern Meets Johnson And Welcomes Support

By CHRISTOPHER LYDON

Special to The New York Times

AUSTIN, Tex., Aug. 22—Senator George McGovern gratefully accepted today the personal, largely private, blessing of an old adversary, former President Lyndon B. Johnson.

Mr. McGovern, whose road to the Democratic Presidential nomination began in his opposition to Mr. Johnson's policies in Vietnam, ate a steak lunch and chatted for about three hours with the former President and his wife, Lady Bird, at the LBJ Ranch about 60 miles east of here.

Sargent Shriver, the Vice-Presidential nominee, whose service to the Johnson Administration in its last days may have been a factor in Mr. Johnson's endorsement of the 1972 Democratic ticket, also took part in the meeting.

Mr. McGovern called the session "friendly and helpful." A spokesman for Mr. Johnson called it "cordial and constructive."

But the political meaning of the event seemed diminished by the exclusion of the press corps traveling with Mr. McGovern from what might have been a public celebration of party unity.

Mr. McGovern's spokesmen said that, "in deference to President Johnson's privacy," they had not asked to take the press corps to the LBJ Ranch.

Robert Hardesty, a writer in the Johnson White House who was a go-between in the arrangements for the meeting today, said that he had suggested excluding the press and explained that Mr. Johnson "isn't feeling well."

But Mr. McGovern said that the former President appeared to be in excellent health—"fit, tanned and vigorous." The Sen-

Continued on Page 29, Column 1

## WAR FOES HARASS G. O. P. DELEGATES

### 3,000 Miami Demonstrators at Convention Hall—216 Seized in Day of Protests

By JOHN KIFNER

Special to The New York Times

MIAMI BEACH, Aug. 22 — Republican delegates entering their convention hall were harassed tonight by a crowd of more than 3,000 antiwar demonstrators, many with their faces painted to represent death masks, who chanted, cursed, jostled and sometimes beat on their cars.

One limousine raced through a crowd of demonstrators, injuring one. Another limousine, stopped by a horde of protesters, was badly damaged.

No delegate or visitor to the convention was reported injured, although Senator James L. Buckley, Conservative-Republican of New York, was chased by a crowd of angry demonstrators.

Tonight's demonstration was the climax of a day that saw a mob of protesters smash windows on Collins Avenue, a march of antiwar veterans to the Fontainebleau Hotel, the headquarters of the Republican National Convention, and the first mass arrests of the week. The police arrested 212 protesters in the afternoon and four

Continued on Page 28, Column 1

## State of Emergency Declared by Allende

By The Associated Press

SANTIAGO, Chile, Aug. 22—President Salvador Allende Gossens declared a state of emergency in Santiago Province last night in an attempt to quell mounting protests against food shortages.

Most of Chile's 150,000 shopkeepers closed yesterday in a one-day protest strike against Mr. Allende's socialist policies. Housewives in Santiago staged a pot-banging demonstration, riot squads clashed with anti-Marxist demonstrators and anti-leftist youths put up flaming barricades along Santiago's elegant Providencia Avenue.

Government troops and the

Continued on Page 2, Column 4

## Rhodesia Out of Olympics After a Dispute on Racism

By NEIL AMDUR

Special to The New York Times

MUNICH, West Germany, Aug. 22—The International Olympic Committee tonight withdrew its invitation to Rhodesia to compete in the Olympic Games. The decision followed a week of objections by black athletes from other African nations to Rhodesia's participation in the Olympics because of that country's racial policies.

The vote, announced by Avery Brundage, the committee president, was 36 in favor of withdrawal, 31 opposed and 3 abstentions, an indication of the philosophical division that marked the two days of intense deliberation.

The racial issue, however, was not offered by the committee as the reason for the ousting. The Rhodesians' failure to produce passports and prove they were British subjects as well as Rhodesian citizens, as stated on their Olympic identity cards, was given by Brundage as the technicality for withdrawing the invitation four days before the opening ceremonies.

But the growing concern of a mass withdrawal by black African nations undoubtedly presented a more realistic threat to the competitive aspect of the Games and overshadowed repeated committee support for Rhodesian participation.

The significance of the decision was best symbolized in

Continued on Page 47, Column 2

## CHURCH UNIT ACTS ON SOUTH AFRICA

### World Council to Liquidate Stocks to Set Example in Fight on Racism

Special to The New York Times

UTRECHT, The Netherlands, Aug. 22—The World Council of Churches voted overwhelmingly tonight to liquidate its financial stake in all corporations doing business with white-ruled African countries.

The decision, made by the council's 120-member policy-making committee, could oblige the church agency to sell off its entire portfolio of $3.5-million in company stocks, the committee's finance unit said.

By its action the committee hoped to set an example for its 250 Protestant and Orthodox member churches in the fight against racism.

A council official said that a preliminary study indicated that the council's holdings in about 18 United States corporations would be affected by the sell-off.

The corporations were not named, but Baldwin Sjollema, head of the council's Program to Combat Racism, later identified the following concerns with investments in South Africa or Angola as being among those in which the council holds shares: Chrysler Corporation, the General Electric Company, the Polaroid Corporation, the Ford Motor Company, Monsanto Company, Squibb Beech-nut, Inc., Merck & Co., Inc., Atlantic Richfield Company, Burroughs Corporation, Black & Decker Manufacturing

Continued on Page 6, Column 1

## 3 SEIZED IN THEFT OF $360,000 BONDS

### Hidden TV Camera Records Act—$400,000 Securities Found in Getaway Car

By ERIC PACE

Three men were arrested in the act of stealing $360,000 in negotiable bonds from the brokerage house where one of them worked, and a separate batch of securities worth more than $400,000 was found in their getaway car, authorities here said yesterday.

"This incident followed the classic pattern of organized crime moving into financial institutions by getting an otherwise honest employe in its debt and then forcing him to do its will," said Chief of Detectives Louis Cottell in an interview.

The chief said one of the arrested men, 27-year-old Rocco Voglio, had agreed to help steal the bonds from the firm, CBWL-Hayden, Stone, Inc., because he owed $1,100 to one of the others, an unemployed truck driver named Louis Malpeso.

The authorities said that state, Federal and city law-enforcement officers, acting on a tip, had watched over closed-circuit television on Monday as Mr. Voglio handed a two-inch-thick manila envelope to Mr. Malpeso in the firm's of-

Continued on Page 25, Column 1

## Russians Suggest Fischer Uses Electronics to Weaken Spassky

By HAROLD C. SCHONBERG

Special to The New York Times

REYKJAVIK, Iceland, Aug. 22—Boris Spassky and Bobby Fischer adjourned the 17th game in their match for the world chess championship tonight amid assertions by the Russians that the Americans might be using "electronic devices and a chemical substance" to weaken Spassky's playing ability.

A long statement to that effect was issued by Efim Geller, the champion's second, in which he demanded that the referee, Lothar Schmid, and the sponsors of the match examine the playing hall "with the assistance of competent experts" to determine whether the Americans are using "non-chess means" to influence Spassky.

"It is surprising that the Americans can be found in the playing hall when the games are not taking place even at night," Geller's statement said. Speaking of Spassky's lackluster performance in the games played thus far Geller said:

"Having known [Spassky] for many years, it is the first time that I observe such unusual slackening of concentration and display of impulsiveness in his playing which I cannot account for by [Fischer's] exclusively impressive playing."

Geller mentioned specifically

Continued on Page 14, Column 4



NEWS INDEX



| | Page | | Page |
|---|---|---|---|
| Books | 39 | Music | 30-34 |
| Bridge | 38 | Obituaries | 44 |
| Business | 53-65 | Op-Ed | 41 |
| Crossword | 39 | Society | 35 |
| Editorials | 40 | Sports | 46-49 |
| Family/Style | 36 | Theaters | 30-34 |
| Financial | 53-65 | Transportation | 82 |
| Going Out Guide | 31 | TV and Radio | 83 |
| Man in the News | 27 | U. N. Proceedings | 2 |
| Movies | 30-34 | Weather | 82 |

News Summary and Index, Page 43

Associated Press

Senator George McGovern visiting with former President Lyndon B. Johnson at the LBJ Ranch in Texas yesterday. The Presidential candidate said he did not expect a "more worthwhile visit with anyone" in the campaign.

## Rockefeller Names Nixon, His Old Rival

By FRANK LYNN

Special to The New York Times

MIAMI BEACH, Aug. 22 — Governor Rockefeller, the man who fought Richard M. Nixon at previous Republican National Conventions, placed in nomination tonight the name of President Nixon as the man who "has brought us to the threshold of a generation of peace."

The Governor was greeted cordially but hardly warmly by the delegates. Eight years ago, he was jeered repeatedly when he spoke from the Republican convention podium.

It was apparent tonight that he was still not a favorite among many Republican delegates as he received considerably less applause than a political rival, Gov. Ronald Rea-

Continued on Page 27, Column 1

"All the News That's Fit to Print"

# The New York Times

**LATE CITY EDITION**

Weather: Hot, humid today; warm tonight. Continued hot tomorrow. Temp. range: today 71-91; Wed. 65-88. Temp.-Hum. Index yesterday 72. Full U.S. report on Page 81.

VOL. CXXI . . . No. 41,851 — NEW YORK, THURSDAY, AUGUST 24, 1972 — 15 CENTS



# NIXON ASKS SUPPORT FOR A 'NEW MAJORITY' AFTER AGNEW IS RENAMED AS RUNNING MATE

## Bank Bandit Slain, 2d Seized at Kennedy, Ending 14-Hour Ordeal for 7 Hostages

John Wojtowicz, foreground, one of two gunmen who held hostages in a Brooklyn bank robbery attempt, being taken for arraignment in Federal Court.

### Code Word Is Signal for Shot by F.B.I. Agent

By ROBERT HANLEY

A 14-hour ordeal for seven bank employes held hostage by a distraught homosexual and his 18-year-old accomplice ended just before sunrise yesterday when a Federal agent shot and killed the accomplice at Kennedy International Airport.

Just after the youth, identified by the Federal Bureau of Investigation as Salvatore Natuarale, was hit with the single bullet in the chest, the other alleged robber, John Wojtowicz, was overpowered and captured.

The seven hostages then walked out onto the tip of a remote runway from a 14-passenger limousine that the gunman had ordered driven to Kennedy from the scene of the holdup Tuesday afternoon of a Chase Manhattan Bank branch in the Flatbush section of Brooklyn.

The agent who fired the shot drove the vehicle. He was part of a strategy that included a code word from another agent during an apparently innocuous conversation about the small jet plane the gunmen had demanded be brought to Kennedy.

The moment the code word was spoken, the driver, who was not identified, grabbed a shotgun Natuarale had aimed at his head. Then he whirled in his seat, pulled out a concealed .38-caliber revolver and shot Natuarale.

The youth was two rows behind the agent and was flanked by two hostages. There was an empty row in between. Wojtowicz, whose rifle was seized through an open window by the agent in charge of the op-

Continued on Page 37, Column 3

Associated Press

Wojtowicz, carrying a rifle, inspecting a limousine brought to the bank to take gunmen and hostages to Kennedy Airport. A Federal agent driving the vehicle fatally wounded Wojtowicz's companion, Salvatore Natuarale, on an airport runway.

United Press International

President Nixon and Vice President Agnew on the podium at the convention hall in Miami Beach last night

## RIVALS ATTACKED

### President Enlists Aid of the Old, the Young and the Disaffected

By MAX FRANKEL

Special to The New York Times

MIAMI BEACH, Aug. 23—President Nixon opened his campaign for re-election here tonight by summoning the nation, and particularly the young, the old and disaffected Democrats, "to join our new majority."

He drew sharp contrasts between himself and his challenger, Senator George McGovern, in economics and taxation and in the handling

*Nixon address and excerpts from Agnew's, Page 47*

of crime and defense preparedness.

But he issued a special appeal to be allowed to continue the works of peace in the world, pledging that he "will not stain the honor" of the country in Vietnam and that he would reject the policies "of those who whine and whimper about our frustrations and call on us to turn inward."

"I ask everyone listening to me tonight, Democrats, Republicans and independents, to join our new majority, not on the basis of the party label you wear on your lapel but what you believe in your hearts," Mr. Nixon said.

**Closing Session**

The President appeared before the closing session of the 30th Republican National Convention after the renomination of his chosen running mate, Vice President Spiro Theodore Agnew.

They flew to the hall in separate helicopters over a city that suffered considerable harassment and vandalism from antiwar protesters and the widespread use of CS irritant gas and Chemical Mace by police forces.

Approximately 900 demonstrators were arrested and scores of delegates were delayed by the confrontations in the street. But the protestors failed in their announced objective of upsetting the schedule of the convention and its candidates.

**One Dissenting Vote**

Mr. Agnew was renamed to the ticket with only one dissenting vote, but this and two abstentions in two states were only surface signs of the feelings of reluctance and opposition in several parts of the hall.

In their first full-scale assault on their Democratic challengers, Mr. McGovern and Sargent Shriver, both the President and Vice President pressed the argument that the nation faces the "clearest choice" of this century.

Mr. Nixon called it a choice

Continued on Page 46, Column 1

## ASIAN HEROIN RING UNCOVERED HERE

### Four Arrests in Chinatown Linked to Gang's Effort to Expand U.S. Sales

By JAMES M. MARKHAM

Federal authorities said yesterday that they had uncovered a "loose-knit" narcotics ring based in Chinatown that had been attempting to move into the distribution system for heroin here and capitalize on shifts in the international market for the drug.

The announcement, by Daniel P. Casey, regional director of the Bureau of Narcotics and Dangerous Drugs, came as he disclosed the arrests on Tuesday night of four Chinese with 20 pounds of Asian heroin. The suspects had allegedly just "sold" the drug to two undercover agents for a briefcase full of $200,000 in cash.

Displaying the heroin and the briefcase laden with $50 and $100 bills, Mr. Casey called the arrests the climax of a five-month investigation of the United States end of the "Asian connection."

Mr. Casey noted that the gradual reduction of Turkish opium cultivation and increasing pressure on French-based heroin refineries had spurred

Continued on Page 81, Column 1

## End to Fixed Stock Fees Is Urged by House Group

By EDWIN L. DALE Jr.

Special to The New York Times

WASHINGTON, Aug. 23 — A unanimous House subcommittee proposed today sweeping changes for the securities industry, including abolition by phases of fixed commission rates for securities transactions.

The panel also recommended permission for institutional investors such as mutual funds and insurance companies to become members, through affiliates, of securities exchanges, but urged that the institutions not be allowed to do any business through their own affiliates.

*Excerpts from subcommittee report are on Page 58.*

The 170-page report, covering nearly all facets of the industry, contained numerous proposals for legislative changes. In a few cases, such as the abolition of fixed commission rates, the subcommittee threatened legislation unless the aim was achieved by the Securities and Exchange Commission and the various stock exchanges.

There is no prospect for sweeping legislation this year, according to subcommittee sources, though one or two bills already in an advanced stage of Congressional consideration may be enacted.

Today's report was issued by the subcommittee on commerce and finance of the House Commerce Committee. The chairman of the group is Representative John E. Moss, Democrat of California.

Its views are important not only because it will originate all securities legislation in the House of Representatives but also because many of the proposals in today's report appear to parallel thinking in a comparable subcommittee in the Senate.

Apart from the abolition of fixed commissions and the support of institutional membership—both opposed by much of the securities industry—today's report included such recommendations as these:

¶More criminal penalties for violations of the securities laws and regulations.

¶A doubling of the staff of the S.E.C. over the next five years.

¶New standards for entry

Continued on Page 58, Column 1

### Chess Game Is Drawn

Bobby Fischer and Boris Spassky agreed to a draw after 45 moves of the 17th game in their world chess championship match in Reykjavik, Iceland. The 18th game will be played today. Details on Page 30.

## POLICE SEIZE 900 IN MIAMI BEACH

### Use Stinging Gas to Scatter Thousands of Protesters Outside Convention

By JOHN KIFNER

Special to The New York Times

MIAMI BEACH, Thursday, Aug. 24—Thousands of antiwar demonstrators roamed through the streets last night, but failed in their major goal—to delay the session of the Republican National Convention at which President Nixon accepted his nomination.

By 1 o'clock this morning, the police had arrested 900 demonstrators and reported that 52 persons had been injured. Twelve of those hurt were policemen, including the only two whose injuries were listed by the police as serious.

From late yesterday into the early hours of the morning today the police tossed canisters of stinging "pepper" gas at groups of demonstrators as large crowds and small bands tried to block traffic by slashing tires, throwing paint or trying to rip out the distributor caps of vehicles.

Most of the delegates and visitors arrived on schedule behind a wall of parked buses, and as the evening session opened at 7:37—only seven minutes late—nearly all of the delegates' seats were occupied and the visitors' gallery was filled.

Early this morning there were still a few small bands of demonstrators on the streets, with the police chasing them, the blue lights of their squad cars flashing.

Shortly after midnight, the

Continued on Page 48, Column 1

## City Picks New Litter Container After 2-Year Search

By DAVID BIRD

After a two-year search, the city's Environmental Protection Administration has finally decided on a new litter container to replace the current wire-mesh model that has been disappearing at the rate of more than 6,000 a year through theft, vandalism and normal wear.

The new container is a 470-pound hexagonal concrete receptacle that will carry advertising on three of its six sides. To empty the new containers, a sanitationman unlocks and lifts a plastic lid to remove a plastic bag liner.

Because of the advertising feature, officials say, the containers will not only be provided free to the city but will also be an added source of revenue as well.

A Florida-based company has agreed to provide and maintain the new containers and to give the city a share of the profits from the advertising.

A contract to put 60,000 of the containers throughout the city within the next five years is awaiting approval of the Corporation Counsel. The contract also requires action by the City Council and the Board of Estimate.

Payments to the city would

Continued on Page 17, Column 1

The New York Times

One of the heavy concrete containers on Madison Avenue

## Expense-Account Padding Vexes Soviet

By HEDRICK SMITH

Special to The New York Times

MOSCOW, Aug. 23—Summer in the Soviet Union brings not only sun to Siberia and near-tropical heat to Moscow but a surge of convention freeloading and expense-account boondoggling that worries the protectors of the state purse and Communist morality.

So frequent are the special summer conferences at Black Sea resorts, so pervasive the expense - account padding, and so common the practice of taking along wives, relatives, friends and even mistresses to resort hotels at state expense that the newspaper Komsomolskaya Pravda commented sarcastically that the time had come "to reserve a special beach area in Sochi for business travelers."

Sochi—like Miami Beach, a magnet for ordinary vacationers — is attracting increasing numbers of expense-account finaglers, but local authorities seem in no mood to crack down on the abuses, according to the paper.

In a long article that provided a rare glimpse of expense-account practices in a state-managed economy, the paper cited the case of a company from Krasnodar in the northern Caucasus that held a three-day seminar at Sochi on the Black Sea, racked up a bill for 4,000 rubles (nearly $5,000), and left no trace of having held any actual business meetings. There were restaurant bills, a charge for a sightseeing excursion, items for a typist and a stenographer, the article said, but no seminar programs or records.

By American standards, the per diem allowance paid to Soviet scholars, state officials, technicians, teachers or workers sent on out-of-town assignments is paltry.

Low-level and middle-level employes often get no more than a ruble or two for their hotel beds (which is what most Soviet hotels charge Russians, though foreigners pay five to ten times the price for the same rooms), and two or three rubles for meals. Allowances for higher officials, though

Continued on Page 10, Column 3

### NEWS INDEX



| | Page | | Page |
|---|---|---|---|
| Books | 38-39 | Music | 50-52 |
| Bridge | 38 | Obituaries | 44 |
| Business | 57-69 | Op-Ed | 41 |
| Crossword | 39 | Society | 52 |
| Editorials | 40 | Sports | 53-57 |
| Family/Style | 36 | Theaters | 50-52 |
| Financial | 57-69 | Transportation | 81 |
| Going Out Guide | 50 | TV and Radio | 82-83 |
| Man in the News | 48 | U. N. Proceedings | 5 |
| Movies | 50-52 | Weather | 81 |

News Summary and Index, Page 43


## G.O.P. Aide Queried on Check In Study of Raid on Democrats

By WALTER RUGABER

Special to The New York Times

MIAMI, Aug. 23—A Republican finance official was summoned from at meeting at President Nixon's closely guarded headquarters hotel today for questioning by Florida officials investigating the break-in at the Democratic headquarters in Washington.

Kenneth H. Dahlberg of Minneapolis, Midwestern regional chairman of the Finance Committee to Re-elect the President, was subsequently questioned under oath by investigators for Richard E. Gerstein, the state attorney here.

Martin Dardis, chief investigator for the state attorney, or local prosecutor, is understood to have called Mr. Dahlberg to the Metropolitan Justice Building in Miami and to have asked him about a $25,000 campaign contribution he collected in cash. The questioning concerned a notarized statement on a check he endorsed that was deposited in a Florida bank.

Mr. Dahlberg has said that he converted the $25,000 into a cashier's check and handed it to Maurice H. Stans, Mr. Nixon's chief fund raiser, at a meeting in Washington. It was later deposited in a Miami bank account controlled by Bernard L. Barker.

Mr. Barker is the alleged leader among five men who were arrested at gunpoint in the offices of the Democratic National Committee in Washington. The men carried copying cameras and electronic bugging equipment.

When Mr. Barker first pre-

Continued on Page 49, Column 5

"All the News That's Fit to Print"

# The New York Times

LATE CITY EDITION

Weather: Cloudy, rain likely today and tonight. Cloudy, cool tomorrow. Temp. range: today 48-60; Tuesday 45-61. Full U.S. report on Page 93.

VOL. CXXII . . No. 41,927



NEW YORK, WEDNESDAY, NOVEMBER 8, 1972

15 CENTS

# NIXON ELECTED IN LANDSLIDE; M'GOVERN IS BEATEN IN STATE; DEMOCRATS RETAIN CONGRESS

## President Loses in City By 81,920-Vote Margin

By FRANK LYNN

President Nixon swept New York State yesterday, but lost to Senator McGovern in New York City by a total of 81,920 votes.

Mr. Nixon's statewide plurality was expected to be about a million votes.

With 11,521 of the 12,948 districts in the state reporting, the tally was:

Nixon . . . . . . . . . . . .3,712,113
McGovern . . . . . . . .2,539,326

With all of the 4,219 districts in the city reporting, the tally was:

Nixon . . . . . . . . . . 1,259,244
McGovern . . . . . . . 1,341,164

The President's strong showing in the state rivaled the 1956 victory of President Dwight D. Eisenhower, who first brought Mr. Nixon to the national ticket 20 years ago.

The Nixon victory did not appear to carry too far down the Republican line. The Legislature remained Republican, but with no indication of substantially increased Republican majorities.

Three Republican candidates for the Court of Appeals held slight leads but returns were still inconclusive.

The President's capture of the state was only the third time a Republican Presidential candidate had won New York since 1928.

Dozens of sample districts showed last night that the President substantially improved his 1968 showing in virtually all ethnic groups and geographic areas in the state and city.

In many cases, particularly in the cities, Mr. Nixon surpassed Governor Rockefeller's victory margins of two years ago.

In New York City, Senator McGovern carried districts that were predominantly black, Puerto Rican and Jewish. But in the Jewish areas, Mr. Nixon doubled his showing of four years before. In a middle class

Continued on Page 36, Column 2

## MANY VOTES SPLIT

### G.O.P. Loses Senate Seats in 6 States and Picks Up 4 Others

By R. W. APPLE Jr.

The Democratic party withstood President Nixon's landslide yesterday to retain control of both houses of Congress.

With voters in all parts of the nation splitting their tickets in huge numbers, the Democrats brought off a series of startling upsets in Senate contests to gain at least two seats, similar to their feat in the face of Dwight D. Eisenhower's sweep of 1956.

The Democrats captured previously Republican Senate seats in six states—Delaware, Iowa, Kentucky, Maine, Colorado and South Dakota. Those pickups more than offset Republican gains in the two Southwestern states of Oklahoma and New Mexico and the two Southern states of Virginia and North Carolina.

**Two Races Open**

Two Senate races remained in doubt this morning—in Alaska and Nebraska. Both seats were held by the Republicans in the last Congress.

The figures for the House were far less complete, but the Republicans were not making the gains they needed to take control. It appeared that they would pick up somewhere in the neighborhood of a dozen seats; they had already gained seven.

At present, the Senate lineup is 54 Democrats, 44 Republicans, one Conservative-Republican and one independent who votes with the Democrats. In the House it is 255 Democrats, 177 Republicans and three vacancies.

Mr. Nixon's coattails proved relatively short this year, as they had in 1968. In state after state, he swept to massive vic-

Continued on Page 34, Column 7

C.B.S. News

Associated Press

President and Mrs. Nixon and Vice President Agnew at the Republican celebration in Washington early today

## MARGIN ABOUT 60%

### Massachusetts Is Only State to Give Vote to the Dakotan

By MAX FRANKEL

Richard Milhous Nixon won re-election by a huge majority yesterday, perhaps the largest ever given a President.

Mr. Nixon scored a stunning personal triumph in all sections of the country, sweeping New York and most other bastions of Democratic strength.

He was gathering more than 60 per cent of the nation's ballots and more than 500 electoral votes. He lost only Massachusetts and the District of Columbia.

The victory was reminiscent of the landslide triumphs of Franklin D. Roosevelt in 1936 and Lyndon B. Johnson in 1964, although it could fall just short of their record proportions.

**Tickets Are Split**

Despite this drubbing of George Stanley McGovern, the Democratic challenger, the voters split their tickets in record numbers to leave the Democrats in control of both houses of Congress and a majority of the nation's governorships. Mr. Nixon thus became the first two-term President to face an opposition Congress at both inaugurals.

The turnout of voters appeared to be unusually low, despite jams at many polling places. Projections indicated a total vote of 76 million out of a voting-age population of 139.6 million, or only about 54 per cent. If accurate, that would be the lowest proportion since 51.4 per cent in 1948. The percentage had been over 60 per cent in every election since then.

**May Claim Mandate**

The President seemed certain, however, to claim a clear mandate for his policies of gradual disengagement from Vietnam, continued strong spending on defense, opposition to busing to integrate the schools and a slowdown in Federal spending for social programs. These are the issues he stressed through the campaign.

The 59-year-old Mr. Nixon, who will be 60 before inauguration on Jan. 20, could also claim a resounding personal vindication against the strong charges of corruption brought against him personally by the opposition.

By coincidence, the greatest triumph of his 26 years in national politics came on the 10th anniversary of his defeat for Governor of California—the time he told newsmen they would not have Nixon to kick around anymore.

**McGovern Concedes**

Mr. McGovern, 50, conceded defeat before midnight in the East with a telegram of support for the President if he leads the nation to peace abroad and justice at home.

The South Dakotan took credit for helping to push the Administration nearer to peace in Indochina and assured his cheering supporters at the Sioux Falls Coliseum that their defeat would bear fruit for years to come.

The President responded in a brief address from the White

Continued on Page 34, Column 1

## Nixon Has a Big Plurality In Jersey and Connecticut

**Case an Easy Winner**

By RONALD SULLIVAN

President Nixon won the overwhelming victory predicted for him in New Jersey in yesterday's Presidential election, defeating Senator George McGovern by a 2-to-1 margin.

At the same time, Senator Clifford P. Case, the liberal Republican, won a fourth term and one of the biggest Senate election victories in New Jersey's history, defeating Paul J. Krebs, the Democratic candidate.

However, incumbent Democratic Representatives survived the G.O.P. onslaught at the top of the ballot in what political leaders described as a remarkable display of ticket-splitting.

The Presidential tally, with 4,142 districts of 5,212 reporting, was:

Nixon . . . . . . . .1,440,420
McGovern . . . . . . 862,582

The tally in the race for the Senate, with 3,657 of 5,212 districts reporting, was:

Case . . . . . . . . . .1,112,754
Krebs . . . . . . . . . . 627,352

With both Mr. Nixon and Senator Case piling up 2-to-1 margins throughout the state, Republican leaders predicted that the President's margin would rival the 800,000-vote plurality achieved by Dwight D.

Continued on Page 37, Column 3

**Hartford Assembly G.O.P.**

By LAWRENCE FELLOWS

Special to The New York Times

HARTFORD, Nov. 7—President Nixon carried Connecticut today in a landslide victory.

The President swept the state's eight electoral votes with a plurality of 252,289, approaching the 306,758-vote margin by which the late President Dwight D. Eisenhower carried the state in 1956.

The Republicans also took control of the General Assembly, winning the State Senate by 23 to 13 and the House of Representatives by 93 to 58.

But widespread ticket-splitting enabled three of the four incumbent Democratic Representatives to keep their seats in Washington.

With all of the 169 towns in the state reporting, the Presidential tally was:

Nixon . . . . . . . . . . . . .799,249
McGovern . . . . . . . . . . .546,960

Representative John G. Schmitz of California, the

Continued on Page 37, Column 7

## Mrs. Smith Defeated For Senate in Maine

By BILL KOVACH

Special to The New York Times

PROVIDENCE, R. I., Wednesday, Nov. 8—The 34-year Congressional career of Senator Margaret Chase Smith, the Senate's only woman member, ended last night in a major upset as Democrats showed unexpected strength in New England Senate and Gubernatorial races.

William D. Hathaway, the Democrat who gave up his Second District Congressional office to challenge the 74-year-old Mrs. Smith despite her near-legendary standing in Maine, won the seat in a hard-fought contest.

Mr. Hathaway's stunning victory was part of a Democratic surge that overcame the general New England sweep by President Nixon, and reflected stubborn ticket-splitting by

Continued on Page 21, Column 1

## Reid Wins as Democrat; Bella Abzug Easy Victor

By RICHARD L. MADDEN

Representative Ogden R. Reid, a former Republican, was re-elected yesterday as a Democrat in Westchester County, and Representative Bella S. Abzug, a one-term Democrat, won a decisive re-election in Manhattan.

In another key Westchester race, Representative Peter A. Peyser, a freshman Republican, claimed victory over his predecessor in the House, Richard L. Ottinger, a Democrat-Liberal, who was seeking to recapture his former seat.

Mrs. Abzug defeated by about a 2-to-1 margin Mrs. Priscilla M. Ryan, a Liberal and widow of the late Representative William F. Ryan, who had defeated Mrs. Abzug in the Democratic primary in the 20th Congressional District last June.

With about 85 per cent of the vote reported in Westchester, but with large numbers of absentee ballots still to be counted, Mr. Reid led Carl A. Vergari, a Republican-Conservative and the county's District Attorney, by more than 8,000 votes.

Despite the strong vote for President Nixon in the state, incumbent Democratic Representatives generally appeared to be withstanding the Republican tide. One exception was Representative John G. Dow, of Newburgh, a liberal Democrat who had strenuously opposed the war in Vietnam.

Mr. Dow, who lost his House seat in the generally conservative Rockland-Orange county area in 1968 and won it back two years ago, was substantially trailing Assemblyman Benjamin A. Gilman, a Middletown Republican.

Representative Otis G. Pike, a six-term Democrat from Suffolk County, won a three-way fight for re-election and another prime target of the Republicans, Representative James M. Hanley of Syracuse, defeated his Republican-Conservative opponent, Leonard C. Koldin.

Representative Lester L. Wolff, a four-term Democrat whose new Nassau County district now takes in part of Queens, led Assemblyman John

Continued on Page 36, Column 6

## Olympic Fund Barred

Voters in Colorado cut off public funds for the 1976 Winter Olympics yesterday. Without the tax money, the International Olympic Committee was all but forced to move the games to another site. Page 31.

## M'GOVERN TO BACK MOVES FOR PEACE

### But Says He Will Continue to Oppose Policies He Had Deplored in Campaign

By JAMES M. NAUGHTON

Special to The New York Times

SIOUX FALLS, S.D., Nov. 7—Senator George McGovern conceded defeat of his Presidential candidacy here tonight but said that he would "shed no tears" because of the effort his campaign had made to draw the nation close to peace.

The Democratic nominee told 1,200 cheering enthusiasts at 10:40 P.M., Central standard time, that he had sent a telegram to President Nixon pledging support for "peace abroad and justice at home."

He said the President had his "full support" in efforts toward such goals.

But he added in his speech, which was televised, that he would, as the leader of the "loyal opposition," continue to oppose any policies that he had deplored during his long campaign.

"Now, the question is to what standards does the loyal

Continued on Page 3, Column 3

*Text of McGovern's comments appears on Page 3*

## A Rockefeller Loses West Virginia Race

By BEN A. FRANKLIN

Special to The New York Times

CHARLESTON, W. Va., Wednesday, Nov. 8—Secretary of State John D. Rockefeller 4th suffered a sharp defeat yesterday in a bid for the West Virginia governorship. The loss appeared, at least, to have postponed a possible role for him in national Democratic politics in 1976.

Mr. Rockefeller's well-financed candidacy had depended heavily on proposals on the environment in this second-ranked coal-mining state. These also suffered a setback through his defeat in a race that eclipsed all others here.

Gov. Arch A. Moore Jr., a Republican former Congressman who is the first Governor here who has been constitutionally able to succeed to a second

Continued on Page 23, Column 1

## The Election at a Glance

**President**

Needed for Election—270 Electoral Votes

| | *Number of States | Electoral Votes |
|---|---|---|
| Nixon | 49 | 521 |
| McGovern | 2 | 17 |

**The Senate**

| Newly Elected Senators | | Make-up of New Senate | |
|---|---|---|---|
| Democrats | 16 | Democrats | 57 |
| Republicans | 15 | Republicans | 41 |
| In Doubt | 2 | In Doubt | 2 |

**The House**

| | |
|---|---|
| Democrats Elected | 218 |
| Republicans Elected | 154 |
| In Doubt | 63 |

*Includes District of Columbia.

## Victory, 10 Years Later

### Spectacular Nixon Vote Considered Vindication in Light of Past Defeats

By JAMES RESTON

News Analysis

It was a spectacular personal victory for Richard Nixon, 10 years to the day, and almost to the hour, after his most humiliating defeat by Pat Brown in the 1962 election for the governorship of California.

Beaten by John Kennedy by the narrowest of margins in the Presidential election of 1960, beaten again for the control of his own state in 1962, finished with American politics by his own angry proclamation exactly a decade ago, here he is now, not only vindicated but triumphant in one of the most decisive victories in the history of American Presidential politics.

In a few days before he will take the oath of office for a second term as President of the United States (Jan. 9), he will be 60 years old. His thirties were a political surprise, even to himself, his forties were an agony of controversy and self-doubt, his fifties were a struggle and at the end a triumph. What now will he do with his sixties? This is the question that even his most intimate associates in Washington cannot answer.

In the world, he has to achieve not only the cease-fire, but the peace he has promised in Vietnam, the "reconciliation and cooperation" with Peking and Moscow that were so central to his victory, the truce in the savage struggle between Israel and the Arab states, and some kind of new economic and political relationship with Japan and the Common Market countries of Europe, who are now challenging the American economic leadership of the modern world.

At home, Mr. Nixon has to deal also now with the minorities who failed to support him in the election: the poor and the blacks who have been left behind in the general prosperity of the nation, the young in the universities who have been over-run but not persuaded or

Continued on Page 34, Column 3

## NIXON ISSUES CALL TO 'GREAT TASKS'

### At Victory Celebration, He Vows to Make Himself 'Worthy' of Victory

By ROBERT B. SEMPLE Jr.

Special to The New York Times

WASHINGTON, Wednesday, Nov. 8 — President Nixon summoned the nation last night "to get on with the great tasks that lie before us" and, in a later statement to a crowd of cheering supporters, pledged to make himself "worthy of this victory."

Mr. Nixon made two statements, both televised.

The first of these was a brief statement from his desk in the Oval Office of the White House in which he pledged himself to secure not only "a peace with honor in Vietnam" but also "a new era of peace" throughout the world; to "prosperity without war and without inflation" at home, and to an America in which all citizens will have "an equal chance."

"I would only hope," he said, "that in these next four years we can so conduct ourselves in

Continued on Page 34, Column 3

*Text of Nixon's remarks is printed on Page 34*

## Summary of Other News

*Following is a summary of major nonelection news. A full report begins on the first page, second part.*

**Canarsie School Boycott**

Leaders of Canarsie parents who have kept their children out of school for two weeks declared yesterday that "the boycott is over" and called on parents to return their children to school. But the prospect of full classes today remained in doubt since more than 1,000 parents shouted down the same call Monday night.

**Bid by Vietcong**

Agents of the National Liberation Front have made several recent contacts with Saigon's anti-Government, non-Communist opposition, according to opposition sources.

**Britons Protest Price Rises**

British Government offices were swamped with complaints of price increases on the first full day of Prime Minister Heath's anti-inflation freeze. But a check of London shops found no wide pattern of violations. Most of the increases involved noncontrolled items.

**Soviet Parades Its Arms**

The Soviet Union, marking the 55th anniversary of the Bolshevik Revolution, paraded its military might in low-key fashion. The unusually deliberate movements of Leonid I. Brezhnev, the party leader, reinforced speculation that he had been ill.

NEWS INDEX


| | Page | | Page |
|---|---|---|---|
| Art | 52 | Movies | 52-57 |
| Books | 45 | Music | 52-57 |
| Bridge | 44 | Obituaries | 50 |
| Business | 69-75 | Op-Ed | 47 |
| Crossword | 45 | Sports | 59-62 |
| Editorials | 46 | Theaters | 52-57 |
| Family/Style | 42 | Transportation | 93 |
| Financial | 69-75 | TV and Radio | 94-95 |
| Going Out Guide | 52 | U. N. Proceedings | 94 |
| Man in the News | 35 | Weather | 93 |


News Summary and Index, Page 49

"All the News That's Fit to Print"

# The New York Times

LATE CITY EDITION
Weather: Sunny, cool today; cold tonight. Chance of rain tomorrow. Temp. range: today 25-37; Saturday 31-52 Full U.S. report on Page 83.

SECTION ONE

VOL. CXXII . . No. 42,001  NEW YORK, SUNDAY, JANUARY 21, 1973 — 75¢ beyond 50-mile zone from New York City, except Long Island. Higher in air delivery cities. — 50 CENTS

# NIXON INAUGURATED FOR HIS SECOND TERM; SEES WORLD ON THRESHOLD OF A PEACE ERA

The New York Times/Mike Lien

President Nixon takes oath of office, administered by Chief Justice Warren E. Burger. Mrs. Nixon holds Bibles. At rear are Senator Marlow W. Cook, inauguration official, and Vice President Agnew.

## SELF-HELP URGED

### President Discerns a 'Better Way' in Shift From Old Policies

By R. W. APPLE Jr.
Special to The New York Times

WASHINGTON, Jan. 20—Richard Milhous Nixon was inaugurated for his second term as President today and appealed to the nation and to its allies to show greater self-reliance "as we stand on the threshold of a new era of peace."

In a ceremony that mingled the martial spirit of brass bands and cannon, the peace prayers of clergymen and the distant shouts of protesters, the 60-year-old President took the oath of office.

*Text of the address, Page 40; a page of pictures, 41.*

Then he embarked on a speech that omitted the words "Vietnam" and "Indochina" but assured the thousands of persons gathered beneath the East Front of the Capitol that "America's longest and most difficult war" was ending. Reading quickly, almost methodically, he sketched his vision of the postwar era.

**Retreat Ruled Out**

"Abroad," Mr. Nixon said, "the shift from old policies to new has not been a retreat from our responsibilities, but a better way to peace. And at home, the shift from old policies to new will not be a retreat from our responsibilities, but a better way to progress."

"Just as we respect the right of each nation to determine its own future," the President said, "we also recognize the responsibility of each nation to secure its own future.

"Just as America's role is indispensable in preserving the world's peace, so is each nation's role indispensable in preserving its own peace."

**Gathering of Republicans**

The President, hatless despite the temperatures in the low 40's and a stiff breeze that threatened to topple the flag standards below him, gave the greatest emphasis to, and received the most enthusiastic applause for, a sentence that reiterated his distrust of many of the Federal Government's social programs:

"Government must learn to take less from people so that people can do more for themselves."

In one of the most striking passages of the speech, Mr. Nixon boldly appropriated the most famous phrase of President Kennedy's 1961 inaugural and turned it to his own devices.

"In our own lives, let each of us ask not just what will Government do for me, but what can I do for myself?"

The President spoke from a temporary portico erected adjacent to the Capitol, with the

Continued on Page 40, Column 4

## Gunmen Holding Out in Brooklyn Siege; Admit Doctor, Free One of 10 Hostages

By ROBERT D. McFADDEN

Hundreds of heavily armed policemen maintained a massive but impotent cordon of firepower around a Brooklyn sporting goods store yesterday as four trapped gunmen holding a group of frightened hostages rejected repeated appeals for a peaceful surrender.

But late in the afternoon, the gunmen—one of whom was seriously wounded—exchanged one of their 10 hostages for a doctor, who made two trips inside the store. The second time, in which he and a nurse remained there for three hours, they took in medical supplies, food, and a telephone line that established the first phone communications between the police and the gunmen.

At a news conference at the scene, Police Commissioner Patrick V. Murphy said he was "encouraged by the better communications." But there were no indications that the gunmen were prepared to surrender without a fight.

Two hostages had been freed previously.

"This is the end, this is glory—we'll go out in a hail of bullets," one gunman was reported to have told a Muslim minister allowed inside for four minutes in the morning.

The gunmen have been holed up in the store since shortly before 6 P.M. Friday, when the police aborted their attempted robbery, aimed at getting both guns and money. One patrolman was killed and two others were wounded Friday night in a fierce batttle of shotguns, rifles and automatic weapons fire.

Expressing fears for the lives of the six men and three women still held inside, the police said no attempt would be made to storm the store, John & Al Sports, Inc., at 927 Broadway on the border of the Bushwick and Bedford-Stuyvesant sections. Instead, the police concentrated their efforts on establishing a dialogue. The gunmen responded with silence or gunfire.

The four, described as young

*A step-by-step account of the siege appears on Page 54.*

black men, rejected communication efforts by Baptist and Muslim ministers. A bullhorn and a walkie-talkie proffered by the police were hurled out onto the sidewalk.

Attempts by the police to talk to them over a loudspeaker from an armored personnel carrier planted like a tank in the street outside were met with bursts of gunfire from the store's shattered display windows.

Late in the afternoon, however, the gunmen allowed a hostage to retrieve a walkie-talkie placed in front of the store. The hostages used it to request cigarettes and sandwiches from the police, and the gunmen used it to negotiate the exchange of a hostage for a doctor.

About 5 P.M., Dr. Thomas W. Matthew, head of the National Economic Growth and Reconstruction Organization (NEGRO)

Continued on Page 54, Column 4

Flushing Ave.
ELEVATED LINE
BROOKLYN
Central Ave.
Bushwick
Evergreen Ave.
Park Ave.
Arion Pl.
Melrose St.
Jefferson St.
Myrtle Ave.
ELEVATED LINE
SITE OF SIEGE
(Not in use west of Broadway)
Sumner Ave.
Lewis Ave.
Stuyvesant Ave.
Bushwick Ave.
Bedford-Stuyvesant
Feet 1000

The New York Times/Jan. 21, 1973

## LAZAR FORESEES IMPROVED TAXIS

### Predicts More Comfort and Safety Soon and an 'End of Gypsy-Cab Problem'

By FRANK J. PRIAL

The chairman of the city's Taxi and Limousine Commission said last week that taxicabs would be safer and more comfortable here within the next two months and that 1973 could bring "an end to the gypsy-cab problem."

In an interview last week with editors and reporters of The New York Times, Michael J. Lazar, the commission chairman, made the following points:

¶About 5,000 livery license plates, the kind used by most operators of the so-called gypsy cabs were not renewed this year. There were an estimated total of 15,000 gypsy cabs here last year.

¶An additional 1,000 non-medallion cabs have been licensed by the city as "limousines," with 3,000 additional appilcations for limousine licenses pending.

¶As many as 1,000 battered, unsafe medallion cabs will be ordered off city streets by March 1.

¶Still another 1,000 cabs, new Chevrolet Novas, have been banned here because they do

Continued on Page 58, Column 1

## HAIG SEES THIEU FOR A FINAL TALK

### Then Flies to South Korea to See Park Before Returning Home to Report to Nixon

By FOX BUTTERFIELD
Special to The New York Times

SAIGON, South Vietnam, Sunday, Jan. 21—Gen. Alexander M. Haig Jr. met for half an hour yesterday with President Nguyen Van Thieu and then left Saigon for South Korea.

[A Canadian Member of Parliament visiting Hanoi said that North Vietnamese officials had said a cease-fire agreement had been reached with the United States, The Globe and Mail of Toronto reported from Peking. Page 2. Military sources said there was fighting in two regions of South Vietnam. Page 3.]

Shortly after General Haig's departure, according to a South Vietnamese official, President Thieu ordered Foreign Minister Tran Van Lam to go to Paris this morning by the first available flight. The official said he did not know the exact reason for Mr. Lam's trip, but added that Mr. Lam "has been very buoyant these last few days—he seems to feel he is going to be passing into history."

This morning, however, Mr.

Continued on Page 4, Column 1

## Congressmen Hail Theme But Ask for More Details

By JAMES M. NAUGHTON
Special to The New York Times

WASHINGTON, Jan. 20—Members of the Congress that has challenged President Nixon to share governmental authority fidgeted through his second inauguration today and then applauded its theme but pleaded for specifics of his program.

"It was a fine speech," Representative Wright Patman, Democrat of Texas, said in a symptomatic reaction. "It included many inspiring things, some of which were first said by Franklin Roosevelt in 1933 and John F. Kennedy in 1961."

Only about half the 435 members of the House of Representatives and the 100 members of the Senate took their places on the Capitol steps to witness Mr. Nixon's recitation of the Presidential oath of office.

The Democrat who lost the election last year to Mr. Nixon, Senator George McGovern of South Dakota, was in Oxford, England, for a series of lectures. Senator Thomas F. Eagleton of Missouri, whose elevation to and departure from the Democratic ticket may have contributed to the scope of its defeat, was also among the missing.

Senator Sam J. Ervin Jr., whose chairmanship of two Senate subcommittees and one committee has placed him at the center of a gathering Congressional demand for a restoration of legislative authority, stayed in his home state of North Carolina to make a series

Continued on Page 42, Column 1

## Washington's 3 Moods: Joy, Anger, Indifference

By JAMES T. WOOTEN
Special to The New York Times

WASHINGTON, Jan. 20—Like Gaul, this old city was divided into three parts today.

From the suburbs to the slums to the bunting-draped downtown streets, the trichotomy was nearly complete: one part joyously celebrated, another stridently protested, and the other stoically ignored the $4-million advent of President Nixon's second term.

They cheered or they jeered or they just stayed home. They threw roses or kisses or rocks or apple cores or they went shopping with the kids. They gaped at the inaugural parade or formed ranks of their own or took a nap in the den. They stood in awe or approval of the Government's grand panoply or they marched shoulder-to-shoulder against it or they thought about it not at all.

It was today, as Mrs. Alice Roosevelt Longworth and other Washingtonians believe it always has been, "a city where some do and some don't and some don't care."

Inauguration Day broke cold and a sharp wind from the south sliced across the dirty Potomac, snapping the

Continued on Page 42, Column 3

## Today's Sections


| Section | | |
|---|---|---|
| Section 1 | (2 Parts) | News |
| Section 2 | | Drama, Movies, TV, Radio |
| Section 3 | | Financial and Business |
| Section 4 | | The Week in Review |
| Section 5 | | Sports |
| Section 6 | | Magazine |
| Section 7 | | Book Review |
| Section 8 | | *Real Estate |
| Section 9 | | *Employment Advertising |
| Section 10 | | Resort & Travel |
| Section 11 | | *Advertising |
| Section 12 | | **Advertising |


## Index to Subjects

*Included in all copies distributed in New York City and the suburban area.
**Included in all copies distributed in Northern Manhattan, the Bronx and Putnam, Westchester, Rockland and Fairfield counties.


| | Section | Page |
|---|---|---|
| Art | 2 | 21-24 |
| Boating | 5 | 10-12 |
| Bridge | 6 | 66 |
| Chess | 1 | 66 |
| Coins | 2 | 31-32 |
| Dance | 2 | 11 |
| Editorials | 4 | 16 |
| Education | 4 | 11 |
| Fashions | 6 | 54 |
| Food | 6 | 48 |
| Gardens | 2 | 33-36 |
| Home Fashion | 6 | 52 |
| Home Improvement | 2 | 35 |
| Letter to the Editor | 4 | 16 |
| Music | 2 | 14-16 |
| News Summary & Index | 1 | 67 |
| Obituaries | 1 | 60-61 |
| Op-Ed | 4 | 17 |
| Photography | 2 | 29-30 |
| Puzzles | 6 | 68 |
| Records | 2 | 25-28 |
| Science | 4 | 8 |
| Society | 1 | 62-66 |
| Stamps | 2 | 31-32 |
| Transportation | 1 | 58 |
| TV (Late Listings) | 1 | 59 |
| Weather | 1 | 67 |

Associated Press

A hostage sent by the gunmen to retrieve first walkie-talkie left on sidewalk by police returns to the Brooklyn sporting goods store carrying device in right hand. It was thrown back. Armored vehicle is visible at left.

## Key to Apartheid Is Complexity of Laws

By CHARLES MOHR
Special to The New York Times

JOHANNESBURG, South Africa—When a black clergyman visited Johannesburg recently, his manner offended a white shopkeeper, who hit him on the head with an ax handle.

The black man had come to the city to attend a conference on "justice and reconciliation."

Such incidents may seem to symbolize the South African racial problem, just as park benches marked "Whites Only" may seem to symbolize apartheid.

But both officially and in the public consciousness, South African racial doctrine has been undergoing change for many years. The changes, some positive and some negative, are continuing today.

It is not ax handles but ideology that causes the most suffering for the black, colored and Asian population here.

It is not lawless brutality, which is relatively rare, but legal bureaucracy—implementing a proposed "solution" of racial problems—that differentiates South Africa from the hatred, discrimination and racial practices common to much of the rest of the world.

Drawing a balance sheet is difficult. Private attitudes of whites toward other races seem to be improving, at least slightly. The Government has moved in some ways toward a more stringent application of its complex racial policies, but in a few matters even it has become more moderate.

One factor that makes the racial situation in South Africa almost unique is that it is so closely linked to political power.

The more than 2.3 million white Afrikaners — descended from early Dutch, French and German settlers and speaking Afrikaans—and the 1.5-million English-speaking whites make up about 17 per cent of the population. There are more than 15 million black Africans, more than 2 million people of mixed blood, known as coloreds,

Continued on Page 28, Column 4

"All the News That's Fit to Print"

# The New York Times

LATE CITY EDITION

Weather: Partly sunny today; cool tonight. Fair and milder tomorrow. Temp. range: today 54-68; Wed. 58-75. Additional details on Page 90.

VOL. CXXIII ... No. 42,264



NEW YORK, THURSDAY, OCTOBER 11, 1973

15 CENTS

# AGNEW QUITS VICE PRESIDENCY AND ADMITS TAX EVASION IN '67; NIXON CONSULTS ON SUCCESSOR

## U.S. Believes Moscow Is Resupplying Arabs by Airlift

### Soviet Could Spur Move to Aid Israel

By JOHN W. FINNEY

Special to The New York Times

WASHINGTON, Oct. 10—Administration officials said today that they believed the Soviet Union was airlifting military equipment to resupply the forces of Egypt and Syria.

The State Department said that if the Russians were in fact engaged in a huge resupply effort, this would put a "new face" on the Middle East conflict. Speaking for the department, Robert J. McCloskey said, however, that he was "not in a position to confirm that any of this is taking place at this time."

But other officials, apparently acting upon instructions laid down by the State Department, readily volunteered information. They did so, however, on a basis that precluded their identification.

The fact that officials who until today had been extremely reluctant to discuss any detail of the Middle East war were now willing to talk openly about indications of a Soviet resupply effort prompted immediate speculation that the Nixon Administration might be laying the groundwork for resupplying the forces of Israel.

There were reports that Israel was flying military supplies from the United States and from American bases in Britain and West Germany, but it was not clear whether the supplies referred to had previously been ordered. Asked about the reports, the Defense Department refused to confirm or deny them.

The exact nature of the reported Soviet airlift remains unclear, United States officials said. All that is known, according to officials, is that in the last day or so, an unusually large number of Soviet transports have been observed landing at Egyptian and Syrian airports. The presumption is that the planes are carrying military equipment.

The airlift, officials reported, was being staged primarily from Hungary, with the planes

Continued on Page 18, Column 1

### A 10-Mile Egyptian Gain

By HENRY TANNER

Special to The New York Times

IN THE SINAI PENINSULA, Oct. 10 — Egyptian soldiers, tanks and equipment are continuing to pour across the Suez Canal, a group of Western correspondents confirmed from the battle area today.

On a three-and-half-mile tour into the Sinai Peninsula, this correspondent also saw evidence that Egyptian forces had reached positions 10 miles or more east of the canal in some parts of the sector.

[In the air war the Egyptians said they had shot down six more Israeli planes. Egyptian aircraft were said to have attacked Israeli command headquarters, units and administrative installations on the northern Sinai coast.]

The Egyptian soldiers in the area toured by the correspondents were in high spirits, often jubilant, and seemed oblivious to Israeli artillery shells bursting near them.

"Don't worry. God is with us!" one of three young soldiers shouted laughingly to the correspondents, who ducked for cover when a shell burst too close for comfort. The Egyptians remained where they were, standing atop a ridge.

Shells fell every few moments but caused no casualties during a half-hour visit to the particular sector. An Egyptian officer said they were from an Israeli battery 15 miles away that was trying to hit a military bridge.

More than 50 trucks interspersed with antiaircraft guns were lined up in open country on the west bank, waiting for their turn to cross the canal. Waved onto the bridge by a young soldier with a yellow flag, they moved quickly, often with three or four vehicles on the bridge simultaneously.

On one truck two young soldiers were dancing. Others clapped their hands rhythmically.

The elation and excitement of returning to Egyptian territory occupied for more than six years by Israel was everywhere.

The loose boards and pontoons that made up the bridge

Continued on Page 18, Column 5

### Israel Claiming Heights

By CHARLES MOHR

Special to The New York Times

TEL AVIV, Thursday, Oct. 11—Israel said last night that the Syrian Army on the Golan heights had been driven back to the 1967 cease-fire line, but Israeli forces fighting the Egyptians clearly seemed to have suspended a counterattack aimed at pushing them from the eastern bank of the Suez Canal.

*Text of Mrs. Meir's address is printed on Page 19.*

A highly informed source said that Israel estimated the Egyptian invasion force at five divisions, which could be close to 75,000 men. The force, he said, crossed with about 600 tanks, and 300 to 400 of these may still be operational.

The Israeli Air Force bombed two air fields in the Nile delta as well as a naval headquarters, fuel installation and power plant in Syria in a day of slackening air action.

The Israeli command announced this morning that for the first time in the war Israeli forces had struck against the opposite bank of the Suez Canal. The command spokesman said that an Israeli force of unannounced size had raided convoys and rear echelon installations of the Egyptian Army.

The wording of the communiqué indicated that the operation was not an attempt to gain a foothold on the other side and that the raiding force

Continued on Page 19, Column 3



### CONGRESS TO VOTE

#### Opposition Is Hinted if Choice Is Possible 1976 Candidate

Special to The New York Times

WASHINGTON, Oct. 10—President Nixon began his search today for a successor to Vice President Agnew amid indications that he will face stiff resistance from Congress if he chooses anyone who might qualify as a strong Republican candidate in 1976.

The Senate majority leader, Mike Mansfield, Democrat of Montana, said the choice of either John B. Connally, the former Treasury Secretary and Texas Governor, or Gov. Ronald Reagan of California—both presumed contenders for the Republican Presidential nomination in 1976—would provoke a fight from Senate Democrats.

Similar warnings had come from Democratic leaders in the House.

**Quick Action Indicated**

Mr. Nixon's first moves today indicated that he wished to move quickly but with some show of bipartisan consultation. Senator Mansfield said after meeting the President that Mr. Nixon had indicated he would submit the name of his nominee to Congress "at the end of this week or the first of next week."

"President Nixon intends to move expeditiously in selecting a nominee and he trusts the Congress will then act promptly to consider the nomination," Ronald L. Ziegler, the President's press secretary, announced shortly after word that the President had accepted Mr. Agnew's resignation spread through the White House.

Mr. Nixon then began meeting with Congressional leaders of both parties and with George Bush, chairman of the Republican National Committee, to reach an understanding on the procedures he will follow in selecting a Vice President ac-

Continued on Page 34, Column 2

Associated Press

Spiro T. Agnew speaking to reporters after appearing at court in Baltimore yesterday

### Agnew Plea Ends 65 Days Of Insisting on Innocence

By BEN A. FRANKLIN

Special to The New York Times

BALTIMORE, Oct. 10—Vice President Agnew ended today 65 days of defiant insistence that he was innocent of any wrongdoing by pleading no contest to a charge of cheating the Government of $13,551.47 on his Federal income tax payment for 1967, his first year as Governor of Maryland. Then he resigned his Federal office.

*Richardson, Agnew, Hoffman statements on Page 35.*

At a dramatic, surprise appearance here before United States District Court Judge Walter E. Hoffman after two days of secret negotiations, Mr. Agnew was confronted in open court by Attorney General Elliot L. Richardson.

The Attorney General said in a prepared statement that the Government's evidence against the former Vice President went far beyond the six-year-old tax violation. But he said that "critical national interests"—the avoidance of the "serious and permanent scars" upon the nation that would have been inflicted by months or years of a criminal prosecution of a sitting Vice President, together with the new and allied dispute over newsmen's sources—justified the agreement with Mr. Agnew. Judge Hoffman then approved the agreement.

Under it, Mr. Agnew in a 40-minute court appearance waived all his rights as a defendant—the right to be indicted and to an arraignment—and was sentenced on the spot to pay a $10,000 fine and to three years of probation. He was admonished by Judge Hoffman to violate no state or Federal laws on pain of having his avoidance of a prison term reconsidered.

A long list of other charges, involving perhaps $100,000 in payoffs by Maryland contrac-

Continued on Page 35, Column 1

### EVIDENCE SHOWS GIFTS TO AGNEW

#### Cites Requests and Receipt of Over $100,000—Denial Also Entered in Record

By ANTHONY RIPLEY

Special to The New York Times

BALTIMORE, Oct. 10—Spiro T. Agnew, in three elective offices including the Vice-Presidency, asked for and accepted cash payments totaling more than $100,000, according to the evidence gathered against him by the United States Attorneys in Baltimore.

That evidence, denied by Mr. Agnew, was entered by Attorney General Elliott L. Richardson in Federal District Court today as part of the agreement between the Justice Department and Mr. Agnew's lawyers.

*Charge and jury information are on Pages 36, 37 and 38.*

It became a permanent part of the record in the case, along with Mr. Agnew's denial and other terms of the agreement that included his resignation and a plea of no contest to a tax charge.

The 40-page document told of

Continued on Page 38, Column 1

### Mets in World Series; Defeat Reds for Flag

By JOSEPH DURSO

The New York Mets completed their six-week odyssey from last place to the National League pennant yesterday when they overpowered the favored Cincinnati Reds, 7-2, in a tumultuous game that rocked and almost ruined Shea Stadium.

In a riotous scene that brought back memories of their "miracle" of 1969, they decided the issue with four runs in the fifth inning of a 2-2 game.

But then, in a swirling scene, thousands of persons in the crowd of 50,323 stormed the field after delaying the game in the ninth inning and clawed huge chunks of fence, sod and fixtures from the arena.

Professional sports may have had more clamorous moments. But New York baseball has had none since the Mets won the World Series four years ago after eight seasons as the comic relief of the leagues.

Their rise this summer carried them from medical history to baseball history, and their public responded yesterday by mobbing Willie Mays, Pete Rose and the 340 police officers struggling to prevent panic.

Repairs on the stadium were started immediately after the crowd had dispersed shortly after 5 o'clock, while the Mets celebrated their victory in champagne and prepared for the next milestone.

They will open the World Series on Saturday in the home park of the Oakland A's or Baltimore Orioles, who will decide the American League pennant this after-

Continued on Page 61, Column 4



NEWS INDEX



| | Page | | Page |
|---|---|---|---|
| Art | 58 | Man in the News | 33 |
| Books | 43 | Movies | 56-59 |
| Bridge | 42 | Music | 56-59 |
| Business | 67-78 | Obituaries | 48 |
| Chess | 42 | Op-Ed | 46 |
| Crossword | 43 | Sports | 61-65 |
| Editorials | 44 | Theaters | 56-59 |
| Family Style | 54 | Transportation | 90 |
| Financial | 67-78 | TV and Radio | 91 |
| Going Out Guide | 58 | U. N. Proceedings | 19 |
| Letters | 44 | Weather | 90 |

News Summary and Index, Page 47

### I.R.S. Sees Nothing to Prevent New Tax Cases Against Agnew

By EILEEN SHANAHAN

Special to The New York Times

WASHINGTON, Oct. 10—Former Vice President Agnew's plea of "no contest" today in the income-tax evasion case against him could mark only the beginning of difficulties for him with the Internal Revenue Service.

An official spokesman for Internal Revenue said that so far as the agency is aware, there was nothing in the agreement leading to Mr. Agnew's resignation that would prohibit Internal Revenue from attempting to collect taxes on every payment to Mr. Agnew that could be documented as having been made but not reported on his tax returns.

The charge of tax evasion to which Mr. Agnew pleaded "nolo contendere" involved $29,500. But a document released by the Justice Department detailing the evidence against the former Vice President alleges payments from contractors and others totaling as much as $100,000. The precise figure is not clear, because some of the allegations of illegal payments are stated in terms of percentages of the value of construction contracts awarded, and the figures for the contracts themselves are not given.

The Internal Revenue spokesman said, however, that it was common in tax-evasion cases for a charge of criminal tax-evasion to be made involving

Continued on Page 33, Column 3



### Judge Orders Fine, 3 Years' Probation

By JAMES M. NAUGHTON

Special to The New York Times

WASHINGTON, Oct. 10—Spiro T. Agnew resigned as Vice President of the United States today under an agreement with the Department of Justice to admit evasion of Federal income taxes and avoid imprisonment.

The stunning development, ending a Federal grand jury investigation of Mr. Agnew in Baltimore and probably terminating his political career, shocked his closest associates and precipitated an immediate search by President Nixon for a successor.

"I hereby resign the office of Vice President of the United States, effective immediately," Mr. Agnew declared in a formal statement delivered at 2:05 P.M. to Secretary of State Kissinger, as provided in the Succession Act of 1792.

Minutes later, Mr. Agnew stood before United States District Judge Walter E. Hoffman in a Baltimore courtroom, hands barely trembling, and read from a statement in which he pleaded nolo contendere, or no contest, to a Government charge that he had failed to report $29,500 of income received in 1967, when he was Governor of Maryland. Such a plea, while not an admission of guilt, subjects a defendant to a judgment of conviction on the charge.

**Tells Court Income Was Taxable**

"I admit that I did receive payments during the year 1967 which were not expended for political purposes and that, therefore, these payments were income taxable to me in that year and that I so knew," the nation's 39th Vice President told the stilled courtroom.

Judge Hoffman sentenced Mr. Agnew to three years' probation and fined him $10,000. The judge declared from the bench that he would have sent Mr. Agnew to prison had not Attorney General Elliot L. Richardson personally interceded, arguing that "leniency is justified."

In his dramatic courtroom statement, Mr. Agnew declared that he was innocent of any other wrongdoing but that it would "seriously prejudice the national interest" to involve himself in a protracted struggle before the courts or Congress.

Mr. Agnew also cited the national interest in a letter to President Nixon saying that he was resigning.

"I respect your decision," the President wrote to Mr. Agnew in a "Dear Ted" letter made public by the White House. The letter hailed Mr. Agnew for "courage and candor," praised his patriotism and dedication, and expressed Mr. Nixon's "great sense of personal loss." But it agreed

Continued on Page 33, Column 1

### Agnew-Nixon Exchange

October 10, 1973

Dear Mr. President:

As you are aware, the accusations against me cannot be resolved without a long, divisive and debilitating struggle in the Congress and in the courts. I have concluded that, painful as it is to me and to my family, it is in the best interests of the nation that I relinquish the Vice Presidency.

Accordingly, I have today resigned the office of Vice President of the United States. A copy of the instrument of resignation is enclosed.

It has been a privilege to serve with you. May I express to the American people, through you, my deep gratitude for their confidence in twice electing me to be Vice President.

Sincerely,
SPIRO T. AGNEW

•

October 10, 1973.

Dear Ted:

The most difficult decisions are often those that are the most personal, and I know your decision to resign as Vice President has been as difficult as any facing a man in public life could be. Your departure from the Administration leaves me with a great sense of personal loss. You have been a valued associate throughout these nearly five years that we have served together. However, I respect your decision, and I also respect the concern for the national interest that led you to conclude that a resolution of the matter in this way, rather than through an extended battle in the courts and the Congress, was advisable in order to prevent a protracted period of national division and uncertainty.

As Vice President, you have addressed the great issues of our times with courage and candor. Your strong patriotism, and your profound dedication to the welfare of the nation, have been an inspiration to all who have served with you as well as to millions of others throughout the country.

I have been deeply saddened by this whole course of events, and I hope that you and your family will be sustained in the days ahead by a well-justified pride in all that you have contributed to the nation by your years of service as Vice President.

Sincerely,
RICHARD NIXON

"All the News That's Fit to Print"

# The New York Times

LATE CITY EDITION

Weather: Mostly sunny, mild today; cloudy, chance of rain tonight. Temp. range: today 56-73. Friday 51-71. Additional details on Page 70.

VOL.CXXIII....No.42,266 · NEW YORK, SATURDAY, OCTOBER 13, 1973 · 15 CENTS



# GERALD FORD NAMED BY NIXON AS THE SUCCESSOR TO AGNEW

## Appeals Court Agrees President Should Give Up Tapes

## Israelis Drive Syrians Back Within 18 Miles of Damascus

### Capture of Capital Thought Unlikely

By CHARLES MOHR

Special to The New York Times

EL QUNEITRA, on the Golan Heights, Oct. 12—Parts of the Syrian Army appeared to be in full retreat today as the Israeli Army advanced to within 18 miles of the Syrian capital of Damascus.

But an Israeli officer said: "We won't be having dinner together tomorrow in Damascus."

[In Tel Aviv, a well-informed Israeli source said that "the latest thinking is that we will not capture Damascus, which would be a terrible headache." An Israeli military spokesman said that Israeli forces had encountered Iraqi troops in the Golan heights for the first time.]

In at least one area of the Syrian front, northeast of the town of El Quneitra, it was apparent that Syrian forces were in retreat, although still fighting delaying actions.

Reporters following the Israeli Army—and clocking distances on the odometers of their rented sedans—could see that the Israeli forward elements were at least 30 kilometers, or 18 miles, past the old 1967 cease-fire line—and thus about 30 kilometers from Damascus.

It was apparent to neutral foreign observers that, in this one area at least, the main Syrian line of resistance had been smashed. The heavy fortifications constructed by Syria on the 1967 cease-fire line were abandoned and many of its bunkers damaged or destroyed.

Great plumes of brown dust rose in the air as Israeli tank companies moved forward over the rolling, hill-dotted terrain east of the cease-fire line.

A heavy Syrian artillery barrage came in on an area about four miles within Syria this afternoon, but journalists had no clear idea what was happening at the spearhead of the Israeli advance and how determined Syrian resistance was in the most forward areas.

On a brief visit to what is now the Israeli rear area on the route of advance, there were

Continued on Page 14, Column 5

### To Our Readers

Distribution of this issue of The New York Times was delayed by work stoppages by the printers' union in defiance of a court order. The stoppages also made it necessary to reduce coverage of the news. Details, Page 24.

### 3 Freighters Sunk

By JUAN de ONIS

Special to The New York Times

DAMASCUS, Syria, Oct. 12 — Syrian air defenses today shot down 35 Israeli planes that attacked military air bases around this capital and other targets, according to a military spokesman.

Three freighters, one Soviet, one Japanese and one Greek, were sunk during attacks by Israeli missile boats on the ports of Latakia and Tartus, an official announcment said today. The Syrian spokesman said eight of the attacking Israeli craft were sunk by Syrian missile boats.

[In Cairo, military communiqués said that Egyptian forces were continuing to pour across the Suez Canal. Page 15.]

On the ground, "fierce fighting" continued all along the Syrian front, said the spokesman. He said more than 40 Israeli tanks and 20 armored vehicles had been destroyed. There was no figure on Syrian losses.

The front, along the occupied Golan Heights, was 24 miles southeast of this city of 840,000 people, which was calm tonight under a nearly full moon.

Traffic in the blacked-out streets consisted mainly of

Continued on Page 15, Column 1

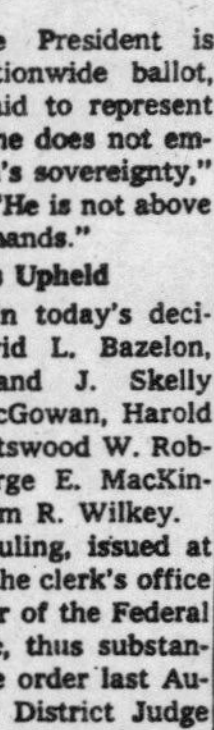

United Press International

Fumes and smoke rise as Israeli artillerymen, on the Syrian border, fire 155-mm. guns

## JUDGES RULE 5-2

### Historic Decision Finds President Not Above Law's Commands

By LESLEY OELSNER

Special to The New York Times

WASHINGTON, Oct. 12—In what it called an "unavoidable" and "extraordinary" ruling, the United States Court of Appeals held tonight that President Nixon must turn over to the Federal District Court here the disputed White House tape recordings possibly bearing on Watergate crimes.

By a 5-to-2 vote, the appeals court said that the District

*Excerpts from court opinions will be found on Page 21.*

Court could then give the Watergate grand jury any relevant material, unless it felt that there was some public interest to be served by withholding "particular" statements or information.

"Though the President is elected by nationwide ballot, and is often said to represent all the people, he does not embody the nation's sovereignty," the court said. "He is not above the law's commands."

**Order Is Upheld**

Participants in today's decision were David L. Bazelon, chief judge, and J. Skelly Wright, Carl McGowan, Harold Leventhal, Spottswood W. Robinson, 3d, George E. MacKinnon and Malcolm R. Wilkey.

The court's ruling, issued at 6 P.M. through the clerk's office on the fifth floor of the Federal Courthouse here, thus substantially upheld the order last August of Federal District Judge John J. Sirica, although it appeared to take an even tougher stance against the President than Judge Sirica had.

The appellate court made its ruling in response to requests by both Mr. Nixon and Archibald Cox, the special Watergate prosecutor, to reverse Judge Sirica. Mr. Cox, who had initiated the proceedings when he had a subpoena issued for the tapes, asked the appeals court to order that the tapes be turned over directly to the grand jury.

Mr. Nixon, for his part, asked

Continued on Page 20, Column 4

United Press International

Gerald R. Ford with President, after Mr. Nixon nominated him for Vice President

## MOVE IS SURPRISE

### House G.O.P. Leader Would Be the 40th Vice President

By JOHN HERBERS

Special to The New York Times

WASHINGTON, Oct. 12 — Gerald Rudolph Ford of Michigan, the 60-year-old minority leader of the House of Representatives, was nominated by President Nixon tonight to be the 40th Vice President of the United States.

Mr. Nixon, making the surprise announcement on national television and radio shortly after 9 P.M., said that he would

*Texts of Nixon and Ford remarks are on Page 19.*

send the nomination to Congress tomorrow. Because of Mr. Ford's long service in that body, 25 years, he was expected to be easily confirmed.

Under the 25th Amendment, ratified in 1967 and never used before tonight, the nomination must be approved by simple majorities of both the House and the Senate before he can take office.

Mr. Ford's selection came two days after Spiro T. Agnew, who had served in the office almost five years, resigned, pleaded no contest to income tax evasion, was fined $10,000 and was placed on probation for three years.

**Move Toward Unity**

In a brief announcement speech in the East Room of the White House, Mr. Nixon made it clear that he had chosen a respected memb of Congress for the post because he considered it essential for national unity to select a person who would not be the subject of a protracted and bitter fight in Congress.

It was learned that Mr. Nixon had given strong consideration to former Treasury Secretary John B. Connally but that leaders in the Democratic-controlled Congress had served notice they would oppose him. They opposed Mr. Connally because he recently switched to the Republican party and because it would have appeared that Mr. Nixon was setting him up for the Presidency in the 1976 elections.

Mr. Ford, the President said, "has earned the respect of both Democrats and Republicans."

**'Unwavering' on Vietnam**

"He is a man also who has been unwavering in his support of the policies that brought peace with honor for America in Vietnam and in support of the policies for a strong national defense," Mr. Nixon said.

Several score Congressional leaders, Cabinet members and other high Government officials burst into cheers and surrounded the baldish, tanned Republican and offered congratulations even before Mr. Nixon uttered his name. They knew he was the nominee when Mr. Nixon said his choice "is a man who has served for 25 years in the House of Representatives with great distinction."

Mr. Ford, the President said, met the three criteria he had set for the nominee—that "the

Continued on Page 19, Column 1

## Amtrak Will Double Fleet Of 'Corridor' Metroliners

By EDWARD C. BURKS

Amtrak, the nationwide rail passenger system, announced yesterday that it would virtually double its fleet of Metroliner cars and extend high-speed Metroliner service from New York to Boston.

It signed contracts in Washington for new equipment valued at $63.5-million including the following:

¶Fifty-seven new Metroliner-type coaches, capable of operation in trains pulled by either electric or diesel locomotives, for service in the Washington-New York-Boston "Northeast Corridor."

¶Eleven new 6,000-horsepower electric locomotives (added to 15 ordered earlier this year) to replace the famed but ancient Penn Central GG-1 electrics that have operated in the corridor since the nineteen-thirties.

¶Seventy new diesel passenger locomotives for other Amtrak routes around the nation.

In Philadelphia, Judge John P. Fullam, who is in charge of the Penn Central Railroad's bankruptcy case in Federal District Court, said he believed there was no immediate need for the carrier to cease its operations. [Details Page 47.]

With the award of yesterday's contracts, Amtrak has now committed more than $110-million this year to new locomotives and passenger cars.

Started in 1969, the high-speed Metroliner service between New York and Washington has been expanded to a train every hour in each direction from early morning until evening on weekdays.

There are somewhat fewer services on the weekends. In addition, some Metroliners go on through New York as far as New Haven.

Although very-high speed service on the New York-Boston line must await the day of extensive track realignment on the curving route, new equipment ordered yesterday can substantially reduce present running times, according to Amtrak.

Bryan Duff, Amtrak's news director, said that the first of the new Metroliner-type coaches with airliner interiors should be delivered in 15 months. They are to be built by the Budd Company at Red Lion, Pa.

The 61 Metroliner cars now in operation are self-propelled and equipped with pantographs on the roof. Their use is thus limited to the relatively short stretches in this country with overhead catenary installations.

The new cars will have the

Continued on Page 70, Column 5

## CHOICE IS PRAISED BY BOTH PARTIES

### Widespread Enthusiasm Is Expressed in Congress—Fast Confirmation Seen

By RICHARD L. MADDEN

Special to The New York Times

WASHINGTON, Oct. 12—Congressional Democrats and Republicans received President Nixon's choice of Gerald R. Ford to be Vice President with widespread enthusiasm tonight.

The reaction indicated that the nomination of Mr. Ford of Michigan, who has been the House Republican leader since 1965, would be confirmed relatively quickly by both houses, barring some unforeseen development.

However, it was expected that the Senate would take more time than the House in considering the nomination.

"My own feeling is Gerry will probably be confirmed," said Speaker Carl Albert of Oklahoma, he added:

"I think I was the first in Congress to tell the President that Gerry would be the easiest candidate to sell to the House. He's a very fine man to work with. I think he earned this."

Senator Robert C. Byrd of West Virginia, the Democratic majority whip and member of the Senate Rules Committee, which will probably handle Mr. Ford's nomination, said he did not think it would be proper

Continued on Page 19, Column 5

## Israel Is Accused in U.N. Of Sinking a Soviet Ship

By ROBERT ALDEN

Special to The New York Times

UNITED NATIONS, N. Y., Oct. 12—The Soviet Union accused Israel today of "barbarous" attacks on nonmilitary targets and demanded that they be stopped at once.

Yakov A. Malik, the Soviet delegate, read to the Security Council a dispatch from Tass, the Soviet press agency, that said the Soviet merchant ship Ilya Mechnikov had been sunk in Tartus, a Syrian port, by an Israeli attack.

Tass demanded "an immediate stop to the bombings of peaceful towns in Syria and Egypt, and the strict observance by Israel of the norms of international law."

"The continuation of criminal acts by Israel will lead to grave consequences for Israel itself," the Tass article added.

Yosef Tekoah, the Israeli representative, said his information on the basis of a news dispatch was that the Soviet merchant ship had been damaged as a result of a naval battle that took place between Syrian and Israeli naval vessels outside the port. He termed the damage "unfortunate."

Reports from Damascus said that the ship had subsequently been sunk, as had a Greek and a Japanese merchant ship during attacks made by Israeli missile boats on the ports of Tartus and Latakia.

"We regret the sinking of

Continued on Page 14, Column 2

## Rival Stadium Plans Stir a Bistate Furor

By FRANK LYNN

A bitter behind-the-scenes struggle has developed between New York and New Jersey over a proposed Sunnyside, Queens, sport complex that has the strong backing of Governor Rockefeller and that could effectively kill a similar New Jersey race track and football stadium.

High New York State sources said that the Governor had approved the announcement of the Queens sports complex last Saturday that forced postponement of the sale of a $280-million bond issue to finance the New Jersey race track and stadium for the New York Football Giants in the Hackensack Meadows.

"We were signaling investors of New York's interest in its

Continued on Page 24, Column 5

## P.S.C. Certifies Shortage Of Fuel Oil on Long Island

### First in the State

By DAVID A. ANDELMAN

The State Public Service Commission certified yesterday that a major shortage in home and industrial fuel oils existed for Long Island—the first region in the state to be declared an "oil insufficient area."

According to the certification, between now and Jan. 15 Long Island will face a shortage of at least 150.1 million gallons of No. 2 home heating oil and 39.5 million gallons of Nos. 4 and 6 industrial fuel oils.

The certification was made to Henry L. Diamond, the State Environmental Conservation Commissioner, who must now decide whether to lift the regulations prohibiting use of high-sulphur fuel oil to ease the anticipated shortage.

Yesterday's certification applies only to fuels distributed through Northville Industries, the largest distributor on Long Island, but reportedly not the only one finding supplies short. As a result, a senior official of the Public Service Commission noted, "there may be other

Continued on Page 36, Column 3

### Federal Controls Ordered

By The Associated Press

WASHINGTON, Oct. 12—The Nixon Administration reluctantly adopted today a mandatory allocation program governing the wholesale distribution of home heating oil.

At the same time, Congress moved steadily closer to forcing a mandatory program for all petroleum products.

The Administration's limited program, which will take effect Nov. 1, requires suppliers to distribute home heating oil, jet fuel, kerosene, diesel fuel, range oil, stove oil and gas oil to their customers in proportion to purchases made in the calendar year 1972.

On Oct. 2, the Administration imposed a similar allocation program on propane gas, but so far there is no Government control over the distribution of crude oil or of gasoline and other petroleum products.

Legislation now before Congress would require mandatory allocation of all petroleum products and crude oil.

The House Rules Committee

Continued on Page 36, Column 5

## Agnew Prosecution Took Pains To Prepare a 'Locked-Up Case'

By AGIS SALPUKAS

Special to The New York Times

BALTIMORE, Oct. 12—It started modestly.

When George Beall, the United States Attorney for Maryland, asked that a grand jury be impaneled last Dec. 4, he recalled in an interview today, the thought was: "If we ended up bringing criminal charges against a couple of building inspectors in Baltimore it would have been justified."

And the inquiry remained focused on lesser political figures, with no hint that it would lead higher, until the beginning of June when several key witnesses began to seek favored treatment from the prosecutors by telling them what they knew about making payments to the then Vice President Agnew.

By the beginning of July, Mr. Beall was convinced that the case against the Vice President was serious and on July 3 he called Attorney General Elliot L. Richardson to inform him of the explosive turn of events.

Mr. Beall comes from a long line of prominent Republicans in Maryland. He is the son of J. Glenn Beall, the former Republican United States Senator, and the brother of J. Glenn Beall Jr., who won election to the Senate in 1970. Today he recalled his feelings at that point last summer when he realized the implication of the inquiry.

"I was turning somersaults," he said as he sat at his neat

Continued on Page 18, Column 2

NEWS INDEX


| | Page | | Page |
|---|---|---|---|
| Antiques | 32 | Man in the News | 19 |
| Art | 27-29 | Movies | 24-26 |
| Books | 33 | Music | 24-26 |
| Bridge | 32 | Obituaries | 38 |
| Business | 45-54 | Op-Ed | 35 |
| Churches | 22 | Society | 31 |
| Crossword | 33 | Sports | 40-44 |
| Editorials | 34 | Theaters | 24-26 |
| Family/Style | 30 | Transportation | 70 |
| Financial | 45-54 | TV and Radio | 70-71 |
| Going Out Guide | 25 | Weather | 70 |


News Summary and Index, Page 37

"All the News That's Fit to Print"

# The New York Times

LATE CITY EDITION

Weather: Mostly sunny today; cold tonight. Sunny and cold tomorrow. Temp. range: today 36-46; Thursday 45-62. Additional details on Page 81.

VOL. CXXIII ... No. 42,321 · © 1973 The New York Times Company · NEW YORK, FRIDAY, DECEMBER 7, 1973 · 15 CENTS

# FORD SWORN AS VICE PRESIDENT AFTER HOUSE APPROVES, 387-35; HE VOWS EQUAL JUSTICE FOR ALL

The New York Times/George Tames

Gerald R. Ford being sworn in as Vice President of the United States as his wife, Elizabeth, held Bible and Chief Justice Warren E. Burger administered oath. Observing were President Nixon, at right, and at rear, Carl Albert, left, Speaker of the House, and James O. Eastland, right, who is the President pro tem of the Senate.

## LOYALTY TO NIXON

### 1,500 Hear Ford Give His Full Support to President

By MARJORIE HUNTER

Special to The New York Times

WASHINGTON, Dec. 6 — Gerald R. Ford, pledging "equal justice for all Americans," took office just after dusk tonight as the 40th Vice President of the United States.

With President Nixon standing right behind him, he was sworn into office in the 116-year-old House chamber, which has been his political home for the last 25 years.

*Transcript of the ceremony and speech are on Page 27; a page of pictures, 26.*

Only an hour earlier, the House completed action on his nomination by voting 387 to 35 for confirmation. He was confirmed Nov. 27 by the Senate by a vote of 92 to 3.

Mr. Ford, 60 years old, resigned his House seat before assuming the Vice-Presidency. He has been minority leader of the House since 1965.

**Jerry Ford's Day**

It was clearly Jerry Ford's day, and not even President Nixon's appearance overshadowed the new Vice President. The waves of applause and the smiles of his colleagues were seemingly beamed at him alone as he stood, in a trim navy blue suit, his right hand held high in recognition of old friends.

And, as he spoke, it was the Jerry Ford many of them had listened to through the years, speaking in a flat tone, declaring his love for his wife and his country and pledging his loyalty to his President.

The historic ceremony ended a Vice-Presidential vacancy that had existed since the resignation on Oct. 10 of Spiro T. Agnew just before he pleaded no contest to a charge of income tax evasion.

**First Use of Amendment**

This is the first time that a Vice President was chosen under the 25th Amendment to the Constitution. The amendment, ratified by the states in 1967, provides for Presidential succession and for filling Vice-Presidential vacancies.

The 25th Amendment was adopted to deal with situations such as that which existed following the assassination of President Kennedy in 1963. At that time, the Vice-Presidency stood vacant 13 months after Vice President Johnson succeeded to the Presidency.

Mr. Ford heard none of today's five hours of House debate, nor did he vote. He arrived in the chamber just minutes after the final vote had been cast and was greeted by thunderous cheers and applause—the first of many such

Continued on Page 27, Column 2

## Governor to Quit and Seek Presidency, His Aides Say

### Expected to Announce the Move Before Christmas—Wilson Would Succeed Him and Address New Legislature

By FRANK LYNN

Governor Rockefeller will resign the governorship and turn it over to Lieut. Gov. Malcolm Wilson so Mr. Rockefeller can devote full time to his Presidential quest, his closest associates said yesterday.

The resignation will be announced before Christmas, to give Mr. Wilson time to prepare a State of the State message when the Legislature convenes Jan. 9, the informants said in interviews with The New York Times.

The decision of the 65-year-old Mr. Rockefeller to resign after 15 years ended months of soul-searching in which he weighed, first, whether to seek a fifth term next year, and, then, whether to resign before his fourth term ends, to give Mr. Wilson maximum exposure and the advantages of an incumbent in next year's gubernatorial election.

The decision appeared to be final, although one Rockefeller associate cautioned that he could change his mind. But even this informant agreed that the Governor's actions pointed to resignation. He said Mr. Rockefeller's demeanor at the Tuesday meeting of his newly formed National Commission on Critical Choices convinced him that "the Governor has something entirely viable with the commission and something he's going to throw himself into heavily."

The Governor, who was in Washington yesterday for a meeting of the National Commission on Water Quality, which he heads, was unavailable for comment, but his press secretary, Ronald Maiorana, said that "there is no point in my speculating on any of the options that Governor has before him."

The Governor himself had signaled a decision to resign at a news conference Tuesday when, speaking of the commis-

Continued on Page 49, Column 5

## M.T.A. TO PROVIDE TWO SUNDAY RIDES FOR PRICE OF ONE

### 5-Week Plan on All Subway, Bus and Train Routes Is Aimed at Luring Riders

By DEIRDRE CARMODY

In a dramatic experiment to lure people to public transportation on "gasless Sundays," the Metropolitan Transportation Authority will provide round-trip transportation for the price of a normal one-way fare on all public transportation in New York City and on all M.T.A. commuter lines for five consecutive Sundays beginning Dec. 16.

"We are really pioneering," said Dr. William J. Ronan, chairman of the authority, when he announced the plans at a news conference yesterday. "As far as I know, it's the first move of its kind that has been made in the country in response to the energy crisis."

Under the plan, which will be in effect from 6 A.M. Sundays to 1 A.M. Mondays, subway riders will be given a token and a return coupon for their 35 cents. The coupon will be good only on that day. Bus riders will be given similar return passes but the coupons may not be used interchangeably on subways and buses.

**Connecticut Accord**

Riders on the M.T.A. commuter lines—Long Island Rail Road and the Harlem, Hudson and New Haven lines of the Penn Central—will be issued round-trip tickets for the price of single fares. These return tickets also will be good only on the date of purchase.

Under an agreement with Gov. Thomas J. Meskill of Connecticut, the special fares will also apply to the Connecticut portion of the New Haven line. Governor Meskill said the plan included the New Canaan, Waterbury and Danbury branches.

The plan will also include Nassau County buses that are operated by the Metropolitan Suburban Bus Authority, a subsidiary of the M.T.A.

Also included in the program is the Staten Island Rapid Transit Operating Authority, a subsidiary of the M.T.A. However, the Staten Island ferry, which is operated by the city's Department of Marine and Aviation and which charges 10 cents

Continued on Page 46, Column 4

## Wholesale Index Up 1.8% On Soaring Prices of Fuel

By EDWIN L. DALE Jr.

Special to The New York Times

WASHINGTON, Dec. 6—Soaring prices for oil products and other fuels were the main element in another big increase in the Government's wholesale price index in November, the Labor Department reported today.

The index rose 1.8 per cent after adjustment for normal seasonal changes in some prices. The increase occurred despite a third consecutive monthly decline for farm and food prices — a decline that may now be over.

The wholesale price index was 17.5 per cent above a year earlier, an unheard of rate of inflation for peacetime in the modern era. This huge rise reflected chiefly an explosion in prices of raw commodities of all kinds, agricultural and nonagricultural, plus the more recent burst in the energy area.

**Labor Doubts Data**

Today's index showed an almost unbelievable increase of 34.7 per cent in prices of refined petroleum products in a single month — but the Labor Department indicated that it doubted its own statistics in this case.

The department said it based its index on prices in "spot markets" which now "appear to represent a declining portion of the transactions taking place in domestic markets." Petroleum products sold on a long-term or medium-term contract basis undoubtedly rose

Continued on Page 61, Column 6

## ARABS CUT FUNDS AT BANKS OF U.S.

### Transfers May Be Spurred by Accord in Cairo to Use Money for Development

By CLYDE H. FARNSWORTH

Special to The New York Times

PARIS, Dec. 6—Arab states are stepping up their economic offensive against the United States by withdrawing funds from American banks.

"The French and Swiss banks ought to be very happy because they are getting the deposits," one American commented.

The transfers may be accelerated as a result of actions by Arab League economic ministers meeting for the last three days in Cairo. They agreed "in principle" that funds should be withdrawn from Western banks to finance development projects in Arab countries.

Mahmoud Riad, secretary general of the Arab League, said that a "gradual withdrawal of deposits" had been agreed on.

"Special planning committees will meet to discuss what percentages would be withdrawn, and how the money would be invested," a spokesman for the league was quoted as having said.

Arab sources in Cairo said that Egypt and Syria would get priority in the development program.

The Arabs, in both official

Continued on Page 63, Column 3

## Con Ed Announces 'Dramatic' Cut Here In the Use of Power

By RICHARD SEVERO

Consolidated Edison yesterday reported a "dramatic decrease" in the electricity, natural gas and steam used by its customers during November, and a company executive hailed it as "strong indication that customers in New York and Westchester County are cooperating in conserving energy."

Con Edison said its November electric output was 0.6 per cent below November, 1972, when a 4 per cent increase would normally have been expected. Natural gas was down 2.1 per cent, compared with a company projection of an 8 per cent increase for "normal" times, and steam output was down 8.4 per cent, compared with an original expectation of a 2.7 per cent increase.

Louis H. Roddis, company vice chairman, added that it was the first time in more than 30 years that electric sales had declined.

Shortly before Con Edison announced the November figures, a fire broke out in its Ravenswood, Queens, plant, knocking out "Big Allis," the giant generator that can produce 10 per cent of the company's total capacity of 10 million kilowatts.

A spokesman said that there was "no immediate problem"

Continued on Page 47, Column 2

## Air Travelers Delayed

Thousands of air travelers were delayed here yesterday as employes of Trans World Airlines, on strike for a month, picketed at the terminals of American Airlines and Pan American World Airways. Operations resumed last night after pickets were removed in compliance with a court order. Page 81.

## WHITE HOUSE BARS ROLE ON TRUCKERS

### Nixon Aide Says Halting of Interstate Road Blockades Is 'Matter for the States'

By PHILIP SHABECOFF

Special to The New York Times

WASHINGTON, Dec. 6—The White House avoided today responsibility for halting the truck driver blockades of interstate highways and instead called on the state Governors to take action.

Asked at a White House briefing why President Nixon was not using the power of the Federal Government against truck drivers illegally snarling traffic on interstate highways in protest over higher fuel prices and lower speed limits, the deputy press secretary, Gerald L. Warren, replied that it was "a matter for the states."

Meanwhile widespread protests by truck drivers took a new form as the blockades that paralyzed traffic at several points for three days were called off and a bid to shut down the entire trucking industry was started.

Mr. Warren was also asked why the Federal Government was able to act against civil rights and peace demonstrators who blocked traffic but not against the wildcatting truckers. He was specifically asked about the mass arrest, without warrants, of more than 10,000 peace demonstrators in May, 1971, by Washington D.C. police acting under the supervision of the then Attorney General, John N. Mitchell.

Mr. Warren, in reply, reiterated that the blockade of the interstate highways was for the

Continued on Page 46, Column 3

## A Watershed for Nixon

### Some Republicans in Congress Hope Ford Will Soon Be the 38th President

By JAMES M. NAUGHTON

Special to The New York Times

News Analysis

WASHINGTON, Dec. 6—Now that Gerald R. Ford has become the nation's 40th Vice President, a number of Republicans in Congress hope that he will soon become the 38th President.

They expect and desire the resignation of President Nixon. His resignation would relieve them of the need to face up to an eventual vote on his impeachment. But if Mr. Nixon does not step down voluntarily by next spring or somehow restore widespread public confidence in his Administration, some of Mr. Ford's old colleagues in the House of Representatives are likely to join in any impeachment move against the President.

The reason, outlined privately in the last few days by typical Republicans, is a basic one: Their own political future is at stake.

"You'd like him to resign, wouldn't you?" a senior Democrat said tauntingly to a Republican colleague in the Speaker's lobby just off the House floor. "The President's an albatross around your neck."

"At least that," the Republican replied.

Similar conversations have become increasingly commonplace as Congress, resolving the issue of Presidential succession, has begun to focus on the question of Presidential conduct. Republicans, though a minority in Congress, are central to any determination of Mr. Nixon's fate. A month ago, they were demanding a verdict on Mr. Ford's nomination. Now, they

Continued on Page 27, Column 5

## Nixon-Dean Tape Will Go To Mitchell Trial Judge

By ARNOLD H. LUBASCH

Federal prosecutors disclosed last night that the White House had agreed to provide the tape recording of a conversation between President Nixon and John W. Dean 3d for the trial of two former Cabinet officers.

The tape recording of the conversation last Feb. 28 between the President and the former White House counsel was demanded yesterday by Judge Lee P. Gagliardi, who is presiding over the trial of former Attorney General John N. Mitchell and former Secretary of Commerce Maurice H. Stans that is scheduled to begin Jan. 9 in Federal District Court here.

Mr. Mitchell and Mr. Stans were indicted last May 10 for allegedly obstructing an investigation of the financial operations of Robert L. Vesco in return for the fugitive financier's secret $200,000 cash contribution to President Nixon's 1972 election campaign.

Meanwhile, Mr. Vesco was granted permission yesterday to live in Argentina and will not be liable to extradition, Reuters reported. [Page 20.]

Two prosecutors in the Mitchell-Stans trial, James W. Rayhill and Kenneth R. Feinberg, told Judge Gagliardi yesterday after his request that J. Fred Buzhardt Jr., a special White House counsel, had informed them that the tape would be provided no later than next Friday for the judge to examine in private.

Judge Gagliardi had indicated earlier that he would not permit Mr. Dean to testify as a

Continued on Page 20, Column 1

## Vizzini Is Indicted In Firemen's Strike

By JOHN SIBLEY

Richard J. Vizzini, president of the Uniformed Firefighters Association, and two other top union officials were arrested yesterday on charges stemming from the first strike by the city's 10,900 firemen exactly one month earlier.

An eight-count indictment handed up by a Manhattan grand jury charges the three with reckless endangerment of life and property, attempted coercion of city officials during bargaining negotiations, obstructing governmental administration and conspiring to commit each of these crimes.

Mr. Vizzini's co-defendants are John O'Sullivan, the U.F.A.'s financial and recording secretary, and Dominick Gentiluomo, sergeant at arms.

All three pleaded not guilty

Continued on Page 14, Column 4

The New York Times/Neal Boenzi

"Big Allis," the million-kilowatt turbine that was damaged by a fire in Con Edison's Ravenswood, Queens, plant, giving off steam, a normal procedure during shutdown. At right are firemen who put out fire. Assessment of damage will take at least two days.

## Level of South Vietnam Fighting Is Fiercest Since Truce Accord

By JAMES M. MARKHAM

Special to The New York Times

SAIGON, South Vietnam, Dec. 6—In the last month, the fighting in South Vietnam has reached its fiercest levels since the January signing of the agreement for an ostensible cease-fire, which has since been shattered.

The North Vietnamese and their Vietcong allies have taken the initiative in most of the actions—though the South Vietnamese Air Force has been bombing at a scorching pace. But it is not clear that the Communists have struck the opening blows of a much-predicted dry-season offensive.

In the eyes of many foreign military analysts here, the intentions of the Communists for 1974 remain uncertain. "They are still looking for a strategy that works," one authority on the Indochinese Communist movement observed.

But there is almost universal agreement that the new year will see more and probably heavier fighting. A few months ago some people were talking about "a momentum to peace." Now they, too, are talking about momentum in the other direction.

South Vietnam's President, Nguyen Van Thieu, himself a former general, has been the most persistent and outspoken on an upcoming all-out Com-

Continued on Page 8, Column 3

## Stock Prices Score Sixth Biggest Rise

The stock market bounded ahead yesterday in a dynamic recovery that saw the sixth biggest point advance ever for the Dow-Jones industrial average. The blue-chip indicator soared 25.81 points to 814.12.

Wall Street labeled the action a technical rally in the absence of any significant news developments. A similar rally with a gain of 22 points occurred on Nov. 28.

The market's latest recovery followed a drop of 198 points in the Dow average within a six-week period. Trading was heavy on the New York Stock Exchange, where 23.26 million shares changed hands.

In the glamour group, Kodak rose 7 points and McDonald's advanced 7½.

Details on Page 61.

NEWS INDEX


| | Page | | Page |
|---|---|---|---|
| About New York | 49 | Movies | 31-37 |
| Art | 32 | Music | 31-37 |
| Books | 38-39 | Obituaries | 44 |
| Bridge | 38 | Op-Ed | 41 |
| Business | 59-67 | Sports | 51-55 |
| Crossword | 39 | Theaters | 31-37 |
| Editorials | 40 | Transportation | 81 |
| Family/Style | 48 | TV and Radio | 82-83 |
| Financial | 59-67 | U. N. Proceedings | 9 |
| Going Out Guide | 32 | Weather | 81 |

News Summary and Index, Page 43

"All the News That's Fit to Print"

# The New York Times

LATE CITY EDITION

Weather: Partly cloudy today; cool tonight. Fair, pleasant tomorrow. Temp. range: today 65-78; Thursday 64-85. Highest Temp.-Hum. Index yesterday: 75. Details on Page 66.

VOL. CXXIII..No. 42,566 · NEW YORK, FRIDAY, AUGUST 9, 1974 · 20c beyond 50-mile radius of New York City, except Long Island. Higher in air delivery cities · 15 CENTS



# NIXON RESIGNS

## *HE URGES A TIME OF 'HEALING'; FORD WILL TAKE OFFICE TODAY*

## 'Sacrifice' Is Praised; Kissinger to Remain

By ANTHONY RIPLEY

Special to The New York Times

WASHINGTON, Aug. 8—Vice President Ford praised President Nixon tonight for "one of the greatest personal sacrifices for the country and one of the finest personal decisions on behalf of all of us as Americans."

Mr. Ford, who will take office as the 38th President at noon tomorrow, vowed to continue Mr. Nixon's foreign policy and announced that Secretary of State Kissinger had agreed to stay on in the new Administration.

"I pledge to you tonight, as I will pledge to you tomorrow and in the future, my best efforts in cooperation, leadership and dedication to what's good for America and good for the world," he said.

The Vice President, who never sought the nation's highest office and disclaimed any intention of seeking it after Mr. Nixon's term, will take the oath of office in a private ceremony at the White House.

Thus will he become the first man to serve as President without being chosen by the American people in an election. Tomorrow night he will address the nation on radio and television. It is expected that he will speak at 6 P.M.

All day today the signs of the historic change were in the air, sensed by the crowds that gathered along Pennsylvania

*Text of Mr. Ford's remarks appears on Page 2.*

Avenue near the White House. Applause rang out from the crowds when Mr. Ford appeared briefly.

After watching Mr. Nixon on television tonight with his family, the Vice President stepped outside into a slight drizzle at his suburban split-level home in nearby Alexandria, Va., to face television cameras and photographers assembled in the street and about 100 cheering neighbors.

**Speaks Outside Home**

Speaking without notes or a prepared text, Mr. Ford pledged to continue the Nixon foreign policy and called the Secretary of State "a very great man" whom he has known for many years.

On domestic policy, he said that he had been "very fortunate in my lifetime" to have adversaries in Congress but said that he did not think he had "a single enemy" there.

President Nixon had cited in his resignation address his lack of support in Congress as one of the major reasons for his resignation.

Mr. Ford said, "The net result is that I think tomorrow I can start out working with Democrats and with Republi-

Continued on Page 4, Column 3

The New York Times/William E. Sauro

Vice President Ford meeting with newsmen last night

United Press International

President Nixon on TV as he announced his resignation

## The 37th President Is First to Quit Post

By JOHN HERBERS

Special to The New York Times

WASHINGTON, Aug. 8—Richard Milhous Nixon, the 37th President of the United States, announced tonight that he had given up his long and arduous fight to remain in office and would resign, effective at noon tomorrow.

At that hour, Gerald Rudolph Ford, whom Mr. Nixon nominated for Vice President last Oct. 12, will be sworn in as the 38th President, to serve out the 895 days remaining in Mr. Nixon's second term.

Less that two years after his landslide re-election victory, Mr. Nixon, in a conciliatory address on national

*Text of the address will be found on Page 2.*

television, said that he was leaving not with a sense of bitterness but with a hope that his departure would start a "process of healing that is so desperately needed in America."

He spoke of regret for any "injuries" done "in the course of the events that led to this decision." He acknowledged that some of his judgments had been wrong.

The 61-year-old Mr. Nixon, appearing calm and resigned to his fate as a victim of the Watergate scandal, became the first President in the history of the Republic to resign from office. Only 10 months earlier Spiro Agnew resigned the Vice-Presidency.

**Speaks of Pain at Yielding Post**

Mr. Nixon, speaking from the Oval Office, where his successor will be sworn in tomorrow, may well have delivered his most effective speech since the Watergate scandals began to swamp his Administration in early 1973.

In tone and content, the 15-minute address was in sharp contrast to his frequently combative language of the past, especially his first "farewell" appearance—that of 1962, when he announced he was retiring from politics after losing the California governorship race and declared that the news media would not have "Nixon to kick around" anymore.

Yet he spoke tonight of how painful it was for him to give up the office.

"I would have preferred to carry through to the finish whatever the personal agony it would have involved, and my family unanimously urged me to do so," he said.

**Puts 'Interests of America First'**

"I have never been a quitter," he said. "To leave office before my term is completed is opposed to every instinct in my body." But he said that he had decided to put "the interests of America first."

Conceding that he did not have the votes in Congress to escape impeachment in the House and conviction in the Senate, Mr. Nixon said, "To continue to fight through the months ahead for my personal vindication would almost totally absorb the time and attention of the President and the Congress in a period when our entire focus should be on the great issues of peace abroad and prosperity without inflation at home."

"Therefore," he continued, "I shall resign the Presidency effective at noon tomorrow. Vice President Ford will be

Continued on Page 3, Column 1

## SPECULATION RIFE ON VICE PRESIDENT

### Some Ford Associates Say Selecting a Successor Could Take Weeks

By CHRISTOPHER LYDON

Special to The New York Times

WASHINGTON, Aug. 8 — Potentially the most revealing and most important decision of Gerald R. Ford's Presidential debut — his choice of a successor in the Vice Presidency — was a much-discussed mystery here today.

Close friends of Mr. Ford continued to feed speculation about more than a dozen possible candidates. But none of the friends claimed to have discussed the Vice-Presidential question with Mr. Ford or to be speaking for him on it. A number of Ford associates thought he might hold off the decision for days or even weeks.

"Everybody's on tenterhooks up here," a Senator remarked this afternoon in a telephone interview from the Republican cloakroom, "but I think they're wasting their time. It's going to be a week or two. So far I'd say he's a loner on this issue."

Former Defense Secretary Melvin R. Laird, a Ford counselor in the House for more than a decade, was being quoted again today as saying he believes that Nelson A. Rocke-

Continued on Page 4, Column 1

## POLITICAL SCENE SHARPLY ALTERED

### G.O.P. Prospects Improved, Ford in Good Spot for '76 and Watergate Fades

By R. W. APPLE Jr.

Special to The New York Times

WASHINGTON, Aug. 8—President Nixon's resignation drastically altered the American political landscape.

It improved Republican prospects for the Congressional elections in November, thrust Vice President Ford into the favorite's role for the 1976 Presidential election, ended the Watergate agony that has served to bind together the heterogeneous Democratic party and removed from the political stage the man who was the dominant Republican for the last 15 years.

In a larger sense, it seemed to presage an era of more open government, of more cooperation and less antagonism between Capitol Hill and the White House and of decline of the White House staff as an independent power center.

**Lives Are Altered**

A kind of "honeymoon" between the executive and legislative branches was widely predicted by Congressional leaders today. Congressmen who knew Mr. Ford for years as a Capitol Hill colleague said that they expected to work closely with him.

At least in the beginning, pragmatic conservatism is expected to remain the dominant ideological tone in the executive branch.

How that will be translated into policies, and how those policies will shape the political dialogue, will not be clear for weeks. But experts in the two fields forecast an essentially unchanged foreign policy and a similar, but more carefully and consistently applied, economic policy.

By his decision, Mr. Nixon

Continued on Page 6, Column 4

## *Rise and Fall*

### Appraisal of Nixon Career

By ROBERT B. SEMPLE Jr.

The central question is how a man who won so much could have lost so much. How could a public figure who so well perceived the instincts of the majority of his countrymen have misused the powers and duties those same countrymen so eagerly ceded him?

The historians will be kept busy on these questions, but for those who spent their time observing Mr. Nixon for the last six years the answer may well be found in a phrase he often applied to himself. "At bottom," he used to say, "I am a political man."

By his own description, he was a man of action rather than contemplation, a tactician rather than a theologian, a student of technique who seemed always impatient with substance, a figure whose exceptional antennae seemed to dwarf and even hide what lay at the core.

To his enemies, he was both manipulative and synthetic; to his friends, a pragmatist unencumbered by inflexible principles; to those who watched him, a man who learned to run before he had learned to walk and who, on reaching his destination, was not always certain what to do when he got there—except, perhaps, to keep going.

That image has only been reinforced and deepened by the transcripts of three conversations with H. R. Haldeman on June 23, 1972, six days after the Watergate break-in, which were released on Aug. 5, and the edited transcripts of White House conversations published April 30. Whatever history's judgment of those tapes, this much was clear: Faced with mounting evidence of deception and wrongdoing in his own official family, he sought not to confront the issue but to manipulate it until he himself became part of the deception.

Mr. Nixon used the words "I am a political man" proudly, as if to challenge the moralists, but in the end they became his epitaph—a possible explanation for both his success and failure.

For if the words implied the presence of a talent for finding opportunities for political prof-

Continued on Page 11, Column 1

## JAWORSKI ASSERTS NO DEAL WAS MADE

### Says Nixon Did Not Ask for and Was Not Given a Way to Avoid Prosecution

By RICHARD D. LYONS

Special to The New York Times

WASHINGTON, Aug. 8—Leon Jaworski, the special Watergate prosecutor, said tonight after President Nixon's resignation speech that no deals had been either made or offered that would have given Mr. Nixon immunity from prosecution on any charges that might stem from the Watergate scandal.

"There has been no agreement or understanding of any sort between the President or his representatives and the special prosecutor relating in any way to the President's resignation," Mr. Jaworski said in a statement issued by his office.

Mr. Jaworski's words, plus the fact that the President made no mention of the immunity issue in his address to the nation, left open the possibility, at least for the moment, that Mr. Nixon might be charged and stand trial.

**No Immunity Sought**

Mr. Nixon did not ask for any immunity assurances from Mr. Jaworski before the resignation speech, the prosecutor said, adding that none had been offered.

As Mr. Jaworski put it, "The special prosecutor's office was not asked for any such agreement or understanding and offered none."

"Although I was informed of the President's decision this afternoon, my office did not participate in any way in the President's decision to resign," the statement concluded.

Mr. Jaworski met earlier today with Gen. Alexander M. Haig Jr., the White House chief of staff, but that meeting was said to have been only for the purpose of informing the special prosecutor of what the President would say later in the evening.

The meeting did not take place in the White House, presumably because Mr. Jaworski would have been recognized there, and his visit would have excited speculation.

Earlier today, there were moves in both houses of Congress to grant Mr. Nixon immunity from prosecution, but

Continued on Page 2, Column 4

## The Other Major News

**Wholesale Prices Up**

A new upward surge of farm prices joined a big jump in industrial prices to produce the year's largest monthly increase in the wholesale price index. The rise for July was 3.7 per cent, seasonally adjusted, and 3.9 per cent before adjustment. Page 45.

**Election Bill Voted**

The House approved by a vote of 355 to 48 a broad campaign-finance reform bill. The measure would set limits on political contributions, restrict candidate spending and provide subsidies for Presidential primaries, conventions and elections. The bill now goes to a House-Senate conference committee. Page 36.

**Cyprus Talks Open**

The foreign ministers of Greece, Turkey and Britain met in Geneva to try to work out an effective cease-fire on Cyprus and to tackle the political problems behind the fighting there. Page 16.

On Cyprus, acting President Glafkos Clerides named a moderate Cabinet stripped of any militant proponents of union with Greece.

Mr. Clerides, who will occupy the key posts of Foreign Affairs and Interior, left for Athens on his way to Geneva for the talks on a political settlement. Page 16.

**10 Police Accused**

Ten New York City police sergeants were arrested for allegedly participating in a "club" that collected more than $250,000 over a decade from legitimate businesses and illegal rackets operations in Queens. Page 68.

**Meskill Named Judge**

Gov. Thomas J. Meskill of Connecticut was nominated by President Nixon to a seat on the Federal bench. Mr. Meskill, a Republican, stunned the state Republican party earlier this year by declining to run for a second term amid reports that he had been offered a judgeship. Page 38.



NEWS INDEX

| | Page | | Page |
|---|---|---|---|
| About New York | 7 | Man in the News | 8 |
| Art | 35 | Movies | 19-25 |
| Books | 31 | Music | 19-25 |
| Bridge | 30 | Obituaries | 36 |
| Business | 43-53 | Op-Ed | 33 |
| Crossword | 31 | Sports | 27-30 |
| Editorials | 32 | Theaters | 19-25 |
| Family/Style | 39 | Transportation | 66 |
| Financial | 43-53 | TV and Radio | 67 |
| Going Out Guide | 22 | Weather | 66 |

News Summary and Index, Page 35




## *A Tiny G.O.P. Bastion Feels Loss and Relief*

By PRANAY GUPTE

Special to The New York Times

SHELTER ISLAND, L.I., Aug. 8—Six years after he put it on his car, Evans K. Griffing sadly stripped off his bold, red-lettered bumper sticker today — the one that said "NIXON."

Mr. Griffing felt a sense of loss. So did hundreds of people in this conservative community 100 miles east of New York City.

In 1968 and 1972, Suffolk County gave Richard M. Nixon the largest single election plurality of any county in the United States. Today all that had changed on Shelter Island.

As the hour of the President's resignation announcement approached, many islanders expressed both a feeling of hurt at having been "betrayed" by Mr. Nixon and relief that he was leaving office.

"We tried to stay by him till the very end," said Thomas L. Jernick, the Town Supervisor. "But when he disclosed on Monday that he had covered up his role in Watergate, we couldn't support him any more. He lied to us, and for a President of the United States to lie is inexcusable."

"We really believed in Mr. Nixon" was a phrase used again and again by dozens of islanders today.

At the same time they spoke hopefully of the Ford Administration and of moving urgently to tasks long neglected—ending the nation's political turmoil and easing its economic distress.

Shelter Island has 1,800 year-round residents, most of whom are registered Republicans.

Only last June interviews with islanders indicated that whatever else Watergate had done, it apparently had not diluted Shelter Island's faith in Mr. Nixon. People said at the time that they felt the President was being vilified by the media

Continued on Page 7, Column 6

## *Only Nixon Is Serene At Sad White House*

By PHILIP SHABECOFF

Special to The New York Times

WASHINGTON, Aug. 8—On his 2,027th and penultimate day as President of the United States, with his staff and family unable to conceal their anguish, Richard M. Nixon went composedly through the schedule of a busy President.

He met with his Vice President and the bipartisan leadership of Congress. He appointed Federal judges, accepted resignations from executive agencies and signed several laws.

He vetoed as inflationary an appropriation bill for the Department of Agriculture and the Environmental Protection Agency.

He also announced, over national television, that tomorrow he would resign his high office.

Mr. Nixon did not loosen his self control even when he talked of his "regret" and his "sadness" at leaving the Presidency. His delivery, with its familiar half-smiles, did not reflect the momentous message he had for his audience: that at noon tomorrow he would become the first healthy, living American President to leave office before his term expired.

At 12:30 this afternoon, the White House press secretary, Ronald L. Ziegler, announced that the President would address the nation at 9 P.M.

Mr. Ziegler did not say what the speech would be about. He did not have to. He choked on his words several times and was struggling visibly to keep himself under control as he left the rostrum of the packed but hushed briefing room at the White House.

The young women who work in the press office went through the motions of their jobs while tears streamed down their faces.

But the President himself, according to his appointments

Continued on Page 3, Column 6

GERALD R. FORD

"All the News That's Fit to Print"

# The New York Times

LATE CITY EDITION

Weather: Partly sunny today; cool tonight. Partly sunny tomorrow. Temp. range: today 65-78; Friday 68-84. Highest Temp.-Hum. Index yesterday: 78. Details on Page 58.

VOL. CXXIII ... No. 42,567  NEW YORK, SATURDAY, AUGUST 10, 1974 — 20c beyond 50-mile radius of New York City except Long Island. Higher in air delivery cities. — 15 CENTS

# FORD SWORN IN AS PRESIDENT; ASSERTS 'NIGHTMARE IS OVER'

## Nixon Bids an Emotional Farewell to Washington

Associated Press

Gerald R. Ford takes the Presidential oath, administered by Chief Justice Warren E. Burger. Mrs. Ford attends the White House ceremony.

### TEARS AT PARTING

#### Ex-President Warns Against Bitterness and Revenge

By JAMES T. WOOTEN
Special to The New York Times

WASHINGTON, Aug. 9 — Richard M. Nixon, his face wet with tears, bade an emotional farewell to the remnants of his broken Administration today, urging its members to be proud of their record in government and warning them against bitterness, self-pity and revenge.

"Always remember, others may hate you," he told mem-

*The text of Nixon's speech is printed on Page 4.*

bers of his Cabinet and staff in a final gathering at the White House, "but those who hate you don't win unless you hate them—and then you destroy yourself."

Shortly thereafter, for the last time as President of the United States, he strode up the ramp of the plane that had taken him to the capitals of the world and was flown home to California, where his career in American politics began nearly thirty years ago.

It was 11:35 A.M. here when President Nixon's letter of resignation was delivered to the office of Secretary of State Kissinger. This is what it said:

"Dear Mr. Secretary: I hereby resign the office of President of the United States. Sincerely, Richard Nixon."

**Greeted by 5,000**

Soon after his departure, while the giant jet was soaring high above the heartland of the country, Gerald R. Ford was sworn in here as the nation's President.

Despite that new status, 5,000 people greeted his arrival in his native state at El Toro Marine Base. They cheered and applauded when, with his wife, Pat, standing nearby, Mr. Nixon stepped to a waiting microphone, squinted into the brilliant midday heat and said, "We're home."

After a few more remarks, a helicopter whisked the former President, Mrs. Nixon, their daughter Tricia and her husband Edward F. Cox, to La Casa Pacifica, the sprawling seaside villa near San Clemente.

Mr. Nixon's day began in the mist and rain of a humid Washington morning, when Manolo Sanchez, his long-time valet, laid out the clothes he would wear during the final hours of

Continued on Page 4, Column 1

### G.M. to Raise Prices 9.5% On 1975 Cars and Trucks

Special to The New York Times

DETROIT, Aug. 9—The General Motors Corporation announced today that it would raise prices of 1975 model cars and trucks by an average of $480 or 9.5 per cent.

The price increase will include about $130, or 2.5 per cent for government-required pollution control equipment—catalytic converters, while $350, or 7 per cent, will be to cover added labor and material costs, the corporation said.

Mack W. Worden, G.M. vice president, made the announcement in a letter sent to dealers Thursday and released publicly today. G.M. is traditionally the price pace-setter for the auto industry. The increases it sets are expected to be matched by its competitors.

**Ford Sending Notices**

The Ford Motor Company has already told its dealers it is sending them advanced billing notices of an average 8 per cent increase above the 1974 prices, which is calculated to mean an increase ranging from about $225 to $800, depending on the model.

Chrysler Corporation officials have indicated their price increases will be in the same area.

A Chrysler spokesman said today that next week "we are going to begin mailing tentative price bulletins on 1975 trucks. They will be in the same ball park as the G.M. and Ford increases. But that is as much as we are going to say at the present time."

Mr. Worden, in charge of the G.M. marketing staff, said that "based on past practice we would expect the Bureau of Labor Statistics will recognize 'the catalytic converter's added value and not consider it a price increase in their published data."

Mr. Worden told the dealers G.M recognized the increases were "substantial" but said the corporation had "no alternative in light of rapidly rising labor and material costs over which we have only limited control and the necessity of complying with 1975 emission standards, which have been mandated by the Government."

As for the other auto com-

Continued on Page 36, Column 4

### Friedmann Case Ends

The third and last person charged with the 1972 murder of Wolfgang Friedmann, Columbia University law professor, pleaded guilty to robbery last night. The others had earlier pleaded guilty to robbery. As a result, none of those who have admitted robbing the professor will be convicted of murdering him. Page 33.

### PAPERS AND TAPES ISSUES IN CAPITAL

#### Impoundment of Nixon Data in White House Is Urged by Some in Congress

By RICHARD D. LYONS
Special to The New York Times

WASHINGTON, Aug. 9—On the heels of Richard M. Nixon's resignation, some members of Congress were urging impoundment of Presidential documents still in the White House. A few even demanded that the Watergate investigations be continued.

But Representative Peter W. Rodino Jr. said after a morning discussion of whether his House Judiciary Committee should make another attempt to obtain the 147 subpoenaed Presidential tape recordings that "we're not an investigative body."

"Our inquiry is at an end," the New Jersey Democrat said in expressing what seemed to be the feeling of the majority of the membership of both houses of Congress.

Yet the disposition and even ownership of the vast amount of Presidential records, some of which could be used as evidence in forthcoming trials, was a recurring question that remained unresolved.

As Representative Jonathan

Continued on Page 7, Column 6

### Aide Doubtful That Ford Would Give Nixon Pardon

By LESLEY OELSNER
Special to The New York Times

WASHINGTON, Aug. 9—The new White House press secretary, J. F. terHorst, suggested today that President Ford was not likely to grant a pardon to former President Nixon. The press secretary was asked at a briefing this afternoon about the prospects of a pardon.

He replied that he had not spoken to Mr. Ford about the question directly, but that the President had apparently stated his position on the matter last fall, during the Senate confirmation hearings into his nomination as Vice President.

"I do not think the public would stand for it," Mr. Ford said then.

Mr. Nixon's prospects for avoiding criminal prosecution thus remained in doubt, with the office of the special Watergate prosecutor saying only that a decision on whether to prosecute had not been made.

Mr. Nixon lost whatever immunity from prosecution that he may have had when he resigned today. According to Mr. terHorst, Mr. Nixon did not try to pardon himself before leaving office, nor did he grant pardons to anyone else.

Some Republican members of Congress urged today that Mr. Nixon not be prosecuted, saying that he had already suffered enough. But even among Republicans, the sentiment was not unanimous.

Senator Edward W. Brooke, Republican of Massachusetts, submitted a resolution to the Senate yesterday expressing the "sense" of the Congress

Continued on Page 5, Column 3

### 4 NAMED TO HELP FORD'S TRANSITION

#### All on New Panel Served in House—President Vows Open Administration

By JOHN HERBERS
Special to The New York Times

WASHINGTON, Aug. 9—Immediately after he was sworn in today as the nation's 38th President, Gerald R. Ford took control of the Presidency and moved to give it a character and shape different from that of his predecessor, Richard M. Nixon.

After declaring in his inaugural speech that "here the people rule," President Ford named a four-member committee composed of former elected officials to oversee the transition and make recommendations for staff changes.

The four are William W. Scranton, former Governor of Pennsylvania; Donald M. Rumsfeld, Ambassador to the North Atlantic Treaty Organization and a former Republican member of Congress from Illinois; Rogers C. B. Morton, Secretary of the Interior and a former

Continued on Page 5, Column 3

### A Plea to Bind Up Watergate Wounds

By MARJORIE HUNTER
Special to The New York Times

WASHINGTON, Aug. 9—Gerald Rudolph Ford became the 38th President of the United States today, declaring that "our long national nightmare is over."

Calling upon the nation to "bind up the internal wounds of Watergate," he said, "Our Constitution works. Our great Republic is a government of laws and not of men. Here the people rule."

And then, his voice filled with emotion, he urged the nation to pray for his predecessor

*The text of Ford's address will be found on Page 3.*

and friend of a quarter century, Richard Milhous Nixon.

"May our former President, who brought peace to millions, find it for himself," he said.

Mr. Ford assumed the powers of the Presidency at 11:35 A.M., the moment that Mr. Nixon's letter of resignation was handed to Secretary of State Kissinger.

Then, at 12:03 P.M., he was administered the oath of office in the historic East Room of the White House by Chief Justice Warren E. Burger before an overflow crowd of friends, the Cabinet and former Congressional colleagues from both parties.

**Wife Holds Bible**

It was in that same room, scarcely two hours earlier, that Mr. Nixon said an emotional good-by to his Cabinet and top aides.

Raising his right hand, Mr. Ford rested his left hand on a Bible held by his wife and opened to one of his favorite passages, the fifth and sixth verses of the third chapter of Proverbs: "Trust in the Lord with all thine heart; and lean not unto thine own understanding. In all thy ways acknowledge Him, and He shall direct thy paths."

Then, in a firm voice, he took the oath of office: "I, Gerald R. Ford, do solemnly swear that I will faithfully execute the office of President of the United States and will to the best of my ability preserve, protect and defend the Constitution of the United States."

As the heavy applause ended, the 61-year-old President began perhaps the most moving speech of his career. Speaking in his flat, Middle Western tone, but with what appeared to be a new sense of self-assurance, he said that he was assuming the Presidency under circumstances never before experienced by Americans.

**Minds Are Troubled**

"This is an hour of history that troubles our minds and hurts our hearts," he said.

"Therefore," he continued, "I feel it is my first duty to make an unprecedented compact with my countrymen. Not an inaugural address, not a fireside chat, not a campaign speech. Just a little straight talk among friends. I intend it to be the first of many."

As the first American to assume the office after the resignation of a President, Mr. Ford said that he was "acutely aware that you have not elected me as your President by your ballots."

"So I ask you to confirm me as your President with your prayers," he added.

He declared that he had not gained office by secret promises, that he had not campaigned either for the Presidency or the Vice-Presidency.

"I have not subscribed to any partisan platform," he said. "I am indebted to no man and only to one woman, my dear wife."

This was reminiscent of his earlier "I am my own man," a declaration that he repeated frequently in recent months as he sought to remain loyal to Mr. Nixon and at the same time hold himself above the spreading taint of the Watergate affair.

He said that while he had not sought the responsibility, he would not shirk it. He said that those who nominated him and confirmed him just eight months ago as Vice President were his friends from both parties.

"It is only fitting then that I

Continued on Page 3, Column 1

### Gains of Watergate

#### Positive and Hopeful Results Found As the Transition Is Made Smoothly

By CLIFTON DANIEL
Special to The New York Times

News Analysis

WASHINGTON, Aug. 9—Watergate has now joined Teapot Dome, Credit Mobilier and the Whisky Ring in the lexicon of political infamy. Yet, in millions of minds it also symbolizes the finest hour of American democracy. A President has been deposed, but the Republic endures. Its institutions have survived, and some are saying they have been strengthened as well. Even the Presidency, which Richard M. Nixon professed to be so anxious to protect, shows no signs of debility. The man in the White House is as powerful today as he was yesterday, although his name has changed from Nixon to Ford.

He is just as powerful, although, as the new President said today, he is "acutely aware" that he was not elected by the votes of the people, whereas his predecessor had the largest popular majority in history.

Under the United States Constitution, removal of the President requires drastic surgery, not just a shift in the political balance, as it does in the parliamentary democracies.

However, the surgery performed on the American Government this week, while agonizing and painful, has done a minimum of visible damage to the body politic.

Mr. Nixon himself has said that one way to judge a country is to see how it effects a transfer of power. Today's transfer was effected without missing a heartbeat.

"Our Constitution works," President Ford proclaimed, after taking the oath of office. "Here the people rule."

"All in all," William P.

Continued on Page 7, Column 2

The New York Times/Mike Lien

President Nixon at ceremony where he bade his Cabinet and staff good-by. At left is his daughter Julie Eisenhower.

### President and Kissinger Confer With the Envoys of 60 Nations

By BERNARD GWERTZMAN
Special to The New York Times

WASHINGTON, Aug. 9 — President Ford undertook to convince foreign governments today that he would pursue the same foreign policy objectives that brought wide respect to Richard M. Nixon.

Two hours after taking the oath as President, Mr. Ford, assisted by Secretary of State Kissinger, who will retain his office, began meeting with about 60 envoys—some in groups and some individually—in brief sessions that lasted into the early evening.

The substance of what was said was, in general, a reaffirmation of well-known American policy positions. But Mr. Ford and Mr. Kissinger believed the exercise to be necessary to emphasize that there would be no significant change during the transition period in which Mr. Ford, who is less experienced in foreign affairs than his predecessor, makes his leadership felt.

Priority was given to a group meeting in the Roosevelt Room of the White House with members of the North Atlantic Treaty Organization. In a pattern followed in the other sessions, Mr. Kissinger and members of his staff met with 13 envoys for about 20 minutes

Continued on Page 6, Column 6



NEWS INDEX


| | Page | | Page |
|---|---|---|---|
| Antiques | 26 | Letters | 28 |
| Art | 25 | Movies | 18-20 |
| Books | 27 | Music | 18-20 |
| Bridge | 26 | Obituaries | 32 |
| Business | 35-44 | Op-Ed | 29 |
| Churches | 27 | Society | 35 |
| Crossword | 27 | Sports | 21-25 |
| Editorials | 28 | Theaters | 18-20 |
| Family/Style | 34 | Transportation | 58 |
| Financial | 35-44 | TV and Radio | 59 |
| Going Out Guide | 20 | Weather | 58 |

News Summary and Index, Page 31

"All the News That's Fit to Print"

# The New York Times

LATE CITY EDITION

Weather: Warm, partly sunny today; partly cloudy tonight, tomorrow. Temp. range: today 62-78; Sunday 58-77. Highest Temp.-Hum. Index yesterday: 72. Details on Page 66.

VOL. CXXIII..No. 42,597 — NEW YORK, MONDAY, SEPTEMBER 9, 1974 — 20 CENTS



Higher in air delivery cities.

# FORD GIVES PARDON TO NIXON, WHO REGRETS 'MY MISTAKES'

## U.S.-Bound Plane With 88 Crashes in Sea Off Greece

### All on T.W.A. Flight From Tel Aviv Are Believed Dead—Wreckage Is Sighted

By The Associated Press

ATHENS, Sept. 8 — A Trans World Airlines jet bound for the United States with 88 persons aboard crashed today in the stormy Ionian Sea off Greece. The Greek Civil Aviation Authority said there appeared to be no survivors.

T.W.A. said that the Boeing 707 fell from an overcast sky after the pilot reported that an engine had failed.

Flight 841 originated in Tel Aviv, stopped in Athens and was scheduled to make stops in Rome and New York.

The airline's Tel Aviv office said 49 passengers boarded the plane there for Rome and the United States. They included 17 Americans, including a baby, 13 Japanese, four Italians, four French, three Indians, two Iranians, two Israelis, two Sri Lankans, an Australian and a Canadian.

The nationalities of 30 other passengers and the nine crew members were not immediately known. [Reuters reported a total of 37 Americans aboard.]

[In Beirut, it was reported that a Palestinian youth organization said it had placed a guerrilla aboard the plane with a bomb. In New York, however, a spokesman for T.W.A. said sabotage was "highly unlikely."]

"All that can be seen by our overflying planes are remnants of the wreckage and bodies floating on the surface," said a Greek aviation official. "The stormy sea in the area is making it difficult for our ships to approach.

"Only when our ships can get nearer will we be able to

Continued on Page 6, Column 1

0 Miles 300 — RUMANIA — YUGOSLAVIA — BULGARIA — ALB. — Athens — GREECE

The New York Times/Sept. 9, 1974

## 'PAIN' EXPRESSED

### Ex-President Cites His Sorrow at the Way He Handled Watergate

By EVERETT R. HOLLES

Special to The New York Times

SAN CLEMENTE, Calif., Sept. 8—President Ford's pardon for Richard M. Nixon evoked today from the former President an expression of "regret and pain at the anguish my mistakes over Watergate have caused the nation and the Presidency."

Within 10 minutes after the Presidential pardon was announced in Washington, Mr. Nixon's statement was released at his Casa Pacifica estate, citing his sorrow in allowing Watergate to become "a national tragedy."

"That the way I tried to deal with Watergate was the wrong way is the burden I shall bear for every day of the life that is left in me," he said.

**Hopes Burden Is Lifted**

In a subsequent statement, given in response to reporters' questions, an aide quoted Mr. Nixon as saying that, in grate fully accepting the Presidential pardon, he hoped Mr. Ford's "compassionate act would contribute to lifting the burdens of Watergate from our country."

When the Nixon statement was released by his adviser and former White House press secretary, Ronald L. Ziegler, Mr. and Mrs. Nixon were already on the way to a new haven of seclusion away from the heavily guarded Casa Pacifica.

They left at 7 A.M., Pacific Coast time, in a large black limousine accompanied by Secret Service agents and Mr. Nixon's military aide, Lieut. Col. Jack Brennan, reportedly for the Palm Desert estate of Walter H. Annenberg, Ambassador to Britain.

A close friend of the Nixons said the former President planned to play golf on the Annenberg private 18-hole course.

[In New York, Mr. Nixon's daughter, Julie Nixon Eisenhower, said that her father had gone to the Annenberg estate "for a rest," The Associated Press reported.]

Mr. Ziegler and Mr. Nixon's appointments secretary, Stephen

Continued on Page 24, Column 1

Richard M. Nixon in a photo made earlier this year

Associated Press

President Ford speaking at the White House yesterday

## The Statement by Nixon

I have been informed that President Ford has granted me a full and absolute pardon for any charges which may be brought against me for actions taken during the time I was the President of the United States. In accepting this pardon, I hope that his compassionate act will contribute to lifting the burden of Watergate from our country.

Here in California, my perspective on Watergate is quite different than it was while I was embattled in the midst of the controversy while I was still subject to the unrelenting daily demand of the Presidency itself.

Looking back on what is still in my mind a complex and confusing maze of events, decisions, pressures, and personalities, one thing I can see clearly now is that I was wrong in not acting more decisively and more forthrightly in dealing with Watergate, particularly when it reached the stage of judicial proceedings and grew from a political scandal into a national tragedy.

No words can describe the depths of my regret and pain at the anguish my mistakes over Watergate have caused the nation and the Presidency, a nation I so deeply love and an institution I so greatly respect.

I know that many fair-minded people believe that my motivation and actions in the Watergate affair were intentionally self-serving and illegal. I now understand how my own mistakes and misjudgments have contributed to that belief and seemed to support it. This burden is the heaviest one of all to bear.

That the way I tried to deal with Watergate was the wrong way is a burden I shall bear for every day of the life that is left to me.

## Proclamation of Pardon

Richard Nixon became the thirty-seventh President of the United States on January 20, 1969, and was re-elected in 1972 for a second term by the electors of forty-nine of the fifty states. His term in office continued until his resignation on August 9, 1974.

Pursuant to resolutions of the House of Representatives, its Committee on the Judiciary conducted an inquiry and investigation on the impeachment of the President extending over more than eight months. The hearings of the committee and its deliberations, which received wide national publicity over television, radio, and in printed media, resulted in votes adverse to Richard Nixon on recommended Articles of Impeachment.

As a result of certain acts or omissions occurring before his resignation from the office of President, Richard Nixon has become liable to possible indictment and trial for offenses against the United States. Whether or not he shall be so prosecuted depends on findings of the appropriate grand jury and on the discretion of the authorized prosecutor. Should an indictment ensue, the accused shall then be entitled to a fair trial by an impartial jury, as guaranteed to every individual by the Constitution.

It is believed that a trial of Richard Nixon, if it became necessary, could not fairly begin until a year or more has elapsed. In the meantime, the tranquility to which this nation has been restored by the events of recent weeks could be irreparably lost by the prospects of bringing to trial a former President of the United States. The prospects of such trial will cause prolonged and divisive debate over the propriety of exposing to further punishment and degradation a man who has already paid the unprecedented penalty of relinquishing the highest elective office in the United States.

NOW, THEREFORE, I, Gerald R. Ford, President of the United States, pursuant to the pardon power conferred upon me by Article II, Section 2, of the Constitution, have granted and by these presents do grant a full, free, and absolute pardon unto Richard Nixon for all offenses against the United States which he, Richard Nixon, has committed or may have committed or taken part in during the period from January 20, 1969, through August 9, 1974.

IN WITNESS WHEREOF, I have hereunto set my hand this 8th day of September in the year of our Lord nineteen hundred seventy-four, and of the independence of the United States of America the 199th.

## NO CONDITIONS SET

### Action Taken to Spare Nation and Ex-Chief, President Asserts

By JOHN HERBERS

Special to The New York Times

WASHINGTON, Sept. 8—President Ford granted former President Richard M. Nixon an unconditional pardon today for all Federal crimes that he "committed or may have committed or taken part in" while in office, an act Mr. Ford said was intended to spare Mr. Nixon and the nation further punishment in the Watergate scandals.

Mr. Nixon, in San Clemente, Calif., accepted the pardon, which exempts him from indictment and trial for, among

*Text of the Ford statement is printed on Page 24.*

other things, his role in the cover-up of the Watergate burglary. He issued a statement saying that he could now see he was "wrong in not acting more decisively and more forthrightly in dealing with Watergate."

**'Act of Mercy'**

Philip W. Buchen, the White House counsel, who advised Mr. Ford on the legal aspects of the pardon, said the "act of mercy" on the President's part was done without making any demands on Mr. Nixon and without asking the advice of the Watergate special prosecutor, Leon Jaworski, who had the legal responsibility to prosecute the case.

Reaction to the pardon was sharply divided, but not entirely along party lines. Most Democrats who commented voiced varying degrees of disapproval and dismay, while most Republican comment backed President Ford.

However, Senators Edward W. Brooke of Massachusetts and Jacob K. Javits of New York disagreed with the action. [Page 25.]

**Dangers Seen in Delay**

Mr. Buchen said that, at the President's request, he had asked Mr. Jaworski how long it would be, in the event Mr. Nixon was indicted, before he could be brought to trial and that Mr. Jaworski had replied it would be at least nine months or more, because of the enormous amount of publicity the charges against Mr. Nixon had received when the House Judiciary Committee recommended impeachment.

This was one reason Mr. Ford cited for granting the pardon, saying he had concluded that "many months and perhaps more years will have to pass before Richard Nixon could obtain a fair trial by jury in any jurisdiction of the United States under governing decisions of the Supreme Court."

"During this long period of delay and potential litigation, ugly passions would again be aroused, our people would

Continued on Page 24, Column 4

## State Panel Charges City Fails to Pursue Fugitives

By SELWYN RAAB

The State Commission of Investigation disclosed yesterday that the backlog of missing bail jumpers and probation violators in the city had risen during the last three years from 82,000 to 130,000.

After sifting through voluminous police and court records, the commission largely blamed the Police Department's warrant division for the 50 per cent increase since 1971 in unexecuted warrants for criminal defendants who fail to appear in court. The police division is primarily responsible for capturing such fugitives.

Sharply criticizing the performance of the division over the last three years, the investigation commission said in a report that it had found that warrant officers rarely worked at night or on weekends and that a typical attempt to track down a fugitive consisted of no more than one or two visits to an often fictitious home address given by the suspect.

The commission described the problem of fugitives here as "critical to the public safety" and called for a major reorganization of the warrant division.

"At the present time the people of New York City are unnecessarily subjected to the risk of grave harm from known criminals because of ineffective warrant enforcement," the commission declared in its report.

In response to the findings, Police Commissioner Michael J. Codd said he was "concerned" by the growing backlog, and he hinted there might be a reorganization of the warrant division.

He also announced the assignment of First Deputy Com-

Continued on Page 21, Column 1

## Jaworski Won't Challenge Pardon, Spokesman Says

By JOHN M. CREWDSON

Special to The New York Times

WASHINGTON, Sept. 8 — Leon Jaworski, the Watergate special prosecutor, apparently has no plans to challenge the validity of the unconditional pardon that President Ford bestowed today on Richard M. Nixon, according to a spokesman for Mr. Jaworski.

The special prosecutor "accepts the decision," said John Barker, the spokesman. "He thinks it's within the President's power to do it. His feeling is that the President is exercising his lawful power, and he accepts it."

Mr. Barker added that Mr. Jaworski had not been consulted in advance on the decision by either Mr. Ford or White House lawyers, and learned of the President's position less than an hour before it was announced.

Some lawyers, including Senator Edmund S. Muskie, Democrat of Maine, questioned the legal and constitutional validity of a Presidential pardon conferred before an indictment had been brought or a conviction obtained.

"It could be challenged," declared Mr. Muskie, adding "there are those who say that it ought to be challenged, lest the precedent be established in an undesirable way."

But the remarks by Mr. Barker and by other lawyers familiar with the Watergate prosecutions indicated strongly that Mr. Jaworski was little inclined to test the pardon by seeking to indict Mr. Nixon, which one authority described as "the way to do it."

The principal Watergate grand jury voted earlier this

Continued on Page 25, Column 6

## Nixon Tapes Must Be Kept 3 Years for Use in Court

By R. W. APPLE Jr.

Special to The New York Times

WASHINGTON, Sept. 8 — Richard M. Nixon and the Ford Administration have reached an agreement under which the former President will ultimately be permitted to destroy the White House tape recordings that led to his downfall.

The agreement, announced today by the White House, also provides that all of Mr. Nixon's Presidential papers and tapes will be preserved for three years for possible use in court cases arising out of the Watergate scandals.

Mr. Nixon signed the agreement in San Clemente, Calif., on Friday; it was countersigned yesterday by Arthur F. Sampson, head of the General Services Administration.

Philip W. Buchen, counsel for President Ford, said at a White House briefing this afternoon that Mr. Ford instructed him about 10 days ago to resolve the controversy over the White House files so the Administration would not find itself "enmeshed for a long time" in jurisdictional disputes.

Although Mr. Buchen denied

Continued on Page 26, Column 1

## CANDIDATES SKIRT LAWS ON FINANCING

### Evidence Shows Big Money Played a Major Role—Voting Is Tomorrow

By FRANK LYNN

Big money—from family fortunes and large contributors—played a major role in the Democratic primary campaigns despite new state and Federal

*Ballot and candidate list appear on Page 28.*

campaign-finance laws that were supposed to have reduced its influence.

The question of how much money was spent and where it came from was being discussed as the primary campaigns drew to a close. The polls will be open tomorrow in the city from 6 A.M. to 9 P.M. and in the rest of the state from noon to 9 P.M.

Interviews with campaign aides and campaign financial reports show that there was considerable evidence of circumventing of the new laws in fact and in spirit, possible unrecorded cash contributions and spending and even "laundering" of campaign contribu-

Continued on Page 28, Column 1

## Knievel Safe as Rocket Falls Into Snake Canyon

By JON NORDHEIMER

Special to The New York Times

TWIN FALLS, Idaho, Sept. 8 —Evel Knievel failed today in an attempt to rocket 1,600 feet across the Snake River Canyon when a tail parachute deployed prematurely on the take-off of his vehicle.

The vehicle, which Mr. Knievel calls the Sky-Cycle X-2, went streaking to about 1,000 feet above the river before floating into the canyon to make a nose-down crash landing on a rocky bank at the river's edge.

Mr. Knievel was pulled from the craft several minutes later by a rescue team. He had superficial cuts and scrapes of the face and legs.

The flight aborted almost as soon as steam exploded from a rear nozzle of the 13-foot-long craft and propelled it along a 108-foot launching track aimed at the cloudless sky.

A drogue parachute designed to slow the rocket at an altitude of 2,800 feet deployed while the vehicle was still on the ramp, whipping in a blast of steam.

Once the vehicle lifted off the ramp, it turned belly up and the main chute, attached to the drogue, was automatically deployed at about 1,000 feet.

A large crowd along the canyon's south rim gasped as a 15-mile-an-hour wind blew the vehicle back toward them, rocking gently in the air nose-down like a red, white and blue Christmas ornament.

For several seconds, it appeared that Mr. Knievel, who could be seen struggling inside the open cockpit, might crash into the crowd on the rim of the canyon.

But the vehicle dropped onto a boulder-strewn ledge, bounced twice on its bottom and came to rest about 20 feet from the water's edge.

The vehicle was obscured from sight from the plateau 540 feet above, and some cries of anguish were heard in the crowd when several minutes went by and there was no sign of the stuntman.

But a helicopter picked him

Continued on Page 50, Column 5

### Chris Evert Beaten

Evonne Goolagong of Australia defeated Chris Evert in the semifinals of the United States Open tennis at Forest Hills, Queens, yesterday, 6-0, 6-7, 6-3, and will meet Billie Jean King in the final today. Details, Page 45.

## Some Mixed Reactions in Foley Square

By PAUL L. MONTGOMERY

A few hours after President Ford's pardon of his predecessor was announced yesterday, Mr. and Mrs. Wilson Wainwright of Olean, N.Y., were strolling in Foley Square in lower Manhattan, looking at the public buildings.

"It's going to make a lot of people mad, but I can see why he did it," Mr. Wainwright said. "It wouldn't look right to the rest of the world to have a President of the United States in jail."

Mr. Wainwright, here on a late-summer vacation, was asked if he had any doubts about former President Richard M. Nixon's guilt.

"None that I can see," his wife, Judy, replied. "I guess some people would say it would have been better to pardon him after the courts decided."

Nearby, at 100 Centre Street, the afternoon session of the arraignment part of Criminal Court was about to begin. In the dingy, crowded room, lawyers and policemen, and defendants and their families lounged on the oak benches, waiting for the judge to return from lunch.

Hal Mayerson and Peter Davis of the Legal Aid Society, which represents indigent defendants, had been discussing the pardon during the break.

"It's a bit unseemly to pardon someone before they're prosecuted," Mr. Davis said. "It doesn't do much for the concept of equal justice under law."

"How about all the young men who refused to serve in an illegal, immoral and vicious war?" Mr. Mayerson asked. "Is he going to pardon them, too? It's like Peter was saying, maybe they should give Nixon a pardon if he does 18 months of alternate service."

Mr. Mayerson looked around the room.

"Seriously, though, it's outrageous," he continued. "You get a lady here who's going to jail for stealing a blouse, or some guy in on assault because he got tired of living with the rats and hit somebody. And here's one of the biggest plun-

Continued on Page 25, Column 6

## terHorst Quits Post To Protest Pardon

Special to The New York Times

WASHINGTON, Sept. 8—J. F. terHorst, whose appointment as White House press secretary was the first in President Ford's new Administration, resigned tonight in what he said was a protest over the granting of an unconditional pardon to former President Nixon.

In a statement released by the White House tonight, Mr. Ford said that he deeply regretted Mr. terHorst's decision.

"I understand his position," the statement said. "I appreciate the fact that good people will differ with me on this very difficult decision. However, it is my judgment that it is in

Continued on Page 28, Column 1

NEWS INDEX



| | Page | | Page |
|---|---|---|---|
| About New York | 62 | Movies | 42-44 |
| Books | 33 | Music | 42-44 |
| Bridge | 32 | Obituaries | 38 |
| Business | 51-56 | Op-Ed | 35 |
| Crossword | 33 | Sports | 45-50 |
| Editorials | 34 | Theaters | 42-44 |
| Family/Style | 40 | Transportation | 66 |
| Financial | 51-56 | TV and Radio | 67-71 |
| Going Out Guide | 43 | U.N. Proceedings | 2 |
| Letters | 34 | Weather | 66 |

News Summary and Index, Page 37

"All the News That's Fit to Print"

# The New York Times

LATE CITY EDITION

Weather: Sunny, warmer today; cold tonight. Chance of rain tomorrow. Temperature range: today 31-47; Thursday 29-38. Details on Page 74.

VOL. CXXIV..No. 42,699 | NEW YORK, FRIDAY, DECEMBER 20, 1974 | Price higher in air delivery cities. | 20 CENTS



# ROCKEFELLER SWORN IN AS VICE PRESIDENT AFTER CONFIRMATION BY HOUSE, 287 TO 128

## Congress Votes $1-Billion For Jobs for Unemployed

By DAVID E. ROSENBAUM

Special to The New York Times

WASHINGTON, Dec. 19 — The House and Senate gave final approval tonight to legislation appropriating $1-billion for jobs for the unemployed next year.

The money was part of a $5-billion appropriations bill that also allocates money for increased unemployment compensation.

President Ford supports the measure and is considered certain to sign it.

It was estimated that the measure would provide 100,000 jobs nationwide at an average salary of $7,500.

More than $2-billion would become available for unemployment compensation, with the exact amount depending on the number of persons out of work next year.

Under the bill, $875-million would be distributed to states and communities to provide public service jobs for the unemployed in such areas as health, education, recreation and sanitation.

The measure specified that $125-million would be distributed through the Economic Development Administration to stimulate public works projects in depressed areas.

Based on the September unemployment statistics and an appropriation of $1-billion, the Labor Department calculated that New York State would get $107-million, of which New York City would get $61-million; New Jersey would get $48-million, and Connecticut $18-million. [Page 4.]

The Senate had authorized $4-billion and the House $2-billion for the public service jobs program. But the authorization figures merely set ceilings on the amount of money that might be made available. The appropriation determines the amount available to be spent.

Meanwhile, today, the Democrats on the House Ways and Means Committee, which has jurisdiction over many of the important economic measures to be considered next year, created six subcommittees and appointed chairmen.

It was the first time the panel formed subcommittees since 1957.

The committee Democrats de-

Continued on Page 10, Column 2

## CITY AND UNIONS SEEK RETIREMENT ON ELECTIVE BASIS

### 510 Workers Who Were to Be Let Go Today Get a Month's Reprieve

By FRED FERRETTI

The city and a group of leaders representing the municipal unions agreed yesterday to seek voluntary retirements of city employes aged 63 to 70 to save the jobs of 860 younger employes. The latter are scheduled to be dismissed in the budget-cutting layoffs recently announced by Mayor Beame.

The agreement is an alternative to an earlier plan, which would have forced the retirement of 860 older Civil Service employes to save the jobs of the younger employes — a plan that on Wednesday was declared illegal by the United States Secretary of Labor, Peter J. Brennan.

First Deputy Mayor James Cavanagh, in announcing the alternative, said that to give union actuaries time to find prospective volunteers, 510 employes scheduled to be dismissed today would get a month's reprieve.

The 510 represented part of the first wave of 1,510 municipal layoffs announced by Mr. Beame on Nov. 22 in an effort to decrease the deficit in the city's $11.1-billion budget.

**The Second Wave**

On Dec. 11 the Mayor called for the discharge of 6,425 more city employes, consisting of 2,200 permanent Civil Service workers, 1,525 appointed provisionals and 2,700 workers aged 65 or older who the Mayor said would not receive renewals of their work extensions and would have to retire by next June 30. In the group of 2,200 were teachers, policemen, firemen and sanitation workers and 350 other permanent Civil Service employes.

The 350, like the first group of 510, are in the New York City Employes Retirement System, one of the city's five pension programs. It was these 860 employes, mostly young members of minority groups and women, who were scheduled to be dismissed and on whom a week's effort was expended in attempts to save their jobs.

After Victor Gotbaum, executive director of the 110,000-member District 37, American Federation of State, County and Municipal Employes, and other union leaders denounced the dismissals, the Mayor met with them and announced a plan to

Continued on Page 25, Column 1

The New York Times/George Tames

Nelson A. Rockefeller being sworn in as Vice President last night by Chief Justice Warren E. Burger. In background from left are Senators Hugh Scott, Jacob K. Javits, Robert C. Byrd, James L. Buckley and Howard W. Cannon.

## SENATE CEREMONY

### He Tells of 'Gratitude for the Privilege of Serving Country'

By LINDA CHARLTON

Special to The New York Times

WASHINGTON, Dec. 19 — Nelson Aldrich Rockefeller was sworn in tonight as the 41st Vice President of the United States.

He was sworn in by Chief Justice Warren E. Burger in a televised ceremony in the Senate chamber.

Mr. Rockefeller became Vice President one day short of four months after his nomination by President Ford. He was escorted to the Senate by Mr. Ford.

*Transcript of the ceremony appears on Page 16.*

Members of Mr. Rockefeller's family, Congress, the Cabinet and New York State dignitaries were among those who witnessed the ceremony.

He took the oath of office with his hand on a family Bible at 10:12 P.M.

The former New York Governor, only the second man to become Vice President without a public vote, took office after the House completed Congressional approval of his nomination by a vote of 287 to 128. The Senate approved him by a vote of 90 to 7 last week.

**Ford Is Pleased**

Immediately after the confirmation vote, the White House issued the following statement by President Ford:

"I am delighted that Nelson Rockefeller has been duly confirmed today to be the 41st Vice President of the United States. I congratulate him and look forward to his participation and assistance in the Administration. I commend the House of Representatives for its confirmation vote today, and the Senate for its vote earlier. Members of the 93d Congress have rendered a service to the nation by filling the constitutional office of the Vice President before adjournment. All Americans will benefit from the distinguished and devoted public service of the new Vice President."

**Oath and Speech**

At just past 10:11 P.M., Mr. Rockefeller raised his right hand to take the oath: "I, Nelson Aldrich Rockefeller, do solemnly swear that I will support and defend the Constitution of the United States . . . ."

When the applause had subsided, Mr. Rockefeller read a short spech to the crowded chamber illuminated by five banks of television lights.

"I feel," he said, "a great sense of gratitude for the privilege of serving the country I love."

He went on to thank all those involved in his nomination—the President, Congress, Betty Ford for "her great warmth and her courage."

"And if you'll forgive me for a personal note, my love and

Continued on Page 16, Column 1

## Cuomo Selected by Carey As His Secretary of State

By FRANCIS X. CLINES

Mario M. Cuomo

Governor-elect Hugh L. Carey announced yesterday that Mario M. Cuomo, a longtime friend, would be appointed Secretary of State, and that Raymond T. Schuler, the incumbent Secretary of Transportation, would be retained in the new administration, which takes office Jan. 1.

Mr. Cuomo, who ran unsuccessfully this year for the Democratic nomination for Lieutenant Governor, will have the responsibilities of his post expanded to include special advisory and trouble-shooting duties, Mr. Carey announced. These include the inquiry into nursing home abuses Mr. Carey charged him with earlier this week, plus executive responsibilities in programs for judicial selection, income disclosure for public officials and the current review of the New York City Charter.

Commissioner Schuler, like Mr. Cuomo, is a Democrat. H has 18 years of career service in the state bureaucracy and was appointed Commissioner two years ago by former Gov. Nelson A. Rockefeller. Under his control, the transportation agency has started to shed its traditional highway-oriented direction and to stress the need for mass transit.

Mr. Cuomo, who is 42 years old, practices law in Brooklyn and lives in Queens with his wife, Matilda, and five children. He is also a law professor at St. John's University Law School. He had been reported concerned about moving to Albany and yesterday he said that in the light of the expanded role being created for Secretary of State, he was not sure whether he would be living upstate. The Department of State, which has headquarters in Albany, oversees the licensing and registration procedures for professions and technical jobs.

Mr. Cuomo said the Governor-elect had emphasized that the post—which politicians in recent years had come to consider a Governor's symbolic Italian-American chamberlain—would not be "an ethnic position."

Mr. Cuomo first came to pub-

Continued on Page 25, Column 2

## Nominee Takes His Oath On the Old Family Bible

By RICHARD L. MADDEN

Special to The New York Times

WASHINGTON, Dec. 19—In a simple but well-organized ceremony in the Senate chamber, Nelson A. Rockefeller held a black family Bible in his left hand tonight and took the oath of office as Vice President.

The oath was administered by Chief Justice Warren E. Burger amid a blaze of lights to accommodate television cameras, the first time they had been allowed in the room. It brought the 66-year-old Mr. Rockefeller within a heartbeat of the Presidency, a job he had been denied three times by the Republican party.

The Bible was the same one that Mr. Rockefeller had used four times when he was sworn in at Albany as Governor of New York, and in it was a note from his father, John D. Rockefeller, Jr., which said:

"This was my mother's Bible, which always lay on the table in the library at 4 West 54th Street, New York. April 1, 1946."

The 25-minute ceremony was a combination of a solemn oath, a brief speech of gratitude, formal expressions of good wishes from Senate leaders and finally hearty applause and handshakes from Representatives who had confirmed Mr. Rockefeller's nomination two hours earlier and from Senators who had done the same last week, as well as some who had

Mr. Rockefeller, wearing a dark blue suit, blue-and-white-striped shirt and dark blue tie, stumbled briefly as he took the first step down to the well of the Senate on entering the chamber. But he recovered his balance quickly, grinned and waved as he strode toward the

Continued on Page 17, Column 1

## Outlook for Rockefeller

### Long Experience in Running Things Is Expected to Reinforce President

By R. W. APPLE Jr.

Special to The New York Times

News Analysis

WASHINGTON, Dec. 19 — Even before Nelson A. Rockefeller was sworn into office, the Washington sharpshooters were reminding him that the principal assignment of most Vice Presidents has been to stay reasonably healthy. In his whimsy for today, for example, Art Buchwald wrote of the Vice President who had to pretend he was the March of Dimes poster child's father just to get into the President's office.

But the fact is that Mr. Rockefeller has the best chance of anyone who has held the Vice-Presidency in recent times to make a real impact on government and politics, despite all the continuing constraints of the No. 2 job.

This is so for two basic reasons.

First, Mr. Rockefeller himself brings to the job a depth of executive experience—years and years of running things, not just talking about them—that is unmatched in this century. He is by disposition and by training an operator, and as one Senator said, "he will find some way to operate."

Second, Mr. Rockefeller joins a President who came to office with no electoral mandate in a time of national crisis, a President who needs reinforcement in a way unique in American political history. That was one of the reasons that Mr. Ford chose him.

Not that it is going to be easy.

Continued on Page 17, Column 3

## 6 SUGAR REFINERS INDICTED BY JURY

### Price-Fixing Conspiracies Alleged in Three Markets in West and Midwest

By HENRY WEINSTEIN

Special to The New York Times

SAN FRANCISCO, Dec. 19—Six major sugar refining companies were indicted today by a Federal Grand Jury on charges of illegal price fixing after an 18-month investigation.

The companies indicted were the Great Western Sugar Company of Denver, the American Crystal Sugar Company, formerly of Denver; the Holly Sugar Corporation of Colorado Springs, Colo.; California and Hawaiian Sugar Company of San Francisco; the Amalgamated Sugar Company of Ogden, Utah; and the Union Sugar Division of the Consolidated Foods Corporation of Chicago. Also named as civil defendants were the National Sugar Beet Growers Federation of Greeley, Colo.; and Utah-Idaho Sugar Company of Salt Lake City, Utah.

The indictments and three companion civil antitrust suits covered acts allegedly committed through the end of 1972. Since then sugar prices have soared, and Robert J. Staal, assistant United States Attorney, stated here today that "the current pricing practices of the sugar industry are still under investigation."

Last month the staff of the Council on Wage and Price Stability said the United States sugar industry had "reaped very large windfall gains" this year from rapidly increasing sugar prices. Mr. Staal declined to state whether a grand jury

Continued on Page 62, Column 4

## TEN ECONOMISTS FAVOR STIMULUS

### Group Meets With Ford's Top Advisers — Details of Some Views Differ

By EDWIN L. DALE Jr.

Special to The New York Times

WASHINGTON, Dec. 19 — Government stimulus for the sliding economy was reported favored by a group of 10 leading private economists at an unpublicized meeting at the White House today.

Participants at the meeting declined to discuss individual views in detail. However, some of the views are well known. But one participant did say, "I can't think of anyone who didn't favor stimulus in some form." The group's members, however, were reported to have differed on numerous important details, including the type of stimulus and how large it should be.

President Ford was not present, but nearly all his chief economic advisers were. Alan Greenspan, chairman of the Council of Economic Advisers, presided.

According to reports, the Government members mainly listened and asked questions and made no attempt to achieve a consensus. Mr. Greenspan had previously pledged to solicit

Continued on Page 54, Column 1

## City's Fire Alarm Boxes Are Called Undependable

By JOHN DARNTON

The city's fire-alarm boxes, connected to a deteriorating network of cables laid more than half a century ago, are becoming dangerously unreliable, according to Fire Department dispatchers, maintenance men and fire fighters.

While some of the old mechanical "pull" boxes have failed in recent months, the new voice-alarm boxes that are replacing them at the rate of 60 a month have developed technological problems of their own. All of these Emergency Response System boxes installed in the city so far—over 1,000—will be replaced by their manufacturer because they have been found to "transmit themselves" during electrical storms.

The scope of the fire-box problem, as the city enters its heavy fire-fatality season, is indicated by the aftereffects of one severe ice storm a year ago. The storm knocked out 2,500 of the department's 15,840 street and building boxes. Most of them were in Queens and many were out of service for weeks.

Since the storm of Dec. 17, 1973, "silent sentries"—alarm boxes that do not work—have been implicated in at least two deaths here so far.

The problem appears most severe in Queens, where aerial cables that have lost their insulation come into contact with tree branches, sometimes grounding entire circuits. In Queens, some circuits carry as many as 80 boxes, contrary to the generally accepted standard of allowing 20 to 30 boxes on a circuit.

But the problem appears in the other boroughs, such as

Continued on Page 38, Column 1

## Export Bank Credit Curbs Are Said to Anger Moscow

By BERNARD GWERTZMAN

Special to The New York Times

WASHINGTON, Dec. 19—The Soviet Union has followed up yesterday's disavowal of a deal on emigration for trade benefits with a private denunciation of Congressional adoption of a ceiling on Export-Import Bank credits to Moscow.

United Press International

According to State Department officials, Ambassador Anatoly F. Dobrynin told Secretary of State Kissinger yesterday that Moscow was angry at what it regarded as the failure of the United States to live up to its side of détente.

Without stating whether the Soviet Union would step up emigration in return for the modest trade benefits approved by Congress, Mr. Dobrynin reportedly was caustic in his complaints, particularly about the credit limitation.

Some officials said that because the additional credits—a ceiling of $300-million over four years, limited to $75-million a year—were lower than Moscow had expected, there was some question whether the Kremlin would go ahead with the informal arrangement to ease emigration restrictions in return for trade concessions. Despite the Soviet denial, the officials insist that such an arrangement exists.

The consensus was that it

Continued on Page 13, Column 1

## Man, 98, Strangled In Brooklyn Robbery

By JOSEPH B. TREASTER

A 98-year-old former yeshiva principal was choked to death with his yarmulke early yesterday morning by thieves who climbed into his ground-floor apartment in the Crown Heights section of Brooklyn as he slept, the police said.

The victim, Nathan Friedler, who was described by neighbors as "a nice, quiet old man," was found tied on his bed, spread-eagled with neckties to the four corner posts. He was found by his daughter, Mrs. Sigmund Schwartz, as she brought him breakfast at about 8 A.M. from her own apartment in the same building at 899 Montgomery Street. The skull cap had been

Continued on Page 74, Column 4

NEWS INDEX


| | Page | | Page |
|---|---|---|---|
| About New York | 25 | Movies | 19-31 |
| Art | 20 | Music | 19-31 |
| Books | 35 | Notes on People | 43 |
| Bridge | 34 | Obituaries | 40 |
| Business | 54-65 | Op-Ed | 37 |
| Crossword | 35 | Society | 45 |
| Editorials | 36 | Sports | 46-53 |
| Family/Style | 44 | Theaters | 19-31 |
| Financial | 54-65 | Transportation | 74 |
| Going Out Guide | 32 | TV and Radio | 75 |
| Man in the News | 2 | Weather | 74 |

News Summary and Index, Page 39




## Watergate Argument

The chief prosecutor at the Watergate cover-up trial began his final argument to the jury yesterday after 46 days of testimony. The prosecutor, James F. Neal, mocked and scorned the five defendants. Page 18.

## Publisher Suspends Luciano Paperback

By NICHOLAS GAGE

New American Library is suspending its plans to publish a paperback edition of "The Last Testament of Lucky Luciano," for which it was going to pay $800,000, according to a company spokesman.

The spokesman, Harold Rosenthal, said the decision was reached following a meeting Wednesday in Boston with executives of Little, Brown & Co., the book's primary publisher.

The New York Times disclosed last Tuesday that an examination of the book, including research into papers and documents concerning Mr. Luciano and more than 20 interviews, produced information that questioned the publisher's

Continued on Page 29, Column 7

"All the News That's Fit to Print"

# The New York Times

LATE CITY EDITION

Weather: Mostly fair, unseasonably mild today, tonight and tomorrow. Temperature range: today 58-71; Monday 57-74. Details on Page 70.

VOL. CXXV . No. 43,018 | NEW YORK, TUESDAY, NOVEMBER 4, 1975 | 25 cents beyond 50-mile zone from New York City, except Long Island. Higher in air delivery cities. | 20 CENTS



# ROCKEFELLER BARS RACE ON FORD TICKET; PRESIDENT NAMES RUMSFELD TO DEFENSE, RICHARDSON TO COMMERCE, BUSH TO C.I.A.

## SWEEPING CHANGE

### Cheney Is White House Staff Chief—General Is Security Adviser

By JAMES M. NAUGHTON

Special to The New York Times

WASHINGTON, Nov. 3 — President Ford tonight confirmed sweeping changes in his national security hierarchy and also announced he would nominate Elliot L. Richardson to succeed Rogers C. B. Morton as Secretary of Commerce.

The President, at a nationally televised news conference, said

*News conference transcript is printed on Page 24.*

that Mr. Morton had expressed a desire some weeks ago to return to the private sector. Mr. Richardson only recently was named Ambassador to Britain. [Opening statement, Page 24.]

The announcement came as the President confirmed the following major changes in his Administration:

¶The nomination of Donald H. Rumsfeld, the White House chief of staff, to succeed James R. Schlesinger as Secretary of Defense.

¶The designation of George Bush, the head of the United States liaison office in Peking, to succeed William E. Colby as Director of Central Intelligence.

¶The elevation of Air Force Lieut. Gen. Brent Scowcroft, the deputy director of the National Security Council, to succeed Henry A. Kissinger, as the White House adviser on national security. Mr. Kissinger will remain Secretary of State.

**For 'Closer Liaison'**

The President also said he would designate Richard B. Cheney to succeed Mr. Rumsfeld as chief of the White House Staff. Mr. Cheney is now a deputy assistant to the President.

Despite what he called a successful foreign policy in his brief Presidency, Mr. Ford explained that he had replaced the Secretary of Defense and the Director of Central Intelligence to provide "closer liaison and cooperation" on national defense and foreign policy matters. [Question 2.]

The President's decision to transfer Mr. Richardson from London to the post of Commerce Secretary was the only element of the Cabinet shuffle

Continued on Page 25, Column 1

The New York Times/Teresa Zabala

President Ford at his televised news session in the White House last night. He told of high-level changes.

The New York Times/Tyrone Dukes

Vice President Rockefeller answering a question during an appearance here Sunday on a television program.

## MUTUAL DECISION

### Vice President's Letter Gives No Reason for His Withdrawal

By PHILIP SHABECOFF

Special to The New York Times

WASHINGTON, Nov. 3—Vice President Rockefeller added today to the sudden upheaval within the Ford Administration by saying that he would not be the President's running mate in 1976.

At his news conference tonight, President Ford said that

*Text of Rockefeller letter appears on Page 27.*

Mr. Rockefeller had not been requested to withdraw as a candidate for election. He said the Vice President had "done a superb job" and had made "a decision on his own" not to seek the election next year.

Mr. Ford said that Mr. Rockefeller had "assured me categorically that he will support me in 1976." [Question 1, Page 24.]

However, the President declined to give any reasons for the Vice President's action. Administration sources said, meanwhile, that the decision had been reached through a mutual understanding between Mr. Ford and Mr. Rockefeller.

**Resignation Not Asked**

These sources said that while the President had not pressed Mr. Rockefeller for a resignation, neither had he asked the Vice President to reconsider. In fact, they said, the President had been aware for about two weeks of Mr. Rockefeller's plan for a public withdrawal from the Vice-Presidential race.

Mr. Rockefeller publicly disclosed the move by releasing a letter to President Ford, which he delivered to the Oval Office of the White House at 10:30 this morning. The President and Vice President met for 20 minutes in an atmosphere described as "extremely cordial" by Ron Nessen, the White House press secretary.

The letter gave no reason for Mr. Rockefeller's action, and aides did not rule out the possibility of his running for President himself.

**'Detrimental' Presence**

One White House source close to the President said that Mr. Rockefeller would have inevitably had to step aside because his presence had become "detrimental" to Mr. Ford's efforts to win the Republican Party nomination.

The White House official said that Mr. Rockefeller had been unable to make his peace with the right wing of the Republican Party. He was, therefore, regarded as a liability by the President Ford Committee, which is seeking to win the party's Presidential nomination for Mr. Ford in the face of an expected strong challenge by former Gov. Ronald Reagan of California, the official explained.

Mr. Reagan is a favorite of the Republican right.

**'The Proper Time'**

President Ford said recently that he would announce "at the proper time" whether or not he wanted Mr. Rockefeller as his running mate in 1976.

Meanwhile, Mr. Rockefeller has grown increasingly uncomfortable in his Vice-Presidential role, according to members of his staff and others familiar with his activities. Senator Jacob K. Javits, Republican of New York, said in a telephone interview today that he had been expecting Mr. Rockefeller's decision for several months.

Senator Javits said that Mr. Rockefeller's position in an Administration tailoring its policies to the most conservative elements in the Republican Party was becoming "untenable." As four-term Governor

Continued on Page 27, Column 1

## House Banking Committee Backs Guarantee for City

### Members Give Measure 50-50 Chance in Vote on Floor Next Week

By MARTIN TOLCHIN

Special to The New York Times

WASHINGTON, Nov. 3—The House Banking Committee today approved, 23 to 16, legislation to authorize $7 billion in loan guarantees to New York City before or after default.

The legislation thus passed its third consecutive test and continued to gain momentum under pressure from the Democratic leadership, despite a threatened Presidential veto and the determined opposition of conservatives and some moderates in both parties.

President Ford, meanwhile, reaffirmed last night his conviction that a New York City default could be avoided, and, if not, that a default would have no significant national repercussions. He also again stated that his differences with Vice President Rockefeller over the New York fiscal crisis were "minimal."

"I believe that New York City can avoid default," the President said. "They can take stronger action than they have

Continued on Page 32, Column 1

### M.A.C. Weighs Proposal for a Trade of Notes for Its Securities

By JOHN DARNTON

Municipal Assistance Corporation officials have scaled down a plan to use union pension funds to borrow money for the city and have combined it with another proposal for averting default—a voluntary exchange of outstanding city notes for M.A.C. bonds.

A similar idea, attempting to persuade holders of short-term notes issued by the city to trade them in for long-term bonds issued by the M.A.C. was proposed several months ago. It did not get far.

Meanwhile, Governor Carey notified the leaders of the State Legislature to "be prepared and on hand" for a special legislative session next Tuesday and Wednesday to deal with the city situation and other urgent matters. [Page 32.]

Because of the possibility of a default by New York City coming as soon as late this month, M.A.C. officials are at least mulling over the hope that holders of city notes would be more receptive now

Continued on Page 32, Column 6

## FORD'S TIMETABLE UPSET IN SHAKEUP

### President's Attempt to Put Imprimatur on His Policies Was Imperiled by Leak

By LESLIE H. GELB

Special to The New York Times

WASHINGTON, Nov. 3—The strategy behind Vice President Rockefeller's withdrawal, the dismissal of Defense Secretary James R. Schlesinger and other possible moves yet to come is to put a distinct Ford imprimatur on his Administration's domestic and foreign policies, Administration sources said today.

The first move was to be the announcement of Mr. Rockefeller's decision not to be Mr. Ford's running mate, a move planned for and made public today, but agreed on between the Vice President and Mr. Ford about two weeks ago. This, the officials said, was to strengthen Mr. Ford's conservative credentials on domestic policy.

The second move—the removal of Mr. Schlesinger and William P. Colby, Director of Central Intelligence, along with Secretary of State Henry A. Kissinger's relinquishing of his job as national security adviser to the President—had been scheduled to be announced this Wednesday. This, the officials

Continued on Page 26, Column 6

## Mixed Impact From Moves Seen

By R. W. APPLE Jr.

Special to The New York Times

News Analysis

WASHINGTON, Nov. 3—The temptation is to say that Vice President Rockefeller's decision not to accept the Vice-Presidential nomination next year has solved one of President Ford's chief problems. That was an interpretation encouraged by officials of the President Ford Committee, one of whom said that "the biggest millstone is off the President's neck now," and some politicians appeared initially to agree.

But the events of the last several days will have wide and subtle ramifications, and many of them may be unfavorable to the President. Trying to gauge them all immediately, as Senator Jesse Helms, Republican of North Carolina said, is "like trying to pick up all the feathers from a busted pillow."

Mr. Rockefeller's decision removed from the 1976 Vice-Presidential competition a man whom the Republican right never forgave, despite his latter-day stylistic and policy changes, for his divisive tactics in 1964 and his espousal of big Government during his long tenure as Governor of New York.

Representative John Ashbrook, the conservative Ohio Republican who challenged President Nixon in 1972, said that the withdrawal would hurt the chances of former Gov. Ronald Reagan of California "because part of Reagan's appeal was the possibility that Rockefeller would be on the ticket."

Governor Reagan said in Florida, where he was campaigning in anticipation of the announcement of his White House candidacy the week of Nov. 17, that Mr. Rockefeller's decision would help President Ford with some Republicans and hurt him with others, but that voters ultimately decided on the basis of the Presidential, not the Vice-Presidential, nominee.

As for himself, he added, "I'm certainly not appeased."

Many other conservative Republicans commented that, taking the development of the Rockefeller withdrawal in its full context, they were unimpressed and thought that Mr.

Continued on Page 26, Column 4

## Behind Shift: Push for Arms Pact

By BERNARD GWERTZMAN

Special to The New York Times

News Analysis

WASHINGTON, Nov. 3—Although President Ford treated the subject of détente cautiously tonight, the dramatic personnel shifts he announced appeared to signal a strengthened determination to strike a new strategic arms agreement with the Soviet Union. Without this accord, the policy of détente would be in serious jeopardy.

In his news conference, Mr. Ford mixed a desire for improved Soviet relations with renewed pledges for a strong national defense, and said that while he wanted a new arms accord, he was not negotiating with Moscow under any "time pressure." [Question 11, Page 24.]

Mr. Ford refused to confirm it, but the dismissal of Secretary of Defense James R. Schlesinger seemed a victory of sorts for Secretary of State Henry A. Kissinger's efforts to seek accommodation with the Russians in the nuclear arms area.

Somewhat surprisingly, given the well-known differences between Mr. Schlesinger and Mr. Kissinger, the President specifically denied in his news conference that the differences were a factor in the dismissal of Mr. Schlesinger [Question 4.]

An unintended consequence of the upheaval may be to give additional arguments to the conservative critics of détente who have been unhappy for some time with Mr. Kissinger.

Senator Henry M. Jackson, a leading "anti-détentist" in Washington, bitterly assailed Mr. Schlesinger's removal as a virtual capitulation to the Russians since he was the best-known Administration skeptic about détente. His voice was not alone.

On the other hand, some advocates of arms control who have been unhappy with the tough negotiating demands of the Pentagon and Mr. Schlesinger tended to see his replacement as an encouraging sign for an accord with Moscow limiting offensive strategic arms.

Insiders insisted that Mr. Schlesinger's dismissal was not due to differences over détente alone and that it would be wrong to attach such a policy motivation to it. As so often happens, however, the perception may be as important as the reality.

If the Kremlin views the dismissal as a forerunner of new concessions on arms control, it may adopt a harder line, waiting for the United States to

Continued on Page 26, Column 1

## Drive for Women's Rights Culminates at Polls Today

By MAURICE CARROLL

"On to the streets! On with the leaflets!" shouted City Council President Paul O'Dwyer, and a crowd of placard-carrying officials swarmed into midday midtown crowds yesterday to urge support of the women's rights amendment that will be on the New York State ballot today.

The supporters, gathered in Bryant Park, first heard Governor Carey offer his endorsement. His five daughters, he said, deserve the same constitutional rights as his seven sons.

"Let us catch up with time," the Governor exhorted a small crowd of paper-bag lunchers and the scowling vagrants who congregate in the park behind the main branch of the Public Library.

It was the major electioneering effort on the final day of a New York campaign that has stirred a minimum of interest.

In New York State, from 6 A.M. until 9 P.M. today, voters will cast ballots on the equal-rights amendment, which bans discrimination on the basis of sex, on six other amendments and on one proposition.

New York City voters will decide whether to adopt 10 amendments to the City Charter.

In New Jersey, from 7 A.M. to 8 P.M., voters will elect their entire 80-member State Assembly, consider an equal-rights amendment similar to New York State's and decide on a $922 million package of spending proposals.

In 158 Connecticut communities, from 6 A.M. to 8 P.M., local officials will be chosen.

New York skies will be cloudy

Continued on Page 20, Column 2

The New York Times/Neal Boenzi

Supporters of New York's equal rights amendment at Bryant Park rally. One woman brought a baby in a carrier.

## Franco Has an Operation To Stem Hemorrhaging

By HENRY GINIGER

Special to The New York Times

MADRID, Tuesday, Nov. 4—Generalissimo Francisco Franco underwent a three-hour emergency operation last night to halt large-scale hemorrhaging in his stomach. Early this morning his doctors said his vital signs had become normal but that the prognosis was "very grave."

The 82-years-old chief of state, who has been battling with great strength against death for more than two weeks, fell into a critical state at 3 P.M. yesterday, when his blood pressure dropped, cardiac insufficiency increased and intense pain set in between his shoulder blades.

The doctors reported that they were unable to halt the internal bleeding and, six-and-one-half hours after it began, the general underwent surgery in the infirmary of the barracks of the palace guard 250 yards from the Pardo Palace.

While Government leaders gathered and Mrs. Franco prayed in the palace chapel, surgeons discovered an acute gastric ulcer that had affected the gastroepploic artery. Both the ulcer and the artery were closed and large amounts of blood were administered.

The general sustained the operation well, the official report said, aside from severe but sporadic electrocardiographic changes that were brought under control.

The Acting Chief of State, Prince Juan Carlos de Borbón had spent much of the day a short distance away in his own Zarzuela Palace trying to deal with the intractable problems of Spanish Sahara, which thousands of Moroccans were approaching, vowing to occupy it. But he too went to the Pardo after the general's condition had taken a turn for the worse.

Although the prognosis had remained grave most of last week, his condition had appeared to stabilize in the last few days and even to show improvement in some aspects.

Attended at the palace by a medical team that had grown to 24, General Franco had amazed both experts and laymen by his resistance.

Yesterday, however, he was reported to have suffered

Continued on Page 23, Column 1

NEWS INDEX


| | Page | | Page |
|---|---|---|---|
| Books | 33 | Movies | 28-31 |
| Bridge | 32 | Music | 28-31 |
| Business | 47-60 | Notes on People | 21 |
| Chess | 32 | Obituaries | 38 |
| Crossword | 33 | Op-Ed | 35 |
| Editorials | 34 | Sports | 42-46 |
| Family/Style | 40-41 | Theaters | 28-31 |
| Financial | 47-60 | Transportation | 70 |
| Going Out Guide | 30 | TV and Radio | 71 |
| Letters | 34 | U.N. Proceedings | 5 |
| Man in the News | 25 | Weather | 70 |

News Summary and Index, Page 37

"All the News That's Fit to Print"

# The New York Times

LATE CITY EDITION

Weather: Partly sunny today; mild tonight. Cloudy, cooler tomorrow. Temperature range: today 45-64; Wednesday 44-70. Details, page 61.

VOL. CXXV ... No. 43,132 | NEW YORK, THURSDAY, FEBRUARY 26, 1976 | 20 CENTS



25 cents beyond 50-mile zone from New York City, except Long Island. Higher in air delivery cities.

# FORD EDGES PAST REAGAN BY 1,300 IN NEW HAMPSHIRE, TAKING 17 OF 21 DELEGATES

## LONG FIGHT LIKELY

### Both Claim Victory in First Formal Test—Carter Is Strong

By R. W. APPLE Jr.

Special to The New York Times

CONCORD, N.H., Feb. 25—President Ford won an exceedingly slender victory over Ronald Reagan in yesterday's New Hampshire Republican primary, one of the closest such elections on record, final returns showed today.

In the first formal test between the two Presidential contenders, Mr. Ford won the nonbinding preferential primary by only about 1,300 votes out of some 108,000 votes — roughly four votes per precinct—over the former California Governor.

In the separate election of delegates to the Republican National Convention, the President apparently won 17 of 21, with some races still in doubt.

**Protracted Struggle**

Neither Mr. Ford nor Mr. Reagan could muster the strength to do any great damage to the other here, and the Reagan camp was reported to be preparing for a protracted struggle between the two candidates.

Among Democrats, Jimmy Carter, the former Governor of Georgia, extended the series of strong showings he had begun in early caucus states, finishing first with about 30 percent of the vote. He also took 13 of the 17 national convention delegates, with the others going to the preferential runner-up, Representative Morris K. Udall of Arizona.

Senator Birch Bayh of Indiana, former Senator Fred R. Harris of Oklahoma, Sargent Shriver and Senator Hubert H. Humphrey of Minnesota, a write-in candidate, trailed Mr. Carter and Mr. Udall in that order.

**Few Surprises**

Despite New Hampshire's reputation as one of the most unpredictable states, voters in both parties provided few surprises yesterday.

Appearing before a meeting of his senior staff in Washington this morning, President Ford said that his victory here would serve as "a great springboard" to nomination on the first ballot and to victory over the Democrats in November.

In Charleston, Ill., where he was seeking votes in the March 16 Illinois primary, Mr. Reagan said that his "virtual tie" with Mr. Ford in the New Hampshire contest was unprecedented in the history of that primary and demonstrated the "viability" of his campaign against an incumbent President. [Page 20.]

But most analysts and most politicians said the results were so close that it provided no great advantage to either competitor. They are in the posi-

Continued on Page 18, Column 1

## Reagan Voters Viewed As Similar to Carter's

By ROBERT REINHOLD

Former Govs. Ronald Reagan of California and Jimmy Carter of Georgia drew support from similar sources in the Presidential primaries in New Hampshire on Tuesday—from those who wanted to cut government services and to decentralize government spending, who were opposed to détente with the Russians and who were generally hostile to the Federal Government.

While there were differences in their constituencies, a poll of voters conducted by The New York Times and CBS News suggested that issues and ideology were becoming clearer in the Presidential race. And Mr. Reagan, a Republican challenging an incumbent President, and Mr. Carter, a Democrat who has elbowed his way toward the front of a large field, appeared to have the most conservative appeal in New Hampshire.

While Mr. Carter was capturing most of the conservative vote, the four other major Democrats split the moderate and liberal vote. Closer analysis of the Times/CBS News poll, in which voters were asked for their second choice, suggests that a head-to-head race between Mr. Carter and Representative Morris K. Udall of Arizona would have been about as tight as was the Ford-Reagan race.

The survey also found the following:

¶On the issue that the voters most often mentioned as influencing their vote — balancing the Federal budget — Mr. Reagan outpolled President Ford by 3 to 2 among those who said that the budget should be balanced by cutting social services. Similarly, on the Democratic side, Mr. Carter, the victor, got a third of the votes, and his closest runner up, Mr. Udall, won only 10 percent.

¶Mr. Reagan carried the vote by 3 to 2 among those favoring decentralization of Federal services, an issue that he introduced, and Mr. Carter won over Mr. Udall by 2 to 1.

¶On détente, the only substantive issue dividing the two Republican contenders, Mr. Reagan won 60 percent of those

Continued on Page 18, Column 5

## MORELAND REPORT ON NURSING HOMES CITES ROCKEFELLER

### It Blames Former Governor for Industry's Poor Care and Political Influence

### OTHERS DRAW CRITICISM

### Wilson, Lefkowitz, Steingut and Blumenthal Are Found to Be Culpable, Too

By JOHN L. HESS

The Moreland Act Commission on Nursing Homes blamed Nelson A. Rockefeller yesterday for the political influence, official neglect and poor care that it said were rife in the industry while he was Governor.

In a 218-page report, it accused a dozen major political figures of interference, negligence or impropriety. Among them were former Gov. Malcolm Wilson, State Attorney General Louis J. Lefkowitz, Assembly Speaker Stanley Steingut, Albert H. Blumenthal, now majority leader of the Assembly, and, to a lesser degree, former Mayor John V. Lindsay and Mayor Beame.

On the other hand, it cleared former Mayor Robert F. Wagner Jr. of allegations that his administration had suppressed a 1960 report that charged large-scale fraud by the city's nursing homes.

**Study Limited**

Morris B. Abram, the Moreland Act Commission chairman, said at a news conference that the panel's study had been limited to a few exemplary areas, explaining: "We have left literally thousands of instances of larceny or worse to Joe Hynes." The reference was to Charles J. Hynes, the special state prosecutor for nursing homes.

The study nevertheless raised new questions about testimony a year ago by Speaker Steingut and Assemblyman James L. Emery, Republican of Livonia, both of whom have been under grand jury investigation. It reported that Grand Brokerage, in which the Speaker and Meade H. Esposito, the Brooklyn Democratic leader, were partners, had insurance business from six of Bernard Bergman's nursing homes, instead of only two, as they had insisted.

And it said that Mr. Emery had earned $12,747 in insurance commissions from Albert Schwartzberg, another promoter, rather than $864, as the Assemblyman had testified.

Mr. Abram described Mr. Lef-

Continued on Page 61, Column 5

Associated Press

IDEOLOGICAL UNREST DESCRIBED: In an explicit and unusual briefing, an official of Tsinghua University in Peking tells Richard M. Nixon about student posters criticizing "capitalist roaders" in government. The sign at rear says, "Fiercely Criticize the Re-emergence of the Demoniacal Rightist Wind." Details page 3.

## RHODESIA REPORTS KILLING 24 REBELS

### Clash, Most Serious in Year, Is Believed to Involve a Thrust Into Mozambique

By MICHAEL T. KAUFMAN

Special to The New York Times

SALISBURY, Rhodesia, Feb. 25—The Rhodesian Government announced today that its security forces had engaged in "hot pursuit" of nationalist guerrillas along the Mozambique border, killing 24 and losing one soldier.

Though the terse communiqué did not pinpoint the location or give the time of the clash—the most serious in more than a year—it was learned that it occurred yesterday at a point south of Umtali, a province capital in southeastern Rhodesia. The term hot pursuit was being openly interpreted here as meaning that the Rhodesian forces crossed over the Mozambique border, which runs for 800 miles to the east and north of this country.

**Challenge to Mozambique**

The fighting came 12 days after President Samora Machel of Mozambique issued a warning that his country would invade Rhodesia in retaliation for possible future violations of its borders. In light of this statement, the hot pursuit is seen here as a challenge to Mozambique, where Soviet arms have recently been reported unloaded and where Rhodesian guerrillas, trained by both the Chinese and the Russians, are encamped.

It is assumed here that the latest combat took place at one of the guerrilla encampments since the communiqué said that a quantity of arms had been seized.

The casualty figures in the Government statement today bring to 769 the number of alleged terrorists who have been killed since the white minority government of Ian D.

Continued on Page 10, Column 2

## Delhi to Penalize Couples For Not Limiting Births

By The Associated Press

NEW DELHI, Feb. 25—The Indian Government, acting to encourage sterilization, has announced a plan to penalize government employees and Delhi residents who do not limit their families to two children. The Indian capital is under federal administration.

The plan, similar to those in state assemblies across the country, also provides incentives to couples with one sterilized spouse or with one who has signed a pledge to undergo sterilization after having two children.

The penalties, which the Government said would become effective "almost immediately," directly or indirectly curtail a couple's access to almost the entire range of government assistance — from government jobs and housing to loans, medical care, schools and drinking water.

The plan does not provide fines or imprisonment for couples who fail to comply, but legislation being drafted in other states does.

The West Bengal government is drafting a bill providing that if a couple has three children, one spouse must be sterilized or face a fine, imprisonment or both.

The current birth rate in West Bengal is 38 per 1,000 population; the population is nearly 50 million, and a baby is born every 19 seconds.

About 22 million babies are now born annually in India, leading to an annual net population increase of 13 million. The population is now about 600 million, and Prime Minister

Continued on Page 7, Column 1

## Pakistanis Resist A Role for Canada At Nuclear Facility

By ROBERT TRUMBULL

Special to The New York Times

OTTAWA, Feb. 25—Pakistan has balked at Canadian demands for a say in how it will use a nuclear reprocessing plant purchased this week from France. The Canadian concern is that wastes from a Canadian-supplied nuclear power reactor at Karachi could be processed into material from which an atomic bomb could be made.

The Pakistani objections were voiced here by Prime Minister Zulfikar Ali Bhutto, who today ended a three-day visit to Ottawa during which he had inconclusive talks on the nuclear issue with Prime Minister Pierre Elliott Trudeau. On departing for Toronto to continue his official visit to Canada, Mr. Bhutto left several senior Pakistani officials in his party behind

Continued on Page 8, Column 6

## High Court Rules States May Curb Illegal Aliens

By LESLEY OELSNER

Special to The New York Times

WASHINGTON, Feb. 25—The Supreme Court ruled unanimously today that states may forbid employers to hire illegal aliens if such hiring would make it harder for lawful resident workers to get jobs.

In so ruling, the Court rejected the views of both the United States Solicitor General and the two California state courts that had ruled on the issue. All had contended that laws on hiring of aliens should be left to the Federal Government rather than the states.

The Supreme Court decision came in a case brought by two migrant farm workers citing a 1971 California statute that banned the hiring of illegal aliens when "such employment would have an adverse effect" on workers legally entitled to reside and work in the state.

The use of illegal aliens, particularly on farms, has been the cause of much controversy and labor unrest in California. The use of illegal aliens as strikebreakers during early unionizing efforts by Cesar Chavez and his union, now the United Farm Workers of America, was a particular complaint of the union.

The Court decision, according to one of the lawyers for the two farm workers involved in the case, could lead to a way for people to challenge through civil lawsuits the use of illegal aliens. Currently, there is no practical way to file a civil suit to challenge the use of illegal aliens, the lawyer, Howard S. Scher of Washington, said.

Also, Federal restrictions regarding illegal aliens are generally agreed to be inadequately enforced, with several million illegal aliens now believed to be living in the country. Conceivably, the Court ruling today could lead to increased enforcement of restrictions against il-

Continued on Page 15, Column 1

## Philharmonic Picks Mehta as Conductor

By HAROLD C. SCHONBERG

Zubin Mehta was named yesterday as the new director of the New York Philharmonic to succeed Pierre Boulez.

The 39-year-old, Bombay-born Mr. Mehta will leave the Los Angeles Philharmonic and assume his new position in September 1978. It was also announced by Carlos Moseley, president of the New York Philharmonic, that the 1977-78 season would be given over to guest conductors.

Thus a new era will start with the Philharmonic some two years from now, and it will be an altogether different one from the rather austere six years in which Mr. Boulez will

Continued on Page 22, Column 1

Camera Press

U.S. Embassy on Tchaikovsky Street, Moscow. Antennas are barely visible from below.

## Moscow Rays Linked to U.S. Bugging

By BERNARD GWERTZMAN

Special to The New York Times

WASHINGTON, Feb. 25 — Soviet officials have privately conceded that microwaves have been beamed at the American Embassy in Moscow, but they justified the possibly harmful activity as necessary to jam American listening devices on the roof of the building.

Congressional and Administration sources said today that, after having denied for some 15 years that there had been such microwave emissions, Soviet officials recently conceded their existence. Soviet diplomats here have discussed the purpose of the microwaves with American reporters and Administration officials.

The American officials said they accepted the Soviet contention that the microwaves were aimed at the embassy to jam the sophisticated monitoring equipment and not to bug the embassy or to harm American personnel.

The listening devices on the embassy roof in Moscow are secret and hardly any Americans in the city know of them. There have been reports that they were able to eavesdrop on Soviet officials riding in limousines, and they presumably monitor Soviet frequencies.

Earlier news reports from Moscow noted speculation that the microwave emissions, which produce low-level electromagnetic radiation of the kind found near radar stations or even radio and television transmitters, were either for recharging listening devices or for picking up conversations from within the embassy.

Two factors have irritated

Continued on Page 4, Column 4

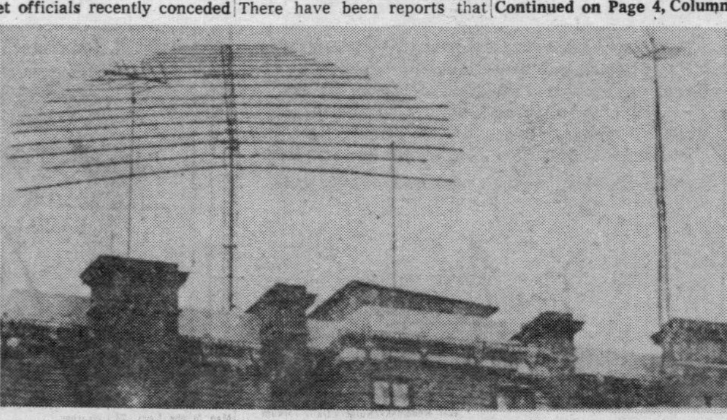

The New York Times

Antennas are more in evidence at Soviet Embassy in Washington, 1125 16th Street N.W.

## CITY MAY BAR AID TO LOCAL BOARDS

### Annual $15,000 to Each Cut From Draft Budget

By FRANCIS X. CLINES

A draft budget proposed by Mayor Beame has eliminated the allocation of $15,000 annually for each of the city's 62 community planning boards.

Officials of the Beame administration said that the deletion was part of an incomplete draft. But Borough President Percy E. Sutton of Manhattan, who notified Manhattan board members on Tuesday that their vouchers could no longer be accepted, indicated that the draft budget was complete, according to board members.

The austerity measure was immediately denounced by the board members as a crippling blow for planning at precisely the time that the local boards are to assume broadened powers under city charter changes.

"This is the worst possible time for this—the moment when the Charter changes are supposed to be in preparation," Mr. Sutton said in an interview. He said that he would fight to see that the boards got their money.

"This causes a loss of faith by the public after expressing their will in the Charter vote,"

Continued on Page 28, Column 5



## 2 Americans Freed By Captors in Beirut

By JAMES M. MARKHAM

Special to The New York Times

BEIRUT, Lebanon, Feb. 25—Two American Government employees who were kidnapped here four months ago were freed tonight, apparently unharmed and in good health.

The two men, Charles D. Gallagher and William R. Dykes Jr., were seized early in the morning of Oct. 22 on the Corniche Mazra in a largely Moslem and Palestinian quarter of the city.

Shortly after they were dragged out of their station-wagon at gunpoint, and as the tempo of street fighting sharply increased, the American Embassy began evacuating its dependents from Beirut and then began reducing its staff to min-

Continued on Page 10, Column 4



## Reagan Puts His Net Worth at $1,455,571

By JON NORDHEIMER

Special to The New York Times

CHARLESTON, Ill., Feb. 25—Ronald Reagan released a financial statement today that placed his net worth at $1,455,571.

The statement by the former two-term California Governor included a list of his real estate and stock holdings and estimated his earnings last year after leaving office at $282,253.

Mr. Reagan, who opposes President Ford for the Republican nomination for the Presidency, made the disclosure after resisting requests for information on his financial holdings since announcing his candidacy. He reportedly acquiesced after campaign advisers said his refusal was politically damaging in view of Mr. Ford's disclosure of his financial status.

A statement issued by the White House on Feb. 12 listed Mr. Ford's personal financial worth at the end of 1975 at $323,489, up slightly more than $67,000 from the figure of $256,378 given at the time he became President in August 1974.

Mr. Reagan's statement showed $822,300 in real and personal holdings, $586,775 in securities and cash on hand and $46,496 as the cash value of life insurance policies and California retirement fund interests.

There was some confusion about details of the document after it was released.

For example, one of the candidate's major holdings of investment property, a single parcel of 771 acres of undeveloped land in Riverside County, Calif., was valued at $417,500.

Peter Hannaford, one of Mr. Reagan's top staff members, said the figure was the official assessment of the land. Later, he said it was the price placed on the property by a professional appraiser and represented the current market value.

A reporter later placed a telephone call to the assessor of Riverside County and was told the figure was the county's official assessment figure. Assessments usually run well under current market values,

Continued on Page 20, Column 4

NEWS INDEX



| | Page | | Page |
|---|---|---|---|
| Books | 29 | Movies | 22-25 |
| Bridge | 28 | Music | 22-25 |
| Business | 41-53 | Notes on People | 23 |
| Chess | 28 | Obituaries | 34 |
| Crossword | 29 | Op-Ed | 31 |
| Editorials | 30 | Sports | 36-40 |
| Family/Style | 26 | Theaters | 22-25 |
| Financial | 41-53 | Transportation | 61 |
| Going Out Guide | 24 | TV and Radio | 63 |
| Letters | 30 | U.N. Proceedings | 2 |
| Man in the News | 22 | Weather | 61 |

News Summary and Index, Page 33

"All the News That's Fit to Print"

# The New York Times

LATE CITY EDITION

Weather: Cloudy, cool with periods of rain and fog through tomorrow. Temperature range: today 32-43; Tuesday 35-41. Details on page 73

VOL. CXXV . . No. 43,138 — NEW YORK, WEDNESDAY, MARCH 3, 1976 — 20 CENTS

25 cents beyond 50-mile zone from New York City, except Long Island. Higher in air delivery cities.



# JACKSON BEATS WALLACE AND UDALL, CARTER IS 4TH IN MASSACHUSETTS VOTE

The New York Times/Neal Boenzi

Felix G. Rohatyn, right, chairman of the Municipal Assistance Corporation; George Gould, chairman of its finance committee, and Donna Shalala, treasurer, discussing the city's fiscal problems at City Hall yesterday.

## GUN CONTROL BILL PUT ON THE SHELF

### House Unit Sends It Back to Subcommittee With No Revision Instructions

By NANCY HICKS

Special to The New York Times

WASHINGTON, March 2—The House Judiciary Committee voted today to return its gun control bill to subcommittee for revisions—a move that will probably kill any chance of firearms control in this Congress.

The committee did not specifically instruct the subcommittee on crime as to which changes to make in the bill, whose strongest feature is a ban on the manufacture and sale of about 70 percent of the handguns produced in this country. Individual members made suggestions for changes.

The bill, sponsored by Representative Martin A. Russo, Democrat of Illinois, was approved by the committee last week, 18 to 14. Today, after a weekend of heavy lobbying by opponents of gun control, the measure was recommitted by a vote of 17 to 16.

**Waning of Interest**

Two attempts to assassinate President Ford last September created new interest in handgun control in the current Congress, but that interest soon waned, resulting in the committee decision today.

"I am personally disappointed by this vote," said the committee chairman, Peter W. Rodino Jr., Democrat of New Jersey, who added he doubted that the bill could be revised and approved so late in an election year. He said that he had hoped that the desired changes could be made on the floor of the House, rather than by return-

Continued on Page 12, Column 3

### Subpoena Dropped

The office of Maurice H. Nadjari, the Special State Prosecutor, has withdrawn a subpoena seeking the appearance of Civil Court Judge Anthony J. Mercorella before a special Manhattan grand jury investigating allegations of corruption in the State Liquor Authority and the Alcoholic Beverage Control Board. Page 41.

## 'Secret' U.S. Pacts Reported by Sadat

By BERNARD GWERTZMAN

Special to The New York Times

WASHINGTON, March 2—President Anwar el-Sadat of Egypt claims that as part of last September's Sinai accord with Israel he concluded "secret agreements" in which the United States pledged that Israel would not attack Syria and that every effort would be made to insure Palestinian participation in a Middle East settlement.

Neither of these agreements was made known publicly during last fall's extensive Congressional hearings on the American role in the Sinai accord. Today, State Department officials seemed reluctant to comment directly on Mr. Sadat's remarks, made at a news

Continued on Page 3, Column 1



## Sweeping Inquiry Planned In House Spy Report Leak

By RICHARD D. LYONS

Special to The New York Times

WASHINGTON, March 2—The House ethics committee requested $350,000 today to pay for its investigation of the leaking of the Pike intelligence report. It prepared to hire a staff of about 20 outside consultants headed by a former inspector of the Federal Bureau of Investigation to conduct the detective and legal work.

The amount of money, the size of the staff and the committee's request for broadened subpoena power raised the expectation that the committee, which has never formally investigated anyone, is preparing to open a major detailed and long inquiry.

In the face of the overwhelming House vote ordering the ethics committee to conduct the investigation, several key representatives said they had little doubt that the money would be approved—although there might be extensive debate on the size of the request.

The committee could spend even more than $350,000 on the investigation. It now has only five regular staff members but is entitled to 30 under the rules of the House. Representative John J. Flynt, the Georgia Democrat who is chairman of the committee, said he intended to fill from available but unspent funds some of the missing 25 positions to augment the special investigation staff.

Theoretically, the extra amount could be as much as $900,000, although there is almost no chance that such an amount would be spent despite the vote for an inquiry.

"We were mandated to conduct a full investigation and we intend to do just that," Mr. Flynt said.

Some indication of the extent of the committee's plans lay in the fact that when the House Select Committee on Intelligence, headed by Representative Otis G. Pike, Democrat of Long Island, began its inquiry into intelligence that resulted in the report that was

Continued on Page 14, Column 3

## Undefeated Rutgers Helps Jersey Forget Its Worries

By JOSEPH F. SULLIVAN

Special to The New York Times

NEW BRUNSWICK, N. J., March 2 — New Jerseyans were diverted today from rising prices, tax problems and crime statistics; they had an all-winning basketball team, which ended its regular season last night with a 26-0 won-lost record.

"People have needed and have wanted something like this for a long time," said Dr. Edward J. Bloustein, the Rutgers president who has been fighting a battle of the budget with state officials for several weeks. "It means something to the morale of people all across the state."

Dr. Bloustein was in the middle of the crowd following last night's 85-to-80 victory over St. Bonaventure, waving a scarlet bandana while crowds of students shouted for him, "Eddie! Eddie!"

"Even the student who has no interest in going for sports himself will be attracted to a school with a successful athletic program," Dr. Bloustein said. "It adds to the image of a well-rounded university."

Following a celebration

Continued on Page 41, Column 1

Walt Redomsky/Rutgers Daily Targum

Rutgers fans surrounding the team bus on the campus Monday night as Mark Conlin, a player, turned to wave

## 2D BOND EXCHANGE WEIGHED BY M.A.C.

### Decision Is Due in 3 Months, Says Rohatyn—Extension of Moratorium Indicated

By EDWARD RANZAL

The Municipal Assistance Corporation is thinking about making a second offer to exchange its bonds for city notes that were placed under a moratorium last fall.

"We're considering it," Felix G. Rohatyn, the corporation chairman, testified at a City Council committee hearing yesterday. "But we have not determined what the terms will be."

Last fall, as part of the intricate fiscal package that staved off a city default, a three-year moratorium was imposed on $1.6 billion in short-term city notes. Those who held them were invited to trade them for 10-year M.A.C. bonds paying 8 percent interest. Holders of about $500 million of the notes did so.

Mr. Rohatyn said that a decision on a similar offer to holders of the remaining $1.1 billion in notes would be made in 30 to 90 days.

He indicated that a long extension was likely for the three-year moratorium.

A holder of those notes, he said, "would have to have a very long life expectancy if he is to get his notes redeemed."

The city's worsening financial condition, he said, has dampened investors' hopes of redeeming their notes and "they may find our bonds more desirable now."

In an unusual open meeting

Continued on Page 74, Column 1

### Miss Hearst Disputed

Patricia Hearst's testimony that she had participated in a bank robbery without knowing if her gun was loaded or in working condition was contradicted by an electronics technician. Page 73.

## BILLS SEEK TO GIVE CHECK PRIVILEGES TO SAVINGS BANKS

### Measure Expected to Pass in Albany Despite Efforts by Commercial Banks

By LINDA GREENHOUSE

Special to The New York Times

ALBANY, March 2—The State Banking Department today asked the Legislature to give checking-account privileges to the state's savings banks. Unless legislative action is taken, the banks will have to close 165,000 so-called "now" accounts under a court order on March 31.

The two bills introduced by the department in the Senate and Assembly banking committees would give checking-account powers to savings banks and state-chartered savings and loan associations immediately, and would phase in expanded personal-loan powers over a four-year period beginning a year from now. The bills also provide for election of savings bank trustees by depositors.

There were early indications that the bills would pass without much difficulty, despite a contention by the state's commercial bankers that checking-account privileges give the savings banks an unfair competitive edge since Federal regulations also allow the savings banks to pay a quarter-point higher interest rate on deposits.

**Issue Defused**

The Assembly voted to give checking accounts to the savings banks last year, but the bill died in the Senate because the Assembly had tied it to a prohibition against "redlining," the alleged banking practice of refusing to write mortgages in certain neighborhoods.

Governor Carey, in effect, defused the redlining issue last month when his Banking Superintendent, John G. Heimann, issued strict administrative regulations requiring disclosure of mortgage investments.

Senator Jay P. Rolison Jr., Republican of Poughkeepsie and chairman of the Senate Banks Committee, said he believed the checking-account bill would receive "substantial support" in the Senate this year.

**Would Not Pay Interest**

Under the bill, the checking accounts at savings banks would not pay interest. The principal benefit to the ordinary depositor would be the convenience of being able to keep both a checking and a savings account at a bank that pays the highest allowable interest on savings.

Late last year, the State Court of Appeals ruled that the "now" accounts being offered by a number of savings banks—identical to commercial bank-checking accounts in all but technical details—were illegal because they had never been authorized by the Legislature. The court said the accounts would have to be closed by March 31 unless the Legislature

Continued on Page 74, Column 8

Associated Press

Senator Henry M. Jackson raising his arms in victory last night at his campaign headquarters in Boston.

## New Political Universe

### In Just Four Years, Domestic Problems Have Replaced War as Key Voter Issue

By R. W. APPLE Jr.

Special to The New York Times

News Analysis

BOSTON, March 2—The returns from Massachusetts' vote tonight showed how much the Democratic political universe had changed in just four years.

Of the four who finished at the top in the state that was Senator George McGovern's best in 1972, only Representative Morris K. Udall of Arizona is a liberal. The others—Senator Henry M. Jackson of Washington, Gov. George C. Wallace of Alabama and former Gov. Jimmy Carter of Georgia—range from moderate to conservative.

What has happened? Most important, the Vietnam war has ended. The economy, disgust with Washington and race-related issues (busing, crime, welfare) have emerged to replace it at the center of voters' concerns. Here in Massachusetts, where the antiwar movement once burned so brightly, the voters are now focusing on domestic issues—notably jobs, with state unemployment at 11.8 percent.

Mr. Jackson spent more than $400,000 in this state, far more than any other candidate, and for the first time in his career he proved that he could win outside his native state of Washington. It was a stunning improvement over the 1.4 percent that he polled here four years ago.

As he said tonight, his success in Massachusetts bodes well for his efforts in the other big Northern industrial states with large convention delegations.

In New Hampshire last Tues-

Continued on Page 17, Column 1

## High Court Limits Press's Protection Against Libel Suits

By LESLEY OELSNER

Special to The New York Times

WASHINGTON, March 2—A divided Supreme Court cut back today on the broad protection that the Court, on First Amendment grounds, has given the press against libel suits brought by so-called "public figures."

The Court did this by applying the designation of "public figure," in a case involving Time magazine, in a way that appears to exclude types of persons who formerly would have been assumed to be public people.

Under Court rulings, public figures are required to make a much stronger case against the publisher of alleged libel than are nonpublic figures. By limiting the application of the "public figure" category the Court thus makes it easier to bring libel cases.

The Court ruled, in the Time case, that a Florida socialite who was often mentioned in society reports in the press, whose divorce proceedings were widely reported, and who herself gave news conferences during those proceedings could not be considered a "public figure" for the purpose of de-

Continued on Page 11, Column 2

NEWS INDEX



| | Page | | Page |
|---|---|---|---|
| About New York | 73 | Movies | 28-32 |
| Art | 38 | Music | 28-32 |
| Books | 35 | Notes on People | 34 |
| Bridge | 34 | Obituaries | 40 |
| Business | 49-62 | Op-Ed | 37 |
| Crossword | 35 | Real Estate | 62-63 |
| Editorials | 36 | Sports | 43-48 |
| Education | 33 | Theaters | 28-32 |
| Family/Style | 18-27 | Transportation | 73 |
| Financial | 49-62 | TV and Radio | 74-75 |
| Going Out Guide | 30 | U.N. Proceedings | 10 |
| Man in the News | 74 | Weather | 73 |

News Summary and Index, Page 39


## JOBLESSNESS IS UP TO 12.2% IN CITY

### Increase Is Laid to Seasonal Factors—Rate Is Worst Since World War II

By MICHAEL STERNE

The city's economy weakened considerably in January as unemployment rose from 11.5 to 12.2 percent, the highest level since World War II, and the number of jobs fell to the lowest January levels since 1950, the State Labor Department reported yesterday.

These new indications of a "severely troubled local economy," according to a senior economist of the department, are a result of seasonal factors—principally the usual December-January declines in employment in retail trade—coming on top of the rapid deterioration of the job market during 1975.

They also reflect the still incomplete process of feeding new annual benchmarks into the complex federally mandated system of computing employment and unemployment. Though the new benchmarks may have exaggerated the January jobless rate somewhat, the senior economist said, they still indicate accurately the trend of what is happening in New York's factories, stores, docks, banks, brokerages and building trades.

The state economy also suffered a further decline from December to January. The jobless rate rose even more sharply than the city rate—eight tenths of a percentage point—

Continued on Page 74, Column 6

## FORD TOPS REAGAN

### Shriver, Bayh, Harris and Shapp Trail in Democratic Race

By JOHN KIFNER

Special to The New York Times

BOSTON, Wednesday, March 3—Senator Henry M. Jackson of Washington won the Massachusetts Democratic primary yesterday as voters went to the polls in relatively light numbers amid snow, sleet and cold.

Gov. George C. Wallace of Alabama, who carried Boston, was locked in a close struggle with Representative Morris K. Udall of Arizona for second place with approximately two-thirds of the precincts reporting early today. Former Gov. Jimmy Carter of Georgia was running fourth.

Bunched far behind the leaders were Sargent Shriver, the party's 1972 Vice-Presidential nominee; Senator Birch Bayh of Indiana, former Senator Fred R. Harris of Oklahoma, Ellen McCormack, the anti-abortion candidate, and Gov. Milton J. Shapp of Pennsylvania.

In a Republican race in which neither candidate visited the state, President Ford won handily, swamping former Gov. Ronald Reagan of California.

With 1,700 of 2,187 precincts totaled, the tally was:

| DEMOCRATS | | |
|---|---|---|
| Jackson | 125,307 | (23%) |
| Wallace | 95,355 | (18%) |
| Udall | 94,086 | (17%) |
| Carter | 78,734 | (14%) |
| Shriver | 41,164 | ( 8%) |
| Harris | 41,021 | ( 8%) |
| Bayh | 25,737 | ( 5%) |
| MsCormack | 18,447 | ( 3%) |
| Shapp | 16,118 | ( 3%) |

With 1,704 precincts reporting, the tally was:

| REPUBLICANS | | |
|---|---|---|
| Ford | 89,005 | (61%) |
| Reagan | 48,186 | ( 36%) |

After the victory, Senator Jackson told reporters he had "gotten the lunch bucket vote and some of the liberals." "You know, this is a working-class state," he added.

He said he had won with a "grand coalition of labor, and ethnic groups that elected Roosevelt, Truman, Kennedy and Johnson."

At the White House, Ron Nessen, the Presidential spokesman, issued a statement expressing Mr. Ford's pleasure at the outcome in Massachusetts and Vermont and saying that

Continued on Page 16, Column 1

### Carter Wins in Vermont

Jimmy Carter won the Democratic Presidential primary in Vermont yesterday, with almost half the votes in a five-candidate race. President Ford was the only Republican on the ballot, with Ronald Reagan receiving a write-in from about one G.O.P. voter in six. Page 17.

## U.S. Ends Firestone And Goodyear Suits

By The Associated Press

WASHINGTON, March 2—The Justice Department today dropped lawsuits intended to break up the Goodyear and Firestone tire companies after officials concluded they could not prove charges of an attempted illegal monopoly.

The civil antitrust suits, filed in 1973 in the United States District Court in Cleveland, were dropped when the Government and the companies submitted a dismissal agreement to the court today.

Under the agreement, the Justice Department agreed to drop the charges "without prejudice," meaning it could reopen the case if it wished.

A department spokesman said

Continued on Page 57, Column 1

"All the News That's Fit to Print"

# The New York Times

LATE CITY EDITION

Weather: Partly sunny today; cold tonight. Fair and cold tomorrow. Temperatue range: today 27-39; Tuesday 31-34. Details on page 77.

VOL. CXXV .. No. 43,145 · NEW YORK, WEDNESDAY, MARCH 10, 1976 · 20 CENTS

25 cents beyond 50-mile zone from New York City, except Long Island. Higher in air delivery cities.



## RHODESIANS FACE A WIDER CONFLICT WITH GUERRILLAS

### Minister Announces Fighting Extends Along 800-Mile Mozambique Border

### FORCES STRENGTHENED

### Salisbury Holds No Hope for End of Combat Even If Current Talks Succeed

By HENRY KAMM

Special to The New York Times

SALISBURY, Rhodesia, March 9—Rhodesia announced today that since late January black nationalist guerrilla forces had extended their area of conflict to the full length of the 800-mile border with Mozambique.

"We don't see it coming to an end, whether we reach a political settlement or not," Edward Sutton-Pryce, a Deputy Minister in the office of Prime Minister Ian D. Smith, said at a news conference. "It would be daydreaming to say it will come to an end."

At the same time, the minister announced that the Rhodesian troop commitment to the combat area had been increased by about three-fifths since January, with an accompanying increase in the number of reserves called to active duty.

Rhodesia does not reveal troop-strength figures, in line with a policy of exceptionally tight military secrecy, but official sources put the number of regular troops in the army, paramilitary police and air force at 12,000 and the organized reserves at 25,000.

**Cuban Presence Denied**

While characterizing the extension of the war as part of a Soviet inspired and manipulated quest for control of the "wealth and strategic value" of southern Africa, Mr. Sutton-Pryce said there was no evidence of any Soviet or Cuban presence in the field.

Reports have been circulated in the West of arrivals of Soviet tanks and other heavy weaponry, as well as Cuban soldiers, in the Mozambican port of Beira for deployment against Rhodesia.

The minister, a man on whom Mr. Smith is said to rely heavily, said the weapons and equipment of the guerrillas—a term the minister and all Rhodesian officials reject in favor of "terrorists"—were of Soviet or Eastern European origin, replacing an earlier flow of military supplies from China. But Mr. Sutton-Pryce said in

Continued on Page 4, Column 3

## Pike Charges C.I.A. Effort At Retaliation for Findings

### Accuses Agency of Seeking to Discredit Him and Congress So as to Gloss Over Report by House Select Committee

By RICHARD D. LYONS

Special to The New York Times

WASHINGTON, March 9 — Representative Otis G. Pike accused the Central Intelligence Agency today of waging a campaign to discredit both himself and Congress in an effort to gloss over the findings of his House Select Committee on Intelligence.

The Suffolk County Democrat took the House floor twice to relate hitherto undisclosed incidents of his dealings with the C.I.A., including a telephone conversation in which he quoted the agency's special counsel as having stated:

"Pike will pay for this, you wait and see—we'll destroy him for this."

According to Mr. Pike, the conversation was between Mitchell Rogovin, special counsel to the Director of the Central Intelligence, and A. Searle Field, the committee's staff director.

United Press International

Representative Otis Pike

Meanwhile the State Department said that Secretary of State Henry A. Kissinger and his top aide, Lawrence S. Eagleburger, were personally conducting the inquiry into the disclosure of highly secret details of Mr. Kissinger's conversations with Middle East leaders. [Page 10.]

Mr. Rogovin, reached in a telephone interview, denied that he had ever threatened Mr. Pike's political standing or said anything that could have been construed as a political threat.

Mr. Rogovin said he called Mr. Pike today after learning of the Congressman's remarks and asked him where he heard about such political threats. He said Mr. Pike had told him that the threat had been relayed to him by Mr. Field. "I told him he was dead wrong and that Field was dead wrong," Mr. Rogovin said. "I flatly deny every inference of Mr. Pike's statement."

Moreover, he said that he has met with Mr. Pike on several occasions since the alleged threat and that Mr. Pike never mentioned it before. "He was always very cordial," Mr. Rogovin said.

Mr. Pike's comments came

Continued on Page 11, Column 1

## 3 Foreign 'Penetrations' Of F.B.I. Offices Indicated

By JOHN M. CREWDSON

Special to The New York Times

WASHINGTON, March 9 — The Federal Bureau of Investigation may have been "penetrated" by hostile foreign intelligence agencies on at least three occasions since the end of World War II, according to a former intelligence official who says he has direct knowledge of all three incidents.

The evidence in each case, which involved bureau agents in New York, Washington and another undisclosed American city, was entirely circumstantial, the former official said, and no criminal charges were ever brought against the three agents thought to have been subverted by foreign governments.

But in one case, he said, the conclusion that an agent assigned to the bureau's Washington field office had become a paid Soviet spy was virtually inescapable, even though the man broke off his alleged relationship with Soviet intelligence after he became aware of an internal F.B.I. investigation of his activities.

Clarence M. Kelley, the F.B.I. director, said through a spokesman that, over the years, "several allegations have come to our attention that attempts have been made to penetrate the F.B.I."

Mr. Kelley said that what he termed "exhaustive investigations" had not "disclosed any evidence that a hostile foreign intelligence service ever successfully recruited or operated an employee of the F.B.I."

The director's statement did not take account, however, of instances in which the bureau's agents might have voluntarily

Continued on Page 12, Column 3

## PUBLIC PENSIONS IN SINGLE SYSTEM URGED IN ALBANY

### $200 Million-a-Year Savings Seen in Unified Setup for State and Local Workers

By LINDA GREENHOUSE

Special to The New York Times

ALBANY, March 9—A special state commission recommended today that all public employees hired since 1973 be brought under a unified pension system that would save state and local governments an estimated total of $200 million a year through a combination of required employee contributions and lower initial benefits.

After age 73, employees who had retired at age 65 would begin to receive higher benefits than in current plans under a proposed clause that would increase benefits by 3 percent a year to compensate for inflation.

At present, staff employees pay nothing into their pension plans. New York City employees pay from 3 to 8 percent into their plans, with the exception of transit employees, who contribute nothing to their pensions.

Under the state panel's proposal, all public employees hired since 1973 would be required to contribute a minimum of 3 percent.

**Difficulty Foreseen**

The proposal was made to the Governor and the Legislature by the Permanent Commission on Public Employee Pension and Retirement Systems, which the Legislature set up in 1971 to study the growing public-employee-pension problem.

Since then the commission's chairman, Otto Kinzel, has not been especially successful in getting his recommendations adopted, and today's proposals seemed likely to face a difficult time in an election-year Legislature.

The recommendations come at a time of increasing public concern about the role that rapidly growing pension costs have played in the city and state fiscal crises. According to the pension commission, the cost to the state's taxpayers of public-employee retirement plans is now $3.5 billion a year, double what it was five years ago.

The recommendations were immediately labeled "totally

Continued on Page 55, Column 3

### 15 Die in Mine Blast

Fifteen coal miners were found dead in a mine in southeastern Kentucky 12 hours after they were trapped by an explosion, a Federal official said. Page 53.

# FORD DEFEATS REAGAN IN FLORIDA; CARTER IS WINNER OVER WALLACE IN DEMOCRATIC VOTE, JACKSON 3D

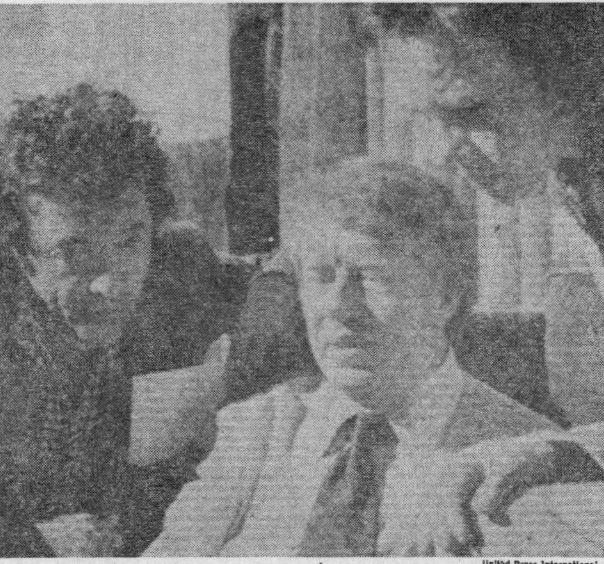

United Press International

Jimmy Carter, his wife, Rosalyn, and an aide watching primary returns in Orlando

## PRESIDENT ELATED

### Loss Seen as Blow to Alabama Governor and Californian

By ROY REED

Special to The New York Times

MIAMI, March 9—President Ford defeated Ronald Reagan in Florida's Republican Presidential primary election today, gaining his fourth victory in as many primaries.

Jimmy Carter, the former Governor of Georgia, won the hotly contested Democratic primary. Gov George C. Wallace of neighboring Alabama finished second, suffering his worst political setback since he was shot and seriously wounded by an assassin while campaigning at a shopping center in Laurel, Md., on May 15, 1972. The shooting ended his 1972 campaign.

Senator Henry M. Jackson of Washington, the winner of the Massachusetts primary a week ago, ran third, well behind Mr. Wallace. Next in order were "no preference," Gov. Milton J. Shapp of Pennsylvania, the only other Democrat who campaigned actively here, and Representative Morris K. Udall of Arizona.

Seven other Democrats brought up the rear.

With 3,308, or 97 percent, of 3,420 precincts reporting, the tally was:

| REPUBLICANS | | |
| --- | --- | --- |
| Ford | 303,975 | (53%) |
| Reagan | 268,607 | (47%) |
| **DEMOCRATS** | | |
| Carter | 429,230 | (35%) |
| Wallace | 385,785 | (31%) |
| Jackson | 285,613 | (23%) |
| No Preference | 36,581 | ( 3%) |
| Shapp | 28,644 | ( 2%) |
| Udall | 25,321 | ( 2%) |

The President's victory seriously damaged the candidacy of the former California Governor as a challenger for the Republican nomination. However, Mr. Reagan has said that he intends to continue campaigning until the Republican National Convention next August in Kansas City, Mo.

**Ford Is 'Overjoyed'**

In Washington, the President said he was "overjoyed" at the outcome, but he declined to tell reporters whether he thought Mr. Reagan should withdraw from the race.

Mr. Ford's campaign advisers were also said to be sending signals to Mr. Reagan to end his insurgency—and perhaps to become the President's running mate. [Page 18].

With 97 percent of the precincts reporting, the contest for Florida delegates to the national conventions looked this way:

Republicans, 66 delegates—Ford 43, Reagan 23; Democrats, 81 delegates—Carter 35, Wallace 26, Jackson 20.

Mr. Carter's showing would seem to re-establish his position as the front-runner of the Democratic Party's center. It helped to counter the one de-

Continued on Page 19, Column 1

## JERSEY BUS STRIKE DISRUPTS 450,000

### Other Carriers Report No Difficulties in Handling Transport's Riders

By FRANK J. PRIAL

About 450,000 daily riders of Transport of New Jersey buses had to find other means of getting to and from work yesterday after the Amalgamated Transit Union struck the company, the largest private bus operator in the country.

Other carriers—bus operators and railroads—reported no difficulty in accommodating the line's commuters. A spokesman for the Penn Central Railroad said that the line had added extra trains between Newark and New York for the morning rush hour, but that the expected demand never materialized.

**No Problems Found**

The Port Authority of New York and New Jersey said that there was no noticeable increase in traffic at bridges and tunnels leading from New Jersey to New York, and that its PATH railroad had no problem handling extra passengers who ordinarily would have used Transport buses.

Union drivers, mechanics and clerks walked out after weeks of bargaining. The 3,400 employees involved voted 2,318 to 708 Monday to reject the company's final offer of a 12 percent wage increase over two years. They had been working without a contract since March 1.

The bus company and state officials said 200,000 commuters to New York were affected by the strike. But a Port Authority official said that normal commuter traffic at its main bus terminal in New York involved 1,100 arrivals and 1,-

Continued on Page 55, Column 1

## Impact of Florida Vote

### Reagan's Prospects Appear Dimmed; Carter Did What He Said He Had to Do

By R. W. APPLE Jr.

Special to The New York Times

**News Analysis**

MIAMI, March 9—President Ford's victory over former Gov. Ronald Reagan of California in Florida's primary today does not guarantee his nomination, but it drastically reduces Mr. Reagan's prospects. If the Californian, even with fierce attacks on the President's policies and leadership, can still go down to defeat in a state once so favorably disposed toward him, it is difficult to think of major states where he can win. He has already downgraded his chances in Illinois, his native state, which holds its primary next Tuesday.

He must win somewhere—despite his assertion this week that he would press on to the Republican national convention come what may—if he is to remain in the race. With only two contestants, a consistent loser soon finds himself without the funds and the campaign workers to keep him fighting.

On the Democratic side, former Gov. Jimmy Carter of Georgia did what he had said for more than a year that he had to do to establish credibility for the long struggle toward the nomination. He cut Gov. George C. Wallace of Alabama down to size in the state that sent the Alabamian on his way four years ago.

Mr. Wallace ran about 10 percentage points behind his 1972 total of 42 percent in Florida, and he was soundly beaten by a fellow Southerner. Together with his failure to win in Massachusetts, even with the busing issue at full

Continued on Page 18, Column 2

## Panel Finds Incompetence In City Day-Care Program

By EDWARD RANZAL

A mayoral task force on the operation of the city's $128 million day-care program has found "incompetence" and "an atmosphere of mistrust" at the highest levels of management.

In making public the report yesterday, First Deputy Mayor John E. Zuccotti said that as many as 16,000 of the 36,200 children enrolled in 410 centers financed by the city, state and Federal governments might be ineligible.

Mr. Zuccotti said that the task force had uncovered no evidence of criminality, but that Nicholas Scoppetta, the Investigation Commissioner, was continuing an independent investigation.

He said he had given J. Henry Smith, the new Human Resources Administrator, two weeks to review the report and make specific plans to follow the recommendations of the task force, including the hiring of an outside consultant to study leasing agreements between the city and operators of the centers.

On the basis of the task force's recommendations, Mr. Zuccotti said, he anticipates personnel changes in the Agency for Child Development, which is in charge of the day-care program.

Top officials of the agency, the task force said, "cannot be held solely and totally responsible for the failure" of efficient operations.

"In some respects [the agency management] has been trapped between a major reorientation in social climate and direction and unclear definition of city attitudes towards day care and a rapidly worsening economic

Continued on Page 54, Column 1

## Canada to Resume Nuclear Aid to India

By ROBERT TRUMBULL

Special to The New York Times

OTTAWA, March 9—India has accepted Canadian demands for certain strictures on its nuclear program, and Canada has agreed in return to resume nuclear aid.

According to a Canadian official, the new agreement, which is expected to be ratified soon by both governments, includes an Indian pledge that the three reactors supplied by Canada will not be used in developing an explosive device.

The official said the three Canadian reactors would be subject to "adequate safeguards" based on current standards of the International Atom-

Continued on Page 5, Column 1

## Modern Gets Huge Matisse Cutout in $1 Million Trade

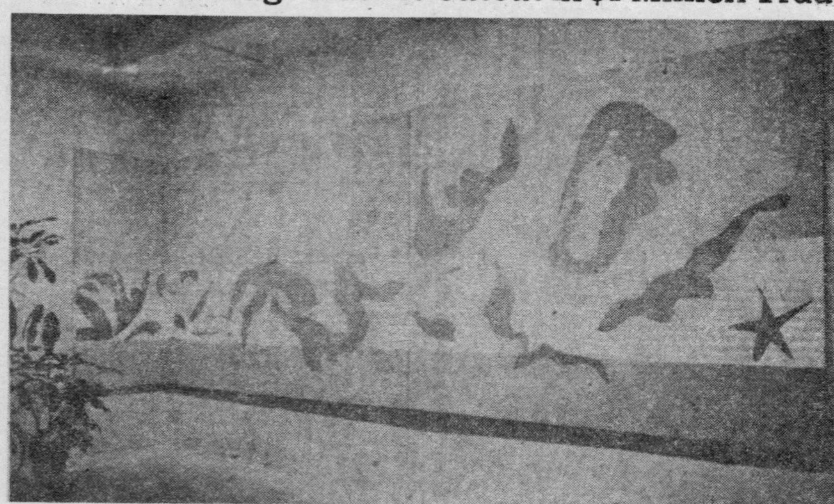

The Museum of Modern Art

Part of the multipaneled work, "The Swimming Pool," by Henri Matisse, bought by the Museum of Modern Art

By GRACE GLUECK

The Museum of Modern Art has acquired a huge "cutout" work by the modern French master Henri Matisse and will exchange objects from its own collection equal to the purchase price, said to be around $1 million.

William Rubin, director of painting and sculpture at the museum, stressed yesterday that neither the price of the Matisse nor of the works to be exchanged had been finally determined. But he said the new acquisition was now in the museum's possession and was undergoing minor restoration.

The multipaneled work, measuring 53 feet 11¾ inches long by 7 feet 6½ inches high, once ran around the four walls of Matisse's own dining room. It is said to be a superb example of the artist's later papiers découpé (paper cutouts)—bold, vividly colored works done with scissors and paper that were the main activity of his last years. Entitled "The Swimming Pool," it portrays big female swimmers cut from blue paper and simplified to the point of abstraction, collaged on a white horizontal band that is in turn collaged on a brownish cloth.

Negotiations to acquire the work, owned by the artist's daughter, Mrs. Georges Duthuit, were begun 4½ years ago, Mr. Rubin said. The museum owns two other Matisse cutouts: "Nuit de Noël," a maquette for a stained-glass window, and "Memories of Oceania," purchased during Mr. Rubin's tenure. "But we didn't have a work from the great series called 'Blue Nudes,' of which

Continued on Page 24, Column 1

## 42 Skiers Are Killed in Italy When Cable Car Falls 200 Feet

By The Associated Press

TRENTO, Italy, March 9—A cable car packed with skiers plunged 200 feet to the ground near this northern Italian city today, and the police reported that 42 people had been killed.

They said that there was only one survivor, a seriously injured woman.

The police said most of the victims were West Germans. The Italian news agency Ansa said 38 of the 41 passengers were part of a large group of skiers from Hamburg. The other passengers and the car's two crewmen were Italians.

The accident took place at Cavalese, a resort in the Fiemme Valley in the Dolomites about 45 miles south of the Austrian border and 20 miles northeast of here.

The passengers were returning in early evening from the slopes of a mountain called Alpe Cermis.

Witnesses at the cableway's lowest station said a cable came loose and the car began to swing and then fell when the cable broke.

When the cable car struck the ground, a heavy metal bar that had connected it to the cable smashed through the car's roof, the witnesses said.

The cable car was only 600 feet from the terminal station when it fell, the police said.

Rescue workers pulled 38

Continued on Page 77, Column 7



### NEWS INDEX


| | Page | | Page |
| --- | --- | --- | --- |
| About New York | 21 | Movies | 23-28 |
| Books | 37 | Music | 23-28 |
| Bridge | 36 | Notes on People | 53 |
| Business | 56-67 | Obituaries | 42 |
| Crossword | 37 | Op-Ed | 39 |
| Editorials | 38 | Real Estate | 65 |
| Education | 22-23 | Sports | 29-32 |
| Family/Style | 44-54 | Theaters | 23-28 |
| Financial | 56-67 | Transportation | 77 |
| Going Out Guide | 24 | TV and Radio | 77-79 |
| Letters | 38 | Weather | 77 |

News Summary and Index, Page 41

"All the News That's Fit to Print"

# The New York Times

LATE CITY EDITION

Weather: Cloudy, windy today; cold tonight. Fair, seasonable tomorrow. Temperature range: today 28-37; Tuesday 36-43. Details on page 82.

VOL. CXXV . No. 43,152



NEW YORK, WEDNESDAY, MARCH 17, 1976

25 cents beyond 50-mile zone from New York City, except Long Island. Higher in air delivery cities.

20 CENTS

## FORD DECISIVELY DEFEATS REAGAN IN ILLINOIS VOTING; CARTER IS A SOLID WINNER

### GEORGIAN BEATS 3

### Daley Choice Is Victor Over Gov. Walker In the Primary

By WILLIAM E. FARRELL

Special to The New York Times

CHICAGO, March 16—President Ford won a decisive victory today in the Illinois Republican Presidential primary, dealing a further blow to the waning prospects of his opponent, Ronald Reagan. It was Mr. Ford's fifth triumph in a row over the former Governor of California.

Jimmy Carter, the former Governor of Georgia, easily won the Democratic preference primary, defeating three other contenders. They were Gov. George C. Wallace of Alabama, who came in second; Sargent Shriver, former director of the Office of Economic Opportunity, who ran third, and Fred R. Harris, former Senator of Oklahoma.

**Incomplete Voting Returns**

With 7,073, or 63 percent, of the 11,272 precincts reported: The tallies were:

REPUBLICANS

Ford ........265,497 (59%)
Reagan ......176,587 (40%)

With 7,137, or 63 percent, of the 11,272 precincts reported:

DEMOCRATS

Carter ......394,041 (48%)
Wallace .....218,599 (27%)
Shriver ......139,466 (17%)
Harris ........65,626 ( 8%)

As the returns rolled in, Mr. Shriver told a group of his followers here that his candidacy was no longer an active one. In effect, Mr. Shriver withdrew from the race.

The powerful Cook County machine of Mayor Richard J. Daley of Chicago achieved its aim of ousting Gov. Daniel Walker, a maverick Democrat long at odds with the Mayor. The machine candidate, Secretary of State Michael J. Howlett, won the Democratic gubernatorial primary.

The machine was less successful, however, in a race in the First Congressional District, where the incumbent Representative, Ralph H. Metcalfe, who broke with the machine a few years ago, beat Mr. Daley's candidate, Erwin A. France, former head of Chicago's Model Cities program. Both candi-

Continued on Page 24, Column 1

Associated Press

Mayor Richard J. Daley after voting in Chicago yesterday

## Foundations of Victory

### Ford Aided by Signs of Economic Rise, Carter by Absence of His Main Rivals

By R. W. APPLE Jr.

Special to The New York Times

News Analysis

CHICAGO, March 16—President Ford's victory over Ronald Reagan in Illinois today was built on three main foundations: his success in pre-empting issues, the belief among Republicans that he is both honest and electable and indications of an improving economy. The scope of Mr. Ford's triumph, based on a New York Times/CBS News poll of 1,060 voters who had cast their ballots, was far more impressive than his narrow New Hampshire and Florida victories. He has now taken five straight.

If Mr. Reagan stays in the race, which most Republicans considered pointless in view of the results in Illinois and elsewhere, he will probably do better, in North Carolina next week, although he trails there.

If the Californian had hoped that conflict-of-interest charges leveled last week against the President's campaign chairman, Howard H. Callaway, would help him here, he was disappointed.

The Times/CBS poll indicated that the Callaway issue had made no difference to voters of this populous state, often called an American microcosm.

Only 5 percent said that the Callaway episode influenced their votes, while 60 percent said that it had not mattered.

Jimmy Carter won his long-sought victory in a Northern industrial state. But he won it under circumstances that foretold little about his prospects in those other industrial states, such as New York, Pennsylvania and Michigan, where he will be tested by his main rivals, Henry M. Jackson and Morris K. Udall.

Neither Mr. Jackson, a Senator from Washington, nor Mr. Udall, a Representative from Arizona, was entered in the preferential "beauty contest" in Illinois. It was unclear, moreover, whether Mr. Carter's dominance in the preferential contest would translate itself into dominance of the delegate contests.

Tabulation of delegate returns was slow, but it seemed likely that many of Illinois' 169 votes at the Democratic National Convention would be controlled by Mayor Richard J. Daley of Chicago and Senator Adlai E. Stevenson 3d. Neither is pro-Carter, Mr. Daley preferring Mr. Jackson and Mr.

Continued on Page 24, Column 3

## DR. X IS IDENTIFIED; JERSEY PLANNING TO SEEK CHARGES

### Mario Jascalevich Is Named in Grand Jury Proceedings on Deaths in 1965-66

By M. A. FARBER

Special to The New York Times

HACKENSACK, N. J., March 16—Joseph C. Woodcock Jr., the Bergen County Prosecutor, plans to seek the indictment of Dr. Mario E. Jascalevich, a New Jersey surgeon, on charges of murdering one or more patients with curare at Riverdell Hospital a decade ago, according to law enforcement officials.

Dr. Jascalevich has been referred to as "Dr. X" in The New York Times, which published on Jan. 7 and 8 the results of its investigation into the "suspicious" deaths of nine or more patients in 1965 and 1966 at the small osteopathic hospital in Oradell at which Dr. Jascalevich was formerly chief surgeon.

However, his name has now emerged in the grand jury proceedings that began yesterday and in legal documents that are publicly available. In addition, his identity appears to be well known in medical circles in the state.

**Interview Declined**

Dr. Jascalevich, a 48-year-old Argentine immigrant who practices in West New York, has declined to be interviewed regarding the case.

His lawyer, James E. Anderson, reiterated at an unusual news conference today that his client was innocent of any wrongdoing and had "nothing to hide."

The lawyer, who had declined to have his own name used in this case until today, would neither confirm his client's identity nor answer specific questions relating to Dr. Jascalevich's use of curare a decade ago.

**Curare Found**

But he said that "a Roman circus spectacle" had been created by the publication of results of chemical tests on five bodies recently exhumed in Mr. Woodcock's new investigation of the case.

In another development today, a chemist who is performing some of those tests for Dr. Richard Coumbis, the chief toxicologist of New Jersey, said that he had found curare in the tissues of each of the four bodies he had examined so far.

In an interview with The New York Times, the chemist, Dr. David P. Beggs of the Hewlett-Packard Company in Avondale, Pa., said he had detected curare in at least one organ

Continued on Page 37, Column 2

## BYRNE CONFIDENT INCOME TAX BILL CAN PASS SENATE

### Merlino, Democratic Chief, Says Votes Will Be There —More Levies Likely

By MARTIN WALDRON

Special to The New York Times

TRENTON, March 16—Governor Byrne and the Senate Democratic leader, Joseph P. Merlino, said today that the billion-dollar state income tax bill approved early this morning by the State Assembly had an excellent chance to become law.

The Governor said he would sign the measure if it was passed by the Senate, which may vote on it as early as Monday.

The tax package "creates a new era, a modern era of sound taxpaying in our state," the Governor said, adding that he was encouraged that Legislators considered the tax to be theirs and not his.

**Earlier Defeats Recalled**

The Governor lost a fight in the Legislature in 1974 and in 1975 for his version of an income tax.

Senator Merlino said he was confident that the votes to pass the bill in the Senate would be there. In the last two years, a state income tax was killed in the Senate five times after passing the Assembly. The State Senate is currently in recess, but the Senate President, Matthew Feldman, who is vacationing in Hawaii, had promised to reconvene the Senate as soon as the Assembly had acted on an income tax.

Governor Byrne raised the possibility of still more new taxes at a news conference today.

**Money Is for Schools**

Money from the income tax is earmarked for public schools and for a cut in local property taxes, and therefore none of it will be available to restore cuts in state budgets, including those of state colleges, the Governor said.

Mr. Byrne said, however, that he would accept an increase in the 5 percent state sales tax or the gasoline tax if the Legislature passed them.

The income tax, which passed the Assembly by a 43-to-33 vote, could provide a windfall of $10 million or more a year for New York State.

Some 80,000 New York res-

Continued on Page 45, Column 4

### Economic Gains Shown

Industrial production increased again in February, housing starts registered a big advance and business began to accumulate inventories, Government statistics showed. Page 59.

## WILSON, STUNNING BRITAIN, QUITS AS PRIME MINISTER; LABORITE LEADER 13 YEARS

United Press International

Prime Minister Wilson at 10 Downing Street yesterday

### 5 IN LINE FOR POST

### Party M.P.'s to Name a Successor in Vote Beginning in Week

By ROBERT B. SEMPLE Jr.

Special to The New York Times

LONDON, March 16—Prime Minister Harold Wilson announced his resignation today, stunning his party and the nation.

The resignation will take effect as soon as the Labor Party members of the House of Commons have chosen a successor. Voting will begin next week.

Mr. Wilson, a fixture in British politics for 30 years—13 of them as Labor Party leader, nearly eight of them as Prime Minister — informed Queen Elizabeth II of his decision early today and then told his Cabinet.

*Excerpts from the Wilson statement are on Page 14.*

In a statement issued shortly before noon from 10 Downing Street, he said in part:

"In March 1974 I decided that I would remain in office for no more than two years. I have not wavered in this decision and it is irrevocable."

**Speculation on Successor**

The decision took the country by complete surprise, and immediately started a round of speculation about his successor. The leading candidates appear to be James Callaghan, the Foreign Secretary, and Denis Healey, Chancellor of the Exchequer, with three others regarded as somewhat longer shots: Roy Jenkins, the Home Secretary, Anthony Crosland, Secretary of the Environment, and Michael Foot, Secretary for Employment.

The decision also raised a host of questions about Mr. Wilson's motives and his sense of timing, since he himself conceded that he had chosen to leave at a critical juncture in his Government's effort to contain inflation and restore health to the nation's economy.

He had apparently confided in very few people. He said that in 1974, when he last came to office, he had written himself a confidential memorandum setting last fall's Labor Party conference as the date on which he would retire; he amended this in order to direct the anti-inflation policy, but on

Continued on Page 14, Column 1

## U.S., Angry Over Angola, To Delay 3 Soviet Meetings

By BERNARD GWERTZMAN

Special to The New York Times

WASHINGTON, March 16—Because of Soviet military involvement in Angola, the United States has decided for the time being against participating in Cabinet-level meetings of various Soviet-American joint commissions set up in recent years when détente was in vogue, State Department officials said today.

There are nine such commissions, but the decision has so far affected only three, dealing in trade, housing and energy. The other commissions are not due to meet until late in the year, and, by then, the United States may decide to participate, officials said.

The United States decision not to take part in the energy commission was first indicated late last night by an Administration official.

Robert L. Funseth, the State Department spokesman, today announced the official decision on the commissions, when he said that "in light of the situation in Angola, we felt we could not conduct our business with the Soviet Union as usual."

At the very moment when the Administration was signaling its irritation with the Soviet Union, 10 Senators, including Henry M. Jackson, the Washington Democrat, introduced a resolution today in the Senate supporting efforts to improve Soviet-American relations.

The Administration's action was clearly a limited one and not meant to disrupt overall Soviet-American relations.

Secretary of State Henry A. Kissinger, testifying before the Senate Foreign Relations Committee, repeated that the Government's anger over Soviet

Continued on Page 4, Column 4

## FORD BILL OPPOSES TAPS ON CITIZENS

### Surveillance Would Require Warrant—Draft by Levi Endorsed by Kennedy

By NICHOLAS M. HORROCK

Special to The New York Times

WASHINGTON, March 16—The Ford Administration is expected to unveil later this week legislation that its framers said would virtually end the practice of Federal electronic surveillance of American citizens without a court order.

This is the first time that a Republican Administration has been willing to support a bill that would require Federal officials to get a warrant from a judge before instituting national security and foreign intelligence electronic surveillance within the United States, senior Administration sources said today.

The bill is not designed to cover foreign intelligence-gathering activities in international communications and foreign communications conducted by the National Security Agency, according to Administration sources.

The draft of the bill, which is now before President Ford for approval, was worked out

Continued on Page 12, Column 4

## Harris's Campaign In State Collapses; Phone Is Shut Off

By FRANK LYNN

The New York Democratic Presidential primary was reduced to an essentially three-way contest yesterday as Fred R. Harris's campaign in the state all but collapsed, with his delegates switching to other candidates. The New York Telephone Company shut off service to his headquarters when a deposit it demanded was not paid.

The demise of the Harris effort here highlighted a day in which dozens of candidates for Democratic National Convention delegates switched sides or declined to run hours before the midnight mailing deadline for delegate candidates to express a Presidential preference under the newly amended state election law.

The clear gainer from the widespread switching, largely by supporters of Mr. Harris and Senator Birch Bayh of Indiana, was Representative Morris K. Udall of Arizona. To a lesser extent, Jimmy Carter, the former Governor of Georgia, also gained.

Both candidates picked up so many new delegate candi-

Continued on Page 24, Column 6



## Miss Hearst's Father, on Stand, Disputes a Psychiatric Witness

By WALLACE TURNER

Special to The New York Times

SAN FRANCISCO, March 16—Randolph A. Hearst, a tall, undemonstrative man who spent $2 million distributing food to the poor in an unsuccessful effort to ransom his daughter from a band of revolutionaries, took the witness stand this afternoon to defend her at her bank robbery trial.

Mr. Hearst, youngest son of William Randolph Hearst, builder of a newspaper empire, spoke to the jury in quiet tones about the 22-year-old defendant, the third of his five daughters:

"She was a very bright girl," he said. "She was strong-willed, and is, I think, pretty independent."

Mr. Hearst, president of The San Francisco Examiner and chairman of the board of directors of the Hearst Corporation, said that he had seen no signs of the resentment or anger in his daughter that were described yesterday by a Government psychiatric witness. "She was fun to be with, as when we went to Mexico," he said.

Then Mr. Hearst gave his version of how Dr. Joel Fort, a

Continued on Page 20, Column 1

NEWS INDEX


| | Page | | Page |
|---|---|---|---|
| About New York | 34 | Movies | 32-37 |
| Art | 36 | Music | 32-37 |
| Books | 39 | Notes on People | 26 |
| Bridge | 38 | Obituaries | 44 |
| Business | 58-71 | Op-Ed | 41 |
| Crossword | 39 | Real Estate | 72 |
| Editorials | 40 | Sports | 26-29 |
| Education | [illegible] | Theaters | 32-37 |
| Family/Style | 46-56 | Transportation | 82 |
| Financial | 58-71 | TV and Radio | 83 |
| Going Out Guide | 36 | U.N. Proceedings | 7 |
| Man in the News | 24 | Weather | 82 |

News Summary and Index, Page 43

Mark Greenberg-Images

Dr. Mario E. Jascalevich outside his office last week

## White Rhodesians Intent On Preserving 'Easy Life'

By HENRY KAMM

Special to The New York Times

SALISBURY, Rhodesia, March 16—"This man Smith has no visible appeal," said Sir Roy Welensky, who calls himself a "bitter opponent" of Prime Minister Ian D. Smith's Government, "it's the appeal of a very easy life."

"For $6,000 a year you can have five servants, a swimming pool and the lot," the 69-year-old Sir Roy, Prime Minister of the former Central African Federation and the elder statesman of Rhodesia, continued.

"That's the secret this man has had: you're going to keep what you have."

The 278,000 white Rhodesians live in a style and comfort ranging, in American terms, from middle-class suburbia to Westchester County estate. There are no visible poor whites, no whites in menial jobs and it seems unlikely that there is a white who has one of this country's 6.1 million blacks as his working superior.

There appear to be few Rhodesians to whom this state of affairs does not seem worth fighting for, although those who are considered moderates say they consider a multiracial society and government inevitable. But they hope, understandably, that such a government would guarantee that in raising the black population to equal opportunity it would not lower

Continued on Page 2, Column 4

## Ford Finds Injury From Steel Imports But Delays Quotas

By EDWIN L. DALE Jr.

Special to The New York Times

WASHINGTON, March 16—President Ford disclosed today his finding that imports were injuring domestic producers of stainless and other "specialty" steels, but he held up imposing import quotas for 90 days pending an effort to negotiate an "orderly marketing agreement" with the main foreign supplying countries.

The President's decision was the first major one under the import-limiting provisions of the 1974 Trade Act. It followed a hearing, a finding of injury and a recommendation of import quotas by the International Trade Commission.

One way or another, import restraints on specialty steel are now all but certain to be imposed, though with a delay. Probably more important, the President disclosed his decision to seek, in current international trade negotiations in Geneva, a special world trade agreement covering all international trade in steel.

In the case of the United States, specialty steel accounts for less than 2 percent of im-

Continued on Page 69, Column 1

"All the News That's Fit to Print"

# The New York Times

LATE CITY EDITION

Weather: Sunny, mild today; cool tonight. Chance of rain tomorrow. Temperature range: today 40-63; Tuesday 30-52. Details on page 78.

VOL. CXXV . . No. 43,159 — NEW YORK, WEDNESDAY, MARCH 24, 1976 — 20 CENTS

25 cents beyond 50-mile zone from New York City, except Long Island. Higher in air delivery cities.



## MRS. PERON OVERTHROWN BY MILITARY IN ARGENTINA AND REPORTED ARRESTED

### JUNTA WILL RULE

### President Is Expected to Be Held During Corruption Inquiry

By JUAN de ONIS

Special to The New York Times

BUENOS AIRES, Wednesday, March 24—Air force officers reportedly arrested President Isabel Martínez de Perón at an air base here early today as the armed forces overthrew Argentina's Peronist Government.

Mrs. Perón, the 45-year-old widow of Juan Domingo Perón, founder of the populist Peronist movement, left the Casa Rosada, the government house, in her presidential helicopter for her residence in suburban Olivos, but the flight ended at the military section of the municipal airport, informed sources said.

Air force troops and heavily armed policemen blocked access to the airport, which is the central Palermo park section of Buenos Aires.

**National Values Cited**

A communiqué broadcast over the national radio network said a three-man junta headed by the army commander, Gen. Jorge Rafael Videla, had taken over the Government "to restore the essential values" of the nation. The other members of the junta are the navy commander, Adm. Emilio Massera, and the air force commander, Brig. Gen. Orlando R. Agosti.

"In the face of institutional, social and administrative chaos that the republic was suffering, the military junta made up of the commanding generals of the armed forces has decided to assume the Government of the Argentine nation," the announcement said.

"The action of the Government will be characterized by the respect of the law within a framework of order and respect for human dignity. The fundamental objective will be to restore the essential values that guide the state."

**Labor Leaders Disperse**

Peronist labor leaders, who had been meeting at the Ministry of Labor, hastily left the building when they received reports that troops were on the way to take control of all ministries. Some sang "Peronista Boys," the movement's marching song, before they dispersed. Others left crying.

The military are reported to be planning to take control of the General Confederation of Labor, arrest some labor leaders, and block union bank accounts.

Diplomatic sources said Mrs. Perón, who succeeded her late husband in the presidency 21 months ago, would be flown to a vacation resort in the western province of Neuquén.

The armed forces commanders have reportedly decided that she should be held in Argentina during an investiga-

Continued on Page 4, Column 4

Associated Press — Isabel Martínez de Perón

United Press International — Gen. Jorge Rafael Videla

## Rhodesian Leader Rebuffs British Proposal on Rule

By Reuters

SALISBURY, Rhodesia, March 23—Prime Minister Ian D. Smith today rejected as extreme Britain's proposals for legalizing Rhodesia's independence based on black majority rule.

Mr. Smith said, in a statement after a Cabinet meeting that Foreign Secretary James Callaghan, who announced the plan to Parliament in London yesterday, had "chosen to disregard the realities and had come forward with proposals no less extreme than those of the African National Council."

Three months of talks between Mr. Smith and Joshua Nkomo, head of the council's internal faction, collapsed on Friday over how long it should take to hand over power to Rhodesia's six million blacks, who outnumber whites by 20 to 1.

Mr. Smith was not prepared to contemplate black rule before 10 to 15 years, but the black nationalists wanted it within a year. The British proposed two years at the most.

Shortly before Mr. Smith spoke, it was announced in Zambia that four African Presidents would meet there tomorrow to work out a new strategy for ending white rule in Rhodesia.

Kenneth D. Kaunda of Zambia, Samora Machel of Mozambique, Julius Nyerere of Tanzania and Sir Seretse Khama of Botswana are expected to be joined by the Rhodesian nationalist leaders, Mr. Nkomo and Bishop Abel Muzorewa.

The Presidents are expected to try to resolve a conflict

Continued on Page 12, Column 4

## Moslem Gunmen In Beirut Advance In Christian Areas

By JAMES M. MARKHAM

Special to The New York Times

BEIRUT, Lebanon, Wednesday, March 24—Moslem militiamen, bolstered by strong help from Palestinian guerrillas, advanced yesterday into downtown sections here traditionally held by Christian Phalangists.

Militiamen of the Phalangist Party were pushed out of the Holiday Inn, and fierce battles were fought around the Starco shopping complex and the unfinished Hilton Hotel.

As the Moslems continued their slow advance, two Syrian colonels, who arrived here Monday night, sought to arrange a cease-fire as a first step toward carrying out a plan the Syrian Government has fostered to ease Lebanon's President, Suleiman Franjieh, out of office.

[Moslem foes of the President shelled his palace at Baabda for the first time, Reuters reported. The shelling came from positions in a Beirut suburb.]

A Phalangist spokesman said his side was still holding the Hilton and that Phalangist representatives had met with the Syrian colonels, Ali al-

Continued on Page 3, Column 1

## U.S. Offers a Plan For Big Tariff Cuts

By VICTOR A. LUSINCHI

Special to The New York Times

GENEVA, March 23—The United States today presented a formula at the world trade negotiations here under which industrialized countries would cut their tariffs as much as 60 percent.

The mathematical formula would reduce tariffs in two ways: It would permit across-the-board, or linear, reductions by an agreed percentage. And it would also narrow the spread between high and low tariff rates.

Washington is seeking a "significant overall reduction" of tariff duties, American sources said. The proposed formula

Continued on Page 57, Column 2

## GOVERNOR ASSAILS SOME BUDGET CUTS AS 'NOT FEASIBLE'

### Says Legislature's Action Poses Threat of Losses in Federal Funds

By LINDA GREENHOUSE

Special to The New York Times

ALBANY, March 23—Governor Carey warned today that the cuts the Legislature made last week in his budget requests for state agencies and departments were "unworkable and counterproductive" and could "make it impossible for us to do the job" of running the state.

Breaking a public silence on the subject six days after the Legislature adopted the $10.78 billion budget, Mr. Carey said that some of the cuts "were simply not feasible" and that others could lead to the loss of accreditation for some state facilities or to the loss of Federal funds for insufficiently staffed departmental programs.

Mr. Carey made his comments at an impromptu news conference in his office. His fiscal aides later said the new budget was under intensive review and that there were few specifics available yet on the impact of the cuts.

**Schuler Gives Warning**

The Governor met yesterday with his department heads, and Raymond T. Schuler, the Commissioner of Transportation, told him that inadequate staffing in the department's planning, design, development and construction programs could lead to the loss of as much as $200 million a year in Federal grants.

On another fiscal matter, meanwhile, Charles J. Hynes, the special nursing-home prosecutor, met here today with legislative fiscal aides and with Burton G. Hecht, the Bronx Democrat who is chairman of the Assembly Ways and Means Committee, to seek restoration of a $2.3 million appropriation for nursing-home auditors.

In a joint news conference with the prosecutor, Mr. Hecht said that the justification Mr. Hynes had presented for the auditing program had been "very helpful" and that the Legislature would decide "strictly on the merits" whether to restore the funds early next week.

Judging from the conciliatory tone adopted by both Assemblyman Hecht and Mr. Hynes, it seemed likely that the money would be restored. Mr. Hynes

Continued on Page 23, Column 1

### Braniff Is Penalized

Braniff Airways has agreed to a record civil penalty of $300,000 resulting from failure to report a Nixon campaign gift and a $1 million ticket discount scheme, the Civil Aeronautics Board announced. Details on Page 55.

## Field Marshal Montgomery Dead at 88

By Reuters

LONDON, Wednesday, March 24 — Field Marshal Viscount Montgomery, the most famous British soldier of modern times, died early today, the Ministry of Defense announced. He was 88 years old.

Lord Montgomery died in his sleep at his country home in the south of England where he had been bedridden for several years. A military funeral will be held at Windsor.

**Controversial Militarist**

General Montgomery's victory over the Germans and Italians at El Alamein in Northern Egypt in November 1942 was a major and decisive battle in history, for before it, the Germans had not lost a major battle in World War II.

But the controversial, cantankerous, and stubborn general bore a major responsibility for one of the war's most tragically executed blunders. It was an operation code-named "Market-Garden," of which he was the major architect, designed to seize from the Germans, in 1944, five major Dutch bridges and cross the Rhine into German territory.

But the bridge at Arnhem, the last in the battle, the one later dubbed by the historian

Imperial War Museum

General Montgomery at El Alamein as commander in 1943

Cornelius Ryan as "A Bridge Too Far," could not be taken, and the result was a major setback with all its consequences, including horrendous casualties. The Allies did not, in fact, cross the Rhine until March 1945.

Although General Montgomery frankly, in his memoirs, abandoned his usual reluctance to admit error and conceded "I take the blame for this mis-

Continued on Page 42, Column 1

## REAGAN TOPS FORD IN N. CAROLINA FOR FIRST TRIUMPH IN A PRIMARY; CARTER EASILY DEFEATS WALLACE

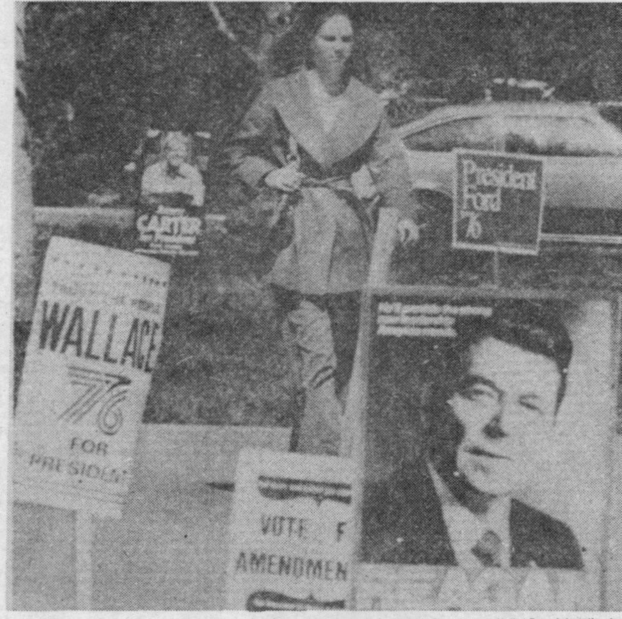



United Press International

Young woman threading her way through posters after voting in Raleigh, N.C., yesterday

### SURPRISE VICTORY

### Gain for Californian Breathes New Life Into His Campaign

By R. W. APPLE Jr.

Special to The New York Times

RALEIGH, N. C., March 23—Ronald Reagan upset President Ford and Jimmy Carter trounced Gov. George C. Wallace of Alabama tonight in the North Carolina Presidential primary.

The former California Governor's victory here, his first after five consecutive primary losses to Mr. Ford, guaranteed that he would remain in the race. It can be expected to help replenish his campaign treasury and to lift his spirit.

But the Republican voters of North Carolina are unusually conservative. Mr. Ford remains the favorite in most of the primaries still to come, and the heavy favorite to win the party's nomination.

An NBC News poll of 600 Republicans as they left their polling places indicated that a fifth of them—an unusually high figure—had made up their minds in the final week. Moreover, the poll showed that Mr. Reagan benefited greatly from a distrust of détente and of Secretary of State Henry A. Kissinger.

**Reagan Strong in Suburbs**

Mr. Reagan carried nearly all of the state's big counties, where suburban Republicans are staunchly conservative. Only in the mountains, where anti-slavery Republicanism is more moderate, did the President manage to win.

The Californian flew home from Wisconsin without claiming victory. He had announced earlier that he would buy network time for a national address next week to raise money and to press his attacks on the Administration.

Mr. Carter's triumph was the former Georgia Governor's third in three weeks over Mr. Wallace, whose campaign is barely alive. And the Georgian was the first Democratic primary victor of the year to win a majority of the vote, with 54 percent.

Complete returns showed Mr. Carter winning every Congressional district, from Cape Hatteras to the Smokies. Even in the most deeply conservative eastern rural counties, where Mr. Wallace piled up huge majorities in winning the 1972 Presidential primary here, Mr. Carter ran strongly.

**Jackson Strategy Noted**

Senator Henry M. Jackson of Washington, a major contender in the Wisconsin and New York primaries two weeks from today, cut off his campaign here earlier this month in an attempt to avoid embarrassment.

With reports in from all of the state's 2,343 precincts, the tally was:

| REPUBLICANS | | |
|---|---|---|
| Reagan | 101,448 | (52%) |
| Ford | 88,924 | (46%) |
| **DEMOCRATS** | | |
| Carter | 321,059 | (54%) |
| Wallace | 209,807 | (35%) |
| Jackson | 25,098 | (4%) |
| No Preference | 22,585 | (4%) |

Mr. Carter swept the black vote. In one predominantly black precinct in Durham, he won 533 votes to 3 for Mr. Wallace.

The defeat was a bitter blow to the Alabamian. But even before the votes were counted, Mr. Wallace had decided to restructure his campaign, de-emphasizing the colorful rallies that helped to build his fame.

Although obviously dispirited by his weak showing, Mr. Wallace vowed at a news conference tonight to move on to Wisconsin, the next state where

Continued on Page 20, Column 1

## KIBBEE PLAN GETS BACKING OF BOARD

### Bulk of City U. Restructuring Approved—Ideas on York and Richmond Altered

By EDWARD B. FISKE

The Board of Higher Education will advise the Emergency Financial Control Board today that it is prepared to accept the bulk of the controversial Kibbee plan for consolidating and restructuring the City University, sources in the board reported yesterday.

The principal exceptions involved Richmond College, which Dr. Robert J. Kibbee, the university's chancellor, proposed closing but which the board has agreed to merge with Staten Island Community College, and York College, which the board wants to retain as a four-year institution rather than make it a two-year institution. There is also no clear consensus yet on whether to close John Jay College or to maintain it as a separate but smaller institution specializing in criminal justice.

There were also reported to be clear-cut majorities to accept other elements of the chancellor's plan—to merge Hostos Community College with Bronx Community College and to reduce Medgar Evers College from a four-year to a two-year institution. In both cases, however, some minor modifications received majority support.

The 10-member board, however, has taken no formal vote on any aspects of the proposed reorganization, and Alfred A. Giardino, the chairman, said that no formal action

Continued on Page 35, Column 6

## House Budget Chief Urges More Spending Than Ford

By EILEEN SHANAHAN

Special to The New York Times

WASHINGTON, March 23 — Representative Brock Adams, Democrat of Washington, who is chairman of the House Budget Committee, proposed today that the Federal Government spend $412.8 billion next year, $18.6 billion more than President Ford recommended.

Mr. Adams said that the increase was necessary to stop

*Excerpts from Adams statement appear on Page 68.*

Mr. Ford's proposed "drastic shifting of priorities from human resource programs to defense" and to make sure that restrictive budget policies do not "arrest the beginning of economic recovery."

The proposed budget targets submitted by Mr. Adams to his committee are expected to set the framework not only for its discussions and votes on budget policy, but also, to a large extent, for the entire Congressional debate on the issue.

To a significant extent, the proposals of the House Budget Committee chairman, rather than those of the President, will become the baseline from which these debates will start.

Mr. Adams's proposals included not only overall spending and revenue figures, but also recommended spending ceilings for each of 16 major subcategories of Federal spending.

The $18.6 billion increase in overall spending recommended by Mr. Adams to his commit-

Continued on Page 68, Column 3

## Court Curbs Federal Suits On Defamation by Officials

By LESLEY OELSNER

Special to The New York Times

WASHINGTON, March 23—Over a strong dissent by three Justices, the Supreme Court ruled today that the Constitution gives citizens only limited protection and recourse against public officials who defame them.

Specifically, the Court ruled that state and local officials, such as policemen who defame a citizen, may not be sued in Federal court for alleged civil rights violations if the defamation resulted merely in injury to the person's reputation.

To file a Federal civil rights suit, the Court indicated, a citizen would have to show some injury in addition to defamation, such as loss of employment.

Today's ruling can apply, according to the Court's decision, even where the defamation takes the form of branding a person as a criminal on the basis of the fact that a person has been arrested for a crime though not convicted of it.

The Court's decision came in a case involving a flyer sent to some 800 merchants in the Louisville, Ky., metropolitan area in December 1972, giving photographs and names of per-

Continued on Page 18, Column 4

## Papal Birth Stand Found to Hurt Church

By KENNETH A. BRIGGS

Overwhelming rejection by the Roman Catholic laity in the United States of the 1968 papal ban on artificial birth control has led to drastic declines in religious devotion and annually costs the church nearly a billion dollars in income, according to a survey of Catholic attitudes released yesterday by the National Opinion Research Center.

The report, issued in a 483-page book entitled "Catholic Schools in a Declining Church," further shows that support for parochial schools remains strong despite the church's general retreat from that field.

The study, a 10-year follow-up of a 1963 survey, raises critical questions about church decisions. It calls the birth-control decision "both a failure and an organizational and religious disaster." At the same time, it notes that "Catholic schools seem substantially more important today than they were a decade ago" but that "fewer resources are allowed them."

The report says that Catholics would have given $5.5 billion to the church in 1974 if they had given at 1963 levels. But even though Catholics were more affluent than they were a decade ago, they gave only $3.8 billion.

Of the $1.7 billion difference, the researchers assert, almost a billion can be accounted for by the alienation from the church created by the Pope's encyclical, "Humanae Vitae."

"It is rare," said the Rev. Andrew Greeley, program di-

Continued on Page 18, Column 5

### NEWS INDEX



| | Page | | Page |
|---|---|---|---|
| About New York | 36 | Movies | 24-28 |
| Art | 26 | Music | 24-28 |
| Books | 37 | Notes on People | 28 |
| Bridge | 36 | Obituaries | 42 |
| Business | 54-68 | Op-Ed | 39 |
| Crossword | 37 | Real Estate | 66 |
| Editorials | 38 | Sports | 29-34 |
| Education | 35 | Theaters | 24-28 |
| Family/Style | 44-53 | Transportation | 78 |
| Financial | 54-68 | TV and Radio | 78-79 |
| Going Out Guide | 25 | Weather | 78 |

News Summary and Index, Page 41